# KEY TO WORLD MA

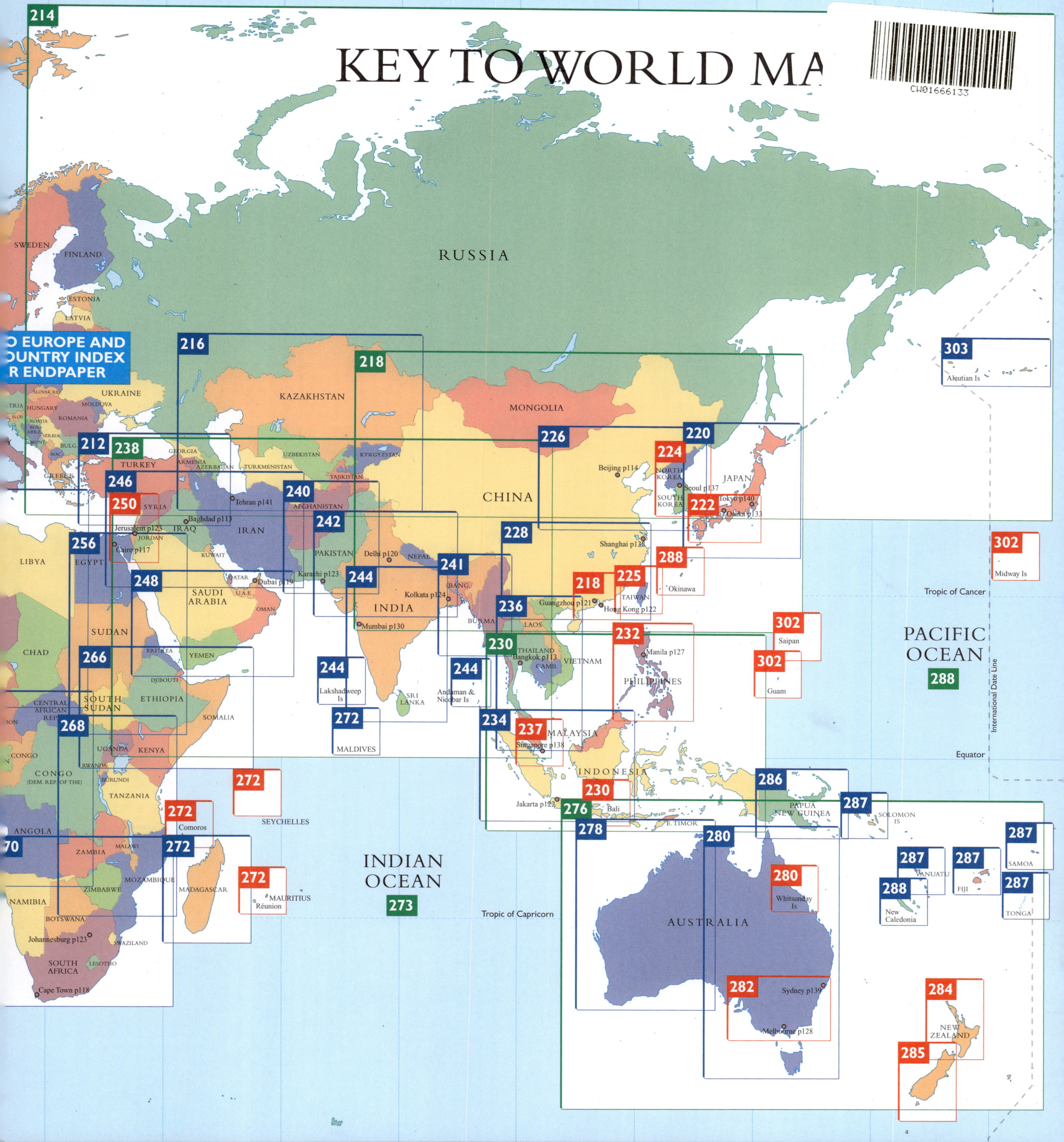

214
RUSSIA
SWEDEN
FINLAND
ESTONIA
LATVIA
O EUROPE AND
OUNTRY INDEX
R ENDPAPER
UKRAINE
MOLDOVA
HUNGARY
ROMANIA
CROATIA
SERBIA
BULG.
GREECE
216
218
KAZAKHSTAN
MONGOLIA
212
238
TURKEY
GEORGIA
ARMENIA
AZERBAIJAN
UZBEKISTAN
TURKMENISTAN
KYRGYZSTAN
TAJIKISTAN
226
220
224
Beijing p114
NORTH KOREA
Seoul p137
JAPAN
SOUTH KOREA
222
Tokyo p140
Osaka p133
246
250
SYRIA
240
Tehran p141
AFGHANISTAN
CHINA
Baghdad p113
IRAQ
IRAN
Jerusalem p123
JORDAN
242
Cairo p117
256
LIBYA
EGYPT
KUWAIT
PAKISTAN
Delhi p120
NEPAL
228
Shanghai p128
288
Okinawa
241
244
248
QATAR
Dubai p119
Karachi p123
BANG.
U.A.E.
SAUDI ARABIA
Kolkata p124
OMAN
INDIA
218
225
TAIWAN
Guangzhou p121
Hong Kong p122
236
BURMA
LAOS
SUDAN
Mumbai p130
230
THAILAND
Bangkok p113
CAMB.
VIETNAM
232
Manila p127
PHILIPPINES
302
Saipan
302
Guam
CHAD
266
ERITREA
YEMEN
DJIBOUTI
ETHIOPIA
SOMALIA
244
Lakshadweep Is
244
Andaman & Nicobar Is
SRI LANKA
CENTRAL AFRICAN REP.
SOUTH SUDAN
268
272
MALDIVES
234
237
Singapore p138
MALAYSIA
CONGO
UGANDA
KENYA
RWANDA
BURUNDI
CONGO (DEM. REP. OF THE)
TANZANIA
272
SEYCHELLES
INDONESIA
230
Jakarta p122
Bali
276
E. TIMOR
286
PAPUA NEW GUINEA
287
SOLOMON IS
272
Comoros
ANGOLA
ZAMBIA
MALAWI
272
MOZAMBIQUE
MADAGASCAR
ZIMBABWE
NAMIBIA
BOTSWANA
272
MAURITIUS
Réunion
INDIAN OCEAN
273
Tropic of Capricorn
Johannesburg p123
SWAZILAND
SOUTH AFRICA
LESOTHO
Cape Town p118
278
280
280
Whitsunday Is
AUSTRALIA
282
Sydney p139
Melbourne p128
287
VANUATU
287
FIJI
288
New Caledonia
287
SAMOA
287
TONGA
284
NEW ZEALAND
285
303
Aleutian Is
302
Midway Is
Tropic of Cancer
PACIFIC OCEAN
288
International Date Line
Equator


## KEY TO WORLD MAP SYMBOLS

### SETTLEMENTS

PARIS · Strasbourg · Livorno · Brugge · Exeter · *Torremolinos* · *Oberammergau* · *Thira*

Settlement symbols and type styles vary according to the scale of each map and indicate the importance of towns on the map rather than specific population figures

*Vaduz* Capital cities have red infills

Urban agglomerations

Ruins or archeological sites

Wells in desert

### ADMINISTRATION

International boundaries

International boundaries (undefined or disputed)

Internal boundaries

National parks

PERU Country names

KENT Administrative area names

International boundaries show the *de facto* situation where there are rival claims to territory

### COMMUNICATIONS

Motorways, freeways and expressways

Principal roads

Other roads

Road tunnels

Principal railways

Railways under construction

Other railways

Railway tunnels

LHR Principal airports (with location identifier)

Other airports

Principal canals

Passes

### PHYSICAL FEATURES

Perennial streams

Intermittent streams

Sand deserts

Intermittent lakes

Swamps and marshes

Permanent ice and glaciers

▲ 8848 Elevations in metres

▼ 8500 Sea depths in metres

*1134* Height of lake surface above sea level in metres

The Royal Geographical Society

# ATLAS OF THE WORLD

PHILIP'S

**Gazetteer of Nations**
Text Keith Lye

**Photographic Acknowledgements**
Robin Aiello (Ocean Antics Consulting) 10 (bottom right);
Alamy /*Peter Barritt* 88 (bottom), /*BrazilPhotos.com* 97, /*Reinhard Dirscherl* 10 (bottom left), /*Everett Collection Historical* 13 (centre), /*Images and Stories* 12, 94, /*Ingolf Pompe 90* 10 (top), /*David Parker* 91;
Corbis /*William Caram* 103, /*P. Deliss* 88 (top), /*Nigel J. Dennis/Gallo Images* 84, /*Jay Dickman* 109 (top), /*Paulo Fridman* 89 (centre), /*Gideon Mendel* 89 (top), /*Liba Taylor* 104, /*David Turnley* 109 (bottom);
© Crown copyright 2007. Published by the Met Office, UK 80;
Galaxy Picture Library /*Robin Scagell* 73;
Getty Images /*Andreas Arnold* 8–9, /*Hannele Lahti* 13 (bottom);
Javier Méndez (ING)/Nik Szymanek (Univ. Herts) 68;
NASA/GSFC 81 (bottom), 98, /*Jacques Descloitres, MODIS Rapid Response Team* 79, /*MODIS Rapid Response Team* 82, /*NASA image by Jesse Allen, using AMSR-E data processed and provided by Chelle Gentemann and Frank Wentz, Remote Sensing Systems* 10 (centre), /*NASA Earth Observatory image by Jesse Allen and Robert Simmon, using Landsat data from the US Geological Survey* 13 (top);
NSIDC courtesy J. Maslanik and M. Tschudi, University of Colorado 81 (top);
NPA Satellite Mapping 14–33, 110–111, 144–145, 156–157, 208–209, 252–253, 274–275, 290–291, 324–325, /*Image provided by the USGS EROS Data Center Satellite Systems Branch* 85;
Plantagon International 89 (bottom);
USGS/Landsat 66–67.

**Star Charts (page 69)**
Wil Tirion

**Cartography by Philip's**

**World Cities**
Page 120, Dublin: The town plan of Dublin is based on Ordnance Survey Ireland by permission of the Government Permit Number 8847. © Ordnance Survey Ireland and Government of Ireland.

Ordnance Survey Page 121, Edinburgh, and Page 125, London:
This product includes mapping data licensed from Ordnance Survey® with the permission of the Controller of Her Majesty's Stationery Office. © Crown copyright 2013. All rights reserved. Licence number 100011710.

Published in Great Britain in 2013 by Philip's,
a division of Octopus Publishing Group Limited
(www.octopusbooks.co.uk)
Endeavour House, 189 Shaftesbury Avenue,
London WC2H 8JY
An Hachette UK Company (www.hachette.co.uk)



ISBN 978-1-84907-296-0

A CIP catalogue record for this book is available from the British Library.



Printed in Thailand

Details of other Philip's titles and services can be found on our website at: **www.philips-maps.co.uk**

## Specialist Geography Consultants

The editors are grateful to the following for their contributions to the '*World Geography*' section in this atlas:

**Dr Dibyesh Anand**
**John Burden**
**Peter Grego**
**Keith Lye**
**Ross Reynolds**
**Robin Scagell**
**John Woodruff**

The editors are especially grateful to **Garrett Nagle** for his invaluable assistance in preparing this section and '*The Future of the Oceans and Seas*' feature.

The specialist consultant for the '*Food Supply*' spread is **Professor Keith W. T. Goulding,** President of the British Society of Soil Science and Head: Department of Sustainable and Grassland Systems, Rothamsted Research, Harpenden, UK (www.rothamsted.ac.uk).

**Rothamsted Research** is an institute of the Biotechnology and Biological Sciences Research Council.

The editors would also like to thank **Richard Chiles** and the staff at **NPA Satellite Mapping, Edenbridge, Kent, UK** (www.npa.cgg.com) for sourcing and processing the satellite imagery that appears in the atlas.

**Royal Geographical Society** with IBG
Advancing geography and geographical learning

Philip's World Atlases are published in association with The Royal Geographical Society (with The Institute of British Geographers).

The Society was founded in 1830 and given a Royal Charter in 1859 for 'the advancement of geographical science'. It holds historical collections of national and international importance, many of which relate to the Society's association with and support for scientific exploration and research from the 19th century onwards. It was pivotal in establishing geography as a teaching and research discipline in British universities close to the turn of the century, and has played a key role in geographical and environmental education ever since.

Today the Society is a leading world centre for geographical learning – supporting education, teaching, research and expeditions, and promoting public understanding of the subject. The Society welcomes those interested in geography as members. For further information, please visit the website at: **www.rgs.org**

# USER GUIDE

The reference maps which form the main body of this atlas have been prepared in accordance with the highest standards of international cartography to provide an accurate and detailed representation of the Earth. The scales and projections used have been carefully chosen to give balanced coverage of the world, while emphasizing the most densely populated and economically significant regions. A hallmark of Philip's mapping is the use of hill shading and relief colouring to create a graphic impression of landforms: this makes the maps exceptionally easy to read. However, knowledge of the key features employed in the construction and presentation of the maps will enable the reader to derive the fullest benefit from the atlas.

## Map Sequence

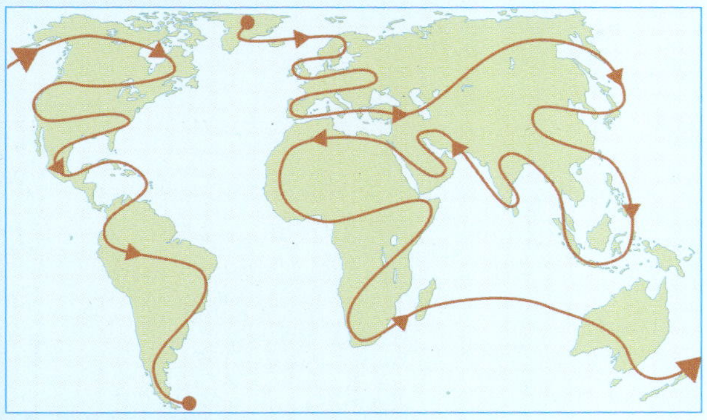

The atlas covers the Earth continent by continent: first Europe; then its land neighbour Asia (mapped north before south, in a clockwise sequence), then Africa, Australia and Oceania, North America and South America. This is the classic arrangement adopted by most cartographers since the 16th century. For each continent, there are maps at a variety of scales. First, physical relief and political maps of the whole continent; then a series of larger-scale maps of the regions within the continent, each followed, where required, by still larger-scale maps of the most important or densely populated areas. The governing principle is that by turning the pages of the atlas, the reader moves steadily from north to south through each continent, with each map overlapping its neighbours.

## Map Presentation

With very few exceptions (for example, for the Arctic and Antarctica), the maps are drawn with north at the top, regardless of whether they are presented upright or sideways on the page. In the borders will be found the map title; a locator diagram showing the area covered; continuation arrows showing the page numbers for maps of adjacent areas; the scale; the projection used; the degrees of latitude and longitude; and the letters and figures used in the index for locating place names and geographical features. Physical relief maps also have a height reference panel identifying the colours used for each layer of contouring.

## Map Symbols

Each map contains a vast amount of detail which can only be conveyed clearly and accurately by the use of symbols. Points and circles of varying sizes locate and identify the relative importance of towns and cities; different styles of type are employed for administrative, geographical and regional place names to aid identification. A variety of pictorial symbols denote landforms such as glaciers, marshes and coral reefs, and man-made structures including roads, railways, airports and canals. International borders are shown by red lines. Where neighbouring countries are in dispute, for example in parts of the Middle East, the maps show the *de facto* boundary between nations, regardless of the legal or historical situation.

The symbols are explained on the front endpapers of the atlas.

336 SOUTHERN CHILE AND ARGENTINA

## Map Scales

1:16 000 000
1 inch = 252 statute miles

The scale of each map is given in the numerical form known as the 'representative fraction'. The first figure is always one, signifying one unit of distance on the map; the second figure, usually in millions, is the number by which the map unit must be multiplied to give the equivalent distance on the Earth's surface. Calculations can easily be made in centimetres and kilometres, by dividing the Earth units figure by 100 000 (i.e. deleting the last five 0s). Thus 1:1 000 000 means 1 cm = 10 km. The calculation for inches and miles is more laborious, but 1 000 000 divided by 63 360 (the number of inches in a mile) shows that 1:1 000 000 means approximately 1 inch = 16 miles. The table below provides distance equivalents for scales down to 1:50 000 000.

LARGE SCALE

| | | |
|---|---|---|
| 1:1 000 000 | 1 cm = 10 km | 1 inch = 16 miles |
| 1:2 500 000 | 1 cm = 25 km | 1 inch = 39.5 miles |
| 1:5 000 000 | 1 cm = 50 km | 1 inch = 79 miles |
| 1:6 000 000 | 1 cm = 60 km | 1 inch = 95 miles |
| 1:8 000 000 | 1 cm = 80 km | 1 inch = 126 miles |
| 1:10 000 000 | 1 cm = 100 km | 1 inch = 158 miles |
| 1:15 000 000 | 1 cm = 150 km | 1 inch = 237 miles |
| 1:20 000 000 | 1 cm = 200 km | 1 inch = 316 miles |
| 1:50 000 000 | 1 cm = 500 km | 1 inch = 790 miles |

SMALL SCALE

## Measuring Distances

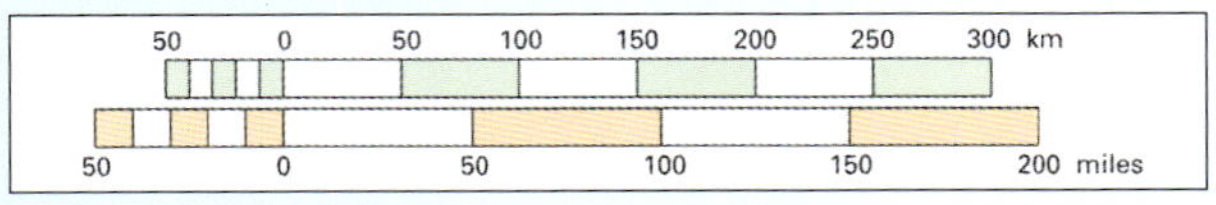
50 0 50 100 150 200 250 300 km
50 0 50 100 150 200 miles

Although each map is accompanied by a scale bar, distances cannot always be measured with confidence because of the distortions involved in portraying the curved surface of the Earth on a flat page. As a general rule, the larger the map scale, the more accurate and reliable will be the distance measured. On small-scale maps such as those of the world and of entire continents, measurement may only be accurate along the 'standard parallels', or central axes, and should not be attempted without considering the map projection.

## Map Projections

CONIC
AZIMUTHAL
CYLINDRICAL

Unlike a globe, no flat map can give a true scale representation of the world in terms of area, shape and position of every region. Each of the numerous systems that have been devised for projecting the curved surface of the Earth on to a flat page involves the sacrifice of accuracy in one or more of these elements. The variations in shape and position of land masses such as Alaska, Greenland and Australia, for example, can be quite dramatic when different projections are compared.

For this atlas, the guiding principle has been to select projections that involve the least distortion of size and distance. The projection used for each map is noted in the border. Most fall into one of three categories – conic, azimuthal or cylindrical – whose basic concepts are shown above. Each involves plotting the forms of the Earth's surface on a grid of latitude and longitude lines, which may be shown as parallels, curves or radiating spokes.

## Latitude and Longitude

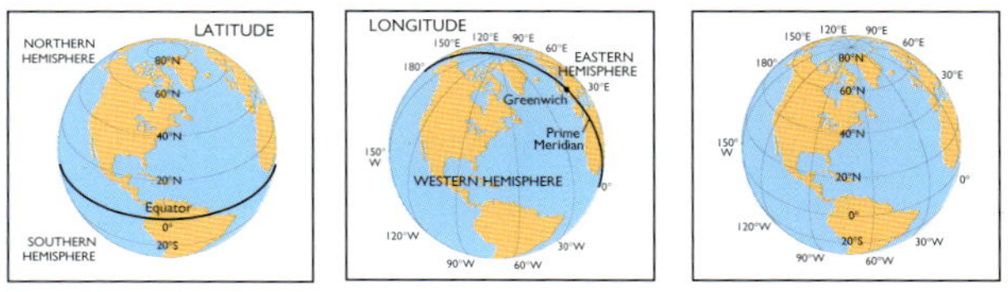
NORTHERN HEMISPHERE
LATITUDE
SOUTHERN HEMISPHERE
Equator
LONGITUDE
EASTERN HEMISPHERE
Greenwich
Prime Meridian
WESTERN HEMISPHERE

Accurate positioning of individual points on the Earth's surface is made possible by reference to the geometrical system of latitude and longitude. Latitude *parallels* are drawn west–east around the Earth and numbered by degrees north and south of the Equator, which is designated 0° of latitude. Longitude *meridians* are drawn north–south and numbered by degrees east and west of the *prime meridian*, 0° of longitude, which passes through Greenwich in England. By referring to these co-ordinates and their subdivisions of minutes (1/60th of a degree) and seconds (1/60th of a minute), any place on Earth can be located to within a few hundred metres. Latitude and longitude are indicated by blue lines on the maps; they are straight or curved according to the projection employed. Reference to these lines is the easiest way of determining the relative positions of places on different maps, and for plotting compass directions.

## Name Forms

For ease of reference, both English and local name forms appear in the atlas. Oceans, seas and countries are shown in English throughout the atlas; country names may be abbreviated to their commonly accepted form (for example, Germany, not The Federal Republic of Germany). Conventional English forms are also used for place names on the smaller-scale maps of the continents. However, local name forms are used on all large-scale and regional maps, with the English form given in brackets only for important cities – the large-scale map of Russia and Northern Asia thus shows Moskva (Moscow). For countries which do not use a Roman script, place names have been transcribed according to the systems adopted by the British and US Geographic Names Authorities. For China, the Pin Yin system has been used, with some more widely known forms appearing in brackets, as with Beijing (Peking). Both English and local names appear in the index, the English form being cross-referenced to the local form.

# CONTENTS


## World Statistics

Countries 6
Cities 7

## The Future of the Oceans and Seas

Overview 10–11
The Issues 12–13

## Images of Earth

London, UK 16
Amsterdam, Netherlands 17
Istanbul, Turkey 18
Mumbai, India 19
Singapore City, Singapore 20
Hong Kong/Shenzhen, China 21
Cairo, Egypt 22
Juba, South Sudan 23
Cape Town, South Africa 24
Sydney, Australia 25
Auckland, New Zealand 26
Vancouver, Canada 27
New York City, USA 28
Washington, DC, USA 29
Panama Canal, Panama 30
Rio de Janeiro, Brazil 31

## Gazetteer of Nations

An A–Z Gazetteer of Countries 34–65

## World Geography

The Universe 68–69
The Solar System 70–71
Seasons, Time and Motion 72–73
Geology of the Earth 74–75
The Atmosphere 76–77
Climate 78–79
Climate Change and Global Warming 80–81
Water and Vegetation 82–83
Biodiversity and the Natural World 84–85
Population 86–87
Food Supply 88–89
Cities 90–91
The Human Family 92–93
Conflict and Co-operation 94–95
Energy 96–97
Minerals 98–99
Employment and Industry 100–101
Trade 102–103
Health 104–105
Wealth 106–107
Standards of Living 108–109

## World Cities

Amsterdam 112
Athens 112
Atlanta 113
Baghdad 113
Bangkok 113
Barcelona 114
Beijing 114
Berlin 115
Boston 116
Brussels 116
Budapest 117
Buenos Aires 117
Cairo 117
Cape Town 118
Copenhagen 118
Chicago 119
Dubai 119
Delhi 120
Dublin 120
Edinburgh 121
Guangzhou 121
Helsinki 121
Hong Kong 122
Istanbul 122
Jakarta 122
Jerusalem 123
Johannesburg 123
Karachi 123
Kolkata 124
Lagos 124
Las Vegas 124
Lima 124
London 125
Lisbon 126
Los Angeles 126
Madrid 127
Manila 127
Melbourne 128
Mexico City 128
Milan 128
Miami 129
Moscow 129
Montréal 130
Mumbai 130
Munich 131
New Orleans 131
New York 132
Orlando 133
Osaka 133
Oslo 133
Paris 134
Prague 135
Rio de Janeiro 135
Rome 136
San Francisco 136
St Petersburg 137
Santiago 137
São Paulo 137
Seoul 137
Shanghai 138
Singapore 138
Stockholm 139
Sydney 139
Tokyo 140
Tehran 141
Toronto 141
Venice 142
Vienna 142
Warsaw 143
Washington 143

## World Maps

### The World

Map Symbols Front Endpaper

The World: Physical 146–147
1:76 000 000

The World: Political 148–149
1:76 000 000

Arctic Ocean 150
1:28 000 000

Antarctica 151
1:28 000 000

Atlantic Ocean 152
1:41 000 000

Islands of the Atlantic 153
Bermuda 1:400 000
New Providence Island 1:400 000
Madeira 1:800 000
Azores 1:1 600 000
Canary Islands 1:1 600 000
Falkland Islands 1:6 400 000
Ascension Island 1:400 000
St Helena 1:400 000
Cape Verde Islands 1:8 000 000

Greenland 154
1:10 000 000

Iceland 155
1:2 000 000

### Europe

Europe: Physical 158
1:16 000 000

Europe: Political 159
1:16 000 000

Scandinavia 160–161
1:4 800 000
Iceland 1:4 800 000
Færoe Islands 1:4 800 000

Denmark and Southern Sweden 162–163
1:2 000 000

Southern Norway 164
1:2 000 000

British Isles 165
1:4 000 000

Ireland 166
1:1 600 000

Scotland 167
1:1 600 000

England and Wales 168–169
1:1 600 000

Netherlands, Belgium and Luxembourg 170
1:2 000 000

France 171
1:4 000 000

Northern France 172–173
1:2 000 000

Southern France 174–175
1:2 000 000

Central Europe 176–177
1:4 000 000

Germany and Switzerland 178–179
1:2 000 000

Austria, Czech Republic and Slovak Republic 180–181
1:2 000 000

Hungary, Romania and the Lower Danube 182–183
1:2 000 000

Poland and the Southern Baltic 184–185
1:2 000 000

Eastern Europe 186–187
1:8 000 000

Baltic States, Belarus and Ukraine 188–189
1:4 000 000

The Volga Basin and the Caucasus 190–191
1:4 000 000

Southern Europe 192–193
1:8 000 000

Western Spain and Portugal 194–195
1:2 000 000

Eastern Spain 196–197
1:2 000 000

Northern Italy, Slovenia and Croatia 198–199
1:2 000 000

Southern Italy 200–201
1:2 000 000

The Balkans 202–203
1:2 000 000

Southern Greece and Western Turkey 204–205
1:2 000 000

Mediterranean Islands 206–207
Ibiza, Majorca, Minorca 1:800 000
Malta 1:400 000
Corfu 1:800 000
Rhodes 1:800 000
Levkas, Zante, Cephalonia 1:800 000
Crete 1:1 000 000
Cyprus 1:1 000 000

### Asia

Asia: Physical 210
1:40 000 000

Asia: Political 211
1:40 000 000

Turkey and Transcaucasia 212–213
1:4 000 000

Russia and Northern Asia 214–215
1:16 000 000

# CONTENTS


Kazakhstan and Central Asia 216–127
1:8 000 000

China and the Far East 218–219
1:12 000 000
Hong Kong, Macau and Shenzhen 1:800 000

Japan 220–221
1:4 000 000
Ryukyu Islands 1:4 000 000

Southern Japan 222–223
1:2 000 000

Korea 224
1:3 100 000
Jeju-do 1:3 100 000

Taiwan 225
1:1 400 000
Chinmen 1:1 400 000
Matsu 1:1 400 000

Northern China and Korea 226–227
1:4 800 000

Southern China and Taiwan 228–229
1:4 800 000
Hainan 1:4 800 000

South-east Asia 230–231
1:10 000 000
Java and Madura 1:6 000 000
Bali 1:1 600 000

Philippines 232–233
1:3 200 000

Western Indonesia and Malaysia 234–235
1:5 600 000

Mainland South-east Asia 236–237
1:4 800 000
Ko Phuket 1:800 000
Ko Samui 1:800 000
Pinang 1:800 000
Singapore 1:800 000

Southern Asia and the Middle East 238–239
1:14 000 000

Afghanistan and Pakistan 240
1:5 600 000

Bangladesh, North-eastern India and Burma 241
1:4 800 000

Northern India, Pakistan and Nepal 242–243
1:4 800 000
Jammu and Kashmir 1:4 800 000

Southern India and Sri Lanka 244–245
1:4 800 000
Lakshadweep Islands 1:4 800 000
Andaman and Nicobar Islands 1:4 800 000

The Middle East 246–247
1:5 600 000

Southern Arabian Peninsula 248–249
1:5 600 000
Emirates of the U.A.E. 1:5 600 000

Eastern Mediterranean 250–251
1:2 000 000


## Africa


Africa: Physical 254
1:33 600 000

Africa: Political 255
1:33 600 000

The Nile Valley 256–257
1:6 400 000
The Nile Delta 1:3 200 000

Central North Africa 258–259
1:6 400 000

North-west Africa 260–261
1:6 400 000

West Africa 262–263
1:6 400 000

Central Africa 264–265
1:6 400 000
São Tomé and Príncipe 1:6 400 000

Ethiopia and the Horn of Africa 266–267
1:6 400 000

East Africa 268–269
1:6 400 000

Southern Africa 270–271
1:6 400 000

Madagascar 272
1:6 400 000
Comoros 1:2 000 000
Mayotte 1:800 000
Seychelles 1:2 000 000
Réunion 1:800 000
Mauritius 1:800 000
Maldives 1:6 400 000

Indian Ocean 273
1:40 000 000


## Australia and Oceania


Australia and Oceania: Physical and Political 276–277
1:16 000 000

Western Australia 278–279
1:6 400 000

Eastern Australia 280–281
1:6 400 000
Whitsunday Group 1:2 000 000
Tasmania 1:6 400 000
Torres Strait 1:6 400 000

South-eastern Australia 282–283
1:3 200 000

New Zealand – North Island 284
1:2 800 000

New Zealand – South Island 285
1:2 800 000
Chatham Islands 1:2 800 000

Papua New Guinea 286
1:5 200 000

Islands of the South-west Pacific 287
Fiji 1:4 000 000
Vanuatu 1:4 000 000
Solomon Islands 1:4 000 000
Tonga 1:4 000 000
Yap 1:830 000
Chuuk 1:830 000
Samoan Islands 1:4 000 000

Pacific Ocean 288–289
1:43 200 000
Okinawa 1:1 550 000
Iwo-Jima 1:200 000
Palau 1:1 550 000
New Caledonia 1:5 750 000
Tahiti 1:1 150 000
French Polynesia 1:26 000 000
Niue 1:830 000
Rarotonga 1:415 000


## North America


North America: Physical 292
1:28 000 000

North America: Political 293
1:28 000 000

Canada 294–295
1:12 000 000
Northern Canada 1:12 000 000

Western Canada 296–297
1:5 600 000

Eastern Canada 298–299
1:5 600 000

United States 300–301
1:12 000 000
Alaska 1:12 000 000
Hawai'i 1:12 000 000

Hawai'i and the U.S. Pacific Islands 302
1:2 500 000
Hawaiian Islands 1:21 000 000
O'ahu 1:500 000
Northern Marianas 1:17 500 000
Wake Island 1:200 000
Midway Islands 1:200 000
Guam 1:800 000
Saipan and Tinian 1:800 000
Tutuila 1:640 000
Manu'a Islands 1:640 000

Alaska 303
1:8 000 000

United States – West 304–305
1:5 360 000

Central and Southern California and Western Washington 306–307
1:2 000 000

United States – Midwest and North-east 308–309
1:5 360 000

Chicago and the Midwest 310–311
1:2 000 000

North-eastern United States 312–313
1:2 000 000

United States – South 314–315
1:5 360 000

South-eastern United States 316–317
1:2 000 000

Mexico 318–319
1:6 400 000

Central America and the West Indies 320–321
1:6 400 000
Puerto Rico and the Virgin Islands 1:1 600 000
Jamaica 1:1 600 000
Panama Canal 1:800 000

Lesser Antilles 322–323
Northern Leewards 1:600 000
Antigua and Barbuda 1:600 000
St Kitts and Nevis 1:600 000
Guadeloupe 1:600 000
ABC Islands 1:600 000
Martinique 1:600 000
Dominica 1:600 000
St Lucia 1:600 000
St Vincent and the Grenadines 1:600 000
Montserrat 1:600 000
Grenada 1:600 000
Barbados 1:600 000
Trinidad and Tobago 1:600 000


## South America


South America: Physical 326
1:28 000 000

South America: Political 327
1:28 000 000

South America – North-west 328–329
1:6 400 000
Margarita 1:600 000

South America – West 330–331
1:6 400 000
Galapagos Islands 1:3 200 000
Easter Island 1:400 000
Robinson Crusoe Island 1:400 000

Eastern Brazil 332–333
1:6 400 000

Central South America 334–335
1:6 400 000

Southern Chile and Argentina 336
1:6 400 000

Geographical Glossary 337–338

Index to World Maps 339–448

# 6 WORLD STATISTICS: COUNTRIES

This alphabetical list includes the principal countries and territories of the world. If a territory is not completely independent, the country it is associated with is named. The area figures give the total area of land, inland water and ice. The population figures are 2012 estimates where available. The annual income is the Gross Domestic Product per capita in US dollars; the figures are the latest available, usually 2012 estimates.

| Country/Territory | Area km² Thousands | Area miles² Thousands | Population Thousands | Capital | Annual Income US $ |
|---|---|---|---|---|---|
| Afghanistan | 652 | 252 | 30,420 | Kabul | 1,000 |
| Albania | 28.7 | 11.1 | 3,003 | Tirana | 8,000 |
| Algeria | 2,382 | 920 | 37,367 | Algiers | 7,500 |
| American Samoa (US) | 0.20 | 0.08 | 55 | Pago Pago | 8,000 |
| Andorra | 0.47 | 0.18 | 85 | Andorra La Vella | 37,200 |
| Angola | 1,247 | 481 | 18,056 | Luanda | 6,200 |
| Anguilla (UK) | 0.10 | 0.04 | 15 | The Valley | 12,200 |
| Antigua & Barbuda | 0.44 | 0.17 | 89 | St John's | 17,500 |
| Argentina | 2,780 | 1,074 | 42,192 | Buenos Aires | 18,200 |
| Armenia | 29.8 | 11.5 | 2,970 | Yerevan | 5,600 |
| Aruba (Netherlands) | 0.19 | 0.07 | 108 | Oranjestad | 21,800 |
| Australia | 7,741 | 2,989 | 22,016 | Canberra | 42,400 |
| Austria | 83.9 | 32.4 | 8,220 | Vienna | 42,500 |
| Azerbaijan | 86.6 | 33.4 | 9,494 | Baku | 10,700 |
| Azores (Portugal) | 2.2 | 0.86 | 236 | Ponta Delgada | 15,000 |
| Bahamas | 13.9 | 5.4 | 316 | Nassau | 31,300 |
| Bahrain | 0.69 | 0.27 | 1,248 | Manama | 28,200 |
| Bangladesh | 144 | 55.6 | 161,084 | Dhaka | 2,000 |
| Barbados | 0.43 | 0.17 | 288 | Bridgetown | 25,500 |
| Belarus | 208 | 80.2 | 9,644 | Minsk | 16,000 |
| Belgium | 30.5 | 11.8 | 10,438 | Brussels | 38,100 |
| Belize | 23.0 | 8.9 | 328 | Belmopan | 8,400 |
| Benin | 113 | 43.5 | 9,599 | Porto-Novo | 1,700 |
| Bermuda (UK) | 0.05 | 0.02 | 69 | Hamilton | 69,900 |
| Bhutan | 47.0 | 18.1 | 717 | Thimphu | 6,500 |
| Bolivia | 1,099 | 424 | 10,290 | La Paz/Sucre | 5,000 |
| Bosnia-Herzegovina | 51.2 | 19.8 | 3,879 | Sarajevo | 8,300 |
| Botswana | 582 | 225 | 2,098 | Gaborone | 16,800 |
| Brazil | 8,514 | 3,287 | 199,321 | Brasília | 12,000 |
| Brunei | 5.8 | 2.2 | 409 | Bandar Seri Begawan | 50,500 |
| Bulgaria | 111 | 42.8 | 7,038 | Sofia | 14,200 |
| Burkina Faso | 274 | 106 | 17,275 | Ouagadougou | 1,400 |
| Burma (Myanmar) | 677 | 261 | 54,585 | Rangoon/Naypyidaw | 1,400 |
| Burundi | 27.8 | 10.7 | 10,557 | Bujumbura | 600 |
| Cambodia | 181 | 69.9 | 14,953 | Phnom Penh | 2,400 |
| Cameroon | 475 | 184 | 20,130 | Yaoundé | 2,300 |
| Canada | 9,971 | 3,850 | 34,300 | Ottawa | 41,500 |
| Canary Is. (Spain) | 7.2 | 2.8 | 1,682 | Las Palmas/Santa Cruz | 19,900 |
| Cape Verde Is. | 4.0 | 1.6 | 524 | Praia | 4,100 |
| Cayman Is. (UK) | 0.26 | 0.10 | 53 | George Town | 43,800 |
| Central African Republic | 623 | 241 | 5,057 | Bangui | 800 |
| Chad | 1,284 | 496 | 10,976 | Ndjaména | 2,000 |
| Chile | 757 | 292 | 17,067 | Santiago | 18,400 |
| China | 9,597 | 3,705 | 1,343,240 | Beijing | 9,100 |
| Colombia | 1,139 | 440 | 45,239 | Bogotá | 10,700 |
| Comoros | 2.2 | 0.86 | 737 | Moroni | 1,300 |
| Congo | 342 | 132 | 4,366 | Brazzaville | 4,700 |
| Congo (Dem. Rep. of the) | 2,345 | 905 | 73,599 | Kinshasa | 400 |
| Cook Is. (NZ) | 0.24 | 0.09 | 11 | Avarua | 9,100 |
| Costa Rica | 51.1 | 19.7 | 4,636 | San José | 12,600 |
| Croatia | 56.5 | 21.8 | 4,480 | Zagreb | 18,100 |
| Cuba | 111 | 42.8 | 11,075 | Havana | 9,900 |
| Curaçao (Netherlands) | 0.44 | 0.17 | 146 | Willemstad | 15,000 |
| Cyprus | 9.3 | 3.6 | 1,138 | Nicosia | 26,900 |
| Czech Republic | 78.9 | 30.5 | 10,177 | Prague | 27,200 |
| Denmark | 43.1 | 16.6 | 5,543 | Copenhagen | 37,700 |
| Djibouti | 23.2 | 9.0 | 774 | Djibouti | 2,700 |
| Dominica | 0.75 | 0.29 | 73 | Roseau | 14,600 |
| Dominican Republic | 48.5 | 18.7 | 10,089 | Santo Domingo | 9,600 |
| East Timor | 14.9 | 5.7 | 1,144 | Dili | 9,500 |
| Ecuador | 284 | 109 | 15,224 | Quito | 8,800 |
| Egypt | 1,001 | 387 | 83,688 | Cairo | 6,600 |
| El Salvador | 21.0 | 8.1 | 6,091 | San Salvador | 7,700 |
| Equatorial Guinea | 28.1 | 10.8 | 685 | Malabo | 20,200 |
| Eritrea | 118 | 45.4 | 6,086 | Asmara | 800 |
| Estonia | 45.1 | 17.4 | 1,275 | Tallinn | 21,200 |
| Ethiopia | 1,104 | 426 | 91,196 | Addis Ababa | 1,200 |
| Falkland Is. (UK) | 12.2 | 4.7 | 3 | Stanley | 55,400 |
| Faroe Is. (Denmark) | 1.4 | 0.54 | 49 | Tórshavn | 30,500 |
| Fiji | 18.3 | 7.1 | 890 | Suva | 4,800 |
| Finland | 338 | 131 | 5,263 | Helsinki | 36,500 |
| France | 552 | 213 | 65,631 | Paris | 35,500 |
| French Guiana (France) | 90.0 | 34.7 | 203 | Cayenne | 8,300 |
| French Polynesia (France) | 4.0 | 1.5 | 275 | Papeete | 18,000 |
| Gabon | 268 | 103 | 1,608 | Libreville | 17,300 |
| Gambia, The | 11.3 | 4.4 | 1,840 | Banjul | 1,900 |
| Georgia | 69.7 | 26.9 | 4,571 | Tbilisi | 5,900 |
| Germany | 357 | 138 | 81,306 | Berlin | 39,100 |
| Ghana | 239 | 92.1 | 24,652 | Accra | 3,300 |
| Gibraltar (UK) | 0.006 | 0.002 | 29 | Gibraltar Town | 43,000 |
| Greece | 132 | 50.9 | 10,768 | Athens | 25,100 |
| Greenland (Denmark) | 2,176 | 840 | 58 | Nuuk | 38,400 |
| Grenada | 0.34 | 0.13 | 109 | St George's | 14,100 |
| Guadeloupe (France) | 1.7 | 0.66 | 453 | Basse-Terre | 7,900 |
| Guam (US) | 0.55 | 0.21 | 160 | Agana | 15,000 |
| Guatemala | 109 | 42.0 | 14,099 | Guatemala City | 5,200 |
| Guinea | 246 | 94.9 | 10,885 | Conakry | 1,100 |
| Guinea-Bissau | 36.1 | 13.9 | 1,629 | Bissau | 1,100 |
| Guyana | 215 | 83.0 | 742 | Georgetown | 8,000 |
| Haiti | 27.8 | 10.7 | 9,802 | Port-au-Prince | 1,300 |
| Honduras | 112 | 43.3 | 8,297 | Tegucigalpa | 4,600 |
| Hungary | 93.0 | 35.9 | 9,958 | Budapest | 19,800 |
| Iceland | 103 | 39.8 | 313 | Reykjavik | 39,400 |
| India | 3,287 | 1,269 | 1,205,074 | New Delhi | 3,900 |
| Indonesia | 1,905 | 735 | 248,645 | Jakarta | 5,000 |
| Iran | 1,648 | 636 | 78,869 | Tehran | 13,100 |
| Iraq | 438 | 169 | 31,129 | Baghdad | 4,600 |
| Ireland | 70.3 | 27.1 | 4,722 | Dublin | 41,700 |
| Israel | 20.6 | 8.0 | 7,591 | Jerusalem | 32,200 |
| Italy | 301 | 116 | 61,261 | Rome | 30,100 |
| Ivory Coast (Côte d'Ivoire) | 322 | 125 | 21,952 | Yamoussoukro | 1,700 |
| Jamaica | 11.0 | 4.2 | 2,889 | Kingston | 9,100 |
| Japan | 378 | 146 | 127,368 | Tokyo | 36,200 |
| Jordan | 89.3 | 34.5 | 6,509 | Amman | 6,000 |
| Kazakhstan | 2,725 | 1,052 | 17,522 | Astana | 13,900 |
| Kenya | 580 | 224 | 43,013 | Nairobi | 1,800 |
| Kiribati | 0.73 | 0.28 | 102 | Tarawa | 5,900 |
| Korea, North | 121 | 46.5 | 24,589 | Pyŏngyang | 1,800 |
| Korea, South | 99.3 | 38.3 | 48,861 | Seoul | 32,400 |
| Kosovo | 10.9 | 4.2 | 1,837 | Pristina | 7,400 |
| Kuwait | 17.8 | 6.9 | 2,646 | Kuwait City | 43,800 |
| Kyrgyzstan | 200 | 77.2 | 5,497 | Bishkek | 2,400 |
| Laos | 237 | 91.4 | 6,586 | Vientiane | 3,000 |
| Latvia | 64.6 | 24.9 | 2,192 | Riga | 18,100 |
| Lebanon | 10.4 | 4.0 | 4,140 | Beirut | 15,900 |
| Lesotho | 30.4 | 11.7 | 1,930 | Maseru | 2,000 |
| Liberia | 111 | 43.0 | 3,888 | Monrovia | 700 |
| Libya | 1,760 | 679 | 5,613 | Tripoli | 13,300 |
| Liechtenstein | 0.16 | 0.06 | 37 | Vaduz | 89,400 |
| Lithuania | 65.2 | 25.2 | 3,526 | Vilnius | 20,100 |
| Luxembourg | 2.6 | 1.0 | 509 | Luxembourg | 80,700 |
| Macedonia (FYROM) | 25.7 | 9.9 | 2,082 | Skopje | 10,900 |
| Madagascar | 587 | 227 | 22,005 | Antananarivo | 1,000 |
| Madeira (Portugal) | 0.78 | 0.30 | 241 | Funchal | 25,800 |
| Malawi | 118 | 45.7 | 16,323 | Lilongwe | 900 |
| Malaysia | 330 | 127 | 29,180 | Kuala Lumpur/Putrajaya | 16,900 |
| Maldives | 0.30 | 0.12 | 394 | Malé | 8,700 |
| Mali | 1,240 | 479 | 15,494 | Bamako | 1,100 |
| Malta | 0.32 | 0.12 | 410 | Valletta | 26,100 |
| Marshall Is. | 0.18 | 0.07 | 68 | Majuro | 2,500 |
| Martinique (France) | 1.1 | 0.43 | 436 | Fort-de-France | 14,400 |
| Mauritania | 1,026 | 396 | 3,359 | Nouakchott | 2,100 |
| Mauritius | 2.0 | 0.79 | 1,313 | Port Louis | 15,600 |
| Mayotte (France) | 0.37 | 0.14 | 231 | Mamoudzou | 4,900 |
| Mexico | 1,958 | 756 | 114,975 | Mexico City | 15,300 |
| Micronesia, Fed. States of | 0.70 | 0.27 | 106 | Palikir | 2,200 |
| Moldova | 33.9 | 13.1 | 3,657 | Kishinev | 3,500 |
| Monaco | 0.001 | 0.0004 | 31 | Monaco | 63,400 |
| Mongolia | 1,567 | 605 | 3,180 | Ulan Bator | 5,400 |
| Montenegro | 14.0 | 5.4 | 657 | Podgorica | 11,700 |
| Montserrat (UK) | 0.10 | 0.39 | 5 | Brades | 8,500 |
| Morocco | 447 | 172 | 32,309 | Rabat | 5,300 |
| Mozambique | 802 | 309 | 23,516 | Maputo | 1,200 |
| Namibia | 824 | 318 | 2,166 | Windhoek | 7,800 |
| Nauru | 0.02 | 0.008 | 9 | Yaren | 5,000 |
| Nepal | 147 | 56.8 | 29,891 | Katmandu | 1,300 |
| Netherlands | 41.5 | 16.0 | 16,731 | Amsterdam/The Hague | 42,300 |
| New Caledonia (France) | 18.6 | 7.2 | 260 | Nouméa | 15,000 |
| New Zealand | 271 | 104 | 4,328 | Wellington | 28,800 |
| Nicaragua | 130 | 50.2 | 5,728 | Managua | 3,300 |
| Niger | 1,267 | 489 | 16,345 | Niamey | 900 |
| Nigeria | 924 | 357 | 170,124 | Abuja | 2,700 |
| Northern Mariana Is. (US) | 0.46 | 0.18 | 51 | Saipan | 12,500 |
| Norway | 324 | 125 | 4,707 | Oslo | 55,300 |
| Oman | 310 | 119 | 3,090 | Muscat | 28,500 |
| Pakistan | 796 | 307 | 190,291 | Islamabad | 2,900 |
| Palau | 0.46 | 0.18 | 21 | Melekeok | 8,100 |
| Panama | 75.5 | 29.2 | 3,510 | Panamá | 15,300 |
| Papua New Guinea | 463 | 179 | 6,310 | Port Moresby | 2,700 |
| Paraguay | 407 | 157 | 6,542 | Asunción | 6,100 |
| Peru | 1,285 | 496 | 29,550 | Lima | 10,700 |
| Philippines | 300 | 116 | 103,775 | Manila | 4,300 |
| Poland | 323 | 125 | 38,415 | Warsaw | 21,000 |
| Portugal | 88.8 | 34.3 | 10,781 | Lisbon | 23,000 |
| Puerto Rico (US) | 8.9 | 3.4 | 3,691 | San Juan | 16,300 |
| Qatar | 11.0 | 4.2 | 1,952 | Doha | 102,800 |
| Réunion (France) | 2.5 | 0.97 | 788 | St-Denis | 6,200 |
| Romania | 238 | 92.0 | 21,849 | Bucharest | 12,800 |
| Russia | 17,075 | 6,593 | 142,518 | Moscow | 17,700 |
| Rwanda | 26.3 | 10.2 | 11,690 | Kigali | 1,400 |
| St Kitts & Nevis | 0.26 | 0.10 | 51 | Basseterre | 15,500 |
| St Lucia | 0.54 | 0.21 | 162 | Castries | 13,300 |
| St Vincent & Grenadines | 0.39 | 0.15 | 104 | Kingstown | 11,900 |
| Samoa | 2.8 | 1.1 | 194 | Apia | 6,200 |
| San Marino | 0.06 | 0.02 | 32 | San Marino | 36,200 |
| São Tomé & Príncipe | 0.96 | 0.37 | 183 | São Tomé | 2,300 |
| Saudi Arabia | 2,150 | 830 | 26,535 | Riyadh | 25,700 |
| Senegal | 197 | 76.0 | 12,970 | Dakar | 1,900 |
| Serbia | 77.5 | 29.9 | 7,277 | Belgrade | 10,500 |
| Seychelles | 0.46 | 0.18 | 90 | Victoria | 26,200 |
| Sierra Leone | 71.7 | 27.7 | 5,486 | Freetown | 1,400 |
| Singapore | 0.68 | 0.26 | 5,353 | Singapore City | 60,900 |
| Slovak Republic | 49.0 | 18.9 | 5,483 | Bratislava | 24,300 |
| Slovenia | 20.3 | 7.8 | 1,997 | Ljubljana | 28,600 |
| Solomon Is. | 28.9 | 11.2 | 585 | Honiara | 3,400 |
| Somalia | 638 | 246 | 10,086 | Mogadishu | 600 |
| South Africa | 1,221 | 471 | 48,810 | Cape Town/Pretoria | 11,300 |
| Spain | 498 | 192 | 47,043 | Madrid | 30,400 |
| Sri Lanka | 65.6 | 25.3 | 21,481 | Colombo | 6,100 |
| Sudan | 1,886 | 728 | 34,207 | Khartoum | 2,400 |
| Sudan, South | 620 | 239 | 10,625 | Juba | 900 |
| Suriname | 163 | 63.0 | 560 | Paramaribo | 12,300 |
| Swaziland | 17.4 | 6.7 | 1,387 | Mbabane | 5,300 |
| Sweden | 450 | 174 | 9,104 | Stockholm | 41,700 |
| Switzerland | 41.3 | 15.9 | 7,926 | Berne | 45,300 |
| Syria | 185 | 71.5 | 22,531 | Damascus | 5,100 |
| Taiwan | 36.0 | 13.9 | 23,235 | Taipei | 38,500 |
| Tajikistan | 143 | 55.3 | 7,768 | Dushanbe | 2,200 |
| Tanzania | 945 | 365 | 46,913 | Dodoma | 1,700 |
| Thailand | 513 | 198 | 67,091 | Bangkok | 10,000 |
| Togo | 56.8 | 21.9 | 6,961 | Lomé | 1,100 |
| Tonga | 0.65 | 0.25 | 106 | Nuku'alofa | 7,500 |
| Trinidad & Tobago | 5.1 | 2.0 | 1,226 | Port of Spain | 20,400 |
| Tunisia | 164 | 63.2 | 10,733 | Tunis | 9,700 |
| Turkey | 775 | 299 | 79,749 | Ankara | 15,000 |
| Turkmenistan | 488 | 188 | 5,055 | Ashkhabad | 8,500 |
| Turks & Caicos Is. (UK) | 0.43 | 0.17 | 46 | Cockburn Town | 11,500 |
| Tuvalu | 0.03 | 0.01 | 11 | Fongafale | 3,300 |
| Uganda | 241 | 93.1 | 33,641 | Kampala | 1,400 |
| Ukraine | 604 | 233 | 44,854 | Kiev | 7,600 |
| United Arab Emirates | 83.6 | 32.3 | 5,314 | Abu Dhabi | 49,000 |
| United Kingdom | 242 | 93.4 | 63,047 | London | 36,700 |
| United States of America | 9,629 | 3,718 | 313,847 | Washington, DC | 49,800 |
| Uruguay | 175 | 67.6 | 3,316 | Montevideo | 15,800 |
| Uzbekistan | 447 | 173 | 28,394 | Tashkent | 3,500 |
| Vanuatu | 12.2 | 4.7 | 256 | Port-Vila | 4,900 |
| Venezuela | 912 | 352 | 28,048 | Caracas | 13,200 |
| Vietnam | 332 | 128 | 91,519 | Hanoi | 3,500 |
| Virgin Is. (UK) | 0.15 | 0.06 | 31 | Road Town | 38,500 |
| Virgin Is. (US) | 0.35 | 0.13 | 105 | Charlotte Amalie | 14,500 |
| Wallis & Futuna Is. (France) | 0.20 | 0.08 | 15 | Mata-Utu | 3,800 |
| Yemen | 528 | 204 | 24,772 | Sana' | 2,200 |
| Zambia | 753 | 291 | 13,817 | Lusaka | 1,700 |
| Zimbabwe | 391 | 151 | 12,620 | Harare | 500 |

This list shows the principal cities with more than 850,000 inhabitants. The figures are taken from the most recent census or estimate available, usually 2012, and as far as possible are the population of the metropolitan area or urban agglomeration. The list includes Metropolitan Statistical Areas from the United States 2010 Census. All the figures are in thousands. Local name forms have been used for the smaller cities (for example, Thessaloniki).

| | |
|---|---|
| **AFGHANISTAN** | |
| Kabul | 3,097 |
| **ALGERIA** | |
| Algiers | 2,916 |
| **ANGOLA** | |
| Luanda | 5,068 |
| Huambo | 1,098 |
| **ARGENTINA** | |
| Buenos Aires | 13,528 |
| Córdoba | 1,556 |
| Rosario | 1,283 |
| Mendoza | 1,072 |
| San Miguel de Tucumán | 868 |
| **ARMENIA** | |
| Yerevan | 1,116 |
| **AUSTRALIA** | |
| Sydney | 4,543 |
| Melbourne | 3,961 |
| Brisbane | 2,039 |
| Perth | 1,649 |
| Adelaide | 1,198 |
| **AUSTRIA** | |
| Vienna | 1,720 |
| **AZERBAIJAN** | |
| Baku | 2,123 |
| **BANGLADESH** | |
| Dhaka | 15,391 |
| Chittagong | 5,239 |
| Khulna | 1,781 |
| Rajshahi | 932 |
| **BELARUS** | |
| Minsk | 1,861 |
| **BELGIUM** | |
| Brussels | 1,949 |
| Antwerpen | 959 |
| **BENIN** | |
| Cotonou | 924 |
| **BOLIVIA** | |
| Santa Cruz | 1,719 |
| La Paz | 1,715 |
| **BRAZIL** | |
| São Paulo | 20,395 |
| Rio de Janeiro | 11,990 |
| Belo Horizonte | 5,910 |
| Pôrto Alegre | 4,115 |
| Salvador | 3,940 |
| Recife | 3,890 |
| Fortaleza | 3,740 |
| Curitiba | 3,490 |
| Campinas | 2,835 |
| Brasília | 2,330 |
| Belém | 2,205 |
| Goiânia | 2,155 |
| Vitória | 1,825 |
| Santos | 1,820 |
| Manaus | 1,802 |
| Natal | 1,315 |
| São Luís | 1,275 |
| Guarulhos | 1,222 |
| Maceió | 1,190 |
| Joinville | 1,065 |
| Florianópolis | 1,040 |
| João Pessoa | 1,010 |
| Teresina | 911 |
| Duque de Caxias | 855 |
| **BULGARIA** | |
| Sofia | 1,174 |
| **BURKINA FASO** | |
| Ouagadougou | 2,053 |
| **BURMA (MYANMAR)** | |
| Rangoon | 4,457 |
| Mandalay | 1,063 |
| Naypyidaw | 1,060 |
| **CAMBODIA** | |
| Phnom Penh | 1,550 |
| **CAMEROON** | |
| Douala | 2,449 |
| Yaoundé | 2,432 |
| **CANADA** | |
| Toronto | 5,573 |
| Montréal | 3,856 |
| Vancouver | 2,267 |
| Calgary | 1,216 |
| Ottawa | 1,208 |
| Edmonton | 1,142 |
| **CHAD** | |
| Ndjamena | 1,079 |
| **CHILE** | |
| Santiago | 6,355 |
| Valparaiso | 931 |
| **CHINA** | |
| Shanghai | 20,208 |
| Beijing | 15,594 |
| Guangzhou, Guangdong | 10,849 |
| Shenzhen | 10,630 |
| Chongqing | 9,977 |
| Wuhan | 9,158 |
| Tianjin | 8,744 |
| Dongguan, Guangdong | 7,280 |
| Hong Kong | 7,122 |
| Chengdu | 6,670 |
| Foshan | 6,486 |
| Nanjing, Jiangsu | 5,866 |
| Harbin | 5,687 |
| Shenyang | 5,568 |
| Hangzhou | 5,448 |
| Xi'an, Shaanxi | 4,975 |
| Shantou | 4,175 |
| Zhengzhou | 3,964 |
| Qingdao | 3,797 |
| Jinan, Shandong | 3,697 |
| Changchun | 3,694 |
| Taiyuan, Shanxi | 3,495 |
| Kunming | 3,472 |
| Suzhou, Jiangsu | 3,463 |
| Wuxi, Jiangsu | 3,366 |
| Dalian | 3,359 |
| Changsha | 3,335 |
| Ürümqi | 3,123 |
| Hefei | 3,012 |
| Fuzhou, Fujian | 2,897 |
| Xiamen | 2,880 |
| Zhongshan | 2,862 |
| Shijiazhuang | 2,841 |
| Zibo | 2,797 |
| Ningbo | 2,755 |
| Wenzhou | 2,733 |
| Lanzhou | 2,555 |
| Guiyang | 2,525 |
| Nanchang | 2,411 |
| Changzhou, Jiangsu | 2,405 |
| Jinxi | 2,268 |
| Xuzhou | 2,242 |
| Nanning | 2,136 |
| Nanchong | 2,046 |
| Wanxian | 1,963 |
| Baotou | 1,953 |
| Jilin | 1,942 |
| Tangshan | 1,927 |
| Huzhou | 1,856 |
| Weifang | 1,752 |
| Anshan | 1,694 |
| Tianmen | 1,676 |
| Shangqiu | 1,650 |
| Lu'an | 1,647 |
| Haikou | 1,624 |
| Qiqihar | 1,616 |
| Daqing | 1,603 |
| Yangzhou | 1,603 |
| Xinghua | 1,587 |
| Luoyang | 1,575 |
| Pingxiang | 1,562 |
| Yantai | 1,557 |
| Xiantao | 1,528 |
| Hohhot | 1,499 |
| Linyi | 1,454 |
| Xianyang | 1,450 |
| Luzhou | 1,447 |
| Neijiang | 1,441 |
| Huainan | 1,436 |
| Changde | 1,429 |
| Suining, Sichuan | 1,401 |
| Datong | 1,390 |
| Liuzhou | 1,390 |
| Fushun | 1,379 |
| Xintai | 1,334 |
| Yancheng | 1,330 |
| Heze | 1,318 |
| Yiyang | 1,318 |
| Huai'an | 1,316 |
| Handan | 1,306 |
| Tai'an | 1,276 |
| Suqian | 1,258 |
| Jining, Shandong | 1,246 |
| Chifeng | 1,238 |
| Jingmen | 1,228 |
| Nanyang | 1,227 |
| Yuzhou | 1,226 |
| Xining | 1,225 |
| Zaozhuang | 1,211 |
| Zaoyang | 1,210 |
| Tianshui | 1,199 |
| Yueyang | 1,184 |
| Yongzhou | 1,182 |
| Baoding | 1,177 |
| Mudanjiang | 1,171 |
| Liupanshui | 1,149 |
| Anyang | 1,144 |
| Leshan | 1,143 |
| Hengyang | 1,135 |
| Jiangmen | 1,130 |
| Xiaoshan | 1,130 |
| Yixing | 1,129 |
| Yinchuan | 1,119 |
| Quanzhou | 1,097 |
| Zigong | 1,087 |
| Putian | 1,084 |
| Zhangjiakou | 1,072 |
| Jinzhou | 1,070 |
| Fuyu | 1,068 |
| Jixi | 1,067 |
| Yulin | 1,060 |
| Mianyang | 1,052 |
| Zhuzhou | 1,047 |
| Xinyang | 1,045 |
| Pingdingshan | 1,041 |
| Zhanjiang | 1,041 |
| Xinyi, Jiangsu | 1,022 |
| Lianyungang | 1,017 |
| Linqing | 1,009 |
| Jiamusi | 1,006 |
| Xiangfan | 1,006 |
| Huaibei | 1,005 |
| Guilin | 992 |
| Dongying | 989 |
| Benxi | 980 |
| Xiangtan | 979 |
| Puning | 945 |
| Xiangxiang | 936 |
| Zhangjiagang | 936 |
| Baoji | 933 |
| Xinyu | 932 |
| Yichun, Heilongjiang | 916 |
| Qinhuangdao | 913 |
| Yichun, Jiangxi | 890 |
| Zhaotong | 879 |
| Yuyao | 876 |
| Jinzhou | 865 |
| Anshun | 864 |
| Shaoguan | 856 |
| Xuanzhou | 851 |
| **COLOMBIA** | |
| Bogotá | 8,743 |
| Medellín | 3,694 |
| Cali | 2,453 |
| Barranquilla | 1,900 |
| Bucaramanga | 1,120 |
| Cartagena | 988 |
| **CONGO** | |
| Brazzaville | 1,611 |
| **CONGO (DEM. REP. OF THE)** | |
| Kinshasa | 8,798 |
| Lubumbashi | 1,556 |
| Mbuji-Mayi | 1,504 |
| Kananga | 888 |
| **COSTA RICA** | |
| San José | 1,511 |
| **CROATIA** | |
| Zagreb | 1,067 |
| **CUBA** | |
| Havana | 2,116 |
| **CZECH REPUBLIC** | |
| Prague | 1,276 |
| **DENMARK** | |
| Copenhagen | 1,206 |
| **DOMINICAN REPUBLIC** | |
| Santo Domingo | 2,191 |
| Santiago de los Caballeros | 804 |
| **ECUADOR** | |
| Guayaquil | 2,287 |
| Quito | 1,622 |
| **EGYPT** | |
| Cairo | 11,169 |
| Alexandria | 4,494 |
| Shubrâ el Kheima | 937 |
| **EL SALVADOR** | |
| San Salvador | 1,605 |
| **ETHIOPIA** | |
| Addis Ababa | 2,979 |
| **FINLAND** | |
| Helsinki | 1,134 |
| **FRANCE** | |
| Paris | 10,620 |
| Marseilles | 1,489 |
| Lyons | 1,488 |
| Lille | 1,042 |
| Nice | 991 |
| Toulouse | 933 |
| Bordeaux | 852 |
| **GEORGIA** | |
| Tbilisi | 1,121 |
| **GERMANY** | |
| Berlin | 3,462 |
| Hamburg | 1,796 |
| Munich | 1,364 |
| Cologne | 1,006 |
| **GHANA** | |
| Accra | 2,573 |
| Kumasi | 2,019 |
| **GREECE** | |
| Athens | 3,414 |
| Thessaloniki | 883 |
| **GUATEMALA** | |
| Guatemala City | 1,168 |
| **GUINEA** | |
| Conakry | 1,786 |
| **HAITI** | |
| Port-au-Prince | 2,207 |
| **HONDURAS** | |
| Tegucigalpa | 1,088 |
| **HUNGARY** | |
| Budapest | 1,737 |
| **INDIA** | |
| Delhi | 22,654 |
| Mumbai | 19,744 |
| Kolkata | 14,402 |
| Chennai | 8,784 |
| Bangalore | 8,614 |
| Hyderabad | 7,837 |
| Ahmedabad | 6,425 |
| Pune | 5,100 |
| Surat | 4,661 |
| Jaipur | 3,102 |
| Kanpur | 2,928 |
| Lucknow | 2,926 |
| Nagpur | 2,511 |
| Indore | 2,188 |
| Coimbatore | 2,180 |
| Patna | 2,059 |
| Bhopal | 1,900 |
| Vadodara | 1,829 |
| Agra | 1,763 |
| Vishakhapatnam | 1,746 |
| Ludhiana | 1,622 |
| Kochi | 1,620 |
| Nashik | 1,579 |
| Vijayawada | 1,511 |
| Madurai | 1,472 |
| Varanasi | 1,443 |
| Meerut | 1,434 |
| Rajkot | 1,406 |
| Jamshedpur | 1,346 |
| Faridabad | 1,330 |
| Srinagar | 1,285 |
| Ghaziabad | 1,277 |
| Jabalpur | 1,273 |
| Asansol | 1,248 |
| Allahabad | 1,223 |
| Aurangabad | 1,201 |
| Dhanbad | 1,200 |
| Amritsar | 1,190 |
| Solapur | 1,155 |
| Jodhpur | 1,149 |
| Raipur | 1,140 |
| Ranchi | 1,137 |
| Gwalior | 1,111 |
| Guwahati | 1,075 |
| Bhilainagar-Durg | 1,069 |
| Chandigarh | 1,034 |
| Thiruvananthapuram | 1,030 |
| Tiruchchirapalli | 1,028 |
| Kota | 1,013 |
| Trivandrum | 1,010 |
| Calicut | 1,007 |
| Mysore | 991 |
| Bareilly | 990 |
| Tiruppur | 982 |
| Hubli-Dharwad | 950 |
| Salem | 925 |
| Aligarh | 919 |
| Moradabad | 900 |
| Bhubaneswar | 891 |
| Jalandhar | 880 |
| Bhiwandi | 859 |
| Jammu | 857 |
| **INDONESIA** | |
| Jakarta | 9,769 |
| Surabaya | 2,787 |
| Bandung | 2,429 |
| Medan | 2,118 |
| Semarang | 1,573 |
| Palembang | 1,455 |
| Makassar | 1,387 |
| Batam | 1,034 |
| Bogor | 978 |
| Pekanbaru | 955 |
| Bandar Lampung | 900 |
| Denpasar | 850 |
| **IRAN** | |
| Tehran | 7,304 |
| Mashhad | 2,713 |
| Karaj | 1,635 |
| Esfahan | 1,781 |
| Tabriz | 1,509 |
| Shiraz | 1,321 |
| Ahvaz | 1,082 |
| Qom | 1,065 |
| Kermanshah | 851 |
| **IRAQ** | |
| Baghdad | 6,036 |
| Mosul | 1,494 |
| Irbil | 1,039 |
| Basra | 942 |
| As Sulaymaniyah | 867 |
| **IRELAND** | |
| Dublin | 1,121 |
| **ISRAEL** | |
| Tel Aviv-Yafo | 3,381 |
| Haifa | 1,054 |
| **ITALY** | |
| Rome | 3,298 |
| Milan | 2,909 |
| Naples | 2,373 |
| Turin | 1,613 |
| Palermo | 915 |
| **IVORY COAST (CÔTE D'IVOIRE)** | |
| Abidjan | 4,288 |
| Yamoussoukro | 966 |
| **JAMAICA** | |
| Kingston | 875 |
| **JAPAN** | |
| Tokyo | 13,159 |
| Yokohama | 3,689 |
| Osaka | 2,665 |
| Nagoya | 2,264 |
| Sapporo | 1,916 |
| Kobe | 1,544 |
| Kyoto | 1,474 |
| Fukuoka | 1,463 |
| Kawasaki | 1,426 |
| Saitama | 1,222 |
| Hiroshima | 1,174 |
| Kitakyushu | 1,011 |
| Sendai | 1,008 |
| Hamamatsu | 1,000 |
| Naha | 970 |
| Chiba | 961 |
| **JORDAN** | |
| Amman | 1,179 |
| **KAZAKHSTAN** | |
| Almaty | 1,426 |
| **KENYA** | |
| Nairobi | 3,363 |
| Mombasa | 1,040 |
| **KOREA, NORTH** | |
| Pyŏngyang | 2,843 |
| **KOREA, SOUTH** | |
| Seoul | 9,888 |
| Busan | 3,372 |
| Incheon | 2,884 |
| Daegu | 2,447 |
| Daejeon | 1,538 |
| Gwangju | 1,503 |
| Seognam | 1,353 |
| Suwon | 1,159 |
| Ulsan | 1,100 |
| Goyang | 988 |
| Bucheon | 932 |
| **KUWAIT** | |
| Kuwait City | 2,406 |
| **LEBANON** | |
| Beirut | 2,022 |
| **LIBYA** | |
| Tripoli | 1,127 |
| Benghazi | 1,114 |
| **MADAGASCAR** | |
| Antananarivo | 1,987 |
| **MALAWI** | |
| Lilongwe | 870 |
| Blantyre | 860 |
| **MALAYSIA** | |
| Kuala Lumpur | 1,556 |
| Klang | 1,190 |
| Johore Bharu | 1,045 |
| **MALI** | |
| Bamako | 2,037 |
| **MEXICO** | |
| Mexico City | 20,446 |
| Guadalajara | 4,525 |
| Monterrey | 4,213 |
| Puebla | 2,335 |
| Tijuana | 1,820 |
| Toluca | 1,748 |
| León | 1,653 |
| Ciudad Juárez | 1,338 |
| Torreón | 1,242 |
| Querétaro | 1,143 |
| San Luis Potosí | 1,061 |
| Mérida | 1,040 |
| Aguascalientes | 957 |
| Mexicali | 957 |
| Acapulco | 883 |
| Chihuahua | 874 |
| **MONGOLIA** | |
| Ulan Bator | 1,184 |
| **MOROCCO** | |
| Casablanca | 3,046 |
| Rabat | 1,843 |
| Fès | 1,088 |
| Marrakesh | 939 |
| **MOZAMBIQUE** | |
| Maputo | 1,150 |
| **NEPAL** | |
| Katmandu | 1,015 |
| **NETHERLANDS** | |
| Amsterdam | 1,056 |
| Rotterdam | 1,014 |
| **NEW ZEALAND** | |
| Auckland | 1,452 |
| **NICARAGUA** | |
| Managua | 1,165 |
| **NIGER** | |
| Niamey | 1,297 |
| **NIGERIA** | |
| Lagos | 11,223 |
| Kano | 3,375 |
| Ibadan | 2,949 |
| Abuja | 2,153 |
| Port Harcourt | 1,894 |
| Kaduna | 1,524 |
| Benin City | 1,359 |
| Ogbomosho | 1,075 |
| Aba | 866 |
| Maiduguri | 851 |
| **NORWAY** | |
| Oslo | 915 |
| **PAKISTAN** | |
| Karachi | 13,876 |
| Lahore | 7,566 |
| Faisalabad | 3,038 |
| Rawalpindi | 2,026 |
| Multan | 1,775 |
| Gujranwala | 1,767 |
| Hyderabad | 1,701 |
| Peshawar | 1,523 |
| Quetta | 903 |
| Islamabad | 856 |
| **PANAMA** | |
| Panamá | 1,426 |
| **PARAGUAY** | |
| Asunción | 2,139 |
| **PERU** | |
| Lima | 9,130 |
| **PHILIPPINES** | |
| Manila | 11,862 |
| Davao | 1,565 |
| Zamboanga | 884 |
| Cebu | 855 |
| **POLAND** | |
| Warsaw | 1,723 |
| Lódz | 910 |
| **PORTUGAL** | |
| Lisbon | 2,843 |
| Porto | 1,367 |
| **PUERTO RICO** | |
| San Juan | 2,475 |
| **ROMANIA** | |
| Bucharest | 1,937 |
| **RUSSIA** | |
| Moscow | 11,621 |
| St Petersburg | 4,866 |
| Novosibirsk | 1,478 |
| Yekaterinburg | 1,355 |
| Nizhniy Novgorod | 1,245 |
| Samara | 1,166 |
| Omsk | 1,156 |
| Kazan | 1,147 |
| Chelyabinsk | 1,135 |
| Rostov | 1,092 |
| Ufa | 1,064 |
| Volgograd | 1,022 |
| Perm | 991 |
| Krasnoyarsk | 980 |
| Voronezh | 894 |
| **RWANDA** | |
| Kigali | 1,004 |
| **SAUDI ARABIA** | |
| Riyadh | 5,451 |
| Jedda | 3,578 |
| Mecca | 1,591 |
| Medina | 1,142 |
| Dammam | 941 |
| **SENEGAL** | |
| Dakar | 3,035 |
| **SERBIA** | |
| Belgrade | 1,135 |
| **SIERRA LEONE** | |
| Freetown | 1,007 |
| **SINGAPORE** | |
| Singapore City | 5,188 |
| **SOMALIA** | |
| Mogadishu | 1,554 |
| **SOUTH AFRICA** | |
| Johannesburg | 3,844 |
| Cape Town | 3,562 |
| Durban | 3,012 |
| Pretoria | 1,501 |
| Vereeniging | 1,200 |
| Port Elizabeth | 1,119 |
| **SPAIN** | |
| Madrid | 6,574 |
| Barcelona | 5,570 |
| **SRI LANKA** | |
| Colombo | 2,115 |
| **SUDAN** | |
| Khartoum | 4,632 |
| **SWEDEN** | |
| Stockholm | 1,385 |
| **SWITZERLAND** | |
| Zürich | 1,194 |
| **SYRIA** | |
| Aleppo | 3,164 |
| Damascus | 2,650 |
| Homs | 1,369 |
| Hamah | 933 |
| **TAIWAN** | |
| Taipei | 2,730 |
| Kaohsiung | 1,560 |
| T'aichung | 1,244 |
| Tainan | 1,205 |
| **TANZANIA** | |
| Dar es Salaam | 3,588 |
| **THAILAND** | |
| Bangkok | 8,426 |
| Samut Prakan | 1,212 |
| **TOGO** | |
| Lomé | 1,524 |
| **TUNISIA** | |
| Tunis | 2,385 |
| **TURKEY** | |
| Istanbul | 11,253 |
| Ankara | 4,194 |
| Izmir | 2,927 |
| Bursa | 1,713 |
| Adana | 1,468 |
| Gaziantep | 1,198 |
| Konya | 1,057 |
| Antalya | 907 |
| **UGANDA** | |
| Kampala | 1,659 |
| **UKRAINE** | |
| Kiev | 2,829 |
| Kharkov | 1,451 |
| Dnepropetrovsk | 1,100 |
| Odessa | 1,010 |
| Donetsk | 959 |
| **UNITED ARAB EMIRATES** | |
| Dubai | 1,978 |
| Abu Dhabi | 942 |
| Sharjah | 983 |
| **UNITED KINGDOM** | |
| London | 9,005 |
| Birmingham | 2,272 |
| Manchester | 2,213 |
| Liverpool | 1,519 |
| Glasgow | 1,137 |
| Newcastle-upon-Tyne | 874 |
| **UNITED STATES OF AMERICA** | |
| New York | 19,016 |
| Los Angeles | 12,945 |
| Chicago | 9,505 |
| Dallas–Fort Worth | 6,527 |
| Houston | 6,087 |
| Philadelphia | 5,992 |
| Washington, DC | 5,704 |
| Miami | 5,670 |
| Atlanta | 5,359 |
| Boston | 4,591 |
| San Francisco | 4,391 |
| San Bernardino | 4,305 |
| Detroit | 4,286 |
| Phoenix–Mesa | 4,263 |
| Seattle | 3,500 |
| Minneapolis–St Paul | 3,318 |
| San Diego | 3,140 |
| Tampa–St Petersburg | 2,825 |
| St Louis | 2,817 |
| Baltimore | 2,729 |
| Denver | 2,600 |
| Pittsburgh | 2,360 |
| Portland | 2,263 |
| San Antonio | 2,195 |
| Sacramento | 2,176 |
| Orlando | 2,171 |
| Cincinnati | 2,138 |
| Cleveland | 2,068 |
| Kansas City | 2,053 |
| Las Vegas | 1,970 |
| San Jose | 1,865 |
| Columbus | 1,858 |
| Charlotte | 1,795 |
| Austin | 1,784 |
| Indianapolis | 1,779 |
| Norfolk–Virginia Beach | 1,680 |
| Nashville | 1,617 |
| Providence | 1,600 |
| Milwaukee | 1,562 |
| Jacksonville | 1,360 |
| Memphis | 1,326 |
| Louisville | 1,295 |
| Oklahoma | 1,278 |
| Richmond | 1,269 |
| Hartford | 1,213 |
| New Orleans | 1,191 |
| Raleigh | 1,163 |
| Salt Lake City | 1,145 |
| Buffalo | 1,134 |
| Birmingham | 1,132 |
| Rochester | 1,055 |
| Tucson | 989 |
| Honolulu | 964 |
| Tulsa | 947 |
| Fresno | 943 |
| Stamford | 926 |
| Albuquerque | 899 |
| Omaha | 877 |
| Albany | 871 |
| New Haven | 861 |
| **URUGUAY** | |
| Montevideo | 1,672 |
| **UZBEKISTAN** | |
| Tashkent | 2,227 |
| **VENEZUELA** | |
| Caracas | 3,242 |
| Maracaibo | 2,310 |
| Valencia | 1,866 |
| Barquisimeto | 1,245 |
| Maracay | 1,115 |
| **VIETNAM** | |
| Ho Chi Minh City | 6,405 |
| Hanoi | 2,955 |
| Can Tho | 1,004 |
| Haiphong | 925 |
| **YEMEN** | |
| Sana' | 2,419 |
| **ZAMBIA** | |
| Lusaka | 1,802 |
| **ZIMBABWE** | |
| Harare | 1,542 |

# THE FUTURE OF THE OCEANS AND SEAS

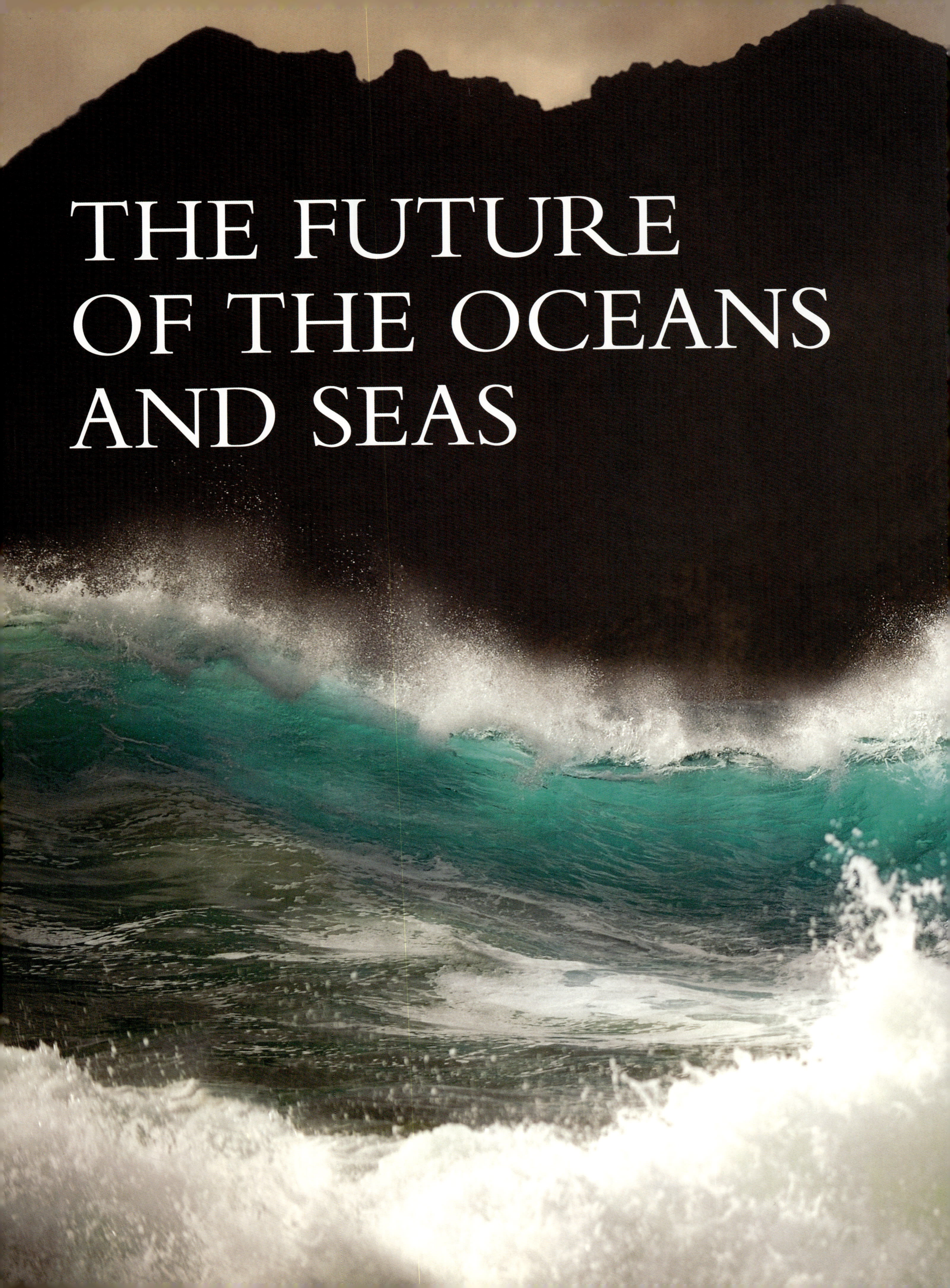

The past 50 years have been described by some as the 'Space Age'. However, another exciting and perhaps even more important area of discovery, proceeding at the same time, has been the start of the exploration and our understanding and appreciation of the oceans, which cover more than 70% of our planet. Ironically, during the same time frame, we have developed global technologies which, used carelessly, will cause irreparable damage to this massive ecosystem. The following pages provide an overview and highlight some of the major issues facing the future of our oceans and seas today.

**For more information:**


79 Temperature and precipitation
80 Climate change and global warming
82 Water distribution
86 Population
98 Minerals


Oceans cover about 70% of the Earth's surface and are of great importance to humans in a number of ways. These include regulating global climates and providing a source of economic materials, such as food resources. In addition, oceans are important for leisure and recreation. They have also been described as the 'highways in the globalized world'. However, anthropogenic (man-made) stresses are changing the oceans faster than at almost any time in our planet's history.

## TEMPERATURE

Temperature varies considerably at the surface of the ocean but there is little variation at depth. In tropical and subtropical areas, sea-surface temperatures in excess of 25°C [77°F] are caused by the warming effects of the Sun, called 'insolation'. From about 300 m to 1,000 m [1,000–3,000 ft] the temperature declines steeply to about 8–10°C [46–50°F]. Below 1,000 m [3,000 ft] the temperature decreases to a more uniform 2°C [36°F].

The temperature profile is similar in the mid-latitudes, although there are clear seasonal variations. Summer temperatures may reach 17°C [63°F], whereas winter sea temperatures are closer to 10°C [50°F]. There is a more gradual decrease in temperature with depth (know as the 'thermocline'). In high latitudes and polar oceans, sea-surface temperatures range between 0°C and 5°C [32–41°F]. In some cases the temperature may be below freezing, but the water does not freeze because of its salinity. Below the surface it reaches the uniform temperature of 2°C [36°F] in the deep ocean.

Temperature, salinity and pressure affect the density of sea water. Large water masses of different densities are important in the layering of the ocean water (the denser water sinks). As temperature increases, water becomes less dense, but as salinity and pressure increase, water becomes more dense. A cold, highly saline, deep mass of water is therefore very dense, whereas a warm, less saline, surface water mass is less dense. When large water masses with different densities meet, the denser water mass slips under the less dense mass. These responses to density are the reason for some of the deep-ocean circulation models.

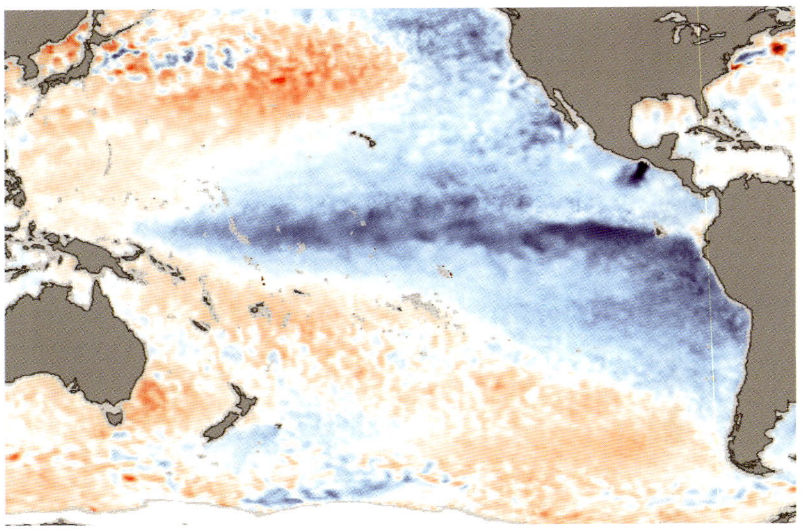

▲ The development of the global monitoring of sea temperatures using satellites within the last 30 years has revolutionized our understanding of the mechanics of the ocean circulatory systems and our ability to predict quite large changes in weather, on a continental scale. This image, derived from data collected by NASA's 'Aqua' satellite in November 2007, clearly shows the cool, blue tongue of 'La Niña' extending from the Pacific coast of South America across to Papua New Guinea and Indonesia. The colours show the 'temperature anomaly' – that is, the amount by which the actual temperatures deviate from previously collected long-term averages for the same date. *(See also the diagram on page 11, opposite.)*

## SALINITY

The predominant minerals in sea water are chloride (54.3%) and sodium (30.2%), which combine to form salt. Oceanic water varies in its salinity and temperature. The average salinity is about 35 parts per thousand (ppt). Concentrations of salt are higher in warm seas, due to the high rates of evaporation of water. In these areas, the commercial production of salt by evaporation is often found and is an important part of the local economy. The freezing and thawing of ice also affects salinity, so the thawing of large icebergs decreases the ocean's salinity.

► Salt collection from evaporation pans near Nha Trang, Vietnam. The pans are flooded and the sea water left to evaporate, producing raw sea salt.

## OCEANIC CONVEYOR BELTS

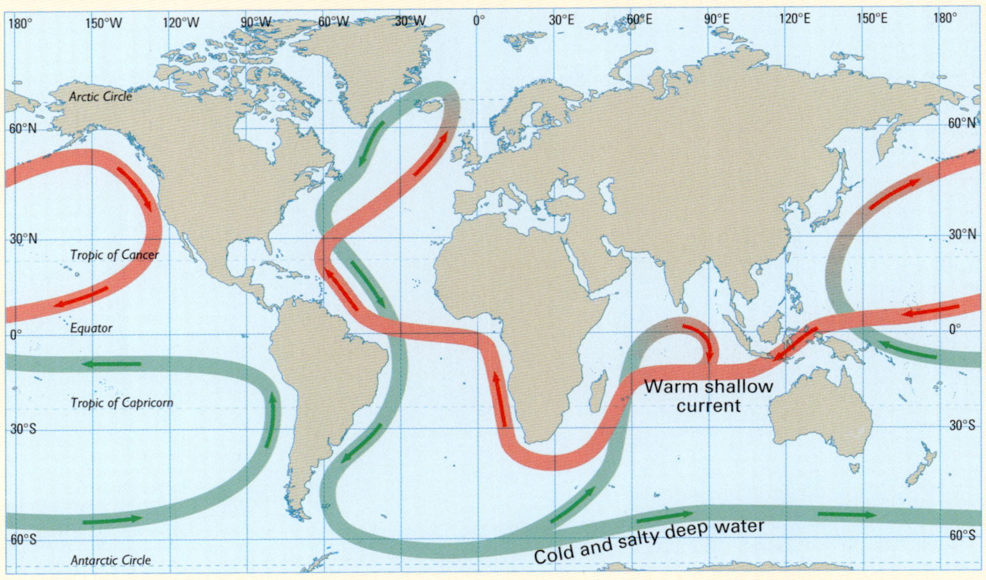
180°
150°W
120°W
90°W
60°W
30°W
0°
30°E
60°E
90°E
120°E
150°E
180°
Arctic Circle
60°N
30°N
Tropic of Cancer
Equator
0°
Tropic of Capricorn
30°S
60°S
Antarctic Circle
Warm shallow current
Cold and salty deep water

Oceanic convection occurs where cold, salty water from polar regions sinks into the depths and makes its way towards the Equator. The densest water is found in the Antarctic area. This cold, dense water sweeps round Antarctica at a depth of about 4 km [2.5 miles]. It then spreads into the deep basins of the Atlantic Ocean, the Pacific Ocean, and the Indian Ocean. Surface currents bring warm water to the North Atlantic from the Indian and Pacific Oceans. These waters give up their heat to cold winds, which blow from Canada across the North Atlantic. This water then sinks and starts the reverse convection of the deep ocean current. The amount of heat given up is about a third of the energy that is received from the Sun. Because the conveyor operates in this way, the North Atlantic is warmer than the North Pacific, so there is proportionally more evaporation there. The water left behind by evaporation contains more salt and it is therefore much denser, which causes it to sink. Eventually, this water is transported into the Pacific Ocean where it picks up more warm water, and thus its salinity and therefore its density is reduced.

## INCREASING PROBLEMS FOR AUSTRALIA'S COASTAL ZONE

Up to 80% of Australians live by the coast. A recent parliamentary report said that US $156 billion worth of property was at risk from rising sea levels and more frequent storms. If sea levels rise by 80 cm [32 in] by 2100, some 711,000 homes, businesses and properties, which sit less than 6 m [20 ft] above sea level and lie within 3 km [2 miles] of the coast, will be vulnerable to flooding, erosion, high tides, and surging storms. The report argued that Australia needs a national policy to respond to sea-level rise brought on by global warming, which could see people forced to abandon homes and banned from building at the beachside. Some estimates predict a 1–2 m [3–6.5 ft] sea-level rise by 2100. The state of Queensland is considered the most at risk, with almost 250,000 buildings vulnerable.

► Coral bleaching (*far right*) occurs when there is a breakdown in the relationship between corals and the microscopic plants that live within their tissue. These plants provide food to the corals and give them their normal healthy colour (*right*). When corals are stressed, they expel these plants, and their corals begin to starve, and their white skeletons become visible. Global climate change may play a role in the increase in coral bleaching and could cause the destruction of major reef tracts such as the Great Barrier Reef, Australia, and the extinction of many coral species. In 1998, a rise in sea temperatures caused by El Niño led to a mass bleaching of the world's coral reefs. Up to 90% of the Indian Ocean's reefs were bleached as a result.

## OCEANS AND CARBON DIOXIDE

**Typical air and sea circulation pattern (La Niña)**

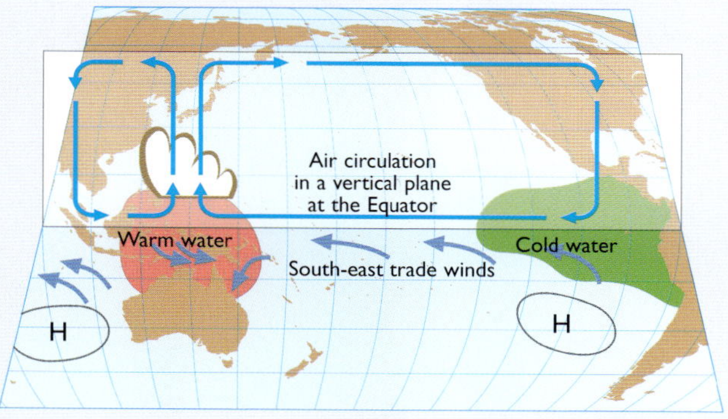
Air circulation
in a vertical plane
at the Equator
Warm water
Cold water
South-east trade winds
H
H

**El Niño air and sea circulation pattern**

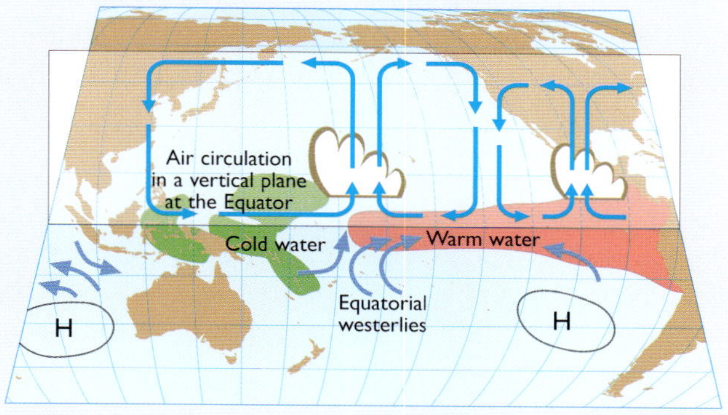
Air circulation
in a vertical plane
at the Equator
Cold water
Warm water
Equatorial
westerlies
H
H

The oceans store a thousand times more heat than the atmosphere and transport enormous amounts of it around the globe. In consequence, they are largely responsible for determining the climate on land. The warm Gulf Stream washing up from the Tropics in the Atlantic Ocean keeps Europe many degrees warmer in winter than the Hudson Bay on the opposite side of the ocean. The oscillation between El Niño and La Niña currents in the tropical Pacific Ocean fundamentally changes the weather across the ocean, flipping Indonesia, Australia, and coastal South America into and out of droughts and floods.

However, all these processes now face disruption from the global scale of human activity, particularly climate change. Currently, the oceans moderate climate change by absorbing a third of the carbon dioxide emitted into the air by human activity, the equivalent of some 2 billion tonnes of carbon. But several studies suggest that global warming will stratify the oceans and reduce their capacity to act as a carbon dioxide 'sink' by 10% to 20% over the next century, accelerating warming.

Until now, the sea has been a buffer against global warming because the heat capacity of water is several times that of air. The oceans have absorbed most of the additional heat, sparing the continents further warming. One effect of the warming ocean, for example, is to increase the density difference between the water surface and the chilly deep, which in turn decreases the mixing of them. This means that less oxygen is making its way down to the depths, reducing the liveability of the oceans. Off the west coast of North America, the upper limit of low-oxygen water is thought to have risen by 100 m [330 ft] in recent years. Where strong winds bring this water nearer to the surface, there are mass die-offs of marine life.

Fish that are under temperature and oxygen stress will reach smaller sizes, will live less long, and will have to devote a bigger fraction of their energy to survival at the cost of growth and reproduction.

## OCEANS AND RESOURCES

Oceans contain a variety of resources. *Biotic resources* are living ones, such as fish and plant life; *abiotic resources* are non-living resources, such as oil. Salt water contains nutrients and minerals, such as salt, magnesia and phosphates, some of which can be recovered when it is converted into fresh water. Oil and gas deposits are found under the continental shelf. The Persian Gulf accounts for 66% of the world's proven oil reserves and 33% of the world's proven gas reserves, while the continental shelf area of the Gulf of Mexico has been explored and developed since the 1940s.

The continental shelf contains sediments such as gravel, sand and mud. These come from the erosion of rocks and transport by rivers to the sea. Diamonds can be found in the continental shelf areas off Africa and Indonesia, while gold and manganese are found on the ocean floor. Ocean-floor sediments are formed of sand, mud and silt. Authigenic sediments are precipitates of chemicals, such as iron oxide, from sea water, in forms such as manganese nodules, which are fist-sized and located on the deep-sea abyssal plain.

Near ocean ridges and rift valleys are rich deposits of sulphur, some associated with hydrothermal vents ('black smokers'). In the future, the biological riches of 'black smokers' face threats from deep-sea mining. The mid-ocean hot springs spew out potentially valuable metal sulphides, such as gold, silver and copper. In the cold water, they are deposited in thick crusts, attracting exploitation. Rights have already been given to prospect for metals on 4,000 sq km [1,500 sq mi] of the Bismarck Sea bed, north of Papua New Guinea.

The oceans provide a valuable supply of fish. The worldwide harvest of fish was 5 million tonnes in 1900 and around 90 million tonnes in 2012. Fish account for about 10% of the protein eaten by people, and it is the only major food source still gathered from the wild.

## OCEAN CURRENTS

**JANUARY CURRENTS**
**(Northern Hemisphere: winter)**

| Cold | Warm | Speed (knots) |
| --- | --- | --- |
| | | Less than 0.5 |
| | | 0.5 – 1.0 |
| | | Over 1.0 |

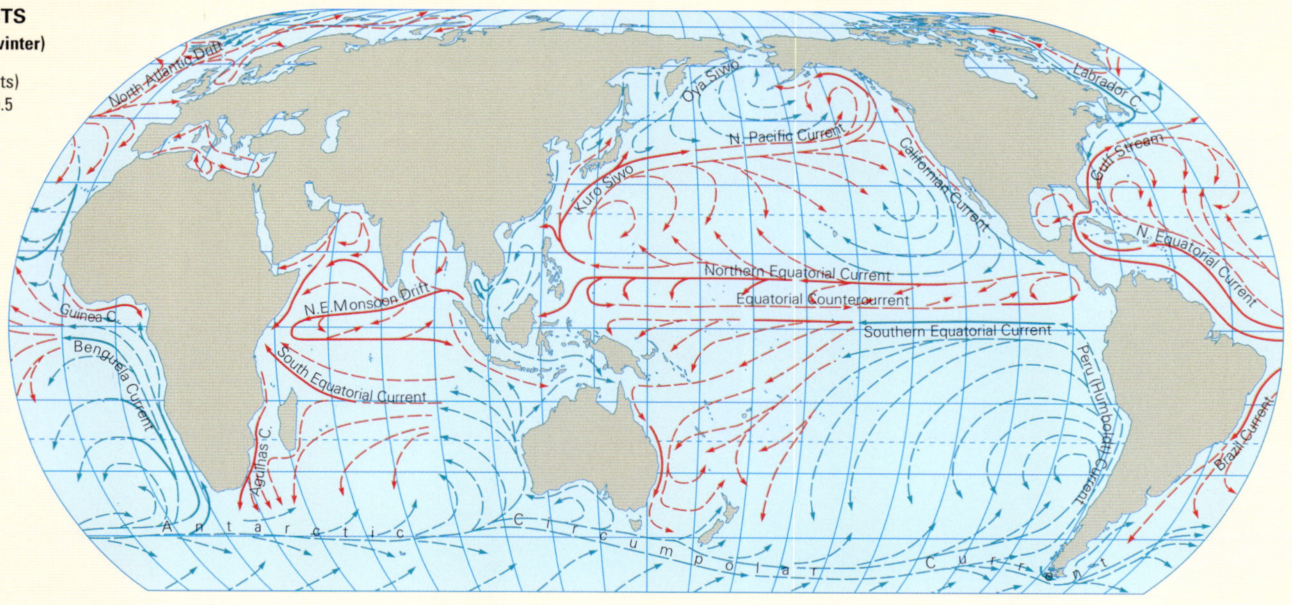
North Atlantic Drift
Oya Siwo
N. Pacific Current
Labrador C.
Kuro Siwo
Californian Current
Gulf Stream
N. Equatorial Current
Northern Equatorial Current
Equatorial Countercurrent
N.E.Monsoon Drift
Guinea C.
Southern Equatorial Current
Benguela Current
South Equatorial Current
Peru (Humboldt) Current
Brazil Current
Agulhas C.
Antarctic Circumpolar Current

**JULY CURRENTS**
**(Northern Hemisphere: summer)**

| Cold | Warm | Speed (knots) |
| --- | --- | --- |
| | | Less than 0.5 |
| | | 0.5 – 1.0 |
| | | Over 1.0 |

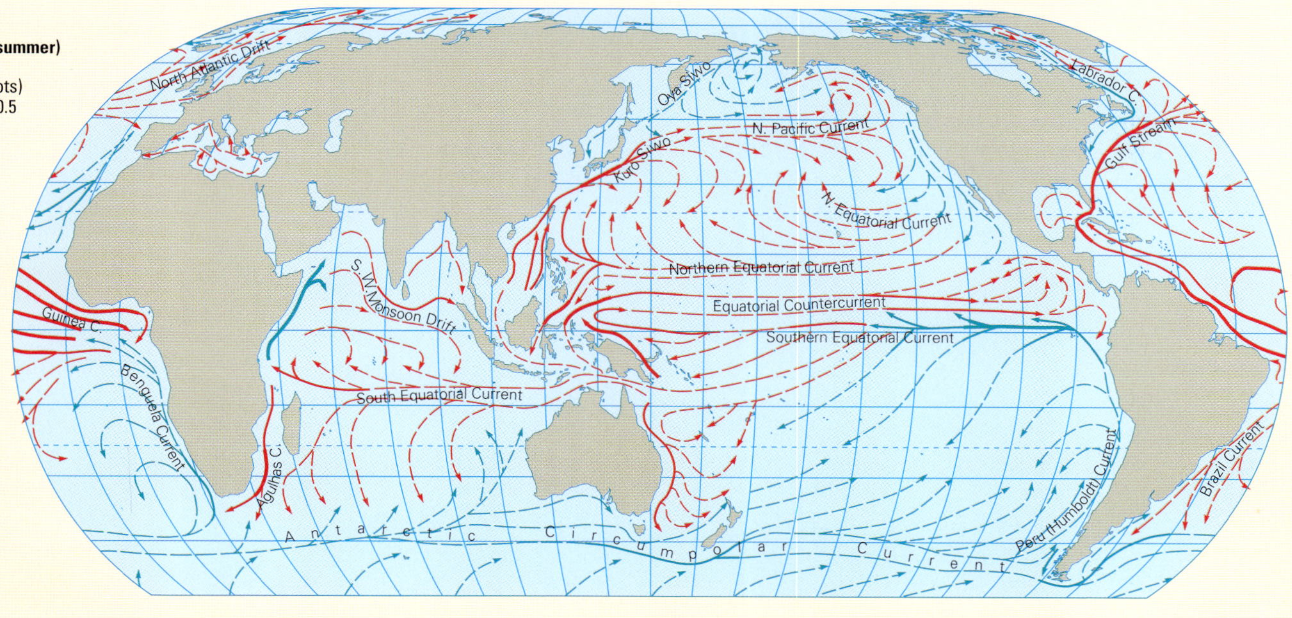
North Atlantic Drift
Oya Siwo
N. Pacific Current
Labrador C.
Kuro Siwo
Gulf Stream
N. Equatorial Current
Northern Equatorial Current
S.W. Monsoon Drift
Equatorial Countercurrent
Guinea C.
Southern Equatorial Current
South Equatorial Current
Benguela Current
Agulhas C.
Peru (Humboldt) Current
Brazil Current
Antarctic Circumpolar Current

Moving immense quantities of energy as well as billions of tonnes of water every hour, the ocean currents are a vital part of the great heat engine that drives the Earth's climate. They themselves are produced by a twofold mechanism. At the surface, winds push huge masses of water before them; in the deep ocean below, an abrupt temperature gradient separates the churning surface waters from the still depths (*see the ocean conveyor belt diagram on the facing page*).

**Coriolis effect**

The pattern of circulation of the great surface currents is determined by the displacement known as the 'Coriolis effect'. As the Earth turns, the vast mass of ocean water is deflected to one side. The deflection is most obvious near the Equator, where the Earth's surface is spinning eastwards at 1,700 km/h; currents moving polewards are curved clockwise in the northern hemisphere and anticlockwise in the southern hemisphere.

**Ocean currents**

The result is a system of spinning circles known as 'gyres'. Warm currents move constantly from the Equator towards the poles, while cold water moves in the reverse direction. In this way, ocean currents act like a thermostat, helping to regulate temperatures around the world.

Depending on the annual movements of the prevailing wind belts, some currents on or near the Equator may reverse their direction in the course of the year, a variation on which Asia's monsoon rains depend and whose occasional failure has brought disaster to millions of people.

**For more information:**
82 Water distribution
83 Natural vegetation
84 Biodiversity and the natural world

Increasingly larger fishing fleets are now catching fewer large predatory fish but greater quantities of the smaller fish that are further down the food chain. The most prized food fish, such as cod and salmon, which tend to be top-level predators, are declining in numbers, leaving smaller, less desirable fish to be caught. Not only does this affect the type of fish available for human consumption, but it could also change marine ecosystems forever.

World fish stocks have declined rapidly – some species have even become extinct. Oceans have lost up to 75% of their megafauna (animals such as whales, dolphins, sharks, rays and turtles). Up to 99% of the stock of American sawfish, members of the ray family, and the 'common' skate of northern Europe have disappeared. With more and more ships chasing fewer fish, prices have risen sharply. Despite many attempts to rescue the fishing industry, for example through quotas and bans, there has been little success.

Nearly 70% of the world's fish stocks are in need of management. Cod stocks in the North Sea are now at less than 10% of the 1970 levels, and more than half of the fish consumed in Europe is now imported. A World Bank and FAO (Food and Agriculture Organization) report in 2008 showed that up to US $50 billion per year is lost in poor management, inefficiency and overfishing in world fisheries.

There are a number of possible strategies for the future, but there are clearly no simple solutions to the problems associated with such a politically, economically, and environmentally sensitive global industry. Fish resources could be conserved in a number of ways – for example, the protection of juveniles as well as policies to encourage breeding and discourage the marketing of illegal catches would help boost stocks. Catches could be restricted in order to match supply with demand and to protect sensitive species. The number of vessels allowed to fish could also be limited. In addition, improved surveillance could monitor landings by vessels, with owners fined for overfishing and illegal landings. Restrictions could be placed on imports. Imposing license fees might restrict the number of vessels, although this is likely to affect the smaller fishing boats rather than the large factory fishing boats.

## DEAD ZONES AND RED TIDES

There are increasingly frequent appearances of dead zones and red tides affecting our oceans. *Dead zones* are areas in the ocean where the water at the bottom is almost completely devoid of oxygen, so marine life suffocates. *Red tides* (or algal bloom) are fed by nutrients brought up from the deep, and regularly form off the Cape coast of South Africa, for example. Nowadays, though, most are associated with a combination of phenomena including overfishing, warmer waters and, often, the washing into the sea of farm fertilizers and sewage.

In shallow coastal waters, as the larger species disappear, so the smaller ones thrive. These smaller organisms are also stimulated by nitrogen and phosphorous nutrients running off the land. The result is an explosion of growth among phytoplankton and other algae, some of which die, sink to the bottom and decompose, combining with dissolved oxygen as they rot. Warmer conditions, and sometimes the loss of mangroves and marshes that once acted as filters, encourage the growth of bacteria in these oxygen-depleted waters.

Red tides do not necessarily last long, nor do they cover much of the surface of the sea. But they are increasing in both size and number – dead zones have now been reported in more than 400 areas. And, increasingly, they affect not only estuaries and inlets, but also continental seas such as the Baltic, the Black and East China Seas, and the Gulf of Mexico. All of these are traditional fishing grounds.

▼ The image below in some ways typifies the problems of regulating fish catches. It was taken in the eastern Mediterranean and shows a Turkish fishing vessel, on the left, unloading its catch of bluefin tunas on to a Japanese factory ship. This threatened species is highly prized in the Far East, where there is now increased demand from China, which makes it the world's most valuable fish. Consequently, this makes international quota controls very difficult to enforce. As the fish become scarcer, their value to the fishermen increases.

## WASTE MATERIAL

The oceans, like the atmosphere, are fundamental to the health of our planet. They dominate many of its cycling processes as well as being the ultimate sink for a variety of pollutants. For example, they disperse an estimated 3 million tonnes of oil spilled or dumped annually from ships and, predominantly, from sources on land.

Over 80% of marine pollution comes from land-based activities. The most toxic waste material dumped into the world's oceans includes dredged material, industrial waste, sewage sludge, and radioactive waste. About 20–22% of dredged material is dumped into the ocean, and dredging contributes about 80% of all waste dumped. Approximately 10% of all dredged material is polluted with heavy metals such as cadmium, mercury and chromium, hydrocarbons such as heavy oils, nutrients including phosphorous and nitrogen, and organochlorines from pesticides. When waste is dumped, it is often close to the coast and very concentrated. Alternatives to ocean dumping include recycling, producing less wasteful products, saving energy, and changing the dangerous material into more benign waste.

Radioactive effluent also makes its way into the oceans. Between 1958 and 1992, the Arctic Ocean was used by the Soviet Union, or its Russian successor, as the resting place for 18 unwanted nuclear reactors, several still containing their nuclear fuel. Radioactive waste is also dumped in the oceans and usually comes from the nuclear power process, medical use of radioisotopes, research use of radioisotopes, and industrial uses. Following the Japanese earthquake and tsunami in March 2011, radiation from the damaged Fukushima Daiichi nuclear power station was transferred by ocean currents towards Canada and the USA.

## FISHING

As stocks are overfished and dwindle, it is important to manage them carefully so that there are sufficient resources for future generations. The Marine Stewardship Council (MSC) is an international, non-profit organization set up to help make the seafood market sustainable. It oversees and manages the distinctive blue labelling system that tells consumers which species of fish they can buy without destroying stocks. This system is popular with large food retailers who wish to be seen supporting sustainable fish catches. It is estimated that over 23% of shoppers worldwide recognize the MSC eco-label. However, only 7% of the world's fisheries are MSC certified.

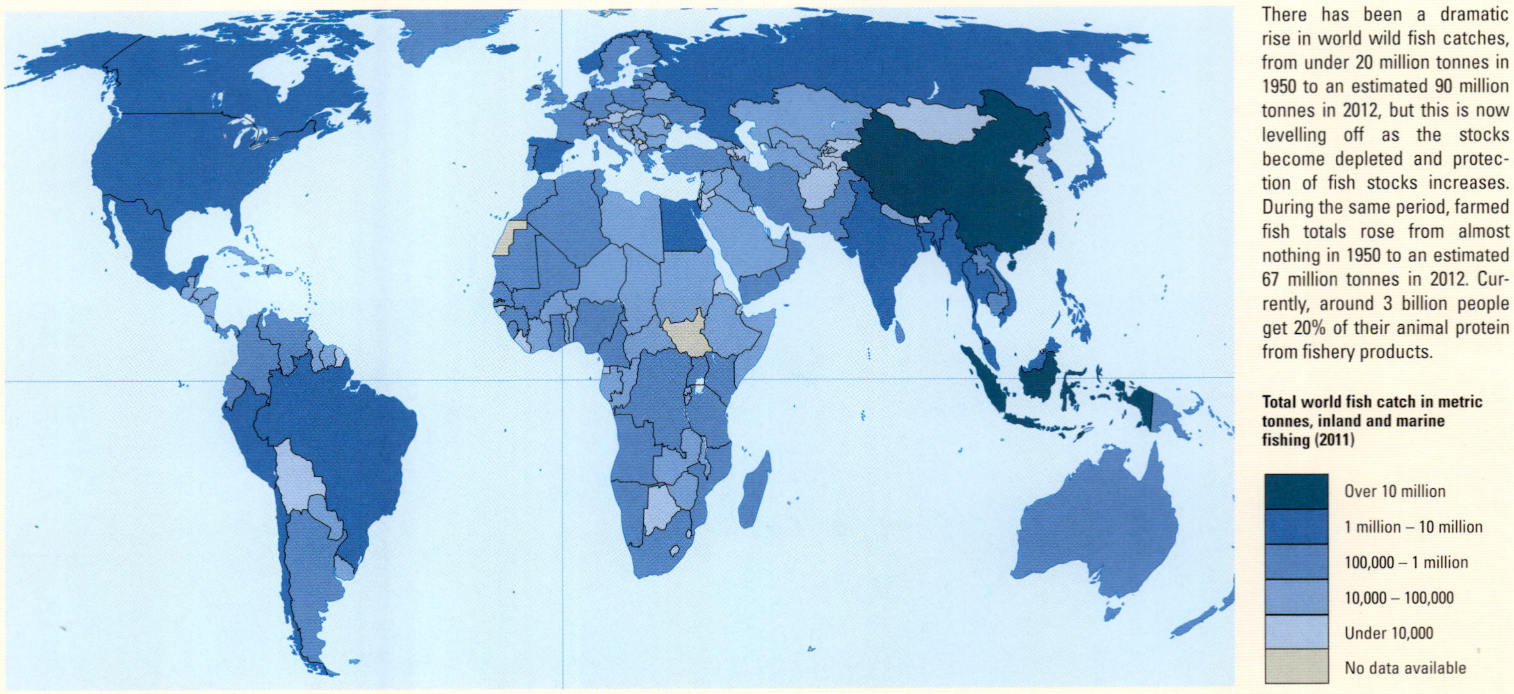
Total world fish catch in metric tonnes, inland and marine fishing (2011)
Over 10 million
1 million – 10 million
100,000 – 1 million
10,000 – 100,000
Under 10,000
No data available

There has been a dramatic rise in world wild fish catches, from under 20 million tonnes in 1950 to an estimated 90 million tonnes in 2012, but this is now levelling off as the stocks become depleted and protection of fish stocks increases. During the same period, farmed fish totals rose from almost nothing in 1950 to an estimated 67 million tonnes in 2012. Currently, around 3 billion people get 20% of their animal protein from fishery products.

## AQUACULTURE

▲ This satellite image shows the rectangular shrimp ponds by the Gulf of Fonseca in Honduras, where large quantities of shrimp are bred for the worldwide market.

Aquaculture involves raising fish commercially, usually for food. In contrast, a fish hatchery releases juvenile fish into the wild for recreational fishing or to supplement a species' natural numbers. The most important fish species raised by fish farms are salmon, carp, tilapia, catfish and cod. Salmon makes up 85% of the total sale of Norwegian fish farming. Farming was introduced when populations of wild Atlantic salmon in the North Atlantic and Baltic Sea crashed due to overfishing.

Technological costs are high, and include using drugs, such as antibiotics to keep fish healthy and steroids to improve growth. Breeding programmes are also expensive. Outputs are high per hectare and per farmer, and efficiency is high also. However, environmental effects can be damaging. Salmon are carnivores and so need to be fed pellets made from other fish. It is possible that farmed salmon actually represent a net loss of protein in the global food supply, as it takes between 2–5 kg [4–11 lbs] of wild fish to grow 1 kg [2 lbs] of salmon. In contrast, most global aquaculture production (*c.* 85%) uses non-carnivorous fish species, such as tilapia and catfish, for domestic markets. Fish like herring, mackerel, sardine and anchovy are used to produce the feed for farmed salmon, and so the production of salmon leads to the depletion of other fish species on a global scale.

Other environmental costs include the sea lice and disease that spread from farmed salmon into wild stocks, and pollution (created by uneaten food, faeces, and chemicals used to treat them) contaminating surrounding waters. Organic debris of this type, with steroids and other chemical waste, can contaminate coastal waters. In addition, the accidental escape of fish can affect local wild fish gene pools, when escaped fish interbreed with wild populations, reducing their genetic diversity, and potentially introducing non-natural genetic variation. In some parts of the world, escapees of farmed fish threaten native wild fish, as salmon is an alien species (for example, the salmon farming industry in British Columbia, Canada, has inadvertently introduced a non-native species – Atlantic salmon – into the Pacific Ocean).

However, the positive environmental benefits of not removing fish from wild stocks, but of growing them in farms, are great. Wild populations are allowed to breed and maintain stocks, whilst the farmed variety provides food.

## OCEAN ACIDIFICATION

Carbon dioxide, which is absorbed by the sea from the atmosphere, turns to carbonic acid, which is a threat to coral, mussels, oysters, and all animals with a shell formed of calcium carbonate.

The oceans are thought to have absorbed about half of the extra carbon dioxide put into the atmosphere during the industrial age. This has lowered its pH by 0.1. Sea water is mildly alkaline with a 'natural' pH of about 8.2. The Intergovernmental Panel on Climate Change (IPCC) forecasts that ocean pH will fall by 'between 0.14 and 0.35 units over the 21st century', adding to the present decrease of 0.1 units since pre-industrial times.

More acidic oceans are beginning to kill off coral reefs and shellfish beds, as well as threatening stocks of fish. Scientists estimate that oceans absorb around a million tonnes of carbon dioxide every hour. As a result, they are now 30% more acidic than they were in the last century.

Early warning signs that have been noticed include:

- the failure of commercial oyster and other shellfish beds on the Pacific coasts of the USA and Canada;
- coral reefs – already bleached by rising global temperatures – have suffered disintegration in many regions;
- at the poles and high latitudes, tiny shellfish called pteropods (the basis of the food chain for fish, whales and seabirds) have suffered noticeable drops in numbers.

Ocean acidification is thought to be involved in all three of these changes.

## RESPONSES TO THE THREATS

In the case of the oceans, a conservative estimate of the cost of climate change is that by the year 2100 it will amount to nearly US $2 trillion annually, or about 0.4% of global GDP. Economists at the Stockholm Environment Institute arrived at the figure by looking at five measures: how much fisheries and tourism stood to lose, and what the economic impact would be of rising sea levels, more storms, and less carbon being absorbed by the oceans.

If the world continues to warm at its present rate and temperatures rise by 4°C [7.2°F] by 2100, the total will come to US $1.98 trillion. However, if drastic measures are taken to cut emissions and they rise by only 2.2°C [4°F], this figure will be US $612 billion. Governments worldwide were urged by the 1972 Stockholm Convention to control the dumping of waste in their oceans by implementing new laws. The United Nations met in London after this recommendation to begin the Convention on the Prevention of Marine Pollution by Dumping of Wastes and Other Matter, which was implemented in 1975. The International Maritime Organization was given responsibility for this convention and a Protocol was finally adopted in 1996, a major step in the regulation of ocean dumping.

The United Nations Convention on the Law of the Sea, signed in 1982 but only entering into force in 1994, established a framework of law for the oceans, including rules for deep-sea mining and economic exclusion zones extending 200 nautical miles around nation states.

## OIL

All over the world, oil spills regularly contaminate coasts. The threats vary, but there is growing evidence of widespread toxic effects on benthic communities. Meanwhile, oil exploration in deep waters using acoustic prospecting may deter or disorientate some marine mammals, including whales.

Countries around the Arctic Ocean are rushing to stake claims on the Polar Basin seabed and its oil and gas reserves. Resolving territorial disputes in the Arctic has gained urgency because scientists believe rising temperatures could leave most of the Arctic ice-free in the summer months in a few decades' time.

According to the US Geological Survey, the Arctic could hold a quarter of the world's undiscovered gas and oil reserves. This amounts to 90 billion barrels of oil and vast amounts of natural gas. Nearly 85% of these deposits, they believe, are offshore. As a result, the bordering five countries (Canada, Denmark, Norway, Russia and the USA) are racing to establish the limits of their territory, stretching far beyond their land borders.

Environmental groups have criticized the scramble for the Arctic, saying it will damage unique animal habitats, and have called for a treaty similar to that regulating Antarctica, which bans military activity and mineral mining.

Shipping itself is a huge cause of pollution. Since ships burn bunker oil, the dirtiest of fuels, this means not just more carbon dioxide is released, but also more 'particulate matter', which may be responsible for about 60,000 deaths each year from chest and lung diseases, including cancer. Most of these occur near coastlines in Europe, East and South Asia.

Some action is being taken, however. Oil spills should become rarer since 2010, when all single-hulled ships were banned. Efforts are also being made to prevent the spread of invasive species through the taking on and discharging of ships' ballast water. Similarly, in 2010 the Rotterdam Convention added tributyltin to the list of hazardous chemicals and pesticides in international trade. Tributyltin is a highly toxic chemical once added to the paint used on almost all ships' hulls in order to kill algae and barnacles.

▲ Oil drilling accidents have devastating consequences for the regions in which they occur. In April 2010, the Deepwater Horizon oil rig exploded and collapsed in the Gulf of Mexico, near the Mississippi River Delta. In total, up to 2.275 million barrels of oil may have entered the waters of the Gulf of Mexico. Over 160 km [100 mi] of coastline were affected, including oyster beds and shrimp farms. In the six months after the spill, more than 8,000 birds, sea turtles and marine animals were found dead or injured, while the long-term damage to the marine habitat caused by the oil and the nearly 2 million gallons of chemical dispersants used to clean up the spill may not be known for many years.

## PLASTIC

Yet more alarming for the health of the oceans and their wildlife is the plague of plastic. The UN Environment Programme estimated in 2006 that every square kilometre of sea held nearly 18,000 pieces of floating plastic. Much of it was, and is, in the central Pacific, where scientists believe as much as 100 million tonnes of plastic jetsam are suspended in two separate 'gyres' of garbage over an area twice the size of the USA. This has been referred to as the Great Pacific Garbage Patch – about 90% of the plastic in the sea has been carried there by wind or water from land. It takes decades to sink or decompose.

Situated on the south-western shore of Lake Michigan, Chicago is the centre of the third largest metropolitan area in the United States, with a population of over 9.5 million people. The central area of the agglomeration, known by some as 'Chicagoland', can be seen on the lake shore. It developed as a major transport focus for the Midwest, with complex road and rail networks radiating out to its rich agricultural hinterland. It also developed as a large port, trading these commodities on a global scale. Chicago boasts the fifth busiest airport in the world, O'Hare International, which handles over 66.6 million passengers a year and which can be seen towards the north-west of the city. [Map page 119]
*Source: USGS Landsat/NPA Satellite Mapping*

IMAGES
OF
EARTH

# 16 LONDON, UNITED KINGDOM

The River Thames snakes from Chelsea Bridge in the west to Tower Bridge in the east in this image covering both the West End and the City of London. Despite having a population in excess of 8 million people, there are still many parks and open spaces around the city centre. St James's Park and Green Park, together with Buckingham Palace and its gardens, can be seen at centre left of the image, and, on the western edge, parts of Hyde Park and Regent's Park can also be seen. Just below the page title, at top centre, the newly developing area around Kings Cross and St Pancras railway stations can be seen. In addition, the low sun shows clearly the shadows of The Shard and the chimney of Tate Modern as well as the many high-rise buildings in the City. [Map page 125]
*Source: GeoEye/NPA Satellite Mapping*

As both the capital and the largest city in the Netherlands, with over 1 million inhabitants, Amsterdam is a major commercial and cultural centre. Its name is derived from its position at the mouth of the River Amstel, flowing in from the south. The urban area is split by the Nordzeekanaal, which connects the Ijsselmeer to the North Sea. There is also the important Rijnkanaal, which links it with the major inland waterways of Europe via the River Rhine. The ancient core of the settlement is to the south, where the concentric rings of the famous canal system can be seen. This network is evidence of city planning to accommodate and service a fast-rising population in the 17th century. [Map page 112]
*Source: RapidEye/NPA Satellite Mapping*

# 18 ISTANBUL, TURKEY

The city of Istanbul was formerly known as Constantinople and, before that, as Byzantium. It is split by the narrow stretch of water running from north to south called the Bosporus. This forms the continental boundary between Europe and Asia, connecting the Black Sea, to the north, to the Sea of Marmara, thence to the Mediterranean. It is because of this strategic position between the east–west (land) and north–south (sea) trade routes that the city has been important for such a long time. Under the Ottoman Empire it was the capital city of Turkey, but in 1923 this was moved to Ankara. Currently, over 11 million people live in Istanbul, the largest city in Turkey. [Map page 122]
*Source: USGS Landsat/NPA Satellite Mapping*

Also known as Bombay, Mumbai is the largest and most important commercial city in India, with a population of 20 million people. Its harbour is the best in the country, and the new port, built in 1989 and called Nhava Sheva (on the right-hand side of the image), handles 65% of the country's total container traffic. The growth of cotton weaving, and the opening of the Suez Canal in 1869, cemented its position as India's most important trading port. Diversifying into areas such as engineering and information technology, the city is also the centre of the highly successful Hindi movie industry, or 'Bollywood', which exports its products around the world. [Map page 130]
*Source: RapidEye/NPA Satellite Mapping*

# 20 SINGAPORE CITY, SINGAPORE

Three countries can be seen in this image. At the top, partially covered by cloud, is the southern end of Malaysia; the large island just below is the independent city state of Singapore; and the islands at the bottom of the image are part of Indonesia. Singapore has developed a fast-growing economy based on being the focus of south-east Asian shipping routes and on the trans-shipment of goods between the Far East and the West. As a result, it is one of the world's major ports and much new development, by reclaiming land from the sea, can be seen in the south. The city state is one of the world's wealthiest countries, with a population of over 5 million people. [Map page 138]
*Source: RapidEye/NPA Satellite Mapping*

This image covers one of the most dynamic areas in the world, Hong Kong, with Shenzhen to its north. Hong Kong became a major port and international financial centre during the period of British rule and retains a special status as a Special Administrative Region (SAR) with a high degree of economic autonomy, including the retention of the Hong Kong dollar. To its north Shenzhen was established by China as a Special Economic Zone (SEZ) in 1979, to attract foreign industry and investment. This has proved very successful and communications between the two have also improved, as can be seen by the sinuous Shenzhen Bay Bridge, at centre left in this image. [Map page 122]
*Source: RapidEye/NPA Satellite Mapping*

# 22 CAIRO, EGYPT

The largest city in Africa, with over 11 million inhabitants, Cairo evolved in a strategic location on the eastern bank of the River Nile just below its delta, 165 km (100 miles) from the Mediterranean Sea. This image clearly shows the differences between the arid desert areas to the south-east and south-west, the fertile lands of the Nile flood plain, and the urban area itself. Air pollution from vehicle emissions and industry is a major concern in this rapidly expanding metropolitan area. To ease congestion, three metro lines have been built. The shadows of the Pyramids on the Giza Plateau can be seen at the bottom left of the image, showing the modern city's links with Ancient Egypt. [Map page 117]
*Source: RapidEye/NPA Satellite Mapping*

The light purple area on the western bank of the White Nile River in this image is the newest capital city in the world. Juba is the capital of the Republic of South Sudan, which gained its independence on 9 July 2011. Its population is over 350,000. The town is situated near to the borders with the Democratic Republic of the Congo, Uganda and Kenya. South Sudan has a less arid climate than Sudan to the north, and there is a wide variety of wildlife. Most of the oilfields in the former Sudan are situated in the new state, but production has been disrupted. The ongoing civil war with Sudan has destroyed much of the transportation infrastructure. [Map page 266]
*Source: USGS Landsat/NPA Satellite Mapping*

# 24 CAPE TOWN, SOUTH AFRICA

The city of Cape Town sits at the northern end of the Cape Peninsula beneath Table Mountain – the port facilities are clearly visible in this image. It developed from the first settlement in the 17th century, founded by the Dutch East India Company, because of its safe north-facing harbour, looking across Table Bay towards Robben Island. The urban area now spreads to the east of the peninsula down to False Bay. As well as being the second largest city in South Africa, after Johannesburg, Cape Town is also the seat of the National Parliament and is the country's legislative capital. To the west of the port can be seen the oval shape of the Cape Town Stadium. [Map page 118]
*Source: RapidEye/NPA Satellite Mapping*

Sydney is the largest city in Australia, with a population of over 4.5 million inhabitants. It was founded at the end of the 18th century at Sydney Cove on the south shore of Port Jackson, the northern of the two enclosed bays seen here. It has since spread inland along the valley of the Parramatta River and to the south, to Botany Bay. The image covers the main central business district from the Sydney Harbour Bridge down to the runways of Australia's busiest airport, Sydney Kingsford Smith. On the Pacific coast, at the southern end of the pointed peninsula, the white sands and sheltered bay of Bondi Beach can be seen. As the financial and commercial centre for the whole country, the city has a vibrant cultural life. [Map page 139]
*Source: RapidEye/NPA Satellite Mapping*

# 26 AUCKLAND, NEW ZEALAND

Situated at the northern end of North Island, the city of Auckland was founded by the Maoris on the narrow isthmus at the top left of this image. It has since grown to become the largest settlement in the country. This is a landscape that has been shaped by volcanic forces – the dark circular shape to the east of the city is Rangitoto Island, the now-extinct remains of a volcano that erupted from the sea some 600 years ago. At the bottom of the image is the town of Hamilton. [Map page 284]
*Source: USGS Landsat/NPA Satellite Mapping*

On the north side of the Fraser River delta, the settlement grew up in the second half of the 19th century around its fine, natural harbour. It developed as the western railhead of the Canadian Pacific Railroad and is now the terminus of the Trans-Canada Highway, which crosses on the easternmost of the two road bridges visible here to the north. Vancouver is the largest cargo port in Canada. The larger metropolitan area of the city is home to over 2.25 million people. Downtown Vancouver is at the southern end of the peninsula which projects northwards and separates Vancouver Harbour from Burrard Inlet. The wooded area at the northern end is Stanley Park, which is connected to West and North Vancouver via the Lions Gate Bridge. [Map page 296]
*Source: RapidEye/NPA Satellite Mapping*

# 28 NEW YORK CITY, USA

This image covers parts of New York City (to the east) and Jersey City (to the west). Flowing from the north, the Hudson River divides them, and the elongated island of Manhattan with Central Park at its heart is clearly visible. It is the centre of the most densely populated metropolitan area in the United States, with a population in excess of 19 million people. To the south-east is the end of Long Island, on which the suburbs of Brooklyn and Queens are situated. South-west of Manhattan are two small islands: the first is Ellis Island, where the early immigrants first disembarked, and beyond that is Liberty Island, where the famous Statue of Liberty is located. [Map page 132]
*Source: RapidEye/NPA Satellite Mapping*

Washington is the capital of the United States and was created in 1790. It is named after George Washington and is in a unique federal district, the District of Columbia, so that it should not fall into any particular state. The city is in the centre of this image, at the confluence of the Potomac and Anacostia rivers, just to the east of the original capital city, Georgetown. As well as being home to the President, in the White House, the majority of foreign embassies in the US are situated here, as are the headquarters of important global organizations such as the World Bank and the International Monetary Fund (IMF). To service the many branches of government and other institutions, over half a million people commute into the city every day. [Map page 143]
*Source: RapidEye/NPA Satellite Mapping*

# 30 PANAMA CANAL, PANAMA

The Panama Canal, originally dug between 1904–14, crosses between the Caribbean Sea, to the north of the image, and the Pacific Ocean in the south. Paradoxically, therefore, the Pacific entrance is to the east of the Caribbean entrance. Panama City, the capital of Panama, is at the Pacific end of the canal. The canal has until recently been able to handle the world's largest cargo vessels, carrying up to 5,000 containers, thus cutting the ocean passage time between Asia and the eastern USA. It is now being upgraded so that by the end of 2015 it will be able to handle the latest vessels – these can carry a maximum load of 12,000 containers. [Map page 320]
*Source: USGS Landsat/NPA Satellite Mapping*

Situated on the west side of the mouth of the Guanabara Bay, Rio de Janeiro is the most visited city in the southern hemisphere. It is famous for its beaches (Copacabana and Ipanema, both at the western entrance to the bay), its carnivals, the Sugar Loaf Mountain, and the famous Cristo Redentor (Christ the Redeemer) statue. It has a hot, humid climate with a mean daily temperature of 24°C (75°F), and was the capital city of Brazil until 1960, when the newly built capital Brasília superseded it. It is the second largest manufacturing centre in Brazil, after São Paulo, and a major port. The metropolitan area has a population of almost 11 million people. [Map page 135]
*Source: USGS Landsat/NPA Satellite Mapping*

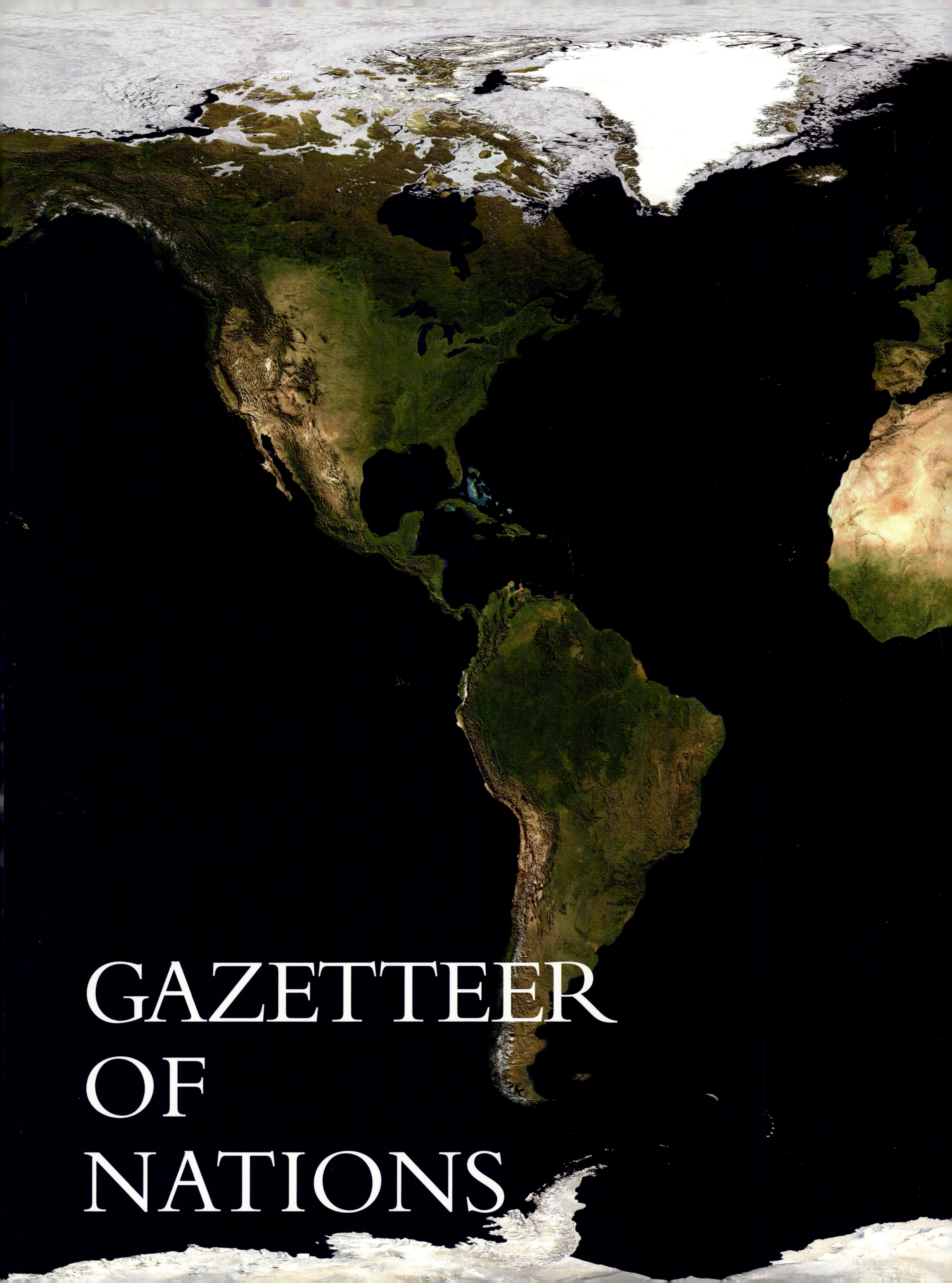
GAZETTEER
OF
NATIONS

## AFGHANISTAN

**GEOGRAPHY** The Republic of Afghanistan is a landlocked, mountainous country in southern Asia. The central highlands reach a height of more than 7,000 m [22,966 ft] in the east and make up nearly three-quarters of Afghanistan. The main range is the Hindu Kush. In winter, northerly winds bring cold, snowy weather to the mountains, but summers are hot and dry.

**POLITICS & ECONOMY** The modern history of Afghanistan began in 1747, when the various tribes in the area united for the first time. In the 19th century, Russia and Britain struggled for control of the country. Following Britain's withdrawal in 1919, Afghanistan became fully independent. Soviet troops invaded in 1979 to support a socialist regime in Kabul, but they withdrew in 1989. By 2001, a group called the Taliban ('Islamic students') controlled 90% of the country. In 2001, following the refusal of the Taliban to hand over the al Qaida terrorist leader Osama bin Laden, an international force invaded Afghanistan. In 2002, a coalition government was set up under Hamid Karzai. In late 2011, President Karzai stated that international support would still be needed after all foreign troops withdraw in 2014.

Afghanistan is a poor country and nearly 79% of its people are farmers or nomadic herders. Natural gas is produced, together with some coal, copper, gold, precious stones and salt.

**AREA** 652,090 sq km [251,772 sq mi]
**POPULATION** 30,420,000 **CAPITAL** Kabul
**GOVERNMENT** Islamic Republic **ETHNIC GROUPS** Pashtun (Pathan) 42%, Tajik 27%, Hazara 9%, Uzbek 9%, others 13%
**LANGUAGES** Pashtu, Dari/Persian (both official), Uzbek
**RELIGIONS** Islam (Sunni Muslim 80%, Shi'ite Muslim 19%), others 1%
**CURRENCY** Afghani = 100 puls

## ALBANIA

**GEOGRAPHY** The Republic of Albania lies in the Balkan peninsula, facing the Adriatic Sea. About 70% of the land is mountainous, but most Albanians live in the west on the coastal lowlands.

The coastal areas of Albania experience a typical Mediterranean climate, with fairly dry, sunny summers and cool, moist winters. The mountains have a severe climate, with heavy winter snowfalls.

**POLITICS & ECONOMY** Albania is one of Europe's poorest nations. A former Communist country, Albania adopted a multi-party system in the early 1990s. The change proved difficult. But after elections in 1997, a socialist government committed to a market system took office. The transition to democracy has been challenging. Elections were held in 2005, and again in 2009 amid accusations of vote-rigging. Violent anti-government demonstrations occurred in January 2011.

In 2012, agriculture employed about 20% of the people. Since 1991, private ownership of land has been encouraged, replacing the former state farm and collective system. Albania has some minerals. Chromite, copper and nickel are exported.

**AREA** 28,748 sq km [11,100 sq mi] **POPULATION** 3,003,000
**CAPITAL** Tirana **GOVERNMENT** Multiparty republic
**ETHNIC GROUPS** Albanian 95%, Greek 3%, Macedonian, Vlachs, Gypsy **LANGUAGES** Albanian (official)
**RELIGIONS** Islam 70%, Christianity 30% (Orthodox 20%, Roman Catholic 10%)
**CURRENCY** Lek = 100 qindars

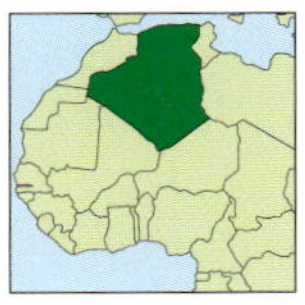

## ALGERIA

**GEOGRAPHY** The People's Democratic Republic of Algeria is Africa's largest country. Most Algerians live in the north, on the fertile coastal plains and hill country bordering the Mediterranean Sea. Four-fifths of Algeria is in the Sahara, the world's largest desert. The coast has a Mediterranean climate but the arid Sahara is hot by day and cold at night.

**POLITICS & ECONOMY** France ruled Algeria from 1830 until 1962, when the socialist FLN (National Liberation Front) formed a one-party government. Following the recognition of opposition parties in 1989, a Muslim group, the FIS (Islamic Salvation Front), won an election in 1991. The FLN cancelled the elections and civil conflict broke out. About 100,000 people were killed in the 1990s. Abdelaziz Bouteflika was elected president in 1999, 2004 and 2009. The scale of violence went down under his leadership. In 2011, protests broke out over food prices and unemployment, but the protests did not lead to the overthrow of the government as elsewhere in North Africa.

Algeria is a developing country, whose chief resources are oil and natural gas, which were discovered in the Sahara in 1956. The natural gas reserves are among the world's largest, and gas and oil account for more than 90% of the exports. Cement, iron and steel, textiles and vehicles are manufactured. Barley, citrus fruits, dates, potatoes and wheat are major crops.

**AREA** 2,381,741 sq km [919,590 sq mi]
**POPULATION** 37,367,000 **CAPITAL** Algiers
**GOVERNMENT** Socialist republic **ETHNIC GROUPS** Arab-Berber 99%
**LANGUAGES** Arabic and Berber (official), French **RELIGIONS** Sunni Muslim 99% **CURRENCY** Algerian dinar = 100 centimes

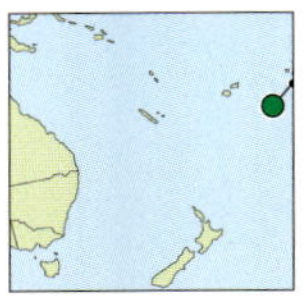

## AMERICAN SAMOA

An 'unincorporated territory' of the United States, American Samoa lies in the south-central Pacific Ocean.

**AREA** 199 sq km [77 sq mi]
**POPULATION** 55,000 **CAPITAL** Pago Pago

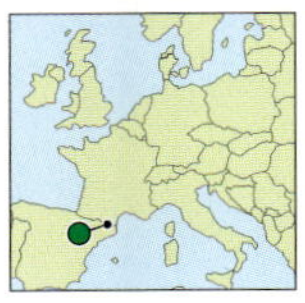

## ANDORRA

A mini-state situated in the Pyrenees Mountains, Andorra is a co-principality whose main activity is tourism. Most Andorrans live in the six valleys (the Valls) that drain into the River Valira.

**AREA** 468 sq km [181 sq mi]
**POPULATION** 85,000 **CAPITAL** Andorra La Vella

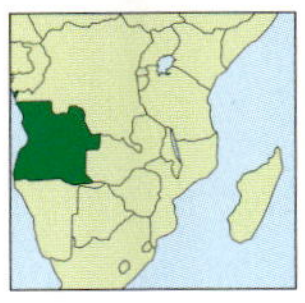

## ANGOLA

**GEOGRAPHY** The Republic of Angola is a large country in south-western Africa. Much of the country is part of the plateau that forms most of southern Africa, with a narrow coastal plain in the west.

Angola has a tropical climate, with temperatures of over 20°C [68°F] throughout the year, though the highest areas are cooler. The coast is dry, but the rainfall increases to the north and east.

**POLITICS & ECONOMY** Bantu-speaking people settled in Angola in the 13th century and later founded large kingdoms, such as the Kongo and Mbundu. Portugal controlled the coastal slave trade from the 17th century and extended its control inland in the 19th century. Angola became independent from Portugal in 1975, after which rival nationalist groups struggled for power. Despite a ceasefire in the mid-1990s, conflict finally ended only in 2002, when the rebel leader, Jonas Savimbi, was killed. Successful parliamentary elections were held in 2008.

Angola is a developing country, where 85% of the people are poor farmers. The main food crops are cassava and maize. Coffee is exported. Angola has important oil reserves and oil is exported. Angola also produces diamonds and has reserves of copper, manganese and phosphates.

**AREA** 1,246,700 sq km [481,351 sq mi]
**POPULATION** 18,056,000 **CAPITAL** Luanda
**GOVERNMENT** Multiparty republic
**ETHNIC GROUPS** Ovimbundu 37%, Kimbundu 25%, Bakongo 13%, others 25% **LANGUAGES** Portuguese (official), many others
**RELIGIONS** Traditional beliefs 47%, Roman Catholic 38%, Protestant 15%
**CURRENCY** Kwanza = 100 lwei

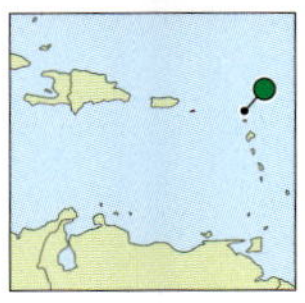

## ANGUILLA

Formerly part of St Kitts and Nevis, Anguilla, the most northerly of the Leeward Islands, became a British dependency (now a British overseas territory) in 1980. The main source of revenue is now tourism, though lobster still accounts for half the island's exports.

**AREA** 96 sq km [37 sq mi]
**POPULATION** 15,000 **CAPITAL** The Valley

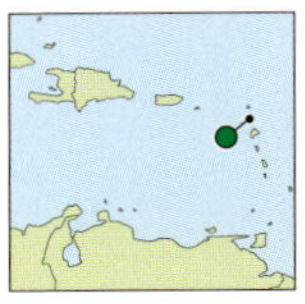

## ANTIGUA & BARBUDA

A former British dependency in the Caribbean, Antigua and Barbuda became independent in 1981. Tourism is the main industry, though sugar is an important product.

**AREA** 442 sq km [171 sq mi]
**POPULATION** 89,000 **CAPITAL** St John's

## ARGENTINA

**GEOGRAPHY** The Argentine Republic is South America's second largest and the world's eighth largest country. The high Andes range in the west contains Mount Aconcagua, the highest peak in the Americas. In southern Argentina, the Andes Mountains overlook Patagonia, a plateau region. In east-central Argentina lies a fertile plain called the pampas.

The climate varies from subtropical in the north to temperate in the south. Rainfall is abundant in the north-east but lower to the west and south. Patagonia is largely desert.

**POLITICS & ECONOMY** The earliest people were American Indians, but 86% of the people are now of European ancestry. Spain took control in the 16th century and ruled until 1816. Argentina later suffered from instability and periods of military rule. In 1982, Argentina's military regime invaded the Falkland (Malvinas) Islands, but Britain regained the islands later that year. Argentina restored civilian rule in 1983. In 2007, Christina Fernández de Kirchner was elected president, succeeding her husband, Néstor Carlos Kirchner, who had served as president from 2003. She was the first woman to be Argentina's directly elected president. She was re-elected in 2011. The dispute with Britain resurfaced in 2012, the 30th anniversary of the Falklands war.

The World Bank classifies Argentina as an 'upper-middle-income' developing country. About 92% of the people live in urban areas. Manufactures include food products, cars, electrical equipment and textiles. Oil is the main resource and the chief farm products are beef, maize and wheat. Exports include oil, meat, wheat, maize, vegetable oils, hides and skins, and wool. In 1991, Argentina, Brazil, Paraguay and Uruguay set up an alliance, Mercosur, aimed at creating a common market.

**AREA** 2,780,400 sq km [1,073,512 sq mi]
**POPULATION** 42,192,000 **CAPITAL** Buenos Aires
**GOVERNMENT** Federal republic **ETHNIC GROUPS** European 97%, Mestizo, Amerindian **LANGUAGES** Spanish (official)
**RELIGIONS** Roman Catholic 92%, Protestant 2%, Jewish 2%, others **CURRENCY** Argentine peso = 100 centavos

## ARMENIA

**GEOGRAPHY** The Republic of Armenia is a landlocked country in south-western Asia. Most of Armenia consists of a rugged plateau, crisscrossed by long faults (cracks). Movements along the faults cause earthquakes. The highest point is Mount Aragats, at 4,090 m [13,419 ft] above sea level.

The height of the land, which averages 1,500 m [4,920 ft] above sea level, gives rise to severe winters and cool summers. The highest peaks are snow-capped, but the total yearly rainfall is generally low.

**POLITICS & ECONOMY** In 1920, Armenia became a Communist republic and, in 1922, it became, with Azerbaijan and Georgia, part of the Transcaucasian Republic within the Soviet Union. But the three territories became separate Soviet Socialist Republics in 1936. After the break-up of the Soviet Union in 1991, Armenia became an independent republic. Fighting broke out over Nagorno-Karabakh, an area enclosed by Azerbaijan where most people are Armenians. In 1992, Armenia occupied the land between it and Nagorno-Karabakh. A ceasefire in 1994 left Armenia in control of about 20% of Azerbaijan's land area. In 2010, Armenia and Azerbaijan agreed to exchange prisoners taken during the Nagorno-Karabakh conflict.

Armenia's economy has suffered because of its former dependency on a centrally planned Soviet system.

**AREA** 29,800 sq km [11,506 sq mi]
**POPULATION** 2,970,000 **CAPITAL** Yerevan
**GOVERNMENT** Multiparty republic
**ETHNIC GROUPS** Armenian 98%, Yezidi 1%
**LANGUAGES** Armenian (official) **RELIGIONS** Armenian Apostolic 95%
**CURRENCY** Dram = 100 luma

**NOTE**: This alphabetical list includes the principal countries and territories of the world. The area figures give the total area of land, inland water and ice. The population figures are 2012 estimates where available.

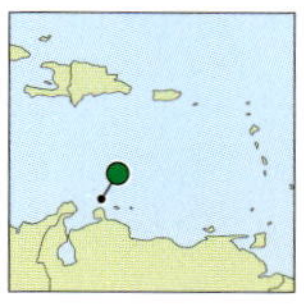

## ARUBA

Formerly part of the Netherlands Antilles, Aruba (the most westerly of the Lesser Antilles) became a separate self-governing Dutch territory in 1986.

**AREA** 193 sq km [75 sq mi]
**POPULATION** 108,000 **CAPITAL** Oranjestad

## AUSTRALIA

**GEOGRAPHY** The Commonwealth of Australia, the world's sixth largest country, is also a continent. Australia is the flattest of the continents and the main highland area is in the east. Here the Great Dividing Range separates the eastern coastal plains from the Central Plains. This range extends from Cape York Peninsula to Victoria in the far south. The longest rivers, the Murray and Darling, drain the south-eastern part of the Central Plains. The Western Plateau makes up two-thirds of Australia. A few mountain ranges break the monotony of the generally flat landscape. Only 10% of Australia, notably the tropical north, the north-east coast and the south-east, has an average annual rainfall of more than 1,000 mm [39 in]. But extreme weather events, including a prolonged drought in the Murray–Darling basin in the early 21st century and severe flooding in Queensland in 2010–12, cause periodic problems.

**POLITICS & ECONOMY** The Aboriginal people of Australia entered the continent from South-east Asia more than 50,000 years ago. The first European explorers were Dutch in the 17th century, but they did not settle. In 1770, the British Captain Cook explored the east coast and, in 1788, the first British settlement was established for convicts on the site of what is now Sydney. Australia has strong ties with the British Isles. But in the last 50 years, people from other parts of Europe and, most recently, from Asia have settled in Australia. Ties with Britain were also weakened by Britain's membership of the European Union. Many Australians believe that they should become more involved with the nations of eastern Asia and the Americas rather than with Europe. In 1999, Australians voted to retain the country's status as a monarchy. In 2003, Australian troops joined in the invasion of Iraq. The Labour Party won the 2007 elections. The prime minister, Kevin Rudd, was succeeded in 2010 by Julia Gillard.

Australia is a prosperous country. Crops can be grown on only 6% of the land, but dry pasture covers another 58%. Yet the country remains a major producer and exporter of farm products, particularly cattle, wheat and wool. Grapes grown for wine-making are also important. The country is a major producer of minerals, including bauxite, coal, copper, diamonds, gold, iron ore, manganese, nickel, silver, tin, tungsten and zinc. Australia also produces oil and natural gas. Metals, minerals and farm products account for the bulk of exports. Australia's imports are mostly manufactured goods, especially machinery, though industry is now important, especially the manufacture of consumer goods.

**AREA** 7,741,220 sq km [2,988,885 sq mi] **POPULATION** 22,016,000
**CAPITAL** Canberra **GOVERNMENT** Federal constitutional monarchy
**ETHNIC GROUPS** Caucasian 92%, Asian 7%, Aboriginal 1%
**LANGUAGES** English (official) **RELIGIONS** Non-Christian 36%, Roman Catholic 26%, Anglican 19%, other Christian 19%
**CURRENCY** Australian dollar = 100 cents

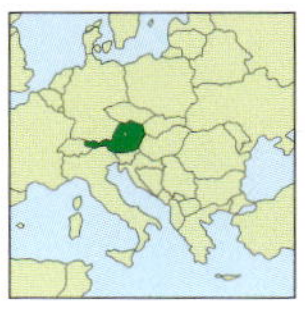

## AUSTRIA

**GEOGRAPHY** Austria is a landlocked country in Europe. Northern Austria contains the valley of the River Danube, which flows from Germany to the Black Sea, and the Vienna basin. Southern Austria contains ranges of the Alps, their highest point at Grossglockner, 3,797 m [12,457 ft] above sea level.

The climate is temperate in the west and more continental in the east. Winters are cold and snowy. Summers are warm and dry in the east.

**POLITICS & ECONOMY** Formerly part of the monarchy of Austria–Hungary, which collapsed in 1918, Austria was annexed by Germany in 1938. After World War II, the Allies partitioned and occupied the country. In 1955, Austria became a neutral federal republic. It joined the European Union in 1995. In 2000, a coalition government was formed by the right-wing People's Party and the extreme right-wing Freedom Party, which lost much of its support in 2002. In 2008, the Social Democratic/People's Party coalition (formed in 2007) collapsed, but the same parties formed another government after elections, in which far-right parties won nearly 29% of the vote.

Austria has a highly developed economy, with plenty of hydroelectric power and some oil, gas and coal reserves. The country's leading economic activity is manufacturing metals and metal products. Crops are grown on 16% of the land, and another 24% is pasture. Dairy and livestock farming are the leading activities. Major crops include barley, potatoes, rye, sugar beet and wheat. Tourism is a major activity in this scenic country.

**AREA** 83,859 sq km [32,378 sq mi] **POPULATION** 8,220,000
**CAPITAL** Vienna **GOVERNMENT** Federal republic
**ETHNIC GROUPS** Austrian 90%, Croatian, Slovene, others
**LANGUAGES** German (official) **RELIGIONS** Roman Catholic 74%, Protestant 5%, Islam and others 21% **CURRENCY** Euro = 100 cents

## AZERBAIJAN

**GEOGRAPHY** The Azerbaijani Republic is a country in the south-west of Asia, facing the Caspian Sea to the east. It includes an area called the Naxçivan Autonomous Republic, which is completely cut off from the rest of Azerbaijan by Armenian territory. The Caucasus Mountains border Russia in the north.

Azerbaijan has hot summers and cool winters. The plains are fairly dry, but the mountains are rainy.

**POLITICS & ECONOMY** After the Russian Revolution of 1917, attempts were made to form a Transcaucasian Federation made up of Armenia, Azerbaijan and Georgia. When this failed, Azerbaijanis set up an independent state. But Russian forces occupied the area in 1920. In 1922, the Communists set up a Transcaucasian Republic consisting of Armenia, Azerbaijan and Georgia under Russian control. In 1936, the three areas became separate Soviet Socialist Republics within the Soviet Union. In 1991, following the break-up of the Soviet Union, Azerbaijan became an independent nation. After independence, Azerbaijan clashed with Armenia over the enclave of Nagorno-Karabakh, a region in Azerbaijan where the majority of the people are Armenian. A ceasefire in 1994 left Armenia in control of 20% of Azerbaijan's area, including Nagorno-Karabakh.

Azerbaijan has huge oil reserves. Oil extraction and manufacturing, including oil refining and the production of chemicals, machinery and textiles are important.

**AREA** 86,600 sq km [33,436 sq mi] **POPULATION** 9,494,000
**CAPITAL** Baku **GOVERNMENT** Federal multiparty republic
**ETHNIC GROUPS** Azeri 90%, Dagestani 2%, Russian 2%, Armenian, others **LANGUAGES** Azerbaijani (official), Lezgi, Russian, Armenian
**RELIGIONS** Islam 93%, Russian Orthodox 2%, Armenian Orthodox 2%
**CURRENCY** Azerbaijani manat = 100 gopik

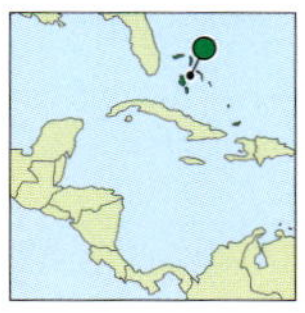

## BAHAMAS

A coral-limestone archipelago off the coast of Florida, the Bahamas became independent from Britain in 1973, and has since developed strong ties with the United States. Tourism and banking are major activities.

**AREA** 13,878 sq km [5,358 sq mi]
**POPULATION** 316,000 **CAPITAL** Nassau

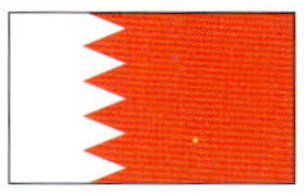
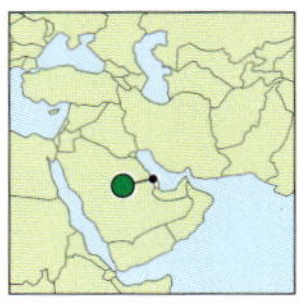

## BAHRAIN

The Kingdom of Bahrain, an island nation in the Persian Gulf, became independent from the UK in 1971. Oil accounts for 80% of its exports.

In early 2011, demonstrators called for reform. Violence occurred, a state of emergency was declared, and troops from other Gulf states arrived to help control the situation. Demonstrations continued in 2012.

**AREA** 694 sq km [268 sq mi]
**POPULATION** 1,248,000 **CAPITAL** Manama

## BANGLADESH

**GEOGRAPHY** The People's Republic of Bangladesh is one of the world's most densely populated countries. Apart from hilly regions in the far north-east and south-east, most of the land is flat and covered by fertile alluvium spread over the land by the Ganges, Brahmaputra and Meghna rivers. These rivers overflow when they are swollen by the annual monsoon rains. Floods also occur along the coast, 575 km [357 mi] long, when cyclones (hurricanes) drive seawater inland. Bangladesh has a tropical monsoon climate. Dry northerly winds blow in winter, but moist southerly winds bring heavy rain in summer.

**POLITICS & ECONOMY** In 1947, British India was partitioned between the mainly Hindu India and the Muslim Pakistan. Pakistan consisted of two parts, West and East Pakistan, which were separated by about 1,600 km [1,000 mi] of Indian territory. Differences developed between West and East Pakistan. In 1971, the East Pakistanis rebelled. After a nine-month civil war, they declared East Pakistan to be a new nation named Bangladesh. A famine in 1974 and a coup in 1975 were followed by political upheavals. The army seized power in 2007, but elections in 2008 returned Sheikh Hasina's Awami League to power.

Bangladesh is one of the world's poorest countries. Its economy depends mainly on agriculture, which employs about 45% of the population. Bangladesh is the world's fourth largest producer of rice.

**AREA** 143,998 sq km [55,598 sq mi]
**POPULATION** 161,084,000 **CAPITAL** Dhaka
**GOVERNMENT** Multiparty republic **ETHNIC GROUPS** Bengali 98%, tribal groups **LANGUAGES** Bengali (official), English
**RELIGIONS** Islam 83%, Hinduism 16% **CURRENCY** Taka = 100 paisas

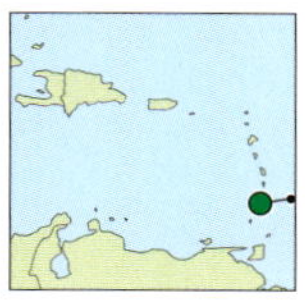

## BARBADOS

The most easterly Caribbean country, Barbados became independent from the UK in 1960. A densely populated island, Barbados is prosperous by comparison with most Caribbean countries.

**AREA** 430 sq km [166 sq mi]
**POPULATION** 288,000 **CAPITAL** Bridgetown

## BELARUS

**GEOGRAPHY** The Republic of Belarus is a landlocked country in Eastern Europe. The land is low-lying and mostly flat. In the south, much of the land is marshy and this area contains Europe's largest marsh and peat bog, the Pripet Marshes. The climate is affected by both the moderating influence of the Baltic Sea and continental conditions to the east. The winters are cold and the summers warm.

**POLITICS & ECONOMY** In 1918, Belarus (White Russia) became an independent republic, but Russia invaded the country and, in 1919, a Communist state was set up. In 1922, Belarus became a founder republic of the Soviet Union. In 1991, Belarus again became an independent republic, and though Belarus continued to support reunification with Russia, any surrender of sovereignty was not expected. President Alexander Lukashenko, who was elected in flawed elections in 1994, 2001, 2006 and 2010, when he won nearly 80% of the vote amid opposition protests, has been criticized for his autocratic rule, his poor record on human rights, and his disregard for freedom of speech.

According to the World Bank, Belarus has an 'upper-middle-income' economy. Most economic activities remain under government control and, from the 1990s, the economy has declined. Mining and manufacturing are the most valuable activities.

**AREA** 207,600 sq km [80,154 sq mi]
**POPULATION** 9,644,000 **CAPITAL** Minsk
**GOVERNMENT** Multiparty republic **ETHNIC GROUPS** Belarusian 84%, Russian 8%, Polish, Ukrainian, others **LANGUAGES** Belarusian, Russian (both official) **RELIGIONS** Eastern Orthodox 80%, others 20% **CURRENCY** Belarusian rouble = 100 kapyeyka

## BELGIUM

**GEOGRAPHY** The Kingdom of Belgium is a densely populated country in western Europe. Behind the coastline on the North Sea, which is 63 km [39 mi] long, lie its coastal plains. Central Belgium consists of low plateaux and the only highland region is the Ardennes in the south-east.

Belgium has a cool, temperate climate. Moist winds from the Atlantic Ocean bring fairly heavy rain, especially in the Ardennes. In January and February much snow falls on the Ardennes.

**POLITICS & ECONOMY** In 1815, Belgium and the Netherlands united as the 'low countries', but Belgium became independent in 1830. Belgium's economy was weakened by the two World

Wars, but, from 1945, the country recovered quickly, first through collaboration with the Netherlands and Luxembourg, which formed a customs union called Benelux, and later through its membership of the European Union.

A central political problem in Belgium has been the tension between the Dutch-speaking Flemings and the French-speaking Walloons. In the 1970s, the government divided the country into three economic regions: Dutch-speaking Flanders, French-speaking Wallonia, and bilingual Brussels. In 1993, Belgium adopted a federal constitution, giving each region its own parliament. In 2010, a coalition government set up in 2009 collapsed because of deep differences between the Flemish- and French-speaking parties. A prime minister was appointed in December 2011, following a world record of 541 days when Belgium had no government.

Belgium is a major trading nation, though most materials used in manufacturing are imported. Major products include chemicals, processed food and steel. The textile industry has existed since medieval times in Flanders. Agriculture employs less than 2% of the people, but farmers produce most of the food the country needs. Barley and wheat are major crops, followed by flax, hops, potatoes and sugar beet. But the most valuable agricultural activities are dairy farming and livestock rearing.

**AREA** 30,528 sq km [11,787 sq mi]
**POPULATION** 10,438,000
**CAPITAL** Brussels
**GOVERNMENT** Federal constitutional monarchy
**ETHNIC GROUPS** Belgian 89% (Fleming 58%, Walloon 31%), others 11% **LANGUAGES** Dutch, French, German (all official)
**RELIGIONS** Roman Catholic 75%, others 25%
**CURRENCY** Euro = 100 cents

## BELIZE

**GEOGRAPHY** Behind the southern coastal plain, the land rises to the Maya Mountains, which reach 1,120 m [3,674 ft] at Victoria Peak. The north is mostly low-lying and swampy. Temperatures are high all year round, while the average annual rainfall ranges from 1,300 mm [51 in] in the north to over 3,800 mm [150 in] in the south. Hurricanes caused much damage in the 1990s and 2000s, but tourist numbers have continued to increase.

**POLITICS & ECONOMY** From 1862, Belize (then called British Honduras) was a British colony. Full independence was achieved in 1981, but Guatemala, which had claimed the area since the early 19th century, opposed Belize's independence and British troops remained to prevent a possible invasion. Relations improved in the early 1990s, when Guatemala agreed to recognize Belize's independence and British troops withdrew. In 2011, the United States added Belize and El Salvador to its list of illegal drug producers or major transit routes into the US.

The World Bank classifies Belize as a 'lower-middle-income' developing country. Its economy is based on agriculture and sugar cane is the chief commercial crop and export. Other crops include bananas, beans, citrus fruits, maize and rice. Forestry, fishing and tourism are other important activities.

**AREA** 22,966 sq km [8,867 sq mi] **POPULATION** 328,000
**CAPITAL** Belmopan **GOVERNMENT** Constitutional monarchy
**ETHNIC GROUPS** Mestizo 49%, Creole 25%, Mayan Indian 11%, Garifuna 6%, others 9%
**LANGUAGES** English (official), Spanish, Creole
**RELIGIONS** Roman Catholic 39%, Protestant 27%, others
**CURRENCY** Belizean dollar = 100 cents

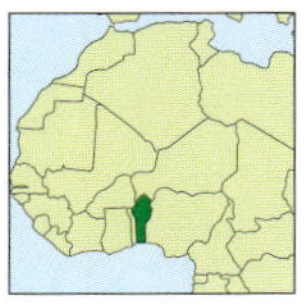

## BENIN

**GEOGRAPHY** The Republic of Benin is one of Africa's smallest countries. It extends north–south for about 620 km [390 mi]. Lagoons line the short coastline, and the country has no natural harbours.

Benin has a hot, wet climate. The average annual temperature on the coast is about 25°C [77°F], and the average rainfall is about 1,330 mm [52 in]. The inland plains are wetter than the coast.

**POLITICS & ECONOMY** After slavery was ended in the 19th century, the French began to gain influence in the area. Benin became self-governing in 1958 and fully independent in 1960. After much instability and many changes of government, a military group took over in 1972. The country, renamed Benin in 1975, became a one-party socialist state. Socialism was abandoned in 1989. Former coup leader Mathieu Kérékou served as president until 2006, when a former banker, Yayi Boni, was elected president. He was re-elected in 2011.

Benin is a poor developing country. About half of the people live by farming, mainly at subsistence level. Exports include cotton, petroleum, and palm products. Cocoa, coffee, groundnuts (peanuts), tobacco and shea nuts are also grown for export.

**AREA** 112,622 sq km [43,483 sq mi]
**POPULATION** 9,599,000 **CAPITAL** Porto-Novo
**GOVERNMENT** Multiparty republic **ETHNIC GROUPS** Fon, Adja, Bariba, Yoruba, Fulani **LANGUAGES** French (official), Fon, Adja, Yoruba
**RELIGIONS** Christianity 43%, traditional beliefs 30%, Islam 27%
**CURRENCY** CFA franc = 100 centimes

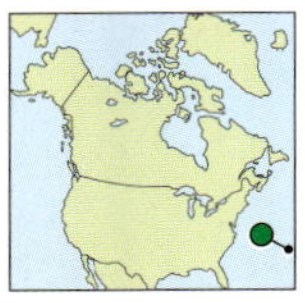

## BERMUDA

A group of about 150 small islands situated 920 km [570 mi] east of the USA. Bermuda remains Britain's oldest overseas territory, but it has a long tradition of self-government.

**AREA** 53 sq km [21 sq mi]
**POPULATION** 69,000 **CAPITAL** Hamilton

## BHUTAN

**GEOGRAPHY** A mountainous, isolated Himalayan country located between India and Tibet. The climate is similar to that of Nepal, being dependent on altitude and affected by monsoonal winds.

**POLITICS & ECONOMY** The monarch of Bhutan is head of both state and government, and this predominantly Buddhist country remains, even in the Asian context, both conservative and poor. In 2008, Bhutan held its first ever democratic elections, ending over a century of absolute royal rule and turning Bhutan into a constitutional monarchy.

**AREA** 47,000 sq km [18,147 sq mi] **POPULATION** 717,000
**CAPITAL** Thimphu **GOVERNMENT** Constitutional monarchy
**ETHNIC GROUPS** Bhutanese 50%, Nepalese 35%
**LANGUAGES** Dzongkha (official) **RELIGIONS** Buddhism 75%, Hinduism 25% **CURRENCY** Ngultrum = 100 chetrum

## BOLIVIA

**GEOGRAPHY** The Plurinational State of Bolivia, as the country is officially called, is a landlocked South American country which straddles the Andes Mountains. The highest point is 6,520 m [21,391 ft] at Nevado Sajaama in the west. About 40% of Bolivians live on a high plateau called the Altiplano in the Andes. The sparsely populated east is a vast lowland plain.

The Bolivian climate is greatly affected by altitude, with the Andean peaks permanently snow-covered and the eastern plains remaining hot and humid.

**POLITICS & ECONOMY** American Indians have lived in Bolivia for at least 10,000 years. The main groups today are the Aymara and Quechua people.

In the last 50 years, Bolivia, an independent country since 1825, has been ruled by a succession of civilian and military governments, which violated human rights. Democracy was restored in 1982. Economic problems led a widening of the gap between rich and poor and, in 2005, Evo Morales, a left-wing Aymara farmer, was elected president. His policies of nationalization and redistributing wealth to peasants aroused opposition especially in the richer east. In 2009, Morales was re-elected president, but his popularity declined in 2010–11 because of food shortages and price rises.

Bolivia is one of South America's poorest countries. Resources include natural gas, silver, tin and zinc, but the main activity is agriculture. Soybeans and soybean products are exported.

**AREA** 1,098,581 sq km [424,162 sq mi]
**POPULATION** 10,290,000 **CAPITAL** La Paz (seat of government); Sucre (legal capital/seat of judiciary)
**GOVERNMENT** Multiparty republic **ETHNIC GROUPS** Mestizo 30%, Quechua 30%, Aymara 25%, White 15% **LANGUAGES** Spanish, Aymara, Quechua (all official) **RELIGIONS** Roman Catholic 95%
**CURRENCY** Boliviano = 100 centavos

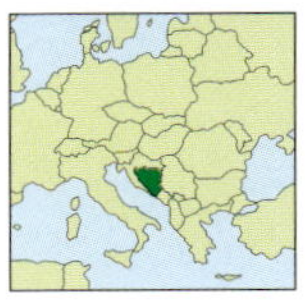

## BOSNIA-HERZEGOVINA

**GEOGRAPHY** The Republic of Bosnia-Herzegovina is one of the five republics to emerge from the former Federal People's Republic of Yugoslavia. Much of the country is mountainous or hilly, with an arid limestone plateau in the south-west. The River Sava, which forms most of the northern border with Croatia, is a tributary of the River Danube. Because of the country's odd shape, the coastline is limited to a short stretch of 20 km [13 mi] on the Adriatic coast.

A Mediterranean climate, with dry, sunny summers and moist, mild winters, prevails only near the coast. Inland, the weather is more severe, with hot, dry summers and bitterly cold, snowy winters.

**POLITICS & ECONOMY** In 1918, Bosnia-Herzegovina became part of the Kingdom of the Serbs, Croats and Slovenes, which was renamed Yugoslavia in 1929. Germany occupied the area during World War II (1939–45). From 1945, Communist governments ruled Yugoslavia as a federation containing six republics, one of which was Bosnia-Herzegovina. In the 1980s, the country faced problems as Communist policies proved unsuccessful.

In 1990, free elections were held in Bosnia-Herzegovina and the non-Communists won a majority. A Muslim, Alija Izetbegovic, was elected president. In 1991, Croatia and Slovenia, other parts of the former Yugoslavia, declared themselves independent. In 1992, Bosnia-Herzegovina held a vote on independence. Most Bosnian Serbs boycotted the vote, while the Muslims and Bosnian Croats voted in favour. Many Bosnian Serbs, opposed to independence, started a war against the non-Serbs. They soon occupied more than two-thirds of the land. The Bosnian Serbs were accused of 'ethnic cleansing' – that is, the killing or expulsion of other ethnic groups from Serb-occupied areas. The war was later extended when Croat forces seized other parts of the country.

In 1995, the country retained its boundaries, but it was divided into two self-governing provinces – one Bosnian Serb and the other Muslim Croat under a central government. Stability was restored with the help of NATO, but the country remained divided along ethnic lines, and in December 2011, Muslim Croat and Serb leaders agreed on the formation of a central government after 14 months of political crisis.

The economy of Bosnia-Herzegovina, the least developed of the six republics of the former Yugoslavia apart from Macedonia, was shattered by the war in the early 1990s. Before the war, manufactures were the main exports, including electrical, machinery and transport equipment, and textiles. Farm products include fruits, maize, tobacco, vegetables and wheat, but food has to be imported.

**AREA** 51,197 sq km [19,767 sq mi]
**POPULATION** 3,879,000 **CAPITAL** Sarajevo
**GOVERNMENT** Federal republic **ETHNIC GROUPS** Bosnian 48%, Serb 37%, Croat 14% **LANGUAGES** Bosnian, Serbian, Croatian
**RELIGIONS** Islam 40%, Serbian Orthodox 31%, Roman Catholic 15%, others 14% **CURRENCY** Convertible marka = 100 convertible pfenniga

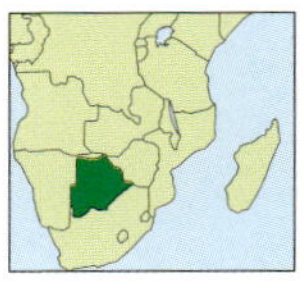

## BOTSWANA

**GEOGRAPHY** The Republic of Botswana is a landlocked country in southern Africa. The Kalahari, a semi-desert area covered mostly by grasses and thorn scrub, covers much of the country. Most of the south has no permanent streams. But large depressions in the north are inland drainage basins. In one of them, the Okavango River, which rises in Angola, forms a large, swampy delta.

Temperatures are high in the summer months (October to April), but the winter months are much cooler. In winter, night-time temperatures sometimes drop below freezing point. The average annual rainfall ranges from over 400 mm [16 in] in the east to less than 200 mm [8 in] in the south-west.

**POLITICS & ECONOMY** The earliest inhabitants of the region were the San, who are also called Bushmen. They had a nomadic way of life, hunting wild animals and collecting wild plant foods.

Britain ruled the area as the Bechuanaland Protectorate between 1885 and 1966. When the country became independent, it was renamed Botswana. Since then, the country has been a stable, multiparty democracy. However, a major setback occurred in the 21st century, when health officials announced that around 25% of the people were infected with HIV/AIDS.

In 1966, Botswana was extremely poor, depending on meat and live cattle for its exports. But the discovery of minerals, including coal, cobalt, copper, diamonds and nickel, has boosted the economy. About 25% of the people now depend on agriculture, raising cattle and growing crops. Industries include the processing of farm products.

**AREA** 581,730 sq km [224,606 sq mi] **POPULATION** 2,098,000
**CAPITAL** Gaborone **GOVERNMENT** Multiparty republic
**ETHNIC GROUPS** Tswana (or Setswana) 79%, Kalanga 11%, Basarwa 3%, others **LANGUAGES** English (official), Setswana
**RELIGIONS** Christianity 72%, Badimo 6%, others 2%
**CURRENCY** Pula = 100 thebe

## BRAZIL

**GEOGRAPHY** The Federative Republic of Brazil is the world's fifth largest country. It contains three main regions. The Amazon basin in the north covers more than half of Brazil. The Amazon, the world's second longest river, has a far greater volume than any other river. The second region, the north-east, consists of a coastal plain and the *sertão*, which is the name for the inland plateaux and hill country. The main river in this region is the São Francisco.

The third region is made up of the plateaux in the south-east. This region, which covers about a quarter of the country, is the most developed and densely populated part of Brazil. Its main river is the Paraná, which flows south through Argentina.

Manaus has high temperatures all through the year. Rainfall is heavy, though the period from June to September is drier than the rest of the year. The capital, Brasília, and the city Rio de Janeiro also have tropical climates, with much more marked dry seasons than Manaus. The far south has a temperate climate. The north-eastern interior is the driest region, with an average annual rainfall of only 250 mm [10 in] in places. Rainfall is also unreliable and severe droughts are common in this region.

**POLITICS & ECONOMY** The Portuguese explorer Pedro Alvarez Cabral claimed Brazil for Portugal in 1500. With Spain occupied in western South America, the Portuguese began to develop their colony, which was more than 90 times as big as Portugal. To do this, they enslaved many local Amerindian people and introduced about 4 million African slaves. Brazil declared itself an independent empire in 1822 and a republic in 1889. From the 1930s, Brazil faced periods of military rule and widespread corruption. Civilian rule was restored in 1985. Brazil adopted a new constitution in 1988.

Brazil is described as a 'rapidly industrializing economy', and in 2012 the government announced that it was the world's sixth largest economy. But many people, including poor farmers and residents of the *favelas* (city slums), do not share in the country's fast economic growth. Poverty led to the election of President Luíz Inácio Lula da Silva (generally called 'Lula') in 2002. His economic policies proved popular. In 2010, he was succeeded by Dilma Roussef, also of Lula's Workers Party. She became Brazil's first female president.

Brazil is South America's leading economy, with industry as the most important economic sector. It is among the world's top producers of bauxite, chrome, diamonds, gold, iron ore, manganese and tin. It is also a major manufacturing country, with products including aircraft, cars, chemicals, processed food, iron and steel, paper and textiles.

Brazil is a major farming nation and agriculture employs 16% of the people. Coffee is a leading export. Other products include bananas, citrus fruits, cocoa, maize, rice, soybeans and sugar cane. Brazil is also South America's top producer of eggs, meat and milk.

Forestry is a major industry, though many people fear that the destruction of the rainforests, which may accelerate global warming, is an impending disaster for the entire world.

**AREA** 8,514,215 sq km [3,287,338 sq mi]
**POPULATION** 199,321,000 **CAPITAL** Brasília
**GOVERNMENT** Federal republic
**ETHNIC GROUPS** White 54%, Mixed 38%, Black 6%, others 2%
**LANGUAGES** Portuguese (official)
**RELIGIONS** Roman Catholic 80%
**CURRENCY** Real = 100 centavos

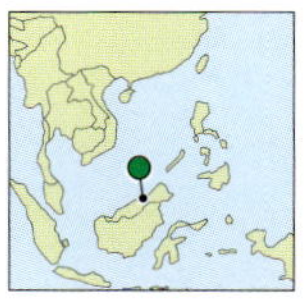

## BRUNEI

The Islamic Sultanate of Brunei, a British protectorate until 1984, lies on the north coast of Borneo. The climate is tropical and rainforests cover large areas. Brunei is a prosperous country because of its oil and natural gas production, and the Sultan is said to be among the world's richest men.

**AREA** 5,765 sq km [2,226 sq mi]
**POPULATION** 409,000 **CAPITAL** Bandar Seri Begawan

## BULGARIA

**GEOGRAPHY** The Republic of Bulgaria is a country in the Balkan peninsula, facing the Black Sea in the east. The heart of Bulgaria is mountainous. The main ranges are the Balkan Mountains in the centre and the Rhodope (or Rhodopi) Mountains in the south.

Summers are hot and winters are cold, though seldom severe. The rainfall is moderate.

**POLITICS & ECONOMY** Ottoman Turks ruled Bulgaria from 1396 and ethnic Turks still form a sizeable minority in the country. In 1879, Bulgaria became a monarchy, and in 1908 it became fully independent. Bulgaria was an ally of Germany in World War I (1914–18) and again in World War II (1939–45). In 1944, Soviet troops invaded Bulgaria and, after the war, the monarchy was abolished and the country became a Communist ally of the Soviet Union. Reforms in the Soviet Union in the late 1980s led Bulgaria's government to introduce a multi-party system in 1990. A non-Communist government was elected in 1991, in the first free elections in 44 years. Throughout the 1990s, Bulgaria faced many problems and it sought to become aligned to the West. Bulgaria became a member of NATO in 2004 and a member of the European Union in 2007. In 2009, the centre-right GERB party, led by Boiko Borisov, who promised to tackle corruption and the economic crisis, won the parliamentary elections.

Bulgaria has an 'upper-middle economy'. It has some mineral deposits, including brown coal, manganese, gold and iron ore. Manufacturing is the leading activity, with principal products including chemicals, processed foods, metal products, machinery and textiles. Manufactures are the leading exports.

**AREA** 110,912 sq km [42,823 sq mi] **POPULATION** 7,038,000
**CAPITAL** Sofia **GOVERNMENT** Multiparty republic
**ETHNIC GROUPS** Bulgarian 77%, Turkish 8%, Roma 4%, Macedonian, Armenian, others **LANGUAGES** Bulgarian (official), Turkish **RELIGIONS** Eastern Orthodox 59%, Islam 8%, others
**CURRENCY** Lev = 100 stotinki

## BURKINA FASO

**GEOGRAPHY** The Democratic People's Republic of Burkina Faso is a landlocked country, a little larger than the United Kingdom, in West Africa. But Burkina Faso has only a quarter of the population of the UK. The country consists of a plateau, between about 300 m and 700 m [650 ft to 2,300 ft] above sea level. The plateau is cut by several rivers.

The capital city, Ouagadougou, in central Burkina Faso, has high temperatures throughout the year. Most of the rain falls between May and September, but the rainfall is erratic and droughts are common.

**POLITICS & ECONOMY** The people of Burkina Faso are divided into two main groups. The Voltaic group includes the Mossi, who form the largest single group, and the Bobo. The French conquered the Mossi capital of Ouagadougou in 1897 and they made the area a protectorate. In 1919, the area became a French colony called Upper Volta. After independence in 1960, Upper Volta became a one-party state. But it was unstable – military groups seized power several times and political killings took place. In 1984, the country's name was changed to Burkina Faso. In 1991, 1998, 2005 and 2010, the former coup leader, Captain Blaise Compaoré, was elected president.

Burkina Faso is one of the world's 20 poorest countries and has become very dependent on foreign aid. Most of Burkina Faso is dry with thin soils. The country's main food crops are beans, maize, millet, rice and sorghum. Cotton, groundnuts (peanuts) and shea nuts, whose seeds produce a fat used to make cooking oil and soap, are grown for sale abroad. Livestock are also an important export.

The country has few resources and manufacturing is on a small scale. There are some deposits of manganese, zinc, lead and nickel in the north of the country, but there is not yet a good enough transport system there. Many young men seek jobs abroad in Ghana and Ivory Coast. The money they send home to their families is important to the country's economy.

**AREA** 274,000 sq km [105,791 sq mi]
**POPULATION** 17,275,000 **CAPITAL** Ouagadougou
**GOVERNMENT** Multiparty republic **ETHNIC GROUPS** Mossi 40%, Gurunsi, Senufo, Lobi, Bobo, Mande, Fulani **LANGUAGES** French (official), Mossi, Fulani **RELIGIONS** Islam 60%, Christianity 24%, traditional beliefs 16% **CURRENCY** CFA franc = 100 centimes

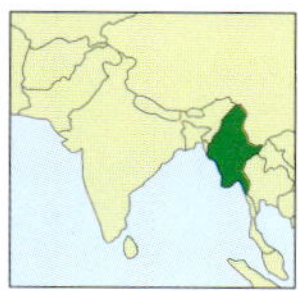

## BURMA (MYANMAR)

**GEOGRAPHY** The Union of Burma has been officially known as the Union of Myanmar since 1989. However, it is more usually referred to as Burma. Mountains border the country in the east and west, with the highest mountains in the north. Burma's highest mountain is Hkakabo Razi, which is 5,881 m [19,294 ft] high. Between these ranges is central Burma, which contains the fertile valleys of the Irrawaddy and Sittang rivers. The Irrawaddy delta is a leading rice-growing area.

Burma has a tropical monsoon climate with three seasons. The rainy season runs from late May to mid-October. A cool, dry season follows, between late October and the middle part of February. The hot season lasts from late February to mid-May. In May 2008, a typhoon devastated the south, including the Irrawaddy delta, killing more than 80,000 people.

**POLITICS & ECONOMY** Many groups settled in Burma in ancient times. Some, called the hill peoples, live in remote mountain areas where they have retained their own cultures. The ancestors of the country's main ethnic group today, the Burmese, arrived in the 9th century AD. Britain conquered Burma in the 19th century and made it a province of British India. But, in 1937, the British granted Burma limited self-government. Japan conquered Burma in 1942, but the Japanese were driven out in 1945. Burma became a fully independent country in 1948.

Revolts by Communists and various hill people led to instability in the 1950s. In 1962, Burma became a military dictatorship and, in 1974, a one-party state. Attempts to control minority liberation movements and the opium trade led to repressive rule. The National League for Democracy led by Aung San Suu Kyi won the elections in 1990, but the military continued their repressive rule.

In 2010, the military released Aung San Suu Kyi from house arrest, but she was not allowed to participate in elections. A military-backed party was victorious in elections in 2010, and in 2011 a civilian government backed by the military took power. In 2012, Aung San Suu Kyi won a parliamentary seat, while her party, the National League for Democracy, won 43 of the 44 contested seats. But the military and their allies held a large majority in parliament. There has been recent rioting in western Burma against the minority Muslim Rohingya population.

Agriculture is the main activity, employing 66% of the people. The chief crop is rice. Maize, pulses, oilseeds and sugar cane are other major products. Forestry is important. Teak and rice together make up about two-thirds of the total value of exports. Burma has many mineral resources, though they are mostly undeveloped, but the country is famous for its precious stones, especially rubies. Manufacturing is mostly on a small scale.

**AREA** 676,578 sq km [261,227 sq mi] **POPULATION** 54,585,000
**CAPITAL** Rangoon (Yangon); Naypyidaw (administrative capital)
**GOVERNMENT** Military regime **ETHNIC GROUPS** Burman 68%, Shan 9%, Karen 7%, Rakhine 4%, Chinese, Indian, Mon
**LANGUAGES** Burmese (official); minority ethnic groups have their own languages **RELIGIONS** Buddhism 89%, Christianity, Islam
**CURRENCY** Kyat = 100 pyas

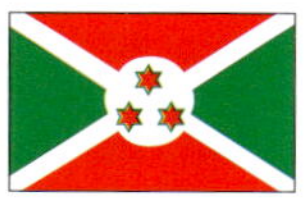

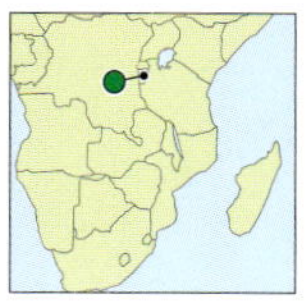

## BURUNDI

**GEOGRAPHY** The Republic of Burundi is the fifth smallest country in mainland Africa. It is also the second most densely populated after its northern neighbour, Rwanda. Part of the Great African Rift Valley, which runs throughout eastern Africa into south-western Asia, lies in western Burundi. It includes part of Lake Tanganyika. Bujumbura, the capital city, lies on the shore of Lake Tanganyika and has a warm climate. A dry season occurs from June to September, but the other months are fairly rainy. The mountains and plateaux to the east are cooler and wetter, but the rainfall generally decreases to the east.

**POLITICS & ECONOMY** The Twa, a pygmy people, were the first known inhabitants of Burundi. About 1,000 years ago, the Hutu, a people who speak a Bantu language, gradually began to settle the area, pushing the Twa into remote areas.

From the 15th century, the Tutsi, a cattle-owning people from the north-east, gradually took over the country. The Hutu, though greatly outnumbering the Tutsi, were forced to serve the Tutsi overlords.

Germany conquered the area that is now Burundi and Rwanda in the late 1890s. The area, called Ruanda-Urundi, was taken by Belgium during World War I (1914–18). In 1961, the people of Urundi voted to become a monarchy, while the people of Ruanda voted to become a republic. The two territories became fully independent as Burundi and Rwanda in 1962. After 1962, the rivalries between the Hutu and Tutsi led to periodic outbreaks of fighting. The Tutsi monarchy was ended in 1966 and Burundi became a republic. Instability continued with coups and massacres as Tutsis and Hutus fought against each other. A power-sharing agreement was reached in 2001. The government of President Pierre Nkurunziza, who was re-elected in 2010, faced many political and economic challenges.

Burundi is one of the world's poorest countries. About 93% of the people live by farming, mostly at subsistence level. Food crops include beans, cassava, maize and sweet potatoes. Livestock are raised and fishing is important. But Burundi has to import food.

**AREA** 27,834 SQ KM [10,747 SQ MI]
**POPULATION** 10,557,000 **CAPITAL** BUJUMBURA
**GOVERNMENT** REPUBLIC **ETHNIC GROUPS** HUTU 85%, TUTSI 14%, TWA (PYGMY) 1% **LANGUAGES** FRENCH AND KIRUNDI (BOTH OFFICIAL)
**RELIGIONS** ROMAN CATHOLIC 62%, TRADITIONAL BELIEFS 23%, ISLAM 10%, PROTESTANT 5% **CURRENCY** BURUNDI FRANC = 100 CENTIMES

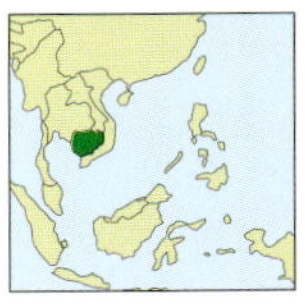

## CAMBODIA

**GEOGRAPHY** The Kingdom of Cambodia is a country in South-east Asia. Low mountains border the country except in the south-east. But most of Cambodia consists of plains drained by the River Mekong, which enters Cambodia from Laos in the north and exits through Vietnam in the south-east. The north-west contains Tonlé Sap (or Great Lake). In the dry season, this lake drains into the River Mekong. But in the wet season, the level of the Mekong rises and water flows in the opposite direction from the river into Tonlé Sap – the lake then becomes the largest freshwater lake in Asia.

Cambodia has a tropical monsoon climate, with high temperatures throughout the year. The dry season, when winds blow from the north or north-east, runs from November to April. During the rainy season (May to October), moist winds blow from the south or south-east. The high humidity and heat often make conditions unpleasant. Rainfall is heaviest near the coast, and rather lower inland.

**POLITICS & ECONOMY** From 802 to 1432, the Khmer people ruled a great empire, which reached its peak in the 12th century. The Khmer capital was at Angkor. The Hindu stone temples built there and at nearby Angkor Wat form the world's largest group of religious buildings. France ruled the country between 1863 and 1954, when the country became an independent monarchy. But the monarchy was abolished in 1970 and Cambodia became a republic.

In 1970, US and South Vietnamese troops entered Cambodia, but left after destroying North Vietnamese Communist camps in the east. The country became involved in the Vietnam War, and then in a civil war as Cambodian Communists of the Khmer Rouge organization fought for power. The Khmer Rouge took over Cambodia in 1975 and launched a reign of terror in which between 1 million and 2.5 million people were killed. In 1979, Vietnamese and Cambodian troops overthrew the Khmer Rouge government. But fighting continued between factions. Vietnam withdrew in 1989, and in 1991 Prince Sihanouk was recognized as head of state. Elections were held in May 1993, and in September 1993 the monarchy was restored. Elections were held in 1998, 2003 and 2008. In 2004, King Sihanouk abdicated because of ill health and his son, Prince Norodom Sihamoni, became king. Between 2008 and December 2011, Cambodian and Thai troops clashed periodically over a border dispute involving an area near the ancient Preah Vihear temple, a World Heritage Site.

Cambodia is a poor country whose economy was wrecked by war. Garment manufacture is the main activity and rice, rubber and maize are leading agricultural products. The discovery of potential oil reserves and an increase in tourism have recently boosted the economy.

**AREA** 181,035 SQ KM [69,898 SQ MI] **POPULATION** 14,953,000
**CAPITAL** PHNOM PENH **GOVERNMENT** CONSTITUTIONAL MONARCHY
**ETHNIC GROUPS** KHMER 90%, VIETNAMESE 5%, CHINESE 1%, OTHERS
**LANGUAGES** KHMER (OFFICIAL), FRENCH, ENGLISH
**RELIGIONS** BUDDHISM 95%, OTHERS 5% **CURRENCY** RIEL = 100 SEN

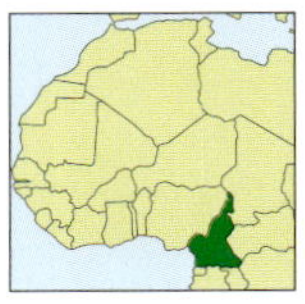

## CAMEROON

**GEOGRAPHY** The Republic of Cameroon in West Africa derived its name from the Portuguese word *camarões*, or prawns. This name was used by Portuguese explorers who fished for prawns along the coast. Behind the narrow coastal plains on the Gulf of Guinea, the land rises to a series of plateaux, with a mountainous region in the south-west where the volcano Mount Cameroun is situated. In the north, the land slopes down towards the Lake Chad basin.

The rainfall is heavy, especially in the highlands, but it becomes drier to the north. Temperatures are high on the coast, while the inland plateaux are cooler.

**POLITICS & ECONOMY** Germany lost Cameroon during World War I (1914–18). The country was then divided into two parts, one ruled by Britain and the other by France. In 1960, French Cameroon became the independent Cameroon Republic. In 1961, after a vote in British Cameroon, part of the territory joined the Cameroon Republic to become the Federal Republic of Cameroon – the other part joined Nigeria. In 1972, Cameroon became a unitary state called the United Republic of Cameroon. It adopted the name Republic of Cameroon in 1984, but the country had two official languages. In 1995, partly to placate the English-speaking people, Cameroon became the 52nd member of the Commonwealth. In 2008, parliament passed a controversial amendment enabling President Paul Biya, who had assumed office in 1982, to run for election for a third term, a contest which he won by a landslide.

Like most countries in tropical Africa, Cameroon's economy is based on agriculture, which employs 70% of the people. The chief food crops include cassava, maize, millet, sweet potatoes and yams. Cocoa and coffee are exported, along with oil and bauxite. In 2002, Cameroon's claim over the disputed oil-rich Bakassi peninsula was upheld and the handover by Nigeria was finally completed in 2008. Cameroon has few manufacturing industries, but it is self-sufficient in food.

**AREA** 475,442 SQ KM [183,568 SQ MI] **POPULATION** 20,130,000
**CAPITAL** YAOUNDÉ **GOVERNMENT** MULTIPARTY REPUBLIC
**ETHNIC GROUPS** CAMEROON HIGHLANDERS 31%, BANTU 27%, KIRDI 11%, FULANI 10%, OTHERS **LANGUAGES** FRENCH AND ENGLISH (BOTH OFFICIAL)
**RELIGIONS** CHRISTIANITY 40%, TRADITIONAL BELIEFS 40%, ISLAM 20%
**CURRENCY** CFA FRANC = 100 CENTIMES

## CANADA

**GEOGRAPHY** Canada is the world's second largest country after Russia. It is thinly populated, however, with much of the land too cold or too mountainous for human settlement. Most Canadians live within 300 km [186 mi] of the southern border.

Western Canada is rugged. It includes the Pacific ranges and the mighty Rocky Mountains. East of the Rockies are the interior plains. In the north lie the bleak Arctic islands, while to the south lie the densely populated lowlands around lakes Erie and Ontario and in the St Lawrence River valley. The melting of Arctic ice, attributed to global warming, has led to concern about international rights over the Arctic waters off northern Canada.

Canada has a cold climate. In winter, temperatures fall below freezing point throughout most of Canada. But the south-western coast has a relatively mild climate. Along the Arctic Circle, mean temperatures are below freezing for seven months a year. The west and south-east have high rainfall, but the prairies are dry with 250 mm to 500 mm [10 in to 20 in] of rain every year.

**POLITICS & ECONOMY** Canada's first people, the ancestors of the Native Americans, or Indians, arrived in North America from Asia around 40,000 years ago. The Inuit (Eskimos) were later arrivals from Asia. Europeans first reached Canada in 1497 and soon Britain and France began to compete for control.

France gained an initial advantage, and the French founded Québec in 1608. But the British later occupied eastern Canada. In 1867, Britain passed the British North America Act, which set up the Dominion of Canada, which was made up of Québec, Ontario, Nova Scotia and New Brunswick. Other areas were added, the last being Newfoundland in 1949. Canada fought alongside Britain in both World Wars and many Canadians feel close ties with Britain. Canada is a constitutional monarchy, and the British monarch is Canada's head of state.

In 1995, the people of Québec voted narrowly against a move to make Québec a sovereign state. In 2006, the national parliament voted to recognize Québec as a nation within a united Canada – a symbolic act of reconciliation. Another major issue concerns the rights of Aboriginal minorities. In 1999, Canada created the territory of Nunavut for the Inuit population. Nunavut covers 64% of what was formerly the eastern part of the Northwest Territories. In 2006, the Conservative Party, led by Stephen Harper, was returned to power, ending 12 years of Liberal Party rule. Stephen Harper was re-elected in 2008 and 2011.

Canada is a highly developed and prosperous country. Although farmland covers only 8% of the country, Canadian farms are highly productive. Canada is one of the world's leading producers of barley, wheat, meat and milk. Forestry and fishing are other important industries. It is rich in natural resources, especially oil and natural gas, and is a major exporter of minerals. The country also produces copper, gold, iron ore, uranium and zinc. Manufacturing is important in the cities, where 58% of the people live. Manufactures include processed mineral and farm products, cars, chemicals, electronic goods, machinery, paper, and timber products.

**AREA** 9,970,610 SQ KM [3,849,653 SQ MI]
**POPULATION** 34,300,000 **CAPITAL** OTTAWA
**GOVERNMENT** FEDERAL MULTIPARTY CONSTITUTIONAL MONARCHY
**ETHNIC GROUPS** BRITISH ORIGIN 28%, FRENCH ORIGIN 23%, OTHER EUROPEAN 15%, AMERINDIAN/INUIT 2%, OTHERS
**LANGUAGES** ENGLISH AND FRENCH (BOTH OFFICIAL)
**RELIGIONS** ROMAN CATHOLIC 43%, PROTESTANT 23%, JUDAISM, ISLAM, HINDUISM **CURRENCY** CANADIAN DOLLAR = 100 CENTS

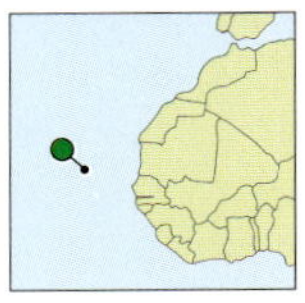

## CAPE VERDE

Cape Verde consists of ten large and five small islands, and is situated 560 km [350 mi] west of Dakar in Senegal. The islands have a tropical climate, with high temperatures all year round. Cape Verde became independent from Portugal in 1975 and is rated as a 'low-income' developing country by the World Bank.

**AREA** 4,033 SQ KM [1,557 SQ MI]
**POPULATION** 524,000 **CAPITAL** PRAIA

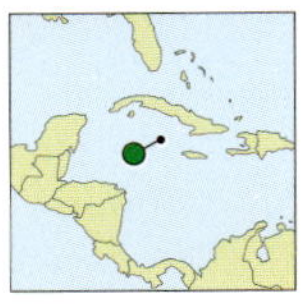

## CAYMAN ISLANDS

The Cayman Islands are an overseas territory of the UK, consisting of three low-lying islands. Financial services are the main economic activity and the islands offer a secret tax haven to many companies and banks.

**AREA** 264 SQ KM [102 SQ MI]
**POPULATION** 53,000 **CAPITAL** GEORGE TOWN

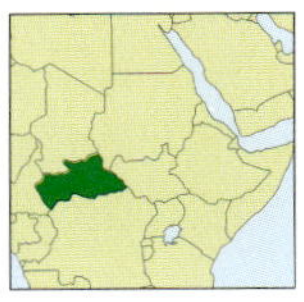

## CENTRAL AFRICAN REPUBLIC

**GEOGRAPHY** The Central African Republic is a remote, landlocked country in the heart of Africa. It consists mostly of a plateau lying between 600 m and 800 m [1,970 ft to 2,620 ft] above sea level. The Ubangi drains the south, while the Chari (or Shari) River flows from the north to the Lake Chad basin. The climate is warm throughout the year, while the annual average rainfall in the capital Bangui totals 1,574 mm [62 in]. The north is drier, with an average annual rainfall of about 800 mm [31 in].

**POLITICS & ECONOMY** France set up an outpost at Bangui in 1889 and ruled the country as a colony from 1894. Known as Ubangi-Shari, the country was ruled by France as part of French Equatorial Africa until it gained independence in 1960.

Central African Republic became a one-party state in 1962, but army officers seized power in 1966. The head of the army, Jean-Bedel Bokassa, made himself emperor in 1976. The country was renamed the Central African Empire, but Bokassa was removed by a military coup in 1979. The country again became a republic.

The republic adopted a new multiparty constitution in 1991, and elections were held in 1993 and 1998. An army uprising in 2002 ended in the overthrow of the government in 2003. General François Bozize took power. He was elected president in 2005 and 2010. In 2006–7, rebel activities led thousands of refugees to flee into Chad and Cameroon, and in 2009 the US-based Fund for Peace classified the country as a 'failed state'.

The World Bank classifies Central African Republic as a 'low-income' developing country. Over 80% of the people are farmers, and most of them produce little more than they need to feed their families. The main crops are bananas, maize, manioc, millet and yams. Coffee, cotton, timber and tobacco are produced for export. Development has been impeded by the country's remote position, its poor transport system, and its untrained workforce. The country depends heavily on aid from France.

**AREA** 622,984 SQ KM [240,534 SQ MI] **POPULATION** 5,057,000
**CAPITAL** BANGUI **GOVERNMENT** MULTIPARTY REPUBLIC
**ETHNIC GROUPS** BAYA 33%, BANDA 27%, MANDJIA 13%, SARA 10%, MBOUM 7%, MBAKA 4%, OTHERS **LANGUAGES** FRENCH (OFFICIAL), SANGHO
**RELIGIONS** TRADITIONAL BELIEFS 35%, PROTESTANT 25%, ROMAN CATHOLIC 25%, ISLAM 15% **CURRENCY** CFA FRANC = 100 CENTIMES

## CHAD

**GEOGRAPHY** The Republic of Chad is a landlocked country in north-central Africa. It is Africa's fifth largest country and is over twice the size of France, the country which once ruled it as a colony.

Ndjamena in central Chad has a hot, tropical climate, with a marked dry season from November to April. The south of the country is wetter, with an average yearly rainfall of around 1,000 mm [39 in]. The burning-hot desert in the north has an average yearly rainfall of less than 130 mm [5 in].

**POLITICS & ECONOMY** Chad straddles two worlds. The north is populated by Muslim Arab and Berber peoples, while black Africans, who follow traditional beliefs or who have converted to Christianity, live in the south. French explorers were active in the area in the late 19th century. France made Chad a colony in 1902.

Chad became independent in 1960, but the 1970s were marked by ethnic conflict that led to civil wars, coups, and conflict with Libya, which supported rebel factions. Chad and Libya agreed a truce in 1987, and in 1994 the International Court of Justice ruled against Libya's claim on the Aozou Strip. From 2004, Chad forces clashed with pro-Sudanese militias as the conflict in Sudan's Darfur province spilled over the border. In 2010 a settlement was agreed with Sudan, and Chad held elections in 2011.

Chad is one of the world's poorest countries. Farming and fishing employ 83% of the people. Food crops include groundnuts, millet, rice and sorghum, but cotton is the chief export crop. Chad has few manufacturing industries, but its oil reserves hold out hope for development. Oil production began in 2003.

**AREA** 1,284,000 sq km [495,752 sq mi]
**POPULATION** 10,976,000 **CAPITAL** Ndjamena
**GOVERNMENT** Multiparty republic **ETHNIC GROUPS** 200 distinct groups: mostly Muslim in the north and centre; mostly Christian or animist in the south **LANGUAGES** French and Arabic (both official), many others **RELIGIONS** Islam 53%, Christianity 34%, animist 7%
**CURRENCY** CFA franc = 100 centimes

## CHILE

**GEOGRAPHY** The Republic of Chile stretches about 4,260 km [2,650 mi] from north to south, although the maximum east–west distance is only about 430 km [267 mi]. The high Andes Mountains form Chile's eastern borders with Argentina and Bolivia. To the west are basins and valleys, with coastal uplands overlooking the shore. Most people live in the central valley, where Santiago is situated. Earthquakes are common. In February 2010, an earthquake with a magnitude of 8.8 (the biggest in 50 years) struck central Chile, killing more than 400 people.

Santiago has a Mediterranean climate with hot, dry summers and mild, moist winters. The Atacama Desert in the north is extremely arid, while the south is cold and stormy.

**POLITICS & ECONOMY** Amerindian people reached the southern tip of South America 8,000 years ago. In 1520, Portuguese navigator Ferdinand Magellan was the first European to sight Chile. The country became a Spanish colony in the 1540s. Chile became independent in 1818. During a war (1879–83), it gained mineral-rich areas from Peru and Bolivia.

In 1970, Salvador Allende became the first Communist leader to be elected democratically. He was overthrown in 1973 by army officers, who were supported by the CIA. General Augusto Pinochet then ruled as a dictator. A new constitution was introduced in 1981. Pinochet remained in power until 1989. In 2006, Michelle Bachelet, a centre-left former torture victim under the Pinochet regime, became president. She was succeeded in 2010 by a right-winger, Sebastian Pinera.

According to the World Bank, Chile has an 'upper-middle-income' economy. Mining, especially copper, is important and minerals dominate exports. But manufacturing is the most valuable activity. Products include processed foods, metals, iron and steel, transport equipment, and textiles. The chief crop is wheat, while beans, fruits, maize and livestock products are also important. Chile's fishing industry is one of the world's largest.

**AREA** 756,626 sq km [292,133 sq mi]
**POPULATION** 17,067,000 **CAPITAL** Santiago
**GOVERNMENT** Multiparty republic **ETHNIC GROUPS** Mestizo 95%, Amerindian 3% **LANGUAGES** Spanish (official)
**RELIGIONS** Roman Catholic 70%, Protestant 17%
**CURRENCY** Chilean peso = 100 centavos

## CHINA

**GEOGRAPHY** The People's Republic of China is the world's third largest country. Most people live in the east – on the coastal plains or in the fertile valleys of the Huang He (Hwang Ho or Yellow River), the Chang Jiang (Yangtse Kiang), which is Asia's longest river at 6,380 km [3,960 mi], and the Xi Jiang (Si Kiang). Western China is thinly populated. It includes the bleak Tibetan plateau, which is bounded by the Himalaya, the world's highest mountain range. Deserts include the Gobi Desert along the Mongolian border and the Taklamakan Desert in the far west. Earthquakes are common. In May 2008, a major earthquake in the south-west killed more than 69,000 people and made millions homeless.

Beijing has cold winters and warm summers with moderate rainfall. To the south, Shanghai has milder winters and more rain. The south-east has a wet, subtropical climate, but the west has a severe climate. Lhasa has very cold winters and a low rainfall.

**POLITICS & ECONOMY** China is one of the world's oldest civilizations, going back 3,500 years. Under the Han dynasty (202 BC to AD 220), the Chinese empire was as large as the Roman empire. Mongols conquered China in the 13th century, but Chinese rule was restored in 1368. The Manchu people of Mongolia ruled the country from 1644 to 1912, when the country became a republic.

War with Japan (1937–45) was followed by civil war between the nationalists and the Communists. The Communists triumphed in 1949, setting up the People's Republic of China. In the 1980s, following the death of the revolutionary leader Mao Zedong (Mao Tse-tung) in 1976, China encouraged formerly forbidden policies, namely private enterprise and foreign investment. But the Communist leaders have not permitted political freedom. Opponents are still harshly treated, while attempts to negotiate some degree of autonomy for Tibet have been rejected.

China's economy has expanded greatly since the 1970s and many new industries have been set up in the east. Between 1989 and 2011, the economy grew by over 9% per year. China has benefited from its admission to the World Trade Organization in 2001. The global financial crisis in 2008 slowed the economic growth rate, though China's grew faster than any other major economy. In early 2011, China overtook Japan to become the world's second largest economy after the United States. But growth dropped below 8% in 2012.

Despite its recent success, China remains a poor country. In 2010, agriculture employed 37% of the workforce, although only 10% of the land is farmed. By 2010, the urban population had reached 53% of the total population. This was the first time that urban dwellers outnumbered the rural population.

Farm products include rice, sweet potatoes, tea and wheat, and many fruits and vegetables. Livestock farming is important, and China has more than a third of the world's pigs. Resources include coal, iron ore, and other metals. Manufactures include cement, chemicals, fertilizers, machinery, telecommunications and recording equipment, and textiles. China is now a major producer of consumer goods, including cameras, computer products, refrigerators and television sets.

**AREA** 9,596,961 sq km [3,705,387 sq mi]
**POPULATION** 1,343,240,000 **CAPITAL** Beijing
**GOVERNMENT** Single-party Communist republic
**ETHNIC GROUPS** Han Chinese 92%, many others
**LANGUAGES** Mandarin Chinese (official) **RELIGIONS** Atheist (official)
**CURRENCY** Renminbi yuan = 10 jiao = 100 fen

## COLOMBIA

**GEOGRAPHY** The Republic of Colombia, in north-eastern South America, is the only country in the continent to have coastlines on both the Pacific Ocean and the Caribbean Sea. Colombia also contains the northernmost ranges of the Andes Mountains.

There is a tropical climate in the lowlands, but the altitude greatly affects the climate in the Andes. The capital, Bogotá, which stands on a plateau in the eastern Andes at about 2,800 m [9,200 ft] above sea level, has mild temperatures throughout the year. Rainfall is heavy, especially on the Pacific coast.

**POLITICS & ECONOMY** Amerindian people have lived in Colombia for thousands of years. But today, only a small proportion of the people are of unmixed Amerindian ancestry. Mestizos (people of mixed white and Amerindian ancestry) form the largest group, followed by whites and mulattos (people of mixed European and African ancestry). Spaniards opened up the area in the early 16th century. They set up a territory known as the Viceroyalty of the New Kingdom of Granada, including Colombia, Ecuador, Panama and Venezuela. In 1819, the area became independent, but Ecuador and Venezuela soon split away, followed by Panama in 1903.

Instability has marked its recent history. Colombia faces economic and security problems, notably combating left-wing guerrillas and right-wing paramilitaries, while controlling the illicit drugs industry. Andrés Pastrana, president in 1998–2002, tried to end the guerrilla war, but peace talks collapsed and conflict resumed. His successors, Alvaro Uribe and, from 2010, Juan Manuel Santos, pursued tough policies against the rebels.

Colombia has an 'upper-middle-income' economy. It exports oil, coffee and chemicals.

**AREA** 1,138,914 sq km [439,735 sq mi] **POPULATION** 45,239,000
**CAPITAL** Bogotá **GOVERNMENT** Multiparty republic
**ETHNIC GROUPS** Mestizo 58%, White 20%, Mulatto 14%, Black 4%
**LANGUAGES** Spanish (official) **RELIGIONS** Roman Catholic 90%
**CURRENCY** Colombian peso = 100 centavos

## COMOROS

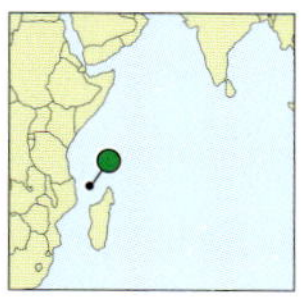

The Union des Isles Comores, as the Comoros is officially called, consists of three large volcanic islands and some smaller ones lying at the north end of the Mozambique Channel in the Indian Ocean. France took over one of the islands, Mayotte, in 1843, and in 1886 the other islands came under French protection. The Comoros became independent in 1974, but Mayotte remained French, becoming fully integrated with France in 2009. In the 1990s, the islands of Anjouan and Mohéli tried to secede, but, in 2004, the large islands were granted autonomy. In 2008, an illegal regime on Anjouan was overthrown. Exports include cloves, perfume oil, and vanilla.

**AREA** 2,235 sq km [863 sq mi] **POPULATION** 737,000 **CAPITAL** Moroni

## CONGO

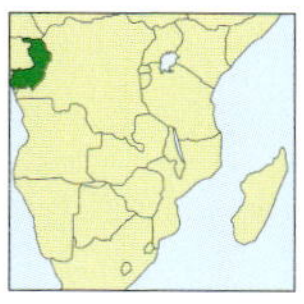

**GEOGRAPHY** The Republic of the Congo is a country on the River Congo in west-central Africa. The equator runs through the centre of the country. Congo has a narrow coastal plain on which its main port, Pointe Noire, stands. Behind the plain are uplands through which the River Niari has carved a fertile valley. Central Congo consists of high plains. The north contains large swampy areas in the valleys of the tributaries of the River Congo.

Congo has a hot, wet equatorial climate. Brazzaville has a dry season between June and September. The coast is drier and cooler than the rest of the Congo, because of the cold offshore Benguela ocean current.

**POLITICS & ECONOMY** Part of the huge Kongo kingdom between the 15th and 18th centuries, the coast of the Congo later became a centre of the European slave trade. The area came under French protection in 1880. It was later governed as part of a larger region called French Equatorial Africa. The country remained under French control until 1960.

Congo became a one-party state in 1964 and a military group took over the government in 1968. In 1970, Congo declared itself a Communist country, though it continued to seek aid from Western countries. The government officially abandoned its Communist policies in 1990. Multiparty elections were held in 1992, but the elected president, Pascal Lissouba, was overthrown in 1997 by former president Denis Sassou-Nguesso. Civil war broke out in 1999 but peace was restored in 2002. Sassou-Nguesso was elected president. He was re-elected in 2009.

The World Bank classifies Congo as a 'lower-middle-income' developing country. Agriculture is the most important activity, employing about 32% of the people. But many farmers produce little more than they need to feed their families. Major food crops include bananas, cassava, maize and rice, while the leading cash crops are coffee and cocoa. Congo's main exports are oil (which makes up more than 90% of the total) and timber. Manufacturing is relatively unimportant at the moment, still hampered by poor transport links, but it is gradually being developed.

**AREA** 342,000 sq km [132,046 sq mi]
**POPULATION** 4,366,000 **CAPITAL** Brazzaville
**GOVERNMENT** Republic **ETHNIC GROUPS** Kongo 48%, Sangha 20%, Teke 17%, M'Bochi 12% **LANGUAGES** French (official), many others **RELIGIONS** Christianity 50%, animist 48%, Islam 2%
**CURRENCY** CFA franc = 100 centimes

## CONGO (DEMOCRATIC REPUBLIC OF THE)

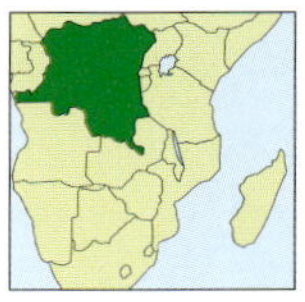

**GEOGRAPHY** The Democratic Republic of the Congo, formerly known as Zaïre, is the world's 12th largest country. Much of the country lies within the drainage basin of the huge River Congo. The river reaches the sea along the country's coastline, which is 40 km [25 mi] long. Mountains rise in the east, where the country's borders run through lakes Tanganyika, Kivu, Edward and Albert. The equatorial region has high temperatures and heavy rainfall throughout the year.

**POLITICS & ECONOMY** Pygmies were the first inhabitants of the region, with Portuguese navigators not reaching the coast until 1482, but the interior was not explored until the late 19th century. In 1885, the country, called Congo Free State, became the personal property of King Léopold II of Belgium. In 1908, the country became a Belgian colony.

The Belgian Congo became independent in 1960 and was renamed Zaïre in 1971. Ethnic rivalries caused instability until 1965, when the country became a one-party state, ruled by President Mobutu. The government allowed the formation of political parties in 1990, but elections were repeatedly postponed. In 1996, fighting broke out in eastern Zaïre, as the Tutsi–Hutu conflict in Burundi and Rwanda spilled over. The rebel leader Laurent Kabila took power in 1997, ousting Mobutu and renaming the country. A rebellion against Kabila broke out in 1998. Rwanda and Uganda supported the rebels, while Angola, Chad, Namibia and Zimbabwe assisted Kabila. A peace treaty was signed in 1999, but fighting continued. Kabila was assassinated in 2001. His son, Major-General Joseph Kabila, became president and was re-elected in 2011, in contentious circumstances. Instability continued as various militias, including Tutsi, Hutu and Ugandan rebels, clashed with government forces in the east.

The World Bank classifies the Democratic Republic of the Congo as a 'low-income' developing country, despite its reserves of copper, the main export, and other minerals. Agriculture, mainly at subsistence level, employs 60% of the people.

**AREA** 2,344,858 sq km [905,350 sq mi]
**POPULATION** 73,599,000 **CAPITAL** Kinshasa
**GOVERNMENT** Single-party republic
**ETHNIC GROUPS** Over 200; the largest are Mongo, Luba, Kongo, Mangbetu-Azande
**LANGUAGES** French (official), tribal languages
**RELIGIONS** Roman Catholic 50%, Protestant 20%, Islam 10%, others
**CURRENCY** Congolese franc = 100 centimes

## COSTA RICA

**GEOGRAPHY** The Republic of Costa Rica in Central America has coastlines on both the Pacific Ocean and the Caribbean Sea. Central Costa Rica consists of mountain ranges and plateaux with many volcanoes.

The coolest months of the year are December and January. The north-east trade winds bring heavy rain to the Caribbean coast, while there are lower amounts of rainfall in the highlands and on the Pacific coastlands.

**POLITICS & ECONOMY** Christopher Columbus reached the Caribbean coast in 1502 and rumours of treasure soon attracted many Spaniards to settle in the country. Spain ruled the country until 1821, when Spain's Central American colonies broke away to join Mexico in 1822. In 1823, the Central American states broke with Mexico and set up the Central American Federation. Later, this large union broke up and Costa Rica became fully independent in 1838.

From the late 19th century onwards, Costa Rica experienced a number of revolutions, with periods of dictatorship alternating with spells of democracy. In 1948, following a revolt, the armed forces were completely abolished. Since that year, Costa Rica has enjoyed a long period of consistent stable democracy. In 2010, Costa Ricans elected their first woman president, Laura Chinchilla.

Costa Rica is classified by the World Bank as an 'upper-middle-income' developing country and one of the most prosperous countries in Central America. There are high educational standards and a high average life expectancy (about 77 years for men and 81 years for women). Agriculture employs 14% of the people. Costa Rica's natural resources include its forests, but it lacks minerals apart from some bauxite and manganese. Manufacturing is increasing. The United States is Costa Rica's main trading partner. Tourism is a fast-growing industry.

**AREA** 51,100 sq km [19,730 sq mi] **POPULATION** 4,636,000
**CAPITAL** San José **GOVERNMENT** Multiparty republic
**ETHNIC GROUPS** White (including Mestizo) 94%, Black 3%, Amerindian 1%, Chinese 1%, others **LANGUAGES** Spanish (official), English **RELIGIONS** Roman Catholic 76%, Evangelical 14%
**CURRENCY** Costa Rican colón = 100 céntimos

## CROATIA

**GEOGRAPHY** The Republic of Croatia was one of the six republics that made up the former Communist country of Yugoslavia until it became independent in 1991. The region bordering the Adriatic Sea is called Dalmatia. It includes the coastal ranges, which contain large areas of bare limestone. Most of the rest of the country consists of the fertile Pannonian plains.

The coastal area has a typical Mediterranean climate, with hot, dry summers and mild, moist winters. Inland, the climate becomes more continental. Winters are cold, while temperatures often soar to 38°C [100°F] in the summer months.

**POLITICS & ECONOMY** Slav people settled in the area around 1,400 years ago. In 803, Croatia became part of the Holy Roman empire and the Croats soon adopted Christianity. Croatia was an independent kingdom in the 10th and 11th centuries. In 1102, the king of Hungary also became king of Croatia, creating a union that lasted 800 years. In 1526, part of Croatia came under the Turkish Ottoman empire, while the rest came under the Austrian Habsburgs.

After Austria–Hungary was defeated in World War I (1914–18), Croatia became part of the new Kingdom of the Serbs, Croats and Slovenes. This kingdom was renamed Yugoslavia in 1929. Germany occupied Yugoslavia during World War II (1939–45). Croatia was proclaimed independent, but it was really ruled by the invaders.

After the war, Communists took power with Josip Broz Tito as the country's leader. Despite ethnic differences between the people, Tito held Yugoslavia together until his death in 1980. In the 1980s, economic and ethnic problems, including a deterioration in relations with Serbia, threatened stability. In the 1990s, Yugoslavia split into five nations, one of which was Croatia, which declared itself independent in 1991.

After Serbia supplied arms to Serbs living in Croatia, war broke out between the two republics, causing great damage. Croatia lost more than 30% of its territory. But in 1992, the United Nations sent a peacekeeping force to Croatia, which effectively ended the war with Serbia.

In 1992, when war broke out in Bosnia-Herzegovina, Bosnian Croats occupied parts of the country. But in 1994, Croatia helped to end Croat–Muslim conflict in Bosnia-Herzegovina and, in 1995, after retaking some areas occupied by Serbs, it helped to draw up the Dayton Peace Accord, ending the civil war. The conflict in the early 1990s disrupted the economy. Croatia's main exports are manufactures. In 2011, Croatia signed an accession treaty, paving the way for it to join the European Union. In 2012, the people voted in a referendum in favour of becoming an EU member; the country is due to join on 1 July 2013.

**AREA** 56,538 sq km [21,829 sq mi] **POPULATION** 4,480,000
**CAPITAL** Zagreb **GOVERNMENT** Multiparty republic
**ETHNIC GROUPS** Croat 90%, Serb 5%, others
**LANGUAGES** Croatian 96% **RELIGIONS** Roman Catholic 88%, Orthodox 4%, Islam 1%, others **CURRENCY** Kuna = 100 lipas

## CUBA

**GEOGRAPHY** The Republic of Cuba is the largest island country in the Caribbean Sea. It consists of one large island, Cuba, the Isle of Youth (Isla de la Juventud), and about 1,600 small islets. Mountains and hills cover about a quarter of Cuba. The highest mountain range, the Sierra Maestra in the south-east, reaches 2,000 m [6,562 ft] above sea level. The rest of the land consists of gently rolling country or coastal plains, crossed by fertile valleys carved by the short, mostly shallow and narrow rivers.

Cuba lies in the tropics. But sea breezes moderate the temperature, warming the land in winter and cooling it in summer.

**POLITICS & ECONOMY** Christopher Columbus discovered the island in 1492 and Spaniards began to settle there from 1511. Spanish rule ended in 1898, when the United States defeated Spain in the Spanish–American War. American influence in Cuba remained strong until 1959, when revolutionary forces under the leadership of Fidel Castro overthrew the dictatorship of Fulgencio Batista.

The United States opposed Castro's policies, when he turned to the Soviet Union for assistance. In 1962, a world crisis occurred when, under intense US pressure, the Soviet Union withdrew missile sites that could have been used to launch nuclear strikes against the United States. The break-up of the Soviet Union in 1991 damaged Cuba's economy. Fidel Castro's brother, Raul, took over the leadership in 2008. He introduced reforms in 2009–12, including the overhaul of the state-run economy and the release of political prisoners. The government runs the Cuban economy, though, in 2011, a new law allowed people to buy and sell private property for the first time in 50 years. Nickel oxide is the main export. Other exports include sugar, cigars, medicines, citrus fruits, fish and rum.

Before 1959, US companies owned most of Cuba's manufacturing industries. But under Fidel Castro, these became government property. After the collapse of Communist governments in the Soviet Union and its allies, Cuba worked to increase its trade with Latin America and China.

**AREA** 110,861 sq km [42,803 sq mi]
**POPULATION** 11,075,000 **CAPITAL** Havana
**GOVERNMENT** Socialist republic
**ETHNIC GROUPS** White 65%, Mulatto 25%, Black 10%
**LANGUAGES** Spanish (official) **RELIGIONS** Christianity
**CURRENCY** Cuban peso = 100 centavos

## CURAÇAO

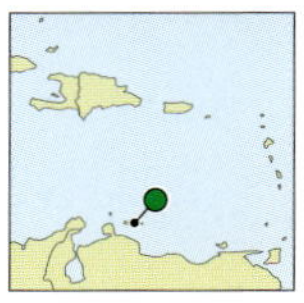

Part of the Netherlands Antilles until 2010, Curaçao is a self-governing territory within the Kingdom of the Netherlands. Oil refining, tourism and trade are important.

**AREA** 444 sq km [171 sq mi]
**POPULATION** 146,000 **CAPITAL** Willemstad

## CYPRUS

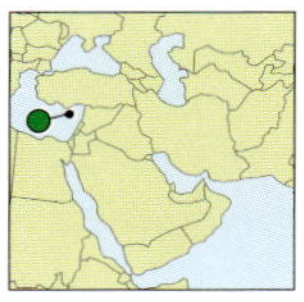

**GEOGRAPHY** The Republic of Cyprus is an island nation in the north-eastern Mediterranean Sea. Geographers regard it as part of Asia, but it resembles southern Europe in many ways. Its scenic mountain ranges include the southern Troodos Mountains, which reach 1,951 m [6,401 ft] at Mount Olympus, and the Kyrenia range in the north. Between them lies the Mesaoria plain. The climate is Mediterranean, with hot, dry summers and mild, moist winters.

**POLITICS & ECONOMY** Greeks settled on Cyprus around 3,200 years ago. From AD 330, the island was part of the Byzantine empire. In the 1570s, Cyprus became part of the Turkish Ottoman empire. Turkish rule continued until 1878 when Cyprus was leased to Britain. Britain annexed the island in 1914 and proclaimed it a colony in 1925. In the 1950s, Greek Cypriots, who made up four-fifths of the population, began a campaign for *enosis* (union) with Greece. Their leader was the Greek Orthodox Archbishop Makarios. A secret guerrilla force called EOKA attacked the British, who exiled Makarios in 1956; he returned to Cyprus in 1959.

Cyprus became an independent country in 1960, although Britain retained two military bases. Independent Cyprus had a constitution which provided for power-sharing between the Greek and Turkish Cypriots. But the constitution proved unworkable and fighting broke out between the two communities. In 1964, the United Nations sent in a peacekeeping force, but communal clashes recurred in 1967.

In 1974, Makarios was overthrown by Greek officers and Turkey invaded northern Cyprus. In 1979, the north was proclaimed the Turkish Republic of Northern Cyprus. The only country to recognize this state was Turkey. In 2002, the European Union invited Cyprus to become a member in 2004. In 2004, the people voted on a UN plan to reunify Cyprus. The Turkish-Cypriots voted in favour, but the Greek-Cypriots voted against, unhappy at limits on their right to return to property located in the north. As a result, only the south was admitted to EU membership on 1 May 2004. Talks on reunification began in 2008, but progress was slow.

Cyprus got its name from the Greek word *kypros*, meaning copper. But little copper remains and the chief minerals today are asbestos and chromium. However, the most valuable activity in Cyprus is tourism. Manufactures include cement, clothes, footwear, tiles and wine.

Problems due to the global financial crisis, and the south joining the euro in 2008, resulted in a contraction of the economy and a bailout from the EU at the beginning of 2013.

**AREA** 9,251 sq km [3,572 sq mi]
**POPULATION** 1,138,000 **CAPITAL** Nicosia
**GOVERNMENT** Multiparty republic **ETHNIC GROUPS** Greek Cypriot 77%, Turkish Cypriot 18%, others **LANGUAGES** Greek and Turkish (both official), English **RELIGIONS** Greek Orthodox 78%, Islam 18%
**CURRENCY** Euro = 100 cents

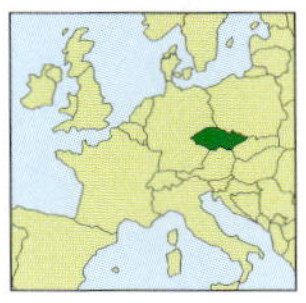

## CZECH REPUBLIC

**GEOGRAPHY** The Czech Republic is the western three-fifths of the former country of Czechoslovakia. It contains two regions: Bohemia in the west and Moravia in the east. Mountains border much of the country in the west. The Bohemian basin in the north-centre is a fertile lowland region, with Prague, the capital city, as its main centre. Highlands cover much of the centre of the country, with lowlands in the south-east.

The climate is influenced by the country's landlocked position in east-central Europe. Summers are warm and winters cold. Rainfall is moderate.

**POLITICS & ECONOMY** After World War I (1914–18), Czechoslovakia was created. Germany seized the country in World War II (1939–45). In 1948, Communist leaders took power and Czechoslovakia was allied to the Soviet Union. When democratic reforms were introduced in the Soviet Union in the late 1980s, the Czechs also demanded reforms. Free elections were held in 1990, but differences between the Czechs and Slovaks led to the partitioning of the country on 1 January 1993. The Czech Republic became a member of NATO in 1999 and a member of the European Union on 1 May 2004. Following elections in 2010, Petr Necas, leader of the conservative Civic Democratic Party, became prime minister.

Under Communist rule the Czech Republic became one of the most industrialized parts of Eastern Europe. The country has deposits of coal, uranium, iron ore, magnesite, tin and zinc. Manufacturing employs about 27% of the Czech Republic's entire workforce. Farming is also important. The main crops include barley, fruit, hops for beer-making, maize, potatoes, sugar beet, vegetables and wheat.

**AREA** 78,866 sq km [30,450 sq mi]
**POPULATION** 10,177,000 **CAPITAL** Prague
**GOVERNMENT** Multiparty republic **ETHNIC GROUPS** Czech 64%, Moravian 5%, Slovak 2%, Polish, German, Silesian, Gypsy, Hungarian, Ukrainian **LANGUAGES** Czech (official) **RELIGIONS** Atheist 40%, Roman Catholic 39%, Protestant 4%, Orthodox 3%, others
**CURRENCY** Czech koruna = 100 haler

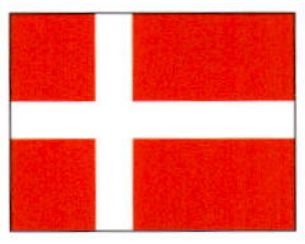

## DENMARK

**GEOGRAPHY** The Kingdom of Denmark is the smallest country in Scandinavia. It consists of a peninsula, called Jutland (or Jylland), which is joined to Germany, and more than 400 islands, 89 of which are inhabited. The land is flat and mostly covered by rocks dropped there by huge ice sheets during the last Ice Age. The highest point in Denmark is on Jutland. It is only 171 m [561 ft] above sea level. Denmark has a mild, moist climate, except during cold spells in winter when the Sound (Øresund) between Sjælland and Sweden may freeze over.

**POLITICS & ECONOMY** Danish Vikings terrorized much of Western Europe for about 300 years after AD 800. In the late 14th century, Denmark formed a union with Norway and Sweden (which included Finland). Sweden broke away in 1523, while Denmark lost Norway to Sweden in 1814. After 1945, Denmark joined NATO and it became a member of the European Union in 1973. In 2010, Greenland, a former Danish territory, became a self-governing territory. In 2011, a centre-left party won parliamentary elections in Denmark. Helle Thorning-Schmidt became the country's first female prime minister.

Denmark is a prosperous country. Resources include some oil and gas. Manufacturing employs 12% of the people. Products include furniture, processed food, machinery, television sets, and textiles. Farming employs 3% of the people, but it is highly scientific. Meat and dairy farming are the chief activities.

**AREA** 43,094 sq km [16,639 sq mi] **POPULATION** 5,543,000
**CAPITAL** Copenhagen **GOVERNMENT** Parliamentary monarchy
**ETHNIC GROUPS** Scandinavian, Inuit, Færoese **LANGUAGES** Danish (official), Greenlandic, English, Færoese **RELIGIONS** Evangelical Lutheran 95% **CURRENCY** Danish krone = 100 øre

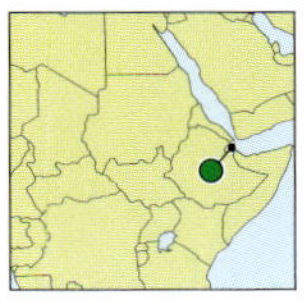

## DJIBOUTI

**GEOGRAPHY** The Republic of Djibouti in eastern Africa occupies a strategic position where the Red Sea meets the Gulf of Aden. Djibouti has one of the world's hottest and driest climates.

**POLITICS & ECONOMY** France set up a territory called French Somaliland in 1888. Its capital, Djibouti, became important when a railway was built to Addis Ababa and Djibouti became the main outlet for Ethiopian trade. In 1967, France renamed the dependency the French Territory of the Afars and Issas, but it was renamed Djibouti on independence in 1977. It became a one-party state in 1981, but a new constitution (1992) permitted four parties which had to maintain a balance between the country's ethnic groups. In 2008, a border dispute led to clashes between Djiboutian and Eritrean troops.

Djibouti is a poor country. Its economy is based largely on the revenue it gets from its port and the railway to Addis Ababa.

**AREA** 23,200 sq km [8,958 sq mi] **POPULATION** 774,000
**CAPITAL** Djibouti **GOVERNMENT** Multiparty republic
**ETHNIC GROUPS** Somali 60%, Afar 35% **LANGUAGES** Arabic and French (both official) **RELIGIONS** Islam 94%, Christianity 6%
**CURRENCY** Djiboutian franc = 100 centimes

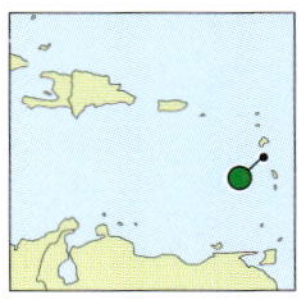

## DOMINICA

The Commonwealth of Dominica, a former British colony, became independent in 1978. The island has a mountainous spine and less than 10% of the land is cultivated. But agriculture employs 40% of the people. The manufacture of coconut-based soap is important, while tourism and mining are other economic activities.

**AREA** 751 sq km [290 sq mi] **POPULATION** 73,000 **CAPITAL** Roseau

## DOMINICAN REPUBLIC

**GEOGRAPHY** Second largest of the Caribbean nations in both area and population, the Dominican Republic shares the island of Hispaniola with Haiti, with the Dominican Republic occupying the eastern two-thirds. The country is mountainous, and the generally hot and humid climate eases with altitude.

**POLITICS & ECONOMY** In 1492, Christopher Columbus landed on Hispaniola and Spaniards soon settled the island, followed by the French, who occupied the western third of the island (which is now Haiti). The island was held by Haitians from 1822 until 1844, when the Dominican Republic was established. Civil war broke out in 1966 but US intervention ended the conflict. Since 1966, the young democracy has survived violent elections under the watchful eye of the United States.

The Dominican Republic is a developing country and agriculture is the chief activity. Sugar cane, rice, bananas and cocoa are leading crops. Food processing is also important and some ferronickel is produced.

**AREA** 48,511 sq km [18,730 sq mi] **POPULATION** 10,089,000
**CAPITAL** Santo Domingo **GOVERNMENT** Multiparty republic
**ETHNIC GROUPS** Mulatto 73%, White 16%, Black 11%
**LANGUAGES** Spanish (official) **RELIGIONS** Roman Catholic 95%
**CURRENCY** Dominican peso = 100 centavos

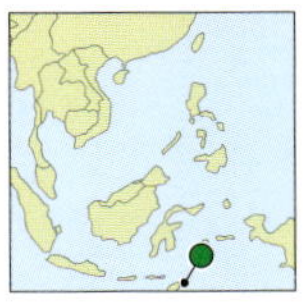

## EAST TIMOR

The Republic of East Timor, also known as Timor-Leste, became fully independent on 20 May 2002. The land is mainly rugged. Temperatures are generally high and the rainfall is moderate. Portugal ruled the area from the late 19th century, when it was called Portuguese Timor. Portugal withdrew in 1975 and Indonesia seized the area. Guerrilla activity mounted under Indonesian rule and, in 1999, the people voted for independence. Agriculture is the main activity and East Timor is the poorest country in South-east Asia. But, in 2006, East Timor and Australia signed a deal to share the revenue from the oil and natural gas deposits under the Timor Sea.

**AREA** 14,874 sq km [5,743 sq mi] **POPULATION** 1,144,000 **CAPITAL** Dili

## ECUADOR

**GEOGRAPHY** The Republic of Ecuador straddles the equator on the west coast of South America. Three ranges of the high Andes Mountains form the backbone of the country. Between the towering, snow-capped peaks of the mountains, some of which are volcanoes, lie a series of high plateaux, or basins. Nearly half of Ecuador's population lives on these plateaux. The coast has a warm tropical climate, despite the cold offshore Peruvian Current. Inland, the altitude gives the plateaux spring-like weather throughout the year.

**POLITICS & ECONOMY** The Inca people of Peru conquered much of what is now Ecuador in the late 15th century. They introduced their language, Quechua, which is widely spoken today. Spanish forces defeated the Incas in 1533 and took control of Ecuador. The country became independent in 1822, following the defeat of a Spanish force in a battle near Quito.

In the 19th and 20th centuries, Ecuador suffered from political instability, while successive governments failed to tackle the country's social and economic problems. A war with Peru in 1941 led to a loss of territory. Disputes continued until 1995, but a border agreement was signed in January 1998. Economic crises in the early 21st century led to the adoption of the US dollar as the official currency. Political instability marred progress. In 2010, a state of emergency was declared following a coup attempt. In 2011, voters approved reforms in a referendum. Critics said the changes enhanced the president's powers even further. In 2013, the leftist Rafael Correa was re-elected president.

The World Bank classifies Ecuador as an 'upper-middle-income' developing country. Agriculture employs 28% of the people and bananas, cocoa and coffee are all important crops. Fishing, forestry, mining and manufacturing are other activities.

**AREA** 283,561 sq km [109,483 sq mi]
**POPULATION** 15,224,000 **CAPITAL** Quito
**GOVERNMENT** Multiparty republic
**ETHNIC GROUPS** Mestizo (mixed White/Amerindian) 72%, Montubio 7%, Afroecuadorian 7%, Amerindian 7%, White 6%
**LANGUAGES** Spanish (official), Quechua, Shuar
**RELIGIONS** Roman Catholic 95%
**CURRENCY** US dollar = 100 cents

## EGYPT

**GEOGRAPHY** The Arab Republic of Egypt is Africa's second largest country by population after Nigeria, though it ranks 13th in area. Most of Egypt is desert. Almost all the people live either in the Nile Valley and its fertile delta or along the Suez Canal, the artificial waterway between the Mediterranean and Red seas. This canal shortens the sea journey between the United Kingdom and India by 9,700 km [6,027 mi]. Recent attempts have been made to irrigate parts of the western desert and thus redistribute the rapidly growing Egyptian population into previously uninhabited regions.

Apart from the Nile Valley, Egypt has three other main regions. The Western and Eastern deserts are parts of the Sahara. The Sinai peninsula (Es Sina), to the east of the Suez Canal, is a mountainous desert region, geographically within Asia. It contains Egypt's highest peak, Gebel Katherîna (2,637 m [8,650 ft]); few people live in this area.

Egypt is a dry country. The low rainfall occurs, if at all, in winter and the country is one of the sunniest places on Earth.

**POLITICS & ECONOMY** Ancient Egypt, which was founded about 5,000 years ago, was one of the great early civilizations. Throughout the country, pyramids, temples and richly decorated tombs are memorials to its great achievements.

After Ancient Egypt declined, the country came under successive foreign rulers. Arabs occupied Egypt in AD 639–42. They introduced the Arabic language and Islam. Their influence was so great that most Egyptians now regard themselves as Arabs.

Egypt came under British rule in 1882, but it gained partial independence in 1922, becoming a monarchy. The monarchy was abolished in 1952, when Egypt became a republic. The creation of Israel in 1948 led Egypt into a series of wars in 1948–9, 1956, 1967 and 1973. Since the late 1970s, Egypt has sought for peace. In 1979, Egypt signed a peace treaty with Israel and regained the Sinai region, which it had lost in a war in 1967. Extremists opposed contacts with Israel and, in 1981, President Sadat, who had signed the treaty, was assassinated.

While Egypt plays a major part in Arab affairs, most of its people are poor. In the 1990s, attacks on foreign visitors caused a decline in the valuable tourist industry. In February 2011, Hosni Mubarak,

Egypt's president since 1981, was forced out of office following huge popular demonstrations. A Supreme Military Council took power and organized elections in 2011–12. President Muhammed Mursi from the formerly banned Muslim Brotherhood was elected in June 2012. Mubarak was sentenced to life imprisonment in 2012 for failing to stop the killing of protesters in the 2011 uprising, but political unrest continues.

Egypt is Africa's second most industrialized country after South Africa, but most people are poor. Oil and textiles are the country's main exports. In 2007, the government announced plans to build several nuclear power stations to generate electricity.

**AREA** 1,001,449 sq km [386,659 sq mi] **POPULATION** 83,688,000
**CAPITAL** Cairo **GOVERNMENT** Republic
**ETHNIC GROUPS** Egyptians/Bedouins/Berbers 99%
**LANGUAGES** Arabic (official), French, English **RELIGIONS** Islam (mainly Sunni Muslim) 90%, Christianity (mainly Coptic Christian) and others 10% **CURRENCY** Egyptian pound = 100 piastres

## EL SALVADOR

**GEOGRAPHY** The Republic of El Salvador is the only country in Central America not to have a coast on the Caribbean Sea. El Salvador has a narrow coastal plain along the Pacific Ocean. Behind the coastal plain, the coastal range is a zone of rugged mountains, including volcanoes, which overlooks a densely populated inland plateau. Beyond the plateau, the land rises to the sparsely populated interior highlands. The coast has a hot tropical climate, but inland this is moderated by the altitude. Rain is heavy between May and October. In October 2011, torrential rains caused flooding that killed more than 30 people in El Salvador.
**POLITICS & ECONOMY** Amerindians have lived in El Salvador for thousands of years. The ruins of Mayan pyramids built between AD 100 and 1000 are still found in the western part of the country. Spanish soldiers conquered the area in 1524 and 1525, and Spain ruled until 1821. In 1823, all the Central American countries, except for Panama, set up the Central American Federation. But El Salvador withdrew in 1840 and declared its independence in 1841. El Salvador suffered from instability throughout the 19th century. The 20th century saw more stable government, but from 1931 military dictatorships alternated with elected governments.

The country remained poor. In the 1970s, protesters demanded that the government introduce reforms to help the poor. Kidnappings and murders committed by left- and right-wing groups caused instability. A civil war broke out in 1979 between the US-backed government forces and left-wing guerrillas. A ceasefire was agreed in 1992. In 2011, the United States added El Salvador and Belize to its list of countries considered to be major producers or transit routes of illegal drugs.

The World Bank classifies El Salvador as a 'lower-middle-income' economy. About three-quarters of the country is farmed. Coffee, grown in the highlands, is the main export, followed by sugar and cotton, which grow on the coastal lowlands. Fishing for lobsters and shrimps is important, but manufacturing is on a small scale.

**AREA** 21,041 sq km [8,124 sq mi]
**POPULATION** 6,091,000 **CAPITAL** San Salvador
**GOVERNMENT** Republic **ETHNIC GROUPS** Mestizo (mixed White and Amerindian) 86%, White 13%, Amerindian 1%
**LANGUAGES** Spanish (official) **RELIGIONS** Roman Catholic 57%, Protestant 21% **CURRENCY** US dollar = 100 cents

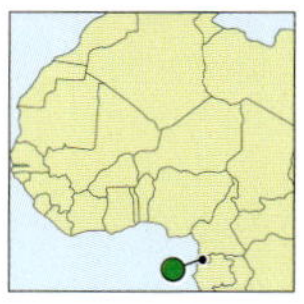

## EQUATORIAL GUINEA

**GEOGRAPHY** The Republic of Equatorial Guinea is a small republic in west-central Africa. It consists of a mainland territory which makes up 90% of the land area, called Rio Muni, between Cameroon and Gabon, and five offshore islands in the Bight of Bonny, the largest of which is Bioko. The island of Annobon lies 560 km [350 mi] south-west of Rio Muni. Rio Muni consists mainly of hills and plateaux behind the coastal plains.

The climate is hot and humid. Bioko is mountainous, with the land rising to 3,008 m [9,869 ft], and hence it is particularly rainy. However, there is a marked dry season between the months of December and February. Mainland Rio Muni has a similar climate, though the rainfall diminishes inland.
**POLITICS & ECONOMY** Portuguese navigators reached the area in 1471. In 1778, Portugal granted Bioko, together with rights over Rio Muni, to Spain.

In 1959, Spain made Bioko and Rio Muni provinces of overseas Spain and, in 1963, it gave the provinces a degree of self-government. Equatorial Guinea became independent in 1968.

The first president of Equatorial Guinea, Francisco Macias Nguema, proved to be a tyrant. He was overthrown in 1979 and a group of officers, led by Lieutenant-Colonel Teodoro Obiang Nguema Mbasogo, set up a Supreme Military Council to rule the country. In 1991, a democratic system was restored, but alleged human rights abuses continued. In 2004, a coup attempt was foiled. In 2011, the corruption watchdog Transparency International placed the country in its list of the 12 most corrupt nations.

Agriculture employs two-thirds of the people. The most valuable crop is coffee. Oil, which has been produced since 1966, accounts for most of the export revenue.

**AREA** 28,051 sq km [10,830 sq mi] **POPULATION** 685,000
**CAPITAL** Malabo **GOVERNMENT** Republic
**ETHNIC GROUPS** Bubi (on Bioko), Fang (in Rio Muni)
**LANGUAGES** Spanish and French (both official)
**RELIGIONS** Christianity **CURRENCY** CFA franc = 100 centimes

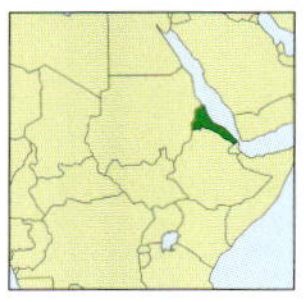

## ERITREA

**GEOGRAPHY** The State of Eritrea consists of a hot, dry coastal plain facing the Red Sea, with a fairly mountainous area in the centre. Most people live in the cooler highland area.
**POLITICS & ECONOMY** From the 1st century AD, Eritrea was part of the ancient Kingdom of Axum, which adopted Christianity in the 4th century AD. It began to decline in the 7th century. The Ottoman Turks took over the area in the 16th century and it became an Italian colony in the 1880s. The Italians were driven out in 1941 and, in 1952, it became part of Ethiopia. A guerrilla struggle launched in 1961 ended in 1993, when Eritrea became independent. Economic recovery was hampered by conflict with Yemen over three islands in the Red Sea. In 1988–9, clashes occurred along the border with Ethiopia. A peace agreement was signed in 2000, but problems continued. In 2011, the UN accused Eritrea of backing the Islamist al-Shabab in Eritrea. Tension between Eritrea and Ethiopia continued, and in 2012 Ethiopia attacked military bases in Eritrea where rebel groups were trained.

The main economic activities are farming and livestock rearing. The few manufacturing industries are based mainly in Asmara.

**AREA** 117,600 sq km [45,405 sq mi] **POPULATION** 6,086,000
**CAPITAL** Asmara **GOVERNMENT** Transitional government
**ETHNIC GROUPS** Tigrinya 55%, Tigre 30%, Saho 4%, Kunama 2%, others 16% **LANGUAGES** Tigrinya, Arabic, English (all official), others **RELIGIONS** Islam, Coptic Christian, Roman Catholic
**CURRENCY** Nakfa = 100 cents

## ESTONIA

**GEOGRAPHY** The Republic of Estonia is the smallest of the three states on the Baltic Sea, which were formerly part of the Soviet Union, but became independent in the early 1990s. Estonia consists of a generally flat plain which was covered by ice sheets during the Ice Age. The land is strewn with moraine (rocks deposited by the ice).

The country is dotted with more than 1,500 small lakes. The large Lake Peipus (Chudskoye Ozero) and the River Narva together make up much of Estonia's eastern border with Russia. The largest of the islands is Saaremaa (Sarema). The climate is fairly mild because of the moderating effects of the sea.
**POLITICS & ECONOMY** The ancestors of the Estonians, who are related to the Finns, settled in the area several thousand years ago. German crusaders, known as the Teutonic Knights, introduced Christianity in the early 13th century. By the 16th century, German noblemen owned much of the land in Estonia. In 1561, Sweden took the northern part of the country and Poland the south. From 1625, Sweden controlled the entire country until Sweden handed it over to Russia in 1721.

Estonian nationalists campaigned for their independence from around the mid-19th century. Finally, Estonia was proclaimed independent in 1918. In 1919, the government began to break up the large estates and distribute land among the peasants.

In 1939, Germany and the Soviet Union agreed to take over parts of Eastern Europe. In 1940, Soviet forces occupied Estonia, but they were driven out by the Germans in 1941. Soviet troops returned in 1944 and Estonia became one of the 15 Soviet Socialist Republics of the Soviet Union. The Estonians strongly opposed Soviet rule. Many of them were deported to Siberia.

Political changes in the Soviet Union in the late 1980s led to renewed demands for freedom. In 1990, the Estonian government declared the country independent and, finally, the Soviet Union recognized this act in September 1991, shortly before the Soviet Union was dissolved. Estonia adopted a new constitution in 1992, and elections were held. In 1994, Russian troops withdrew, but anti-Russian sentiment continued. On 1 January 2011, Estonia became the 17th member of the eurozone.

Under Soviet rule, Estonia was the most prosperous of the three Baltic states. Since 1988, Estonia has worked to restructure its economy. Turning increasingly to the West, it became a member of both the North Atlantic Treaty Organization and the European Union in 2004. Estonia's resources include oil shale and its forests. Industries produce fertilizers, processed food, machinery, petrochemical products, wood products and textiles. Agriculture and fishing are also important activities.

**AREA** 45,100 sq km [17,413 sq mi] **POPULATION** 1,275,000
**CAPITAL** Tallinn **GOVERNMENT** Multiparty republic
**ETHNIC GROUPS** Estonian 69%, Russian 26%, Ukrainian 2%, Belarusian 1%, Finnish 1% **LANGUAGES** Estonian (official), Russian
**RELIGIONS** Lutheran, Russian and Estonian Orthodox, Methodist, Baptist, Roman Catholic **CURRENCY** Euro = 100 cents

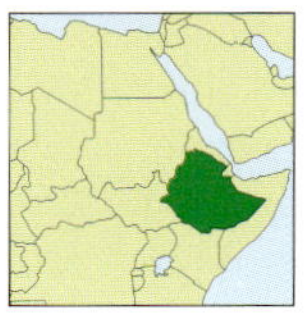

## ETHIOPIA

**GEOGRAPHY** Ethiopia is a landlocked country in north-eastern Africa. The land is mainly mountainous, though there are extensive plains in the east, bordering southern Eritrea, and in the south, bordering Somalia. The highlands are divided into two blocks by an arm of the Great Rift Valley which runs throughout eastern Africa. North of the Rift Valley, the land is especially rugged, rising to 4,533 m [14,872 ft] at Ras Dashen. South-east of Ras Dashen is Lake Tana, source of the River Abay (Blue Nile). The climate is affected by the altitude. The rainfall in the highlands is generally more than 1,000 mm [39 in]. The lowlands are hot and arid.
**POLITICS & ECONOMY** Ethiopia was the home of an ancient monarchy, which became Christian in the 4th century. In the 7th century, Muslims gained control of the lowlands, but Christianity survived in the highlands. Ethiopia resisted attempts to colonize it, but Italy invaded the country in 1935. The Italians were driven out in 1941 during World War II.

In 1952, Eritrea, on the Red Sea coast, was federated with Ethiopia. But in 1961, Eritrean nationalists demanded their freedom and began a struggle that ended in their independence in 1993. In 1995, because of Ethiopia's great ethnic diversity, the country was divided into nine provinces, each with its own regional assembly. In 1998, boundary disputes with Eritrea led to conflict. A peace agreement was reached in 2001, but tensions mounted in 2005–6 when Ethiopia failed to accept an international ruling over Badme, a border settlement. In 2006, Ethiopian troops intervened in Somalia on behalf of its provisional government. Ethiopian troops defeated the Islamists, who had taken control of Mogadishu. Ethiopia withdrew its forces in 2009. In 2011, Ethiopian troops returned to Somalia in support of the African Union troops combating the Islamist al-Shabab forces.

Ethiopia is one of the world poorest countries. It is heavily dependent on aid. Agriculture is the main activity. Coffee and the drug khat are leading exports.

**AREA** 1,104,300 sq km [426,370 sq mi]
**POPULATION** 91,196,000 **CAPITAL** Addis Ababa
**GOVERNMENT** Federation of nine provinces
**ETHNIC GROUPS** Oromo 34%, Amhara 27%, Somali 6%, Tigraway 6%, Sidama 4% **LANGUAGES** Amharic (official), many others **RELIGIONS** Ethiopian Orthodox 43%, Islam 34%, Protestant 19% **CURRENCY** Birr = 100 santim

## FALKLAND ISLANDS

Comprising two main islands and over 200 small ones, the Falkland Islands (or the Islas Malvinas, as they are called in Argentina) lie 480 km [300 mi] from South America. Sheep farming is the main activity, though the search for oil and diamonds holds out hope for the future. A referendum held early in 2013 voted overwhelmingly to stay British.

**AREA** 12,173 sq km [4,700 sq mi]
**POPULATION** 3,000 **CAPITAL** Stanley

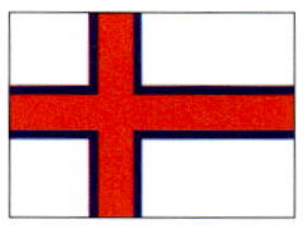
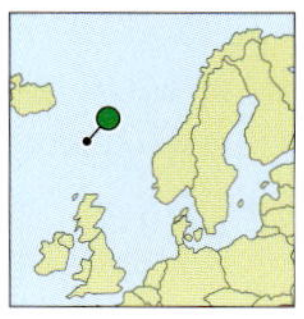

## FÆROE ISLANDS

The Færoe Islands are a group of 18 volcanic islands and some reefs in the North Atlantic Ocean. The islands have been Danish since the 1380s, but they became largely self-governing in 1948. In 2001, a referendum on independence was called off after Denmark said that subsidies would end soon after independence.

**AREA** 1,399 sq km [540 sq mi]
**POPULATION** 49,000 **CAPITAL** Tórshavn

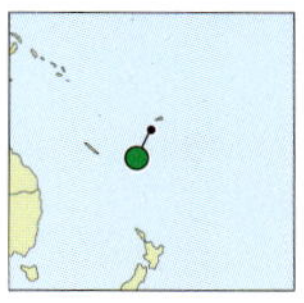

## FIJI

The Republic of Fiji (the official name of Fiji since February 2011) consists of more than 800 Melanesian islands, the biggest being Viti Levu and Vanua Levu. The climate is tropical. A former British colony, Fiji became independent in 1970. Its recent history has been marred by efforts of ethnic Fijians to impose their rule, stopping members of the ethnic Indian community from holding senior cabinet posts. Coups have occurred in 1987, 2000 and 2006.

**AREA** 18,274 sq km [7,056 sq mi] **POPULATION** 890,000 **CAPITAL** Suva

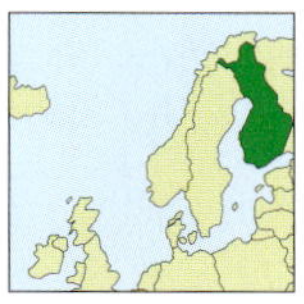

## FINLAND

**GEOGRAPHY** The Republic of Finland is a beautiful country in northern Europe. In the south, behind the coastal lowlands where most Finns live, lies a region of sparkling lakes worn out by ice sheets in the Ice Age. The thinly populated northern uplands cover about two-fifths of the country.

Helsinki, the capital city, has warm summers, but the average temperatures between the months of December and March are below freezing point. Snow covers the land in winter. The north has less precipitation than the south, but it is much colder.

**POLITICS & ECONOMY** Between 1150 and 1809, Finland was under Swedish rule. The close links between the countries continue today. Swedish remains an official language in Finland and many towns have Swedish as well as Finnish names.

In 1809, Finland became a grand duchy of the Russian empire. It finally declared itself independent in 1917, after the Russian Revolution and the collapse of the Russian empire. But during World War II (1939–45), the Soviet Union declared war on Finland and took part of Finland's territory. Finland allied itself with Germany, but it lost more land to the Soviet Union at the end of the war.

After World War II, Finland became a neutral country and negotiated peace treaties with the Soviet Union. Finland also strengthened its relations with other northern European countries and became an associate member of the European Free Trade Association (EFTA) in 1961. Finland became a full member of EFTA in 1986, but then became a member of the European Union on 1 January 1995. It adopted the euro as its currency in 2002. In 2000 and 2006, Tarja Halonen was elected Finland's first woman president, while, in 2010, Mari Kiviniemi became its second woman prime minister. Sauli Niinistö was elected president in 2012.

Forests are the chief resource and wood, wood products and paper once dominated the economy. They still make up about a quarter of exports, but, since World War II, Finland has set up many new industries, which employ around 17% of the workforce. Major exports include telecommunications equipment, paper products, and iron and steel.

**AREA** 338,145 sq km [130,558 sq mi]
**POPULATION** 5,263,000 **CAPITAL** Helsinki
**GOVERNMENT** Multiparty republic **ETHNIC GROUPS** Finnish 93%, Swedish 6% **LANGUAGES** Finnish and Swedish (both official)
**RELIGIONS** Evangelical Lutheran 83% **CURRENCY** Euro = 100 cents

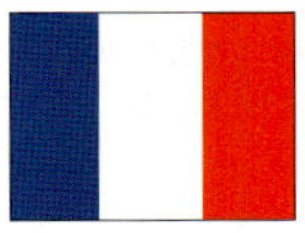
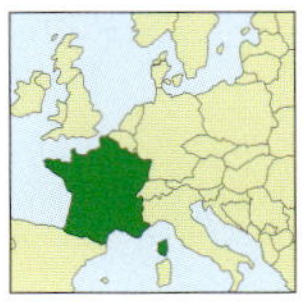

## FRANCE

**GEOGRAPHY** The Republic of France is the largest country in Western Europe. The scenery is extremely varied. The Vosges Mountains overlook the Rhine valley in the north-east, the Jura Mountains and the Alps form the borders with Switzerland and Italy in the south-east, while the Pyrenees straddle France's border with Spain. The only large highland area entirely within France is the Massif Central between the Rhône-Saône valley and the basin of Aquitaine in southern France.

Brittany (Bretagne) and Normandy (Normande) form a scenic hill region. Fertile lowlands cover most of northern France, including the densely populated Paris basin. Another major lowland area, the Aquitanian basin, is in the south-west, while the Rhône-Saône valley and the Mediterranean lowlands are in the south-east.

The climate of France varies from west to east and from north to south. The west comes under the moderating influence of the Atlantic Ocean, giving generally mild weather. To the east, summers are warmer and winters colder. The climate also becomes warmer as one travels from north to south. The Mediterranean Sea coast has hot, dry summers and mild, moist winters. The Alps, Jura and Pyrenees mountains have snowy winters. Winter sports centres are found in all three areas. Large glaciers occupy high valleys in the Alps.

**POLITICS & ECONOMY** The Romans conquered France (then called Gaul) in the 50s BC. Roman rule began to decline in the 5th century AD and, in 486, the Frankish realm (as France was called) became independent under a Christian king, Clovis. In 800, Charlemagne, who had been king since 768, became emperor of the Romans. He extended France's boundaries, but in 843 his empire was divided into three parts and the area of France contracted. After the Norman invasion of England in 1066, large areas of France came under English rule, but this was all but ended in 1453.

France later became a powerful monarchy. But the French Revolution (1789–99) ended absolute rule by French kings. In 1799, Napoleon Bonaparte took power and fought a series of brilliant military campaigns before his final defeat in 1815. The monarchy was restored until 1848, when the Second Republic was founded. In 1852, Napoleon's nephew became Napoleon III, but the Third Republic was established in 1875. France was the scene of much fighting during World War I (1914–18) and World War II (1939–45), causing great loss of life and much damage to the economy.

In 1946, France adopted a new constitution, establishing the Fourth Republic. But political instability and costly colonial wars slowed France's post-war recovery. In 1958, Charles de Gaulle was elected president and he introduced a new constitution, giving the president extra powers and inaugurating the Fifth Republic.

Since the 1960s, France has made rapid economic progress, becoming one of the most prosperous nations in the European Union. But France's government faced a number of problems, including unemployment, pollution, and the growing number of elderly people. In 2011–12, France faced economic difficulties linked to the problems of some eurozone member nations. A social issue concerns the large numbers of immigrants, including Muslims from North Africa.

In 2002, the euro became France's sole unit of currency, replacing the franc. In 2005, France was rocked by inter-ethnic violence and, in 2007, the right-wing Nicolas Sarkozy was elected president. In 2009, he announced that France would rejoin NATO, from which President de Gaulle had withdrawn in 1966. François Hollande, a socialist, was elected president in 2012.

France is one of the world's most developed countries. Its natural resources include its fertile soil, together with deposits of bauxite, coal, iron ore, oil and natural gas, and potash. France is also one of the world's top manufacturing nations, and it has often innovated in bold and imaginative ways. The TGV and hypermarkets are typical examples. Paris is a world centre of fashion industries, but France has many other industrial towns and cities. Major manufactures include aircraft, cars, chemicals, electronic and metal products, machinery, processed food, steel and textiles.

Agriculture employs about 4% of the people, but France is the largest producer of farm products in Western Europe, producing most of the food it needs. Wheat is the leading crop and livestock farming is of major importance. Fishing and forestry are leading industries, while tourism is a major activity.

**AREA** 551,500 sq km [212,934 sq mi] **POPULATION** 65,631,000
**CAPITAL** Paris **GOVERNMENT** Multiparty republic
**ETHNIC GROUPS** Celtic, Latin, Arab, Teutonic, Slavic
**LANGUAGES** French (official) **RELIGIONS** Roman Catholic 85%, Islam 8%, others **CURRENCY** Euro = 100 cents

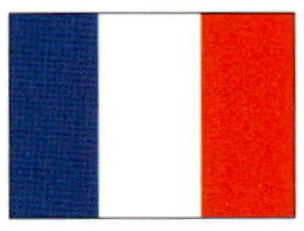

## FRENCH GUIANA

**GEOGRAPHY** French Guiana is the smallest country in mainland South America. The coastal plain is swampy in places, but some dry areas are cultivated. Inland lies a plateau, with the low Tumachumac Mountains in the south. Most of the rivers run north towards the Atlantic Ocean.

French Guiana has a hot, equatorial climate, with high temperatures throughout the year. The rainfall is heavy, especially between December and June, but the climate is dry between August and October. The north-east trade winds blow constantly across the country.

**POLITICS & ECONOMY** The first people to live in what is now French Guiana were Amerindians. Today, only a few of them survive in the interior. The first Europeans to explore the coast arrived in 1500, and they were followed by adventurers seeking El Dorado, the mythical city of gold. Cayenne was founded in 1637 by a group of French merchants. The area became a French colony in the late 17th century.

France used the colony as a penal settlement for political prisoners from the times of the French Revolution in the 1790s. From the 1850s to 1945, the country became notorious as a place where prisoners were harshly treated. Many of them died, unable to survive in the tropical conditions.

In 1946, French Guiana became an overseas department of France, and in 1974 it also became an administrative region. An independence movement developed in the 1980s, but most people want to retain their links with France. In 2010, the people voted in a referendum to reject plans for increased autonomy.

Although it has rich forest and mineral resources, such as bauxite (aluminium ore), French Guiana is a developing country. It depends greatly on France for money to run its services and the government is the country's biggest employer. Since 1968, Kourou in French Guiana, the European Space Agency's rocket-launching site, has earned money for France by sending communications satellites into space.

**AREA** 90,000 sq km [34,749 sq mi]
**POPULATION** 203,000 **CAPITAL** Cayenne
**GOVERNMENT** Overseas department of France
**ETHNIC GROUPS** Black or Mulatto 66%, East Indian/Chinese and Amerindian 12%, White 12%, others 10% **LANGUAGES** French (official) **RELIGIONS** Roman Catholic **CURRENCY** Euro = 100 cents

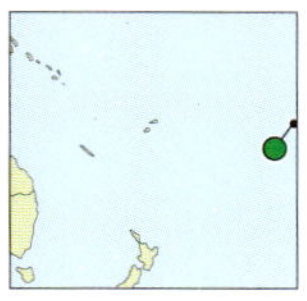

## FRENCH POLYNESIA

French Polynesia consists of 130 islands, scattered over 4 million sq km [1.5 million sq mi] of the Pacific Ocean. Tribal chiefs in the area agreed to a French protectorate in 1843. They gained increased autonomy in 1984, but the links with France ensure a high standard of living.

**AREA** 4,000 sq km [1,544 sq mi]
**POPULATION** 275,000 **CAPITAL** Papeete

## GABON

**GEOGRAPHY** The Gabonese Republic lies on the equator in west-central Africa. In area, it is a little larger than the United Kingdom, with a coastline 800 km [500 mi] long. Behind the narrow, partly lagoon-lined coastal plain, the land rises to hills, plateaux and mountains divided by deep valleys carved by the River Ogooué and its tributaries.

Most of Gabon has an equatorial climate, with high temperatures and humidity throughout the year. Rainfall is heavy and the skies are often cloudy.

**POLITICS & ECONOMY** Gabon became a French colony in the 1880s, but it achieved full independence in 1960. In 1964, an attempted coup was put down when French troops intervened and crushed the revolt. In 1967, Bernard-Albert Bongo, who later renamed himself El Hadj Omar Bongo, became president. He declared Gabon a one-party state in 1968. Opposition parties were legalized in 1991, but Bongo was re-elected president in 1993. Following his death in 2008, he was succeeded by his son Ali Ben Bongo, who was elected in 2009.

Gabon's natural resources include its forests, oil and gas deposits, manganese and uranium. Its mineral deposits make it one of Africa's better-off countries. But agriculture still employs about 30% of the people and many farmers produce little more than they need to support their families.

**AREA** 267,668 sq km [103,347 sq mi]
**POPULATION** 1,608,000 **CAPITAL** Libreville
**GOVERNMENT** Multiparty republic
**ETHNIC GROUPS** Four major Bantu tribes: Fang, Bapounou, Nzebi and Obamba **LANGUAGES** French (official), Fang, Myene, Nzebi, Bapounou/Eschira, Bandjabi
**RELIGIONS** Christianity 65%, animist, Islam
**CURRENCY** CFA franc = 100 centimes

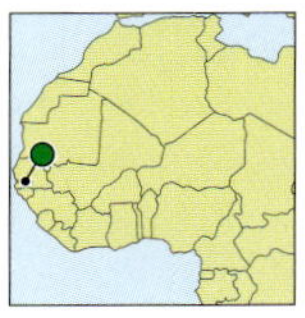

## GAMBIA, THE

**GEOGRAPHY** The Republic of The Gambia is the smallest country in mainland Africa. It consists of a narrow strip of land bordering the River Gambia. The Gambia is almost entirely enclosed by Senegal, except along the short Atlantic coastline.

The Gambia has hot and humid summers, but winter temperatures (November to May) drop to around 16°C [61°F]. In the summer, moist south-westerlies bring rain, which is heaviest on the coast.

**POLITICS & ECONOMY** English traders bought rights to trade on the River Gambia in 1588, and in 1664 the English established a settlement on an island in the river estuary. In 1765, the British founded Senegambia, which included parts of The Gambia and Senegal. In 1783, Britain handed this colony over to France. In the 19th century, Britain and France discussed the exchange of The Gambia for some other French territory, but an agreement was reached and Britain made The Gambia a British colony in 1888.

The Gambia achieved independence in 1965 and it became a republic in 1970. In 1981, an attempted coup in The Gambia was put down with the help of Senegalese troops. In 1982, The Gambia and Senegal set up a defence alliance, called the Confederation of Senegambia. But this alliance was dissolved in 1989. In 1994, a military group led by Captain Yahya Jammeh overthrew the government of Sir Dawda Jawara. Jammeh became president and was re-elected in 1996, 2001, 2006 and 2011.

Agriculture is the chief activity. Food crops include cassava, millet and sorghum, but groundnuts (peanuts) and groundnut products are the main exports. Tourism is growing and offshore oilfields were discovered in 2004. In the early 21st century, The Gambia became a transit point for drugs from Latin America.

**AREA** 11,295 sq km [4,361 sq mi]
**POPULATION** 1,840,000 **CAPITAL** Banjul
**GOVERNMENT** Republic
**ETHNIC GROUPS** Mandinka 42%, Fula 18%, Wolof 16%, Jola 10%, Serahuli 9%, others
**LANGUAGES** English (official), Mandinka, Wolof, Fula
**RELIGIONS** Islam 90%, Christianity 8%, traditional beliefs 2%
**CURRENCY** Dalasi = 100 butut

## GEORGIA

**GEOGRAPHY** Georgia is a country on the borders of Europe and Asia, facing the Black Sea. The land is rugged with the Caucasus Mountains forming its northern border. The highest mountain in this range, Mount Elbrus (5,642 m [18,510 ft]), lies over the border in Russia. The Black Sea plains have hot summers and mild winters. The rainfall is heavy, though inland areas are drier.

**POLITICS & ECONOMY** The first Georgian state was set up nearly 2,500 years ago. But for much of its history, the area was ruled by various conquerors. Christianity was introduced in AD 330. Georgia freed itself of foreign rule in the 11th and 12th centuries, but Mongol armies attacked in the 13th century. From the 16th to the 18th centuries, Persia and the Turkish Ottoman empire struggled for control of the area, and in the late 18th century Georgia sought the protection of Russia. By the early 19th century, it was part of the Russian empire. After the Russian Revolution of 1917, Georgia declared its independence, but Russia invaded, making the country part of the Soviet regime. Georgia declared itself independent in 1991. It became a separate country when the Soviet Union was dissolved in December 1991.

Georgia contains three regions containing minority peoples: Abkhazia in the north-west, South Ossetia in north-central Georgia, and Adjaria (also spelled Adzharia) in the south-west. Civil war broke out in South Ossetia in the early 1990s, while fierce fighting continued in Abkhazia until the late 1990s. In 2000, Georgia agreed to recognize Adjaria's autonomy in the country's constitution. In 2003, the pro-Western Mikhail Saakashvili was elected president following the 'Rose Revolution'. Following Saakashvili's re-election in 2008, relations with Russia deteriorated. In August 2008, Georgia tried to retake South Ossetia by force. Russian troops counter-attacked and drove Georgian troops out of South Ossetia and Abkhazia. Parliamentary elections in 2012 resulted in the defeat of Saakashvili's party and, until presidential elections in 2013, power is being shared.

Georgia is a developing country. Agriculture, food processing and perfume-making are important activities. Products include barley, citrus fruits, grapes for wine-making, maize, tea, tobacco and vegetables. Sheep and cattle are reared.

**AREA** 69,700 sq km [26,911 sq mi]
**POPULATION** 4,571,000 **CAPITAL** Tbilisi
**GOVERNMENT** Multiparty republic
**ETHNIC GROUPS** Georgian 84%, Azeri 7%, Armenian 6%, Russian 1%, others 2%
**LANGUAGES** Georgian (official), Russian, Armenian, Azeri
**RELIGIONS** Georgian Orthodox 84%, Islam 10%, Armenian Gregorian 4% **CURRENCY** Lari = 100 tetri

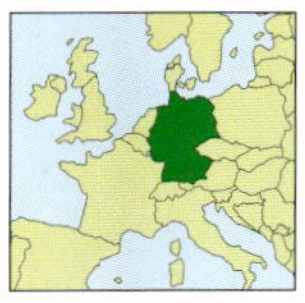

## GERMANY

**GEOGRAPHY** The Federal Republic of Germany is the fourth largest country in Western Europe, after France, Spain, and Sweden. The North German Plain borders the North Sea in the north-west and the Baltic Sea in the north-east. Major rivers draining the plain include the Weser, Elbe and Oder.

The central highlands include the Harz Mountains, the Thuringian Forest (Thüringer Wald), the Ore Mountains (Erzgebirge), and the Bohemian Forest (Böhmerwald) on the Czech border. The Bavarian Alps in the south contain Germany's highest peak, Zugspitze, at 2,962 m [9,718 ft] above sea level. The Black Forest (Schwarzwald) in the south-west overlooks the River Rhine. North-western Germany has a mild climate, but the Baltic coasts are cooler. To the south, the climate becomes more continental, especially in the highlands. Precipitation is greatest on the uplands, with snow in winter.

**POLITICS & ECONOMY** Germany and its allies were defeated in World War I (1914–18) and the country became a republic. Adolf Hitler came to power in 1933 and ruled as a dictator. His order to invade Poland led to the start of World War II (1939–45), which ended with Germany in ruins.

In 1945, Germany was divided into four military zones. In 1949, the American, British and French zones were amalgamated to form the Federal Republic of Germany (West Germany), while the Soviet zone became the German Democratic Republic (East Germany), a Communist state. Berlin, which had also been partitioned, became a divided city. West Berlin was part of West Germany, while East Berlin became the capital of East Germany. Bonn was the capital of West Germany.

Tension between East and West mounted during the Cold War, but West Germany rebuilt its economy quickly. In East Germany, the recovery was less rapid. In the late 1980s, reforms in the Soviet Union led to unrest in East Germany. Free elections were held in East Germany in 1990 and, on 3 October 1990, Germany was reunited.

The united Germany adopted West Germany's official name, the Federal Republic of Germany. In the 1990s, the government faced many problems, especially those arising from reunification. In 1999, the parliament moved from Bonn to the reconstructed Reichstag building in Berlin. In 2005, Angela Merkel became Germany's first female Chancellor. She was swept back into power in elections in 2009.

West Germany's 'economic miracle' after World War II was greatly helped by foreign aid. Today, Germany is one of the world's leading economic powers. It is a leading member of the European Union and the 17-member eurozone. In 2011–12, it helped to maintain the eurozone in supporting debt-ridden countries, such as Greece. The mainstay of its export-led economy is manufacturing. Exports include machinery, metals, chemicals and vehicles. Germany has some coal, potash and rock salt deposits, but it imports many industrial raw materials. Germany also imports food. Leading agricultural products include fruits, grapes for wine-making, potatoes, sugar beet and vegetables. Livestock include beef and dairy cattle.

**AREA** 357,022 sq km [137,846 sq mi]
**POPULATION** 81,306,000 **CAPITAL** Berlin
**GOVERNMENT** Federal multiparty republic
**ETHNIC GROUPS** German 92%, Turkish 2%, Serbo-Croatian, Italian, Greek, Polish, Spanish **LANGUAGES** German (official)
**RELIGIONS** Protestant (mainly Lutheran) 34%, Roman Catholic 34%, Islam 4%, others **CURRENCY** Euro = 100 cents

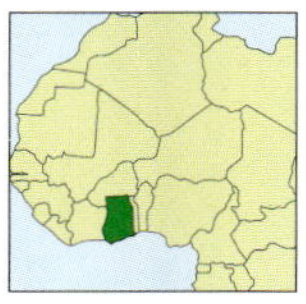

## GHANA

**GEOGRAPHY** The Republic of Ghana faces the Gulf of Guinea in West Africa. This hot country, just north of the equator, was formerly called the Gold Coast. Behind the thickly populated southern coastal plains, which are lined with lagoons, lies a plateau region in the south-west.

Accra has a hot, tropical climate. Rain occurs all through the year, though Accra is drier than areas inland.

**POLITICS & ECONOMY** Portuguese explorers reached the area in 1471 and named it the Gold Coast. The area became a centre of the slave trade in the 17th century. The slave trade was ended in the 1860s and, gradually, the British took control of the area. After independence in 1957, attempts were made to develop the economy by creating large state-owned manufacturing industries. But debt and corruption, together with falls in the price of cocoa, the chief export, caused economic problems. This led to instability and frequent coups. In 1981, power was invested in a Provisional National Defence Council, led by Flight-Lieutenant Jerry Rawlings.

The government steadied the economy and introduced reforms. In 1992, a new constitution allowing for multiparty elections was adopted. Rawlings was elected president in 1992 and 1996. He retired in 2002 and was succeeded as president by John Ageykum Kufuor. In 2008, opposition leader John Atta-Mills was narrowly elected president. He was succeeded in 2012 by John Dramani Mahama.

The World Bank classifies Ghana as a 'lower-middle-income' developing country. Most people are poor and farming employs 56% of the population.

**AREA** 238,533 sq km [92,098 sq mi] **POPULATION** 24,652,000
**CAPITAL** Accra **GOVERNMENT** Republic
**ETHNIC GROUPS** Akan 47%, Mole-Dagbon 17%, Ewe 14%, Ga-Dangme 7%, Gurma 3% **LANGUAGES** English (official), Asante, Ewe, Fante, Boron, Dagomba **RELIGIONS** Christianity 71%, Islam 18%, traditional beliefs 5% **CURRENCY** Cedi = 100 pesewas

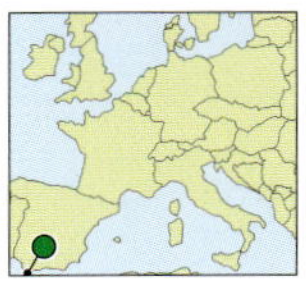

## GIBRALTAR

Gibraltar occupies a strategic position on the south coast of Spain where the Mediterranean meets the Atlantic. It was recognized as a British possession in 1713 and, despite Spanish claims, its population has consistently voted to retain its contacts with Britain.

**AREA** 6 sq km [2.3 sq mi]
**POPULATION** 29,000 **CAPITAL** Gibraltar Town

## GREECE

**GEOGRAPHY** The Hellenic Republic, as Greece is officially called, is a rugged country situated at the southern end of the Balkan peninsula. Olympus, at 2,917 m [9,570 ft], is the highest peak. Islands make up about a fifth of the land area.

Low-lying areas in Greece have mild, moist winters and hot, dry summers. The east coast has more than 2,700 hours of sunshine a year and only about half of the rainfall of the west. The mountains have a much more severe climate, with snow on the higher slopes in winter.

**POLITICS & ECONOMY** Around 2,500 years ago, Greece became the birthplace of Western civilization, and Ancient Greek ruins and art still attract millions of tourists to the country. The first civilization, the Minoan, was centred on Crete. It flourished between about 3000 and 1400 BC. Following the end of the related Mycaenean period on the mainland (1580–1100 BC), a 'dark age' lasted until about 800 BC. But from 750 BC, Greeks became rich traders and the city-state of Athens reached its peak in 461–431 BC. Greece became a Roman province in 146 BC and, in AD 365, it became part of the Byzantine empire.

The Byzantine empire fell to the Turks in 1453. But Greece became an independent monarchy in 1830. After World War II (1939–45), when Germany ruled Greece, a civil war broke out between Greek Communists and nationalists. It ended in 1949 and a military dictatorship seized power in 1967. The monarchy was abolished in 1973 and democracy was restored in 1974. Greece joined the European Community (now the European Union) in 1981 and, on 1 January 2002, the euro became the sole unit of currency. In 2010–12, its government faced a debt crisis and was forced to take drastic emergency economic cuts, amidst growing public unrest.

Greece is one of the EU's less economically developed members. Manufactured products include processed food, cement, chemicals, metal products, textiles and tobacco. Greece also mines lignite (brown coal), bauxite and chromite. Crops include barley, grapes, dried fruits, olives, potatoes, sugar beet and wheat. Livestock farming is important and tourism is a major industry.

**AREA** 131,957 sq km [50,949 sq mi]
**POPULATION** 10,768,000 **CAPITAL** Athens
**GOVERNMENT** Multiparty republic **ETHNIC GROUPS** Greek 98%
**LANGUAGES** Greek (official) **RELIGIONS** Greek Orthodox 98%
**CURRENCY** Euro = 100 cents

## GREENLAND

Greenland is the world's largest island. Settlements are confined to the coast, because an ice sheet covers four-fifths of the land. Greenland became a Danish possession in 1380. Full internal self-government was granted in 1981 and, in 2009, Greenland became a self-governing territory, though it remains dependent on Danish subsidies.

**AREA** 2,175,600 sq km [838,999 sq mi]
**POPULATION** 58,000 **CAPITAL** Nuuk

## GRENADA

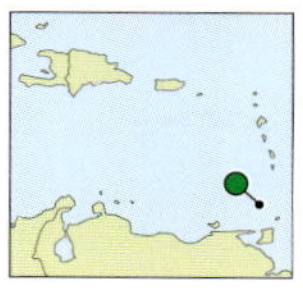

The most southerly of the Windward Islands in the Caribbean Sea, Grenada became independent from the UK in 1974. A military group seized power in 1983, when the prime minister was killed. US troops intervened and restored order and constitutional government.

**AREA** 344 sq km [133 sq mi]
**POPULATION** 109,000 **CAPITAL** St George's

## GUADELOUPE

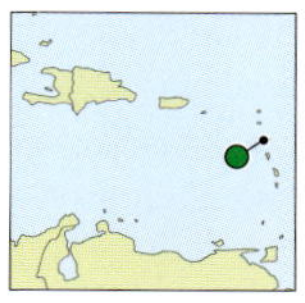

Guadeloupe is a French overseas department which includes seven Caribbean islands, the largest of which is Basse-Terre. French aid has helped to maintain a reasonable standard of living for the people.

**AREA** 1,705 sq km [658 sq mi]
**POPULATION** 453,000 **CAPITAL** Basse-Terre

## GUAM

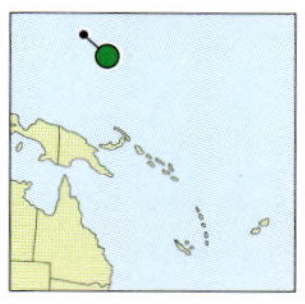

Guam, a strategically important 'unincorporated territory' of the USA, is the largest of the Mariana Islands in the Pacific Ocean. It is composed of a coralline limestone plateau.

**AREA** 549 sq km [212 sq mi]
**POPULATION** 160,000 **CAPITAL** Agana

## GUATEMALA

**GEOGRAPHY** The Republic of Guatemala in Central America contains a densely populated mountain region, with fertile soils. The mountains, which run in an east–west direction, contain many volcanoes, some of which are active. Volcanic eruptions and earthquakes are common in the highlands. South of the mountains lie the thinly populated Pacific coastlands, while a large inland plain occupies the north.

The lowlands of Guatemala are hot and rainy, but the central highlands are cooler and drier. Guatemala City has a pleasant, warm climate with a dry season between November and April.

**POLITICS & ECONOMY** Much of what is now Guatemala was part of the Maya empire which thrived between AD 300 and 900. Spain ruled the area from the 1520s until 1821. In 1823, Guatemala joined the Central American Federation. But it became fully independent in 1839. Instability and periodic violence have marred its progress. Guatemala has a long-standing claim over Belize, but this was reduced in 1983 to the southern fifth of the country. Between 1960 and 1996, civil war occurred between left-wing groups, including many Amerindians, and government forces. The war claimed perhaps 200,000 lives. In 2011, former army general Otto Perez Molina of the right-wing Patriotic Party was elected president.

Guatemala is ranked as a 'lower-middle-income' economy. Agriculture employs 38% of the population. Coffee, sugar, bananas and beef are exported, and the spice cardamom and cotton are also important. Maize is the main food crop.

**AREA** 108,889 sq km [42,042 sq mi]
**POPULATION** 14,099,000 **CAPITAL** Guatemala City
**GOVERNMENT** Republic **ETHNIC GROUPS** Ladino (mixed Hispanic and Amerindian) 55%, Amerindian 43%, others 2%
**LANGUAGES** Spanish (official), Amerindian languages
**RELIGIONS** Roman Catholic, indigenous Mayan beliefs
**CURRENCY** US dollar; Quetzal = 100 centavos

## GUINEA

**GEOGRAPHY** The Republic of Guinea faces the Atlantic Ocean in West Africa. A flat, swampy plain borders the coast. Behind this plain, the land rises to a plateau region called Fouta Djalon. The Upper Niger Plains, named after one of Africa's longest rivers, the Niger, which rises there, are in the north-east.

Guinea has a tropical climate and Conakry has its rainy period between May and November, the coolest season. In the dry season, hot harmattan winds blow from the Sahara.

**POLITICS & ECONOMY** Guinea came under the influence of several medieval African states, including Ancient Ghana and Ancient Mali. France began to control the area in the late 19th century. Guinea became independent in 1958. Its leaders pursued socialist policies but resorted to repressive measures to hold on to power. A military regime under Lansana Conté took over in 1984, but a multiparty system was restored in 1992. Conté was elected president in 1993, 1998 and 2002. But following his death in 2008, an army group led by Captain Mousa Dadis Camara seized power. But in 2010, Alpha Condé was elected president in Guinea's first democratic election since independence.

Guinea is a 'low-income' developing country. Its resources include bauxite (aluminium ore), diamonds, gold, iron ore and uranium. Bauxite and alumina (processed bauxite) account for more than half of the country's exports. Agriculture employs more than 70% of the people, but most farmers are poor. Manufactures include alumina, processed food and textiles.

**AREA** 245,857 sq km [94,925 sq mi]
**POPULATION** 10,885,000 **CAPITAL** Conakry
**GOVERNMENT** Multiparty republic
**ETHNIC GROUPS** Peuhl 40%, Malinke 30%, Soussou 20%, others 10% **LANGUAGES** French (official)
**RELIGIONS** Islam 85%, Christianity 8%, traditional beliefs 7%
**CURRENCY** Guinean franc = 100 cauris

## GUINEA-BISSAU

**GEOGRAPHY** The Republic of Guinea-Bissau, formerly known as Portuguese Guinea, is a small country in West Africa. The land is mostly low-lying, with a broad, swampy coastal plain and many flat offshore islands. The country has a tropical climate, with a dry season (December to May) and a wet season (June to November).

**POLITICS & ECONOMY** Portuguese explorers reached Guinea-Bissau in 1446 and the area became a centre of the slave trade. From 1836, Portugal administered Guinea-Bissau with the Cape Verde Islands, but in 1879 the territories were separated. Guinea-Bissau became a separate colony called Portuguese Guinea. But economic development in the colony was slow.

In 1956, African nationalists in Portuguese Guinea and Cape Verde founded the African Party for the Independence of Guinea and Cape Verde (PAIGC). The PAIGC began a guerrilla war in 1963 and, by 1968, it held two-thirds of the country. In 1972, a rebel National Assembly, elected by the people in the PAIGC-controlled area, voted to make the country independent as Guinea-Bissau.

In 1974, newly independent Guinea-Bissau faced many problems arising from its underdeveloped economy and its lack of trained people to work in the administration. One objective of the leaders of Guinea-Bissau was to unite their country with Cape Verde. But, in 1980, army leaders overthrew Guinea-Bissau's government. The Revolutionary Council, which took over, opposed unification with Cape Verde. Guinea-Bissau ceased to be a one-party state in 1991 and multiparty elections were held in 1994. Civil war broke out in 1998 and a military coup occurred in 1999. Elections were held in 2000. Another coup occurred in 2003, but civilian government was restored in 2004. In 2005, Joao Bernardo Vieira became president but he was assassinated in 2009. Malam Bacai Sanha was elected president in July 2009 but died in 2012, followed by a military coup and appointment of a Transitional National Council.

Agriculture employs 82% of the people. Crops include coconuts, groundnuts (peanuts), maize and rice. The country is a major hub for drug trafficking between Latin America and Europe.

**AREA** 36,125 sq km [13,948 sq mi] **POPULATION** 1,629,000
**CAPITAL** Bissau **GOVERNMENT** 'Interim' government
**ETHNIC GROUPS** Balanta 30%, Fula 20%, Manjaca 14%, Mandinga 13%, Papel 7% **LANGUAGES** Portuguese (official), Crioulo
**RELIGIONS** Traditional beliefs 50%, Islam 40%, Christianity 10%
**CURRENCY** CFA franc = 100 centimes

## GUYANA

**GEOGRAPHY** The Co-operative Republic of Guyana is a country facing the Atlantic Ocean in north-eastern South America. The coastal plain is flat and much of it is below sea level.

The climate is hot and humid, though the interior highlands are cooler than the coast. Rainfall is heavy, occurring on more than 200 days a year.

**POLITICS & ECONOMY** Britain gained control of the area in 1814 and ruled British Guiana until it became independent as Guyana in 1966. A black lawyer, Forbes Burnham, was the first prime minister. Under a new constitution adopted in 1980, the president's powers were increased. Burnham became president and served in this post until he died in 1985. He was succeeded by Hugh Desmond Hoyte, who was defeated in 1993 by an ethnic Indian, Cheddi Jagan. Jagan died in 1997 and was succeeded by his wife, Janet. In 1999, Bharrat Jagdeo was elected president. He was succeeded by Donald Ramotar in 2011.

Guyana is a poor country. Its resources include gold, bauxite (aluminium ore) and other minerals, forests and fertile soils. Sugar cane and rice are leading crops. Guyana has potential for producing hydroelectricity from its many rivers.

**AREA** 214,969 sq km [83,000 sq mi]
**POPULATION** 742,000 **CAPITAL** Georgetown
**GOVERNMENT** Multiparty republic
**ETHNIC GROUPS** East Indian 43%, Black 30%, Amerindian 9%, others 18% **LANGUAGES** English (official), Creole, Hindi, Urdu
**RELIGIONS** Christianity 57%, Hinduism 28%, Islam 7%, others 8%
**CURRENCY** Guyanese dollar = 100 cents

## HAITI

**GEOGRAPHY** The Republic of Haiti occupies the western third of Hispaniola in the Caribbean. The land is mainly mountainous. The climate is hot and humid, though the northern highlands, with about 200 mm [79 in], have more than twice as much rainfall as the southern coast.

**POLITICS & ECONOMY** Visited by Christopher Columbus in 1492, Haiti was later developed by the French. The African slaves revolted in 1791 and the country became independent in 1804. Haiti subsequently suffered from instability, violence and dictatorial rule. Elections in 1990 returned Jean-Bertrand Aristide as president, but he was overthrown in 1991. In 1995, René Préval was elected president, but Aristide was again elected president in 2000. In 2004, rebel activity forced Aristide to flee the country. Michel Martelly was elected president in 2011.

In January 2010, an earthquake hit Port-au-Prince, killing up to 230,000 people and devastating the economy. Thousands were made homeless and cholera killed several thousand people.

**AREA** 27,750 sq km [10,714 sq mi]
**POPULATION** 9,802,000 **CAPITAL** Port-au-Prince
**GOVERNMENT** Multiparty republic **ETHNIC GROUPS** Black 95%, Mulatto/White 5% **LANGUAGES** French and Creole (both official)
**RELIGIONS** Roman Catholic 80%, Protestant 16%, Voodoo
**CURRENCY** Gourde = 100 centimes

## HONDURAS

**GEOGRAPHY** The Republic of Honduras is the second largest country in Central America. The northern coast, on the Caribbean Sea, extends more than 600 km [373 mi], but the Pacific coast in the south-east is only about 80 km [50 mi] long. Honduras has a tropical climate, but the highlands are cooler. The rainiest months are between May and November. Hurricanes often hit the north coast. Hurricane Mitch in 1998 caused the worst destruction in modern times.

**POLITICS & ECONOMY** Western Honduras was part of the Maya empire which flourished between AD 300 and 900. Christopher Columbus claimed the area for Spain in 1502 and Spain ruled from 1625 until 1821. Honduras became part of the Central American Federation but withdrew in 1838.

In the 1890s, American companies developed plantations to grow bananas and Honduras became known as a 'banana state'. But instability slowed economic progress. Since 1980, civilian governments friendly towards the United States have ruled Honduras, but in 2008 it joined the 'Bolivarian Alternative to the Americas', a left-wing alliance headed by Venezuelan President Hugo Chavez. A military coup in 2009 removed

President Manuel Zelaya from office. In elections in November 2009, Porfiro Lobo was elected president.

Honduras is a developing country. Its few resources include silver, lead and zinc. Agriculture is the main activity. Bananas and coffee are exported and maize is the chief food crop. Honduras is one of Central America's least industrialized countries. Products include processed food, textiles and wood products.

**AREA** 112,088 sq km [43,277 sq mi]
**POPULATION** 8,297,000 **CAPITAL** Tegucigalpa
**GOVERNMENT** Republic **ETHNIC GROUPS** Mestizo 90%, Amerindian 7%, Black (including Black Carib) 2%, White 1% **LANGUAGES** Spanish (official), Amerindian dialects **RELIGIONS** Roman Catholic 97%
**CURRENCY** Honduran lempira = 100 centavos

## HUNGARY

**GEOGRAPHY** Hungary is a landlocked country in central Europe. The land is mostly low-lying and drained by the Danube (Duna) and its tributary, the Tisza. Most of the land east of the Danube belongs to a region called the Great Plain (Nagyalföld), which covers about half of Hungary.

Hungary lies far from the moderating influence of the sea. As a result, summers are warmer and sunnier, and the winters colder than in Western Europe.

**POLITICS & ECONOMY** Hungary entered World War II (1939–45) in 1941, as an ally of Germany, but the Germans occupied the country in 1944. The Soviet Union invaded Hungary in 1944 and, in 1946, the country became a republic. The Communists gradually took over the government, taking complete control in 1949. From this time, Hungary was an ally of the Soviet Union. In 1956, Soviet troops crushed an anti-Communist revolt. But in the 1980s, reforms in the Soviet Union led to the growth of anti-Communist groups in Hungary. In 1989, Hungary adopted a new constitution making it a multiparty state. Elections held in 1990 led to a victory for the non-Communist Democratic Forum. In 2002, the Hungarian Socialist Party, in alliance with the liberal Free Democrats, won a majority in parliament. In 2004, Hungary became a member of both the North Atlantic Treaty Organization and the European Union.

Before World War II, Hungary's economy was based mainly on agriculture. But the Communists set up many manufacturing industries. From the late 1980s, private ownership increased. This caused problems, including inflation and high rates of unemployment. Elections in 2010 resulted in victory for the centre-right Fidezs Party led by Viktor Orban. In 2011–12, government austerity measures caused unrest.

Leading manufactures include aluminium, chemicals, electrical and electronic goods, and telecommunications equipment.

**AREA** 93,032 sq km [35,920 sq mi]
**POPULATION** 9,958,000 **CAPITAL** Budapest
**GOVERNMENT** Multiparty republic
**ETHNIC GROUPS** Magyar 92%, Gypsy, German, Serb, Romanian, Slovak **LANGUAGES** Hungarian (official)
**RELIGIONS** Roman Catholic 52%, Calvinist 16%, Lutheran 3%, others **CURRENCY** Forint = 100 fillér

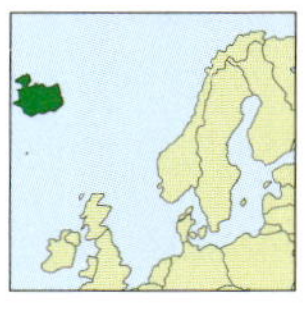

## ICELAND

**GEOGRAPHY** The Republic of Iceland, in the North Atlantic Ocean, is closer to Greenland than Scotland. Iceland sits astride the Mid-Atlantic Ridge. It is slowly getting wider as the ocean is being stretched apart by continental drift.

Iceland has around 200 volcanoes, and eruptions are frequent. An eruption under the Vatnajökull ice cap in 1996 created a subglacial lake which subsequently burst, causing severe flooding. Geysers and hot springs are common, and in 2010 a volcanic eruption and its resulting ash cloud disrupted international air services. Ice caps and glaciers cover about an eighth of the land. The only habitable regions are the coastal lowlands. Despite its northerly position, Iceland's climate is moderated by the warm waters of the Gulf Stream. The port of Reykjavik is ice-free all year round.

**POLITICS & ECONOMY** Norwegian Vikings colonized Iceland in AD 874, and in 930 the settlers founded the world's oldest parliament, the Althing.

Iceland united with Norway in 1262. But when Norway united with Denmark in 1380, Iceland came under Danish rule. Iceland became a self-governing kingdom, united with Denmark, in 1918. It became a fully independent republic in 1944, following a referendum in which 97% of the people voted to break their country's ties with Denmark. Iceland has played a leading part in European affairs and is a member of the North Atlantic Treaty Organization. But it has been involved in fishing and whaling disputes. Iceland has few resources besides its fishing grounds, and fishing and fish processing dominate Iceland's overseas trade. Barely 1% of the land is used to grow crops, but 23% of the country can be used for grazing sheep and cattle. Vegetables and fruit are grown in greenhouses, heated by water from the hot springs. Iceland's economy was hit by the global financial crisis of 2008–9, causing the collapse of its currency and banking system. In 2009, Johanna Sigurdardottir became Iceland's first female prime minister and Iceland started negotiations for membership of the European Union.

**AREA** 103,000 sq km [39,768 sq mi]
**POPULATION** 313,000 **CAPITAL** Reykjavik
**GOVERNMENT** Multiparty republic
**ETHNIC GROUPS** Icelandic 97%, Danish 1%
**LANGUAGES** Icelandic (official) **RELIGIONS** Evangelical Lutheran 87%, other Protestant 4%, Roman Catholic 2%, others
**CURRENCY** Icelandic króna = 100 aurar

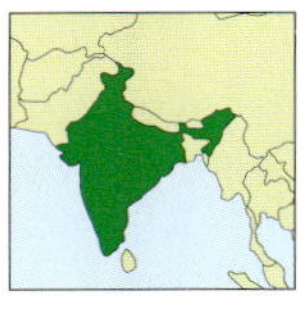

## INDIA

**GEOGRAPHY** The Republic of India is the world's seventh largest country. In population, it ranks second only to China. The north is mountainous, with mountains and foothills of the Himalayan range. Rivers, such as the Brahmaputra and Ganges (Ganga), rise in the Himalaya and flow across the fertile northern plains. Southern India consists of a large plateau, called the Deccan. The Deccan is bordered by two mountain ranges, the Western Ghats and the Eastern Ghats.

India has three main seasons. The cool season runs from October to February. The hot season runs from March to June. The rainy monsoon season starts in the middle of June and continues into September. Delhi has moderate rainfall, with about 640 mm [25 in] a year. The south-western coast and the north-east have far more rain. Darjeeling in the north-east has an average annual rainfall of 3,040 mm [120 in]. But parts of the Thar Desert in the north-west have only 50 mm [2 in] of rain per year.

**POLITICS & ECONOMY** In southern India, most of the people are descendants of the dark-skinned Dravidians, who were among India's earliest people. Most northerners are descendants of lighter-skinned Aryans who arrived around 3,500 years ago.

India was the birthplace of several major religions, including Hinduism, Buddhism and Sikhism. Islam was introduced from about AD 1000. The Muslim Mughal empire was founded in 1526. From the 17th century, Britain began to gain influence. From 1858 to 1947, India was ruled as part of the British empire. An independence movement began after the Sepoy Rebellion (1857–9), and in 1885 the Indian National Congress was formed. In 1920, Mohandas K. Gandhi became its leader and it soon became a mass movement. When independence was finally achieved in 1947, British India was divided into modern India and Muslim Pakistan. Partition was marred by mass slaughter as Hindus and Sikhs fled from Pakistan, and Indian Muslims poured into Pakistan. In the ensuing disputes, some 1 million people were killed.

India has 15 major languages and hundreds of minor ones, together with many religions. The country remains the world's largest democracy. It has faced many problems, especially with Pakistan, over the disputed territory of Jammu and Kashmir. Two wars in 1965 and 1972 failed to alter greatly the 1948 ceasefire lines. In the late 1980s, Kashmiri nationalists in the Indian-controlled area waged a campaign, demanding either integration into Pakistan or independence. India sent in troops and accused Pakistan of intervention. In the 1990s, Pakistani-backed guerrillas fought to break India's hold on the Srinagar valley, Kashmir's most populous region. Tension mounted following the testing of nuclear devices by both countries in 1998. Relations improved, but an attack on buildings in Mumbai in 2008, allegedly by Pakistanis, caused tension. In 2009–11, the dispute with Maoists in central and eastern India flared up again.

The World Bank classifies India as a developing country and a large number of people are poor. However, since 2004, under a government led by the United Progressive Alliance, led by Manmohan Singh, the national economy developed rapidly. By 2010–11, India's economy was the world's second fastest growing after China, but growth has since slowed.

Agriculture employs 53% of the people. Crops include rice, wheat, millet, sorghum, peas and beans. India has more cattle than any other country. Milk is produced, but Hindus do not eat beef. Resources include coal, iron ore and oil. Manufacturing has expanded greatly since 1947. Iron and steel, machinery, refined petroleum, textiles and transport equipment are major products.

**AREA** 3,287,263 sq km [1,269,212 sq mi]
**POPULATION** 1,205,074,000 **CAPITAL** New Delhi
**GOVERNMENT** Multiparty federal republic
**ETHNIC GROUPS** Indo-Aryan (Caucasoid) 72%, Dravidian 25%, others (mainly Mongoloid) 3%
**LANGUAGES** Hindi, English, Telugu, Bengali, Marathi, Tamil, Urdu, Gujarati, Malayalam, Kannada, Oriya, Punjabi, Assamese, Kashmiri, Sindhi and Sanskrit are all official languages
**RELIGIONS** Hinduism 80%, Islam 13%, Christianity 2%, Sikhism 2%, Buddhism and others **CURRENCY** Indian rupee = 100 paisa

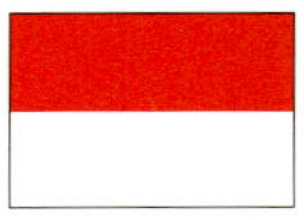

## INDONESIA

**GEOGRAPHY** The Republic of Indonesia is an island nation in South-east Asia. In all, Indonesia contains about 13,600 islands, fewer than 6,000 of which are inhabited. Three-quarters of the country is made up of five main areas: the islands of Sumatra, Java and Sulawesi (Celebes), together with Kalimantan (southern Borneo) and Irian Jaya (western New Guinea). The islands are generally mountainous and volcanic. The larger islands have extensive coastal lowlands. The climate is hot and humid, with a high rainfall. Only Java and the Sunda Islands have relatively dry seasons.

**POLITICS & ECONOMY** Indonesia is the world's most populous Muslim nation, though Islam was introduced as recently as the 15th century. The Dutch became active in the area in the early 17th century and Indonesia became a Dutch colony in 1799. After a long struggle, the Netherlands recognized Indonesia's independence in 1949. The economy has expanded, but ethnic and religious conflict have slowed down economic progress.

In the early 21st century, Indonesia was facing many problems, arising from widespread corruption in the government and the army. Separatists were operating in Aceh province in northern Sumatra and in West Papua (formerly Irian Jaya), Christian-Muslim clashes led to loss of life in the Moluccas, and East (formerly Portuguese) Timor became an independent country. Terrorist incidents occurred in the early 21st century. In December 2004, a tsunami killed more than 100,000 people. Aceh province was granted autonomy in 2006.

In 2011, separatists in the Papua region demonstrated in favour of independence. Indonesia, a developing country, has a growing industrial sector. It exports oil and natural gas, and mines tin and other minerals. Timber, textiles, rubber, coffee and tea are also exported. Rice is the main food crop.

**AREA** 1,904,569 sq km [735,354 sq mi]
**POPULATION** 248,645,000 **CAPITAL** Jakarta
**GOVERNMENT** Multiparty republic
**ETHNIC GROUPS** Javanese 41%, Sundanese 15%, Madurese 3%, Minangkabau 3%, Betawi 2%, Bugis 2%, Banten 2%, others 32%
**LANGUAGES** Bahasa Indonesian (official), many others
**RELIGIONS** Islam 86%, Protestant 6%, Roman Catholic 3%, Hinduism 2%, Buddhism 1%
**CURRENCY** Indonesian rupiah = 100 sen

## IRAN

**GEOGRAPHY** The Republic of Iran contains a barren central plateau which covers about half of the country. It includes the Dasht-e-Kavir (Great Salt Desert) and the Dasht-e-Lut (Great Sand Desert). The Elburz Mountains north of the plateau contain Iran's highest peak, Damavand, while narrow lowlands lie between the mountains and the Caspian Sea. West of the plateau are the Zagros Mountains, beyond which the land descends to the plains bordering the Persian Gulf.

Much of Iran has a severe, dry climate, with hot summers and cold winters. In Tehran, rain falls on only about 30 days in the year and the annual temperature range is more than 25°C [45°F]. The climate in the lowlands, however, is generally milder.

**POLITICS & ECONOMY** Iran was called Persia until 1935. The empire of Ancient Persia flourished between 550 and 350 BC, when it fell to Alexander the Great. Islam was introduced in AD 641.

Britain and Russia competed for influence in the area in the 19th century, and in the early 20th century the British began to develop the country's oil resources. In 1925, the Pahlavi family took power.

Reza Khan became shah (king) and worked to modernize the country. The Pahlavi dynasty was ended in 1979 when a religious leader, Ayatollah Ruhollah Khomeini, made Iran an Islamic republic. In 1980–8, Iran and Iraq fought a war over disputed borders. Khomeini died in 1989, but his fundamentalist views and anti-Western attitudes continued to dominate politics. In 2005, a hardliner, Mahmoud Ahmadinejad, was elected president. Iran's nuclear policies led to the application of international sanctions against Iran in 2009–12. The more moderate Hassan Rouhani was elected president in June 2013.

Iran's prosperity is based on its oil production and oil accounts for more than 80% of the country's exports. However, the economy was severely damaged by the Iran–Iraq war in the 1980s. Oil revenues have been used to develop a growing manufacturing sector. Agriculture is important even though farms cover only a tenth of the land. The main crops are wheat and barley. Livestock farming and fishing are other important activities, although Iran has to import much of the food it needs.

**AREA** 1,648,195 sq km [636,368 sq mi]
**POPULATION** 78,869,000 **CAPITAL** Tehran
**GOVERNMENT** Islamic republic **ETHNIC GROUPS** Persian 53%, Azeri 16%, Kurd 10%, Lur 6%, Arab 2%, Baloch 2%, Turkmen 2%
**LANGUAGES** Persian, Turkic, Kurdish
**RELIGIONS** Islam 98% (Shi'ite Muslim 89%)
**CURRENCY** Iranian rial = 100 dinars

## IRAQ

**GEOGRAPHY** The Republic of Iraq is a south-west Asian country at the head of the Persian Gulf. Rolling deserts cover western and south-western Iraq, with part of the Zagros Mountains in the north-east, where farming can be practised without irrigation. The northern plains, across which flow the rivers Euphrates (Nahr al Furat) and Tigris (Nahr Dijlah), are dry. But the southern plains, including Mesopotamia and the delta of the Shatt al Arab, contain irrigated farmland, together with marshland.

The climate of Iraq ranges from temperate in the north to subtropical in the south. Baghdad, in central Iraq, has cool winters, with occasional frosts, and hot summers. The rainfall is generally low.

**POLITICS & ECONOMY** Mesopotamia was the home of several great civilizations, including Sumer, Babylon and Assyria. It later became part of the Persian empire. Islam was introduced in AD 637 and Baghdad became the brilliant capital of the powerful Arab empire. But Mesopotamia declined after the Mongols invaded it in 1258. From 1534, Mesopotamia became part of the Turkish Ottoman empire. Britain invaded the area in 1916. In 1921, Britain renamed the country Iraq and set up an Arab monarchy. Iraq finally became independent in 1932.

By the 1950s, oil dominated Iraq's economy. In 1952, Iraq agreed to take 50% of the profits of the foreign oil companies. This revenue enabled the government to pay for welfare services and development projects. But many Iraqis felt that they should benefit more from their oil. Since 1958, when army officers killed the king and made Iraq a republic, Iraq has undergone turbulent times. In the 1960s, the Kurds, who live in northern Iraq and also in Iran, Turkey, Syria and Armenia, asked for self-rule. The government rejected their demands and war broke out. A peace treaty was signed in 1975, but conflict has continued.

In 1979, Saddam Hussein became Iraq's president. Under his leadership, Iraq invaded Iran in 1980, starting an eight-year war. Iraqi Kurds supported Iran and the Iraqi government attacked Kurdish villages with poison gas. In 1990, Iraqi troops occupied Kuwait, but an international force drove them out in 1991. From 1991, Iraqi troops attacked Shi'ite Marsh Arabs and Kurds. In 1998, Iraq's failure to permit UN inspectors, charged with disposing of Iraq's deadliest weapons, access to suspect sites led to the Western bombardment of Iraqi military sites. Another major offensive occurred in 2001. In 2002–3, pressure mounted on Iraq to dispose of its alleged weapons of mass destruction. In March–April 2003, a coalition force headed by the United States invaded Iraq, overthrowing Saddam Hussein's regime. Despite ongoing violence, elections were held in 2005, and again in 2010. Following a period of deadlock, Nouri al-Maliki continued as prime minister. Political disputes and an upsurge of violence occurred in 2011–12.

Civil war, war damage, mismanagement and UN sanctions have damaged the economy. Oil remains the main resource. Farmland, including pasture, covers about a fifth of the land. Products include barley, cotton, dates, fruit, livestock, wheat and wool. But Iraq still has to import food. Manufactures include refined oil, petrochemicals and consumer goods.

**AREA** 438,317 sq km [169,235 sq mi]
**POPULATION** 31,129,000 **CAPITAL** Baghdad
**GOVERNMENT** Parliamentary Democracy **ETHNIC GROUPS** Arab 77%, Kurdish 19%, Assyrian and others **LANGUAGES** Arabic (official), Kurdish (official in Kurdish areas), Assyrian, Armenian **RELIGIONS** Islam 97% (Shi'ite Muslim 63%) **CURRENCY** Iraqi dinar = 100 fils

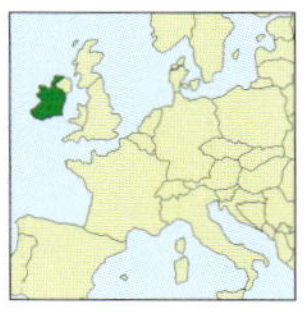

## IRELAND

**GEOGRAPHY** Ireland occupies five-sixths of the island which is also called Ireland. The country consists of a large lowland region surrounded by a broken rim of low mountains. The uplands include the Mountains of Kerry where Carrauntoohill, Ireland's highest peak at 1,041 m [3,415 ft], is situated. The River Shannon is the longest in Ireland, flowing through three large lakes, loughs Allen, Ree and Derg.

Ireland has a mild, rainy climate influenced by the warm Gulf Stream current, whose effects are greatest in the west. However, Dublin in the east is cooler than places on the west coast.

**POLITICS & ECONOMY** In 1801, the Act of Union created the United Kingdom of Great Britain and Ireland. But Irish discontent intensified in the 1840s when a potato blight caused a famine in which a million people died and nearly a million emigrated. Britain was blamed for not having done enough to help. In 1916, an uprising in Dublin was crushed, but between 1919 and 1922 civil war occurred. In 1922, the Irish Free State was created as a Dominion in the British Commonwealth. But Northern Ireland remained part of the UK.

Ireland became a republic in 1949. In 1973, it became a member of the European Community (now the European Union) and, until the global financial crisis of 2008–9, it prospered. In 1998, Ireland took part in the negotiations to produce a constitutional settlement in Northern Ireland. Ireland agreed to give up its claim on Northern Ireland and, in 2007, a power-sharing government was set up in the north.

Major farm products in Ireland include barley, cattle and dairy products, pigs, potatoes, poultry, sheep, sugar beet and wheat, while fishing is also important. But manufacturing is the leading activity. In 2010, the economy worsened and Ireland sought assistance from the EU and the IMF. Following elections in 2011, a coalition government was set up by two opposition parties, Fine Gael and the centre-left Labour Party.

**AREA** 70,273 sq km [27,132 sq mi]
**POPULATION** 4,722,000 **CAPITAL** Dublin
**GOVERNMENT** Multiparty republic **ETHNIC GROUPS** Irish 94%
**LANGUAGES** Irish (Gaelic) and English (both official)
**RELIGIONS** Roman Catholic 92%, Protestant 3%
**CURRENCY** Euro = 100 cents

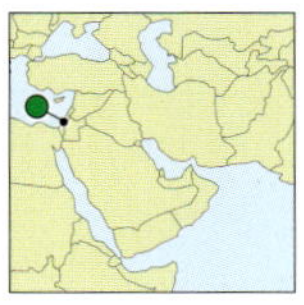

## ISRAEL

**GEOGRAPHY** The State of Israel is a small country in the eastern Mediterranean. It includes a fertile coastal plain, where Israel's main industrial cities, Haifa (Hefa) and Tel Aviv-Jaffa, are situated. Inland lie the Judaeo-Galilean highlands, which run from northern Israel to the northern tip of the Negev Desert. To the east lies part of the Great Rift Valley, which contains the River Jordan, the Sea of Galilee, and the Dead Sea. Summers are hot and dry. Winters on the coast are mild and moist, but rainfall decreases from west to east and from north to south.

**POLITICS & ECONOMY** Israel is part of a region called Palestine. Some Jews have always lived in the area, though most modern Israelis are descendants of immigrants who began to settle there from the 1880s. Britain ruled Palestine from 1917. Large numbers of Jews escaping Nazi persecution arrived in the 1930s, provoking an Arab uprising against British rule. In 1947, the UN agreed to partition Palestine into an Arab and a Jewish state. Fighting broke out after Arabs rejected the plan. The State of Israel came into being in May 1948, but fighting continued into 1949. Other Arab-Israeli wars in 1956, 1967 and 1973 led to land gains for Israel.

In 1978, Israel signed a treaty with Egypt which led to the return of the occupied Sinai peninsula to Egypt in 1979. But conflict continued between Israel and the PLO (Palestine Liberation Organization). In 1993, the PLO and Israel agreed to establish Palestinian self-rule in two areas: the occupied Gaza Strip, and in the town of Jericho in the occupied West Bank. The agreement was extended in 1995 to include more than 30% of the West Bank. Israel's prime minister, Yitzhak Rabin, was assassinated in 1995. In 1996, Benjamin Netanyahu was elected prime minister. The peace process stalled until Ehud Barak defeated Netanyahu in 1999. In 2001, Ariel Sharon became prime minister. In 2005, he handed over the Gaza Strip to the Palestinian Authority. Sharon formed a new political party, Kadima. After Sharon suffered a stroke, Ehud Olmert became prime minister. Israeli forces clashed with Palestinians in Gaza and southern Lebanon in 2005–9. In 2010, talks between Israel and the Palestinian Authority collapsed. Clashes between Israel and Gaza continued into 2013. Benjamin Netanyahu was re-elected prime minister in 2013.

Manufacturing is the most valuable activity. Products include chemicals, electronic equipment, plastics, processed food, scientific instruments and textiles. Fruit and vegetables are major exports.

**AREA** 20,600 sq km [7,954 sq mi] **POPULATION** 7,591,000
**CAPITAL** Jerusalem **GOVERNMENT** Multiparty republic
**ETHNIC GROUPS** Jewish 76%, Arab and others 24%
**LANGUAGES** Hebrew and Arabic (both official)
**RELIGIONS** Judaism 76%, Islam (mostly Sunni) 17%, Christianity 2%, Druze and others 5% **CURRENCY** New Israeli shekel = 100 agorot

## ITALY

**GEOGRAPHY** The Republic of Italy is famous for its history and traditions, its art and culture, and its beautiful scenery. Northern Italy is bordered in the north by the high Alps, with their many climbing and skiing resorts. The Alps overlook the northern plains – Italy's most fertile and densely populated region – drained by the River Po. The rugged Apennines form the backbone of southern Italy. Bordering the range are scenic hilly areas and coastal plains. Southern Italy contains a string of volcanoes, stretching from Vesuvius, through the Lipari Islands, to Etna on Sicily, the largest Mediterranean island. Northern Italy has cold, often snowy, winters, but the summer months are warm and sunny, with brief summer thunderstorms. Rainfall is abundant. The south has mild, moist winters and warm, dry summers.

**POLITICS & ECONOMY** Magnificent ruins throughout Italy testify to the glories of the ancient Roman empire, which was founded, according to legend, in 753 BC. It reached its peak in the AD 100s. It finally collapsed in the 400s, although the Eastern Roman empire, also called the Byzantine empire, survived for another 1,000 years.

In the Middle Ages, Italy was split into many tiny states. These states made a great contribution to the revival of art and learning, called the Renaissance, in the 14th to 16th centuries. Beautiful cities, such as Florence (Firenze) and Venice (Venézia), testify to the artistic achievements of this period.

Italy finally became a united kingdom in 1861, although the Papal Territories (a large area ruled by the Roman Catholic Church) was not added until 1870. The Pope and his successors disputed the takeover of the Papal Territories. The dispute was finally resolved in 1929, when the Vatican City was set up in Rome as a fully independent state.

Italy fought in World War I (1914–18) alongside the Allies – Britain, France and Russia. In 1922, the dictator Benito Mussolini, leader of the Fascist Party, took power. Under Mussolini, Italy conquered Ethiopia. During World War II (1939–45), Italy at first fought on Germany's side against the Allies. But in late 1943, Italy declared war on Germany. Italy became a republic in 1946. It has played an important part in European affairs. It was a founder member of the North Atlantic Treaty Organization (NATO) in 1949 and also, in 1958, of what has since become the European Union.

After the setting up of the European Union, Italy's economy developed quickly. But the country faced many problems. For example, much of the economic development was in the north. This forced many people to leave the poor south to find jobs in the north or abroad. Social problems, corruption at high levels of society, and a succession of weak coalition governments all contributed to instability. From 1998, power shifted between centre-left coalitions led by Romano Prodi and centre-right coalitions led by media tycoon Silvio Berlusconi. Berlusconi won elections in 2008. In 2011, faced with a major economic crisis, Berlusconi resigned and was succeeded by Mario Monti, who himself resigned in December 2012, to be replaced by a political coalition, led by Enrico Letta, in 2013.

Only 50 years ago, Italy was a mainly agricultural society. But today it is a leading industrial power. It lacks mineral resources, and imports most of the raw materials used in industry. Manufactures include textiles and clothing, processed food, machinery, cars and chemicals. The chief industrial region is in the north-west.

Farmland covers around 42% of the land, pasture 17%, and forest and woodland 22%. Major crops include citrus fruits, grapes which are used to make wine, olive oil, sugar beet and vegetables. Livestock farming is important, though meat is imported.

**AREA** 301,318 sq km [116,339 sq mi]
**POPULATION** 61,261,000 **CAPITAL** Rome
**GOVERNMENT** Multiparty republic **ETHNIC GROUPS** Italian 94%, German, French, Albanian, Slovene, Greek **LANGUAGES** Italian (official), German, French, Slovene **RELIGIONS** Predominantly Roman Catholic **CURRENCY** Euro = 100 cents

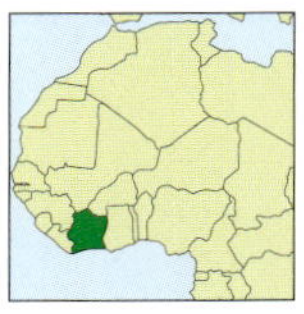

## IVORY COAST

**GEOGRAPHY** The Republic of the Ivory Coast, in West Africa, is officially known as Côte d'Ivoire. The south-east coast is bordered by sand bars that enclose lagoons. The south-west coast is lined by rocky cliffs.

Ivory Coast has a hot and humid tropical climate, with high temperatures all year. The south has two rainy seasons: between May and July, and from October to November. Inland, the rainfall decreases and the north has one dry and one rainy season.

**POLITICS & ECONOMY** From 1895, Ivory Coast was governed as part of French West Africa, which also included what are now Benin, Burkina Faso, Guinea, Mali, Mauritania, Niger and Senegal. In 1946, Ivory Coast became a territory in the French Union.

Ivory Coast became fully independent in 1960. Its first president, Félix Houphouët-Boigny, became the longest serving head of state in Africa with an uninterrupted period in office which ended with his death in 1993. Houphouët-Boigny, a pro-Western leader, made Ivory Coast a one-party state. In 1983, the National Assembly voted to make Yamoussoukro, the president's birthplace, the new capital. In 1999, a military coup occurred, but civilian rule was restored in 2000, when Laurent Gbagbo was elected president. An army rebellion began in 2002. By 2004, the government held the south, while mainly Muslim rebels held the north. A peace deal was agreed in 2007. Elections held in 2010 were won by opposition leader Alassane Ouattara, but President Laurent Gbagbo refused to stand down. After much fighting, Gbagbo was finally arrested in April 2011.

Agriculture employs 68% of the people. Cocoa beans, farm products, and petroleum products are exported.

**AREA** 322,463 sq km [124,503 sq mi]
**POPULATION** 21,952,000 **CAPITAL** Yamoussoukro
**GOVERNMENT** Multiparty republic **ETHNIC GROUPS** Akan 42%, Voltaiques 18%, Northern Mandes 16%, Krous 11%, Southern Mandes 10% **LANGUAGES** French (official), many native dialects **RELIGIONS** Islam 39%, Christianity 33%, traditional beliefs 12%
**CURRENCY** CFA franc = 100 centimes

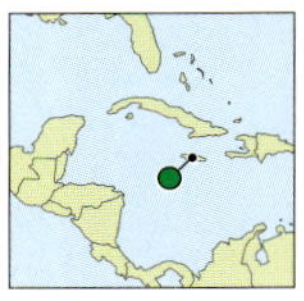

## JAMAICA

**GEOGRAPHY** The third largest of the Caribbean islands, half of Jamaica lies above 300 m [1,000 ft] and moist south-east trade winds bring rain to the central mountain range.

The 'cockpit country' in the north-west of the island is an inaccessible limestone area of steep broken ridges and isolated basins.

**POLITICS & ECONOMY** Britain took Jamaica from Spain in the 17th century, and the island did not gain its independence until 1962. Power has alternated between the People's National Party (PNP) and Jamaica Labour Party. In 2006, Portia Simpson-Miller became prime minister. She was defeated in elections in 2007, but returned as prime minister in 2011. Tourism and sugar-cane farming are important, but alumina and bauxite are the main exports.

**AREA** 10,991 sq km [4,244 sq mi]
**POPULATION** 2,889,000 **CAPITAL** Kingston
**GOVERNMENT** Constitutional monarchy
**ETHNIC GROUPS** Black 91%, Mixed 7%, East Indian 1%
**LANGUAGES** English (official), patois English
**RELIGIONS** Protestant 65%, Roman Catholic 3%
**CURRENCY** Jamaican dollar = 100 cents

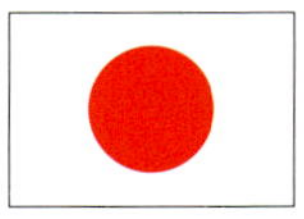

## JAPAN

**GEOGRAPHY** Japan's four largest islands – Honshu, Hokkaido, Kyushu and Shikoku – make up 98% of the country. But Japan contains thousands of small islands. The four largest islands are mainly mountainous, while many of the small islands are the tips of volcanoes. Japan has more than 150 volcanoes, about 60 of which are active. Volcanic eruptions, earthquakes and tsunamis (powerful sea waves) are common. In March 2011, a massive earthquake. the most powerful recorded in Japan (magnitude 9.0) struck Honshu in the north-east. The tremors and a tsunami caused great loss of life and severe damage to nuclear reactors at Fukushima, shutting down all nuclear power generation.

The climate of Japan varies greatly from north to south. Hokkaido in the north has cold, snowy winters. At Sapporo, temperatures below –20°C [4°F] have been recorded between December and March. But summers are warm, with temperatures sometimes exceeding 30°C [86°F]. Rain falls throughout the year, though Hokkaido is one of the driest parts of Japan. Tokyo has higher rainfall and temperatures, while the southern islands of Shikoku and Kyushu have warm temperate climates. Summers are long and hot; winters are cold.

**POLITICS & ECONOMY** In the late 19th century, Japan began a programme of modernization. Under its new imperial leaders, it began to look for lands to conquer. In 1894–5, it fought a war with China and, in 1904–5, it defeated Russia. Soon its overseas empire included Korea and Taiwan. In 1930, Japan invaded Manchuria (north-east China), and in 1937 it began a war against China. In 1941, Japan launched an attack on the US base at Pearl Harbor in Hawai'i. This drew both Japan and the United States into World War II.

Japan surrendered in 1945 when the Americans dropped atomic bombs on two cities, Hiroshima and Nagasaki. The United States occupied Japan until 1952. During this period, Japan adopted a democratic constitution. The emperor, who had previously been regarded as a god, became a constitutional monarch. Power was vested in the prime minister and cabinet, who are chosen from the Diet (elected parliament).

From the 1960s, Japan experienced many changes as the country rapidly built up new industries, becoming the world's second richest economic power after the United States. But economic success has brought problems. For example, the rapid growth of cities has led to housing shortages and pollution. Another problem is that the proportion of people over 65 years of age is steadily increasing. In 2011, China overtook Japan as the world's second largest economy after the US. Japan had held second place since 1968, and, although its economy grew by nearly 4% in 2010, it was insufficient to keep it in second place.

The leading activity is manufacturing. Japan imports most of the materials and fuels it needs, and its success has been based on its use of the latest technology, its skilled workforce, its vigorous export policies, and the relatively low expenditure on defence. Exports include machinery, electrical and electronic equipment, iron and steel, chemicals, textiles and ships. Japan's economy suffered a stagnation in the 1990s. Signs of recovery from 2005 were shattered by the global financial crisis in 2008–9, when exports greatly declined. The economy has gone back into recession following the 2011 earthquake and tsunami, and the consequent extensive reconstruction work that is required.

Japan is one of the world's top fishing nations and fish is an important source of protein. Because the land is so rugged, only 15% of the country can be farmed. Yet Japan produces about 70% of the food it needs. Rice is the chief crop, taking up about half of the total farmland.

**AREA** 377,829 sq km [145,880 sq mi] **POPULATION** 127,368,000
**CAPITAL** Tokyo **GOVERNMENT** Constitutional monarchy
**ETHNIC GROUPS** Japanese 99%, Chinese, Korean, Brazilian and others
**LANGUAGES** Japanese (official) **RELIGIONS** Shintoism and Buddhism 84% (most Japanese consider themselves to be both Shinto and Buddhist), others **CURRENCY** Yen = 100 sen

## JORDAN

**GEOGRAPHY** The Hashemite Kingdom of Jordan is an Arab country in south-western Asia. The Great Rift Valley in the west contains the River Jordan and the Dead Sea, which Jordan shares with Israel. East of the Rift Valley is the Transjordan plateau, where most Jordanians live. To the east and south lie vast areas of desert.

Amman has a much lower rainfall and longer dry season than the Mediterranean lands to the west. The Transjordan plateau, on which Amman stands, is a transition zone between the Mediterranean climate zone and the desert climate to the east.

**POLITICS & ECONOMY** In 1921, Britain created a territory called Transjordan east of the River Jordan. In 1923, Transjordan became self-governing, but Britain retained control of its defences, finances and foreign affairs. This territory became fully independent as Jordan in 1946. Jordan has suffered from instability arising from the Arab–Israeli conflict since the creation of the State of Israel in 1948. After the first Arab–Israeli War in 1948–9, Jordan acquired East Jerusalem and a fertile area called the West Bank. In 1967, Israel occupied this area. In Jordan, the presence of Palestinian refugees led to civil war in 1970–1.

In 1974, Arab leaders declared that the PLO (Palestine Liberation Organization) was the sole representative of the Palestinian people. In 1988, King Hussein of Jordan renounced Jordan's claims to the West Bank and passed responsibility for it to the PLO. Opposition parties were legalized in 1991 and elections were held in 1993. In October 1994, Jordan and Israel signed a peace treaty, ending a state of war that had lasted more than 40 years. Jordan's King Hussein commanded respect for his role in Middle Eastern affairs until his death in 1999. He was succeeded by his eldest son, who became Abdullah II. Jordan supported the US-led war on terrorism. In 2005, suicide bombings on hotels in Amman damaged Jordan's reputation as a stable country. In 2009, the king dissolved parliament. Parliamentary elections were held in 2010, and again in January 2013.

Jordan has an 'upper-middle-income' economy. It lacks natural resources, apart from phosphates and potash, and depends on substantial aid. Less than 6% of the land is farmed or used as pasture. The country is currently having to absorb high numbers of refugees from neighbouring Syria.

**AREA** 89,342 sq km [34,495 sq mi]
**POPULATION** 6,509,000 **CAPITAL** Amman
**GOVERNMENT** Constitutional monarchy **ETHNIC GROUPS** Arab 98%, of which Palestinians make up roughly half **LANGUAGES** Arabic (official) **RELIGIONS** Islam (mostly Sunni) 92%, Christianity (mostly Greek Orthodox) 6% **CURRENCY** Jordanian dinar = 100 piastre

## KAZAKHSTAN

**GEOGRAPHY** Kazakhstan is a large country in west-central Asia. In the west, the Caspian Sea lowlands include the Karagiye depression, which reaches 132 m [433 ft] below sea level. The lowlands extend eastwards through the Aral Sea area. The north contains high plains, but the highest land is along the eastern and southern borders. These areas include parts of the Altai and Tian Shan mountain ranges. Eastern Kazakhstan contains several freshwater lakes, the largest of which is Lake Balkhash. The water in the rivers has been used for irrigation, causing ecological problems. For example, the Aral Sea, deprived of water, shrank from 66,900 sq km [25,830 sq mi] in 1960 to 33,642 sq km [12,989 sq mi] in 1993. Large areas are now barren desert.

Kazakhstan has an extreme climate. Winters are cold and snowy. The rainfall is generally low.

**POLITICS & ECONOMY** After the Russian Revolution of 1917, many Kazakhs wanted to make their country independent. But the Communists prevailed and in 1936 Kazakhstan became a republic of the Soviet Union, called the Kazakh Soviet Socialist Republic. During World War II and also after the war, the Soviet government moved many people from the west into Kazakhstan. From the 1950s, people were encouraged to work on a 'Virgin Lands' project, which involved bringing large areas of grassland under cultivation.

Reforms in the Soviet Union in the 1980s led to its break-up in December 1991. Kazakhstan maintained contacts with Russia through the Commonwealth of Independent States (CIS). In 1997, the government moved its capital from Almaty to Aqmola (later renamed Astana), a town in the north. By the mid-2000s, the economy was in better shape than the other ex-Soviet republics in Central Asia. But President Nursultan Nazarbaev was criticized for his authoritarian rule. In 2007, constitutional changes enabled Nazarbaev to stand for the presidency as many times as he wished. In 2011, he was re-elected, despite opposition protests that he had given them no time to prepare.

The World Bank classifies Kazakhstan as an 'upper-middle-income' developing country. Livestock farming, especially sheep and cattle, is an important activity, and major crops include barley, cotton, rice and wheat. The country is rich in mineral resources, including coal and oil reserves, together with bauxite, copper, lead, tungsten and zinc. Manufactures include chemicals, food products, machinery and textiles. Oil is exported via a pipeline through Russia. However, to reduce the country's dependence on Russia, another pipeline to China was inaugurated in 2009. Other exports include metals, chemicals, grain, wool and meat.

**AREA** 2,724,900 sq km [1,052,084 sq mi] **POPULATION** 17,522,000
**CAPITAL** Astana **GOVERNMENT** Multiparty republic
**ETHNIC GROUPS** Kazakh 63%, Russian 24%, Uzbek 3%, Ukrainian 2%, others 8% **LANGUAGES** Kazakh (official); Russian, the former official language, is widely spoken **RELIGIONS** Islam 47%, Russian Orthodox 44% **CURRENCY** Tenge = 100 tiyn

## KENYA

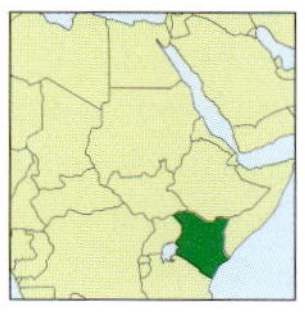

**GEOGRAPHY** The Republic of Kenya is a country in East Africa which straddles the equator. Behind the narrow coastal plain on the Indian Ocean, the land rises to high plains and highlands, broken by volcanic mountains, including Mount Kenya, the country's highest peak at 5,199 m [17,057 ft]. Crossing the country is an arm of the Great Rift Valley, on the floor of which are several lakes, including Baringo, Magadi, Naivasha, Nakuru and, on the northern frontier, Lake Turkana (formerly Lake Rudolf). Nairobi, in the south-western highlands, has summer temperatures which are about 18°C [10°F] lower than humid Mombasa. Only about 15% of Kenya has a reliable annual rainfall of 800 mm [31 in].

**POLITICS & ECONOMY** The Kenyan coast has been a trading centre for more than 2,000 years. Britain took over the coast in 1895 and soon extended its influence inland. In the 1950s, a secret movement, called Mau Mau, launched an armed struggle against British rule. Although Mau Mau was eventually defeated, Kenya became independent in 1963.

Kenya was a one-party state for much of the time after 1963. Democracy was restored in 1992. Elections in 2007 led to inter-ethnic violence when the opposition refused to accept the declared results. A deal was agreed by President Mwai Kibaki and Raila Odinga, who became prime minister. In 2011, Somali attacks and kidnappings in northern Kenya provoked Kenya to send forces into Somalia to combat the Islamist al-Shabab group. In March 2013, Uhuru Kenyatta was elected president.

Kenya remains a 'low-income' developing country. Many Kenyans are subsistence farmers. The chief food crop is maize. The main cash crops and the leading exports are coffee and tea. Manufactures include chemicals, leather and footwear, processed food, petroleum products, and textiles.

**AREA** 580,367 sq km [224,080 sq mi]
**POPULATION** 43,013,000 **CAPITAL** Nairobi
**GOVERNMENT** Multiparty republic **ETHNIC GROUPS** Kikuyu 22%, Luhya 14%, Luo 13%, Kalenjin 12%, Kamba 11%, others
**LANGUAGES** Kiswahili and English (both official)
**RELIGIONS** Protestant 47%, Roman Catholic 23%, Islam 11%, others 19% **CURRENCY** Kenyan shilling = 100 cents

## KIRIBATI

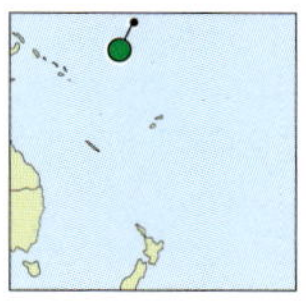

The Republic of Kiribati comprises three groups of coral atolls scattered over about 5 million sq km [2 million sq mi]. Kiribati straddles the equator and temperatures are high and the rainfall is abundant.

Formerly part of the British Gilbert and Ellice Islands, Kiribati became independent in 1979. The main export is copra and the country depends heavily on foreign aid.

**AREA** 726 sq km [280 sq mi] **POPULATION** 102,000 **CAPITAL** Tarawa

## KOREA, NORTH

**GEOGRAPHY** The Democratic People's Republic of Korea occupies the northern part of the Korean peninsula, which extends south from north-eastern China. Mountains form the heart of the country, with the highest peak, Paektu-san, reaching 2,744 m [9,003 ft] on the northern border. North Korea has a fairly severe climate, with cold, snowy winters. In summer, moist winds from the oceans bring rain.

**POLITICS & ECONOMY** North Korea was created in 1945, when the peninsula, which had been a Japanese colony since 1910, was divided into two parts. Soviet forces occupied the north, with US forces in the south. Soviet occupation led to a Communist government being established in 1948 under the leadership of Kim Il Sung, who effectively became a dictator.

The Korean War began in June 1950 when North Korean troops invaded the south. North Korea, aided by China and the Soviet Union, fought with South Korea, which was supported by troops from the United States and other UN members. The war ended in July 1953. An armistice was signed but no permanent peace treaty was agreed. The end of the Cold War in the late 1990s eased the situation. North and South Korea joined the United Nations in 1991, though North Korea remained isolated from most other countries. In 1993, North Korea withdrew from the Nuclear Non-Proliferation Treaty, arousing suspicions that it was developing nuclear weapons. Kim Il Sung died in 1994 and was succeeded by his son, Kim Jong Il. From 2003, the United States accused North Korea of developing nuclear weapons, and in 2006, 2009 and 2013 it conducted nuclear tests, resulting in increased international isolation and tension. Kim Jong Il died in 2011. His son, Kim Jong-Un, succeeded him.

North Korea's resources include coal, copper, iron ore, lead, tin, tungsten and zinc. Under Communism, the country developed heavy, state-owned industries. Manufactures include chemicals, iron and steel, machinery, processed food, and textiles. Agriculture employs 35% of the people. Rice is the chief food crop, but food shortages have occurred in recent years.

**AREA** 120,538 sq km [46,540 sq mi]
**POPULATION** 24,589,000 **CAPITAL** Pyŏngyang
**GOVERNMENT** Single-party people's republic
**ETHNIC GROUPS** Korean 99%
**LANGUAGES** Korean (official)
**RELIGIONS** Buddhism and Confucianism
**CURRENCY** North Korean won = 100 chon

## KOREA, SOUTH

**GEOGRAPHY** The Republic of Korea, as South Korea is officially known, occupies the southern part of the Korean peninsula. Mountains cover much of the country. The southern and western coasts are major farming regions. Many islands are found along the west and south coasts. The largest of these is Cheju-do, which contains South Korea's highest peak, Hallasan, which rises to 1,950 m [6,398 ft].

Like North Korea, South Korea is chilled in winter by cold, dry winds from central Asia. Summers are hot and wet, especially in July and August.

**POLITICS & ECONOMY** After Japan's defeat in World War II (1939–45), North Korea was occupied by troops from the Soviet Union, while South Korea was occupied by United States forces. A National Assembly elected in 1948 in South Korea created the Republic of Korea, while North Korea became a Communist state. North Korea invaded the South in June 1950, sparking off the Korean War (1950–3). Despite the destruction caused by the war, South Korea under a series of rather authoritarian governments began to industrialize the economy between the 1960s and 1980s. In 1987, a new constitution permitted the election of presidents every five years. In the 2000s, South Korea worked for closer contacts with the North, but tension continued into 2013.

Until the onset of the global financial crisis in 2008, South Korea had one of the world's fastest growing economies. Its main manufactures are processed food and textiles. Heavy industries produce chemicals, fertilizers, and iron and steel, together with a wide range of consumer products, such as computers, cars and television sets.

Farming remains important in South Korea. Rice is the chief crop, together with fruits, grains and vegetables, while fishing provides a major source of protein.

**AREA** 99,268 sq km [38,327 sq mi]
**POPULATION** 48,861,000 **CAPITAL** Seoul
**GOVERNMENT** Multiparty republic **ETHNIC GROUPS** Korean 99%
**LANGUAGES** Korean (official) **RELIGIONS** No affiliation 43%, Christianity 32%, Buddhism 24%, others 1%
**CURRENCY** South Korean won = 100 jeon

## KOSOVO

**GEOGRAPHY** The Republic of Kosovo, formerly part of Serbia and, before 2003, part of Yugoslavia, declared its independence in February 2008. Its independence was recognized by the United States and major EU countries. But Serbia and its ally Russia refused recognition. It is a landlocked country, consisting of a river basin bounded by uplands in the north and south-west. It has cold, snowy winters and hot, dry summers.

**POLITICS & ECONOMY** Most people are Albanian-speakers who are Muslims, but there is an important Christian Serb minority. In the early 13th century, Kosovo was part of the Serbian empire but, after 1389, it came under Muslim Turkish Ottoman rule. Serbia regained control of Kosovo in 1912 and, in 1918, it became part of the Kingdom of Serbia. In 1946, it became part of the Socialist Federal Republic of Yugoslavia, becoming an autonomous province within the Republic of Serbia. In 1989, Serbia curtailed Kosovo's autonomy, while Albanian speakers declared their province independent. In 1995, the Albanian speakers set up the Kosovo Liberation Army, which launched an uprising against Serbia. In 1998, Serbia began repressive measures against Kosovo, resulting in massacres and ethnic cleansing of Albanian-speaking Kosovars. In 1999, NATO forces bombed Serbia and placed Kosovo under a temporary administration. Finally, the Kosovo Assembly declared its independence on 17 February 2008. In 2011, Kosovo and Serbia resolved a border dispute.

Kosovo is a poor country, with the lowest per capita income in Europe. Many people are subsistence farmers and its industries have declined because of lack of investment. The economy is highly dependent on international aid.

**AREA** 10,887 sq km [4,203 sq mi]
**POPULATION** 1,837,000 **CAPITAL** Pristina
**GOVERNMENT** Republic
**ETHNIC GROUPS** Albanian 92%, others 8%
**LANGUAGES** Albanian and Serbian (both official), Turkish
**RELIGIONS** Islam, Serbian Orthodox, Roman Catholic
**CURRENCY** Euro = 100 cents

## KUWAIT

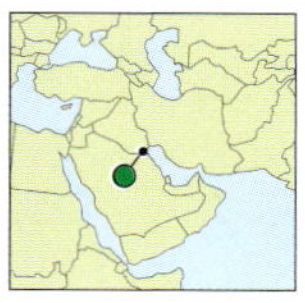

**GEOGRAPHY** The State of Kuwait at the north end of the Persian Gulf is an emirate (ruled by an emir, or amir). The land is low-lying and largely desert in nature. Summer temperatures are high but winters are cooler. Rainfall is low.

**POLITICS & ECONOMY** British influence began in 1775 and, in 1899, the local ruler concluded a treaty with Britain, agreeing to support British interests in return for British protection. Kuwait became independent in 1961. Its revenue from its oil exports made it highly prosperous. Iraq invaded Kuwait in 1990, but it was liberated in 1991 by a coalition force. In 2004, the government announced legislation for women to vote and stand for parliament. Women stood in the 2008 elections, but none was elected.

**AREA** 17,818 sq km [6,880 sq mi]
**POPULATION** 2,646,000 **CAPITAL** Kuwait City

## KYRGYZSTAN

**GEOGRAPHY** The Republic of Kyrgyzstan is a landlocked country between China, Tajikistan, Uzbekistan and Kazakhstan. The country is mountainous, with spectacular scenery. The highest mountain, Pik Pobedy in the Tian Shan range, reaches 7,439 m [24,406 ft] in the east. The lowlands have warm summers and cold winters. But January temperatures in the mountains plummet to –28°C [–18°F]. Kyrgyzstan has a low annual rainfall.

**POLITICS & ECONOMY** In 1876, Kyrgyzstan became a province of Russia and Russian settlement in the area began. In 1916, Russia crushed a rebellion among the Kyrgyz, and many subsequently fled to China. In 1922, the area became an autonomous oblast (self-governing region) of the newly formed Soviet Union, but in 1936 it became one of the Soviet Socialist Republics. Under Communist rule, local customs and religious worship were suppressed, but education and health services were greatly improved.

In 1991, Kyrgyzstan became an independent country following the break-up of the Soviet Union. The Communist Party was dissolved, but the country maintained ties with Russia through an organization called the Commonwealth of Independent States. Elections were held under a new constitution adopted in 1994. Massive protests followed elections in 2005. President Askar Akayev fled the country. His successor, Kurmanbek Bakiyev, faced huge protests in 2010 and he also fled. In 2011, Almazbek Atambayev was elected president.

In the 1990s, Kyrgyzstan sought to reform its Soviet-style economy. Now classified as a 'lower-middle income' developing country, agriculture is the main activity. Major products include cotton, eggs, fruits, grain, tobacco, vegetables and wool, but food is imported. Most industries are concentrated around the capital Bishkek.

**AREA** 199,900 sq km [77,181 sq mi]
**POPULATION** 5,497,000 **CAPITAL** Bishkek
**GOVERNMENT** Multiparty republic
**ETHNIC GROUPS** Kyrgyz 65%, Uzbek 13%, Russian 12%
**LANGUAGES** Kyrgyz and Russian (both official)
**RELIGIONS** Islam 75%, Russian Orthodox 20%
**CURRENCY** Kyrgyzstani som = 100 tyiyn

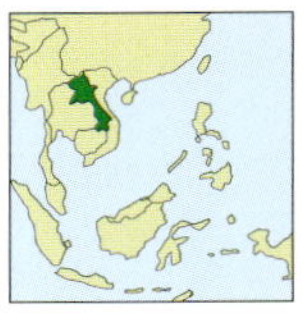

## LAOS

**GEOGRAPHY** The Lao People's Democratic Republic is a landlocked country in South-east Asia. Mountains and plateaux cover much of the country. Most people live on the plains bordering the River Mekong and its tributaries. This river, one of Asia's longest, forms much of the country's north-western and south-western borders.

Laos has a tropical monsoon climate. Winters are dry and sunny with winds blowing from the north-east. From April, the monsoon season starts with the arrival of moist south-westerly winds.

**POLITICS & ECONOMY** France made Laos a protectorate in the late 19th century and ruled it, with Cambodia and Vietnam, as part of French Indo-China. Laos became an independent kingdom in 1954. After independence, a power struggle between royalist government forces and a pro-Communist group called Pathet Lao caused instability. A civil war broke out and continued into the 1970s. The Pathet Lao took control in 1975 and the king abdicated. In the 1990s, Laos started to open to the world and began tentative reforms. In 2011, a stock exchange was opened in Vientiane, as part of a gradual move towards capitalism.

Laos is one of the world's poorest countries. Agriculture employs nearly 75% of the population and accounts for 26% of the gross domestic product. Rice is the main crop. Timber and coffee are exported. But the most valuable export is electricity, which is produced at hydroelectric power stations on the River Mekong and is exported to Thailand. Laos also produces opium.

**AREA** 236,800 sq km [91,428 sq mi]
**POPULATION** 6,586,000 **CAPITAL** Vientiane
**GOVERNMENT** Single-party republic
**ETHNIC GROUPS** Lao 55%, Khmou 11%, Hmong 8%, others 26%
**LANGUAGES** Lao (official), French, English **RELIGIONS** Buddhism 67%, traditional beliefs and others 33% **CURRENCY** Kip = 100 att

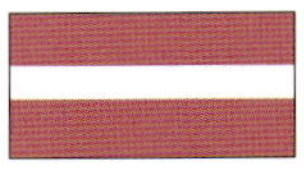

## LATVIA

**GEOGRAPHY** The Republic of Latvia is one of three states on the south-eastern corner of the Baltic Sea which were ruled as parts of the Soviet Union between 1940 and 1991. Latvia consists mainly of flat plains separated by low hills, composed of moraine (ice-worn rocks).

Riga has warm summers, but the winter months are subzero. The rainfall is moderate.

**POLITICS & ECONOMY** In 1800, Russia was in control of Latvia, but Latvians declared their independence after World War I. In 1940, under a German-Soviet pact, Soviet troops occupied Latvia, but they were driven out by the Germans in 1941. Soviet troops returned in 1944 and Latvia became part of the Soviet Union. Under Soviet rule, many Russian immigrants settled in Latvia and many Latvians feared that the Russians would become the dominant ethnic group.

In the late 1980s, when reforms were being introduced in the Soviet Union, Latvia's government ended absolute Communist rule and made Latvian the official language. In 1990, it declared the country to be independent, an act which was finally recognized by the Soviet Union in September 1991.

Latvia held the first free elections to its parliament (the Saeima) in 1993. Voting was limited only to citizens of Latvia on 17 June 1940, and their descendants. This meant that about 34% of Latvian residents were unable to vote. In 1994, Latvia restricted the naturalization of non-Latvians, including many Russian settlers, who were not allowed to vote or own land. However, in 1998, the government agreed that all children born since independence should have automatic citizenship. In 2004, Latvia became a member of the North Atlantic Treaty Organization and the European Union. Latvia was hit hard by the global financial crisis in 2009. In 2011, a new coalition government was formed, excluding a pro-Russian party that had won the most votes.

The World Bank classifies Latvia as an 'upper-middle-income' country. Manufactures include electronic goods, farm machinery, fertilizers, processed food, plastics, radios and vehicles. Latvia produces only about a tenth of the electricity it needs. It imports the rest from Belarus, Russia and Ukraine.

**AREA** 64,600 sq km [24,942 sq mi] **POPULATION** 2,192,000
**CAPITAL** Riga **GOVERNMENT** Multiparty republic
**ETHNIC GROUPS** Latvian 59%, Russian 28%, Belarusian, Ukrainian, Polish, Lithuanian
**LANGUAGES** Latvian (official), Russian, Lithuanian
**RELIGIONS** Lutheran, Russian Orthodox, Roman Catholic
**CURRENCY** Latvian lats = 10 santimi

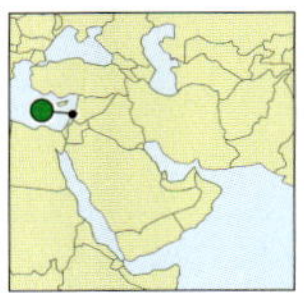

## LEBANON

**GEOGRAPHY** The Republic of Lebanon is a country on the eastern shores of the Mediterranean Sea. Behind the coastal plain are the rugged Lebanon Mountains (Jabal Lubnan), which rise to 3,088 m [10,131 ft]. Another range, the Anti-Lebanon Mountains (Al Jabal Ash Sharqi), forms the eastern border with Syria. Between the two ranges is the Bekaa (Beqaa) Valley, a fertile farming region. The coast has hot, dry summers and mild, wet winters. Heavy rain falls on the mountains, with snow at high altitudes.

**POLITICS & ECONOMY** Lebanon was ruled by Turkey from 1516 until World War I. France ruled the country from 1923, but Lebanon became independent in 1946. After independence, the Muslims and Christians agreed to share power, and Lebanon made rapid economic progress. But from the late 1950s, development was slowed by periodic conflict between Sunni and Shia Muslims, Druze and Christians. The situation was further complicated by the presence of Palestinian refugees, who used bases in Lebanon to attack Israel.

In 1975, civil war broke out as private armies representing the many factions struggled for power. This led to intervention by Israel in the south and Syria in the north. UN peacekeeping forces arrived in 1978, but violence continued in the 1980s. Peace was restored in the 1990s, but, in 2005, the assassination of Rafik Hariri, former prime minister, was blamed on Syria. Under pressure, Syria withdrew its forces from Lebanon. In 2006, a 34-day conflict between Israeli troops and Hezbollah guerrillas caused devastation in southern Lebanon. In 2011, a new cabinet was formed with the militant Hezbollah holding a majority of the seats. Large numbers of refugees crossed from Syria in 2012–13.

Lebanon's civil war almost destroyed valuable trade and financial services that had been Lebanon's chief source of income, together with tourism. Manufacturing, formerly a major activity, was badly hit.

**AREA** 10,400 sq km [4,015 sq mi]
**POPULATION** 4,140,000 **CAPITAL** Beirut
**GOVERNMENT** Multiparty republic **ETHNIC GROUPS** Arab 95%, Armenian 4%, others **LANGUAGES** Arabic (official), French, English, Armenian **RELIGIONS** Islam 60%, Christianity 39%
**CURRENCY** Lebanese pound = 100 piastres

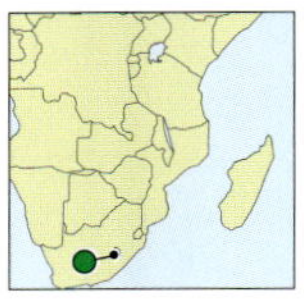

## LESOTHO

**GEOGRAPHY** The Kingdom of Lesotho is a landlocked country, completely enclosed by South Africa. The land is mountainous, rising to 3,482 m [11,424 ft] on the north-eastern border. The Drakensberg range covers most of the country.

The climate of Lesotho is greatly affected by the altitude, because most of the country lies above 1,500 m [4,920 ft]. Summers are warm but winters are cold. The rainfall averages about 700 mm [28 in].

**POLITICS & ECONOMY** The Basotho nation was founded in the 1820s by King Moshoeshoe I, who united various groups fleeing from tribal wars in southern Africa. Britain made the area a protectorate in 1868 and, in 1871, placed it under the British Cape Colony in South Africa. But in 1884, Basutoland, as the area was called, was reconstituted as a British protectorate, where whites were not allowed to own land.

The country finally became independent in 1966 as the Kingdom of Lesotho, with Moshoeshoe II, great-grandson of Moshoeshoe I, as its king. Since independence, Lesotho has suffered instability. The military seized power in 1986 and stripped Moshoeshoe II of his powers in 1990, installing his son, Letsie III, as monarch. After elections in 1993, Moshoeshoe II was restored to office in 1995. But after his death in a car crash in 1996, Letsie III again became king. In 1998, an army revolt, following an election in which the ruling party won 79 out of the 80 seats, caused much damage to the economy. Lesotho has faced many problems, including drought, while 23% of the adult population were reported in 2011 to be infected with the HIV virus.

Lesotho lacks natural resources, and the UN has stated that 40% of the people are 'ultra-poor'. Agriculture employs 18% of the people, mostly at subsistence level. Remittances sent home by Basotho working abroad are important to the economy.

**AREA** 30,355 sq km [11,720 sq mi]
**POPULATION** 1,930,000 **CAPITAL** Maseru
**GOVERNMENT** Constitutional monarchy
**ETHNIC GROUPS** Sotho 99% **LANGUAGES** Sesotho and English (both official) **RELIGIONS** Christianity 80%, traditional beliefs 20%
**CURRENCY** Loti = 100 lisente

## LIBERIA

**GEOGRAPHY** The Republic of Liberia is a country in West Africa. Behind the coastline, 500 km [311 mi] long, lies a narrow coastal plain. Beyond, the land rises to a plateau region, with the highest land along the border with Guinea. Liberia has a tropical climate with high temperatures and high humidity all through the year. Rainfall is abundant all year round, but there is a particularly wet period from June to November. Rainfall generally increases from east to west.

**POLITICS & ECONOMY** In the late 18th century, some white Americans in the United States wanted to help freed black slaves to return to Africa. In 1816, they set up the American Colonization Society, which bought land in what is now Liberia.

In 1822, the Society landed former slaves at a settlement on the coast which they named Monrovia. In 1847, Liberia became a fully independent republic with a constitution much like that of the United States. For many years, Americo-Liberians controlled the country's government. US influence remained strong and the American Firestone Company, which ran the rubber plantations, was especially influential. Foreign companies were also involved in exploiting Liberia's mineral resources, including its huge iron-ore deposits.

In 1980, a military group composed of people from the local population killed the Americo-Liberian president, William R. Tolbert. An army sergeant, Samuel K. Doe, was made president of Liberia. Elections held in 1985 resulted in victory for Doe. From 1989, the country was plunged into civil war between various ethnic groups. Doe was assassinated in 1990 and the struggle with rebel groups continued. West African peacekeeping forces arrived in Liberia and, in 1995, a ceasefire was agreed. A council of state, composed of former warlords, was set up in 1997 and Charles Taylor became president. Taylor fled the country in 2003, and in 2006 he was extradited and faced war crimes charges, on several of which he was convicted in 2012. Following elections in 2005, Ellen Sirleaf-Johnson was elected president. She became Africa's first woman president. She was re-elected in 2011.

Liberia's economy was devastated by the civil war. Agriculture is important, but most farmers live at subsistence level. Food crops include cassava, rice and sugar cane, while rubber, cocoa and coffee are exported. The most valuable export is rubber.

Liberia also obtains revenue from its 'flag of convenience', which is used by about one-sixth of the world's commercial shipping, exploiting low taxes.

**AREA** 111,369 sq km [43,000 sq mi]
**POPULATION** 3,888,000 **CAPITAL** Monrovia
**GOVERNMENT** Multiparty republic **ETHNIC GROUPS** Indigenous African tribes 95% (including Kpelle, Bassa, Grebo, Gio, Kru, Mano)
**LANGUAGES** English (official), ethnic languages
**RELIGIONS** Christianity 86%, Islam 12%, traditional beliefs and others 2% **CURRENCY** Liberian dollar = 100 cents

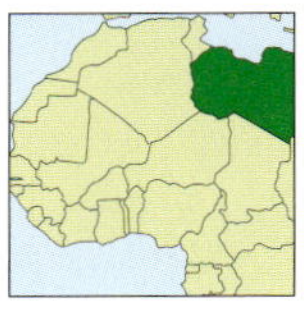

## LIBYA

**GEOGRAPHY** The Socialist People's Libyan Arab Jamahiriya, as Libya is officially called, is a large country in North Africa. Most people live on the coastal plains in the north-east and north-west. The Sahara, the world's largest desert, which occupies 95% of Libya, reaches the Mediterranean coast along the Gulf of Sidra (Khalij Surt).

The coastal plains in the north-east and north-west have Mediterranean climates, with hot, dry summers and mild, sometimes wet winters. Hot desert conditions prevail inland.

**POLITICS & ECONOMY** Italy took over Libya in 1911, but lost it during World War II. Britain and France jointly ruled Libya until 1951, when the country became an independent kingdom.

In 1969, a military group headed by Colonel Muammar Gaddafi deposed the king and set up a military government. Under Gaddafi, the government took control of the economy and used money from oil exports to finance welfare services and development projects. Gaddafi was criticized for supporting terrorist groups around the world, and Libya became isolated from the mid-1980s.

From 2004, relations with the West improved and diplomatic relations were restored with many nations, including the United States. However, in February 2011, the arrest of a human rights campaigner sparked off protests in Benghazi. The protests rapidly spread to other cities. As the fighting intensified, the UN sanctioned Western governments to impose a no-fly zone over Libya to protect civilians. In October, Gaddafi was killed and a National Transition Council was set up as the *de facto* government. In August 2012, the first post-Gaddafi elections resulted in a 200-member National Congress and a new prime minister.

The discovery of oil and natural gas in 1959 led to a transformation of Libya's economy. This formerly poor country soon became Africa's richest in terms of its per capita income. But it remains a developing country, because oil accounts for nearly all its export revenues. Agriculture is important, although Libya imports food. Crops include barley, citrus fruits, dates, olives, potatoes and wheat, while cattle, sheep and poultry are raised. Libya has oil refineries and petrochemical plants. Other manufactures include cement and steel.

**AREA** 1,759,540 sq km [679,358 sq mi] **POPULATION** 5,613,000 **CAPITAL** Tripoli **GOVERNMENT** Transitional **ETHNIC GROUPS** Libyan Arab and Berber 97% **LANGUAGES** Arabic (official), Berber **RELIGIONS** Islam (Sunni Muslim) 97% **CURRENCY** Libyan dinar = 1,000 dirhams

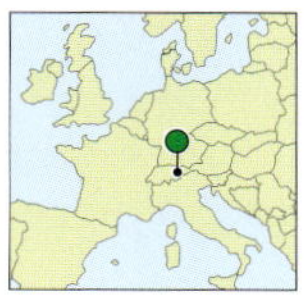

## LIECHTENSTEIN

The tiny Principality of Liechtenstein is sandwiched between Switzerland and Austria. The River Rhine flows along its western border, while Alpine peaks rise in the east and south. The climate is relatively mild. Since 1924, Liechtenstein has been in a customs union with Switzerland. Taxation is low and the country is a haven for foreign companies. In 2004, the head of state Prince Hans-Adam II handed over the running of the country to his son, Prince Alois, though he remained titular head of state. In 2009, Liechtenstein agreed to share tax information with a number of countries, including Germany, the UK and the US.

**AREA** 160 sq km [62 sq mi] **POPULATION** 37,000 **CAPITAL** Vaduz

## LITHUANIA

**GEOGRAPHY** The Republic of Lithuania is the southernmost of the three Baltic states which were ruled as part of the Soviet Union between 1940 and 1991. Much of the land is flat or gently rolling, with the highest land in the south-east.

Winters are cold and summers warm. The annual rainfall in the west is about 630 mm [25 in]. Eastern areas are drier.

**POLITICS & ECONOMY** The Lithuanian people were united into a single nation in the 12th century, and later joined a union with Poland. In 1795, Lithuania came under Russian rule. After World War I (1914–18), Lithuania declared itself independent, and in 1920 it signed a peace treaty with the Russians, though Poland held Vilnius until 1939. In 1940, the Soviet Union occupied Lithuania, but the Germans invaded in 1941. Soviet forces returned in 1944, and Lithuania was integrated into the Soviet Union. In 1988, when the Soviet Union was introducing reforms, the Lithuanians demanded independence. Their language is one of the oldest in the world, and the country was always the most homogenous of the Baltic states, staunchly Catholic and resistant of attempts to suppress its culture. Pro-independence groups won the national elections in 1990 and, in 1991, the Soviet Union recognized Lithuania's independence.

Since 1991, Lithuania has sought to reform its economy and introduce a private enterprise system. Lithuania has also drawn closer to the West and, in 2004, it became a member of both the North Atlantic Treaty Organization and the European Union.

The World Bank classifies Lithuania as a 'lower-middle-income' developing country. Lithuania lacks natural resources, but manufacturing, based on imported materials, is the most valuable activity.

**AREA** 65,200 sq km [25,174 sq mi] **POPULATION** 3,526,000 **CAPITAL** Vilnius **GOVERNMENT** Multiparty republic **ETHNIC GROUPS** Lithuanian 84%, Polish 6%, Russian 5%, Belarusian 1% **LANGUAGES** Lithuanian (official), Russian, Polish **RELIGIONS** Mainly Roman Catholic **CURRENCY** Litas = 100 centu

## LUXEMBOURG

**GEOGRAPHY** The Grand Duchy of Luxembourg is one of the smallest and oldest countries in Europe. The north belongs to an upland region which includes the Ardenne in Belgium and Luxembourg, and the Eifel highlands in Germany.

Luxembourg has a temperate climate. The south has warm summers and autumns, when grapes ripen in sheltered south-eastern valleys. Winters are sometimes severe, especially in upland areas.

**POLITICS & ECONOMY** Germany occupied Luxembourg in World Wars I and II. In 1944–5, northern Luxembourg was the scene of the Battle of the Bulge. In 1948, Luxembourg joined Belgium and the Netherlands in a union called Benelux. In the 1950s, it was one of the six founders of what is now the European Union. Its capital is a major financial centre and contains several international agencies. In 2008, parliament restricted the monarch to a ceremonial role following the grand duke's refusal to sign a law allowing euthanasia.

Luxembourg has iron-ore reserves and is a major steel producer. It also has many high-technology industries, producing electronic goods and computers. Steel and other manufactures, including chemicals, rubber products, glass and aluminium, dominate the country's exports. Other major activities include tourism and financial services.

**AREA** 2,586 sq km [998 sq mi] **POPULATION** 509,000 **CAPITAL** Luxembourg **GOVERNMENT** Constitutional monarchy (Grand Duchy) **ETHNIC GROUPS** Luxembourger 63%, Portuguese 13%, Italian, French, Belgian, Slavs **LANGUAGES** Luxembourgish (official), French, German **RELIGIONS** Roman Catholic 87%, others 13% **CURRENCY** Euro = 100 cents

## MACEDONIA (FYROM)

**GEOGRAPHY** The Republic of Macedonia is a country in south-eastern Europe, which was once one of the six republics that made up the former Federal People's Republic of Yugoslavia. This landlocked country is largely mountainous or hilly. Macedonia has hot summers, though highland areas are cooler. Winters are cold and snowfalls are often heavy. The climate is fairly continental in character and rain occurs throughout the year.

**POLITICS & ECONOMY** Until the 20th century, Macedonia's history was closely tied to a larger area, also called Macedonia, which included parts of northern Greece and south-western Bulgaria. This region reached its peak in power at the time of Philip II (382–336 BC) and his son Alexander the Great (336–323 BC). After Alexander's death, his empire was split up and it gradually declined. The area became a Roman province in the 140s BC and part of the Byzantine empire from AD 395. In the 6th century, Slavs from eastern Europe settled in the area, followed by Bulgars from central Asia in the 9th century. The Byzantine empire regained control in 1018, but Serbia took Macedonia in the early 14th century. In 1371, the Ottoman Turks conquered the area and ruled it for more than 500 years.

In 1913, at the end of the Balkan Wars, the area was divided between Serbia, Bulgaria and Greece. At the end of World War I, Serbian Macedonia became part of the Kingdom of the Serbs, Croats and Slovenes, which was renamed Yugoslavia in 1929. After World War II, Yugoslavia became a Communist country under ex-partisan leader Josip Broz Tito.

Tito died in 1980 and, in the early 1990s, the country broke up into five separate republics. Macedonia declared its independence in September 1991. Greece objected to this territory using the name Macedonia, which it considered to be a Greek name. It also objected to a symbol on Macedonia's flag and a reference in the constitution to the desire to reunite the three parts of the old Macedonia.

Macedonia adopted a new clause in its constitution rejecting any Macedonian claims on Greek territory and, in 1993, the United Nations accepted the new republic as a member under the name of the Former Yugoslav Republic of Macedonia (FYROM). By the end of 1993, all the countries of the EU, except Greece, were establishing diplomatic relations with the FYROM. In 1995, Greece lifted its trade ban when Macedonia agreed to redesign its flag, though the issue over its name remained unresolved. In 2001, fighting along the Kosovo border was attributed to people who wanted to create a Greater Albania. The uprising ended when Macedonia granted its Albanian-speakers increased rights. In 2011, the International Court of Justice ruled that Greece was wrong to block Macedonia's bid to join NATO in 2008 because of the dispute over its name.

The World Bank describes Macedonia as an 'upper-middle-income' economy. Manufactures dominate the country's exports. Coal is mined, but oil and natural gas are imported. The country is self-sufficient in its basic food needs.

**AREA** 25,713 sq km [9,928 sq mi] **POPULATION** 2,082,000 **CAPITAL** Skopje **GOVERNMENT** Multiparty republic **ETHNIC GROUPS** Macedonian 64%, Albanian 25%, Turkish 4%, Romanian 3%, Serb 2% **LANGUAGES** Macedonian and Albanian (official) **RELIGIONS** Macedonian Orthodox 65%, Islam 33% **CURRENCY** Macedonian denar = 100 deni

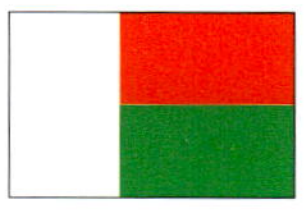

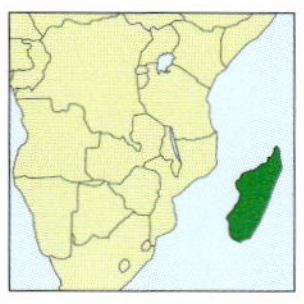

## MADAGASCAR

**GEOGRAPHY** The Democratic Republic of Madagascar, in south-eastern Africa, is an island nation, which has a larger area than France. Behind the narrow coastal plains in the east lies a highland zone, mostly between 610 m and 1,220 m [2,000 ft to 4,000 ft] above sea level. Broad plains border the Mozambique Channel in the west.

Temperatures in the highlands are moderated by the altitude. The winters (from April to September) are dry, but heavy rains occur in summer. The eastern coastlands are warm and humid. The west is drier, and the south and south-west are hot and dry.

**POLITICS & ECONOMY** People from South-east Asia began to settle on Madagascar around 2,000 years ago. Subsequent influxes from Africa and Arabia added to the island's diverse heritage, culture and language.

French troops defeated a Malagasy army in 1895 and Madagascar became a French colony. In 1960, it achieved full independence as the Malagasy Republic. In 1972, army officers seized control and, in 1975, under the leadership of Lieutenant-Commander Didier Ratsiraka, the country was renamed Madagascar. In 2002, the country came close to civil war when Ratsiraka and his opponent Marc Ravalomanana both claimed victory in presidential elections. Ravalomanana became president, but he was deposed in 2009 by Andry Rajoelina, who became *de facto* president. In 2010, a new constitution was adopted in a referendum, enabling Rajoelina to run for president.

Madagascar is a poor country. Poverty and population growth impose pressure on the dwindling forests and the unique wildlife, as well as causing severe soil erosion. Farming, fishing and forestry employ about 80% of the people. Food crops include bananas, cassava, rice and sweet potatoes. Coffee is exported.

**AREA** 587,041 sq km [226,657 sq mi] **POPULATION** 22,005,000 **CAPITAL** Antananarivo **GOVERNMENT** Republic **ETHNIC GROUPS** Merina, Betsimisaraka, Betsileo, Tsimihety, Sakalava and others **LANGUAGES** Malagasy and French (both official) **RELIGIONS** Traditional beliefs 52%, Christianity 41%, Islam 7% **CURRENCY** Malagasy ariary = 5 iraimbilanja

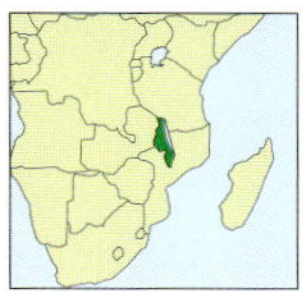

## MALAWI

**GEOGRAPHY** The Republic of Malawi includes part of Lake Malawi, which is drained by the River Shire, a tributary of the River Zambezi. The land is mostly mountainous. The highest peak, Mulanje, reaches 3,002 m [9,849 ft] in the south-east.

While the low-lying areas of Malawi are hot and humid all year round, the uplands have a pleasant climate. Lilongwe has a warm and sunny climate. Frosts sometimes occur in July and August, in the middle of the long dry season.

**POLITICS & ECONOMY** Malawi, then called Nyasaland, became a British protectorate in 1891. In 1953, Britain established the Federation of Rhodesia and Nyasaland, which also included what are now Zambia and Zimbabwe. Black African opposition, led in Nyasaland by Dr Hastings Kamuzu Banda, led to the dissolution of the federation in 1963. In 1964, Nyasaland became independent as Malawi, with Banda as prime minister. Banda became president when the country became a republic in 1966, and in 1971 he was made president for life. Banda was an autocrat, ruling through the only party, the Malawi Congress Party. But a multiparty system was restored in 1993. Bakili Muluzi became president, and in 2004 he was succeeded by Bingu wa Mutharika, leader of the United Democratic Front (UDF). In 2005, he resigned from the UDF and set up the Democratic Progressive Party. Mutharika died in 2012 and was succeeded by Vice President Joyce Banda.

Malawi is one of the world's poorest countries. More than 90% of the people are farmers, but many grow little more than they need to feed their families.

**AREA** 118,484 sq km [45,747 sq mi] **POPULATION** 16,323,000 **CAPITAL** Lilongwe **GOVERNMENT** Multiparty republic **ETHNIC GROUPS** Chewa, Lomwe, Yao, Ngoni, Tumbuka, Nyanja, Sena, Tonga, Ngonde and others **LANGUAGES** Chichewa and English (both official) **RELIGIONS** Protestant 55%, Roman Catholic 20%, Islam 20% **CURRENCY** Malawian kwacha = 100 tambala

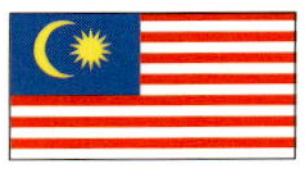

## MALAYSIA

**GEOGRAPHY** The Federation of Malaysia consists of two main parts. Peninsular Malaysia, which is joined to mainland Asia, contains about 80% of the population. The other main regions, Sabah and Sarawak, are in northern Borneo, an island which Malaysia shares with Indonesia. Behind the coastal lowlands, the interior is mountainous.

Malaysia has a hot equatorial climate. The temperatures are high all through the year, though the mountains are much cooler than the lowland areas. Rainfall is heavy throughout the year.

**POLITICS & ECONOMY** Around 1,200 years ago, Indian traders introduced Hinduism and Buddhism into the Malay peninsula, while Arabs introduced Islam in the 15th century. Portuguese traders reached Melaka in 1509, but the Dutch took over in 1641. Britain became established in the area in 1786.

Japan occupied the area during World War II (1939–45), but the area reverted to British rule in 1945. In the 1940s and 1950s, Communist guerrillas battled unsuccessfully for power. Malaya (Peninsular Malaysia) became independent in 1957. Malaysia was created in 1963, when Malaya, Singapore, Sabah and Sarawak agreed to unite, but Singapore withdrew in 1965.

From 1981, Malaysia achieved rapid economic progress, but it experienced an economic recession in 1997. The government took action to restore confidence. In 2003, Mahathir bin Mohamad was succeeded by Abdullah Ahmad Badawi, who stood down in 2009. His deputy, Najib Razak, took over as prime minister.

The World Bank classifies Malaysia as an 'upper-middle-income' developing country. Palm oil, rubber and tin are major products. Manufactures include cars, chemicals, a wide range of electronic goods, plastics, textiles, rubber, and wood products.

**AREA** 329,758 sq km [127,320 sq mi] **POPULATION** 29,180,000
**CAPITAL** Kuala Lumpur; Putrajaya (administrative capital awaiting completion)
**GOVERNMENT** Federal constitutional monarchy
**ETHNIC GROUPS** Malay and other indigenous groups 61%, Chinese 24%, Indian 7%, others **LANGUAGES** Malay (official), Chinese, English **RELIGIONS** Islam, Buddhism, Daoism, Hinduism, Christianity, Sikhism **CURRENCY** Ringgit = 100 sen

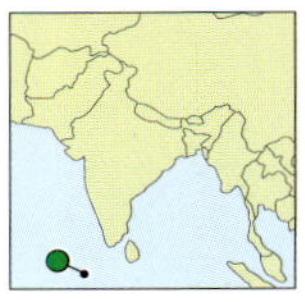

## MALDIVES

The Republic of the Maldives consists of about 1,200 low-lying coral islands, south of India. The highest point is 24 m [79 ft], but most of the land is only 1.8 m [6 ft] above sea level. The islands became a British territory in 1887 and independence was achieved in 1965. Tourism and fishing are the main industries.

**AREA** 298 sq km [115 sq mi] **POPULATION** 394,000 **CAPITAL** Malé

## MALI

**GEOGRAPHY** The Republic of Mali is a landlocked country in northern Africa. The land is generally flat, with the highest land in the north. Northern Mali is hot and practically rainless. The south has enough rain for farming.

**POLITICS & ECONOMY** Between the 4th and 16th centuries, Mali was part of three African empires – Ancient Ghana, Ancient Mali and Songhay. However, after 1591, when Songhay was defeated by Morocco, the area was divided into small kingdoms. France ruled the area, then known as French Sudan, from 1893 until the country became independent as Mali in 1960.

The first socialist government was overthrown in 1968 by an army group led by Moussa Traoré, but he was ousted in 1991. Multiparty democracy was restored in 1992 and Alpha Oumar Konaré was elected president. Konaré stood down in 2002 and Ahmadou Toure, who had restored democracy in 1992, was elected president. In 2012, an army coup overthrew Toure, followed by three successive 'unity cabinets'. The coup leaders said that the government was failing to give them enough arms to tackle a rebellion by ethnic Tuaregs in northern Mali, many of whom had returned from Libya.

Mali is one of the world's poorest countries and 70% of the land is desert or semi-desert. Only about 2% of the land is used for growing crops, while 25% is used for grazing animals. Agriculture employs more than one-third of the people, many of whom subsist by nomadic livestock rearing.

**AREA** 1,240,192 sq km [478,838 sq mi]
**POPULATION** 15,494,000 **CAPITAL** Bamako
**GOVERNMENT** Multiparty republic **ETHNIC GROUPS** Mande 50% (Bambara, Malinke, Soninke), Peul 17%, Voltaic 12%, Songhai 6%, Tuareg and Moor 10%, others **LANGUAGES** French (official), many African languages **RELIGIONS** Islam 95%, traditional beliefs 3%, Christianity 2% **CURRENCY** CFA franc = 100 centimes

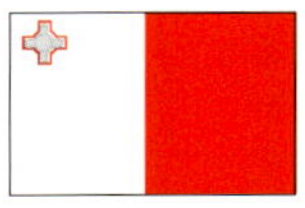

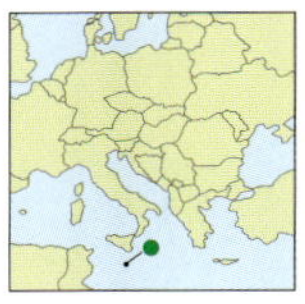

## MALTA

**GEOGRAPHY** The Republic of Malta consists of two main islands, Malta and Gozo, with a third, much smaller island called Comino lying between the two large islands and two islets. The climate is typically Mediterranean, with hot, dry summers and mild, moist winters.

**POLITICS & ECONOMY** Malta has fascinating Stone Age and Bronze Age remains. The islands later came under Phoenician, Greek, Carthaginian, Roman and Arab rule. In about 1090, Malta came under the Norman kings of Sicily and, from 1530, the Knights Hospitallers (also called the Knights of St John of Jerusalem). France took the islands in 1798, but the British drove them out in 1800. British rule was officially recognized in 1815.

During World War I (1914–18), Malta was an important naval base. In World War II (1939–45), Italian and German aircraft bombed the islands. In recognition of the islanders' bravery, the British King George VI awarded the George Cross to Malta in 1942. In 1953, Malta became a base for NATO (North Atlantic Treaty Organization). Malta became independent in 1964 and a republic in 1974. In 1979, Malta ceased to be a British military base. Malta was declared a neutral country in the 1980s. It became a member of the European Union on 1 May 2004, and adopted the euro as its official currency in 2008.

The World Bank classifies Malta as a 'high-income' developing country. It lacks natural resources, and most people work in the former naval dockyards, which are now used for commercial shipbuilding and repair, in manufacturing industries, and in the tourist industry.

Manufactures include processed food and chemicals. Farming is difficult, because of the rocky soils. Crops include barley, fruits, potatoes and wheat. Malta also has a small fishing industry.

**AREA** 316 sq km [122 sq mi] **POPULATION** 410,000
**CAPITAL** Valletta **GOVERNMENT** Multiparty republic
**ETHNIC GROUPS** Maltese 96%, British 2% **LANGUAGES** Maltese and English (both official) **RELIGIONS** Roman Catholic 98%
**CURRENCY** Euro = 100 cents

## MARSHALL ISLANDS

The Republic of the Marshall Islands, a former US territory, became fully independent in 1991. This island nation, lying north of Kiribati in a region known as Micronesia, is heavily dependent on US aid. The main activities are agriculture and tourism.

**AREA** 181 sq km [70 sq mi]
**POPULATION** 68,000 **CAPITAL** Majuro

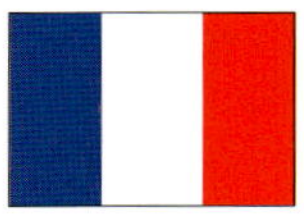

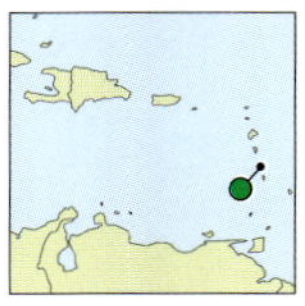

## MARTINIQUE

Martinique, a volcanic island nation in the Caribbean, was colonized by France in 1635. It became a French overseas department in 1946. Tourism and agriculture are major activities. About 70% of Martinique's gross domestic product is provided by the French government, allowing for a good standard of living.

**AREA** 1,102 sq km [425 sq mi]
**POPULATION** 436,000 **CAPITAL** Fort-de-France

## MAURITANIA

**GEOGRAPHY** The Islamic Republic of Mauritania in north-western Africa is nearly twice the size of France. But France has almost 20 times as many people. Part of the world's largest desert, the Sahara, covers northern Mauritania and most Mauritanians live in the south-west. The amount of rainfall and the length of the rainy season increase from north to south. Much of the land is desert, but south-westerly winds bring summer rain to the south.

**POLITICS & ECONOMY** Originally part of the great African empires of Ghana and Mali, Mauritania became a French protectorate in 1903. In 1920, the country became a territory of French West Africa and a French colony. French West Africa included present-day Benin, Burkina Faso, Guinea, Ivory Coast, Mali, Niger and Senegal, as well as Mauritania. Mauritania finally became independent in 1960.

In 1976, Spain withdrew from Spanish (now Western) Sahara, a territory bordering Mauritania to the north. Morocco occupied the northern two-thirds of this territory, while Mauritania took the rest. But Saharan guerrillas belonging to POLISARIO (the Popular Front for the Liberation of Saharan Territories) began an armed struggle for independence. In 1979, Mauritania withdrew from the southern part of Western Sahara, which was then occupied by Morocco. Democracy was restored after a new constitution was adopted in 1991. A military group seized power in 2005, but democratic elections were held in 2007. The military again seized control in 2008, and in 2009 its leader, Mohamad Ould Abdel Aziz, was elected president. In 2010–11, al Qaida militants committed terrorist acts in Mauritania.

Mauritania is a 'low-income' developing country. Nearly half of the people are engaged in agriculture. In 2006, Mauritania became Africa's newest oil producer, when an offshore platform came online for the first time.

**AREA** 1,025,520 sq km [395,953 sq mi]
**POPULATION** 3,359,000 **CAPITAL** Nouakchott
**GOVERNMENT** Multiparty Islamic republic
**ETHNIC GROUPS** Mixed Moor/Black 40%, Moor 30%, Black 30%
**LANGUAGES** Arabic (official), Pulaar, Soninke, Wolof, French
**RELIGIONS** Islam
**CURRENCY** Ouguiya = 5 khoums

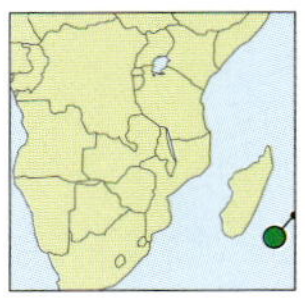

## MAURITIUS

The Republic of Mauritius, an Indian Ocean nation lying east of Madagascar, was previously ruled by France and Britain until it achieved independence in 1968. It became a republic in 1992. Sugar production is in decline but tourism is vital to the economy.

**AREA** 2,040 sq km [788 sq mi]
**POPULATION** 1,313,000 **CAPITAL** Port Louis

## MEXICO

**GEOGRAPHY** The United Mexican States, as Mexico is officially named, is the world's most populous Spanish-speaking country. Much of the land is mountainous, although most people live on the central plateau. Mexico contains two large peninsulas: Lower (or Baja) California in the north-west, and the flat Yucatán peninsula in the south-east.

The climate varies according to the altitude. The resort of Acapulco on the south-west coast has a dry and sunny climate. Mexico City, at about 2,300 m [7,546 ft] above sea level, is much cooler. Most rain occurs between June and September. Rainfall decreases north of Mexico City and northern Mexico is mainly arid.

**POLITICS & ECONOMY** In the mid-19th century, Mexico lost land to the United States, and between 1910 and 1921 violent revolutions created chaos. Reforms were introduced in the 1920s and, in 1929, the Institutional Revolutionary Party (PRI) was formed. The PRI ruled Mexico effectively as a one-party state until it was finally defeated in 2001. The new president, Vicente Fox, faced many problems. He was succeeded by Felipe Calderón in 2006, and at the end of 2012 Enrique Peña Nieto was elected president. Between 2008–13, killings associated with the illegal drug traffic increased dramatically.

The World Bank classifies Mexico as an 'upper-middle-income' developing country. Agriculture is important. Food crops include beans, maize, rice and wheat, while cash crops include coffee, cotton, fruits and vegetables. Beef cattle, dairy cattle and other livestock are raised, and fishing is also important.

However, oil and oil products are the chief exports, while manufacturing is the most valuable activity. Mexico is the world's leading silver producer, and it also mines copper, gold, lead, zinc and other minerals. Many factories near the northern border assemble goods, such as car parts and electrical products, for US companies.

Hopes for the future lie in increasing co-operation with the US and Canada. However, problems with the United States mounted as drug cartels carried out large numbers of killings, mostly along the US border.

**AREA** 1,958,201 sq km [756,061 sq mi]
**POPULATION** 114,975,000 **CAPITAL** Mexico City
**GOVERNMENT** Federal republic
**ETHNIC GROUPS** Mestizo 60%, Amerindian 30%, White 9%
**LANGUAGES** Spanish (official)
**RELIGIONS** Roman Catholic 83%, Protestant 2%, others 15%
**CURRENCY** Mexican peso = 100 centavos

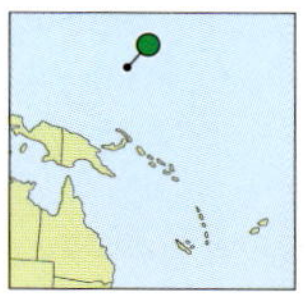

## MICRONESIA

The Federated States of Micronesia, a former US territory covering a vast area in the western Pacific Ocean, became fully independent in 1991. The main export is copra. Fishing and tourism are also important.

**AREA** 702 sq km [271 sq mi]
**POPULATION** 106,000 **CAPITAL** Palikir

## MOLDOVA

**GEOGRAPHY** The Republic of Moldova is a small country sandwiched between Ukraine and Romania. It was formerly one of the 15 republics that made up the Soviet Union. Much of the land is hilly and the highest areas are near the centre of the country.

Moldova has a moderately continental climate, with warm summers and fairly cold winters when temperatures dip below freezing point. Most of the rain comes in the warmer months.

**POLITICS & ECONOMY** In the 14th century, the Moldavians formed a state called Moldavia. It included part of Romania and Bessarabia (now the modern country of Moldova). The Ottoman Turks took the area in the 16th century, but in 1812 Russia took over Bessarabia. In 1861, Moldavia and Walachia united to form Romania. Russia retook southern Bessarabia in 1878. After World War I (1914–18), all of Bessarabia was returned to Romania, but the Soviet Union did not recognize this act. From 1944, the Moldovan Soviet Socialist Republic was part of the Soviet Union.

In 1989, the Moldovans asserted their independence and ethnicity by making Romanian the official language and, at the end of 1991, Moldova became an independent nation. But Trans-Dniester, an area east of the River Dniester, has sought autonomy. In 2006, its people voted for independence and union with Russia. This vote was not recognized internationally.

In 2001, Moldovans returned the Communist Party to power in a general election. Under President Vladimir Voronin, Moldova enjoyed a period of economic growth. The Communist Party was re-elected in 2005 and 2009. Following allegations of fraud, further elections were held in 2010. In 2012, Nicolae Timoftu was elected president, after several inconclusive votes.

In terms of its GNP per capita, Moldova is one of Europe's poorest countries. Agriculture is the leading activity and products include fruits, maize, tobacco and wine. Moldova has few natural resources and it imports materials and fuels for its industries. Light industries, such as food processing and factories making household appliances, are increasing.

**AREA** 33,851 sq km [13,070 sq mi]
**POPULATION** 3,657,000 **CAPITAL** Kishinev
**GOVERNMENT** Multiparty republic
**ETHNIC GROUPS** Moldovan/Romanian 78%, Ukrainian 8%, Russian 6%, Gagauz 4%, others
**LANGUAGES** Moldovan/Romanian (official), Gagauz, Russian
**RELIGIONS** Eastern Orthodox 98%
**CURRENCY** Moldovan leu = 100 bani

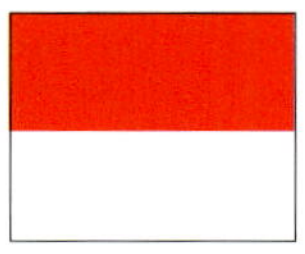

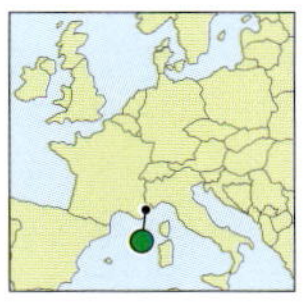

## MONACO

The tiny Principality of Monaco consists of a narrow strip of coastline and a rocky peninsula on the French Riviera. Its considerable wealth is derived largely from banking, finance, gambling, recreation and tourism. Monaco's citizens do not pay any state tax. From 2005, the reigning prince is Albert II. His family, the Grimaldis, have ruled the country for over 700 years.

**AREA** 1 sq km [0.4 sq mi] **POPULATION** 31,000 **CAPITAL** Monaco

## MONGOLIA

**GEOGRAPHY** The State of Mongolia is the world's largest landlocked country. It consists mainly of high plateaux, with the Gobi Desert in the south-east.

Ulan Bator lies on the northern edge of a desert plateau. It has bitterly cold winters. Summer temperatures are moderated by the altitude.

**POLITICS & ECONOMY** In the 13th century, Genghis Khan united the Mongolian peoples and built up a great empire. Under his grandson, Kublai Khan, the Mongol empire extended from Korea and China to eastern Europe and present-day Iraq.

The Mongol empire broke up in the late 14th century. In the early 17th century, Inner Mongolia came under Chinese control, and by the late 17th century Outer Mongolia had become a Chinese province. In 1911, the Mongolians drove the Chinese out of Outer Mongolia and made the area a Buddhist kingdom. But in 1924, under Russian influence, the Communist Mongolian People's Republic was set up. From the 1950s, Mongolia supported the Soviet Union in its disputes with China. In 1990, the people demonstrated for more freedom, and free elections in June 1990 were won by the Communist Mongolian People's Revolutionary Party (MPRP). The Democratic Union coalition won power in 1996, but the MPRP regained power in 2000. In 2004, after disputed elections, a coalition government was set up. In 2009, the Democratic Union candidate, Tsakhiagiin Elbegdorj, was elected president.

The World Bank classifies Mongolia as a 'lower-middle-income' developing country. Most people were once nomads, who moved around with their herds of sheep, cattle, goats and horses. Under Communist rule, most people were moved into permanent homes on government-owned farms. Livestock and animal products remain important, but minerals and fuels now account for more than three-fifths of Mongolia's exports.

**AREA** 1,566,500 sq km [604,826 sq mi]
**POPULATION** 3,180,000 **CAPITAL** Ulan Bator
**GOVERNMENT** Multiparty republic **ETHNIC GROUPS** Khalkha Mongol 95%, Kazakh 5% **LANGUAGES** Khalkha Mongolian (official), Turkic, Russian **RELIGIONS** Tibetan Buddhist Lamaism 96%
**CURRENCY** Mongolian tögrög = 100 möngös

## MONTENEGRO

The Republic of Montenegro became a fully independent nation in 2006. It was formerly part of the Union of Serbia and Montenegro and, before 2003, part of Yugoslavia.

The coastal region has a Mediterranean climate. However, inland, the Dinaric Alps, which reach a height of 2,522 m [8,274 ft], have a more severe climate.

Serbia fell under Turkish rule in the 14th century, but Montenegro remained Christian. Montenegro was absorbed into Serbia in 1918. It became part of the Kingdom of the Serbs, Croats and Slovenes, which was renamed Yugoslavia in 1929. After World War II, Montenegro was recognized as one of the six republics in the Federal Republic of Yugoslavia.

Elections were held in 2009 and 2012. The current prime minister, Milo Djukanovic, is serving his fourth term. The presidential election held in April 2013 was won by the incumbent Filip Vujanovic.

Manufacturing is the leading activity, and steel and aluminium are major products. But farming remains important. Forests cover more than half of the land.

**AREA** 14,026 sq km [5,415 sq mi] **POPULATION** 657,000
**CAPITAL** Podgorica **GOVERNMENT** Republic
**ETHNIC GROUPS** Montenegrin 43%, Serb 32%, Bosnian 8%, Albanian 5%, others **LANGUAGES** Serbian and Montenegrin (both official), Bosnian, Albanian **RELIGIONS** Orthodox, Islam, Roman Catholic
**CURRENCY** Euro = 100 cents

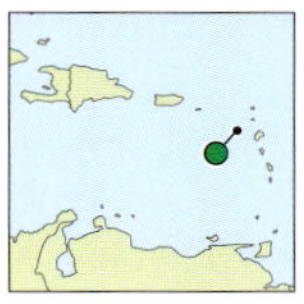

## MONTSERRAT

Montserrat is a British overseas territory in the Caribbean Sea. The climate is tropical and hurricanes often cause much damage. Intermittent eruptions of the Soufrière Hills volcano between 1995 and 1998, and again in 2003, led to the emigration of many people and the virtual destruction of Plymouth, the then capital. A new airport was opened in 2005.

**AREA** 102 sq km [39 sq mi] **POPULATION** 5,000 **CAPITAL** Brades

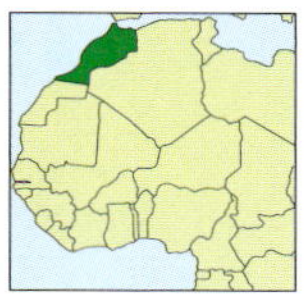

## MOROCCO

**GEOGRAPHY** The Kingdom of Morocco lies in north-western Africa. Its name comes from the Arabic Maghreb-el-Aksa, meaning 'the farthest west'. Behind the western coastal plain the land rises to a broad plateau and ranges of the Atlas Mountains. The High (Haut) Atlas contains the highest peak, Djebel Toubkal, at 4,165 m [13,665 ft]. East of the mountains, the land descends to the Sahara. The Canaries Current cools the Atlantic coast. Inland, summers are hot and dry. Winters are mild, with moderate rainfall. Snow often falls on the High Atlas Mountains.

**POLITICS & ECONOMY** The original people of Morocco were the Berbers. But in the 680s, Arab invaders introduced Islam and the Arabic language. By the early 20th century, France and Spain controlled Morocco, which became an independent kingdom in 1956. Although Morocco is a constitutional monarchy, King Hassan II ruled the country in a generally authoritarian way from the time of his accession to the throne in 1961 to his death in 1999. His successor, Mohamed VI, faced several problems, including that of Western Sahara, which he claimed for Morocco, and the activities of Islamist extremists. In 2011, the people approved a new constitution, granting the prime minister more power.

Morocco is classified as a 'lower-middle-income' developing country. It is the world's third largest producer of phosphate rock, which is used to make fertilizer. One of the reasons why Morocco wants to keep Western Sahara is that it, too, has large phosphate reserves. Farming employs about 45% of Moroccans. Chief crops include barley, beans, citrus fruits, maize, olives, sugar beet and wheat. Processed phosphates are exported, but most of Morocco's manufactures are for home consumption. Fishing and tourism are also important.

**AREA** 446,550 sq km [172,413 sq mi]
**POPULATION** 32,309,000 **CAPITAL** Rabat
**GOVERNMENT** Constitutional monarchy
**ETHNIC GROUPS** Arab-Berber 99%
**LANGUAGES** Arabic (official), Berber dialects, French
**RELIGIONS** Islam 99% **CURRENCY** Moroccan dirham = 100 centimes

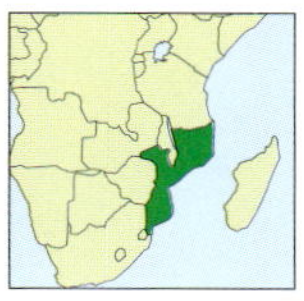

## MOZAMBIQUE

**GEOGRAPHY** The Republic of Mozambique borders the Indian Ocean in south-eastern Africa. The coastal plains are narrow in the north but broaden in the south. Inland lie plateaux and hills, which make up another two-fifths of the country. Mozambique has a mostly tropical climate. The capital Maputo, which lies outside the tropics, has hot and humid summers, though the winters are mild and fairly dry.

**POLITICS & ECONOMY** In 1885, when the European powers divided Africa, Mozambique was recognized as a Portuguese colony. But black African opposition to European rule gradually increased. In 1961, the Front for the Liberation of Mozambique (FRELIMO) was founded to oppose Portuguese rule. In 1964, FRELIMO launched a guerrilla war, which continued for ten years. Mozambique became independent in 1975.

After independence, Mozambique became a one-party state. Its government aided African nationalists in Rhodesia (now Zimbabwe) and South Africa. But the white governments of these countries helped an opposition group, the Mozambique National Resistance Movement (RENAMO) to lead an armed struggle against Mozambique's government. Civil war, combined with droughts, caused much suffering in the 1980s. In 1989, FRELIMO ended one-party rule. The war ended in 1992 and multiparty elections were held in 1994. In 1995 Mozambique became the 53rd member of the Commonwealth. In 2004, and again in 2009, FRELIMO leader Antonio Guebuza was elected president.

In the early 1990s, the UN rated Mozambique as one of the world's poorest countries. The second half of the 1990s saw the start of renewed economic growth, but floods in 2000–1, 2007, and 2008, and prolonged droughts in the mid-2000s and 2008, were major setbacks. About 80% of the people are poor farmers. Crops include cassava, cotton, maize, rice and tea.

**AREA** 801,590 sq km [309,494 sq mi]
**POPULATION** 23,516,000 **CAPITAL** Maputo
**GOVERNMENT** Multiparty republic **ETHNIC GROUPS** Indigenous tribal groups (Shangaan, Chokwe, Manyika, Sena, Makua, others) 99%
**LANGUAGES** Portuguese (official), many others
**RELIGIONS** Roman Catholic 28%, Protestant 28%, Islam 18%
**CURRENCY** Metical = 100 centavos

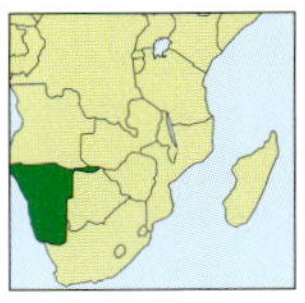

## NAMIBIA

**GEOGRAPHY** The Republic of Namibia was formerly ruled by South Africa, which called it South West Africa. The country became independent in 1990. The coastal region contains the arid Namib Desert, which is virtually uninhabited. Inland is a central plateau, bordered by a rugged spine of mountains stretching north–south. Eastern Namibia contains part of the Kalahari Desert, a semi-desert area extending into Botswana. Namibia has a warm and arid climate. Windhoek has an average annual rainfall of 370 mm [15 in], which often occurs in thunderstorms during the hot summer.

**POLITICS & ECONOMY** During World War I, South African troops defeated the Germans who ruled what is now Namibia. After World War II, many people challenged South Africa's right to govern the territory, and a civil war began in the 1960s between African guerrillas and South African troops. A ceasefire was agreed in 1989 and Namibia became independent in 1990. In the 1990s, the government pursued a policy of 'national reconciliation'. An enclave on the coast, called Walvis Bay (Walvisbaai), remained part of South Africa until 1994, when it was transferred to Namibia. In 2004, the nationalist leader, Sam Nujoma, president since 1990, retired. He was succeeded by Hifikepunye Pohamba, who was re-elected in 2009.

Namibia has reserves of diamonds, uranium, zinc and copper. Minerals make up the bulk of exports, though agriculture employs 16% of the people. Fishing is important. Namibia has few industries. Oil has been discovered and tourism is expanding.

**AREA** 824,292 sq km [318,259 sq mi]
**POPULATION** 2,166,000 **CAPITAL** Windhoek
**GOVERNMENT** Multiparty republic **ETHNIC GROUPS** Ovambo 50%, Kavango 9%, Herero 7%, Damara 7%, White 6%, Nama 5%
**LANGUAGES** English (official), Afrikaans, German, indigenous dialects **RELIGIONS** Christianity 90% (Lutheran 51%)
**CURRENCY** Namibian dollar = 100 cents

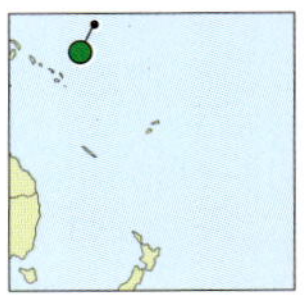

## NAURU

Nauru is the world's smallest republic, located in the western Pacific Ocean, close to the equator. Independent since 1968, Nauru's prosperity is based on phosphate mining, but the reserves are running out.

**AREA** 21 sq km [8 sq mi]
**POPULATION** 9,000 **CAPITAL** Yaren

## NEPAL

**GEOGRAPHY** Over three-quarters of Nepal lies in the Himalayan region, culminating in the world's highest peak (Mount Everest, or Chomolongma in Nepali) at 8,850 m [29,035 ft]. As a result, climatic conditions vary widely according to the altitude.

**POLITICS & ECONOMY** Nepal was united in the late 18th century, although its complex topography has ensured that it remains a diverse patchwork of peoples. From the mid-19th century to 1951, power was held by the royal Rana family. The first democratic elections in 32 years were held in 1991, but, by the early 21st century, Nepal faced many problems, including an uprising of Maoist guerrillas. In 2005, King Gyanendra seized power but failed to stop the conflict. In 2006, the Maoists joined a provisional coalition government. In elections in April 2008, the Maoists became the largest single party. In May, Nepal became a republic and the Maoist leader, named Prachanda, became prime minister in August. He resigned in 2009. In 2011, a Maoist, Baburam Bhattari, became prime minister.

Agriculture is the main activity in this overwhelmingly rural country, and Nepal is heavily dependent on aid. Tourism, based on the attractions of the high Himalaya, is growing in importance. There are also ambitious plans to exploit the hydroelectric potential offered by the ferocious Himalayan rivers.

**AREA** 147,181 sq km [56,827 sq mi] **POPULATION** 29,891,000
**CAPITAL** Katmandu **GOVERNMENT** Multiparty republic
**ETHNIC GROUPS** Brahman, Chetri, Newar, Gurung, Magar, Tamang, Sherpa and others
**LANGUAGES** Nepali (official), local languages
**RELIGIONS** Hinduism 81%, Buddhism 11%, Islam 4%
**CURRENCY** Nepalese rupee = 100 paisa

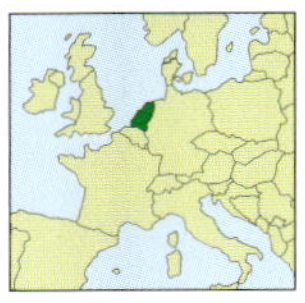

## NETHERLANDS

**GEOGRAPHY** The Netherlands lies at the western end of the North European Plain, which extends to the Ural Mountains in Russia. Except for the far south-eastern corner, the Netherlands is flat and about 40% lies below sea level at high tide. To prevent flooding, the Dutch have built dykes (sea walls) to hold back the waves. Large areas which were once under the sea, but which have been reclaimed, are called polders. Because of its position on the North Sea, the Netherlands has a temperate climate, with mild, rainy winters.

**POLITICS & ECONOMY** Before the 16th century, the area that is now the Netherlands was under a succession of foreign rulers, including the Romans, the Germanic Franks, the French and the Spanish. The Dutch declared their independence from Spain in 1581 and their status was finally recognized by Spain in 1648. In the 17th century, the Dutch built up a great overseas empire, especially in South-east Asia. But in the early 18th century, the Dutch lost control of the seas to England.

France controlled the Netherlands from 1795 to 1813. In 1815, the Netherlands, then containing Belgium and Luxembourg, became an independent kingdom. Belgium broke away in 1830 and Luxembourg followed in 1890.

The Netherlands was neutral in World War I (1914–18), but was occupied by Germany in World War II (1939–45). After the war, the Netherlands Indies became independent as Indonesia. The Netherlands became active in West European affairs. With Belgium and Luxembourg, it formed a customs union called Benelux in 1948. In 1949, it joined NATO (the North Atlantic Treaty Organization), and the European Coal and Steel Community (ECSC) in 1953. In 1957, it became a founder member of the European Economic Community (now the European Union), and in 2002 it adopted the euro as its sole unit of currency. Since 2002, five coalition governments have collapsed, the latest in early 2012 when the right-wing Freedom Party refused to back the coalition's austerity measures.

In 2013, Queen Beatrix abdicated in favour of her son, Prince Willem Alexander, after a 33-year reign.

In 2010, the Netherlands Antilles, an island territory in the Caribbean, was dissolved. Curaçao and St Maarten became nations in the Kingdom of the Netherlands. The small islands of Bonaire, St Eustatius and Saba became special municipalities of the Netherlands.

The Netherlands is a highly industrialized country, and industry and commerce are the most valuable activities. Its resources include natural gas, some oil, salt and china clay. But the Netherlands imports many of the materials needed by its industries and it is, therefore, a major trading country. Industrial products are wide-ranging, including aircraft, chemicals, electronic equipment, machinery, textiles and vehicles. Farming is scientific and yields are high. Dairy farming is the leading farming activity. Major products include barley, flowers and bulbs, potatoes, sugar beet and wheat.

**AREA** 41,526 sq km [16,033 sq mi] **POPULATION** 16,731,000
**CAPITAL** Amsterdam; The Hague (seat of government)
**GOVERNMENT** Constitutional monarchy
**ETHNIC GROUPS** Dutch 83%, Indonesian, Turkish, Moroccan, and others **LANGUAGES** Dutch and Frisian (both official)
**RELIGIONS** Roman Catholic 30%, Protestant 20%, Islam 6%, others
**CURRENCY** Euro = 100 cents

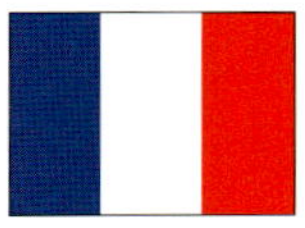

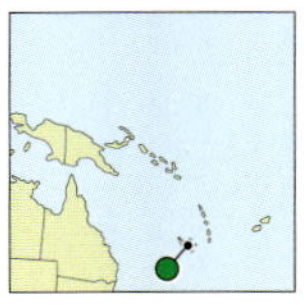

## NEW CALEDONIA

New Caledonia is the most southerly of the Melanesian countries in the Pacific. It has been a French possession since 1853 and an Overseas Territory since 1958. In 1998, France announced that a vote on independence would be postponed until between 2014 and 2018. The country is rich in mineral resources, especially nickel.

**AREA** 18,575 sq km [7,172 sq mi] **POPULATION** 260,000 **CAPITAL** Nouméa

## NEW ZEALAND

**GEOGRAPHY** New Zealand lies about 1,600 km [994 mi] south-east of Australia. It consists of two main islands and several other small ones. Much of North Island is volcanic. Active volcanoes include Ngauruhoe and Ruapehu. Hot springs and geysers are common, and steam from the ground is used to produce electricity. The Southern Alps, which contain the country's highest peak, Aoraki Mount Cook, at 3,753 m [12,313 ft], form the backbone of South Island. This island also has some large, fertile plains.

New Zealand lies on the geologically active 'Pacific ring of fire'. Most of the 14,000 earthquakes that occur every year have a magnitude of less than 5.0. But, in 2010 and 2011, two earthquakes, with magnitudes of 7.0 and 6.3 respectively, struck Christchurch on South Island, causing great damage. The 2011 earthquake resulted in a death toll of more than 180.

Auckland in the north has a warm, humid climate throughout the year. Wellington has cooler summers, while in Dunedin, in the south-east, temperatures sometimes dip below freezing in winter. The rainfall is heaviest on the western highlands.

**POLITICS & ECONOMY** Evidence suggests that early Maori settlers arrived in New Zealand more than 1,000 years ago. The Dutch navigator Abel Tasman reached New Zealand in 1642, but his discovery was not followed up. In 1769, the British Captain James Cook rediscovered the islands. In the early 19th century, British settlers arrived and, in 1840, under the Treaty of Waitangi, Britain took possession of the islands. From the 1870s, the Maoris were gradually integrated into colonial society.

In 1907, New Zealand became a self-governing dominion in the British Commonwealth. The country's economy developed quickly and the people became increasingly prosperous. However, after Britain joined the European Economic Community in 1973, New Zealand's exports to Britain shrank and the country had to reassess its economic and defence strategies and seek new markets. The world recession led the government to cut back on welfare spending in the 1990s. The preservation of Maori culture and Maori rights are major issues. The Maoris, a Polynesian people, make up about 13% of the population. Other mainly Polynesian Pacific people make up another 6%. Ties with Britain have been reduced. Helen Clark, leader of the Labour Party and prime minister from 1999–2008, has expressed the view that New Zealand will eventually abolish the monarchy and become a republic. In November 2008, the centre-right National Party defeated the Labour Party in elections. John Key became prime minister and he was re-elected in 2011.

The economy once depended on agriculture, but manufacturing now employs twice as many people as farming. Meat and dairy products are leading commodities. Sheep rearing has declined as the area under cattle, deer and vines has expanded. Crops include barley, fruits, potatoes and other vegetables, and wheat. In 2008–9, New Zealand's economy entered a period of recession. Full recovery was expected to be slow.

**AREA** 270,534 sq km [104,453 sq mi]
**POPULATION** 4,328,000 **CAPITAL** Wellington
**GOVERNMENT** Constitutional monarchy
**ETHNIC GROUPS** European 57%, Asian 8%, Maori 7%, Polynesian 5%
**LANGUAGES** English and Maori (both official)
**RELIGIONS** Anglican 24%, Presbyterian 18%, Roman Catholic 15%, others
**CURRENCY** New Zealand dollar = 100 cents

## NICARAGUA

**GEOGRAPHY** The Republic of Nicaragua is a large country in Central America. In the east is a broad plain bordering the Caribbean Sea. The plain is drained by rivers that flow from the Central Highlands. The fertile western Pacific region contains about 40 volcanoes, many of which are active, and earthquakes are common.

Nicaragua has a tropical climate. Managua is hot throughout the year and there is a marked rainy season from May to October. In October 1998, Hurricane Mitch caused great devastation in Nicaragua. The Central Highlands and Caribbean region are cooler and wetter. The wettest region is the humid Caribbean plain.

**POLITICS & ECONOMY** In 1502, Christopher Columbus claimed the area for Spain, which ruled Nicaragua until 1821. By the early 20th century, the United States had considerable influence in the country and, in 1912, US forces entered Nicaragua to protect US interests. From 1927 to 1933, rebels under General Augusto César Sandino tried to drive US forces out of the country. In 1933, US marines set up a Nicaraguan army, the National Guard, to help to defeat the rebels. Its leader, Anastasio Somoza Garcia, had Sandino murdered in 1934, and from 1937 Somoza ruled as a dictator.

In the mid-1970s, many people began to protest against Somoza's rule. Many joined a guerrilla force, called the Sandinista National Liberation Front, named after General Sandino. The rebels defeated the Somoza regime in 1979. In the 1980s, US-supported forces, called the 'Contras', launched a campaign against the Sandinista government. The US government opposed the Sandinista regime, under Daniel José Ortega Saavedra, claiming that it was a Communist dictatorship. A coalition, the National Opposition Union, defeated the Sandinistas in 1990. In 2001, the Sandinista candidate, Ortega, was defeated in presidential elections, but he was re-elected in 2006. In 2009, he announced plans to change the constitution so that he could stand for another term. He was re-elected president in 2011.

In the early 1990s, Nicaragua faced many problems in rebuilding its shattered economy. Agriculture employs about 28% of the people. Coffee, cotton, sugar and bananas are grown for export, while rice is the main food crop.

**AREA** 130,000 SQ KM [50,193 SQ MI]
**POPULATION** 5,728,000 **CAPITAL** MANAGUA
**GOVERNMENT** MULTIPARTY REPUBLIC
**ETHNIC GROUPS** MESTIZO 69%, WHITE 17%, BLACK 9%, AMERINDIAN 5%
**LANGUAGES** SPANISH (OFFICIAL)
**RELIGIONS** ROMAN CATHOLIC 59%, PROTESTANT 23%, OTHERS
**CURRENCY** NICARAGUAN CÓRDOBA = 100 CENTAVOS

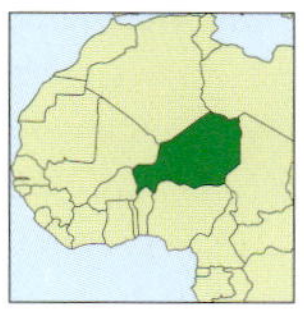

## NIGER

**GEOGRAPHY** The Republic of Niger is a landlocked nation in north-central Africa. The northern plateaux lie in the Sahara Desert, while Central Niger contains the rugged Aïr Mountains. The most fertile, densely populated region is the Niger valley in the south-west.

Niger has a tropical climate and the south has a rainy season between June and September. The north is practically rainless.

**POLITICS & ECONOMY** Since independence in 1960, Niger, a French territory from 1900, has suffered severe droughts. Food shortages and the collapse of the traditional nomadic way of life of some of Niger's people have caused political instability. After a period of military rule, a multiparty constitution was adopted in 1992, but the military again seized power in 1996. Later that year, the coup leader, Colonel Ibrahim Barre Mainassara, was elected president. He was assassinated in 1999, but parliamentary rule was restored and Mamadou Tandja was elected president. He was overthrown in a coup in 2010 and a military regime took power. But democratic elections took place in 2011.

Niger's chief resource is uranium and the country is the world's fifth largest producer. Some tin and tungsten are also mined, though other mineral reserves are largely untouched. Despite its considerable resources, Niger remains one of the world's poorest countries. Only 3% of the land can be used for growing crops.

**AREA** 1,267,000 SQ KM [489,189 SQ MI] **POPULATION** 16,345,000
**CAPITAL** NIAMEY **GOVERNMENT** MULTIPARTY REPUBLIC
**ETHNIC GROUPS** HAUSA 56%, DJERMA 22%, TUAREG 8%, FULA 8%, OTHERS **LANGUAGES** FRENCH (OFFICIAL), HAUSA, DJERMA
**RELIGIONS** ISLAM 80%, INDIGENOUS BELIEFS, CHRISTIANITY
**CURRENCY** CFA FRANC = 100 CENTIMES

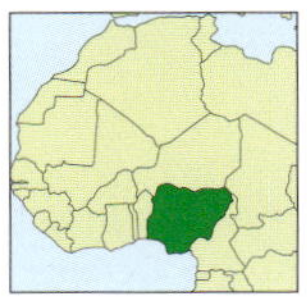

## NIGERIA

**GEOGRAPHY** The Federal Republic of Nigeria is the most populous nation in Africa. The country's main rivers are the Niger and Benue, which meet in central Nigeria. North of the two river valleys are high plains and plateaux. The Lake Chad basin is in the north-east, with the Sokoto plains in the north-west. The south contains hilly uplands and plains. The south has a hot, rainy climate. The north is drier and often hotter than the south.

**POLITICS & ECONOMY** Nigeria has a long artistic tradition. Major cultures include the Nok (500 BC to AD 200), the Ife, a major Yoruba culture which developed about 1,000 years ago, and the Benin (15th to 17th centuries). Britain gradually extended its influence over the area in the second half of the 19th century.

Nigeria became independent in 1960 and a federal republic in 1963. A federal constitution dividing the country into regions was necessary because Nigeria contains more than 250 ethnic and linguistic groups, as well as several religious ones. Local rivalries have long been a threat to national unity, and six new states were created in 1996 in an attempt to overcome this. Civil war occurred between 1967 and 1970, when the people of the south-east attempted unsuccessfully to secede during the Biafran War. Between 1960 and 1998, Nigeria had only nine years of civilian government.

In 1998–9, civilian rule was restored and Olusegun Obasanjo became president. Nigeria faced many problems, including violence in the Niger delta region and religious conflict. In 2011–12, northern Nigeria was hit by a series of violent attacks made by an Islamist organization called Boko Haram, a Hausa term meaning 'Western education is a sin'. In late 2011, Nigeria's President Goodluck Jonathan declared an emergency in some areas.

Nigeria is a developing country with great potential. Its chief natural resource is oil, which accounts for most of its exports. Agriculture employs 70% of the people and the country is a major producer of cocoa, palm oil and palm kernels, groundnuts (peanuts) and rubber. Industry is increasing and manufactures include cement, chemicals, fertilizers, textiles and timber.

**AREA** 923,768 SQ KM [356,667 SQ MI] **POPULATION** 170,124,000
**CAPITAL** ABUJA **GOVERNMENT** FEDERAL MULTIPARTY REPUBLIC
**ETHNIC GROUPS** HAUSA AND FULANI 29%, YORUBA 21%, IBO (OR IGBO) 18%, IJAW 10%, KANURI 4%, MANY OTHERS
**LANGUAGES** ENGLISH (OFFICIAL), HAUSA, YORUBA, IBO
**RELIGIONS** ISLAM 50%, CHRISTIANITY 40%, TRADITIONAL BELIEFS 10%
**CURRENCY** NAIRA = 100 KOBO

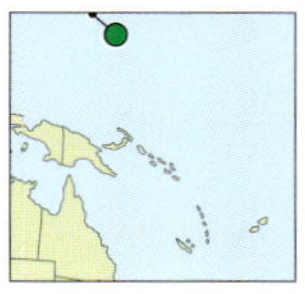

## NORTHERN MARIANA ISLANDS

The Commonwealth of the Northern Mariana Islands contains 16 mountainous islands north of Guam in the western Pacific Ocean. In a 1975 plebiscite, the islanders voted for Commonwealth status in union with the United States, and in 1986 they were granted US citizenship.

**AREA** 464 SQ KM [179 SQ MI] **POPULATION** 51,000 **CAPITAL** SAIPAN

## NORWAY

**GEOGRAPHY** The Kingdom of Norway forms the western part of the rugged Scandinavian peninsula. The deep inlets along the highly indented coastline were worn out by glaciers during the Ice Age. The warm North Atlantic Drift off the coast of Norway moderates the climate, with mild winters and cool summers. Nearly all the ports are ice-free throughout the year. Inland, winters are colder and snow cover lasts for at least three months a year.

**POLITICS & ECONOMY** Between about AD 800 and 1100, Norwegian Vikings ravaged western Europe. In 1380, Norway was united with Denmark. But in 1814, Denmark handed Norway over to Sweden, though it kept Norway's colonies – Greenland, Iceland and the Færoe Islands. Norway briefly became independent, but Swedish forces defeated the Norwegians and Norway had to accept Sweden's king as its ruler. The union with Sweden ended in 1903. Germany occupied Norway during World War II (1939–45). Norway recovered quickly after the war and it now has one of the world's highest standards of living. In 1960, Norway and six other countries formed the European Free Trade Association (EFTA). But, in 1994, Norway voted against joining the European Union. In 2009, the centre-left coalition led by Prime Minister Jens Stoltenberg was narrowly re-elected.

Norway's chief resources and exports are oil and natural gas which come from wells under the North Sea. Farmland covers only 3% of the land. Dairy farming and meat production are important, but Norway has to import food. Norway has many industries powered by cheap hydroelectricity.

**AREA** 323,877 SQ KM [125,049 SQ MI]
**POPULATION** 4,707,000 **CAPITAL** OSLO
**GOVERNMENT** CONSTITUTIONAL MONARCHY
**ETHNIC GROUPS** NORWEGIAN 94%
**LANGUAGES** NORWEGIAN (OFFICIAL)
**RELIGIONS** EVANGELICAL LUTHERAN 86%
**CURRENCY** NORWEGIAN KRONE = 100 ØRE

## OMAN

**GEOGRAPHY** The Sultanate of Oman occupies the south-eastern corner of the Arabian peninsula. It also includes the tip of the Musandam peninsula, overlooking the strategic Strait of Hormuz.

Oman has a hot tropical climate. In Muscat, temperatures may reach 47°C [117°F] in the summer months.

**POLITICS & ECONOMY** British influence in Oman dates back to the end of the 18th century, but the country became fully independent in 1971. Since then, using revenue from oil, which was discovered in 1964, the absolute ruler, Qaboos ibn Said, and his government have sought to modernize Oman. In 2000, Oman held elections to its consultative parliament. In 2004, the Sultan appointed Oman's first woman minister without portfolio. In 2011, following anti-government demonstrations, Sultan Qaboos ibn Said promised jobs and benefits.

Oil and natural gas make up about 80% of Oman's exports. Agriculture and fishing remain important. Crops include alfalfa, bananas, coconuts, dates, limes, tobacco, vegetables and wheat. However, Oman has to import food.

**AREA** 309,500 SQ KM [119,498 SQ MI]
**POPULATION** 3,090,000 **CAPITAL** MUSCAT
**GOVERNMENT** MONARCHY WITH CONSULTATIVE COUNCIL
**ETHNIC GROUPS** ARAB, BALUCHI, INDIAN, PAKISTANI
**LANGUAGES** ARABIC (OFFICIAL), BALUCHI, ENGLISH
**RELIGIONS** ISLAM (MAINLY IBADHI), HINDUISM
**CURRENCY** OMANI RIAL = 1,000 BAISA

## PAKISTAN

**GEOGRAPHY** The Islamic Republic of Pakistan contains high mountains, fertile plains, and rocky deserts. The Karakoram range, which contains K2, the world's second highest peak, lies in the northern part of Jammu and Kashmir, which is occupied by Pakistan but claimed by India. Other mountains rise in the west. Plains, drained by the River Indus and its tributaries, occupy much of eastern Pakistan. Arid areas include the Thar Desert and the Baluchistan plateau. Most of Pakistan has hot summers and mild winters, though the mountains have cold winters. The rainfall is generally sparse.

**POLITICS & ECONOMY** Pakistan was the site of the Indus Valley civilization which developed about 4,500 years ago. But Pakistan's modern history dates from 1947, when British India was divided into India and Pakistan. Muslim Pakistan was divided into two parts: East and West Pakistan, but East Pakistan broke away in 1971 to become Bangladesh. In 1948–9, 1965, and 1971, Pakistan and India clashed over Kashmir. In 1998, Pakistan responded in kind to India's nuclear weapons tests, but, in 2003–7, Pakistan and India launched a series of initiatives aimed at achieving peace.

Pakistan has been subject to several periods of military rule, but elections in 1988 led to Benazir Bhutto becoming prime minister. She was removed from office in 1990, but she returned as prime minister between 1993 and 1996. In 1997, Narwaz Sharif was elected prime minister, but a military coup in 1999 brought General Pervez Musharraf to power. The security situation deteriorated in 2006–7. In 2007, in the run-up to elections in February 2008, Benazir Bhutto was assassinated, but in the elections, the opposition parties heavily defeated Musharraf's supporters. Musharraf resigned in August 2008 and was succeeded as president by Benazir Bhutto's widower, Asif Ali Zardari. In 2011, relations with the United States deteriorated after the US accused Pakistan's government of supporting militants. In May 2013, Narwaz Sharif was elected prime minister for a third term.

According to the World Bank, Pakistan is a 'lower-middle-income' developing country. The economy is based on farming and rearing goats and sheep. Agriculture employs 45% of the people. Major crops include cotton, fruits, rice, sugar cane and wheat.

**AREA** 796,095 SQ KM [307,372 SQ MI]
**POPULATION** 187,343,000 **CAPITAL** ISLAMABAD
**GOVERNMENT** MILITARY REGIME **ETHNIC GROUPS** PUNJABI, SINDHI, PASHTUN (PATHAN), BALUCHI, MUHAJIR
**LANGUAGES** ARABIC (OFFICIAL), MANY OTHERS
**RELIGIONS** ISLAM 97%, CHRISTIANITY, HINDUISM
**CURRENCY** PAKISTANI RUPEE = 100 PAISA

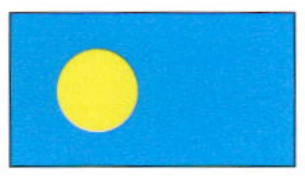

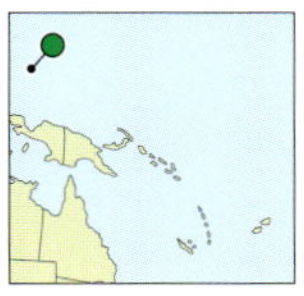

## PALAU

The Republic of Palau became fully independent in 1994, after the USA refused to accede to a 1979 referendum that declared this island nation a nuclear-free zone. In December 1994 Palau joined the United Nations. The economy relies heavily on US aid, tourism, fishing and subsistence agriculture. The main crops include cassava, coconuts and copra.

**AREA** 459 SQ KM [177 SQ MI] **POPULATION** 21,000 **CAPITAL** MELEKEOK

## PANAMA

**GEOGRAPHY** The Republic of Panama forms an isthmus linking Central America to South America. The Panama Canal, which is 81.6 km [50.7 mi] long, cuts across the isthmus. It has made the country a major transport centre.

Panama has a tropical climate. Temperatures are high, though the mountains are much cooler than the coastal plains. The main rainy season is between May and December.

**POLITICS & ECONOMY** Christopher Columbus landed in Panama in 1502 and Spain soon took the area. In 1821, Panama became independent from Spain and a province of Colombia.

In 1903, Colombia refused a request by the United States to build a canal. Panama then revolted against Colombia, and became independent. The United States then began to build the canal, which was opened in 1914. The United States administered the Panama Canal Zone, a strip of land along the canal. But many Panamanians resented US influence and, in 1979, the Canal Zone was returned to Panama. Control of the canal itself was handed over by the USA to Panama on 31 December 1999.

Panama's government has changed many times since independence, and there have been periods of military dictatorships, including that of General Manuel Antonio Noriega in the 1980s. He was finally convicted of drug offences in the United States in 1992. In May 2009, Ricardo Marinelli of the conservative Alliance for Change coalition was elected president. In 2011, the US Congress approved a long-stalled free-trade agreement with Panama.

The World Bank classifies Panama as an 'upper-middle-income' developing country. The Panama Canal is an important source of revenue and, in 2006, work began on widening the canal to take giant container ships. Away from the canal, the main activity is agriculture, which employs 17% of the people.

**AREA** 75,517 sq km [29,157 sq mi] **POPULATION** 3,510,000
**CAPITAL** Panamá **GOVERNMENT** Multiparty republic
**ETHNIC GROUPS** Mestizo 70%, Black and Mulatto 14%, White 10%, Amerindian 6% **LANGUAGES** Spanish (official), English **RELIGIONS** Roman Catholic 85%, Protestant 15%
**CURRENCY** US dollar; Balboa = 100 centésimos

## PARAGUAY

**GEOGRAPHY** The Republic of Paraguay is a landlocked country and rivers, notably the Paraná, Pilcomayo (Brazo Sur) and Paraguay, form most of its borders. A flat region called the Gran Chaco lies in the north-west, while the south-east contains plains, hills and plateaux. Northern Paraguay lies in the tropics, while the south is subtropical. Most of the country has a warm, humid climate.

**POLITICS & ECONOMY** In 1776, Paraguay became part of a large colony called the Viceroyalty of La Plata, with Buenos Aires as the capital. Paraguayans opposed this move and the country declared its independence in 1811.

For many years, Paraguay was torn by internal strife and conflict with its neighbours. A war against Brazil, Argentina, and Uruguay (1865–70) led to the deaths of more than half of Paraguay's population, and a great loss of territory.

General Alfredo Stroessner took power in 1954 and ruled as a dictator. His government imprisoned many opponents. Stroessner was overthrown in 1989 (he died in exile in Brazil in 2006). However, the return of democracy in the years that followed often seemed precarious, because of rivalries between politicians and army leaders, together with economic problems arising partly from the severe problems experienced in neighbouring Argentina and Brazil in 1999. In 2008, a former Roman Catholic bishop, Fernando Lugo, who was regarded as a champion of the poor, was elected president. His victory ended more than six decades of rule by the Colorado Party. However, the 2013 presidential election was won by the Colorado Party's representative, Horacio Cartes.

The World Bank classifies Paraguay as a 'lower-middle-income' developing country. Agriculture and forestry, employing about a third of the population, are important. Paraguay produces hydroelectricity and exports power to its neighbours.

**AREA** 406,752 sq km [157,047 sq mi] **POPULATION** 6,542,000
**CAPITAL** Asunción **GOVERNMENT** Multiparty republic
**ETHNIC GROUPS** Mestizo 95% **LANGUAGES** Spanish and Guaraní (both official) **RELIGIONS** Roman Catholic 90%, Protestant 6%
**CURRENCY** Guaraní = 100 céntimos

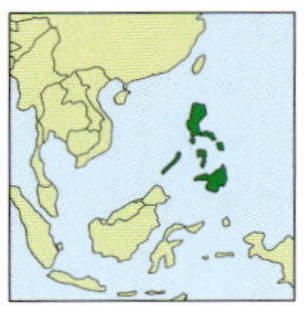

## PHILIPPINES

**GEOGRAPHY** The Republic of the Philippines is an island country in south-eastern Asia. It includes about 7,100 islands, of which 2,770 are named and about 1,000 are inhabited. Luzon and Mindanao, the two largest islands, make up more than two-thirds of the country. The land is mainly mountainous.

The country has a hot tropical climate. The dry season runs from December to April. The rest of the year is wet. Much of the rainfall comes from the typhoons which periodically strike the east coast. In November 2006, a powerful typhoon struck Luzon in the Philippines. The typhoon triggered mudslides on the slopes of Mount Mayon, one of the country's many volcanoes. The mudslides destroyed several villages and killed around 1,000 people.

**POLITICS & ECONOMY** The first European to reach the Philippines was the Portuguese navigator Ferdinand Magellan in 1521. Spanish explorers claimed the region in 1565 when they established a settlement on Cebu. The Spaniards ruled the country until 1898, when the United States took over at the end of the Spanish–American War. Japan invaded the Philippines in 1941, but US forces returned in 1944. The country became fully independent as the Republic of the Philippines in 1946.

Since independence, the country's problems have included armed uprisings by left-wing guerrillas demanding land reform, Muslim separatist groups, crime, corruption and unemployment. The dominant figure in recent times was Ferdinand Marcos, who ruled in a dictatorial manner from 1965 to 1986. His successors were Corazon Aquino (1986–92), Fidel Ramos (1992–8), and Joseph Estrada, who resigned following accusations of corruption. He was succeeded by Vice President Gloria Arroyo, who was re-elected president in 2004. In 2010, Benigno Aquino was elected president. Fighting, killings and kidnappings continued throughout the 2000s, while the government attempted to agree a peace settlement with rebel groups.

The Philippines is a developing country. Agriculture employs around 32% of the people. The main foods are rice and maize, while bananas, cocoa, coffee, sugar cane and tobacco are grown commercially. Shellfish and sea fishing in coastal waters are also important, while manufacturing plays an increasingly significant part in the economy.

**AREA** 300,000 sq km [115,830 sq mi]
**POPULATION** 103,775,000 **CAPITAL** Manila
**GOVERNMENT** Multiparty republic
**ETHNIC GROUPS** Tagalog 28%, Cebuano 14%, Ilocano 9%, Bisaya 7%, and others **LANGUAGES** Filipino (Tagalog) and English (both official), and eight major dialects
**RELIGIONS** Roman Catholic 83%, Protestant 9%, Islam 5%
**CURRENCY** Philippine peso = 100 centavos

## PAPUA NEW GUINEA

**GEOGRAPHY** Papua New Guinea is an independent country in the Pacific Ocean, north of Australia. It is part of a Pacific island region called Melanesia. Papua New Guinea includes the eastern part of New Guinea, the Bismarck Archipelago, the northern Solomon Islands, the D'Entrecasteaux Islands and the Louisiade Archipelago. The land is largely mountainous.

Papua New Guinea has a tropical climate, with high temperatures. Most of the rain occurs during the monsoon season (December–April), when north-westerly winds blow. In the dry season, winds blow from the south-east.

**POLITICS & ECONOMY** The Dutch took western New Guinea (now part of Indonesia) in 1828, but it was not until 1884 that Germany took north-eastern New Guinea and Britain took the south-east. In 1906, Britain handed the south-east over to Australia. It then became known as the Territory of Papua. When World War I broke out in 1914, Australia took German New Guinea, and in 1921 the League of Nations gave Australia a mandate to rule the area, which was named the Territory of New Guinea. Japan invaded New Guinea in 1942, but the Allies reconquered the area in 1944. In 1949, Papua and New Guinea were combined into the Territory of Papua and New Guinea. Papua New Guinea became fully independent in 1975.

Mining is important. An important mine was on Bougainville, where a secessionist group declared the island independent. Under a peace treaty in 2001, Bougainville became autonomous and held elections in 2005. A crisis occurred in 2011–12, when Prime Minister Michael Somare was replaced by Peter O'Neill, following Somare's absence abroad for medical treatment. O'Neill was finally elected prime minister in August 2012.

The country has a 'lower-middle-income' economy. Agriculture employs 85% of the people, mostly at subsistence level. Petroleum and minerals, notably copper, are major exports.

**AREA** 462,840 sq km [178,703 sq mi] **POPULATION** 6,310,000
**CAPITAL** Port Moresby **GOVERNMENT** Constitutional monarchy
**ETHNIC GROUPS** Papuan, Melanesian, Micronesian **LANGUAGES** English, Tok Pisin, Hiri Motu (all official); more than 800 indigenous languages **RELIGIONS** Traditional beliefs 34%, Roman Catholic 22%, Lutheran 16% **CURRENCY** Kina = 100 toea

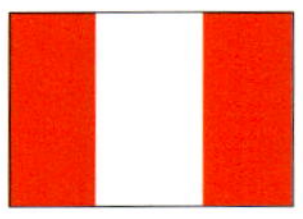

## PERU

**GEOGRAPHY** The Republic of Peru lies in the tropics in western South America. A narrow coastal plain borders the Pacific Ocean in the west. Inland are ranges of the Andes Mountains, which rise to 6,768 m [22,205 ft] at Nevado Huascarán, an extinct volcano. East of the Andes lies the Amazon basin.

Lima, on the coastal plain, has an arid climate. The coastal region is chilled by the cold, offshore Humboldt Current. Rainfall increases inland and many mountains in the high Andes are snow-capped.

**POLITICS & ECONOMY** Spanish *conquistadores* conquered Peru in the 1530s. In 1820, an Argentinian, José de San Martín, led an army into Peru and declared it independent. But Spain still held large areas. In 1823, the Venezuelan Simon Bolívar led another army into Peru and, in 1824, one of his generals defeated the Spaniards at Ayacucho. The Spaniards surrendered in 1826. Peru suffered much instability throughout the 19th century.

Instability continued in the 20th century. In 1980, when civilian rule was restored, a left-wing group called the Sendero Luminoso, or the 'Shining Path', began guerrilla warfare against the government. In 1990, Alberto Fujimori, son of Japanese immigrants, became president. In 1992, he suspended the constitution and dismissed the legislature. The guerrilla leader, Abimael Guzmán, was arrested in 1992 and, in 2006, he was sentenced to life imprisonment. Fujimori left Peru but was later extradited, and in 2009 he was found guilty of ordering killings and kidnapping during the conflict and sentenced to 25 years in jail. In 2006, Alan Garcia was elected president. In 2011, Ollanta Humala won presidential elections in a run-off, defeating Keiko Fujimori.

The World Bank classifies Peru as an 'upper-middle-income' developing country. Major food crops include beans, maize, potatoes and rice. Fish products are exported, but the most valuable export is copper. Peru also produces lead, silver, zinc and iron ore.

**AREA** 1,285,216 sq km [496,222 sq mi]
**POPULATION** 29,550,000 **CAPITAL** Lima
**GOVERNMENT** Constitutional republic **ETHNIC GROUPS** Amerindian 45%, Mestizo 37%, White 15% **LANGUAGES** Spanish and Quechua (both official), Aymara, other Amazonian languages **RELIGIONS** Roman Catholic 81% **CURRENCY** Peruvian sol = 100 centavos

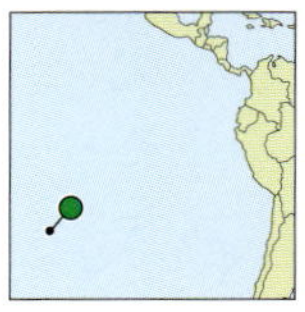

## PITCAIRN

Pitcairn Island is a British overseas territory in the Pacific Ocean. Its inhabitants are descendants of the original settlers – nine mutineers from HMS *Bounty* and 18 Tahitians who arrived in 1790.

**AREA** 55 sq km [21 sq mi]
**POPULATION** 48 **CAPITAL** Adamstown

## POLAND

**GEOGRAPHY** The Republic of Poland faces the Baltic Sea and behind its lagoon-fringed coast lies a broad plain. A plateau lies in the south-east, while the Sudeten Highlands straddle part of the border with the Czech Republic. Part of the Carpathian Range (the Tatra) lies in the south-east.

Poland's climate is influenced by its position in Europe. Warm, moist air masses come from the west, while cold air masses come from the north and east. Summers are warm, but winters are cold and snowy.

**POLITICS & ECONOMY** Poland's boundaries have changed several times in the last 200 years, partly as a result of its geographical location between the powers of Germany and Russia. It disappeared from the map in the late 18th century, when a Polish state called the Grand Duchy of Warsaw was set up. But in 1815, the country was partitioned between Austria, Prussia and Russia. Poland became independent in 1918, but in 1939 it was divided between Germany and the Soviet Union. The country again became independent in 1945, when it lost land to Russia but gained some from Germany. Communists took power in 1948, but opposition mounted and eventually became focused through an organization called Solidarity.

Solidarity was led by a trade unionist, Lech Walesa. A coalition government was formed between Solidarity and the Communists in 1989. In 1990, the Communist Party was dissolved and Walesa became president. But he faced many problems in turning Poland towards a market economy, and was defeated in presidential elections in 1995. But his successor followed westwards-looking policies. Poland joined NATO in 1999 and the European Union in 2004. In 2005, a nationalist, Lech Kaczynski, was elected president. But, along with other prominent Poles, he was killed in a plane crash in Russia in 2010. In 2011, Prime Minister Donald Tusk's centre-right Civic Platform Party won parliamentary elections.

Poland has reserves of coal and various minerals which are used in its industries. Manufactures include chemicals, food, machinery, ships, steel and textiles.

**AREA** 323,250 sq km [124,807 sq mi]
**POPULATION** 38,415,000 **CAPITAL** Warsaw
**GOVERNMENT** Multiparty republic
**ETHNIC GROUPS** Polish 97%, Belarusian, Ukrainian, German
**LANGUAGES** Polish (official) **RELIGIONS** Roman Catholic 90%, Eastern Orthodox **CURRENCY** Zloty = 100 groszy

## PORTUGAL

**GEOGRAPHY** The Republic of Portugal is the most westerly of Europe's mainland countries. The land rises from the coastal plains on the Atlantic Ocean to the western edge of the huge plateau, or Meseta, which occupies most of the Iberian peninsula. The climate is moderated by winds blowing from the Atlantic Ocean. Summers are cooler and winters are milder than in other Mediterranean lands. Portugal also contains two autonomous regions: the Azores and Madeira island groups.

**POLITICS & ECONOMY** Portugal became a separate country, independent of Spain, in 1143. In the 15th century, Portugal led the 'Age of European Exploration'. This led to the growth of a large Portuguese empire, with colonies in Africa, Asia, and, most valuable of all, Brazil in South America. Portuguese power began to decline in the 16th century and, between 1580 and 1640, Portugal was ruled by Spain. Portugal lost Brazil in 1822, and in 1910 Portugal became a republic. Instability hampered progress and army officers seized power in 1926. In 1928, they chose Antonio de Salazar to be minister of finance.

Salazar became prime minister in 1932 and ruled as a dictator from 1933 until 1968. In 1974, army officers mounted a coup. The new regime made most of Portugal's colonies independent and held free elections in 1978. Portugal joined the European Community (now the European Union) in 1986, and in 2002 the euro became the sole unit of currency. In 2011–12, Portugal experienced many problems when it sought to introduce austerity measures so that it could obtain a huge bailout to help its weak economy. Public protests against the cuts increased.

Agriculture and fishing were the mainstays of the economy until the mid-20th century, when manufacturing became the most valuable activity.

**AREA** 88,797 sq km [34,285 sq mi]
**POPULATION** 10,781,000 **CAPITAL** Lisbon
**GOVERNMENT** Multiparty republic **ETHNIC GROUPS** Portuguese 99%
**LANGUAGES** Portuguese (official) **RELIGIONS** Roman Catholic 84%, Protestant **CURRENCY** Euro = 100 cents

## PUERTO RICO

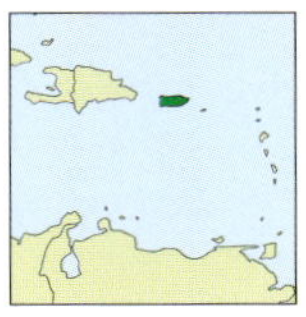

The Commonwealth of Puerto Rico, a mainly mountainous island, is the easternmost of the Greater Antilles chain. The climate is hot and wet. Puerto Rico is a dependent territory of the United States and the people are US citizens. In 2012, the population voted in a referendum on possible statehood to maintain the status quo.

Puerto Rico is the most industrialized country in the Caribbean. Tax exemptions attract US companies to the island and manufacturing is expanding. The chief exports are chemicals and chemical products, machinery and food.

**AREA** 8,875 sq km [3,427 sq mi]
**POPULATION** 3,691,000 **CAPITAL** San Juan

## QATAR

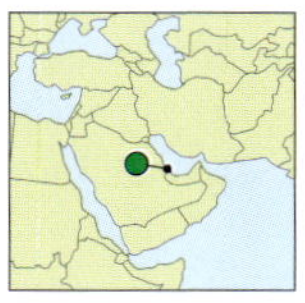

The State of Qatar occupies a low, barren peninsula that extends northwards from the Arabian peninsula into the Persian Gulf. The climate is hot and dry. Qatar became a British protectorate in 1916, but it became fully independent in 1971. Oil, first discovered in 1939, is the mainstay of the economy of this prosperous nation.

**AREA** 11,000 sq km [4,247 sq mi] **POPULATION** 1,952,000 **CAPITAL** Doha

## RÉUNION

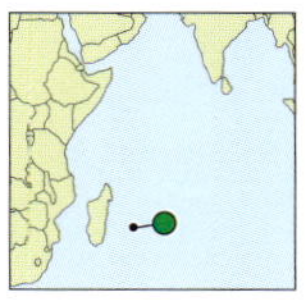

Réunion is a French overseas department in the Indian Ocean. The land is mainly mountainous, though the lowlands are intensely cultivated. Sugar and sugar products are the main exports, but French aid, given to the island in return for its use as a military base, is important to the economy.

**AREA** 2,510 sq km [969 sq mi]
**POPULATION** 788,000 **CAPITAL** St-Denis

## ROMANIA

**GEOGRAPHY** Romania is a country on the Black Sea in eastern Europe. Eastern and southern Romania form part of the Danube river basin. The delta region, near the mouths of the Danube, where the river flows into the Black Sea, is one of Europe's finest wetlands. The southern part of the coast contains several resorts. The heart of the country is called Transylvania. It is ringed in the east, south, and west by scenic mountains which are part of the Carpathian mountain system. Romania has hot summers and cold winters. Rainfall is heaviest in spring and early summer.

**POLITICS & ECONOMY** From the late 18th century, the Turkish empire began to break up. The modern history of Romania began in 1861 when Walachia and Moldavia united. After World War I (1914–18), Romania, which had fought on the side of the victorious Allies, obtained large areas, including Transylvania, where most people were Romanians. This almost doubled the country's size and population. In 1939, Romania lost territory to Bulgaria, Hungary and the Soviet Union. Romania fought alongside Germany in World War II, and Soviet troops occupied the country in 1944. Hungary returned northern Transylvania to Romania in 1945, but Bulgaria and the Soviet Union kept former Romanian territory. In 1947, Romania officially became a Communist country.

In 1990, Romania held its first free elections since the end of World War II. The National Salvation Front, led by Ion Iliescu and containing many former Communist leaders, won a large majority. A new constitution, approved in 1991, made the country a democratic republic. Elections held under this constitution in 1992 again resulted in victory for Ion Iliescu, whose party was renamed the Party of Social Democracy in 1993. Iliescu was defeated in 1996, but he served again as president in 2000–4. Romania joined NATO in 2004 and the European Union in 2007. In 2010, the European Union called on Romania to take urgent action to combat crime and corruption.

Romania has an 'upper-middle-income' economy. Under Communist rule, industry, including mining and manufacturing, became more important than farming.

**AREA** 238,391 sq km [92,043 sq mi]
**POPULATION** 21,849,000 **CAPITAL** Bucharest
**GOVERNMENT** Multiparty republic
**ETHNIC GROUPS** Romanian 89%, Hungarian 7%, Roma 2%, Ukrainian **LANGUAGES** Romanian (official), Hungarian, Romany **RELIGIONS** Eastern Orthodox 87%, Protestant 7%, Roman Catholic 5% **CURRENCY** Leu = 100 bani

## RUSSIA

**GEOGRAPHY** Russia is the world's largest country. About 25% lies west of the Ural Mountains in European Russia, where 80% of the population lives. It is mostly flat or undulating, but the land rises to the Caucasus Mountains in the south, where Russia's highest peak, Elbrus, at 5,642 m [18,510 ft], is found. Asian Russia, or Siberia, contains vast plains and plateaux, with mountains in the east and south. The Kamchatka peninsula in the far east has many active volcanoes. Russia contains several of the world's longest rivers. It also includes part of the world's largest inland body of water, the Caspian Sea, and Lake Baikal, the world's deepest lake.

Moscow has a continental climate, with cold, snowy winters and hot summers. Siberia has a harsher, drier climate. In 2010, during a long heat wave, devastating wildfires swept over large areas.

**POLITICS & ECONOMY** In the 9th century AD, a state called Kievan Rus was formed by a group of people called the East Slavs. Kiev, now capital of Ukraine, became a major trading centre, but, in 1237, Mongol armies conquered Russia and destroyed Kiev. Russia was part of the Mongol empire until the late 15th century. Under Mongol rule, Moscow became the leading Russian city.

In the 16th century, Moscow's grand prince was retitled 'tsar'. The first tsar, Ivan the Terrible, expanded Russian territory. In 1613, after a period of civil war, Michael Romanov became tsar, founding a dynasty which ruled until 1917. In the early 18th century, Tsar Peter the Great began to westernize Russia and, by 1812, when Napoleon failed to conquer the country, Russia was a major European power. But during the 19th century, many Russians demanded reforms and discontent was widespread.

In World War I (1914–18), the Russian people suffered great hardships and, in 1917, Tsar Nicholas II was forced to abdicate. In November 1917, the Bolsheviks seized power under Vladimir Lenin. The Bolsheviks set up the Union of Soviet Socialist Republics (also called the USSR or the Soviet Union).

From 1924, Joseph Stalin introduced a socialist economic programme, suppressing all opposition. In 1939, the Soviet Union and Germany signed a non-aggression pact, but Germany invaded the Soviet Union in 1941. Soviet forces pushed the Germans back, occupying eastern Europe. They reached Berlin in May 1945. From the late 1940s, tension between the Soviet Union and its allies and Western nations developed into a 'Cold War'. This continued until 1991, when the Soviet Union was dissolved.

The Soviet Union collapsed because of the failure of its economic policies. From 1991, President Boris Yeltsin introduced democratic and economic reforms. Yeltsin retired in 1999 and, in 2000, was succeeded by Vladimir Putin. Putin, who was re-elected in 2004, sought to develop contacts with the West. He supported the US-declared 'war on terrorism', though he opposed the invasion of Iraq in 2003. The secessionist conflict in Chechenia, including the occupation of a school by Muslim extremists in 2004, causing more than 330 deaths, provoked outrage. In 2005, violent incidents in the republics of Dagestan, Ingushetia and Kabardino-Balkaria further confirmed that Russia's size and diversity make national unity hard to achieve. From 2006, relations with the West appeared to deteriorate, with Russia criticizing the expansion of NATO in Eastern Europe.

In 2008, Putin, having served two terms as president, was replaced by Dmitry Medvedev, but Putin was again re-elected to the presidency in 2012. In August 2008, Russia fought a short war against Georgia, which had attacked the secessionist region of South Ossetia. In 2010, Muslim militants from the troubled region of the North Caucasus were accused of bomb attacks on the Moscow Metro.

Russia's economy was thrown into disarray after the collapse of the Soviet Union, and in the early 1990s the World Bank described Russia as a 'lower-middle-income' economy. Russia was admitted to the Council of Europe in 1997 and was also invited to attend the G7 summit in 1997, which then became known as the G8. Industry is Russia's leading economic activity. Resources include oil and natural gas, coal, timber, metal ores and hydroelectric power.

Russia is a major producer of farm products, though it imports grains. Major crops include barley, flax, fruits, oats, rye, potatoes, sugar beet, sunflower seeds, vegetables and wheat.

**AREA** 17,075,400 sq km [6,592,812 sq mi]
**POPULATION** 142,518,000 **CAPITAL** Moscow
**GOVERNMENT** Federal multiparty republic
**ETHNIC GROUPS** Russian 82%, Tatar 4%, Ukrainian 3%, Chuvash 1%, more than 100 others **LANGUAGES** Russian (official), many others
**RELIGIONS** Mainly Russian Orthodox, Islam, Judaism
**CURRENCY** Russian ruble = 100 kopeks

## RWANDA

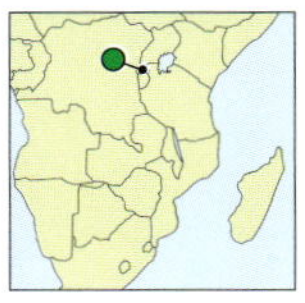

**GEOGRAPHY** The Republic of Rwanda is a small, landlocked country in east-central Africa. Lake Kivu and the River Ruzizi in the Great African Rift Valley form the country's western border.

Kigali stands on the central plateau of Rwanda. Here, temperatures are moderated by the altitude. Rainfall is abundant, but much heavier rain falls on the western uplands, while the Rift Valley floor is drier and warmer than the rest of Rwanda.

**POLITICS & ECONOMY** Germany conquered the area, called Ruanda-Urundi, in the 1890s. However, Belgium occupied the region during World War I (1914–18) and ruled it until 1961, when the people of Ruanda voted for their country to become a republic, called Rwanda. This decision followed a rebellion by the majority Hutu people against the Tutsi monarchy. About 150,000 deaths resulted from this conflict. Many Tutsis fled to Uganda, where they formed a rebel army. Relations between Hutus and Tutsis deteriorated and, in 1994, between 500,000 and 800,000 people were massacred in Rwanda. After the Tutsis had restored order, Hutu rebels fled into the Democratic Republic of the Congo. Rwanda intervened in the Congo in 1996, 2002 and again in 2009. In 2009, Rwanda became the 54th member of the Commonwealth.

According to the World Bank, Rwanda is a 'low-income' developing country. Most people are poor farmers. Food crops include bananas, beans, cassava and sorghum. Some cattle are raised.

**AREA** 26,338 sq km [10,169 sq mi]
**POPULATION** 11,690,000 **CAPITAL** Kigali
**GOVERNMENT** Republic **ETHNIC GROUPS** Hutu 84%, Tutsi 15%, Twa 1% **LANGUAGES** French, English and Kinyarwanda (all official) **RELIGIONS** Roman Catholic 57%, Protestant 26%, Adventist 11%, Islam 5% **CURRENCY** Rwandan franc = 100 centimes

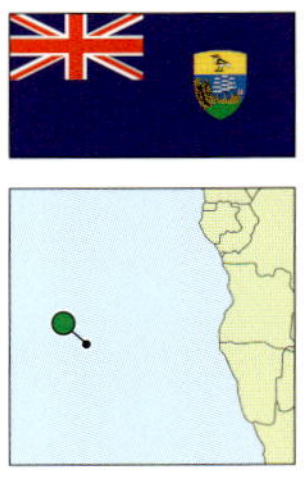

## ST HELENA

St Helena, which became a British colony in 1834, is an isolated volcanic island in the South Atlantic Ocean. Now a British overseas territory, it is also the administrative centre of Ascension and Tristan da Cunha.

**AREA** 122 sq km [47 sq mi]
**POPULATION** 4,000 **CAPITAL** Jamestown

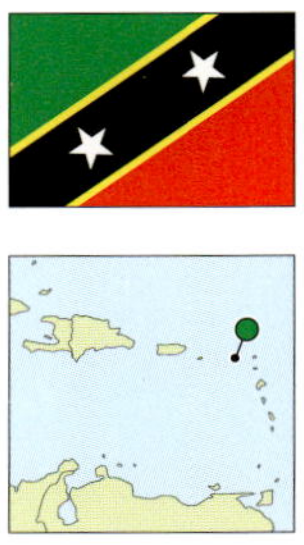

## ST KITTS AND NEVIS

The Federation of St Kitts and Nevis comprises two well-watered volcanic islands, whose highest mountain rises to 1,156 m [3,793 ft]. The islands were the first in the Caribbean to be colonized by Britain (in 1623 and 1628), and they became an independent country in 1983. In 1998, a vote for the secession of Nevis fell short of the two-thirds majority required. Tourism has replaced sugar as the principal earner.

**AREA** 261 sq km [101 sq mi]
**POPULATION** 51,000 **CAPITAL** Basseterre

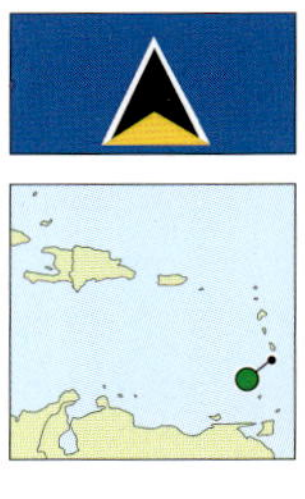

## ST LUCIA

St Lucia, which became independent from Britain in 1979, is a mountainous, forested island of extinct volcanoes. It exports bananas and coconuts, and now attracts many tourists.

**AREA** 539 sq km [208 sq mi]
**POPULATION** 162,000 **CAPITAL** Castries

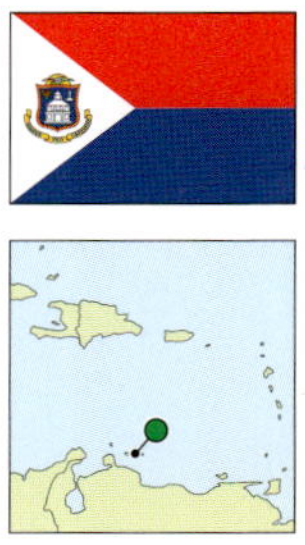

## ST MAARTEN

Part of the Netherlands Antilles until 2010, the southern part of the island of St Maarten (called Sint Maarten in Dutch) is a self-governing territory within the Kingdom of the Netherlands.

**AREA** 34 sq km [13 sq mi]
**POPULATION** 39,000 **CAPITAL** Philipsburg

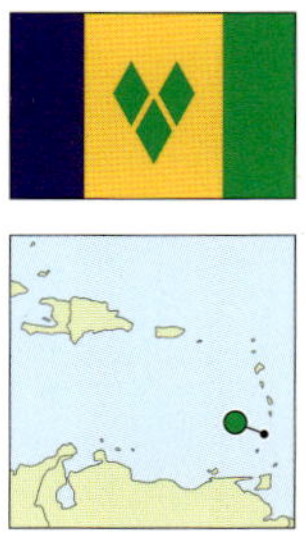

## ST VINCENT AND THE GRENADINES

St Vincent and the Grenadines achieved its independence from Britain in 1979. Tourism is growing, but the territory is less prosperous than its neighbours.

**AREA** 388 sq km [150 sq mi]
**POPULATION** 104,000 **CAPITAL** Kingstown

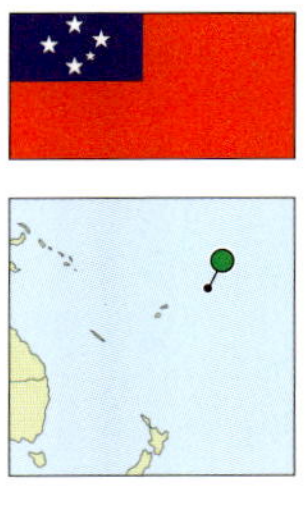

## SAMOA

The Independent State of Samoa (formerly Western Samoa) comprises two islands in the south Pacific Ocean. Governed by New Zealand from 1920, the territory became independent in 1962. Exports include coconut cream and beer.

**AREA** 2,831 sq km [1,093 sq mi]
**POPULATION** 194,000 **CAPITAL** Apia

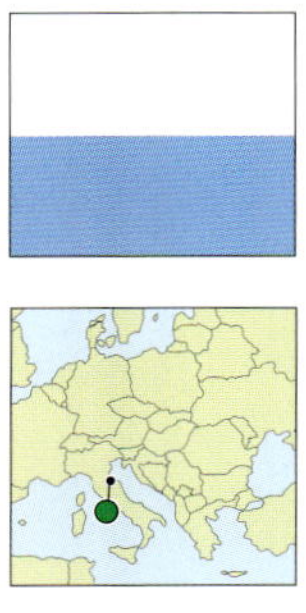

## SAN MARINO

San Marino in northern Italy has been independent since 885 and a republic since the 14th century. It is the world's oldest republic. It has a friendship and co-operation treaty with Italy dating back to 1862. The state is governed by an elected council and has its own legal system. It has no armed forces and the police are 'hired' from the Italian constabulary. The chief occupations are tourism, limestone quarrying, textiles and wine-making.

**AREA** 61 sq km [24 sq mi] **POPULATION** 32,000 **CAPITAL** San Marino

## SÃO TOMÉ AND PRÍNCIPE

The Democratic Republic of São Tomé and Príncipe, a mountainous island territory west of Gabon, became a Portuguese colony in 1522. Following independence in 1975, the islands became a one-party Marxist state, but multiparty elections were held from 1991.

**AREA** 964 sq km [372 sq mi] **POPULATION** 183,000 **CAPITAL** São Tomé

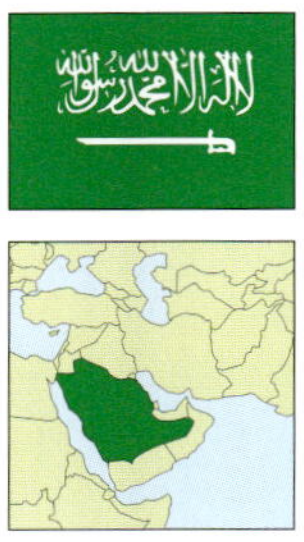

## SAUDI ARABIA

**GEOGRAPHY** The Kingdom of Saudi Arabia occupies about three-quarters of the Arabian peninsula in south-west Asia. Deserts cover most of the land. Mountains border the Red Sea plains in the west. In the north is the sandy Nafud Desert (An Nafud). In the south is the Rub' al Khali (the 'Empty Quarter'), one of the world's bleakest deserts. Saudi Arabia has a hot dry climate. Summer temperatures in Riyadh often exceed 40°C [104°F]. The nights are cool.

**POLITICS & ECONOMY** Saudi Arabia contains the two holiest places in Islam – Mecca (or Makka), the birthplace of the Prophet Muhammad in AD 570, and Medina (Al Madinah) where Muhammad went in 622. These places are visited by many pilgrims.

Since 1933, oil has been the mainstay of the economy. The monarch has supreme authority. Many of the terrorists involved in attacks on the US on 11 September 2001, were Saudi nationals. Saudi Arabia condemned the violence and, from 2003, Islamists launched attacks in Saudi Arabia. In 2011, King Abdullah announced more rights for women, including the rights to vote and to stand in municipal elections.

Saudi Arabia has about 25% of the world's known oil reserves and oil products make up about 90% of the exports. Irrigation and desalination projects have increased crop production.

**AREA** 2,149,690 sq km [829,995 sq mi]
**POPULATION** 26,535,000 **CAPITAL** Riyadh
**GOVERNMENT** Absolute monarchy with consultative assembly
**ETHNIC GROUPS** Arab 90%, Afro-Asian 10%
**LANGUAGES** Arabic (official)
**RELIGIONS** Islam 100%
**CURRENCY** Saudi riyal = 100 halalas

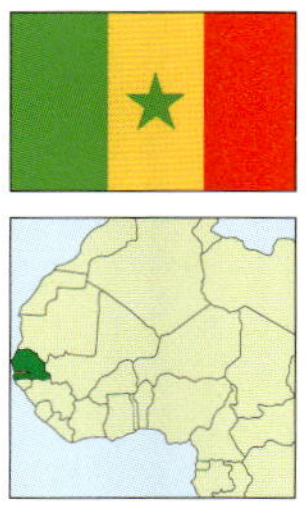

## SENEGAL

**GEOGRAPHY** The Republic of Senegal is on the north-west coast of Africa. The volcanic Cape Verde (Cap Vert), on which Dakar stands, is the most westerly point in Africa. Plains cover most of Senegal, though the land rises gently in the south-east.

Dakar has a tropical climate, with a short rainy season between July and October.

**POLITICS & ECONOMY** In 1882, Senegal became a French colony, and from 1895 it was ruled as part of French West Africa, the capital of which, Dakar, developed as a major port and city.

In 1959, Senegal joined French Sudan (now Mali) to form the Federation of Mali. But Senegal withdrew in 1960 and became the separate Republic of Senegal. Its first president, Léopold Sédar Senghor, served until 1981, when he was succeeded by Abdou Diouf. However, in 2000, Diouf was defeated in elections by Abdoulaye Wade. Wade served until 2012, when, controversially seeking a third term in office, he was defeated by a former prime minister, Macky Sall.

According to the World Bank, Senegal is a 'lower-middle-income' developing country. It was badly hit in the 1960s and 1970s by droughts, which caused starvation. Agriculture still employs 77% of the population, though many farmers produce little more than they need to feed their families. Food crops include groundnuts (peanuts), millet and rice. Phosphates are the country's chief resource, but Senegal also refines oil, which it imports from Gabon and Nigeria. Dakar is a busy port and has many industries.

**AREA** 196,722 sq km [75,954 sq mi]
**POPULATION** 12,970,000 **CAPITAL** Dakar
**GOVERNMENT** Multiparty republic
**ETHNIC GROUPS** Wolof 44%, Pular 24%, Serer 15%
**LANGUAGES** French (official), tribal languages
**RELIGIONS** Islam 94%, Christianity (mainly Roman Catholic) 5%, traditional beliefs 1%
**CURRENCY** CFA franc = 100 centimes

## SERBIA

**GEOGRAPHY** The Republic of Serbia lies in the central Balkan peninsula. A landlocked country, it contains large, fertile lowlands drained by the River Danube and its tributaries, with uplands in the south. Most of Serbia has a continental climate, with cold, snowy winters and hot, dry summers. Heavy rains occur in the spring and the autumn.

**POLITICS & ECONOMY** Around 1,500 years ago, South Slavs moved into the Balkan peninsula, and each group founded its own state. Serbia came under the Turkish Ottoman empire in the 15th century. In the 19th century, many Slavs worked for independence and Slavic unity. In 1914, Austria–Hungary declared war on Serbia, blaming it for the assassination of Archduke Franz Ferdinand of Austria–Hungary. In 1918, the South Slavs united in the Kingdom of the Serbs, Croats and Slovenes, which was renamed Yugoslavia in 1929. Germany invaded in 1941, but Communist partisans, led by Josip Broz Tito, took power in 1945.

From 1945, the country became the Federal People's Republic of Yugoslavia. In 1991–2, the country split apart, with Bosnia-Herzegovina, Croatia, Macedonia and Slovenia proclaiming their independence. The remaining republics, Serbia and Montenegro, retained the name Yugoslavia. In 2003, these two republics agreed to form the loose Union of Serbia and Montenegro. In 2006, the Montenegrins voted for full independence, and Serbia and Montenegro became separate republics. In 2008, the province of Kosovo declared itself independent. Serbia did not recognize this act. In 2011, the European Commission recommended Serbia for European Union candidate status, but said talks could start only after it normalized ties with Kosovo.

Serbia's resources include bauxite, coal, copper and other metals, together with oil and natural gas. Manufactured products include aluminium, machinery, plastics, steel, textiles and vehicles. Crops include fruits, maize, potatoes, tobacco and wheat. Livestock include cattle, pigs and sheep.

**AREA** 77,474 sq km [29,913 sq mi]
**POPULATION** 7,277,000 **CAPITAL** Belgrade
**GOVERNMENT** Republic
**ETHNIC GROUPS** Serb 83%, Hungarian 4%, others
**LANGUAGES** Serbian (official), Hungarian
**RELIGIONS** Serbian Orthodox, Roman Catholic, Islam, Protestant
**CURRENCY** New dinar = 100 paras

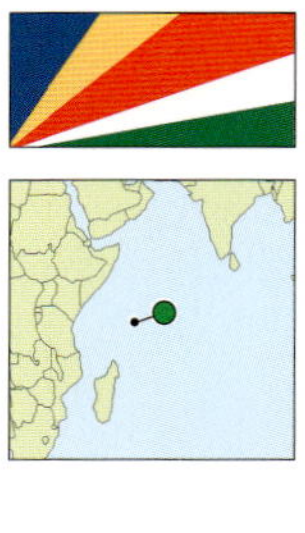

## SEYCHELLES

The Republic of Seychelles in the western Indian Ocean achieved independence from Britain in 1976. Coconuts are the main cash crop, and fishing and tourism are important to the country's economy.

**AREA** 455 sq km [176 sq mi]
**POPULATION** 90,000 **CAPITAL** Victoria

## SIERRA LEONE

**GEOGRAPHY** The Republic of Sierra Leone in West Africa is about the same size as the country of Ireland. The coast contains several deep estuaries in the north, with lagoons in the south. The most prominent feature is the mountainous Freetown (or Sierra Leone) peninsula.

Sierra Leone has a tropical climate, with heavy rainfall between April and November.

**POLITICS & ECONOMY** A former British territory, Sierra Leone became independent in 1961 and a republic in 1971. It became a one-party state in 1978, but, in 1991, the people voted for the restoration of democracy. The military seized power in 1992 and a civil war caused much destruction in 1994–5. Elections in 1996 were followed by another military coup. In 1998, the West African Peace Force restored the deposed President Ahmed Tejan Kabbah. In 1999, a peace agreement followed further conflict. As part of this agreement, Foday Sankoh, one of the rebel leaders, became vice president. However, he was arrested in 2000 and charged with war crimes. Another ceasefire was agreed in 2004. The last of the UN troops left the country in 2005, and national elections were held in 2007. In 2010, the UN Security Council lifted the last remaining sanctions against Sierra Leone.

Sierra Leone has a 'low-income' economy. About 59% of the people live by farming, mainly at subsistence level. The leading exports are minerals, including diamonds, bauxite and rutile (titanium ore). The country has few manufacturing industries.

**AREA** 71,740 sq km [27,699 sq mi]
**POPULATION** 5,486,000 **CAPITAL** Freetown
**GOVERNMENT** Single-party republic **ETHNIC GROUPS** Native African tribes 90% **LANGUAGES** English (official), Mende, Temne, Limba
**RELIGIONS** Islam 60%, traditional beliefs 30%, Christianity 10%
**CURRENCY** Leone = 100 cents

## SINGAPORE

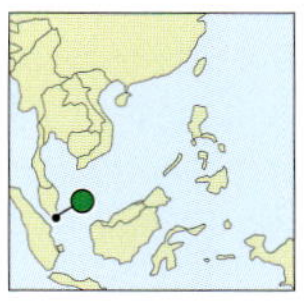

**GEOGRAPHY** The Republic of Singapore is an island country at the southern tip of the Malay peninsula. It consists of the large Singapore Island and 58 small islands, 20 of which are inhabited. The climate is hot and humid. Temperatures are high and rainfall is heavy throughout the year.

**POLITICS & ECONOMY** In 1819, Sir Thomas Stamford Raffles (1781–1826), agent of the British East India Company, made a treaty with the Sultan of Johor allowing the British to build a settlement on Singapore Island. Singapore soon became the leading British trading centre in South-east Asia and it later became a naval base. Japanese forces seized the island in 1942, but British rule was restored in 1945.

In 1963, Singapore became part of the Federation of Malaysia, which also included Malaya and the territories of Sabah and Sarawak on Borneo. In 1965, Singapore broke away and became independent.

The People's Action Party (PAP) has ruled Singapore since 1959. Its leader, Lee Kuan Yew, served as prime minister from 1959 until 1990, when he resigned and was succeeded by Goh Chok Tong. In 2004, Lee Hsien Loong, son of Lee Kuan Yew, became prime minister. He was re-elected in 2006 and 2011.

The World Bank classifies Singapore as a 'high-income' economy, where a skilled workforce has created a fast-growing economy. Trade and finance are major activities. The global financial crisis in 2008–9 caused great concern, but recovery was rapid. Manufactures include electronic products, machinery, scientific instruments, textiles and ships. Petroleum products and manufactures are the main exports.

**AREA** 683 sq km [264 sq mi]
**POPULATION** 5,353,000 **CAPITAL** Singapore City
**GOVERNMENT** Multiparty republic
**ETHNIC GROUPS** Chinese 77%, Malay 14%, Indian 8%
**LANGUAGES** Chinese, Malay, Tamil and English (all official)
**RELIGIONS** Buddhism, Islam, Christianity, Hinduism
**CURRENCY** Singapore dollar = 100 cents

## SLOVAK REPUBLIC

**GEOGRAPHY** The Slovak Republic is a predominantly mountainous country, consisting of part of the Carpathian range. The highest peak is Gerlachovsky in the Tatra Mountains, which reaches 2,655 m [8,711 ft]. The south is a fertile lowland. The Slovak Republic has cold winters and warm summers. Kosice, in the east, has average temperatures ranging from –3°C [27°F] in January to 20°C [68°F] in July. The highland areas are much colder. Snow or rain falls throughout the year. Kosice has an average annual rainfall of 600 mm [24 in], the wettest months being July and August.

**POLITICS & ECONOMY** Slavic peoples settled in the region in the 5th century AD. They were subsequently conquered by Hungary, beginning a millennium of Hungarian rule and suppression of Slovak culture.

In 1867, Hungary and Austria united to form Austria–Hungary, of which the present-day Slovak Republic was a part. Austria–Hungary collapsed at the end of World War I (1914–18). The Czech and Slovak people then united to form a new nation, Czechoslovakia. But Czech domination led to resentment by many Slovaks. In 1939, the Slovak Republic declared itself independent, but Germany occupied the country. At the end of World War II, the Slovak Republic again became part of Czechoslovakia.

The Communist Party took control in 1948. In the 1960s, many people sought reform, but they were crushed by the Russians. In the late 1980s, demands for democracy mounted and a non-Communist government took office in 1990. Elections in 1992 led to victory for the Movement for a Democratic Slovakia headed by a former Communist and nationalist, Vladimir Meciar, and the independent Slovak Republic came into existence on 1 January 1993.

Independence raised national aspirations among Slovakia's Magyar-speaking community, but relations with Hungary deteriorated when the Magyars felt that administrative changes under-represented them politically. The government also made Slovak the only official language. The Slovak Republic became a member of NATO and the European Union in 2004. On 1 January 2009, it became the 16th country to adopt the euro as its official currency. In 2012, the opposition party Smer, led by former Prime Minister Robert Fico, won a landslide victory in a general election, taking over half of the seats in parliament.

Before 1948, the Slovak Republic's economy was based on farming, but Communist governments developed manufacturing industries, producing such things as chemicals, machinery, steel and weapons. Since the late 1980s, many state-run businesses have been handed over to private owners.

**AREA** 49,012 sq km [18,924 sq mi]
**POPULATION** 5,483,000 **CAPITAL** Bratislava
**GOVERNMENT** Multiparty republic
**ETHNIC GROUPS** Slovak 86%, Hungarian 11%
**LANGUAGES** Slovak (official), Hungarian
**RELIGIONS** Roman Catholic 69%, Protestant 11%, others
**CURRENCY** Euro = 100 cents

## SLOVENIA

**GEOGRAPHY** The Republic of Slovenia was one of the six republics which made up the former Yugoslavia. Much of the land is mountainous, rising to 2,864 m [9,396 ft] at Mount Triglav in the Julian Alps (Julijske Alpe) in the north-west. Central Slovenia contains the limestone Karst region. The Postojna caves near Ljubljana are among the largest in Europe.

The coast has a mild Mediterranean climate, but inland the climate is more continental. The mountains are snow-capped in winter.

**POLITICS & ECONOMY** In the last 2,000 years, the Slovene people have been independent as a nation for less than 50 years. The Austrian Habsburgs ruled over the region from the 13th century until World War I. Slovenia became part of the Kingdom of the Serbs, Croats and Slovenes (later called Yugoslavia) in 1918. During World War II, Slovenia was invaded and partitioned between Italy, Germany, and Hungary, but, after the war, Slovenia again became part of Yugoslavia.

From the late 1960s, some Slovenes demanded independence, but the central government opposed the break-up of the country. In 1990, when Communist governments had collapsed throughout Eastern Europe, elections were held and a non-Communist coalition government was set up. Slovenia then declared itself independent. This led to fighting between Slovenes and the federal army, but Slovenia did not become a battlefield. Slovenia's independence was recognized in 1992 and a coalition led by the Liberal Democrats was elected in 1992, 1996 and 2000. In 2004, Slovenia became a member of the North Atlantic Treaty Organization and the European Union. In 2009, Slovenia became the first former Communist country to assume the presidency of the European Union. In 2011, the newly formed Positive Slovenia Party scored a surprise win in parliamentary elections. The former ruling Social Democrats dropped to third place.

The reform of the formerly state-run economy caused problems for Slovenia. However, since 1993, the country has made considerable economic progress.

Manufacturing is the leading activity and manufactures are the main exports. Manufactures include chemicals, machinery and transport equipment, metal goods, and textiles. Slovenia mines some iron ore, lead, lignite and mercury. Agriculture and forestry employ 9% of the people. Fruits, maize, potatoes and wheat are major crops, and many farmers raise animals.

**AREA** 20,256 sq km [7,821 sq mi] **POPULATION** 1,997,000
**CAPITAL** Ljubljana **GOVERNMENT** Multiparty republic
**ETHNIC GROUPS** Slovene 83%, Croat 2%, Serb 2%, Hungarian, Bosniak
**LANGUAGES** Slovenian (official), Serbo-Croatian
**RELIGIONS** Mainly Roman Catholic
**CURRENCY** Euro = 100 cents

## SOLOMON ISLANDS

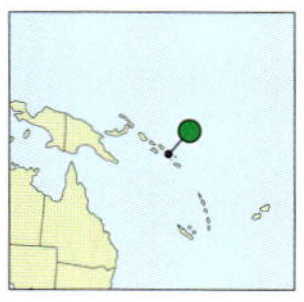

The Solomon Islands, a chain of mainly volcanic islands in the Pacific Ocean, were a British territory between 1893 and 1978. The chain extends for some 2,250 km [1,400 mi]. They were the scene of fierce fighting during World War II. Most people are Melanesians, and the islands have a young population profile, with 40% of the people aged under 15. Fish, coconuts, and cocoa are leading products, though development is hampered by mountainous, forested terrain.

**AREA** 28,896 sq km [11,157 sq mi]
**POPULATION** 585,000 **CAPITAL** Honiara

## SOMALIA

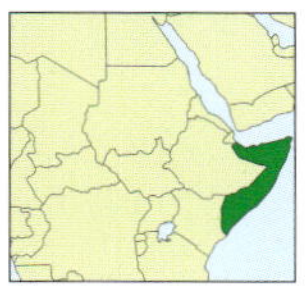

**GEOGRAPHY** The Somali Democratic Republic, or Somalia, is in a region known as the 'Horn of Africa'. It is more than twice the size of Italy, the country which once ruled the southern part of Somalia. The most mountainous part of the country is in the north, behind the narrow coastal plains that border the Gulf of Aden. Rainfall is sparse, with the wettest regions in the south and northern mountains. Droughts are common and temperatures are generally high.

**POLITICS & ECONOMY** European powers became interested in the Horn of Africa in the 19th century. In 1884, Britain made the northern part of what is now Somalia a protectorate, while Italy took the south in 1905. The new boundaries divided the Somalis into five areas: the two Somalilands, Djibouti (which was taken by France in the 1880s), Ethiopia, and Kenya. Since then, many Somalis have wanted to create a Greater Somalia. Italy invaded British Somaliland in 1940, but was defeated in 1941. Britain ruled both Somalilands until 1950, when the United Nations asked Italy to take over the former Italian Somaliland for ten years. In 1960, the two Somalilands united to become Somalia.

Somalia has faced many problems. Economic difficulties led a military group to seize power in 1969. In the 1970s, Somalia supported an uprising of Somali-speaking people in the Ogaden region of Ethiopia. But, in 1988, Somalia and Ethiopia signed a peace treaty. In the 1990s, Somalia gradually broke apart. In 1991, the people in what was once British Somaliland set up the 'Somaliland Republic', but it failed to get international recognition. The north-east, called Puntland, also seceded, while the south was riven by clan warfare. In 2004–5, a Somali parliament was set up in Kenya. In 2006, it moved to Baidoa, in Somalia (Mogadishu was regarded as unsafe). In 2006, Mogadishu was taken over by the Islamist Union of Islamic Courts, but government forces backed by Ethiopian troops defeated the Islamists. Ethiopia finally withdrew all its troops in January 2009. In 2012, the militant group al-Shabab was driven out of central and southern Somalia. Parliament met for the first time in 20 years and a president was elected.

Somalia's economy has been shattered by war, droughts and periodic floods. Many Somalis are nomads, who raise livestock. Live animals, meat, and hides and skins are exported. Crops include bananas, citrus fruits, cotton, maize and sugar cane. Mining and manufacturing are relatively unimportant.

**AREA** 637,657 sq km [246,199 sq mi] **POPULATION** 10,086,000
**CAPITAL** Mogadishu **GOVERNMENT** Single-party republic, military dominated **ETHNIC GROUPS** Somali 85%, Bantu, Arab
**LANGUAGES** Somali (official), Arabic **RELIGIONS** Islam (Sunni Muslim)
**CURRENCY** Somali shilling = 100 cents

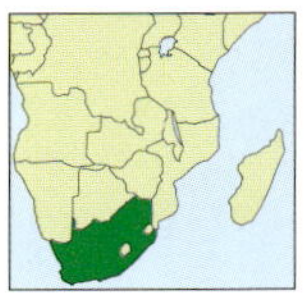

## SOUTH AFRICA

**GEOGRAPHY** The Republic of South Africa is made up largely of the southern part of the huge plateau which makes up most of southern Africa. The highest peaks are in the Drakensberg range. Part of the Namib Desert is in the north-west. The area around Cape Town has a sunny climate with mild, rainy winters. Inland, large areas of the plateau are arid.

**POLITICS & ECONOMY** Early inhabitants in South Africa were the Khoisan. In the last 2,000 years, Bantu-speaking people moved into the area. Their descendants include the Zulu, Xhosa, Sotho and Tswana. The Dutch founded a settlement at the Cape in 1652, but Britain took over in the early 19th century, making the area a colony. The Dutch, called Boers or Afrikaners, resented British rule and moved inland. Rivalry between the groups led to Anglo-Boer Wars in 1880–1 and 1899–1902.

In 1910, the country was united as the Union of South Africa. In 1948, the National Party won power and introduced a policy known as apartheid, under which non-whites had no votes and their human rights were strictly limited. In 1990, Nelson Mandela, leader of the African National Congress (ANC), was released from prison. Multi-racial elections were held in 1994 and Mandela became president. After Mandela retired, the ANC won elections in 1999 and 2004, led by Thabo Mbeki, and in 2009 when Jacob Zuma became president. The government has faced many problems, including a health crisis – South Africa has more people infected with the HIV virus than any other country.

South Africa is Africa's most developed country. However, most of the black people are poor, with low standards of living. Natural resources include diamonds, gold, and many other metals. Mining and manufacturing are the most valuable activities.

**AREA** 1,221,037 SQ KM [471,442 SQ MI] **POPULATION** 48,810,000
**CAPITAL** CAPE TOWN (LEGISLATIVE); PRETORIA/TSHWANE (ADMINISTRATIVE); BLOEMFONTEIN (JUDICIARY) **GOVERNMENT** MULTIPARTY REPUBLIC
**ETHNIC GROUPS** BLACK 79%, WHITE 10%, COLOURED 9%, ASIAN 2%
**LANGUAGES** AFRIKAANS, ENGLISH, NDEBELE, PEDI, SOTHO, SWAZI, TSONGA, TSWANA, VENDA, XHOSA AND ZULU (ALL OFFICIAL)
**RELIGIONS** CHRISTIANITY 68%, ISLAM 2%, HINDUISM 1%
**CURRENCY** RAND = 100 CENTS

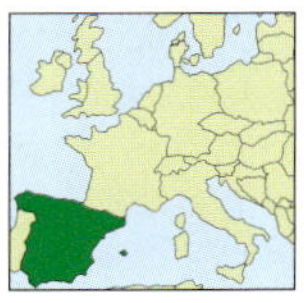

## SPAIN

**GEOGRAPHY** The Kingdom of Spain is the second largest country in Western Europe after France. It shares the Iberian peninsula with Portugal. A large plateau, called the Meseta, covers most of Spain. Much of the Meseta is flat, but it is crossed by several mountain ranges, called sierras.

The northern highlands include the Cantabrian Mountains (Cordillera Cantabrica) and the high Pyrenees, which form Spain's border with France. But Mulhacén, the highest peak on the Spanish mainland, is in the Sierra Nevada in the south-east. Spain also contains fertile coastal plains. Other major lowlands are the Ebro river basin in the north-east and the Guadalquivir river basin in the south-west. Spain also includes the Balearic Islands in the Mediterranean Sea and the Canary Islands off the north-west coast of Africa.

The Meseta has a continental climate, with hot summers and cold winters, when temperatures often fall below freezing point. Snow frequently covers the mountain ranges on the Meseta. The Mediterranean coasts have hot, dry summers and mild winters.

**POLITICS & ECONOMY** In the 16th century, Spain became a world power. At its peak, it controlled much of Central and South America, parts of Africa, and the Philippines in Asia. Spain began to decline in the late 16th century. Its sea power was destroyed by a British fleet in the Battle of Trafalgar (1805). By the 20th century, it was a poor country.

Spain became a republic in 1931, but the republicans were defeated in the Spanish Civil War (1936–9). General Francisco Franco became the country's dictator, though technically Spain remained a monarchy. After Franco died in 1975, Prince Juan Carlos became king.

Spain has several groups with their own languages and cultures. Some of these people want to run their own regional affairs. In the northern Basque region, some nationalists have waged a terrorist campaign. A truce in 1998 was ended in 1999 when talks failed to produce results.

Since the 1970s, regional parliaments with a large degree of autonomy have been set up in the Basque Country, in Catalonia in the north-east, and in Galicia in the north-west. From the 1960s, ETA, a Basque terrorist group, waged a violent campaign for the secession of the Basque Country. In 2011, ETA declared an end to shootings and bombings.

Spain has been badly affected since the global recession of 2008. An unemployment rate of 26% in 2012 and sluggish economic growth make the government's task a difficult one. Agriculture employs 4% of the people, as compared with 14% in mining and manufacturing. Farmland makes up two-thirds of Spain, with forests covering most of the rest. Crops include barley, citrus fruits, grapes for wine-making, olives, potatoes and wheat. Spain lacks natural resources apart from some high-grade iron ore in the north. Manufactures include cars, chemicals, electronic goods, food, metal goods, and textiles.

**AREA** 497,548 SQ KM [192,103 SQ MI] **POPULATION** 47,043,000
**CAPITAL** MADRID **GOVERNMENT** CONSTITUTIONAL MONARCHY
**ETHNIC GROUPS** COMPOSITE OF MEDITERRANEAN AND NORDIC TYPES
**LANGUAGES** CASTILIAN SPANISH (OFFICIAL) 74%, CATALAN 17%, GALICIAN 7%, BASQUE 2% **RELIGIONS** ROMAN CATHOLIC 94%, OTHERS 6% **CURRENCY** EURO = 100 CENTS

## SRI LANKA

**GEOGRAPHY** The Democratic Socialist Republic of Sri Lanka is an island nation, separated from the south-east coast of India by the Palk Strait. The land is mostly low-lying, but a mountain region dominates the south-central part of the country.

The western part of Sri Lanka has a wet equatorial climate. Temperatures are high and the rainfall is heavy.

**POLITICS & ECONOMY** From the early 16th century, Ceylon (as Sri Lanka was then known) was ruled successively by the Portuguese, Dutch and British. Independence was achieved in 1948 and the country was renamed Sri Lanka in 1972.

After independence, rivalries between the two main ethnic groups, the Sinhalese and Tamils, marred progress. In the 1950s, the government made Sinhala the official language. Following protests, the prime minister made provisions for Tamil to be used in some areas. In 1959, the prime minister was assassinated by a Sinhalese extremist and he was succeeded by Sirimavo Bandanaraike, the world's first woman prime minister.

Conflict between Tamils and Sinhalese continued in the 1970s and 1980s. In 1987, India helped to engineer a ceasefire. Indian troops arrived to enforce the agreement, but withdrew in 1990 after failing to subdue the main guerrilla group, the Tamil Tigers, who wanted to set up an independent Tamil homeland in northern Sri Lanka. The Tamil Tigers were finally defeated in May 2009 and, in 2010, Mahinda Rajapaksa was re-elected president of Sri Lanka.

In late 2004, a natural disaster occurred when a tsunami, caused by a sudden movement of the plates underlying the eastern Indian Ocean, struck parts of the coast of Sri Lanka. killing more than 30,000 people.

Sri Lanka is classed as a 'lower-middle-income' economy. Agriculture employs about 30% of the people. Coconuts, rubber and tea are exported, but rice is the main food crop. Factories process farm products and manufacture textiles.

**AREA** 65,610 SQ KM [25,332 SQ MI]
**POPULATION** 21,481,000 **CAPITAL** COLOMBO
**GOVERNMENT** MULTIPARTY REPUBLIC
**ETHNIC GROUPS** SINHALESE 74%, TAMIL 9%, MOOR 7%
**LANGUAGES** SINHALA AND TAMIL (BOTH OFFICIAL)
**RELIGIONS** BUDDHISM 69%, ISLAM 8%, HINDUISM 7%, CHRISTIANITY 6%
**CURRENCY** SRI LANKAN RUPEE = 100 CENTS

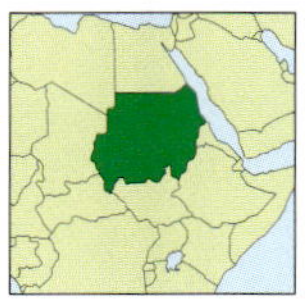

## SUDAN

**GEOGRAPHY** The Republic of Sudan was Africa's largest country until 2011, when the people in the south voted to secede and set up a new nation called South Sudan. Sudan is mainly arid, with part of the vast Sahara in the north. The main feature is the fertile River Nile valley, where most people live.

**POLITICS & ECONOMY** In the 19th century, Egypt gradually took over Sudan. In 1881, a Muslim religious teacher, the Mahdi ('divinely appointed guide'), led an uprising. Britain and Egypt put the rebellion down in 1898. In 1899, they agreed to rule Sudan jointly as a condominium. After independence in 1952, the black Africans in the south, who were either Christians or followers of traditional religions, feared domination by the Muslim north. They objected to Arabic becoming the sole official language and, in 1964, civil war broke out. The war ended in 1972, when the south was granted regional self-government.

In 1983, the announcement that Islamic law would apply throughout Sudan sparked off further resistance from the rebel Sudan People's Liberation Army (SPLA) in the south. In 1998, Sudan's government announced that it accepted the idea of a referendum in the south. In 2005, a peace agreement was signed, bringing peace to the south. The referendum took place in January 2011, when around 99% of the people in the south voted to set up their own country, South Sudan.

Since 2003, another conflict has raged in the western province of Darfur, where government-backed militias battled with local rebel forces. In 2008, the International Criminal Court charged President al-Bashir with war crimes, but he was re-elected president in national elections in 2010.

Cotton is the chief crop in Sudan. Cotton, gum arabic and sesame seeds are exported, but the most valuable exports are oil and oil products. More than 80% of the oil is produced in South Sudan, but Sudan has the infrastructure to exploit and export it.

**AREA** 1,886,086 SQ KM [728,222 SQ MI] **POPULATION** 34,207,000
**CAPITAL** KHARTOUM **GOVERNMENT** FEDERAL PRESIDENTIAL DEMOCRATIC REPUBLIC **ETHNIC GROUPS** ARAB, BLACK, BEJA, OTHERS
**LANGUAGES** ARABIC AND ENGLISH (BOTH OFFICIAL), NUBIAN, BEJA
**RELIGIONS** ISLAM, TRADITIONAL BELIEFS
**CURRENCY** SUDANESE POUND = 100 PIASTRES

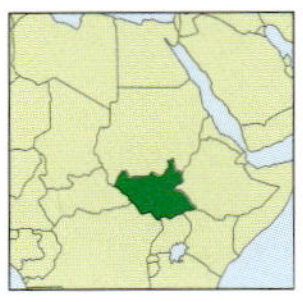

## SUDAN, SOUTH

**GEOGRAPHY** The Republic of South Sudan is a landlocked country in north-eastern Africa. Much of the land is low-lying and drained by the White Nile and its tributaries. Mountains lie in the far south. The country has a wet tropical climate. Forests, swamps and grasslands cover large areas.

**POLITICS & ECONOMY** South Sudan has about 200 ethnic groups. Each group has its own traditional beliefs and languages. The South's deep cultural differences with the mainly Arab-Muslim north led to civil war (1964–1972 and 1983–2005). In January 2011, as part of the peace agreement, a referendum was held in which the vast majority of the people in the south voted for independence on 9 July 2011. After independence, South Sudan and Sudan clashed along disputed borders, while ethnic conflicts occurred in South Sudan.

Most people depend on agriculture and forestry, but South Sudan has many mineral resources, including oil.

**AREA** 619,745 SQ KM [239,285 SQ MI] **POPULATION** 10,625,000
**CAPITAL** JUBA **GOVERNMENT** REPUBLIC
**ETHNIC GROUPS** DINKA, KAKWA, BARI, AZANDE, SHILLUK, OTHERS
**LANGUAGES** ENGLISH AND ARABIC (BOTH OFFICIAL), LOCAL LANGUAGES
**RELIGIONS** TRADITIONAL BELIEFS, CHRISTIANITY
**CURRENCY** SUDANESE POUND = 100 PIASTRES

## SURINAME

**GEOGRAPHY** The Republic of Suriname is sandwiched between French Guiana and Guyana in north-eastern South America. The narrow coastal plain was once swampy, but it has been drained and now consists mainly of farmland. Inland lie hills and low mountains, which rise to 1,230 m [4,035 ft].

Suriname has a hot, wet and humid climate. Temperatures are high throughout the year.

**POLITICS & ECONOMY** In 1667, the British handed Suriname to the Dutch in return for New Amsterdam, an area that is now the state of New York. Slave revolts and Dutch neglect hampered development. In the early 19th century, Britain and the Netherlands disputed the ownership of the area. The British gave up their claims in 1813. Slavery was abolished in 1863 and, soon afterwards, Indian and Indonesian labourers were introduced to work on the plantations.

Suriname became fully independent in 1975, but the economy was weakened when thousands of skilled people emigrated from Suriname to the Netherlands. Following a coup in 1980, Suriname was ruled by a military dictator, Desiré ('Dési') Bouterse. The adoption of a new constitution led to the restoration of democracy in 1988, though another military coup occurred in 1990. Ronald Venetiaan was elected president in 2000, and his government replaced the guilder with the Surinamese dollar in 2004. In 2010, the Mega Combination coalition, led by Desiré Bouterse, won parliamentary elections and Bouterse became president.

The World Bank classifies Suriname as an 'upper-middle-income' developing country. Its economy is based on mining and metal processing. Suriname is a leading producer of bauxite, from which the metal aluminium is made.

**AREA** 163,265 sq km [63,037 sq mi]
**POPULATION** 560,000 **CAPITAL** Paramaribo
**GOVERNMENT** Multiparty republic
**ETHNIC GROUPS** Hindustani/East Indian 37%, Creole (mixed White and Black) 31%, Javanese 15%, Black 10%, Amerindian 2%, Chinese 2%, others **LANGUAGES** Dutch (official), Sranang Tongo
**RELIGIONS** Hinduism 27%, Protestant 25%, Roman Catholic 23%, Islam 20% **CURRENCY** Surinamese dollar= 100 cents

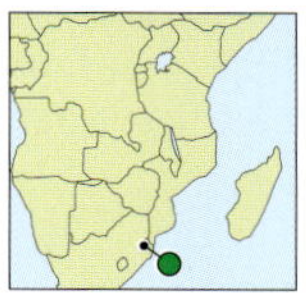

## SWAZILAND

**GEOGRAPHY** The Kingdom of Swaziland is a small, landlocked country in southern Africa. The country has four regions which run north–south. In the west, the Highveld, with an average height of 1,200 m [3,950 ft], makes up 30% of Swaziland. The Middleveld, between 350 m and 1,000 m [1,150 ft to 3,280 ft], covers 28% of the country. The Lowveld, with an average height of 270 m [886 ft], covers another 33%. Finally, the Lebombo Mountains reach 800 m [2,600 ft] along the eastern border. The Lowveld is almost tropical, with average temperatures of 22°C [72°F] and low rainfall.

**POLITICS & ECONOMY** In 1894, Britain and the Boers of South Africa agreed to put Swaziland under the control of the South African Republic (the Transvaal). But at the end of the Anglo–Boer War (1899–1902), Britain took control of the country. In 1968, when Swaziland became fully independent as a constitutional monarchy, the head of state was King Sobhuza II. Sobhuza died in 1982 and was succeeded by his son, who, in 1986, became King Mswati III. Political parties were banned in elections in 1993 and 1998. Mswati ruled by decree. In 2005, Mswati signed a new constitution, but Swaziland remained an absolute monarchy.

Swaziland is a developing country. Farm products and processed food and drink, sugar, wood pulp, citrus fruits and canned fruit are the leading exports. Many farmers live at subsistence level. Swaziland is heavily dependent on South Africa and it shares two problems with its large neighbour – widespread poverty and a high incidence of HIV/AIDS.

**AREA** 17,364 sq km [6,704 sq mi]
**POPULATION** 1,387,000 **CAPITAL** Mbabane
**GOVERNMENT** Monarchy **ETHNIC GROUPS** African 97%, European 3% **LANGUAGES** Siswati and English (both official)
**RELIGIONS** Zionist (a mix of Christianity and traditional beliefs) 40%, Roman Catholic 20%, Islam 10% **CURRENCY** Lilangeni = 100 cents

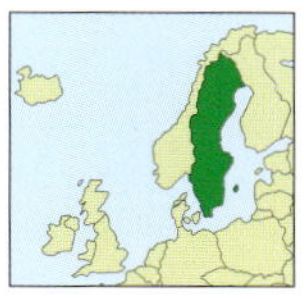

## SWEDEN

**GEOGRAPHY** The Kingdom of Sweden is the largest of the countries of Scandinavia in both area and population. It shares the Scandinavian peninsula with Norway. The western part of the country, along the border with Norway, is mountainous. The highest point is Kebnekaise, which reaches 2,114 m [6,936 ft] in the north-west. The climate becomes increasingly severe from south to north.

**POLITICS & ECONOMY** Swedish Vikings plundered areas to the south and east between the 9th and 11th centuries. Sweden, Denmark, and Norway were united in 1397, but Sweden regained its independence in 1523. In 1809, Sweden lost Finland to Russia, but, in 1814, it gained Norway from Denmark. The union between Sweden and Norway was dissolved in 1905. Sweden was neutral in World Wars I and II. Since 1945, Sweden has become a prosperous country. In 1995, it joined the European Union. However, it did not adopt the euro in 1999.

Sweden has wide-ranging welfare services. But many people are concerned about the high cost of these services and the high taxes they must pay. In 2006, a centre-right alliance defeated the Social Democrats, who had ruled Sweden for 65 of the previous 74 years. Fredrik Reinfeldt replaced Göran Persson as prime minister.

Sweden is a highly developed industrial country. Major products include steel and steel goods. Steel is used in the engineering industry to manufacture aircraft, cars, machinery and ships. Sweden has some of the world's richest iron ore deposits. They are located near Kiruna in the far north. But most of this ore is exported, and Sweden imports most of the materials needed by its industries. Forestry is also important and hydroelectricity is a major source of energy. In 1996, Sweden announced the decommissioning of its nuclear power stations. The first reactor closed in 1999, followed by a second in 2005. But in 2009, the government, under pressure to diversify from fossil fuels, reversed this policy.

**AREA** 449,964 sq km [173,731 sq mi]
**POPULATION** 9,104,000 **CAPITAL** Stockholm
**GOVERNMENT** Constitutional monarchy **ETHNIC GROUPS** Swedish 91%, Finnish, Sami **LANGUAGES** Swedish (official), Finnish, Sami
**RELIGIONS** Lutheran 87%, Roman Catholic, Orthodox
**CURRENCY** Swedish krona = 100 öre

## SWITZERLAND

**GEOGRAPHY** The Swiss Confederation is a landlocked country in Western Europe. Much of the land is mountainous. The Jura Mountains lie along Switzerland's western border with France, while the Swiss Alps make up about 60% of the country in the south and east. Four-fifths of the people of Switzerland live on the fertile Swiss plateau, which contains most of Switzerland's large cities.

The climate of Switzerland varies greatly according to the altitude. The plateau has warm summers and cold, snowy winters. Rain occurs throughout the year.

**POLITICS & ECONOMY** In 1291, three small cantons (states) united to defend their freedom against the Habsburg rulers of the Holy Roman empire. They were Schwyz, Uri and Unterwalden, and they called the confederation they formed 'Switzerland'. Switzerland expanded and, in the 14th century, defeated Austria in three wars of independence. After a defeat by the French in 1515, the Swiss adopted a policy of neutrality, which they still follow. In 1815, the Congress of Vienna expanded Switzerland to 22 cantons and guaranteed its neutrality. Switzerland's 23rd canton, Jura, was created in 1979 from part of Bern.

Neutrality combined with the vigour and independence of its people have made Switzerland prosperous. In 2002, Switzerland became a member of the United Nations, though it still maintained its tradition of neutrality. In 2010, a fourth female minister was elected by the Federal Assembly to the seven-member Federal Council. For the first time, women were in the majority in the country's cabinet.

Although lacking in natural resources, Switzerland is a wealthy, industrialized country. Products include chemicals, electrical equipment, machinery and machine tools, precision instruments, processed food, watches and textiles. Farmers produce about three-fifths of the country's food – the rest is imported. Crops include fruits, potatoes and wheat. Tourism and banking are also important. Swiss banks attract investors from all over the world.

**AREA** 41,284 sq km [15,940 sq mi] **POPULATION** 7,926,000
**CAPITAL** Berne **GOVERNMENT** Federal republic
**ETHNIC GROUPS** German 65%, French 18%, Italian 10%, Romansch 1%, others **LANGUAGES** German, French, Italian and Romansch (all official) **RELIGIONS** Roman Catholic 42%, Protestant 35% **CURRENCY** Swiss franc = 100 centimes

## SYRIA

**GEOGRAPHY** The Syrian Arab Republic is a country in south-western Asia. The narrow coastal plain is overlooked by a low mountain range which runs north–south. Another range, the Jabal ash Sharqi, runs along the border with Lebanon. South of this range is the Golan Heights, which Israel has occupied since 1967.

The coast has a Mediterranean climate, with dry, warm summers and wet, mild winters. The low mountains cut off Damascus from the sea. It has less rainfall than the coastal areas. To the east, the land becomes drier.

**POLITICS & ECONOMY** After the collapse of the Turkish Ottoman empire in World War I, Syria was ruled by France. Since independence in 1946, Syria has been involved in the Arab–Israeli wars, and in 1967 it lost a strategic border area, the Golan Heights, to Israel. In 1970, Lieutenant-General Hafez al-Assad took power, establishing a stable but repressive regime. Syria sent troops into Lebanon in 1976 in an effort to halt the civil war there, but, in 2005, following demonstrations, Syria withdrew its troops. Hafez al-Assad died in 2000 and was succeeded by his son, Bashar al-Assad. Between 2011–13, more than 60,000 people have died in what is now a civil war. Over 130 countries recognize the opposition groups as the sole legitimate representatives of the Syrian people.

The World Bank classifies Syria as a 'lower-middle-income' developing country. Its main resources are oil, hydroelectricity and fertile land. Oil was the main export. However, the economy has been crippled by the civil war and the consequent effects of mass emigration into neighbouring states.

**AREA** 185,180 sq km [71,498 sq mi]
**POPULATION** 22,531,000 **CAPITAL** Damascus
**GOVERNMENT** Multiparty republic **ETHNIC GROUPS** Arab 90%, Kurdish, Armenian, others **LANGUAGES** Arabic (official), Kurdish, Armenian **RELIGIONS** Sunni Muslim 74%, other Islam 16%
**CURRENCY** Syrian pound = 100 piastres

## TAIWAN

**GEOGRAPHY** High mountain ranges run down the length of the island, with dense forest in many areas. The climate is warm, moist, and suitable for agriculture.

**POLITICS & ECONOMY** Chinese settlers occupied Taiwan from the 7th century. In 1895, Japan seized the territory from the Portuguese, who had named it Isla Formosa, or 'beautiful island'. China regained the island after World War II. In 1949, it became the refuge of the Nationalists who had been driven out of China by the Communists. They set up the Republic of China, which, with US help, began to expand its economy. Today, it is a dynamic economy and produces a wide range of manufactured goods.

In the early 21st century, the Taiwanese declared full nationhood for Taiwan. But the government of mainland China threatened to attack the territory if it did not accept the fact that it was a self-governing province of China. However, in 2010, Taiwan and China signed a free-trade pact.

**AREA** 36,000 sq km [13,900 sq mi]
**POPULATION** 23,235,000 **CAPITAL** Taipei
**GOVERNMENT** Unitary multiparty republic
**ETHNIC GROUPS** Taiwanese 84%, mainland Chinese 14%
**LANGUAGES** Mandarin Chinese (official), Min, Hakka
**RELIGIONS** Buddhism, Taoism, Confucianism
**CURRENCY** New Taiwan dollar = 100 cents

## TAJIKISTAN

**GEOGRAPHY** The Republic of Tajikistan is one of the five central Asian republics that formed part of the former Soviet Union. Only 7% of the land is below 1,000 m [3,280 ft], while almost all of eastern Tajikistan is above 3,000 m [9,840 ft]. The highest point is Pik Imeni Ismail Samani (formerly known as Communism Peak or Pik Kommunizma), which reaches 7,495 m [24,590 ft]. The main ranges are the westwards extension of the Tian Shan Range in the north and the snow-capped Pamirs in the south-east. Earthquakes are common throughout the country. The climate is continental, with hot, dry summers in the lower valleys and bitterly cold winters, especially in the mountains.

**POLITICS & ECONOMY** Russia conquered parts of Tajikistan in the late 19th century, and by 1920 Russia took complete control. In 1924, Tajikistan became part of the Uzbek Soviet Socialist Republic, but, in 1929, it was expanded, taking in some areas populated by Uzbeks, becoming the Tajik Soviet Socialist Republic.

While the Soviet Union began to introduce reforms during the 1980s, many Tajiks demanded freedom. In 1989, the Tajik government made Tajik the official language instead of Russian and, in 1990, it stated that its local laws overruled Soviet ones. Tajikistan became fully independent in 1991, following the break-up of the Soviet Union. In 1992, civil war broke out between the government, which was run by former Communists, and an alliance of democrats and Islamic forces. A ceasefire was agreed in 1996. In 2006, President Emomali Rahmon, president since 1994, was re-elected. In 2010, his party won parliamentary elections amid accusations of fraud.

The World Bank classifies Tajikistan as a 'low-income' developing country and, in 2009, an international think tank warned that it risked becoming a failed state, with 70% of its people living in abject poverty. Agriculture, mainly on irrigated land, is the main activity and cotton is the chief product. Other crops include fruits, grains and vegetables. The country has large hydroelectric resources and it produces aluminium.

**AREA** 143,100 sq km [55,521 sq mi]
**POPULATION** 7,768,000 **CAPITAL** Dushanbe
**GOVERNMENT** Republic
**ETHNIC GROUPS** Tajik 80%, Uzbek 15%, Russian 1%, Kyrgyz 1%
**LANGUAGES** Tajik (official), Russian
**RELIGIONS** Islam (Sunni Muslim 85%, Shia Muslim 15%)
**CURRENCY** Somoni = 100 dirams

## TANZANIA

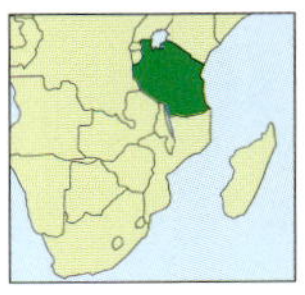

**GEOGRAPHY** The United Republic of Tanzania consists of the former mainland country of Tanganyika and the island nation of Zanzibar, which also includes the island of Pemba. Behind a narrow coastal plain, most of Tanzania is a plateau, which is broken by arms of the Great African Rift Valley. In the west, this valley contains lakes Nyasa and Tanganyika. The highest peak is Kilimanjaro, Africa's tallest mountain at 5,895 m [19,340 ft].

The coast has a hot and humid climate, with the greatest rainfall in April and May. The inland plateaux and mountains are cooler and less humid.

**POLITICS & ECONOMY** Mainland Tanganyika became a German territory in the 1880s, while Zanzibar and Pemba became a British protectorate in 1890. Following Germany's defeat in World War I, Britain took over Tanganyika, which remained a British territory until its independence in 1961. In 1964, Tanganyika and Zanzibar united to form the United Republic of Tanzania. The country's president, Julius Nyerere, pursued socialist policies of self-help (*ujamaa*) and egalitarianism. Many of its social reforms were successful, though the country failed to make economic progress. Nyerere resigned as president in 1985. His successors followed more liberal economic policies. In 2009, Tanzania joined with Burundi, Kenya, Rwanda and Uganda in a common market agreement, allowing free movement of goods and people between them.

Tanzania is a poor country. Crops are grown on only 4% of the land, yet agriculture employs about 75% of the people. Food crops include bananas, cassava, maize, millet and rice. Minerals, including gold, as well as cashews, tobacco, coffee and tea are exported.

**AREA** 945,090 SQ KM [364,899 SQ MI]
**POPULATION** 46,913,000 **CAPITAL** DODOMA
**GOVERNMENT** MULTIPARTY REPUBLIC
**ETHNIC GROUPS** NATIVE AFRICAN 99% (OF WHICH 95% ARE BANTU CONSISTING OF MORE THAN 130 TRIBES)
**LANGUAGES** SWAHILI (KISWAHILI) AND ENGLISH (BOTH OFFICIAL)
**RELIGIONS** ISLAM 35% (99% IN ZANZIBAR), TRADITIONAL BELIEFS 35%, CHRISTIANITY 30% **CURRENCY** TANZANIAN SHILLING = 100 CENTS

## THAILAND

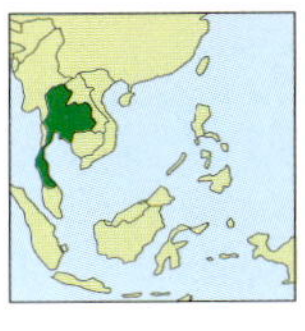

**GEOGRAPHY** The Kingdom of Thailand is one of the ten countries in South-east Asia. The highest land is in the north, where Doi Inthanon, the highest peak, reaches 2,565 m [8,415 ft]. The Khorat plateau, in the north-east, makes up about 30% of the country and is the most heavily populated part of Thailand. In the south, Thailand shares the finger-like Malay peninsula with Burma and Malaysia.

Thailand has a tropical climate. Monsoon winds from the south-west bring heavy rains in May to October. Mountains shelter the central plains from the rain-bearing winds.

**POLITICS & ECONOMY** The first Thai state was set up in the 13th century. By 1350, it included most of what is now Thailand. European contact began in the early 16th century. But, in the late 17th century, the Thais, fearing interference in their affairs, forced all Europeans to leave. This policy continued for 150 years. In 1782, a Thai General, Chao Phraya Chakkri, became king, founding a dynasty which continues today. The country became known as Siam, and Bangkok became its capital. From the mid-19th century, contacts with the West were restored. In World War I, Siam supported the Allies against Germany and Austria–Hungary. But in 1941, the country was conquered by Japan and became its ally. After 1945, it became an ally of the United States.

After 1967, when Thailand became a member of ASEAN (Association of South-east Asian Nations), its economy expanded rapidly, especially in manufacturing and service industries. In 1997, with other eastern Asian economies, it suffered an economic recession. Thailand has also faced conflict in southern Thailand, where the government has clashed with Muslim groups who feel that the government discriminates against them. In 2001, Thaksin Shinawatra, a businessman, became prime minister. In 2006, his party won a majority, the result of a boycott of opposition parties. Following mass protests, a military *junta* took power. Civilian rule was restored in 2007. In 2011, Thaksin's sister, Yingluck Shinawatra, was elected prime minister. She became the first Thai woman to be prime minister.

Agriculture employs 41% of the people and rice is the chief crop. Cassava, cotton, maize, rubber, sugar cane and tobacco are also grown. Tin is mined, but the chief exports are manufactures and food products. Tourism is also important.

**AREA** 513,115 SQ KM [198,114 SQ MI]
**POPULATION** 67,091,000 **CAPITAL** BANGKOK
**GOVERNMENT** CONSTITUTIONAL MONARCHY
**ETHNIC GROUPS** THAI 75%, CHINESE 14%, OTHERS 11%
**LANGUAGES** THAI (OFFICIAL), ENGLISH, ETHNIC AND REGIONAL DIALECTS
**RELIGIONS** BUDDHISM 95%, ISLAM, CHRISTIANITY
**CURRENCY** THAI BAHT = 100 SATANG

## TOGO

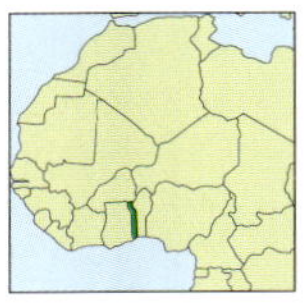

**GEOGRAPHY** The Republic of Togo is a long, narrow country in West Africa. From north to south, it extends about 500 km [311 mi]. Its coastline on the Gulf of Guinea is only 64 km [40 mi] long and it is only 145 km [90 mi] at its widest point.

Togo has high temperatures all through the year. The main wet season is from March to July, with a minor wet season in October and November.

**POLITICS & ECONOMY** Togo became a German protectorate in 1884, but, in 1919, Britain took over the western third of the territory, while France took over the eastern two-thirds. In 1956, the people of British Togoland voted to join Ghana, while French Togoland became an independent republic in 1960.

A military regime took power in 1963. In 1967, General Gnassingbé Eyadéma became head of state and suspended the constitution. Under a new constitution adopted in 1992, multiparty elections were held in 1994. However, in 1998, the count in the presidential elections was stopped when it became clear that Eyadéma had been defeated. The opposition boycotted subsequent elections. Eyadéma died in 2005. His son, Faure Gnassingbé, took over as president, but international pressure forced him to step down. However, he was elected president in 2005 and 2010.

Togo is a poor, developing country dependent on agriculture. Major food crops include cassava, maize, millet and yams. Phosphate rock is the leading export.

**AREA** 56,785 SQ KM [21,925 SQ MI]
**POPULATION** 6,961,000 **CAPITAL** LOMÉ
**GOVERNMENT** MULTIPARTY REPUBLIC **ETHNIC GROUPS** NATIVE AFRICAN 99% (LARGEST TRIBES ARE EWE, MINA AND KABRE) **LANGUAGES** FRENCH (OFFICIAL), AFRICAN LANGUAGES **RELIGIONS** TRADITIONAL BELIEFS 51%, CHRISTIANITY 29%, ISLAM 20% **CURRENCY** CFA FRANC = 100 CENTIMES

## TONGA

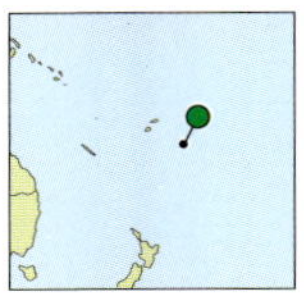

The Kingdom of Tonga, a former British protectorate, became independent in 1970. Situated in the south Pacific Ocean, it contains more than 170 islands, 36 of which are inhabited. In 2010, Tonga held its first election for a popularly elected parliament. Agriculture is the main activity.

**AREA** 650 SQ KM [251 SQ MI] **POPULATION** 106,000 **CAPITAL** NUKU'ALOFA

## TRINIDAD AND TOBAGO

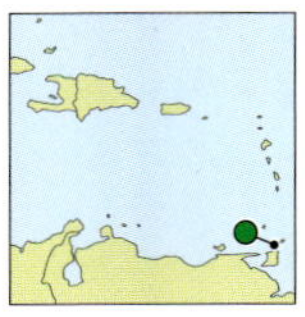

The Republic of Trinidad and Tobago became independent from Britain in 1962. These tropical islands, populated by people of African, Asian (mainly Indian) and European origin, are hilly and forested, though there are some fertile plains. Oil production is the mainstay of the economy.

**AREA** 5,130 SQ KM [1,981 SQ MI]
**POPULATION** 1,226,000 **CAPITAL** PORT OF SPAIN

## TUNISIA

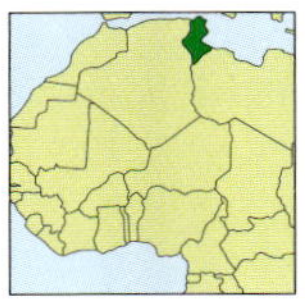

**GEOGRAPHY** The Republic of Tunisia is the smallest country in North Africa. The mountains in the north are an eastwards and comparatively low extension of the Atlas Mountains. To the north and east of the mountains lie fertile plains, especially between Sfax, Tunis, and Bizerte. In the south, low-lying regions contain a vast salt pan, called the Chott Djerid, and part of the Sahara Desert.

Northern Tunisia has a Mediterranean climate, with dry, sunny summers, and mild winters with a moderate rainfall. The average yearly rainfall decreases towards the south.

**POLITICS & ECONOMY** In 1881, France established a protectorate over Tunisia and ruled the country until 1956. The new parliament abolished the monarchy and declared Tunisia to be a republic in 1957, with the nationalist leader, Habib Bourguiba, as president. His government introduced many reforms, including votes for women, but various problems arose, including unemployment among the middle class and fears that Western values introduced by tourists might undermine Muslim values. In 1987, the prime minister, Zine el Abidine Ben Ali, removed Bourguiba, and became president. He was re-elected to a fifth term in 2009. In 2011, anti-government demonstrations forced the president to flee the country. Elections were won by the moderate Islamist party Ennahda, though without an absolute majority.

The World Bank classifies Tunisia as an 'upper-middle-income' developing country. The main resources and chief exports are phosphates and oil. Most industries are concerned with food processing. Barley, dates, grapes, olives and wheat are major crops. Fishing is important, as also is tourism.

**AREA** 163,610 SQ KM [63,170 SQ MI] **POPULATION** 10,733,000
**CAPITAL** TUNIS **GOVERNMENT** MULTIPARTY REPUBLIC
**ETHNIC GROUPS** ARAB 98%, EUROPEAN 1% **LANGUAGES** ARABIC (OFFICIAL), FRENCH **RELIGIONS** ISLAM 98%, CHRISTIANITY 1%, OTHERS
**CURRENCY** TUNISIAN DINAR = 1,000 MILLIMES

## TURKEY

**GEOGRAPHY** The Republic of Turkey lies in two continents. European Turkey, also called Thrace, lies west of a waterway linking the Mediterranean and Black seas. Most of Asian Turkey consists of plateaux and mountains, which rise to 5,165 m [16,945 ft] at Mount Ararat, near the border with Armenia. Earthquakes are common. Central Turkey has a dry climate, with hot, sunny summers and cold winters. The west has a Mediterranean climate, but the Black Sea coast has cooler summers.

**POLITICS & ECONOMY** In AD 330, the Roman empire moved its capital to Byzantium, which it renamed Constantinople. Constantinople became capital of the East Roman (or Byzantine) empire in 395. Muslim Seljuk Turks from central Asia invaded Anatolia in the 11th century. In the 14th century, another group of Turks, the Ottomans, conquered the area. In 1453, the Ottoman Turks took Constantinople, which they called Istanbul. The Ottomans built up a vast empire which finally collapsed during World War I (1914–18). Turkey became a republic in 1923. Its leader, Mustafa Kemal, or Atatürk ('father of the Turks'), began to modernize and secularize the country.

Since the 1940s, Turkey has sought to strengthen its ties with Western powers. It joined NATO (North Atlantic Treaty Organization) in 1951 and it applied to join the European Economic Community in 1987. But Turkey's conflict with Greece, together with its invasion of northern Cyprus in 1974, have led many Europeans to treat Turkey's aspirations with caution. Political instability, military coups, conflict with Kurdish nationalists in eastern Turkey, and concern about the country's record on human rights are other problems.

Turkey has enjoyed democracy since 1983, though, in 1998, the government banned the Islamist Welfare Party, which it accused of violating secular principles. In 1999, the Muslim Virtue Party (successor to the Islamist Welfare Party) lost ground. The largest numbers of parliamentary seats were won by the ruling Democratic Left Party and the far-right National Action Party. However, in the elections in 2002, the moderate Islamic Justice and Development Party (AKP) won 362 of the 500 seats in parliament. Despite concerns about its Islamist roots, the AKP was re-elected in 2007. In 2007–8, the activities of the separatist Kurdish Workers Party (PKK) guerrillas provoked Turkey to bomb its bases in northern Iraq. Between 2009–13, tensions increased along the Syrian border, with over 250,000 refugees crossing into Turkey.

Turkey came close to economic collapse in 2002, but its recovery enabled it to withstand the global financial crisis in 2008, and its economy bounced back in 2010–11. Agriculture employs 21% of the people. Barley, cotton, fruits, maize, tobacco and wheat are major crops. But manufactures, including textiles, cars, machinery and paper products, are among the leading exports.

**AREA** 774,815 SQ KM [299,156 SQ MI]
**POPULATION** 79,749,000 **CAPITAL** ANKARA
**GOVERNMENT** MULTIPARTY REPUBLIC **ETHNIC GROUPS** TURKISH 80%, KURDISH 20% **LANGUAGES** TURKISH (OFFICIAL), KURDISH, ARABIC
**RELIGIONS** ISLAM (MAINLY SUNNI MUSLIM) 99%
**CURRENCY** NEW TURKISH LIRA = 100 KURUS

## TURKMENISTAN

**GEOGRAPHY** The Republic of Turkmenistan is one of the five central Asian republics which once formed part of the former Soviet Union. Most of the land is low-lying, with mountains lying on the southern and south-western borders. In the west lies the salty Caspian Sea. Most of Turkmenistan is arid and the Garagum, Asia's largest sand desert, covers about 80% of the country. Turkmenistan has a continental climate, with average annual rainfall varying from 80 mm [3 in] in the desert to 300 mm [12 in] in the mountains. Summer months are hot, but winter temperatures drop well below freezing point.

**POLITICS & ECONOMY** Just over 1,000 years ago, Turkic people settled in the lands east of the Caspian Sea and the name 'Turkmen' comes from this time. Mongol armies conquered the area in the 13th century and Islam was introduced in the 14th century. Russia took over the area in the 1870s and 1880s. The area came under Communist rule in 1917 and, in 1924, it became the Turkmen Soviet Socialist Republic. The Communists controlled all aspects of life, but they raised living standards.

In the 1980s, when the Soviet Union began to introduce reforms, the Turkmen began to demand more freedom. In 1990, the Turkmen government stated that its laws overruled Soviet ones. In 1991, Turkmenistan became fully independent after the break-up of the Soviet Union. But the country kept ties with Russia through the Commonwealth of Independent States (CIS).

In 1992, Turkmenistan adopted a new constitution, allowing for the setting up of political parties, providing that they were not ethnic or religious in character. But, effectively, Turkmenistan remained a one-party state and, in 1992, Saparmurad Niyazov, the former Communist and at that time Democratic Party leader, was the only presidential candidate. In 1999, parliament declared Niyazov president for life. Niyazov died in 2006 and was succeeded by Gurbanguly Berdymukhamedov. In 2012, he was re-elected, winning more than 97% of the vote.

Faced with many economic problems, Turkmenistan began to look south rather than to the CIS for support. As part of this policy, it joined the Economic Co-operation Organization, which had been set up in 1985 by Iran, Pakistan and Turkey. In 1996, the completion of a rail link from Turkmenistan to the Iranian coast was an important step in the development of Central Asia. Oil and natural gas are the chief resources, and gas pipelines to China and Iran were opened in 2009 and 2010. But agriculture is the main activity. Cotton is the main commercial crop. Manufactures include cement, glass, petrochemicals and textiles.

**AREA** 488,100 sq km [188,455 sq mi] **POPULATION** 5,055,000
**CAPITAL** Ashkhabad **GOVERNMENT** Single-party republic
**ETHNIC GROUPS** Turkmen 85%, Uzbek 5%, Russian 4%
**LANGUAGES** Turkmen (official), Russian, Uzbek **RELIGIONS** Islam 89%, Eastern Orthodox 9% **CURRENCY** Turkmen manat = 100 tennesi

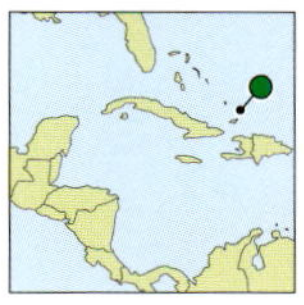

## TURKS AND CAICOS ISLANDS

The Turks and Caicos Islands, a British territory in the Caribbean since 1776, are a group of about 30 islands. Fishing and tourism are major activities.

**AREA** 430 sq km [166 sq mi]
**POPULATION** 46,000 **CAPITAL** Cockburn Town

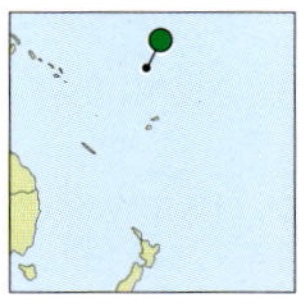

## TUVALU

Tuvalu, formerly called the Ellice Islands, was a British territory from the 1890s until it became independent in 1978. It consists of nine low-lying coral atolls in the southern Pacific Ocean. Copra is the chief export.

**AREA** 26 sq km [10 sq mi]
**POPULATION** 11,000 **CAPITAL** Fongafale

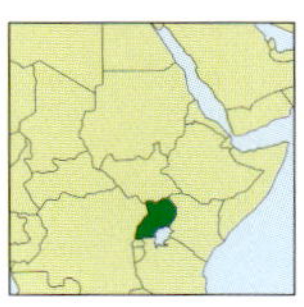

## UGANDA

**GEOGRAPHY** The Republic of Uganda is a landlocked country on the East African plateau. It contains part of Lake Victoria, Africa's largest lake and a source of the River Nile, which occupies a shallow depression in the plateau.

The equator runs through Uganda and the country is warm throughout the year, though the high altitude moderates the temperature. The wettest regions are the lands to the north of Lake Victoria, where Kampala is situated, and the western mountains, especially the high Ruwenzori range.

**POLITICS & ECONOMY** Little is known of the early history of Uganda. When Europeans first reached the area in the 19th century, many of the people were organized in kingdoms, the most powerful of which was Buganda, the home of the Baganda people. Britain took over the country between 1894 and 1914, and ruled it until independence in 1962.

In 1967, Uganda became a republic and Buganda's Kabaka (king), Sir Edward Mutesa II, was made president. But tensions between the Kabaka and the prime minister, Apollo Milton Obote, led to the dismissal of the Kabaka in 1966. Obote also abolished the traditional kingdoms, including Buganda. Obote was overthrown in 1971 by an army group led by General Idi Amin Dada. Amin ruled as a dictator. He forced most of the Asians who lived in Uganda to leave the country and had many of his opponents killed.

In 1978, a border dispute between Uganda and Tanzania led Tanzanian troops to enter Uganda. With help from Ugandan opponents of Amin, they overthrew Amin's government. In 1980, Obote led his party to victory in national elections. But after charges of fraud, Obote's opponents began guerrilla warfare. A military group overthrew Obote in 1985, though strife continued until 1986, when Yoweri Museveni's National Resistance Movement seized power. In 1993, Museveni restored the traditional kingdoms. Elections were held in 1994, but political parties were forbidden. Museveni was elected in 1996, 2001, 2006 and 2011. In recent years, Uganda has faced the rebel Lord's Resistance Army (LRA) in the north. The LRA extended its activities into the Central African Republic, the Democratic Republic of the Congo, and Sudan. In 2010, two bombings in Kampala, killing 74 people, were carried out by a Somali Islamist group, al-Shabab, which said it was a response to Uganda's role in supplying troops to the African Union mission in Somalia.

Agriculture dominates the economy, employing 66% of the people. The chief export is coffee.

**AREA** 241,038 sq km [93,065 sq mi]
**POPULATION** 33,641,000 **CAPITAL** Kampala
**GOVERNMENT** Republic
**ETHNIC GROUPS** Baganda 17%, Ankole 8%, Basogo 8%, Iteso 8%, Bakiga 7%, Langi 6%, Rwanda 6%, Bagisu 5%, Acholi 4%, Lugbara 4%, and others
**LANGUAGES** English and Swahili (both official), Ganda
**RELIGIONS** Roman Catholic 42%, Protestant 42%, Islam 12%, traditional beliefs 4%
**CURRENCY** Ugandan shilling = 100 cents

## UKRAINE

**GEOGRAPHY** Ukraine is the second largest country in Europe after Russia. It was formerly part of the Soviet Union, which split apart in 1991. This mostly flat country faces the Black Sea in the south. The Crimean peninsula includes a highland region overlooking Yalta. Ukraine has warm summers, but the winters are cold, becoming more severe from west to east. In the summer, the east is often warmer than the west. Most rain comes in summer.

**POLITICS & ECONOMY** Kiev was the original capital of the early Slavic civilization known as Kievan Rus. In the 17th and 18th centuries, parts of Ukraine came under Polish and Russian rule. But Russia gained most of Ukraine in the late 18th century. In 1918, Ukraine became independent, but in 1922 it became part of the Soviet Union.

In the 1980s, Ukrainian people demanded more say over their affairs. The country became independent in 1991. Leonid Kuchma, who became president in 1994, came under fire in the early 2000s for maladministration and for his alleged involvement in the murder of a journalist. In 2005, the pro-Western leader Viktor Yushchenko was elected president. Economic problems and political infighting led to a Russian-leaning party, led by Viktor Yanukovych, winning most seats in parliament in 2006. Yanukovych became prime minister, but an election in 2007 resulted in a pro-Western coalition government led by a former prime minister, Yulia Tymoshenko. In 2010, the pro-Russian Viktor Yanukovych was declared winner of the presidential election. Tymoshenko was later accused of exceeding her powers when she signed a gas deal with Russia. She was sentenced to seven years in prison.

The World Bank classifies Ukraine as a 'lower-middle-income' economy. Agriculture is important. Wheat and sugar are exported. Barley, maize, potatoes, sunflowers and tobacco are also grown. Livestock rearing and fishing are also important.

Manufacturing is the chief economic activity. Major manufactures include iron and steel, machinery and vehicles. Ukraine has large coalfields. The country imports oil and natural gas, but it has hydroelectric and nuclear power stations.

**AREA** 603,700 sq km [233,089 sq mi]
**POPULATION** 44,854,000 **CAPITAL** Kiev
**GOVERNMENT** Multiparty republic
**ETHNIC GROUPS** Ukrainian 78%, Russian 17%, Belarusian, Moldovan, Bulgarian, Hungarian, Polish
**LANGUAGES** Ukrainian (official), Russian
**RELIGIONS** Mostly Ukrainian Orthodox
**CURRENCY** Hryvnia = 100 kopiykas

## UNITED ARAB EMIRATES

The United Arab Emirates were formed in 1971 when the seven Trucial States of the Persian Gulf (Abu Dhabi, Dubai, Sharjah, Ajman, Umm al Qawayn, Ra's al Khaymah and Al Fujayrah) opted to join together and form an independent country. The economy of this hot and dry country depends on oil production, and oil revenues give the United Arab Emirates one of the highest per capita GDPs in Asia.

**AREA** 83,600 sq km [32,278 sq mi]
**POPULATION** 5,314,000 **CAPITAL** Abu Dhabi

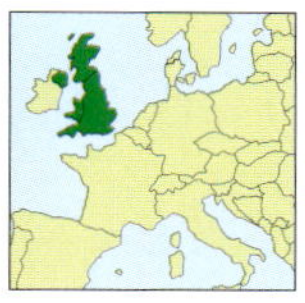

## UNITED KINGDOM

**GEOGRAPHY** The United Kingdom (or UK) is a union of four countries. Three of them – England, Scotland and Wales – make up Great Britain. The fourth country is Northern Ireland. The Isle of Man and the Channel Islands, including Jersey and Guernsey, are not part of the UK. They are self-governing British dependencies.

The land is highly varied. Much of Scotland and Wales is mountainous, and the highest peak is Scotland's Ben Nevis at 1,344 m [4,409 ft]. England has some highland areas, including the Cumbrian Mountains (or Lake District) and the Pennine range in the north. But England also has large areas of fertile lowland. Northern Ireland is also a mixture of lowlands and uplands. It contains the UK's largest lake, Lough Neagh.

The UK has a mild climate, influenced by the warm Gulf Stream which flows across the Atlantic from the Gulf of Mexico, then past the British Isles. Moist winds from the south-west bring rain, but the rainfall decreases from west to east. Winds from the east and north bring cold weather in winter.

**POLITICS & ECONOMY** In ancient times, Britain was invaded by many peoples, including Iberians, Celts, Romans, Angles, Saxons, Jutes, Norsemen, Danes and the Normans, who arrived in 1066. The evolution of the United Kingdom spanned hundreds of years. The Normans finally overcame Welsh resistance in 1282, when King Edward I annexed Wales and united it with England. Union with Scotland was achieved by the Act of Union of 1707. This created a country known as the United Kingdom of Great Britain.

Ireland came under Norman rule in the 11th century, and much of its later history was concerned with a struggle against English domination. In 1801, Ireland became part of the United Kingdom of Great Britain and Ireland. But in 1921, southern Ireland broke away to become the Irish Free State. Most of the people in the Irish Free State were Roman Catholics. In Northern Ireland, where the majority of the people were Protestants, most people wanted to remain citizens of the United Kingdom. As a result, the country's official name changed to the United Kingdom of Great Britain and Northern Ireland.

The modern history of the UK began in the 18th century when the British empire began to develop, despite the loss in 1783 of its 13 North American colonies, which became the core of the modern United States. The other major event occurred in the late 18th century, when the UK became the first country to industrialize its economy.

The British empire broke up after World War II (1939–45), though the UK still administers many small, mainly island, territories around the world. The empire was transformed into the Commonwealth of Nations, a free association of independent countries which numbered 54 in 2013.

The UK has retained an important world role. For example, in 2001, it played a prominent role in creating a broad alliance to counter international terrorism following the attacks on the United

States. It was also a prominent member of the coalition force which invaded Iraq in 2003. However, the UK has recognized that its economic future lies within Europe. It became a member of the European Economic Community (now the European Union) in 1973. Membership of the EU has been important to the British economy, but some people fear a loss of British identity should the EU ever evolve into a political union. Another matter of public concern is large-scale immigration, both from the EU and outside.

The UK is a major industrial and trading nation. It lacks natural resources apart from coal, iron ore, oil and natural gas, and has to import most of the materials it needs for its industries. The UK also has to import food, because it produces only about two-thirds of the food it needs. In the first half of the 20th century, Britain was a major exporter of cars, ships, steel and textiles. But many industries have suffered from competition from other countries, with lower labour costs. From 2008, Britain's economy was hit by a global financial crisis, which led the country into recession. Severe austerity measures were introduced.

The UK is one of the world's most urbanized countries, and agriculture employs only 1% of the people. Production is high because of the use of scientific methods and modern machinery. However, in the early 21st century, especially following the outbreak of foot-and-mouth disease in 2001, questions were raised about the future of rural industries. Major crops include barley, potatoes, sugar beet and wheat. Sheep are the leading livestock, but beef and dairy cattle, pigs and poultry are also important. Fishing is another major activity and the UK is one of the largest fishing countries in the EU. Important catches include cod, haddock, plaice and mackerel.

Service industries play a major part in the UK's economy. Financial and insurance services bring in much-needed foreign exchange, while tourism has become a major earner.

**AREA** 241,857 sq km [93,381 sq mi]
**POPULATION** 63,047,000 **CAPITAL** London
**GOVERNMENT** Constitutional monarchy
**ETHNIC GROUPS** English 84%, Scottish 9%, Welsh 5%, Ulster 3%, West Indian, Indian, Pakistani and others
**LANGUAGES** English (official), Welsh, Gaelic
**RELIGIONS** Christianity (Anglican, Roman Catholic, Presbyterian, Methodist), Islam, Sikhism, Hinduism, Judaism
**CURRENCY** Pound sterling = 100 pence

## UNITED STATES OF AMERICA

**GEOGRAPHY** The United States of America is the world's fourth largest country in area and the third largest in population. It contains 50 states, 48 of which lie between Canada and Mexico, plus Alaska in north-western North America, and Hawai'i, a group of volcanic islands in the north Pacific Ocean. Densely populated coastal plains lie to the east and south of the Appalachian Mountains. The central lowlands, drained by the Mississippi–Missouri rivers, stretch from the Appalachians to the Rocky Mountains in the west. The Pacific region contains fertile valleys, separated by mountain ranges.

The climate varies greatly, ranging from the Arctic cold of Alaska to the intense heat of Death Valley, a bleak desert in California. Of the 48 states between Canada and Mexico, winters are cold and snowy in the north, but mild in the south, a region which is often called the 'Sun Belt'.

**POLITICS & ECONOMY** The first people in North America, the ancestors of the Native Americans (or American Indians) arrived perhaps 40,000 years ago from Asia. Although Vikings probably reached North America 1,000 years ago, European exploration proper did not begin until the late 15th century.

The first Europeans to settle in large numbers were the British, who founded settlements on the eastern coast in the early 17th century. British rule ended in the War of Independence (1775–83). The country expanded in 1803 when a vast territory in the south and west was acquired through the Louisiana Purchase, while the border with Mexico was fixed in the mid-19th century. The Civil War (1861–5) ended slavery and the serious threat that the nation might split into two parts. In the late 19th century, the West was opened up, while immigrants flooded in from Europe and elsewhere.

During the late 19th and early 20th centuries, industrialization led to the United States becoming the world's leading economic superpower and a pioneer in science and technology. It took on the mantle of the champion of Western democracy and, following the break-up of the former Soviet Union, it became the world's only superpower. But the attacks on the country on 11 September 2001, revealed its vulnerability to terrorists and rogue states. The response was vigorous. In 2001, it attacked the Taliban government in Afghanistan, which was protecting al Qaida terrorists. Then, in 2003, it led a coalition force to invade Iraq and overthrow Saddam Hussein. President George W. Bush was re-elected in 2004, and the conflicts in Afghanistan and Iraq continued. In 2008, the Democratic Party candidate, Barack Obama, defeated the Republican John McCain in the presidential elections. Obama, the first black president in US history, faced many challenges, including those arising from the global financial crisis and the conflicts in south-western Asia. He was re-elected in 2012.

The United States has the world's largest economy in terms of the total value of its production. Although agriculture employs only about 0.7% of the people, farming is highly mechanized and scientific, and the United States leads the world in farm production. Major products include beef and dairy cattle, together with such crops as cotton, fruits, groundnuts (peanuts), maize, potatoes, soybeans, tobacco and wheat.

Natural resources include oil, natural gas, coal, a wide range of metal ores, and timber, especially from the Pacific north-west. Manufacturing is the single most valuable activity, employing 10.3% of the people. Major products include vehicles, food products, chemicals, machinery, printed goods, metal products, and scientific instruments. California, with its high-tech electronics industries, is the top manufacturing state.

**AREA** 9,629,091 sq km [3,717,792 sq mi]
**POPULATION** 313,847,000 **CAPITAL** Washington, DC
**GOVERNMENT** Federal republic
**ETHNIC GROUPS** White 80%, African American 13%, Asian 4%, Amerindian 1%, others **LANGUAGES** English, Spanish, more than 30 others **RELIGIONS** Protestant 51%, Roman Catholic 24%, Judaism 2%, Mormon 2%, Islam 1%
**CURRENCY** US dollar = 100 cents

## URUGUAY

**GEOGRAPHY** Uruguay is South America's second smallest independent country after Suriname. The land consists mainly of flat plains and hills. The River Uruguay, which forms the country's western border, flows into the Río de la Plata, a large estuary which leads into the South Atlantic Ocean.

Uruguay has a mild climate, with rain in every month, though droughts sometimes occur. Summers are pleasantly warm and winters relatively mild.

**POLITICS & ECONOMY** In 1726, Spanish settlers founded Montevideo in order to halt the Portuguese gaining influence in the area. By the late 18th century, Spaniards had settled in most of the country. Uruguay became part of a colony called the Viceroyalty of La Plata, which also included Argentina, Paraguay, and parts of Bolivia, Brazil and Chile. In 1820 Brazil annexed Uruguay, ending Spanish rule. In 1825, Uruguayans, supported by Argentina, began a struggle for independence. Finally, in 1828, Brazil and Argentina recognized Uruguay as an independent republic. Social and economic developments were slow, but, from 1903, Uruguay became stable and democratic.

From the 1950s, economic problems caused unrest. Terrorist groups, notably the Tupumaros, carried out murders and kidnappings. The army crushed the Tupamaros in 1972, and took over the government in 1973. Military rule continued until 1984 when elections were held. In the early 21st century, Uruguay faced many economic problems, many of which were the result of the economic crisis in its neighbour, Argentina, and its imposition of banking controls. In 2009, the former left-wing rebel-turned-moderate Jose Mujica, of the governing Broad Front, was elected president.

The World Bank classifies Uruguay as an 'upper-middle-income' developing country. Agriculture employs 13% of the people, but farm products, notably hides and leather goods, beef, and wool, are the main exports, while many manufacturing industries process farm products. Crops include maize, potatoes, wheat and sugar beet. Uruguay depends largely on hydroelectric power for energy. In 2008, Uruguay announced the discovery of an offshore natural gas field, which is being developed.

**AREA** 175,016 sq km [67,574 sq mi]
**POPULATION** 3,316,000 **CAPITAL** Montevideo
**GOVERNMENT** Multiparty republic
**ETHNIC GROUPS** White 88%, Mestizo 8%, Mulatto or Black 4%
**LANGUAGES** Spanish (official)
**RELIGIONS** Christianity 58% (Roman Catholic 47%), others
**CURRENCY** Uruguayan peso = 100 centésimos

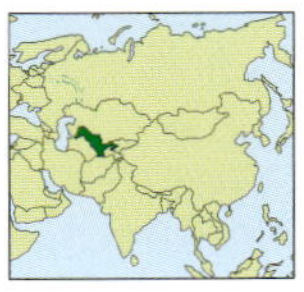

## UZBEKISTAN

**GEOGRAPHY** The Republic of Uzbekistan is one of the five republics in Central Asia which were once part of the Soviet Union. Plains cover most of western Uzbekistan, with highlands in the east. The main rivers, the Amu (or Amu Darya) and Syr (or Syr Darya), drain into the Aral Sea. So much water has been taken from these rivers to irrigate the land that the Aral Sea has now shrunk to about a quarter of its size in 1960. The former lake area is now desert. Uzbekistan has cold winters and hot summers. The largely uninhabited Kyzyl Kum Desert lies in central Uzbekistan.

**POLITICS & ECONOMY** Russia took the area in the 19th century. After the Russian Revolution of 1917, the Communists took over and, in 1924, they set up the Uzbek Soviet Socialist Republic. Under Communism, all aspects of Uzbek life were controlled and religious worship was discouraged. But education, health, housing and transport were improved. In the late 1980s, the people demanded more freedom, and in 1990 the government stated that its laws overruled those of the Soviet Union. Uzbekistan became independent in 1991 when the Soviet Union broke up, but it continued to retain links with Russia through the Commonwealth of Independent States.

Islom Karimov, leader of the People's Democratic Party (formerly the Communist Party), was elected president in December 1991. In 1992–3, many opposition leaders were arrested because the government said that they threatened national stability. In 1994–5, the PDP was victorious in national elections. Karimov was re-elected in 2001 and 2007. Initially, his government allowed the US to use bases in Uzbekistan for its military campaign in Afghanistan. It asked the US to remove its troops in 2005, but, in 2009, it allowed the US to transport supplies through Uzbekistan to its troops in Afghanistan. In 2010, the United Nations called on Uzbekistan to improve its human rights record.

The World Bank classifies Uzbekistan as a 'lower-middle-income' developing country and the government still controls most economic activity. The country produces coal, copper, gold, oil and natural gas.

**AREA** 447,400 sq km [172,741 sq mi]
**POPULATION** 28,394,000 **CAPITAL** Tashkent
**GOVERNMENT** Socialist republic **ETHNIC GROUPS** Uzbek 80%, Russian 5%, Tajik 5%, Kazakh 3%, Tatar 2%, Kara-Kalpak 2%
**LANGUAGES** Uzbek (official), Russian **RELIGIONS** Islam 88%, Eastern Orthodox 9% **CURRENCY** Uzbekistani sum = 100 tyiyn

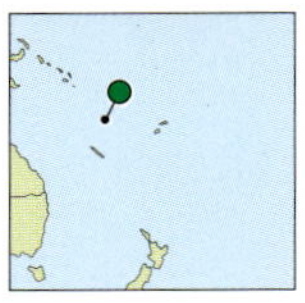

## VANUATU

The Republic of Vanuatu, formerly the Anglo-French Condominium of the New Hebrides, became independent in 1980. It consists of a chain of 80 islands in the south Pacific Ocean. Its economy is based on agriculture, and it exports copra, beef and veal, timber and cocoa.

**AREA** 12,189 sq km [4,706 sq mi]
**POPULATION** 256,000 **CAPITAL** Port-Vila

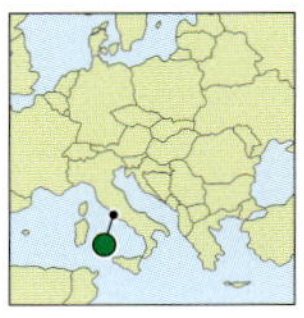

## VATICAN CITY

Vatican City State, the world's smallest independent nation, is an enclave on the west bank of the River Tiber in Rome. It forms an independent base for the Holy See, the governing body of the Roman Catholic Church.

**AREA** 0.44 sq km [0.17 sq mi]
**POPULATION** 832

## VENEZUELA

**GEOGRAPHY** The Bolivarian Republic of Venezuela, in northern South America, contains the Maracaibo lowlands around the oil-rich Lake Maracaibo in the west. Andean ranges enclose the lowlands and extend across most of the northern part of the country. The Orinoco river basin, containing tropical grasslands called *llanos*, lies between the northern highlands and the Guiana Highlands in the south-east. The Orinoco is Venezuela's longest river.

Venezuela has a tropical climate. Temperatures are high throughout the year on the lowlands, though the mountains are cooler. Rainfall is heaviest in the mountains. But much of the country has a dry season between December and April.

**POLITICS & ECONOMY** In the early 19th century, Venezuelans, such as Simón Bolívar and Francisco de Miranda, began a struggle against Spanish rule. Venezuela declared its independence in 1811. But it only became truly independent in 1821, when the Spanish were defeated in a battle near Valencia.

The development of Venezuela in the 19th and the first half of the 20th centuries was marred by instability, violence and periods of harsh dictatorial rule. But Venezuela has had elected governments since 1958. The country has greatly benefited from its oil resources, which were first exploited in 1917. In 1960, Venezuela helped to form OPEC (the Organization of Petroleum Exporting Countries) and, in 1976, the government of Venezuela took control of the country's entire oil industry. In 1999, Hugo Chavez, who had staged an unsuccessful coup in 1992, was elected president. In 2004, he won a majority in a referendum that had been intended by the opposition to remove him from office. His left-wing policies continued to arouse US hostility. He was re-elected again, but died in March 2013, to be succeeded by the socialist Nicolás Maduro.

With oil accounting for about 95% of its exports, Venezuela has an 'upper-middle-income' economy. Other exports include bauxite and aluminium, iron ore and farm products. Beef cattle, dairy cattle and poultry are raised. Crops include bananas, cassava, citrus fruits, coffee and rice. The main industry is petroleum refining. Cement, steel and textiles are also produced.

**AREA** 912,050 sq km [352,143 sq mi] **POPULATION** 28,048,000
**CAPITAL** Caracas **GOVERNMENT** Federal republic
**ETHNIC GROUPS** Spanish, Italian, Portuguese, Arab, German, African, indigenous people **LANGUAGES** Spanish (official), indigenous dialects **RELIGIONS** Roman Catholic 96%
**CURRENCY** Bolívar = 100 céntimos

## VIETNAM

**GEOGRAPHY** The Socialist Republic of Vietnam occupies an S-shaped strip of land facing the South China Sea in South-east Asia. The coastal plains include two densely populated, fertile delta regions: the Red (Hong) delta facing the Gulf of Tonkin in the north and the Mekong delta in the south.

Vietnam has a tropical climate, though the driest months of January to March are a little cooler than the wet, hot summer months, when monsoon winds blow from the south-west. Typhoons (cyclones or hurricanes) sometimes hit the coast, causing extensive flooding and much damage.

**POLITICS & ECONOMY** China dominated Vietnam for a thousand years before AD 939, when a Vietnamese state was founded. The French took over the area between the 1850s and 1880s. They ruled Vietnam as part of French Indo-China, which also included Cambodia and Laos.

Japan conquered Vietnam during World War II (1939–45). In 1946, war broke out between a nationalist group, called the Vietminh, and the French colonial government. France withdrew in 1954 and Vietnam was divided into a Communist North Vietnam, led by the Vietminh leader, Ho Chi Minh, and a non-Communist South.

A force called the Viet Cong rebelled against South Vietnam's government in 1957 and a war began, which gradually increased in intensity. The United States aided the South, but after it withdrew in 1975, South Vietnam surrendered. In 1976, the united Vietnam became a socialist republic. Vietnamese troops intervened in Cambodia in 1978 to defeat the Khmer Rouge government, but it withdrew its troops in 1989. Following reforms in Vietnam, the US opened an embassy in Hanoi in 1995, and, in 2002, trade relations with the US were normalized. In 2007, Vietnam became a member of the World Trade Organization. By 2011, economic reforms were continuing, but Vietnam resisted calls for increased human rights.

Agriculture remains the main activity and rice the main food crop. Vietnam produces chromium, tin and phosphates.

**AREA** 331,689 sq km [128,065 sq mi]
**POPULATION** 91,519,000 **CAPITAL** Hanoi
**GOVERNMENT** Socialist republic
**ETHNIC GROUPS** Vietnamese 87%, Chinese, Hmong, Thai, Khmer, Cham, mountain groups **LANGUAGES** Vietnamese (official), English, Chinese **RELIGIONS** Buddhism, Christianity, indigenous beliefs
**CURRENCY** Dong = 10 hao = 100 xu

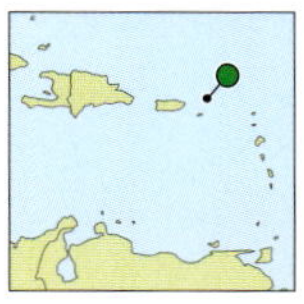

## VIRGIN ISLANDS, BRITISH

The British Virgin Islands, the most northerly of the Lesser Antilles, are a British overseas territory, with a substantial measure of self-government.

**AREA** 151 sq km [58 sq mi]
**POPULATION** 31,000 **CAPITAL** Road Town

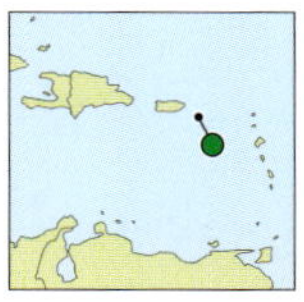

## VIRGIN ISLANDS, US

The Virgin Islands of the United States, a group of three islands and 65 small islets, are a self-governing US territory, which was purchased from Denmark in 1917. Its residents are US citizens and they elect a non-voting delegate to the US House of Representatives.

**AREA** 347 sq km [134 sq mi]
**POPULATION** 105,000 **CAPITAL** Charlotte Amalie

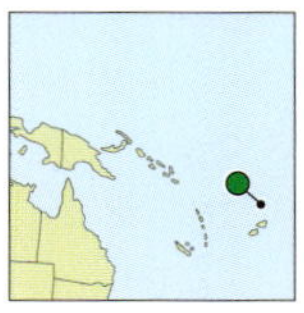

## WALLIS AND FUTUNA

Wallis and Futuna, in the south Pacific Ocean, is the smallest and the poorest of France's overseas territories. French aid remains vital to an economy based on subsistence agriculture.

**AREA** 200 sq km [77 sq mi]
**POPULATION** 15,000 **CAPITAL** Mata-Utu

## YEMEN

**GEOGRAPHY** The Republic of Yemen faces the Red Sea and the Gulf of Aden in the south-western corner of the Arabian peninsula. Behind the narrow coastal plain along the Red Sea, the land rises to a mountain region called High Yemen. The climate ranges from hot and often humid conditions on the coast to the cooler highlands. Most of the country is arid. The south coasts are particularly hot and humid.

**POLITICS & ECONOMY** After World War I, northern Yemen, which had been ruled by Turkey, began to evolve into a separate state from the south, where Britain was in control. Britain withdrew in 1967 and a left-wing government took power in the south. In North Yemen, the monarchy was abolished in 1962 and the country became a republic.

Clashes occurred between the traditionalist Yemen Arab Republic in the north and the formerly British Marxist People's Democratic Republic of Yemen, but, in 1990, the two Yemens merged to form a single country. Further conflict occurred in 1994, when southern secessionists were defeated. However, in the 2000s, the government faced conflict with Shi'ite northern rebels, called Houthis, al Qaida supporters, and southern separatists. In 2011, protesters in the cities called on President Ali Abdullah Saleh to resign. He pledged not to run at the next election and to introduce constitutional reforms, including the introduction of a parliamentary system, but the violent protests continued. In 2012, Saleh left the country and the vice president, Abd Rabbuh Mansour Hadi, became president.

Yemen is a developing country and agriculture employs about half of the people. Sheep are reared and such crops as barley, fruits, wheat and vegetables are grown in highland valleys and around oases. Cash crops include coffee and cotton. Since the 1980s, petroleum extraction has been important in the economy. Manufactures include handicrafts, leather goods, and textiles. Remittances from Yemenis abroad are a major source of revenue.

**AREA** 527,968 sq km [203,848 sq mi] **POPULATION** 24,772,000
**CAPITAL** Sana' **GOVERNMENT** Multiparty republic
**ETHNIC GROUPS** Predominantly Arab **LANGUAGES** Arabic (official)
**RELIGIONS** Islam **CURRENCY** Yemeni rial = 100 fils

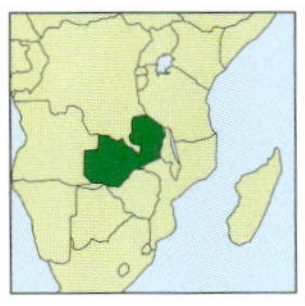

## ZAMBIA

**GEOGRAPHY** The Republic of Zambia is a landlocked country in southern Africa. Zambia lies on the plateau that makes up most of southern Africa. Much of the land is between 900 m and 1,500 m [2,950 ft to 4,920 ft] above sea level. The Muchinga Mountains in the north-east rise above this flat land. Lakes include Bangweulu, which is entirely within Zambia, together with parts of lakes Mweru and Tanganyika in the north. Zambia lies in the tropics, but temperatures are moderated by the altitude.

**POLITICS & ECONOMY** European contact with Zambia began in the 19th century, when the explorer David Livingstone crossed the River Zambezi. In the 1890s, the British South Africa Company, set up by Cecil Rhodes (1853–1902), the British financier and statesman, made treaties with local chiefs and gradually took over the area. In 1911, the Company named the area Northern Rhodesia. In 1924, Britain took over the government of the country.

In 1953, Britain formed a federation of Northern Rhodesia, Southern Rhodesia (now Zimbabwe) and Nyasaland (now Malawi). Because of African opposition, the federation was dissolved in 1963 and Northern Rhodesia became independent as Zambia in 1964. Kenneth Kaunda became president and one-party rule was introduced in 1972. Under a new constitution, Frederick Chiluba was elected president in 1996. He stood down in 2001 and Levy Mwanawasa became president. In 2011, Michael Sata was elected president, defeating the incumbent Rupiah Banda.

Copper, the main resource, accounts for about 64% of the country's exports. Zambia also produces cobalt, lead, zinc and gemstones. Agriculture employs about 85% of the people, as compared with less than 4% in industry and mining. Food crops include cassava, fruits and vegetables, maize, millet and sorghum. Cash crops include coffee, sugar cane and tobacco.

**AREA** 752,618 sq km [290,586 sq mi]
**POPULATION** 13,817,000 **CAPITAL** Lusaka
**GOVERNMENT** Multiparty republic **ETHNIC GROUPS** Native African (Bemba, Tonga, Maravi/Nyanja) **LANGUAGES** English, Bemba, Kaonda, Nyanja and about 70 others **RELIGIONS** Christianity 62%, Islam, Hinduism **CURRENCY** Zambian kwacha = 100 ngwee

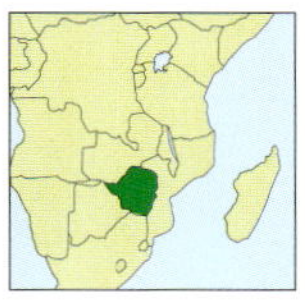

## ZIMBABWE

**GEOGRAPHY** The Republic of Zimbabwe is a landlocked country in southern Africa. Most of the country lies on a high plateau between the Zambezi and Limpopo rivers, ranging from 900 m to 1,500 m [2,950 ft to 4,920 ft] above sea level. From October to March, the weather is hot and wet, but in the winter, daily temperatures can vary greatly.

**POLITICS & ECONOMY** The Shona people became dominant in the region about 1,000 years ago. The British South Africa Company, under the statesman Cecil Rhodes (1853–1902), occupied the area in the 1890s, after obtaining mineral rights from local chiefs. The area was named Rhodesia and later Southern Rhodesia. It became a self-governing British colony in 1923. Between 1953 and 1963, Southern and Northern Rhodesia (now Zambia) were joined to Nyasaland (Malawi) in the Central African Federation.

In 1965, the European government of Southern Rhodesia (then called Rhodesia) declared their country independent, but Britain refused to accept this. Finally, after a civil war, the country became legally independent in 1980, though rivalries between the Shona and Ndebele people threatened stability. Order was restored when the Shona prime minister, Robert Mugabe, brought his Ndebele rivals into his government. In 1987, Mugabe became the country's executive president, and in 1991 the government renounced its Marxist ideology. Mugabe was re-elected president in 1990 and 1996.

From the late 1990s, Mugabe's government seized white-owned farms and landless 'war veterans' began to occupy them. In 2002, Mugabe was re-elected amid accusations of electoral irregularities. In elections in 2008, Mugabe's party was defeated and Mugabe lost to Morgan Tsvangirai in the presidential election. A presidential run-off was ordered, but intimidation of opposition supporters led Tsvangirai to withdraw. In September 2008, a power-sharing agreement was signed and a power-sharing government was set up, with Mugabe as president and Tsvangirai as prime minister. But relations between them proved difficult.

In the 2000s, the economy collapsed. Hyperinflation occurred and many people starved, while the breakdown of public services led to a cholera epidemic. Zimbabwe has valuable mineral reserves and minerals are important exports. Agriculture employs 85% of the people. Maize is the main food crop. Cash crops include cotton, sugar and tobacco. Cattle ranching is also important.

**AREA** 390,757 sq km [150,871 sq mi]
**POPULATION** 12,620,000 **CAPITAL** Harare
**GOVERNMENT** Multiparty republic **ETHNIC GROUPS** Shona 82%, Ndebele 14%, other African groups 2%, mixed and Asian 1%
**LANGUAGES** English (official), Shona, Ndebele
**RELIGIONS** Christianity, traditional beliefs
**CURRENCY** Zimbabwean new dollar = 100 cents [suspended in 2009]

# WORLD GEOGRAPHY

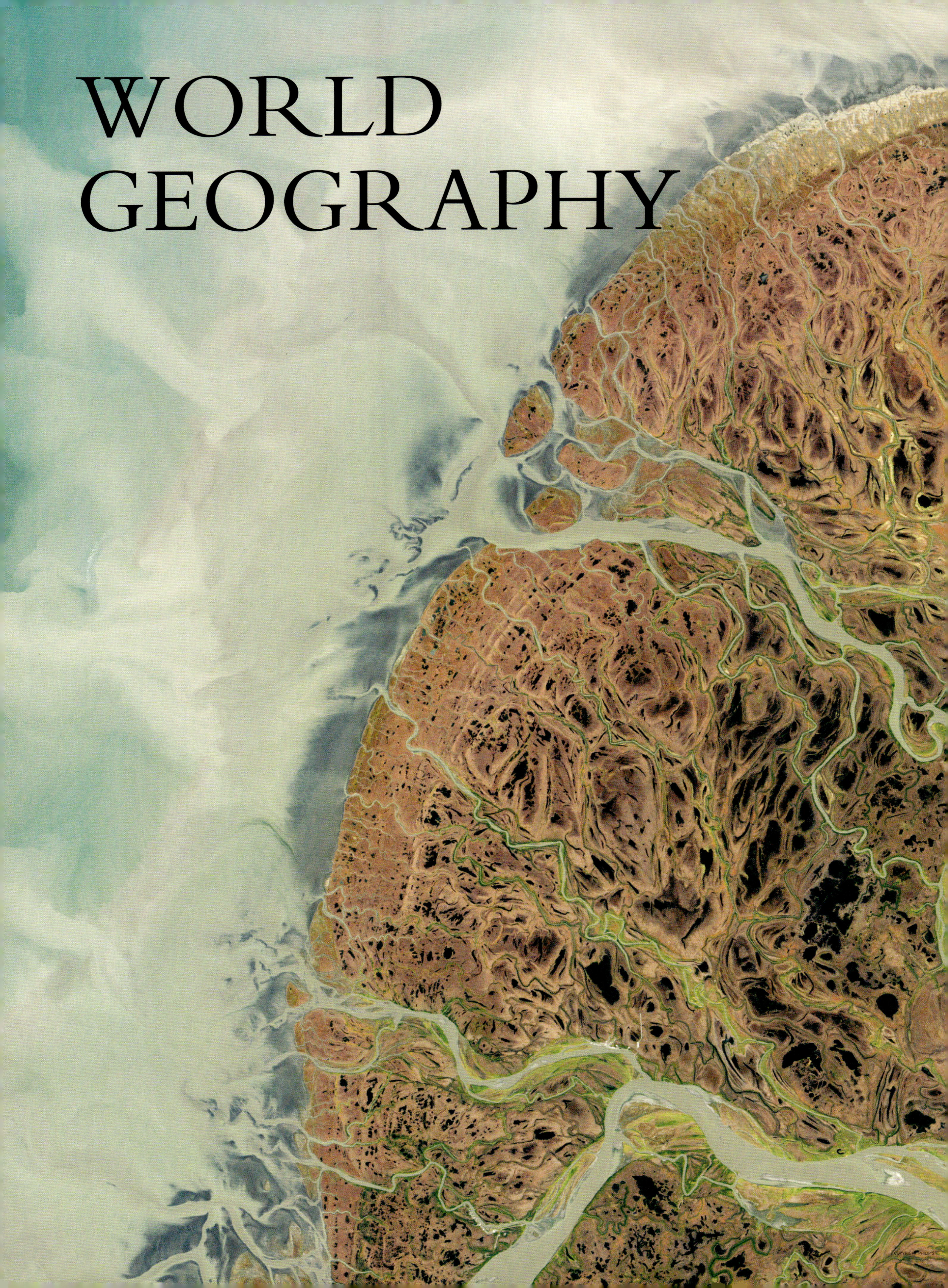

The Yukon River is the fifth longest river in the whole of North America, flowing 3,185 km (1,980 miles) from its source, the Llewellyn Glacier in British Columbia, Canada, to the delta in Alaska where it enters Norton Sound in the Bering Sea. By that stage in its course it has been joined by the Kuskokwim River, and the river meanders slowly over the low-lying coastal plain, dropping its heavy load of sediment and forming the cauliflower-like delta as it enters the sea. The land across which it flows is tundra and is frozen for most of the year, with only the top few centimetres thawing out in the short subarctic summer. [Map page 303]

**For more information:**
70 Orbits of the planets
Planetary data

About 13.7 billion years ago, time and space began with the most colossal explosion in cosmic history: the so-called Big Bang that is believed to have initiated the Universe. According to current theory, in the first millionth of a second of its existence it expanded from a dimensionless point of infinite mass and density into a fireball about the size of our present Solar System – and it has been expanding ever since.

It took about 300,000 years for the primal fireball to cool enough for atoms to form. They were mostly hydrogen which is still the most abundant material in the Universe. The radiation from this era still pervades the Universe, though its subsequent expansion means that we see it at about 3° above absolute zero instead of its original 3,000°C. Observations of this faint background glow reveal slight fluctuations. It is these which appear to have become, over the next billion years or so, the large-scale structures in the present Universe. As well as the matter which we can see, there is evidence of a much greater quantity of dark matter whose nature remains unknown. Within knots of this dark matter, the first stars and galaxies formed, probably within the first billion years of the life of the Universe. Our own Galaxy was among them.

There were several generations of stars, each feeding on the wreckage of its extinct predecessors as well as the original galactic gas swirls. With each new generation, progressively larger atoms were forged in stellar furnaces, and the Galaxy's range of elements, once restricted to hydrogen and helium, grew larger. About 9 billion years after the Big Bang, a star formed on the outskirts of our Galaxy with enough matter left over to create a retinue of planets. Nearly 5 billion years after that, human beings evolved.

The Sun is one of more than 100 billion stars in the Home Galaxy alone. Our Galaxy, in turn, forms part of a local group consisting of approximately 30 similar structures, mostly small 'dwarf' galaxies but a few large ones, and one – the Andromeda Galaxy – larger than our own. There are at least 100 billion galaxies in the Universe, many of which are members of huge galaxy clusters.

## LIFE OF A STAR

For most of its existence, a star produces energy by the nuclear fusion of hydrogen into helium at its core. The duration of this hydrogen-burning period – known as the *main sequence* – depends on the star's mass; the greater the mass, the higher the core temperatures and the sooner the star's supply of hydrogen is exhausted. Dim, dwarf stars consume their hydrogen slowly, eking it out over billions of years. The Sun, like other stars of its mass, should spend about 10 billion years on the main sequence; since it was formed less than 5 billion years ago, it still has half its life left.

Once all of a star's core hydrogen has been fused into helium, nuclear activity moves outwards into layers of unconsumed hydrogen. For a time, energy production sharply increases: the star grows hotter and expands enormously, turning into a so-called red giant. Its energy output will increase a thousandfold, and it will swell to a hundred times its former diameter.

After a few hundred million years, helium in the core will become sufficiently compressed to initiate a new cycle of nuclear fusion: from helium to carbon. The star will contract somewhat, before beginning its last expansion, in the Sun's case engulfing the Earth and perhaps Mars. In this bloated condition, the Sun's outer layers will break off into space, leaving a tiny inner core, mainly of carbon, that shrinks progressively under its own gravity. The white dwarf star thus formed can attain a density more than 10,000 times that of normal matter, with crushing surface gravity to match. Gradually, the nuclear fires will die down, and the Sun will reach its terminal stage: a black dwarf, emitting insignificant amounts of energy.

**Black holes**

However, stars more massive than the Sun may undergo a different transformation. The additional mass allows gravitational collapse to continue indefinitely: eventually, all the star's remaining matter shrinks to a point, and its density approaches infinity – a state that will not permit even subatomic structures to survive.

The star has become a *black hole*: an anomalous 'singularity' in the fabric of space and time. Although vast coruscations of radiation will be emitted by any matter falling into its grasp, the singularity itself has an escape velocity that exceeds the speed of light, and nothing can ever be released from it. Within the boundaries of the black hole, the laws of physics are suspended.

## GALACTIC STRUCTURES

Many of the Universe's 100 billion galaxies show clear structural patterns, originally classified by the American astronomer Edwin Hubble in 1925. Spiral galaxies like our own have a central, almost spherical bulge and a surrounding disk composed of spiral arms. Barred spirals have a central bar of stars across the nucleus, with spiral arms trailing from the ends of the bar. Elliptical galaxies have a more uniform appearance, ranging from a flattened disk to a near sphere.

▲ M51, the Whirlpool Nebula, comprises the large spiral galaxy NGC 5194 and its smaller, barred companion NGC 5195. M51 was the first astronomical object in which a spiral structure was identified, in 1845. Although smaller and less massive than our own Galaxy, M51 is much brighter, due to recent star formation.

Most galaxies, however, have no obvious structure at all. Galaxies also vary enormously in size, from dwarf galaxies only 2,000 light-years across to great assemblies of stars 80 or more times larger.

## THE HOME GALAXY

The Sun and its planets are located in one of the spiral arms of the Galaxy, about 26,000 light-years from the galactic centre and orbiting around it in a period of about 220 million years. The centre is invisible from the Earth, masked by vast, light-absorbing clouds of interstellar dust.

The Galaxy is probably around 12 billion years old and, like other spiral galaxies, has three distinct regions. The central bulge is about 30,000 light-years in diameter. The disk in which the Sun is located is not much more than 1,000 light-years thick, but approximately 100,000 light-years from end to end. Around the Galaxy is the halo, a spherical zone 300,000 light-years across, studded with globular star clusters and sprinkled with individual suns.

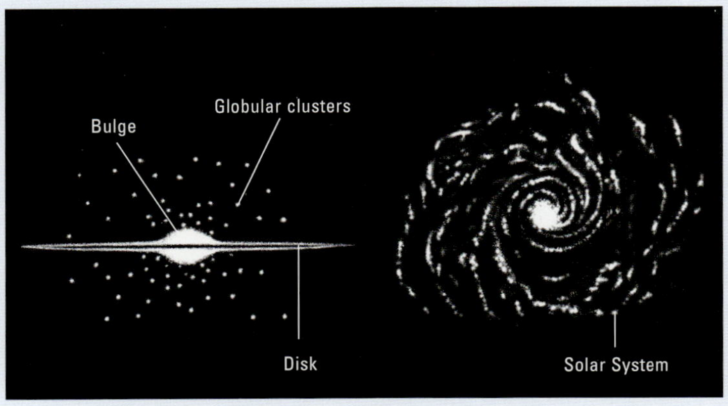
Globular clusters
Bulge
Disk
Solar System

## THE END OF THE UNIVERSE

The likely fate of the Universe is disputed. According to one theory (*top of diagram, below*), the expansion begun at the time of the Big Bang will continue 'indefinitely', with ageing galaxies moving further and further apart in an immense, dark graveyard.

Alternatively, gravity may overcome the expansion (*bottom of diagram*). Galaxies will fall back together until everything is again concentrated at a single point, followed by a new Big Bang and a new expansion, in an endlessly repeated cycle.

The first theory is supported by the amount of visible matter in the Universe; the second theory assumes that there is enough dark material in the Universe to bring about the gravitational collapse.

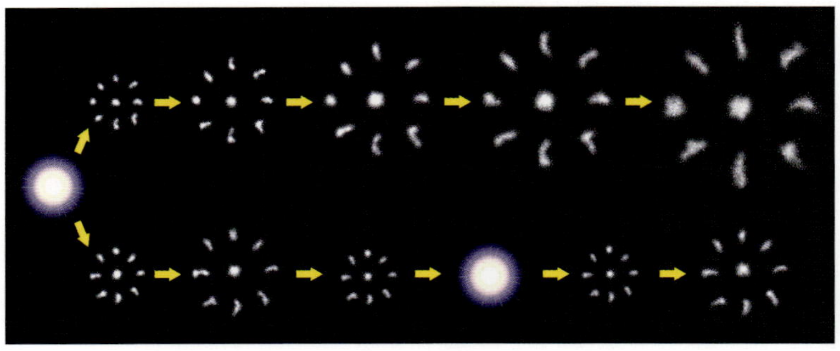

## THE NEAREST STARS

**The 22 nearest stars, excluding the Sun, with their distance from Earth in light-years***

| | | | | | |
|---|---|---|---|---|---|
| Proxima Centauri | 4.2 | UV Ceti A | 8.7 | 61 Cygni A | 11.4 |
| Alpha Centauri A | 4.4 | UV Ceti B | 8.7 | Procyon A | 11.4 |
| Alpha Centauri B | 4.4 | Ross 154 | 9.7 | Procyon B | 11.4 |
| Barnard's Star | 5.9 | Ross 248 | 10.3 | 61 Cygni B | 11.4 |
| Wolf 359 | 7.8 | Epsilon Eridani | 10.5 | HD 173740 | 11.5 |
| Lalande 21185 | 8.3 | HD 217987 | 10.7 | HD 173739 | 11.7 |
| Sirius A | 8.6 | Ross 128 | 10.9 | | |
| Sirius B | 8.6 | L789-6 | 11.2 | | |

* A light-year is about 9,500 billion km [5,900 billion miles]

Many of the nearest stars, like Alpha Centauri A and B, are double stars, orbiting about their common centre of gravity and to all intents and purposes equidistant from Earth. Many of them are dim objects, with no name other than the designation given to them by the astronomers who first investigated them.

However, they include Sirius, the brightest star in the sky, and Procyon, the seventh brightest. Both are larger than the Sun; of the nearest stars, only Epsilon Eridani is similar in size and luminosity. Most of the other bright stars in the sky are within 500 light-years of the Sun – a small fraction of the diameter of our Galaxy.

## STAR CHARTS

### NORTHERN HEMISPHERE SKY

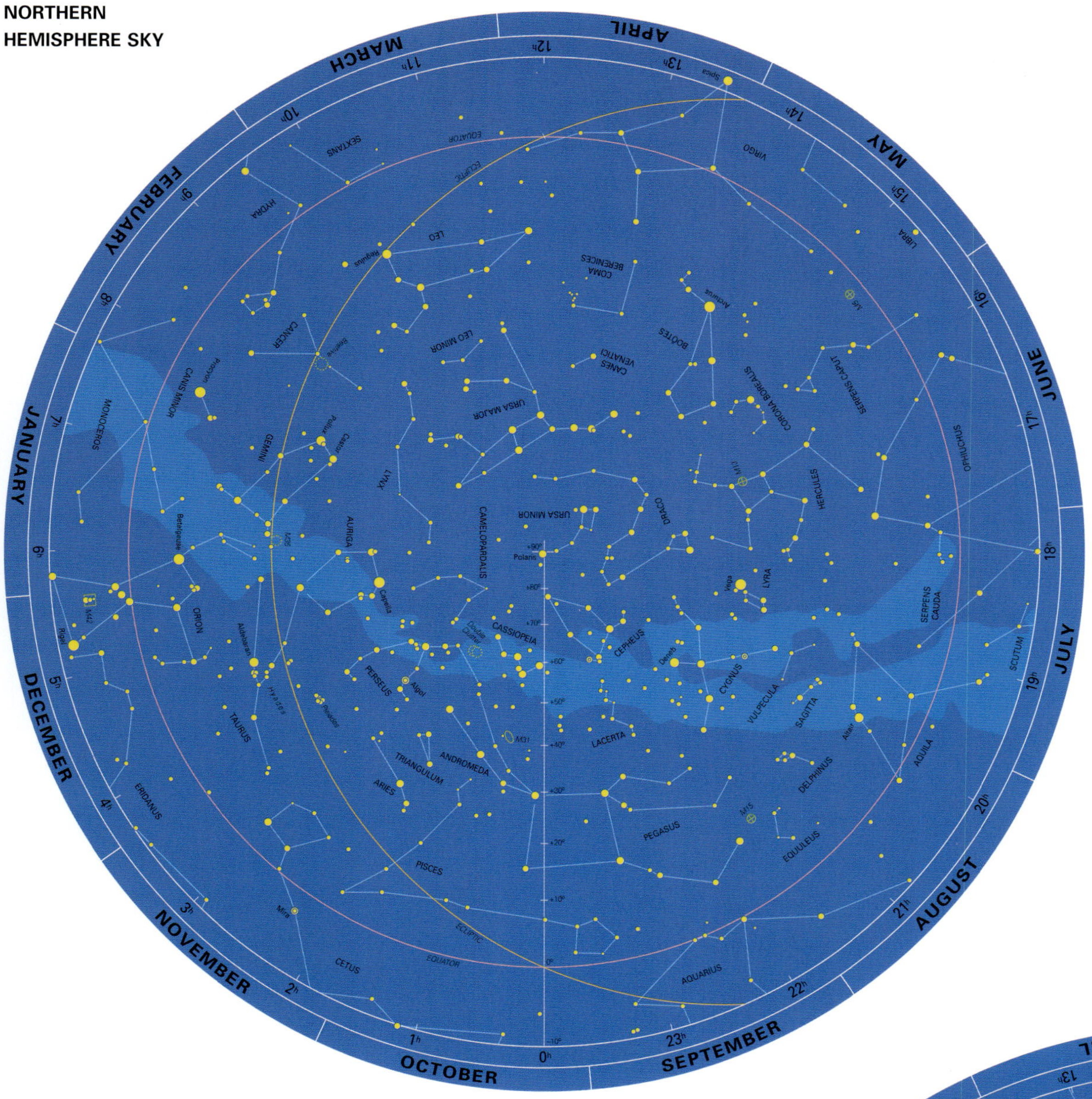
MARCH
APRIL
MAY
JUNE
JULY
AUGUST
SEPTEMBER
OCTOBER
NOVEMBER
DECEMBER
JANUARY
FEBRUARY
URSA MINOR
URSA MAJOR
CASSIOPEIA
CYGNUS
PEGASUS
ANDROMEDA

### THE CONSTELLATIONS

**The constellations and their English names**

| | | | |
|---|---|---|---|
| Andromeda | Andromeda | Lacerta | Lizard |
| Antlia | Air Pump | Leo | Lion |
| Apus | Bird of Paradise | Leo Minor | Little Lion |
| Aquarius | Water Carrier | Lepus | Hare |
| Aquila | Eagle | Libra | Scales |
| Ara | Altar | Lupus | Wolf |
| Aries | Ram | Lynx | Lynx |
| Auriga | Charioteer | Lyra | Lyre |
| Boötes | Herdsman | Mensa | Table Mountain |
| Caelum | Chisel | Microscopium | Microscope |
| Camelopardalis | Giraffe | Monoceros | Unicorn |
| Cancer | Crab | Musca | Fly |
| Canes Venatici | Hunting Dogs | Norma | Level |
| Canis Major | Great Dog | Octans | Octant |
| Canis Minor | Little Dog | Ophiuchus | Serpent Bearer |
| Capricornus | Sea Goat | Orion | Orion |
| Carina | Ship's Keel | Pavo | Peacock |
| Cassiopeia | Cassiopeia | Pegasus | Winged Horse |
| Centaurus | Centaur | Perseus | Perseus |
| Cepheus | Cepheus | Phoenix | Phoenix |
| Cetus | Whale | Pictor | Easel |
| Chamaeleon | Chameleon | Pisces | Fishes |
| Circinus | Compasses | Piscis Austrinus | Southern Fish |
| Columba | Dove | Puppis | Ship's Stern |
| Coma Berenices | Berenice's Hair | Pyxis | Mariner's Compass |
| Corona Australis | Southern Crown | Reticulum | Net |
| Corona Borealis | Northern Crown | Sagitta | Arrow |
| Corvus | Crow | Sagittarius | Archer |
| Crater | Cup | Scorpius | Scorpion |
| Crux | Southern Cross | Sculptor | Sculptor |
| Cygnus | Swan | Scutum | Shield |
| Delphinus | Dolphin | Serpens | Serpent |
| Dorado | Swordfish | Sextans | Sextant |
| Draco | Dragon | Taurus | Bull |
| Equuleus | Little Horse | Telescopium | Telescope |
| Eridanus | River Eridanus | Triangulum | Triangle |
| Fornax | Furnace | Triangulum Australe | Southern Triangle |
| Gemini | Twins | Tucana | Toucan |
| Grus | Crane | Ursa Major | Great Bear |
| Hercules | Hercules | Ursa Minor | Little Bear |
| Horologium | Clock | Vela | Ship's Sails |
| Hydra | Water Snake | Virgo | Virgin |
| Hydrus | Sea Serpent | Volans | Flying Fish |
| Indus | Indian | Vulpecula | Fox |

### SOUTHERN HEMISPHERE SKY

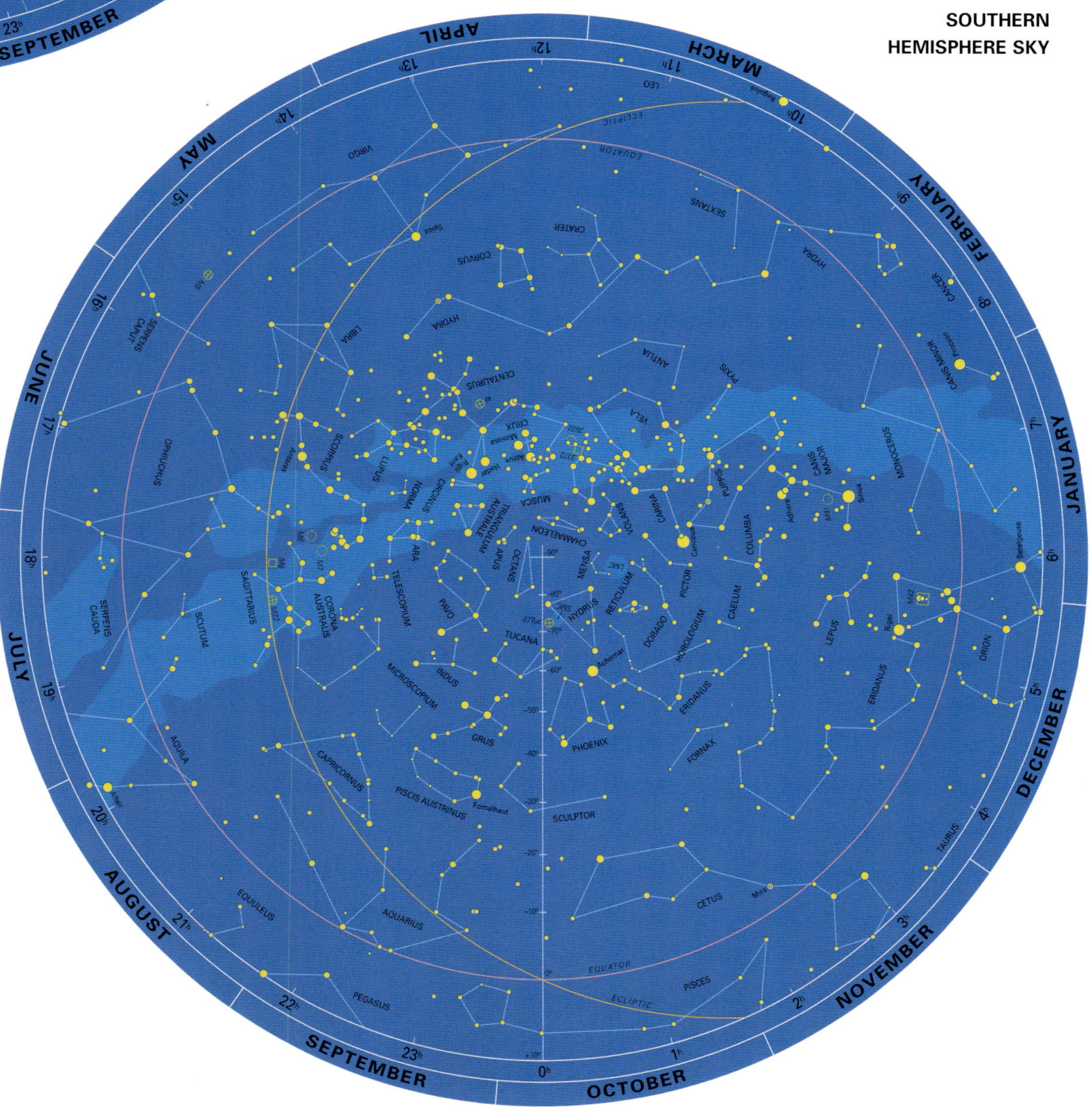
APRIL
MARCH
FEBRUARY
JANUARY
DECEMBER
NOVEMBER
OCTOBER
SEPTEMBER
AUGUST
JULY
JUNE
MAY

The charts on this page show the entire heavens divided into northern and southern hemispheres, with 10° of overlap between them around the perimeter of each one. However, the view from any particular location on Earth will be different, and will change both hourly as the Earth turns, and throughout the year as the Earth goes around the Sun.

The Sun's annual path through the heavens is known as the 'ecliptic', and is shown here by an orange line. When the Sun is in the sky its light drowns out our view of the stars, so only that part of the heavens opposite the Sun is visible at a particular time. The sky's equivalent of longitude is known as 'right ascension'. As the stars appear to rotate around the Earth once every 24 hours, right ascension is measured eastwards in hours and minutes, and is marked around the edge of the maps. The equivalent of latitude is 'declination', measured in degrees north or south of the celestial equator, and shown by the vertical line on each chart.

**Using the charts**

At any place and time you can see half of the whole sky, assuming a flat horizon. If you were at one of the poles your view would be shown as a circle centred on the middle of the map for the appropriate hemisphere, with the horizon marked by the celestial equator. From all other locations the centre of your view (your overhead point) will be at some other point on the map whose location changes with time. The closer you are to Earth's equator, the closer the centre will be to the edge of the map and more stars in the opposite hemisphere will be visible.

So first choose the appropriate chart for your hemisphere and hold it with the month at the bottom. At 11 p.m., not allowing for Daylight Saving Time (Summer Time), your overhead point will be at the same declination as your geographical latitude and stars lower on the map will be due south (or north in the southern hemisphere). From latitude 50° in mid August, for example, your overhead point will be close to the star Deneb in the constellation of Cygnus. Stars on the opposite side of the map will be below your northern horizon, while stars below Deneb will be due south.

### STAR MAGNITUDES

**Apparent visual magnitudes**

The magnitude scale of star brightnesses is developed from the system used by the Ancient Greeks in which the brightest stars were first magnitude and the faintest visible to the naked eye were sixth. Today the scale has a mathematical basis and extends, at the brightest end, through to negative magnitudes.

The Milky Way is shown in light blue on these charts.

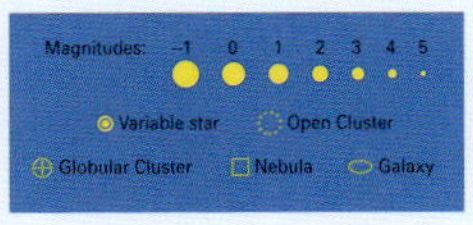
Magnitudes: -1 0 1 2 3 4 5
Variable star
Open Cluster
Globular Cluster
Nebula
Galaxy

**For more information:**
68 The Home Galaxy
72 The seasons
Day and night
73 The Moon

Lying about halfway from the centre of one of billions of galaxies that populate the observable Universe, our Solar System contains eight planets and their moons, five dwarf planets, innumerable asteroids, comets and other icy bodies, and a miscellany of dust and gas, all tethered by the immense gravitational field of the Sun, the star whose thermonuclear furnaces provide them all with heat and light.

The Solar System was formed about 5 billion years ago, when a spinning cloud of gas, mostly hydrogen but seeded with other heavier elements, condensed enough to ignite a nuclear reaction and create a star. The Sun still accounts for almost 99.9% of the system's total mass.

By composition as well as distance, the planetary array divides quite neatly in two: an inner system of four small, solid planets, including the Earth, and an outer system, from Jupiter to Neptune, of four much larger planets composed of lighter materials, such as gas, liquid and ice. Lying mostly between the two groups is a scattering of rocky asteroids, numbering perhaps a million or more. They may be debris left over from the formation of the inner Solar System. In 2006, Pluto was demoted from its former status as a planet and is now regarded as a member of the Kuiper Belt of icy bodies at the fringes of the Solar System.

Much of the early history of science is the story of people trying to make sense of the wandering points of light that were all they knew of the planets. Now, men have stood on the Earth's Moon, space probes have landed on Mars and Venus, and distant landscapes have been mapped with astonishing accuracy, transforming our knowledge of our celestial environment.

In the 1980s, the Voyager space probes skimmed all four major planets of the outer Solar System, bringing new revelations with each close approach. The Magellan (Venus), Galileo (Jupiter) and Cassini–Huygens (Saturn) missions have transformed our knowledge of those planets and the giants' moons, and a host of orbiters and landers have shown us Mars in a new light. A spacecraft is also on its way to visit Pluto.

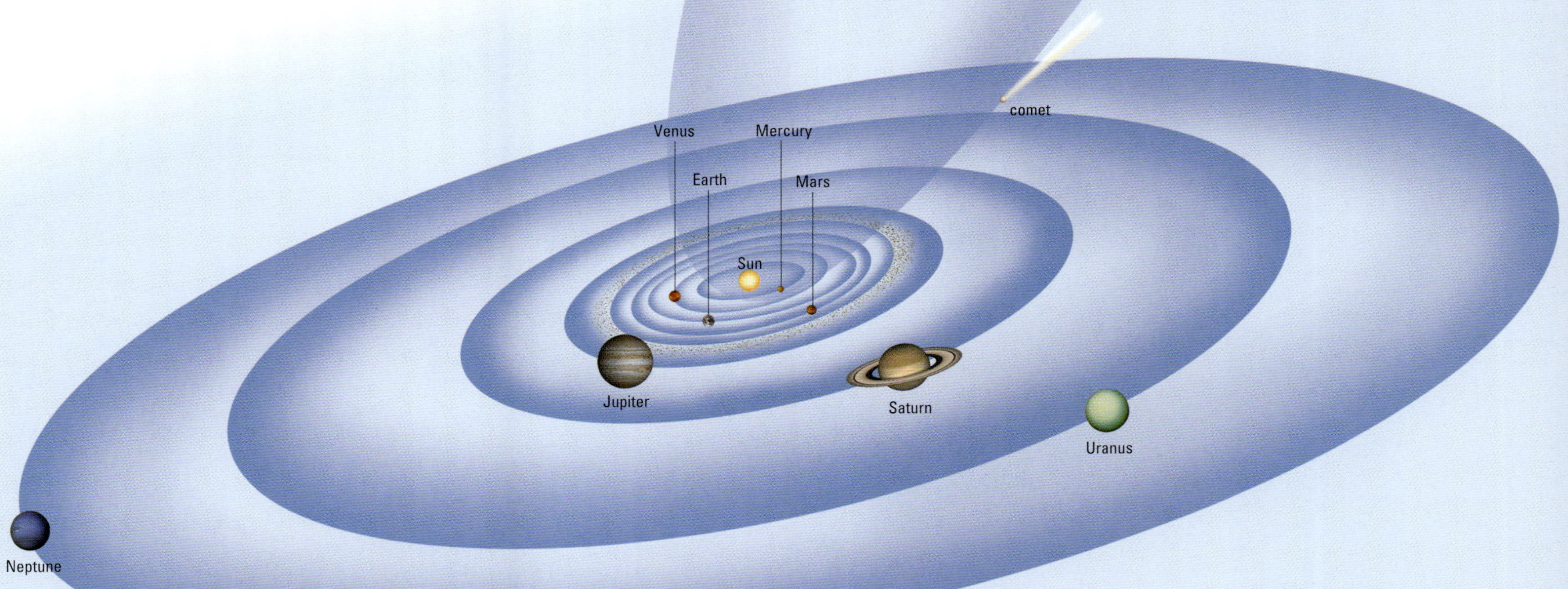
comet
Venus
Mercury
Earth
Mars
Sun
Jupiter
Saturn
Uranus
Neptune

*Diagram not drawn to scale*

## ORBITS OF THE PLANETS

The diagram above shows the Solar System as it might appear to an observer a few light-hours away in the direction of the constellation Hercules. Seen from such a position, above the plane of the ecliptic, all the planets revolve about the Sun in an anticlockwise direction. The perspective view exaggerates the elliptical form of all the planetary orbits: only Mercury follows a path that deviates noticeably from circularity.

The diagram also shows the main swarm of asteroids between Mars and Jupiter, and the orbit of a comet. Comets reside in a vast spherical halo beyond the Solar System, and are occasionally diverted towards the Sun on highly elliptical orbits which may take many thousands of years to complete. Most, therefore, still await discovery, though there are a number of shorter-period comets which return regularly, such as Halley's Comet.

## PLANETARY DATA

| | Mean distance from Sun (million km) | Mass (Earth = 1) | Period of orbit (Earth days/years) | Period of rotation (Earth days) | Equatorial diameter (km) | Average density (water = 1) | Surface gravity (Earth = 1) | Number of known satellites* |
|---|---|---|---|---|---|---|---|---|
| *Sun* | *–* | *332,946* | *–* | *25.38* | *1,392,000* | *1.41* | *27.9* | *–* |
| **Mercury** | 57.9 | 0.06 | 87.97d | 58.65 | 4,879 | 5.43 | 0.38 | 0 |
| **Venus** | 108.2 | 0.82 | 224.7d | 243.02 | 12,104 | 5.24 | 0.91 | 0 |
| **Earth** | 149.6 | 1.00 | 365.3d | 1.00 | 12,756 | 5.52 | 1.00 | 1 |
| **Mars** | 227.9 | 0.11 | 687.0d | 1.029 | 6,792 | 3.94 | 0.38 | 2 |
| **Jupiter** | 483.7 | 317.8 | 11.86y | 0.411 | 142,984 | 1.33 | 2.36 | 67 |
| **Saturn** | 778 | 95.2 | 29.45y | 0.428 | 120,536 | 0.69 | 0.91 | 62 |
| **Uranus** | 2,871 | 14.5 | 84.02y | 0.720 | 51,118 | 1.27 | 0.89 | 27 |
| **Neptune** | 4,498 | 17.2 | 164.8y | 0.673 | 49,528 | 1.64 | 1.13 | 13 |

Planetary days are given in sidereal days – that is, with respect to the stars rather than the Sun. The difference is caused by the movement of the planet in its orbit, so the interval between successive noons is slightly different from that between the rising of a particular star. The Earth's own sidereal day is 23h 56m in solar time. The equatorial diameters of most planets differ from their polar diameters as a consequence of their rotation, which is most marked in the case of Jupiter and Saturn, which are very noticeably flattened at the poles. Strictly speaking, the figures for surface gravity apply to the four inner planets only, as the outer planets have no solid surfaces. In their case, the figure is given for an arbitrary point in the atmosphere where the pressure is 1 bar.

** Number of known satellites at mid-2013*

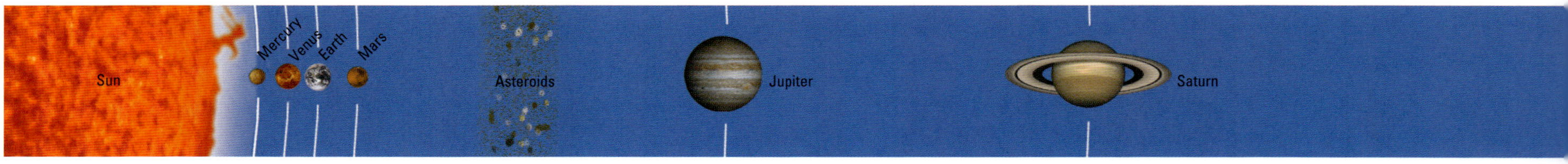
Sun
Mercury
Venus
Earth
Mars
Asteroids
Jupiter
Saturn

## THE PLANETS

**Mercury** is the closest planet to the Sun and hence the fastest-moving. It is very hot, with a cratered, wrinkled surface very similar to that of Earth's Moon. It is small and has low gravity, so there is no significant atmosphere.

**Venus** has much the same physical dimensions as Earth. Its dense atmosphere is composed of 97% carbon dioxide resulting in a runaway greenhouse effect that makes the surface, at 477°C, the hottest of all the planets in the Solar System. Radar mapping revealed a terrain consisting of highland regions and vast, rolling plains crossed by volcanic flows and dotted with craters. Discharges from volcanic regions could explain the sulphuric-acid rain detected by spacecraft. Soft-landers last less than an hour in Venus's fierce climate.

**Earth** seen from space is easily the most beautiful of the inner planets; it is also, and more objectively, the largest, as well as the only known home of life. Living things are the main reason why the Earth is able to retain a substantial proportion of reactive oxygen in its atmosphere; the oxygen in turn supports the life that constantly regenerates it. The Earth's natural satellite, the Moon, is believed to have been created when an asteroid struck our planet in its infancy.

**Mars**, smaller and cooler than the Earth, is nevertheless the most likely planet other than Earth where life may have formed. The planet was until recently (in astronomical terms) a geologically active world with water on its surface: rivers, lakes, and even an ocean. Liquid water may well exist today, but trapped beneath its dusty, boulder-strewn surface. The Martian landscape features huge extinct volcanoes, a giant canyon system, craters, and sand dunes. Its thin atmosphere is mostly carbon dioxide, and its polar caps are of frozen carbon dioxide and water ice. It has two tiny moons, probably captured asteroids.

**Jupiter** has about three times the mass of all the other planets combined. The planet is mostly gas, under intense pressure in the lower atmosphere above a core of fiercely compressed hydrogen and helium. The upper layers form strikingly coloured rotating belts, the outward sign of the intense storms created by Jupiter's rapid rotation. The Great Red Spot is a storm feature that has persisted for at least 170 years. Jupiter has at least 67 moons. Most are very small, but the four largest – Io, Europa, Ganymede and Callisto – are fascinating worlds in their own right. Io is the most volcanically active world known, and Europa possesses an ocean deep below its icy surface. The planet also has a system of rings, though nowhere near as prominent as Saturn's.

**Saturn** is structurally similar to Jupiter, rotating fast enough to produce an obvious bulge at its equator. It is composed of 89% hydrogen and 11% helium, and has wind velocities in the outer atmosphere of 500 m/sec. Ever since the invention of the telescope, Saturn's rings have been the feature that has most attracted observers. The rings consist of thousands of individual ringlets, composed of icy particles ranging in size from 10 metres down to microscopic. Titan, the largest of Saturn's 62 known moons, has a dense atmosphere.

**Uranus** was unknown to the ancients. Although it is faintly visible to the naked eye, it was not established as a planet until 1781. In its interior is probably a rocky core surrounded by frozen methane, water, and ammonia; the atmosphere is of hydrogen, helium, and some methane, which gives the planet its greenish-blue colour. There is a system of thin, dark rings and a retinue of 27 moons, all but five of which are small.

**Neptune** is always more than 4,000 billion km from Earth, and despite its diameter of over 49,000 km, it can only be seen by telescope. Its discovery in 1846 was the result of mathematical predictions by astronomers seeking to explain irregularities in the orbit of Uranus. Like Uranus, it has a ring system; recent observations have revealed a total of 13 moons.

In 2006, following an increasing number of discoveries of objects orbiting the Sun of similar size to Pluto but at a greater distance, the International Astronomical Union issued for the first time a definition of a planet. A planet is defined as 'a body orbiting the Sun, which is essentially round as a consequence of its gravity, and which does not share its orbital neighbourhood with similar bodies'. On this definition, Pluto is no longer classified as a planet, but is instead a member of a new category of 'dwarf planet', which relaxes the last criterion but excludes bodies in orbit around another one.

Mean distance from the Sun in millions of kilometres
Mercury
57.9 Mercury
Venus
108.2 Venus
Earth
149.6 Earth
Mars
227.9 Mars
Jupiter
778 Jupiter
Saturn
1,427 Saturn
Uranus
2,871 Uranus
Neptune
4,498 Neptune
Diagrams not drawn to scale

Uranus
Neptune

**For more information:**


11 Ocean currents

70 Orbits of the planets

76 Circulation of the air

78 Climate


The basic units of time measurement are the day and the year. The day is one rotation of the Earth on its axis. Our present calendar is based on the solar year of 365.24 days, the time taken by the Earth to orbit the Sun. Calendars based on the movements of the Sun and Moon have been used since ancient times. The length of the year, reckoned by the Julian Calendar introduced by Julius Caesar, was about 11 minutes too long. The cumulative error was rectified in 1582 by the Gregorian Calendar, when Pope Gregory XIII decreed that the day following 4 October was 15 October, and that century years did not count as leap years unless they were divisible by 400. England finally adopted the reformed calendar in 1752, when it was 11 days behind the European mainland.

The rotation of the Earth on its axis causes day and night. The Earth rotates through 360° every 24 hours, and the world is divided into 24 time zones centred on lines of longitude at 15° intervals.

The tilt of the Earth's axis, which is also called the 'obliquity of the ecliptic', accounts for the seasons which are so familiar in the middle latitudes. However, geological evidence shows that, over long periods of time, climates change, and the advances and retreats of the ice during the Pleistocene Ice Age may have been caused by regular variations in the Earth's tilt, its orbit around the Sun, and changes in the season when it is closest to the Sun (perihelion).

## THE SEASONS

Seasons occur because the Earth's axis is tilted at an angle of approximately 23½°. When the northern hemisphere is tilted to a maximum extent towards the Sun, on 21 June, the Sun is overhead at the Tropic of Cancer (latitude 23½° North). This is midsummer, or the summer solstice, in the northern hemisphere.

On 22 or 23 September, the Sun is overhead at the equator, and day and night are of equal length throughout the world. This is the autumnal equinox in the northern hemisphere.

On 21 or 22 December, the Sun is overhead at the Tropic of Capricorn (23½° South), the winter solstice in the northern hemisphere. The overhead Sun then tracks north until, on 21 March, it is overhead at the equator. This is the spring (vernal) equinox in the northern hemisphere.

In the southern hemisphere, the seasons are the reverse of those in the north.

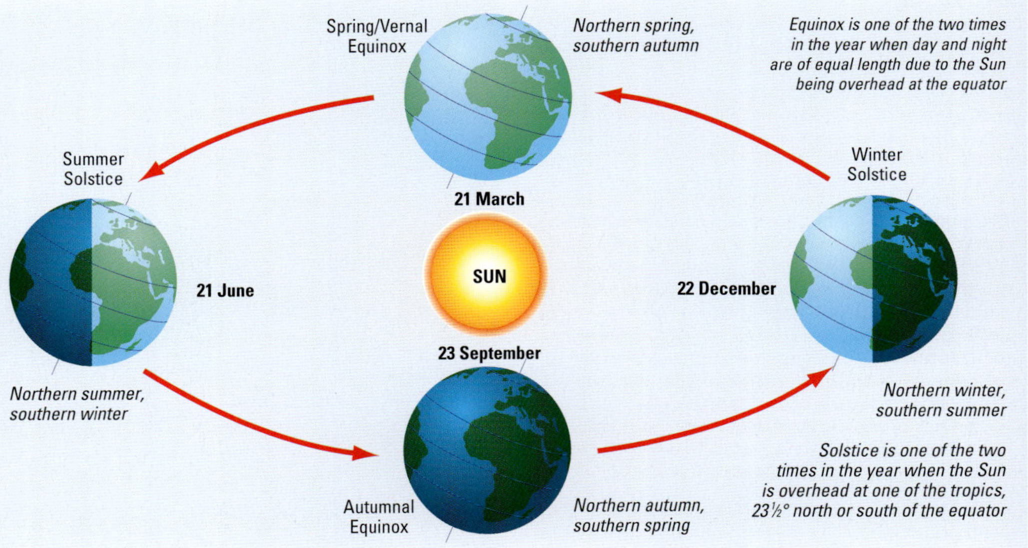

Spring/Vernal Equinox
Northern spring, southern autumn
Equinox is one of the two times in the year when day and night are of equal length due to the Sun being overhead at the equator
Summer Solstice
21 March
Winter Solstice
21 June
SUN
22 December
23 September
Northern summer, southern winter
Northern winter, southern summer
Solstice is one of the two times in the year when the Sun is overhead at one of the tropics, 23½° north or south of the equator
Autumnal Equinox
Northern autumn, southern spring


## DAY AND NIGHT

The Sun appears to rise in the east, reach its highest point at noon, and then set in the west, to be followed by night. In reality, it is not the Sun that is moving but the Earth rotating from west to east. The moment when the Sun's upper limb first appears above the horizon is termed sunrise; the moment when the Sun's upper limb disappears below the horizon is sunset.

At the summer solstice in the northern hemisphere (21 June), the Arctic has total daylight and the Antarctic total darkness. The opposite occurs at the winter solstice (21 or 22 December). At the equator, the length of day and night are almost equal all year.

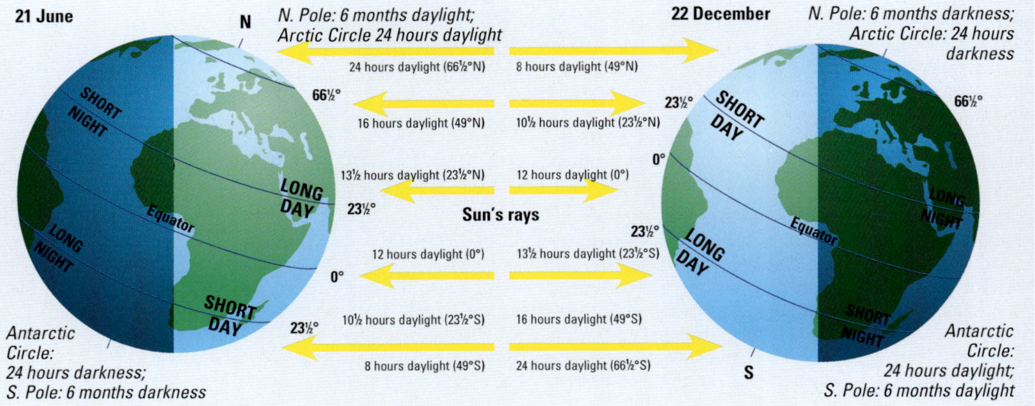

21 June
N
N. Pole: 6 months daylight; Arctic Circle 24 hours daylight
22 December
N. Pole: 6 months darkness; Arctic Circle: 24 hours darkness
SHORT NIGHT
LONG DAY
LONG NIGHT
SHORT DAY
Equator
24 hours daylight (66½°N)
8 hours daylight (49°N)
16 hours daylight (49°N)
10½ hours daylight (23½°N)
13½ hours daylight (23½°N)
12 hours daylight (0°)
Sun's rays
12 hours daylight (0°)
13½ hours daylight (23½°S)
10½ hours daylight (23½°S)
16 hours daylight (49°S)
8 hours daylight (49°S)
24 hours daylight (66½°S)
66½°
23½°
0°
S
Antarctic Circle: 24 hours darkness; S. Pole: 6 months darkness
Antarctic Circle: 24 hours daylight; S. Pole: 6 months daylight


## EARTH DATA

| | | | | | |
|---|---|---|---|---|---|
| **Aphelion (maximum distance from Sun):** | 152,096,150 km | **Length of year:** | 365 days, 5 hours, 48 minutes, 46 seconds of mean solar time | **Polar circumference:** | 40,008 km |
| **Perihelion (minimum distance from Sun):** | 147,099,590 km | **Superficial area:** | 510,000,000 sq km | **Equatorial diameter:** | 12,756 km |
| **Angle of tilt (obliquity of the ecliptic):** | 23° 27′ 08″ | **Land surface:** | 149,000,000 sq km (29.2%) | **Polar diameter:** | 12,714 km |
| **Length of year – solar tropical (equinox to equinox):** | 365.24 days | **Water surface:** | 361,000,000 sq km (70.8%) | **Equatorial radius:** | 6,378 km |
| | | **Equatorial circumference:** | 40,074 km | **Polar radius:** | 6,357 km |
| | | | | **Volume of the Earth:** | 1,083,230 × $10^6$ cu km |
| | | | | **Mass of the Earth:** | 5.97 × $10^{24}$ kg |

## SUNRISE AND SUNSET

The term 'equinox' comes from the Latin for 'equal night'. At the spring and autumnal equinoxes, the Sun is vertically overhead at midday at the equator and all places on Earth have 12 hours of darkness and 12 hours of daylight. The graphs of sunrise and sunset show that these occasions occur on 21 March and on 22 or 23 September. The graphs also show that, because the Sun remains high in the sky at the equator throughout the year, the length of day and night there remains roughly the same throughout the year, with sunrise around 6 a.m. and sunset around 6 p.m.

The further north or south one travels, the greater the difference between the number of hours of daylight and darkness. For example, the graph (*right*) shows that at latitude 60°N sunrise varies from just after 9 a.m. in midwinter (on 22 or 23 December) to about 2.30 a.m. in midsummer (around the summer solstice on 21 June). By contrast, the second graph (*far right*) shows that sunset at latitude 60°N occurs at about 2.45 p.m. in midwinter and 9.20 p.m. in midsummer.

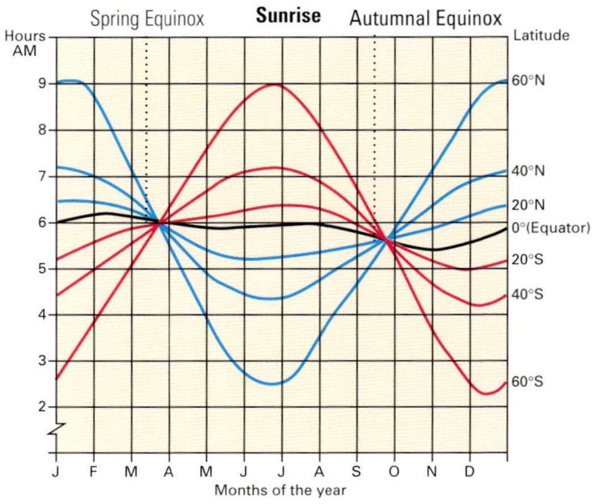

Spring Equinox
Sunrise
Autumnal Equinox
Hours AM
Latitude
9
8
7
6
5
4
3
2
60°N
40°N
20°N
0°(Equator)
20°S
40°S
60°S
J F M A M J J A S O N D
Months of the year


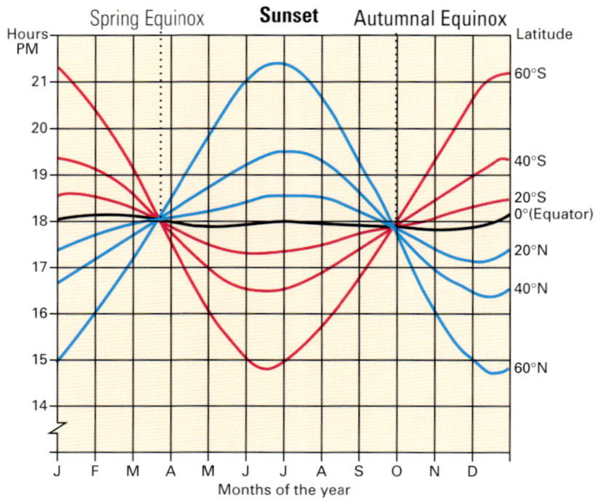

Spring Equinox
Sunset
Autumnal Equinox
Hours PM
Latitude
21
20
19
18
17
16
15
14
60°S
40°S
20°S
0°(Equator)
20°N
40°N
60°N
J F M A M J J A S O N D
Months of the year

## THE MOON

The Moon rotates more slowly than the Earth, taking just over 27 days to make one complete rotation on its axis. This corresponds to the Moon's orbital period around the Earth, and therefore the Moon always presents the same hemisphere towards us; some 41% of the Moon's far side is never visible from the Earth. The interval between one New Moon and the next is 29½ days – this is called a lunation, or lunar month. The Moon shines only by reflected sunlight, and emits no light of its own. During each lunation the Moon displays a complete cycle of phases, caused by the changing angle of illumination from the Sun.

## PHASES OF THE MOON

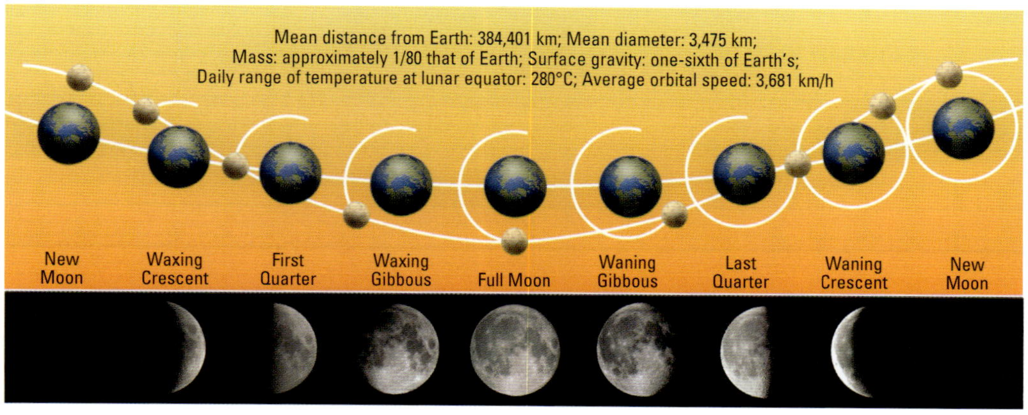
Mean distance from Earth: 384,401 km; Mean diameter: 3,475 km;
Mass: approximately 1/80 that of Earth; Surface gravity: one-sixth of Earth's;
Daily range of temperature at lunar equator: 280°C; Average orbital speed: 3,681 km/h
New Moon
Waxing Crescent
First Quarter
Waxing Gibbous
Full Moon
Waning Gibbous
Last Quarter
Waning Crescent
New Moon

## MOON DATA

**Distance from Earth**
The Moon orbits at a mean distance of 384,401 km, at an average speed of 3,681 km/h in relation to the Earth.

**Size and mass**
The average diameter of the Moon is 3,475 km. It is 400 times smaller than the Sun but is about 400 times closer to the Earth, so we see them as the same size. The Moon has a mass of $7.35 \times 10^{22}$ kg, with a density 3.344 times that of water.

**Visibility**
Only 59% of the Moon's surface is visible from the Earth over time. Sunlight reflected from the Moon takes 1.3 seconds to reach the Earth (the Sun itself is around 8½ light-minutes away).

**Temperature**
With the Sun overhead, the temperature on the lunar equator can reach 117°C [243°F]. At night it can sink to −163°C [−261°F].

## ECLIPSES

When the Moon passes between the Sun and the Earth, the Sun becomes partially eclipsed (1). A partial eclipse becomes a total eclipse if the Moon proceeds to cover the Sun completely (2) and the dark central part of the lunar shadow touches the Earth. The broad geographical zone covered by the Moon's outer shadow (P) has only a very small central area (often less than 100 km wide) that experiences totality. Totality can never last for more than 7½ minutes at maximum, but is usually much briefer than this. Lunar eclipses take place when the Moon moves through the shadow of the Earth, and can be partial or total. Any single location on Earth can experience a maximum of four solar and three lunar eclipses in any single year, while a total solar eclipse occurs an average of once every 360 years for any given location.

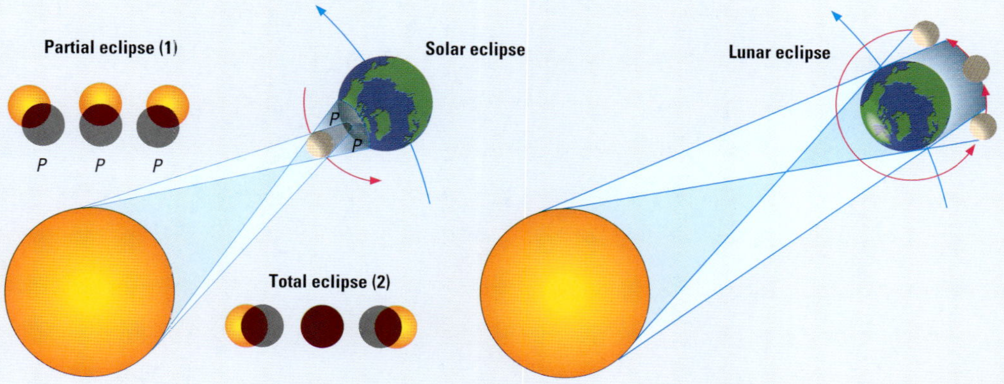
Partial eclipse (1)
P
P
P
Solar eclipse
P
P
Lunar eclipse
Total eclipse (2)

## TIDES

The daily rise and fall of the ocean's tides are the result of the gravitational pull of the Moon and that of the Sun, though the effect of the latter is not as strong as that of the Moon. This effect is greatest on the hemisphere facing the Moon and causes a tidal 'bulge'. Spring tides occur when the Sun, Earth and Moon are aligned; high tides are at their highest, and low tides fall to their lowest. When the Moon and Sun are furthest out of line (near the Moon's First and Last Quarters), neap tides occur, producing the smallest range between high and low tides.

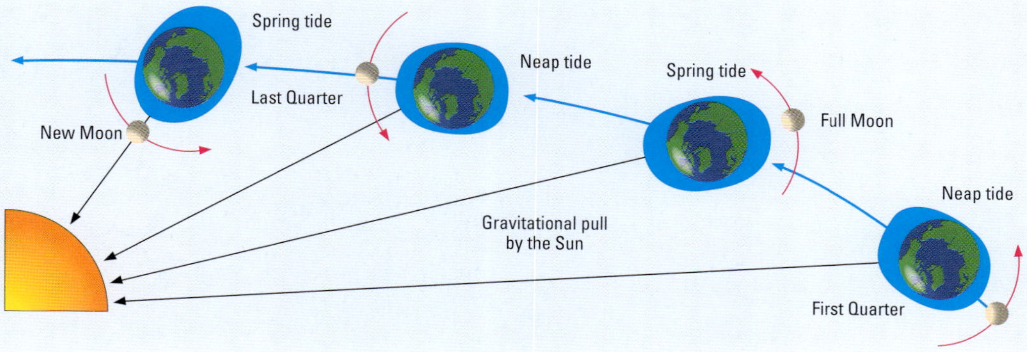
Spring tide
Last Quarter
New Moon
Neap tide
Spring tide
Full Moon
Neap tide
Gravitational pull by the Sun
First Quarter

## TIME ZONES

The Earth rotates through 360° in 24 hours, and so moves 15° every hour. The world is divided into 24 standard time zones, each centred on lines of longitude at 15° intervals. At the centre of the first zone is the prime meridian, or Greenwich meridian. All places to the west of Greenwich are one hour behind for every 15° of longitude; places to the east are ahead by one hour for every 15°.

**International Date Line**
When it is 12 noon on the Greenwich meridian, 180° east it is midnight of the same day – while 180° west the day is just beginning. To overcome this, the International Date Line was established, approximately following the 180° meridian. Thus, if you were to travel eastwards from Japan (140°E) to Hawai'i (160°W), you would pass from Sunday night into Sunday morning.

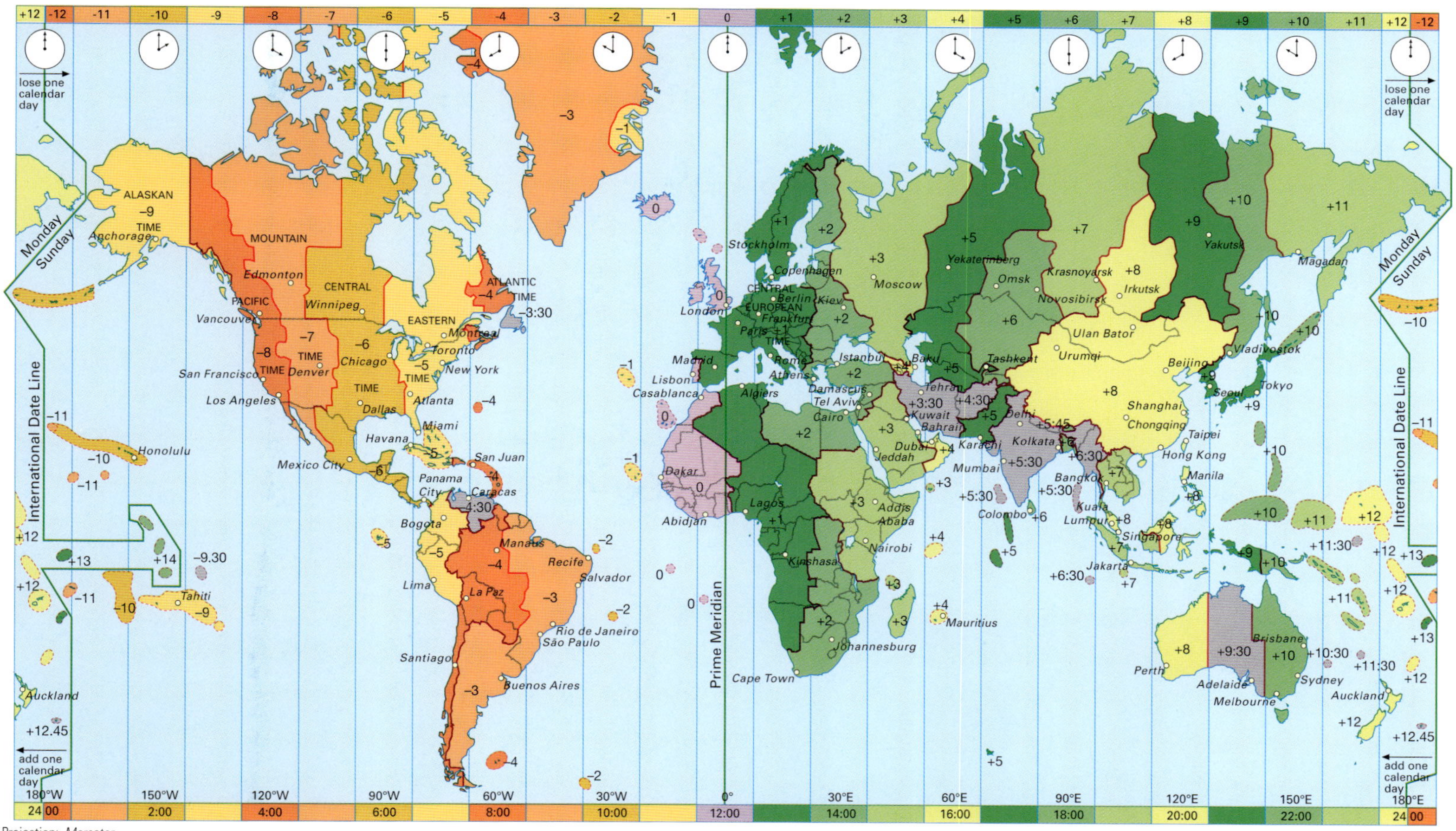
+12
-12
-11
-10
-9
-8
-7
-6
-5
-4
-3
-2
-1
0
+1
+2
+3
+4
+5
+6
+7
+8
+9
+10
+11
+12
-12
lose one calendar day
lose one calendar day
Monday
Sunday
Monday
Sunday
ALASKAN -9 TIME
Anchorage
MOUNTAIN
Edmonton
PACIFIC
CENTRAL
Winnipeg
Vancouver
EASTERN
ATLANTIC TIME
-3:30
Montreal
Toronto
New York
Chicago
Denver
San Francisco
Los Angeles
Dallas
Atlanta
Miami
Havana
Mexico City
Honolulu
San Juan
Panama City
Caracas
-4:30
Bogota
Manaus
Recife
Salvador
Lima
La Paz
Rio de Janeiro
São Paulo
Santiago
Buenos Aires
Tahiti
-9.30
Auckland
+12.45
Stockholm
Copenhagen
CENTRAL EUROPEAN TIME
Berlin
Frankfurt
Paris
London
Madrid
Lisbon
Casablanca
Rome
Athens
Algiers
Istanbul
Kiev
Moscow
Tel Aviv
Damascus
Cairo
Baku
Tehran
+3:30
+4:30
Kuwait
Bahrain
Jeddah
Dubai
Karachi
Mumbai
+5:30
Delhi
+5:45
Kolkata
+6:30
Colombo
Addis Ababa
Nairobi
Dakar
Abidjan
Lagos
Kinshasa
Mauritius
Johannesburg
Cape Town
Prime Meridian
Yekaterinburg
Omsk
Novosibirsk
Krasnoyarsk
Irkutsk
Yakutsk
Magadan
Tashkent
Ulan Bator
Urumqi
Beijing
Vladivostok
Seoul
Tokyo
Shanghai
Chongqing
Taipei
Hong Kong
Manila
Bangkok
Kuala Lumpur
Singapore
Jakarta
Perth
Adelaide
Melbourne
Brisbane
Sydney
Auckland
+9:30
+10:30
+11:30
+12.45
International Date Line
180°W
150°W
120°W
90°W
60°W
30°W
0°
30°E
60°E
90°E
120°E
150°E
180°E
add one calendar day
add one calendar day
24 00
2:00
4:00
6:00
8:00
10:00
12:00
14:00
16:00
18:00
20:00
22:00
24 00

Projection: *Mercator*

| | |
|---|---|
| 10 | Hours behind or ahead of UT or Co-ordinated Universal Time |
| | Zones using UT (GMT) |
| | Zones behind UT (GMT) |
| | International boundaries |
| | Zones ahead of UT (GMT) |
| | Half-hour zones |
| | Time-zone boundaries |
| | International Date Line |
| | Actual solar time when time at Greenwich is 12:00 (noon) |

**Note:** Some of the above time zones are affected by the incidence of Daylight Saving Time in countries where it is adopted.

**For more information:**
98 Minerals

Every year, earthquakes and volcanic eruptions cause much destruction throughout the world. Such phenomena were once thought to be unconnected, but since the late 1960s, scientists have understood that these events are surface manifestations of the tremendous forces operating in the Earth's interior that are slowly but constantly changing the face of our planet.

The Earth is divided into three zones. The crust, a brittle, low-density zone, overlies the dense mantle. Separating the crust from the mantle is a distinct boundary called the Mohorovičić (or Moho) discontinuity. Enclosed by the mantle is the Earth's core, which consists mainly of iron and nickel.

Temperatures inside the Earth range from about 870°C in the upper mantle to perhaps 5,000°C in the core. Heat creates convection currents in a semi-molten part of the mantle called the asthenosphere. Above the asthenosphere is the lithosphere, a solid layer about 70 km thick, consisting of the crust and part of the mantle. The lithosphere is divided into rigid plates, moved around by the currents in the asthenosphere, a process named plate tectonics.

The Earth was formed around 4.6 billion years ago. Lighter elements floated towards the surface, where they formed crustal rocks. The oldest rocks so far discovered are about 4 billion years old, while the oldest fossils occur in rocks formed around 3.5 billion years ago. An explosion of life occurred at the start of the Cambrian period, 570 million years ago. The fossil record since the start of the Cambrian has enabled scientists to piece together the story of life on Earth.

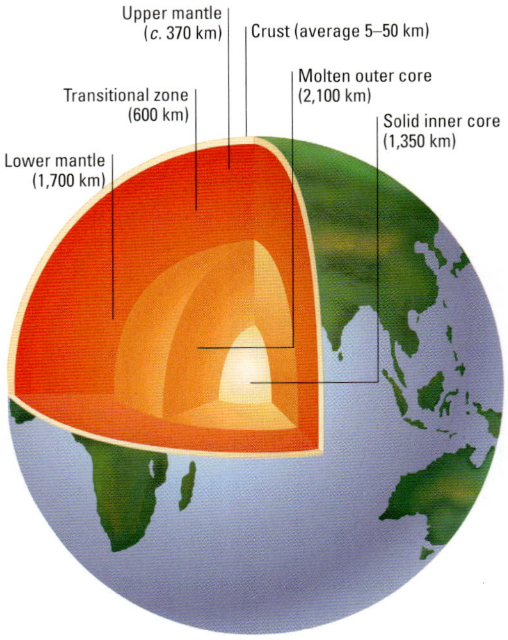
Upper mantle
(*c.* 370 km)
Crust (average 5–50 km)
Molten outer core
(2,100 km)
Transitional zone
(600 km)
Solid inner core
(1,350 km)
Lower mantle
(1,700 km)

## CONTINENTAL DRIFT

Trench
Rift
New ocean floor
Zones of slippage

In 1915, Alfred Wegener produced a series of world maps proposing that, around 200 million years ago, the continents had been joined together in a supercontinent that he called Pangaea. This land mass started to break up about 180 million years ago and the parts drifted to their present positions. In the 1950s and 1960s, evidence from studies of the ocean floor suggested that the low-density continents rest on huge slow-moving plates. The arrows on the present-day world map (*below*) show that the continents are still on the move.

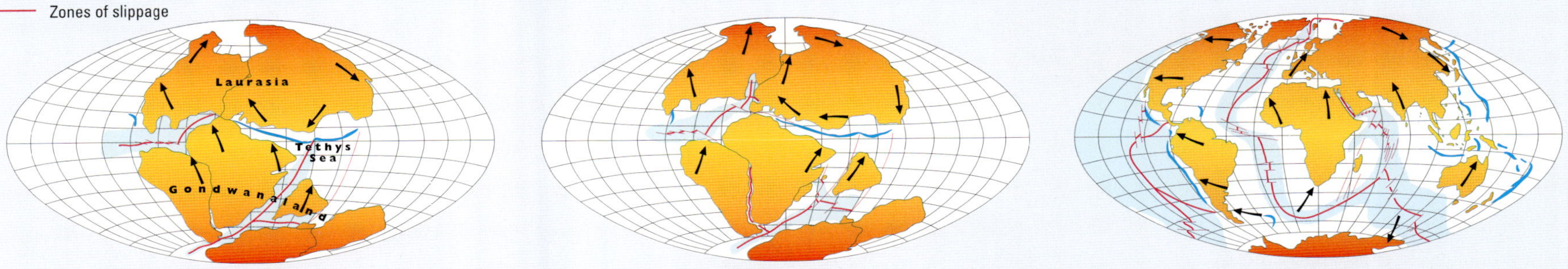
Laurasia
Tethys Sea
Gondwanaland

**180 million years ago** **135 million years ago** **Present day**

## DISTRIBUTION OF VOLCANOES

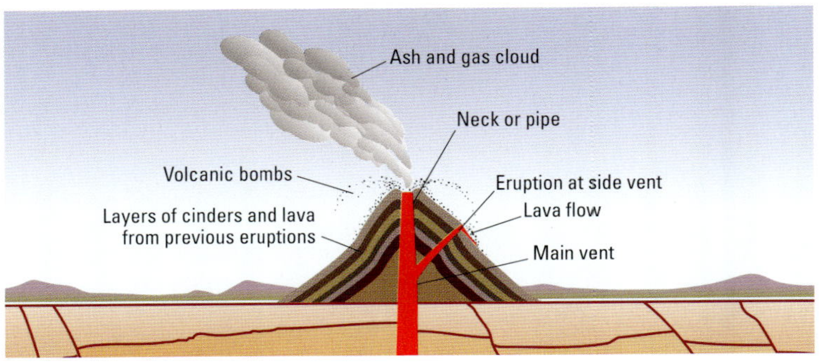
Ash and gas cloud
Neck or pipe
Volcanic bombs
Eruption at side vent
Lava flow
Layers of cinders and lava from previous eruptions
Main vent

Volcanoes occur when hot liquefied rock beneath the Earth's crust is pushed up by pressure to the surface as molten lava. There are some 550 known active volcanoes, around 20 of which are erupting at any one time.

Submarine volcanoes
Land volcanoes active since 1700
Boundaries of tectonic plates

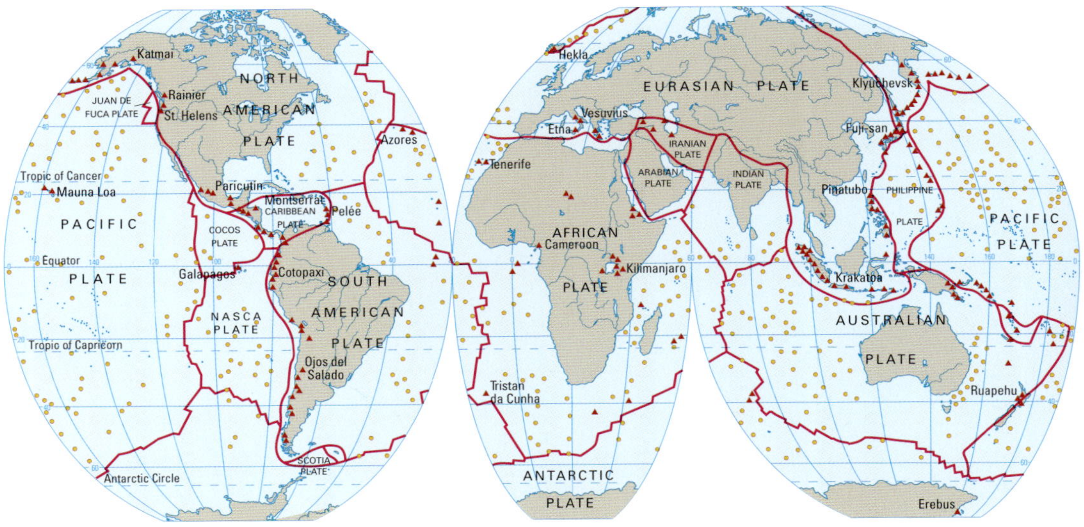
Katmai
Rainier
St. Helens
JUAN DE FUCA PLATE
NORTH AMERICAN PLATE
Azores
Tropic of Cancer
Mauna Loa
Paricutin
Montserrat
CARIBBEAN PLATE
Pelée
PACIFIC
COCOS PLATE
Equator
PLATE
Galapagos
Cotopaxi
SOUTH AMERICAN PLATE
NASCA PLATE
Tropic of Capricorn
Ojos del Salado
SCOTIA PLATE
Antarctic Circle
Hekla
EURASIAN PLATE
Vesuvius
Etna
Tenerife
IRANIAN PLATE
ARABIAN PLATE
INDIAN PLATE
AFRICAN PLATE
Cameroon
Kilimanjaro
Tristan da Cunha
ANTARCTIC PLATE
Klyuchevsk
Fuji-san
Pinatubo
PHILIPPINE PLATE
PACIFIC PLATE
Krakatoa
AUSTRALIAN PLATE
Ruapehu
Erebus

## PLATE TECTONICS

The huge ridges that run through the oceans represent boundaries between plates. Here plates are diverging and molten magma from the mantle rises along a central rift valley to form new crustal rock. These ocean ridges, which are active zones where earthquakes and volcanic eruptions are common, are called constructive plate margins. Destructive plate margins, which occur when two contrasting plates converge, are marked by deep-ocean trenches as one plate is forced under the other. The descending plate is melted to produce the magma that fuels volcanoes alongside the trenches. Movements of descending plates are often sudden, triggering earthquakes in overlying continental areas.

**Sea-floor spreading in the Atlantic Ocean and plate collision**

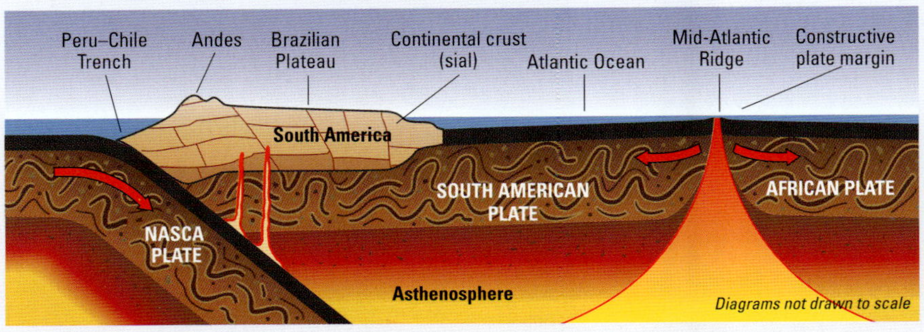
Peru–Chile Trench
Andes
Brazilian Plateau
Continental crust (sial)
Atlantic Ocean
Mid-Atlantic Ridge
Constructive plate margin
South America
SOUTH AMERICAN PLATE
AFRICAN PLATE
NASCA PLATE
Asthenosphere
Diagrams not drawn to scale

**Sea-floor spreading in the Indian Ocean and continental plate collision**

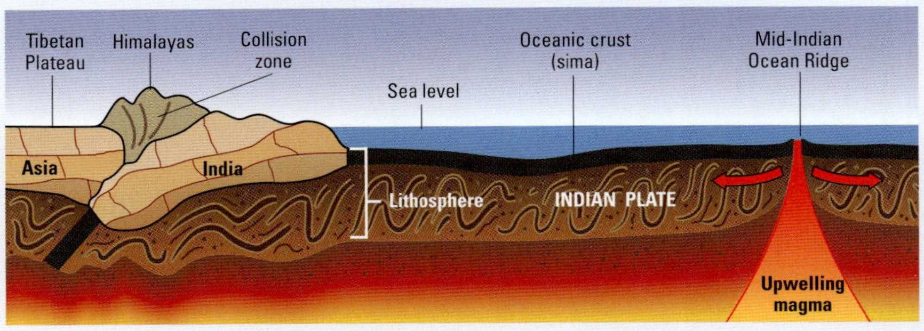
Tibetan Plateau
Himalayas
Collision zone
Sea level
Oceanic crust (sima)
Mid-Indian Ocean Ridge
Asia
India
Lithosphere
INDIAN PLATE
Upwelling magma

## GEOLOGICAL TIME

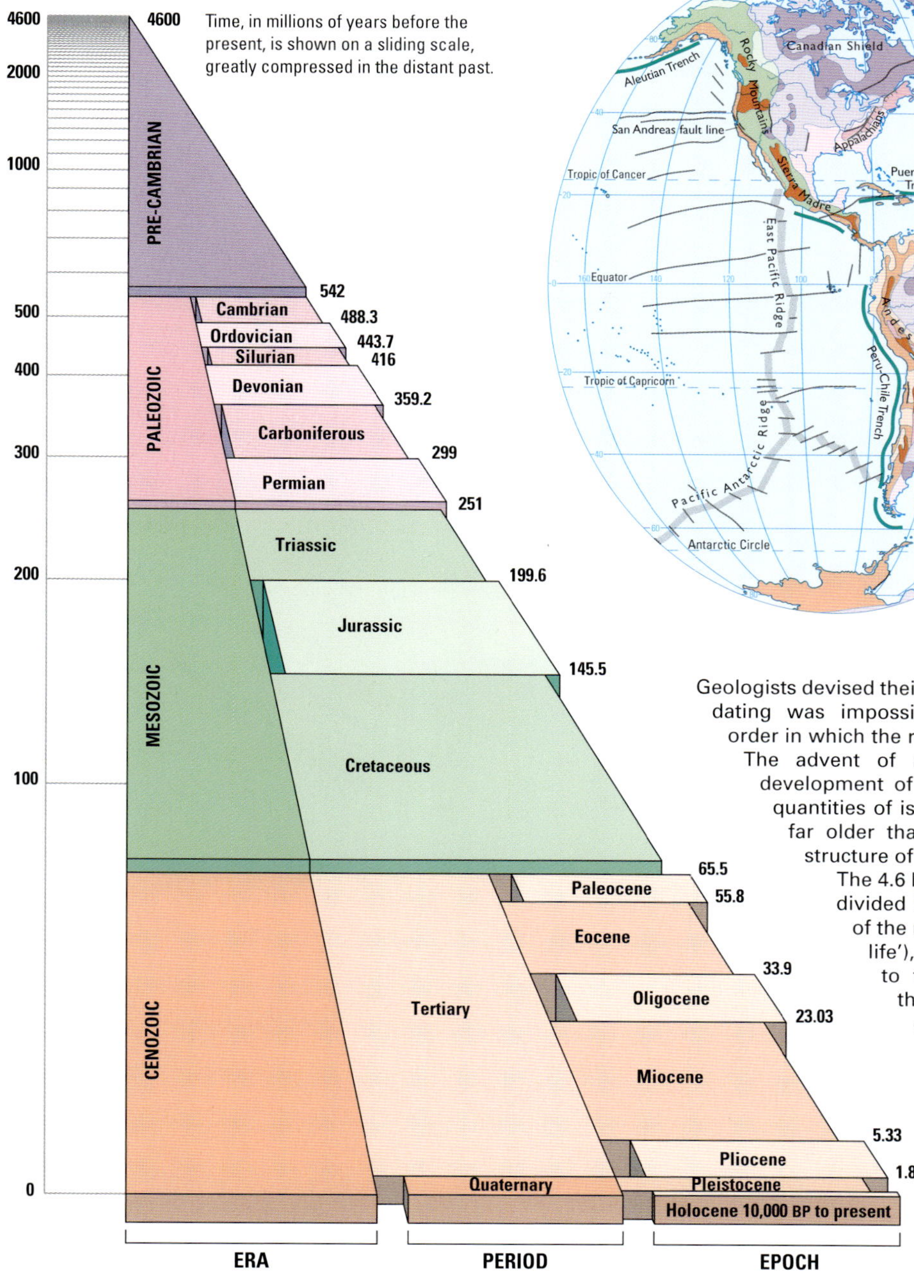

4600
2000
1000
500
400
300
200
100
0
4600
Time, in millions of years before the present, is shown on a sliding scale, greatly compressed in the distant past.
PRE-CAMBRIAN
542
PALEOZOIC
Cambrian
488.3
Ordovician
443.7
Silurian
416
Devonian
359.2
Carboniferous
299
Permian
251
MESOZOIC
Triassic
199.6
Jurassic
145.5
Cretaceous
65.5
CENOZOIC
Tertiary
Paleocene
55.8
Eocene
33.9
Oligocene
23.03
Miocene
5.33
Pliocene
1.81
Quaternary
Pleistocene
Holocene 10,000 BP to present
ERA
PERIOD
EPOCH


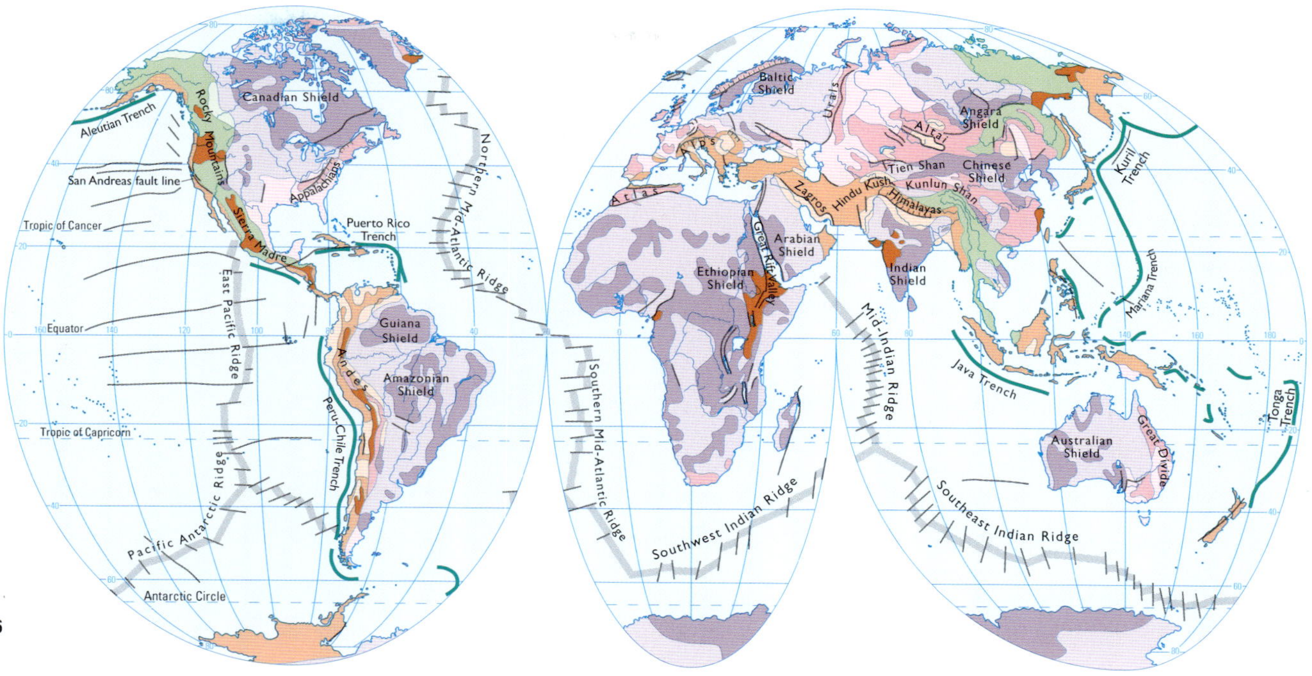

Aleutian Trench
Canadian Shield
Rocky Mountains
San Andreas fault line
Appalachians
Tropic of Cancer
Sierra Madre
Puerto Rico Trench
Northern Mid-Atlantic Ridge
East Pacific Ridge
Equator
Guiana Shield
Amazonian Shield
Andes
Peru-Chile Trench
Tropic of Capricorn
Pacific Antarctic Ridge
Antarctic Circle
Southern Mid-Atlantic Ridge
Southwest Indian Ridge
Baltic Shield
Urals
Alps
Atlas
Angara Shield
Altai
Tien Shan
Chinese Shield
Hindu Kush
Kunlun Shan
Zagros
Himalayas
Arabian Shield
Great Rift Valley
Ethiopian Shield
Indian Shield
Kuril Trench
Mariana Trench
Mid-Indian Ridge
Java Trench
Australian Shield
Great Divide
Tonga Trench
Southeast Indian Ridge


Pre-Cambrian shields
Sedimentary cover on Pre-Cambrian shields
Paleozoic (Caledonian and Hercynian) folding
Sedimentary cover on Paleozoic folding
Mesozoic folding
Sedimentary cover on Mesozoic folding
Cenozoic (Alpine) folding
Sedimentary cover on Cenozoic folding
Intensive Mesozoic and Cenozoic vulcanism
Principal faults
Oceanic marginal troughs
Mid-oceanic ridges
Overthrust faults

Geologists devised their timescale on the basis of relative, not calendar, ages. Accurate dating was impossible and estimates were often bitterly disputed, but the order in which the rocks were formed could be deduced from careful observation. The advent of radioactive dating – culminating in the 1950s with the development of a mass spectrometer capable of accurately measuring tiny quantities of isotopes – appears to have settled the arguments. The Earth is far older than geologists first imagined, but their painstakingly-created structure of geological time has withstood the advent of high technology.

The 4.6 billion (4,600 million) years since the formation of the Earth are divided into four great eras, further split into periods and, in the case of the most recent era, epochs. The present era is the Cenozoic ('new life'), extending backwards through 'middle life' and 'ancient life' to the Pre-Cambrian, named after the Latin word for Wales, the location of some of the earliest known fossils. Most of the Earth's geological history is encompassed by the Pre-Cambrian: though traces of ancient life have since been found, it was largely the proliferation of fossils from the beginning of the Paleozoic era onwards, some 570 million years ago, which first allowed precise subdivisions to be made.

Like the Cambrian, most are named after regions exemplifying a period's geology. Others – such as the Carboniferous ('coal-bearing') or the Cretaceous ('chalk-bearing') – are more directly descriptive.

## EARTHQUAKES

Earthquake magnitude is usually rated according to either the Richter scale or the Modified Mercalli scale, both devised by seismologists in the 1930s. The Richter scale measures absolute earthquake power with mathematical precision: each step upwards represents a tenfold increase in the amplitude of the shockwave. Theoretically, there is no upper limit, but most of the largest earthquakes measured have been rated at between 8.8 and 8.9. The 12-point Mercalli scale, based on observed effects, is often more meaningful, ranging from I (earthquakes noticed only by seismographs) to XII (total destruction); intermediate points include V (people awakened at night; unstable objects overturned), VII (collapse of ordinary buildings; chimneys and monuments fall), and IX (conspicuous cracks in ground; serious damage to reservoirs).

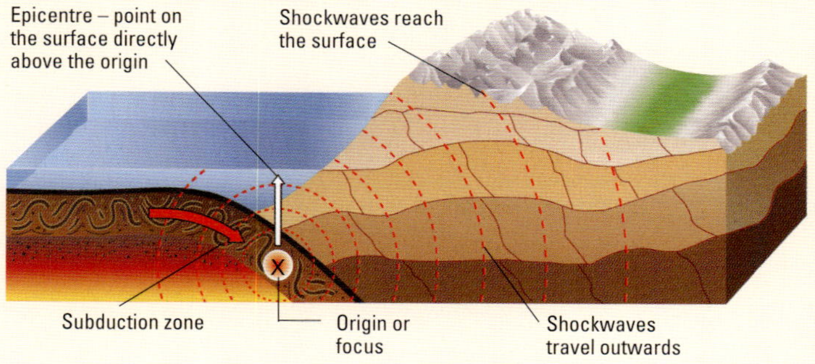

Epicentre – point on the surface directly above the origin
Shockwaves reach the surface
Subduction zone
Origin or focus
Shockwaves travel outwards


Mobile land areas
Submarine zones of mobile land areas
Stable land platforms
Submarine extensions of land platforms
Mid-oceanic volcanic ridges
Oceanic platforms
1976 Principal earthquakes and dates (since 1900)

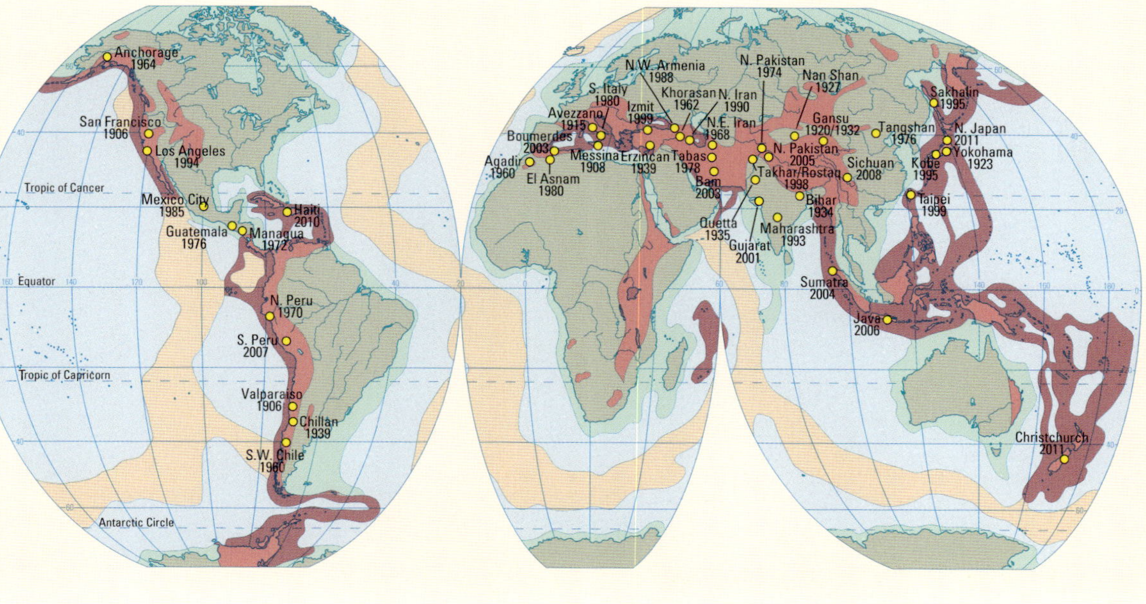

Anchorage 1964
San Francisco 1906
Los Angeles 1994
Tropic of Cancer
Mexico City 1985
Haiti 2010
Guatemala 1976
Managua 1972
Equator
N. Peru 1970
S. Peru 2007
Tropic of Capricorn
Valparaiso 1906
Chillan 1939
S.W. Chile 1960
Antarctic Circle
N.W. Armenia 1988
N. Pakistan 1974
Nan Shan 1927
S. Italy 1980
Khorasan 1962
N. Iran 1990
Izmit 1999
Avezzano 1915
N.E. Iran 1968
Gansu 1920/1932
Tangshan 1976
Sakhalin 1995
N. Japan 2011
Boumerdes 2003
Messina 1908
Erzincan 1939
Tabas 1978
N. Pakistan 2005
Takhar/Rostaq 1998
Sichuan 2008
Kobe 1995
Yokohama 1923
Agadir 1960
El Asnam 1980
Bam 2003
Bihar 1934
Taipei 1999
Quetta 1935
Maharashtra 1993
Gujarat 2001
Sumatra 2004
Java 2006
Christchurch 2011


Earthquakes are a series of rapid vibrations originating from the slipping or faulting of parts of the Earth's crust when stresses within build up to breaking point. They usually happen at depths varying from 8 km to 30 km. Severe earthquakes cause extensive damage when they take place in populated areas, destroying structures and severing communications. Most initial loss of life occurs due to secondary causes such as falling masonry, fires and flooding.

**Notable Earthquakes Since 1900**

| Year | Location | Mag. | Deaths |
|---|---|---|---|
| 1906 | San Francisco, USA | 8.3 | 3,000 |
| 1906 | Valparaiso, Chile | 8.6 | 22,000 |
| 1908 | Messina, Italy | 7.5 | 83,000 |
| 1915 | Avezzano, Italy | 7.5 | 30,000 |
| 1920 | Gansu (Kansu), China | 8.6 | 180,000 |
| 1923 | Yokohama, Japan | 8.3 | 143,000 |
| 1927 | Nan Shan, China | 8.3 | 200,000 |
| 1932 | Gansu (Kansu), China | 7.6 | 70,000 |
| 1933 | Sanriku, Japan | 8.9 | 2,990 |
| 1934 | Bihar, India/Nepal | 8.4 | 10,700 |
| 1935 | Quetta, India* | 7.5 | 60,000 |
| 1939 | Chillan, Chile | 8.3 | 28,000 |
| 1939 | Erzincan, Turkey | 7.9 | 30,000 |
| 1960 | S. W. Chile | 9.5 | 2,200 |
| 1960 | Agadir, Morocco | 5.8 | 12,000 |
| 1962 | Khorasan, Iran | 7.1 | 12,230 |
| 1964 | Anchorage, USA | 9.2 | 125 |
| 1968 | N. E. Iran | 7.4 | 12,000 |
| 1970 | N. Peru | 7.8 | 70,000 |
| 1972 | Managua, Nicaragua | 6.2 | 5,000 |
| 1974 | N. Pakistan | 6.3 | 5,200 |
| 1976 | Guatemala | 7.5 | 22,500 |
| 1976 | Tangshan, China | 8.2 | 255,000 |
| 1978 | Tabas, Iran | 7.7 | 25,000 |
| 1980 | El Asnam, Algeria | 7.3 | 20,000 |
| 1980 | S. Italy | 7.2 | 4,800 |
| 1985 | Mexico City, Mexico | 8.1 | 4,200 |
| 1988 | N.W. Armenia | 6.8 | 55,000 |
| 1990 | N. Iran | 7.7 | 36,000 |
| 1993 | Maharashtra, India | 6.4 | 30,000 |
| 1994 | Los Angeles, USA | 6.6 | 51 |
| 1995 | Kobe, Japan | 7.2 | 5,000 |
| 1995 | Sakhalin, Russia | 7.5 | 2,000 |
| 1998 | Takhar, Afghanistan | 6.1 | 4,200 |
| 1998 | Rostaq, Afghanistan | 7.0 | 5,000 |
| 1999 | Izmit, Turkey | 7.4 | 15,000 |
| 1999 | Taipei, Taiwan | 7.6 | 1,700 |
| 2001 | Gujarat, India | 7.7 | 14,000 |
| 2003 | Boumerdes, Algeria | 6.8 | 2,200 |
| 2003 | Bam, Iran | 6.6 | 30,000 |
| 2004 | Sumatra, Indonesia | 9.0 | 250,000 |
| 2005 | N. Pakistan | 7.6 | 74,000 |
| 2006 | Java, Indonesia | 6.4 | 6,200 |
| 2007 | S. Peru | 8.0 | 600 |
| 2008 | Sichuan, China | 7.9 | 70,000 |
| 2010 | Haiti | 7.0 | 230,000 |
| 2011 | Christchurch, NZ | 6.3 | 182 |
| 2011 | N. Japan | 9.0 | 20,000 |

* now Pakistan

**For more information:**


11 El Niño phenomenon
11 Ocean currents
79 Beaufort wind scale
Monsoon
80 Climate change
Global warming


The atmosphere is a meteor shield, a radiation deflector, a thermal blanket, and a source of chemical energy for the Earth's diverse life forms. Five-sixths of its mass is in the lowest layer, the troposphere, which ranges in thickness from 18–10 km between the equator and the poles. Powered by the Sun, the air is always on the move, flowing generally from high- to low-pressure areas. The troposphere is the layer where virtually all weather phenomena, including clouds, precipitation and winds, occur. Above the troposphere is the stratosphere, which contains the important ozone layer and extends to about 50 km above the Earth's surface. Beyond 100 km, atmospheric density is lower than most laboratory vacuums.

## STRUCTURE OF THE ATMOSPHERE

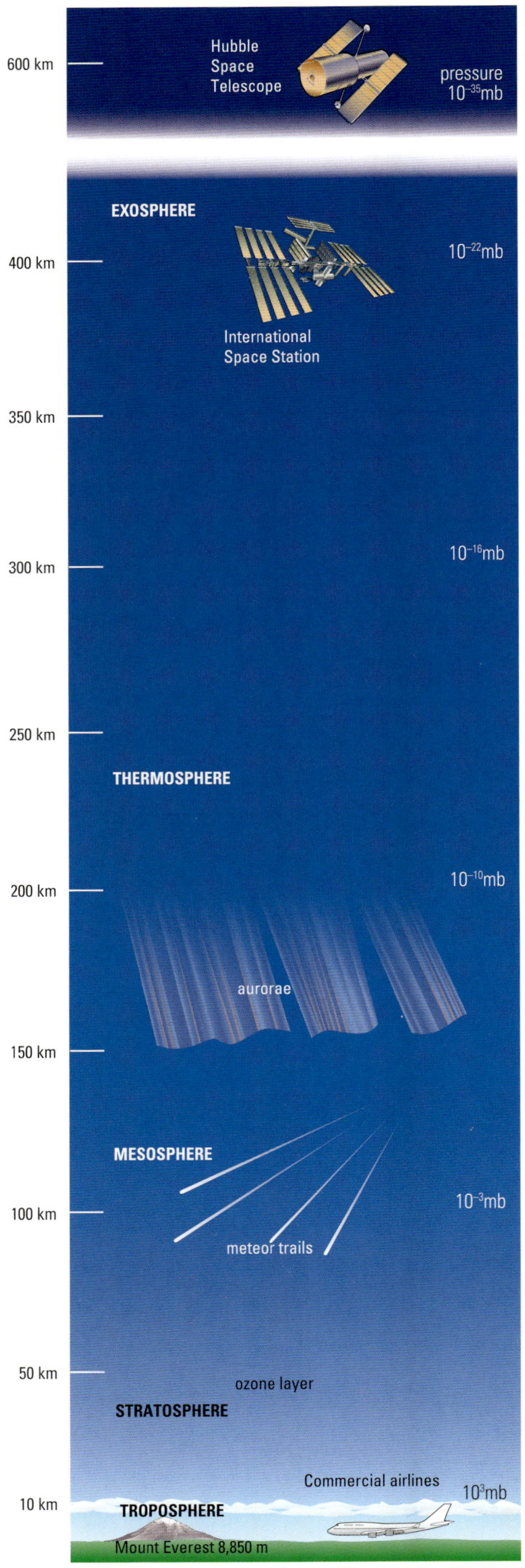

600 km
Hubble Space Telescope
pressure $10^{-35}$mb
EXOSPHERE
400 km
$10^{-22}$mb
International Space Station
350 km
300 km
$10^{-16}$mb
250 km
THERMOSPHERE
200 km
$10^{-10}$mb
aurorae
150 km
MESOSPHERE
100 km
$10^{-3}$mb
meteor trails
50 km
ozone layer
STRATOSPHERE
10 km
Commercial airlines
$10^{3}$mb
TROPOSPHERE
Mount Everest 8,850 m


## CIRCULATION OF THE AIR

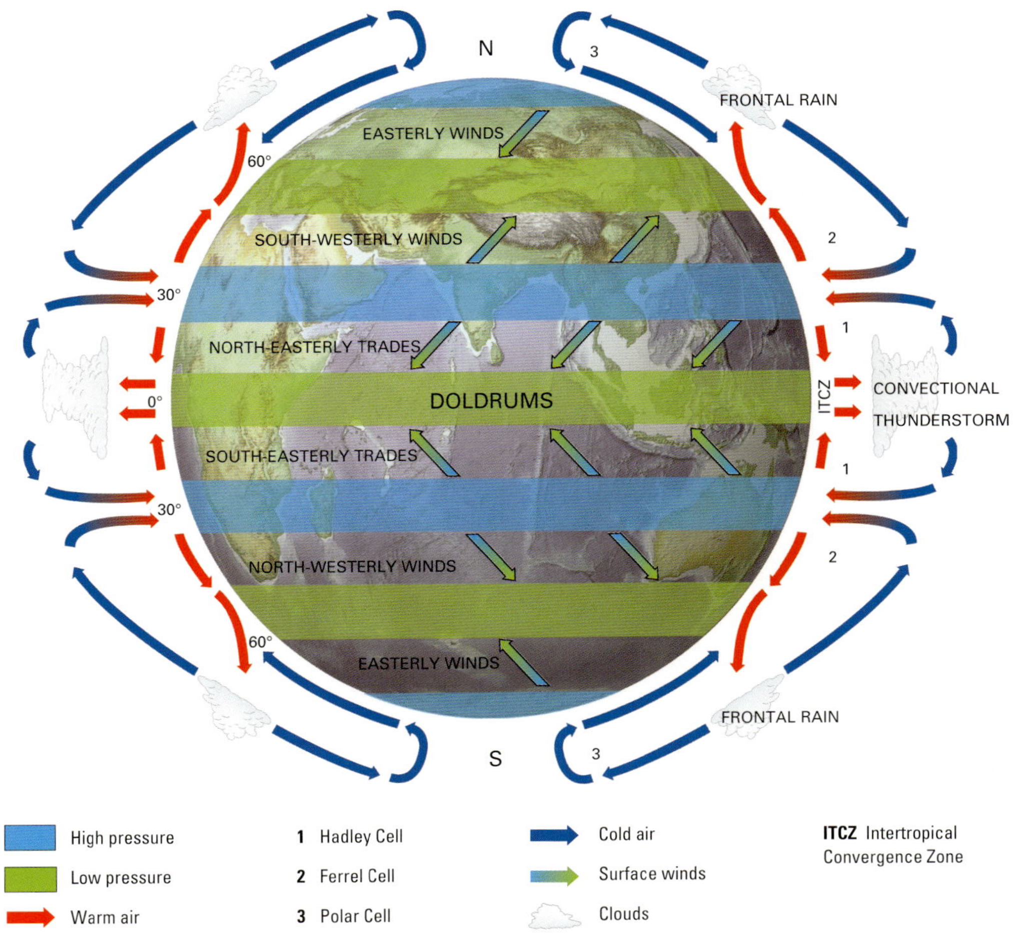

N
S
EASTERLY WINDS
SOUTH-WESTERLY WINDS
NORTH-EASTERLY TRADES
DOLDRUMS
SOUTH-EASTERLY TRADES
NORTH-WESTERLY WINDS
EASTERLY WINDS
60°
30°
0°
30°
60°
FRONTAL RAIN
CONVECTIONAL THUNDERSTORM
ITCZ
1
2
3
High pressure
Low pressure
Warm air
1 Hadley Cell
2 Ferrel Cell
3 Polar Cell
Cold air
Surface winds
Clouds
ITCZ Intertropical Convergence Zone


## FRONTAL SYSTEMS

Depressions, also known as cyclones or lows, form on the polar front where relatively cold and dry polar air flows alongside warmer, moister subtropical air. They occur when the flow high above the polar front generates a surface inward-swirling circulation that moves along the polar front as a wave.

The warm front is the leading edge of the subtropical air that glides up and over the cooler air ahead of it. This gently ascending flow produces a characteristic sequence of clouds ahead of the warm front and a band of precipitation a few hundred kilometres wide immediately in advance it. Conditions within the warm sector are often overcast with layer cloud and generally light rain or drizzle. The cloud sometimes breaks up downwind of hills.

Another band of precipitation often occurs just ahead of the cold front that is the leading edge of the cooler polar air. Cumulus clouds tend to occur in the air behind the cold front, producing scattered showers. The changes of temperature, wind direction, and cloud, etc, are illustrated by the diagram below.

## CHEMICAL COMPOSITION

**Gaseous composition of the principal atmospheric layers**

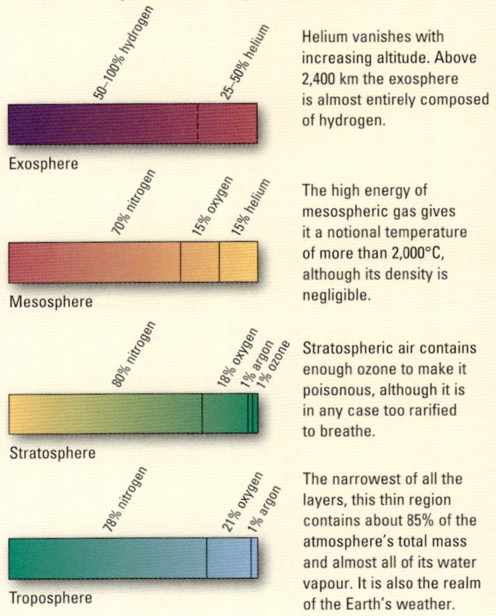

50–100% hydrogen
25–50% helium
Exosphere
Helium vanishes with increasing altitude. Above 2,400 km the exosphere is almost entirely composed of hydrogen.
70% nitrogen
15% oxygen
15% helium
Mesosphere
The high energy of mesospheric gas gives it a notional temperature of more than 2,000°C, although its density is negligible.
80% nitrogen
18% oxygen
1% argon
1% ozone
Stratosphere
Stratospheric air contains enough ozone to make it poisonous, although it is in any case too rarified to breathe.
78% nitrogen
21% oxygen
1% argon
Troposphere
The narrowest of all the layers, this thin region contains about 85% of the atmosphere's total mass and almost all of its water vapour. It is also the realm of the Earth's weather.


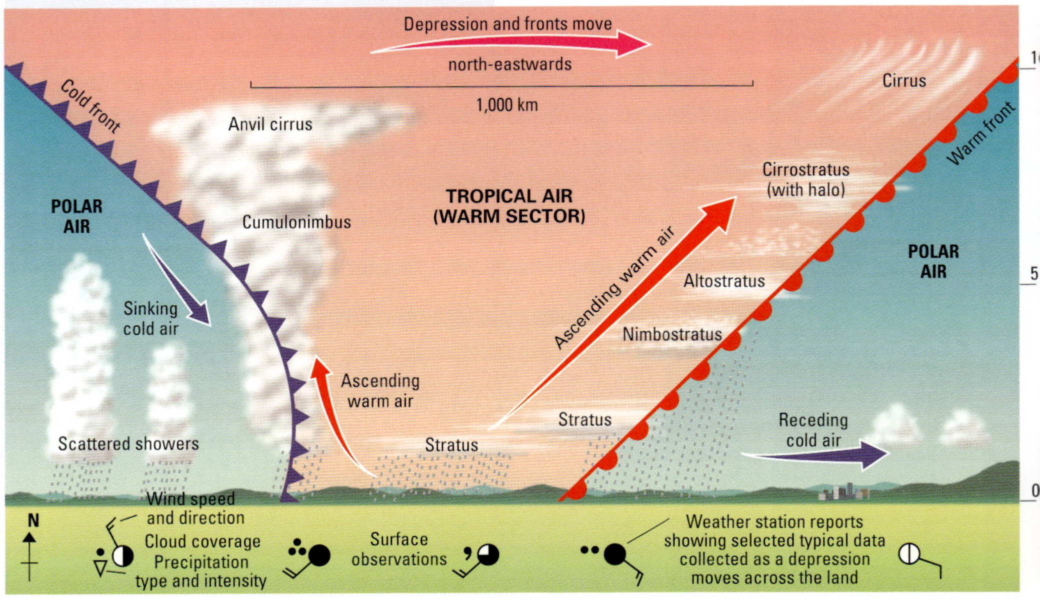

Depression and fronts move
north-eastwards
1,000 km
Cold front
Warm front
Anvil cirrus
Cirrus
POLAR AIR
Cumulonimbus
TROPICAL AIR (WARM SECTOR)
Cirrostratus (with halo)
POLAR AIR
Ascending warm air
Altostratus
Sinking cold air
Nimbostratus
Ascending warm air
Stratus
Receding cold air
Scattered showers
Stratus
Wind speed and direction
Cloud coverage
Precipitation type and intensity
Surface observations
Weather station reports showing selected typical data collected as a depression moves across the land
N

## AIR MASSES

Air masses are large bodies of air where the variations of the main physical properties (that is, temperature and humidity) are relatively gentle. The term is generally applied only to the lower layers of the atmosphere, although air masses can cover areas of tens of thousands of square kilometres.

Air masses derive their temperature and humidity from the regions over which they lie. These regions are known as 'source regions'. The principal ones are:

- areas of relative calm, such as semi-permanent high-pressure areas;
- areas where the surface is relatively uniform, including deserts, oceans and ice-fields.

These are the 'highs' marked on the map below.

As air masses move from their source regions, they may be changed due to the effects of the surface over which they move. These changes create 'secondary air masses'. For example, a warm air mass that travels over a cold surface is cooled and becomes more stable. Hence, it may form low cloud or fog, but is unlikely to produce much rain. By contrast, a cold air mass that passes over a warm surface is warmed and becomes less stable. The rising air is likely to produce more rain.

When two contrasting air masses meet, they form a 'front'. As warm air is lighter than cold, dense air, it begins to rise over it, condensing as it rises to form cloud and rain.

## CLASSIFICATION OF CLOUDS

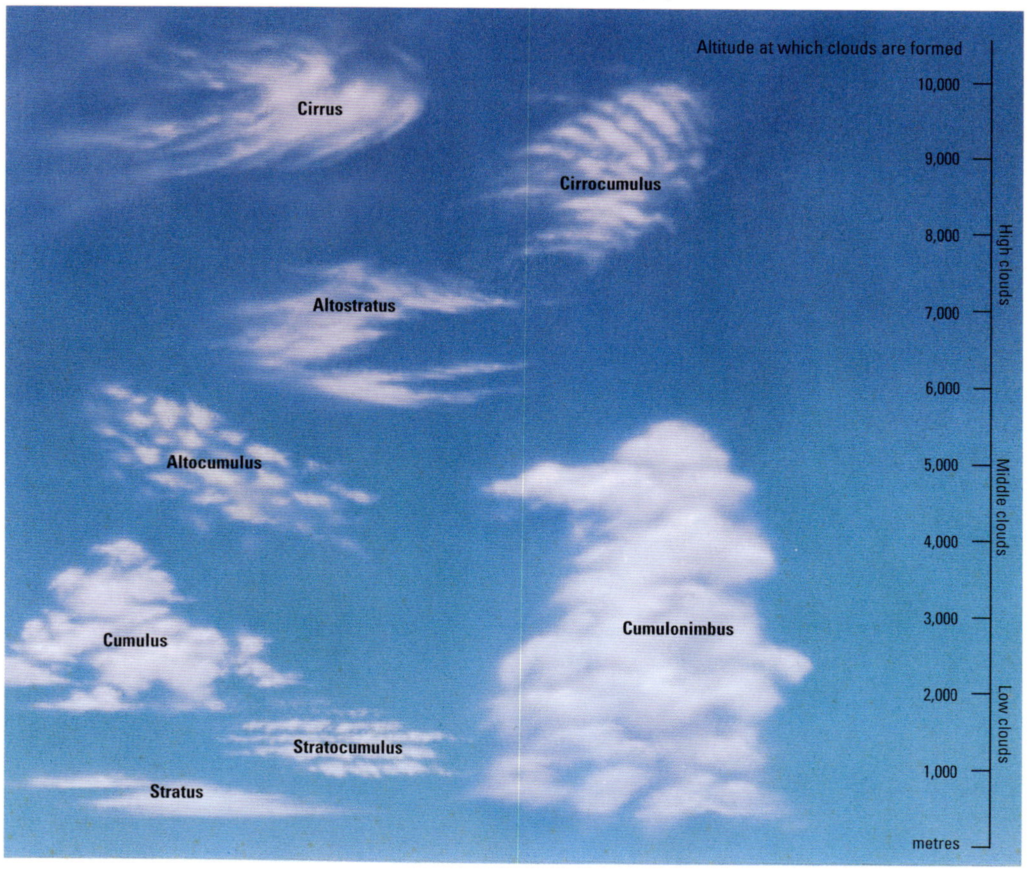
Altitude at which clouds are formed
10,000
9,000
8,000
7,000
6,000
5,000
4,000
3,000
2,000
1,000
metres
High clouds
Middle clouds
Low clouds
Cirrus
Cirrocumulus
Altostratus
Altocumulus
Cumulus
Cumulonimbus
Stratocumulus
Stratus

Clouds form when damp, usually rising, air is cooled. Thus they form when a wind rises to cross hills or mountains; when a mass of air rises over, or is pushed up by, another mass of denser air; or when local heating of the ground causes convection currents.

The first classification of clouds was developed by a London chemist, Luke Howard, in 1803, and it was later modified by the World Meteorological Organization. The types of clouds are classified according to altitude as high, middle or low. The high ones, composed of ice crystals, are cirrus, cirrostratus and cirrocumulus.

The middle clouds are altostratus – a grey or bluish striated, fibrous or uniform sheet producing light drizzle – and altocumulus, a thicker and fluffier version of cirrocumulus.

Low clouds include nimbostratus, a dark grey layer that brings rain or snow; cumulus, a detached heap, dark at the base; stratus, which forms dull, overcast skies at low levels; and stratocumulus, which consists of fluffy greyish-white layers.

Cumulonimbus, associated with storms and rains, heavy and dense with a flat base and a high, fluffy outline, can be tall enough to occupy middle as well as low altitudes.

## PRESSURE AND SURFACE WINDS

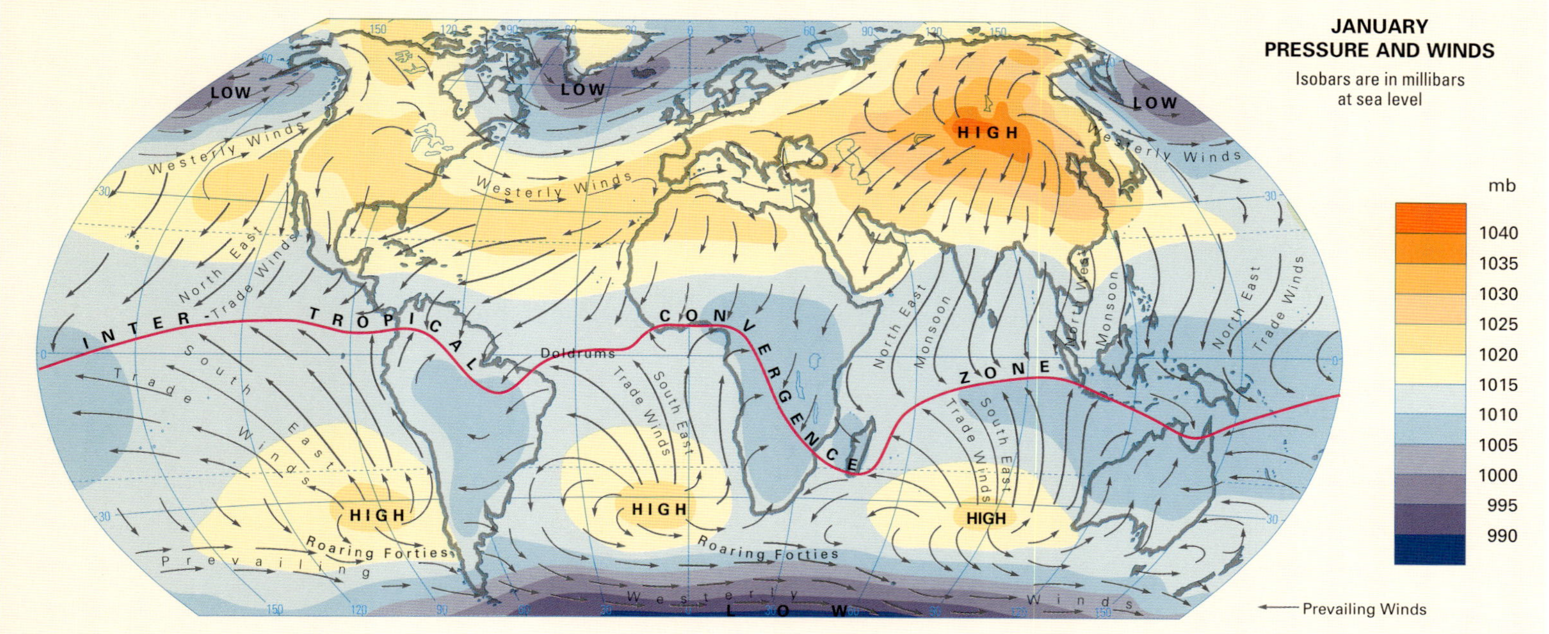
JANUARY
PRESSURE AND WINDS
Isobars are in millibars at sea level
mb
1040
1035
1030
1025
1020
1015
1010
1005
1000
995
990
Prevailing Winds
LOW
LOW
LOW
HIGH
HIGH
HIGH
HIGH
Westerly Winds
Westerly Winds
North East Trade Winds
INTER-TROPICAL CONVERGENCE ZONE
Doldrums
South East Trade Winds
North East Monsoon
North West Monsoon
Roaring Forties
Prevailing Westerly Winds

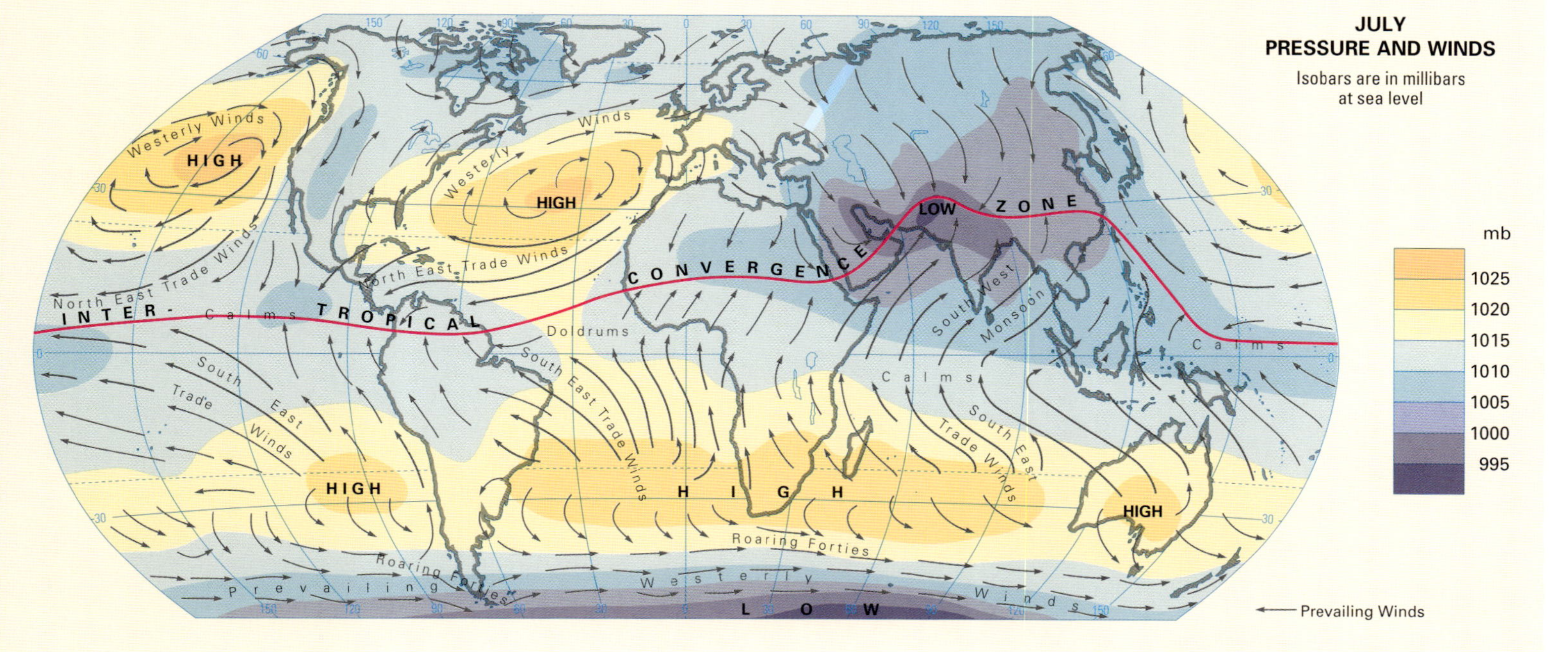
JULY
PRESSURE AND WINDS
Isobars are in millibars at sea level
mb
1025
1020
1015
1010
1005
1000
995
Prevailing Winds
HIGH
HIGH
HIGH
HIGH
HIGH
LOW
Westerly Winds
North East Trade Winds
INTER-TROPICAL CONVERGENCE ZONE
Calms
Doldrums
South East Trade Winds
South West Monsoon
Roaring Forties
Prevailing Westerly Winds
LOW

## WEATHER RECORDS

### Pressure and winds

**Highest barometric pressure:**
Agata, Siberia, 1,083.8 mb at altitude 262 m [862 ft], 31 December 1968.

**Lowest barometric pressure:**
Typhoon Tip, 480 km [300 mi] west of Guam, Pacific Ocean, 870 mb, 12 October 1979.

**Highest recorded wind speed:**
Bridge Creek, Oklahoma, USA, 512 km/h [318 mph], 3 May 1999. Measured by Doppler radar monitoring a tornado.

**Windiest place:**
Port Martin, Antarctica, where winds of more than 64 km/h [40 mph] occur for not less than 100 days a year.

**Worst recorded storm:**
Bangladesh (then East Pakistan) cyclone, November 13, 1970 – over 300,000 dead or missing. The 1991 cyclone, Bangladesh's and the world's second worst in terms of loss of life, killed an estimated 138,000 people.

**Worst recorded tornado:**
Tri-state tornado – Missouri/Illinois/Indiana, USA, 18 March 1925 – 695 deaths, lasted 3 hours with 352 km [219 mi] path length. A suspected tornado in Bangladesh on 26 April 1989 killed approximately 1,300 people.

**For more information:**
11 Ocean currents
76 Circulation of the air
77 Classification of clouds
Pressure and winds
80 Climate change
Global warming
82 Hydrological cycle
83 Natural vegetation

Weather is the day-to-day or hour-to-hour condition of the air, while climate is weather in the long term – the seasonal pattern of hot and cold, wet and dry, averaged over a long period.

Most classifications of climate are based on a system developed in the early 19th century by Vladimir Köppen, a Russian meteorologist. Using a code based on letters and a classification centred on two main features, temperature and precipitation, he identified five main climatic types: tropical (A), dry (B), warm temperate (C), cold temperate (D), and polar (E). A highland mountain climate (H) was added later to account for the variety of altitudinal climatic zones on high mountains. Each of these main regions was then further subdivided.

Latitude is a major factor in determining climate, but other factors add to the complexity. These include the differential heating of land and sea, the distance from the sea, the effect of mountains on winds, and the influence of ocean currents. For example, New York City, Naples and the Gobi Desert share almost the same latitude, but their climates are very different.

During the last Ice Age, the Earth underwent alternating cold periods, called glacials, separated by warm interglacials. The Milankovich theory suggests such cycles may be caused by variations in the Earth's path around the Sun, changing from almost circular to elliptical every 95,000 years, and variations in the Earth's tilt from 21.5° to 24.5° every 42,000 years. Another factor is that the Earth is now closest to the Sun in the middle of winter in the northern hemisphere and furthest away in summer. But 12,000 years ago, at the height of the last glacial period, the northern winter fell with the Sun at its most distant.

Studies of these cycles suggest that we are now in an interglacial with a new glacial period on the way. However, scientists believe that global warming, largely a result of burning fossil fuels and deforestation, may be occurring much faster than the great, slow cycles of the Solar System.

**Tropical rainy climates**
All mean monthly temperatures above 18°C [64°F].
- Af Rainforest climate
- Am Monsoon climate
- Aw Savanna climate

**Dry climates**
Low rainfall combined with a wide range of temperatures.
- BS Steppe climate
- BW Desert climate

**Warm temperate rainy climates**
The mean temperature is below 18°C [64°F] but above –3°C [26°F] and that of the warmest month is over 10°C [50°F].
- Cw Dry winter climate
- Cs Dry summer climate
- Cf Climate with no dry season

**Cold temperate rainy climates**
The mean temperature of the coldest month is below –3°C [26°F] but that of the warmest month is still over 10°C [50°F].
- Dw Dry winter climate
- Df Climate with no dry season

**Polar climates**
The mean temperature of the warmest month is below 10°C [50°F], giving permanently frozen subsoil.
- ET Tundra climate

The mean temperature of the warmest month is below 0°C [32°F], giving permanent ice and snow.
- EF Polar climate

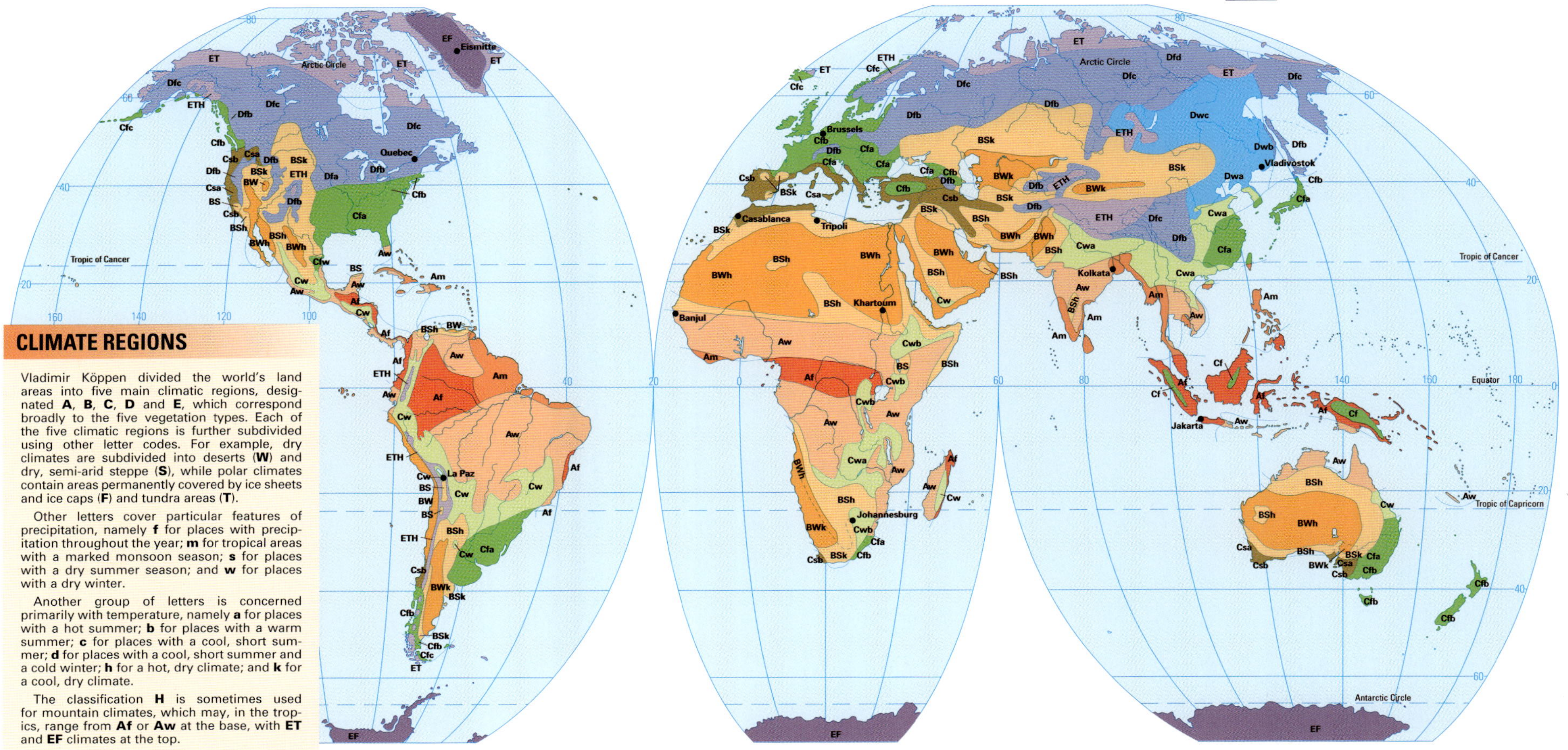
Arctic Circle
Tropic of Cancer
Equator
Tropic of Capricorn
Antarctic Circle
Eismitte
Quebec
La Paz
Brussels
Casablanca
Tripoli
Banjul
Khartoum
Johannesburg
Kolkata
Vladivostok
Jakarta

## CLIMATE REGIONS

Vladimir Köppen divided the world's land areas into five main climatic regions, designated **A**, **B**, **C**, **D** and **E**, which correspond broadly to the five vegetation types. Each of the five climatic regions is further subdivided using other letter codes. For example, dry climates are subdivided into deserts (**W**) and dry, semi-arid steppe (**S**), while polar climates contain areas permanently covered by ice sheets and ice caps (**F**) and tundra areas (**T**).

Other letters cover particular features of precipitation, namely **f** for places with precipitation throughout the year; **m** for tropical areas with a marked monsoon season; **s** for places with a dry summer season; and **w** for places with a dry winter.

Another group of letters is concerned primarily with temperature, namely **a** for places with a hot summer; **b** for places with a warm summer; **c** for places with a cool, short summer; **d** for places with a cool, short summer and a cold winter; **h** for a hot, dry climate; and **k** for a cool, dry climate.

The classification **H** is sometimes used for mountain climates, which may, in the tropics, range from **Af** or **Aw** at the base, with **ET** and **EF** climates at the top.

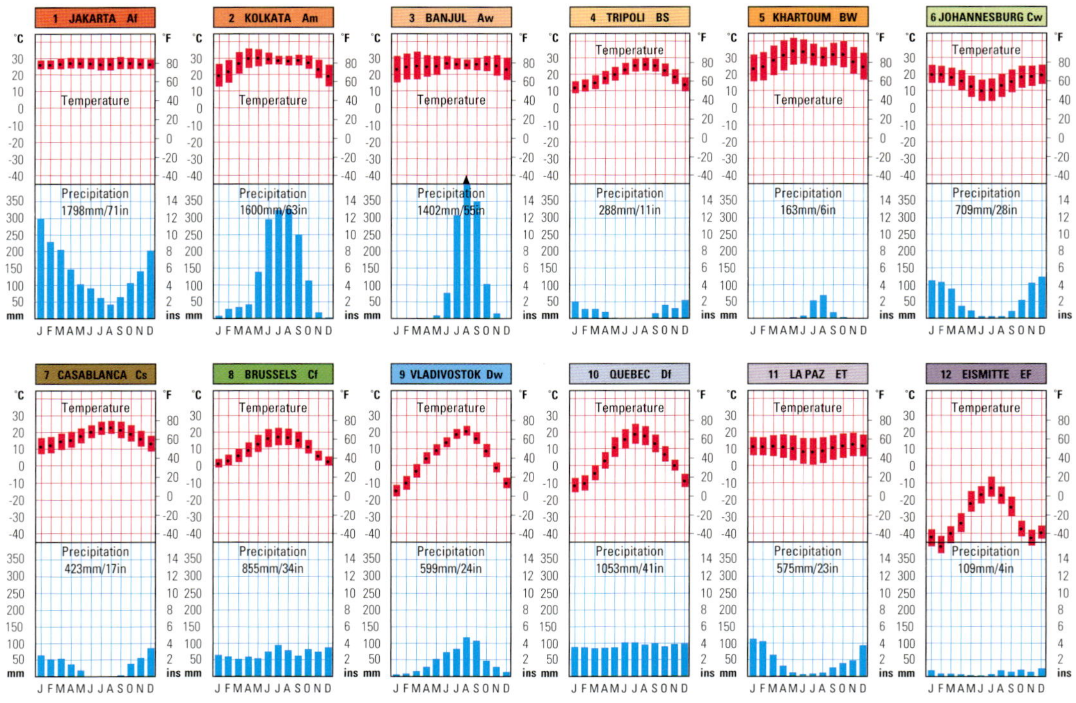
1 JAKARTA Af
Precipitation 1798mm/71in
2 KOLKATA Am
Precipitation 1600mm/63in
3 BANJUL Aw
Precipitation 1402mm/55in
4 TRIPOLI BS
Precipitation 288mm/11in
5 KHARTOUM BW
Precipitation 163mm/6in
6 JOHANNESBURG Cw
Precipitation 709mm/28in
7 CASABLANCA Cs
Precipitation 423mm/17in
8 BRUSSELS Cf
Precipitation 855mm/34in
9 VLADIVOSTOK Dw
Precipitation 599mm/24in
10 QUEBEC Df
Precipitation 1053mm/41in
11 LA PAZ ET
Precipitation 575mm/23in
12 EISMITTE EF
Precipitation 109mm/4in
Temperature
°C
°F
mm
ins
J F M A M J J A S O N D

## CLIMATE AND WEATHER TERMS

**Anticyclone:** area of high pressure with light winds and generally quiet weather.
**Absolute humidity:** mass of water vapour contained in a given volume of air.
**Cloud cover:** amount of cloud in the sky; measured in oktas (from 0–9), with 0 clear, and 9 'sky obscured'.
**Condensation:** the conversion of water vapour into liquid.
**Cyclone:** violent storm resulting from anticlockwise rotation of winds in the northern hemisphere and clockwise in the southern: called hurricane in North America, typhoon in the Far East.
**Depression:** large area of low barometric pressure, a few thousand kilometres across.
**Dew:** deposition of small water droplets on the Earth's surface by direct condensation of water vapour.
**Dew point:** the temperature at which air becomes saturated by cooling at constant barometric pressure and absolute humidity
**Drizzle:** precipitation drops between 0.2 and 0.5 mm [0.01–0.02 in] in diameter.
**Evaporation:** conversion of water from liquid into vapour or moisture in the air.
**Front:** the dividing line between two air masses.
**Frost:** the surface deposition of water vapour as minute ice crystals, when temperature reaches the frost point.
**Hail:** variably-sized pieces of ice that fall in downdrafts from cumulonimbus clouds.
**Humidity:** amount of water vapour in the air.
**Isobar:** line joining places with the same barometric pressure.
**Isotherm:** line connecting places of equal temperature.
**Lightning:** massive electrical discharge released in thunderstorm from cloud to cloud or cloud to ground, the result of the top becoming positively charged and the bottom negatively charged.
**Precipitation:** measurable rain, snow, sleet or hail.
**Prevailing wind:** most common direction of wind at a given location.
**Rain:** precipitation of liquid particles with diameter larger than 0.5 mm [0.02 in].
**Relative humidity:** observed quantity of water vapour in a mass of air over the saturation value at a given temperature (as a percentage).
**Snow:** flake-like coagulations of ice crystals that fall from clouds in subzero temperatures.
**Thunder:** sound produced by the rapid expansion of air heated by lightning.
**Tornado:** rapidly-rotating funnel-shaped cloud or debris column that must reach the surface and be attached to a parent cumulonimbus cloud.

## BEAUFORT WIND SCALE

Named after Admiral Sir Francis Beaufort, the 19th-century British naval officer who devised it, the Beaufort Scale assesses wind speed according to its effects. It was originally designed as an aid for sailors, but has since been adapted for use on the land. It is used internationally.

| Scale | Wind speed mph | Wind speed km/h | Effect |
|---|---|---|---|
| 0 | 0–1 | 0–1 | **Calm** Smoke rises vertically |
| 1 | 1–3 | 1–5 | **Light air** Wind direction shown only by smoke drift |
| 2 | 4–7 | 6–11 | **Light breeze** Wind felt on face; leaves rustle; vanes moved by wind |
| 3 | 8–12 | 12–19 | **Gentle breeze** Leaves and small twigs in constant motion; wind extends small flag |
| 4 | 13–18 | 20–28 | **Moderate** Raises dust and loose paper; small branches move |
| 5 | 19–24 | 29–38 | **Fresh** Small trees in leaf sway; crested wavelets on inland waters |
| 6 | 25–31 | 39–49 | **Strong** Large branches move; difficult to use umbrellas; overhead wires whistle |
| 7 | 32–38 | 50–61 | **Near gale** Whole trees in motion; difficult to walk against wind |
| 8 | 39–46 | 62–74 | **Gale** Twigs break from trees; walking very difficult |
| 9 | 47–54 | 75–88 | **Strong gale** Slight structural damage |
| 10 | 55–63 | 89–102 | **Storm** Trees uprooted; serious structural damage |
| 11 | 64–72 | 103–117 | **Violent storm** Widespread damage |
| 12 | 73+ | 118+ | **Hurricane** |

▲ On 14 September 2003, Hurricane Isabel was located over the Atlantic Ocean, 640 km [400 miles] north of Puerto Rico. It moved in a north-westwards direction with maximum winds of 250 km/h [155 mph], making it a Category 5 hurricane, which is 12 on the Beaufort Scale.

## THE MONSOON

Monsoon is the term given to the seasonal reversal of wind direction, most noticeably in South-east Asia. It results from a combination of factors: the extreme heating and cooling of large land masses in relation to the less marked changes in temperature of the adjacent seas; the northwards movement of the Intertropical Convergence Zone (ITCZ); and the effect of the Himalayas on the circulation of the air.

In March, winds blow outwards from the mainland. But as the Sun and the ITCZ move northwards, the land is intensely heated, and a low-pressure system develops. The south-east trade winds change direction and are sucked into the interior to become south-westerlies, bringing heavy rain. By November, the Sun and the ITCZ have again moved south and the wind directions are again reversed. Cool winds blow from the Asian interior to the sea, losing any moisture on the Himalayas before descending to the coast.

## TEMPERATURE

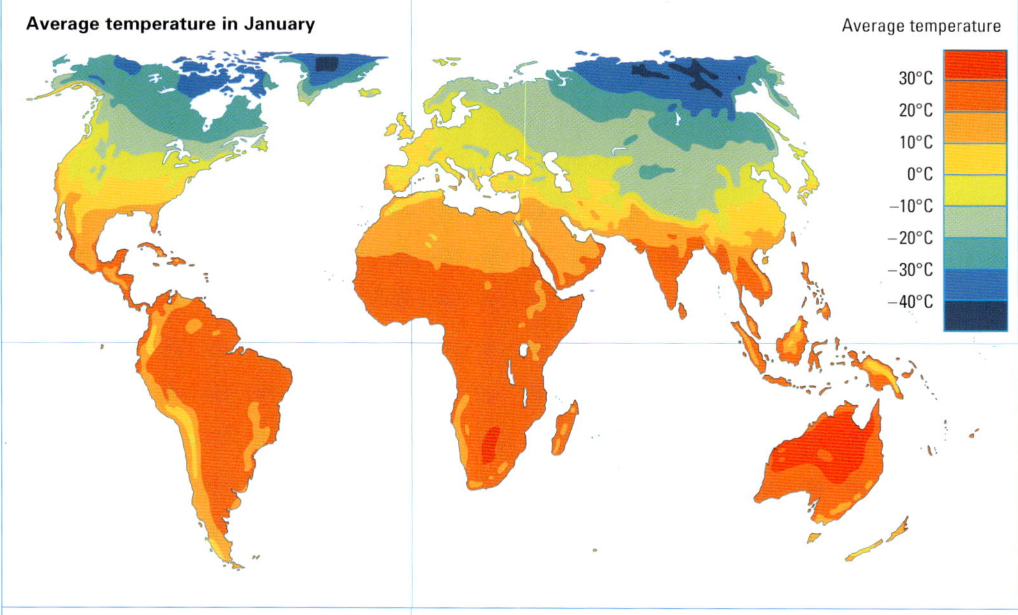
Average temperature in January
Average temperature
30°C
20°C
10°C
0°C
–10°C
–20°C
–30°C
–40°C

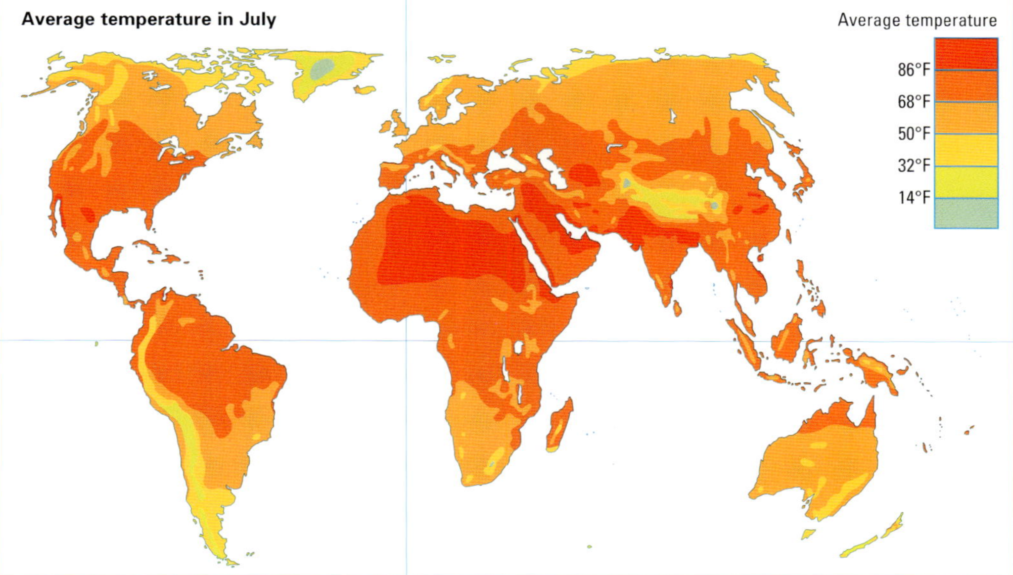
Average temperature in July
Average temperature
86°F
68°F
50°F
32°F
14°F

## PRECIPITATION (RAINFALL AND SNOW)

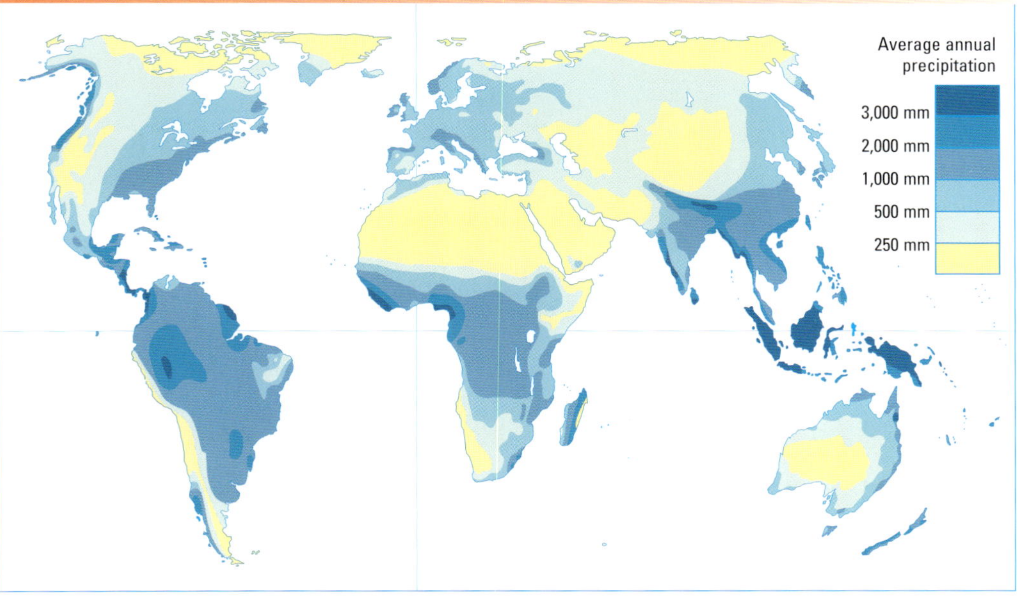
Average annual precipitation
3,000 mm
2,000 mm
1,000 mm
500 mm
250 mm

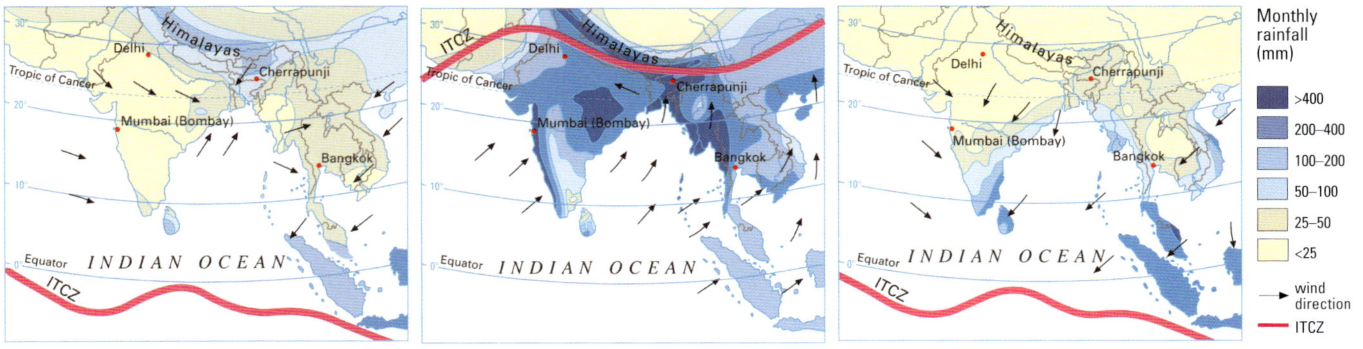
Himalayas
Delhi
Cherrapunji
Tropic of Cancer
Mumbai (Bombay)
Bangkok
Equator
INDIAN OCEAN
ITCZ
Monthly rainfall (mm)
>400
200–400
100–200
50–100
25–50
<25
wind direction
ITCZ

**March** – Start of the hot, dry season. The ITCZ is over the southern Indian Ocean.

**July** – The rainy season. The ITCZ has migrated northwards; winds blow onshore.

**November** – The ITCZ has returned south. The offshore winds are cool and dry.

## CLIMATE RECORDS

### TEMPERATURE

**Highest recorded temperature:** Al Aziziyah, Libya, 57.7°C [135.9°F], 13 September 1922.

**Highest mean annual temperature:** Dallol, Ethiopia, 34.4°C [94°F], 1960–6.

**Longest heatwave:** Marble Bar, W. Australia, 162 days over 38°C [100°F], 23 October 1923 to 7 April 1924.

**Lowest recorded temperature (outside poles):** Verkhoyansk, Siberia, –69.8°C [–93.6°F], 7 February 1982. Verkhoyansk also registered the greatest annual range of temperature: –68°C to 37°C [–90°F to 98°F].

**Lowest mean annual temperature:** Polus Nedostupnosti, Pole of Cold, Antarctica, –57.8°C [–72°F].

### PRECIPITATION

**Driest place:** Quillagua, N. Chile, mean annual rainfall 0.5 mm [0.02 in], 1964–2001.

**Wettest place (average):** Mt Wai'ale'ale, Hawai'i, USA, mean annual rainfall 11,680 mm [459.8 in].

**Wettest place (12 months):** Cherrapunji, Meghalaya, N.E. India, 26,461 mm [1,042 in], August 1860 to August 1861. Cherrapunji also holds the record for rainfall in one month: 2,930 mm [115 in], July 1861. (*See Monsoon maps below.*)

**Wettest place (24 hours):** Fac Fac, Réunion, Indian Ocean, 1,825 mm [71.9 in], 15–16 March 1952.

**Heaviest hailstones:** Gopalganj, Bangladesh, up to 1.02 kg [2.25 lb], 14 April 1986 (killed 92 people).

**Heaviest snowfall (continuous):** Bessans, Savoie, France, 1,730 mm [68 in] in 19 hours, 5–6 April 1969.

**Heaviest snowfall (season/year):** Mt Baker, Washington, USA, 28,956 mm [1,140 in], June 1998 to June 1999.

**For more information:**

11 Ocean currents
76 Atmosphere
78 Climate

Ever since the Industrial Revolution began, the amount of carbon dioxide in the atmosphere has steadily increased. It is the result of burning fossil fuels (coal, oil and natural gas), and also the destruction of forests which absorb carbon dioxide. In the late 18th century, carbon dioxide made up about 280 parts per million by volume (ppmv). Since 1958, regular measurements have been made at the Mauna Kea Observatory, Hawai'i, to avoid local pollution. It has since risen from 316 ppmv to 390 ppmv in 2010.

Carbon dioxide is one of the 'greenhouse gases', which also include CFCs (which also cause ozone depletion in the upper atmosphere), methane, and nitrous oxides. Water vapour is another greenhouse gas. The volume of vapour in the atmosphere is not changing significantly, though it may increase if the atmosphere warms up, causing an increase in the evaporation of surface waters.

Greenhouse gases are so-called because they slow the escape of heat that is reradiated from the Earth's surface, in much the same way the glass walls and roof of a greenhouse block the escape of heat. The greenhouse effect is essential for life on Earth. Without it, our planet would be some 30°C [54°F] colder than it is. But the increase in the volume of carbon dioxide in particular has caused global temperatures to rise. These changes were detailed by the Intergovernmental Panel on Climate Change (IPCC) report in 2007. While computer projections are difficult to make, the IPCC report concluded that a rise in temperatures of 4°C [7°F] was likely by 2100. Global warming will almost certainly alter weather patterns, causing extreme food and water shortages in vulnerable parts of the world, massive floods, and a rise in sea levels of between 18 cm and 59 cm [7–23 in].

While an international ban has been imposed on some greenhouse gases, their residence time in the atmosphere may have long-lasting consequences.

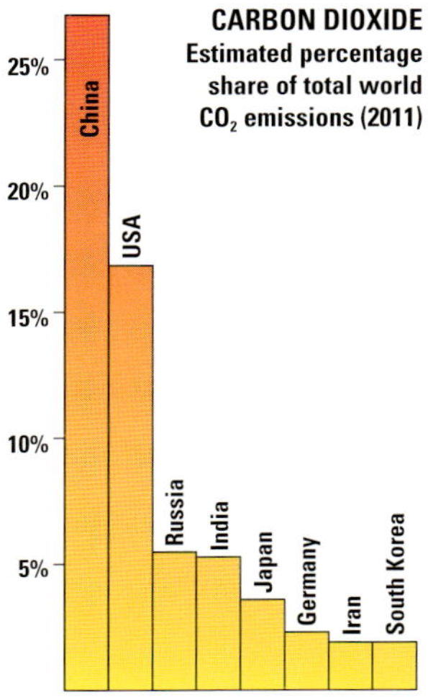
CARBON DIOXIDE
Estimated percentage share of total world $CO_2$ emissions (2011)
25%
20%
15%
10%
5%
China
USA
Russia
India
Japan
Germany
Iran
South Korea

In 2010 it was estimated that China was generating almost 80% of its electricity from coal-fired power stations to support its economic boom. It has since overtaken the USA to become the world's biggest producer of carbon dioxide.

## GLOBAL WARMING

High atmospheric concentrations of heat-absorbing gases appear to be causing a rise in average temperatures worldwide – up by approximately 1.5°C [3°F] by the year 2020, according to some estimates. Global warming is also likely to bring about a rise in sea levels that may flood some of the world's densely populated coastal areas.

Evidence of global warming is attributed mainly to the 'greenhouse effect', caused by the emission of certain gases, notably carbon dioxide, into the atmosphere. Despite international action to control emissions of some greenhouse gases, carbon dioxide levels are still rising.

**Carbon dioxide emissions in tonnes per capita (2011)**

- Over 15
- 10 – 15
- 5 – 10
- 1 – 5
- Under 1
- No data available

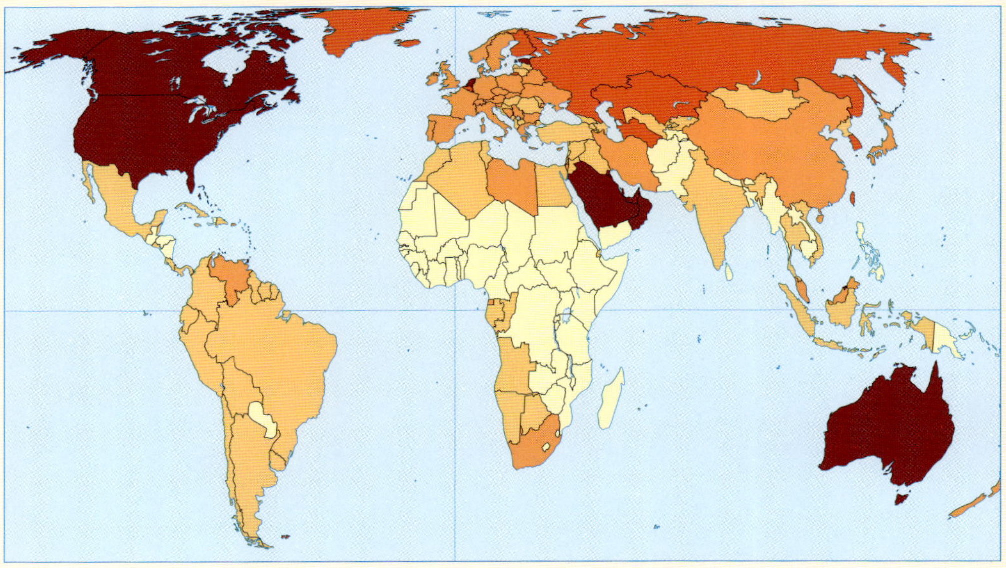

## CLIMATE CHANGE

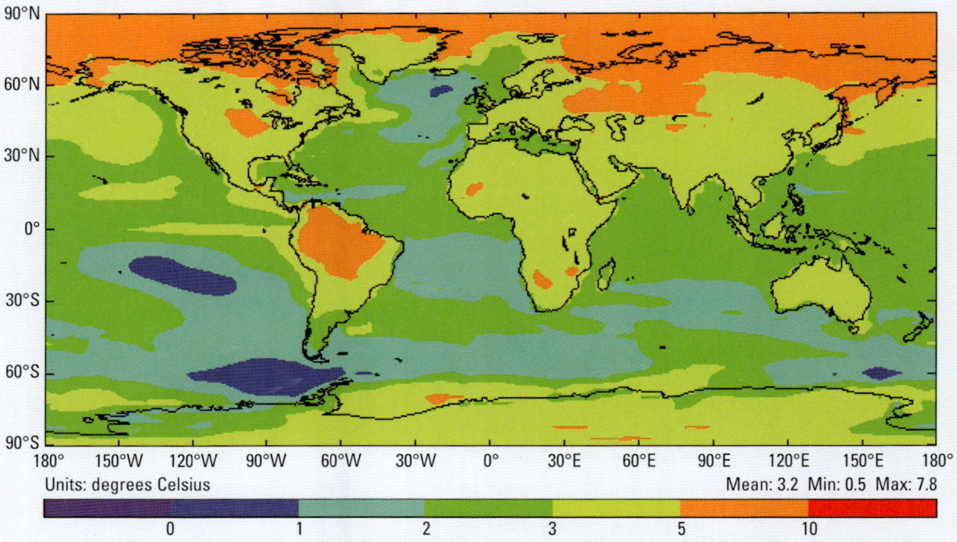
90°N
60°N
30°N
0°
30°S
60°S
90°S
180° 150°W 120°W 90°W 60°W 30°W 0° 30°E 60°E 90°E 120°E 150°E 180°
Units: degrees Celsius
Mean: 3.2 Min: 0.5 Max: 7.8
0 1 2 3 5 10

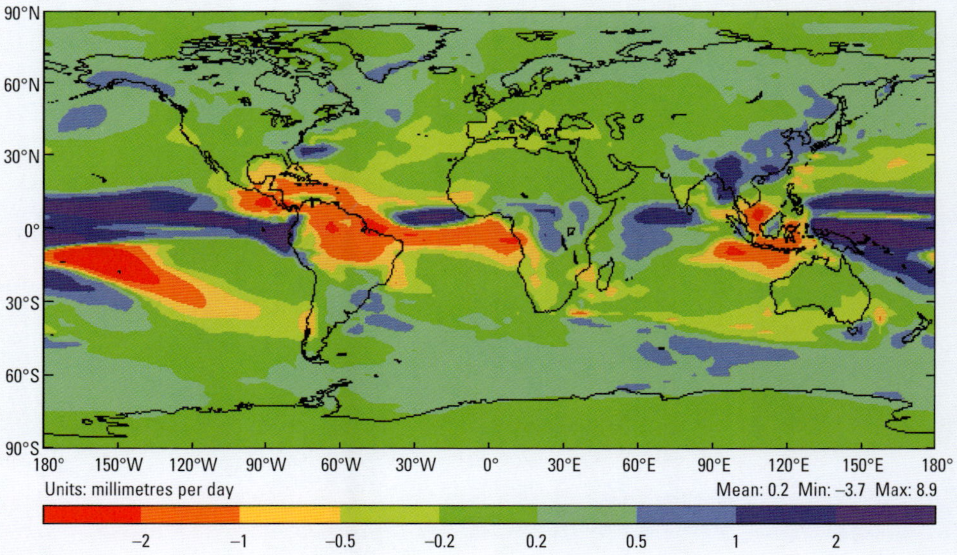
90°N
60°N
30°N
0°
30°S
60°S
90°S
180° 150°W 120°W 90°W 60°W 30°W 0° 30°E 60°E 90°E 120°E 150°E 180°
Units: millimetres per day
Mean: 0.2 Min: –3.7 Max: 8.9
–2 –1 –0.5 –0.2 0.2 0.5 1 2

### Annual average surface air temperature

The map summarizes the change in long-term mean values between the predicted average for the period from 2070 to 2100, and the observed average for 1960 to 1990. The predictions are from a long-term 'run' of a 'coupled' atmosphere-ocean computer model that represents the complex processes in the Earth's climate system. It assumes that the atmospheric concentration of carbon dioxide will increase more than twofold during the 21st century, assuming 'medium growth' of the global economy, and that no measures to combat the emission of greenhouse gases are taken. Note that the predicted increase in average surface temperature suggests a warming across Britain and Ireland of between 2°C [3.6°F] in the north and west to possibly 4°C [7.2°F] in the south-east. Very broadly, the oceans and some adjacent continental areas are likely to see the smaller increases.

### Annual average precipitation

Predictions from climate models always involve some degree of uncertainty. This is because our understanding of the climate system and its complex workings are imperfect, as are the model representations of the physical system. Additionally, we are unsure quite how the world will evolve economically and politically over the coming decades – although different scenarios are used in this regard. The map of predicted precipitation change indicates broadly, for example, an increase across Britain and Ireland. The largest increases of some 0.2–0.5 mm [0.01–0.02 in] a day are anticipated to be over northern and western areas. This equates to some 75–180 mm [3–7 in] a year.

It should be noted that both these maps mask quite significant seasonal detail, which is also predicted by the models.

## ARCTIC SEA ICE

The fact that the Arctic sea ice is disappearing has been known for decades. The underlying cause is believed by all but a handful of climatologists to be global warming, brought about by greenhouse-gas emissions. At current rates of shrinkage, this looks likely to happen some time between 2020 and 2050.

The reason is that Arctic air is warming twice as fast as the atmosphere as a whole. While some of the causes of this are understood, others are not. The darkness of land and water compared to the reflectiveness of snow and ice means that when the snow and ice melt to reveal land or water, the area exposed absorbs more heat from the Sun and reflects less of it back into space. The result is a feedback loop that accelerates local warming.

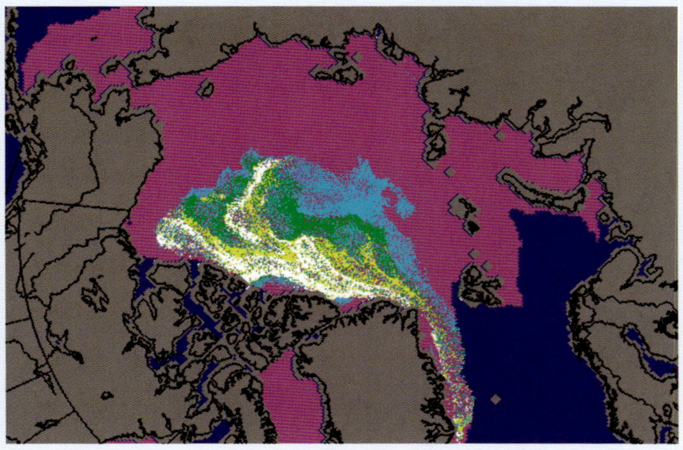

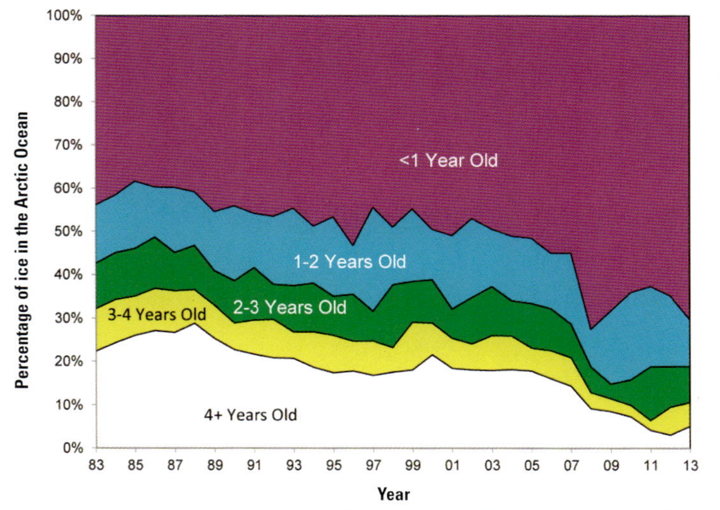

100%
90%
80%
70%
60%
50%
40%
30%
20%
10%
0%
Percentage of ice in the Arctic Ocean
<1 Year Old
1-2 Years Old
2-3 Years Old
3-4 Years Old
4+ Years Old
83 85 87 89 91 93 95 97 99 01 03 05 07 09 11 13
Year


The diagram and map show that ice older than 1 year, which used to cover up to 60% of the Arctic Ocean, now covers only 30%. The oldest ice, over 4 years old, now comprises only 5% of the ice in the Arctic Ocean, whereas during the 1980s it covered roughly 25% of the region.

NSIDC courtesy J. Maslanik and M. Tschudi, University of Colorado

## TEMPERATURE CHANGE

Climate modellers have produced simulations of global and continental surface temperature changes over the last century. This is done using only 'natural forcing' by modelling the impact on atmospheric temperatures from known solar variability and volcanic eruptions. In addition, the same period of time is simulated by adding to natural forcing the impact of anthropogenic (human) influence due to measured changes in the concentration of greenhouse gases, particulate matter, etc.

The separate model 'runs' are then compared with the observed temperature changes to illustrate which of the simulations matches the observations best.

This is a powerful means of verifying the relative roles of natural and human induced changes in atmospheric composition, and known solar output fluctuations on climate change.

► Climate model simulations for 1906 to 2005 using 'natural forcings only' (blue bands) and 'natural plus anthropogenic forcings' (pink bands). Regional decadal averages of observed temperature (black lines) are plotted as anomalies with respect to the 1901 to 1950 average. Blue and pink bands define the 5% to 95% range of possibilities for 19 runs produced by five models (natural forcing), and 58 simulations from 14 models (natural plus anthropogenic forcing).

Models using only natural forcings

Models using both natural and anthropogenic forcings

Observations
(dashed when spatial coverage is less than 50%)

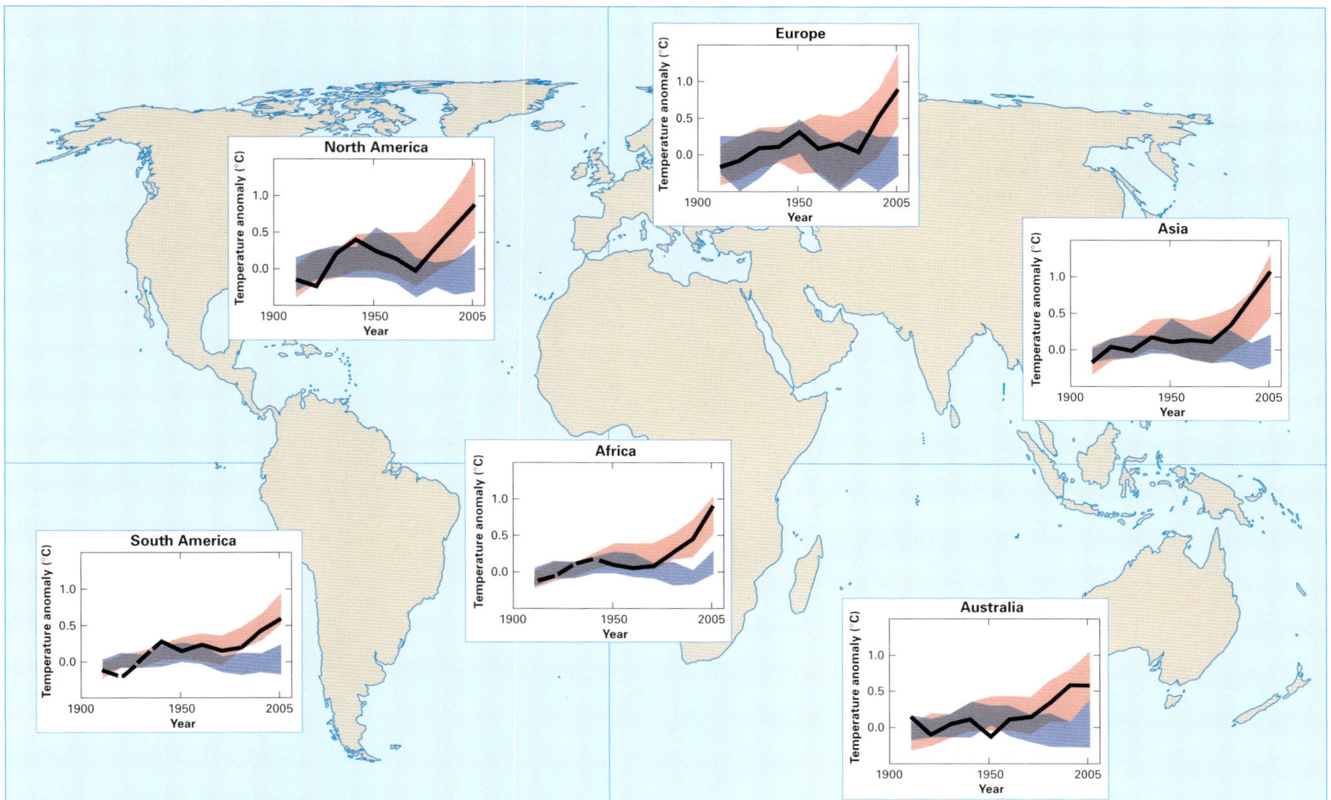

Europe
North America
Asia
Africa
South America
Australia
Temperature anomaly (°C)
1.0
0.5
0.0
1900
1950
2005
Year


Source: Intergovernmental Panel on Climate Change (IPCC)

## PROJECTED CHANGE IN GLOBAL WARMING

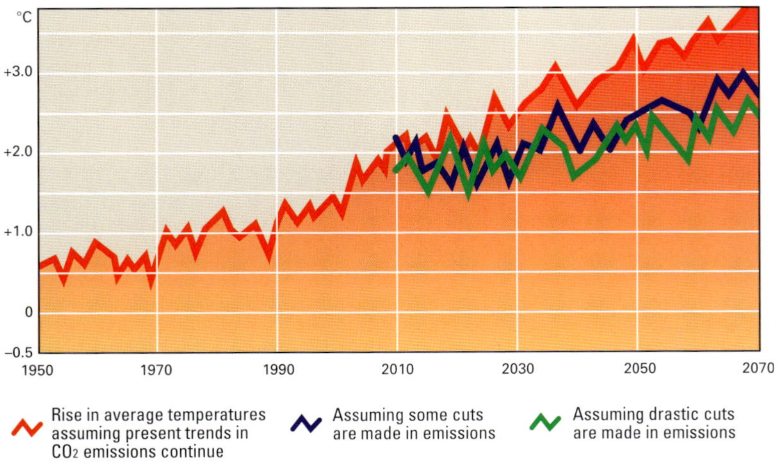

°C
+3.0
+2.0
+1.0
0
–0.5
1950 1970 1990 2010 2030 2050 2070
Rise in average temperatures assuming present trends in CO2 emissions continue
Assuming some cuts are made in emissions
Assuming drastic cuts are made in emissions


Climate models are used to provide the best scientifically-based estimates of the future global climate. A typical method is to run the models for some decades ahead and then to compare the predicted average with a past 30-year period. A range of climate models are used, run with different scenarios that express the breadth of possibilities of, for example, industrial development and the degree of atmospheric pollution 'clean-up' by industrial nations.

The diagram above shows global observed and predicted surface mean temperature change from 1950 to 2070 with three prediction scenarios. The first (red) assumes rapid economic growth and continued population increases. The second (blue) assumes some attempts are made to cut greenhouse gas emissions, while the green line involves the greater use of cleaner technologies, with global population peaking mid-century then declining.

## THE OZONE LAYER

**Total atmospheric ozone concentration in the southern hemisphere**

In 1985, scientists working in Antarctica discovered a thinning of the ozone layer, resulting in what is commonly known as the 'ozone hole'. This caused immediate alarm because the ozone layer absorbs most of the Sun's dangerous ultraviolet radiation, which is believed to cause an increase in skin cancer, cataracts, and damage to the immune system.

Between 1985 and 2001 the ozone depletion increased and, by 2002, the ozone hole over the South Pole was estimated to be three times as large as the USA. These false-colour images show the total atmospheric ozone concentration in the southern hemisphere in November 1985 and 2012, with the ozone hole in the former clearly identifiable in purple and blue at the centre. The data is from NASA's Aura satellite, ESA's ERS-2 satellite, and the NOAA-16 weather-forecasting satellite. The colours represent the ozone concentration in Dobson Units (DU).

Scientists agree that ozone depletion is caused by CFCs, a group of manufactured chemicals that were used in refrigerators and air-conditioning systems. In the Montreal Protocol in 1987, industrial nations agreed to phase out CFCs, and a complete ban on most CFCs was agreed after the end of 1995.

Since 2001 the amount of ozone in the atmosphere has stabilized and so too has the hole. While scientists believe that the chemicals may remain in the atmosphere for 50 to 100 years, if current trends are maintained it is possible that ozone levels may recover by 2050.

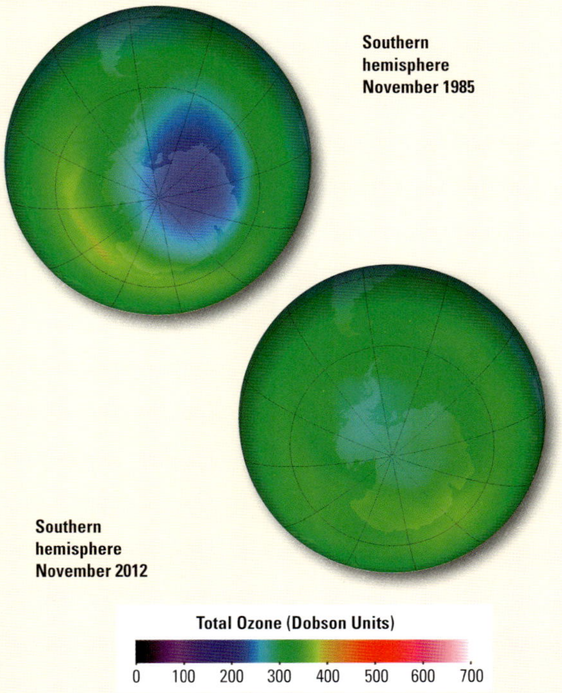

Southern hemisphere November 1985
Southern hemisphere November 2012
Total Ozone (Dobson Units)
0 100 200 300 400 500 600 700

**For more information:**
78 Climate regions
79 Precipitation
84 Biodiversity

Without the hydrological cycle, by which water is constantly recycled between the oceans, the atmosphere and the land, the continents would be barren. Precipitation enables plants to grow and soils to form, creating the world's natural vegetation regions and the ecosystems that support animal life.

Running water also plays a major role in shaping landforms. Yet in many parts of the world, people do not have safe water to drink and suffer from diseases caused by water-borne organisms and pollution. It is estimated that 780 million people lack access to safe water and more people have a mobile phone than a toilet.

Experts argue that world demand for water is increasing at about twice the rate of population growth. It is predicted that, by 2025, half the world's population will face water shortages. This could lead to conflict and even boundary wars – 300 major rivers cross national frontiers and access to their water is likely to be disputed.

## THE HYDROLOGICAL CYCLE

The world's water balance is regulated by the constant recycling of water between the oceans, the atmosphere and the land. The movement of water between these three reservoirs is known as the 'hydrological cycle'. The oceans play a vital role in the hydrological cycle: 74% of the total precipitation falls over the oceans and 84% of the total evaporation comes from the oceans. Water vapour in the atmosphere circulates around the planet, transporting energy as well as the water itself. When the vapour cools, it falls as rain or snow. The whole cycle is driven by the Sun.

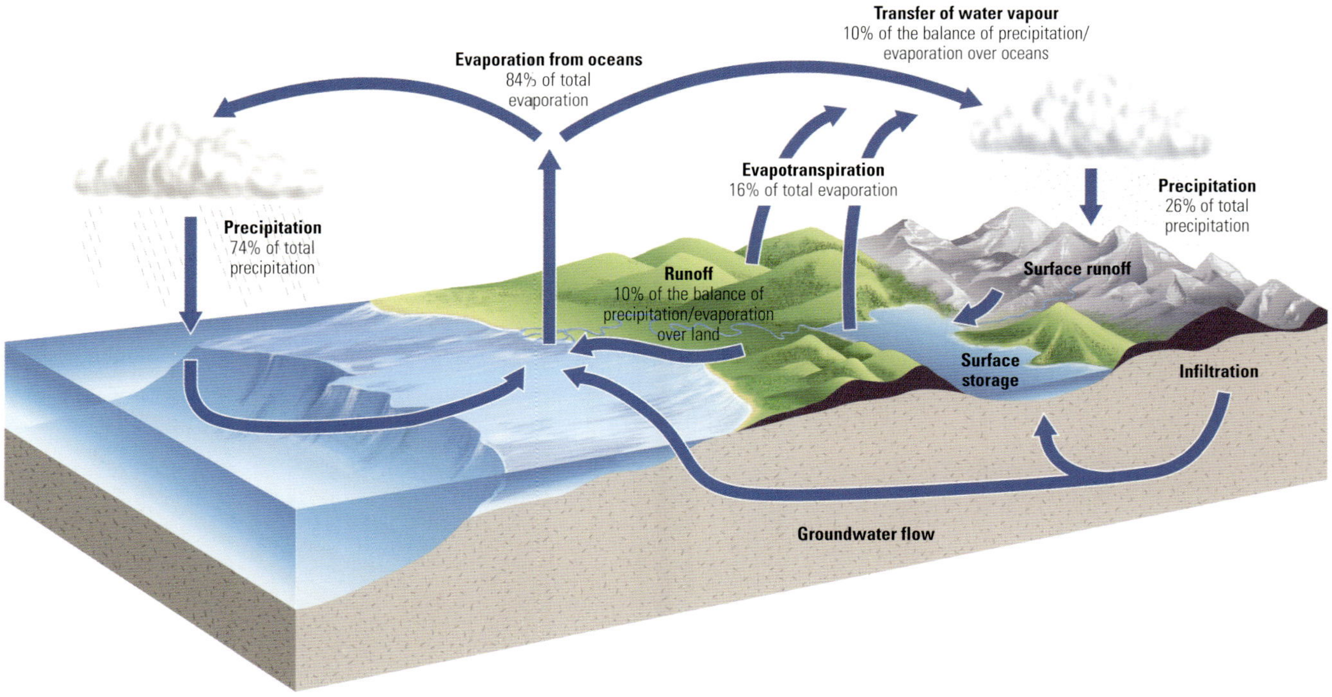
Transfer of water vapour
10% of the balance of precipitation/ evaporation over oceans
Evaporation from oceans
84% of total evaporation
Evapotranspiration
16% of total evaporation
Precipitation
26% of total precipitation
Precipitation
74% of total precipitation
Runoff
10% of the balance of precipitation/evaporation over land
Surface runoff
Surface storage
Infiltration
Groundwater flow

## WATER DISTRIBUTION

The distribution of planetary water is shown by percentage. Oceans and ice caps together account for more than 99% of the total; the breakdown of the remainder is estimated.

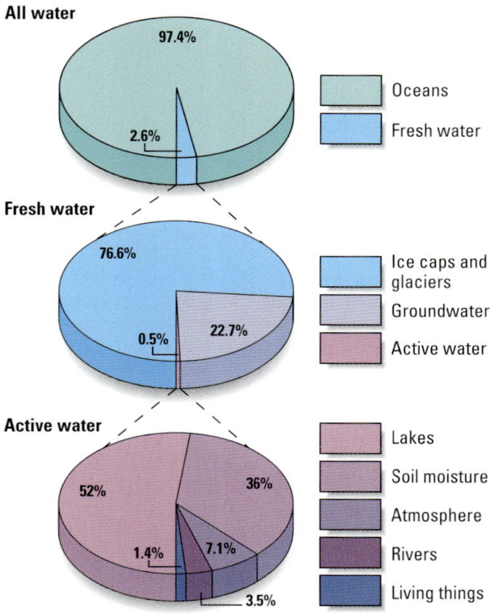
All water
97.4%
2.6%
Oceans
Fresh water
Fresh water
76.6%
0.5%
22.7%
Ice caps and glaciers
Groundwater
Active water
Active water
52%
36%
1.4%
7.1%
3.5%
Lakes
Soil moisture
Atmosphere
Rivers
Living things

Almost all the world's water is 3,000 million years old, and all of it cycles endlessly through the hydrosphere, though at different rates. Water vapour circulates over days, even hours; deep-ocean water circulates over millennia; and ice-cap water remains solid for millions of years.

## ANNUAL SEDIMENT YIELD

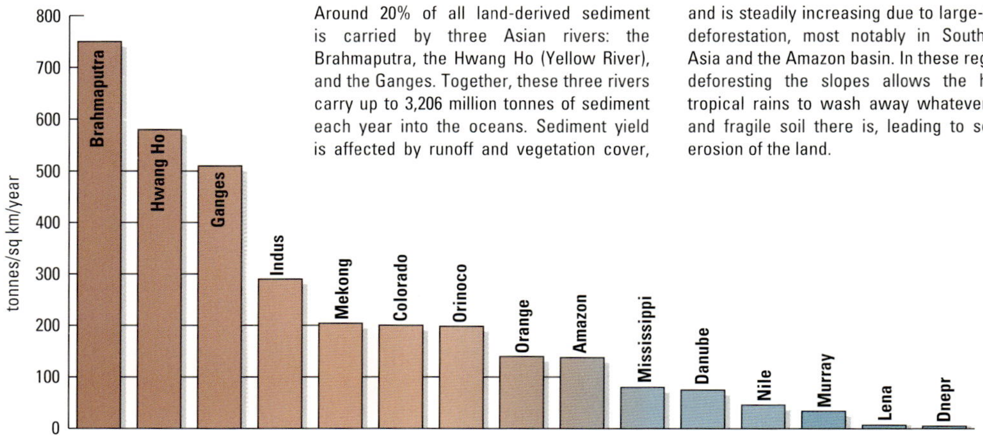
tonnes/sq km/year
800
700
600
500
400
300
200
100
0
Brahmaputra
Hwang Ho
Ganges
Indus
Mekong
Colorado
Orinoco
Orange
Amazon
Mississippi
Danube
Nile
Murray
Lena
Dnepr

Around 20% of all land-derived sediment is carried by three Asian rivers: the Brahmaputra, the Hwang Ho (Yellow River), and the Ganges. Together, these three rivers carry up to 3,206 million tonnes of sediment each year into the oceans. Sediment yield is affected by runoff and vegetation cover, and is steadily increasing due to large-scale deforestation, most notably in South-east Asia and the Amazon basin. In these regions, deforesting the slopes allows the heavy tropical rains to wash away whatever thin and fragile soil there is, leading to severe erosion of the land.

## WATER RUNOFF

**Annual fresh water runoff by continent in cubic kilometres**

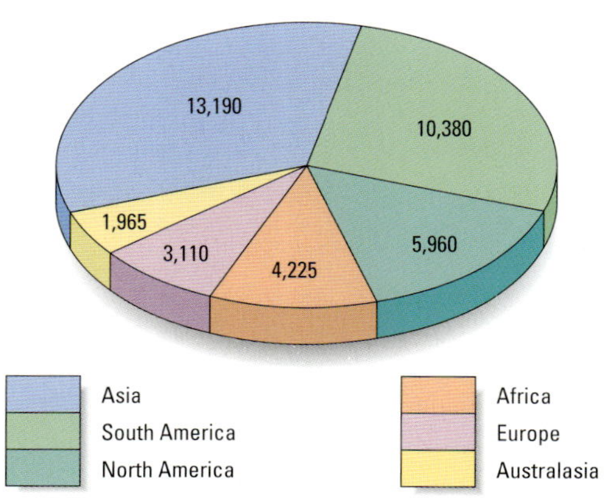
13,190
10,380
1,965
3,110
4,225
5,960
Asia
South America
North America
Africa
Europe
Australasia

► The River Amazon is the world's second-longest river (after the River Nile), draining the vast rainforest basin of northern South America. The Amazon carries by far the greatest volume of water of any river in the world: the average rate of discharge is approximately 95,000 cu m [3,355,000 cu ft] per second, nearly three times as much as its nearest rival, the Congo. The flow is so great that its silt discolours the water up to 200 km [125 miles] into the Atlantic. At approximately 7 million sq km [2.7 million sq miles], the Amazon basin comprises nearly 40% of the whole of South America. Nevertheless, in 2010 large parts of the Amazon rainforest were at their driest in living memory. Rainfall was significantly below average and some Amazon tributaries, such as the Rio Negro, were at their lowest levels for over 100 years. Rivers and lakes began to dry up, revealing huge sandbanks and making navigation difficult for boats. The image shows the Rio Negro joining the Amazon from the north.

## WATER SCARCITY

Human populations require fresh water for many purposes – drinking, cooking, washing, farming, industry, recreation and energy production. Given population growth and rising standards of living in some areas, there will inevitably be increased pressure on this resource in certain places. Water scarcity can be physical and/or economic.

- Areas with little or no water scarcity – less than 25% of water from rivers is withdrawn for agriculture, industry and domestic purposes
- Areas with physical water scarcity – more than 75% of water from rivers is withdrawn for agriculture, industry and domestic purposes
- Areas approaching physical water scarcity – more than 60% of water from rivers is withdrawn and scarcity is expected in the near future
- Areas with economic water scarcity – less than 25% of water from rivers is withdrawn but human, institutional and financial problems limit access to water
- No data available

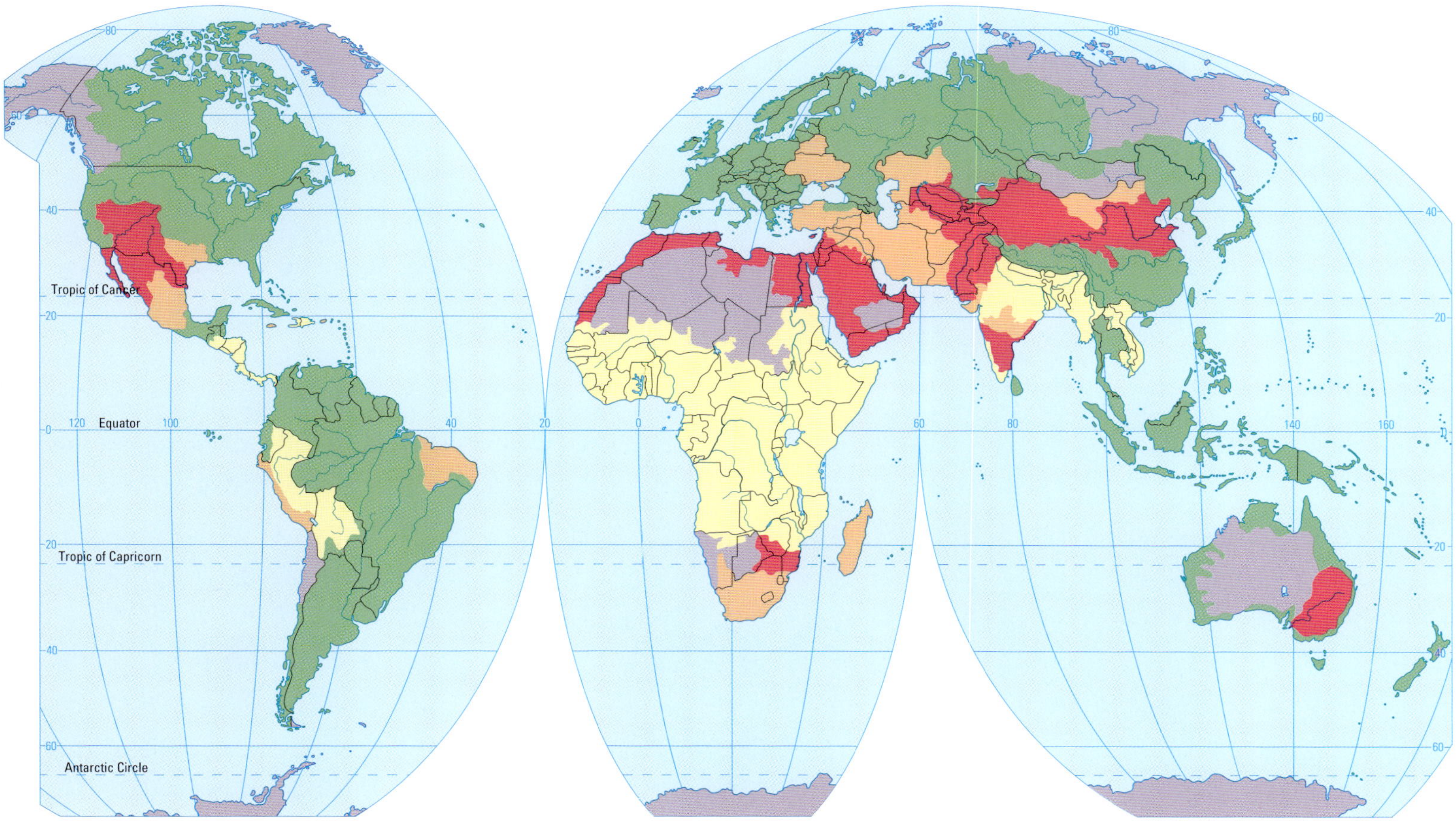

Tropic of Cancer
Equator
Tropic of Capricorn
Antarctic Circle


## NATURAL VEGETATION

The map below illustrates the natural 'climax vegetation' of a region, as dictated by its climate and topography. In most cases, human agricultural activity has drastically altered the pattern of the vegetation. The various vegetation regions support different kinds of animals and wildlife, and, in an undisturbed state, they are highly developed biological communities, or 'biomes'.

The blue line on the map represents the northern limit of tree growth, and the red lines indicate the northern and southern limits of palm growth. The majority of the numerous species are tropical or subtropical. Some, such as the coconut, date, sago, and oil palms, are important economically.

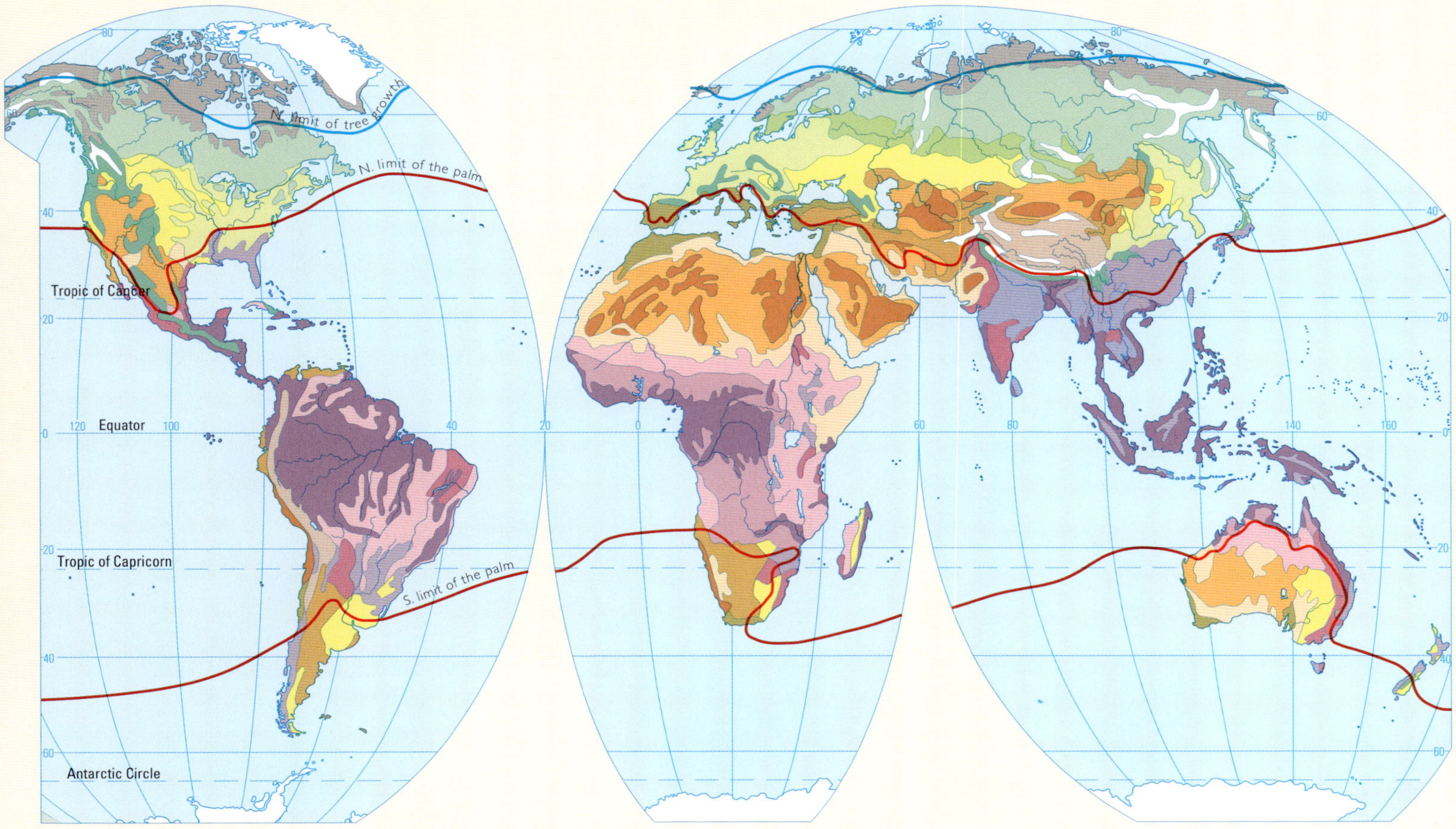

N. limit of tree growth
N. limit of the palm
S. limit of the palm
Tropic of Cancer
Equator
Tropic of Capricorn
Antarctic Circle


- Tropical rainforest
- Subtropical and temperate rainforest
- Monsoon woodland and open jungle
- Subtropical and temperate woodland, scrub and bush
- Tropical savanna, with low trees and bush
- Tropical savanna and grasslands
- Dry semi-desert, with shrub and grass
- Desert shrub
- Desert
- Dry steppe and shrub
- Temperate grasslands, prairie and steppe
- Mediterranean hardwood forest and scrub
- Temperate deciduous forest and meadow
- Temperate deciduous and coniferous forest
- Northern coniferous forest (taïga)
- Mountainous forest, mainly coniferous
- High plateau steppe and tundra
- Arctic tundra
- Polar and mountainous ice desert

**For more information:**
78 Climate
80 Climate change
Global warming
83 Natural vegetation

Biodiversity refers to the variety of living material. It includes the variety of species, the variety within the same species, and the variety of ecosystems within which species operate. Estimates of the number of species in the world vary from between 7 million and 80 million. The currently accepted total is about 14 million, yet only 2 million species have been formally identified.

Biodiversity is vital for human survival. It remains the basis for our food and most of our medicine. In less economically developed countries (LEDCs), over 20% of the food consumed is gathered from natural sources. At a global level, over 15% of animal protein consumed is from sea fish caught in the wild. More than 60% of the world's population rely on traditional medicines for their health care. In Mexico, the Popoluca Indians 'farm' over 250 species of plant. Many medicines come from natural sources. Aspirin, for example, comes from an acid taken from the bark of willow trees. The anti-cancer drug 'taxol' originates from the wild Pacific yew tree. It is estimated that the pharmaceuticals industry gains US $32 billion per year in profits from traditional remedies.

However, the loss of biodiversity is increasing at an accelerating rate. Up to 27,000 species a year may be lost, and the United Nations Environment Programme (UNEP) suggests that the current rate of extinction is 50–100 times greater than 'normal', and believes that up to 25% of all the world's species may be lost by 2025. The main reasons for the decline are the introduction of alien species and habitat destruction. Human impact on biodiversity has brought about more extinctions than any other single factor since the extinction of the dinosaurs (65 million years ago).

Since 1600, 39% of animal extinctions have been due to the introduction of alien species, 36% from habitat destruction, and 23% from hunting or deliberate extermination. The introduction of rats, cats and other species has led to the extinction of many flightless birds in Polynesia. Plantation crops, such as rubber, often thrive best when taken away from their natural homes, since in the new lands there may not be the pests to control them. One noted example of extinction was caused by the introduction of the Nile perch into Lake Victoria, East Africa: introduced in the 1960s, it led to the extinction of some 50 species of cichlid fish within 20 years.

In 2012, a report by the International Union for the Conservation of Nature listed 20,219 organisms facing extinction. Up to 46% of primates are said to be at risk of extinction. Overall, some 25% of mammals are endangered – including 'charismatic' species such as the tiger and the panda, but equally less recognizable species of bats, rodents and marsupials. Up to one-fifth of reptiles, one-third of amphibians and one-third of bird species are at risk of extinction. The most threatened group are fish (one-third are at risk), largely as a result of overfishing. The IUCN also reported that 8% of mammals were threatened in the US, compared with 32% in the Philippines and 44% in Madagascar, two countries where habitat destruction has been proceeding on a large scale.

**THREATENED SPECIES**
**Total number of threatened species for selected countries in each continent**

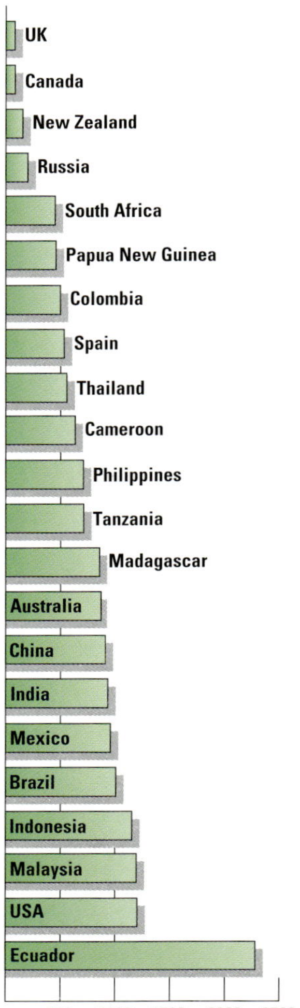
UK
Canada
New Zealand
Russia
South Africa
Papua New Guinea
Colombia
Spain
Thailand
Cameroon
Philippines
Tanzania
Madagascar
Australia
China
India
Mexico
Brazil
Indonesia
Malaysia
USA
Ecuador
500
1000
1500
2000
2500

Source: IUCN Red List 2012

## THREATENED MAMMAL SPECIES

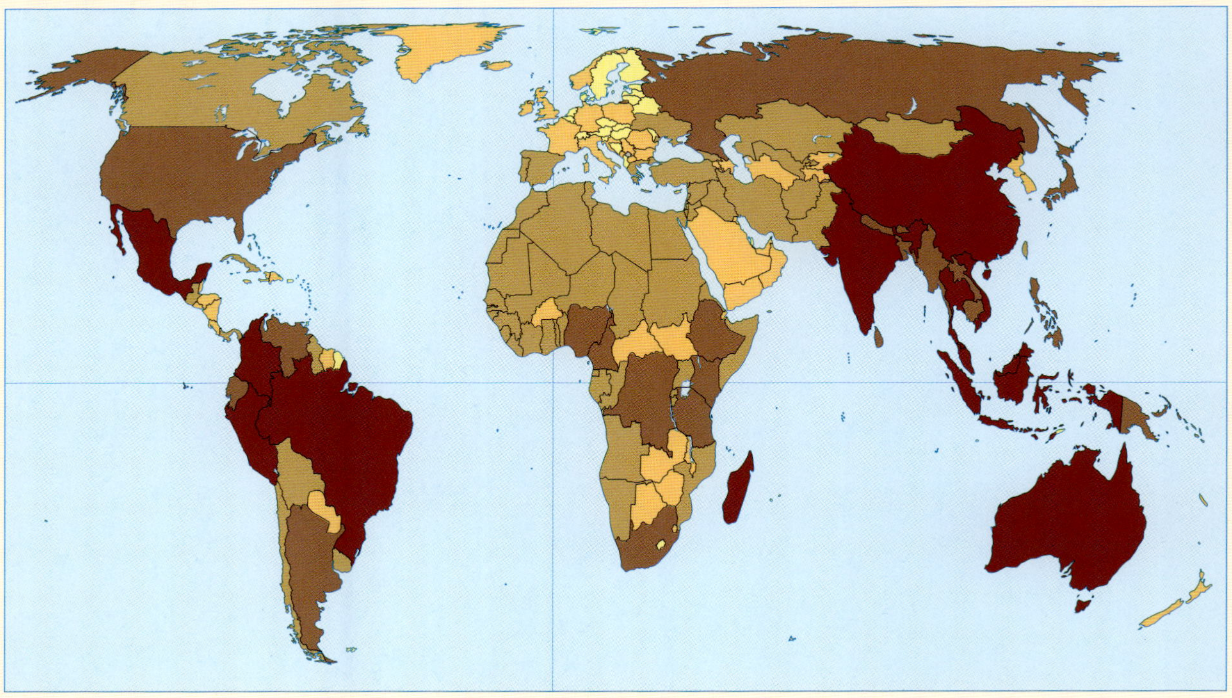

**Mammal species threatened with extinction (2011)**

- Over 50
- 25 – 50
- 10 – 25
- 5 – 10
- 0 – 5
- No data

**Countries with the highest number of mammal species threatened with extinction (2011)**

| | |
|---|---|
| Indonesia | 184 |
| Mexico | 100 |
| India | 94 |
| Brazil | 81 |
| China | 75 |
| Malaysia | 70 |
| Madagascar | 65 |
| Thailand | 57 |
| Australia | 55 |
| Peru | 54 |
| Vietnam | 54 |
| Colombia | 52 |

## THREATENED NATIVE ('ENDEMIC') SPECIES (SELECTED COUNTRIES)

| Country | Mammals | | Birds | | Amphibians | |
|---|---|---|---|---|---|---|
| | Total endemic | Threatened endemic | Total endemic | Threatened endemic | Total endemic | Threatened endemic |
| Argentina | 82 | 13 | 12 | 0 | 36 | 21 |
| Australia | 241 | 49 | 322 | 27 | 209 | 47 |
| Bolivia | 22 | 4 | 15 | 5 | 64 | 27 |
| Brazil | 185 | 54 | 203 | 71 | 529 | 26 |
| China | 82 | 17 | 59 | 17 | 169 | 74 |
| Colombia | 37 | 9 | 68 | 43 | 333 | 154 |
| Congo (Dem. Rep.) | 25 | 4 | 12 | 8 | 42 | 4 |
| Cuba | 21 | 12 | 22 | 8 | 59 | 49 |
| Ecuador | 30 | 12 | 34 | 19 | 156 | 98 |
| Ethiopia | 32 | 18 | 15 | 10 | 24 | 9 |
| India | 44 | 29 | 54 | 16 | 150 | 61 |
| Indonesia | 257 | 114 | 378 | 70 | 172 | 21 |
| Japan | 41 | 16 | 15 | 6 | 45 | 17 |
| Kenya | 12 | 7 | 8 | 6 | 14 | 4 |
| Madagascar | 186 | 58 | 107 | 28 | 242 | 67 |
| Malaysia | 19 | 3 | 7 | 0 | 45 | 22 |
| Mexico | 158 | 80 | 88 | 22 | 245 | 171 |
| Panama | 13 | 4 | 8 | 3 | 27 | 13 |
| Papua New Guinea | 69 | 20 | 84 | 16 | 174 | 9 |
| Peru | 55 | 19 | 106 | 36 | 223 | 70 |
| Philippines | 111 | 25 | 196 | 59 | 79 | 48 |
| South Africa | 31 | 11 | 16 | 4 | 42 | 16 |
| Tanzania | 22 | 18 | 24 | 15 | 72 | 48 |
| USA | 104 | 20 | 67 | 35 | 182 | 49 |
| Venezuela | 19 | 6 | 39 | 14 | 142 | 63 |

▲ Madagascar has developed in isolation since it split from Africa 150 million years ago. As a result of this isolation, a unique range of plants and animals has evolved, adapted to its own specific conditions. Over 95% of Madagascar's mammals, 90% of its reptiles, over 66% of its plants, and over 40% of its breeding birds do not exist anywhere else in the world.

Madagascar is home to all of the world's lemurs (all of which are endangered, such as the aye-aye pictured above) and two-thirds of the world's chameleons. Its plant species include pitcher plants, orchids, and the Madagascar rosy periwinkle (the most effective known treatment for childhood leukemia). However, large-scale deforestation since the 1970s has reduced Madagascar's cover of rainforest to less than 10% of the island's original forest cover.

## ENVIRONMENTAL HOTSPOTS

Up to 75% of the world's most threatened mammals, birds and amphibians live in an area covering just 2.3% of the Earth's surface, and roughly half of all flowering plant species and 42% of land-based vertebrates exist in 34 biological hotspots.

Scientists argue that, with limited financial resources, governments and conservationists should prioritize by protecting the small total land areas that account for a very high percentage of global biodiversity. In 1999, scientists identified 25 such areas, mostly in the tropics, which were the centre of global biodiversity.

The number of hotspots has risen to 34. These include the mountains of central Asia, the whole of Japan, the Horn of Africa including the Ethiopian highlands, and the Himalayas region. The hotspots once covered 15.7% of the Earth's surface, an area roughly the size of Russia and Australia combined – now they cover only 2.3% of the Earth's surface, an area slightly larger than India.

Over 70% of all mammals, 86% of all birds, and 92% of all amphibians are crammed into this small area of the world's total land mass. Madagascar and the Indian Ocean Islands hotspot was found to have very high concentrations of plant and vertebrate families that are found nowhere else on the globe.

Global warming could have a devastating effect on biodiversity hotspots such as the Amazonian and Indonesian rainforests. By 2100, between 12% and 39% of the land surface of the Earth will have a new climate. There are numerous species that will be unable to move in order to stay within their preferred climate range. These species will either have to evolve rapidly or die out.

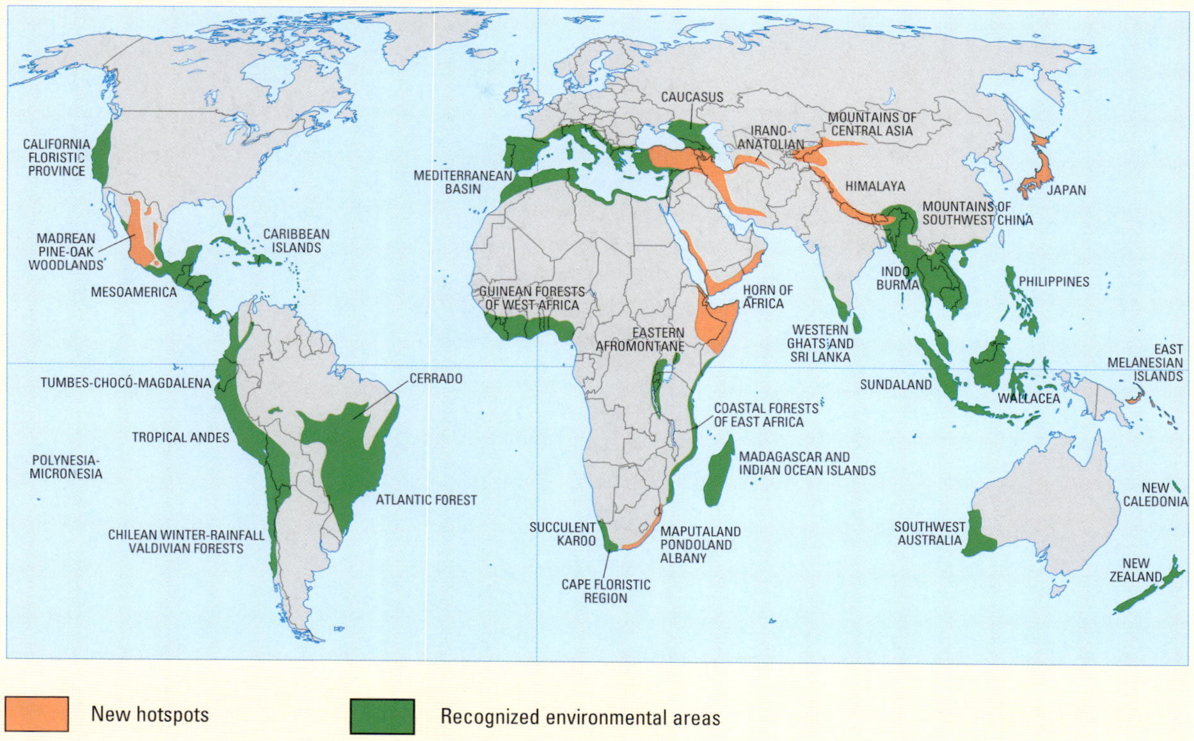
CALIFORNIA FLORISTIC PROVINCE
MADREAN PINE-OAK WOODLANDS
CARIBBEAN ISLANDS
MESOAMERICA
TUMBES-CHOCÓ-MAGDALENA
CERRADO
POLYNESIA-MICRONESIA
TROPICAL ANDES
ATLANTIC FOREST
CHILEAN WINTER-RAINFALL VALDIVIAN FORESTS
MEDITERRANEAN BASIN
CAUCASUS
IRANO-ANATOLIAN
MOUNTAINS OF CENTRAL ASIA
HIMALAYA
JAPAN
MOUNTAINS OF SOUTHWEST CHINA
INDO BURMA
PHILIPPINES
GUINEAN FORESTS OF WEST AFRICA
HORN OF AFRICA
EASTERN AFROMONTANE
WESTERN GHATS AND SRI LANKA
SUNDALAND
WALLACEA
EAST MELANESIAN ISLANDS
COASTAL FORESTS OF EAST AFRICA
MADAGASCAR AND INDIAN OCEAN ISLANDS
NEW CALEDONIA
SUCCULENT KAROO
MAPUTALAND PONDOLAND ALBANY
SOUTHWEST AUSTRALIA
NEW ZEALAND
CAPE FLORISTIC REGION
New hotspots
Recognized environmental areas

## AUSTRALIA'S INTRODUCED SPECIES

Australia's native plants and animals adapted to life on an isolated continent over millions of years. Since European settlement in the 18th century they have had to compete with a range of species introduced by the settlers, which impact on the native species by predation, competition for food and shelter, destroying habitat, and by spreading diseases. Introduced species typically have few predators or fatal diseases, and some have very high reproductive rates.

Management and the prevention of the introduction of new invasive species are key environmental and agricultural policy issues for the Australian federal and state governments.

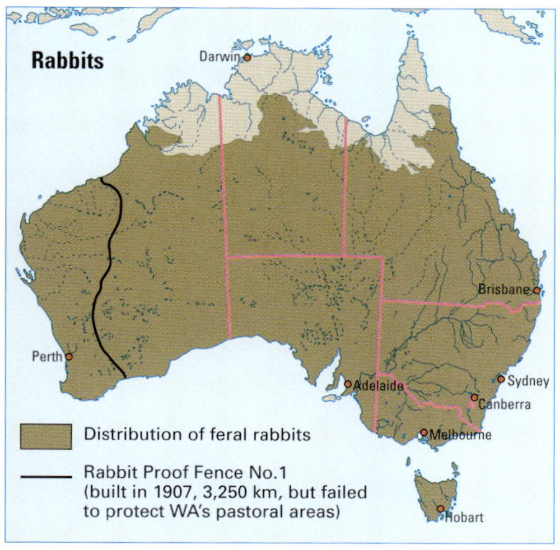
Rabbits
Darwin
Brisbane
Perth
Adelaide
Sydney
Canberra
Melbourne
Hobart
Distribution of feral rabbits
Rabbit Proof Fence No.1 (built in 1907, 3,250 km, but failed to protect WA's pastoral areas)

▲ Rabbits were introduced to Australia from England in 1859 for hunting, and quickly spread throughout the country. They are one of the most destructive introduced species in Australia, competing with native wildlife, damaging vegetation, and degrading the land.

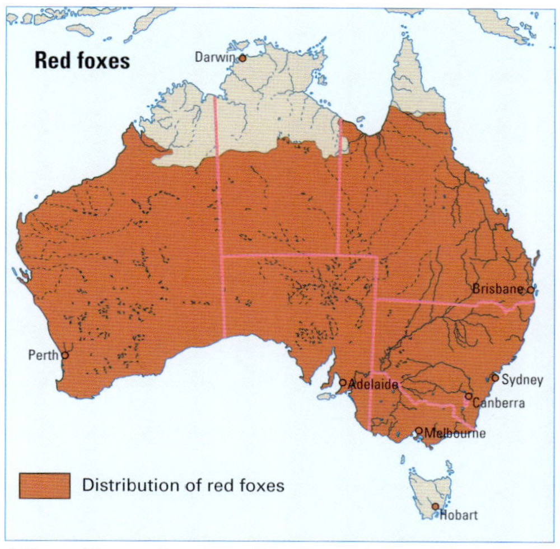
Red foxes
Darwin
Brisbane
Perth
Adelaide
Sydney
Canberra
Melbourne
Hobart
Distribution of red foxes

▲ The red fox was introduced from Europe for recreational hunting in 1855 and populations became established in the wild within 15 years. They prey on newborn lambs and have also been responsible for the decline of a number of native species.

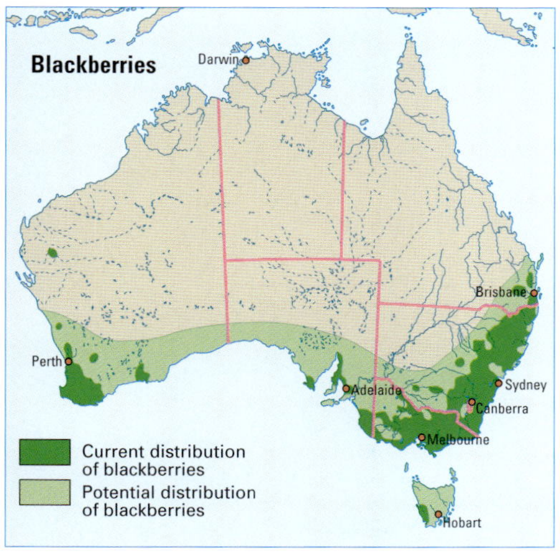
Blackberries
Darwin
Brisbane
Perth
Adelaide
Sydney
Canberra
Melbourne
Hobart
Current distribution of blackberries
Potential distribution of blackberries

▲ The blackberry was introduced from Europe as a source of fresh fruit. It is now regarded as one of the worst weeds in Australia because of its invasiveness, spreading through farmland, forests and scrub. It out-competes many native plants, prevents light reaching the ground below, and provides food and shelter for pests.

Cane toads
Darwin
Brisbane
Perth
Adelaide
Sydney
Canberra
Melbourne
Hobart
Distribution of cane toads

▲ Cane toads were introduced in 1935 to control beetles which were threatening the sugar-cane industry. However, this was a failure and both the toad and the beetle are still thriving. They adapted well to the Australian environment and with no natural predators they quickly spread. They eat small native wildlife and poison any predators.

## ESTIMATED VALUE OF WILD RESOURCES IN LESS ECONOMICALLY DEVELOPED COUNTRIES

| | |
|---|---|
| Tropical non-coniferous forest product exports | US $11 billion per year |
| Fruit/latex harvesting, Peru | US $6,330 per hectare |
| Sustainable timber harvesting, Peru | US $490 per hectare |
| Buffalo range ranching, Zimbabwe | US $3.5–4.5 per hectare |
| Wetlands fish and fuelwood, Nigeria | US $38–59 per hectare |
| Viewing value of elephants, Kenya | US $25 million per year |
| Ecotourism, Costa Rica | US $1,250 per hectare |
| Tourism, Thailand | US $385,000–860,000 per year |
| Research/education, Thailand | US $38,000–77,000 per year |
| Tourism, Cameroon | US $10 per hectare |
| Genetic value, Cameroon | US $7 per hectare |
| Pharmaceutical prospecting, Costa Rica | US $4,981 million per product |

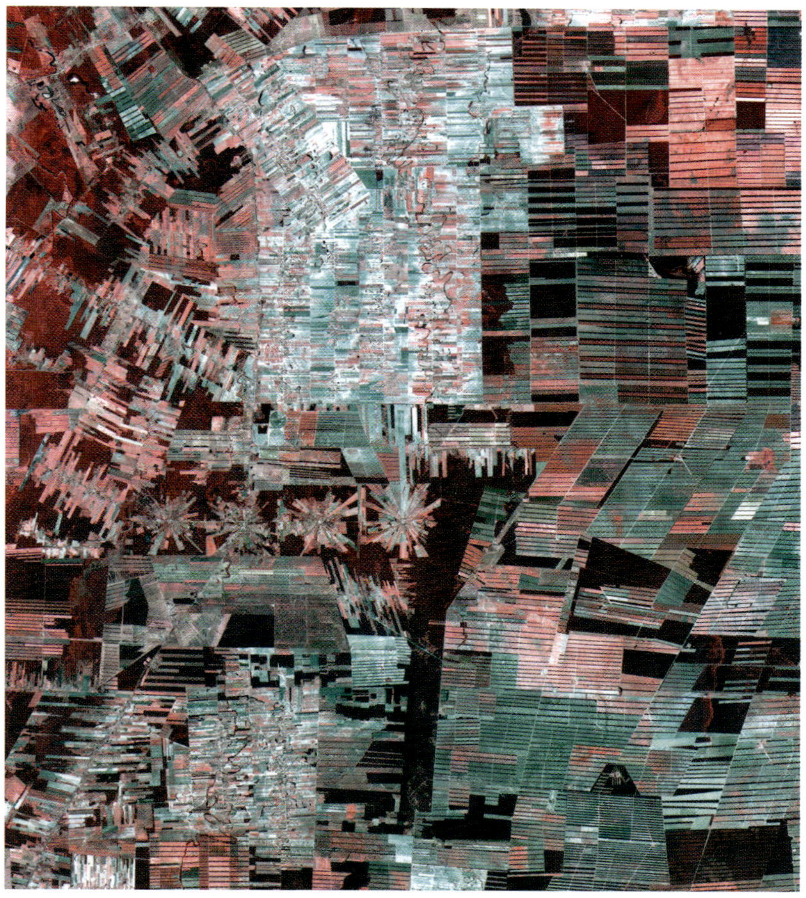

▲ Bolivia has over 250,000 sq km [100,000 sq miles] of dry tropical forest, home to animals such as jaguars and ocelots. It is, however, being cleared at a rate of over 2% per annum. This false-colour image shows an area that has been almost completely cleared. The darkest areas are remnants of the original forest, some of which have been retained as wind-breaks between newly created arable fields. The radial patterns are fields with new villages at their centres, part of a government resettlement scheme.

**For more information:**

89 Food and population
90 Urbanization of the Earth
Urban population
91 Largest cities

## LARGEST NATIONS

**The world's most populous nations, in millions (2012)**

| | | |
|---|---|---|
| 1. | China | 1,343 |
| 2. | India | 1,205 |
| 3. | USA | 314 |
| 4. | Indonesia | 248 |
| 5. | Brazil | 206 |
| 6. | Pakistan | 190 |
| 7. | Nigeria | 170 |
| 8. | Bangladesh | 161 |
| 9. | Russia | 138 |
| 10. | Japan | 127 |
| 11. | Mexico | 115 |
| 12. | Philippines | 104 |
| 13. | Ethiopia | 94 |
| 14. | Vietnam | 92 |
| 15. | Egypt | 84 |
| 16. | Germany | 81 |
| 17. | Turkey | 80 |
| 18. | Iran | 79 |
| 19. | Congo (Dem. Rep.) | 74 |
| 20. | Thailand | 67 |
| 21. | France | 66 |
| 22. | UK | 63 |
| 23. | Italy | 61 |
| 24. | Burma (Myanmar) | 55 |
| 25. | Korea, South | 49 |

## MOST CROWDED NATIONS

**Population per square km (2012)**

| | | |
|---|---|---|
| 1. | Monaco | 31,000 |
| 2. | Singapore | 7,872 |
| 3. | Gaza Strip (OPT) | 4,750 |
| 4. | Bahrain | 1,468 |
| 5. | Maldives | 1,313 |
| 6. | Malta | 1,281 |
| 7. | Bangladesh | 1,119 |
| 8. | Barbados | 670 |
| 9. | Mauritius | 657 |
| 10. | Taiwan | 642 |

## LEAST CROWDED

**Population per square km (2012)**

| | | |
|---|---|---|
| 1. | Western Sahara | 2.0 |
| 2. | Mongolia | 2.0 |
| 3. | Namibia | 2.6 |
| 4. | Australia | 2.8 |
| 5. | Iceland | 3.0 |
| 6. | Mauritania | 3.3 |
| 7. | Suriname | 3.4 |
| 8. | Canada | 3.4 |
| 9. | Guyana | 3.5 |
| 10. | Botswana | 3.6 |

In 8000 BC, following the development of agriculture, the world had an estimated population of 8 million and by AD 1000 it was about 300 million. The onset of the Industrial Revolution in the late 18th century led to a population explosion. The 1,000 million mark was passed by 1850, it doubled by the 1920s, and doubled again to 4,000 million by 1975.

In the 1990s, demographers estimated that the world's population, which passed the 7 billion mark in 2012, would reach 9.3 billion by 2050 and only level out in 2200, at a peak of around 11 billion. However, in the early 21st century, after the rate of population growth had shown signs of decline, the Institute for Applied Systems Analysis suggested that the world's population might peak at about 9 billion in 2070. Whatever the global projections, everyone agreed that the greatest population growth would be in the developing countries.

The developing world includes what the World Bank (2011) describes as low-income economies (per capita GNI of US $1,025 or less), lower-middle-income economies (per capita GNI of US $1,026 to US $4,035), and upper-middle-income economies (per capita GNI of US $4,036 to US $12,745). Most developing countries are in Africa, Asia and Latin America. The developed world, made up of high-income, industrialized economies (per capita GNI of US $12,746 or more), contains Australasia, most of Europe and North America, and Japan.

In developing countries, a high proportion of the population is young and so these countries face high expenditure on health and education. In developed countries, the population pyramids are becoming top-heavy, with increasingly ageing populations.

## POPULATION DENSITY

The places marked on the map reflect the size of the urban agglomerations and conurbations, rather than the actual city limits. San Francisco itself, for example, has an official population of less than a million people. All cities with more than 5 million inhabitants are named on the map.

Toronto
Chicago
New York
Philadelphia
Washington D.C.
Los Angeles
Dallas-Ft. Worth
Atlanta
Houston
Miami
Tropic of Cancer
Mexico
Bogotá
Equator
Lima
Belo Horizonte
Rio de Janeiro
São Paulo
Tropic of Capricorn
Santiago
Buenos Aires

**Inhabitants per square kilometre**

- Over 200
- 100 – 200
- 50 – 100
- 25 – 50
- 6 – 25
- 3 – 6
- 1 – 3
- Under 1

**Urban population**

- ■ Over 10,000,000
- ● 5,000,000 – 10,000,000
- • 1,000,000 – 5,000,000

## POPULATION CHANGE

**The projected population change for the years 2004–2050**

- Over 125% population gain
- 100 – 125% population gain
- 50 – 100% population gain
- 25 – 50% population gain
- 0 – 25% population gain
- No change or population loss
- No data available

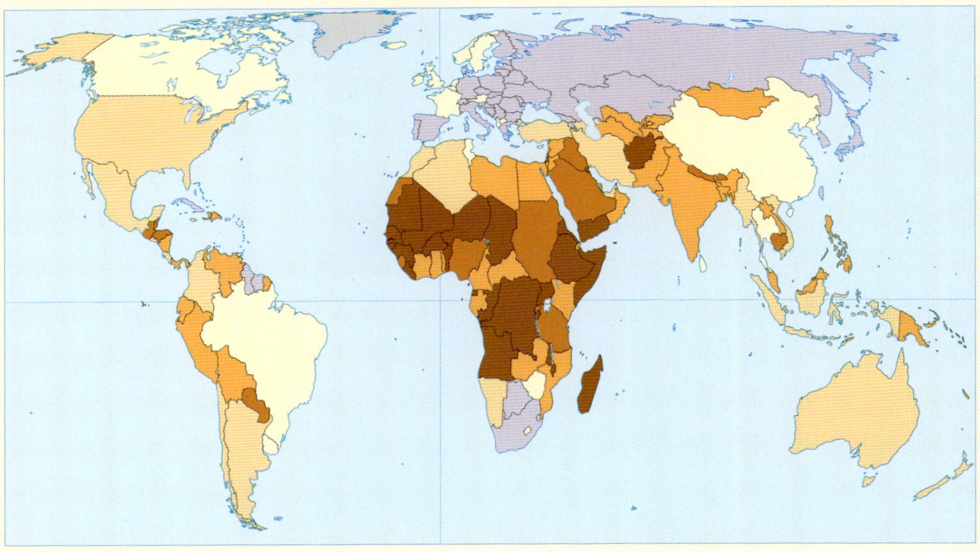

**Based on estimates for the year 2050, below are listed the ten most populous nations in the world, in millions:**

| | | |
|---|---|---|
| 1. India | 1,628 | |
| 2. China | 1,437 | |
| 3. USA | 420 | |
| 4. Indonesia | 308 | |
| 5. Nigeria | 307 | |
| 6. Pakistan | 295 | |
| 7. Bangladesh | 280 | |
| 8. Brazil | 221 | |
| 9. Congo (Dem. Rep.) | 181 | |
| 10. Ethiopia | 173 | |

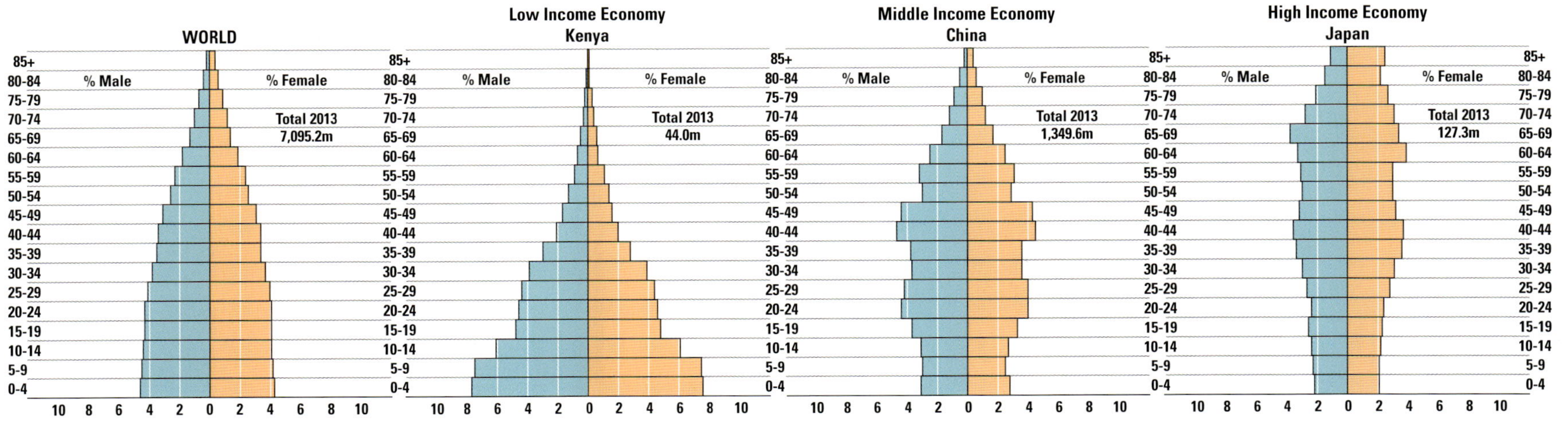
WORLD
Low Income Economy
Kenya
Middle Income Economy
China
High Income Economy
Japan
% Male
% Female
Total 2013
7,095.2m
Total 2013
44.0m
Total 2013
1,349.6m
Total 2013
127.3m
85+
80-84
75-79
70-74
65-69
60-64
55-59
50-54
45-49
40-44
35-39
30-34
25-29
20-24
15-19
10-14
5-9
0-4
10 8 6 4 2 0 2 4 6 8 10

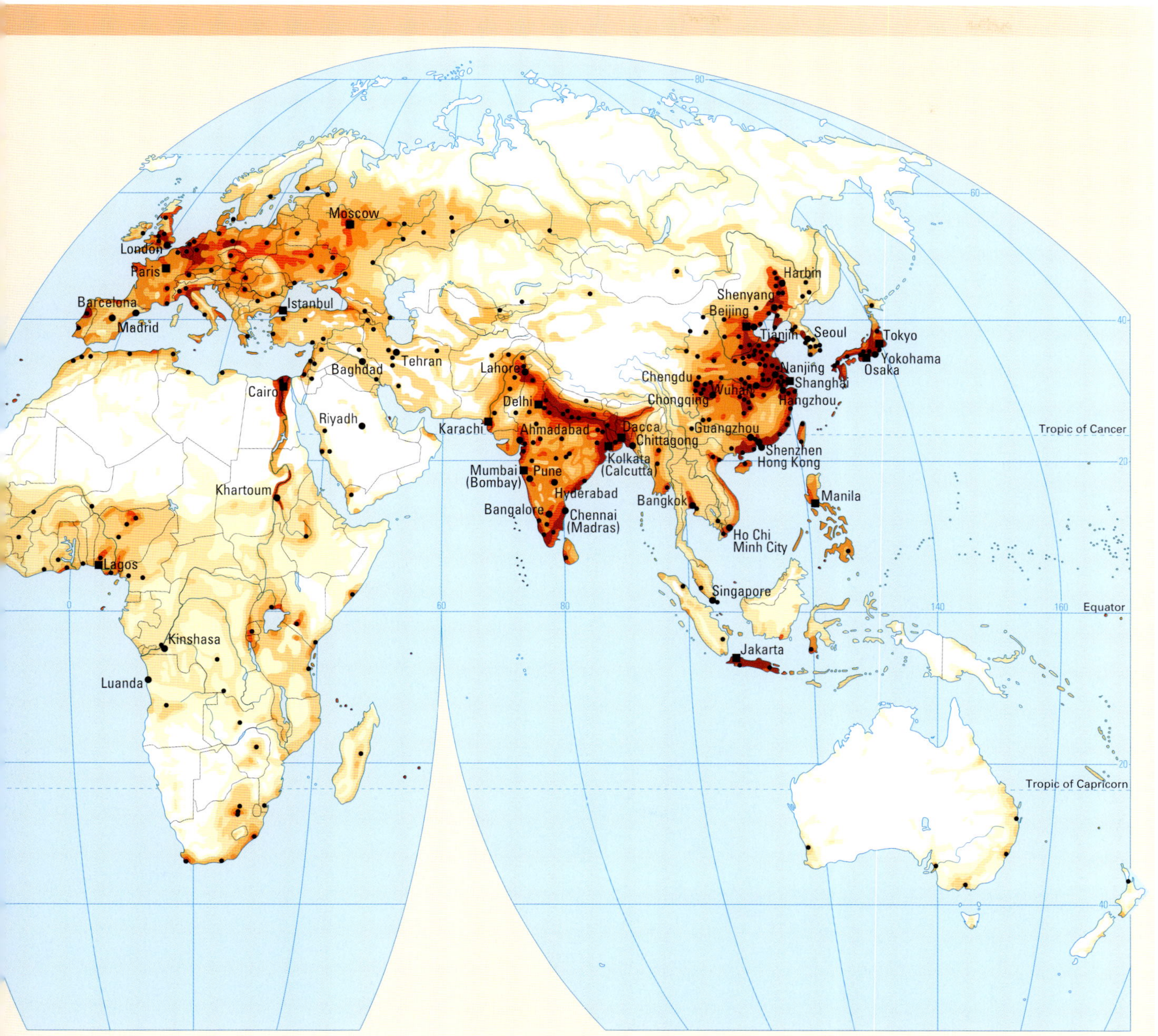

Moscow
London
Paris
Barcelona
Madrid
Istanbul
Baghdad
Tehran
Cairo
Riyadh
Khartoum
Lagos
Kinshasa
Luanda
Lahore
Delhi
Karachi
Ahmadabad
Mumbai (Bombay)
Pune
Hyderabad
Bangalore
Chennai (Madras)
Dacca
Chittagong
Kolkata (Calcutta)
Chengdu
Chongqing
Wuhan
Bangkok
Ho Chi Minh City
Singapore
Jakarta
Manila
Guangzhou
Shenzhen
Hong Kong
Hangzhou
Shanghai
Nanjing
Tianjin
Beijing
Shenyang
Harbin
Seoul
Tokyo
Yokohama
Osaka
Tropic of Cancer
Equator
Tropic of Capricorn


## FASTEST GROWING POPULATIONS

**Average annual growth (2012)**

| | | |
|---|---|---|
| 1. | Libya | 4.85% |
| 2. | Zimbabwe | 4.38% |
| 3. | Qatar | 4.19% |
| 4. | Uganda | 3.32% |
| 5. | Niger | 3.32% |
| 6. | Burundi | 3.08% |
| 7. | Burkina Faso | 3.06% |
| 8. | Gaza Strip (OPT) | 3.01% |
| 9. | Mali | 3.01% |
| 10. | Western Sahara | 2.96% |

## FASTEST DECLINING POPULATIONS

**Average annual decline (2012)**

| | | |
|---|---|---|
| 1. | Cook Islands | –3.07% |
| 2. | Moldova | –1.02% |
| 3. | Bulgaria | –0.81% |
| 4. | Estonia | –0.66% |
| 5. | Ukraine | –0.63% |
| 6. | Latvia | –0.61% |
| 7. | Montenegro | –0.56% |
| 8. | US Virgin Islands | –0.53% |
| 9. | Puerto Rico | –0.47% |
| 10. | Serbia | –0.46% |

## JAPAN'S AGEING POPULATION

A reduction in the birth rate, due to later marriages and more career-focused women, together with one of the highest life expectancy rates in the world, has meant that Japan has an increasingly ageing population. In 2050, if the birth rate remains the same, people older than 65 will make up 30% of the population. This means there will be one elderly person for every two people in the workforce, leaving Japan with the highest old-age dependency ratio in the industrialized world. Consequently, higher social security expenditure, in terms of pensions and medical care, will lead to more public debt and put a strain on Japan's economic growth.

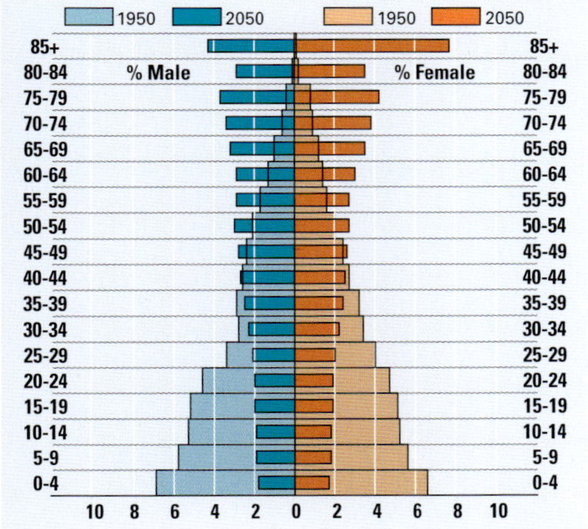

1950
2050
1950
2050
% Male
% Female
85+
80-84
75-79
70-74
65-69
60-64
55-59
50-54
45-49
40-44
35-39
30-34
25-29
20-24
15-19
10-14
5-9
0-4
10 8 6 4 2 0 2 4 6 8 10


## POPULATION BY CONTINENT

**Each square in the diagram below represents 1% of the world's total population**

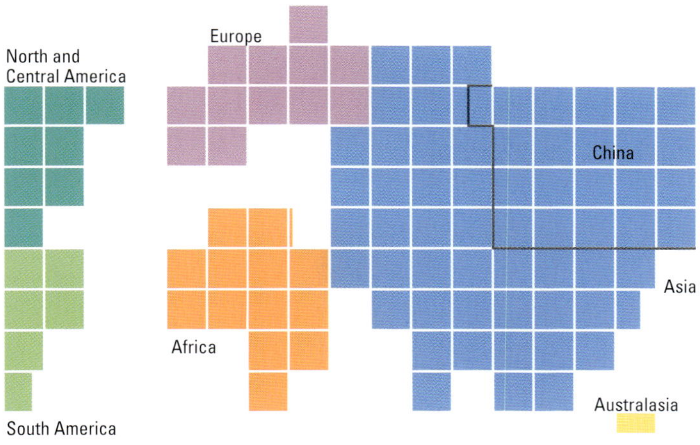

North and Central America
Europe
China
Asia
Africa
Australasia
South America


The graph below shows the extraordinary explosion of the world's population that has occurred in the last 250 years, with projections showing the predicted rate of growth in the 21st century. Projections of current growth rates become increasingly speculative as they advance into the future and projections have to be constantly revised. Very contrasting predictions can be made. For example, high birth rates and fast-declining death rates could give the world a population of 23 billion by 2100. Another scenario, based on such assumptions as rampant disease and falling birth rates, would indicate a fall in world population.

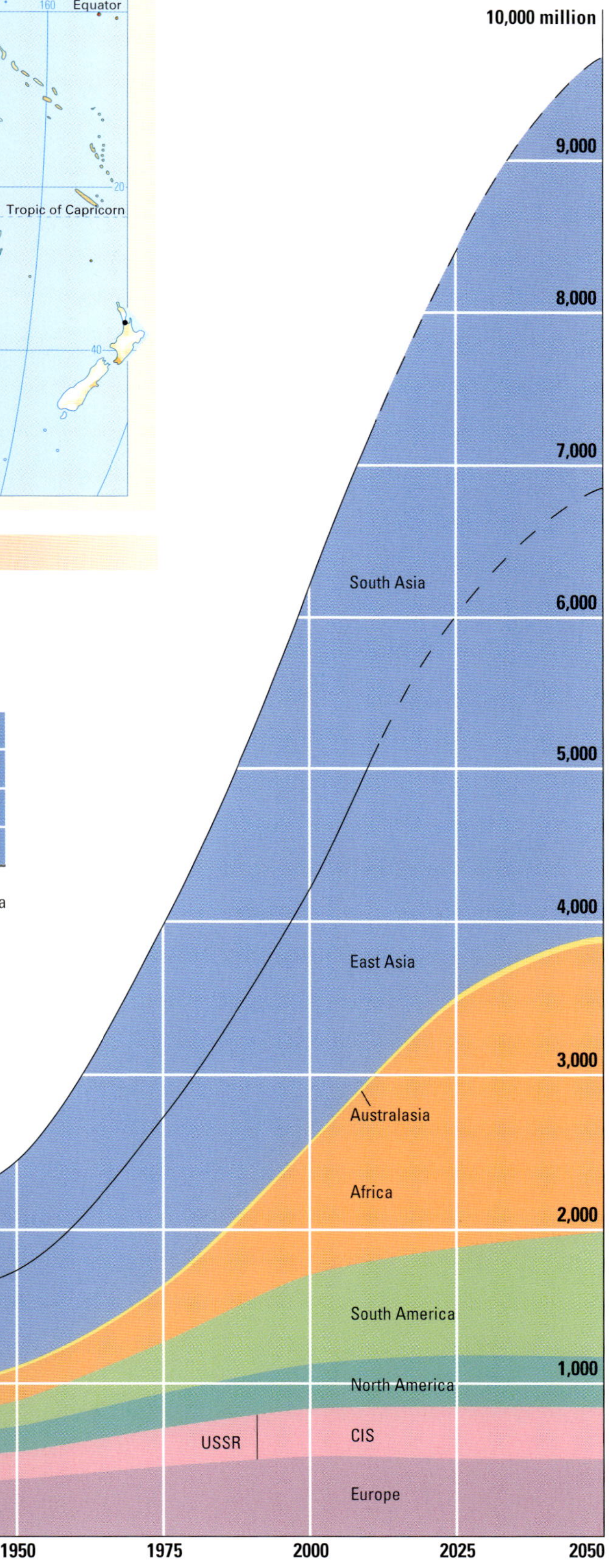

10,000 million
9,000
8,000
7,000
6,000
5,000
4,000
3,000
2,000
1,000
South Asia
East Asia
Australasia
Africa
South America
North America
USSR
CIS
Europe
1750
1775
1800
1825
1850
1875
1900
1925
1950
1975
2000
2025
2050

**For more information:**


78 Temperature and precipitation
80 Climate change and global warming
82 Water distribution
86 Population
98 Minerals


At current rates of growth, the world's population will increase to 9 billion people by 2050, from just over 7 billion today. To sustain this population there will have to be a 40% increase in food production which, as now, will have to be grown on the fertile soils irregularly distributed across just 11% of the Earth's surface. In addition, the fast-growing and increasingly better-off economies, such as China and India, are demanding a wider variety and better food in their diets, with many people eating more meat. However, the global trend in population is for people to move off the land towards the cities, resulting in fewer people actually producing the food.

Sixty years ago there was a food crisis in the developing world, which was tackled by the so-called 'Green Revolution'. This combined the breeding of sturdy disease-resistant dwarf crop varieties with the use of irrigation, synthetic fertilizers, and chemical pesticides. Productivity per acre increased by up to 300%, but the benefits of the Green Revolution levelled out in the 1990s.

The issues in the developed world revolve around the quality and quantity of what we eat. The range of food available to consumers in a modern supermarket shows the extent to which food products are transported from around the world, the issue of 'food miles', to satisfy the perceived need for such a wide variety of choice.

Additionally, there are also huge economic pressures from parts of the processed food industry enticing people in the developed world to eat more than is actually good for them. By comparison, in the developing world many struggle to achieve the minimum food intake to sustain life. Globally, about 1 billion people are malnourished and 1 billion are overweight. One of the biggest problems society faces is balancing this inequality of distribution, not only of food, but also of wealth.

► Supermarkets in the developed world carry a huge variety of fresh foods from all over the world, much of it out of season. A modern supermarket can often stock in excess of 130 varieties of vegetables and fruit for sale at any one time, much of it flown in chilled from abroad. As well as being extremely costly, these flights produce $CO_2$ emissions and, because of the high water content of fruit and vegetables, effectively export water and nutrients from countries that can often ill afford to do so. However, they do provide much needed income and employment for the producing country. By comparison, the market in the photograph (below right) only sells produce which can be grown locally and carried there, with no consequent $CO_2$ cost.

## WATER

Since over 71% of the Earth's surface is covered in water, it can hardly be said to be in short supply. However, less than 3% of this is fresh water and, of that, over two-thirds is frozen in ice caps and glaciers. The world, therefore, will never run out of water as such, but its overexploitation in developed areas and availability in regions where it is scarce are major problems. By 2030 there will be a 30% increase in water demand to support the world's population and its value will soar, so more efficient methods of collection and delivery will have to be developed.

## DEMAND FOR MEAT

Currently, over a third of the world's grain is fed to livestock for intensive stock raising, rising to 70% in developed countries where there is higher meat consumption per person. Animals (and humans) are very inefficient in their utilization of nutrients – generally less than 20% of the nitrogen in their food is used; the rest is excreted, causing problems for recycling and the risk of environmental impact. Methane emissions from cattle are also a major contributor to greenhouse gases in the atmosphere. Additionally, meat is very expensive in terms of water consumption; for example, 0.5 kg [1 lb] of beef requires 8,442 litres [1,857 gallons] of water to produce it, taking account of the water used to grow feed, etc.

### WORLD LIVESTOCK PRODUCTION

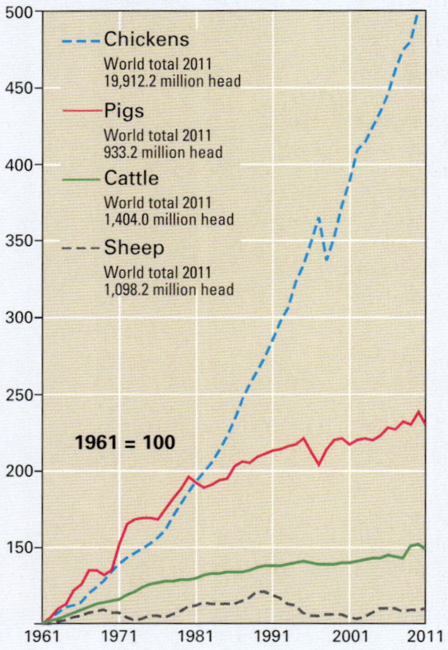

Chickens
World total 2011
19,912.2 million head
Pigs
World total 2011
933.2 million head
Cattle
World total 2011
1,404.0 million head
Sheep
World total 2011
1,098.2 million head
1961 = 100
500
450
400
350
300
250
200
150
1961
1971
1981
1991
2001
2011


## FERTILIZERS

By 1909, the process to make synthetic nitrogen fertilizer from ammonia had been developed. This has been a major factor in enabling the world's population to grow to today's levels. The process uses less than 2% of the world's total energy demand to produce more than 100 million tonnes of nitrogen fertilizer, which helps feed about 40% of the world's population. Without the application of fertilizers, we would have been unable to sustain our historic growth rates of agricultural production. Yet the production of these is under pressure. The supply of phosphate rock, which occurs naturally and is currently the major source of phosphorus fertilizer (an essential plant nutrient), is predicted by some to peak in the 2030s, though others say that there are still hundreds of years of reserves.

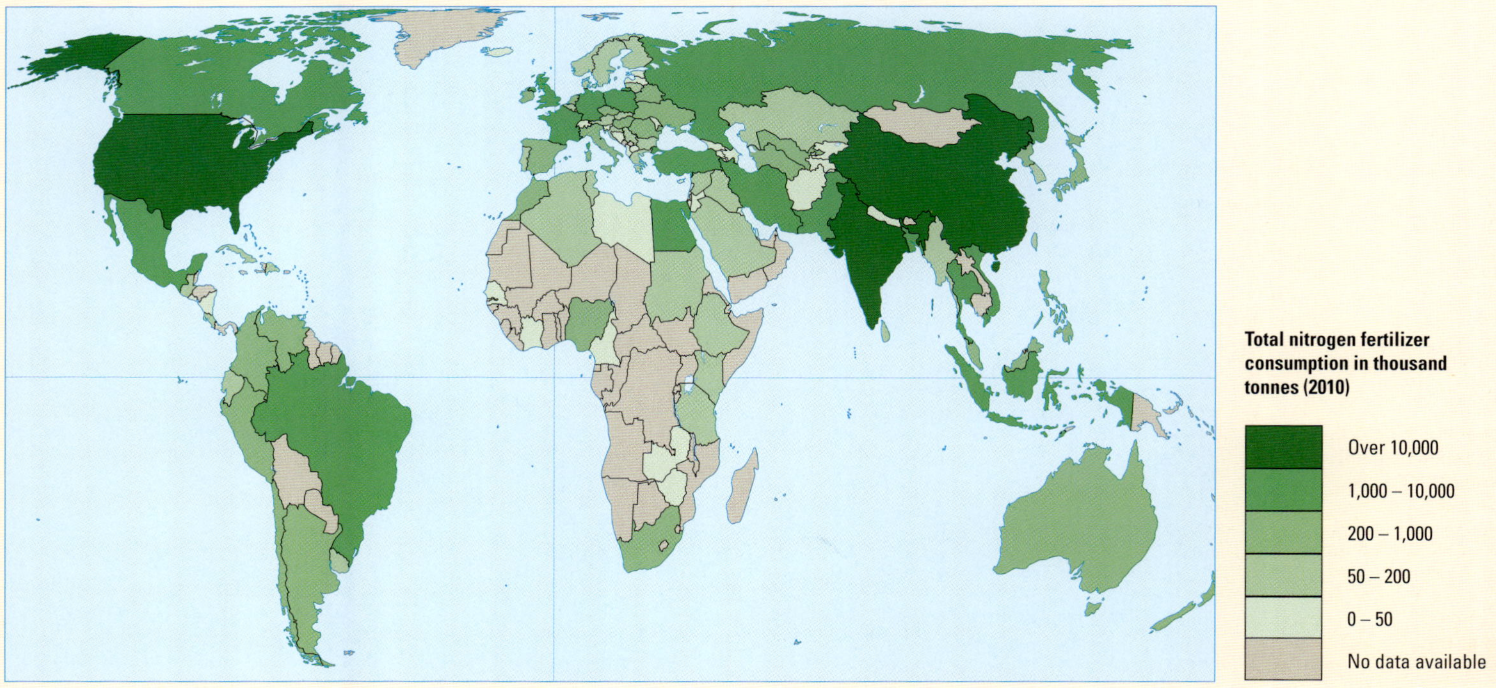

Total nitrogen fertilizer consumption in thousand tonnes (2010)
Over 10,000
1,000 – 10,000
200 – 1,000
50 – 200
0 – 50
No data available

## PESTS, DISEASES AND WEEDS

Currently, 30% of the world's crop yield is lost because of the effects of pests, diseases and weeds. Chemical controls (such as herbicides and fungicides) continue to be effective but are disliked by many. Because of this, research is focusing on isolating pest- and disease-resistant characteristics, using molecular methods. Breeding for resistance in both crops and animals can be done using conventional plant-breeding methods but is much quicker using GM methods. Crop rotations can be used to control pests, diseases and weeds, as can mechanical methods, cultivations, and inter-cropping (that is, mixing crops) and trap crops (which protect the main crop from pests).

Changing weather patterns have already caused the movement of pests and diseases around the world. For example, 'bluetongue', a disease that affects livestock, has been spread by a species of tiny biting midge from sub-Saharan Africa into north-west Europe since 2006, before which it was never recorded in Europe.

## WORLD CROP PRODUCTION

### ROOTS AND TUBERS

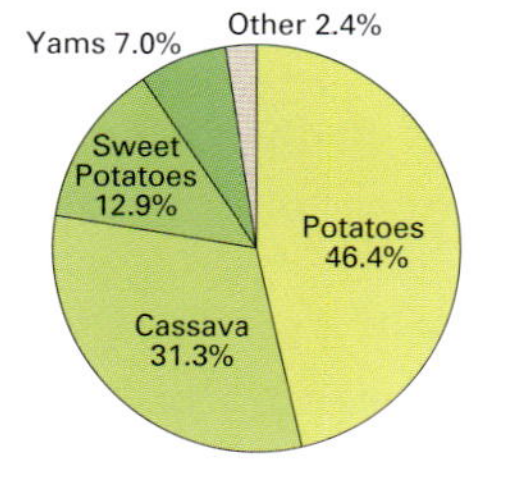
Yams 7.0%
Other 2.4%
Sweet Potatoes 12.9%
Potatoes 46.4%
Cassava 31.3%

World total (2011): 806.9 million tonnes

### OIL CROPS

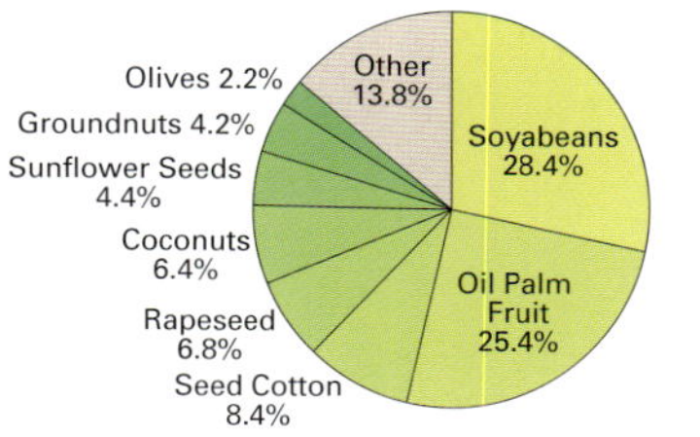
Olives 2.2%
Other 13.8%
Groundnuts 4.2%
Sunflower Seeds 4.4%
Soyabeans 28.4%
Coconuts 6.4%
Oil Palm Fruit 25.4%
Rapeseed 6.8%
Seed Cotton 8.4%

World total (2011): 919.0 million tonnes

### CEREALS

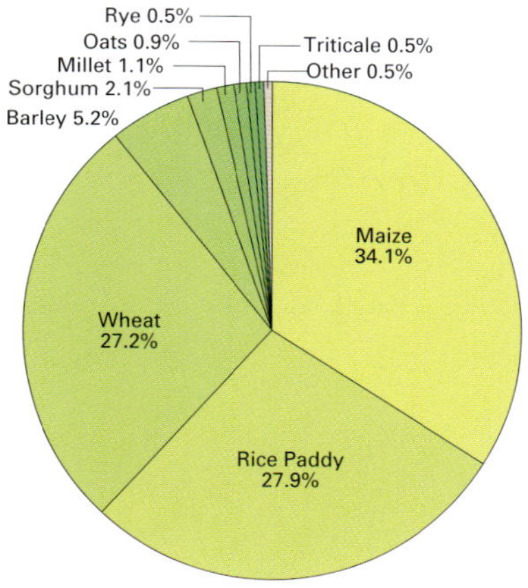
Rye 0.5%
Oats 0.9%
Millet 1.1%
Sorghum 2.1%
Barley 5.2%
Triticale 0.5%
Other 0.5%
Maize 34.1%
Wheat 27.2%
Rice Paddy 27.9%

World total (2011): 2,587.1 million tonnes

▼ These two images illustrate the opposite sides of world agriculture. The farmers with the plough in southern Africa (top) are engaged in subsistence agriculture, in which they can only produce enough food to feed themselves. There is, therefore, no surplus to sell and no money to spend on equipment to make the farm more productive. The second photograph (bottom) is of a commercial grain farm in Brazil, where fertilizers and pesticides are used. This, combined with huge field sizes that enable large machinery to be used for sowing and harvesting the crops, results in very high crop yields per person employed. The crops are then all sold on the open market.

## GLOBAL LAND USAGE

Most suitable land for agriculture is already in use and much is lost to development and erosion each year. The amount of extra land for agriculture is very limited unless we cut down forests or plough up old grasslands, which results in the release of $CO_2$ into the atmosphere.

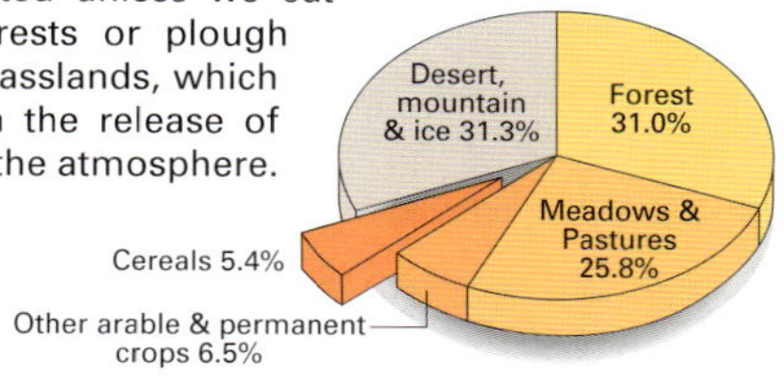
Desert, mountain & ice 31.3%
Forest 31.0%
Meadows & Pastures 25.8%
Cereals 5.4%
Other arable & permanent crops 6.5%

World total (2011): 13,003.4 million hectares

## GENETIC MODIFICATION (GM)

In the past 20–30 years, molecular genetics has increasingly been used to guide crop breeding. Biotechnological tools, such as genetic modification (GM), can complement conventional breeding processes to improve almost all important characteristics, including yield, plant structure, tolerance to salinity, cold and acidity, disease resistance, nutritional quality, and market preference.

GM critics suggest that there may be unforeseen effects on human health and the environment. However, in Europe and elsewhere, detailed risk analysis of potential effects of GM crops is made before licences to release the technology are granted. This has shown that the species of crop grown (that is, beet, maize or rape) had a greater impact on biodiversity than whether the crop was GM or conventional. Some would claim proven benefits, and GM crops are currently grown in more than 29 countries, on over 150 million hectares worldwide, equivalent to about 7% of global cultivated land. These include seven EU states: Spain, Czech Republic, Portugal, Poland, Germany, Slovak Republic and Romania.

## USING EXISTING TECHNOLOGY

How can we feed 9 billion people adequately and sustainably? Most agree that we should not be taking more land from forest and other uncropped areas into production because of the release of carbon dioxide that would result and the adverse impacts on predicted climate change and biodiversity. Using existing science and technology to enable those producing the lowest yields to produce national average yields, and those producing average yields to equal the best, would transform agriculture. This is likely to involve better pest and disease control, and more widespread and effective use of fertilizers. The Alliance for the Green Revolution in Africa (AGRA), with initial support from the Rockefeller Foundation and the Bill and Melinda Gates Foundation, is looking to achieve this.

## IMPROVED LAND MANAGEMENT

Many soils have been compacted through the use of heavy machinery or by regular ploughing, which causes a 'plough pan' (a thin compacted layer of soil) to develop just below the bottom of the plow. Other soils have been allowed to become acid or saline through acid rain, the inappropriate use of fertilizers, or polluted by toxic metals such as cadmium, nickel and copper, or by organic pollutants through the use of human and animal 'wastes'. However, these soils can be reclaimed.

Conservation agriculture that includes 'no-till' and 'min-till' has many benefits in terms of allowing a stable and good soil structure to develop, which retains organic matter, nutrients and moisture. But perennial weeds can be a problem on 'heavy' clay soils, requiring a greater use of herbicides. Strip tillage (cultivating only a narrow strip in which the crop is planted) saves energy use, maintains a soil cover (preventing erosion), and generally carries the benefits of conservation tillage. In the longer-term, 'controlled traffic' in which tractors and other equipment travel along fixed paths, or in which equipment is run from gantries, all linked to GPS, are precision farming systems that would contribute to a high-tech solution to food security.

In addition, it is important to control pests and diseases in growing crops, but post-harvest crop losses from moulds, insects, rodents and birds are 10–40% of the total, according to the UN Food and Agriculture Organization (FAO). The application of existing technologies could avoid these and make a significant impact on food supplies. Finally, the avoidance of food waste would also make an important contribution in developed countries.

## FOOD VERSUS FUEL

At the same time as the demand for food has increased, the demand for so-called 'green' biofuels, derived from plant products, has also increased. Industrialized countries, looking to reduce their reliance on fossil fuels, are setting targets for 'bioenergy' production from renewable sources such as maize, sugar cane, potatoes or manioc. The EU has decided that 10% of its fuel for transport should be from these sources – mostly bioethanol – by 2020. This demand is resulting in both developed and developing countries converting food crops into bioethanol, jeopardizing food supplies. A major push by the US for bioethanol, coupled with poor harvests in Europe, Australia and the other grain-exporting countries, pushed grain prices up to unusually high levels in late 2007 and 2011; the poor suffered as a result.

## FOOD & POPULATION

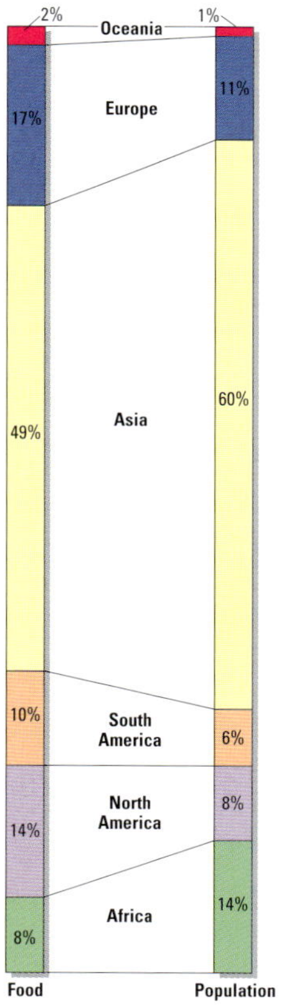
2%
Oceania
1%
17%
Europe
11%
49%
Asia
60%
10%
South America
6%
14%
North America
8%
8%
Africa
14%
Food
Population

► **Comparison of food production and population by continent**

The left column indicates the proportion of world food production and the right shows population in proportion.

## THE FUTURE

If we adopt and develop appropriate techniques and practices, and modify our behaviour, we stand a good chance of feeding the future, predominantly urban, world population. However, some see a very different future for agriculture. The image (right) shows one of several proposals for a new development currently under discussion: the 'vertical farm' as envisaged by Plantagon International and due for completion by 2014 in Linköping in Sweden. It consists of a giant self-contained production unit, enabling crop production to take place in a controlled environment, regardless of climatic variations, and situated within an urban area, where consumption is greatest. Its proponents also claim that crops will be able to be grown throughout the year, making 1 acre in the controlled environment the equivalent of many times more acres grown outdoors. They also say that the units would grow the crops organically, would reduce runoff pollution, and would also ease the pressure on water demand by recycling the water used from evapotranspiration.

**For more information:**


80 Greenhouse gases
82 Water distribution
86 Population density
102 World trade


In 2008, for the first time in history, more than half of the world's population lived in urban areas. By 2050, it is thought that 5.3 billion people in the developing world will be living in an urban environment, with Asia having over 60% of the world's urban population and Africa almost 25%.

Urbanization is greatest in industrialized countries. For example, in 2010, 82% of the people in the US lived in urban areas; but in low-income countries, which had nearly 40% of the world's population in the early 21st century, only 31% lived in urban areas.

A typical city in a developing country contains millions of people living, often illegally, in shanty towns (or 'informal settlements'), while thousands live on the streets. Yet many of these shanty towns are healthier than the industrial cities of 19th-century Europe and North America. Indeed, surveys have shown that migrants to cities in developing countries are less likely to face poverty than they are in rural areas, while benefiting from greater access to healthcare services and education.

Modern cities face many problems today, including pollution, unemployment and crime. Yet, with competent government, they are capable of generating the wealth they need to solve them, as well as making a major contribution to the nation's economy.

Megacities are cities with a population of over 10 million people. Megacities grow as a result of economic growth, rural to urban migration, and high rates of natural increase. As the cities grow, they swallow up rural areas and nearby towns. Some of these cities have populations that are bigger than those of entire countries – Mumbai, for example, has more people than Sweden and Norway combined.

Nevertheless, megacities contain between 4% and 7% of the world's total population, and grow at relatively slow rates, perhaps 1.5% per year. The first megacity was Tokyo, which now has a population of about 37 million (larger than Canada's population). By 2017, other megacities will include Mumbai, Delhi, Mexico City, São Paulo, New York, Dhaka, Jakarta and Lagos. Lagos has been growing at a very fast rate of 5% per annum and is expected to increase at this rate until after 2020. Usually, very large cities grow more slowly than medium-sized cities.

By 2020, all but four of the world's megacities will be in developing regions, 12 of them in Asia alone. The impact of megacities on their region is huge. For example, rapid economic growth and urbanization in China has had a negative impact on the urban environment. China contains 16 of the 20 most polluted cities in the world and is the largest producer of greenhouse gases.

Megacities are important for the generation of wealth – in more economically developed countries (MEDCs) urban areas generate over 80% of national economic output, while in less economically developed countries (LEDCs) it is over 40%. However, there are some aspects of megacities, such as crime and environmental issues, where they are less than attractive.

## URBAN POPULATION

**Percentage of total population living in towns and cities (2012)**

- Over 80%
- 60 – 80%
- 40 – 60%
- 20 – 40%
- Under 20%
- No data available

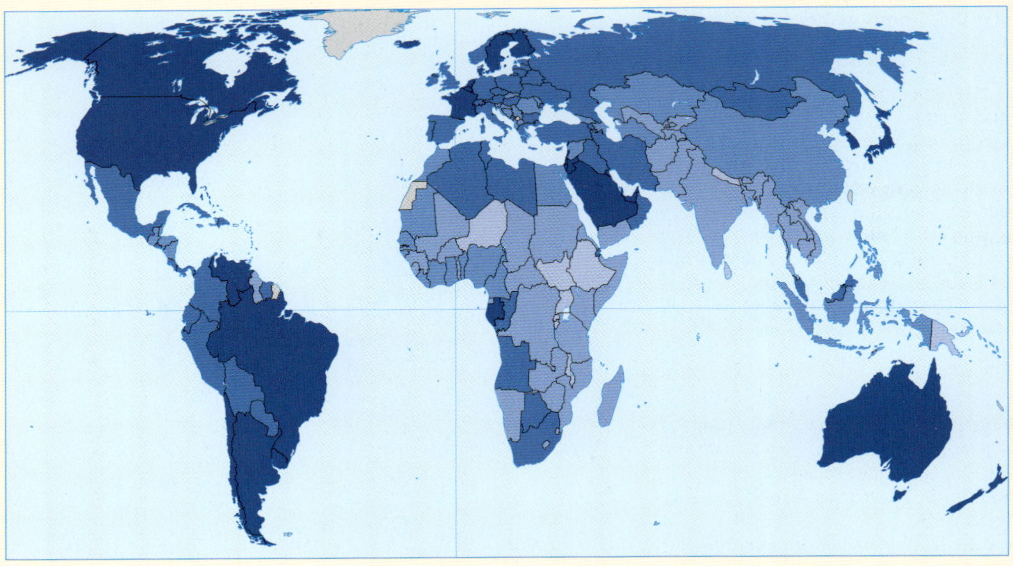

| **Most urbanized** | | **Least urbanized** | |
|---|---|---|---|
| Singapore | 100% | Burundi | 11% |
| Qatar | 99% | Papua New Guinea | 13% |
| Kuwait | 98% | Trinidad & Tobago | 14% |
| Belgium | 97% | Sri Lanka | 15% |
| Malta | 95% | Uganda | 16% |

## THE URBANIZATION OF THE EARTH

**City-building, 1900–2005; each white spot represents a city of at least 1 million inhabitants**

**1900**

**1950**

**1975**

**2005**

## URBANIZATION

The urban population of 3.7 billion people in 2012 was larger than the entire global population in 1947, 65 years earlier. Cities and urban areas are gaining an estimated 60 million people per year – over 1 million every week.

Urbanization rates vary across the world; the US and UK have far lower rates of urbanization compared to less developed countries. This is because a high proportion of their populations already live in cities. The largest percentage increases in the urban population in the next decade will be in Africa and Asia. For example, Lagos in Nigeria increased from 675,000 inhabitants in 1960 to 12,090,000 in 2013.

Rapid urban growth reflects three factors:

1. Migration to cities from rural areas.
2. Natural population increases (births minus deaths).
3. Reclassification of previously rural areas as urban as they become built up and engulfed by urban sprawl.

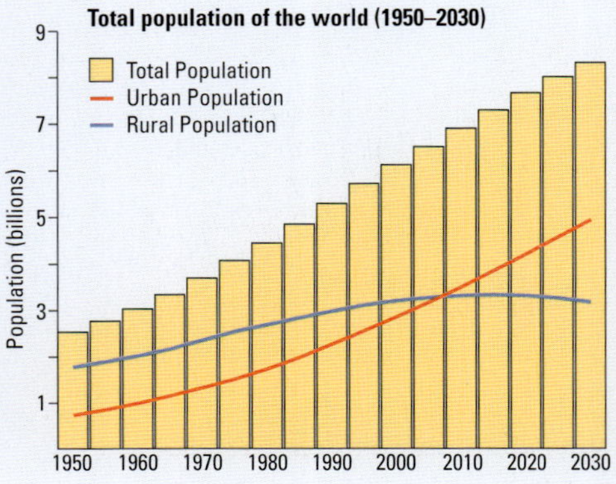

Total population of the world (1950–2030)
Total Population
Urban Population
Rural Population
Population (billions)
1
3
5
7
9
1950
1960
1970
1980
1990
2000
2010
2020
2030

## SLUM CITIES

The total number of slum dwellers in the world reached 1 billion in 2007, with one in every three city residents living in inadequate housing, with no or few basic services.

Urbanization in most developing countries has been proceeding so rapidly that local governments have been unable to provide the necessary services and housing to meet demand.

In some cities, many people make their homes in squatter settlements, or slums, which are frequently without basic services such as power, water, and sanitation. They are often on hazardous, dangerous or polluted land, and the building structures are inadequate and sometimes unsafe. Slum dwellers have limited access to credit and formal job markets due to stigmatization, discrimination, and geographical isolation.

Slums have a high concentration of poverty and social and economic deprivation, which may include broken families, unemployment, and economic, physical and social exclusion. Yet these communities are often a dynamic part of the city's economy, keeping the wheels of the city turning in many different ways. Their inhabitants often take the initiative in setting up their own local government and self-help associations.

Some of the world's richest cities also have a homeless underclass, although calculating the numbers of people involved is problematic. Yet it is the case that homelessness and unemployment are currently affecting an increasing number of people in the developed world.

The locus of poverty is moving from the countryside to cities, in a process now recognized as the 'urbanization of poverty'.

Efforts to improve the living conditions of slum dwellers peaked during the 1980s. However, renewed concern about poverty has recently led governments to adopt specific targets on slums in the United Nations Millennium Declaration, which aims to improve the lives of at least 100 million slum dwellers by the year 2020.

## SLUM FACTBOX

- A slum is defined by the UN as 'a dilapidated area of a city characterized by substandard housing, squalor, and lacking in tenure security'.
- 78% of the urban population in developing countries live in slums.
- More than 41% of Kolkata's slum households have lived there for more than 30 years.
- In most African cities between 40% and 70% of the city's population live in slums or squatter settlements.
- Slum populations in some parts of the world often include university lecturers, students, civil servants, and formal private-sector employees.
- The majority of slum households in Bangkok have a colour television.
- Singapore is one of the few countries that successfully practises comprehensive public-sector housing development.
- Slums are the fastest growing human habitat in the world.

## SUSTAINABLE CITIES

Large sprawling cities are often considered unsustainable because they consume huge amounts of resources and produce vast amounts of waste. The concept of 'Sustainable Urban Development' is designed to meet the needs of the present generation without compromising the needs of future generations.

In the 'compact' sustainable city, inputs are smaller and there is more recycling. Compact cities minimize the amount of distance travelled, use less space, require less infrastructure (pipes, cables, roads, etc), reduce urban sprawl, and the provision of public transport is easier. But if the compact city covers too large an area, it becomes congested, overcrowded, overpriced, and polluted. As a result, it then becomes unsustainable.

In order to achieve sustainability, a number of options are available:

- reducing the use of fossil fuels, e.g. by promoting public transport;
- keeping waste production to within levels that can be treated locally;
- providing sufficient green spaces;
- reusing and reclaiming land, e.g. brownfield sites;
- active involvement of the local community;
- conservation of non-renewable resources;
- using renewable resources.

## CITY GROWTH

**The growth of some of the world's largest cities in millions, 1950–2015**

Comparisons of city populations over time are problematic due to changes in the definition of the city limits. These figures attempt to take such changes into consideration.

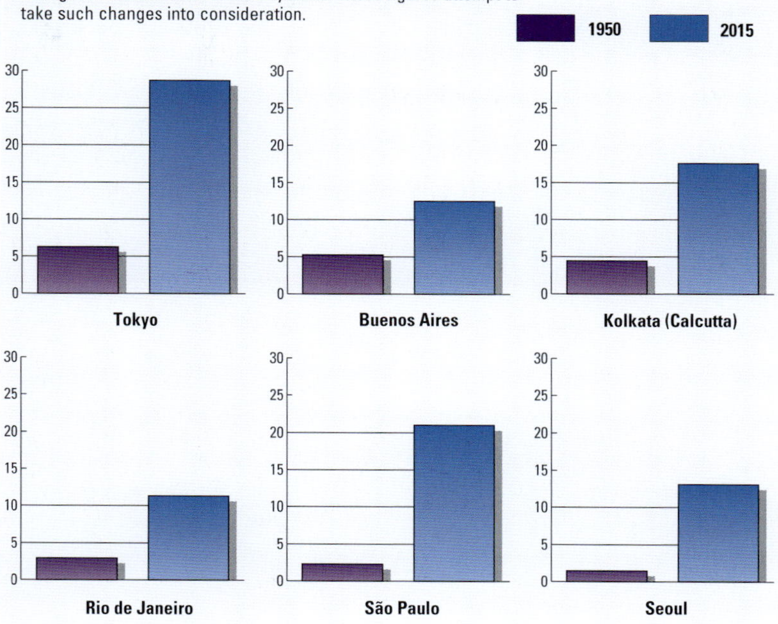
1950
2015
0
5
10
15
20
25
30
Tokyo
Buenos Aires
Kolkata (Calcutta)
Rio de Janeiro
São Paulo
Seoul

## LARGEST CITIES

◀ Originally a fishing village, Shanghai's skyscrapers and modern lifestyle are often seen as representing China's recent economic development. It is now the fifth largest city in the world and home to many of China's tallest buildings.

**In 2008, for the first time in history, the majority of the world's population lived in cities. Below is a list of the urban areas in the world with over 10 million inhabitants in 2012.**

| | | |
|---|---|---|
| 1. | Tokyo–Yokohama | 37.2 |
| 2. | Jakarta | 26.7 |
| 3. | Seoul–Incheon | 22.9 |
| 4. | Delhi | 22.8 |
| 5. | Shanghai | 21.8 |
| 6. | Manila | 21.2 |
| 7. | Karachi | 20.9 |
| 8. | New York | 20.7 |
| 9. | São Paulo | 20.6 |
| 10. | Mexico City | 20.0 |
| 11. | Beijing | 18.2 |
| 12. | Guangzhou–Foshan | 17.7 |
| 13. | Mumbai | 17.3 |
| 14. | Osaka–Kobe–Kyoto | 17.2 |
| 15. | Moscow | 15.8 |
| 16. | Cairo | 15.1 |
| 17. | Los Angeles | 15.1 |
| 18. | Kolkata | 14.6 |
| 19. | Bangkok | 14.5 |
| 20. | Dhaka | 14.4 |
| 21. | Buenos Aires | 13.8 |
| 22. | Tehran | 13.3 |
| 23. | Istanbul | 12.9 |
| 24. | Shenzhen | 12.5 |
| 25. | Lagos | 12.1 |
| 26. | Rio de Janeiro | 11.6 |
| 27. | Paris | 10.9 |
| 28. | Nagoya | 10.2 |

The city populations above are based on urban agglomerations rather than legal city limits. In some cases, where two adjacent cities have merged into one concentration, such as Tokyo–Yokohama, they have been regarded as a single unit.

## URBAN ADVANTAGES

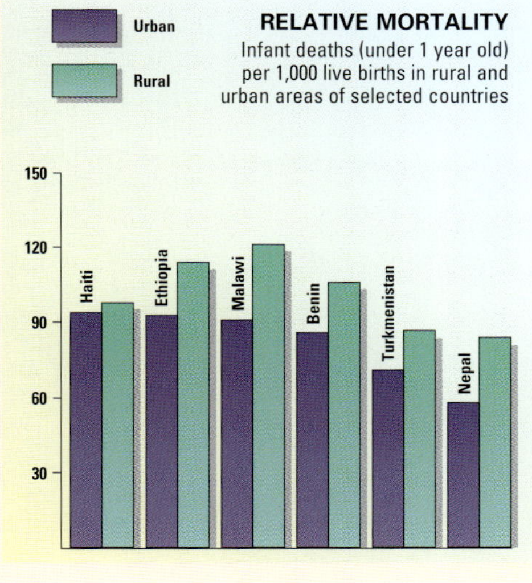
Urban
Rural
RELATIVE MORTALITY
Infant deaths (under 1 year old) per 1,000 live births in rural and urban areas of selected countries
150
120
90
60
30
Haiti
Ethiopia
Malawi
Benin
Turkmenistan
Nepal

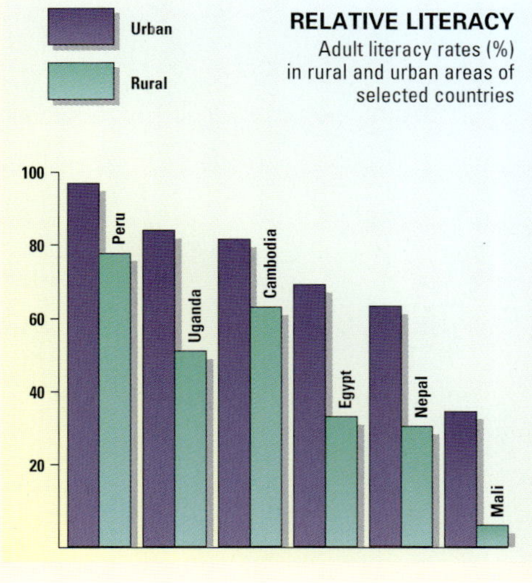
Urban
Rural
RELATIVE LITERACY
Adult literacy rates (%) in rural and urban areas of selected countries
100
80
60
40
20
Peru
Uganda
Cambodia
Egypt
Nepal
Mali

Despite overcrowding and poor housing, living standards in the developing world's cities are almost invariably better than in the surrounding countryside. Resources – financial, material and administrative – are concentrated in the towns, which are usually also the centres of political activity and pressure. Governments – frequently unstable, and rarely established on a solid democratic base – are usually more responsive to urban discontent than to rural misery.

In many developing countries, especially in Africa, food prices are kept artificially low, thus appeasing the underemployed urban masses at the expense of agricultural development.

This imbalance encourages further cityward migration, helping to account for the astonishing rate of post-1950 urbanization and putting great strain on the ability of many nations to provide even modest improvements for their people.

**For more information:**
86 Population density
94 Conflict
95 United Nations International organizations

Migration is the permanent or semi-permanent change in residence. Migration can be voluntary or forced, international or internal, long- or short-distance. Most voluntary migrants are people moving either for work (this is especially true for young people), to retire to a small town or coastal area (this is especially true in some rich countries), or to live in a smaller urban area for a better quality of life than they had in a large urban area. Others may migrate for educational or health reasons. In contrast, forced migrations may be due to civil conflict, environmental damage, or some form of persecution.

According to the World Bank's Migration and Remittances Factbook, more than 215 million people, or 3% of the world's population, live outside their countries of birth. However, current migration flows, relative to population, are weaker than those of the last decades of the 19th century.

The top migrant destination countries are the United States, Russia, Germany, Saudi Arabia and Canada. The top immigration countries, relative to population, are Qatar (87%), the United Arab Emirates (70%), Kuwait (69%), Andorra (64%), Cayman Islands (63%) and Northern Mariana Islands (62%).

The United States has seen the largest inflows of migrants between 2005 and 2010, despite the global financial crisis. The expansion of the European Union led to a surge of migrant flows to Spain, Italy and the United Kingdom, with a large share from Eastern Europe. The Middle Eastern countries of Saudi Arabia, United Arab Emirates, Bahrain, Qatar, Oman and Kuwait have also seen a significant increase in migrant flows in the last few years, mostly from South Asia and East Asia. However, immigrant stocks in all regions started to plateau in 2009–10 because of the global financial crisis.

The Mexico–United States migration corridor is the largest in the world, accounting for 11.6 million migrants in 2010. Migration corridors in the former Soviet Union (Russia–Ukraine, and Ukraine–Russia) are the next largest, followed by Bangladesh–India. In these corridors, some people have become migrants without moving when new international boundaries were drawn.

Smaller countries tend to have higher rates of skilled emigration. For example, almost all physicians trained in Grenada and Dominica have emigrated abroad. St Lucia, Cape Verde, Fiji, São Tomé and Príncipe, and Liberia are also among the countries with the highest emigration rates of physicians.

Worldwide remittance flows are estimated to have exceeded US $414 billion in 2009, of which developing countries received US $307 billion. The true size, including unrecorded flows through formal and informal channels, is believed to be significantly larger. Recorded remittances are more than twice as large as official aid and nearly two-thirds of foreign direct investment (FDI) flows to developing countries.

In 2009, the top recipient countries of recorded remittances were India, China, Mexico, the Philippines and Poland. As a share of GDP, however, smaller countries such as Tajikistan (50%), Tonga (38%), Moldova (31%), Kyrgyzstan (28%) and Lesotho (27%) were the largest recipients in 2008.

Rich countries are the main source of remittances. The United States is by far the largest, with US $46 billion in recorded outward flows in 2008. Russia ranks as the second largest, followed by Switzerland and Saudi Arabia.

## WORLD MIGRATION

**MIGRATION**
**International migrants as a percentage of the population (2010)**

- Over 20%
- 10 – 20%
- 5 – 10%
- 1 – 5%
- 0 – 1%
- No data available

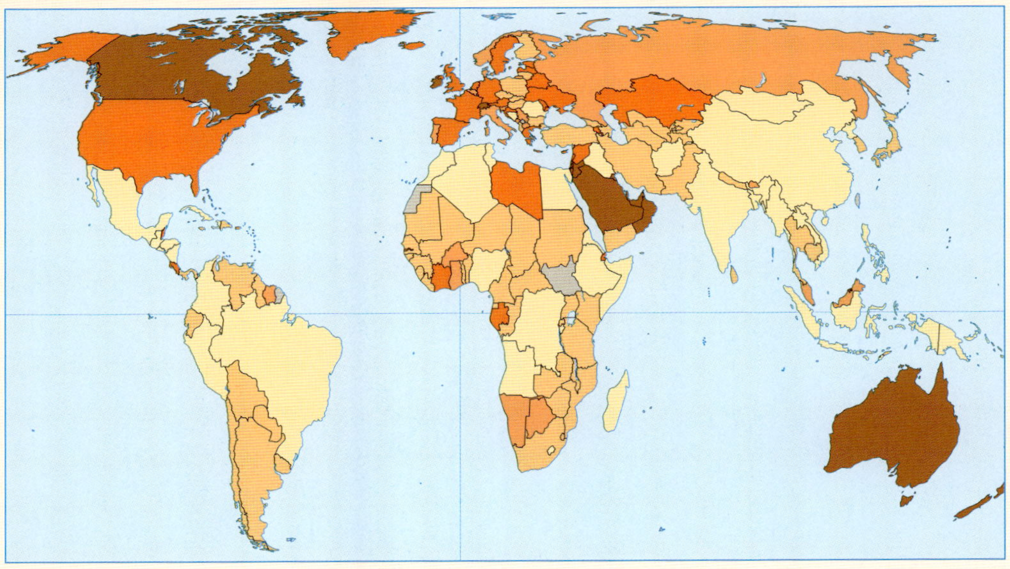

**MONEY SENT HOME BY MIGRANTS**
**Remittances as a percentage share of GDP (2010)**

- Over 10%
- 5 – 10%
- 2.5 – 5%
- 1 – 2.5%
- Under 1%
- No data available

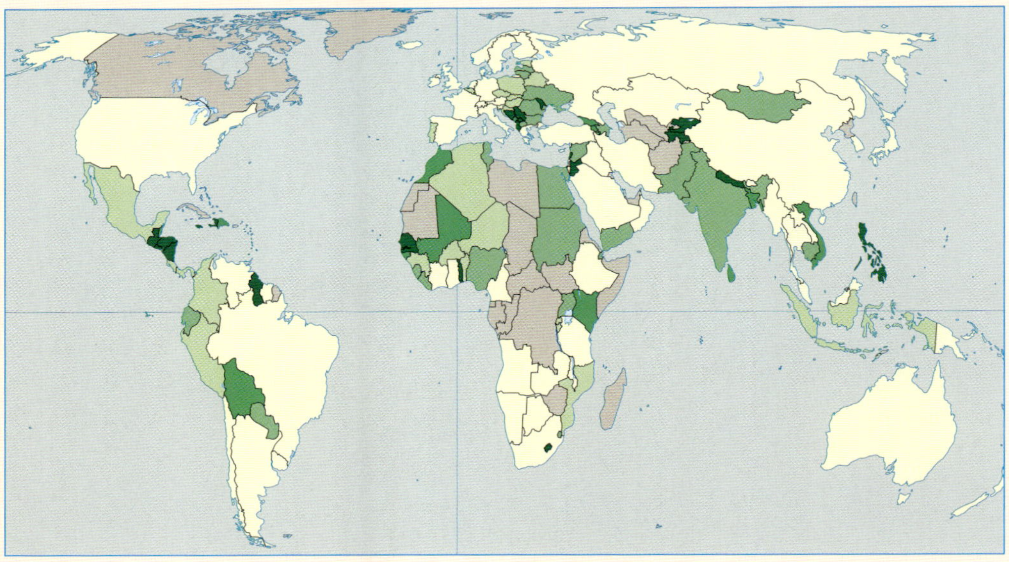

**REFUGEES**
**Total refugees* as a percentage of the population (2011)**

- Over 1%
- 0.10 – 1%
- 0.01 – 0.09%
- Under 0.01%
- No data available

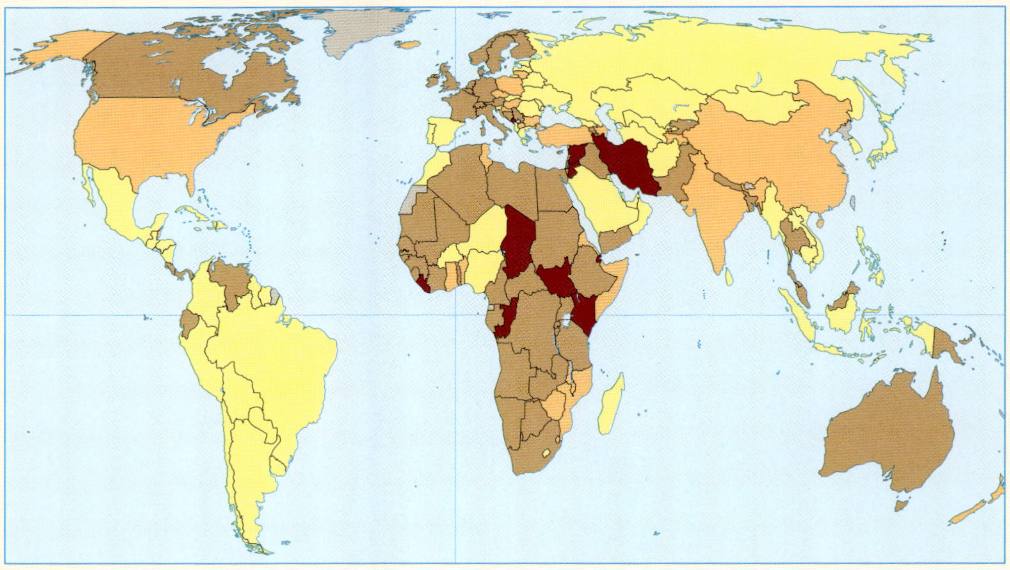

*includes people in a refugee-like situation

*See also Refugees graph at the top of page 94.*

According to the United Nations High Commission for Refugees (UNHCR) in 2011 there were 10.4 million refugees. However, the UNHCR definition of a refugee, 'a person who has left or remains outside their own country because they have a well-founded fear of persecution, or because their safety is threatened by events seriously disturbing public order', does not include people who are in a refugee-like situation but who have not been formally recognized. In 2011, there were a further 26.4 million people who were internally displaced, and a total 'population of concern' of 42.5 million people, worldwide.

All but a few who cross international boundaries seek asylum in neighbouring countries, which are often the least equipped to deal with them. Lacking any rights or power, they frequently become an unwelcome burden to their hosts. Usually, the best any refugee can hope for is rudimentary food and shelter in temporary camps. Many Palestinians, for example, have been forced to live in camps since 1948.

In 2011, according to the UNHCR, Afghanistan produced more refugees than any other country – 3.1 million – followed by Iraq and Somalia. Up to 4.3 million people were newly displaced, and in many countries, the majority of people 'of concern' to the UNHCR were children aged under 18. In Eritrea children account for 72% of those 'causing concern'.

## PREDOMINANT LANGUAGES

**INDO-EUROPEAN FAMILY**

- 1 Balto-Slavic group (incl. Russian, Ukrainian)
- 2 Germanic group (incl. English, German)
- 3 Celtic group
- 4 Greek
- 5 Albanian
- 6 Iranian group
- 7 Armenian
- 8 Romance group (incl. Spanish, Portuguese, French, Italian)
- 9 Indo-Aryan group (incl. Hindi, Bengali, Urdu, Punjabi, Marathi)

- 10 **CAUCASIAN FAMILY**

**AFRO-ASIATIC FAMILY**

- 11 Semitic group (incl. Arabic)
- 12 Kushitic group
- 13 Berber group

- 14 **KHOISAN FAMILY**
- 15 **NIGER-CONGO FAMILY**
- 16 **NILO-SAHARAN FAMILY**
- 17 **URALIC FAMILY**

**ALTAIC FAMILY**

- 18 Turkic group (incl. Turkish)
- 19 Mongolian group
- 20 Tungus-Manchu group
- 21 Japanese and Korean

**SINO-TIBETAN FAMILY**

- 22 Sinitic (Chinese) languages (incl. Mandarin, Wu, Yue)
- 23 Tibetic-Burmic languages

- 24 **TAI FAMILY**

**AUSTRO-ASIATIC FAMILY**

- 25 Mon-Khmer group
- 26 Munda group
- 27 Vietnamese

**DRAVIDIAN FAMILY**

- 28 (incl. Telugu, Tamil)

**AUSTRONESIAN FAMILY**

- 29 (incl. Malay-Indonesian, Javanese)

- 30 **OTHER LANGUAGES**

**First-language speakers, in millions**

| | |
|---|---|
| Mandarin Chinese | 845 |
| Spanish | 329 |
| English | 328 |
| Arabic | 221 |
| Hindi | 182 |
| Bengali | 181 |
| Portuguese | 178 |
| Russian | 144 |
| Japanese | 122 |
| German | 90 |
| Javanese | 85 |
| Wu Chinese | 77 |
| Tegulu | 70 |
| Vietnamese | 69 |
| Marathi | 68 |
| French | 68 |
| Korean | 66 |
| Tamil | 66 |
| Punjabi | 63 |
| Italian | 62 |

**Languages** form a kind of tree of development, splitting from a few ancient proto-tongues into branches that have grown apart and further divided with the passage of time. English and Hindi, for example, both belong to the great Indo-European family, although the relationship is only apparent after much analysis and comparison with non-Indo-European languages such as Chinese or Arabic. Hindi is part of the Indo-Aryan subgroup, whereas English is a member of Indo-European's Germanic branch. French, another Indo-European tongue, traces its descent through the Latin, or Romance, branch. A few languages – Basque is one example – have no apparent links with any other, living or dead. Most modern languages, of course, have acquired enormous quantities of vocabulary from each other.

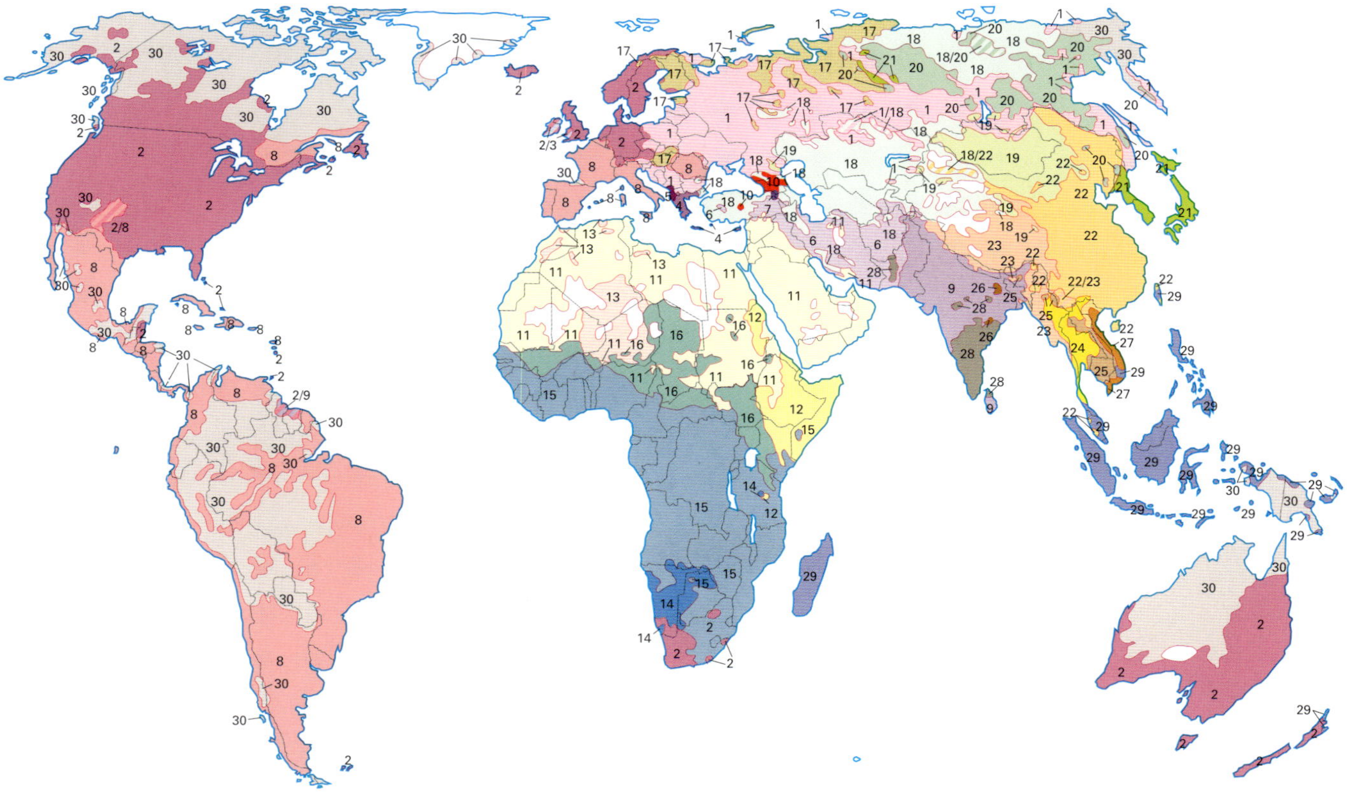

## DISTRIBUTION OF LIVING LANGUAGES

**The figures refer to the number of languages currently in use in the regions shown**

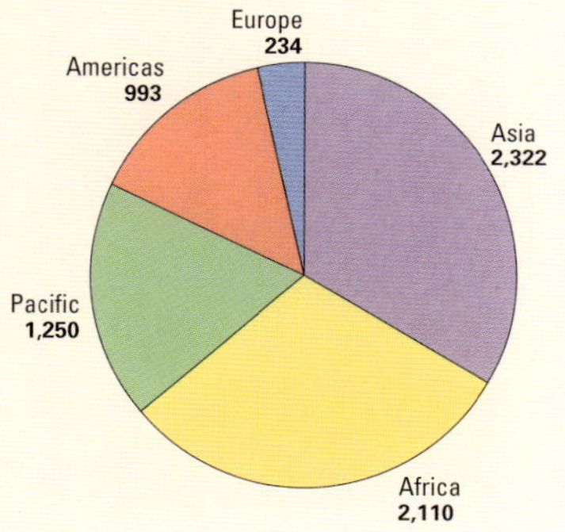

Europe
234
Asia
2,322
Americas
993
Pacific
1,250
Africa
2,110


## PREDOMINANT RELIGIONS

- ▲ Roman Catholicism
- Orthodox and other Eastern Churches
- ● Protestantism
- Sunni Islam
- Shia Islam
- Buddhism
- Hinduism
- Confucianism
- ✱ Judaism
- Shintoism
- Tribal Religions

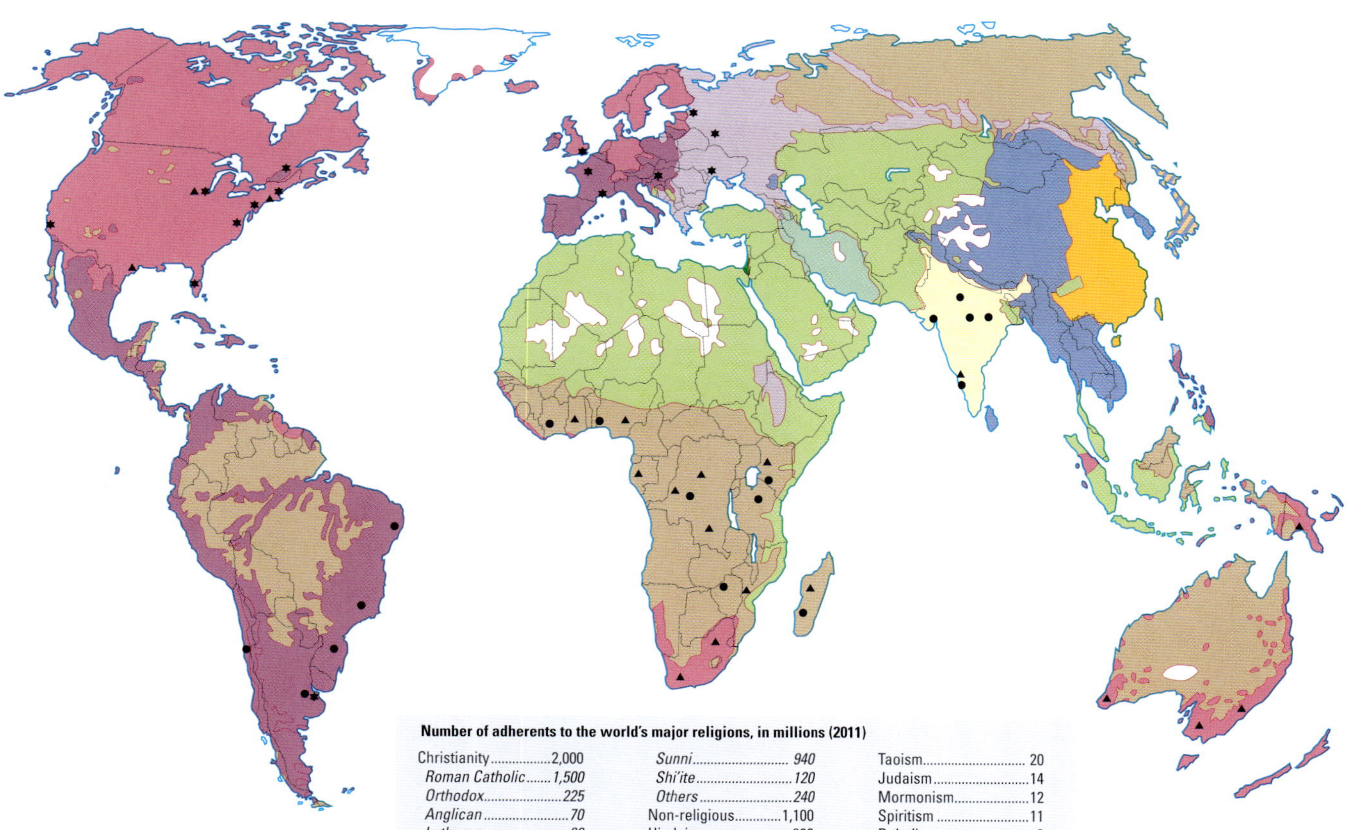

**Religions** are not as easily mapped as the physical contours of the land. Divisions are often blurred and frequently overlapping: most nations include people of many different faiths – or no faith at all. Some religions, like Islam and Christianity, have proselytes worldwide; others, like Hinduism and Confucianism, are restricted to a particular area, though modern migrations have taken some Indians and Chinese very far from their cultural origins. It is also difficult to show the degree to which religion controls daily life: Christian Western Europe, for example, is now far less dominated by its religion than are the Islamic nations of the Middle East. Similarly, figures for the major faiths' adherents make no distinction between nominal believers enrolled at birth and those for whom religion is a vital part of their existence.

**Number of adherents to the world's major religions, in millions (2011)**

| | | | | | |
|---|---|---|---|---|---|
| Christianity | 2,000 | *Sunni* | *940* | Taoism | 20 |
| *Roman Catholic* | *1,500* | *Shi'ite* | *120* | Judaism | 14 |
| *Orthodox* | *225* | *Others* | *240* | Mormonism | 12 |
| *Anglican* | *70* | Non-religious | 1,100 | Spiritism | 11 |
| *Lutheran* | *66* | Hinduism | 900 | Baha'i | 6 |
| *Methodist* | *8* | Chinese traditional | 394 | Confucianism | 5 |
| *Others* | *131* | Buddhism | 360 | Jainism | 4 |
| Islam | 1,300 | Sikhism | 23 | Shintoism | 4 |

**For more information:**
92 Migration
93 Religion

In the late 1980s, many people hoped that the end of the Cold War, following the collapse of Communist regimes in the former Soviet Union and Eastern Europe, would herald a new era of international stability. Instead, old ethnic and religious antagonisms surfaced in many areas, leading to civil war in such places as Chechenia, in Russia, and the former Yugoslavia. Nationalist rivalries, suppressed under Communist rule, replaced ideological factors as the major cause of conflict. Since, 2010, there has been accelerated political change, especially across North Africa and the Middle East.

Some countries are more likely to fail than others. Demographic stress is a major factor. Where there are large numbers of unemployed youths concentrated in large cities and a lack of growth, the chances of conflict escalate. Young men 'out of school, out of work, and charged with hatred' are the lifeblood of deadly conflict.

The causes of state failure and civil disintegration are multiple, but certain characteristics increase vulnerability. Extreme income and gender inequality increase the risk of discord. Corrupt governments that are widely regarded as illegitimate and ineffective are 'at risk'. Democracy, especially with a strong parliament, lowers the risk of state failure; autocracy increases it. Population pressure, exacerbated by internally displaced people, refugees and food scarcity, contribute to state failure and civil unrest. Governments that fail to protect human rights are especially prone to fail.

The Arab Spring, a term given to the Arab Revolution, is a wave of demonstrations, protests and wars that began in December 2010. A number of rulers have been forced from power in Tunisia, Egypt, Libya and Yemen. In addition, there have been civil uprisings in Bahrain and Syria. However, the major oil-rich nations (Saudi Arabia, UAE, Qatar, Kuwait and Oman) have managed to keep their ruling families in power.

The protests have shared techniques of civil resistance in sustained campaigns involving strikes, demonstrations, marches and rallies, but were also noticeable for their use of social media to organize, communicate, and raise awareness of the situation.

Despite the words of John F. Kennedy, US President 1961–3, that 'Mankind must put an end to war or war will put an end to mankind', in 2013 military conflicts were taking place around the world in countries such as Colombia, Afghanistan, Somalia, Yemen, Pakistan, Mexico (the 'drugs war') South Sudan and Sudan, Syria, Iraq, Libya and Mali.

## REFUGEES

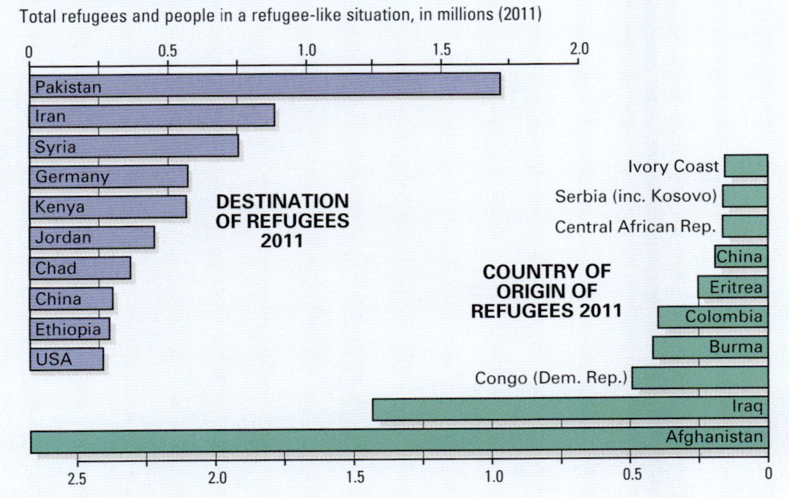
Total refugees and people in a refugee-like situation, in millions (2011)
0
0.5
1.0
1.5
2.0
Pakistan
Iran
Syria
Germany
Kenya
Jordan
Chad
China
Ethiopia
USA
DESTINATION OF REFUGEES 2011
COUNTRY OF ORIGIN OF REFUGEES 2011
Ivory Coast
Serbia (inc. Kosovo)
Central African Rep.
China
Eritrea
Colombia
Burma
Congo (Dem. Rep.)
Iraq
Afghanistan
2.5
2.0
1.5
1.0
0.5
0

▲ Part of the extensive Badbaado refugee camp, situated outside Mogadishu in Somalia. The camp was started when famine struck the north-east of Africa, after a drought in 2011. It subsequently expanded further after the civil war intensified. There was a breakdown of law and order, and people fled there for safety. The United Nations Refugee Agency, also known as UNHCR, estimated that there were 1,373,080 internally displaced persons in Somalia in January 2013.

## MILITARY SPENDING

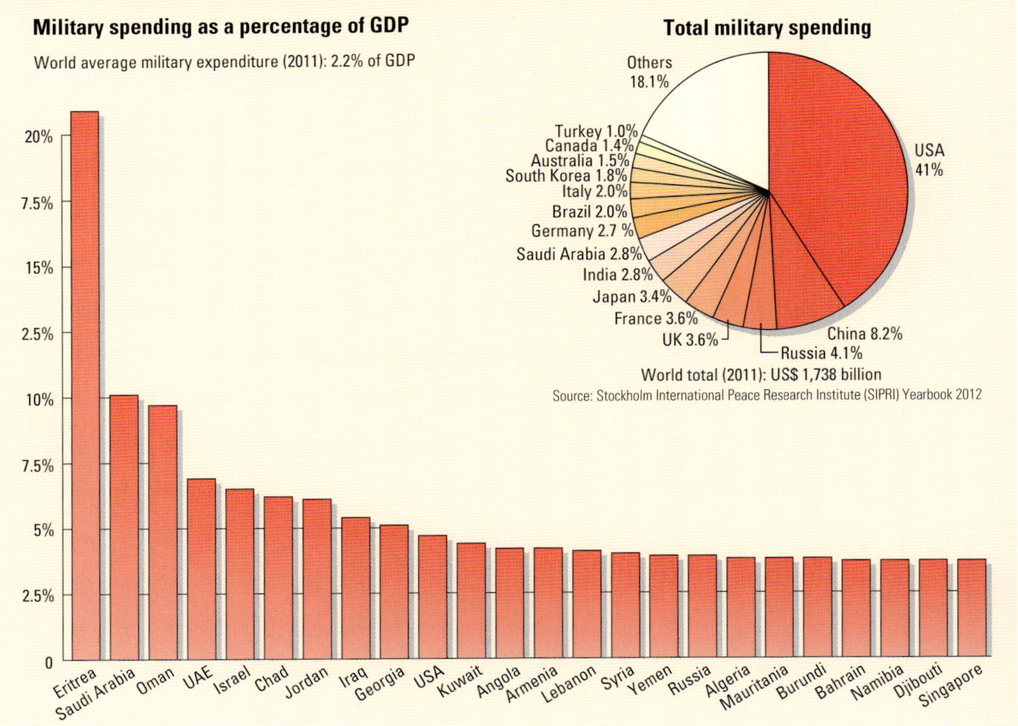
Military spending as a percentage of GDP
World average military expenditure (2011): 2.2% of GDP
Total military spending
Others 18.1%
USA 41%
Turkey 1.0%
Canada 1.4%
Australia 1.5%
South Korea 1.8%
Italy 2.0%
Brazil 2.0%
Germany 2.7 %
Saudi Arabia 2.8%
India 2.8%
Japan 3.4%
France 3.6%
UK 3.6%
China 8.2%
Russia 4.1%
World total (2011): US$ 1,738 billion
Source: Stockholm International Peace Research Institute (SIPRI) Yearbook 2012
20%
15%
10%
5%
2.5%
0
Eritrea
Saudi Arabia
Oman
UAE
Israel
Chad
Jordan
Iraq
Georgia
USA
Kuwait
Angola
Armenia
Lebanon
Syria
Yemen
Russia
Algeria
Mauritania
Burundi
Bahrain
Namibia
Djibouti
Singapore

## GLOBAL PEACE INDEX

The Global Peace Index (GPI) is an attempt to measure the relative position of nations' and regions' peacefulness. First published in May 2007, it is published annually. It currently ranks 158 countries (up from 121 in 2007). Iceland is considered to be the most peaceful country at the present time.

**Global Peace Index (2012)**

- Under 1.500 (most peaceful)
- 1.501 – 2.000
- 2.001 – 2.500
- 2.501 – 3.000
- Over 3.001 (least peaceful)
- No data available

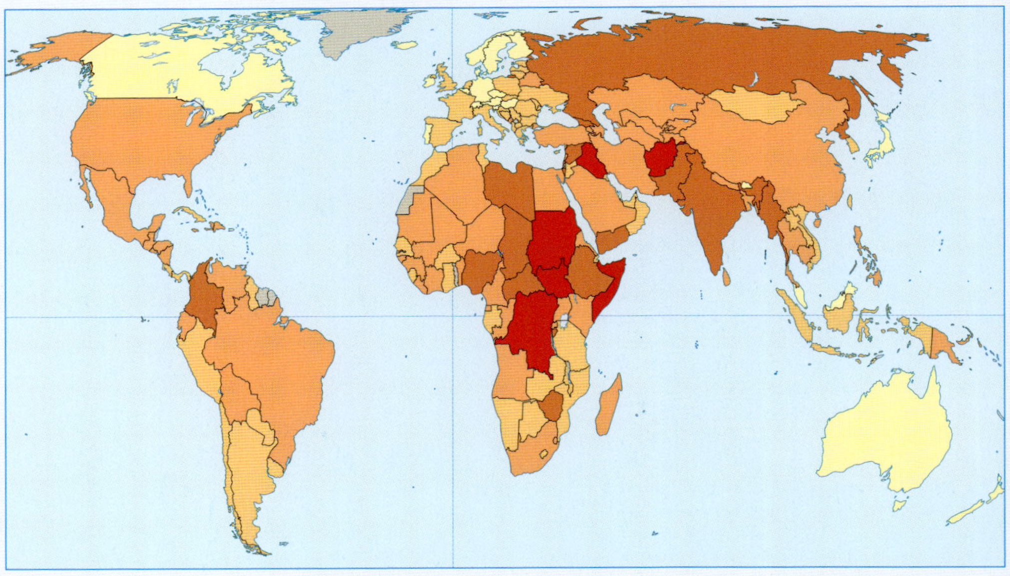

| **Five most peaceful countries** | | **Five least peaceful countries** | |
|---|---|---|---|
| Iceland | 1.113 | Somalia | 3.392 |
| Denmark | 1.239 | Afghanistan | 3.252 |
| New Zealand | 1.239 | Sudan | 3.193 |
| Canada | 1.317 | Iraq | 3.192 |
| Japan | 1.326 | Congo (Dem. Rep.) | 3.073 |

## INTERNATIONAL ORGANIZATIONS

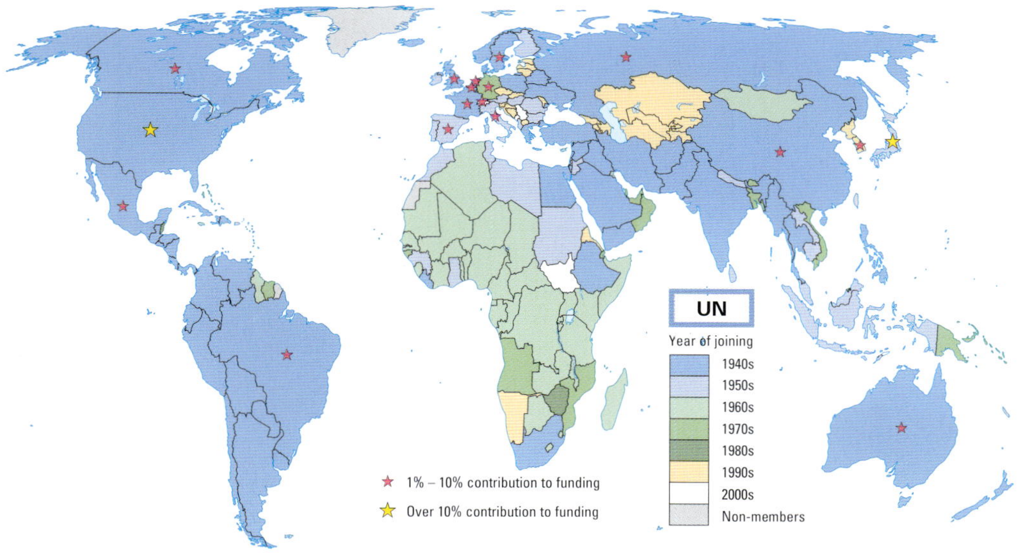

UN
Year of joining
1940s
1950s
1960s
1970s
1980s
1990s
2000s
Non-members
1% – 10% contribution to funding
Over 10% contribution to funding


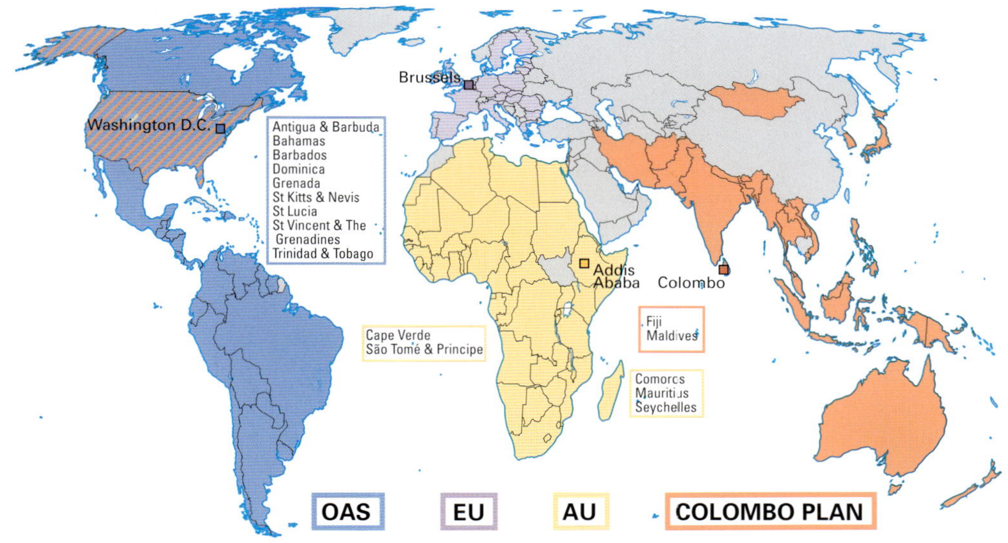

Brussels
Washington D.C.
Antigua & Barbuda
Bahamas
Barbados
Dominica
Grenada
St Kitts & Nevis
St Lucia
St Vincent & The Grenadines
Trinidad & Tobago
Addis Ababa
Colombo
Fiji
Maldives
Cape Verde
São Tomé & Principe
Comoros
Mauritius
Seychelles
OAS
EU
AU
COLOMBO PLAN


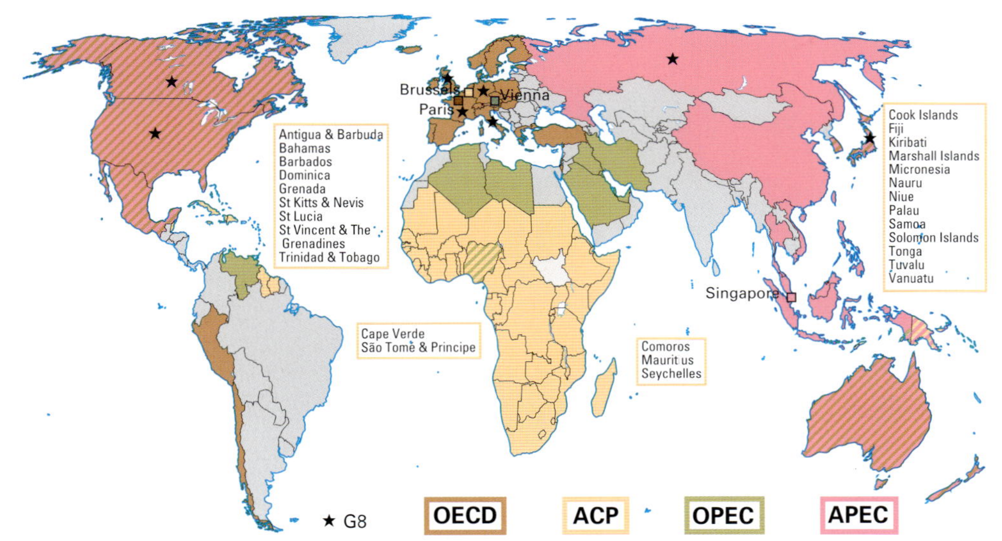

Paris
Vienna
Antigua & Barbuda
Bahamas
Barbados
Dominica
Grenada
St Kitts & Nevis
St Lucia
St Vincent & The Grenadines
Trinidad & Tobago
Cook Islands
Fiji
Kiribati
Marshall Islands
Micronesia
Nauru
Niue
Palau
Samoa
Solomon Islands
Tonga
Tuvalu
Vanuatu
Singapore
Cape Verde
São Tomé & Principe
Comoros
Mauritius
Seychelles
★ G8
OECD
ACP
OPEC
APEC


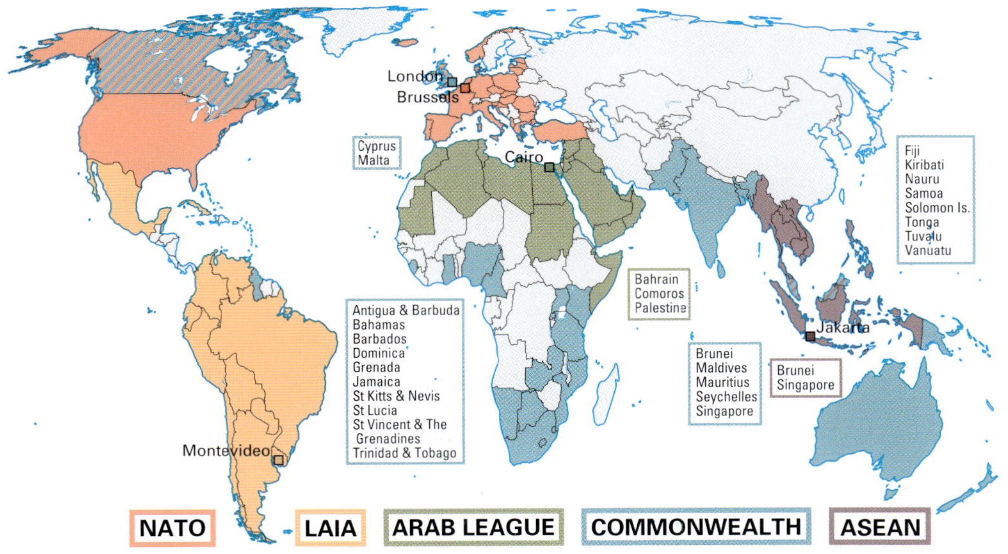

London
Brussels
Cyprus
Malta
Cairo
Fiji
Kiribati
Nauru
Samoa
Solomon Is.
Tonga
Tuvalu
Vanuatu
Bahrain
Comoros
Palestine
Jakarta
Brunei
Maldives
Mauritius
Seychelles
Singapore
Brunei
Singapore
Antigua & Barbuda
Bahamas
Barbados
Dominica
Grenada
Jamaica
St Kitts & Nevis
St Lucia
St Vincent & The Grenadines
Trinidad & Tobago
Montevideo
NATO
LAIA
ARAB LEAGUE
COMMONWEALTH
ASEAN


## UNITED NATIONS

The creation of the United Nations in 1945 held out hope that the world's nations, tired of war, would have the means to control humanity's aggressive instincts. Although the UN lacks the power to halt conflicts, it has often helped to achieve negotiation. Economic pressures have led to another kind of co-operation, resulting in the creation of common markets and economic unions, such as ASEAN in South-east Asia, the European Union, and NAFTA in North America.

The United Nations Organization was born as World War II drew to its conclusion. That body would replace the League of Nations, which, since its inception in 1920, had failed to curb the aggression of some of its member nations. At the United Nations Conference on International Organization held in San Francisco, the United Nations Charter was drawn up. Ratified by the Security Council and signed by the 51 original members, it came into effect on 24 October 1945.

The Charter set out the aims of the organization: to maintain peace and security, and to develop friendly relations between nations; to achieve international co-operation in solving economic, social, cultural and humanitarian problems; to promote respect for human rights and fundamental freedoms; and to harmonize the activities of nations in order to achieve these common goals.

**Membership** From the original 51, membership of the UN has now grown to 193. There are only two independent states that are not members – Taiwan and the Vatican City. Official languages are Chinese, English, French, Russian, Spanish and Arabic.

**Funding** The UN budget for 2012–13 was US $5.4 billion. Contributions are assessed by the members' ability to pay, with the maximum 22% of the total (the USA's share), and the minimum 0.001%. The 27-member EU pays approximately 35% of the budget.

**Peacekeeping** The UN has been involved in 67 peacekeeping operations worldwide since 1948.

**OAS** The **Organization of American States** was formed in 1948. It aims to promote social and economic co-operation between countries in the developed North America and developing Latin America.

**EU** The **European Union** evolved from the European Community in 1993. Cyprus, the Czech Republic, Estonia, Hungary, Latvia, Lithuania, Malta, Poland, the Slovak Republic and Slovenia joined the EU in May 2004; Bulgaria and Romania joined in 2007. The other 15 members of the EU are Austria, Belgium, Denmark, Finland, France, Germany, Greece, Ireland, Italy, Luxembourg, Netherlands, Portugal, Spain, Sweden and the UK. Together, the 27 members aim to integrate economies, co-ordinate social developments, and bring about political union. Croatia is due to become the 28th member of the EU in July 2013.

**AU** The **African Union** was set up in 2002, taking over from the Organization of African Unity (1963). It has 54 members. The main objectives of the OAU were, *inter alia*, to rid the continent of the remaining vestiges of colonization and apartheid; to promote unity and solidarity among African states; to co-ordinate and intensify co-operation for development; to safeguard the sovereignty and territorial integrity of member states; and to promote international co-operation within the framework of the United Nations.

**COLOMBO PLAN** Formed in 1951, its 25 members aim to promote economic and social development in Asia and the Pacific.

**G8** Group of eight leading industrialized nations, comprising Canada, France, Germany, Italy, Japan, Russia, the UK and the USA. Periodic meetings are held to discuss major world issues, such as world recessions.

**OECD** The **Organization for Economic Co-operation and Development** (formed in 1961) comprises 34 major free-market economies. The 'G8' is its 'inner group' of leading industrial nations, comprising Canada, France, Germany, Italy, Japan, Russia, the UK and the USA. The mission of the OECD is to promote policies that will improve the economic and social well-being of people around the world.

**ACP** The **African, Caribbean and Pacific Group of States** was formed in 1963. Members enjoy economic ties with the EU. The ACP Group's main objectives are sustainable development of its member states and their gradual integration into the global economy, which entails making poverty reduction a matter of priority; co-ordination of the activities of the ACP Group in the framework of the implementation of ACP–EU Partnership Agreements; establishment and consolidation of peace and stability in a free and democratic society.

**OPEC** The **Organization of Petroleum Exporting Countries** was formed in 1960. It controls about three-quarters of the world's oil supply. Its mission is to co-ordinate and unify the petroleum policies of its member countries, and to ensure the stabilization of oil markets in order to secure an efficient, economic, and regular supply of petroleum to consumers, a steady income to producers, and a fair return on capital for those investing in the petroleum industry. Gabon formally withdrew from OPEC in August 1996.

**APEC** Formed in 1989, the **Asia–Pacific Economic Co-operation** aims to enhance economic growth and prosperity for the region and to strengthen the Asia–Pacific community. APEC is the only intergovernmental grouping in the world operating on the basis of non-binding commitments, open dialogue, and equal respect for the views of all participants. There are 21 member economies.

**NATO** The **North Atlantic Treaty Organization** (formed in 1949) continues despite the winding-up of the Warsaw Pact in 1991. Bulgaria, Estonia, Latvia, Lithuania, Romania, the Slovak Republic and Slovenia became members in 2004, and Albania and Croatia in 2009. Its main aim is to provide peace and security to its North Atlantic members through collective defence – an attack on one country is seen as an attack on all of NATO.

**LAIA** The **Latin American Integration Association** (formed in 1980) superceded the Latin American Free Trade Association formed in 1961. Its aim is to promote freer regional trade.

**ARAB LEAGUE** Formed in 1945, the Arab League aims to promote economic, social, political and military co-operation. There are 22 member nations.

**COMMONWEALTH** The **Commonwealth of Nations** evolved from the British Empire. Pakistan was suspended in 1999, but reinstated in 2004. Zimbabwe was suspended in 2002 and, in response to its continued suspension, Zimbabwe left the Commonwealth in 2003. Fiji was suspended in 2006 following a military coup. Rwanda joined the Commonwealth in 2009, as the 54th member state, becoming only the second country that was not formerly a British colony to be admitted to the group. Their objective is to build stronger democratic institutions and processes across the Commonwealth and to support economic growth in their member countries.

**ASEAN** The **Association of South-east Asian Nations** was formed in 1967. Cambodia joined in 1999. The aims of ASEAN include: to accelerate the economic growth, social progress, and cultural development in the region; to promote regional peace and stability; and to collaborate more effectively for the greater utilization of their agriculture and industries, the expansion of their trade, including the study of the problems of international commodity trade, the improvement of their transportation and communications facilities, and the raising of the living standards of their peoples.

**For more information:**
80 Global warming
Carbon dioxide
98 Minerals

Every year, the world's energy consumption is about the equivalent of what would come from burning 12,000 million tonnes of oil (12,000 MtOe) – a 20-fold increase since 1850. Two-fifths of this total actually comes from burning oil and most of the rest comes from coal and natural gas.

The oil crises in the 1970s precipitated concern over dependence on finite fossil fuels as the primary source of energy, and growing environmental awareness has added impetus to the search for alternative energy resources. Fossil fuel combustion damages the environment through the release of gases and particulate matter, but two other major sources of energy, hydroelectricity and nuclear power, are also controversial. Hydroelectricity production involves flooding large areas to create reservoirs, while nuclear power stations generate dangerous radioactive wastes and can cause major disasters. Nuclear power has been a growing source of energy, but the 2011 Japanese earthquake, with the consequent serious damage to the Fukushima nuclear power station, has caused many countries to rethink their energy strategies.

Alternative energy resources may soon provide a much larger proportion of the world's energy consumption. Solar and wind energy may become important in such countries as China and India, while tidal, wave and geothermal energy all have potential in appropriate areas. Experts calculate that solar power could, in theory, supply between five and ten times the present electricity supply of developing countries.

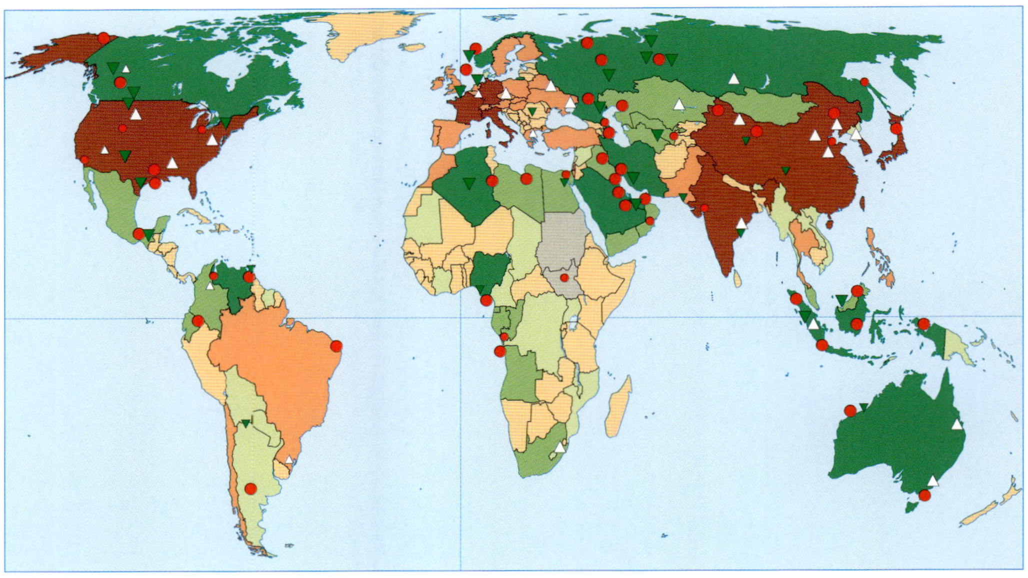

## ENERGY BALANCE

**Difference between energy production and consumption in millions of tonnes of oil equivalent (MtOe) (2011)**

- Over 100 MtOe surplus
- 10 – 100 MtOe surplus
- 0 – 10 MtOe surplus
- 0 – 10 MtOe deficit
- 10 – 100 MtOe deficit
- Over 100 MtOe deficit
- No data available

- Principal oilfields
- Secondary oilfields
- Principal gasfields
- Secondary gasfields
- Principal coalfields
- Secondary coalfields

## ENERGY CONSUMPTION

Energy consumed by world regions, measured in million tonnes of oil equivalent in 2011. Total world consumption was 12,275 MtOe. Only energy from oil, natural gas, coal, nuclear and hydroelectric sources are included. Excluded are biomass fuels such as wood, peat and animal waste, and wind, solar and geothermal energy which, though important locally in some countries, are not always reliably documented statistically.

**World energy consumption, by source (2011)**

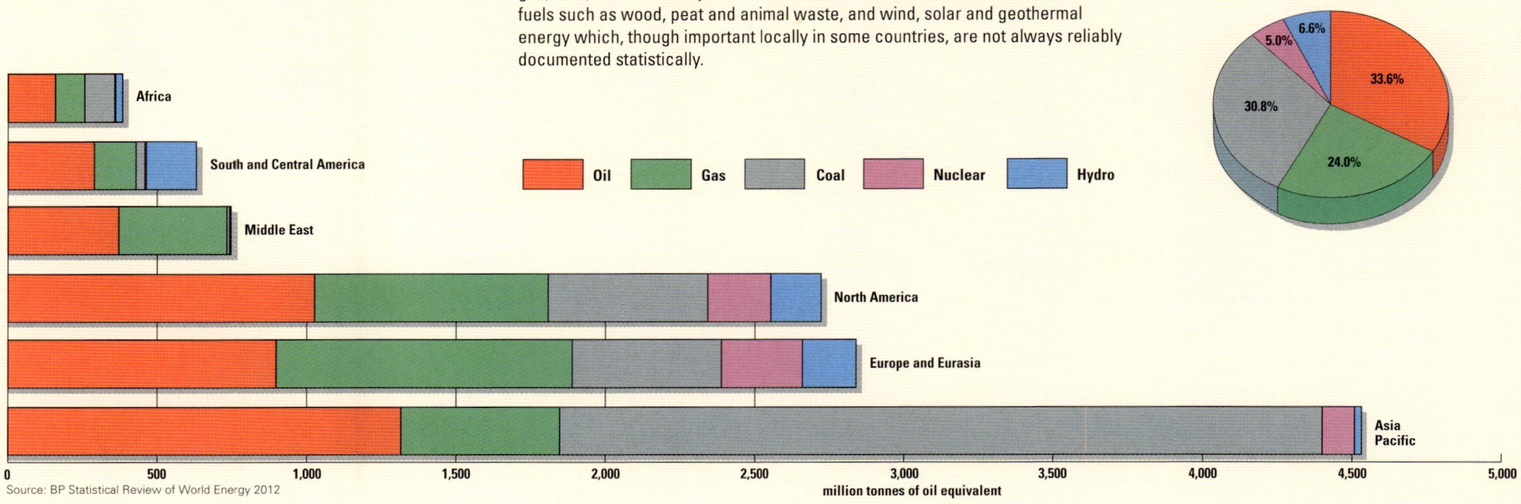
33.6%
24.0%
30.8%
5.0%
6.6%
Oil
Gas
Coal
Nuclear
Hydro
Africa
South and Central America
Middle East
North America
Europe and Eurasia
Asia Pacific
0
500
1,000
1,500
2,000
2,500
3,000
3,500
4,000
4,500
5,000
million tonnes of oil equivalent

Source: BP Statistical Review of World Energy 2012

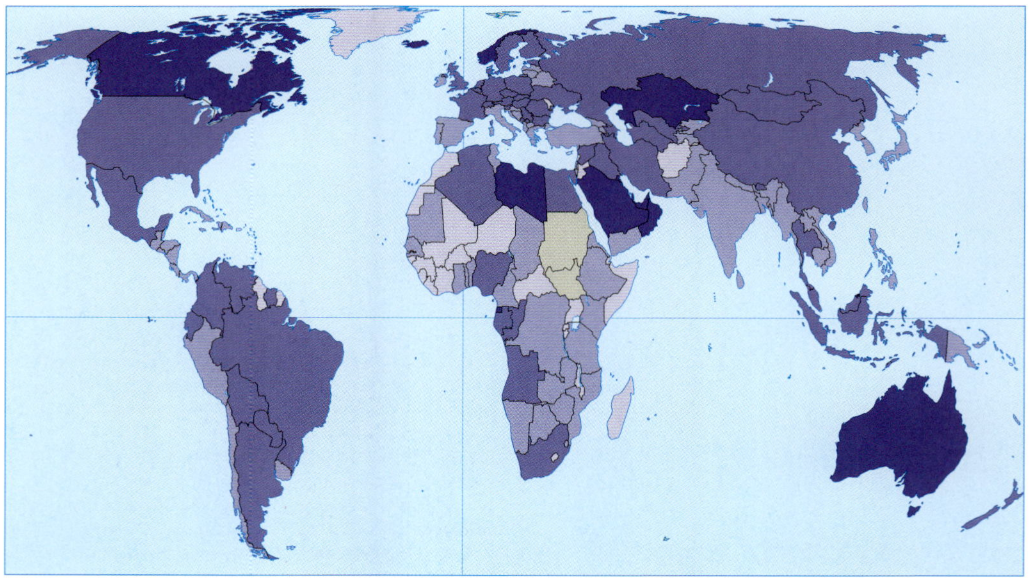

## ENERGY PRODUCTION

**Energy production in tonnes of oil equivalent per capita (2011)**

- Over 10
- 1 – 10
- 0.1 – 1
- 0 – 0.1
- No data available

**Highest energy producers, tonnes of oil equivalent per capita (2011)**

| | |
|---|---|
| Qatar | 205.3 |
| Kuwait | 51.6 |
| Brunei | 47.0 |
| Norway | 41.8 |
| Trinidad & Tobago | 36.6 |

## OIL MOVEMENTS

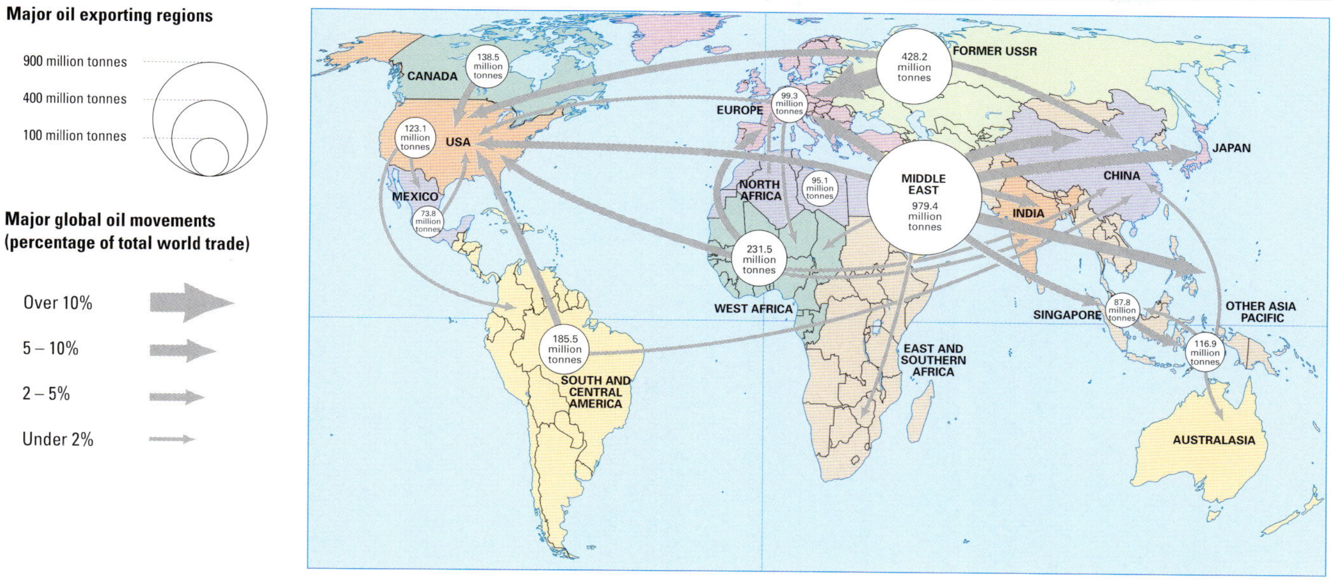

Major oil exporting regions
900 million tonnes
400 million tonnes
100 million tonnes
Major global oil movements (percentage of total world trade)
Over 10%
5 – 10%
2 – 5%
Under 2%
CANADA
138.5 million tonnes
USA
123.1 million tonnes
MEXICO
73.8 million tonnes
EUROPE
99.3 million tonnes
FORMER USSR
428.2 million tonnes
JAPAN
CHINA
MIDDLE EAST
979.4 million tonnes
INDIA
NORTH AFRICA
95.1 million tonnes
WEST AFRICA
231.5 million tonnes
SOUTH AND CENTRAL AMERICA
185.5 million tonnes
EAST AND SOUTHERN AFRICA
SINGAPORE
87.8 million tonnes
OTHER ASIA PACIFIC
116.9 million tonnes
AUSTRALASIA

▲ Two Liquefied Natural Gas (LNG) carriers, named *Excelsior* and *Excalibur*, moored at Guanabara Bay, near Rio de Janeiro. These two vessels together hold enough gas to provide the whole of Brazil's needs for approximately 2.5 days. The gas is cooled to –162°C [–260°F], which turns it into a liquid, 1/600th of its original volume, allowing it to be transported to markets around the world.

## ENERGY RESERVES

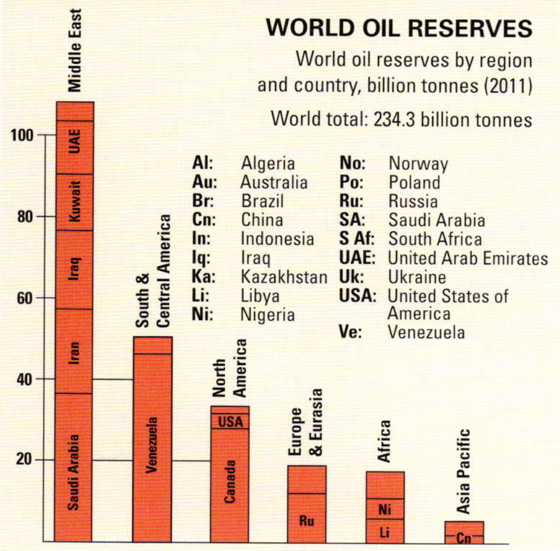

WORLD OIL RESERVES
World oil reserves by region and country, billion tonnes (2011)
World total: 234.3 billion tonnes
Al: Algeria
Au: Australia
Br: Brazil
Cn: China
In: Indonesia
Iq: Iraq
Ka: Kazakhstan
Li: Libya
Ni: Nigeria
No: Norway
Po: Poland
Ru: Russia
SA: Saudi Arabia
S Af: South Africa
UAE: United Arab Emirates
Uk: Ukraine
USA: United States of America
Ve: Venezuela
Middle East
UAE
Kuwait
Iraq
Iran
Saudi Arabia
South & Central America
Venezuela
North America
USA
Canada
Europe & Eurasia
Ru
Africa
Ni
Li
Asia Pacific
Cn
100
80
60
40
20


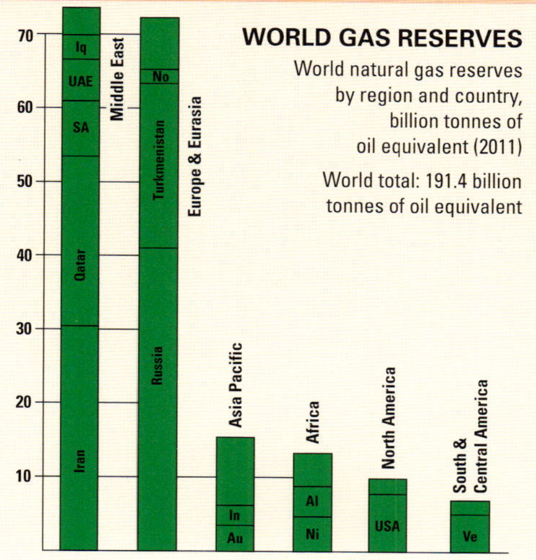

WORLD GAS RESERVES
World natural gas reserves by region and country, billion tonnes of oil equivalent (2011)
World total: 191.4 billion tonnes of oil equivalent
70
60
50
40
30
20
10
Iq
UAE
SA
Qatar
Iran
Middle East
No
Turkmenistan
Russia
Europe & Eurasia
Asia Pacific
In
Au
Africa
Al
Ni
North America
USA
South & Central America
Ve


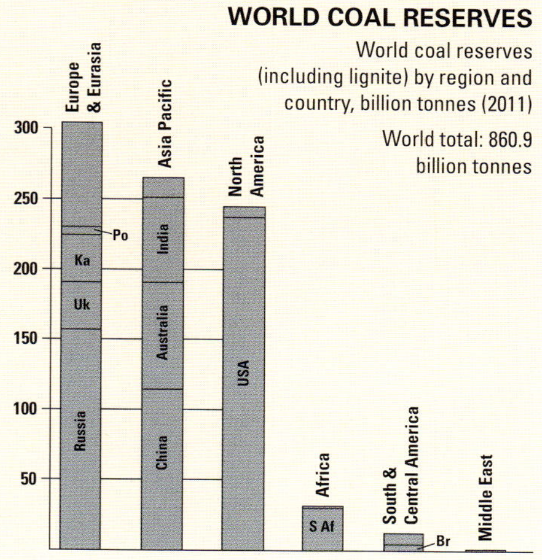

WORLD COAL RESERVES
World coal reserves (including lignite) by region and country, billion tonnes (2011)
World total: 860.9 billion tonnes
300
250
200
150
100
50
Europe & Eurasia
Po
Ka
Uk
Russia
Asia Pacific
India
Australia
China
North America
USA
Africa
S Af
South & Central America
Br
Middle East


## NUCLEAR POWER

**Major producers by percentage of world total and by percentage of domestic electricity generation (2011)**

| *Country* | *% of world total production* | *Country* | *% of nuclear as proportion of domestic electricity* |
|---|---|---|---|
| 1. United States | 31.4 | 1. France | 78.3 |
| 2. France | 16.7 | 2. Belgium | 56.9 |
| 3. Russia | 6.5 | 3. Slovak Republic | 53.7 |
| 4. Japan | 6.2 | 4. Ukraine | 46.5 |
| 5. Korea, South | 5.7 | 5. Hungary | 43.4 |
| 6. Germany | 4.1 | 6. Sweden | 39.8 |
| 7. Canada | 3.6 | 7. Switzerland | 38.8 |
| 8. Ukraine | 3.4 | 8. Bulgaria | 32.4 |
| 9. China | 3.3 | 9. Czech Republic | 32.3 |
| 10. UK | 2.6 | 10. Finland | 32.0 |

Although the 1980s were a bad time for the nuclear power industry, the industry picked up in the early 1990s. Despite this, growth has recently been curtailed whilst countries review their energy mix, in light of the March 2011 Japanese earthquake and tsunami that seriously damaged the Fukushima nuclear power station. Germany, for example, is phasing out its nuclear power production.

## PEAK OIL

'Peak oil' refers to the peak of oil production. We depend on oil for many things: we use it for fuel, transport and heating, as a raw material in the plastics industry, and for fertilizer in food production. But as oil production decreases after peak oil, so will all of these, unless we can find new materials and alternatives.

Peak oil varies by country. The peak of oil discovery occurred in the 1960s, and by the 1980s the world was using more oil than was being discovered. Since then, the gap between use and discovery has been increasing, and many countries have now passed their peak oil production.

The International Energy Agency suggests that global peak oil will occur between 2013 and 2037. In contrast, the US Geological Survey suggests it will not occur until 2059. M. King Hubbert, who popularized the theory of peak oil, predicted that it would occur in 1995. It is claimed that in 1950 the world consumed 4 billion barrels of oil per annum, while the average discovery was 30 billion barrels per annum. Now, however, research suggests the figures are reversed: new discoveries are around 4 billion barrels per year, with an annual consumption of 30 billion barrels.

## FRACKING

Hydraulic fracturing, commonly known as 'fracking', releases natural gas or oil that is trapped in shale rock and is unobtainable by conventional techniques. This is accomplished by boring holes into the rock and injecting a liquid mix of chemicals under pressure, thus fracturing the rock and forcing the trapped oil or gas to the surface.

Just as nuclear scientists in the 1950s and 1960s believed that nuclear energy was going to be the answer to the world's energy needs, oil and gas producers believe that gas derived from shale could provide a plentiful supply of low-cost energy. As a result, shale gas could transform the pattern of energy trade in the world. Nevertheless, fracking has its critics and there may be problems related to the extraction of shale gas.

Shale is one of the most common forms of sedimentary rock on Earth. Significant reserves have been found in China, Argentina, the USA and South Africa, and these are therefore having a new geopolitical influence. The world's gas trade has long been dominated by Russia, Qatar and Algeria, but shale gas development has since taken off in the USA. In 2010, the USA replaced Russia as the world's largest gas producer and a new wave of gas producers may soon emerge.

However, as with the nuclear dawn, there are potential drawbacks with fracking. It may pollute soil and ground water, release methane, produce toxic byproducts that have to be disposed of, and it may also trigger earthquakes.

## HYDROELECTRICITY

**Major producers by percentage of world total and by percentage of domestic electricity generation (2011)**

| *Country* | *% of world total production* | *Country* | *% of hydroelectric as proportion of domestic electricity* |
|---|---|---|---|
| 1. China | 19.8 | 1. Norway | 95.3 |
| 2. Brazil | 12.3 | 2. Brazil | 85.7 |
| 3. Canada | 10.8 | 3. Colombia | 82.3 |
| 4. United States | 9.4 | 4. Venezuela | 68.0 |
| 5. Russia | 4.7 | 5. Canada | 62.0 |
| 6. India | 3.8 | 6. New Zealand | 58.2 |
| 7. Norway | 3.5 | 7. Peru | 55.5 |
| 8. Japan | 2.4 | 8. Ecuador | 49.2 |
| 9. Venezuela | 2.4 | 9. Switzerland | 48.2 |
| 10. Sweden | 1.9 | 10. Austria | 46.3 |

Countries heavily reliant on hydroelectricity are usually small and non-industrial: a high proportion of hydroelectric power more often reflects a modest energy budget than vast hydroelectric resources. The USA, for instance, produces only 6% of its domestic power requirements from hydroelectricity; yet that 6% amounts to almost half the hydropower generated by the whole of Africa.

## ALTERNATIVE ENERGY RESOURCES

**Solar:** Each year the Sun bestows upon the Earth almost a million times as much energy as is locked up in all the planet's oil reserves, but only an insignificant fraction is trapped and used commercially. In a few installations around the world, mirrors focus the Sun's rays on to boilers, whose steam generates electricity by spinning turbines, and the use of photovoltaic panels in sunny climates has also started to become established.

**Wind:** Caused by uneven heating of the Earth, winds are themselves a form of solar energy. Windmills have been long used for wind power; recent models are often arranged in banks on wind-swept high ground or situated off coastlines. Wind-power figures are given in the table (*right*). Wind power contributes 19% of all electricity generated in Denmark.

**Tidal:** The energy from tides is potentially enormous, although only a few installations have so far been built to exploit it. In theory, at least, waves and currents could also provide almost unimaginable power, and the thermal differences in the ocean depths are another huge well of potential energy. But work on extracting it is still at the experimental stage.

**Geothermal:** The Earth's temperature rises by 1°C for every 30 metres descent, with much steeper temperature gradients in geologically active areas. El Salvador, for example, produces 25% of its electricity from geothermal power stations, whilst the USA is the world's leading producer. Some of the oldest and most successful applications are in Iceland, where 86% of all households are heated by geothermal energy.

**Biomass:** The oldest of human fuels ranges from animal dung, still burned in cooking fires in much of North Africa and elsewhere, to sugar-cane plantations feeding high-technology distilleries to produce ethanol for motor-vehicle engines. In Brazil and South Africa, plant ethanol provides up to 25% of motor fuel. Throughout the developing world, most biomass energy comes from firewood: although accurate figures are impossible to obtain, it may yield as much as 10% of the world's total energy consumption.

## WIND POWER

**World wind energy generating capacity, in megawatts**

| | |
|---|---|
| 1984 | 600 |
| 1986 | 1,270 |
| 1988 | 1,580 |
| 1990 | 1,930 |
| 1992 | 2,510 |
| 1994 | 3,710 |
| 1996 | 6,115 |
| 1998 | 9,600 |
| 2000 | 17,800 |
| 2002 | 31,000 |
| 2003 | 39,300 |
| 2004 | 47,671 |
| 2005 | 58,982 |
| 2006 | 74,151 |
| 2007 | 93,927 |
| 2008 | 121,188 |
| 2009 | 157,899 |
| 2010 | 196,653 |
| 2011 | 238,035 |
| 2012 | 282,482 |

**For more information:**

74 Geology
103 Globalization

The use of metals played a vital part in the evolving technologies of early peoples. Copper first came into use around 10,000 years ago, bronze about 5,000 years ago, and iron 3,300 years ago. In the early stages of the Industrial Revolution, the location of coal, iron ore, and water power usually determined the location of new industries. But due to continuing improvements in transport, including oil pipelines, industries can now be located almost anywhere.

Minerals are distributed unevenly and some industrial countries, lacking their own mineral resources, import most of the raw materials they need. Some imports come from mineral-rich countries, such as Australia, but others come from developing countries, especially in Africa and South America. Most developing countries export unprocessed ores, losing out on the higher revenues gained from exporting metals.

Most minerals come from land deposits, because undersea deposits, with the exception of oil reserves under the continental shelves, have been inaccessible. But shortages of terrestrial minerals may one day encourage exploitation of the ocean floor.

► Bingham Canyon Mine in Utah, USA, is the largest open-pit mine in the world. It measures over 4 km [2.5 miles] wide and 1,200 m [3,900 ft] deep. Copper-containing rocks are excavated from the surface downwards in terraces. These terraces are 15–25 m [50–80 ft] high and provide access for equipment to work the rock face whilst maintaining stability of the sloping pit walls.

Today's copper market is booming due to global demands from construction, telecommunications, and electronics companies. Over 17 million tonnes of copper have been mined from Bingham Canyon Mine to date, as well as gold, silver and other minerals.

## URANIUM

Uranium was first discovered by the German chemist Martin Klaproth in 1789. In its pure state, uranium is an immensely heavy, white metal. Its main use is as a fuel in nuclear reactors and in nuclear weaponry, although depleted uranium is employed as a projectile in anti-missile cannons, where its mass ensures a lethal punch.

Uranium is very scarce: the main source is the rare ore pitchblende, which itself contains only 0.2% uranium oxide. This blackish, lustrous ore occurs in quartz veins. Only a minute fraction of that is the radioactive $U^{235}$ isotope, though so-called breeder reactors can transmute the more common $U^{238}$ into highly radioactive plutonium.

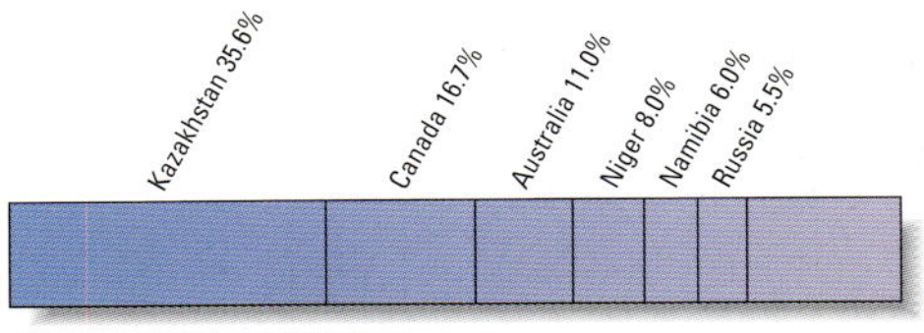
Kazakhstan 35.6%
Canada 16.7%
Australia 11.0%
Niger 8.0%
Namibia 6.0%
Russia 5.5%

World total (2012): 54,610 tonnes

## DIAMOND

Most of the world's diamond is found in kimberlite, or 'blue ground', a basic igneous rock; erosion may wash the diamond from its kimberlite matrix and deposit it with sand or gravel on river beds. Only a small proportion of the world's diamond, the most flawless, is cut into gemstones – 'diamonds'; most are used in industry, where the material's remarkable hardness and abrasion resistance finds a use in cutting tools, drills and dies. In 2012, the world's major producers were Botswana (30.8%), the Democratic Republic of the Congo (20.5%), Russia (19.2%), Australia (10.3%) and South Africa (5.1%). Natural diamonds now account for less than 10% of all industrial diamond output. Synthetic diamond production in centres such as Ireland, Japan, Russia and the USA far exceeds it.

## BLOOD DIAMONDS

Blood Diamonds, or 'Conflict Diamonds', are stones that are produced in areas controlled by rebel forces that are opposed to internationally recognized governments. The rebels sell these diamonds, using the money to purchase arms or to fund their military actions. These diamonds are often the main source of funding for the rebels – however, arms merchants, smugglers and dishonest diamond traders facilitate their actions.

The flow of Blood Diamonds originated mainly from Sierra Leone, Angola, Democratic Republic of Congo, Liberia and Ivory Coast. In 2003, the United Nations and other groups introduced a certification procedure known as the 'Kimberley Process', to try to eradicate this practice. This procedure requires each nation to certify that all rough diamond exports are produced through legitimate mining and sales activity.

Over 70 countries participate in the agreement.

**Aluminium:** Produced mainly from its oxide, bauxite, which yields 25% of its weight in aluminium. The cost of refining and production is often too high for producer-countries to bear, so bauxite is largely exported. Lightweight and corrosion resistant, aluminium alloys are widely used in aircraft, vehicles, cans and packaging.

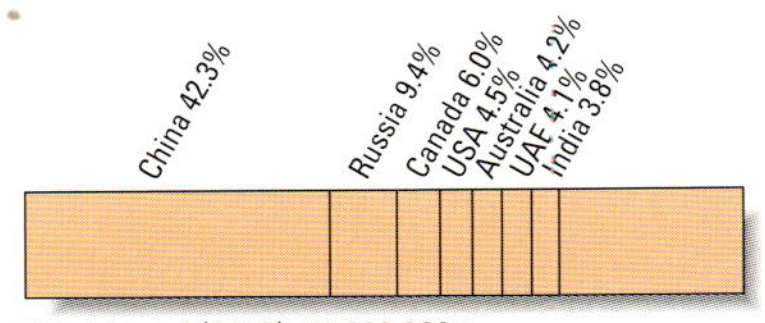
China 42.3%
Russia 9.4%
Canada 6.0%
USA 4.5%
Australia 4.2%
UAE 4.1%
India 3.8%

World total (2012): 44,900,000 tonnes

**Lead:** A soft metal, obtained mainly from galena (lead sulphide), which occurs in veins associated with iron, zinc and silver sulphides. Its use in vehicle batteries accounts for the USA's prime consumer status; lead is also made into sheeting and piping. Its use as an additive to paints and petrol is decreasing.

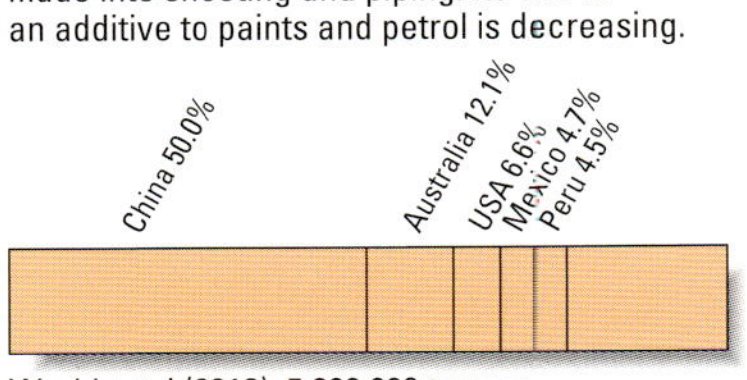
China 50.0%
Australia 12.1%
USA 6.6%
Mexico 4.7%
Peru 4.5%

World total (2012): 5,200,000 tonnes

**Tin:** Soft, pliable and non-toxic, used to coat 'tin' (tin-plated steel) cans, in the manufacture of foils and in alloys. The principal tin-bearing mineral is cassiterite ($SnO_2$), found in ore formed from molten rock.

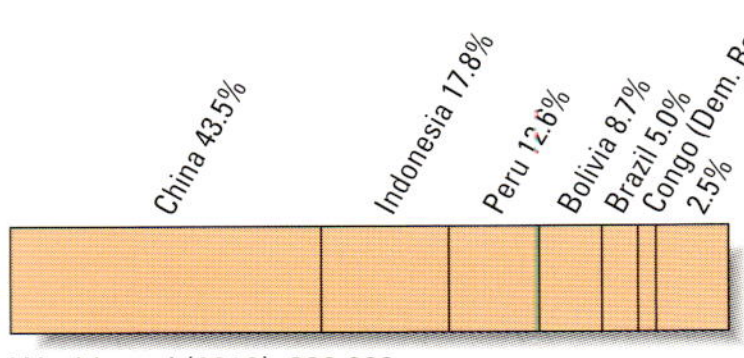
China 43.5%
Indonesia 17.8%
Peru 12.6%
Bolivia 8.7%
Brazil 5.0%
Congo (Dem. Rep.) 2.5%

World total (2012): 230,000 tonnes

**Gold:** Regarded for centuries as the most valuable metal in the world and used to make coins, gold is still recognized as the monetary standard. A soft metal, it is alloyed to make jewellery; the electronics industry values its corrosion resistance and conductivity.

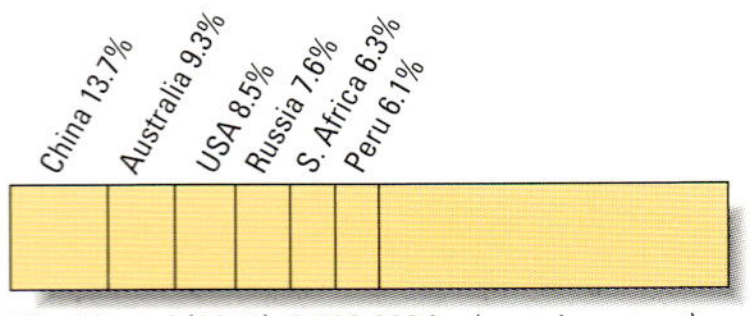
China 13.7%
Australia 9.3%
USA 8.5%
Russia 7.6%
S. Africa 6.3%
Peru 6.1%

World total (2012): 2,700,000 kg (metal content)

**Copper:** Derived from low-yielding sulphide ores, copper is an important export for several developing countries. An excellent conductor of heat and electricity, it forms part of most electrical items, and is used in the manufacture of brass and bronze. Major importers include Japan and Germany.

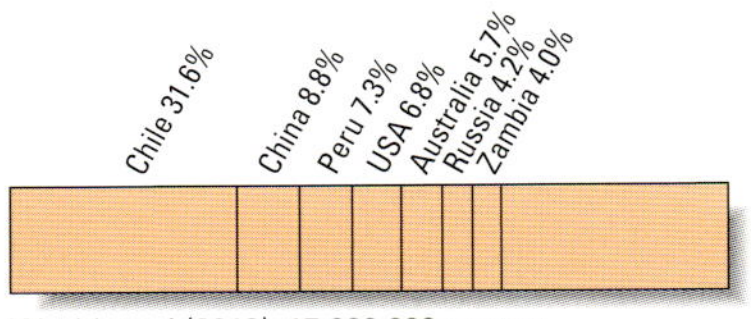
Chile 31.6%
China 8.8%
Peru 7.3%
USA 6.8%
Australia 5.7%
Russia 4.2%
Zambia 4.0%

World total (2012): 17,000,000 tonnes

**Mercury:** The only metal that is liquid at normal temperatures, most is derived from its sulphide, cinnabar, found only in small quantities in volcanic areas. Apart from its value in thermometers and other instruments, most mercury production is used in anti-fungal and anti-fouling preparations, and to make detonators.

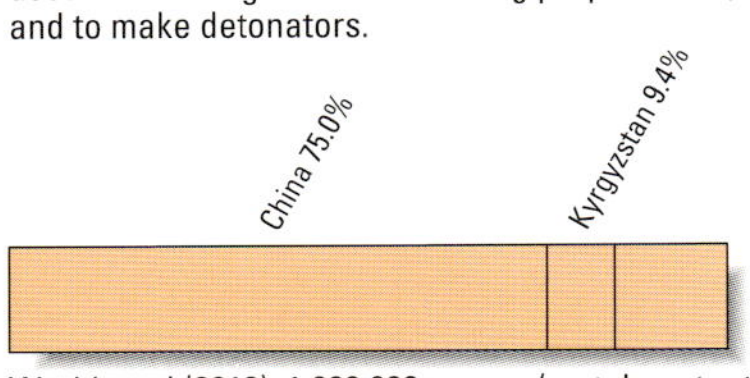
China 75.0%
Kyrgyzstan 9.4%

World total (2012): 1,600,000 tonnes (metal content)

**Zinc:** Often found in association with lead ores, zinc is highly resistant to corrosion, and about 40% of the refined metal is used to plate sheet steel, particularly vehicle bodies – a process known as galvanizing. Zinc is also used in dry batteries, paints and dyes.

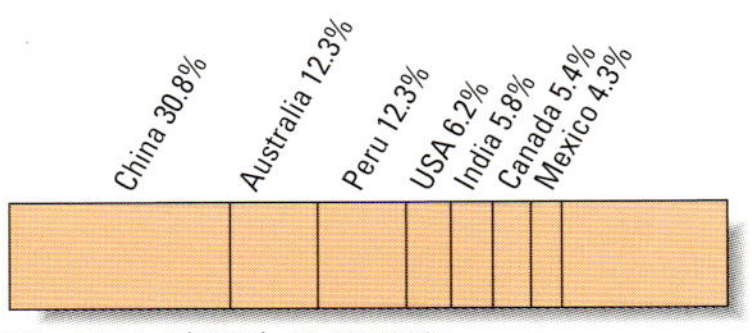
China 30.8%
Australia 12.3%
Peru 12.3%
USA 6.2%
India 5.8%
Canada 5.4%
Mexico 4.3%

World total (2012): 12,000,000 tonnes

**Silver:** Most silver comes from ores mined and processed for other metals (including lead and copper). Pure or alloyed with harder metals, it is used for jewellery and ornaments. Industrial use includes dentistry, electronics, photography and as a chemical catalyst.

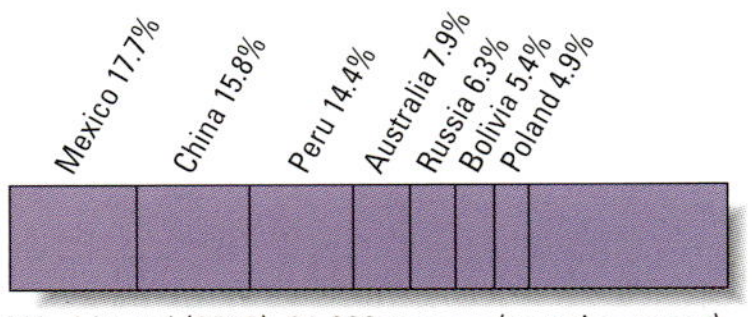
Mexico 17.7%
China 15.8%
Peru 14.4%
Australia 7.9%
Russia 6.3%
Bolivia 5.4%
Poland 4.9%

World total (2012): 24,000 tonnes (metal content)

## DISTRIBUTION OF MINERALS

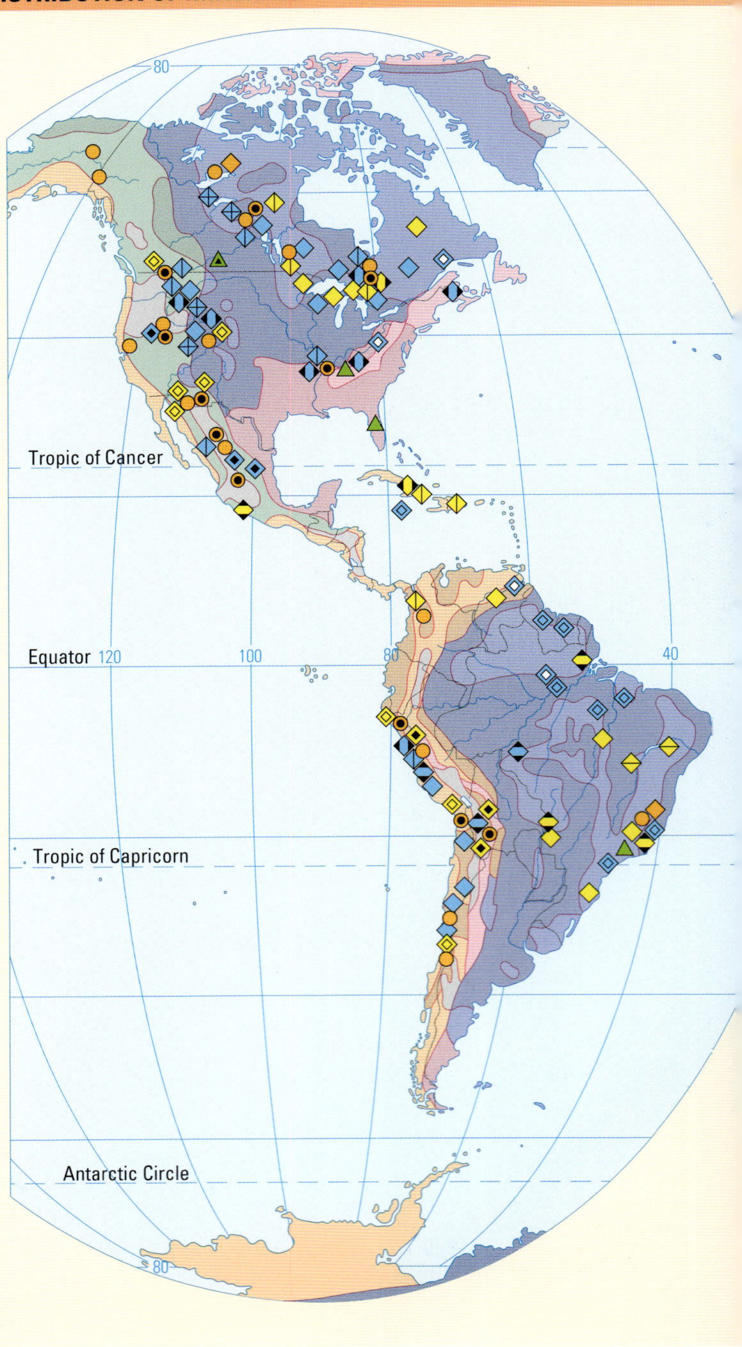
80
Tropic of Cancer
Equator
120
100
80
40
Tropic of Capricorn
Antarctic Circle
80

## IRON ORE

Ever since the art of high-temperature smelting was discovered, some time in the second millennium BC, iron has been by far the most important metal known to man. The earliest iron ploughs transformed primitive agriculture and led to the first human population explosion, while iron weapons – or the lack of them – ensured the rise or fall of entire cultures.

Widely distributed around the world, iron ores usually contain 25–60% iron; blast furnaces process the raw product into pig-iron, which is then alloyed with carbon and other minerals to produce steels of various qualities. From the time of the Industrial Revolution, steel has been almost literally the backbone of modern civilization, the prime structural material on which all else is built.

Iron smelting usually developed close to the sources of ore and, later, to the coalfields that fuelled the furnaces. Today, most ore comes from a few richly-endowed locations where large-scale mining is possible.

Iron and steel plants are generally built at coastal sites so that giant ore carriers, which account for a sizeable proportion of the world's merchant fleet, can more easily discharge their cargoes.

**World production of pig-iron (2012)**

**Total world production: 1.100 million tonnes**

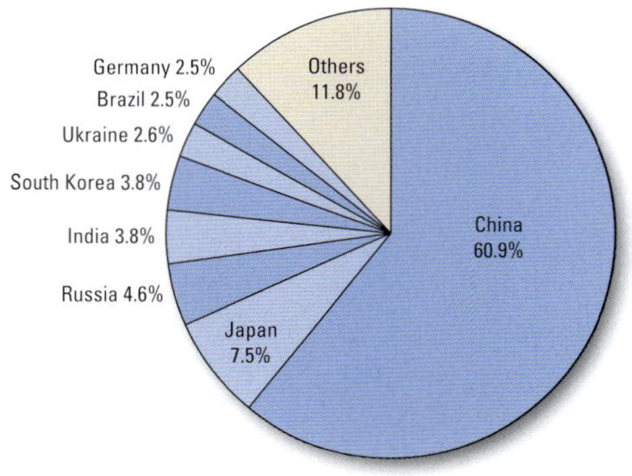
Germany 2.5%
Brazil 2.5%
Ukraine 2.6%
South Korea 3.8%
India 3.8%
Russia 4.6%
Japan 7.5%
Others 11.8%
China 60.9%

**Iron ore**

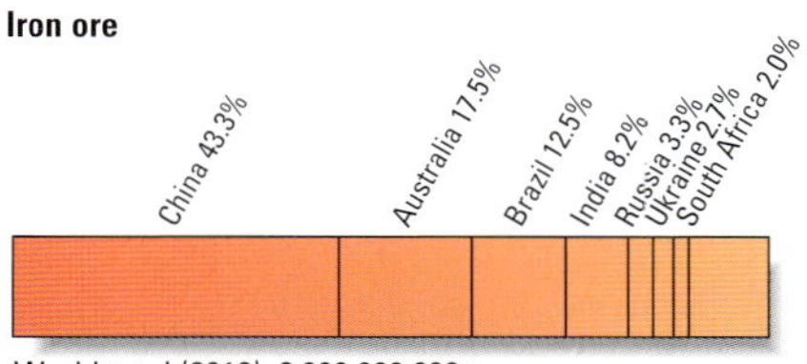
China 43.3%
Australia 17.5%
Brazil 12.5%
India 8.2%
Russia 3.3%
Ukraine 2.7%
South Africa 2.0%

World total (2012): 3,000,000,000 tonnes

## RARE EARTHS

Rare earth elements, or rare earth metals, are a set of 17 chemical elements, specifically the 15 lanthanides plus scandium and yttrium. Despite their name, rare earth elements are relatively plentiful, but are typically dispersed and not often found concentrated in economically exploitable ore deposits.

Until 1948, most of the world's rare earths were sourced from sand deposits in India and Brazil. Between the 1960s and the 1980s, the leading producer was California, USA. Today, China produces over 90% of the world's rare earth supply, although it only has less than 25% of proven reserves. The US Geological Survey is currently actively surveying southern Afghanistan for rare earth deposits under the protection of US military forces.

New demand has recently strained supply, and there is a growing concern that the world may soon face a shortage of the rare earths. In 2009, China announced plans to reduce its export quota between 2010 and 2015, in order to conserve scarce resources and protect the environment.

A recently developed source of rare earths is electronic waste, and other wastes have rare earth components. Advances in recycling technology have made extraction of rare earths from these materials more feasible.

Rare earths are used as follows:

- **Neodymium** To make powerful magnets in loudspeakers and computer hard drives; also used in wind turbines and hybrid cars.
- **Lanthanum** In camera and telescope lenses.
- **Cerium** In catalytic converters in cars, and in the refining of oil.
- **Praseodymium** As an alloy, to create strong metals in aircraft engines.
- **Gadolinium** For X-ray machines, MRI scanning systems, and television screens.
- **Yttrium, terbium, europium** For television and computer screens, and for visual display units.

## SCRAP METAL

Scrap metal has been an important source material for the manufacturing industry in domestic markets for decades, its value fluctuating according to the state of the local economy. Recently, however, with growing concern for the global environment and the rapid development of the economies in the Far East, the industry has become far more globalized. Container loads of processed-metal scrap from time-expired machinery in the Western world are now being exported to the Far East to be recycled. Processed-steel scrap accounts for almost half of the requirements for 'furnace feed' for the world's steelmakers, and 40% of the world's copper requirements are derived from scrap.

Two major advantages of using scrap rather than refining mined ore are the energy and raw material savings that can be made. If 1 tonne of steel scrap is recycled, it saves 54 kg [120 lb] of limestone, 1,130 kg [2,500 lb] of iron ore and 635 kg [1,400 lb] of coal, with a consequent 86% reduction in air pollution, 40% saving in water use, and 76% reduction in water pollution. Huge energy savings, with consequent cuts in greenhouse-gas emissions, can also be made by using scrap.

As well as bulk minerals, such as those quoted above, alloys using nickel, chromium, tungsten, molybdenum, cobalt and titanium, which are often only available in limited supplies and are expensive to produce, can also be recycled. The techniques involved to do this work are often very sophisticated, involving X-ray spectrometry and other computer-controlled methods, in order to recover high-value but low-volume metals from devices such as computers and televisions.

With companies having to take increased responsibility for their products, from manufacturing to sale and thence to their ultimate disposal at the end of their useful life, recycling scrap metals will become a much more important method of conserving the world's raw materials and preserving the environment in the future.

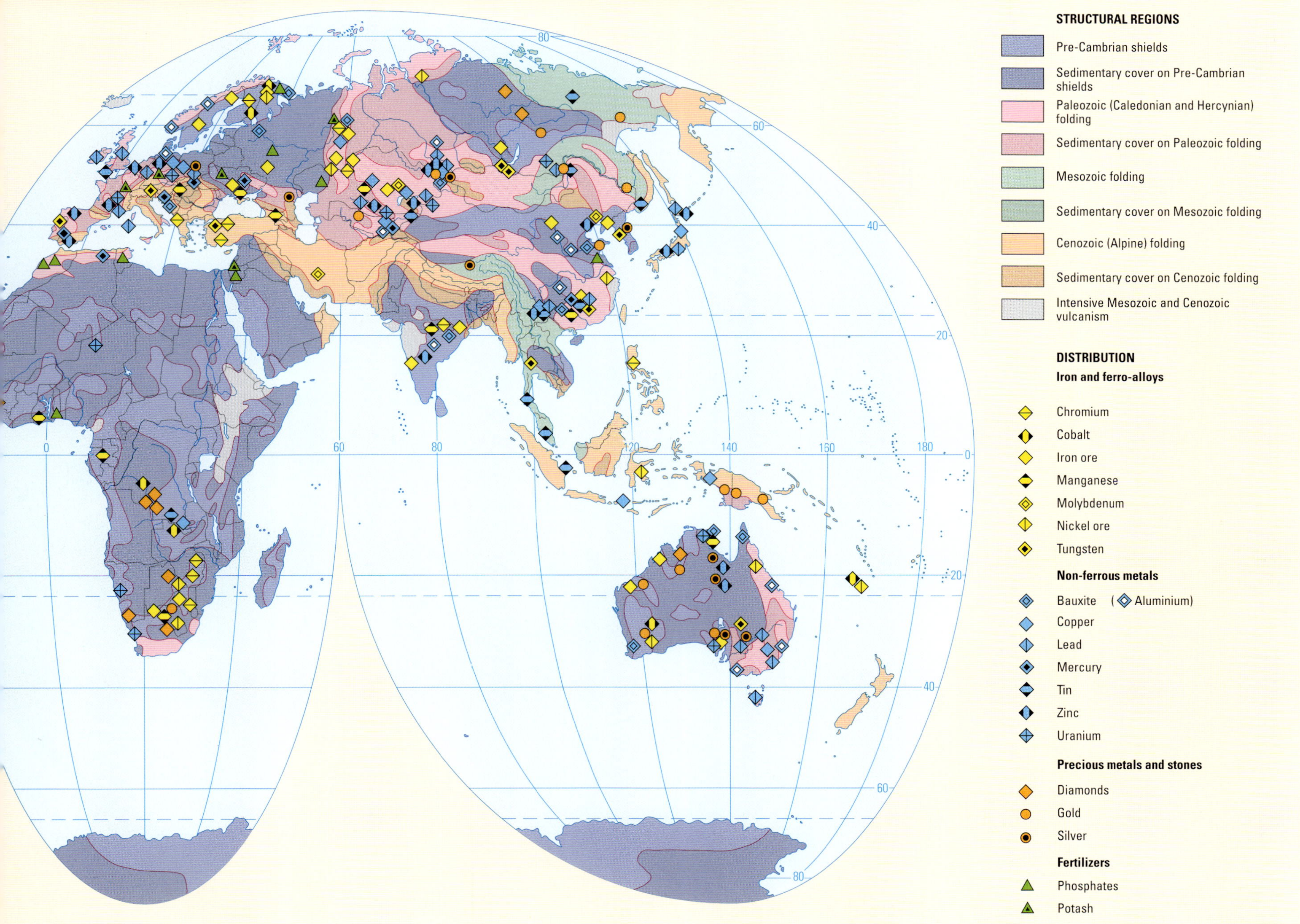
STRUCTURAL REGIONS
Pre-Cambrian shields
Sedimentary cover on Pre-Cambrian shields
Paleozoic (Caledonian and Hercynian) folding
Sedimentary cover on Paleozoic folding
Mesozoic folding
Sedimentary cover on Mesozoic folding
Cenozoic (Alpine) folding
Sedimentary cover on Cenozoic folding
Intensive Mesozoic and Cenozoic vulcanism
DISTRIBUTION
Iron and ferro-alloys
Chromium
Cobalt
Iron ore
Manganese
Molybdenum
Nickel ore
Tungsten
Non-ferrous metals
Bauxite (Aluminium)
Copper
Lead
Mercury
Tin
Zinc
Uranium
Precious metals and stones
Diamonds
Gold
Silver
Fertilizers
Phosphates
Potash

**For more information:**
82 Water distribution
98 Minerals
102 World trade
103 Globalization

The Industrial Revolution, which began in Britain in the late 18th century, represented a major technological advance in the evolution of human society. It enabled a group of countries to become prosperous by replacing expensive human labour with increasingly sophisticated machinery. In economic terms, manufacturing is the transformation of raw materials, energy, labour and machines into finished goods, which have a higher value than the various elements used in production.

The economies of countries can be compared by reference to their per capita Gross Domestic Products (GDPs), namely, the total value of goods and services produced within a country in a year, divided by the population. The industrialized, or developed, countries accounted for 19% of the world's population in 2011 with an average per capita GDP of more than US $41,000. On the other hand, low-income developing countries, with small industrial sectors, accounted for 39% of the world's population. Their per capita GDPs are less than $600, with some as low as $230.

Kenya, with its low-income economy, had a per capita GDP in 2012 of US $1,800. Agriculture employs 75% of the people, while industry together with services employs 25%. The main industries are the processing of agricultural imports and import substitution (making such necessities as cement, footwear and textiles). Heavy industry plays only a small part. By contrast, Germany had a per capita GDP in 2012 of $39,100. Agriculture employs only 1% of the population, with 28% in industry and 71% in services. Germany's industrial sector differs greatly from Kenya's, with its emphasis on vehicles, machinery, chemicals and electronics.

Since the 1970s, some former developing countries in eastern Asia achieved rapid economic growth through industrialization. Despite setbacks in the late 1990s, they demonstrated that a developing industrial sector can transform an economy, which starts off with certain advantages, such as low labour costs. But economic success also depends on such factors as education to provide skills, and regulations that attract foreign investors. China, whose economy grew by more than 9.3% per year between 2001 and 2011, satisfies many of these criteria, though its record on human rights leaves much to be desired.

## EMPLOYMENT

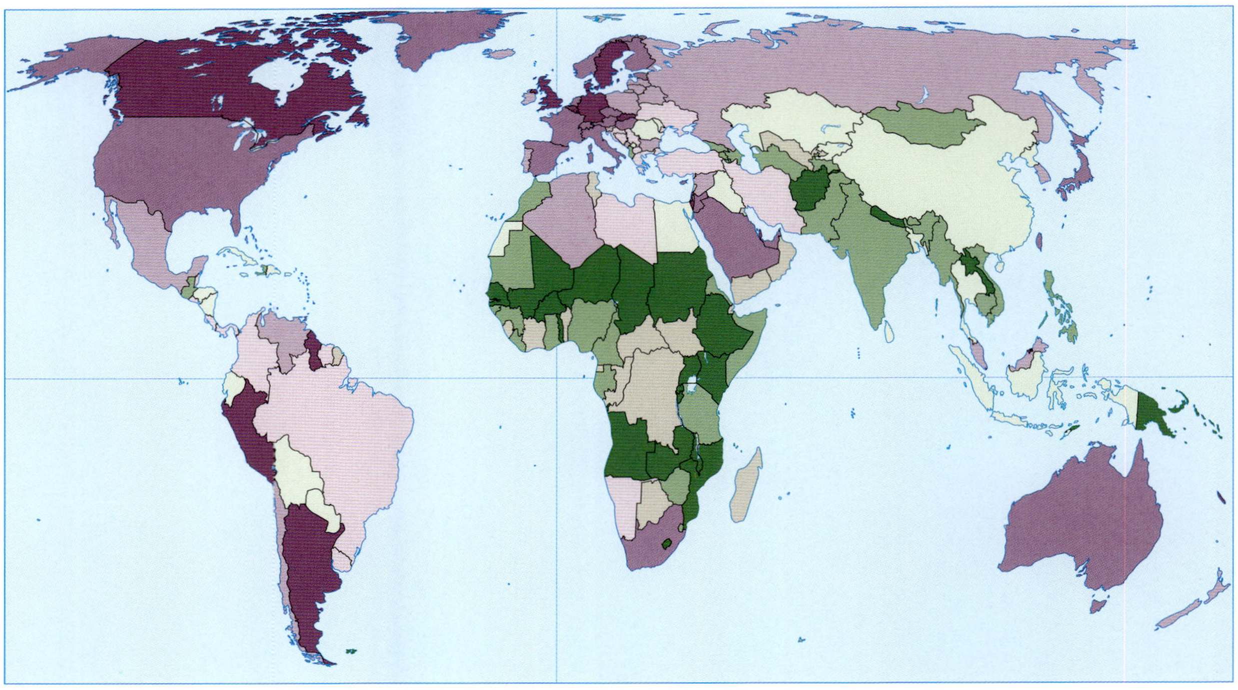

**The number of workers employed in manufacturing for every 100 workers engaged in agriculture (2011)**

Over 1000
500 – 1000
200 – 500
100 – 200
(Mainly industrial countries)

50 – 100
10 – 50
0 – 10
(Mainly agricultural countries)

No data available

**Countries with the highest number of workers employed in manufacturing per 100 workers in agriculture (2011)**

| | |
|---|---|
| Bahrain | 7,900 |
| Qatar | 5,400 |
| Micronesia, Fed. States of | 3,500 |
| Argentina | 2,400 |
| Malta | 2,400 |
| Peru | 2,400 |
| Belgium | 2,300 |
| Canada | 2,200 |
| Singapore | 2,200 |
| Liechtenstein | 2,150 |
| Guyana | 1,900 |
| United Kingdom | 1,900 |

## DIVISION OF EMPLOYMENT

**Distribution of workers between agriculture, industry and services, selected countries**

The six countries selected illustrate the usual stages of economic development, from dependence on agriculture through industrial growth to the expansion of the service sector.

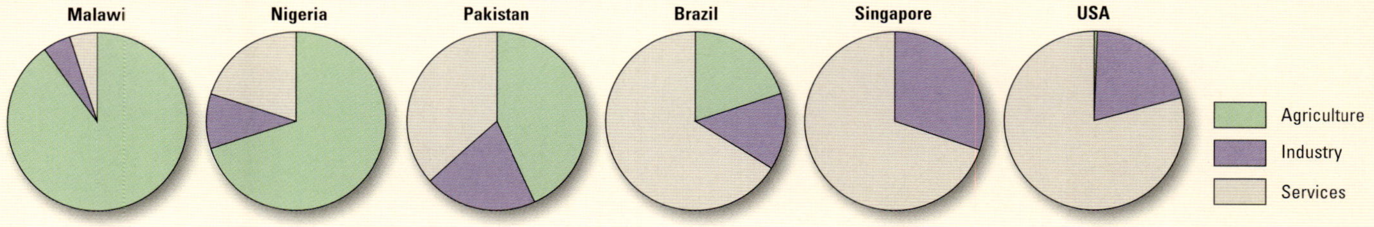
Malawi
Nigeria
Pakistan
Brazil
Singapore
USA
Agriculture
Industry
Services

## THE WORKFORCE

**Percentages of men and women between 15 and 64 in employment (selected countries)**

The figures include employees and the self-employed, who in developing countries are often subsistence farmers. People in full-time education are excluded. Because of the population age structure in developing countries, the employed population has to support a far larger number of non-workers than its industrial equivalent. For example, more than 52% of Kenya's people are under 15, an age group that makes up less than a tenth of the UK population.

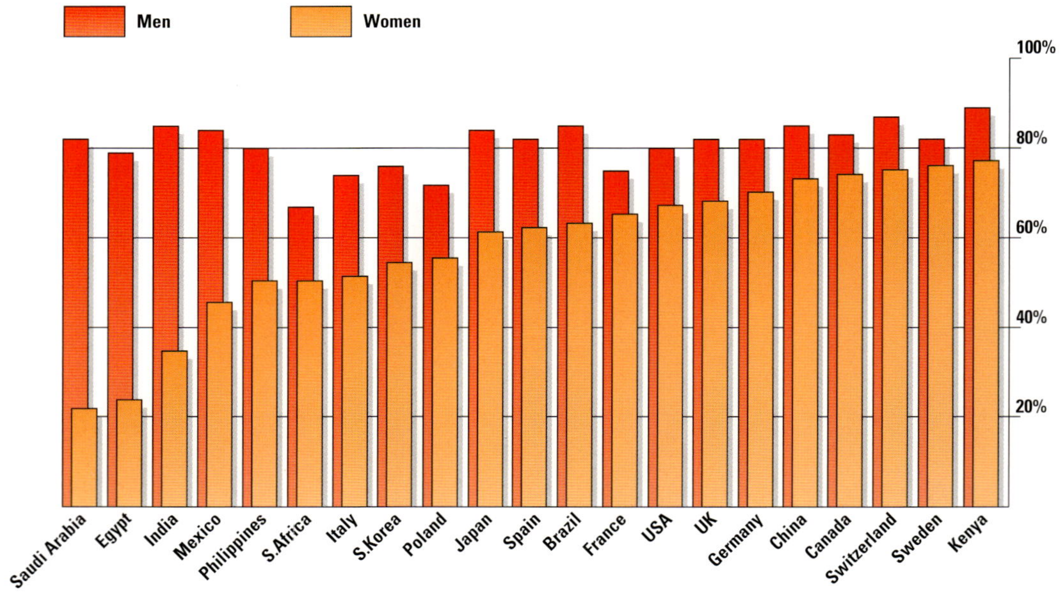
Men
Women
100%
80%
60%
40%
20%
Saudi Arabia
Egypt
India
Mexico
Philippines
S.Africa
Italy
S.Korea
Poland
Japan
Spain
Brazil
France
USA
UK
Germany
China
Canada
Switzerland
Sweden
Kenya

## INDUSTRIAL OUTPUT

**Largest industrial output (mining, manufacturing, construction and energy), US $ billion (2011)**

| | | |
|---|---|---|
| 1. | China | 3,416 |
| 2. | USA | 3,336 |
| 3. | Japan | 1,409 |
| 4. | Germany | 1,005 |
| 5. | Russia | 685 |
| 6. | Brazil | 671 |
| 7. | Italy | 554 |
| 8. | UK | 522 |
| 9. | France | 514 |
| 10. | Canada | 477 |
| 11. | India | 441 |
| 12. | South Korea | 438 |
| 13. | Saudi Arabia | 390 |
| 14. | Indonesia | 389 |
| 15. | Spain | 387 |
| 16. | Australia | 381 |
| 17. | Mexico | 379 |
| 18. | UAE | 214 |
| 19. | Turkey | 209 |
| 20. | Netherlands | 203 |
| 21. | Iran | 196 |
| 22. | Norway | 185 |
| 23. | Switzerland | 175 |
| 24. | Poland | 173 |
| 25. | Taiwan | 149 |
| 26. | Sweden | 145 |
| 27. | Argentina | 137 |
| 28. | South Africa | 129 |
| 29. | Colombia | 125 |
| 30. | Austria | 124 |
| 31. | Thailand | 118 |
| 32. | Algeria | 117 |
| 33. | Belgium | 111 |
| 34. | Malaysia | 111 |
| 35. | Venezuela | 110 |
| 36. | Chile | 104 |
| 37. | Egypt | 93 |
| 38. | Czech Rep. | 83 |
| 39. | Finland | 78 |
| 40. | Israel | 76 |
| 41. | Philippines | 71 |
| 42. | Singapore | 69 |

## INDUSTRY AND TRADE

**Manufactured goods (including machinery and transport) as a percentage of total exports (2011)**

- Over 75%
- 50 – 75%
- 25 – 50%
- 10 – 25%
- Under 10%
- No data available

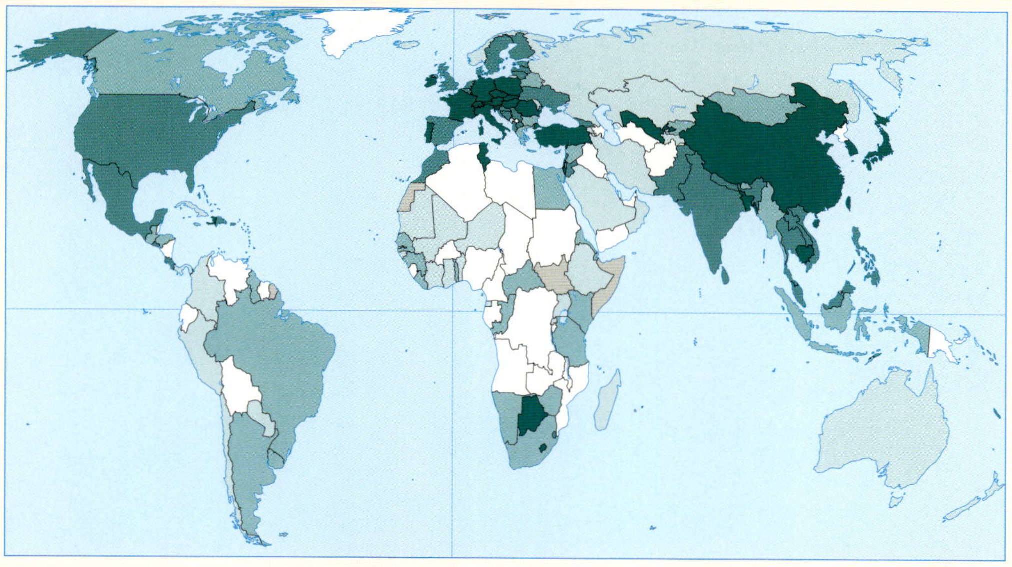

**Countries most dependent on the export of manufactured goods**

| | |
|---|---|
| Cambodia | 96% |
| China | 93% |
| Israel | 93% |
| Japan | 89% |
| St Kitts & Nevis | 89% |
| Bangladesh | 88% |

## UNEMPLOYMENT

**Highest rates of unemployment, percentage of the labour force (2011)**

| | | |
|---|---|---|
| 1. | Zimbabwe | 95% |
| 2. | Nauru | 90% |
| 3. | Burkina Faso | 77% |
| 4. | Turkmenistan | 60% |
| 5. | Djibouti | 59% |
| 6. | Namibia | 51% |
| 7. | Senegal | 48% |
| 8. | Nepal | 46% |
| 9. | Kosovo | 45% |
| 10. | Lesotho | 45% |
| 11. | Bosnia & Herzegovina | 43% |
| 12. | Haiti | 41% |
| 13. | Swaziland | 40% |
| 14. | Gaza Strip | 40% |
| 15. | Kenya | 40% |
| 16. | Afghanistan | 35% |
| 17. | Yemen | 35% |
| 18. | Cameroon | 30% |
| 19. | Libya | 30% |
| 20. | Mali | 30% |

## IMPORTANCE OF SERVICE SECTOR

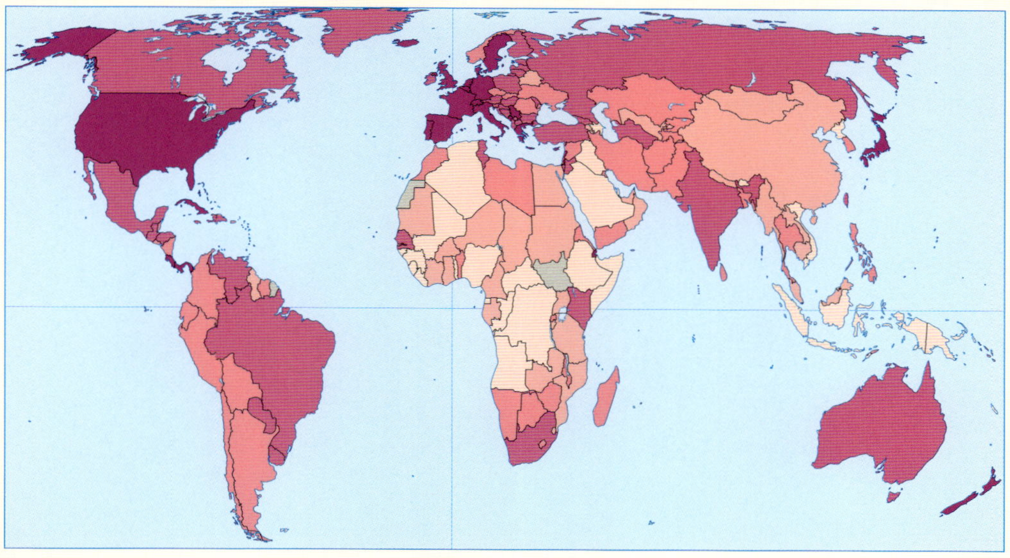

**Percentage of total GDP from service sector (2012)**

- Over 70%
- 60 – 70%
- 50 – 60%
- 40 – 50%
- Under 40%
- No data available

The service sector involves those parts of business such as accountancy, advertising, financial services, tourism, etc. No actual goods are produced, but high levels of income may be generated.

## TOURISM AND TRAVEL

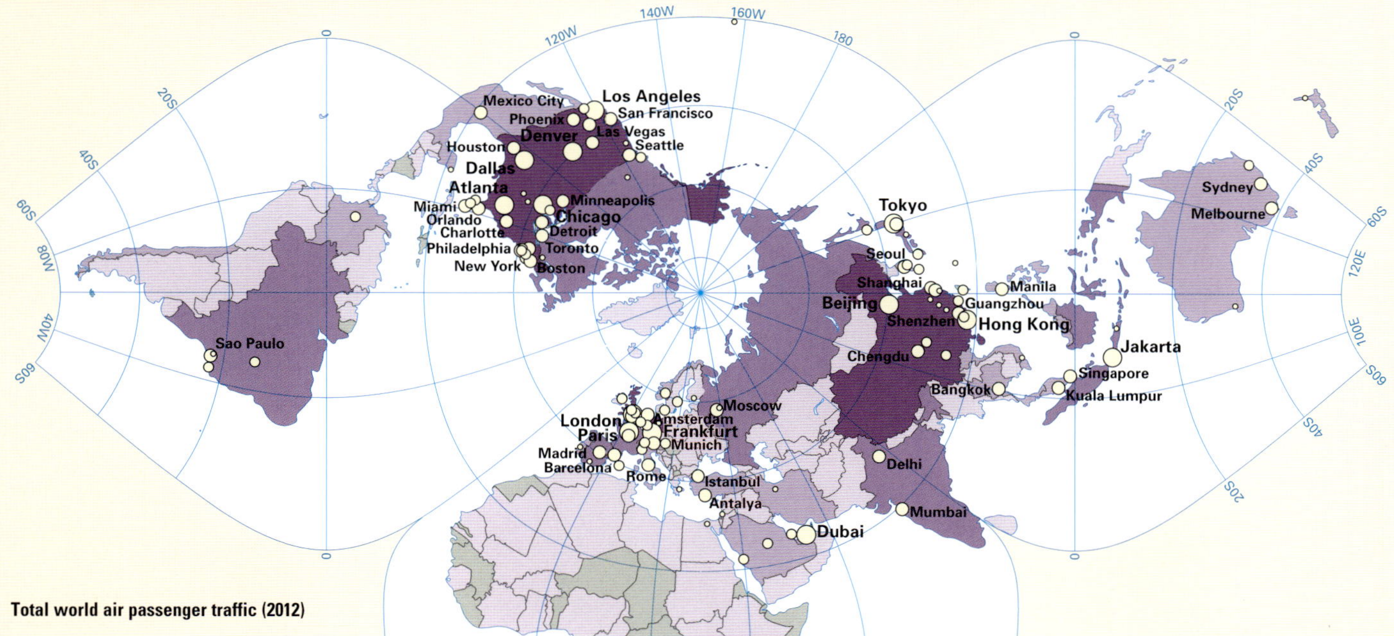

Los Angeles
San Francisco
Mexico City
Phoenix
Denver
Las Vegas
Seattle
Houston
Dallas
Atlanta
Miami
Orlando
Charlotte
Minneapolis
Chicago
Detroit
Toronto
Philadelphia
New York
Boston
Sao Paulo
Tokyo
Seoul
Shanghai
Beijing
Manila
Guangzhou
Shenzhen
Hong Kong
Chengdu
Jakarta
Singapore
Kuala Lumpur
Bangkok
Delhi
Mumbai
Dubai
Moscow
London
Amsterdam
Paris
Frankfurt
Munich
Madrid
Barcelona
Rome
Istanbul
Antalya
Sydney
Melbourne
Projection: Peirce


**Total world air passenger traffic (2012)**

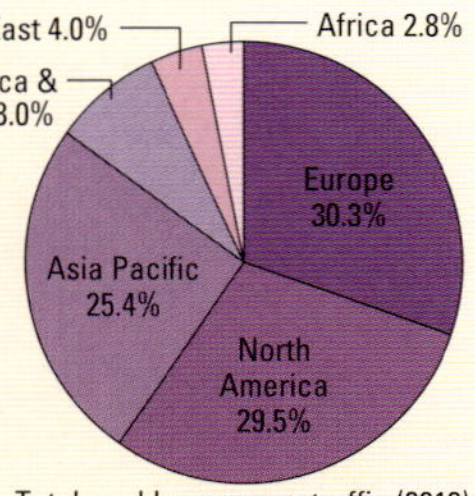

Middle East 4.0%
Africa 2.8%
Latin America & Caribbean 8.0%
Europe 30.3%
Asia Pacific 25.4%
North America 29.5%


Total world passenger traffic (2012) 3,873,600,000

**Passenger traffic**
Number of passengers carried (domestic and international, 2011)

- Over 100 million
- 50 – 100 million
- 10 – 50 million
- Under 10 million
- No data available

**Major airports**
Number of passengers (international and domestic, 2011)

- Over 50 million
- 25 – 50 million
- 15 – 25 million
- 10 – 15 million

Air freight accounts for 35% of all international freight handled by value.

Leisure and tourism is the world's second largest industry in terms of revenue generated. Small economies in attractive areas are often completely dominated by tourism: in some Caribbean islands, for example, tourist spending provides over 90% of the total income and is the biggest foreign-exchange earner.

In cash terms, the United States is the world leader: its 2012 earnings were US $164 billion, although that sum amounted to approximately 1.1% of its total GNI. Of the 60 million visitors to the US, 31% came from Canada and 25% came from Mexico. The United States also spends the most on overseas tourism; this amounts to US $110 billion. The next biggest spenders are Germany, the UK and China.

**WORLD'S BUSIEST AIRPORTS**
**Total passengers in millions (2012)**

| | | |
|---|---|---|
| 1. | Atlanta Hartsfield Intl. (ATL) | 95.5 |
| 2. | Beijing Capital Intl. (PEK) | 81.9 |
| 3. | London Heathrow (LHR) | 70.0 |
| 4. | Tokyo Haneda (HND) | 66.8 |
| 5. | Chicago O'Hare Intl. (ORD) | 66.6 |
| 6. | Los Angeles Intl. (LAX) | 63.7 |
| 7. | Paris Charles de Gaulle (CDG) | 61.6 |
| 8. | Dallas/Fort Worth Intl. (DFW) | 58.6 |
| 9. | Jakarta Intl. (CGK) | 57.8 |
| 10. | Dubai Intl. (DXB) | 57.7 |

London's Heathrow handles the most international passengers (65.9 million in 2012), followed by Paris Charles de Gaulle (55.7 million).

**For more information:**

95 International organizations
97 Movements of oil
98 Minerals
101 Industry and trade
Tourism and travel
107 Inflation

Trade played a vital role in the growth of early civilizations and it was later a spur to European exploration and colonization. The colonial powers grew rich by exporting cheap manufactures, such as clothing and footwear, while obtaining primary products from their colonies.

From the late 19th century to the early 1950s, as transport technology improved, primary products, especially oil in the later stages of this period, dominated world trade. However, since that time, manufactures have become the chief commodities in world trade, which is dominated by the industrialized countries. Nearly half of all world trade flows between the developed market economies of the European Union, the United States and Japan, although a number of Asian economies, notably China, India, Malaysia, Singapore, South Korea, Taiwan and Thailand, have dramatically increased their share since the 1990s.

China's remarkable growth means that it has rapidly overtaken countries such as Japan, Mexico and Germany, to become the second biggest exporter to the United States. China's low production costs, especially its cheap labour, were estimated to be one-twentieth of those of Japan, making its high-quality exports highly competitive in price. Growth in world trade is regarded as a sign of economic health, as is a favorable balance of trade (or trade surplus) in any country.

## WORLD TRADE

**Percentage share of total world exports by value (2012)**

- Over 10% of world trade
- 1 – 10% of world trade
- 0.1 – 1.0% of world trade
- 0 – 0.1% of world trade
- No world trade
- No data available

International trade is dominated by a handful of powerful maritime nations: the members of 'G8' (Canada, France, Germany, Italy, Japan, Russia, UK and USA) and the 'BRIC' nations (Brazil, Russia, India and China).

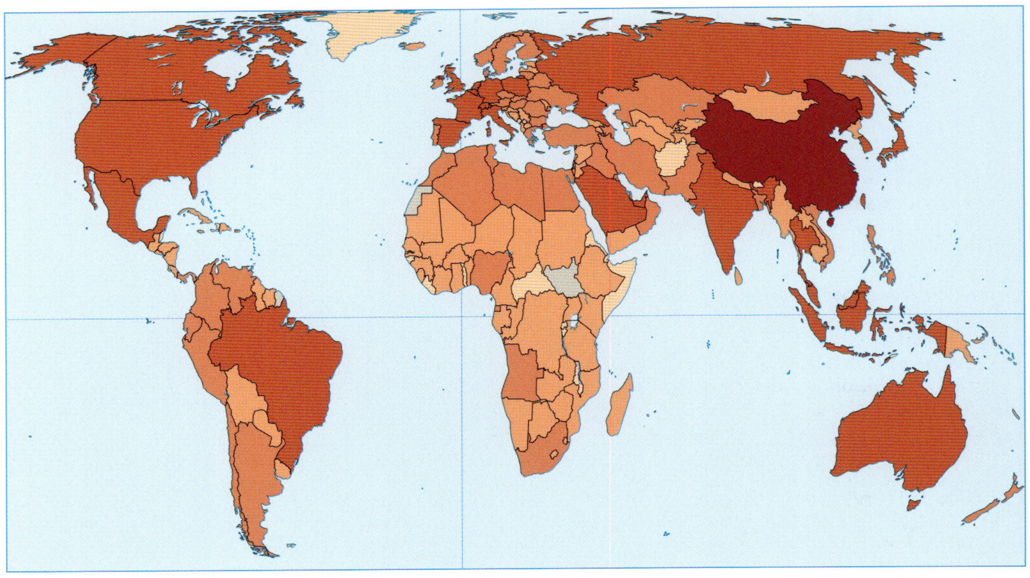

## DEPENDENCE ON TRADE

**Exports as a percentage of GDP (2012)**

- Over 50%
- 25 – 50%
- 10 – 25%
- 0 – 10%
- No data available

The character of world trade has changed a great deal in the last 60 years or so. While many developing countries still remain heavily dependent on exporting mineral ores, fossil fuels or farm products, such as coffee or cocoa, world trade is now dominated by manufactured goods. Since the 1980s, high-tech products, such as computer equipment, telecommunications gear and transistors, have become increasingly important.

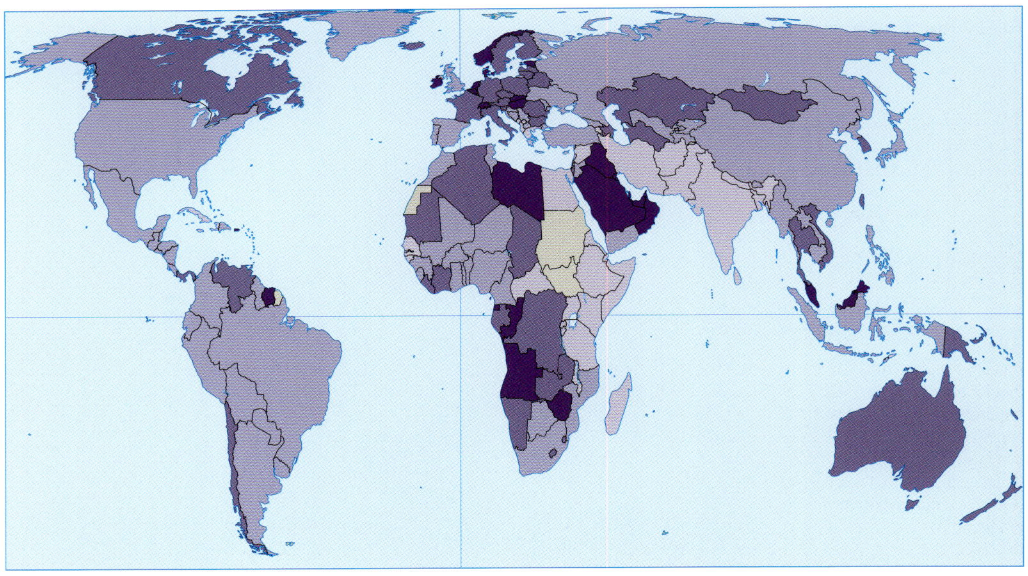

## TRADED PRODUCTS

**World merchandise exports by product, percentage of total value (2011)**

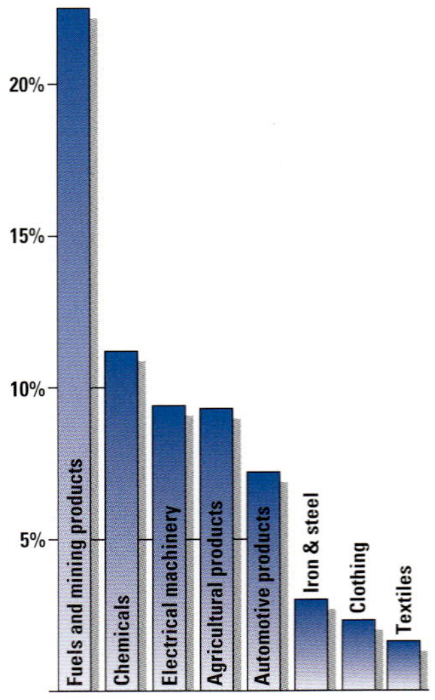
20%
15%
10%
5%
Fuels and mining products
Chemicals
Electrical machinery
Agricultural products
Automotive products
Iron & steel
Clothing
Textiles

## MAJOR EXPORTS

**Leading manufactured items and their exporters**

**Motor Vehicles**
World total (2012): US$ 4,068,895 million

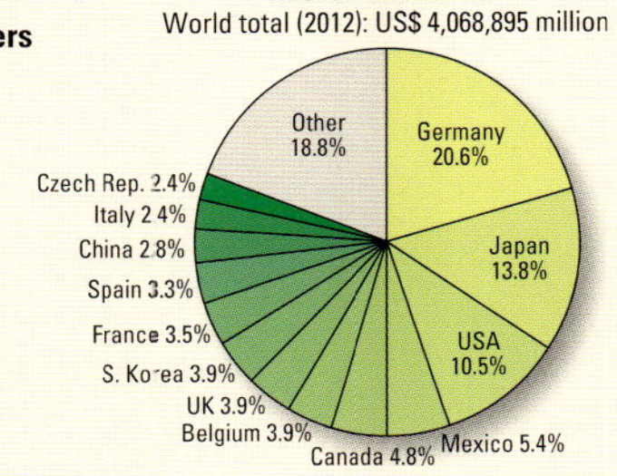
Germany 20.6%
Japan 13.8%
USA 10.5%
Mexico 5.4%
Canada 4.8%
Belgium 3.9%
UK 3.9%
S. Korea 3.9%
France 3.5%
Spain 3.3%
China 2.8%
Italy 2.4%
Czech Rep. 2.4%
Other 18.8%

**Telecommunications Gear**
World total (2012): US$ 2,140,743 million

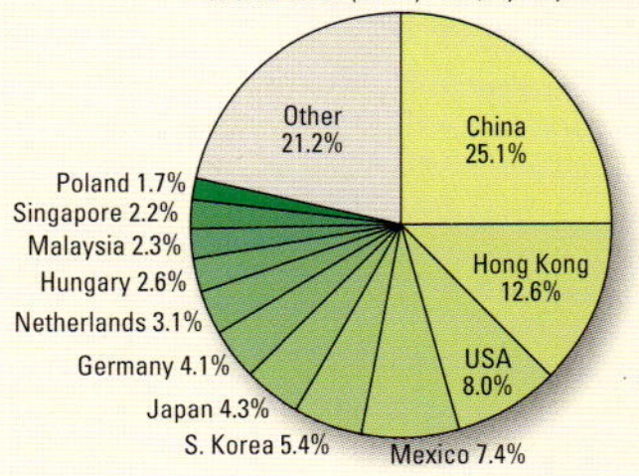
China 25.1%
Hong Kong 12.6%
USA 8.0%
Mexico 7.4%
S. Korea 5.4%
Japan 4.3%
Germany 4.1%
Netherlands 3.1%
Hungary 2.6%
Malaysia 2.3%
Singapore 2.2%
Poland 1.7%
Other 21.2%

**Petrol Products**
World total (2012): US$ 2,510,843 million

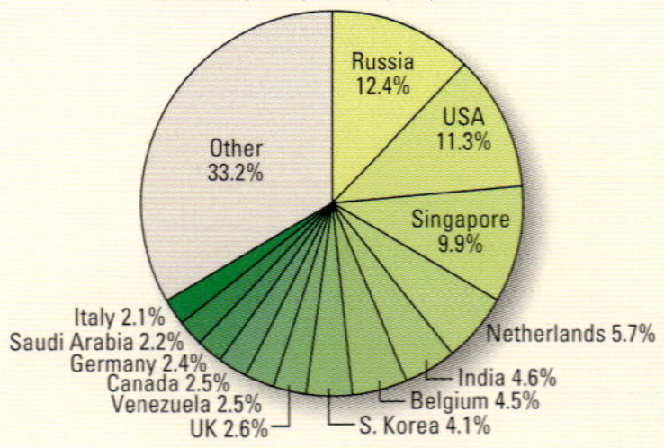
Russia 12.4%
USA 11.3%
Singapore 9.9%
Netherlands 5.7%
India 4.6%
Belgium 4.5%
S. Korea 4.1%
UK 2.6%
Venezuela 2.5%
Canada 2.5%
Germany 2.4%
Saudi Arabia 2.2%
Italy 2.1%
Other 33.2%

**Computers**
World total (2012): US$ 1,788,510 million

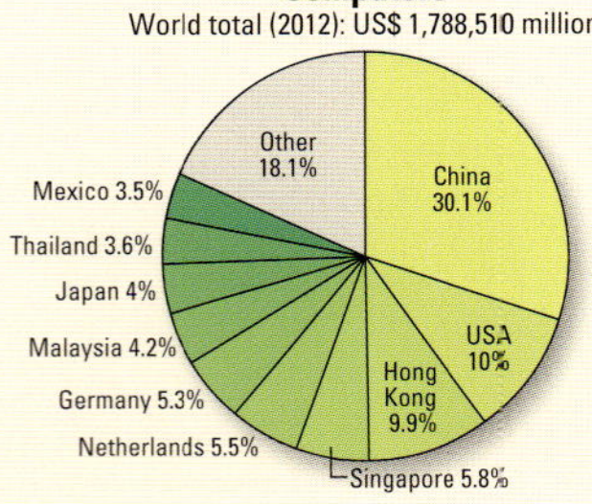
China 30.1%
USA 10%
Hong Kong 9.9%
Singapore 5.8%
Netherlands 5.5%
Germany 5.3%
Malaysia 4.2%
Japan 4%
Thailand 3.6%
Mexico 3.5%
Other 18.1%

**Electrical Components**
World total (2012): US$ 6,742,402 million

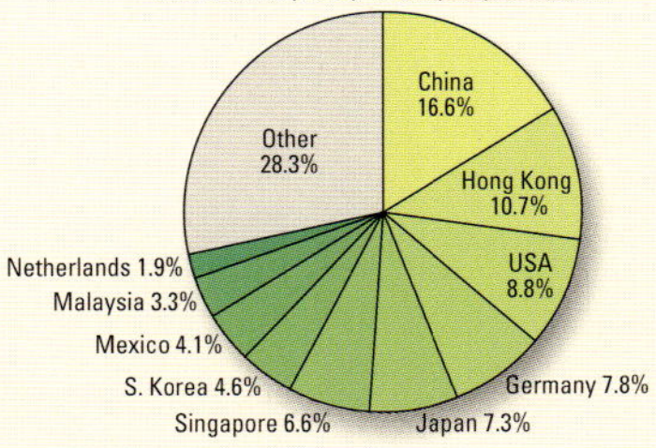
China 16.6%
Hong Kong 10.7%
USA 8.8%
Germany 7.8%
Japan 7.3%
Singapore 6.6%
S. Korea 4.6%
Mexico 4.1%
Malaysia 3.3%
Netherlands 1.9%
Other 28.3%

**Pharmaceuticals**
World total (2012): US$ 1,530,424 million

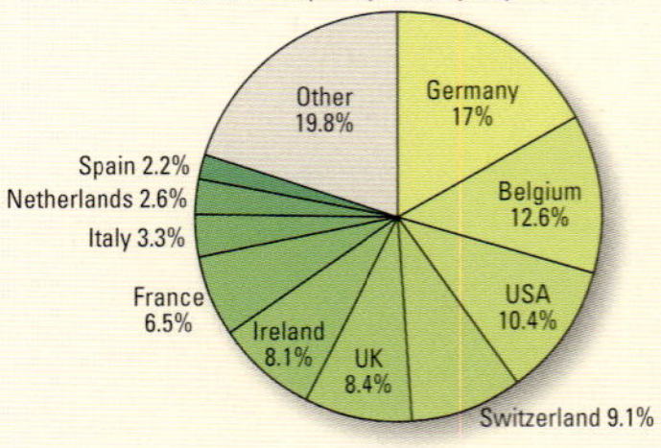
Germany 17%
Belgium 12.6%
USA 10.4%
Switzerland 9.1%
UK 8.4%
Ireland 8.1%
France 6.5%
Italy 3.3%
Netherlands 2.6%
Spain 2.2%
Other 19.8%

## GLOBALIZATION

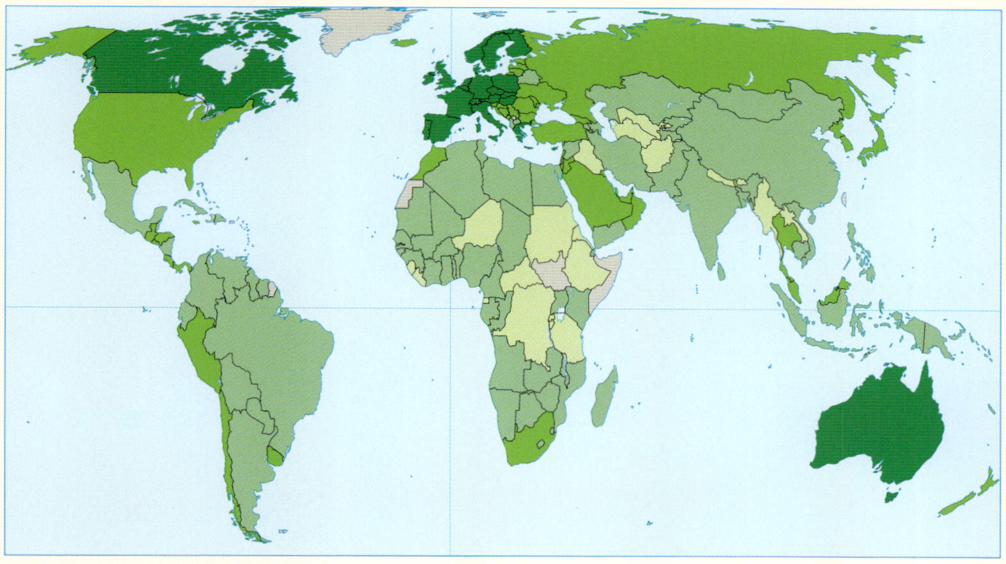

**GLOBALIZATION INDEX**

**KOF index of globalization (2009)**

- Over 80
- 60 – 80
- 40 – 60
- 20 – 40
- No data available

The KOF index of globalization is named after the Swiss Federal Institute of Technology in Zürich, Switzerland, which devised it. Countries are scored on each of the three criteria below:

• **economic globalization**, characterized as long-distance flows of goods, capital and services, as well as information and perceptions that accompany market exchanges (this accounts for 38% of the globalization index);

• **political globalization**, characterized by a diffusion of government policies (this accounts for 23% of the globalization index);

• **social globalization**, expressed as the spread of ideas, information, images and people (this accounts for the remaining 39% of the globalization index).

The higher values denote a greater level of globalization.

The concept of globalization developed in the 1960s after the Canadian academic Marshall McLuhan used the term 'global village' to describe the breakdown of spatial barriers around the world. He argued that the similarities between places were greater than the differences between them, and that much of the world had been caught up in the same economic and social processes. He suggested that economic activities operated at a global scale and that other scales were becoming less important.

Today, globalization is defined by the International Monetary Fund (IMF) as 'the growing interdependence of countries worldwide through the increasing volume and variety of cross-border transactions in goods and services and of international capital flows, and through the more rapid and widespread diffusion of technology'. Essentially, it means that all countries, with the possible exception of North Korea, are increasingly bound in a global network of migration, trade, products and services, investment, and the diffusion of ideas and culture.

Globalization has occurred as a result of many factors, such as:

- improvements in transport and ICT, leading to a 'shrinking' world;
- the desire to reach new markets;
- the attempt to tap cheap sources of labour;
- the expansion of economic activity to use resources from a wide range of locations;
- the rise of free-market economies and the spread of democratic governments;
- the role of trading blocs, free trade, and the impact of the World Trade Organization;
- the importance of multinational companies.

▲ A container ship being unloaded in the port of Melbourne, Australia. World trade depends on transport. Containerization, introduced in the 1950s, reduced the risk of damage to cargo and cut the time and cost of loading and unloading.

## TRADE IN PRIMARY EXPORTS

**Primary exports as a percentage of total export value**

- Over 75%
- 50 – 75%
- 20 – 50%
- Under 20%
- No data available

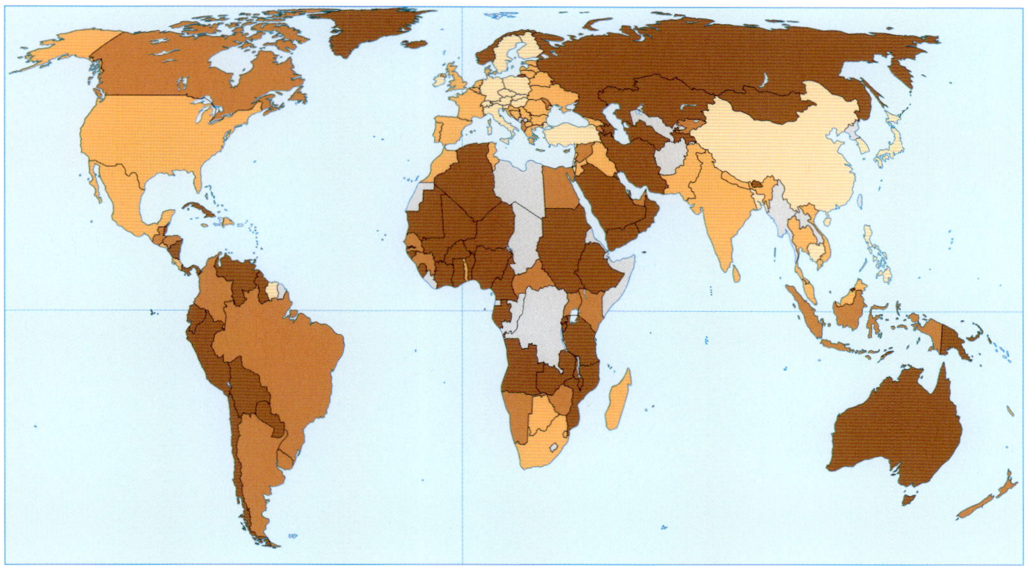

Primary exports are raw materials or partly processed products that form the basis for manufacturing. They are the necessary requirements of industries and include agricultural products, minerals, fuels and timber, as well as many semi-manufactured goods such as cotton, which has been spun but not woven, wood pulp, or flour. Many developed countries have few natural resources and rely on imports for the majority of their primary products. The countries of South-east Asia export hardwoods to the rest of the world, while many South American countries are heavily dependent on coffee exports.

## BALANCE OF TRADE

**Value of exports in proportion to the value of imports (2012)**

Exports exceed imports:
- More than 50%
- 25 – 50%
- 0 – 25%

Imports exceed exports:
- 0 – 25%
- 25 – 50%
- More than 50%

- No data available

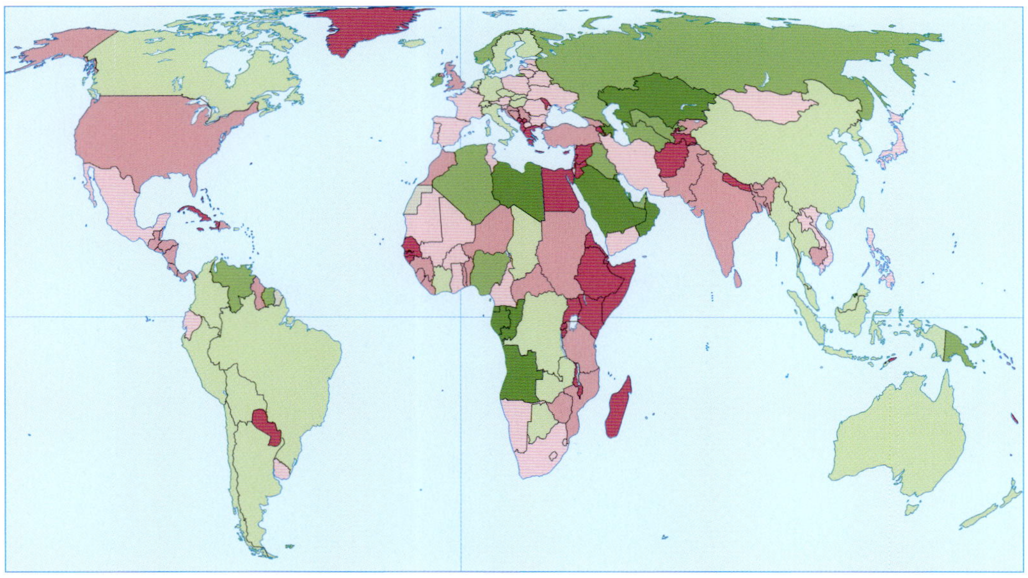

The total world trade balance should amount to zero, since exports must equal imports on a global scale. In practice, though, at least US $100 billion in exports go unrecorded, leaving the world with an apparent deficit and many countries in a better position than public accounting reveals. However, a favorable trade balance is not necessarily a sign of prosperity: many poorer countries must maintain a high surplus in order to service debts, and do so by restricting imports below the levels needed to sustain successful economies.

**For more information:**

82 Water distribution
91 Slum cities
Urban advantages
109 Distribution of spending

Until the late 1990s, when the full extent of the AIDS crisis emerged, average life expectancies at birth were rising almost everywhere. By 2010, they ranged from 80 years in high-income economies to 54 in sub-Saharan Africa. These figures represented an enormous advance on the situation in 1880, when citizens of Berlin had an estimated life expectancy of 30 years.

The ravages of AIDS have been greatest in southern Africa. One of the worst affected countries is Swaziland, where over 25% of the adult population were thought to be infected in 2009. Life expectancy fell from 61 years in 2000, to 32 years in 2009, but recovered to 50 years in 2013. In much of the world, average life expectancies are still increasing. The rises are attributed to improvements in agriculture and, hence, nutrition, as well as health education, improved sanitation and the quality of drinking water, together with advances in medicine.

Besides AIDS, the people of the developing world are subject to another affliction – malnutrition. The map below shows that in most of Africa, Asia, and Latin America, the average daily calorie supply per person is so low as to cause malnutrition. Malnutrition is a serious condition – among pregnant women it causes high rates of child mortality.

Deficiency diseases occur when people do not have a balanced diet. Protein deficiency causes stunting and kwashiorkor, which can be fatal, especially among young children, while vitamin deficiencies cause such illnesses as beri beri, pellagra, scurvy and rickets. Iron deficiency causes anemia, while a lack of iodine causes mental retardation.

Infectious diseases, in association with deficient diets, continue to affect people in developing countries. Around the turn of the century, a WHO report stated that infectious diseases cause over 16 million deaths a year. Most of the victims are young and otherwise fit people in developing countries. The major killers are AIDS, cholera, dysentery, malaria, measles, pneumonia, respiratory infections, tuberculosis and typhoid.

Infectious diseases are much less important as causes of death in developed countries, where cancer and circulatory diseases, such as atherosclerosis and hypertension, which cause strokes and heart attacks, are the most common causes of fatality. Because these diseases tend to kill older people, they are relatively less important in the developing countries where people have shorter lifespans.

Harmful habits are also generally practiced more by the rich than the poor. For example, smoking is an important cause of death in developed countries, while poor diet and high alcohol consumption can badly affect health.

▲ Almost 20% of the world's population does not have access to safe water (the diagram at the bottom left-hand corner of page 105 shows how this breaks down by region). This places a huge strain on the millions of mainly women and children who have to walk, collect, and carry drinkable water in order to survive. UNICEF is dedicated to help improve this situation and to react swiftly in the case of emergencies such as civil war, as with the case of this man in Liberia.

## MILLENNIUM DEVELOPMENT GOALS

The eight Millennium Development Goals (MDGs) were formulated by the United Nations in 2000. The target date to achieve the MDGs is 2015. Many of the Goals have a direct link to health. For example, MDG 1, *'Eradicate extreme poverty and hunger'*, has as its aim to reduce by 50% the proportion of people suffering from hunger. MDG 4, *'Reduce child mortality'*, aims to reduce by two-thirds the under-five mortality rate, and to provide universal child immunization against measles. The fifth MDG, *'Improve maternal health'*, has a target to reduce the maternal mortality ratio by 75%, while MDG 6, *'Combat HIV/AIDS, malaria, and other diseases'*, is attempting to halt and begin to reverse the spread of HIV/AIDS, malaria and tuberculosis. Others are more indirect: MDG 7, *'Ensure environmental sustainability'*, aims to halve the proportion without improved drinking water in urban and rural areas, and to halve the proportion without sanitation in urban and rural areas.

Progress towards the goals has been somewhat uneven, but there have been some successes. According to the UN, in north-east Brazil, stunting, an indicator of child malnutrition, decreased from 22.2% to 5.9% between 1996 and 2007, while in Ghana, between 1991 and 2004, the number of people who suffered from undernourishment fell by 34%, to 9% of the population. Rwanda is very likely to meet – and possibly even surpass – the MDG targets for child and maternal mortality by 2015, in part thanks to the government's successful health insurance programme. The under-five child mortality rate has fallen by 40% or more since 1990 in Ethiopia, Malawi, Mozambique and Niger. New HIV infections and AIDS-related deaths have declined significantly in sub-Saharan Africa, thanks to education programmes, prevention policies and the wider availability of anti-retroviral medicines. South Africa successfully achieved the MDG target of halving the proportion of people lacking access to safe water, as lack of access to improved drinking water was reduced from 19% in 1990 to 7% in 2006.

## MATERNAL MORTALITY RATE

**The number of mothers who died during pregnancy or childbirth per 100,000 live births (2010)**

| Countries with highest maternal mortality rate | | Countries with lowest maternal mortality rate | |
|---|---|---|---|
| Chad | 1,100 | Estonia | 2 |
| Somalia | 1,000 | Singapore | 3 |
| Sierra Leone | 890 | Greece | 3 |
| Central African Republic | 890 | Italy | 4 |
| Burundi | 800 | Austria | 4 |
| Guinea-Bissau | 790 | Sweden | 4 |
| Liberia | 770 | Finland | 5 |
| Sudan | 730 | Iceland | 5 |
| Cameroon | 690 | Poland | 5 |
| Nigeria | 630 | Czech Republic | 5 |

The maternal mortality rate is the annual number of female deaths per 100,000 live births from any cause related to or aggravated by pregnancy or its management (excluding accidental or incidental causes). It includes deaths during pregnancy, childbirth, or within 42 days of termination of pregnancy, irrespective of the duration and site of the pregnancy, for a specified year.

## FOOD CONSUMPTION

**Average daily food intake in calories per person (2009)**

Over 3,500 calories
3,000 – 3,500 calories
2,500 – 3,000 calories
2,000 – 2,500 calories
Under 2,000 calories
No data available

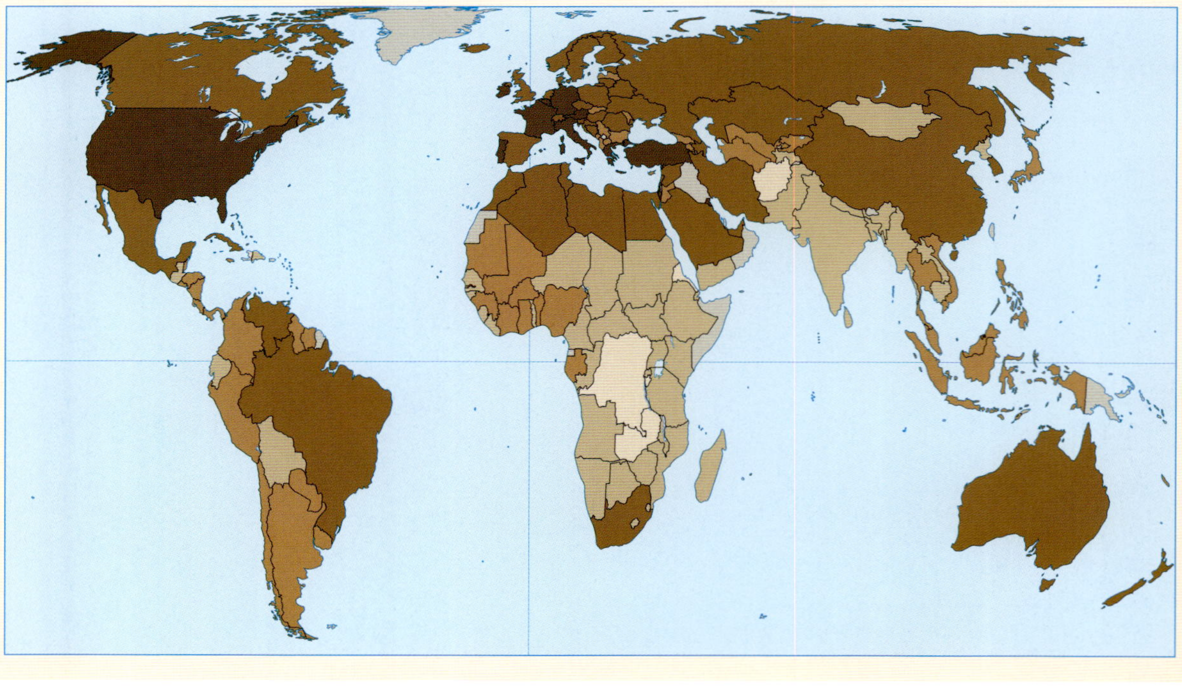

The daily food intake rated adequate by the World Health Organization is between 2,300 and 2,500 calories per day. Approximately 6 million children under the age of 5 years die of starvation each year, the vast majority in Africa. In 2012, the FAO estimated that 870 million people were undernourished, contrasting sharply with the overconsumption of food in some Western cultures.

## INFANT MORTALITY

**Number of babies who died under the age of one, per 1,000 live births (2012)**

- Over 100 deaths
- 50 – 100 deaths
- 20 – 50 deaths
- 10 – 20 deaths
- Under 10 deaths
- No data available

**Highest infant mortality**

| | |
|---|---|
| Afghanistan | 122 deaths |
| Niger | 110 deaths |
| Mali | 109 deaths |

**Lowest infant mortality**

| | |
|---|---|
| Japan | 2 deaths |
| Singapore | 3 deaths |
| Sweden | 3 deaths |

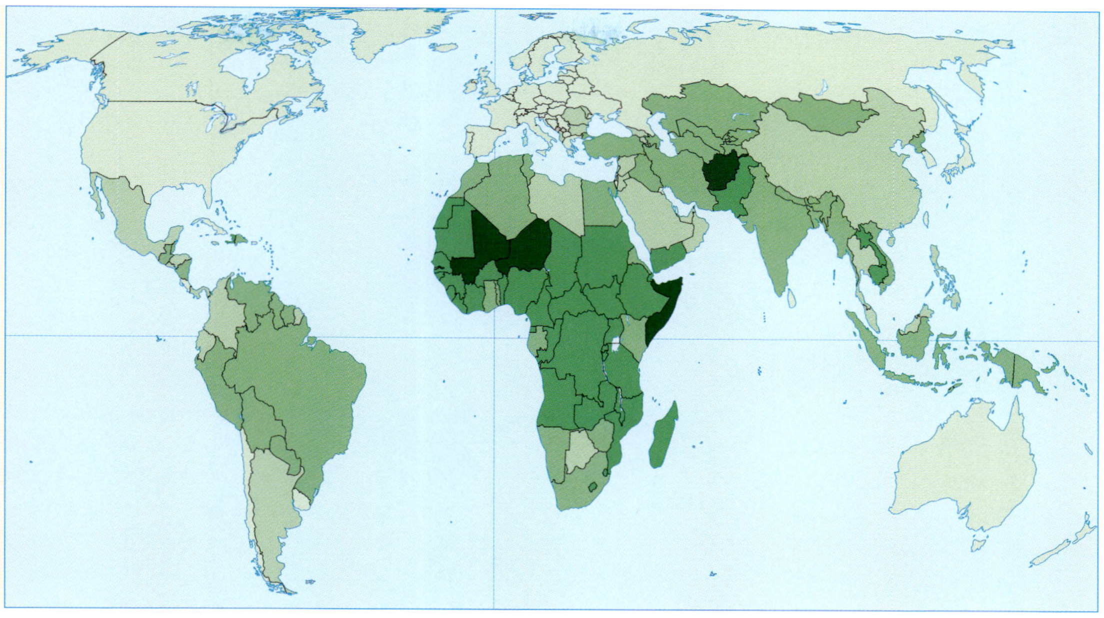

## THE AIDS CRISIS

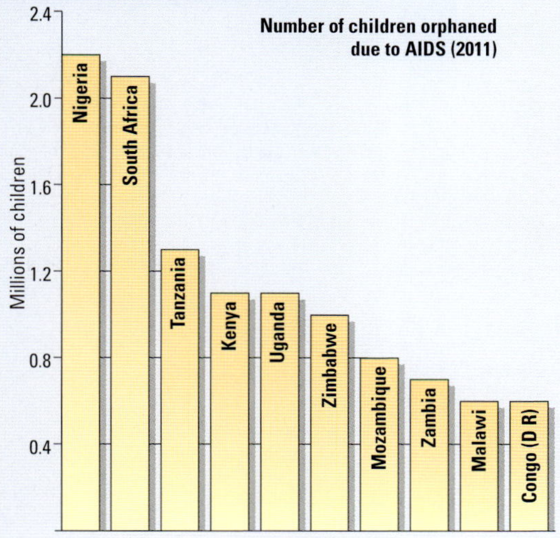
Number of children orphaned due to AIDS (2011)
Millions of children
2.4
2.0
1.6
1.2
0.8
0.4
Nigeria
South Africa
Tanzania
Kenya
Uganda
Zimbabwe
Mozambique
Zambia
Malawi
Congo (D R)

**Percentage of adults living with HIV/AIDS (2011)**

- Over 10 %
- 1 – 10 %
- 0.5 – 1 %
- 0.2 – 0.5 %
- Under 0.2 %
- No data available

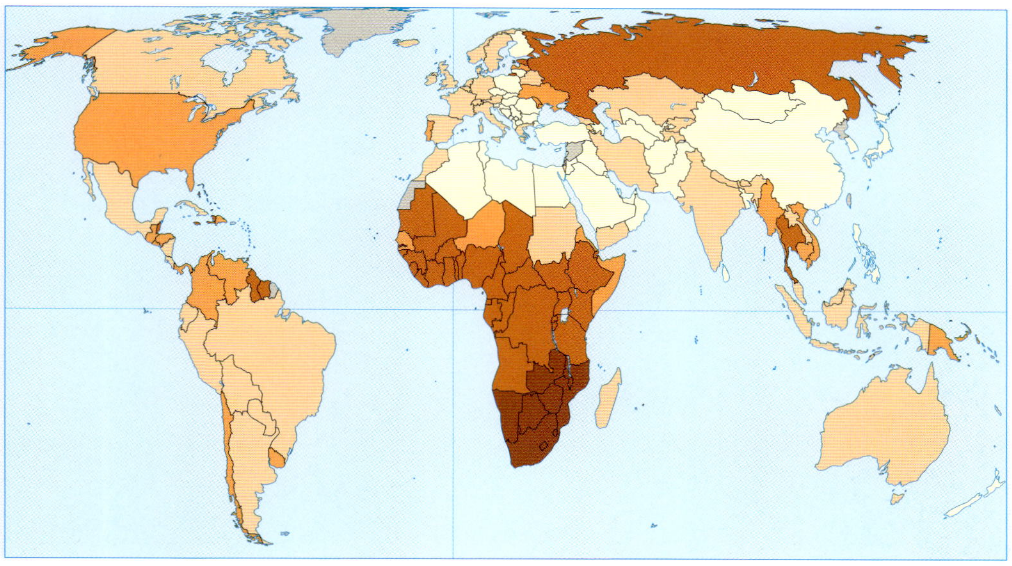

## EXPENDITURE ON HEALTH

**Public health expenditure per capita, in US $ (2010)**

| Countries with the highest spending | | Countries with the lowest spending | |
|---|---|---|---|
| USA | $8,361 | Eritrea | $12 |
| Luxembourg | $8,181 | Ethiopia | $16 |
| Norway | $8,091 | Congo (Democratic Republic) | $16 |
| Switzerland | $7,812 | Madagascar | $16 |
| Denmark | $6,421 | Burma (Myanmar) | $17 |
| Monaco | $6,325 | Central African Republic | $18 |
| Netherlands | $5,593 | Niger | $18 |
| Canada | $5,222 | Burundi | $21 |
| Austria | $4,958 | Mozambique | $21 |
| Australia | $4,774 | Pakistan | $22 |

The allocation of limited funds for health care in developing countries is rarely evenly spread – for example, the quality of treatment can vary enormously from place to place within the same country. Urban dwellers tend to have much better access to health provisions than those living in rural areas.

## CAUSES OF DEATH

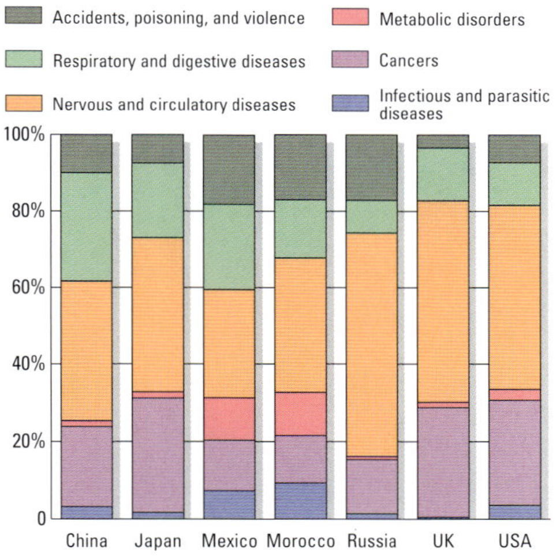
Accidents, poisoning, and violence
Metabolic disorders
Respiratory and digestive diseases
Cancers
Nervous and circulatory diseases
Infectious and parasitic diseases
100%
80%
60%
40%
20%
0
China
Japan
Mexico
Morocco
Russia
UK
USA

## MEDICAL PROVISION

**Doctors per 100,000 population, selected countries (2010)**

Although the ratio of people to doctors gives a good approximation of a country's health provision, it is not an absolute indicator. Raw numbers may mask inefficiency and other weaknesses. The definition of a doctor also varies from nation to nation.

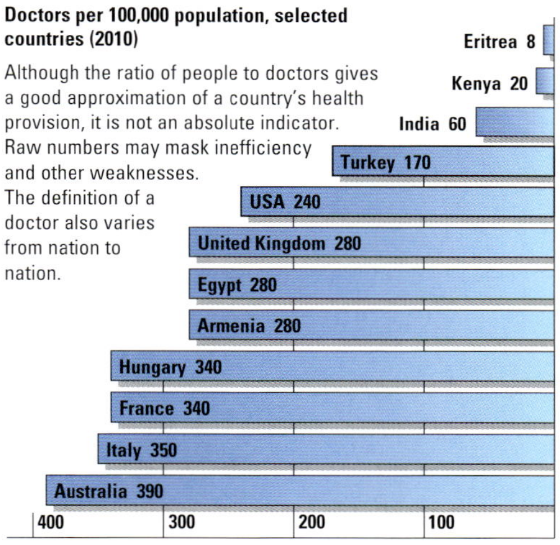
Eritrea 8
Kenya 20
India 60
Turkey 170
USA 240
United Kingdom 280
Egypt 280
Armenia 280
Hungary 340
France 340
Italy 350
Australia 390
400
300
200
100

## ACCESS TO SAFE WATER

Percentage of urban and rural population with access to safe water, by region (2010)

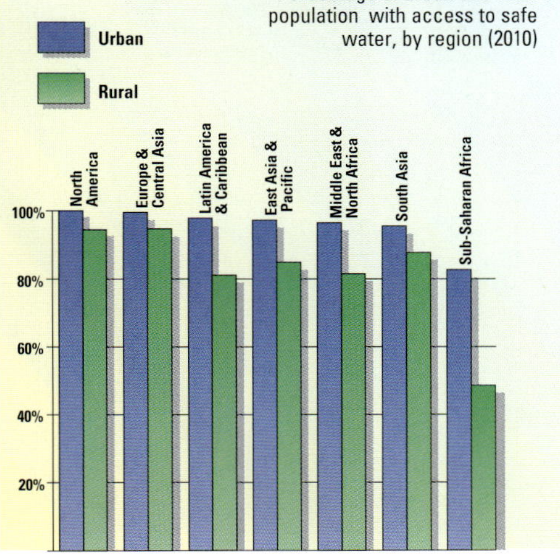
Urban
Rural
100%
80%
60%
40%
20%
North America
Europe & Central Asia
Latin America & Caribbean
East Asia & Pacific
Middle East & North Africa
South Asia
Sub-Saharan Africa

## SANITATION

Percentage of population with access to sanitation services, selected countries (2010)

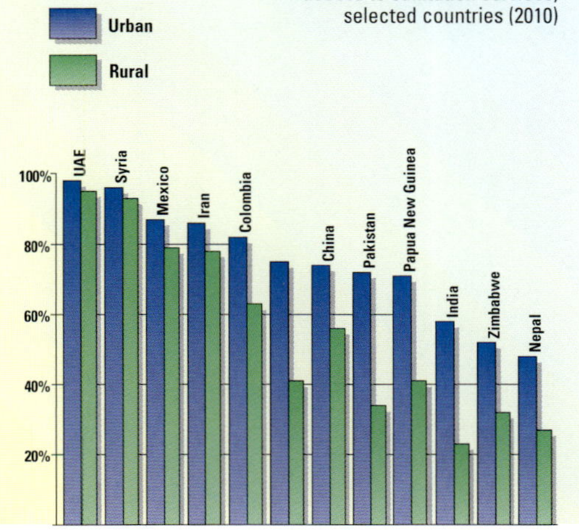
Urban
Rural
100%
80%
60%
40%
20%
UAE
Syria
Mexico
Iran
Colombia
China
Pakistan
Papua New Guinea
India
Zimbabwe
Nepal

## MALARIA

Cases of malaria per 100,000 people exposed to malaria-infected environments (2009)

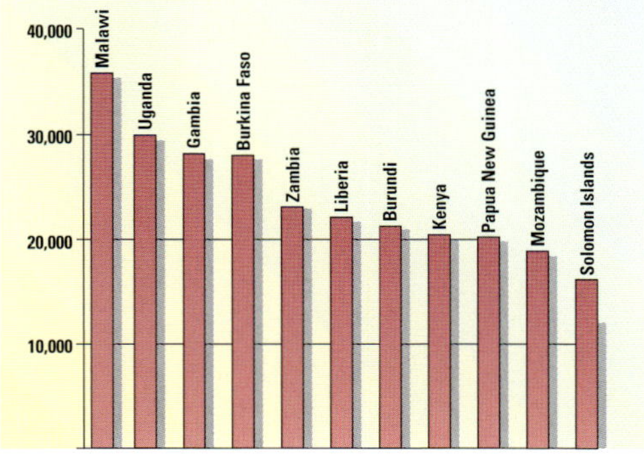
40,000
30,000
20,000
10,000
Malawi
Uganda
Gambia
Burkina Faso
Zambia
Liberia
Burundi
Kenya
Papua New Guinea
Mozambique
Solomon Islands

**For more information:**
100 Industrial output
102 World trade
Major exports
103 Balance of trade
104 Millennium Development Goals
109 Distribution of spending

Perhaps the most glaring differences in the world today are those between the rich and the poor. The World Bank divides countries into three main groups based on average economic production expressed in terms of per capita GNI (Gross National Income). They are the low-income economies (most African countries and much of Asia), the middle-income economies (most of Latin America and most of the former USSR), and the high-income economies of Canada, the United States, Western Europe, Japan and Australia.

Per capita GNIs are a measure of the total goods and services produced by a country divided by the population, and then converted into US dollars at official exchange rates. They are useful indicators of a country's prosperity, though, like all statistics, they must be treated with care. For example, the prices for goods and services in China are far cheaper than they are in the United States. China's per capita GNI in 2011 was $4,940 (as compared with $48,450 in the US), but the PPP (Purchasing Power Parity, which adjusts the figure for cost-of-living differences) estimate of China's per capita GNI was considerably higher at $8,450. Another problem with per capita GNIs is that they are averages, which often conceal wide internal variations.

The pattern of poverty varies from region to region. In Latin America, much progress has been made through industrialization, though startling inequalities still exist between rich and poor. China and other countries in eastern Asia, including South Korea and Taiwan, have followed Japan's example in pursuing export-led industrial policies. The success of China's Special Economic Zones, where foreign investment is encouraged, has led to a huge rise in China's per capita GNI.

In contrast to the dynamism of Asia, Africa lags behind as an impoverished continent. Corrupt governments, wasteful expenditures, civil wars, natural disasters, faulty national and international policy environments, high population growth, and the failure to break away from the neo-colonial trading patterns – all these contribute to keeping the majority of Africans impoverished. An initiative in some African countries has been to improve the infrastructure and develop tourism, creating employment and providing much-needed foreign currency. But the social and environmental cost of mass tourism needs to be taken seriously too.

The International Monetary Fund and the World Bank argue that real economic progress in Africa will be achieved only when African countries create market-friendly economies that encourage trade through export-led manufacturing, while at the same time strictly controlling public spending.

## CONTINENTAL SHARES

**Shares of population and of wealth (GNI) by continent (2011)**

These generalized continental figures show the startling difference between rich and poor, but mask the successes or failures of individual countries. Japan, for example, with less than 4% of Asia's population, produces almost 19% of the continent's output. Within countries, the difference between rich and poor can also be startling. In Brazil, for example, the richest 20% of the population own 60% of the wealth.

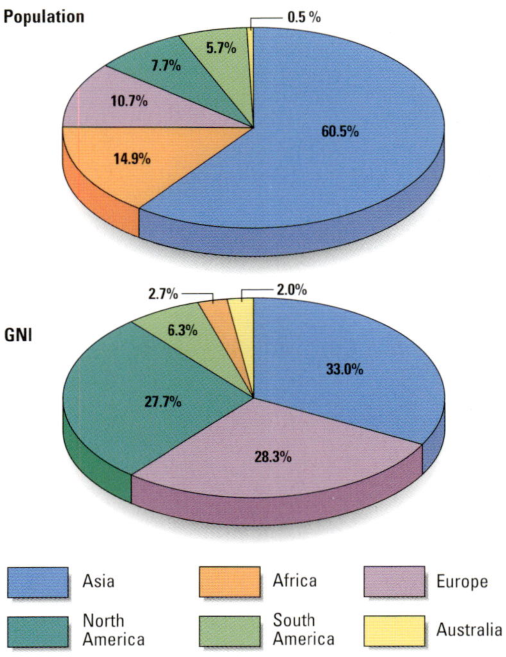
Population
0.5 %
5.7%
7.7%
10.7%
14.9%
60.5%
GNI
2.7%
2.0%
6.3%
33.0%
27.7%
28.3%
Asia
Africa
Europe
North America
South America
Australia

## LEVELS OF INCOME

**Gross National Income per capita: the value of total production divided by the population (2011)**

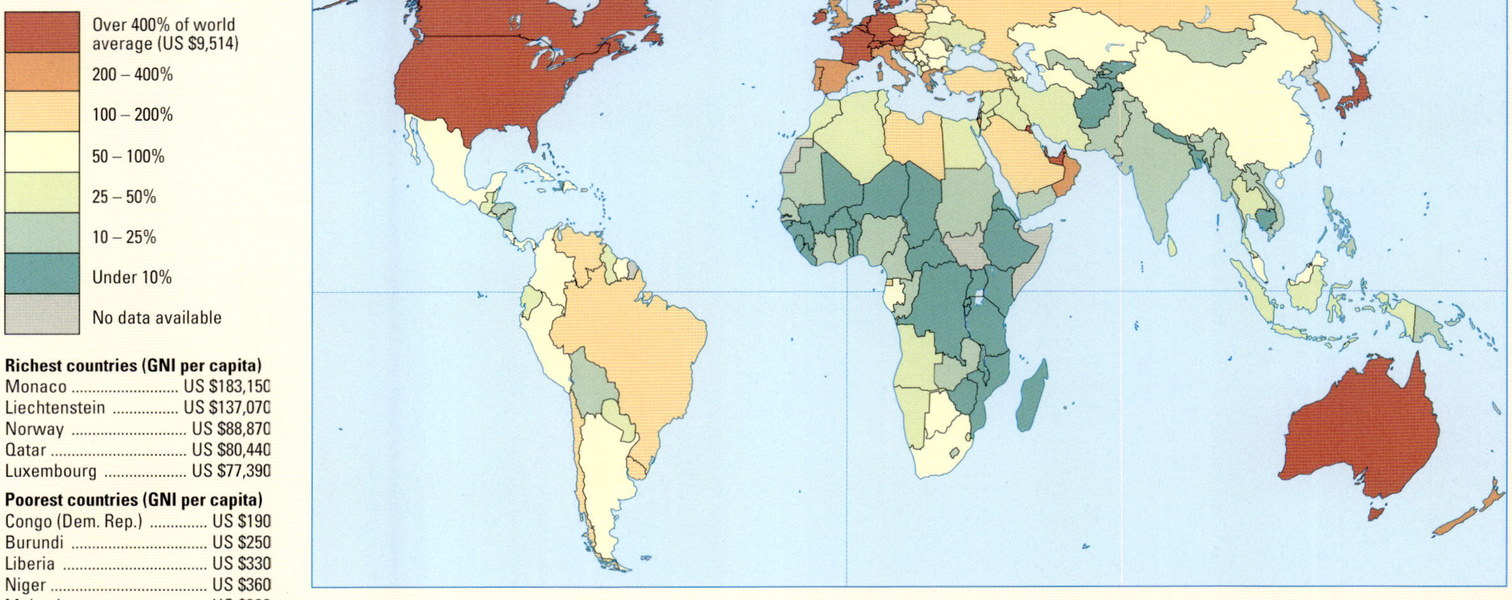
Over 400% of world average (US $9,514)
200 – 400%
100 – 200%
50 – 100%
25 – 50%
10 – 25%
Under 10%
No data available

**Richest countries (GNI per capita)**

| | |
|---|---|
| Monaco | US $183,150 |
| Liechtenstein | US $137,070 |
| Norway | US $88,870 |
| Qatar | US $80,440 |
| Luxembourg | US $77,390 |

**Poorest countries (GNI per capita)**

| | |
|---|---|
| Congo (Dem. Rep.) | US $190 |
| Burundi | US $250 |
| Liberia | US $330 |
| Niger | US $360 |
| Malawi | US $360 |

## INDICATORS

The gap between the world's rich and poor is now so great that it is difficult to illustrate on a single graph. Within each income group (as defined by the World Bank), however, comparisons have some meaning. The wealth gap in many developing countries, though, is wide, with a small, rich class and a large, impoverished majority, while many high-income countries contain an underclass of unemployed and homeless people.

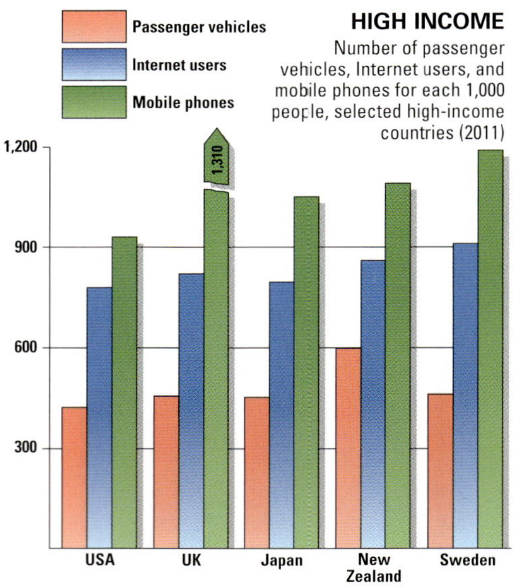
Passenger vehicles
Internet users
Mobile phones
HIGH INCOME
Number of passenger vehicles, Internet users, and mobile phones for each 1,000 people, selected high-income countries (2011)
1,200
900
600
300
1,310
USA
UK
Japan
New Zealand
Sweden

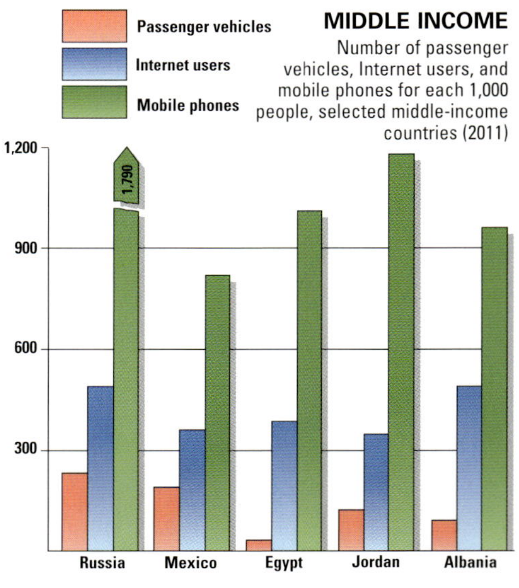
Passenger vehicles
Internet users
Mobile phones
MIDDLE INCOME
Number of passenger vehicles, Internet users, and mobile phones for each 1,000 people, selected middle-income countries (2011)
1,200
900
600
300
1,790
Russia
Mexico
Egypt
Jordan
Albania

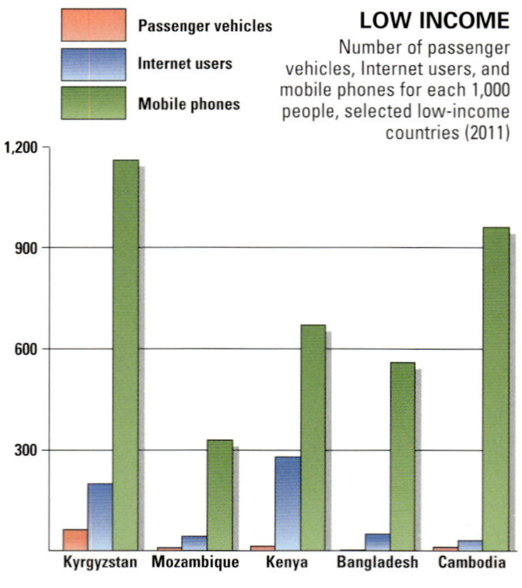
Passenger vehicles
Internet users
Mobile phones
LOW INCOME
Number of passenger vehicles, Internet users, and mobile phones for each 1,000 people, selected low-income countries (2011)
1,200
900
600
300
Kyrgyzstan
Mozambique
Kenya
Bangladesh
Cambodia

## STATE FINANCE

Inflation rates (*shown on the map, right*) are an indication of a country's financial stability and, usually, of its prosperity. Annual inflation rates above 20% are usually marked by slow or even negative growth of the GNI. Above 50%, it becomes hyperinflation and an economy is left reeling.

In the late 1980s and early 1990s, many high-income countries had to contend with annual inflation rates of 10% or more, while Japan, the growth leader, had an average inflation rate of just 1.3% between 1985 and 1994.

Market-friendly policies, including low taxes and state spending, liberal trade policies, and a warm welcome for foreign investors, are major factors in countries that have enjoyed rapid economic growth in the decades since 1980. For example, the setting-up of Special Economic Zones in eastern China has led to a spectacular rise in that country's per capita GNI. However, an effective government remains a crucial factor in economic growth in most countries.

Other successful countries include South Korea and Singapore, although an Asian market crash in 1997 temporarily halted the dramatic economic expansion of these countries.

## INFLATION

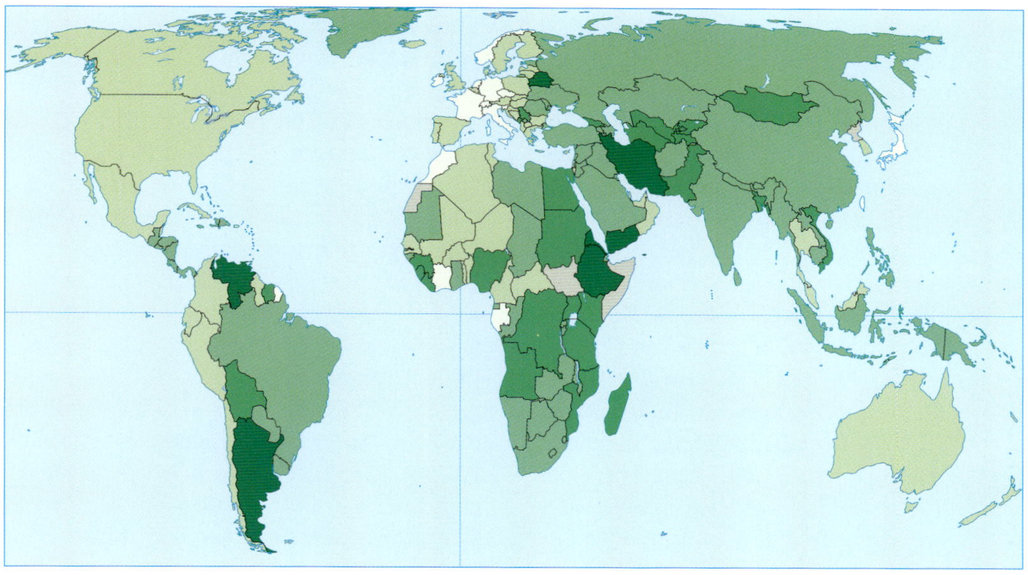

**Average annual rate of inflation (2011)**

- Over 20%
- 10 – 20%
- 5 – 10%
- 2.5 – 5%
- Under 2.5%
- No data available

**Highest average inflation**

| | |
|---|---|
| Belarus | 41% |
| Venezuela | 29% |
| Ethiopia | 29% |

**Lowest average inflation**

| | |
|---|---|
| Bahrain | 0.3% |
| Switzerland | 0.4% |
| Japan | 0.4% |

## GROWTH IN GNI

**GNI average annual change (1999–2011)**

- Over 50%
- 25 – 50%
- 10 – 25%
- 5 – 10%
- Under 5%
- No data available

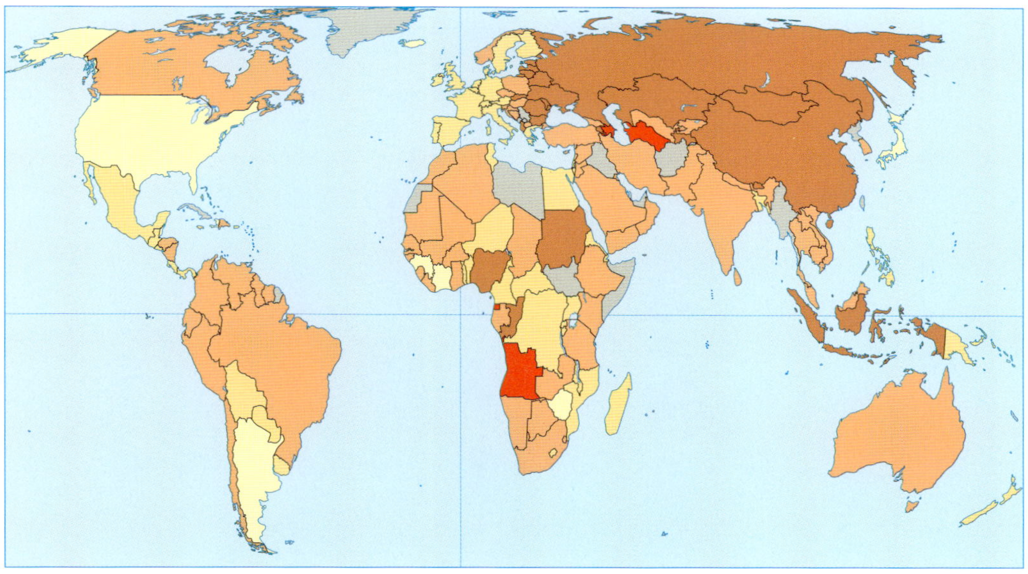

**Countries with the highest rate of change**

| | |
|---|---|
| Equatorial Guinea | 151% |
| Azerbaijan | 69% |
| Angola | 66% |
| Turkmenistan | 57% |
| Kazakhstan | 45% |

## TACKLING POVERTY – MILLENNIUM DEVELOPMENT GOAL 1

Formulated by the United Nations in 2000, Millennium Development Goal 1 is to *'Eradicate extreme poverty and hunger'*. The target for 2015 is to reduce the proportion of people living on less than $1.25 a day by 50%.

However, the world has made unprecedented progress against poverty and, as a result mainly of economic growth in China and India, the first MDG target has been met.

According to the 2012 Millennium Development Goals Report, the poverty rates and the number of people living in extreme poverty fell in every developing region – including in sub-Saharan Africa, where rates are highest. In the developing regions, the proportion of people living on less than $1.25 a day fell from 47% in 1990 to 24% in 2008. In 2008, about 110 million fewer people than in 2005 lived in conditions of extreme poverty. The number of extreme poor in the developing regions fell from over 2 billion in 1990 to less than 1.4 billion in 2008.

Thus, the MDG target for poverty reduction has been met. Estimates suggest that the global poverty rate at $1.25 a day fell in 2010 to less than half the 1990 rate.

While high food and fuel prices, and deep economic recession since 2008, have hurt vulnerable populations and slowed the rate of poverty reduction in some countries, global poverty rates have continued to fall.

But even at the current rate of progress, estimates indicate that about 1 billion people will still be living on less than $1.25 a day in 2015, corresponding to a global extreme poverty rate of just below 16%. Four out of every five people living in extreme poverty will live in sub-Saharan Africa and Southern Asia.

Some regions have seen greater progress than others. A remarkable rate of progress was sustained in China: after the extreme poverty rate had dropped from 60% in 1990 to 16% in 2005, the incidence fell further by 2008 to 13%. In India and in the Southern Asian region excluding India, poverty rates fell from 51% to 37% and from 52% to 26%, respectively, between 1990 and 2008.

On the other hand, poverty remains widespread in sub-Saharan Africa and in Southern Asia, despite significant progress. The sub-Saharan African poverty fell by almost 5%, to less than 48%, between 2005 and 2008. For the first time, the absolute number of people living in extreme poverty also fell in the region, from 395 million in 2005 to 386 million in 2008. This drop reversed the long-term trend of increase since 1981.

### EXTREME POVERTY

The percentage of people living on less than $1.25 a day, for selected regions, for 1990, 2005 and 2008.

One of the Millennium Development Goals (MDG) is to halve, between 1990 and 2015, the percentage of people whose income is less than $1.25 per day.

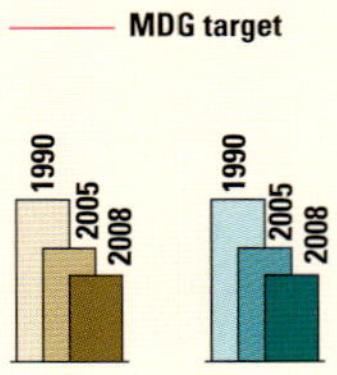
MDG target
1990
2005
2008
1990
2005
2008

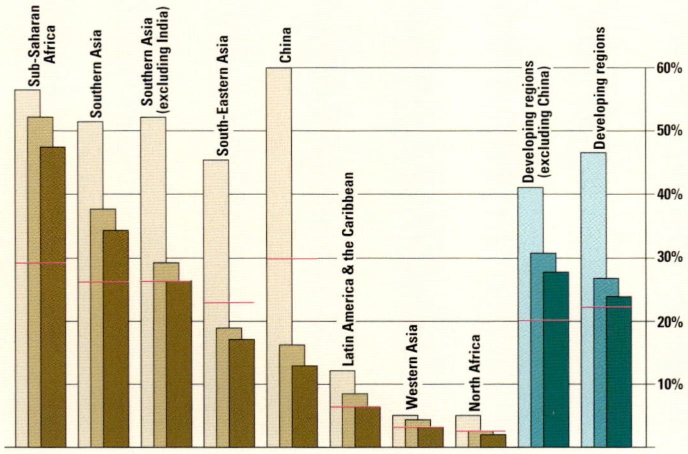
Sub-Saharan Africa
Southern Asia
Southern Asia (excluding India)
South-Eastern Asia
China
Latin America & the Caribbean
Western Asia
North Africa
Developing regions (excluding China)
Developing regions
60%
50%
40%
30%
20%
10%

**For more information:**
82 Water supply
86 Population density
90 Urban population
91 Urban advantages
92 World's refugees
100 Employment
The workforce
105 Infant mortality
106 Wealth

Wealth is a basic factor in determining standards of living. Everywhere, the rich have more of everything, including higher average life expectancies, while the poor have to spend most of their income on basic human needs, such as food and clothing. Yet poverty and wealth are relative terms: slum dwellers living on social security in an industrial society feel their poverty acutely, but have far more resources than an average African living in a rural area.

In 1990 the United Nations Development Programme published its first Human Development Index (HDI), an attempt to construct a comparative scale by which a simplified form of well-being might be measured. The HDI, expressed as a value between 0 and 0.999, combines figures for life expectancy and literacy with a wealth scale, based on Purchasing Power Parity.

The world's countries are divided into three groups: those with a high HDI (0.8 and above); those with a medium HDI (0.5 to 0.799); and those with a low HDI (below 0.5). In 2011, Norway and Australia were top in the world rankings and Congo DR was bottom. In fact, 29 of the 32 countries with a low HDI were from Africa. Besides having low per capita GNIs, the average life expectancy in these countries was 58 years, while the adult literacy rate was 36%. By comparison, the average life expectancy at birth in countries in the high HDI group was 72 years, while the literacy rate was 94%.

Comparisons between countries with similar per capita GNIs reveal the effects of government actions. For example, the World Bank classifies both India and China as low-income economies, but India's HDI at 0.547 is much lower than that of China, at 0.687. This reflects not only China's economic progress in the 1980s and 1990s, but also differences in average life expectancies (67 years in India and 75 years in China) and adult literacy rates (66% in India and 93% in China).

Disparities in standards of living exist not only between countries but also between individuals, groups and regions within countries. For example, income distribution figures show that, in the United States, the poorest 10% of households receive less than 2% of the income.

Other contrasts exist in developing countries between rural communities, where incomes are low and basic services are often in short supply, and urban areas, where even those living in slums are generally better off than their rural neighbours. Other striking differences exist between men and women. For example, while adult literacy rates for men and women living in developed countries are more or less the same, large differences exist in many developing countries. In countries in the lowest HDI category, only 36% of women were literate, as compared with 58% of men.

Female education is a factor in population control, especially as women's fertility rates appear to fall in direct proportion to the amount of secondary education they receive. This point was acknowledged in 2004 by the UN Population Fund, which defined four main objectives relating to women and population control: the reduction of maternal, infant and child mortality; better education, especially for girls; universal access to reproductive health services; and gender equality.

Statistical analysis presents many problems of interpretation, especially when trying to define such intangible factors as a sense of well-being. For example, education helps create wealth; but are rich countries wealthy because their people are well educated, or are they well educated because they are rich?

## HUMAN DEVELOPMENT INDEX

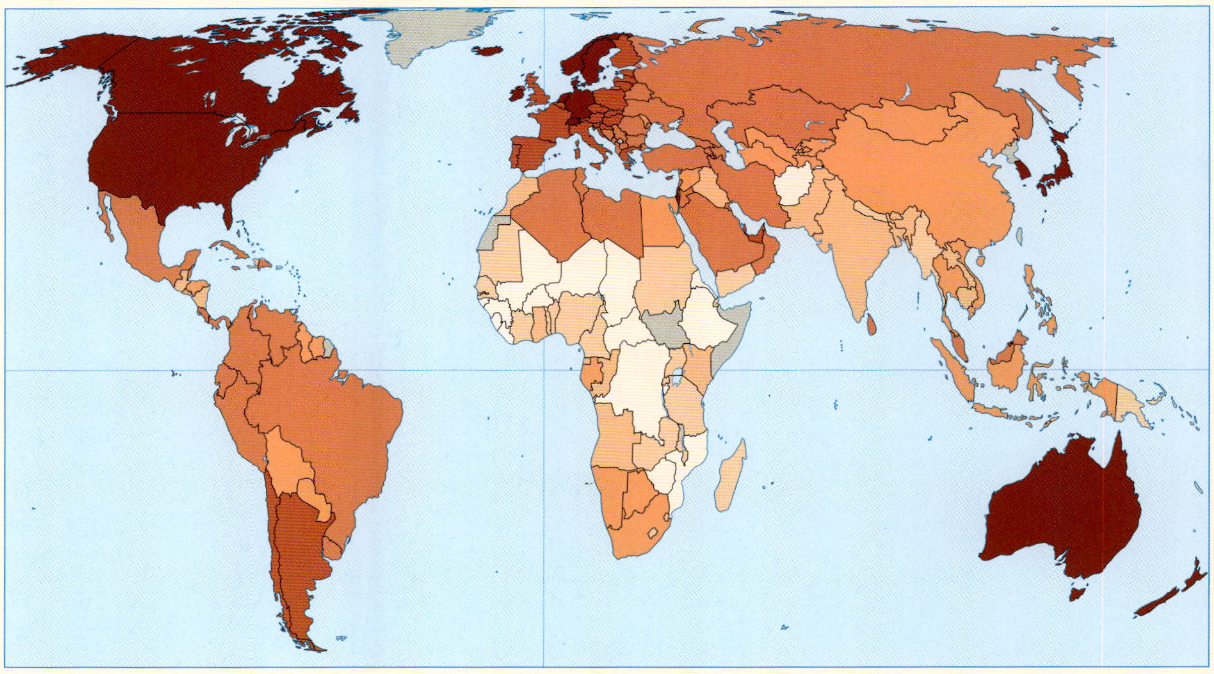

**The Human Development Index (HDI), calculated by the UN Development Programme (UNDP), gives a value to countries using indicators of life expectancy, education and standards of living (2012).**

Over 0.9
0.8 – 0.9
0.7 – 0.8
0.6 – 0.7
0.5 – 0.6
0.4 – 0.5
Under 0.4
No data available

**Highest values**

| | |
|---|---|
| Norway | 0.955 |
| Australia | 0.938 |
| USA | 0.937 |
| Netherlands | 0.921 |
| Germany | 0.919 |

**Lowest values**

| | |
|---|---|
| Congo (Dem. Rep) | 0.304 |
| Niger | 0.304 |
| Mozambique | 0.327 |
| Chad | 0.340 |
| Burkina Faso | 0.343 |

## EDUCATION

The developing countries made great efforts in the 1970s and 1980s to bring at least a basic education to their people. In all but the poorest nations, primary school enrolments rose above 60%. However, figures often include teenagers or young adults, and there are still 300 million children worldwide who receive no schooling at all. A lack of resources has restricted the development of secondary and higher education. Most primary school education is free in the poorer countries, but fees are often paid for secondary and higher education, thus heightening the differences between rich and poor.

**PRIMARY**
Percentage of age group in primary school, selected countries (2011)

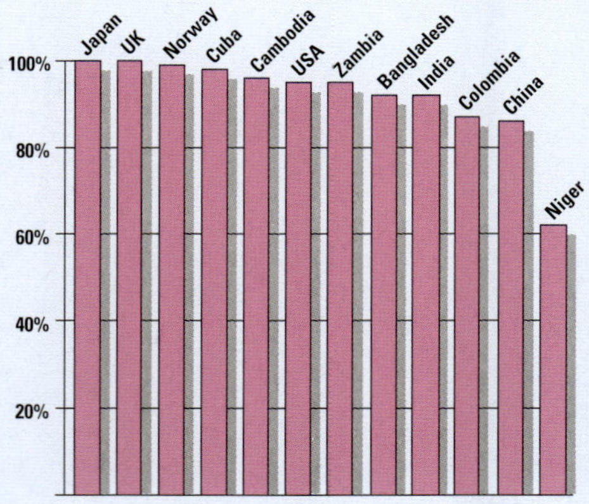
100%
80%
60%
40%
20%
Japan
UK
Norway
Cuba
Cambodia
USA
Zambia
Bangladesh
India
Colombia
China
Niger

**SECONDARY**
Percentage of age group in secondary school, selected countries (2011)

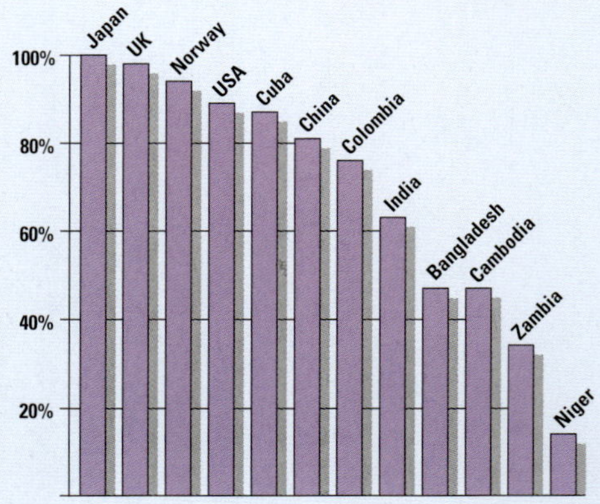
100%
80%
60%
40%
20%
Japan
UK
Norway
USA
Cuba
China
Colombia
India
Bangladesh
Cambodia
Zambia
Niger

**HIGHER**
Percentage of age group in higher education, selected countries (2011)

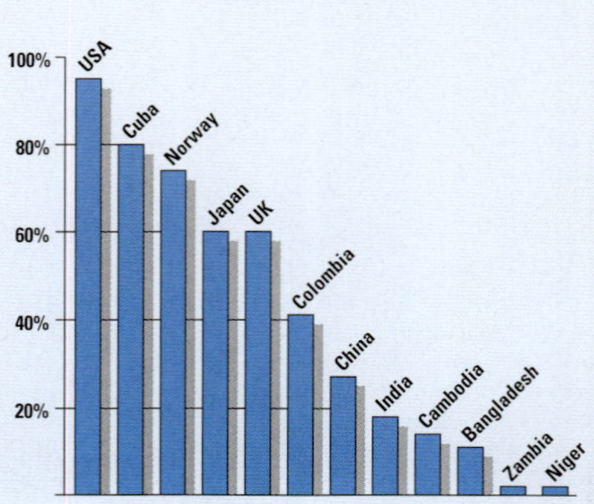
100%
80%
60%
40%
20%
USA
Cuba
Norway
Japan
UK
Colombia
China
India
Cambodia
Bangladesh
Zambia
Niger

## DISTRIBUTION OF SPENDING

**Percentage share of household spending**

A high proportion of the average income of households in developing nations is spent on basic needs such as food and clothing. In most Western countries food and clothing account for less than 25% of expenditure.

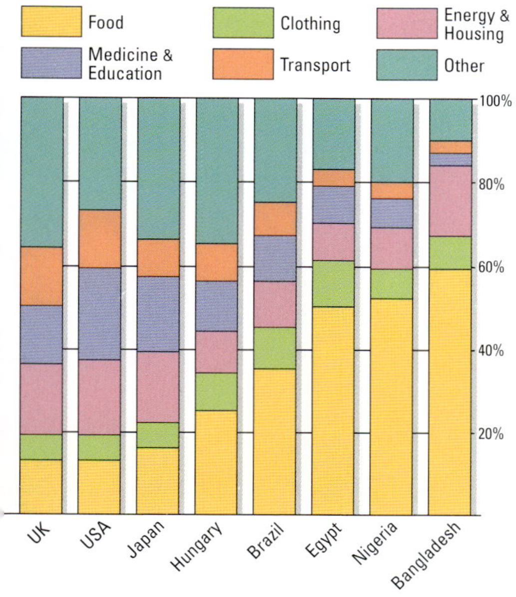
Food
Clothing
Energy & Housing
Medicine & Education
Transport
Other
100%
80%
60%
40%
20%
UK
USA
Japan
Hungary
Brazil
Egypt
Nigeria
Bangladesh

▲ These two images illustrate the reality of suburban life for people at either end of the economic scale. At the top is part of a huge area of 'tract housing' in California, where large houses of a similar design are laid out by a developer, complete with gardens, drives and swimming pools. Below, is a much more haphazard arrangement of home-built, rudimentary shelters, many without sanitation and most with no electricity, in Crossroads Township, outside Cape Town in South Africa.

## FERTILITY AND EDUCATION

**Fertility rates compared with female education, selected countries**

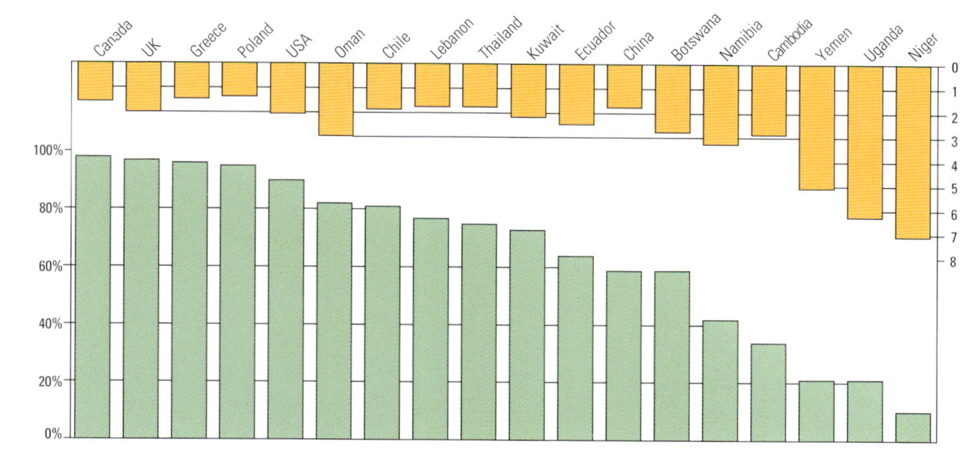
Canada
UK
Greece
Poland
USA
Oman
Chile
Lebanon
Thailand
Kuwait
Ecuador
China
Botswana
Namibia
Cambodia
Yemen
Uganda
Niger
0
1
2
3
4
5
6
7
8
100%
80%
60%
40%
20%
0%

There seems to be a strong link between access to secondary education and the fertility rate. In developed countries, young girls have a high access to education and a low fertility rate. In contrast, in many developing countries women have a high fertility rate but lack access to education. This can be for a complex mix of social, economic and cultural reasons. Despite a few high-profile examples of female politicians in different parts of the world, all evidence points to the continuing marginalization of women from the political and economic processes of decision-making. Female wages are, on average, only two-thirds of those of men.

Fertility rate: average number of children borne per woman

Percentage of females aged 12–17 in secondary education

## GENDER INEQUALITY INDEX

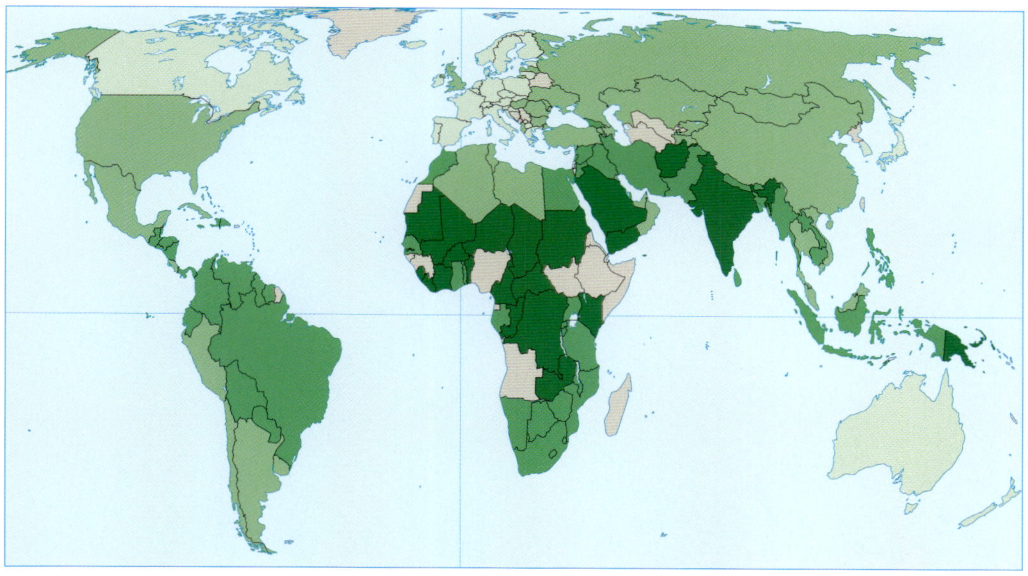

The Gender Inequality Index is a composite measure reflecting inequality in achievements between women and men in three categories: reproductive health, empowerment, and the labour market. It varies between 0, when women and men fare equally, and 1, when women or men fare poorly compared to the other in all categories (2012).

Over 0.6
0.4 – 0.6
0.2 – 0.4
Under 0.2
No data available

**Most equal**

| | |
|---|---|
| Netherlands | 0.045 |
| Sweden | 0.055 |
| Switzerland | 0.057 |

**Least equal**

| | |
|---|---|
| Yemen | 0.747 |
| Chad | 0.735 |
| Afghanistan | 0.712 |

## GENDER EQUALITY

The UN's Millennium Development Goal 3 is to *'Eliminate gender disparity in primary and secondary education'* in all levels of education no later than 2015. According to the 2012 Millennium Development Goal Report, achieving parity in education is an important step towards equal opportunity for men and women in the social, political and economic domains. The Gender Parity Index (GPI) shows the ratio between the enrolment rate of girls and that of boys. The GPI grew from 91% in 1999 to 97% in 2010 for the developing regions as a whole – falling within the +/– 3-point margin of 100% that is the accepted measure for parity.

While most of the developing world had reached a GPI of at least 95% at the primary level by 2010, the Index was only 93% in Western Asia and sub-Saharan Africa. These two regions, however, have recorded the greatest progress.

Between 1999 and 2010, girls' participation in primary education increased from 72% to 96% in sub-Saharan Africa, and from 87% to 97% in Western Asia.

Girls face greater barriers at the secondary level of education than at the primary level. The GPI for secondary education in the developing world as a whole was 96% in 2010, compared with 97% for primary education. By 2010, sub-Saharan Africa had only 82 girls enrolled per 100 boys. But in Latin America and the Caribbean, enrolment rates in secondary school were actually higher for girls than for boys, with a GPI of 108%.

In general, countries with lower levels of national wealth tend to have more men enrolled in tertiary education than women, while the opposite occurs in countries with higher average incomes.

The GPI measures the rate of girls' school enrolment as a percentage of boys' enrolment in primary, secondary and tertiary education.

### GENDER PARITY INDEX (GPI)

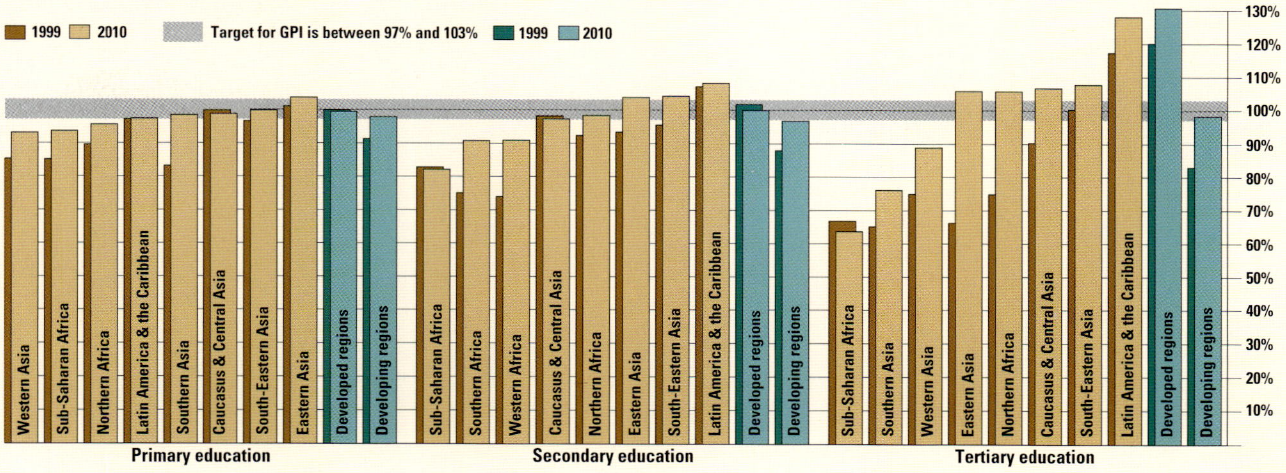
1999
2010
Target for GPI is between 97% and 103%
1999
2010
130%
120%
110%
100%
90%
80%
70%
60%
50%
40%
30%
20%
10%
Western Asia
Sub-Saharan Africa
Northern Africa
Latin America & the Caribbean
Southern Asia
Caucasus & Central Asia
South-Eastern Asia
Eastern Asia
Developed regions
Developing regions
Sub-Saharan Africa
Southern Africa
Western Africa
Caucasus & Central Asia
Northern Africa
Eastern Asia
South-Eastern Asia
Latin America & the Caribbean
Developed regions
Developing regions
Sub-Saharan Africa
Southern Asia
Western Asia
Eastern Asia
Northern Africa
Caucasus & Central Asia
South-Eastern Asia
Latin America & the Caribbean
Developed regions
Developing regions
Primary education
Secondary education
Tertiary education

# WORLD CITIES

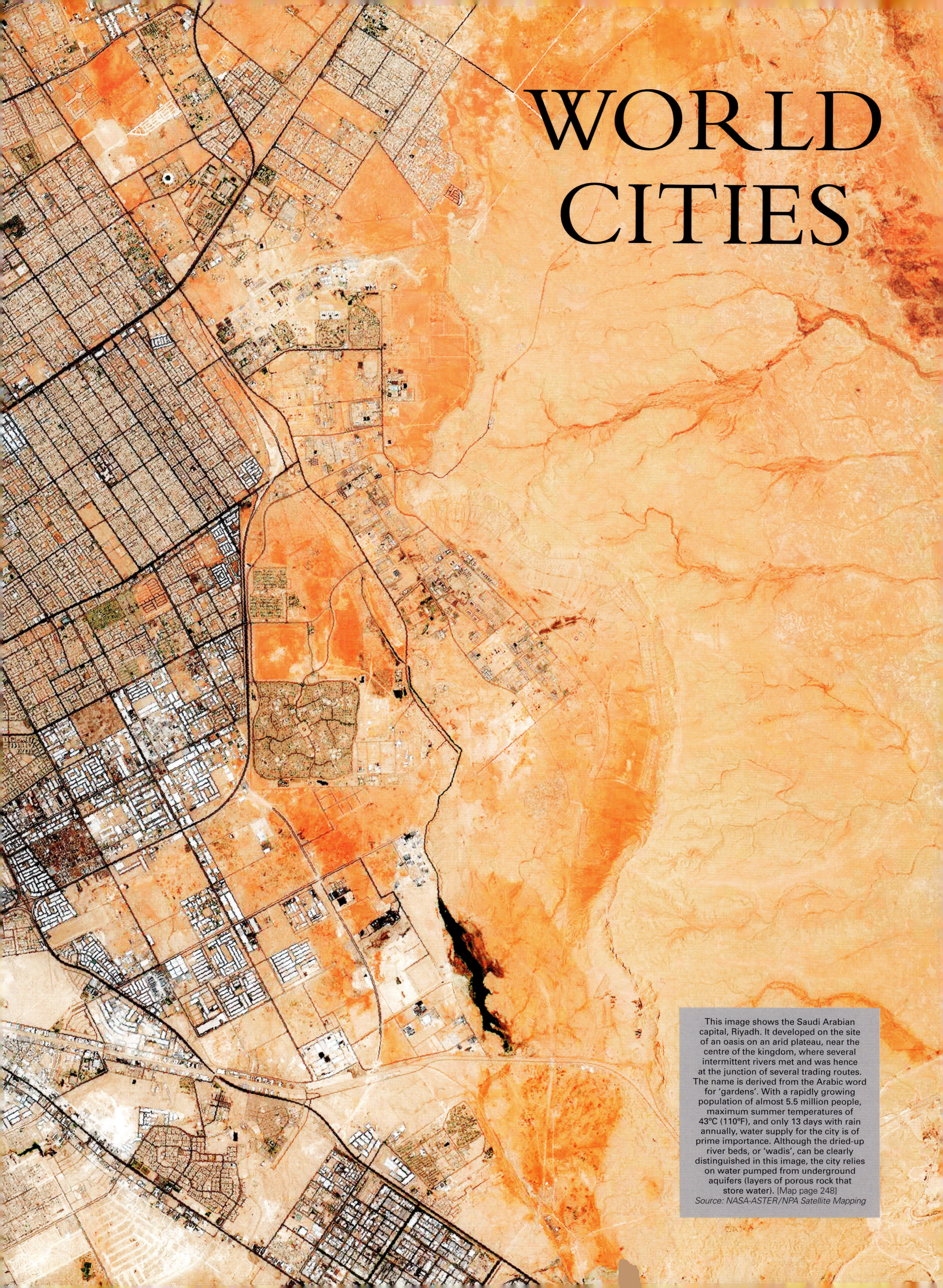

This image shows the Saudi Arabian capital, Riyadh. It developed on the site of an oasis on an arid plateau, near the centre of the kingdom, where several intermittent rivers met and was hence at the junction of several trading routes. The name is derived from the Arabic word for 'gardens'. With a rapidly growing population of almost 5.5 million people, maximum summer temperatures of 43°C (110°F), and only 13 days with rain annually, water supply for the city is of prime importance. Although the dried-up river beds, or 'wadis', can be clearly distinguished in this image, the city relies on water pumped from underground aquifers (layers of porous rock that store water). [Map page 248]
*Source: NASA-ASTER/NPA Satellite Mapping*

## AMSTERDAM, NETHERLANDS

1 0 1 km 2 3 4 5
1 0 miles 1 2 3
Assendelft
Zaandijk
Westzaan
Zaanstad
Zaandam
Wijde Wormer
Ilpendam
Monnickendam
Het Twiske
Oostzaan
Den Ilp
Waterland
Broek in Waterland
Noordzeekanaal
Landsmeer
Zuiderwoude
AMSTERDAM
Oostzaan Tuindorp
Buiksloot
Zunderdorp
Holysloot
Nieuwendam
Ransdorp
Sloterdijk
Zwanenburg
Het IJ
Central Station
Anne Frankhuis
Artis Zoo
IJ-meer
Rijksmuseum
Van Gogh museum
Osdorp
Watergraafsmeer
IJburg
Diemen
Sloten
Badhoevedorp
Muiden
Het Nieuwe Meer
Duivendrecht
Bijlmermeer
Buitenveldert
Amsterdamse Bos
Amsterdam Zuidoost
AMSTERDAM SCHIPHOL (AMS)
Amstelveen
Weesp
Bovenkerk
Ouderkerk
Abcoude
Aalsmeer
Bovenkerker Polder
Amsterdam
Nederhorst
Uithoorn
Baambrugge
Westeinder Plassen
Vinkeveense Plassen
East from Greenwich
A
B
1
2
3

## CENTRAL AMSTERDAM

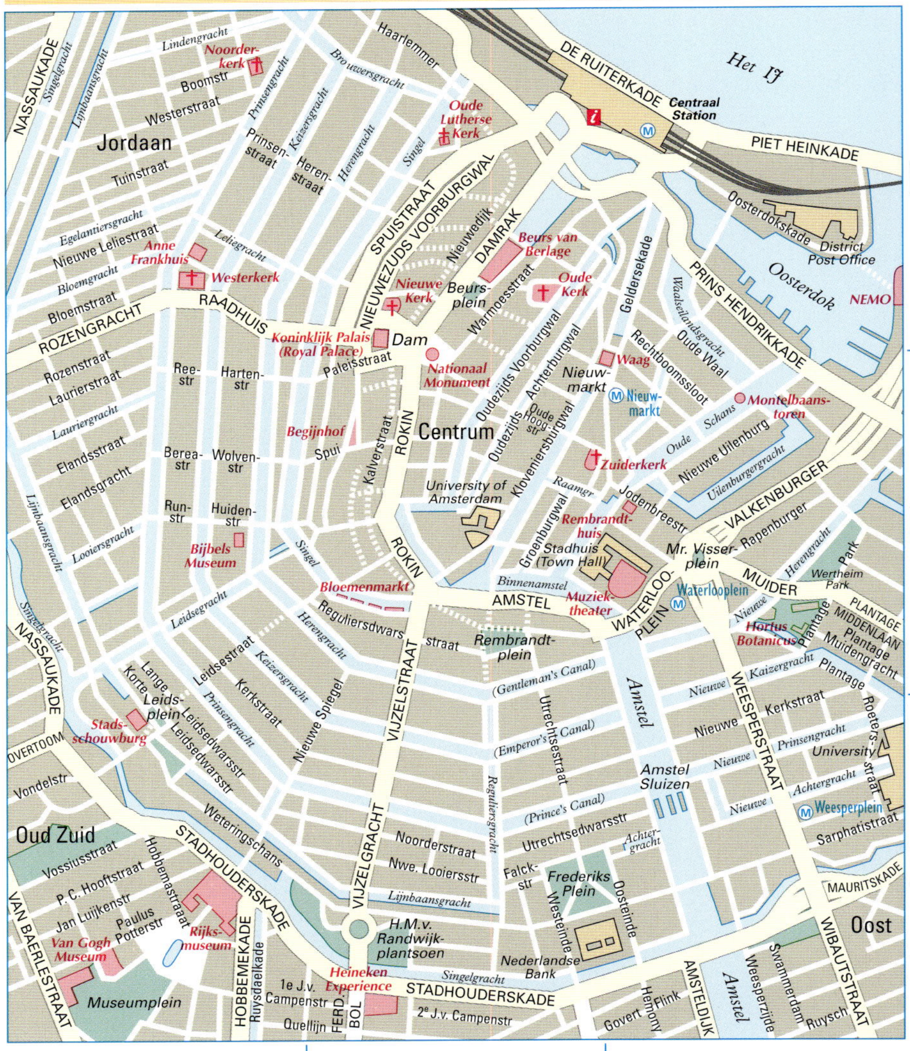
0 km 0.5
0 miles 0.25
Het IJ
DE RUITERKADE
Centraal Station
PIET HEINKADE
Jordaan
Noorderkerk
Oude Lutherse Kerk
Anne Frankhuis
Westerkerk
ROZENGRACHT
RAADHUIS
Koninklijk Paleis (Royal Palace)
Dam
Beurs van Berlage
Oude Kerk
Nieuwe Kerk
Nationaal Monument
District Post Office
Oosterdok
NEMO
PRINS HENDRIKKADE
DAMRAK
Nieuwmarkt
Waag
Montelbaanstoren
Begijnhof
Centrum
University of Amsterdam
Zuiderkerk
Rembrandthuis
Stadhuis (Town Hall)
VALKENBURGER
Mr. Visserplein
Bijbels Museum
Bloemenmarkt
AMSTEL
Muziektheater
Waterlooplein
MUIDER
Hortus Botanicus
PLANTAGE
Rembrandtplein
Amstel
Amstel Sluizen
Stadsschouwburg
Leidseplein
VIJZELSTRAAT
Oud Zuid
STADHOUDERSKADE
Frederiksplein
Oost
Rijksmuseum
Van Gogh Museum
Museumplein
H.M.v. Randwijkplantsoen
Heineken Experience
Nederlandsche Bank
Weesperplein
WIBAUTSTRAAT
1
2
3

## ATHENS, GREECE

1 0 1 km 2 3 4 5
1 0 miles 1 2 3
Diflistiria
Petroupolis
Nea Liosia
Nea Ionia
TO ATHINA ELEFTHERIOS VENIZELOS (ATH)
Filadelfia
Patisia
Chalandri
Dafni
Filothei
Skaramangas
Chaidari
Sepolia
Psichiko
Peristeri
Galatsi
Aghia Paraskevi
Kolokinthou
Kipseli
Liouni
Kolonos
Neapoli
Cholargos
Glyka Nera
Koridalos
Egaleo
Ambelokipi
ATHINA
Zografou
Neapoli
Tavros
Kouponia
Perama
Damarakia
Aghios Ioannis Rendis
Keratsini
Nikea
Gargareta
Kesariani
Drapetsona
Moschato
Kalithea
Pangrati
Vironas
Dafni
Peania
Faliro
Nea Smirni
Imitos
Ilioupoli
Pireas
Aghios Dimitrios
Paleo Faliro
Nea Alexandria
Kalamaki
Saronikos Kolpos
Alimos
Argiroupoli
Elliniko Olympic Complex
Glifada
Iraklio, Chania, Kithnos, Kos, Mykonos, Milos, Naxos, Paros, Rhodes, Samos
Voula
Kitsi
Vouliagmeni
Idrousa
Vari
C. Kavouri
Varkiza
Athens
Aghia Marina
East from Greenwich
A
B
C
1
2
3

## CENTRAL ATHENS

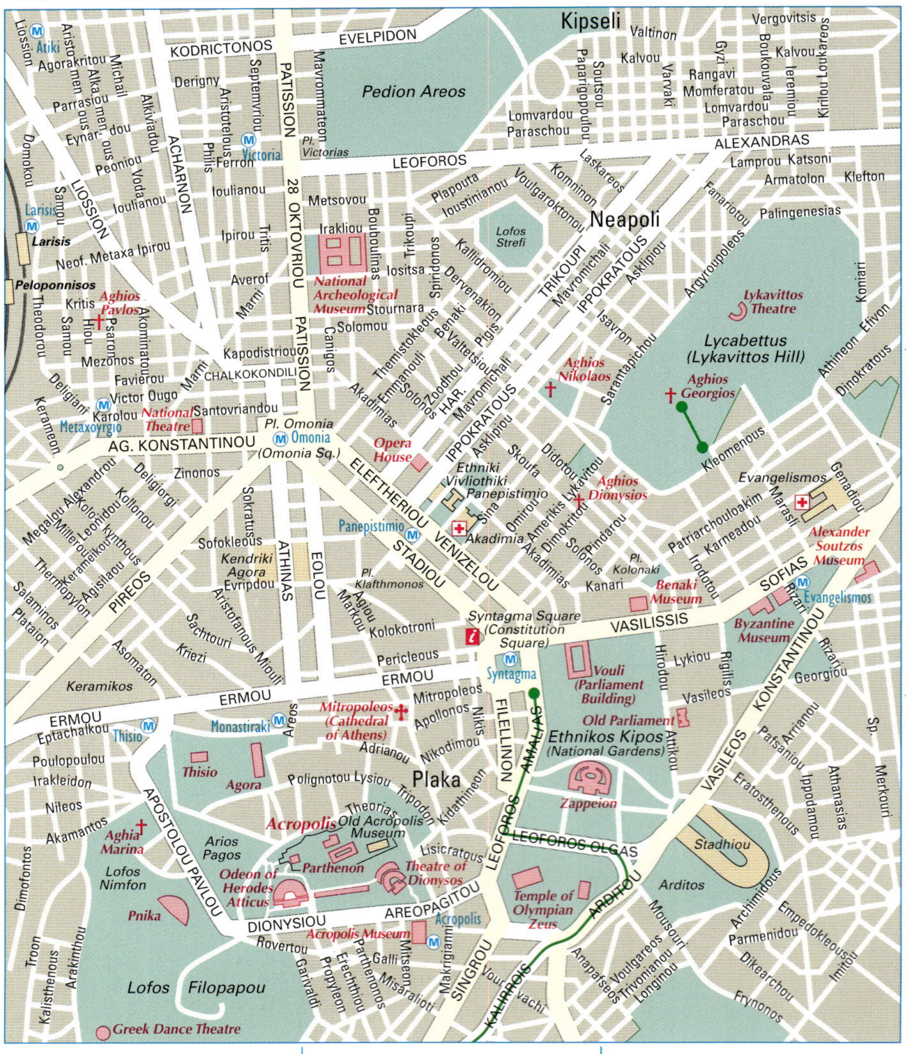
0 km 1
0 miles 0.5
Kipseli
EVELPIDON
Pedion Areos
KODRICTONOS
ALEXANDRAS
LEFOROS
Larisis
Peloponnisos
Neapoli
National Archeological Museum
Lycabettus (Lykavittos Hill)
Lykavittos Theatre
Aghios Georgios
Aghios Nikolaos
CHALKOKONDILI
National Theatre
Omonia (Omonia Sq.)
AG. KONSTANTINOU
Opera House
Aghios Dionysios
Panepistimio
Akadimia
Benaki Museum
VASILISSIS SOFIAS
Byzantine Museum
Alexander Soutzos Museum
Evangelismos
PIREOS
Syntagma Square (Constitution Square)
Vouli (Parliament Building)
Old Parliament
ERMOU
Keramikos
Mitropoleos (Cathedral of Athens)
Monastiraki
Thisio
Agora
Plaka
Ethnikos Kipos (National Gardens)
Zappeion
Acropolis
Old Acropolis Museum
Parthenon
Theatre of Dionysos
Odeon of Herodes Atticus
Aghia Marina
Arios Pagos
Lofos Nimfon
Pnika
Temple of Olympian Zeus
Stadhiou
Arditos
DIONYSIOU AREOPAGITOU
Acropolis Museum
LEFOROS OLGAS
Lofos Filopapou
Greek Dance Theatre
1
2
3

## ATLANTA, GEORGIA

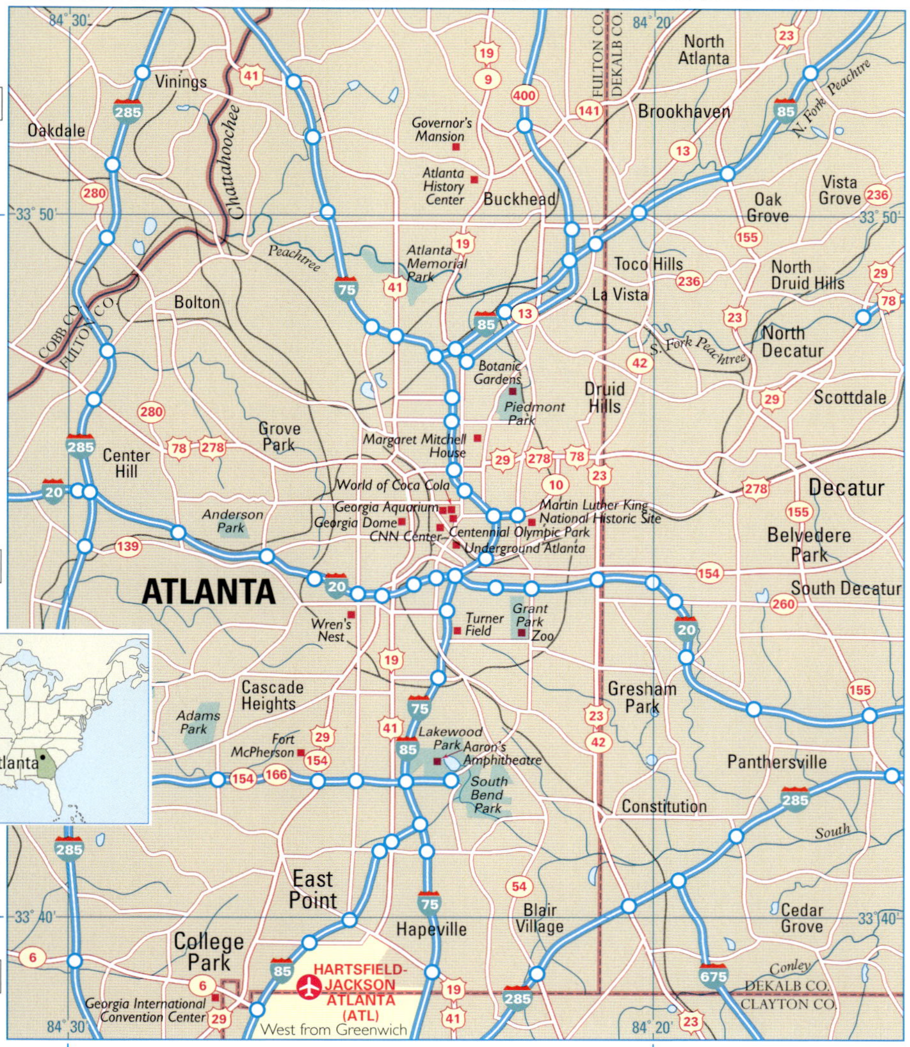
0 1 km 2 3 4 5
0 miles 1 2 3
84° 30'
84° 20'
33° 50'
33° 40'
Vinings
Oakdale
Chattahoochee
North Atlanta
Brookhaven
Governor's Mansion
Atlanta History Center
Buckhead
Oak Grove
Vista Grove
Peachtree
Atlanta Memorial Park
Toco Hills
North Druid Hills
La Vista
Bolton
North Decatur
Botanic Gardens
Piedmont Park
Druid Hills
Scottdale
Grove Park
Margaret Mitchell House
Center Hill
World of Coca Cola
Georgia Aquarium
Georgia Dome
CNN Center
Centennial Olympic Park
Underground Atlanta
Martin Luther King National Historic Site
Decatur
Anderson Park
Belvedere Park
ATLANTA
South Decatur
Wren's Nest
Turner Field
Grant Park Zoo
Cascade Heights
Adams Park
Fort McPherson
Lakewood Park
Aaron's Amphitheatre
Gresham Park
South Bend Park
Panthersville
Constitution
East Point
Hapeville
Blair Village
Cedar Grove
College Park
Georgia International Convention Center
HARTSFIELD-JACKSON ATLANTA (ATL)
West from Greenwich
DEKALB CO.
CLAYTON CO.
FULTON CO.
Atlanta

1 2 3

85 Interstate route numbers 29 U.S. route numbers 166 State route numbers

## BAGHDAD, IRAQ

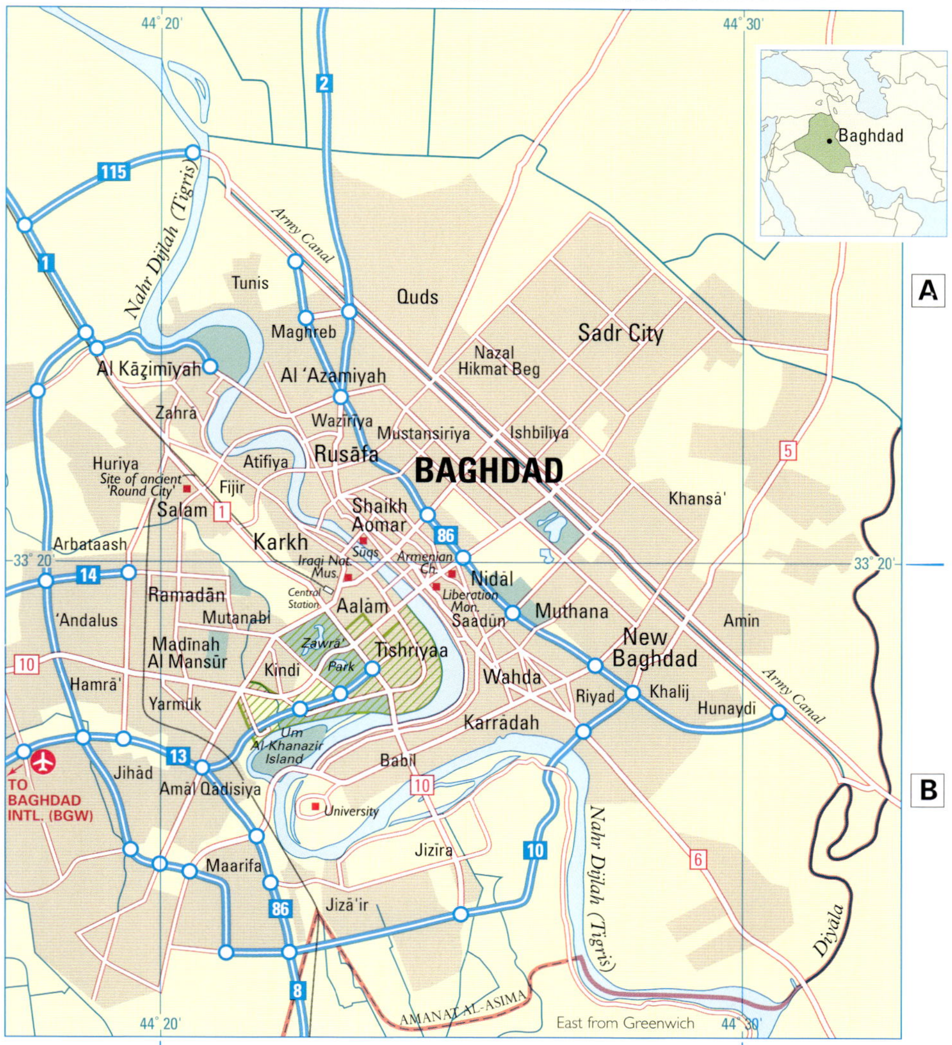
0 1 km 2 3 4 5
0 miles 1 2 3
44° 20'
44° 30'
33° 20'
Baghdad
Nahr Dijlah (Tigris)
Army Canal
Tunis
Quds
Sadr City
Maghreb
Al Kāzimiyah
Al 'Azamiyah
Nazal Hikmat Beg
Zahra
Waziriya
Mustansiriya
Ishbiliya
Huriya
Site of ancient Round City
Atifiya
Rusāfa
BAGHDAD
Fijir
Salam
Shaikh Aomar
Khansā'
Karkh
Arbataash
Iraqi Nat. Mus.
Armenian Ch.
Nidal
Ramadān
Mutanabi
Central Station
Aalam
Liberation Mon.
Saadūn
Muthana
'Andalus
Madinah Al Mansūr
Zawra Park
Tishriyaa
New Baghdad
Amin
Hamrā'
Kindi
Wahda
Riyad
Khalij
Yarmuk
Hunaydi
Karradah
Um Al-Khanazir Island
TO BAGHDAD INTL. (BGW)
Jihād
Babil
Amal Qadisiya
University
Jizira
Maarifa
Jizā'ir
Diyala
AMANAT AL-ASIMA
East from Greenwich

1 2 3

International Zone (Green Zone)

## BANGKOK, THAILAND

0 1 km 2 3 4 5
0 miles 1 2 3
100° 30'
13° 50'
13° 40'
DON MUANG
Bangkhen
Nonthaburi
Laksi
Klong Prem Prachakorn
Klong Bang Bua
Chao Phraya
Bung Kum
Bangsu
Lad Phrao
Chatuchak Park
Chatuchak
NONTHABURI
BANGKOK
Dusit
Huay Khwang
Klong Lat Phrao
Bang Kapi
Bang Phlad
Phaya Thai
BANGKOK (KRUNG THEP)
Bangkok Noi
Thon Buri
Royal Chitralada Palace
Victory Mon.
Ramkhamhaeng University
National Museum
Phra Nakhon
Pomprap
Grand Palace
Wat Pho
Samphan Thawong
Hua Lamphong
Chulalongkorn University
Pathumwan
Bangkok Yai
Lumphini Park
Bangrak
Klhong Toey
Wong Wian Yai
Khlong San
Thon Buri
Sathorn
K. Phra Khanong
Bang Kholaem
Samut Prakan
Phra Khanong
Yannawa
Chom Thong
Bang Na
TO BANGKOK SUVARNABHUMI (BKK)
BANGKOK SAMUT PRAKAN
East from Greenwich
Phra Pradaeng
Bangkok

1 2

## CENTRAL BANGKOK

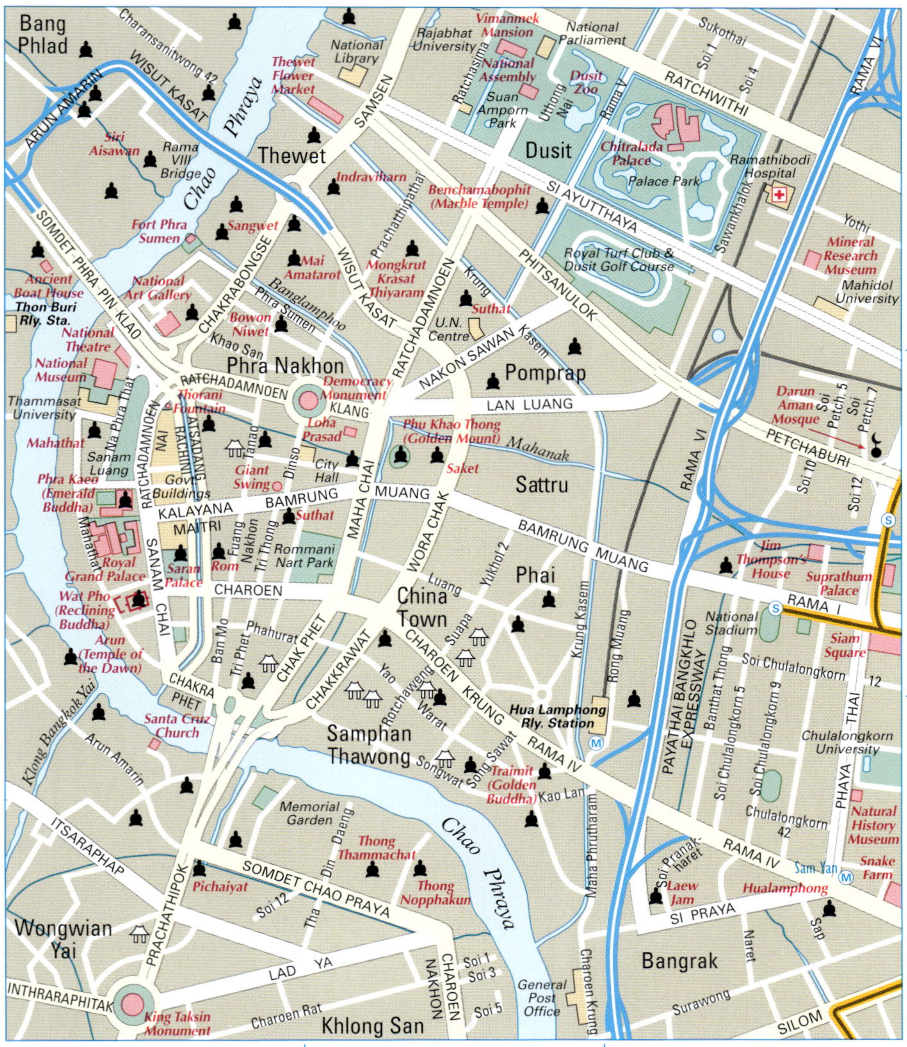
0 km 1
0 miles 0.5
Bang Phlad
WISUT KASAT
National Library
Rajabhat University
Vimanmek Mansion
National Parliament
Sukothai
RATCHWITHI
Thewet Flower Market
National Assembly
Suan Amporn Park
Dusit Zoo
Dusit
Chitralada Palace
Palace Park
Ramathibodi Hospital
Siri Aisawan
Rama VIII Bridge
Chao Phraya
Thewet
SAMSEN
Indravihan
Benchamabophit (Marble Temple)
SI AYUTTHAYA
Fort Phra Sumen
Sangwet
Royal Turf Club & Dusit Golf Course
Mineral Research Museum
Mahidol University
Ancient Boat House
Thon Buri Rly. Sta.
National Art Gallery
Mai Amatarot
Mongkrut Krasat Thiyaram
National Theatre
Bowon Niwet
U.N. Centre
PHITSANULOK
National Museum
Phra Nakhon
Pomprap
Thammasat University
RATCHADAMNOEN
Democracy Monument
NAKON SAWAN
LAN LUANG
Mahathat
Loha Prasad
Phu Khao Thong (Golden Mount)
Darun Aman Mosque
Sanam Luang
Mahanak
PETCHABURI
Phra Kaeo (Emerald Buddha)
Giant Swing
City Hall
Saket
Sattru
Gov. Buildings
BAMRUNG MUANG
Suthat
KALAYANA
MAITRI
Royal Grand Palace
Saran Palace
Rommani Nart Park
Phai
Jim Thompson's House
Wat Pho (Reclining Buddha)
CHAROEN
China Town
RAMA I
Suprathum Palace
Arun (Temple of the Dawn)
National Stadium
Siam Square
Soi Chulalongkorn
Santa Cruz Church
Samphan Thawong
Hua Lamphong Rly. Station
RAMA IV
PAYATHAI BANGKLO EXPRESSWAY
Chulalongkorn University
Klong Bangkok Yai
Arun Amarin
Traimit (Golden Buddha)
Memorial Garden
Natural History Museum
Snake Farm
ITSARAPHAP
Thong Thammachat
Thong Nopphakun
Pichaiyat
SOMDET CHAO PRAYA
Plaew Jam
Hualamphong
SI PRAYA
Wongwian Yai
PRACHATHIPOK
LAD YA
Bangrak
INTHARAPHITAK
General Post Office
Surawong
King Taksin Monument
Charoen Rat
Khlong San
CHAROEN NAKHON
SILOM

1 2 3

Skytrain Shrine Temple

## BARCELONA, SPAIN

Rubí
Cerdanyola del Vallès
Ripollet
Montcada i Reixac
Valldoreix
Sant Cugat del Vallès
La Floresta
El Papiol
Santa Cruz de Olorde
Tibidabo 512
Molins de Rei
Vallvidrera
Sant Vicenç dels Horts
Sant Just Desvern
Sant Feliu de Llobregat
Esplugas
Pedralbes
Sarrià
Putxet
Gràcia
Les Corts
La França
Sants
Cornellà
Sant Joan Despí
Colonia Güell
La Ribera
Beri
Sant Boi de Llobregat
L'Hospitalet de Llobregat
Hostafranchs
Montjuïc
Castell de Montjuïc
El Prat de Llobregat
BARCELONA (EL PRAT) (BCN)
Viladecans
Gavà
Gavamar
Estany de la Ricarda
Estany del Rémola
Riu Llobregat
Llano de Can Gineu
C'an San Joan
La Puntigala 151
Sta. Coloma de Gramanet
Badalona
Sant Adrià de Besòs
San Andrés
Santa Eulalia
La Sagrera
Vallcarca
La Taxonera
Guinardó
La Llacuna
San Martin
El Poblenou
Sagrada Família
Templo de Toros Monumental
La Barceloneta
BARCELONA
Museu Marítim
Palau Nacional Museu d'Art
Camp Nou FC Barcelona
Universitat
Est. Central
Est. de França
Gènova
Maó, Palma de Mallorca, Eivissa
MEDITERRANEAN SEA
Barcelona
East from Greenwich
Turó de Galceran 477
Madrona 336
2° 00'
2° 10'
41° 20'
A
B
1
2

## CENTRAL BARCELONA

Gràcia
Sagrada Família
Plaça Glòries Catalanes
AVINGUDA DIAGONAL
La Pedrera (Casa Milà)
Les Saleses
Temple de Toros Monumental
PASSEIG DE GRÀCIA
RAMBLA DE CATALUNYA
GRAN VIA DE LES CORTS CATALANES
L'Eixample
Hospital Clínic i Provincial
Universitat Industrial
Universidad
Plaça de Catalunya
Palau de la Música Catalana
Barrio Gòtico
Catedral
Parlament de Catalunya
Parc de la Ciutadella
Parc Zoològic
Estació de França
Museu d'Art Contemporani (MACBA)
Hospital Santa Creu
Liceu
Teatre del Liceu
Palau de la Virreina
La Ribera
El Raval
Sant Pau del Camp
Museu Marítim
Monument a Colón (Columbus Monument)
Museu d'Història de Catalunya
L'Aquarium Barcelona
La Barceloneta
Port Vell
World Trade Centre
Dàrsena de Sant Bertràn
Mediterranean Sea
AVINGUDA DEL PARAL·LEL
Plaça d'Espanya
Palau Nacional Museu d'Art (National Palace)
Poble Espanyol
Palau de Victoria Eugenia
Palau de la Metal·lurgia
Museu Arqueològic
Fundació Joan Miró
Estadi Olympic
Palau Sant Jordi
Parc de Montjuïc
Montjuïc
Castell de Montjuïc
Miramar
Parc J. Miró
Tarragona
La França
1
2
3

## BEIJING, CHINA

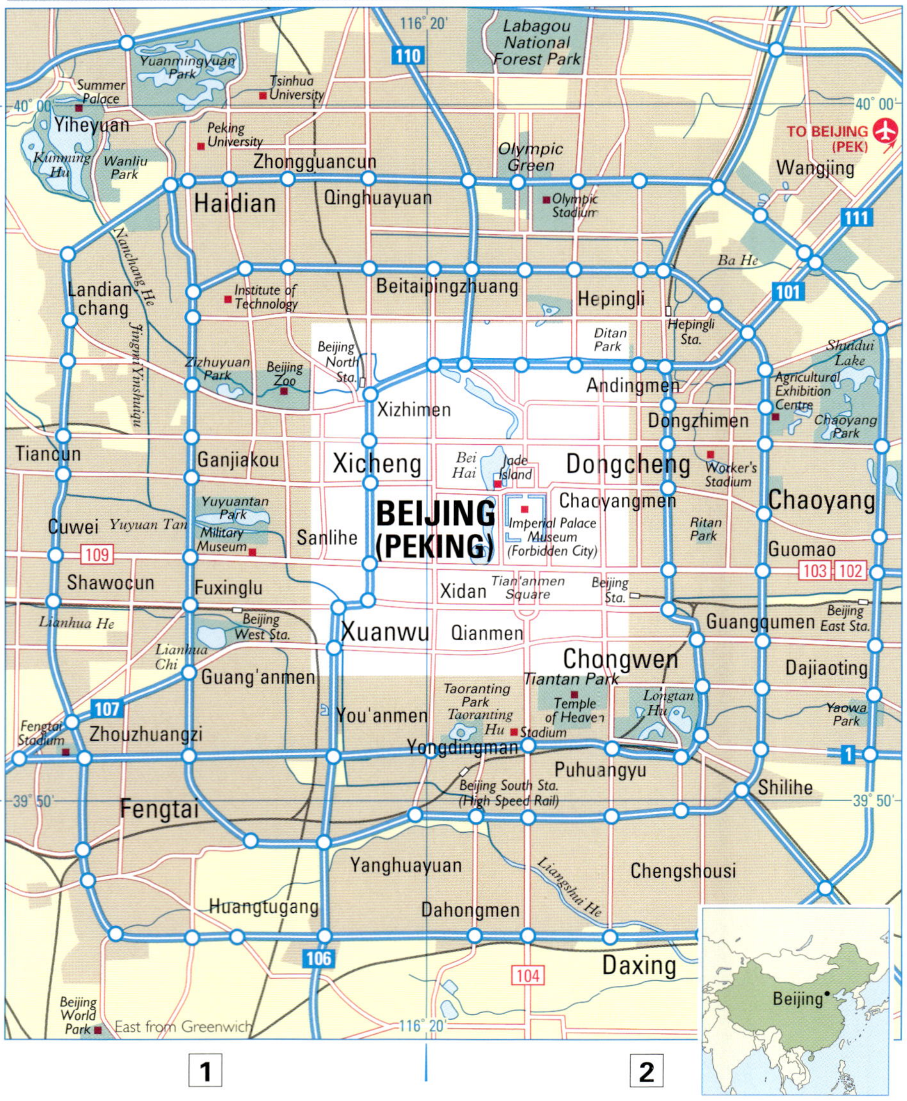
Labagou National Forest Park
Summer Palace
Yuanmingyuan Park
Tsinhua University
Yiheyuan
Kunming Hu
Wanliu Park
Peking University
Zhongguancun
Olympic Green
Olympic Stadium
TO BEIJING (PEK)
Wangjing
Haidian
Qinghuayuan
Landianchang
Institute of Technology
Beitaipingzhuang
Hepingli
Beijing North Sta.
Beijing Zoo
Xizhimen
Andingmen
Dongzhimen
Agricultural Exhibition Centre
Chaoyang Park
Tiancun
Ganjiakou
Xicheng
Dongcheng
Workers Stadium
Chaoyangmen
Chaoyang
BEIJING (PEKING)
Imperial Palace Museum (Forbidden City)
Cuiwei
Military Museum
Sanlihe
Ritan Park
Guomao
Shawocun
Fuxinglu
Xidan
Tian'anmen Square
Beijing Sta.
Beijing West Sta.
Xuanwu
Qianmen
Guangqumen
Beijing East Sta.
Guang'anmen
Chongwen
Tiantan Park
Temple of Heaven
Dajiaoting
Zhouzhuangzi
You'anmen
Taoranting Park
Yongdingmen
Puhuangyu
Shilihe
Fengtai
Beijing South Sta. (High Speed Rail)
Yanghuayuan
Chengshousi
Huangtugang
Dahongmen
Daxing
Beijing World Park
Beijing
East from Greenwich
116° 20'
40° 00'
39° 50'
A
B
C
1
2

## CENTRAL BEIJING

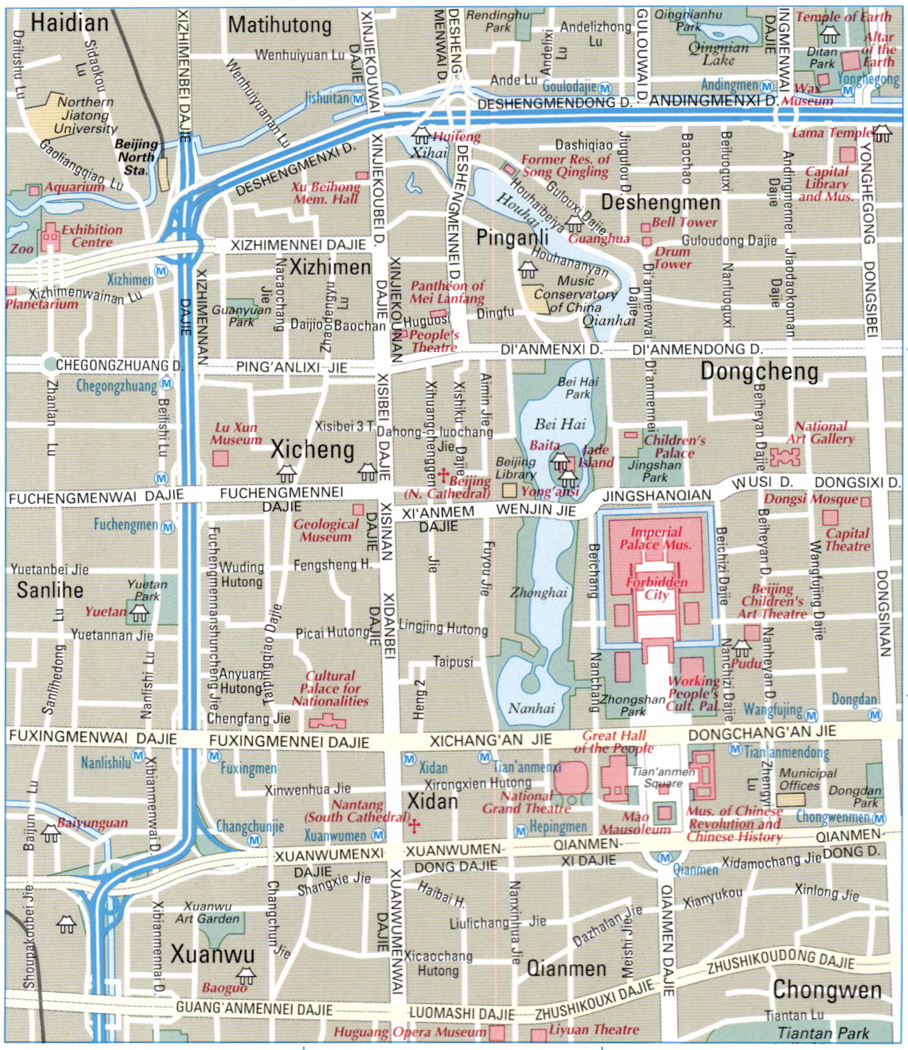
Haidian
Matihutong
Temple of Earth
Northern Jiatong University
Beijing North Sta.
DESHENGMENDONG D.
ANDINGMENXI D.
Aquarium
Exhibition Centre
Zoo
Planetarium
Xu Beihong Mem. Hall
Former Res. of Song Qingling
Deshengmen
Lama Temple
Capital Library and Mus.
Bell Tower
Drum Tower
Pinganli
Xizhimen
Pantheon of Mei Lanfang
People's Theatre
Music Conservatory of China
Qianhai
DI'ANMENXI D.
DI'ANMENDONG D.
PING'ANLIXI JIE
Dongcheng
Lu Xun Museum
Xicheng
Bei Hai
Beijing Library
Children's Palace
Jingshan Park
National Art Gallery
FUCHENGMENWAI DAJIE
FUCHENGMENNEI DAJIE
XI'ANMEN DAJIE
WENJIN JIE
JINGSHANQIAN
WUSI D.
DONGSIXI D.
Geological Museum
Imperial Palace Mus.
Forbidden City
Dongsi Mosque
Capital Theatre
Sanlihe
Yuetan Park
Zhonghai
Nanhai
Cultural Palace for Nationalities
Working People's Cult. Pal.
FUXINGMENWAI DAJIE
FUXINGMENNEI DAJIE
XICHANG'AN JIE
DONGCHANG'AN JIE
Great Hall of the People
Tian'anmen
Tian'anmen Square
Xidan
Nantang (South Cathedral)
National Grand Theatre
Mao Mausoleum
Mus. of Chinese Revolution and Chinese History
XUANWUMENXI DAJIE
XUANWUMEN DONG DAJIE
QIANMENXI DAJIE
QIANMENDONG D.
Xuanwu
Qianmen
Chongwen
Tiantan Park
GUANG'ANMENNEI DAJIE
LUOMASHI DAJIE
ZHUSHIKOUXI DAJIE
ZHUSHIKOUDONG DAJIE
Huguang Opera Museum
Liyuan Theatre
1
2
3

Temple

## BERLIN, GERMANY

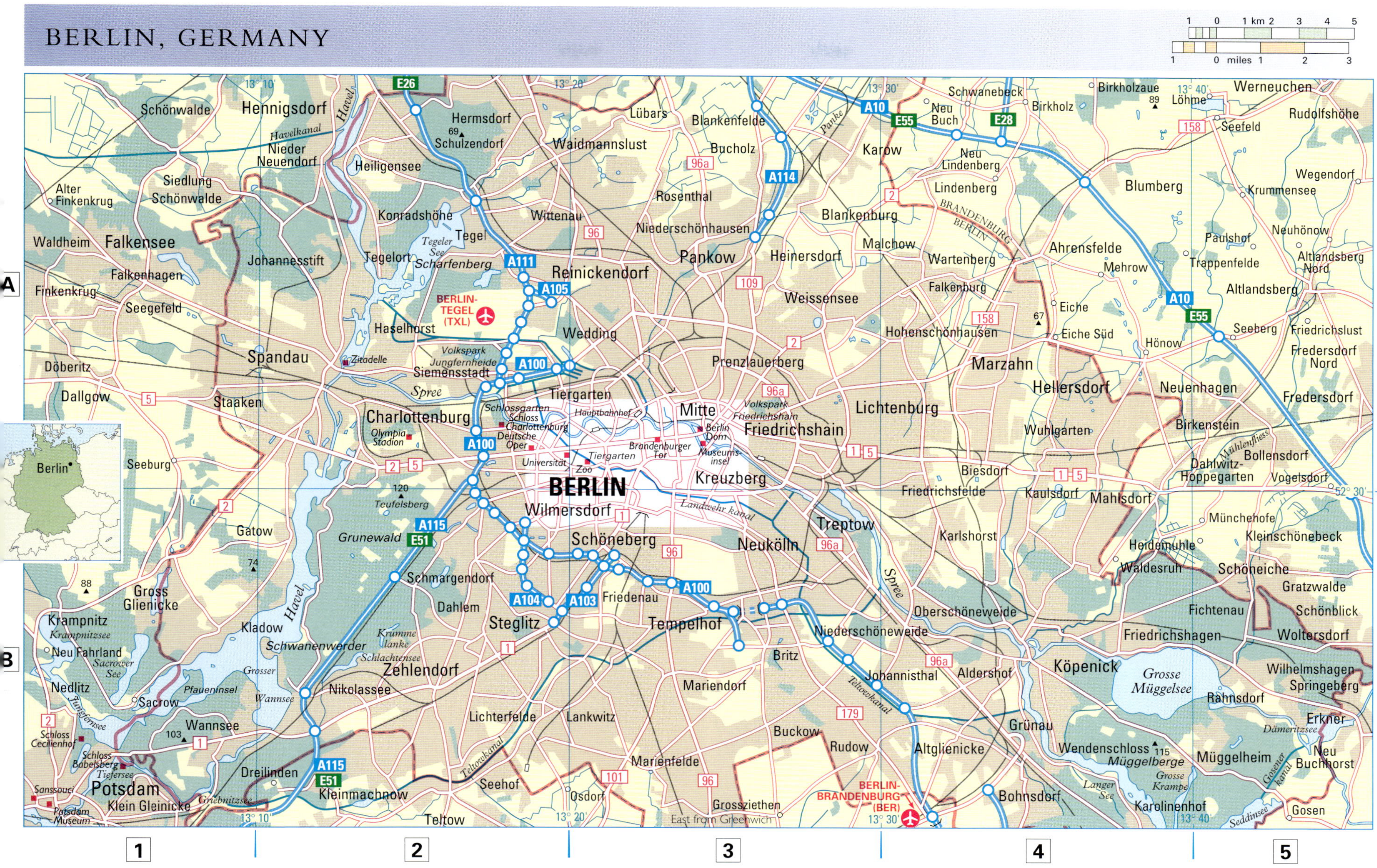
BERLIN
Mitte
Friedrichshain
Kreuzberg
Wilmersdorf
Schöneberg
Neukölln
Tempelhof
Steglitz
Zehlendorf
Charlottenburg
Spandau
Reinickendorf
Pankow
Prenzlauerberg
Weissensee
Lichtenburg
Marzahn
Hellersdorf
Treptow
Köpenick
Wedding
Tiergarten
Potsdam
Wannsee
Dahlem
Falkensee
Hennigsdorf
Tegel
BERLIN-TEGEL (TXL)
BERLIN-BRANDENBURG (BER)
Grosse Müggelsee
Grunewald
Havel
Spree
Teltow
Kleinmachnow
Blumberg
Ahrensfelde
Hohenschönhausen
Friedrichshagen
Grünau
Altglienicke
Rudow
Britz
Mariendorf
Lichterfelde
Nikolassee
Gatow
Kladow
Staaken
Dallgow
Seeburg
Erkner
Müggelheim
East from Greenwich

## CENTRAL BERLIN

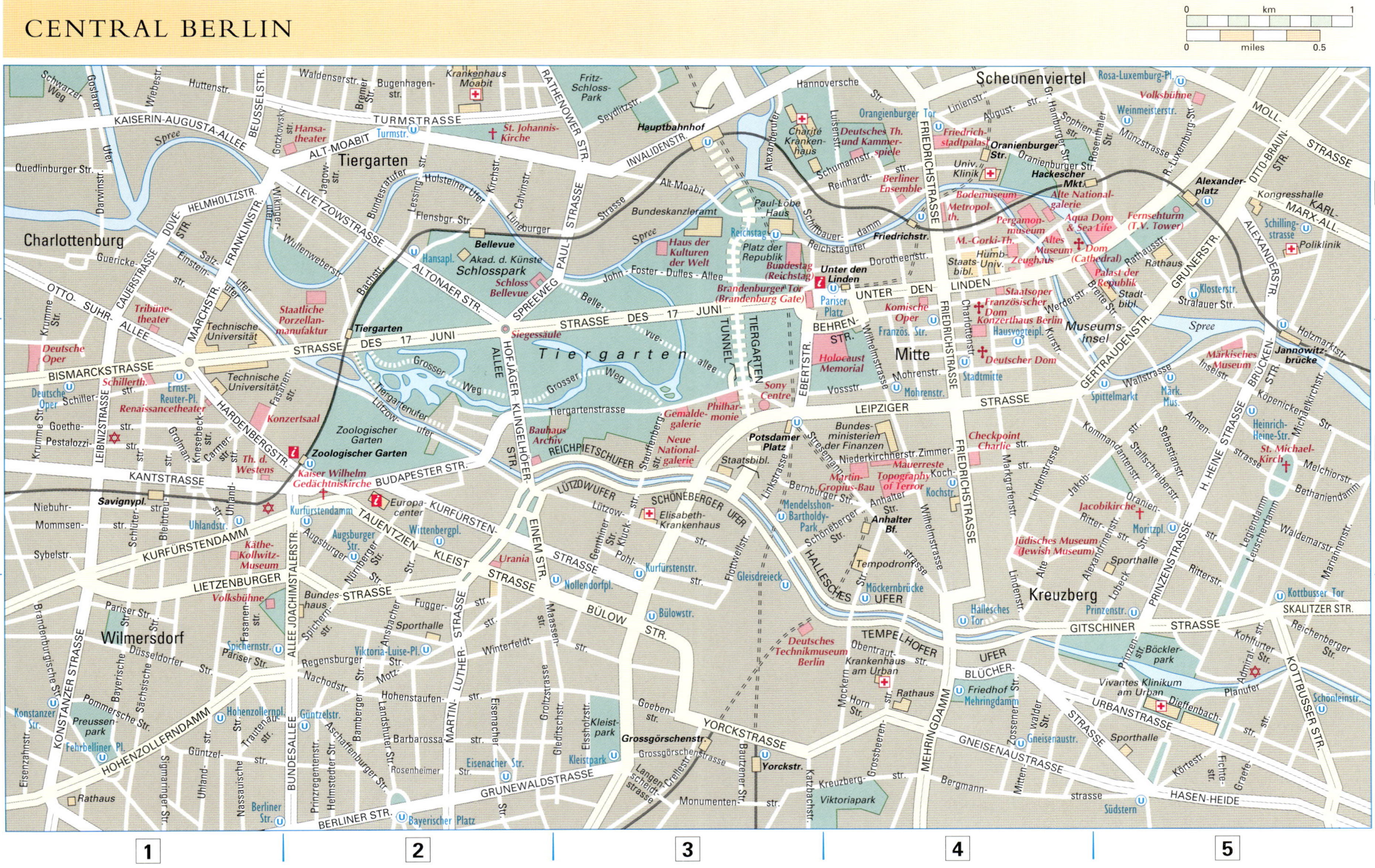
Charlottenburg
Tiergarten
Mitte
Kreuzberg
Wilmersdorf
Scheunenviertel
Hauptbahnhof
Tiergarten
Zoologischer Garten
Brandenburger Tor (Brandenburg Gate)
Reichstag
Unter den Linden
Potsdamer Platz
Museumsinsel
Alexanderplatz
Fernsehturm (T.V. Tower)
Checkpoint Charlie
Kaiser Wilhelm Gedächtniskirche
KURFÜRSTENDAMM
STRASSE DES 17 JUNI
LEIPZIGER STRASSE
FRIEDRICHSTRASSE
Jüdisches Museum (Jewish Museum)
Deutsches Technikmuseum Berlin
Viktoriapark
Spree

## BOSTON, MASSACHUSETTS

Bedford
Burlington
Woburn
Wakefield
North Saugus
Lynn Woods Reservation
Stoneham
Greenwood
North Lexington
Hancock-Clarke House
Winchester
Melrose
Saugus
Cliftondale
Lexington
Arlington Heights
West Medford
Malden
East Lexington
Medford
Revere
Concord Turnpike
Arlington
East Arlington
Tufts Univ.
Wellington
Everett
Belmont
Somerville
Chelsea
Orient Heights
Waltham
Waverley
Harvard University
Charlestown
East Boston
Watertown
Cambridge
BOSTON LOGAN INTL. (BOS)
Charles R.
Allston
Mass. Inst. of Tech.
BOSTON
Brandeis Univ.
Auburndale
Brighton
Massachusetts State House
Newtonville
John F. Kennedy Nat. Hist. Site
Museum of Fine Arts
Northeastern University
South Boston
Newton
Boston College
Chestnut Hill
Roxbury
Spectacle Island
Brookline
Wellesley Hills
Jamaica Plain
Grove Hall
Thompson Island
Dorchester Bay
Needham Heights
Oak Hill
Franklin Park
Fields Corner
Roslindale
Dorchester
Squantum
Needham
West Roxbury
North Quincy
Quincy Bay
Mattapan
Hyde Park
Wollaston
Boston
Dedham
Milton
Quincy
A
B
1
2

95 Interstate route numbers 20 U.S. route numbers 109 State route numbers

## CENTRAL BOSTON

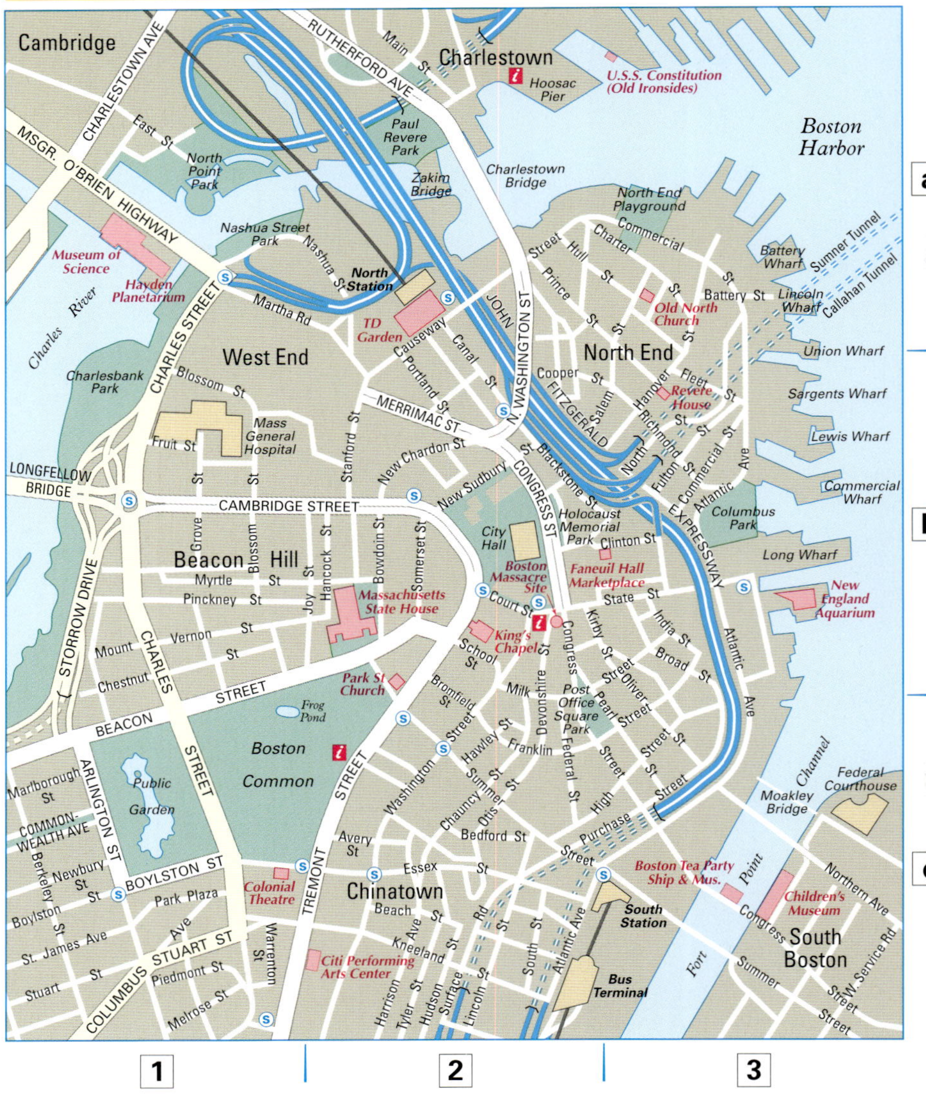
Cambridge
Charlestown
U.S.S. Constitution (Old Ironsides)
Boston Harbor
Charlestown Bridge
Museum of Science
Hayden Planetarium
North Station
TD Garden
North End
West End
Mass General Hospital
Old North Church
Paul Revere House
Union Wharf
Sargents Wharf
Lewis Wharf
Commercial Wharf
Long Wharf
New England Aquarium
CAMBRIDGE STREET
Beacon Hill
City Hall
Faneuil Hall Marketplace
Holocaust Memorial Park
Boston Massacre Site
King's Chapel
Massachusetts State House
Park St Church
Boston Common
Public Garden
BEACON STREET
Chinatown
Colonial Theatre
Citi Performing Arts Center
South Station
Bus Terminal
Boston Tea Party Ship & Mus.
Children's Museum
South Boston
Federal Courthouse
Moakley Bridge
1
2
3

## BRUSSELS, BELGIUM

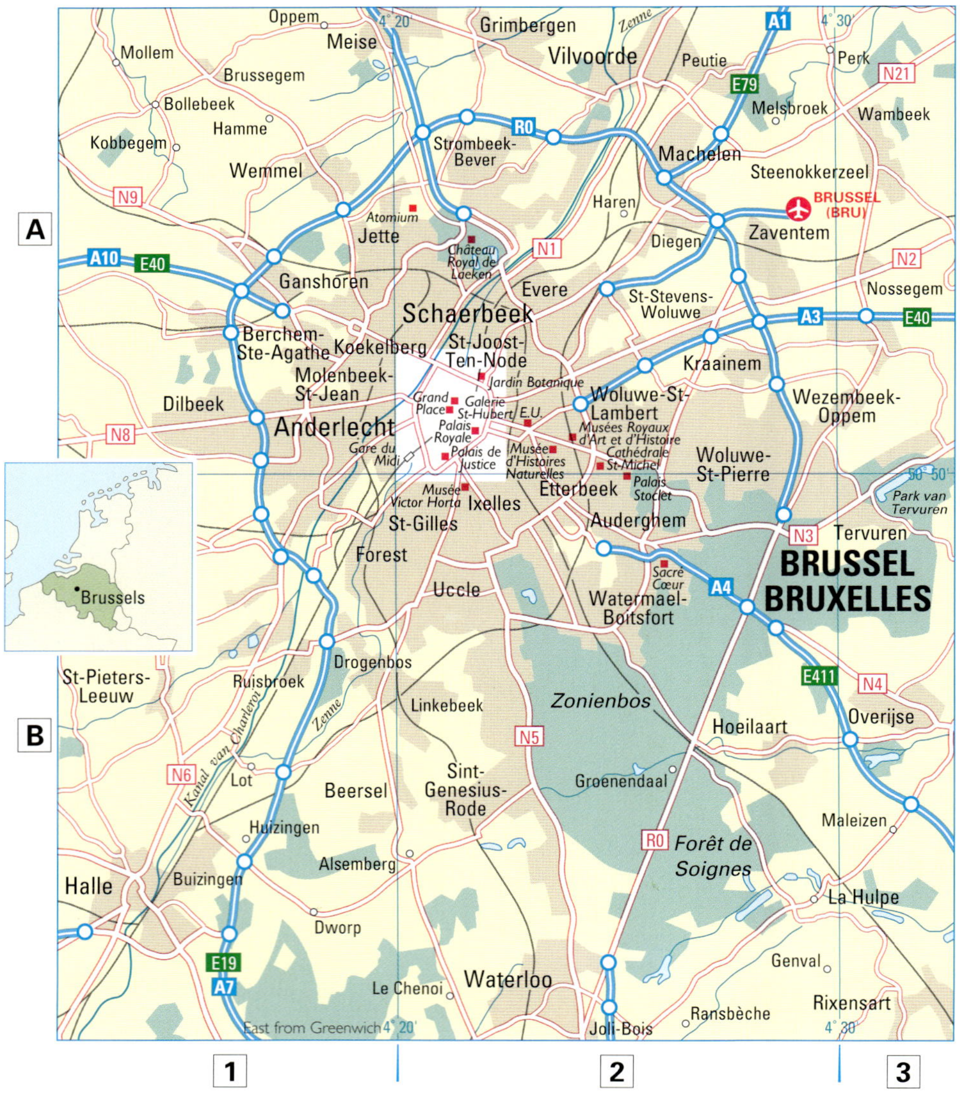
Oppem
Meise
Grimbergen
Vilvoorde
Mollem
Brussegem
Bollebeek
Hamme
Kobbegem
Wemmel
Strombeek-Bever
Machelen
Melsbroek
Wambeek
Steenokkerzeel
BRUSSEL (BRU)
Zaventem
Jette
Ganshoren
Diegem
Evere
Schaerbeek
Nossegem
Berchem-Ste-Agathe
Koekelberg
St-Joost-Ten-Node
Molenbeek-St-Jean
Dilbeek
Anderlecht
Woluwe-St-Lambert
Kraainem
Wezembeek-Oppem
Woluwe-St-Pierre
Etterbeek
Ixelles
Auderghem
St-Gilles
Forest
Tervuren
BRUSSEL BRUXELLES
Uccle
Watermael-Boitsfort
Brussels
St-Pieters-Leeuw
Ruisbroek
Drogenbos
Linkebeek
Zonienbos
Hoeilaart
Overijse
Beersel
Sint-Genesius-Rode
Groenendaal
Lot
Huizingen
Forêt de Soignes
Maleizen
Alsemberg
Halle
Buizingen
La Hulpe
Dworp
Genval
Le Chenoi
Waterloo
Rixensart
Joli-Bois
Ransbèche
A
B
1
2
3

## CENTRAL BRUSSELS

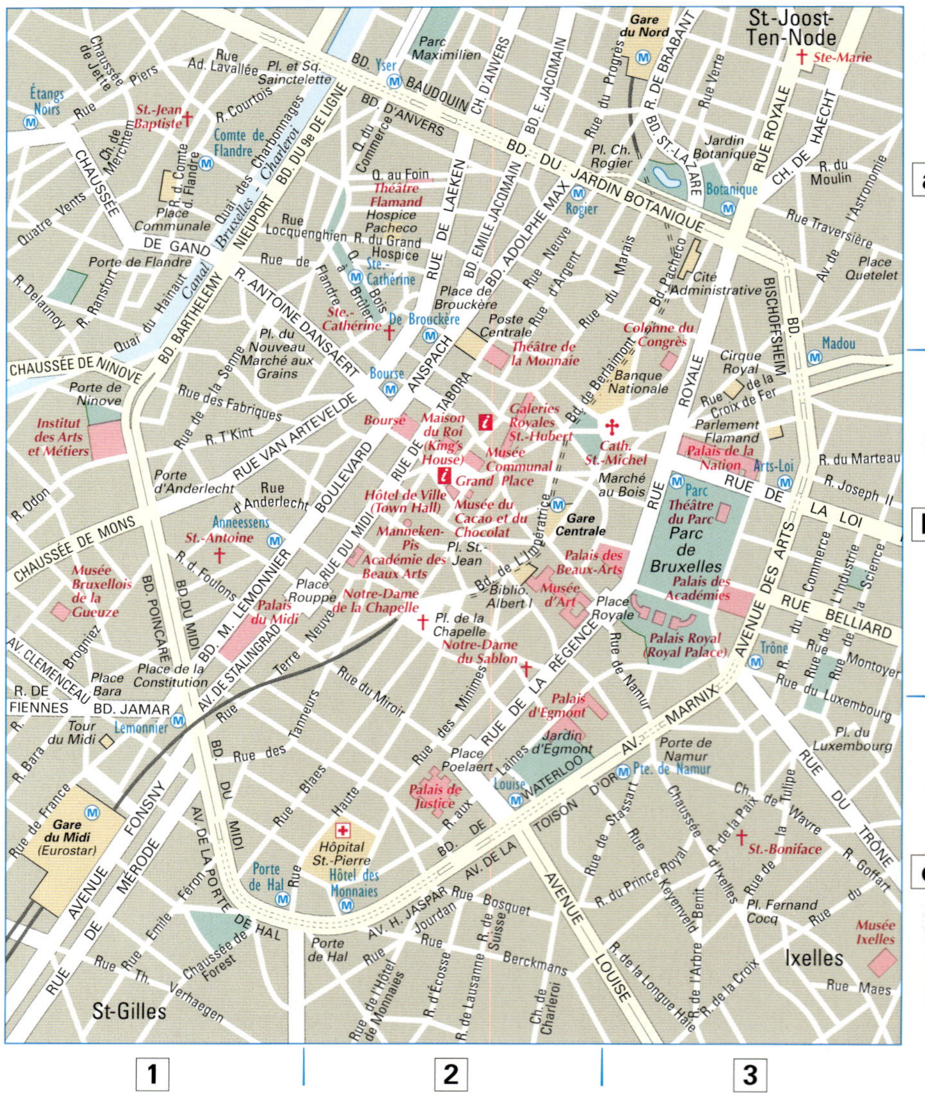
Gare du Nord
St-Joost-Ten-Node
Parc Maximilien
BD. DU JARDIN BOTANIQUE
Jardin Botanique
Comte de Flandre
Place Communale
Porte de Flandre
Théâtre Flamand
Ste-Catherine
Place de Brouckère
Poste Centrale
Théâtre de la Monnaie
Colonne du Congrès
Cité Administrative
Madou
CHAUSSÉE DE NINOVE
Institut des Arts et Métiers
Bourse
Galeries Royales St-Hubert
Cath. St-Michel
Banque Nationale
Palais de la Nation
Arts-Loi
Grand Place
Maison du Roi (King's House)
Hôtel de Ville (Town Hall)
Manneken-Pis
Gare Centrale
Parc de Bruxelles
Palais des Académies
Palais Royal (Royal Palace)
Trône
Porte d'Anderlecht
Anneessens
Palais du Midi
Notre-Dame de la Chapelle
Notre-Dame du Sablon
Palais d'Egmont
Place Royale
Musée d'Art
Place Bara
Lemonnier
Gare du Midi (Eurostar)
Palais de Justice
Louise
Porte de Namur
Hôpital St-Pierre
Porte de Hal
St-Gilles
Ixelles
Musée Ixelles
1
2
3

## BUDAPEST, HUNGARY

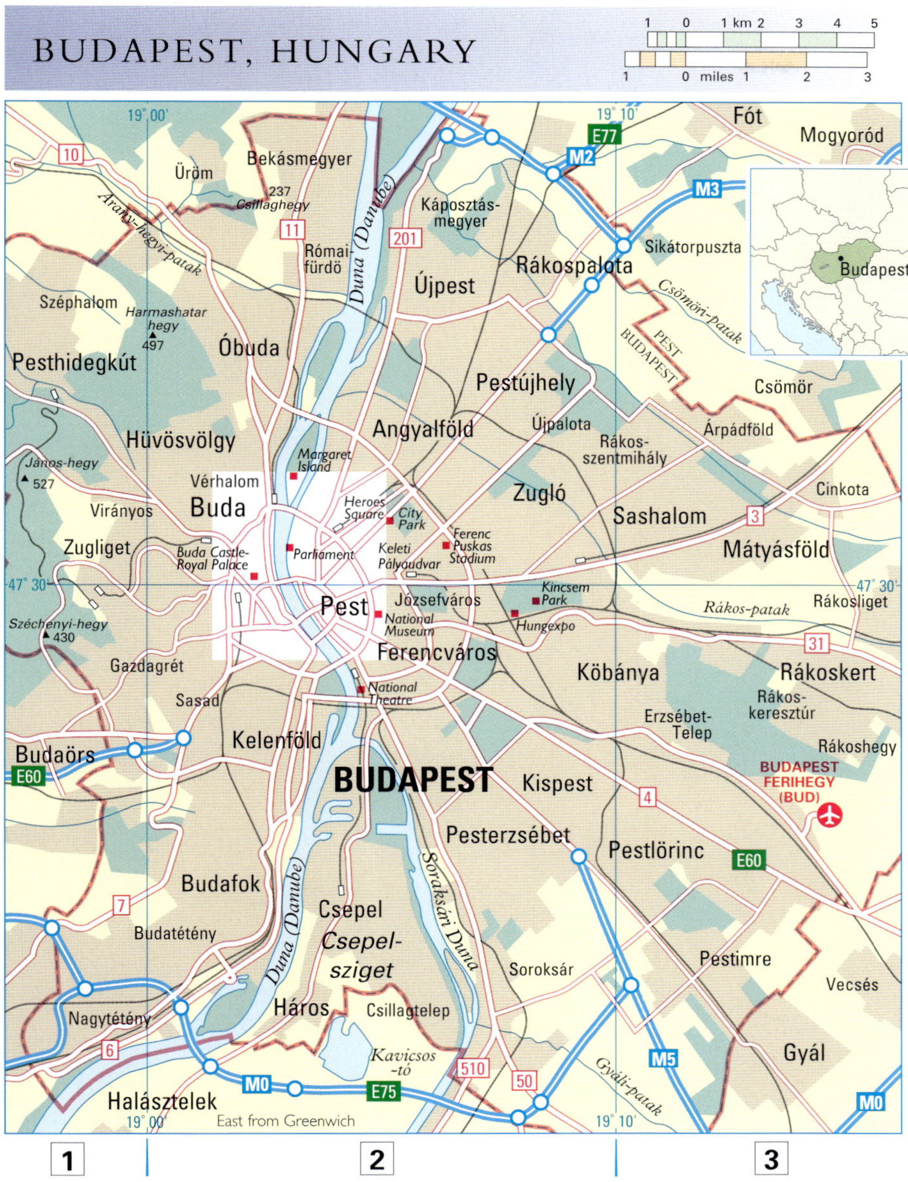

Fót
Mogyoród
Üröm
Békásmegyer
Káposztásmegyer
Római-fürdő
Újpest
Rákospalota
Sikátorpuszta
Budapest
Széphalom
Óbuda
Pesthidegkút
Pestújhely
Csömör
Hűvösvölgy
Angyalföld
Újpalota
Rákosszentmihály
Árpádföld
Cinkota
Vérhalom
Buda
Zugló
Sashalom
Virányos
Zugliget
Mátyásföld
Pest
Józsefváros
Rákosliget
Rákos-patak
Gazdagrét
Ferencváros
Kőbánya
Rákoskert
Sasad
Rákoskeresztúr
Erzsébet-Telep
Kelenföld
Rákoshegy
Budaörs
BUDAPEST
Kispest
BUDAPEST FERIHEGY (BUD)
Pesterzsébet
Pestlőrinc
Budafok
Csepel
Csepel-sziget
Budatétény
Soroksár
Pestimre
Nagytétény
Háros
Csillagtelep
Vecsés
Gyál
Halásztelek
Duna (Danube)
East from Greenwich


## CENTRAL BUDAPEST

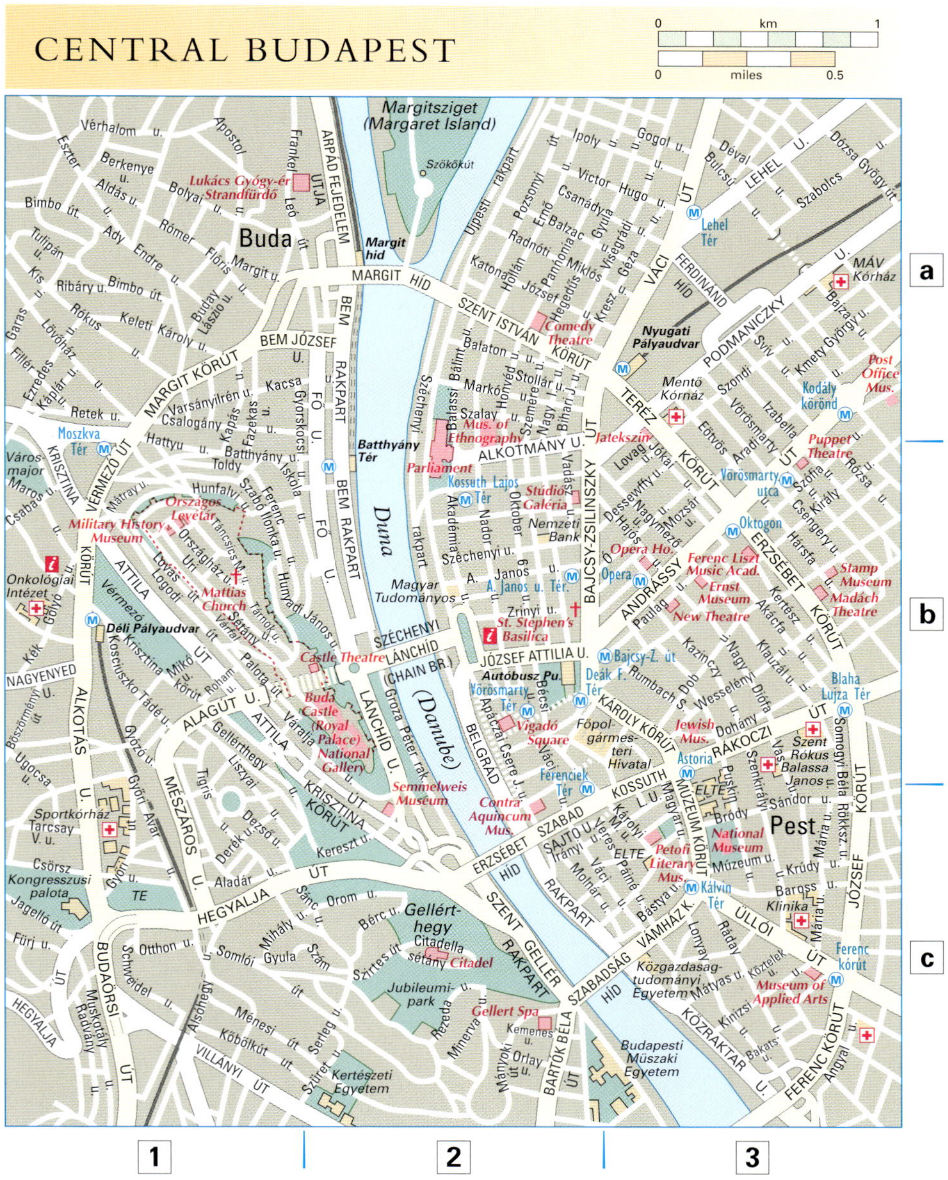

Margitsziget (Margaret Island)
Buda
Margit híd
MARGIT KÖRÚT
Batthyány Tér
Parliament
Duna
(Danube)
Magyar Tudományos
SZÉCHENYI LÁNCHÍD (CHAIN BR.)
Castle Theatre
Buda Castle (Royal Palace) National Gallery
Mátyás Church
Déli Pályaudvar
Nyugati Pályaudvar
St. Stephen's Basilica
Opera
Vigadó Square
Semmelweis Museum
Gellért-hegy Citadella
Gellért Spa
Jubileumi-park
National Museum
Museum of Applied Arts
Budapesti Műszaki Egyetem
Közgazdaság-tudományi Egyetem
Pest


## BUENOS AIRES, ARGENTINA

Acassuso
Juan Anchorena
Martinez
La Lucila
Olivos
Rio de la Plata
Buenos Aires
Villa Adelina
Vicente Lopez
Carapachay
Munro
Florida
Ciudad Universitaria
Saavedra
Nuñez
JORGE NEWBERY
Villa Ballester
BUENOS AIRES
Belgrano
General San Martin
Villa Urquiza
Colegiales
Chacarrita
Palermo
Puerto Retiro
Villa Bosch
Villa Lynch
Recoleta
Retiro
La Paternal
San Nicolás
Villa Devota
Almagro
Monserrat
Balvanera
San Telmo
Puerto Madero
Floresta
Caballito
Constitución
Villa Ciudadela
Versailles
Boedo
San Cristobal
Flores
Parque Chacabuco
Parque Patricios
La Boca
Ramos Mejia
Liniers
Mataderos
Nueva Pompeya
Barracas
Avellaneda
San Justo
Villa Diamante
Sarandi
Villa Dominico
Tablada
Villa Madero
Villa Lugano
Gerli
Villa C. Colon
Tapiales
Caraza
Ciudad General Belgrano
Aldo Bonzi
Lanús
Villa Barilari
TO BUENOS AIRES EZEIZA (EZE)
La Salada
Remedios de Escalada
Monte Chingolo
West from Greenwich


## CAIRO, EGYPT

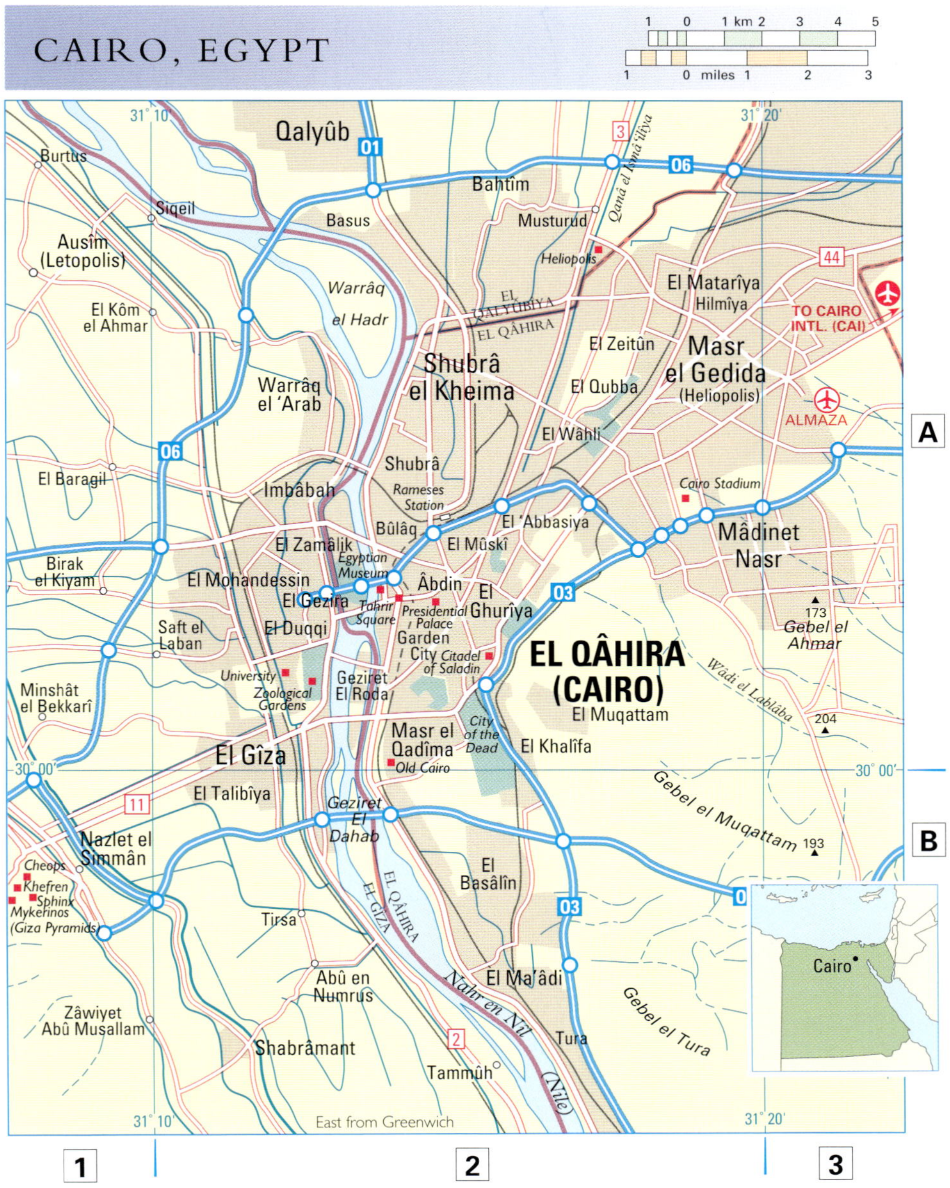

Qalyûb
Burtus
Bahtîm
Sigeil
Basus
Mustur
Ausîm (Letopolis)
Heliopolis
El Matarîya
El Kôm el Ahmar
Warrâq el Hadr
TO CAIRO INTL. (CAI)
El Zeitûn
Shubrâ el Kheima
Mars el Gedida (Heliopolis)
Warrâq el 'Arab
El Qubba
ALMAZA
El Wâhli
El Baragil
Shubrâ
Imbâbah
Cairo Stadium
Bûlâq
El 'Abbasiya
El Zamâlik
Mâdinet Nasr
Birak el Kiyam
El Mohandessin
El Mûski
Âbdîn
El Gezîra
El Ghurîya
El Duqqi
Saft el Laban
Citadel of Saladin
EL QÂHIRA (CAIRO)
Gezîret El Rôda
El Muqattam
Minshât el Bekkarî
Masr el Qadîma
El Khalîfa
El Gîza
El Talibîya
Gezîret El Dahab
Gebel el Muqattam
Nazlet el Simmân
El Basâtîn
Tirsa
El Ma'âdi
Abû en Numrus
Zâwiyet Abû Musallam
Shabrâmant
Tamûh
Tura
Gebel el Tura
Nahr en Nîl (Nile)
Cairo
East from Greenwich

## CAPE TOWN, SOUTH AFRICA

ATLANTIC OCEAN
Table Bay
CAPE TOWN
Milnerton
Tijgerhof
Goodwood
Parow
Vasco
Elsies-rivier
Brooklyn
Windermere
Maitland
Green Point
Sea Point
Signal Hill
Woodstock
Salt River
Thornton
Tamboers-kloof
Zonnebloem
Clifton
Vredehoek
Pinelands
Langa
Bishop Lavis
Bonteheuwel
Camps Bay
Devil's Peak
Table Mountain
Rondebosch
Athlone
Bridge-town
Heideveld
CAPE TOWN INTERNATIONAL (CPT)
Twelve Apostles
Cape Peninsula Nat. Park
Claremont
Crawford
Manenberg
Bishops-court
Kenilworth
Lansdowne
Nyanga
Llandudno
Wynberg
Constantia
Youngsfield
Wetton
Ottery
Plumstead
Hout Bay
Constantiaberg
Diep-rivier
Parkwood
Lotus River
Mitchell's Plain
Tokai Plantation
Bergvliet
Heathfield
Grassy Park
Cape Flats
Retreat
Strandfontein
Westlake
Lakeside
Silvermine Nature Reserve
Kalkbaaiberg
Muizenberg
False Bay
Noordhoek
East from Greenwich
Cape Town
1


## CENTRAL CAPE TOWN

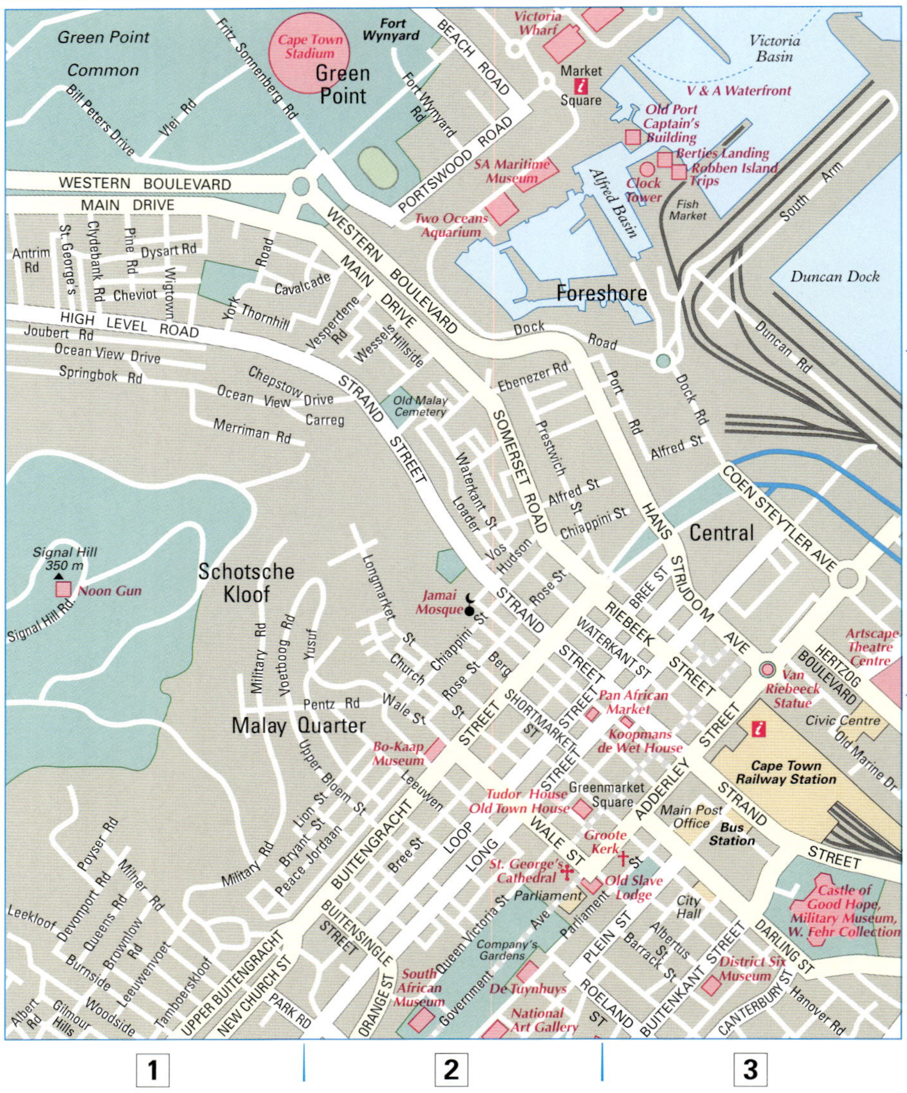

Green Point Common
Cape Town Stadium
Green Point
Fort Wynyard
Victoria Wharf
Victoria Basin
V & A Waterfront
Market Square
Old Port Captain's Building
Robben Island Trips
Clock Tower
Fish Market
SA Maritime Museum
Two Oceans Aquarium
Alfred Basin
Duncan Dock
WESTERN BOULEVARD
MAIN DRIVE
HIGH LEVEL ROAD
Foreshore
Signal Hill 350 m
Noon Gun
Schotsche Kloof
Jamai Mosque
Central
Malay Quarter
Bo-Kaap Museum
Pan African Market
Koopmans de Wet House
Greenmarket Square
Old Town House
St. George's Cathedral
Groote Kerk
Old Slave Lodge
Parliament
Company's Gardens
City Hall
Cape Town Railway Station
Castle of Good Hope, Military Museum, W. Fehr Collection
District Six Museum
South African Museum
De Tuynhuys
National Art Gallery
Artscape Theatre Centre
Van Riebeeck Statue
Civic Centre
Main Post Office
Bus Station
1
2
3


## COPENHAGEN, DENMARK

Furesø
Lille Værløse
Kirke Værløse
Virum
Brede
Jægersborg Dyrehave
Tårbæk
Klampenborg
Øresund
Frederiksdal
Kongens Lyngby
Store Hareskov
Bagsværd Sø
Ordrup
Jonstrup
Hareskovby
Bagsværd
Jægersborg
Skovshoved
Måløv
Hjortespring
Vangede
Gentofte
Charlottenlund
Oslo
Pederstrup
Buddinge
Hellerup
Ballerup
Herlev
Gladsakse
Søborg
Ågerup
Svanemøllen
Rønne Swinoujscie Klaipeda
Skovlunde
Husum
Bispebjerg
KØBENHAVN
Ejby
Brønshøj
Fælledparken
Refshaleøen
Vestskoven
Islev
Risby
Herstedøster
Vanløse
Rosenborg Slot
Amalienborg Slot
Rødovre
Frederiksberg
Christianshavn
Tivoli
Carlsberg Brewery
Glostrup
Brøndbyøster
Valby
Sundbyerne
Albertslund
Taastrup
Hvidovre
Ørestad
Kastrup
Øresund Bridge
Vallensbæk
Tranegilde
Brøndby-vester
Avedøre
Kalveboderne
Tårnby
KØBENHAVN KASTRUP (CPH)
Ishøj
Amager
Ishøj Strand
Brøndby Strand
Vallensbæk Strand
Hundige
Kalvebod Fælled
Store Magleby
Dragør
Hundige Strand
Ullerup
Greve Strand
Køge Bugt
Copenhagen
Kongelunden (Kings Forest)
Sydstranden
Søvang
East from Greenwich
Aflandshage
1
2
3


## CENTRAL COPENHAGEN

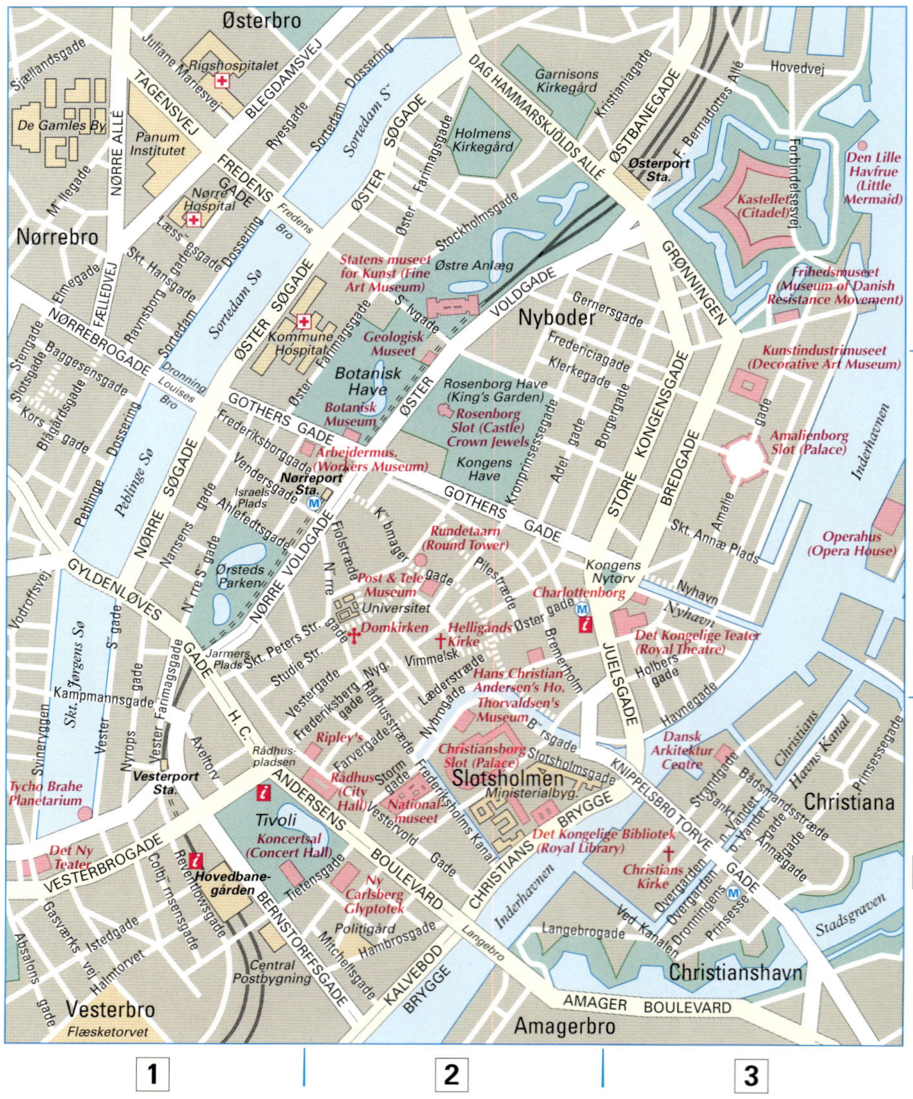

Østerbro
Rigshospitalet
Garnisons Kirkegård
Hovedvej
De Gamles By
Panum Instituttet
Holmens Kirkegård
Østerport Sta.
Den Lille Havfrue (Little Mermaid)
Kastellet (Citadel)
Nørrebro
Statens museet for Kunst (Fine Art Museum)
Østre Anlæg
Frihedsmuseet (Museum of Danish Resistance Movement)
Nyboder
Kommune Hospital
Geologisk Museet
Botanisk Have
Kunstindustrimuseet (Decorative Art Museum)
Rosenborg Have (King's Garden)
Rosenborg Slot (Castle) Crown Jewels
Amalienborg Slot (Palace)
Arbejdermus. (Workers Museum)
Nørreport Sta.
Kongens Have
Ørsteds Parken
Rundetaarn (Round Tower)
Operahus (Opera House)
Kongens Nytorv
Post & Tele Museum
Universitet
Charlottenborg
Domkirken
Helligånds Kirke
Det Kongelige Teater (Royal Theatre)
Hans Christian Andersen's Ho.
Thorvaldsen's Museum
Christiansborg Slot (Palace)
Slotsholmen
Dansk Arkitektur Centre
Tycho Brahe Planetarium
Vesterport Sta.
Rådhus (City Hall)
Nationalmuseet
Ripley's
Det Kongelige Bibliotek (Royal Library)
Christiana
Tivoli
Koncerthal (Concert Hall)
Christians Kirke
Det Ny Teater
Hovedbanegården
Ny Carlsberg Glyptotek
Central Postbygning
Christianshavn
Vesterbro
Fløsketorvet
Amagerbro
AMAGER BOULEVARD
1
2
3

## CENTRAL CHICAGO

0 km 0.5
0 miles 0.25
DIVISION ST
E DIVISION ST
Oak St Beach
Gold Coast
Outer Harbor
John Hancock Center
Water Tower Place
Lake Shore Park
W CHICAGO AVENUE
E CHICAGO AVE
Northwestern Memorial Hosp.
Near North
River North
W ONTARIO ST
E ONTARIO ST
W OHIO ST
E OHIO ST
Water Purification Plant
Olive Park
Ohio St Beach
Lake Point Tower
Navy Pier
Children's Museum
Ogden Slip
Wrigley Bldg.
Tribune Tower
Trump Tower
Merchandise Mart
Chicago River
E WACKER DRIVE
W WACKER DR
GEORGE HALAS DRIVE
AON Center
One Prudential Plaza
E RANDOLPH DRIVE
W RANDOLPH ST
City Hall & County Bldg.
Macy's on State St
Cultural Center
Jay Pritzker Pavilion
Ogilvie Transportation Center
Civic Opera Ho.
The Loop
Millennium Park
Grant Park
Art Institute of Chicago
Petrillo Music Shell
Chicago Yacht Club
Union Sta.
Willis Tower (Sears Tower)
E JACKSON DR
W JACKSON BLVD
Van Buren Sta.
Buckingham Fountain
Chicago Harbor
LAKE MICHIGAN
Main Post Office
LaSalle St. Sta.
CONGRESS PKWY
HARRISON ST
Printer's Row
S LAKE SHORE DRIVE
S MICHIGAN AVE
S COLUMBUS DRIVE
S CANAL ST
S Wells Street
1
2
3

Elevated rail lines

## CHICAGO, ILLINOIS

1 0 1 km 2 3 4 5
1 0 miles 1 2 3
Northbrook Historical Society Museum
Glencoe
Northbrook
Skokie Lakes
Winnetka
Kenilworth
Glenview
Northfield
Chicago
Baha'i Temple
Wilmette
Grosse Point Lighthouse & Lakefront
Mitchell Museum of the American Indian
Northwestern University
Evanston
Glenview Countryside
Golf
Golf Mill Shopping Center
Morton Grove
Skokie
Skokie Heritage Museum
Charles Gates Dawes House
Niles
Edison Park
Lincolnwood Town Center
Park Ridge
Lincolnwood
Rogers Park
LAKE
MICHIGAN
Loyola University
CHICAGO-O'HARE INTL.(ORD)
Norwood Park
Smith Forest Preserve
Jefferson Park
Rosemont
Swedish American Museum
Harwood Heights
Uptown
Norridge
Irving Park
Harlem Irving Plaza
Lincoln Park
Schiller Woods
Dunning
Portage Park
Avondale
Wrigley Field
Belmont Harbor
River Grove
The Brickyard
Belmont Cragin
Lakeview
Logan Square
De Paul Univ.
Old Town
Lincoln Park Zoo
Elmwood Park
Maywood Park Race Track
Chicago History Museum
Humboldt Park
Steppenwolf Theatre
Gold Coast
River Forest
Concordia Univ.
Oak Park
Austin
John Hancock Center
Near North
Navy Pier
Frank Lloyd Wright Home
West Town
Millennium Park
Garfield Park
Ogilvie Transportation Center
United Center
Chicago Harbor
Art Institute
Maywood
Union Sta.
Dwight D. Eisenhower Expwy.
Grant Park
LaSalle St. Sta.
Field Museum
Forest Park
Univ. of Illinois at Chicago
Adler Planetarium
Broadview
Douglas Park
Soldier Field
Miller Meadow
Cicero
Chinatown
CHICAGO
Burnham Park Harbor
Brookfield Zoo
North Riverside
Berwyn
Lawndale
Bridgeport
Illinois Inst. of Tech.
Riverside
Hawthorne Racecourse
U.S. Cellular Field
Stickney
Chicago Sanitary and Ship Canal
McKinley Park
Burnham Park
Forest View
Lyons
A.E. Stevenson Expwy.
Brighton Park
Dan Ryan Expwy.
Chicago Portage Nat. Hist. Site
McCook
Gage Park
Sherman Park
Washington Park
Hyde Park
Mus. of Science & Industry
Summit
CHICAGO-MIDWAY (MDW)
Chicago Lawn
Ogden Park
Univ. of Chicago
Jackson Park
Bedford Park
Englewood
Toyota Park
Marquette Park
South Shore
Bridgeview
Ford City Mall
Hayford
Ashburn
Chatham
Justice
Burbank
Chicago Skyway
Dan Ryan Woods
Hickory Hills
Hometown
Evergreen Park
Chicago Ridge Mall
Oak Lawn
St. Xavier University
The Plaza
Beverly
Chicago State University
Roseland
Palos Hills
Chicago Ridge
Mount Greenwood
Beverly Hills - Morgan Park Historic District
South Deering
Morgan Park
Pullman Historic District
Merrionette Park
Beverly Arts Center
Lake Calumet
Worth
Calumet Sag Channel
Tri-State Tollway
Alsip
Stony Creek
Bishop Ford Mem. Expwy.
Palos Park
Calumet Park
Palos Heights
Robbins
Blue Island
Little Calumet
Crestwood
Standard Bank Stadium
Posen
Riverdale
Chicago Gaelic Park
Midlothian
Dolton
Oak Forest
Dixmoor
Calumet City
Orland Park
Harvey
Phoenix
South Holland
Markham
West from Greenwich
87° 50'
87° 40'
42° 00'
41° 50'
41° 40'
A
B
C
D
1
2
3

Interstate route numbers U.S. route numbers State route numbers

## DUBAI, U.A.E.

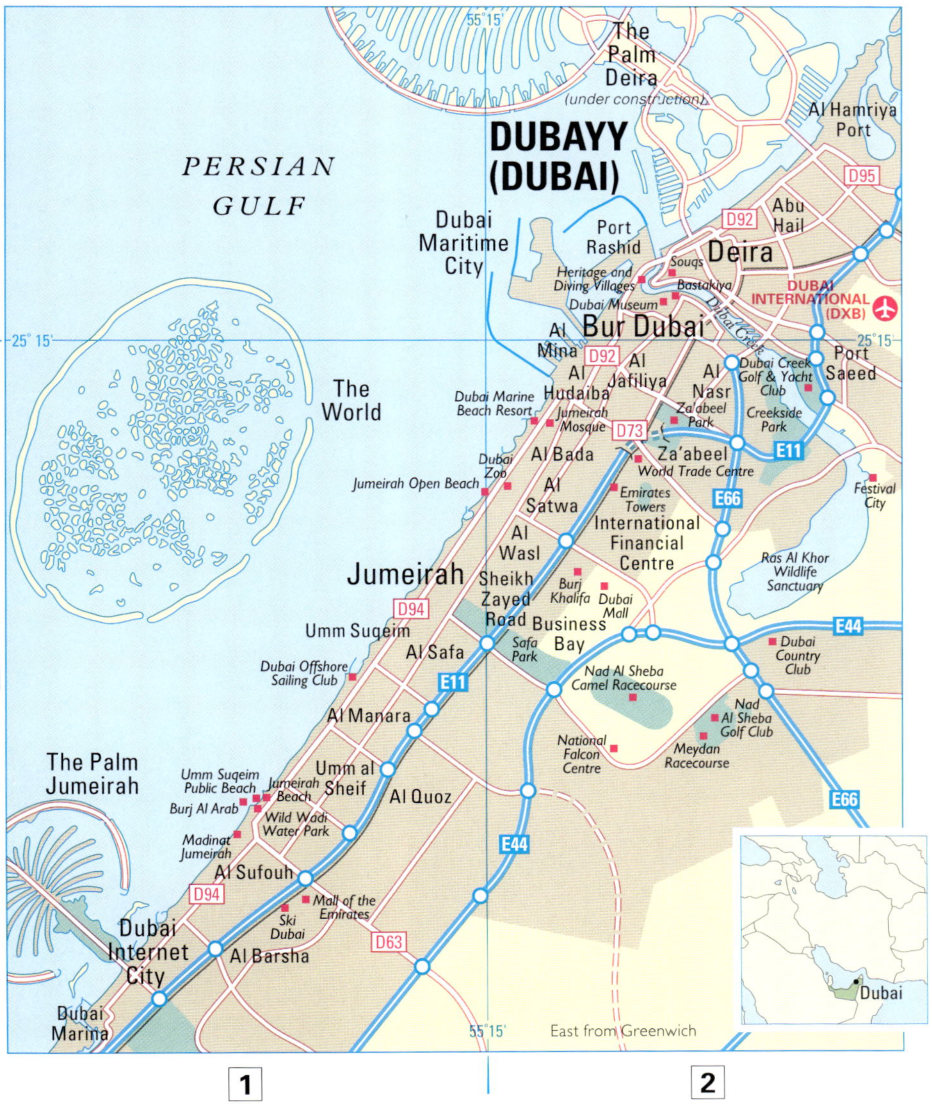
1 0 1 km 2 3 4 5
1 0 miles 1 2 3
The Palm Deira (under construction)
Al Hamriya Port
PERSIAN GULF
DUBAYY (DUBAI)
Dubai Maritime City
Port Rashid
Abu Hail
Deira
Souqs
Heritage and Diving Villages
Bastakiya
Dubai Museum
DUBAI INTERNATIONAL (DXB)
Bur Dubai
Al Mina
Port Saeed
Dubai Creek
The World
Al Hudaiba
Al Jafiliya
Al Nasr
Dubai Creek Golf & Yacht Club
Dubai Marine Beach Resort
Jumeirah Mosque
Za'abeel Park
Creekside Park
Al Bada
Za'abeel
Dubai Zoo
World Trade Centre
Jumeirah Open Beach
Al Satwa
Emirates Towers
Festival City
International Financial Centre
Al Wasl
Ras Al Khor Wildlife Sanctuary
Jumeirah
Sheikh Zayed Road
Burj Khalifa
Dubai Mall
Business Bay
Umm Suqeim
Al Safa
Safa Park
Dubai Country Club
Dubai Offshore Sailing Club
Nad Al Sheba Camel Racecourse
Al Manara
Nad Al Sheba Golf Club
The Palm Jumeirah
Umm Suqeim Public Beach
Jumeirah Beach
Umm al Sheif
National Falcon Centre
Meydan Racecourse
Burj Al Arab
Wild Wadi Water Park
Al Quoz
Madinat Jumeirah
Al Sufouh
Mall of the Emirates
Ski Dubai
Dubai Internet City
Al Barsha
Dubai Marina
Dubai
East from Greenwich
55° 15'
25° 15'
A
B
1
2

## DELHI, INDIA

1 0 1 km 2 3 4 5
1 0 miles 1 2 3
A
B
1
2
Daulatpur
Shamapur
Bhalswa Lake
Subhepur
Loni
NH1
Badli
Mukandpur
Jagatpur
Rampur
Bhalswa
Jahangirpuri
Wazirabad
UTTAR PRADESH
DELHI
Rithala
Haidarpur
Coronation Memorial
Outer Ring Road
Western Yamuna Canal
Grand Trunk Road
Pitampura
Saboli
Mangolpuri
University
Ghonda
Mandoli
Shakurbasti
Wazirpur
Babarpur
NH10
Rohtak Road
Shastrinagar
Rajpura
Civil Lines
Grand Trunk Road
Punjabi Bagh
Sabzi Mandi
Mutiny Meml.
ISBus Terminal
NH24
Jwalahari
Silampur
Shahdara
Najafgarh Drain
Delhi Station
Red Fort
Patel Nagar
Karol Bagh
DELHI
New Delhi Station
Tilak Nagar
Ring Road
Connaught Place
IG Stadium
Ghazipur
Jamakpuri
263
Mandaoli
NH24
The Ridge
Khichripur
India Gate
Commonwealth Games Village
Kondli
New Delhi
National Stadium
Noida
Naraina
Lodi Estate
Safdar Jang's Tomb
Humayun's Tomb
Chilla Saroda
Chanakyapuri
SAFDAR JANG
Yamuna
Mehram Nagar
Nehru Stadium
Kilokri
DELHI INDIRA GANDHI INTL. (DEL)
Moti Bagh
Mujahidpur
Okhla
Agra Canal
Ramakrishna Puram
Hauz Khas
Lotus Temple
Siri Fort
Mahipalpur
NH2
Kalkaji
Rangpuri
Qutb Minar
Mahrauli
NH8
East from Greenwich
77°10'
28°40'
Tughlakabad
Delhi

## CENTRAL DELHI

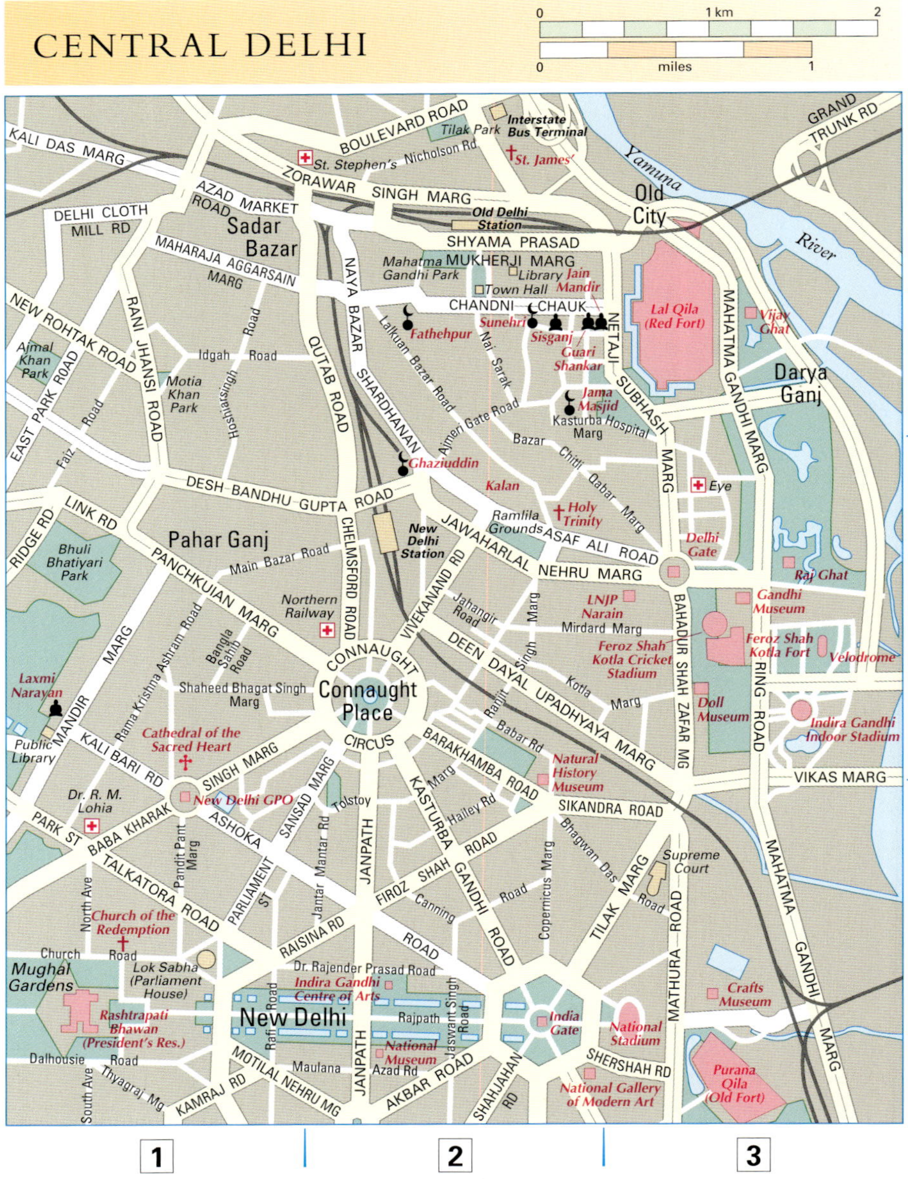
0 1 km 2
0 miles 1
1
2
3
KALI DAS MARG
BOULEVARD ROAD
Tilak Park
Interstate Bus Terminal
St. Stephen's
Nicholson Rd
St. James'
GRAND TRUNK RD
ZORAWAR SINGH MARG
Yamuna
Old City
AZAD MARKET ROAD
DELHI CLOTH MILL RD
Sadar Bazar
Old Delhi Station
SHYAMA PRASAD MUKHERJI MARG
River
MAHARAJA AGGARSAIN MARG
Mahatma Gandhi Park
Library
Jain Mandir
Town Hall
Lal Qila (Red Fort)
CHANDNI CHAUK
Vijay Ghat
Fatehpur
Sunehri
Sisganj
Gauri Shankar
NEW ROHTAK ROAD
RANI JHANSI ROAD
QUTAB ROAD
NAYA BAZAR
Jama Masjid
Darya Ganj
Ajmal Khan Park
Idgah
Motia Khan Park
SHARDHANAND
Kasturba Hospital
NETAJI SUBHASH MARG
MAHATMA GANDHI MARG
EAST PARK ROAD
Ghaziuddin
DESH BANDHU GUPTA ROAD
Kalan
Eye
LINK RD
Holy Trinity
RIDGE RD
Pahar Ganj
New Delhi Station
Ramlila Grounds
ASAF ALI ROAD
Delhi Gate
Bhuli Bhatiyari Park
Main Bazar Road
JAWAHARLAL NEHRU MARG
Raj Ghat
PANCHKUIAN MARG
CHELMSFORD ROAD
LNJP Narain
Gandhi Museum
Northern Railway
Mirdard Marg
Feroz Shah Kotla Cricket Stadium
Feroz Shah Kotla Fort
Velodrome
Laxmi Narayan
Shaheed Bhagat Singh Marg
Connaught Place
DEEN DAYAL UPADHYAYA MARG
Doll Museum
Indira Gandhi Indoor Stadium
Public Library
Cathedral of the Sacred Heart
CIRCUS
BARAKHAMBA ROAD
Natural History Museum
VIKAS MARG
Dr. R. M. Lohia
New Delhi GPO
SIKANDRA ROAD
BAHADUR SHAH ZAFAR MG
RING ROAD
PARK ST
BABA KHARAK SINGH MARG
ASHOKA
Tolstoy
KASTURBA GANDHI ROAD
Supreme Court
TILAK MARG
MAHATMA GANDHI MARG
TALKATORA ROAD
Church of the Redemption
FIROZ SHAH ROAD
JANPATH
RAISINA RD
Mughal Gardens
Lok Sabha (Parliament House)
Dr. Rajender Prasad Road
Indira Gandhi Centre of Arts
Crafts Museum
Rashtrapati Bhawan (President's Res.)
New Delhi
Rajpath
India Gate
National Stadium
MATHURA ROAD
Dalhousie Road
National Museum
SHERSHAH RD
Purana Qila (Old Fort)
Maulana Azad Rd
National Gallery of Modern Art
KAMRAJ RD
MOTILAL NEHRU MG
AKBAR ROAD
SHAHJAHAN RD

Shrine Mosque

## DUBLIN, IRELAND

1 0 1 km 2 3 4 5
1 0 miles 1 2 3
A
B
1
2
3
6°20'
6°10'
53°20'
Swords
Malahide
IRISH SEA
N1
Cloghran
DUBLIN (DUB)
Kinsaley
Portmarnock
St. Margaret's
Dublin
M50
N32
Carrigeen Bay
Ireland's Eye
Poppintree
Santry
M1
Darndale
Baldoyle
Howth
Corduff
Finglas
Ballymun
Kilmore
Donaghmede
N3
Glasnevin
Beaumont
Edenmore
Sutton
Coolock
Kilbarrack
Howth Head
Whitehall
Artane
Raheny
National Botanic Gardens
Killester
Ashtown
Cabra
Drumcondra
Marino
Clontarf
Dollymount
North Bull Island
Castleknock
Croke Park
Phoenix Park
Dublin Zoo
Dublin Harbour
Isle of Man
Liffey
Chapelizod
Heuston Sta.
Connolly Sta.
Palmerston
Kilmainham Gaol
Kilmainham
Trinity College
Holyhead Liverpool
Ballyfermot
Inchicore
Guinness Hop Store
Ringsend
Aviva Stadium
Grand Canal
Dolphin's Barn
Ranelagh
Sandymount
DUBLIN
Drimnagh
The Shaw Birthplace
Dublin Bay
Bluebell
Harolds Cross
Donnybrook
Merrion
M50
Crumlin
Walkinstown
Clonskeagh
N7
Milltown
Booterstown
Kimmage
N11
Blackrock
Greenhills
Rathfarnham
Windy Arbour
Mount Merrion
Holyhead
Kilnamanagh
N31
Scotsman's Bay
Tymon North
Templeogue
Churchtown
Monkstown
Dún Laoghaire
Tallaght
Willbrook
Dundrum
Kilmacud
Stillorgan
Glasthule
Ballyboden
Deans Grange
Dalkey
Firhouse
Oldbawn
Dodder
Edmondstown
Ballinteer
Sandyford
Foxrock
Sallynoggin
Dalkey Island
M50
Leopardstown
Killiney
Friarstown
Kilmashogue Mt.
Stepaside
Cabinteely
Killiney Bay
Carrickmines
Ballybrack
Loughlinstown
Killakee
Tibradden Mt.
536
Two Rock Mt.
Kilternan
Glenasmole Reservoirs
Cruagh Mt.
Shankill
582
Glendoo Mt.
275
Ballymorefinn Hill
Glencullen
M11
Bray
West from Greenwich

## CENTRAL DUBLIN

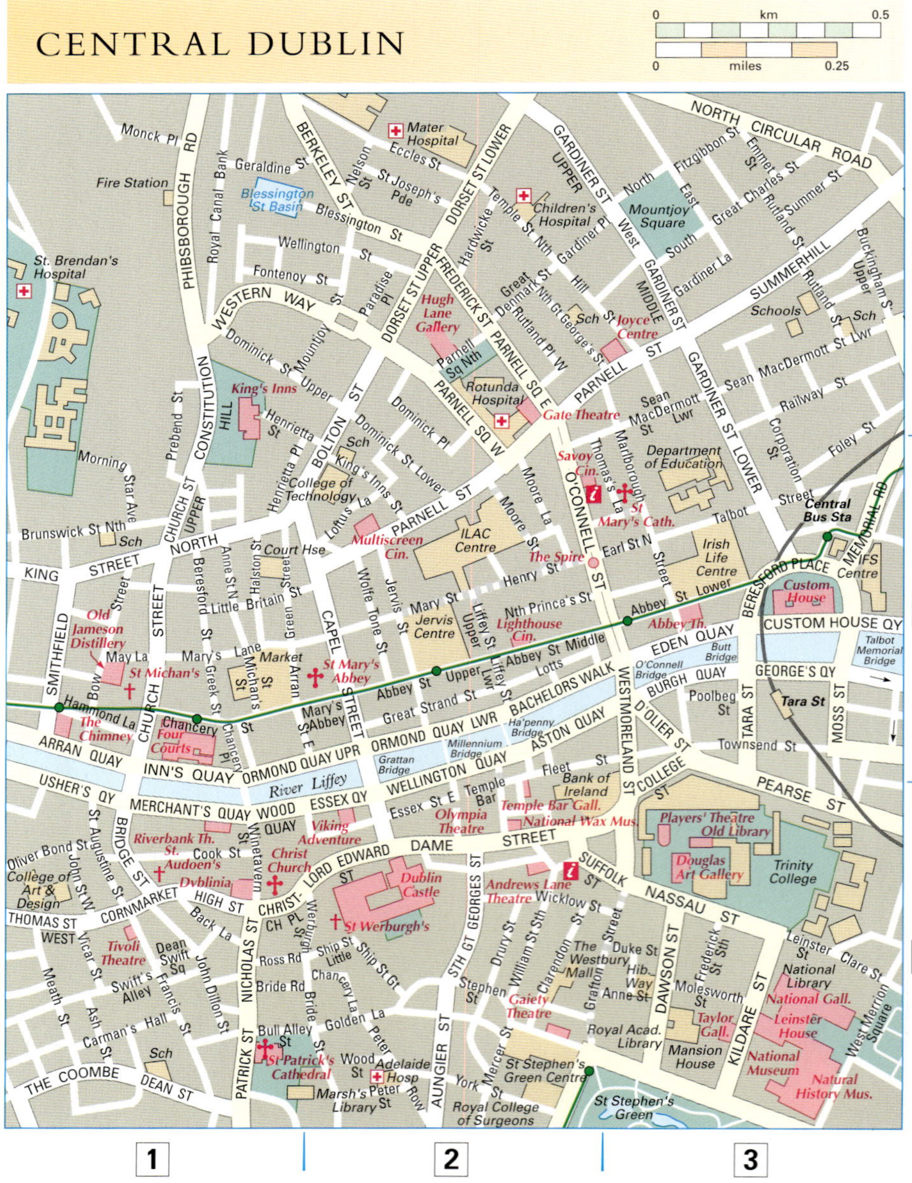
0 km 0.5
0 miles 0.25
1
2
3
NORTH CIRCULAR ROAD
Monck Pl
Mater Hospital
Eccles St
Geraldine St
Fire Station
St. Joseph's Pde
Children's Hospital
Mountjoy Square
Blessington St Basin
Blessington St
St. Brendan's Hospital
Wellington St
Fontenoy St
WESTERN WAY
Hugh Lane Gallery
Joyce Centre
Schools
SUMMERHILL
King's Inns
Rotunda Hospital
Gate Theatre
Department of Education
College of Technology
Savoy Cin.
St Mary's Cath.
Central Bus Sta
Multiscreen Cin.
ILAC Centre
The Spire
Irish Life Centre
Talbot
Brunswick St Nth
KING STREET NORTH
Court Hse
Jervis Centre
Lighthouse Cinema
Abbey Th.
Custom House
CUSTOM HOUSE QY
Old Jameson Distillery
St Mary's Abbey
EDEN QUAY
GEORGE'S QY
St Michan's
Abbey St Upper
Abbey St Middle
BACHELORS WALK
BURGH QUAY
Tara St
Four Courts
ORMOND QUAY UPR
The Chimney
Ha'penny Bridge
ASTON QUAY
ARRAN QUAY
INN'S QUAY
River Liffey
WELLINGTON QUAY
PEARSE ST
USHER'S QY
MERCHANT'S QUAY
WOOD QUAY
ESSEX QY
Temple Bar
Bank of Ireland
Players' Theatre
Old Library
Olympia Theatre
Temple Bar Gall.
National Wax Mus.
Riverbank Th.
Viking Adventure
DAME STREET
Douglas Art Gallery
Trinity College
St Audoen's
Christ Church
Dublin Castle
Andrews Lane Theatre
NASSAU ST
College of Art & Design
Dublinia
HIGH ST
LORD EDWARD
St Werburgh's
THOMAS ST WEST
CORNMARKET
Tivoli Theatre
The Westbury Mall
National Library
National Gall.
Leinster House
Gaiety Theatre
Molesworth
Royal Acad. Library
Mansion House
National Museum
Natural History Mus.
St Patrick's Cathedral
Marsh's Library
Adelaide Hosp
St Stephen's Green Centre
Royal College of Surgeons
St Stephen's Green
THE COOMBE
DEAN ST
PATRICK ST
AUNGIER ST
DAWSON ST
KILDARE ST

Light Rail (LUAS)

## EDINBURGH, U.K.

1 0 1 km 2 3 4 5
1 0 miles 1 2 3
Dunfermline
FIFE
Aberdour Castle
Aberdour
Burntisland
Kinghorn
Pettycur
Rosyth
Hillend
Dalgety Bay
Inverkeithing
Inchcolm
Inchkeith
Edinburgh
Firth of Forth
Forth Road Bridge
North Queensferry
Forth Rail Bridge
Inchmickery
Queensferry
Cramond I.
Dalmeny House
Dalmeny
Cramond
Granton
Newhaven
HMY Britannia
Leith
Trinity
Davidson's Mains
Pilton
Kirkliston
Cramond Bridge
Braepark
Drylaw
Royal Botanic Gardens
Warriston
EDINBURGH
Turnhouse
Clermiston
Duddingston
Portobello
Joppa
Palace of Holyroodhouse
Scottish Parliament
Arthur's Seat
EDINBURGH (EDI)
Ravelston
Ingliston
North Gyle
Murrayfield
Haymarket
Castle
Gogar
Corstorphine
Murrayfield
Newington
Craigmillar
Newcraighall
Ratho Station
Edinburgh Park
Sighthill
Gorgie
Morningside
Niddrie
Ratho
Union Canal
Royal Observatory
Danderhall
Millerhill
Bonnington
Hermiston
Wester Hailes
Craiglockhart
Braid
Colinton
Fairmilehead
Gilmerton
Wilkieston
Juniper Green
Oxgangs
Kaimes
Liberton
WEST LOTHIAN
Burnwynd
Dalkeith
Kirknewton
Currie
Straiton
Eskbank
Balerno
Allermuir Hill
Loanhead
Newbattle
Water of Leith
Malleny Mills
Harlaw Reservoir
Bilston
Bonyrigg and Lasswade
Woodhouselee
Polton
Easter Howgate
Roslin
Newtongrange
Glencorse Reservoir
Milton Bridge
Threipmuir Reservoir
North Esk
Rosewell
Harperrig Reservoir
Scald Law
Penicuik
Auchendinny
MIDLOTHIAN
Silverburn
Kirkhill
Carrington
West from Greenwich
3°20'
3°10'
56°00'
55°50'
1
2
3
A823
M90
A921
A904
A90
M9
A8
M8
A720
A71
A70
A702
A701
A7
A1
A768
A720

## CENTRAL EDINBURGH

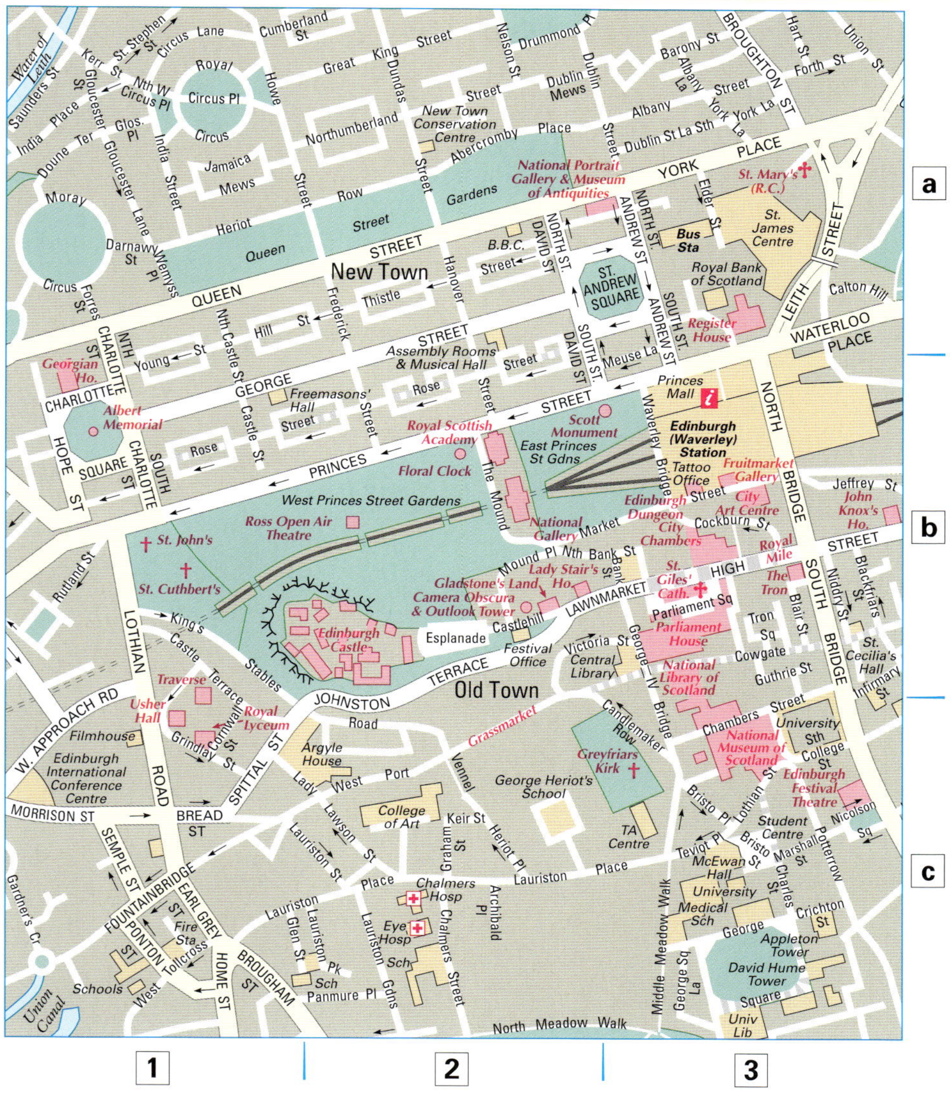
0 km 0.5
0 miles 0.25
Circus Lane
Royal Circus
Cumberland St
Great King Street
Drummond Pl
Barony St
Broughton St
Hart St
Union St
Northumberland
New Town Conservation Centre
Abercromby
Dublin Mews
Albany
York La
Forth St
Dublin St La Sth
Place
Heriot Row
Queen Street
Jamaica Mews
National Portrait Gallery & Museum of Antiquities
York Place
St. Mary's (R.C.)
St. James Centre
Bus Sta
Royal Bank of Scotland
St. Andrew Square
Queen Street
New Town
Thistle
B.B.C.
Young St
George
Street
Assembly Rooms & Musical Hall
Rose
Freemasons' Hall
Register House
Waterloo Place
Calton Hill
Georgian Ho.
Albert Memorial
Charlotte Square
Royal Scottish Academy
Scott Monument
East Princes St Gdns
Princes Mall
Edinburgh (Waverley) Station
Fruitmarket Gallery
Princes Street
Floral Clock
West Princes Street Gardens
Ross Open Air Theatre
Tattoo Office
City Art Centre
John Knox's Ho.
Edinburgh Dungeon
City Chambers
Royal Mile
St. John's
St. Cuthbert's
National Gallery
Market
Mound Pl
Lady Stair's Ho.
Gladstone's Land
Camera Obscura & Outlook Tower
St. Giles' Cath.
Parliament Sq
Parliament House
The Tron
High Street
Edinburgh Castle
Esplanade
Castlehill
Lawnmarket
Festival Office
Victoria St
Central Library
National Library of Scotland
Cowgate
St. Cecilia's Hall
Usher Hall
Traverse
Royal Lyceum
Johnston Terrace
Old Town
Grassmarket
Greyfriars Kirk
Chambers Street
National Museum of Scotland
University
Edinburgh Festival Theatre
Filmhouse
Edinburgh International Conference Centre
Argyle House
West Port
George Heriot's School
College of Art
Student Centre
Morrison St
Bread St
Lothian Road
Lauriston Place
TA Centre
Teviot Pl
McEwan Hall
University Medical Sch
Chalmers Hosp
Eye Hosp
Sch
Fire Sta
Tollcross
Ponton St
Fountainbridge
Earl Grey St
Home St
Brougham St
Schools
Union Canal
Appleton Tower
David Hume Tower
George Square
Univ Lib
Middle Meadow Walk
North Meadow Walk
a
b
c
1
2
3

## GUANGZHOU, CHINA

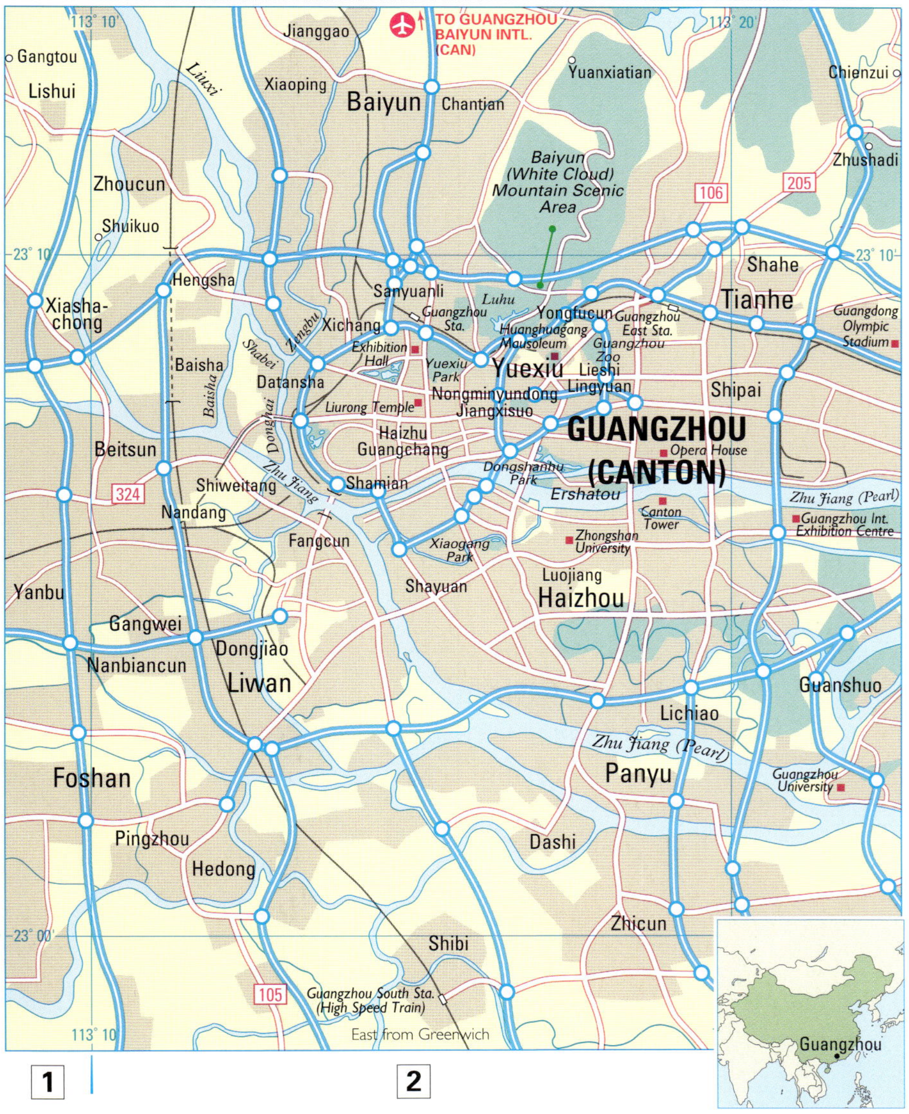
1 0 1 km 2 3 4 5
1 0 miles 1 2 3
TO GUANGZHOU BAIYUN INTL. (CAN)
Gangtou
Jianggao
Lishui
Liuxi
Xiaoping
Baiyun
Chantian
Yuanxiatian
Chienzui
Zhushadi
Zhoucun
Baiyun (White Cloud) Mountain Scenic Area
Shuikuo
Shahe
Hengsha
Sanyuanli
Guangzhou Sta.
Luhu
Tianhe
Xiasha-chong
Xichang
Yongfucun
Guangzhou East Sta.
Guangdong Olympic Stadium
Exhibition Hall
Huanghuagang Mausoleum
Guangzhou Zoo
Baisha
Yuexiu Park
Yuexiu
Liesh
Shipai
Datansha
Nongminyundong
Lingyuan
Liurong Temple
Jiangxisuo
GUANGZHOU (CANTON)
Beitsun
Haizhu Guangchang
Opera House
Shiweitang
Shamian
Dongshanhu Park
Ershatou
Zhu Jiang (Pearl)
Guangzhou Int. Exhibition Centre
Nandang
Canton Tower
Fangcun
Xiaogang Park
Zhongshan University
Luojiang
Haizhou
Yanbu
Shayuan
Gangwei
Dongjiao
Nanbiancun
Liwan
Guanshuo
Lichiao
Foshan
Zhu Jiang (Pearl)
Panyu
Guangzhou University
Pingzhou
Dashi
Hedong
Shibi
Zhicun
Guangzhou South Sta. (High Speed Train)
East from Greenwich
Guangzhou
113°10'
113°20'
23°10'
23°00'
106
205
324
105
1
2

## HELSINKI, FINLAND

1 0 1 km 2 3 4 5
1 0 miles 1 2 3
Kongo
Linna
Seutula
Mäkiniitty
Maantiekylä
Ketunkorpi
Vestra
Keimola
Hanala
Rekola
HELSINKI-VANTAA (HEL)
Lahnus
Kivistö
Koivupää
Harjusuo
Vantaa
Odilampi
Petas
Vantaanpuisto
Hiekkaharju
Röylä
Simonkylä
Ita Hakkila
Perusmaki
Vantaankoski
Vantaa
Ylästö
Askisto
Niiperi
Tikkurila
Gobbacka
Martinkylä
Silvolanteko järvi
Puistola
Haltiala
Tapanila
Hakunila
Hämeenkylä
Friherrs
Haltiavuori
Kaivoksela
Pitkäjärvi
Paloheinä
Malmi
TATTARISUO
Rastaala
Laaksolahti
Pakila
Pukinmäki
Rajakylä
Mellunmäki
Konala
Lintuvaara
Pirkkola
Pihlajamäki
Oulunkylä
Mellunkylä
Haaga
Myllypuro
Vartiokylä
Kauniainen
Käpylä
Viikki
Kilo
Leppävaara
Puotila
Pasila
Herttoniemi
Rastila
Nuijala
Munkkiniemi
HELSINKI
Roihuvuori
Tuomarila
Henttaa
Laajalahti
Otaniemi
Olympic Stadium
Tammisalo
Mankkaa
Vartiosaari
Friluftsmuseum
Parliament and National Museum
Kulosaari
Olari
Tapiola
Lehtisaari
Temppeliaukio Church
Laajasalo
Nöykkiö
Hietaniemi
Cathedral
Jollas
Westend
Villinki
Lauttasaari
Suomenlinna
Nokkala
Pihlajasaari
Santahamina
Miessaari
Melkki
Svinö
Stockholm, Lubeck, Travemund, Tallinn, Rostock
Vallisaari
Helsinki
Harmaja
East from Greenwich
24°50'
25°00'
60°20'
60°10'
E12
E18
E75
A
B
C
1
2
3

## HONG KONG, CHINA

1 0 1 km 2 3 4 5
1 0 miles 1 2 3
Shenzhen Wan (Deep Bay)
Hung Shui Kiu
Ha Pak Nai
Lam Tei
Ching Chung Koon Temple
Black Point
Castle Peak 583
Tuen Mun
Tai Tong Tsuen
Tai Lam Country Park
Tai Lam Chung Reservoir
506
New Territories
Shek Kong
Tai Mo Shan 957
Grassy Hill 645
Cheung Shue Ta
Ma On Shan
Three Fathoms Cove
Kei Ling Ha
Pak Tam
Shan Mei
Sheung Fa Shan
Chuen Lung
Shing Mun Country Park
Shing Mun Res.
Needle Hill 532
Fo Tan
Temple of the 10 000 Buddhas
Tai Shui Hang
Ma On Shan 702
Wong Chuk Yeung
Wong Chuk Wan
Lung Kwu Tan
Tap Shek Kok
Lung Kwu Chau
Urmston Road
Lo Wai
Wo Yi Hop
Sha Tin
Lung Mei
Inner Port Shelter
Sai Kung
Chai Wan Kok
Tai Wai
Ma On Shan Country Park
Shek Kok Mei
So Kwun Wat
Ting Kau
Tsuen Wan
Kwai Chung
Hin Keng
Mau Tso Ngam
Pak Kong
Sham Tseng
Ngau Kok Wan
Tai Wo Hau
Kam Shan Country Park
Lion Rock Country Park
Tai Lo Shan 577
Ho Chung
Sharp Island
Hebe Haven
Kau Sai Chau
Castle Peak Bay
Pearl Island
Pillar Point
Tsing Lung Tau
Beacon Hill 452
Tsz Wan Shan
Ma Nam Wat
Pak Chau
Sha Chau
Kap Shui Mun
Ma Wan
Ma Wan Channel
Tsing Yi
Rambler Channel
Cheung Sha Wan
Kowloon Peak 602
Ngau Chi Wan
Wo Mei
Chuk Kok
Port Shelter
Tai Po Tsai
Zhujiang Kou (Mouth of the Pearl R.)
The Brothers
Sunny Bay
22° 20'
Sham Shui Po
Kowloon Tong
San Po Kong
Tseng Lan Shue
Ngau Tau Kok
Tseung Kwan
Silverstrand
Hang Hau
Shelter Island
Stonecutters Island (Ngong Shuen Chau)
Mong Kok
Kowloon Bay
Kwun Tong
AsiaWorld-Expo
HONG KONG INTERNATIONAL (HKG)
Chek Lap Kok
Siu Ho
Disneyland Hong Kong
HONG KONG (XIANGGANG)
Kowloon
To Kwa Wan
Hung Hom
Cha Kwo Ling
Lam Tin
Tiu Keng Leng
Mang Kung Uk
Discovery Bay
Lo Fu Tau 465
Union Square
Tsim Sha Tsui
High Junk Peak 344
Tai Wan Tau
Pearl River Bridge
Sha Lo Wan
San Tau
Tung Chung Bay
Tai Ho
Siu Kau Yi Chau
Kau Yi Chau
Green Island
Sai Ying Pun
Kennedy Town
Victoria Harbour
North Point
Sai Wan Ho
Junk Bay
Chik Sha
Clear Water Bay
Tung Chung
Lantau North Country Park
Tai Shui Hang
Peng Chau
Sulphur Channel
Hong Kong Univ.
Sheung Wan
Man Mo Temple
Wan Chai
Victoria
Shau Kei Wan
Lei Yue Mun
Sheung Lau Wan
Po Toi O
Sai Tso Wan
Sham Wat
Lantau Island
Sunset Peak 869
Mui Wo
Silver Mine Bay
Victoria Peak 554
Happy Valley
528
Sai Wan
Joss House Bay
Tei Tong Tsui
Tai O
Big Buddha
Ngong Ping
Sunshine Island
Pok Fu Lam
Aberdeen Country Park
Chai Wan
Lantau Peak 934
Hei Ling Chau
Hong Kong Island
Wong Chuk Hang
Violet Hill
Tai Tam Tuk Res.
Shek O Country Park
Tung Lung Chau
Wah Fu
Aberdeen
Keung Shan
Chi Ma Wan
Chung Hau
Boulder Pt.
433
Tai Tam Country Park
Tai Long Wan
Tathong Channel
Lantau South Country Park
Shek Pik Reservoir
Tong Fuk
Pui O Wan
Pak Kok
Ap Lei Chau
Deep Water Bay
Repulse Bay
Shek O
Tathong Pt.
Yi O San Tsuen
Cheung Sha
Chi Ma Wan Peninsula
Luk Chau Wan
East Lamma Channel
George Island (Luk Chau)
Ocean Park
Middle Island
The Twins 386
466
Tai Long
Tai Hom Wan Tsuen Sham
Shek Pik
Tong Fuk Miu Wan
Shui Hau
Tai Long Wan
Cha Kwo Chau
Adamasta Channel
Cheung Chau
West Lamma Channel
Yung Shue Wan
Lo So Shing
Round Island
Stanley
D'Aguilar Peninsula
Tai Tam Bay
Hok Tsui
Kau Pai Chau
Fan Lau
Shek Kwu Chau
Ha Mei Wan
Picnic Bay
Sok Kwu Wan
Lamma Island
Tung O Wan
Tung O
353
Stanley Peninsula
Sheung Sze Mun
Beaufort Island
Bluff Head
Po Toi Islands
Soko Islands
South China Sea
114° 00'
114° 10'
East from Greenwich
Hong Kong
A
B
1
2
3


## ISTANBUL, TURKEY

1 0 1 km 2 3 4 5
1 0 miles 1 2 3
A
B
C
Göktürk
Bahçeköy
29° 00'
Anadolukavağı
41° 10'
Pirinçi
010
Sarıyer
Yuşa Tepesi 197
Kemerburgaz
Büyükdere
Beykoz
Alibey Barajı
Kâğıthane
Tarabya
Cebecci
Yeniköy
Paşabahçe
Ayazağa
İstanbul Technical University
İstinye
Emirgan
Bosporus
020
Türk Telekom Arena
Boyacıköy
Çubuklu
Kanlıca
Göz Tepe 285
Gaziosmanpaşa
E80
O-2
Rumelihisarı
Rumeli Hisarı
Elmalı Barajı
128
Levent
Bebek
Anadoluhisarı
Alibeyköy
Kâğıthane
Mecidiyeköy
Arnavutköy
Kandilli
E80
Küçükköy
020
O-1
Küçüksu
O-3
Şişli
Ortaköy
Vaniköy
Atışalen
Eyüp Mosque
Beşiktaş
Yıldız Park
Çengelköy
Bayrampaşa
O-3
Esenler
Eyüp
Hasköy
Taksim
Beylerbeyi
İnkilap
Dolmabahçe Palace
Bağcılar
Fener
Beyoğlu
Galata
Kuzguncuk
Topkapı
Galata Tower
Leander's Tower
Çamlıca
020
Güngören
Golden Horn
Eminönü
Üsküdar
Kısıklı
Ümraniye
Bahçelievler
Topkapı Palace
Grand Bazaar
Hagia Sophia
Fatih
Blue Mosque
Selimiye
O-4
O-2
TO İSTANBUL ATATÜRK (IST)
E5
Esat Paşa
41° 00'
100
Samatya
Yenikapı
Yedikule
İSTANBUL
Kadıköy
O-1
TO İSTANBUL SABHA GÖKÇEN (SAW)
Bakırköy
Zeytinburnu
Kızıltoprak
E5
Fenerbahçe
Erenköy
İçerenköy
Marmara Denizi (Sea of Marmara)
100
Bostancı
İstanbul
29° 00'
1
2


## JAKARTA, INDONESIA

1 0 1 km 2 3 4 5
1 0 miles 1 2 3
106° 50'
JAVA SEA
Jakarta
Waduk Pluit
Teluk Jakarta
Koja Utara
TO JAKARTA SUKARNO-HATTA (CGK)
Sunda Kelapa Harbour
Taman Impian Jaya Ancol
Aquarium
Cilincing
Penjaringan
Ancol
Tanjung Priok
Koja
Angke
Kota
Jakarta Museum
Kapuk
International Trade Centre
Sunter
Jelambar
Tambora
Cengkareng
Taman Sari
Sawah Besar
JAKARTA
Grogol Petamburan
Gambir
Istiqlal Mosque
Kemayoran
Kelapa Gading
6° 10'
Kedoya
Tanjung Daren
Merdeka Palace
Cathedral
National Monument
National Museum
Gambir Station
Kayu Putih
Orchid Palace
Senen
Cempaka Putih
Race Course
Slipi
Kampung Bali
Menteng
Taman Ismail Marzuki
Welcome Monument
University
Pulo Gadung
Kebon Jeruk
Tanah Abang
Matraman
Rawamangun
Joglo
Parliament House
Setia Budi
Klender
Gelora Bung Karno Stadium
Jatinegara
Duren Sawit
Kebayoran Lama
Kuningan
JAKARTA
BANTEN
Kebayoran Baru
Tebet
Ciliwung
Pondok Kelapa
Tanah Kusir
Kemang
Halim
Bintaro Jaya
Mampang Prapatan
Jatiwaringin
Kramat Jati
Makasar
Cipete
Pondok Indah
Pasar Minggu
JAKARTA HALIM PERDANA KUSUMA (HLP)
Pondok Gede
Cilandak
Condet
East from Greenwich
1
2

## JERUSALEM, ISRAEL / W. BANK

Beitin
Deir Dibwan
Deir Ibzi'e
Ein Arik
Rām Allāh
El Bira
Pesagot
Beit Ghur at-Taht
Beit Ur al-Fawqa
Burqa
Khirbet el Misbah
Beitunya
Bet Horon
Kafr 'Aqab
Kokhav Ya'akov
Ma'ale Mikhmas
Mukhmas
Beit Liqya
Tira
Beit Duqu
Giv'at Ze'ev
Atarot
Qalandiya
Judeira
Jaba
Sha'ar Binymain
Beit I'nan
Giv'on
Jib
Ar Ram
Geva Binyamin
Khirbet Batin Abu Lihyah
Qubeiba
Beitlj'za
Bir Nabala
Ram
Neve Ya'akov
Beit Hanina
Pisgat Ze'ev
Hizma
Qatane
Bidu
Ma'ale Ha-Khamisha
Har Adar
Beit Surik
Ramot Allon
Pisgat O'mer
Almon
Beit Iksa
Shu'afat
Abu Ghosh
Kiryat Anavim
Beit Nekofa
Mevaseret Zion
WEST BANK
ISRAEL
Ramat Shafat
Ramat Eshkol
Anata
Mt. Scopus
TO TEL AVIV BEN GURION INTL. (TLV)
Ein Naquba
Ein Rafa
Motsa
Romema
JERUSALEM (Yerushalayim) (Al Quds)
Motsa Ilit
Har Nof
Kiryat Moshe
Giv'at Ye'arim
Tsova
Beit Zayit
Holocaust Memorial
Knesset
Israel Museum
National Hebrew University
Old City
Mt. of Olives
Ma'ale Adumim
Eizariya
Ramat Razi'el
Kiryat Ha Yovel
Bayit Va-Gan
Teddy Stadium
Abu Dis
Even Sapir
Ora
Aminadav
Manakhat
Malha Railway Sta.
Gonen
East Talpiyot
Kedar
Beit Safafa
Khirbet Jub e-Rum
Bar Giyora
Mevo Beitar
Al Walaja
Gilo
Sur Bahr
Har Homa
Wadi al Arayis
Ubeidiya
Batir
Rachel's Tomb
Bethlehem (Bayt Lahm)
Beit Lekhem
Mata
Tsur Hadassa
Har Gilo
Husan
Beit Jala
Beit Sahur
Basilica of Nativity
Juhdum
El Khadr
Wadi Fukin
Beitar Ilit
Daheisha
As Shawawra
Nahalin
Artas
East from Greenwich
Jerusalem

1 2

1949 Cease-fire line — Israeli security fence

## CENTRAL JERUSALEM

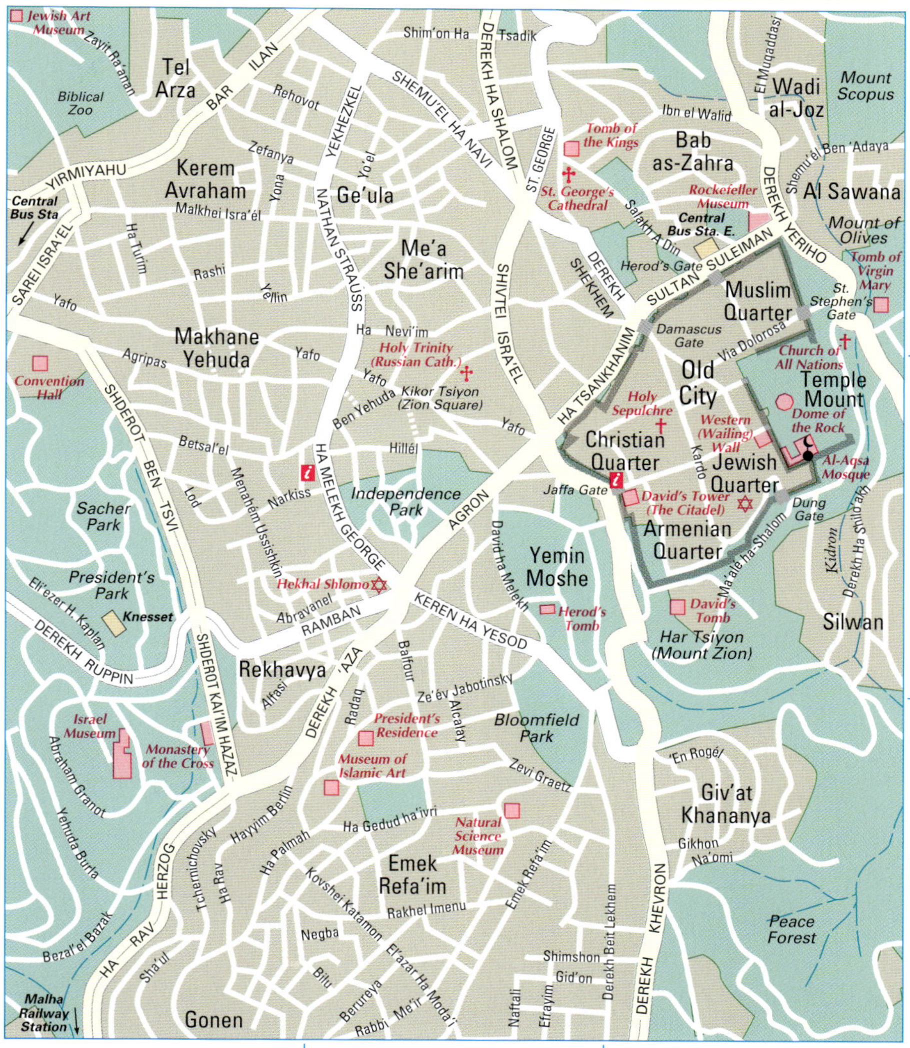
Jewish Art Museum
Tel Arza
Biblical Zoo
Kerem Avraham
Ge'ula
Tomb of the Kings
Wadi al-Joz
Mount Scopus
Bab as-Zahra
Central Bus Sta
St. George's Cathedral
Rockefeller Museum
Central Bus Sta E.
Al Sawana
Mount of Olives
Me'a She'arim
Herod's Gate
Muslim Quarter
Tomb of Virgin Mary
St. Stephen's Gate
Makhane Yehuda
Damascus Gate
Church of All Nations
Holy Trinity (Russian Cath.)
Old City
Temple Mount
Convention Hall
Kikor Tsiyon (Zion Square)
Holy Sepulchre
Christian Quarter
Western (Wailing) Wall
Dome of the Rock
Jewish Quarter
Al-Aqsa Mosque
Jaffa Gate
David's Tower (The Citadel)
Dung Gate
Sacher Park
Independence Park
Armenian Quarter
Yemin Moshe
President's Park
Knesset
Hekhal Shlomo
Herod's Tomb
David's Tomb
Har Tsiyon (Mount Zion)
Silwan
Rekhavya
Israel Museum
Monastery of the Cross
President's Residence
Bloomfield Park
Museum of Islamic Art
Giv'at Khananya
Natural Science Museum
Emek Refa'im
Peace Forest
Malha Railway Station
Gonen

1 2 3

a b c

## JOHANNESBURG, S. AFRICA

Bryanston
Randburg
Morningside
Kelvin
Randpark Ridge
Sandton
Modderfontein
Linbropark
Parkmore
Ferndale
Sandown
Lakeside
Weltevreden Park
Fontainebleau
Blairgowrie
Alexandra
Hyde Park
Lombardy East
Florence Bloom Bird Sanctuary
Craighall Park
Atholl
Bramley
Windsor
Fairland
Linden
Parkhurst
Waverley
Edenvale
Rosebank
Highlands North
Dunvegan
Northcliff
Parkwood
TO O.R. TAMBO INTL. (JNB)
Quellerina
Emmarentia
Herman Eckstein Park
Norwood
Sydenham
Parkview
Zoo
Houghton
Linksfield
Florida
Newlands
West Park
Westcliff
Observatory
Westdene
Melville
The Wilds
Bezuidenhout Park
Bedfordview
Bosmont
Parktown
Hillbrow Tower
Auckland Park
Univ. of Johannesburg
Univ. of Witwatersrand
JOHANNESBURG
Primrose
Industria
Crosby
Mayfair
Doornfontein
Kensington
Central Sta.
Ellis Park
Museum Africa and Market Theatre
Malvern
New Canada Dam
Riverlea
Selby
New Canada
Germiston
Crown Mine
Simmer and Jack Mines
Noordgesig
Ophirton
Wemmer Pan
Rosherville Dam
Victoria Lake
Soweto
Soccer City Stadium
Race Course
Orlando East
Diepkloof
National Exhibition Centre
Gold Reef City
RAND
Regents Park
Turffontein
South Hills
Orlando Dam
Robertsham
Rosettenville
Linmeyer
Alberton
Mondeor
Randhart
Florentia
Meredale
Glenvista
Kibler Park
Klipriviersberg Nature Reserve
Mulbarton
Meyersdal
Alrode
East from Greenwich
Johannesburg

1 2

## KARACHI, PAKISTAN

Super Highway
North Nazimabad
Chauki
Orangi
Gulshan-e Iqbal
Baldia
Nazimabad
Lolokhet
Pinjrapur
JINNAH INTERNATIONAL (KHI)
Goth Goli Mar
National Stadium
Zoological Garden
Goth Sher Shah
Gulbai
Drigh Road
Mauripur
Layari
Gandhi Zoo
Quaid-i-Azam Mausoleum
FAISAL
Sadr
M.A. Jinnah Rd
Malir
Mahmoodabad
Quaid-i-Azam
City Sta.
Tower of Silence
Phihai
KARACHI
Cantonment Sta.
Race Course
West Wharf
Napier Mole
Bath I.
China Cr.
Bhambo Khan Qarmati
Baba I.
Bhit I.
Kiamari
Ghizri
Sandspit
Baba Channel
Bunker I.
Clifton
Chhota Andai
Oyster Rocks
Clifton Beach
Barra Andai
DHA Phase VIII
Manora
Manora Pt.
Korangi
Gizri Creek
Korangi Creek
ARABIAN SEA
Karachi
East from Greenwich

1 2

A B

## KOLKATA, INDIA

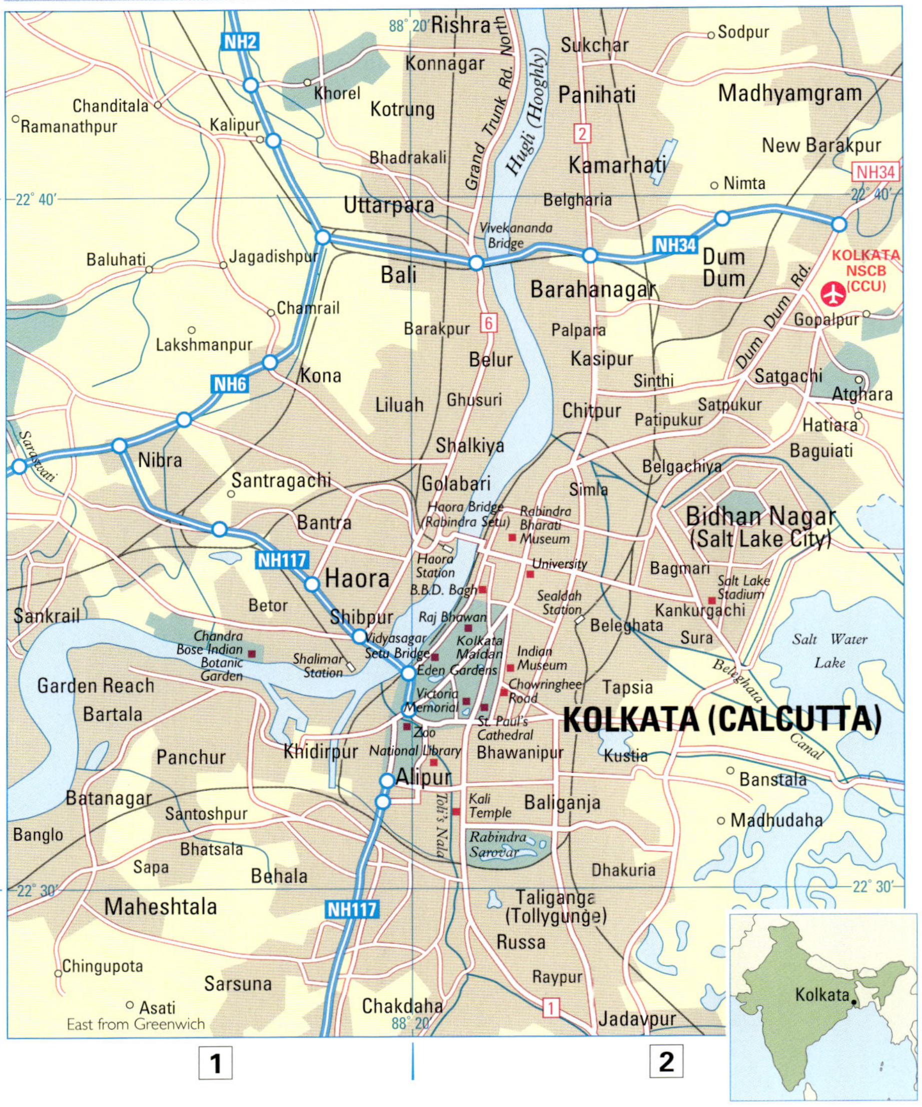

1 0 1 km 2 3 4 5
1 0 miles 1 2 3
Rishra
Konnagar
Sukchar
Sodpur
Chanditala
Ramanathpur
Khorel
Kotrung
Panihati
Madhyamgram
Kalipur
Bhadrakali
Kamarhati
New Barakpur
Nimta
Uttarpara
Belgharia
Baluhati
Jagadishpur
Bali
Barahanagar
Dum Dum
KOLKATA NSCB (CCU)
Chamrail
Gopalpur
Lakshmanpur
Barakpur
Belur
Palpara
Kasipur
Kona
Liluah
Ghusuri
Sinthi
Satgachi
Atghara
Chitpur
Patipukur
Satpukur
Hatiara
Nibra
Shalkiya
Baguiati
Santragachi
Golabari
Simla
Belgachiya
Bantra
Bidhan Nagar (Salt Lake City)
Haora
Bagmari
Betor
Shibpur
Kankurgachi
Sankrail
Beleghata
Sura
Salt Water Lake
Garden Reach
Tapsia
Bartala
KOLKATA (CALCUTTA)
Panchur
Khidirpur
Alipur
Kustia
Batanagar
Santoshpur
Baliganja
Banstala
Banglo
Bhatsala
Madhudaha
Sapa
Behala
Dhakuria
Maheshtala
Taliganja (Tollygunge)
Russa
Chingupota
Sarsuna
Raypur
Asati
Chakdaha
Jadavpur
Kolkata
East from Greenwich


## LAGOS, NIGERIA

1 0 1 km 2 3 4 5
1 0 miles 1 2 3
Erunkan
Ikeja
Oregun
Onisigun
Ikorodu
MURTALA MOHAMMED INT. (LOS)
Ojota
Oruba
Ogudu
Shogunle
Oshodi
Ejigbo
Ewu
Ibese
Osorun
Oworonsoki
Shomolu
Ofin
Isolo
Mushin
Isagatedo
Idi-Oro
Igbobi
University of Lagos
LAGOS LAGOON
Yaba
Ijesa-Tedo
Surulere
Oke-Ira
Iganmu
Iponri
Ebute-Metta
Coker
Iddo
LAGOS
Banana Island
Lekki Peninsula
Ijora
Lagos Island
Kirikiri
Ajegunle
Apapa
Obalende
Ikoyi
Moba
Falomo
Tin Can Island
Apapa Quays
Victoria Island
Lekki
Ogoyo
Ogogoro
Igbologun
Ikuata
Alaguntan
Okeogbe
Tarqua Bay
Lagos
BIGHT OF BENIN
East from Greenwich


## LAS VEGAS, NEVADA

1 0 1 km 2 3 4 5
1 0 miles 1 2 3
North Las Vegas
NELLIS AFB
City View Park
NORTH LAS VEGAS (VGT)
Zoological Botanical Park
Las Vegas Natural History Museum
Cashman Field
Nevada State Museum & Historical Society
Lorenzi Park
LAS VEGAS
Sunrise Mountain Natural Area
The Meadows Mall
Court Ho.
Sunrise Manor
Stratosphere Tower
The Strip
Las Vegas Country Club
Convention Center
Fashion Show Mall
Desert Wetlands Park
Winchester
Spring Valley
Whitney (East Las Vegas)
Paradise
Sam Boyd Stadium
LAS VEGAS McCARRAN INTL. (LAS)
Mandalay Bay
Town Square Mall
Sunset Park
Civic Center
Galleria at Sunset
Las Vegas Outlet Center
Henderson
Enterprise
West from Greenwich


## LIMA, PERU

1 0 1 km 2 3 4 5
1 0 miles 1 2 3
Independencia
Los Olivos
Huascar
San Juan de Lurigancho
Chavarria
Bocanegra
LIMA JORGE CHAVEZ (LIM)
San Martin de Porras
Rimac
Lima
Carmen de la Legua-Reynosa
El Agustino
Callao
Bellavista
LIMA
La Victoria
La Perla
La Punta
Breña
Jesus Maria
San Miguel
Pueblo Libre
San Luis
Lince
Magdalena
San Borja
Isla San Lorenzo
San Isidro
Isla Frontón
Surquillo
Miraflores
PACIFIC OCEAN
Santiago de Surco
Barranco
Vista Alegre
LAS PALMAS
La Campiña
Chorrillos
La Encantada
West from Greenwich


Interstate route numbers — U.S. route numbers — State route numbers

## LONDON, U.K.

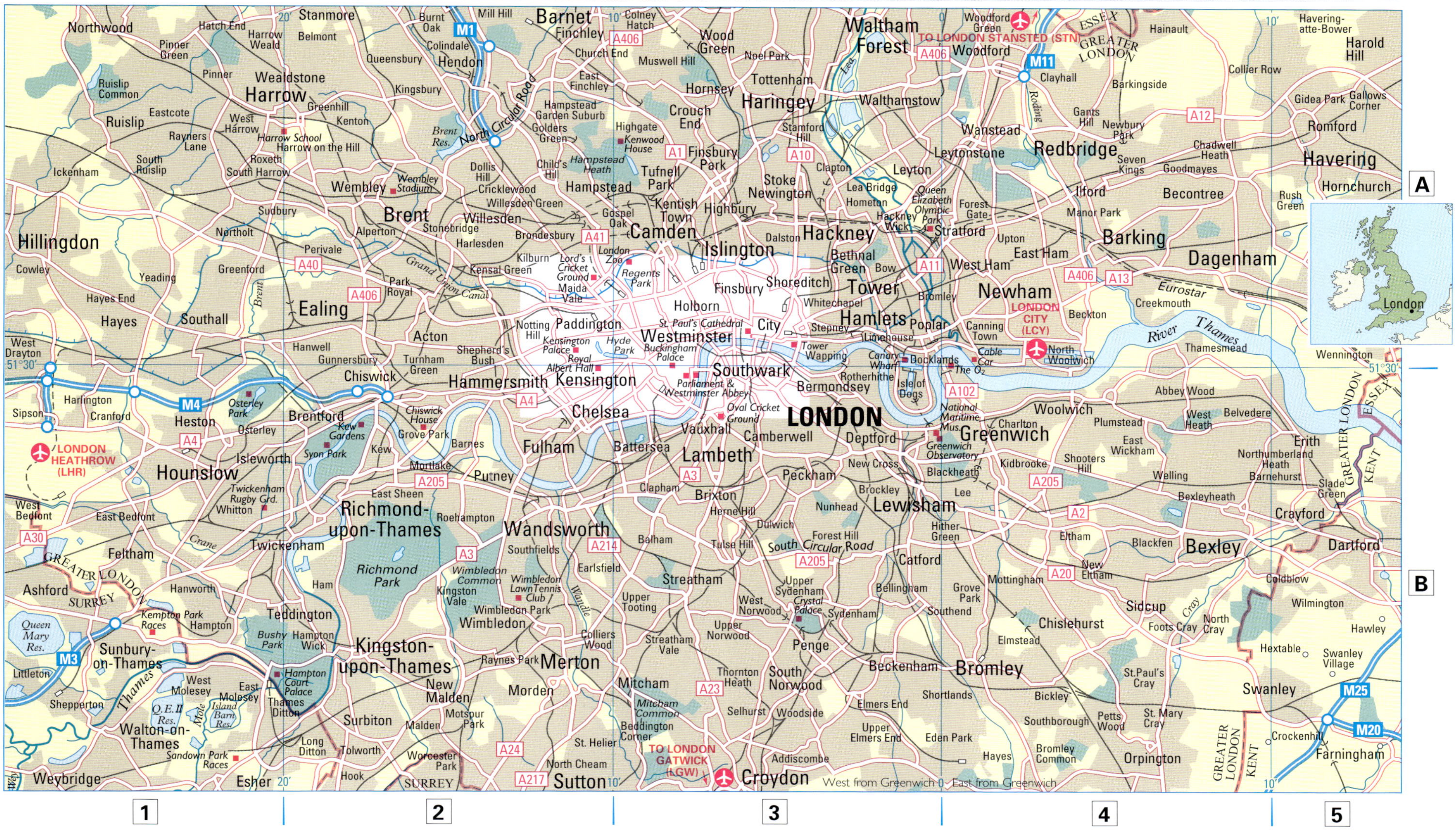
1 0 1 km 2 3 4 5
1 0 miles 1 2 3
Barnet
Harrow
Waltham Forest
Haringey
Redbridge
Havering
Hillingdon
Brent
Camden
Islington
Hackney
Barking
Dagenham
Ealing
Tower Hamlets
Newham
Westminster
City
Hammersmith
Kensington
Southwark
Chelsea
LONDON
Fulham
Lambeth
Greenwich
Hounslow
Richmond-upon-Thames
Wandsworth
Lewisham
Bexley
Kingston-upon-Thames
Merton
Bromley
Sutton
Croydon
LONDON HEATHROW (LHR)
TO LONDON STANSTED (STN)
LONDON CITY (LCY)
TO LONDON GATWICK (LGW)
River Thames
London
West from Greenwich 0 East from Greenwich
A
B
1
2
3
4
5

## CENTRAL LONDON

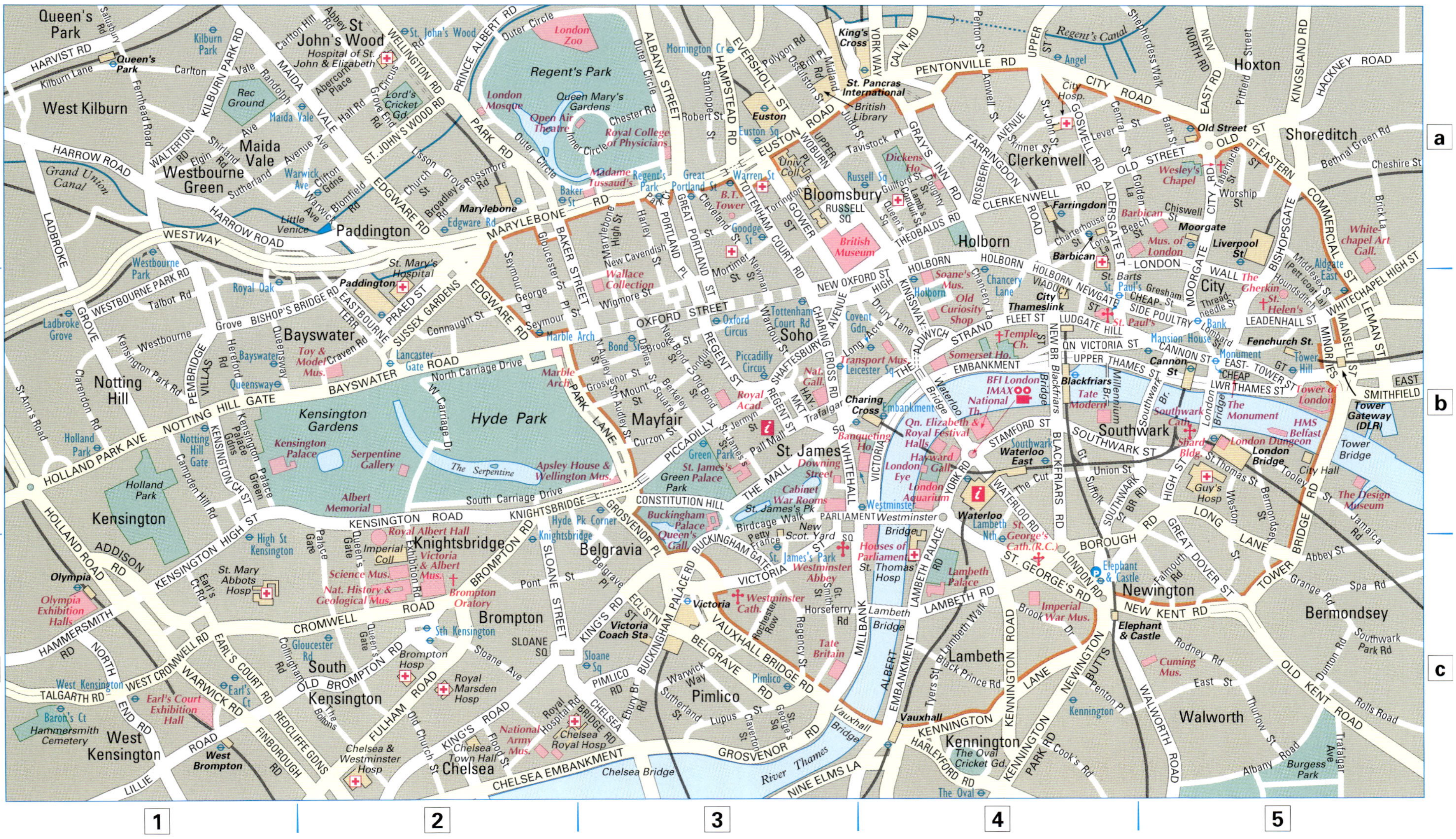
0 1 km 2
0 miles 1
Regent's Park
Paddington
Marylebone
Bloomsbury
Clerkenwell
Shoreditch
Holborn
Barbican
City
Bayswater
Notting Hill
Kensington Gardens
Hyde Park
Mayfair
Soho
St. James's
Southwark
Knightsbridge
Belgravia
Kensington
Brompton
South Kensington
Chelsea
Pimlico
Lambeth
Kennington
Walworth
Bermondsey
Newington
West Kensington
River Thames
a
b
c
1
2
3
4
5

Congestion Charging Zone

## LISBON, PORTUGAL

1 0 1 km 2 3 4 5
1 0 miles 1 2 3
Almargem do Bispo
Botica Sete
São Juliao do Tojal
Santo Antão do Tojal
Santa Iria da Azóia
Sabugo
Piedade
Tapada
Montemor
Camaroes
Loures
Unhos
Apelação
Caneças
Povoa de Santo Adriao
Boavista
Camarate
Telhal
Amoreira
Famões
Ada Beja
Odivelas
Sacavém
Ponte Vasco de Gama
Venda Seca
Charneca
Moscavide
Parque das Nações (Park of Nations)
Rio de Mouro
Belas
Casal da Mira
Lumiar
Ameixoeira
LISBOA PORTELA (LIS)
Agualva-Cacem
Pontinha
Olivais
Cotao
Massamá
Amadora
Carnide
Alvalade
Queluz
Benfica
Campo Grande
Matinha
Damaia
Campo Pequeno
Talaide
Rib. de Barcarena
Monsanto
Alto do Pina
Beato
Barcarena
Parque Florestal de Monsanto
Xabregas
Leião
Carnaxide
Campolide
Bairro Lopes
LISBOA
Rato
Tejo
Linda-a-Pastora
Ajuda
Alcantara
Castelo de S. Jorge
Estação Santa Apolónia
Terrugem
Caxias
Algés
Santo Amaro
Mosteiro dos Jerónimos
Praça do Comércio
Belém
Estação Cais do Sodré
Paco de Arcos
Torre de Belém
Padrão dos Descobrimentos
Ponte 25 de Abril
Cacilhas
Oeiras
Porto Brandão
Almada
Rio
ATLANTIC
Trafaria
Banática
Cristo Rei
Lavradio
Raposo
Ccva de Piedade
Caparica
Barreiro
Bugio
OCEAN
Sobreda
Laranjeiro
Coina
Quinta de Santo António
Corroios
Costa da Caparica
Capuchos
Seixal
Santo André
Amora
Cruz de Pau
Palhais
Lisbon
West from Greenwich
Charneca
Arrentela
38°40'
9°10'
A
B
1
2


## CENTRAL LISBON

0 km 1
0 miles 0.5
Palacio de Justica
Penitenciária
Parque Eduardo VII
Pavilhão dos Desportos
Maternidade
Estefânia
Instituto Superior Técnico
RUA PASCOAL DE MELO
Praça Marquês de Pombal
Amoreiros
Penha França
Hospital M. Bombarda
Anjos
Hospital de Santa Marta
Rato
Academia das Ciências
Jardin Botanico
AVENIDA DA LIBERDADE
Instituto de Medicina Legal
Graça
Bairro Lopes
Palácio de Assembleia Nacional
Estação do Rossio
Teatro Nac. de Dona Maria II
Igreja da Graça
Bairro Alto
Museu do Arqueologia
Castelo de São Jorge (St. George's Castle)
Museu de Arte Decorativas
Igreja Sta. Engrácia
Estação Santa Apolónia
Elevador de Santa Justa
Theatro Nac. de São Carlos
Museu Antoniano (St. Anthony Mus.)
Military Museum
Alfama
Sé Catedral
Biblioteca Nacional
Museu do Chiado
Praça do Comércio
Dom José I
Baixa
RUA DO ARSENAL
AV. RIBEIRA DAS NAUS
AVENIDA INFANTE DOM HENRIQUE
Estação Cais do Sodré
Estação Fluvial
Rio Tejo (Tagus)
1
2
3


## LOS ANGELES, CALIFORNIA

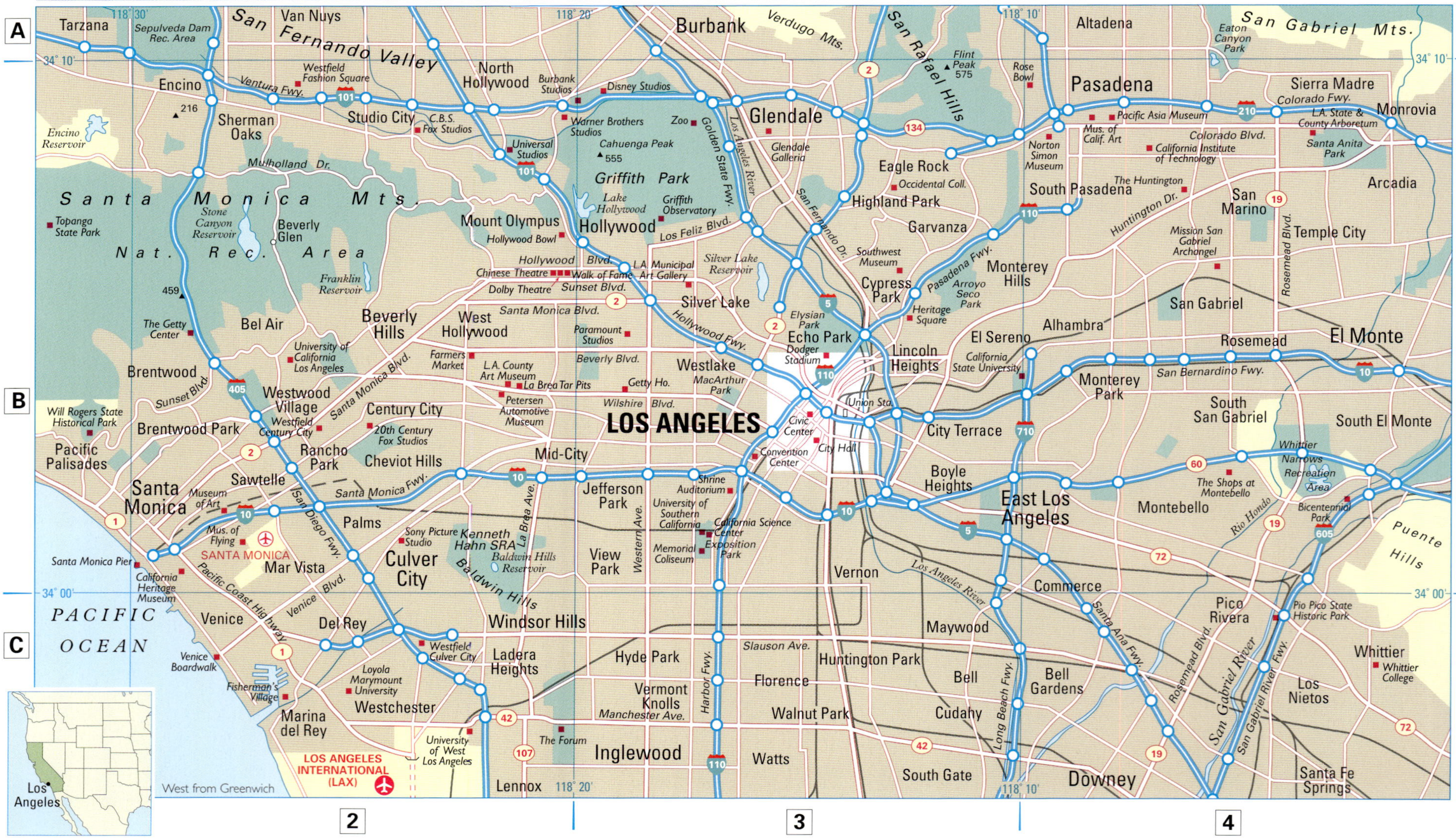

1 0 1 km 2 3 4 5
1 0 miles 1 2 3
Tarzana
Sepulveda Dam Rec. Area
Van Nuys
San Fernando Valley
Burbank
Verdugo Mts.
San Rafael Hills
Altadena
San Gabriel Mts.
Encino
Westfield Fashion Square
North Hollywood
Disney Studios
Flint Peak 575
Pasadena
Sierra Madre
Monrovia
Sherman Oaks
Studio City
Universal Studios
Warner Brothers Studios
Glendale
Pacific Asia Museum
Encino Reservoir
Mulholland Dr.
Griffith Park
Eagle Rock
California Institute of Technology
Santa Anita Park
Santa Monica Mts.
Highland Park
South Pasadena
The Huntington
Arcadia
Topanga State Park
Nat. Rec. Area
Beverly Glen
Mount Olympus
Hollywood
Griffith Observatory
Garvanza
San Marino
Temple City
Hollywood Bowl
Chinese Theatre
Walk of Fame
Silver Lake Reservoir
Mission San Gabriel Archangel
Southwest Museum
Cypress Park
Monterey Hills
The Getty Center
Silver Lake
San Gabriel
Bel Air
Beverly Hills
West Hollywood
Echo Park
Alhambra
Lincoln Heights
El Sereno
Rosemead
El Monte
Brentwood
University of California Los Angeles
L.A. County Art Museum
Dodger Stadium
Westlake
California State University
Monterey Park
Will Rogers State Historical Park
Westwood Village
Century City
LOS ANGELES
South San Gabriel
Brentwood Park
Petersen Automotive Museum
Union Sta.
City Terrace
South El Monte
Pacific Palisades
Rancho Park
20th Century Fox Studios
Cheviot Hills
Mid-City
City Hall
Boyle Heights
Sawtelle
Whittier Narrows Recreation Area
Santa Monica
Jefferson Park
Shrine Auditorium
The Shops at Montebello
Palms
University of Southern California
California Science Center
East Los Angeles
Montebello
Puente Hills
Santa Monica Pier
SANTA MONICA
Kenneth Hahn SRA
Exposition Park
Memorial Coliseum
View Park
Vernon
PACIFIC
Mar Vista
Culver City
Commerce
OCEAN
Venice
Del Rey
Windsor Hills
Maywood
Pico Rivera
Pio Pico State Historic Park
Venice Boardwalk
Westfield Culver City
Ladera Heights
Hyde Park
Huntington Park
Whittier
Whittier College
Loyola Marymount University
Florence
Bell
Bell Gardens
Los Nietos
Marina del Rey
Westchester
Vermont Knolls
Walnut Park
Cudahy
Los Angeles
LOS ANGELES INTERNATIONAL (LAX)
University of West Los Angeles
The Forum
Inglewood
Watts
South Gate
Downey
Santa Fe Springs
West from Greenwich
Lennox
34° 10'
34° 00'
118° 20'
118° 10'
A
B
C
2
3
4


Interstate route numbers State route numbers

## MADRID, SPAIN

1 0 1 km 2 3 4 5
1 0 miles 1 2 3
Monte de El Pardo
El Pardo
Valdelatas
Alcobendas
La Moraleja
El Encinar de los Reyes
MADRID-BARAJAS (MAD)
Fuencarral
Aravaca
Barajas
Hortaleza
Tetuán
Chamartín
Canillas
La Estación
Universidad
Ciudad Lineal
Ciudad Fin de Semana
Pozuelo de Alarcón
Humera
Chamberí
Canillejas
Casa de Campo
Salamanca
MADRID
Pueblo Nuevo
Coslada
Latina
Retiro
Moratalaz
Vicálvaro
Arganzuela
Campamento
Carabanchel Bajo
Legazpi
Mediodia
Palomeras
Cuatro Vientos
Usera
Entrevías
Vallecas
Carabanchel Alto
Mercamadrid
La Fortuna
Villaverde
Villaverde Bajo
Alcorcón
Canteras de Vallecas
Cumbres de Vallecas
Leganés
Parque de Polvoranca
Perales del Rio
Getafe
Cerro de los Angeles
Salmedina
Fuenlabrada
GETAFE
West from Greenwich
Madrid
1
2

## CENTRAL MADRID

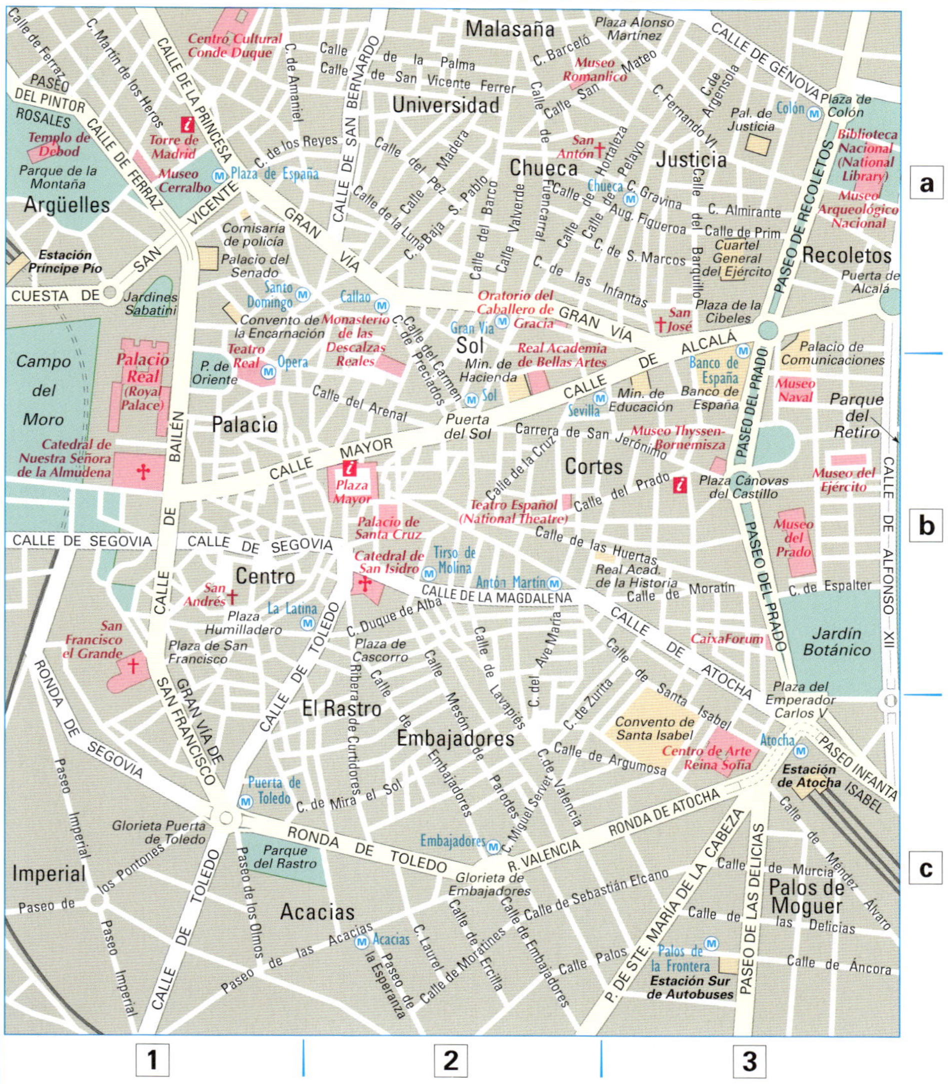
0 kms 1
0 miles 0.5
Malasaña
Universidad
Chueca
Justicia
Argüelles
Recoletos
Sol
Palacio
Cortes
Centro
El Rastro
Embajadores
Imperial
Acacias
Palos de Moguer
Plaza Mayor
Palacio Real (Royal Palace)
Catedral de Nuestra Señora de la Almudena
Museo del Prado
Jardín Botánico
Estación de Atocha
Estación Sur de Autobuses
Puerta del Sol
Gran Vía
Calle Mayor
Paseo del Prado
a
b
c
1
2
3

## CENTRAL LOS ANGELES

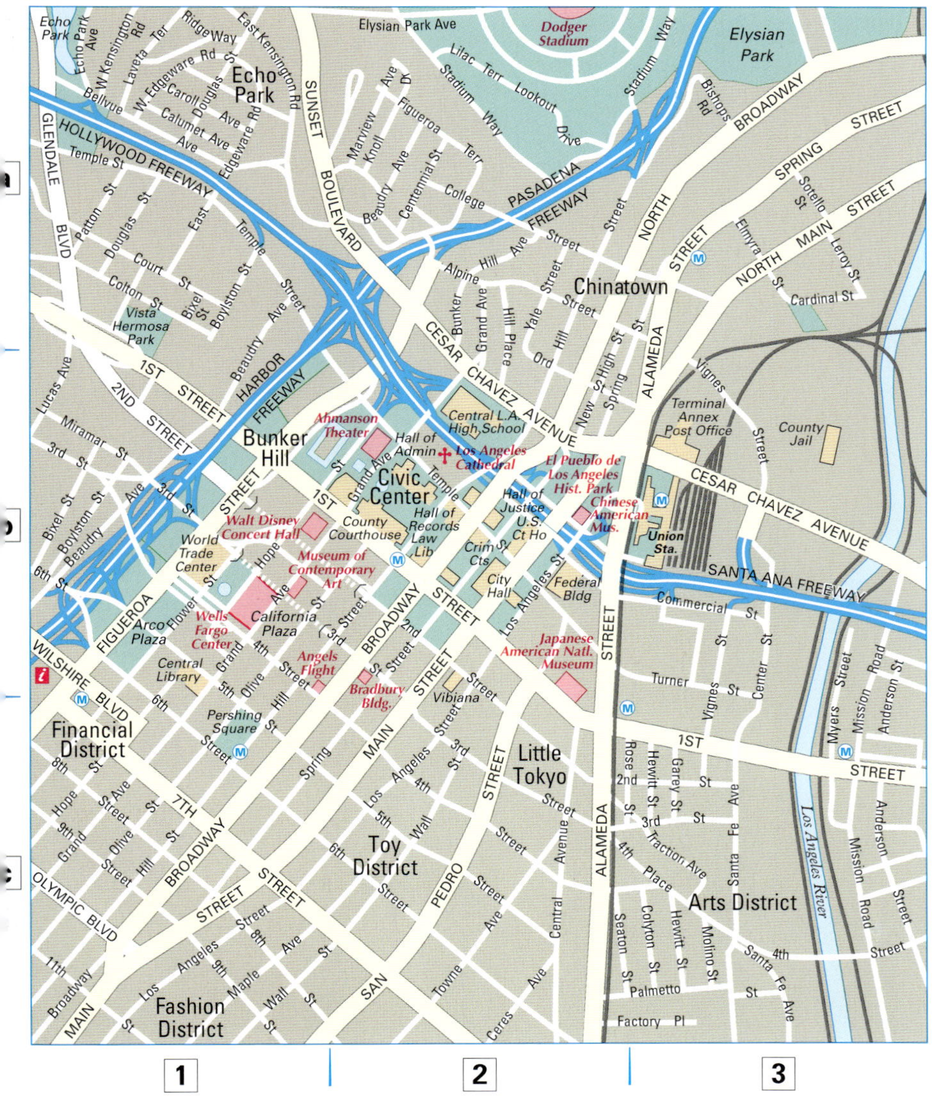
0 km 1
0 miles 0.5
Dodger Stadium
Elysian Park
Echo Park
Chinatown
Bunker Hill
Civic Center
Union Sta.
Little Tokyo
Financial District
Toy District
Arts District
Fashion District
Hollywood Freeway
Harbor Freeway
Santa Ana Freeway
Pasadena Freeway
Los Angeles River
1
2
3

## MANILA, PHILIPPINES

1 0 1 km 2 3 4 5
1 0 miles 1 2 3
Malabon
Talipapa
Navotas
Caloocan
Quezon City
Balara
Marikina
Cubao
Tondo
San Juan del Monte
MANILA
Mandaluyong
Intramuros
Paco
Ermita
Malate
Santa Ana
Pasig
Makati
Guadalupe
Pasay
Pateros
Taguig
Manila Bay
Baclaran
MANILA NINOY AQUINO INTL. (MNL)
Hagonoy
Sangley Pt.
Cañacao Bay
Las Piñas
Bicutan
Cavite
Parañaque
Bacoor
Bacoor Bay
Zapote
Laguna de Bay
Binacayan
Habay
Muntinlupa
Kawit
East from Greenwich
A
B
C
1
2

## MEXICO CITY, MEXICO

1 0 1 km 2 3 4 5
1 0 miles 1 2 3
A
B
C
1
2
Naucalpan de Juárez
Azcapotzalco
Gustavo A. Madero
Venustiano Carranza
Miguel Hidalgo
Cuauhtémoc
CIUDAD DE MÉXICO
Benito Juárez
Iztacalco
Iztapalapa
Álvaro Obregón
Coyoacán
Magdalena Contreras
Tlalpan
Ciudad Satélite
Tacuba
Tacubaya
Mixcoac
San Ángel
Tizapán
Pantitlán
Tepalcates
Ticomán
Progreso Nacional
San Pedro Zacatenco
Villa de Guadalupe
San Juan de Aragón
Xochimilco
Nueva Atzacoalco
Tlatelolco
Zócalo
MÉXICO BENITO JUÁREZ INTL. (MEX)
Parque Nacional de los Remedios
Bosque de Chapultepec
Ciudad Universitaria
West from Greenwich
Mexico City
Federal route numbers


## CENTRAL MEXICO CITY

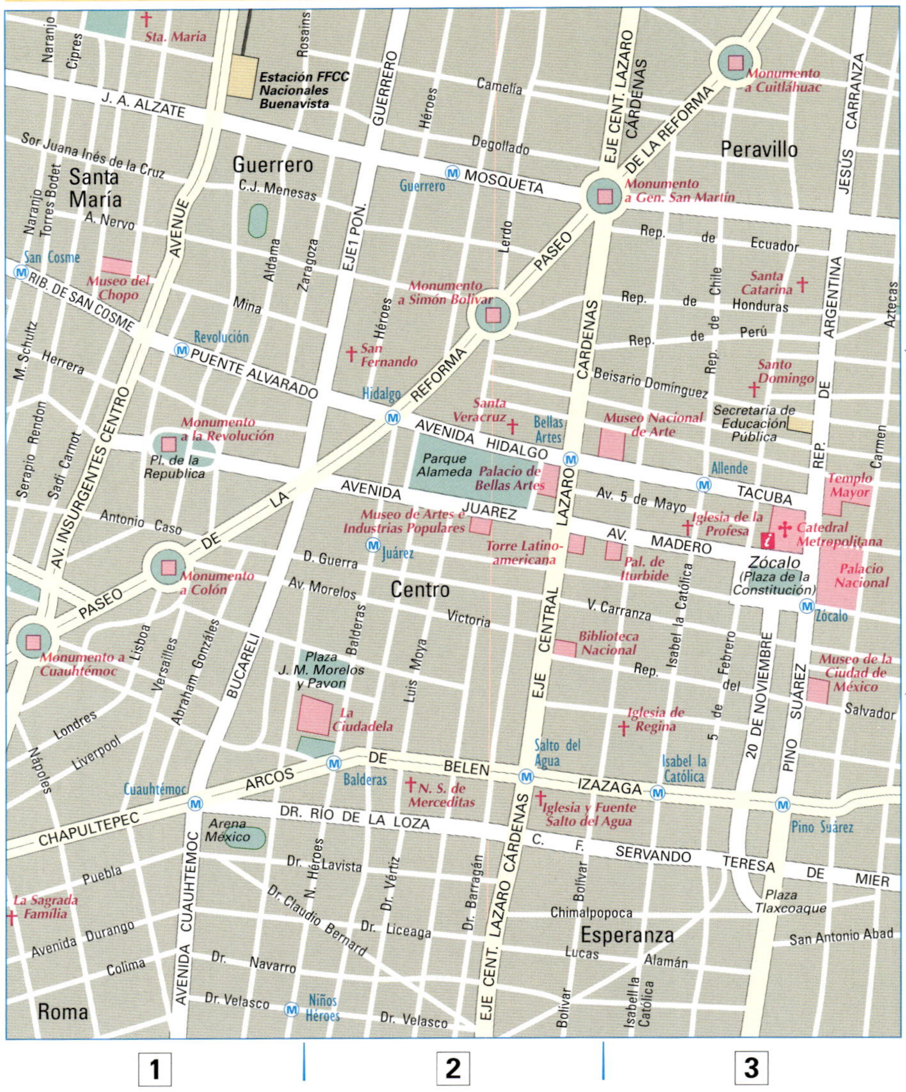

0 km 1
0 miles 0.5
1
2
3
Guerrero
Santa María
Peravillo
Centro
Esperanza
Roma
Tabacalera
Zócalo
PASEO DE LA REFORMA
AV. INSURGENTES CENTRO
EJE CENTRAL LÁZARO CÁRDENAS
AVENIDA HIDALGO
AVENIDA JUÁREZ
Palacio Nacional
Catedral Metropolitana
Templo Mayor
Palacio de Bellas Artes
Torre Latino-americana
Monumento a la Revolución
Monumento a Colón
Monumento a Cuauhtémoc
Parque Alameda
La Ciudadela
Estación FFCC Nacionales Buenavista


## MELBOURNE, AUSTRALIA

1 0 1 km 2 3 4 5
1 0 miles 1 2 3
A
B
1
2
MELBOURNE
MELBOURNE (MEL)
ESSENDON
Broadmeadows
Tullamarine
Keilor
Coburg
Brunswick
Preston
Heidelberg
Kew
Balwyn
Footscray
Sunshine
Williamstown
Port Melbourne
Hobsons Bay
Port Phillip Bay
St. Kilda
Brighton
Caulfield
Malvern
Camberwell
Richmond
Oakleigh
Altona
Yarra R.
West Gate Freeway
East from Greenwich
Melbourne


## MILAN, ITALY

1 0 1 km 2 3 4 5
1 0 miles 1 2 3
1
2
MILANO
Monza
Sesto San Giovanni
Cinisello Balsamo
Bollate
Rho
Cormano
Bresso
Novate Milanese
Pero
Bovisa
Greco
Lambrate
Città degli Studi
San Siro
Quinto Romano
Bággio
Cesano Boscone
San Cristoforo
Corsico
Assago
Rozzano
Vigentino
Linate
San Donato Milanese
San Giuliano Milanese
Segrate
TO MILAN MALPENSA (MXP)
MILAN LINATE (LIN)
Tangenziale Ovest
Tangenziale Est
Parco Regionale
East from Greenwich
Milan

## MIAMI, FLORIDA

The Everglades
Tamarac
FORT LAUDERDALE EXECUTIVE AIRPORT
Pompano Beach
Lockhart Stadium
Florida Atlantic University
Oakland Park
Lauderdale Lakes
Wilton Manors
Sunrise
Sawgrass Mills Mall
Mills Pond Park
Lazy Lake
Lauderhill
Fort Lauderdale
Hugh Taylor Birch S.R.A.
Plantation
Holiday Park
Galleria
Bonnet House
F.L. Mus. of Art
Mus. of Discovery & Science
Old Ft. Lauderdale
Mosaic Theatre
Westfield Broward
North New River Canal
Melrose Park
Young at Art Children's Mus.
Jungle Queen Riverboat
Plantation Isles
Pine Island
Broadview Park
John U Lloyd Beach S.P.
Port Everglades
Nova Southeastern University
Flamingo Gardens
Tree Tops Park
Davie
Davie Rodeo Arena
FORT LAUDERDALE HOLLYWOOD INTERNATIONAL (FLL)
South New River Canal
Florida's Turnpike
Tiger Tail Lake Park
Dania
Dania Jai-Alai
Dania Beach
Cooper City
Seminole Indian Res.
Anne Kolb Nature Center
C.B. Smith Park
Pembroke Pines
Pembroke Lakes Mall
Sunshine Park
Hollywood
Art and Culture Center of Hollywood
NORTH PERRY AIRPORT
Pembroke Park
Gulfstream Race Track
Miramar
West Park
Hallandale Beach
Toll
Calder Race Course
Ives Estates
Aventura
Aventura Mall
BROWARD CO.
MIAMI-DADE CO.
Snake Creek Canal
Sun Life Stadium
Norland
Golden Beach
Ulleta
Greynolds Park
Spanish Monastery
Ojus
Sunny Isles Beach
Carol City
North Miami Beach
Miami Gardens
St. Thomas University
Oleta River State Rec. Area
North Miami
Miami Lakes
OPA-LOCKA
Opa-Locka
Florida Intl. Univ. (Biscayne Bay)
Museum of Contemporary Art
Bay Harbor Islands
Bal Harbour
Surfside
Amelia Earhart Park
Gratigny Pkwy.
Biscayne Park
Pinewood Park
Barry University
Indian Creek Village
Westland Mall
Hialeah
Hialeah Race Track
Miami Amtrak Station
Miami Shores
El Portal
Atlantic Ocean
Little Haiti
North Bay Village
Biscayne Bay
Carl Fisher Mon.
Miami Beach
Miami River
Palmetto Expressway
Brownsville
Virginia Gardens
Miami Springs
Metrorail
Art Deco Historic District
Florida Int. Univ.
MIAMI INTERNATIONAL (MIA)
Venetian Islands
Bass Mus. of Art
Dolphin Expressway
Little Havana
Jungle Island
Miami Beach Convention Center
L. Mahar
Blue Lagoon Lake
Miami Art Museum
American Airlines Arena
Wolfsonian Museum
South Beach
Jewish Museum
Mall of the Americas
Port of Miami
MIAMI
Fisher Island
West Miami
Coral Gables
Museum of Science & Planetarium
Venetian Pool
Vizcaya Museum and Gardens
Virginia Key
Coconut Grove
Coconut Grove Convention Center
Seaquarium
University of Miami
Lowe Art Museum
Barnacle State Historic Site
Crandon Park
South Miami
Coral Gables
Biscayne Bay
Key Biscayne
Dadeland Mall
Kendall
Pinecrest
Fairchild Tropical Botanic Garden
Biscayne Bay Aquatic Reserve
Bill Baggs Cape Florida State Rec. Area
Miami
West from Greenwich
1 2 3

Interstate route numbers · U.S. route numbers · State route numbers

## MOSCOW, RUSSIA

TO MOSCOW SHEREMETYEVO INTL. (SVO)
Degunino
Vladykino
Khimki-Khovrino
Babushkin
Moskva Oblast
Gorod Moskva
Nikolskiy
Petrovsko-Razumovskoye
Dzerzhinskiy Park
Losiny Ostrov National Park
Abramtsevo
Timiryazev Park
Ostankino
Moscow
Leningradskiy Prospekt
Galyanovo
Bogorodskoye
Petrovskiy Park
Third Ring Road
Sokolniki Park
Sokolniki
Izmaylovo
Frunze
Dzerzhinskiy
Khorosovo
Sverdlov
Leningrad Station
Yaroslavl Station
Kazan Station
Izmaylovskiy Park
Moscow Ring Road
Mnevniki
MOSKVA
Leportovo
Krasno-Presnenskaya
Bolshoi Theatre
Bauman
Kursk Station
Novogireyevo
Moskva Siti
Naberezhnaya Tower
Kremlin
Red Square
St. Basil's Cath.
Lenin Museum
Perovo
Kuskovo
Fili-Mazilovo
Kiev Station
Tretiakov Art Gallery
Zhdanov
Plyushchevo
Veshnyaki
Garden Ring
International House of Music
Davydkovo
Novodevichy Convent
Gorky Park
Pavelet Station
Luzhniki Sports Centre, Lenin Stadium
Moskvoretskiy
Vykhino
Volgogradskiy Prospekt
Lomonosov Moscow State University
Third Ring Road
Tekstilshchik
Kuzyminki
Leninskiye Gory
Moscow Circus
Oktyabrskiy
Ramenki
Prospekt
Nogatino
Lyublino
MKAD
Cheryomushki
Leninskiy
Yugo-Zarad
Maryino
Dyakovo
Moskva (Moscow)
Volkhonka-Zil
Troparevo
Zyuzino
Kuryanovo
Kapotnya
Belyayevo Bogorodskoye
Bittsevsky Forest Park
Chertanovka
Brateyevo
TO MOSCOW DOMODEDOVO INTL. (DME)
Lenino
Chertanovo
Borisovo
East from Greenwich
1 2 3
A B C

## CENTRAL MOSCOW

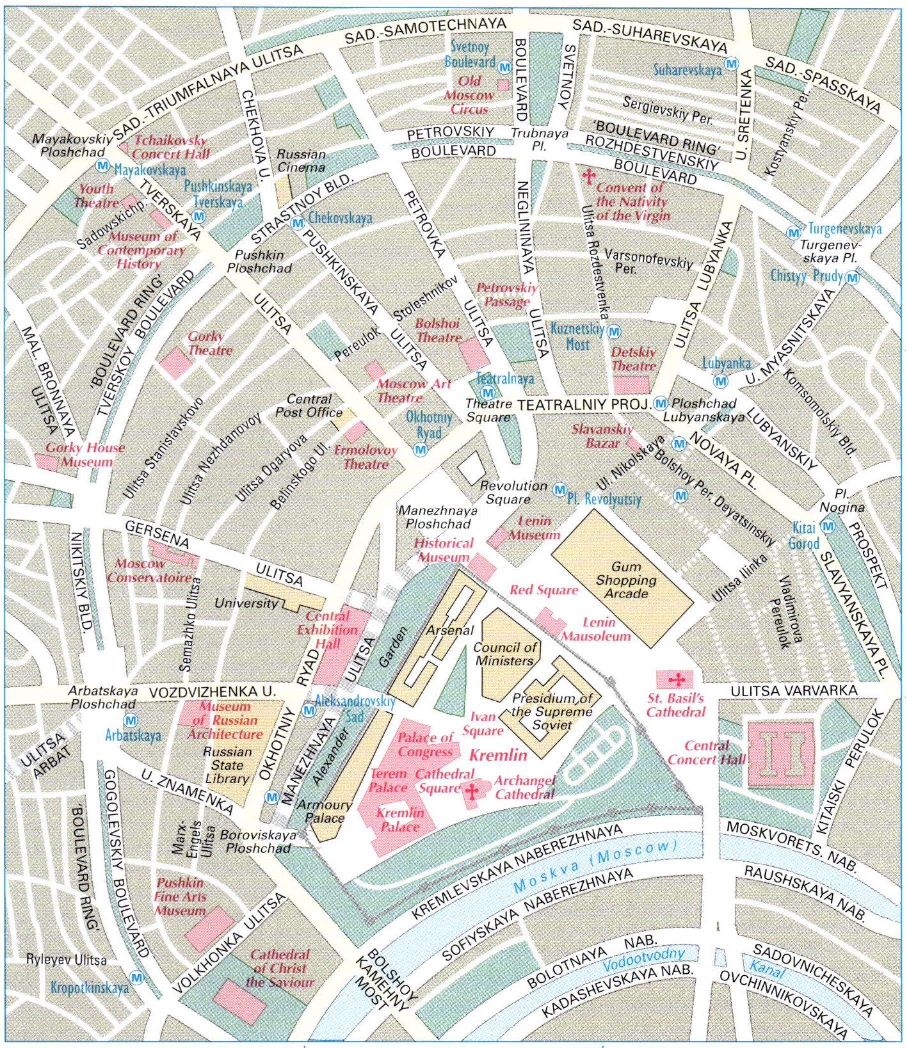
SAD.-SAMOTECHNAYA
SAD.-SUHAREVSKAYA
SAD.-SPASSKAYA
SAD.-TRIUMFALNAYA ULITSA
Svetnoy Boulevard
Old Moscow Circus
BOULEVARD
SVETNOY
Suharevskaya
Sergievskiy Per.
Mayakovskiy Ploshchad
Tchaikovsky Concert Hall
Mayakovskaya
CHEKHOVA U.
PETROVSKIY BOULEVARD
Trubnaya Pl.
'BOULEVARD RING' ROZHDESTVENSKIY BOULEVARD
U. SRETENKA
Russian Cinema
Youth Theatre
Pushkinskaya
Tverskaya
Convent of the Nativity of the Virgin
TVERSKAYA
STRASTNOY BLD.
Chekhovskaya
Turgenevskaya
Turgenev-skaya Pl.
Chistye Prudy
Museum of Contemporary History
Pushkin Ploshchad
PETROVKA
NEGLINNAYA
Varsonofevskiy Per.
LUBYANKA
MYASNITSKAYA
'BOULEVARD RING' TVERSKOI BOULEVARD
Gorky Theatre
ULITSA
PUSHKINSKAYA
Stoleshnikov
Petrovskiy Passage
Bolshoi Theatre
Kuznetskiy Most
Detskiy Theatre
MAL. BRONNAYA ULITSA
Moscow Art Theatre
Teatralnaya
Theatre Square
TEATRALNIY PROJ.
Lubyanka
Ploshchad Lubyanskaya
Central Post Office
Okhotniy Ryad
Gorky House Museum
Ermolova Theatre
Slavanskiy Bazar
NOVAYA PL.
LUBYANSKIY
Revolution Square
Pl. Revolyutsiy
Pl. Nogina
Kitai Gorod
GERSENA
Manezhnaya Ploshchad
Lenin Museum
Historical Museum
Moscow Conservatoire
Red Square
Gum Shopping Arcade
NIKITSKIY BLD.
University
Central Exhibition Hall
Lenin Mausoleum
Arsenal
Council of Ministers
St. Basil's Cathedral
ULITSA VARVARKA
Arbatskaya Ploshchad
VOZDVIZHENKA U.
Museum of Russian Architecture
Aleksandrovskiy Sad
Presidium of the Supreme Soviet
Ivan Square
Arbatskaya
Russian State Library
Palace of Congress
Kremlin
Central Concert Hall
ULITSA ARBAT
GOGOLEVSKIY BOULEVARD
U. ZNAMENKA
Terem Palace
Cathedral Square
Archangel Cathedral
MOSKVORETS. NAB.
Kremlin Palace
Armoury Palace
Borovitskaya Ploshchad
Pushkin Fine Arts Museum
KREMLEVSKAYA NABEREZHNAYA
Moskva (Moscow)
RAUSHSKAYA NAB.
SOFIYSKAYA NABEREZHNAYA
Ryleyev Ulitsa
VOLKHONKA ULITSA
Cathedral of Christ the Saviour
BOLSHOY KAMENNY MOST
BOLOTNAYA NAB.
Vodootvodny Kanal
SADOVNICHESKAYA
OVCHINNIKOVSKAYA
KADASHEVSKAYA NAB.
Kropotkinskaya
1 2 3
a b c

## MONTRÉAL, CANADA

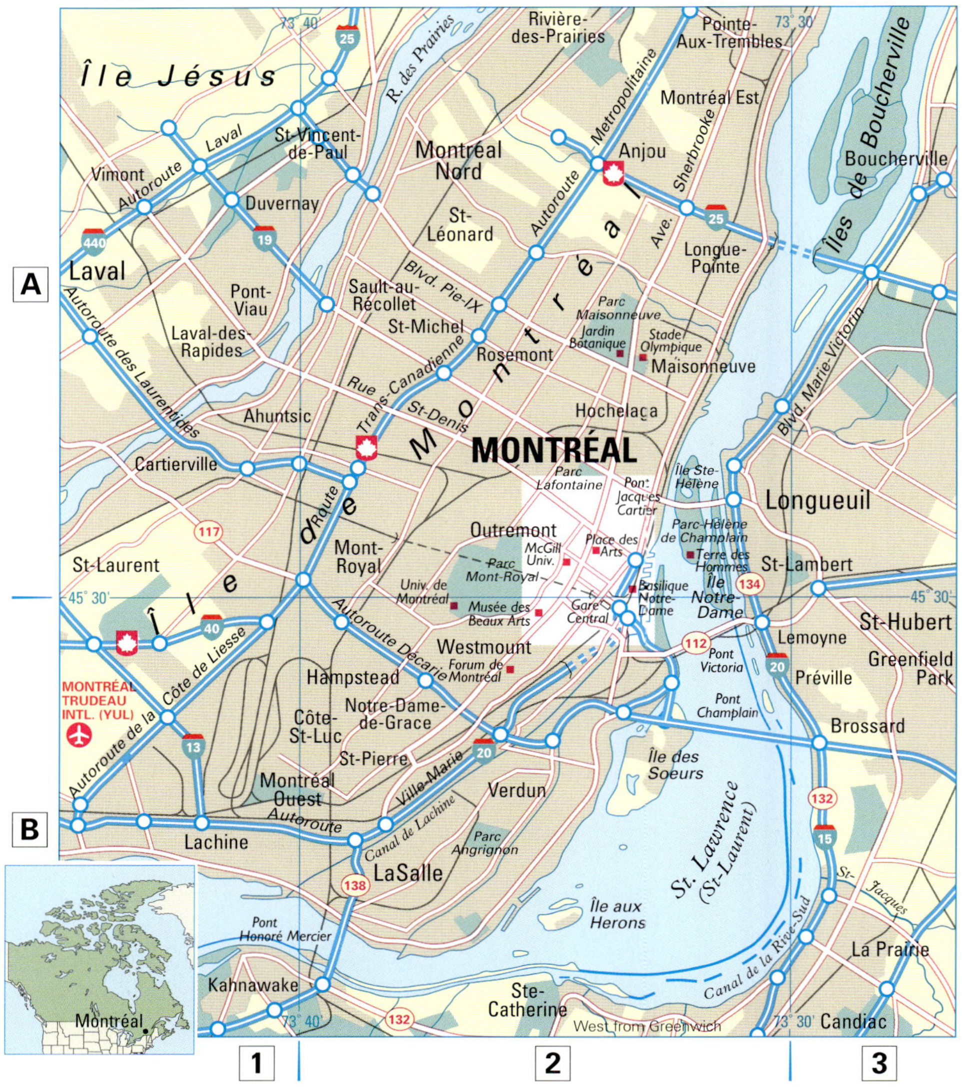
Île Jésus
Rivière-des-Prairies
Pointe-aux-Trembles
Montréal Est
Vimont
Laval
St-Vincent-de-Paul
Montréal Nord
Anjou
Boucherville
Îles de Boucherville
Duvernay
St-Léonard
Longue-Pointe
Pont-Viau
Sault-au-Récollet
St-Michel
Laval-des-Rapides
Parc Maisonneuve
Jardin Botanique
Stade Olympique
Maisonneuve
Rosemont
Ahuntsic
Hochelaga
Cartierville
MONTRÉAL
Parc Lafontaine
Île Ste-Hélène
Longueuil
Outremont
McGill Univ.
Place des Arts
Parc-Hélène de Champlain
Terre des Hommes
St-Laurent
Mont-Royal
Parc Mont-Royal
Univ. de Montréal
Musée des Beaux Arts
Basilique Notre-Dame
Île Notre Dame
St-Lambert
Gare Central
Westmount
Forum de Montréal
Lemoyne
St-Hubert
MONTRÉAL TRUDEAU INTL. (YUL)
Hampstead
Pont Victoria
Préville
Greenfield Park
Côte-St-Luc
Notre-Dame-de-Grace
Pont Champlain
Brossard
St-Pierre
Montréal Ouest
Verdun
Île des Soeurs
Lachine
Parc Angrignon
St. Lawrence (St-Laurent)
LaSalle
Île aux Herons
Pont Honoré Mercier
La Prairie
Kahnawake
Ste-Catherine
Canal de la Rive-Sud
Candiac
Autoroute des Laurentides
Autoroute Décarie
Autoroute Métropolitaine
Autoroute de la Côte de Liesse
Bvd. Marie-Victorin
Île de Montréal
West from Greenwich
45° 30'
73° 40'
73° 30'
A
B
1
2
3
Montréal

Trans-Canada route · Canadian autoroute numbers · Provincial route numbers

## CENTRAL MONTRÉAL

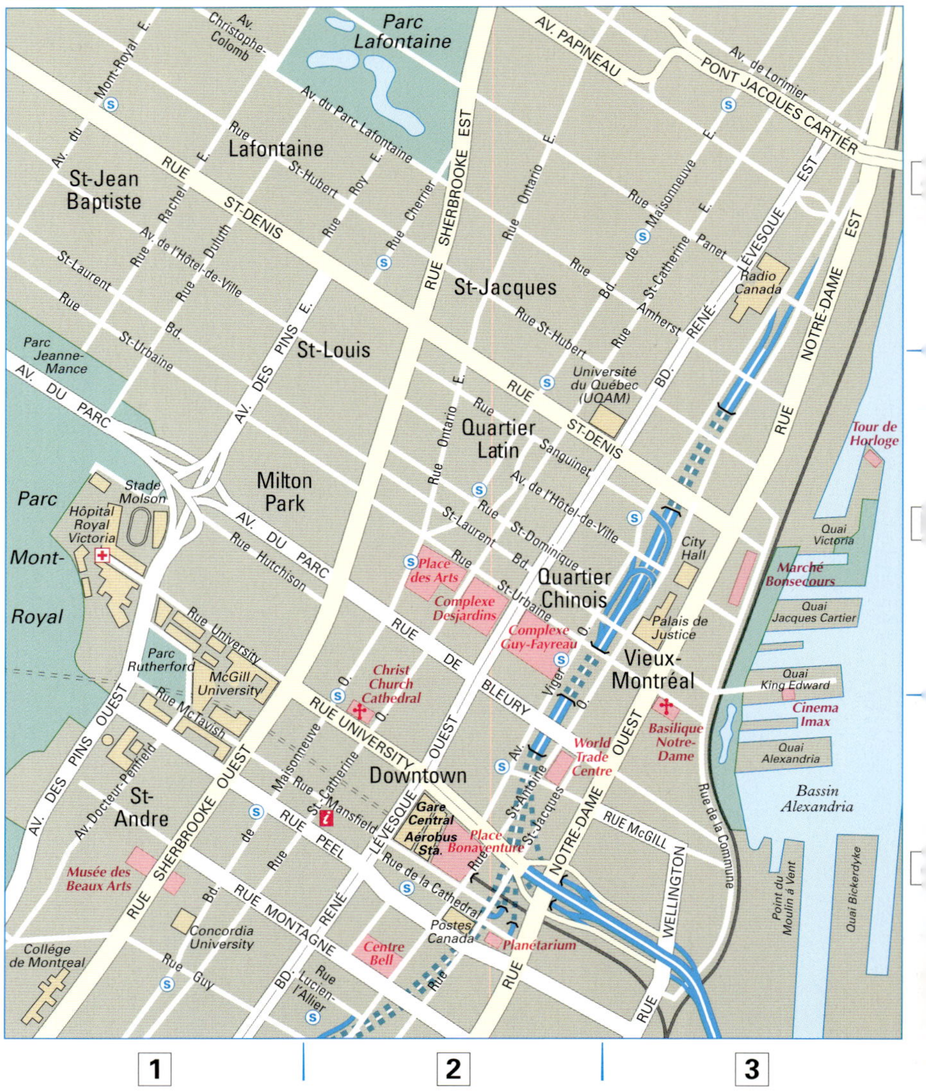
Parc Lafontaine
AV. PAPINEAU
PONT JACQUES CARTIER
St-Jean Baptiste
Lafontaine
RUE SHERBROOKE EST
St-Jacques
Radio Canada
St-Louis
Université du Québec (UQAM)
Parc Jeanne-Mance
AV. DU PARC
Quartier Latin
Tour de l'Horloge
Parc Mont-Royal
Stade Molson
Hôpital Royal Victoria
Milton Park
Place des Arts
Complexe Desjardins
Quartier Chinois
City Hall
Marché Bonsecours
Quai Victoria
Quai Jacques Cartier
Complexe Guy-Fayreau
Palais de Justice
Parc Rutherford
McGill University
Christ Church Cathedral
Vieux-Montréal
Quai King Edward
Cinema Imax
Basilique Notre-Dame
World Trade Centre
Quai Alexandria
Bassin Alexandria
St-Andre
Downtown
Gare Central
Aerobus Sta.
Place Bonaventure
Musée des Beaux Arts
Postes Canada
Planetarium
Collège de Montréal
Concordia University
Centre Bell
RUE SHERBROOKE OUEST
RUE STE-CATHERINE
BD. RENÉ LEVESQUE
RUE NOTRE-DAME
RUE ST-DENIS
1
2
3

## MUMBAI, INDIA

Andheri
Salsette Island
Vikhroli
Juhu Beach
Juhu
Vile Parle
Tara
MUMBAI CHHATRAPATI SHIVAJI (BOM)
Ghatkopar
Koparkhairna
Navi Mumbai (New Mumbai)
Santa Cruz
Kurmuri
University of Mumbai
Khar
Kurla
Thane Creek
Vashi
Bandra
Naupada
Sion
Chembur
Mankhurd
Mahim Creek
Govandi
Bandra Point
Mahim Bay
Mahim
Dharavi
Maraoli
Trombay
Worli Fort
Worli
Matunga
Wadala
Anik
Dadar
Naigaon
Mahul
Nanole
Sewri
Parel
Nehru Planetarium & Science Centre
Haji Ali Mosque
Race Course
Victoria Gardens
MUMBAI (BOMBAY)
Mumbai Harbour
Central Station
Elephanta Island (Gharapuri)
Imperial Towers
Byculla
Nhava
Malabar Hill
Mazagaon
Butcher Island (Dia Deva)
Shet Bandar
Elephanta Caves
Tardeo
Hanging Gardens
Bhuleshwar
Chowpatty Beach
Kalbadevi
Gharapuri
Cross Island
Back Bay
Mandvi
Sheva
Nhava Sheva (Jawaharlal Nehru Port)
Crawford Market
Chhatrapati Shivaji Terminus
Malabar Point
Churchgate Station
Nariman Point
Fort
Gateway of India
Saltpans
Colaba
Mora
Parje
Sonari
Jaskhar
Oyster Rock
Kharavli
Dongri
Pagote
Colaba Point
ARABIAN SEA
Ranvad
Punde
Uran
Bhendkhal
East from Greenwich
72°50'
73°00'
19°00'
A
B
1
2
Mumbai

## CENTRAL MUMBAI

Haji Ali Mosque
Causeway
Mahalaxmi Race Course
Mahalaxmi
Mahalaxmi Temple
Jijamata Udyan (Victoria Gardens)
Byculla
Breach Candy
Willingdon Sports Club
R. C. Cathedral
Mazagaon
Cumballa Hill
Mumbai Central Station
State Road Transport Terminus
Imperial Towers
Tardeo
Mani Bhavan (Gandhi Museum)
Raudat Tahera Mosque
Umerkhadi
Hanging Gardens
Babulnath Temple
SARDAR VALLABHBHAI PATEL RD
Bhuleshwar
Mandvi
Prince's Dock
Chowpatty Beach
Mumbadevi Temple
Victoria Dock
Kalbadevi
Taraporewala Aquarium
Girgaum
Jama Masjid Mosque
Crawford Market
Mahatma Phule
Cross Island
Pydhuni
Back Bay
St. George's Hospital
Albless & Cama Hospital
Azad Maidan
Chhatrapati Shivaji (Victoria) Terminus
Indira Docks
Wankhede Stadium
Mumbai Harbour
Churchgate Station
Brabourne Stadium
Oval Maidan
Fort
Rajabai Twr.
University
Town Hall
The Mint
Custom Basin
Jehangir Art Gallery
Chhatrapati Shivaji Museum
West Basin
National Gallery of Modern Art
Nariman Point
National Centre for Performing Arts
Colaba
Gateway of India
MARINE DRIVE
SIR JAMSHEDJI JIJIBHOY MARG
BARRISTER NATH PAI MARG
1
2
3

## MUNICH, GERMANY

1 0 1 km 2 3 4 5
1 0 miles 1 2 3
Udlding
Dachau-Ost
Dachau
Obermoos Schwaige
Oberschleissheim
TO MÜNCHEN FRANZ JOSEF STRAUSS (MUC)
Fischerhäuser
Garching
Lustheim
Hochbrück
Rothschmaige
Karlsfeld
Dirnismaning
Ismaning
Gröbenried
Eschenried
Ludwigsfeld
Neuherberg
Am Hasenbergl
Feldmoching
Allianz Arena
Deutsches Theater
Speicher-See
Gerberau
Allach
Fasanerie-Nord
Gross-Lappen
Freimann
Untermenzing
Langwald
Moosach
Milbertshofen
Unterföhring
Aschheim
Lochhausen
Obermenzing
Johanneskirchen
Oberföhring
Olympic Park
Gern
Schwabing
Aubing
Blutenberg
Nymphenburg
MÜNCHEN
Neu Aubing
Schloss Nymphenburg
Neuhausen
Bogenhausen
Dornach
Zamdorf
Daglfing
Riem
Freiham
Pasing
Frauenkirche
Residenz
Altes Rathaus
Haidhausen
Lochham
Laim
Deutsches Museum
Kirchtrudering
Gräfelfing
Sendling
Gronsdorf
Gross-Hadern
Berg am Laim
Ramersdorf
Strasstrudering
Planegg
Martinsried
Thalkirchen
Giesing
Neuperlach
Haar
Waldtrudering
Krailling
Perlach
Neuried
Forstenried
Fasangarten
Solalinden
Öden-Stockach
Harlaching
Waldperlach
Maxhof
Solln
Perlacher
Unterbiberg
Warnberg
Forst
Neubiberg
Forstenrieder
Gross-hesselohe
Unterhaching
Geiselgasteig
Pullach
Westerham
Ottobrunn
Park
Am Wald
Hohenbrunn
Höllriegelskreuth
Taufkirchen
Winning
Buchenhain
Grünwalder
Bergham
Wachterhof
Grünwald
Furth
Potzham
Forst
Kirchstockbach
Oberhaching
Munich
East from Greenwich
1 2 3


## CENTRAL MUNICH

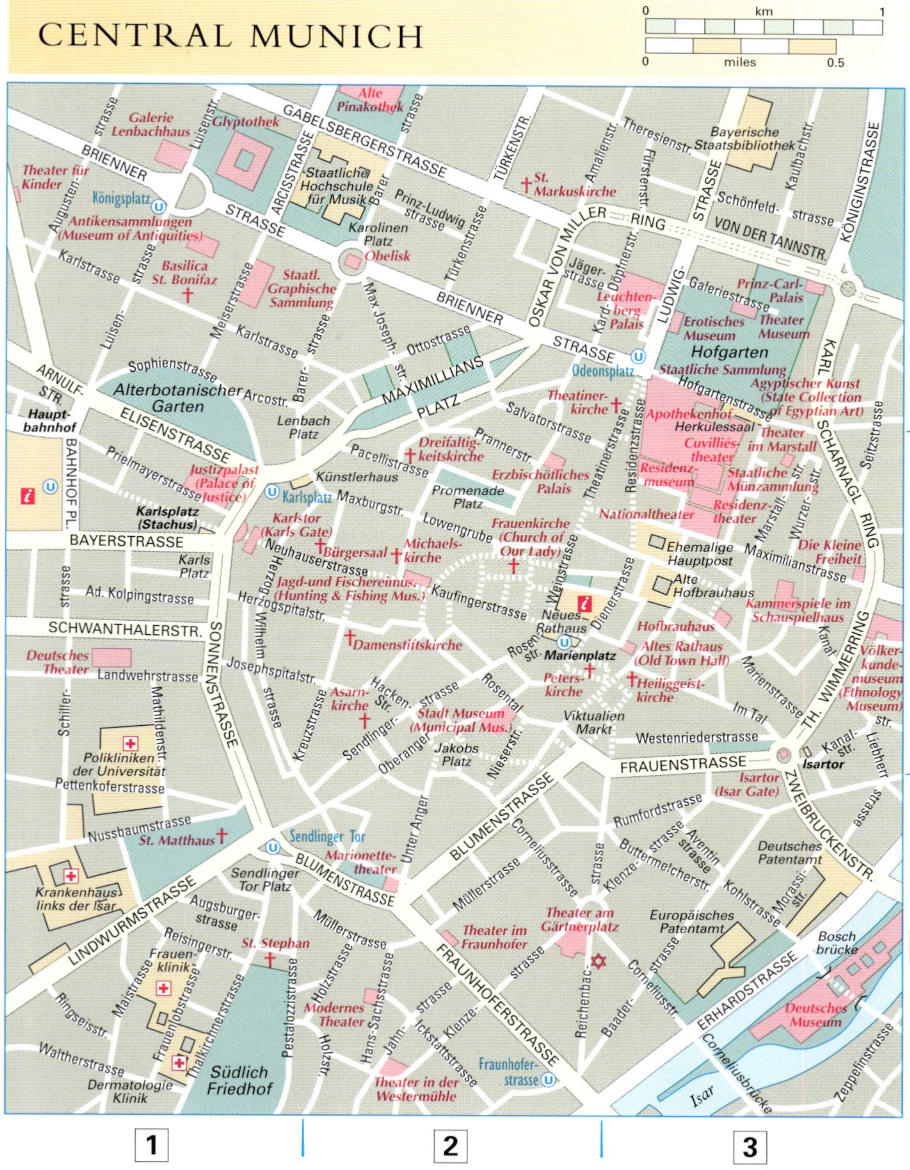

0 km 1
0 miles 0.5
Alte Pinakothek
Galerie Lenbachhaus
Glyptothek
GABELSBERGERSTRASSE
Bayerische Staatsbibliothek
Theater für Kinder
Königsplatz
Staatliche Hochschule für Musik
Karolinenplatz
Obelisk
Antikensammlungen (Museum of Antiquities)
Basilica St. Bonifaz
Staatl. Graphische Sammlung
BRIENNER STRASSE
St. Markuskirche
Prinz-Carl-Palais
Leuchtenberg Palais
Erotisches Museum
Theater Museum
Hofgarten
Odeonsplatz
Staatliche Sammlung Ägyptischer Kunst (State Collection of Egyptian Art)
Alterbotanischer Garten
MAXIMILLIANS PLATZ
Theatinerkirche
Haupt-bahnhof
Lenbach Platz
Apothekenhof
Herkulessaal
Theater im Marstall
Cuvilliés-theater
Residenz-museum
Staatliche Münzsammlung
Dreifaltig-keitskirche
Erzbischöfliches Palais
Justizpalast (Palace of Justice)
Künstlerhaus
Promenade Platz
Karlsplatz (Stachus)
Karlstor (Karls Gate)
Frauenkirche (Church of Our Lady)
Nationaltheater
Residenz-theater
Die Kleine Freiheit
BAYERSTRASSE
Bürgersaal
Michaels-kirche
Jagd-und Fischereimus. (Hunting & Fishing Mus.)
Neues Rathaus
Marienplatz
Ehemalige Hauptpost
Alte Hofbrauhaus
Kammerspiele im Schauspielhaus
SCHWANTHALERSTR.
Damenstiftskirche
Hofbrauhaus
Altes Rathaus (Old Town Hall)
Völker-kunde-museum (Ethnology Museum)
Deutsches Theater
Peters-kirche
Heiliggeist-kirche
Asam-kirche
Stadt Museum (Municipal Mus.)
Viktualien Markt
Polikliniken der Universität
Jakobs Platz
Westenriederstrasse
FRAUENSTRASSE
Isartor (Isar Gate)
St. Matthaus
Sendlinger Tor
Sendlinger Tor Platz
Marionette-theater
Deutsches Patentamt
Krankenhaus links der Isar
BLUMENSTRASSE
Theater im Fraunhofer
Theater am Gärtnerplatz
Europäisches Patentamt
Bosch brücke
St. Stephan
Frauen-klinik
Modernes Theater
Deutsches Museum
LINDWURMSTRASSE
FRAUNHOFERSTRASSE
ERHARDSTRASSE
Dermatologie Klinik
Südlich Friedhof
Theater in der Westermühle
Fraunhofer-strasse
Isar
1 2 3
a b c


## NEW ORLEANS, LOUISIANA

1 0 1 km 2 3 4 5
1 0 miles 1 2 3
Lake Pontchartrain
Lake Pontchartrain Causeway (Toll)
JEFFERSON PARISH
ORLEANS PARISH
NEW ORLEANS LAKEFRONT
Kenner
Treasure Chest Casino
Kiefer UNO Lakefront Arena
Southern Yacht Club
Univ. of New Orleans
The Esplanade
Bissonet Plaza
Southern Univ. at New Orleans
New Orleans Baptist Theological Sem.
Toll
Bucktown
Lakeside Shop. Ctr.
Bonnabel Place
City Park
Southwest Univ.
Willowdale
Gentilly
Lakeview
Westgate
Lafreniere Park
Clearview Shop. Ctr.
Dillard University
LOUIS ARMSTRONG NEW ORLEANS INTL. (MSY)
Metairie
New Orleans Mus. of Art
Fairgrounds Racetrack
Bywater
NEW ORLEANS
Longue Vue House
Mid City
Central Sta.
Rivertown
Zephyr Field
Elmwood Center
French Quarter (Vieux Carre)
River Ridge
South-port
Jefferson
St Louis Cath.
Mississippi
Live Oak Manor
Elmwood
Carrollton
Mercedes-Benz Superdome
Huey P. Long Bridge
Tulane University
Union Station
Algiers
Bridge City
Loyola University
Harahan
Audubon Park
Garden District
Waggaman
Audubon Zoological Gardens
Oakwood Shop. Ctr.
Avondale
Gretna
Harvey
Terrytown
Alario Ctr.
Bayou Segnette State Park
Gretna City Park
Westwego
Marrero
New Orleans
Jean Lafitte Natl. Historical Park
Estelle
(Bayou Boeuf)
Boomtown Casino Westbank
Lake Cataouatche
JEFFERSON PARISH
ST CHARLES PARISH
JEFFERSON PAR.
PLAQUEMINES PAR.
ALVIN CALLENDAR NAVAL AIR STATION
West from Greenwich
1 2


## CENTRAL NEW ORLEANS

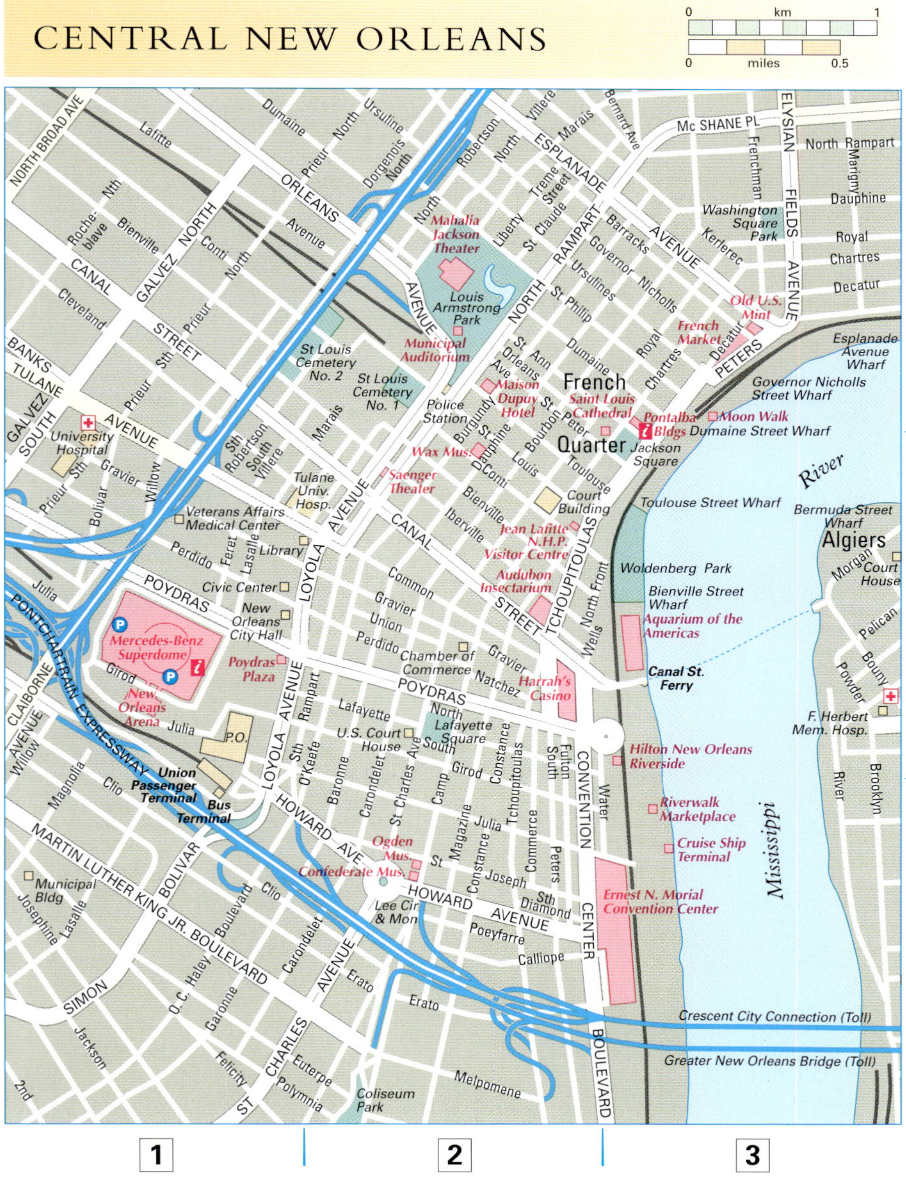

0 km 1
0 miles 0.5
NORTH BROAD AVE
ESPLANADE
Mc SHANE PL
ELYSIAN FIELDS AVENUE
Mahalia Jackson Theater
Washington Square Park
Louis Armstrong Park
Municipal Auditorium
Old U.S. Mint
French Market
Esplanade Avenue Wharf
St Louis Cemetery No. 2
St Louis Cemetery No. 1
French Quarter
Governor Nicholls Street Wharf
Police Station
Maison Dupuy Hotel
Saint Louis Cathedral
Pontalba Bldgs
Moon Walk
Dumaine Street Wharf
Jackson Square
University Hospital
Wax Mus.
Saenger Theater
Tulane Univ. Hosp.
Court Building
Toulouse Street Wharf
River
Bermuda Street Wharf
Algiers
Veterans Affairs Medical Center
Jean Lafitte N.H.P. Visitor Centre
Woldenberg Park
Library
Civic Center
Audubon Insectarium
Bienville Street Wharf
Aquarium of the Americas
Court House
New Orleans City Hall
Mercedes-Benz Superdome
Poydras Plaza
Chamber of Commerce
Harrah's Casino
Canal St. Ferry
New Orleans Arena
F. Herbert Mem. Hosp.
U.S. Court House
Lafayette Square
Hilton New Orleans Riverside
Union Passenger Terminal
Bus Terminal
Riverwalk Marketplace
Cruise Ship Terminal
PONTCHARTRAIN EXPRESSWAY
Ogden Mus.
Confederate Mus.
Mississippi
Municipal Bldg
MARTIN LUTHER KING JR. BOULEVARD
Lee Cir & Mon
Ernest N. Morial Convention Center
CONVENTION CENTER BOULEVARD
Crescent City Connection (Toll)
Greater New Orleans Bridge (Toll)
Coliseum Park
1 2 3
a b c


Interstate route numbers   U.S. route numbers   State route numbers

## NEW YORK, NEW YORK

## CENTRAL NEW YORK

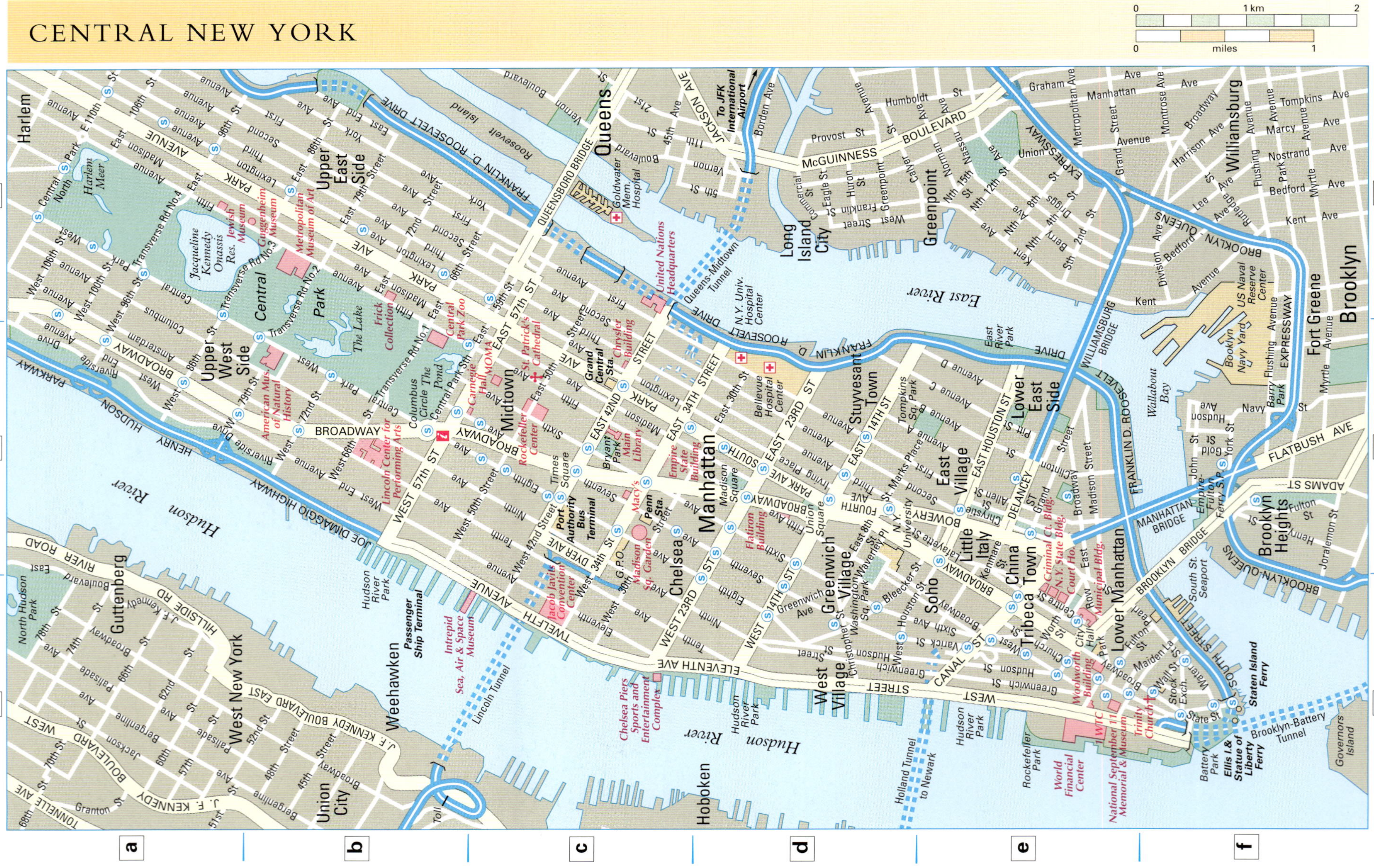

## ORLANDO, FLORIDA

Lake Apopka
Clarcona
Lockhart
Eatonville
Maitland
Winter Park
Winter Garden
Ocoee
Fairview Shores
Pine Hills
ORLANDO
ORLANDO EXECUTIVE
Beulah
Gotha
Orlovista
Windermere
Summerport Beach
Lake Cain Hills
Edgewood
Conway
Belle Isle
Pine Castle
Bay Hill
Tangelo Park
Sky Lake
Doctor Phillips
Morningside Park
ORLANDO INTERNATIONAL (MCO)
Taft
Vineland
Williamsburg
Walt Disney World
Lake Buena Vista
Hunter's Creek
Flamingo
Florida's Turnpike
ORANGE CO.
West from Greenwich
Orlando
1
2

Interstate route numbers U.S. route numbers State route numbers

## OSAKA, JAPAN

Takarazuka
Chūgoku-Jidosha Expressway
Senriyama
Yamada
Itami
OSAKA ITAMI (ITM)
Toyonaka
Settsu
Meishin-Kosuku Expressway
Suita
Hirota
Nishinomiya
Kadoma
Higashiyodogawa
Moriguchi
Naruo
Amagasaki
Asahi
Jūsō
Miyakojima
Umeda
Jōtō
Nishiyodogawa
Fukushima
Kita
Higashi
Higashinari
Konohana
Minami
Maishima (Sports Island)
Minato
Nishi
Ikuno
Yumeshima Island
Naniwa
ŌSAKA
Osaka Harbour
Tennōji
Abeno
Taishō
Kyūhōji
Kizuri
Sakishima Island
Nishinari
Setonaiki (Inland Sea)
Higashisumiyoshi
Sakai Harbour
Sumiyoshi
Tainaka
Ikeuchi
Matsubara
Sakai
TO OSAKA KANSAI INTL. (KIX)
Osaka
A
B
1
2

## OSLO, NORWAY

Nordmarka
Maridalen
Holmenkollen
Kjelsås
Bærums Verk
Gorud
Røa
Ris
OSLO
Ullevål
Rødtvet
Lijordet
Østerås
Ullern
Sinsen
Rykkinn
Haslum
Skøyen
Alna
Kolsås
Bekkestua
Tøyen
TO OSLO (OSL)
Stabekk
Lysaker
Bærum
Bygdøy
Høvik
Hovedøya
Tanum
Sandvika
Lindøya
Oppsal
Bøler
Slependen
Fornebu
Bekkelaget
Nesøya
Ormøya
Nesbru
Hvalstad
Nesoddtangen
Malmøya
Nordstrand
Asker
Flaskebekk
Ljabru
Holmenfjorden
Oksval
Hauketo
Konglungen
Ljan
Skoklefall
Hellvik
Oslofjorden
Bunnefjorden
Holmlia
Klemetsrud
Blakstad
Ingierstrand
Torvvik
Kolbotn
Nesodden
Vollen
Fjellstrand
Bomansvik
Svestad
Svartskog
Granerud
Blylaget
Oppegård
Nærsnes
East from Greenwich
Oslo
2
3
4

## CENTRAL OSLO

Rikshospitalet
Vår Frelsers Gravlund
Slotts parken (Royal Park)
ST. OLAVS GATE
Slottet (Royal Palace)
Dronningparken
DRAMMENSVEIEN
Universitet
Nasjonalgalleriet (National Gallery)
HAMMERSBORG TUNNELEN
Nationaltheatret
Det Norske Teater
Stortinget (Parliament)
Rådhus (City Hall)
Nobel Peace Center
KARL JOHANS GATE
Domkirke (Cathedral)
GRENSEN
MØLLERGATA
Oslo Spektrum
STENERSGATA
Sentralstasjon
Akershus Slott og festning (Akerhus Castle)
Forsvarsmuseet (Defence Museum)
Hjemmefrontmuseet (Resistance Museum)
Museet for samtidskunst (Museum of Contemporary Art)
Operahuset (Oslo Opera House)
OPERATUNNELEN
BISPEGATA
NYLANDSVEIEN
Pipervika
Bjørvika
Bispevika
Oslofjorden
a
b
c
1
2
3

## PARIS, FRANCE

Carrières-sous-Poissy
Achères
Maisons-Laffitte
Sartrouville
Argenteuil
VAL-D'OISE
Gennevilliers
Villeneuve-la-Garenne
St-Denis
Stains
TO PARIS CHARLES-DE-GAULLE (CDG)
Le Blanc-Mesnil
Aulnay-sous-Bois
Sevran
Tremblay-en-France
Villeparisis
Claye-Souilly
Forêt de St-Germain
Le Mesnil-le-Roi
Poissy
Carrières-sous-Bois
Houilles
Bezons
Colombes
Bois-Colombes
Asnières
La Courneuve
Le Bourget
Drancy
Livry-Gargan
Vaujours
Coubron
Courtry
Le Pin
Villevaudé
Montjay-la-Tour
St-Germain-en-Laye
Chambourcy
Aigremont
Montesson
Carrières-sur-Seine
La Garenne-Colombes
Clichy
St-Ouen
Aubervilliers
SEINE-ST-DENIS
Bobigny
Les Pavillons-sous-Bois
Clichy-sous-Bois
Montfermeil
Forêt de Bondy
Le Vésinet
Courbevoie
Levallois-Perret
Pantin
Bondy
Le Raincy
Chelles
Brou-sur-Chantereine
Chantereine
Fourqueux
Le Pecq
Chatou
Puteaux
La Défense
Sacré Cœur
Le Pré-St-Gervais
Les Lilas
Noisy-le-Sec
Gagny
Forêt de Marly-le-Roi
Mareil-Marly
Le Port-Marly
Croissy-sur-Seine
Nanterre
Neuilly-sur-Seine
Gare du Nord
Gare de l'Est
Romainville
Villemomble
Rosny-sous-Bois
Neuilly-sur-Marne
Vaires-sur-Marne
L'Étang-la-Ville
Marly-le-Roi
Rueil-Malmaison
Suresnes
Bois de Boulogne
Arc de Triomphe
Place de la Concorde
PARIS
Bagnolet
Montreuil
Canal de Chelles
Marne
Torcy
Bougival
Garches
Hippodrome de Longchamp
Tour Eiffel
Invalides
Musée du Louvre
Notre Dame
Gare de Lyon
Fontenay-sous-Bois
Neuilly-Plaisance
Gournay-sur-Marne
Noisiel
St-Nom-la-Bretèche
Noisy-le-Roi
Louveciennes
La Celle-St-Cloud
St-Cloud
Vaucresson
Roland Garros
Gare Montparnasse
Gare d'Austerlitz
Vincennes
St-Mandé
Nogent-sur-Marne
Bry-sur-Marne
Noisy-le-Grand
Champs-sur-Marne
Marne-la-Vallée
Bailly
Rennemoulin
YVELINES
Ville-d'Avray
Boulogne-Billancourt
Parc des Princes
Vanves
Bois de Vincennes
Charenton-le-Pont
St-Maurice
Joinville-le-Pont
Le Perreux-sur-Marne
Villiers-sur-Marne
Fontenay-le-Fleury
Le Chesnay
Sèvres
Issy-les-Moulineaux
Malakoff
Montrouge
Gentilly
Ivry-sur-Seine
Le Kremlin-Bicêtre
Maisons-Alfort
Champigny-sur-Marne
Cœuilly
Bois St-Martin
Émerainville
LOGNES ÉMERAINVILLE
St-Cyr-l'École
Versailles
Château de Versailles
HAUTS-DE-SEINE
Meudon
Clamart
Châtillon
Arcueil
Alfortville
St-Maur-des-Fossés
Le Plessis-Trévise
Combault
SEINE-ET-MARNE
Roissy-en-Brie
Bois d'Arcy
Chaville
Bagneux
Cachan
Villejuif
Vitry-sur-Seine
Créteil
VAL-DE-MARNE
Chennevières-sur-Marne
La Queue-en-Brie
Étang de St-Quentin
Viroflay
Vélizy-Villacoublay
Le Plessis-Robinson
Fontenay-aux-Roses
L'Haÿ-les-Roses
Chevilly-Larue
Thiais
Choisy-le-Roi
Ormesson-sur-Marne
Pontault-Combault
Bouviers
Guyancourt
Montigny-le-Bretonneux
Buc
Jouy-en-Josas
Sceaux
Châtenay-Malabry
Bourg-la-Reine
Bonneuil-sur-Marne
Sucy-en-Brie
Noiseau
Forêt de Notre-Dame
Ozoir-la-Ferrière
TOUSSUS-LE-NOBLE
Toussus-le-Noble
Les Loges-en-Josas
Bièvres
Verrières-le-Buisson
Antony
Fresnes
Rungis
Orly
PARIS-ORLY (ORY)
Valenton
Limeil-Brévannes
Boissy-St-Léger
Marolles-en-Brie
Lésigny
Magny-les-Hameaux
Châteaufort
Étang de Saclay
Le Christ de Saclay
Igny
Vauhallan
Massy
Wissous
Villeneuve-le-Roi
Villeneuve-St-Georges
Grosbois
Santeny
St-Lambert
Milon-la-Chapelle
Saclay
Villiers-le-Bâcle
ESSONNE
Chilly-Mazarin
Paray-Vieille Poste
Athis-Mons
Ablon-sur-Seine
Crosne
Villecresnes
Yerres
Cressely
St-Aubin
Rhodon
Palaiseau
East from Greenwich


## CENTRAL PARIS

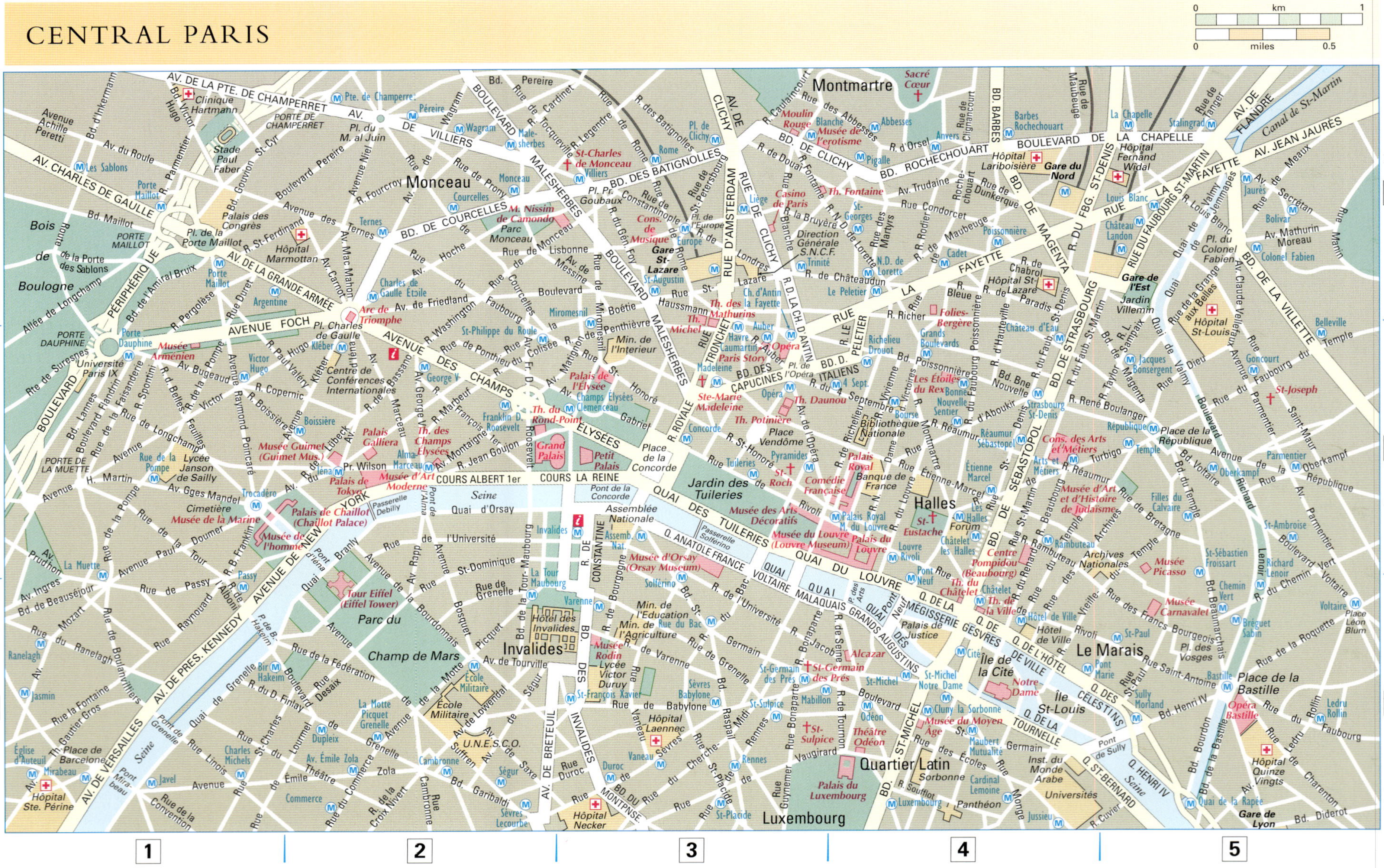

Montmartre
Sacré Cœur
Moulin Rouge
Musée de l'érotisme
Monceau
Parc Monceau
St-Charles de Monceau
M. Nissim de Camondo
Stade Paul Faber
Palais des Congrès
Porte Maillot
Bois de Boulogne
Avenue Foch
Arc de Triomphe
Pl. Charles de Gaulle
Gare St-Lazare
Opéra
Gare du Nord
Gare de l'Est
Hôpital Lariboisière
Hôpital Fernand Widal
Canal de St-Martin
Musée Marmottan
Musée Arménien
Musée Guimet (Guimet Mus.)
Palais Galliera
Grand Palais
Petit Palais
Palais de l'Élysée
Champs Élysées
Place de la Concorde
Madeleine
Place Vendôme
Jardin des Tuileries
Musée du Louvre (Louvre Museum)
Palais Royal
Halles
Forum des Halles
Centre Pompidou (Beaubourg)
Cons. des Arts et Métiers
Place de la République
Hôpital St-Louis
Musée Picasso
Musée Carnavalet
Le Marais
Place de la Bastille
Opéra Bastille
Hôpital Quinze Vingts
Palais de Chaillot (Chaillot Palace)
Musée de l'homme
Musée de la Marine
Tour Eiffel (Eiffel Tower)
Parc du Champ de Mars
École Militaire
U.N.E.S.C.O.
Invalides
Hôtel des Invalides
Musée Rodin
Assemblée Nationale
Musée d'Orsay (Orsay Museum)
Quai d'Orsay
Seine
Île de la Cité
Notre-Dame
Île St-Louis
St-Germain des Prés
St-Sulpice
Théâtre Odéon
Quartier Latin
Sorbonne
Panthéon
Palais du Luxembourg
Luxembourg
Hôpital Necker
Hôpital Laennec
Hôpital Ste. Périne
Gare de Lyon
Institut du Monde Arabe
Universités
Boulevard Haussmann
Boulevard de Clichy
Boulevard de la Chapelle
Boulevard de Magenta
Boulevard de Strasbourg
Boulevard de Sébastopol
Quai du Louvre
Quai Voltaire
Av. de Pres. Kennedy
Av. de New York
Bd. Saint-Germain
Bd. St-Michel
Rue de Rivoli

## PRAGUE, CZECH REPUBLIC

1 0 1 km 2 3 4 5
1 0 miles 1 2 3

Vodochodny
Klíčany
Bašt
Měšice
Mratín
Turkso
Libčice nad Vltavou
Libeznice
Sluhy
Hovorčovice
Brázdim
Řež
Vltava
Klecany
Veleň
Úholičky
Žalov
Zdiby
Třeboradice
Přezletice
Velké Přílepy
Roztoky
Dolní Chabry
Čakovice
Vinoř
Statenice
Suchdol
Čimice
Ďáblice
Letňany
Kbely
Horoměřice
Lysolaje
Kobylisy
Střížkov
Prosek
Satalice
Tuchoměřice
Podbaba
Zoo
Troja
Kyje
Nebušice
Libeň
Horní Počernice
PRAHA-RUZYNĚ (PRG)
Vokovice
Dejvice
Bubeneč
Holešovice
Vysočany
Hloubětín
Hradčany
Castle
Karlín
Dolní Počernice
Střešovice
Ruzyně
Veleslavin
Břevnov
Staré Město
Žižkov
Vinohrady
PRAHA
Malešice
Malá Strana
Nové Město
Strašnice
Repy
Motol
Smíchov
Vršovice
Běchovice
Zličín
Košíře
Vyšehrad
Radlice
Nusle
Záběhlice
Dubeč
Kopanina
Stodůlky
Jinonice
Podolí
Michle
Hostivař
Měcholupy
Řeporyje
Spořilov
Petrovice
Jinočany
Hlubočepy
Krč
Chodov
Uhříněves
Zbuzany
Braník
Kunratice
Slivenec
Lhotka
Šeberov
Lochkov
Velká Chuchle
Modřany
Libuš
Průhonice
Písnice
Radotín
Cholupice
Třebotov
Černošice
Zbraslav
Točná
Jesenice
East from Greenwich
Prague
1
2
3


## CENTRAL PRAGUE

0 km 1
0 miles 0.5

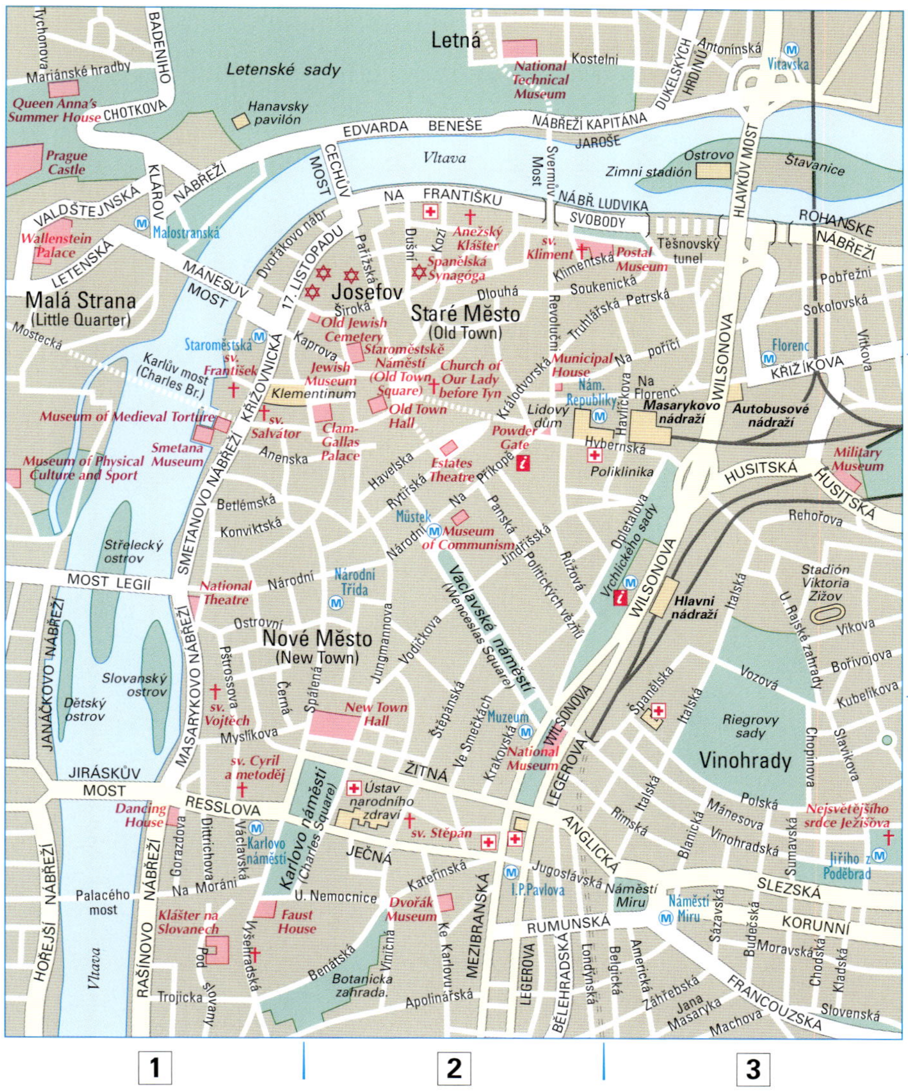

Letná
Letenské sady
Hanavský pavilón
National Technical Museum
Queen Anne's Summer House
Prague Castle
Wallenstein Palace
Malostranská
Malá Strana (Little Quarter)
Vltava
Josefov
Staré Město (Old Town)
Old Jewish Cemetery
Jewish Museum
Staroměstské Náměstí (Old Town Square)
Church of Our Lady before Týn
Old Town Hall
Karlův most (Charles Br.)
Klementinum
Museum of Medieval Torture
Smetana Museum
Clam-Gallas Palace
Estates Theatre
Powder Gate
Municipal House
Masarykovo nádraží
Autobusové nádraží
Florenc
Military Museum
Museum of Physical Culture and Sport
Střelecký ostrov
Museum of Communism
Národní Třída
National Theatre
Slovanský ostrov
Dětský ostrov
Nové Město (New Town)
Václavské náměstí (Wenceslas Square)
Hlavní nádraží
Stadion Viktoria Žižkov
New Town Hall
National Museum
Muzeum
Riegrovy sady
Vinohrady
Dancing House
Karlovo náměstí (Charles Square)
Faust House
Dvořák Museum
Botanická zahrada
Náměstí Míru
Nejsvětějšího srdce Ježíšova
Jiřího z Poděbrad
I.P.Pavlova
Palackého most
Klášter na Slovanech
a
b
c
1
2
3


## RIO DE JANEIRO, BRAZIL

1 0 1 km 2 3 4 5
1 0 miles 1 2 3

Duque de Caxias
Vigário Geral
Ilha do Governador
RIO DE JANEIRO GALEÃO (GIG)
Moneró
Freguesia
Cocotá
Jardim Guanabara
Zumbi
Penha
Ribeira
Ilha dos Tavares
Porto Novo
Olaria
Cosmos
Ramos
Bonsucesso
Baía de Guanabara
Serra da Misericórdia
Ilha do Fundão
Cidade Universitária
Inhaúma
Ilha do Engenho
Neves
Ilha de Santa Cruz
Pilares
Piedade
Benfica
Caju
Ponte Presidente Costa e Silva
Ilha da Conceição
Barreto
São Cristóvão
Armação
Encantado
Estádio Olímpico João Havelange
Méier
Jacaré
Ilha das Cobras
Palácio do Governo
Niterói
Água Santa
Gamboa
Gragoatá
SANTOS DUMONT (SDU)
Icaraí
Sa. dos Pretos Forros
Vila Isabel
Estádio Maracanã
Maracanã
Isabel
RIO DE JANEIRO
Catete
Glória
Lapa
Enseada de Jurujuba
Rio Comprido
Serra dos Três Rios
Andaraí
Laranjeiras
Morro do Macaco
Pico da Tijuca
Tijuca
Flamengo
Usina
Botafogo
Urca
Pão de Açúcar (Sugar Loaf Mt.)
Alto da Boa Vista
Parque Nacional da Tijuca
Corcovado
Cristo Redentor
Jd. Mar Azul
Lagoa
Leme
Ilha de Cotunduba
Itanhanga
Gávea
Copacabana
Leblon
Ilha do Pai
Ipanema
Forte de Copacabana
Ponta do Arpoador
Pedra da Gávea
Joá
São Conrado
ATLANTIC OCEAN
Barra de Tijuca
West from Greenwich
Rio de Janeiro
1
2


## CENTRAL RIO DE JANEIRO

0 km 0.25
0 miles 0.125

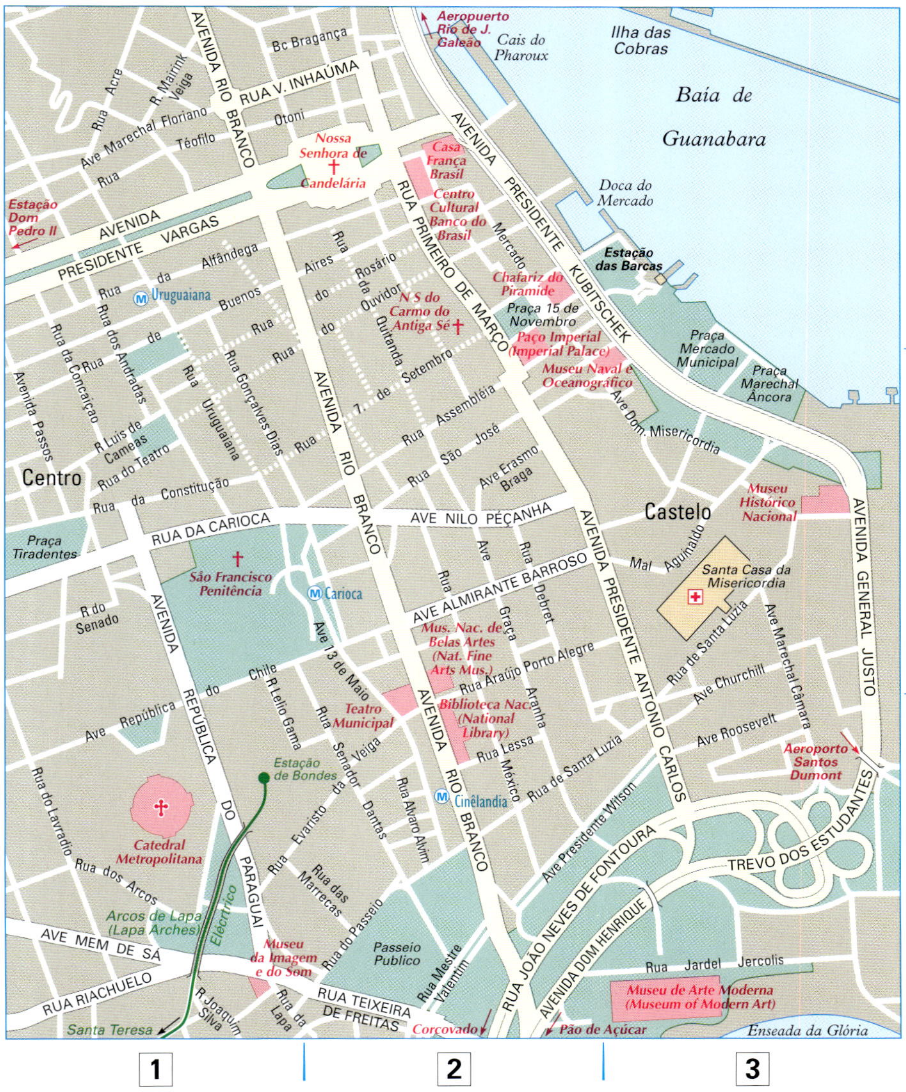

Aeropuerto Rio de J. Galeão
Cais do Pharoux
Ilha das Cobras
Baía de Guanabara
Doca do Mercado
Estação Dom Pedro II
Nossa Senhora de Candelária
Casa França Brasil
Centro Cultural Banco do Brasil
Estação das Barcas
Avenida Presidente Vargas
Uruguaiana
N.S. do Carmo da Antiga Sé
Chafariz do Piramide
Praça 15 de Novembro
Paço Imperial (Imperial Palace)
Museu Naval e Oceanográfico
Mercado Municipal
Praça Marechal Âncora
Centro
Praça Tiradentes
Rua da Carioca
Ave Nilo Peçanha
Castelo
Museu Histórico Nacional
São Francisco Penitência
Carioca
Ave Almirante Barroso
Santa Casa da Misericórdia
Mus. Nac. de Belas Artes (Nat. Fine Arts Mus.)
Teatro Municipal
Biblioteca Nac. (National Library)
Estação de Bondes
Cinelândia
Aeroporto Santos Dumont
Catedral Metropolitana
Arcos de Lapa (Lapa Arches)
Passeio Publico
Trevo dos Estudantes
Museu da Imagem e do Som
Museu de Arte Moderna (Museum of Modern Art)
Santa Teresa
Corcovado
Pão de Açúcar
Enseada da Glória
Avenida Rio Branco
Avenida Presidente Antonio Carlos
Avenida General Justo
a
b
c
1
2
3

## ROME, ITALY

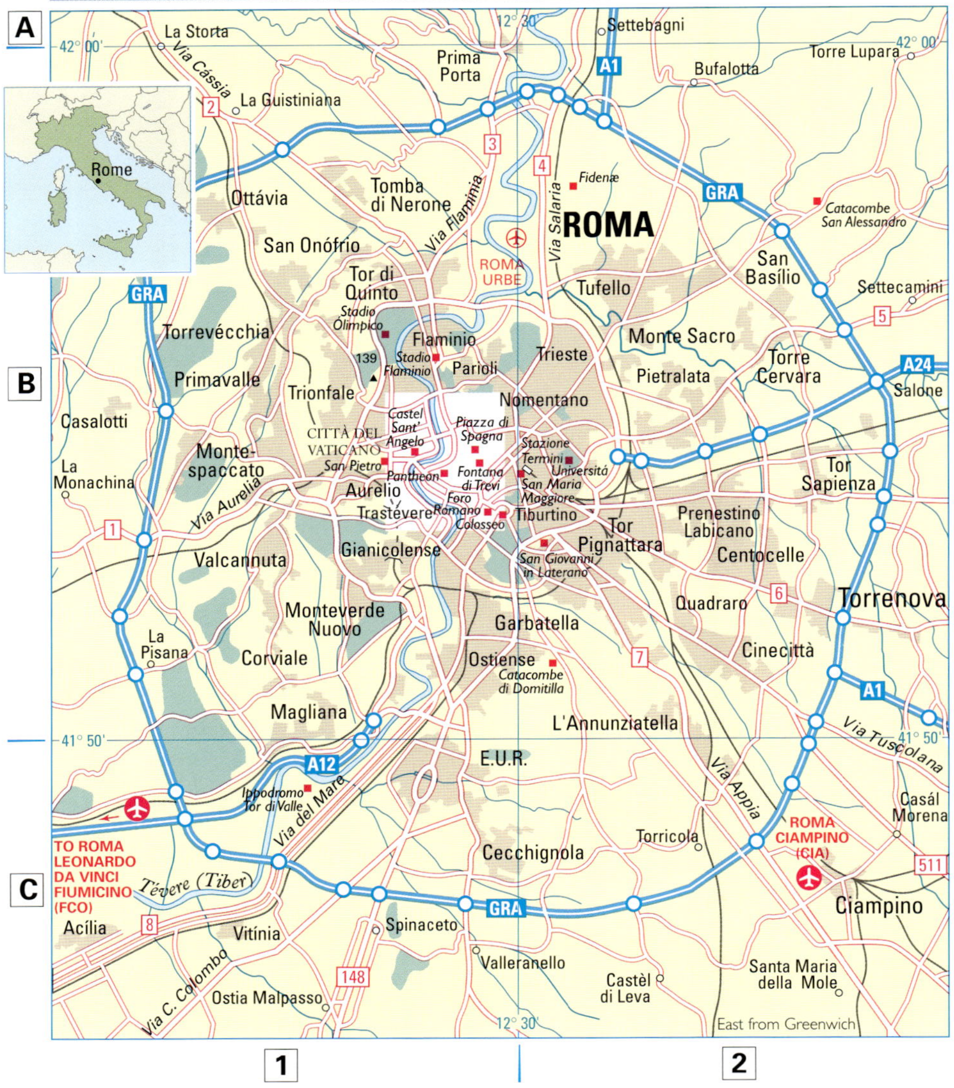
A
B
C
1
2
La Storta
Via Cássia
La Guistiniana
Prima Porta
Settebagni
Bufalotta
Torre Lupara
Rome
Ottávia
Tomba di Nerone
Via Flaminia
Via Salaria
Fidenæ
ROMA
GRA
Catacombe San Alessandro
San Onófrio
Tor di Quinto
Stadio Olimpico
ROMA URBE
Tufello
San Basilio
Settecamini
Torrevécchia
Primavalle
Flaminio
Parioli
Trieste
Monte Sacro
Pietralata
Torre Cervara
A24
Salone
Casalotti
Trionfale
CITTÀ DEL VATICANO
Nomentano
La Monachina
Monte-spaccato
Aurelio
Via Aurelia
Trastevere
Tiburtino
Tor Pignattara
Prenestino Labicano
Tor Sapienza
Valcannuta
Gianicolense
Centocelle
Monteverde Nuovo
Garbatella
Quadraro
Torrenova
La Pisana
Corviale
Ostiense
Catacombe di Domitilla
Cinecittà
A1
Magliana
L'Annunziatella
Via Tuscolana
A12
E.U.R.
Via Appia
Casál Morena
TO ROMA LEONARDO DA VINCI FIUMICINO (FCO)
Via del Mare
ROMA CIAMPINO (CIA)
Tévere (Tiber)
Cecchignola
Torricola
Ciampino
Acilia
Vitinia
Spinaceto
Vallerანello
Santa Maria della Mole
Castèl di Leva
Via C. Colombo
Ostia Malpasso
East from Greenwich

## CENTRAL ROME

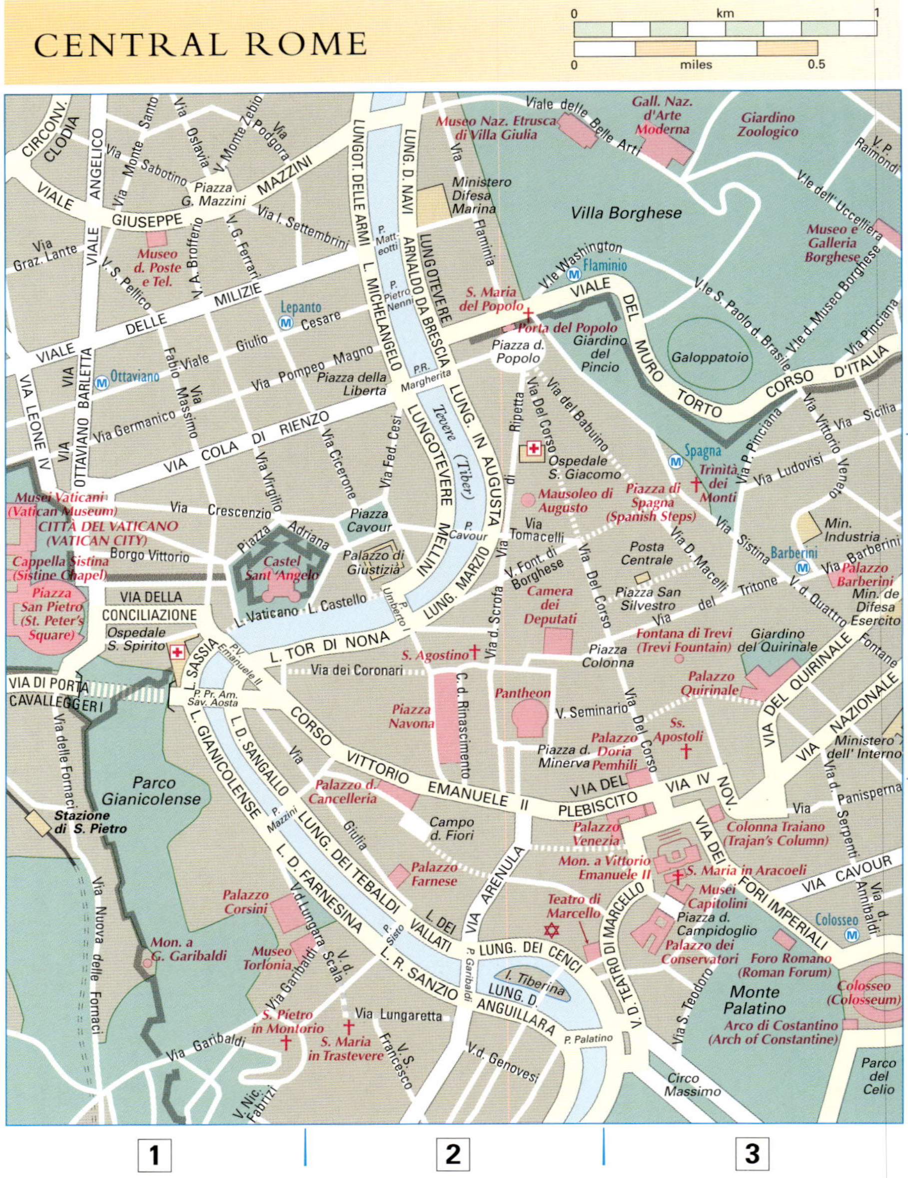
km
miles
0.5
1
2
3
Villa Borghese
Galoppatoio
Giardino Zoologico
Gall. Naz. d'Arte Moderna
Museo Naz. Etrusco di Villa Giulia
Museo e Galleria Borghese
Piazza del Popolo
S. Maria del Popolo
Porta del Popolo
Flaminio
Lepanto
Ottaviano
Musei Vaticani (Vatican Museum)
CITTÀ DEL VATICANO (VATICAN CITY)
Cappella Sistina (Sistine Chapel)
Piazza San Pietro (St. Peter's Square)
Castel Sant'Angelo
Palazzo di Giustizia
Piazza Cavour
Mausoleo di Augusto
Piazza di Spagna (Spanish Steps)
Trinità dei Monti
Spagna
Barberini
Palazzo Barberini
Fontana di Trevi (Trevi Fountain)
Palazzo Quirinale
Pantheon
Piazza Navona
Piazza Colonna
Palazzo Venezia
Colonna Traiano (Trajan's Column)
Campo d. Fiori
Palazzo Farnese
Palazzo Corsini
Parco Gianicolense
Stazione di S. Pietro
Teatro di Marcello
Foro Romano (Roman Forum)
Colosseo (Colosseum)
Monte Palatino
Arco di Costantino (Arch of Constantine)
Circo Massimo
S. Maria in Trastevere
S. Pietro in Montorio
I. Tiberina
VIA DELLA CONCILIAZIONE
CORSO VITTORIO EMANUELE II
VIA DEL PLEBISCITO
VIA CAVOUR
VIA NAZIONALE

## SAN FRANCISCO, CALIF.

A
B
C
1
2
3
122° 30'
122° 20'
37° 50'
37° 40'
Marin City
Belvedere
Tiburon
Angel Island State Park
Berkeley
Marin Peninsula
Sausalito
Blunt Point
MARIN CO.
San Francisco Bay
Emeryville
Golden Gate National Rec. Area
Alcatraz I.
Treasure Island
Golden Gate Bridge
Oakland
Yerba Buena I.
Presidio
Pacific Hts.
Western Addition
Alameda Point
Alameda
Richmond
Haight Ashbury
Golden Gate Park
Sunset
Castro
Mission
Potrero Hill
Twin Peaks
Forest Hill
Bernal Heights
Bayview
SAN FRANCISCO
Parkside
West of Twin Peaks
Outer Mission
Visitacion Valley
Hunters Point
Candlestick Park San Francisco 49ers
SAN FRANCISCO CO.
SAN MATEO CO.
Daly City
Bayshore
Westlake
Broadmoor
Sterling Park
Brisbane
San Bruno Mountain State Park
Colma
Serramonte
South San Francisco
Point San Bruno
Edgemar
Pacifica
Pacific Manor
TO SAN FRANCISCO INTL. (SFO)
PACIFIC OCEAN
San Francisco
West from Greenwich

## CENTRAL SAN FRANCISCO

km
miles
0.25
0.125
1
2
3
Hyde Street Pier
Fisherman's Wharf
Bay Cruises
Pier 39 Aquarium of the Bay
Cruise Ship Terminal
San Francisco Bay
National Maritime Museum
The Cannery
Fort Mason Center
Ghirardelli Square
Telegraph Hill
Coit Tower
Russian Hill
North Beach
St. Peter & St.Paul
THE EMBARCADERO
COLUMBUS AVE
Chinatown
Ferry Terminal
Trans-Bay Tube (BART)
Transamerica Pyramid
Embarcadero Center
Justin Herman Plaza
Haas-Lilienthal House
Nob Hill
Cable Car Barn
Grace Cathedral
Financial District
Transbay Terminal
Lafayette Park
Union Square
Powell St. Cable Car Turntable
Yerba Buena Gardens
Museum of Modern Art
Japan Center
St. Mary's Cath.
Moscone Convention Center
Civic Center
City Hall
Main Library
South of Market
South Beach Harbor
AT&T Park
China Basin
Opera Ho.
Symphony Hall
Hall of Justice
Caltrain Depot
Mission Creek Marina
VAN NESS AVENUE
MARKET STREET
GEARY STREET
CALIFORNIA STREET

Interstate route numbers — U.S. route numbers — State route numbers — Cable Car route

## ST PETERSBURG, RUSSIA

Gulf of Finland
SANKT-PETERBURG
Olgino
Lakhtinskiy
Dolgoe Ozero
Kolomyag
Udelnaya
Sosnovka
Murino
Grazhdanka
Rybatskaya
Rzhevka
Staraya Derevnya
Novaya Derevnya
Udelnoe
Ostrova Krestovskiye
Ostrov Trudyashchikhsya
Apterkarskiya Ostrov
Petrogradskaya Storona
Vyborgskaya Storona
Stoyka
Polyustrovo
Ostrov Dekabristov
Ostrov Vasilyevskiy
Neva
Admiralteyskaya Storona
Bolshaya-Okhta
Zhernovka
Zanevka
Malaya-Okhta
Kudrovo
Vesolyy Posolok
Volodarskoye
Obukhovo
Farforovskaya
Utkina Zavod
Lesnozavodskaya
Ostrov Kanonerskiy
Ostrov Gutuyevskiy
Volynkina-Derevnya
Avtovo
Aleksandrovskoye
Kupchino
Novoaleksandrovskoye
Novosaratovka
Rybatskoye
Ust-Slavyanka
Uritsk
Ulyanka
Dakhnoye
Srednaya Rogatka
Ligovo
ST. PETERSBURG PULKOVO (LED)
Sassnitz
Moskovskiy Prospekt
Karla Marksa Prospekt
St Petersburg
East from Greenwich
1
2
3


## SANTIAGO, CHILE

Santiago
SANTIAGO
Cerros de Conchalí
Carmen de Huechuraba
Cerro Manquehue 1638
La Dehesa
El Carmen
Quilicura
Santa Teresa de lo Ovalle
Lo Boza
El Cortijo
Huechuraba
El Salto
Lo Aranguiz
Conchalí
Recoleta
Vitacura
Apoquindo
Renca
Independencia
Sta. Rosa de Locobe
Cerro Navia
Carrascal
Quinta Normal
Providencia
La Reina
TO SANTIAGO BENITEZ INTL. (SCL)
Lo Prado
Las Rejas
Ñuñoa
Santa Elena del Gomero
Peñalolén
Lo Hermida
Cerrillos
LOS CERRILLOS
San Miguel
San Joaquin
Santa Julia
Vista Alegre
Maipú
La Blanca
Macul
Lo Espejo
La Granja
Bellavista
La Florida
La Cisterna
El Bosque
Avda. Américo-Vespucio
Río Mapocho
West from Greenwich
A
B
C
1
2


## SÃO PAULO, BRAZIL

SÃO PAULO
São Paulo
Jaraguá
Pico de Jaraguá 1133
Brasilândia
Tucuruvi
Imirim
Casa Verde
TO SÃO PAULO GUARULHOS INTL. (GRU)
Pirituba
Vila Jaguára
Nossa Senhora do Ó
Santana
Vila Guilherme
CAMPO DE MARTE
Vila Maria
Tietê
Osasco
Lapa
Bom Retiro
Barra Funda
Pari
Tatuapé
Belènzinho
Perdizes
Sta. Efigênia
Brás
Vila Madalena
Consolação
Bela Vista
Liberdade
Cambuci
Móoca
Butantã
América
Aclimação
Alto da Móoca
Jardins
Vila Mariana
Vila Prudente
Rod. Raposo Tavares
Taboão de Serra
Morumbi
Indianópolis
Ipiranga
Saúde
Sacomã
São Caetano do Sul
SÃO PAULO CONGONHAS (CGH)
Ibirapuera
Santo Amaro
Capão Redondo
Socorro
Interlagos
Diadema
Represa Guarapiranga
West from Greenwich
1
2


## SEOUL, SOUTH KOREA

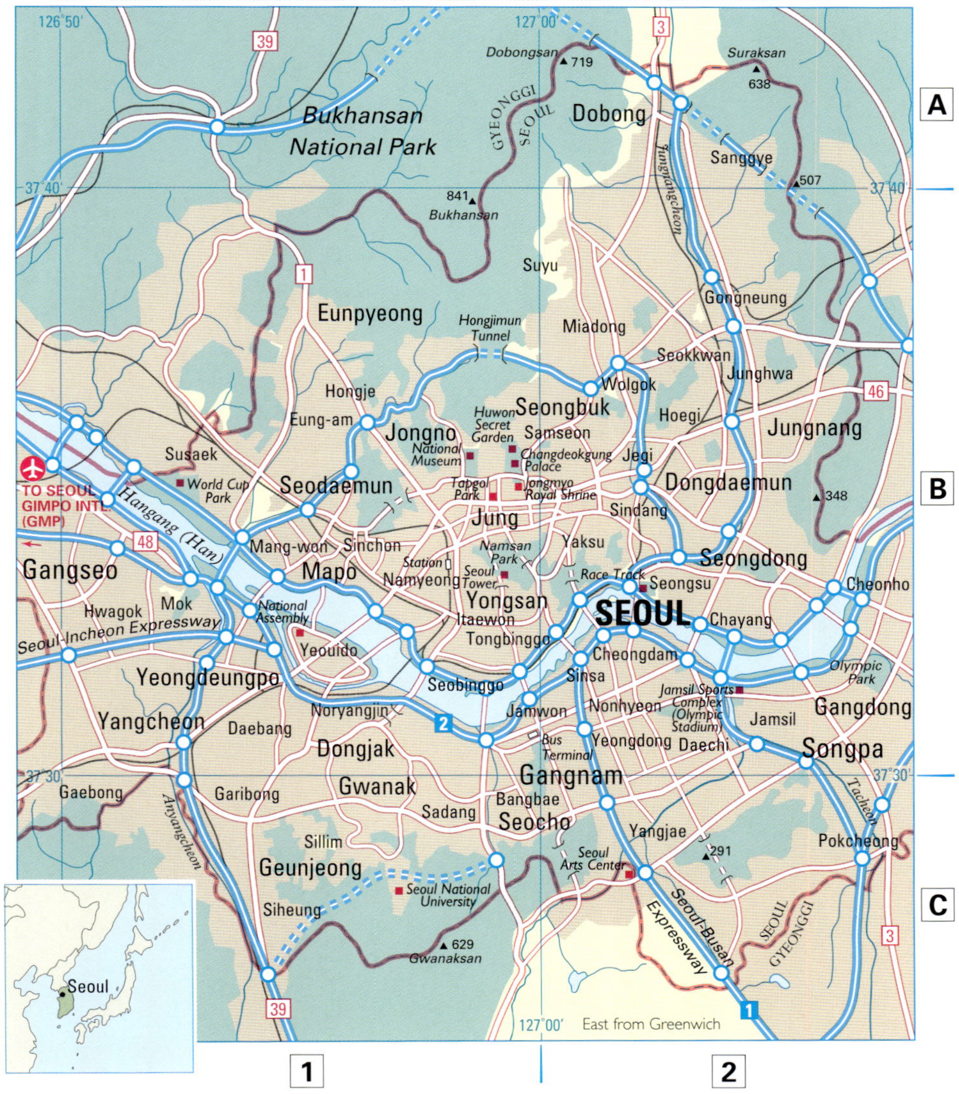

SEOUL
Seoul
Bukhansan National Park
Dobongsan 719
Dobong
Suraksan 638
Sanggye
Bukhansan 841
Suyu
Eunpyeong
Miadong
Gongneung
Seokkwan
Junghwa
Hongje
Jongno
Seongbuk
Wolgok
Hoegi
Jungnang
Eung-am
Susaek
Seodaemun
Jung
Dongdaemun
TO SEOUL GIMPO INTL. (GMP)
Hangang (Han)
Mang-won
Sinchon
Mapo
Yaksu
Seongdong
Gangseo
Yongsan
Chayang
Cheonho
Hwagok
Mok
Yeouido
Seongsu
Seoul-Incheon Expressway
Yeongdeungpo
Seobinggo
Sinsa
Gangdong
Yangcheon
Daebang
Noryangjin
Jamsil
Songpa
Dongjak
Gangnam
Gaebong
Garibong
Gwanak
Sadang
Bangbae
Seocho
Yangjae
Pokcheong
Sillim
Geunjeong
Siheung
Gwanaksan 629
Seoul-Busan Expressway
East from Greenwich
A
B
C
1
2

## SHANGHAI, CHINA

Gucun
Yangjiazhuang
Wusong
SHANGHAI
Chang Jiang (Yangtze)
Baoshan
Tangqiao
Gaoqiao
Huangpu Jiang
Yinhangzhen
Gaohang
DACHANG
Jiangwan
Wujiaochang
Dachang
Donggou
Lu Xun Park
Hongkou Stadium
Heping Park
Yangpu Park
Yangpu
Fuxing Dao
Zhenru
Shanghai West
Zhabei
Hongkou
Dingningsi
Zhoujiazhen
Tilanqiao
Jinqiao
Putuo
Shanghai University
Oriental Pearl Tower
Lujiazui
Jin Mao Tower
World Financial Centre
Shanghai Tower
Yangjing
Jade Buddha Temple
Jingan
Huangpu
People's Park
People's Square
Shanghai Museum
Yuyuan Garden
SHANGHAI
Science & Technology Museum
Century Park
Shanghai International Expo Centre
Changning
Fuxing Park
Old City
Pudong New Area
Puxi
Sun Yat Sen's Former Residence
Luwan
Nanshi
Shanghai Zoo
Hongqiao
Xujiahui
Xuhui
Nanpu Bridge
Beicai
TO SHANGHAI PUDONG (PVG)
TO SHANGHAI HONGQIAO (SHA)
Shanghai Stadium
Lupu Bridge
Zhoujiadu Expo Centre
Longhua Park
Longhua Pagoda
Nanshi
Caohejing
LONGHUA
Sanlintang
Botanical Gardens
Shanghai South
Sanlin
Gangkou
East from Greenwich 121°30'
A20
312
318
31°20'
31°10'
121°30'
Shanghai


A B C 1 2

Magnetic Levitation (Maglev) Railway

## CENTRAL SINGAPORE

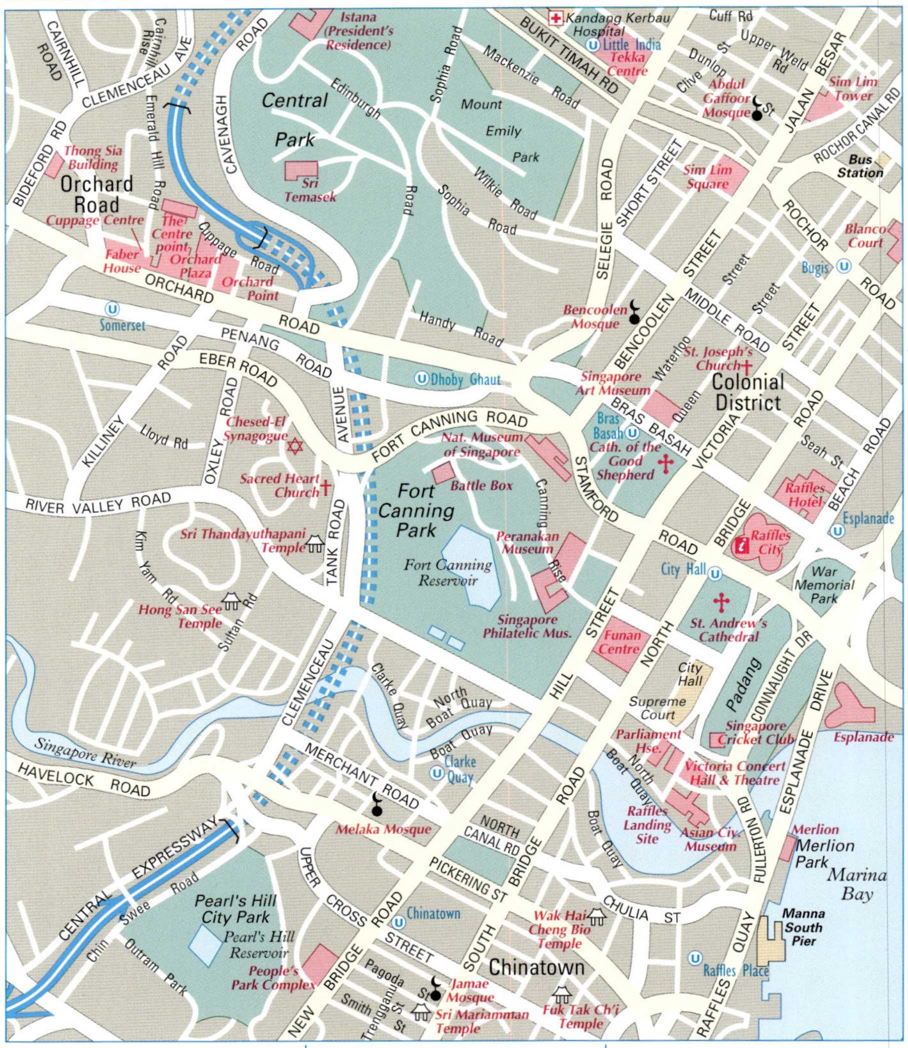

Istana (President's Residence)
Kandang Kerbau Hospital
Little India
Tekka Centre
Central Park
Abdul Gaffoor Mosque
Sim Lim Tower
Orchard Road
Thong Sia Building
Cuppage Centre
The Centre point
Orchard Plaza
Orchard Point
Faber House
Sri Temasek
Mount Emily Park
Sim Lim Square
Bus Station
Blanco Court
Bugis
ORCHARD ROAD
Somerset
PENANG ROAD
Dhoby Ghaut
Bencoolen Mosque
Singapore Art Museum
St. Joseph's Church
Colonial District
Chesed-El Synagogue
Sacred Heart Church
FORT CANNING ROAD
Nat. Museum of Singapore
Cath. of the Good Shepherd
Battle Box
RIVER VALLEY ROAD
Fort Canning Park
Raffles Hotel
Raffles City
Esplanade
Sri Thandayuthapani Temple
Peranakan Museum
Fort Canning Reservoir
City Hall
War Memorial Park
Hong San See Temple
Singapore Philatelic Mus.
Funan Centre
St. Andrew's Cathedral
City Hall
Supreme Court
Padang
Parliament Hse.
Singapore Cricket Club
Esplanade
Singapore River
HAVELOCK ROAD
Clarke Quay
Victoria Concert Hall & Theatre
Raffles Landing Site
Asian Civ. Museum
Melaka Mosque
Merlion
Merlion Park
Marina Bay
CENTRAL EXPRESSWAY
Pearl's Hill City Park
Pearl's Hill Reservoir
Chinatown
Wak Hai Cheng Bio Temple
Manna South Pier
People's Park Complex
Chinatown
Jamae Mosque
Sri Mariamman Temple
Fuk Tak Ch'i Temple
Raffles Place


1 2 3

## SINGAPORE

103°40'E
103°50'E
104°00'E
1°20'N
Johor Bahru
Senoko Ind. Est.
Sembawang
Selat Johor
Pasir Gudang
Sungei Buloh Nature Park
Kranji Ind. Est.
WTCP
Causeway
Woodlands
Chong Pang
Pulau Seletar
MALAYSIA
SINGAPORE
Lim Chu Kang
Sarimbun Res.
Kranji Reservoir
Yishun
Punggol Point
Singapore Turf Club
Mandai
Sungai Kadut Ind. Est.
Sungai Seletar Reservoir
SELETAR
Seletar Golf Course
Pulau Serangoon (Coney I.)
Pulau Ubin
Pulau Tekong Kechil
Pulau Tekong
Tg. Ladang
Sarimbun
Murai Res.
Ama Keng
Singapore Zoo
Seletar Reservoir
Nee Soon
Jalan Kayu
Punggol
Pulau Ketam
TENGAH
BKE
SLE
TPE
Sengkang
Serangoon Harbour
Central Catchment Nature Reserve
Choa Chu Kang
Bukit Panjang
Lower Peirce Reservoir
Yio Chu Kang
Seletar
Hougang
Pasir Ris Park
Pasir Ris
Loyang Ind. Est.
Changi
Upper Peirce Reservoir
Ang Mo Kio
SINGAPORE CHANGI (SIN)
KJE
Bt. Panjang
Bukit Timah Nature Reserve
Serangoon
Chia Keng
PAYA LEBAR
Yan Kit
Changi Prison Museum
Tengeh Res.
Nanyang University
Bishan
Bedok Reservoir
Tampines
Reclaimed Land
MacRitchie Reservoir
PIE
Bukit Batok Nature Parks
Jurong West
Air View Park
Raffles Park
CTE
Toa Payoh
Paya Lebar
Simei
South End Res.
Raffles Golf Course & Country Club
Boon Lay
Chinese & Japanese Gardens
Snow City
Jurong East
Tai Seng
Geylang Serai
Kg Landang
Singapore Expo
Tanah Merah Golf Course
Singapore Discovery Centre
Tuas
Tang Dynasty Museum
Dunearn
Chai Chee
Bedok
Tuas Second Link
Jurong Industrial Estate
Jurong
Jurong Bird Park
Clementi
Maryland
Victoria Park
Frankel
Pandan Res.
Holland Village
Botanic Gardens
National Stadium
Kallang Park
Singapore Indoor Stadium
Katong
ECP
East Coast Park
Selat Jurong
Kg Tanjong Penjuru
AYE
N.U.S.
Queenstown
Pasir Panjang
Telok Blangah
National Museum
St Andrew's Cathedral
City Hall
Singapore Flyer and F1 track
Marina Bay Golf Course
ArtScience Mus.
Pulau Jurong
Seraya
Pasir Panjang Terminal
Buona Vista Park
Mt. Faber
Harbour Front Centre
Thian Hock Keng Temple
Marina Bay Sands
SINGAPORE
Reclaimed Land
Sakra
Siloso Pt.
Cable Car
Imbiah Lookout
P. Brani
Keppel Harbour
Universal Studios
Straits of Singapore
Reclaimed Land
Selat Pandan
Pulau Busing
Pulau Bukum
Sentosa
Tanjong Golf Course
East from Greenwich
Singapore


A B 1 2 3 4

## STOCKHOLM, SWEDEN

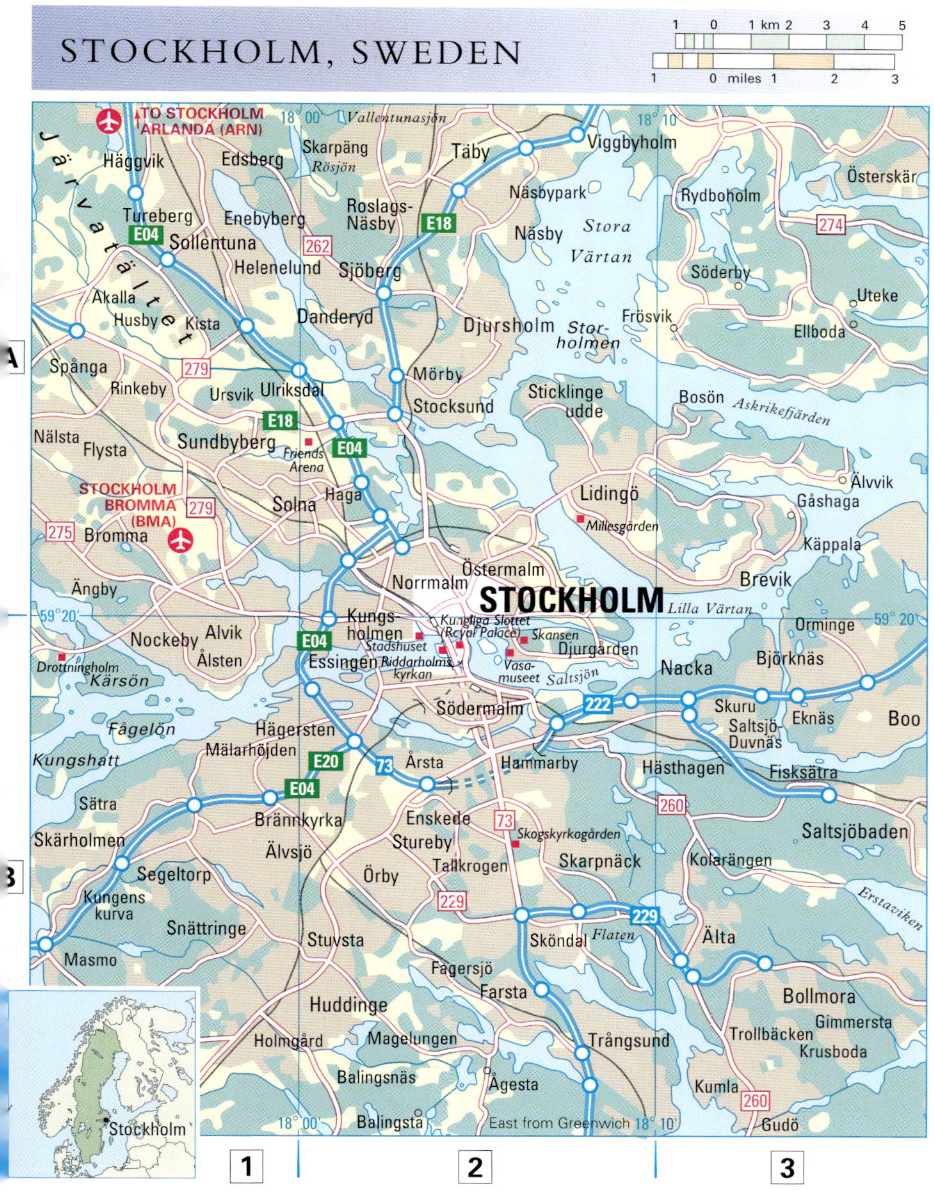
km
miles
TO STOCKHOLM ARLANDA (ARN)
Vallentunasjön
Järvafältet
Häggvik
Edsberg
Skarpäng
Täby
Viggbyholm
Österskär
Tureberg
Enebyberg
Roslags-Näsby
Näsbypark
Rydboholm
Sollentuna
Helenelund
Sjöberg
Näsby
Stora Värtan
Söderby
Akalla
Husby
Kista
Danderyd
Djursholm
Stor-holmen
Frösvik
Uteke
Ellboda
Spånga
Rinkeby
Ursvik
Ulriksdal
Mörby
Stocksund
Sticklinge udde
Bosön
Askrikefjärden
Nälsta
Flysta
Sundbyberg
Friends Arena
Haga
STOCKHOLM BROMMA (BMA)
Solna
Lidingö
Millesgården
Ålvvik
Gåshaga
Bromma
Käppala
Ängby
Norrmalm
Östermalm
STOCKHOLM
Brevik
Lilla Värtan
Nockeby
Alvik
Kungs-holmen
Kungliga Slottet (Royal Palace)
Skansen
Orminge
Drottningholm
Ålsten
Stadshuset
Djurgården
Björknäs
Kärsön
Essingen
Riddarholms-kyrkan
Vasa-museet
Saltsjön
Nacka
Fågelön
Södermalm
Skuru
Saltsjö-Duvnäs
Eknäs
Boo
Kungshatt
Hägersten
Mälarhöjden
Årsta
Hammarby
Hästhagen
Fisksätra
Sätra
Brännkyrka
Enskede
Skogskyrkogården
Saltsjöbaden
Skärholmen
Älvsjö
Stureby
Tallkrogen
Skarpnäck
Kolarängen
Segeltorp
Örby
Kungens kurva
Snättringe
Stuvsta
Skondal
Flaten
Älta
Erstaviken
Masmo
Fagersjö
Farsta
Bollmora
Huddinge
Gimmersta
Trollbäcken
Krusboda
Holmgård
Magelungen
Trångsund
Balingsnäs
Ågesta
Kumla
Balingsta
Gudö
East from Greenwich
Stockholm

## CENTRAL STOCKHOLM

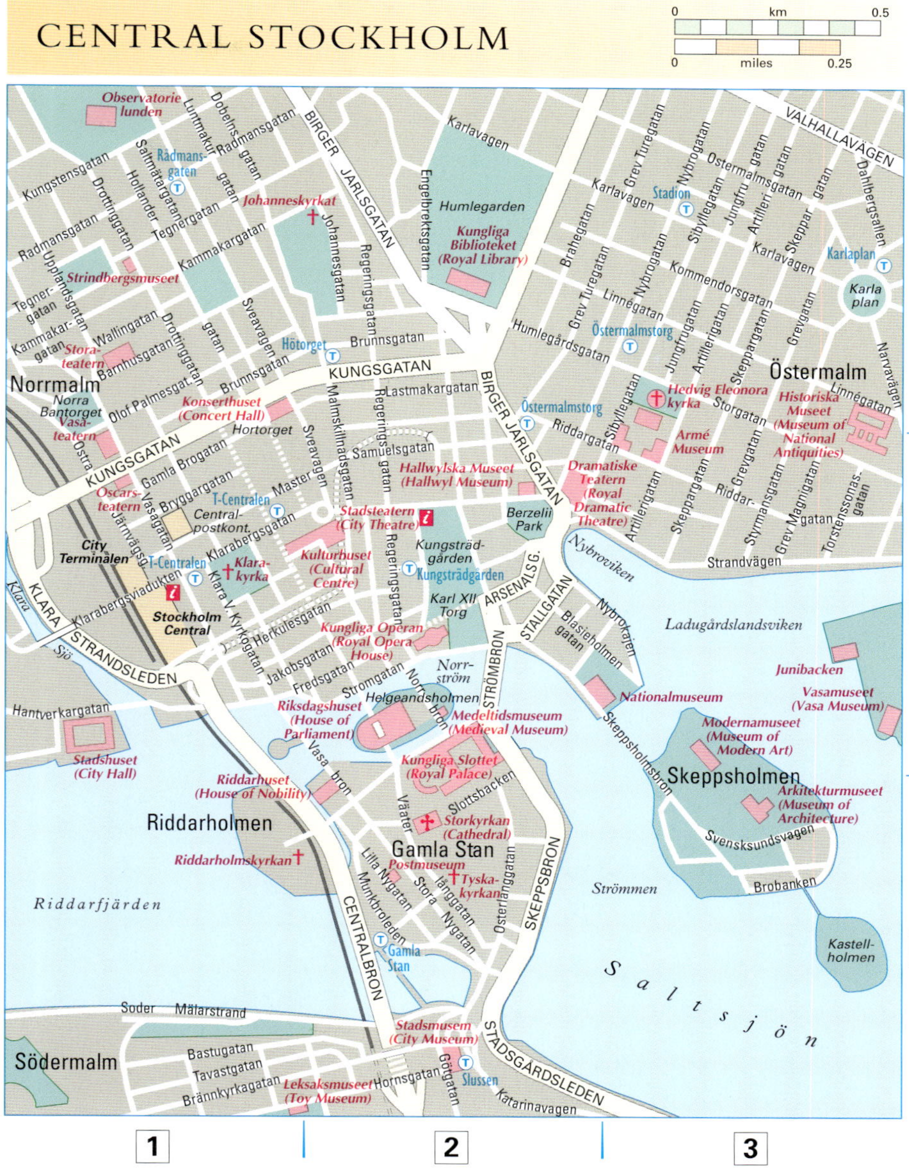
km
miles
Observatorielunden
Karlavägen
VALHALLAVÄGEN
Humlegården
Kungliga Biblioteket (Royal Library)
Johanneskyrkan
Strindbergsmuseet
Stadion
Karlaplan
Stora teatern
Hötorget
Östermalmstorg
Östermalm
Historiska Museet (Museum of National Antiquities)
Hedvig Eleonora kyrka
Armé Museum
Norrmalm
KUNGSGATAN
Konserthuset (Concert Hall)
Hallwylska Museet (Hallwyl Museum)
Dramatiska Teatern (Royal Dramatic Theatre)
Oscars-teatern
Stadsteatern (City Theatre)
Berzelii Park
Centralpostkont.
Kulturhuset (Cultural Centre)
Kungsträdgården
Strandvägen
City Terminalen
Klara kyrka
Kungliga Operan (Royal Opera House)
Karl XII Torg
Nybroviken
Stockholm Central
KLARA STRANDSLEDEN
Ladugårdslandsviken
Junibacken
Nationalmuseum
Vasamuseet (Vasa Museum)
Hantverkargatan
Riksdagshuset (House of Parliament)
Medeltidsmuseum (Medieval Museum)
Modernamuseet (Museum of Modern Art)
Skeppsholmen
Stadshuset (City Hall)
Riddarhuset (House of Nobility)
Kungliga Slottet (Royal Palace)
Arkitekturmuseet (Museum of Architecture)
Riddarholmen
Storkyrkan (Cathedral)
Gamla Stan
Riddarholmskyrkan
Postmuseum
Tyska-kyrkan
Strömmen
Riddarfjärden
CENTRALBRON
SKEPPSBRON
Kastell-holmen
Saltsjön
Söder Mälarstrand
Stadsmuseum (City Museum)
Södermalm
Leksaksmuseet (Toy Museum)
Slussen
STADSGÅRDSLEDEN

## SYDNEY, AUSTRALIA

km
miles
Epping
Macquarie Park
Eastwood
Denistone Heights
Lane Cove National Park
Pacific Highway
Allambie Heights
Queenscliff
Balgowlah
Chatswood
North Ryde
Willoughby
Seaforth
Manly
Ryde
Field of Mars Wildlife Refuge
Gore Hill Fwy
Northbridge
Clontarf
Meadowbank Park
Ermington
Boronia Park
Lane Cove
Northbridge Park
Balgowlah Heights
Sydney Harbour Nat. Park
Gladesville
Gore Hill
Spit Junction
Rhodes
Crows Nest
Middle Head
North Hd.
Hunters Hill
Mosman
Sydney Harbour Nat. Park
South Head
Bicentennial Park
Mortlake
North Sydney
Taronga Zoological Park
Watsons Bay
Sydney Olympic Park
Port Jackson
ANZ Stadium
Hen & Chicken Bay
Drummoyne
Sydney Harbour Bridge
Balmain
Opera House
Government House
Vaucluse House
Vaucluse
Concord
Observatory
Royal Botanic Gdns.
Five Dock
Darling Point
Strathfield
Gt. Western Hwy.
Sydney Tower
Dover Heights
Burwood
Leichhardt
SYDNEY
Paddington
Camperdown
Central Sta.
Surry Hills
Allianz Stadium
Woollahra
Bondi
Enfield
Ashfield
Univ. of Sydney
Newtown
Sydney C.G.
Redfern
Fox Studios Centennial Park
Waverley
Croydon Park
Canterbury Racecourse
Enmore
Erskineville
Kensington
Randwick
Marrickville
St. Peters
Randwick Racecourse
Univ. of N.S.W.
Clovelly
PACIFIC OCEAN
Belmore
Canterbury
Rosebery
Kingsford
Lakemba
Earlwood
Mascot
Coogee
Punchbowl
Arncliffe
SYDNEY KINGSFORD SMITH (SYD)
Astrolabe Park
Beverley Hills
Bexley
Barton Park
Botany
Pagewood
Maroubra
Riverwood
Rockdale
Banksmeadow
Peakhurst
Hurstville
Kogarah
Brighton-Le-Sands
Malabar
Beverley Park
Port Botany
Phillip Bay
Long Bay
Oatley
Blakehurst
Ramsgate
Monterey
Botany Bay
Little Bay
Botany Bay Nat. Park
La Perouse
San Souci
Georges River Bridge
Towra Point
Sylvania
Captain Cook Bridge
Woolooware B.
Kurnell
Captain Cook's Landing Place
Cape Banks
East from Greenwich
Sydney

## CENTRAL SYDNEY

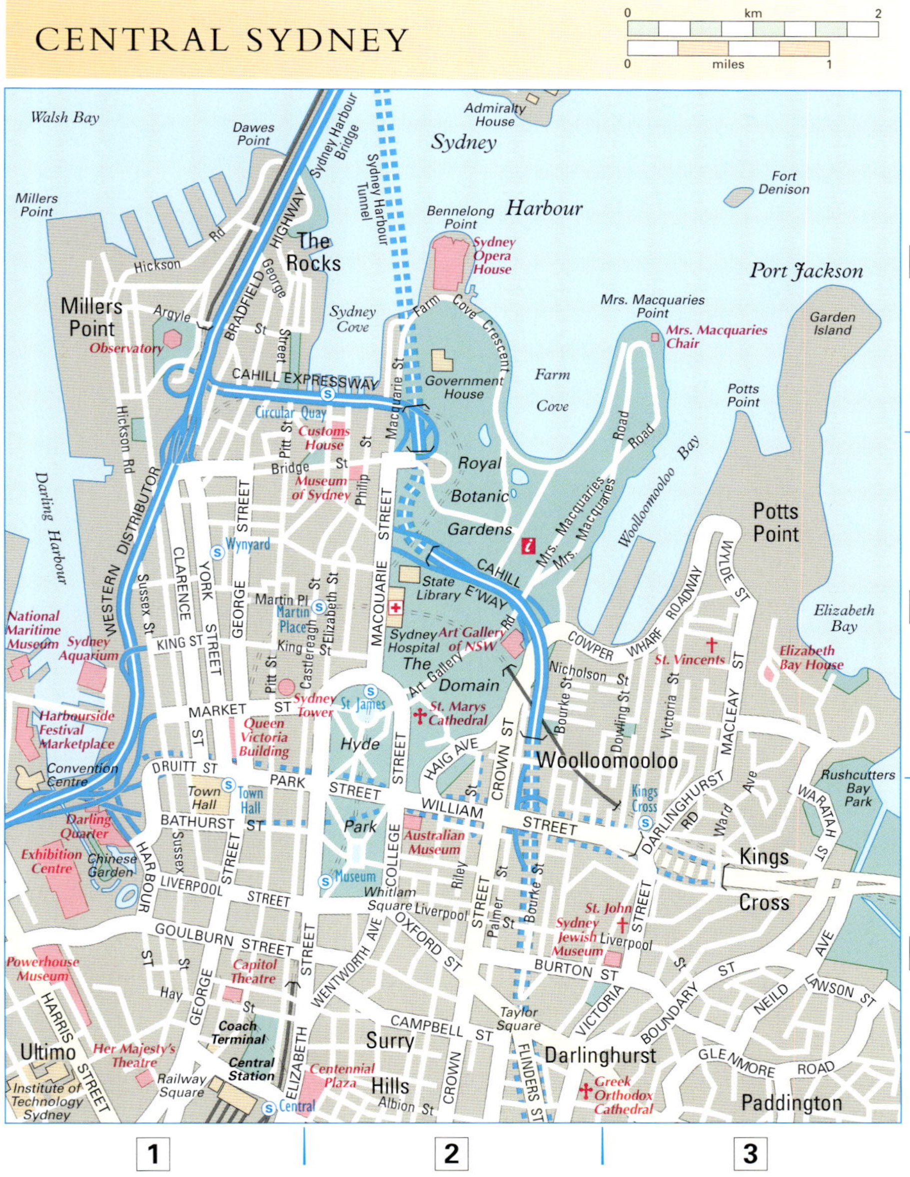
km
miles
Walsh Bay
Dawes Point
Sydney Harbour Bridge
Admiralty House
Sydney
Fort Denison
Millers Point
Bennelong Point
Harbour
Sydney Opera House
The Rocks
Hickson Rd
Port Jackson
Millers Point
Sydney Cove
Mrs. Macquaries Point
Mrs. Macquaries Chair
Garden Island
Observatory
CAHILL EXPRESSWAY
Government House
Farm Cove
Potts Point
Circular Quay
Customs House
Royal Botanic Gardens
Museum of Sydney
Darling Harbour
WESTERN DISTRIBUTOR
Woolloomooloo Bay
Potts Point
Wynyard
State Library
National Maritime Museum
Sydney Aquarium
Sydney Hospital
Art Gallery of NSW
Elizabeth Bay
Elizabeth Bay House
St. Vincents
The Domain
Sydney Tower
Harbourside Festival Marketplace
Queen Victoria Building
St. Marys Cathedral
Woolloomooloo
Rushcutters Bay Park
Convention Centre
Hyde Park
Town Hall
Darling Quarter
Australian Museum
Kings Cross
Exhibition Centre
Chinese Garden
Museum
Sydney Jewish Museum
Powerhouse Museum
Capitol Theatre
Coach Terminal
Central Station
Surry Hills
Darlinghurst
Ultimo
Her Majesty's Theatre
Centennial Plaza
Railway Square
Institute of Technology Sydney
Greek Orthodox Cathedral
Paddington

## TOKYO, JAPAN

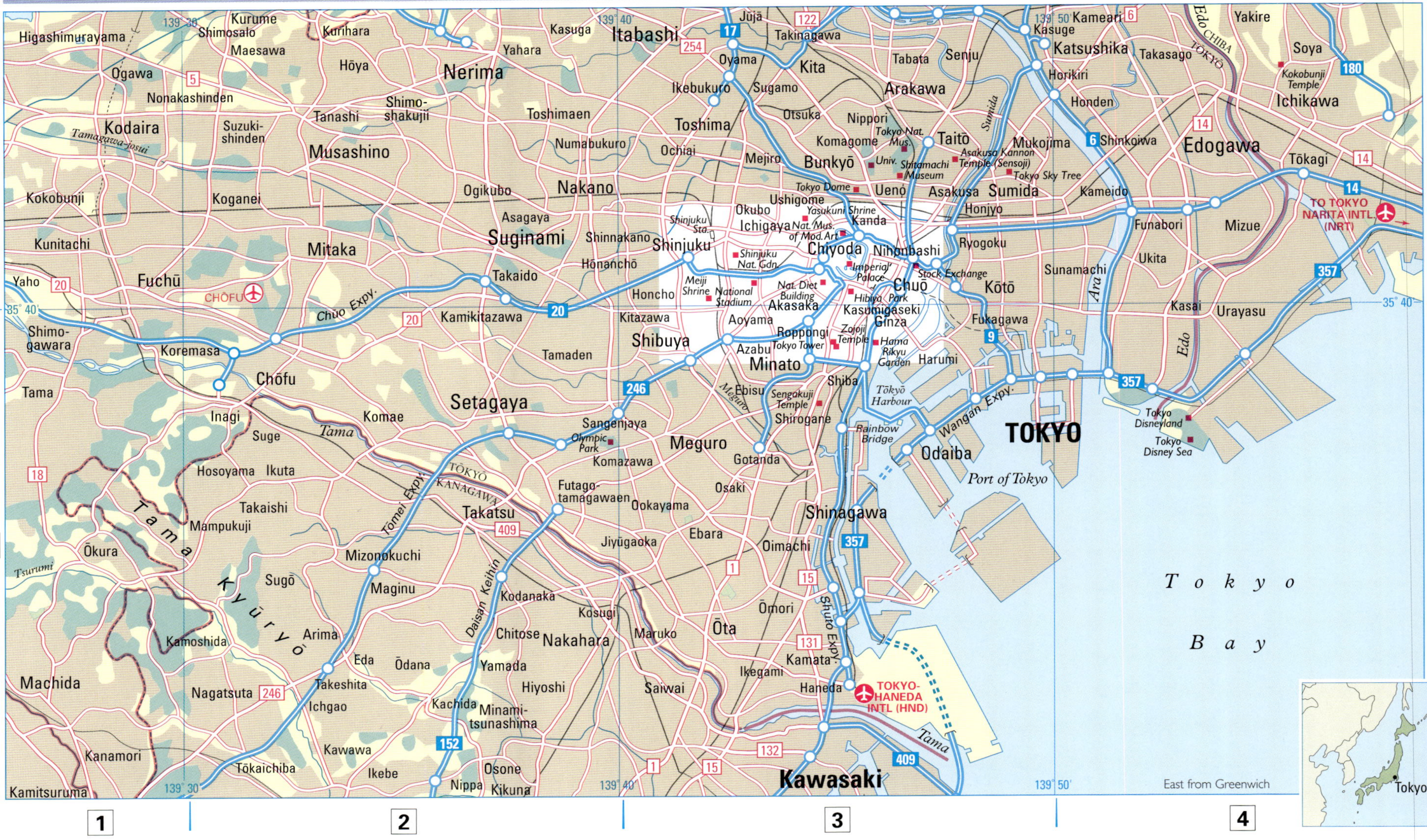

Higashimurayama
Kurume
Shimosato
Kurihara
Maesawa
Hōya
Nerima
Yahara
Kasuga
Itabashi
Jūjō
Takinogawa
Kita
Tabata
Senju
Kameari
Kasuge
Katsushika
Takasago
Yakire
Soya
Ogawa
Nonakashinden
Kodaira
Suzuki-shinden
Tanashi
Shimo-shakujii
Musashino
Toshimaen
Ikebukuro
Sugamo
Oyama
Arakawa
Horikiri
Honden
Ichikawa
Edogawa
Kokobunji
Koganei
Ogikubo
Nakano
Numabukuro
Ochiai
Toshima
Mejiro
Bunkyō
Ueno
Taitō
Asakusa
Sumida
Mukojima
Shinkoiwa
Tōkagi
Kunitachi
Mitaka
Asagaya
Suginami
Shinjuku
Ichigaya
Chiyoda
Nihonbashi
Ryogoku
Kameido
Funabori
Mizue
TO TOKYO NARITA INTL (NRT)
Yaho
Fuchū
CHŌFU
Takaido
Kamikitazawa
Honcho
Chuō
Kōtō
Sunamachi
Ukita
Kasai
Urayasu
Shimo-gawara
Koremasa
Chōfu
Tamaden
Kitazawa
Shibuya
Aoyama
Akasaka
Ginza
Minato
Harumi
Fukagawa
Tama
Inagi
Komae
Setagaya
Sangenjaya
Meguro
Shiba
Shirogane
Odaiba
TOKYO
Tokyo Disneyland
Tokyo Disney Sea
Suge
Hosoyama
Ikuta
Komazawa
Gotanda
Port of Tokyo
Takaishi
Mampukuji
Futago-tamagawaen
Takatsu
Ookayama
Osaki
Shinagawa
Ōkura
Mizonokuchi
Jiyūgaoka
Ebara
Oimachi
Tokyo Bay
Sugō
Maginu
Kodanaka
Kosugi
Ōmori
Kamoshida
Arima
Chitose
Nakahara
Maruko
Ōta
Kamata
Eda
Ōdana
Yamada
Ikegami
Machida
Nagatsuta
Takeshita
Ichgao
Kachida
Hiyoshi
Minami-tsunashima
Saiwai
Haneda
TOKYO-HANEDA INTL (HND)
Kanamori
Kawawa
Ikebe
Tōkaichiba
Osone
Kawasaki
Kamitsuruma
Nippa
Kikuna
East from Greenwich
Tokyo


## CENTRAL TOKYO

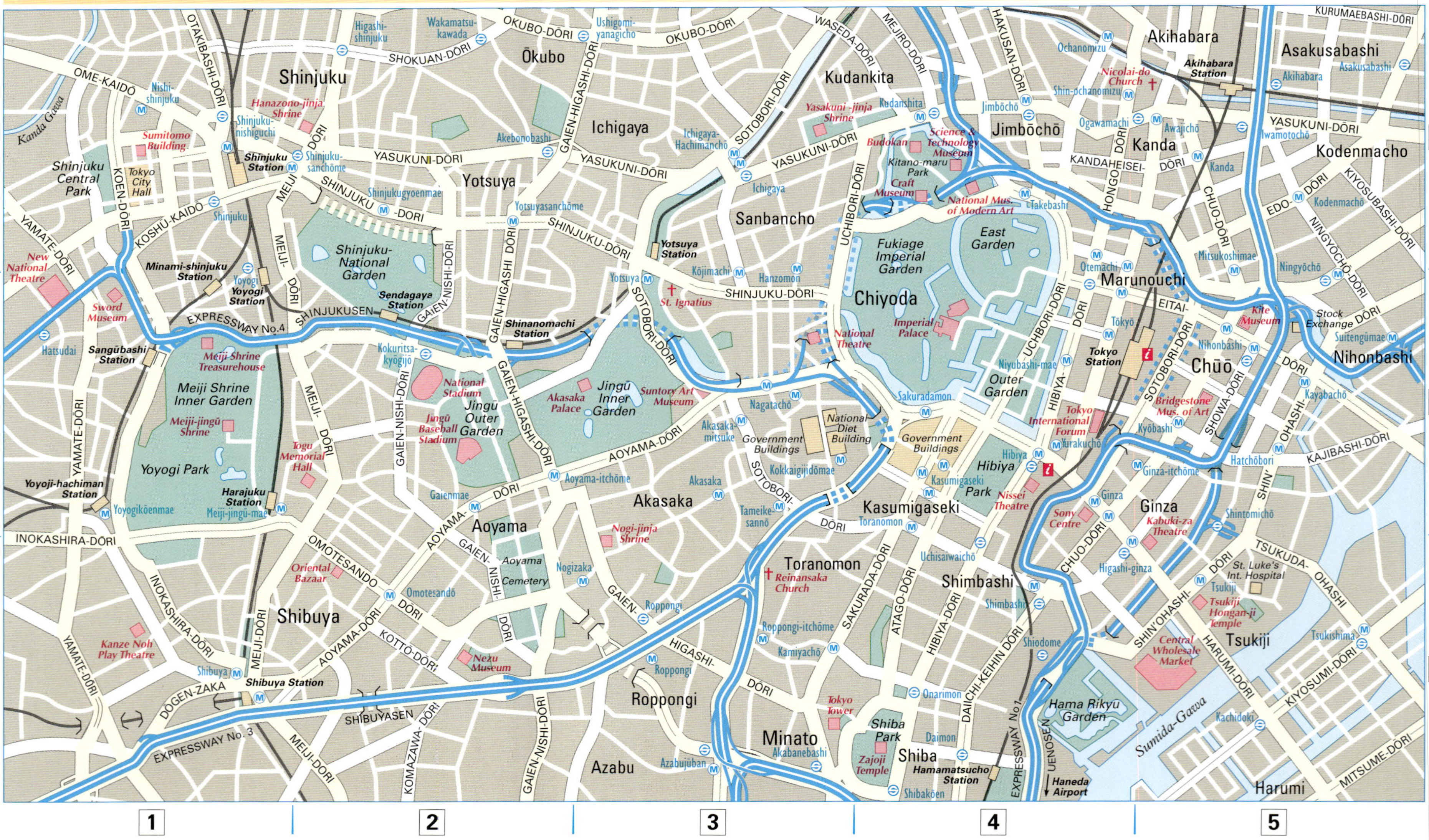

Shinjuku
Ōkubo
Kudankita
Akihabara
Asakusabashi
Shinjuku Central Park
Tokyo City Hall
Ichigaya
Jimbōchō
Kanda
Kodenmacho
Yotsuya
Sanbancho
Shinjuku National Garden
East Garden
Fukiage Imperial Garden
Chiyoda
Imperial Palace
Marunouchi
Nihonbashi
Chūō
Tokyo Station
Meiji Shrine Inner Garden
Jingū Outer Garden
Akasaka Palace
Jingū Inner Garden
National Diet Building
Outer Garden
Hibiya Park
Yoyogi Park
Akasaka
Kasumigaseki
Ginza
Aoyama
Toranomon
Shimbashi
Tsukiji
Shibuya
Shibuya Station
Roppongi
Hama Rikyu Garden
Minato
Shiba Park
Shiba
Azabu
Harumi
Toei Subway
Tokyo Metro

## TEHRAN, IRAN

Reshteh-ye Kūhhā-ye Alborz (Elburz Mts.)
Tehran
Darakeh
Darband
Niāvarān
Sowhānak
Evin
Tajrīsh
Sa'ādatābād
International Trade Fair
Hesārak
Qolhak
Lavīzān
Darrūs
Shahrak-e Qods (Gharb)
Pūnak
Vanak
Dāvūdīyeh
Qāsemābād
Hasanābād
Bāgh-e Feyz
Pardisan Nature Park
Milad Tower
Tehrān Pārs
Yūsofābād
Amīrābād
Nārmak
Karaj Expwy.
Tehran West Bus Terminal
Jamshīdīyeh
Carpet Mus.
Tehrān Now
TEHRAN MEHRĀBĀD (THR)
Freedom Tower
University
City Theatre
Museum of Glass and Ceramics
TEHRĀN
Farahābād
Jey
National Mus. of Iran
Golestan Palace (Ethnographical Mus.)
Akbarābād
Shah Mosque
Bāzār
Dūlāb
Qasr-e Fīrūzeh
Tehran Station
Javādīyeh
Vasfenārd
Qal'eh Morghī
Tehran South Bus Terminal
Afsarīyeh
Yaftābād
N'ematābād
Dowlatābād
Park-e Azadegan
Shahrak-e Golshahr
Āzādegān Expwy.
Shahr-e Rey (Rey)
TO TEHRAN IMAM KHOMEINI INTL. (IKA)
Qom Expwy.
Mesgarābād
East from Greenwich

## CENTRAL TORONTO

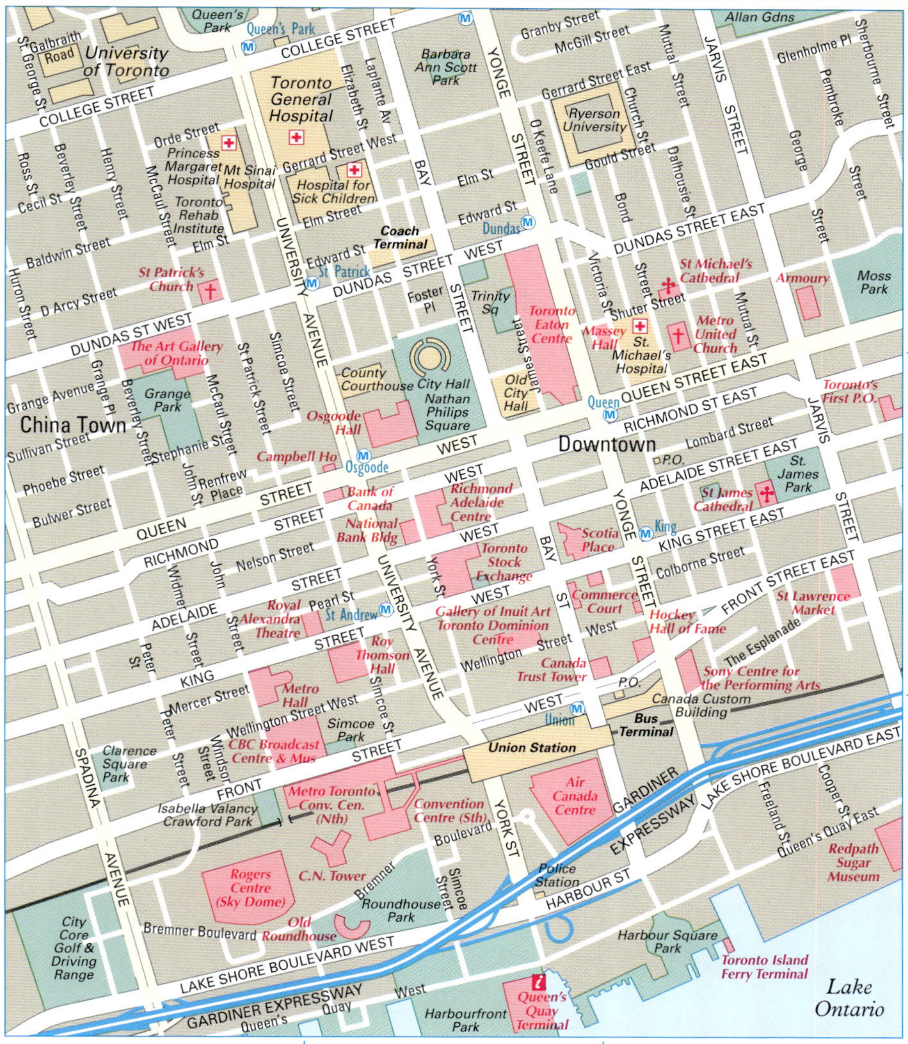
University of Toronto
COLLEGE STREET
Toronto General Hospital
Queen's Park
Barbara Ann Scott Park
YONGE STREET
Ryerson University
Gerrard Street East
JARVIS STREET
Allan Gdns
Princess Margaret Hospital
Mt Sinai Hospital
Hospital for Sick Children
Toronto Rehab Institute
Coach Terminal
UNIVERSITY AVENUE
BAY STREET
DUNDAS STREET EAST
St Michael's Cathedral
Armoury
Moss Park
St Patrick's Church
DUNDAS ST WEST
The Art Gallery of Ontario
Grange Park
Trinity Sq
Toronto Eaton Centre
Massey Hall
St. Michael's Hospital
Metro United Church
China Town
County Courthouse
City Hall Nathan Philips Square
Old City Hall
QUEEN STREET EAST
Toronto's First P.O.
Osgoode Hall
Campbell Ho
Downtown
Bank of Canada
National Bank Bldg
Richmond Adelaide Centre
ADELAIDE STREET EAST
St James Cathedral
St. James Park
KING STREET EAST
Scotia Plaza
Toronto Stock Exchange
Royal Alexandra Theatre
Roy Thomson Hall
Gallery of Inuit Art
Toronto Dominion Centre
Commerce Court
Hockey Hall of Fame
St Lawrence Market
FRONT STREET EAST
Canada Trust Tower
Sony Centre for the Performing Arts
Metro Hall
CBC Broadcast Centre & Mus
Simcoe Park
Union Station
Bus Terminal
Canada Custom Building
Clarence Square Park
Isabella Valancy Crawford Park
Metro Toronto Conv. Cen. (Nth)
Convention Centre (Sth)
Air Canada Centre
GARDINER EXPRESSWAY
LAKE SHORE BOULEVARD EAST
Redpath Sugar Museum
SPADINA AVENUE
Rogers Centre (Sky Dome)
C.N. Tower
Roundhouse Park
Police Station
HARBOUR ST
City Core Golf & Driving Range
Old Roundhouse
Bremner Boulevard
LAKE SHORE BOULEVARD WEST
Harbour Square Park
Toronto Island Ferry Terminal
Lake Ontario
Queen's Quay Terminal
Harbourfront Park

## TORONTO, CANADA

Boyd Conservation Area
Vaughan
Thornhill
The Promenade
Concord
Markham
Brown
Toronto Zoo
Rouge Hill
Fairport
West Rouge
Glen Rouge Park
Pine Grove
Edgeley
Newtonbrook
Agincourt
Malvern
Port Union
Woodbridge
Fisherville
G. Ross Lord Park
Willowdale
East Don Parkland
Fairview Mall
Highland Creek
Northmount
Macdonald-Cartier Frwy.
Scarborough Town Centre
Morningside Park
Black Creek Pioneer Village
York University
Humber Summit
Lansing
Bendale
Woburn
West Hill
North York
Beaumonte Heights
Armour Heights
York Mills
Wexford
Creek Hague Park
Eastpoint Park
Thistletown
Downsview Park
Don Mills
Scarborough
Claireville Reservoir
Humberwood Park
Kipling Heights
Downsview
Lawrence Heights
Yorkdale Shopping Centre
York Univ.
Sunnybrook Health Science Centre
Wilket Creek Park
Cliffside
Malton
Woodbine Centre
Rexdale
Humberlea
Ontario Science Centre
Danforth
Woodbine Race Track
Weston
Forest Hill
Leaside
Thorncliffe
Bluffers Park
Cedarvale Park
Dentonia Park
Scarborough Bluffs
TORONTO LESTER B. PEARSON INTL. (YYZ)
York
Don Valley Pkwy.
East York
Birch Cliff
Casa Loma
Royal Ontario Museum
Riverdale Park
Kew Gardens
Humber Valley Village
Mount Dennis
Parliament Buildings
University of Toronto
Old City Hall
Ashbridge's Bay Park
Hanlon
Etobicoke
Swansea
Lambton Mills
C.N. Tower & Rogers Centre
Union Sta.
Islington
Kingsway
High Park
Old Fort York
TORONTO
Markland Wood
Humber Bay
Parkdale
Exhibition Place
Gardiner Expy.
TORONTO CITY (ISLAND)
Toronto Harbour
Tommy Thompson Park
Ontario Place
Burnhamthorpe
Summerville
Humber Bay Park
Toronto Islands
Island Park
Mimico
Gibraltar Point
LAKE ONTARIO
New Toronto
Square One
Dixie Mall
Humber College
Samuel Smith Park
Cooksville
Mississauga
Long Branch
West from Greenwich
Toronto

427 Provincial route numbers

## CENTRAL VENICE

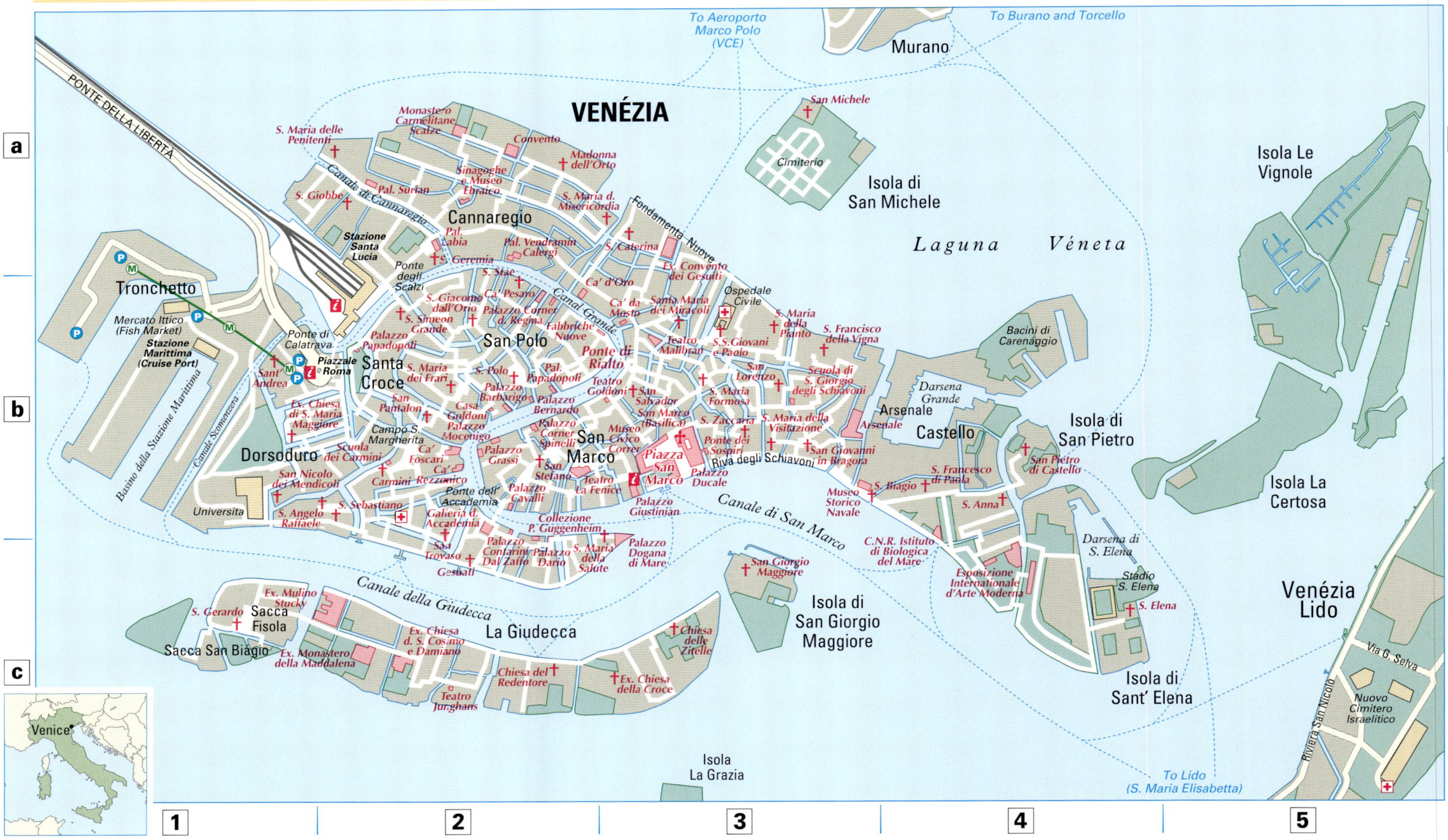

0 km 1
0 miles 0.5
To Aeroporto Marco Polo (VCE)
To Burano and Torcello
Murano
VENÉZIA
PONTE DELLA LIBERTÀ
San Michele
Cimiterio
Isola di San Michele
Laguna Véneta
Isola Le Vignole
Cannaregio
Canale di Cannaregio
Stazione Santa Lucia
Fondamenta Nuove
Tronchetto
Mercato Ittico (Fish Market)
Stazione Marittima (Cruise Port)
Piazzale Roma
Santa Croce
San Polo
Canal Grande
Ponte di Rialto
Castello
Arsenale
Bacini di Carenaggio
Darsena Grande
Isola di San Pietro
Isola La Certosa
Dorsoduro
San Marco
Piazza San Marco
Palazzo Ducale
Riva degli Schiavoni
Canale di San Marco
Universitá
Canale della Giudecca
La Giudecca
Sacca Fisola
Sacca San Biagio
Isola di San Giorgio Maggiore
Darsena di S. Elena
Stadio S. Elena
Isola di Sant' Elena
Venézia Lido
Via G. Selva
Riviera San Nicolò
Nuovo Cimitero Israelitico
Isola La Grazia
To Lido (S. Maria Elisabetta)
Venice
a
b
c
1
2
3
4
5


Car parks    Vaporetti (water buses)    Monorail (Venice People Mover)

## VIENNA, AUSTRIA

0 1 km 2 3 4 5
0 miles 1 2 3
Kritzendorf
Kierling
Klosterneuburg
Weidling
Wienerwald
Hagenbrunn
Langenzersdorf
Stammersdorf
Föhrenhain
Kapellerfeld
Gerasdorf bei Wien
Strebersdorf
Oberlisse
Donau
Aderklaa
Parbasdorf
Neusüssenbrunn
Süssenbrunn
Floridsdorf
Jedlesee
Grinzing
Nussdorf
Salmannsdorf
Sievering
Döbling
Währing
Breitenlee
Neuessling
Raasdorf
Hirschstetten
Kagran
Donaustadt
Brigittenau
UNO City
Hernals
Leopoldstadt
Ottakring
Alsergrund
WIEN
Stadlau
Aspern
Essling
Gross-Enzersdorf
Penzing
Rudolfsheim
Landstrasse
Fünfhaus
Margareten
Wieden
Simmering
Hietzing
Meidling
Favoriten
Mühlleiten
Lobau
Donau (Danube)
Albern
Kaiserebersdorf
Mannswörth
Schwechat
Wienerberg
Mauer
Atzgersdorf
Liesing
Inzersdorf
Oberlaa
Rothneusiedl
Unterlaa
Kledering
Rannersdorf
Neukettenhof
Perchtoldsdorf
Vösendorf
Leopoldsdorf
Zwölfaxing
Himberg
Mödling
WIEN SCHWECHAT (VIE)
Vienna
East from Greenwich
A
B
1
2
3


## CENTRAL VIENNA

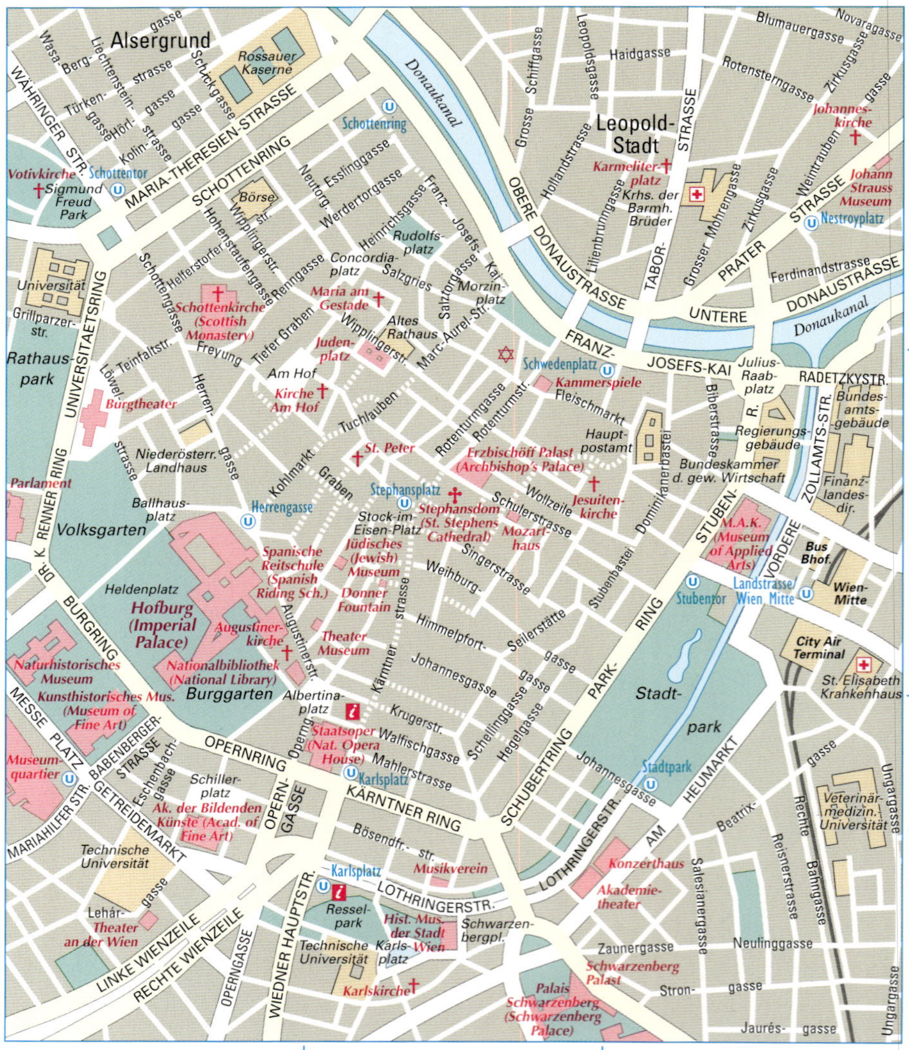

0 km 0.5
0 miles 0.25
Alsergrund
Rossauer Kaserne
Donaukanal
Leopold-Stadt
Votivkirche
Sigmund Freud Park
Schottenring
Börse
Universität
Rathaus-park
Schottenkirche (Scottish Monastery)
Burgtheater
Parlament
Volksgarten
Hofburg (Imperial Palace)
Heldenplatz
Spanische Reitschule (Spanish Riding Sch.)
Nationalbibliothek (National Library)
Augustinerkirche
Burggarten
Albertina
Staatsoper (Nat. Opera House)
Naturhistorisches Museum
Kunsthistorisches Mus. (Museum of Fine Art)
Museumsquartier
Stephansdom (St. Stephens Cathedral)
Jüdisches Museum
Mozarthaus
Schwedenplatz
Stadtpark
Karlsplatz
Karlskirche
Musikverein
Konzerthaus
Akademietheater
Palais Schwarzenberg (Schwarzenberg Palace)
Technische Universität
Ak. der Bildenden Künste (Acad. of Fine Art)
Schwarzenbergplatz
Ressel-park
OPERNRING
KÄRNTNER RING
SCHUBERTRING
PARKRING
STUBENRING
LOTHRINGERSTR.
LINKE WIENZEILE
RECHTE WIENZEILE
WIEDNER HAUPTSTR.
M.A.K. (Museum of Applied Arts)
City Air Terminal
Wien-Mitte
St. Elisabeth Krankenhaus
Veterinärmedizin. Universität
Johann Strauss Museum
1
2
3

## WARSAW, POLAND

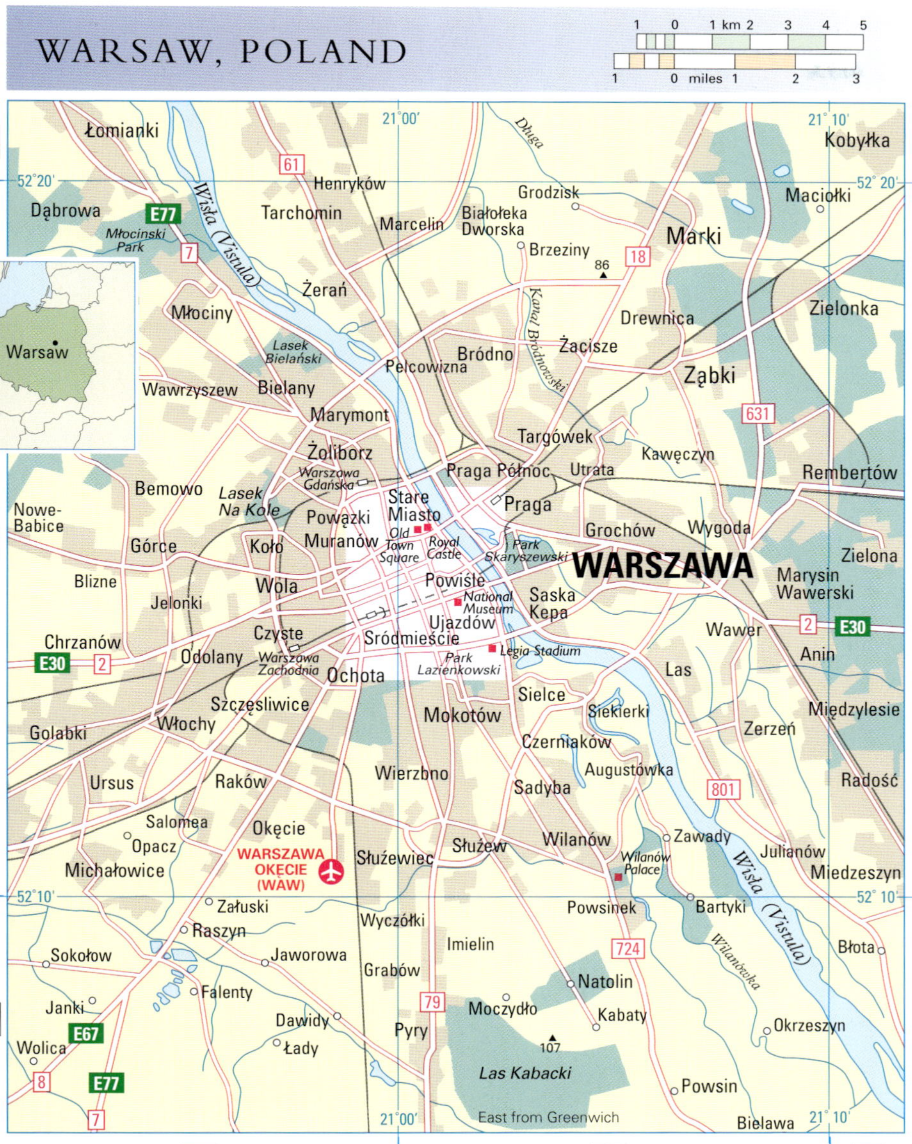

0 1 km 2 3 4 5
0 miles 1 2 3
Łomianki
Kobyłka
Henryków
Dąbrowa
Tarchomin
Marcelin
Białołęka Dworska
Grodzisk
Maciołki
Młocinski Park
Brzeziny
Marki
Warsaw
Żerań
Zielonka
Młociny
Drewnica
Lasek Bielański
Żacisze
Bródno
Pelcowizna
Ząbki
Wawrzyszew
Bielany
Marymont
Targówek
Kawęczyn
Żoliborz
Bemowo
Lasek Na Kole
Praga Północ
Utrata
Rembertów
Nowe-Babice
Stare Miasto
Praga
Powązki
Grochów
Wygoda
Górce
Koło
Muranów
WARSZAWA
Zielona
Blizne
Wola
Powiśle
Saska Kępa
Marysin Wawerski
Jelonki
Czyste
Ujazdów
Wawer
Chrzanów
Odolany
Śródmieście
Ochota
Las
Anin
Szczęśliwice
Sielce
Golabki
Włochy
Mokotów
Siekierki
Międzylesie
Czerniaków
Zerzeń
Ursus
Raków
Wierzbno
Augustówka
Radość
Salomea
Sadyba
Opacz
Okęcie
WARSZAWA OKĘCIE (WAW)
Michałowice
Służewiec
Służew
Wilanów
Zawady
Julianów
Miedzeszyn
Załuski
Powsinek
Bartyki
Raszyn
Wyczółki
Wisła (Vistula)
Imielin
Błota
Sokołów
Jaworowa
Grabów
Natolin
Falenty
Janki
Moczydło
Kabaty
Dawidy
Pyry
Okrzeszyn
Wolica
Łady
Las Kabacki
Powsin
East from Greenwich
Bielawa
E77
E30
E67
1
2
3


## CENTRAL WARSAW

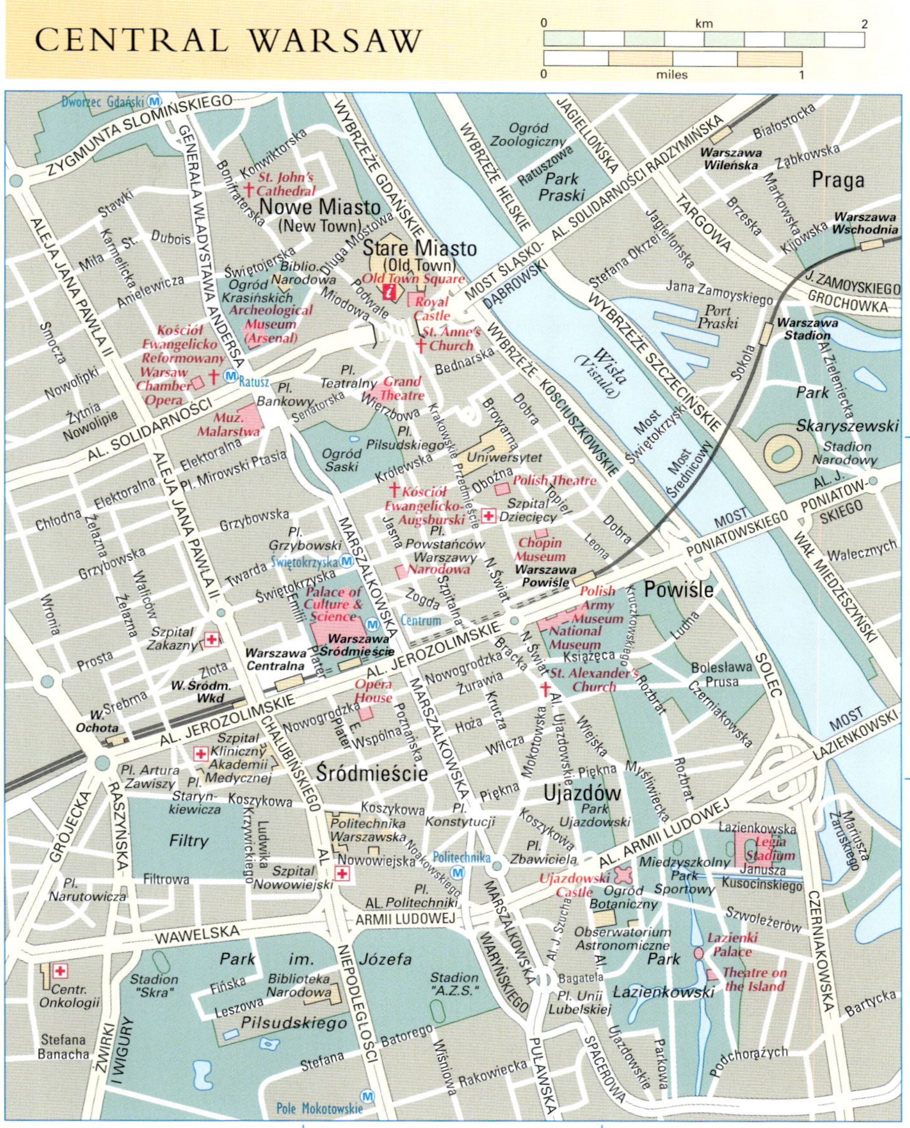

0 km 2
0 miles 1
Dworzec Gdański
ZYGMUNTA SŁOMIŃSKIEGO
Ogród Zoologiczny
Park Praski
Praga
Warszawa Wileńska
Nowe Miasto (New Town)
St. John's Cathedral
Stare Miasto (Old Town)
Old Town Square
Royal Castle
St. Anne's Church
Warszawa Wschodnia
Kościół Ewangelicko Reformowany
Archeological Museum (Arsenal)
Warsaw Chamber Opera
Grand Theatre
Warszawa Stadion
Skaryszewski
Stadion Narodowy
Muz. Malarstwa
Ogród Saski
Uniwersytet
Polish Theatre
AL. SOLIDARNOŚCI
Kościół Ewangelicko Augsburski
Palace of Culture & Science
Chopin Museum
Warszawa Powiśle
Powiśle
Polish Army Museum
National Museum
Warszawa Centralna
Warszawa Śródmieście
AL. JEROZOLIMSKIE
St. Alexander's Church
Opera House
W. Śródm. Wkd
W. Ochota
Śródmieście
Ujazdów
Politechnika Warszawska
Filtry
Ujazdowski Castle
Ogród Botaniczny
Legia Stadium
Obserwatorium Astronomiczne
Łazienki Palace
Theatre on the Island
Park Łazienkowski
Stadion "Skra"
Park im. Józefa Piłsudskiego
Stadion "A.Z.S."
Biblioteka Narodowa
Centr. Onkologii
Stefana Banacha
WAWELSKA
Pole Mokotowskie
a
b
c
1
2
3


## WASHINGTON D.C.

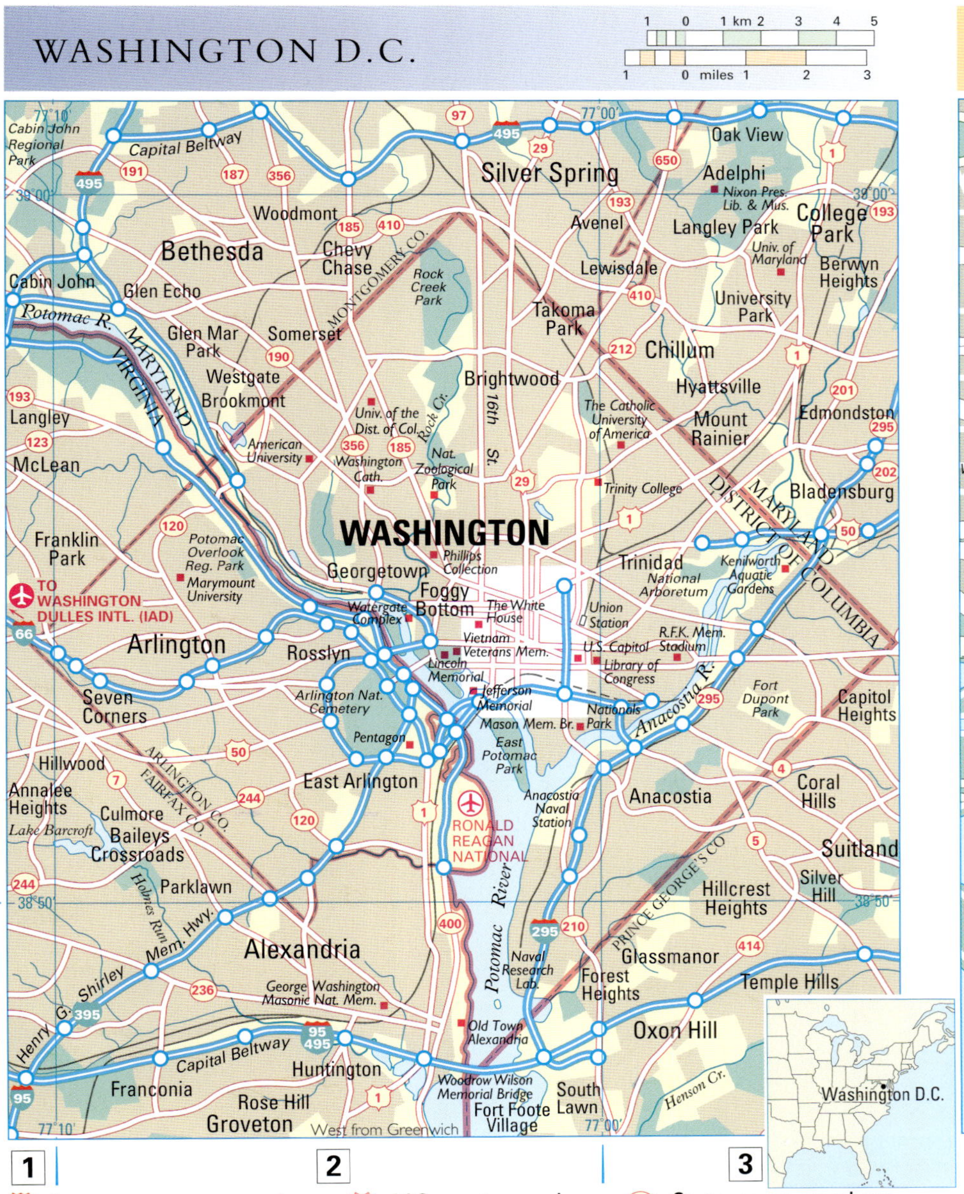

0 1 km 2 3 4 5
0 miles 1 2 3
Cabin John Regional Park
Capital Beltway
Silver Spring
Oak View
Adelphi
Woodmont
College Park
Bethesda
Chevy Chase
Avenel
Langley Park
Lewisdale
Berwyn Heights
Cabin John
Glen Echo
Rock Creek Park
Takoma Park
University Park
Potomac R.
Glen Mar Park
Somerset
Chillum
Westgate
Brookmont
Brightwood
Hyattsville
Langley
McLean
Mount Rainier
Edmondston
Bladensburg
WASHINGTON
Franklin Park
Georgetown
TO WASHINGTON DULLES INTL. (IAD)
Foggy Bottom
Trinidad
Arlington
Rosslyn
Seven Corners
Fort Dupont Park
Capitol Heights
Pentagon
East Arlington
Anacostia
Coral Hills
Annalee Heights
Culmore
Baileys Crossroads
RONALD REAGAN NATIONAL
Suitland
Parklawn
Hillcrest Heights
Silver Hill
Alexandria
Glassmanor
Forest Heights
Temple Hills
Oxon Hill
Huntington
Franconia
Rose Hill
Groveton
South Lawn
Fort Foote Village
West from Greenwich
Washington D.C.
1
2
3


## CENTRAL WASHINGTON

0 km 1
0 miles 0.5
North West
Logan Circle
Scott Circle
Thomas Circle
Washington Convention Center
Mt. Vernon Sq.-UDC
Farragut North
Mount Vernon Square
Franklin Square
Farragut West
McPherson Sq.
Renwick Gallery
Lafayette Square
Metro Center
Gallery Place
Union Station
World Bank
The White House
Nat. Mus. of American Art
Nat. Mus. of Crime
Judiciary Sq.
Columbus Circle
F.B.I. Bldg.
Ford's Theatre
Dept. of the Interior
Zero Milestone
The Ellipse
Federal Triangle
Dept. of Commerce
Ronald Reagan Bldg.
Dept. of Justice
Newseum
U.S. Courthouse
Union Station Plaza
Archives-Navy Memorial
Nat. Museum of American History
Nat. Museum of Natural History
National Gallery of Art
Supreme Court
Reflecting Pool
Washington Monument
The Mall
National Air & Space Museum
Grant Statue
U.S. Capitol
Library of Congress
W.W. II Memorial
Smithsonian
Smithsonian Institution
D. C. War Memorial
Hirshhorn Museum
National American Indian Museum
Botanic Gardens
US Holocaust Memorial Museum
Federal Center SW
Capitol South
Kutz Bridge
Tidal Basin
L'Enfant Plaza
Roosevelt Memorial
Jefferson Memorial
Outlet Bridge
Potomac Park
SOUTHWEST FREEWAY
South West
Francis Case Meml. Bridge
Washington Channel
Potomac River
East Potomac Park
Waterfront
Navy Yard
a
b
c
1
2
3


Interstate route numbers   U.S. route numbers   State route numbers

# WORLD MAPS

Equatorial Scale 1:76 000 000

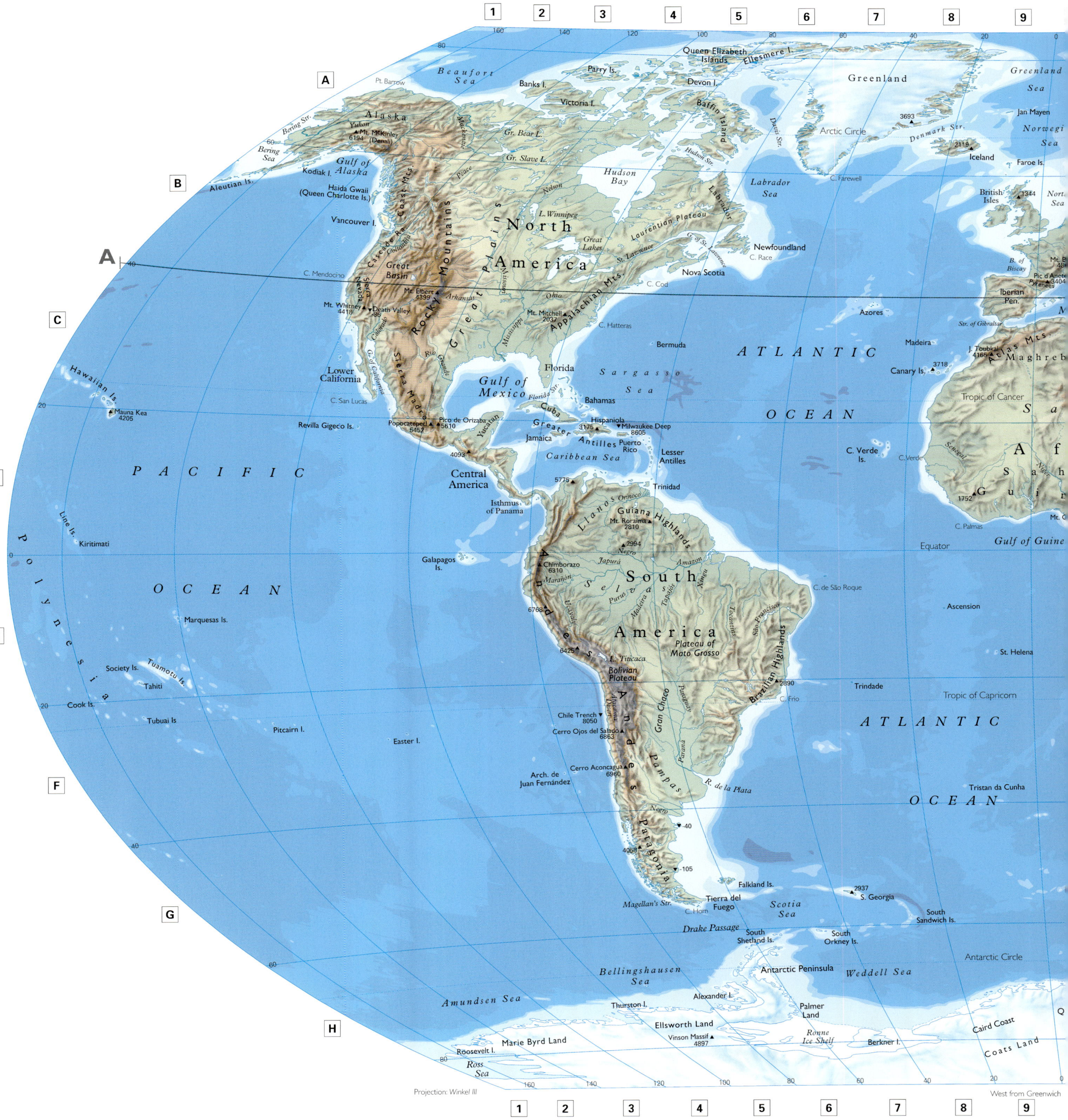

Beaufort Sea
Pt. Barrow
Queen Elizabeth Islands
Ellesmere I.
Parry Is.
Banks I.
Devon I.
Victoria I.
Baffin Island
Greenland
Greenland Sea
Jan Mayen
Norwegian Sea
Denmark Str.
Iceland
Faroe Is.
Arctic Circle
Davis Str.
Hudson Str.
C. Farewell
Bering Str.
Bering Sea
Alaska
Yukon
Mt. McKinley 6194 (Denali)
Mackenzie
Gr. Bear L.
Gr. Slave L.
Kodiak I.
Gulf of Alaska
Aleutian Is.
Haida Gwaii (Queen Charlotte Is.)
Coast Mts.
Peace
Hudson Bay
Nelson
Labrador Sea
Labrador
Vancouver I.
L. Winnipeg
North America
Great Lakes
Laurentian Plateau
Newfoundland
C. Race
British Isles
North Sea
Cascade Ra.
Columbia
Great Basin
Rocky Mountains
Great Plains
St. Lawrence
G. of St. Lawrence
Nova Scotia
C. Cod
C. Mendocino
Sierra Nevada
Mt. Elbert 4399
Mt. Whitney 4418
Death Valley -86
Arkansas
Missouri
Ohio
Appalachian Mts.
Mt. Mitchell 2037
C. Hatteras
Iberian Pen.
B. of Biscay
Pic d'Aneto 3404
Pyrenees
Azores
Str. of Gibraltar
Madeira
Atlas Mts.
J. Toubkal 4165
Maghreb
Canary Is.
3718
Bermuda
ATLANTIC OCEAN
Sargasso Sea
Mississippi
Rio Grande
Colorado
Sierra Madre
G. of California
Lower California
Hawaiian Is.
Mauna Kea 4205
C. San Lucas
Gulf of Mexico
Florida
Florida Str.
Bahamas
Cuba
Greater Antilles
Hispaniola
3175
Milwaukee Deep -8605
Jamaica
Puerto Rico
Lesser Antilles
Caribbean Sea
Tropic of Cancer
Revilla Gigedo Is.
Popocatepetl 5452
Pico de Orizaba 5610
Yucatan
4093
C. Verde Is.
C. Verde
Senegal
Niger
Africa
Sahara
PACIFIC
Central America
5775
Trinidad
Isthmus of Panama
Llanos
Orinoco
Guiana Highlands
Mt. Roraima 2810
2994
Negro
1752
C. Palmas
Gulf of Guinea
Line Is.
Kiritimati
Polynesia
Galapagos Is.
Equator
Chimborazo 6310
Marañon
Japurá
Amazon
Xingu
Tapajós
Madeira
Purus
Selvas
South America
C. de São Roque
Ascension
OCEAN
Andes
6768
Ucayali
Tocantins
São Francisco
Marquesas Is.
Plateau of Mato Grosso
Brazilian Highlands
L. Titicaca
6425
Bolivian Plateau
St. Helena
Society Is.
Tuamotu Is.
Tahiti
2890
C. Frio
Trindade
Tropic of Capricorn
Cook Is.
Tubuai Is.
Gran Chaco
Paraguay
Paraná
Atacama Desert
Chile Trench -8050
Cerro Ojos del Salado 6863
Pitcairn I.
Easter I.
ATLANTIC
Arch. de Juan Fernández
Cerro Aconcagua 6960
Pampas
R. de la Plata
Tristan da Cunha
OCEAN
Negro
-40
Patagonia
4058
-105
Falkland Is.
2937
S. Georgia
Magellan's Str.
C. Horn
Tierra del Fuego
Scotia Sea
South Sandwich Is.
Drake Passage
South Shetland Is.
South Orkney Is.
Antarctic Circle
Bellingshausen Sea
Antarctic Peninsula
Weddell Sea
Amundsen Sea
Alexander I.
Thurston I.
Palmer Land
Ellsworth Land
Vinson Massif 4897
Ronne Ice Shelf
Berkner I.
Caird Coast
Coats Land
Marie Byrd Land
Roosevelt I.
Ross Sea
Projection: Winkel III
West from Greenwich


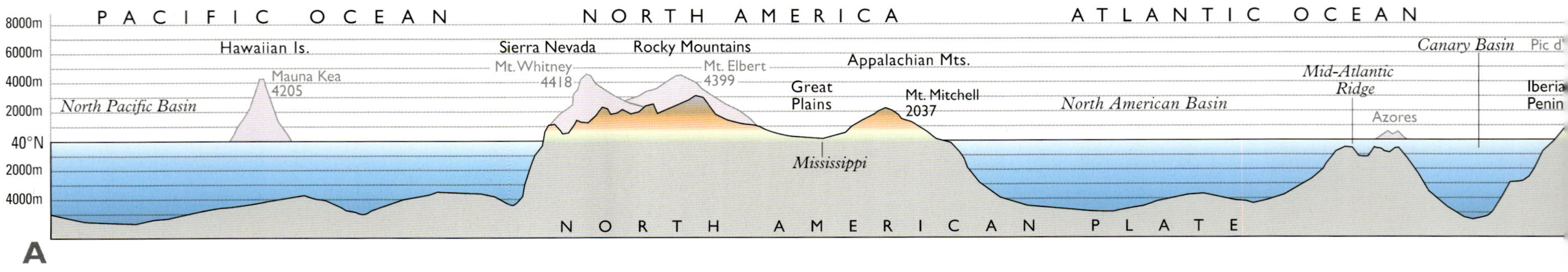

8000m
6000m
4000m
2000m
40°N
2000m
4000m
PACIFIC OCEAN
NORTH AMERICA
ATLANTIC OCEAN
Hawaiian Is.
Mauna Kea 4205
North Pacific Basin
Sierra Nevada
Mt. Whitney 4418
Rocky Mountains
Mt. Elbert 4399
Appalachian Mts.
Great Plains
Mt. Mitchell 2037
Mississippi
North American Basin
Canary Basin
Mid-Atlantic Ridge
Azores
NORTH AMERICAN PLATE
A

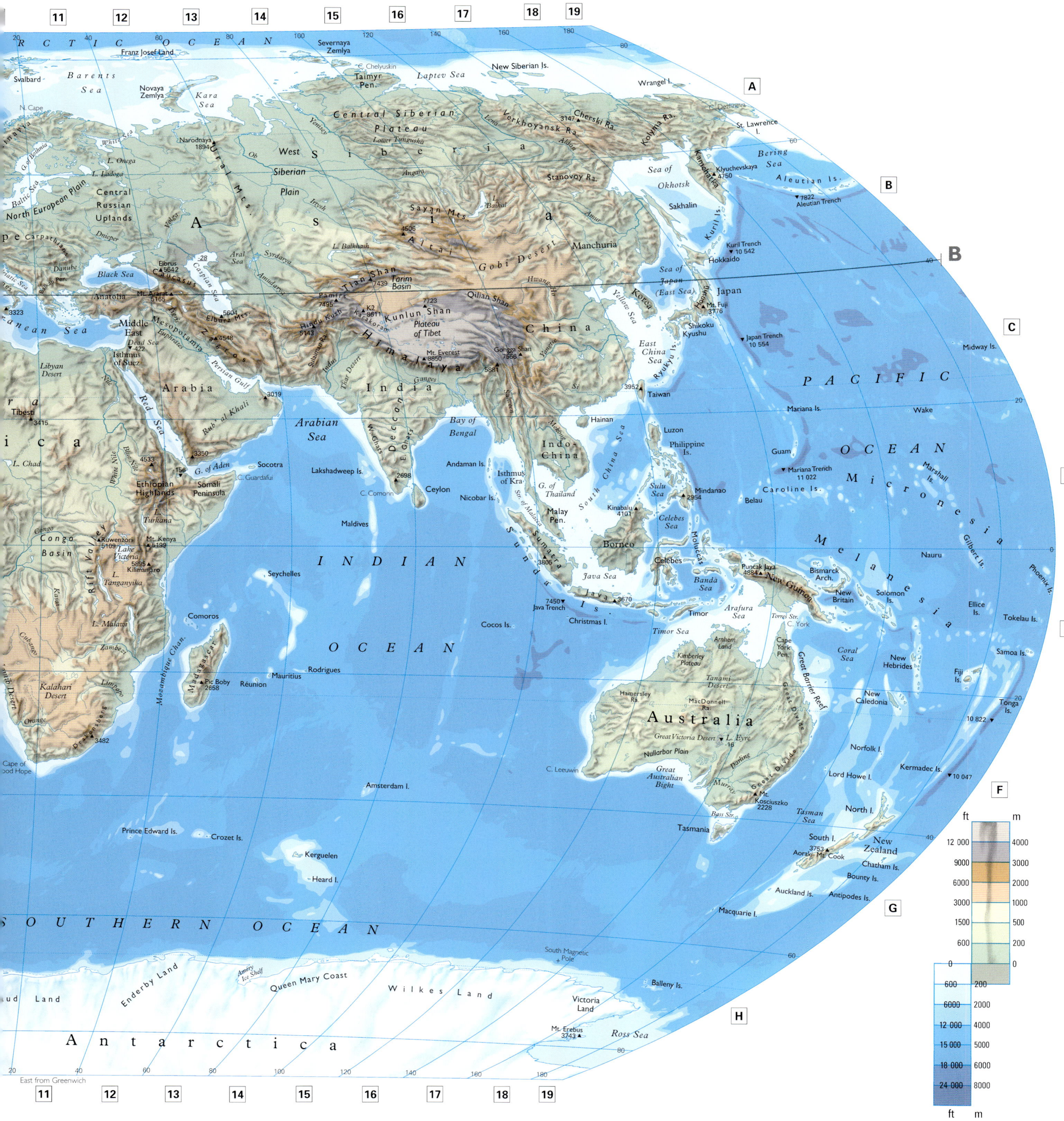
Franz Josef Land
Svalbard
Barents Sea
Novaya Zemlya
Kara Sea
Severnaya Zemlya
Taimyr Pen.
Laptev Sea
New Siberian Is.
Wrangel I.
Central Siberian Plateau
Verkhoyansk Ra.
Cherski Ra.
Kolyma Ra.
St. Lawrence I.
Bering Sea
Aleutian Is.
Aleutian Trench
West Siberian Plain
Central Russian Uplands
North European Plain
Ural Mts.
Sea of Okhotsk
Sakhalin
Kamchatka
Klyuchevskaya 4750
Stanovoy Ra.
Sayan Mts.
Altai
Gobi Desert
Manchuria
Kuril Is.
Kuril Trench
Hokkaido
Sea of Japan (East Sea)
Japan
Mt. Fuji 3776
Japan Trench
Korea
Yellow Sea
Shikoku
Kyushu
Black Sea
Caspian Sea
Aral Sea
L. Balkhash
Tian Shan
Tarim Basin
Qilian Shan
Kunlun Shan
Plateau of Tibet
K2 8611
Mt. Everest 8850
Gongga Shan 7556
Himalaya
Hindu Kush
Pamirs
Caucasus
Elbrus 5642
Anatolia
Elburz Mts.
Zagros Mts.
Mesopotamia
Middle East
Arabia
Persian Gulf
Red Sea
Rub' al Khali
Arabian Sea
G. of Aden
Socotra
India
Bay of Bengal
Lakshadweep Is.
Ceylon
Maldives
Andaman Is.
Nicobar Is.
China
East China Sea
Taiwan
Hainan
Indo-China
South China Sea
Luzon
Philippine Is.
Mindanao
G. of Thailand
Malay Pen.
Borneo
Kinabalu 4101
Sulu Sea
Celebes Sea
Celebes
Moluccas
Banda Sea
Java Sea
Java
Sumatra
Java Trench
Christmas I.
Cocos Is.
Timor
Timor Sea
Arafura Sea
New Guinea
Puncak Jaya 4884
Bismarck Arch.
New Britain
Solomon Is.
PACIFIC OCEAN
Mariana Is.
Mariana Trench 11 022
Guam
Caroline Is.
Micronesia
Melanesia
Marshall Is.
Gilbert Is.
Nauru
Midway Is.
Wake
Ellice Is.
Tokelau Is.
Phoenix Is.
Samoa Is.
Fiji Is.
Tonga Is.
New Hebrides
New Caledonia
Coral Sea
Great Barrier Reef
Cape York Pen.
Australia
Great Victoria Desert
Nullarbor Plain
Great Australian Bight
Tanami Desert
MacDonnell Ra.
Hamersley Ra.
Kimberley Plateau
Arnhem Land
Great Dividing Range
Mt. Kosciuszko 2228
Tasmania
Tasman Sea
Lord Howe I.
Norfolk I.
Kermadec Is.
New Zealand
North I.
South I.
Aoraki Mt. Cook 3753
Chatham Is.
Bounty Is.
Antipodes Is.
Auckland Is.
Macquarie I.
INDIAN OCEAN
Seychelles
Comoros
Madagascar
Mauritius
Réunion
Rodrigues
Amsterdam I.
Prince Edward Is.
Crozet Is.
Kerguelen
Heard I.
Africa
Tibesti
L. Chad
Libyan Desert
Ethiopian Highlands
Somali Peninsula
Congo Basin
Rift Valley
Mt. Kenya 5199
Kilimanjaro 5895
L. Victoria
L. Tanganyika
L. Malawi
Kalahari Desert
Drakensberg
SOUTHERN OCEAN
Enderby Land
Queen Mary Coast
Wilkes Land
Victoria Land
Ross Sea
Mt. Erebus 3743
Balleny Is.
South Magnetic Pole
Antarctica
East from Greenwich
ft m
12 000 4000
9000 3000
6000 2000
3000 1000
1500 500
600 200
0 0
600 200
6000 2000
12 000 4000
15 000 5000
18 000 6000
24 000 8000

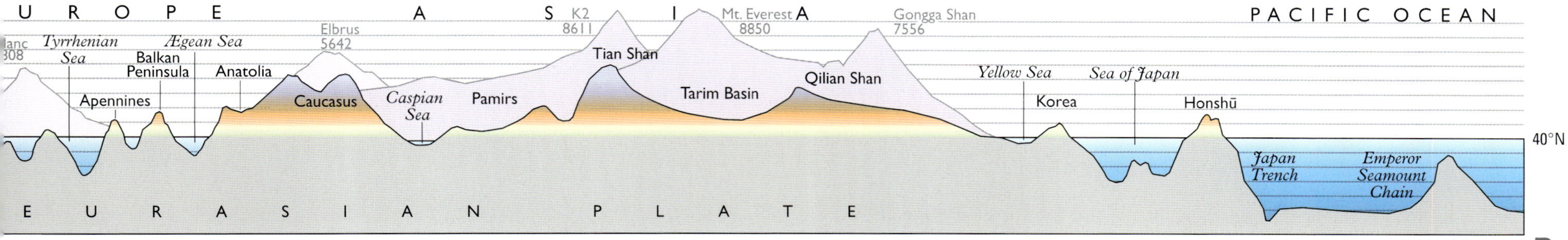
EUROPE
ASIA
PACIFIC OCEAN
Tyrrhenian Sea
Ægean Sea
Balkan Peninsula
Apennines
Anatolia
Elbrus 5642
Caucasus
Caspian Sea
Pamirs
K2 8611
Tian Shan
Mt. Everest 8850
Tarim Basin
Qilian Shan
Gongga Shan 7556
Yellow Sea
Korea
Sea of Japan
Honshū
Japan Trench
Emperor Seamount Chain
40°N
EURASIAN PLATE


B

Equatorial Scale 1·76 000 000

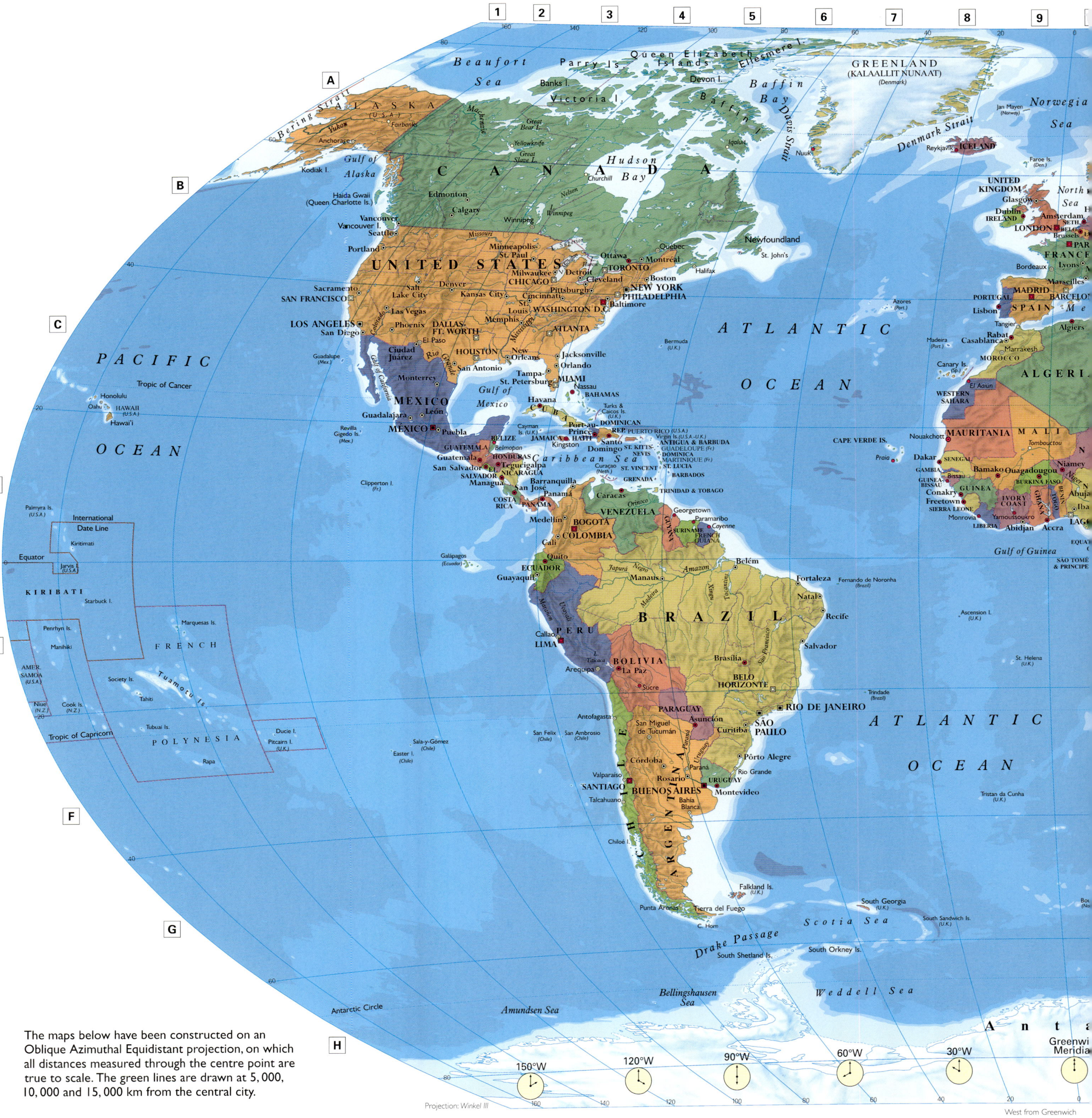

Beaufort Sea
Parry Is.
Queen Elizabeth Islands
Ellesmere I.
GREENLAND (KALAALLIT NUNAAT) (Denmark)
Banks I.
Victoria I.
Devon I.
Baffin Bay
Baffin I.
Davis Strait
Denmark Strait
Norwegian Sea
Jan Mayen (Norway)
Reykjavík
ICELAND
Bering Strait
ALASKA (U.S.A.)
Yukon
Fairbanks
Anchorage
Mackenzie
Great Bear L.
Yellowknife
Great Slave L.
Gulf of Alaska
Kodiak I.
CANADA
Hudson Bay
Churchill
Nuuk
Iqaluit
Faroe Is. (Den.)
UNITED KINGDOM
Glasgow
North Sea
Dublin
IRELAND
Amsterdam
LONDON
Brussels
PARIS
FRANCE
Haida Gwaii (Queen Charlotte Is.)
Edmonton
Calgary
Nelson
Winnipeg
Vancouver
Vancouver I.
Seattle
Missouri
Portland
Minneapolis-St. Paul
Ottawa
Québec
Montréal
TORONTO
Newfoundland
St. John's
Halifax
Bordeaux
Lyons
UNITED STATES
Milwaukee
CHICAGO
Detroit
Cleveland
Boston
NEW YORK
PHILADELPHIA
Baltimore
Pittsburgh
Denver
Salt Lake City
Kansas City
Cincinnati
St. Louis
WASHINGTON D.C.
Sacramento
SAN FRANCISCO
Las Vegas
Memphis
LOS ANGELES
San Diego
Phoenix
DALLAS-FT. WORTH
ATLANTA
El Paso
Azores (Port.)
PORTUGAL
Lisbon
MADRID
SPAIN
BARCELONA
Marseilles
Tangier
Rabat
Casablanca
Algiers
Marrakesh
MOROCCO
ALGERIA
Madeira (Port.)
ATLANTIC OCEAN
Bermuda (U.K.)
PACIFIC OCEAN
Guadalupe (Mex.)
Ciudad Juárez
HOUSTON
New Orleans
Jacksonville
Orlando
San Antonio
Monterrey
Tampa-St. Petersburg
MIAMI
Nassau
BAHAMAS
Gulf of Mexico
Tropic of Cancer
Honolulu
Oahu
HAWAII (U.S.A.)
Hawai'i
Havana
CUBA
Turks & Caicos Is. (U.K.)
Canary Is. (Sp.)
El Aaiún
WESTERN SAHARA
MEXICO
León
Guadalajara
MEXICO
Puebla
Revilla Gigedo Is. (Mex.)
Cayman Is. (U.K.)
JAMAICA
Kingston
HAITI
Port-au-Prince
DOMINICAN REP.
Santo Domingo
PUERTO RICO (U.S.A.)
Virgin Is. (U.S.A.-U.K.)
ANTIGUA & BARBUDA
GUADELOUPE (Fr.)
DOMINICA
MARTINIQUE (Fr.)
ST. LUCIA
ST. KITTS-NEVIS
ST. VINCENT
BARBADOS
GRENADA
TRINIDAD & TOBAGO
BELIZE
Belmopan
GUATEMALA
Guatemala
HONDURAS
Tegucigalpa
EL SALVADOR
San Salvador
NICARAGUA
Managua
Caribbean Sea
Curaçao (Neth.)
CAPE VERDE IS.
Praia
Nouakchott
MAURITANIA
MALI
Tombouctou
Dakar
SENEGAL
GAMBIA
GUINEA-BISSAU
Bissau
GUINEA
Conakry
Freetown
SIERRA LEONE
Monrovia
LIBERIA
IVORY COAST
Yamoussoukro
Abidjan
Accra
GHANA
Bamako
Ouagadougou
BURKINA FASO
Niamey
Clipperton I. (Fr.)
Barranquilla
COSTA RICA
San José
PANAMA
Panamá
Caracas
VENEZUELA
Orinoco
Georgetown
GUYANA
Paramaribo
SURINAME
Cayenne
FRENCH GUIANA
Medellín
BOGOTÁ
COLOMBIA
Cali
Palmyra Is. (U.S.A.)
International Date Line
Kiritimati
Equator
Jarvis I. (U.S.A.)
KIRIBATI
Starbuck I.
Galápagos (Ecuador)
Quito
ECUADOR
Guayaquil
Japurá
Negro
Manaus
Amazon
Belém
Fortaleza
Natal
Recife
Fernando de Noronha (Brazil)
Gulf of Guinea
SÃO TOMÉ & PRINCIPE
Marquesas Is.
Penrhyn Is.
Manihiki
FRENCH POLYNESIA
Ascension I. (U.K.)
BRAZIL
Madeira
Xingu
Tocantins
São Francisco
Callao
PERU
LIMA
Ucayali
Marañón
Salvador
St. Helena (U.K.)
AMER. SAMOA (U.S.A.)
Society Is.
Tahiti
Tuamotu Is.
Niue (N.Z.)
Cook Is. (N.Z.)
Arequipa
BOLIVIA
La Paz
Titicaca
Sucre
Brasília
BELO HORIZONTE
Trindade (Brazil)
RIO DE JANEIRO
SÃO PAULO
Curitiba
PARAGUAY
Asunción
Antofagasta
Tubuai Is.
Tropic of Capricorn
Ducie I.
Pitcairn I. (U.K.)
Rapa
Sala-y-Gómez (Chile)
Easter I. (Chile)
San Felix (Chile)
San Ambrosio (Chile)
San Miguel de Tucumán
Paraná
Uruguay
Pôrto Alegre
Rio Grande
URUGUAY
Montevideo
Córdoba
Rosario
Valparaíso
SANTIAGO
BUENOS AIRES
Talcahuano
Bahía Blanca
CHILE
ARGENTINA
Chiloé I.
Tristan da Cunha (U.K.)
Falkland Is. (U.K.)
Punta Arenas
Tierra del Fuego
C. Horn
South Georgia (U.K.)
South Sandwich Is. (U.K.)
Scotia Sea
Drake Passage
South Shetland Is.
South Orkney Is.
Bellingshausen Sea
Weddell Sea
Amundsen Sea
Antarctic Circle
Antarctica
Greenwich Meridian
150°W
120°W
90°W
60°W
30°W
Projection: Winkel III
West from Greenwich


The maps below have been constructed on an Oblique Azimuthal Equidistant projection, on which all distances measured through the centre point are true to scale. The green lines are drawn at 5,000, 10,000 and 15,000 km from the central city.

MEXICO CITY
19° 26'N 99° 04'W

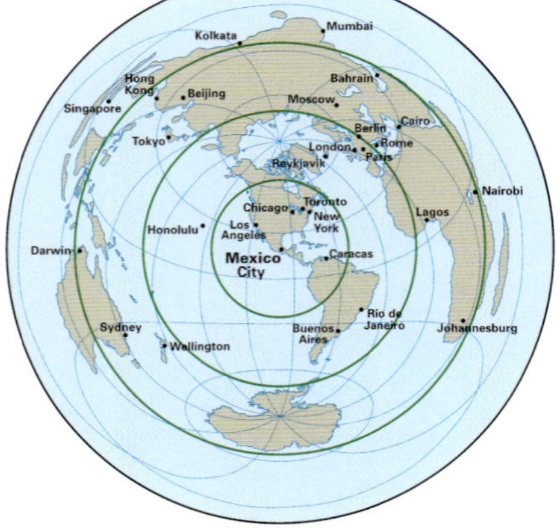

Kolkata
Mumbai
Hong Kong
Beijing
Bahrain
Singapore
Moscow
Cairo
Tokyo
Berlin
Rome
London
Paris
Reykjavik
Nairobi
Chicago
Toronto
New York
Honolulu
Los Angeles
Lagos
Mexico City
Caracas
Darwin
Sydney
Rio de Janeiro
Johannesburg
Wellington
Buenos Aires


NEW YORK
40° 43'N 74° 00'W

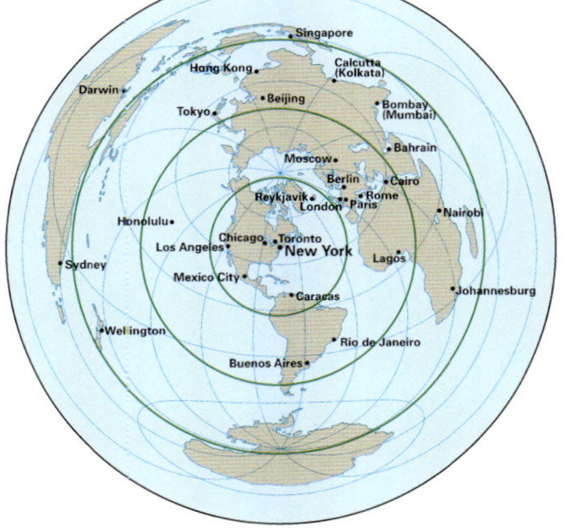

Singapore
Hong Kong
Calcutta (Kolkata)
Darwin
Beijing
Tokyo
Bombay (Mumbai)
Bahrain
Moscow
Berlin
Cairo
Reykjavik
London
Rome
Paris
Nairobi
Honolulu
Chicago
Toronto
New York
Los Angeles
Sydney
Mexico City
Lagos
Caracas
Johannesburg
Wellington
Rio de Janeiro
Buenos Aires


RIO DE JANEIRO
22° 50'S 43° 15'W

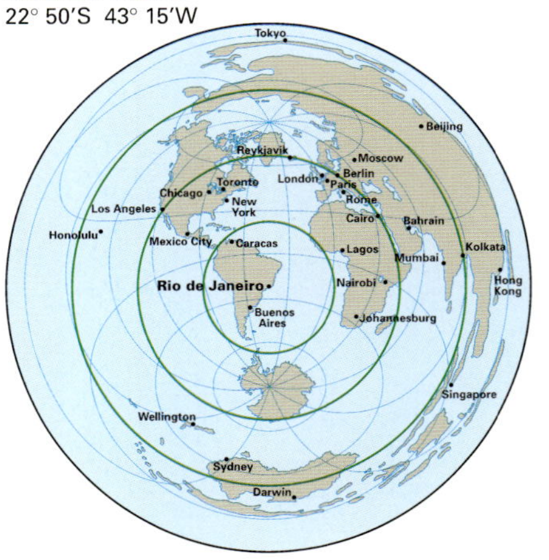

Tokyo
Beijing
Reykjavik
Moscow
Chicago
Toronto
London
Berlin
Paris
New York
Rome
Los Angeles
Cairo
Bahrain
Honolulu
Mexico City
Caracas
Kolkata
Lagos
Mumbai
Rio de Janeiro
Nairobi
Hong Kong
Buenos Aires
Johannesburg
Singapore
Wellington
Sydney
Darwin


LONDON
51° 28'N 00° 27'W

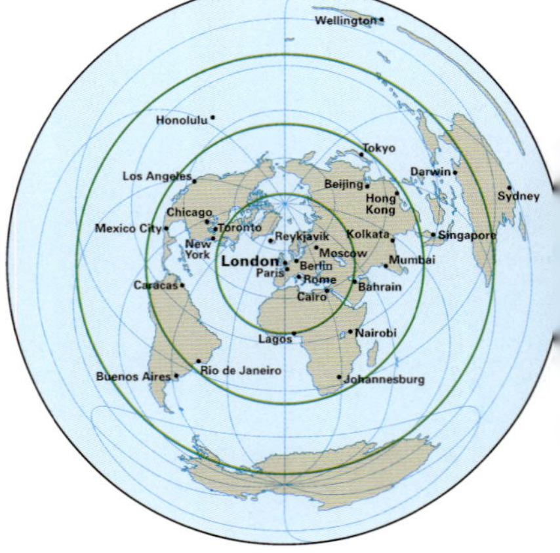

Wellington
Honolulu
Tokyo
Darwin
Los Angeles
Beijing
Hong Kong
Sydney
Chicago
Toronto
Reykjavik
Kolkata
Mexico City
New York
Singapore
London
Berlin
Moscow
Paris
Mumbai
Rome
Caracas
Cairo
Bahrain
Lagos
Nairobi
Buenos Aires
Rio de Janeiro
Johannesburg

11
12
13
14
15
16
17
18
19
A
B
C
D
E
F
G
H
0 0
600 200
6 000 2000
12 000 4000
15 000 5000
18 000 6000
24 000 8000
ft m
ARCTIC OCEAN
Severnaya Zemlya
Franz Josef Land (Russia)
Barents Sea
Kara Sea
Laptev Sea
New Siberian Is.
East Siberian Sea
Wrangel I.
Novaya Zemlya
Arctic Circle
R U S S I A
Bering Sea
Aleutian Is. (U.S.A.)
Sea of Okhotsk
K A Z A K H S T A N
M O N G O L I A
C H I N A
T I B E T
Black Sea
Caspian Sea
T U R K E Y
I R A N
IRAQ
AFGHANISTAN
P A K I S T A N
I N D I A
S A U D I A R A B I A
E G Y P T
S U D A N
E T H I O P I A
S O M A L I A
K E N Y A
T A N Z A N I A
Z A M B I A
MADAGASCAR
SOUTH AFRICA
BOTSWANA
ANGOLA
CHAD
Bay of Bengal
BURMA
THAILAND
VIETNAM
PHILIPPINES
M A L A Y S I A
I N D O N E S I A
PAPUA NEW GUINEA
SOLOMON IS.
TUVALU
KIRIBATI
VANUATU
FIJI
TONGA
SAMOA
NEW CALEDONIA (Fr.)
A U S T R A L I A
NEW ZEALAND
Tasman Sea
J A P A N
East China Sea
South China Sea
P A C I F I C O C E A N
NORTHERN MARIANAS (U.S.A.)
FED. STATES OF MICRONESIA
MARSHALL IS.
PALAU
I N D I A N O C E A N
S O U T H E R N O C E A N
Tropic of Cancer
Equator
Tropic of Capricorn
International Date Line
Antarctic Circle
Ross Sea
30°E
60°E
90°E
120°E
150°E
IDL
30°W
The time at this longitude when it is 12.00 (noon) at Greenwich
East from Greenwich

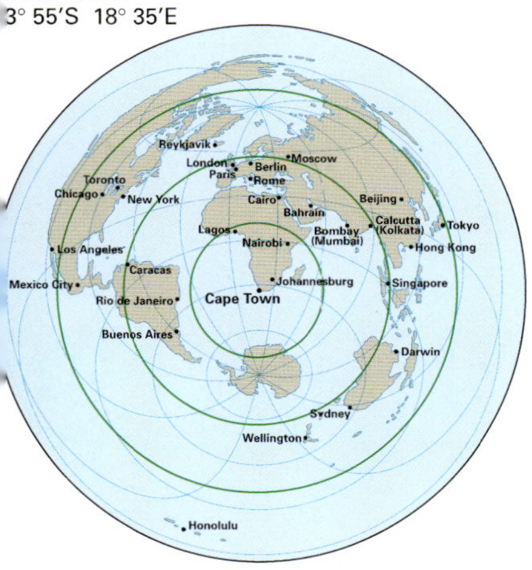

APE TOWN
3° 55'S 18° 35'E

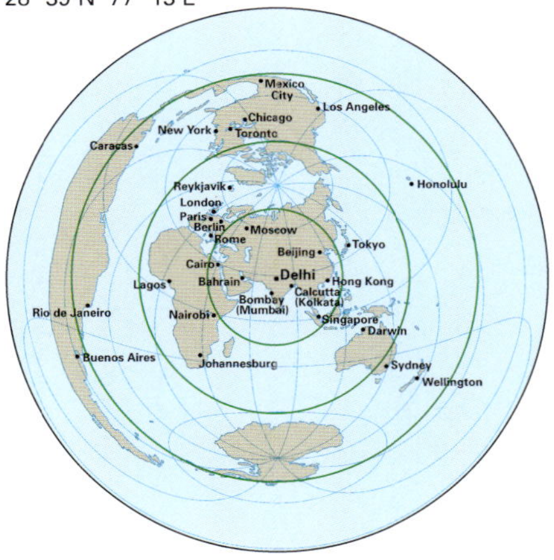

DELHI
28° 39'N 77° 13'E

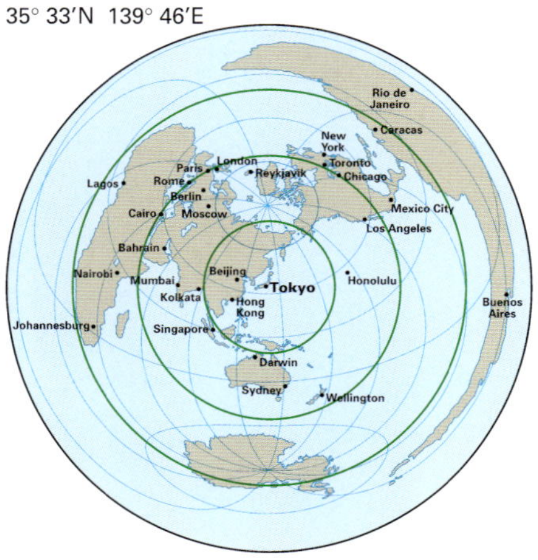

TOKYO
35° 33'N 139° 46'E

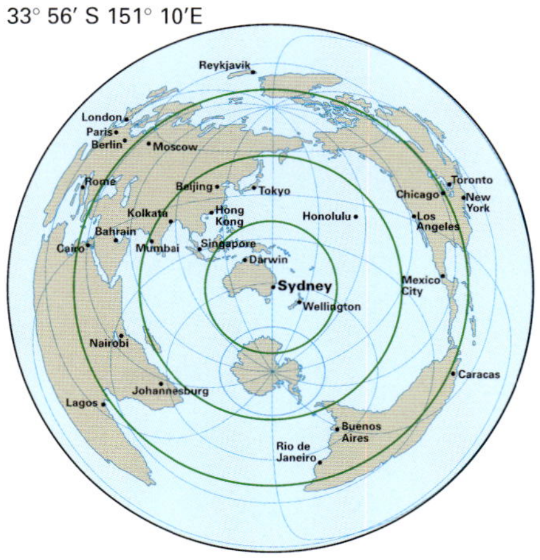

SYDNEY
33° 56' S 151° 10'E

1:28 000 000
km
miles
18
17
16
15
1
2
3
4
5
6
7
8
9
A
B
C
D
PACIFIC OCEAN
Tufts Abyssal Plain
Gilbert Seamounts
Aleutian Trench
Aleutian Islands (U.S.A.)
Aleutian Basin
Bowers Basin
Bowers Ridge
Near Is. (U.S.A.)
7822
Dutch Harbor
Unimak I.
2857
Bering Sea
Pribilof Is. (U.S.A.)
42
Komandorskiye Ostrova
Petropavlovsk-Kamchatskiy
Klyuchevskaya Sopka 4750
Ust-Kamchatsk
Ostrov Karaginskiy
International Date Line
Mys Olyutorskiy
Mys Lopatka
Kurilskiye Ostrova (Russia)
La Perouse Str.
Kuril Basin
JAPAN
Hokkaido
SAPPORO
Yuzhno-Sakhalinsk
Sakhalin (Russia)
1609
Sea of Okhotsk
Sakhalinskiy Zaliv
Vanino
Amur
Khabarovsk
Nikolayevsk
Komsomolsk-na-Amur
Udskaya Guba
Tauiskaya Guba
Magadan
Okhotsk
Stanovoy Khrebet
Aldan
Poluostrov Kamchatka
Penzhinskaya G.
Gizhiginskaya Guba
Kolymskoye Nagorye
Omolon
Kolyma
Srednekolymsk
3147
Nizhne Kolymsk
Indigirka
Bristol Bay
Alaska Pen.
Kodiak I.
1362
Cook Inlet
G. of Alaska
Seward
Prince William Sd.
Anchorage
Cordova
Mt. McKinley 6194
Kuskokwim
Yukon
Nunivak
St. Matthew (U.S.A.)
Mys Navarin
St. Lawrence I. (U.S.A.)
Anadyrskiy Zaliv
Anadyr
2453
Norton Sd.
Nome
Bering Str.
Provideniya
Mys Dezhneva
C. Prince of Wales
Chukotskoye Nagorye
Kotzebue Sd.
Pt. Hope
C. Lisburne
Proliv Longa
Pevek
Chukchi Sea
Ostrov Vrangelya (Russia)
1096
Chaunskaya G.
Haida Gwaii (Queen Charlotte Is.)
Alexander Arch.
Prince Rupert
Mt. St. Elias 5489
Mt. Logan 5959
4949
Fairbanks
ALASKA (U.S.A.)
Juneau
Skagway
Skeena
4019
Whitehorse
Dawson
Stewart
Peel
Noatak
Koyukuk
Fort Yukon
Porcupine
Rocky Mountains
Dawson Creek
2762
Prudhoe Bay
2761
Pt. Barrow
C. Halkett
Harrison Bay
Fort McPherson
Herschel I.
Fort Simpson
Liard
Mackenzie
Tulita
Fort Good Hope
Peace
Fort Vermilion
Great Bear Lake
Mackenzie Bay
2882
Tuktoyaktuk
C. Bathurst
Beaufort Sea
Canada Abyssal Plain
Canada Basin
Chukchi Plateau
Mendeleyev Ridge
East Siberian Sea
46
O. Delonga
Novosibirskiye Ostrova
Lyakhovskiye Ostrova
374
O. Kotelnyy
Laptev Sea
Verkhoyansk
Yana
Kazachye
Verkhoyanskiy Khrebet
2295
Yakutsk
Lena
Olekma
Vilyuy
Zhigansk
Bulun
Tiksi
Olenek
North
Athabasca
Yellowknife
Great Slave Lake
Athabasca Lake
Coppermine
Kugluktuk
Dolphin & Union Sd.
Banks I.
C. Kellett
C. Prince Alfred
371
Prince Albert Pen.
Wollaston Pen.
Coronation G.
America
NUNAVUT
Victoria Island
M'Clure Str.
Prince Patrick I.
Queen Elizabeth Islands
Melville I.
Viscount Melville Sd.
M'Clintock Chan.
Parry Is.
Borden I.
3700
North Magnetic Pole 2011
3327
ARCTIC OCEAN
3546
3849
Ostrova Petra
Nordvik
Anabar
Kharanga
Poluostrov Taymyr
Kotuy
Kheta
Gory Putorana
Nizhnyaya Tunguska
Podkamennaya Tunguska
Ozero Taymyr
Pyasina
Mys Chelyuskin
Severnaya Zemlya
O. Oktyabrskoy Revolyutsii
965
Alpha Ridge
Makarov Basin
4007
Lomonosov Ridge
4100
Amundsen Basin
4484
Arctic Mid-Ocean Ridge
NORTH POLE
4346
Gakkel Ridge
King William I.
Back
Chesterfield Inlet
Churchill
Hudson Bay
Roes Welcome Sd.
Southampton I.
Coats I.
Mansel I.
Boothia Pen.
Gulf of Boothia
Prince of Wales I.
Bathurst I.
Somerset I.
Prince Regent Inlet
Barrow Str.
Lancaster Sd.
Resolute
Devon I.
Jones Sound
Axel Heiberg I.
Ellef Ringnes I.
Sverdrup Is.
Nansen Sd.
2104
Eureka
Ellesmere I. (Canada)
Alert
2616
C. Columbia
Lincoln Sea
Melville Pen.
Nanisivik
Bylot I.
Foxe Basin
Foxe Chan.
Prince Charles I.
Fury & Hecla Str.
Smith Sd.
Nares Str.
Kane Basin
Robeson Chan.
Qaanaaq
Uummannaq
K. York
2469
Baffin Bay
Baffin I.
Knud Rasmussen Land
Kronprins Frederik Land
2170
Peary Land
K. Morris Jesup
Independence Fjord
Kong Frederik VIII.s Land
McKinley Sea
3741
Nansen Basin
3910
O. Ushakova
O. Vise
O. Uedineniya
Dikson
Yenisey
Igarka
Norilsk
Dudinka
Gydanskiy Poluostrov
Taz
Novyy Urengoy
Novyy Port
Nadym
Nizhnevartovsk
Surgut
Nefteyugansk
Poluostrov Yamal
Baydaratskaya Guba
Kara Sea
O. Belyy
Zemlya Frantsa Iosifa (Russia)
O. Greem-Bell
Z. Vilcheka
Z. Aleksandry
90
Novaya Zemlya
1547
1342
Belushya Guba
Nordaustlandet
Nordkapp
2571
Spitsbergen
Svalbard (Norway)
1717
Longyearbyen
Edgeøya
Barents Sea
O. Kolguyev
Vorkuta
Amderma
Salekhard
Ob
Tobolsk
Berezovo
1894
Narodnaya
Uralskie Gory
Naryan-Mar
Pechora
Ukhta
YEKATERINBURG
Perm
Syktyvkar
UFA
Mys Kanin Nos
Mezen
Arkhangelsk
Sev. Dvina
Severodvinsk
Onega
Onezhskoye Ozero
Belomorsk
Kandalaksha
Beloye More
Kolskiy Poluostrov
Murmansk
Kirkenes
Vardø
Varangerfjorden
Nettilling L.
Cumberland Sd.
Iqaluit
2147
Frobisher B.
Hudson Str.
C. Wolstenholme
Feuilles
Ungava Bay
Resolution I.
C. Chidley
Labrador
2276
C. Dyer
Davis Str.
Upernavik
Qeqertarsuaq
Uummannaq
Qeqertarsuaq
GREENLAND (KALAALLIT NUNAAT) (Denmark)
3238
Kong Frederik IX.s Land
Kong Christian X.s Land
Kejser Franz Joseph Fd.
Kong Oscar Fjord
Ittoqqortoormiit
Nuuk
2850
Mt. Forel 3360
Kong Christian IX.s Land
3693
Gunnbjørn Fjeld
Kong Frederik VI.s Kyst
Paamiut
Qaqortoq
Alluitsup Paa
Nunap Isua (Kap Farvel)
Tasiilaq
Kangikajik
Greenland Sea
Mohns Ridge
2277
Jan Mayen (Norway)
Bjørnøya (Norway)
480
Nordkapp
Hammerfest
Tromsø
Lofoten
Narvik
Icelandic Plateau
Denmark Str.
Horn
Fontur
Breiðafjörður
Reykjavík
ICELAND
Öræfajökull 2119
Norwegian Sea
Arctic Circle
Norwegian Basin
3800
Labrador Sea
Hamilton Inlet
Northwest Atlantic Mid-Ocean Canyon
Charlie Gibbs Fracture Zone
4563
Mid-Atlantic Ridge
Iceland Basin
ATLANTIC OCEAN
King's Trough
Rockall Trough
Rockall (U.K.)
Hebrides (U.K.)
Føroyar (Den.)
Shetland Is. (U.K.)
Orkney Is. (U.K.)
UNITED KINGDOM
Edinburgh
GLASGOW
North Sea
Belfast
DUBLIN
IRELAND
C. Clear
LONDON
AMSTERDAM
NETH.
GERMANY
Elbe
HAMBURG
BERLIN
POLAND
WARSZAWA
Wisla
Kraków
PRAHA
Lviv
UKRAINE
MOLDOVA
ROMANIA
ODESA
Black Sea
Sea of Azov
Donetsk
ROSTOV
KHARKIV
KYYIV
BELARUS
Vilnius
LITHUANIA
Kaliningrad (Russia)
LATVIA
Riga
ESTONIA
Tallinn
G. of Finland
HELSINKI
Chudskoye Ozero
ST. PETERBURG
Ladozhskoye Ozero
MOSKVA
Volga
NIZHNIY NOVGOROD
SAMARA
Saratov
VOLGOGRAD
RUSSIA
FINLAND
Oulu
Tornio
Gulf of Bothnia
SWEDEN
NORWAY
Trondheim
2469
Bergen
Oslo
STOCKHOLM
Skagerrak
KØBENHAVN
DENMARK
Baltic Sea
Maximum extent of sea ice
Minimum extent of sea ice (September 2011)
Ice caps and permanent ice shelf
Projection : Zenithal Equidistant
West from Greenwich
East from Greenwich
COPYRIGHT PHILIP'S

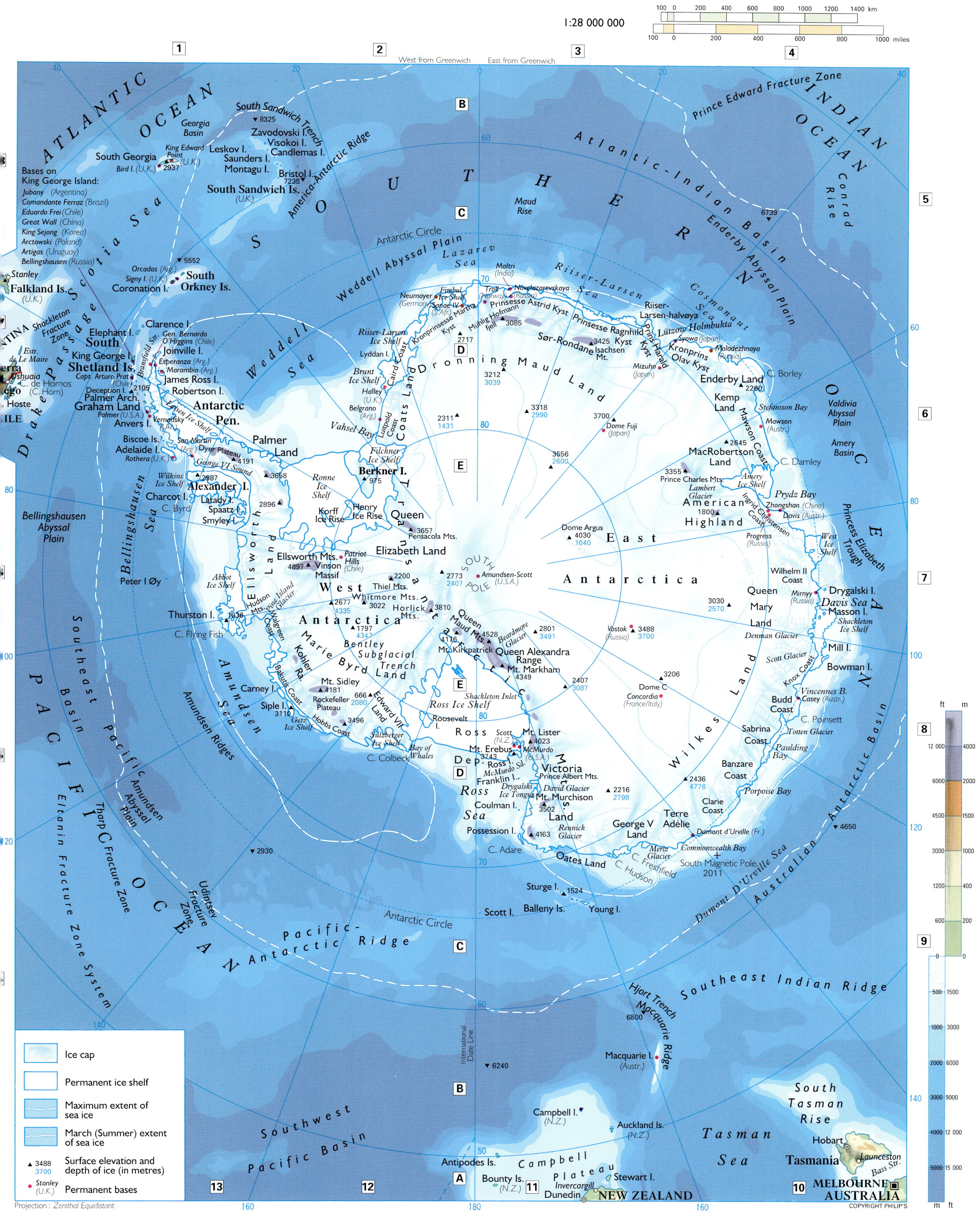
1:28 000 000
km
miles
West from Greenwich
East from Greenwich
ATLANTIC OCEAN
INDIAN OCEAN
PACIFIC OCEAN
SOUTHERN OCEAN
Weddell Sea
Scotia Sea
Drake Passage
Lazarev Sea
Riiser-Larsen Sea
Cosmonaut Sea
Davis Sea
Amundsen Sea
Bellingshausen Sea
Ross Sea
Tasman Sea
Dumont D'Urville Sea
Antarctic Circle
South Georgia
South Sandwich Is.
South Orkney Is.
Falkland Is.
South Shetland Is.
Antarctic Pen.
Graham Land
Palmer Land
Alexander I.
Ellsworth Land
Queen Elizabeth Land
Coats Land
Dronning Maud Land
Enderby Land
Kemp Land
MacRobertson Land
American Highland
Queen Mary Land
Wilkes Land
Terre Adélie
George V Land
Oates Land
Victoria Land
Marie Byrd Land
West Antarctica
East Antarctica
Transantarctic Mts.
Ronne Ice Shelf
Filchner Ice Shelf
Ross Ice Shelf
Amery Ice Shelf
Shackleton Ice Shelf
Berkner I.
Vinson Massif
Ellsworth Mts.
SOUTH POLE
Amundsen-Scott (U.S.A.)
Vostok (Russia)
Dome Argus
Dome C
Dome Fuji (Japan)
Concordia (France/Italy)
McMurdo (U.S.A.)
Scott (N.Z.)
Mt. Erebus
Mt. Kirkpatrick
Prydz Bay
South Magnetic Pole 2011
Macquarie I.
Campbell I.
Auckland Is.
Antipodes Is.
Bounty Is.
Tasmania
Hobart
NEW ZEALAND
MELBOURNE AUSTRALIA
Invercargill
Dunedin
Stewart I.
Pacific-Antarctic Ridge
Southeast Indian Ridge
Atlantic-Indian Basin
Weddell Abyssal Plain
Enderby Abyssal Plain
Southeast Pacific Basin
Southwest Pacific Basin
Bases on King George Island:
Jubany (Argentina)
Comandante Ferraz (Brazil)
Eduardo Frei (Chile)
Great Wall (China)
King Sejong (Korea)
Arctowski (Poland)
Artigas (Uruguay)
Bellingshausen (Russia)
Ice cap
Permanent ice shelf
Maximum extent of sea ice
March (Summer) extent of sea ice
3488 3700 Surface elevation and depth of ice (in metres)
Stanley (U.K.) Permanent bases
COPYRIGHT PHILIP'S
Projection: Zenithal Equidistant

The Antarctic Treaty was signed in Washington in 1959 so that scientific and technical research could continue unhampered by international politics.

All territorial claims covering land areas south of latitude 60°S have been suspended. Those claims were:

| | | | | | |
|---|---|---|---|---|---|
| Norwegian claim (Dronning Maud Land) | 45°E - 20°W | French claim (Terre Adélie) | 136°E - 142°E | British claim | 80°W - 20°W |
| Australian claims | 45°E - 136°E<br>142°E - 160°E | New Zealand claim (Ross Dependency) | 160°E - 150°W | Argentine claim | 74°W - 53°W |
| | | | | Chilean claim | 90°W - 53°W |

Equatorial Scale 1:41 000 000

ATLANTIC OCEAN
PACIFIC OCEAN
GREENLAND
ICELAND
CANADA
UNITED STATES
Hudson Bay
Labrador Sea
Davis Strait
Denmark Strait
Norwegian Sea
North Sea
Newfoundland
Grand Banks of Newfoundland
Flemish Cap
Charlie Gibbs Fracture Zone
Reykjanes Ridge
Northwest Atlantic Mid-Ocean Canyon
Mid-Atlantic Ridge
Porcupine Abyssal Plain
Rockall Trough
Celtic Sea
Bay of Biscay
Biscay Abyssal Plain
Azores-Biscay Rise
King's Trough
Açores
Ponta Delgada
New England Seamounts
Corner Seamounts
Sohm Abyssal Plain
Bermuda
Bermuda Rise
Hatteras Abyssal Plain
Sargasso Sea
Gulf of Mexico
Tropic of Cancer
Nares Abyssal Plain
West Indies
Puerto Rico Trench
Caribbean Sea
Colombian Basin
Leeward Is.
Windward Is.
Demerara Abyssal Plain
Ceara Rise
Ceara Abyssal Plain
Equator
Pernambuco Abyssal Plain
Brazil Basin
Sierra Leone Rise
Sierra Leone Basin
Cape Verde Abyssal Plain
Cape Verde Plateau
CAPE VERDE IS.
Is. Canarias
Madeira
Saharan Seamounts
Gulf of Guinea
Guinea Basin
Angola Basin
Angola Abyssal Plain
Ascension I.
St. Helena
Walvis Ridge
Cape Basin
Nambia Abyssal Plain
Agulhas Ridge
Discovery Seamount
Tristan da Cunha
Gough I.
Inaccessible I.
Tropic of Capricorn
Rio Grande Rise
Hotspur Seamount
Vitória Seamount
Banco Abrolhos
Argentine Basin
Argentine Abyssal Plain
Falkland Plateau
Falkland Ridge
Falkland Is.
Georgia Basin
South Georgia
South Sandwich Trench
Bouvetøya
Chile Basin
Chile Rise
Nasca Ridge
Peru-Chile Trench
BRAZIL
ARGENTINA
CHILE
PERU
BOLIVIA
PARAGUAY
URUGUAY
COLOMBIA
VENEZUELA
ECUADOR
GUYANA
SURINAME
FRENCH GUIANA
MEXICO
CUBA
BAHAMAS
NORWAY
UNITED KINGDOM
IRELAND
FRANCE
SPAIN
PORTUGAL
ITALY
GERMANY
POLAND
DENMARK
MOROCCO
ALGERIA
WESTERN SAHARA
MAURITANIA
MALI
NIGER
NIGERIA
SENEGAL
GUINEA
GHANA
Sahara
Mediterranean Sea
Andes
Amazonas
Patagonia
Pampas
Gran Chaco
West from Greenwich
Projection: Mollweide
COPYRIGHT PHILIP'S

BERMUDA
a
1:400 000
2 0 5 km
2 0 5 miles
St. George
St. Catherine Point
St. Georges I.
St. Georges Harb.
BDA
St. David's I.
Castle Harbour
Castle Roads
Harrington Sound
Tuckers Town
Ireland I.
Commissioner's Pt.
Ireland Island
Flatts Village
Spanish Boaz I. Pt
Somerset
Somerset I.
Hamilton
Great Sound
Little Sound
Clermont
Bermuda
(U.K.)
ATLANTIC OCEAN
64° 40'
64° 50'
32° 20'
NEW PROVIDENCE
b
on same scale as Bermuda
North Cay
Long Cay
Salt Cay
Paradise I.
Athol I.
Gambier Village
Cable Beach
Nassau
Dick's Point
NAS
Lake Killarney
Harold Pond
Sandilands
East End Point
Coral Heights
Carmichael Village
Bonefish Pond
Long Point
Adelaide
South West Bay
Coral Heights
South Beach
Coral Harbour
Cay Point
Providence
ATLANTIC OCEAN
77° 30'
77° 20'
25
MADEIRA
c
1:800 000
5 0 10 km
5 0 5 10 miles
Porto Moniz
Seixal
Pta. de São Jorge
Ponta do Pargo
São Vicente
Santana
Faial
1320
1640
Pico Ruivo
1861
Porto da Cruz
São Roque
Pta. de São Lourenço
Calheta
MADEIRA
Caniçal
Machico
Ponta do Sol
Santa Cruz
Campanário
FNC
Madeira
(Portugal)
Ribeira Brava
Câmara de Lobos
Camacha
Funchal
ATLANTIC OCEAN
17
AZORES
d1
1:1 600 000
10 0 10 20 30 km
10 0 10 20 miles
d2
Ponta Torrais
718
Corvo
Vila Nova do Corvo
Ponta Delgada
913
Fajã Grande
Santa Cruz das Flores
Lajedo
Lajes das Flores
Flores
39° 30'
31
29
28
39
Graciosa
Santa Cruz da Graciosa
Praia
Luz
Terceira
Biscoitos
Serra de Santa Bárbara
1021
Lajes
Praia da Vitória
Ponta de São Jorge
Santa Barbara
São Sebastião
Angra do Heroísmo
Ponta das Contendas
Ponta dos Rosais
São Jorge
Velas
Norte Grande
Faial
Cedros
Praia do Norte
Ponta dos Capelinhos
1043
Flamengos
Manadas
1083
Calheta
Topo
Ponta do Topo
Castelo Branco
Horta
Madalena
São Roque do Pico
2351
Ponta do Pico
Prainha
Canal do Faial
Canal de São Jorge
São Mateus
Lajes do Pico
Pico
Ponta da Ilha
Calheta de Nesquim
Ponta da Queimada
AÇORES (AZORES)
(Portugal)
ATLANTIC OCEAN
d4
Santa Maria
Santa Barbara
Ponta do Norte
587
Maia
Vila do Porto
Ponta do Castelo
25
37
38
d3
São Miguel
Ponta da Bretanha
Mosteiros
Lagoa Azul
Ribeira Grande
Porto Formoso
Ponta da Ajuda
Nordeste
Capelas
1103
Pico da Vara
PDL
Lagoa
Furnas
Povoação
Ponta Delgada
Ponta da Galera
Vila Franca do Campo
26
25
36
27
Corvo
Flores
Graciosa
São Jorge
Terceira
Faial
Pico
São Miguel
ATLANTIC OCEAN
Santa Maria
CANARY ISLANDS
1:1 600 000
10 0 10 20 30 km
10 0 10 20 miles
ATLANTIC OCEAN
La Palma
Lanzarote
Tenerife
Gomera
Fuerteventura
Hierro
Gran Canaria
AFRICA
Garafía
Pta. Cumplida
Barlovento
Roque de los Muchachos
2423
CALDERA TABURIENTE
Santa Cruz de la Palma
Los Llanos
SPC
El Pueblo
La Palma
Volcán Teneguía
Fuencaliente
Pta. Fuencaliente
ATLANTIC OCEAN
Punta del Hidalgo
Pta. de Anaga
Bajamar
San Cristóbal de La Laguna
Santa Cruz de Tenerife
Tenerife
Puerto de la Cruz
TFN
Garachico
La Orotava
Pta. de Teno
Icod
Realejo Alto
Candelaria
Santiago del Teide
Pico del Teide
3718
Güímar
Guía de Isora
LAS CAÑADAS DEL TEIDE
Arico
Adeje
Arona
Playa de las Americas
Granadilla de Abona
TFS
El Medano
Los Cristianos
Pta. de la Rasca
Pta. de los Organos
Vallehermoso
Agulo
Gomera
Garajonay
1487
Valle Gran Rey
GARAJONAY
San Sebastián de la Gomera
Alajeró
Santiago
Pta. del Norte
Valverde
Pico Tenerife
1417
Taibique
La Restinga
ISLAS CANARIAS
(Spain)
Pta. Sardina
Gáldar
Pta. El Roque
Agaete
Guía
Arucas
Las Palmas de Gran Canaria
Pta. de la Aldea
San Nicolás
Pico de las Nieves
1949
Telde
San Bartolomé de Tirajana
LPA
Pta. Gando
Ingenio
Mogán
Santa Lucía de Tirajana
Agüimes
Playa de Mogán
Cruce de Sardina
Puerto Rico
San Agustín
Arguineguín
Maspalomas
Pta. Maspalomas
Playa del Inglés
Gran Canaria
e2
I. Alegranza
259
I. Montaña Clara
I. Graciosa
Pta. Fariones
ARCHIPIÉLAGO CHINIJO
Haría
Lanzarote
La Santa
671
Peñas del Chache
Tinajo
Teguise
San Bartolomé
Costa Teguise
TIMANFAYA
Janubio
Yaiza
Tías
Arrecife
Atalaya de Femés
679
Puerto del Carmen
Pta. Pechiguera
Playa Blanca
I. de Lobos
Corralejo
Pta. de Tostón
El Cotillo
La Oliva
Muda
689
Fuerteventura
Puerto del Rosario
Pta. de la Herradura
Betancuria
Betancuria
724
Antigua
FUE
Pájara
Tuineje
Pozo Negro
Gran Tarajal
JANDÍA
Tarajalejo
Cofete
Jandía
807
Costa Calma
Morro del Jable
Pta. de Jandía
Pta. de Morro Jable
ft m
4500 1500
3000 1000
1800 600
1200 400
600 200
300 100
0 0
200 600
1000 3000
2000 6000
3000 9000
4000 12 000
m ft
FALKLAND IS.
f
1:6 400 000
50 0 50 km
50 0 50 miles
ATLANTIC OCEAN
West Falkland
Jason Is.
Pebble I.
C. Dolphin
King George Bay
Queen Charlotte B.
Mt. Adam
700
Mt. Usborne
705
Weddell I.
Falkland Sound
MPN
Port Darwin
Stanley
C. Meredith
East Falkland
Falkland Is.
(U.K.)
Beauchêne I.
52
60
ASCENSION I.
g
on same scale as Bermuda
ATLANTIC OCEAN
English Bay
North Pt.
Porpoise Pt.
Pyramid Pt.
North East Bay
Clarence Bay
Sisters Peak
Georgetown
446
Two Boats Village
Boatswain Bird I.
The Peak
859
Whale Pt.
Payne Pt.
South West Bay
South East Bay
Portland Pt.
ASI
Mars Bay
South Pt.
Pillar Bay
Ascension Island
(U.K.)
7° 55'
8°
14° 25'
14° 20'
ST. HELENA
h
on same scale as Bermuda
ATLANTIC OCEAN
Sugar Loaf Pt.
Flagstaff Bay
688
The Barn
Jamestown
616
Half Tree Hollow
Briars
Prosperous Bay
NAPOLEON'S TOMB
St. Pauls
Longwood
Saddle Pt.
Egg I.
820
High Peak
798
Diana's Peak
Gill Pt.
694
George I.
South West Pt.
Manati Bay
Sandy Bay
Speery I.
Castle Rock Pt.
St. Helena
(U.K.)
15° 55'
16°
5° 45'
5° 40'
West from Greenwich
CAPE VERDE IS.
j
1:8 000 000
50 0 100 km
50 0 50 miles
Barlovento
Ribeira Grande
Santo Antão
1979
Mindelo
São Vicente
Santa Luzia
79
Sal
Pedra Lume
Santa Maria
São Nicolau
Vila da Ribeira Brava
Sal Rei
Boa Vista
ATLANTIC OCEAN
Curral Velho
CAPE VERDE IS.
4270
São Tiago
Tarrafal
Maio
Vila Nova Sintra
2829
1392
RAI
Vila do Maio
Brava
São Filipe
Fogo
Praia
Sotavento
16

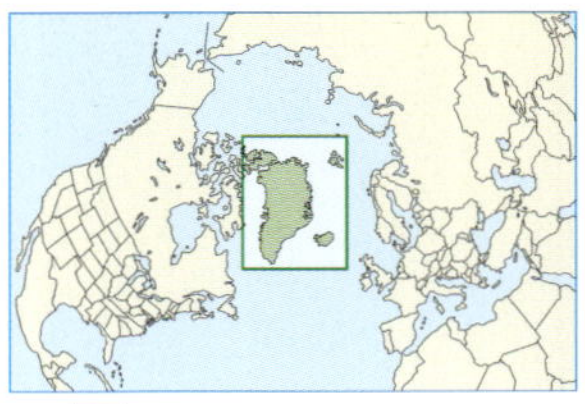

1:10 000 000

ARCTIC OCEAN
Lincoln Sea
Cape Columbia
Alert
Robeson Chan.
Kennedy Chan.
Nares Str.
Smith Sound
Kane Basin
CANADA
Ellesmere Island
Axel Heiberg I.
Meighen I.
Nansen Sound
QUTTINIRPAAQ NAT. PARK
Lake Hazen
Eureka
Hans I.
Grise Fiord
Jones Sd.
Coburg I.
Devon Island
Washington Land
Hall Land
Petermann Gletscher
Nyeboe Land
Wulff Land
Warming Land
Victoria Fjord
Nansen Land
J.P. Koch Fjord
Peary Land
Kap Morris Jesup
Oodaaq
Frederick E. Hyde Fjord
Jørgen Brønlund Fjord
Heilprin Land
Independence Fjord
Mylius Erichsen Land
Academy Gletscher
Kronprins Frederik Land
Danmark Fjord
Kronprins Christian Land
Station Nord
Nordostrundingen
Ingolf Fjord
Mallemukfjeld
Lambert Land
Hovgaard Ø
Nioghalvfjerdsfjorden
Norske Øer
Jøkelbugten
Franske Øer
Île de France
Germania Land
Danmarkshavn
Storstrømmen
Dove Bugt
Store Koldewey
Hochstetter Forland
Shannon Ø
Dronning Margrethe II Land
Kong Frederik VIII.s Land
GRØNLANDS NATIONALPARK
Kong Christian X.s Land
Ole Rømer Land
Waltershausen Gletscher
Daneborg
Zackenberg
Wollaston Forland
Clavering Ø
Andrée Land
Ymer Ø
Kejser Franz Joseph Fd.
Petermann Bjerg
Geographical Society Ø
Traill Ø
Mestersvig
Kong Oscar Fjord
Stauning Alper
Uunartoq Qeqertoq (Warming I.)
Renland
Jameson Land
Ittoqqortoormiit (Scoresbysund)
Uunarteq
Milne Land
Ittaajimmiit (Kangertittivaq)
Scoresby Sund
Kangikajik (Kap Brewster)
Kap Dalton
Blosseville Kyst
Kong Christian IX.s Land
Gunnbjørn Fjeld
Kangerdlugssuaq
Kap Gustav Holm
Mt. Forel
Helheim Gletscher
Kuummiut
Kulusuk
Ikkatteq
Isortoq
Tasiilaq (Ammassalik)
Gyldenløve Fjord
Kap Møsting
Kap Moltke
Kap Skjold
Timmiarmiut
Mogens Heinesen Fjord
Kong Frederik VI.s Kyst
KUJALLEQ
Lindenow Fjord
Prins Christian Sund
Nunap Isua (Kap Farvel)
Nanortalik
Narsarmijit
Alluitsup Paa (Sydprøven)
Qaqortoq (Julianehåb)
Narsaq
Narsarsuaq
Ivittuut
Arsuk
Kangilinnguit (Grønnedal)
Narsalik
Paamiut (Frederikshåb)
Qeqertarsuatsiaat (Fiskenæsset)
Kangerluarsoruseq (Færingehavn)
Nuuk (Godthåb)
Kapisillit
Dronning Ingrid Land
Maniitsoq (Sukkertoppen)
Kangaamiut
Søndre Strømfjord
Itilleq
Sisimiut (Holsteinsborg)
Kangerlussuaq (Søndre Strømfjord)
Kong Frederik IX.s Land
Nordre Strømfjord
QEQQATA
SERMERSOOQ
GREENLAND (KALAALLIT NUNAAT)
(Denmark)
Kangaatsiaq
Aasiaat (Egedesminde)
Ikamiut
Qasigiannguit (Christianshåb)
Ilulissat (Jakobshavn)
Disko Bugt
Qeqertarsuaq (Godhavn)
Qeqertarsuaq (Disko)
Kangerluk
Saqqaq
Ikerasak
Uummannaq
Maarmorilik
Illorsuit
Nunavik
Upernavik Kujalleq
Kangersuatsiaq
Upernavik
Nuussuaq (Kraulshavn)
QAASUITSUP
Steenstrup Gletscher
Melville Bugt
Kap York
Uummannaq (Dundas) (Thule Air Base)
Lauge Koch Kyst
Kap Atholl
Qeqertarsuaq
Qaanaaq (Thule)
Siorapaluk
Inglefield Land
Knud Rasmussen Land
Sermersuaq (Humboldt Gletscher)
Baffin Bay
Clyde River (Kangiqtugaapik)
Baffin I.
C. Dyer
Davis Strait
Labrador Sea
ATLANTIC OCEAN
Reykjanes Ridge
Denmark Strait
Icelandic Plateau
Arctic Circle
GREENLAND SEA
Mohns Ridge
Jan Mayen (Norway)
Beerenberg
McKinley Sea
Nansen Basin
Svalbard (Spitsbergen) (Norway)
Nordaustlandet
Kvitøya
Kong Karls Land
Sjuøyane
Nordkapp
Olgastredet
Barentsøya
Edgeøya
Storfjorden
Longyearbyen
Newtontoppen
Barentsburg
Prins Karls Forland
Sørkapp
ICELAND
Reykjavík
Ísafjörður
Horn
Húnaflói
Eyjafjörður
Húsavík
Akureyri
Neskaupstaður
Blönduós
Breiðafjörður
Faxaflói
Vatnajökull
Öræfajökull
Höfn
Vestmannaeyjar
Heimaey
Surtsey
Projection: Conic with two standard parallels
West from Greenwich
COPYRIGHT PHILIP'S


Underlined towns give their name to the administrative area in which they stand.

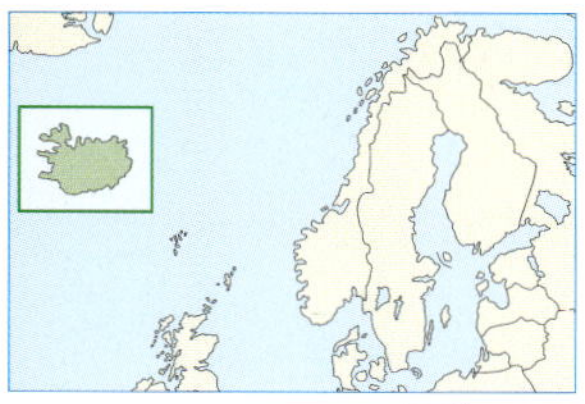

1:2 000 000

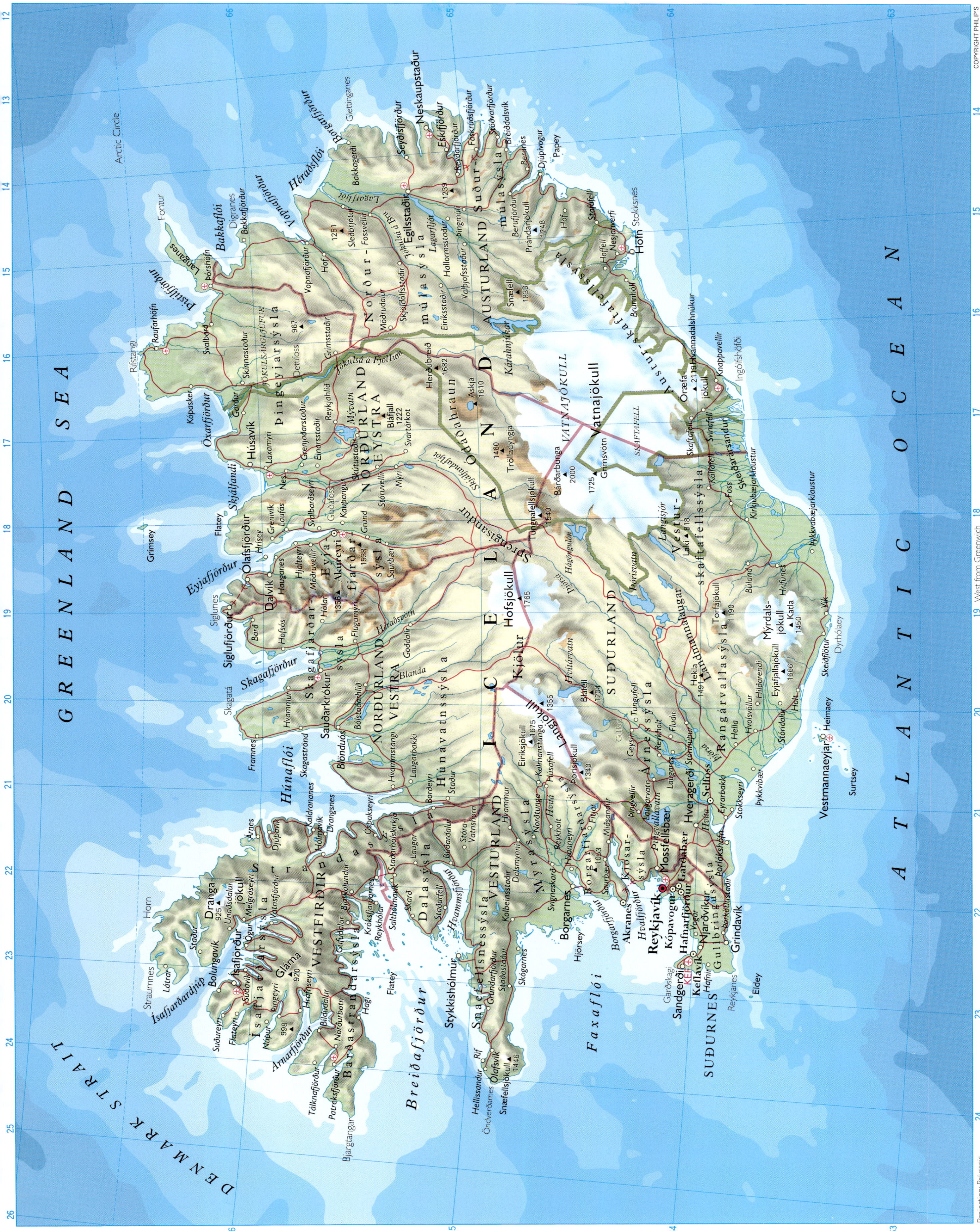
GREENLAND SEA
ATLANTIC OCEAN
DENMARK STRAIT
ICELAND
Vatnajökull
Hofsjökull
Langjökull
Mýrdalsjökull
Reykjavík
Akureyri
Ísafjörður
Húsavík
Egilsstaðir
Höfn
Vestmannaeyjar
Faxaflói
Breiðafjörður
Húnaflói
Skagafjörður
Eyjafjörður
Skjálfandi
Öxarfjörður
Þistilfjörður
Bakkaflói
Vopnafjörður
Héraðsflói
VESTFIRÐIR
VESTURLAND
SUÐURLAND
AUSTURLAND
SUÐURNES
Arctic Circle
Grímsey
Surtsey
Heimaey
Keflavík
Hafnarfjörður
Kópavogur
Selfoss
Akranes
Borgarnes
Stykkishólmur
Sauðárkrókur
Siglufjörður
Dalvík
Ólafsfjörður
Blönduós
Seyðisfjörður
Neskaupstaður
Eskifjörður
Vík
Grindavík
Sandgerði
Hveragerði
Mosfellsbær
Garðabær
Njarðvík
Kjölur
Sprengisandur
Askja
Hekla
Katla
Eyjafjallajökull
Öræfajökull
Langanes
Raufarhöfn
Þórshöfn
West from Greenwich
Projection: Polyconic
COPYRIGHT PHILIP'S

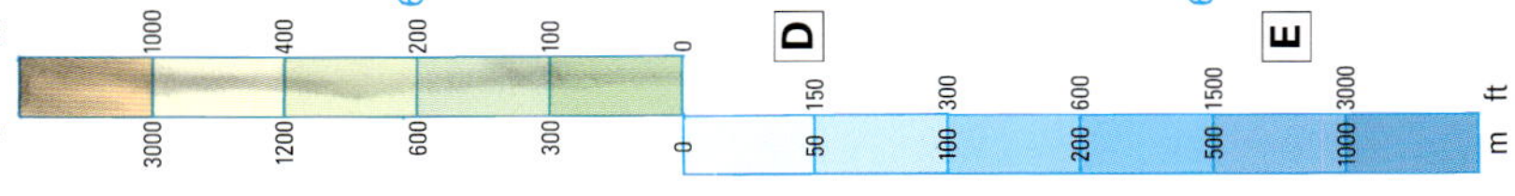

# EUROPE

1:16 000 000

Norwegian Sea
North Sea
Baltic Sea
Black Sea
Caspian Sea
Mediterranean Sea
ATLANTIC OCEAN
Bay of Biscay
Celtic Sea
English Channel
Adriatic Sea
Tyrrhenian Sea
Ionian Sea
Barents Sea
White Sea
G. of Bothnia
G. of Finland
Sea of Azov
Ural Mountains
West Siberian Lowlands
Timan Ridge
Northern Uvals
Volga Hts.
Caspian Depression
Central Russian Uplands
North European Plain
Ukraine
Donets Basin
Finland
Lapland
Scandinavia
Carpathians
Plain of Hungary
Alps
Jura
Massif Central
Pyrenees
Apennines
Dinaric Alps
Balkans
Rhodope
Pindus
Caucasus
Transcaucasia
Armenia
Kurdistan
Mesopotamia
Anatolia (Asia Minor)
Pontine Mts.
Taurus Mts.
Iberian Peninsula
Old Castile
New Castile
Sierra Morena
Sierra Nevada
Andalusia
Cantabrian Mts.
Iceland
British Isles
Great Britain
Ireland
Corsica
Sardinia
Sicily
Crete
Cyprus
Majorca
Minorca
Balearic Is.
Africa
Plateau of the Shotts
Sea areas named in weather forecasts
ROCKALL
COPYRIGHT PHILIP'S
Projection: Bonne
West from Greenwich
East from Greenwich

1:16 000 000

100 0 100 200 300 400 500 600 700 800 km

100 0 100 200 300 400 500 miles

Norwegian Sea
North Sea
Baltic Sea
G. of Bothnia
White Sea
Black Sea
Caspian Sea
Adriatic Sea
Tyrrhenian Sea
Ionian Sea
Aegean Sea
Mediterranean Sea
Bay of Biscay
English Channel
ATLANTIC OCEAN
Skagerrak
Kattegat
ICELAND
Reykjavik
Faroe Is. (Den.)
Tórshavn
Shetland Is.
Orkney Is.
Hebrides
UNITED KINGDOM
SCOTLAND
ENGLAND
WALES
LONDON
IRELAND
Dublin
NORWAY
Oslo
SWEDEN
Stockholm
FINLAND
Helsinki
DENMARK
Copenhagen
ESTONIA
Tallinn
LATVIA
Riga
LITHUANIA
Vilnius
BELARUS
Minsk
POLAND
Warsaw
GERMANY
Berlin
NETHERLANDS
Amsterdam
BELGIUM
Brussels
Luxembourg
FRANCE
PARIS
SWITZERLAND
Bern
AUSTRIA
Vienna
CZECH REP.
Prague
SLOVAK REP.
Bratislava
HUNGARY
Budapest
SLOVENIA
Ljubljana
CROATIA
Zagreb
BOSNIA-HERZ.
Sarajevo
SERBIA
Belgrade
MONTENEGRO
Podgorica
KOSOVO
Pristina
MACEDONIA
Skopje
ALBANIA
Tirana
GREECE
Athens
BULGARIA
Sofia
ROMANIA
Bucharest
MOLDOVA
Kishinev
UKRAINE
Kiev
CRIMEA
RUSSIA
MOSCOW
St. Petersburg
KARELIA
KOMI
KALMYKIA
DAGESTAN
CHECHNIA
GEORGIA
Tbilisi
ARMENIA
Yerevan
AZERBAIJAN
Baku
KAZAKHSTAN
TURKEY
Ankara
Istanbul
CYPRUS
Nicosia
SYRIA
IRAQ
BAGHDAD
IRAN
ITALY
Rome
SAN MARINO
MONACO
MALTA
Valletta
Corsica
Sardinia
Sicily
SPAIN
MADRID
ANDORRA
PORTUGAL
Lisbon
Balearic Is.
Gibraltar (U.K.)
Str. of Gibraltar
MOROCCO
Rabat
ALGERIA
Algiers
TUNISIA
Tunis
Africa
Arctic Circle
LONDON Capital Cities
Projection: Bonne
West from Greenwich
East from Greenwich
COPYRIGHT PHILIP'S

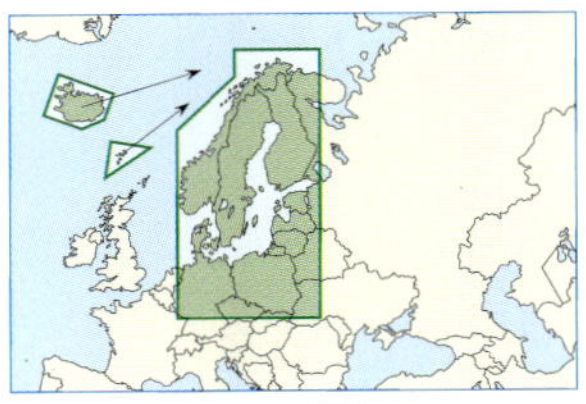

50 0 25 50 75 100 125 150 175 km

50 0 25 50 75 100 125 miles

1:4 800 000

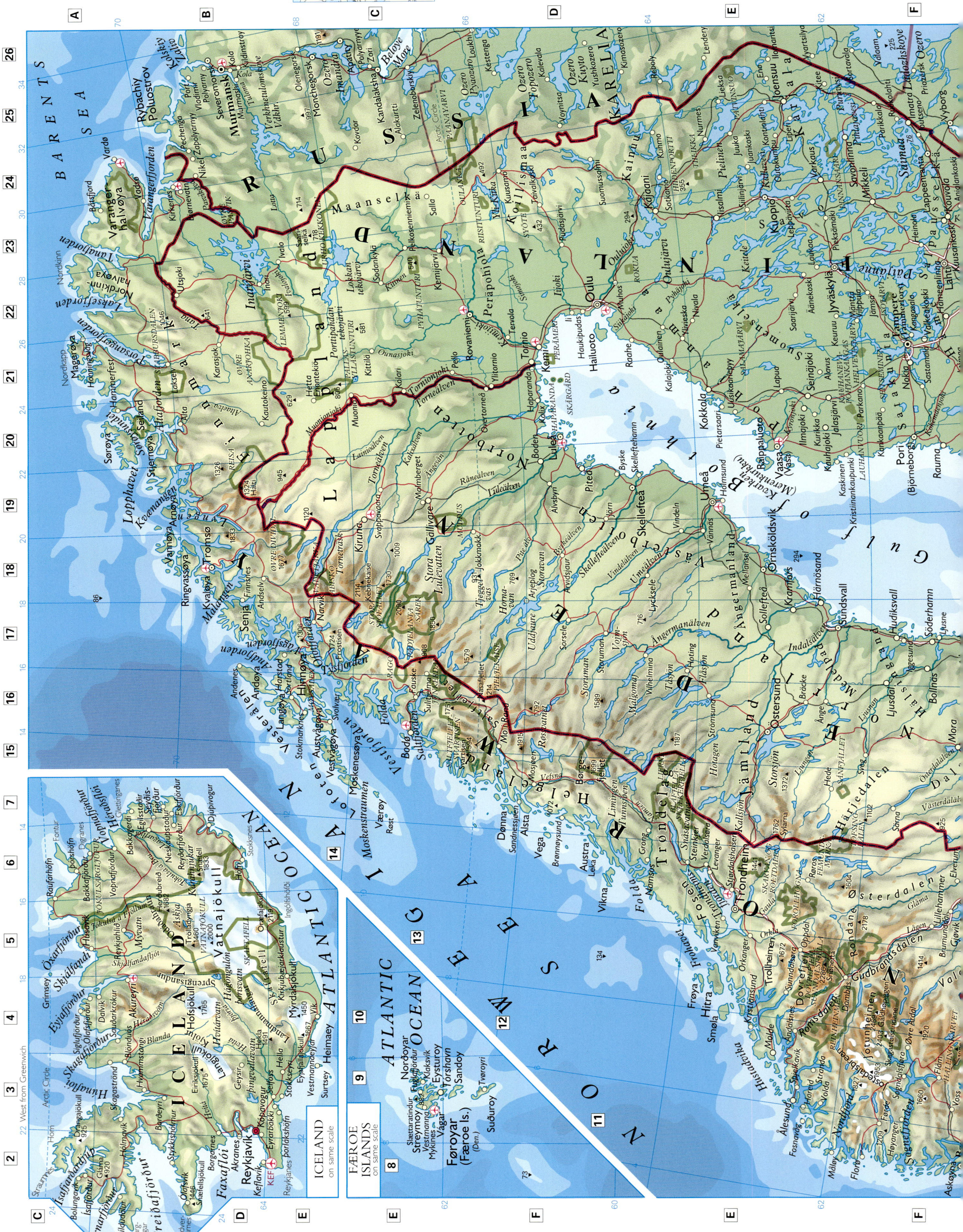
BARENTS SEA
NORWEGIAN SEA
ATLANTIC OCEAN
Gulf of Bothnia
Gulf of Finland
RUSSIA
KARELIA
FINLAND
SWEDEN
NORWAY
ICELAND on same scale
FÆROE ISLANDS on same scale
Lapland
Finnmark
Lofoten
Vesterålen
Tromsø
Bodø
Narvik
Kiruna
Luleå
Oulu
Umeå
Vaasa
Kuopio
Tampere
Trondheim
Östersund
Ålesund
Murmansk
Kandalaksha
Reykjavík
Akureyri
Vatnajökull
Tórshavn
Føroyar (Færoe Is.) (Den.)
Arctic Circle
22 West from Greenwich

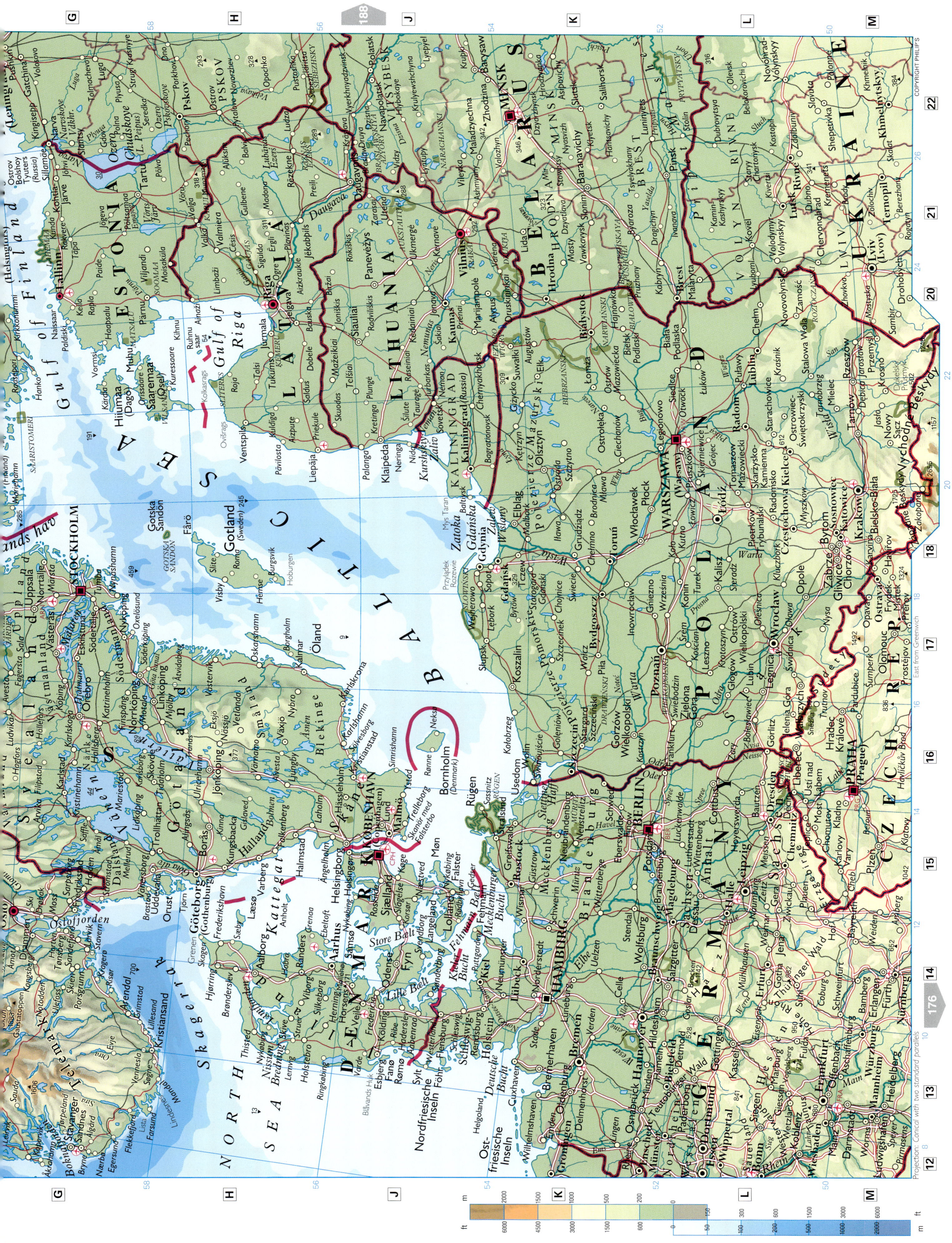
NORTH SEA
Skagerrak
Kattegat
BALTIC SEA
Gulf of Finland
Gulf of Riga
DENMARK
ESTONIA
LATVIA
LITHUANIA
BELARUS
POLAND
GERMANY
CZECH REP.
UKRAINE
KALININGRAD (Russia)
STOCKHOLM
KØBENHAVN
Tallinn
Riga
Vilnius
MINSK
WARSZAWA (Warsaw)
BERLIN
PRAHA (Prague)
HAMBURG
Göteborg (Gothenburg)
Gotland (Sweden)
Öland
Bornholm (Denmark)
Rügen
Hiiumaa (Dago)
Saaremaa (Ösel)
Projection: Conical with two standard parallels
East from Greenwich
COPYRIGHT PHILIP'S

10 0 10 20 30 40 50 60 70 80 90 km

10 0 10 20 30 40 50 60 miles

1:2 000 000

Gulf of Bothnia
STOCKHOLM
Uppsala
Oslo
Trondheim
Östersund
Sundsvall
Härnösand
Hudiksvall
Söderhamn
Bollnäs
Gävle
Sandviken
Falun
Borlänge
Mora
Ludvika
Avesta
Sala
Västerås
Köping
Eskilstuna
Örebro
Lindesberg
Karlskoga
Kristinehamn
Karlstad
Norrtälje
Södertälje
Nacka
Lillehammer
Hamar
Gjøvik
Røros
Kongsvinger
Drammen
Hønefoss
Kongsberg
Tønsberg
Sandefjord
Fredrikstad
Sarpsborg
Halden
JÄMTLANDS LÄN
GÄVLEBORGS LÄN
DALARNAS LÄN
VÄSTMANLANDS LÄN
UPPSALA LÄN
STOCKHOLMS LÄN
ÖREBRO LÄN
HEDMARK
OPPLAND
BUSKERUD
AKERSHUS
ØSTFOLD
VESTFOLD
TELEMARK
SØR-TRØNDELAG
Klarälven
Siljan
Mjøsa
Jotunheimen
Rondane
Dovrefjell

A B C D E

1 2 3 4 5 6 7 8 9 10 11 12 13

160
161
164

m 2000 1500 1000 500 200 0

ft 6000 4500 3000 1500 600 0

B A L T I C
S E A
S k a g e r r a k
K a t t e g a t
D E N M A R K
G E R M A N Y
P O L A N D
Öland (Sweden)
Gotland (Sweden)
Bornholm (Denmark)
Læsø (Denmark)
Anholt (Denmark)
KØBENHAVN
Göteborg
Malmö
Aarhus
Odense
Aalborg
Helsingborg
Halmstad
Jönköping
Växjö
Kalmar
Visby
Linköping
Norrköping
Karlskrona
Lund
Flensburg
Kiel
Fehmarn Belt
Store Bælt
Hanöbukten
Bornholmsgattet
SJÆLLAND
FYN
LOLLAND
FALSTER
178
184
East from Greenwich
Projection: Lambert's Conformal Conic
COPYRIGHT PHILIP'S

# SOUTHERN NORWAY

1:2 000 000

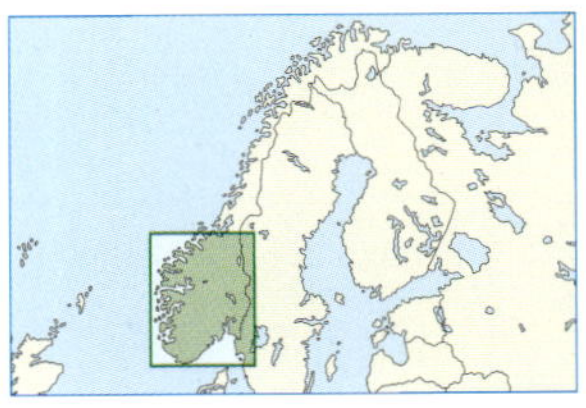

NORWEGIAN SEA
Norskerenna
Skagerrak
Trondheim
Kristiansund
Molde
Ålesund
Bergen
Stavanger
Kristiansand
Oslo
Drammen
Lillehammer
Hamar
Gjøvik
Fredrikstad
Sarpsborg
Halden
Moss
Tønsberg
Larvik
Sandefjord
Skien
Porsgrunn
Arendal
Egersund
Haugesund
Karmøy
Florø
Førde
Lista
Lindesnes
Trollhättan
Uddevalla
Strömstad
Bohuslän
Vänersborg
SØR-TRØNDELAG
MØRE OG ROMSDAL
SOGN OG FJORDANE
HORDALAND
ROGALAND
VEST-AGDER
AUST-AGDER
TELEMARK
BUSKERUD
VESTFOLD
ØSTFOLD
AKERSHUS
OPPLAND
HEDMARK
NORWAY
SWEDEN
Jotunheimen
Hardangervidda
Dovrefjell
Trollheimen
Rondane
Jostedalsbreen
Sognefjorden
Hardangerfjorden
Nordfjord
Gudbrandsdalen
Østerdalen
Femunden
Mjøsa
Sunnmøre
Nordmøre
Romsdal
Ryfylke
Jæren
Sunnhordland
Hitra
Smøla
Stadlandet
Utsira
Projection: Lambert's Conformal Conic
East from Greenwich
COPYRIGHT PHILIP'S


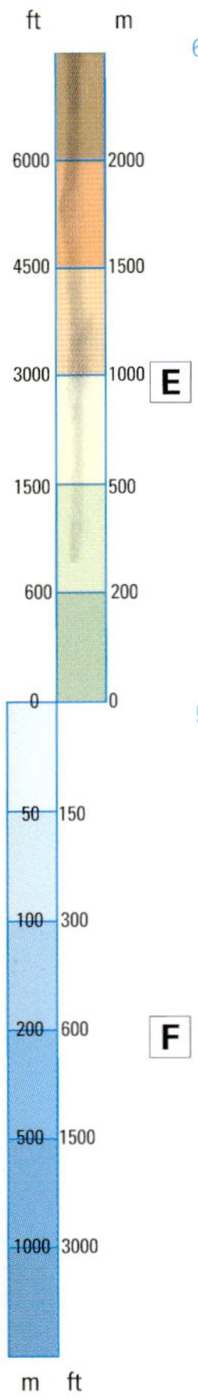

ft
m
6000
4500
3000
1500
600
0
2000
1500
1000
500
200
0
150
300
600
1500
3000

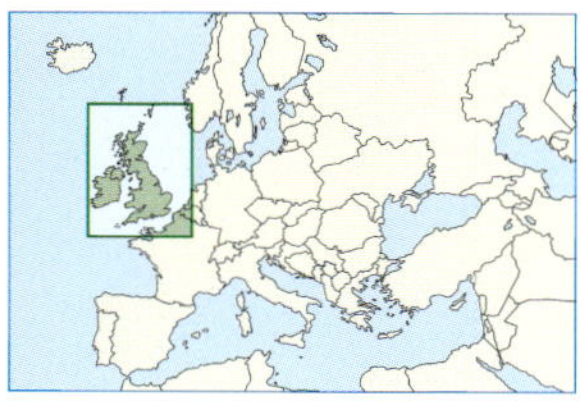

1:4 000 000

50 0 25 50 75 100 125 150 175 km
50 0 25 50 75 100 125 miles
1 2 3 4 5 6 7 8 9
A C D G
ATLANTIC OCEAN
NORTH SEA
CELTIC SEA
IRISH SEA
English Channel
Shetland Is. (U.K.)
Yell
Unst
Fetlar
Mainland
Lerwick
Foula
Fair Isle
Orkney Is.
Westray
Sanday
Stronsay
Mainland
Kirkwall
Hoy
South Ronaldsay
Pentland Firth
Thurso
Wick
C. Wrath
Helmsdale
Moray Firth
Outer Hebrides
Lewis
Stornoway
Harris
North Uist
Benbecula
South Uist
Barra
St. Kilda (U.K.)
Inner Hebrides
Sea of the Hebrides
North Minch
Skye
Portree
Rum
Eigg
Coll
Tiree
Mull
Tobermory
Iona
Colonsay
Jura
Islay
Ullapool
North West Highlands
Lairg
Golspie
Tain
Invergordon
Dingwall
Inverness
Nairn
Elgin
Buckie
Banff
Fraserburgh
Peterhead
Huntly
Inverurie
Aberdeen
Stonehaven
CAIRNGORMS
Aviemore
Glen Mor
L. Ness
Mallaig
Fort William
Ben Nevis
Grampian Mts.
SCOTLAND
Ballater
Montrose
Arbroath
Forfar
Dundee
St. Andrews
Perth
Oban
L. Lomond
Stirling
Glenrothes
Kirkcaldy
Dunfermline
Dunbar
Edinburgh
Dumbarton
Greenock
GLASGOW
Paisley
Motherwell
Hamilton
East Kilbride
Irvine
Kilmarnock
Ayr
Arran
Campbeltown
Firth of Clyde
North Channel
Girvan
Southern Uplands
Galashiels
Jedburgh
Hawick
Cheviot Hills
Berwick-upon-Tweed
Alnwick
Dumfries
Kirkcudbright
Stranraer
Mull of Galloway
Malin Hd.
Buncrana
Derry/Londonderry
Coleraine
Ballymena
Larne
Antrim
Bangor
Belfast
Lisburn
Lurgan
Portadown
Armagh
Newry
Omagh
Lough Neagh
NORTHERN IRELAND
Letterkenny
Lifford
Arranmore
Donegal
Bundoran
Sligo
Enniskillen
Lower L. Erne
Ballina
Castlebar
Westport
Achill I.
L. Conn
Lough Mask
Lough Corrib
Connemara
Roscommon
Longford
Lough Ree
Athlone
Mullingar
Cavan
Kells
Dundalk
Drogheda
Dundalk
DUBLIN
Dun Laoghaire
Bray
Wicklow Mts.
Arklow
Galway
Galway B.
Aran Is.
Ballinasloe
Tullamore
Lough Derg
Ennis
Shannon
Limerick
Portlaoise
Nenagh
Thurles
Kilkenny
Carlow
Athy
Tipperary
Clonmel
Waterford
Wexford
Rosslare
Dungarvan
Youghal
Listowel
Tralee
Dingle
Killarney
Macgillycuddy's Reeks
Mallow
Cork
Cobh
Kinsale
Bantry
Bandon
C. Clear
IRELAND
UNITED KINGDOM
Douglas
I. of Man
Whitehaven
Workington
Carlisle
Cumbrian Mts.
LAKE DISTRICT
Barrow-in-Furness
Lancaster
Blackpool
Preston
Blackburn
Burnley
Keighley
Bolton
Hexham
Gateshead
Newcastle-upon-Tyne
South Shields
Sunderland
Durham
Hartlepool
Redcar
Middlesbrough
Stockton-on-Tees
Darlington
Pennines
NORTH YORK MOORS
Scarborough
Bridlington
Harrogate
York
Leeds
Bradford
Halifax
Huddersfield
Barnsley
Kingston upon Hull
Scunthorpe
Grimsby
Doncaster
Rotherham
Sheffield
MANCHESTER
Oldham
Stockport
LIVERPOOL
Warrington
Chester
Wrexham
Anglesey
Holyhead
Bangor
Colwyn Bay
Snowdon
SNOWDONIA
Pwllheli
Cardigan Bay
Aberystwyth
Cambrian Mts.
Shrewsbury
Telford
Stoke-on-Trent
Crewe
Chesterfield
Mansfield
Nottingham
Derby
Stafford
Lincoln
Louth
Skegness
Boston
The Wash
Grantham
Leicester
Nuneaton
Wolverhampton
BIRMINGHAM
Coventry
Rugby
Redditch
Worcester
Hereford
Leamington Spa
Northampton
Peterborough
Corby
Cromer
King's Lynn
Norwich
THE BROADS
Great Yarmouth
Lowestoft
Thetford
Ely
Bury St. Edmunds
Cambridge
Bedford
Milton Keynes
Ipswich
Felixstowe
Harwich
Colchester
Chelmsford
Stevenage
Luton
Harlow
Watford
Basildon
Southend-on-Sea
ENGLAND
WALES
Carmarthen
BRECON BEACONS
Brecon
Haverfordwest
Milford Haven
Pembroke
PEMBROKESHIRE COAST
Llanelli
Swansea
Neath
Merthyr Tydfil
Rhondda
Port Talbot
Barry
Cardiff
Newport
Cheltenham
Gloucester
Cotswold Hills
Oxford
Hemel Hempstead
High Wycombe
Swindon
Bristol
Bath
Newbury
Reading
Slough
LONDON
Chatham
Margate
Canterbury
Maidstone
Dover
Ashford
Folkestone
Basingstoke
Guildford
Reigate
Crawley
Winchester
Salisbury
SOUTH DOWNS
Hastings
Eastbourne
Brighton
Worthing
Portsmouth
Havant
Fareham
Southampton
NEW FOREST
Isle of Wight
Bournemouth
Poole
Weymouth
Yeovil
Taunton
Weston-super-Mare
Bristol Channel
Exmoor
Barnstaple
Bude
Exeter
Exmouth
Dartmoor
Torbay
Plymouth
St. Austell
Truro
Falmouth
Newquay
Penzance
Land's End
Isles of Scilly
Str. of Dover
St. George's Channel
Fishguard
Alderney
C. de la Hague
Guernsey
St. Peter Port
Sark
Channel Is. (U.K.)
St. Helier
Jersey
Pte. de Barfleur
Cherbourg-Octeville
Valognes
Cotentin
Bayeux
Caen
Lisieux
Le Havre
Trouville-sur-Mer
Fécamp
Pays de Caux
Bolbec
Rouen
Elbeuf
Seine
Dieppe
Le Tréport
Abbeville
Amiens
Picardie
FRANCE
Dunkerque
Calais
C. Gris Nez
Boulogne-sur-Mer
Le Touquet-Paris-Plage
St-Omer
Béthune
Bruay-la-Buissière
Lens
LILLE
Tourcoing
Villeneuve d'Ascq
Valenciennes
Tournai
Cambrai
St.-Quentin
Laon
Oostende
Zeebrugge
Brugge
Gent
Antwerpen
Mechelen
BRUSSEL (Bruxelles)
BELGIUM
Vlissingen
NETHERLANDS
Texel
Den Helder
Alkmaar
Haarlem
's-Gravenhage (Den Haag)
Hoek van Holland
ROTTERDAM
Dordrecht
NORWAY
Askøyna
Bergen
Os
Stord
Bømlo
Leirvik
Haugesund
Kopervik
Åkrahamn
Boknafjorden
Stavanger
Sandnes
Bryne
Nærbø
Projection: Conical with two standard parallels
West from Greenwich
East from Greenwich
161
176
171

1:1 600 000
km
miles
ATLANTIC OCEAN
CELTIC SEA
IRISH SEA
North Channel
St. George's Channel
SCOTLAND
Kintyre
Arran
Campbeltown
Mull of Kintyre
Firth of Clyde
Stranraer
WALES
St. David's Hd.
St. Brides Bay
NORTHERN IRELAND
IRELAND
Ulster
Connaught
Leinster
Munster
DUBLIN (Baile Átha Cliath)
Belfast
Derry/Londonderry
Cork (Corcaigh)
Limerick (Luimneach)
Galway (Gaillimh)
Waterford (Port Láirge)
Dundalk (Dún Dealgan)
Drogheda (Droichead Átha)
Sligo
Donegal
DONEGAL
LONDONDERRY
ANTRIM
TYRONE
FERMANAGH
ARMAGH
DOWN
MONAGHAN
CAVAN
LEITRIM
SLIGO
MAYO
ROSCOMMON
LONGFORD
WESTMEATH
MEATH
LOUTH
GALWAY
OFFALY
KILDARE
WICKLOW
LAOIS
CARLOW
KILKENNY
WEXFORD
CLARE
TIPPERARY
LIMERICK
KERRY
CORK
WATERFORD
Lough Neagh
Lough Corrib
Lough Mask
Lough Ree
Lough Derg
Lower L. Erne
Upper Erne
Shannon
Aran Is.
Galway Bay
Donegal Bay
Dingle Bay
Bantry Bay
Achill I.
Clew Bay
Connemara
Macgillycuddy's Reeks
Mourne Mts.
Wicklow Mts.
Sperrin Mts.
Slieve Bloom
Galty Mts.
Knockmealdown Mts.
Boggeragh Mts.
Nagles Mts.
Silvermine Mts.
Mizen Hd.
Fastnet Rock
Carnsore Pt.
Projection : Lambert's Conformal Conic
West from Greenwich
COPYRIGHT PHILIP'S

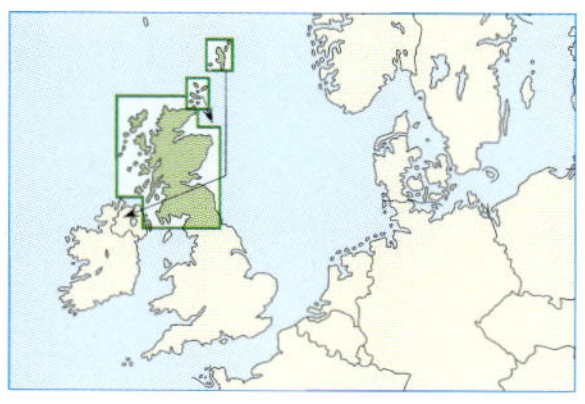

1:1 600 000

Key to Scottish unitary authorities on map
1 CITY OF ABERDEEN
2 DUNDEE CITY
3 WEST DUNBARTONSHIRE
4 EAST DUNBARTONSHIRE
5 CITY OF GLASGOW
6 INVERCLYDE
7 RENFREWSHIRE
8 EAST RENFREWSHIRE
9 NORTH LANARKSHIRE
10 FALKIRK
11 CLACKMANNANSHIRE
12 WEST LOTHIAN
13 CITY OF EDINBURGH
14 MIDLOTHIAN
ORKNEY IS. on same scale
SHETLAND IS. on same scale
SCOTLAND
ENGLAND
NORTHERN IRELAND
ATLANTIC OCEAN
NORTH SEA
North Channel
Pentland Firth
Moray Firth
Firth of Forth
Firth of Clyde
Solway Firth
Sea of the Hebrides
Little Minch
North Minch
Outer Hebrides
Inner Hebrides
EILEAN SIAR (WESTERN ISLES)
HIGHLAND
MORAY
ABERDEENSHIRE
ANGUS
PERTH AND KINROSS
ARGYLL AND BUTE
STIRLING
FIFE
EAST LOTHIAN
SCOTTISH BORDERS
DUMFRIES & GALLOWAY
SOUTH AYRSHIRE
EAST AYRSHIRE
NORTH AYRSHIRE
SOUTH LANARKSHIRE
NORTHUMBERLAND
CUMBRIA
DURHAM
Grampian Mountains
Cairngorm Mts.
Monadhliath Mts.
North West Highlands
Southern Uplands
Cheviot Hills
Lammermuir Hills
Sidlaw Hills
Ochil Hills
Pentland Hills
Cuillin Hills
Glen Mor
Ben Nevis 1344
Ben Macdhui 1309
Lochnagar 1154
Ben Lawers 1214
Ben More 1174
The Cheviot 816
Glasgow
Edinburgh
Aberdeen
Dundee
Inverness
Perth
Stirling
Fort William
Oban
Stornoway
Kirkwall
Lerwick
Thurso
Wick
Ayr
Dumfries
Carlisle
Newcastle-upon-Tyne
Belfast
Berwick-upon-Tweed
Lewis
Harris
North Uist
South Uist
Benbecula
Barra
Skye
Rùm (Rhum)
Eigg
Mull
Coll
Tiree
Islay
Jura
Arran
Kintyre
Orkney
Mainland
Hoy
Shetland
Yell
Unst
Fetlar
Foula
Projection : Lambert's Conformal Conic
West from Greenwich
COPYRIGHT PHILIP'S
166
168

1:1 600 000
km
miles
Key to English unitary authorities on map
25 HARTLEPOOL
26 DARLINGTON
27 STOCKTON-ON-TEES
28 MIDDLESBROUGH
29 REDCAR AND CLEVELAND
30 BLACKPOOL
31 BLACKBURN WITH DARWEN
32 HALTON
33 WARRINGTON
34 KINGSTON UPON HULL
35 NORTH EAST LINCOLNSHIRE
36 STOKE-ON-TRENT
37 TELFORD AND WREKIN
38 DERBY CITY
39 CITY OF NOTTINGHAM
40 LEICESTER CITY
41 RUTLAND
42 PETERBOROUGH
43 MILTON KEYNES
44 LUTON
45 NORTH SOMERSET
46 CITY OF BRISTOL
47 BATH AND NORTH EAST SOMERSET
48 SWINDON
49 READING
50 WOKINGHAM
51 WINDSOR AND MAIDENHEAD
52 SLOUGH
53 BRACKNELL FOREST
54 THURROCK
55 SOUTHEND-ON-SEA
56 MEDWAY
57 PLYMOUTH
58 TORBAY
59 POOLE
60 BOURNEMOUTH
61 SOUTHAMPTON
62 PORTSMOUTH
63 BRIGHTON AND HOVE
64 BEDFORD
65 CENTRAL BEDFORDSHIRE
66 CHESHIRE WEST AND CHESTER
67 CHESHIRE EAST
Key to Welsh unitary authorities on map
15 SWANSEA
16 NEATH PORT TALBOT
17 BRIDGEND
18 RHONDDA CYNON TAFF
19 MERTHYR TYDFIL
20 CAERPHILLY
21 BLAENAU GWENT
22 TORFAEN
23 CARDIFF
24 NEWPORT
NORTH SEA
IRISH SEA
NORTHERN IRELAND
ISLE OF MAN
North Channel
167
166

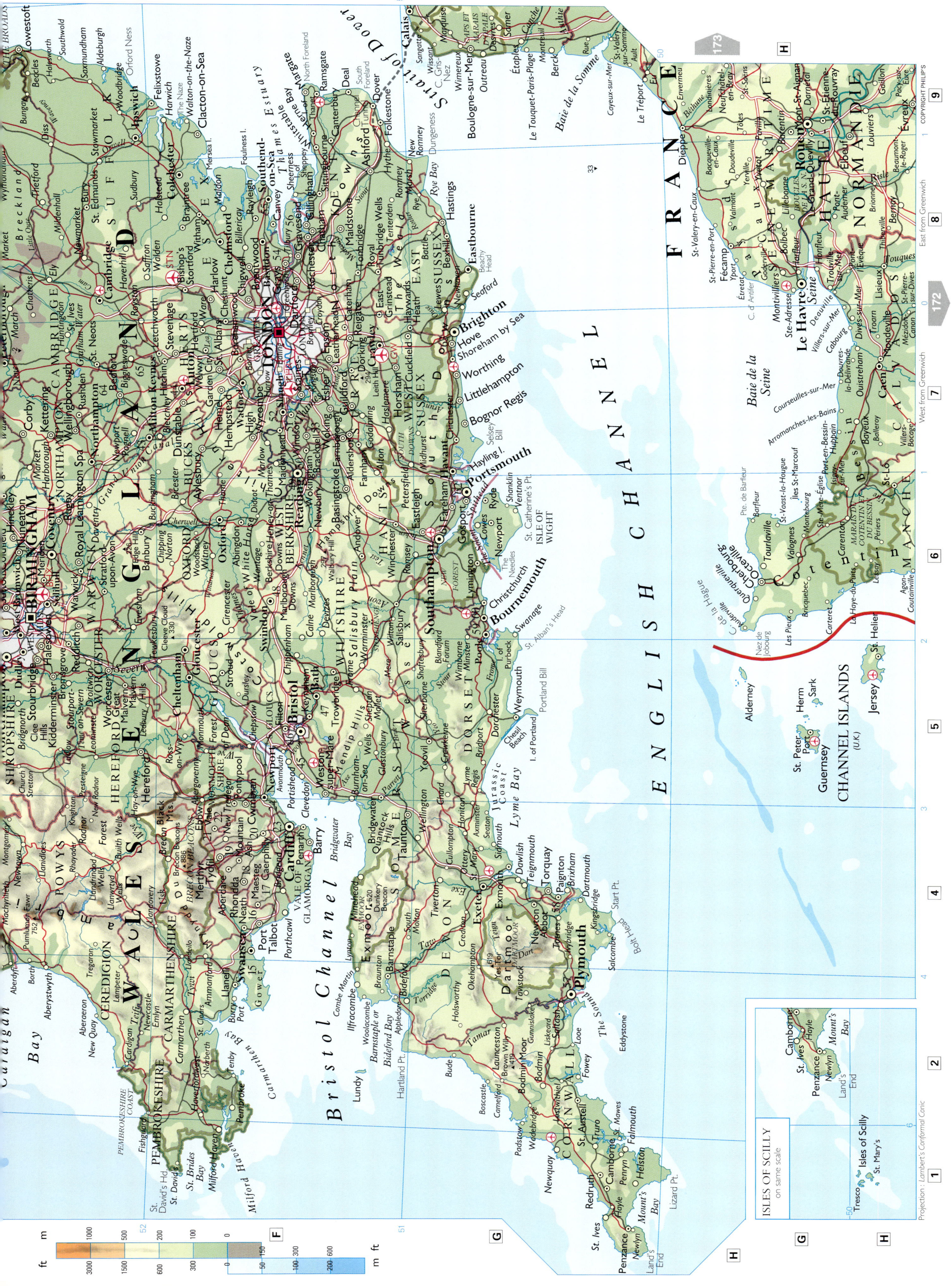
ENGLAND
WALES
FRANCE
ENGLISH CHANNEL
Bristol Channel
Strait of Dover
CHANNEL ISLANDS (U.K.)
ISLES OF SCILLY on same scale
LONDON
BIRMINGHAM
Bristol
Cardiff
Southampton
Portsmouth
Bournemouth
Brighton
Plymouth
Exeter
Swansea
Oxford
Cambridge
Reading
Dover
Calais
Dieppe
Le Havre
Rouen
Caen
Cherbourg
Guernsey
Jersey
Alderney
Sark
Herm
Lyme Bay
Baie de la Seine
Cardigan Bay
Carmarthen Bay
Projection: Lambert's Conformal Conic
COPYRIGHT PHILIP'S
West from Greenwich
East from Greenwich
172
173

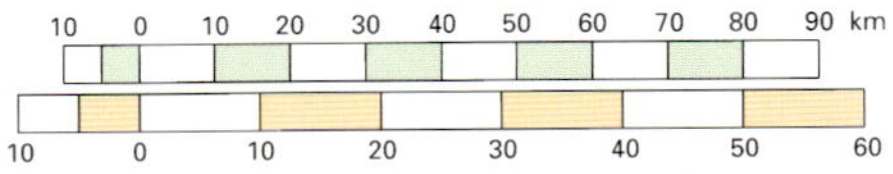

1:2 000 000

NORTH SEA
UNITED KINGDOM
NETHERLANDS
BELGIUM
LUXEMBOURG
GERMANY
FRANCE
Waddeneilanden
Waddenzee
Ostfriesische Inseln
AMSTERDAM
ROTTERDAM
's-Gravenhage (Den Haag)
Utrecht
Groningen
Antwerpen
BRUSSEL (Bruxelles)
Gent
Brugge
Liège
Namur
Charleroi
Luxembourg
Köln
Düsseldorf
Essen
Dortmund
Lille
PARIS
Reims
Metz
Nancy
Calais
Dunkerque
Oostende
Great Yarmouth
Norwich
Lowestoft
169
173
COPYRIGHT PHILIP'S

Underlined towns give their name to the administrative area in which they stand.

High-speed rail routes

1:4 000 000

FRANCE
PARIS
LYON
MARSEILLE
BELGIUM
BRUSSELS
LUXEMBOURG
GERMANY
SWITZERLAND
ZÜRICH
ITALY
MILANO
TORINO
MONACO
ANDORRA
UNITED KINGDOM
English Channel
Bay of Biscay
Golfe de Gascogne
Golfe du Lion
MEDITERRANEAN SEA
Corse
Channel Is. (U.K.)
Massif Central
Pyrénées
Alpes
Bretagne
Normandie
Bourgogne
Provence
Projection: Conical with two standard parallels
COPYRIGHT PHILIP'S

# NORTHERN FRANCE

1:2 000 000

UNITED KINGDOM
DEVON
DORSET
CORNWALL
ISLE OF WIGHT
Southampton
Portsmouth
Plymouth
Exeter
Brighton
English Channel
CHANNEL ISLANDS (U.K.)
Alderney
Guernsey
Sark
Herm
Jersey
St. Helier
St. Peter Port
Golfe de St-Malo
Cherbourg-Octeville
Baie de la Seine
Le Havre
Dieppe
Caen
BASSE-NORMANDIE
HAUTE-NORMANDIE
MANCHE
CALVADOS
BRETAGNE
FINISTÈRE
CÔTES-D'ARMOR
MORBIHAN
ILLE-ET-VILAINE
Brest
Quimper
St-Brieuc
Rennes
Lorient
Vannes
St-Malo
Mer d'Iroise
Belle-Île
PAYS DE LA LOIRE
LOIRE-ATLANTIQUE
MAYENNE
SARTHE
MAINE-ET-LOIRE
VENDÉE
Nantes
St-Nazaire
Angers
Le Mans
Laval
Cholet
Tours
Poitiers
Niort
La Rochelle
Angoulême
Limoges
POITOU-CHARENTES
DEUX-SÈVRES
VIENNE
CHARENTE
CHARENTE-MARITIME
Île de Ré
Île d'Oléron
Île d'Yeu
Île de Noirmoutier
Baie de Bourgneuf
ATLANTIC OCEAN
Projection : Lambert's Conformal Conic
West from Greenwich
169
174

DÉPARTEMENTS IN THE PARIS AREA

1 Ville de Paris
2 Seine-St-Denis
3 Val-de-Marne
4 Hauts-de-Seine

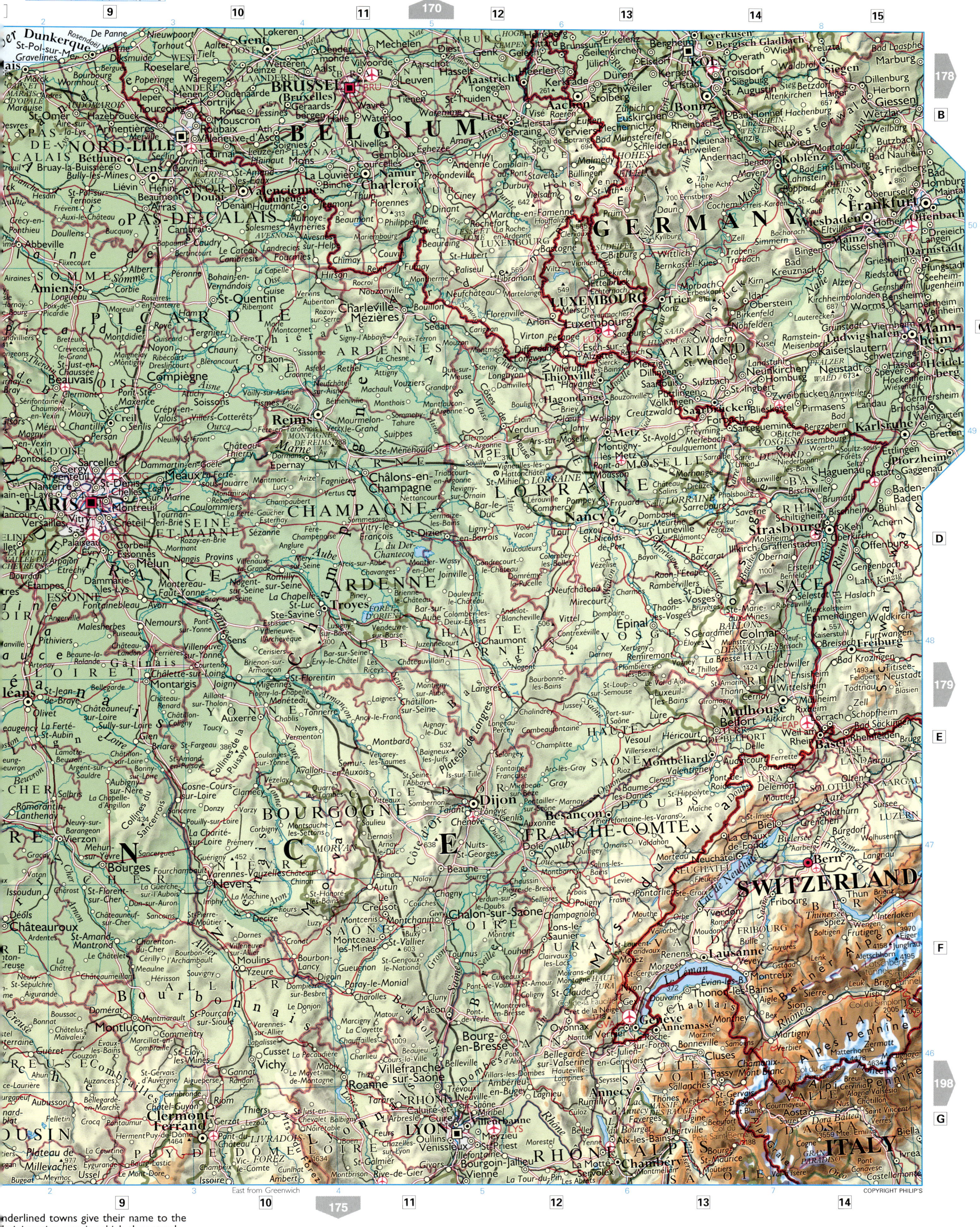

BELGIUM
GERMANY
LUXEMBOURG
SWITZERLAND
ITALY
PARIS
BRUSSEL (Bruxelles)
NORD-LILLE
PAS-DE-CALAIS
PICARDIE
CHAMPAGNE
LORRAINE
ALSACE
BOURGOGNE
FRANCHE-COMTÉ
ARDENNE
SAARLAND
Dijon
Strasbourg
Reims
Nancy
Metz
Lyon
Genève
Bern
Frankfurt
Köln
Luxembourg
Mulhouse
Basel
Besançon
East from Greenwich
COPYRIGHT PHILIP'S
170
175
178
179
198
B
C
D
E
F
G
9
10
11
12
13
14
15


nderlined towns give their name to the
lministrative area in which they stand.

TGV (Train à Grande Vitesse)

1:2 000 000

172
196
ATLANTIC
OCEAN
Golfe de
Gascogne
Golfe du Lion
Costa Brava
Cholet
Poitiers
Niort
La Rochelle
Île de Ré
Île d'Oléron
Rochefort
Pertuis Breton
Pertuis d'Antioche
Pertuis de Maumusson
Côte Sauvage
Côte de Lumière
Côte de Jade
Côte d'Argent
Côte Basque
Les Sables-d'Olonne
VENDÉE
DEUX-SÈVRES
POITOU-CHARENTES
CHARENTE
CHARENTE-MARITIME
HAUTE-VIENNE
VIENNE
Angoulême
Limoges
LIMOUSIN
Plateau de Millevaches
CORRÈZE
Brive-la-Gaillarde
Tulle
Périgueux
DORDOGNE
Bergerac
Bordeaux
Arcachon
Bassin d'Arcachon
Lac de Lacanau
GIRONDE
Gironde
Royan
Saintes
Cognac
Libourne
LANDES DE GASCOGNE
LANDES
AQUITAINE
LOT-ET-GARONNE
Agen
Marmande
Villeneuve-sur-Lot
Mont-de-Marsan
Dax
Bayonne
Biarritz
Anglet
Hendaye
Pau
Tarbes
Lourdes
PYRÉNÉES-ATLANTIQUES
HAUTES-PYRÉNÉES
GERS
Auch
Condom
TARN-ET-GARONNE
Montauban
Toulouse
Colomiers
Blagnac
Muret
HAUTE-GARONNE
ARIÈGE
Foix
Pamiers
Cahors
LOT
Rodez
AVEYRON
Millau
Albi
TARN
Castres
Carcassonne
AUDE
Narbonne
Béziers
Perpignan
PYRÉNÉES-ORIENTALES
Côte Vermeille
Roussillon
LANGUEDOC-ROUSSILLON
MIDI-PYRÉNÉES
CANTAL
Aurillac
Saint-Flour
AUVERGNE
PUY-DE-DÔME
Clermont-Ferrand
Vichy
Montluçon
ALLIER
Moulins
Bourges
CHER
Nevers
NIÈVRE
INDRE
Châteauroux
Issoudun
Châtellerault
BRENNE
CREUSE
Guéret
Aubusson
Mende
LOZÈRE
CÉVENNES
Causses
Montagne Noire
Corbières
ANDORRA
Andorra la Vella
Pic d'Estats
Pic de Aneto
Donostia-San Sebastián
Pamplona-Iruña
NAVARRA
Huesca
Zaragoza
Lleida (Lérida)
CATALUÑA
Barcelona
Sabadell
Terrassa
Badalona
Mataró
Girona
Figueres
Manresa
Vic
Olot
Sierra de Guara
C. de Creus
G. de Roses
Roses
Ebro
SPAIN
FRANCE
Projection : Lambert's Conformal Conic
West from Greenwich
East from Greenwich

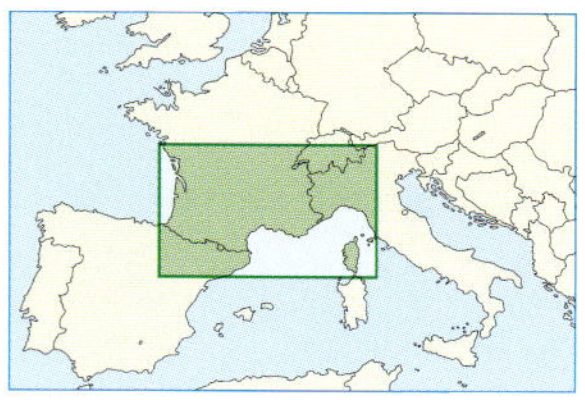

SWITZERLAND
ITALY
PROVENCE
CÔTE D'AZUR
RHÔNE-ALPES
LOMBARDIA
PIEMONTE
LIGURIA
CORSE
MONACO
LIGURIAN SEA
MEDITERRANEAN SEA
Golfo di Génova
Riviera di Ponente
Riviera di Levante
Lyon
Marseille
Toulon
Nice
Cannes
Avignon
Grenoble
Genève
Lausanne
Bern
Torino
Milano
Genova
Ajaccio
Bastia
Elba
Arcipelago Toscano
Livorno
Pisa
La Spezia
Annecy
Chambéry
St-Étienne
Valence
Montélimar
Aix-en-Provence
Arles
Sanremo
Is. d'Hyères
Alpes-Maritimes
Mont Blanc
Matterhorn
Lago Maggiore
L. di Como
L. Léman
Bouches de Bonifacio
173
198
TGV (Train à Grande Vitesse)

1:4 000 000
NORTH SEA
BALTIC SEA
ADRIATIC SEA
Golfo di Venézia
Golfo di Génova
UNITED KINGDOM
NETHERLANDS
BELGIUM
LUXEMBOURG
GERMANY
DENMARK
CZECH
FRANCE
SWITZERLAND
AUSTRIA
ITALY
SLOVENIA
SAN MARINO
MONACO
AMSTERDAM
ROTTERDAM
BRUSSELS (Bruxelles)
PARIS
BERLIN
HAMBURG
Bremen
Hannover
Frankfurt
KÖLN (Cologne)
Düsseldorf
Dortmund
Essen
Leipzig
Dresden
PRAHA (Prague)
MÜNCHEN (Munich)
Stuttgart
Nürnberg
ZÜRICH
Bern
Genève
Lausanne
LYON
MARSEILLE
Nice
TORINO (Turin)
MILANO
Venézia (Venice)
Bologna
Firenze (Florence)
Génova
Ljubljana
Trieste
Salzburg
Innsbruck
Graz
Linz
Strasbourg
Metz
Nancy
Dijon
Lille
Reims
Mannheim
Würzburg
Magdeburg
Rostock
Kiel
Lübeck
Szczecin
Rügen
Fehmarn Bælt
Kieler Bucht
Mecklenburger Bucht
Deutsche Bucht
Nordfriesische Inseln
Ostfriesische Inseln
Niedersachsen
Nordrhein-Westfalen
Hessen
Rheinland-Pfalz
Thüringer Wald
Bayern
Baden-Württemberg
Schwäbische Alb
Sachsen
Sachsen-Anhalt
Brandenburg
Mecklenburg
Böhmerwald
Erzgebirge
Vosges
Jura
Massif Central
Alpes Maritimes
Dolomiti
Karnische Alpen
Istra
Provence
Dauphiné
Bourgogne
Lorraine
Champagne
Picardie
Île-de-France
Piemonte
Liguria
Lombardia
Projection: Conical with two standard parallels
ft
m
12000
9000
6000
4500
3000
1500
600
0
4000
3000
2000
1500
1000
500
200
150
300
600
1500
3000
6000
50
25
75
100
125
150
175 km
25 miles
161
165
171
192

LITHUANIA
BELARUS
MINSK
Vilnius
Kaliningrad (Russia)
POLAND
WARSZAWA (Warsaw)
Gdańsk
Gdynia
Zatoka Gdańska
Olsztyn
Białystok
Bydgoszcz
Toruń
Łódź
Radom
Lublin
Kielce
Kraków
Wrocław
Katowice
Rzeszów
Brest
Pinsk
Homyel
Babruysk
Hrodna
UKRAINE
KYIV (Kiev)
Zhytomyr
Rivne
Lutsk
Lviv (Lvov)
Ternopil
Khmelnytskyy
Vinnytsya
Chernivtsi
Ivano-Frankivsk
Uzhhorod
MOLDOVA
Chişinău (Kishinev)
Tiraspol
SLOVAK REP.
Bratislava
Košice
HUNGARY
BUDAPEST
Debrecen
Miskolc
Szeged
Pécs
Balaton
ROMANIA
BUCUREŞTI (Bucharest)
Cluj-Napoca
Timişoara
Braşov
Iaşi
Constanţa
Galaţi
Craiova
SERBIA
BEOGRAD (Belgrade)
Novi Sad
Vojvodina
BOSNIA-HERZEGOVINA
Sarajevo
BULGARIA
Varna
Ruse
Carpathians
Transilvania
Moldavia
Dunărea (Danube)
Wisła
Dnister
Pripet
East from Greenwich
COPYRIGHT PHILIP'S

1:2 000 000
km
miles
BALTIC SEA
NORTH SEA
DENMARK
POLAND
MECKLENBURG-VORPOMMERN
BRANDENBURG
SCHLESWIG-HOLSTEIN
NIEDERSACHSEN
SACHSEN-ANHALT
SACHSEN
THÜRINGEN
NORDRHEIN-WESTFALEN
HESSEN
NETHERLANDS
GERMANY
BERLIN
HAMBURG
Hannover
Bremen
Kiel
Rostock
Magdeburg
Leipzig
Dresden
Erfurt
Düsseldorf
Köln
Bonn
Szczecin
Mecklenburger Bucht
Kieler Bucht
Deutsche Bucht
Fehmarn
Rügen
Ostfriesische Inseln
Nordfriesische Inseln
Elbe
Weser
Ems
Oder
163
170
184

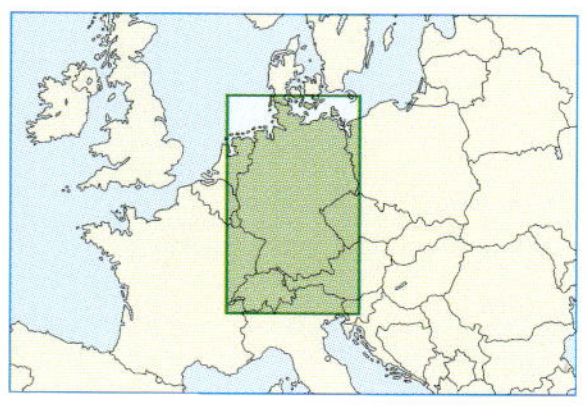

Underlined towns give their name to the administrative area in which they stand.
High-speed rail routes
Projection: Lambert's Conformal Conic
East from Greenwich
COPYRIGHT PHILIP'S
FRANCE
LUXEMBOURG
SWITZERLAND
AUSTRIA
ITALY
SLOVENIA
CZECH REP.
BADEN-WÜRTTEMBERG
BAYERN
München
Stuttgart
Zürich
Bern
Praha
Frankfurt
Nürnberg
Strasbourg
Innsbruck
Salzburg
Linz
180
198
199
175

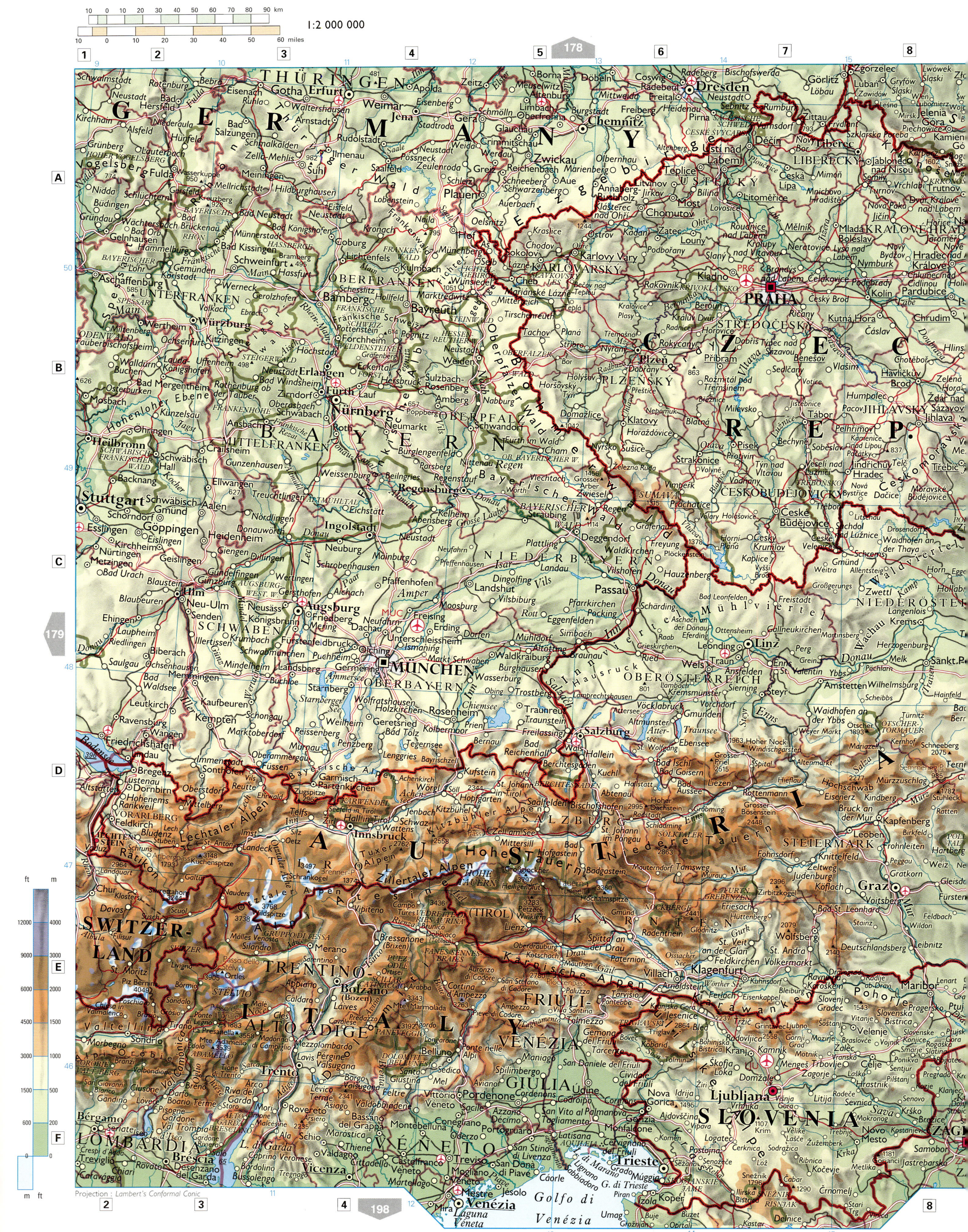
1:2 000 000
km
miles
178
179
198
Projection : Lambert's Conformal Conic
ft
m
GERMANY
CZECH REP.
AUSTRIA
SWITZERLAND
ITALY
SLOVENIA
THÜRINGEN
BAYERN
OBERBAYERN
SCHWABEN
OBERFRANKEN
UNTERFRANKEN
MITTELFRANKEN
OBERPFALZ
NIEDERBAYERN
OBERÖSTERREICH
NIEDERÖSTERREICH
SALZBURG
STEIERMARK
KÄRNTEN
TIROL
VORARLBERG
TRENTINO-ALTO ADIGE
FRIULI-VENEZIA GIULIA
VENETO
LOMBARDIA
STŘEDOČESKÝ
PLZEŇSKÝ
JIHOČESKÝ
KARLOVARSKÝ
LIBERECKÝ
KRÁLOVÉHRADECKÝ
JIHLAVSKÝ
PRAHA
Dresden
Chemnitz
Erfurt
Würzburg
Nürnberg
Regensburg
Stuttgart
Augsburg
MÜNCHEN
Ingolstadt
Linz
Salzburg
Innsbruck
Graz
Klagenfurt
Ljubljana
Bolzano
Trento
Venézia
Trieste
Plzeň
České Budějovice
Ústí nad Labem
Liberec
Golfo di Venézia

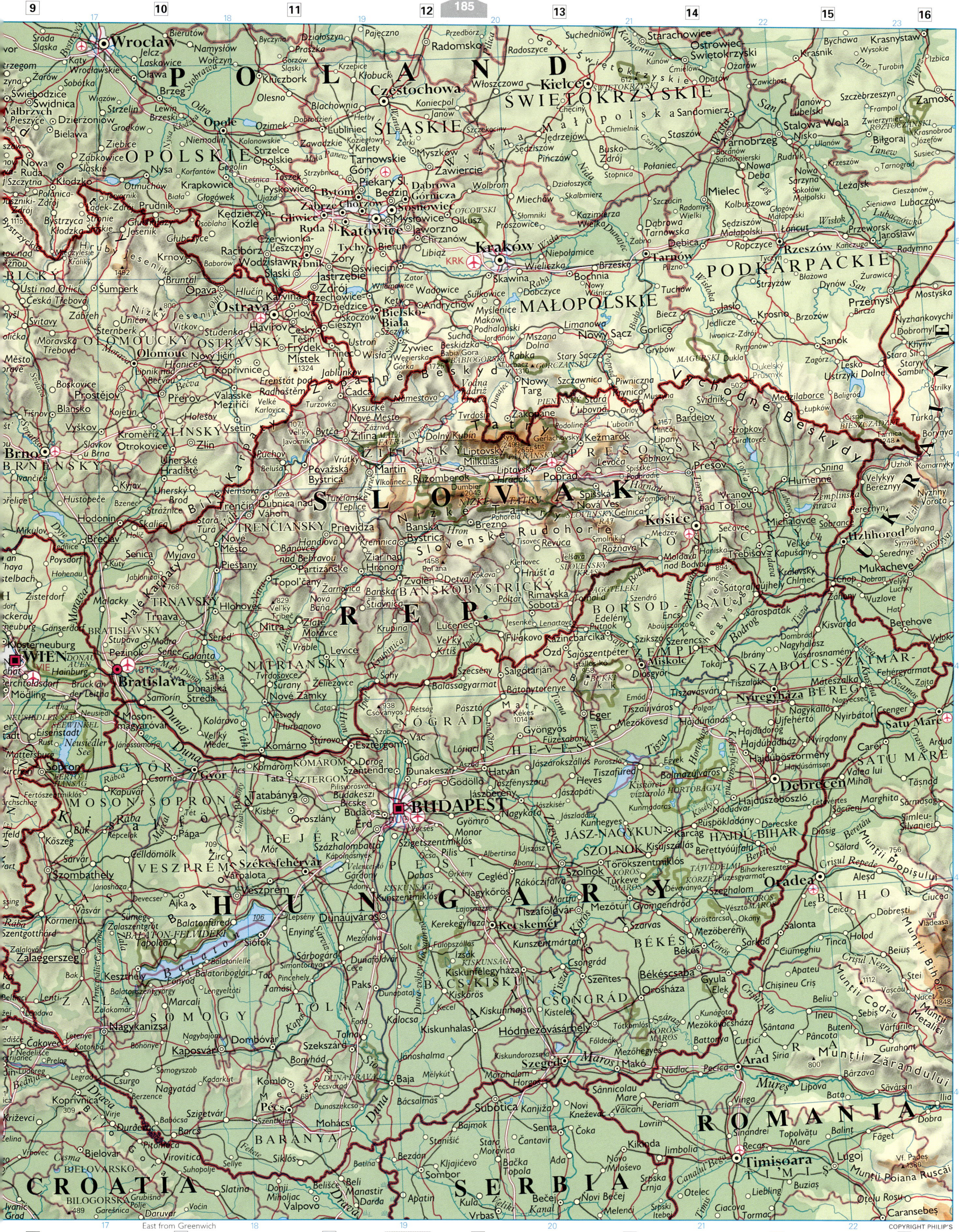
185
187
183
182
POLAND
SLOVAK REP.
HUNGARY
ROMANIA
CROATIA
SERBIA
UKRAINE
ŚWIĘTOKRZYSKIE
ŚLĄSKIE
OPOLSKIE
MAŁOPOLSKIE
PODKARPACKIE
OLOMOUCKÝ
MORAVSKOSLEZSKÝ
ZLÍNSKÝ
ŽILINSKÝ
PREŠOVSKÝ
KOŠICKÝ
BANSKOBYSTRICKÝ
TRENČIANSKY
TRNAVSKÝ
NITRIANSKY
BRATISLAVSKÝ
BORSOD-ABAÚJ-ZEMPLÉN
SZABOLCS-SZATMÁR-BEREG
HAJDÚ-BIHAR
JÁSZ-NAGYKUN-SZOLNOK
PEST
NÓGRÁD
HEVES
KOMÁROM-ESZTERGOM
GYŐR-MOSON-SOPRON
VESZPRÉM
FEJÉR
VAS
ZALA
SOMOGY
TOLNA
BARANYA
BÁCS-KISKUN
CSONGRÁD
BÉKÉS
BIHOR
SATU MARE
ARAD
TIMIŞ
BJELOVARSKO-BILOGORSKA
Wrocław
Częstochowa
Kielce
Kraków
Katowice
Opole
Rzeszów
Tarnów
Przemyśl
Ostrava
Olomouc
Brno
Bratislava
WIEN
Žilina
Prešov
Košice
Banská Bystrica
Nitra
Miskolc
Debrecen
Nyíregyháza
BUDAPEST
Győr
Székesfehérvár
Veszprém
Kecskemét
Szeged
Pécs
Oradea
Arad
Timişoara
Uzhhorod
Balaton
Tatry
Dunaj
Duna
Tisza
Maros
Mureş
Munţii Apuseni
East from Greenwich
COPYRIGHT PHILIP'S

Underlined towns give their name to the administrative area in which they stand.

1:2 000 000

SLOVAK REP.
HUNGARY
ROMANIA
CROATIA
BOSNIA-HERZEGOVINA
SERBIA
AUSTRIA
UKRAINE
FEDERACIJA BOSNA I HERCEGOVINA
REPUBLIKA SRPSKA
VOJVODINA
BUDAPEST
WIEN
Bratislava
BEOGRAD (Belgrade)
Sarajevo
Debrecen
Szeged
Timişoara
Oradea
Novi Sad
Pécs
Osijek
Košice
Miskolc
Kecskemét
Arad
Subotica
Banja Luka
Tuzla
Kragujevac
Nyíregyháza
Győr
Székesfehérvár
Szolnok
Dunaj
Duna
Dunav
Tisza
Sava
Drava
Mureş
Balaton
Projection : Lambert's Conformal Conic
East from Greenwich

Administrative divisions in Croatia:
1 Brodsko-Posavska
2 Koprivničko-Križevačka
4 Međimurska
5 Osječko-Baranjska
6 Požeško-Slavonska
8 Virovitičko-Podravska
9 Vukovarsko-Srijemska

ROMANIA
MOLDOVA
UKRAINE
BULGARIA
BLACK SEA
Carpathian Mountains
Transilvania
Walachia
Moldova
Dobrogea
BUCUREŞTI (Bucharest)
Chişinău (Kishinev)
Ivano-Frankivsk
Chernivtsi
Cluj-Napoca
Iaşi
Braşov
Ploieşti
Galaţi
Brăila
Constanţa
Craiova
Piteşti
Sibiu
Ruse
Pleven
Tiraspol
Bălţi
Dunărea
Delta Dunării
Prut
Siret
Nistru
189
203
COPYRIGHT PHILIP'S


Underlined towns give their name to the administrative area in which they stand.

1:2 000 000

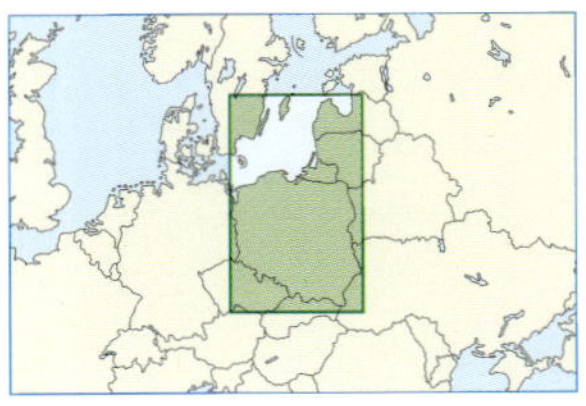

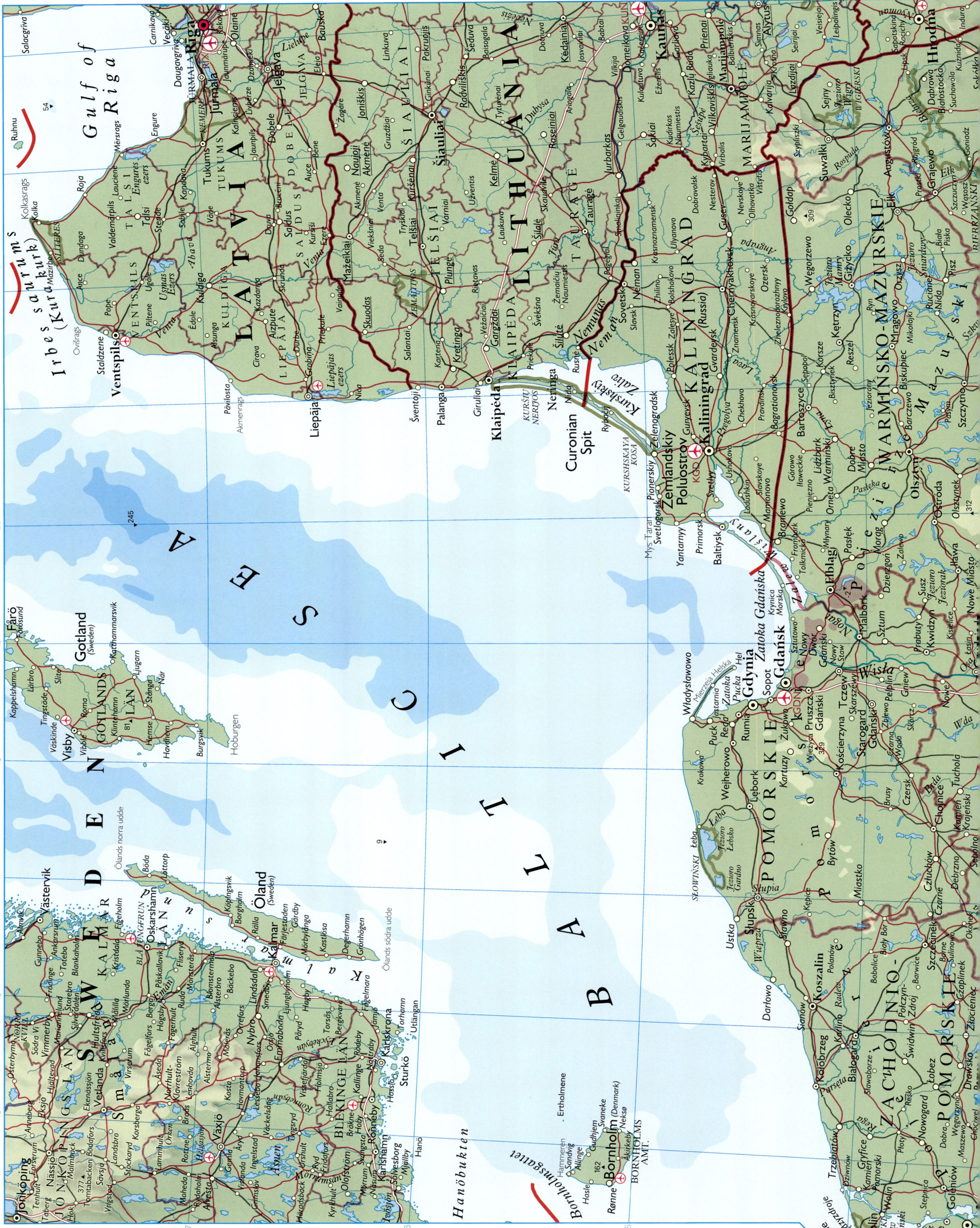
BALTIC SEA
Gulf of Riga
LATVIA
LITHUANIA
KALININGRAD (Russia)
SWEDEN
Gotland (Sweden)
Öland (Sweden)
Bornholm (Denmark)
Curonian Spit
Zatoka Gdańska
Hanöbukten
POMORSKIE
WARMIŃSKO-MAZURSKIE
ZACHODNIO-POMORSKIE
Riga
Jūrmala
Jelgava
Ventspils
Liepāja
Šiauliai
Klaipėda
Kaunas
Kaliningrad
Gdańsk
Gdynia
Elbląg
Olsztyn
Suwałki
Hrodna
Słupsk
Koszalin
Szczecin
Visby
Kalmar
Karlskrona
Växjö
Jönköping

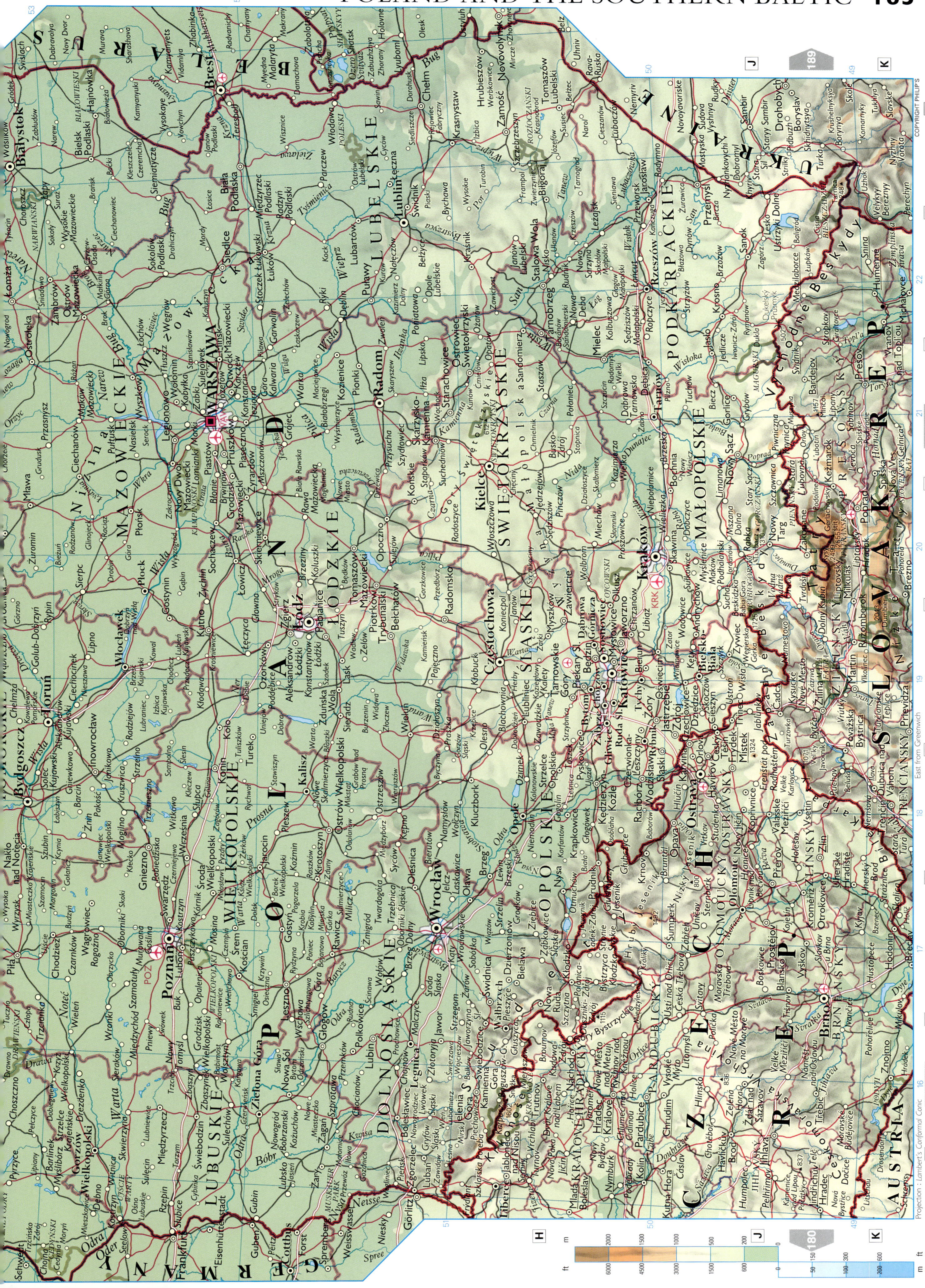
POLAND
CZECH REPUBLIC
SLOVAK REPUBLIC
UKRAINE
BELARUS
GERMANY
AUSTRIA
Warszawa
Kraków
Wrocław
Poznań
Łódź
Katowice
Lublin
Białystok
Bydgoszcz
Toruń
Kielce
Radom
Częstochowa
Opole
Rzeszów
Brest
Ostrava
Brno
Olomouc
MAZOWIECKIE
ŁÓDZKIE
ŚWIĘTOKRZYSKIE
LUBELSKIE
PODKARPACKIE
MAŁOPOLSKIE
ŚLĄSKIE
OPOLSKIE
DOLNOŚLĄSKIE
LUBUSKIE
WIELKOPOLSKIE
Underlined towns give their name to the administrative area in which they stand.
Projection: Lambert's Conformal Conic
East from Greenwich
COPYRIGHT PHILIP'S

50 0 100 200 300 400 km

1:8 000 000

50 0 50 100 150 200 250 miles

214
BARENTS SEA
Beloye More (White Sea)
Poluostrov Kanin
Ostrov Kolguyev
Pechorskaya Guba
Cheshskaya Guba
Kolskiy Poluostrov
Murmansk
Arkhangelsk
Severodvinsk
Onezhskaya Guba
Onezhskoye Ozero
Ladozhskoye Ozero
KARELIA
KOMI
Timanskiy Kryazh
Ural'skiye Gory
Severnyye Uvaly
Vorkuta
Ukhta
Syktyvkar
Kotlas
Vologda
Petrozavodsk
Sankt-Peterburg
Velikiy Novgorod
Pskov
Tver'
Yaroslavl'
Kostroma
Ivanovo
Nizhniy Novgorod
Kazan'
Izhevsk
Perm'
Kirov
Samara
Orenburg
Ufa
Ryazan'
Tula
Kaluga
Smolensk
Penza
Saransk
MOSKVA (Moscow)
R U S S I A
UDMURTIYA
TATARSTAN
BASHKORTOSTAN
CHUVASHIYA
MARIY EL
MORDVINIYA
FINLAND
Helsinki
Oulu
Tampere
Turku
Kuopio
Gulf of Finland
Gulf of Bothnia
SWEDEN
NORWAY
Lappland
Luleå
Umeå
ESTONIA
Tallinn
Tartu
LATVIA
Rīga
Gulf of Riga
LITHUANIA
Vilnius
Kaunas
Klaipėda
Kaliningrad (Russia)
BELARUS
Minsk
Homyel'
Mahilyow
Vitsyebsk
Hrodna
Brest
POLAND
Warszawa (Warsaw)
BALTIC SEA
Hiiumaa
Saaremaa
Åland

KAZAKHSTAN
CASPIAN SEA
BLACK SEA
Sea of Azov
MEDITERRANEAN SEA
UKRAINE
ROMANIA
BULGARIA
MOLDOVA
GEORGIA
ARMENIA
AZERBAIJAN
TURKMENISTAN
TURKEY
SYRIA
IRAQ
IRAN
LEBANON
CYPRUS
CRIMEA
KALMYKIA
DAGESTAN
CHECHENIA
Caucasus Mountains
Ustyurt Plateau
Caspian Depression
KYYIV (Kiev)
BUCUREŞTI (Bucharest)
TBILISI
YEREVAN
BAKI (Baku)
ANKARA
İSTANBUL
TEHRAN
DIMASHQ
BAYRŪT (Beirut)
Nicosia
VOLGOGRAD
ROSTOV
ODESA
KHARKIV
DNIPROPETROVSK
KONYA
ADANA
GAZIANTEP
TABRIZ
İZMIR
BURSA
Projection: Conical with two standard parallels
East from Greenwich
COPYRIGHT PHILIP'S

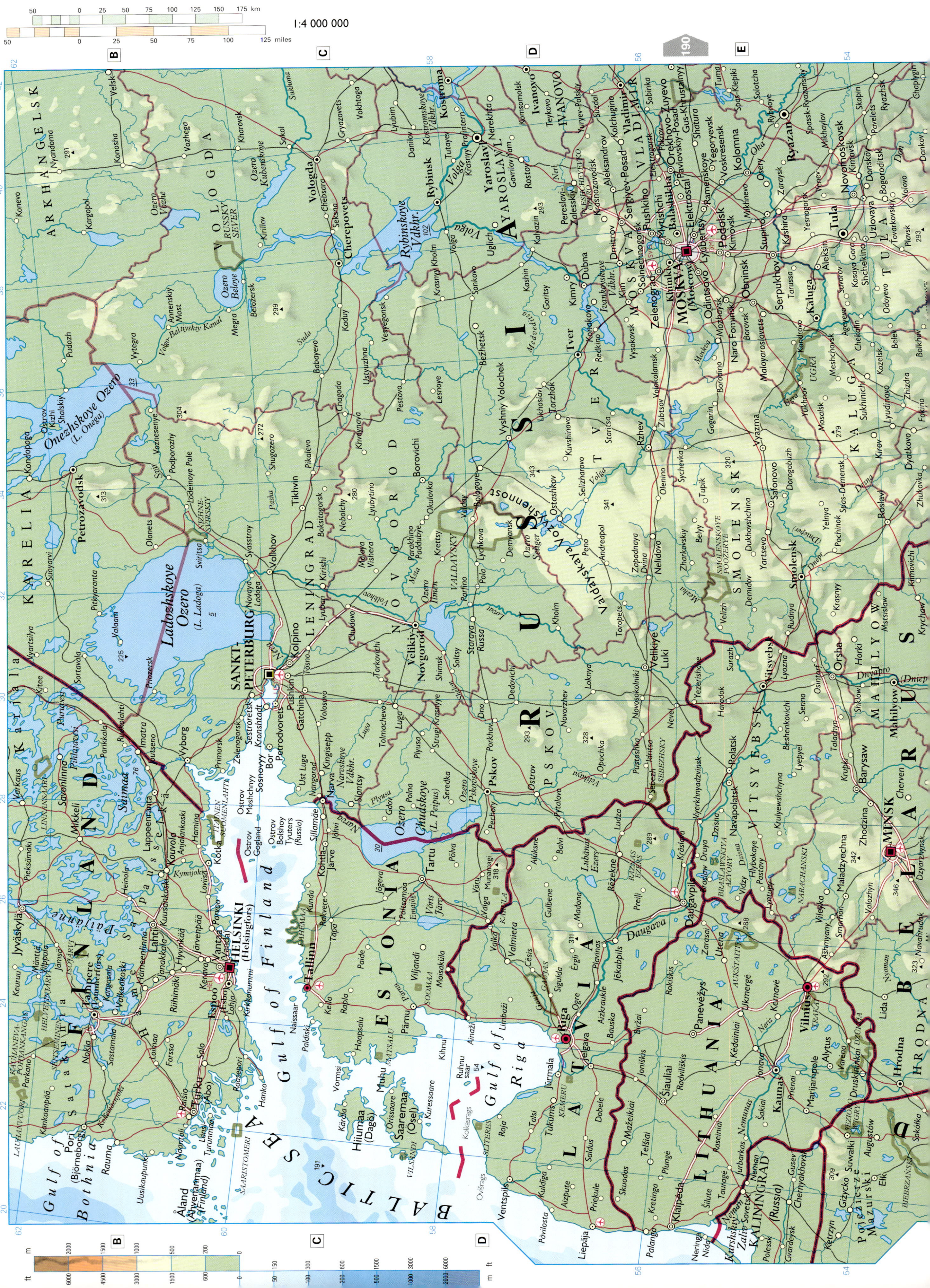
1:4 000 000
km
miles
BALTIC SEA
Gulf of Finland
Gulf of Riga
Gulf of Bothnia
FINLAND
ESTONIA
LATVIA
LITHUANIA
BELARUS
RUSSIA
KALININGRAD (Russia)
KARELIA
LENINGRAD
NOVGOROD
PSKOV
TVER
SMOLENSK
VITSYEBSK
MAHILYOW
HRODNA
VOLOGDA
YAROSLAVL
KALUGA
TULA
ARKHANGELSK
MOSKVA
SANKT-PETERBURG
HELSINKI (Helsingfors)
Tallinn
Riga
Vilnius
MINSK
Ladozhskoye Ozero (L. Ladoga)
Onezhskoye Ozero (L. Onega)
Ozero Chudskoye (L. Peipus)
Rybinskoye Vdkhr.
Petrozavodsk
Vologda
Cherepovets
Yaroslavl
Tver
Velikiy Novgorod
Pskov
Tartu
Pärnu
Daugavpils
Kaunas
Klaipėda
Šiauliai
Panevėžys
Liepāja
Ventspils
Smolensk
Vitsyebsk
Mahilyow
Hrodna
Turku (Åbo)
Tampere (Tammerfors)
Lahti
Kotka
Vyborg
Narva
Hiiumaa (Dagö)
Saaremaa (Ösel)
Åland (Ahvenanmaa) (Finland)
Valdayskaya Vozvyshennost
Daugava
Volga
186
190
160

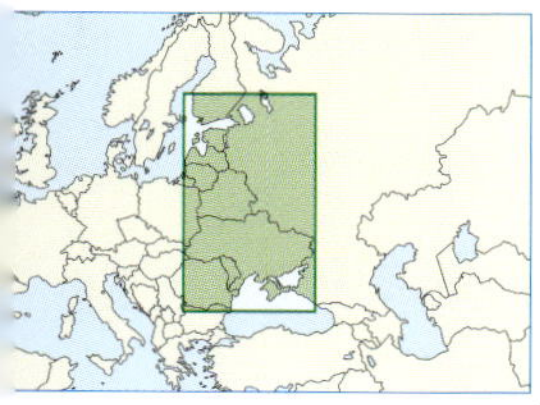

BLACK SEA
Sea of Azov
UKRAINE
MOLDOVA
ROMANIA
BULGARIA
KYYIV (Kiev)
ODESA
KHARKIV (Kharkov)
DNIPROPETROVSK
BUCUREŞTI (Bucharest)
CHIŞINĂU (Kishinev)
ROSTOV
Projection: Conical with two standard parallels
East from Greenwich
COPYRIGHT PHILIP'S

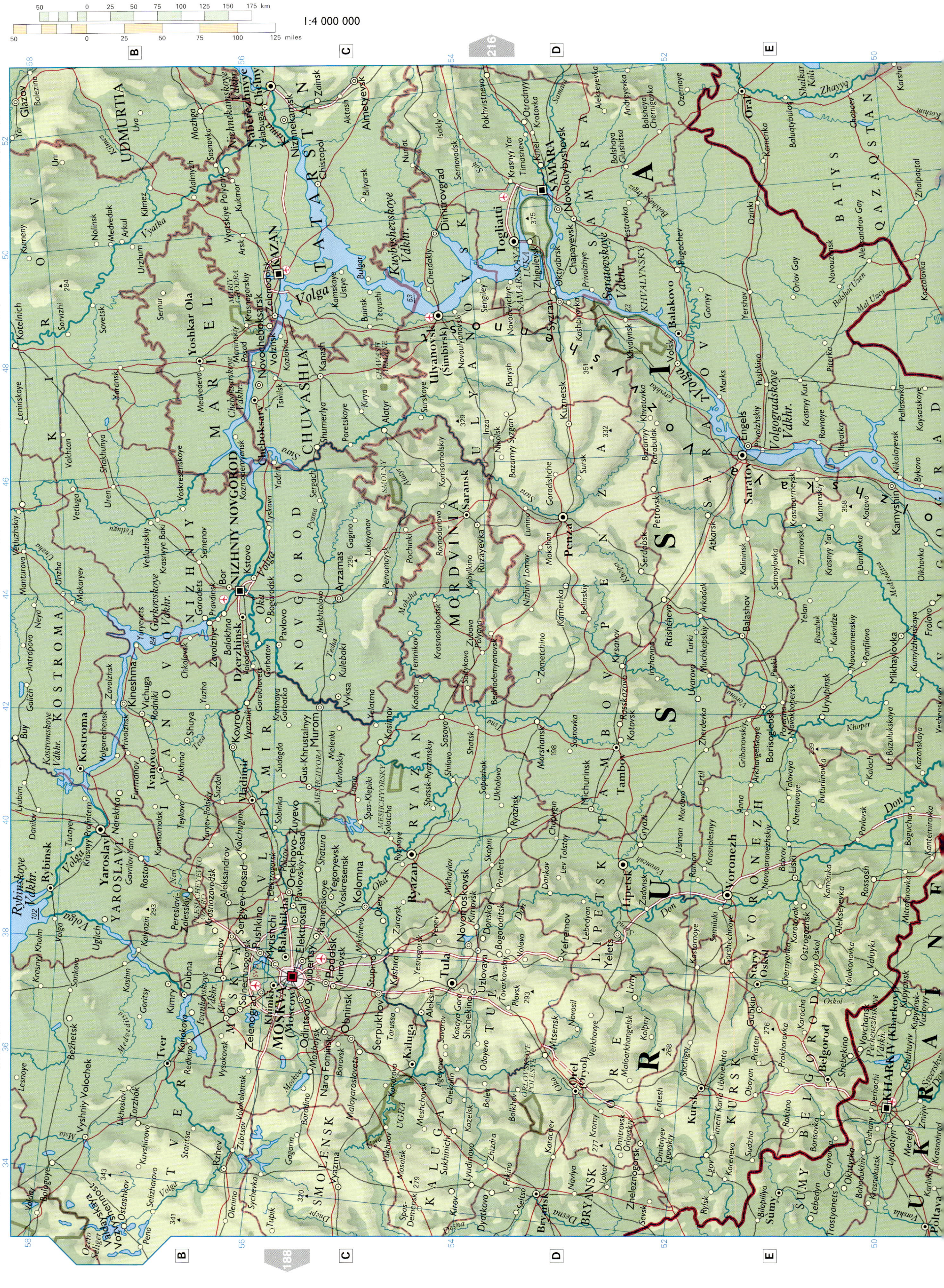
1:4 000 000
0 25 50 75 100 125 150 175 km
0 25 50 75 100 125 miles
UDMURTIA
TATARSTAN
MARI EL
CHUVASHIA
NIZHNIY NOVGOROD
MORDVINIA
ULYANOVSK
SAMARA
SARATOV
PENZA
KOSTROMA
IVANOVO
YAROSLAVL
VLADIMIR
RYAZAN
MOSKVA
TULA
TAMBOV
LIPETSK
VORONEZH
OREL
KURSK
BELGOROD
BRYANSK
KALUGA
SMOLENSK
TVER
KIROV
RUSSIA
BATYS QAZAQSTAN
SUMY
KHARKIV (KHARKOV)
Moskva
Kazan
Samara
Saratov
Nizhniy Novgorod
Voronezh
Yaroslavl
Ulyanovsk (Simbirsk)
Penza
Tula
Ryazan
Kursk
Orel (Oryol)
Kaluga
Bryansk
Tambov
Lipetsk
Cheboksary
Yoshkar Ola
Saransk
Togliatti
Engels
Kostroma
Ivanovo
Vladimir
Tver
Rybinskoye Vdkhr.
Kuybyshevskoye Vdkhr.
Saratovskoye Vdkhr.
Volgogradskoye Vdkhr.
Gorkovskoye Vdkhr.
Volga
Oka
Don
Sura
Khoper
Vyatka
Kama
Moksha
Desna

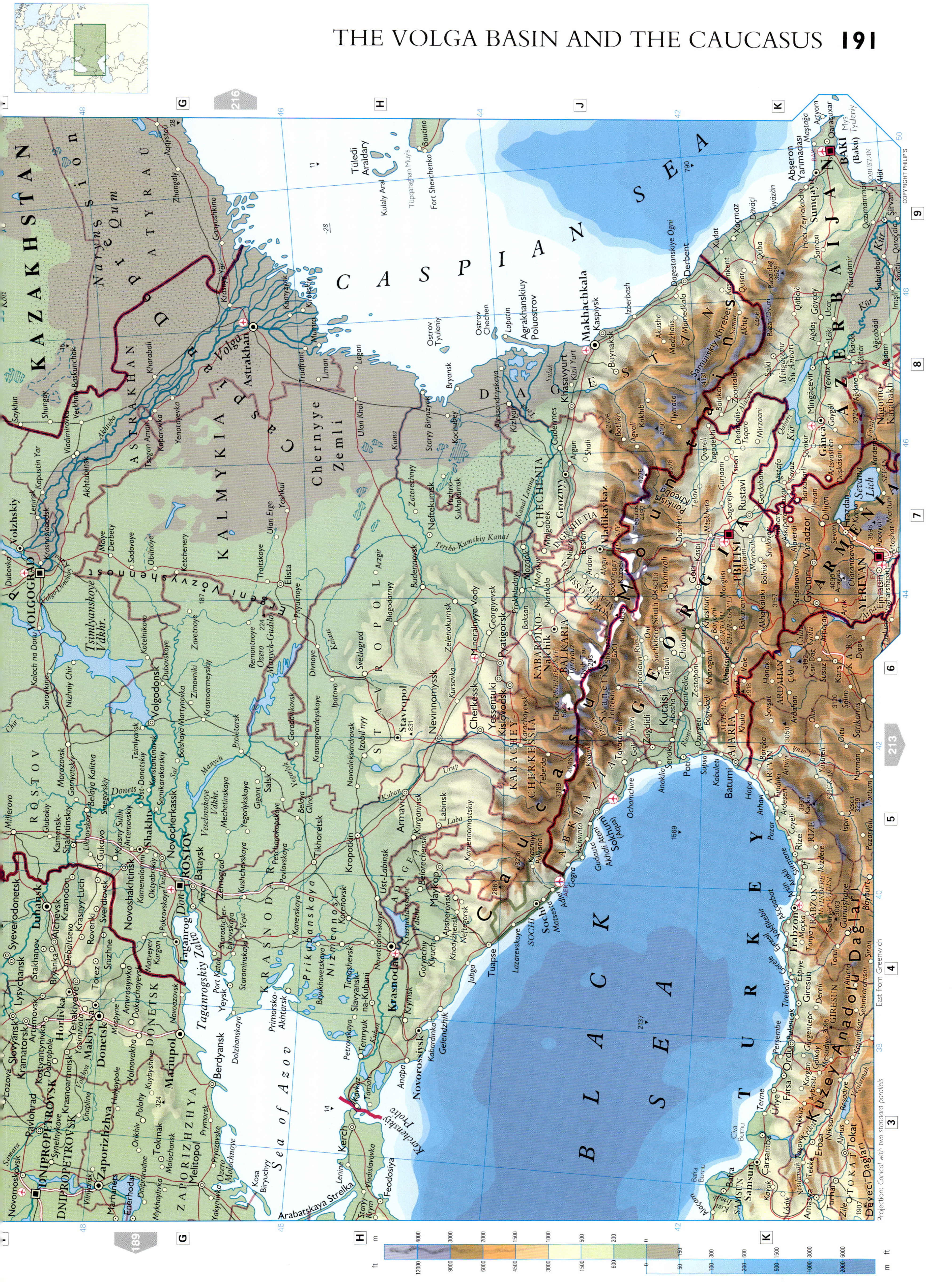
KAZAKHSTAN
CASPIAN SEA
BLACK SEA
Sea of Azov
KALMYKIA
DAGESTAN
CHECHENIA
GEORGIA
ARMENIA
AZERBAIJAN
TURKEY
VOLGOGRAD
ROSTOV
Astrakhan
Volga
Makhachkala
Derbent
Grozny
Vladikavkaz
Elista
Stavropol
Krasnodar
Novorossiysk
Sochi
Sokhumi
Batumi
TBILISI
YEREVAN
BAKI (Baku)
Gəncə
Trabzon
Samsun
Kerch
Taganrog
Donetsk
Luhansk
Mariupol
Caucasus
Chernyye Zemli
Projection: Conical with two standard parallels
East from Greenwich
COPYRIGHT PHILIP'S

1:8 000 000

50 0 100 200 300 400 km
50 0 50 100 150 200 250 miles
ATLANTIC OCEAN
Bay of Biscay
Golfe de Gascogne
English Channel
Str. of Dover
Isles of Scilly
Channel Is. (U.K.)
Jersey
Ouessant
Pte. de Penmarch
Belle-Île
U.K.
LONDON
Bristol
Exeter
Southampton
Portsmouth
Plymouth
Penzance
Brighton
Folkestone
Dover
NETHERLANDS
AMSTERDAM
ROTTERDAM
Haarlem
's-Gravenhage
Vlissingen
BELGIUM
BRUSSEL
Antwerpen
Liège
Oostende
GERMANY
Osnabrück
Hannover
Potsdam
Münster
Magdeburg
Essen
Dortmund
Düsseldorf
KÖLN
Bonn
Kassel
Halle
Erfurt
Leipzig
Chemnitz
Plauen
Fulda
Aachen
Koblenz
Wiesbaden
Frankfurt
Darmstadt
Mainz
Trier
Mannheim
Heidelberg
Würzburg
Nürnberg
Regensburg
Karlsruhe
Stuttgart
Augsburg
Ulm
MÜNCHEN
Freiburg
LUXEMBOURG
Luxembourg
FRANCE
PARIS
Calais
Dunkerque
Boulogne-sur-Mer
LILLE
Arras
Douai
Amiens
St-Quentin
Rouen
Dieppe
Le Havre
Cherbourg-Octeville
Caen
Reims
Verdun
Metz
Nancy
Strasbourg
Châlons-en-Champagne
Troyes
Épinal
Mulhouse
Belfort
Besançon
Dijon
Versailles
Brest
Quimper
Lorient
Vannes
St-Brieuc
St-Malo
Rennes
Laval
Alencon
Le Mans
Angers
Tours
Orléans
St-Nazaire
Nantes
Bourges
Le Creusot
Chalon-sur-Saône
Mâcon
Vichy
La Rochelle
Rochefort
Poitiers
Limoges
Angoulême
Clermont-Ferrand
St-Étienne
LYON
Chambéry
Grenoble
Valence
Périgueux
Bordeaux
Massif Central
Cévennes
Montauban
Toulouse
Montpellier
Béziers
Nîmes
Avignon
Aix-en-Provence
MARSEILLE
Toulon
Sète
Narbonne
Perpignan
Pau
Bayonne
Biarritz
Nice
Cannes
MONACO
Menton
Golfe du Lion
SWITZERLAND
Bern
Basel
ZÜRICH
Lausanne
Genève
LIECHTENSTEIN
AUSTRIA
Innsbruck
Salzburg
ITALY
TORINO
MILANO
Novara
Como
Bergamo
Brescia
Verona
Vicenza
Padova
Venézia
Trieste
Udine
Bolzano
Trento
Pavia
Alessandria
Génova
Parma
Reggio nell'Emilia
Modena
Ferrara
Bologna
Ravenna
Forlì
Rímini
SAN MARINO
La Spezia
Pisa
Livorno
Firenze
Arezzo
Siena
Perugia
Grosseto
Elba
Terni
Civitavécchia
ROMA
Latina
NÁPOLI
Golfo di Venézia
Golfo di Génova
LIGURIAN SEA
Corse (France)
Bastia
Ajaccio
Bonifacio
Sardegna (Italy)
Sássari
Ólbia
Oristano
Cágliari
Porto Tórres
TYRRHENIAN SEA
MEDITERRANEAN SEA
SPAIN
MADRID
Santiago de Compostela
A Coruña (La Coruña)
Ferrol
C. Ortegal
C. Finisterre
Oviedo
Gijón (Xixón)
Santander
Bilbao
Donostia-San Sebastián
Vitoria-Gasteiz
Pamplona-Iruña
Logroño
Burgos
León
Ponferrada
Ourense (Orense)
Pontevedra
Vigo
Cordillera Cantábrica
Picos de Europa
Palencia
Valladolid
Salamanca
Zamora
Ciudad Rodrigo
Sierra de Gata
Sierra de Guadarrama
Guadalajara
Zaragoza
Huesca
Lleida (Lérida)
Girona
BARCELONA
Tarragona
Tortosa
ANDORRA
Pyrénées
Pico de Aneto
Teruel
Cuenca
Toledo
Cáceres
Badajoz
Ciudad Real
Puertollano
La Mancha
Albacete
Castelló de la Plana
Valencia
Alicante (Alacant)
Elche (Elx)
Benidorm
Murcia
Cartagena
Lorca
Sierra Morena
Córdoba
Linares
Jaén
Granada
Guadix
Sierra Nevada
Mulhacén
Almería
Málaga
Marbella
Sevilla
Huelva
Jerez de la Frontera
Cádiz
Algeciras
Gibraltar (U.K.)
Str. of Gibraltar
C. Trafalgar
C. de Gata
Islas Baleares (Spain)
Mallorca
Menorca
Palma de Mallorca
Eivissa
Formentera
Cabrera
Maó
PORTUGAL
LISBOA
PORTO
Braga
Bragança
Coimbra
Serra da Estrela
Évora
Faro
C. de São Vicente
MOROCCO
RABAT
Kenitra
Meknès
FÈS
Tanger
Larache
Ceuta (Sp.)
Tétouan
Ksar el Kebir
Al Hoceima
Melilla (Sp.)
Nador
Ouezzane
Taza
Oujda
Azrou
Moyen Atlas
Beni Mellal
Haut Atlas
Bouârfa
Er Rachidia
Figuig
ALGERIA
ALGER (Algiers)
Oran
Mostaganem
Ech Chéliff
Blida
Médéa
Tizi-Ouzou
Bejaïa
Skikda
Annaba
Sétif
Constantine
Batna
Tébessa
Biskra
Ksar el Boukhari
M'sila
Chott el Hodna
Djelfa
Laghouat
Tiaret
Saïda
Sidi-bel-Abbès
Tlemcen
Chott ech Chergui
Hauts Plateaux
Atlas Saharien
Mecheria
Aïn-Sefra
Béchar
Beni Ounif
Abadla
Beni Abbès
Grand Erg Occidental
El Goléa
Ghardaïa
Ouargla
Touggourt
El Oued
Hassi Messaoud
Chott Melrhir
Grand Erg Oriental
Timimoun
Sahara
TUNISIA
TUNIS
Bizerte
Béja
Nabeul
Hammamet
Golfe de Hammamet
Sousse
Kairouan
Mahdia
Kasserine
Sfax
Gafsa
Tozeur
Chott Djerid
Îles Kerkenna
Golfe de Gabès
Gabès
Djerba
Zarzis
Médenine
Tataouine
Dehibat
Trápani
Marsala
Agrigento
Caltanissetta
Pantelleria (Italy)
Lampedusa (Italy)
Ísole Égadi
Zuwārah
Az Zawiyah
Al-Khums
Gharyān
Nālūt
Mizdah
Ṭarābulus (Tripolitania)
Projection: Conical with two standard parallels
West from Greenwich 0 East from Greenwich


260

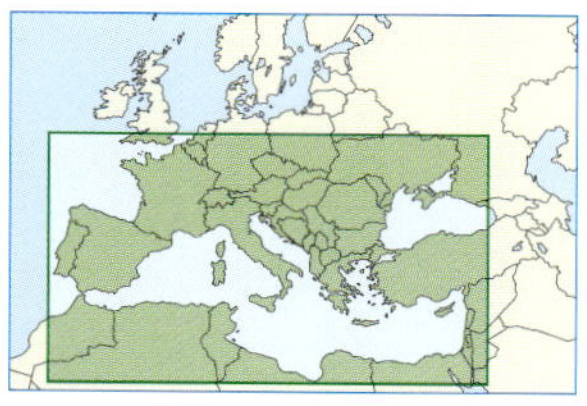

POLAND
UKRAINE
RUSSIA
SLOVAK REP.
HUNGARY
ROMANIA
MOLDOVA
CROATIA
BOSNIA-HERZEGOVINA
SERBIA
MONTENEGRO
KOSOVO
BULGARIA
MACEDONIA
ALBANIA
GREECE
TURKEY
CYPRUS
SYRIA
LEBANON
ISRAEL
EGYPT
LIBYA
BLACK SEA
Sea of Azov
CRIMEA
AEGEAN SEA
IONIAN SEA
MEDITERRANEAN SEA
Khalīj Surt
(Gulf of Sidra)
WARSZAWA
(Warsaw)
KYYIV
(Kiev)
BUDAPEST
BEOGRAD
BUCUREŞTI
(Bucharest)
SOFIYA
ISTANBUL
ANKARA
ATHINA
(Athens)
Chişinău
Sarajevo
Skopje
Tiranë
Podgorica
Priština
ZAGREB
Nicosia
BAYRŪT
(Beirut)
DIMASHQ
TEL AVIV-YAFO
Jerusalem
AMMAN
EL QÂHIRA
(Cairo)
EL ISKANDARÎYA
(Alexandria)
BANGHĀZĪ
Kriti (Crete)
Dodekanisa
Kyklades
Peloponnesos
Anadolu
Toros Dağları
Kuzey Anadolu Dağlari
Stara Planina
Rhodopi Planina
Carpaţii Meridionali
Barqah
(Cyrenaica)
Munkhafed el Qattâra
Odesa
Constanţa
Varna
Burgas
Thessaloniki
İzmir
(Smyrna)
Antalya
Rhodes
Iraklio
COPYRIGHT PHILIP'S

186
187
246
256

1:2 000 000

Bay of Biscay
Costa Verde
Donostia-San Sebastián
Bilbao
Vitoria-Gasteiz
PAÍS VASCO
LA RIOJA
Logroño
Santander
CANTABRIA
Gijón (Xixón)
Oviedo
ASTURIAS
León
Burgos
Palencia
Valladolid
CASTILLA Y LEÓN
Zamora
Salamanca
Segovia
Ávila
Soria
Guadalajara
MADRID
Alcalá de Henares
Toledo
Talavera de la Reina
Plasencia
A Coruña (La Coruña)
Ferrol
Lugo
GALICIA
Santiago de Compostela
Pontevedra
Vigo
Ourense (Orense)
Ponferrada
Bragança
VILA REAL
BRAGA
PORTO
VISEU
GUARDA
AVEIRO
COIMBRA
CASTELO BRANCO
Figueira da Foz
Sierra de Gredos
Sierra de Guadarrama
Douro
Duero
Ebro
Tajo

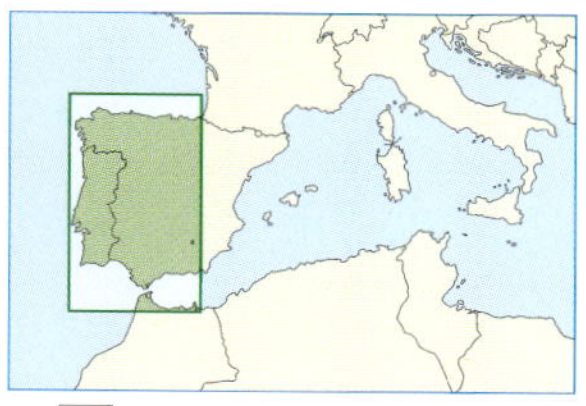

ATLANTIC OCEAN
MEDITERRANEAN SEA
Alboran Sea
Golfo de Cádiz
Costa de la Luz
Costa del Sol
Strait of Gibraltar
EXTREMADURA
CASTILLA-LA MANCHA
ANDALUCÍA
CIUDAD REAL
BADAJOZ
CÓRDOBA
SEVILLA
HUELVA
CÁDIZ
MÁLAGA
GRANADA
JAÉN
ALMERÍA
PORTUGAL
LISBOA
SETÚBAL
ÉVORA
BEJA
FARO
Algarve
MOROCCO
LISBOA
Sevilla
Córdoba
Granada
Málaga
Cádiz
Huelva
Jaén
Almería
Badajoz
Cáceres
Ciudad Real
Jerez de la Frontera
Algeciras
Gibraltar (U.K.)
Ceuta (Sp.)
Tanger (Tangier)
Tétouan
Larache
Melilla (Sp.)
Nador
Marbella
Faro
Évora
Beja
Setúbal
Guadiana
Guadalquivir
Sierra Nevada
Sierra Morena
Projection : Lambert's Conformal Conic
West from Greenwich
AVE (Alta Velocidad Española)
COPYRIGHT PHILIP'S
197
260
F
G
H
J
K
1
2
3
4
5
6
7
m
ft
3000
2000
1500
1000
500
200
0
50
100
200
500
1000
2000
3000
4000
9000
6000
4500
3000
1500
600
150
300
600
1500
3000
6000
9000
12 000

1:2 000 000

FRANCE
SPAIN
ANDORRA
BARCELONA
Zaragoza
Tarragona
Toulouse
Pamplona-Iruña
Vitoria-Gasteiz
Donostia-San Sebastián
Bilbao
Burgos
Logroño
Lleida
Huesca
Teruel
Castelló de la Plana
Cuenca
Guadalajara
MADRID
Perpignan
Carcassonne
Narbonne
Béziers
Pau
Bayonne
Tarbes
Agen
Montauban
Golfe de Gascogne
Côte d'Argent
Côte Basque
MENORCA
Maó (Mahón)
Cuitadella de Menorca
MALLORCA
Delta del Ebre
Costa Brava
Costa Daurada
Golfo de Valencia
ARAGÓN
CATALUNYA
NAVARRA
LA RIOJA
PAÍS VASCO
CASTILLA Y LEÓN
PYRÉNÉES-ATLANTIQUES
HAUTES-PYRÉNÉES
PYRÉNÉES-ORIENTALES
ARIÈGE
AUDE
GERS
LANDES
BALEARES
Ebro
Sierra de Albarracín
Montes Universales
Sierra de Gúdar

174
194

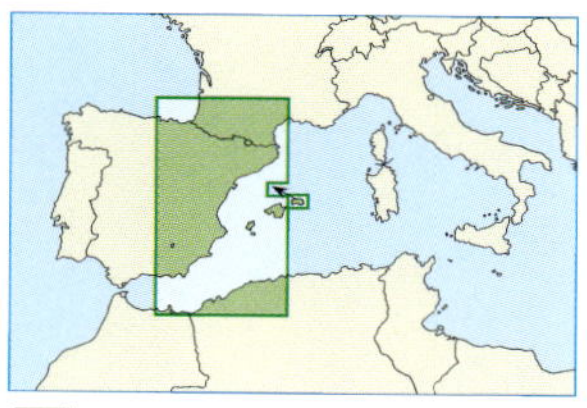

MEDITERRANEAN SEA
Valencia
Golfo de Valencia
Costa Blanca
Alicante (Alacant)
Elche (Elx)
Murcia
Cartagena
Torrevieja
Albacete
CASTILLA-LA MANCHA
CIUDAD REAL
ALBACETE
MURCIA
ALICANTE
ALMERÍA
GRANADA
Granada
Almería
G. de Almería
Costa Cálida
Costa del Sol
Sierra Nevada
Eivissa (Ibiza)
Formentera
Palma
Cabrera
Alborán (Sp.)
Melilla (Sp.)
Islas Chafarinas (Sp.)
ALGER (Algiers)
Oran (Ouahran)
Mostaganem
Relizane
Mascara
Tiaret
Sidi-bel-Abbès
Aïn Temouchent
Blida
Médéa
Ech Chélif
Golfe d'Arzew
ALGERIA
COPYRIGHT PHILIP'S
Projection: Lambert's Conformal Conic
East from Greenwich
West from Greenwich
195
260
261
ft
m
12000
9000
6000
4500
3000
1500
600
4000
3000
2000
1500
1000
500
200
0
50
100
200
500
1000
2000
3000
150
300
600
1500
3000
6000
9000

10 0 10 20 30 40 50 60 70 80 90 km

10 0 10 20 30 40 50 60 miles

1:2 000 000

SWITZERLAND
FRANCE
LIGURIAN SEA
Golfo di Génova
Riviera di Ponente
Riviera di Levante
Côte d'Azur
CORSE
Arcipelago Toscano
LOMBARDIA
PIEMONTE
PROVENCE-ALPES-CÔTE D'AZUR
RHÔNE-ALPES
Bern
Genève
Lausanne
TORINO
MILANO
Genova
Nice
MONACO
MARSEILLE
Toulon
LYON
Grenoble
Avignon
Bastia
Ajaccio
Livorno
Elba
Piacenza
Parma
Cremona
Brescia
Bergamo
Alpi Pennine
Mts du Jura
Alpes Maritimes
179
200
174

Projection : Lambert's Conformal Conic

East from Greenwich

m 4000 3000 2000 1500 1000 500 200 0

ft 12 000 9000 6000 4500 3000 1500 600

150 300 600 1500 3000 6000 ft

50 100 200 500 1000 2000 m

Underlined towns give their name to the administrative area in which they sta

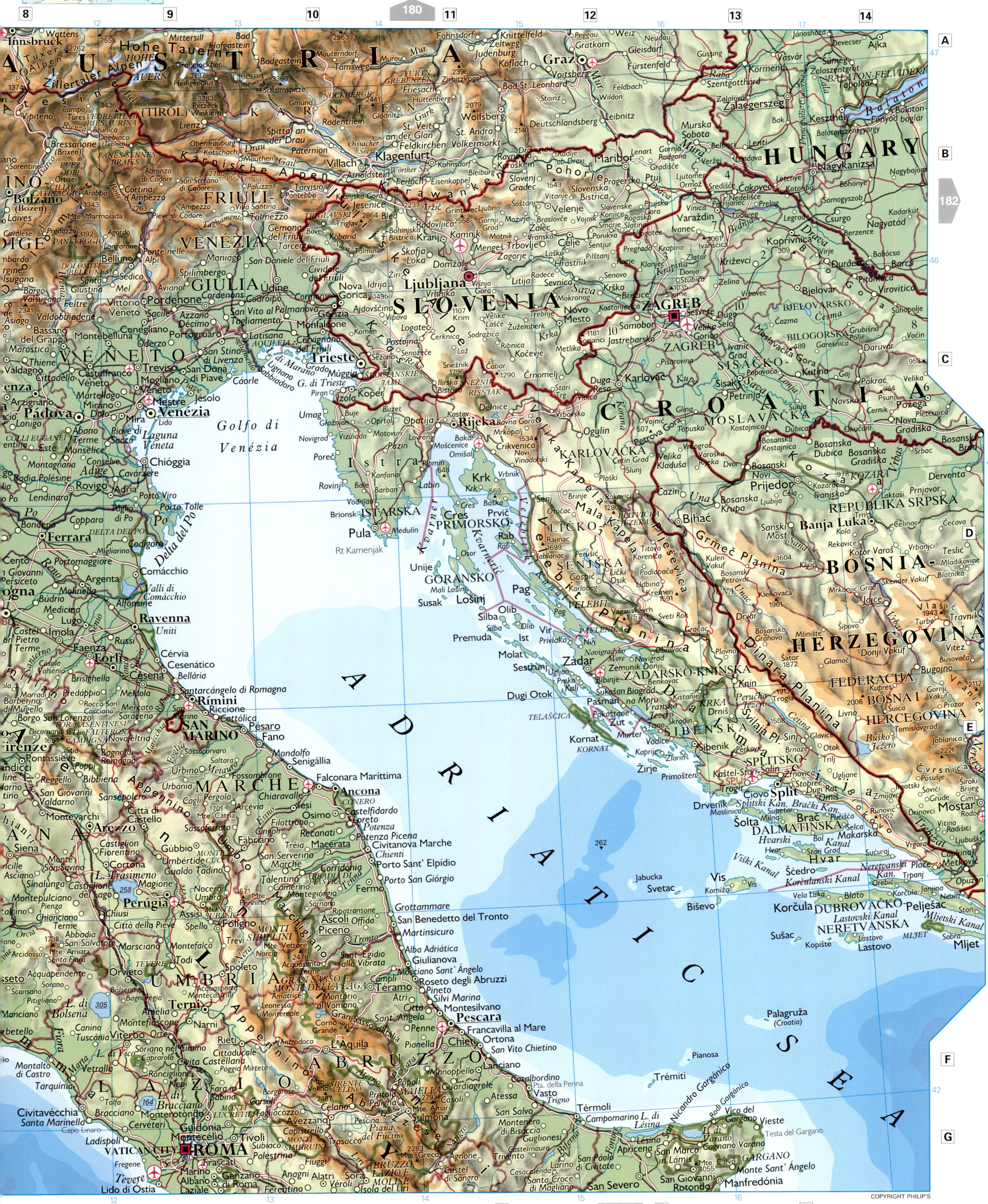
AUSTRIA
SLOVENIA
CROATIA
HUNGARY
BOSNIA-HERZEGOVINA
SAN MARINO
ADRIATIC SEA
Golfo di Venézia
Ljubljana
Zagreb
Trieste
Venézia
Pádova
Rijeka
Zadar
Split
Ancona
Pescara
Ravenna
Rímini
Ferrara
Perúgia
ROMA
Graz
Klagenfurt
Maribor
Sarajevo
Banja Luka
Dubrovnik
Pula
Bologna
Firenze
Arezzo
Terni
L'Aquila
Chieti
Foggia
Brčko
Bihać
Karlovac
Osijek
Kranj
Celje
Villach
Lienz
Udine
Pordenone
Treviso
Rovigo
Chióggia
Fano
Pésaro
Urbino
Macerata
Ascoli Piceno
Térmoli
Vasto
Palagruža (Croatia)
Vis
Korčula
Lastovo
Mljet
Krk
Cres
Lošinj
Pag
Dugi Otok
Kornat
Brač
Hvar
Šolta
Šibenik
Makarska
Mostar
Livno
Travnik
Zenica
Prijedor
Sisak
Varaždin
Koprivnica
Bjelovar
Nagykanizsa
Zalaegerszeg
Balaton
Keszthely
Pécs
Alpi Dináriche
Velebit
Dinara Planina
Appennino
Monti Sibillini
Gran Sasso d'Italia
Lago Trasimeno
Lago di Bolsena
Gargano
Manfredónia
Trémiti
Pianosa
Vieste
Monte Sant' Angelo
San Severo
Civitavecchia
Fiumicino
Lido di Ostia
Tívoli
Frosinone
Sulmona
Avezzano
Isernia
Campobasso
COPYRIGHT PHILIP'S

Administrative divisions in Croatia:

odsko-Posavska
privničko-Križevačka
apinsko-Zagorska
4 Medimurska
6 Požeško-Slavonska
7 Varaždinska
8 Virovitičko-Podravska
10 Zagreba čka

TAV (Treno Alta Velocità)

1:2 000 000

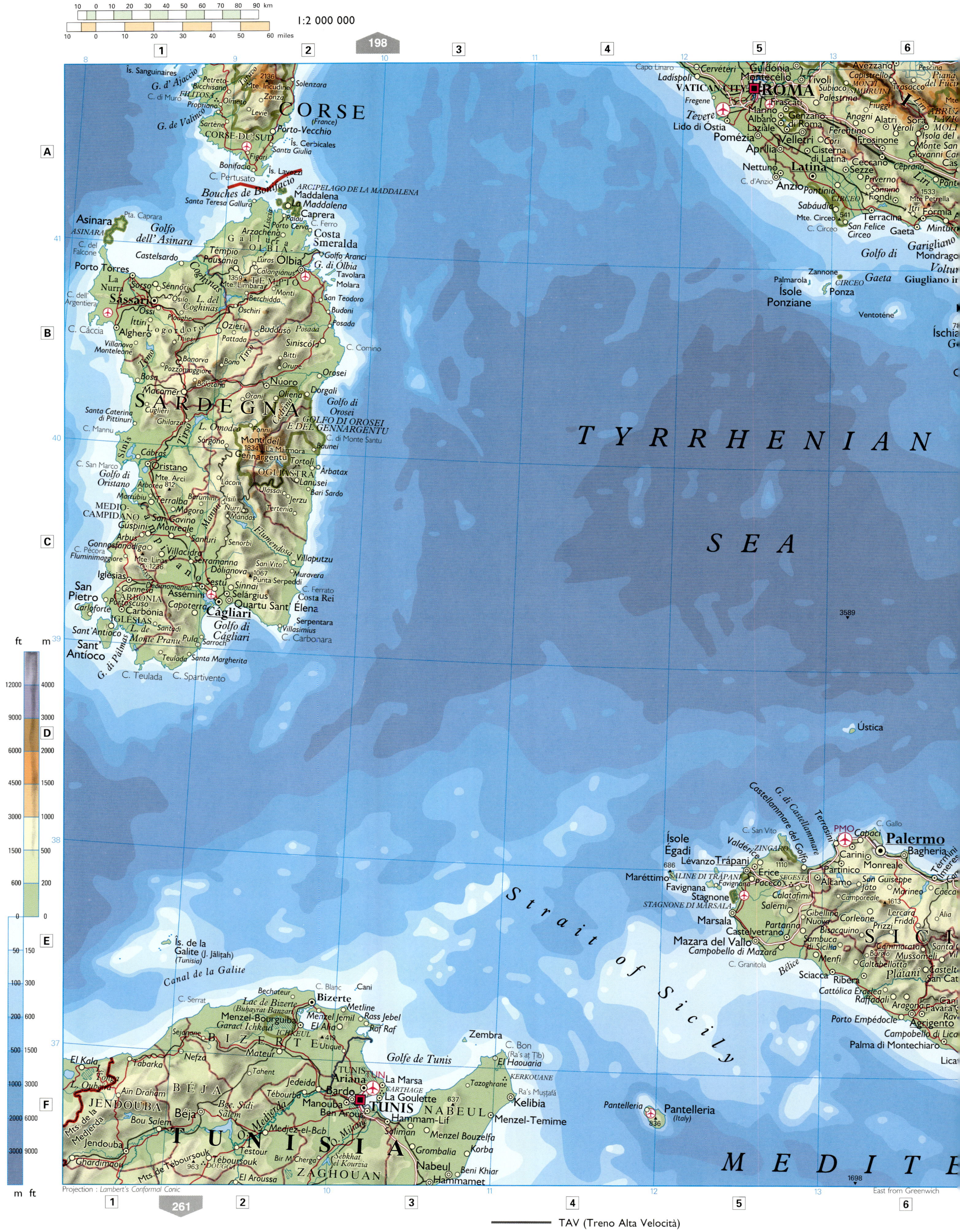
198
CORSE
(France)
Porto-Vecchio
Bonifacio
Bouches de Bonifacio
ARCIPELAGO DE LA MADDALENA
Maddalena
Caprera
Asinara
Golfo dell' Asinara
Porto Torres
Costa Smeralda
Olbia
G. di Olbia
Sassari
Alghero
Nuoro
SARDEGNA
Golfo di Orosei
GOLFO DI OROSEI E DEL GENNARGENTU
Oristano
Golfo di Oristano
MEDIO-CAMPIDANO
Iglesias
San Pietro
Carbonia
Sant' Antíoco
Cágliari
Golfo di Cágliari
C. Teulada
C. Spartivento
ROMA
VATICAN CITY
Tívoli
Frascati
Lido di Óstia
Pomézia
Aprilia
Latina
Nettuno
Anzio
Sabáudia
Terracina
Gaeta
Golfo di Gaeta
Ponza
Ìsole Ponziane
Ventoténe
TYRRHENIAN SEA
3589
Ústica
Palermo
Bagheria
Tràpani
Ìsole Égadi
Favignana
Marèttimo
Marsala
Mazara del Vallo
Castelvetrano
Sciacca
Agrigento
Porto Empédocle
SICI
Strait of Sicily
Pantelleria
(Italy)
Ìs. de la Galite
(Tunisia)
Canal de la Galite
Bizerte
BIZERTE
Golfe de Tunis
Zembra
C. Bon
TUNIS
La Goulette
La Marsa
Kelibia
Menzel-Temime
Hammamet
Nabeul
NABEUL
Béja
BÉJA
JENDOUBA
Jendouba
ZAGHOUAN
TUNISIA
MEDITE
1698
261

Projection : Lambert's Conformal Conic

East from Greenwich

TAV (Treno Alta Velocità)

ADRIATIC SEA
IONIAN SEA
RANEAN SEA
Strait of Otranto
Golfo di Táranto
Golfo di Manfredónia
Golfo di Salerno
Golfo di Policastro
Golfo di Sant' Eufémia
Golfo di Squillace
Golfo di Gióia
Golfo di Catánia
Golfo di Noto
Str. di Messina
BASILICATA
CALÁBRIA
GREECE
Ísole Eólie
Strómboli
Vulcano
Lipari
Salina
Filicudi
Alicudi
Panarea
Monti Nébrodi
Etna
Bari
Táranto
Brindisi
Lecce
Fóggia
Campobasso
Potenza
Matera
Cosenza
Catanzaro
Crotone
Messina
Réggio di Calábria
Catánia
Siracusa
Ragusa
Enna
Benevento
Avellino
Salerno
Barletta
Andria
Trani
Molfetta
Monópoli
Otranto
Gallipoli
C. Santa Maria di Léuca
Vieste
Capri
Sorrento
Lamezia Terme
Vibo Valentia
Isola di Capo Rizzuto
Durrës
Tiranë
Vlorë
Kerkyra (Corfu)
Paxi
Othoni
Stenon Kerkyras
Sazanit
Karaburun
7
8
9
10
11
12
A
B
C
D
E
F
199
202
204
15
16
17
18
19
20
37
38
39
40
41
COPYRIGHT PHILIP'S

Underlined towns give their name to the administrative area in which they stand.

1:2 000 000

182
199
201
204
BOSNIA-HERZEGOVINA
CROATIA
SERBIA
KOSOVO
MONTENEGRO
ALBANIA
MACEDONIA
ITALY
ADRIATIC SEA
Strait of Otranto
VOJVODINA
BEOGRAD (Belgrade)
Sarajevo
Podgorica
Prishtinë (Priština)
Skopje
Tiranë
SOFIYA
Thessaloniki (Salonica)
KENTRIKI MAKEDONIA
DYTIKI MAKEDONIA
Thessaloniki Kolpos
Kerkyra (Corfu)
Brindisi
Lecce
Craiova
Novi Sad
Niš
Durrës
Shkodër
Ohrid
Bitola
Prilep
Projection : Lambert's Conformal Conic
East from Greenwich

BLACK SEA
ROMANIA
BULGARIA
TURKEY
BUCUREŞTI (Bucharest)
Constanţa
Varna
Burgas
Ruse
Pleven
Plovdiv
Edirne
ISTANBUL
Bursa
Çanakkale
Tekirdağ
Galaţi
Brăila
Ploieşti
Piteşti
Dunărea
Marmara Denizi (Sea of Marmara)
Sea of Thrace
Saros Körfezi
Thasos
Samothraki
Limnos
Gökçeada (Imroz)
Istanbul Boğazi (Bosporus)
Çanakkale Boğazi (Dardanelles)
DELTA DUNĂRII
Lacul Razim
Stara Zagora
Kazanlăk
Sliven
Yambol
Shumen
Dobrich
Silistra
Kărdzhali
Smolyan
Alexandroupoli
Komotini
Xanthi
Kavala
Lüleburgaz
Kırklareli
Çorlu
Gebze
İzmit
İnegöl
Bandırma
Mudanya
Yalova
Gemlik
Tulcea
Călăraşi
Slobozia
Buzău
Târgovişte
Giurgiu
Alexandria
Veliko Tărnovo
Gabrovo
Lovech
Khaskovo
Pazardzhik
Asenovgrad
Dimitrovgrad
Svilengrad
Harmanli
Keşan
Gelibolu
Marmara
Erdek
Mustafakemalpaşa
COPYRIGHT PHILIP'S




Underlined towns give their name to the administrative area in which they stand.

1:2 000 000

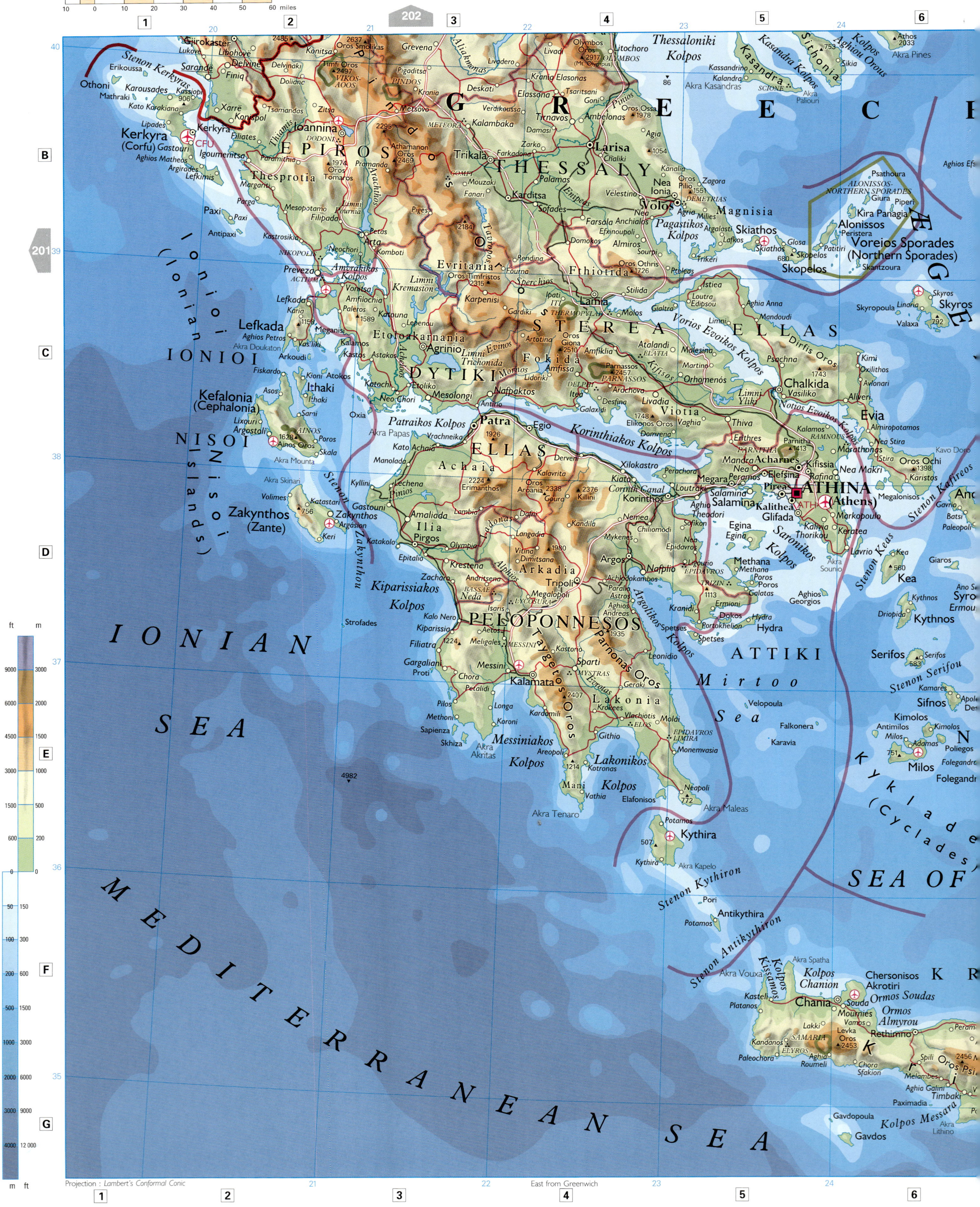
km
miles
GREECE
EPIROS
THESSALY
STEREA ELLAS
DYTIKI ELLAS
PELOPONNESOS
ATTIKI
IONIOI NISOI (Ionian Islands)
Voreios Sporades (Northern Sporades)
IONIAN SEA
MEDITERRANEAN SEA
SEA OF
Mirtoo Sea
Kyklades (Cyclades)
Kerkyra (Corfu)
Ioannina
Larisa
Volos
Lamia
Lefkada
Kefalonia (Cephalonia)
Zakynthos (Zante)
Patra
Korinthiakos Kolpos
Patraikos Kolpos
ATHINA (Athens)
Pireas
Salamina
Chalkida
Evia
Korinthos
Argos
Tripoli
Kalamata
Sparti
Kiparissiakos Kolpos
Messiniakos Kolpos
Lakonikos Kolpos
Argolikos Kolpos
Saronikos Kolpos
Kythira
Antikythira
Stenon Kythiron
Stenon Antikythiron
Chania
Rethimno
Gavdos
Milos
Kea
Kythnos
Serifos
Sifnos
Skiathos
Skopelos
Alonissos
Skyros
Thessaloniki Kolpos
Pagastikos Kolpos
Projection: Lambert's Conformal Conic
East from Greenwich

7
8
9
10
11
12
203
212
B
C
D
E
F
G
MEDITERRANEAN SEA
AIGAIO
VOREIO AIGAIO
Dodecanese (Dodekanisos)
TURKEY
Stenon Karpathou
Stenon Kasou
Çanakkale
Gökçeada (Imroz)
Bozcaada
Limnos
Lesbos
Mitilini
Edremit Körfezi
Edremit
Ayvalık
Bergama
Balıkesir
Bursa
İnegöl
Mustafakemalpaşa
Eskişehir
Kütahya
Tavşanlı
Simav
Gediz
Uşak
Afyon (Afyonkarahisar)
Akhisar
Manisa
Aliağa
Foça
Menemen
İzmir (Smyrna)
Çandarlı Körfezi
Chios
Psara
Çeşme
Torbalı
Ödemiş
Salihli
Alaşehir
Kuşadası
Samos
Ikaria
Mykonos
Naxos
Amorgos
Thira
Aydın
Nazilli
Denizli
Söke
Milas
Didim (Yenihisar)
Bodrum
Kos
Kalimnos
Leros
Patmos
Astipalea
Tilos
Nissiros
Simi
Muğla
Marmaris
Dalaman
Fethiye
Rhodes
Lindos
Karpathos
Kasos
Saria
Gökova Körfezi
Burdur
Isparta
Eğirdir
Antalya
Kaş
Kalkan
Finike
Megisti (Kastelorizo)
Sitia
Lasithi
Ierapetra
Koufonisi
Gaidouronisi
Kolpos Mirabello
Elmalı
Beydağları
Babadağ
Acıpayam
Tavas
Pamukkale
Buldan
Tire
Selçuk
Ephesus
Aydın Dağları
Boz Dağları
Simav Dağları
Kaz Dağı

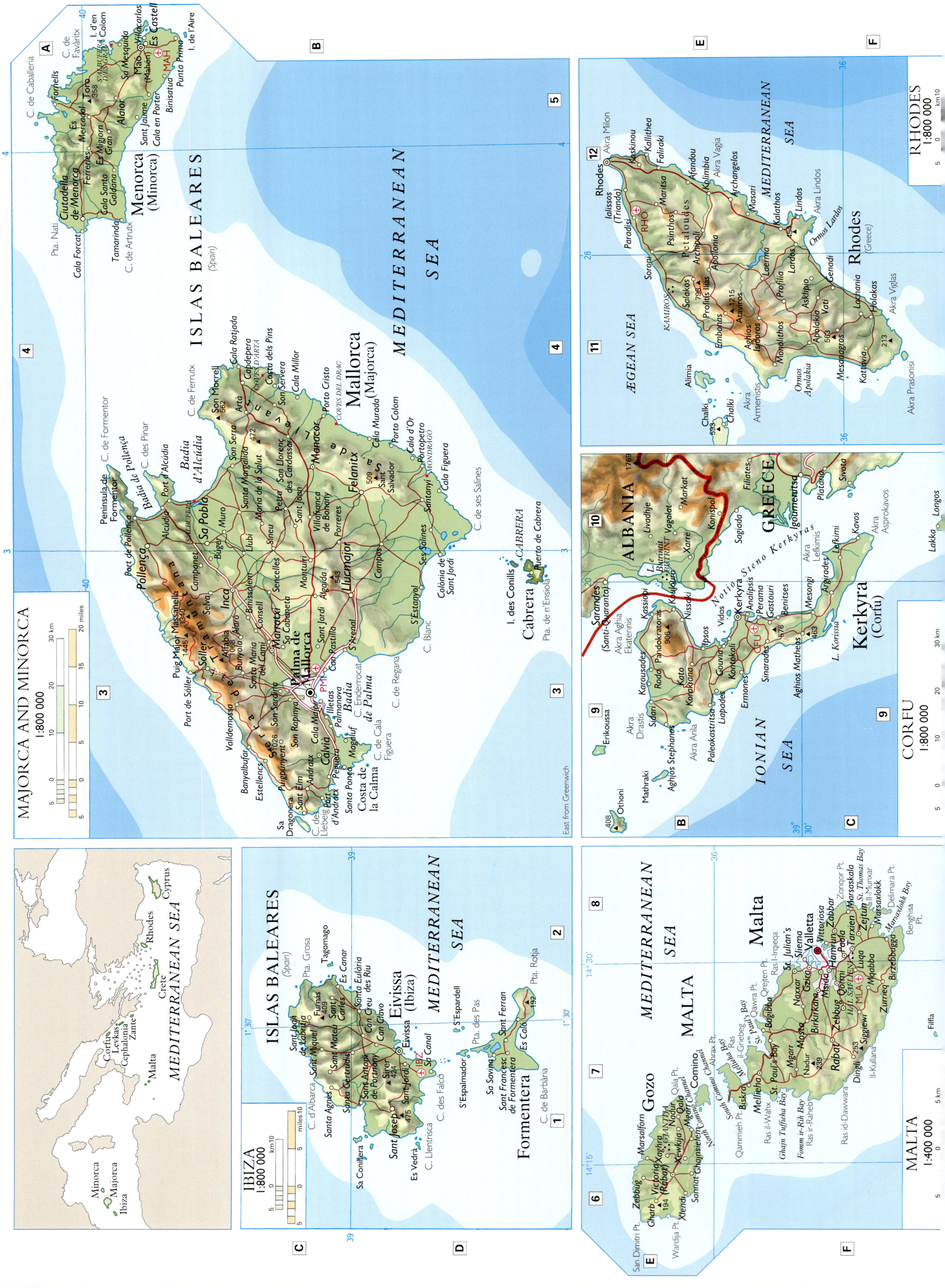
MAJORCA AND MINORCA
1:800 000
ISLAS BALEARES
(Spain)
MEDITERRANEAN SEA
Menorca
(Minorca)
Mallorca
(Majorca)
Palma de Mallorca
Cabrera
East from Greenwich
IBIZA
1:800 000
Eivissa
(Ibiza)
Formentera
MALTA
1:400 000
Malta
Gozo
Comino
Valletta
CORFU
1:800 000
Kerkyra
(Corfu)
IONIAN SEA
ALBANIA
GREECE
RHODES
1:800 000
Rhodes
(Greece)
ÆGEAN SEA
Minorca
Majorca
Ibiza
Corfu
Levkas
Cephalonia
Zante
Malta
Crete
Rhodes
Cyprus

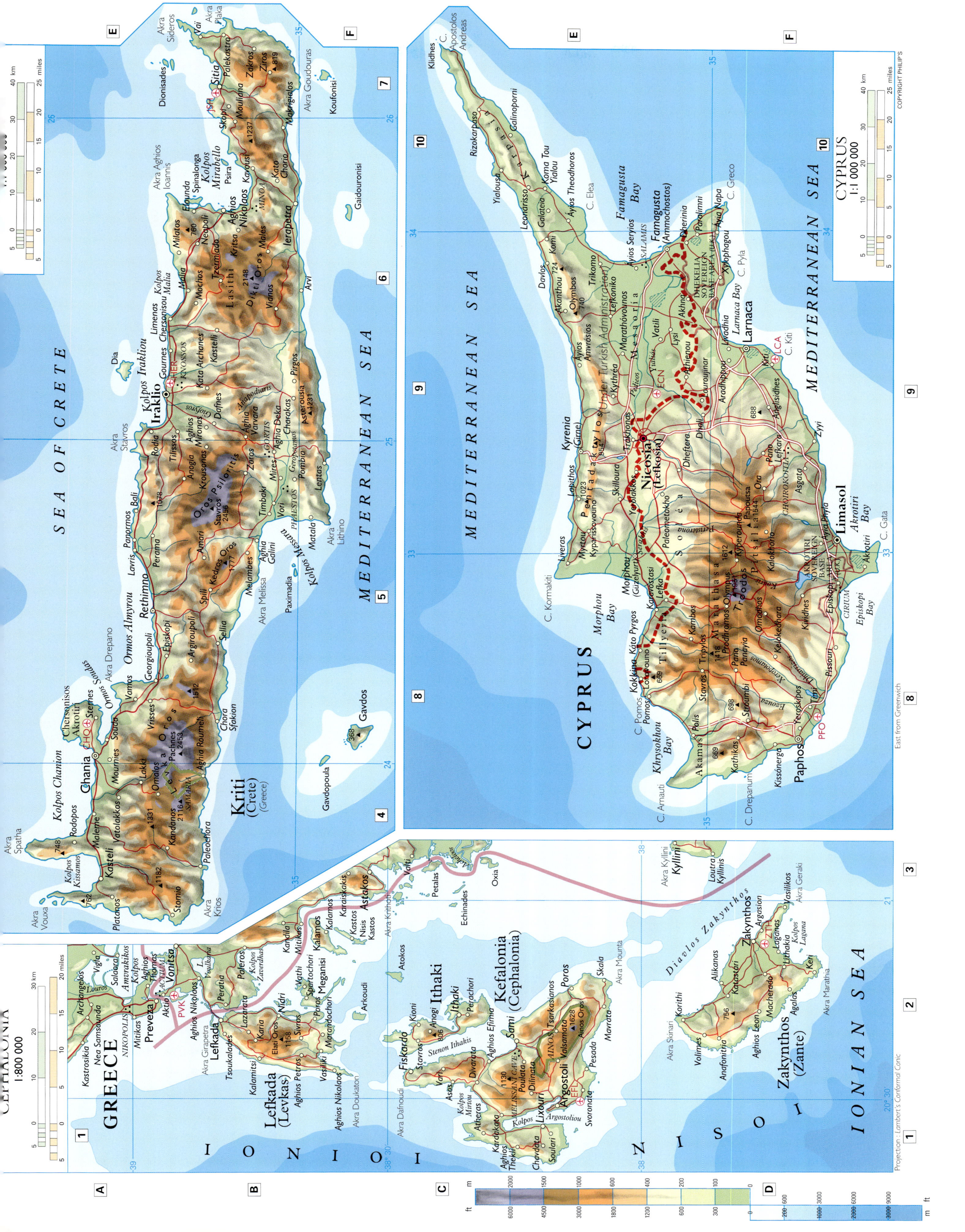
SEA OF CRETE
MEDITERRANEAN SEA
Kriti
(Crete)
(Greece)
Gavdos
Chania
Rethimno
Iraklio
Agios Nikolaos
Ierapetra
Sitia
CYPRUS
CYPRUS
1:1 000 000
Nicosia
(Lefkosia)
Kyrenia
(Girne)
Famagusta
(Ammochostos)
Larnaca
Limasol
Paphos
MEDITERRANEAN SEA
GREECE
Lefkada
(Levkas)
Ithaki
Kefalonia
(Cephalonia)
Zakynthos
(Zante)
IONIAN SEA
IONIOI NISOI
Preveza
Argostoli
Projection : Lambert's Conformal Conic
East from Greenwich
COPYRIGHT PHILIP'S

# ASIA

1:40 000 000

ARCTIC OCEAN
PACIFIC OCEAN
INDIAN OCEAN
Bering Sea
Sea of Okhotsk
Sea of Japan
East China Sea
South China Sea
Philippine Sea
Bay of Bengal
Arabian Sea
Caspian Sea
Black Sea
Mediterranean Sea
Red Sea
Persian Gulf
Barents Sea
Kara Sea
Laptev Sea
Norwegian Sea
Baltic Sea
North Sea
Adriatic Sea
West Siberian Plain
Central Siberian Plateau
North European Plain
Ural Mts.
Verkhoyansk Ra.
Plateau of Tibet
Kunlun Shan
Tien Shan
Himalaya
Hindu Kush
Pamirs
Karakoram Ra.
Gobi
Plateau of Mongolia
Takla Makan
Kara Kum
Kyzyl Kum
Caucasus
Zagros Mts.
Anatolia
Arabia
Rub' al Khali (Empty Quarter)
India
Deccan
Indo-China
Malay Peninsula
Borneo
Sumatra
Java
New Guinea
Philippines
Japan
Korea
Sri Lanka
Africa
Australia
COPYRIGHT PHILIP'S
East from Greenwich
Projection: Bonne

1:40 000 000

RUSSIA
1 Adygea
2 Karachey-Cherkessia
3 Kabardino-Balkaria
4 North Ossetia-Alaniya
5 Ingushetia
6 Chechenia
7 Dagestan
8 Mordvinia
9 Chuvashia
10 Mari El
11 Tatarstan
12 Udmurtia
AZERBAIJAN
13 Naxçivan
GEORGIA
14 Ajaria
15 Abkhazia
RUSSIA
KAZAKHSTAN
MONGOLIA
CHINA
INDIA
PAKISTAN
AFGHANISTAN
IRAN
TURKEY
SAUDI ARABIA
JAPAN
PHILIPPINES
INDONESIA
MALAYSIA
THAILAND
BURMA
VIETNAM
LAOS
CAMBODIA
NEPAL
BHUTAN
SRI LANKA
OMAN
YEMEN
Caspian Sea
Black Sea
Arabian Sea
Bay of Bengal
South China Sea
East China Sea
Sea of Japan
Sea of Okhotsk
Bering Sea
Kara Sea
Barents Sea
Laptev Sea
Red Sea
Mediterranean Sea
PACIFIC OCEAN
INDIAN OCEAN
Hanoi Capital Cities
Projection: Bonne
COPYRIGHT PHILIP'S

50 0 25 50 75 100 125 150 175 km

50 0 25 50 75 100 125 miles

1: 4 000 000

1 2 3 4 5 6 7
189
203
204
256
A B C D E F G
BLACK SEA
MEDITERRANEAN SEA
BULGARIA
GREECE
CYPRUS
LEBANON
ISRAEL
WEST BANK
TURKEY
Anadolu
İSTANBUL
İstanbul Boğazi (Bosporus)
Marmara Denizi (Sea of Marmara)
Edirne
Tekirdağ
Çanakkale
Bursa
Balıkesir
İzmir (Smyrna)
Manisa
Aydın
Denizli
Muğla
Uşak
Kütahya
Eskişehir
ANKARA
Zonguldak
Bolu
Kastamonu
Sinop
Samsun
Amasya
Tokat
Çorum
Yozgat
Kırşehir
Kırıkkale
Sivas
Kayseri
Nevşehir
Aksaray
Niğde
Konya
Afyon (Afyonkarahisar)
Isparta
Burdur
Antalya
Antalya Körfezi
Karaman (Laranda)
İçel (Mersin)
Tarsus
Adana
Osmaniye
Kahramanmaraş
Gaziantep (Antep)
İskenderun
Antakya
Halab (Alep)
Al Lādhiqīyah (Latakia)
Hamāh
Hims (Homs)
Tarābulus (Tripoli)
Bayrūt (Beirut)
Saydā
Sūr
Dimashq (Damascus)
Hefa (Haifa)
Tel Aviv-Yafo
Jerusalem
'Ammān
Nicosia
Famagusta
Larnaca
Limassol
Paphos
Troodos
Lesbos
Chios
Samos
Ikaria
Rhodes
Karpathos
Kasos
Dodekanisa
Tuz Gölü
Toros Dağları
Köroğlu Dağları
Küre Dağları
Projection: Conical with two standard parallels

CASPIAN SEA
Caucasus Mountains
RUSSIA
DAGESTAN
GEORGIA
ARMENIA
AZERBAIJAN
TURKEY
IRAN
IRAQ
SYRIA
Kurdistan
Al Jazīrah
Syrian Desert
(Mesopotamia)
Anadolu Dağlari
Güneydoğu Toroslar
Bingöl Dağlari
Van Gölü
Sevana Lich
Daryācheh-ye Orūmīyeh
Sochi
Gagra
Sokhumi (Aqua)
Kutaisi
Batumi
Poti
TBILISI
Rustavi
Vladikavkaz
Groznyy
Makhachkala
Derbent
Gyumri
Vanadzor
YEREVAN
Gäncä
Mingäçevir
Sumqayit
BAKI (Baku)
Nagorno-Karabakh (Under Armenian Control)
NAXÇIVAN
Lankäran
Rize
Trabzon
Giresun
Erzurum
Erzincan
Kars
Ağri
Van
Muş
Bitlis
Siirt
Batman
Diyarbakır
Elâzığ
Malatya
Şanlıurfa (Urfa)
Mardin
Cizre
Hakkâri
Tabrīz
Ardabīl
Rasht
Orūmīyeh (Urmia)
Zanjān
Hamadān
Kermānshāh (Bākhtarān)
Sanandaj
Khorramābād
Borūjerd
Dezfūl
Al Qāmishlī
Al Ḩasakah
Ar Raqqah
Dayr az Zawr
Al Mawşil (Mosul)
Arbil (Irbil)
Dahūk
As Sulaymānīyah
Kirkūk
Tikrīt
Sāmarrā'
Ba'qūbah
BAGHDĀD
Ar Ramādī
Al Fallūjah
Karbalā'
Al Ḩillah
An Najaf
Ad Dīwānīyah
Al Kūt
Al 'Amārah
Nahr al Furāt (Euphrates)
Nahr Dijlah (Tigris)
Kür
Araks
East from Greenwich
COPYRIGHT PHILIP'S

191
216
247
246

Underlined towns give their name to the administrative area in which they stand

1:16 000 000

RUSSIA
1 Adygea
2 Karachey-Cherkessia
3 Kabardino-Balkaria
4 North Ossetia-Alaniya
5 Ingushetia
6 Chechenia
7 Dagestan
8 Mordvinia
9 Chuvashia
10 Mari El
11 Tatarstan
12 Udmurtia
13 Khakassia
AZERBAIJAN
14 Naxçıvan
GEORGIA
15 Ajaria
16 Abkhazia
UKRAINE
17 Crimea
Norwegian Sea
Barents Sea
Kara Sea
Black Sea
Caspian Sea
Gulf of Bothnia
Baltic Sea
North Sea
RUSSIA
KAZAKHSTAN
UKRAINE
BELARUS
POLAND
FINLAND
SWEDEN
NORWAY
TURKMENISTAN
UZBEKISTAN
KYRGYZSTAN
TAJIKISTAN
AFGHANISTAN
IRAN
IRAQ
TURKEY
MOSKVA
ST PETERSBURG
ASTANA
ALMATY
TASHKENT
BAKI (Baku)
TEHRAN
Projection: Conical Orthomorphic with two standard parallels
East from Greenwich


238
239

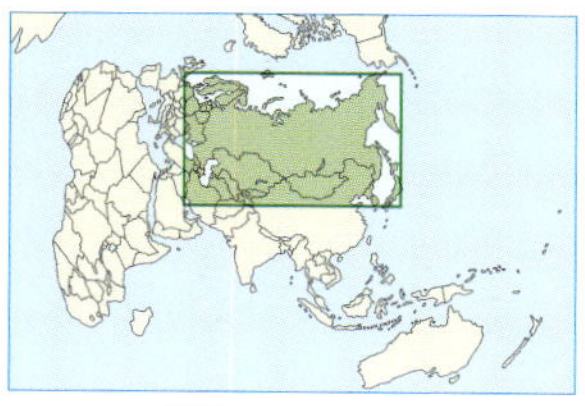

150
A
B
C
D
E
F
9
10
11
12
13
14
15
16
17
18
19
OCEAN
Laptev Sea
East Siberian Sea
Chukchi Sea
Bering Sea
Bering Str.
Sea of Okhotsk
Sea of Japan (East Sea)
Severnaya Zemlya
Poluostrov Taymyr
Byrranga Gory
Novosibirskiye Ostrova
Ostrov Kotelnyy
Ostrov Vrangelya
Chukotskoye Nagorye
Chukotskiy Poluostrov
Koryakskoye Nagorye
Sredinnyy Khrebet
Poluostrov Kamchatka
Kolymskoye Nagorye
Khrebet Cherskogo
Verkhoyanskiy Khrebet
DALNEVOSTOCHNY
Khrebet Dzhugdzur
Stanovoy Khrebet
Yablonovyy Khrebet
Khrebet Sikhote Alin
Sakhalin
Kurilskiye Ostrova
Hokkaidō
Honshū
RUSSIA
MONGOLIA
CHINA
NORTH KOREA
SOUTH KOREA
JAPAN
Dongbei (Manchuria)
Gobi
Da Hinggan Ling
Oz. Baykal
Lena
Kolyma
Amur
Tiksi
Yakutsk
Magadan
Okhotsk
Khabarovsk
Vladivostok
Petropavlovsk-Kamchatskiy
Yuzhno-Sakhalinsk
Komsomolsk-na-Amure
Blagoveshchensk
Chita
Ulan Ude
Irkutsk
Bratsk
Krasnoyarsk
Norilsk
ULAANBAATAR
HARBIN
CHANGCHUN
SHENYANG
BEIJING
PYONGYANG
SEOUL
SAPPORO
KYOTO
OSAKA
KOBE
Arctic Circle
International Date Line


218
219

50 0 100 200 300 400 km
50 0 50 100 150 200 250 miles
1:8 000 000
191
214
187
247
1 2 3 4 5 6
B C D F
ft m
18 000 6000
12 000 4000
9000 3000
6000 2000
4500 1500
3000 1000
1500 500
600 200
0 0
100 300
200 600
500 1500
m ft
Projection : Modified Miller oblated stereographic
MORDVINIA
Saransk
Ryazhsk
Morshansk
Yelets
Michurinsk
Lipetsk
Tambov
Penza
Kirsanov
Usman
Voronezh
Rtishchevo
Petrovsk
Balashov
Borisoglebsk
Liski
Pavlovsk
Buturlinovka
Kalach
Mikhaylovka
Don
UKRAINE
Luhansk
VOLGOGRAD
Volzhskiy
Dubovka
Kamyshin
Nikolayevsk
Saratov
Engels
Pugachev
Yershov
Pushkino
Krasnyy Kut
Balakovo
Volsk
Syzran
Chapayevsk
Novokuybyshevsk
SAMARA
Togliatti
Ulyanovsk
Dimitrovgrad
Kuznetsk
Inza
Almetyevsk
Leninogorsk
Tuymazy
Oktyabrskiy
Belebey
Bugulma
Abdulino
Buguruslan
Buzuluk
Sorochinsk
BASHKORTOSTAN
UFA
Sterlitamak
Salavat
Ishimbay
Meleuz
Kumertau
Orenburg
Ural
Mednogorsk
Novotroitsk
Orsk
Gay
Akbulak
Sol-Iletsk
Magnitogorsk
Beloretsk
Uralskie Gory
Zlatoust
Miass
CHELYABINSK
Kopeysk
Korkino
Yemanzhelinsk
Yuzhnouralsk
Troitsk
KURGAN
Plast
Kartaly
Sibay
Baymak
Bredy
Qarabalyq
Fedorovka
Kachar
Qostanay
Rudnyy
Lisakovsk
Denisovka
Zhetiqara
Torghay
Ustirti
Zhayylma
Yasnyy
Svetlyy
Domborovskiy
Oral
Aqsay
Zhympity
Zashaghan
Chapaev
Kirgiziya Steppe
BATYS QAZAQSTAN
Zhanibek
Aralsor Köli
Zhangaqala
Novouzensk
Aleksandrov Gay
Qobda
Aqtöbe
Khromtau
Komsomolskoe
Alga
Qandyaghash
Shubarqudyq
Temir
Embi
Shubarshi
AQTÖBE
Mughalzhar Taūy
Qarabutaq
Yrghyz
Shalqar
Aral Mangy Qaraqumy
Sekseūil
Aral
Qaraoba
Ülken Borsyq Qumy
Northern Aral Sea
Qazaly
Zhangaqazaly
Baygonyr (Baikonur)
Zhosaly
Southern Aral Sea
Aralqum
Zhaslyk
Muynak
QORAQALPOGHISTAN
Qüngirot
Chimboy
Nukus
Beruni
Urganch
Xiva
Dasoguz
UZBEKISTAN
Uchquduq
Kyz
Zarafsho
BUXORO
Buxoro (Bukhara)
Gazli
Kogon
Qarakol
Navo
Türkmenabat (Chardzhou)
Amudarya
Amudar
Atamyrat
Garabil Belentligi
Andkhoy
Meymaneh
Bayramaly
Mary
Yolöten
MARY
Dashköpri
Serhetabat
Torghay
Narn Qum
Caspian Depression
ATYRAŪ
Atyraū
Inderbor
Maqat
Qulsary
Balyqshy
Oyyl
Astrakhan
Kosshaghyl
Boranku
Beyneu
MANGGHYSTAU
CASPIAN SEA
Tüledi Araldary
Fort Shevchenko
Mangghystaū
Aqtaū
Zhangaözen
Shetpe
Ustyurt Plateau
Bekdash
Garabogazköl Aylagy
BALKAN
Türkmenbashi
Hazar (Cheleken)
Ogurja Ada
Balkanabat (Nebitdag)
Gumdag
Bereket
Serdar (Gyzylarbat)
Etrek
Esenguly
Garrygala
Ashgabat (Ashkhabad)
Tejen
Sarakhs
MASHHAD
Neyshabur
Sabzevar
Bojnurd
Kopet Dag
TURKMENISTAN
Garagum
DAŞOGUZ
Ahal
Baherden
Kāh-e Sorkh
Mangghystaū
Makhachkala
Kaspiysk
Derbent
Xaçmaz
Quba
Sumqayit
BAKI (Baku)
Älät
Salyan
Neftçala
Lankäran
Astara
Tälesh
Bandar-e Anzali
Rasht
GILAN
MAZANDARAN
Babol
Sari
Gorgan
Amol
Gonbad-e Kāvus
GOLESTAN
KHORASAN-E SHEMALI
KHORASAN-E RAZAVI
Dāmghān
Semnān
SEMNAN
Dasht-e Kavir
IRAN
TEHRAN
Qazvin
KARAJ
QOM
Kāshān
Arāk
ESFAHAN
YAZD
Herat
BADGHIS
Safid Kuh
Torghay
Elista
KALMYKIA
Divnoye
Salsk
Tikhoretsk
Kropotkin
Armavir
Stavropol
Nevinnomyssk
Blagodarnyy
Budennovsk
Neftekumsk
Georgiyevsk
Pyatigorsk
Kislovodsk
Cherkessk
Nalchik
Mozdok
CHECHENIA
Grozny
Kizlyar
DAGESTAN
Caucasus Mountains
GEORGIA
TBILISI
Rustavi
Kutaisi
Poti
Sokhumi
Black Sea
Batumi
Gori
Telavi
Mingäçevir
AZERBAIJAN
Gäncä
Şäki
ARMENIA
YEREVAN
Vanadzor
Gyumri
Kars
TURKEY
Van Gölü
Van
Ağrı
Naxçıvan
Khvoy
Salmās
Orumiyeh
Marand
Ahar
TABRIZ
Ardabil
Maragheh
Miyaneh
Mahābād
Zanjan
Saqqez
KORDESTAN
Sanandaj
HAMADAN
Hamadan
Kermānshāh
Malāyer
Borujerd
LORESTAN
Khorramābād
Dezful
Zagros
Kuhha-ye Alborz
Reshteh-ye Alborz
AL MAWSIL
NINAWA
Arbil
Kirkuk
As Sulaymaniyah
BAGHDAD
IRAQ
Al Kut
Al Hayy
Ba'qubah
Dahuk
ROSTOV
Novocherkassk
Novoshakhtinsk
Shakhty
Volgodonsk
Kotelnikovo
Tsimlyanskoye Vdkhr.
Volga
Akhtuba
Privolzhskaya Vozvyshennost
Yergeni Vozvyshennost
Caspian

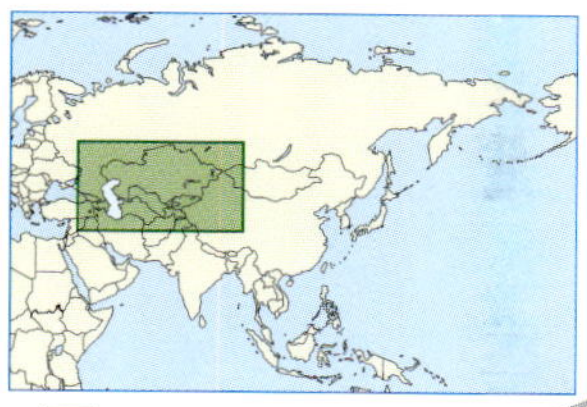

7
214
8
9
10
11
12
13
B
C
D
E
F
218
217
242
50
45
40
35
70
75
80
85
OMSK
NOVOSIBIRSK
Petropavl
Tatarsk
Berdsk
Barnaul
Novokuznetsk
Biysk
Gorno-Altaysk
Abakan
Minusinsk
Kyzyl
Pavlodar
Ekibastuz
Semey (Semipalatinsk)
Öskemen
Rubtsovsk
Kökshetau
Astana
Qaraghandy (Karaghanda)
Temirtaū
Balqash
Balqash Köli (L. Balkhash)
Zaysan Köli (Oz. Zaysan)
Alakol
Ebinur Hu
Taldyqorghan
Qapshaghay
ALMATY (Alma Ata)
Bishkek (Frunze)
Ysyk-Köl
Tokmak
Naryn
Osh
Jalal-Abad
Andijon
Namangan
Farghona
TOSHKENT (Tashkent)
Samarqand
Dushanbe
Khujand
Qŭrghonteppa
Kŭlob
Termiz
Mazar-e Sharif
KABUL
Jalalabad
Peshawar
Mardan
Abbottabad
SRINAGAR
Gilgit
Leh
Kashi (Kashgar)
Shache (Yarkand)
Yecheng
Hotan
Aksu
Kuqa
Korla
Yining (Gulja)
Karamay
ÜRÜMQI
Turpan
Hami
Altay
K A Z A K H S T A N
R U S S I A
M O N G O L I A
C H I N A
K Y R G Y Z S T A N
T A J I K I S T A N
A F G H A N I S T A N
P A K I S T A N
I N D I A
U Z B E K I S T A N
XINJIANG UYGUR ZIZHIQU (SINKIANG)
XIZANG ZIZHIQU (TIBET)
JAMMU & KASHMIR
Betpaqdala
Saryesik-Atyraū Qumy
Moyynqum
Usaqshoqylygh
Qazaqtyng
Tarim Pendi
Taklamakan Shamo
Junggar Pendi
Gurbantünggüt Shamo
Turpan Pendi
Kuruktag
T'ien Shan
Borohoro Shan
Bogda Shan
Karateki Shan
Halik Shan
Khrebet Tarbagatay
Altay
Altun Shan
Kunlun Shan
Karakoram Range
Pamir
Hindu Kush
Alai Range
Fergana Range
Talas Ala Too
Kungey Ala Too
Terskey Ala Too
Ili
Ertis (Irtysh)
Ob
Syrdarya
Yenisey
Tarim He
Hotan He
Yarkant He
Indus
Lop Nur
Bosten Hu
Aksai Chin
Underlined towns give their name to the administrative area in which they stand.
COPYRIGHT PHILIP'S

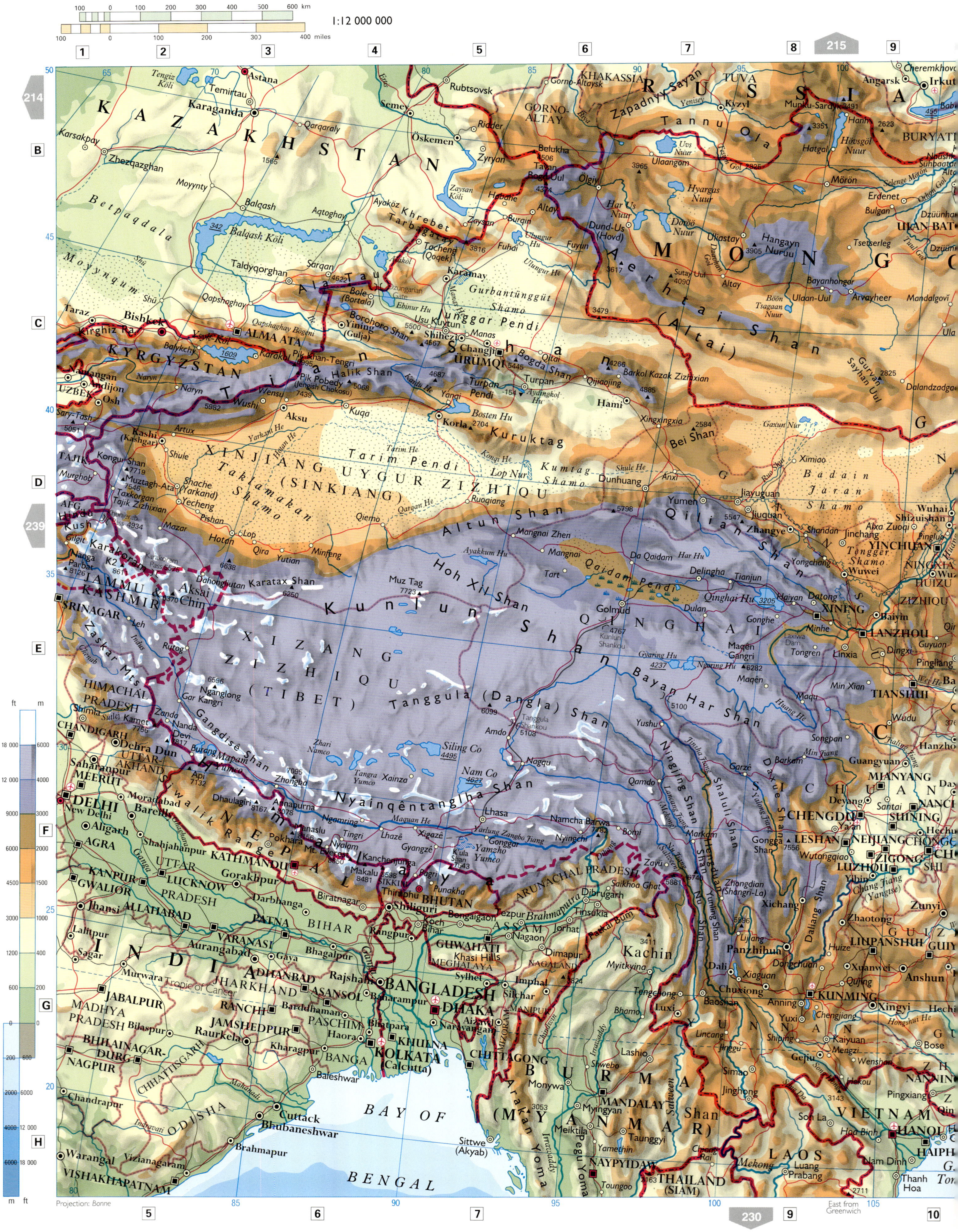
1:12 000 000
Projection: Bonne
East from Greenwich
KAZAKHSTAN
RUSSIA
MONGOLIA
KYRGYZSTAN
UZBEK.
TAJIK.
AFG.
INDIA
NEPAL
BHUTAN
BANGLADESH
BURMA (MYANMAR)
LAOS
VIETNAM
THAILAND (SIAM)
XINJIANG UYGUR ZIZHIQU (SINKIANG)
XIZANG ZIZHIQU (TIBET)
QINGHAI
SICHUAN
GANSU
YUNNAN
JAMMU & KASHMIR
HIMACHAL PRADESH
UTTARAKHAND
UTTAR PRADESH
BIHAR
JHARKHAND
MADHYA PRADESH
CHHATTISGARH
ODISHA
ARUNACHAL PRADESH
MEGHALAYA
NAGALAND
TUVA
KHAKASSIA
GORNO ALTAY
BURYATIA
Astana
Karaganda
Almaty
Bishkek
Ürümqi
Kashi (Kashgar)
Lhasa
Xining
Lanzhou
Chengdu
Kunming
Delhi
New Delhi
Kathmandu
Thimphu
Dhaka
Kolkata (Calcutta)
Hanoi
Naypyidaw
Mandalay
Srinagar
Irkutsk
Tarim Pendi
Taklamakan Shamo
Kunlun Shan
Tian Shan
Altun Shan
Qilian Shan
Tanggula (Dangla) Shan
Nyainqêntanglha Shan
Gangdise Shan
Bayan Har Shan
Karakoram
Himalaya
Hoh Xil Shan
Qaidam Pendi
Gurbantünggüt Shamo
Badain Jaran Shamo
Tengger Shamo
Aerhtai Shan (Altai)
Hangayn Nuruu
Tannu Ola
Zapadnyy Sayan
Balqash Köli
Betpaqdala
Moyynqum
Bay of Bengal
Tropic of Cancer
Brahmaputra
Yarlung Zangbo Jiang
Mt. Everest 8850
K2 8611
Siling Co
Nam Co
Qinghai Hu
Bosten Hu

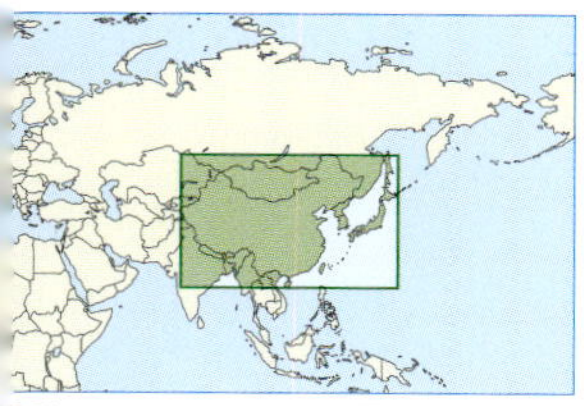

RUSSIA
Sakhalin
Yuzhno-Sakhalinsk
Khabarovsk
Komsomolsk-na-Amur
Blagoveshchensk
La Perouse Str.
Tatarskiy Proliv
Khrebet Sikhote Alin
Hokkaidō
SAPPORO
Vladivostok
Nakhodka
HARBIN
CHANGCHUN
SHENYANG
JILIN
QIQIHAR
MONGOLIA
NEI MONGOL ZIZHIQU (INNER MONGOLIA)
HOHHOT
BEIJING (Peking)
TIANJIN
DALIAN
P'YONGYANG
NORTH KOREA
SEOUL
SOUTH KOREA
BUSAN
SEA OF JAPAN (EAST SEA)
YELLOW SEA
HIROSHIMA
KŌBE
ŌSAKA
KYŌTO
NAGOYA
TŌKYŌ
YOKOHAMA
KAWASAKI
SENDAI
Honshū
Shikoku
Kyūshū
FUKUOKA
KITAKYUSHU
JAPAN
Korea Strait
Jeju-do
PACIFIC OCEAN
EAST CHINA SEA
Ryūkyū-Rettō
Okinawa-Jima
SHANGHAI
NANJING
HANGZHOU
WUHAN
ZHENGZHOU
JINAN
QINGDAO
TAIYUAN
CHANGSHA
NANCHANG
FUZHOU
XIAMEN
GUANGZHOU (Canton)
SHENZHEN
HONG KONG (Xianggang)
Macau
T'AIPEI
TAIWAN
KAOHSIUNG
Taiwan Strait
Tropic of Cancer
SOUTH CHINA SEA
HAINAN
Hainan Dao
HAIKOU
ZHANJIANG
PHILIPPINES
Babuyan Is.
HONG KONG, MACAU AND SHENZHEN
1:800 000
SHENZHEN
Lantau Island (Tai Yue Shan)
Kowloon (Jiulong)
Victoria
HONG KONG (Xianggang)
Macau (Aomen)
ZHUHAI
ZHONGSHAN
Lingding Yang
Zhujiang Kou (Mouth of the Pearl)
Zhu Jiang (Pearl River)
GUANGDONG
New Territories
COPYRIGHT PHILIP'S
232

1:4 000 000
50 0 25 50 75 100 125 150 175 km
50 0 25 50 75 100 125 miles
SEA OF OKHOTSK
Sakhalin
La Perouse Strait
(Sōya-Kaikyō)
HOKKAIDŌ
SAPPORO
Hakodate
Tsugaru-Kaikyō
TOHOKU
Honshū
SENDAI
Akita
Niigata
Sado
SEA OF JAPAN
(EAST SEA)
Yamato Rise
RUSSIA
PRIMORSKIY KRAY
SIKHOTE ALIN
Vladivostok
Nakhodka
Ussuriysk
Lake Khanka
Zaliv Petra Velikogo
CHINA
HEILONGJIANG
JILIN
NORTH KOREA
Najin
Rason
219
227

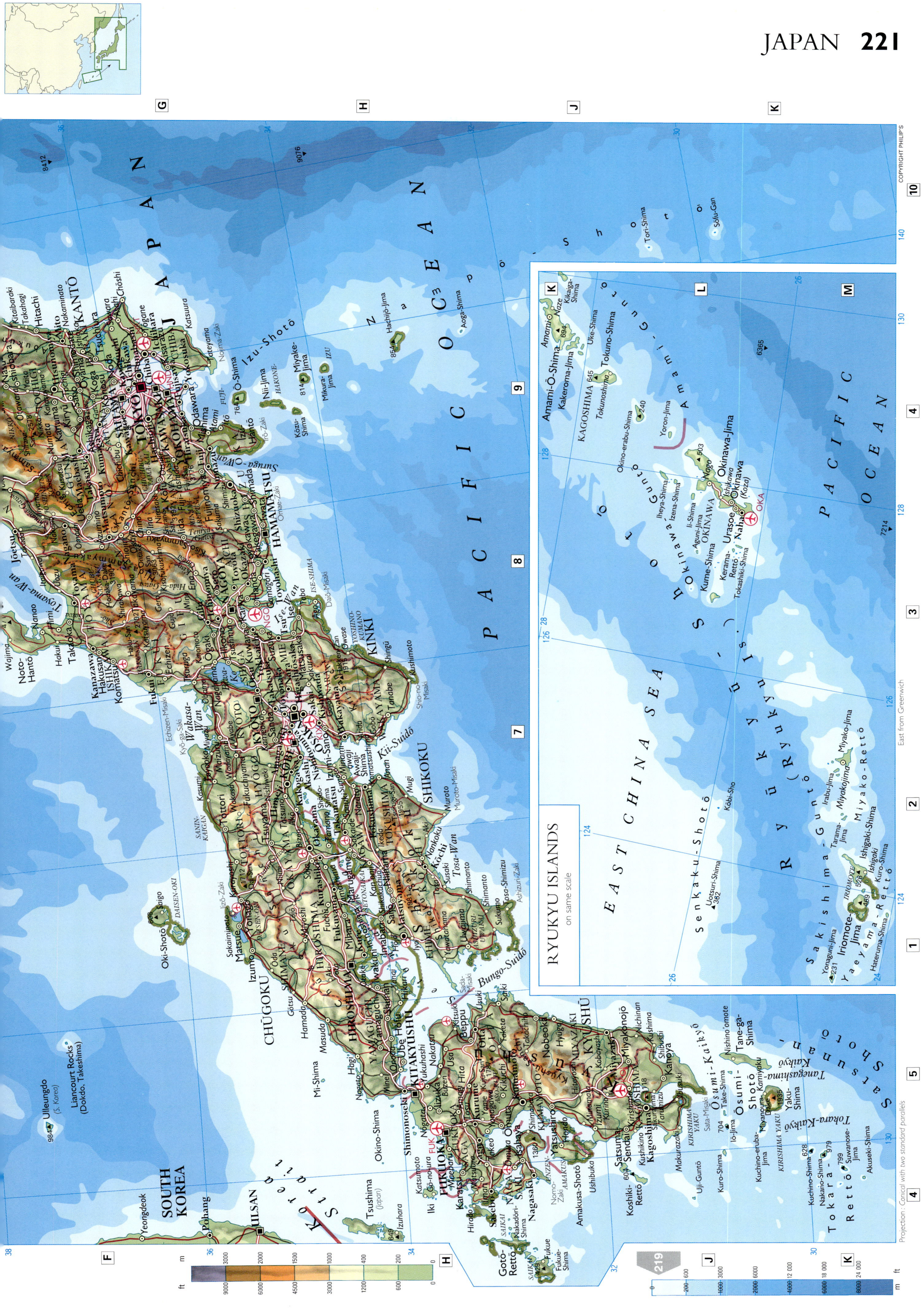
RYUKYU ISLANDS
on same scale
PACIFIC OCEAN
EAST CHINA SEA
Ryūkyū (Ryukyu) Shotō
Amami-Guntō
Okinawa-Jima
Sakishima-Guntō
Miyako-Rettō
Yaeyama-Rettō
Senkaku-Shotō
Nansei-Shotō
JAPAN
SHIKOKU
KYŪSHŪ
CHŪGOKU
KINKI
KANTŌ
Izu-Shotō
SOUTH KOREA
Korea Strait
Tsushima
Ulleungdo
Liancourt Rocks (Dokdo, Takeshima)
Oki-Shotō
Satsunan-Shotō
Tokara-Rettō
TOKYO
OSAKA
KYOTO
NAGOYA
HIROSHIMA
FUKUOKA
Projection: Conical with two standard parallels
East from Greenwich
COPYRIGHT PHILIP'S
219

1:2 000 000
km
miles
SEA OF JAPAN
(EAST SEA)
Oki-Shotō
Daimanji-San
Dōgo
608
Saigō
Dōzen
DAISEN-OKI
Yeongdeok
Heunghae
Pohang
SOUTH KOREA
Honshū
Korea Strait
Kara-Saki
Kamigata
Kamitsushima
Tsushima
Mitsushima
Izuhara
649
Kō-Saki
Higashi-Suidō
Katsumoto
Iki
Gō-no-ura
Iki-Kaikyō
Genkai-Nada
Hibiki-Nada
Mi-Shima
Tsuno-Shima
Ōmi-Shima
Hagi
CHŪGOKU-DISTRICT
Chūgoku-Sanchi
Shimane-Hantō
Jizō-Zaki
Hi-no-Misaki
Hirata
Matsue
Sakaiminato
Yonago
Taisha
Izumo
Shinji
Yasugi
Daitō
Kisuki
Dai-Sen
1729
TOTTORI
Kurayoshi
Tottori
Iwami
Kasumi
Toyooka
SANIN-KAIGAN
Oda
Sanbe-San
1126
Yunotsu
Gōtsu
Hamada
SHIMANE
Gō-Gawa
Dōgo-San
1269
Katsuyama
Niimi
Tsuyama
Ochiai
Bingo-Ochiai
Tōjō
Shōbara
OKAYAMA
Takahashi
Miyoshi
HIROSHIMA
Akiōta
Yoshida
Masuda
Kanmuri-Yama
1339
Aono-Yama
908
Atō
Nagato
YAMAGUCHI
Yamaguchi
Mine
Ogōri
San'yō
Hōfu
Tokuji
Shin-Nan'yō
Shūnan
Kudamatsu
Hikari
Yanai
Iwakuni
Ōtake
Hatsukaichi
HIROSHIMA
Kaita
Kure
Takehara
Higashi-Hiroshima
Fuchū
Fukuyama
Mihara
Onomichi
Kasaoka
Ibara
Yakage
Sōja
Okayama
Kurashiki
Bizen
Saidaiji
Tamano
Shōdo-Shima
Tonoshō
Kojima
Sakaide
Takamatsu
Marugame
Tadotsu
Zentsūji
Kotohira
KAGAWA
Miki
Sanuki
Higashi-kagawa
Naruto
Itano
Tokushima
Komatsushima
Anan
Awaji-Shima
Sumoto
Harima-Nada
Ieshima-Shotō
Himeji
Tatsuno
Aioi
Ako
Takasago
Kakogawa
Sayo
Yamasaki
HYOGO
Wakasa
Chizu
Hidaka
Suga-no-Sen
1510
Wadayama
Ikuno
Nishiwaki
Kasai
Yanahara
Wake
Ōmi-Shima
In'noshima
Kurahashi-Jima
Ondo
Aki-Nada
Hiroshima-Wan
Yashiro-Jima
Heigun-Tō
Iyo-Nada
Hiuchi-Nada
Kan'onji
Onohara
Shikokuchūō
Mima
Ikeda
Mishima
Imabari
Niihama
Saijō
Iyo
Hōjō
Tōyo
Matsuyama
Ishizuchi-Yama
1981
Shikoku-Sanchi
TOKUSHIMA
Tsurugi-San
1955
1423
Otoyo
KŌCHI
Kuma
EHIME
Nagahama
Ōzu
Uchiko
1562
Yawatahama
Uwa
Sada-Misaki-Hantō
Sada-Misaki
Uwajima
Kihoku
Tsushima
Mishō
Nishi-Tosa
Sukumo
865
Tosa-Shimizu
Ashizuri-Zaki
ASHIZURI-UWAKAI
Shimanto
Saga
Susaki
Sakawa
Ino
Nankoku
Kōchi
Kami
Noichi
Aki
Tosa
Tosa-Wan
Tōyō
Muroto
Muroto-Misaki
Mugi
Gamō-Saki
Shikoku
SHIKOKU-DISTRICT
Hōgo-Kaikyō
Bungo-Suidō
Tsurumi-Saki
Oki-no-Shima
Shimonoseki
Onoda
Ube
Suō-Nada
Naga-Shima
Iwai-Jima
Hime-Jima
KITAKYŪSHŪ
Nakama
Ō-Shima
Munakata
Fukuma
Koga
Nōgata
Miyata
Iizuka
Yukuhashi
Tagawa
FUKUOKA
Maebaru
Dazaifu
Kama
Buzen
Nakatsu
Kasuga
Chikushino
Amagi
Futago-Yama
721
Kunisaki
Bungotakada
Kitsuki
Usa
Hiji
Yufu-Dake
1584
Beppu
Beppu-Wan
Tsurusaki
Ōita
Saganoseki
Usuki
ŌITA
Kuju-San
1787
Hita
Kusu
Tsukumi
Taketa
Mie
Saiki
Kamae
Aso
Ichinomiya
Aso-Zan
1592
Sobo-Yama
1758
Takachiho
Hinokage
Nobeoka
Hyūga
Shiiba
MIYAZAKI
Kyūshū-Sanchi
Kunimi-Dake
1739
Kyūshū
KYŪSHŪ-DISTRICT
Saito
Takanabe
Sadowara
Miyazaki
Kobayashi
Kirishima-Yama
1700
KIRISHIMA YAKU
Miyakonojō
Nichinan
Aburatsu
Sōo
Shibushi
Shibushi-Wan
Kushima
Ōsaki
Kanoya
Tarumizu
Kōyama
968
Ōsumi-Hantō
Sata-Misaki
KIRISHIMA YAKU
Kagoshima
KAGOSHIMA
Sakurajima
1118
On-Take
Hayato
Kirishima
Aira
Kagoshima-Wan
Ibusuki
Kiire
Yamagawa
Kaimon-Dake
924
Satsuma-Hantō
Makurazaki
Bō-no-Misaki
Kawanabe
Kaseda
Fukiage
Noma-Saki
Ijūin
Satsuma-Sendai
Kushikino
Miyanojō
Kurino
Yoshimatsu
Ebino
Ōkuchi
Izumi
Akune
Minamata
Hitoyoshi
Taragi
Itsuki
Yatsushiro
Yatsushiro-Kai
Matsubase
Uto
Misumi
KUMAMOTO
Kumamoto
Ozu
Mashiki
Kikuchi
Kōshi
Tamana
Yamaga
Arao
Ōmuta
Setaka
Yame
Kurume
Chikugo
Saga
Ogōri
Tosu
Sefuri-San
1055
SAGA
Takeo
Taku
Ogi
Kashima
Ureshino
Yanagawa
Ariake-Kai
Kurogi
Karatsu
Yobuko
Imari
Matsuura
Arita
Hirado
Hirado-Shima
Ikitsuki-Shima
Ō-Shima
SAIKAI
Saza
Sasebo
Nishi-Sonogi-Hantō
Ōmura-Wan
Ōmura
Isahaya
Tara-Dake
1076
NAGASAKI
Nagayo
Nagasaki
Unzen-Dake
1360
Shimabara
Obama
UNZEN-AMAKUSA
Tachibana-Wan
Nomo-Zaki
Kuchinotsu
Amakusa-Nada
Amakusa-Shotō
Hondo
Matsushima
Kami-Jima
Shimo-Jima
Ushibuka
Naga-Shima
Kami-Koshiki-Jima
Koshiki-Rettō
604
Shimo-Koshiki-Jima
Koshiki-Kaikyō
Kyūshū Trench
5737
Projection: Lambert's Conformal Conic
Shinkansen lines
224

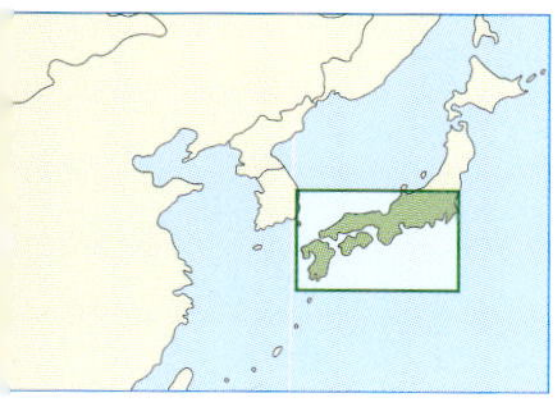

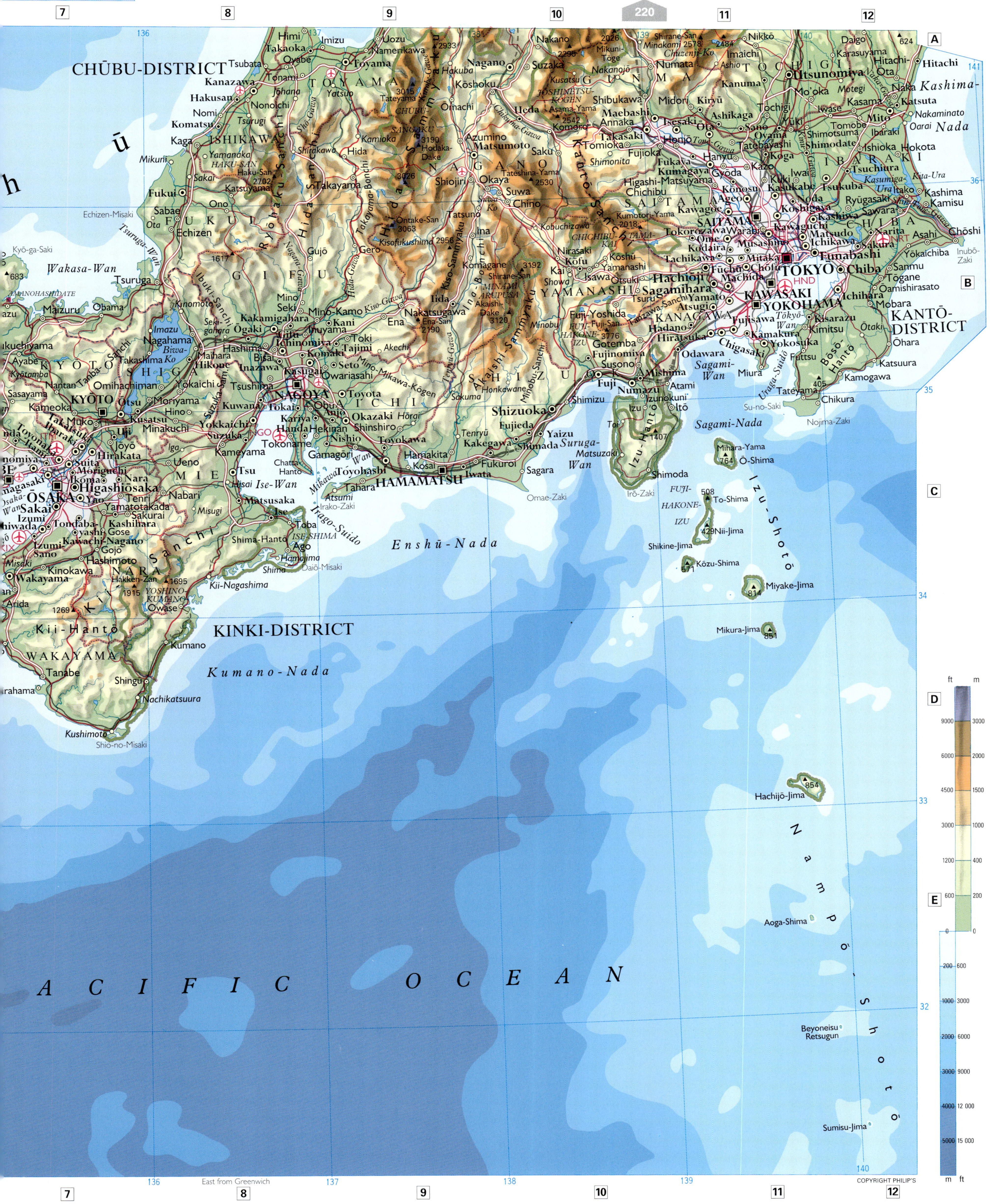
CHŪBU-DISTRICT
KINKI-DISTRICT
KANTŌ-DISTRICT
PACIFIC OCEAN
Enshū-Nada
Kumano-Nada
Sagami-Nada
Suruga-Wan
Ise-Wan
Wakasa-Wan
Kashima-Nada
Izu-Shotō
Nampō-Shotō
Kii-Hantō
Izu-Hantō
TOKYO
YOKOHAMA
KAWASAKI
NAGOYA
ŌSAKA
KYOTO
HAMAMATSU
Shizuoka
Nagano
Toyama
Kanazawa
Fukui
Gifu
Tsu
Nara
Wakayama
Chiba
Utsunomiya
Maebashi
Kōfu
Mito
Saitama
Hachiōji
Sagamihara
Fuji
Numazu
Toyohashi
Okazaki
Toyota
Hachijō-Jima
Miyake-Jima
Ō-Shima
Mikura-Jima
Aoga-Shima
Sumisu-Jima
Beyoneisu Retsugun
East from Greenwich
COPYRIGHT PHILIP'S

1:3 100 000
km
miles
CHINA
NORTH KOREA
SOUTH KOREA
RUSSIA
JAPAN
Dongbei (Manchuria)
LIAONING
JILIN
SEA OF JAPAN (EAST SEA)
YELLOW SEA (HUANG HAI)
Korea Bay
Korea Strait
Tongjosŏn-man
Gyeonggi-man
Changbai Shan
Hamgyong-sanmaek
Nangnim-sanmaek
Longgang Shan
SHENYANG
FUSHUN
Anshan
Liaoyang
Benxi
Dandong
Tonghua
Meihekou
Tumen
Ch'ŏngjin
Rasŏn
Hamhŭng
Hŭngnam
P'YŎNGYANG
NAMP'O
Sinŭiju
Kaesŏng
Haeju
Wŏnsan
SEOUL
INCHEON
SUWON
SEONGNAM
GOYANG
Bucheon
Chuncheon
Gangneung
Sokcho
DAEJEON
Cheongju
Cheonan
DAEGU
Pohang
ULSAN
BUSAN
GWANGJU
Jeonju
Mokpo
Yeosu
Chang-won
Masan
Ulleungdo
Tsushima
JEJU-DO on same scale
Jeju
Jeju-do
Seogwipo
HALLASAN
Projection : Conical with two standard parallels
East from Greenwich
COPYRIGHT PHILIP'S

Korea Train eXpress (KTX)

1:1 400 000

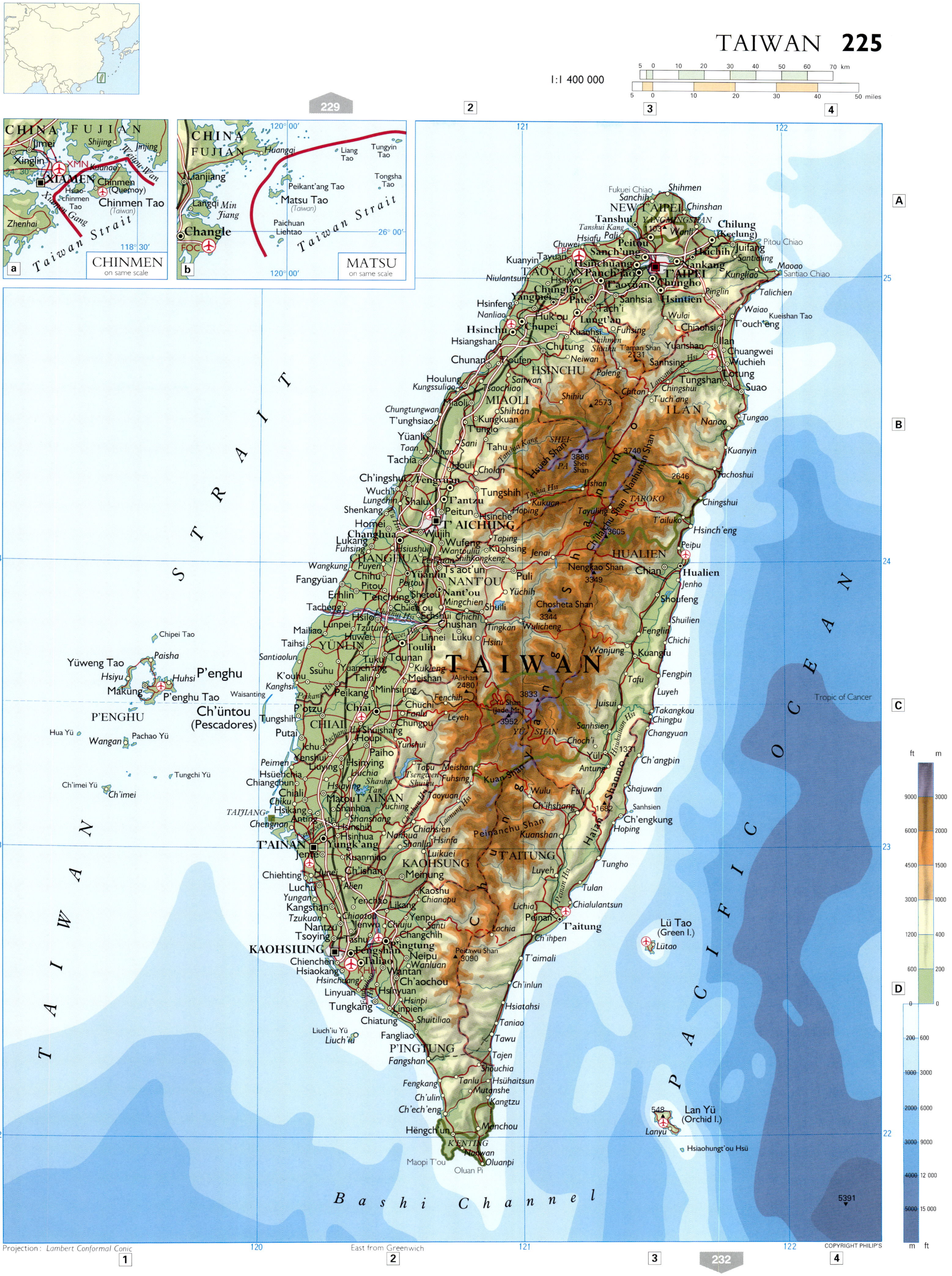
0 10 20 30 40 50 60 70 km
0 10 20 30 40 50 miles
CHINMEN
on same scale
CHINA FUJIAN
Jimei
Shijing
Jinjing
Xinglin
XIAMEN
Chinmen (Quemoy)
Chinmen Tao
(Taiwan)
Zhenhai
Taiwan Strait
MATSU
on same scale
Lianjiang
Langqi
Min Jiang
Changle
Huangqi
Liang Tao
Tungyin Tao
Tongsha Tao
Peikant'ang Tao
Matsu Tao
(Taiwan)
Paichuan Liehtao
Fukuei Chiao
Shihmen
NEW T'AIPEI
Tanshui
YANGMINGSHAN
Chilung (Keelung)
Pitou Chiao
Santiao Chiao
T'AIPEI
Panch'iao
T'aoyuan
TAOYUAN
Hsinchu
HSINCHU
Chunan
MIAOLI
Ilan
ILAN
Suao
Hsueh Shan
3886
Nanhunta Shan
3740
TAROKO
T'AICHUNG
Changhua
CHANGHUA
Hualien
HUALIEN
NANT'OU
Puli
Yüanlin
YÜNLIN
Touliu
CHIAI
Chiai
T A I W A N
Yü Shan (Jade Mt.)
3952
YU SHAN
Chungyang Shanmo
T'AINAN
T'AITUNG
T'aitung
KAOHSIUNG
Fengshan
P'INGTUNG
KENTING
Oluanpi
Hengch'un
Lü Tao (Green I.)
Lan Yü (Orchid I.)
P'enghu
P'ENGHU
Ch'üntou (Pescadores)
Makung
Wangan
TAIWAN STRAIT
PACIFIC OCEAN
Bashi Channel
Tropic of Cancer
5391
ft m
9000 3000
6000 2000
4500 1500
3000 1000
1200 400
600 200
0 0
200 600
1000 3000
2000 6000
3000 9000
4000 12 000
5000 15 000
Projection: Lambert Conformal Conic
East from Greenwich
COPYRIGHT PHILIP'S

Taiwan High Speed Rail (THSR)

1:4 800 000

MONGOLIA
ÖVÖRHANGAY
DUNDGOVĬ
DORNOGOVĬ
SÜHBAATAR
ÖMNÖGOVĬ
Gurvan Sayhan Uul
Galbin Govĭ
Gobi
NEI MONGOL
Badrain Jaran Shamo
Tengger Shamo
Mu Us Shamo (Ordos)
Lang Shan
Daqing Shan
Helan Shan
Lüliang Shan
Taihang Shan
Qinling Shandi
Liupan Shan
Funiu Shan
Zhongtiao Shan
NINGXIA HUIZU ZIZHIQU
SHANXI
SHAANXI
HENAN
HEBEI
GANSU
Huang He (Yellow River)
Mandalgovĭ
Ulaanbaatar
Sonid Zuoqi
Erenhot
Xilinhot
Dalai Nur
Duolun
Wuhai
Linhe
BAOTOU
HOHHOT
Jining
DATONG
ZHANGJIAKOU (Kalgan)
BEIJING (PEKING)
YINCHUAN
Shizuishan
Wuzhong
Zhongwei
LANZHOU
Baiyin
Dongsheng
Yulin
TAIYUAN
Yangquan
SHIJIAZHUANG
BAODING
Xingtai
HANDAN
ANYANG
Changzhi
Jincheng
Linfen
Houma
Yuncheng
Sanmenxia
LUOYANG
ZHENGZHOU
Kaifeng
Xinxiang
Jiaozuo
PINGDINGSHAN
Xuchang
NANYANG
SHANGQIU
XIANYANG
XI'AN
Baoji
TIANSHUI
Pingliang
Yan'an
Tongchuan
Weinan
Hanzhong
Ankang
Guangyuan
Projection: Conical with two standard parallels

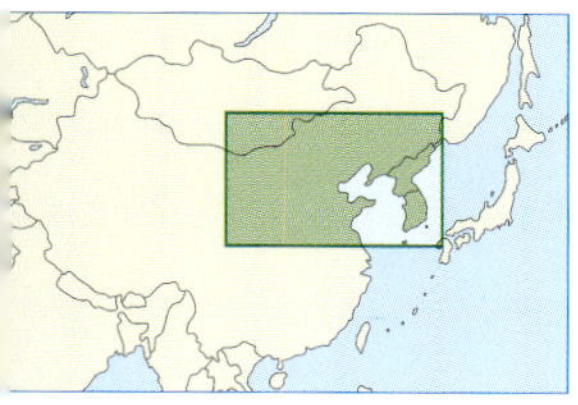

9 10 11 12 13 14 15 16
219
B
C
D
E
F
G
H
220
229
HARBIN
Bin Xian
Acheng
Shuangcheng
Horqin Youyi Qianqi (Ulanhot)
Baicheng
Taonan
Zhenlai
Da'an
Tongyu
Huolin Gol
Qian Gorlos
FUYU
Changchunling
Wuchang
Shangzhi
Yanshou
Linkou
Muling
Jixi
Novokachalinsk
Lake Khanka
MUDANJIANG
Hailin
Ning'an
Dongning
Suifenhe
Pogranichnyy
Ussuriysk
Nong'an
Dehui
Yushu
Shulan
Jiutai
CHANGCHUN
JILIN
Jiaohe
Gongzhuling
Siping
Liaoyuan
Dunhua
Yanji
Tumen
Hunchun
Vladivostok
Artem
Nakhodka
Tongliao
Xi Ujimqin Qi
Ar Horqin Qi
Bairin Zuoqi
Linxi
Bairin Youqi
CHIFENG (Ulanhad)
Kangping
Tieling
Faku
Kaiyuan
Meihekou
Fuxin
Heishui
Beipiao
Chaoyang
SHENYANG
FUSHUN
Benxi
Liaoyang
ANSHAN
Haicheng
Panjin
Jinzhou
Xingcheng
Huludao
Yingkou
Dandong
Sinŭiju
Qinhuangdao
Changli
TIANJIN
Tanggu
Hangu
Liaodong Wan
Wafangdian
Pulandian
DALIAN (Lüda)
Lüshun
Zhuanghe
BO HAI
Bo Hai Haixia
Korea Bay
P'YŎNGYANG
NAMP'O
Sariwŏn
Haeju
Kaesŏng
Hamhŭng
Hŭngnam
Wŏnsan
Tongjosŏn-man
Kanggye
Hyesan
Chongjin
Kimch'aek
Paektu-san
Changbai Shan
NORTH KOREA
SEA OF JAPAN (EAST SEA)
SEOUL
INCHEON
SUWON
SEONGNAM
Chuncheon
Gangneung
Donghae
Samcheok
Wonju
Chungju
Cheongju
DAEJEON
Gunsan
Iksan
Jeonju
DAEGU
Pohang
Gyeongju
ULSAN
BUSAN
Masan
Changwon
Jinju
GWANGJU
Mokpo
Suncheon
Yeosu
SOUTH KOREA
Ulleungdo (S. Korea)
Gyeonggi-man
Korea Strait
Tsushima (Japan)
Izuhara
Jeju Haehyop
Jeju-do (S. Korea)
Jeju
Hallasan
Seogwipo
JAPAN
Karatsu
Sasebo
Nagasaki
Fukue-Shima
Nakadōri-Shima
Iki
YANTAI
Penglai
Longkou
Weihai
Wendeng
Rongcheng
Laizhou Wan
Shandong Bandao
WEIFANG
ZIBO
QINGDAO
Jimo
Jiaozhou
Rizhao
XINTAI
Linyi
YELLOW SEA (HUANG HAI)
LIANYUNGANG
HUAI'AN
YANCHENG
XINGHUA
Sheyang
Bengbu
Fengyang
Hongze Hu
Dongtai
East from Greenwich
COPYRIGHT PHILIP'S

50 0 50 100 150 200 km
50 0 50 100 150 miles
1:4 800 000

1 2 3 4 226 5 6 7

A
B
C
D
E
F
G
H
ft m
12 000 4000
9000 3000
6000 2000
4500 1500
3000 1000
1200 400
600 200
0 0
200 600
2000 6000
m ft
241
236
GANSU
SHAANXI
SICHUAN
Sichuan Pendi
CHENGDU
CHONGQING
Chongqing
WANXIAN
NANCHONG
SUINING
ZIGONG
LESHAN
NEIJIANG
LUZHOU
MIANYANG
GUIZHOU
GUIYANG
Zunyi
Anshun
YUNNAN
KUNMING
Qujing
Dali
Lijiang
Panzhihua
Xichang
Gejiu
Xishuangbanna
GUANGXI
NANNING
LIUZHOU
Qinzhou
Beihai
VIETNAM
HANOI
HAIPHONG
LAOS
BURMA (MYANMAR)
KACHIN
SHAN
THAILAND
Gulf of Tonkin
Hengduan Shan
Shaluli Shan
Daxue Shan
Qionglai Shan
Daliang Shan
Wumeng Shan
Dalou Shan
Ningjing Shan
Nu Shan
Wuliang Shan
Ailao Shan
Dabashan
Miao Ling
Hanzhong
Guangyuan
Bazhong
Dazhou
Yibin
Chishui
Bijie
Zhaotong
Xingyi
Baise
Bose
Yulong Xueshan
Kangding
Litang
Batang
Barkam
Songpan
Mekong
Salween
Red River
Sanxia Shuiku (Three Gorges Res.)
Projection: Conical with two standard parallels
32
30
28
26
24
22
20
98
100
102
104
106
108

2 3 4 236 5 6 7

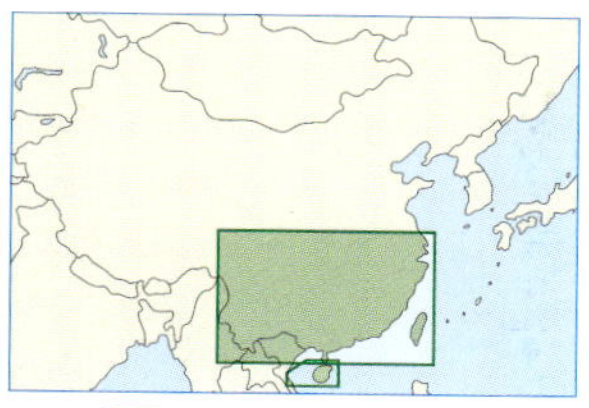

227
A
B
C
D
E
F
G
H
8
9
10
11
12
13
14
HENAN
ANHUI
JIANGSU
HUBEI
HUNAN
JIANGXI
ZHEJIANG
FUJIAN
GUANGDONG
SHANGHAI SHI
NANYANG
XINYANG
HUAINAN
HEFEI
NANJING
YANGZHOU
CHANGZHOU
WUXI
SUZHOU
SHANGHAI
HUZHOU
HANGZHOU
XIAOSHAN
NINGBO
WUHAN
HUANGSHI
JINGZHOU
XIANTAO
TIANMEN
JINGMEN
XIANGFAN
ZAOYANG
SHIYAN
YUEYANG
CHANGDE
YIYANG
CHANGSHA
XIANGTAN
ZHUZHOU
PINGXIANG
HENGYANG
YONGZHOU
NANCHANG
TAIZHOU
WENZHOU
FUZHOU
QUANZHOU
XIAMEN (Amoy)
SHANTOU
GUANGZHOU (CANTON)
HUIZHOU
DONGGUAN
SHENZHEN
JIANGMEN
ZHONGSHAN
FOSHAN
ZHUHAI
Macau
HONG KONG (XIANGGANG)
ZHANJIANG (Xiashan)
T'AIPEI
T'AICHUNG
T'AINAN
KAOHSIUNG
TAIWAN
Taiwan Strait
Luzon Strait
SOUTH CHINA SEA
Tropic of Cancer
Qiongzhou Haixia (Hainan Str.)
Chang Jiang (Yangtse)
Poyang Hu
Dongting Hu
Tai Hu
CHINA
HAIKOU
HAINAN
Hainan Dao (China)
Gulf of Tonkin
VIETNAM
Sanya
HAINAN a on same scale
East from Greenwich
COPYRIGHT PHILIP'S

1:10 000 000
km
miles
Projection: Mercator
East from Greenwich
218
239
BURMA
RANGOON (Yangon)
(MYANMAR)
G. of Martaban
Moulmein
Tavoy (Dawei)
Mergui (Myeik)
Myeik Kyunzu (Mergui Arch.)
Kho Khot Kra (Isthmus of Kra)
ANDAMAN SEA
THAILAND
BANGKOK (Krung Thep)
SAMUT PRAKAN
Chiang Mai
Nakhon Ratchasima
Udon Thani
Khon Kaen
Ubon Ratchathani
Phitsanulok
Nakhon Sawan
Pattaya
Chon Buri
Hua Hin
Surat Thani
Nakhon Si Thammarat
Phuket
Songkhla
Hat Yai
Gulf of Thailand
LAOS
Vientiane (Viangchan)
Savannakhet
Pakxe
VIETNAM
Hue
Da Nang
Quang Ngai
Qui Nhon
Nha Trang
Da Lat
Phan Thiet
Buon Me Thuot
THANH PHO HO CHI MINH (Saigon)
Vung Tau
CAN THO
Ca Mau
Rach Gia
CAMBODIA
PHNOM PENH
Siemreab
Batdambang
Kampong Cham
Kampot
Tonlé Sap
Paracel Islands
Amphitrite Group
Crescent Group
Macclesfield Bank
SOUTH CHINA SEA
Spratly Islands
Dao Con Son
Malay Peninsula
MALAYSIA
PENINSULAR MALAYSIA
KUALA LUMPUR
Kota Bharu
Kuala Terengganu
George Town
Butterworth
Ipoh
Kuantan
Seremban
Melaka
Johor Bahru
SINGAPORE
BATAM
Straits of Malacca
Alor Setar
Kepulauan Natuna Besar
Kepulauan Anambas
Kepulauan Natuna Selatan
BRUNEI
Bandar Seri Begawan
Kota Kinabalu
SABAH
SARAWAK
Kuching
Sibu
Bintulu
Miri
LABUAN
INDONESIA
Banda Aceh
ACEH
MEDAN
SUMATERA UTARA
Pekanbaru
RIAU
Padang
SUMATERA BARAT
Jambi
JAMBI
PALEMBANG
SUMATERA SELATAN
Bengkulu
BENGKULU
Bandar Lampung
LAMPUNG
Simeulue
Nias
Siberut
Kepulauan Mentawai
Kepulauan Batu
Bangka
Belitung
Pontianak
KALIMANTAN BARAT
KALIMANTAN TENGAH
KALIMANTAN SELATAN
KALIMANTAN TIMUR
Palangkaraya
Banjarmasin
Selat Karimata
Greater Sunda Islands
JAVA SEA
JAKARTA
Bandung
Bogor
Cirebon
Semarang
Yogyakarta
Surakarta
SURABAYA
Malang
Madura
BALI
Denpasar
NUSA TENGG. BARAT
Mataram
Lombok
Jawa (Java)
INDIAN OCEAN
Java Trench
Enggano
Selat Sunda
Krakatau

JAVA AND MADURA
1:6 000 000
BALI
1:1 600 000
JAKARTA
Bogor
BANDUNG
Semarang
SURABAYA
Yogyakarta
Madura
Jawa
Bali
Denpasar
Singaraja
Lombok
Mataram
Nusa Penida
INDIAN OCEAN
Luzon
MANILA
Quezon City
Mindoro
Samar
Leyte
Cebu
Negros
Mindanao
DAVAO
Zamboanga
Puerto Princesa
SULU SEA
CELEBES SEA
PACIFIC OCEAN
Minda nao Trench
Halmahera
Ternate
Manado
Sulawesi (Celebes)
MOLUCCA SEA
Seram (Ceram)
Ambon
Buru
BANDA SEA
Flores
Sumba
Sawu Sea
Timor
Dili
EAST TIMOR
Kupang
Kepulauan Aru
Kepulauan Tanimbar
ARAFURA SEA
Pegunungan Maoke
IRIAN JAYA
PAPUA NEW GUINEA
Jayapura
Merauke
Equator
COPYRIGHT PHILIP'S

1:3 200 000

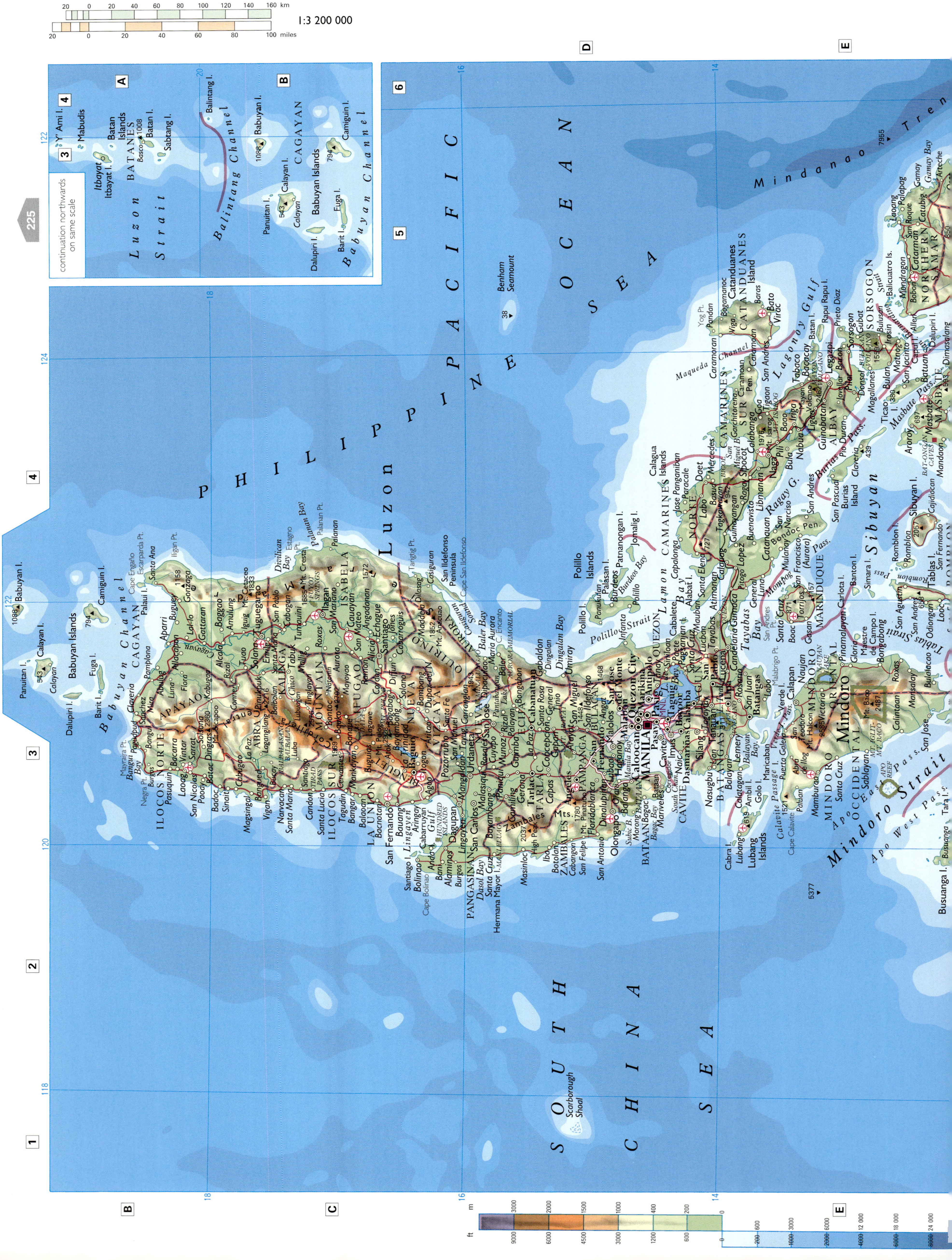
P H I L I P P I N E   S E A
P A C I F I C   O C E A N
S O U T H   C H I N A   S E A
Luzon
MANILA
Luzon Strait
Balintang Channel
Babuyan Channel
Babuyan Islands
Batan Islands
BATANES
CAGAYAN
ISABELA
ILOCOS NORTE
ILOCOS SUR
LA UNION
PANGASINAN
ZAMBALES
BATAAN
TARLAC
PAMPANGA
BULACAN
CAVITE
BATANGAS
QUEZON
AURORA
QUIRINO
NUEVA VIZCAYA
NUEVA ECIJA
CAMARINES NORTE
CAMARINES SUR
CATANDUANES
ALBAY
SORSOGON
MASBATE
MARINDUQUE
ROMBLON
Mindoro
MINDORO ORIENTAL
MINDORO OCCIDENTAL
Mindoro Strait
Sibuyan Sea
Lamon Bay
Lagonoy Gulf
Ragay G.
Tayabas Bay
Lingayen Gulf
Manila Bay
Polillo Islands
Polillo Strait
Catanduanes Island
Maqueda Channel
Mindanao Trench
NORTHERN SAMAR
Lubang Islands
Scarborough Shoal
Benham Seamount
Dingalan Bay
Baler Bay
Palanan Bay
continuation northwards on same scale
225

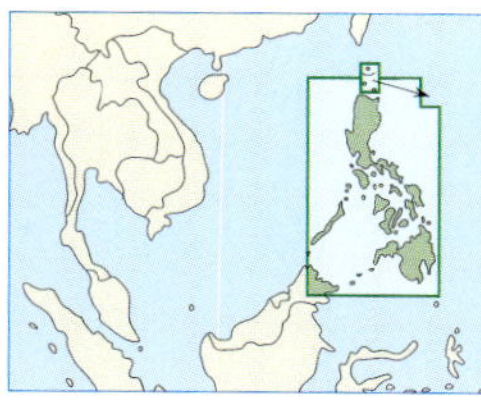

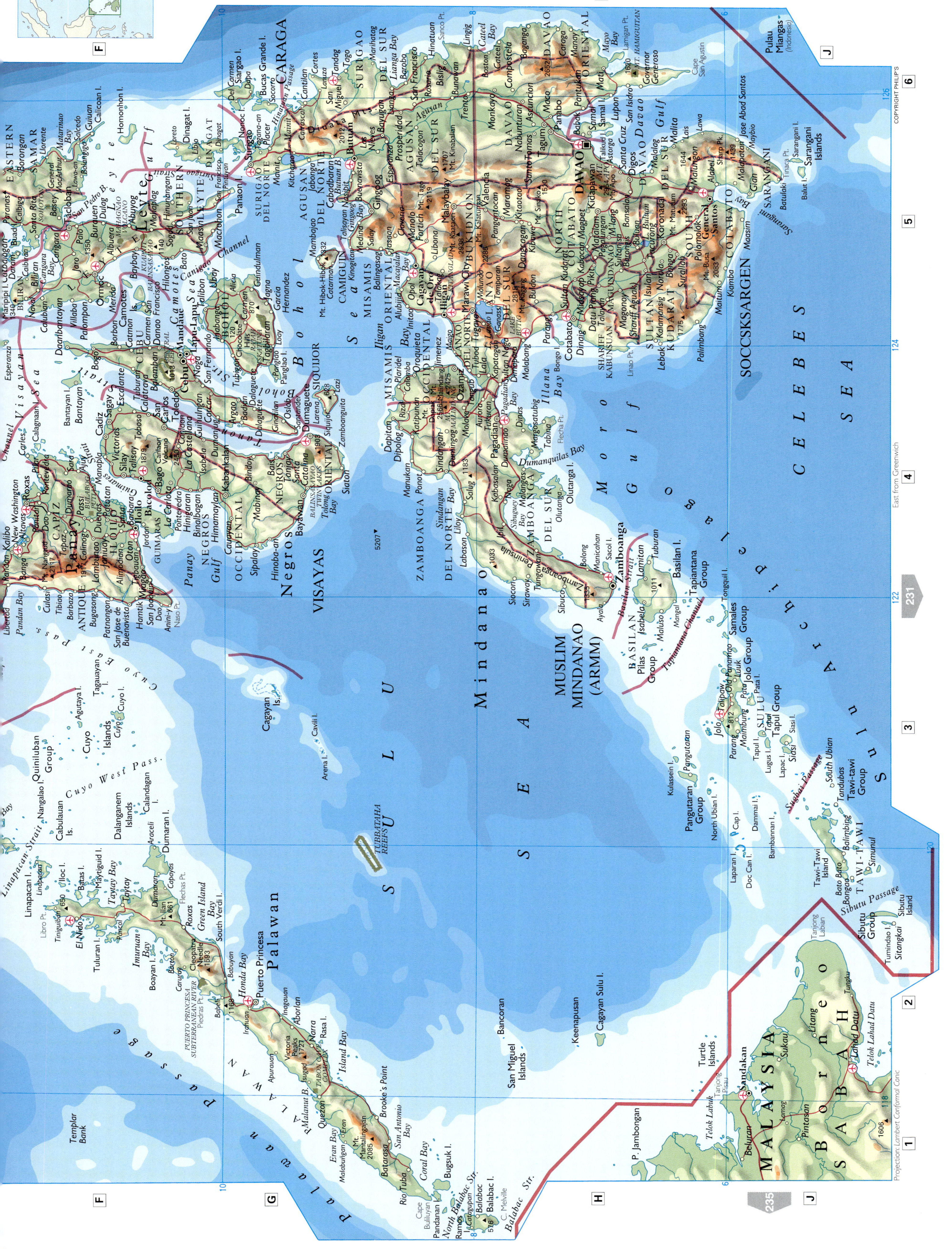
SULU SEA
CELEBES SEA
Mindanao
Palawan
PALAWAN PASSAGE
Negros
Panay
Leyte Gulf
Bohol Sea
Visayan Sea
Moro Gulf
Sulu Archipelago
VISAYAS
MUSLIM MINDANAO (ARMM)
SOCCSKSARGEN
CARAGA
Zamboanga
DAVAO
Puerto Princesa
Sandakan
MALAYSIA
SABAH
Borneo
Basilan I.
TAWI-TAWI
SULU
Cagayan Sulu I.
Turtle Islands
Projection: Lambert Conformal Conic
COPYRIGHT PHILIPS

1:5 600 000
245
237
THAILAND
PENINSULAR MALAYSIA
KUALA LUMPUR
SINGAPORE
Straits of Malacca
SUMATERA UTARA
SUMATERA BARAT
SUMATERA SELATAN
ACEH
RIAU
JAMBI
BENGKULU
LAMPUNG
KEPULAUAN RIAU
BANGKA-BELITUNG
BANTEN
Banda Aceh
Medan
Padang
Pekanbaru
Palembang
Bengkulu
Bandar Lampung
Jambi (Telanaipura)
Johor Bahru
Kuala Terengganu
Kuantan
George Town
Ipoh
Melaka
Simeulue
Nias
Siberut
Kepulauan Mentawai
Enggano
Bangka
Selat Sunda
Selat Mentawai
Danau Toba
Java Trench
Equator
INDIAN OCEAN
Projection: Mercator
East from Gr

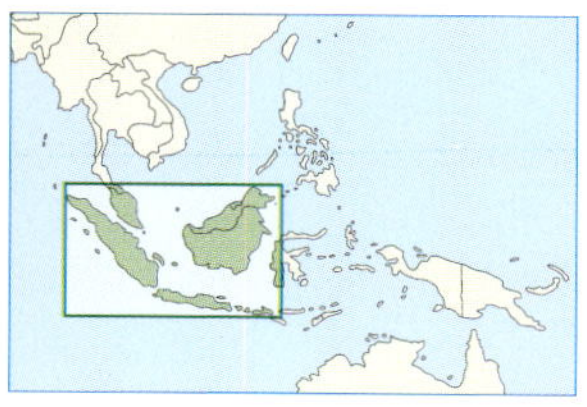

CHINA SEA
MALAYSIA
BRUNEI
Bandar Seri Begawan
SABAH
Kota Kinabalu
Sandakan
SULU SEA
PHILIPPINES
CELEBES SEA
SARAWAK
Kuching
Sibu
Miri
Bintulu
Natuna Besar
Kepulauan Natuna Selatan (Indonesia)
Selat Serasan
KALIMANTAN BARAT
Pontianak
KALIMANTAN TIMUR
Samarinda
Balikpapan
Tarakan
KALIMANTAN TENGAH
Palangkaraya
KALIMANTAN SELATAN
Banjarmasin
Kalimantan (Borneo)
Pegunungan Schwaner
Pegunungan Muller
Equator
Selat Makassar
Sulawesi (Celebes)
SULAWESI BARAT
MAKASSAR (Ujung Pandang)
Palu
Selat Karimata
Belitung
Kepulauan Karimata
INDONESIA
Greater Sunda Islands
JAVA SEA
Bawean
KEPULAUAN KARIMUNJAWA
Madura
JAWA TENGAH
JAWA TIMUR
SURABAYA
Semarang
BANDUNG
Yogyakarta
YOGYAKARTA
Malang
BALI SEA
Bali
Denpasar
Lombok
Mataram
Sumbawa
Flores
NUSA TENGGARA BARAT
Lesser Sunda Islands
FLORES SEA
Jawa (Java)
Selat Madura
Kepulauan Laut Kecil
Kepulauan Masalembo
Kepulauan Kangean
A
B
C
D
4
5
110
115
233
231
COPYRIGHT PHILIP'S

50 0 50 100 150 200 km

1:4 800 000

50 0 50 100 150 miles

Gulf of Tonkin
HAINAN
Hainan Dao
(China)
HAIKOU
Sanya
ZHANJIANG
NANNING
HANOI
HAIPHONG
Da Nang
Hue
BANGKOK
SAMUT PRAKAN
Bight of Bangkok
NAY PYI TAW
MANDALAY
Moulmein
G. of Martaban
ANDAMAN SEA
Tonle Sap
Mekong
228
241

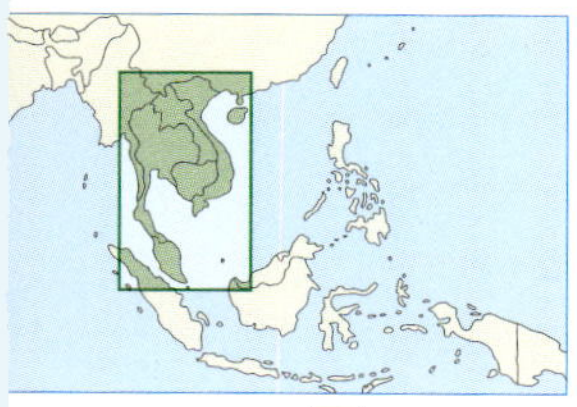

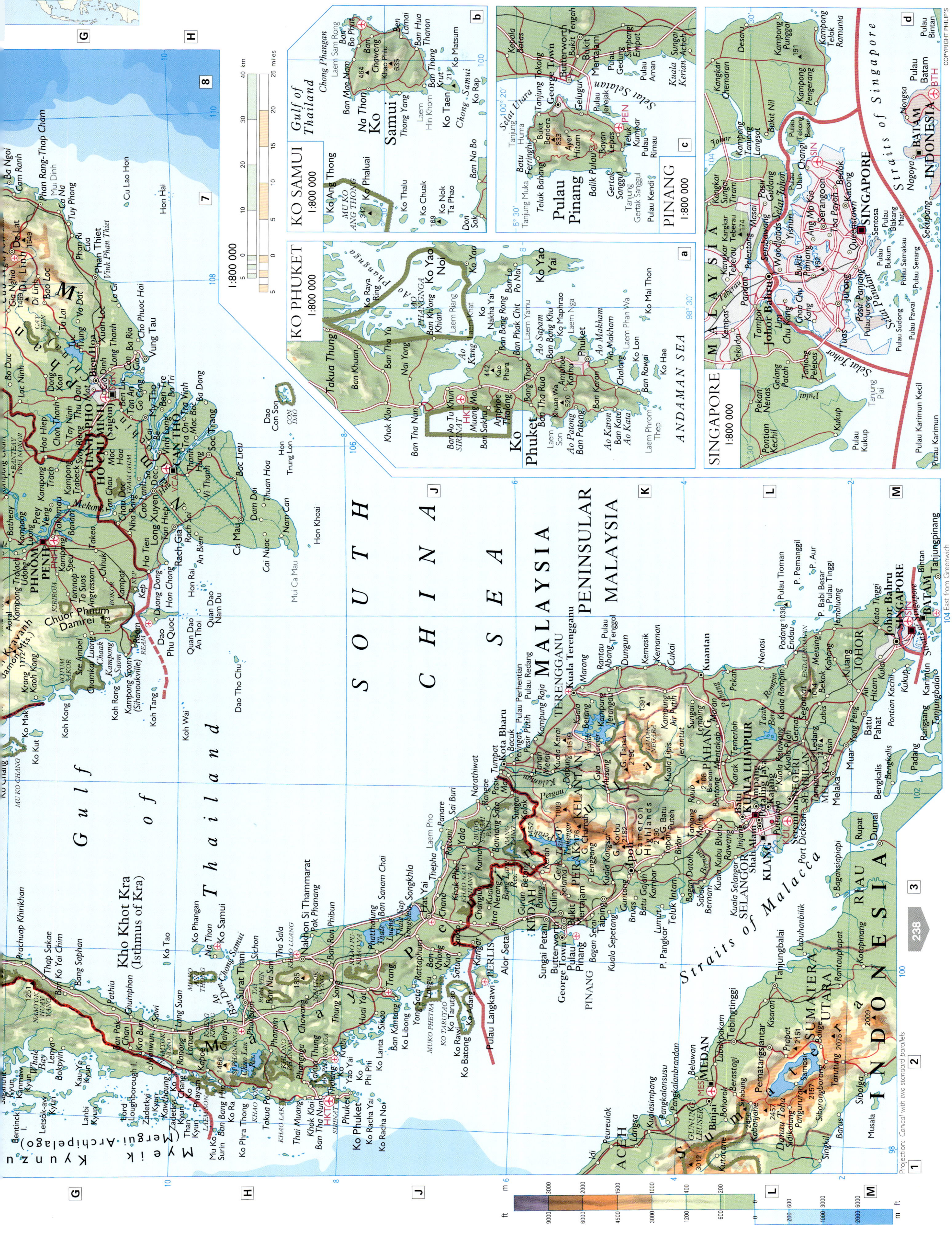
SOUTH CHINA SEA
Gulf of Thailand
MALAYSIA
PENINSULAR MALAYSIA
INDONESIA
Straits of Malacca
SUMATERA UTARA
RIAU
ACEH
Kho Khot Kra (Isthmus of Kra)
Myeik Kyunzu (Mergui Archipelago)
KO PHUKET 1:800 000
KO SAMUI 1:800 000
PINANG 1:800 000
SINGAPORE 1:800 000
ANDAMAN SEA
Straits of Singapore
Pulau Pinang
PHNOM PENH
KUALA LUMPUR
SINGAPORE
MEDAN
Kota Bharu
Kuala Terengganu
Kuantan
Johor Bahru
Ipoh
Melaka
Phuket
Songkhla
Hat Yai
Nakhon Si Thammarat
Surat Thani
Chumphon
Ranong
Vung Tau
Can Tho
Phan Thiet
Ca Mau
Cameron Highlands
1:800 000
Projection: Conical with two standard parallels
104 East from Greenwich
238
COPYRIGHT PHILIP'S

1:14 000 000
216
217
256
257
266
Projection: Bonne
East from Greenwich
Black Sea
Caspian Sea
Mediterranean Sea
Red Sea
Persian Gulf
Gulf of Oman
Gulf of Aden
ARABIAN SEA
INDIA
TURKEY
GEORGIA
ARMENIA
AZERBAIJAN
TURKMENISTAN
UZBEKISTAN
AFGHANISTAN
PAKIS
SYRIA
LEBANON
ISRAEL
JORDAN
IRAQ
IRAN
KUWAIT
SAUDI ARABIA
BAHRAIN
QATAR
UNITED ARAB EMIRATES
OMAN
YEMEN
EGYPT
SUDAN
ERITREA
DJIBOUTI
ETHIOPIA
SOMALIA
KENYA
CYPRUS
RUSSIA
ISTANBUL
ANKARA
TBILISI
YEREVAN
BAKI (Baku)
TEHRAN
MASHHAD
HALAB (Aleppo)
DIMASHQ (Damascus)
BAYRUT (Beirut)
ʽAMMAN
BAGHDAD
AL KUWAYT (Kuwait)
AR RIYAD (Riyadh)
MAKKAH (Mecca)
AL MADINAH (Medina)
JIDDAH (Jedda)
SANʽA'
ʽAdan (Aden)
Masqat (Muscat)
DUBAYY (Dubai)
Abū Zaby (Abu Dhabi)
Ad Dawhah (Doha)
Al Manāmah
KARACHI
ADDIS ABEBA (Addis Ababa)
Djibouti
MUQDISHO (Mogadishu)
EL QAHIRA (Cairo)
Rub' al Khali (Empty Quarter)
An Nafūd (Nafud Desert)
Dasht-e Kavir (Great Salt Desert)
Dasht-e Lūt
Socotra (Yemen)
Tropic of Cancer

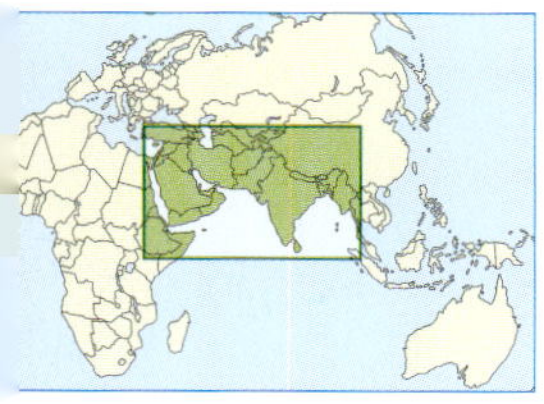

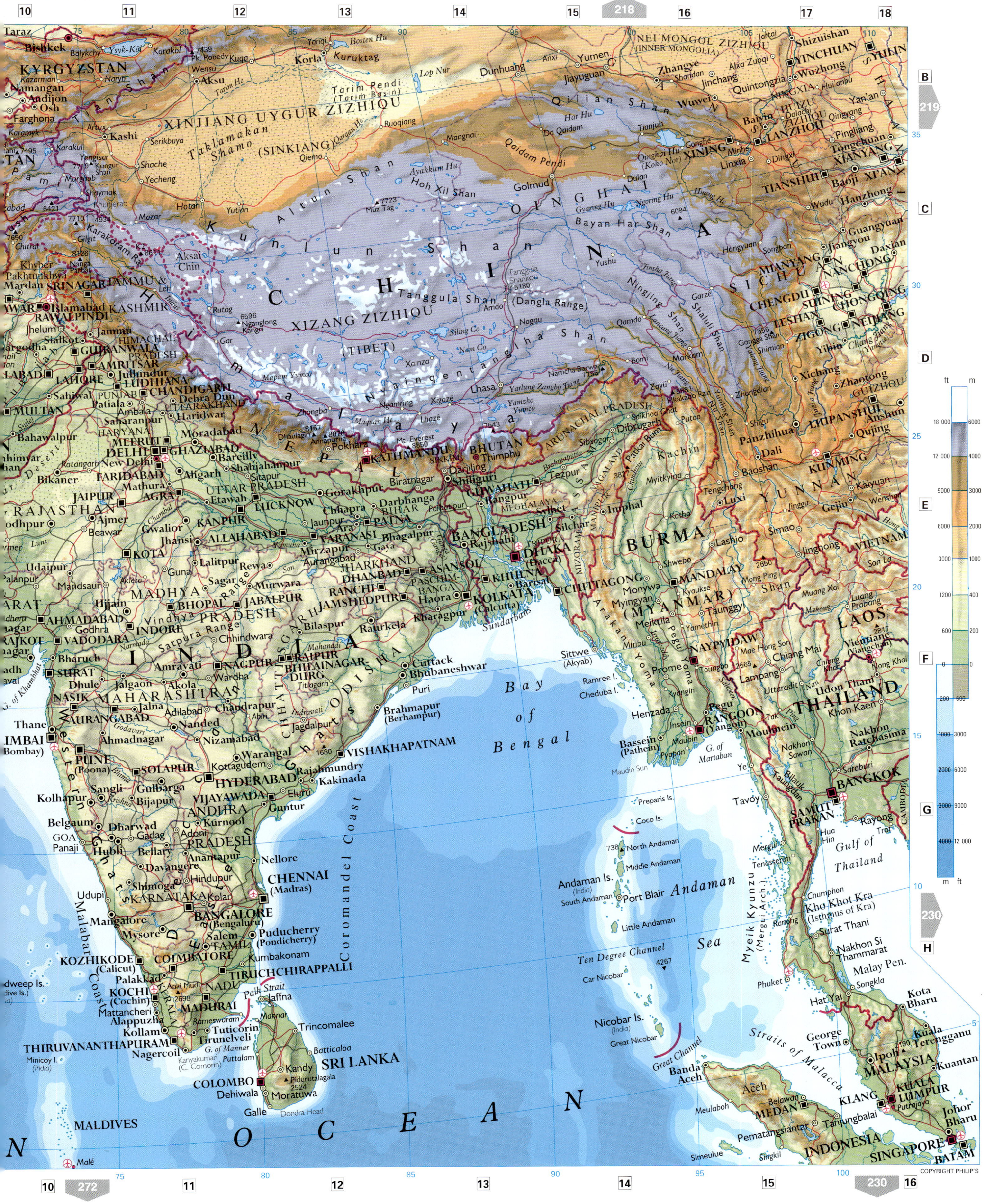

KYRGYZSTAN
Bishkek
XINJIANG UYGUR ZIZHIQU
(SINKIANG)
Taklamakan Shamo
Tarim Pendi (Tarim Basin)
Kunlun Shan
Altun Shan
Qilian Shan
Qaidam Pendi
QINGHAI
Bayan Har Shan
CHINA
XIZANG ZIZHIQU
(TIBET)
Tanggula Shan
Nyainqentanglha Shan
Himalaya
NEI MONGOL ZIZHIQU (INNER MONGOLIA)
NINGXIA HUIZU ZIZHIQU
SICHUAN
YUNNAN
GUIZHOU
CHENGDU
CHONGQING
LANZHOU
XINING
KUNMING
Lhasa
JAMMU & KASHMIR
SRINAGAR
Islamabad
RAWALPINDI
LAHORE
AMRITSAR
LUDHIANA
CHANDIGARH
HIMACHAL PRADESH
UTTARAKHAND
HARYANA
DELHI
New Delhi
UTTAR PRADESH
LUCKNOW
KANPUR
AGRA
RAJASTHAN
JAIPUR
NEPAL
KATHMANDU
Mt. Everest
SIKKIM
BHUTAN
Thimphu
ARUNACHAL PRADESH
ASSAM
MEGHALAYA
NAGALAND
MANIPUR
MIZORAM
TRIPURA
BIHAR
PATNA
JHARKHAND
RANCHI
WEST BENGAL
KOLKATA (Calcutta)
BANGLADESH
DHAKA (Dacca)
CHITTAGONG
MADHYA PRADESH
BHOPAL
INDORE
JABALPUR
INDIA
CHHATTISGARH
RAIPUR
ODISHA
Bhubaneshwar
Cuttack
GUJARAT
AHMADABAD
VADODARA
SURAT
MAHARASHTRA
NAGPUR
PUNE (Poona)
MUMBAI (Bombay)
ANDHRA PRADESH
HYDERABAD
VISHAKHAPATNAM
KARNATAKA
BANGALORE (Bengaluru)
CHENNAI (Madras)
Puducherry (Pondicherry)
TAMIL NADU
MADURAI
KERALA
KOCHI (Cochin)
KOZHIKODE (Calicut)
THIRUVANANTHAPURAM
GOA
Western Ghats
Eastern Ghats
Malabar Coast
Coromandel Coast
SRI LANKA
COLOMBO
Kandy
Jaffna
Trincomalee
Palk Strait
G. of Mannar
MALDIVES
Malé
Lakshadweep Is.
Bay of Bengal
INDIAN OCEAN
BURMA (MYANMAR)
MANDALAY
NAYPYIDAW
RANGOON (Yangon)
G. of Martaban
Andaman Sea
Andaman Is. (India)
Port Blair
Ten Degree Channel
Nicobar Is. (India)
Great Channel
LAOS
Vientiane
THAILAND
BANGKOK
Gulf of Thailand
Kho Khot Kra (Isthmus of Kra)
Malay Pen.
MALAYSIA
KUALA LUMPUR
Straits of Malacca
SINGAPORE
INDONESIA
MEDAN
Banda Aceh
VIETNAM
CAMBODIA
COPYRIGHT PHILIP'S

# AFGHANISTAN AND PAKISTAN

1:5 600 000

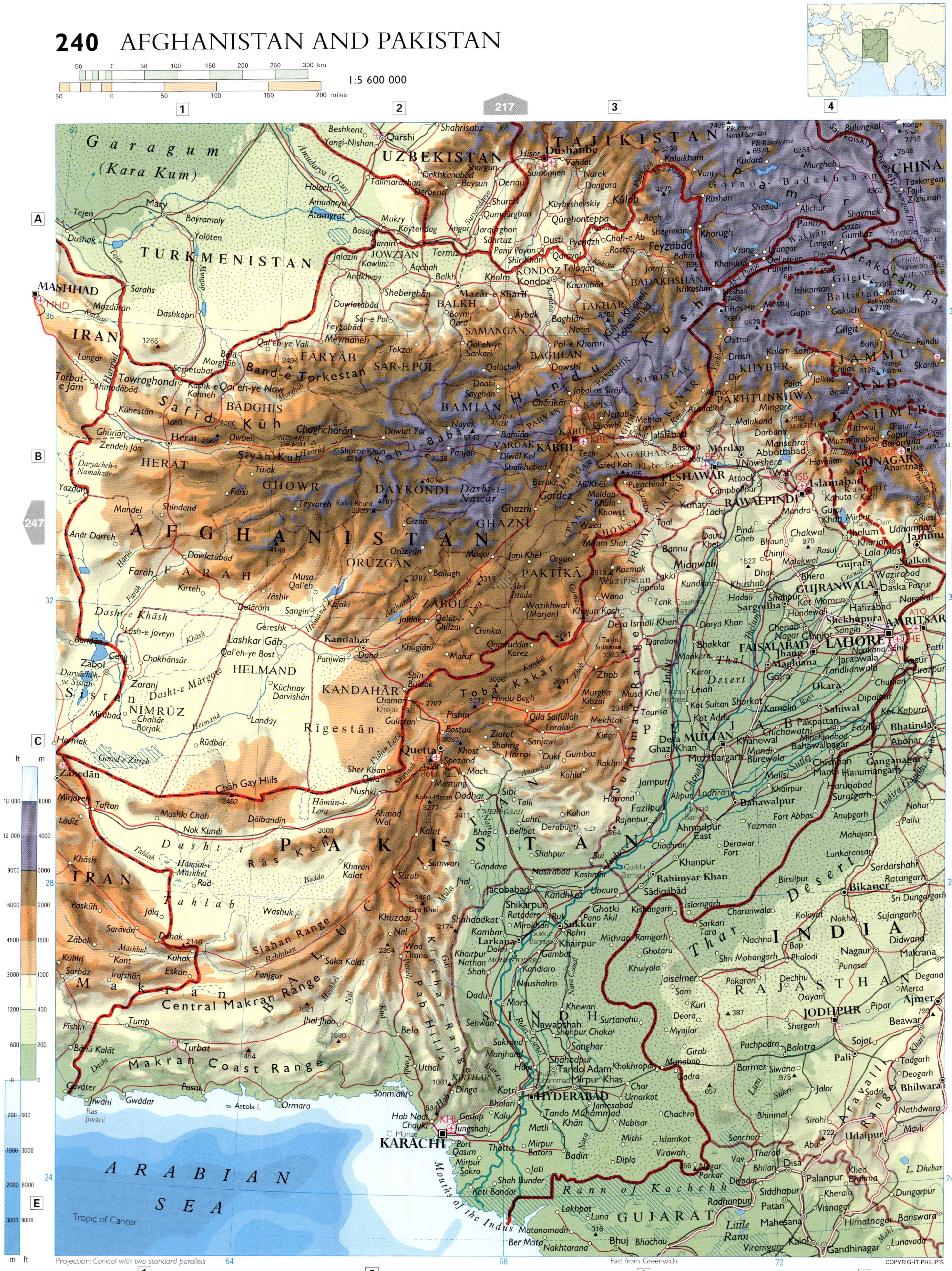
50 0 50 100 150 200 250 300 km
50 0 50 100 150 200 miles
217
247
Garagum (Kara Kum)
TURKMENISTAN
UZBEKISTAN
TAJIKISTAN
CHINA
IRAN
AFGHANISTAN
PAKISTAN
INDIA
JAMMU AND KASHMIR
Hindu Kush
Pamir
Karakoram Ra.
Band-e Torkestan
Safid Kuh
Koh-i-Baba
Dasht-e Margow
Rigestan
Chagai Hills
Kharan
Central Makran Range
Makran Coast Range
Kirthar Range
Sulaiman Range
Thar Desert
Rann of Kachchh
ARABIAN SEA
Tropic of Cancer
Mouths of the Indus
Mashhad
Herat
Kabul
Kandahar
Mazar-e Sharif
Peshawar
Islamabad
Rawalpindi
Lahore
Faisalabad
Multan
Quetta
Hyderabad
Karachi
Amritsar
Srinagar
Jammu
Bikaner
Jodhpur
Dushanbe
Zahedan
Gwadar
GUJARAT
RAJASTHAN
SINDH
PUNJAB
BALUCHISTAN
ft m
18 000 6000
12 000 4000
9000 3000
6000 2000
4500 1500
3000 1000
1200 400
600 200
0 0
200 600
1000 3000
2000 6000
3000 9000
m ft
Projection: Conical with two standard parallels
East from Greenwich
COPYRIGHT PHILIP'S

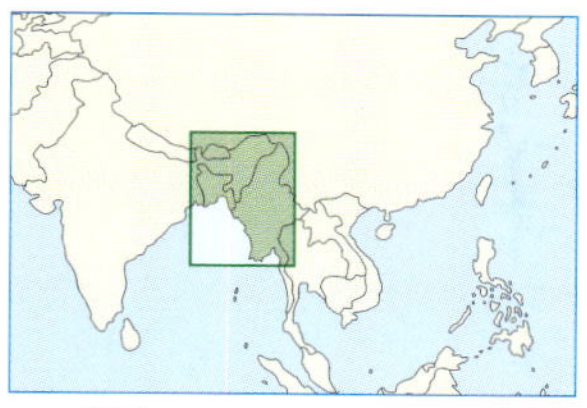

1:4 800 000

218
228
236
A
B
C
D
E
F
1
2
3
4
5
6
7
XIZANG ZIZHIQU (TIBET)
CHINA
NEPAL
SIKKIM
BHUTAN
INDIA
ARUNACHAL PRADESH
ASSAM
NAGALAND
MANIPUR
MEGHALAYA
TRIPURA
MIZORAM
BANGLADESH
DHAKA
KOLKATA
CHITTAGONG
GUWAHATI
Shillong
Imphal
Aizawl
Agartala
Thimphu
KACHIN
SAGAING
CHIN
MANDALAY
BURMA (MYANMAR)
NAYPYIDAW
MAGWE
RAKHINE
SHAN
KAYAH
KAYIN
PEGU
IRRAWADDY
RANGOON (YANGON)
YUNNAN
CHINA
THAILAND
Mouths of the Ganges
BAY OF BENGAL
INDIAN OCEAN
Arakan Coast
G. of Martaban
Mouths of the Irrawaddy
Tropic of Cancer
Projection: Conical with two standard parallels
East from Greenwich
COPYRIGHT PHILIP'S

1:4 800 000
Projection: Conical with two standard parallels
217
243
240
AFGHANISTAN
PAKISTAN
BALUCHISTAN
SINDH
RAJASTHAN
PUNJAB
HARYANA
HIMACHAL PRADESH
JAMMU & KASHMIR
MADHYA PRADESH
ARABIAN SEA
Gulf of Kachchh
Rann of Kachchh
Little Rann
Mouths of the Indus
Tropic of Cancer
Thar (Great Indian) Desert
Thal Desert
KABUL
PESHAWAR
Islamabad
RAWALPINDI
LAHORE
AMRITSAR
FAISALABAD
MULTAN
GUJRANWALA
SRINAGAR
Quetta
Kandahar
HYDERABAD
KARACHI
Sukkur
Bikaner
JODHPUR
JAIPUR
DELHI
New Delhi
AHMADABAD
VADODARA
RAJKOT
INDORE
BHOPAL
KOTA
LUDHIANA
CHANDIGARH
Jamnagar
Bhavnagar
Udaipur
Ajmer
Bahawalpur
Jalandhar
Kirthar Range
Sulaiman Range
Toba Kakar
Pab Hills
Aravalli Range
Indus
Chenab
Sutlej
Jhelum
Ravi
Beas
Indira Gandhi Canal
Narmada
Tapti

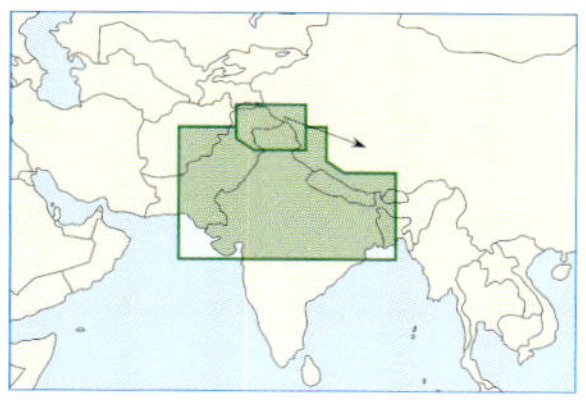

JAMMU AND KASHMIR
on same scale
CHINA
C H I N A
XIZANG ZIZHIQU (TIBET)
NEPAL
BHUTAN
BANGLADESH
KHYBER PAKHTUNKHWA (N.W. FRONTIER)
PUNJAB
HIMACHAL PRADESH
UTTARAKHAND
UTTAR PRADESH
BIHAR
JHARKHAND
WEST BENGAL
CHHATTISGARH
ODISHA
MADHYA PRADESH
SIKKIM
ASSAM
AFGHANISTAN
Gilgit-Baltistan (Northern Areas)
Kunlun Shan
Aksai Chin
Karakoram
Zaskar Mountains
Deosai Mts.
Gangdisê Shan
Mahabharat Lekh
Siwalik Range
Kaimur Hills
Rajmahal Hills
Mouths of the Ganges
The Sandheads
ISLAMABAD
RAWALPINDI
SRINAGAR
Leh
KATHMANDU
Thimphu
LUCKNOW
KANPUR
ALLAHABAD
VARANASI
PATNA
JABALPUR
RANCHI
JAMSHEDPUR
DHANBAD
ASANSOL
KOLKATA
DHAKA
RAJSHAHI
KHULNA
Mt. Everest (Chomolungma or Sagarmatha)
Kanchenjunga
East from Greenwich
COPYRIGHT PHILIP'S

50 0 50 100 150 200 km

1:4 800 000

50 0 50 100 150 miles

A
B
C
D
E
F
1
2
3
4
5
6
7
8
241
242
243
JAIPUR
JODHPUR
AJMER
KOTA
GWALIOR
AGRA
KANPUR
LUCKNOW
ALLAHABAD
VARANASI
PATNA
RANCHI
JAMSHEDPUR
DHANBAD
ASANSOL
BHOPAL
INDORE
UJJAIN
JABALPUR
RAIPUR
BHILAINAGAR-DURG
NAGPUR
AHMADABAD
VADODARA
SURAT
NASIK
AURANGABAD
MUMBAI (BOMBAY)
PUNE
SOLAPUR
HYDERABAD
VISHAKHAPATNAM
CUTTACK
BHUBANESWAR
UTTAR PRADESH
MADHYA PRADESH
JHARKHAND
CHHATTISGARH

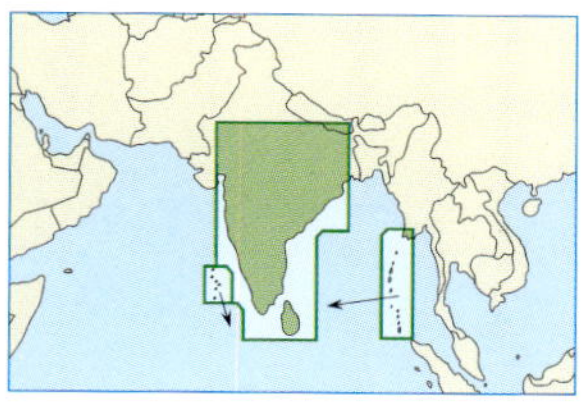

SRI LANKA (CEYLON)
BAY OF BENGAL
ARABIAN SEA
INDIAN OCEAN
ANDAMAN SEA
ANDAMAN AND NICOBAR ISLANDS
LAKSHADWEEP ISLANDS
on same scale
CHENNAI (MADRAS)
BENGALURU (BANGALORE)
COLOMBO
KOCHI (Cochin)
KOZHIKODE
THIRUVANANTHAPURAM
Port Blair
Gulf of Mannar
Projection: Conical with two standard parallels
COPYRIGHT PHILIP'S

1:5 600 000
km
miles
1
2
3
213
4
5
212
B
C
D
256
E
F
ft
m
18 000
6000
12 000
4000
9000
3000
6000
2000
4500
1500
3000
1000
1200
400
600
200
0
0
200
600
1000
3000
2000
6000
T U R K E Y
KONYA
Kayseri
ADANA
Erzurum
YEREVAN
ARMENIA
TABRIZ
GAZIANTEP
Diyarbakır
Malatya
Elazığ
Van Gölü
Toros Dağları (Taurus Mts.)
MEDITERRANEAN SEA
CYPRUS
Nicosia
Limassol
Larnaca
Famagusta
LEBANON
BAYRŪT (Beirut)
ISRAEL
TEL AVIV-YAFO
Jerusalem
Gaza
HEFA (Haifa)
ʿAMMĀN
DIMASHQ (Damascus)
S Y R I A
HALAB (Aleppo)
HIMS (Homs)
Hamāh
Al Lādhiqīyah (Latakia)
Dayr az Zawr
Ar Raqqah
Tudmur (Palmyra)
AL MAWSIL (Mosul)
Arbīl
As Sulaymānīyah
Kirkūk
BAGHDĀD
I R A Q
Karbalāʾ
An Najaf
Al Hillah
Ar Ramādī
AL ANBĀR
An Nāsirīyah
AL BASRA
AL MUTHANNĀ
Kermānshāh
E G Y P T
Es Sînâ (Sinai)
Elat
Al ʿAqabah
Gulf of Aqaba
RED SEA
Hurghada
Tabūk
S A U D I   A R A B I A
AL JAWF
Sakākah
Hāʾil
Jabal Shammar
Buraydah
AL QASĪM
AL MADĪNAH (Medina)
Yanbu ʿal Bahr
Ar Rutbah
Badiyat ash Sham
Hafar al Bātin
AR RIYĀD
AR RIYAD (Riyadh)
AL HUDŪD ASH SHAMĀLĪYAH
An Nafūd
Ad Dahnāʾ
ASH SHARQĪYAH
Projection: Conical with two standard parallels
248
3
40
4
44
5
Underlined towns in Iraq give their name to the administrative area in which they stand
Lava fields

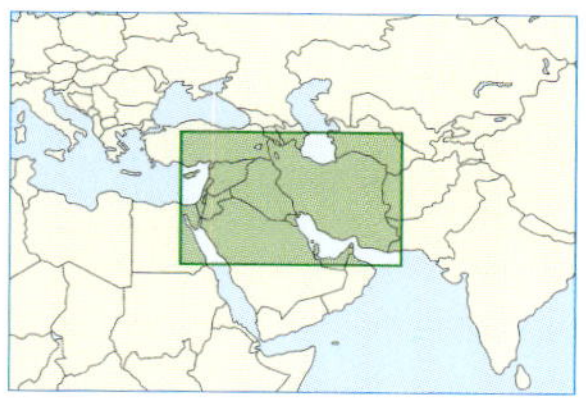

216
240
249
TURKMENISTAN
Garagum (Kara Kum)
Aşgabat
Türkmenbashi
Balkanabat (Nebitdag)
Türkmenabat (Chardzhou)
Mary
Bayramaly
Tejen
Serdar
Gumdag
Kopet Dag
BAKI (Baku)
Länkäran
CASPIAN SEA
-28
Rasht
Bandar-e Anzalī
Gorgān
GOLESTĀN
MĀZANDARĀN
Reshteh-ye Kūhhā-ye Alborz (Elburz Mts.)
Damāvand 5604
Sārī
Bābol
Āmol
Qazvin
QAZVIN
KARAJ
TEHRĀN
TEHRAN
Qom
QOM
Semnān
SEMNĀN
Shāhrūd
Bojnūrd
KHORĀSĀN-E SHEMĀLĪ
MASHHAD
KHORĀSĀN-E RAZAVĪ
Neyshābūr
Sabzevār
Torbat-e Heydārīyeh
Kāshmar
Dasht-e Kavīr (Great Salt Desert)
Arāk
MARKAZĪ
Hamadān
Malāyer
Borūjerd
Khorramābād
Kāshān
Eşfahān
EŞFAHĀN
Najafābād
Shahr-e Kord
CHAHĀR MAHĀLL VA BAKHTĪĀRĪ
Dezfūl
Shūshtar
Ahvāz
KHŪZESTĀN
Ābādān
Khorramshahr
Bandar-e Māh'shur
KOHKĪLŪYEH VA BŪYER AHMADĪ
Yāsūj
Shīrāz
FĀRS
Būshehr
BŪSHEHR
IRAN
Zagros Mts.
Yazd
YAZD
Dasht-e Lūt
Kermān
KERMĀN
Sīrjān
Rafsanjān
Bam
Jiroft
Zāhedān
SĪSTĀN VA BALŪCHESTĀN
Zābol
Īrānshahr
Chāh Bahār
Bandar-e Abbās
HORMOZGĀN
Qeshm
Strait of Hormuz
Bīrjand
KHORĀSĀN-E JANŪBĪ
Tabas
AFGHANISTAN
Herāt
HERAT
FARĀH
Farāh
NĪMRŪZ
Safīd Kūh
PAKISTAN
Gowd-e Zereh
Hāmūn-i-Māshkel
KUWAIT
Al Kuwayt (Kuwait)
Shatt al Arab
PERSIAN GULF
Gulf of Oman
BAHRAIN
Al Manāmah
QATAR
Ad Dawhah (Doha)
Ad Dammām
Al Khubar
Az Zahran (Dhahran)
Al Jubayl
Al Hufūf
UNITED ARAB EMIRATES
Abū Zaby (Abu Dhabi)
Dubayy (Dubai)
Ash Shāriqah (Sharjah)
Ra's al Khaymah
Al Fujayrah
OMAN
Musandam (Oman)
Al Ayn
East from Greenwich
COPYRIGHT PHILIP'S

# SOUTHERN ARABIAN PENINSULA

1:5 600 000

246
257
267
1
2
3
4
A
B
C
D
50 0 50 100 150 200 250 300 km
50 0 50 100 150 200 miles
EGYPT
SUDAN
ERITREA
ETHIOPIA
YEMEN
DJIBOUTI
HALAIB TRIANGLE
RED SEA
Gulf of Aden
Tropic of Cancer
Quseir
Port Ghalib
Marsa Alam
Berenice
Bûr Sûdân (Port Sudan)
Suakin
Suakin Arch. (Sudan)
Kassala
Keren
Asmera (Asmara)
Mitsiwa (Massawa)
Dahlak Kebir (Dahlak Arch.)
Danakil Depression
Danakil Desert
Gonder
L. Tana
Aksum
Mekele
Aseb
Tabūk
Al Wajh
Umm Lajj
Yanbu 'al Bahr
AL MADĪNAH (Medina)
Buraydah
'Unayzah
AR RIYĀḌ (Riyadh)
JIDDAH (Jedda)
MAKKAH (Mecca)
At Ṭā'if
Al Bāḥah
Al Qunfudhah
Abhā
Khamis Mushayt
Najrān
Jīzān
Jazā'ir Farasān (Farasān Is.)
Ṣa'dah
ṢAN'Ā'
Al Ḥudaydah (Hodeida)
Ma'rib
Dhamār
Ibb
Ta'izz
Al Mukhā
'Adan (Aden)
Shuqrā'
Ramlat as Sab'atayn
Harrat Khaybar
Harrat al Kishb
Harrat Nawāṣif
As Sulayyil
NAJRĀN
AL JAWF
SHABWAH
ABYĀN
LAHIJ
Es Sahrâ esh Sharqîya


Projection: Conical with two standard parallels

Lava fields

PERSIAN GULF
Gulf of Oman
ARABIAN SEA
UNITED ARAB EMIRATES
QATAR
BAHRAIN
OMAN
IRAN
HORMOZGĀN
SISTAN VA BALUCHESTAN
MUSANDAM
MASQAT
ASH SHARQĪYAH
AD DĀKHILĪYAH
AẒ ẒĀHIRAH
AL WUSṬĀ
ẒUFĀR
AL MAHRAH
HADRAMAWT
AL BĀṬINAH
Ar Rub' al Khālī (Empty Quarter)
Al Jafūrah
Al 'Uruq al Mu'tariḍah
Jiddat al Ḥarāsīs
ARABIAN ORYX SANCTUARY
Ad Dawḥah (Doha)
Abū Ẓaby (Abū Dhabi)
DUBAYY (Dubai)
Ash Shāriqah (Sharjah)
'Ajmān
Umm al Qaywayn
Ra's al Khaymah
Al Fujayrah
Masqaṭ (Muscat)
Maṭraḥ (Mutruh)
Ṣuḥār (Sohar)
Nizwá
Ṣūr
Jazīrat Maṣīrah
Ad Duqm
Ṣalālah
Mirbāṭ
Jazā'ir al Ḥallānīyāt (Kuria Muria Is.)
Al Ghayḍah
Al Mukallā
Socotra (Yemen)
The Brothers (Yemen)
'Abd al Kūrī (Yemen)
Al Dammām
Al Khobar
Al Hufūf
Jāsk
Chāh Bahār
Qeshm
Tropic of Cancer
EMIRATES OF THE U.A.E.
on same scale as main map
RA'S AL KHAYMAH
UMM AL QAYWAYN
AJMĀN
ASH SHĀRIQAH (SHARJAH)
DUBAYY (DUBAI)
AL FUJAYRAH
AL FUJAYRAH/SHARJAH
OMAN/AJMĀN
ABŪ ẒABY (ABŪ DHABI)
SAUDI ARABIA
East from Greenwich

10 0 10 20 30 40 50 60 70 80 90 km

10 0 10 20 30 40 50 60 miles

1:2 000 000

246

CYPRUS
MEDITERRANEAN SEA
LEBANON
SYRIA
TURKEY
Nicosia (Lefkosia)
Famagusta (Ammochostos)
Larnaca
Limassol
Paphos
Kyrenia
BAYRŪT (Beirut)
DIMASHQ (Damascus)
HALAB (Aleppo)
HIMS (Homs)
Ḩamāh
Al Lādhiqīyah (Latakia)
Ţarābulus (Tripoli)
Şaydā (Sidon)
Şūr (Tyre)
ADANA
Tarsus
İçel (Mersin)
İskenderun
GAZİANTEP
Antalya
Alanya
Anamur
Antalya Körfezi
İskenderun Körfezi
Morphou Bay
Larnaca Bay
Famagusta Bay
Akrotiri Bay
Episkopi Bay


212

193

ISRAEL
JORDAN
EGYPT
SAUDI ARABIA
TEL AVIV-YAFO
Jerusalem
'AMMĀN
EL QÂHIRA (Cairo)
Bûr Sa'îd (Port Said)
El Suweis (Suez)
Gulf of Aqaba
Khalîg el Suweis (Gulf of Suez)
Sînâ' (Sinai)
GAZA STRIP
WEST BANK
Dead Sea
Nile Delta
Hanegev (Negev Desert)
Es Sahrâ Esh Sharqîya (Eastern Desert)
Tabūk
Al 'Aqabah
Elat
Sharm el Sheikh
Lava fields
1974 Cease Fire Lines
Projection : Polyconic
East from Greenwich
COPYRIGHT PHILIP'S

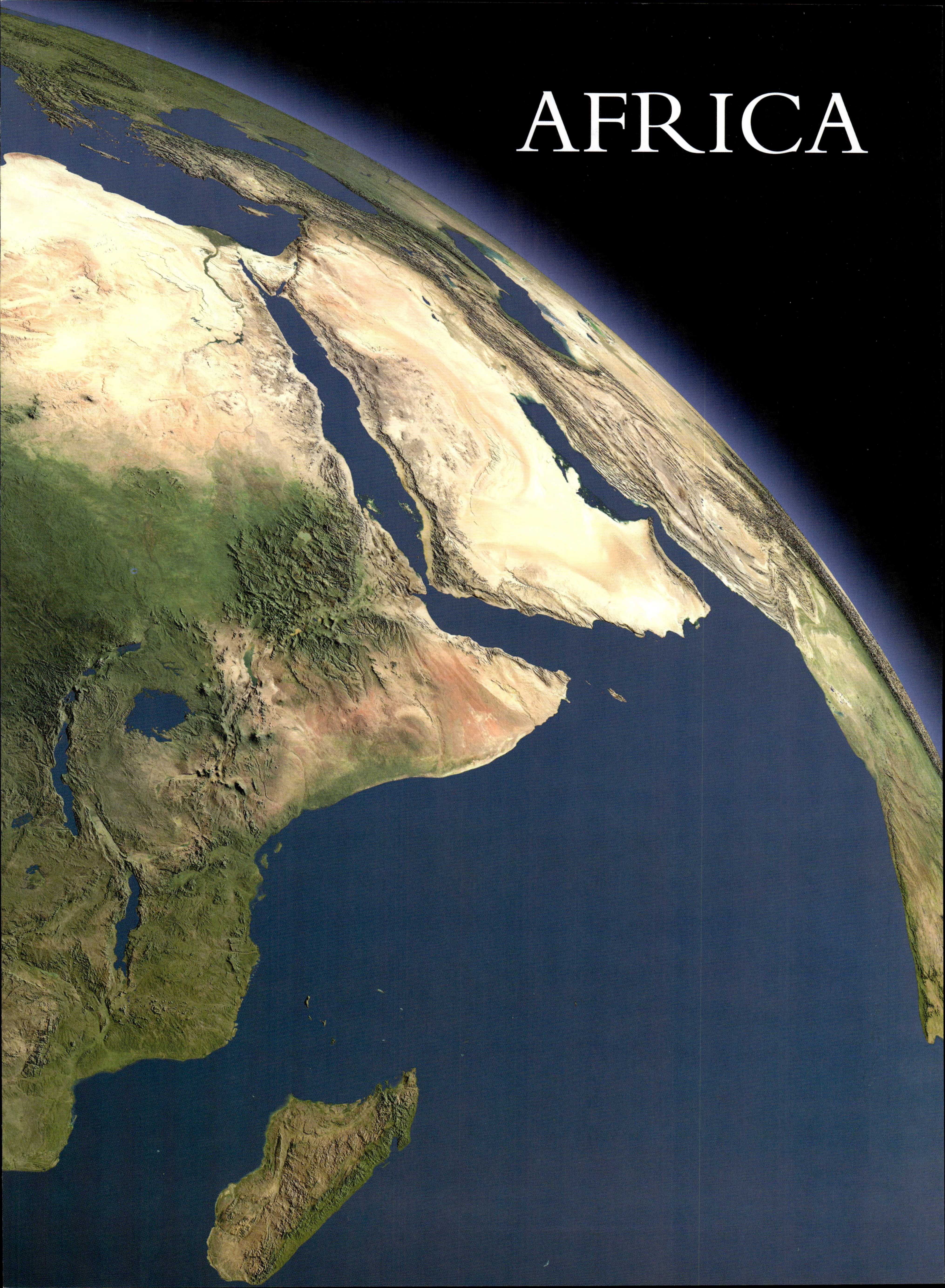
AFRICA

1:33 600 000
km
miles
Projection: Azimuthal Equidistant
West from Greenwich
East from Greenwich
COPYRIGHT PHILIP'S
ft
m
Equator
Tropic of Cancer
Tropic of Capricorn
Europe
Asia
ATLANTIC OCEAN
INDIAN OCEAN
British Isles
B. of Biscay
Carpathians
Alps
Mont Blanc 4808
Dinaric Alps
Apennines
Adriatic Sea
Black Sea
Caucasus
Elbrus 5633
Caspian Sea
Aral Sea
Azores
Pyrénées
Iberian Peninsula
Corsica
Sardinia
Balearic Is.
Sicily
Malta
Crete
Cyprus
Str. of Gibraltar
Madeira
Mediterranean Sea
Levant
Syrian Desert
Dead Sea
Mesopotamia
Tigris
Euphrates
Persian Gulf
Arabia
Hejaz
Red Sea
Canary Is.
Tenerife 3718
C. Juby
C. Bojador
Middle Atlas
High Atlas
Toubkal
High Plateaux
Saharan Atlas
Chott Melrhir
Chott Djerid
G. of Gabès
Djerba
Maghreb
Great Western Erg
Great Eastern Erg
Tripolitania
G. of Sidra
Cyrenaica
Nile Delta
Suez Canal
Mt. Sinai 2285
Siwa Oasis
Egypt
Libyan Desert
Eastern Desert
Nile
El Khârga
Al Kufrah
L. Nasser
Nubian Desert
Nubia
Ras Banâs
Erg Iguidi
Erg Chech
Oued Saoura
Tasili Plateau
Hoggar 2918
Sahara
El Djouf
Adrar 485
Ras Nouâdhibou
C. Timiris
Adrar des Iforas 598
Aïr 2022
Ténéré
Bilma
Tibesti 3415
Cape Verde Is.
2829
C. Vert
El Mreyye
L. Faguibine
Senegal
Senegambia
Gambia
Bijagos Is.
Fouta Djallon
Niger
L. Débo
Bani
Black Volta
White Volta
Sahel
L. Chad
Hadejia
Bahr el Ghazal
Wadai
Dârfûr 3088
Kordofân
1310
Dahlak Is.
Ras Dashen 4533
L. Tana
Barim
Bab el Mandeb
G. of Aden
Ras Asir
Ras Xaafuun
3350
Ethiopian Highlands
Somali Peninsula
Ogaden
Shaballe
Juba
L. Abbé
L. Abaya
4307
Omo
Sobat
Blue Nile
White Nile
'Atbara
Sudd
Bahr el Arab
Bahr el Ghazal
Bahr el Jebel
Guinea
Sherbro I.
Grain Coast
Ivory Coast
C. Palmas
L. de Kossou
Gold Coast
L. Volta
C. Three Points
Slave Coast
Bight of Benin
Niger Delta
Kainji Res. 1780
Benue
Adamawa Highlands
Mt. Cameroon 4070
Bioko 3008
Bight of Bonny
I. de Principe
São Tomé
Annobón
C. Lopez
Gulf of Guinea
Ogooué
Chari
Ouham
Bahr Aouk
1330
Dar Banda
Bomu
Uele
Sangha
Sanaga
Oubangi
Congo
Congo Basin
L. Mai-Ndombe
Chutes Boyoma
Kasai
Sankuru
Lomami
Lualaba
Cuango
Ruwenzori 5109
L. Albert
L. Edward
L. Kivu
L. Kyoga
Mt. Elgon 4321
L. Victoria
1134
L. Turkana
Lach Dera
Tana
Mt. Kenya 5199
Kilimanjaro 5895
Meru 4564
Pangani
Rift Valley
Mitumba Mts.
L. Tanganyika
L. Rukwa
Rungwe 2961
Great Ruaha
L. Mweru
Lukuga
Katanga
L. Bangweulu
Luapula
L. Malawi (L. Nyasa)
Pemba I.
Zanzibar I.
Aldabra Is.
Comoros
2361
Mayotte
C. Delgado
C. d'Ambre
Ruvuma
Lúrio
Luangwa
Shire
Zambezi
L. Cabora Bassa
L. Kariba
Victoria Falls
Kafue
Cuando
Zambezi
Cubango
Cunene
Cuanza
Palmeirinhas Pt.
Bié Plateau 2619
C. Fria
Skeleton Coast
Etosha Pan
Okavango Delta
Makgadikgadi Salt Pans
2483
2593
Limpopo
Walvis Bay
Namib Desert
Nossob
Kalahari
Vaal
High Veld
Orange
Thabana Ntlenyana 3492
Drakensberg
Maputo Bay
St. Helena Bay
Great Nuweveldberge
Compass Mt. 2502
Karoo
Swartberge
C. of Good Hope
C. Agulhas
Algoa B.
Mozambique Channel
Madagascar
Ihopa
Mangoky
2643
2658
C. Ste. Marie
Réunion
Seych
Ascension I.
St. Helena
Tristan da Cunha
6578
5121
-125
-156
1752

1:33 600 000
200 0 200 400 600 800 1000 1200 1400 1600 1800 km
200 0 200 400 600 800 1000 1200 miles
ATLANTIC OCEAN
Azores (Port.)
Ponta Delgada
Madeira (Port.)
Funchal
Canary Is. (Sp.)
Santa Cruz de Tenerife
Las Palmas
B. of Biscay
UNITED KINGDOM
LONDON
NETH.
BELG.
PARIS
FRANCE
GERMANY
POLAND
Warsaw
Prague
CZECH REP.
SLOVAK REP.
Vienna
AUSTRIA
HUNGARY
SWITZ.
UKRAINE
Kiev
RUSSIA
Volgograd
KAZAKHSTAN
Aral Sea
ROMANIA
Odessa
CROATIA
BOS.-HERZ.
SERBIA
MONT.
KOS.
MAC.
ALB.
BULGARIA
GREECE
Athens
Black Sea
Caspian Sea
GEORGIA
ARM.
AZER.
Baku
TURKMEN.
ISTANBUL
Ankara
TURKEY
TEHRAN
Esfahan
IRAN
Mosul
BAGHDAD
IRAQ
Basra
KUWAIT
Persian Gulf
BAHRAIN
QATAR
RIYADH
SAUDI ARABIA
Medina
Jedda
Mecca
Aleppo
SYRIA
Damascus
LEB.
Tel Aviv-Jaffa
Jerusalem
ISRAEL
JORDAN
Syrian Desert
Euphrates
Tigris
CYPRUS
Crete
Marseilles
Corsica
BARCELONA
MADRID
SPAIN
PORTUGAL
Lisbon
ITALY
Rome
Sardinia
Sicily
Adriatic Sea
MALTA
Mediterranean Sea
Gibraltar (U.K.)
Ceuta (Sp.)
Melilla (Sp.)
Oran
Algiers
Annaba
Constantine
Tunis
Sfax
TUNISIA
Chott Djerid
Tripoli
Misratah
Benghazi
Alexandria
Port Said
CAIRO
Suez
El Faiyûm
Asyût
EGYPT
Aswân
Nile
Red Sea
Rabat
Casablanca
Fès
MOROCCO
Marrakesh
El Aaiún
WESTERN SAHARA
Dakhla
ALGERIA
In Salah
LIBYA
Sabhâ
Al Jawf
Sahara
Tropic of Cancer
Fdérik
Ras Nouâdhibou
MAURITANIA
Nouakchott
St-Louis
Senegal
C. Vert
Dakar
SENEGAL
GAMBIA
Banjul
GUINEA-BISSAU
Bissau
GUINEA
Conakry
Freetown
SIERRA LEONE
LIBERIA
Monrovia
IVORY COAST
Yamoussoukro
Bouaké
Abidjan
GHANA
Kumasi
Accra
Sekondi-Takoradi
TOGO
Lomé
BENIN
Porto Novo
MALI
Tombouctou
Bamako
BURKINA FASO
Ouagadougou
Bobo-Dioulasso
Niger
Niamey
NIGER
Agadès
Kano
Kaduna
NIGERIA
Abuja
Maiduguri
Ibadan
LAGOS
Benin City
Enugu
Benue
Port Harcourt
Bight of Benin
Gulf of Guinea
CHAD
L. Chad
Abéché
Ndjamena
Chari
CAMEROON
Douala
Yaoundé
Rey Malabo
EQUATORIAL GUINEA
SÃO TOMÉ & PRÍNCIPE
Annobón (Eq. Guinea)
Libreville
GABON
C. Lopez
Equator
CONGO
Oubangui
Brazzaville
Pointe-Noire
CABINDA (Angola)
KINSHASA
Matadi
CENTRAL AFRICAN REP.
Bangui
Mbandaka
Kisangani
CONGO (DEM. REP. OF THE)
Kasai
Lualaba
Kananga
Mbuji-Mayi
Kolwezi
Likasi
Lubumbashi
SUDAN
Wadi Halfa
Port Sudan
Atbara
Omdurmân
KHARTOUM
Wad Medani
White Nile
Blue Nile
El Fasher
El Obeid
Malakal
SOUTH SUDAN
Wau
Juba
Bahr el Jebel
ERITREA
Massawa
Asmera
YEMEN
Sana'
G. of Aden
Socotra (Yemen)
Ras Asir
DJIBOUTI
Djibouti
Berbera
SOMALILAND
ETHIOPIA
Addis Ababa
Harer
L. Tana
Shabeelle
SOMALIA
Mogadishu
Juba
Kismayu
L. Turkana
KENYA
Nairobi
Kisumu
Mombasa
UGANDA
Kampala
L. Albert
L. Edward
L. Victoria
L. Kivu
RWANDA
Kigali
BURUNDI
Bujumbura
TANZANIA
Dodoma
Zanzibar
Dar es Salaam
L. Tanganyika
L. Mweru
L. Malawi
MALAWI
Lilongwe
Blantyre
INDIAN OCEAN
SEYCHELLES
Victoria
Aldabra Is. (Seychelles)
C. Delgado
COMOROS
Moroni
Mamoudzou
Mayotte (Fr.)
Antsiranana
Mahajanga
Toamasina
Antananarivo
MADAGASCAR
Fianarantsoa
MAURITIUS
Port Louis
St-Denis
Réunion (Fr.)
Mozambique Channel
MOZAMBIQUE
Moçambique
Beira
Maputo
Luanda
ANGOLA
Lobito
Huambo
Namibe
Cuango
Cubango
Cunene
C. Fria
ZAMBIA
Ndola
Lusaka
Zambezi
Livingstone
ZIMBABWE
Harare
Bulawayo
Limpopo
NAMIBIA
Windhoek
BOTSWANA
Gaborone
Pretoria (Tshwane)
Johannesburg
Mbabane
SWAZ.
Vaal
Orange
Kimberley
Maseru
LESOTHO
Durban
SOUTH AFRICA
Cape Town
C. of Good Hope
C. Agulhas
East London
Port Elizabeth
Ascension I. (U.K.)
St. Helena (U.K.)
Tristan da Cunha (U.K.)
Tropic of Capricorn
Projection: Azimuthal Equidistant
West from Greenwich
East from Greenwich
COPYRIGHT PHILIP'S
Dakar Capital Cities

1:6 400 000

THE NILE DELTA
1:3 200 000
MEDITERRANEAN SEA
EGYPT
SAUDI ARABIA
JORDAN
ISRAEL
RED SEA
EL QAHIRA (Cairo)
EL ISKANDARIYA (Alexandria)
EL GIZA
Bur Sa'id (Port Said)
El Suweis (Suez)
Aswan
El Uqsur (Luxor)
Buheirat en Nasser (Lake Nasser)
Wadi Halfa
JIDDAH (Jedda)
MAKKAH (Mecca)
AL MADINAH (Medina)
'AMMAN
Jerusalem (Al Quds)
TEL AVIV-YAFO
Bur Sudan (Port Sudan)
HALAIB TRIANGLE
BIR TAWIL
Es Sahra el Gharbiya (Western Desert)
Sahra en Nubiya (Nubian Desert)

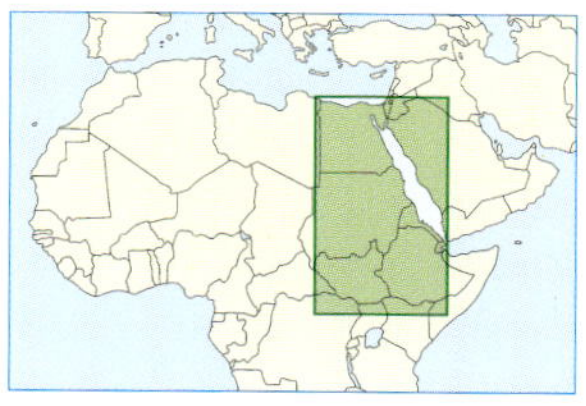

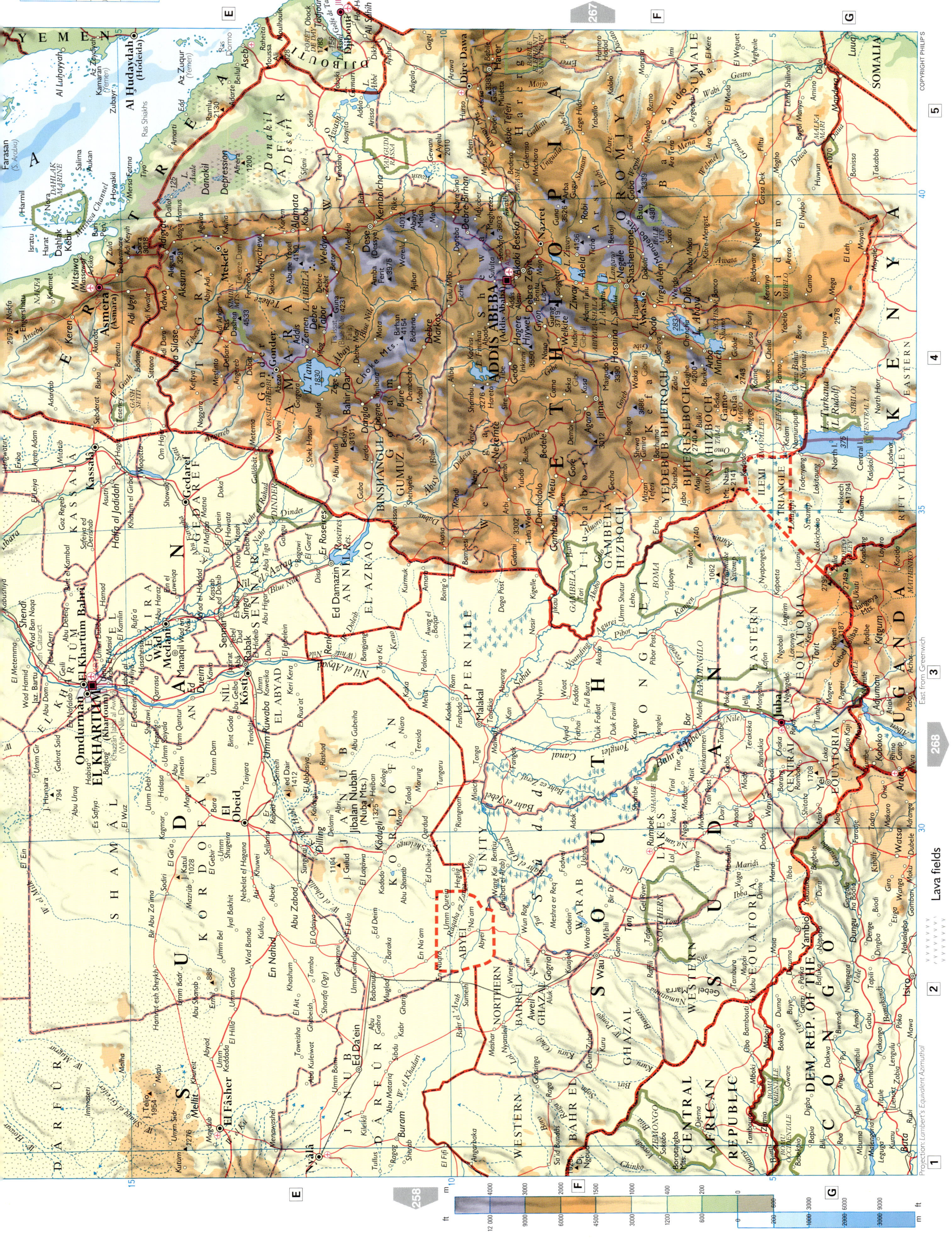
YEMEN
ERITREA
ETHIOPIA
SUDAN
SOUTH SUDAN
KENYA
UGANDA
DJIBOUTI
SOMALIA
CENTRAL AFRICAN REPUBLIC
DEM. REP. OF THE CONGO
ADDIS ABABA
EL KHARTUM (Khartoum)
Omdurman
El Khartûm Bahri
Asmera (Asmara)
Djibouti
Juba
L. Tana
L. Turkana (L. Rudolf)
ILEMI TRIANGLE
ABYEI
Lava fields
Projection: Lambert's Equivalent Azimuthal
COPYRIGHT PHILIP'S
East from Greenwich
257
258
267
268

50 0 50 100 150 200 250 300 km

1:6 400 000

50 0 50 100 150 200 miles

A
B
C
D
256
193
192
261
1
2
3
4
5
MEDITERRANEAN SEA
IONIAN SEA
GREECE
ITALY
MALTA
Valletta
Sicilia
Str. of Sicily
Kriti (Crete)
Irakleio
Chania
Peloponnesos
Kalamata
Tripoli
Kyklades
Dodekanisa
Karpathos
Ierapetra
Catánia
Siracusa
Ragusa
Agrigento
Caltanissetta
Pantelleria
Lampedusa
Linosa
Gozo
TUNIS
Sousse
Monastir
Mahdia
Sfax
Gabès
Djerba
Zarzis
Medenine
Tataouine
Kairouan
Gafsa
Tozeur
Nefta
Kebili
Îles Kerkenna
G. de Gabès
G. de Hammamet
TÙNISIA
Annaba
Constantine
Skikda
Tebessa
El Oued
Biskra
EL OUED
KEBILI
TATAOUINE
TARĀBULUS
(Tripoli)
Zuwārah
Az Zāwiyah
Al Khums
Mişrātah
Zlīţan
Gharyān
Yafran
Nālūt
Ghadāmis
Surt
BANGHĀZĪ
(Benghazi)
Al Marj
Al Bayḑā'
Darnah
Ţubruq
Ajdābiyā
Khalīj Surt
(Gulf of Sidra)
Barqa
(Cyrenaica)
Ad Diffah
(Libyan Plateau)
Ed Déffa
Al Jaghbūb
Jālū
Awjilah
Marādah
Zillah
Waddān
Hūn
Sabhā
Murzūq
Awbārī
Ghāt
Al Jawf
Al Kufrah
Tāzirbū
Ramlat Zaltan
Sarīr Calanscio
Ṣaḥrā' Rabiānah
Ṣaḥrā' Marzūq
Idehan Awbārī
Idehan Murzūq
Al Ḥamādah al Ḥamrā'
Hamadat Tinghert
Al Harūj al Aswad
Fezzan
WĀDĪ ASH SHĀṬI'
WĀDĪ AL ḤAYĀT
AL JUFRAH
SURT
MIŞRĀTAH
AL WĀḤĀT
AL BUṬNĀN
DARNAH
AL MARJ
BANGHĀZĪ
AL KUFRAH
MURZŪQ
SABHĀ
GHĀT
NĀLŪT
AL JABAL AL GHARBĪ
AL JABAL AL AKHḌAR
Tarābulus
(Tripolitania)
LIBYA
EGYPT
Great Sand Sea
Libyan Desert
Siwa
Sahara
ALGERIA
Grand Erg Oriental
Tassili n'Ajjer
Erg d'Admer
Djanet
Illizi
In Amenas
Tropic of Cancer
Sarīr Tibastī
Mesach Mellet
Erg Tin Merzouga
Hadabat el Gilf el Kebir

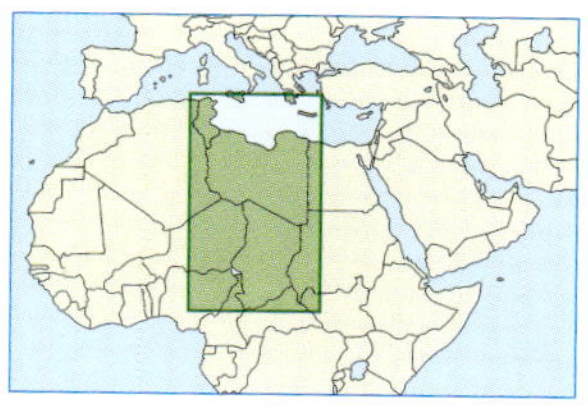

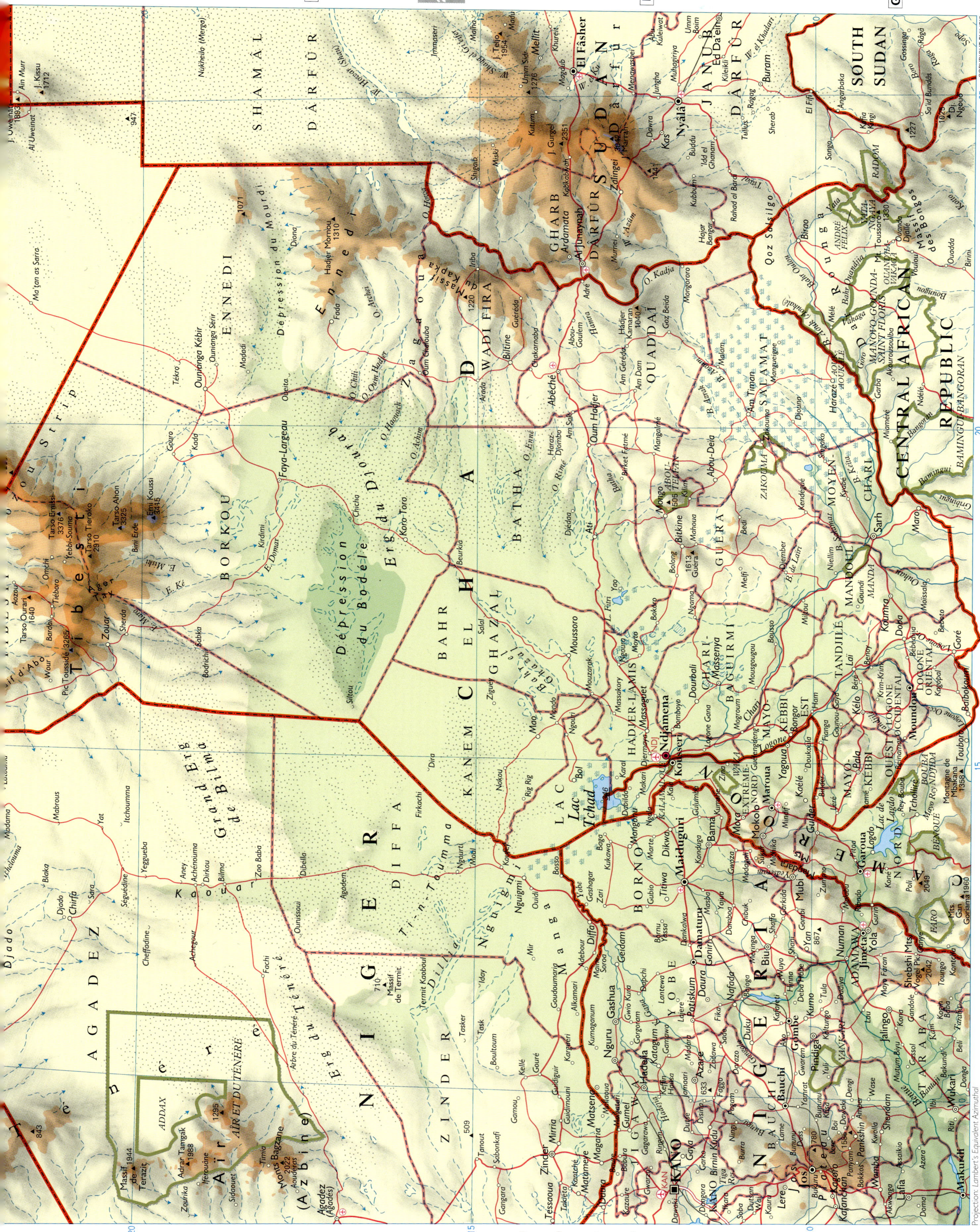

E
F
G
1
2
3
4
5
257
263
264
20
15
10
25
TIBESTI
BORKOU
ENNEDI
Dépression du Bodélé
Erg du Djourab
Grand Erg de Bilma
Ténéré
Aïr
AGADEZ
ZINDER
DIFFA
NIGER
NIGERIA
CHAD
KANEM
LAC
BAHR EL GHAZAL
BATHA
WADI FIRA
OUADDAÏ
GUÉRA
SALAMAT
CHARI-BAGUIRMI
HADJER-LAMIS
MAYO-KEBBI EST
LOGONE OCCIDENTAL
LOGONE ORIENTAL
MANDOUL
MOYEN-CHARI
TANDJILÉ
BORNO
YOBE
KANO
JIGAWA
BAUCHI
GOMBE
ADAMAWA
TARABA
PLATEAU
SHAMÂL DÂRFÛR
GHARB DÂRFÛR
JANUB DÂRFÛR
SUDAN
SOUTH SUDAN
CENTRAL AFRICAN REPUBLIC
CAMEROON
EXTRÊME-NORD
NORD
Lac Tchad
Ndjamena
Maiduguri
Kano
Zinder
Agadez
Abéché
Sarh
Moundou
Nyala
El Fasher
Faya-Largeau
Yola
Jos
Bauchi
Garoua
Maroua
Lava fields
Projection: Lambert's Equivalent Azimuthal
COPYRIGHT PHILIP'S


Underlined towns give their name to the administrative area in which they stand.

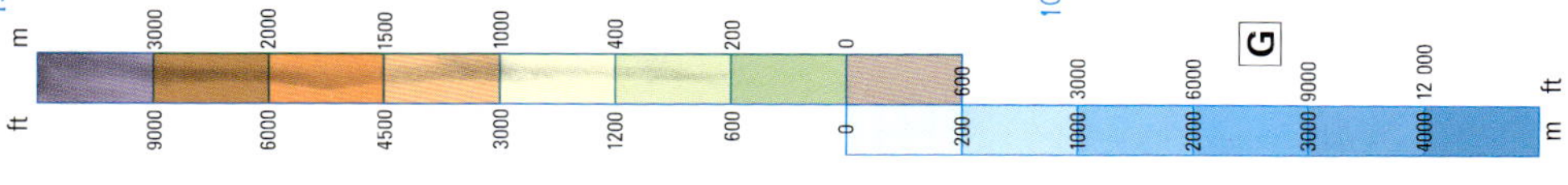

m
3000
2000
1500
1000
400
200
0
ft
9000
6000
4500
3000
1200
600
0
200
1000
2000
3000
4000
600
3000
6000
9000
12 000

1:6 400 000

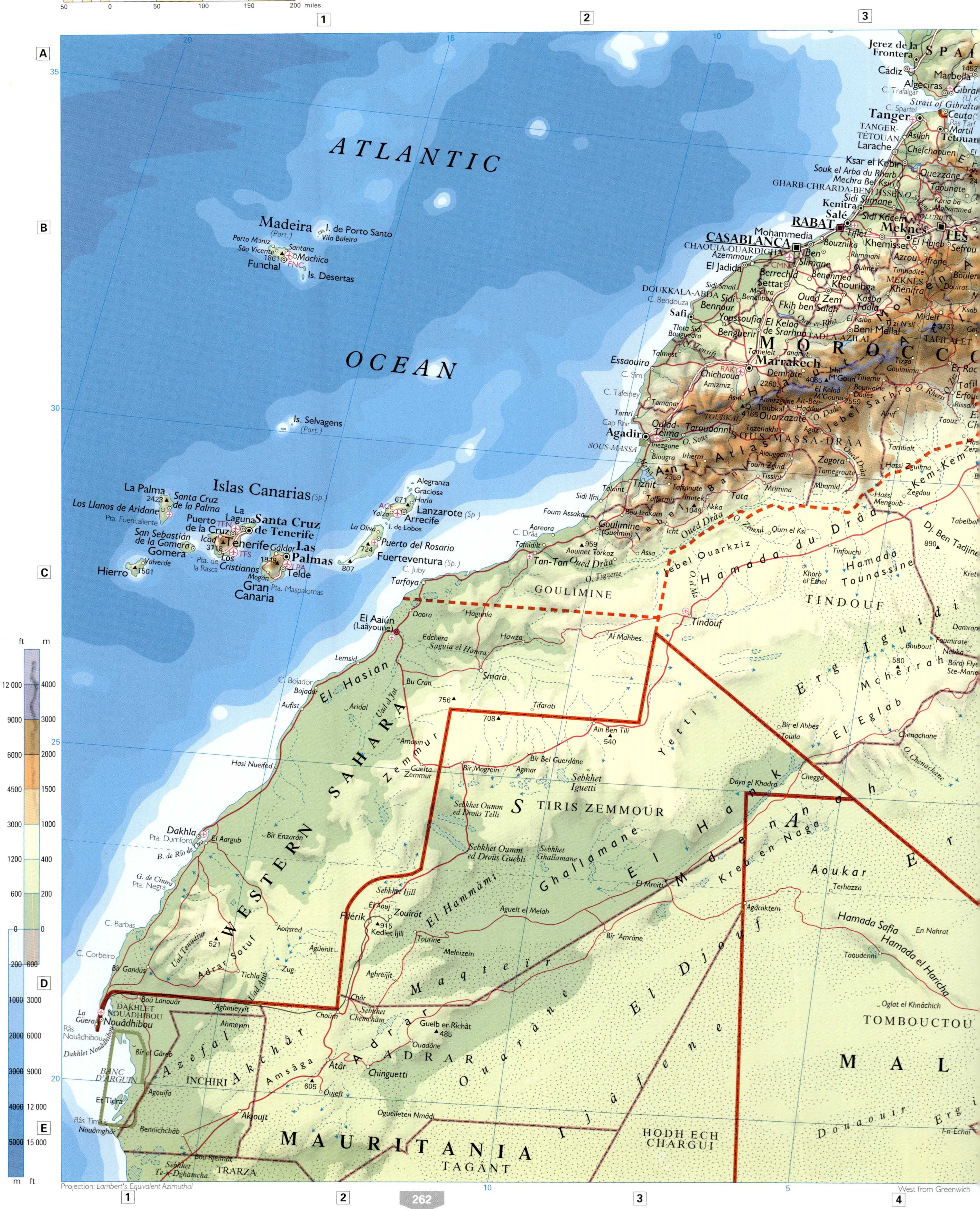
ATLANTIC
OCEAN
Madeira (Port.)
I. de Porto Santo
Funchal
Is. Desertas
Is. Selvagens (Port.)
Islas Canarias (Sp.)
La Palma
Santa Cruz de la Palma
Santa Cruz de Tenerife
Tenerife
Gomera
Hierro
Las Palmas
Gran Canaria
Lanzarote (Sp.)
Arrecife
Fuerteventura (Sp.)
Puerto del Rosario
MOROCCO
RABAT
CASABLANCA
Tanger
Fès
Meknès
Marrakech
Agadir
Essaouira
Safi
El Jadida
Kenitra
Salé
Ouarzazate
Tiznit
Goulimine
Tan-Tan
Tarfaya
GOULIMINE
SOUS-MASSA-DRÂA
Jebel Toubkal 4165
Anti Atlas
Tindouf
TINDOUF
Hamada du Drâa
Hamada Tounassine
Erg Iguidi
El Aaiún (Laayoune)
Smara
WESTERN SAHARA
El Hasian
Zemmour
Dakhla
Nouâdhibou
TIRIS ZEMMOUR
El Hank
Mdenah
Aoukar
Hamada Safia
TOMBOUCTOU
MALI
El Djouf
Ouarâne
Adrar
Atâr
Chinguetti
Akjoujt
Fdérik
Zouîrât
INCHIRI
MAURITANIA
TAGANT
HODH ECH CHARGUI
TRARZA
Bou Rjeimât

Projection: Lambert's Equivalent Azimuthal

West from Greenwich

262

Underlined towns give their name to the administrative area in which they stand

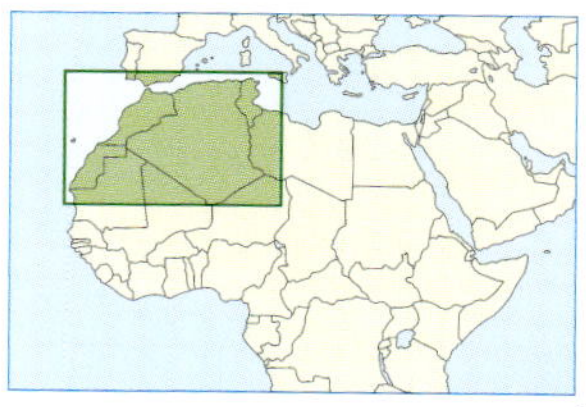

4 192 5 6 7 192

MEDITERRANEAN SEA
ALGER (Algiers)
Oran (Ouahran)
TUNIS
TARĀBULUS (Tripoli)
Sicilia (It.)
Pantelleria (It.)
Lampedusa (It.)
Îles Kerkenna
G. de Gabès
Golfe de Tunis
G. de Hammamet
Bizerte (Binzert)
Annaba
Constantine
Skikda
Bejaïa
Sétif
Batna
Biskra
Blida
Médéa
Mostaganem
Relizane
Mascara
Sidi-bel-Abbès
Tlemcen
Oujda
Saïda
Tiaret
Djelfa
Laghouat
Ghardaïa
Ouargla
Touggourt
El Oued
Béchar
Tindouf
Sfax
Sousse
Kairouan
Gafsa
Gabès
Medenine
Tataouine
Zuwārah
Ghadāmis
Gharyān
Yafran
Nālūt
Tébessa
Guelma
Souk Ahras
El Goléa (El Ménia)
Timimoun
Adrar
In Salah
Reggane
Illizi
In Amenas
Djanet
Ghāt
Tamanrasset
Bordj Mokhtar
Tessalit
Agadez
ALGERIA
TUNISIA
LIBYA
NIGER
Atlas Saharien
Hauts Plateaux
Grand Erg Occidental
Grand Erg Oriental
Plateau du Tademaït
Plateau du Tinrhert
Tassili n'Ajjer
Ahaggar
Atakor
Tassili-Oua-n-Ahaggar
Tanezrouft
Erg Chech
Adrar des Iforas
Aurès
Chott Melrhir
Chott el Hodna
Chott Djerid
Erg Issaouane
Hamada de Tinrhert
Al Hamādah al Hamrā'
Idehān Awbārī
Idehān Murzūq
Tahat 2918
Tropic of Cancer
Plateau du Djado
Hamada Manguéni
Massif de Termit
Aïr et Ténéré
East from Greenwich
COPYRIGHT PHILIP'S

A B C D E 258 5 263 6 7

50 0 50 100 150 200 250 300 km

50 0 50 100 150 200 miles

1:6 400 000

1 2 260 3

ADRAR
INCHIRI
MAURITANIA
TAGÂNT
SAHARA
TRARZA
BRAKNA
ASSÂBA
HODH EL GHARBI
HODH ECH CHARGUI
Aoukâr Depression
El Mreyyé
TOMBOUCTOU
Nouakchott
NKC
SENEGAL
ST-LOUIS
St-Louis
LOUGA
MATAM
DAKAR
Thiès
Diourbel
Kaolack
TAMBACOUNDA
KOLDA
ZIGUINCHOR
KEDOUGOU
GAMBIA
Banjul
GUINEA-BISSAU
Arquipélago dos Bijagós
Bissau
BOKÉ
LABÉ
Fouta Djallon
MAMOU
KINDIA
GUINEA
FARANAH
KANKAN
NZÉRÉKORÉ
CONAKRY
FREETOWN
SIERRA LEONE
NORTHERN
EASTERN
SOUTHERN
WESTERN
LIBERIA
Monrovia
MALI
KAYES
KOULIKORO
BAMAKO
SÉGOU
SIKASSO
MOPTI
Mopti
Tombouctou
Bobo-Dioulasso
IVORY COAST
SAVANES
DENGUÉLÉ
WORODOUGOU
VALLÉE DU BANDAMA
ZANZAN
LACS
Yamoussoukro
Bouaké
ABIDJAN
BAS-SASSANDRA
San Pédro
ATLANTIC OCEAN
Grain Coast
Ivory Coast
GULF


Projection : Lambert's Equivalent Azimuthal



Underlined towns give their name to the administrative area in which they stand.

Administrative divisions in Ivory Coast:

1 Dix-Huit Montagnes
2 Fromager
3 Haut-Sassandra
4 Lagunes
5 Marahoué
6 Moyen-Cavally
7 Moyen-Comoé
8 Sud-Bandama
9 Sud-Comoé

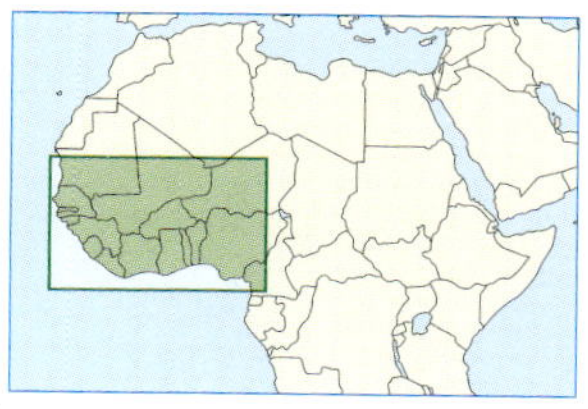

261
259
264
ALGERIA
Adrar des Iforas
KIDAL
GAO
TILLABÉRI
NIAMEY
Aïr (Azbine)
AGADEZ
Agadez (Agadès)
ADDAX
AÏR ET TÉNÉRÉ
Ténéré
Talak
TAHOUA
Azaouak
NIGER
TADRÈS
MARADI
ZINDER
DIFFA
Manga
DOSSO
OUAGADOUGOU
BURKINA
W DU BENIN
BENIN
TOGO
GHANA
Lake Volta
VOLTA
ACCRA
LOMÉ
Cotonou
Porto-Novo
LAGOS
IBADAN
OGBOMOSHO
Sokoto
Katsina
KANO
JIGAWA
YOBE
Maiduguri
BORNO
GOMBE
Bauchi
KADUNA
Jos
Plateau
PLATEAU
ABUJA
FED. CAP. TERR.
NIGERIA
ZAMFARA
KEBBI
KOGI
BENUE
ENUGU
Enugu
BENIN CITY
EDO
DELTA
PORT HARCOURT
RIVERS
BAYELSA
CROSS RIVER
Calabar
ADAMAWA
TARABA
Adamaoua
CAMEROON
DOUALA
YAOUNDÉ
LITTORAL
CENTRE
Bioko
EQUATORIAL GUINEA
Rey Malabo
Bight of Bonny
Bight of Benin
Slave Coast
Niger Delta
GULF OF GUINEA
Lac Tchad
CHAD
N. E. NIGERIA on same scale
East from Greenwich
COPYRIGHT PHILIP'S

1:6 400 000
257
268
259
263
CENTRAL AFRICAN REPUBLIC
DEM. REP. OF THE CONGO
CONGO
GABON
CAMEROON
CHAD
NIGERIA
SOUTH SUDAN
SUDAN
EQUATORIAL GUINEA
Bangui
Yaoundé
Douala
Libreville
Kisangani
Mbandaka
Bight of Bonny
Malabo
Sarh
Garoua
Ngaoundéré
Berbérati
Bambari
Bossangoa
Bouar
Franceville
Port-Gentil
Ouesso
Impfondo
Gemena
Lisala
Bumba
Buta
Bandundu
ORIENTALE
EQUATEUR
ADAMAOUA
Massif des Bongos
Congo
Ubangi
Sangha
Lualaba
Bioko

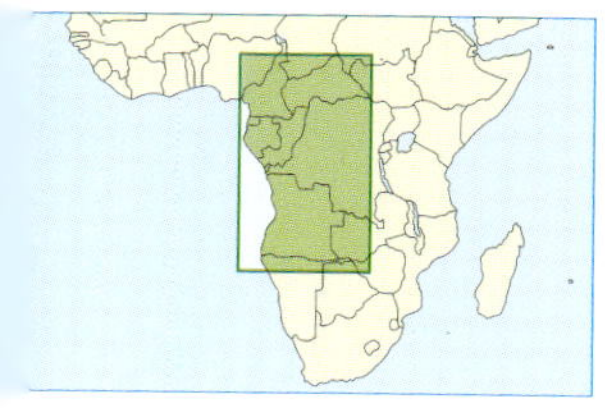

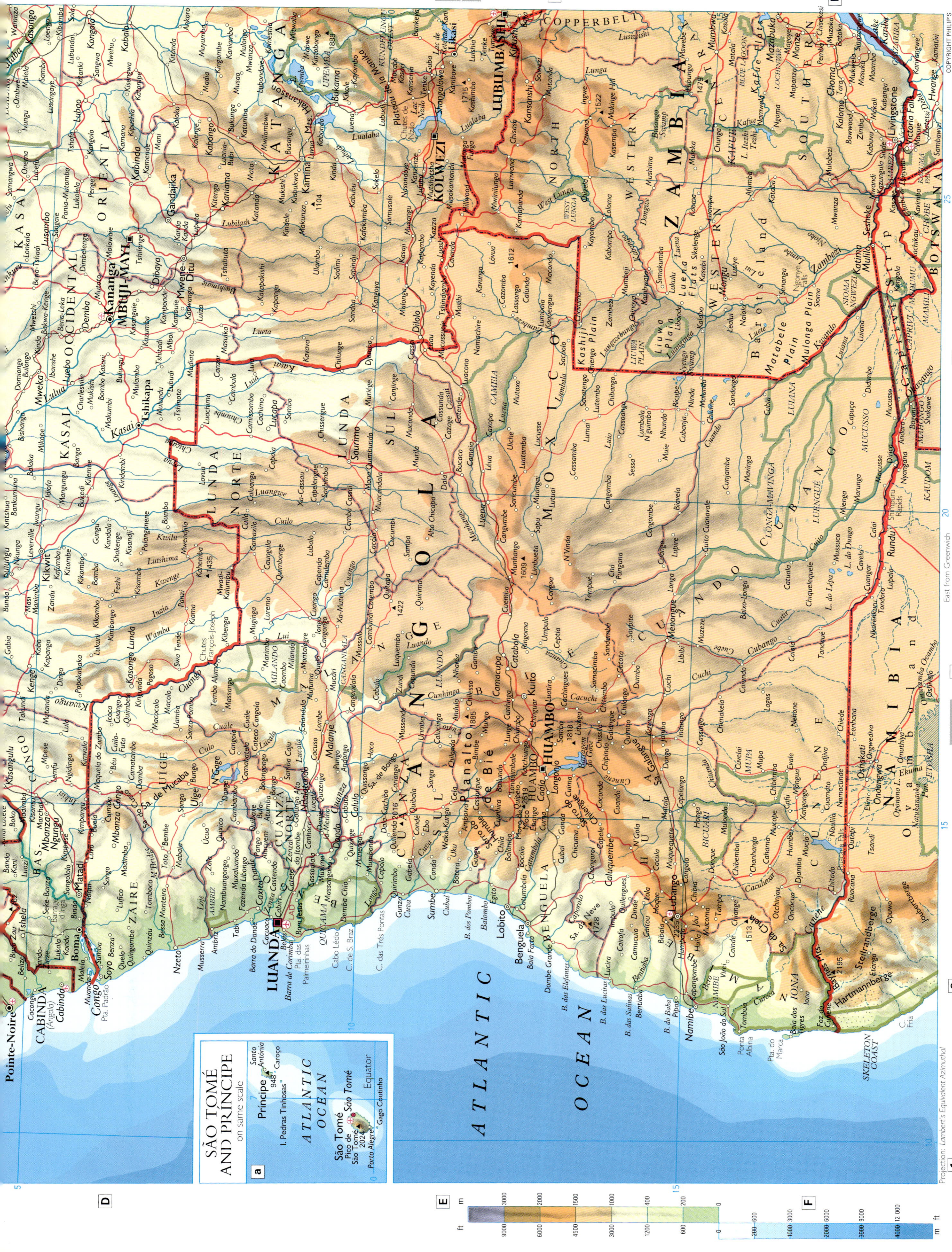
ANGOLA
ZAMBIA
NAMIBIA
BOTSWANA
ATLANTIC OCEAN
LUANDA
HUAMBO
LUBUMBASHI
KOLWEZI
Kananga
Tshikapa
MBUJI-MAYI
Lobito
Benguela
Lubango
Namibe
Livingstone
Pointe-Noire
Cabinda
SÃO TOMÉ AND PRÍNCIPE
on same scale
São Tomé
Príncipe
Equator
SKELETON COAST
269
270
Projection: Lambert's Equivalent Azimuthal
COPYRIGHT PHILIP'S

# ETHIOPIA AND THE HORN OF AFRICA

1:6 400 000

257
259
268
SHAMÂL DÂRFÛR
SHAMÂL KORDOFÂN
JANUB DÂRFÛR
JANUB KORDOFÂN
SUDAN
SOUTH SUDAN
ABYEI
UNITY
UPPER NILE
JONGLEI
NORTHERN BAHR EL GHAZAL
WESTERN BAHR EL GHAZAL
WARAB
LAKES
WESTERN EQUATORIA
CENTRAL EQUATORIA
EASTERN EQUATORIA
CENTRAL AFRICAN REPUBLIC
DEM. REP. OF THE CONGO
ORIENTALE
NORD KIVU
UGANDA
KENYA
ETHIOPIA
ILEMI TRIANGLE
EL KHARTUM
Omdurman
El Khartum Bahri
(Khartoum)
KASSALA
Kassala
GEZIRA
Wad Medani
SENNAR
Sennar
EL ABYAD
Kosti
NIL EL AZRAQ
Ed Damazin
GEDAREF
Gedaref
El Obeid
El Fasher
Nyala
Malakal
Wau
Juba
Kisangani
KAMPALA
NAIROBI
ADDIS ABEBA
Asmera
Lake Victoria
L. Turkana (L. Rudolf)
L. Tana
GAMBELA
BINSHANGUL GUMUZ
YEDEBUB BIHEROCH BIHERESEBOCH NA HIZBOCH
Projection: Lambert's Equivalent Azimuthal

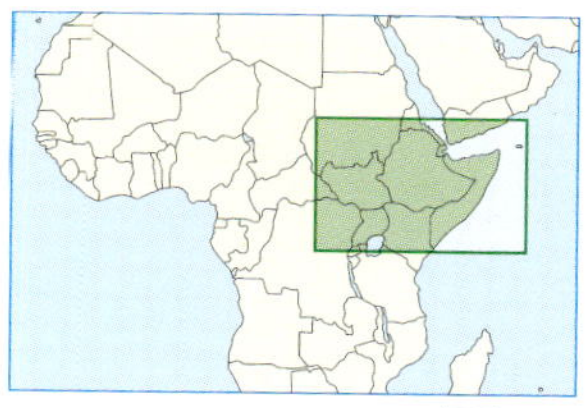

249

RED SEA
YEMEN
Hadramawt
SAN'A'
Al Hudaydah (Hodeida)
Dhamar
Ibb
Ta'izz
Al Mukalla
Ash Shihr
Shuqrā
Shaykh Uthmān
Adan (Aden)
Gulf of Aden
Bab el Mandeb
Socotra (Yemen)
Hadiboh
The Brothers (Yemen)
'Abd al Kūri (Yemen)
Ras Asir (C. Guardafui)
Danakil Depression
AFAR
Danakil Desert
DJIBOUTI
Djibouti
Tadjoura
Golfe de Tadjoura
Obock
Dire Dawa
Harer
Jijiga
Hargeisa
Berbera
Burco (Burao)
Ceerigaabo (Erigavo)
Boosaaso (Bosaso)
Qardho (Gardo)
Garoowe
Las Anod (Laascaanood)
Somaliland
Puntland
AWDAL
TOGDHEER
SANAAG
SOOL
BARI
NUGAAL
MUDUG
Galmudug
GALGUDUUD
HIIRAAN
BAKOOL
BAY
GEDO
SHABEELLAHA DHEXE
SHABEELLAHA HOOSE
BANAADIR
JUBBADA DHEXE
JUBBADA HOOSE
Haud
Ogaden
SUMALE
OROMIYA
Hararge
Bale
Galkacyo (Galcaio)
Gode
Kebri Dehar
Degeh Bur
Beledweyne (Belet Uen)
Baydhabo (Baidoa)
Buurhakaba (Bur Acaba)
Wanleweyne (Uanle Uen)
Afgooye
MUQDISHO (Mogadishu)
Marka (Merca)
Baraawe (Brava)
Jilib (Gelib)
Jamaame (Giamama)
Kismaayo (Chisimaio)
Hobyo (Obbia)
Eyl
Mandera
Garissa
Wajir
NORTH EASTERN
INDIAN OCEAN
East from Greenwich
40
45
50
15
10
5
0
5
6
7
A
B
C
D
E

50 0 50 100 150 200 250 300 km

50 0 50 100 150 200 miles

1:6 400 000

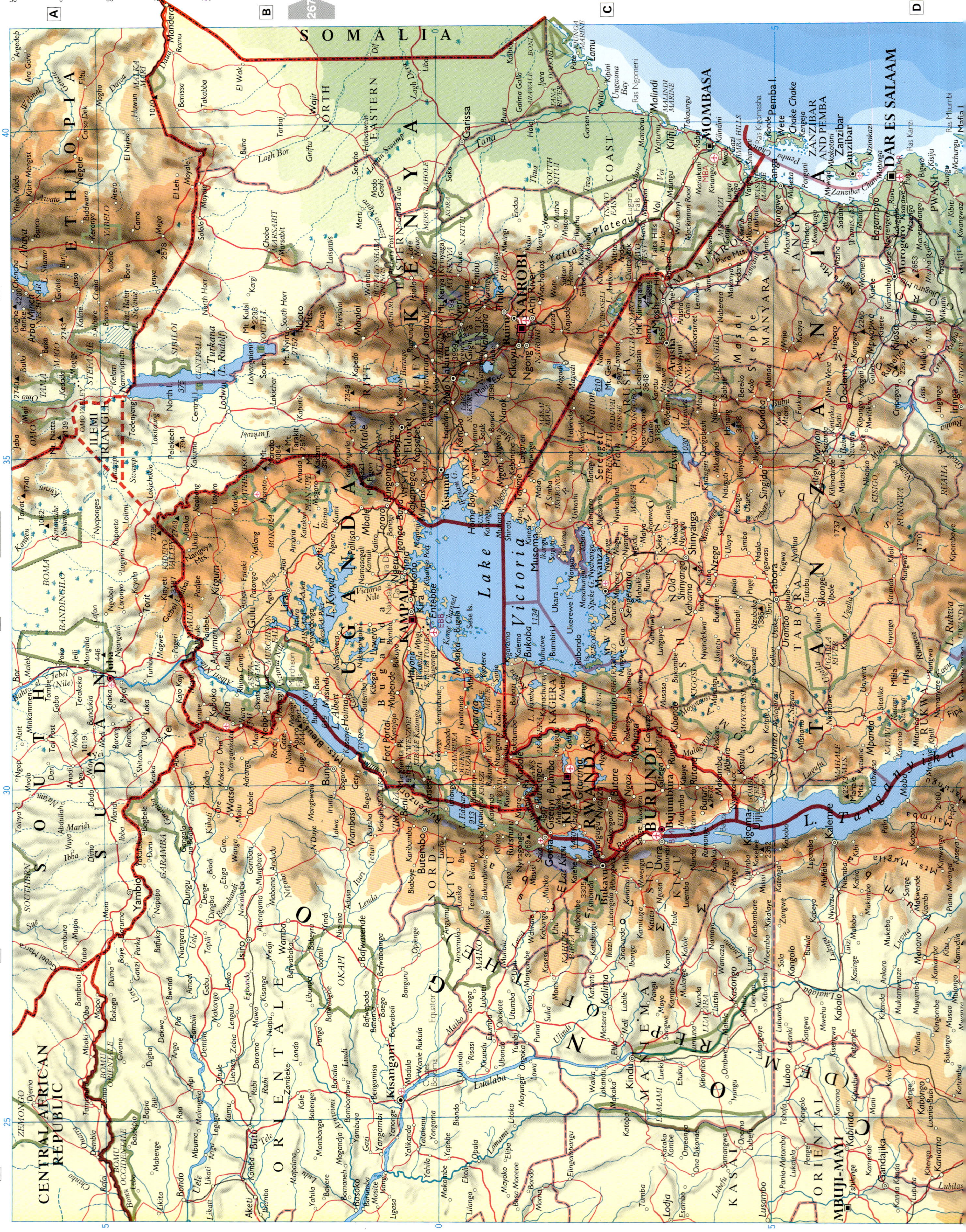
SOMALIA
ETHIOPIA
KENYA
UGANDA
TANZANIA
RWANDA
BURUNDI
SOUTH SUDAN
CENTRAL AFRICAN REPUBLIC
NAIROBI
MOMBASA
DAR ES SALAAM
KAMPALA
KIGALI
Bujumbura
Dodoma
Juba
Kisangani
MBUJI-MAYI
ZANZIBAR AND PEMBA
Zanzibar
Pemba I.
Lake Victoria
L. Turkana (L. Rudolf)
L. Albert
L. Kivu
L. Tanganyika
L. Rukwa
ILEMI TRIANGLE
Serengeti Plain
Masai Steppe
Yatta Plateau
Arusha
Moshi
Tabora
Mwanza
Kisumu
Eldoret
Nakuru
Gulu
Entebbe
Goma
Bukavu
Kigoma
Garissa
Lamu
Malindi
Marsabit
Moyale
Lodwar
Isiro
Bunia
Butembo
Uvira
Kindu
Kabinda
Kalemie
Singida
Shinyanga
Morogoro
Iringa

257
264
267

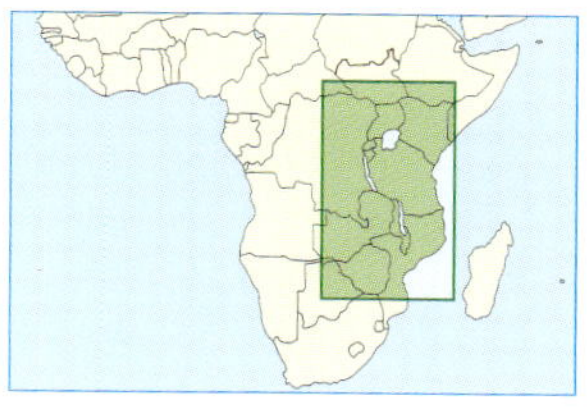

INDIAN OCEAN
MOZAMBIQUE
ZAMBIA
ZIMBABWE
BOTSWANA
SOUTH AFRICA
ANGOLA
NAMIBIA
L. Nyasa
L. Malawi
HARARE
LUSAKA
Projection: Lambert's Equivalent Azimuthal
COPYRIGHT PHILIP'S
East from Greenwich

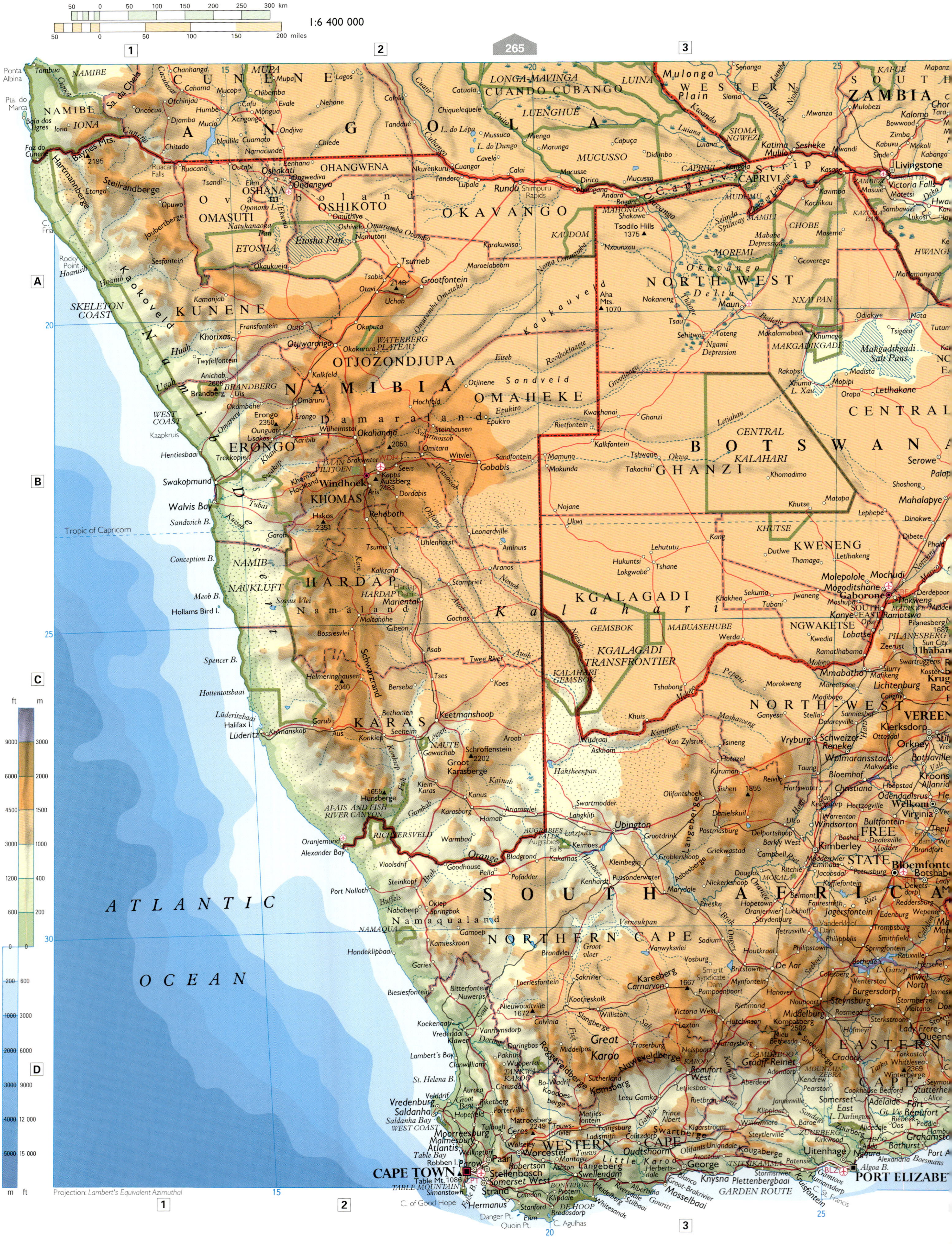
1:6 400 000
km
miles
265
ZAMBIA
NAMIBIA
BOTSWANA
SOUTH AFRICA
ATLANTIC OCEAN
Tropic of Capricorn
Projection: Lambert's Equivalent Azimuthal
KUNENE
OTJOZONDJUPA
OMAHEKE
ERONGO
KHOMAS
HARDAP
KARAS
OKAVANGO
OSHIKOTO
OHANGWENA
OMUSATI
OSHANA
CAPRIVI
NORTH-WEST
CENTRAL
GHANZI
KGALAGADI
KWENENG
NGWAKETSE
NORTHERN CAPE
WESTERN CAPE
EASTERN CAPE
FREE STATE
SKELETON COAST
Kalahari
Great Karoo
Namaqualand
Damaraland
Windhoek
Swakopmund
Walvis Bay
Lüderitz
Keetmanshoop
Rundu
Tsumeb
Gobabis
Maun
Gaborone
Molepolole
Mahalapye
Serowe
Livingstone
Victoria Falls
Kimberley
Bloemfontein
Upington
Oranjemund
Alexander Bay
Saldanha
Vredenburg
Worcester
Paarl
Stellenbosch
George
Knysna
Mossel Bay
CAPE TOWN
PORT ELIZABETH
Etosha Pan
Makgadikgadi Salt Pans
C. of Good Hope
C. Agulhas
Orange
Okavango Delta
Kaokoveld
Namib Desert

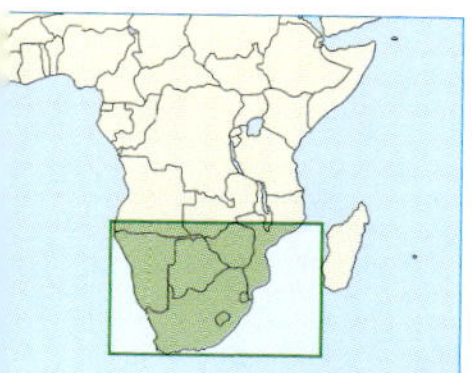

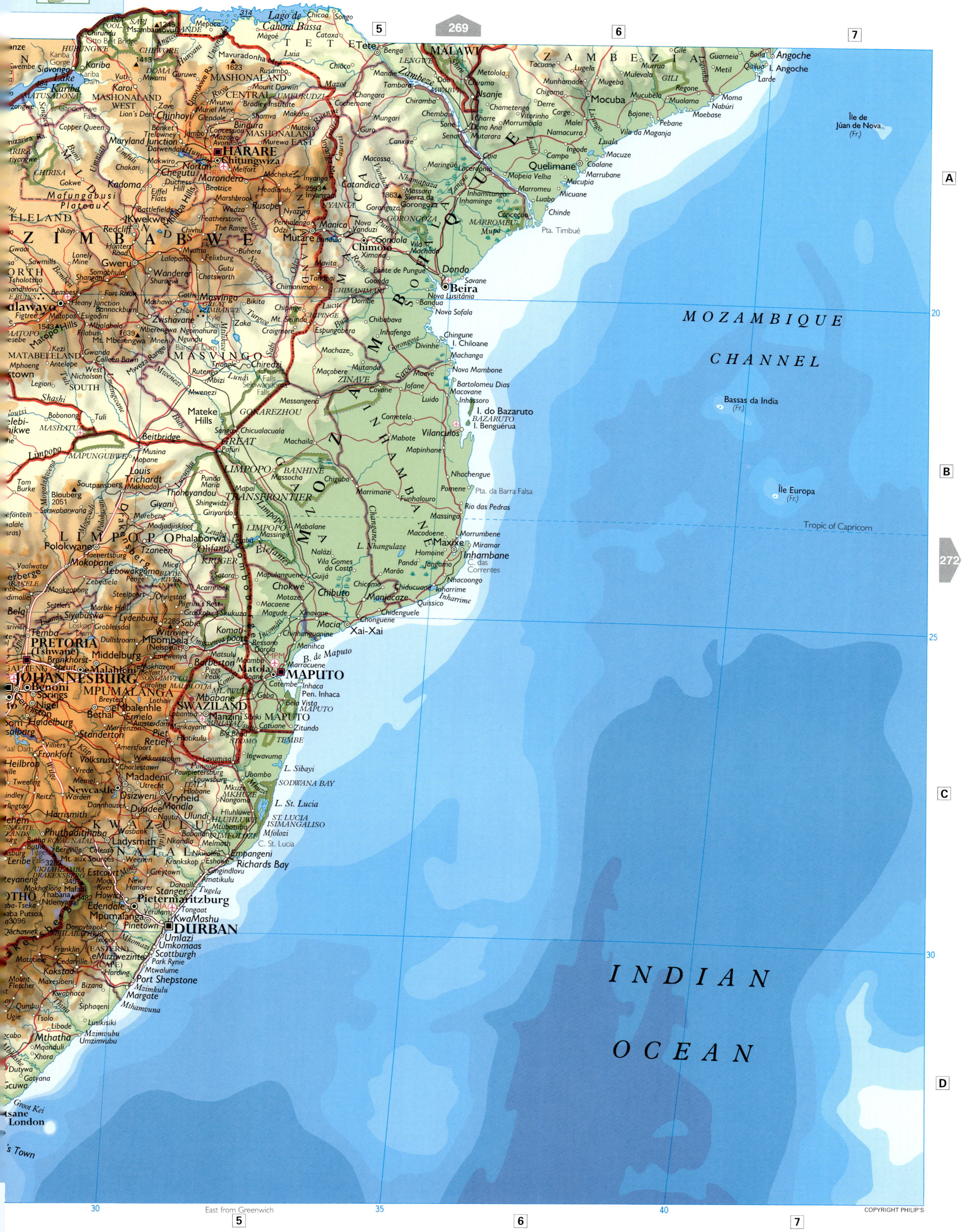

269
272
5
6
7
A
B
C
D
20
25
30
35
40
East from Greenwich
MOZAMBIQUE
CHANNEL
INDIAN
OCEAN
Tropic of Capricorn
Bassas da India
Île Europa
Île de Júan de Nova
(Fr.)
Lago de Cahora Bassa
MALAWI
ZAMBEZIA
ZIMBABWE
MOZAMBIQUE
MANICA
SOFALA
INHAMBANE
GAZA
MASVINGO
MPUMALANGA
LIMPOPO
SWAZILAND
KWAZULU NATAL
MASHONALAND
HARARE
Chitungwiza
Mutare
Gweru
Masvingo
Bulawayo
Beira
Dondo
Chimoio
Quelimane
Mocuba
Angoche
I. Angoche
Tete
Vilanculos
I. do Bazaruto
I. Benguérua
Inhambane
Maxixe
Xai-Xai
Chibuto
Chókwè
MAPUTO
Matola
Mbabane
Manzini
PRETORIA
(Tshwane)
JOHANNESBURG
Benoni
Springs
Middelburg
Mbombela
Polokwane
Phalaborwa
Louis Trichardt
Beitbridge
Newcastle
Ladysmith
Pietermaritzburg
DURBAN
Richards Bay
Port Shepstone
Margate
Mthatha
East London
Umlazi
KwaMashu
Pinetown
Inhaca
Pen. Inhaca
B. de Maputo
L. St. Lucia
L. Sibayi
Pta. da Barra Falsa
Rio das Pedras
C. das Correntes
Pta. Timbué
Chinde
Nova Mambone
Nova Sofala
Chiloane
Mateke Hills
COPYRIGHT PHILIP'S

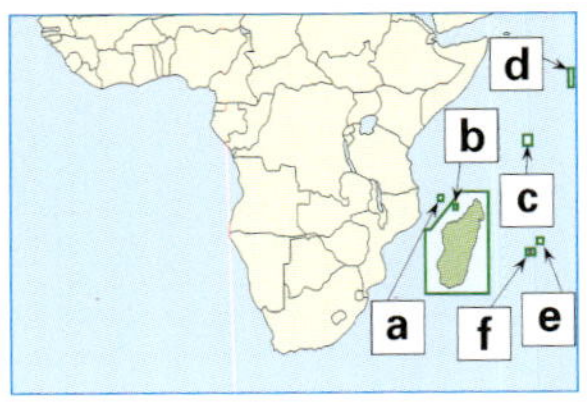
a
b
c
d
e
f

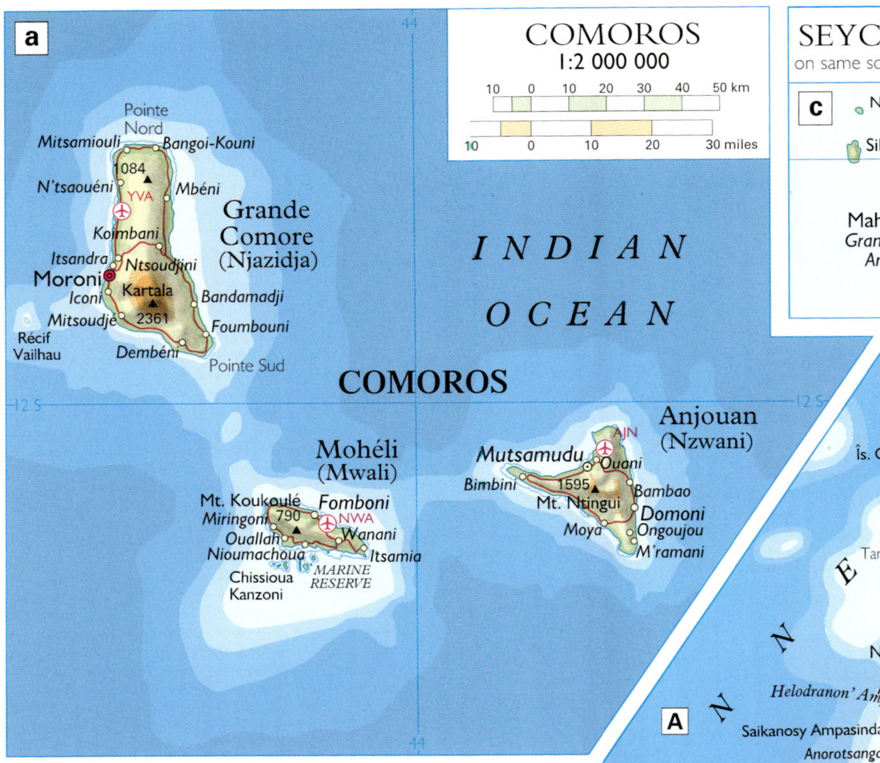
COMOROS
1:2 000 000
COMOROS
INDIAN OCEAN
Grande Comore (Njazidja)
Moroni
Mitsamiouli
Bangoi-Kouni
Pointe Nord
N'tsaouéni
Mbéni
Koimbani
Itsandra
Ntsoudjini
Kartala
2361
Iconi
Mitsoudjé
Bandamadji
Foumbouni
Récif
Vaihau
Dembéni
Pointe Sud
Mohéli (Mwali)
Mt. Koukoulé
Fomboni
Miringoni
Ouallah
Nioumachoua
Wanani
Itsamia
Chissioua
Kanzoni
MARINE RESERVE
Anjouan (Nzwani)
Mutsamudu
Ouani
Bimbini
Mt. Ntingui
1595
Bambao
Domoni
Moya
Ongoujou
M'ramani

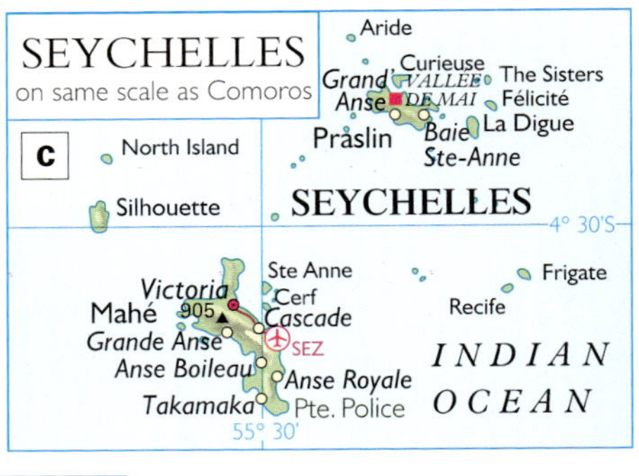
SEYCHELLES
on same scale as Comoros
c
SEYCHELLES
Aride
Curieuse
Grand Anse
The Sisters
Félicité
Praslin
La Digue
Baie Ste-Anne
North Island
Silhouette
Victoria
Mahé
Grande Anse
Anse Boileau
Takamaka
Ste Anne
Cerf
Cascade
Anse Royale
Pte. Police
Recife
Frigate
INDIAN OCEAN
4° 30'S
55° 30'

MALDIVES
on same scale as Madagascar
d
MALDIVES
INDIAN OCEAN
Ihavandiffulu Atoll
Tiladummati Atoll
Kulhudhuffushi
Makunudu Atoll
Miladummadulu Atoll
North Malosmadulu Atoll
Ugoofaaru
Naifaru
Fadiffolu Atoll
South Malosmadulu Atoll
Eydhafushi
Kaashidhoo Channel
Kaashidhoo Atoll
Gaa Faru Atoll
Goidu Atoll
North Malé Atoll
Toddu Atoll
Rasdu Atoll
Rasdhoo
Malé
South Malé Atoll
Ari Atoll
Maafushi
Mahibadhoo
Felidhoo
Felidu Atoll
North Nilandu Atoll
Vattaru Atoll
Mulaku Atoll
South Nilandu Atoll
Muli
Kudahuvadhoo
Kudahuvadhoo Channel
Kolumadulu Atoll
Veimandu Channel
Haddumati Atoll
One and a Half Degree Channel
Thinadhoo
Huvadu Atoll
Equator
Equatorial Channel
Fua Mulaku
Hithadhoo
Addu Atoll
GAN

MAYOTTE
1: 800 000
b
Île Mtsamboro
C. Douamougo
Mtsamboro
B. de Longoni
Bandraboua
Koungou
Acoua
Mtsapéré
Pamandzi (Petite Terre)
Grande Terre
Mtsangamouji
Mamoudzou
Dzaoudzi
DZA
Chingoni
Chiconi
Dembéni
Sada
Ouangani
Bénara
653
B. de Bouéni
Bandrélé
Bouéni
Chirongui
Kani-Kéli
Choungui
594
Mayotte (France)

MADAGASCAR
1:6 400 000
MOZAMBIQUE CHANNEL
INDIAN OCEAN
ANTANANARIVO
Antananarivo
Antsiranana (Diego Suarez)
Mahajanga
Toamasina (Tamatave)
Fianarantsoa
Toliara
Taolanaro (Fort Dauphin)
Antsirabe
Morondava
Îs. Glorieuses (Fr.)
Nosy Bé
Nosy Boraha (Île Ste-Marie)
Tropic of Capricorn
Tanjon' i Vohimena
East from Greenwich
Projection: Lambert's Equivalent Azimuthal
COPYRIGHT PHILIP'S

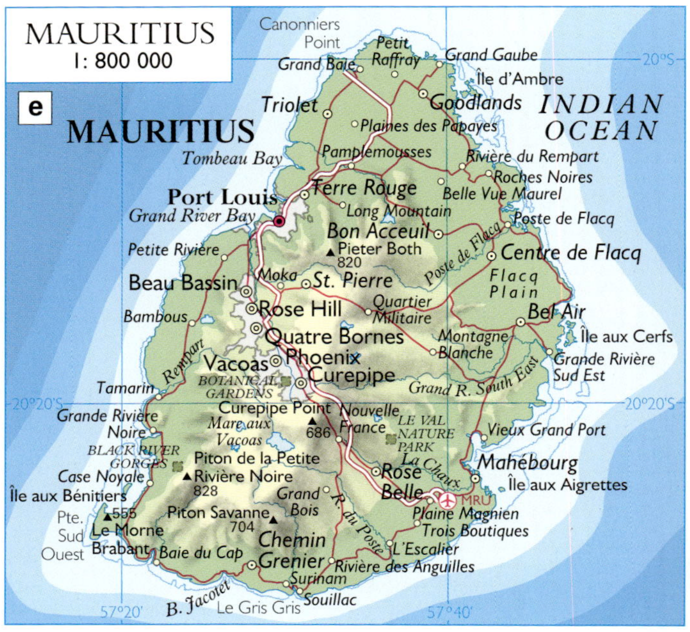
MAURITIUS
1: 800 000
e
MAURITIUS
INDIAN OCEAN
Port Louis
Canonniers Point
Grand Baie
Triolet
Goodlands
Pamplemousses
Terre Rouge
Beau Bassin
Rose Hill
Quatre Bornes
Vacoas
Phoenix
Curepipe
Centre de Flacq
Mahébourg
Rose Belle
Chemin Grenier
Souillac
Le Morne Brabant
Le Gris Gris

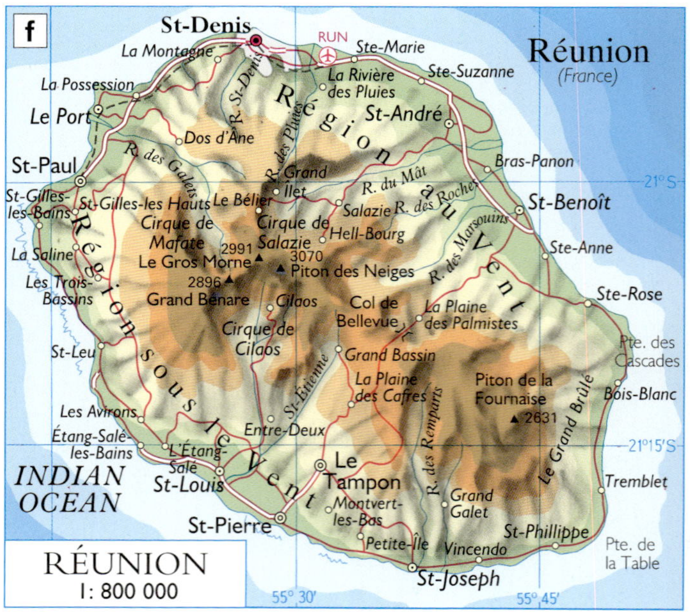
Réunion
(France)
f
St-Denis
Ste-Marie
Ste-Suzanne
St-André
St-Benoît
Ste-Anne
Ste-Rose
Le Port
St-Paul
St-Gilles-les-Bains
Cilaos
Piton des Neiges
3070
Salazie
St-Louis
St-Pierre
Le Tampon
St-Philippe
St-Joseph
Piton de la Fournaise
2631
INDIAN OCEAN
RÉUNION
1: 800 000

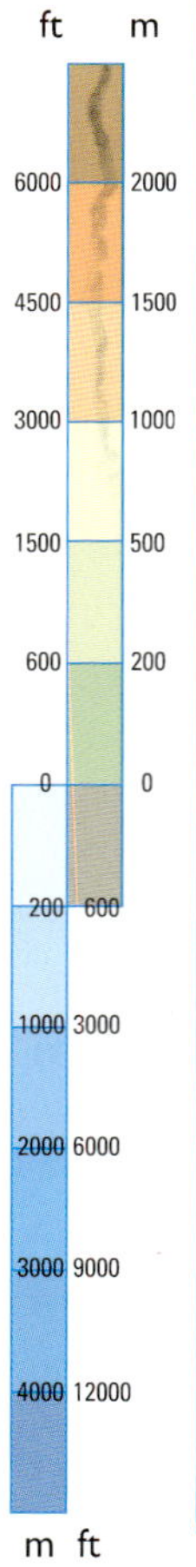
ft
m
6000
2000
4500
1500
3000
1000
1500
500
600
200
0
0
200
600
1000
3000
2000
6000
3000
9000
4000
12000
m
ft

1:800 000

TURKEY
Mediterranean Sea
Athína
Izmir
CYPRUS
Kriti
SYRIA
Bayrūt
LEB.
Dimashq
ISRAEL
Tel Aviv-Yafo
Jerusalem
JORDAN
Banghāzī
El Iskandarîya
El Qâhira (Cairo)
Bûr Sa'îd
El Suweis (Suez)
Asyût
EGYPT
LIBYA
Aswân
B. en Naser
Wadi Halfa
Bûr Sûdân
CHAD
Omdurmân
El Khartûm
SUDAN
ERITREA
Mitsiwa
Asmera
DJIBOUTI
Djibouti
Berbera
Addis Abeba
ETHIOPIA
Batu 4307
SOUTH SUDAN
Wau
Juba
CENTRAL AFRICAN REP.
SOMALIA
Muqdisho
UGANDA
Kampala
KENYA
Mt. Kenya 5199
Nairobi
L. Turkana
L. Albert
L. Edward
L. Victoria
Kisangani
RWANDA
BURUNDI
Mwanza
Kilimanjaro 5895
Mombasa
Pemba I.
Zanzibar
Dar es Salaam
Tabora
TANZANIA
L. Tanganyika
CONGO (DEM. REP. OF THE)
Lualaba
Likasi
Lubumbashi
L. Mweru
L. Bangweulu
ZAMBIA
Lusaka
Lilongwe
L. Malawi
MALAWI
Blantyre
ANGOLA
Harare
ZIMBABWE
Bulawayo
Beira
MOZAMBIQUE
Quelimane
Moçambique
NAMIBIA
BOTSWANA
Gaborone
Pretoria (Tshwane)
Johannesburg
SWAZI.
Maputo
Kimberley
Orange
Bloemfontein
LES.
Durban
SOUTH AFRICA
Cape Town
East London
Port Elizabeth
C. of Good Hope
Cape Agulhas
Baghdād
Tehrān
IRAQ
IRAN
Eşfahān
Al Başrah
Ābādān
KUWAIT
Kuwait
Persian Gulf
SAUDI ARABIA
Ar Riyāḍ
Al Madīnah
Tropic of Cancer
Jiddah
Makkah (Mecca)
Red Sea
BAHRAIN
QATAR
UNITED ARAB EMIRATES
Dubayy
Gulf of Oman
Masqat
OMAN
YEMEN
Şan'ā'
'Adan
Gulf of Aden
Socotra (Yemen)
Ras Asir
Zāhedān
AFGHANISTAN
Kābul
Kandahār
Quetta
PAKISTAN
Islamabad
Lahore
Multan
Karachi
Indus
G. of Kachchh
New Delhi
Delhi
Agra
Kanpur
Varanasi
Ganga
INDIA
Ahmadabad
Narmada
Kolkata (Calcutta)
Cuttack
Mumbai (Bombay)
Pune
Godavari
Krishna
Hyderabad
Bangalore (Bengaluru)
Chennai (Madras)
Madurai
Palk Str.
Lakshadweep Is. (India)
C. Comorin
SRI LANKA
Pidurutalagala 2524
Colombo
MALDIVES
Malé
NEPAL
Kathmandu
Mt. Everest 8850
BHUTAN
Brahmaputra
BANGLADESH
Dhaka
Chittagong
BURMA (MYANMAR)
Mandalay
Naypyidaw
Rangoon
Bay of Bengal
Andaman Is. (India)
Port Blair
Andaman Sea
Nicobar Is. (India)
TIBET
CHINA
Hotan
Lanzhou
Zhengzhou
Xi'an
Jinan
Zibo
Nanjing
Shanghai
Hangzhou
Wuhan
Chang Jiang
Chengdu
Chongqing
Changsha
Nanchang
Kunming
Guiyang
Guangzhou
Fuzhou
TAIWAN
Hong Kong
Hanoi
G. of Tonkin
Hainan
Paracel Is.
LAOS
VIETNAM
Chiang Mai
THAILAND
Bangkok
Mergui Arch.
CAMBODIA
Phnom Penh
Thanh Pho Ho Chi Minh
G. of Thailand
Isthmus of Kra
PHILIPPINES
Manila
South China Sea
MALAYSIA
George Town
Kuala Lumpur
Str. of Malacca
Singapore
Natuna
BRUNEI
SABAH
SARAWAK
Kuching
Borneo
Banda Aceh
Medan
Sumatera
Nias
Mentawai
Bangka
Palembang
INDONESIA
Java Sea
Selat Sunda
Jakarta
Semarang
Bandung
Jawa
Surabaya
Bali
Lombok
Sumbawa
Java Trench
7125
Christmas I. (Austral.)
Sunda Islands
North Australian Basin
Exmouth Plateau
Onslow
North West C.
Shark Bay
AUSTRALIA
Geraldton
Perth
Perth Basin
5746
Naturaliste Plateau
Albany
Arabian Sea
Arabian Basin
2758
5827
Carlsberg Ridge
Chain Ridge
2194
Somali Basin
Equator
Mid-Indian Ridge
Chagos-Laccadive Ridge
Ceylon Plain
Cocos Basin
Victoria
Mahé
Amirante Is.
SEYCHELLES
Coëtivy I.
6402
Aldabra Is. (Seych.)
Farquhar Is. (Seych.)
Agalega Is. (Mauritius)
Mascarene Plateau
C. Delgado
COMOROS
Moroni
Mayotte (Fr.)
Mozambique Channel
Mahajanga
MADAGASCAR
Toamasina
Antananarivo
2643
Toliara
Bassas da India (Fr.)
Europa (Fr.)
Mascarene Plain
Î. Tromelin (Fr.)
Cargados Carajos (Mauritius)
Port Mathurin
Rodrigues (Mauritius)
MAURITIUS
5194
Port Louis
St-Denis
3070
RÉUNION (Fr.)
Mascarene Is.
Chagos Arch. (U.K.)
Diego Garcia
Mid-Indian Ocean Basin
INDIAN OCEAN
Osborn Plateau
Ninetyeast Ridge
Cocos Is. (Austral.)
Investigator Ridge
6327
Wharton Basin
Tropic of Capricorn
Madagascar Basin
Madagascar Ridge
Mozambique Basin
Mozambique Plateau
Thabana Ntlenyana 3482
5778
Southwest Indian Ridge
Broken Ridge
1104
1491
5371
Agulhas Plateau
Crozet Basin
Î. Nouvelle Amsterdam (Fr.)
Î. St. Paul (Fr.)
Southeast Indian Ridge
2899
Agulhas Basin
Del Caño Rise
Prince Edward Is. (S. Africa)
Marion I.
Îs. Crozet (Fr.)
4590
Kerguelen (Fr.)
1850
Port-aux-Français
Kerguelen Plateau
McDonald Is. (Austral.)
Heard I. (Austral.)
2745
Mawson Pk.
3902
Atlantic-Indian Ridge
Conrad Rise
Atlantic-Indian Basin
6739
SOUTHERN OCEAN
Enderby Abyssal Plain
4691
Princess Elizabeth Trough
Australian-Antarctic Basin
South Indian Abyssal Basin
Maud Rise
Antarctic Circle
Antarctica
Enderby Land
Wilkes Land
Projection: Mollweide
East from Greenwich
COPYRIGHT PHILIP'S
ft m
12000 4000
9000 3000
6000 2000
3000 1000
1500 500
600 200
0 0
200 600
1000 3000
2000 6000
4000 12000
6000 18000
8000 24000
m ft

# AUSTRALIA AND OCEANIA

1:16 000 000
km
miles
Projection: Lambert's Equivalent Azimuthal
East from Greenwich
Equator
Maluku (Moluccas)
Sulawesi (Celebes)
Palu
Mamuju
Palopo
Kendari
Parepare
Watampone
Butung
MAKASSAR (Ujung Pandang)
Kep. Sula
Buru
Seram Sea
Seram (Ceram)
Ambon
Banda Sea
Weber Basin
Kep. Kai
Kep. Tanimbar
Kep. Aru
Pulau Dolak
Misool
Sorong
Waigeo
Vogelkop Peninsula
Fakfak
Biak
Yapen
Jayapura
Papua
Pegunungan Maoke
Puncak Jaya
New Guinea
I N D O N E S I A
Bismarck Sea
Wewak
Bismarck Archipelago
Kavieng
Kokopo
New Ireland
New Britain
PAPUA NEW GUINEA
Madang
Mount Hagen
Mt. Wilhelm
Lae
Owen Stanley Range
Port Moresby
Gulf of Papua
Fly
D'Entrecasteaux Islands
Louisiade Archipelago
Solomon Sea
New Britain Trench
Coral Sea Basin
Coral Sea
Queensland Plateau
Torres Strait
Badu I.
Moa I.
C. York
Prince of Wales I.
Flores Sea
Sumbawa
Raba
Flores
Ende
Alor
Wetar
Dili
EAST TIMOR
Timor
Kupang
Roti
Savu Sea
Sumba
Leti
Babar
Timor Sea
Arafura Sea
North Australian Basin
Ashmore and Cartier Is.
Melville I.
Bathurst I.
C. Croker
Coburg Pen.
Darwin
Wessel Is.
C. Arnhem
Arnhem Land
Groote Eylandt
Gulf of Carpentaria
Katherine
Larrimah
Joseph Bonaparte Gulf
C. Londonderry
Bonaparte Archipelago
Wyndham
Kununurra
L. Argyle
Kimberley
Halls Creek
Daly Waters
Derby
Broome
Tanami Desert
NORTHERN TERRITORY
Barkly Tableland
Tennant Creek
Wellesley Is.
Normanton
Forsayth
Cape York Peninsula
Weipa
Cooktown
Mitchell
Cairns
Bartle Frere
Great Barrier Reef
Townsville
Charters Towers
Whitsunday Is.
Mackay
L. Dalrymple
Flinders
Kajabbi
Cloncurry
Mount Isa
Dajarra
Hughenden
Winton
Great Dividing Range
QUEENSLAND
Longreach
Emerald
Rockhampton
Gladstone
Yaraka
Maryborough
Gympie
Roma
Charleville
Quilpie
Toowoomba
BRISBANE
Port Hedland
Dampier
Karratha
Great Sandy Desert
L. Mackay
MacDonnell Ranges
Mt. Zeil
Alice Springs
A U S T R A L I A
N. W. Cape
Pannawonica
Mt. Meharry
Hamersley Range
Newman
Lake Disappointment
Gibson Desert
Paraburdoo
Pilbara
Uluru (Ayers Rock)
Mt. Woodroffe
Musgrave Ranges
Simpson Desert
Sturt Stony Desert
Cooper Creek
Diamantina
Grey Range
Warrego
Paroo
Cunnamulla
Dirranbandi
Thargomindah
Carnarvon
Gascoyne
WESTERN AUSTRALIA
L. Carnegie
Great Victoria Desert
SOUTH AUSTRALIA
Coober Pedy
Lake Eyre
Marree
Bourke
Walgett
Moree
Shark Bay
Meekatharra
Murchison
Mount Magnet
Leonora
Lake Barlee
Kalgoorlie-Boulder
Nullarbor Plain
Tarcoola
Lake Torrens
St. Mary Pk.
Flinders Ranges
Lake Gairdner
Broken Hill
NEW SOUTH WALES
Cobar
Darling
Tamworth
Round Mt.
Dubbo
Newcastle
Gosford
Bathurst
Orange
SYDNEY
Wollongong
Geraldton
INDIAN OCEAN
Darling Range
PERTH
Northam
Rockingham
Bunbury
Norseman
Esperance
Penong
Port Augusta
Whyalla
Eyre Pen.
Port Pirie
Spencer Gulf
Yorke Pen.
ADELAIDE
Murray Bridge
Gulf St. Vincent
Port Lincoln
Kangaroo I.
Encounter B.
Great Australian Bight
Murray
Mildura
Hay
Griffith
Murrumbidgee
Wagga Wagga
Goulburn
Canberra
A.C.T.
Swan Hill
Shepparton
Albury-Wodonga
Mt. Kosciuszko
Snowy Mts.
Bombala
C. Howe
Bendigo
Horsham
VICTORIA
Ballarat
MELBOURNE
Geelong
Sale
Wilsons Promontory
Mount Gambier
Warrnambool
Bass Strait
King I.
Flinders I.
Furneaux Group
Naturaliste Plateau
C. Leeuwin
Augusta
Albany
South Australian Basin
S O U T H E R N   O C E A N
Burnie
Devonport
Launceston
Mt. Ossa
TASMANIA
Hobart
S.E.Cape
Tasman Abyssal
South Tasman Plateau

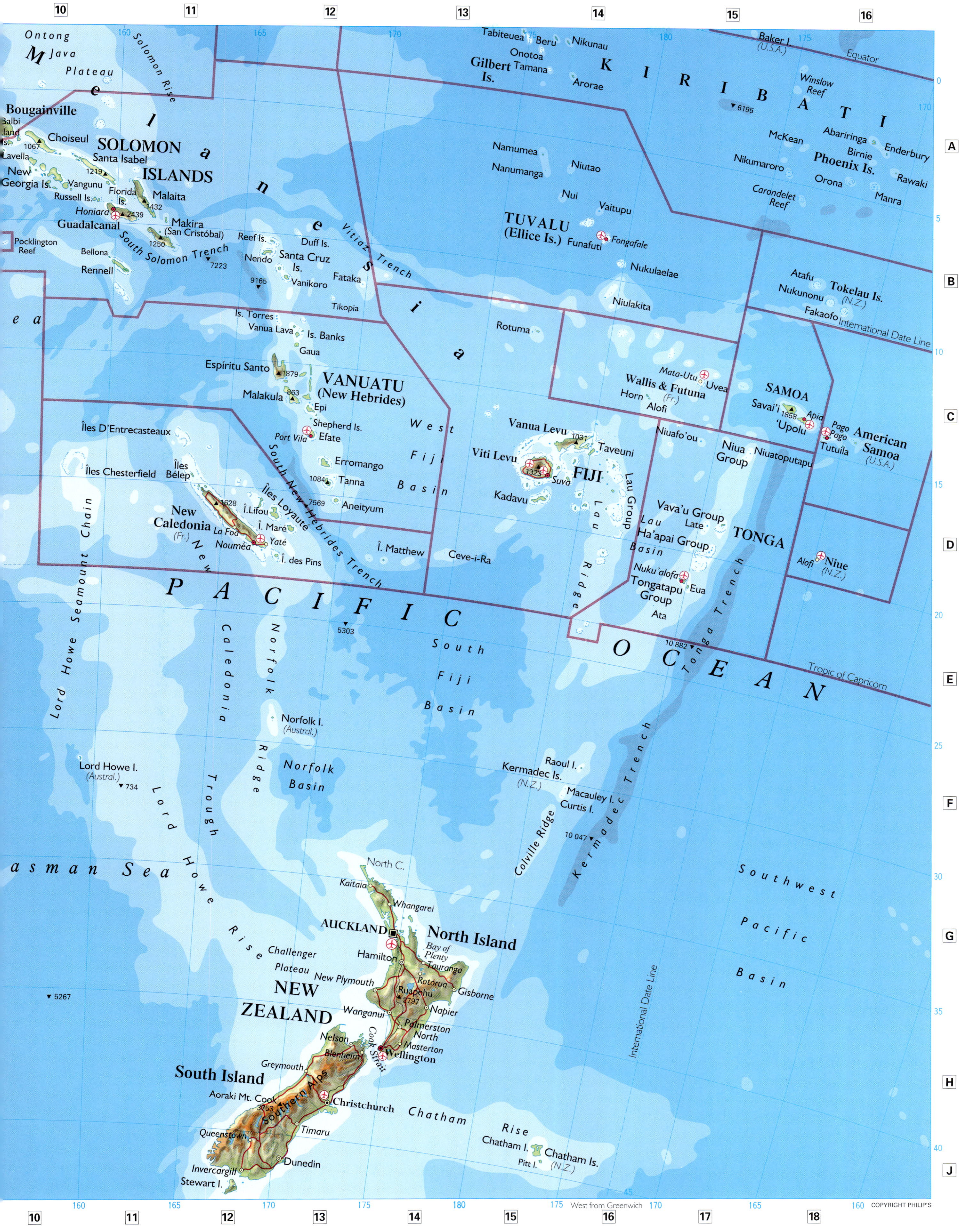

Ontong Java Plateau
Solomon Rise
Melanesia
Bougainville
Choiseul
SOLOMON ISLANDS
Santa Isabel
New Georgia Is.
Vangunu
Russell Is.
Florida Is.
Malaita
Honiara
Guadalcanal
Makira (San Cristóbal)
Pocklington Reef
Bellona
Rennell
South Solomon Trench
Reef Is.
Duff Is.
Nendo
Santa Cruz Is.
Vanikoro
Fataka
Tikopia
Vitiaz Trench
Is. Torres
Vanua Lava
Is. Banks
Gaua
Espíritu Santo
Malakula
VANUATU (New Hebrides)
Epi
Shepherd Is.
Port Vila
Efate
Erromango
Tanna
Aneityum
Îles D'Entrecasteaux
Îles Chesterfield
Îles Bélep
New Caledonia (Fr.)
La Foa
Nouméa
Yaté
Î. Lifou
Î. Maré
Î. des Pins
Îles Loyauté
South New Hebrides Trench
Î. Matthew
Ceve-i-Ra
West Fiji Basin
Tabiteuea
Beru
Nikunau
Onotoa
Gilbert Is.
Tamana
Arorae
KIRIBATI
Baker I. (U.S.A.)
Equator
Winslow Reef
Abariringa
McKean
Birnie
Enderbury
Phoenix Is.
Nikumaroro
Rawaki
Orona
Manra
Carondelet Reef
Namumea
Nanumanga
Niutao
Nui
Vaitupu
TUVALU (Ellice Is.)
Funafuti
Fongafale
Nukulaelae
Niulakita
Atafu
Nukunonu
Tokelau Is. (N.Z.)
Fakaofo
International Date Line
Rotuma
Mata-Utu
Uvea
Wallis & Futuna (Fr.)
Horn
Alofi
SAMOA
Savai'i
'Upolu
Apia
Pago Pago
American Samoa (U.S.A.)
Tutuila
Niuafo'ou
Niua Group
Niuatoputapu
Vanua Levu
Taveuni
Viti Levu
Suva
FIJI
Kadavu
Lau Group
Lau Ridge
Vava'u Group
Late
Lau Basin
Ha'apai Group
TONGA
Nuku'alofa
Tongatapu Group
Eua
Ata
Alofi
Niue (N.Z.)
Tonga Trench
PACIFIC OCEAN
Tropic of Capricorn
South Fiji Basin
Lord Howe Seamount Chain
New Caledonia Trough
Norfolk Ridge
Norfolk I. (Austral.)
Norfolk Basin
Lord Howe I. (Austral.)
Lord Howe Rise
Tasman Sea
Raoul I.
Kermadec Is. (N.Z.)
Macauley I.
Curtis I.
Colville Ridge
Kermadec Trench
Southwest Pacific Basin
North C.
Kaitaia
Whangarei
AUCKLAND
North Island
Hamilton
Bay of Plenty
Tauranga
Challenger Plateau
New Plymouth
Rotorua
Ruapehu
Gisborne
NEW ZEALAND
Wanganui
Napier
Palmerston North
Nelson
Blenheim
Cook Strait
Masterton
Wellington
Greymouth
South Island
Southern Alps
Aoraki Mt. Cook
Christchurch
Chatham Rise
Timaru
Queenstown
Dunedin
Invercargill
Stewart I.
Chatham I.
Chatham Is. (N.Z.)
Pitt I.
West from Greenwich
COPYRIGHT PHILIP'S

50 0 50 100 150 200 250 300 km

50 0 50 100 150 200 miles

1:6 400 000

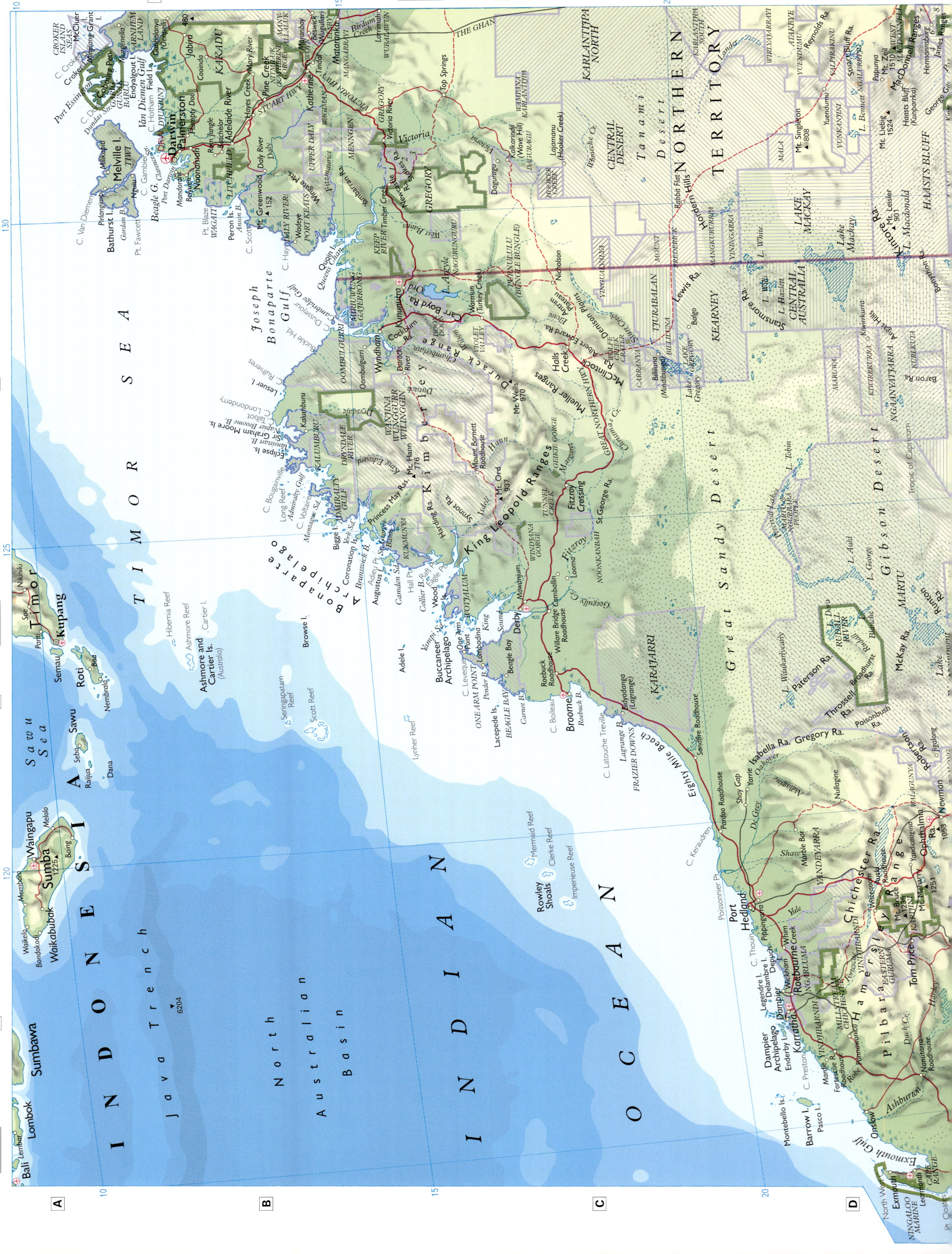
280
231
235
INDONESIA
TIMOR SEA
INDIAN OCEAN
Sawu Sea
Java Trench
North Australian Basin
Joseph Bonaparte Gulf
Bonaparte Archipelago
Timor
Kupang
Roti
Sawu
Sumba
Waingapu
Waikabubak
Sumbawa
Lombok
Bali
Melville I.
Bathurst I.
Darwin
Palmerston
Jabiru
KAKADU
Katherine
Victoria
GREGORY
NORTHERN TERRITORY
Tanami Desert
CENTRAL DESERT
KARLANTIJPA NORTH
LAKE MACKAY
CENTRAL AUSTRALIA
Lake Mackay
KEARNEY
Kununurra
Wyndham
Kimberley
Durack Range
King Leopold Ranges
Halls Creek
Fitzroy Crossing
Derby
Broome
Eighty Mile Beach
Great Sandy Desert
Gibson Desert
Port Hedland
Karratha
Dampier
Roebourne
Hamersley Range
Pilbara
Tom Price
Newman
Onslow
Exmouth
Exmouth Gulf
Barrow I.
Montebello Is.
Rowley Shoals
Browse I.
Ashmore and Cartier Is. (Australia)
Scott Reef
Buccaneer Archipelago
Chichester Ra.
Paterson Ra.
Tropic of Capricorn
A
B
C
D
2
3
4
5

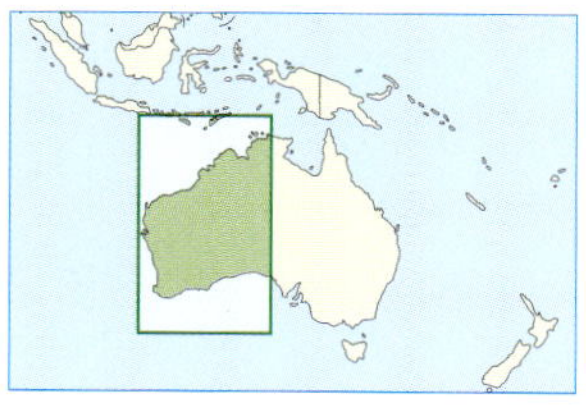

WESTERN AUSTRALIA
SOUTH AUSTRALIA
INDIAN OCEAN
SOUTHERN OCEAN
Great Australian Bight
Great Victoria Desert
Nullarbor Plain
PERTH
Kalgoorlie-Boulder
Geraldton
Albany
Esperance
Bunbury
Mandurah
Rockingham
Fremantle
Norseman
Carnarvon
Kalbarri
Meekatharra
Laverton
Leonora
Southern Cross
Merredin
Coolgardie
Wiluna
Busselton
Archipelago of the Recherche
Robinson Ra.
Musgrave Ranges
Petermann Ranges
Hampton Tableland
TRANS AUSTRALIAN RWY
EYRE HWY
GREAT NORTHERN HWY
NORTHWEST COASTAL HWY
Aboriginal lands
1. NGALIWURRU / NUNGALI
2. WANIMIRI
3. WAMBARDI
4. LIALAUTUMA
5. RODNA
6. NTARIA
7. ROULPMAULPMA
8. URUNA
Projection: Bonne
East from Greenwich
COPYRIGHT PHILIP'S

1:6 400 000

CORAL SEA
Great Barrier Reef
Gulf of Carpentaria
Cape York Peninsula
Great Dividing Range
QUEENSLAND
NORTHERN TERRITORY
Barkly Tableland
Arnhem Land
Simpson Desert
Channel Country
Townsville
Cairns
Mackay
Rockhampton
Mount Isa
Alice Springs
Tennant Creek
Capricorn Coast
PAPUA NEW GUINEA
Gulf of Papua
Torres Strait
TORRES STRAIT on same scale as main map
WHITSUNDAY ISLANDS
1:2 000 000
Whitsunday I.
CUMBERLAND ISLANDS
Clarke Ra.
Wellesley Is.
Mornington I.
Groote Eylandt
Sir Edward Pellew Group
286
231
278

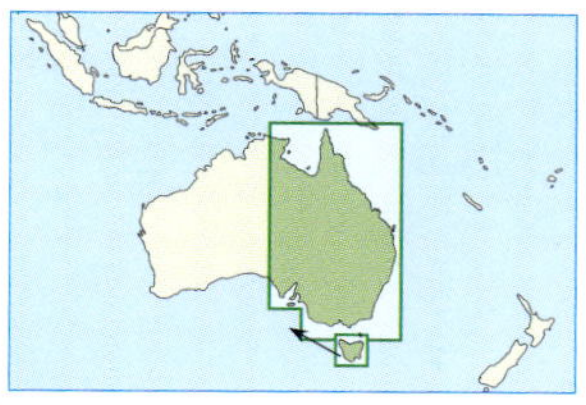

NEW SOUTH WALES
SOUTH AUSTRALIA
TASMAN SEA
Bass Strait
SYDNEY
MELBOURNE
BRISBANE
ADELAIDE
Canberra
Newcastle
Wollongong
Gold Coast
Sunshine Coast
Toowoomba
Broken Hill
Mildura
Dubbo
Tamworth
Wagga Wagga
Geelong
Ballarat
Bendigo
Port Augusta
Whyalla
Port Pirie
Sturt Stony Desert
Strzelecki Desert
Kangaroo I.
King Island
Flinders Island
TASMANIA
Launceston
Hobart
Aboriginal lands
East from Greenwich
COPYRIGHT PHILIP'S
Projection: Bonne

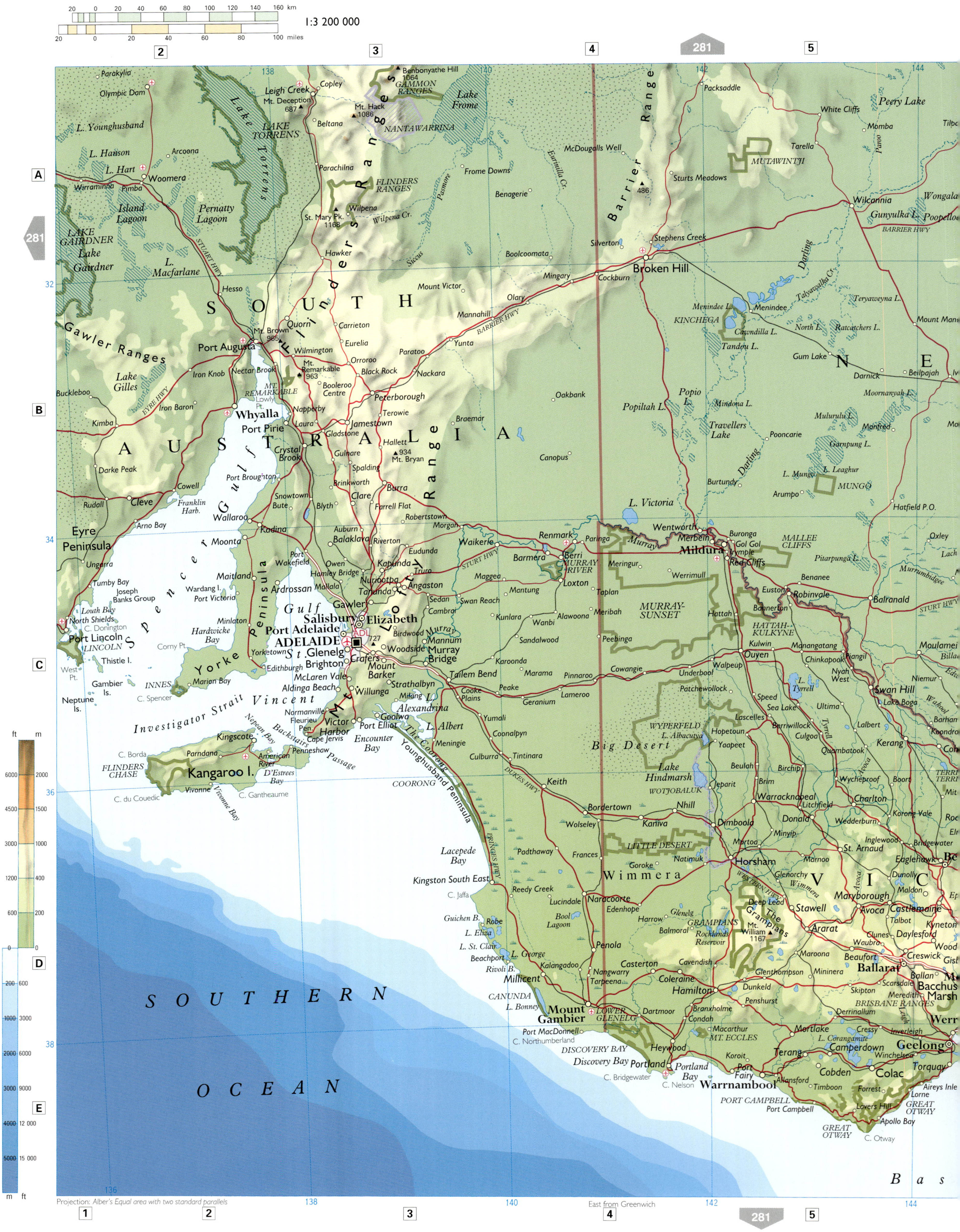

1:3 200 000
km
miles
Projection: Alber's Equal area with two standard parallels
East from Greenwich
281
SOUTH AUSTRALIA
N S W
V I C
SOUTHERN OCEAN
Bass
Flinders Ranges
Gawler Ranges
Barrier Range
Mt. Lofty Ranges
Lake Torrens
LAKE TORRENS
Lake Frome
L. Younghusband
L. Hanson
L. Hart
Island Lagoon
Pernatty Lagoon
LAKE GAIRDNER
Lake Gairdner
L. Macfarlane
Lake Gilles
Eyre Peninsula
Spencer Gulf
Gulf St Vincent
Yorke Peninsula
Investigator Strait
Backstairs Passage
Kangaroo I.
FLINDERS CHASE
Encounter Bay
The Coorong
Younghusband Peninsula
COORONG
Lacepede Bay
Discovery Bay
DISCOVERY BAY
Portland Bay
Big Desert
Wimmera
The Grampians
GRAMPIANS
Murray
Darling
MURRAY-SUNSET
HATTAH-KULKYNE
WYPERFELD
LITTLE DESERT
MUNGO
KINCHEGA
MUTAWINTJI
MALLEE CLIFFS
NANTAWARRINA
GAMMON RANGES
FLINDERS RANGES
INNES
LINCOLN
CANUNDA
LOWER GLENELG
MT. ECCLES
PORT CAMPBELL
GREAT OTWAY
BRISBANE RANGES
Broken Hill
Port Augusta
Whyalla
Port Pirie
Port Lincoln
ADELAIDE
Port Adelaide
Elizabeth
Salisbury
Gawler
Glenelg
Brighton
Victor Harbor
Murray Bridge
Mount Gambier
Mildura
Horsham
Hamilton
Warrnambool
Portland
Ballarat
Geelong
Colac
Ararat
Stawell
Swan Hill
Kerang
Wentworth
Renmark
Berri
Loxton
Bordertown
Naracoorte
Kingston South East
Robe
Millicent
Wilcannia
Menindee
Balranald
Robinvale
Ouyen
Hawker
Quorn
Peterborough
Burra
Clare
Kadina
Moonta
Wallaroo
Cleve
Cowell
Tumby Bay
Woomera
Leigh Creek
Copley
Beltana
Parachilna
Wilpena
Olary
Cockburn
Silverton
Kingscote
Penneshaw
Cape Jervis
Goolwa
Port Elliot
Strathalbyn
Tailem Bend
Meningie
Keith
Dimboola
Warracknabeal
Nhill
Kaniva
Casterton
Coleraine
Heywood
Port Fairy
Terang
Camperdown
Cobden
Timboon
Torquay
Lorne
Apollo Bay
C. Otway
Maryborough
Castlemaine
Daylesford
Bacchus Marsh
Werribee

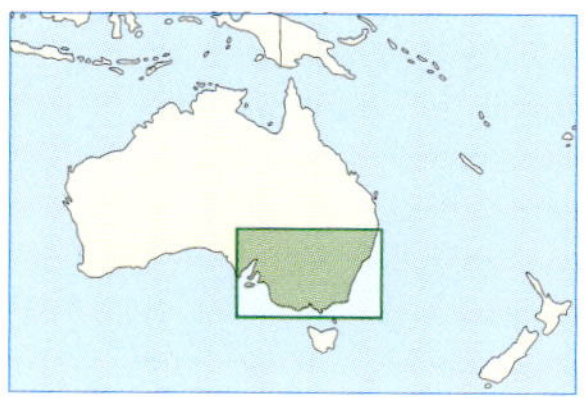

281

6
7
8
9
10
A
B
C
D
E
NEW SOUTH WALES
VICTORIA
TASMAN SEA
Strait
Great Dividing Range
Liverpool Range
Liverpool Plains
Hastings Range
Hunter Range
Cullarin Range
Gourock Range
Snowy Mts.
Gippsland
SYDNEY
Canberra
MELBOURNE
Newcastle
Wollongong
Coffs Harbour
Armidale
Tamworth
Port Macquarie
Dubbo
Orange
Bathurst
Wagga Wagga
Albury
Wodonga
Goulburn
Queanbeyan
Cobar
Nyngan
Parkes
Forbes
Cowra
Young
Griffith
Shepparton
Wangaratta
Benalla
Dandenong
Sale
Bairnsdale
Lakes Entrance
Batemans Bay
Nowra
Kiama
Shellharbour
Port Kembla
Campbelltown
Sutherland
Liverpool
Parramatta
Penrith
Hornsby
Manly
Gosford
Maitland
Cessnock
Taree
Forster
Tuncurry
Mudgee
Gunnedah
Coonabarabran
Narromine
Cootamundra
Tumut
Cooma
Jindabyne
Eden
Merimbula
Bega
Narooma
Moruya
Ulladulla
Bowral
Mittagong
Katoomba
Lithgow
Singleton
Muswellbrook
Scone
Deniliquin
Moama
Wilsons Promontory
Traralgon
Morwell
Moe
Warragul
Pakenham
Kosciuszko
Mt. Kosciuszko 2228
Aboriginal lands
East from Greenwich
146
148
150
152
32
34
36
38

Aboriginal lands

# NEW ZEALAND - NORTH ISLAND

1:2 800 000

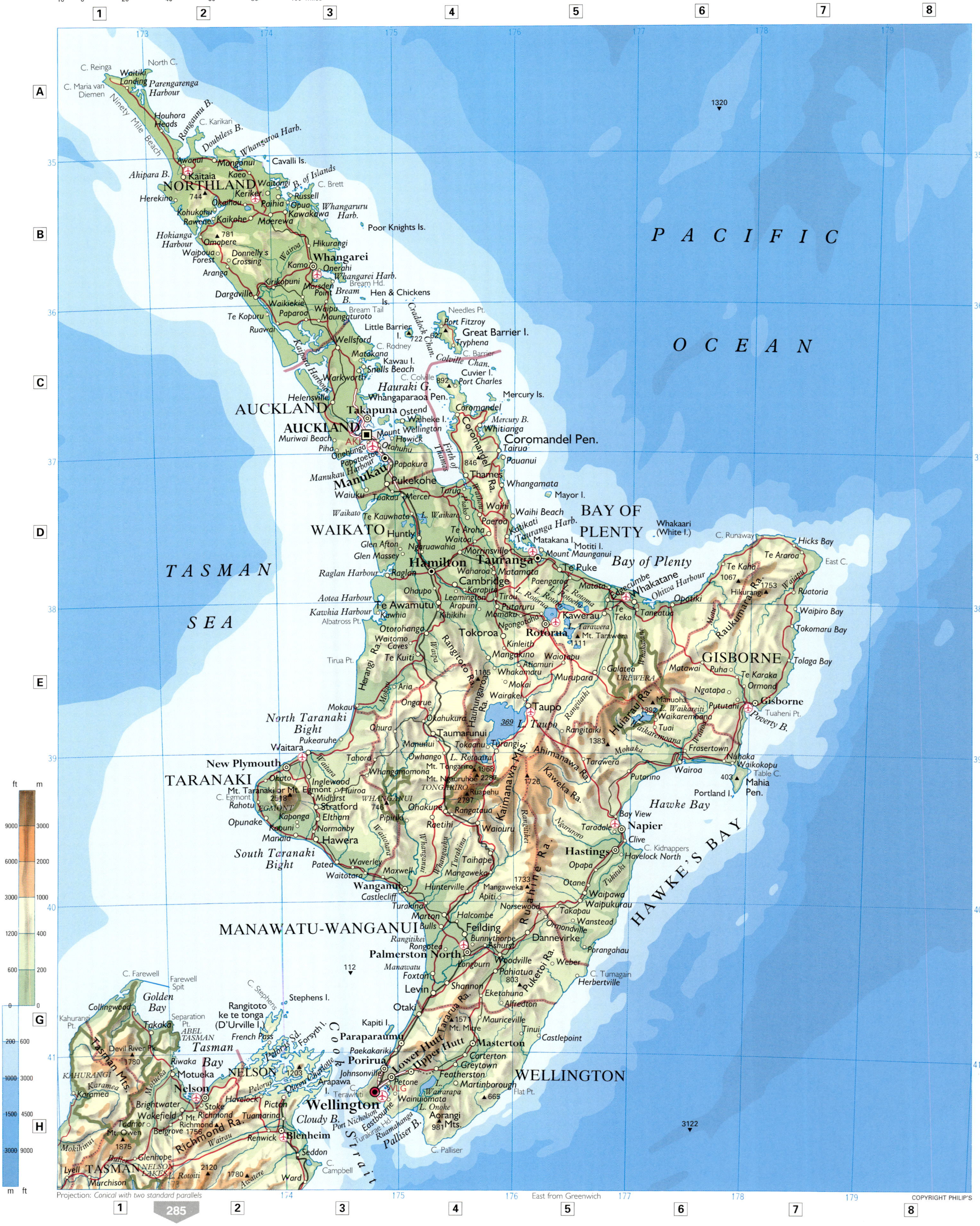
PACIFIC OCEAN
TASMAN SEA
NORTHLAND
AUCKLAND
WAIKATO
BAY OF PLENTY
GISBORNE
TARANAKI
HAWKE'S BAY
MANAWATU-WANGANUI
WELLINGTON
NELSON
TASMAN
C. Reinga
North C.
C. Maria van Diemen
Parengarenga Harbour
Houhora Heads
Ninety Mile Beach
Rangaunu B.
C. Karikari
Doubtless B.
Whangaroa Harb.
Cavalli Is.
Ahipara B.
Kaitaia
B. of Islands
Russell
Paihia
Kerikeri
Kawakawa
Whangaruru Harb.
Poor Knights Is.
Hokianga Harbour
Waipoua Forest
Dargaville
Whangarei
Whangarei Harb.
Bream Hd.
Bream B.
Hen & Chickens Is.
Needles Pt.
Great Barrier I.
Little Barrier I.
Cradock Chan.
Colville Chan.
Wellsford
Kaipara Harbour
Warkworth
Hauraki G.
Whangaparaoa Pen.
Helensville
Takapuna
AUCKLAND
Manukau
Manukau Harbour
Waiheke I.
Firth of Thames
Coromandel
Coromandel Pen.
Coromandel Ra.
Mercury Is.
Thames
Whangamata
Mayor I.
Waihi
Tauranga
Tauranga Harb.
Motiti I.
Bay of Plenty
Whakaari (White I.)
C. Runaway
Hicks Bay
East C.
Te Araroa
Raukumara Ra.
Hikurangi
Ruatoria
Waipiro Bay
Tokomaru Bay
Tolaga Bay
Gisborne
Poverty B.
Mahia Pen.
Table C.
Whakatane
Opotiki
Ohiwa Harbour
Rotorua
L. Rotorua
L. Tarawera
Mt. Tarawera
Kawerau
Hamilton
Huntly
Raglan Harbour
Raglan
Aotea Harbour
Kawhia Harbour
Te Awamutu
Cambridge
Tokoroa
Otorohanga
Waitomo Caves
Te Kuiti
Tirua Pt.
Taupo
L. Taupo
Turangi
Taumarunui
Urewera
Huiarau Ra.
L. Waikaremoana
Wairoa
Kaimanawa Mts.
Kaweka Ra.
Ruahine Ra.
Ahimanawa Ra.
Mt. Tongariro
Mt. Ruapehu
Tongariro
Waiouru
North Taranaki Bight
Waitara
New Plymouth
Mt. Taranaki or Mt. Egmont
C. Egmont
Egmont
Stratford
Hawera
Opunake
South Taranaki Bight
Wanganui
Hawke Bay
Napier
Hastings
C. Kidnappers
Waipukurau
Dannevirke
C. Turnagain
Feilding
Palmerston North
Levin
Tararua Ra.
Masterton
Castlepoint
Kapiti I.
Paraparaumu
Porirua
Lower Hutt
Upper Hutt
Wellington
Cook Strait
Palliser B.
C. Palliser
Aorangi Mts.
Martinborough
Flat Pt.
Farewell Spit
C. Farewell
Golden Bay
Tasman Bay
Rangitoto ke te tonga (D'Urville I.)
French Pass
Stephens I.
Nelson
Motueka
Takaka
Collingwood
Tasman Mts.
Richmond Ra.
Picton
Blenheim
Seddon
C. Campbell
Ward
Cloudy B.
Kahurangi Pt.
Murchison
Nelson Lakes
1320
3122
Projection: Conical with two standard parallels
East from Greenwich
COPYRIGHT PHILIP'S

285

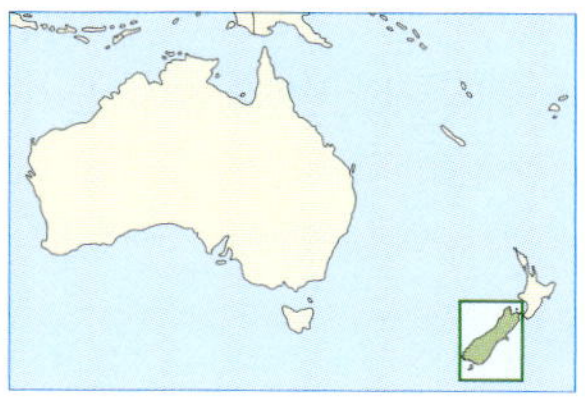

1:2 800 000

TASMAN SEA
Westland Bight
Karamea Bight
Golden Bay
Tasman Bay
Cloudy B.
Pegasus Bay
Canterbury Bight
PACIFIC OCEAN
Foveaux Str.
C. Farewell
Farewell Spit
Collingwood
Takaka
Nelson
Motueka
Richmond
Blenheim
Picton
Havelock
Seddon
Ward
Kaikoura
Westport
Greymouth
Hokitika
Ross
Reefton
Hanmer Springs
Culverden
Rangiora
Kaiapoi
Christchurch
Lyttelton
Banks Pen.
Akaroa
Ashburton
Methven
Geraldine
Temuka
Timaru
Waimate
Oamaru
Palmerston
Dunedin
Mosgiel
Balclutha
Milton
Gore
Invercargill
Bluff
Riverton
Queenstown
Arrowtown
Cromwell
Alexandra
Wanaka
Te Anau
Manapouri
Stewart I. (Rakiura)
Port Pegasus
Solander I.
NELSON
TASMAN
MARLBOROUGH
WEST COAST
CANTERBURY
OTAGO
SOUTHLAND
FIORDLAND
Southern Alps
Canterbury Plains
Mackenzie Plains
Richmond Ra.
Inland Kaikoura Ra.
Seaward Kaikoura Ra.
Victoria Ra.
Paparoa Ra.
Spenser Mts.
Two Thumbs Ra.
Kakanui Mts.
Dunstan Mts.
The Remarkables
Eyre Mts.
Takitimu Mts.
Aoraki Mount Cook 3753
Mt. Aspiring 3033
Mt. Tasman 3497
L. Tekapo
L. Pukaki
L. Ohau
L. Wanaka
L. Hawea
L. Wakatipu
L. Te Anau
L. Manapouri
L. Ellesmere
Milford Sd.
Doubtful Sd.
Dusky Sd.
Otago Pen.
Projection: Conical with two standard parallels
East from Greenwich
CHATHAM ISLANDS
on same scale
PACIFIC OCEAN
The Sisters
C. Young
Chatham I. (Rekohu)
Waitangi
Te One
Owenga
The Forty Fours
Pitt Strait
Pitt I.
Mangere I.
Star Keys
Rangatira I.
The Pyramid
Chatham Islands (Wharekauri)
West from Greenwich
COPYRIGHT PHILIP'S

# PAPUA NEW GUINEA

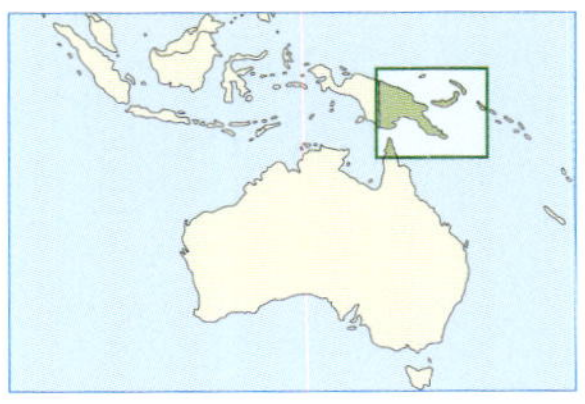

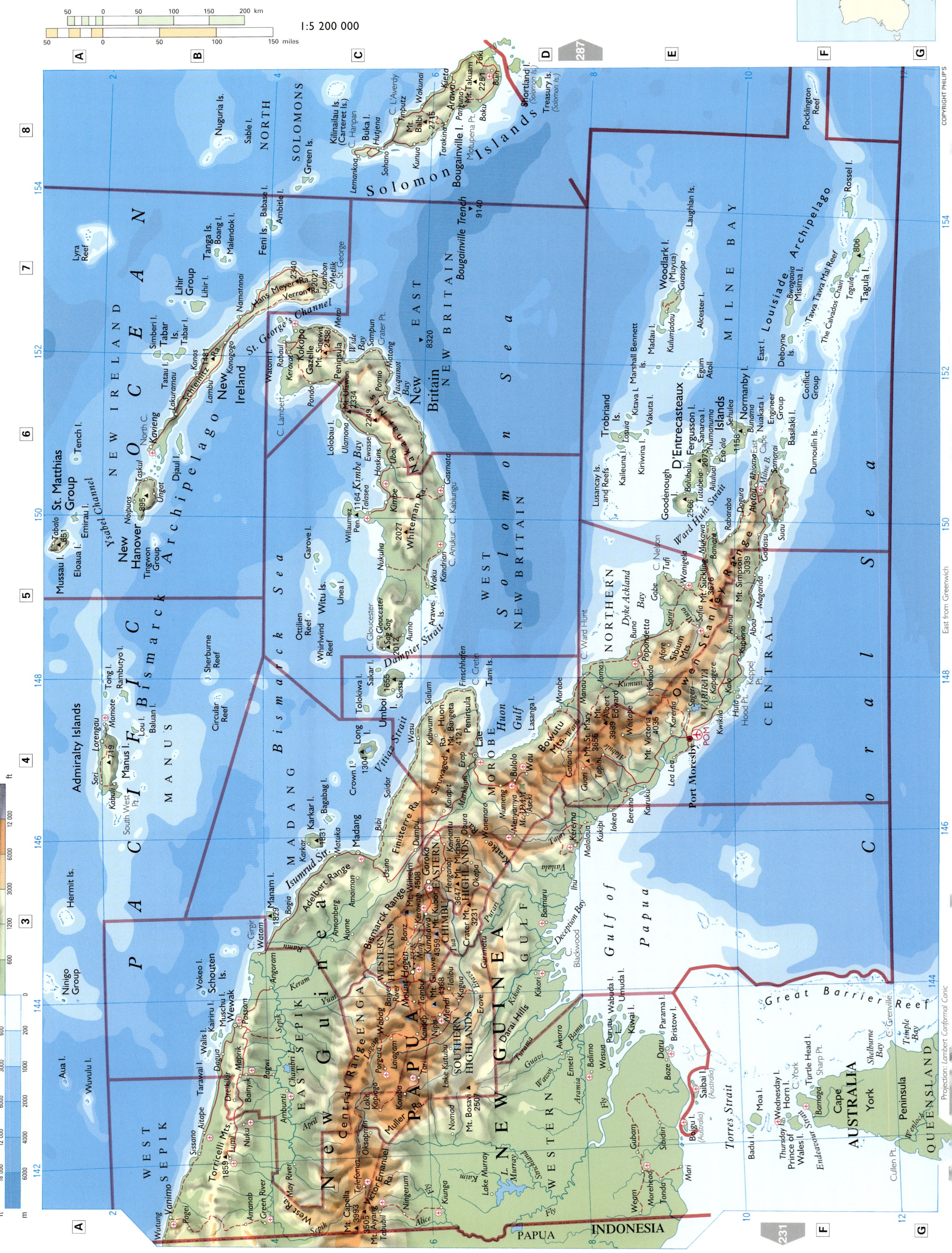

1:5 200 000
km
miles
COPYRIGHT PHILIP'S
287
231
PACIFIC OCEAN
Bismarck Sea
Bismarck Archipelago
Admiralty Islands
Manus I.
MANUS
NEW IRELAND
New Ireland
New Hanover
St. Matthias Group
St. George's Channel
NORTH SOLOMONS
Solomon Islands
Bougainville I.
Buka I.
Solomon Sea
EAST NEW BRITAIN
WEST NEW BRITAIN
New Britain
Dampier Strait
Vitiaz Strait
Huon Gulf
MADANG
Madang
MOROBE
Lae
EAST SEPIK
WEST SEPIK
Wewak
Vanimo
New Guinea
Central Range
Bismarck Range
Owen Stanley Range
NORTHERN
CENTRAL
Port Moresby
MILNE BAY
D'Entrecasteaux Islands
Trobriand Is.
Woodlark I.
Louisiade Archipelago
Coral Sea
Gulf of Papua
GULF
WESTERN
Torres Strait
Great Barrier Reef
Cape York Peninsula
AUSTRALIA
QUEENSLAND
PAPUA
INDONESIA
Projection: Lambert Conformal Conic
East from Greenwich

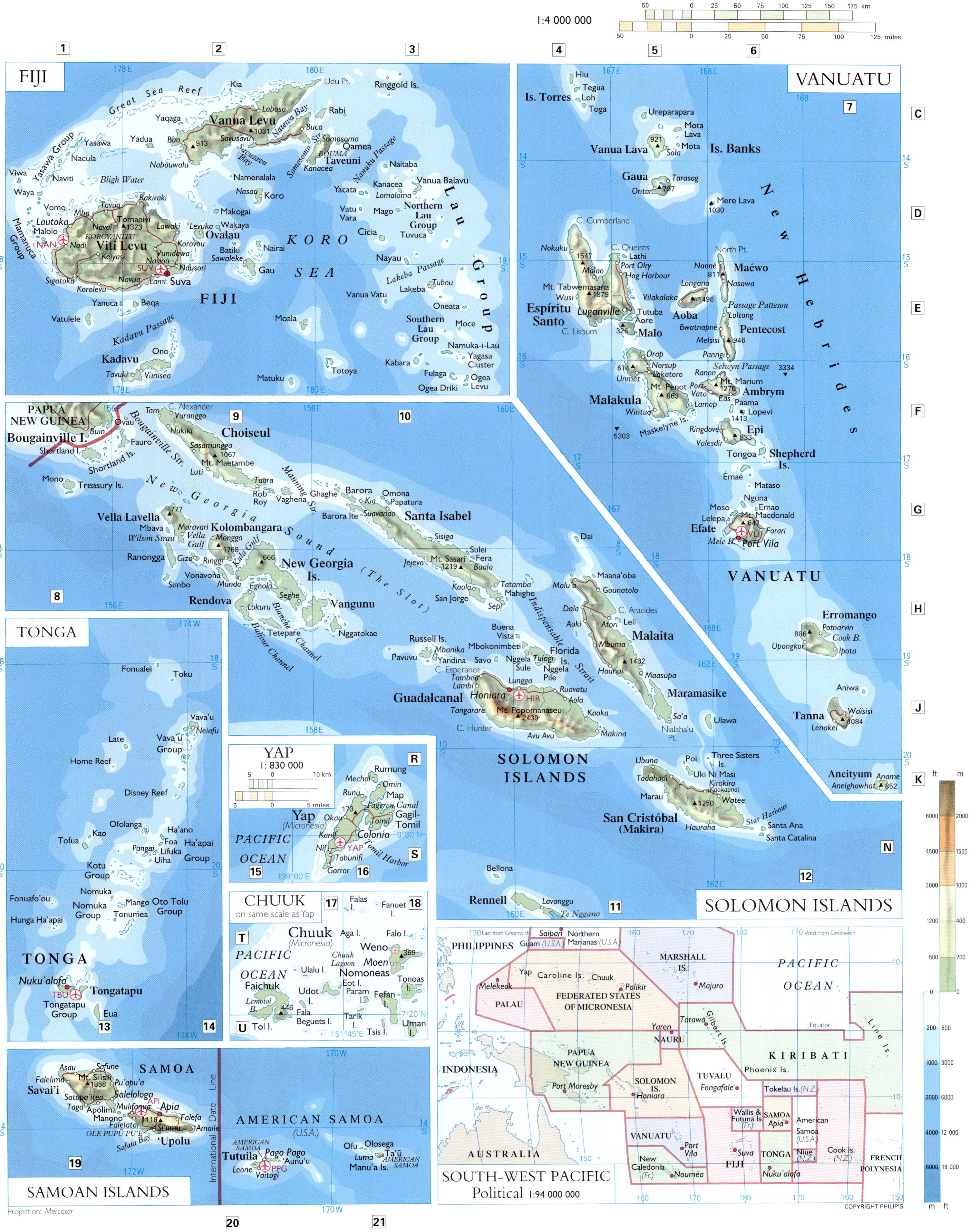
1:4 000 000
FIJI
Great Sea Reef
Vanua Levu
Taveuni
Viti Levu
Suva
Kadavu
Ovalau
KORO SEA
FIJI
Lau Group
Northern Lau Group
Southern Lau Group
Yasawa Group
Mamanuca Group
Bligh Water
Lakeba Passage
Kadavu Passage
Nanuku Passage
Ringgold Is.
Udu Pt.
Labasa
Savusavu
Natewa Bay
Somosomo Str.
Qamea
Koro
Gau
Moala
Totoya
Matuku
Vatulele
Beqa
Yanuca
Lautoka
Nadi
Nausori
Sigatoka
Tomanivi
Vanua Balavu
Lakeba
Vanua Vatu
Kabara
Fulaga
Ogea Levu
Ogea Driki
Yagasa Cluster
Namuka-i-Lau
Moce
Oneata
Tuvuca
Cicia
Nayau
Vatu Vara
Mago
VANUATU
Is. Torres
Hiu
Tegua
Loh
Toga
Ureparapara
Mota Lava
Mota
Vanua Lava
Is. Banks
Gaua
Mere Lava
New Hebrides
C. Cumberland
Espíritu Santo
Luganville
Malo
Aoba
Maéwo
Pentecost
Malakula
Ambrym
Epi
Shepherd Is.
Tongoa
Émaé
Efate
Port Vila
VANUATU
Erromango
Tanna
Aniwa
Aneityum
Selwyn Passage
PAPUA NEW GUINEA
Bougainville I.
Bougainville Str.
Shortland Is.
Treasury Is.
Choiseul
New Georgia
New Georgia Sound (The Slot)
Vella Lavella
Kolombangara
Ranongga
Rendova
Vangunu
Santa Isabel
Manning Str.
Indispensable Strait
Malaita
Florida Is.
Russell Is.
Guadalcanal
Honiara
Mt. Popomanaseu 2439
Maramasike
Ulawa
San Cristóbal (Makira)
Santa Ana
Santa Catalina
Rennell
Bellona
SOLOMON ISLANDS
SOLOMON ISLANDS
TONGA
Fonualei
Toku
Vava'u Group
Late
Home Reef
Disney Reef
Ha'apai Group
Tofua
Kao
Kotu Group
Nomuka Group
Otu Tolu Group
Hunga Ha'apai
TONGA
Nuku'alofa
Tongatapu
Tongatapu Group
Eua
YAP
1:830 000
Yap (Micronesia)
Colonia
PACIFIC OCEAN
CHUUK
on same scale as Yap
Chuuk (Micronesia)
Chuuk Lagoon
Weno
Moen
Tol I.
PACIFIC OCEAN
SAMOA
Savai'i
Upolu
Apia
AMERICAN SAMOA
(U.S.A.)
Tutuila
Pago Pago
Manu'a Is.
International Date Line
SAMOAN ISLANDS
SOUTH-WEST PACIFIC
Political 1:94 000 000
PHILIPPINES
PALAU
FEDERATED STATES OF MICRONESIA
MARSHALL IS.
PACIFIC OCEAN
NAURU
KIRIBATI
INDONESIA
PAPUA NEW GUINEA
SOLOMON IS.
TUVALU
VANUATU
AUSTRALIA
New Caledonia (Fr.)
FIJI
TONGA
SAMOA
American Samoa (U.S.A.)
Cook Is. (N.Z.)
FRENCH POLYNESIA
Projection: Mercator
COPYRIGHT PHILIP'S

Equatorial Scale 1:43 200 000

OKINAWA
on same scale as Palau
a
Hedo-misaki
Hedo
Kunigami
Okinawa
(Japan)
EAST CHINA SEA
Iheya-shima
Kouri-shima
Yagaji-shima
Yonaha-Dake
Nakijin
Motobu
Seseko-shima
Minna-shima
Nago-wan
Nago
Arume-wan
Banno-saki
Onna
Ishikawa
Kin-wan
Ikei-shima
Kadena
Uruma
Takabanare-shima
Okinawa (Koza)
Henna
Ginowan
Heanza-shima
Urasoe
Tsuken-jima
Naha
Nakagusuku-wan
OKA
Shuri
Kudaka-shima
PACIFIC OCEAN
Rukan-sho
Gushikami
Itoman
Kyan-zaki
128° E
26° 30' N
b
Kangoku Iwa
Kitano Hana
COAST GUARD STATION
Iwo-Jima
(Japan)
Hanare Iwa
108
IWO JIMA AIRFIELD
Kama Iwa
PACIFIC OCEAN
Suribachi Yama
167
Fatatsu Ne
Tobiishi Hana
141° 20' E
24° 45' N
IWO-JIMA
1: 200 000
3 km
2 m
PALAU
c
Ngaregur
Konrei
Ngardmau Bay
Ngardmau
218
Babelthuap I.
Namai Bay
Melekeok
Komebail Lagoon
ROR
Koror
Garusuun
Malakal Harbor
Garreru
Koror I.
Aulong
Apurashokoru
Ngobasangel
Urukthapel I.
Sar Passage
Orukuizui
Eil Malk I.
Shonian Harbor
(Mecherchar)
Ngeregong
Barnum Bay
Ngergoi
Ngesebus I.
Kongauru I.
Ngardololok
Peleliu I.
PACIFIC OCEAN
Angaur I.
134° 30' E
7° 30' N
1: 1 550 000
30 km
20 miles
R U S S I A
Okhotsk
Sea of Okhotsk
Poluostrov Kamchatka
Komandorskiye Ostrova
(Russia)
Aleutian Basin
Near Is.
(U.S.A.)
Andreanof
Petropavlovsk-Kamchatskiy
Aleutian Trench
Lena
Irkutsk
Oz. Baykal
Chita
Amur
Sakhalin
Kurilskiye Ostrova
(Russia)
Kuril-Kamchatka Trench
Blagoveshchensk
Khabarovsk
Ulaanbaatar
Harbin
La Perouse Str.
10,542
Emperor Seamount Chain
Emperor Trough
Chinook Trough
Ürümqi
MONGOLIA
Changchun
Sapporo
Hokkaido
Hakodate
Shenyang
Vladivostok
Sea of Japan
N o r t h w e s t
Beijing
Tianjin
NORTH KOREA
Honshū
Sendai
C H I N A
Taiyuan
Huang He
Dalian
Seoul
SOUTH KOREA
Fuji-San 3776
Tōkyō
Nagoya
Kyōto
Yokohama
Shatsky Rise
P a c i f i c
Kunlun Shan
Lanzhou
Qingdao
Xi'an
Ōsaka
JAPAN
XIZANG
Kitakyūshū
Yellow Sea
Shikoku
Kyūshū
10,554
Japan Trench
Nanjing
Shanghai
Chengdu
Wuhan
Lhasa
Chongqing
Hangzhou
East China Sea
Chang Jiang
Changsha
Okinawa
Brahmaputra
Iwo-Jima
(Japan)
Ogasawara Gunto
(Japan)
B a s i n
Midway Is.
(U.S.A.)
Kunming
Fuzhou
Taipei
Ryūkyū-rettō
(Japan)
Kyushu-Palau Ridge
Izu-Ogasawara Trench
Minami-Tori-Shima
(Japan)
Lisianski I.
(U.S.A.)
Dhaka
Mandalay
Guangzhou
TAIWAN
Kazan-Rettō
(Japan)
Irrawaddy
BURMA
Hong Kong
Macau
Hanoi
LAOS
Philippine Sea
Kyushu-Palau Ridge
Mid-Pacific Seamounts
Wake I.
(U.S.A.)
International Date Line
Hainan
C. Engano
NORTHERN MARIANAS
(U.S.A.)
Saipan
Tinian
West Mariana Basin
East Mariana Basin
Rangoon
THAILAND
Mekong
Luzon
Paracel Is.
Manila
Philippine Basin
GUAM
(U.S.A.)
Mariana Trench
MARSHALL IS.
Bangkok
CAMBODIA
Phnom Penh
VIETNAM
PHILIPPINES
Challenger Deep
11,022
South China Sea
Mindoro
Samar
10,497
G. of Thailand
Thanh Pho Ho Chi Minh
Palawan
M i c r o n e s i a
Bikini Atoll
Enewetak Atoll
Kwajalein
Ralik Chain
Ratak Chain
Majuro
SRI LANKA
Nicobar Is.
(India)
Yap
Caroline Is.
Chuuk
Colombo
MALAYSIA
Sea
Sulu Sea
Mindanao
Davao
Philippine Trench
Melekeok
FED. STATES OF MICRONESIA
Pohnpei
Palikir
Jaluit I.
Kuala Lumpur
PEN. MALAYSIA
BRUNEI
SABAH
SARAWAK
Celebes Sea
PALAU
West Caroline Basin
East Caroline Basin
Solomon Rise
Melanesian Basin
Butaritari
Tarawa
Gilbert Is.
Eauripik Rise
M e l a n e s i a
Singapore
Maluku
Sumatera
Borneo
Halmahera
PAPUA NEW GUINEA
Yaren
NAURU
Banaba
Howland I.
Baker I.
Phoenix Is.
I N D O N E S I A
Sulawesi
Seram
Admiralty Is.
New Ireland
Palembang
Buru
Puncak Jaya
PAPUA
4884
New Guinea
Bismarck Arch.
Kokopo
Makassar
Banda Sea
Java Sea
8940
Bougainville
Jakarta
Flores Sea
7440
Lae
New Britain
SOLOMON IS.
Jawa
Surabaya
Flores
Dili
EAST TIMOR
Arafura Sea
Torres Strait
Port Moresby
Honiara
Guadalcanal
Fongafale
TUVALU
Selat Sunda
Sunda Trench
(Java Trench)
Bali
Sumbawa
Sumba
Louisiade Arch.
Santa Cruz Is.
9165
Tokelau
Christmas I.
(Austral.)
Cocos Is.
(Austral.)
S u n d a I s l a n d s
C. York
C. Arnhem
Rotuma
Is. Wallis & Futuna
(Fr.)
Darwin
Gulf of Carpentaria
Coral Sea Basin
Espíritu Santo
North Australian Basin
Great Barrier Reef
VANUATU
Port Vila
Coral Sea
West Fiji Basin
Vanua Levu
Viti Levu
FIJI
Suva
I N D I A N
Ninetyeast Ridge
Cairns
Is. Chesterfield
Townsville
7570
Nuku'alofa
TONGA
Broome
Exmouth Plateau
Wharton Basin
North West C.
Mount Isa
A U S T R A L I A
NEW CALEDONIA
(Fr.)
Nouméa
Is. Loyauté
Rockhampton
10,822
O C E A N
Alice Springs
Great Dividing Ra.
Middleton
Brisbane
South Fiji Basin
L. Eyre
Basin
Lord Howe Rise
Norfolk Ridge
New Caledonia Trough
Norfolk I.
(Austral.)
Geraldton
Darling
Broken Ridge
Perth Basin
Lord Howe I.
(Austral.)
Kermadec Is.
(N.Z.)
Kermadec Trench
Perth
10,047
Sydney
Naturaliste Plateau
Great Australian Bight
Murray
Canberra
Mt. Kosciuszko
2228
Tasman Sea
NEW ZEALAND
Albany
Adelaide
Auckland
Cook Strait
South Australian Basin
Melbourne
Bass Str.
Wellington
Tasmania
Hobart
Aoraki
Mt. Cook
3753
Christchurch
Chatham Rise
Chatham
(N.Z.)
East Tasman Plateau
Tasman Basin
Dunedin
Bounty Trough
Bounty Is.
(N.Z.)
South Tasman Rise
Invercargill
Antipodes Is.
(N.Z.)
Campbell Plateau
Auckland Is.
(N.Z.)
Campbell I.
(N.Z.)
S O U T H E R N O C E A N
Macquarie I.
(Austral.)
Projection: Mollweide's Homolographic
East from Greenwich
110
120
130
140
150
160
170
180
Îles Belep
Récif de Cook
Île Art
Récif de l' Astrolabe
NEW CALEDONIA
1: 5 750 000
100 km
50 miles
d
Île Balabio
Nouvelle-Calédonie
(France)
Poum
Ouégoa
Pouébo
Mt. Panié
1628
Koumac
Hienghène
Kaala-Gomen
Île Ouvéa
Fayaoué
Îles Loyauté
Chépénéhé
C. Escarpé
7570
Poindimié
Voh
Ponérihouen
Koné
Houailou
Île Lifou
Wé
Nou
C. de Flotte
Île Tiga
3566
Poya
Canala
Tadine
La Roche
C. Boyer
Île Maré
Bourail
Thio
CORAL SEA
La Foa
Boulouparis
1618
Mt. Humbolt
2212
Dumbéa
Yaté
Nouméa
Mont Dore
Païta
C. Ndoua
Grand Récif Sud
Île des Pins
Vao
165° E
166° E
167° E
168° E
20° S
21° S
22° S

Arctic Circle
ALASKA
(U.S.A.)
Anchorage
Bristol Bay
Gulf of Alaska
Juneau
5959
CANADA
Prince of Wales I.
(U.S.A.)
Prince Rupert
Haida Gwaii
(Queen Charlotte Is.)
(Canada)
Tufts
Abyssal
Plain
Edmonton
Calgary
Vancouver
Vancouver I.
Victoria
Seattle
Portland
Rocky Mts
Snake
Boise
Salt Lake City
Denver
Colorado
Northeast
Mendocino Fracture Zone
C. Mendocino
Sacramento
San Francisco
4418
6741
Murray Fracture Zone
Los Angeles
San Diego
Pacific
UNITED STATES
Oklahoma City
Memphis
Atlanta
Phoenix
Dallas
Mississippi
Jacksonville
Houston
New Orleans
San Antonio
Ciudad Juárez
Guadalupe
(Mex.)
Baja California
Golfo de California
Molokai Fracture Zone
Gulf of Mexico
Miami
BAHAMAS
Monterrey
MEXICO
3504
Sigsbee Deep
La Habana
CUBA
Canal de Yucatán
Tropic of Cancer
Ridge
Honolulu
O'ahu
HAWAI'I
(U.S.A.)
4205
Hawai'i
Basin
C. San Lucas
Guadalajara
Mexico
Puebla
5610
Mérida
7680
HAITI
JAMAICA
Kingston
Is. de Revillagigedo
(Mex.)
Clarion Fracture Zone
Acapulco
BELIZE
GUATEMALA
Guatemala
HONDURAS
Caribbean Sea
Middle America Trench
San Salvador
EL SALVADOR
NICARAGUA
Managua
Barranquilla
COSTA RICA
San José
Colón
Panamá
PANAMA
Guatemala Basin
I. Clipperton
(Fr.)
Clipperton Fracture Zone
Cocos Ridge
Panama Basin
I. del Coco
(Costa Rica)
Medellín
I. de Malpelo
(Colombia)
Cali
COLOMBIA
PACIFIC
Cooper Ridge
Palmyra Is.
(U.S.A.)
Teraina
Tabuaeran
Kiritimati
Line Islands
Equator
OCEAN
Jarvis I.
(U.S.A.)
Galapagos Fracture Zone
Galápagos
(Ecuador)
Carnegie Ridge
Quito
ECUADOR
Guayaquil
Malden I.
Starbuck I.
C. Pariñas
East Pacific Rise
Penrhyn
(Tongareva)
Manihiki
Pukapuka
Manihiki
Plateau
Caroline I.
(Millennium I.)
Vostok I.
Flint I.
Nuku Hiva
Îs. Marquises
Hiva Oa
Marquesas Fracture Zone
Trujillo
6369
PERU
Lima
Cusco
Yupanqui Basin
Mendaña Fracture Zone
Galapagos Rise
Suwarrow Is.
Îs. de la Société
Bora Bora
Huahine
Raiatea
Papeete
Tahiti
Rangiroa
Îs. Tuamotu
Cook Is.
(N.Z.)
Aitutaki
Atiu
Rarotonga
Mangaia
FRENCH POLYNESIA
Îs. Gambier
Mururoa
Îs. Tubuai
Austral Seamount Chain
Tuamotu Ridge
Peru Basin
L. Titicaca
Nevado Ancohuma
6550
La Paz
BOLIVIA
Arequipa
6866
Peru-Chile Trench
Arica
Iquique
Chile
Nazca Ridge
Chile Basin
Antofagasta
8064
PARAGUAY
Asunción
San Miguel de Tucumán
Oeno I.
Henderson I.
Ducie I.
Pitcairn I.
(U.K.)
Rapa
Tropic of Capricorn
Easter Fracture Zone
Sala y Gómez Ridge
Sala-y-Gómez
(Chile)
I. de Pascua
(Chile)
Easter Fracture Zone
San Félix
(Chile)
San Ambrosio
(Chile)
Porto Alegre
Roggeveen Basin
Arch. de Juan Fernández
(Chile)
Valparaíso
Aconcagua
6962
Santiago
Córdoba
Rosario
Buenos Aires
URUGUAY
Montevideo
Río de la Plata
Challenger Fracture Zone
Chile Rise
Concepción
ARGENTINA
Argentine Basin
Southwest
Pacific
Basin
Nemo Point
(furthest point from any land)
East Pacific Antarctic Ridge
Menard Fracture Zone
Patagonia
ANDES
ATLANTIC OCEAN
114
6212
Falkland Plateau
Falkland Is.
(U.K.)
Georgia Basin
Punta Arenas
Est. de Magallanes
Tierra del Fuego
C. de Hornos
South Georgia Ridge
4402
South Georgia
(U.K.)
Southeast Pacific Basin
Drake Passage
West from Greenwich
COPYRIGHT PHILIP'S
TAHITI
1:1 150 000
Pte. Aroa
B. de Matavai
Pte. Vénus
Mahina
Papetoai
Papeete
Arue
Papenoo
Tiarei
Tahiti
(France)
Hitiaa
Mt. Tohiea
1207
Afareaitu
Pirae
Faaa
Haapiti
Moorea
Pte. Nuupere
Punaauia
Mt. Aorai
2066
Mt. Orohena
2241
Mt. Tetufera
1799
Lac Vaihiria
Taravao
Isthme de Taravao
Paea
Papara
Afaahiti
Pte. Tatatua
Pueu
Tautira
Maraa
Atimaono
Mataiea
Vairao
Mt. Rooniu
1332
Teahupoo
Presqu'île de Taiarapu
PACIFIC OCEAN
FRENCH POLYNESIA
1:26 000 000
Hatutu
Eiao
Îles Marquises
Nuku Hiva
Ua Huka
Ua Pu
Hiva Oa
Tahuata
Motane
4884
Flint I.
(Kiribati)
6513
Îles Tuamotu
Îles du Roi-Georges
Îles du Désappointement
Tikehau
Manihi
Takaroa
Puka Puka
Îles Sous-le-Vent
Rangiroa
Tikei
Takume
Fangatau
Maupiti
Bora Bora
Îles du Vent
Apataki
Kauehi
Raroia
Huahine
Raraka
Makemo
Maupihaa
Raiatea
Tahiti
Anaa
Tekokota
Tatakoto
Îles de la Société
Moorea
Papeete
Méhétia
Marokau
Amanu
Puka Ruha
Hereheretue
4616
Ravahere
Nengonengo
Hao
Paraoa
Vahitahi
Reao
Ahunui
Vairaatea
Îles du Duc-de-Gloucester
Vanavana
Tureia
Groupe Actéon
Îles Maria
Rurutu
Tematagi
Mururoa
Fangataufa
Rimatara
Tubuai
Raivavae
Tropic of Capricorn
Îles Gambier
Morane
Îles Tubuai (Îles Australes)
Récif Président-Thiers
Récif Portland
PACIFIC OCEAN
Récif Neilson
Rapa
Îlots de Bass
NIUE
1:830 000
Hikutavake
Mutalau
Namukulu
Tuapa
Toi
Makefu
Lakepa
Niue
(N.Z.)
Alofi Bay
Alofi
Liku
Halangingie Pt.
IUE
Fonuakula
Tamakautoga
Avatele
Tepa Pt.
Vaiea
Hakupu
PACIFIC OCEAN
RAROTONGA
1:415 000
Rarotonga
(N.Z.)
RAR
Avarua Harbour
Nikao
Avatiu
Avarua
Pue
Matavera
509
Te Manga
653
588
Ngatangiia
Arorangi
Maungaroa
222
Te Kou
Maungatongaiti
Motu Tapu
Oneroa
329
Muri
Koromiri
Taakoka
Titikaveka
PACIFIC OCEAN

# NORTH AMERICA

1:28 000 000
ARCTIC OCEAN
Lincoln Sea
Beaufort Sea
Chukchi Sea
Bering Sea
Asia
Greenland
Iceland
Denmark Strait
Baffin Bay
Davis Strait
Baffin Island
Queen Elizabeth Is.
Ellesmere I.
Axel Heiberg I.
Devon I.
Melville I.
Banks I.
Victoria I.
Labrador Sea
Hudson Strait
Hudson Bay
Southampton I.
Canadian Shield
Great Lakes
Newfoundland
Alaska
Alaska Range
Brooks Ra.
Mackenzie Mts.
Gulf of Alaska
Rocky Mountains
Great Plains
Coast Mountains
Columbia Plateau
Great Basin
Colorado Plateau
Appalachian Mts.
Piedmont
Florida
Mississippi River Delta
Gulf of Mexico
ATLANTIC OCEAN
Sargasso Sea
Bahamas
Cuba
Greater Antilles
West Indies
Caribbean Sea
Hispaniola
Jamaica
Yucatán Peninsula
Mexican Plateau
Western Sierra Madre
Eastern Sierra Madre
Baja California
Gulf of California
Tropic of Cancer
PACIFIC OCEAN
Clarion Fracture Zone
Isthmus of Tehuantepec
Guatemala Trench
Central America
Andes
Projection: Bonne
West from Greenwich
COPYRIGHT PHILIP'S

1:28 000 000

ARCTIC OCEAN
Beaufort Sea
Bering Sea
Bering Strait
International Date Line
RUSSIA
Asia
ALASKA (USA)
Fairbanks
Anchorage
Gulf of Alaska
Kodiak I.
Yukon
Porcupine
YUKON TERRITORY
Whitehorse
Juneau
NORTHWEST TERRITORIES
Arctic Circle
Mackenzie
Great Bear L.
Great Slave L.
Yellowknife
Queen Elizabeth Is.
Victoria I.
Ellesmere I.
Baffin Island
Baffin Bay
NUNAVUT
Iqaluit
Hudson Strait
Hudson Bay
GREENLAND (Denmark)
Nuuk
Davis Strait
Denmark Strait
ICELAND
Reykjavík
CANADA
BRITISH COLUMBIA
ALBERTA
Edmonton
Calgary
SASKATCHEWAN
Regina
MANITOBA
Winnipeg
L. Winnipeg
Churchill
Nelson
Athabasca
Peace
Fraser
Skeena
ONTARIO
QUÉBEC
Eastmain
NEWFOUNDLAND & LABRADOR
St. John's
St.-Pierre et Miquelon (Fr.)
PRINCE EDWARD I.
Charlottetown
NEW BRUNSWICK
NOVA SCOTIA
Halifax
Fredericton
Québec
Montréal
Ottawa
TORONTO
Vancouver
Victoria
UNITED STATES
WASHINGTON
Seattle
Olympia
Portland
Salem
OREGON
Columbia
IDAHO
Boise
Snake
MONTANA
Helena
Missouri
NORTH DAKOTA
Bismarck
SOUTH DAKOTA
MINNESOTA
Minneapolis-St. Paul
WISCONSIN
Madison
Milwaukee
L. Superior
L. Michigan
L. Huron
L. Erie
L. Ontario
MICHIGAN
Lansing
Detroit
Toledo
Cleveland
Buffalo
NEW YORK
Hartford
Boston
Providence
Concord
Augusta
MAINE
NEW YORK
PHILADELPHIA
PA.
Pittsburgh
Baltimore
WASHINGTON D.C.
Richmond
VIRGINIA
W.V.
Raleigh
NORTH CAROLINA
Charlotte
SOUTH CAROLINA
Columbia
Charleston
WYOMING
NEBRASKA
Lincoln
IOWA
CHICAGO
ILLINOIS
INDIANA
Indianapolis
OHIO
Columbus
Cincinnati
KENTUCKY
Nashville
TENNESSEE
Memphis
Springfield
St. Louis
MISSOURI
Kansas City
Topeka
KANSAS
COLORADO
Denver
UTAH
Salt Lake City
NEVADA
Carson City
Sacramento
SAN FRANCISCO
San Jose
CALIFORNIA
Las Vegas
LOS ANGELES
San Diego
Tijuana
Mexicali
ARIZONA
Phoenix
Tucson
NEW MEXICO
Santa Fe
Albuquerque
El Paso
Ciudad Juárez
OKLAHOMA
Oklahoma City
DALLAS-FT. WORTH
TEXAS
Austin
HOUSTON
San Antonio
ARKANSAS
Little Rock
MISSISSIPPI
Jackson
Mississippi
LOUISIANA
Baton Rouge
New Orleans
ALABAMA
Birmingham
Montgomery
GEORGIA
ATLANTA
Tallahassee
Jacksonville
FLORIDA
Orlando
Tampa-St. Petersburg
MIAMI
Florida Str.
Bermuda (U.K.)
ATLANTIC OCEAN
PACIFIC OCEAN
Guadalupe (Mex.)
Tropic of Cancer
Gulf of Mexico
MEXICO
Hermosillo
Culiacán
Torreón
Monterrey
Rio Grande
San Luis Potosí
León
Querétaro
Guadalajara
MÉXICO
Toluca
Puebla
Acapulco
Mérida
Revilla Gigedo Is. (Mex.)
BAHAMAS
Nassau
Turks & Caicos Is. (U.K.)
CUBA
Havana
Cayman Is. (U.K.)
JAMAICA
Kingston
HAITI
Port-au-Prince
DOMINICAN REP.
Santo Domingo
PUERTO RICO (U.S.A.)
San Juan
Caribbean Sea
BELIZE
Belmopan
GUATEMALA
Guatemala
HONDURAS
Tegucigalpa
San Salvador
EL SALVADOR
NICARAGUA
Managua
L. Nicaragua
COSTA RICA
San José
PANAMA
Panamá
Barranquilla
Maracaibo
VENEZUELA
COLOMBIA
Medellín
South America
Projection: Bonne
West from Greenwich
COPYRIGHT PHILIP'S
MÉXICO Capital Cities

1:12 000 000
km
miles
Beaufort Sea
Banks Island
Victoria Island
Melville Island
Viscount Melville Sound
Prince of Wales I.
Amundsen Gulf
Coronation Gulf
Great Bear Lake
Great Slave Lake
Lake Athabasca
Reindeer Lake
Lake Winnipeg
Lake Manitoba
L. Winnipegosis
Gulf of Alaska
PACIFIC OCEAN
Alexander Archipelago
Haida Gwaii (Queen Charlotte Is.)
Vancouver Island
ALASKA
Alaska Range
YUKON TERRITORY
NORTHWEST TERRITORIES
BRITISH COLUMBIA
ALBERTA
SASKATCHEWAN
MANITOBA
WASHINGTON
OREGON
IDAHO
MONTANA
WYOMING
NORTH DAKOTA
SOUTH DAKOTA
NEBRASKA
MINNESOTA
IOWA
NEVADA
CALIFORNIA
UNITED STATES
Rocky Mountains
Mackenzie Mountains
Selwyn Mts.
Cassiar Mountains
Coast Mountains
Anchorage
Fairbanks
Whitehorse
Dawson City
Yellowknife
Inuvik
Tuktoyaktuk
Fort Simpson
Fort Smith
Uranium City
Prince Rupert
Prince George
Kamloops
VANCOUVER
Victoria
Edmonton
CALGARY
Lethbridge
Medicine Hat
Saskatoon
Regina
Moose Jaw
Prince Albert
Flin Flon
Thompson
Churchill
Winnipeg
Brandon
SEATTLE
Spokane
PORTLAND
Boise
Helena
Great Falls
Billings
Bismarck
Fargo
MINNEAPOLIS
ST. PAUL
SACRAMENTO
SAN FRANCISCO
SALT LAKE CITY
Projection: Bonne
West from Greenwich

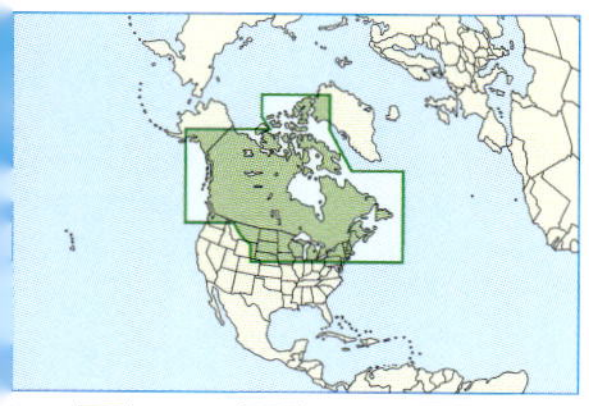

150
154
301
NORTHERN CANADA
continuation northwards on same scale as main map
ARCTIC OCEAN
Queen Elizabeth Islands
Parry Islands
Melville Island
Axel Heiberg Island
Ellesmere Island
Devon Island
Prince of Wales I.
Somerset Island
Bathurst Island
Jones Sound
Lancaster Sound
Baffin Bay
GREENLAND (KALAALLIT NUNAAT)
Nares Strait
Kane Basin
NUNAVUT
Baffin Island
Davis Strait
Foxe Basin
Hudson Strait
Ungava Bay
Labrador Sea
ATLANTIC OCEAN
Péninsule d'Ungava
James Bay
NEWFOUNDLAND & LABRADOR
Newfoundland
Gulf of St. Lawrence
PRINCE EDWARD I.
NEW BRUNSWICK
NOVA SCOTIA
Cabot Strait
B. of Fundy
Iqaluit
Québec
MONTRÉAL
OTTAWA
TORONTO
DETROIT
BUFFALO
ROCHESTER
CLEVELAND
BOSTON
PROVIDENCE
HARTFORD
St. John's
Halifax
MAINE
VERMONT
NEW HAMPSHIRE
NEW YORK
MASS.
PENNSYLVANIA
L. Superior
L. Huron
L. Ontario
L. Erie
L. Michigan
COPYRIGHT PHILIP'S

1:5 600 000

km 50 0 50 100 150 200 250 300
miles 50 0 50 100 150 200
303
294
304
YUKON TERRITORY
NORTHWEST TERRITORIES
BRITISH COLUMBIA
ALBERTA
ALASKA (USA)
WASHINGTON
IDAHO
UNITED STATES
PACIFIC OCEAN
GREAT SLAVE LAKE
Haida Gwaii (Queen Charlotte Is.)
Alexander Archipelago
Vancouver Island
Queen Charlotte Sound
Hecate Strait
Dixon Entrance
Coast Mountains
Rocky Mountains
Skeena Mountains
Cariboo Mts.
Monashee Mts.
Purcell Mts.
Caribou Mts.
Swan Hills
Clear Hills
Birch Mountains
Whitehorse
Yellowknife
Juneau
EDMONTON
CALGARY
VANCOUVER
Victoria
SEATTLE
Prince George
Prince Rupert
Kamloops
Kelowna
Red Deer
Lethbridge
Grande Prairie
Fort St. John
Fort Nelson
Dawson Creek
Surrey
Coquitlam
Nanaimo
Chilliwack
Bellingham
Everett
Hay River
Peace River
Fort Smith
Projection: Lambert's Equivalent Azimuthal
West from Greenwich

NUNAVUT
HUDSON BAY
MANITOBA
SASKATCHEWAN
ONTARIO
NORTH DAKOTA
MINNESOTA
MONTANA
LAKE WINNIPEG
Lake Winnipegosis
Lake Manitoba
Cedar Lake
Lake Athabasca
Reindeer Lake
Lake of the Woods
Wollaston L.
Winnipeg
Regina
Saskatoon
Brandon
Churchill
Thompson
Flin Flon
The Pas
Prince Albert
North Battleford
Moose Jaw
Swift Current
Yorkton
Dauphin
Portage la Prairie
Kenora
Dryden
Lloydminster
Estevan
Weyburn
Minot
Grand Forks
Bemidji
Duluth
Uranium City
Arviat (Eskimo Point)
Whale Cove (Tikirarjuaq)
Dawson Inlet
Hubbart Pt.
C. Churchill
C. Tatnam
CARIBOU RIVER PARK RESERVE
WAPUSK NATIONAL PARK
SAND LAKES PROV. PARK
NUMAYKOOS LAKE PROV. PARK
ATHABASCA SAND DUNES PROV. PARK
PRINCE ALBERT NAT. PARK
GRASSLANDS NAT. PARK
RIDING MOUNTAIN NAT. PARK
OPASQUIA PROV. PARK
WOODLAND CARIBOU PROV. PARK
ATIKAKI PROV. WILDERNESS PARK
GRASS RIVER PROV. PARK
CLEARWATER PROV. PARK
NARROW HILLS PROV. PARK
LAC LA RONGE PROV. PARK
MEADOW LAKE PROV. PARK
NOPIMING PROV. PARK
WHITESHELL PROV. PARK
DUCK MT. PROV. PARK
MOOSE MT. PROV. PARK
GREENWATER LAKE PROV. PARK
QUETICO PROV. PARK
VOYAGEURS NAT. PARK
Cypress Hills
A
B
C
D
7
8
9
10
11
110
105
100
95
90
60
55
50
298
308
COPYRIGHT PHILIP'S

1:5 600 000

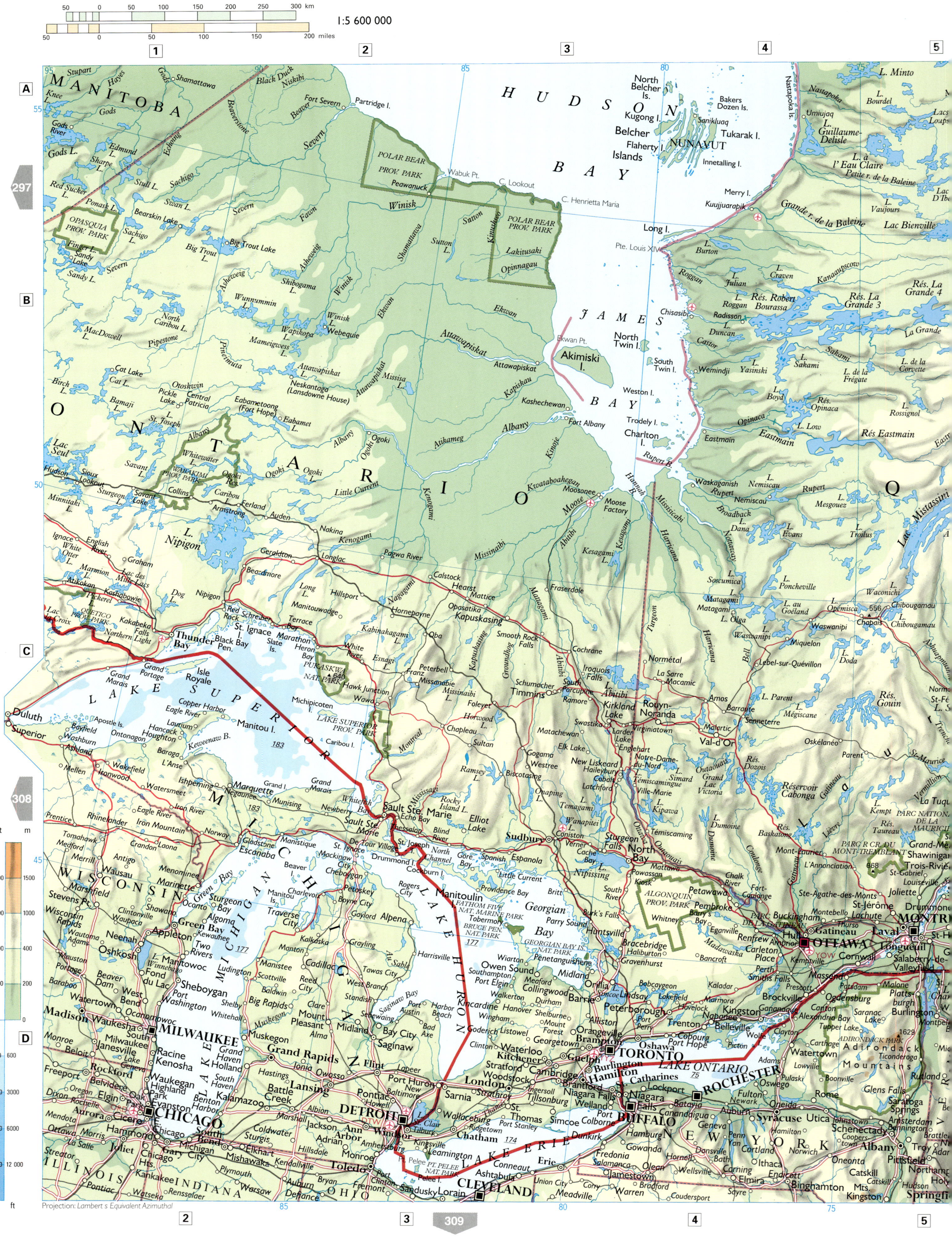
50 0 50 100 150 200 250 300 km
50 0 50 100 150 200 miles
1 2 3 4 5
A B C D
297
308
309
HUDSON BAY
JAMES BAY
MANITOBA
ONTARIO
NUNAVUT
WISCONSIN
MICHIGAN
ILLINOIS
INDIANA
OHIO
NEW YORK
LAKE SUPERIOR
LAKE MICHIGAN
LAKE HURON
LAKE ONTARIO
LAKE ERIE
Georgian Bay
Belcher Islands
Akimiski I.
POLAR BEAR PROV. PARK
OPASQUIA PROV. PARK
WABAKIMI PROV. PARK
QUETICO PROV. PARK
PUKASKWA NAT. PARK
LAKE SUPERIOR PROV. PARK
ALGONQUIN PROV. PARK
FATHOM FIVE NAT. MARINE PARK
BRUCE PEN. NAT. PARK
GEORGIAN BAY IS. NAT. PARK
PT. PELEE NAT. PARK
ADIRONDACK PARK
Adirondack Mountains
L. Nipigon
L. Mistassini
Réservoir Cabonga
Isle Royale
Manitoulin
Duluth
Superior
Thunder Bay
Sault Ste. Marie
Marquette
Sudbury
North Bay
Timmins
Kapuskasing
Hearst
Cochrane
Moosonee
Chisasibi
Val-d'Or
Rouyn-Noranda
OTTAWA
Gatineau
MONTRÉAL
Laval
Kingston
Peterborough
Barrie
TORONTO
Hamilton
Burlington
Brampton
Kitchener
Waterloo
Guelph
London
Windsor
Sarnia
DETROIT
Flint
Lansing
Grand Rapids
Green Bay
MILWAUKEE
Madison
CHICAGO
Toledo
CLEVELAND
BUFFALO
Niagara Falls
ROCHESTER
Syracuse
Utica
Albany
Schenectady
Binghamton
Erie
Projection: Lambert's Equivalent Azimuthal

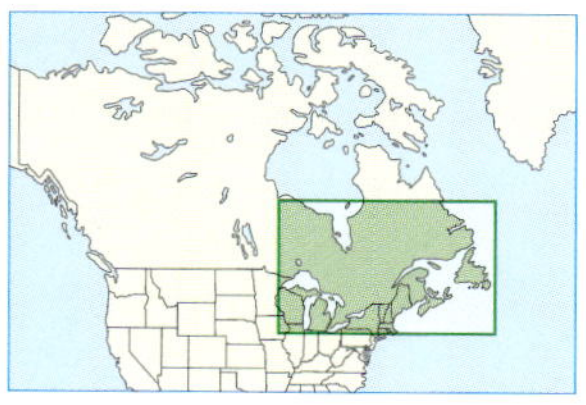



6 295 7 8 9

LABRADOR SEA
NEWFOUNDLAND & LABRADOR
Labrador
Newfoundland
Q U É B E C
Smallwood Reservoir
Churchill Falls
Happy Valley-Goose Bay
North West River
Nain
Hopedale
Makkovik
Postville
Cartwright
Mealy Mts.
Labrador City
Wabush
Fermont
Schefferville
Mts. Otish
Rés. Manicouagan
Sept-Îles
Port-Cartier
Baie-Comeau
Havre-St.-Pierre
Natashquan
Kegaska
La Romaine
St-Augustin
Blanc-Sablon
Str. of Belle Isle
Belle Isle
St. Anthony
L'Anse aux Meadows
Long Range Mts.
Gros Morne Nat. Park
Deer Lake
Corner Brook
Stephenville
Port aux Basques
Channel-Port aux Basques
Cabot Strait
Grand Falls-Windsor
Gander
Lewisporte
Botwood
Terra Nova Nat. Park
Clarenville
Bonavista
Trinity
Carbonear
St. John's
Mount Pearl
Conception B.
Avalon Peninsula
Placentia
Marystown
Burin
Grand Bank
Fortune
ST-PIERRE-ET-MIQUELON (France)
Île d'Anticosti
GULF OF ST. LAWRENCE
Îs. de la Madeleine
St. Lawrence
Pén. de la Gaspésie
Gaspé
Percé
Chic-Chocs
Matane
Rimouski
Chicoutimi
Jonquière
La Baie
Rivière-du-Loup
Edmundston
Lévis
Charny
Thetford Mines
St-Georges
Sherbrooke
Coaticook
NEW BRUNSWICK
Bathurst
Campbellton
Dalhousie
Miramichi
Moncton
Fredericton
Saint John
Bay of Fundy
PRINCE EDWARD ISLAND
Charlottetown
Summerside
Northumberland Str.
Cape Breton Highlands Nat. Park
Cape Breton Island
Sydney
North Sydney
Glace Bay
NOVA SCOTIA
Halifax
Dartmouth
Truro
New Glasgow
Antigonish
Yarmouth
Kejimkujik Nat. Park
Sable I. (Nova Scotia)
ATLANTIC OCEAN
MAINE
Bangor
Augusta
Portland
Lewiston
Auburn
Biddeford
Portsmouth
Manchester
Nashua
Lowell
BOSTON
Quincy
Brockton
UNITED STATES
West from Greenwich

1:12 000 000
PACIFIC OCEAN
Anchorage
Washington D.C.
San Francisco
Honolulu
3363 miles
5412 km
2010 miles
3234 km
2438 miles
3923 km
2785 miles
4482 km
2395 miles
3854 km
Tropic of Cancar
BRITISH COLUMBIA
VANCOUVER
SEATTLE
PORTLAND
SACRAMENTO
SAN FRANCISCO
SAN JOSE
LOS ANGELES
SAN DIEGO
TIJUANA
LAS VEGAS
PHOENIX
SALT LAKE CITY
SAN BERNARDINO
WASHINGTON
OREGON
IDAHO
NEVADA
ARIZONA
UTAH
Great Basin
Columbia Plateau
Colorado Plateau
Mojave Desert
Sonoran Desert
West from Greenwich
ALASKA
on same scale
RUSSIA
ARCTIC OCEAN
CHUKCHI SEA
BERING SEA
Bering Strait
International Date Line
Gulf of Alaska
Aleutian Islands
Alaska Peninsula
Brooks Range
Alaska Range
North Slope
Seward Peninsula
Yukon Flats
Kuskokwim Mountains
Fairbanks
Anchorage
Kodiak I.
Nunivak I.
St. Lawrence I.
Pribilof Is.
Koryakskoye Nagorye
Chukotskoye Nagorye
Projection: Albers' Equal Area with two standard parallels

GULF OF MEXICO
ATLANTIC OCEAN
PACIFIC OCEAN
HAWAI'I
on same scale
HAWAI'I
CHICAGO
NEW YORK
PHILADELPHIA
WASHINGTON D.C.
BOSTON
DETROIT
TORONTO
MONTRÉAL
OTTAWA
ST. LOUIS
MEMPHIS
ATLANTA
DALLAS
HOUSTON
SAN ANTONIO
NEW ORLEANS
MIAMI
JACKSONVILLE
ORLANDO
TAMPA
BIRMINGHAM
NASHVILLE
LOUISVILLE
INDIANAPOLIS
COLUMBUS
CLEVELAND
PITTSBURGH
BALTIMORE
RICHMOND
NORFOLK
CHARLOTTE
RALEIGH
KANSAS CITY
OKLAHOMA CITY
MINNEAPOLIS
ST. PAUL
MILWAUKEE
BUFFALO
DENVER
AUSTIN
Winnipeg
Honolulu
Hilo
BAHAMAS
Nassau
NORTH DAKOTA
SOUTH DAKOTA
NEBRASKA
KANSAS
OKLAHOMA
MINNESOTA
IOWA
MISSOURI
ARKANSAS
LOUISIANA
MISSISSIPPI
ALABAMA
GEORGIA
TENNESSEE
KENTUCKY
ILLINOIS
INDIANA
OHIO
WISCONSIN
MICHIGAN
NORTH CAROLINA
SOUTH CAROLINA
FLORIDA
WEST VIRGINIA
VIRGINIA
MAINE
MANITOBA
ONTARIO
QUÉBEC
West from Greenwich
Tropic of Cancer
COPYRIGHT PHILIP'S

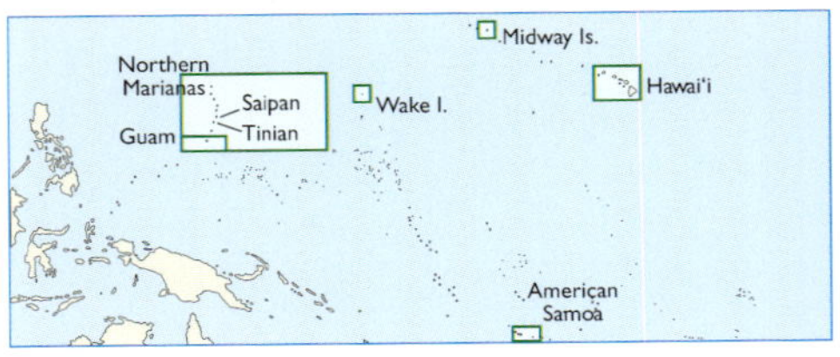
Midway Is.
Northern Marianas
Saipan
Tinian
Guam
Wake I.
Hawai'i
American Samoa

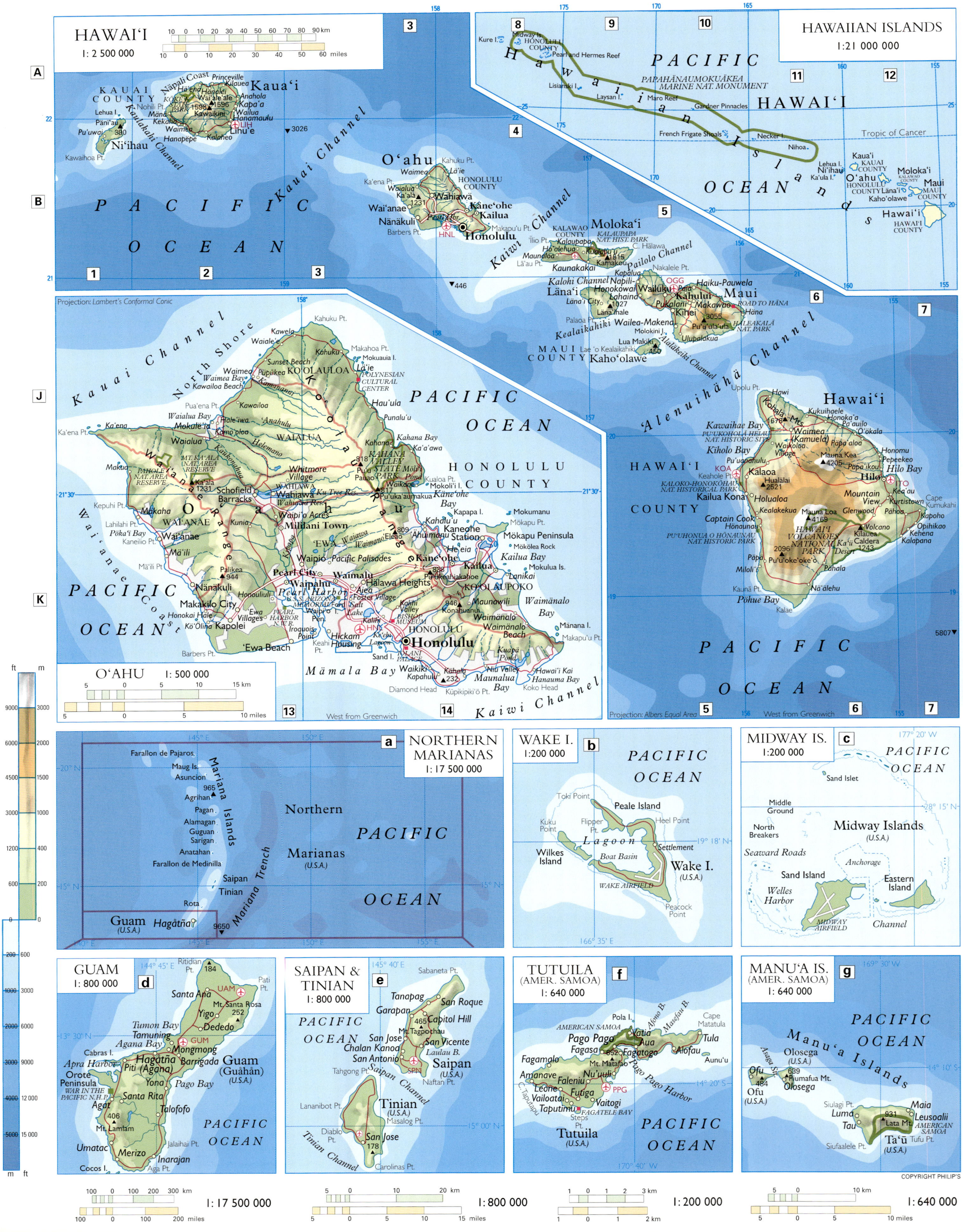
HAWAI'I
1: 2 500 000
HAWAIIAN ISLANDS
1:21 000 000
PACIFIC OCEAN
Hawaiian Islands
PAPAHĀNAUMOKUĀKEA MARINE NAT. MONUMENT
Tropic of Cancer
Kure I.
Midway Is.
Pearl and Hermes Reef
Lisianski I.
Laysan I.
Maro Reef
Gardner Pinnacles
French Frigate Shoals
Necker I.
Nihoa
Kaua'i
Ni'ihau
O'ahu
Moloka'i
Lāna'i
Maui
Kaho'olawe
Hawai'i
KAUAI COUNTY
HONOLULU COUNTY
KALAWAO COUNTY
MAUI COUNTY
HAWAI'I COUNTY
Kaua'i Channel
Kaulakahi Channel
Kaiwi Channel
Pailolo Channel
Kalohi Channel
Kealaikahiki Channel
'Alenuihāhā Channel
Alalākeiki Channel
Līhu'e
Honolulu
Kāne'ohe
Kailua
Wahiawā
Wai'anae
Kaunakakai
Kahului
Wailuku
Lahaina
Kīhei
Hilo
Kailua Kona
Waimea
Mauna Kea 4205
Mauna Loa 4169
Hualālai 2521
HAWAI'I VOLCANOES NATIONAL PARK
HALEAKALĀ NAT. PARK
KALAUPAPA NAT. HIST. PARK
Ka Lae
Projection: Lambert's Conformal Conic
O'AHU 1: 500 000
Kauai Channel
North Shore
Ko'olau Range
Wai'anae Range
Wai'anae Coast
Pearl Harbor
Mililani Town
Pearl City
Waipahu
Kapolei
'Ewa Beach
Māmala Bay
Waikīkī
Diamond Head
Koko Head
Hanauma Bay
Waimānalo Bay
Kailua Bay
Mōkapu Peninsula
Kahuku Pt.
Ka'ena Pt.
Barbers Pt.
Makapu'u Pt.
West from Greenwich
Projection: Albers Equal Area
NORTHERN MARIANAS
1: 17 500 000
Northern Marianas (U.S.A.)
Mariana Islands
Mariana Trench
Farallon de Pajaros
Maug Is.
Asuncion
Agrihan
Pagan
Alamagan
Guguan
Sarigan
Anatahan
Farallon de Medinilla
Saipan
Tinian
Rota
Guam (U.S.A.)
Hagåtña
9650
WAKE I.
1:200 000
Peale Island
Wilkes Island
Wake I. (U.S.A.)
Lagoon
Boat Basin
WAKE AIRFIELD
Toki Point
Kuku Point
Heel Point
Peacock Point
MIDWAY IS.
1:200 000
Midway Islands (U.S.A.)
Sand Islet
Sand Island
Eastern Island
Welles Harbor
Seaward Roads
North Breakers
Middle Ground
Anchorage
MIDWAY AIRFIELD
Channel
GUAM
1: 800 000
Guam (Guåhån) (U.S.A.)
Ritidian Pt.
Pati Pt.
Santa Ana
Mt. Santa Rosa
Yigo
Dededo
Tumon Bay
Tamuning
Agana Bay
Hagåtña (Agana)
Mongmong
Barrigada
Apra Harbor
Orote Peninsula
Piti
Yona
Pago Bay
Santa Rita
Agat
Talofofo
Mt. Lamlam
Umatac
Merizo
Inarajan
Cocos I.
SAIPAN & TINIAN
1: 800 000
Saipan (U.S.A.)
Tinian (U.S.A.)
Saipan Channel
Tinian Channel
Tanapag
Garapan
San Roque
Capitol Hill
San Jose
Chalan Kanoa
San Antonio
San Vicente
Sabaneta Pt.
Naftan Pt.
TUTUILA (AMER. SAMOA)
1: 640 000
Tutuila (U.S.A.)
AMERICAN SAMOA
Pago Pago
Fagatogo
Pago Pago Harbor
Aua
Vatia
Fagasa
Fagamalo
Amanave
Leone
Vailoatai
Taputimu
Faleniu
Futiga
Nu'uuli
Alofau
Tula
Aunu'u
Cape Matatula
FAGATELE BAY
MANU'A IS. (AMER. SAMOA)
1: 640 000
Manu'a Islands
Ofu (U.S.A.)
Olosega (U.S.A.)
Ta'ū (U.S.A.)
Lata Mt.
Lumā
Tau
Maia
Leusoalii
Fitiuta
Siufaalele Pt.
COPYRIGHT PHILIP'S
1: 17 500 000
1: 800 000
1: 200 000
1: 640 000

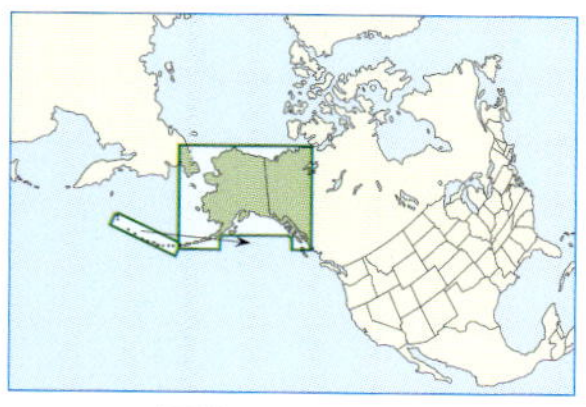

1:8 000 000
ARCTIC OCEAN
BEAUFORT SEA
CHUKCHI SEA
BERING SEA
PACIFIC OCEAN
Gulf of Alaska
Bristol Bay
Norton Sound
Kotzebue Sd.
Bering Strait
Seward Peninsula
Kodiak I.
Nunivak I.
St. Lawrence I.
St. Matthew I.
Pribilof Is.
Aleutian Islands
Alaska Peninsula
Alexander Archipelago
Brooks Range
Alaska Range
Mackenzie Mountains
Yukon
Anchorage
Fairbanks
Juneau
Nome
Whitehorse
Kotzebue
Bethel
RUSSIA
Chukotskiy Poluostrov
NORTHWEST TERRITORIES
YUKON TERRITORY
BRITISH COLUMBIA
CANADA
ALASKA (U.S.A.)
1 ANCHORAGE
2 BRISTOL BAY
3 HAINES
4 SKAGWAY-HOONAH-ANGOON
5 KETCHIKAN GATEWAY
continuation westwards on same scale
West from Greenwich
East from Greenwich
Projection: Bipolar oblique conic conformal

1:5 360 000

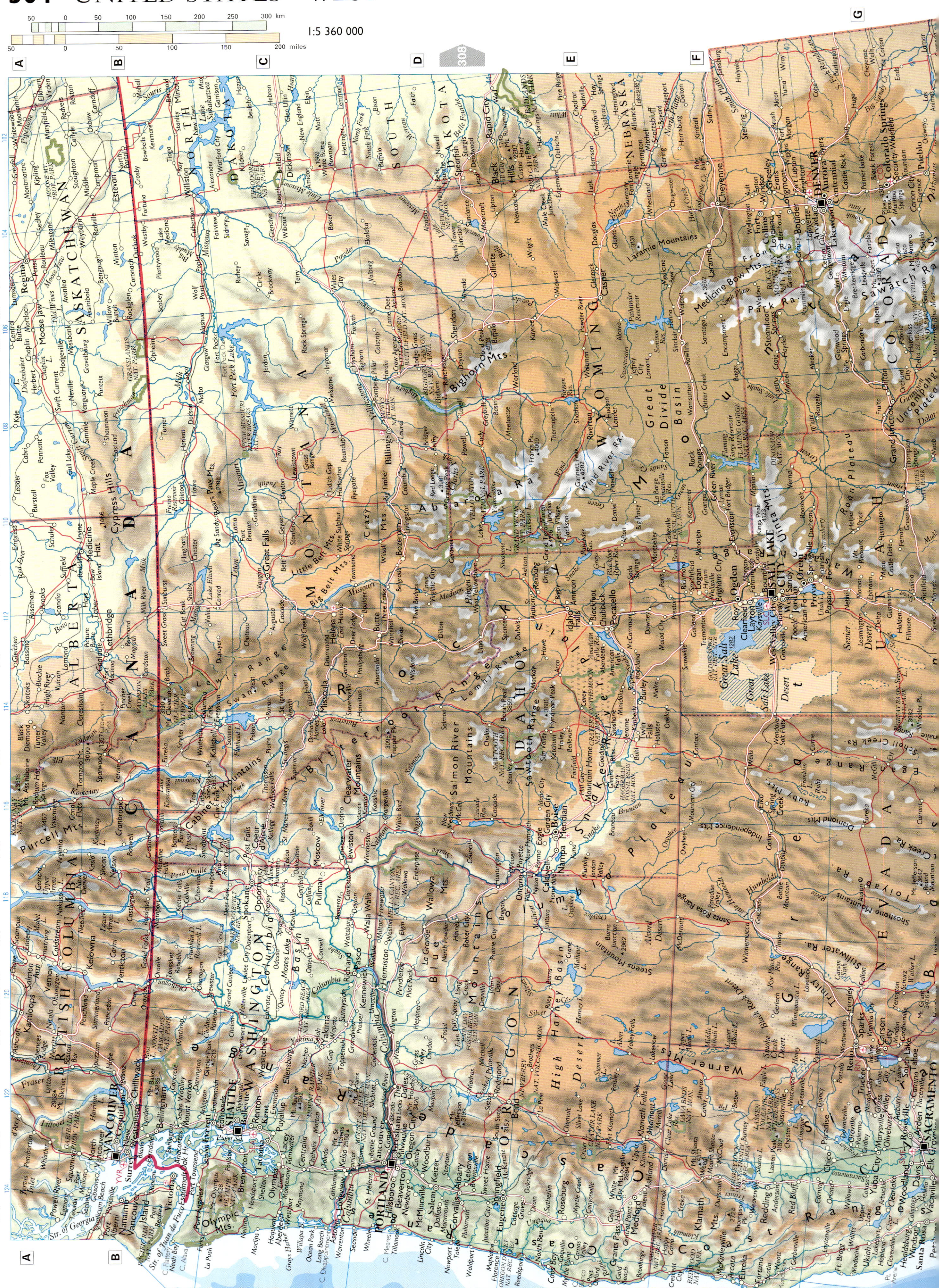

308
297
296
MONTANA
WYOMING
IDAHO
OREGON
WASHINGTON
NEVADA
UTAH
COLORADO
NEBRASKA
SOUTH DAKOTA
NORTH DAKOTA
ALBERTA
SASKATCHEWAN
BRITISH COLUMBIA
CANADA
Great Divide Basin
Bighorn Mts.
Wind River Ra.
Great Salt Lake
Snake River Plain
High Desert
Harney Basin
Salmon River Mountains
Columbia Basin
Great Falls
Billings
Helena
Boise
Spokane
Seattle
Portland
Cheyenne
Denver
Salt Lake City
Casper
Sacramento
Reno
Vancouver
Regina
Moose Jaw
Lethbridge

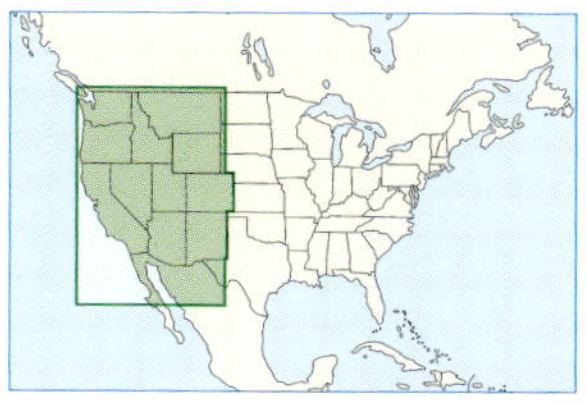

PACIFIC OCEAN
ARIZONA
NEW MEXICO
TEXAS
MEXICO
SONORA
CHIHUAHUA
BAJA CALIFORNIA
BAJA CALIFORNIA SUR
Golfo de California
Colorado Plateau
Mojave Desert
Llano Estacado
Sacramento Mts.
Cedros Trench
LOS ANGELES
SAN DIEGO
TIJUANA
PHOENIX
Tucson
LAS VEGAS
CIUDAD JUÁREZ
El Paso
Albuquerque
Santa Fe
Hermosillo
Chihuahua
Isla Guadalupe (Mexico)
Lava fields
COPYRIGHT PHILIP'S
Projection: Albers' Equal Area with two standard parallels
West from Greenwich

1:2 000 000

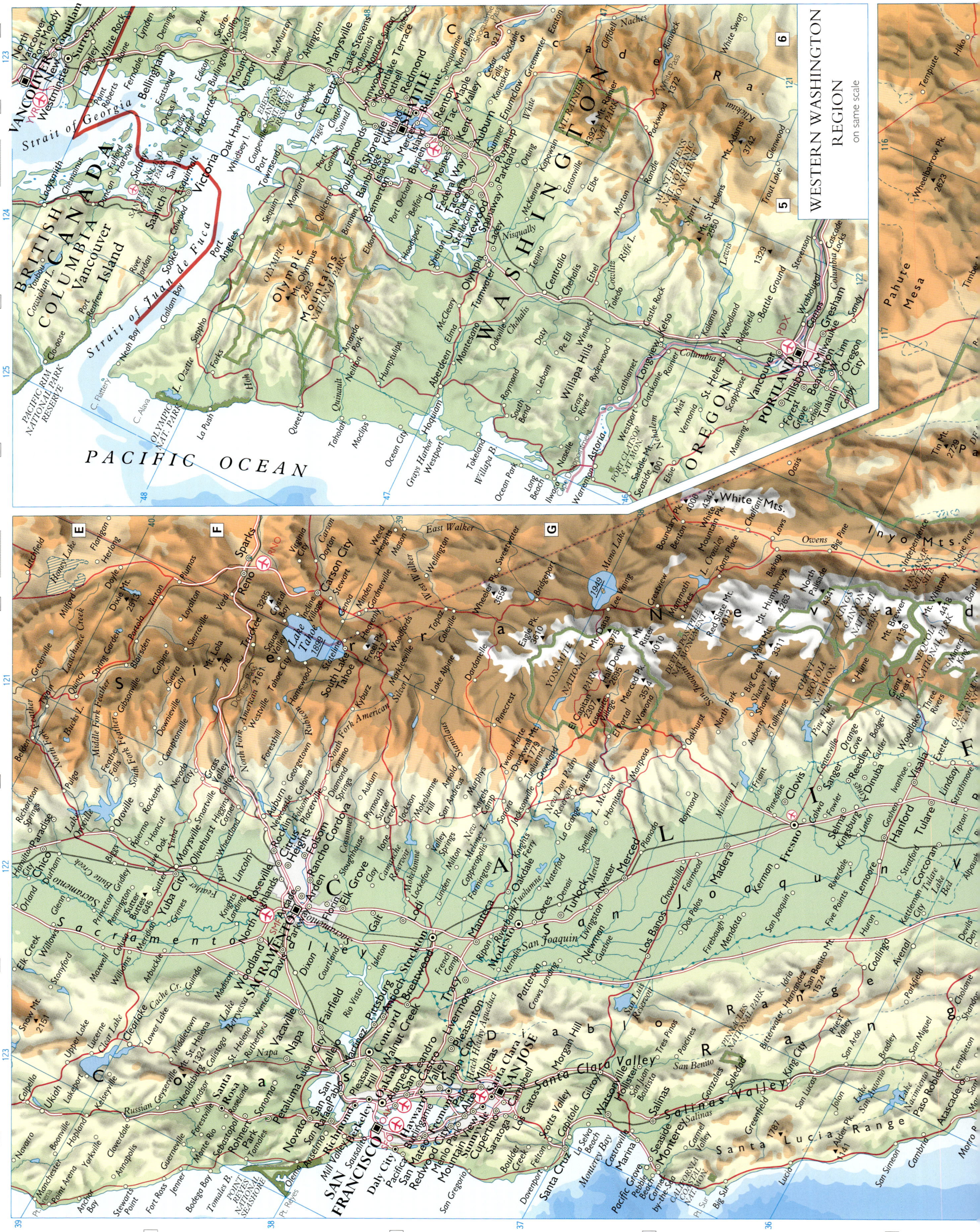
WESTERN WASHINGTON REGION
on same scale
BRITISH COLUMBIA
CANADA
Vancouver Island
Strait of Georgia
Strait of Juan de Fuca
PACIFIC OCEAN
WASHINGTON
OREGON
Olympic Mountains
VANCOUVER
Victoria
SEATTLE
Tacoma
Olympia
PORTLAND
Mt. Rainier 4392
Mt. St. Helens 2550
Mt. Adams 3742
Lake Tahoe
Mono Lake
SACRAMENTO
SAN FRANCISCO
Oakland
SAN JOSE
Stockton
Modesto
Fresno
Reno
Carson City
Santa Cruz
Monterey
Salinas
Sacramento Valley
San Joaquin
Santa Clara Valley
Salinas Valley
Santa Lucia Range
White Mts.
Inyo Mts.
Pahute Mesa

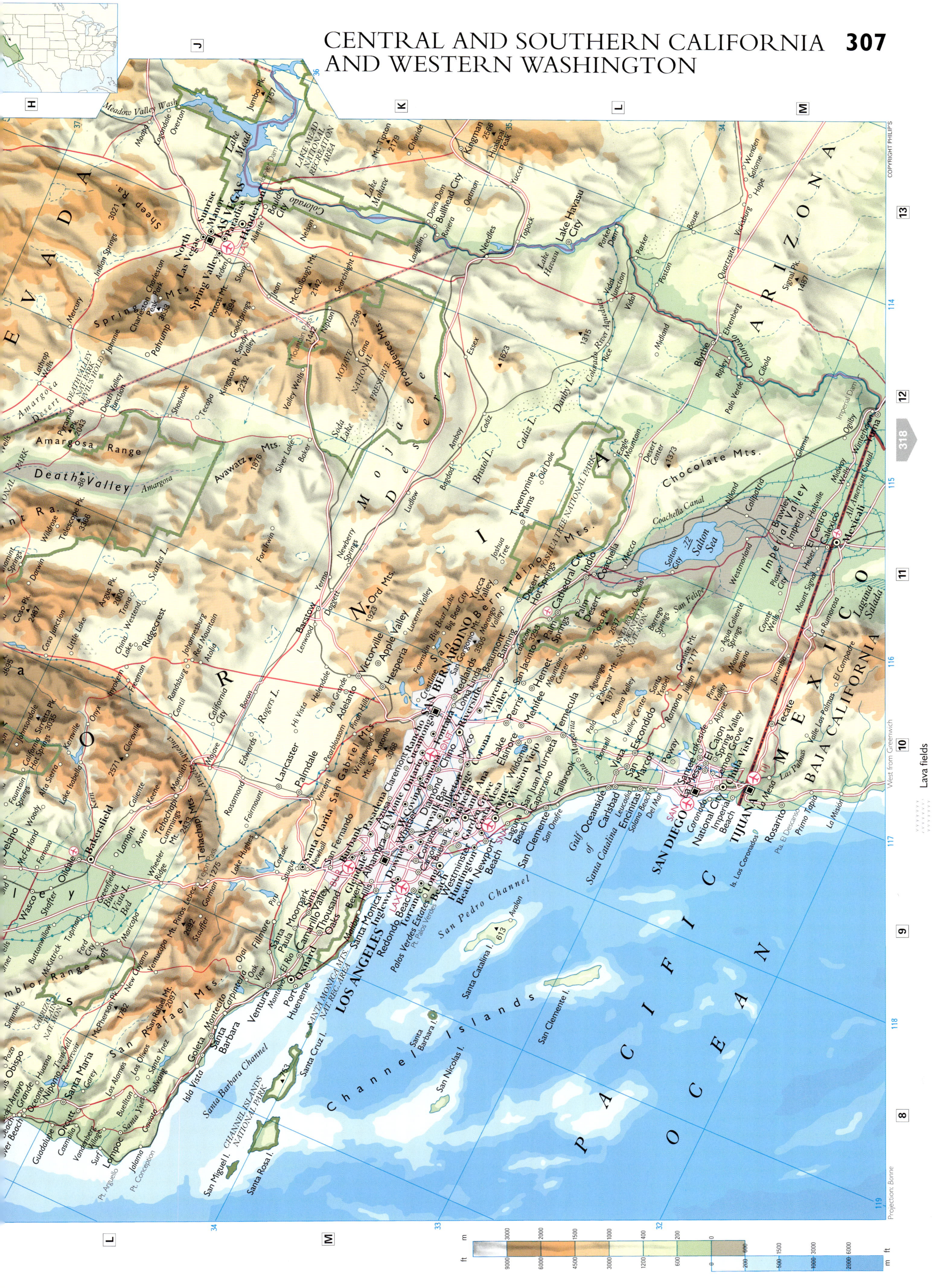
NEVADA
ARIZONA
MEXICO
BAJA CALIFORNIA
PACIFIC OCEAN
Mojave Desert
Death Valley
Amargosa Range
Spring Mts.
Sheep Ra.
Chocolate Mts.
Salton Sea
Imperial Valley
San Bernardino Mts.
San Gabriel Mts.
Tehachapi Mts.
Channel Islands
Santa Barbara Channel
San Pedro Channel
Gulf of Santa Catalina
LAS VEGAS
Henderson
Boulder City
Lake Mead
Lake Havasu City
Bullhead City
Kingman
Needles
Blythe
Barstow
Victorville
Hesperia
Apple Valley
Lancaster
Palmdale
Bakersfield
Santa Clarita
LOS ANGELES
Long Beach
Santa Ana
Anaheim
Riverside
SAN BERNARDINO
Palm Springs
Indio
Temecula
Oceanside
Escondido
SAN DIEGO
Chula Vista
TIJUANA
Mexicali
El Centro
Calexico
Tecate
Rosarito
Oxnard
Ventura
Santa Barbara
Santa Maria
Lompoc
San Miguel I.
Santa Rosa I.
Santa Cruz I.
Santa Catalina I.
San Clemente I.
San Nicolas I.
Santa Barbara I.
Colorado
Coachella Canal
All American Canal
Lava fields
West from Greenwich
Projection: Bonne
COPYRIGHT PHILIP'S
318
m
ft

1:5 360 000
50 0 50 100 150 200 250 300 km
50 0 50 100 150 200 miles
NORTH DAKOTA
SOUTH DAKOTA
NEBRASKA
KANSAS
OKLAHOMA
MINNESOTA
IOWA
MISSOURI
ARKANSAS
WISCONSIN
ILLINOIS
MISSISSIPPI
LAKE SUPERIOR
Bismarck
Fargo
Pierre
Sioux Falls
Omaha
Lincoln
Topeka
Kansas City
Wichita
Oklahoma City
Tulsa
Minneapolis
St. Paul
Des Moines
St. Louis
Chicago
Milwaukee
Memphis
Little Rock
Duluth
Thunder Bay
Sand Hills
Smoky Hills
Ozark Plateau
Boston Mts.
Black Hills
Badlands
Lake Sakakawea

Projection: Albers' Equal Area with two standard parallels

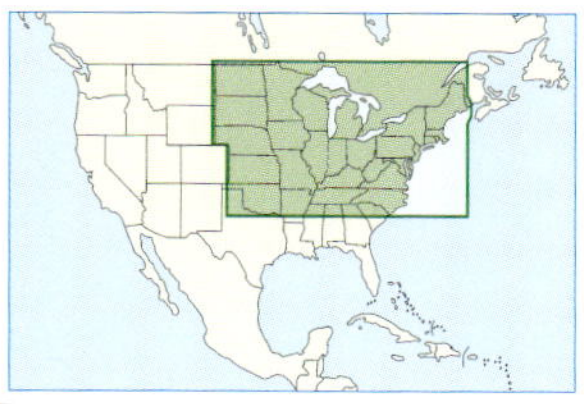

ONTARIO
QUEBEC
LAKE HURON
LAKE ONTARIO
LAKE ERIE
Georgian Bay
OTTAWA
MONTREAL
TORONTO
DETROIT
CLEVELAND
PITTSBURGH
BUFFALO
ROCHESTER
NEW YORK
PHILADELPHIA
BALTIMORE
WASHINGTON D.C.
BOSTON
PROVIDENCE
HARTFORD
RICHMOND
NORFOLK
CHARLOTTE
RALEIGH
COLUMBUS
CINCINNATI
ATLANTA
OHIO
PENNSYLVANIA
NEW YORK
WEST VIRGINIA
VIRGINIA
MARYLAND
DELAWARE
NEW JERSEY
VERMONT
NEW HAMPSHIRE
MAINE
MA.
CT.
R.I.
NORTH CAROLINA
SOUTH CAROLINA
GEORGIA
KENTUCKY
Gulf of Maine
ATLANTIC OCEAN
COPYRIGHT PHILIP'S
298
299
315

1:2 000 000

km
miles
Projection: Bonne
ft
m
1200
600
400
200
0
A
B
C
D
E
F
G
1
2
3
4
5
6
7
308
43
42
41
40
38
95
94
93
92
91
90
IOWA
WISCONSIN
ILLINOIS
MISSOURI
KANSAS
Mississippi
Missouri
Des Moines
Iowa
Cedar
Illinois
Rock
Chicago
EFFIGY MOUNDS NAT. MONUMENT
HERBERT HOOVER NAT. HIST. SITE
Emmetsburg
Algona
Mason City
Charles City
Clear Lake
Fort Dodge
Webster City
Waterloo
Cedar Falls
Dubuque
Ames
Boone
Marshalltown
Cedar Rapids
Iowa City
Des Moines
West Des Moines
Ankeny
Saylorville L.
Newton
Grinnell
Clinton
Davenport
Bettendorf
Rock Island
Moline
East Moline
Muscatine
Burlington
Ottumwa
Oskaloosa
Pella
Keokuk
Fort Madison
Mount Pleasant
Fairfield
Galesburg
Peoria
East Peoria
Quincy
Hannibal
Springfield
Jacksonville
Kirksville
Moberly
Columbia
Jefferson City
Sedalia
St. Joseph
Kansas City
Independence
Blue Springs
Lee's Summit
Raytown
Liberty
Gladstone
Shawnee
Prairie Village
Leawood
Grandview
Belton
Harry S. Truman Reservoir
Lake of the Ozarks
Mark Twain Lake
Thomas Hill Reservoir
Rathbun Lake
Coralville Lake
Rolla
Lebanon
Camdenton
Fulton
Mexico
Boonville
Marshall
St. Charles
St. Peters
O'Fallon
Florissant
ST. LOUIS
East St. Louis
Alton
Granite City
Collinsville
Belleville
Edwardsville
Kirkwood
Chesterfield
Washington
Festus
Farmington
Carbondale
Freeport
Rockford
Sterling
Dixon
Kewanee
Macomb
Canton
Pekin
Lincoln
Beardstown
Madison
Janesville
Monroe
Platteville
Prairie du Chien
Waukesha
Decorah
Independence
Manchester
Maquoketa
Anamosa
Marion
Washington
Knoxville
Indianola
Creston
Red Oak
Atlantic
Carroll
Jefferson
Perry
Chillicothe
Trenton
Maryville
Cameron
Excelsior Springs
Warrensburg
Clinton
Osceola
Warsaw
Nevada
Lamar
Bolivar
Hermann
Union
Pacific
Eureka
Arnold
Hillsboro
De Soto
Potosi
Sullivan
Cuba
St. James
Ste. Genevieve
Perryville
Chester
Sparta
Red Bud
Waterloo
Columbia
Highland
Litchfield
Hillsboro
Carlinville
Jerseyville
Pittsfield
Mount Sterling
Rushville
Havana
Lewistown
Clinton
Davenport
Dubuque
Galena
Savanna
Mount Carroll
Morrison
Princeton
Bradford
Toulon
Wyoming
Monmouth
Aledo
Keithsburg
Oquawka
Carthage
Nauvoo
Warsaw
Hamilton
Alexandria
Kahoka
Memphis
Lancaster
Bloomfield
Centerville
Chariton
Osceola
Leon
Corydon
Bethany
Albany
Gallatin
Princeton
Milan
Macon
Brookfield
Carrollton
Richmond
Lexington
Higginsville
Concordia
Sweet Springs
Pilot Grove
California
Versailles
Eldon
Tuscumbia
Linn
Owensville
Vienna
Belle
St. Robert
Waynesville
Richland
Buffalo
Humansville
Stockton
Weaubleau
El Dorado Springs
Collins
Hermitage
Preston
Cross Timbers
Lowry City
Appleton City
Butler
Adrian
Harrisonville
Freeman
Garden City
Pleasant Hill
Odessa
Holden
Knob Noster
Windsor
Cole Camp
La Monte
Otterville
Tipton
Jamestown
Holts Summit
Mokane
Chamois
Gasconade
New Haven
Montgomery City
Wellsville
Vandalia
Bowling Green
Louisiana
Clarksville
Elsberry
Troy
Moscow Mills
Wentzville
Hawk Point
Jonesburg
Warrenton
Auxvasse
Kingdom City
Centralia
Paris
Madison
Huntsville
Salisbury
Keytesville
Glasgow
Fayette
New Franklin
Brunswick
Slater
Marshall
Waverly
Wellington
Norborne
Polo
Hamilton
Braymer
Lathrop
Lawson
Kearney
Smithville
Platte City
Plattsburg
Dearborn
Stewartsville
Maysville
Union Star
Savannah
King City
Stanberry
Rosendale
Ravenwood
Grant City
Hopkins
Bedford
Lenox
Corning
Villisca
Clarinda
Shenandoah
Sidney
Eagleville
Lamoni
Mount Ayr
Grand River
Humeston
Lineville
Mercer
Unionville
Green City
Novinger
La Plata
Atlanta
Bucklin
Marceline
Clarence
Shelbina
Shelbyville
Monroe City
Palmyra
Canton
La Grange
Lewistown
Monticello
Edina
Baring
La Belle
Novelty
Ewing

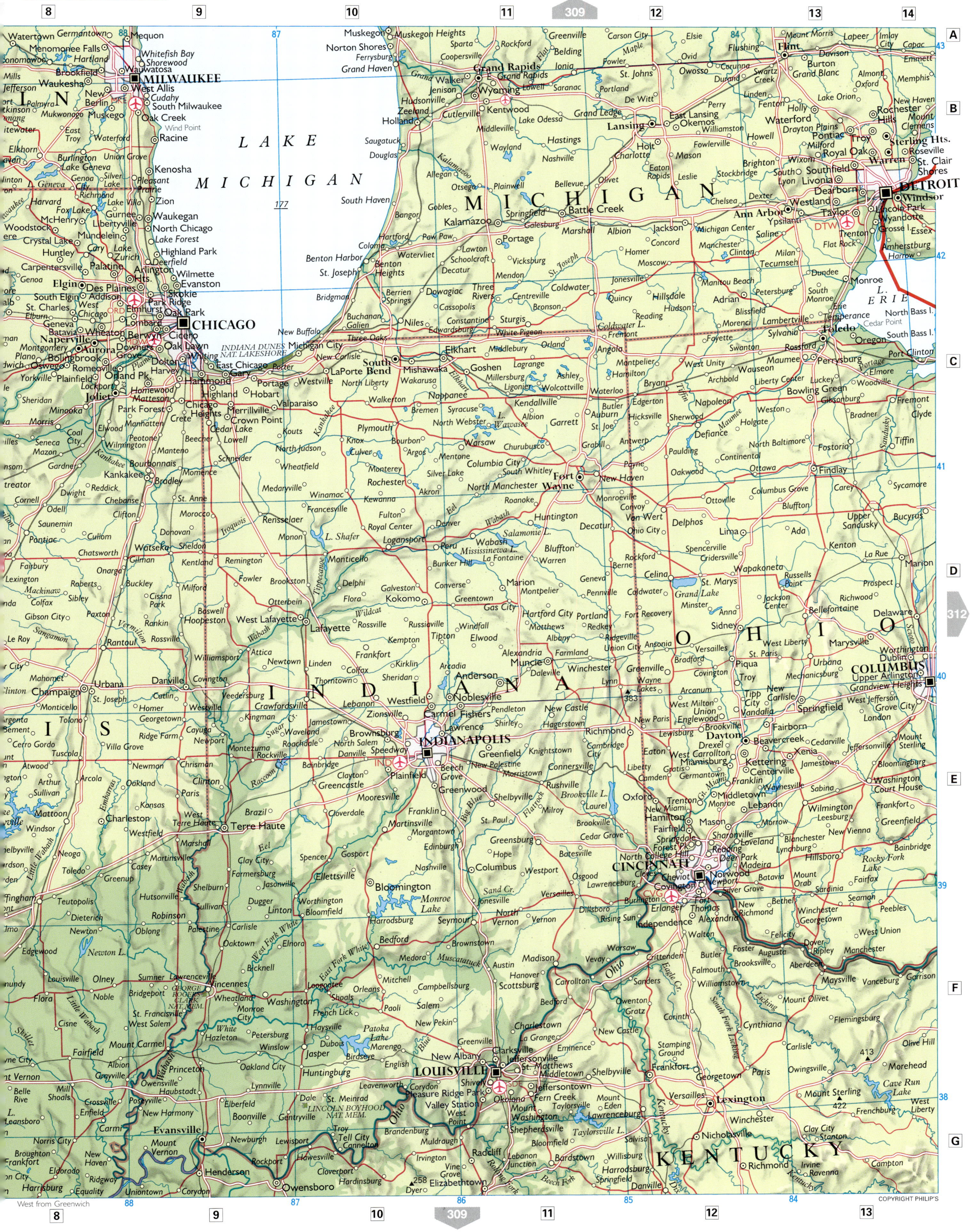

LAKE MICHIGAN
MICHIGAN
INDIANA
OHIO
ILLINOIS
KENTUCKY
L. ERIE
MILWAUKEE
CHICAGO
DETROIT
INDIANAPOLIS
COLUMBUS
CINCINNATI
LOUISVILLE
Lansing
Grand Rapids
Fort Wayne
Toledo
Dayton
Lexington
Evansville
Terre Haute
Lafayette
South Bend
Kalamazoo
Ann Arbor
Flint
Windsor
Gary
Joliet
Springfield
Champaign
Bloomington
Muncie
Lima
Findlay
Owensboro
INDIANA DUNES NAT. LAKESHORE
GEORGE ROGERS CLARK NAT. HIST. PARK
LINCOLN BOYHOOD NAT. MEM.
Ohio
Wabash
West from Greenwich
COPYRIGHT PHILIP'S

1:2 000 000

Georgian Bay
Bruce Peninsula
BRUCE PENINSULA NAT. PARK
FATHOM FIVE NAT. MARINE PARK
Main Channel
GEORGIAN BAY ISLANDS NAT. PARK
ALGONQUIN PROVINCIAL PARK
LAKE HURON
LAKE ONTARIO
LAKE ERIE
L. Simcoe
Nottawasaga Bay
C A N A D A
O N T A R I O
MICHIGAN
O H I O
P E N N S Y L V A N I A
N E W
Allegheny Plateau
Allegheny Mountains
TORONTO
Mississauga
Hamilton
BUFFALO
ROCHESTER
DETROIT
Windsor
CLEVELAND
PITTSBURGH
Akron
Erie
London
Kitchener
Waterloo
Guelph
Oakville
Burlington
St. Catharines
Niagara Falls
Oshawa
Barrie
Peterborough
Orillia
Owen Sound
Sarnia
Port Huron
Youngstown
Canton
Chatham
Brantford
Cambridge
RONDEAU PROV. PARK
POINT PELEE NAT. PARK
CUYAHOGA VALLEY NAT. REC. AREA
Projection: Bonne


298
311
309

298
309
OTTAWA
MONTREAL
QUEBEC
VERMONT
NEW HAMPSHIRE
MAINE
MASSACHUSETTS
CONNECTICUT
RHODE ISLAND
NEW YORK
NEW JERSEY
ADIRONDACK PARK
Adirondack Mountains
Green Mountains
White Mountains
Catskill Mts.
L. Champlain
Long Island
ATLANTIC OCEAN
BOSTON
PROVIDENCE
HARTFORD
Albany
Syracuse
Springfield
Worcester
Manchester
Burlington
Montpelier
PHILADELPHIA
Trenton
Schenectady
Utica
Binghamton
Scranton
Allentown
Bridgeport
New Haven
New London
Stamford
Newark
Jersey City
Yonkers
Martha's Vineyard
Block I.
Block Island Sound
Long Island Sound
Cape Ann
Mt. Washington 1917
Mt. Marcy 1629
Mt. Mansfield 1339
Killington Pk. 1293
Mt. Monadnock 965
Mt. Greylock 1064
Slide Mt. 1281
Stratton Mt. 1176
Mt. Kearsarge 895
Mt. Moosilauke 1466
Mt. Cabot 1244
Snow Mt. 1203
Lake George
Lake Placid
Saranac Lakes
Ashokan Res.
FIRE ISLAND NAT. SEASHORE
GATEWAY NAT. REC. AREA
DELAWARE WATER GAP NAT. REC. AREA
SARATOGA NAT. HIST. PARK
Kittatinny Mt.
Shawangunk Mts.
Tug Hill Plateau
COPYRIGHT PHILIP'S
8
9
10
11
12
13
14
A
B
C
D
E
F
G
45
44
43
42
41
40
76
75
74
73
72
71

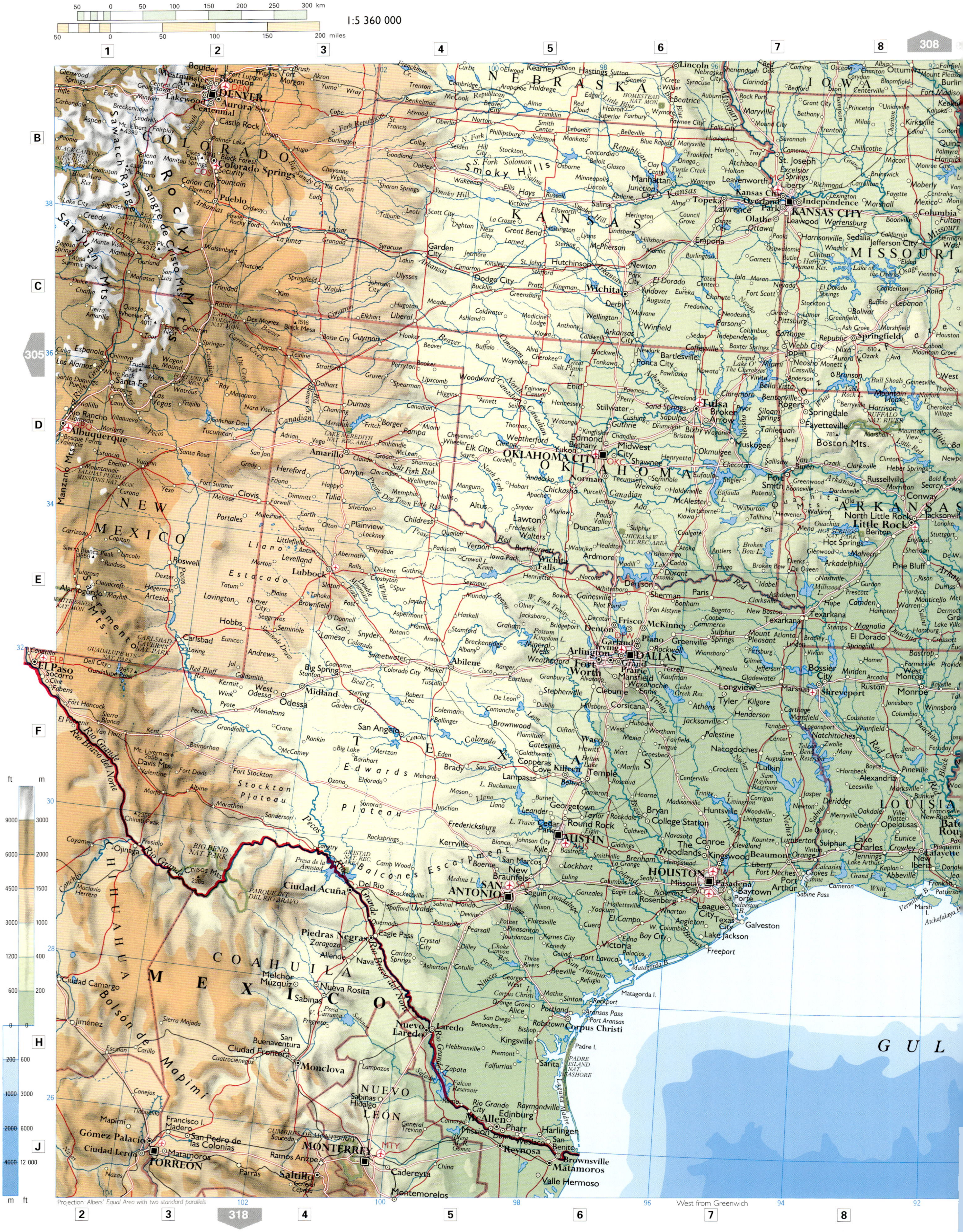
1:5 360 000
NEBRASKA
KANSAS
IOWA
MISSOURI
COLORADO
OKLAHOMA
ARKANSAS
NEW MEXICO
TEXAS
LOUISIANA
MEXICO
COAHUILA
NUEVO LEÓN
CHIHUAHUA
Rocky Mts.
Smoky Hills
Llano Estacado
Edwards Plateau
Stockton Plateau
Balcones Escarpment
Bolsón de Mapimí
Boston Mts.
GULF
DENVER
Colorado Springs
Pueblo
Albuquerque
Santa Fe
El Paso
Lubbock
Amarillo
OKLAHOMA CITY
Tulsa
Wichita
KANSAS CITY
Springfield
Little Rock
Shreveport
DALLAS
Fort Worth
AUSTIN
SAN ANTONIO
HOUSTON
Corpus Christi
Laredo
MONTERREY
TORREÓN
Brownsville
Matamoros
Galveston
Projection: Albers' Equal Area with two standard parallels
West from Greenwich

305
308
318

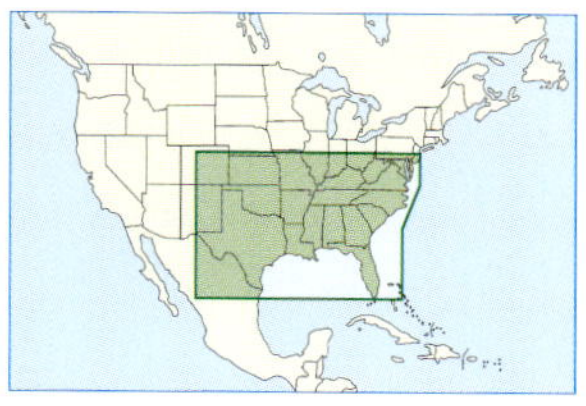

309
320
ILLINOIS
INDIANA
OHIO
PENNSYLVANIA
MARYLAND
DELAWARE
WEST VIRGINIA
VIRGINIA
KENTUCKY
TENNESSEE
NORTH CAROLINA
SOUTH CAROLINA
GEORGIA
ALABAMA
MISSISSIPPI
FLORIDA
BAHAMAS
ATLANTIC OCEAN
GULF OF MEXICO
Appalachian Mountains
Cumberland Plateau
PITTSBURGH
PHILADELPHIA
BALTIMORE
WASHINGTON D.C.
INDIANAPOLIS
COLUMBUS
CINCINNATI
LOUISVILLE
RICHMOND
NORFOLK
NASHVILLE
MEMPHIS
RALEIGH
CHARLOTTE
ATLANTA
BIRMINGHAM
NEW ORLEANS
JACKSONVILLE
ORLANDO
TAMPA
MIAMI
Florida Keys
Str. of Florida
Florida Bay
Mississippi River Delta
COPYRIGHT PHILIP'S

1:2 000 000

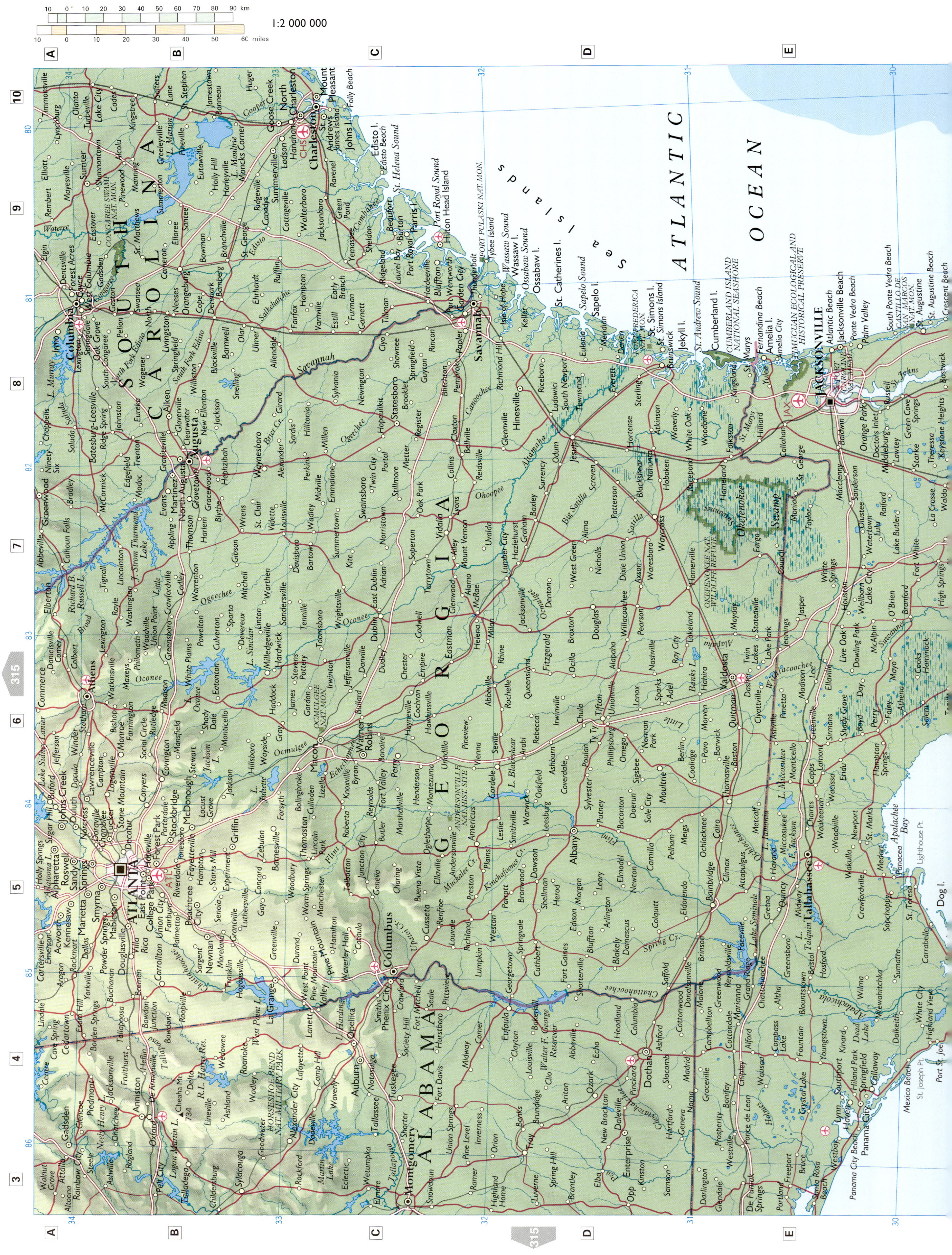
ATLANTIC
OCEAN
SOUTH CAROLINA
GEORGIA
ALABAMA
Sea Islands
ATLANTA
Columbia
Charleston
Savannah
Augusta
Athens
Macon
Columbus
Albany
Valdosta
Tallahassee
JACKSONVILLE
Montgomery
Dothan
Okefenokee Swamp
Savannah
Chattahoochee
315

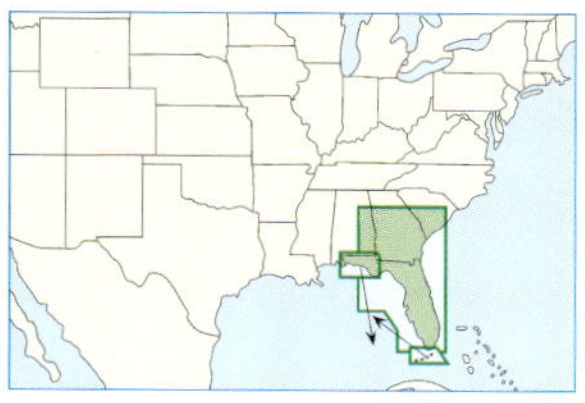

GULF OF MEXICO
FLORIDA
ORLANDO
TAMPA
St. Petersburg
MIAMI
West Palm Beach
Fort Lauderdale
Hollywood
Hialeah
Daytona Beach
Melbourne
Sarasota
Fort Myers
Cape Coral
Naples
Lakeland
Kissimmee
Sanford
Ocala
Lake Okeechobee
Everglades
Big Cypress
Ten Thousand Is.
CANAVERAL NATIONAL SEASHORE
KENNEDY SPACE CENTER
BISCAYNE NAT. PARK
EVERGLADES NATIONAL PARK
BIG CYPRESS NAT. PRESERVE
Florida Keys
Straits of Florida
Florida Bay
Key West
Marathon
Key Largo
ALABAMA
Pensacola
Panama City
Tallahassee
Apalachicola
GULF ISLANDS NAT. SEASHORE
Continuation southwards on same scale
Continuation westwards on same scale
Projection: Albers Equal Area
West from Greenwich
COPYRIGHT PHILIPS
320
315

1:6 400 000
305
314
TIJUANA
Mexicali
Ensenada
Yuma
San Luis Río Colorado
ORGAN PIPE CACTUS NAT. MON.
A R I Z O N A
Tucson
Nogales
Bisbee
Douglas
Agua Prieta
N E W M E X I C O
Las Cruces
Lordsburg
Deming
CIUDAD JUAREZ
El Paso
Roswell
Carlsbad
Hobbs
Lubbock
Llano Estacado
Midland
Odessa
Big Spring
Sweetwater
Edward Plateau
Stockton Plateau
U N I T E
Golfo de California
Puerto Peñasco
Caborca
GRAN DESIERTO DEL PINACATE
Hermosillo
Guaymas
Empalme
Ciudad Obregón
Navojoa
Huatabampo
Los Mochis
Guasave
Guamúchil
Culiacán
Mazatlán
S O N O R A
C H I H U A H U A
Chihuahua
Cuauhtémoc
Delicias
Ciudad Camargo
Hidalgo del Parral
Jiménez
Ojinaga
Nuevo Casas Grandes
Madera
Ciudad Guerrero
Sierra Madre Occidental
BIG BEND NAT. PARK
Ciudad Acuña
Del Rio
Piedras Negras
COAHUILA
Nueva Rosita
Monclova
Saltillo
MONTERREY
Gómez Palacio
Ciudad Lerdo
TORREÓN
Matamoros
San Pedro de las Colonias
Parras
D U R A N G O
Durango
Santiago Papasquiaro
Bolsón de Mapimí
BAJA CALIFORNIA
BAJA CALIFORNIA SUR
Sierra de San Pedro Mártir
Bahía Sebastián Vizcaíno
Guerrero Negro
Desierto de Vizcaíno
Santa Rosalía
Mulegé
Loreto
Ciudad Constitución
La Paz
Todos Santos
Cabo San Lucas
San José del Cabo
I. Cedros
Cedros Trench
I. Ángel de la Guarda
I. Tiburón
Tropic of Cancer
P A C I F I C   O C E A N
Islas Marías
Is. de Revillagigedo (Mexico)
I. San Benedicto
I. Socorro
I. Roca Partida
I. Clarión (Mexico)
S I N A L O A
N A Y A R I T
Tepic
Compostela
Puerto Vallarta
B. de Banderas
C. Corrientes
Z A C A T E C A S
Zacatecas
Fresnillo
Sombrerete
Aguascalientes
Jalisco
GUADALAJARA
Zapopan
Tlaquepaque
Tonalá
L. de Chapala
León
Irapuato
Celaya
Morelia
Uruapan
Zamora
Colima
Manzanillo
Tecomán
Lázaro Cárdenas
Zihuatanejo
Tecpan de Galeana
Acapulco Trench
San Luis Potosí
Projection: Bi-polar oblique Conical Orthomorphic
West from Greenwich
110
105
30
25
20

State names in Central Mexico

| | | | |
|---|---|---|---|
| 1 DISTRITO FEDERAL | 3 GUANAJUATO | 5 MÉXICO | 7 QUERÉTARO |
| 2 AGUASCALIENTES | 4 HIDALGO | 6 MORELOS | 8 TLAXCALA |

5
6
7
8
315
A
B
C
D
E
320
320
ARKANSAS
MISSISSIPPI
ALABAMA
GEORGIA
FLORIDA
LOUISIANA
STATES
Texarkana
El Dorado
Camden
Greenville
Tuscaloosa
Opelika
Phenix City
Columbus
Selma
Montgomery
Americus
Cordele
Troy
Albany
Tifton
Waycross
Meridian
Jackson
Vicksburg
Monroe
Shreveport
Tallulah
Natchez
Laurel
Hattiesburg
Brewton
Dothan
Valdosta
Chattahoochee
Tallahassee
Lake City
Alexandria
McComb
Bogalusa
Baton Rouge
Hammond
Biloxi
Mobile
Pensacola
Panama City
Gulfport
Mobile Bay
Apalachee Bay
C. San Blas
Suwannee
Lake Charles
Lafayette
NEW ORLEANS
L. Pontchartrain
Breton Sd.
Mississippi River Delta
Atchafalaya Bay
Terrebonne Bay
Port Arthur
Beaumont
Galveston
Clearwater
Wichita Falls
Denison
Sherman
Paris
Denton
Greenville
DALLAS
Fort Worth
Cleburne
Marshall
Longview
Tyler
Corsicana
Palestine
Hillsboro
Waco
Brownwood
Nacogdoches
Sam Rayburn Reservoir
Toledo Bend Res.
Lufkin
Temple
Bryan
Huntsville
College Station
AUSTIN
Navasota
HOUSTON
Rosenberg
SAN ANTONIO
Victoria
Dilley
Alice
Laredo
Kingsville
Corpus Christi
Nuevo Laredo
PADRE ISLAND
NAT. SEASHORE
Laguna Madre
McAllen
Harlingen
Brownsville
Reynosa
Río Bravo
Matamoros
Valle Hermoso
San Fernando
GULF OF MEXICO
Sigsbee Deep
3750
32
35
82
75
47
Tropic of Cancer
Banco Campeche
I. Desterrada
I. Pérez (Mexico)
Canal de Yucatán
CUBA
La Esperanza
Guane
C. San Antonio
C. Corrientes
C. Catoche
Isla Mujeres
Cancún
Puerto Morelos
Playa del Carmen
Isla Cozumel
Yucatan Basin
Progreso
MÉRIDA
Motul
Izamal
Tizimín
Espita
Valladolid
Río Lagartos
YUCATAN
Maxcanú
Ticul
Peto
Tekax
Tenabo
Campeche
Hopelchén
Champotón
Felipe Carrillo Puerto
QUINTANA ROO
Costa Maya
B. de la Ascensión
SIAN KA'AN
B. del Espíritu Santo
Banco Chinchorro
Bacalar
Chetumal
B. de Chetumal
Corozal
Orange Walk
Ambergris Cay
Belize City
Belize Barrier Reef
Turneffe Is.
BELIZE
Belmopan
Dangriga
Golfo de Campeche
Ciudad del Carmen
L. de Términos
Escárcega
CAMPECHE
CALAKMUL
Frontera
Paraíso
Comalcalco
TABASCO
Villahermosa
Macuspana
Cárdenas
Palenque
Tenosique
Balancán
Flores
San Luis
Coatzacoalcos
Minatitlán
Acayucan
San Andrés Tuxtla
Alvarado
Veracruz
Boca del Río
Tampico
Ciudad Madero
Altamira
Aldama
Tuxpan
Poza Rica
Papantla
Xalapa
Córdoba
Orizaba
Pico de Orizaba
PUEBLA
Tehuacán
Oaxaca
Tuxtla Gutiérrez
Tapachula
Acapulco
Chilpancingo
Puerto Escondido
Golfo de Tehuantepec
Salina Cruz
Istmo de Tehuantepec
CHIAPAS
San Cristóbal de las Casas
Comitán de Domínguez
GUATEMALA
Huehuetenango
Cobán
Puerto Barrios
Golfo de Honduras
Puerto Cortés
San Pedro Sula
La Ceiba
Tela
Trujillo
HONDURAS
TEGUCIGALPA
Roatán
Is. de la Bahía
Guanaja
Sigsbee Deep

JAMAICA
1:1 600 000
CARIBBEAN SEA
Montego Bay
St. Ann's Bay
Kingston
Spanish Town
Port Antonio
CORNWALL
MIDDLESEX
SURREY
Mandeville
Savanna-la-Mar
May Pen
Old Harbour
FLORIDA
U. S. A.
MIAMI
West Palm Beach
Fort Lauderdale
Fort Myers
Naples
Cape Coral
Hialeah
EVERGLADES NAT. PARK
Florida Keys
Key West
Straits of Florida
Great Bahama Bank
Nassau
New Providence
Andros Island
LA HABANA (Havana)
CUBA
Matanzas
Pinar del Río
Cienfuegos
Santa Clara
Camagüey
Las Tunas
Bayamo
Manzanillo
Nueva Gerona
I. de la Juventud
Gulf of Mexico
MÉRIDA
YUCATÁN
Cancún
Cozumel
Playa del Carmen
Campeche
CAMPECHE
MEXICO
QUINTANA ROO
Chetumal
Ciudad del Carmen
Canal de Yucatán
Yucatan Basin
Cayman Islands (U.K.)
George Town
Cayman Trench
Misteriosa Bank
BELIZE
Belmopan
Belize City
GUATEMALA
Guatemala
Quetzaltenango
Gulfo de Honduras
HONDURAS
TEGUCIGALPA
San Pedro Sula
La Ceiba
Choluteca
Mosquitia
EL SALVADOR
SAN SALVADOR
Santa Ana
San Miguel
NICARAGUA
MANAGUA
León
Granada
Matagalpa
Lago de Nicaragua
Bluefields
Puerto Cabezas
Costa de Mosquitos
COSTA RICA
SAN JOSÉ
Limón
Puntarenas
PANAMÁ
Colón
David
Golfo de Panamá
Isthmus of Panama
Guatemala Trench
PACIFIC OCEAN
Pedro Bank
Rosalind Bank
Serranilla Bank
Banco Gorda
CARIBBEAN
Is. Santanilla (Swan Islands) (Honduras)
I. de Providencia (Colombia)
I. de San Andrés (Colombia)
PANAMA CANAL
1:800 000
Gatún
Lago Gatún
Balboa
PANAMA
Place of interest
Projection: Conical with two standard parallels
1:6 400 000

PUERTO RICO AND THE VIRGIN IS.
1:1 600 000
ATLANTIC OCEAN
CARIBBEAN SEA
VIRGIN ISLANDS (U.K.)
VIRGIN ISLANDS (U.S.A.)
SAN JUAN
PUERTO RICO
Puerto Rico Trench
Hispaniola
Antilles
HAITI
PORT-AU-PRINCE
DOMINICAN REP.
SANTO DOMINGO
Venezuelan Basin
Lesser Antilles
Leeward Islands
Windward Islands
Aves Ridge
Beata Ridge
ANTIGUA & BARBUDA
ST. KITTS & NEVIS
GUADELOUPE (Fr.)
DOMINICA
MARTINIQUE (Fr.)
ST. LUCIA
ST. VINCENT & THE GRENADINES
BARBADOS
GRENADA
TRINIDAD & TOBAGO
COLOMBIA
VENEZUELA
CARACAS
MARACAIBO
COPYRIGHT PHILIP'S

1:600 000
5 0 5 10 15 20 25 30 km
5 0 5 10 15 20 miles
a
Anguilla
(U.K.)
Prickly Pear Cays
Seal I.
Scrub I.
Grafton's Pt.
Snake Pt.
Island Harbour
The Quarter
The Valley
Crocus Bay
Sandy I.
Sandy Ground Village
Sandy Hill Bay
South Hill Village
West End Village
Blowing Point Village
Anguillita I.
Blowing Rock
Anguilla Channel
Île Tintamarre
Anegada Passage
Grand Case
Cul de Sac
Saint Martin
(France)
Pte. du Canonnier
Marigot
Quartier d'Orléans
Simpson Bay
Colombier
Mulletbaai
Cul-de-Sac
Sentry Hill
SXM
Simsonbaai
Philipsburg
St. Maarten
(Netherlands)
Pte. Blanche
Saint Barthélemy Channel
Île Fourchue
Île Chevreau
Flamands
St-Jean
Lorient
Corossol
Toiny
Gustavia
Grand Fond
Saint Barthélemy
(St. Barts)
(France)
CARIBBEAN SEA
Saba
(Netherlands)
Mt. Scenery
The Bottom
Hells Gate
Windward Side
Fort Bay
St. Eustatius (Statia)
(Netherlands)
Zeelandia
Oranjestad
The Quill
NORTHERN LEEWARDS
Northern Leewards
West from Greenwich
b
ANTIGUA AND BARBUDA
ATLANTIC OCEAN
Antigua
Dickinson Bay
Boon Pt.
Beggars Pt.
Long I.
Runaway Bay
St. Johnston Village
Crabs Pen
Guiana I.
St. John's
ANU
Potters Village
Five I. Harbour
Willikies
Indian Town Pt.
DEVIL'S BRIDGE
Nonsuch Bay
Mt. Obama
Freetown
Green I.
York I.
English Harbour Town
Soldier Pt.
Willoughby Bay
Johnsons Pt.
Old Road Bluff
NELSON'S DOCKYARD
Nanton Pt.
c
Billy Pt.
Goat Pt.
Goat
Kid I.
Hog Pt.
Cedar Tree Pt.
Codrington Lagoon
The Highlands
Low Bay
Codrington
Dulcina
Palmetto Pt.
Barbuda
Cocoa Point
Spanish Pt.
d
ST. KITTS AND NEVIS
ATLANTIC OCEAN
Helden's Pt.
Dieppe Bay Town
Sadlers
Tabernacle
Sandy Point Town
Mt. Liamuiga
BRIMSTONE HILL FORT
Cayon
Middle Island
Old Road Town
St. Kitts
Palmetto Pt.
SKB
Basseterre
Frigate Bay
Sand Bank Bay
Friar's Bay
Gt. Salt Pond
CARIBBEAN SEA
Nags Head
The Narrows
Round Hill
Nevis Peak
Cotton Ground
Nevis
Charlestown
Bath
Fig Tree
Saddle
St. Kitts & Nevis
Barbuda
Antigua
e
Guadeloupe Passage
Pte. de la Grande Vigie
Pte. du Piton
Anse-Bertrand
Haut de la Montagne
Campêche
Pte. d'Antigues
Port-Louis
Beauport
Gros Cap
Les Mangles
Petit-Canal
Ste-Marguerite
Îlet à Kahouanne
Pointe Allègre
Grand Cul-de-Sac Marin
Îlet à Fajou
Pte. Macou
Bazin
Morne-à-l'Eau
Château Gaillard
Le Moule
L'Autre Bord
MAISON COLONIALE
Grande Anse
Deshaies
Ste-Rose
MUSÉE DU RHUM
Sofaia
Vieux Bourg
Grande-Terre
Zévallos
ATLANTIC OCEAN
La Désirade
Le Souffleur
Baie-Mahault
Lamentin
PTP
Les Abymes
Les Grands Fonds
Plaine de la Simonière
Pte. des Colibris
Beausejour
Bailles Argent
Pointe-Noire
Castel
Pointe-à-Pitre
Douville
Ste-Marthe
Kahouanne
Deshauteur
St-François
Pointe des Châteaux
Morne Jeanneton
Ravine Chaude
Bas du Fort
Ste-Anne
Mahaut
Petit-Bourg
Le Gosier
Petit Cul-de-Sac Marin
Terre de Bas
Îles de la Petite Terre
Vernou
Basse-Terre
Pigeon
Pitons (ou Sauts) de Bouillante
Montebello
Guadeloupe
(France)
Bouillante
Goyave
Pte. de la Rivière à Goyave
PARC NATIONAL DE LA GUADELOUPE
Morne Moustique
Ste-Marie
Marigot
Vieux-Habitants
Pte. de la Capesterre
Canal de Marie-Galante
Matouba
CHUTES DU CARBET
Capesterre-Belle-Eau
Baillif
St-Claude
Soufrière
Basse-Terre
Gourbeyre
Bananier
Grosse Pointe
Vieux Fort
Pte. Pisou
Marie-Galante
Monts Caraïbes
Grande Pte.
Vieux-Fort
Trois-Rivières
Pte. du Vieux Fort
St-Louis
LE TROU À DIABLE
Pte. de Folle Anse
Canal des Saintes
Grand-Bourg
Capesterre-de-Marie-Galante
CHÂTEAU MURAT
Pte. des Basses
Îles des Saintes
FORT NAPOLÉON
Terre-de-Bas
Terre-de-Haute
Petites-Anses
Le Chameau
Grand Îlet
Dominica Passage
GUADELOUPE
Guadeloupe
Martinique
f
Kudarebe
Malmok
CARIBBEAN SEA
Palm Beach
Noord
Eagle Beach
BUBALI BIRD SANCTUARY
Bushiribana
Noordkaap
Oranjestad
Paradera
AUA
Santa Cruz
ARIKOK
Jamanota
Spaans Lagoen
Pos Chiquito
Savaneta
Aruba
(Netherlands)
Sint Nicolaas
Seroe Colorado
Punta Basora
West from Greenwich
Aruba
Curaçao
Bonaire
h
CARIBBEAN SEA
Noordpunt
Washington
Boca Slagbaai
Brandaris
WASHINGTON SLAGBAAI
Gotomeer
Onima
Bonaire
(Netherlands)
Wekoewa Pt.
Rincon
Noord Saliña
Punt Blanco
Klein Bonaire
Hato
Antriol
Kralendijk
Nikiboko
Tera Kora
Bachelor's Beach
Vierkant Pt.
Hoop
Wanapa
Lac Bay
Pink Beach
Witte Pan (Salt Flats)
Lacre Punt
West from Greenwich
ABC ISLANDS
g
Noordpunt
Westpunt
BOKA TABLA
Savonet
CHRISTOFFEL
Lagún
St. Christoffelberg
B. Santa Cruz
Santa Cruz
Bartolbaai
Soto
St. Nicolaas
St. Marthabaai
Barber
San Juan
Pt. Halve Dag
Siberië
St. Willibrordus
Curaçao (Netherlands)
K. St. Marie
Bullenbaai
Hato
HATO CAVES
CUR
Stenen Koraal
Julianadorp
Brievengat
Buena Vista
St. Michiel
Gasparito
Emmastad
St. Jorisbaai
Schottegat
Otrobanda
Punda
Santa Rosa
St. Annabaai
Willemstad
Bottelier
Santa Barbara
SEAQUARIUM
Spaanse Water
Tafelberg
Nieuwpoort
Lagún Blanku
Oostpunt
CARIBBEAN SEA
West from Greenwich
Projection: Conical with two standard parallels
j
MARTINIQUE
Martinique Passage
Grand' Rivière
Macouba
Basse-Pointe
Cap St-Martin
GORGES DE LA FALAISE
Le Lorrain
Le Marigot
Montagne Pelée
Ajoupa-Bouillon
ATLANTIC OCEAN
Le Prêcheur
Pte. Lamare
Le Morne Rouge
Ste-Marie
Pte. du Diable
Havre de Trinité
CHÂTEAU DUBUC
Presqu'île de la Caravelle
Tartane
Pte. Caracoli
Rade de St-Pierre
St-Pierre
Fonds-St-Denis
Morne des Esses
Beauséjour
La Trinité
Baie du Galion
Le Carbet
Le Morne-Vert
Gros-Morne
Îlet Chancel ou Ramville
Pitons du Carbet
JARDIN DE BALATA
Le Robert
Bellefontaine
St-Joseph
Havre du Robert
Pte. Larose
Case-Pilote
Fort-de-France
B. du François
Fond Rousseau
Schœlcher
Le François
Îlet Long
Pte. des Nègres
FDF
Le Lamentin
Baie de Fort-de-France
Pte. du Bout
B. de Génipa
Ducos
Montagne du Vauclin
Pte. de Vauclin
Martinique
(France)
L'Anse Mitan
L'Anse à l'Âne
Les Trois-Îlets
LA PAGERIE
Le St-Esprit
Le Vauclin
Pte. Ducassous
Cap Salomon
Rivière-Salée
Grande Anse
Les Anses-d'Arlet
Le Diamant
Rivière-Pilote
Le Marin
Barrière-la-Croix
Trois-Rivières
Cap Ferré
Petite Anse
Ste-Luce
Pte. Borgnesse
Pte. du Diamant
Rocher du Diamant
Ste-Anne
Îlet Chevalier
CARIBBEAN SEA
Cul-de-Sac du Marin
Étang des Salines
Pte. Baham
Pte. d'Enfer
Pte. des Salines
Îlet Cabrits
St. Lucia Channel
West from Greenwich
ft m
3000 1000
1200 400
600 200
0 0
100 300
200 600
500 1500
1000 3000
2000 6000
m ft
Place of interest
Mangrove

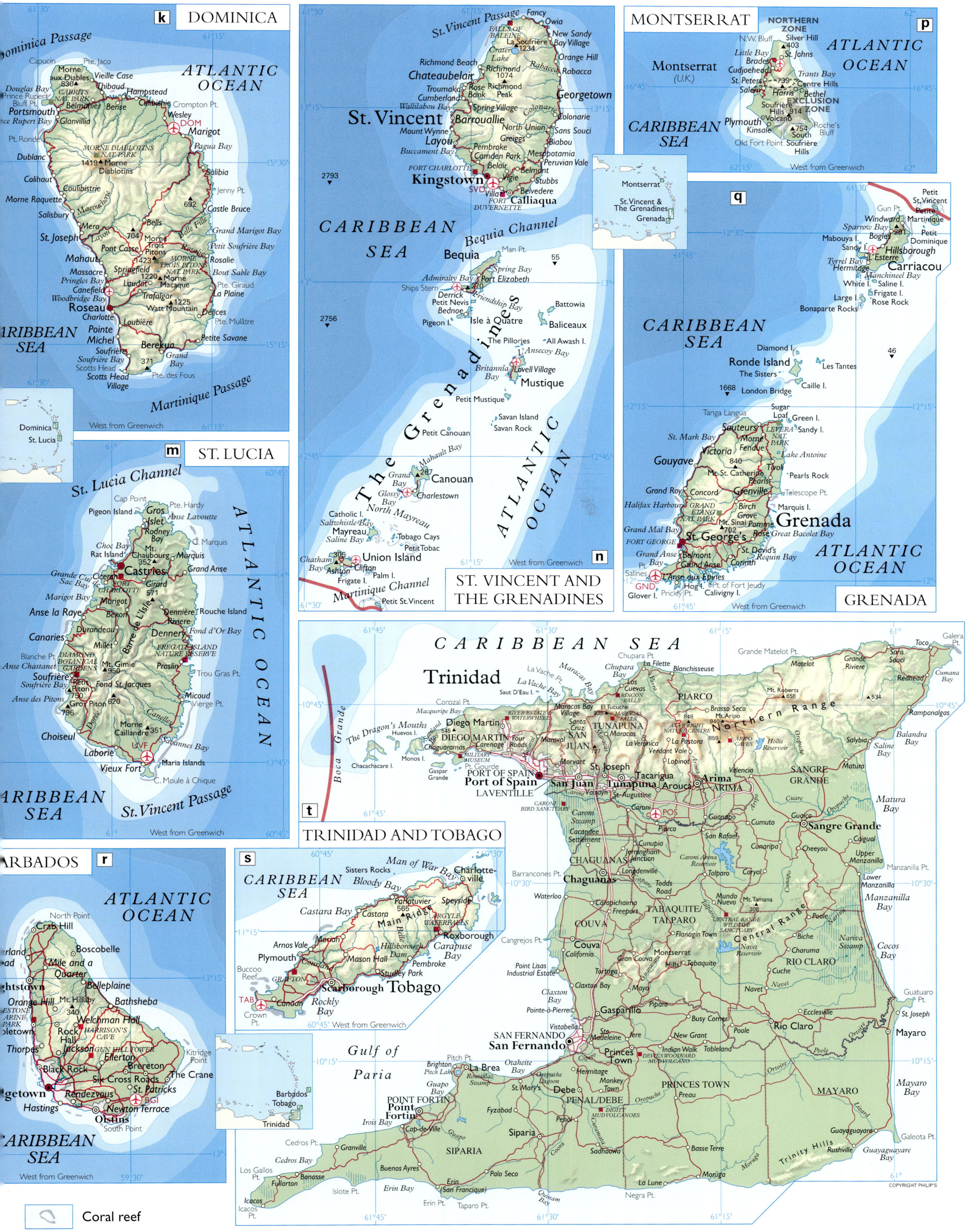
k DOMINICA
ATLANTIC OCEAN
CARIBBEAN SEA
Roseau
Portsmouth
Marigot
Dominica Passage
Martinique Passage
West from Greenwich
ST. VINCENT AND THE GRENADINES
n
St. Vincent
Kingstown
CARIBBEAN SEA
ATLANTIC OCEAN
The Grenadines
Bequia
Mustique
Canouan
Union Island
Bequia Channel
St. Vincent Passage
Martinique Channel
MONTSERRAT
p
Montserrat
(U.K.)
ATLANTIC OCEAN
CARIBBEAN SEA
Plymouth
EXCLUSION ZONE
NORTHERN ZONE
q
GRENADA
Grenada
St. George's
Carriacou
Hillsborough
m
ST. LUCIA
Castries
St. Lucia Channel
St. Vincent Passage
ATLANTIC OCEAN
CARIBBEAN SEA
r
BARBADOS
ATLANTIC OCEAN
CARIBBEAN SEA
t
TRINIDAD AND TOBAGO
s
Tobago
Scarborough
Trinidad
CARIBBEAN SEA
Gulf of Paria
Port of Spain
San Fernando
Northern Range
Central Range
COPYRIGHT PHILIP'S

Coral reef

SOUTH
AMERICA

1:28 000 000
km
miles
Caribbean Sea
ATLANTIC OCEAN
PACIFIC OCEAN
Greater Antilles
West Indies
Lesser Antilles
Central America
Guiana Highlands
Amazon Basin
Llanos
Andes
Brazilian Highlands
Plateau of Mato Grosso
Plat. of Borborema
Altiplano (Bolivian Plateau)
Atacama Desert
Chaco Boreal
Gran Chaco
Chaco Austral
Pampas
Patagonia
Peru-Chile Trench
Chile Rise
Argentine Abyssal Plain
Galapagos Is.
Falkland Is.
West Falkland
East Falkland
Tierra del Fuego
South Georgia
Arch. de Juan Fernández
Amazon
Orinoco
Paraná
Río de la Plata
L. Titicaca
Mt. Aconcagua
6962
Chimborazo
6267
Cotopaxi
5897
Huascarán
6768
Nevado Coropuna
6425
Nevado Ancohuma
6550
Cerro Ojos del Salado
6893
Monte Pissis
6793
Cerro Bonete
6759
Cerro Mercedario
6720
Pico de Neblina
2994
Mt. Roraima
2810
Pico da Bandeira
2890
Mt. Paget
2937
Tropic of Cancer
Tropic of Capricorn
Equator
Projection: Lambert's Azimuthal Equal Area
West from Greenwich

1:28 000 000
ATLANTIC OCEAN
PACIFIC OCEAN
Caribbean Sea
CUBA
Havana
BAHAMAS
Turks & Caicos Is. (U.K.)
Cayman Is. (U.K.)
HAITI
DOMINICAN REP.
Port-au-Prince
Santo Domingo
San Juan
PUERTO RICO (U.S.A.)
JAMAICA
Kingston
MEXICO
BELIZE
GUATEMALA
Guatemala
HONDURAS
Tegucigalpa
San Salvador
EL SALVADOR
NICARAGUA
Managua
COSTA RICA
San José
PANAMA
Panamá
Virgin Is. (U.S.A. - U.K.)
Anguilla (U.K.)
St. Martin (Fr. - Neth.)
ST. KITTS & NEVIS
ANTIGUA & BARBUDA
Basse-Terre
GUADELOUPE (Fr.)
DOMINICA
Fort-de-France
MARTINIQUE (Fr.)
Castries
ST. LUCIA
ST. VINCENT
Kingstown
BARBADOS
Bridgetown
GRENADA
St. George's
ARUBA (Neth.)
CURAÇAO (Neth.)
Oranjestad
Willemstad
Port of Spain
TRINIDAD & TOBAGO
Barranquilla
Cartagena
G. of Darién
Maracaibo
Barquisimeto
Caracas
Valencia
Cúcuta
San Cristóbal
Orinoco
Ciudad Guayana
VENEZUELA
Bucaramanga
Medellín
BOGOTÁ
Cali
COLOMBIA
Magdalena
Gulf of Panama
I. del Coco (Costa Rica)
I. de Malpelo (Colombia)
Georgetown
GUYANA
Paramaribo
SURINAME
Cayenne
FRENCH GUIANA
C. Orange
Boa Vista
RORAIMA
Branco
Essequibo
AMAPÁ
Macapá
Equator
Marajó I.
Belém
Galapagos Is. (Ecuador)
Quito
ECUADOR
Guayaquil
G. of Guayaquil
Napo
Putumayo
Japurá
Iquitos
Marañón
Amazon
Manaus
Santarém
AMAZONAS
PARÁ
São Luís
Fortaleza
Teresina
MARANHÃO
CEARÁ
Imperatriz
Tocantins
Xingu
Tapajós
Madeira
Purus
Juruá
Ucayali
RIO G. DO NORTE
Natal
PARAÍBA
João Pessoa
Campina Grande
Recife
PERNAMBUCO
ALAGOAS
Maceió
SERGIPE
Aracaju
Chiclayo
Trujillo
Chimbote
PERU
Callao
LIMA
Cusco
ACRE
Rio Branco
Pôrto Velho
RONDÔNIA
Madre de Dios
Mamoré
BRAZIL
Palmas
TOCANTINS
Araguaia
PIAUÍ
Parnaíba
São Francisco
BAHIA
Salvador
MATO GROSSO
Cuiabá
GOIÁS
DIS. FED.
Brasília
Goiânia
MINAS GERAIS
L. Titicaca
Arequipa
La Paz
BOLIVIA
Cochabamba
Santa Cruz
Sucre
Paraguay
MATO GROSSO DO SUL
Campo Grande
BELO HORIZONTE
ESPIRITO SANTO
Vitória
Ribeirão Prêto
Juiz de Fora
Campos
SÃO PAULO
Campinas
R. DE J.
Niterói
RIO DE JANEIRO
Santos
Iquique
Antofagasta
PARAGUAY
Pilcomayo
Asunción
Paraná
PARANÁ
Curitiba
SANTA CATARINA
Florianópolis
Tropic of Capricorn
San Félix (Chile)
San Ambrosio (Chile)
Salta
San Miguel de Tucumán
Resistencia
Corrientes
Uruguay
RIO GRANDE DO SUL
Pôrto Alegre
Pelotas
Salado
Córdoba
San Juan
Santa Fé
Paraná
Rosario
URUGUAY
Montevideo
Mendoza
Viña del Mar
Valparaíso
SANTIAGO
Arch. de Juan Fernández (Chile)
Robinson Crusoe
BUENOS AIRES
La Plata
Rio de la Plata
Talca
Concepción
CHILE
ARGENTINA
Neuquén
Colorado
Bahía Blanca
Mar del Plata
Valdivia
Negro
Viedma
Puerto Montt
Chubut
Comodoro Rivadavia
Gulf of San Jorge
Gulf of Penas
West Falkland
FALKLAND IS. (U.K.)
Stanley
East Falkland
Magellan's Str.
Punta Arenas
Tierra del Fuego
C. Horn
South Georgia (U.K.)
Tropic of Cancer
West from Greenwich
Projection: Lambert's Azimuthal Equal Area
COPYRIGHT PHILIP'S
LIMA Capital Cities

50 0 50 100 150 200 250 300 km

50 0 50 100 150 200 miles

1:6 400 000

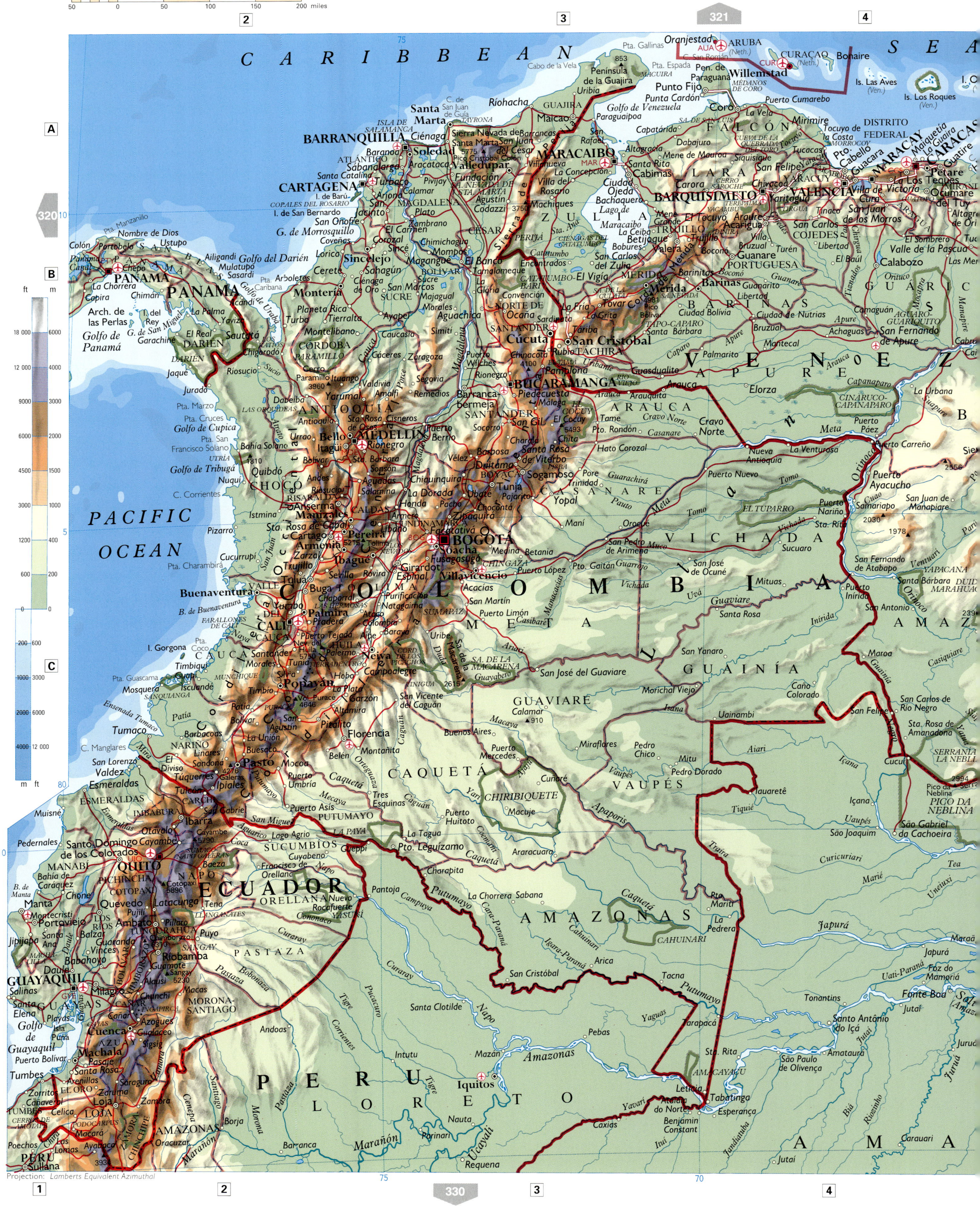
2
3
4
321
320
330
C A R I B B E A N S E A
PACIFIC OCEAN
C O L O M B I A
V E N E Z U E L A
ECUADOR
P E R U
PANAMA
ARUBA
(Neth.)
CURAÇAO
(Neth.)
Bonaire
Oranjestad
Willemstad
Is. Las Aves
(Ven.)
Is. Los Roques
(Ven.)
Peninsula de la Guajira
Golfo de Venezuela
Paraguaipoa
Punto Fijo
Punta Cardón
Coro
Puerto Cumarebo
Maracaibo
MARACAIBO
Lago de Maracaibo
Cabimas
Ciudad Ojeda
BARQUISIMETO
VALENCIA
MARACAY
CARACAS
Maiquetía
La Guaira
Los Teques
Petare
San Felipe
Puerto Cabello
Barinas
Mérida
San Cristóbal
Cúcuta
Valera
Trujillo
Guanare
Acarigua
Araure
Calabozo
San Fernando de Apure
Puerto Ayacucho
Puerto Carreño
Puerto Páez
Riohacha
Santa Marta
BARRANQUILLA
Ciénaga
Soledad
Valledupar
CARTAGENA
Sincelejo
Montería
Magangué
El Banco
Ocaña
Bucaramanga
BUCARAMANGA
Barrancabermeja
MEDELLÍN
Bello
Itagüí
Rionegro
Quibdó
Manizales
Pereira
Armenia
Ibagué
BOGOTÁ
Soacha
Zipaquirá
Tunja
Sogamoso
Yopal
Villavicencio
Girardot
Neiva
Buenaventura
CALI
Palmira
Tuluá
Popayán
Pasto
Tumaco
Ipiales
Florencia
Mocoa
Puerto Asís
Leticia
Tabatinga
San José del Guaviare
Mitú
Inírida
Puerto Inírida
ANTIOQUIA
CHOCÓ
CALDAS
CAUCA
HUILA
NARIÑO
PUTUMAYO
CAQUETÁ
AMAZONAS
VAUPÉS
GUAVIARE
GUAINÍA
VICHADA
META
CASANARE
ARAUCA
BOYACÁ
SANTANDER
CÓRDOBA
SUCRE
BOLÍVAR
ATLÁNTICO
MAGDALENA
CESAR
GUAJIRA
ZULIA
FALCÓN
LARA
BARINAS
APURE
Golfo del Darién
Golfo de Urabá
Golfo de Panamá
Arch. de las Perlas
Colón
Panamá
La Chorrera
Chimán
DARIÉN
Esmeraldas
QUITO
Santo Domingo de los Colorados
Ibarra
Otavalo
Latacunga
Ambato
Riobamba
Cuenca
Machala
GUAYAQUIL
Portoviejo
Manta
Salinas
Golfo de Guayaquil
Tumbes
Puerto Bolívar
Loja
Macas
Puyo
Tena
SUCUMBÍOS
ORELLANA
NAPO
PASTAZA
MORONA-SANTIAGO
Iquitos
Nauta
Requena
LORETO
Amazonas
Putumayo
Caquetá
Orinoco
Meta
Guaviare
Vaupés
Japurá
Marañón
Ucayali
Napo
Tigre
Pastaza
Magdalena
Cauca
Atrato
Santo Antônio do Içá
São Paulo de Olivença
Benjamin Constant
Fonte Boa
São Gabriel da Cachoeira
PICO DA NEBLINA
Sierra Nevada de Santa Marta
Cordillera Oriental
Cordillera Central
Cordillera Occidental
CHIRIBIQUETE
1
2
3
4
A
B
C
75
70
10
5
0
80
ft
m
18 000
6000
12 000
4000
9000
3000
6000
2000
4500
1500
3000
1000
1200
400
600
200
0
0
200 600
1000 3000
2000 6000
4000 12 000
m
ft

Projection: *Lamberts Equivalent Azimuthal*

a

MARGARITA
1:600 000
CARIBBEAN SEA
NUEVA ESPARTA
Isla de Margarita
(Venezuela)
Isla Cubagua
Isla Coche
La Asunción
Porlamar
Pampatar
Juangriego
Península de Macanao
Isla Los Frailes
West from Greenwich
The Grenadines
St. George's
GRENADA
Blanquilla
Is Los Hermanos
Is. Los Testigos
I. de Margarita
Tobago
Scarborough
TRINIDAD AND TOBAGO
Port of Spain
San Fernando
Trinidad
Cumaná
Barcelona
Maturín
SUCRE
MONAGAS
ANZOÁTEGUI
DELTA
Delta del Orinoco
Tucupita
Ciudad Guayana
Ciudad Bolívar
El Tigre
AMACURO
Embalse de Guri
Sa. Pacaraima
Serra Parima
Serra Curupira
GUYANA
Georgetown
New Amsterdam
Linden
ATLANTIC OCEAN
SURINAME
Paramaribo
FRENCH GUIANA
Cayenne
Kourou
Saint-Laurent du Maroni
Serra Tumucumaque
MONTANHAS DO TUMUCUMAQUE
AMAPÁ
Macapá
Ilha de Marajó
RORAIMA
Boa Vista
Represa de Balbina
MANAUS
Santarém
Óbidos
Amazonas
Negro
Xingu
Tapajós
BRAZIL
PARÁ
AMAZONAS
Equator
5
6
7
A
B
C
D
60
55
50

331
332

1:6 400 000
km
miles
328
ECUADOR
LORETO
PERU
Cordillera Central
Cordillera Occidental
Cordillera Oriental
AMAZONAS
SAN MARTÍN
LA LIBERTAD
HUÁNUCO
ANCASH
PASCO
JUNÍN
LIMA
HUANCAVELICA
AYACUCHO
APURÍMAC
CUSCO
MADRE DE DIOS
PUNO
AREQUIPA
MOQUEGUA
TACNA
ICA
ACRE
AMAZONAS
PANDO
LA PAZ
ORURO
TARAPACÁ
ANTOFAGASTA
CHILE
Tumbes
Piura
Chiclayo
Trujillo
Chimbote
Cajamarca
Iquitos
Pucallpa
Huánuco
Cerro de Pasco
Huancayo
Ayacucho
Cusco
Puno
Juliaca
Arequipa
Tacna
Arica
Iquique
Calama
La Paz
Oruro
Rio Branco
Cruzeiro do Sul
Cobija
Puerto Maldonado
Lago Titicaca
Peru Basin
Peru-Chile Trench
PACIFIC OCEAN
Projection: Lamberts Equivalent Azimuthal
Arch. de Colón (Is. Galápagos)
(Ecuador)
Isla Isabela (Albemarle)
Isla Santa Cruz (Indefatigable)
Isla San Cristóbal (Chatham)
Isla Fernandina (Narborough)
Isla Santiago
Isla Española (Hood)
GALAPAGOS IS.
1:3 200 000
West from Greenwich
Isla de Pascua (Easter I., Rapa Nui)
(Chile)
Hanga Roa
EASTER ISLAND
1:400 000
Isla Robinson Crusoe
(Chile)
Isla Santa Clara
ROBINSON CRUSOE I.
1:400 000

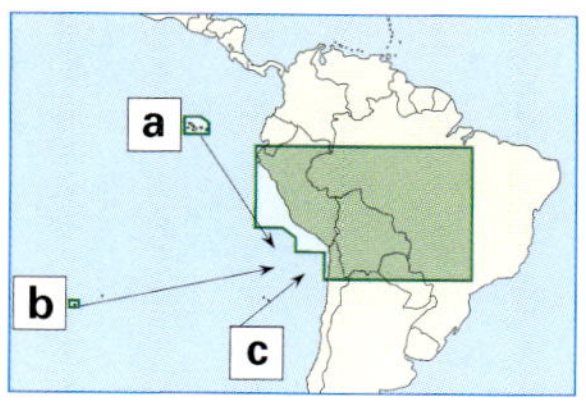
a
b
c

5
329
6
7
A
B
C
D
E
332
333
334
335
West from Greenwich
COPYRIGHT PHILIP'S
Coari
Lima
Andrade
Paricatuba
Purus
Arumã
Borba
Canumã
Maués
Itaituba
AMAZÔNIA
São Luís do Tapajós
Tapajós
Rurópolis
Iriri
Bacajá
Itanhauã
Hevelândia
Novo Aripuanã
Madeira
Jaburu
Itatuba
Tapauá
Democracia
Manicoré
Santa Maria dos Marmelos
Capoeira
Tucunaré
Entre Rios
Canutama
Caranapatuba
Três Casas
Canumã
Miriti
Sai-Cinza
Lábrea
Humaitá
Prainha Nova
Barra de São Manuel
São Félix do Xingu
Xingu
Calama
Samaúma
Aripuanã
Juruena
Teles Pires
Serra do Cachimbo
Porto Velho
Tabajara
Jaci-Paraná
Caritionas
Abunã
S. Benedito
Cachimbo
Ariquemes
Nova Vida
Jaru
Aripuanã
Alta Floresta
Guarantã do Norte
Serra dos Apiacás
Guajará-Mirim
Guayaramerín
Ouro Preto do Oeste
Ji-Paraná
Peixoto Azevedo
São José do Xingu
Presidente Médici
Cacoal
PACAÁS NOVOS
RONDÔNIA
Pimenta Bueno
Colíder
Manitsauá-Missu
Marco Rondon
Juruena
Juína
Porto dos Gaúchos
Sinop
Serra Formosa
Príncipe da Beira
Vilhena
Nhambiquara
Serra do Tombador
Serra dos Caiabis
Sorriso
Liquilândia
Pedras Negras
Mategua
Versalles
Magdalena
Puerto Siles
San Joaquín
Utiariti
Pimenteiras
Puerto Villazón
San Ramón
Baures
El Carmen
NOEL KEMPFF MERCADO
Serrania de Huanchaca
São José do Rio Claro
Nova Mutum
Planalto do Mato Grosso
Trinidad
San Javier
Perseverancia
Nortelândia
Arenápoli
Diamantino
Alto Paraguai
Tangará da Serra
Rosário Oeste
Barra do Bugres
Paranatinga
Nova Xavantina
Serra Azul
Loreto
Vila Bela da Santíssima Trindade
Pontes e Lacerda
Acorizal
Chapada dos Guimarães
Aruanã
Britânia
Añez
Santa Rosa de la Roca
Porto Esperidião
Várzea Grande
Cuiabá
Nossa Senhora do Livramento
Cáceres
Santo Antônio do Leverger
Coronel Ponce
Barra do Garças
Aragarças
Aguapeí
San Javier
Concepción
San Ignacio
San Matías
Poconé
Barão de Melgaço
Jaciara
Poxoréo
Tesouro
Guiratinga
Rondonópolis
Ponte Branca
Santa Rosa del Palmar
San Miguel
San Rafael
SANTA CRUZ
Caiapônia
Iporá
Montero
Warnes
Cotoca
El Cerro
Laguna Concepción
Lagoa Uberaba
São Lourenço
Itiquira
Alto Garças
Alto Araguaia
Santa Rita do Araguaia
GOIÁS
SANTA CRUZ
El Palmar
Buena Vista
Portachuelo
San Carlos
AMBORÓ
CARRASCO
San José de Chiquitos
Santo Corazón
Porto Jofre
Pantanal do São Lourenço
Mineiro
Rio Verde
Jataí
Santiago de Chiquitos
Roboré
La Cal
Lagoa Mandioré
Pantanal do Rio Negro
EMAS
Baús
Serranópolis
Santa Ana
Puerto Suárez
Corumbá
Ladário
Nhecolândia
MATO GROSSO DO SUL
Coxim
Rio Verde de Mato Grosso
KAA-IYA
OTUQUIS
Fortín General Pando
Albuquerque
Porto Esperança
Paraíso
Cassilândia
Itarumã
Cachoeira Alta
Mayor Pablo Lagerenza
Coimbra
Corguinho
Rochedo
Camapuã
Alto Sucuriú
Paranaíba
Inocência
General Eugenio A. Garay
Chaco Boreal
DEFENSORES DEL CHACO
Bahía Negra
Miranda
Aquidauana
Terenos
Campo Grande
Ribas do Rio Pardo
Água Clara
Aparecida do Taboado
Rubinéia
Pereira Barreto
Andradina
ALTO PARAGUAY
Fortín Madrejón
Fuerte Olimpo
PARAGUAY
Puerto Guaraní
Bonito
Nioaque
Sidrolândia
Três Lagoas
Garcias
Fortín Teniente Primero Ramiro Espínola
TTE. AGRIPINO ENCISO
BOQUERÓN
Porto Murtinho
Jardim
Guia Lopes da Laguna
Maracaju
Nova Alvorada do Sul
Xavantina
Mirandópolis
Panorama
Sucre
Yotala
Tarabuco
Zudañez
Padilla
Sopachuy
Monteagudo
Azurduy
CHUQUISACA
Camargo
Tarija
Uriondo
Padcaya
Villa Montes
Yacuiba
Tartagal
Dr. Pedro P. Peña
SALTA
TARIJA
Camiri
Boyuibe
Carandaiti
Huacaya
Cuevo
Charagua
Lagunillas
Gutiérrez
Abapó
Pucará
Vallegrande
Samaipata
Comarapa
Aiquile
Pasorapa
Presto
Totora
Pampa Grande
Llanos de Chiquitos
Bañados de Izozog
BENI
BOLIVIA
BRAZIL
PARÁ
AMAZONAS
San Ignacio
Llanos de Mojos
Mato Grosso

1:6 400 000

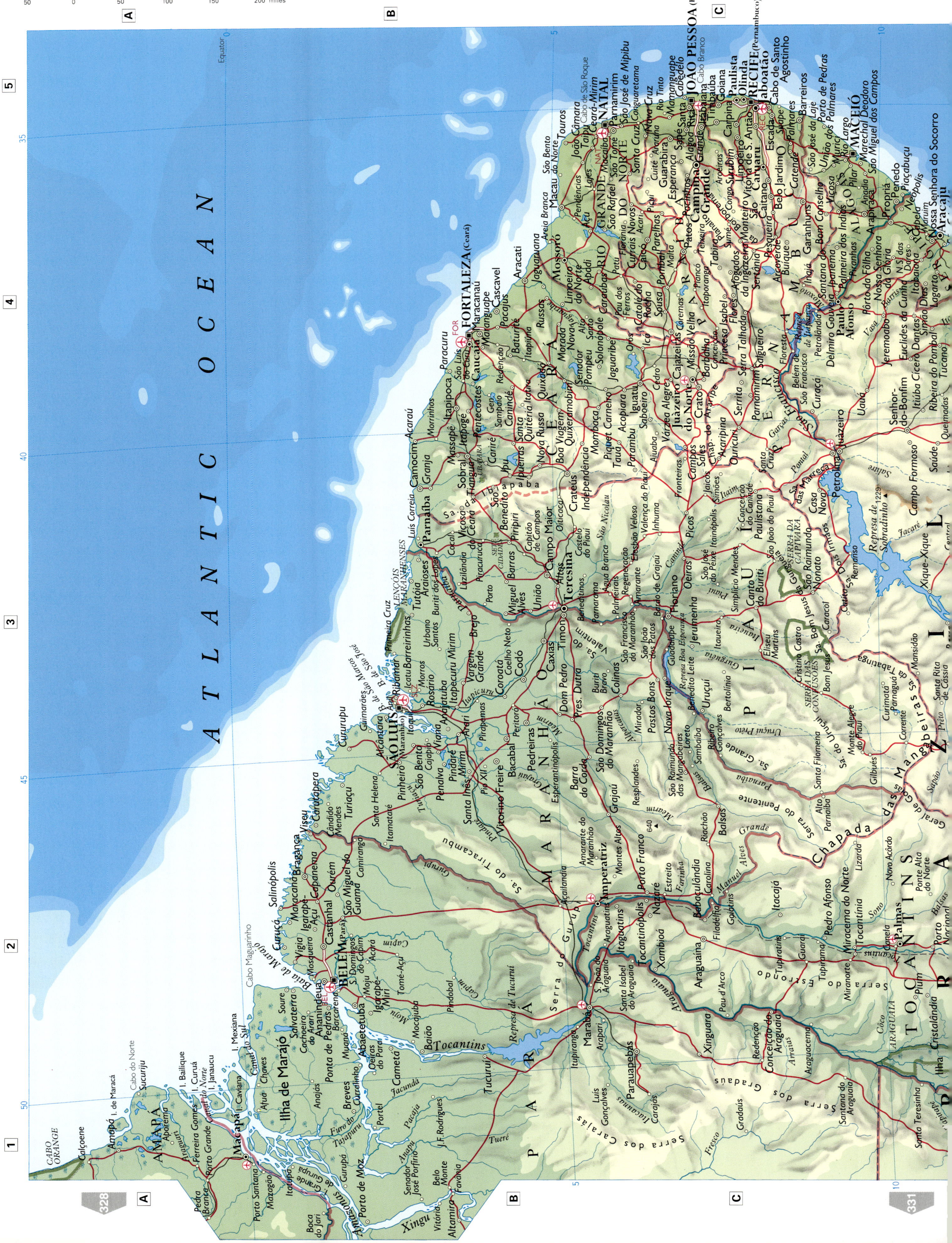
ATLANTIC OCEAN
Equator
FORTALEZA (Ceará)
NATAL
JOÃO PESSOA (Paraíba)
RECIFE (Pernambuco)
MACEIÓ
Aracaju
SÃO LUÍS
BELÉM
Teresina
MACAPÁ
Palmas
Ilha de Marajó
Imperatriz
Marabá
Petrolina
Juazeiro
Caxias
Campina Grande
Mossoró
Parnaíba
Tocantins
Xingu
Represa de Tucuruí
Represa de Sobradinho
Chapada das Mangabeiras
Serra dos Carajás
CEARÁ
MARANHÃO
PIAUÍ
PARÁ
TOCANTINS
AMAPÁ
RIO GRANDE DO NORTE
Cabo Orange
Cabo do Norte
Cabo Maguarinho
Cabo Branco
Cabo de Santo Agostinho
328
331

ATLANTIC OCEAN
BAHIA
MINAS GERAIS
ESPÍRITO SANTO
GOIÁS
SÃO PAULO
PARANÁ
RIO DE JANEIRO
DISTRITO FEDERAL
SALVADOR (Bahia)
BRASÍLIA
BELO HORIZONTE
VITÓRIA
GOIÂNIA
SÃO PAULO
CURITIBA
CAMPINAS
SANTOS
Tropic of Capricorn
West from Greenwich
Projection : Lambert's Equivalent Azimuthal
COPYRIGHT PHILIP'S
D
E
F
G
1
2
3
4
5
15
20
25
35
40
45
50
331
335


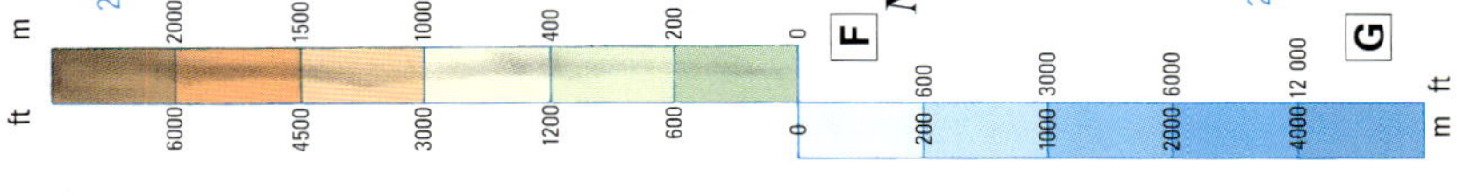

m
ft
6000
4500
3000
1200
600
0
2000
1500
1000
400
200
0
200
600
3000
6000
12 000
200
1000
2000
4000

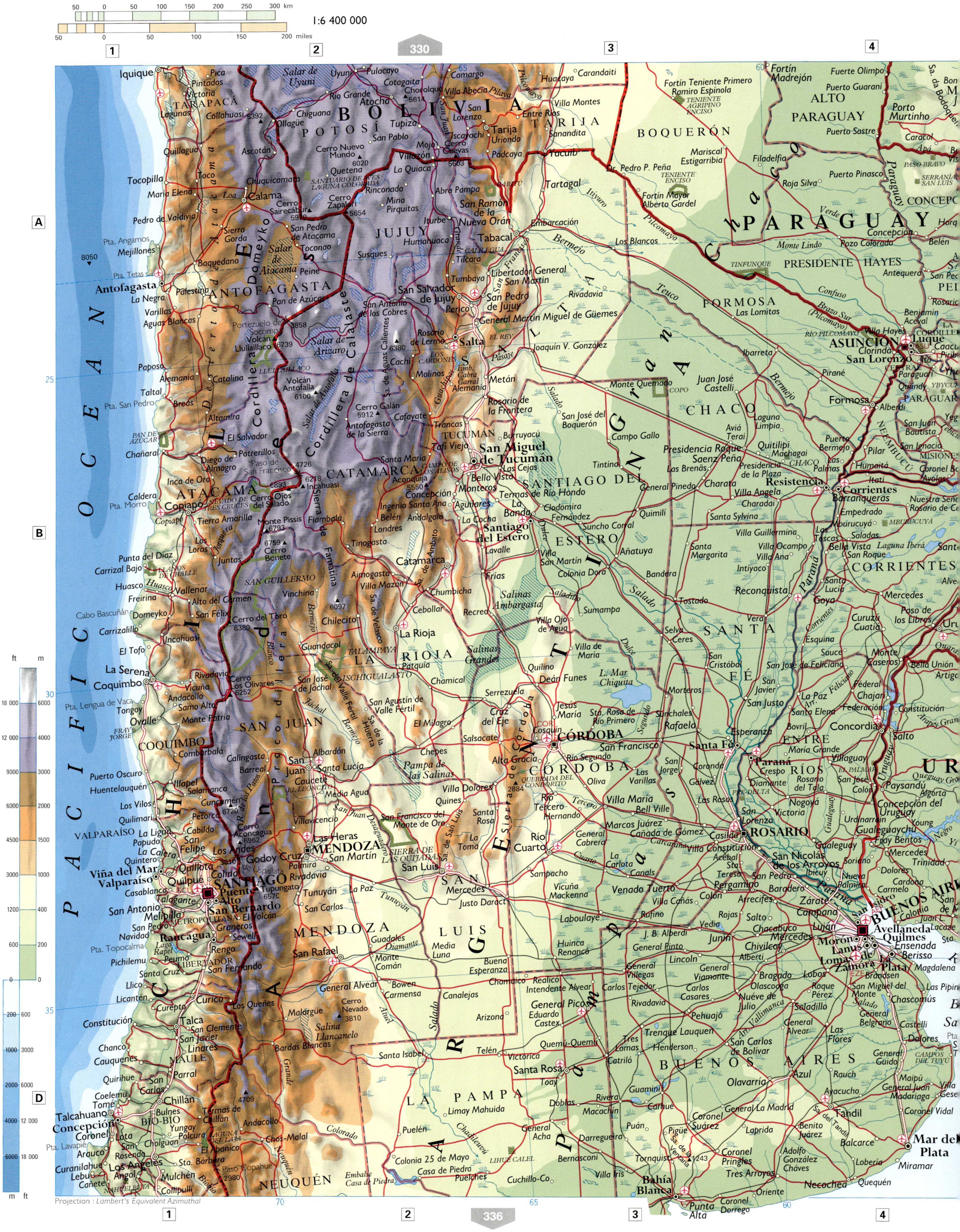

1:6 400 000
330
336
PACIFIC OCEAN
BOLIVIA
PARAGUAY
ALTO PARAGUAY
BOQUERÓN
PRESIDENTE HAYES
FORMOSA
CHACO
Gran Chaco
SALTA
JUJUY
TUCUMÁN
CATAMARCA
SANTIAGO DEL ESTERO
SANTA FÉ
CORRIENTES
ENTRE RÍOS
CÓRDOBA
LA RIOJA
SAN JUAN
SAN LUIS
MENDOZA
LA PAMPA
BUENOS AIRES
NEUQUÉN
ANTOFAGASTA
ATACAMA
COQUIMBO
TARAPACÁ
POTOSÍ
TARIJA
CHILE
ARGENTINA
Pampas
Desierto de Atacama
Cordillera Domeyko
Cordillera de los Andes
Iquique
Antofagasta
La Serena
Coquimbo
Valparaíso
Viña del Mar
SANTIAGO
Rancagua
Talca
Concepción
ASUNCIÓN
Corrientes
Resistencia
Santa Fé
Paraná
ROSARIO
CÓRDOBA
MENDOZA
San Juan
San Miguel de Tucumán
Salta
BUENOS AIRES
La Plata
Mar del Plata
Bahía Blanca
Projection : Lambert's Equivalent Azimuthal

5
6
7
333
A
B
C
D
BELO HORIZONTE
VITÓRIA
RIO DE JANEIRO
SÃO PAULO
CAMPINAS
SANTOS
CURITIBA
JOINVILLE
FLORIANÓPOLIS
PORTO ALEGRE
B R A Z I L
P A R A N Á
S Ã O P A U L O
SANTA CATARINA
R I O G R A N D E D O S U L
RIO DE JANEIRO
Tropic of Capricorn
A T L A N T I C
O C E A N
Lagoa dos Patos
Lagoa Mirim
Lagoa Mangueira
Ilha de São Sebastião
Ilha de Santa Catarina
Cabo Frio
Cabo Santa Marta Grande
Rio Grande
Pelotas
Londrina
Maringá
Cascavel
Foz do Iguaçu
Ciudad del Este
Ponta Grossa
Paranaguá
Blumenau
Itajaí
Criciúma
Caxias do Sul
Santa Maria
Passo Fundo
Campos
Juiz de Fora
Petrópolis
Niterói
Volta Redonda
Ribeirão Prêto
Sorocaba
Bauru
Presidente Prudente
Três Lagoas
Dourados
Pedro Juan Caballero
Maldonado
MONTEVIDEO
MISIONES
5304
West from Greenwich
55
50
45
40
25
30
35

# SOUTHERN CHILE AND ARGENTINA

1:6 400 000

50 0 50 100 150 200 250 300 km
50 0 50 100 150 200 miles
334
335
LA PAMPA
BUENOS AIRES
NEUQUÉN
RÍO NEGRO
CHUBUT
SANTA CRUZ
TIERRA DEL FUEGO
LA ARAUCANIA
LOS RÍOS
LOS LAGOS
MAGALLANES Y ANTÁRTICA CHILENA
CHILE
ARGENTINA
ATLANTIC OCEAN
PACIFIC OCEAN
FALKLAND ISLANDS (U.K.)
(ISLAS MALVINAS)
West Falkland
East Falkland
Stanley
Jason Is.
Pebble I.
C. Dolphin
Mt. Adam
Mt. Usborne
Port Darwin
Weddell I.
C. Meredith
Beauchêne I.
Golfo San Matías
Golfo San Jorge
Bahía Grande
Golfo de Penas
Isla de Chiloé
Archipiélago de los Chonos
Península de Taitao
Archipiélago Guayaneco
Isla Grande de Tierra del Fuego
Estrecho de Magallanes
Magellan's Strait
Canal Beagle
Estr. de Le Maire
I. de los Estados (Staten I.)
Cabo de Hornos (Cape Horn)
Islas Diego Ramirez
Islas Wollaston
I. Navarino
Nueva
I. Lennox
Ushuaia
Puerto Williams
Río Grande
Porvenir
Punta Arenas
Puerto Natales
Río Gallegos
El Calafate
Puerto Santa Cruz
Puerto San Julián
Puerto Deseado
Caleta Olivia
Comodoro Rivadavia
Rawson
Trelew
Puerto Madryn
Península Valdés
Viedma
Carmen de Patagones
San Antonio Oeste
Bahía Blanca
Necochea
Neuquén
Cipolletti
General Roca
San Carlos de Bariloche
Esquel
Coihaique
Puerto Aisén
Puerto Montt
Osorno
Valdivia
Temuco
Angol
Ancud
Castro
Chaitén
Quellón
Cochrane
Mte. San Valentín 4058
Cerro Fitz Roy 3405
Mt. Darwin 2488
Mte. Sarmiento 2246
Projection : Lambert s Equivalent Azimuthal
West from Greenwich

# GEOGRAPHICAL GLOSSARY

This is a list of the geographical terms from various foreign languages that are found in the place names on the maps and in the index. Each is followed by the language and its English meaning.

*Afr.* Afrikaans
*Alb.* Albanian
*Amh.* Amharic
*Ar.* Arabic
*Belo.* Belorussian
*Berb.* Berber
*Bulg.* Bulgarian
*Burm.* Burmese
*Cam.* Cambodian
*Cat.* Catalan
*Chin.* Chinese
*Czec.* Czech
*Dan.* Danish
*Dut.* Dutch
*Est.* Estonian
*Fin.* Finnish
*Fr.* French
*Gae.* Gaelic
*Ger.* German
*Gr.* Greek
*Heb.* Hebrew
*Hin.* Hindi
*Hung.* Hungarian
*I.-C.* Indo-Chinese
*Ice.* Icelandic
*It.* Italian
*Indo.* Indonesian
*Jap.* Japanese
*Kaz.* Kazakh
*Kor.* Korean
*Kyrg.* Kyrgyz
*Lapp.* Lapp (Sami)
*Lat.* Latvian
*Lith.* Lithuanian
*Malag.* Malagasy
*Mong.* Mongolian
*Nor.* Norway
*Pash.* Pashto
*Per.* Persian
*Pol.* Polish
*Port.* Portuguese
*Rom.* Romanian
*Russ.* Russian
*Sin.* Sinhalese
*Ser.-Cr.* Serbo-Croat
*Slov.* Slovene
*Som.* Somali
*Span.* Spanish
*Swe.* Swedish
*Tib.* Tibetan
*Turk.* Turkish
*Ukr.* Ukrainian
*Viet.* Vietnamese

-á *Ice.* river
-å *Dan., Nor., Swe.* stream
-abad *Farsi, Russ.* town
Abyad *Ar.* white mountain
Ada, Adasi *Turk.* island
Addis *Amh.* new
Adrar *Ar., Berb.* mountains
Aiguille *Fr.* peak
Aïn, Aîn (A.) *Ar.* spring
Ákra *Gr.* cape, point
Akrotiri *Gr.* cape, point
Alb *Ger.* mountains
Albufera *Span.* lagoon
-ålen *Nor.* islands
Alpen *Ger.* mountain ranges
Alpes *Fr.* mountains
Alpi *It.* mountains
Alt *Ger.* old
Alta, Alto *Port.* high, upper
Altos *Span.* mountains
-älv, -älven *Swe.* stream, river
Amtskommune (Amt.) *Dan.* first-order administrative division
-ån *Swe.* river
Anse *Fr.* bay
Ao *Thai* bay
Appennino *It.* mountain range
Archipel *Fr.* archipelago
Archipiélago (Arch.) *Span.* archipelago
Arcipélago *It.* archipelago
Arquipélago (Arq.) *Port.* archipelago
Arrecife *Span.* reef
Arroyo (Arr.) *Span.* stream
-ås, -åsen *Nor., Swe.* hill
Ayios *Gr.* island
Ayn *Ar.* well, waterhole

Baai, -baai *Afr., Dut.* bay
Bāb *Ar.* gate, strait
Bäck, -bäcken *Swe.* stream
Back, -backen, *Swe.* hill
Bad, -baden *Ger.* spa
Badia *Cat.* bay
Bādiyah, Bādiyat *Ar.* desert
Bæk *Dan.* stream
Bælt *Dan.* strait
Baharu *Malay* new
Bahía (B.) *Span.* bay
Bahiret *Ar.* lagoon
Bahr *Ar.* sea, lake, river
Bahra Bahrat *Ar.* lake
Baía (B.) *Port.* bay
Baie (B.) *Fr.* bay
Baixa, Baixo *Port.* lower
Baja, Bajo *Span.* lower
Bakke *Nor.* hill
Bala *Farsi* upper
Ballon *Fr.* dome
Baltă *Rom.* marsh, lake
Ban *Lao, Thai* village
-Bana *Jap.* cape
Banc *Fr.* bank
Banco *Span.* bank
Bandao *Chin.* peninsula
Bandar *Ar., Malay* port, harbour
Bandar *Farsi* bay
Banja *Ser.-Cr.* spa, resort
Banjaran *Malay* mountain range
Baraji *Turk.* dam
Barat *Indo., Malay* western
Barrage (Barr.) *Fr.* dam
Barragem (Barr.) *Port.* dam, reservoir
Bas, basse *Fr.* lower
Bassin *Fr.* basin
-batang *Indo.* river
Baţlaq *Farsi* marsh
Batu *Malay* mountain
Bayt *Heb.* house, village
Bazar *Hin.* market, bazaar
-beek *Afr., Dut.* river
Be'er *Heb.* well
Bei *Chin.* north, northern
Beinn, Ben *Gae.* mountain
Beit *Heb.* village
Belaya, Belo, Beloye, Belyy *Russ.* white
Belogorye *Russ.* hills, mountain range
Bender *Som.* harbour
Berg(e), -berg(e) *Afr., Ger.* mountain(s)
-berg, -en, -et *Nor., Swe.* hill, mountain, rock
Besar *Indo., Malay* big
Bet *Heb.* house, village
Bir, Bîr, Bi'r *Ar.* well
Birkat, Birket *Ar.* lake, marsh, well
Bishti *Alb.* cape
-bjerg *Dan.* hill, point
Blaenau *Welsh* upland
-bo *Chin.* lake
Boca *Port., Span.* river mouth, inlet
Bodden *Ger.* bay, inlet
Bogaz, Boğazı *Turk.* channel, strait
Bogd *Mong.* mountain range
Bois *Fr.* woods
Boka *Ser.-Cr.* gulf, inlet
Bolshoi, Bolshaya, Bolshoye (Bol.) *Russ.* great, large
Bordj (Bj.) *Ar.* fort
-borg *Dan., Nor., Swe.* castle, fort
Bory *Pol.* woods
Bosque *Span.* woods
-botn *Nor.* valley floor
Bouche(s) *Fr.* mouth(s)
Braţul *Rom.* distributary stream, branch
-bre, -breen *Nor.* glacier
Bredning *Dan.* bay
Brücke *Ger.* bridge
-brug *Dut.* bridge
-brunn *Swe.* well, spring
Bucht *Ger.* bay
Bugt *Dan.* bay
-bugten *Dan.* bay
Buheirat *Ar.* lake, reservoir
Bukit *Malay* hill
-bukt, -a *Nor.* bay
-bukten *Swe.* bay
-bulag *Mong.* spring
Bulag *Chin.* lake
Bulu *Malay* mountain
Bum *Burm.* mountain
Bûr *Ar.* port
Burg. *Ar.* fort
Burg, -burg *Ger.* castle
Burnu, Burun *Turk.* cape
Butt *Gae.* promontory
Büyük *Turk.* big
-by *Dan., Nor., Swe.* town
-byen *Nor., Swe.* town

Cabeza *Span.* peak, hill
Cabo (C.) *Port., Span.* headland, cape
Cachoeira *Port.* waterfall
Cala Cat. *It.* bay
Camp Port. *Span.* land, field
Câmpia *Rom.* plain
Campo *It., Port., Span.* plain
Campos *Span.* upland
Canal (Can.) *Fr., Port., Span.* canal, channel
Canale (Can.) *It.* channel
Canalul (Can.) *Ser.-Cr.* canal
Cao Nguyen *Thai* plateau, tableland
Cap (C.) *Cat., Fr.* cape
Capo (C) *It.* cape
Carn *Gae.* hill
Carse *Gae.* valley
Catarata *Port., Span.* cataract
Cauce *Span.* intermittent stream
Causse *Fr.* limestone plateau
Cay, Cayi, -cay, -cayi *Turk.* river
Cayo(s) *Span.* rock(s), islet(s)
Cefn *Welsh* hill
Cerro *Span.* hill, peak
Česká, Český, České *Czec.* Czech
Chaco *Span.* jungle
Chaîne(s) *Fr.* mountain range(s)
Chang *Chin.* mountain
Chapa *Span.* hills, upland
Chapada *Port.* hills, upland
Chaung *Burm.* stream, river
Chi *Chin.* small lake
-ch'ŏn *Kor.* river
-chŏsuji *Kor.* reservoir
Chott *Ar.* salt lake, depression
Chu *Tib.* river
Chute *Fr.* waterfall
Città *It.* city
Ciudad *Span.* city
Co *Tib.* lake
Cochilla (Coch.) *Port.* hills
Col *Fr., It.* pass
Colina(s) *Span.* hill(s)
Colle *It.* pass
Colline(s) *Fr.* hill(s)
Conca *It.* plain, basin
Cordillera (Cord.) *Span.* mountain range
Costa *It., Port., Span.* coast
Côte *Fr.* coast, slope, hill
Coteaux *Fr.* hills
Cuchilla *Span.* hills
Cuenca *Span.* river basin
Cu-Lao *Viet.* island

Da *Chin.* big
Da *Viet.* river
Daban *Mong.* pass
Dağ(ı) *Turk.* mountain(s)
Dāgh *Farsi* mountain
Dağlari *Turk.* mountain range
-dai, -daichi *Jap.* plateau
-Dake *Jap.* mountain
-dal, -e *Dan., Swe.* valley
-dal, -en *Swe., Nor.* valley, stream
Dalay Mong. large lake
-dalir, -dalur *Ice.* valley
-damm, -en *Swe.* lake
Danau *Malay* lake
Dao *Chin., Viet.* island
Dar *Ar.* region
Darya *Russ.* river
Daryācheh *Farsi* marshy lake, lake
Dasht *Farsi* desert, steppe
Daung *Burm.* mountain, hill
Dayr *Ar.* monastery
Debre *Amh.* hill
Deli *Ser.-Cr.* mountain
Deniz, -i *Turk.* sea
Département (Dépt.) *Fr.* first-order administrative division
Dere *Turk.* stream
Desierto (Des.) *Span.* desert
Détroit *Fr.* strait
Dhar *Ar.* region, mountain range
Diep *Dut.* channel
Dijk *Dut.* dyke
Ding *Chin.* mountain
Dingzi *Chin.* hill, mountain
Djebel (Dj.) *Ar.* mountain
-djúp *Ice.* fjord
-djupet *Swe.* channel, sound
-Do *Jap., Kor.* island
Dolina *Russ.* valley
Dolna, Dolni *Bulg.* lower
Dolna, Dolne, Dolny *Russ.* lower
Dolní *Czec.* lower
Dolok (D.) *Malay* mountain
-dong *Kor.* village, town
Dong *Chin.* east, eastern
Donja, Donji *Ser.-Cr.* lower
-dorf *Ger.* village
-dorp *Afr.* village
-drif *Afr.* ford
-dybet *Dan.* marine channel
Dzong *Tib.* town, settlement
Dzüün *Mong.* east, eastern

-egga *Nor.* peak
-eiland, -en (eil.) *Afr., Dut.* island(s)
Eilean *Gae.* island
-elv, -a *Nor.* river
Embalse *Span.* reservoir
'Emeq *Heb.* plain, valley
Ensenada *Span.* bay
Erg *Ar.* sand desert
Estero *Span.* estuary
Estrada *Span.* bay
Estrecho *Span.* strait
Estuaire *Fr.* estuary
Estuario *Span.* estuary
Étang *Fr.* lagoon, lake
-ey, -jar *Ice.* island(s)
-ežeras *Lith.* lake
-ezers *Lat.* lake

Falaise *Fr.* cliff
-fallet *Swe.* waterfall
Farihy *Malag.* lake
Faro *Span.* lighthouse
-feld *Ger.* field
-fell *Ice.* mountain, hill
Feng *Chin.* mountain range
Fiume (F.) *It.* river
-fjäll, -en, -et *Swe.* hill(s), mountain(s), ridge
-fjärden *Swe.* fjord
Fjeld *Dan.* mountain
-fjell, -et *Nor.* mountain range
-fjord, -en *Dan., Nor., Swe.* fjord
-fjorður *Ice.* fjord, bay, inlet
Fleuve (Fl.) *Fr.* river
-flói *Ice.* bay, marshy country
Fluss (F.) *Ger.* river
Foce, Foci *It.* mouth(s)
Folyó (F.) *Hung.* river
-fonn *Nor.* glacier
-fontein *Afr.* fountain, spring
Forêt *Fr.* forest
-fors, -en *Swe.* waterfall, rapids
-foss, -en *Ice., Nor.* waterfall
Forst *Ger.* forest
Foum *Ar.* pass
Fuente *Span.* source
-furt *Ger.* ford
Fylke *Nor.* first-order administrative division

-gang *Chin.* bay, harbour
-gang *Kor.* river
Ganga *Hin., Sin.* river
Gangri *Tib.* mountain
Gaoyuan *Chin.* plateau
-gat *Dan.* sound
-Gata *Jap.* lake
-gau *Ger.* district
-Gawa *Jap.* river
Gebel (G.) *Ar.* mountain
Gebirge (Geb.) *Ger.* hills, mountains
Gezirat, Geziret *Ar.* island
Ghat *Hin.* range of hills
Ghiol *Rom.* lake
Ghubbat *Ar.* bay, inlet
Gjiri *Alb.* bay
Gjol *Alb.* lagoon, lake
Glava (Gl.) *Ser.-Cr.* mountain, peak
Glen *Gae.* valley
Gletscher (Gl.) *Ger.* glacier
Gobi *Mong.* desert
Gol *Mong.* river
Göl *Azeri, Turk.* lake
Golfe (G.) *Fr.* gulf
Golfo (G.) *It., Span.* gulf
Gölü *Turk.* lake
Gomba *Tib.* settlement
Gora, Góra *Bulg., Russ., Ser.-Cr., Pol.* mountain
Gorje *Ser.-Cr.* hills, mountains
Gorno *Russ.* mountainous
-gorod *Russ.* small town
Gory, Góry *Pol., Russ.* mountain
-grad *Bulg. Russ., Ser.-Cr.* town, city
-grada *Russ.* ridge
Gran *It., Span.* big, great
Grand, -e *Fr.* big, great
Groot (Gt.) *Afr., Dut.* big, great
Gross, -e, -en, -er *Ger.* big, great(er)
Grupo *Span.* group
Gruppo *It.* group
Guan *Chin.* pass
Guba (G.) *Russ.* bay
-Guntō *Jap.* island group
Gunong, Gunung (G.) *Indo., Malay* mountain
Gură *Rom.* passage

Hadabat *Ar.* plateau
Hadjer *Ar.* mountain
-hafen *Ger.* harbour, port
Haff *Ger.* bay, lagoon
Hai *Chin.* lake, sea
Haixia *Chin.* channel, strait
Halbinsel *Ger.* peninsula
Halvø *Dan.* peninsula
Halvøya *Nor.* peninsula
Hāmad, Hamada, Hammādah, Hammādat *Ar.* stony desert, plateau
-hamn *Swe., Nor.* harbour, anchorage
Hāmūn *Farsi* marsh, lake
-Hantō *Jap.* peninsula
Har(e) *Heb.* hill(s), mountain(s)
Hassi (Hi.) *Ar.* well
-haug *Nor.* hill
Hav, Havet *Nor., Swe.* sea
-havn *Dan., Nor.* bay, harbour
Havre *Fr.* harbour
Hawd *Ar.* oasis
Hawr *Ar.* lake, marsh
He *Chin.* river
-hegység *Hung.* hills, forest
Heide *Ger.* heath, moor
Helodranon' *Malag.* bay
Higashi *Jap.* east, eastern
-ho *Kor.* lake
-hø *Nor.* peak
Hoch *Ger.* high
Hochland *Afr.* highland
Hoek, -hoek *Afr., Dut.* cape, point
-höfn *Ice.* harbour, port
-hög, -en, -högar, -högarna *Swe.* hill(s), peak, mountain
Höhe *Ger.* height
Hohen *Ger.* high, upper
-hoi *Chin.* bay
-høj, -e *Dan.* hills
-holm, -holme, -holmen *Dan., Nor., Swe.* island
Hon *Viet.* island
Hoog *Dut.* high
Hora *Czec., Ukr.* mountain
-horn *Ger.* peak
Hory *Czec.* mountains, hills
-hot *Mong.* town
-hoved *Dan.* point, headland, peninsula
-hrad *Czec.* town
Hráun *Ice.* lava
-hsi *Chin.* river
-hsia *Chin.* gorge, strait
-hsien *Chin.* district
Hu *Chin.* lake, reservoir
Huk *Dan., Ger.* cape
-huk *Swe.* cape
Huken *Nor.* cape

Idd *Ar.* well
Idehan *Ar., Berb.* sandy plain, dunes
-ike *Jap.* lake
Île(s) (I(s).) *Fr.* island(s)
Ilha(s) (I(s).) *Port.* island(s)
imeni *Russ.* 'in the name of'
Inish *Gae.* island
Insel(n) (I.) *Ger.* island(s)
Irmak *Turk.* river
'Irq *Ar.* dunes
Isla(s) (I(s).) *Span.* island(s)
Iso *Fin.* big, great
Isol, -a, -e (I.) *It.* island(s)
Isthme *Fr.* isthmus
Istmo *Span.* isthmus
-iwa *Jap.* island

Jabal *Ar.* mountain range
Järv *Est.* lake
järvi *Fin.* lake, bay, pond
-jaur, -javre *Lapp.* lake
Jazā'ir *Ar.* islands
Jazīra, jazīrat *Ar.* island
Jazireh *Farsi* island
Jebel *Ar.* mountain
Jezero *Ser.-Cr.* lake
Jezioro *Pol.* lake
Jiang *Chin.* river
Jiao *Chin.* cape
-Jima *Jap.* island
Jøkulen *Nor.* glacier, ice cap
-joki *Fin.* river
-jökull *Ice.* glacier, ice cap
Jūras Līcis *Lat.* bay, gulf

Kaap (K.) *Afr.* cape
-kai *Jap.* bay, channel, sea
-kaikyō *Jap.* strait
-kaise *Lapp.* mountain
kalnas *Lith.* hill
Kamennyy *Russ.* stony
Kampong *Cam.* village
Kampung *Malay* village
-kanaal *Dut.* canal
Kanal *Dan.* channel, gulf
Kanal *Ger., Swe.* canal
-kanal *Ser.-Cr.* channel, canal
Kanava *Fin.* canal
Kang *Kor.* river, bay
Kap (K.) *Dan., Ger.* cape, point
-kapp *Nor.* cape, point
-kaupstaður *Ice.* market town
-kaupunki *Fin.* town
Kavīr *Farsi* salt desert
Kébir *Ar.* great
Kecil *Malay* lesser, little
Kefar *Heb.* village, hamlet
-Ken *Jap.* first-order administrative division
Kep, -i (K.) *Alb.* cape
Kepulauan (Kep.) *Indo., Malay* archipelago
Keski- *Fin.* middle, central
Khalīg, Khalīj *Ar.* gulf
-khamba *Tib.* source, spring
Khawr *Ar.* bay, channel, wadi
Khlong *Thai* river
Kho Khot *Thai* isthmus
Khôr *Farsi* bay, estuary
Khrebet *Russ.* mountain range
Kita- *Jap.* north
Klein,-e, -er *Ger.* small
-klint *Dan.* cliff
Klintar *Swe.* hills
-kloof *Afr.* gorge, pass
Knude *Dan.* point
-Ko *Jap.* lake
Ko *Thai* island
-kōchi *Jap.* mountainous region
-kōgen *Jap.* plateau
Kohi *Pash.* mountains
Kol *Kaz., Kyrg.* lake
Kólpos *Gr., Turk.* gulf, bay
Kolymskoye *Russ.* mountain range
Kompong *Malay* landing place
-kop *Afr.* hill
-kopf *Ger.* hill
-köping *Swe.* market town
Körfäzi *Azeri* gulf
Körfezi *Turk.* gulf
Kosa *Russ., Ukr.* spit
-koski *Fin.* rapids
-kraal *Afr.* native village
-kraj *Czec., Pol., Ser.-Cr.* region
Krasnyy *Russ.* red
Kryazh *Russ.* ridge, hills
Kuala *Malay* bay
-kuan *Chin.* pass
Kūh(ha) *Farsi* mountain(s)
Kul *Russ.* lake
-kulle *Swe.* hill
Kum *Russ.* sandy desert
Kumpu *Fin.* hill
Kwe *Burm.* bay, gulf
-kylä *Fin.* village
Kyst, -en *Dan., Nor.* coast
Kyun(zu) *Burm.* island(s)

La *Tib.* pass
-laagte *Afr.* watercourse

Lääni *Fin.* first-order administrative division
Lac (L.) *Fr.* lake
Lacul (L.) *Rom.* lake, lagoon
Lago (L.) *It., Port., Span.* lake, lagoon
Lagoa (L.) *Port.* lagoon
Lagos *Port., Span.* lakes
Laguna (L.) *It., Span.* lagoon, lake
Lagune (L.) *Fr.* lake
-laht *Est.* bay
Lahti *Fin.* bay, gulf, cove
Lakhti *Russ.* bay, gulf
Lam *Thai* river
Lampi *Fin.* lake
Län *Swe.* first-order administrative division
Land *Ger.* first-order administrative division
-land *Dan.* region
-land *Afr., Nor.* land, province
Lande *Fr.* heath
Laut *Indo.* sea
Law *Gae.* hill, mountain
Līcis *Lat.* gulf
Lido *It.* beach, shore
Liedao *Chin.* islands
Lilla *Swe.* small
Lille *Dan., Nor.* small
Liman *Russ.* bay, gulf
Límni (L.) *Gr.* lake
Ling *Chin.* mountain range
-linna *Fin.* fort
Llano *Span.* prairie, plain
Llyn *Welsh* lake
Loch (L.) *Gae.* lake, inlet
Lough (L.) *Gae.* lake, inlet
Lum *Alb.* river
Lund *Dan.* forest
-lund, -en *Swe.* wood(s)
-luoto *Fin.* island

-maa *Est.* island
Madīnat *Ar.* town, city
Madiq *Ar.* strait
Maja *Alb.* mountains
-mäki *Fin.* hill, hillside
Mal *Alb.* mountain
Maloye, Malyy, Malyya *Russ.* little, small
Mala, Mali, Malo *Ser.-Cr.* little, small
Malaya *Belo.* small
Malé *Czec., Slovak* small
Mali *Alb.* mountain
-man *Kor.* bay
Mar *Span.* lagoon, sea
Marais *Fr.* marsh
Mare *It.* sea
Mare *Rom.* great
Marisma *Span.* marsh
-mark *Dan., Nor.* land
Marsâ *Ar.* anchorage, bay, inlet
Masabb *Ar.* river mouth, estuary
Massif *Fr.* upland, mountains
Mato *Port.* forest
Mazar *Farsi* shrine, tomb
Meer, -meer *Afr., Dut., Ger.* lake, sea
-men *Chin.* bay, gorge, channel
Mesto *Ser.-Cr., Czec.* town
Mezzo *It.* middle
Midbar *Heb.* wilderness
Mierzeja *Pol.* spit
Mifraz *Heb.* bay
Mina *Ar.* port
Minami *Jap.* south, southern
-misaki *Jap.* cape, point
Mittel *Ger.* central, middle
-mo *Nor., Swe.* heath, island
-mon *Swe.* heath
Mong *Burm.* town
Mont(s) (Mt(s).) *Fr.* hill(s), mountain(s)
Montagna (Mt.) *It.* mountain
Montagne(s) (Mt(s).) *Fr.* hill(s), mountain(s)
Montaña(s) (Mt(s).) *Span.* mountain(s)
Montanyes *Cat.* mountains
Monte(s) (Mte(s).) *It., Port., Span.* mountain(s)
Monti (Mti.) *It.* mountains
More *Russ.* sea
Mörön *Mong.* river
Moyen *Fr.* central, middle
Muang *Malay* town
Mui *Viet.* cape
Mull *Gae.* promontory
Mund, -mund *Afr.* mouth
Munkhafed *Ar.* depression
Munte (Mte.) *Rom.* mount
Munţi (Mţi.) *Rom.* mountain(s)
Muong *Malay* village
Myit *Burm.* river
Myitwanya *Burm.* mouths of river
Mynydd *Welsh* mountain
-myr *Nor., Swe.* swamp
-mýri *Ice.* swamp
Mys (M.) *Russ.* cape

-Nada *Jap.* bay, gulf
-næs *Dan.* point, cape
Nafūd *Ar.* sandy desert
Nagorye *Russ.* hills, mountains
Nagy *Hung.* big
Nahal (N.) *Heb.* river
Nahr (N.) *Ar.* river, stream
Najd *Ar.* plateau, pass
Nakhon *Thai* town
Nam *Kor., Viet.* river
-nam *Kor.* south
Namakzār *Per.* salt flat
Nan *Chin.* south, southern
-nao *Chin.* lake
-näs *Swe.* cape
Neder *Dut.* lower
Nedre *Nor.* lower
Nei *Chin.* inner
Nek *Afr.* pass
-nes *Ice., Nor.* cape
Ness, -ness *Gae.* promontory, cape
Nevada, Nevado *Span.* snow-capped mountain
Nez *Fr.* cape
Nieder *Ger.* lower
-niemi *Fin.* cape, point, peninsula, island
Nieuw, -e *Dut.* new
Nishi *Jap.* west, western
Nisos, Nisoi *Gr.* island(s)
Nizhneye, Nizhniy *Russ.* lower
Nizina *Belo., Pol.* lowland
Nizmennost *Russ.* plain, lowland
Nizni *Czec.* lower
Noord *Dut.* north, northern
Nord *Fr.* north, northern
Norra *Swe.* north, northern
Nørre *Dan.* north, northern
Norte *Port., Span.* north, northern
Nos *Bulg., Russ.* cape, point
Nosy *Malag.* island
Nouveau, Nouvelle *Fr.* new
Nova, Novi *Bulg., Port., Serb.-Cr.* new
Novaya, Novo, Novoye, Novyy *Russ.* new
Nové, Novy *Czec., Slovak* new
Novo *Port.* new
Nowa, Nowe, Nowy *Pol.* new
Nudo *Span.* mountain
Nueva, Nuevo *Span.* new
Nur *Chin.* lake
Nur *Tib.* peak
Nuruu *Mong.* mountain range
Nusa *Indo.* island
Nuur *Mong.* lake
Ny *Dan., Nor., Swe.* new

-ø *Dan., Nor.* island
-ö *Swe.* island,
-öar, -na *Swe.* islands
Ober *Ger., Ukr.* upper
Oblast *Russ.* administrative division
Öbor *Mong.* inner
Occidental *Fr., Span.* western
-odde *Dan., Nor.* point, peninsula, cape
Oeste *Span.* west, western
Oglat *Ar.* well
Oji *Alb.* bay
Ojo *Span.* spring
-Oki *Jap.* bay
-ön *Swe.* island
Ondör *Mong.* upper
Oost(er) *Dut.* east(ern)
Oraşu *Rom.* city
Ord *Gae.* point
Óri *Gr.* mountains
Oriental, -e *Fr., Span.* east, eastern
Órmos *Gr.* bay
Óros *Gr.* mountain(s)
Ort *Ger.* point, cape
Ost *Ger.* east
Øst(er) *Den., Nor.* east(ern)
Öst(ra) *Swe.* east(ern)
Ostriv *Ukr.* island
Ostrov(a) *Russ.* island(s)
Otok(i) *Ser.-Cr.* island(s)
Ouabi, Ouadi (O.) *Ar.* dry watercourse, wadi
Oud, -e *Dut.* old
Oued, -i (O.) *Ar.* watercourse
Ouest *Fr.* west, western
Ouzan *Farsi* river
Ova, -si *Turk.* plains, lowlands
Over- *Dan., Dut.* upper
Över-, Övre *Nor., Swe.* upper
-øy, -a *Nor.* island(s)
Oya *Hin.* point
Oya *Sin.* river
Ozero, Ozera (Oz.) *Russ., Ukr.* lake(s)

-pää *Fin.* hill(s), mountain
Pahta *Lapp.* hill
Pampa(s) *Span.* plain(s)
Pantanal *Port.* marsh
Pantano *Span.* reservoir
Pantao *Chin.* peninsula
Parbat *Urdu* mountain
Pas *Fr.* strait
Paso (P.) *Span.* pass
Passage *Fr.* channel
Passe *Fr.* channel
Passo (P.) *It.* pass
Pasul (P.) *Rom.* pass
Patam *Hin.* small village
Patna, -patnam *Hin.* small village
Pegunungan *Indo., Malay* mountain range
Pei, -pei *Chin.* north
Pélagos *Gr.* sea
Pen *Welsh* hill
Peña *Span.* rock, peak
Pendi *Chin.* basin, depression
Péninsule *Fr.* peninsula
Penisola (Pen.) *It.* peninsula
Pereval (Per.) *Russ.* pass
Pervo-, Pervyy- *Russ.* first
Pertuis *Fr.* channel, strait
Peski *Russ.* sand desert
Petit, -e *Fr.* small
Phanom *Thai* mountain
Phnum *Cam.* mountain
Phou *Lao.* mountain
Phu *Thai, Viet.* mountain
Piano *It.* plain
Pic *Cat., Fr.* peak
Pico(s) *Span.* peak(s)
-piggen *Dan.* peak
Pik *Russ.* peak
Pingyuan *Chin.* plain
Pique *Fr.* peak
Piton *Fr.* peak
Pivostriv *Ukr.* peninsula
Piz, Pizzo *It.* peak
Plage *Fr.* beach
Plaine *Fr.* plain
Planalto *Port.* plateau
Planina (Pl.) *Bulg., Ser.-Cr.* mountain range
Plato *Russ., Bulg.* plateau
Playa *Span.* beach
-po *Chin.* lake, wetland
Pointe (Pte.) *Fr.* point, cape
Pojezierze *Pol.* lakes
Polder *Dut.* reclaimed farmland
-pólis *Gr.* city, town
Poluostrov (Pov.) *Russ.* peninsula
Połwysep *Pol.* peninsula
Pont *Fr.* bridge
Ponta (Pta.) *Port.* point, cape
Ponte *Port.* bridge
Poort *Afr.* passage, gate
-poort *Dut.* port
Porta *Port.* pass
Porţile *Rom.* gate
Portillo *Span.* pass
Porto *It., Port., Span.* port
Potámi, Potamós *Gr.* river
Pradesh *Hin.* state
Praia *Port.* beach, shore
Presa *Span.* reservoir
Presqu'île *Fr.* peninsula
Prokhod *Bulg.* pass
Proliv *Russ.* strait
Promontorio *Span.* promontory
Průsmyk (Pr.) *Czec.* pass
Pueblo *Span.* village
Puerto (Pto.) *Span.* port
Puig *Cat.* peak
Pulau (P.) *Indo., Malay* island
Puna *Span.* desert plateau
Puncak *Indo.* peak
Punta (Pta.) *It., Span.* point, peak
Puy *Fr.* peak

Qal'at *Ar.* fort
Qanat *Ar.* canal
Qasr *Ar.* fort
Qiryat *Heb.* town
Qiuling *Chin.* plateau
Qolleh *Farsi* mountain
-qundao *Chin.* islands

Rach *Viet.* river
Rags *Lat.* cape
Rambla *Cat.* river
Ramlat *Ar.* sandy desert
Rão (R.) *Port.* river
Rann *Hin.* swampy region
Rao *I.-C.* river
Ras *Amh., Ar., Farsi* cape, point
Récif(s) *Fr.* reef(s)
Recife(s) *Port.* reef(s)
Reka *Bulg.* river
Repede *Rom.* rapids
Reprêsa *Port.* reservoir
Reshteh *Farsi* mountain range
-rettō *Jap.* group of islands, chain
Ria *Port., Span.* estuary, bay
Ribeirão (R.) *Port.* river
Ribera (R.) *Span.* river bank
Rijeka *Ser.-Cr.* river
Rio (R.) *Port., Span.* river
Rivier (R.) *Afr., Dut.* river
Riviera *It.* coastal plain, coast
Rivière (R.) *Fr.* river
Roca *Span.* rock
Rocca *It.* rock, peak
Roche *Fr.* rock
Rt *Ser.-Cr.* cape, point
Rubh', Rubha *Gae.* cape, point
-rück *Ger.* ridge
Rūd *Farsi* stream, river
Rudohorie *Slovak* mountains
Rzeka (R.) *Pol.* river

-saar *Est.* island
-saari *Fin.* island
Sabkhat, Sabkhet *Ar.* salt flats
Sadd *Ar.* dam
Sagar,-a *Hin., Urdu* lake
Sahrâ *Ar.* desert
-Saki *Jap.* cape, point
Salar *Span.* salt flat
Salina(s) *Span.* salt marsh(es)
-salmi *Fin.* strait, sound, lake, channel
Saltsjöbad *Swe.* resort
-Sammyaku *Jap.* mountain range
Samut *Thai* gulf
San (S.) *It., Port., Span.* saint
-San *Jap., Kor.* hill, mountain
-Sanchi *Jap.* mountain range
Sankt (St.) *Ger., Russ.* saint
-sanmaek *Kor.* mountain range
-sanmyaku *Jap.* mountain range
Santa (Sta.) *It., Port., Span.* saint
Santo (Sto.) *It. Port., Span.* saint
São (S.) *Port.* saint
Sarīr *Ar.* desert
Sasso *It.* mountain
Satu *Rom.* village
Saurums *Lat.* strait
Sebkha, Sebkhet *Ar.* salt flat
See, -see *Ger.* lake
-şehir *Turk.* town
Selat *Indo., Malay* strait
Selatan *Indo.* southern
-selkä *Fin.* bay, lake, ridge, hills
Selo *Ser.-Cr., Russ.* village
Selva *Port., Span.* forest, wood
Seno *Span.* bay, sound
Serir *Ar.* stony desert
Serra (Sa.) *Cat., Port.* range of hills
Serrania *Span.* mountain ridge
Severo, Severnaya, Severnoye, Severnyy (Sev.) *Russ.* north, northern
Sfântu *Rom.* saint
Shahr, -shahr *Farsi* city, town
Shamo *Chin.* desert
Shan *Chin.* hills, mountains
Shankou *Chin.* pass
Shanmo *Chin.* mountain range
Sharm *Ar.* bay
Shatt *Ar.* river mouth, estuary
-Shima *Jap.* island
Shimāli *Ar.* northern
-Shotō *Jap.* group of islands
-shui *Chin.* river
-shuiku *Chin.* reservoir
Sierra (Sa.) *Span.* mountain range
-sjö, -sjön, -sjø *Swe., Nor.* lake
-sjøen *Dan.* sea
-sjór *Ice.* lake
-sker *Ice.* island
-skär *Swe.* island, rock, cape
-skog, -skogen *Nor., Swe.* wood(s)
-skov *Dan.* forest
Slieve *Gae.* hill, mountain
Sø *Dan., Nor.* lake
Söder, Södra *Swe.* south, southern
Sør *Nor.* south, southern
Solonchak *Russ.* salt lake, marsh
Sønder, Søndra *Dan.* south, southern
Song *Viet.* river
Souk *Ar.* market
-spitze *Ger.* peak, mountain
-spruit *Afr.* stream
Sredna, Sredno *Bulg.* middle, central
Sredne, Sredneye *Russ.* middle, central
Srednja *Ser.-Cr.* middle, central
-stad *Afr., Nor., Swe.* town
-stadt *Ger.* town
-staður *Ice.* town
Stara, Stari *Ser.-Cr.* old
Stará, Staré, Stary *Czec.* old
Staraya, Staroye, Staryy *Russ.* old
Stare, Staro, Stary *Ukr.* old
Stausee *Ger.* reservoir
Stenón *Gr.* strait, pass
Step *Russ.* steppe
Stor, -a *Swe.* big
Store *Dan.* big
-strand *Dan., Ger., Nor., Swe.* beach
-strede *Nor.* straits
Strelka *Russ.* spit
-strete *Nor.* straits
Stretto (Str.) *It.* strait
Strædet (Str.) *Dan.* strait
-ström, -strömmen *Swe.* stream(s)
-stroom *Afr.* large river
Sud *Fr.* south, southern
Süd, -er *Ger.* south, southern
Suid *Afr.* south, southern
-Suidō *Jap.* strait, channel
Sul *Port.* south, southern
Sûn *Burm.* cape
-sund, -et *Swe., Nor.* sound, estuary, inlet
Sungai *Indo., Malay* river
Sur *Span.* south, southern
Sveti *Bulg.* saint
Syd *Dan., Swe.* south, southern
Sýsla *Ice.* first-order administrative division

-tag *Uighur* mountain
Tai -tai *Chin.* tower
-Take *Jap.* mountain
Tal *Mong.* plain, steppe
-tal *Ger.* valley
Tall *Ar.* hills
Tanjona *Malag.* cape, point
Tanjung, Tanjong (Tg.) *Indo., Malay.* cape, point
Tao *Chin.* island
Tasik *Malay* lake
Tassili *Ar.* rocky plateau
Tau *Russ.* mountain range
Taung *Burm.* mountain
Taungdan. *Burm.* mountain range
Taunggya *Burm.* pass
-tekojärvi *Fin.* reservoir
Teluk *Indo., Malay* bay, gulf
Ténéré *Berb.* desert
Tengah *Indo.* middle, central
-thal *Ger.* valley
Thok *Tib.* town
Tien *Chin.* lake, marsh
Tierra *Span.* land, country
Timur *Indo.* eastern
-tind *Nor.* peak
-ting *Chin.* mountain
Tjärn, -en, -et *Swe.* lake
-Tō *Jap.* island
Tong *Kor.* village, town
Tong *Burm., Thai, Kor.* mountain range
Tonlé *Cam.* lake
Top *Dut.* peak
-topp, -en *Nor.* peak
-träsk *Swe.* lake, swamp
Tsangpo *Tib.* large river
Tso *Tib.* lake
Tsu *Jap.* entrance, bay
Tsui *Chin.* cape, point
Tulur *Ar.* hill
-tunturi *Fin.* hill(s), mountain(s), ridge

Uad *Ar.* dry watercourse, wadi
Über *Ger.* upper
-udde, -udden *Swe.* point, cape
Uebi *Som.* river
Ujung *Indo., Malay* cape
Unter- *Ger.* lower
Us *Mong.* water
Ust, Ustye *Russ.* river mouth
Utara *Indo.* north, northern
Uttar *Hin.* north, northern
Uul *Mong., Russ.* mountain range

-vaara *Fin.* hill, mountain ridge, peak
Vaart *Dut.* canal
-våg *Nor.* bay
Val *Fr., Port., Span.* valley
Valea *Rom.* valley
-vall, -en *Swe.* mountain
Valle *It., Span.* valley
Vallée *Fr.* valley
Valli *It.* lake, lagoon
-város *Hung.* town
-varre *Nor.* mountain
Väst, Västra *Swe.* west, western
-vatn *Ice., Nor.* lake
-vatnet *Nor.* lake
-vatten, vattnet *Swe.* lake
-vecchio *It.* old
Vechi *Rom.* old
-ved, -veden *Swe.* hills
Veld, -veld *Afr.* field
Velha, Velho *Port.* old
Velika, Velike, Veliki, Veliko *Ser.-Cr., Slov.* big, large
Velikaya, Velikiy *Russ.* big, large
Velká, Velké, Velký *Czec.* big, large
Verkhne, Verkhniy *Russ.* upper
-vesi *Fin.* water, lake, bay, sound, strait
Vest, Vester, Vestre *Dan., Nor.* west, western
-vidda *Nor.* plateau
Vieille, Vieux *Fr.* old
Vieja, Vejo *Span.* old
Vig *Dan.* bay, inlet, cove, lagoon, lake
-vik *Ice.* bay
-vik, -a, -en *Nor., Swe.* bay, gulf, inlet, lake
Vila *Port.* small town
Villa *Span.* town
Ville *Fr.* town
Vinh *Viet.* bay
Vîrful (Vf.) *Rom.* peak, mountain
-viz *Hung.* river
-víztároló *Hung.* reservoir
-vlei *Afr.* lake, salt pan
-vliet *Dut.* canal
-vloer *Afr.* salt pan
Vodokhranilishche (Vdkhr.) *Russ.* reservoir
Vodoskovyshche (Vdskh.) *Ukr.* reservoir
Volcán (Vol.) *Span.* volcano, mountain
Vorota *Russ.* pass, channel, strait
Vostochno, Vostochnyy *Russ.* east, eastern
-vötn *Ice.* lakes
Vozvyshennost *Russ.* heights, uplands
Vozyera *Belo.* lake
Vrata *Bulg.* gate, pass
Vrchovina *Czec.* mountainous country
Vrch(y) *Czec.* mountain (range)
Vung *Viet.* bay, gulf
-vuori *Fin.* mountain, hill
Vychodné *Slovak* east, eastern
Vysochyna *Ukr.* upland

-waard *Dut.* polder
Wadi (W.) *Ar.* dry watercourse
Wāhât *Ar.* oasis
Wald *Ger.* forest, mountains
-Wan *Chin., Jap.* bay, harbour
Wāw *Ar.* well
Webi *Amh.* river
Wes *Afr.* west, western
Wielka, Wielki, Wielko *Pol.* big, large
Woestyn *Afr.* desert
Wysoka, Wysoki *Pol.* upper
Wyżyna *Pol.* plateau

Xi *Chin.* river
Xia *Chin.* gorge, strait
Xiao *Chin.* small

Yam *Heb.* sea
-Yama *Jap.* mountain
-yan *Chin.* gorge, island
Yang *Chin.* bay, sea, sound
Yangi *Russ.* new
Yazovir *Bulg.* reservoir
Yeni *Turk.* new
Yli *Fin.* upper
Ynys *Welsh* island
Yoma *Burm.* mountain range
Ytre-, Ytter- *Nor., Swe.* outer
-yuan *Chin.* stream
Yugo- *Ser.-Cr.* south, southern
Yunhe *Chin.* canal
Yuzhni, Yuzhno *Russ.* south, southern

-Zaki *Jap.* point
Zalew *Pol.* lagoon, swamp
Zaliv *Russ.* bay, gulf
-Zan *Jap.* mountain
Zangbo *Tib.* stream, river
Zapadnaya, Zapadno, Zapadnyi (Zap.) *Russ.* west, western
Zatoka *Pol., Ukr.* bay, gulf
-zee *Dut.* lake, sea
Zemlya *Russ.* land, island(s)
Zhang *Chin.* mountain
-zhou *Chin.* island
Zhong *Chin.* middle, central
Zhou *Chin.* island
Zizhiqu *Chin.* autonomous region
Zuid, Zuider *Dut.* south, southern

# INDEX TO WORLD MAPS

## HOW TO USE THE INDEX

The index contains the names of all the principal places and features shown on the World and City Maps. Each name is followed by an additional entry in italics giving the country or region within which it is located. The alphabetical order of names composed of two or more words is governed primarily by the first word, then by the second, and then by the country or region name that follows. This is an example of the rule:

| | | | |
|---|---|---|---|
| **Mir** *Niger* | 14°5N 11°59E | **259** | F2 |
| **Mīr Kūh** *Iran* | 26°22N 58°55E | **247** | E8 |
| **Mīr Shahdād** *Iran* | 26°15N 58°29E | **247** | E8 |
| **Mira** *Italy* | 45°26N 12°8E | **199** | C9 |

Physical features composed of a proper name (Erie) and a description (Lake) are positioned alphabetically by the proper name. The description is positioned after the proper name and is usually abbreviated:

**Erie, L.** *N. Amer.* 42°15N 81°0W **312** D4

Where a description forms part of a settlement or administrative name, however, it is always written in full and put in its true alphabetical position:

**Mount Olive** *U.S.A.* 39°4N 89°44W **310** E7

Names beginning with M' and Mc are indexed as if they were spelled Mac. Names beginning St. are alphabetized under Saint, but Sankt, Sint, Sant', Santa and San are all spelt in full and are alphabetized accordingly. If the same place name occurs two or more times in the index and all are in the same country, each is followed by the name of the administrative subdivision in which it is located.

The geographical co-ordinates which follow each name in the index give the latitude and longitude of each place. The first co-ordinate indicates latitude – the distance north or south of the Equator. The second co-ordinate indicates longitude – the distance east or west of the Greenwich Meridian. Both latitude and longitude are measured in degrees and minutes (there are 60 minutes in a degree). Latitude and longitude references are not used on the Central Area City Maps.

The latitude is followed by N(orth) or S(outh) and the longitude by E(ast) or W(est).

The number in bold type which follows the geographical co-ordinates refers to the number of the map page where that feature or place will be found. This is usually the largest scale at which the place or feature appears.

The letter and figure that are immediately after the page number give the grid square on the map page, within which the feature is situated. The letter represents the latitude and the figure the longitude. A lower-case letter immediately after the page number refers to an inset map on that page.

In some cases the feature itself may fall within the specified square, while the name is outside. This is usually the case only with features that are larger than a grid square.

Rivers are indexed to their mouths or confluences, and carry the symbol ➙ after their names. The following symbols are also used in the index: ■ country, ⊠ overseas territory or dependency, □ first-order administrative area, ☆ U.S. county, △ national park, ⌓ other park (provincial park, nature reserve or game reserve), ❂ Australian aboriginal land, ▲ U.S. Indian reservation ✈ (LHR) principal airport (and location identifier).

## HOW TO PRONOUNCE PLACE NAMES

English-speaking people usually have no difficulty in reading and pronouncing correctly English place names. However, foreign place name pronunciations may present many problems. Such problems can be minimized by following some simple rules. However, these rules cannot be applied to all situations, and there will be many exceptions.

1. In general, stress each syllable equally, unless your experience suggests otherwise.
2. Pronounce the letter 'a' as a broad 'a' as in 'arm'.
3. Pronounce the letter 'e' as a short 'e' as in 'elm'.
4. Pronounce the letter 'i' as a cross between a short 'i' and long 'e', as the two 'i's in 'California'.
5. Pronounce the letter 'o' as an intermediate 'o' as in 'soft'.
6. Pronounce the letter 'u' as an intermediate 'u' as in 'sure'.
7. Pronounce consonants hard, except in the Romance-language areas where 'g's are likely to be pronounced softly like 'j' in 'jam'; 'j' itself may be pronounced as 'y'; and 'x's may be pronounced as 'h'.
8. For names in mainland China, pronounce 'q' like the 'ch' in 'chin', 'x' like the 'sh' in 'she', 'zh' like the 'j' in 'jam', and 'z' as if it were spelled 'dz'. In general, pronounce 'a' as in 'father', 'e' as in 'but', 'i' as in 'keep', 'o' as in 'or', and 'u' as in 'rule'.

Moreover, English has no diacritical marks (accent and pronunciation signs), although some languages do. The following is a brief and general guide to the pronunciation of those most frequently used in the principal Western European languages.

| | | **Pronunciation as in** |
|---|---|---|
| **French** | é | day and shows that the 'e' is to be pronounced; e.g. Orléans. |
| | è | mare |
| | î | used over any vowel and does not affect pronunciation; shows contraction of the name, usually omission of 's' following a vowel. |
| | ç | 's' before 'a', 'o' and 'u'. |
| | ë, ï, ü | over 'e', 'i' and 'u' when they are used with another vowel and shows that each is to be pronounced. |
| **German** | ä | fate |
| | ö | fur |
| | ü | no English equivalent; like French 'tu'. |
| **Italian** | à, é | over vowels and indicates stress. |
| **Portuguese** | ã, õ | vowels pronounced nasally. |
| | ç | boss |
| | á | shows stress. |
| | ô | shows that a vowel has an 'i' or 'u' sound combined with it. |
| **Spanish** | ñ | canyon |
| | ü | pronounced as 'w' and separately from adjoining vowels. |
| | á | usually indicates that this is a stressed vowel. |

## ABBREVIATIONS

*A.C.T.* – Australian Capital Territory
*A.R.* – Autonomous Region
*Afghan.* – Afghanistan
*Afr.* – Africa
*Ala.* – Alabama
*Alta.* – Alberta
*Amer.* – America(n)
*Ant.* – Antilles
*Arch.* – Archipelago
*Ariz.* – Arizona
*Ark.* – Arkansas
*Atl. Oc.* – Atlantic Ocean
*B.* – Baie, Bahía, Bay, Bucht, Bugt
*B.C.* – British Columbia
*Bangla.* – Bangladesh
*Barr.* – Barrage
*Bos.-H.* – Bosnia-Herzegovina
*C.* – Cabo, Cap, Cape, Coast
*C.A.R.* – Central African Republic
*C. Prov.* – Cape Province
*Calif.* – California
*Cat.* – Catarata
*Cent.* – Central
*Chan.* – Channel
*Colo.* – Colorado
*Conn.* – Connecticut
*Cord.* – Cordillera
*Cr.* – Creek
*Czech.* – Czech Republic
*D.C.* – District of Columbia
*Del.* – Delaware
*Dem.* – Democratic
*Dep.* – Dependency
*Des.* – Desert
*Dét.* – Détroit
*Dist.* – District
*Dj.* – Djebel
*Dom. Rep.* – Dominican Republic
*E.* – East
*El Salv.* – El Salvador
*Eq. Guin.* – Equatorial Guinea
*Est.* – Estrecho
*Falk. Is.* – Falkland Is.
*Fd.* – Fjord
*Fla.* – Florida
*Fr.* – French
*G.* – Golfe, Golfo, Gulf, Guba, Gebel
*Ga.* – Georgia
*Gt.* – Great, Greater
*Guinea-Biss.* – Guinea-Bissau
*H.K.* – Hong Kong
*H.P.* – Himachal Pradesh
*Hants.* – Hampshire
*Harb.* – Harbor, Harbour
*Hd.* – Head
*Hts.* – Heights
*I.(s).* – Île, Ilha, Insel, Isla, Island, Isle
*Ill.* – Illinois
*Ind.* – Indiana
*Ind. Oc.* – Indian Ocean
*Ivory C.* – Ivory Coast
*J.* – Jabal, Jebel
*Jaz.* – Jazīrah
*Junc.* – Junction
*K.* – Kap, Kapp
*Kans.* – Kansas
*Kep.* – Kepulauan
*Ky.* – Kentucky
*L.* – Lac, Lacul, Lago, Lagoa, Lake, Limni, Loch, Lough
*La.* – Louisiana
*Ld.* – Land
*Liech.* – Liechtenstein
*Lux.* – Luxembourg
*Mad. P.* – Madhya Pradesh
*Madag.* – Madagascar
*Man.* – Manitoba
*Mass.* – Massachusetts
*Md.* – Maryland
*Me.* – Maine
*Medit. S.* – Mediterranean Sea
*Mich.* – Michigan
*Minn.* – Minnesota
*Miss.* – Mississippi
*Mo.* – Missouri
*Mont.* – Montana
*Mozam.* – Mozambique
*Mt.(s)* – Mont, Montaña, Mountain
*Mte.* – Monte
*Mti.* – Monti
*N.* – Nord, Norte, North, Northern, Nouveau, Nahal, Nahr
*N.B.* – New Brunswick
*N.C.* – North Carolina
*N. Cal.* – New Caledonia
*N. Dak.* – North Dakota
*N.H.* – New Hampshire
*N.I.* – North Island
*N.J.* – New Jersey
*N. Mex.* – New Mexico
*N.S.* – Nova Scotia
*N.S.W.* – New South Wales
*N.W.T.* – North West Territory
*N.Y.* – New York
*N.Z.* – New Zealand
*Nac.* – Nacional
*Nat.* – National
*Nebr.* – Nebraska
*Neths.* – Netherlands
*Nev.* – Nevada
*Nfld & L..* – Newfoundland and Labrador
*Nic.* – Nicaragua
*O.* – Oued, Ouadi
*Occ.* – Occidentale
*Okla.* – Oklahoma
*Ont.* – Ontario
*Or.* – Orientale
*Oreg.* – Oregon
*Os.* – Ostrov
*Oz.* – Ozero
*P.* – Pass, Passo, Pasul, Pulau
*P.E.I.* – Prince Edward Island
*Pa.* – Pennsylvania
*Pac. Oc.* – Pacific Ocean
*Papua N.G.* – Papua New Guinea
*Pass.* – Passage
*Peg.* – Pegunungan
*Pen.* – Peninsula, Péninsule
*Phil.* – Philippines
*Pk.* – Peak
*Plat.* – Plateau
*Prov.* – Province, Provincial
*Pt.* – Point
*Pta.* – Ponta, Punta
*Pte.* – Pointe
*Qué.* – Québec
*Queens.* – Queensland
*R.* – Rio, River
*R.I.* – Rhode Island
*Ra.* – Range
*Raj.* – Rajasthan
*Recr.* – Recreational, Récréatif
*Reg.* – Region
*Rep.* – Republic
*Res.* – Reserve, Reservoir
*Rhld-Pfz.* – Rheinland-Pfalz
*S.* – South, Southern, Sur
*Si. Arabia* – Saudi Arabia
*S.C.* – South Carolina
*S. Dak.* – South Dakota
*S.I.* – South Island
*S. Leone* – Sierra Leone
*Sa.* – Serra, Sierra
*Sask.* – Saskatchewan
*Scot.* – Scotland
*Sd.* – Sound
*Sev.* – Severnaya
*Sib.* – Siberia
*Sprs.* – Springs
*St.* – Saint
*Sta.* – Santa
*Ste.* – Sainte
*Sto.* – Santo
*Str.* – Strait, Stretto
*Switz.* – Switzerland
*Tas.* – Tasmania
*Tenn.* – Tennessee
*Terr.* – Territory, Territoire
*Tex.* – Texas
*Tg.* – Tanjung
*Trin. & Tob.* – Trinidad & Tobago
*U.A.E.* – United Arab Emirates
*U.K.* – United Kingdom
*U.S.A.* – United States of America
*Univ.* – University, Université, Universidad
*Ut. P.* – Uttar Pradesh
*Va.* – Virginia
*Vdkhr.* – Vodokhranilishche
*Vdskh.* – Vodoskhovyshche
*Vf.* – Vîrful
*Vic.* – Victoria
*Vol.* – Volcano
*Vt.* – Vermont
*W.* – Wadi, West
*W. Va.* – West Virginia
*Wall. & F. Is.* – Wallis and Futuna Is.
*Wash.* – Washington
*Wis.* – Wisconsin
*Wlkp.* – Wielkopolski
*Wyo.* – Wyoming
*Yorks.* – Yorkshire

# A


A ʻÂli an Nîl = Upper Nile □ South Sudan 9°30N 33°0E 257 F3
A Baiuca Spain 43°19N 8°29W 194 B2
A Baña = San Vicenzo Spain 42°58N 8°46W 194 C2
A Cañiza Spain 42°13N 8°16W 194 C2
A Carballa Spain 43°13N 8°54W 194 B2
A Carreira Spain 43°21N 8°12W 194 B2
A Coruña Spain 43°20N 8°25W 194 B2
A Coruña □ Spain 43°10N 8°30W 194 B2
A Cruz do Incio Spain 42°39N 7°21W 194 C3
A Estrada Spain 42°43N 8°27W 194 C2
A Feira do Monte Spain 43°12N 7°34W 194 B3
A Fonsagrada Spain 43°8N 7°4W 194 B3
A Guarda Spain 41°56N 8°52W 194 D2
A Gudiña Spain 42°4N 7°8W 194 C3
A Pobre Spain 42°58N 7°3W 194 C3
A Ramallosa Spain 42°45N 8°30W 194 C2
A Rúa Spain 42°24N 7°6W 194 C3
A Serra de Outes Spain 42°52N 8°55W 194 C2
A Shau Vietnam 16°6N 107°22E 236 D6
A.N.Z. Stadium Sydney, Australia 33°51S 151°5E 139 B1
A.R.M.M. = Muslim Mindanao □ Phil. 8°0N 123°0E 233 H3
Aabenraa Denmark 55°3N 9°25E 163 J3
Aabybro Denmark 57°10N 9°44E 163 G3
Aachen Germany 50°45N 6°6E 178 E2
Aalām Iraq 33°19N 44°23E 113 B2
Aalborg Denmark 57°2N 9°54E 163 G3
Aalborg Bugt Denmark 56°50N 10°35E 163 H4
Aalen Germany 48°51N 10°6E 179 G6
Aalestrup Denmark 56°42N 9°29E 163 H3
Aalsmeer Neths. 52°16N 4°46E 112 B1
Aalst Belgium 50°56N 4°2E 170 D4
Aalten Neths. 51°56N 6°35E 170 C6
Aalter Belgium 51°5N 3°28E 170 C3
Äänekoski Finland 62°36N 25°44E 160 E21
Aarau Switz. 47°23N 8°4E 179 H4
Aarberg Switz. 47°2N 7°16E 179 H3
Aare → Switz. 47°33N 8°14E 179 H4
Aargau □ Switz. 47°26N 8°10E 179 H4
Aarhus Denmark 56°8N 10°11E 163 H4
Aarlen = Arlon Belgium 49°42N 5°49E 170 E5
Aars Denmark 56°48N 9°30E 163 H3
Aarschot Belgium 50°59N 4°49E 170 D4
Aasiaat Greenland 68°43N 52°56W 154 D5
Ab-i-Istada Afghan. 32°29N 67°55E 240 B3
Ab-i-Panja = Pyandzh → Asia 37°6N 68°20E 240 A2
Aba Sichuan, China 32°59N 101°42E 228 A3
Aba Dem. Rep. of the Congo 3°58N 30°17E 268 B3
Aba Nigeria 5°10N 7°19E 263 D6
Âbâ, Jazîrat Sudan 13°30N 32°31E 257 E3
Abacaxis → Brazil 3°54S 58°47W 329 D6
Abaco I. Bahamas 26°25N 77°10W 320 A4
Abadab, J. Sudan 18°54N 35°56E 256 D4
Ābādān Iran 30°22N 48°20E 247 D6
Abade Ethiopia 9°22N 38°3E 257 F4
Ābādeh Iran 31°8N 52°40E 247 D7
Abadín Spain 43°21N 7°29W 194 B3
Abadla Algeria 31°2N 2°45W 261 B4
Abaeté Brazil 19°9S 45°27W 333 E2
Abaeté → Brazil 18°2S 45°12W 333 E2
Abaetetuba Brazil 1°40S 48°50W 332 B2
Abagnar Qi = Xilinhot China 43°52N 116°2E 226 C9
Abah, Tanjung Indonesia 8°46S 115°38E 231 K18
Abai Paraguay 25°58S 55°54W 335 B4
Abakaliki Nigeria 6°22N 8°2E 263 D6
Abakan Russia 53°40N 91°10E 217 B12
Abala Congo 1°17S 15°35E 264 C3
Abala Niger 14°56N 3°22E 263 C5
Abalak Niger 15°22N 6°21E 263 B6
Abalemma Algeria 20°51N 5°59E 261 D6
Abalemma Niger 16°12N 7°50E 263 B6
Abalessa Algeria 22°58N 4°47E 261 D5
Abana Turkey 41°59N 34°1E 212 B6
Abancay Peru 13°35S 72°55W 330 C3
Abang, Gunung Indonesia 8°16S 115°25E 231 J18
Abanga → Gabon 0°20S 10°30E 264 C2
Abano Terme Italy 45°22N 11°46E 199 C8
Abapó Bolivia 18°48S 63°25W 331 D5
Abarán Spain 38°12N 1°23W 197 G3
Abariringa Kiribati 2°50S 171°40W 277 A16
Abarqū Iran 31°10N 53°20E 247 D7
Abasha Georgia 42°11N 42°13E 191 J6
Abashiri Japan 44°0N 144°15E 220 B12
Abashiri-Wan Japan 44°0N 144°30E 220 C12
Abau Papua N. G. 10°11S 148°46E 286 F5
Abaújszántó Hungary 48°16N 21°12E 182 B6
Abava → Latvia 57°6N 21°54E 184 A8
Ābay = Nîl el Azraq → Sudan 15°38N 32°31E 257 D3
Abay Kazakhstan 49°38N 72°53E 217 C8
Abaya, L. Ethiopia 6°30N 37°50E 257 F4
Abaza Russia 52°39N 90°6E 217 B12
Abba C.A.R. 5°20N 15°11E 264 A3
Abbadia di Fiastra ⌂ Italy 43°12N 13°24E 199 E10
Abbadia San Salvatore Italy 42°53N 11°41E 199 F8
ʻAbbāsābād Iran 33°34N 58°23E 247 C8
Abbay = Nîl el Azraq → Sudan 15°38N 32°31E 257 D3
Abbaye, Pt. U.S.A. 46°58N 88°8W 308 B9
Abbazia = Opatija Croatia 45°21N 14°17E 199 C11
Abbé, L. Ethiopia 11°8N 41°47E 257 E5
Abbeville Somme, France 50°6N 1°49E 173 B8
Abbeville Ala., U.S.A. 31°34N 85°15W 316 D4
Abbeville Ga., U.S.A. 31°59N 83°18W 316 D6
Abbeville La., U.S.A. 29°58N 92°8W 314 G8
Abbeville S.C., U.S.A. 34°11N 82°23W 316 A7
Abbey Wood U.K. 51°29N 0°7E 125 B4
Abbeyfeale Ireland 52°23N 9°18W 166 D2
Abbeyleix Ireland 52°54N 7°22W 166 D4
Abbiategrasso Italy 45°24N 8°54E 198 C5
Abbot Ice Shelf Antarctica 73°0S 92°0W 151 D16
Abbotsford Canada 49°5N 122°20W 296 D4
Abbottabad Pakistan 34°10N 73°15E 242 B5
Abbou, O. ben → Algeria 28°32N 5°14E 261 C6
ABC Islands W. Indies 12°15N 69°0W 322 g
Abcoude Neths. 52°17N 4°59E 112 B2
Abd al Kūrī Yemen 12°5N 52°20E 249 D6
Ābdānān Iran 32°56N 47°28E 213 F12
Ābdar Iran 30°16N 55°19E 247 D7
Âbdin Egypt 30°2N 31°14E 117 A2
ʻAbdolābād Iran 34°12N 56°30E 247 C8
Abdulino Russia 53°42N 53°40E 216 B4
Abdullah South Sudan 5°30N 29°55E 257 F3
Abdulpur Bangla. 24°15N 88°59E 243 G13
Abéché Chad 13°50N 20°35E 259 F4
Abejar Spain 41°48N 2°47W 196 D2
Abekr Sudan 12°45N 28°50E 257 E2
Abel Tasman △ N.Z. 40°59S 173°3E 285 A8
Abengourou Ivory C. 6°42N 3°27W 262 D4
Abeno Japan 34°38N 135°31E 133 B2
Abenójar Spain 38°53N 4°21W 195 G6
Åbenrå = Aabenraa Denmark 55°3N 9°25E 163 J3
Abensberg Germany 48°48N 11°51E 179 G7
Abeokuta Nigeria 7°3N 3°19E 263 D5
Aberaeron U.K. 52°15N 4°15W 169 E3
Aberayron = Aberaeron U.K. 52°15N 4°15W 169 E3
Aberchirder U.K. 57°34N 2°37W 167 D6
Abercorn = Mbala Zambia 8°46S 31°24E 269 D3
Abercorn Australia 25°12S 151°5E 281 D5
Abercrombie River △ Australia 34°5S 149°40E 283 C8
Aberdare U.K. 51°43N 3°27W 169 F4
Aberdare △ Kenya 0°22S 36°44E 268 C4
Aberdare Ra. Kenya 0°15S 36°50E 268 C4
Aberdaugleddau = Milford Haven U.K. 51°42N 5°7W 169 F2
Aberdeen N.S.W., Australia 32°9S 150°56E 283 B9
Aberdeen Sask., Canada 52°20N 106°8W 297 C7
Aberdeen Hong Kong, China 22°14N 114°8E 122 B2
Aberdeen Eastern Cape, S. Africa 32°28S 24°2E 270 D3
Aberdeen C. of Aberd., U.K. 57°9N 2°5W 167 D6
Aberdeen Idaho, U.S.A. 42°57N 112°50W 304 E7
Aberdeen Md., U.S.A. 39°31N 76°10W 309 F15
Aberdeen Miss., U.S.A. 33°49N 88°33W 315 E10
Aberdeen Ohio, U.S.A. 38°39N 83°46W 311 F13
Aberdeen S. Dak., U.S.A. 45°28N 98°29W 308 C4
Aberdeen Wash., U.S.A. 46°59N 123°50W 306 D3
Aberdeen, City of □ U.K. 57°10N 2°10W 167 D6
Aberdeen Country Park ⌂ Hong Kong, China 22°16N 114°9E 122 B2
Aberdeen L. Canada 64°30N 99°0W 294 E12
Aberdeenshire □ U.K. 57°17N 2°36W 167 D6
Aberdour U.K. 56°3N 3°18W 121 A2
Aberdour Castle U.K. 56°3N 3°18W 121 A2
Aberdovey = Aberdyfi U.K. 52°33N 4°3W 169 E3
Aberdyfi U.K. 52°33N 4°3W 169 E3
Aberfeldy U.K. 56°37N 3°51W 167 E5
Aberfoyle U.K. 56°11N 4°23W 167 E4
Abergavenny U.K. 51°49N 3°1W 169 F4
Abergele U.K. 53°17N 3°35W 168 D4
Abergwaun = Fishguard U.K. 52°0N 4°58W 169 E3
Aberhonddu = Brecon U.K. 51°57N 3°23W 169 F4
Abermaw = Barmouth U.K. 52°44N 4°4W 168 E3
Abernathy U.S.A. 33°50N 101°51W 314 E4
Aberpennar = Mountain Ash U.K. 51°40N 3°23W 169 F4
Abert, L. U.S.A. 42°38N 120°14W 304 E3
Abertawe = Swansea U.K. 51°37N 3°57W 169 F4
Aberteifi = Cardigan U.K. 52°5N 4°40W 169 E3
Aberystwyth U.K. 52°25N 4°5W 169 E3
Abfanggraben → Germany 48°10N 11°41E 131 A3
Abhā Si. Arabia 18°0N 42°34E 248 C3
Abhar Iran 36°9N 49°13E 213 D13
Abhayapuri India 26°24N 90°38E 241 B3
Abia □ Nigeria 5°30N 7°35E 263 D6
Abide Turkey 38°55N 29°20E 205 C11
Abidiya Sudan 18°18N 34°3E 256 D3
Abidjan Ivory C. 5°26N 3°58W 262 D4
Abilene Kans., U.S.A. 38°55N 97°13W 308 F5
Abilene Tex., U.S.A. 32°28N 99°43W 314 E5
Abingdon Oxon., U.K. 51°40N 1°17W 169 F6
Abingdon Ill., U.S.A. 40°48N 90°24W 310 D6
Abingdon Va., U.S.A. 36°43N 81°59W 309 G13
Abingdon, I. = Pinta, I. Ecuador 0°35N 90°44W 330 a
Abington Reef Australia 18°0S 149°35E 280 B4
Abiod, Remel el Tunisia 31°45N 9°35E 261 B6
Abisko △ Sweden 68°18N 18°44E 160 B18
Abitau → Canada 59°53N 109°3W 297 B7
Abitibi → Canada 51°3N 80°55W 298 B3
Abitibi, L. Canada 48°40N 79°40W 298 C4
Abiy Adi Ethiopia 13°39N 39°3E 257 E4
Abiyata, L. Ethiopia 7°37N 38°36E 266 C4
Abiyata-Shala △ Ethiopia 7°40N 38°37E 257 F4
Abkhaz Republic = Abkhazia □ Georgia 43°12N 41°5E 191 J5
Abkhazia □ Georgia 43°12N 41°5E 191 J5
Ablon-sur-Seine France 48°43N 2°25E 134 B3
Abminga Australia 26°8S 134°51E 281 D1
Abnûb Egypt 27°18N 31°4E 256 B3
Åbo = Turku Finland 60°30N 22°19E 188 B2
Abo, Massif d' Chad 21°41N 16°8E 259 D3
Abohar India 30°10N 74°10E 242 D6
Aboisso Ivory C. 5°30N 3°5W 262 D4
Abolo Congo 0°8N 14°16E 264 B2
Abomey Benin 7°10N 2°5E 263 D5
Abong-Mbang Cameroon 4°0N 13°8E 264 B2
Abongabong Indonesia 4°15N 96°48E 234 B1
Abonnema Nigeria 4°41N 6°49E 263 E6
Abony Hungary 47°12N 20°3E 182 C5
Abor Hills India 28°25N 94°46E 241 A5
Aborlan Phil. 9°26N 118°33E 233 G2
Aboso Ghana 5°23N 1°57W 262 D4
Abou-Deïa Chad 11°20N 19°20E 259 F3
Abou-Goulem Chad 13°37N 21°38E 259 F4
Abou-Telfan ⌂ Chad 12°2N 18°58E 259 F3
Abovyan Armenia 40°16N 44°37E 191 K7
Aboyne U.K. 57°4N 2°47W 167 D6
Abra □ Phil. 17°35N 120°45E 232 C3
Abra de Ilog Phil. 13°27N 120°44E 232 E3
Abra Pampa Argentina 22°43S 65°42W 334 A2
Abraham L. Canada 52°15N 116°35W 296 C5
Abramtsevo Russia 55°49N 37°49E 129 B3
Abrantes Portugal 39°24N 8°7W 195 F2
Abreojos, Pta. Mexico 26°50N 113°40W 318 B2
Abri Esh Shamâliya, Sudan 20°50N 30°27E 256 C3
Abri Janub Kordofân, Sudan 11°40N 30°21E 257 E3
Abrolhos, Banco dos Brazil 18°0S 38°0W 333 E4
Abrud Romania 46°19N 23°5E 182 D8
Abruzzo □ Italy 42°15N 14°0E 199 F10
Absaroka Range U.S.A. 44°45N 109°50W 304 D9
Abşeron Yarımadası Azerbaijan 40°28N 49°57E 191 K9
Abtenau Austria 47°33N 13°21E 180 D6
Abu India 24°41N 72°50E 242 G5
Abū aḍ Ḍuhūr Syria 35°44N 37°2E 250 C8
Abū al Abyad U.A.E. 24°11N 53°50E 247 E7
Abū al Khaşīb Iraq 30°25N 48°0E 246 D5
Abū ʻAlī Si. Arabia 27°20N 49°27E 247 E6
Abū ʻAlī → Lebanon 34°25N 35°50E 250 D6
Abū ʻArīsh Si. Arabia 16°53N 42°48E 248 C3
Abu ʻAweigîla Egypt 30°50N 34°7E 251 H5
Abû Ballas Egypt 24°26N 27°36E 256 C2
Abu Deleiq Sudan 15°57N 33°48E 257 D3
Abu Dhabi = Abū Ẓāby U.A.E. 24°28N 54°22E 247 E7
Abu Dis Sudan 19°12N 33°38E 256 D3
Abu Dis West Bank 31°46N 35°16E 123 B2
Abu Dom Sudan 16°18N 32°25E 257 D3
Abū Du'ān Syria 36°25N 38°15E 213 D8
Abu el Gaīn, W. → Egypt 29°35N 33°30E 251 J4
Abû en Numrus Egypt 29°57N 31°12E 117 B2
Abu Fatma, Ras Sudan 22°25N 36°25E 256 C4
Abu Gabra Sudan 11°2N 26°50E 257 E2
Abu Ga'da, W. → Egypt 29°15N 32°53E 251 J3
Abu Gelba Sudan 13°11N 31°52E 257 E3
Abu Ghosh Israel 31°48N 35°6E 123 B1
Abu Gubeiha Sudan 11°30N 31°15E 257 E3
Abu Habl, Khawr → Sudan 12°37N 31°0E 257 E3
Abū Ḥadrīyah Si. Arabia 27°20N 48°58E 247 E6
Abu Hail U.A.E. 25°17N 55°20E 119 A2
Abu Hamed Sudan 19°32N 33°13E 256 D3
Abu Haraz An Nîl el Azraq, Sudan 18°1N 33°58E 256 D3
Abu Haraz El Gezira, Sudan 14°35N 33°30E 257 E3
Abu Haraz Esh Shamâliya, Sudan 19°8N 32°18E 256 D3
Abu Higar Sudan 12°50N 33°59E 257 E3
Abū Kamāl Syria 34°30N 41°0E 213 E9
Abu Kebîr Egypt 30°43N 31°40E 251 H2
Abu Kuleiwat Sudan 12°20N 26°0E 257 E2
Abū Madd, Ra's Si. Arabia 24°50N 37°7E 246 E3
Abu Matariq Sudan 10°59N 26°9E 257 E2
Abu Mena = Abu Mina Egypt 30°51N 29°40E 256 H6
Abu Mendi Ethiopia 11°48N 35°42E 257 E4
Abu Mina Egypt 30°51N 29°40E 256 H6
Abū Mūsā U.A.E. 25°52N 55°3E 247 E7
Abū Nujaym Libya 30°35N 15°24E 258 B3
Abū Qaşr Si. Arabia 30°21N 38°34E 246 D3
Abu Qireiya Egypt 24°5N 35°28E 256 C4
Abu Qurqâs Egypt 28°1N 30°44E 256 B3
Abū Raşāş, Ra's Oman 20°10N 58°38E 249 B7
Abu Rudeis Egypt 28°54N 33°11E 251 K4
Abu Shagara, Ras Sudan 21°4N 37°19E 256 C4
Abu Shanab Janub Kordofân, Sudan 10°47N 29°32E 266 B2
Abu Shanab Shamâl Kordofân, Sudan 13°58N 27°49E 257 E2
Abu Simbel Egypt 22°18N 31°40E 256 C3
Abu Soma, Râs Egypt 26°51N 33°58E 256 B3
Abū Şukhayr Iraq 31°54N 44°30E 213 G11
Abu Sultân Egypt 30°24N 32°21E 256 H8
Abu Tabari Sudan 17°32N 28°32E 256 D2
Abu Tig Egypt 27°4N 31°15E 256 B3
Abu Tiga Sudan 12°47N 34°12E 257 E3
Abu Tineitin Sudan 14°24N 31°1E 257 E3
Abu Uruq Sudan 15°52N 30°25E 257 D3
Abu Zabad Sudan 12°25N 29°10E 257 E2
Abū Ẓāby U.A.E. 24°28N 54°22E 247 E7
Abū Zeydābād Iran 33°54N 51°45E 247 C6
Abufari Brazil 5°25S 62°59W 331 B5
Abuja Nigeria 9°5N 7°32E 263 D6
Abukuma-Gawa → Japan 38°6N 140°52E 220 E10
Abukuma-Sammyaku Japan 37°30N 140°45E 220 F10
Abulug Phil. 18°27N 121°27E 232 B3
Abumombazi Dem. Rep. of the Congo 3°42N 22°10E 264 B4
Abunã Brazil 9°40S 65°20W 331 B4
Abunã → Brazil 9°41S 65°20W 331 B4
Abune Yosef Ethiopia 12°5N 39°12E 257 E4
Aburatsu Japan 31°34N 131°24E 222 F3
Aburo Dem. Rep. of the Congo 2°4N 30°53E 268 B3
Abut Hd. N.Z. 43°7S 170°15E 285 D5
Abuye Meda Ethiopia 10°30N 39°49E 257 E4
Abuyog Phil. 10°45N 125°0E 233 F5
Abwong South Sudan 9°2N 32°14E 257 F3
Åby Sweden 58°40N 16°10E 163 F10
Aby, Lagune Ivory C. 5°15N 3°14W 262 D4
Abyad Sudan 13°47N 26°24E 257 E2
Abyān □ Yemen 13°50N 46°0E 248 D4
Abyei Sudan 9°36N 28°26E 257 F2
Abyei ⊠ Sudan 9°30N 28°30E 257 F2
Ābyek Iran 36°4N 50°33E 247 B6
Acacías Colombia 3°59N 73°46W 328 C3
Acacias Madrid, Spain 127 c2
Academy Gletscher Greenland 82°2N 34°0W 154 A7
Acadia △ U.S.A. 44°20N 68°13W 309 C19
Açailândia Brazil 4°57S 47°30W 332 B2
Acajutla El Salv. 13°36N 89°50W 320 D2
Acámbaro Mexico 20°2N 100°44W 318 D4
Acandí Colombia 8°32N 77°14W 328 B2
Acanthus Greece 40°27N 23°47E 202 F7
Acaponeta Mexico 22°30N 105°22W 318 C3
Acapulco Mexico 16°51N 99°55W 319 D5
Acapulco Trench Pac. Oc. 12°0N 88°0W 320 D2
Acará Brazil 1°57S 48°11W 332 B2
Acaraí, Serra Brazil 1°50N 57°50W 329 C6
Acaraú Brazil 2°53S 40°7W 332 B3
Acari Brazil 6°31S 36°38W 332 C4
Acarí Peru 15°25S 74°36W 330 D3
Acarigua Venezuela 9°33N 69°12W 328 B4
Acassuso Argentina 34°29S 58°30W 117 A2
Acatlán Mexico 18°12N 98°3W 319 D5
Acayucán Mexico 17°57N 94°55W 319 D6
Accademia, Galleria dell' Venice, Italy 142 b2
Accademia, Ponte dell' Venice, Italy 142 b2
Accéglio Italy 44°28N 7°0E 198 D4
Accomac U.S.A. 37°43N 75°40W 309 G16
Accous France 43°0N 0°36W 174 E3
Accra Ghana 5°35N 0°6W 263 D4
Accrington U.K. 53°45N 2°22W 168 D5
Acebal Argentina 33°20S 60°50W 334 C3
Aceh □ Indonesia 4°15N 97°30E 234 B1
Acerra Italy 40°57N 14°22E 201 B7
Aceuchal Spain 38°39N 6°30W 195 G4
Achacachi Bolivia 16°3S 68°43W 330 D4
Achaguas Venezuela 7°46N 68°14W 328 B4
Achaia Greece 38°5N 21°45E 204 C3
Achalpur India 21°22N 77°32E 244 D3
Achao Chile 42°28S 73°30W 336 B2
Acharnes Greece 38°5N 23°44E 204 C5
Achegour Niger 19°10N 11°54E 259 E2
Acheloos → Greece 38°19N 21°7E 204 C3
Achelouma Niger 22°12N 12°50E 259 D2
Achelouma, Enneri → Niger 21°55N 13°35E 259 D2
Acheng China 45°30N 126°58E 227 B14
Achenkirch Austria 47°32N 11°45E 180 D4
Achénouma Niger 19°7N 12°55E 259 E2
Achensee Austria 47°26N 11°45E 180 D4
Achentrias Greece 34°59N 25°13E 205 G7
Acher India 23°10N 72°32E 242 H5
Achères France 48°57N 2°3E 134 A1
Achern Germany 48°37N 8°4E 179 G4
Acheron → N.Z. 42°16S 173°4E 285 C8
Achill Hd. Ireland 53°58N 10°15W 166 C1
Achill I. Ireland 53°58N 10°1W 166 C1
Achim Germany 53°1N 9°3E 178 B5
Achinsk Russia 56°20N 90°20E 215 D10
Achladokambos Greece 37°31N 22°35E 204 D4
Achouka Gabon 0°52S 9°45E 264 C2
Acıgöl Turkey 37°50N 29°50E 205 D11
Acília Italy 41°47N 12°21E 136 C1
Acıpayam Turkey 37°26N 29°22E 205 D11
Acireale Italy 37°37N 15°10E 201 E8
Ackerman U.S.A. 33°19N 89°11W 315 E10
Ackley U.S.A. 42°33N 93°3W 310 B3
Acklins I. Bahamas 22°30N 74°0W 321 B5
Aclimação Brazil 23°34S 46°37W 137 B2
Acme Alta., Canada 51°33N 113°30W 296 C6
Acme Pa., U.S.A. 40°8N 79°26W 312 F5
Acobamba Peru 12°52S 74°35W 330 C3
Acomayo Peru 13°55S 71°38W 330 C3
Aconcagua, Cerro Argentina 32°39S 70°0W 334 C2
Aconquija, Mt. Argentina 27°0S 66°0W 334 B2
Acopiara Brazil 6°6S 39°27W 332 C4
Açores, Is. dos Atl. Oc. 38°0N 27°0W 153 d1
Acorizal Brazil 15°12S 56°22W 331 D6
Acornhoek S. Africa 24°37S 31°2E 271 B5
Acoua Mayotte 12°43S 45°4E 272 b
Acquapendente Italy 42°44N 11°52E 199 F8
Acquasanta Terme Italy 42°46N 13°24E 199 F10
Acquasparta Italy 42°41N 12°33E 199 F9
Acquaviva delle Fonti Italy 40°54N 16°50E 201 B9
Ácqui Terme Italy 44°41N 8°28E 198 D5
Acraman, L. Australia 32°2S 135°23E 281 E2
Acre = ʻAkko Israel 32°55N 35°4E 250 F6
Acre □ Brazil 9°1S 71°0W 330 B3
Acre → Brazil 8°45S 67°22W 330 B4
Acri Italy 39°29N 16°23E 201 C9
Acropolis Athens, Greece 112 c2
Acs Hungary 47°42N 18°2E 182 C3
Actæon Mt. = Diana's Peak St. Helena 15°58S 5°42W 153 h
Actéon, Groupe French Polynesia 21°20S 136°30W 289 f
Actinolite Canada 44°32N 77°19W 312 B7
Actium Greece 38°57N 20°45E 207 B2
Acton Ont., Canada 43°38N 80°3W 312 C4
Acton London, U.K. 51°30N 0°16W 125 A2
Açu Brazil 5°34S 36°54W 332 C4
Açúcar, Pão de Brazil 22°56S 43°9W 135 B2
Acul = Vidin Bulgaria 43°59N 22°50E 202 C6
Acworth U.S.A. 34°4N 84°41W 316 A5
Ad Dafinah Si. Arabia 23°18N 41°58E 248 B3
Aḑ Ḑafrah U.A.E. 23°30N 54°30E 249 B6
Ad Daghghāran Iraq 32°8N 44°55E 213 G11
Aḑ Ḑahī Yemen 15°13N 43°4E 248 D3
Ad Dahnā Si. Arabia 24°30N 48°10E 249 A5
Ad Dākhilīyah □ Oman 22°30N 57°30E 249 B7
Aḑ Ḑālīʼ Yemen 13°42N 44°44E 248 D4
Aḑ Ḑālīʻ □ Yemen 13°42N 44°44E 248 D4
Ad Dammām Si. Arabia 26°20N 50°5E 247 E6
Ad Dāmūr Lebanon 33°43N 35°27E 250 E6
Ad Darb Si. Arabia 18°2N 43°7E 248 C3
Ad Dawādimī Si. Arabia 24°35N 44°15E 246 E5
Ad Dawḩah Qatar 25°15N 51°35E 247 E6
Ad Dawr Iraq 34°27N 43°47E 213 E10
Ad Dhakhīrah Qatar 25°44N 51°33E 247 E6
Aḑ Ḑiffah Libya 30°30N 24°30E 258 B4
Ad Dilam Si. Arabia 23°55N 47°10E 248 B4
Ad Dirʻīyah Si. Arabia 24°44N 46°35E 246 E5
Ad Dīwānīyah Iraq 32°0N 45°0E 213 F11
Ad Dujayl Iraq 33°51N 44°14E 213 F11
Ad Duqm Oman 19°39N 57°42E 249 C7
Ad Duwayd Si. Arabia 30°15N 42°17E 246 D4
Ada Ghana 5°44N 0°40E 263 D5
Ada Serbia 45°49N 20°9E 182 E5
Ada Minn., U.S.A. 47°18N 96°31W 308 B5
Ada Ohio, U.S.A. 40°46N 83°49W 311 D13
Ada Okla., U.S.A. 34°46N 96°41W 314 D6
Ada Beja Portugal 38°47N 9°13W 126 A1
Adad Somalia 9°27N 46°49E 267 C6
Adado, Ras Somalia 11°19N 48°39E 267 B6
Adair, C. Canada 71°30N 71°34W 295 C17
Adaja → Spain 41°32N 4°52W 194 D6
Adak U.S.A. 51°45N 176°45W 303 L3
Adak I. U.S.A. 51°45N 176°45W 303 L3
Ådalsbruk Norway 60°43N 11°19E 164 D8
Adam Oman 22°15N 57°28E 249 B7
Adam, Mt. Falk. Is. 51°34S 60°4W 153 f
Adamantina Brazil 21°42S 51°4W 333 F1
Adamaoua □ Cameroon 6°30N 13°30E 263 D7
Adamaoua, Massif de l' Cameroon 7°20N 12°20E 263 D7
Adamasta Channel Hong Kong, China 22°14N 114°1E 122 B2
Adamawa □ Nigeria 9°20N 12°30E 263 D7
Adamawa Highlands = Adamaoua, Massif de l' Cameroon 7°20N 12°20E 263 D7
Adamello, Mte. Italy 46°9N 10°30E 198 B7
Adamello ⌂ Italy 46°4N 10°28E 198 B7
Adami Tulu Ethiopia 7°53N 38°41E 257 F4
Adaminaby Australia 36°0S 148°45E 283 D8
Adams Mass., U.S.A. 42°38N 73°7W 313 D11
Adams N.Y., U.S.A. 43°49N 76°1W 313 C8
Adams Wis., U.S.A. 43°57N 89°49W 308 D9
Adams, Mt. U.S.A. 46°12N 121°30W 306 D5
Adam's Bridge Sri Lanka 9°15N 79°40E 245 K4
Adams L. Canada 51°10N 119°40W 296 C5
Adams Park U.S.A. 33°43N 84°27W 113 B2
Adam's Peak Sri Lanka 6°48N 80°30E 245 L5
Adamuz Spain 38°2N 4°32W 195 G6
ʻAdan Yemen 12°45N 45°0E 248 D4
Adana Turkey 37°0N 35°16E 250 B6
Adana □ Turkey 37°0N 35°30E 250 B6
Adanero Spain 40°56N 4°36W 194 E6
Adang, Ko Thailand 6°33N 99°18E 237 J2
Adapazarı = Sakarya Turkey 40°48N 30°25E 212 B4
Adar Gwagwa, J. Sudan 22°15N 35°20E 256 C4
Adarama Sudan 17°10N 34°52E 257 D3
Adare Ireland 52°34N 8°47W 166 D3
Adare, C. Antarctica 71°0S 171°0E 151 D11
Adarte Eritrea 13°18N 42°8E 257 E5
Adaut Indonesia 8°8S 131°7E 231 F8
Adavale Australia 25°52S 144°32E 281 D3
Adda → Italy 45°8N 9°53E 198 C6
Addatigala India 17°31N 82°3E 244 F6
Addax ⌂ Niger 19°17N 9°22E 259 E1
Addis Ababa = Addis Abeba Ethiopia 9°2N 38°42E 257 F4
Addis Abeba Ethiopia 9°2N 38°42E 257 F4
Addis Alem Ethiopia 9°0N 38°17E 257 F4
Addis Zemen Ethiopia 12°7N 37°47E 257 E4
Addiscombe U.K. 51°22N 0°4W 125 B3
Addison Ill., U.S.A. 41°55N 88°0W 311 C8
Addison N.Y., U.S.A. 42°1N 77°14W 312 D7
Addo S. Africa 33°32S 25°45E 270 D4
Addo △ S. Africa 33°30S 25°50E 270 D4
Addu Atoll Maldives 0°38S 73°10E 272 d
Adebour Niger 13°17N 11°50E 259 F2
Ādeh Iran 37°42N 45°11E 246 B5
Adeje Canary Is. 28°7N 16°43W 153 e1
Adel Ga., U.S.A. 31°8N 83°25W 316 D6
Adel Iowa, U.S.A. 41°37N 94°1W 310 C2
Adel Bagrou Mauritania 15°29N 6°57W 262 B3
Adelaide S. Austral., Australia 34°52S 138°30E 282 C3
Adelaide Eastern Cape, S. Africa 32°42S 26°20E 270 D4
Adelaide I. Antarctica 67°15S 68°30W 151 C17
Adelaide Pen. Canada 68°15N 97°30W 294 D12
Adelaide River Australia 13°15S 131°7E 278 B5
Adelaide Village Bahamas 25°0N 77°31W 153 b
Adelanto U.S.A. 34°35N 117°22W 307 L9
Adelaye C.A.R. 7°7N 22°49E 264 A4
Adele I. Australia 15°32S 123°9E 278 C3
Adélie, Terre Antarctica 68°0S 140°0E 151 C10
Adelie Land = Adélie, Terre Antarctica 68°0S 140°0E 151 C10
Adelong Australia 35°16S 148°4E 283 C8
Adelphi U.S.A. 39°0N 76°58W 143 A3
Adelsk Belarus 53°24N 23°47E 184 E10
Ademuz Spain 40°5N 1°13W 196 E3
Aden = ʻAdan Yemen 12°45N 45°0E 248 D4
Aden, G. of Ind. Oc. 12°30N 47°30E 267 B6
Adendorp S. Africa 32°15S 24°30E 270 D3
Aderbissinat Niger 15°34N 7°54E 263 B6
Aderklaa Austria 48°17N 16°32E 142 A3
Adh Dhayd U.A.E. 25°17N 55°53E 247 E7
Adhoi India 23°26N 70°32E 242 H4
Adi Indonesia 4°15S 133°30E 231 E8
Adi Arkai Ethiopia 13°35N 37°57E 257 E4
Adi Daro Ethiopia 14°20N 38°14E 257 E4
Adi Keyih Eritrea 14°51N 39°22E 257 E4
Adi Kwala Eritrea 14°38N 38°48E 257 E4
Adi Ugri Eritrea 14°58N 38°48E 257 E4
Adieu, C. Australia 32°0S 132°10E 279 F5
Adieu Pt. Australia 15°14S 124°35E 278 C3
Adigala Ethiopia 10°24N 42°15E 257 E5
Adige → Italy 45°9N 12°20E 199 C9
Adigrat Ethiopia 14°20N 39°26E 257 E4
Adıgüzel Barajı Turkey 38°13N 29°14E 205 C11
Adilabad India 19°33N 78°20E 244 E4
Adilcevaz Turkey 38°47N 42°43E 213 C10
Adīrī Libya 27°32N 13°2E 258 C2
Adirondack ⌂ U.S.A. 44°0N 74°20W 313 C10
Adirondack Mts. U.S.A. 44°0N 74°0W 313 C10
Adis Abeba = Addis Abeba Ethiopia 9°2N 38°42E 257 F4
Adıyaman Turkey 37°45N 38°16E 213 D8
Adıyaman □ Turkey 37°30N 38°10E 213 D8
Adjim Tunisia 33°47N 10°50E 258 B2
Adjohon Benin 6°41N 2°32E 263 D5
Adjud Romania 46°7N 27°10E 183 D12
Adjumani Uganda 3°20N 31°50E 268 B3
Adjuntas Puerto Rico 18°10N 66°43W 321 b
Adlavik Is. Canada 55°0N 58°40W 299 B8
Adler Russia 43°28N 39°52E 191 J4
Adler Planetarium Chicago, U.S.A. 41°51N 87°36W 119 B3
Admer Algeria 20°21N 5°27E 261 D6
Admer, Erg d' Algeria 24°0N 9°5E 261 D6
Admiralteyskaya Storona Russia 59°56N 30°20E 137 B2
Admiralty G. Australia 14°20S 125°55E 278 B4
Admiralty Gulf ☼ Australia 14°16S 125°52E 278 B4
Admiralty I. U.S.A. 57°30N 134°30W 296 B2
Admiralty Inlet Canada 72°30N 86°0W 295 C14
Admiralty Is. Papua N. G. 2°0S 147°0E 286 B4
Admiralty Island ⌂ U.S.A. 57°40N 134°10W 303 H14
Adnan Menderes, İzmir ✈ (ADB) Turkey 38°23N 27°6E 205 C9
Ado Nigeria 6°36N 2°56E 263 D5
Ado-Ekiti Nigeria 7°38N 5°12E 263 D6
Adok South Sudan 8°10N 30°20E 257 F3
Adola Ethiopia 11°14N 41°44E 257 E5
Adolfo González Chaves Argentina 38°2S 60°5W 334 D3
Adolfo Ruiz Cortines, Presa Mexico 27°15N 109°6W 318 B3
Adonara Indonesia 8°15S 123°5E 231 F6
Adoni India 15°33N 77°18E 245 G3
Adony Hungary 47°6N 18°52E 182 C3
Adour → France 43°32N 1°32W 174 E2
Adra India 23°30N 86°42E 243 H12
Adra Spain 36°43N 3°3W 195 J7
Adrano Italy 37°40N 14°50E 201 E7
Adrar Algeria 27°51N 0°19W 261 C4
Adrar □ Algeria 25°45N 1°0E 261 C5
Adrar □ Mauritania 20°10N 10°0W 260 D3
Adrar des Iforas Africa 19°40N 1°40E 261 D5
Adré Chad 13°40N 22°20E 259 F4
Ádria Italy 45°3N 12°3E 199 C9
Adrian Ga., U.S.A. 32°33N 82°35W 316 C7
Adrian Mich., U.S.A. 41°54N 84°2W 311 C12
Adrian Mo., U.S.A. 38°24N 94°21W 310 F2
Adrian Tex., U.S.A. 35°16N 102°40W 314 D3
Adrianople = Edirne Turkey 41°40N 26°34E 203 E10
Adriatic Sea Medit. S. 43°0N 16°0E 193 C7
Adua Indonesia 1°45S 129°50E 231 E7
Adung Long Burma 28°7N 97°42E 241 A6
Adur India 9°8N 76°40E 245 K3
Adwa Ethiopia 14°15N 38°52E 257 E4
Adygea □ Russia 45°0N 40°0E 191 H5
Adzhar Republic = Ajaria □ Georgia 41°30N 42°0E 191 K6
Adzhibakul = Qazımämmäd Azerbaijan 40°3N 49°0E 191 K9
Adzopé Ivory C. 6°7N 3°49W 262 D4
Aegae = Aigai Greece 40°28N 22°19E 202 F6
Ægean Sea Medit. S. 38°30N 25°0E 205 C7
Aerhtai Shan Mongolia 46°40N 92°45E 217 C12
Ærø Denmark 54°52N 10°25E 163 K4
Ærøskøbing Denmark 54°53N 10°24E 163 K4
Aetdia-Akarnania = Etoloakarnania Greece 38°45N 21°18E 204 C3
Aetos Greece 37°15N 21°50E 204 D3
Afaahiti Tahiti 17°45S 149°17W 289 e
Afafi, Massif d' Niger 22°11N 15°10E 259 D3
ʻAfak Iraq 32°4N 45°15E 213 F11
Afandou Greece 36°18N 28°12E 206 E12
Afar □ Ethiopia 12°0N 41°0E 257 E5
Afarag, Erg Algeria 23°50N 2°47E 261 D5
Afareaitu Moorea 17°33S 149°47W 289 e
Åfarnes Norway 62°40N 7°32E 164 B4
Afdega Ethiopia 6°4N 43°30E 267 C5
Afdem Ethiopia 9°28N 41°0E 267 C5
Áffori Italy 45°31N 9°10E 128 A2
Affton U.S.A. 38°33N 90°20W 310 F6
Afghanistan ■ Asia 33°0N 65°0E 240 B2
Afgooye Somalia 2°7N 44°59E 267 D5
ʻAfif Si. Arabia 23°53N 42°56E 248 B3
Afikpo Nigeria 5°53N 7°54E 263 D6
Aflandshage Denmark 55°33N 12°35E 118 B3
Aflisses, O. → Algeria 28°40N 0°50E 261 C5
Aflou Algeria 34°7N 2°3E 261 B5
Afmadow Somalia 0°31N 42°4E 267 D5
Afogados da Ingàzeira Brazil 7°45S 37°39W 332 C4
Afognak I. U.S.A. 58°15N 152°30W 303 G9
Afono B. Amer. Samoa 14°15S 170°38W 302 f
Afore Papua N. G. 9°9S 148°23E 286 E5
Afragóla Italy 40°55N 14°18E 201 B7
Afram → Ghana 7°0N 0°52W 263 D4
Afrera Ethiopia 13°16N 41°5E 257 E5
Africa 10°0N 20°0E 254 E6
ʻAfrīn Syria 36°32N 36°50E 250 B7
ʻAfrīn → Syria 36°20N 36°35E 250 B7
Afşar → Turkey 37°2N 32°35E 250 A3
Afsarīyeh Iran 35°39N 51°30E 141 B2
Afşin Turkey 38°14N 36°55E 212 C7
Afton Iowa, U.S.A. 41°2N 94°12W 310 C2
Afton N.Y., U.S.A. 42°14N 75°32W 313 D9
Afton Wyo., U.S.A. 42°44N 110°56W 304 E8
Afuá Brazil 0°15S 50°20W 329 D7
ʻAfula Israel 32°37N 35°17E 250 F6
Afumba Zambia 15°38S 24°56E 265 F4
Afyon Turkey 38°45N 30°33E 205 C12
Afyon □ Turkey 38°25N 30°30E 205 C12
Afyonkarahisar = Afyon Turkey 38°45N 30°33E 205 C12
Aga Egypt 30°55N 31°10E 256 H7
Aga I. Micronesia 7°29N 151°43E 287 T18
Āgā Jarī Iran 30°42N 49°50E 247 D6
Agadem Niger 16°50N 13°11E 259 E2
Agadés = Agadez Niger 16°58N 7°59E 259 E1
Agadez Niger 16°58N 7°59E 259 E1
Agadir Morocco 30°28N 9°55W 260 B3
Agaete Canary Is. 28°6N 15°43W 153 e1
Agaie Nigeria 9°1N 6°18E 263 D6
Agalas Greece 37°43N 20°47E 207 D2
Agalega Is. Mauritius 11°0S 57°0E 273 F4
Agana = Hagåtña Guam 13°28N 144°45E 302 d
Agana B. Guam 13°29N 144°45E 302 d
Ağapınar Turkey 39°48N 30°47E 205 B12
Agar India 23°40N 76°2E 242 H7
Agar → India 21°0N 82°57E 244 D6
Agâraktem Mali 23°8N 6°22W 260 D3
Agaro Ethiopia 7°50N 36°38E 257 F4
Agartala India 23°50N 91°23E 241 D3
Agăş Romania 46°28N 26°15E 183 D11
Agassiz Canada 49°14N 121°46W 296 D4
Agassiz Icecap Canada 80°15N 76°0W 295 A16
Agat Guam 13°25N 144°40E 302 d
Agats Indonesia 5°33S 138°0E 231 F9
Agatti I. India 10°50N 72°12E 245 J1
Agattu I. U.S.A. 52°25N 173°35E 303 K1
Agawam U.S.A. 42°5N 72°37W 313 D12
Agbélouvé Togo 6°35N 1°14E 263 D5
Agboville Ivory C. 5°55N 4°15W 262 D4
Agboyi Cr. → Nigeria 6°33N 3°24E 124 A2
Ağcabädi Azerbaijan 40°5N 47°27E 191 K8
Ağdam Azerbaijan 40°0N 46°58E 191 K8
Ağdara Azerbaijan 40°13N 46°49E 191 K8
Ağdaş Azerbaijan 40°44N 47°22E 191 K8
Agde France 43°19N 3°28E 174 E7
Agde, C. d' France 43°16N 3°28E 174 E7
Agdz Morocco 30°47N 6°30W 260 B3
Agdzhabedi = Ağcabädi Azerbaijan 40°5N 47°27E 191 K8
Agen France 44°12N 0°38E 174 D4
Ageo Japan 35°58N 139°36E 223 B11
Ager Tay Chad 20°0N 17°41E 259 E3
Agerbæk Denmark 55°36N 8°48E 163 J2
Agersø Denmark 55°13N 11°12E 163 J5
Ågerup Denmark 55°43N 12°19E 118 A1
Ågesta Sweden 59°12N 18°6E 139 B2
Ageyevo Russia 54°10N 36°27E 188 E9
Aggteleki △ Hungary 48°27N 20°36E 182 B5
Āgh Kand Iran 37°15N 48°4E 213 D13
Aghathonisi Greece 37°28N 27°0E 205 D8
Aghia Anna Greece 38°52N 23°24E 204 C5
Aghia Deka Greece 35°3N 24°58E 207 E5
Aghia Ekaterinis, Akra Greece 39°50N 19°50E 206 B9
Aghia Galini Greece 35°6N 24°41E 207 E5
Aghia Marina Athina, Greece 37°48N 23°51E 112 C3
Aghia Marina Kasos, Greece 35°27N 26°53E 205 F8
Aghia Marina Leros, Greece 37°11N 26°48E 205 D8
Aghia Paraskevi Athina, Greece 38°1N 23°49E 112 A2
Aghia Paraskevi Voreio Aigaio, Greece 39°14N 26°21E 205 B8
Aghia Roumeli Greece 35°14N 23°58E 207 E4
Aghia Varvara Greece 35°8N 25°1E 207 E6
Aghiasos Greece 39°5N 26°23E 205 B8
Aghio Theodori Greece 37°55N 23°9E 204 D5
Aghion Oros = Athos Greece 40°9N 24°22E 203 F8
Aghion Oros □ Greece 40°25N 24°6E 203 F8
Aghios Andreas Greece 37°21N 22°45E 204 D4
Aghios Dimitrios Greece 37°53N 23°44E 112 B2
Aghios Efimia Greece 38°18N 20°36E 207 C2
Aghios Efstratios Greece 39°34N 24°58E 204 B6
Aghios Georgios Greece 37°28N 23°57E 204 D5
Aghios Ioannis, Akra Greece 35°20N 25°40E 207 E6
Aghios Ioannis Rendis Greece 37°57N 23°39E 112 B1
Aghios Isidoros Greece 36°9N 27°51E 206 E11
Aghios Kirikos Greece 37°34N 26°17E 205 D8
Aghios Leon Greece 37°47N 20°43E 207 D2
Aghios Matheos Greece 39°30N 19°47E 206 C9
Aghios Mironas Greece 35°15N 25°1E 207 E6
Aghios Nikolaos Etoloakarnania, Greece 38°52N 20°48E 207 B2
Aghios Nikolaos Kriti, Greece 35°11N 25°41E 207 E6
Aghios Nikolaos Lefkada, Greece 38°36N 20°34E 207 B2
Aghios Petros Greece 38°40N 20°36E 207 B2
Aghios Stephanos Greece 39°46N 19°39E 206 B9
Aghios Thekli Greece 38°15N 20°23E 207 C1
Aghios Thomas Greece 38°58N 20°47E 207 B2
Aghiou Orous, Kolpos Greece 40°6N 24°0E 202 F7
Aghireşu Romania 46°53N 23°15E 183 D8
Aghoueyyît Mauritania 21°10N 15°6W 260 D1
Aghreïjît Mauritania 21°58N 12°11W 260 D2
Agia Greece 39°43N 22°45E 204 B4
Agincourt Canada 43°47N 79°16W 141 A3
Aginskoye Russia 51°6N 114°32E 215 D12
Agjert Mauritania 16°23N 9°17W 262 B3
Ağlasun Turkey 37°39N 30°31E 205 D12
Agly → France 42°46N 3°3E 174 F7
Agmar Mauritania 25°18N 10°50W 260 C2
Agnéby □ Ivory C. 6°0N 4°15W 262 D4
Agnew Australia 28°1S 120°31E 279 E3
Agnibilékrou Ivory C. 7°10N 3°11W 262 D4
Agnita Romania 45°59N 24°40E 183 E9
Agnone Italy 41°48N 14°22E 199 G11
Ago Japan 34°20N 136°51E 223 C8
Ago-Are Nigeria 8°30N 3°25E 263 D5
Agofie Ghana 8°27N 0°15E 263 D5
Agogna → Italy 45°4N 8°54E 198 C5
Agoitz = Aoiz Spain 42°46N 1°22W 196 C3
Agön Sweden 61°34N 17°23E 162 C11
Agon-Coutainville France 49°2N 1°34W 172 C5
Agoo Phil. 16°20N 120°22E 232 C3
Agora Athens, Greece 112 c1
Ágordo Italy 46°18N 12°2E 199 B9
Agori India 24°33N 82°57E 243 G10
Agouifa Mauritania 19°57N 16°10W 260 E1
Agouna Benin 7°39N 1°47E 263 D5
Agout → France 43°47N 1°41E 174 E5
Agra India 27°17N 77°58E 242 F7
Agra Canal India 28°33N 77°17E 120 B2
Agrakhanskiuy Poluostrov Russia 43°42N 47°36E 191 J8
Agram = Zagreb Croatia 45°50N 15°58E 199 C12
Agramunt Spain 41°48N 1°6E 196 D6
Ágreda Spain 41°51N 1°55W 196 D3
Ağri Turkey 39°44N 43°3E 213 C10
Ağri □ Turkey 39°45N 43°5E 213 C10
Agri → Italy 40°13N 16°44E 201 B9
Ağrı Dağı Turkey 39°50N 44°15E 213 C11
Ağri Karakose = Ağri Turkey 39°44N 43°3E 213 C10
Agria Greece 39°20N 23°1E 204 B5
Agricola Oriental Mexico 19°23N 99°4W 128 B2
Agrigento Italy 37°19N 13°34E 200 E6
Agrihan N. Marianas 18°46N 145°40E 302 a
Agrinio Greece 38°37N 21°27E 204 C3
Agrópoli Italy 40°21N 14°59E 201 B7
Ağstafa Azerbaijan 41°7N 45°27E 191 K7
Água Branca Brazil 5°50S 42°40W 332 C3
Agua Caliente Mexico 32°29N 116°59W 307 N10
Agua Caliente Springs U.S.A. 32°56N 116°19W 307 N10
Água Clara Brazil 20°25S 52°45W 331 E7
Água Espraiada → Brazil 23°36S 46°41W 137 B2
Agua Fria ⌂ U.S.A. 34°14N 112°0W 305 J8
Agua Hechicera Mexico 32°28N 116°15W 307 N10
Água Preta → Brazil 1°41S 63°48W 329 D5
Agua Prieta Mexico 31°18N 109°34W 318 A3
Aguachica Colombia 8°19N 73°38W 328 B3
Aguada Puerto Rico 18°23N 67°11W 321 b
Aguada Cecilio Argentina 40°51S 65°51W 336 B3
Aguadas Colombia 5°40N 75°38W 328 B2
Aguadilla Puerto Rico 18°26N 67°10W 321 C6
Aguadulce Panama 8°15N 80°32W 320 E3
Agualva-Cacem Portugal 38°46N 9°15W 126 A1
Aguanga U.S.A. 33°27N 116°51W 307 M10
Aguanish Canada 50°14N 62°2W 299 B7
Aguanish → Canada 50°13N 62°5W 299 B7
Aguapeí Brazil 16°12S 59°43W 331 D6
Aguapeí → Brazil 21°0S 51°0W 333 F1
Aguapey → Argentina 29°7S 56°36W 334 B4
Aguaray Guazú → Paraguay 24°47S 57°19W 334 A4
Aguarico → Ecuador 0°59S 75°11W 328 D2

Aguaro-Guariquito △ *Venezuela* 8°20N 66°35W 328 B4
Aguas ➜ *Spain* 41°20N 0°30W 196 D4
Aguas Blancas *Chile* 24°15S 69°55W 334 A2
Aguas Calientes, Sierra de *Argentina* 25°26S 66°40W 334 B2
Águas Formosas *Brazil* 17°5S 40°57W 333 E3
Águas Lindas de Goiás *Brazil* 15°46S 48°15W 333 E2
Aguascalientes *Mexico* 21°53N 102°18W 318 C4
Aguascalientes ☐ *Mexico* 22°0N 102°20W 318 C4
Agudo *Spain* 38°59N 4°52W 195 G6
Águeda *Portugal* 40°34N 8°27W 194 E2
Agueda ➜ *Spain* 41°2N 6°56W 194 D4
Aguelhok *Mali* 19°29N 0°52E 261 E5
Aguelt el Melah *Mauritania* 23°3N 10°40W 260 D2
Agüenit *W. Sahara* 22°11N 13°8W 260 D2
Aguié *Niger* 13°31N 7°46E 263 C6
Aguila, Punta *Puerto Rico* 17°57N 67°13W 321 b
Aguilafuente *Spain* 41°13N 4°7W 194 D6
Aguilar de Campóo *Spain* 42°47N 4°15W 194 C6
Aguilar de la Frontera *Spain* 37°31N 4°40W 195 H6
Aguilares *Argentina* 27°26S 65°35W 334 B2
Águilas *Spain* 37°23N 1°35W 197 H3
Agüimes *Canary Is.* 27°58N 15°27W 153 e1
Aguja, C. de la *Colombia* 11°18N 74°12W 328 A3
Agujereada, Pta. *Puerto Rico* 18°30N 67°8W 321 b
Agulaa *Ethiopia* 13°40N 39°40E 257 E4
Agulhas, C. *S. Africa* 34°52S 20°0E 270 D3
Agulhas Ridge *Atl. Oc.* 42°0S 15°0E 152 L13
Agulo *Canary Is.* 28°11N 17°12W 153 e1
Agung, Gunung *Indonesia* 8°20S 115°28E 231 J18
Aguni-Jima *Japan* 26°30N 127°10E 221 L3
Agur *Uganda* 2°28N 32°55E 268 B3
Agurei ➜ *South Sudan* 7°45N 33°0E 257 F3
Agusan ➜ *Phil.* 9°0N 125°30E 233 G5
Agusan del Norte ☐ *Phil.* 9°20N 125°10E 233 G5
Agusan del Sur ☐ *Phil.* 8°30N 125°30E 233 G5
Agustín Codazzi *Colombia* 10°2N 73°14W 328 A3
Agutaya I. *Phil.* 11°9N 120°58E 233 F3
Ağva *Turkey* 41°8N 29°51E 203 E13
Agvali *Russia* 42°36N 46°8E 191 J8
Aha Mts. *Botswana* 19°45S 21°0E 270 A3
Ahad Rifaydah *Si. Arabia* 17°50N 42°50E 248 C3
Ahaggar *Algeria* 23°0N 6°30E 261 D6
Ahaggar △ *Algeria* 23°0N 4°50E 261 D5
Ahai Dam *China* 27°21N 100°30E 228 D3
Ahal ☐ *Turkmenistan* 37°0N 57°0E 216 E5
Ahamansu *Ghana* 7°38N 0°35E 263 D5
Ahar *Iran* 38°35N 47°0E 213 C12
Ahat *Turkey* 38°39N 29°47E 205 C11
Ahaura ➜ *N.Z.* 42°21S 171°34E 285 C6
Ahaus *Germany* 52°4N 7°0E 178 C2
Ahé *French Polynesia* 14°30S 146°18W 289 f
Åheim *Norway* 62°2N 5°13E 164 B2
Ahelledjem *Algeria* 26°37N 6°58E 261 C6
Ahimanawa Ra. *N.Z.* 39°3S 176°30E 284 F5
Ahioma *Papua N. G.* 10°20S 150°33E 286 F6
Ahipara B. *N.Z.* 35°5S 173°5E 284 B2
Ahir Dağı *Turkey* 38°45N 30°10E 205 C12
Ahiri *India* 19°30N 80°0E 244 E5
Ahlat *Turkey* 38°45N 42°29E 213 C10
Ahlen *Germany* 51°45N 7°53E 178 D3
Ahmad Wal *Pakistan* 29°18N 65°58E 242 E1
Ahmadabad *India* 23°0N 72°40E 242 H5
Aḥmadābād *Khorāsān, Iran* 35°3N 60°50E 247 C9
Aḥmadābād *Khorāsān, Iran* 35°49N 59°42E 247 C8
Aḥmadī *Iran* 27°56N 56°42E 247 E8
Ahmadnagar *India* 19°7N 74°46E 244 E2
Ahmadpur *India* 18°40N 76°57E 244 E3
Ahmadpur East *Pakistan* 29°12N 71°10E 242 E4
Ahmadpur Lamma *Pakistan* 28°19N 70°3E 242 E4
Ahmanson Theater *Los Angeles, U.S.A.* 127 b2
Ahmar, Mts. *Ethiopia* 9°20N 41°15E 257 F5
Ahmedabad = Ahmadabad *India* 23°0N 72°40E 242 H5
Ahmednagar = Ahmadnagar *India* 19°7N 74°46E 244 E2
Ahmetbey *Turkey* 41°26N 27°34E 203 E11
Ahmetler *Turkey* 38°28N 29°5E 205 C11
Ahmetli *Turkey* 38°32N 27°57E 205 C9
Ahmeyim *Mauritania* 20°51N 14°25W 260 D2
Ahoada *Nigeria* 5°8N 6°36E 263 D6
Ahome *Mexico* 25°55N 109°11W 318 B3
Ahon, Tarso *Chad* 20°23N 18°18E 259 D3
Ahoskie *U.S.A.* 36°17N 76°59W 315 C16
Ahr ➜ *Germany* 50°32N 7°16E 178 E3
Ahram *Iran* 28°52N 51°16E 247 D6
Ahrax Pt. *Malta* 36°0N 14°22E 206 F7
Ahrensbök *Germany* 54°2N 10°35E 178 A6
Ahrensburg *Germany* 53°40N 10°13E 178 B6
Ahrensfelde *Germany* 52°34N 13°34E 115 A4
Ahu Akivi *Chile* 27°7S 109°24W 330 b
Ahu Tepeu *Chile* 27°6S 109°25W 330 b
Ahu Tongariki *Chile* 27°8S 109°17W 330 b
Ahu Vinapu *Chile* 27°10S 109°25W 330 b
Ahuachapán *El Salv.* 13°54N 89°52W 320 D2
'Āhuimanu *U.S.A.* 21°26N 157°50W 302 K14
Ahun *France* 46°4N 2°5E 173 F9
Ahuntsic *Canada* 45°32N 73°41W 130 A1
Ahunui *French Polynesia* 19°39S 140°25W 289 f
Ahuriri ➜ *N.Z.* 44°31S 170°12E 285 E5
Åhus *Sweden* 55°56N 14°18E 163 J8
Ahvāz *Iran* 31°20N 48°40E 247 D6
Ahvenanmaa = Åland *Finland* 60°15N 20°0E 161 F19
Aḥwar *Yemen* 13°30N 46°40E 248 D4
Ahzar ➜ *Mali* 15°30N 3°20E 263 B5
Ai ➜ *India* 26°26N 90°44E 241 B3
Ai ➜ *Ōsaka, Japan* 34°46N 135°35E 133 A2
Ai-Ais *Namibia* 27°54S 17°59E 270 C2
Ai-Ais and Fish River Canyon △ *Namibia* 24°45S 17°15E 270 B2
Aiari ➜ *Brazil* 1°22N 68°36W 328 C4
Aichach *Germany* 48°27N 11°8E 179 G7
Aichi ☐ *Japan* 35°0N 137°15E 223 G9
'Aiea *U.S.A.* 21°23N 157°56W 302 K14
Aigai *Greece* 40°28N 22°19E 202 F6
Aigle *Switz.* 46°18N 6°58E 179 J2
Aignay-le-Duc *France* 47°40N 4°43E 173 E11
Aigoual, Mt. *France* 44°8N 3°35E 174 D7
Aigre *France* 45°54N 0°1E 174 C4
Aigremont *France* 48°54N 2°1E 134 A1
Aigrettes, Île aux *Mauritius* 20°25S 57°43E 272 e
Aiguá *Uruguay* 34°13S 54°46W 335 C5
Aigueperse *France* 46°3N 3°13E 173 F10
Aigues ➜ *France* 44°7N 4°43E 175 D8
Aigues-Mortes *France* 43°35N 4°12E 175 E8
Aigues-Mortes, G. d' *France* 43°31N 4°3E 175 E8
Aigües-Tortes i Estany de St. Maurici △ *Spain* 42°38N 0°31E 196 C4
Aiguilles *France* 44°47N 6°51E 175 D10
Aiguillon *France* 44°18N 0°21E 174 D4
Aigurande *France* 46°27N 1°49E 173 F8
Aihui = Heihe *China* 50°10N 127°30E 219 A14
Aija *Peru* 9°50S 77°45W 330 B2
Aikawa *Japan* 38°2N 138°15E 220 E9
Aiken *U.S.A.* 33°34N 81°43W 316 B8
Ailao Shan *China* 24°0N 101°20E 228 F3
Aileron *Australia* 22°39S 133°20E 280 C1
Ailey *U.S.A.* 32°11N 82°34W 316 C7
Ailigandi *Panama* 9°14N 78°1W 328 B2
Aillant-sur-Tholon *France* 47°52N 3°20E 173 E10
Aillik *Canada* 55°11N 59°18W 299 A8
Ailsa Craig *Ont., Canada* 43°8N 81°33W 312 C3
Ailsa Craig *S. Ayrs., U.K.* 55°15N 5°6W 167 F3
Ailuluai *Papua N. G.* 9°38S 150°35E 286 E6
Aim *Russia* 59°0N 133°55E 215 D14
Aimogasta *Argentina* 28°33S 66°50W 334 B2
Aimorés *Brazil* 19°30S 41°4W 333 E3
Ain ☐ *France* 46°5N 5°20E 173 F12
Ain ➜ *France* 45°45N 5°11E 175 C9
Aïn Beïda *Algeria* 35°50N 7°29E 261 A6
Aïn Ben Khellil *Algeria* 33°15N 0°49W 261 B4
Aïn Ben Tili *Mauritania* 25°59N 9°27W 260 C3
Aïn Beni Mathar *Morocco* 34°1N 2°0W 261 B4
Aïn Benian *Algeria* 36°48N 2°55E 261 A5
Ain Dalla *Egypt* 27°20N 27°23E 256 B2
Aïn Defla *Algeria* 36°16N 1°58E 261 A5
Aïn Defla ☐ *Algeria* 36°10N 2°10E 261 A5
Ain el Akhḍar *Egypt* 28°50N 33°55E 251 K4
Ain el Mafki *Egypt* 27°30N 28°15E 256 B2
Ain Girba *Egypt* 29°20N 25°14E 256 B2
Aïn M'lila *Algeria* 36°2N 6°35E 261 A6
Ain Murr *Sudan* 21°50N 25°9E 256 C2
Ain Qeiqab *Egypt* 29°42N 24°55E 256 B1
Aïn Salah = In Salah *Algeria* 27°10N 2°32E 261 C5
Aïn Sefra *Algeria* 32°47N 0°37W 261 B4
Ain Sheikh Murzûk *Egypt* 26°47N 27°45E 256 B2
Ain Sudr *Egypt* 29°50N 33°6E 251 J4
Ain Sukhna *Egypt* 29°32N 32°20E 256 J8
Aïn Tédelès *Algeria* 36°0N 0°21E 261 A5
Aïn Témouchent *Algeria* 35°16N 1°8W 261 A4
Aïn Témouchent ☐ *Algeria* 35°20N 1°5W 261 A4
Aïn Tikkidine *Algeria* 25°33N 1°24E 261 C5
Aïn Touta *Algeria* 35°26N 5°54E 261 A6
Ain Zeitûn *Egypt* 29°10N 25°48E 256 B2
Aïn Zorah *Morocco* 34°37N 3°32W 261 B4
Ainaži *Latvia* 57°50N 24°24E 188 D3
Ainos Oros *Greece* 38°9N 20°40E 207 C2
Ainsworth *U.S.A.* 42°33N 99°52W 308 D4
Aintab = Gaziantep *Turkey* 37°6N 37°23E 250 A8
Aioi *Japan* 34°48N 134°28E 222 C6
Aiome *Papua N. G.* 5°8S 144°44E 286 C3
Aipe *Colombia* 3°13N 75°15W 328 C2
Aiquile *Bolivia* 18°10S 65°10W 331 D4
Aïr *Niger* 18°30N 8°0E 259 E1
Air Canada Centre *Toronto, Canada* 141 c2
Aïr et Ténéré △ *Niger* 18°12N 9°56E 263 B6
Air Force I. *Canada* 67°58N 74°5W 295 D17
Air Hitam *Malaysia* 1°55N 103°11E 237 M4
Air View Park *Singapore* 1°20N 103°46E 138 A2
Aira *Japan* 31°43N 130°43E 222 F2
Airaines *France* 49°58N 1°55E 173 C8
Airão *Brazil* 1°56S 61°22W 329 D5
Airbangis *Indonesia* 0°12N 99°22E 234 B1
Airdrie *Alta., Canada* 51°18N 114°2W 296 C6
Airdrie *N. Lanarks., U.K.* 55°52N 3°57W 167 F5
Aire ➜ *Meuse, France* 49°18N 4°49E 173 C11
Aire ➜ *N. Yorks., U.K.* 53°43N 0°55W 168 D7
Aire, I. de l' *Spain* 39°48N 4°16E 206 B5
Aire-sur-la-Lys *France* 50°37N 2°22E 173 B9
Aire-sur-l'Adour *France* 43°42N 0°15W 174 E3
Aireys Inlet *Australia* 38°29S 144°52E 282 E6
Airlie Beach *Australia* 20°16S 148°43E 280 b
Airport West *Australia* 37°42S 144°52E 128 A1
Airvault *France* 46°50N 0°8W 172 F6
Aisch ➜ *Germany* 49°49N 10°58E 179 F6
Aisen ☐ *Chile* 46°30S 73°0W 336 C2
Aisne ☐ *France* 49°42N 3°40E 173 C10
Aisne ➜ *France* 49°26N 2°50E 173 C9
Ait *India* 25°54N 79°14E 243 G8
Ait Ben Haddou *Morocco* 31°3N 7°7W 260 B3
Aitana, Sierra de *Spain* 38°35N 0°24W 197 G4
Aitape *Papua N. G.* 3°11S 142°22E 286 B2
Aitkin *U.S.A.* 46°32N 93°42W 308 B7
Aitutaki *Cook Is.* 18°52S 159°45W 289 J12
Aiuaba *Brazil* 6°38S 40°7W 332 C3
Aiud *Romania* 46°19N 23°44E 183 D8
Aix-en-Provence *France* 43°32N 5°27E 175 E9
Aix-la-Chapelle = Aachen *Germany* 50°45N 6°6E 178 E2
Aix-les-Bains *France* 45°41N 5°53E 175 C9
Aixe-sur-Vienne *France* 45°47N 1°9E 174 C5
Aiyang, Mt. *Papua N. G.* 5°10S 141°20E 286 C1
Aiyina = Egina *Greece* 37°45N 23°26E 204 D5
Aizawl *India* 23°40N 92°44E 241 D4
Aizenay *France* 46°44N 1°38W 172 F5
Aizkraukle *Latvia* 56°36N 25°11E 188 D3
Aizpute *Latvia* 56°43N 21°40E 188 D2
Aizuwakamatsu *Japan* 37°30N 139°56E 220 F9
Ajabshir *Iran* 37°28N 45°54E 213 D11
Ajaccio *France* 41°55N 8°40E 175 G12
Ajaccio, G. d' *France* 41°52N 8°40E 175 G12
Ajai △ *Uganda* 2°52N 31°16E 268 B3
Ajaigarh *India* 24°52N 80°16E 243 G9
Ajajú ➜ *Colombia* 0°59N 72°20W 328 C3
Ajalpan *Mexico* 18°22N 97°15W 319 D5
Ajanta *India* 20°30N 75°48E 244 D2
Ajanta Ra. *India* 20°28N 75°50E 244 D2
Ajaokuta *Nigeria* 7°28N 6°42E 263 D6
Ajari Rep. = Ajaria ☐ *Georgia* 41°30N 42°0E 191 K6
Ajaria ☐ *Georgia* 41°30N 42°0E 191 K6
Ajax *Canada* 43°50N 79°1W 312 C5
Ajax, Mt. *N.Z.* 42°35S 172°5E 285 C7
Ajdābiyā *Libya* 30°54N 20°4E 258 B4
Ajdovščina *Slovenia* 45°54N 13°54E 199 C10
Ajegunle *Nigeria* 6°26N 3°20E 124 B2
Aji *Japan* 34°40N 135°27E 133 A1
Ajibar *Ethiopia* 10°35N 38°36E 257 E4
Ajka *Hungary* 47°4N 17°31E 182 C2
'Ajlūn *Jordan* 32°18N 35°47E 251 F6
'Ajmān *U.A.E.* 25°25N 55°30E 247 E7
Ajmer *India* 26°28N 74°37E 242 F6
Ajnala *India* 31°50N 74°48E 242 D6
Ajo *U.S.A.* 32°22N 112°52W 305 K7
Ajo, C. de *Spain* 43°31N 3°35W 194 B7
Ajoupa-Bouillon *Martinique* 14°49N 61°7W 322 j
Ajuda *Portugal* 38°42N 9°12W 126 A1
Ajuda, Pta. da *Azores* 37°52N 25°19W 153 d3
Ajuy *Phil.* 11°10N 123°1E 233 F4
Ak Dağ *Turkey* 36°30N 29°32E 205 E11
Ak Dağlar *Turkey* 39°32N 36°12E 212 C7
Ak Dağları *Turkey* 36°30N 29°30E 205 E11
Ak-Dovurak *Russia* 51°11N 90°36E 217 B12
Ak-Mechet = Qyzylorda *Kazakhstan* 44°48N 65°28E 216 D7
Ak-Mednet = Chornomorske *Ukraine* 45°31N 32°40E 189 K7
Ak-Sheikh = Razdolnoye *Ukraine* 45°46N 33°29E 189 K7
Akaba *Togo* 8°10N 1°2E 263 D5
Akabira *Japan* 43°33N 142°5E 220 C11
Akabli *Algeria* 26°49N 1°31E 261 C5
Akademika Obrucheva, Khrebet *Russia* 51°50N 96°0E 217 B13
Akagera △ *Rwanda* 1°31S 30°33E 268 C3
Akaishi-Dake *Japan* 35°27N 138°9E 223 B10
Akaishi-Sammyaku *Japan* 35°25N 138°10E 223 B10
Akaki Beseka *Ethiopia* 8°55N 38°45E 257 F4
Akākūs, J. *Libya* 25°20N 10°30E 258 C2
Akalkot *India* 17°32N 76°13E 244 F3
Akalla *Sweden* 59°24N 17°55E 139 A1
Akamas *Cyprus* 35°3N 32°18E 207 E8
Akan △ *Japan* 43°20N 144°20E 220 C12
Akanthou *Cyprus* 35°22N 33°45E 207 E9
Akarca *Turkey* 38°35N 29°35E 205 C11
Akaroa *N.Z.* 43°49S 172°59E 285 D7
Akaroa Harbour *N.Z.* 43°50S 172°55E 285 D7
Akasaka *Tokyo, Japan* 140 b3
Akasha *Sudan* 21°10N 30°32E 256 C3
Akashi *Japan* 34°45N 134°58E 222 C6
Akbarābād *Iran* 35°40N 51°20E 141 A2
Akbarpur *Bihar, India* 24°39N 83°58E 243 G10
Akbarpur *Ut. P., India* 26°25N 82°32E 243 F10
Akbou *Algeria* 36°31N 4°31E 261 A5
Akbulak *Russia* 51°1N 55°37E 216 B5
Akçaabat *Turkey* 41°1N 39°34E 213 B8
Akçadağ *Turkey* 38°27N 37°43E 212 C7
Akçakale *Turkey* 36°41N 38°56E 213 D8
Akçakoca *Turkey* 41°5N 31°8E 212 B4
Akçalı Dağları *Turkey* 36°18N 33°21E 250 B4
Akçaova *Turkey* 41°3N 29°57E 203 E13
Akçay *Turkey* 36°36N 29°45E 205 E11
Akçay ➜ *Turkey* 37°50N 28°15E 205 D10
Akchâr *Mauritania* 20°20N 14°28W 260 D2
Akchi-Karasu = Toktogul *Kyrgyzstan* 41°50N 72°50E 217 D8
Akdağ *Antalya, Turkey* 37°0N 32°0E 250 B3
Akdağ *Izmir, Turkey* 38°33N 26°30E 205 C8
Akdağmadeni *Turkey* 39°39N 35°53E 212 C6
Akdere *Turkey* 36°14N 33°46E 250 B4
Akdoğan = Lysi *Cyprus* 35°6N 33°41E 207 E9
Akechi *Japan* 35°18N 137°23E 223 B9
Akelamo *Indonesia* 1°35N 129°40E 231 D7
Åkernes = Åknes *Norway* 58°45N 7°30E 164 F4
Åkers styckebruk *Sweden* 59°15N 17°5E 162 E11
Åkersberga *Sweden* 59°29N 18°18E 162 E12
Akershus ☐ *Norway* 60°0N 11°10E 164 D8
Akershus Slott *Oslo, Norway* 133 c1
Akeru ➜ *India* 17°25N 80°5E 244 F5
Aketi *Dem. Rep. of the Congo* 2°38N 23°47E 264 B4
Akhali Atoni *Georgia* 43°7N 40°50E 191 J5
Akhalkalaki *Georgia* 41°27N 43°25E 191 K6
Akhaltsikhe *Georgia* 41°40N 43°0E 191 K6
Akhḍar, W. al ➜ *Si. Arabia* 28°36N 36°36E 251 K7
Akhiok *U.S.A.* 56°57N 154°10W 303 H9
Akhisar *Turkey* 38°56N 27°48E 205 C9
Akhmîm *Egypt* 26°31N 31°47E 256 B3
Akhna *Cyprus* 35°3N 33°47E 207 E9
Akhnur *India* 32°52N 74°45E 243 C6
Akhtarīn *Syria* 36°31N 37°20E 250 B8
Akhtopol *Bulgaria* 42°6N 27°56E 203 D11
Akhtuba ➜ *Russia* 47°41N 46°55E 191 G8
Akhtubinsk *Russia* 48°13N 46°7E 191 F8
Akhty *Russia* 41°30N 47°45E 191 K8
Akhtyrka = Okhtyrka *Ukraine* 50°25N 35°0E 189 G8
Aki *Japan* 33°30N 133°54E 222 D5
Aki-Nada *Japan* 34°5N 132°40E 222 C4
Akiachak *U.S.A.* 60°55N 161°26W 303 F7
Akiak *U.S.A.* 60°55N 161°13W 303 F7
Akiéni *Gabon* 1°11S 13°53E 264 C2
Akihabara *Tokyo, Japan* 140 a5
Akimiski I. *Canada* 52°50N 81°30W 298 B3
Akıncı Burnu *Turkey* 36°19N 35°46E 250 B6
Akıncılar = Louroujina *Cyprus* 35°0N 33°28E 207 F9
Akiōta *Japan* 34°36N 132°19E 222 C4
Åkirkeby *Denmark* 55°4N 14°55E 163 J8
Akita *Japan* 39°45N 140°7E 220 E10
Akita ☐ *Japan* 39°40N 140°30E 220 E10
Akjoujt *Mauritania* 19°45N 14°15W 262 B2
Akka *Mali* 15°24N 4°11W 262 B4
Akka *Morocco* 29°22N 8°9W 260 C3
Akkaraipattu *Sri Lanka* 7°13N 81°51E 245 L5
Akkaya Tepesi *Turkey* 37°25N 29°38E 205 D11
Akkerman = Bilhorod-Dnistrovskyy *Ukraine* 46°11N 30°23E 189 J6
Akkeshi *Japan* 43°2N 144°51E 220 C12
'Akko *Israel* 32°55N 35°4E 250 F6
Akköy *Turkey* 37°29N 27°15E 205 D9
Akkuş *Turkey* 40°47N 37°0E 212 B7
Aklampa *Benin* 8°15N 2°10E 263 D5
Aklan ☐ *Phil.* 11°50N 122°30E 233 F4
Aklavik *Canada* 68°12N 135°0W 294 D4
Aklera *India* 24°26N 76°32E 242 G7
Akmenė *Lithuania* 56°15N 22°45E 184 B9
Akmenrags *Latvia* 56°50N 21°4E 184 B8
Akmolinsk = Astana *Kazakhstan* 51°10N 71°30E 217 B8
Akmonte = Almonte *Spain* 37°13N 6°38W 195 H4
Åknes *Norway* 58°45N 7°30E 164 F4
Aknoul *Morocco* 34°40N 3°55W 261 B4
Akō *Japan* 34°45N 134°24E 222 C6
Ako *Nigeria* 10°19N 10°48E 263 C7
Akobo *South Sudan* 7°47N 33°1E 257 F3
Akobo ➜ *Ethiopia* 7°48N 33°3E 257 F3
Akola *Maharashtra, India* 20°42N 77°2E 244 D3
Akola *Maharashtra, India* 19°32N 74°3E 244 E2
Akolmiut *U.S.A.* 60°55N 162°20W 303 F7
Akonolinga *Cameroon* 3°50N 12°18E 263 E7
Akor *Mali* 14°59N 6°58W 262 C3
Akordat *Eritrea* 15°30N 37°40E 257 D4
Akosombo Dam *Ghana* 6°20N 0°5E 263 D5
Akot *India* 21°10N 77°10E 244 D3
Akot *South Sudan* 6°31N 30°9E 257 F3
Akoupé *Ivory C.* 6°23N 3°54W 262 D4
Akourousoulba *C.A.R.* 8°58N 20°46E 264 A4
Akpatok I. *Canada* 60°25N 68°8W 295 E18
Åkrahamn *Norway* 59°15N 5°10E 164 E2
'Akramah *Libya* 32°2N 23°41E 258 B4
Akranes *Iceland* 64°19N 22°5W 155 C4
Akrēījit *Mauritania* 18°19N 9°11W 262 B3
Akritas, Akra *Greece* 36°43N 21°54E 204 E3
Akron *Colo., U.S.A.* 40°10N 103°13W 304 F12
Akron *Ind., U.S.A.* 41°2N 86°1W 311 C10
Akron *Ohio, U.S.A.* 41°5N 81°31W 312 E3
Akrotiri *Cyprus* 34°36N 32°57E 207 F8
Akrotiri, Akra *Greece* 40°26N 25°27E 203 F9
Akrotiri Bay *Cyprus* 34°35N 33°10E 207 F8
Aksai Chin *China* 35°15N 79°55E 243 B8
Aksaray *Turkey* 38°25N 34°2E 212 C6
Aksaray ☐ *Turkey* 38°20N 33°45E 212 C5
Aksay = Aqsay *Kazakhstan* 51°11N 53°0E 187 D9
Akşehir *Turkey* 38°18N 31°30E 212 C4
Akşehir Gölü *Turkey* 38°30N 31°25E 212 C4
Akseki *Turkey* 37°2N 31°47E 250 A2
Akstafa = Ağstafa *Azerbaijan* 41°7N 45°27E 191 K7
Aksu *Xinjiang Uygur, China* 41°5N 80°10E 217 D10
Aksu *Turkey* 36°57N 30°50E 250 B1
Aksu ➜ *Turkey* 36°52N 30°57E 250 B1
Aksu He ➜ *China* 40°26N 80°59E 217 D10
Aksum *Ethiopia* 14°5N 38°40E 257 E4
Aktash *Russia* 55°2N 52°0E 190 C11
Aktepe *Turkey* 36°42N 36°27E 250 B7
Aktio *Greece* 38°57N 20°46E 207 B2
Akto *China* 39°5N 75°59E 217 E9
Aktsyabrski *Belarus* 52°38N 28°53E 177 B15
Aktyubinsk = Aqtöbe *Kazakhstan* 50°17N 57°10E 187 D10
Aku *Nigeria* 6°40N 7°18E 263 D6
Akula *Dem. Rep. of the Congo* 2°22N 20°12E 264 B4
Akun I. *U.S.A.* 54°11N 165°32W 303 J6
Akune *Japan* 32°1N 130°12E 222 E2
Akure *Nigeria* 7°15N 5°5E 263 D6
Akurenan *Eq. Guin.* 1°2N 10°40E 264 B2
Akuressa *Sri Lanka* 6°5N 80°29E 245 L5
Akureyri *Iceland* 65°40N 18°6W 155 B8
Akuseki-Shima *Japan* 29°27N 129°37E 221 K4
Akusha *Russia* 42°18N 47°30E 191 J8
Akutan *U.S.A.* 54°8N 165°46W 303 J6
Akutan I. *U.S.A.* 54°7N 165°55W 303 J6
Akwa-Ibom ☐ *Nigeria* 4°30N 7°30E 263 E6
Akwanga *Nigeria* 8°55N 8°23E 263 D6
Akyab = Sittwe *Burma* 20°18N 92°45E 241 E4
Akyazı *Turkey* 40°40N 30°38E 212 B4
Ål *Norway* 60°38N 8°33E 164 D5
Al Abyaḍ *Libya* 26°49N 14°1E 258 C2
Al Abyār *Libya* 32°9N 20°29E 258 B4
Al 'Adam *Libya* 31°51N 23°55E 258 B4
Al 'Adan = 'Adan *Yemen* 12°45N 45°0E 248 D4
Al Aḥsā = Hasa *Si. Arabia* 25°50N 49°0E 247 E6
Al Ajfar *Si. Arabia* 27°26N 43°0E 246 E4
Al Akhḍar, al Jabal *Libya* 32°30N 21°30E 258 B4
Al Amādīyah *Iraq* 37°5N 43°30E 213 D10
Al 'Amārah *Iraq* 31°55N 47°15E 213 G12
Al Anbār ☐ *Iraq* 33°25N 42°0E 246 C4
Al 'Aqabah *Jordan* 29°31N 35°0E 251 J6
Al 'Aqabah ☐ *Jordan* 29°30N 35°0E 251 J6
Al 'Aqīq *Si. Arabia* 20°39N 41°25E 248 B3
Al Arak *Syria* 34°38N 38°35E 213 E8
Al 'Aramah *Si. Arabia* 25°30N 46°0E 246 E5
Al 'Ariḍah *Si. Arabia* 17°3N 43°5E 248 C3
Al 'Arṭāwīyah *Si. Arabia* 26°31N 45°20E 246 E5
Al Ashkhara *Oman* 21°50N 59°30E 249 B7
Al 'Āṣimah = 'Ammān ☐ *Jordan* 31°40N 36°30E 251 G7
Al 'Assāfiyah *Si. Arabia* 28°17N 38°59E 246 D3
Al Atārib *Syria* 36°9N 36°49E 250 B7
Al 'Awdah *Si. Arabia* 25°32N 45°41E 246 E5
Al 'Ayn *Si. Arabia* 25°4N 38°6E 246 E3
Al 'Ayn *U.A.E.* 24°15N 55°45E 247 E7
Al 'Azamīyah *Iraq* 33°22N 44°22E 113 A2
Al 'Azīzīyah *Iraq* 32°54N 45°4E 213 F11
Al 'Azīzīyah *Libya* 32°30N 13°1E 258 B2
Al Bāb *Syria* 36°23N 37°29E 250 B8
Al Bad' *Si. Arabia* 28°28N 35°1E 246 D2
Al Bada *U.A.E.* 25°13N 55°16E 119 B2
Al Bada'i' *Si. Arabia* 26°2N 43°33E 246 E4
Al Bādī *Iraq* 35°56N 41°32E 246 C4
Al Badī' *Si. Arabia* 22°0N 46°35E 248 B4
Al Bāḥah *Si. Arabia* 20°1N 41°28E 256 C5
Al Bāḥah ☐ *Si. Arabia* 20°30N 41°30E 248 B3
Al Baḥrah *Kuwait* 29°40N 47°52E 246 D5
Al Baḥral Mayyit = Dead Sea *Asia* 31°30N 35°30E 251 G6
Al Balqā' ☐ *Jordan* 32°5N 35°45E 251 F6
Al Barkāt *Libya* 24°56N 10°14E 258 D2
Al Barsha *U.A.E.* 25°6N 55°11E 119 B1
Al Bārūk, J. *Lebanon* 33°39N 35°40E 250 E6
Al Başrah *Iraq* 30°30N 47°50E 246 D5
Al Baṭḥā *Iraq* 31°6N 45°53E 246 D5
Al Bāṭinah ☐ *Oman* 24°0N 57°0E 249 B7
Al Batrūn *Lebanon* 34°15N 35°40E 250 D6
Al Bayaḍ *Si. Arabia* 22°0N 47°0E 248 B4
Al Bayḍā *Libya* 32°50N 21°44E 258 B4
Al Bayḍā' *Yemen* 14°5N 45°42E 248 D4
Al Bayḍā' ☐ *Yemen* 14°5N 45°42E 248 D4
Al Bi'ār *Si. Arabia* 22°39N 39°40E 248 B2
Al Biqā *Lebanon* 34°10N 36°10E 250 D7
Al Biqā ☐ *Lebanon* 34°0N 36°5E 250 E7
Al Bi'r *Si. Arabia* 28°51N 36°16E 251 K7
Al Birk *Si. Arabia* 18°13N 41°33E 248 C3
Al Bu'ayrāt al Ḥasūn *Libya* 31°24N 15°44E 258 B3
Al Bukayrīyah *Si. Arabia* 26°9N 43°40E 246 E4
Al Bumbah *Libya* 32°24N 23°8E 258 B4
Al Burayj *Syria* 34°15N 36°46E 250 D7
Al Buṭnān ☐ *Libya* 31°40N 24°30E 258 B4
Al Buwayqāt *Yemen* 15°22N 48°30E 249 D5
Al Faḍilī *Si. Arabia* 26°58N 49°10E 247 E6
Al Fallūjah *Iraq* 33°20N 43°55E 213 F10
Al Fatḥah *Iraq* 35°3N 43°33E 213 E10
Al Fāw *Iraq* 30°0N 48°30E 247 D6
Al Faydamī *Yemen* 16°25N 52°26E 249 C6
Al Fujayrah *U.A.E.* 25°7N 56°18E 247 E8
Al Ghadaf, W. ➜ *Jordan* 31°26N 36°43E 251 G7
Al Ghammās *Iraq* 31°45N 44°37E 246 D5
Al Gharīb *Libya* 32°35N 21°11E 258 B4
Al Ghayḍah *Yemen* 16°13N 52°11E 249 C6
Al Ghayl *Yemen* 15°30N 50°54E 249 D5
Al Ghazālah *Si. Arabia* 26°48N 41°19E 246 E4
Al Ghuwayfāt *U.A.E.* 24°10N 51°38E 247 E6
Al Ḥadd *Oman* 22°32N 59°48E 249 B7
Al Ḥaddār *Si. Arabia* 21°58N 45°57E 248 B4
Al Ḥadīthah *Iraq* 34°0N 41°13E 213 E10
Al Ḥadīthah *Si. Arabia* 31°28N 37°8E 246 D3
Al Ḥaḍr *Iraq* 35°35N 42°44E 213 E10
Al Ḥaffah *Syria* 35°36N 36°1E 250 C7
Al Ḥājānah *Syria* 33°20N 36°33E 250 E7
Al Ḥajar al Gharbī *Oman* 24°10N 56°15E 247 E8
Al Ḥallānīyah *Oman* 17°30N 56°1E 249 C7
Al Ḥāmad *Si. Arabia* 31°30N 39°30E 246 D3
Al Ḥamar *Si. Arabia* 22°26N 46°12E 248 B4
Al Ḥamdānīyah *Syria* 35°25N 36°50E 250 C7
Al Ḥāmī *Yemen* 14°48N 49°49E 249 D5
Al Ḥamīdīyah *Syria* 34°42N 35°57E 250 D6
Al Ḥammār *Iraq* 30°57N 46°51E 246 D5
Al Ḥamrā' *Si. Arabia* 24°2N 38°55E 246 E3
Al Ḥamrā' *Syria* 35°19N 37°5E 250 C8
Al Ḥamrā', al Ḥamādah *Libya* 29°30N 12°0E 258 C2
Al Hamriya Port *U.A.E.* 25°18N 55°20E 119 A2
Al Ḥamzah *Iraq* 31°43N 44°58E 246 D5
Al Ḥanākīyah *Si. Arabia* 24°51N 40°31E 246 E4
Al Ḥarīq *Si. Arabia* 23°29N 46°27E 248 B4
Al Ḥarūj al Aswad *Libya* 27°0N 17°10E 258 C3
Al Ḥasakah *Syria* 36°35N 40°45E 213 D9
Al Ḥasakah ☐ *Syria* 36°40N 40°50E 213 D9
Al Ḥāshimīyah *Iraq* 32°22N 44°39E 213 G11
Al Ḥāsikīyah *Oman* 17°28N 55°36E 249 C6
Al Hawīyah *Ash Sharqīyah, Si. Arabia* 24°45N 49°6E 249 A5
Al Ḥawīyah *Makkah, Si. Arabia* 21°26N 40°30E 248 B3
Al Ḥawrah *Yemen* 13°50N 47°35E 248 D4
Al Ḥawṭah = Laḥij *Yemen* 13°4N 44°53E 248 D4
Al Ḥawṭah *Si. Arabia* 23°30N 47°0E 248 B4
Al Ḥayy *Iraq* 32°5N 46°5E 213 F12
Al Ḥazm = Al Jawf *Yemen* 16°10N 44°37E 248 C4
Al Ḥijārah *Asia* 30°0N 44°0E 246 D4
Al Ḥillah *Iraq* 32°30N 44°25E 213 F11
Al Ḥillah *Si. Arabia* 23°35N 46°50E 248 B4
Al Hindīyah *Iraq* 32°30N 44°10E 213 F11
Al Hirmil *Lebanon* 34°26N 36°24E 250 D7
Al Hoceïma *Morocco* 35°8N 3°58W 261 A4
Al Ḥudaiba *U.A.E.* 25°14N 55°16E 119 B2
Al Ḥudaydah *Yemen* 14°50N 43°0E 248 D3
Al Ḥudaydah ☐ *Yemen* 14°50N 43°0E 248 D3
Al Ḥudūd ash Shamālīyah ☐ *Si. Arabia* 29°10N 42°30E 246 D4
Al Ḥufrah *Libya* 25°32N 14°1E 258 C2
Al Hufūf *Si. Arabia* 25°25N 49°45E 247 E6
Al Ḥulwah *Si. Arabia* 23°24N 46°48E 248 B4
Al Ḥumaydah *Si. Arabia* 29°14N 34°56E 251 J5
Al Ḥunayy *Si. Arabia* 25°58N 48°45E 247 E6
Al Ḥuraydah *Yemen* 15°36N 48°11E 249 D5
Al Ḥusayyāt *Libya* 30°24N 20°37E 258 B4
Al Ḥuwaymī *Yemen* 14°5N 47°32E 248 D4
Al 'Irqah *Yemen* 13°39N 47°22E 248 D4
Al 'Isāwīyah *Si. Arabia* 30°43N 37°59E 246 D3
Al Ittihad = Madīnat ash Sha'b *Yemen* 12°50N 45°0E 248 D4
Al Jabal al Akhḍar ☐ *Libya* 32°30N 21°41E 258 B4
Al Jabal al Gharbī ☐ *Libya* 31°26N 12°59E 258 B2
Al Jafiliya *U.A.E.* 25°13N 55°16E 119 B2
Al Jafr *Jordan* 30°18N 36°14E 251 H7
Al Jāfūrah *Si. Arabia* 25°0N 50°15E 247 E7
Al Jaghbūb *Libya* 29°42N 24°38E 258 C4
Al Jahrah *Kuwait* 29°25N 47°40E 246 D5
Al Jalāmīd *Si. Arabia* 31°20N 40°6E 246 D3
Al Jamalīyah *Qatar* 25°37N 51°5E 247 E6
Al Janūb ☐ *Lebanon* 33°20N 35°20E 250 E6
Al Jawf *Libya* 24°10N 23°24E 258 D4
Al Jawf *Si. Arabia* 29°55N 39°40E 246 D3
Al Jawf *Yemen* 16°10N 44°37E 248 C4
Al Jawf ☐ *Si. Arabia* 29°30N 39°30E 246 D3
Al Jawf ☐ *Yemen* 16°15N 45°0E 248 C4
Al Jazair = Algeria ■ *Africa* 28°30N 2°0E 261 C5
Al Jazirah *Iraq* 33°30N 44°0E 213 E10
Al Jithāmīyah *Si. Arabia* 27°41N 41°43E 246 E4
Al Jubayl *Si. Arabia* 27°0N 49°50E 247 E6
Al Jubaylah *Si. Arabia* 24°55N 46°25E 246 E5
Al Jubb *Si. Arabia* 27°11N 42°17E 246 E4
Al Jufrah *Libya* 29°10N 16°0E 258 C3
Al Jufrah ☐ *Libya* 27°30N 17°30E 258 C3
Al Jumūm *Si. Arabia* 21°37N 39°42E 248 B2
Al Junaynah *Sudan* 13°27N 22°45E 259 F4
Al Kabā'ish *Iraq* 30°58N 47°0E 246 D5
Al Kāmil *Oman* 22°13N 59°12E 249 B7
Al Karak *Jordan* 31°11N 35°42E 251 G6
Al Karak ☐ *Jordan* 31°0N 36°0E 251 H7
Al Kāẓimīyah *Iraq* 33°22N 44°18E 213 F11
Al Khābūrah *Oman* 23°57N 57°5E 247 F8
Al Khafji *Si. Arabia* 28°24N 48°29E 247 E6
Al Khalīl *West Bank* 31°32N 35°6E 251 G6
Al Khāliṣ *Iraq* 33°49N 44°32E 213 F11
Al Khamāsīn *Si. Arabia* 20°29N 44°46E 248 B4
Al Kharj *Si. Arabia* 24°0N 47°0E 248 B4
Al Kharsānīyah *Si. Arabia* 27°13N 49°18E 247 E6
Al Khaṣab *Oman* 26°14N 56°15E 247 E8
Al Khāṣirah *Si. Arabia* 23°30N 43°47E 248 B3
Al Khawr *Qatar* 25°41N 51°30E 247 E6
Al Khiḍr *Iraq* 31°12N 45°33E 246 D5
Al Khiyām *Lebanon* 33°20N 35°36E 250 E6
Al Khubar *Si. Arabia* 26°17N 50°12E 247 E6
Al Khums *Libya* 32°40N 14°17E 258 B2
Al Khurmah *Si. Arabia* 21°54N 42°3E 248 B3
Al Kifl *Iraq* 32°13N 44°22E 213 G11
Al Kiswah *Syria* 33°23N 36°14E 250 E7
Al Kūfah *Iraq* 32°2N 44°24E 213 F11
Al Kufrah *Libya* 24°17N 23°15E 258 D4
Al Kuhayfiyah *Si. Arabia* 27°12N 43°3E 246 E4
Al Kumayt *Iraq* 32°2N 46°52E 213 G12
Al Kūt *Iraq* 32°30N 46°0E 213 F11
Al Kuwayt *Kuwait* 29°30N 48°0E 246 D5
Al Labwah *Lebanon* 34°11N 36°20E 250 D7
Al Lādhiqīyah *Syria* 35°30N 35°45E 250 C6
Al Lādhiqīyah ☐ *Syria* 35°45N 36°0E 250 C7
Al Līth *Si. Arabia* 20°9N 40°15E 248 B3
Al Liwā' *Oman* 24°31N 56°36E 247 E8
Al Luḥayyah *Yemen* 15°45N 42°40E 248 D3
Al Madīnah *Iraq* 30°57N 47°16E 246 D5
Al Madīnah *Si. Arabia* 24°35N 39°52E 246 E3
Al Madīnah ☐ *Si. Arabia* 23°50N 40°30E 248 B3
Al Mafraq *Jordan* 32°17N 36°14E 251 F7
Al Mafraq ☐ *Jordan* 32°17N 36°15E 251 F7
Al Maghreb = Morocco ■ *N. Afr.* 32°0N 5°50W 260 B3
Al Maḥābishah *Yemen* 15°55N 43°24E 248 D3
Al Mahbes *W. Sahara* 27°10N 9°50W 260 C3
Al Maḥfidh *Yemen* 14°5N 46°55E 248 D4
Al Maḥmūdīyah *Iraq* 33°3N 44°21E 213 F11
Al Mahrah *Yemen* 16°0N 51°20E 249 D5
Al Mahrah ☐ *Yemen* 17°0N 52°0E 249 C6
Al Maḥwīt *Yemen* 15°29N 43°33E 248 D3
Al Majma'ah *Si. Arabia* 25°57N 45°22E 246 E5
Al Makhruq, W. ➜ *Jordan* 31°28N 37°0E 251 G8
Al Makḥūl *Si. Arabia* 26°37N 42°39E 246 E4
Al Mālikīyah *Syria* 37°10N 42°8E 213 D10
Al Manāmah *Bahrain* 26°10N 50°30E 247 E6
Al Manara *U.A.E.* 25°9N 55°14E 119 B1
Al Maqwa' *Kuwait* 29°10N 47°59E 246 D5
Al Marāḥ *Si. Arabia* 25°35N 49°35E 247 E6
Al Marāwi'ah *Yemen* 14°50N 43°9E 248 D3
Al Marj *Libya* 32°25N 20°30E 258 B4
Al Marj ☐ *Libya* 32°0N 21°0E 258 B4
Al Marqab ☐ *Libya* 32°32N 14°35E 258 B2
Al Masana'a *Oman* 23°46N 57°39E 249 B7
Al Maṭlā *Kuwait* 29°24N 47°40E 246 D5
Al Mawṣil *Iraq* 36°15N 43°5E 213 D10
Al Mayādin *Syria* 35°1N 40°27E 213 E9
Al Mazār *Jordan* 31°4N 35°41E 251 G6
Al Midhnab *Si. Arabia* 25°50N 44°18E 246 E5
Al Minā' *Lebanon* 34°24N 35°49E 250 D6
Al Mina *U.A.E.* 25°15N 55°16E 119 B2
Al Miqdādīyah *Iraq* 34°0N 45°0E 213 E11
Al Mubarraz *Si. Arabia* 25°30N 49°40E 247 E6
Al Mudawwarah *Jordan* 29°19N 36°0E 251 J7
Al Muḍaybī *Oman* 22°34N 58°7E 249 B7
Al Mughayrā' *U.A.E.* 24°5N 53°32E 247 E7
Al Muḥarraq *Bahrain* 26°15N 50°40E 247 E6
Al Mukallā *Yemen* 14°33N 49°2E 249 D5
Al Mukhā *Yemen* 13°18N 43°15E 248 D3
Al Mukhaylī *Libya* 32°10N 22°17E 258 B4
Al Musayjīd *Si. Arabia* 24°5N 39°5E 246 E3
Al Musayyib *Iraq* 32°49N 44°20E 213 F11
Al Muthannā ☐ *Iraq* 30°30N 45°15E 246 D5
Al Muwayh *Si. Arabia* 22°41N 41°37E 256 C5
Al Muwayliḥ *Si. Arabia* 27°40N 35°30E 246 E2
Al Muzāḥimīyah *Si. Arabia* 24°29N 46°18E 248 A4
Al Nasr *U.A.E.* 25°14N 55°18E 119 B2
Al Owuho = Otukpa *Nigeria* 7°9N 7°41E 263 D6
Al Qaddāḥīyah *Libya* 31°15N 15°9E 258 B3
Al Qaḍīmah *Si. Arabia* 22°20N 39°13E 248 B2
Al Qādisīyah ☐ *Iraq* 32°0N 45°0E 246 D5
Al Qadmūs *Syria* 35°5N 36°10E 250 C7
Al Qaḥmah *Si. Arabia* 18°0N 41°40E 248 C3
Al Qā'idah *Yemen* 13°45N 44°10E 248 D4
Al Qā'im *Iraq* 34°21N 41°7E 213 E9
Al Qā'īyah *Si. Arabia* 24°33N 43°15E 248 A3
Al Qalībah *Si. Arabia* 28°24N 37°42E 246 D3
Al Qāmishlī *Syria* 37°2N 41°14E 213 D9
Al Qardāḥah *Syria* 35°27N 36°3E 250 C7
Al Qaryah ash Sharqīyah *Libya* 30°28N 13°40E 258 B2
Al Qaryatayn *Syria* 34°12N 37°13E 250 D8
Al Qaṣabāt *Libya* 32°39N 14°1E 258 B2
Al Qaṣīm ☐ *Si. Arabia* 26°0N 43°0E 246 E4
Al Qaṭ'ā *Syria* 34°40N 40°48E 213 E9
Al Qaṭīf *Si. Arabia* 26°35N 50°0E 247 E6
Al Qaṭn *Yemen* 15°51N 48°26E 249 D5
Al Qatrānah *Jordan* 31°12N 36°6E 251 G7
Al Qaṭrūn *Libya* 24°56N 15°3E 258 D3
Al Qawz *Si. Arabia* 18°58N 41°26E 248 C3
Al Qayṣūmah *Si. Arabia* 28°20N 46°7E 246 D5
Al Qiblīyah *Oman* 17°30N 56°20E 249 C7
Al Quds = Jerusalem *Israel/West Bank* 31°47N 35°10E 123 B2
Al Qunayṭirah *Syria* 33°5N 35°45E 250 E6
Al Qunfudhah *Si. Arabia* 19°3N 41°4E 248 C3
Al Quoz *U.A.E.* 25°8N 55°14E 119 B1
Al Qurayyāt *Oman* 23°17N 58°53E 249 B7
Al Qurayyāt *Si. Arabia* 31°20N 37°20E 251 G8
Al Qurḥ *Yemen* 16°44N 51°29E 249 C6
Al Qurnah *Iraq* 31°1N 47°25E 246 D5
Al Quṣayr *Iraq* 30°39N 45°50E 246 D5
Al Quṣayr *Syria* 34°31N 36°34E 250 D7
Al Quṭayfah *Syria* 33°44N 36°36E 250 E7
Al Quway'īyah *Si. Arabia* 24°3N 45°15E 248 A4
Al Quwaysimah *Jordan* 31°55N 35°57E 251 G6
Al Safa *U.A.E.* 25°10N 55°14E 119 B1
Al Satwa *U.A.E.* 25°13N 55°16E 119 B2
Al Seeb = As Sīb *Oman* 23°41N 58°11E 249 B7
Al Sufouh *U.A.E.* 25°7N 55°12E 119 B1
Al 'Ubaylah *Si. Arabia* 21°59N 50°57E 249 B5
Al 'Uḍaylīyah *Si. Arabia* 25°8N 49°18E 247 E6
Al 'Ulā *Si. Arabia* 26°35N 38°0E 246 E3
Al 'Ulayyah *Si. Arabia* 19°39N 41°54E 248 C3
Al Uqaylah ash Sharqīgah *Libya* 30°12N 19°10E 258 B3
Al 'Uqayr *Si. Arabia* 25°40N 50°15E 247 E6
Al 'Urūq al Mutariḍah *Si. Arabia* 21°0N 53°30E 249 B6
Al 'Uwaynāt *Libya* 25°47N 10°34E 261 C7
Al 'Uwaynid *Si. Arabia* 24°50N 46°0E 246 E5
Al 'Uwayqīlah *Si. Arabia* 30°30N 42°10E 246 D4
Al Uweinat *Libya* 21°34N 24°50E 259 D4
Al 'Uyūn *Ḥijāz, Si. Arabia* 24°33N 39°35E 246 E3
Al 'Uyūn *Najd, Si. Arabia* 26°30N 43°50E 246 E4
Al 'Uzayr *Iraq* 31°19N 47°25E 246 D5
Al Wāhāt ☐ *Libya* 29°0N 22°0E 258 C4
Al Wajh *Si. Arabia* 26°10N 36°30E 246 E3
Al Wakrah *Qatar* 25°10N 51°40E 247 E6
Al Walaja *West Bank* 31°44N 35°9E 123 B1
Al Waqbah *Si. Arabia* 28°48N 45°33E 246 D5
Al Wari'āh *Si. Arabia* 27°51N 47°25E 246 E5
Al Wasl *U.A.E.* 25°12N 55°16E 119 B2
Al Waṭīyah *Libya* 32°28N 11°57E 258 B2
Al Wīgh *Libya* 24°16N 15°30E 258 D3
Al Wusṭā ☐ *Oman* 20°0N 57°0E 249 C7
Al Yaman = Yemen ■ *Asia* 15°0N 44°0E 248 D4
Ala *Italy* 45°45N 11°0E 198 C8
Ala Archa △ *Kyrgyzstan* 42°32N 74°28E 217 D8
Ala Dağ *Turkey* 37°44N 35°9E 246 B2
Ala Dağları *Turkey* 39°15N 43°33E 213 C10
Ala Tau *Asia* 45°30N 80°40E 217 C10
Ala Tau Shankou = Dzungarian Gate *Asia* 45°10N 82°0E 217 C10
Alabama ☐ *U.S.A.* 33°0N 87°0W 315 E11
Alabama ➜ *U.S.A.* 31°8N 87°57W 315 F11
Alabaster *U.S.A.* 33°15N 86°49W 315 E11
Alabat I. *Phil.* 14°7N 122°3E 232 D4
Alabel *Phil.* 6°4N 125°16E 233 H5
Alabule ➜ *Papua N. G.* 8°31S 146°56E 286 E4
Alaca *Turkey* 40°10N 34°51E 212 B6
Alacaatlı *Turkey* 39°15N 28°3E 205 B10
Alaçam *Turkey* 41°36N 35°36E 212 B6
Alaçam Dağları *Turkey* 39°18N 28°49E 205 B10
Alacant = Alicante *Spain* 38°23N 0°30W 197 G4
Alaçatı *Turkey* 38°15N 26°22E 205 C8
Alachua *U.S.A.* 29°47N 82°30W 316 F7
Alaejos *Spain* 41°18N 5°13W 194 D5
Alagir *Russia* 43°3N 44°14E 191 J7
Alagna Valsésia *Italy* 45°51N 7°56E 198 C4
Alagoa de Baixo = Sertânia *Brazil* 8°5S 37°20W 332 C4
Alagoa Grande *Brazil* 7°3S 35°35W 332 C4
Alagoas = Marechal Deodoro *Brazil* 9°43S 35°54W 332 C4
Alagoas ☐ *Brazil* 9°0S 36°0W 332 C4
Alagoinhas *Brazil* 12°7S 38°20W 333 D4
Alagón *Spain* 41°46N 1°12W 196 D3
Alagón ➜ *Spain* 39°44N 6°53W 194 F4
Alaguntan *Nigeria* 6°25N 3°29E 124 B2
Alagyoz = Aragats *Armenia* 40°30N 44°15E 191 K7
Alahan *Turkey* 36°46N 33°19E 250 B4
Alaheaieatnu = Altaelva ➜ *Norway* 69°54N 23°17E 160 B20
Alai Range *Asia* 39°45N 72°0E 217 E8
Alaior *Spain* 39°57N 4°8E 206 B5
Alajero *Canary Is.* 28°3N 17°13W 153 e1
Alajuela *Costa Rica* 10°2N 84°8W 320 D3
Alajuela, L. *Panama* 9°14N 79°34W 320 c
Alakamisy *Madag.* 21°19S 47°14E 272 C2
Alakanuk *U.S.A.* 62°41N 164°37W 303 E6
Alaknanda ➜ *India* 30°8N 78°36E 243 D8
Alaköl *Kazakhstan* 46°0N 81°5E 217 C10
Alakurtti *Russia* 66°58N 30°25E 160 C24
'Alalākeiki Channel *U.S.A.* 20°30N 156°30W 302 C5
Alalapura *Suriname* 2°20N 56°25W 329 C6
Alalaú ➜ *Brazil* 0°30S 61°9W 329 D5
Alamagan *N. Marianas* 17°36N 145°50E 302 a
Alamarvdasht *Iran* 27°37N 52°59E 247 E7
Alamata *Ethiopia* 12°25N 39°33E 257 E4
Alameda *Calif., U.S.A.* 37°46N 122°15W 136 B3
Alameda *N. Mex., U.S.A.* 35°11N 106°37W 305 J10
Alameda, Parque *Mexico City, Mexico* 128 b2
Alameda Memorial State Beach Park *U.S.A.* 37°45N 122°16W 136 B3
Alaminos *Phil.* 16°10N 119°59E 232 C2
Alamo *Ga., U.S.A.* 32°9N 82°47W 316 C7
Alamo *Nev., U.S.A.* 37°22N 115°10W 307 H11
Alamogordo *U.S.A.* 32°54N 105°57W 305 K11
Alamos *Mexico* 27°1N 108°56W 318 B3
Alamosa *U.S.A.* 37°28N 105°52W 305 H11
Alampur *India* 15°55N 78°6E 245 G4
Åland *Finland* 60°15N 20°0E 161 F19
Aland *India* 17°36N 76°35E 244 F3
Alandroal *Portugal* 38°41N 7°24W 195 G3
Ålands hav *Europe* 60°0N 19°30E 161 G18
Ålandsbro *Sweden* 62°40N 17°51E 162 B11
Alandur *India* 13°0N 80°15E 245 H5
Alang *Indonesia* 4°7N 117°0E 235 B5
Alange, Embalse d' *Spain* 38°45N 6°18W 195 G4
Alanís *Spain* 38°3N 5°43W 195 G5
Alaniya = North Ossetia-Alaniya ☐ *Russia* 43°30N 44°30E 191 J7
Alaniya ➜ *Russia* 42°55N 44°30E 191 J7
Alanya *Turkey* 36°38N 32°0E 250 B3
Alaotra, Farihin' *Madag.* 17°30S 48°30E 272 B2
Alapaha *U.S.A.* 31°23N 83°13W 316 D6
Alapayevsk *Russia* 57°52N 61°42E 214 D7
Alappuzha *India* 9°30N 76°28E 245 K3
'Alāqān *Si. Arabia* 29°10N 35°21E 251 J6
Alar del Rey *Spain* 42°38N 4°20W 194 C6
Alara ➜ *Turkey* 36°38N 31°39E 250 B2
Alaraz *Spain* 40°45N 5°17W 194 E5
Alarcón, Embalse de *Spain* 39°36N 2°10W 196 F2
Alaró *Spain* 39°42N 2°47E 206 B3
Alarobia-Vohiposa *Madag.* 20°59S 47°9E 272 C2
Alas *Indonesia* 8°29S 117°0E 235 D5
Alas, Selat *Indonesia* 8°40S 116°40E 235 D5
Alaşehir *Turkey* 38°23N 28°30E 205 C10
Alashtar *Iran* 33°51N 48°15E 213 F13
Alaska ☐ *U.S.A.* 64°0N 154°0W 303 D9
Alaska, G. of *Pac. Oc.* 58°0N 145°0W 303 G11
Alaska Maritime Nat. Wildlife Refuge △ *U.S.A.* 52°0N 174°0W 303 L4
Alaska Peninsula *U.S.A.* 56°0N 159°0W 303 H8
Alaska Peninsula Nat. Wildlife Refuge △ *U.S.A.* 56°0N 159°0W 303 J8
Alaska Range *U.S.A.* 62°50N 151°0W 303 E10
Alássio *Italy* 44°0N 8°10E 198 E5
Ālāt *Azerbaijan* 39°58N 49°25E 191 L9
Alatau Shan = Ala Tau *Asia* 45°30N 80°40E 217 C10
Alatri *Italy* 41°43N 13°21E 199 G10
Alatyr *Russia* 54°55N 46°35E 190 C8
Alatyr ➜ *Russia* 54°52N 46°36E 190 C8
Alaungdaw Kathapa △ *Burma* 22°30N 94°30E 241 D5
Alausí *Ecuador* 2°0S 78°50W 328 D2
Álava ☐ *Spain* 42°48N 2°28W 196 C2
Alava, C. *U.S.A.* 48°10N 124°44W 306 B2
Alaverdi *Armenia* 41°15N 44°37E 191 K7
Alavo = Alavus *Finland* 62°35N 23°36E 160 E20
Alavus *Finland* 62°35N 23°36E 160 E20
Alawa ◎ *Australia* 15°42S 134°39E 280 B1

Alawoona Australia 34°45S 140°30E 282 C4
Alayawarra ☼ Australia 22°0S 134°30E 280 C1
'Alayh Lebanon 33°46N 35°33E 250 E6
Alayköy = Yerolakkos Cyprus 35°11N 33°15E 207 E9
Alazani → Azerbaijan 41°5N 46°40E 191 K8
Alba Italy 44°42N 8°2E 198 D5
Alba □ Romania 46°10N 23°30E 183 D8
Alba Adriática Italy 42°50N 13°56E 199 F10
Alba de Tormes Spain 40°50N 5°30W 194 E5
Alba-Iulia Romania 46°8N 23°39E 183 D8
Albac Romania 46°28N 22°58E 182 D7
Albacete Spain 39°0N 1°50W 197 F3
Albacete □ Spain 38°50N 2°0W 197 G3
Albacutya, L. Australia 35°45S 141°58E 282 C4
Ålbæk Denmark 57°36N 10°25E 163 G4
Ålbæk Bugt Denmark 57°35N 10°40E 163 G4
Albaida Spain 38°51N 0°31W 197 G4
Albalate de las Nogueras Spain 40°22N 2°18W 196 E2
Albalate del Arzobispo Spain 41°6N 0°31W 196 D4
Alban France 43°53N 2°28E 174 E6
Albanel, L. Canada 50°55N 73°12W 298 B5
Albania ■ Europe 41°0N 20°0E 202 E4
Albano Laziale Italy 41°44N 12°39E 199 G9
Albany W. Austral., Australia 35°1S 117°58E 279 G2
Albany Ga., U.S.A. 31°35N 84°10W 316 D5
Albany Ind., U.S.A. 40°18N 85°14W 311 D11
Albany Mo., U.S.A. 40°15N 94°20W 310 D2
Albany N.Y., U.S.A. 42°39N 73°45W 313 D11
Albany Oreg., U.S.A. 44°38N 123°6W 304 D2
Albany Tex., U.S.A. 32°44N 99°18W 314 E5
Albany Wis., U.S.A. 42°42N 89°26W 310 B7
Albany → Canada 52°17N 81°31W 298 B3
Albarca, C. d' Spain 39°4N 1°22E 206 C1
Albardón Argentina 31°20S 68°30W 334 C2
Albarracín Spain 40°25N 1°26W 196 E3
Albarracín, Sierra de Spain 40°30N 1°30W 196 E3
Albatera Spain 38°11N 0°52W 197 G4
Albâtre, Côte d' France 49°55N 0°50E 172 C7
Albatross B. Australia 12°45S 141°30E 280 A3
Albatross Pt. N.Z. 38°7S 174°44E 284 E3
Albay □ Phil. 13°13N 123°33E 232 E4
Albegna → Italy 42°30N 11°11E 199 F8
Albemarle U.S.A. 35°21N 80°12W 315 D14
Albemarle, I. = Isabela, I. Ecuador 0°30S 91°4W 330 a
Albemarle, Pta. Ecuador 0°11N 91°21W 330 a
Albemarle Sd. U.S.A. 36°5N 76°0W 315 C16
Albenga Italy 44°3N 8°13E 198 D5
Alberche → Spain 39°58N 4°46W 194 F6
Alberdi Paraguay 26°14S 58°20W 334 B4
Albères, Mts. France 42°28N 2°56E 174 F6
Ålberga Sweden 58°44N 16°35E 163 F10
Alberga → Australia 27°6S 135°33E 281 D2
Albern Austria 48°9N 16°29E 142 B2
Albersdorf Germany 54°8N 9°17E 178 A5
Albert France 50°0N 2°38E 173 C9
Albert, L. Africa 1°30N 31°0E 268 B3
Albert, L. S. Austral., Australia 35°30S 139°10E 282 C3
Albert Edward, Mt. Papua N. G. 8°20S 147°24E 286 E4
Albert Edward Ra. Australia 18°17S 127°57E 278 C4
Albert Lea U.S.A. 43°39N 93°22W 308 D7
Albert Nat. Park = Virunga △ Dem. Rep. of the Congo 0°5N 29°38E 268 B2
Albert Nile → Uganda 3°36N 32°2E 268 B3
Albert Park Australia 37°51S 144°58E 128 B1
Albert Town Bahamas 22°37N 74°33W 321 B5
Albert Town Jamaica 18°17N 77°33W 320 a
Alberta □ Canada 54°40N 115°0W 296 C6
Alberti Argentina 35°1S 60°16W 334 D3
Albertinia S. Africa 34°11S 21°34E 270 D3
Albertirsa Hungary 47°14N 19°37E 182 C4
Alberto de Agostini △ Chile 54°38S 71°37W 336 D2
Alberton P.E.I., Canada 46°50N 64°0W 299 C7
Alberton Gauteng, S. Africa 26°15S 28°7E 123 B2
Albertslund Denmark 55°39N 12°21E 118 B2
Albertville = Kalemie Dem. Rep. of the Congo 5°55S 29°9E 268 D2
Albertville Savoie, France 45°40N 6°22E 175 C10
Albertville Ala., U.S.A. 34°16N 86°13W 315 D11
Albi France 43°56N 2°9E 174 E6
Albia U.S.A. 41°2N 92°48W 310 C4
Albina Suriname 5°37N 54°15W 329 B7
Albina, Ponta Angola 15°52S 11°44E 265 F2
Albino Italy 45°46N 9°47E 198 C6
Albion Ill., U.S.A. 38°23N 88°4W 311 F8
Albion Ind., U.S.A. 41°24N 85°25W 311 C11
Albion Mich., U.S.A. 42°15N 84°45W 311 B12
Albion Nebr., U.S.A. 41°42N 98°0W 308 E4
Albion Pa., U.S.A. 41°53N 80°22W 312 E4
Albocásser Spain 40°21N 0°1E 196 E5
Albolote Spain 37°14N 3°39W 195 H7
Alborán Medit. S. 35°57N 3°0W 195 K7
Alboran Sea Medit. S. 36°0N 3°30W 195 K7
Alborea Spain 39°17N 1°24W 197 F3
Ålborg = Aalborg Denmark 57°2N 9°54E 163 G3
Ålborg Bugt = Aalborg Bugt Denmark 56°50N 10°35E 163 H4
Alborz, Reshteh-ye Kūhhā-ye Iran 36°0N 52°0E 247 C7
Albox Spain 37°23N 2°8W 197 H2
Albuera Phil. 10°55N 124°42E 233 F5
Albufeira Portugal 37°5N 8°15W 195 H2
Albula → Switz. 46°38N 9°28E 179 J5
Albuñol Spain 36°48N 3°11W 195 J7
Albuquerque Brazil 19°23S 57°26W 331 D6
Albuquerque N. Mex., U.S.A. 35°5N 106°39W 305 J10
Albuquerque, Cayos de Caribbean 12°10N 81°50W 320 D3
Alburg U.S.A. 44°59N 73°18W 313 B11
Alburno, Mte. Italy 40°33N 15°17E 201 B8
Alburquerque Spain 39°15N 6°59W 195 F4
Albury Australia 36°3S 146°56E 283 D7
Alby Sweden 62°30N 15°28E 162 B9
Alcácer do Sal Portugal 38°22N 8°33W 195 G2
Alcáçovas Portugal 38°23N 8°9W 195 G2
Alcala Phil. 17°54N 121°39E 232 C3
Alcalá de Guadaira Spain 37°20N 5°50W 195 H5
Alcalá de Henares Spain 40°28N 3°22W 194 E7
Alcalá de los Gazules Spain 36°29N 5°43W 195 J5
Alcalá de Xivert Spain 40°19N 0°13E 196 E5
Alcalá del Júcar Spain 39°12N 1°26W 197 F3
Alcalá del Río Spain 37°31N 5°59W 195 H5
Alcalá del Valle Spain 36°54N 5°10W 195 J5
Alcalá la Real Spain 37°27N 3°57W 195 H7
Álcamo Italy 37°59N 12°55E 200 E5
Alcanadre Spain 42°24N 2°7W 196 C2
Alcanadre → Spain 41°43N 0°12W 196 D4
Alcanar Spain 40°33N 0°28E 196 E5
Alcanede Portugal 39°25N 8°49W 195 F2
Alcanena Portugal 39°27N 8°40W 195 F2
Alcañices Spain 41°41N 6°21W 194 D4
Alcañiz Spain 41°2N 0°8W 196 D4
Alcântara Brazil 2°20S 44°30W 332 B3
Alcantara Lisboa, Portugal 38°43N 9°10W 126 A1
Alcántara Spain 39°41N 6°57W 194 F4
Alcántara, Embalse de Spain 39°44N 6°50W 194 F4
Alcantarilla Spain 37°59N 1°12W 197 H3
Alcaracejos Spain 38°24N 4°58W 195 G6
Alcaraz Spain 38°40N 2°29W 197 G2
Alcaraz, Sierra de Spain 38°40N 2°20W 197 G2
Alcatraz I. U.S.A. 37°49N 122°25W 136 B2
Alcaudete Spain 37°35N 4°5W 195 H6
Alcázar de San Juan Spain 39°24N 3°12W 195 F7
Alcazarquivir = Ksar el Kebir Morocco 35°0N 6°0W 260 B3
Alcedo, Volcán Ecuador 0°24S 91°6W 330 a
Alchevsk Ukraine 48°30N 38°45E 189 H10
Alcira = Alzira Spain 39°9N 0°30W 197 F4
Alcobaça = Tucuruí Brazil 3°42S 49°44W 332 B2
Alcobaça Portugal 39°32N 8°58W 195 F2
Alcobendas Spain 40°32N 3°38W 127 A2
Alcolea del Pinar Spain 41°2N 2°28W 196 D2
Alcoma U.S.A. 27°54N 81°29W 317 H8
Alcorcón Spain 40°20N 3°48W 127 B1
Alcoutim Portugal 37°25N 7°28W 195 H3
Alcova U.S.A. 42°34N 106°43W 304 E10
Alcoy Spain 38°43N 0°30W 197 G4
Alcubierre, Sierra de Spain 41°45N 0°22W 196 D4
Alcublas Spain 39°48N 0°43W 196 F4
Alcúdia Spain 39°51N 3°7E 206 B4
Alcúdia, B. d' Spain 39°47N 3°15E 206 B4
Alcúdia, Sierra de la Spain 38°34N 4°30W 195 G6
Aldabra Is. Seychelles 9°22S 46°28E 255 G8
Aldama Mexico 22°55N 98°4W 319 C5
Aldan Russia 58°40N 125°30E 215 D13
Aldan → Russia 63°28N 129°35E 215 C13
Aldea, Pta. de la Canary Is. 28°0N 15°50W 153 e1
Aldeburgh U.K. 52°10N 1°37E 169 E9
Alden Norway 61°19N 4°45E 164 C1
Alder Pk. U.S.A. 35°53N 121°22W 306 K5
Alderney U.K. 49°42N 2°11W 169 H5
Aldershof Germany 52°26N 13°33E 115 B4
Aldershot U.K. 51°15N 0°44W 169 F7
Aldinga Beach Australia 35°17S 138°27E 282 C3
Aldo Bonzi Argentina 34°42S 58°31W 117 C1
Åled Sweden 56°44N 12°57E 163 H6
Aledo U.S.A. 41°12N 90°45W 310 C6
Alefa Ethiopia 11°55N 36°55E 257 E4
Aleg Mauritania 17°3N 13°55W 262 B2
Alegranza Canary Is. 29°23N 13°32W 260 C2
Alegranza, I. Canary Is. 29°23N 13°32W 153 e2
Alegre Brazil 20°50S 41°30W 333 F3
Alegrete Brazil 29°40S 56°0W 335 B4
Aleknagik U.S.A. 59°17N 158°36W 303 G8
Aleksandriya = Oleksandriya Kirovohrad, Ukraine 48°42N 33°3E 189 H7
Aleksandriya = Oleksandriya Rivne, Ukraine 50°37N 26°19E 177 C14
Aleksandriyskaya Russia 43°58N 47°14E 191 J8
Aleksandropol = Gyumri Armenia 40°47N 43°50E 191 K6
Aleksandrov Russia 56°23N 38°44E 188 D10
Aleksandrov Gay Russia 50°9N 48°34E 190 E9
Aleksandrovac Serbia 43°28N 21°3E 202 C5
Aleksandrovac Serbia 44°23N 21°13E 202 B5
Aleksandrovka = Oleksandrivka Ukraine 48°55N 32°20E 189 H7
Aleksandrovka = Ordzhonikidze Ukraine 47°39N 34°3E 189 J8
Aleksandrovo Bulgaria 43°14N 24°51E 203 C8
Aleksandrovsk = Belogorsk Russia 51°0N 128°20E 215 D13
Aleksandrovsk = Polyarny Russia 69°8N 33°20E 160 B25
Aleksandrovsk = Zaporizhzhya Ukraine 47°50N 35°10E 189 J8
Aleksandrovsk-Grushevsky = Shakhty Russia 47°40N 40°16E 191 G5
Aleksandrovsk-Sakhalinskiy Russia 50°50N 142°20E 219 A17
Aleksandrovskoye Russia 59°51N 30°20E 137 B2
Aleksandrów Kujawski Poland 52°53N 18°43E 185 F5
Aleksandrów Łódźki Poland 51°49N 19°17E 185 G6
Aleksandry, Zemlya Russia 80°25N 48°0E 214 A5
Alekseyevka Samara, Russia 52°35N 51°17E 190 D10
Alekseyevka Voronezh, Russia 50°43N 38°40E 189 G10
Alekseyevsk = Svobodnyy Russia 51°20N 128°0E 215 D13
Alekseyevskoye = Qazyghurt Kazakhstan 41°45N 69°23E 217 D7
Aleksin Russia 54°31N 37°9E 188 E9
Aleksinac Serbia 43°31N 21°42E 202 C5
Além Paraíba Brazil 21°52S 42°41W 333 F3
Alemania Argentina 25°40S 65°30W 334 B2
Alemania Chile 25°10S 69°55W 334 B2
Alen Eq. Guin. 1°58N 11°19E 264 B2
Alençon France 48°27N 0°4E 172 D7
'Alenuihähä Channel U.S.A. 20°30N 156°0W 302 C5
Alépé Ivory C. 5°29N 3°40W 262 D4
Aleppo = Ḥalab Syria 36°10N 37°15E 250 B8
Alerce Andino △ Chile 41°33S 72°29W 336 B2
Alerce Costero △ Chile 40°10S 73°30W 336 B2
Aléria France 42°5N 9°26E 175 F13
Alert Canada 83°2N 60°0W 295 A20
Aleru India 17°39N 79°3E 244 F4
Alès France 44°9N 4°5E 175 D8
Aleşd Romania 47°3N 22°22E 182 C7
Alessándria Italy 44°54N 8°37E 198 D5
Ålesund Norway 62°28N 6°12E 164 B3
Alet-les-Bains France 42°59N 2°14E 174 F6
Aletschhorn Switz. 46°28N 8°0E 179 J4
Aleutian Basin Pac. Oc. 57°0N 177°0E 288 B9
Aleutian Is. Pac. Oc. 52°0N 175°0W 303 K3
Aleutian Range U.S.A. 60°0N 154°0W 303 G9
Aleutian Trench Pac. Oc. 48°0N 180°0E 150 D17
Alexander Ga., U.S.A. 33°1N 81°53W 316 B8
Alexander N. Dak., U.S.A. 47°51N 103°39W 308 B2
Alexander, C. Solomon Is. 6°34S 156°32E 287 L9
Alexander, Mt. Australia 28°58S 120°16E 279 E3
Alexander Arch. U.S.A. 56°0N 136°0W 303 J14
Alexander Bay S. Africa 28°40S 16°30E 270 C2
Alexander City U.S.A. 32°56N 35°58W 316 C4
Alexander I. Antarctica 69°0S 70°0W 151 C17
Alexander Nevsky Abbey Russia 59°54N 30°23E 137 B2
Alexander Soutzos Museum Athens, Greece 112 b3
Alexandra Vic., Australia 37°8S 145°40E 283 D6
Alexandra N.Z. 45°14S 169°25E 285 F4
Alexandra Singapore, Singapore 1°17N 103°49E 138 B2
Alexandra Gauteng, S. Africa 26°6S 28°5E 123 A2
Alexandra Channel Burma 14°7N 93°13E 245 G11
Alexandra Falls Canada 60°29N 116°18W 296 A5
Alexandretta = İskenderun Turkey 36°32N 36°10E 250 B7
Alexandria = El Iskandarîya Egypt 31°13N 29°58E 256 H6
Alexandria B.C., Canada 52°35N 122°27W 296 C4
Alexandria Ont., Canada 45°19N 74°38W 313 A10
Alexandria Romania 43°57N 25°24E 183 G10
Alexandria Eastern Cape, S. Africa 33°38S 26°28E 270 D4
Alexandria W. Dunb., U.K. 55°59N 4°35W 167 F4
Alexandria Ind., U.S.A. 40°16N 85°41W 311 D11
Alexandria Ky., U.S.A. 38°58N 84°23W 311 F12
Alexandria La., U.S.A. 31°18N 92°27W 314 F8
Alexandria Minn., U.S.A. 45°53N 95°22W 308 C6
Alexandria Mo., U.S.A. 40°27N 91°28W 310 D5
Alexandria S. Dak., U.S.A. 43°39N 97°47W 308 D5
Alexandria Va., U.S.A. 38°49N 77°5W 143 C2
Alexandria Bay U.S.A. 44°20N 75°55W 313 B9
Alexandrina, L. Australia 35°25S 139°10E 282 C3
Alexandroupoli Greece 40°50N 25°54E 203 F9
Alexis U.S.A. 41°4N 90°33W 310 C6
Alexis → Canada 52°33N 56°8W 299 B8
Alexis Creek Canada 52°10N 123°20W 296 C4
Aley → Russia 52°51N 83°36E 217 B10
Aleysk Russia 52°40N 83°0E 217 B10
Alfabia Spain 39°44N 2°44E 206 B3
Alfama Lisbon, Portugal 126 c3
Alfambra Spain 40°33N 1°5W 196 E3
Alfândega da Fé Portugal 41°20N 6°59W 194 D4
Alfaro Spain 42°10N 1°50W 196 C3
Alfatar Bulgaria 43°59N 27°13E 203 C11
Alfeld Germany 51°59N 9°50E 178 D5
Alfenas Brazil 21°20S 46°10W 335 A6
Alföld Hungary 46°30N 20°0E 182 D5
Alfonsine Italy 44°30N 12°3E 199 D9
Alford Aberds., U.K. 57°14N 2°41W 167 D6
Alford Lincs., U.K. 53°15N 0°10E 168 D8
Alford Fla., U.S.A. 30°42N 85°24W 316 E4
Alfortville France 48°48N 2°24E 134 B3
Ålfotbreen Norway 61°45N 5°39E 164 C2
Ålfoten Norway 61°51N 5°41E 164 C2
Alfred Maine, U.S.A. 43°29N 70°43W 313 C14
Alfred N.Y., U.S.A. 42°16N 77°48W 312 D7
Alfredton N.Z. 40°41S 175°54E 284 G4
Alfreton U.K. 53°6N 1°24W 168 D6
Alfta Sweden 61°21N 16°4E 162 C10
Algaida Spain 39°33N 2°53E 206 B3
Algar Spain 36°40N 5°39W 195 J5
Ålgård Norway 58°46N 5°53E 164 F2
Algarinejo Spain 37°19N 4°9W 195 H6
Algarve Portugal 36°58N 8°20W 195 J2
Algeciras Spain 36°9N 5°28W 195 J5
Algemesí Spain 39°11N 0°27W 197 F4
Alger Algeria 36°42N 3°8E 261 A5
Alger □ Algeria 36°45N 3°10E 197 J8
Alger ✈ (ALG) Algeria 36°39N 3°13E 197 J8
Algeria ■ Africa 28°30N 2°0E 261 C5
Algés Portugal 38°42N 9°13W 126 A1
Algha Kazakhstan 49°53N 57°20E 187 E10
Alghero Italy 40°33N 8°19E 200 B1
Älghult Sweden 57°0N 15°35E 163 G9
Algiers = Alger Algeria 36°42N 3°8E 261 A5
Algiers U.S.A. 29°56N 90°2W 131 B2
Algoa B. S. Africa 33°50S 25°45E 270 D4
Algodonales Spain 36°54N 5°24W 195 J5
Algodor → Spain 39°55N 3°53W 194 F7
Algoma U.S.A. 44°36N 87°26W 308 C10
Algona U.S.A. 43°4N 94°14W 310 A2
Algonac U.S.A. 42°37N 82°32W 312 D2
Algonquin ⌓ Canada 45°50N 78°30W 298 C4
Algorta Spain 43°21N 2°59W 196 B2
Algorta Uruguay 32°25S 57°24W 334 C4
Alhama de Almería Spain 36°57N 2°34W 195 J8
Alhama de Aragón Spain 41°18N 1°54W 196 D3
Alhama de Granada Spain 37°0N 3°59W 195 H7
Alhama de Murcia Spain 37°51N 1°25W 197 H3
Alhambra U.S.A. 34°5N 118°7W 126 B4
Alhaurín el Grande Spain 36°39N 4°41W 195 J6
Alhucemas = Al Hoceïma Morocco 35°8N 3°58W 261 A4
'Alī al Gharbī Iraq 32°30N 46°45E 213 F12
'Alī ash Sharqī Iraq 32°7N 46°44E 213 F12
Äli Bayramlı = Şirvan Azerbaijan 39°59N 48°52E 191 L9
'Alī Khēl Afghan. 33°57N 69°43E 242 C3
Ali Sahîh Djibouti 11°10N 42°44E 257 E5
Alī Shāh Iran 38°9N 45°50E 246 B5
Ália Italy 37°47N 13°43E 200 E6
'Alīābād Golestān, Iran 36°40N 54°33E 247 B7
'Alīābād Khorāsān, Iran 32°30N 57°30E 247 C8
'Alīābād Kordestān, Iran 35°4N 46°58E 246 C5
'Alīābād Yazd, Iran 31°41N 53°49E 247 D7
Aliade Nigeria 7°18N 8°29E 263 D6
Aliaga Spain 40°40N 0°42W 196 E4
Aliağa Turkey 38°47N 26°59E 205 C8
Aliakmonas → Greece 40°30N 22°36E 202 F6
Alibag India 18°38N 72°56E 244 E1
Alibey → Turkey 41°3N 28°56E 122 B1
Alibey Barajı Turkey 41°8N 28°53E 122 B1
Alibeyköy Turkey 41°4N 28°56E 122 B1
Alibo Ethiopia 9°52N 37°5E 257 F4
Alibori → Benin 11°56N 3°17E 263 C5
Alibunar Serbia 45°5N 20°57E 182 E5
Alicante Spain 38°23N 0°30W 197 G4
Alicante □ Spain 38°30N 0°37W 197 G4
Alicante ✈ (ALC) Spain 38°14N 0°36W 197 G4
Alice Eastern Cape, S. Africa 32°48S 26°55E 270 D4
Alice Tex., U.S.A. 27°45N 98°5W 314 H5
Alice → Queens., Australia 24°2S 144°50E 280 C3
Alice → Queens., Australia 15°35S 142°20E 280 B3
Alice → Papua N. G. 6°10S 141°8E 286 D1
Alice, Punta Italy 39°24N 17°9E 201 C10
Alice Arm Canada 55°29N 129°31W 296 B3
Alice Springs Australia 23°40S 133°50E 280 C1
Alicedale S. Africa 33°15S 26°4E 270 D4
Aliceville U.S.A. 33°8N 88°9W 315 E10
Alicia Bohol, Phil. 9°54N 124°26E 233 G5
Alicia Isabela, Phil. 16°46N 121°42E 232 C3
Alicudi Italy 38°33N 14°20E 201 D7
Alien Taiwan 22°52N 120°19E 225 D2
Aliganj India 27°30N 79°10E 243 F8
Aligarh Raj., India 25°55N 76°15E 242 G7
Aligarh Ut. P., India 27°55N 78°10E 242 F8
Alīgūdarz Iran 33°25N 49°45E 247 C6
Alijó Portugal 41°16N 7°27W 194 D3
Alikanas Greece 37°51N 20°47E 207 D2
Alima → Congo 1°35S 16°37E 264 C3
Alimia Greece 36°16N 27°43E 206 E11
Alimodian Phil. 10°49N 122°26E 233 F4
Alimos Greece 37°52N 23°43E 112 B2
Alindao C.A.R. 5°2N 21°13E 264 A4
Alingsås Sweden 57°56N 12°31E 163 G6
Alipur Paschimbanga, India 22°43N 88°12E 124 B1
Alipur Pakistan 29°25N 70°55E 242 E4
Alipur Duar India 26°30N 89°35E 241 B2
Aliquippa U.S.A. 40°37N 80°15W 312 F4
Alishan Taiwan 23°31N 120°48E 225 C2
Aliste → Spain 41°34N 5°58W 194 D5
Alitus = Alytus Lithuania 54°24N 24°3E 188 E3
Aliveri Greece 38°24N 24°2E 204 C6
Aliwal North S. Africa 30°45S 26°45E 270 D4
Alix Canada 52°24N 113°11W 296 C6
Aljezur Portugal 37°18N 8°49W 195 H2
Aljustrel Portugal 37°55N 8°10W 195 H2
Alkamari Niger 13°27N 11°10E 259 F2
Alkhanay △ Russia 51°0N 113°30E 215 D12
Alkmaar Neths. 52°37N 4°45E 170 B4
All American Canal U.S.A. 32°45N 115°15W 307 N11
Allacapan Phil. 18°15N 121°35E 232 B3
Allach Germany 48°11N 11°27E 131 A1
Allada Benin 6°41N 2°9E 263 D5
Allagadda India 15°8N 78°30E 245 G4
Allagash → U.S.A. 47°5N 69°3W 309 B19
Allah Dad Pakistan 25°38N 67°34E 242 G2
Allahabad India 25°25N 81°58E 243 G9
Allakaket U.S.A. 66°34N 152°39W 303 C9
Allambie Heights Australia 33°46S 151°15E 139 A2
Allan Canada 51°53N 106°4W 297 C7
Allanche France 45°14N 2°57E 174 C6
Allanmyo Burma 19°30N 95°17E 241 F5
Allanridge S. Africa 27°45S 26°40E 270 C4
Allansford Australia 38°26S 142°39E 282 E5
Allanton N.Z. 45°55S 170°15E 285 F5
Allaqi, Wadi → Egypt 23°7N 32°47E 256 C3
Allariz Spain 42°11N 7°50W 194 C3
Allassac France 45°15N 1°29E 174 C5
Allatoona L. U.S.A. 34°10N 84°44W 316 A5
Ålleberg Sweden 58°8N 13°36E 163 F7
Allegan U.S.A. 42°32N 85°51W 311 B11
Allegany U.S.A. 42°6N 78°30W 312 D6
Allegheny → U.S.A. 40°27N 80°1W 312 F5
Allegheny Mts. U.S.A. 38°15N 80°10W 309 F13
Allegheny Plateau U.S.A. 41°30N 78°30W 309 E14
Allegheny Res. U.S.A. 41°50N 79°0W 312 E6
Allègre France 45°12N 3°41E 174 C7
Allègre, Pte. Guadeloupe 16°22N 61°46W 322 e
Allen Argentina 38°58S 67°50W 336 A3
Allen Phil. 12°30N 124°17E 232 E5
Allen, Bog of Ireland 53°15N 7°0W 166 C5
Allen, L. Ireland 54°8N 8°4W 166 B3
Allendale U.S.A. 33°1N 81°18W 316 B8
Allende Mexico 28°20N 100°51W 318 B4
Allenstein = Olsztyn Poland 53°48N 20°29E 184 E7
Allentown U.S.A. 40°37N 75°29W 313 F9
Allentsteig Austria 48°41N 15°20E 180 C8
Alleppey = Alappuzha India 9°30N 76°28E 245 K3
Allepuz Spain 40°29N 0°44W 196 E4
Aller → Germany 52°56N 9°12E 178 C5
Allermuir Hill U.K. 55°53N 3°14W 121 B2
Alley, The Jamaica 17°48N 77°17W 320 a
Alliance Suriname 5°50N 54°50W 329 B7
Alliance Nebr., U.S.A. 42°6N 102°52W 308 D2
Alliance Ohio, U.S.A. 40°55N 81°6W 312 F3
Allianz Arena Munich, Germany 48°13N 11°37E 131 A2
Allier □ France 46°25N 2°40E 173 F9
Allier → France 46°57N 3°4E 173 F10
Alliford Bay Canada 53°12N 131°58W 296 C2
Alligator Pond Jamaica 17°52N 77°34W 320 a
Allinagaram India 10°2N 77°30E 245 J3
Allinge Denmark 55°17N 14°50E 163 J8
Allison U.S.A. 42°45N 92°48W 310 B4
Alliston Canada 44°9N 79°52W 312 B5
Alloa U.K. 56°7N 3°47W 167 E5
Allones France 48°20N 1°40E 172 D8
Allora Australia 28°2S 152°0E 281 D5
Allos France 44°15N 6°38E 175 D10
Allston U.S.A. 42°21N 71°7W 116 A2
Alluitsup Paa Greenland 60°30N 45°35W 154 E6
Allur India 14°40N 80°4E 245 G5
Alluru Kottapatnam India 15°24N 80°7E 245 G5
Alma Qué., Canada 48°35N 71°40W 299 C5
Alma Ga., U.S.A. 31°33N 82°28W 316 D7
Alma Kans., U.S.A. 39°1N 96°17W 308 F5
Alma Mich., U.S.A. 43°23N 84°39W 309 D11
Alma Nebr., U.S.A. 40°6N 99°22W 308 E4
Alma Wis., U.S.A. 44°20N 91°55W 308 C8
Alma Ata = Almaty Kazakhstan 43°15N 76°57E 217 D9
Alma Hill U.S.A. 42°2N 78°0W 312 D7
Almacelles Spain 41°43N 0°27E 196 D5
Almada Portugal 38°41N 9°8W 126 A2
Almaden Queens., Australia 17°22S 144°40E 280 B3
Almadén Spain 38°49N 4°52W 195 G6
Almagro Argentina 34°38S 58°24W 117 B2
Almagro I. Phil. 11°55N 124°18E 233 F5
Almalyk = Olmaliq Uzbekistan 40°50N 69°35E 217 D7
Almanor, L. U.S.A. 40°14N 121°9W 304 F3
Almansa Spain 38°51N 1°5W 197 G3
Almanza Spain 42°39N 5°3W 194 C5
Almanzor, Pico Spain 40°15N 5°18W 194 E5
Almanzora → Spain 37°14N 1°46W 197 H3
Almargem do Bispo Portugal 38°49N 9°17W 126 A1
Almas Brazil 11°33S 47°9W 333 D2
Almaş, Munţii Romania 44°49N 22°12E 182 F7
Almaty Kazakhstan 43°15N 76°57E 217 D9
Almaty □ Kazakhstan 44°30N 78°0E 217 D9
Almazán Spain 41°30N 2°30W 196 D2
Almazora Spain 39°57N 0°3W 196 F4
Almeirim Brazil 1°30S 52°34W 329 D7
Almeirim Portugal 39°12N 8°37W 195 F2
Almelo Neths. 52°22N 6°42E 170 B6
Almenar de Soria Spain 41°43N 2°12W 196 D2
Almenara Brazil 16°11S 40°42W 333 E3
Almenara Spain 39°46N 0°14W 196 F4
Almenara, Sierra de Spain 37°34N 1°32W 197 H3
Almendra, Embalse de Spain 41°10N 6°5W 194 D4
Almendralejo Spain 38°41N 6°26W 195 G4
Almere Neths. 52°20N 5°15E 170 B5
Almería Spain 36°52N 2°27W 195 J8
Almería □ Spain 37°20N 2°20W 197 H2
Almería, G. de Spain 36°41N 2°28W 197 J2
Almetyevsk Russia 54°53N 52°20E 190 C11
Älmhult Sweden 56°33N 14°8E 163 H8
Almirante Panama 9°10N 82°30W 320 E3
Almirante G. Brown, Parque Argentina 34°40S 58°28W 117 C2
Almirante Montt, G. Chile 51°52S 72°50W 336 D2
Almiropotamos Greece 38°16N 24°11E 204 C6
Almiros Greece 39°11N 22°45E 204 B4
Almodôvar Portugal 37°31N 8°2W 195 H2
Almodóvar del Campo Spain 38°43N 4°10W 195 G6
Almodóvar del Río Spain 37°48N 5°1W 195 H5
Almon West Bank 31°49N 35°17E 123 B2
Almond U.S.A. 42°19N 77°44W 312 D7
Almond → U.K. 55°58N 3°18W 121 B2
Almont U.S.A. 42°55N 83°3W 312 D1
Almonte Ont., Canada 45°14N 76°12W 313 A8
Almonte Spain 37°13N 6°38W 195 H4
Almora India 29°38N 79°40E 243 E8
Almoradí Spain 38°7N 0°46W 197 G4
Almorox Spain 40°14N 4°24W 194 E6
Almoustarat Mali 17°35N 0°8E 263 B5
Älmsta Sweden 59°58N 18°50E 162 E12
Almudévar Spain 42°3N 0°35W 196 C4
Almuñécar Spain 36°43N 3°41W 195 J7
Almunge Sweden 59°53N 18°3E 162 E12
Almuradiel Spain 38°32N 3°28W 195 G7
Almus Turkey 40°22N 36°54E 212 B7
Almvik Sweden 57°49N 16°30E 163 G10
Almyrou, Ormos Greece 35°23N 24°20E 207 E5
Alna Norway 59°55N 10°50E 133 A4
Alness U.K. 57°41N 4°16W 167 D4
Alnif Morocco 31°10N 5°8W 260 B3
Alnmouth U.K. 55°24N 1°37W 168 B6
Alnsjøen Norway 59°57N 10°51E 133 A4
Alnwick U.K. 55°24N 1°42W 168 B6
Alofau Amer. Samoa 14°16S 170°36W 302 f
Alofi Niue 19°1S 169°55W 289 g
Alofi, I. Wall. & F. Is. 14°27S 178°5W 277 C15
Alofi B. Niue 19°1S 169°56W 289 g
Aloi Uganda 2°16N 33°10E 268 B3
Alon Burma 22°12N 95°5E 241 D5
Along India 28°10N 94°46E 241 A5
Alonissos Greece 39°12N 23°50E 204 B5
Alonissos-Northern Sporades △ Greece 39°15N 24°5E 204 B6
Alor Indonesia 8°15S 124°30E 231 F6
Alor Setar Malaysia 6°7N 100°22E 237 J3
Álora Spain 36°49N 4°46W 195 J6
Alosno Spain 37°33N 7°7W 195 H3
Alost = Aalst Belgium 50°56N 4°2E 170 D4
Alot India 23°56N 75°40E 242 H6
Alotau Papua N. G. 10°16S 150°30E 286 F6
Alougoum Morocco 30°17N 6°56W 260 B3
Aloum Cameroon 2°16N 10°34E 264 B2
Aloysius, Mt. Australia 26°0S 128°38E 279 E4
Alpaugh U.S.A. 35°53N 119°29W 306 K7
Alpe Apuane ⌓ Italy 44°4N 10°15E 198 D7
Alpedrinha Portugal 40°6N 7°27W 194 E3
Alpena U.S.A. 45°4N 83°27W 312 A1
Alpercatas → Brazil 6°2S 44°19W 332 C3
Alperton U.K. 51°32N 0°17W 125 A2
Alpes-de-Haute-Provence □ France 44°8N 6°10E 175 D10
Alpes-Maritimes □ France 43°55N 7°10E 175 E11
Alpha Queens., Australia 23°39S 146°37E 280 C4
Alpha Ill., U.S.A. 41°12N 90°23W 310 C6
Alpha Ridge Arctic 84°0N 118°0W 150 A2
Alpharetta U.S.A. 34°5N 84°18W 316 A5
Alphen aan den Rijn Neths. 52°7N 4°40E 170 B4
Alphios → Greece 37°40N 21°33E 204 D3
Alpiarça Portugal 39°15N 8°35W 195 F2
Alpine Ariz., U.S.A. 33°51N 109°9W 305 K9
Alpine Calif., U.S.A. 32°50N 116°46W 307 N10
Alpine N.J., U.S.A. 40°57N 73°57W 132 A2
Alpine Tex., U.S.A. 30°22N 103°40W 314 F3
Alpine △ Australia 36°56S 148°10E 283 D7
Alps Europe 46°30N 9°30E 176 E5
Alpu Turkey 39°46N 30°58E 212 C4
Alpurrurulam Australia 20°59S 137°50E 280 C2
Alqueta, Barragem do Portugal 38°20N 7°25W 195 G3
Alrø Denmark 55°52N 10°5E 163 J4
Alrode S. Africa 26°17S 28°7E 123 B2
Als Denmark 54°59N 9°55E 163 K3
Alsace □ France 48°15N 7°25E 173 D14
Alsask Canada 51°21N 109°59W 297 C7
Alsasua Spain 42°54N 2°10W 196 C2
Alsek → U.S.A. 59°10N 138°12W 296 B1
Alsemberg Belgium 50°44N 4°20E 116 B2
Alsergrund Austria 48°13N 16°21E 142 A2
Alsfeld Germany 50°44N 9°16E 178 E5
Alsip U.S.A. 41°40N 87°44W 119 C2
Alsta Norway 65°58N 12°40E 160 D15
Ålsten Sweden 59°19N 17°57E 139 B1
Alsterbro Sweden 56°57N 15°55E 163 H9
Alstermo Sweden 56°58N 15°38E 163 H9
Alston U.K. 54°49N 2°25W 168 C5
Alta Finnmark, Norway 69°57N 23°10E 160 B20
Älta Sweden 59°15N 18°11E 139 B3
Alta, Sierra Spain 40°31N 1°30W 196 E3
Alta Floresta Brazil 9°57S 55°58W 331 B6
Alta Gracia Argentina 31°40S 64°30W 334 C3
Alta Murgia △ Italy 40°55N 16°30E 201 B9
Alta Sierra U.S.A. 35°42N 118°33W 307 K8
Altadena U.S.A. 34°11N 118°8W 126 A4
Altaelva → Norway 69°54N 23°17E 160 B20
Altafjorden Norway 70°5N 23°5E 160 A20
Altagracia Nueva Esparta, Venezuela 11°6N 63°57W 329 a
Altagracia Zulia, Venezuela 10°45N 71°30W 328 A3
Altagracia de Orituco Venezuela 9°52N 66°23W 328 B4
Altai = Aerhtai Shan Mongolia 46°40N 92°45E 217 C12
Altai = Gorno-Altay □ Russia 51°0N 86°0E 217 B11
Altai △ Russia 50°30N 85°30E 217 B11
Altamachi → Bolivia 16°8S 66°50W 330 D4
Altamaha → U.S.A. 31°20N 81°20W 316 D8
Altamira Brazil 3°12S 52°10W 329 D7
Altamira Chile 25°47S 69°51W 334 B2
Altamira Colombia 2°3N 75°47W 328 C2
Altamira Tamaulipas, Mexico 22°24N 97°55W 319 C5
Altamira, Cuevas de Spain 43°20N 4°5W 194 B6
Altamont Ill., U.S.A. 39°4N 88°45W 311 E8
Altamont N.Y., U.S.A. 42°42N 74°2W 313 D10
Altamura Italy 40°49N 16°33E 201 B9
Altanbulag Mongolia 50°16N 106°30E 218 A10
Altar Mexico 30°43N 111°44W 318 A2
Altar, Gran Desierto de Mexico 31°50N 114°10W 318 B2
Altata Mexico 24°40N 107°55W 318 C3
Altavas Phil. 11°32N 122°29E 233 F4
Altavista U.S.A. 37°6N 79°17W 309 G14
Altay Xinjiang Uygur, China 47°48N 88°10E 217 C11
Altay Mongolia 46°22N 96°15E 218 B8
Altdorf Switz. 46°52N 8°36E 179 J4
Alte-Donau → Austria 48°14N 16°25E 142 A2
Alte Mellum Germany 53°43N 8°10E 178 B4
Altea Spain 38°38N 0°2W 197 G4
Altenberg Germany 50°45N 13°45E 178 E9
Altenbruch Germany 53°49N 8°46E 178 B4
Altenburg Germany 50°59N 12°25E 178 E8
Altenkirchen Mecklenburg-Vorpommern, Germany 54°38N 13°22E 178 A9
Altenkirchen Rhld-Pfz., Germany 50°41N 7°39E 178 E3
Altenmarkt Austria 47°43N 14°39E 180 D7
Alter do Chão Brazil 2°31S 54°57W 329 D6
Alter do Chão Portugal 39°12N 7°40W 195 F3
Alter Finkenkrug Germany 52°35N 13°3E 115 A1
Altes Rathaus Munich, Germany 131 b3
Altglienicke Germany 52°25N 13°32E 115 B4
Altha U.S.A. 30°34N 85°8W 316 E4
Altınkaya Barajı Turkey 41°18N 35°30E 212 B6
Altınoluk Turkey 39°34N 26°45E 205 B8
Altınova Turkey 39°12N 26°47E 205 B8
Altınözü Turkey 36°7N 36°14E 250 B7
Altıntaş Turkey 39°4N 30°7E 205 B12
Altınyaka Turkey 36°33N 30°20E 205 E12
Altınyayla Turkey 37°0N 29°33E 205 D11
Altiplano Bolivia 17°0S 68°0W 330 D4
Altkirch France 47°37N 7°15E 173 E14
Altlandsberg Germany 52°33N 13°43E 115 A5
Altlandsberg Nord Germany 52°34N 13°43E 115 A5
Altmannsdorf Austria 48°9N 16°18E 142 B1
Altmark Germany 52°45N 11°30E 178 C7
Altmühl → Germany 48°54N 11°52E 179 G7
Altmühltal ⌓ Germany 48°55N 11°15E 179 G7
Altmunster Austria 47°54N 13°45E 180 D6
Alto Adige = Trentino-Alto Adige □ Italy 46°30N 11°20E 199 B8
Alto Alegre Brazil 2°50N 61°20W 329 C5
Alto Araguaia Brazil 17°15S 53°20W 331 D7
Alto Chicapa Angola 10°52S 19°17E 265 E3
Alto Cuchumatanes = Cuchumatanes, Sierra de los Guatemala 15°35N 91°25W 320 C1
Alto Cuito = Tempué Angola 13°27S 18°49E 265 E3
Alto da Boa Vista Brazil 22°57S 43°16W 135 B1
Alto da Moóca Brazil 23°34S 46°33W 137 B2
Alto del Carmen Chile 28°46S 70°30W 334 B1
Alto do Pina Portugal 38°44N 9°7W 126 A2
Alto Douro Portugal 41°6N 7°47W 194 D3
Alto Garças Brazil 16°56S 53°32W 331 D7
Alto Garda Bresciano ⌓ Italy 45°42N 10°38E 198 C7
Alto Iriri → Brazil 8°50S 53°25W 331 B7
Alto Ligonha Mozam. 15°30S 38°11E 269 F4
Alto Molocue Mozam. 15°50S 37°35E 269 F4
Alto Paraguai Brazil 14°30S 56°31W 331 C6
Alto Paraguay □ Paraguay 21°0S 58°30W 334 A4
Alto Paraiso de Goiás Brazil 14°7S 47°31W 333 D2
Alto Paraná □ Paraguay 25°30S 54°50W 335 B5
Alto Parnaíba Brazil 9°6S 45°57W 332 C2
Alto Purús → Peru 9°12S 70°28W 330 B3
Alto Río Senguerr Argentina 45°2S 70°50W 336 C2
Alto Santo Brazil 5°31S 38°15W 332 C4
Alto Sucuriú Brazil 19°19S 52°47W 331 D7
Alto Tajo ⌓ Spain 40°44N 2°30W 196 E2
Alton Ont., Canada 43°54N 80°5W 312 C4
Alton Hants., U.K. 51°9N 0°59W 169 F7
Alton Ill., U.S.A. 38°53N 90°11W 310 F6
Alton N.H., U.S.A. 43°27N 71°13W 313 C13
Altona Vic., Australia 37°51S 144°49E 128 B1
Altona Man., Canada 49°6N 97°33W 297 D9
Altoona Ala., U.S.A. 34°2N 86°20W 316 A3
Altoona Iowa, U.S.A. 41°39N 93°28W 310 C3
Altoona Pa., U.S.A. 40°31N 78°24W 312 F6
Altos Brazil 5°3S 42°28W 332 C3
Altötting Germany 48°12N 12°39E 179 G8
Altsasu = Alsasua Spain 42°54N 2°10W 196 C2
Altstätten Switz. 47°22N 9°33E 179 H5
Altun Kupri Iraq 35°45N 44°9E 213 E11
Altun Shan China 38°30N 88°0E 217 E11
Alturas U.S.A. 41°29N 120°32W 304 F3
Altus U.S.A. 34°38N 99°20W 314 D5
Altyn-Emel △ Kazakhstan 44°40N 78°26E 217 D9
Alubijid Phil. 8°35N 124°29E 233 G5
Alucra Turkey 40°22N 38°47E 213 B8
Aluk South Sudan 8°25N 27°30E 257 F2
Alūksne Latvia 57°24N 27°3E 188 D4
Alunda Sweden 60°4N 18°5E 162 D12
Alunite U.S.A. 35°59N 114°55W 307 K12
Aluoro → Ethiopia 8°26N 33°24E 257 F3
Alupka Ukraine 44°23N 34°2E 189 K8
Alur India 15°24N 77°15E 245 E3
Alur Gajah Malaysia 2°23N 102°13E 234 B2
Alushta Ukraine 44°40N 34°25E 189 K8
Alusi Indonesia 7°35S 131°40E 231 F8
Alustante Spain 40°36N 1°40W 196 E3
Alutgama Sri Lanka 6°26N 79°59E 245 L4
Alutnuwara Sri Lanka 7°19N 80°59E 245 L5
Aluva = Alwaye India 10°8N 76°24E 245 J3
Alva U.S.A. 36°48N 98°40W 314 C5
Alvaiázere Portugal 39°49N 8°23W 194 F2
Alvalade Portugal 38°45N 9°8W 126 A2
Älvängen Sweden 57°58N 12°8E 163 G6
Alvão ⌓ Portugal 41°22N 7°48W 194 D3
Alvarado Veracruz, Mexico 18°46N 95°46W 319 D5
Alvarado Tex., U.S.A. 32°24N 97°13W 314 E6
Alvarães Brazil 3°12S 64°50W 329 D5
Alvaro Obregón, Presa Mexico 27°52N 109°52W 318 B3
Alvdal Norway 62°6N 10°37E 164 B7
Älvdalen Sweden 61°13N 14°4E 162 C8
Alvear Argentina 29°5S 56°30W 334 B4
Alverca Portugal 38°56N 9°1W 195 G1
Alvesta Sweden 56°54N 14°35E 163 H8
Alvik Sweden 59°19N 17°58E 139 B1
Alvin Callendar Naval Air Station U.S.A. 29°50N 90°1W 131 B2
Alvinston Canada 42°49N 81°52W 312 D3
Alvito Portugal 38°15N 7°58W 195 G3
Älvkarleby Sweden 60°34N 17°26E 162 D11
Alvorado Brazil 12°28S 49°6W 333 D2
Alvord Desert U.S.A. 42°30N 118°25W 304 E4
Älvros Sweden 62°3N 14°38E 162 B8
Älvsbyn Sweden 65°40N 21°0E 160 D19
Älvsjo Sweden 59°16N 18°0E 139 B2
Ålvundeid Norway 62°45N 8°33E 164 B5
Älvvik Sweden 59°21N 18°15E 139 A3
Alwar India 27°38N 76°34E 242 F7
Alwaye India 10°8N 76°24E 245 J3
Alxa Zuoqi China 38°50N 105°40E 226 E3
Alyangula Australia 13°55S 136°30E 280 A2
Alyata = Älät Azerbaijan 39°58N 49°25E 191 L9
Alyth U.K. 56°38N 3°13W 167 E5
Alytus Lithuania 54°24N 24°3E 188 E3
Alzada U.S.A. 45°2N 104°25W 304 D11
Alzamay Russia 55°33N 98°39E 215 D10
Alzey Germany 49°45N 8°7E 179 F4
Alzira Spain 39°9N 0°30W 197 F4
Am Dam Chad 12°40N 20°35E 259 F4
Am Géréda Chad 12°53N 21°14E 259 F4
Am Hasenbergl Germany 48°12N 11°33E 131 A2
Am Sak Chad 13°39N 20°8E 259 F4
Am Steinhof Austria 48°12N 16°17E 142 A1
Am Timan Chad 11°0N 20°10E 259 F4
Am Wald Germany 48°3N 11°36E 131 B2
Ama Keng Singapore 1°23N 103°41E 138 A2
Amacayacu △ Colombia 3°21S 70°8W 328 D3
Amada Gaza C.A.R. 4°46N 15°9E 264 B3
Amådalen Sweden 61°20N 14°44E 162 C8
Amadeus, L. Australia 24°54S 131°0E 279 D5
Amadi Dem. Rep. of the Congo 3°40N 26°40E 268 B2
Amadi South Sudan 5°29N 30°25E 257 F3
Amadjuak L. Canada 65°0N 71°8W 295 E17
Amadora Portugal 38°45N 9°13W 126 A1
Amagansett U.S.A. 40°59N 72°9W 313 F12
Amagasaki Japan 34°42N 135°23E 133 A1
Amager Denmark 55°36N 12°35E 118 B3
Amagi Japan 33°25N 130°39E 222 D2
Amagunze Nigeria 6°20N 7°40E 263 D6
Amahai Indonesia 3°20S 128°55E 231 E7
Amaile Samoa 13°59S 171°22W 287 V20
Amaimon Papua N. G. 5°12S 145°30E 286 C3
Amaiun-Maia Spain 43°12N 1°29W 196 B3
Amakusa = Hondo Japan 32°27N 130°12E 222 E2
Amakusa-Nada Japan 32°35N 130°5E 222 E2
Amakusa-Shotō Japan 32°15N 130°10E 222 E2
Amal Oman 18°21N 55°39E 249 C6
Åmål Sweden 59°3N 12°42E 162 E6
Amāl Qādisiya Iraq 33°16N 44°20E 113 B2
Amalapuram India 16°35N 81°55E 245 F5
Amalfi Colombia 6°55N 75°4W 328 B2
Amalfi Italy 40°38N 14°36E 201 B7
Amaliada Greece 37°47N 21°22E 204 D3
Amalienborg Slot Copenhagen, Denmark 118 b3
Amalner India 21°5N 75°5E 244 D2
Amamapare Indonesia 4°53S 136°38E 231 E9
Amambaí Brazil 23°5S 55°13W 335 A4
Amambaí → Brazil 23°22S 53°56W 335 A5
Amambay □ Paraguay 23°0S 56°0W 335 A4
Amambay, Cordillera de S. Amer. 23°0S 55°45W 335 A4
Amami Japan 28°22N 129°27E 221 K4
Amami-Guntō Japan 27°16N 129°21E 221 L4
Amami-Ō-Shima Japan 28°16N 129°21E 221 K4
Aman, Pulau Malaysia 5°16N 100°24E 237 c
Amana → Venezuela 9°45N 62°39W 329 B5
Amaná, L. Brazil 2°35S 64°40W 329 D5
Amanab Papua N. G. 3°40S 141°14E 286 B1
Amanat → India 24°7N 84°4E 243 G11
Amanave Amer. Samoa 14°20S 170°50W 302 f
Amanda Park U.S.A. 47°28N 123°55W 306 C3
Amankeldi Kazakhstan 50°10N 65°10E 216 B7
Amanohashidate Japan 35°40N 135°15E 223 B7
Amantea Italy 39°8N 16°4E 201 C9
Amanu French Polynesia 17°48S 140°46W 289 f
Amapá Brazil 2°5N 50°50W 329 C7
Amapá □ Brazil 1°40N 52°0W 329 C7

Amapari = Ferreira Gomes Brazil 0°48N 51°8W 329 C7
Amara Sudan 10°25N 34°10E 257 E3
Amara □ Ethiopia 12°30N 37°30E 257 E4
Amaração = Luís Correia Brazil 3°0S 41°35W 332 B3
Amarante Brazil 6°14S 42°50W 332 C3
Amarante Portugal 41°16N 8°5W 194 D2
Amarante do Maranhão Brazil 5°36S 46°45W 332 C2
Amaranth Canada 50°36N 98°43W 297 C9
Amarapura Burma 21°54N 96°3E 241 E6
Amaravati → India 11°0N 78°15E 245 J4
Amareleja Portugal 38°12N 7°13W 195 G3
Amargosa Brazil 13°2S 39°36W 333 D4
Amargosa → U.S.A. 36°14N 116°51W 307 J10
Amargosa Desert U.S.A. 36°40N 116°30W 307 J10
Amargosa Range U.S.A. 36°20N 116°45W 307 J10
Amari Greece 35°13N 24°40E 207 E5
Amarillo U.S.A. 35°13N 101°50W 314 D4
Amarkantak India 22°40N 81°45E 243 H9
'Amârna, Tell el Egypt 27°38N 30°52E 256 B3
Amarnath India 19°12N 73°22E 244 E1
Amaro, Mte. Italy 42°5N 14°5E 199 F11
Amarpur Bihar, India 25°5N 87°0E 243 G12
Amarpur Tripura, India 23°31N 91°39E 241 D3
Amarti Eritrea 14°17N 41°6E 257 E5
Amarwara India 22°18N 79°10E 243 H8
Amasin W. Sahara 25°45N 13°20W 260 C2
Amasra Turkey 41°45N 32°23E 212 B5
Amassama Nigeria 5°1N 6°2E 263 D6
Amasya Turkey 40°40N 35°50E 212 B6
Amasya □ Turkey 40°40N 35°50E 212 B6
Amata S. Austral., Australia 26°9S 131°9E 279 E5
Amata Piemonte, Italy 45°34N 9°8E 128 A1
Amataurá Brazil 3°29S 68°6W 328 D4
Amatignak I. U.S.A. 51°16N 179°6W 303 L3
Amatikulu S. Africa 29°3S 31°33E 271 C5
Amatitlán Guatemala 14°29N 90°38W 320 D1
Amatrice Italy 42°38N 13°17E 199 F10
Amau Papua N. G. 10°2S 148°34E 286 F5
Amay Belgium 50°33N 5°19E 170 D5
Amazon = Amazonas → S. Amer. 0°5S 50°0W 329 D8
Amazonas □ Brazil 5°0S 65°0W 331 B5
Amazonas □ Peru 5°0S 78°0W 330 B2
Amazonas □ Venezuela 3°30N 66°0W 328 C4
Amazonas → S. Amer. 0°5S 50°0W 329 D8
Amba Ferit Ethiopia 10°55N 38°50E 257 E4
Ambad India 19°38N 75°50E 244 E2
Ambae = Aoba Vanuatu 15°25S 167°50E 287 E5
Ambagarh Chowki India 20°47N 80°43E 244 D5
Ambah India 26°43N 78°13E 242 F8
Ambahakily Madag. 21°36S 43°41E 272 C1
Ambahita Madag. 24°1S 45°16E 272 C2
Ambajogai India 18°44N 76°23E 244 E3
Ambala India 30°23N 76°56E 242 D7
Ambalangoda Sri Lanka 6°15N 80°5E 245 L5
Ambalanta Sri Lanka 6°7N 81°1E 245 L5
Ambalapulai India 9°25N 76°25E 245 K3
Ambalavao Madag. 21°50S 46°56E 272 C2
Ambam Cameroon 2°20N 11°15E 264 B2
Ambanja Madag. 13°40S 48°27E 272 A2
Ambararata Madag. 15°3S 48°33E 272 B2
Ambarchik Russia 69°40N 162°20E 215 C17
Ambarijeby Madag. 14°56S 47°41E 272 A2
Ambaro, Helodranon' Madag. 13°23S 48°38E 272 A2
Ambasamudram India 8°43N 77°25E 245 K3
Ambato Ecuador 1°5S 78°42W 328 D2
Ambato Madag. 13°24S 48°29E 272 A2
Ambato, Sierra de Argentina 28°25S 66°10W 334 B2
Ambato Boeny Madag. 16°28S 46°43E 272 B2
Ambatofinandrahana Madag. 20°33S 46°48E 272 C2
Ambatolampy Madag. 19°20S 47°35E 272 B2
Ambatomainty Madag. 17°41S 45°40E 272 B2
Ambatomanoina Madag. 18°18S 47°37E 272 B2
Ambatondrazaka Madag. 17°55S 48°28E 272 B2
Ambatosoratra Madag. 17°37S 48°31E 272 B2
Ambelokipi Greece 37°58N 23°47E 112 B2
Ambelonas Greece 39°45N 22°22E 204 B4
Ambenja Madag. 15°17S 46°58E 272 B2
Amberg Germany 49°26N 11°52E 179 F7
Ambergris Cay Belize 18°0N 87°55W 320 C2
Ambérieu-en-Bugey France 45°57N 5°20E 175 C9
Amberley Ont., Canada 44°2N 81°42W 312 B3
Amberley N.Z. 43°9S 172°44E 285 D7
Ambert France 45°33N 3°44E 174 C7
Ambidédi Mali 14°35N 11°47W 262 C2
Ambikapur India 23°15N 83°15E 243 H10
Ambikol Sudan 21°20N 30°50E 256 C3
Ambil I. Phil. 13°48N 120°18E 232 E3
Ambilobé Madag. 13°10S 49°3E 272 A2
Ambinanindrano Madag. 20°5S 48°23E 272 C2
Ambinanitelo Madag. 15°21S 49°35E 272 B2
Ambinda Madag. 16°25S 45°52E 272 B2
Ambitle I. Papua N. G. 4°5S 153°37E 286 C7
Amble U.K. 55°20N 1°36W 168 B6
Ambler U.S.A. 67°5N 157°52W 303 C8
Ambleside U.K. 54°26N 2°58W 168 C5
Ambo Peru 10°5S 76°10W 330 C2
Amboahangy Madag. 24°15S 46°22E 272 C2
Amboasary Madag. 25°1S 46°45E 272 D2
Ambodifototra Madag. 16°59S 49°52E 272 B2
Ambodilazana Madag. 18°6S 49°10E 272 B2
Ambodiriana Madag. 17°55S 49°18E 272 B2
Ambohidratrimo Madag. 18°50S 47°26E 272 B2
Ambohidray Madag. 18°36S 48°18E 272 B2
Ambohimahamasina Madag. 21°56S 47°11E 272 C2
Ambohimahasoa Madag. 21°7S 47°13E 272 C2
Ambohimanga Antananarivo, Madag. 18°45S 47°33E 272 B2
Ambohimanga Fianarantsoa, Madag. 20°52S 47°36E 272 C2
Ambohimitombo Madag. 20°43S 47°26E 272 C2
Ambohitra Madag. 12°30S 49°10E 272 A2
Amboise France 47°24N 1°2E 172 E8
Amboiva Angola 11°33S 14°43E 265 E2
Ambon Indonesia 3°43S 128°12E 231 E7
Ambondro Madag. 25°13S 45°44E 272 D2
Amboró △ Bolivia 17°39S 64°3W 331 D5
Amboseli, L. Kenya 2°40S 37°10E 268 C4
Amboseli △ Kenya 2°37S 37°13E 268 C4
Ambositra Madag. 20°31S 47°25E 272 C2
Ambovombe Madag. 25°11S 46°5E 272 D2
Amboy Calif., U.S.A. 34°33N 115°45W 307 L11
Amboy Ill., U.S.A. 41°44N 89°20W 310 C7
Amboyna Cay S. China Sea 7°50N 112°50E 230 C4
Ambre, Île d' Mauritius 20°2S 57°41E 272 e
Ambridge U.S.A. 40°36N 80°14W 312 F4
Ambriz Angola 7°48S 13°8E 265 D2
Ambriz △ Angola 7°56S 13°0E 265 D2
Ambrolauri Georgia 42°31N 43°9E 213 A10
Ambrym Vanuatu 16°15S 168°10E 287 F6
Ambulong I. Phil. 12°13N 121°1E 232 E3
Ambunti Papua N. G. 4°13S 142°52E 286 C2
Ambur India 12°48N 78°43E 245 H4
Amchitka I. U.S.A. 51°32N 179°0E 303 L2
Amderma Russia 69°45N 61°30E 214 C7
Amdhi India 23°51N 81°27E 243 H9
Amdo China 32°20N 91°40E 238 E3
Ameca Mexico 20°33N 104°2W 318 C4
Ameca → Mexico 20°41N 105°18W 318 C3
Amecameca de Juárez Mexico 19°8N 98°46W 319 D5
Amed Indonesia 8°19S 115°39E 231 J18
Ameixoeira Portugal 38°46N 9°8W 126 A2
Ameland Neths. 53°27N 5°45E 170 A5
Amélia Italy 42°33N 12°25E 199 F9
Amelia City U.S.A. 30°35N 81°28W 316 E8
Amelia Earhart Park U.S.A. 25°53N 80°16W 129 C1
Amelia I. U.S.A. 30°40N 81°25W 316 E8
Amendolara Italy 39°57N 16°35E 201 C9
Amenia U.S.A. 41°51N 73°33W 313 E11
América Brazil 23°35S 46°41W 137 B1
America-Antarctica Ridge S. Ocean 59°0S 16°0W 151 B2
American Falls U.S.A. 42°47N 112°51W 304 E7
American Falls Res. U.S.A. 42°47N 112°52W 304 E7
American Fork U.S.A. 40°23N 111°48W 304 F8
American Highland Antarctica 73°0S 75°0E 151 D6
American Indian Museum Washington, D.C., U.S.A. 143 b3
American Museum of Natural History New York, U.S.A. 132 b2
American River Australia 35°47S 137°46E 282 C2
American Samoa ☑ Pac. Oc. 14°20S 170°0W 302 f
American Samoa △ Amer. Samoa 14°15S 170°28W 302 g
American Univ. U.S.A. 38°56N 77°5W 143 B2
Americana Brazil 22°45S 47°20W 335 A6
Americus U.S.A. 32°4N 84°14W 316 C5
Amerigo Vespucci, Firenze ✗ (FLR) Italy 43°49N 11°13E 199 E8
Amerika = Nakhodka Russia 42°53N 132°54E 220 C6
Amersfoort Neths. 52°9N 5°23E 170 B5
Amersfoort Mpumalanga, S. Africa 26°59S 29°53E 271 C4
Amery Basin S. Ocean 68°15S 74°30E 151 C6
Amery Ice Shelf Antarctica 69°30S 72°0E 151 C6
Amerzgane Morocco 31°4N 7°14W 260 B3
Ames = Bertamirans Spain 42°54N 8°38W 194 C2
Ames U.S.A. 42°2N 93°37W 310 C3
Amesbury U.S.A. 42°51N 70°56W 313 D14
Amet India 25°18N 73°56E 242 G5
Amfiklia Greece 38°38N 22°35E 204 C4
Amfilochia Greece 38°52N 21°9E 204 C3
Amfipoli Greece 40°48N 23°52E 202 F7
Amfissa Greece 38°32N 22°22E 204 C4
Amga Russia 60°50N 132°0E 215 C14
Amga → Russia 62°38N 134°32E 215 C14
Amgaon India 21°22N 80°22E 244 D5
Amgu Russia 45°45N 137°15E 220 B8
Amguid Algeria 26°26N 5°22E 261 C6
Amgun → Russia 52°56N 139°38E 215 D14
Amherst = Kyaikkami Burma 16°4N 97°34E 241 G6
Amherst N.S., Canada 45°48N 64°8W 299 C7
Amherst Mass., U.S.A. 42°23N 72°31W 313 D12
Amherst N.Y., U.S.A. 42°59N 78°48W 312 D6
Amherst Ohio, U.S.A. 41°24N 82°14W 312 E2
Amherst I. Canada 44°8N 76°43W 313 B8
Amherstburg Canada 42°6N 83°6W 311 B13
Amiata, Mte. Italy 42°53N 11°37E 199 F8
Amidon U.S.A. 46°29N 103°19W 308 B2
Amiens France 49°54N 2°16E 173 C9
Amik Gölü Turkey 36°22N 36°17E 250 B7
Amili India 28°25N 95°52E 241 A5
Amin Iraq 33°19N 44°29E 113 B2
Aminadav Israel 31°45N 35°8E 123 B1
Amindeo Greece 40°42N 21°42E 202 F5
Amindivi Is. India 11°23N 72°23E 245 J1
Amingaon India 26°11N 91°40E 241 B3
Amini I. India 11°6N 72°45E 245 J1
Amino Ethiopia 4°25N 41°52E 257 G5
Aminuis Namibia 23°43S 19°21E 270 B2
Āmīr, Ra's Libya 32°57N 21°43E 258 B4
Amīrābād Īlām, Iran 33°20N 46°16E 246 C5
Amīrābād Tehrān, Iran 35°43N 51°24E 141 A2
Amirante Is. Seychelles 6°0S 53°0E 210 J7
Amisk △ Canada 56°43N 98°0W 297 B9
Amisk L. Canada 54°35N 102°15W 297 C8
Amistad, Presa de la Mexico 29°26N 101°3W 318 B4
Amistad △ U.S.A. 29°32N 101°12W 314 G4
Amite U.S.A. 30°44N 90°30W 315 F9
Amizmiz Morocco 31°12N 8°15W 260 B3
Amla India 21°56N 78°7E 242 J8
Amlapura Indonesia 8°27S 115°37E 231 J18
Åmli Norway 58°45N 8°32E 164 F5
Amlia I. U.S.A. 52°4N 173°30W 303 K4
Amlwch U.K. 53°24N 4°20W 168 D3
Amm Adam Sudan 16°20N 36°1E 257 D4
'Ammān Jordan 31°57N 35°52E 251 G6
'Ammān □ Jordan 31°40N 36°30E 251 G7
Ammanford U.K. 51°48N 3°59W 169 F4
Ammassalik = Tasiilaq Greenland 65°40N 37°20W 154 D7
Ammerån → Sweden 63°9N 16°13E 162 A10
Ammersee Germany 48°0N 11°7E 179 G7
Ammochostos = Famagusta Cyprus 35°8N 33°55E 207 E9
Ammon U.S.A. 43°28N 111°58W 304 E8
Amnat Charoen Thailand 15°51N 104°38E 236 E5
Amnura Bangla. 24°37N 88°25E 243 G13
Amo Jiang → China 23°0N 101°50E 228 F3
Āmol Iran 36°23N 52°20E 247 B7
Amora Portugal 38°37N 9°6W 126 B2
Amoreira Portugal 38°48N 9°11W 126 A1
Amoret U.S.A. 38°15N 94°35W 310 F2
Amorgos Greece 36°50N 25°57E 205 E7
Amory U.S.A. 33°59N 88°29W 315 E10
Amos Canada 48°35N 78°5W 298 C4
Åmot Buskerud, Norway 59°57N 9°54E 164 E6
Åmot Oppland, Norway 61°0N 10°2E 164 D7
Åmot Telemark, Norway 59°34N 8°0E 164 E5
Åmot Sweden 60°58N 16°27E 162 D10
Åmotfors Sweden 59°47N 12°22E 166 E6
Åmotsdal Norway 59°37N 8°26E 164 E5
Amour, Djebel Algeria 33°42N 1°37E 261 B5
Amoy = Xiamen China 24°25N 118°4E 229 E12
Ampah Indonesia 1°46S 115°7E 235 C5
Ampanavoana Madag. 15°41S 50°22E 272 B3
Ampang Malaysia 3°8N 101°45E 237 L3
Ampangalana, Lakandranon' Madag. 22°48S 47°50E 272 C2
Ampani India 19°35N 82°38E 244 E6
Ampanihy Madag. 24°40S 44°45E 272 C1
Amparafaravola Madag. 17°35S 48°13E 272 B2
Ampasinambo Madag. 20°31S 48°0E 272 C2
Ampasindava, Helodranon' Madag. 13°40S 48°15E 272 A2
Ampasindava, Saikanosy Madag. 13°42S 47°55E 272 A2
Ampato, Nevado Peru 15°40S 71°56W 330 D3
Ampenan Indonesia 8°34S 116°4E 231 K18
Amper Nigeria 9°25N 9°40E 263 D6
Amper → Bayern, Germany 48°29N 11°55E 179 G7
Amper → Oberbayern, Germany 48°14N 11°25E 131 A1
Ampezzo Italy 46°25N 12°48E 199 B9
Amphitrite Group S. China Sea 16°50N 112°20E 230 A4
Amphoe Kathu Thailand 7°55N 98°21E 237 a
Amphoe Thalang Thailand 8°1N 98°20E 237 a
Ampitsikinana Madag. 12°57S 49°49E 272 A2
Ampombiantambo Madag. 12°42S 48°57E 272 A2
Amposta Spain 40°43N 0°34E 196 E5
Ampotaka Madag. 25°3S 44°41E 272 D1
Ampoza Madag. 22°20S 44°44E 272 C1
Amqui Canada 48°28N 67°27W 299 C6
Amrabad India 16°23N 78°50E 245 F4
'Amrān Yemen 15°41N 43°55E 248 D3
'Amrān □ Yemen 15°41N 43°55E 248 D3
Amraoti = Amravati India 20°55N 77°45E 244 D3
Amravati India 20°55N 77°45E 244 D3
Amreli India 21°35N 71°17E 242 J4
Amrenene el Kasba Algeria 22°10N 0°30E 261 D5
Amritsar India 31°35N 74°57E 242 D6
Amroha India 28°53N 78°30E 243 E8
Amrum Germany 54°38N 8°22E 178 A4
Amsâga Mauritania 20°7N 14°10W 260 D2
Amsel Algeria 22°47N 5°29E 261 D6
Amstel Amsterdam, Neths. 112 b2
Amstel → Amsterdam, Neths. 112 b3
Amstel-Drecht-Kanaal Neths. 52°18N 4°54E 112 B2
Amstelveen Neths. 52°18N 4°51E 112 B2
Amsterdam Neths. 52°23N 4°54E 112 A2
Amsterdam N.Y., U.S.A. 42°56N 74°11W 313 D10
Amsterdam ✗ (AMS) Neths. 52°18N 4°45E 112 B1
Amsterdam Arena Neths. 52°19N 4°56E 112 B2
Amsterdam I. = Nouvelle Amsterdam, Î. Ind. Oc. 38°30S 77°30E 273 H6
Amsterdam-Rijnkanaal Neths. 52°17N 5°1E 112 B3
Amsterdam Zuidoost Neths. 52°18N 4°58E 112 B2
Amsterdamse Bos Neths. 52°19N 4°50E 112 B1
Amstetten Austria 48°7N 14°51E 180 C7
'Amūdah Syria 37°6N 40°55E 213 D9
Amudarya Turkmenistan 37°53N 65°15E 216 E7
Amudarya → Uzbekistan 43°58N 59°34E 216 D5
Amukta I. U.S.A. 52°30N 171°16W 303 K5
Amukta Pass U.S.A. 52°0N 171°0W 303 K5
Amulung Phil. 17°50N 121°43E 232 C3
Amund Ringnes I. Canada 78°20N 96°25W 295 B12
Amundsen Abyssal Plain S. Ocean 65°0S 125°0W 151 C14
Amundsen Basin Arctic 87°30N 80°0E 150 A
Amundsen Gulf Canada 71°0N 124°0W 294 C7
Amundsen Ridges S. Ocean 69°15S 123°0W 151 C14
Amundsen-Scott Antarctica 90°0S 166°0E 151 E
Amundsen Sea Antarctica 72°0S 115°0W 151 D15
Amungen Sweden 61°10N 15°40E 162 C9
Amuntai Indonesia 2°28S 115°25E 235 C5
Amur → Russia 52°56N 141°10E 215 D15
Amur, W. → Sudan 18°56N 33°34E 256 D3
Amurang Indonesia 1°5N 124°40E 231 D6
Amurrio Spain 43°3N 3°0W 196 B1
Amursk Russia 50°14N 136°54E 215 D14
Amusco Spain 42°10N 4°28W 194 C6
Amvrakikos Kolpos Greece 39°0N 20°55E 204 C2
Amvrosiyivka Ukraine 47°43N 38°30E 189 J10
Amyderya = Amudarya → Uzbekistan 43°58N 59°34E 216 D5
An Bang, Dao = Amboyna Cay S. China Sea 7°50N 112°50E 230 C4
An Bien Vietnam 9°45N 105°0E 237 H5
An Hoa Vietnam 15°40N 108°5E 236 E7
An Khe Vietnam 13°57N 108°51E 236 F7
An Nabatīyah at Tahta Lebanon 33°23N 35°27E 250 E6
An Nabk Syria 34°2N 36°44E 250 D7
An Nafūd Si. Arabia 28°15N 41°0E 246 D4
An Nāḥiyah Iraq 34°26N 41°33E 213 E9
An Najaf Iraq 32°3N 44°15E 213 G11
An Namāṣ Si. Arabia 19°7N 42°8E 248 C3
An Nāṣirīyah Iraq 31°0N 46°15E 246 D5
An Nawfalīyah Libya 30°54N 17°58E 258 B3
An Nhon = Binh Dinh Vietnam 13°55N 109°7E 236 F7
An Nīl □ Sudan 19°30N 33°0E 256 D3
An Nîl el Abyad □ Sudan 14°0N 32°15E 257 E3
An Nîl el Azraq □ Sudan 11°30N 34°30E 257 E3
An Nu'ayrīyah Si. Arabia 27°30N 48°30E 247 E6
An Nu'mānīyah Iraq 32°32N 45°25E 213 F11
An Nuqat al Khams □ Libya 32°42N 11°57E 258 B2
An Ros = Rush Ireland 53°31N 6°6W 166 C5
An Thoi, Quan Dao Vietnam 9°58N 104°0E 237 H5
Åna-Sira Norway 58°17N 6°25E 164 F3
Anaa French Polynesia 17°25S 145°30W 289 f
Anabar → Russia 73°8N 113°36E 215 B12
Anaco Venezuela 9°27N 64°28W 329 B5
Anaconda U.S.A. 46°8N 112°57W 304 C7
Anacortes U.S.A. 48°30N 122°37W 306 B4
Anacostia U.S.A. 38°51N 76°59W 143 B3
Anacostia → U.S.A. 38°52N 77°1W 143 B3
Anacuao, Mt. Phil. 16°16N 121°53E 232 C3
Anadarko U.S.A. 35°4N 98°15W 314 D5
Anadia Brazil 9°42S 36°18W 332 C4
Anadia Portugal 40°26N 8°27W 194 E2
Anadolu Turkey 39°0N 30°0E 212 C5
Anadoluhisarı Turkey 41°4N 29°3E 122 B2
Anadolukavaği Turkey 41°10N 29°7E 122 A2
Anadyr Russia 64°35N 177°20E 215 C18
Anadyr → Russia 64°55N 176°5E 215 C18
Anadyrskiy Zaliv Russia 64°0N 180°0E 215 C19
Anafi Greece 36°22N 25°48E 205 E7
Anafonitria Greece 37°51N 20°39E 207 D2
Anaga, Pta. de Canary Is. 28°34N 16°9W 153 e1
Anagni Italy 41°44N 13°9E 199 G10
'Ānah Iraq 34°25N 42°0E 213 E10
Anaheim U.S.A. 33°50N 117°55W 307 M9
Anahim Lake Canada 52°28N 125°18W 296 C3
Anahola U.S.A. 22°9N 159°19W 302 A2
'Anahulu → U.S.A. 21°37N 158°6W 302 J13
Anai Mudi India 10°12N 77°4E 245 J3
Anaichak △ U.S.A. 56°50N 158°15W 303 H8
Anaimalai Hills India 10°20N 76°40E 245 J3
Anajás Brazil 0°59S 49°57W 332 B2
Anajatuba Brazil 3°16S 44°37W 332 B3
Anakao Madag. 23°40S 43°39E 272 C1
Anakapalle India 17°42N 83°6E 244 F6
Anakena Chile 27°5S 109°20W 330 b
Anakie Australia 23°32S 147°45E 280 C4
Anaklia Georgia 42°22N 41°35E 191 J5
Anaktuvuk Pass U.S.A. 68°8N 151°45W 303 B10
Analalava Madag. 14°35S 48°0E 272 A2
Analavoka Madag. 22°23S 46°30E 272 C2
Analipsis Greece 39°36N 19°55E 206 B9
Anamã Brazil 3°35S 61°22W 329 D5
Anambar → Pakistan 30°15N 68°50E 242 D3
Anambas, Kepulauan Indonesia 3°20N 106°30E 234 B3
Anambas Is. = Anambas, Kepulauan Indonesia 3°20N 106°30E 234 B3
Anambra □ Nigeria 6°20N 7°0E 263 D6
Aname Vanuatu 20°8S 169°47E 287 K7
Anamosa U.S.A. 42°7N 91°17W 310 B5
Anamur Turkey 36°8N 32°58E 250 B3
Anamur → Turkey 36°5N 32°53E 250 B3
Anamur Burnu Turkey 36°2N 32°47E 250 B3
Anan Japan 33°54N 134°40E 222 D6
Anand India 22°32N 72°59E 242 H5
Anandapuram India 14°5N 75°12E 245 G2
Anandpur India 21°16N 86°13E 244 D8
Ananes Greece 36°33N 24°9E 204 E6
Anangu Pitjantjatjara ✪ Australia 27°0S 132°0E 279 E5
Ananindeua Brazil 1°22S 48°22W 332 B2
Anantapur India 14°39N 77°42E 245 G3
Anantnag India 33°45N 75°10E 243 C6
Ananyiv Ukraine 47°44N 29°58E 183 C14
Anapa Russia 44°55N 37°25E 189 K9
Anapodiaris → Greece 34°59N 25°20E 207 F6
Anápolis = Simão Dias Brazil 10°44S 37°49W 332 D4
Anápolis Brazil 16°15S 48°50W 333 E2
Anapu → Brazil 1°53S 50°53W 329 D7
Anār Iran 30°55N 55°13E 247 D7
Anār Darreh Afghan. 32°46N 61°39E 240 B1
Anārak Iran 33°25N 53°40E 247 C7
Anarisfjällen Sweden 63°6N 13°10E 162 A7
Anas → India 23°26N 74°0E 242 H5
Añasco Puerto Rico 18°17N 67°8W 321 b
Anata West Bank 31°49N 35°16E 123 B2
Anatahan N. Marianas 16°21N 145°40E 302 a
Anatolia = Anadolu Turkey 39°0N 30°0E 212 C5
Anatoliki Makedonia kai Thraki □ Greece 41°10N 24°30E 203 E8
Anatsogno Madag. 23°33S 43°46E 272 C1
Añatuya Argentina 28°20S 62°50W 334 B3
Anatye ✪ Australia 22°29S 137°3E 280 C2
Anauá → Brazil 0°58N 61°21W 329 C5
Anaunethad L. Canada 60°55N 104°25W 297 A8
Anavilhanas, Arquipélago das Brazil 2°42S 60°45W 329 D5
Anbyŏn N. Korea 39°1N 127°35E 224 C3
Ancares, Sierra dos Spain 42°51N 6°52W 194 C4
Ancares △ Spain 42°50N 6°40W 194 C4
Ancash □ Peru 9°30S 77°45W 330 B2
Ancaster Canada 43°13N 79°59W 312 C5
Ancenis France 47°21N 1°10W 172 E5
Anchieta = Piatã Brazil 13°9S 41°48W 333 D3
Anch'ing = Anqing China 30°30N 117°3E 229 B11
Ancho, Canal Chile 50°0S 74°20W 336 D2
Anchor Bay U.S.A. 38°48N 123°34W 306 G3
Anchorage U.S.A. 61°13N 149°54W 303 F10
Anchorage ✗ (ANC) U.S.A. 61°10N 150°0W 303 F10
Anchuras Spain 39°29N 4°50W 195 F6
Anchuthengu India 8°40N 76°46E 245 K3
Anci China 39°20N 116°40E 226 E9
Ancohuma, Nevado Bolivia 16°0S 68°50W 330 D4
Ancol Indonesia 6°7S 106°49E 122 A1
Ancón Peru 11°50S 77°10W 330 C2
Ancona Italy 43°38N 13°30E 199 E10
Ancud Chile 42°0S 73°50W 336 B2
Ancud, G. de Chile 42°0S 73°0W 336 B2
Ancy-le-Franc France 47°46N 4°10E 173 E11
Anda Heilongjiang, China 46°24N 125°19E 219 B14
Anda Phil. 16°17N 119°57E 232 C2
Andacollo Argentina 37°10S 70°42W 334 D1
Andacollo Chile 30°14S 71°6W 334 C1
Andahuaylas Peru 13°40S 73°25W 330 C3
Andaingo Madag. 18°12S 48°17E 272 B2
Andalgalá Argentina 27°40S 66°30W 334 B2
Åndalsnes Norway 62°35N 7°43E 164 B4
Andalucía □ Spain 37°35N 5°0W 195 H6
'Andalus Iraq 33°19N 44°18E 113 B1
Andalusia = Andalucía □ Spain 37°35N 5°0W 195 H6
Andalusia U.S.A. 31°18N 86°29W 315 F11
Andaman & Nicobar Is. □ India 10°0N 93°0E 245 K11
Andaman Is. Ind. Oc. 12°30N 92°45E 245 H11
Andaman Sea Ind. Oc. 13°0N 96°0E 230 B1
Andamooka Australia 30°27S 137°9E 281 E2
Andapa Madag. 14°39S 49°39E 272 A2
Andara Namibia 18°2S 21°9E 270 A3
Andaraí Bahia, Brazil 12°48S 41°20W 333 D3
Andaraí Rio de J., Brazil 22°56S 43°14W 135 B1
Andelot-Blancheville France 48°15N 5°18E 173 D12
Andenes Norway 69°19N 16°18E 160 B17
Andenne Belgium 50°28N 5°5E 170 D5
Andéranboukane Mali 15°26N 3°2E 263 B5
Anderlecht Belgium 50°50N 4°19E 116 A1
Andermatt Switz. 46°38N 8°35E 179 J4
Andernach Germany 50°26N 7°24E 178 E3
Andernos-les-Bains France 44°44N 1°6W 174 D2
Andersen Air Force Base ✗ (UAM) Guam 13°35N 144°55E 302 d
Anderslöv Sweden 55°26N 13°19E 163 J7
Anderson Vic., Australia 38°31S 145°26E 283 E6
Anderson Alaska, U.S.A. 64°25N 149°15W 303 D10
Anderson Calif., U.S.A. 40°27N 122°18W 304 F2
Anderson Ind., U.S.A. 40°10N 85°41W 311 D11
Anderson Mo., U.S.A. 36°39N 94°27W 308 G6
Anderson S.C., U.S.A. 34°31N 82°39W 315 D13
Anderson → Canada 69°42N 129°0W 294 C6
Anderson I. India 12°46N 92°43E 245 H11
Anderson Park U.S.A. 33°45N 84°27W 113 B2
Andersonville U.S.A. 32°12N 84°9W 316 C5
Andersonville △ U.S.A. 32°12N 84°9W 316 C5
Anderstorp Sweden 57°19N 13°39E 163 G7
Andes Colombia 5°39N 75°54W 328 B2
Andes N.Y., U.S.A. 42°12N 74°47W 313 D10
Andes, Cord. de los S. Amer. 20°0S 68°0W 330 E4
Andfjorden Norway 69°10N 16°20E 160 B17
Andhra, L. India 18°54N 73°32E 244 E1
Andhra Pradesh □ India 18°0N 79°0E 244 F4
Andijon Uzbekistan 41°10N 72°15E 217 D8
Andijon □ Uzbekistan 41°0N 72°0E 217 D8
Andikíthira = Antikythira Greece 35°52N 23°15E 204 F5
Andilamena Madag. 17°1S 48°35E 272 B2
Andīmeshk Iran 32°27N 48°21E 213 F13
Andimilos = Antimilos Greece 36°47N 24°12E 204 E6
Anding = Anting Taiwan 23°7N 120°14E 225 C2
Andingmen China 39°55N 116°23E 114 B2
Andiparos = Antiparos Greece 37°0N 25°3E 205 D7
Andipaxoi = Antipaxi Greece 39°9N 20°13E 204 B2
Andipsara Greece 38°30N 25°29E 205 C7
Andizhan = Andijon Uzbekistan 41°10N 72°15E 217 D8
Andkhvoy Afghan. 36°52N 65°8E 240 A2
Andoain Spain 43°13N 2°1W 196 B2
Andoany Madag. 13°25S 48°16E 272 A2
Andoas Peru 2°55S 76°25W 328 D2
Andohahela △ Madag. 24°4S 46°44E 272 C2
Andol India 17°51N 78°4E 244 F4
Andola India 16°57N 76°50E 244 F3
Andong S. Korea 36°40N 128°43E 224 D4
Andorra Spain 40°59N 0°28W 196 E4
Andorra ■ Europe 42°30N 1°30E 174 F5
Andorra La Vella Andorra 42°31N 1°32E 174 F5
Andover Hants., U.K. 51°12N 1°29W 169 F6
Andover Kans., U.S.A. 37°43N 97°7W 308 G5
Andover Maine, U.S.A. 44°38N 70°45W 313 B14
Andover Mass., U.S.A. 42°40N 71°8W 313 D13
Andover N.J., U.S.A. 40°59N 74°45W 313 F10
Andover N.Y., U.S.A. 42°10N 77°48W 312 D7
Andover Ohio, U.S.A. 41°36N 80°34W 312 E4
Andøya Norway 69°10N 15°50E 160 B16
Andrade Brazil 4°40S 63°45W 329 D5
Andradina Brazil 20°54S 51°23W 333 F1
Andrahary Madag. 13°37S 49°17E 272 A2
Andramasina Madag. 19°11S 47°35E 272 B2
Andranopasy Madag. 21°17S 43°44E 272 C1
Andranovory Madag. 23°8S 44°10E 272 C1
Andratx Spain 39°39N 2°25E 206 B3
André Félix △ C.A.R. 9°29N 23°18E 264 A4
Andreanof Is. U.S.A. 51°30N 176°0W 303 L4
Andreapol Russia 56°40N 32°17E 188 D7
Andrée Land Greenland 73°40N 26°0W 154 C8
Andrews S.C., U.S.A. 33°27N 79°34W 315 E15
Andrews Tex., U.S.A. 32°19N 102°33W 314 E3
Andreyev = Jędrzejów Poland 50°35N 20°15E 185 H7
Andreyevka Russia 52°19N 51°55E 190 D10
Ándria Italy 41°13N 16°17E 201 A9
Andriamena Madag. 17°26S 47°30E 272 B2
Andriandampy Madag. 22°45S 45°41E 272 C2
Andriba Madag. 17°30S 46°58E 272 B2
Andrijevica Montenegro 42°45N 19°48E 202 D3
Andringitra △ Madag. 22°13S 46°55E 272 C2
Andritsena Greece 37°29N 21°52E 204 D3
Androka Madag. 24°58S 44°2E 272 C1
Andropov = Rybinsk Russia 58°5N 38°50E 188 C10
Andros Greece 37°50N 24°57E 204 D6
Andros I. Bahamas 24°30N 78°0W 320 B4
Andros Town Bahamas 24°43N 77°47W 320 B4
Androth I. India 10°50N 73°41E 245 J1
Andrychów Poland 49°51N 19°18E 185 J6
Andselv Norway 69°4N 18°34E 160 B18
Andújar Spain 38°3N 4°5W 195 G6
Andulo Angola 11°25S 16°45E 265 E3
Åneby Akershus, Norway 60°5N 10°51E 164 D7
Aneby Sweden 57°48N 14°49E 163 G8
Anéfis Mali 18°2N 0°36E 263 B5
Anegada Br. Virgin Is. 18°45N 64°20W 321 C7
Anegada, B. Argentina 40°20S 62°20W 336 B4
Anegada Passage W. Indies 18°15N 63°45W 321 C7
Aného Togo 6°12N 1°34E 263 D5
Aneityum Vanuatu 20°12S 169°45E 287 K7
Anelghowhat Vanuatu 20°19S 169°43E 287 K7
Añelo Argentina 38°20S 68°45W 336 A3
Anenni-Noi Moldova 46°53N 29°15E 183 D14
Aneto, Pico de Spain 42°37N 0°40E 196 C5
Anew Turkmenistan 37°52N 58°31E 216 E5
Aney Niger 19°15N 12°50E 259 E2
Añez Bolivia 15°40S 63°10W 331 D5
Anfu China 27°21N 114°40E 229 D10
Ang Mo Kio Singapore 1°23N 103°50E 138 A3
Ang Thong Thailand 14°35N 100°31E 236 E3
Ang Thong, Ko Thailand 9°37N 99°41E 237 b
Ang Thong, Mu Ko △ Thailand 9°40N 99°43E 237 b
Angadanan Phil. 16°45N 121°45E 232 C3
Angamos, Punta Chile 23°1S 70°32W 334 A1
Angara → Russia 58°5N 94°20E 215 D10
Angara-Débou Benin 11°19N 3°3E 263 C5
Angarbaka South Sudan 9°44N 24°44E 257 F1
Angarsk Russia 52°30N 104°0E 218 A9
Angas Hills Australia 23°0S 127°50E 278 D4
Angaston Australia 34°30S 139°8E 282 C3
Angat Phil. 14°56N 121°2E 232 D3
Angaur I. Palau 6°54N 134°9E 288 c
Ånge Sweden 62°31N 15°35E 162 B9
Ángel, Salto = Angel Falls Venezuela 5°57N 62°30W 329 B5
Ángel de la Guarda, I. Mexico 29°20N 113°25W 318 B2
Angel Falls Venezuela 5°57N 62°30W 329 B5
Angel I. U.S.A. 37°52N 122°25W 136 A2
Angel Island State Park △ U.S.A. 37°52N 122°25W 136 A2
Angeles Phil. 15°9N 120°33E 232 D3
Ängelholm Sweden 56°15N 12°50E 163 H6
Angels Camp U.S.A. 38°4N 120°32W 306 G6
Ängelsberg Sweden 59°58N 16°0E 162 E10
Anger → Ethiopia 9°37N 36°6E 257 F4
Angerburg = Węgorzewo Poland 54°13N 21°43E 184 D8
Angereb Ethiopia 13°11N 37°7E 257 E4
Angereb → Ethiopia 13°45N 36°40E 257 E4
Ångermanälven → Sweden 63°0N 17°20E 162 A11
Ångermanland Sweden 63°36N 17°45E 160 E17
Angermünde Germany 53°0N 14°0E 178 B9
Angers Qué., Canada 45°31N 75°29W 313 A9
Angers Maine-et-Loire, France 47°30N 0°35W 172 E6
Angerville France 48°19N 2°0E 173 D9
Ångesån → Sweden 66°16N 22°47E 160 C20
Angical Brazil 12°0S 44°42W 333 D3
Angikuni L. Canada 62°12N 99°59W 297 A9
Angke, Kali → Indonesia 6°6S 106°46E 122 A1
Angkor Cambodia 13°22N 103°50E 236 F4
Angledool Australia 29°5S 147°55E 281 D4
Anglem, Mt. N.Z. 46°45S 167°53E 285 G2
Anglès Spain 41°57N 2°38E 196 D7
Anglesey U.K. 53°17N 4°20W 168 D3
Anglesey, Isle of □ U.K. 53°16N 4°18W 168 D3
Anglet France 43°29N 1°31W 174 E2
Angleton U.S.A. 29°10N 95°26W 314 G7
Anglin → France 46°42N 0°52E 174 B4
Anglisidhes Cyprus 34°51N 33°27E 207 F9
Anglure France 48°35N 3°50E 173 D10
Angmagssalik = Tasiilaq Greenland 65°40N 37°20W 154 D7
Ango Dem. Rep. of the Congo 4°10N 26°5E 268 B2
Angoche Mozam. 16°8S 39°55E 269 F4
Angoche, I. Mozam. 16°20S 39°50E 269 F4
Angol Chile 37°56S 72°45W 334 D1
Angola Ind., U.S.A. 41°38N 85°0W 311 C12
Angola N.Y., U.S.A. 42°38N 79°2W 312 D5
Angola ■ Africa 12°0S 18°0E 265 E3
Angola Abyssal Plain Atl. Oc. 15°0S 2°0E 152 H12
Angola Basin Atl. Oc. 15°0S 3°0E 152 H12
Angoon U.S.A. 57°30N 134°35W 303 H14
Angora = Ankara Turkey 39°57N 32°54E 212 C5
Angoram Papua N. G. 4°4S 144°4E 286 C3
Angoulême France 45°39N 0°10E 174 C4
Angoumois France 45°50N 0°25E 174 C4
Angra do Heroismo Azores 38°39N 27°13W 153 d1
Angra dos Reis Brazil 23°0S 44°10W 335 A7
Angren Uzbekistan 41°1N 70°12E 217 D8
Angtassom Cambodia 11°1N 104°41E 237 G5
Angu Dem. Rep. of the Congo 3°23N 24°30E 264 B4
Anguang China 45°15N 123°45E 227 B12
Anguilla ☑ W. Indies 18°14N 63°5W 322 a
Anguillita I. Anguilla 18°9N 63°11W 322 a
Angul India 20°51N 85°6E 244 D7
Anguo China 38°28N 115°15E 226 E8
Angurugu Australia 14°0S 136°25E 280 A2
Angus Canada 44°19N 79°53W 312 B5
Angus □ U.K. 56°46N 2°56W 167 E6
Angwa → Zimbabwe 16°0S 30°23E 271 A5
Angyalföld Hungary 47°32N 19°5E 117 A2
Anhanduí → Brazil 21°46S 52°9W 335 A5
Anholt Denmark 56°42N 11°33E 163 H5
Anhua China 28°23N 111°12E 229 C8
Anhui □ China 32°0N 117°0E 229 B11
Anhwei = Anhui □ China 32°0N 117°0E 229 B11
Aniak U.S.A. 61°35N 159°32W 303 F8
Anichab Namibia 21°0S 14°46E 270 B1
Anicuns Brazil 16°28S 49°58W 333 E2
Anidros Greece 36°38N 25°43E 205 E7
Anié Togo 7°42N 1°8E 263 D5
Anik India 19°1N 72°53E 130 A2
Anil Brazil 2°32S 44°14W 332 B3
Animas → U.S.A. 36°43N 108°13W 305 H9
Anin Burma 15°36N 97°50E 236 E1
Anin Warszawa, Poland 52°13N 21°9E 143 B2
Anina Romania 45°6N 21°51E 182 E6
Anini India 28°47N 95°53E 241 A5
Anini-y Phil. 10°25N 121°55E 233 F3
Añisoc Eq. Guin. 1°51N 10°46E 264 B2
Anita U.S.A. 41°27N 94°46W 310 C2
Anivorano Antsiranana, Madag. 12°44S 49°14E 272 A2
Anivorano Toamasina, Madag. 18°44S 48°58E 272 B2
Aniwa Vanuatu 19°17S 169°35E 287 J7
Anjalankoski Finland 60°45N 26°51E 188 B4
Anjangaon India 21°10N 77°20E 244 D3
Anjar = Hawsh Mūssá Lebanon 33°45N 35°55E 250 E6
Anjar India 23°6N 70°10E 242 H4
Anjengo = Anchuthengu India 8°40N 76°46E 245 K3
Anji China 30°46N 119°40E 229 B12
Anjidiv I. India 14°40N 74°10E 245 G2
Anjō Japan 34°57N 137°5E 223 C9
Anjou Qué., Canada 45°36N 73°33W 130 A2
Anjou Maine-et-Loire, France 47°20N 0°15W 172 E6
Anjouan Comoros Is. 12°15S 44°20E 272 a
Anjouan ✗ (AJN) Comoros Is. 12°9S 44°26E 272 a
Anjozorobe Madag. 18°22S 47°52E 272 B2
Anju N. Korea 39°36N 125°40E 224 C2
Anka Nigeria 12°13N 5°58E 263 C6
Ankaboa, Tanjona Madag. 21°58S 43°20E 272 C1
Ankang China 32°40N 109°1E 226 H5
Ankara Turkey 39°57N 32°54E 212 C5
Ankara □ Turkey 39°55N 32°50E 212 C5
Ankarafantsika △ Madag. 16°8S 47°5E 272 B2
Ankaramena Madag. 21°57S 46°39E 272 C2
Ankarata Madag. 19°20S 47°30E 272 B2
Ankarsrum Sweden 57°41N 16°20E 163 G10
Ankasakasa Madag. 16°21S 44°52E 272 B1
Ankavandra Madag. 18°46S 45°18E 272 B2
Ankazoabo Madag. 22°18S 44°31E 272 C1
Ankazobe Madag. 18°20S 47°10E 272 B2
Ankeny U.S.A. 41°44N 93°36W 310 C3
Ankhialo = Pomorie Bulgaria 42°32N 27°41E 203 D11
Ankilimalinika Madag. 22°58S 43°45E 272 C1
Ankilizato Madag. 20°25S 45°1E 272 C2
Anking = Anqing China 30°30N 117°3E 229 B11
Ankisabe Madag. 19°17S 46°29E 272 B2
Anklam Germany 53°51N 13°41E 178 B9
Ankleshwar India 21°38N 73°3E 244 D1
Ankober Ethiopia 9°35N 39°40E 257 F4
Ankola India 14°40N 74°18E 245 G2
Ankoro Dem. Rep. of the Congo 6°45S 26°55E 268 D2
Ankororoka Madag. 25°30S 45°11E 272 D2
Ankpa Nigeria 7°22N 7°38E 263 D6
Anlong China 25°2N 105°27E 228 E5
Anlong Veng Cambodia 14°14N 104°5E 236 E5
Anlu China 31°15N 113°45E 229 B9
Anmyeondo S. Korea 36°25N 126°25E 224 D3
Ann Burma 19°48N 94°0E 241 F5
Ann Sweden 63°19N 12°33E 162 A6
Ann, C. U.S.A. 42°38N 70°35W 313 D14
Ann Arbor U.S.A. 42°17N 83°45W 311 B13
Anna Russia 51°28N 40°23E 190 E5
Anna Ill., U.S.A. 37°28N 89°15W 308 G9
Anna Ohio, U.S.A. 40°24N 84°11W 311 D12
Anna Regina Guyana 7°10N 58°30W 329 B6
Annaba Algeria 36°50N 7°46E 261 A6
Annaba □ Algeria 36°50N 7°46E 261 A6
Annaberg-Buchholz Germany 50°34N 13°0E 178 E9
Annai Guyana 3°57N 59°8W 329 C6
Annaka Japan 36°19N 138°54E 223 A10
Annalee → Ireland 54°2N 7°24W 166 B4
Annalee Heights U.S.A. 38°51N 77°10W 143 B1
Annam = Trung-Phan Vietnam 17°0N 109°0E 236 D6
Annamitique, Chaîne Asia 17°0N 106°0E 236 D6
Annan U.K. 54°59N 3°16W 167 G5
Annan → U.K. 54°58N 3°16W 167 G5
Annanberg Papua N. G. 4°52S 144°42E 286 C3
Annapolis U.S.A. 38°59N 76°30W 309 F15
Annapolis Royal Canada 44°44N 65°32W 299 D6
Annapurna Nepal 28°34N 83°50E 243 E10
Anne Frankhuis Amsterdam, Neths. 112 a1
Annean, L. Australia 26°54S 118°14E 279 E2
Anneberg Sweden 57°44N 14°49E 163 G8
Annecy France 45°55N 6°8E 175 C10
Annecy, Lac d' France 45°52N 6°10E 175 C10
Annemasse France 46°12N 6°16E 173 F13
Annenfeld = Şämkir Azerbaijan 40°50N 46°0E 191 K8
Annenskiy Most Russia 60°45N 37°10E 188 B9
Annette I. U.S.A. 55°9N 131°28W 296 B2
Annette Island ▲ U.S.A. 55°9N 131°28W 303 J15
Annigeri India 15°26N 75°26E 245 G2
Anning China 24°55N 102°26E 228 E4
Anniston U.S.A. 33°39N 85°50W 316 B4
Annobón Atl. Oc. 1°25S 5°36E 255 G4
Annonay France 45°15N 4°40E 175 C8
Annot France 43°58N 6°38E 175 E10
Annotto B. Jamaica 18°17N 76°45W 320 a
Annotto Bay Jamaica 18°16N 76°47W 320 a
Annsjön Sweden 63°19N 12°34E 162 A6
Annville U.S.A. 40°20N 76°31W 313 F8
Annweiler Germany 49°12N 7°57E 179 F3
Ano Poroia Greece 41°17N 23°2E 202 E7
Ano Syros Greece 37°29N 24°56E 204 D6
Anogi Greece 38°25N 20°40E 207 C2
Anogia Greece 35°16N 24°52E 207 E5
Anorotsangana Madag. 13°56S 47°55E 272 A2
Anosibe Madag. 19°26S 48°13E 272 B2
Anou Mellene Mali 17°52N 0°31E 263 B5
Anoumaba Ivory C. 6°23N 4°38W 262 D4
Anping Hebei, China 38°15N 115°30E 226 E8
Anping Liaoning, China 41°5N 123°30E 224 B1
Anpu Gang China 21°25N 109°50E 228 G7
Anqing China 30°30N 117°3E 229 B11
Anqiu China 36°25N 119°10E 227 F10
Anren China 26°43N 113°18E 229 D9
Ansager Denmark 55°43N 8°45E 163 J2
Ansai China 36°50N 109°20E 226 F5
Ansan S. Korea 37°21N 126°52E 224 D3
Ansbach Germany 49°28N 10°34E 179 F6
Anse-Bertrand Guadeloupe 16°28N 61°32W 322 e
Anse Boileau Seychelles 4°43S 55°29E 272 c
Anse la Raye St. Lucia 13°55N 61°3W 323 m
Anse Royale Seychelles 4°44S 55°31E 272 c
Anseba → Eritrea 16°0N 38°30E 257 D4
Anseong S. Korea 37°0N 127°16E 224 D3
Anserma Colombia 5°13N 75°48W 328 B2
Ansfelden Austria 48°12N 14°17E 180 C7
Anshan China 41°5N 122°58E 224 B1
Anshun China 26°18N 105°57E 228 D5
Ansião Portugal 39°56N 8°27W 194 F2

Ansley U.S.A. 41°18N 99°23W 308 E4
Ansó Spain 42°51N 0°48W 196 C4
Ansoáin Spain 42°50N 1°38W 196 C3
Anson U.S.A. 32°45N 99°54W 314 E5
Anson B. Australia 13°20S 130°6E 278 B5
Ansongo Mali 15°25N 0°35E 263 B5
Ansongo-Ménaka ⌂ Mali 15°3N 1°37E 263 B5
Ansonia Conn., U.S.A. 41°21N 73°5W 313 E11
Ansonia Ohio, U.S.A. 40°13N 84°38W 311 D12
Anstruther U.K. 56°14N 2°41W 167 E6
Ansudu Indonesia 2°11S 139°22E 231 E9
Antabamba Peru 14°40S 73°0W 330 C3
Antagarh India 20°6N 81°9E 244 D5
Antakya = Hatay Turkey 36°14N 36°10E 250 B7
Antalaha Madag. 14°57S 50°20E 272 A3
Antalāt Libya 31°8N 20°42E 258 B4
Antalya Turkey 36°52N 30°45E 250 B1
Antalya □ Turkey 36°50N 30°45E 250 B1
Antalya Körfezi Turkey 36°15N 31°30E 250 B2
Antambohobe Madag. 22°20S 46°47E 272 C2
Antanambao-Manampotsy Madag. 19°29S 48°34E 272 B2
Antanambe Madag. 16°26S 49°52E 272 B2
Antananarivo Madag. 18°55S 47°31E 272 B2
Antananarivo □ Madag. 19°0S 47°0E 272 B2
Antanifotsy Madag. 19°39S 47°19E 272 B2
Antanimbaribe Madag. 21°30S 44°48E 272 C1
Antanimora Madag. 24°49S 45°40E 272 C2
Antarctic Pen. Antarctica 67°0S 60°0W 151 C18
Antarctica 90°0S 0°0 151 E3
Antécume Pata Fr. Guiana 3°17N 54°4W 329 C7
Antelope Zimbabwe 21°2S 28°31E 269 G2
Antep = Gaziantep Turkey 37°6N 37°23E 250 A8
Antequera Paraguay 24°8S 57°7W 334 A4
Antequera Spain 37°5N 4°33W 195 H6
Antero, Mt. U.S.A. 38°41N 106°15W 304 G10
Antevamena Madag. 21°2S 44°8E 272 C1
Anthony Fla., U.S.A. 29°18N 82°7W 317 F7
Anthony Kans., U.S.A. 37°9N 98°2W 308 G4
Anthony N. Mex., U.S.A. 32°0N 106°36W 305 K10
Anti Atlas Morocco 30°0N 8°30W 260 C3
Anti-Lebanon = Sharqi, Al Jabal ash Lebanon 33°40N 36°10E 250 E7
Antibes France 43°34N 7°6E 175 E11
Antibes, C. d' France 43°31N 7°7E 175 E11
Anticosti, Î. d' Canada 49°30N 63°0W 299 C7
Antifer, C. d' France 49°41N 0°10E 172 C7
Antigo U.S.A. 45°9N 89°9W 308 C9
Antigonish Canada 45°38N 61°58W 299 C7
Antigua Canary Is. 28°24N 14°1W 153 e2
Antigua Guatemala 14°34N 90°41W 320 D1
Antigua W. Indies 17°0N 61°50W 322 b
Antigua & Barbuda ■ W. Indies 17°20N 61°48W 322 b
Antigua Int. ✈ (ANU) Antigua & B. 17°8N 61°47W 322 b
Antigues, Pte. d' Guadeloupe 16°26N 61°32W 322 e
Antikythira Greece 35°52N 23°15E 204 F5
Antilla Cuba 20°40N 75°50W 320 B4
Antilles = West Indies Cent. Amer. 15°0N 65°0W 321 D7
Antimilos Greece 36°47N 24°12E 204 E6
Anting Taiwan 23°7N 120°14E 225 C2
Antioch = Hatay Turkey 36°14N 36°10E 250 B7
Antioch U.S.A. 38°1N 121°48W 306 G5
Antioche, Pertuis d' France 46°6N 1°20W 174 B2
Antioquia Colombia 6°40N 75°55W 328 B2
Antioquia □ Colombia 7°0N 75°30W 328 B2
Antiparos Greece 37°0N 25°3E 205 D7
Antipaxi Greece 39°9N 20°13E 204 B2
Antipodes Is. Pac. Oc. 49°45S 178°40E 288 M9
Antipolo Phil. 14°35N 121°10E 232 D3
Antique □ Phil. 11°10N 122°5E 233 F4
Antirio Greece 38°20N 21°46E 204 C3
Antlers U.S.A. 34°14N 95°37W 314 D7
Antoetra Madag. 20°46S 47°20E 272 C2
Antofagasta Chile 23°50S 70°30W 334 A1
Antofagasta □ Chile 24°0S 69°0W 334 A2
Antofagasta de la Sierra Argentina 26°5S 67°20W 334 B2
Antofalla Argentina 25°30S 68°5W 334 B2
Antofalla, Salar de Argentina 25°40S 67°45W 334 B2
Antoine, L. Grenada 12°11N 61°36W 323 q
Anton U.S.A. 33°49N 102°10W 314 E3
Antongila, Helodrano Madag. 15°30S 49°50E 272 B2
Antonibé Madag. 15°7S 47°24E 272 B2
Antonina Brazil 25°26S 48°42W 335 B6
Antonio B. Won Pat Int. ✈ (GUM) Guam 13°29N 144°48E 302 d
António Enes = Angoche Mozam. 16°8S 39°55E 269 F4
Antony France 48°44N 2°17E 134 B2
Antrain France 48°28N 1°30W 172 D5
Antrim Antrim, U.K. 54°43N 6°14W 166 B5
Antrim Ohio, U.S.A. 40°7N 81°21W 312 F3
Antrim □ U.K. 54°56N 6°25W 166 B5
Antrim, Mts. of U.K. 55°3N 6°14W 166 A5
Antrim Plateau Australia 18°8S 128°20E 278 C4
Antriol Bonaire 12°12N 68°16W 322 h
Antrodoco Italy 42°25N 13°5E 199 F10
Antropovo Russia 58°24N 43°6E 190 A6
Antsakabary Madag. 15°3S 48°56E 272 B2
Antsalova Madag. 18°40S 44°37E 272 B1
Antsenavolo Madag. 21°24S 48°3E 272 C2
Antsiafabositra Madag. 17°18S 46°57E 272 B2
Antsirabe Antananarivo, Madag. 19°55S 47°2E 272 B2
Antsirabe Antsiranana, Madag. 14°0S 49°59E 272 A2
Antsirabe Mahajanga, Madag. 15°57S 48°58E 272 B2
Antsiranana Madag. 12°25S 49°20E 272 A2
Antsiranana □ Madag. 12°16S 49°17E 272 A2
Antsohihy Madag. 14°50S 47°59E 272 A2
Antsohimbondrona Seranana Madag. 13°7S 48°48E 272 A2
Antu China 42°30N 128°20E 227 C15
Antufash Yemen 15°42N 42°25E 248 D3
Antung Taiwan 23°18N 121°20E 225 C3
Antwerp = Antwerpen Belgium 51°13N 4°25E 170 C4
Antwerp N.Y., U.S.A. 44°12N 75°37W 313 B9
Antwerp Ohio, U.S.A. 41°11N 84°45W 311 C12
Antwerpen Belgium 51°13N 4°25E 170 C4
Antwerpen □ Belgium 51°15N 4°40E 170 C4
Anukur, C. Papua N. G. 6°18S 149°37E 286 D5
Anupgarh India 29°10N 73°10E 242 E5
Anuppur India 23°6N 81°41E 243 H9
Anuradhapura Sri Lanka 8°22N 80°28E 245 K5
Anurrete ✪ Australia 20°50S 135°38E 280 C2
Anveh Iran 27°23N 54°11E 247 E7
Anvers = Antwerpen Belgium 51°13N 4°25E 170 C4
Anvers I. Antarctica 64°30S 63°40W 151 C17
Anvik U.S.A. 62°39N 160°13W 303 E7
Anwen China 29°4N 120°26E 229 C13
Anxi Fujian, China 25°2N 118°12E 229 E12
Anxi Gansu, China 40°30N 95°43E 218 C8
Anxian China 31°40N 104°25E 228 B5
Anxiang China 29°27N 112°11E 229 C9
Anxious B. Australia 33°24S 134°45E 281 E1
Anyama Ivory C. 5°30N 4°3W 262 D4
Anyang Henan, China 36°5N 114°21E 226 F8
Anyang S. Korea 37°23N 126°55E 224 D3
Anyer Indonesia 6°4S 105°53E 234 D3
Anyi Jiangxi, China 28°49N 115°25E 229 C10
Anyi Shanxi, China 35°2N 111°2E 226 G6
Anyuan China 25°9N 115°21E 229 E10
Anyue China 30°9N 105°50E 228 B5
Anza U.S.A. 33°35N 116°39W 307 M10
Anze China 36°10N 112°12E 226 F7
Anzeglouf Algeria 26°50N 0°1E 261 C5
Anzhero-Sudzhensk Russia 56°10N 86°0E 214 D9
Ánzio Italy 41°27N 12°37E 200 A5
Anzoátegui □ Venezuela 9°0N 64°30W 329 B5
Ao Makham Thailand 7°50N 98°24E 237 a
Ao Phangnga △ Thailand 8°10N 98°32E 237 a
Aoba Vanuatu 15°25S 167°50E 287 E5
Aoga-Shima Japan 32°28N 139°46E 223 E11
Aohan Qi China 43°18N 119°43E 227 C10
Aoiz Spain 42°46N 1°22W 196 C3
Aoji N. Korea 42°31N 130°23E 224 A5
Aola Solomon Is. 9°30S 160°30E 287 M11
Aomen = Macau China 22°12N 113°33E 229 F9
Aomori Japan 40°45N 140°45E 220 D10
Aomori □ Japan 40°45N 140°40E 220 D10
AON Center Chicago, U.S.A. 119 b2
tAonach, An = Nenagh Ireland 52°52N 8°11W 166 D3
Aonla India 28°16N 79°11E 243 E8
Aono-Yama Japan 34°28N 131°48E 222 C3
Aorai, Mt. Tahiti 17°34S 149°30W 289 e
Aoraki Mount Cook N.Z. 43°36S 170°9E 285 D5
Aoral, Phnum Cambodia 12°0N 104°15E 237 G5
Aorangi Ra. N.Z. 41°28S 175°22E 284 H4
Aore Vanuatu 15°35S 167°10E 287 E5
Aoreora Morocco 28°51N 10°53W 260 C2
Aosta Italy 45°45N 7°20E 198 C4
Aotea Harbour N.Z. 38°0S 174°50E 284 E3
Aotearoa = New Zealand ■ Oceania 40°0S 176°0E 284 G5
Aoudéras Niger 17°45N 8°20E 259 E1
Aouinet Torkoz Morocco 28°31N 9°46W 260 C3
Aouk, Bahr → Africa 8°51N 18°53E 259 G3
Aouk-Aoukalé ⌂ C.A.R. 9°52N 21°25E 264 A4
Aoukar Mali 23°50N 2°45W 260 D4
Aoukâr Mauritania 17°40N 10°0W 262 B3
Aoulef el Arab Algeria 26°55N 1°2E 261 C5
Aousred W. Sahara 22°32N 14°17W 260 D2
Aoyama Tokyo, Japan 140 b2
Aozou Chad 21°45N 17°28E 259 D3
Aozou, Couloir d' Chad 22°0N 19°0E 259 D3
Ap Lei Chau Hong Kong, China 22°14N 114°9E 122 B2
Apá → S. Amer. 22°6S 58°2W 334 A4
Apache U.S.A. 34°54N 98°22W 314 D5
Apache Junction U.S.A. 33°25N 111°33W 305 K8
Apalachee B. U.S.A. 30°0N 84°0W 316 E5
Apalachicola U.S.A. 29°43N 84°59W 316 F5
Apalachicola → U.S.A. 29°43N 84°58W 316 F5
Apalachicola B. U.S.A. 29°40N 85°0W 316 F3
Apam Ghana 5°19N 0°42W 263 D4
Apamea Syria 35°31N 36°28E 250 C7
Apapa Nigeria 6°26N 3°21E 124 B2
Apapa Quays Nigeria 6°26N 3°23E 124 B2
Apaporis → Colombia 1°23S 69°25W 328 D4
Aparados da Serra △ Brazil 29°10S 50°8W 335 B5
Aparecida = Bertolínia Brazil 7°38S 43°57W 332 C3
Aparecida de Goiânia Brazil 16°45S 49°16W 333 E2
Aparecida do Taboado Brazil 20°5S 51°5W 333 F1
Aparri Phil. 18°22N 121°38E 232 B3
Aparurén Venezuela 5°6N 62°8W 329 B5
Apataki French Polynesia 15°26S 146°20W 289 f
Apateu Romania 46°36N 21°47E 182 D6
Apatin Serbia 45°40N 19°0E 182 E4
Apatity Russia 67°34N 33°22E 160 C25
Apatou Fr. Guiana 5°9N 54°20W 329 B7
Apatula = Finke Australia 25°34S 134°35E 280 D1
Apatzingán Mexico 19°5N 102°21W 318 D4
Apayao □ Phil. 18°10N 121°10E 232 B3
Apelacão Portugal 38°48N 9°7W 126 A2
Apeldoorn Neths. 52°13N 5°57E 170 B5
Apen Germany 53°13N 7°48E 178 B3
Apennines = Appennini Italy 44°30N 10°0E 198 D7
Apenrade = Aabenraa Denmark 55°3N 9°25E 163 J3
Apere → Bolivia 13°44S 65°18W 331 C4
Aphrodisias Turkey 37°42N 28°46E 205 D10
Api Nepal 30°0N 80°57E 218 F5
Apia Samoa 13°50S 171°50W 287 V20
Apiacás, Serra dos Brazil 9°50S 57°0W 331 B6
Apiaí Brazil 24°31S 48°50W 333 F2
Apiaú → Brazil 2°39N 61°12W 329 C5
Apiaú, Serra do Brazil 2°30N 62°0W 329 C5
Apidiá → Brazil 11°39S 61°11W 331 C5
Apies → S. Africa 25°15S 28°8E 271 C4
Apinajé Brazil 11°31S 48°18W 333 D2
Apiti N.Z. 39°58S 175°54E 284 F4
Apizaco Mexico 19°25N 98°8W 319 D5
Aplao Peru 16°0S 72°40W 330 D3
Apo, Mt. Phil. 6°53N 125°14E 233 H5
Apo East Pass. Phil. 12°40N 120°40E 232 E3
Apo Reef △ Phil. 12°50N 120°50E 232 E3
Apo West Pass. Phil. 12°31N 120°22E 232 E3
Apodi Brazil 5°39S 37°48W 332 C4
Apoera Suriname 5°12N 57°10W 329 B6
Apolakia Greece 36°5N 27°48E 206 E11
Apolakia, Ormos Greece 36°5N 27°45E 206 E11
Apolda Germany 51°2N 11°32E 178 D7
Apolima Samoa 13°49S 172°9W 287 V19
Apollo Bay Australia 38°45S 143°40E 282 E5
Apollonia = Sūsah Libya 32°52N 21°59E 258 B4
Apollonia Greece 36°15N 27°58E 206 E11
Apolo Bolivia 14°30S 68°30W 330 C4
Apolonia Greece 36°58N 24°43E 204 E6
Apónguao → Venezuela 4°48N 61°36W 329 C5
Apopa El Salv. 13°48N 89°10W 320 D2
Apopka U.S.A. 28°40N 81°31W 317 G8
Apopka, L. U.S.A. 28°37N 81°37W 133 A1
Apoquindo Chile 33°24S 70°32W 137 B2
Aporé Brazil 18°58S 52°1W 331 D7
Aporé → Brazil 19°27S 50°57W 333 E1
Aporema Brazil 1°14N 50°49W 332 A1
Apostle Is. U.S.A. 47°0N 90°40W 308 B8
Apostle Islands ⌂ U.S.A. 46°55N 91°0W 308 B8
Apóstoles Argentina 28°0S 56°0W 335 B4
Apostolos Andreas, C. Cyprus 35°42N 34°35E 207 E10
Apostolovo Ukraine 47°39N 33°39E 189 J7
Apoteri Guyana 4°2N 58°32W 329 C6
Appalachian Mts. U.S.A. 38°0N 80°0W 309 G14
Äppelbo Sweden 60°29N 14°1E 162 D8
Appenino Lucano-Val d'Agri-Lagonegrese ⌂ Italy 40°5N 16°10E 201 B9
Appenino Tosco-Emiliano ⌂ Italy 44°10N 10°25E 198 D7
Appennini Italy 44°30N 10°0E 198 D7
Appennino Ligure Italy 44°30N 9°0E 198 D6
Appenzell-Ausser Rhoden □ Switz. 47°23N 9°23E 179 H5
Appenzell-Inner Rhoden □ Switz. 47°20N 9°25E 179 H5
Appiano Italy 46°28N 11°15E 199 B8
Apple Hill Canada 45°13N 74°46W 313 A10
Apple Valley U.S.A. 34°32N 117°14W 307 L9
Appleby-in-Westmorland U.K. 54°35N 2°29W 168 C5
Appledore U.K. 51°3N 4°13W 169 F3
Appleton U.S.A. 44°16N 88°25W 308 C9
Appleton City U.S.A. 38°11N 94°2W 310 F2
Appleton Rum Distillery Jamaica 18°10N 77°44W 320 a
Appling U.S.A. 33°33N 82°19W 316 B7
Approuague Fr. Guiana 4°20N 52°0W 329 C7
Apra Harbor Guam 13°26N 144°40E 302 d
Apricena Italy 41°47N 15°27E 199 G12
April → Papua N. G. 4°18S 142°26E 286 C2
Aprília Italy 41°36N 12°39E 200 A5
Apsheronsk Russia 44°28N 39°42E 191 H4
Apsley Canada 44°45N 78°6W 312 B6
Apt France 43°53N 5°24E 175 E9
Apterkarskiy Ostrov Russia 59°57N 30°20E 137 B2
Apuane, Alpi Italy 44°7N 10°14E 198 D7
Apuaú Brazil 2°25S 60°53W 329 D5
Apucarana Brazil 23°55S 51°33W 335 A5
Apulia = Púglia □ Italy 41°15N 16°15E 201 A9
Apurashokoru Palau 7°16N 134°17E 288 c
Apurauan Phil. 9°35N 118°20E 233 G2
Apure □ Venezuela 7°10N 68°50W 328 B4
Apure → Venezuela 7°37N 66°25W 328 B4
Apurímac □ Peru 14°0S 73°0W 330 C3
Apurímac → Peru 12°17S 73°56W 330 C3
Apuseni, Munţii Romania 46°30N 22°45E 182 D7
Āq Qālā Iran 37°10N 54°30E 247 B7
Aqaba = Al 'Aqabah Jordan 29°31N 35°0E 251 J6
Aqaba, G. of Red Sea 29°0N 34°40E 251 K5
'Aqabah, Khalīj al = Aqaba, G. of Red Sea 29°0N 34°40E 251 K5
Aqadyr Kazakhstan 48°17N 74°50E 217 C8
Āqchah Afghan. 36°56N 66°11E 240 A2
'Aqdā Iran 32°26N 53°37E 247 C7
Aqîq Sudan 18°14N 38°12E 256 D4
Aqîq, Khalîg Sudan 18°20N 38°10E 256 D4
'Aqīq, W. al → Si. Arabia 20°16N 41°40E 248 B3
Aqköl Kazakhstan 51°59N 70°56E 217 B8
Aqmola = Astana Kazakhstan 51°10N 71°30E 217 B8
Aqmola □ Kazakhstan 51°30N 70°0E 217 B8
'Aqrah Iraq 36°46N 43°45E 213 D10
Aqsay Kazakhstan 51°11N 53°0E 187 D9
Aqshataū Kazakhstan 47°59N 74°3E 217 C8
Aqsū Ongtüstik Qazaqstan, Kazakhstan 42°25N 69°50E 217 D7
Aqsū Pavlodar, Kazakhstan 52°2N 76°55E 217 B9
Aqsügek Kazakhstan 44°37N 74°30E 217 D8
Aqtaū Mangghystaū, Kazakhstan 43°39N 51°12E 187 F9
Aqtaū Qaraghandy, Kazakhstan 50°14N 73°3E 217 B8
Aqtöbe Kazakhstan 50°17N 57°10E 187 D10
Aqtoghay Kazakhstan 46°57N 79°40E 217 C9
Aqua = Sokhumi Georgia 43°0N 41°0E 191 J5
Aquarium of the Americas New Orleans, U.S.A. 131 b3
Aquidauana Brazil 20°30S 55°50W 331 E6
Aquidauana → Brazil 19°44S 56°50W 331 D6
Aquila Mexico 18°36N 103°30W 318 D4
Aquileia Italy 45°46N 13°22E 199 C10
Aquiles Serdán Mexico 28°36N 105°53W 318 B3
Aquin Haiti 18°16N 73°24W 321 C5
Aquitain, Bassin France 44°0N 0°30W 171 D3
Aquitaine □ France 44°25N 0°30W 174 D3
Ar Horqin Qi China 43°45N 120°0E 227 C11
Ar Kazimiyah Iraq 33°22N 44°20E 113 B1
Ar Rafid Syria 32°57N 35°52E 250 F6
Ar Raḥḥālīyah Iraq 32°44N 43°23E 213 F10
Ar Rāhidah Yemen 13°23N 44°19E 248 D4
Ar Ram West Bank 31°51N 35°15E 123 A2
Ar Ramādī Iraq 33°25N 43°20E 213 F10
Ar Raml Libya 26°45N 19°40E 258 C3
Ar Ramthā Jordan 32°34N 36°0E 251 F7
Ar Raqqah Syria 35°59N 39°8E 213 E8
Ar Raqqah □ Syria 36°20N 39°10E 213 D8
Ar Rashidiya = Er Rachidia Morocco 31°58N 4°20W 260 B4
Ar Rass Si. Arabia 25°50N 43°40E 246 E4
Ar Rastan Syria 34°55N 36°43E 250 D7
Ar Rawḍah Si. Arabia 21°16N 42°50E 248 B3
Ar Rawḍah Ṣan'ā', Yemen 15°26N 44°13E 248 D4
Ar Rawḍah Shabwah, Yemen 14°28N 47°17E 248 D4
Ar Rayyan Qatar 25°17N 51°25E 247 E6
Ar Rifā'ī Iraq 31°50N 46°10E 246 D5
Ar Riyāḍ Si. Arabia 24°41N 46°42E 246 E5
Ar Riyāḍ □ Si. Arabia 23°0N 45°50E 248 B4
Ar Riyān Yemen 14°39N 49°19E 267 B6
Ar Rmās, W. → Syria 35°47N 36°50E 250 C7
Ar Ru'ays Qatar 26°8N 51°12E 247 E6
Ar Rukhaymīyah Iraq 29°22N 45°38E 246 D5
Ar Rumaythah Iraq 31°31N 45°12E 246 D5
Ar Ruṣāfah Syria 35°45N 38°49E 213 E8
Ar Ruṣayfah Jordan 32°1N 36°3E 251 F7
Ar Rustāq Oman 23°23N 57°26E 249 B7
Ar Ruṭbah Iraq 33°0N 40°15E 213 F9
Ar Ruwayḍah Si. Arabia 23°40N 44°40E 248 B4
Ara India 25°35N 84°32E 243 G11
Ara → Japan 35°41N 139°50E 140 A4
Ara Goro Ethiopia 5°48N 41°18E 257 F5
Ara Tera Ethiopia 6°38N 40°57E 257 F5
Arab U.S.A. 34°19N 86°30W 315 D11
'Arab, Bahr el → South Sudan 9°0N 29°30E 257 F2
Arab, Khalîg el Egypt 30°55N 29°0E 256 A2
Arab, Shatt al → Asia 29°57N 48°34E 247 D6
'Araba, W. → Egypt 28°19N 33°31E 256 J8
'Arabābād Iran 33°2N 57°41E 247 C8
'Arabah, W. → Yemen 18°5N 51°26E 249 C5
Araban Turkey 37°28N 37°44E 212 D7
Arabatskaya Strelka Ukraine 45°40N 35°0E 189 K8
Arabba Italy 46°30N 11°52E 199 B8
Arabelo Venezuela 4°55N 64°13W 329 C5
Arabi U.S.A. 31°50N 83°44W 316 D6
Arabia Asia 25°0N 45°0E 210 F6
Arabian Basin Ind. Oc. 11°30N 65°0E 273 C5
Arabian Desert = Es Sahrâ' Esh Sharqîya Egypt 27°30N 32°30E 256 B3
Arabian Gulf = Persian Gulf Asia 27°0N 50°0E 247 E6
Arabian Sea Ind. Oc. 16°0N 65°0E 238 F9
Arabistan = Khūzestān □ Iran 31°0N 49°0E 247 D6
Araç Turkey 41°15N 33°21E 212 B5
Aracaju Brazil 10°55S 37°4W 332 D4
Aracataca Colombia 10°38N 74°9W 328 A3
Aracati Brazil 4°30S 37°44W 332 B4
Araçatuba Brazil 21°10S 50°30W 335 A5
Araceli Phil. 10°33N 119°59E 233 F2
Aracena Spain 37°53N 6°38W 195 H4
Aracena, Sierra de Spain 37°50N 6°50W 195 H4
Arachova Greece 38°28N 22°35E 204 C4
Arachthos → Greece 39°20N 21°4E 204 B3
Aracides, C. Solomon Is. 8°21S 161°0E 287 M11
Aračinovo Macedonia 42°1N 21°34E 202 D5
Araçuaí Brazil 16°52S 42°4W 333 E3
Araçuaí → Brazil 16°46S 42°2W 333 E3
'Arad Israel 31°15N 35°12E 251 G6
Arad Romania 46°10N 21°20E 182 D6
Arad □ Romania 46°20N 22°0E 182 D6
Arada Chad 15°0N 20°20E 259 F4
Arādān Iran 35°21N 52°30E 247 C7
Aradhippou Cyprus 34°57N 33°36E 207 F9
Arafura Sea E. Indies 9°0S 135°0E 288 H5
Aragarças Brazil 15°55S 52°15W 331 D7
Aragats Armenia 40°30N 44°15E 191 K7
Aragon U.S.A. 34°2N 85°3W 316 A4
Aragón □ Spain 41°25N 0°40W 196 D4
Aragón → Spain 42°13N 1°44W 196 C3
Aragona Italy 37°24N 13°27E 200 E6
Aragua □ Venezuela 10°0N 67°10W 328 B4
Aragua de Barcelona Venezuela 9°28N 64°49W 329 B5
Araguacema Brazil 8°50S 49°20W 332 C2
Araguaçu = Paraguaçu Paulista Brazil 22°22S 50°35W 335 A5
Araguaçu Brazil 12°49S 49°51W 333 D2
Araguaia → Brazil 5°21S 48°41W 332 C2
Araguaia △ Brazil 10°30S 50°0W 332 D2
Araguaiana Brazil 15°43S 51°51W 331 D7
Araguaína Brazil 7°12S 48°12W 332 C2
Araguari Brazil 18°38S 48°11W 333 E2
Araguari → Brazil 1°15N 49°55W 329 C8
Araguatins Brazil 5°38S 48°7W 332 C2
Arahal Spain 37°15N 5°33W 195 H5
Arain India 26°27N 75°2E 242 F6
Araioses Brazil 2°53S 41°55W 332 B3
Arak Algeria 25°20N 3°45E 261 C5
Arāk Iran 34°0N 49°40E 247 C6
Araka South Sudan 4°20N 30°23E 257 G3
Arakan = Rakhine □ Burma 19°0N 94°15E 241 F5
Arakan Coast Burma 19°0N 94°0E 241 F4
Arakan Yoma Burma 20°0N 94°40E 241 F5
Arakawa Japan 35°44N 139°48E 140 A3
Arakkonam India 13°7N 79°43E 245 H4
Araklı Turkey 41°6N 40°2E 213 B9
Araks = Aras, Rūd-e → Asia 40°5N 48°29E 213 B13
Araks → Iran 39°10N 47°10E 216 E3
Aral Kazakhstan 46°41N 61°45E 216 C6
Aral Mangy Qaraqumy Kazakhstan 46°50N 63°10E 216 C6
Aral Sea Asia 45°0N 58°20E 216 C5
Aral Tengizi = Aral Sea Asia 45°0N 58°20E 216 C5
Aralık Turkey 39°52N 44°31E 213 C11
Aralkum Asia 44°30N 60°35E 216 D6
Aralsk = Aral Kazakhstan 46°41N 61°45E 216 C6
Aralskoye More = Aral Sea Asia 45°0N 58°20E 216 C5
Aralsor, Ozero = Aralsor Köli Kazakhstan 49°5N 48°12E 191 F9
Aralsor Köli Kazakhstan 49°5N 48°12E 191 F9
Aramac Australia 22°58S 145°14E 280 C4
Aramia → Papua N. G. 7°55S 143°22E 286 D2
Aran → India 19°55N 78°12E 244 E4
Aran, Val de Spain 42°50N 0°55E 196 C5
Aran Areh Ethiopia 9°2N 43°54E 267 C5
Aran I. = Arranmore Ireland 55°0N 8°30W 166 A3
Aran Is. Ireland 53°6N 9°38W 166 C2
Aranda de Duero Spain 41°39N 3°42W 194 D7
Arandān Iran 35°23N 46°55E 246 C5
Aranđelovac Serbia 44°18N 20°34E 202 B4
Aranga N.Z. 35°44S 173°40E 284 B2
Arani Bolivia 17°34S 65°46W 331 D4
Arani India 12°43N 79°19E 245 H4
Aranjuez Spain 40°1N 3°40W 194 E7
Aranos Namibia 24°9S 19°7E 270 B2
Aransas Pass U.S.A. 27°55N 97°9W 314 H6
Arany-hegyi-patak → Hungary 47°34N 19°4E 117 A2
Aranyaprathet Thailand 13°41N 102°30E 236 F4
Arao Japan 32°59N 130°25E 222 E2
Araouane Mali 18°55N 3°30W 262 B4
Arapahoe U.S.A. 40°18N 99°54W 308 E4
Arapari Brazil 5°34S 49°15W 332 C2
Arapawa I. N.Z. 41°11S 174°17E 285 B9
Arapey Grande → Uruguay 30°55S 57°49W 334 C4
Arapgir Turkey 39°5N 38°30E 213 C8
Arapiraca Brazil 9°45S 36°39W 332 C4
Arapis, Akra Greece 40°27N 24°0E 203 F8
Arapongas Brazil 23°29S 51°28W 335 A5
Arapuni N.Z. 38°4S 175°39E 284 E4
Ar'ar Si. Arabia 30°59N 41°2E 246 D4
Araracuara Colombia 0°24S 72°17W 328 D3
Araranguá Brazil 29°0S 49°30W 335 B6
Araraquara Brazil 21°50S 48°0W 333 F2
Araras Brazil 22°22S 47°23W 333 F2
Ararás, Serra das Brazil 25°0S 53°10W 335 B5
Ararat Armenia 39°48N 44°50E 213 C11
Ararat Vic., Australia 37°16S 142°58E 282 D5
Ararat, Mt. = Ağrı Dağı Turkey 39°50N 44°15E 213 C11
Arari Brazil 3°28S 44°47W 332 B3
Araria India 26°9N 87°33E 243 F12
Araripe, Chapada do Brazil 7°20S 40°0W 332 C4
Araripina Brazil 7°33S 40°34W 332 C3
Araruama, L. de Brazil 22°53S 42°12W 333 F3
Araruna Brazil 6°52S 35°44W 332 C4
Aras, Rūd-e → Asia 40°5N 48°29E 213 B13
Aratāne Mauritania 18°24N 8°32W 262 B3
Araticu = Oeiras do Para Brazil 1°58S 49°51W 329 D8
Arauca Colombia 7°0N 70°40W 328 B3
Arauca □ Colombia 6°40N 71°0W 328 B3
Arauca → Venezuela 7°24N 66°35W 328 B4
Arauco Chile 37°16S 73°25W 334 D1
Araújos Brazil 19°56S 45°14W 333 E2
Arauquita Colombia 7°2N 71°25W 328 B3
Araure Venezuela 9°34N 69°13W 328 B4
Aravaca Spain 40°27N 3°47W 127 B1
Aravalli Range India 25°0N 73°30E 242 G5
Arawa Ethiopia 9°57N 41°58E 257 F5
Arawale ⌂ Kenya 1°24S 40°9E 268 C5
Arawe Is. Papua N. G. 6°6S 149°0E 286 D5
Arawhata → N.Z. 44°0S 168°40E 285 E3
Araxá Brazil 19°35S 46°55W 333 E2
Araya, Pen. de Venezuela 10°40N 64°0W 329 A5
Arayat Phil. 15°10N 120°46E 232 D3
Arba Gugu Ethiopia 8°40N 40°15E 257 F5
Arba Minch Ethiopia 6°0N 37°30E 257 F4
Arbat Iraq 35°25N 45°35E 213 E11
Arbataash Iraq 33°20N 44°19E 113 A1
Árbatax Italy 39°56N 9°42E 200 C2
Arbi Ethiopia 9°4N 35°7E 257 F4
Arbīl Iraq 36°15N 44°5E 213 D11
Arbīl □ Iraq 36°20N 44°20E 213 D11
Arboga Sweden 59°24N 15°52E 162 E9
Arbois France 46°55N 5°46E 173 F12
Arboletes Colombia 8°51N 76°26W 328 B2
Arbore Ethiopia 5°3N 36°50E 257 F4
Arboréa Italy 39°46N 8°35E 200 C1
Arborfield Canada 53°6N 103°39W 297 C8
Arborg Canada 50°54N 97°13W 297 C9
Arbre du Ténéré Niger 17°50N 10°4E 259 E2
Arbroath U.K. 56°34N 2°35W 167 E6
Arbuckle U.S.A. 39°1N 122°3W 306 F4
Arbus Italy 39°30N 8°33E 200 C1
Arc → France 45°34N 6°12E 175 C10
Arc de Triomphe Paris, France 134 a2
Arc-lès-Gray France 47°28N 5°34E 173 E12
Arcachon France 44°40N 1°10W 174 D2
Arcachon, Bassin d' France 44°42N 1°10W 174 D2
Arcade U.S.A. 42°32N 78°25W 312 D6
Arcadia = Arkadia Greece 37°30N 22°20E 204 D4
Arcadia Calif., U.S.A. 34°7N 118°1W 126 B4
Arcadia Fla., U.S.A. 27°13N 81°52W 317 H8
Arcadia Ind., U.S.A. 40°11N 86°1W 311 D10
Arcadia Iowa, U.S.A. 42°5N 95°3W 310 B1
Arcadia La., U.S.A. 32°33N 92°55W 314 E8
Arcadia Pa., U.S.A. 40°47N 78°51W 312 F6
Arcanum U.S.A. 39°59N 84°33W 311 E12
Arcata U.S.A. 40°52N 124°5W 304 F1
Arcévia Italy 43°30N 12°56E 199 E9
Archanes Greece 35°16N 25°11E 205 F7
Archangel = Arkhangelsk Russia 64°38N 40°36E 186 B7
Archangelos Preveza, Greece 39°6N 20°42E 207 A2
Archangelos Rhodes, Greece 36°13N 28°7E 206 E12
Archar Bulgaria 43°50N 22°54E 202 C6
Archbald U.S.A. 41°30N 75°32W 313 E9
Archbold U.S.A. 41°31N 84°18W 311 C12
Archena Spain 38°9N 1°16W 197 G3
Archenu, J. Libya 22°15N 24°45E 259 D4
Archer U.S.A. 29°32N 82°32W 317 F7
Archer → Australia 13°28S 141°41E 280 A3
Archer B. Australia 13°20S 141°30E 280 A3
Archer Bend = Mungkan Kandju △ Australia 13°35S 142°52E 280 A3
Archers Post Kenya 0°35N 37°35E 268 B4
Arches △ U.S.A. 38°45N 109°25W 304 G9
Archidona Spain 37°6N 4°22W 195 H6
Archipel-de-Mingan △ Canada 50°13N 63°10W 299 B7
Archipiélago Chinijo △ Canary Is. 29°20N 13°30W 153 e2
Archipiélago Los Roques △ Venezuela 11°50N 66°44W 321 D6
Archives Navy Memorial Washington, D.C., U.S.A. 143 b2
Arci, Mte. Italy 39°47N 8°45E 200 C1
Arcidosso Italy 42°52N 11°33E 199 F8
Arcila = Asilah Morocco 35°29N 6°0W 260 A3
Arcipelago de la Maddalena △ Italy 41°14N 9°24E 200 A2
Arcipelago Toscano △ Italy 42°45N 10°15E 198 F7
Arcis-sur-Aube France 48°32N 4°10E 173 D11
Arckaringa Cr. → Australia 28°10S 135°22E 281 D2
Arco Italy 45°55N 10°53E 198 C7
Arco Idaho, U.S.A. 43°38N 113°18W 304 E7
Arco Plaza Los Angeles, U.S.A. 127 b1
Arcola U.S.A. 39°41N 88°19W 311 E8
Arcoona Australia 31°2S 137°1E 282 A2
Arcos de Jalón Spain 41°12N 2°16W 196 D2
Arcos de la Frontera Spain 36°45N 5°49W 195 J5
Arcos de Valdevez Portugal 41°55N 8°22W 194 D2
Arcot India 12°53N 79°20E 245 H4
Arcoverde Brazil 8°25S 37°4W 332 C4
Arcozelo Portugal 40°32N 7°47W 194 E3
Arctic Bay Canada 73°1N 85°7W 295 C14
Arctic Mid-Ocean Ridge Arctic 87°0N 90°0E 150 A
Arctic Ocean Arctic 78°0N 160°0W 150 B18
Arctic Red River = Tsiigehtchic Canada 67°15N 134°0W 294 D5
Arctic Village U.S.A. 68°8N 145°32W 303 B11
Arctowski Antarctica 62°30S 58°0W 151 C18
Arcueil France 48°48N 2°19E 134 B2
Arda → Bulgaria 41°40N 26°30E 203 E10
Arda → Italy 45°2N 10°2E 198 C7
Ardabīl Iran 38°15N 48°18E 213 C13
Ardabīl □ Iran 38°15N 48°20E 247 B6
Ardahan Turkey 41°7N 42°41E 213 B10
Ardahan □ Turkey 41°10N 42°50E 213 B10
Ardakān = Sepīdān Iran 30°20N 52°5E 247 D7
Ardakān Iran 32°19N 53°59E 247 C7
Ardala Sweden 58°22N 13°19E 163 F7
Ardales Spain 36°53N 4°51W 195 J6
Årdalstangen Norway 61°14N 7°43E 164 C4
Ardamata Sudan 13°29N 22°28E 259 F4
Ardara Ireland 54°46N 8°25W 166 B3
Ardas → Greece 41°40N 26°30E 203 E10
Ardèche □ France 44°42N 4°16E 175 D8
Ardèche → France 44°16N 4°39E 175 D8
Ardee Ireland 53°52N 6°33W 166 C5
Arden Ont., Canada 44°43N 76°56W 312 B8
Arden Denmark 56°46N 9°52E 163 H3
Arden Calif., U.S.A. 38°36N 121°33W 306 G5
Arden Nev., U.S.A. 36°1N 115°14W 307 J11
Ardenne Belgium 49°50N 5°5E 170 E5
Ardennes = Ardenne Belgium 49°50N 5°5E 170 E5
Ardennes □ France 49°35N 4°40E 173 C11
Ardentes France 46°45N 1°50E 173 F8
Arderin Ireland 53°2N 7°39W 166 C4
Ardeşen Turkey 41°12N 41°2E 213 B9
Ardestān Iran 33°20N 52°25E 247 C7
Ardfert Ireland 52°20N 9°47W 166 D2
Ardglass U.K. 54°16N 5°36W 166 B6
Ardhéa = Aridea Greece 40°58N 22°3E 202 F6
Ardila → Portugal 38°12N 7°28W 195 G3
Ardino Bulgaria 41°34N 25°9E 203 E9
Ardivachar Pt. U.K. 57°23N 7°26W 167 D1
Ardlethan Australia 34°22S 146°53E 283 C7
Ardmore Okla., U.S.A. 34°10N 97°8W 314 D6
Ardmore Pa., U.S.A. 40°2N 75°17W 313 F9
Ardnamurchan, Pt. of U.K. 56°43N 6°14W 167 E2
Ardnave Pt. U.K. 55°53N 6°20W 167 F2
Ardon Russia 43°10N 44°18E 191 J7
Ardore Italy 38°11N 16°10E 201 D9
Ardres France 50°50N 1°59E 173 B8
Ardrossan S. Austral., Australia 34°26S 137°53E 282 C2
Ardrossan N. Ayrs., U.K. 55°39N 4°49W 167 F4
Ards Pen. U.K. 54°33N 5°34W 166 B6
Arduan Sudan 19°54N 30°20E 256 D3
Ardud Romania 47°37N 22°52E 182 C7
Åre Sweden 63°22N 13°15E 162 A7
Arecibo Puerto Rico 18°29N 66°43W 321 C6
Areia Branca Brazil 5°0S 37°0W 332 B4
Arena, Pt. U.S.A. 38°57N 123°44W 306 G3
Arena I. Phil. 9°14N 120°45E 233 G3
Arenal Honduras 15°21N 86°50W 320 C2
Arenales, Cerro Chile 47°5S 73°40W 336 C2
Arenápolis Brazil 14°26S 56°49W 331 C6
Arenas = Las Arenas Spain 43°17N 4°50W 194 B6
Arenas, Pta. Venezuela 10°58N 64°24W 329 a
Arenas de San Pedro Spain 40°12N 5°5W 194 E5
Arendal Norway 58°28N 8°46E 164 F5
Arendsee Germany 52°52N 11°27E 178 C7
Arenillas Ecuador 3°33S 80°10W 328 D1
Arensburg = Kuressaare Estonia 58°15N 22°30E 188 C2
Arenys de Mar Spain 41°35N 2°33E 196 D7
Arenzano Italy 44°24N 8°41E 198 D5
Arenzville U.S.A. 39°53N 90°22W 310 E6
Areopoli Greece 36°40N 22°22E 204 E4
Arequipa Peru 16°20S 71°30W 330 D3
Arequipa □ Peru 16°0S 72°50W 330 D3
Arere Brazil 0°16S 53°52W 329 D7
Arero Ethiopia 4°41N 38°50E 257 G4
Arès France 44°47N 1°8W 174 D2
Arese Italy 45°32N 9°4E 128 A1
Arévalo Spain 41°3N 4°43W 194 D6
Arezzo Italy 43°25N 11°53E 199 E8
Arga Turkey 38°21N 37°59E 246 B3
Arga → Spain 42°18N 1°47W 196 C3
Argalasti Greece 39°13N 23°13E 204 B5
Argamasilla de Alba Spain 39°8N 3°5W 195 F7
Argamasilla de Calatrava Spain 38°44N 4°4W 195 G6
Arganda del Rey Spain 40°19N 3°26W 194 E7
Arganil Portugal 40°13N 8°3W 194 E2
Arganzuela Spain 40°23N 3°42W 127 B1
Argao Phil. 9°52N 123°36E 233 G4
Argarapa ✪ Australia 22°20S 134°58E 280 C1
Argasi Greece 37°45N 20°56E 207 D2
Argedeb Ethiopia 6°11N 41°13E 257 F5
Argelès-Gazost France 43°0N 0°6W 174 E3
Argelès-sur-Mer France 42°34N 3°1E 174 F7
Argens → France 43°24N 6°44E 175 E10
Argent, Côte d' France 44°15N 1°30W 174 D2
Argent-sur-Sauldre France 47°33N 2°25E 173 E9
Argenta = North Little Rock U.S.A. 34°45N 92°16W 314 D8
Argenta B.C., Canada 50°11N 116°56W 296 C5
Argenta Italy 44°37N 11°50E 199 D8
Argenta Ill., U.S.A. 39°59N 88°49W 311 E8
Argentan France 48°45N 0°1W 172 D6
Argentário, Mte. Italy 42°24N 11°9E 199 F8
Argentat France 45°6N 1°56E 174 C5
Argentera Italy 44°12N 7°5E 198 D4
Argenteuil France 48°56N 2°15E 134 A2
Argentia Canada 47°18N 53°58W 299 C9
Argentiera, C. dell' Italy 40°44N 8°8E 200 B1
Argentina ■ S. Amer. 35°0S 66°0W 327 G4
Argentine Abyssal Plain Atl. Oc. 46°0S 52°0W 152 L6
Argentine Basin Atl. Oc. 45°0S 45°0W 152 L7
Argentino, L. Argentina 50°10S 73°0W 336 D2
Argenton-les-Vallées France 46°59N 0°27W 172 F6
Argenton-sur-Creuse France 46°36N 1°30E 173 F8
Argeş □ Romania 45°0N 24°45E 183 F9
Argeş → Romania 44°5N 26°38E 183 F11
Arghandab → Afghan. 31°30N 64°15E 242 D1
Argheile Ethiopia 5°19N 42°4E 257 F5
Argirades Greece 39°27N 19°58E 206 C9
Argiroupoli Athina, Greece 37°52N 23°44E 112 B2
Argiroupoli Kriti, Greece 35°17N 24°20E 207 E5
Argo Sudan 19°28N 30°30E 256 D3
Argolikos Kolpos Greece 37°20N 22°52E 204 D4
Argonne France 49°10N 5°0E 173 C12
Argos Greece 37°40N 22°43E 204 D4
Argos Ind., U.S.A. 41°14N 86°15W 311 C10
Argos Orestiko Greece 40°27N 21°18E 202 F5
Argostoli Greece 38°11N 20°29E 207 C2
Argostoliou, Kolpos Greece 38°10N 20°27E 207 C1
Arguedas Spain 42°11N 1°36W 196 C3
Argüelles Madrid, Spain 127 a1
Arguello, Pt. U.S.A. 34°35N 120°39W 307 L6
Arguineguín Canary Is. 27°46N 15°41W 153 e1
Argun Russia 43°18N 45°52E 191 J7
Argun → Russia 53°20N 121°28E 219 A13
Argungu Nigeria 12°40N 4°31E 263 C5
Argus Pk. U.S.A. 35°52N 117°26W 307 K9
Argyle, L. Australia 16°20S 128°40E 278 C4
Argyle Waterfalls Trin. & Tob. 11°15N 60°35W 323 s
Argyll & Bute □ U.K. 56°13N 5°28W 167 E3
Arhavi Turkey 41°21N 41°18E 213 B9
Århus = Aarhus Denmark 56°8N 10°11E 163 H4
Ari Atoll Maldives 3°53N 72°50E 272 d
Aria N.Z. 38°33S 175°0E 284 E4
Ariadnoye Russia 45°8N 134°25E 220 B7
Ariamsvlei Namibia 28°9S 19°51E 270 C2
Ariana Tunisia 36°52N 10°12E 258 A2
Ariana □ Tunisia 36°50N 9°52E 261 A6
Ariano Irpino Italy 41°9N 15°5E 201 A8
Ariari → Colombia 2°35N 72°47W 328 C3
Aribinda Burkina Faso 14°17N 0°52W 263 C4
Arica Chile 18°32S 70°20W 330 D3
Arica Colombia 2°0S 71°50W 328 D3
Arica y Parinacota □ Chile 17°40S 69°50W 330 D4
Arico Canary Is. 28°9N 16°29W 153 e1
Arid, C. Australia 34°1S 123°10E 279 F3
Arida Japan 34°5N 135°8E 223 C7
Aridal W. Sahara 25°59N 13°54W 260 C2
Aride Seychelles 4°13S 55°40E 272 c
Aridea Greece 40°58N 22°3E 202 F6
Ariège □ France 42°56N 1°30E 174 F5
Ariège → France 43°30N 1°25E 174 E5
Arieş → Romania 46°24N 23°20E 183 D8
Arigat el Fersig Algeria 27°35N 2°7W 261 C4
Arihā Israel 31°51N 35°27E 256 A4
Arīḥā Syria 35°49N 36°35E 250 C7
Arikok △ Aruba 12°31N 69°56W 322 f
Arila, Akra Greece 39°43N 19°39E 206 B9
Arilje Serbia 43°44N 20°7E 202 C4
Arima Kanagawa, Japan 35°33N 139°33E 140 B2
Arima Trin. & Tob. 10°38N 61°17W 323 t
Arima → Trin. & Tob. 10°35N 61°16W 323 t
Aringay Phil. 16°26N 120°21E 232 C3
Arinos → Brazil 10°25S 58°20W 331 C6
Ario de Rosales Mexico 19°12N 101°43W 318 D4
Ariogala Lithuania 55°16N 23°28E 184 C10
Arios Pagos Athens, Greece 112 c1
Aripo → Trin. & Tob. 10°35N 61°14W 323 t
Aripo, Mt. Trin. & Tob. 10°45N 61°15W 323 t
Aripo Caves Trin. & Tob. 10°43N 61°14W 323 t
Aripuanã Brazil 9°25S 60°30W 331 B5
Aripuanã → Brazil 5°7S 60°25W 331 B5
Ariquemes Brazil 9°55S 63°6W 331 B5
Arisaig U.K. 56°55N 5°51W 167 E3
Arîsh, W. el → Egypt 31°9N 33°49E 256 A3
Arissa Ethiopia 11°10N 41°35E 257 E5
Aristazabal I. Canada 52°40N 129°10W 296 C3
Arita Japan 33°11N 129°54E 222 D1
Aritao Phil. 16°18N 121°2E 232 C3
Ariton U.S.A. 31°36N 85°43W 316 D4
Arivonimamo Madag. 19°1S 47°11E 272 B2
Ariyalur India 11°8N 79°8E 245 J4
Ariza Spain 41°19N 2°3W 196 D2
Arizaro, Salar de Argentina 24°40S 67°50W 334 A2
Arizona Argentina 35°45S 65°25W 334 D2
Arizona □ U.S.A. 34°0N 112°0W 305 J8
Arizpe Mexico 30°20N 110°10W 318 A2
'Arjah Si. Arabia 24°43N 44°17E 246 E5
Årjäng Sweden 59°24N 12°8E 162 E6
Arjeplog Sweden 66°3N 17°54E 160 C17
Arjepluovve = Arjeplog Sweden 66°3N 17°54E 160 C17
Arjona Colombia 10°14N 75°22W 328 A2
Arjona Spain 37°56N 4°4W 195 H6
Arjuna Indonesia 7°49S 112°34E 235 D4
Arka Russia 60°15N 142°0E 215 C15
Arkadak Russia 51°58N 43°30E 190 E6
Arkadelphia U.S.A. 34°7N 93°4W 314 D8
Arkadia Greece 37°30N 22°20E 204 D4
Arkaig, L. U.K. 56°59N 5°10W 167 E3
Arkalgud India 12°46N 76°3E 245 H3
Arkalyk = Arqalyk Kazakhstan 50°13N 66°50E 217 B7
Arkansas □ U.S.A. 35°0N 92°30W 314 D8
Arkansas → U.S.A. 33°47N 91°4W 314 E9
Arkansas City U.S.A. 37°4N 97°2W 308 G5
Arkaroola Australia 30°20S 139°22E 281 E2
Arkavāz Iran 33°22N 46°35E 213 F12
Arkhangelsk Russia 64°38N 40°36E 186 B7
Arkhangelskoye Russia 51°32N 40°58E 190 E5
Arki Greece 37°24N 26°44E 205 D8
Arki India 31°9N 76°58E 242 D7
Arkiko Eritrea 15°33N 39°30E 257 D4
Arklow Ireland 52°48N 6°10W 166 D5
Arkona, Kap Germany 54°42N 13°26E 178 A9

**Arkösund** *Sweden* 58°29N 16°56E **163** F10
**Arkoudi** *Greece* 38°33N 20°43E **207** B2
**Arkport** *U.S.A.* 42°24N 77°42W **312** D7
**Arkticheskiy, Mys** *Russia* 81°10N 95°0E **215** A10
**Arkul** *Russia* 57°17N 50°3E **190** B10
**Arkville** *U.S.A.* 42°9N 74°37W **313** D10
**Ärla** *Sweden* 59°17N 16°40E **162** E10
**Arlanda, Stockholm ✈ (ARN)** *Sweden* 59°41N 17°56E **139** A1
**Arlanza ➔** *Spain* 42°6N 4°9W **194** C6
**Arlanzón ➔** *Spain* 42°3N 4°17W **194** C6
**Arlbergpass** *Austria* 47°9N 10°12E **180** D3
**Arlbergtunnel** *Austria* 47°9N 10°12E **180** D3
**Arles** *France* 43°41N 4°40E **175** E8
**Arli** *Burkina Faso* 11°35N 1°28E **263** C5
**Arli ⌓** *Burkina Faso* 11°35N 1°28E **263** C5
**Arlington** *Free State, S. Africa* 28°1S 27°53E **271** C4
**Arlington** *Ga., U.S.A.* 31°26N 84°44W **316** D5
**Arlington** *Mass., U.S.A.* 42°24N 71°10W **116** A1
**Arlington** *N.Y., U.S.A.* 41°42N 73°54W **313** E11
**Arlington** *Oreg., U.S.A.* 45°43N 120°12W **304** D3
**Arlington** *S. Dak., U.S.A.* 44°22N 97°8W **308** C5
**Arlington** *Tex., U.S.A.* 32°44N 97°6W **314** E6
**Arlington** *Va., U.S.A.* 38°53N 77°7W **143** B2
**Arlington** *Vt., U.S.A.* 43°5N 73°9W **313** C11
**Arlington** *Wash., U.S.A.* 48°12N 122°8W **306** B4
**Arlington Heights** *Ill., U.S.A.* 42°5N 87°59W **311** B9
**Arlington Heights** *Mass., U.S.A.* 42°25N 71°10W **116** A1
**Arlington Nat. Cemetery** *U.S.A.* 38°52N 77°4W **143** B2
**Arlon** *Belgium* 49°42N 5°49E **170** E5
**Arlparra** *Australia* 22°11S 134°30E **280** C1
**Arltunga** *Australia* 23°26S 134°41E **280** C1
**Armação** *Brazil* 22°52S 43°6W **135** B2
**Armação de Pêra** *Portugal* 37°6N 8°22W **195** H2
**Armadale** *Vic., Australia* 37°51S 145°0E **128** B2
**Armadale** *W. Austral., Australia* 32°9S 116°0E **279** F2
**Armagh** *U.K.* 54°21N 6°39W **166** B5
**Armagh □** *U.K.* 54°18N 6°37W **166** B5
**Armagnac** *France* 43°50N 0°10E **174** E4
**Armançon ➔** *France* 47°59N 3°30E **173** E10
**Armando Bermudez ⌓** *Dom. Rep.* 19°3N 71°0W **321** C5
**Armant** *Egypt* 25°37N 32°32E **256** B3
**Armatree** *Australia* 31°26S 148°28E **283** A8
**Armavir** *Russia* 45°2N 41°7E **191** H5
**Armenia** *Colombia* 4°35N 75°45W **328** C2
**Armenia ■** *Asia* 40°20N 45°0E **191** K7
**Armenian Quarter** *Jerusalem* **123** b3
**Armeniş** *Romania* 45°13N 22°17E **182** E7
**Armenistis, Akra** *Greece* 36°8N 27°42E **206** E11
**Armentières** *France* 50°40N 2°50E **173** B9
**Armero** *Colombia* 4°58N 74°54W **328** C3
**Armidale** *Australia* 30°30S 151°40E **283** A9
**Armilla** *Spain* 37°9N 3°37W **195** H7
**Armori** *India* 20°28N 79°59E **244** D4
**Armorique ⌓** *France* 48°22N 3°50W **172** D3
**Armour** *U.S.A.* 43°19N 98°21W **308** D4
**Armour Heights** *Canada* 43°45N 79°25W **141** A2
**Armstrong** *B.C., Canada* 50°25N 119°10W **296** C5
**Armstrong** *Ont., Canada* 50°18N 89°4W **298** B2
**Armur** *India* 18°48N 78°16E **244** E4
**Armutlu** *Bursa, Turkey* 40°31N 28°50E **203** F12
**Armutlu** *İzmir, Turkey* 38°24N 27°34E **205** C9
**Arnarfjörður** *Iceland* 65°48N 23°40W **155** B3
**Arnaud ➔** *Canada* 59°59N 69°46W **295** F18
**Arnauti, C.** *Cyprus* 35°6N 32°17E **207** E8
**Arnay-le-Duc** *France* 47°10N 4°27E **173** E11
**Arncliffe** *Australia* 33°56S 151°8E **139** B1
**Arnea** *Greece* 40°30N 23°38E **202** F7
**Arnedillo** *Spain* 42°13N 2°14W **196** C2
**Arnedo** *Spain* 42°12N 2°5W **196** C2
**Årnes** *Iceland* 66°1N 21°31W **155** A5
**Årnes** *Akershus, Norway* 60°7N 11°28E **164** D8
**Árnessýsla** *Iceland* 64°15N 20°30W **155** C6
**Arnett** *U.S.A.* 36°8N 99°46W **314** C5
**Arnhem** *Neths.* 51°58N 5°55E **170** C5
**Arnhem, C.** *Australia* 12°20S 137°30E **280** A2
**Arnhem B.** *Australia* 12°20S 136°10E **280** A2
**Arnhem Land** *Australia* 13°10S 134°30E **280** A1
**Arnhem Land ◎** *Australia* 12°50S 134°50E **280** A1
**Arnissa** *Greece* 40°47N 21°49E **202** F5
**Arno ➔** *Italy* 43°41N 10°17E **198** E7
**Arno Bay** *Australia* 33°54S 136°34E **282** B2
**Arnold** *Notts., U.K.* 53°1N 1°7W **168** D6
**Arnold** *Calif., U.S.A.* 38°15N 120°21W **306** G6
**Arnold** *Mo., U.S.A.* 38°26N 90°23W **310** F6
**Arnold Arboretum** *U.S.A.* 42°18N 71°8W **116** B2
**Arnoldstein** *Austria* 46°33N 13°43E **180** E6
**Arnon ➔** *France* 47°13N 2°1E **173** E9
**Arnos Vale** *Trin. & Tob.* 11°13N 60°45W **323** s
**Arnot** *Canada* 55°56N 96°41W **297** B9
**Arnøya** *Norway* 70°9N 20°40E **160** A19
**Arnprior** *Canada* 45°26N 76°21W **313** A8
**Arnsberg** *Germany* 51°24N 8°5E **178** D4
**Arnsberger Wald ⌓** *Germany* 51°25N 8°20E **178** D4
**Arnstadt** *Germany* 50°50N 10°56E **178** E6
**Arnswalde = Choszczno** *Poland* 53°7N 15°25E **185** E2
**Aro ➔** *Venezuela* 8°1N 64°11W **329** B5
**Aroa, Pte.** *Moorea* 17°28S 149°46W **289** e
**Aroab** *Namibia* 26°41S 19°39E **270** C2
**Aroania Oros** *Greece* 37°56N 22°12E **204** D4
**Aroche** *Spain* 37°56N 6°57W **195** H4
**Arochuku** *Nigeria* 5°21N 7°54E **263** D6
**Aroeiras** *Brazil* 7°31S 35°41W **332** C4
**Arolsen** *Germany* 51°23N 9°2E **178** D5
**Aron** *India* 25°57N 77°56E **242** G6
**Aron ➔** *France* 46°50N 3°28E **173** F10
**Arona** *Canary Is.* 28°6N 16°40W **153** e1
**Arona** *Italy* 45°46N 8°34E **198** C5
**Arorae** *Kiribati* 2°38S 176°49E **277** A14
**Arorangi** *Cook Is.* 21°13S 159°49W **289** h
**Aroroy** *Phil.* 12°31N 123°24E **232** E4
**Aros ➔** *Mexico* 29°9N 107°57W **318** B3
**Arouca** *Trin. & Tob.* 10°38N 61°20W **323** t
**Arousa, Ría de ➔** *Spain* 42°28N 8°57W **194** C2
**Årøysund** *Norway* 59°10N 10°27E **164** E7
**Arpa ➔** *Asia* 39°28N 44°56E **213** C11
**Arpaçay** *Turkey* 40°50N 43°19E **213** B10
**Árpádföld** *Hungary* 47°32N 19°8E **117** A3
**Arpajon** *France* 48°36N 2°15E **173** D9
**Arpajon-sur-Cère** *France* 44°53N 2°28E **174** D6
**Arpaşu de Jos** *Romania* 45°47N 24°37E **183** E9
**Arqalyk** *Kazakhstan* 50°13N 66°50E **217** B7
**Arque** *Bolivia* 17°48S 66°23W **330** D4
**Arrah = Ara** *India* 25°35N 84°32E **243** G11
**Arrah** *Ivory C.* 6°40N 3°58W **262** D4
**Arraias** *Brazil* 12°56S 46°57W **333** D2
**Arraias ➔** *Mato Grosso, Brazil* 11°10S 53°35W **331** C7
**Arraias ➔** *Pará, Brazil* 7°30S 49°20W **332** C2
**Arraijan** *Panama* 8°56N 79°36W **320** c
**Arraiolos** *Portugal* 38°44N 7°59W **195** G3
**Arran** *U.K.* 55°34N 5°12W **167** F3
**Arranmore** *Ireland* 55°0N 8°30W **166** A3
**Arras** *France* 50°17N 2°46E **173** B9
**Arrasate** *Spain* 43°4N 2°30W **196** B2
**Arrats ➔** *France* 44°6N 0°52E **174** D4
**Arreau** *France* 42°54N 0°22E **174** F4
**Arrecife** *Canary Is.* 28°57N 13°37W **153** e2
**Arrecifes** *Argentina* 34°6S 60°9W **334** C3
**Arrée, Mts. d'** *France* 48°26N 3°55W **172** D3
**Arrentela** *Portugal* 38°37N 9°6W **126** B2
**Arresø** *Denmark* 55°58N 12°6E **163** J6
**Arriaga** *Mexico* 16°14N 93°54W **319** D6
**Arribes del Duero ⌓** *Spain* 41°11N 6°39W **194** D4
**Arrilalah** *Australia* 23°43S 143°54E **280** C3
**Arrino** *Australia* 29°30S 115°40E **279** E2
**Arriondas** *Spain* 43°23N 5°11W **194** B5
**Arrojado ➔** *Brazil* 13°24S 44°20W **333** D3
**Arromanches-les-Bains** *France* 49°20N 0°38W **172** C6
**Arronches** *Portugal* 39°8N 7°16W **195** F3
**Arros ➔** *France* 43°40N 0°2W **174** E3
**Arrow, L.** *Ireland* 54°3N 8°19W **166** B3
**Arrowsmith, Mt.** *N.Z.* 43°20S 170°55E **285** D5
**Arrowtown** *N.Z.* 44°57S 168°50E **285** E3
**Arroyo de la Luz** *Spain* 39°30N 6°38W **195** F4
**Arroyo del Puerco = Arroyo de la Luz** *Spain* 39°30N 6°38W **195** F4
**Arroyo Grande** *U.S.A.* 35°7N 120°35W **307** K6
**Arroyo Seco Park** *U.S.A.* 34°6N 118°11W **126** B3
**Ars** *Iran* 37°9N 47°46E **246** B5
**Ars-sur-Moselle** *France* 49°5N 6°4E **173** C13
**Arsenale** *Venice, Italy* **142** b4
**Arsenault L.** *Canada* 55°6N 108°32W **297** B7
**Arsenev** *Russia* 44°10N 133°15E **220** B6
**Arsi** *Ethiopia* 7°45N 39°0E **257** F4
**Arsiero** *Italy* 45°48N 11°21E **199** C8
**Arsikere** *India* 13°15N 76°15E **245** H3
**Arsin** *Turkey* 41°8N 39°55E **213** B8
**Arsk** *Russia* 56°10N 49°50E **190** B9
**Arslanköy** *Turkey* 37°0N 34°17E **250** B5
**Årsta** *Sweden* 59°17N 18°3E **139** B2
**Årsunda** *Sweden* 60°31N 16°45E **162** D10
**Art, Î.** *N. Cal.* 19°43S 163°38E **288** d
**Arta** *Greece* 39°8N 21°2E **204** B3
**Artà** *Spain* 39°41N 3°21E **206** B4
**Artà, Coves d'** *Spain* 39°40N 3°24E **206** B4
**Artane** *Ireland* 53°22N 6°12W **120** A2
**Artas** *West Bank* 31°41N 35°11E **123** B2
**Artashat** *Armenia* 40°0N 44°35E **213** B11
**Arteaga** *Mexico* 18°28N 102°25W **318** D4
**Arteche** *Phil.* 12°17N 125°22E **232** E5
**Arteixo = A Baiuca** *Spain* 43°19N 8°29W **194** B2
**Artem = Artyom** *Azerbaijan* 40°28N 50°20E **191** K10
**Artem** *Russia* 43°22N 132°13E **220** C6
**Artemovsk** *Sib., Russia* 54°45N 93°35E **215** D10
**Artemovsk** *Ukraine* 48°35N 38°0E **189** H9
**Artemovskiy** *Russia* 47°45N 40°16E **191** G5
**Artenay** *France* 48°5N 1°50E **173** D8
**Artern** *Germany* 51°22N 11°18E **178** D7
**Artesa de Segre** *Spain* 41°54N 1°3E **196** D6
**Artesia = Mosomane** *Botswana* 24°2S 26°19E **270** B4
**Artesia** *U.S.A.* 32°51N 104°24W **305** K11
**Arthington** *Liberia* 6°35N 10°45W **262** D2
**Arthur** *Ont., Canada* 43°50N 80°32W **312** C4
**Arthur** *Ill., U.S.A.* 39°43N 88°28W **311** E8
**Arthur ➔** *Australia* 41°2S 144°40E **281** G3
**Arthur Cr. ➔** *Australia* 22°30S 136°25E **280** C2
**Arthur Pt.** *Australia* 22°7S 150°3E **280** C5
**Arthur River** *Australia* 33°20S 117°2E **279** F2
**Arthur's Pass** *N.Z.* 42°54S 171°35E **285** C6
**Arthur's Pass ⌓** *N.Z.* 42°53S 171°42E **285** C6
**Arthur's Seat** *U.K.* 55°56N 3°9W **121** B3
**Arthur's Town** *Bahamas* 24°38N 75°42W **321** B4
**Artigas = Río Branco** *Uruguay* 32°40S 53°40W **335** C5
**Artigas** *Antarctica* 62°30S 58°0W **151** C18
**Artigas** *Uruguay* 30°20S 56°30W **334** C4
**Artik** *Armenia* 40°38N 43°58E **191** K6
**Artillery L.** *Canada* 63°9N 107°52W **297** A7
**Artois** *France* 50°20N 2°30E **173** B9
**Artotina** *Greece* 38°42N 22°2E **204** C4
**Artova** *Turkey* 40°5N 36°28E **212** B7
**Artrutx, C. de** *Spain* 39°55N 3°49E **206** B4
**Arts, Place des** *Montréal, Canada* **130** b2
**Arts Bogd Uul** *Mongolia* 44°40N 102°20E **226** B2
**Artsvashen** *Armenia* 40°38N 45°30E **213** B11
**Artsyz** *Ukraine* 46°4N 29°26E **183** D14
**Artux** *China* 39°40N 76°10E **217** E9
**Artvin** *Turkey* 41°14N 41°44E **213** B9
**Artvin □** *Turkey* 41°10N 41°50E **213** B9
**Artyk** *Russia* 64°12N 145°6E **215** C15
**Artyom** *Azerbaijan* 40°28N 50°20E **191** K10
**Aru, Kepulauan** *Indonesia* 6°0S 134°30E **231** F8
**Aru Is. = Aru, Kepulauan** *Indonesia* 6°0S 134°30E **231** F8
**Arua** *Uganda* 3°1N 30°58E **268** B3
**Aruanã** *Brazil* 14°54S 51°10W **333** D1
**Aruba ☑** *W. Indies* 12°30N 70°0W **322** f
**Arudy** *France* 43°7N 0°28W **174** E3
**Arué** *Tahiti* 17°31S 149°30W **289** e
**Arumã** *Brazil* 4°44S 62°8W **329** D5
**Arume-wan** *Japan* 26°35N 128°8E **288** a
**Arumpo** *Australia* 33°48S 142°55E **282** B5
**Arun** *Bangkok, Thailand* **113** b1
**Arun ➔** *Nepal* 26°55N 87°10E **243** F12
**Arun ➔** *W. Susx., U.K.* 50°49N 0°33W **169** G7
**Arunachal Pradesh □** *India* 28°0N 95°0E **241** B5
**Aruppukkottai** *India* 9°31N 78°8E **245** K4
**Arusha** *Tanzania* 3°20S 36°40E **268** C4
**Arusha □** *Tanzania* 3°20S 36°30E **268** C4
**Arusha ⌓** *Tanzania* 3°16S 36°47E **268** C4
**Arusha Chini** *Tanzania* 3°32S 37°20E **268** C4
**Arut ➔** *Indonesia* 2°42S 111°34E **235** C4
**Aruvi ➔** *Sri Lanka* 8°48N 79°53E **245** K4
**Aruwimi ➔** *Dem. Rep. of the Congo* 1°13N 23°36E **264** B4
**Arvada** *Colo., U.S.A.* 39°48N 105°5W **304** G11
**Arvada** *Wyo., U.S.A.* 44°39N 106°8W **304** D10
**Arvakalu** *Sri Lanka* 8°20N 79°58E **245** K4
**Arvayheer** *Mongolia* 46°15N 102°48E **218** B9
**Arve ➔** *France* 46°11N 6°8E **173** F13
**Arvi** *Kriti, Greece* 34°59N 25°28E **207** F6
**Arvi** *India* 20°59N 78°16E **244** D4
**Arviat** *Canada* 61°6N 93°59W **297** A10
**Arvidsjaur** *Sweden* 65°35N 19°10E **160** D18
**Arvika** *Sweden* 59°40N 12°36E **162** E6
**Arvin** *U.S.A.* 35°12N 118°50W **307** K8
**Arwad** *Syria* 34°51N 35°51E **250** D6
**Arwal** *India* 25°15N 84°41E **243** G11
**Arxan** *China* 47°11N 119°57E **219** B12
**Åryd** *Sweden* 56°49N 14°59E **163** H8
**Arys** *Kazakhstan* 42°26N 68°48E **217** D7
**Arzachena** *Italy* 41°5N 9°23E **200** A2
**Arzamas** *Russia* 55°27N 43°55E **190** C6
**Arzanah** *U.A.E.* 24°47N 52°34E **247** E7
**Arzew** *Algeria* 35°50N 0°23W **261** A4
**Arzgir** *Russia* 45°18N 44°23E **191** H7
**Arzignano** *Italy* 45°31N 11°20E **199** C8
**Arzúa** *Spain* 42°56N 8°9W **194** C2
**Aš** *Czech Rep.* 50°13N 12°12E **180** A5
**Ås** *Akershus, Norway* 59°40N 10°48E **164** E7
**Ås** *Sweden* 63°15N 14°34E **162** A8
**As Pontes de García Rodríguez** *Spain* 43°27N 7°50W **194** B3
**As Sa'an** *Syria* 35°16N 37°22E **250** C8
**Aş Şafā** *Syria* 33°10N 37°0E **250** E8
**As Saffānīyah** *Si. Arabia* 27°55N 48°50E **247** E6
**As Safīrah** *Syria* 36°5N 37°21E **250** B8
**Aş Şahm** *Oman* 24°10N 56°53E **247** E8
**Aş Şa'īd** *Yemen* 14°15N 46°50E **248** E4
**As Sājir** *Si. Arabia* 25°11N 44°36E **246** E5
**As Salamīyah** *Syria* 35°1N 37°2E **250** C8
**Aş Şalif** *Yemen* 15°18N 42°41E **248** D3
**As Salmān** *Iraq* 30°30N 44°32E **246** D5
**As Salt** *Jordan* 32°2N 35°43E **251** F6
**As Sal'w'a** *Qatar* 24°23N 50°50E **247** E6
**As Samāwah** *Iraq* 31°15N 45°15E **246** D5
**As Sanamayn** *Syria* 33°3N 36°10E **250** E7
**As Sawāḏah** *Si. Arabia* 22°24N 44°28E **248** B4
**Aş Şawma'ah** *Yemen* 14°5N 45°48E **248** D4
**As Sayl al Kabīr** *Si. Arabia* 21°38N 40°25E **248** B3
**As Shawawra** *West Bank* 31°41N 35°15E **123** B2
**As Sīb** *Oman* 23°41N 58°11E **249** B7
**As Sila'** *U.A.E.* 24°4N 51°45E **247** E6
**As Sukhnah** *Syria* 34°52N 38°52E **213** E8
**As Sulaymānīyah** *Iraq* 35°35N 45°29E **213** E11
**As Sulaymānīyah** *Si. Arabia* 24°9N 47°18E **248** A4
**As Sulaymānīyah □** *Iraq* 35°50N 45°30E **213** E11
**As Sulaymī** *Si. Arabia* 26°17N 41°21E **246** E4
**As Sulayyil** *Si. Arabia* 20°27N 45°34E **248** B4
**As Sulṭān** *Libya* 31°4N 17°8E **258** B3
**As Summān** *Si. Arabia* 25°0N 47°0E **246** E5
**Aş Şurrah** *Yemen* 13°57N 46°14E **248** D4
**Aş Şuwar** *Syria* 35°30N 40°38E **213** E9
**As Suwaydā'** *Syria* 32°40N 36°30E **250** F7
**As Suwaydā' □** *Syria* 32°45N 36°45E **250** F7
**As Suwayq** *Oman* 23°51N 57°26E **247** F8
**Aş Şuwayrah** *Iraq* 32°55N 45°0E **213** F11
**Åsa** *Sweden* 57°21N 12°8E **163** G6
**Asa Wright Nature Centre** *Trin. & Tob.* 10°43N 61°17W **323** t
**Asab** *Namibia* 25°30S 18°0E **270** C2
**Asaba** *Nigeria* 6°12N 6°38E **263** D6
**Asad, Buḥayrat al** *Syria* 36°0N 38°15E **213** D8
**Asadābād** *Iran* 34°47N 48°7E **213** E13
**Asafo** *Ghana* 6°20N 2°40W **262** D4
**Asaga Str.** *Amer. Samoa* 14°10S 169°37W **302** g
**Asagaya** *Japan* 35°41N 139°38E **140** A2
**Asahi** *Chiba, Japan* 35°43N 140°39E **223** B12
**Asahi** *Ōsaka, Japan* 34°43N 135°31E **133** A2
**Asahi-Gawa ➔** *Japan* 34°36N 133°58E **222** C5
**Asahigawa = Asahikawa** *Japan* 43°46N 142°22E **220** C11
**Asahikawa** *Japan* 43°46N 142°22E **220** C11
**Asakusa** *Japan* 35°42N 139°47E **140** A3
**Asakusabashi** *Tokyo, Japan* **140** a5
**Asale, L.** *Ethiopia* 14°0N 40°20E **257** E5
**Asaluyeh** *Iran* 27°29N 52°37E **247** E7
**Asama-Yama** *Japan* 36°24N 138°31E **223** A10
**Asamankese** *Ghana* 5°50N 0°40W **263** D4
**Asan** *S. Korea* 36°48N 127°1E **224** D3
**Asan ➔** *India* 26°37N 78°24E **243** F8
**Asansol** *India* 23°40N 87°1E **243** H12
**Åsarna** *Sweden* 62°39N 14°22E **162** B8
**Asati** *India* 22°28N 88°15E **124** C1
**Asau** *Samoa* 13°27S 172°33W **287** V19
**Asayita** *Ethiopia* 11°35N 41°23E **257** E5
**Asba Littoria = Asbe Teferi** *Ethiopia* 9°4N 40°49E **257** F5
**Asbe Teferi** *Ethiopia* 9°4N 40°49E **257** F5
**Asbesberge** *S. Africa* 29°0S 23°0E **270** C3
**Asbestos** *Canada* 45°47N 71°58W **299** C5
**Asbury Park** *U.S.A.* 40°13N 74°1W **313** F10
**Åsby** *Sweden* 57°14N 12°18E **163** G6
**Ascea** *Italy* 40°8N 15°11E **201** B8
**Ascensión** *Mexico* 31°6N 107°59W **318** A3
**Ascensión, B. de la** *Mexico* 19°40N 87°30W **319** D7
**Ascension I.** *Atl. Oc.* 7°57S 14°23W **153** g
**Ascension I. ✈ (ASI)** *Ascension I.* 7°58S 14°23W **153** g
**Aschach an der Donau** *Austria* 48°22N 14°2E **180** C7
**Aschaffenburg** *Germany* 49°58N 9°6E **179** F5
**Aschendorf** *Germany* 53°3N 7°19E **178** B3
**Aschersleben** *Germany* 51°45N 11°29E **178** D7
**Aschheim** *Germany* 48°10N 11°42E **131** A3
**Asciano** *Italy* 43°14N 11°33E **199** E8
**Áscoli Piceno** *Italy* 42°51N 13°34E **199** F10
**Áscoli Satriano** *Italy* 41°11N 15°32E **201** A8
**Ascope** *Peru* 7°46S 79°8W **330** B2
**Ascot Vale** *Australia* 37°46S 144°53E **128** A1
**Ascotán** *Chile* 21°45S 68°17W **334** A2
**Ascuncion** *Phil.* 7°35N 125°45E **233** H5
**Aseb** *Eritrea* 13°0N 42°40E **257** E5
**Åseda** *Sweden* 57°10N 15°20E **163** G9
**Asedjrad** *Algeria* 24°51N 1°29E **261** D5
**Aseki** *Papua N. G.* 7°21S 146°12E **286** D4
**Asela** *Ethiopia* 8°0N 39°0E **257** F4
**Åsen** *Sweden* 61°17N 13°50E **162** C7
**Asenovgrad** *Bulgaria* 42°1N 24°51E **203** D8
**Asfeld** *France* 49°27N 4°5E **173** C11
**Asfûn el Matâ'na** *Egypt* 25°26N 32°30E **256** B3
**Aşgabat = Ashgabat** *Turkmenistan* 37°58N 58°24E **247** B8
**Åsgårdstrand** *Norway* 59°22N 10°27E **164** E7
**Asgata** *Cyprus* 34°46N 33°15E **207** F9
**Ash Fork** *U.S.A.* 35°13N 112°29W **305** J7
**Ash Grove** *U.S.A.* 37°19N 93°35W **308** G7
**Ash Shabakah** *Iraq* 30°49N 43°39E **246** D4
**Ash Shafa** *Si. Arabia* 21°27N 39°49E **248** B2
**Ash Shamāl □** *Lebanon* 34°25N 36°0E **250** D7
**Ash Shāmīyah** *Iraq* 31°55N 44°35E **213** G11
**Ash Sha'rā'** *Si. Arabia* 24°16N 44°11E **248** A4
**Ash Shāriqah** *U.A.E.* 25°23N 55°26E **247** E7
**Ash Sharmah** *Si. Arabia* 28°1N 35°16E **251** K6
**Ash Sharqāt** *Iraq* 35°27N 43°16E **213** E10
**Ash Sharqīyah □** *Oman* 21°30N 59°0E **249** B7
**Ash Sharqīyah □** *Si. Arabia* 23°0N 50°30E **249** B6
**Ash Shaṭrah** *Iraq* 31°30N 46°10E **246** D5
**Ash Shawbak** *Jordan* 30°32N 35°34E **246** D2
**Ash Shaykh Ḥumayd** *Si. Arabia* 28°6N 34°33E **251** K5
**Ash Shifā'** *Si. Arabia* 28°30N 35°30E **251** K6
**Ash Shiḥr** *Yemen* 14°45N 49°36E **249** D5
**Ash Shināfīyah** *Iraq* 31°35N 44°39E **246** D5
**Ash Shu'bah** *Si. Arabia* 28°54N 44°44E **246** D5
**Ash Shumlūl** *Si. Arabia* 26°31N 47°20E **246** E5
**Ash Shuqayq** *Si. Arabia* 17°44N 42°1E **248** C3
**Ash Shūr'a** *Iraq* 35°58N 43°13E **246** C4
**Ash Shurayf** *Si. Arabia* 25°43N 39°14E **246** E3
**Ash Shuwayfāt** *Lebanon* 33°45N 35°30E **250** E6
**Ash Shuwayrif** *Libya* 29°59N 14°16E **258** C2
**Asha** *Russia* 55°0N 57°16E **186** D10
**Ashanti □** *Ghana* 7°30N 1°30W **263** D4
**Ashbourne** *U.K.* 53°2N 1°43W **168** D6
**Ashbridge's Bay Park** *Canada* 43°40N 79°18W **141** B3
**Ashburn** *Ga., U.S.A.* 31°43N 83°39W **316** D6
**Ashburn** *Ill., U.S.A.* 41°45N 87°43W **119** C2
**Ashburton** *Vic., Australia* 37°51S 145°4E **128** B2
**Ashburton** *N.Z.* 43°53S 171°48E **285** D6
**Ashburton ➔** *Australia* 21°40S 114°56E **278** D1
**Ashburton, North Branch ➔** *N.Z.* 43°54S 171°44E **285** D6
**Ashburton, South Branch ➔** *N.Z.* 43°54S 171°44E **285** D6
**Ashcroft** *Canada* 50°40N 121°20W **296** C4
**Ashdod** *Israel* 31°49N 34°35E **251** G3
**Ashdown** *U.S.A.* 33°40N 94°8W **314** E7
**Asheboro** *U.S.A.* 35°43N 79°49W **315** D15
**Åsheim** *Norway* 61°42N 11°11E **164** C8
**Ashern** *Canada* 51°11N 98°21W **297** C9
**Asherton** *U.S.A.* 28°27N 99°46W **314** G5
**Asheville** *U.S.A.* 35°36N 82°33W **315** D13
**Ashewat** *Pakistan* 31°22N 68°32E **242** D3
**Asheweig ➔** *Canada* 54°17N 87°12W **298** B2
**Ashfield** *Australia* 33°53S 151°7E **139** B1
**Ashford** *N.S.W., Australia* 29°15S 151°3E **281** D5
**Ashford** *Kent, U.K.* 51°8N 0°53E **169** F8
**Ashford** *Surrey, U.K.* 51°25N 0°26W **125** B1
**Ashford** *Ala., U.S.A.* 31°11N 85°14W **316** D4
**Ashgabat** *Turkmenistan* 37°58N 58°24E **247** B8
**Ashhurst** *N.Z.* 40°16S 175°45E **284** G4
**Ashibetsu** *Japan* 43°31N 142°11E **220** C11
**Ashikaga** *Japan* 36°28N 139°29E **223** A11
**Ashington** *U.K.* 55°11N 1°33W **168** B6
**Ashio** *Japan* 36°38N 139°27E **223** A11
**Ashizuri-Uwakai ⌓** *Japan* 32°56N 132°32E **222** E4
**Ashizuri-Zaki** *Japan* 32°44N 133°0E **222** E5
**Ashkarkot** *Afghan.* 33°3N 67°58E **242** C2
**Ashkhabad = Ashgabat** *Turkmenistan* 37°58N 58°24E **247** B8
**Āshkhāneh** *Iran* 37°26N 56°55E **247** B8
**Ashland** *Ala., U.S.A.* 33°16N 85°50W **316** B4
**Ashland** *Ill., U.S.A.* 39°53N 90°1W **310** E7
**Ashland** *Kans., U.S.A.* 37°11N 99°46W **308** G4
**Ashland** *Ky., U.S.A.* 38°28N 82°38W **309** F12
**Ashland** *Maine, U.S.A.* 46°38N 68°24W **309** B19
**Ashland** *Mont., U.S.A.* 45°36N 106°16W **304** D10
**Ashland** *Ohio, U.S.A.* 40°52N 82°19W **312** F2
**Ashland** *Oreg., U.S.A.* 42°12N 122°43W **304** E2
**Ashland** *Pa., U.S.A.* 40°45N 76°22W **313** F8
**Ashland** *Va., U.S.A.* 37°46N 77°29W **309** G15
**Ashland** *Wis., U.S.A.* 46°35N 90°53W **308** B8
**Ashley** *Ill., U.S.A.* 38°20N 89°11W **310** F7
**Ashley** *Ind., U.S.A.* 41°32N 85°4W **311** C11
**Ashley** *N. Dak., U.S.A.* 46°2N 99°22W **308** B4
**Ashley** *Pa., U.S.A.* 41°12N 75°55W **313** E9
**Ashley ➔** *N.Z.* 43°17S 172°44E **285** D7
**Ashmore and Cartier Is.** *Ind. Oc.* 12°15S 123°0E **278** B3
**Ashmore Reef** *Australia* 12°14S 123°5E **278** B3
**Ashmûn** *Egypt* 30°18N 30°58E **251** H1
**Ashmyany** *Belarus* 54°26N 25°52E **177** A13
**Ashokan Res.** *U.S.A.* 41°56N 74°13W **313** E10
**Ashoknagar** *India* 24°34N 77°43E **244** B3
**Ashqelon** *Israel* 31°42N 34°35E **251** G3
**Ashraf = Behshahr** *Iran* 36°45N 53°35E **247** B7
**Ashta** *India* 23°1N 76°43E **242** H7
**Ashtabula** *U.S.A.* 41°52N 80°47W **312** E4
**Ashti** *Maharashtra, India* 21°12N 78°11E **244** D4
**Ashti** *Maharashtra, India* 18°50N 75°15E **244** E2
**Āshtiyān** *Iran* 34°31N 50°0E **247** C6
**Ashton** *Western Cape, S. Africa* 33°50S 20°5E **270** D3
**Ashton** *Idaho, U.S.A.* 44°4N 111°27W **304** D8
**Ashtown** *Ireland* 53°22N 6°19W **120** A2
**Ashuanipi, L.** *Canada* 52°45N 66°15W **299** B6
**Ashuapmushuan ➔** *Canada* 48°37N 72°20W **298** C5
**Ashur = Assur** *Iraq* 35°27N 43°15E **213** E10
**Ashville** *Ala., U.S.A.* 33°50N 86°15W **316** B3
**Ashville** *Fla., U.S.A.* 30°37N 83°39W **316** E6
**Ashville** *Pa., U.S.A.* 40°34N 78°33W **312** F6
**'Āṣī ➔** *Asia* 36°1N 35°59E **250** B6
**Asia** 45°0N 75°0E **210** E9
**Asia, Kepulauan** *Indonesia* 1°0N 131°13E **231** D8
**Asiago** *Italy* 45°52N 11°30E **199** C8
**AsiaWorld-Expo** *Hong Kong, China* 22°19N 113°57E **122** B1
**Asid G.** *Phil.* 12°10N 123°29E **232** E4
**Asidonhoppo** *Suriname* 3°50N 55°30W **329** C6
**Asifabad** *India* 19°20N 79°24E **244** E4
**Asilah** *Morocco* 35°29N 6°0W **260** A3
**Asinara** *Italy* 41°4N 8°16E **200** A1
**Asinara, G. dell'** *Italy* 41°0N 8°30E **200** A1
**Asino** *Russia* 57°0N 86°0E **214** D9
**Asipovichy** *Belarus* 53°19N 28°33E **177** B15
**'Asīr** *Si. Arabia* 18°40N 42°30E **248** C3
**Asir, Ras** *Somalia* 11°55N 51°10E **267** B7
**Aska** *India* 19°2N 84°42E **244** E7
**Aşkale** *Turkey* 39°55N 40°41E **213** C9
**Asker** *Norway* 59°50N 10°29E **164** E7
**Askersund** *Sweden* 58°53N 14°55E **163** F8
**Askham** *S. Africa* 26°59S 20°47E **270** C3
**Askī Mawşil** *Iraq* 36°30N 42°44E **213** D10
**Askim** *Norway* 59°35N 11°10E **164** E8
**Askio, Oros** *Greece* 40°25N 21°35E **202** F5
**Askisto** *Finland* 60°16N 24°47E **121** B1
**Askja** *Iceland* 65°3N 16°48W **155** B10
**Asklipio** *Greece* 36°4N 27°56E **206** E11
**Askøyna** *Norway* 60°29N 5°10E **164** D2
**Askrikefjärden** *Sweden* 59°22N 18°13E **139** A3
**Askvoll** *Norway* 61°21N 5°4E **164** C2
**Asl** *Egypt* 29°33N 32°44E **256** B3
**Aslan Burnu** *Turkey* 38°44N 26°45E **205** C8
**Aslanapa** *Turkey* 39°13N 29°52E **205** B11
**Asländuz** *Iran* 39°26N 47°24E **213** C12
**Āsmār** *Afghan.* 35°10N 71°27E **240** B3
**Asmara = Asmera** *Eritrea* 15°19N 38°55E **257** D4
**Asmera** *Eritrea* 15°19N 38°55E **257** D4
**Asnæs** *Denmark* 55°40N 11°0E **163** J5
**Åsnen** *Sweden* 56°37N 14°45E **163** H8
**Asni** *Morocco* 31°17N 7°58W **260** B3
**Asnières** *France* 48°54N 2°16E **134** A2
**Aso** *Japan* 32°55N 131°5E **222** E3
**Aso Kujū ⌓** *Japan* 32°53N 131°6E **222** E3
**Aso-Zan** *Japan* 32°53N 131°6E **222** E3
**Asola** *Italy* 45°13N 10°24E **198** C7
**Asos** *Greece* 38°22N 20°33E **207** C2
**Asosa** *Ethiopia* 10°3N 34°32E **257** E3
**Asoteriba, Jebel** *Sudan* 21°51N 36°30E **256** C4
**Asouf, O. ➔** *Algeria* 25°40N 2°8E **261** C5
**Aspatria** *U.K.* 54°47N 3°19W **168** C4
**Aspe** *Spain* 38°20N 0°40W **197** G4
**Aspen** *U.S.A.* 39°11N 106°49W **304** G10
**Aspendos** *Turkey* 36°54N 31°7E **250** B3
**Aspermont** *U.S.A.* 33°8N 100°14W **314** E4
**Aspern** *Austria* 48°13N 16°29E **142** A2
**Aspet** *France* 43°1N 0°48E **174** E4
**Aspiring, Mt.** *N.Z.* 44°23S 168°46E **285** E3
**Aspres-sur-Buëch** *France* 44°32N 5°44E **175** D9
**Asprokavos, Akra** *Greece* 39°21N 20°6E **206** C10
**Aspromonte ⌓** *Italy* 38°9N 15°58E **201** D8
**Aspur** *India* 23°58N 74°7E **242** H6
**Asquith** *Canada* 52°8N 107°13W **297** C7
**Assa** *Morocco* 28°35N 9°6W **260** C3
**Assab = Aseb** *Eritrea* 13°0N 42°40E **257** E5
**Assâba □** *Mauritania* 16°40N 11°40W **262** B2
**Assâba, Massif de l'** *Mauritania* 16°10N 11°45W **262** B2
**Assagny ⌓** *Ivory C.* 5°10N 4°48W **262** D4
**Assago** *Italy* 45°24N 9°7E **128** B1
**Assaikio** *Nigeria* 8°34N 8°55E **263** D6
**Assal, L.** *Djibouti* 11°40N 42°26E **257** E5
**Assam □** *India* 26°0N 93°0E **241** C4
**Assamakka** *Niger* 19°21N 5°38E **263** B6
**Assateague Island ⌓** *U.S.A.* 38°15N 75°10W **309** F16
**Assaye** *India* 20°15N 75°53E **244** D2
**Asse** *Belgium* 50°24N 4°10E **170** D4
**Assekrem** *Algeria* 23°16N 5°49E **261** D6
**Assémini** *Italy* 39°17N 9°0E **200** C1
**Assen** *Neths.* 53°0N 6°35E **170** A6
**Assendelft** *Neths.* 52°28N 4°45E **112** A1
**Assens** *Denmark* 55°16N 9°55E **163** J3
**Assiano** *Italy* 45°27N 9°3E **128** B1
**Assini** *Ivory C.* 5°9N 3°17W **262** D4
**Assiniboia** *Canada* 49°40N 105°59W **297** D7
**Assiniboine ➔** *Canada* 49°53N 97°8W **297** D9
**Assiniboine, Mt.** *Canada* 50°52N 115°39W **296** C5
**Assiou** *Algeria* 21°7N 7°36E **261** D6
**Assis** *Brazil* 22°40S 50°20W **335** A5
**Assis Brasil** *Brazil* 10°55S 69°32W **330** C4
**Assisi** *Italy* 43°4N 12°37E **199** E9
**Åsskard** *Norway* 63°1N 8°30E **164** A5
**Assok Ngoum** *Gabon* 1°45N 11°39E **264** B2
**Assumption** *U.S.A.* 39°31N 89°3W **310** E7
**Assur** *Iraq* 35°27N 43°15E **213** E10
**Assynt, L.** *U.K.* 58°10N 5°3W **167** C3
**Astaffort** *France* 44°4N 0°40E **174** D4
**Astakida** *Greece* 35°53N 26°50E **205** F8
**Astakos** *Greece* 38°32N 21°5E **207** B3
**Astana** *Kazakhstan* 51°10N 71°30E **217** B8
**Āstāneh** *Iran* 37°17N 49°59E **247** B6
**Astapovo = Lev Tolstoy** *Russia* 53°13N 39°29E **188** F10
**Astara** *Azerbaijan* 38°30N 48°50E **213** C13
**Āstārā** *Iran* 38°20N 48°52E **213** C13
**Astarabad = Gorgān** *Iran* 36°55N 54°30E **247** B7
**Asterousia** *Greece* 34°59N 25°3E **207** F6
**Asti** *Italy* 44°54N 8°12E **198** D5
**Astipalea** *Greece* 36°32N 26°22E **205** E8
**Astola I.** *Pakistan* 25°7N 63°51E **240** D1
**Astorga** *Davao del S., Phil.* 6°54N 125°27E **233** H5
**Astorga** *Spain* 42°29N 6°8W **194** C4
**Astoria** *Ill., U.S.A.* 40°14N 90°21W **310** D6
**Astoria** *N.Y., U.S.A.* 40°46N 73°55W **132** B2
**Astoria** *Oreg., U.S.A.* 46°11N 123°50W **306** D3
**Åstorp** *Sweden* 56°6N 12°55E **163** H6
**Astrakhan** *Russia* 46°25N 48°5E **191** G9
**Astrakhan □** *Russia* 47°45N 46°20E **191** G8
**Astrebla Downs** *Australia* 24°12S 140°34E **280** C3
**Astrolabe, Récifs de l'** *N. Cal.* 19°48S 165°37E **288** d
**Astrolabe Park** *Australia* 33°57S 151°12E **139** B2
**Astudillo** *Spain* 42°12N 4°22W **194** C6
**Asturias □** *Spain* 43°15N 6°0W **194** B5
**Asturias ✈ (OVD)** *Spain* 43°33N 6°3W **194** B4
**Asumman** *S. Korea* 37°4N 126°40E **224** D3
**Asunción** *Bolivia* 11°46S 67°50W **330** C4
**Asunción** *N. Marianas* 19°40N 145°24E **302** a
**Asunción** *Paraguay* 25°10S 57°30W **334** B4
**Asunción Nochixtlán** *Mexico* 17°28N 97°14W **319** D5
**Åsunden** *Sweden* 58°0N 15°51E **163** F9
**Asutri** *Sudan* 15°25N 35°45E **257** D4
**Aswa ➔** *Uganda* 3°43N 31°55E **268** B3
**Aswa-Lolim ⌓** *Uganda* 2°43N 31°35E **268** B3
**Aswad, Ra's al** *Si. Arabia* 21°20N 39°0E **248** B2
**Aswân** *Egypt* 24°4N 32°57E **256** C3
**Aswan High Dam = Sadd el Aali** *Egypt* 23°54N 32°54E **256** C3
**Asyût** *Egypt* 27°11N 31°4E **256** B3
**Asyûti, Wadi ➔** *Egypt* 27°11N 31°16E **256** B3
**Aszód** *Hungary* 47°39N 19°28E **182** C4
**At-Bashy** *Kyrgyzstan* 41°10N 75°48E **217** D9
**Aṭ Ṭafīlah** *Jordan* 30°45N 35°30E **251** H6
**Aṭ Ṭafīlah □** *Jordan* 30°45N 35°30E **251** H6
**Aṭ Ṭā'if** *Si. Arabia* 21°5N 40°27E **248** B3
**Aṭ Ṭāj** *Libya* 24°13N 23°18E **258** D4
**At Ta'mīm □** *Iraq* 35°30N 44°20E **246** C5
**At Tamīmī** *Libya* 32°20N 23°4E **258** B4
**Aṭ Ṭirāq** *Si. Arabia* 27°19N 44°33E **246** E5
**Aṭ Ṭubayq** *Si. Arabia* 29°30N 37°0E **251** J8
**At Tuhaytah** *Yemen* 14°18N 43°15E **248** D3
**Aṭ Ṭunayb** *Jordan* 31°48N 35°57E **251** G6
**At Turbah** *Lahij, Yemen* 12°40N 43°30E **248** D3
**At Turbah** *Ta'izz, Yemen* 13°13N 44°7E **248** D4
**Atabey** *Turkey* 37°57N 30°39E **205** D12
**Atacama □** *Chile* 27°30S 70°0W **334** B2
**Atacama, Desierto de** *Chile* 24°0S 69°20W **334** A2
**Atacama, Salar de** *Chile* 23°30S 68°20W **334** A2
**Ataco** *Colombia* 3°35N 75°23W **328** C2
**Atafu** *Pac. Oc.* 8°32S 172°31W **277** B16
**Atakeye ◎** *Australia* 22°30S 133°45E **278** D5
**Atakor** *Algeria* 23°27N 5°31E **261** D6
**Atakpamé** *Togo* 7°31N 1°13E **263** D5
**Atalaia do Norte** *Brazil* 4°20S 70°12W **328** D3
**Atalandi** *Greece* 38°39N 22°58E **204** C4
**Atalaya** *Peru* 10°45S 73°50W **330** C3
**Atalaya de Femes** *Canary Is.* 28°56N 13°47W **153** e2
**Ataléia** *Brazil* 18°3S 41°6W **333** E3
**Atami** *Japan* 35°5N 139°4E **223** B11
**Atamyrat** *Turkmenistan* 37°50N 65°12E **217** E7
**Atankawng** *Burma* 25°50N 97°47E **241** C6
**Atap** *Indonesia* 3°51N 117°1E **235** B5
**Atapuerca, Cueva de** *Spain* 42°22N 3°32W **194** C7
**Atapupu** *Indonesia* 9°0S 124°51E **231** F6
**'Ataq** *Yemen* 14°33N 46°47E **248** D4
**Atâr** *Mauritania* 20°30N 13°5W **260** D2
**Ataram, Erg n-** *Algeria* 23°57N 2°0E **261** D5
**Atarfe** *Spain* 37°13N 3°40W **195** H7
**Atari** *Pakistan* 30°56N 74°2E **242** D6
**Atarot** *West Bank* 31°52N 35°13E **123** A2
**Atarot ✈ (JRS)** *West Bank* 31°52N 35°14E **123** A2
**Atascadero** *U.S.A.* 35°29N 120°40W **306** K6
**Atasū** *Kazakhstan* 48°30N 71°0E **217** C8
**Atatürk, İstanbul ✈ (IST)** *Turkey* 40°59N 28°49E **203** F12
**Atatürk Barajı** *Turkey* 37°28N 38°30E **213** D8
**Atauro** *E. Timor* 8°10S 125°30E **231** F7
**Ataviros** *Greece* 36°12N 27°50E **206** E11
**Atbara** *Sudan* 17°42N 33°59E **256** D3
**'Atbara, Nahr ➔** *Sudan* 17°40N 33°56E **256** D3
**Atbasar** *Kazakhstan* 51°48N 68°20E **217** B7
**Atbashi = At-Bashy** *Kyrgyzstan* 41°10N 75°48E **217** D9
**Atça** *Turkey* 37°53N 28°13E **205** D10
**Atchafalaya B.** *U.S.A.* 29°25N 91°25W **314** G9
**Atchison** *U.S.A.* 39°34N 95°7W **308** F6
**Atebubu** *Ghana* 7°47N 1°0W **263** D4
**Ateca** *Spain* 41°20N 1°49W **196** D3
**Aterno ➔** *Italy* 42°11N 13°51E **199** F10
**Āteshān** *Iran* 35°35N 52°37E **247** C7
**Atesine, Alpi** *Italy* 46°55N 11°30E **199** B8
**Atessa** *Italy* 42°4N 14°27E **199** F11
**Atfih** *Egypt* 29°25N 31°15E **256** J7
**Atghara** *India* 22°37N 88°26E **124** B2
**Ath** *Belgium* 50°38N 3°47E **170** D3
**Athabasca** *Canada* 54°45N 113°20W **296** C6
**Athabasca ➔** *Canada* 58°40N 110°50W **297** B6
**Athabasca, L.** *Canada* 59°15N 109°15W **297** B7
**Athabasca Sand Dunes ⌓** *Canada* 59°4N 108°43W **297** B7
**Athagarh** *India* 20°32N 85°37E **244** D7
**Athamanon Oros** *Greece* 39°30N 21°26E **204** B3
**Athboy** *Ireland* 53°36N 6°56W **166** C5
**Athena** *U.S.A.* 29°59N 83°30W **316** F6
**Athenry** *Ireland* 53°18N 8°44W **166** C3
**Athens = Athina** *Greece* 37°58N 23°43E **112** B2
**Athens** *Ala., U.S.A.* 34°48N 86°58W **315** D11
**Athens** *Ga., U.S.A.* 33°57N 83°23W **316** B6
**Athens** *N.Y., U.S.A.* 42°16N 73°49W **313** D11
**Athens** *Ohio, U.S.A.* 39°20N 82°6W **309** F12
**Athens** *Pa., U.S.A.* 41°57N 76°31W **313** E8
**Athens** *Tenn., U.S.A.* 35°27N 84°36W **315** D12
**Athens** *Tex., U.S.A.* 32°12N 95°51W **314** E7
**Atheras** *Greece* 38°19N 20°25E **207** C1
**Atherley** *Canada* 44°37N 79°20W **312** B5
**Atherton** *Australia* 17°17S 145°30E **280** B4
**Athi River** *Kenya* 1°28S 36°58E **268** C4
**Athiéme** *Benin* 6°37N 1°40E **263** D5
**Athienou** *Cyprus* 35°3N 33°32E **207** E9
**Athina** *Greece* 37°58N 23°43E **112** B2
**Athina ✈ (ATH)** *Greece* 37°56N 23°56E **112** A3
**Athínai = Athina** *Greece* 37°58N 23°43E **112** B2
**Athis-Mons** *France* 48°42N 2°23E **134** B3
**Athlone** *Westmeath, Ireland* 53°25N 7°56W **166** C4
**Athlone** *Western Cape, S. Africa* 33°57S 18°30E **118** A2
**Athmalik** *India* 20°43N 84°32E **244** D7
**Athni** *India* 16°44N 75°6E **244** F2
**Athol** *N.Z.* 45°30S 168°35E **285** F3
**Athol** *Mass., U.S.A.* 42°36N 72°14W **313** D12
**Athol I.** *Bahamas* 25°5N 77°16W **153** b
**Athol** *S. Africa* 26°7S 28°3E **123** A2
**Atholl, Forest of** *U.K.* 56°51N 3°50W **167** E5
**Atholl, Kap** *Greenland* 76°25N 69°30W **154** B4
**Atholville** *Canada* 47°59N 66°43W **299** C6
**Athos** *Greece* 40°9N 24°22E **203** F8
**Athy** *Ireland* 53°0N 7°0W **166** C5
**Ati** *Chad* 13°13N 18°20E **259** F3
**Ati** *Sudan* 13°5N 29°2E **257** E2
**Ati, J.** *Libya* 23°24N 14°21E **258** D2
**Atiak** *Uganda* 3°12N 32°2E **268** B3
**Atiamuri** *N.Z.* 38°24S 176°5E **284** E5
**Atico** *Peru* 16°14S 73°40W **330** D3
**Atienza** *Spain* 41°12N 2°52W **196** D2
**Aṭīfiya** *Iraq* 33°21N 44°21E **113** A2
**Atiit** *South Sudan* 6°10N 30°35E **257** F3
**Atik L.** *Canada* 55°15N 96°0W **297** B9
**Atikaki ⌓** *Canada* 51°30N 95°31W **297** C9
**Atikameg ➔** *Canada* 52°30N 82°46W **298** B3
**Atikokan** *Canada* 48°45N 91°37W **298** C1
**Atikonak L.** *Canada* 52°40N 64°32W **299** B7
**Atimaono** *Tahiti* 17°46S 149°28W **289** e
**Atimonan** *Phil.* 14°0N 121°55E **232** D3
**'Ātinah, W. ➔** *Oman* 18°23N 53°28E **249** C6
**Atirampattinam** *India* 10°28N 79°20E **245** J4
**Atişalen** *Turkey* 41°3N 28°52E **122** B1
**Atitlán ⌓** *Guatemala* 14°38N 91°10W **320** D1
**Atiu** *Cook Is.* 20°0S 158°10W **289** J12
**Atka** *Russia* 60°50N 151°48E **215** C16
**Atka** *Alaska, U.S.A.* 52°12N 174°12W **303** K4
**Atka I.** *U.S.A.* 52°7N 174°30W **303** K4
**Atkarsk** *Russia* 51°55N 45°2E **190** E7
**Atkinson** *Ga., U.S.A.* 31°13N 81°47W **316** D8
**Atkinson** *Ill., U.S.A.* 41°25N 90°1W **310** C6
**Atkinson** *Nebr., U.S.A.* 42°32N 98°59W **308** D4
**Atlanta** *Ga., U.S.A.* 33°45N 84°23W **113** B2
**Atlanta** *Ill., U.S.A.* 40°16N 89°14W **310** D7
**Atlanta** *Mo., U.S.A.* 39°54N 92°29W **310** E4
**Atlanta** *Tex., U.S.A.* 33°7N 94°10W **314** E7
**Atlanta Hartsfield-Jackson Int. ✈ (ATL)** *U.S.A.* 33°38N 84°26W **113** C2
**Atlanta History Center** *U.S.A.* 33°45N 84°22W **113** B2
**Atlanta Zoo** *U.S.A.* 33°44N 84°22W **113** B2
**Atlantic** *U.S.A.* 41°24N 95°1W **310** C2
**Atlantic Beach** *U.S.A.* 30°20N 81°24W **316** E8
**Atlantic City** *U.S.A.* 39°21N 74°27W **309** F16
**Atlantic-Indian Basin** *Antarctica* 60°0S 30°0E **151** B4
**Atlantic Ocean** 0°0 20°0W **152** F8
**Atlántico □** *Colombia* 10°45N 75°0W **328** A3
**Atlantis** *S. Africa* 33°34S 18°29E **270** D2
**Atlas Mts. = Haut Atlas** *Morocco* 32°30N 5°0W **260** B4
**Atlin** *Canada* 59°31N 133°41W **296** B2
**Atlin, L.** *Canada* 59°26N 133°45W **296** B2
**Atlin ⌓** *Canada* 59°10N 134°30W **296** B2
**Atløyna** *Norway* 61°21N 4°58E **164** C1
**Atmakur** *Andhra Pradesh, India* 18°45N 78°39E **244** E4
**Atmakur** *Andhra Pradesh, India* 14°37N 79°40E **245** G4
**Atmakur** *Andhra Pradesh, India* 15°53N 78°35E **245** G4
**Atmore** *U.S.A.* 31°2N 87°29W **317** D2
**Atna** *Norway* 61°44N 10°49E **164** C7
**Atna ➔** *Norway* 61°44N 10°49E **164** C7
**Atō** *Japan* 34°25N 131°40E **222** C3
**Atocha** *Bolivia* 20°56S 66°14W **330** E4
**Atok** *Phil.* 16°35N 120°41E **232** C3
**Atoka** *U.S.A.* 34°23N 96°8W **314** D6
**Atokos** *Greece* 38°28N 20°49E **207** C2
**Atolia** *U.S.A.* 35°19N 117°37W **307** K9
**Atomium** *Belgium* 50°54N 4°20E **116** A2
**Atongo-Bakari** *C.A.R.* 5°49N 21°35E **264** A4
**Atori** *Solomon Is.* 8°42S 160°59E **287** M11
**Atqasuk** *U.S.A.* 70°28N 157°24W **303** A8
**Atqasuk ➔** *U.S.A.* 70°52N 155°55W **303** A9
**Atrå** *Norway* 59°59N 8°45E **164** E5
**Atrai ➔** *Bangla.* 24°7N 89°22E **241** C2
**Atrak = Atrek ➔** *Turkmenistan* 37°35N 53°58E **247** B8
**Ätran** *Sweden* 57°7N 12°57E **163** G6
**Ätran ➔** *Sweden* 56°53N 12°30E **163** H6
**Atrato ➔** *Colombia* 8°17N 76°58W **328** B2
**Atrauli** *India* 28°2N 78°20E **242** E8
**Atrek ➔** *Turkmenistan* 37°35N 53°58E **247** B8
**Atri** *Italy* 42°35N 13°58E **199** F10
**Atsiki** *Greece* 39°56N 25°13E **205** B7
**Atsoum, Mts.** *Cameroon* 6°41N 12°57E **263** D7
**Atsugi** *Japan* 35°25N 139°21E **223** B11
**Atsumi** *Japan* 34°35N 137°4E **223** D9
**Atsuta** *Japan* 43°24N 141°26E **220** C10
**Attalla** *U.S.A.* 34°1N 86°6W **316** A3
**Attapeu** *Laos* 14°48N 106°50E **236** E6
**Attapulgus** *U.S.A.* 30°45N 84°29W **316** E5
**Attawapiskat** *Canada* 52°56N 82°24W **298** B3
**Attawapiskat ➔** *Canada* 52°57N 82°18W **298** B3
**Attawapiskat L.** *Canada* 52°18N 87°54W **298** B2
**Attersee** *Austria* 47°55N 13°32E **180** D6
**Attica = Attiki □** *Greece* 37°10N 23°40E **204** D5
**Attica** *Ind., U.S.A.* 40°18N 87°15W **311** D9
**Attica** *Ohio, U.S.A.* 41°4N 82°53W **312** E2
**Attichy** *France* 49°25N 3°3E **173** C10
**Attigny** *France* 49°28N 4°35E **173** C11
**Attikamagen L.** *Canada* 55°0N 66°30W **299** B6
**Attiki** *Greece* 38°0N 23°45E **112** A2
**Attiki □** *Greece* 37°10N 23°40E **204** D5
**Attleboro** *U.S.A.* 41°57N 71°17W **313** E13
**Attock** *Pakistan* 33°52N 72°20E **242** C5
**Attopu = Attapeu** *Laos* 14°48N 106°50E **236** E6
**Attu** *U.S.A.* 52°56N 173°15E **303** K1
**Attu I.** *U.S.A.* 52°55N 172°55E **303** K1
**Attunga** *Australia* 30°55S 150°50E **283** A9
**Attur** *India* 11°35N 78°30E **245** J4
**'Atūd** *Yemen* 14°53N 48°10E **249** D5
**Atuel ➔** *Argentina* 36°17S 66°50W **334** D2
**Atura** *Uganda* 2°7N 32°20E **268** B3
**Åtvidaberg** *Sweden* 58°12N 16°0E **163** F10
**Atwater** *U.S.A.* 37°21N 120°37W **306** H6
**Atwood** *Ont., Canada* 43°40N 81°1W **312** C3
**Atwood** *Ill., U.S.A.* 39°48N 88°28W **311** E8
**Atwood** *Kans., U.S.A.* 39°48N 101°3W **308** F3
**Atyraū** *Kazakhstan* 47°5N 52°0E **187** E9
**Atzgersdorf** *Austria* 48°8N 16°18E **142** B1
**Au Sable** *U.S.A.* 44°25N 83°20W **312** B1
**Au Sable ➔** *U.S.A.* 44°25N 83°20W **309** C12
**Au Sable Forks** *U.S.A.* 44°27N 73°41W **313** B11
**Au Sable Pt.** *U.S.A.* 44°20N 83°20W **312** B1
**Au Vent, Région** *Réunion* 21°0S 55°35E **272** f
**Aua** *Amer. Samoa* 14°17S 170°40W **302** f
**Auas** *Honduras* 15°29N 84°20W **320** C3
**Auasberg** *Namibia* 22°37S 17°13E **270** B2
**Aubagne** *France* 43°17N 5°37E **175** E9
**Aube □** *France* 48°15N 4°10E **173** D11
**Aube ➔** *France* 48°34N 3°43E **173** D10
**Aubenas** *France* 44°37N 4°24E **175** D8
**Aubenton** *France* 49°50N 4°12E **173** C11
**Auberry** *U.S.A.* 37°7N 119°29W **306** H7
**Aubervilliers** *France* 48°54N 2°22E **134** A3
**Aubigny-sur-Nère** *France* 47°30N 2°24E **173** E9
**Aubin** *France* 44°33N 2°15E **174** D6
**Aubing** *Germany* 48°9N 11°25E **131** B1
**Aubrac, Mts. d'** *France* 44°40N 3°2E **174** D7
**Auburn** *S. Austral., Australia* 34°1S 138°42E **282** C3

Auburn Ala., U.S.A. 32°36N 85°29W 316 C4
Auburn Calif., U.S.A. 38°54N 121°4W 306 G5
Auburn Ill., U.S.A. 39°36N 89°45W 310 E7
Auburn Ind., U.S.A. 41°22N 85°4W 311 C11
Auburn Maine, U.S.A. 44°6N 70°14W 309 C18
Auburn N.Y., U.S.A. 42°56N 76°34W 313 D8
Auburn Nebr., U.S.A. 40°23N 95°51W 308 E6
Auburn Pa., U.S.A. 40°36N 76°6W 313 F8
Auburn Wash., U.S.A. 47°18N 122°14W 306 C4
Auburn Ra. Australia 25°15S 150°30E 281 D5
Auburndale Fla., U.S.A. 28°4N 81°48W 317 G8
Auburndale Mass., U.S.A. 42°20N 71°14W 116 A1
Aubusson France 45°57N 2°11E 174 C6
Auce Latvia 56°28N 22°53E 184 B9
Auch France 43°39N 0°36E 174 E4
Auchendinny U.K. 55°51N 3°11W 121 B2
Auchi Nigeria 7°6N 6°13E 263 D6
Auchterarder U.K. 56°18N 3°41W 167 E5
Auchtermuchty U.K. 56°18N 3°13W 167 E5
Auckland N.Z. 36°52S 174°46E 284 C3
Auckland □ N.Z. 36°50S 175°0E 284 C3
Auckland Is. Pac. Oc. 50°40S 166°5E 288 N8
Auckland Park S. Africa 26°11S 28°0E 123 B2
Aude □ France 43°8N 2°28E 174 E6
Aude → France 43°13N 3°14E 174 E7
Auden Canada 50°14N 87°53W 298 B2
Auderghem Belgium 50°49N 4°26E 116 B2
Auderville France 49°43N 1°57W 172 C5
Audierne France 48°1N 4°34W 172 D2
Audincourt France 47°30N 6°50E 173 E13
Audo Ra. Ethiopia 6°20N 41°50E 257 F5
Audomarois ⌓ France 50°50N 2°30E 173 B9
Audubon U.S.A. 41°43N 94°56W 310 C2
Audubon Park U.S.A. 29°55N 90°8W 131 B2
Aue Germany 50°35N 12°41E 178 E8
Auerbach Germany 50°30N 12°24E 178 E8
Aufist W. Sahara 25°44N 14°39W 260 C2
Augathella Australia 25°48S 146°35E 281 D4
Aughnacloy U.K. 54°25N 6°59W 166 B5
Aughrim Ireland 53°18N 8°19W 166 C3
Augrabies Falls S. Africa 28°35S 20°20E 270 C3
Augrabies Falls △ S. Africa 28°40S 20°22E 270 C3
Augsburg Germany 48°25N 10°52E 179 G6
Augsburg-Westliche Wälder ⌓ Germany 48°22N 10°40E 179 G6
August Town Jamaica 17°59N 76°44W 320 a
Augusta W. Austral., Australia 34°19S 115°9E 279 F2
Augusta Italy 37°13N 15°13E 201 E8
Augusta Ark., U.S.A. 35°17N 91°22W 314 D9
Augusta Ga., U.S.A. 33°28N 81°58W 316 B8
Augusta Ill., U.S.A. 40°14N 90°57W 310 D6
Augusta Kans., U.S.A. 37°41N 96°59W 308 G5
Augusta Ky., U.S.A. 38°47N 84°0W 311 F12
Augusta Maine, U.S.A. 44°19N 69°47W 309 C19
Augusta Mont., U.S.A. 47°30N 112°24W 304 C7
Augusta, Mausoleo di Rome, Italy 136 b2
Augustenborg Denmark 54°57N 9°53E 163 K3
Augustine I. U.S.A. 59°22N 153°26W 303 G9
Augusto Cardosa = Metangula Mozam. 12°40S 34°50E 269 E3
Augustów Poland 53°51N 23°0E 184 E9
Augustówka Poland 52°11N 21°5E 143 B2
Augustus, Mt. Australia 24°20S 116°50E 279 D2
Augustus I. Australia 15°20S 124°30E 278 C3
Aujuittuq = Grise Fiord Canada 76°25N 82°57W 295 B15
Aukan Eritrea 15°29N 40°50E 257 D5
Auki Solomon Is. 8°45S 160°42E 287 M11
Aukra Norway 62°47N 6°55E 164 B3
Aukrug ⌓ Germany 54°5N 9°45E 178 A5
Aukštaitija △ Lithuania 55°15N 26°0E 161 J22
Aukum U.S.A. 38°34N 120°43W 306 G6
Aul India 20°41N 86°39E 244 D8
Aulavik △ Canada 73°42N 119°55W 294 C8
Auld, L. Australia 22°25S 123°50E 278 D3
Äūlīeköl Kazakhstan 52°32N 62°45E 216 B6
Aulifeltet Norway 60°30N 11°21E 162 D5
Auliye-Ata = Taraz Kazakhstan 42°54N 71°22E 217 D8
Aulla Italy 44°12N 9°58E 198 D6
Aulnay France 46°2N 0°22W 174 B3
Aulnay-sous-Bois France 48°56N 2°29E 134 A3
Aulne → France 48°17N 4°16W 172 D2
Aulnoye-Aymeries France 50°12N 3°50E 173 B10
Aulong Palau 7°16N 134°17E 288 c
Ault Somme, France 50°8N 1°26E 172 B8
Ault Colo., U.S.A. 40°35N 104°44W 304 F11
Aulus-les-Bains France 42°49N 1°19E 174 F5
Aumale = Sour el Ghozlane Algeria 36°10N 3°45E 261 A5
Aumale France 49°46N 1°46E 173 C8
Aumo Papua N. G. 5°44S 148°30E 286 C5
Aumont-Aubrac France 44°43N 3°17E 174 D7
Auna Nigeria 10°9N 4°42E 263 C5
Aundah India 19°32N 77°3E 244 E3
Aundh India 17°33N 74°23E 244 F2
Auning Denmark 56°26N 10°22E 163 H4
Aunis France 46°5N 0°50W 174 B3
Aunu'u Amer. Samoa 14°20S 170°31W 302 f
Auponhia Indonesia 1°58S 125°27E 231 E7
Aups France 43°37N 6°15E 175 E10
Aur, Pulau Malaysia 2°35N 104°10E 237 L5
Aura Burma 26°59N 97°57E 241 B6
Auraiya India 26°28N 79°33E 243 F8
Aurangabad Bihar, India 24°45N 84°18E 243 G11
Aurangabad Maharashtra, India 19°50N 75°23E 244 E2
Auray France 47°40N 2°59W 172 E4
Aurdal Norway 60°55N 9°26E 164 D6
Aure Norway 63°16N 8°33E 164 A5
Aurelio Italy 41°54N 12°26E 136 B1
Aurès Algeria 35°8N 6°30E 261 A6
Aurich Germany 53°28N 7°28E 178 B3
Aurilândia Brazil 16°44S 50°28W 333 E1
Aurillac France 44°55N 2°26E 174 D6
Aurlandsfjorden Norway 61°3N 7°1E 164 C4
Aurlandsvangen Norway 60°55N 7°12E 164 D4
Auronzo di Cadore Italy 46°33N 12°26E 199 B9
Aurora = Maéwo Vanuatu 15°10S 168°10E 287 E6
Aurora = San Francisco Phil. 13°21N 122°31E 232 E4
Aurora Ont., Canada 44°0N 79°28W 312 C5
Aurora Isabela, Phil. 16°59N 121°38E 232 C3
Aurora Zamboanga del S., Phil. 7°57N 123°36E 233 H4
Aurora Western Cape, S. Africa 32°40S 18°29E 270 D2
Aurora Colo., U.S.A. 39°43N 104°49W 304 G11
Aurora Ill., U.S.A. 41°45N 88°19W 311 C8
Aurora Mo., U.S.A. 36°58N 93°43W 308 G7
Aurora N.Y., U.S.A. 42°45N 76°42W 313 D8
Aurora Nebr., U.S.A. 40°52N 98°0W 308 E5
Aurora Ohio, U.S.A. 41°21N 81°20W 312 E3
Aurora □ Phil. 15°30N 121°30E 232 D3
Aurora Memorial △ Phil. 15°40N 121°20E 232 D3
Aursmoen Norway 59°55N 11°26E 164 E8
Aursunden Norway 62°40N 11°40E 164 B8
Aurukun Australia 13°20S 141°45E 280 A3
Aurukun ⚙ Australia 13°36S 141°48E 280 A3
Aus Namibia 26°35S 16°12E 270 C2
Ausa India 18°15N 76°30E 244 E3
Ausable → Canada 43°19N 81°46W 312 C3
Auschwitz = Oświęcim Poland 50°2N 19°11E 185 H6
Ausîm Egypt 30°7N 31°8E 117 A1
Auski Roadhouse Australia 22°22S 118°41E 278 D2
Auspitz = Hustopeče Czech Rep. 48°57N 16°43E 181 C9
Aussig = Ústí nad Labem Czech Rep. 50°41N 14°3E 180 A7
Aust-Agder □ Norway 58°45N 8°0E 164 F4
Austad Norway 58°58N 7°37E 164 F4
Austen Harbour India 12°55N 92°45E 245 H11
Austerlitz = Slavkov u Brna Czech Rep. 49°10N 16°52E 181 B9
Austerlitz, Gare d' Paris, France 48°50N 2°22E 134 A3
Austevoll Norway 60°5N 5°13E 164 D2
Austin Ill., U.S.A. 41°53N 87°45W 119 B2
Austin Ind., U.S.A. 38°45N 85°49W 311 F11
Austin Minn., U.S.A. 43°40N 92°58W 308 D7
Austin Nev., U.S.A. 39°30N 117°4W 304 G5
Austin Pa., U.S.A. 41°38N 78°6W 312 E6
Austin Tex., U.S.A. 30°17N 97°45W 314 F6
Austin, L. Australia 27°40S 118°0E 279 E2
Austin I. Canada 61°10N 94°0W 297 A10
Austmarka Norway 60°6N 12°21E 164 D9
Austnes Norway 62°38N 6°16E 164 B3
Austra Norway 65°8N 11°55E 160 D14
Austral Is. = Tubuaï, Îs. French Polynesia 25°0S 150°0W 289 f
Austral Seamount Chain Pac. Oc. 24°0S 150°0W 289 K13
Australia ■ Oceania 23°0S 135°0E 276 E3
Australian-Antarctic Basin S. Ocean 60°0S 120°0E 151 C9
Australian Capital Territory □ Australia 35°30S 149°0E 283 C8
Australind Australia 33°17S 115°42E 279 F2
Austria ■ Europe 47°0N 14°0E 180 E7
Austur-skaftafellssýsla Iceland 64°15N 16°0W 155 C10
Austurland □ Iceland 64°55N 15°30W 155 C11
Austvågøya Norway 68°20N 14°40E 160 B16
Autazes Brazil 3°35S 59°8W 329 D6
Auterive France 43°21N 1°29E 174 E5
Authie → France 50°22N 1°38E 173 B8
Authon-du-Perche France 48°12N 0°54E 172 D7
Autlán de Navarro Mexico 19°46N 104°22W 318 D4
Autun France 46°58N 4°17E 173 F11
Auvergne □ France 45°20N 3°15E 174 C7
Auvergne, Mts. d' France 45°20N 2°55E 174 C6
Auvézère → France 45°12N 0°50E 174 C4
Auxerre France 47°48N 3°32E 173 E10
Auxi-le-Château France 50°15N 2°8E 173 B9
Auxonne France 47°10N 5°20E 173 E12
Auxvasse U.S.A. 39°1N 91°54W 310 E5
Auyuittuq △ Canada 67°30N 66°0W 295 D18
Auzances France 46°2N 2°30E 173 F9
Auzangate, Nevado Peru 13°47S 71°13W 330 C3
Av-Dovurak Russia 51°17N 91°35E 215 D10
Ava Ill., U.S.A. 37°53N 89°30W 310 G7
Ava Mo., U.S.A. 36°57N 92°40W 308 G7
Avachinskaya Sopka Russia 53°15N 158°50E 215 D16
Avaldsnes Norway 59°21N 5°20E 164 E2
Avallon France 47°30N 3°53E 173 E10
Avalon U.S.A. 33°21N 118°20W 307 M8
Avalon Pen. Canada 47°30N 53°20W 299 C9
Avana → Cook Is. 21°14S 159°43W 289 h
Avanavero Suriname 4°51N 57°22W 329 C6
Avanigadda India 16°0N 80°56E 245 G5
Avanos Turkey 38°43N 34°51E 212 C6
Avantas Greece 40°57N 25°56E 203 F9
Avaré Brazil 23°4S 43°58W 335 A6
Avarua Cook Is. 21°12S 159°46W 289 h
Avarua Harb. Cook Is. 21°12S 159°46W 289 h
Avatele Cook Is. 19°6S 169°55W 289 g
Avatiu Cook Is. 21°12S 159°47W 289 h
Avawatz Mts. U.S.A. 35°40N 116°30W 307 K10
Avdan Dağı Turkey 40°23N 29°46E 203 F13
Avedøre Denmark 55°37N 12°27E 118 B2
Aveiro Brazil 3°10S 55°5W 329 D6
Aveiro Portugal 40°37N 8°38W 194 E2
Aveiro □ Portugal 40°40N 8°35W 194 E2
Āvej Iran 35°40N 49°15E 247 C6
Avellaneda Argentina 34°40S 58°22W 117 C2
Avellino Italy 40°54N 14°47E 201 B7
Avenal U.S.A. 36°0N 120°8W 306 K6
Avenel U.S.A. 38°59N 76°59W 143 B3
Aventura U.S.A. 25°57N 80°8W 129 C3
Averøya Norway 63°0N 7°35E 164 A4
Aversa Italy 40°58N 14°12E 201 B7
Avery U.S.A. 47°15N 115°49W 304 C6
Aves, I. de W. Indies 15°45N 63°55W 321 C7
Aves, Is. las Venezuela 12°0N 67°30W 321 D6
Aves Laguna Colorada, Santuario de ⌓ Bolivia 22°30S 67°30W 330 E4
Aves Ridge W. Indies 14°0N 63°30W 321 D7
Avesnes-sur-Helpe France 50°8N 3°55E 173 B10
Avesnois ⌓ France 50°10N 3°45E 173 B10
Avesta Sweden 60°9N 16°10E 162 D10
Aveyron □ France 44°22N 2°45E 174 D6
Aveyron → France 44°5N 1°16E 174 D5
Avezzano Italy 42°2N 13°25E 199 F10
Avgo Greece 35°33N 25°37E 205 F7
Aviá Terai Argentina 26°45S 60°50W 334 B3
Aviano Italy 46°4N 12°36E 199 B9
Aviatu → Cook Is. 21°12S 159°49W 289 h
Aviemore U.K. 57°12N 3°50W 167 D5
Aviemore, L. N.Z. 44°37S 170°18E 285 E5
Avigliana Italy 45°5N 7°23E 198 C4
Avigliano Italy 40°44N 15°43E 201 B8
Avignon France 43°57N 4°50E 175 E8
Ávila Spain 40°39N 4°43W 194 E6
Ávila □ Spain 40°30N 5°0W 194 E6
Ávila, Sierra de Spain 40°40N 5°15W 194 E5
Avila Beach U.S.A. 35°11N 120°44W 307 K6
Avilés Spain 43°35N 5°57W 194 B5
Aviño Spain 43°36N 8°8W 194 B2
Avintes Portugal 41°7N 8°33W 194 D2
Avis Portugal 39°4N 7°53W 195 F3
Avis Pa., U.S.A. 41°11N 77°19W 312 E7
Avísio → Italy 46°7N 11°5E 198 B8
Avissawella Sri Lanka 6°56N 80°11E 245 L5
Aviston U.S.A. 38°36N 89°36W 310 F7
Aviva Stadium Dublin, Ireland 53°20N 6°13W 120 A2
Aviz = Avis Portugal 39°4N 7°53W 195 F3
Avize France 48°59N 4°1E 173 D11
Avlona = Vlorë Albania 40°32N 19°28E 202 F3
Avlonari Greece 38°31N 24°8E 204 C6
Avlum Denmark 56°16N 8°47E 163 H2
Avoca Vic., Australia 37°5S 143°26E 282 D5
Avoca N.Y., U.S.A. 42°25N 77°25W 312 D7
Avoca → Vic., Australia 35°40S 143°43E 282 C5
Avoca → Wicklow, Ireland 52°48N 6°10W 166 D5
Avola B.C., Canada 51°45N 119°19W 296 C5
Avola Italy 36°56N 15°7E 201 F8
Avon Ill., U.S.A. 40°40N 90°25W 310 D6
Avon N.Y., U.S.A. 42°55N 77°45W 312 D7
Avon → W. Austral., Australia 31°40S 116°7E 279 F2
Avon → Bristol, U.K. 51°29N 2°41W 169 F5
Avon → Dorset, U.K. 50°44N 1°46W 169 G6
Avon → Warks., U.K. 52°0N 2°3W 169 E5
Avon Park U.S.A. 27°36N 81°31W 317 H8
Avondale Ill., U.S.A. 41°56N 87°41W 119 B2
Avondale La., U.S.A. 29°54N 90°12W 131 B1
Avondale Zimbabwe 17°43S 30°58E 269 F3
Avondale Heights Australia 37°45S 144°52E 128 A1
Avonlea Canada 50°0N 105°0W 297 D8
Avonmore Canada 45°10N 74°58W 313 A10
Avonmouth U.K. 51°30N 2°42W 169 F5
Avramov Bulgaria 42°45N 26°38E 203 D10
Avranches France 48°40N 1°20W 172 D5
Avre → France 48°47N 1°22E 172 D8
Avrig Romania 45°43N 24°21E 183 E9
Avrillé France 47°30N 0°35W 172 E6
Avtovac Bos.-H. 43°9N 18°35E 202 C2
Avtovo Russia 59°51N 30°16E 137 B1
Avu Avu Solomon Is. 9°50S 160°22E 287 M11
Awa-Shima Japan 38°27N 139°14E 220 E9
Awag el Baqar South Sudan 10°10N 33°10E 257 E3
A'waj → Syria 33°23N 36°20E 250 E7
Awaji Japan 34°28N 134°56E 222 C6
Awaji-Shima Japan 34°30N 134°50E 222 C6
'Awālī Bahrain 26°0N 50°30E 247 E6
Awantipur India 33°55N 75°3E 243 C6
Awanui N.Z. 35°4S 173°17E 284 B2
Aware Ethiopia 8°16N 44°9E 267 C5
Awarja → India 17°5N 76°15E 244 F3
Awarua B. N.Z. 44°28S 168°4E 285 E3
Awarua Pt. N.Z. 44°15S 168°5E 285 E3
Awasa Ethiopia 7°2N 38°28E 257 F4
Awasa, L. Ethiopia 7°0N 38°30E 257 F4
Awash Ethiopia 9°1N 40°10E 257 F5
Awash → Ethiopia 11°45N 41°5E 257 E5
Awash △ Ethiopia 9°8N 40°0E 257 F5
Awaso Ghana 6°15N 2°22W 262 D4
Awat China 40°35N 80°24E 217 D10
Awatere → N.Z. 41°37S 174°10E 285 B9
Awbārī Libya 26°46N 12°57E 258 C2
Awbārī, Idehan Libya 27°10N 11°30E 258 C2
Awdal □ Somalia 10°30N 43°30E 267 B5
Awdheegle Somalia 1°59N 44°50E 267 D5
Awe, L. U.K. 56°17N 5°16W 167 E3
Aweil South Sudan 8°42N 27°20E 257 F2
Awgu Nigeria 6°4N 7°24E 263 D6
Awjilah Libya 29°8N 21°7E 258 C4
Awka Nigeria 6°12N 7°5E 263 D6
Aworro Papua N. G. 7°43S 143°11E 286 D2
Awsard Mauritania 22°37N 14°22W 260 D2
Ax-les-Thermes France 42°44N 1°50E 174 F5
Axat France 42°48N 2°13E 174 F6
Axe → U.K. 50°42N 3°4W 169 F5
Axel Heiberg I. Canada 80°0N 90°0W 295 B14
Axim Ghana 4°51N 2°15W 262 E4
Axinim Brazil 4°2S 59°22W 329 D6
Axintele Romania 44°37N 26°47E 183 F11
Axioma Brazil 6°45S 64°31W 331 B5
Axios → Greece 40°57N 22°35E 202 F6
Axminster U.K. 50°46N 3°0W 169 G4
Axson U.S.A. 31°17N 82°44W 316 D7
Axvall Sweden 58°23N 13°34E 163 F7
Ay France 49°3N 4°1E 173 C11
Ayaantang Eq. Guin. 1°58N 10°24E 264 B2
Ayabaca Peru 4°40S 79°53W 330 A2
Ayabe Japan 35°20N 135°20E 223 B7
Ayacucho Argentina 37°5S 58°20W 334 D4
Ayacucho Peru 13°0S 74°0W 330 C3
Ayacucho □ Peru 14°0S 74°0W 330 C3
Ayaguz = Ayaköz Kazakhstan 48°10N 80°10E 217 C10
Ayakkum Hu China 37°30N 89°20E 217 E11
Ayaköz Kazakhstan 48°10N 80°10E 217 C10
Ayaköz → Kazakhstan 46°40N 79°14E 217 C9
Ayakudi India 10°28N 77°56E 245 J3
Ayala Phil. 6°57N 121°57E 233 H3
Ayamé Ivory C. 5°35N 3°9W 262 D4
Ayamonte Spain 37°12N 7°24W 195 H3
Ayan Russia 56°30N 138°16E 215 D14
Ayancık Turkey 41°57N 34°35E 212 B6
Ayangba Nigeria 7°31N 7°8E 263 D6
Ayapel Colombia 8°19N 75°9W 328 B2
Ayas Turkey 40°2N 32°21E 212 B5
Ayaviri Peru 14°50S 70°35W 330 C3
Ayazağa Turkey 41°6N 28°59E 122 B1
Āybak Afghan. 36°15N 68°5E 240 A3
Aybastı Turkey 40°41N 37°23E 212 B7
Aydarköl Uzbekistan 40°50N 67°10E 217 D7
Aydın Turkey 37°51N 27°51E 212 D2
Aydin □ Turkey 37°50N 28°0E 205 D9
Aydin Dağları Turkey 38°0N 28°0E 205 D10
Aydıncık Turkey 36°9N 33°21E 250 B4
Aydingkol Hu China 42°40N 89°15E 217 D11
Ayelu Ethiopia 10°5N 40°42E 257 E5
Ayenngré Togo 8°40N 1°1E 263 D5
Ayer U.S.A. 42°34N 71°35W 313 D13
Ayer Chawan, Pulau Singapore 1°16N 103°41E 138 B2
Ayer Hitam Malaysia 5°24N 100°16E 237 c
Ayer Merbau, Pulau Singapore 1°16N 103°42E 138 B2
Ayerbe Spain 42°17N 0°41W 196 C4
Ayer's Cliff Canada 45°10N 72°3W 313 A12
Ayers Rock = Uluru Australia 25°23S 131°5E 279 E5
Ayeyarwady = Irrawaddy → Burma 15°50N 95°6E 241 G5
Áyia Napa Cyprus 34°59N 34°0E 207 F10
Áyia Phyla Cyprus 34°43N 33°1E 207 F9
Áyios Amvrósios Cyprus 35°20N 33°35E 207 E9
Áyios Seryios Cyprus 35°12N 33°53E 207 E9
Áyios Theodhoros Cyprus 35°22N 34°1E 207 E10
Áyios Yeóryios = Aghios Georgios Greece 37°28N 23°57E 204 D5
Aykhal Russia 66°0N 111°30E 215 C12
Aykino Russia 62°15N 49°56E 186 B8
Aykirikçi Turkey 39°8N 30°9E 205 B12
Aylesbury U.K. 51°49N 0°49W 169 F7
Aylmer Canada 42°46N 80°59W 312 D4
Aylmer, L. Canada 64°5N 108°30W 294 E10
'Ayn al Ghazālah Libya 32°10N 23°20E 258 B4
Ayn Dār Si. Arabia 25°55N 49°10E 247 E7
Ayn Sifnī Iraq 36°41N 43°20E 213 D10
Ayn Zālah Iraq 36°45N 42°35E 213 D10
Ayna Spain 38°34N 2°3W 197 G2
Aynāt Yemen 16°4N 49°9E 249 C5
'Aynūnah Si. Arabia 28°5N 35°8E 251 K6
Ayod South Sudan 8°7N 31°26E 257 F3
Ayolas Paraguay 27°10S 56°59W 334 B4
Ayon, Ostrov Russia 69°50N 169°0E 215 C17
Ayora Spain 39°3N 1°3W 197 F3
Ayorou Niger 14°53N 1°0E 263 C5
Ayos Cameroon 3°53N 12°31E 264 B2
'Ayoûn el 'Atroûs Mauritania 16°38N 9°37W 262 B3
Ayr Queens., Australia 19°35S 147°25E 280 B4
Ayr Ont., Canada 43°17N 80°27W 312 C4
Ayr S. Ayrs., U.K. 55°28N 4°38W 167 F4
Ayr → U.K. 55°28N 4°38W 167 F4
Ayrancı Turkey 37°21N 33°41E 212 D5
Ayrancılar Turkey 38°15N 27°18E 205 C9
Ayre, Pt. of I. of Man 54°25N 4°21W 168 C3
Ayribaba Turkmenistan 37°50N 66°34E 217 E7
Aysha Ethiopia 10°50N 42°23E 257 E5
Ayton Australia 15°56S 145°22E 280 B4
Aytos Bulgaria 42°42N 27°16E 203 D11
Aytoska Planina Bulgaria 42°45N 27°30E 203 D11
Ayu, Kepulauan Indonesia 0°35N 131°5E 231 D8
Ayutla Guatemala 14°40N 92°10W 320 D1
Ayutla de los Libres Mexico 16°54N 99°13W 319 D5
Ayutthaya = Phra Nakhon Si Ayutthaya Thailand 14°25N 100°30E 236 E3
Ayvacık Turkey 39°36N 26°24E 212 C2
Ayvalık Turkey 39°20N 26°46E 205 B8
Az Zabadānī Syria 33°43N 36°5E 250 E7
Aẓ Ẓāhirah □ Oman 22°40N 56°0E 249 B7
Aẓ Ẓāhirīyah West Bank 31°25N 34°58E 251 G5
Aẓ Ẓahrān Si. Arabia 26°10N 50°7E 247 E6
Az Zarqā Jordan 32°5N 36°4E 251 F7
Az Zarqā' U.A.E. 24°53N 53°4E 247 E7
Az Zāwiyah Libya 32°52N 12°56E 258 B2
Az Zāwiyah □ Libya 32°44N 12°43E 261 B7
Az Zaydīyah Yemen 15°20N 43°1E 248 D3
Az Zībār Iraq 36°52N 44°4E 213 D11
Az Zilfī Si. Arabia 26°12N 44°52E 246 E5
Az Zubayr Iraq 30°26N 47°40E 246 D5
Az Zuhrah Yemen 15°44N 43°0E 248 D3
Az Zuqur Yemen 14°0N 42°45E 248 D3
Az Zuwaytīnah Libya 30°58N 20°7E 258 B4
Azabu Tokyo, Japan 140 c3
Azad Kashmir □ Pakistan 33°50N 73°50E 243 C5
Azahar, Costa del Spain 40°0N 0°5E 196 F5
Azambuja Portugal 39°4N 8°51W 195 F2
Azamgarh India 26°5N 83°13E 243 F10
Azangaro Peru 14°55S 70°13W 330 C3
Azaoua Niger 15°50N 4°0E 263 B5
Azaouad Mali 19°0N 3°0W 262 B4
Azaouak → Mali 15°30N 3°18E 263 B5
Azaouak, Vallée de l' Mali 15°50N 3°20E 263 B5
Āzār Shahr Iran 37°45N 45°59E 213 D11
Azara Nigeria 8°22N 9°12E 263 D6
Azarān Iran 37°25N 47°16E 213 D12
Azärbayjan = Azerbaijan ■ Asia 40°20N 48°0E 191 K9
Āzarbāyjān-e Gharbī □ Iran 37°0N 44°30E 246 B5
Āzarbāyjān-e Sharqī □ Iran 37°20N 47°0E 246 B5
Azare Nigeria 11°55N 10°10E 263 C7
Azay-le-Rideau France 47°16N 0°30E 172 E7
A'zāz Syria 36°36N 37°4E 250 B8
Azazga Algeria 36°48N 4°22E 261 A5
Azbine = Aïr Niger 18°30N 8°0E 259 E1
Azcapotzalco Mexico 19°28N 99°10W 128 B1
Azefal Mauritania 21°0N 14°45W 260 D2
Azeffoun Algeria 36°51N 4°26E 261 A5
Azemmour Morocco 33°20N 9°20W 260 B3
Azennezal Algeria 22°58N 0°43E 261 D5
Azerbaijan ■ Asia 40°20N 48°0E 191 K9
Azezo Ethiopia 12°28N 37°15E 257 E4
Azkoien = Peralta Spain 42°20N 1°48W 196 C3
Aznalcóllar Spain 37°32N 6°17W 195 H4
Azogues Ecuador 2°35S 78°0W 328 D2
Azores = Açores, Is. dos Atl. Oc. 38°0N 27°0W 153 d1
Azores-Biscay Rise Atl. Oc. 42°0N 20°0W 152 B9
Azoum, B. → Chad 10°53N 20°15E 259 F4
Azov Russia 47°3N 39°25E 191 G4
Azov, Sea of Europe 46°0N 36°30E 189 J9
Azovskoye More = Azov, Sea of Europe 46°0N 36°30E 189 J9
Azpeitia Spain 43°12N 2°19W 196 B2
Azrak, B. → Chad 10°52N 20°35E 259 F4
Azraq ash Shīshān Jordan 31°50N 36°49E 251 G7
Azrou Morocco 33°28N 5°19W 260 B3
Aztec U.S.A. 36°49N 107°59W 305 H10
Azteca, Estadia Mexico 19°19N 99°9W 128 C2
Azua de Compostela Dom. Rep. 18°25N 70°44W 321 C5
Azuaga Spain 38°16N 5°39W 195 G5
Azuara Spain 41°15N 0°53W 196 D4
Azuay □ Ecuador 2°55S 79°0W 328 D2
Azucar, Cerro Pan de Chile 33°19S 70°41W 137 A1
Azuer → Spain 39°8N 3°36W 195 F7
Azuero, Pen. de Panama 7°30N 80°30W 320 E3
Azuga Romania 45°27N 25°33E 183 E10
Azul Argentina 36°42S 59°43W 334 D4
Azul, Lagoa Azores 37°52N 25°47W 153 d3
Azul, Serra Brazil 14°50S 54°50W 331 C7
Azumino Japan 36°20N 137°50E 223 A9
Azur, Côte d' France 43°25N 7°10E 175 E11
Azurduy Bolivia 19°59S 64°29W 331 D5
Azusa U.S.A. 34°8N 117°52W 307 L9
Azzaba Algeria 36°48N 7°6E 261 A6
Azzano Décimo Italy 45°52N 12°56E 199 C9
Azzel Matti, Sebkra Algeria 26°10N 0°43E 261 C5


## B


Ba Be △ Vietnam 22°25N 105°37E 236 A5
Ba Don Vietnam 17°45N 106°26E 236 D6
Ba Dong Vietnam 9°40N 106°33E 237 H6
Ba Ngoi Vietnam 11°54N 109°10E 237 G7
Ba Ria Vietnam 10°30N 107°10E 237 G6
Ba Tri Vietnam 10°2N 106°36E 237 G6
Ba Vi △ Vietnam 21°1N 105°22E 236 B5
Ba Xian = Bazhou China 39°8N 116°22E 226 E9
Baa Indonesia 10°50S 123°0E 278 B3
Baalbek = Ba'labakk Lebanon 34°0N 36°10E 250 E7
Baambrugge Neths. 52°15N 4°59E 112 B2
Baamonde Spain 43°7N 7°44W 194 B3
Baao Phil. 13°27N 123°22E 232 E4
Baardheere Somalia 2°20N 42°27E 267 D5
Baarle-Nassau Belgium 51°27N 4°56E 170 C4
Bab el Mandeb Red Sea 12°35N 43°25E 248 D3
Baba Bulgaria 42°44N 23°59E 202 D7
Baba, B. do Angola 14°50S 12°14E 265 E2
Bābā, Koh-i- Afghan. 34°30N 67°0E 240 B2
Baba Budan Hills India 13°30N 75°44E 245 H2
Baba Burnu Turkey 39°29N 26°2E 205 B8
Baba Channel Pakistan 24°48N 66°58E 123 B1
Baba dag Azerbaijan 41°0N 48°19E 191 K9
Baba I. Pakistan 24°49N 66°57E 123 B1
Bābā Kalū Iran 30°7N 50°49E 247 D6
Babaçulândia Brazil 7°13S 47°46W 332 C2
Babadag Romania 44°53N 28°44E 183 F13
Babadağ Turkey 37°49N 28°52E 205 D10
Babaeski Turkey 41°26N 27°6E 203 E11
Babahoyo Ecuador 1°40S 79°30W 328 D2
Babai = Sarju → India 27°21N 81°23E 243 F9
Babai → Nepal 28°10N 82°21E 243 E10
Babak Phil. 7°8N 125°41E 233 H5
Babana Nigeria 10°31N 3°46E 263 C5
Babanusa Sudan 11°20N 27°48E 257 E2
Babar Algeria 35°10N 7°6E 261 A6
Babar Indonesia 8°0S 129°30E 231 F7
Babar Pakistan 31°7N 69°32E 242 D3
Babarkach Pakistan 29°45N 68°0E 242 E3
Babarpur India 28°41N 77°16E 120 A2
Babase I. Papua N. G. 4°0S 153°42E 286 B7
Babayevo Russia 59°24N 35°55E 188 C8
Babb U.S.A. 48°51N 113°27W 304 B7
Babelthuap Palau 7°30N 134°30E 288 c
Babenhausen Germany 49°57N 8°57E 179 F4
Băbeni Romania 44°59N 24°11E 183 F9
Baberu India 25°33N 80°43E 243 G9
Babi Indonesia 2°5N 96°39E 234 B1
Babi Besar, Pulau Malaysia 2°25N 103°59E 237 L4
Babia Gora Europe 49°38N 19°38E 185 J6
Babian Jiang → China 22°55N 101°47E 228 F3
Bābil □ Iraq 32°30N 44°30E 246 C5
Babile Ethiopia 9°16N 42°11E 257 F5
Babile ⌓ Ethiopia 8°45N 42°20E 267 C5
Babimost Poland 52°10N 15°49E 185 F2
Babinda Australia 17°20S 145°56E 280 B4
Babine Canada 55°22N 126°37W 296 B3
Babine → Canada 55°45N 127°44W 296 B3
Babine L. Canada 54°48N 126°0W 296 C3
Babiogórski △ Poland 49°38N 19°39E 185 J6
Babo Indonesia 2°30S 133°30E 231 E8
Babócsa Hungary 46°2N 17°21E 182 D2
Bābol Iran 36°40N 52°50E 247 B7
Bābol Sar Iran 36°45N 52°45E 247 B7
Babor, Dj. Algeria 36°31N 5°25E 261 A6
Baborów Poland 50°7N 18°1E 185 H5
Baboua C.A.R. 5°49N 14°58E 264 A2
Babruysk Belarus 53°10N 29°15E 177 B15
Babson Park U.S.A. 27°49N 81°32W 317 H8
Babuhri India 26°49N 69°43E 242 F3
Babuna Macedonia 41°30N 21°40E 202 E5
Babura Nigeria 12°51N 8°59E 263 C6
Babusar Pass Pakistan 35°12N 73°59E 243 B5
Babushkin Russia 55°51N 37°42E 129 A3
Babušnica Serbia 43°7N 22°27E 202 C6
Babuyan Phil. 10°0N 118°54E 233 F2
Babuyan Chan. Phil. 18°40N 121°30E 232 B3
Babuyan I. Phil. 19°32N 121°57E 232 B3
Babuyan Is. Phil. 19°10N 121°40E 232 B3
Babylon Iraq 32°34N 44°22E 213 F11
Bač Serbia 45°29N 19°17E 182 E4
Bâc → Moldova 46°55N 29°26E 183 D14
Bac Can Vietnam 22°8N 105°49E 228 F5
Bac Giang Vietnam 21°16N 106°11E 228 G6
Bac Lieu Vietnam 9°17N 105°43E 237 H5
Bac Ninh Vietnam 21°13N 106°4E 228 G6
Bac Phan Vietnam 22°0N 105°0E 228 G5
Bacaadweyn Somalia 7°15N 47°40E 267 C6
Bacabal Brazil 4°15S 44°45W 332 B3
Bacacay Phil. 13°18N 123°47E 232 E4
Bacajá → Brazil 3°25S 51°50W 329 D7
Bacalar Mexico 18°43N 88°27W 319 D7
Bacan, Kepulauan Indonesia 0°35S 127°30E 231 E7
Bacarra Phil. 18°15N 120°37E 232 B3
Bacău Romania 46°35N 26°55E 183 D11
Bacău □ Romania 46°30N 26°45E 183 D11
Baccarat France 48°28N 6°42E 173 D13
Bacchus Marsh Australia 37°43S 144°27E 282 D6
Bacerac Mexico 30°18N 108°50W 318 A3
Băceşti Romania 46°50N 27°11E 183 D12
Bach Long Vi, Dao Vietnam 20°10N 107°40E 236 B6
Bach Ma △ Vietnam 16°11N 107°49E 236 D6
Bachaquero Venezuela 9°56N 71°8W 328 B3
Bacharach Germany 50°3N 7°44E 179 E3
Bachelor's Beach Bonaire 12°11N 68°18W 322 h
Bachhwara India 25°35N 85°54E 243 G11
Bachu China 39°46N 78°34E 217 E9
Bachuma Ethiopia 6°48N 35°53E 257 F4
Bačina Serbia 43°42N 21°23E 202 C5
Back → Canada 65°10N 104°0W 294 D11
Back B. India 18°56N 72°48E 130 B1
Bačka Palanka Serbia 45°17N 19°27E 182 E4
Bačka Topola Serbia 45°49N 19°39E 182 E4
Bäckebo Sweden 56°53N 16°4E 163 H10
Bäckefors Sweden 58°48N 12°9E 163 F6
Bäckhammar Sweden 59°10N 14°11E 162 E8
Bački Petrovac Serbia 45°29N 19°32E 182 E4
Backnang Germany 48°56N 9°26E 179 G5
Backstairs Passage Australia 35°40S 138°5E 282 C3
Baclaran Phil. 14°31N 121°0E 127 B2
Bacnotan Phil. 16°43N 120°21E 232 C3
Baco, Mt. Phil. 12°49N 121°10E 232 E3
Bacolod Phil. 10°40N 122°57E 233 F4
Bacon Phil. 13°3N 124°3E 232 E5
Baconton U.S.A. 31°23N 84°10W 316 D5
Bacoor Phil. 14°27N 120°56E 127 C1
Bacoor B. Phil. 14°27N 120°54E 127 C1
Bacqueville-en-Caux France 49°47N 1°0E 172 C8
Bács-Kiskun □ Hungary 46°43N 19°30E 182 D4
Bácsalmás Hungary 46°8N 19°17E 182 D4
Bacuag = Placer Phil. 9°36N 125°38E 233 G5
Bacuit = El Nido Phil. 11°10N 119°25E 233 F2
Bacuk Malaysia 6°4N 102°25E 237 J4
Bácum Mexico 27°33N 110°5W 318 B2
Bād Iran 33°41N 52°1E 247 C7
Bad → U.S.A. 44°21N 100°22W 308 C3
Bad Aussee Austria 47°43N 13°45E 180 D6
Bad Axe U.S.A. 43°48N 83°0W 312 C2
Bad Bergzabern Germany 49°6N 7°59E 179 F3
Bad Berleburg Germany 51°2N 8°26E 178 D4
Bad Bevensen Germany 53°5N 10°35E 178 B6
Bad Bramstedt Germany 53°55N 9°53E 178 B5
Bad Brückenau Germany 50°18N 9°47E 179 E5
Bad Doberan Germany 54°6N 11°53E 178 A7
Bad Driburg Germany 51°43N 9°1E 178 D5
Bad Ems Germany 50°20N 7°43E 179 E3
Bad Frankenhausen Germany 51°21N 11°5E 178 D7
Bad Freienwalde Germany 52°46N 14°1E 178 C10
Bad Goisern Austria 47°38N 13°38E 180 D6
Bad Harzburg Germany 51°52N 10°34E 178 D6
Bad Hersfeld Germany 50°52N 9°42E 178 E5
Bad Hofgastein Austria 47°17N 13°6E 180 D6
Bad Homburg Germany 50°13N 8°38E 179 E4
Bad Honnef Germany 50°38N 7°13E 178 E3
Bad Iburg Germany 52°10N 8°3E 178 C4
Bad Ischl Austria 47°44N 13°38E 180 D6
Bad Kissingen Germany 50°11N 10°4E 179 E6
Bad Königshofen Germany 50°17N 10°28E 179 E6
Bad Kreuznach Germany 49°50N 7°51E 179 F3
Bad Krozingen Germany 47°54N 7°42E 179 H3
Bad Kudowa = Kudowa-Zdrój Poland 50°27N 16°15E 185 H3
Bad Laasphe Germany 50°56N 8°25E 178 E4
Bad Landeck = Lądek-Zdrój Poland 50°21N 16°53E 185 H3
Bad Langensalza Germany 51°5N 10°38E 178 D6
Bad Lauterberg Germany 51°38N 10°28E 178 D6
Bad Leonfelden Austria 48°31N 14°18E 180 C7
Bad Liebenwerda Germany 51°31N 13°24E 178 D9
Bad Mergentheim Germany 49°28N 9°42E 179 F5
Bad Münstereifel Germany 50°33N 6°46E 178 E2
Bad Nauheim Germany 50°21N 8°43E 179 E4
Bad Neuenahr-Ahrweiler Germany 50°32N 7°5E 178 E3
Bad Neustadt Germany 50°18N 10°13E 179 E6
Bad Oeynhausen Germany 52°12N 8°46E 178 C4
Bad Oldesloe Germany 53°48N 10°22E 178 B6
Bad Orb Germany 50°12N 9°22E 179 E5
Bad Polzin = Polanica-Zdrój Poland 50°24N 16°32E 185 H3
Bad Pyrmont Germany 51°59N 9°16E 178 D5
Bad Reichenhall Germany 47°43N 12°54E 179 H8
Bad Reinerz = Duszniki-Zdrój Poland 50°24N 16°24E 185 H3
Bad Säckingen Germany 47°33N 7°56E 179 H3
Bad Salzuflen Germany 52°5N 8°45E 178 C4
Bad Salzungen Germany 50°48N 10°14E 178 E6
Bad Sankt Leonhard Austria 46°58N 14°47E 180 E7
Bad Schönfliess = Trzcińsko Zdrój Poland 52°58N 14°35E 185 F1
Bad Schwartau Germany 53°55N 10°41E 178 B6
Bad Segeberg Germany 53°56N 10°17E 178 B6
Bad Tölz Germany 47°45N 11°34E 179 H7
Bad Urach Germany 48°29N 9°23E 179 G5
Bad Vöslau Austria 47°58N 16°12E 181 D9
Bad Waldsee Germany 47°55N 9°45E 179 H5
Bad Wildungen Germany 51°6N 9°7E 178 D5
Bad Wimpfen Germany 49°13N 9°11E 179 F5
Bad Windsheim Germany 49°36N 10°25E 179 F6
Bad Zwischenahn Germany 53°12N 8°1E 178 B4
Bada Barabil India 22°7N 85°24E 243 H11
Badagara = Vadakara India 11°35N 75°40E 245 J2
Badagri Nigeria 6°25N 2°55E 263 D5
Badain Jaran Shamo China 40°23N 102°0E 218 C9
Badajós, L. Brazil 3°15S 62°50W 329 D5
Badajoz Spain 38°50N 6°59W 195 G4
Badajoz □ Spain 38°40N 6°30W 195 G4
Badakhshān □ Afghan. 36°30N 71°0E 240 A3
Badaling China 40°20N 116°0E 226 D9
Badalona Spain 41°26N 2°15E 114 A2
Badalzai Afghan. 29°50N 65°35E 242 E1
Badami India 15°55N 75°41E 245 G2
Badampahar India 22°10N 86°10E 244 C8
Badanah Si. Arabia 30°58N 41°30E 246 D4
Badarinath India 30°45N 79°30E 243 D8
Badarpur India 24°54N 92°36E 241 C4
Badas, Kepulauan Indonesia 0°45N 107°5E 234 B3
Baddo → Pakistan 28°0N 64°20E 240 D2
Bade = Pate Taiwan 24°56N 121°17E 225 B3
Bade Indonesia 7°10S 139°35E 231 F9
Badeggi Nigeria 9°1N 6°8E 263 D6
Badéguichéri Niger 14°30N 5°22E 263 C6
Baden Austria 48°1N 16°13E 181 C9
Baden Switz. 47°28N 8°18E 179 H4
Baden Pa., U.S.A. 40°38N 80°14W 312 F4
Baden-Baden Germany 48°44N 8°13E 179 G4
Baden-Württemberg □ Germany 48°20N 8°40E 179 G4
Badgam India 34°1N 74°45E 243 B6
Badgastein Austria 47°7N 13°9E 180 D6
Badger Nfld. & L., Canada 49°0N 56°4W 299 C8
Badger Calif., U.S.A. 36°38N 119°1W 306 J7
Bādghīs □ Afghan. 35°0N 63°0E 240 B1
Badgingarra △ Australia 30°23S 115°22E 279 F2
Badhoevedorp Neths. 52°20N 4°47E 112 A1
Badia Polésine Italy 45°5N 11°29E 199 C8
Badian Phil. 9°55N 123°24E 233 G4
Badiar △ Guinea 13°37N 13°11W 262 C2
Badin Pakistan 24°38N 68°54E 242 G3
Badinka ⌓ Mali 13°31N 9°28W 262 C3
Badjokola Dem. Rep. of the Congo 3°54N 20°17E 264 B4
Badlands U.S.A. 43°55N 102°30W 308 D2
Badlands △ U.S.A. 43°38N 102°56W 308 D2
Badli India 28°44N 77°8E 120 A1
Badme N. Afr. 14°43N 37°48E 248 D2
Badnera India 20°48N 77°44E 244 D3
Badoc Phil. 17°56N 120°28E 232 C3
Badogo Mali 11°2N 8°13W 262 C3
Badoumbé Mali 13°42N 10°15W 262 C2
Badr Ḥunayn Si. Arabia 23°44N 38°46E 248 B2
Badrah Iraq 33°6N 45°58E 213 F11
Badrain Jaran Shamo China 40°40N 103°20E 226 D2
Badrinath India 30°44N 79°29E 243 D8
Badu Australia 10°7S 142°11E 280 a
Badulla Sri Lanka 7°1N 81°7E 245 L5
Badung, Bukit Indonesia 8°49S 115°10E 231 K18
Badung, Selat Indonesia 8°40S 115°22E 231 K18
Badvel India 14°45N 79°3E 245 G4
Baena Spain 37°37N 4°20W 195 H6
Baengnyeongdo S. Korea 37°57N 124°40E 224 D2
Baerami Australia 32°27S 150°27E 283 B9
Bærum Norway 59°54N 10°36E 133 A2
Baetov Kyrgyzstan 41°13N 74°54E 217 D8
Baeza Ecuador 0°25S 77°53W 328 D2
Baeza Spain 37°57N 3°25W 195 H7
Bafang Cameroon 5°9N 10°11E 263 D7
Bafatá Guinea-Biss. 12°8N 14°40W 262 C2
Baffin B. N. Amer. 72°0N 64°0W 292 B13
Baffin I. Canada 68°0N 75°0W 295 D17
Bafia Cameroon 4°40N 11°10E 263 E7
Bafilo Togo 9°22N 1°22E 263 D5
Bafing □ Ivory C. 8°20N 7°40W 262 D3
Bafing → Mali 13°49N 10°50W 262 C2
Bafing △ Mali 12°38N 10°28W 262 C2
Bafliyūn Syria 36°37N 36°59E 246 B3
Bafoulabé Mali 13°50N 10°55W 262 C2
Bafoussam Cameroon 5°28N 10°25E 263 D7
Bāfq Iran 31°40N 55°25E 247 D7
Bafra Turkey 41°34N 35°54E 212 B6
Bafra Burnu Turkey 41°45N 36°2E 212 B7
Bāft Iran 29°15N 56°38E 247 D8
Bafut Cameroon 6°6N 10°2E 263 D7
Bafwasende Dem. Rep. of the Congo 1°3N 27°5E 268 B2
Bagabag Phil. 16°30N 121°15E 232 C3
Bagabag I. Papua N. G. 4°48S 146°14E 286 C4
Bagac Phil. 14°36N 120°23E 232 D3
Bagac B. Phil. 14°36N 120°20E 232 D3
Bagaha India 27°6N 84°5E 244 A7
Bagalkot India 16°10N 75°40E 245 F2
Bagam Niger 15°43N 6°35E 263 B6
Bagamanoc Phil. 13°57N 124°17E 232 E5
Bagamoyo Tanzania 6°28S 38°55E 268 D4
Bagan = Pagan Burma 21°10N 94°52E 241 E5
Bagan Datoh Malaysia 3°59N 100°47E 237 L3
Bagan Serai Malaysia 5°1N 100°32E 237 K3
Baganga Phil. 7°34N 126°33E 233 H6
Bagani Namibia 18°7S 21°41E 270 A3
Bagansiapiapi Indonesia 2°12N 100°50E 234 B2
Bagasra India 21°30N 71°0E 242 J4
Bagata Dem. Rep. of the Congo 3°44S 17°57E 264 C3
Bagaud India 22°19N 75°53E 242 H6
Bagawi Sudan 12°20N 34°18E 257 E3
Bagbag Sudan 15°23N 31°30E 257 D3
Bağcılar Turkey 41°2N 28°49E 122 B1
Bagdad Calif., U.S.A. 34°35N 115°53W 307 L11
Bagdad Fla., U.S.A. 30°36N 87°2W 317 E2
Bagdarin Russia 54°26N 113°36E 215 D12
Bagé Brazil 31°20S 54°15W 335 C5
Bagenalstown Ireland 52°42N 6°58W 166 D5
Bagepalli India 13°47N 77°47E 245 H3
Bagerhat Bangla. 22°40N 89°47E 241 D2
Bageshwar India 29°51N 79°46E 243 E8
Bagevadi India 16°35N 75°58E 244 F2
Baggao Phil. 17°56N 121°46E 232 C3
Bággio Italy 45°27N 9°6E 128 B1
Baggs U.S.A. 41°2N 107°39W 304 F10
Bagh Pakistan 33°59N 73°45E 243 C5
Bāgh-e-Feyz Iran 35°44N 51°19E 141 A1
Baghain → India 25°32N 81°1E 243 G9
Baghdād Iraq 33°20N 44°23E 113 A2
Baghdad Int. ✈ (BGW) Baghdad, Iraq 33°15N 44°14E 113 B1
Baghdadi Georgia 42°5N 42°49E 213 A10
Bagheria Italy 38°5N 13°30E 200 D6
Baghlān Afghan. 32°12N 68°46E 240 A3
Baghlān □ Afghan. 36°0N 68°30E 240 B3
Bagley U.S.A. 47°32N 95°24W 308 B6
Baglung Nepal 28°16N 83°36E 243 E10
Bagmari India 22°34N 88°23E 124 B2
Bagn Norway 60°49N 9°34E 164 D6
Bagnara Cálabra Italy 38°17N 15°48E 201 D8
Bagnasco Italy 44°18N 8°2E 198 D5
Bagnell Dam U.S.A. 38°14N 92°36W 310 F4
Bagnères-de-Bigorre France 43°5N 0°9E 174 E4
Bagnères-de-Luchon France 42°47N 0°38E 174 F4
Bagneux France 48°47N 2°18E 134 B2
Bagni di Lucca Italy 44°1N 10°35E 198 D7
Bagno di Romagna Italy 43°50N 11°57E 199 E8
Bagnoles-de-l'Orne France 48°32N 0°25W 172 D6

**Bagnolet** *France* 48°52N 2°25E **134** A3
**Bagnols-sur-Cèze** *France* 44°10N 4°36E **175** D8
**Bagnorea = Bagnoregio** *Italy* 42°37N 12°5E **199** F9
**Bagnorégio** *Italy* 42°37N 12°5E **199** F9
**Bago = Pegu** *Burma* 17°20N 96°29E **241** G6
**Bago** *Phil.* 10°32N 122°50E **233** F4
**Bagodar** *India* 24°5N 85°52E **243** G11
**Bagram ✕ (OAI)** *Afghan.* 34°57N 69°16E **240** B3
**Bagrationovsk** *Russia* 54°23N 20°39E **184** D7
**Bagrdan** *Serbia* 44°5N 21°11E **202** B5
**Bagsværd** *Denmark* 55°45N 12°27E **118** A2
**Bagsværd Sø** *Denmark* 55°46N 12°28E **118** A2
**Bagua** *Peru* 5°35S 78°22W **330** B2
**Baguiati** *India* 22°36N 88°25E **124** B2
**Baguio** *Phil.* 16°26N 120°34E **232** C3
**Bagumbayan** *Phil.* 14°28N 121°3E **127** C2
**Bağyurdu** *Turkey* 38°25N 27°41E **205** C9
**Bagzane, Monts** *Niger* 17°43N 8°45E **259** E1
**Bahabón de Esgueva** *Spain* 41°52N 3°43W **194** D7
**Bahadurabad Ghat** *Bangla.* 25°11N 89°44E **241** C2
**Bahadurganj** *India* 26°16N 87°49E **243** F12
**Bahadurgarh** *India* 28°40N 76°57E **242** E7
**Baha'i Temple** *U.S.A.* 42°4N 87°41W **119** A2
**Bahaja** *Somalia* 11°16N 49°50E **267** B6
**Baham, Pte.** *Martinique* 14°24N 60°50W **322** j
**Bahama, Canal Viejo de** *W. Indies* 22°10N 77°30W **320** B4
**Bahamas ■** *N. Amer.* 24°0N 75°0W **321** B5
**Bahār** *Iran* 34°54N 48°26E **213** E13
**Bahārak** *Afghan.* 37°0N 70°53E **240** A3
**Baharampur** *India* 24°2N 88°27E **243** G13
**Bahariya, El Wâhât al** *Egypt* 28°0N 28°50E **256** B2
**Baharu Pandan = Pandan** *Malaysia* 1°32N 103°46E **237** d
**Bahawalnagar** *Pakistan* 30°0N 73°15E **242** E5
**Bahawalpur** *Pakistan* 29°24N 71°40E **242** E4
**Bahçe** *Turkey* 37°13N 36°34E **212** D7
**Bahçecik** *Turkey* 40°41N 29°44E **203** F13
**Bahçeköy** *Turkey* 41°10N 28°59E **122** A1
**Bahçelievler** *Turkey* 41°0N 28°50E **122** B1
**Baheli** *Phil.* 10°0N 118°47E **233** F2
**Bäherden** *Turkmenistan* 38°25N 57°26E **247** B8
**Baheri** *India* 28°45N 79°34E **243** E8
**Bahgul →** *India* 27°45N 79°36E **243** F8
**Bahi** *Tanzania* 5°58S 35°21E **268** D4
**Bahi Swamp** *Tanzania* 6°10S 35°0E **268** D4
**Bahia = Salvador** *Brazil* 13°0S 38°30W **333** D4
**Bahia □** *Brazil* 12°0S 42°0W **333** D3
**Bahía, Is. de la** *Honduras* 16°45N 86°15W **320** C2
**Bahía Blanca** *Argentina* 38°35S 62°13W **334** D3
**Bahía de Caráquez** *Ecuador* 0°40S 80°27W **328** D1
**Bahía de Los Angeles** *Mexico* 28°56N 113°34W **318** B2
**Bahía Honda** *Cuba* 22°54N 83°10W **320** B3
**Bahía Kino** *Mexico* 28°47N 111°58W **318** B2
**Bahía Laura** *Argentina* 48°10S 66°30W **336** C3
**Bahía Mansa** *Chile* 40°33S 73°46W **336** B2
**Bahía Negra** *Paraguay* 20°5S 58°5W **331** E6
**Bahía Solano** *Colombia* 6°14N 77°25W **328** B2
**Bahir Dar** *Ethiopia* 11°37N 37°10E **257** E4
**Bahlā'** *Oman* 22°58N 57°18E **249** B7
**Bahmanzād** *Iran* 31°15N 51°47E **247** D6
**Bahmer** *Algeria* 27°32N 0°10W **261** C4
**Bahr el Ahmar □** *Egypt* 28°40N 31°30E **251** K2
**Bahr el Ahmar □** *Sudan* 20°0N 35°0E **256** D4
**Bahr el Ghazal = Kanem □** *Chad* 15°0N 15°0E **259** F3
**Bahr el Jebel = Central Equatoria □** *South Sudan* 4°0N 31°0E **257** G3
**Bahraich** *India* 27°38N 81°37E **243** F9
**Bahrain ■** *Asia* 26°0N 50°35E **247** E6
**Bahror** *India* 27°51N 76°20E **242** F7
**Bahtîm** *Egypt* 30°8N 31°16E **117** A2
**Bāhū Kalāt** *Iran* 25°43N 61°25E **247** E9
**Bai** *Mali* 13°35N 3°28W **262** C4
**Bai Bung, Mui = Ca Mau, Mui** *Vietnam* 8°38N 104°44E **237** H5
**Bai Thuong** *Vietnam* 19°54N 105°23E **236** C5
**Baia de Aramă** *Romania* 45°0N 22°50E **182** E7
**Baía dos Tigres** *Angola* 16°40S 11°47E **265** F2
**Baía Farta** *Angola* 12°40S 13°11E **265** E2
**Baia Mare** *Romania* 47°40N 23°35E **183** C8
**Baia-Sprie** *Romania* 47°41N 23°43E **183** C8
**Baião** *Brazil* 2°40S 49°40W **332** B2
**Baïbokoum** *Chad* 7°46N 15°43E **259** G2
**Baicheng** *Jilin, China* 45°38N 122°42E **227** B12
**Baicheng** *Xinjiang Uygur, China* 41°46N 81°52E **217** D10
**Băicoi** *Romania* 45°3N 25°52E **183** E10
**Baidoa = Baydhabo** *Somalia* 3°8N 43°30E **267** D5
**Baie-Comeau** *Canada* 49°12N 68°10W **299** C6
**Baie du Cap** *Mauritius* 20°29S 57°22E **272** e
**Baie-Mahault** *Guadeloupe* 16°16N 61°35W **322** e
**Baie-St-Paul** *Canada* 47°28N 70°32W **299** C5
**Baie Ste-Anne** *Seychelles* 4°18S 55°45E **272** c
**Baie-Trinité** *Canada* 49°25N 67°20W **299** C6
**Baie Verte** *Canada* 49°55N 56°12W **299** C8
**Baignes-Ste-Radegonde** *France* 45°23N 0°25W **174** C3
**Baigneux-les-Juifs** *France* 47°31N 4°39E **173** E11
**Baihar** *India* 22°6N 80°33E **243** H9
**Baihe = Paiho** *Taiwan* 23°21N 120°25E **225** C2
**Baihe** *Hubei, China* 32°50N 110°5E **229** A8
**Baihe** *Jilin, China* 42°27N 128°9E **227** C15
**Baihetan Dam** *China* 27°11N 102°54E **228** D4
**Ba'ījī** *Iraq* 35°0N 43°30E **213** E10
**Baijnath** *India* 29°55N 79°37E **243** E8
**Baikal, L. = Baykal, Oz.** *Russia* 53°0N 108°0E **215** D11
**Baikonur = Bayqonyr** *Kazakhstan* 45°40N 63°20E **216** C6
**Baikunthpur** *India* 23°15N 82°33E **243** H10
**Bailadila, Mt.** *India* 18°43N 81°15E **244** E5
**Baile Átha Cliath = Dublin** *Ireland* 53°21N 6°15W **120** A2
**Baile Átha Fhirdhia = Ardee** *Ireland* 53°52N 6°33W **166** C5
**Baile Átha Í = Athy** *Ireland* 53°0N 7°0W **166** C5
**Baile Átha Luain = Athlone** *Ireland* 53°25N 7°56W **166** C4
**Baile Átha Troim = Trim** *Ireland* 53°33N 6°48W **166** C5
**Baile Brigín = Balbriggan** *Ireland* 53°37N 6°11W **166** C5
**Băile Govora** *Romania* 45°5N 24°11E **183** E9
**Băile Herculane** *Romania* 44°53N 22°26E **182** F7
**Băile Olăneşti** *Romania* 45°12N 24°14E **183** E9
**Baile Sear = Baleshare** *U.K.* 57°31N 7°22W **167** D1
**Băile Tuşnad** *Romania* 46°9N 25°51E **183** D10
**Bailén** *Spain* 38°8N 3°48W **195** G7
**Băileşti** *Romania* 44°1N 23°20E **183** F8
**Baileys Crossroads** *U.S.A.* 38°50N 77°6W **143** B2
**Bailhongal** *India* 15°55N 74°53E **245** G2
**Bailieborough** *Ireland* 53°56N 6°59W **166** C5
**Bailique, Ilha** *Brazil* 1°2N 49°58W **332** A2
**Baille-Argent** *Guadeloupe* 16°15N 61°48W **322** e
**Baillif** *Guadeloupe* 16°1N 61°44W **322** e
**Bailly** *France* 48°50N 2°4E **134** A1
**Bailugh** *Afghan.* 32°40N 66°47E **240** B2
**Bailundo = Luau** *Angola* 10°40S 22°10E **265** E4
**Bailundo** *Angola* 12°10S 15°50E **265** E3
**Baima** *China* 33°0N 100°26E **228** A3
**Baimuru** *Papua N. G.* 7°35S 144°51E **286** D3
**Bain-de-Bretagne** *France* 47°50N 1°40W **172** E5
**Bainbridge** *Ga., U.S.A.* 30°55N 84°35W **316** E5
**Bainbridge** *Ind., U.S.A.* 39°46N 86°49W **311** E10
**Bainbridge** *N.Y., U.S.A.* 42°18N 75°29W **313** D9
**Bainbridge** *Ohio, U.S.A.* 39°14N 83°16W **311** E13
**Bainbridge Island** *U.S.A.* 47°38N 122°32W **306** C4
**Baine** *China* 42°0N 128°0E **219** C14
**Baing** *Indonesia* 10°14S 120°34E **231** F6
**Bainiu** *China* 32°50N 112°15E **229** A9
**Bainyik** *Papua N. G.* 3°40S 143°4E **286** B2
**Baiona** *Spain* 42°6N 8°52W **194** C2
**Bā'ir** *Jordan* 30°45N 36°55E **251** H7
**Bā'ir, W. →** *Jordan* 30°59N 37°24E **251** H8
**Baird Mts.** *U.S.A.* 67°0N 160°0W **303** C7
**Bairiki = Tarawa** *Kiribati* 1°30N 173°0E **288** G9
**Bairin Youqi** *China* 43°30N 118°35E **227** C10
**Bairin Zuoqi** *China* 43°58N 119°15E **227** C10
**Bairnsdale** *Australia* 37°48S 147°36E **283** D7
**Bairro Alto** *Lisbon, Portugal* **126** c1
**Bairro Lopes** *Lisbon, Portugal* **126** b3
**Bais** *Phil.* 9°35N 123°7E **233** G4
**Baisha** *Guangdong, China* 23°8N 113°11E **121** B2
**Baisha** *Henan, China* 34°20N 112°32E **226** G7
**Baisha Li** *China* 19°12N 109°20E **229** a
**Baishan = Hunjiang** *China* 41°54N 126°26E **224** B3
**Baishan** *China* 42°43N 127°14E **227** C14
**Baissa** *Nigeria* 7°14N 10°38E **263** D7
**Baitadi** *Nepal* 29°35N 80°25E **243** E9
**Baitarani →** *India* 20°45N 86°48E **244** D8
**Baixa** *Lisbon, Portugal* **126** c2
**Baixa Grande** *Brazil* 11°57S 40°11W **333** D3
**Baixa Limia-Sierra do Xurés △** *Spain* 41°59N 8°2W **194** D2
**Baixo-Longa** *Angola* 15°41S 18°45E **265** F3
**Baiyer River** *Papua N. G.* 5°32S 144°9E **286** C3
**Baiyin** *China* 36°45N 104°14E **226** F3
**Baiyü** *China* 31°16N 98°50E **228** B2
**Baiyu Shan** *China* 37°15N 107°30E **226** F4
**Baiyuda** *Sudan* 17°35N 32°07E **256** D3
**Baiyun** *China* 23°11N 113°16E **121** A2
**Baiyun Mountain Scenic Area** *China* 23°11N 113°17E **121** A2
**Baj Baj** *India* 22°30N 88°5E **243** H13
**Baja** *Hungary* 46°12N 18°59E **182** D3
**Baja, Pta.** *Easter I., Chile* 27°10S 109°22W **330** b
**Baja, Pta.** *Baja Calif., Mexico* 29°58N 115°49W **318** B1
**Baja California** *Mexico* 31°10N 115°12W **318** A1
**Baja California □** *Mexico* 30°0N 115°0W **318** B2
**Baja California Sur □** *Mexico* 25°50N 111°50W **318** B2
**Bajag** *India* 22°40N 81°21E **243** H9
**Bajamar** *Canary Is.* 28°33N 16°20W **153** e1
**Bajana** *India* 23°7N 71°49E **242** H4
**Bajatrejo** *Indonesia* 8°29S 114°19E **231** J17
**Bajawa** *Indonesia* 8°47S 120°59E **231** F6
**Bajera** *Indonesia* 8°31S 115°2E **231** J18
**Bājgīrān** *Iran* 37°36N 58°24E **247** B8
**Bājil** *Yemen* 15°4N 43°17E **248** D3
**Bajimba, Mt.** *Australia* 29°17S 152°6E **281** D5
**Bajina Bašta** *Serbia* 43°58N 19°35E **202** C3
**Bajmok** *Serbia* 45°57N 19°24E **182** E4
**Bajo Boquete** *Panama* 8°46N 82°27W **320** E3
**Bajo Caracoles** *Argentina* 47°27S 70°56W **336** C2
**Bajo Nuevo** *Caribbean* 15°40N 78°50W **320** C4
**Bajoga** *Nigeria* 10°57N 11°20E **263** C7
**Bajool** *Australia* 23°40S 150°35E **280** C5
**Bak** *Hungary* 46°43N 16°51E **182** D1
**Bakala** *C.A.R.* 6°15N 20°20E **264** A4
**Bakar** *Croatia* 45°18N 14°32E **199** C11
**Bakassi Pen.** *Cameroon* 4°42N 8°20E **263** E6
**Bakel** *Senegal* 14°56N 12°20W **262** C2
**Baker** *Calif., U.S.A.* 35°16N 116°4W **307** K10
**Baker** *Fla., U.S.A.* 30°48N 86°41W **317** E3
**Baker** *Mont., U.S.A.* 46°22N 104°17W **304** C11
**Baker, Canal** *Chile* 47°45S 74°45W **336** C2
**Baker, L.** *Canada* 64°0N 96°0W **294** E12
**Baker, Mt.** *U.S.A.* 48°50N 121°49W **304** B3
**Baker City** *U.S.A.* 44°47N 117°50W **304** D5
**Baker I.** *Pac. Oc.* 0°10N 176°35W **277** A15
**Baker I.** *Alaska, U.S.A.* 55°20N 133°40W **296** B2
**Baker L.** *Australia* 26°54S 126°5E **279** E4
**Baker Lake** *Canada* 64°20N 96°3W **294** E12
**Bakere** *Dem. Rep. of the Congo* 1°36N 23°50E **264** B4
**Bakerhill** *U.S.A.* 31°47N 85°18W **316** D4
**Bakers Creek** *Australia* 21°13S 149°7E **280** C4
**Bakers Dozen Is.** *Canada* 56°45N 78°45W **298** A4
**Bakersfield** *Calif., U.S.A.* 35°23N 119°1W **307** K8
**Bakersfield** *Vt., U.S.A.* 44°45N 72°48W **313** B12
**Bakharden = Bäherden** *Turkmenistan* 38°25N 57°26E **247** B8
**Bakhchysaray** *Ukraine* 44°40N 33°45E **189** K7
**Bakhmach** *Ukraine* 51°10N 32°45E **189** G7
**Bakhmut = Artemovsk** *Ukraine* 48°35N 38°0E **189** H9
**Bākhtarān = Kermānshāh** *Iran* 34°23N 47°0E **213** E12
**Bākhtarān = Kermānshāh □** *Iran* 34°0N 46°30E **246** C5
**Bakhtegān, Daryācheh-ye** *Iran* 29°40N 53°50E **247** D7
**Bakhtegān △** *Iran* 29°51N 53°40E **247** D7
**Baki = Krasnyye Baki** *Russia* 57°8N 45°10E **190** B7
**Bakı** *Azerbaijan* 40°29N 49°56E **191** K9
**Baki** *Somalia* 10°30N 43°8E **267** B5
**Bakır →** *Turkey* 38°55N 27°0E **205** C9
**Bakırdağı** *Turkey* 38°13N 35°46E **212** C6
**Bakırköy** *Turkey* 40°58N 28°52E **122** C1
**Bakkafjörður** *Iceland* 66°2N 14°48W **155** A12
**Bakkaflói** *Iceland* 66°10N 14°45W **155** A12
**Bakkagerði** *Iceland* 65°31N 13°49W **155** B13
**Baklan** *Turkey* 38°0N 29°36E **205** C11
**Bako** *Ethiopia* 5°51N 36°23E **257** F4
**Bako** *Ivory C.* 9°8N 7°40W **262** D3
**Bako △** *Malaysia* 1°43N 110°28E **235** B4
**Bakony** *Hungary* 47°10N 17°30E **182** C2
**Bakony Forest = Bakony** *Hungary* 47°10N 17°30E **182** C2
**Bakool □** *Somalia* 4°0N 44°0E **267** D5
**Bakori** *Nigeria* 11°34N 7°25E **263** C6
**Bakouma** *C.A.R.* 5°40N 22°56E **264** A4
**Baksan** *Russia* 43°42N 43°32E **191** J6
**Bakswaho** *India* 24°15N 79°18E **243** G8
**Baku = Bakı** *Azerbaijan* 40°29N 49°56E **191** K9
**Bakun Dam** *Malaysia* 2°50N 113°50E **235** B4
**Bakundi** *Nigeria* 8°2N 10°45E **263** D7
**Bakung** *Indonesia* 0°5N 104°26E **234** B2
**Bakungan** *Indonesia* 2°55N 97°28E **234** B1
**Bakuriani** *Georgia* 41°44N 43°31E **213** B10
**Bakutis Coast** *Antarctica* 74°0S 120°0W **151** D15
**Bakwa-Kenge** *Dem. Rep. of the Congo* 4°51S 22°4E **265** C4
**Bakwanga = Mbuji-Mayi** *Dem. Rep. of the Congo* 6°9S 23°40E **265** D4
**Baky = Bakı** *Azerbaijan* 40°29N 49°56E **191** K9
**Bal Harbor** *U.S.A.* 25°53N 80°7W **129** C3
**Bala** *Ont., Canada* 45°1N 79°37W **312** A5
**Bala** *Senegal* 14°1N 13°8W **262** C2
**Bala** *Turkey* 39°32N 33°6E **212** C5
**Bala** *Gwynedd, U.K.* 52°54N 3°36W **168** E4
**Bala, L.** *U.K.* 52°53N 3°37W **168** E4
**Bālā Morghāb** *Afghan.* 35°35N 63°20E **240** B1
**Balabac** *Phil.* 7°59N 117°4E **233** H1
**Balabac I.** *Phil.* 8°0N 117°0E **233** H1
**Balabac Str.** *E. Indies* 7°53N 117°5E **230** C5
**Balabagh** *Afghan.* 34°25N 70°12E **242** B4
**Ba'labakk** *Lebanon* 34°0N 36°10E **250** E7
**Balabalangan, Kepulauan** *Indonesia* 2°20S 117°30E **235** C5
**Balabio, Î.** *N. Cal.* 20°7S 164°11E **288** d
**Bălăciţa** *Romania* 44°23N 23°8E **183** F8
**Balad** *Iraq* 34°0N 44°9E **213** F11
**Balad Rūz** *Iraq* 33°42N 45°5E **213** F11
**Bālādeh** *Fārs, Iran* 29°17N 51°56E **247** D6
**Bālādeh** *Māzandaran, Iran* 36°12N 51°48E **247** B6
**Balaghat** *India* 21°49N 80°12E **244** D5
**Balaghat Ra.** *India* 18°50N 76°30E **244** E3
**Balaguer** *Spain* 41°50N 0°50E **196** D5
**Balaikarangan** *Indonesia* 0°49N 110°25E **235** B4
**Balaipungut** *Indonesia* 1°3N 101°17E **234** B2
**Balaisabut** *Indonesia* 0°28N 110°49E **235** B4
**Balaka** *Dem. Rep. of the Congo* 4°52S 19°57E **265** C3
**Balakän** *Azerbaijan* 41°43N 46°24E **191** K8
**Balakété** *C.A.R.* 6°56N 19°54E **264** A3
**Balakhna** *Russia* 56°25N 43°32E **190** B6
**Balaklava** *S. Austral., Australia* 34°7S 138°22E **282** C3
**Balaklava** *Ukraine* 44°30N 33°30E **189** K7
**Balakliya** *Ukraine* 49°28N 36°55E **189** H9
**Balakovo** *Russia* 52°4N 47°55E **190** D8
**Balamau** *India* 27°10N 80°21E **243** F9
**Balamban** *Phil.* 10°30N 123°43E **233** F4
**Balambangan, Pulau** *Malaysia* 7°17N 116°55E **235** A5
**Bălan** *Romania* 46°39N 25°49E **183** D10
**Balancán** *Mexico* 17°48N 91°32W **319** D6
**Balanda = Kalininsk** *Russia* 51°30N 44°40E **190** E7
**Balandra B.** *Trin. & Tob.* 10°42N 61°0W **323** t
**Balanga** *Phil.* 14°41N 120°32E **232** D3
**Balangala** *Dem. Rep. of the Congo* 0°30N 19°56E **264** B3
**Balangiga** *Phil.* 11°7N 125°23E **233** F5
**Balangir** *India* 20°43N 83°35E **244** D6
**Balaoan** *Phil.* 16°49N 120°24E **232** C3
**Balapur** *India* 20°40N 76°45E **244** D3
**Balara** *Phil.* 14°39N 121°3E **127** B2
**Balashikha** *Russia* 55°48N 37°58E **188** E9
**Balashov** *Russia* 51°30N 43°10E **190** E6
**Balasinor** *India* 22°57N 73°23E **242** H5
**Balasore = Baleshwar** *India* 21°35N 87°3E **244** D8
**Balassagyarmat** *Hungary* 48°4N 19°15E **182** B4
**Balât** *Egypt* 25°36N 29°19E **256** B2
**Balaton** *Hungary* 46°50N 17°40E **182** D2
**Balaton-Felvidéki △** *Hungary* 46°52N 17°30E **182** D2
**Balatonboglár** *Hungary* 46°46N 17°40E **182** D2
**Balatonfüred** *Hungary* 46°58N 17°54E **182** D2
**Balatonszentgyörgy** *Hungary* 46°41N 17°19E **182** D2
**Balayan** *Phil.* 13°57N 120°44E **232** E3
**Balayan B.** *Phil.* 13°51N 120°48E **232** E3
**Balazote** *Spain* 38°54N 2°9W **197** G2
**Balbalan** *Phil.* 17°27N 121°12E **232** C3
**Balbalasang-Balbalan △** *Phil.* 17°23N 121°8E **232** C3
**Balbi, Mt.** *Papua N. G.* 5°55S 154°58E **286** C8
**Balbieriškis** *Lithuania* 54°32N 23°53E **184** D10
**Balbigny** *France* 45°49N 4°11E **175** C8
**Balbina** *Brazil* 1°58S 59°29W **329** D6
**Balbina, Represa de** *Brazil* 2°0S 59°30W **329** D6
**Balboa** *Panama* 8°57N 79°34W **320** c
**Balbriggan** *Ireland* 53°37N 6°11W **166** C5
**Balcarce** *Argentina* 38°0S 58°10W **334** D4
**Balcarres** *Canada* 50°50N 103°35W **297** C8
**Bălceşti** *Romania* 44°37N 23°57E **183** F8
**Balchik** *Bulgaria* 43°28N 28°11E **203** C12
**Balclutha** *N.Z.* 46°15S 169°45E **285** G4
**Balcones Escarpment** *U.S.A.* 29°30N 99°15W **314** G5
**Balçova** *Turkey* 38°22N 27°4E **205** C9
**Bald I.** *Australia* 34°57S 118°27E **279** F2
**Bald Knob** *U.S.A.* 35°19N 91°34W **314** D9
**Baldenburg = Biały Bór** *Poland* 53°53N 16°51E **184** E3
**Baldia** *Pakistan* 24°54N 66°58E **123** A1
**Baldock L.** *Canada* 56°33N 97°57W **297** B9
**Baldoyle** *Ireland* 53°24N 6°8W **120** A3
**Baldwin** *Fla., U.S.A.* 30°18N 81°59W **316** E8
**Baldwin** *Mich., U.S.A.* 43°54N 85°51W **309** D11
**Baldwin** *Pa., U.S.A.* 40°21N 79°58W **312** F5
**Baldwin, L.** *U.S.A.* 28°34N 81°19W **133** A3
**Baldwin Hills** *U.S.A.* 34°0N 118°21W **126** B2
**Baldwin Hills Res.** *U.S.A.* 34°0N 118°21W **126** B2
**Baldwinsville** *U.S.A.* 43°10N 76°20W **313** C8
**Baldy Peak** *U.S.A.* 33°54N 109°34W **305** K9
**Bale** *Croatia* 45°4N 13°46E **199** C10
**Bale** *Oromiya, Ethiopia* 6°57N 40°8E **257** F5
**Bale** *Oromiya, Ethiopia* 6°20N 41°30E **257** F5
**Bale Mts. △** *Ethiopia* 6°59N 39°52E **257** F4
**Baleares, Is.** *Spain* 39°30N 3°0E **206** B4
**Balearic Is. = Baleares, Is.** *Spain* 39°30N 3°0E **206** B4
**Baleh →** *Malaysia* 2°1N 113°1E **235** B4
**Baleia, Pta. da** *Brazil* 17°40S 39°7W **333** E4
**Baleine →** *Canada* 58°15N 67°40W **299** A6
**Baleine, Petite R. de la →** *Canada* 56°0N 76°45W **298** A4
**Băleni** *Romania* 45°48N 27°51E **183** E12
**Baler** *Phil.* 15°46N 121°34E **232** D3
**Baler B.** *Phil.* 15°50N 121°35E **232** D3
**Baleshare** *U.K.* 57°31N 7°22W **167** D1
**Baleshwar** *India* 21°35N 87°3E **244** D8
**Balestrand** *Norway* 61°11N 6°31E **164** C3
**Baley** *Russia* 51°36N 116°37E **215** D12
**Balezino** *Russia* 58°2N 53°6E **190** B11
**Balfate** *Honduras* 15°48N 86°25W **320** C2
**Balfour Channel** *Solomon Is.* 8°43S 157°27E **287** M9
**Balgo** *Australia* 20°9S 127°58E **278** D4
**Balgowlah** *Australia* 33°47S 151°16E **139** A2
**Balgowlah Heights** *Australia* 33°48S 151°16E **139** A2
**Balham** *U.K.* 51°26N 0°8W **125** B3
**Balharshah** *India* 19°50N 79°23E **244** E4
**Bali** *Cameroon* 5°54N 10°0E **263** D7
**Bali** *Dem. Rep. of the Congo* 2°50S 16°12E **264** C3
**Bali** *Kriti, Greece* 35°25N 24°47E **207** E5
**Bali** *Paschimbanga, India* 22°39N 88°20E **124** B1
**Bali** *Raj., India* 25°11N 73°17E **242** G5
**Bali** *Indonesia* 8°20S 115°0E **231** J18
**Bali □** *Indonesia* 8°20S 115°0E **231** J17
**Bali, Selat** *Indonesia* 8°18S 114°25E **231** J17
**Bali Barat △** *Indonesia* 8°12S 114°35E **231** J17
**Bali Sea** *Indonesia* 8°0S 115°0E **231** J17
**Balia** *S. Leone* 9°22N 11°9W **262** D2
**Baliapal** *India* 21°40N 87°17E **243** J12
**Baliceaux** *St. Vincent* 12°57N 61°8W **323** n
**Balicuatro Is.** *Phil.* 12°39N 124°24E **232** E5
**Baliganja** *India* 22°31N 88°22E **124** B2
**Balige** *Indonesia* 2°14N 99°7E **234** B1
**Baligród** *Poland* 49°20N 22°17E **185** J9
**Baliguda** *India* 20°12N 83°55E **244** D6
**Balik Pulau** *Malaysia* 5°21N 100°14E **237** c
**Balıkeşir** *Turkey* 39°39N 27°53E **205** B9
**Balıkeşir □** *Turkey* 39°45N 28°0E **205** B9
**Balīkh →** *Syria* 35°52N 39°12E **213** E8
**Balıklıçeşme** *Turkey* 40°18N 27°5E **203** F11
**Balikpapan** *Indonesia* 1°10S 116°55E **235** C5
**Balimbing** *Phil.* 5°5N 119°58E **233** J2
**Balimo** *Papua N. G.* 8°6S 142°57E **286** E2
**Baling** *Malaysia* 5°41N 100°55E **237** K3
**Balingasag** *Phil.* 8°45N 124°47E **233** G5
**Bälinge** *Sweden* 59°57N 17°33E **162** E11
**Balingen** *Germany* 48°16N 8°51E **179** G4
**Balingsnäs** *Sweden* 59°13N 18°0E **139** B2
**Balingsta** *Sweden* 59°12N 18°3E **139** B2
**Balinsasayao Twin Lakes △** *Phil.* 9°21N 123°9E **233** G4
**Balinţ** *Romania* 45°48N 21°54E **182** E6
**Balintang Channel** *Phil.* 19°49N 121°40E **232** B3
**Balintang I.** *Phil.* 19°58N 122°9E **232** B4
**Balintawak** *Phil.* 14°39N 120°59E **127** B1
**Baliza** *Brazil* 16°0S 52°20W **331** D7
**Baljurashī** *Si. Arabia* 19°51N 41°33E **248** C3
**Balkan □** *Turkmenistan* 40°0N 54°30E **216** D5
**Balkan Mts. = Stara Planina** *Bulgaria* 43°15N 23°0E **202** C7
**Balkanabat** *Turkmenistan* 39°30N 54°22E **247** B7
**Balkh** *Afghan.* 36°44N 66°47E **217** E7
**Balkh □** *Afghan.* 36°50N 67°0E **240** A2
**Balkhash = Balqash** *Kazakhstan* 46°50N 74°50E **214** E8
**Balkhash, Ozero = Balqash Köli** *Kazakhstan* 46°0N 74°50E **217** C8
**Balkonda** *India* 18°52N 78°21E **244** E4
**Ballachulish** *U.K.* 56°41N 5°8W **167** E3
**Balladonia** *Australia* 32°27S 123°51E **279** F3
**Ballaghaderreen** *Ireland* 53°55N 8°34W **166** C3
**Ballan** *Australia* 37°35S 144°13E **282** D6
**Ballarat** *Australia* 37°33S 143°50E **282** D5
**Ballard, L.** *Australia* 29°20S 120°40E **279** E3
**Ballater** *U.K.* 57°3N 3°3W **167** D5
**Ballé** *Mali* 15°18N 8°33W **262** B3
**Ballena, Pta.** *Venezuela* 11°11N 63°47W **329** a
**Ballenas, Canal de** *Mexico* 29°10N 113°29W **318** B2
**Balleny Is.** *Antarctica* 66°30S 163°0E **151** C11
**Balleroy** *France* 49°11N 0°50W **172** C6
**Ballerup** *Denmark* 55°43N 12°21E **118** A2
**Ballestas, Is.** *Peru* 13°44S 76°25W **330** C2
**Ballı** *Turkey* 40°50N 27°3E **203** F11
**Ballia** *India* 25°46N 84°12E **243** G11
**Ballina** *N.S.W., Australia* 28°50S 153°31E **281** D5
**Ballina** *Mayo, Ireland* 54°7N 9°9W **166** B2
**Ballinasloe** *Ireland* 53°20N 8°13W **166** C3
**Ballincollig** *Ireland* 51°53N 8°33W **166** E3
**Ballinger** *U.S.A.* 31°45N 99°57W **314** F5
**Ballinrobe** *Ireland* 53°38N 9°13W **166** C2
**Ballinskelligs B.** *Ireland* 51°48N 10°13W **166** E1
**Ballinteer** *Ireland* 53°17N 6°15W **120** B2
**Ballon** *France* 48°10N 0°14E **172** D7
**Ballons des Vosges △** *France* 48°0N 7°0E **173** E14
**Ballsh** *Albania* 40°36N 19°44E **202** F3
**Ballston Spa** *U.S.A.* 43°0N 73°51W **313** D11
**Ballyboden** *Ireland* 53°17N 6°18W **120** B2
**Ballyboghil** *Ireland* 53°32N 6°16W **166** C5
**Ballybrack** *Ireland* 53°15N 6°7W **120** B3
**Ballybunion** *Ireland* 52°31N 9°40W **166** D2
**Ballycanew** *Ireland* 52°37N 6°19W **166** D5
**Ballycastle** *U.K.* 55°12N 6°15W **166** A5
**Ballyclare** *U.K.* 54°46N 6°0W **166** B5
**Ballycroy △** *Ireland* 54°5N 9°50W **166** B2
**Ballydehob** *Ireland* 51°34N 9°28W **166** E2
**Ballyfermot** *Ireland* 53°20N 6°21W **120** A1
**Ballygawley** *U.K.* 54°27N 7°2W **166** B4
**Ballyhaunis** *Ireland* 53°46N 8°46W **166** C3
**Ballyheige** *Ireland* 52°23N 9°49W **166** D2
**Ballymena** *U.K.* 54°52N 6°17W **166** B5
**Ballymoney** *U.K.* 55°5N 6°31W **166** A5
**Ballymorefinn Hill** *Ireland* 53°14N 6°22W **120** B1
**Ballymote** *Ireland* 54°5N 8°31W **166** B3
**Ballymun** *Ireland* 53°23N 6°16W **120** A2
**Ballynahinch** *U.K.* 54°24N 5°54W **166** B6
**Ballyporeen** *Ireland* 52°16N 8°6W **166** D3
**Ballyquintin Pt.** *U.K.* 54°20N 5°30W **166** B6
**Ballyshannon** *Ireland* 54°30N 8°11W **166** B3
**Balmaceda** *Chile* 46°0S 71°50W **336** C2
**Balmain** *Australia* 33°51S 151°11E **139** B2
**Balmaseda** *Spain* 43°11N 3°12W **196** B1
**Balmazújváros** *Hungary* 47°37N 21°21E **182** C6
**Balmertown** *Canada* 51°4N 93°41W **297** C10
**Balmoral** *Australia* 37°15S 141°48E **282** D4
**Balmorhea** *U.S.A.* 30°59N 103°45W **314** F3
**Balneário Camboriú** *Brazil* 26°59S 48°38W **335** B6
**Balochistan = Baluchistan □** *Pakistan* 27°30N 65°0E **240** D2
**Balod** *India* 20°44N 81°13E **244** D5
**Balombo** *Angola* 12°21S 14°46E **265** E2
**Balombo →** *Angola* 11°57S 13°46E **265** E2
**Balonne →** *Australia* 28°47S 147°56E **281** D4
**Balotra** *India* 25°50N 72°14E **242** G5
**Balpyq Bī** *Kazakhstan* 44°52N 78°12E **217** D9
**Balqash** *Kazakhstan* 46°50N 74°50E **214** E8
**Balqash Köli** *Kazakhstan* 46°0N 74°50E **217** C8
**Balrampur** *India* 27°30N 82°20E **243** F10
**Balranald** *Australia* 34°38S 143°33E **282** C5
**Balş** *Romania* 44°22N 24°5E **183** F9
**Balsapuerto** *Peru* 5°48S 76°33W **330** B2
**Balsas →** *Maranhão, Brazil* 7°15S 44°35W **332** C3
**Balsas →** *Tocantins, Brazil* 9°58S 47°52W **332** C2
**Balsas →** *Michoacan, Mexico* 17°55N 102°10W **318** D4
**Bálsas del Norte** *Mexico* 18°0N 99°46W **319** D5
**Bålsta** *Sweden* 59°35N 17°30E **162** E11
**Balta** *Romania* 44°54N 22°38E **182** F7
**Balta** *Ukraine* 47°56N 29°45E **183** C14
**Baltakōl** *Kazakhstan* 43°37N 67°46E **217** D7
**Baltanás** *Spain* 41°56N 4°15W **194** D6
**Bălţi** *Moldova* 47°48N 27°58E **183** C12
**Baltic Sea** *Europe* 57°0N 19°0E **161** H18
**Baltîm** *Egypt* 31°35N 31°10E **256** H7
**Baltimore** *Cork, Ireland* 51°29N 9°22W **166** E2
**Baltimore** *Md., U.S.A.* 39°17N 76°36W **309** F15
**Baltimore** *Ohio, U.S.A.* 39°51N 82°36W **312** G2
**Baltinglass** *Ireland* 52°56N 6°43W **166** D5
**Baltit** *Pakistan* 36°15N 74°40E **243** A6
**Baltiysk** *Russia* 54°41N 19°58E **184** D6
**Baltiyskiy = Paldiski** *Estonia* 59°23N 24°9E **188** C3
**Baltra, I.** *Ecuador* 0°26S 90°16W **330** a
**Baltrum** *Germany* 53°43N 7°24E **178** B3
**Baluan I.** *Papua N. G.* 2°33S 147°17E **286** B4
**Baluchistan □** *Pakistan* 27°30N 65°0E **240** D2
**Balud** *Phil.* 12°2N 123°12E **232** E4
**Baluhati** *India* 22°39N 88°15E **124** B1
**Baluqtybulaq** *Kazakhstan* 50°51N 51°8E **190** E10
**Baluran △** *Indonesia* 7°50S 114°23E **235** D4
**Balurghat** *India* 25°15N 88°44E **241** C2
**Balut I.** *Phil.* 5°24N 125°23E **233** J5
**Balvanera** *Argentina* 34°37S 58°23W **117** B2
**Balvi** *Latvia* 57°8N 27°15E **188** D4
**Balwyn** *Australia* 37°48S 145°4E **128** A2
**Balwyn North** *Australia* 37°47S 145°4E **128** A2
**Balya** *Turkey* 39°44N 27°35E **205** B9
**Balykchy** *Kyrgyzstan* 42°26N 76°12E **217** D9
**Balyqshy** *Kazakhstan* 47°4N 51°52E **191** G9
**Balzar** *Ecuador* 2°2S 79°54W **328** D2
**Bam** *Iran* 29°7N 58°14E **247** D8
**Bama** *Guangxi Zhuangzu, China* 24°8N 107°12E **228** E6
**Bama** *Nigeria* 11°33N 13°41E **263** C7
**Bamaga** *Australia* 10°50S 142°25E **280** A3
**Bamaji L.** *Canada* 51°9N 91°25W **298** B1
**Bamako** *Mali* 12°34N 7°55W **262** C3
**Bamba** *Dem. Rep. of the Congo* 5°45S 18°23E **265** D3
**Bamba** *Mali* 17°5N 1°24W **263** B4
**Bambama** *Congo* 2°32S 13°32E **264** C2
**Bambamarca** *Peru* 6°36S 78°32W **330** B2
**Bambang** *Phil.* 16°23N 121°6E **232** C3
**Bambannan I.** *Phil.* 5°37N 120°17E **233** J3
**Bambao** *Comoros Is.* 12°11S 44°31E **272** a
**Bambara Maoundé** *Mali* 13°26N 4°3W **262** B4
**Bambari** *C.A.R.* 5°40N 20°35E **264** A4
**Bambaroo** *Australia* 18°50S 146°10E **280** B4
**Bambaya** *Guinea* 10°55N 13°38W **262** D2
**Bamberg** *Bayern, Germany* 49°54N 10°54E **179** F6
**Bamberg** *S.C., U.S.A.* 33°18N 81°2W **316** B8
**Bambesi** *Ethiopia* 9°45N 34°40E **257** F3
**Bambey** *Senegal* 14°42N 16°28W **262** C1
**Bambili** *Dem. Rep. of the Congo* 3°40N 26°0E **268** B2
**Bambinga** *Dem. Rep. of the Congo* 3°43S 18°53E **264** C3
**Bambio** *C.A.R.* 3°55N 16°57E **264** B3
**Bamboi** *Ghana* 8°13N 2°1W **262** D4
**Bamboo Avenue** *Jamaica* 18°6N 77°47W **320** a
**Bambous** *Mauritius* 20°15S 57°24E **272** e
**Bambouti** *C.A.R.* 5°24N 27°12E **264** A5
**Bambuí** *Brazil* 20°1S 45°58W **333** F2
**Bamburgh** *U.K.* 55°37N 1°43W **168** B6
**Bamenda** *Cameroon* 5°57N 10°11E **263** D7
**Bamendjing, L. de** *Cameroon* 5°50N 10°30E **263** D7
**Bamfield** *Canada* 48°45N 125°10W **296** D3
**Bāmīān** *Afghan.* 34°49N 67°49E **240** B2
**Bāmīān □** *Afghan.* 35°0N 67°0E **240** B2
**Bamiancheng** *China* 43°15N 124°2E **227** C13
**Bamingui** *C.A.R.* 7°34N 20°11E **264** A4
**Bamingui →** *C.A.R.* 8°33N 19°5E **264** A3
**Bamingui-Bangoran □** *C.A.R.* 8°30N 20°0E **264** A4
**Bamingui-Bangoran △** *C.A.R.* 8°30N 19°46E **264** A3
**Bamkin** *Cameroon* 6°3N 11°27E **263** D7
**Bamou △** *Iran* 29°45N 52°35E **247** D7
**Bampūr** *Iran* 27°15N 60°21E **247** E9
**Bampūr →** *Iran* 27°24N 59°0E **247** E8
**Bamu →** *Papua N. G.* 8°1S 143°3E **286** E2
**Ban** *Burkina Faso* 14°5N 2°27W **262** C4
**Ban Ao Tu Khun** *Thailand* 8°9N 98°20E **237** a
**Ban Ban** *Laos* 19°31N 103°30E **236** C4
**Ban Bang Hin** *Thailand* 9°32N 98°35E **237** H2
**Ban Bang Khu** *Thailand* 7°57N 98°23E **237** a
**Ban Bang Rong** *Thailand* 8°3N 98°25E **237** a
**Ban Bo Phut** *Thailand* 9°33N 100°2E **237** b
**Ban Chaweng** *Thailand* 9°32N 100°3E **237** b
**Ban Chiang** *Thailand* 17°30N 103°10E **236** D4
**Ban Chiang Klang** *Thailand* 19°25N 100°55E **236** C3
**Ban Choho** *Thailand* 15°2N 102°9E **236** E4
**Ban Dan Lan Hoi** *Thailand* 17°0N 99°35E **236** D2
**Ban Don = Surat Thani** *Thailand* 9°6N 99°20E **237** H2
**Ban Don** *Vietnam* 12°53N 107°48E **236** F6
**Ban Don, Ao →** *Thailand* 9°20N 99°25E **237** H2
**Ban Dong** *Thailand* 19°30N 100°59E **236** C3
**Ban Hong** *Thailand* 18°18N 98°50E **236** C2
**Ban Hua Thanon** *Thailand* 9°26N 100°1E **237** b
**Ban Kantang** *Thailand* 7°25N 99°31E **237** J2
**Ban Karon** *Thailand* 7°51N 98°18E **237** a
**Ban Kata** *Thailand* 7°50N 98°18E **237** a
**Ban Keun** *Laos* 18°22N 102°35E **236** C4
**Ban Khai** *Thailand* 12°46N 101°18E **236** F3
**Ban Kheun** *Laos* 20°13N 101°7E **236** B3
**Ban Khlong Khian** *Thailand* 8°10N 98°26E **237** a
**Ban Khlong Kua** *Thailand* 6°57N 100°8E **237** J3
**Ban Khuan** *Thailand* 8°20N 98°25E **237** a
**Ban Ko Yai Chim** *Thailand* 11°17N 99°26E **237** G2
**Ban Laem** *Thailand* 13°13N 99°59E **236** F2
**Ban Lamai** *Thailand* 9°28N 100°3E **237** b
**Ban Lao Ngam** *Laos* 15°28N 106°10E **236** E6
**Ban Le Kathe** *Thailand* 15°49N 98°53E **236** E2
**Ban Lo Po Noi** *Thailand* 8°1N 98°34E **237** a
**Ban Mae Chedi** *Thailand* 19°11N 99°31E **236** C2
**Ban Mae Nam** *Thailand* 9°34N 100°0E **237** b
**Ban Mae Sariang** *Thailand* 18°10N 97°56E **236** C1
**Ban Mê Thuôt = Buon Ma Thuot** *Vietnam* 12°40N 108°3E **236** F7
**Ban Mi** *Thailand* 15°3N 100°32E **236** E3
**Ban Muang Mo** *Laos* 19°4N 103°58E **236** C4
**Ban Na Bo** *Thailand* 9°19N 99°41E **237** b
**Ban Na San** *Thailand* 8°53N 99°52E **237** H2
**Ban Na Tong** *Laos* 20°56N 101°47E **236** B3
**Ban Nam Bac** *Laos* 20°38N 102°20E **236** B4
**Ban Nammi** *Laos* 17°7N 105°40E **236** D5
**Ban Nong Bok** *Laos* 17°5N 104°48E **236** D5
**Ban Nong Pling** *Thailand* 15°40N 100°10E **236** E3
**Ban Pak Chan** *Thailand* 10°32N 98°51E **237** G2
**Ban Patong** *Thailand* 7°54N 98°18E **237** a
**Ban Phai** *Thailand* 16°4N 102°44E **236** D4
**Ban Phak Chit** *Thailand* 8°0N 98°24E **237** a
**Ban Pong** *Thailand* 13°50N 99°55E **236** F2
**Ban Rawai** *Thailand* 7°47N 98°20E **237** a
**Ban Ron Phibun** *Thailand* 8°9N 99°51E **237** H2
**Ban Sakhu** *Thailand* 8°4N 98°18E **237** a
**Ban Sanam Chai** *Thailand* 7°33N 100°25E **237** J3
**Ban Tak** *Thailand* 17°2N 99°4E **236** D2
**Ban Tako** *Thailand* 14°5N 102°40E **236** E4
**Ban Tha Nun** *Thailand* 8°12N 98°18E **237** a
**Ban Tha Rua** *Thailand* 7°59N 98°22E **237** a
**Ban Tha Yu** *Thailand* 8°17N 98°22E **237** a
**Ban Thong Krut** *Thailand* 9°25N 99°57E **237** b
**Ban Xien Kok** *Laos* 20°54N 100°39E **236** B3
**Ban Yen Nhan** *Vietnam* 20°57N 106°2E **236** B6
**Banā, W. →** *Yemen* 13°3N 45°24E **248** D4
**Banaadir □** *Somalia* 2°7N 45°24E **267** D6
**Banaba** *Kiribati* 0°45S 169°50E **288** H8
**Banagher** *Ireland* 53°11N 7°59W **166** C3
**Banalia** *Dem. Rep. of the Congo* 1°32N 25°5E **268** B2
**Banam** *Cambodia* 11°20N 105°17E **237** G5
**Banamba** *Mali* 13°29N 7°22W **262** C3
**Banana Is.** *S. Leone* 8°7N 13°15W **262** D2
**Banana Island** *Nigeria* 6°28N 3°27E **124** B2
**Bananal, I. do** *Brazil* 11°30S 50°30W **333** D1
**Bananga** *India* 6°57N 93°54E **245** L11
**Bananier** *Guadeloupe* 16°0N 61°36W **322** e
**Banaras = Varanasi** *India* 25°22N 83°0E **243** G10
**Banas →** *Gujarat, India* 23°45N 71°25E **242** H4
**Banas →** *Mad. P., India* 24°15N 81°30E **243** G9
**Bânâs, Ras** *Egypt* 23°57N 35°59E **256** C4
**Banática** *Portugal* 38°40N 9°11W **126** A1
**Banaue** *Phil.* 16°55N 121°4E **232** C3
**Banaz** *Turkey* 38°46N 29°46E **205** C11
**Banaz →** *Turkey* 38°12N 29°14E **205** C11
**Banbridge** *U.K.* 54°22N 6°16W **166** B5
**Banbury** *U.K.* 52°4N 1°20W **169** E6
**Banc d'Arguin △** *Mauritania* 20°10N 16°20W **260** D1
**Banchory** *U.K.* 57°3N 2°29W **167** D6
**Banco** *Ethiopia* 6°12N 38°13E **257** F4
**Banco do Brasil, Centro Cultural** *Rio de J., Brazil* **135** a2
**Bancoran** *Phil.* 7°45N 118°30E **233** H2
**Bancroft = Chililabombwe** *Zambia* 12°18S 27°43E **269** E2
**Bancroft** *Canada* 45°3N 77°51W **312** A7
**Band** *Romania* 46°30N 24°25E **183** D9
**Band Bonī** *Iran* 25°30N 59°33E **247** E8
**Band-e-Amīr** *Afghan.* 34°50N 67°10E **240** B2
**Band-e Torkestan** *Afghan.* 35°30N 64°0E **240** B2
**Band Qīr** *Iran* 31°39N 48°53E **247** D6
**Banda** *Cameroon* 3°58N 14°32E **264** B2
**Banda** *Mad. P., India* 24°3N 78°57E **243** G8
**Banda** *Maharashtra, India* 15°49N 73°52E **245** G1
**Banda** *Ut. P., India* 25°30N 80°26E **243** G9
**Banda, Kepulauan** *Indonesia* 4°37S 129°50E **231** E7
**Banda Aceh** *Indonesia* 5°35N 95°20E **234** A1
**Banda Banda, Mt.** *Australia* 31°10S 152°28E **283** A10
**Banda Elat** *Indonesia* 5°40S 133°5E **231** F8
**Banda Is. = Banda, Kepulauan** *Indonesia* 4°37S 129°50E **231** E7
**Banda Kani** *Dem. Rep. of the Congo* 4°48S 13°52E **265** C2
**Banda Sea** *Indonesia* 6°0S 130°0E **231** F8
**Bandai-Asahi △** *Japan* 37°38N 140°5E **220** F10
**Bandai-San** *Japan* 37°36N 140°4E **220** F10
**Bandak** *Norway* 59°23N 8°29E **164** E5
**Bandama →** *Ivory C.* 6°32N 4°30W **262** D3
**Bandama Blanc →** *Ivory C.* 6°55N 5°30W **262** D4
**Bandama Rouge →** *Ivory C.* 6°55N 5°30W **262** D4
**Bandamadji** *Comoros Is.* 11°47S 43°26E **272** a
**Bandān** *Iran* 31°23N 60°44E **247** D9
**Bandanaira** *Indonesia* 4°32S 129°54E **231** E7
**Bandanwara** *India* 26°9N 74°38E **242** F6
**Bandar = Machilipatnam** *India* 16°12N 81°8E **245** F5
**Bandar-e Abbās** *Iran* 27°15N 56°15E **247** E8
**Bandar-e Anzalī** *Iran* 37°30N 49°30E **213** D13
**Bandar-e Bushehr = Būshehr** *Iran* 28°55N 50°55E **247** D6
**Bandar-e Chārak** *Iran* 26°45N 54°20E **247** E7
**Bandar-e Deylam** *Iran* 30°5N 50°10E **247** D6
**Bandar-e Emām Khomeynī** *Iran* 30°30N 49°5E **247** D6
**Bandar-e Lengeh** *Iran* 26°35N 54°58E **247** E7
**Bandar-e Maqām** *Iran* 26°56N 53°29E **247** E7
**Bandar-e Ma'shur** *Iran* 30°35N 49°10E **247** D6
**Bandar-e Rīg** *Iran* 29°29N 50°38E **247** D6
**Bandar-e Torkeman** *Iran* 37°0N 54°10E **247** B7
**Bandar Labuan** *Malaysia* 5°20N 115°14E **235** A5
**Bandar Lampung** *Indonesia* 5°20S 105°10E **234** D3
**Bandar Maharani = Muar** *Malaysia* 2°3N 102°34E **237** L4
**Bandar Penggaram = Batu Pahat** *Malaysia* 1°50N 102°56E **237** M4
**Bandar Seri Begawan** *Brunei* 4°52N 115°0E **235** B4
**Bandar Shahid Rajaee** *Iran* 27°7N 56°4E **247** E8
**Bandar Sri Aman** *Malaysia* 1°15N 111°32E **235** B4
**Bandawe** *Malawi* 11°58S 34°5E **269** E3
**Bande** *Spain* 42°3N 7°58W **194** C3
**Bandeira, Pico da** *Brazil* 20°26S 41°47W **333** F3
**Bandeirante** *Brazil* 13°41S 50°48W **333** D1
**Bandera** *Argentina* 28°55S 62°20W **334** B3
**Banderas, B. de** *Mexico* 20°40N 105°25W **318** C3
**Bandhavgarh** *India* 23°40N 81°2E **243** H9
**Bandhavgarh △** *India* 23°45N 81°10E **244** C5
**Bandi →** *India* 26°12N 75°47E **242** F6
**Bandia →** *India* 19°2N 80°28E **244** E5
**Bandiagara** *Mali* 14°12N 3°29W **262** C4
**Bandikui** *India* 27°3N 76°34E **242** F7
**Bandingilo △** *South Sudan* 5°26N 32°17E **257** F3
**Bandipur △** *India* 11°45N 76°30E **245** J3
**Bandırma** *Turkey* 40°20N 28°0E **203** F11
**Bandjarmasin = Banjarmasin** *Indonesia* 3°20S 114°35E **235** C4
**Bandol** *France* 43°8N 5°46E **175** E9
**Bandon** *Ireland* 51°44N 8°44W **166** E3
**Bandon →** *Ireland* 51°43N 8°37W **166** E3
**Bandra** *India* 19°3N 72°49E **130** A1
**Bandra Pt.** *India* 19°2N 72°49E **130** A1
**Bandraboua** *Mayotte* 12°42S 45°8E **272** b
**Bandrélé** *Mayotte* 12°54S 45°11E **272** b
**Bandula** *Mozam.* 19°0S 33°7E **269** F3
**Bandundu** *Dem. Rep. of the Congo* 3°15S 17°22E **264** C3
**Bandundu □** *Dem. Rep. of the Congo* 3°30S 17°30E **264** C3
**Bandung** *Indonesia* 6°54S 107°36E **235** D3
**Bané** *Burkina Faso* 11°42N 0°15W **263** C4
**Băneasa** *Romania* 45°56N 27°55E **183** E12
**Bāneh** *Iran* 35°59N 45°53E **213** E11
**Banes** *Cuba* 21°0N 75°42W **320** B4
**Banff** *Alta., Canada* 51°10N 115°34W **296** C5
**Banff** *Aberds., U.K.* 57°40N 2°33W **167** D6
**Banff △** *Canada* 51°30N 116°15W **296** C5
**Banfora** *Burkina Faso* 10°40N 4°40W **262** C4
**Bang Fai →** *Laos* 16°57N 104°45E **236** D5
**Bang Hieng →** *Laos* 16°10N 105°10E **236** D5
**Bang Kapi** *Thailand* 13°45N 100°38E **113** B2
**Bang Krathum** *Thailand* 16°34N 100°18E **236** D3
**Bang Lamung** *Thailand* 13°3N 100°56E **236** F3
**Bang Lang △** *Thailand* 5°58N 101°19E **237** K3
**Bang Lang Res.** *Thailand* 6°6N 101°17E **237** J3
**Bang Mun Nak** *Thailand* 16°2N 100°23E **236** D3
**Bang Na** *Thailand* 13°40N 100°35E **113** B2
**Bang Pa In** *Thailand* 14°14N 100°35E **236** E3
**Bang Phlad** *Bangkok, Thailand* **113** a1
**Bang Rakam** *Thailand* 16°45N 100°7E **236** D3
**Bang Saphan** *Thailand* 11°14N 99°28E **237** G2
**Bang Thao** *Thailand* 7°59N 98°18E **237** a
**Banga** *Angola* 8°43S 15°13E **265** D3
**Banga** *Dem. Rep. of the Congo* 5°25S 20°28E **265** D4
**Banga** *Aklan, Phil.* 11°38N 122°20E **233** F4
**Banga** *S. Cotabato, Phil.* 6°21N 124°47E **233** H5
**Bangaduni I.** *India* 21°34N 88°52E **241** E2
**Bangala Dam** *Zimbabwe* 21°7S 31°25E **269** G3
**Bangalore** *India* 12°59N 77°40E **245** H3
**Banganapalle** *India* 15°19N 78°14E **245** G4
**Banganga →** *India* 27°6N 77°25E **242** F6
**Bangangté** *Cameroon* 5°8N 10°32E **263** D7
**Bangaon** *India* 23°0N 88°47E **243** H13
**Bangar** *Brunei* 4°43N 115°4E **235** B4
**Bangar** *La Union, Phil.* 16°54N 120°25E **232** C3
**Bangassou** *C.A.R.* 4°55N 23°7E **264** B4
**Bangbae** *S. Korea* 37°29N 126°59E **137** C1
**Bangeta, Mt.** *Papua N. G.* 6°21S 147°3E **286** D4
**Banggai** *Indonesia* 1°34S 123°30E **231** E6
**Banggai, Kepulauan** *Indonesia* 1°40S 123°30E **231** E6
**Banggai Arch. = Banggai, Kepulauan** *Indonesia* 1°40S 123°30E **231** E6
**Banggi, Pulau** *Malaysia* 7°17N 117°12E **235** A5
**Banghāzī** *Libya* 32°11N 20°3E **258** B4
**Banghāzī □** *Libya* 32°7N 20°4E **258** B4
**Bangil** *Indonesia* 7°36S 112°50E **235** D4
**Bangjang** *South Sudan* 11°23N 32°41E **257** E3
**Bangka** *Sulawesi, Indonesia* 1°50N 125°5E **231** D7
**Bangka** *Sumatera, Indonesia* 2°0S 105°50E **234** C3
**Bangka, Selat** *Indonesia* 2°30S 105°30E **234** C3
**Bangka-Belitung □** *Indonesia* 2°30S 107°0E **234** C3
**Bangkalan** *Indonesia* 7°2S 112°46E **235** D4
**Bangkang** *Burma* 22°4N 99°1E **228** F2
**Bangkaru** *Indonesia* 2°4N 97°7E **234** B1
**Bangkhen** *Thailand* 13°52N 100°36E **113** A2
**Bangkinang** *Indonesia* 0°18N 101°5E **234** B2
**Bangko** *Indonesia* 2°5S 102°9E **234** C2
**Bangkok** *Thailand* 13°45N 100°35E **113** B2
**Bangkok, Bight of** *Thailand* 12°55N 100°30E **236** F3
**Bangkok Don Muang Int. ✕ (BKK)** *Thailand* 13°53N 100°36E **113** A2
**Bangkok Noi** *Thailand* 13°45N 100°28E **113** B1
**Bangkok Yai** *Thailand* 13°43N 100°29E **113** B1

Bangla = Paschimbanga □ India 23°0N 88°0E 243 H13
Bangladesh ■ Asia 24°0N 90°0E 241 D3
Bangli Indonesia 8°27S 115°21E 231 J18
Banglo India 22°31N 88°14E 124 B1
Bangoi-Kouni Comoros Is. 11°22S 43°21E 272 a
Bangolo Ivory C. 7°1N 7°29W 262 D3
Bangong Co China 33°45N 78°43E 243 C8
Bangor Down, U.K. 54°40N 5°40W 166 B6
Bangor Gwynedd, U.K. 53°14N 4°8W 168 D3
Bangor Maine, U.S.A. 44°48N 68°46W 309 C19
Bangor Mich., U.S.A. 42°18N 86°7W 311 B10
Bangor Pa., U.S.A. 40°52N 75°13W 313 F9
Bangoran → C.A.R. 8°42N 19°6E 264 A3
Bangrak Thailand 13°43N 100°31E 113 B2
Bangsamoro = Muslim Mindanao □ Phil. 8°0N 123°0E 233 H3
Bangsu Thailand 13°49N 100°31E 113 B2
Bangu Dem. Rep. of the Congo 0°3S 19°12E 264 C3
Bangued Phil. 17°40N 120°37E 232 C3
Bangui C.A.R. 4°23N 18°35E 264 B3
Bangui Phil. 18°32N 120°46E 232 B3
Bangui B. Phil. 18°33N 120°43E 232 B3
Banguru Dem. Rep. of the Congo 0°30N 27°10E 268 B2
Bangweulu, L. Zambia 11°0S 30°0E 269 E3
Bangweulu Swamp Zambia 11°20S 30°15E 269 E3
Banhine △ Mozam. 22°49S 32°55E 271 B5
Bani Burkina Faso 13°43N 0°10W 263 C4
Bani C.A.R. 7°6N 22°50E 264 A4
Baní Dom. Rep. 18°16N 70°22W 321 C5
Bani Phil. 16°11N 119°52E 232 C2
Bani → Mali 14°30N 4°12W 262 C4
Bani, Jebel Morocco 29°16N 8°0W 260 C3
Bani Bangou Niger 15°3N 2°42E 263 B5
Banī Sa'd Iraq 33°34N 44°32E 213 F11
Banī Walīd Libya 31°36N 13°53E 258 B2
Bania C.A.R. 4°1N 16°7E 264 B3
Bania Ivory C. 9°4N 3°6W 262 D4
Baniara Papua N. G. 9°44S 149°54E 286 E5
Banihal Pass India 33°30N 75°12E 243 C6
Banikoara Benin 11°18N 2°26E 263 C5
Banīnah Libya 32°0N 20°12E 258 B4
Banissa Kenya 3°55N 40°19E 257 G5
Bāniyās Syria 35°10N 36°0E 250 C7
Banja Luka Bos.-H. 44°49N 17°11E 182 F2
Banjar India 31°38N 77°21E 242 D7
Banjar → India 22°36N 80°22E 243 H9
Banjarbaru Indonesia 3°25S 114°49E 235 C4
Banjarmasin Indonesia 3°20S 114°35E 235 C4
Banjul Gambia 13°28N 16°40W 262 C1
Bank London, U.K. 125 b5
Banka India 24°53N 86°55E 243 G12
Bankas Mali 14°4N 3°31W 262 C4
Bankeryd Sweden 57°53N 14°6E 163 G8
Banket Zimbabwe 17°27S 30°19E 269 F3
Bankilaré Niger 14°35N 0°44E 263 C5
Bankot India 17°58N 73°2E 244 F1
Banks U.S.A. 31°49N 85°51W 316 D4
Banks, C. Australia 34°0S 151°16E 139 C2
Banks I. = Moa Australia 10°11S 142°16E 280 a
Banks I. B.C., Canada 53°20N 130°0W 296 C3
Banks I. N.W.T., Canada 73°15N 121°30W 294 C7
Banks Is. Vanuatu 13°50S 167°30E 287 C5
Banks L. U.S.A. 31°2N 83°6W 316 D6
Banks Pen. N.Z. 43°45S 173°15E 285 D8
Banks Str. Australia 40°40S 148°10E 281 G4
Banksmeadow Australia 33°57S 151°12E 139 B2
Bankumuna Dem. Rep. of the Congo 4°28S 19°57E 265 C3
Bankura India 23°11N 87°18E 243 H12
Bankya Bulgaria 42°43N 23°8E 202 D7
Banmankhi India 25°53N 87°11E 243 G12
Banmauk Burma 24°24N 95°51E 241 C5
Bann → Armagh, U.K. 54°30N 6°31W 166 B5
Bann → L'derry., U.K. 55°8N 6°41W 166 A5
Bannaanka Saraar Somalia 9°25N 46°17E 267 C6
Bannalec France 47°57N 3°42W 172 E3
Bannang Sata Thailand 6°16N 101°16E 237 J3
Bannerton Australia 34°42S 142°47E 282 C5
Banning U.S.A. 33°56N 116°53W 307 M10
Banningville = Bandundu Dem. Rep. of the Congo 3°15S 17°22E 264 C3
Banno Ethiopia 4°51N 37°24E 257 G4
Banno-saki Japan 26°33N 128°8E 288 a
Bannockburn Ont., Canada 44°39N 77°33W 312 B7
Bannockburn Stirling, U.K. 56°5N 3°55W 167 E5
Bannockburn Zimbabwe 20°17S 29°48E 269 G2
Bannu Pakistan 33°0N 70°18E 240 B3
Bano India 22°40N 84°55E 243 H11
Bañolas = Banyoles Spain 42°16N 2°44E 196 C7
Banon France 44°2N 5°38E 175 D9
Baños de la Encina Spain 38°10N 3°46W 195 G7
Baños de Molgas Spain 42°15N 7°40W 194 C3
Bánovce nad Bebravou Slovak Rep. 48°44N 18°16E 181 C11
Banovići Bos.-H. 44°25N 18°32E 182 F3
Banqiao = Panch'iao Taiwan 25°1N 121°27E 225 A3
Bansagar Dam India 24°11N 81°17E 244 B5
Bansalan Phil. 6°55N 125°13E 233 H5
Bansgaon India 26°33N 83°21E 243 F10
Banská Bystrica Slovak Rep. 48°46N 19°14E 181 C12
Banská Štiavnica Slovak Rep. 48°25N 18°55E 181 C11
Bansko Bulgaria 41°52N 23°28E 202 E7
Banskobystrický □ Slovak Rep. 48°20N 19°0E 181 C12
Banstala India 22°31N 88°24E 124 B2
Banswara India 23°32N 74°24E 242 H6
Bantaeng Indonesia 5°32S 119°56E 235 D5
Bantaji → Nigeria 8°6N 10°5E 263 D7
Bantayan Phil. 11°10N 123°43E 233 F4
Bantayan I. Phil. 11°13N 123°44E 233 F4
Banteay Prei Nokor Cambodia 11°56N 105°40E 237 G5
Banten Indonesia 6°5S 106°8E 234 D3
Banten □ Indonesia 6°30S 106°0E 234 D3
Banton I. Phil. 12°56N 122°4E 232 E4
Bantra India 22°35N 88°18E 124 B1
Bantry Ireland 51°41N 9°27W 166 E2
Bantry B. Ireland 51°37N 9°44W 166 E2
Bantva India 21°29N 70°12E 242 J4
Bantval India 12°55N 75°0E 245 H2
Banya Bulgaria 42°33N 24°50E 203 D8
Banya, Pta. de la Spain 40°33N 0°36E 196 E5
Banyak, Kepulauan Indonesia 2°10N 97°10E 234 B1
Banyalbufar Spain 39°42N 2°31E 206 B3
Banyeres de Mariola Spain 38°44N 0°38W 197 G4
Banyo Cameroon 6°52N 11°45E 263 D7
Banyoles Spain 42°16N 2°44E 196 C7
Banyuls-sur-Mer France 42°28N 3°8E 174 F7
Banyuwangi Indonesia 8°13S 114°21E 231 J17
Banz Papua N. G. 5°47S 144°37E 286 C3
Banza Dem. Rep. of the Congo 0°28N 20°10E 264 B4
Banzare Coast Antarctica 68°0S 125°0E 151 C9
Banzyville = Mobayi Dem. Rep. of the Congo 4°15N 21°8E 264 B4
Bao Ha Vietnam 22°11N 104°21E 228 F5
Bao Lac Vietnam 22°57N 105°40E 236 A5
Bao Loc Vietnam 11°32N 107°48E 237 G6
Bao'an China 22°34N 113°52E 219 a
Baocheng China 33°12N 106°56E 228 A6
Baode China 39°1N 111°5E 226 E6
Baodi China 39°38N 117°20E 227 E9
Baoding China 38°50N 115°28E 226 E8
Baoji China 34°20N 107°5E 226 G4
Baojing China 28°45N 109°41E 228 C7
Baokang China 31°54N 111°12E 229 B8
Baoro C.A.R. 5°40N 15°58E 264 A3
Baoshan Shanghai, China 31°24N 121°28E 138 A1
Baoshan Yunnan, China 25°10N 99°5E 228 E2
Baotou China 40°32N 110°2E 226 D6
Baotow = Baotou China 40°32N 110°2E 226 D6
Baoulé → Mali 12°36N 9°45W 262 C3
Baoxing China 30°24N 102°50E 228 B4
Baoying China 33°17N 119°20E 227 H10
Baoyou = Ledong China 18°41N 109°5E 229 a
Bap India 27°23N 72°18E 242 F5
Bapatla India 15°55N 80°30E 245 G5
Bapaume France 50°7N 2°50E 173 B9
Baqar, Bahr el → Egypt 31°7N 32°6E 251 G3
Bāqerābād Iran 33°2N 51°58E 247 C6
Ba'qūbah Iraq 33°45N 44°50E 213 F11
Baquedano Chile 23°20S 69°52W 334 A2
Bar Montenegro 42°3N 19°6E 202 D3
Bar Ukraine 49°4N 27°40E 177 D14
Bar Bigha India 25°21N 85°47E 243 G11
Bar Giyora Israel 31°45N 35°5E 123 B1
Bar Harbor U.S.A. 44°23N 68°13W 309 C19
Bar-le-Duc France 48°47N 5°10E 173 D12
Bar-sur-Aube France 48°14N 4°40E 173 D11
Bar-sur-Seine France 48°7N 4°20E 173 D11
Bara India 25°16N 81°43E 243 G9
Bâra Romania 47°2N 27°3E 183 C12
Bara Sudan 13°42N 30°22E 266 B3
Bara Banki India 26°55N 81°12E 243 F9
Baraawe Somalia 1°20N 44°8E 267 D5
Barabai Indonesia 2°32S 115°34E 235 C5
Baraboo U.S.A. 43°28N 89°45W 308 D9
Baracoa Cuba 20°20N 74°30W 321 B5
Baradā → Syria 33°33N 36°34E 250 E7
Baradero Argentina 33°52S 59°29W 334 C4
Baradine Australia 30°56S 149°4E 283 A8
Baraga U.S.A. 46°47N 88°30W 308 B9
Bărăganul Romania 44°49N 27°31E 183 F12
Baragoi Kenya 1°47N 36°47E 268 B4
Barah → India 27°42N 77°5E 242 F6
Barahanagar India 22°39N 88°22E 124 B2
Barahona Dom. Rep. 18°13N 71°7W 321 C5
Barail Range India 25°15N 93°20E 241 C4
Barajas Spain 40°28N 3°34W 127 B2
Barajas, Madrid ✕ (MAD) Spain 40°26N 3°34W 127 B2
Barak → India 24°52N 92°30E 241 C4
Baraka Sudan 10°59N 27°59E 257 E2
Baraka → Sudan 18°13N 37°35E 256 D4
Barakaldo Spain 43°18N 2°59W 196 B2
Barakar → India 24°7N 86°14E 243 G12
Barakee △ Australia 31°37S 151°53E 283 A9
Barakī Afghan. 33°56N 68°55E 240 B3
Barakot India 21°33N 84°59E 243 J11
Barakpur India 22°47N 88°21E 124 A2
Baralaba Australia 24°13S 149°50E 280 C4
Baralla Spain 42°53N 7°15W 194 C3
Baralzon L. Canada 60°0N 98°3W 297 B9
Baram → Malaysia 4°35N 113°58E 235 B4
Baramati India 18°11N 74°33E 244 E2
Baramba India 20°25N 85°23E 244 D7
Barameiya Sudan 18°32N 36°38E 256 D4
Baramula India 34°15N 74°20E 243 B6
Baran India 25°9N 76°40E 242 G7
Baran → Pakistan 25°13N 68°17E 242 G3
Barañain Spain 42°48N 1°40W 196 C3
Baranavichy Belarus 53°10N 26°0E 177 B14
Barani Burkina Faso 13°9N 3°51W 262 C4
Baranoa Colombia 10°48N 74°55W 328 A3
Baranof U.S.A. 57°5N 134°50W 296 B2
Baranof I. U.S.A. 57°0N 135°0W 303 H14
Baranów Sandomierski Poland 50°29N 21°30E 185 H8
Baranowicze = Baranavichy Belarus 53°10N 26°0E 177 B14
Baranya □ Hungary 46°0N 18°15E 182 E3
Barão de Cocais Brazil 19°56S 43°28W 333 E3
Barão de Grajaú Brazil 6°45S 43°1W 332 C3
Barão de Melgaço Mato Grosso, Brazil 16°14S 55°52W 331 D6
Barão de Melgaço Rondônia, Brazil 11°50S 60°45W 331 C5
Baraolt Romania 46°5N 25°34E 183 D10
Baraona Spain 41°17N 2°39W 196 D2
Barapasi Indonesia 2°15S 137°5E 231 E9
Barapina = Panguna Papua N. G. 6°21S 155°25E 286 D8
Baras Phil. 13°40N 124°22E 232 E5
Barasat India 22°46N 88°31E 243 H13
Barat Daya, Kepulauan Indonesia 7°30S 128°0E 231 F7
Baratang I. India 12°13N 92°45E 245 H11
Barataria B. U.S.A. 29°20N 89°55W 315 G10
Barauda India 23°33N 75°15E 242 H6
Baraut India 29°13N 77°7E 242 E7
Baraya Colombia 3°10N 75°4W 328 C2
Barbacan = Roxas Phil. 10°20N 119°21E 233 F2
Barbacena Brazil 21°15S 43°56W 333 F3
Barbacoas Colombia 1°45N 78°0W 328 C2
Barbados ■ W. Indies 13°10N 59°30W 323 r
Barbalha Brazil 7°19S 39°17W 332 C4
Barban Croatia 45°5N 14°2E 199 C11
Barbària, C. de Spain 38°39N 1°24E 206 D1
Barbarigo, Palazzo Venice, Italy 142 b2
Barbaros Turkey 40°54N 27°27E 203 F11
Barbas, C. W. Sahara 22°20N 16°42W 260 D1
Barbastro Spain 42°2N 0°5E 196 C5
Barbate Spain 36°13N 5°56W 195 J5
Barbaza Phil. 11°12N 122°2E 233 F4
Barbeau Pk. Canada 81°54N 75°1W 295 A16
Barber Curaçao 12°17N 69°4W 322 g
Barberini, Palazzo Rome, Italy 136 b3
Barberino di Mugello Italy 44°0N 11°15E 199 E8
Barbers Pt. U.S.A. 21°18N 158°7W 302 K13
Barberton Mpumalanga, S. Africa 25°42S 31°2E 271 C5
Barberton Ohio, U.S.A. 41°1N 81°39W 312 E3
Barberville U.S.A. 29°11N 81°26W 317 F8
Barbezieux-St-Hilaire France 45°28N 0°9W 174 C3
Barbican London, U.K. 125 a4
Barbosa Colombia 5°57N 73°37W 328 B3
Barbourville U.S.A. 36°52N 83°53W 309 G12
Barbuda W. Indies 17°30N 61°40W 322 c
Bârca Romania 43°59N 23°36E 183 G8
Barcaldine Australia 23°43S 145°6E 280 C4
Barcarena Brazil 1°30S 48°40W 332 B2
Barcarena Lisboa, Portugal 38°43N 9°16W 126 A1
Barcarena, Rib. de → Portugal 38°41N 9°16W 126 A1
Barcarrota Spain 38°31N 6°51W 195 G4
Barce = Al Marj Libya 32°25N 20°30E 258 B4
Barcellona Pozzo di Gotto Italy 38°9N 15°13E 201 D8
Barcelona Spain 41°22N 2°10E 114 A2
Barcelona Venezuela 10°10N 64°40W 329 A5
Barcelona □ Spain 41°30N 2°0E 196 D7
Barcelona ✕ (BCN) Spain 41°18N 2°5E 114 B1
Barceloneta Puerto Rico 18°27N 66°32W 321 b
Barcelonette France 44°23N 6°40E 175 D10
Barcelos Brazil 1°0S 63°0W 329 D5
Barcin Poland 52°52N 17°55E 185 F4
Barclayville Liberia 4°48N 8°10W 262 E3
Barcoo → Australia 25°30S 142°50E 280 D3
Barcroft, L. U.S.A. 38°52N 77°9W 143 B2
Barcs Hungary 45°58N 17°28E 182 E2
Barczewo Poland 53°50N 20°42E 184 E7
Bärdä Azerbaijan 40°25N 47°10E 191 K8
Barda del Medio Argentina 38°45S 68°11W 336 A3
Bardaï Chad 21°25N 17°0E 259 D3
Bardas Blancas Argentina 35°49S 69°45W 334 D2
Bardawîl, Sabkhet el Egypt 31°10N 33°15E 251 G4
Barddhaman India 23°14N 87°39E 243 H12
Bardejov Slovak Rep. 49°18N 21°15E 181 B14
Bardera = Baardheere Somalia 2°20N 42°27E 267 D5
Barð Iceland 66°3N 19°8W 155 A7
Bárðarbunga Iceland 64°38N 17°32W 155 C9
Barðastrandarsýsla Iceland 65°40N 23°0W 155 B3
Bardi Italy 44°38N 9°44E 198 D6
Bardīyah Libya 31°45N 25°5E 258 B5
Bardoli India 21°12N 73°5E 244 D1
Bardolino Italy 45°33N 10°43E 198 C7
Bardonécchia Italy 45°5N 6°42E 198 C3
Bardsey I. U.K. 52°45N 4°47W 168 E3
Bardstown U.S.A. 37°49N 85°28W 311 G11
Bare Ethiopia 4°37N 42°43E 267 D5
Bareilly India 28°22N 79°27E 243 E8
Barela India 23°6N 80°3E 243 H9
Barellan Australia 34°16S 146°24E 283 C7
Barentin France 49°33N 0°58E 172 C7
Barenton France 48°38N 0°50W 172 D6
Barents Sea Arctic 73°0N 39°0E 150 B9
Barentsøya Svalbard 78°25N 21°20E 154 B13
Barentu Eritrea 15°2N 37°35E 257 D4
Barfleur France 49°40N 1°17W 172 C5
Barfleur, Pte. de France 49°42N 1°16W 172 C5
Barfurush = Bābol Iran 36°40N 52°50E 247 B7
Barga Italy 44°4N 10°29E 198 D7
Bargaal Somalia 11°25N 51°0E 267 B7
Bargara Australia 24°50S 152°25E 280 C5
Bargarh India 21°20N 83°37E 244 D6
Bargas Spain 39°56N 4°3W 194 F6
Barge Italy 44°43N 7°20E 198 D4
Bargi Dam India 22°59N 80°0E 244 C5
Bargo Australia 34°18S 150°35E 283 C9
Bargteheide Germany 53°44N 10°14E 178 B6
Barguzin Russia 53°37N 109°37E 215 D11
Barh India 25°29N 85°46E 243 G11
Barhaj India 26°18N 83°44E 243 F10
Barham Australia 35°36S 144°8E 282 C6
Barharwa India 24°52N 87°47E 243 G12
Barhi India 24°15N 85°25E 243 G11
Bari Dem. Rep. of the Congo 3°20N 19°25E 264 B3
Bari India 26°39N 77°39E 242 F7
Bari Italy 41°8N 16°51E 201 A9
Bari □ Somalia 10°0N 50°0E 267 B6
Bari Doab Pakistan 30°20N 73°0E 242 D5
Bari Sadri India 24°28N 74°30E 242 G6
Bari Sardo Italy 39°50N 9°38E 200 C2
Barīdī, Ra's Si. Arabia 24°17N 37°31E 246 E3
Barīm Yemen 12°39N 43°25E 248 D3
Barima → Guyana 8°33N 60°25W 329 B5
Barinas Venezuela 8°36N 70°15W 328 B3
Barinas □ Venezuela 8°10N 69°50W 328 B4
Baring U.S.A. 40°15N 92°12W 310 D4
Baring, C. Canada 70°0N 117°30W 294 D8
Baringa Dem. Rep. of the Congo 0°45N 20°52E 264 B4
Baringo Kenya 0°38N 36°16E 266 D4
Baringo, L. Kenya 0°47N 36°16E 268 B4
Barinitas Venezuela 8°45N 70°25W 328 B3
Baripada India 21°57N 86°45E 244 D8
Bariri Brazil 22°4S 48°44W 333 F2
Bârîs Egypt 24°42N 30°31E 256 C3
Barisal Bangla. 22°45N 90°20E 241 D3
Barisal □ Bangla. 22°45N 90°20E 241 D3
Barisan, Pegunungan Indonesia 3°30S 102°15E 234 C2
Barit I. Phil. 18°51N 121°15E 232 B3
Barito → Indonesia 4°0S 114°50E 235 C4
Baritú △ Argentina 23°43S 64°40W 334 A3
Barjac France 44°20N 4°22E 175 D8
Barjols France 43°34N 6°2E 175 E10
Barjūj, Wadi → Libya 25°26N 12°12E 258 C2
Bark L. Canada 45°27N 77°51W 312 A7
Barka = Baraka → Sudan 18°13N 37°35E 256 D4
Barkā' Oman 23°40N 58°0E 249 B7
Barkakana India 23°37N 85°29E 243 H11
Barkal, J. Sudan 18°32N 31°50E 256 D3
Barkald Norway 61°59N 10°53E 164 C7
Barkam China 31°51N 102°28E 228 B4
Barker U.S.A. 43°20N 78°33W 312 C6
Barking U.K. 51°32N 0°5E 125 A4
Barkingside U.K. 51°35N 0°4E 125 A4
Barkley, L. U.S.A. 37°1N 88°14W 315 C10
Barkley Sound Canada 48°50N 125°10W 296 D3
Barkly East S. Africa 30°58S 27°33E 270 D4
Barkly Homestead Australia 19°52S 135°50E 280 B2
Barkly Tableland Australia 17°50S 136°40E 280 B2
Barkly West S. Africa 28°5S 24°31E 270 C3
Barkol Kazak Zizhixian China 43°37N 93°2E 218 C7
Barla Dağı Turkey 38°5N 30°40E 205 C12
Bârlad Romania 46°15N 27°38E 183 D12
Bârlad → Romania 45°38N 27°32E 183 E12
Barlee, L. Australia 29°15S 119°30E 279 E2
Barlee, Mt. Australia 24°38S 128°13E 279 D4
Barletta Italy 41°19N 16°17E 201 A9
Barlinek Poland 53°0N 15°15E 185 F2
Barlovento Canary Is. 28°48N 17°48W 153 e1
Barlovento C. Verde Is. 17°0N 25°0W 153 j
Barlow L. Canada 62°0N 103°0W 297 A8
Barmedman Australia 34°9S 147°21E 283 C7
Barmer India 25°45N 71°20E 242 G4
Barmera Australia 34°15S 140°28E 282 C4
Barmouth U.K. 52°44N 4°4W 168 E3
Barmstedt Germany 53°47N 9°46E 178 B5
Barn, The St. Helena 15°55S 5°40W 153 h
Barna → India 25°21N 83°3E 243 G10
Barnagar India 23°7N 75°19E 242 H6
Barnala India 30°23N 75°33E 242 D6
Barnard → Australia 31°34S 151°25E 283 A9
Barnard Castle U.K. 54°33N 1°55W 168 C6
Barnato Australia 31°38S 145°0E 283 A6
Barnaul Russia 53°20N 83°40E 217 B10
Barnes N.S.W., Australia 36°2S 144°49E 282 D6
Barnes London, U.K. 51°28N 0°14W 125 B2
Barnesville Ga., U.S.A. 33°3N 84°9W 316 B5
Barnesville Minn., U.S.A. 46°43N 96°28W 308 B5
Barnet U.K. 51°39N 0°11W 125 A2
Barnet □ U.K. 51°38N 0°9W 169 F7
Barneveld Neths. 52°7N 5°36E 170 B5
Barneville-Cartevert France 49°23N 1°46W 172 C5
Barnhart U.S.A. 31°8N 101°10W 314 F4
Barnsley U.K. 53°34N 1°27W 168 D6
Barnstable U.S.A. 41°42N 70°18W 309 E18
Barnstaple U.K. 51°5N 4°4W 169 F3
Barnstaple Bay = Bideford Bay U.K. 51°5N 4°20W 169 F3
Barnum B. Palau 7°6N 134°15E 288 c
Barnwell U.S.A. 33°15N 81°23W 316 B8
Baro Nigeria 8°35N 6°18E 263 D6
Baro → Ethiopia 8°26N 33°13E 257 F3
Barobo Phil. 8°33N 126°7E 233 G6
Baroda = Vadodara India 22°20N 73°10E 242 H5
Baroda India 25°29N 76°35E 242 G7
Baroe S. Africa 33°13S 24°33E 270 D3
Baron Ra. Australia 23°30S 127°45E 278 D4
Barong China 31°3N 99°20E 228 B2
Barora Solomon Is. 7°30S 158°20E 287 L10
Barora Ite Solomon Is. 7°36S 158°24E 287 L10
Barotse = Western □ Zambia 15°0S 24°4E 265 F4
Barotseland Zambia 15°0S 24°0E 265 F4
Barouéli Mali 13°4N 6°50W 262 C3
Barpali India 21°11N 83°35E 244 D6
Barpathar India 26°17N 93°53E 241 B4
Barpeta India 26°20N 91°10E 241 B3
Barqa Libya 27°0N 23°0E 258 B4
Barqin Libya 27°33N 13°34E 258 C2
Barques, Pt. Aux U.S.A. 44°4N 82°58W 312 B2
Barquísimeto Venezuela 10°4N 69°19W 328 A4
Barr, Ras el Egypt 31°32N 31°50E 256 H7
Barr Smith Range Australia 27°4S 120°20E 279 E3
Barra Brazil 11°5S 43°10W 332 D3
Barra Gambia 13°28N 16°32W 262 C1
Barra W. Isles, U.K. 57°0N 7°29W 167 E1
Barra, Sd. of U.K. 57°4N 7°25W 167 D1
Barra Andai Pakistan 24°47N 66°59E 123 B2
Barra Bonita = Ibaiti Brazil 23°50S 50°10W 333 F1
Barra da Estiva Brazil 13°38S 41°19W 333 D3
Barra de Navidad Mexico 19°12N 104°41W 318 D4
Barra de São Manuel Brazil 7°19S 58°5W 331 B6
Barra do Bugres Brazil 15°0S 57°11W 331 D6
Barra do Corda Brazil 5°30S 45°10W 332 C2
Barra do Dande Angola 8°28S 13°22E 265 D2
Barra do Garças Brazil 15°54S 52°16W 331 D7
Barra do Mendes Brazil 11°43S 42°4W 333 D3
Barra do Piraí Brazil 22°30S 43°50W 333 F3
Barra Falsa, Pta. da Mozam. 22°58S 35°37E 271 B6
Barra Funda Brazil 23°31S 46°39W 137 B2
Barra Hd. U.K. 56°47N 7°40W 167 E1
Barra Mansa Brazil 22°35S 44°12W 333 F3
Barraba Australia 30°21S 150°35E 283 A9
Barracão do Barreto Brazil 8°48S 58°24W 331 B6
Barracas Argentina 34°39S 58°24W 117 B2
Barracas al Sur = Avellaneda Argentina 34°40S 58°22W 117 C2
Barrackpur = Barakpur India 22°47N 88°21E 124 A2
Barrafranca Italy 37°22N 14°12E 201 E7
Barrāmīya Egypt 25°4N 33°47E 256 B3
Barranca Lima, Peru 10°45S 77°50W 330 C2
Barranca Loreto, Peru 4°50S 76°50W 328 D2
Barranca del Cobre ⌓ Mexico 27°18N 107°40W 318 B3
Barrancabermeja Colombia 7°0N 73°50W 328 B3
Barrancas Colombia 10°57N 72°50W 328 A3
Barrancas Venezuela 8°55N 62°5W 329 B5
Barranco Peru 12°9S 77°2W 124 B2
Barrancones Pt. Trin. & Tob. 10°31N 61°28W 323 t
Barrancos Portugal 38°10N 6°58W 195 G4
Barranqueras Argentina 27°30S 59°0W 334 B4
Barranquilla Colombia 11°0N 74°50W 328 A3
Barranquitas Puerto Rico 18°11N 66°19W 321 b
Barras Brazil 4°15S 42°18W 332 B3
Barras Colombia 1°45S 73°13W 328 D3
Barraute Canada 48°26N 77°38W 298 C4
Barre Mass., U.S.A. 42°25N 72°6W 313 D12
Barre Vt., U.S.A. 44°12N 72°30W 313 B12
Barre de L'Isle Ridge St. Lucia 13°55N 60°58W 323 m
Barreal Argentina 31°33S 69°28W 334 C2
Barrei Ethiopia 6°10N 42°49E 267 C5
Barreiras Brazil 12°8S 45°0W 333 D3
Barreirinha Brazil 2°47S 57°3W 329 D6
Barreirinhas Brazil 2°30S 42°50W 332 B3
Barreiro Portugal 38°39N 9°5W 126 B2
Barreiros Brazil 8°49S 35°12W 332 C4
Barrême France 43°57N 6°23E 175 E10
Barren, Nosy Madag. 18°25S 43°40E 272 B1
Barren I. India 12°16N 93°51E 245 H11
Barren Is. U.S.A. 58°55N 152°15W 303 G9
Barreto Brazil 22°50S 43°5W 135 B2
Barretos Brazil 20°30S 48°35W 333 F2
Barrhead Canada 54°10N 114°24W 296 C6
Barrie Canada 44°24N 79°40W 312 B5
Barrier, C. N.Z. 36°25S 175°32E 284 C4
Barrier Ra. N.S.W., Australia 31°0S 141°30E 282 A4
Barrier Ra. Otago, N.Z. 44°15S 169°32E 285 E4
Barrier Ra. W. Coast, N.Z. 44°30S 168°30E 285 E3
Barrière Canada 51°12N 120°7W 296 C4
Barrière-la-Croix Martinique 14°27N 60°51W 322 j
Barrigada Guam 13°28N 144°48E 302 d
Barrineau Park U.S.A. 30°42N 87°26W 317 E2
Barrington U.S.A. 41°44N 71°18W 313 E13
Barrington, I. = Santa Fé, I. Ecuador 0°49S 90°5W 330 a
Barrington L. Canada 56°55N 100°15W 297 B8
Barrington Tops Australia 32°6S 151°28E 283 B9
Barrington Tops △ Australia 32°4S 151°25E 283 B9
Barringun Australia 29°1S 145°41E 281 D4
Barrit-Luluno = Luba Phil. 17°19N 120°42E 232 C3
Barron U.S.A. 45°24N 91°51W 308 C8
Barrouallie St. Vincent 13°14N 61°17W 323 n
Barroui = Salisbury Dominica 15°26N 61°27W 323 k
Barrow U.S.A. 71°18N 156°47W 303 A8
Barrow → Ireland 52°25N 6°58W 166 D5
Barrow, Pt. U.S.A. 71°23N 156°29W 303 A8
Barrow Creek Australia 21°30S 133°55E 280 C1
Barrow I. Australia 20°45S 115°20E 278 D2
Barrow-in-Furness U.K. 54°7N 3°14W 168 C4
Barrow Pt. Australia 14°20S 144°40E 280 A3
Barrow Ra. Australia 26°0S 127°40E 279 E4
Barrow Str. Canada 74°20N 95°0W 295 C13
Barruecopardo Spain 41°4N 6°40W 194 D4
Barruelo de Santullán Spain 42°54N 4°17W 194 C6
Barry V. of Glam., U.K. 51°24N 3°16W 169 F4
Barry Ill., U.S.A. 39°42N 91°2W 310 E5
Barry's Bay Canada 45°29N 77°41W 312 A7
Barsalogho Burkina Faso 13°25N 1°3W 263 C4
Barsat Pakistan 36°10N 72°45E 243 A5
Barsham Syria 35°21N 40°33E 213 E9
Barshatas Kazakhstan 48°10N 78°39E 217 C9
Barsi India 18°10N 75°50E 244 E2
Barsinghausen Germany 52°18N 9°28E 178 C5
Barsoi India 25°48N 87°57E 241 C1
Barstow U.S.A. 34°54N 117°1W 307 L9
Bartala India 22°32N 88°15E 124 B1
Bartenstein = Bartoszyce Poland 54°15N 20°55E 184 D7
Bartfeld = Bardejov Slovak Rep. 49°18N 21°15E 181 B14
Barth Germany 54°22N 12°42E 178 A8
Bartica Guyana 6°25N 58°40W 329 B6
Bartin Turkey 41°38N 32°21E 212 B5
Bartle Frere Australia 17°27S 145°50E 280 B4
Bartlesville U.S.A. 36°45N 95°59W 314 C7
Bartlett Calif., U.S.A. 36°29N 118°2W 306 J8
Bartlett Tenn., U.S.A. 35°12N 89°52W 315 D10
Bartlett, L. Canada 63°5N 118°20W 296 A5
Bartolbaai Curaçao 12°20N 69°2W 322 g
Bartolo = Betanzos Bolivia 19°34S 65°27W 331 D4
Bartolomeu Dias Mozam. 21°10S 35°8E 269 G4
Barton Phil. 10°24N 119°8E 233 F2
Barton Vt., U.S.A. 44°45N 72°11W 313 B12
Barton Park Australia 33°56S 151°9E 139 B1
Barton upon Humber U.K. 53°41N 0°25W 168 D7
Bartonville U.S.A. 40°39N 89°39W 310 D7
Bartoszyce Poland 54°15N 20°55E 184 D7
Bartow Fla., U.S.A. 27°54N 81°50W 317 H8
Bartow Ga., U.S.A. 32°53N 82°29W 316 C7
Bartyki Poland 52°10N 21°6E 143 C2
Barú, I. de Colombia 10°15N 75°35W 328 A2
Barú, Volcan Panama 8°55N 82°35W 320 E3
Barumba Dem. Rep. of the Congo 1°3N 23°37E 268 B1
Barumbu Dem. Rep. of the Congo 1°14N 23°31E 264 B4
Barúmini Italy 39°42N 8°59E 200 C1
Barung, Nusa Indonesia 8°30S 113°30E 235 D4
Barus Indonesia 2°0N 98°24E 234 B1
Baruth Germany 52°4N 13°30E 178 C9
Baruun Urt Mongolia 46°46N 113°15E 219 B11
Baruunsuu Mongolia 43°43N 105°35E 226 C3
Barvinkove Ukraine 48°57N 37°0E 189 H9
Bärwalde = Barwice Poland 53°44N 16°21E 184 E3
Barwani India 22°2N 74°57E 242 H6
Barwice Poland 53°44N 16°21E 184 E3
Barwick U.S.A. 30°54N 83°44W 316 E6
Barxudarlı Azerbaijan 41°0N 45°14E 213 B11
Barycz → Poland 51°42N 16°15E 185 G3
Barysaw Belarus 54°17N 28°28E 177 A15
Barysh Russia 53°39N 47°8E 190 D8
Barzān Iraq 36°55N 44°3E 246 B5
Bârzava Romania 46°7N 21°59E 182 D6
Bas-Congo □ Dem. Rep. of the Congo 5°0S 15°0E 265 D2
Bas du Fort Guadeloupe 16°13N 61°30W 322 e
Bas-Kouilou Congo 4°28S 11°42E 265 C2
Bas-Rhin □ France 48°40N 7°30E 173 D14
Bas-Sassandra □ Ivory C. 5°30N 7°0W 262 D3
Bašaid Serbia 45°38N 20°25E 182 E5
Bāsa'idū Iran 26°35N 55°20E 247 E7
Basal Pakistan 33°33N 72°13E 242 C5
Basankusa Dem. Rep. of the Congo 1°5N 19°50E 264 B3
Basarabeasca Moldova 46°21N 28°58E 183 D13
Basarabi Romania 44°10N 28°26E 183 F13
Basarabia = Bessarabiya Moldova 47°0N 28°10E 177 E15
Basauri Spain 43°13N 2°53W 196 B2
Basawa Afghan. 34°15N 70°50E 242 B4
Basco Phil. 20°27N 121°58E 232 A3
Bascuñán, C. Chile 28°52S 71°35W 334 B1
Basekpio Dem. Rep. of the Congo 4°43N 24°36E 264 B4
Basel Switz. 47°35N 7°35E 179 H3
Basel Euroairport ✕ (EAP) France 47°36N 7°33E 173 E14
Basel-Landschaft □ Switz. 47°26N 7°45E 179 H3
Basento → Italy 40°20N 16°49E 201 B9
Baserah Indonesia 0°25S 101°43E 234 C2
Basey Phil. 11°17N 125°4E 233 F5
Bashākerd, Kūhhā-ye Iran 26°42N 58°35E 247 E8
Bashanta = Gorodovikovsk Russia 46°8N 41°58E 191 G5
Bashaw Canada 52°35N 112°58W 296 C6
Bāshī Iran 28°41N 51°4E 247 D6
Bashi Channel Asia 21°25N 121°30E 225 E2
Bashkand = Artsvashen Armenia 40°38N 45°30E 213 B11
Bashkir Republic = Bashkortostan □ Russia 54°0N 57°0E 186 D10
Bashkiriya △ Russia 52°58N 56°30E 216 B5
Bashkortostan □ Russia 54°0N 57°0E 186 D10
Bashtanivka Ukraine 45°46N 29°29E 183 E14
Basibasy Madag. 22°10S 43°40E 272 C1
Basilaki I. Papua N. G. 10°35S 151°0E 286 F6
Basilan □ Phil. 6°33N 122°4E 233 H3
Basilan I. Phil. 6°35N 122°0E 233 H4
Basilan Str. Phil. 6°50N 122°0E 233 H4
Basildon U.K. 51°34N 0°28E 169 F8
Basilé Eq. Guin. 3°42N 8°48E 263 E6
Basilé, Pico de Eq. Guin. 3°36N 8°49E 263 E6
Basilicata □ Italy 40°30N 16°30E 201 B9
Basim = Washim India 20°3N 77°0E 244 D3
Basin U.S.A. 44°23N 108°2W 304 D9
Basinger U.S.A. 27°23N 81°2W 317 H8
Basingstoke U.K. 51°15N 1°5W 169 F6
Basirhat Bangla. 22°40N 88°54E 241 D2
Basīţ, Ra's al Syria 35°51N 35°48E 250 C6
Baška Croatia 44°58N 14°45E 199 D11
Başkale Turkey 38°2N 43°59E 213 C10
Baskatong, Rés. Canada 46°46N 75°50W 298 C4
Basle = Basel Switz. 47°35N 7°35E 179 H3
Başmakçı Turkey 37°54N 30°1E 205 D12
Basmat India 19°15N 77°12E 244 E3
Basoda India 23°52N 77°54E 242 H7
Basoko Dem. Rep. of the Congo 1°16N 23°40E 264 B4
Basongo Dem. Rep. of the Congo 4°15S 20°20E 265 C4
Basora, Pta. Aruba 12°25N 69°51W 322 f
Basque, Côte France 43°50N 2°0W 174 E2
Basque, Pays France 43°15N 1°20W 174 E2
Basque Provinces = País Vasco □ Spain 42°50N 2°45W 196 C2
Basra = Al Başrah Iraq 30°30N 47°50E 246 D5
Bass, Îs. de French Polynesia 27°55S 143°26W 289 f
Bass Str. Australia 39°15S 146°30E 281 F4
Bassae Greece 37°26N 21°53E 204 D3
Bassano Canada 50°48N 112°20W 296 C6
Bassano del Grappa Italy 45°46N 11°44E 199 C8
Bassar Togo 9°19N 0°57E 263 D5
Bassas da India Ind. Oc. 22°0S 39°0E 269 G4
Basse-Kotto □ C.A.R. 5°0N 21°30E 264 A4
Basse-Normandie □ France 48°45N 0°30W 172 D6
Basse-Pointe Martinique 14°52N 61°8W 322 j
Basse Santa-Su Gambia 13°13N 14°15W 262 C2
Basse-Terre Guadeloupe 16°0N 61°44W 322 e
Basse Terre Trin. & Tob. 10°7N 61°19W 323 t
Bassein Burma 16°45N 94°30E 241 G5
Basses, Pte. des Guadeloupe 15°52N 61°17W 322 e
Basses-Alpes = Alpes-de-Haute-Provence □ France 44°8N 6°10E 175 D10
Basses-Pyrénées = Pyrénées-Atlantiques □ France 43°10N 0°50W 174 E3
Basseterre St. Kitts & Nevis 17°17N 62°43W 322 d
Bassett U.S.A. 42°35N 99°32W 308 D4
Bassi India 30°44N 76°21E 242 D7
Bassigny France 48°0N 5°30E 173 E12
Bassikounou Mauritania 15°55N 6°1W 262 B3
Bassila Benin 9°1N 1°46E 263 D5
Bassum Germany 52°50N 8°40E 178 C4
Båstad Sweden 56°25N 12°51E 163 H6
Bastak Iran 27°15N 54°25E 247 E7
Baştām Iran 36°29N 55°4E 247 B7
Bastar India 19°15N 81°40E 244 E5
Bastelica France 42°1N 9°3E 175 F13
Basti India 26°52N 82°55E 243 F10
Bastia France 42°40N 9°30E 175 F13
Bastille, Place de la Paris, France 134 c5
Bastogne Belgium 50°1N 5°43E 170 D5
Bastrop La., U.S.A. 32°47N 91°55W 314 E9
Bastrop Tex., U.S.A. 30°7N 97°19W 314 F6
Basu Indonesia 0°18S 103°36E 234 C2
Basud Phil. 14°4N 122°58E 232 D4
Basuo = Dongfang China 18°50N 108°33E 229 a
Basus Egypt 30°7N 31°12E 117 A2
Basutoland = Lesotho ■ Africa 29°40S 28°0E 271 C4
Başyayla Turkey 36°45N 32°40E 250 B3
Bat al Khutm & Al 'Ayn Oman 23°16N 56°44E 249 B7
Bat-ongan Caves Phil. 12°20N 123°15E 232 E4
Bat Yam Israel 32°2N 34°44E 251 F5
Bata Eq. Guin. 1°57N 9°50E 264 B1
Bata Romania 46°1N 22°4E 182 D7
Bataan □ Phil. 14°40N 120°25E 232 D3
Bataan △ Phil. 14°45N 120°27E 232 D3
Batabanó Cuba 22°41N 82°18W 320 B3
Batabanó, G. de Cuba 22°30N 82°30W 320 B3
Batac Phil. 18°3N 120°34E 232 B3
Batagai Russia 67°38N 134°38E 215 C14
Batajnica Serbia 44°54N 20°17E 202 B4
Batak Bulgaria 41°57N 24°12E 203 E8
Batakan Indonesia 4°4S 114°37E 235 C4
Batala India 31°48N 75°12E 242 D6
Batalha Portugal 39°40N 8°50W 194 F2
Batalpashinsk = Cherkessk Russia 44°15N 42°5E 191 H6
Batam Indonesia 1°10N 104°2E 237 d
Batama Dem. Rep. of the Congo 0°58N 26°33E 268 B2
Batamay Russia 63°30N 129°15E 215 C13
Batan I. Albay, Phil. 13°15N 124°0E 232 E4
Batan I. Batanes, Phil. 20°26N 121°58E 232 A3
Batan Is. Phil. 20°30N 122°0E 232 A3
Batanagar India 22°31N 88°15E 124 B1
Batanes □ Phil. 20°40N 121°55E 232 A3
Batang Sichuan, China 30°1N 99°0E 228 B2
Batang Indonesia 6°55S 109°45E 235 D3
Batang Ai △ Malaysia 1°32N 112°2E 235 B4
Batang Gadis △ Indonesia 0°28N 99°12E 234 B1
Batanga Gabon 0°21S 9°18E 264 C1
Batangafo C.A.R. 7°25N 18°20E 264 A3
Batangas Phil. 13°35N 121°10E 232 E3
Batangas □ Phil. 13°40N 121°5E 232 E3
Batanta Indonesia 0°55S 130°40E 231 E8
Batarasa Phil. 8°40N 117°37E 233 G1
Batas I. Phil. 11°10N 119°36E 233 F2
Batatais Brazil 20°54S 47°37W 335 A6
Batavia = Jakarta Indonesia 6°9S 106°52E 122 A2
Batavia Ill., U.S.A. 41°51N 88°19W 311 C8
Batavia N.Y., U.S.A. 43°0N 78°11W 312 D6
Batavia Ohio, U.S.A. 39°5N 84°11W 311 E12
Bataysk Russia 47°3N 39°45E 189 J10
Batbakara = Amankeldi Kazakhstan 50°10N 65°10E 216 B7
Batchelor Australia 13°4S 131°1E 278 B5
Batdambang Cambodia 13°7N 103°12E 236 F4
Batéké, Plateau Congo 3°30S 15°45E 264 C3
Batemans B. Australia 35°40S 150°12E 283 C9
Batemans Bay Australia 35°44S 150°11E 283 C9
Batesburg-Leesville U.S.A. 33°54N 81°33W 316 B8
Batesville Ark., U.S.A. 35°46N 91°39W 314 D9
Batesville Ind., U.S.A. 39°18N 85°13W 311 E11
Batesville Miss., U.S.A. 34°19N 89°57W 315 D10
Batesville Tex., U.S.A. 28°58N 99°37W 314 G5
Bath Ont., Canada 44°11N 76°47W 313 B8
Bath St. Kitts & Nevis 17°8N 62°37W 322 d
Bath Bath & N.E. Somerset, U.K. 51°23N 2°22W 169 F5
Bath Maine, U.S.A. 43°55N 69°49W 309 D19
Bath N.Y., U.S.A. 42°20N 77°19W 312 D7
Bath & North East Somerset □ U.K. 51°21N 2°27W 169 F5
Bath Beach U.S.A. 40°36N 74°0W 132 C1
Bath I. Pakistan 24°49N 67°1E 123 B2
Batha □ Chad 14°0N 19°0E 259 F3
Batha → Chad 12°47N 17°34E 259 F3
Batheay Cambodia 11°59N 104°57E 237 G5
Bathsheba Barbados 13°13N 59°32W 323 r
Bathurst = Banjul Gambia 13°28N 16°40W 262 C1
Bathurst N.S.W., Australia 33°25S 149°31E 283 B8
Bathurst N.B., Canada 47°37N 65°43W 299 C6
Bathurst Eastern Cape, S. Africa 33°30S 26°50E 270 D4
Bathurst, C. Canada 70°34N 128°0W 294 C6
Bathurst B. Australia 14°16S 144°25E 280 A3
Bathurst Harb. Australia 43°15S 146°10E 281 G4
Bathurst I. N. Terr., Australia 11°30S 130°10E 278 B5
Bathurst I. Nunavut, Canada 76°0N 100°30W 295 B11
Bathurst Inlet Canada 66°50N 108°1W 294 D10
Bati Ethiopia 11°10N 40°0E 257 E5
Batie Burkina Faso 9°53N 2°53W 262 D4
Batiki Fiji 17°48S 179°10E 287 A2
Batir West Bank 31°43N 35°8E 123 B1
Batken Kyrgyzstan 40°3N 70°50E 217 D8
Batken □ Kyrgyzstan 39°50N 71°0E 217 E8
Batlow Australia 35°31S 148°9E 283 C8
Batman Turkey 37°55N 41°5E 213 D9
Baţn al Ghūl Jordan 29°36N 35°56E 251 J6
Batna Algeria 35°34N 6°15E 261 A6
Batna □ Algeria 35°30N 5°55E 261 A6
Batnfjordsøra Norway 62°53N 7°42E 164 B4
Bato Catanduanes, Phil. 13°36N 124°18E 232 E5
Bato Leyte, Phil. 10°13N 124°48E 233 F5
Bato Bato Phil. 5°6N 119°49E 233 J2
Batoala Gabon 0°48N 13°27E 264 B2
Batobato = San Isidro Phil. 6°50N 126°5E 233 H6
Batočina Serbia 44°7N 21°5E 202 B5
Batok, Bukit Singapore 1°21N 103°46E 138 A2
Batoka Zambia 16°45S 27°15E 269 F2
Baton Rouge U.S.A. 30°27N 91°11W 314 F9
Batong, Ko Thailand 6°32N 99°12E 237 J2
Bátonyterenye Hungary 47°59N 19°50E 182 C4
Batopilas Mexico 27°1N 107°44W 318 B3
Batouri Cameroon 4°30N 14°25E 264 B2
Batovany = Partizánske Slovak Rep. 48°38N 18°23E 181 C11
Båtsfjord Norway 70°38N 29°39E 160 A23
Batsi Greece 37°52N 24°47E 204 D6
Battambang = Batdambang Cambodia 13°7N 103°12E 236 F4
Battersea U.K. 51°28N 0°9W 125 B3
Battery Park New York, U.S.A. 132 f1
Batti Malv India 8°50N 92°51E 245 K11
Batticaloa Sri Lanka 7°43N 81°45E 245 L5
Battipáglia Italy 40°37N 14°58E 201 B7
Battle U.K. 50°55N 0°30E 169 G8
Battle → Canada 52°43N 108°15W 297 C7
Battle Creek U.S.A. 42°19N 85°11W 311 B11
Battle Ground U.S.A. 45°47N 122°32W 306 E4
Battle Harbour Canada 52°16N 55°35W 299 B8
Battle Lake U.S.A. 46°17N 95°43W 308 B6
Battle Mountain U.S.A. 40°38N 116°56W 304 F5
Battlefields Zimbabwe 18°37S 29°47E 269 F2
Battleford Canada 52°45N 108°15W 297 C7
Battonya Hungary 46°16N 21°3E 182 D6
Batu Ethiopia 6°55N 39°45E 257 F4
Batu Malaysia 3°15N 101°40E 237 L3
Batu, Bukit Malaysia 2°16N 113°43E 235 B4
Batu, Kepulauan Indonesia 0°30S 98°25E 234 C1
Batu Bora, Bukit Malaysia 2°43N 114°43E 235 B4
Batu Ferringhi Malaysia 5°28N 100°15E 237 c

Batu Gajah Malaysia 4°28N 101°3E 237 K3
Batu Is. = Batu, Kepulauan Indonesia 0°30S 98°25E 234 C1
Batu Pahat Malaysia 1°50N 102°56E 237 M4
Batu Puteh Malaysia 5°25N 117°55E 235 A5
Batu Puteh, Gunung Malaysia 4°15N 101°31E 237 K3
Batuan Phil. 12°25N 123°46E 232 E4
Batuata Indonesia 6°12S 122°42E 231 F6
Batugondang, Tanjung Indonesia 8°6S 114°29E 231 J17
Batukaru, Gunung Indonesia 8°20S 115°5E 231 J18
Batulaki Phil. 5°34N 125°19E 233 J5
Batuli = San Isidro Phil. 6°50N 126°5E 233 H6
Batumi Georgia 41°39N 41°44E 191 K5
Batuputih Indonesia 1°24N 118°28E 235 B5
Batur, Gunung Indonesia 8°14S 115°23E 231 J18
Batura Sar Pakistan 36°30N 74°31E 243 A6
Baturaja Indonesia 4°11S 104°15E 234 C2
Baturité Brazil 4°28S 38°45W 332 B4
Baturiti Indonesia 8°19S 115°11E 231 J18
Batusangkar Indonesia 0°27S 100°35E 234 C2
Batys Qazaqstan □ Kazakhstan 50°0N 50°0E 216 C3
Bau Malaysia 1°25N 110°9E 235 B4
Bauang Phil. 16°31N 120°20E 232 C3
Baubau Indonesia 5°25S 122°38E 231 F6
Baucau E. Timor 8°27S 126°27E 231 F7
Bauchi Nigeria 10°22N 9°48E 263 C6
Bauchi □ Nigeria 10°30N 10°0E 263 C7
Baud France 47°52N 3°1W 172 E3
Bauda India 20°50N 84°25E 244 D7
Baudette U.S.A. 48°43N 94°36W 308 A6
Bauer, C. Australia 32°44S 134°4E 281 E1
Bauerwitz = Baborów Poland 50°7N 18°1E 185 H5
Bauguen = Salcedo Phil. 11°9N 125°40E 233 F5
Bauhinia Australia 24°35S 149°18E 280 C4
Baukau = Baucau E. Timor 8°27S 126°27E 231 F7
Bauko Phil. 17°0N 120°52E 232 C3
Baulai → Bangla. 24°22N 91°1E 241 C3
Bauld, C. Canada 51°38N 55°26W 295 G20
Bauman Russia 55°45N 37°40E 129 B3
Baume-les-Dames France 47°22N 6°22E 173 E13
Baumgarten Austria 48°12N 16°17E 142 A1
Baunatal Germany 51°14N 9°24E 178 D5
Baunei Italy 40°2N 9°40E 200 B2
Baure Nigeria 12°52N 8°50E 263 C6
Baures Bolivia 13°35S 63°35W 331 C5
Bauru Brazil 22°10S 49°0W 335 A6
Baús Brazil 18°22S 52°47W 331 D7
Bausi India 24°48N 87°1E 243 G12
Bauska Latvia 56°24N 24°15E 184 B11
Bautino Kazakhstan 44°35N 50°14E 191 H10
Bautzen Germany 51°10N 14°26E 178 D10
Bauya S. Leone 8°12N 12°38W 262 D2
Bavānāt Iran 30°28N 53°27E 247 D7
Bavanište Serbia 44°49N 20°55E 182 F5
Bavaria = Bayern □ Germany 48°50N 12°0E 179 G7
Båven Sweden 59°0N 16°56E 162 E10
Bavispe → Mexico 29°15N 109°11W 318 B3
Baw Baw △ Australia 37°50S 146°17E 283 D7
Bawal Indonesia 7°52S 111°13E 235 D4
Bawan Indonesia 1°42S 113°55E 235 C4
Bawdwin Burma 23°5N 97°20E 241 D6
Bawean Indonesia 5°46S 112°35E 235 D4
Bawku Ghana 11°3N 0°19W 263 C4
Bawlakhe Burma 19°11N 97°21E 241 F6
Bawolung China 28°50N 101°16E 228 C3
Bawomataluwo Indonesia 0°38N 97°44E 234 B1
Baxley U.S.A. 31°47N 82°21W 316 D7
Baxter Iowa, U.S.A. 41°49N 93°9W 310 C3
Baxter Minn., U.S.A. 46°21N 94°17W 308 B6
Baxter Springs U.S.A. 37°2N 94°44W 308 G6
Baxter State ⌓ U.S.A. 46°5N 68°57W 309 B19
Bay □ Somalia 3°0N 43°30E 267 D5
Bay, L. U.S.A. 28°25N 81°34W 133 A2
Bay, Laguna de Phil. 14°20N 121°11E 232 D3
Bay City Mich., U.S.A. 43°36N 83°54W 309 D12
Bay City Tex., U.S.A. 28°59N 95°58W 314 G7
Bay Harbor Islands U.S.A. 25°53N 80°7W 129 C3
Bay Hill U.S.A. 28°28N 81°30W 133 B1
Bay Minette U.S.A. 30°53N 87°46W 315 F11
Bay of Plenty □ N.Z. 38°0S 177°0E 284 D5
Bay Ridge U.S.A. 40°37N 74°1W 132 C1
Bay Roberts Canada 47°36N 53°16W 299 C9
Bay St. Louis U.S.A. 30°19N 89°20W 315 F10
Bay Springs U.S.A. 31°59N 89°17W 315 F10
Bay View N.Z. 39°25S 176°50E 284 F5
Baya Dem. Rep. of the Congo 11°53S 27°25E 269 E2
Bayambang Phil. 15°49N 120°27E 232 D3
Bayamo Cuba 20°20N 76°40W 320 B4
Bayamón Puerto Rico 18°24N 66°9W 321 C6
Bayan Har Shan China 34°0N 98°0E 218 E8
Bayan Hot = Alxa Zuoqi China 38°50N 105°40E 226 E3
Bayan Lepas Malaysia 5°17N 100°16E 237 c
Bayan Obo China 41°52N 109°59E 226 D5
Bayan-Ovoo = Erdenetsogt Mongolia 42°55N 106°5E 226 C4
Bayan-Tumen = Choybalsan Mongolia 48°4N 114°30E 219 B11
Bayana India 26°55N 77°18E 242 F7
Bayanaūyl Kazakhstan 50°45N 75°45E 217 B9
Bayanhongor Mongolia 46°8N 102°43E 218 B9
Bayard N. Mex., U.S.A. 32°46N 108°8W 305 K9
Bayard Nebr., U.S.A. 41°45N 103°20W 308 E2
Bayawan Phil. 9°46N 122°45E 233 G4
Baybay Phil. 10°40N 124°55E 233 F5
Bayburt Turkey 40°15N 40°20E 213 B9
Bayburt □ Turkey 40°35N 39°25E 213 B8
Baydaratskaya Guba Russia 69°0N 67°30E 214 C7
Baydhabo Somalia 3°8N 43°30E 267 D5
Bayelsa □ Nigeria 4°30N 6°0E 263 E6
Bayerische Alpen Germany 47°35N 11°30E 179 H7
Bayerische Rhön ⌓ Germany 50°15N 10°5E 179 E6
Bayerischer Spessart ⌓ Germany 49°58N 10°15E 179 F6
Bayerischer Wald Germany 48°56N 12°50E 179 G8
Bayern □ Germany 48°50N 12°0E 179 G7
Bayeux France 49°17N 0°42W 172 C6
Bayfield Ont., Canada 43°34N 81°42W 312 C3
Bayfield Wis., U.S.A. 46°49N 90°49W 308 B8
Bayḥān al Qiṣāb Yemen 15°48N 45°44E 248 D4
Bayındır Turkey 38°13N 27°39E 205 C9
Bayit Va-Gan Israel 31°46N 35°11E 123 B2
Baykal, Oz. Russia 53°0N 108°0E 215 D11
Baykan Turkey 38°7N 41°44E 213 C9
Baymak Russia 52°36N 58°19E 186 D10
Baynes Mts. Namibia 17°15S 13°0E 270 A1
Bayombong Phil. 16°30N 121°10E 232 C3
Bayon France 48°30N 6°20E 173 D13
Bayona = Baiona Spain 42°6N 8°52W 194 C2
Bayonet Point U.S.A. 28°20N 82°41W 317 G7
Bayonne Pyrénées-Atlantiques, France 43°30N 1°28W 174 E2
Bayonne N.J., U.S.A. 40°40N 74°6W 132 B1
Bayou Boeuf U.S.A. 29°50N 90°10W 131 B1
Bayou Segnette State Park ⌓ U.S.A. 29°53N 90°10W 131 B2
Bayovar Peru 5°50S 81°0W 330 B1
Bayport U.S.A. 28°32N 82°39W 317 G7
Bayqonyr Kazakhstan 45°40N 63°20E 216 C6
Bayram-Ali = Baýramaly Turkmenistan 37°37N 62°10E 247 B9
Baýramaly Turkmenistan 37°37N 62°10E 247 B9
Bayramiç Turkey 39°48N 26°36E 205 B8
Bayrampaşa Turkey 41°1N 28°56E 122 B1
Bayreuth Germany 49°56N 11°35E 179 F7
Bayrischzell Germany 47°41N 12°0E 179 H8
Bayrūt Lebanon 33°53N 35°31E 250 E6
Bays, L. of Canada 45°15N 79°4W 312 A5
Bayshore Calif., U.S.A. 37°42N 122°24W 136 B2
Bayshore Fla., U.S.A. 26°43N 81°50W 317 J8
Baysville Canada 45°9N 79°7W 312 A5
Bayswater London, U.K. 125 b2
Bayt al Faqīh Yemen 14°31N 43°19E 248 D3
Bayt Lahm West Bank 31°43N 35°12E 123 B2
Baytik Shan China 45°15N 90°50E 217 C12
Baytown U.S.A. 29°43N 94°59W 314 G7
Bayugan Phil. 8°43N 125°42E 233 G5
Bayuquan China 40°16N 122°8E 227 D12
Bayview U.S.A. 37°44N 122°23W 136 B2
Bayville = Kirkwood S. Africa 33°22S 25°15E 270 D4
Bayy al Kabir, W. Libya 31°10N 15°53E 258 B3
Bayy al Khā'ib, Wādī → Libya 30°55N 15°29E 258 B3
Bayzo Niger 13°52N 4°35E 263 C5
Baza Spain 37°30N 2°47W 195 H8
Bāzār Iran 35°40N 51°25E 141 A2
Bazar Dyuzi Russia 41°12N 47°50E 191 K8
Bazardüzü = Bazar Dyuzi Russia 41°12N 47°50E 191 K8
Bāzargān Iran 39°22N 44°26E 213 C11
Bazargic = Dobrich Bulgaria 43°37N 27°49E 203 C11
Bazarny Karabulak Russia 52°20N 46°29E 190 D8
Bazarnyy Syzgan Russia 53°45N 46°40E 190 D8
Bazaruto, I. do Mozam. 21°40S 35°28E 271 B6
Bazaruto △ Mozam. 21°42S 35°26E 271 B6
Bazas France 44°27N 0°13W 174 D3
Bazhong China 31°52N 106°46E 228 B6
Bazhou China 39°8N 116°22E 226 E9
Bazin Guadeloupe 16°22N 61°26W 322 e
Bazmān, Kūh-e Iran 28°4N 60°1E 247 D9
Baztan = Elizondo Spain 43°12N 1°30W 196 B3
Bé, Nosy Madag. 13°25S 48°15E 272 A2
Beach U.S.A. 46°58N 104°0W 308 B2
Beach City U.S.A. 40°39N 81°35W 312 F3
Beachport Australia 37°29S 140°0E 282 D4
Beachville Canada 43°5N 80°49W 312 C4
Beachy Hd. U.K. 50°44N 0°15E 169 G8
Beacon W. Austral., Australia 30°26S 117°52E 279 F2
Beacon N.Y., U.S.A. 41°30N 73°58W 313 E11
Beacon Hill Hong Kong, China 22°21N 114°10E 122 A3
Beacon Hill Boston, U.S.A. 116 b1
Beaconsfield Australia 41°11S 146°48E 281 G4
Beagle, Canal S. Amer. 55°0S 68°30W 336 E3
Beagle Bay Australia 16°58S 122°40E 278 C3
Beagle Bay ☼ Australia 16°53S 122°40E 278 C3
Beagle G. Australia 12°15S 130°25E 278 B5
Béal an Átha = Ballina Ireland 54°7N 9°9W 166 B2
Béal Átha na Sluaighe = Ballinasloe Ireland 53°20N 8°13W 166 C3
Bealanana Madag. 14°33S 48°44E 272 A2
Beals Cr. → U.S.A. 32°10N 100°51W 314 E4
Beamsville Canada 43°12N 79°28W 312 C5
Bear → Calif., U.S.A. 38°56N 121°36W 306 G5
Bear → Utah, U.S.A. 41°30N 112°8W 300 G17
Béar, C. France 42°31N 3°8E 174 F7
Bear I. = Bjørnøya Arctic 74°30N 19°0E 150 B8
Bear I. Ireland 51°38N 9°50W 166 E2
Bear L. Man., Canada 55°8N 96°0W 297 B9
Bear L. Utah, U.S.A. 41°59N 111°21W 304 F8
Bear Lake Canada 45°27N 79°35W 312 A5
Beardmore Canada 49°36N 87°57W 298 C2
Beardmore Glacier Antarctica 84°30S 170°0E 151 E11
Beardstown U.S.A. 40°1N 90°26W 310 E6
Bearma → India 24°20N 79°51E 243 G8
Béarn France 43°20N 0°30W 174 E3
Bearpaw Mts. U.S.A. 48°12N 109°30W 304 B9
Bearskin Lake Canada 53°58N 91°2W 298 B1
Beas → India 31°10N 74°59E 242 D6
Beas de Segura Spain 38°15N 2°53W 195 G8
Beasain Spain 43°3N 2°11W 196 B2
Beata, C. Dom. Rep. 17°40N 71°30W 321 C5
Beata, I. Dom. Rep. 17°34N 71°31W 321 C5
Beata Ridge W. Indies 16°0N 72°30W 321 C5
Beato Portugal 38°44N 9°5W 126 A2
Beatrice Nebr., U.S.A. 40°16N 96°45W 308 E5
Beatrice Zimbabwe 18°15S 30°55E 269 F3
Beatrice, C. Australia 14°20S 136°55E 280 A2
Beatton → Canada 56°15N 120°45W 296 B4
Beatton River Canada 57°26N 121°20W 296 B4
Beatty U.S.A. 36°54N 116°46W 306 J10
Beau Bassin Mauritius 20°13S 57°27E 272 e
Beauaraba = Pittsworth Australia 27°41S 151°37E 281 D5
Beaucaire France 43°48N 4°39E 175 E8
Beauce, Plaine de la France 48°10N 1°45E 173 D8
Beauceville Canada 46°13N 70°46W 299 C5
Beauchêne, I. Falk. Is. 52°55S 59°15W 153 f
Beaudesert Australia 27°59S 153°0E 281 D5
Beaufort Vic., Australia 37°25S 143°25E 282 D5
Beaufort Savoie, France 45°44N 6°34E 175 C10
Beaufort Malaysia 5°30N 115°40E 235 A5
Beaufort N.C., U.S.A. 34°43N 76°40W 315 D16
Beaufort S.C., U.S.A. 32°26N 80°40W 316 C9
Beaufort Sea Arctic 72°0N 140°0W 292 B5
Beaufort West S. Africa 32°18S 22°36E 270 D3
Beaugency France 47°47N 1°38E 173 E8
Beauharnois Canada 45°20N 73°52W 313 A11
Beaujeu France 46°10N 4°35E 173 F11
Beaujolais France 46°0N 4°22E 173 F11
Beaulieu → Canada 62°3N 113°11W 296 A6
Beaulieu-sur-Dordogne France 44°58N 1°50E 174 D5
Beaulieu-sur-Mer France 43°42N 7°20E 175 E11
Beauly U.K. 57°30N 4°28W 167 D4
Beauly → U.K. 57°29N 4°27W 167 D4
Beaumaris U.K. 53°16N 4°6W 168 D3
Beaumont Belgium 50°15N 4°14E 170 D4
Beaumont Dublin, Ireland 53°23N 6°13W 120 A2
Beaumont N.Z. 45°50S 169°33E 285 F4
Beaumont Calif., U.S.A. 33°57N 116°59W 307 M9
Beaumont Tex., U.S.A. 30°5N 94°6W 314 F7
Beaumont-de-Lomagne France 43°53N 1°0E 174 E5
Beaumont-du-Périgord France 44°45N 0°46E 174 D4
Beaumont-le-Roger France 49°4N 0°47E 172 C7
Beaumont-sur-Sarthe France 48°13N 0°8E 172 D7
Beaumonte Heights Canada 43°45N 79°34W 141 A1
Beaune France 47°2N 4°50E 173 E11
Beaune-la-Rolande France 48°4N 2°25E 173 D9
Beauport Guadeloupe 16°25N 61°30W 322 e
Beaupré Canada 47°3N 70°54W 299 C5
Beaupréau France 47°12N 1°0W 172 E6
Beauraing Belgium 50°7N 4°57E 170 D4
Beaurepaire France 45°22N 5°1E 175 C9
Beausejour Man., Canada 50°5N 96°35W 297 C9
Beauséjour Guadeloupe 16°18N 61°4W 322 e
Beauséjour Martinique 14°44N 60°57W 322 j
Beauvais France 49°25N 2°8E 173 C9
Beauval Canada 55°9N 107°37W 297 B7
Beauvoir-sur-Mer France 46°55N 2°2W 172 F4
Beauvoir-sur-Niort France 46°12N 0°30W 174 B3
Beaver Alaska, U.S.A. 66°22N 147°24W 303 C11
Beaver Okla., U.S.A. 36°49N 100°31W 314 C4
Beaver Pa., U.S.A. 40°42N 80°19W 312 F4
Beaver Utah, U.S.A. 38°17N 112°38W 304 G7
Beaver → B.C., Canada 59°52N 124°20W 296 B4
Beaver → Ont., Canada 55°55N 87°48W 298 A2
Beaver → Sask., Canada 55°26N 107°45W 297 B7
Beaver → Okla., U.S.A. 36°35N 99°30W 314 C5
Beaver City U.S.A. 40°8N 99°50W 308 E4
Beaver Creek Canada 63°0N 141°0W 294 E3
Beaver Dam U.S.A. 43°28N 88°50W 308 D9
Beaver Falls U.S.A. 40°46N 80°20W 312 F4
Beaver Hill L. Canada 54°5N 94°50W 297 C10
Beaver I. U.S.A. 45°40N 85°33W 309 C11
Beavercreek U.S.A. 39°43N 84°11W 311 E12
Beaverhill L. Canada 53°27N 112°32W 296 C6
Beaverlodge Canada 55°11N 119°29W 296 B5
Beaverstone → Canada 54°59N 89°25W 298 B2
Beaverton Ont., Canada 44°26N 79°9W 312 B5
Beaverton Oreg., U.S.A. 45°29N 122°48W 306 E4
Beawar India 26°3N 74°18E 242 F6
Bebedouro Brazil 21°0S 48°25W 335 A6
Bebek Turkey 41°4N 29°2E 122 B2
Bebera, Tanjung Indonesia 8°44S 115°51E 231 K18
Beboa Madag. 17°22S 44°33E 272 B1
Beboto Chad 8°16N 16°56E 259 G3
Bebra Germany 50°58N 9°48E 178 E5
Becán Mexico 18°34N 89°31W 319 D7
Bécancour Canada 46°20N 72°26W 309 B17
Beccles U.K. 52°27N 1°35E 169 E9
Bečej Serbia 45°36N 20°3E 182 E5
Beceni Romania 45°23N 26°48E 183 E11
Becerreá Spain 42°51N 7°10W 194 C3
Béchar Algeria 31°38N 2°18W 261 B4
Béchar □ Algeria 30°15N 3°5E 261 B5
Becharof L. U.S.A. 57°56N 156°23W 303 H8
Becharof Nat. Wildlife Refuge ⌓ U.S.A. 58°0N 156°15W 303 H8
Becharre = Bsharri Lebanon 34°15N 36°0E 250 D7
Běchovice Czech Rep. 50°4N 14°36E 135 B3
Bechuanaland = Botswana ■ Africa 22°0S 24°0E 270 B3
Bechyně Czech Rep. 49°17N 14°29E 180 B7
Beckenham U.K. 51°24N 0°1W 125 B3
Bečkerek = Zrenjanin Serbia 45°22N 20°23E 182 E5
Beckley U.S.A. 37°47N 81°11W 309 G13
Beckton U.K. 51°30N 0°4E 125 A4
Beckum Germany 51°45N 8°3E 178 D4
Beclean Romania 47°11N 24°11E 183 C9
Becontree U.K. 51°33N 0°7E 125 A4
Bečov nad Teplou Czech Rep. 50°5N 12°49E 180 A5
Bečva → Czech Rep. 49°31N 17°20E 181 B10
Bédar Spain 37°11N 1°59W 197 H3
Bédarieux France 43°37N 3°10E 174 E7
Beddington Corner U.K. 51°23N 0°9W 125 B3
Beddouza, C. Morocco 32°33N 9°9W 260 B3
Bedeau = Râs el Ma Algeria 34°26N 0°50W 261 B4
Bedele Ethiopia 8°31N 36°23E 257 F4
Bederkesa Germany 53°37N 8°50E 178 B4
Bederwanak Somalia 9°34N 44°23E 267 C5
Bedeso Ethiopia 9°58N 40°52E 257 F5
Bedford Qué., Canada 45°7N 72°59W 313 A12
Bedford Eastern Cape, S. Africa 32°40S 26°10E 270 D4
Bedford Beds., U.K. 52°8N 0°28W 169 E7
Bedford Ind., U.S.A. 38°52N 86°29W 311 F10
Bedford Iowa, U.S.A. 40°40N 94°44W 310 D2
Bedford Ky., U.S.A. 38°36N 85°19W 311 F11
Bedford Mass., U.S.A. 42°27N 71°15W 116 A1
Bedford Ohio, U.S.A. 41°23N 81°32W 312 E3
Bedford Pa., U.S.A. 40°1N 78°30W 312 F6
Bedford Va., U.S.A. 37°20N 79°31W 309 G14
Bedford □ U.K. 52°4N 0°28W 169 E7
Bedford, C. Australia 15°14S 145°21E 280 B4
Bedford Park Ill., U.S.A. 41°46N 87°46W 119 C2
Bedford Park N.Y., U.S.A. 40°52N 73°52W 132 A2
Bedford Stuyvesant U.S.A. 40°41N 73°56W 132 B2
Bedford View S. Africa 26°10S 28°7E 123 B2
Bedi Chad 11°6N 18°33E 259 F3
Będków Poland 51°36N 19°44E 185 G6
Bednja → Croatia 46°20N 16°52E 199 B13
Bednodemyanovsk Russia 53°55N 43°15E 190 D6
Bedok Singapore 1°19N 103°56E 138 B3
Bedok, Res. Singapore 1°20N 103°56E 138 A3
Bedónia Italy 44°30N 9°38E 198 D6
Bedourie Australia 24°30S 139°30E 280 C2
Bedti → India 14°50N 74°44E 245 G2
Bedugul Indonesia 8°17S 115°10E 231 J18
Bedum Neths. 53°18N 6°36E 170 A6
Będzin Poland 50°19N 19°7E 185 H6
Bee Ridge U.S.A. 27°17N 82°29W 317 H7
Beebe Plain Canada 45°1N 72°9W 313 A12
Beech Creek U.S.A. 41°5N 77°36W 312 E7
Beech Fork → U.S.A. 37°46N 85°41W 311 G11
Beech Grove U.S.A. 39°43N 86°5W 311 E10
Beecher U.S.A. 41°21N 87°38W 311 C9
Beechey Point U.S.A. 70°29N 149°9W 303 A10
Beechworth Australia 36°22S 146°43E 283 D7
Beechy Canada 50°53N 107°24W 297 C7
Beed = Bir India 19°4N 75°46E 244 E2
Beef I. Br. Virgin Is. 18°26N 64°30W 321 b
Beelitz Germany 52°14N 12°58E 178 C8
Beenleigh Australia 27°43S 153°10E 281 D5
Be'er Menuha Israel 30°19N 35°8E 246 D2
Be'er Sheva Israel 31°15N 34°48E 251 G5
Beerenberg Norway 71°0N 8°20W 154 C10
Beersel Belgium 50°46N 4°18E 116 B1
Beersheba = Be'er Sheva Israel 31°15N 34°48E 251 G5
Beeskow Germany 52°10N 14°15E 178 C10
Beestekraal S. Africa 25°23S 27°38E 271 C4
Beeston U.K. 52°56N 1°14W 168 E6
Beeton Canada 44°5N 79°47W 312 B5
Beetzendorf Germany 52°42N 11°6E 178 C7
Beeville U.S.A. 28°24N 97°45W 314 G6
Befale Dem. Rep. of the Congo 0°25N 20°45E 264 B4
Befandriana Mahajanga, Madag. 15°16S 48°32E 272 B2
Befandriana Toliara, Madag. 21°55S 44°0E 272 C1
Befasy Madag. 20°33S 44°23E 272 C1
Befori Dem. Rep. of the Congo 0°8N 22°22E 264 B4
Befotaka Antsiranana, Madag. 13°15S 48°16E 272 A2
Befotaka Fianarantsoa, Madag. 23°49S 47°0E 272 C2
Bega Australia 36°41S 149°51E 283 D8
Bega, Canalul Romania 45°37N 20°46E 182 E5
Begamganj Bangla. 22°56N 91°6E 241 D3
Bégard France 48°38N 3°18W 172 D3
Beğendik Turkey 40°55N 26°34E 203 F10
Beggars Pt. Antigua & B. 17°10N 61°48W 322 b
Begndal Norway 60°49N 9°46E 164 D6
Begoro Ghana 6°23N 0°23W 263 D4
Begusarai India 25°24N 86°9E 243 G12
Behābād Iran 32°24N 59°47E 247 C8
Behala India 22°30N 88°18E 124 B1
Behara Madag. 24°55S 46°20E 272 C2
Behbehān Iran 30°30N 50°15E 247 D6
Behcheco Canada 62°49N 116°4W 296 A5
Beheloka Madag. 23°54S 43°40E 272 C1
Behm Canal U.S.A. 55°10N 131°0W 296 B2
Behshahr Iran 36°45N 53°35E 247 B7
Bei Hai Beijing, China 114 b2
Bei Hai Park Beijing, China 114 b2
Bei Jiang → China 23°2N 112°58E 229 F9
Bei Shan China 41°30N 96°0E 218 C8
Bei'an China 48°10N 126°20E 219 B14
Beibei China 29°47N 106°22E 228 C6
Beicai China 31°11N 121°32E 138 B2
Beichuan China 31°55N 104°39E 228 B5
Beigang = Peikang Taiwan 23°34N 120°18E 225 C2
Beihai China 21°28N 109°6E 228 G7
Beijing China 39°53N 116°21E 114 B1
Beijing □ China 39°55N 116°20E 226 E9
Beijing Zoo Beijing, China 114 a1
Beilau = Pilawa Poland 51°57N 21°32E 185 G8
Beilen Neths. 52°52N 6°27E 170 B6
Beiliu China 22°41N 110°21E 229 F8
Beilngries Germany 49°2N 11°28E 179 F7
Beilpajah Australia 32°54S 143°52E 282 B5
Beilul Eritrea 13°2N 42°20E 257 E5
Béinamar Chad 8°40N 15°23E 259 G3
Beinan = Peinan Taiwan 22°47N 121°7E 225 D3
Beinn na Faoghla = Benbecula U.K. 57°26N 7°21W 167 D1
Beipan Jiang → China 24°55N 106°5E 228 E6
Beipiao China 41°52N 120°32E 227 D11
Beira Mozam. 19°50S 34°52E 269 F3
Beirut = Bayrūt Lebanon 33°53N 35°31E 250 E6
Beiseker Canada 51°23N 113°32W 296 C6
Beit Duqu West Bank 31°51N 35°6E 123 A1
Beit Ghur at-Taht West Bank 31°54N 35°5E 123 A1
Beit Ghur el-Fawqa West Bank 31°53N 35°5E 123 A1
Beit Hanina West Bank 31°50N 35°12E 123 B2
Beit Ij'za West Bank 31°51N 35°9E 123 A1
Beit Iksa West Bank 31°49N 35°11E 123 B2
Beit I'nan West Bank 31°51N 35°7E 123 A1
Beit Jala West Bank 31°43N 35°11E 123 B2
Beit Lāhīyā Gaza Strip 31°33N 34°30E 251 G5
Beit Lekhem = Bayt Lahm West Bank 31°43N 35°12E 123 B2
Beit Liqya West Bank 31°52N 35°4E 123 A1
Beit Nekofa Israel 31°49N 35°7E 123 B1
Beit Sahur West Bank 31°42N 35°13E 123 B2
Beit Sofafa West Bank 31°45N 35°12E 123 B2
Beit Surik West Bank 31°50N 35°9E 123 B1
Beit Ur al-Fawqa West Bank 31°53N 35°7E 123 A1
Beit Zayit Israel 31°47N 35°9E 123 B1
Beitaipingzhuan China 39°57N 116°20E 114 B1
Beitaolaizhao China 44°58N 125°58E 227 B13
Beitar Ilit West Bank 31°42N 35°7E 123 B1
Beitbridge Zimbabwe 22°12S 30°0E 269 G3
Beitin West Bank 31°56N 35°14E 123 A2
Beitou = Peitou Taiwan 25°11N 121°27E 225 A3
Beitsun China 23°7N 113°10E 121 B2
Beitunya West Bank 31°53N 35°10E 123 A2
Beiuş Romania 46°40N 22°21E 182 D7
Beixing Jing Park China 31°14N 121°21E 138 B1
Beizhen = Binzhou China 37°20N 118°2E 227 F10
Beizhen China 41°38N 121°54E 227 D11
Beizhengzhen China 44°31N 123°30E 227 B12
Beja Portugal 38°2N 7°53W 195 G3
Béja Tunisia 36°43N 9°12E 258 A1
Beja □ Portugal 37°55N 7°55W 195 H3
Béja □ Tunisia 36°40N 9°29E 261 A6
Bejaïa Algeria 36°42N 5°2E 261 A6
Bejaïa □ Algeria 36°40N 4°55E 261 A5
Béjar Spain 40°23N 5°46W 194 E5
Bejestān Iran 34°30N 58°5E 247 C8
Bek-Budi = Qarshi Uzbekistan 38°53N 65°48E 217 E7
Bekaa Valley = Al Biqā Lebanon 34°10N 36°10E 250 D7
Bekasi Indonesia 6°14S 106°59E 234 D3
Békásmegyer Hungary 47°35N 19°3E 117 A2
Bekçiler Turkey 36°56N 29°44E 205 E11
Bekdash Turkmenistan 41°34N 52°32E 216 D4
Békés Hungary 46°47N 21°9E 182 D6
Békés □ Hungary 46°45N 21°0E 182 D6
Békéscsaba Hungary 46°40N 21°5E 182 D6
Bekilli Turkey 38°17N 29°27E 205 C11
Bekily Madag. 24°13S 45°19E 272 C2
Bekisopa Madag. 21°40S 45°54E 272 C2
Bekitro Madag. 24°33S 45°18E 272 C2
Bekkelaget Norway 59°53N 10°47E 133 A3
Bekkestua Norway 59°55N 10°35E 133 A2
Bekodoka Madag. 16°58S 45°7E 272 B2
Bekoji Ethiopia 7°40N 39°17E 257 F4
Bekok Malaysia 2°20N 103°7E 237 L4
Bekopaka Madag. 19°9S 44°48E 272 B1
Bekwai Ghana 6°30N 1°34W 263 D4
Bel Air Mauritius 20°15S 57°44E 272 e
Bel Air Calif., U.S.A. 34°4N 118°27W 126 B2
Bela India 25°50N 82°0E 243 G10
Bela Pakistan 26°12N 66°20E 242 F2
Bela Aliança = Rio do Sul Brazil 27°13S 49°37W 335 B6
Bela Bela S. Africa 24°51S 28°19E 271 B4
Bela Crkva Serbia 44°55N 21°27E 182 F6
Bela Palanka Serbia 43°13N 22°17E 202 C6
Bela Vista Mato Grosso do Sul, Brazil 22°12S 56°20W 334 A4
Bela Vista São Paulo, Brazil 23°33S 46°38W 137 B2
Bela Vista Mozam. 26°10S 32°44E 271 C5
Bélabo Cameroon 4°56N 13°18E 264 B2
Bélâbre France 46°34N 1°8E 174 B5
Belaga Malaysia 2°42N 113°47E 235 B4
Belalcázar Spain 38°35N 5°10W 195 G5
Belan → India 24°2N 81°45E 243 G9
Bélanger Canada 45°35N 73°42W 130 A1
Belanovica Serbia 44°15N 20°23E 202 B4
Belarus ■ Europe 53°30N 27°0E 177 B14
Belas Angola 8°55S 13°9E 265 D2
Belas Lisboa, Portugal 38°46N 9°17W 126 A1
Belau = Palau ■ Palau 7°30N 134°30E 288 c
Belavenona Madag. 24°50S 47°4E 272 C2
Belawan Indonesia 3°33N 98°32E 234 B1
Belaya Ethiopia 11°25N 36°8E 257 E4
Belaya → Russia 54°40N 56°0E 186 C9
Belaya Glina Russia 46°5N 40°48E 191 G5
Belaya Kalitva Russia 48°13N 40°50E 191 F5
Belaya Tserkov = Bila Tserkva Ukraine 49°45N 30°10E 177 D16
Belaya Zemlya, Ostrova Russia 81°36N 62°18E 214 A7
Belayan → Indonesia 0°14S 116°36E 235 C5
Belceşti Romania 47°19N 27°7E 183 C12
Bełchatów Poland 51°21N 19°22E 185 G6
Belcher Is. Canada 56°15N 78°45W 298 A3
Belchite Spain 41°18N 0°43W 196 D4
Belden U.S.A. 40°2N 121°17W 306 E5
Beldibi Turkey 36°25N 32°26E 250 B3
Belding U.S.A. 43°6N 85°14W 311 A11
Belebey Russia 54°7N 54°7E 186 D9
Beledweyne Somalia 4°30N 45°5E 267 D6
Beleghata India 22°33N 88°22E 124 B2
Belém = Palmeirais Brazil 6°0S 43°0W 332 C3
Belém Brazil 1°20S 48°30W 332 B2
Belém Lisboa, Portugal 38°41N 9°12W 126 A1
Belém, Torre de Portugal 38°41N 9°12W 126 A1
Belém de São Francisco Brazil 8°46S 38°58W 332 C4
Belén Argentina 27°40S 67°5W 334 B2
Belén Colombia 1°26N 75°56W 328 C2
Belén Paraguay 23°30S 57°6W 334 A4
Belen Turkey 36°31N 36°10E 250 B7
Belen N. Mex., U.S.A. 34°40N 106°46W 305 J10
Belene Bulgaria 43°39N 25°10E 203 C9
Belènzinho Brazil 23°32S 46°34W 137 B2
Belep, Îs. N. Cal. 19°45S 163°40E 288 d
Bélesta France 42°55N 1°56E 174 F5
Belet Uen = Beledweyne Somalia 4°30N 45°5E 267 D6
Belev Russia 53°50N 36°5E 188 F9
Belevi Turkey 38°0N 27°28E 205 C9
Belfair U.S.A. 47°27N 122°50W 306 C4
Belfast = eMakhazeni S. Africa 25°42S 30°2E 271 C5
Belfast N.Z. 43°27S 172°39E 285 D7
Belfast Antrim, U.K. 54°37N 5°56W 166 B6
Belfast Maine, U.S.A. 44°26N 69°1W 309 C19
Belfast N.Y., U.S.A. 42°21N 78°7W 312 D6
Belfast L. U.K. 54°40N 5°50W 166 B6
Belfield U.S.A. 46°53N 103°12W 308 B2
Belfort France 47°38N 6°50E 173 E13
Belfort, Territoire de □ France 47°40N 6°55E 173 E13
Belfry U.S.A. 45°9N 109°1W 304 D9
Belgachiya India 22°36N 88°23E 124 B2
Belgard = Białogard Poland 54°2N 15°58E 184 D2
Belgaum India 15°55N 74°35E 245 G2
Belgavi = Belgaum India 15°55N 74°35E 245 G2
Belgharia India 22°39N 88°22E 124 B2
Belgian Congo = Congo, Dem. Rep. of the ■ Africa 3°0S 23°0E 265 C4
Belgioioso Italy 45°10N 9°19E 198 C6
Belgium ■ Europe 50°30N 5°0E 170 D4
Belgodère France 42°35N 9°1E 175 F13
Belgorod Russia 50°35N 36°35E 189 G9
Belgorod □ Russia 50°45N 36°45E 189 G9
Belgorod-Dnestrovskiy = Bilhorod-Dnistrovskyy Ukraine 46°11N 30°23E 189 J6
Belgrade = Beograd Serbia 44°50N 20°37E 202 B4
Belgrade U.S.A. 45°47N 111°11W 304 D8
Belgrano Antarctica 77°52S 34°37W 151 D1
Belgrano B. Aires, Argentina 34°33S 58°27W 117 B2
Belgravia London, U.K. 125 c3
Belgrove N.Z. 41°27S 172°59E 285 B7
Belhaven U.S.A. 35°33N 76°37W 315 D16
Béli Guinea-Biss. 11°51N 13°56W 262 C2
Beli Nigeria 7°52N 10°55E 263 D7
Beli Drim → Europe 42°6N 20°25E 202 D4
Beli Manastir Croatia 45°45N 18°36E 182 E3
Beli Timok → Serbia 43°53N 22°14E 202 C6
Bélice → Italy 37°35N 12°55E 200 E5
Belimbing Indonesia 8°24S 115°2E 231 J18
Bélinga Gabon 1°10N 13°2E 264 B2
Belinskiy Russia 53°0N 43°25E 190 D6
Belinyu Indonesia 1°35S 105°50E 234 C3
Beliton Is. = Belitung Indonesia 3°10S 107°50E 235 C3
Belitung Indonesia 3°10S 107°50E 235 C3
Beliu Romania 46°30N 22°0E 182 D6
Belize Angola 4°39S 12°46E 265 C2
Belize ■ Cent. Amer. 17°0N 88°30W 320 C2
Belize Barrier Reef Belize 17°9N 88°3W 319 D7
Belize City Belize 17°25N 88°10W 320 C2
Beljakovci Macedonia 42°6N 21°59E 202 D5
Beljanica Serbia 44°8N 21°43E 202 B5
Belkovskiy, Ostrov Russia 75°32N 135°44E 215 B14
Bell Calif., U.S.A. 33°58N 118°11W 126 C3
Bell Fla., U.S.A. 29°45N 82°52W 316 F7
Bell → Canada 49°48N 77°38W 298 C4
Bell Gardens U.S.A. 33°58N 118°9W 126 C4
Bell I. Canada 50°46N 55°35W 299 B8
Bell-Irving → Canada 56°12N 129°5W 296 B3
Bell Peninsula Canada 63°50N 82°0W 295 E15
Bell Tower Beijing, China 114 a3
Bell Ville Argentina 32°40S 62°40W 334 C3
Bella Italy 40°45N 15°32E 201 B8
Bella Bella Canada 52°10N 128°10W 296 C3
Bella Coola Canada 52°25N 126°40W 296 C3
Bella Flor Bolivia 11°9S 67°49W 330 C4
Bella Unión Uruguay 30°15S 57°40W 334 C4
Bella Vista Corrientes, Argentina 28°33S 59°0W 334 B4
Bella Vista Tucuman, Argentina 27°10S 65°25W 334 B2
Bella Vista Ark., U.S.A. 36°28N 94°16W 308 G6
Bellac France 46°7N 1°3E 174 B5
Bellágio Italy 45°59N 9°15E 198 C6
Bellaire U.S.A. 40°1N 80°45W 312 F4
Bellária Italy 44°9N 12°28E 199 D9
Bellary India 15°10N 76°56E 245 G3
Bellata Australia 29°53S 149°46E 281 D4
Bellavista Santiago, Chile 33°31S 70°35W 137 C2
Bellavista Galápagos Is., Ecuador 0°41S 90°18W 330 a
Bellavista Lima, Peru 12°4S 77°8W 124 B2
Belle U.S.A. 38°17N 91°43W 310 F5
Belle → Trin. & Tob. 11°14N 60°37W 323 s
Belle Fille → Dominica 15°25N 61°16W 323 k
Belle Fourche U.S.A. 44°40N 103°51W 308 C2
Belle Fourche → U.S.A. 44°26N 102°18W 308 C2
Belle Glade U.S.A. 26°41N 80°40W 317 J9
Belle Harbor U.S.A. 40°34N 73°51W 132 C2
Belle-Île France 47°20N 3°10W 172 E3
Belle Isle Nfld. & L., Canada 51°57N 55°25W 299 B8
Belle Isle Fla., U.S.A. 28°27N 81°12W 317 G8
Belle Isle, Str. of Canada 51°30N 56°30W 299 B8
Belle Plaine U.S.A. 41°54N 92°17W 310 C4
Belle Rive U.S.A. 38°14N 88°45W 311 F8
Belle River Canada 42°18N 82°43W 312 D2
Belle Vue Maurel Mauritius 20°7S 57°39E 272 e
Belle Yella Liberia 7°24N 10°0W 262 D3
Belledonne France 45°20N 6°10E 175 C10
Bellefontaine Martinique 14°39N 61°10W 322 j
Bellefontaine Ohio, U.S.A. 40°22N 83°46W 311 D13
Bellefonte U.S.A. 40°55N 77°47W 312 F7
Bellegarde France 47°59N 2°26E 173 E9
Bellegarde-en-Marche France 45°59N 2°18E 174 C6
Bellegarde-sur-Valserine France 46°4N 5°50E 173 F12
Bellême France 48°22N 0°34E 172 D7
Belleoram Canada 47°31N 55°25W 299 C8
Belleplaine Barbados 13°15N 59°34W 323 r
Belleview U.S.A. 29°4N 82°3W 317 F7
Belleville Ont., Canada 44°10N 77°23W 312 B7
Belleville Rhône, France 46°7N 4°45E 173 F11
Belleville Ill., U.S.A. 38°31N 89°59W 310 F7
Belleville Kans., U.S.A. 39°50N 97°38W 308 F5
Belleville N.J., U.S.A. 40°47N 74°9W 313 F10
Belleville N.Y., U.S.A. 43°46N 76°10W 313 C8
Belleville-sur-Vie France 46°46N 1°25W 172 F5
Bellevue Idaho, U.S.A. 43°28N 114°16W 304 E6
Bellevue Iowa, U.S.A. 42°16N 90°26W 310 B6
Bellevue Mich., U.S.A. 42°27N 85°1W 311 B11
Bellevue Nebr., U.S.A. 41°9N 95°54W 308 E6
Bellevue Ohio, U.S.A. 41°17N 82°51W 312 E2
Bellevue Wash., U.S.A. 47°37N 122°12W 306 C4
Bellevue, Col de Réunion 21°9S 55°36E 272 f
Bellevue, Schloss Berlin, Germany 115 a2
Belley France 45°46N 5°41E 175 C9
Bellin = Kangirsuk Canada 60°0N 70°0W 295 F18
Bellinge Denmark 55°20N 10°20E 163 J4
Bellingen Australia 30°25S 152°50E 283 A10
Bellingham London, U.K. 51°25N 0°1W 125 B3
Bellingham Wash., U.S.A. 48°46N 122°29W 306 B4
Bellingshausen Abyssal Plain S. Ocean 64°0S 90°0W 151 C16
Bellingshausen Sea Antarctica 66°0S 80°0W 151 C17
Bellinzona Switz. 46°11N 9°1E 179 J5
Bello Colombia 6°20N 75°33W 328 B2
Bellona Solomon Is. 11°17S 159°47E 287 N10
Bellows Falls U.S.A. 43°8N 72°27W 313 C12
Bellpat Pakistan 29°0N 68°5E 242 E3
Bellpuig Spain 41°37N 1°1E 196 D6
Bells Dominica 15°25N 61°21W 323 k
Belluno Italy 46°9N 12°13E 199 B9
Bellville U.S.A. 32°9N 81°59W 316 C8
Bellwood U.S.A. 40°36N 78°20W 312 F6
Belmanier Dominica 15°35N 61°24W 323 k
Bélmez Spain 38°17N 5°17W 195 G5
Belmond U.S.A. 42°51N 93°37W 310 B3
Belmont N.S.W., Australia 33°4S 151°42E 283 B9
Belmont Ont., Canada 42°53N 81°5W 312 D3
Belmont Grenada 12°2N 61°45W 323 q
Belmont Northern Cape, S. Africa 29°28S 24°22E 270 C3
Belmont London, U.K. 51°36N 0°18W 125 A2
Belmont Mass., U.S.A. 42°23N 71°10W 116 A1
Belmont N.Y., U.S.A. 42°14N 78°2W 312 D6
Belmont Cragin U.S.A. 41°55N 87°45W 119 B2
Belmont Harbor U.S.A. 41°56N 87°38W 119 B3
Belmonte Brazil 16°0S 39°0W 333 E4
Belmonte Portugal 40°21N 7°20W 194 E3
Belmonte Spain 39°34N 2°43W 197 F2
Belmopan Belize 17°18N 88°30W 320 C2
Belmore Australia 33°55S 151°5E 139 B1
Belmullet Ireland 54°14N 9°58W 166 B2
Belo Dem. Rep. of the Congo 0°32S 23°13E 264 C4
Belo Madag. 20°44S 44°0E 272 C1
Belo Horizonte Brazil 19°55S 43°56W 333 E3
Belo Jardim Brazil 8°20S 36°26W 332 C4
Belo Monte Brazil 3°5S 51°46W 329 D7
Belo-Tsiribihina Madag. 19°40S 44°30E 272 B1
Belogorsk = Bilohirsk Ukraine 45°3N 34°35E 189 K8
Belogorsk Russia 51°0N 128°20E 215 D13
Belogradchik Bulgaria 43°53N 22°42E 202 C6
Belogradets Bulgaria 43°22N 27°18E 203 C11
Beloha Madag. 25°10S 45°3E 272 D2
Beloit Kans., U.S.A. 39°28N 98°6W 308 F4
Beloit Wis., U.S.A. 42°31N 89°2W 310 B7
Belokalitvenskaya = Belaya Kalitva Russia 48°13N 40°50E 191 F5
Belokorovichi Ukraine 51°7N 28°2E 177 C15
Belomorsk Russia 64°35N 34°54E 186 B5
Belondo Dem. Rep. of the Congo 0°19S 19°31E 264 C3
Belonge Dem. Rep. of the Congo 2°7S 19°33E 264 C3
Belonia India 23°15N 91°30E 241 D3
Belopolye = Bilopillya Ukraine 51°14N 34°20E 189 G8
Belorechensk Russia 44°46N 39°52E 191 H4
Beloretsk Russia 53°58N 58°24E 186 D10
Belorussia = Belarus ■ Europe 53°30N 27°0E 177 B14
Beloshchelye = Naryan-Mar Russia 67°42N 53°12E 186 A9
Beloslav Bulgaria 43°11N 27°42E 203 C11
Belotsarsk = Kyzyl Russia 51°50N 94°30E 217 B12
Beloūsovka Kazakhstan 50°8N 82°31E 217 B10
Belovezhskaya Pushcha = Białowieski △ Poland 52°43N 23°50E 185 F10
Belovo Bulgaria 42°13N 24°1E 203 D8
Belovo Russia 54°30N 86°0E 217 B11
Beloyarskiy Russia 63°42N 66°40E 214 C7
Beloye, Ozero Russia 60°10N 37°35E 188 B9
Beloye More Russia 66°30N 38°0E 186 A6
Belozem Bulgaria 42°12N 25°2E 203 D9
Belozersk Russia 60°1N 37°45E 188 B9
Belpasso Italy 37°35N 14°58E 201 E7
Belpre U.S.A. 39°17N 81°34W 309 F13
Belrain India 28°23N 80°55E 243 E9
Belt U.S.A. 47°23N 110°55W 304 C8
Beltana Australia 30°48S 138°25E 282 A3
Belterra Brazil 2°45S 55°0W 329 D7
Beltinci Slovenia 46°37N 16°20E 199 B13
Belton Mo., U.S.A. 38°49N 94°32W 310 F2
Belton Tex., U.S.A. 31°3N 97°28W 314 F6
Belton L. U.S.A. 31°6N 97°28W 314 F6
Beltsy = Bălţi Moldova 47°48N 27°58E 183 C12
Belturbet Ireland 54°6N 7°26W 166 B4
Belukha Russia 49°50N 86°50E 217 C11
Belur India 22°37N 88°21E 124 B2
Beluran Malaysia 5°48N 117°35E 235 A5
Beluša Slovak Rep. 49°5N 18°17E 181 B11
Belushya Guba Russia 71°32N 52°19E 214 B6
Belušić Serbia 43°50N 21°10E 202 C5
Belvedere St. Vincent 13°8N 61°11W 323 n
Belvedere London, U.K. 51°29N 0°9E 125 B4
Belvedere Calif., U.S.A. 37°52N 122°27W 136 A2
Belvedere Maríttimo Italy 39°37N 15°52E 201 C8
Belvedere Park U.S.A. 33°45N 84°16W 113 B3
Belvès France 44°46N 1°0E 174 D5
Belvidere Ill., U.S.A. 42°15N 88°50W 311 B8
Belvidere N.J., U.S.A. 40°50N 75°5W 313 F9
Belvís de la Jara Spain 39°45N 4°57W 194 F6
Bely Bychek = Chagoda Russia 59°10N 35°15E 188 C8
Belyando → Australia 21°38S 146°50E 280 C4
Belyando Crossing Australia 21°32S 146°51E 280 C4
Belyayevo Bogorodskoye Russia 55°39N 37°31E 129 C2
Belyuen Australia 12°34S 130°42E 278 B5
Belyy Russia 55°49N 33°3E 188 E7
Belyy, Ostrov Russia 73°30N 71°0E 214 B8
Belyy Yar Russia 58°26N 84°39E 214 D9
Belyye Vody = Aqsū Kazakhstan 42°25N 69°50E 217 D7
Belz Ukraine 50°23N 24°1E 185 H11
Bełżec Poland 50°23N 23°26E 185 H10
Belzig Germany 52°8N 12°35E 178 C8
Belzoni U.S.A. 33°11N 90°29W 315 E9
Bełżyce Poland 51°11N 22°17E 185 G9
Bemaraha, Lembalemban' i Madag. 18°40S 44°45E 272 B1
Bemarivo Madag. 21°45S 44°45E 272 C1
Bemarivo → Antsiranana, Madag. 14°9S 50°9E 272 A3
Bemarivo → Mahajanga, Madag. 15°27S 47°40E 272 B2
Bemavo Madag. 21°33S 45°25E 272 C2
Bembe Angola 7°3S 14°25E 265 D2
Bembéréke Benin 10°11N 2°43E 263 C5
Bembesi Zimbabwe 20°0S 28°58E 269 G2
Bembesi → Zimbabwe 18°57S 27°47E 269 F2
Bembézar → Spain 37°45N 5°13W 195 H5
Bembibre Spain 42°37N 6°25W 194 C4
Bemboka △ Australia 36°35S 149°41E 283 D8
Bement U.S.A. 39°55N 88°34W 311 E8
Bemetara India 21°42N 81°32E 243 J9
Bemidji U.S.A. 47°28N 94°53W 308 B6

Bemolanga Madag. 17°44S 45°6E 272 B2
Bemowo Poland 52°15N 20°53E 143 B1
Ben Iran 32°32N 50°45E 247 C6
Ben Boyd △ Australia 37°0S 149°55E 283 D8
Ben Cruachan U.K. 56°26N 5°8W 167 E3
Ben Dearg U.K. 57°47N 4°56W 167 D4
Ben En △ Vietnam 19°37N 105°30E 236 C5
Ben Gardane Tunisia 33°11N 11°11E 258 B2
Ben Halls Gap △ Australia 31°37S 151°1E 283 A9
Ben Hope U.K. 58°25N 4°36W 167 C4
Ben Lawers U.K. 56°32N 4°14W 167 E4
Ben Lomond N.S.W., Australia 30°1S 151°43E 281 E5
Ben Lomond Tas., Australia 41°38S 147°42E 281 G4
Ben Lomond Stirling, U.K. 56°11N 4°38W 167 E4
Ben Lomond △ Australia 41°33S 147°39E 281 G4
Ben Luc Vietnam 10°39N 106°29E 237 G6
Ben Macdhui U.K. 57°4N 3°40W 167 D5
Ben Mhor U.K. 57°15N 7°18W 167 D1
Ben More Argyll & Bute, U.K. 56°26N 6°1W 167 E2
Ben More Stirling, U.K. 56°23N 4°32W 167 E4
Ben More Assynt U.K. 58°8N 4°52W 167 C4
Ben Nevis U.K. 56°48N 5°1W 167 E3
Ben Ohau Ra. N.Z. 44°1S 170°4E 285 E5
Ben Quang Vietnam 17°3N 106°55E 236 D6
Ben Slimane Morocco 33°38N 7°7W 260 B3
Ben Tadjine, Djebel Algeria 29°0N 3°30W 260 C4
Ben Tre Vietnam 10°14N 106°23E 237 G6
Ben Vorlich U.K. 56°21N 4°14W 167 E4
Ben Wyvis U.K. 57°40N 4°35W 167 D4
Bena Nigeria 11°20N 5°50E 263 C6
Bena-Dibele Dem. Rep. of the Congo 4°4S 22°50E 265 C4
Bena-Leka Dem. Rep. of the Congo 5°8S 22°10E 265 D4
Bena-Tshadi Dem. Rep. of the Congo 4°40S 22°49E 265 C4
Benaco, L. di = Garda, L. di Italy 45°40N 10°41E 198 C7
Benagerie Australia 31°25S 140°22E 282 A4
Benahmed Morocco 33°4N 7°9W 260 B3
Benaki Museum Athens, Greece 112 b3
Benalla Australia 36°30S 146°0E 283 D7
Benalmádena Spain 36°36N 4°34W 195 J6
Benambra, Mt. Australia 36°31S 147°34E 283 D7
Benanee Australia 34°31S 142°52E 282 C5
Benangin Indonesia 0°58S 115°19E 235 C5
Bénara Mayotte 12°53S 45°9E 272 b
Benares = Varanasi India 25°22N 83°0E 243 G10
Bénat, C. France 43°5N 6°22E 175 E10
Benavente Portugal 38°59N 8°49W 195 G2
Benavente Spain 42°2N 5°43W 194 C5
Benavides U.S.A. 27°36N 98°25W 314 H5
Benavides de Órbigo Spain 42°30N 5°54W 194 C5
Benbecula U.K. 57°26N 7°21W 167 D1
Benbonyathe Hill Australia 30°25S 139°11E 282 A3
Bend U.S.A. 44°4N 121°19W 304 D3
Bendale Canada 43°45N 79°13W 141 A3
Bendela Dem. Rep. of the Congo 3°18S 17°36E 264 C3
Bendemeer Australia 30°53S 151°8E 283 A9
Bender Beyla Somalia 9°30N 50°48E 267 C7
Bendery = Tighina Moldova 46°50N 29°30E 183 D14
Bendigo Australia 36°40S 144°15E 282 D6
Bendin = Będzin Poland 50°19N 19°7E 185 H6
Bendorf Germany 50°25N 7°35E 178 E3
Bendsburg = Będzin Poland 50°19N 19°7E 185 H6
Benē Beraq Israel 32°6N 34°51E 251 F5
Beneditinos Brazil 5°27S 42°22W 332 C3
Benedito Leite Brazil 7°13S 44°34W 332 C3
Benefica Brazil 22°52S 43°14W 135 B1
Bénéna Mali 13°9N 4°17W 262 C4
Benenitra Madag. 23°27S 45°5E 272 C2
Benešov Czech Rep. 49°46N 14°41E 180 B7
Benevento Italy 41°8N 14°45E 201 A7
Benfeld France 48°22N 7°34E 173 D14
Benfica Portugal 38°45N 9°11W 126 A1
Beng Mealea Cambodia 13°28N 104°14E 236 F5
Benga Mozam. 16°11S 33°40E 269 F3
Bengal = Paschimbanga □ India 23°0N 88°0E 243 H13
Bengal, Bay of Ind. Oc. 15°0N 90°0E 239 F14
Bengaluru = Bangalore India 12°59N 77°40E 245 H3
Bengbis Cameroon 3°27N 12°36E 263 E7
Bengbu China 32°58N 117°20E 229 A11
Benghazi = Banghāzī Libya 32°11N 20°3E 258 B4
Benghisa Point Malta 35°49N 14°33E 206 F8
Bengkalis Indonesia 1°30N 102°10E 237 M4
Bengkayang Indonesia 0°49N 109°28E 235 B3
Bengkulu Indonesia 3°50S 102°12E 234 C2
Bengkulu □ Indonesia 3°48S 102°16E 234 C2
Bengo Dem. Rep. of the Congo 2°11S 19°5E 264 C3
Bengo □ Angola 9°0S 13°10E 265 D2
Bengough Canada 49°25N 105°10W 297 D7
Bengtsfors Sweden 59°2N 12°14E 162 E6
Benguela Angola 12°37S 13°25E 265 E2
Benguela □ Angola 13°0S 13°30E 265 E2
Benguerir Morocco 32°16N 7°56W 260 B3
Benguérua, I. Mozam. 21°58S 35°28E 271 B6
Benguet □ Phil. 16°30N 120°40E 232 C3
Benha Egypt 30°26N 31°8E 256 H7
Benham Seamount Pac. Oc. 15°40N 124°30E 232 D5
Beni Dem. Rep. of the Congo 0°30N 29°27E 268 B2
Beni □ Bolivia 14°0S 65°0W 331 C5
Beni → Bolivia 10°23S 65°24W 331 C4
Beni Abbès Algeria 30°5N 2°5W 261 B4
Beni Hammad Algeria 35°49N 4°47E 261 A5
Beni Haoua Algeria 36°30N 1°30E 261 A5
Beni Mazâr Egypt 28°32N 30°44E 256 B3
Beni Mellal Morocco 32°21N 6°21W 260 B3
Beni Ounif Algeria 32°0N 1°10W 261 B4
Beni Saf Algeria 35°17N 1°15W 261 A4
Beni Suef Egypt 29°5N 31°6E 256 J7
Beniah L. Canada 63°23N 112°17W 296 A6
Benicarló Spain 40°23N 0°23E 196 E5
Benicássim Spain 40°3N 0°4E 196 E5
Benidorm Spain 38°33N 0°9W 197 G4
Benin ■ Africa 10°0N 2°0E 263 D5
Benin → Nigeria 5°45N 5°4E 263 D6
Benin, Bight of W. Afr. 5°0N 3°0E 263 E5
Benin City Nigeria 6°20N 5°31E 263 D6
Benissa Spain 38°43N 0°3E 197 G5
Benitez Int. ✕ (SCL) Santiago, Chile 33°33S 70°42W 137 B1
Bénitiers, Île aux Mauritius 20°24S 57°20E 272 e
Benito Juárez Argentina 37°40S 59°43W 334 D4
Benito Juárez, Int. ✕ (MEX) Mexico 19°25N 99°5W 128 B2
Benitses Greece 39°32N 19°55E 206 B9
Benjamin Aceval Paraguay 24°58S 57°34W 334 A4
Benjamin Constant Brazil 4°40S 70°15W 328 D3
Benjamin Hill Mexico 30°9N 111°7W 318 A2
Benkelman U.S.A. 40°3N 101°32W 308 E3
Benkovac Croatia 44°2N 15°37E 199 D12
Benmore Pk. N.Z. 44°25S 170°8E 285 E5
Bennett Canada 59°51N 135°0W 296 B2
Bennett, L. Australia 22°50S 131°2E 278 D5
Bennetta, Ostrov Russia 76°21N 148°56E 215 B15
Bennettsville U.S.A. 34°37N 79°41W 315 D15
Bennichchāb Mauritania 19°32N 15°12W 262 B1
Bennington N.H., U.S.A. 43°0N 71°55W 313 D11
Bennington Vt., U.S.A. 42°53N 73°12W 313 D11
Beno Dem. Rep. of the Congo 3°41S 17°49E 264 C3
Bénodet France 47°53N 4°7W 172 E2
Benom Malaysia 3°50N 102°6E 237 L4
Benoni S. Africa 26°11S 28°18E 271 C4
Benoud Algeria 32°20N 0°16E 261 B5
Bénoué △ Cameroon 8°30N 13°55E 264 A2
Benoy Chad 8°59N 16°19E 259 G3
Benque Viejo del Carmen Belize 17°5N 89°8W 320 C2
Bense Dominica 15°35N 61°22W 323 k
Bensheim Germany 49°40N 8°38E 179 F4
Benson Ariz., U.S.A. 31°58N 110°18W 305 L8
Benson Minn., U.S.A. 45°19N 95°36W 308 C6
Bensonhurst U.S.A. 40°35N 73°59W 132 C2
Bent Iran 26°20N 59°31E 247 E8
Benteng Indonesia 6°10S 120°30E 231 F6
Bentiaba Angola 14°15S 12°21E 265 E2
Bentinck I. Queens., Australia 17°3S 139°35E 280 B2
Bentinck I. Burma 11°45N 98°3E 237 G2
Bentiu South Sudan 9°10N 29°55E 257 F2
Bentley Subglacial Trench Antarctica 80°0S 115°0W 151 E15
Bento Gonçalves Brazil 29°10S 51°31W 335 B5
Benton Ark., U.S.A. 34°34N 92°35W 314 D8
Benton Calif., U.S.A. 37°48N 118°32W 306 H8
Benton Ill., U.S.A. 38°0N 88°55W 310 G8
Benton Pa., U.S.A. 41°12N 76°23W 313 E8
Benton Harbor U.S.A. 42°6N 86°27W 311 B10
Benton Heights U.S.A. 42°7N 86°24W 311 B10
Bentong Malaysia 3°31N 101°55E 237 L3
Bentonville U.S.A. 36°22N 94°13W 314 C7
Bentu Liben Ethiopia 8°32N 38°21E 257 F4
Benue □ Nigeria 7°20N 8°45E 263 D6
Benue → Nigeria 7°48N 6°46E 263 D6
Benxi China 41°20N 123°48E 224 B1
Benza Dem. Rep. of the Congo 4°49S 13°17E 265 D2
Benzdorp Suriname 3°44N 54°5W 329 C7
Beo Indonesia 4°25N 126°50E 231 D7
Beograd Serbia 44°50N 20°37E 202 B4
Beograd ✕ (BEG) Serbia 43°49N 20°17E 202 C4
Beolgyo S. Korea 34°51N 127°21E 224 E3
Beoumi Ivory C. 7°45N 5°23W 262 D3
Beppu Japan 33°15N 131°30E 222 D3
Beppu-Wan Japan 33°18N 131°34E 222 D3
Beqa Fiji 18°23S 178°8E 287 B2
Beqaa Valley = Al Biqā Lebanon 34°10N 36°10E 250 D7
Bequia St. Vincent 13°0N 61°15W 323 n
Ber Mota India 23°27N 68°34E 242 H3
Bera, Tasik Malaysia 3°5N 102°38E 237 L4
Berach → India 25°15N 75°2E 242 G6
Beraketa Madag. 23°7S 44°25E 272 C1
Béran-Djoko Congo 3°15N 17°0E 264 B3
Berane Montenegro 42°51N 19°52E 202 D3
Berastagi Indonesia 3°11N 98°31E 237 L2
Berat Albania 40°43N 19°59E 202 F3
Berau = Tanjungredeb Indonesia 2°9N 117°29E 235 B5
Berau → Indonesia 2°10N 117°42E 235 B5
Berau, Teluk Indonesia 2°30S 132°30E 231 E8
Beravina Madag. 18°10S 45°14E 272 B2
Berbak △ Indonesia 1°27S 104°19E 234 C2
Berber Sudan 18°0N 34°0E 256 D3
Berbera Somalia 10°30N 45°2E 267 B6
Berbérati C.A.R. 4°15N 15°40E 264 B3
Berbice → Guyana 6°20N 57°32W 329 B6
Berceto Italy 44°31N 9°51E 198 D6
Berchem-Ste-Agathe Belgium 50°52N 4°17E 116 A1
Berchidda Italy 40°47N 9°10E 200 B2
Berchtesgaden Germany 47°38N 13°0E 179 H8
Berchtesgaden △ Germany 47°34N 12°55E 179 H8
Berck France 50°25N 1°36E 173 B8
Berdaale Bay, Somalia 7°4N 47°51E 267 C6
Berdaale Mudug, Somalia 3°14N 43°11E 267 D5
Berdichev = Berdychiv Ukraine 49°57N 28°30E 177 D15
Berdsk Russia 54°47N 83°2E 217 B10
Berdyansk Ukraine 46°45N 36°50E 189 J9
Berdychiv Ukraine 49°57N 28°30E 177 D15
Béré Chad 9°20N 16°9E 259 G3
Berea U.S.A. 37°34N 84°17W 309 G11
Berebere Indonesia 2°25N 128°45E 231 D7
Bereeda Somalia 11°45N 51°0E 267 B7
Berehomet Ukraine 48°10N 25°19E 183 B10
Berehove Ukraine 48°15N 22°35E 182 B7
Bereina Papua N. G. 8°39S 146°30E 286 E4
Bereket Turkmenistan 39°16N 55°32E 247 B7
Berekua Dominica 15°14N 61°19W 323 k
Berekum Ghana 7°29N 2°34W 262 D4
Berenice Egypt 24°2N 35°25E 256 C4
Berens → Canada 52°25N 97°2W 297 C9
Berens I. Canada 52°18N 97°18W 297 C9
Berens River Canada 52°25N 97°0W 297 C9
Beresfield Australia 32°50S 151°40E 283 B9
Beresford U.S.A. 43°5N 96°47W 308 D5
Berestechko Ukraine 50°22N 25°5E 177 C13
Bereşti Romania 46°6N 27°50E 183 D12
Beretău → Romania 47°10N 21°50E 182 C6
Berettyó → Hungary 46°59N 21°7E 182 D6
Berettyóújfalu Hungary 47°13N 21°33E 182 C6
Berevo Mahajanga, Madag. 17°14S 44°17E 272 B1
Berevo Toliara, Madag. 19°44S 44°58E 272 B1
Bereza = Byaroza Belarus 52°31N 24°51E 177 B13
Berezhany Ukraine 49°26N 24°58E 177 D13
Berezina = Byarezina → Belarus 52°33N 30°14E 177 B16
Berezivka Ukraine 47°14N 30°55E 189 J6
Berezna Ukraine 51°35N 31°46E 189 G6
Berezniki Russia 62°51N 42°40E 186 B7
Berezniki Russia 59°24N 56°46E 186 C10
Berezovo Russia 64°0N 65°0E 214 C7
Berezyne Ukraine 46°14N 29°12E 183 D14
Berg am Laim Germany 48°7N 11°38E 131 B2
Berga Spain 42°6N 1°48E 196 C6
Berga Kalmar, Sweden 57°14N 16°3E 163 G10
Bergama Turkey 39°8N 27°11E 205 B9
Bérgamo Italy 45°41N 9°43E 198 C6
Bergaon India 20°41N 80°27E 244 D5
Bergara Spain 43°9N 2°28W 196 B2
Bergby Sweden 60°57N 17°2E 162 D11
Berge Norway 59°34N 8°10E 162 E2
Bergedorf Germany 53°28N 10°16E 178 B6
Bergeforsen Sweden 62°32N 17°23E 162 B11
Bergen Mecklenburg-Vorpommern, Germany 54°25N 13°25E 178 A9
Bergen Niedersachsen, Germany 52°49N 9°57E 178 C5
Bergen Neths. 52°40N 4°43E 170 B4
Bergen Hordaland, Norway 60°20N 5°20E 164 D2
Bergen N.Y., U.S.A. 43°5N 77°57W 312 C7
Bergen ✕ (BGO) Norway 60°17N 5°19E 164 D2
Bergen op Zoom Neths. 51°28N 4°18E 170 C4
Bergenfield U.S.A. 40°55N 73°59W 132 A2
Bergerac France 44°51N 0°30E 174 D4
Bergham Germany 48°2N 11°37E 131 B2
Bergheim Germany 50°57N 6°38E 178 E2
Bergholz U.S.A. 40°31N 80°53W 312 F4
Bergisch Gladbach Germany 50°59N 7°8E 178 E3
Bergisches Land △ Germany 51°0N 7°30E 178 E3
Bergkamen Germany 51°37N 7°38E 178 D3
Bergkvara Sweden 56°23N 16°5E 163 H10
Bergshamra Sweden 59°38N 18°37E 162 E12
Bergsjö Sweden 61°59N 17°3E 162 C11
Bergstadt = Leśnica Poland 50°26N 18°11E 185 H5
Bergstrasse-Odenwald △ Germany 49°45N 5°55E 179 F1
Bergues France 50°58N 2°24E 173 B9
Bergviken Sweden 61°15N 16°40E 162 C10
Bergville S. Africa 28°52S 29°18E 271 C4
Bergvliet S. Africa 34°2S 18°27E 118 B1
Berhala, Selat Indonesia 1°0S 104°15E 234 C2
Berhampore = Baharampur India 24°2N 88°27E 243 G13
Berhampur = Brahmapur India 19°15N 84°54E 244 E7
Berheci → Romania 45°58N 27°28E 183 E12
Beri Spain 41°20N 2°1E 114 A1
Berikat, Tanjung Indonesia 2°34S 106°52E 234 C3
Bering Glacier U.S.A. 60°20N 143°30W 303 F12
Bering Land Bridge △ U.S.A. 66°20N 165°0W 303 C6
Bering Sea Pac. Oc. 58°0N 171°0W 292 D2
Bering Strait Pac. Oc. 65°30N 169°0W 303 D5
Beringovskiy Russia 63°3N 179°19E 215 C18
Berisso Argentina 34°56S 57°50W 334 C4
Berja Spain 36°50N 2°56W 195 J8
Berkåk Norway 62°50N 10°0E 164 B6
Berkane Morocco 34°52N 2°20W 261 B4
Berkeley U.S.A. 37°51N 122°16W 136 A3
Berkeley, C. Ecuador 0°1N 91°35W 330 a
Berkner I. Antarctica 79°30S 50°0W 151 D18
Berkovitsa Bulgaria 43°16N 23°8E 202 C7
Berkshire U.S.A. 42°19N 76°11W 313 D8
Berkshire Downs U.K. 51°33N 1°29W 169 F6
Berlanga Spain 38°17N 5°50W 195 G5
Berlenga, I. Portugal 39°25N 9°30W 195 F1
Berlengas = Valença do Piauí Brazil 6°20S 41°45W 332 C3
Berlin = Kitchener Canada 43°27N 80°29W 312 C4
Berlin Berlin, Germany 52°31N 13°23E 115 A3
Berlin Ga., U.S.A. 31°4N 83°37W 316 D6
Berlin Md., U.S.A. 38°20N 75°13W 309 F16
Berlin N.H., U.S.A. 44°28N 71°11W 313 B13
Berlin N.Y., U.S.A. 42°42N 73°23W 313 D11
Berlin Wis., U.S.A. 43°58N 88°57W 308 D9
Berlin □ Germany 52°30N 13°20E 178 C9
Berlin Brandenburg ✕ (BER) Germany 52°22N 13°30E 115 B4
Berlin Dom Germany 52°31N 13°24E 115 A3
Berlin L. U.S.A. 41°3N 81°0W 312 E4
Berlin Tegel sa (TXL) Berlin, Germany 52°35N 13°14E 115 A2
Berlinchen = Barlinek Poland 53°0N 15°15E 185 F2
Bermagui Australia 36°25S 150°4E 283 D9
Bermeja, Sierra Spain 36°30N 5°11W 195 J5
Bermejo → Formosa, Argentina 26°51S 58°23W 334 B4
Bermejo → San Juan, Argentina 32°30S 67°30W 334 C2
Bermejo, Paso = Uspallata, P. de Argentina 32°37S 69°22W 334 C2
Bermen, L. Canada 53°35N 68°55W 299 B6
Bermeo Spain 43°25N 2°47W 196 B2
Bermillo de Sayago Spain 41°22N 6°8W 194 D4
Bermondsey U.K. 51°29N 0°3W 125 B3
Bermuda ☑ Atl. Oc. 32°18N 64°45W 153 a
Bermuda Int. ✕ (BDA) Bermuda 32°22N 64°41W 153 a
Bermuda Rise Atl. Oc. 32°30N 65°0W 152 C5
Bern Switz. 46°57N 7°28E 179 J3
Bern □ Switz. 46°45N 7°40E 179 J3
Bernabeu, Estadio Spain 40°27N 3°41W 127 B1
Bernal Heights U.S.A. 37°44N 122°24W 136 B2
Bernalda Italy 40°24N 16°41E 201 B9
Bernalillo U.S.A. 35°18N 106°33W 305 J10
Bernam → Malaysia 3°45N 101°5E 234 B2
Bernardo, Palazzo Venice, Italy 142 b2
Bernardo de Irigoyen Argentina 26°15S 53°40W 335 B5
Bernardo O'Higgins △ Chile 48°50S 75°36W 336 C1
Bernardsville U.S.A. 40°43N 74°34W 313 F10
Bernasconi Argentina 37°55S 63°44W 334 D3
Bernau Bayern, Germany 47°47N 12°22E 179 H8
Bernau Brandenburg, Germany 52°40N 13°35E 178 C9
Bernay France 49°5N 0°35E 172 C7
Bernburg Germany 51°47N 11°44E 178 D7
Berndorf Austria 47°59N 16°1E 180 D9
Berne = Bern Switz. 46°57N 7°28E 179 J3
Berne = Bern □ Switz. 46°45N 7°40E 179 J3
Berne U.S.A. 40°39N 84°57W 311 D12
Berner Alpen Switz. 46°27N 7°35E 179 J3
Berneray U.K. 57°43N 7°11W 167 D1
Bernier I. Australia 24°50S 113°12E 279 D1
Bernina, Piz Switz. 46°20N 9°54E 179 J5
Bernkastel-Kues Germany 49°55N 7°3E 179 F3
Bernstadt = Bierutów Poland 51°7N 17°32E 185 G4
Bernstein = Pełczyce Poland 53°3N 15°16E 185 E2
Bero → Angola 15°10S 12°9E 265 F2
Beroroha Madag. 21°40S 45°10E 272 C2
Béroubouay Benin 10°34N 2°46E 263 C5
Beroun Czech Rep. 49°57N 14°5E 180 B7
Berounka → Czech Rep. 50°0N 14°22E 180 B7
Berovo Macedonia 41°38N 22°51E 202 E6
Berre, Étang de France 43°27N 5°5E 175 E9
Berre-l'Étang France 43°27N 5°10E 175 E9
Berrechid Morocco 33°18N 7°36W 260 B3
Berri Australia 34°14S 140°35E 282 C4
Berriane Algeria 32°50N 3°46E 261 B5
Berridale Australia 36°22S 148°48E 283 D8
Berrien Springs U.S.A. 41°57N 86°20W 311 C10
Berrigan Australia 35°38S 145°49E 283 C6
Berriwillock Australia 35°36S 142°59E 282 C5
Berrouaghia Algeria 36°10N 2°53E 261 A5
Berry N.S.W., Australia 34°46S 150°43E 283 C9
Berry Indre, France 46°50N 2°0E 173 F8
Berry Is. Bahamas 25°40N 77°50W 320 A4
Berrydale U.S.A. 30°53N 87°3W 317 E2
Berryessa, L. U.S.A. 38°31N 122°6W 306 G4
Berryville U.S.A. 36°22N 93°34W 314 C8
Berseba Namibia 26°0S 17°46E 270 C2
Bersenbrück Germany 52°34N 7°56E 178 C3
Bershad Ukraine 48°22N 29°31E 183 B14
Bertamirans Spain 42°54N 8°38W 194 C2
Berthold U.S.A. 48°19N 101°44W 308 A3
Berthoud U.S.A. 40°19N 105°5W 304 F11
Bertincourt France 50°5N 2°58E 173 B9
Bertolinia Brazil 7°38S 43°57W 332 C3
Bertoua Cameroon 4°30N 13°45E 264 B2
Bertraghboy B. Ireland 53°22N 9°54W 166 C2
Bertraghboy B. Ireland 53°22N 9°54W 166 C2
Berts = Balqash Kazakhstan 46°50N 74°50E 214 E8
Beru Kiribati 1°20S 176°0E 277 A14
Berufjörður Iceland 64°48N 14°29W 155 C12
Berunes Iceland 64°42N 14°16W 155 C12
Beruni Uzbekistan 41°41N 60°45E 216 D6
Beruri Brazil 3°54S 61°22W 329 D5
Beruwala Sri Lanka 6°30N 80°0E 245 L4
Berwick U.S.A. 41°3N 76°14W 313 E8
Berwick-upon-Tweed U.K. 55°46N 2°0W 168 B6
Berwyn U.S.A. 41°50N 87°47W 119 B2
Berwyn Heights U.S.A. 38°59N 76°55W 143 B3
Berwyn Mts. U.K. 52°54N 3°26W 168 E4
Berzasca Romania 44°39N 21°58E 182 F6
Berzence Hungary 46°12N 17°11E 182 D2
Berzence Hungary 46°12N 17°11E 182 D2
Besal Pakistan 35°4N 73°56E 243 B5
Besalampy Madag. 16°43S 44°29E 272 B1
Besançon France 47°15N 6°2E 173 E13
Besar Indonesia 2°40S 116°0E 235 C5
Besar, Gunung Malaysia 5°10N 101°18E 234 A2
Beshenkovichi Belarus 55°2N 29°29E 188 E5
Besianë Kosovo 42°54N 21°10E 202 D5
Besiktas Turkey 41°2N 29°0E 122 B2
Beška Serbia 45°8N 20°6E 182 E5
Beslan Russia 43°15N 44°28E 191 J7
Besna Kobila Serbia 42°31N 22°10E 202 D6
Besnard L. Canada 55°25N 106°0W 297 B7
Besni Turkey 37°41N 37°52E 212 D7
Besor, N. → Egypt 31°28N 34°22E 251 G5
Besòs → Spain 41°24N 2°13E 114 A2
Bessa Monteiro Angola 7°7S 13°44E 265 D2
Bessarabiya Moldova 47°0N 28°10E 177 E15
Bessarabka = Basarabeasca Moldova 46°21N 28°58E 183 D13
Bessèges France 44°18N 4°8E 175 D8
Bessemer Ala., U.S.A. 33°24N 86°58W 315 E11
Bessemer Mich., U.S.A. 46°29N 90°3W 308 B8
Bessemer Pa., U.S.A. 40°59N 80°30W 312 F4
Bessie, L. U.S.A. 28°29N 81°31W 133 B1
Bessin France 49°18N 1°0W 172 C6
Bessines-sur-Gartempe France 46°6N 1°22E 174 B5
Beswick Australia 14°34S 132°53E 278 B5
Beswick ✪ Australia 14°31S 132°51E 278 B5
Bet Horon West Bank 31°52N 35°7E 123 A1
Bet She'an Israel 32°30N 35°30E 251 F6
Bet Shemesh Israel 31°44N 35°0E 251 G6
Betafo Madag. 19°50S 46°51E 272 B2
Betamba Dem. Rep. of the Congo 2°17S 21°24E 264 C4
Betancuria Canary Is. 28°25N 14°3W 153 e2
Betancuria, Mt. Canary Is. 28°25N 14°6W 153 e2
Betania Colombia 4°22N 72°54W 328 C3
Betanzos Bolivia 19°34S 65°27W 331 D4
Betanzos Spain 43°15N 8°12W 194 B2
Bétaré Oya Cameroon 5°40N 14°5E 264 A2
Betatao Madag. 18°11S 47°52E 272 B2
Betera Spain 39°35N 0°28W 197 F4
Bétérou Benin 9°12N 2°16E 263 D5
Bethal S. Africa 26°27S 29°28E 271 C4
Bethalto U.S.A. 38°55N 90°2W 310 F6
Bethanien Namibia 26°31S 17°8E 270 C2
Bethany Ont., Canada 44°11N 78°34W 312 B6
Bethany Ill., U.S.A. 39°39N 88°45W 311 E8
Bethany Mo., U.S.A. 40°16N 94°2W 310 D2
Bethany Okla., U.S.A. 35°31N 97°38W 314 D6
Bethel Montserrat 16°44N 62°9W 323 p
Bethel Alaska, U.S.A. 60°48N 161°45W 303 F7
Bethel Conn., U.S.A. 41°22N 73°25W 313 E11
Bethel Maine, U.S.A. 44°25N 70°47W 313 B14
Bethel Ohio, U.S.A. 38°58N 84°5W 311 F12
Bethel Vt., U.S.A. 43°50N 72°38W 313 C12
Bethel Park U.S.A. 40°19N 80°2W 312 F4
Béthenville France 49°18N 4°23E 173 C11
Bethesda U.S.A. 38°59N 77°6W 143 B2
Bethlehem = Bayt Lahm West Bank 31°43N 35°12E 123 B2
Bethlehem Free State, S. Africa 28°14S 28°18E 271 C4
Bethlehem Pa., U.S.A. 40°37N 75°23W 313 F9
Bethnal Green U.K. 51°31N 0°2W 125 A3
Bethulie S. Africa 30°30S 25°59E 270 D4
Béthune France 50°30N 2°38E 173 B9
Béthune → France 49°53N 1°9E 172 C8
Bethungra Australia 34°45S 147°51E 283 C7
Betijoque Venezuela 9°23N 70°44W 328 B3
Betim Brazil 19°58S 44°7W 333 E3
Betioky Toliara, Madag. 23°48S 44°20E 272 C1
Betioky Toliara, Madag. 22°27S 43°42E 272 C1
Betong Malaysia 1°24N 111°31E 235 B4
Betong Thailand 5°45N 101°5E 237 K3
Betoota Australia 25°45S 140°42E 280 D3
Betor Ethiopia 11°37N 39°22E 257 E4
Betor Paschimbanga, India 22°34N 88°17E 124 B1
Bétou Congo 3°3N 18°32E 264 B3
Betpaqdala Kazakhstan 45°45N 70°30E 217 C8
Betroka Madag. 23°16S 46°0E 272 C2
Betsiamites Canada 48°56N 68°40W 299 C6
Betsiamites → Canada 48°56N 68°38W 299 C6
Betsiboka → Madag. 16°3S 46°36E 272 B2
Bettendorf U.S.A. 41°32N 90°30W 310 C6
Bettiah India 26°48N 84°33E 243 F11
Bettna Sweden 58°55N 16°38E 163 F10
Béttola Italy 44°47N 9°36E 198 D6
Betul India 21°58N 77°59E 244 D3
Betung Indonesia 3°58S 104°34E 234 C2
Betung Kerihun △ Indonesia 1°11N 113°28E 235 B4
Betws-y-Coed U.K. 53°5N 3°48W 168 D4
Betxí Spain 39°56N 0°12W 196 F4
Betzdorf Germany 50°46N 7°52E 178 E3
Béu Angola 6°15S 15°32E 265 D3
Beuil France 44°6N 6°59E 175 D10
Beulah Vic., Australia 35°58S 142°29E 282 C5
Beulah Fla., U.S.A. 28°32N 81°34W 133 A1
Beulah Mich., U.S.A. 44°38N 86°6W 308 C10
Beulah N. Dak., U.S.A. 47°16N 101°47W 308 B3
Beulah, L. U.S.A. 28°32N 81°33W 133 A1
Beurkia Chad 15°20N 17°56E 259 E3
Beurs van Berlage Amsterdam, Neths. 112 a2
Beuthen = Bytom Poland 50°25N 18°54E 185 H5
Beuthen an der Oder = Bytom Odrzański Poland 51°44N 15°48E 185 G2
Beuvron → France 47°29N 1°15E 172 E8
Beveren Belgium 51°12N 4°16E 170 C4
Beverley W. Austral., Australia 32°9S 116°56E 279 F2
Beverley E. Riding, U.K. 53°51N 0°26W 168 D7
Beverley Hills Australia 33°56S 151°5E 139 B1
Beverley Park Australia 33°58S 151°8E 139 B1
Beverly Ill., U.S.A. 41°42N 87°39W 119 C3
Beverly Mass., U.S.A. 42°33N 70°53W 313 D14
Beverly Arts Center U.S.A. 41°41N 87°40W 119 C2
Beverly Glen U.S.A. 34°6N 118°26W 126 B2
Beverly Hills Calif., U.S.A. 34°5N 118°24W 126 B2
Beverly Hills Fla., U.S.A. 28°55N 82°28W 317 G7
Beverly Hills -Morgan Park Historic District U.S.A. 41°41N 87°40W 119 C2
Beverungen Germany 51°39N 9°22E 178 D5
Bevoalavo Madag. 25°13S 44°26E 272 D2
Bewas → India 23°59N 79°21E 243 H8
Bewdley Canada 44°5N 78°19W 312 B6
Bex Switz. 46°15N 7°0E 179 J3
Bexhill U.K. 50°51N 0°29E 169 G8
Bexley Australia 33°56S 151°7E 139 B1
Bexley □ U.K. 51°27N 0°8E 125 B4
Bexleyheath U.K. 51°27N 0°8E 125 B4
Bexon St. Lucia 13°57N 60°59W 323 m
Bey Dağları Turkey 36°38N 30°29E 205 E12
Beyānlū Iran 36°0N 47°51E 246 C5
Beyazköy Turkey 41°21N 27°42E 203 E11
Beyçayırı Turkey 40°15N 26°55E 203 F10
Beydağ Turkey 38°5N 28°13E 205 C10
Beyğ̇ağ Turkey 37°14N 28°53E 205 D10
Beyin Ghana 5°1N 2°41W 262 D4
Beykoz Turkey 41°7N 29°7E 122 B2
Beyla Guinea 8°30N 8°38W 262 D3
Beylerbeyi Turkey 41°2N 29°2E 122 B2
Beynat France 45°8N 1°44E 174 C5
Beyneu Kazakhstan 45°18N 55°9E 187 E10
Beyoba Turkey 38°48N 27°47E 205 C9
Beyoğlu Turkey 41°1N 28°58E 122 B1
Beyoneisu Retsugan Japan 31°55N 139°55E 223 F11
Beypazarı Turkey 40°10N 31°56E 212 B4
Beypore → India 11°10N 75°47E 245 J2
Beyra Somalia 6°57N 47°19E 267 C6
Beyşehir Turkey 37°41N 31°43E 212 D4
Beyşehir Gölü Turkey 37°41N 31°33E 212 D4
Beytüşşebap Turkey 37°35N 43°10E 213 D10
Bezdan Serbia 45°50N 18°57E 182 E3
Bezhetsk Russia 57°47N 36°39E 188 D9
Béziers France 43°20N 3°12E 174 E7
Bezons France 48°56N 2°13E 134 A2
Bezuidenhout Park S. Africa 26°10S 28°5E 123 B2
Bezwada = Vijayawada India 16°31N 80°39E 244 F5
Bhabua India 25°3N 83°37E 243 G10
Bhachau India 23°20N 70°16E 242 H4
Bhadar → Gujarat, India 22°17N 72°20E 242 H5
Bhadar → Gujarat, India 21°27N 69°47E 242 J3
Bhadarwah India 32°58N 75°46E 243 C6
Bhadgaon = Bhaktapur Nepal 27°38N 85°24E 243 F11
Bhadohi India 25°25N 82°34E 243 G10
Bhadra India 29°8N 75°14E 242 E6
Bhadra → India 14°0N 75°20E 245 H2
Bhadrachalam India 17°40N 80°53E 244 F5
Bhadrak India 21°10N 86°30E 244 D8
Bhadrakali India 22°40N 88°20E 124 A2
Bhadran India 22°19N 72°6E 242 H5
Bhadravati India 13°49N 75°40E 245 H2
Bhag Pakistan 29°2N 67°49E 242 E2
Bhagalpur India 25°10N 87°0E 243 G12
Bhagirathi → Paschimbanga, India 23°25N 88°23E 243 H13
Bhagirathi → Uttarakhand, India 30°8N 78°35E 243 D8
Bhainsa India 19°10N 77°58E 244 E3
Bhairab → Bangla. 22°51N 89°34E 243 H13
Bhairab Bazar Bangla. 24°4N 90°58E 241 C3
Bhakkar Pakistan 31°40N 71°5E 242 D4
Bhakra Dam India 31°30N 76°45E 242 D7
Bhaktapur Nepal 27°38N 85°24E 243 F11
Bhalki India 18°2N 77°13E 244 E3
Bhalswa India 28°44N 77°10E 120 A2
Bhambo Khan Qarmati Pakistan 24°49N 67°7E 123 B2
Bhamo Burma 24°15N 97°15E 241 C6
Bhamragarh India 19°30N 80°40E 244 E5
Bhandara India 21°5N 79°42E 244 D4
Bhanpura India 24°31N 75°44E 242 G6
Bhanrer Ra. India 23°40N 79°45E 243 H8
Bhaptiahi India 26°19N 86°44E 243 F12
Bharat = India ■ Asia 20°0N 78°0E 239 F11
Bharatpur Chhattisgarh, India 23°44N 81°46E 243 H9
Bharatpur Raj., India 27°15N 77°30E 242 F7
Bharatpur Nepal 27°34N 84°10E 243 F11
Bharno India 23°14N 84°53E 243 H11
Bharraig = Barra U.K. 57°0N 7°29W 167 E1
Bharraig, Caolas = Barra, Sd. of U.K. 57°4N 7°25W 167 D1
Bharuch India 21°47N 73°0E 244 D1
Bhatarsaigh = Vatersay U.K. 56°55N 7°32W 167 E1
Bhatghar L. India 18°10N 73°48E 244 E1
Bhatiapara Ghat Bangla. 23°13N 89°42E 241 D2
Bhatinda India 30°15N 74°57E 242 D6
Bhatkal India 13°58N 74°35E 245 H2
Bhatpara India 22°50N 88°25E 243 H13
Bhatsala India 22°30N 88°16E 124 B1
Bhattu India 29°36N 75°19E 242 E6
Bhaun Pakistan 32°55N 72°40E 242 C5
Bhaunagar = Bhavnagar India 21°45N 72°10E 244 D1
Bhavani India 11°27N 77°43E 245 J3
Bhavnagar India 21°45N 72°10E 244 D1
Bhawanipatna India 19°55N 83°10E 244 E6
Bhawanipur India 22°32N 88°21E 124 B2
Bhawari India 25°42N 73°4E 242 G5
Bhayavadar India 21°51N 70°15E 242 J4
Bhearnaraigh = Berneray U.K. 57°43N 7°11W 167 D1
Bhendkhal India 18°52N 72°59E 130 B2
Bhera Pakistan 32°29N 72°57E 242 C5
Bheri → Nepal 28°47N 81°18E 243 E9
Bhikangaon India 21°52N 75°57E 242 J6
Bhilai = Bhilainagar-Durg India 21°13N 81°26E 244 D5
Bhilainagar-Durg India 21°13N 81°26E 244 D5
Bhilsa = Vidisha India 23°28N 77°53E 242 H7
Bhilwara India 25°25N 74°38E 242 G6
Bhima → India 16°25N 77°17E 244 F3
Bhimavaram India 16°30N 81°30E 245 F5
Bhimbar Pakistan 32°59N 74°3E 243 C6
Bhind India 26°30N 78°46E 243 F8
Bhinga India 27°43N 81°56E 243 F9
Bhinmal India 25°0N 72°15E 242 G5
Bhisho S. Africa 32°50S 27°23E 270 D4
Bhit I. Pakistan 24°49N 67°0E 123 B1
Bhiwandi India 19°20N 73°0E 244 E1
Bhiwani India 28°50N 76°9E 242 E7
Bhogava → India 22°26N 72°20E 242 H5
Bhojpur Nepal 27°10N 87°3E 243 F12
Bhokardan India 20°16N 75°46E 244 D2
Bhola Bangla. 22°45N 90°35E 241 D3
Bholari Pakistan 25°19N 68°13E 242 G3
Bhongir India 17°30N 78°56E 244 F4
Bhopal India 23°20N 77°30E 242 H7
Bhopalpatnam India 18°52N 80°23E 244 E5
Bhor India 18°12N 73°53E 244 E1
Bhuban India 20°53N 85°50E 244 D7
Bhubaneshwar India 20°15N 85°50E 244 D7
Bhuj India 23°15N 69°49E 242 H3
Bhuleshwar Mumbai, India 130 b2
Bhumiphol Res. Thailand 17°20N 98°40E 236 D2
Bhusawal India 21°3N 75°46E 244 D2
Bhutan ■ Asia 27°25N 90°30E 241 B3
Biá → Brazil 3°28S 67°23W 328 D4
Biafra, B. of = Bonny, Bight of Africa 3°30N 9°20E 263 E6
Biak Indonesia 1°10S 136°6E 231 E9
Biała Poland 50°24N 17°40E 185 H4
Biała → Poland 50°3N 20°55E 185 H7
Biała Piska Poland 53°37N 22°5E 184 E9
Biała Podlaska Poland 52°4N 23°6E 185 F10
Biała Rawska Poland 51°48N 20°29E 185 G7
Białobrzegi Poland 51°39N 20°58E 185 G7
Białogard Poland 54°2N 15°58E 184 D2
Białołęka Dworska Poland 52°19N 21°1E 143 B2
Białowieski △ Poland 52°43N 23°50E 185 F10
Białowieża Poland 52°41N 23°49E 185 F10
Biały Bór Poland 53°53N 16°51E 184 E3
Białystok Poland 53°10N 23°10E 185 E10
Biancavilla Italy 37°38N 14°52E 201 E7
Bianco Italy 38°5N 16°9E 201 D9
Biankouma Ivory C. 7°50N 7°40W 262 D3
Biaora India 23°56N 76°56E 242 H7
Bīārjmand Iran 36°6N 55°53E 247 B7
Biaro Indonesia 2°5N 125°26E 231 D7
Biarritz France 43°29N 1°33W 174 E2
Biasca Switz. 46°22N 8°58E 179 J4
Biavela Angola 14°43S 19°47E 265 E3
Biba Egypt 28°55N 31°0E 256 J7
Bibai Japan 43°19N 141°52E 220 C10
Bibala Angola 14°44S 13°24E 265 E2
Bibane, Bahiret el Tunisia 33°16N 11°13E 258 B2
Bibassé Gabon 1°27N 11°37E 264 B2
Bibbiena Italy 43°42N 11°49E 199 E8
Bibby I. Canada 61°55N 93°0W 297 A10
Bibei → Spain 42°24N 7°13W 194 C3
Biberach Germany 48°5N 9°47E 179 G5
Bibi Papua N. G. 5°30S 146°2E 286 C4
Bibiani Ghana 6°30N 2°8W 262 D4
Bibile Sri Lanka 7°10N 81°25E 245 L5
Bibungwa Dem. Rep. of the Congo 2°40S 28°15E 268 C2
Bicaj Albania 41°58N 20°25E 202 E4
Bicaz Romania 46°53N 26°5E 183 D11
Bicazu Ardelean Romania 46°51N 25°56E 183 D10
Biccari Italy 41°23N 15°12E 201 A8
Bicentennial Park N.S.W., Australia 33°51S 151°5E 139 B1
Bicentennial Park Calif., U.S.A. 34°1N 118°1W 126 B4
Bicester U.K. 51°54N 1°9W 169 F6
Biche Trin. & Tob. 10°26N 61°8W 323 t
Bichena Ethiopia 10°28N 38°10E 257 E4
Bicheno Australia 41°52S 148°18E 281 G4
Bichia India 22°27N 80°42E 243 H9
Bichvinta Georgia 43°9N 40°21E 191 J5
Bickerton I. Australia 13°45S 136°10E 280 A2
Bickley U.K. 51°23N 0°3E 125 B4
Bicknell U.S.A. 38°47N 87°19W 311 F9
Bicol △ Phil. 13°55N 122°58E 232 E4
Bicske Hungary 47°29N 18°38E 182 C3
Bicuari △ Angola 15°14S 14°45E 265 F2
Bicutan Phil. 14°30N 121°3E 127 C2
Bid = Bir India 19°4N 75°46E 244 E2
Bida Dem. Rep. of the Congo 4°55N 19°56E 264 B3
Bida Nigeria 9°3N 5°58E 263 D6
Bidar India 17°55N 77°35E 244 F3
Bidde Somalia 0°58N 42°37E 267 D5
Biddeford U.S.A. 43°30N 70°28W 309 D18
Biddwara Ethiopia 5°11N 38°34E 257 F4
Bideford U.K. 51°1N 4°13W 169 F3
Bideford Bay U.K. 51°5N 4°20W 169 F3
Bidhan Nagar India 22°35N 88°25E 124 B2
Bidhuna India 26°49N 79°31E 243 F8
Bīdokht Iran 34°20N 58°46E 247 C8
Bidor Malaysia 4°6N 101°15E 237 K3
Bidu West Bank 31°50N 35°9E 123 B1
Bidyadanga Australia 18°45S 121°43E 278 C3
Bidzar Cameroon 9°54N 14°7E 264 A2
Bie Sweden 59°5N 16°12E 162 E10
Bié □ Angola 12°30S 17°0E 265 E3
Bié, Planalto de Angola 12°0S 16°0E 265 E3
Bieber U.S.A. 41°7N 121°8W 304 F3
Biebrza → Poland 53°13N 22°25E 185 E9
Biebrzański △ Poland 53°36N 22°45E 184 E9
Biecz Poland 49°44N 21°15E 185 J8
Biel Switz. 47°8N 7°14E 179 H3
Bielany Poland 52°17N 20°57E 143 B1
Bielawa Dolnośląskie, Poland 50°43N 16°37E 185 H3
Bielawa Warszawa, Poland 52°8N 21°9E 143 C2
Bielefeld Germany 52°1N 8°33E 178 C4
Bielersee Switz. 47°6N 7°5E 179 H3
Bielitz = Bielsko-Biała Poland 49°50N 19°2E 185 J6
Biella Italy 45°34N 8°3E 198 C5
Bielsk Podlaski Poland 52°47N 23°12E 185 F10
Bielsko-Biała Poland 49°50N 19°2E 185 J6
Bien Hoa Vietnam 10°57N 106°49E 237 G6
Bienne = Biel Switz. 47°8N 7°14E 179 H3
Bienvenida Spain 38°18N 6°12W 195 G4
Bienvenue Fr. Guiana 3°0N 52°30W 329 C7
Bienville, L. Canada 55°5N 72°40W 298 A5
Bierné France 47°48N 0°33W 172 E6
Bierun Poland 50°6N 19°6E 185 H6
Bierutów Poland 51°7N 17°32E 185 G4
Biesbosch △ Neths. 51°45N 4°48E 170 C4
Biescas Spain 42°37N 0°20W 196 C4
Biesdorf Germany 52°30N 13°33E 115 A4
Biese → Germany 52°53N 11°46E 178 C7
Biesiesfontein S. Africa 30°57S 17°58E 270 D2
Bieszczadzki △ Poland 49°5N 22°43E 185 J9
Bietigheim-Bissingen Germany 48°58N 9°8E 179 G5
Bièvre → France 48°44N 2°9E 134 B1
Bièvres France 48°45N 2°13E 134 B2
Bieżuń Poland 52°58N 19°55E 185 F6
Biferno → Italy 41°59N 15°2E 199 G12
Bifoum Gabon 0°20S 10°23E 264 C2
Big → Nfld. & L., Canada 54°50N 58°55W 299 B8
Big → Mo., U.S.A. 38°28N 90°37W 310 F6
Big B. = Awarua B. N.Z. 44°28S 168°4E 285 E3
Big B. Canada 55°43N 60°35W 299 A7
Big Bear City U.S.A. 34°16N 116°51W 307 L10
Big Bear Lake U.S.A. 34°15N 116°56W 307 L10
Big Belt Mts. U.S.A. 46°30N 111°25W 304 C8
Big Bend Swaziland 26°50S 31°58E 271 C5
Big Bend △ U.S.A. 29°20N 103°5W 314 G3
Big Black → U.S.A. 32°3N 91°4W 315 E9
Big Blue → Ind., U.S.A. 39°12N 85°56W 311 E11
Big Blue → Kans., U.S.A. 39°35N 96°34W 308 F5
Big Buddha Hong Kong, China 22°15N 113°54E 124 B1
Big Buddha Hong Kong, China 22°15N 113°54E 219 a
Big Creek U.S.A. 37°11N 119°14W 306 H7
Big Cypress △ U.S.A. 26°0N 81°10W 317 J8
Big Cypress Swamp U.S.A. 26°15N 81°30W 317 J8
Big Delta U.S.A. 64°10N 145°51W 303 D11
Big Desert Australia 35°45S 141°10E 281 F3
Big Falls U.S.A. 48°12N 93°48W 308 A7
Big Fork → U.S.A. 48°31N 93°43W 308 A7
Big Horn Mts. = Bighorn Mts. U.S.A. 44°25N 107°0W 304 D10
Big I. Canada 61°7N 116°45W 296 A5
Big Lake Alaska, U.S.A. 61°20N 150°0W 303 F10
Big Lake Tex., U.S.A. 31°12N 101°28W 314 F4
Big Moose U.S.A. 43°49N 74°58W 313 C10
Big Muddy → U.S.A. 37°33N 89°32W 310 G8
Big Muddy Cr. → U.S.A. 48°8N 104°36W 304 B11
Big Pine U.S.A. 37°10N 118°17W 306 H8
Big Pine Key U.S.A. 24°40N 81°21W 317 L8
Big Piney U.S.A. 42°32N 110°7W 304 E8
Big Quill L. Canada 51°55N 104°30W 297 C8
Big Rapids U.S.A. 43°42N 85°29W 309 D11
Big Rideau L. Canada 44°40N 76°15W 313 B8
Big River Canada 53°50N 107°0W 297 C7
Big Run U.S.A. 40°57N 78°55W 312 F6
Big Sable Pt. U.S.A. 44°3N 86°1W 308 C10
Big Salmon → Canada 61°52N 134°55W 296 A2
Big Sand L. Man., Canada 57°45N 99°45W 297 B9
Big Sand L. Fla., U.S.A. 28°25N 81°29W 133 B2
Big Sandy U.S.A. 48°11N 110°7W 304 B8
Big Sandy → U.S.A. 38°25N 82°36W 309 F12
Big Sandy Cr. = Sandy Cr. → U.S.A. 41°51N 109°47W 304 F9
Big Sandy Cr. → U.S.A. 38°7N 102°29W 304 G12
Big Satilla Cr. → U.S.A. 31°27N 82°3W 316 D7
Big Sioux → U.S.A. 42°29N 96°27W 308 D5
Big South Fork △ U.S.A. 36°27N 84°47W 315 C12
Big Spring U.S.A. 32°15N 101°28W 314 E4
Big Stone City U.S.A. 45°18N 96°28W 308 C5
Big Stone Gap U.S.A. 36°52N 82°47W 309 G12
Big Stone L. U.S.A. 45°18N 96°27W 308 C5
Big Sur U.S.A. 36°15N 121°48W 306 J5
Big Timber U.S.A. 45°50N 109°57W 304 D9
Big Trout L. Canada 53°40N 90°0W 298 B2
Big Trout Lake Canada 53°45N 90°0W 298 B2

Biğa Turkey 40°13N 27°14E 203 F11
Biga → Turkey 40°20N 27°14E 203 F11
Bigadiç Turkey 39°22N 28°7E 205 B10
Biganos France 44°39N 0°59W 174 D3
Bigeumdo S. Korea 34°45N 126°56E 224 E3
Biggar Sask., Canada 52°4N 108°0W 297 C7
Biggar S. Lanarks., U.K. 55°38N 3°32W 167 F5
Bigge I. Australia 14°35S 125°10E 278 B4
Biggenden Australia 25°31S 152°4E 281 D5
Biggleswade U.K. 52°5N 0°14W 169 E7
Biggs U.S.A. 39°25N 121°43W 306 F5
Bighorn U.S.A. 46°10N 107°27W 304 C10
Bighorn → U.S.A. 46°10N 107°28W 304 C10
Bighorn Canyon ⌓ U.S.A. 45°10N 108°0W 304 D10
Bighorn L. U.S.A. 44°55N 108°15W 304 D9
Bighorn Mts. U.S.A. 44°25N 107°0W 304 D10
Bigi Dem. Rep. of the Congo 3°2N 22°25E 264 B4
Bignona Senegal 12°52N 16°14W 262 C1
Bigorre France 43°10N 0°5E 174 E4
Bigstone L. Canada 53°42N 95°44W 297 C9
Biguglia, Étang de France 42°36N 9°29E 175 F13
Bigwa Tanzania 7°10S 39°10E 268 D4
Bihać Bos.-H. 44°49N 15°57E 199 D12
Bihar India 25°5N 85°40E 243 G11
Bihar □ India 25°0N 86°0E 243 G12
Biharamulo Tanzania 2°25S 31°25E 268 C3
Biharamulo ⌓ Tanzania 2°24S 31°26E 268 C3
Bihariganj India 25°44N 86°59E 243 G12
Biharkeresztes Hungary 47°8N 21°44E 182 C6
Bihor □ Romania 47°0N 22°10E 182 D7
Bihor, Munţii Romania 46°29N 22°47E 182 D7
Bijagós, Arquipélago dos Guinea-Biss. 11°15N 16°10W 262 C1
Bijaipur India 26°2N 77°20E 242 F7
Bijapur Chhattisgarh, India 18°50N 80°50E 244 E5
Bijapur Karnataka, India 16°50N 75°55E 244 F2
Bījār Iran 35°52N 47°35E 213 E12
Bijauri Nepal 28°6N 82°20E 243 E10
Bijawar India 24°38N 79°30E 243 G8
Bijbels Museum Amsterdam, Neths. 112 b1
Bijela Montenegro 42°28N 18°39E 202 D2
Bijeljina Bos.-H. 44°46N 19°14E 182 F4
Bijelo Polje Montenegro 43°1N 19°45E 202 C3
Bijie China 27°20N 105°16E 228 D5
Bijlmermeer Amsterdam, Neths. 52°19N 4°59E 112 B2
Bijnor India 29°27N 78°11E 242 E8
Bikaner India 28°2N 73°18E 242 E5
Bikapur India 26°30N 82°7E 243 F10
Bikeqi China 40°43N 111°20E 226 D6
Bikfayyā Lebanon 33°55N 35°41E 250 E6
Bikié Congo 3°7S 13°52E 264 C2
Bikin Russia 46°50N 134°20E 220 A7
Bikin → Russia 46°51N 134°2E 220 A7
Bikini Atoll Marshall Is. 12°0N 167°30E 288 F8
Bikita Zimbabwe 20°6S 31°41E 271 B5
Bīkkū Bīttī Libya 22°0N 19°12E 259 D3
Bikoro Dem. Rep. of the Congo 0°48S 18°15E 264 C3
Bikoué Cameroon 3°55N 11°50E 263 E7
Bila Tserkva Ukraine 49°45N 30°10E 177 D16
Bilād Banī Bū 'Alī Oman 22°1N 59°19E 249 B7
Bilanga Burkina Faso 12°40N 0°1W 263 C4
Bilara India 26°14N 73°53E 242 F5
Bilasipara India 26°13N 90°14E 241 B3
Bilaspur Chhattisgarh, India 22°2N 82°15E 243 H10
Bilaspur Punjab, India 31°19N 76°50E 242 D7
Biläsuvar Azerbaijan 39°27N 48°32E 213 C13
Bilauk Taungdan Thailand 13°0N 99°0E 236 F2
Bilauri Nepal 28°41N 80°21E 243 E9
Bilbao Spain 43°16N 2°56W 196 B2
Bilbao ✈ (BIO) Spain 43°18N 2°57W 196 B2
Bilbeis Egypt 30°25N 31°34E 256 H7
Bilbo = Bilbao Spain 43°16N 2°56W 196 B2
Bilbor Romania 47°6N 25°30E 183 C10
Bilche-Zolote Ukraine 48°47N 25°53E 183 B10
Bilciureşti Romania 44°44N 25°48E 183 F10
Bíldudalur Iceland 65°41N 23°36W 155 B3
Bílé Karpaty Europe 49°5N 18°0E 181 B11
Bileća Bos.-H. 42°53N 18°27E 202 D2
Bilecik Turkey 40°5N 30°5E 212 B4
Bilecik □ Turkey 40°0N 30°0E 212 B3
Bilećko Jezero Bos.-H. 42°48N 18°28E 202 D2
Bileh Savār Iran 39°21N 48°21E 213 C13
Biłgoraj Poland 50°33N 22°42E 185 H9
Bilgram India 27°11N 80°2E 243 F9
Bilhaur India 26°51N 80°5E 243 F9
Bilhorod-Dnistrovskyy Ukraine 46°11N 30°23E 189 J6
Bili → Dem. Rep. of the Congo 4°9N 22°29E 264 B4
Bilibino Russia 68°3N 166°20E 215 C17
Bilibiza Mozam. 12°30S 40°20E 269 E5
Bilimora India 20°45N 72°57E 244 D1
Bilin Burma 17°14N 97°15E 241 G6
Biliran Phil. 11°28N 124°28E 233 F5
Biliran □ Phil. 11°35N 124°28E 233 F5
Bilisht Albania 40°37N 21°2E 202 F5
Bill Baggs Cape Florida State Recr. Area ⌓ U.S.A. 25°40N 80°9W 129 D3
Billabong Cr. → Australia 35°5S 144°2E 282 C6
Billdal Sweden 57°35N 11°57E 163 G5
Billiluna Australia 19°37S 127°41E 278 C4
Billings U.S.A. 45°47N 108°30W 304 D9
Billiton Is. = Belitung Indonesia 3°10S 107°50E 235 C3
Billsta Sweden 63°20N 18°28E 162 A12
Billund Denmark 55°44N 9°6E 163 J3
Billy Pt. Antigua & B. 17°44N 61°52W 322 c
Bilma Niger 18°50N 13°30E 259 E2
Bilma, Grand Erg de Niger 18°30N 14°0E 259 E2
Bilo Gora Croatia 45°53N 17°15E 182 E2
Biloela Australia 24°24S 150°31E 280 C5
Bilohirsk Ukraine 45°3N 34°35E 189 K8
Biloku Guyana 1°50N 58°25W 329 C6
Biloli India 18°46N 77°44E 244 E3
Bilopillya Ukraine 51°14N 34°20E 189 G8
Bilovodsk Ukraine 49°13N 39°36E 189 H10
Biloxi U.S.A. 30°24N 88°53W 315 F10
Bilpa Morea Claypan Australia 25°0S 140°0E 280 D3
Bilqâs Qism Auwal Egypt 31°12N 31°21E 251 G2
Bilston U.K. 55°52N 3°10W 121 B2
Biltine Chad 14°40N 20°50E 259 F4
Bilugyun Burma 16°24N 97°32E 241 G6
Bilyarsk Russia 54°58N 50°22E 190 C10
Bim Son Vietnam 20°4N 105°51E 236 B5
Bima Indonesia 8°22S 118°49E 235 D5
Bimban Egypt 24°24N 32°54E 256 C3
Bimbe Angola 11°50S 15°50E 265 E3
Bimberi Pk. Australia 35°44S 148°51E 283 C8
Bimbila Ghana 8°54N 0°5E 263 D5
Bimbini Comoros Is. 12°11S 44°14E 272 a
Bimbo C.A.R. 4°15N 18°33E 264 B3
Bimini Is. Bahamas 25°42N 79°25W 320 A4
Bin Ghunaymah, Jabal Libya 25°0N 15°30E 258 D3
Bin Jawwād Libya 30°47N 18°4E 258 B3
Bin Xian Heilongjiang, China 45°42N 127°32E 227 B14
Bin Xian Shaanxi, China 35°2N 108°4E 226 G5
Bin Yauri Nigeria 10°46N 4°45E 263 C5
Bina-Etawah India 24°13N 78°14E 242 G8
Binacayan Phil. 14°27N 120°55E 127 C1
Binalbagan Phil. 10°12N 122°50E 233 F4
Binalong Australia 34°40S 148°39E 283 C8
Bīnālūd, Kūh-e Iran 36°30N 58°30E 247 B8
Binanga Indonesia 1°24N 99°46E 234 B1
Binangonan de Lampon = Infanta Phil. 14°45N 121°39E 232 D3
Binatang = Bintangau Malaysia 2°10N 111°40E 235 B4
Binche Belgium 50°26N 4°10E 170 D4
Binchuan China 25°42N 100°38E 228 E3
Binda Dem. Rep. of the Congo 5°52S 13°14E 265 D2
Binder Chad 9°56N 14°27E 259 G2
Bindki India 26°2N 80°36E 243 F9
Bindloe, I. = Marchena, I. Ecuador 0°19N 90°29W 330 a
Bindoy Phil. 9°48N 123°5E 233 G4
Bindslev Denmark 57°33N 10°11E 163 G4
Bindura Zimbabwe 17°18S 31°18E 269 F3
Binéfar Spain 41°51N 0°18E 196 D5
Bingara Australia 29°52S 150°36E 281 D5
Bingaram I. India 10°56N 72°17E 245 J1
Bingen Germany 49°57N 7°55E 179 F3
Bingerau = Węgrów Poland 52°24N 22°0E 185 F9
Bingerville Ivory C. 5°18N 3°49W 262 D4
Bingham U.S.A. 45°3N 69°53W 309 C19
Binghamton U.S.A. 42°6N 75°55W 313 D9
Bingo-Ochiai Japan 34°59N 133°8E 222 C4
Bingöl Turkey 38°53N 40°29E 213 C9
Bingöl □ Turkey 38°55N 40°30E 213 C9
Bingöl Dağları Turkey 39°16N 41°9E 213 C9
Bingsjö Sweden 61°1N 15°39E 162 C9
Binh Dinh Vietnam 13°55N 109°7E 236 F7
Binh Son Vietnam 15°20N 108°40E 236 E7
Binhai China 34°2N 119°49E 227 G10
Bini Erde Chad 20°6N 18°1E 259 D3
Binic France 48°46N 2°50W 172 D4
Binisatua Spain 39°50N 4°11E 206 B5
Binissalem Spain 39°41N 2°50E 206 B3
Binjai Kepulauan Riau, Indonesia 3°48N 108°13E 235 B3
Binjai Sumatera Utara, Indonesia 3°20N 98°30E 234 B1
Binji Nigeria 13°10N 4°55E 263 C5
Binka India 21°2N 83°48E 244 D6
Binnah, Ras Somalia 11°9N 51°10E 267 B7
Binnaway Australia 31°28S 149°24E 283 A8
Binondo Phil. 14°36N 120°58E 127 B1
Binongko Indonesia 5°57S 124°2E 231 F6
Binscarth Canada 50°37N 101°17W 297 C8
Binshangul Gumuz □ Ethiopia 11°0N 35°30E 257 E4
Bint Goda Sudan 13°17N 31°33E 257 E3
Bintan Indonesia 1°0N 104°0E 234 B2
Bintangau Malaysia 2°10N 111°40E 235 B4
Bintaro Jaya Indonesia 6°16S 106°44E 122 B1
Bintuhan Indonesia 4°48S 103°22E 234 C2
Bintulu Malaysia 3°10N 113°0E 235 B4
Bintuni Indonesia 2°7S 133°32E 231 E8
Binyang China 23°12N 108°47E 228 F7
Binz Germany 54°24N 13°35E 178 A9
Binza Dem. Rep. of the Congo 4°21S 15°14E 265 C3
Binzert = Bizerte Tunisia 37°15N 9°50E 258 A1
Binzhou China 37°20N 118°2E 227 F10
Bío Bío □ Chile 37°35S 72°0W 334 D1
Bíobío → Chile 36°49S 73°10W 334 D1
Biograd na Moru Croatia 43°56N 15°29E 199 E12
Biogradska Gora △ Montenegro 42°55N 19°40E 202 D3
Bioko Eq. Guin. 3°30N 8°40E 263 E6
Biokovo Croatia 43°23N 17°0E 199 E14
Biougra Morocco 30°15N 9°14W 260 B3
Bipindi Cameroon 3°6N 10°30E 263 E7
Bir India 19°4N 75°46E 244 E2
Bir, Ras Djibouti 12°0N 43°20E 257 E5
Bîr Abu Hashim Egypt 23°42N 34°6E 256 C3
Bîr Abu Minqar Egypt 26°33N 27°33E 256 B2
Bîr Abu Muḩammad Egypt 29°44N 34°14E 251 J5
Bîr Abu Sandûq Egypt 29°24N 32°30E 251 J3
Bîr Adal Deib Sudan 22°35N 36°10E 256 C4
Bi'r al Butayyihāt Jordan 29°47N 35°20E 251 J6
Bi'r al Ḩamḑah Si. Arabia 28°30N 34°55E 251 K5
Bi'r al Mārī Jordan 30°4N 35°33E 251 H6
Bi'r al Musallam Si. Arabia 28°56N 35°38E 251 K6
Bi'r al Qattār Jordan 29°47N 35°32E 251 J6
Bir 'Ali Yemen 14°1N 48°20E 249 D5
Bîr 'Amrâne Mauritania 22°45N 8°39W 260 D3
Bir Aouine Tunisia 32°25N 9°18E 258 B1
Bîr 'Asal Egypt 25°55N 34°20E 256 B3
Bi'r ash Shakkūsīyah Syria 35°23N 37°26E 250 C8
Bîr Atrun Sudan 18°15N 26°40E 256 D2
Bîr Beiḍa Egypt 30°25N 34°29E 251 H5
Bîr Bel Guerdâne Mauritania 25°24N 10°31W 260 C2
Bîr Bireida Egypt 29°8N 32°7E 251 J3
Bîr Buerât Egypt 28°59N 32°11E 251 K3
Bi'r Dhu'fān Libya 31°59N 14°32E 258 B2
Bir Di South Sudan 7°34N 28°49E 257 F2
Bîr Diqnash Egypt 31°3N 25°23E 256 A2
Bir el Abbes Algeria 26°7N 6°9W 260 C3
Bîr el 'Abd Egypt 31°2N 33°0E 251 G4
Bîr el 'Agramîya Egypt 29°38N 31°50E 251 J2
Bir el Ater Algeria 34°46N 8°3E 261 B6
Bîr el Basur Egypt 29°51N 25°49E 256 B2
Bîr el Biarât Egypt 29°30N 34°43E 251 J5
Bîr el Dakhal Egypt 28°39N 32°23E 251 K3
Bîr el Duweidar Egypt 30°56N 32°32E 251 H3
Bîr el Garârât Egypt 31°3N 33°34E 251 G4
Bîr el Gâreb Mauritania 20°33N 16°12W 260 D1
Bîr el Gellaz Egypt 30°50N 26°40E 256 A2
Bîr el Ghamr Egypt 28°43N 31°20E 251 K2
Bîr el Heisi Egypt 29°22N 34°36E 251 J5
Bîr el Jafir Egypt 30°50N 32°41E 251 H3
Bîr el Mâlḥi Egypt 30°38N 33°19E 251 H4
Bîr el Manâyif Egypt 30°31N 32°12E 251 H3
Bîr el-Naşb Egypt 29°3N 33°2E 251 J4
Bîr el Şafra Egypt 28°45N 34°21E 251 K5
Bîr el-Saura Egypt 29°9N 34°30E 251 J5
Bîr el Shaqqa Egypt 30°54N 25°1E 256 A2
Bîr el Thamâda Egypt 30°12N 33°27E 251 H4
Bîr Enzarán W. Sahara 23°53N 14°32W 260 D2
Bîr Fuad Egypt 30°35N 26°28E 256 A2
Bîr Gandús W. Sahara 21°36N 16°30W 260 D1
Bîr Gebeil Ḥişn Egypt 30°2N 33°18E 251 H4
Bi'r Ghadīr Syria 34°6N 37°3E 250 D8
Bîr Ghalla Egypt 28°23N 32°19E 251 K3
Bi'r Gharr Si. Arabia 28°7N 35°32E 251 K6
Bîr Gindali Egypt 29°55N 31°40E 251 J2
Bîr Haimur Egypt 22°45N 33°40E 256 C3
Bîr Ḥasana Egypt 30°29N 33°46E 251 H4
Bîr Hööker Egypt 30°22N 30°21E 256 H7
Bi'r Īdimah Si. Arabia 18°31N 44°12E 248 C4
Bi'r Jadīd Si. Arabia 29°10N 35°6E 251 J6
Bîr Kanayis Egypt 24°59N 33°15E 256 C3
Bîr Kaseiba Egypt 31°0N 33°17E 251 H4
Bîr Kerawein Egypt 27°10N 28°25E 256 B2
Bîr Lahfân Egypt 31°0N 33°51E 251 H4
Bir Lahrache Algeria 32°1N 8°12E 261 B6
Bîr Madkûr Egypt 30°44N 32°33E 251 H3
Bîr Maql Egypt 23°7N 33°40E 256 C3
Bîr Mîneiga Sudan 22°47N 35°12E 256 C4
Bîr Misaha Egypt 22°13N 27°59E 256 C2
Bîr Mogreïn Mauritania 25°10N 11°25W 260 C2
Bîr Mureir Egypt 28°25N 31°15E 251 K2
Bîr Murr Egypt 23°28N 30°10E 256 C3
Bi'r Muţribah Kuwait 29°54N 47°17E 246 D5
Bîr Nabala West Bank 31°51N 35°12E 123 A2
Bîr Nakheila Egypt 24°1N 30°50E 256 C3
Bîr Nakhul Egypt 29°5N 33°16E 251 J4
Bîr Qaţia Egypt 30°58N 32°45E 251 H3
Bîr Qatrani Egypt 30°55N 26°10E 256 A2
Bîr Ranga Egypt 24°25N 35°15E 256 C4
Bîr Sahara Egypt 22°54N 28°40E 256 C2
Bîr Sa'îd Egypt 29°38N 31°24E 251 J2
Bîr Seiyâla Egypt 26°10N 33°50E 256 B3
Bîr Shalatein Egypt 23°5N 35°25E 256 C4
Bîr Shebb Egypt 22°25N 29°40E 256 C2
Bîr Shût Egypt 23°50N 35°15E 256 C4
Bîr Sidri Egypt 28°53N 33°28E 251 K4
Bîr Tâba Egypt 29°29N 34°53E 251 J5
Bîr Terfawi Egypt 22°57N 28°55E 256 C2
Bîr Umm Qubûr Egypt 24°35N 34°2E 256 C3
Bîr Ungât Egypt 22°8N 33°48E 256 C3
Bîr Wuseit Egypt 29°14N 33°1E 251 J4
Bîr Za'farâna Egypt 29°10N 32°40E 256 J8
Bîr Zeidûn Egypt 25°45N 33°40E 256 B3
Birāk Libya 27°31N 14°20E 258 C2
Birak el Kiyam Egypt 30°2N 31°9E 117 A1
Biramféro Guinea 11°40N 9°10W 262 C3
Birao C.A.R. 10°20N 22°47E 264 A4
Biratnagar Nepal 26°27N 87°17E 243 F12
Birawa Dem. Rep. of the Congo 2°20S 28°48E 268 C2
Birch → Canada 58°28N 112°17W 296 B6
Birch Cliff Canada 43°41N 79°16W 141 A3
Birch Grove Grenada 12°6N 61°40W 323 q
Birch Hills Canada 52°59N 105°25W 297 C7
Birch I. Canada 52°26N 99°54W 297 C9
Birch L. N.W.T., Canada 62°4N 116°33W 296 A5
Birch L. Ont., Canada 51°23N 92°18W 298 B1
Birch Mts. Canada 57°30N 113°10W 296 B6
Birch River Canada 52°24N 101°6W 297 C8
Birchip Australia 35°56S 142°55E 282 C5
Birchiş Romania 45°58N 22°9E 182 E7
Birchwood N.Z. 45°55S 167°53E 285 F2
Birchwood Alaska, U.S.A. 61°24N 149°28W 303 F10
Bird Canada 56°30N 94°13W 297 B10
Bird I. = Aves, I. de W. Indies 15°45N 63°55W 321 C7
Bird I. S. Georgia 54°0S 38°3W 151 B1
Birds Creek Canada 45°6N 77°52W 312 A7
Birdseye U.S.A. 38°19N 86°42W 311 F10
Birdsville Australia 25°51S 139°20E 280 D2
Birdum Cr. → Australia 15°14S 133°0E 278 C5
Birdwood Australia 34°51S 138°58E 282 C3
Birecik Turkey 37°2N 38°0E 213 D8
Birein Israel 30°50N 34°28E 251 H5
Bireuen Indonesia 5°14N 96°39E 234 A1
Birganj Nepal 27°1N 84°52E 243 F11
Birgu = Vittoriosa Malta 35°54N 14°31E 206 F8
Birhan Ethiopia 10°45N 38°4E 266 B4
Biri Norway 60°58N 10°35E 164 D7
Biri → South Sudan 7°56N 26°33E 257 F2
Birifo Gambia 13°30N 14°0W 262 C2
Birigüi Brazil 21°18S 50°16W 335 A5
Birini C.A.R. 7°51N 22°24E 264 A4
Bīrjand Iran 32°53N 59°13E 247 C8
Birka Sweden 59°20N 17°32E 162 E11
Birkeland Norway 58°24N 7°12E 164 F4
Birkenfeld Germany 49°38N 7°9E 179 F3
Birkenhead U.K. 53°23N 3°2W 168 D4
Birkenstein Germany 52°31N 13°40E 115 A5
Birkerød Denmark 55°50N 12°25E 163 J6
Birket Fatmé Chad 12°55N 19°7E 259 F3
Birket Qârûn Egypt 29°30N 30°40E 256 J7
Birkfeld Austria 47°21N 15°45E 180 D8
Birkhadem Algeria 36°43N 3°3E 261 A5
Birkholz Germany 52°37N 13°34E 115 A4
Birkholzaue Germany 52°38N 13°36E 115 A4
Birkirkara Malta 35°54N 14°28E 206 F7
Bîrlad = Bârlad Romania 46°15N 27°38E 183 D12
Birmingham W. Mids., U.K. 52°29N 1°52W 169 E6
Birmingham Ala., U.S.A. 33°31N 86°48W 315 E11
Birmingham Iowa, U.S.A. 40°53N 91°57W 310 D5
Birmingham Int. ✈ (BHX) U.K. 52°26N 1°45W 169 E6
Birmitrapur India 22°24N 84°46E 244 C7
Birni Ngaouré Niger 13°5N 2°51E 263 C5
Birni Nkonni Niger 13°55N 5°15E 263 C6
Birnie Kiribati 3°35S 171°31W 277 A16
Birnin Gwari Nigeria 11°0N 6°45E 263 C6
Birnin Kebbi Nigeria 12°32N 4°12E 263 C5
Birnin Kudu Nigeria 11°30N 9°29E 263 C6
Birobidzhan Russia 48°50N 132°50E 219 B15
Birougou, Mts. Gabon 1°51S 12°20E 264 C2
Birr Ireland 53°6N 7°54W 166 C4
Birrarrung Park Australia 37°45S 145°4E 128 A2
Birrie → Australia 29°43S 146°37E 281 D4
Birsilpur India 28°11N 72°15E 242 E5
Birsk Russia 55°25N 55°30E 186 C10
Birtle Canada 50°30N 101°5W 297 C8
Biryuchiy Ukraine 46°10N 35°0E 189 J8
Biržai Lithuania 56°11N 24°45E 188 D3
Birzebbugga Malta 35°50N 14°32E 206 F8
Birzhi = Madona Latvia 56°53N 26°5E 188 D4
Birzula = Kotovsk Ukraine 47°45N 29°35E 177 E15
Bisa Indonesia 1°15S 127°28E 231 E7
Bisáccia Italy 41°1N 15°22E 201 A8
Bisacquino Italy 37°42N 13°15E 200 E6
Bisai Japan 35°16N 136°44E 223 B8
Bisalpur India 28°14N 79°48E 243 E8
Bisbee U.S.A. 31°27N 109°55W 305 L9
Biscarrosse France 44°22N 1°20W 174 D2
Biscarrosse et de Parentis, Étang de France 44°21N 1°10W 174 D2
Biscay, B. of Atl. Oc. 45°0N 2°0W 171 D1
Biscay Abyssal Plain Atl. Oc. 45°0N 8°0W 152 B11
Biscayne ⌓ U.S.A. 25°25N 80°12W 317 K9
Biscayne B. U.S.A. 25°40N 80°12W 317 K9
Biscayne Bay Aquatic Reserve U.S.A. 25°40N 80°16W 129 E2
Biscayne Park U.S.A. 25°52N 80°10W 129 C2
Biscéglie Italy 41°14N 16°30E 201 A9
Bischheim France 48°37N 7°46E 173 D14
Bischoflack = Škofja Loka Slovenia 46°9N 14°19E 199 B11
Bischofsburg = Biskupiec Poland 53°53N 20°58E 184 E7
Bischofshofen Austria 47°26N 13°14E 180 D6
Bischofstal = Ujazd Poland 50°23N 18°21E 185 H5
Bischofstein = Bisztynek Poland 54°8N 20°53E 184 D7
Bischofswerda Germany 51°7N 14°10E 178 D10
Bischwiller France 48°46N 7°50E 173 D14
Biscoe Is. Antarctica 66°0S 67°0W 151 C17
Biscoitos Azores 38°47N 27°15W 153 d1
Biscotasing Canada 47°18N 82°9W 298 C3
Biševo Croatia 42°57N 16°3E 199 F13
Bisha Eritrea 15°30N 37°31E 257 D4
Bishah, W. → Si. Arabia 21°24N 43°26E 248 B3
Bishan China 29°33N 106°12E 228 C6
Bishanga Dem. Rep. of the Congo 4°31S 21°2E 265 C4
Bishkek Kyrgyzstan 42°54N 74°46E 217 D8
Bishnath India 26°40N 93°10E 241 B4
Bishnupur India 23°8N 87°20E 243 H12
Bisho = Bhisho S. Africa 32°50S 27°23E 270 D4
Bishop Calif., U.S.A. 37°22N 118°24W 306 H8
Bishop Ga., U.S.A. 33°49N 83°26W 316 B6
Bishop Tex., U.S.A. 27°35N 97°48W 314 H6
Bishop Auckland U.K. 54°39N 1°40W 168 C6
Bishop Lavis S. Africa 33°56S 18°35E 118 A2
Bishop Museum U.S.A. 21°20N 157°52W 302 K14
Bishop's Falls Canada 49°2N 55°30W 299 C8
Bishop's Stortford U.K. 51°52N 0°10E 169 F8
Bishopscourt S. Africa 33°59S 18°27E 118 A1
Bisignano Italy 39°31N 16°17E 201 C9
Bisina, L. Uganda 1°38N 33°56E 268 B3
Biskra Algeria 34°50N 5°44E 261 B6
Biskra Malta 35°58N 14°21E 206 F7
Biskra □ Algeria 34°40N 5°25E 261 B6
Biskupiec Poland 53°53N 20°58E 184 E7
Bislig Phil. 8°12N 126°18E 233 G6
Bismarck Mo., U.S.A. 37°46N 90°38W 310 G6
Bismarck N. Dak., U.S.A. 46°48N 100°47W 308 B3
Bismarck Arch. Papua N. G. 2°30S 150°0E 286 B6
Bismarck Ra. Papua N. G. 5°35S 145°0E 286 C3
Bismarck Sea Papua N. G. 4°10S 146°50E 286 C4
Bismarckburg = Kasanga Tanzania 8°30S 31°10E 269 D3
Bismark Germany 52°40N 11°33E 178 C7
Bismil Turkey 37°51N 40°40E 213 D9
Bismo Norway 61°54N 8°15E 164 C5
Biso Uganda 1°44N 31°26E 268 B3
Bison U.S.A. 45°31N 102°28W 308 C2
Bīsotūn Iran 34°23N 47°26E 213 E12
Bispebjerg Denmark 55°42N 12°31E 118 A3
Bispgården Sweden 63°2N 16°40E 162 A10
Bissagos = Bijagós, Arquipélago dos Guinea-Biss. 11°15N 16°10W 262 C1
Bissam Cuttack India 19°31N 83°31E 244 E6
Bissau Guinea-Biss. 11°45N 15°45W 262 C1
Bissaula Nigeria 7°0N 10°27E 263 D7
Bissigh, Lach → Somalia 0°45N 41°33E 267 D5
Bissikrima Guinea 10°50N 10°58W 262 C2
Bissonet Plaza U.S.A. 30°1N 90°13W 131 A1
Bissorã Guinea-Biss. 12°16N 15°35W 262 C1
Bistcho L. Canada 59°45N 118°50W 296 B5
Bistreţ Romania 43°54N 23°23E 183 G8
Bistrica = Ilirska-Bistrica Slovenia 45°34N 14°14E 199 C11
Bistriţa Romania 47°9N 24°35E 183 C9
Bistriţa → Romania 46°30N 26°57E 183 D11
Bistriţa Năsăud □ Romania 47°15N 24°30E 183 C9
Bistriţei, Munţii Romania 47°15N 25°40E 183 C10
Biswan India 27°29N 81°2E 243 F9
Bisztynek Poland 54°8N 20°53E 184 D7
Bita → C.A.R. 6°26N 24°43E 264 A4
Bitam Gabon 2°5N 11°25E 264 B2
Bitburg Germany 49°58N 6°31E 179 F2
Bitche France 49°2N 7°25E 173 C14
Bithynia Turkey 40°40N 31°0E 212 B4
Bitkine Chad 11°59N 18°13E 259 F3
Bitlis Turkey 38°20N 42°3E 213 C10
Bitlis □ Turkey 38°20N 42°5E 213 C10
Bitola Macedonia 41°1N 21°20E 202 E5
Bitolj = Bitola Macedonia 41°1N 21°20E 202 E5
Bitonto Italy 41°6N 16°41E 201 A9
Bitra I. India 11°33N 72°9E 245 J1
Bitter Creek U.S.A. 41°33N 108°33W 304 F9
Bitter L. = Buheirat-Murrat-el-Kubra Egypt 30°18N 32°26E 256 H8
Bitterfeld Germany 51°37N 12°20E 178 D8
Bitterfontein S. Africa 31°1S 18°32E 270 D2
Bitterroot → U.S.A. 46°52N 114°7W 304 C6
Bitterroot Range U.S.A. 46°0N 114°20W 304 C6
Bitterwater U.S.A. 36°23N 121°0W 306 J6
Bitti Italy 40°29N 9°23E 200 B2
Bittou Burkina Faso 11°17N 0°18W 263 C4
Bittsevsky Forest Park Russia 55°38N 37°35E 129 C2
Biu Nigeria 10°40N 12°3E 263 C7
Bivolari Romania 47°31N 27°27E 183 C12
Bivolu, Vf. Romania 47°16N 25°58E 183 C10
Biwa-Ko Japan 35°15N 136°10E 223 B8
Biwabik U.S.A. 47°32N 92°21W 308 B7
Bixad Romania 47°56N 23°28E 183 C8
Bixby U.S.A. 35°57N 95°53W 314 D7
Biya → Russia 52°25N 85°0E 217 B11
Biyala Egypt 31°10N 31°13E 251 G2
Biyang China 32°38N 113°21E 229 A9
Biysk Russia 52°40N 85°0E 217 B11
Bizana S. Africa 30°50S 29°52E 271 D4
Bizen Japan 34°43N 134°8E 222 C6
Bizerte Tunisia 37°15N 9°50E 258 A1
Bizerte □ Tunisia 37°5N 9°35E 261 A6
Bjåen fjellstove Norway 59°37N 7°26E 164 E4
Bjargtangar Iceland 65°30N 24°30W 155 B2
Bjarkalundur Iceland 65°33N 22°9W 155 B4
Bjärnum Sweden 56°17N 13°43E 163 H7
Bjästa Sweden 63°12N 18°29E 162 A12
Bjelasica Montenegro 42°50N 19°40E 202 D3
Bjelašnica Bos.-H. 43°43N 18°9E 182 G3
Bjelland Norway 58°23N 7°32E 164 F4
Bjelovar Croatia 45°56N 16°49E 199 C13
Bjerringbro Denmark 56°23N 9°39E 163 H3
Bjervamoen Norway 59°17N 9°5E 164 E6
Bjøberg Norway 60°56N 8°13E 164 D5
Björbo Sweden 60°27N 14°44E 162 D8
Bjørkelangen Norway 59°53N 11°34E 164 E8
Björklinge Sweden 60°2N 17°33E 162 D11
Björknas Sweden 59°19N 18°12E 139 B3
Björkö Sweden 59°52N 19°2E 162 E13
Bjørnafjorden Norway 60°7N 5°28E 164 D2
Björneborg = Pori Finland 61°29N 21°48E 188 B1
Björneborg Sweden 59°14N 14°16E 162 E8
Bjørnevatn Norway 69°40N 30°0E 160 B24
Bjørnøya Arctic 74°30N 19°0E 150 B8
Bjursås Sweden 60°44N 15°25E 162 D9
Bjuv Sweden 56°5N 12°55E 163 H6
Bla Mali 12°56N 5°47W 262 C3
Blå Jungfrun △ Sweden 57°16N 16°47E 163 G10
Blace Serbia 43°18N 21°17E 202 C5
Blachownia Poland 50°49N 18°56E 185 H5
Black = Da → Vietnam 21°15N 105°20E 228 G5
Black → Ont., Canada 44°42N 79°19W 312 B5
Black → Alaska, U.S.A. 66°42N 144°42W 303 C11
Black → Ariz., U.S.A. 33°44N 110°13W 305 K8
Black → Ark., U.S.A. 35°38N 91°20W 314 D9
Black → La., U.S.A. 31°16N 91°50W 314 F9
Black → Mich., U.S.A. 42°59N 82°27W 312 D2
Black → N.Y., U.S.A. 43°59N 76°4W 313 C8
Black → Wis., U.S.A. 43°57N 91°22W 308 D8
Black Bay Pen. Canada 48°38N 88°21W 298 C2
Black Birch L. Canada 56°53N 107°45W 297 B7
Black Canyon of the Gunnison ⌓ U.S.A. 38°40N 107°35W 304 G10
Black Cr. → Canada 43°40N 79°30W 141 A2
Black Creek Pioneer Village Canada 43°46N 79°30W 141 A1
Black Diamond = Pittsburg U.S.A. 38°2N 121°53W 306 G5
Black Diamond Canada 50°45N 114°14W 296 C6
Black Duck → Canada 56°51N 89°2W 298 A2
Black Forest = Schwarzwald Germany 48°30N 8°20E 179 G4
Black Forest U.S.A. 39°0N 104°43W 304 G11
Black Hd. Ireland 53°9N 9°16W 166 C2
Black Hills U.S.A. 44°0N 103°45W 308 D2
Black I. Canada 51°12N 96°30W 297 C9
Black L. Sask., Canada 59°12N 105°15W 297 B7
Black L. Mich., U.S.A. 45°28N 84°16W 309 C11
Black L. N.Y., U.S.A. 44°31N 75°36W 313 B9
Black Lake Canada 59°11N 105°20W 297 B7
Black Mesa U.S.A. 36°58N 102°58W 314 C3
Black Mountain Australia 30°18S 151°39E 283 A9
Black Mt. = Mynydd Du U.K. 51°52N 3°50W 169 F4
Black Mt. Bhutan 27°20N 90°25E 241 B3
Black Mts. U.K. 51°55N 3°7W 169 F4
Black Range U.S.A. 33°15N 107°50W 305 K10
Black River Jamaica 18°0N 77°50W 320 a
Black River N.Y., U.S.A. 44°0N 75°47W 313 C9
Black River B. Jamaica 18°0N 77°51W 320 a
Black River Falls U.S.A. 44°18N 90°51W 308 C8
Black River Gorges Mauritius 20°24S 57°25E 272 e
Black Rock S. Austral., Australia 32°50S 138°44E 282 B3
Black Rock Barbados 13°7N 59°37W 323 r
Black Rock Desert U.S.A. 41°10N 118°50W 304 F4
Black Sea Eurasia 43°30N 35°0E 187 F6
Black Tickle Canada 53°28N 55°45W 299 B8
Black Volta → Africa 8°41N 1°33W 262 D4
Black Warrior → U.S.A. 32°32N 87°51W 315 E11
Blackall Australia 24°25S 145°45E 280 C4
Blackball N.Z. 42°22S 171°26E 285 C6
Blackbraes △ Australia 19°10S 144°10E 280 B3
Blackbull Australia 17°55S 141°45E 280 B3
Blackburn U.K. 53°45N 2°29W 168 D5
Blackburn, Mt. U.S.A. 61°44N 143°26W 303 F12
Blackburn with Darwen □ U.K. 53°45N 2°29W 168 D5
Blackdown Tableland △ Australia 23°52S 149°8E 280 C4
Blackfen U.K. 51°26N 0°6E 125 B4
Blackfoot U.S.A. 43°11N 112°21W 304 E7
Blackfoot → U.S.A. 46°52N 113°53W 304 C7
Blackfoot Res. U.S.A. 42°55N 111°39W 304 E8
Blackheath U.K. 51°28N 0°0 125 B4
Blackman U.S.A. 30°56N 86°38W 317 E3
Blackpool U.K. 53°49N 3°3W 168 D4
Blackpool □ U.K. 53°49N 3°3W 168 D4
Blackriver U.S.A. 44°46N 83°17W 312 B1
Blackrock Ireland 53°18N 6°11W 120 B2
Blacks Harbour Canada 45°3N 66°49W 299 C6
Blacksburg U.S.A. 37°14N 80°25W 309 G13
Blackshear U.S.A. 31°18N 82°14W 316 D7
Blackshear, L. U.S.A. 31°51N 83°56W 316 D6
Blacksod B. Ireland 54°6N 10°0W 166 B1
Blackstairs Mt. Ireland 52°33N 6°48W 166 D5
Blackstone U.S.A. 37°5N 78°0W 309 G14
Blackstone Ra. Australia 26°0S 128°30E 279 E4
Blackville U.S.A. 33°22N 81°16W 316 B8
Blackwater = West Road → Canada 53°18N 122°53W 296 C4
Blackwater Australia 23°35S 148°53E 280 C4
Blackwater → Meath, Ireland 53°39N 6°41W 166 C4
Blackwater → Waterford, Ireland 52°4N 7°52W 166 D4
Blackwater → Armagh, U.K. 54°31N 6°35W 166 B5
Blackwater → Fla., U.S.A. 30°36N 87°2W 317 E2
Blackwater → Mo., U.S.A. 38°56N 92°57W 310 F4
Blackwell U.S.A. 36°48N 97°17W 314 C6
Blackwells Corner U.S.A. 35°37N 119°47W 307 K7
Blackwood, C. Papua N. G. 7°49S 144°31E 286 D3
Bladensburg U.S.A. 38°55N 76°55W 143 B3
Bladensburg △ Australia 22°30S 142°59E 280 C3
Blaenau Ffestiniog U.K. 53°0N 3°56W 168 E4
Blaenau Gwent □ U.K. 51°48N 3°12W 169 F4
Bláfell Iceland 64°30N 19°51W 155 C7
Bláfjall Iceland 65°26N 16°50W 155 B10
Blåfjella-Skjækerfjella △ Norway 64°15N 13°8E 160 D15
Blagaj Bos.-H. 43°16N 17°55E 202 C1
Blagnac France 43°37N 1°23E 174 E5
Blagnac, Toulouse ✈ (TLS) France 43°37N 1°22E 174 E5
Blagodarnyy Russia 45°7N 43°37E 191 H6
Blagoevgrad Bulgaria 42°2N 23°5E 202 D7
Blagoevgrad □ Bulgaria 42°2N 23°5E 202 D7
Blagoveshchensk Russia 50°20N 127°30E 219 A14
Blahkiuh Indonesia 8°31S 115°12E 231 J18
Blain Loire-Atlantique, France 47°29N 1°45W 172 E5
Blain Pa., U.S.A. 40°20N 77°31W 312 F7
Blaine Minn., U.S.A. 45°10N 93°13W 308 C7
Blaine Wash., U.S.A. 48°59N 122°45W 306 B4
Blaine Lake Canada 52°51N 106°52W 297 C7
Blair U.S.A. 41°33N 96°8W 308 E5
Blair Athol Australia 22°42S 147°31E 280 C4
Blair Atholl U.K. 56°46N 3°50W 167 E5
Blair Village U.S.A. 33°40N 84°23W 113 C2
Blairgowrie Gauteng, S. Africa 26°6S 28°0E 123 A2
Blairgowrie Perth & Kinr., U.K. 56°35N 3°21W 167 E5
Blairsden U.S.A. 39°47N 120°37W 306 F6
Blairsville U.S.A. 40°26N 79°16W 312 F5
Blaj Romania 46°10N 23°57E 183 D8
Blaka Niger 21°21N 12°47E 259 D2
Blakang Mati, Pulau Singapore 1°15N 103°50E 237 d
Blake House U.S.A. 42°19N 71°3W 116 B2
Blake Pt. U.S.A. 48°11N 88°25W 308 A9
Blakehurst Australia 33°59S 151°6E 139 B1
Blakely Ga., U.S.A. 31°23N 84°56W 316 D5
Blakely Pa., U.S.A. 41°28N 75°37W 313 E9
Blakesburg U.S.A. 40°58N 92°38W 310 D4
Blakstad Akershus, Norway 59°49N 10°28E 133 B1
Blakstad Aust-Agder, Norway 58°30N 8°39E 164 F5
Blambangan, Semenanjung Indonesia 8°42S 114°29E 231 K17
Blâmont France 48°35N 6°50E 173 D13
Blanc, C. Spain 39°21N 2°51E 206 B3
Blanc, C. Tunisia 37°15N 9°56E 258 A1
Blanc, Mont Europe 45°48N 6°50E 175 C10
Blanca, B. Argentina 39°10S 61°30W 336 A4
Blanca, Costa Spain 38°25N 0°10W 197 G4
Blanca Peak U.S.A. 37°35N 105°29W 305 H11
Blanchardville U.S.A. 42°49N 89°52W 310 B7
Blanche, C. Australia 33°1S 134°9E 281 E1
Blanche, L. S. Austral., Australia 29°15S 139°40E 281 D2
Blanche, L. W. Austral., Australia 22°25S 123°17E 278 D3
Blanche, L. Fla., U.S.A. 28°28N 81°30W 133 B1
Blanche, Pte. St. Lucia 13°53N 61°5W 323 m
Blanche, Pte. St.-Maarten 18°0N 63°2W 322 a
Blanche Channel Solomon Is. 8°30S 157°30E 287 M9
Blanchester U.S.A. 39°17N 83°59W 311 E13
Blanchisseuse Trin. & Tob. 10°48N 61°18W 323 t
Blanco Western Cape, S. Africa 33°55S 22°23E 270 D3
Blanco Tex., U.S.A. 30°6N 98°25W 314 F5
Blanco → Argentina 30°20S 68°42W 334 C2
Blanco → Bolivia 12°30S 64°18W 331 C5
Blanco, C. Costa Rica 9°34N 85°8W 320 E2
Blanco, C. Oreg., U.S.A. 42°51N 124°34W 304 E1
Blanco, Pta. Bonaire 12°13N 68°14W 322 h
Blanda → Iceland 65°37N 20°9W 155 B6
Blandford Forum U.K. 50°51N 2°9W 169 G5
Blanding U.S.A. 37°37N 109°29W 305 H9
Blandinsville U.S.A. 40°33N 90°52W 310 D6
Blanes Spain 41°40N 2°48E 196 D7
Blangkejeren Indonesia 3°59N 97°20E 234 B1
Blangpidie Indonesia 3°44N 96°49E 234 B1
Blangy-sur-Bresle France 49°55N 1°37E 173 C8
Blanice → Czech Rep. 49°10N 14°5E 180 B7
Blankaholm Sweden 57°36N 16°31E 163 G10
Blankenberge Belgium 51°20N 3°9E 170 C3
Blankenburg Berlin, Germany 52°35N 13°27E 115 A3
Blankenburg Sachsen-Anhalt, Germany 51°47N 10°57E 178 D6
Blankenfelde Germany 52°37N 13°23E 115 A3
Blanku, L. Curaçao 12°2N 68°47W 322 g
Blanquefort France 44°55N 0°38W 174 D3
Blanquilla, I. Venezuela 11°51N 64°37W 321 D7
Blanquillo Uruguay 32°53S 55°37W 335 C4
Blansko Czech Rep. 49°22N 16°40E 181 B9
Blantyre Malawi 15°45S 35°0E 269 F4
Blarney Ireland 51°56N 8°33W 166 E3
Blasdell U.S.A. 42°48N 78°50W 312 D6
Blåsjø Norway 59°20N 6°50E 164 E3
Błaszki Poland 51°38N 18°30E 185 G5
Blatná Czech Rep. 49°25N 13°52E 180 B6
Blato Croatia 42°56N 16°48E 199 F13
Blaubeuren Germany 48°24N 9°46E 179 G5
Blaustein Germany 48°25N 9°53E 179 G5
Blåvands Huk Denmark 55°33N 8°4E 163 J2
Blaydon U.K. 54°58N 1°42W 168 C6
Blaye France 45°8N 0°40W 174 C3
Blaye-les-Mines France 44°1N 2°8E 174 D6
Blayney Australia 33°32S 149°14E 283 B8
Blaze, Pt. Australia 12°56S 130°11E 278 B5
Błażowa Poland 49°53N 22°7E 185 J9
Blechhammer = Blachownia Poland 50°49N 18°56E 185 H5
Bleckede Germany 53°17N 10°43E 178 B6
Bled Slovenia 46°27N 14°7E 199 B11
Blefjell Norway 59°48N 9°10E 164 E6
Bleiburg Austria 46°35N 14°49E 180 E7
Blejeşti Romania 44°19N 25°27E 183 F10
Blekinge Sweden 56°25N 15°20E 161 H16
Blekinge län □ Sweden 56°20N 15°20E 163 H9
Blenheim Ont., Canada 42°20N 82°0W 312 D3
Blenheim N.Z. 41°38S 173°57E 285 B8
Bléone → France 44°5N 6°0E 175 D10
Blérancourt France 49°31N 3°9E 173 C10
Bletchley U.K. 51°59N 0°44W 169 F7
Bleus, Monts Dem. Rep. of the Congo 1°30N 30°30E 268 B3
Blida Algeria 36°30N 2°49E 261 A5
Blida □ Algeria 36°35N 3°0E 261 A5
Blidet Amor Algeria 32°59N 5°58E 261 B6
Blidö Sweden 59°37N 18°53E 162 E12
Blidsberg Sweden 57°56N 13°30E 163 G7
Blieskastel Germany 49°14N 7°12E 179 F3
Bligh Sound N.Z. 44°47S 167°32E 285 E2
Bligh Water Fiji 17°0S 178°0E 287 A2
Blind River Canada 46°10N 82°58W 298 C3
Blinisht Albania 41°52N 19°59E 202 E3
Bliss Idaho, U.S.A. 42°56N 114°57W 304 E6
Bliss N.Y., U.S.A. 42°34N 78°15W 312 D6
Blissfield Mich., U.S.A. 41°50N 83°52W 311 C13
Blissfield Ohio, U.S.A. 40°24N 81°58W 312 F3
Blitar Indonesia 8°5S 112°11E 235 D4
Blitchton U.S.A. 32°12N 81°26W 316 C8
Blitta Togo 8°23N 1°6E 263 D5
Blizne Poland 52°14N 20°52E 143 B1
Block I. U.S.A. 41°11N 71°35W 313 E13
Block Island Sd. U.S.A. 41°15N 71°40W 313 E13
Bloemenmarkt Amsterdam, Neths. 112 b2
Bloemfontein S. Africa 29°6S 26°7E 270 C4
Bloemhof S. Africa 27°38S 25°32E 270 C4
Blois France 47°35N 1°20E 172 E8
Blomskog Sweden 59°16N 12°2E 162 E6
Blomstermåla Sweden 56°59N 16°21E 163 H10
Blomvåg Norway 60°32N 4°50E 164 D1
Blönduós Iceland 65°40N 20°12W 155 B6
Blongas Indonesia 8°53S 116°2E 231 K19
Błonie Poland 52°12N 20°37E 185 F7
Bloodvein → Canada 51°47N 96°43W 297 C9
Bloody B. Trin. & Tob. 11°18N 60°38W 323 s
Bloody Foreland Ireland 55°10N 8°17W 166 A3
Bloom = Chicago Heights U.S.A. 41°30N 87°38W 311 C9
Bloomer U.S.A. 45°6N 91°29W 308 C8
Bloomfield Ont., Canada 43°59N 77°14W 312 C7
Bloomfield Ind., U.S.A. 39°1N 86°57W 311 E10
Bloomfield Iowa, U.S.A. 40°45N 92°25W 310 D4
Bloomfield Ky., U.S.A. 37°55N 85°19W 311 G11
Bloomfield N. Mex., U.S.A. 36°43N 107°59W 305 H10
Bloomfield Nebr., U.S.A. 42°36N 97°39W 308 D5
Bloomingburg U.S.A. 39°36N 83°24W 311 E13
Bloomington Ill., U.S.A. 40°28N 89°0W 310 D8
Bloomington Ind., U.S.A. 39°10N 86°32W 311 E10
Bloomington Minn., U.S.A. 44°50N 93°17W 308 C7
Bloomington Wis., U.S.A. 42°53N 90°55W 310 B6
Bloomsburg U.S.A. 41°0N 76°27W 313 F8
Bloomsbury Australia 20°48S 148°38E 280 b
Bloomsbury London, U.K. 125 a3
Blora Indonesia 6°57S 111°25E 235 D4
Blossburg U.S.A. 41°41N 77°4W 312 E7
Blosseville Kyst Greenland 68°50N 26°30W 154 D8
Błota Poland 52°9N 21°11E 143 C3
Blouberg S. Africa 23°8S 28°59E 271 B4
Blountstown U.S.A. 30°27N 85°3W 316 E4
Blowing Point Village Anguilla 18°11N 63°6W 322 a
Blowing Rock Anguilla 18°9N 63°10W 322 a
Bludenz Austria 47°10N 9°50E 180 D2
Blue → U.S.A. 38°11N 86°19W 311 F10
Blue Cypress L. U.S.A. 27°44N 80°45W 317 H9
Blue Earth U.S.A. 43°38N 94°6W 308 D6
Blue Hole Jamaica 18°10N 76°24W 320 a
Blue Hole △ Belize 17°24N 87°30W 320 C2
Blue Island U.S.A. 41°40N 87°40W 119 D2
Blue Lagoon △ Zambia 15°28S 27°26E 269 F2
Blue Lagoon L. U.S.A. 25°46N 80°17W 129 D1
Blue Mesa Res. U.S.A. 38°28N 107°20W 304 G10
Blue Mosque = Sultanahme Camil Turkey 41°0N 28°58E 122 B1
Blue Mound U.S.A. 39°42N 89°7W 310 E7
Blue Mountain Lake U.S.A. 43°51N 74°27W 313 C10
Blue Mountain Pk. Jamaica 18°3N 76°36W 320 a
Blue Mountains and John Crow Mountains △ Jamaica 18°5N 76°34W 320 a
Blue Mt. U.S.A. 40°30N 76°30W 313 F8
Blue Mts. N.S.W., Australia 33°40S 150°15E 283 B9
Blue Mts. Jamaica 18°3N 76°36W 320 a
Blue Mts. Maine, U.S.A. 44°50N 70°35W 313 B14
Blue Mts. Oreg., U.S.A. 45°0N 118°20W 304 D4
Blue Mts. △ Australia 34°2S 150°15E 283 C9
Blue Mud B. Australia 13°30S 136°0E 280 A2
Blue Mud Bay ☼ Australia 13°25S 136°2E 280 A2
Blue Nile = Nîl el Azraq → Sudan 15°38N 32°31E 257 D3
Blue Nile Falls = Tis Issat Ethiopia 11°25N 37°45E 257 E4
Blue Rapids U.S.A. 39°41N 96°39W 308 F5
Blue Ridge U.S.A. 36°40N 80°50W 309 G13
Blue River Canada 52°6N 119°18W 296 C5
Blue Springs U.S.A. 39°1N 94°17W 310 E2
Bluebell Ireland 53°19N 6°21W 120 B1
Bluefield U.S.A. 37°15N 81°17W 309 G13
Bluefields Nic. 12°20N 83°50W 320 D3
Bluevale Canada 43°51N 81°15W 312 C3
Bluff Queens., Australia 23°35S 149°4E 280 C4
Bluff N.Z. 46°37S 168°20E 285 G3
Bluff Utah, U.S.A. 37°17N 109°33W 305 H9
Bluff Harbour N.Z. 46°36S 168°21E 285 G3
Bluff Hd. Hong Kong, China 22°11N 114°12E 122 B3

Bluff Knoll Australia 34°24S 118°15E 279 F2
Bluff Pt. Australia 27°50S 114°5E 279 E1
Bluffers Park Canada 43°43N 79°14W 141 A3
Bluffs U.S.A. 39°45N 90°32W 310 E6
Bluffton Ga., U.S.A. 31°31N 84°52W 316 D5
Bluffton Ind., U.S.A. 40°44N 85°11W 311 D11
Bluffton Ohio, U.S.A. 40°54N 83°54W 311 D13
Bluffton S.C., U.S.A. 32°14N 80°52W 316 C9
Blumberg Germany 52°36N 13°39E 115 A4
Blumenau = Stettler Canada 52°19N 112°40W 296 C6
Blumenau Brazil 27°0S 49°0W 335 B6
Blunt U.S.A. 44°31N 99°59W 308 C4
Blunt Pt. U.S.A. 37°51N 122°25W 136 A2
Blutenberg Germany 48°9N 11°27E 131 B1
Bly U.S.A. 42°24N 121°3W 304 E3
Blyde River Canyon ⌓ S. Africa 24°37S 31°2E 271 B5
Blylaget Norway 59°46N 10°41E 133 B3
Blyth S. Austral., Australia 33°49S 138°28E 282 B3
Blyth Ont., Canada 43°44N 81°26W 312 C3
Blyth Northumberland, U.K. 55°8N 1°31W 168 B6
Blythe Calif., U.S.A. 33°37N 114°36W 307 M12
Blythe Ga., U.S.A. 33°17N 82°12W 316 B7
Blytheville U.S.A. 35°56N 89°55W 315 D10
Bø Telemark, Norway 59°25N 9°3E 164 E6
Bo S. Leone 7°55N 11°50W 262 D2
Bo Duc Vietnam 11°58N 106°50E 237 G6
Bo-eun S. Korea 36°29N 127°43E 224 D3
Bo Hai China 39°0N 119°0E 227 E10
Bo Hai Haixia Asia 38°25N 121°10E 227 E11
Bo-Kaap Museum Cape Town, S. Africa 118 c2
Bō-no-Misaki Japan 31°15N 130°13E 222 F2
Bo Xian = Bozhou China 33°55N 115°41E 226 H8
Boa Esperança Brazil 3°21N 61°23W 329 C5
Boa Esperança, Represa Brazil 6°50S 43°50W 332 C3
Boa Nova Brazil 14°22S 40°10W 333 D3
Boa Viagem Brazil 5°7S 39°44W 332 C4
Boa Vista = Tocantinópolis Brazil 6°20S 47°25W 332 C2
Boa Vista Brazil 2°48N 60°30W 329 C5
Boa Vista C. Verde Is. 16°0N 22°49W 153 j
Boa Vista, Alto do Brazil 22°58S 43°16W 135 B1
Boa Vista do Erechim = Erechim Brazil 27°35S 52°15W 335 B5
Boac Phil. 13°27N 121°50E 232 E3
Boaco Nic. 12°29N 85°35W 320 D2
Bo'ai China 35°10N 113°3E 226 G7
Boal Spain 43°25N 6°49W 194 B4
Boali C.A.R. 4°48N 18°7E 264 B3
Boalsburg U.S.A. 40°47N 77°49W 312 F7
Boane Mozam. 26°6S 32°19E 271 C5
Boang I. Papua N. G. 3°23S 153°18E 286 B7
Boao China 19°8N 110°34E 229 a
Boardman U.S.A. 41°2N 80°40W 312 E4
Boardwalk U.S.A. 40°34N 73°49W 132 C3
Boath India 19°20N 78°20E 244 E4
Boatswain Bird I. Ascension I. 7°56S 14°18W 153 g
Boavista Portugal 38°48N 9°8W 126 A2
Boayan I. Phil. 10°34N 119°9E 233 F2
Boaz I. Bermuda 32°18N 64°51W 153 a
Bob Marley Mausoleum Jamaica 18°18N 77°18W 320 a
Bobadah Australia 32°19S 146°41E 283 B7
Bobai China 22°17N 109°59E 228 F7
Bobbili India 18°35N 83°30E 244 E6
Bóbbio Italy 44°46N 9°23E 198 D6
Bobcaygeon Canada 44°33N 78°33W 312 B6
Bobigny France 48°54N 2°26E 134 A3
Boblad India 17°13N 75°26E 244 F2
Böblingen Germany 48°40N 9°1E 179 G5
Bobo-Dioulasso Burkina Faso 11°8N 4°13W 262 C4
Bobolice Poland 53°58N 16°37E 184 E3
Bobon Phil. 12°32N 124°34E 232 E5
Bobonaza → Ecuador 2°36S 76°38W 328 D2
Bobonong Botswana 21°58S 28°20E 271 B4
Boboshevo Bulgaria 42°9N 23°0E 202 D7
Bobov Dol Bulgaria 42°20N 23°0E 202 D6
Bóbr → Poland 52°4N 15°4E 185 F2
Bobraomby, Tanjon' i Madag. 12°40S 49°10E 272 A2
Bobrov Russia 51°5N 40°2E 190 E5
Bobrovytsya Ukraine 50°45N 31°23E 189 G6
Bobruysk = Babruysk Belarus 53°10N 29°15E 177 B15
Bobrynets Ukraine 48°4N 32°5E 189 H7
Bobures Venezuela 9°15N 71°11W 328 B3
Boby, Pic Madag. 22°12S 46°55E 272 C2
Boca de Pozo Venezuela 11°0N 64°23W 329 a
Boca del Río Veracruz, Mexico 19°5N 96°4W 319 D5
Boca del Río Venezuela 10°58N 64°11W 329 a
Boca do Acre Brazil 8°50S 67°27W 330 B4
Boca do Jari Brazil 1°7S 51°58W 329 D7
Boca Grande Fla., U.S.A. 26°45N 82°16W 317 J7
Boca Grande Venezuela 8°40N 60°40W 329 B5
Boca Raton U.S.A. 26°21N 80°5W 317 J9
Boca Slagbaai Bonaire 12°16N 68°24W 322 h
Bocaiúva Brazil 17°7S 43°49W 333 E3
Bocanda Ivory C. 7°5N 4°31W 262 D4
Bocanegra Peru 12°1S 77°7W 124 B2
Bocaranga C.A.R. 7°0N 15°35E 264 A3
Bocas del Dragón = Dragon's Mouths Trin. & Tob. 11°0N 61°50W 323 t
Bocas del Toro Panama 9°15N 82°20W 320 E3
Boceguillas Spain 41°20N 3°39W 194 D7
Bochkarevo = Belogorsk Russia 51°0N 128°20E 215 D13
Bochmanivka Ukraine 47°40N 29°34E 183 C14
Bochnia Poland 49°58N 20°27E 185 J7
Bocholt Germany 51°50N 6°36E 178 D2
Bochum = Senwabarana S. Africa 23°17S 29°7E 271 B4
Bochum Germany 51°28N 7°13E 178 D3
Bockenem Germany 52°1N 10°8E 178 C6
Boćki Poland 52°39N 23°3E 185 F10
Bocognano France 42°5N 9°4E 175 F13
Bocoio Angola 12°28S 14°10E 265 E2
Boconó Venezuela 9°15N 70°16W 328 B3
Boconó → Venezuela 8°43N 69°34W 328 B4
Bocoyna Mexico 27°52N 107°35W 318 B3
Bocşa Romania 45°21N 21°47E 182 E6
Boda C.A.R. 4°19N 17°26E 264 B3
Boda Dalarna, Sweden 61°1N 15°13E 162 C9
Böda Kalmar, Sweden 57°15N 17°3E 163 G11
Boda Västernorrland, Sweden 62°52N 16°39E 162 B10
Bodafors Sweden 57°48N 14°23E 163 G8
Bodaybo Russia 57°50N 114°0E 215 D12
Boddam U.K. 59°56N 1°17W 167 B7
Boddington Australia 32°50S 116°30E 279 F2
Bode Sadu Nigeria 9°0N 4°47E 263 D5
Bodega Bay U.S.A. 38°20N 123°3W 306 G3
Boden Sweden 65°50N 21°42E 160 D19
Bodensee Europe 47°35N 9°25E 179 H5
Bodenteich Germany 52°50N 10°42E 178 C6
Bodh Gaya India 24°41N 84°59E 243 G11
Bodhan India 18°40N 77°44E 244 E3
Bodinayakkanur India 10°2N 77°10E 245 J3
Bodinga Nigeria 12°58N 5°10E 263 C6
Bodmin U.K. 50°28N 4°43W 169 G3
Bodmin Moor U.K. 50°33N 4°36W 169 G3
Bodø Norway 67°17N 14°24E 160 C16
Bodoquena, Serra da Brazil 21°0S 56°50W 331 E6
Bodoupa C.A.R. 5°43N 17°36E 264 A3
Bodrichi Chad 19°11N 15°54E 259 E3
Bodrog → Hungary 48°11N 21°22E 182 B6
Bodrum Turkey 37°3N 27°30E 205 D9
Boduna Dem. Rep. of the Congo 5°5N 19°44E 264 A3
Bódva → Hungary 48°19N 20°45E 182 B5
Boedo Argentina 34°38S 58°26W 117 B2
Boembé Congo 2°54S 15°39E 264 C3
Boën France 45°44N 4°1E 175 C8
Boende Dem. Rep. of the Congo 0°24S 21°12E 264 C4
Boeotia = Viotia Greece 38°20N 23°0E 204 C5
Boerne U.S.A. 29°47N 98°44W 314 G5
Boesmans → S. Africa 33°42S 26°39E 270 D4
Boffa Guinea 10°16N 14°3W 262 C2
Bog Walk Jamaica 18°6N 77°1W 320 a
Bogal, Lagh → Kenya 0°41N 40°57E 267 D5
Bogale Burma 16°17N 95°24E 241 G5
Bogalusa U.S.A. 30°47N 89°52W 315 F10
Bogan → Australia 30°20S 146°55E 283 A7
Bogan Gate Australia 33°7S 147°49E 283 B7
Bogandé Burkina Faso 13°2N 0°8W 263 C4
Bogangolo C.A.R. 5°34N 18°15E 264 A3
Bogantungan Australia 23°41S 147°17E 280 C4
Bogata U.S.A. 33°28N 95°13W 314 E7
Bogatić Serbia 44°51N 19°30E 202 B3
Boğazkale Turkey 40°2N 34°37E 212 B6
Boğazlıyan Turkey 39°11N 35°14E 212 C6
Bogbonga Dem. Rep. of the Congo 1°36N 19°24E 264 B3
Bogda Shan China 43°35N 89°40E 217 D11
Bogen Sweden 60°4N 12°33E 162 D6
Bogenhausen Germany 48°8N 11°36E 131 B2
Bogense Denmark 55°34N 10°5E 163 J4
Bogetići Montenegro 42°41N 18°58E 202 D2
Boggabilla Australia 28°36S 150°24E 281 D5
Boggabri Australia 30°45S 150°5E 283 A9
Boggeragh Mts. Ireland 52°2N 8°55W 166 D3
Boghari = Ksar el Boukhari Algeria 35°51N 2°52E 261 A5
Bogia Papua N. G. 4°9S 145°0E 286 C3
Bogildo S. Korea 34°9N 126°32E 224 E3
Boglan = Solhan Turkey 38°57N 41°3E 213 C9
Bogles Grenada 12°30N 61°26W 323 q
Bognor Regis U.K. 50°47N 0°40W 169 G7
Bogo Phil. 11°3N 124°0E 233 F4
Bogodukhov = Bohodukhiv Ukraine 50°9N 35°33E 189 G8
Bogol Manya Ethiopia 4°34N 41°29E 257 G5
Bogong, Mt. Australia 36°47S 147°17E 283 D7
Bogor Indonesia 6°36S 106°48E 234 D3
Bogoroditsk Russia 53°47N 38°8E 188 F10
Bogorodsk Russia 56°4N 43°30E 190 B6
Bogorodskoye = Kamskoye Ustye Russia 55°10N 49°20E 190 C9
Bogorodskoye = Leninskoye Russia 58°23N 47°3E 190 A8
Bogorodskoye Russia 55°48N 37°42E 129 B3
Bogoslovsky = Karpinsk Russia 59°45N 60°1E 186 C11
Bogoso Ghana 5°38N 2°3W 262 D4
Bogotá Colombia 4°34N 74°0W 328 C3
Bogota N.J., U.S.A. 40°52N 74°2W 132 A1
Bogotol Russia 56°15N 89°50E 214 D9
Bogou Togo 10°40N 0°12E 263 C5
Bogra Bangla. 24°51N 89°22E 241 C2
Bogstadvatnet Norway 59°58N 10°37E 133 A2
Boguchany Russia 58°40N 97°30E 215 D10
Boguchar Russia 49°55N 40°32E 190 F5
Bogué Mauritania 16°45N 14°10W 262 B2
Boguszów-Gorce Poland 50°45N 16°12E 185 H3
Bohain-en-Vermandois France 49°59N 3°28E 173 C10
Bohdan Ukraine 48°2N 24°22E 183 B9
Bohemian Forest = Böhmerwald Germany 49°8N 13°14E 179 F9
Bohena Cr. → Australia 30°17S 149°42E 283 A8
Bohinjska Bistrica Slovenia 46°17N 14°1E 199 B11
Böhmerwald Germany 49°8N 13°14E 179 F9
Böhmisch-Brod = Český Brod Czech Rep. 50°4N 14°52E 180 A7
Böhmisch-Leipa = Česká Lípa Czech Rep. 50°45N 14°30E 180 A7
Böhmisch-Trübau = Česká Třebová Czech Rep. 49°54N 16°27E 181 B9
Bohmte Germany 52°22N 8°19E 178 C4
Bohnsdorf Germany 52°23N 13°34E 115 B4
Bohodukhiv Ukraine 50°9N 35°33E 189 G8
Bohol Somalia 5°45N 46°9E 267 C6
Bohol □ Phil. 9°50N 124°10E 233 G5
Bohol Sea Phil. 9°0N 124°0E 233 G5
Bohol Str. Phil. 9°45N 123°40E 233 G4
Bohongou Burkina Faso 12°30N 0°40E 263 C5
Böhönye Hungary 46°25N 17°28E 182 D2
Bohorodchany Ukraine 48°48N 24°32E 183 B9
Bohorok Indonesia 3°30N 98°12E 237 L2
Böhöt Mongolia 45°13N 108°16E 226 B5
Bohu China 41°58N 86°37E 217 D11
Bohuslän Sweden 58°25N 12°0E 163 F5
Bohuslev Ukraine 49°33N 30°56E 189 H6
Boi Nigeria 9°35N 9°27E 263 D6
Boi, Pta. do Brazil 23°55S 45°15W 335 A6
Boiaçu Brazil 0°27S 61°46W 329 D5
Boigu Australia 9°16S 142°13E 280 a
Boigu I. Australia 9°15S 142°14E 286 E2
Boileau, C. Australia 17°40S 122°7E 278 C3
Boim Brazil 2°49S 55°10W 329 D6
Boing'o South Sudan 9°58N 33°44E 257 F3
Boipariguda India 18°46N 82°26E 244 E6
Boipeba, I. de Brazil 13°39S 38°55W 333 D4
Boiro Spain 42°39N 8°54W 194 C2
Bois → Brazil 18°35S 50°2W 333 E1
Bois-Blanc Réunion 21°11S 55°49E 272 f
Bois-Colombes France 48°55N 2°16E 134 A2
Bois-d'Arcy France 48°48N 2°1E 134 B1
Boise U.S.A. 43°37N 116°13W 304 E5
Boise City U.S.A. 36°44N 102°31W 314 C3
Boissevain Canada 49°15N 100°5W 297 D8
Boissy-St-Léger France 48°44N 2°31E 134 B4
Bóite → Italy 46°5N 12°5E 199 B9
Boitzenburg Germany 53°16N 13°35E 178 B9
Boizenburg Germany 53°23N 10°43E 178 B6
Bojador W. Sahara 23°56N 15°49W 260 D1
Bojador, C. W. Sahara 26°0N 14°30W 260 C2
Bojana → Albania 41°52N 19°22E 202 E3
Bojano Italy 41°29N 14°29E 201 A7
Bojanowo Poland 51°43N 16°42E 185 G3
Bøjden Denmark 55°6N 10°7E 163 J4
Bojnūrd Iran 37°30N 57°20E 247 B8
Bojonegoro Indonesia 7°11S 111°54E 235 D4
Boju Nigeria 7°22N 7°55E 263 D6
Boka Serbia 45°22N 20°52E 182 E5
Boka Kotorska Montenegro 42°23N 18°32E 202 D2
Boka Tabla Curaçao 12°22N 69°8W 322 g
Bokada Dem. Rep. of the Congo 4°8N 19°23E 264 B3
Bokala Dem. Rep. of the Congo 3°8S 17°4E 264 C3
Bokala Ivory C. 8°31N 4°33W 262 D4
Bokani Nigeria 9°28N 5°10E 263 D6
Bokaro India 23°46N 85°55E 243 H11
Bokatola Dem. Rep. of the Congo 0°38S 18°46E 264 C3
Boké Guinea 10°56N 14°17W 262 C2
Bokela Dem. Rep. of the Congo 1°10S 21°59E 264 C4
Bokenda Dem. Rep. of the Congo 1°16N 21°22E 264 B4
Bokhara → Australia 29°55S 146°42E 281 D4
Bokkos Nigeria 9°17N 9°1E 263 D6
Boklar Dağları Turkey 37°5N 33°55E 250 A4
Boknafjorden Norway 59°14N 5°40E 164 E2
Boko Congo 4°46S 14°36E 265 C2
Bokode Dem. Rep. of the Congo 3°55N 19°30E 264 B3
Bokolo Gabon 2°40S 10°10E 264 C2
Bokondo Dem. Rep. of the Congo 0°15N 22°32E 264 B4
Bokor △ Cambodia 10°50N 104°1E 237 G5
Bokora ⌓ Uganda 2°12N 31°32E 268 B3
Bokoro Chad 12°25N 17°14E 259 F3
Bokota Dem. Rep. of the Congo 0°56S 22°24E 264 C4
Bokote Dem. Rep. of the Congo 0°12S 21°8E 264 C4
Bokpyin Burma 11°18N 98°42E 237 G2
Boksitogorsk Russia 59°22N 33°50E 188 C7
Boku Papua N. G. 6°34S 155°21E 286 D8
Bokungu Dem. Rep. of the Congo 0°35S 22°50E 264 C4
Bol Chad 13°30N 14°40E 259 F2
Bol Croatia 43°18N 16°38E 199 E13
Bolama Guinea-Biss. 11°30N 15°30W 262 C1
Bolan → Pakistan 28°38N 67°42E 242 E2
Bolan Pass Pakistan 29°50N 67°20E 240 C2
Bolaños → Mexico 21°12N 104°5W 318 C4
Bolaños de Calatrava Spain 38°54N 3°40W 195 G7
Bolayır Turkey 40°31N 26°45E 203 F10
Bolbec France 49°30N 0°30E 172 C7
Boldājī Iran 31°56N 51°3E 247 D6
Boldeşti-Scăeni Romania 45°3N 26°2E 183 E11
Boldinasco Italy 45°29N 9°8E 128 B1
Bole Xinjiang Uygur, China 44°55N 81°37E 217 C10
Bole Ethiopia 6°36N 37°20E 257 F4
Bole Ghana 9°3N 2°23W 262 D4
Bolekhiv Ukraine 49°0N 23°57E 177 D12
Boleko Dem. Rep. of the Congo 1°35S 19°50E 264 C3
Bøler Norway 59°53N 10°50E 133 A4
Bolesławiec Poland 51°17N 15°37E 185 G2
Bolgatanga Ghana 10°44N 0°53W 263 C4
Bolgrad = Bolhrad Ukraine 45°40N 28°32E 183 E13
Bolhrad Ukraine 45°40N 28°32E 183 E13
Bolia Dem. Rep. of the Congo 1°36S 18°22E 264 C3
Bolinao Phil. 16°23N 119°54E 232 C2
Bolinao, C. Phil. 16°23N 119°55E 232 C2
Bolingbroke U.S.A. 32°57N 83°48W 316 C6
Bolingbrook U.S.A. 41°42N 88°4W 311 C8
Bolingo Dem. Rep. of the Congo 3°31S 21°43E 264 C4
Bolintin-Vale Romania 44°27N 25°46E 183 F10
Bolívar Antioquía, Colombia 5°50N 76°1W 328 B2
Bolívar Cauca, Colombia 2°0N 77°0W 328 C2
Bolívar Peru 7°18S 77°48W 330 B2
Bolivar Mo., U.S.A. 37°37N 93°25W 308 G7
Bolivar N.Y., U.S.A. 42°4N 78°10W 312 D6
Bolivar Tenn., U.S.A. 35°12N 89°0W 315 D10
Bolívar □ Colombia 9°0N 74°40W 328 B3
Bolívar □ Ecuador 1°15S 79°5W 328 D2
Bolívar □ Venezuela 6°20N 63°30W 329 B5
Bolivia ■ S. Amer. 17°6S 64°0W 331 D5
Bolivian Plateau = Altiplano Bolivia 17°0S 68°0W 330 D4
Boljevac Serbia 43°51N 21°58E 202 C5
Bolkhov Russia 53°25N 36°0E 188 F9
Bolków Poland 50°55N 16°6E 185 H3
Bollate Italy 45°32N 9°7E 128 A1
Bollebeek Belgium 50°55N 4°14E 116 A1
Bollebygd Sweden 57°40N 12°35E 163 G6
Bollène France 44°18N 4°45E 175 D8
Bollensdorf Germany 52°30N 13°42E 115 A5
Bollmora Sweden 59°14N 18°14E 139 B3
Bollnäs Sweden 61°21N 16°24E 162 C10
Bollon Australia 28°2S 147°29E 281 D4
Bollstabruk Sweden 62°59N 17°40E 162 B11
Bolmen Sweden 56°55N 13°40E 163 H7
Bolnisi Georgia 41°26N 44°32E 191 K7
Bolobo Dem. Rep. of the Congo 2°6S 16°20E 264 C3
Bologna Italy 44°29N 11°20E 199 D8
Bologna ✈ (BLQ) Italy 44°34N 11°16E 199 D8
Bologoye Russia 57°55N 34°5E 188 D8
Bolomba Dem. Rep. of the Congo 0°35N 19°0E 264 B3
Bolombo → Dem. Rep. of the Congo 1°32N 21°14E 264 B4
Bolonchén Mexico 20°1N 89°45W 319 D7
Bolondo Dem. Rep. of the Congo 2°12S 18°42E 264 C3
Bolong Chad 12°3N 17°45E 259 F3
Bolong Phil. 7°6N 122°14E 233 H4
Bolongongo Angola 8°28S 15°16E 265 D3
Bolótana Italy 40°20N 8°52E 200 B1
Boloven, Cao Nguyen Laos 15°10N 106°30E 236 E6
Bolpur India 23°40N 87°45E 243 H12
Bolsena Italy 42°39N 11°59E 199 F8
Bolsena, L. di Italy 42°36N 11°56E 199 F8
Bolshakovo Russia 54°53N 21°40E 184 D8
Bolshaya Chernigovka Russia 52°6N 50°52E 190 D10
Bolshaya Garmanda = Evensk Russia 62°12N 159°30E 215 C16
Bolshaya Glushitsa Russia 52°28N 50°30E 190 D10
Bolshaya Martynovka Russia 47°19N 41°37E 191 G5
Bolshaya Okhta Russia 59°56N 30°26E 137 B2
Bolshaya Tsaryovshchina = Volzhskiy Russia 48°56N 44°46E 191 F7
Bolshaya Vradiyevka Ukraine 47°50N 30°40E 189 J6
Bolshevik, Ostrov Russia 78°30N 102°0E 215 B11
Bolshoi Theatre Moscow, Russia 129 b2
Bolshoy Anyuy → Russia 68°30N 160°49E 215 C17
Bolshoy Begichev, Ostrov Russia 74°20N 112°30E 215 B12
Bolshoy Kamen Russia 43°7N 132°19E 220 C6
Bolshoy Kavkas = Caucasus Mountains Eurasia 42°50N 44°0E 191 J7
Bolshoy Lyakhovskiy, Ostrov Russia 73°35N 142°0E 215 B15
Bolshoy Tokmak = Tokmak Kyrgyzstan 42°49N 75°15E 217 D9
Bolshoy Tyuters, Ostrov Russia 59°51N 27°13E 188 C4
Bólstaðarhlíð Iceland 65°31N 19°49W 155 B7
Bolsward Neths. 53°3N 5°32E 170 A5
Bolt Head U.K. 50°12N 3°48W 169 G4
Boltaña Spain 42°28N 0°4E 196 C5
Boltigen Switz. 46°38N 7°24E 179 J3
Bolton Ont., Canada 43°54N 79°45W 312 C5
Bolton Gt. Man., U.K. 53°35N 2°26W 168 D5
Bolton Georgia, U.S.A. 33°48N 84°28W 113 B2
Bolton Landing U.S.A. 43°32N 73°35W 313 C11
Bolu Turkey 40°45N 31°35E 212 B4
Bolu □ Turkey 40°40N 31°30E 212 B4
Bolubolu Papua N. G. 9°21S 150°20E 286 E6
Bolungavík Iceland 66°9N 23°15W 155 A3
Boluo China 23°3N 114°21E 229 F10
Bolvadin Turkey 38°45N 31°4E 212 C4
Bolzano Italy 46°31N 11°22E 199 B8
Bom Comércio Brazil 9°45S 65°54W 331 B4
Bom Conselho Brazil 9°10S 36°41W 332 C4
Bom Despacho Brazil 19°43S 45°15W 333 E2
Bom Jesus Angola 9°11S 13°34E 265 D2
Bom Jesus Brazil 9°4S 44°22W 332 C3
Bom Jesus da Gurguéia, Serra Brazil 9°0S 43°0W 332 C3
Bom Jesus da Lapa Brazil 13°15S 43°25W 333 D3
Bom Retiro Brazil 23°31S 46°38W 137 B2
Boma Dem. Rep. of the Congo 5°50S 13°4E 265 D2
Boma △ South Sudan 7°0N 34°0E 257 F3
Bomaderry Australia 34°52S 150°37E 283 C9
Bomandjokou Congo 0°34N 14°23E 264 B2
Bomaneh Dem. Rep. of the Congo 1°18N 23°47E 264 B4
Bomassa Congo 2°12N 16°12E 264 B3
Bomate Dem. Rep. of the Congo 2°14N 25°15E 264 C3
Bombala Australia 36°56S 149°15E 283 D8
Bombarral Portugal 39°15N 9°9W 195 F1
Bombay = Mumbai India 18°56N 72°50E 130 B2
Bombay U.S.A. 44°56N 74°34W 313 B10
Bombedor, Pta. Venezuela 9°53N 61°37W 329 G9
Bomberai, Semenanjung Indonesia 3°0S 133°0E 231 E8
Bombo Kasani Dem. Rep. of the Congo 5°51S 21°54E 265 D4
Bomboma Dem. Rep. of the Congo 2°25N 18°55E 264 B3
Bombombwa Dem. Rep. of the Congo 1°40N 25°40E 268 B2
Bomboyo Chad 12°1N 15°28E 259 F3
Bomdila India 27°18N 92°22E 241 B4
Bomdo India 28°44N 94°54E 241 A5
Bomet Kenya 0°47S 35°21E 266 E4
Bomi China 29°50N 95°45E 218 F8
Bomi Hills Liberia 7°1N 10°38W 262 D2
Bomili Dem. Rep. of the Congo 1°45N 27°5E 268 B2
Bømlo Norway 59°37N 5°13E 164 E2
Bomokandi → Dem. Rep. of the Congo 3°39N 26°8E 268 B2
Bomongo Dem. Rep. of the Congo 1°27N 18°21E 264 B3
Bompoka India 8°15N 93°13E 245 K11
Bomputu Dem. Rep. of the Congo 0°23S 20°6E 264 C4
Bomst = Babimost Poland 52°10N 15°49E 185 F2
Bomu → C.A.R. 4°40N 22°30E 264 B4
Bomu Occidentale ⌓ Dem. Rep. of the Congo 4°48N 24°17E 264 B4
Bomu Orientale ⌓ Dem. Rep. of the Congo 5°0N 25°50E 264 B2
Bon, C. = Ra's aţ Tib Tunisia 37°1N 11°2E 258 A2
Bon Acceuil Mauritius 20°10S 57°39E 272 e
Bon Echo ⌓ Canada 44°55N 77°16W 312 B7
Bon Sar Pa Vietnam 12°24N 107°35E 236 F6
Bona, Mt. U.S.A. 61°23N 141°45W 303 F12
Bonāb Āzarbājān-e Sharqī, Iran 37°20N 46°4E 213 D12
Bonāb Zanjān, Iran 36°35N 48°41E 213 D13
Bonaigarh India 21°50N 84°57E 243 J11
Bonaire Ga., U.S.A. 32°33N 83°36W 316 C6
Bonaire W. Indies 12°10N 68°15W 322 h
Bonampak Mexico 16°44N 91°5W 319 D6
Bonang Australia 37°11S 148°41E 283 D8
Bonanza Nic. 13°54N 84°35W 320 D3
Bonaparte Arch. Australia 14°0S 124°30E 278 B3
Bonaparte Rocks Grenada 12°24N 61°30W 323 q
Boñar Spain 42°52N 5°19W 194 C5
Bonar Bridge U.K. 57°54N 4°20W 167 D4
Bonasse Trin. & Tob. 10°5N 61°54W 323 t
Bonaventure Canada 48°5N 65°32W 299 C6
Bonaventure, Place Montréal, Canada 130 c2
Bonavista Canada 48°40N 53°5W 299 C9
Bonavista, C. Canada 48°42N 53°5W 299 C9
Bonavista B. Canada 48°45N 53°25W 299 C9
Bondeno Italy 44°53N 11°25E 199 D8
Bondi Australia 33°53S 151°16E 139 B2
Bondo Équateur, Dem. Rep. of the Congo 1°22S 23°54E 264 C4
Bondo Orientale, Dem. Rep. of the Congo 3°55N 23°53E 264 B4
Bondoc Pen. Phil. 13°26N 122°33E 232 E4
Bondokodi Indonesia 9°33S 119°0E 278 A2
Bondoukou Ivory C. 8°2N 2°47W 262 D4
Bondowoso Indonesia 7°55S 113°49E 235 D4
Bondy France 48°54N 2°28E 134 A3
Bondy, Forêt de France 48°54N 2°33E 134 A4
Bône = Annaba Algeria 36°50N 7°46E 261 A6
Bone, Teluk Indonesia 4°10S 120°50E 231 E6
Bonefish Pond Bahamas 24°59N 77°23W 153 b
Bonerate Indonesia 7°25S 121°5E 231 F6
Bonerate, Kepulauan Indonesia 6°30S 121°10E 231 F6
Bo'ness U.K. 56°1N 3°37W 167 E5
Bonete, Cerro Argentina 27°55S 68°40W 334 B2
Bonfim = Senhor-do-Bonfim Brazil 10°30S 40°10W 332 D3
Bonfim Brazil 3°33N 59°25W 329 C6
Bong Son = Hoai Nhon Vietnam 14°28N 109°1E 236 E7
Bonga Ethiopia 7°15N 36°14E 257 F4
Bongabon Phil. 15°38N 121°8E 232 D3
Bongabong Phil. 12°45N 121°29E 232 E3
Bongaigaon India 26°28N 90°34E 241 B3
Bongandanga Dem. Rep. of the Congo 1°24N 21°3E 264 B4
Bongao Phil. 5°2N 119°46E 233 J2
Bongo Dem. Rep. of the Congo 1°47S 17°41E 264 C3
Bongo, Sa. de Angola 10°3S 15°15E 265 E3
Bongo I. Phil. 7°20N 124°3E 233 H5
Bongor Chad 10°35N 15°20E 259 F3
Bongos, Massif des C.A.R. 8°40N 22°25E 264 A4
Bongouanou Ivory C. 6°42N 4°15W 262 D4
Bonham U.S.A. 33°35N 96°11W 314 E6
Boni Mali 15°3N 2°10W 262 B4
Boni ⌓ Kenya 1°35S 41°18E 268 C5
Bonifacio France 41°24N 9°10E 175 G13
Bonifacio, Bouches de Medit. S. 41°12N 9°15E 200 A2
Bonifacio Monument Phil. 14°38N 120°58E 127 B1
Bonifay U.S.A. 30°47N 85°41W 316 E4
Bonin Is. = Ogasawara Gunto Pac. Oc. 27°0N 142°0E 288 E6
Bonita Springs U.S.A. 26°21N 81°47W 317 J8
Bonito Brazil 21°8S 56°28W 331 E6
Bonjol Indonesia 0°1S 100°13E 234 C2
Bonke Ethiopia 6°5N 37°16E 257 F4
Bonkoukou Niger 14°0N 3°15E 263 C5
Bonn Germany 50°46N 7°6E 178 E3
Bonnabel Place U.S.A. 30°0N 90°8W 131 A2
Bonnat France 46°20N 1°54E 173 F8
Bonne Terre U.S.A. 37°55N 90°33W 310 G6
Bonneau U.S.A. 33°16N 79°58W 316 B10
Bonners Ferry U.S.A. 48°42N 116°19W 304 B5
Bonnétable France 48°11N 0°25E 172 D7
Bonneuil-sur-Marne France 48°46N 2°30E 134 B4
Bonneval France 45°22N 7°3E 175 C11
Bonneval-sur-Arc France 48°11N 1°24E 172 D8
Bonneville France 46°4N 6°24E 173 F13
Bonney, L. Australia 37°50S 140°20E 282 D4
Bonnie Doon Australia 37°2S 145°53E 283 D6
Bonnie Rock Australia 30°29S 118°22E 279 F2
Bonnington U.K. 55°54N 3°25W 121 B1
Bonny Nigeria 4°25N 7°13E 263 E6
Bonny → Nigeria 4°20N 7°10E 263 E6
Bonny, Bight of Africa 3°30N 9°20E 263 E6
Bonny Hills Australia 31°36S 152°51E 283 A10
Bonny-sur-Loire France 47°33N 2°50E 173 E9
Bonnyrigg U.K. 55°53N 3°6W 167 F5
Bonnyrigg and Lasswade U.K. 55°52N 3°6W 121 B3
Bonnyville Canada 54°20N 110°45W 297 C6
Bono Italy 40°25N 9°2E 200 B2
Bonoi Indonesia 1°45S 137°41E 231 E9
Bonorva Italy 40°25N 8°46E 200 B1
Bonsall U.S.A. 33°16N 117°14W 307 M9
Bonsucesso Brazil 22°51S 43°15W 135 B1
Bontang Indonesia 0°10N 117°30E 235 B5
Bontebok △ S. Africa 34°5S 20°28E 270 D3
Bonteheuwel S. Africa 33°57S 18°33E 118 A2
Bonthe S. Leone 7°30N 12°33W 262 D2
Bontoc Phil. 17°7N 120°58E 232 C3
Bontosunggu Indonesia 5°41S 119°42E 235 D5
Bonyeri Ghana 5°1N 2°46W 262 D4
Bonyhád Hungary 46°18N 18°32E 182 D3
Bonython Ra. Australia 23°40S 128°45E 278 D4
Boo Sweden 59°20N 18°16E 139 A3
Booderee △ Australia 35°12S 150°42E 283 C9
Boodjamulla △ Australia 18°15S 138°6E 280 B2
Bookabie Australia 31°50S 132°41E 279 F5
Booke Dem. Rep. of the Congo 2°34S 22°3E 264 C4
Booker U.S.A. 36°27N 100°32W 314 C4
Bool Lagoon Australia 37°7S 140°40E 282 D4
Boola Guinea 8°22N 8°41W 262 D3
Boolcoomata Australia 31°57S 140°33E 282 A4
Booleroo Centre Australia 32°53S 138°21E 282 B3
Booligal Australia 33°58S 144°53E 283 B6
Boon Pt. Antigua & B. 17°10N 61°50W 322 b
Böön Tsagaan Nuur Mongolia 45°35N 99°9E 218 B8
Boonah Australia 27°58S 152°41E 281 D5
Boone Iowa, U.S.A. 42°4N 93°53W 310 B3
Boone N.C., U.S.A. 36°13N 81°41W 315 C14
Booneville Ark., U.S.A. 35°8N 93°55W 314 D8
Booneville Miss., U.S.A. 34°39N 88°34W 315 D10
Boonville Calif., U.S.A. 39°1N 123°22W 306 F3
Boonville Ind., U.S.A. 38°3N 87°16W 311 F9
Boonville Mo., U.S.A. 38°58N 92°44W 310 F4
Boonville N.Y., U.S.A. 43°29N 75°20W 313 C9
Boorabbin △ Australia 31°30S 120°10E 279 F3
Boorama Somalia 9°55N 43°7E 267 C5
Boorindal Australia 30°22S 146°11E 281 E4
Boorowa Australia 34°28S 148°44E 283 C8
Boort Australia 36°7S 143°46E 282 D5
Boosaaso Somalia 11°12N 49°18E 267 B6
Booterstown Ireland 53°19N 6°12W 120 B2
Boothia, Gulf of Canada 71°0N 90°0W 294 C14
Boothia Pen. Canada 71°0N 94°0W 294 C13
Bootle U.K. 53°28N 3°1W 168 D4
Booué Gabon 0°5S 11°55E 264 C2
Bopako Dem. Rep. of the Congo 1°53N 21°13E 264 B4
Boppard Germany 50°13N 7°35E 179 E3
Boquerón □ Paraguay 23°0S 60°0W 331 E6
Boquilla, Presa de la Mexico 27°31N 105°30W 318 B3
Boquillas del Carmen Mexico 29°11N 102°58W 318 B4
Bor Czech Rep. 49°41N 12°45E 180 B5
Bor Russia 56°28N 43°59E 190 B7
Bor Serbia 44°5N 22°7E 202 B6
Bor South Sudan 6°10N 31°40E 257 F3
Bor Sweden 57°9N 14°10E 163 G8
Bor Turkey 37°54N 34°32E 212 D6
Bor, Lagh → Kenya 1°18N 40°40E 267 D5
Bor Mashash Israel 31°7N 34°50E 251 G5
Bor u Ceske Lipy = Nový Bor Czech Rep. 50°46N 14°35E 180 A7
Bora Bora French Polynesia 16°30S 151°45W 289 f
Borah Peak U.S.A. 44°8N 113°47W 304 D7
Boraha, Nosy Madag. 16°50S 49°55E 272 B2
Borang South Sudan 4°50N 30°59E 257 G3
Borangapara India 25°14N 90°14E 241 C3
Borankul Kazakhstan 46°11N 54°25E 216 C4
Borås Sweden 57°43N 12°56E 163 G6
Borāzjān Iran 29°22N 51°10E 247 D6
Borba Brazil 4°12S 59°34W 329 D6
Borba Portugal 38°50N 7°26W 195 G3
Borbon Phil. 10°50N 124°2E 233 F5
Borborema, Planalto da Brazil 7°0S 37°0W 332 C4
Borcea Romania 44°20N 27°45E 183 F12
Borchalo = Marneuli Georgia 41°30N 44°48E 191 K7
Borçka Turkey 41°25N 41°41E 213 B9
Bord Khūn-e Now Iran 28°3N 51°28E 247 D6
Borda, C. Australia 35°45S 136°34E 282 C2
Bordeaux France 44°50N 0°36W 174 D3
Bordeaux ✈ (BOD) France 44°50N 0°35W 174 D3
Borden Australia 34°3S 118°12E 279 F2
Borden-Carleton Canada 46°18N 63°47W 299 C7
Borden I. Canada 78°30N 111°30W 295 B9
Borden Pen. Canada 73°0N 83°0W 295 C15
Borden Springs U.S.A. 33°56N 85°28W 316 B4
Border Ranges △ Australia 28°24S 152°56E 281 D5
Borders = Scottish Borders □ U.K. 55°35N 2°50W 167 F6
Bordertown Australia 36°19S 140°45E 282 D4
Borðeyri Iceland 65°12N 21°6W 155 B5
Bordighera Italy 43°46N 7°39E 198 E4
Bordj bou Arreridj Algeria 36°4N 4°45E 261 A5
Bordj Bourguiba Tunisia 32°12N 10°2E 258 B2
Bordj Flye Ste-Marie Algeria 27°19N 2°32W 260 C4
Bordj in Eker Algeria 24°9N 5°3E 261 D6
Bordj Menaïel Algeria 36°46N 3°43E 261 A5
Bordj Messouda Algeria 30°12N 9°25E 261 B6
Bordj Mokhtar Algeria 21°20N 0°56E 261 D5
Bordj Nili Algeria 33°28N 3°2E 261 B5
Bordj Omar Driss Algeria 28°10N 6°40E 261 C6
Bordj Sif Fatima Algeria 31°6N 8°41E 261 B6
Bordj Tarat Algeria 25°55N 9°3E 261 C6
Borduttighat India 26°57N 93°58E 241 B4
Bore Ethiopia 4°39N 37°39E 257 G4
Borehamwood U.K. 51°40N 0°15W 169 F7
Borek Wielkopolski Poland 51°54N 17°11E 185 G4
Borensberg Sweden 58°34N 15°17E 163 F9
Borgå = Porvoo Finland 60°24N 25°40E 188 B3
Borgampad India 17°39N 80°52E 244 F5
Borgarfjarðarsýsla Iceland 64°30N 21°30W 155 C5
Borgarfjörður Austurland Iceland 65°33N 13°47W 155 B13
Borgarfjörður Vesturland Iceland 64°30N 22°0W 155 C4
Borgarnes Iceland 64°32N 21°55W 155 C5
Børgefjellet Norway 65°20N 13°45E 160 D15
Borger Neths. 52°54N 6°44E 170 B6
Borger Tex., U.S.A. 35°39N 101°24W 314 D4
Borgholm Sweden 56°52N 16°39E 163 H10
Bórgia Italy 38°49N 16°30E 201 D9
Borgnesse, Pte. Martinique 14°26N 60°54W 322 j
Borgo San Dalmazzo Italy 44°20N 7°30E 198 D4
Borgo San Donnino = Fidenza Italy 44°52N 10°3E 198 D7
Borgo San Lorenzo Italy 43°57N 11°23E 199 E8
Borgo Val di Taro Italy 44°29N 9°46E 198 D6
Borgo Valsugana Italy 46°3N 11°27E 199 B8
Borgomanero Italy 45°42N 8°28E 198 C5
Borgorose Italy 42°11N 13°13E 199 F10
Borgosésia Italy 45°43N 8°16E 198 C5
Borgotaro = Borgo Val di Taro Italy 44°29N 9°46E 198 D6
Borgund Norway 61°3N 7°48E 164 C4
Borhoyn Tal Mongolia 43°50N 111°58E 226 C6
Bori Nigeria 4°42N 7°21E 263 E6
Borigumma India 19°3N 82°33E 244 E6
Borikhane Laos 18°33N 103°43E 236 C4
Borisoglebsk Russia 51°27N 42°5E 190 E6
Borisov = Barysaw Belarus 54°17N 28°28E 177 A15
Borisovgrad = Pŭrvomay Bulgaria 42°8N 25°17E 203 D9
Borisovka Russia 50°36N 36°1E 189 G9
Borisovo Russia 55°38N 37°44E 129 C3
Borj Jeneïn Tunisia 31°45N 10°9E 258 B2
Borja Peru 4°20S 77°40W 328 D2
Borja Spain 41°48N 1°34W 196 D3
Borjas Blancas = Les Borges Blanques Spain 41°31N 0°52E 196 D5
Borjomi Georgia 41°48N 43°28E 191 K6
Børkop Denmark 55°39N 9°39E 163 J3
Borkou Chad 18°15N 18°50E 259 E3
Borkou □ Chad 18°0N 18°0E 259 E3
Borkum Germany 53°34N 6°40E 178 B2
Borlänge Sweden 60°29N 15°26E 162 D9
Borle India 19°2N 72°54E 130 A2
Borley, C. Antarctica 66°15S 52°30E 151 C5
Borlu Turkey 38°44N 28°27E 205 C10
Bormida → Italy 44°23N 8°13E 198 D5
Bórmio Italy 46°28N 10°22E 198 B7
Borna Germany 51°7N 12°29E 178 D8
Borne Sulinowo Poland 53°32N 16°36E 184 E3
Borneo E. Indies 1°0N 115°0E 235 B4
Bornholm Denmark 55°10N 15°0E 163 J8
Bornholmsgattet Europe 55°15N 14°20E 163 J8
Borno □ Nigeria 11°30N 13°0E 263 C7
Bornos Spain 36°48N 5°42W 195 J5
Bornova Turkey 38°27N 27°14E 205 C9
Bornu Yassa Nigeria 12°14N 12°25E 263 C7
Boro → South Sudan 8°52N 26°11E 257 F2
Borobudur △ Indonesia 7°36S 110°12E 231 G14
Borobudur Indonesia 7°40S 110°11E 235 D4
Borocay I. Phil. 11°58N 121°55E 233 F3
Borodino Russia 55°31N 35°40E 188 E8
Borodino Ukraine 46°18N 29°15E 183 D14
Borogontsy Russia 62°42N 131°8E 215 C14
Borohoro Shan China 44°6N 83°10E 217 D10
Boromo Burkina Faso 11°45N 2°58W 262 C4
Boron U.S.A. 35°0N 117°39W 307 L9
Boronga Is. Burma 19°58N 93°6E 241 F4
Borongan Phil. 11°37N 125°26E 233 F5
Boronia Park Australia 33°49S 151°8E 139 A1
Borotangba Mts. C.A.R. 6°30N 25°0E 257 F2
Borotou Ivory C. 8°46N 7°30W 262 D3
Borovan Bulgaria 43°27N 23°45E 202 C7
Borovichi Russia 58°25N 33°55E 188 C7
Borovsk Russia 55°12N 36°24E 188 E9
Borovskoy Kazakhstan 53°48N 64°9E 216 B6
Borrby Sweden 55°27N 14°10E 163 J8
Borrego Springs U.S.A. 33°15N 116°23W 307 M10
Borriol Spain 40°4N 0°4W 196 E4
Borrisokane Ireland 53°0N 8°7W 166 D3
Borroloola Australia 16°4S 136°17E 280 B2
Borşa Cluj, Romania 46°56N 23°40E 183 D8
Borşa Maramureş, Romania 47°41N 24°50E 183 C9
Borsad India 22°25N 72°54E 242 H5
Borsec Romania 46°57N 25°34E 183 D10
Borshchiv Ukraine 48°48N 26°3E 183 B11
Borsod-Abaúj-Zemplén □ Hungary 48°20N 21°0E 182 B6
Bort-les-Orgues France 45°24N 2°29E 174 C6
Bortala = Bole China 44°55N 81°37E 217 C10
Borth U.K. 52°29N 4°2W 169 E3
Börtnan Sweden 62°45N 13°50E 162 B7
Borūjerd Iran 33°55N 48°50E 213 F13
Boryeong S. Korea 36°21N 126°36E 224 D3
Borynya Ukraine 49°4N 23°0E 185 J10
Boryslav Ukraine 49°18N 23°28E 185 J10
Boryspil Ukraine 50°21N 30°59E 189 G6
Borzhomi = Borjomi Georgia 41°48N 43°28E 191 K6
Borzna Ukraine 51°18N 32°26E 189 G7
Borzya Russia 50°24N 116°31E 219 A12
Bosa Italy 40°18N 8°30E 200 B1
Bosa Monene Dem. Rep. of the Congo 1°16S 23°40E 264 C4
Bosaga Turkmenistan 37°33N 65°41E 240 A2
Bosambi Dem. Rep. of the Congo 2°24N 22°39E 264 B4
Bosanska Dubica Bos.-H. 45°10N 16°50E 199 C13
Bosanska Gradiška Bos.-H. 45°10N 17°15E 182 E2
Bosanska Kostajnica Bos.-H. 45°11N 16°33E 199 C13
Bosanska Krupa Bos.-H. 44°53N 16°10E 199 D13
Bosanski Brod Bos.-H. 45°10N 18°0E 182 E2
Bosanski Novi Bos.-H. 45°2N 16°22E 199 C13
Bosanski Petrovac Bos.-H. 44°35N 16°21E 199 D13
Bosanski Šamac Bos.-H. 45°3N 18°29E 182 E3
Bosansko Grahovo Bos.-H. 44°12N 16°26E 199 D13
Bosavi, Mt. Papua N. G. 6°30S 142°49E 286 D2
Boscastle U.K. 50°41N 4°42W 169 G3
Boscobel U.S.A. 43°8N 90°42W 310 A6
Boscobelle Barbados 13°17N 59°35W 323 r
Bose China 23°53N 106°35E 228 F6
Boseki Dem. Rep. of the Congo 2°34S 19°38E 264 C3
Boseong S. Korea 34°46N 127°5E 224 E3
Boshan China 36°28N 117°49E 227 F9
Boshof S. Africa 28°31S 25°13E 270 C4
Boshrūyeh Iran 33°50N 57°30E 247 C8
Bosilegrad Serbia 42°30N 22°27E 202 D6
Boskovice Czech Rep. 49°29N 16°40E 181 B9
Bosmont S. Africa 26°10S 27°57E 123 B1
Bosna → Bos.-H. 45°4N 18°29E 182 E3
Bosna i Hercegovina = Bosnia-Herzegovina ■ Europe 44°0N 18°0E 182 G2
Bosnia-Herzegovina ■ Europe 44°0N 18°0E 182 G2
Bosnik Indonesia 1°5S 136°10E 231 E9
Bōsō-Hantō Japan 35°20N 140°20E 223 B12
Bosobolo Dem. Rep. of the Congo 4°15N 19°50E 264 B3
Bosön Sweden 59°22N 18°11E 139 A3
Bosporus = İstanbul Boğazı Turkey 41°5N 29°3E 122 B2
Bosque Farms U.S.A. 35°51N 106°42W 305 J10
Bosra = Buşra ash Shām Syria 32°30N 36°25E 251 F7
Bossangoa C.A.R. 6°35N 17°30E 264 A3
Bossé Bangou Niger 13°20N 1°18E 263 C5
Bossembélé C.A.R. 5°25N 17°40E 264 A3
Bossemtélé C.A.R. 5°41N 16°38E 264 A3
Bossier City U.S.A. 32°31N 93°44W 314 E8
Bossiesvlei Namibia 25°1S 16°44E 270 C2
Bosso Niger 13°43N 13°19E 259 F2
Bosso, Dallol → Niger 12°25N 2°50E 263 C5
Bostan Pakistan 30°26N 67°2E 242 D2
Bostānābād Iran 37°50N 46°50E 213 D12
Bostancı Turkey 40°57N 29°5E 122 C2
Bosten Hu China 41°55N 87°40E 217 D11
Boston Phil. 7°52N 126°22E 233 H6
Boston Lincs., U.K. 52°59N 0°2W 168 E7
Boston Ga., U.S.A. 30°47N 83°47W 316 E6
Boston Mass., U.S.A. 42°22N 71°3W 116 A2
Boston Bar Canada 49°52N 121°30W 296 D4
Boston Bay Jamaica 18°9N 76°22W 320 a
Boston Common Boston, U.S.A. 116 c1

Boston Logan Int. ✕ (BOS) U.S.A. 42°22N 71°1W 116 A2
Boston Mts. U.S.A. 35°42N 93°15W 314 D8
Boston Tea Party Ship & Museum Boston, U.S.A. 116 c3
Bostwick U.S.A. 29°46N 81°38W 316 F8
Bosumtwi, L. Ghana 6°30N 1°25W 263 D4
Bosusulu Dem. Rep. of the Congo 0°50N 20°45E 264 B4
Bosut → Croatia 45°20N 18°45E 182 E3
Boswell B.C., Canada 49°28N 116°45W 296 D5
Boswell Ind., U.S.A. 40°31N 87°23W 311 D9
Boswell Pa., U.S.A. 40°10N 79°2W 312 F5
Bosworth U.S.A. 39°28N 93°20W 310 E3
Botad India 22°15N 71°40E 242 H4
Botafogo Brazil 22°56S 43°10W 135 B1
Botan → Turkey 37°57N 42°2E 213 D10
Botanic Gardens Washington, D.C., U.S.A. 143 b3
Botanisk Have Copenhagen, Denmark 118 b2
Botany Australia 33°56S 151°12E 139 B2
Botany B. Australia 33°58S 151°11E 139 B2
Botany Bay △ Australia 34°0S 151°14E 139 B2
Botene Laos 17°35N 101°12E 236 D3
Botera Angola 11°37S 14°16E 265 E2
Botev Bulgaria 42°44N 24°52E 203 D8
Botevgrad Bulgaria 42°55N 23°47E 202 D7
Bothaville S. Africa 27°23S 26°34E 270 C4
Bothnia, G. of Europe 62°0N 20°0E 160 F19
Bothwell Tas., Australia 42°20S 147°1E 281 G4
Bothwell Ont., Canada 42°38N 81°52W 312 D3
Botič → Czech Rep. 50°4N 14°26E 135 B3
Botica Sete Portugal 38°49N 9°10W 126 A1
Boticas Portugal 41°41N 7°40W 194 D3
Botletle → Botswana 20°10S 23°15E 270 B3
Botlikh Russia 42°39N 46°11E 191 J8
Botna → Moldova 46°45N 29°34E 183 D14
Botola Dem. Rep. of the Congo 1°17S 18°13E 264 C3
Botolan Phil. 15°17N 120°1E 232 D3
Botoroaga Romania 44°8N 25°32E 183 F10
Botoşani Romania 47°42N 26°41E 183 C11
Botoşani □ Romania 47°50N 26°50E 183 C11
Botou Burkina Faso 12°42N 1°59E 263 C5
Botou China 38°4N 116°34E 226 E9
Botricello Italy 38°56N 16°51E 201 D9
Botro Ivory C. 7°51N 5°19W 262 D3
Botshabelo S. Africa 29°14S 26°44E 270 C4
Botswana ■ Africa 22°0S 24°0E 270 B3
Bottelier Curaçao 12°6N 68°54W 322 g
Bottineau U.S.A. 48°50N 100°27W 308 A3
Bottnaryd Sweden 57°47N 13°50E 163 G7
Bottom, The Saba 17°38N 63°15W 322 a
Bottopassi Suriname 4°14N 55°27W 329 C6
Bottrop Germany 51°31N 6°58E 178 D2
Botucatu Brazil 22°55S 48°30W 335 A6
Botum Sakor △ Cambodia 11°5N 103°15E 237 G4
Botwood Canada 49°6N 55°23W 299 C8
Bou Alam Algeria 33°50N 1°26E 261 B5
Bou Ali Algeria 27°11N 0°4W 261 C4
Bou Djébéha Mali 18°25N 2°45W 262 B4
Bou Guema Algeria 28°49N 0°19E 261 C5
Bou Ismaïl Algeria 36°38N 2°42E 261 A5
Bou Izakarn Morocco 29°12N 9°46W 260 C3
Boû Lanouâr Mauritania 21°12N 16°34W 260 D1
Boû Naga Mauritania 18°49N 13°20W 262 B2
Bou Noura Algeria 32°29N 3°43E 261 B5
Boû Rjeïmât Mauritania 19°4N 15°3W 262 B1
Bou Saâda Algeria 35°11N 4°9E 261 A5
Bou Salem Tunisia 36°45N 9°2E 258 A1
Bouaflé Ivory C. 7°1N 5°47W 262 D3
Bouaké Ivory C. 7°40N 5°2W 262 D3
Bouanga Congo 2°7S 16°8E 264 C3
Bouar C.A.R. 6°0N 15°40E 264 A3
Bouârfa Morocco 32°32N 1°58W 261 B4
Bouba Ndjida △ Cameroon 8°50N 14°45E 264 A2
Boubout Algeria 27°26N 4°30W 260 C4
Bouca C.A.R. 6°45N 18°25E 264 A3
Boucaut B. Australia 12°0S 134°25E 280 A1
Boucherville Canada 45°36N 73°28W 130 A3
Boucherville, Îs. de Canada 45°36N 73°28W 130 A3
Bouches-du-Rhône □ France 43°37N 5°2E 175 E9
Boucle de Baoulé △ Mali 13°53N 9°0W 262 C3
Boucles de la Seine Normande ⌂ France 49°32N 0°35E 172 C7
Bouctouche Canada 46°30N 64°45W 299 C7
Bouda Algeria 27°50N 0°27W 261 C4
Boudenib Morocco 31°59N 3°31W 260 B4
Bouéni Mayotte 12°54S 45°4E 272 b
Bouéni, B. de Mayotte 12°55S 45°7E 272 b
Bouenza □ Congo 4°30S 13°0E 264 C2
Boufarik Algeria 36°34N 2°58E 261 A5
Bougainville, C. Australia 13°57S 126°4E 278 B4
Bougainville I. Papua N. G. 6°0S 155°0E 287 L8
Bougainville Reef Australia 15°30S 147°5E 280 B4
Bougainville Str. Solomon Is. 6°40S 156°10E 287 L9
Bougaroun, C. Algeria 37°6N 6°30E 261 A6
Bougie = Bejaïa Algeria 36°42N 5°2E 261 A6
Bougival France 48°51N 2°8E 134 A1
Bougouni Mali 11°30N 7°20W 262 C3
Bougtob Algeria 34°2N 0°5E 261 B5
Bouillante Guadeloupe 16°8N 61°46W 322 e
Bouillante, Pitons de Guadeloupe 16°8N 61°43W 322 e
Bouillon Belgium 49°44N 5°3E 170 E5
Bouïra Algeria 36°20N 3°59E 261 A5
Bouïra □ Algeria 36°15N 3°55E 261 A5
Boukombé Benin 10°13N 1°9E 263 C5
Boulal Mali 15°8N 8°21W 262 B3
Boulazac France 45°10N 0°47E 174 C4
Boulder Colo., U.S.A. 40°1N 105°17W 304 F11
Boulder Mont., U.S.A. 46°14N 112°7W 304 C7
Boulder City U.S.A. 35°58N 114°49W 307 K12
Boulder Creek U.S.A. 37°7N 122°7W 306 H4
Boulder Dam = Hoover Dam U.S.A. 36°1N 114°44W 307 K12
Boulder Pt. Hong Kong, China 22°14N 114°6E 122 B2
Boulembo Gabon 1°26S 12°0E 264 C2
Bouli Mauritania 15°17N 12°18W 262 B2
Boulia Australia 22°52S 139°51E 280 C2
Bouligny France 49°17N 5°45E 173 C12
Boulogne → France 47°12N 1°47W 172 E5
Boulogne, Bois de France 48°51N 2°14E 134 A2
Boulogne-Billancourt France 48°50N 2°14E 134 A2
Boulogne-sur-Gesse France 43°18N 0°38E 174 E4
Boulogne-sur-Mer France 50°42N 1°36E 173 B8
Bouloire France 47°59N 0°45E 172 E7
Boulou → C.A.R. 6°45N 24°16E 264 A4
Boulouli Mali 15°30N 9°25W 262 B3
Bouloupari N. Cal. 21°52S 166°4E 288 d
Bouloupesse Congo 1°58S 12°40E 264 C2
Boulsa Burkina Faso 12°39N 0°34W 263 C4
Boultoum Niger 14°45N 10°25E 259 F2
Bouma △ Fiji 16°50S 179°52W 287 A2
Boumaine Dadès Morocco 31°25N 6°0W 260 B3
Boumba → Cameroon 2°2N 15°12E 264 B2
Boumbé → C.A.R. 4°4N 15°23E 264 B3
Boûmdeïd Mauritania 17°25N 11°50W 262 B2
Boumerdès Algeria 36°46N 3°28E 261 A5
Boumerdès □ Algeria 36°45N 3°40E 261 A5
Boun Neua Laos 21°38N 101°54E 236 B3
Boun Tai Laos 21°23N 101°58E 236 B3
Bouna Ivory C. 9°10N 3°0W 262 D4
Boundary U.S.A. 64°5N 141°1W 303 D12
Boundary Peak U.S.A. 37°51N 118°21W 306 H8
Boundiali Ivory C. 9°30N 6°20W 262 D3
Boungou → C.A.R. 8°21N 23°48E 264 A4
Bountiful U.S.A. 40°53N 111°52W 304 F8
Bounty Is. Pac. Oc. 48°0S 178°30E 288 M9
Bounty Trough Pac. Oc. 46°0S 178°0E 288 M9
Boura Mali 12°25N 4°33W 262 C4
Bourail N. Cal. 21°34S 165°30E 288 d
Bourbeuse → U.S.A. 38°24N 90°53W 310 F6
Bourbon U.S.A. 41°18N 86°7W 311 C10
Bourbon-Lancy France 46°37N 3°45E 173 F10
Bourbon-l'Archambault France 46°36N 3°4E 173 F10
Bourbon Street New Orleans, U.S.A. 131 b2
Bourbonnais Allier, France 46°28N 3°0E 173 F10
Bourbonnais Ill., U.S.A. 41°9N 87°52W 311 C9
Bourbonne-les-Bains France 47°54N 5°45E 173 E12
Bourbourg France 50°56N 2°12E 173 B9
Bourdel L. Canada 56°43N 74°10W 298 A5
Bourem Mali 17°0N 0°24W 263 B4
Bouressa Mali 20°0N 2°15E 261 E5
Bourg France 45°3N 0°34W 174 C3
Bourg-Argental France 45°18N 4°32E 175 C8
Bourg-de-Péage France 45°2N 5°3E 175 C9
Bourg-en-Bresse France 46°13N 5°12E 173 F12
Bourg-la-Reine France 48°46N 2°19E 134 B2
Bourg-Lastic France 45°39N 2°35E 174 C6
Bourg-Madame France 42°26N 1°55E 174 F5
Bourg-St-Andéol France 44°23N 4°39E 175 D8
Bourg-St-Maurice France 45°35N 6°46E 175 C10
Bourganeuf France 45°57N 1°45E 174 C5
Bourgas = Burgas Bulgaria 42°33N 27°29E 203 D11
Bourges France 47°9N 2°25E 173 E9
Bourget Canada 45°26N 75°9W 313 A9
Bourget, Lac du France 45°44N 5°52E 175 C9
Bourgneuf, B. de France 47°3N 2°10W 172 E4
Bourgneuf-en-Retz France 47°2N 1°58W 172 E5
Bourgogne □ France 47°0N 4°50E 173 F11
Bourgoin-Jallieu France 45°36N 5°17E 175 C9
Bourgueil France 47°17N 0°10E 172 E7
Bourke Australia 30°8S 145°55E 281 E4
Bourne U.K. 52°47N 0°22W 168 E7
Bournemouth U.K. 50°43N 1°52W 169 G6
Bournemouth □ U.K. 50°43N 1°52W 169 G6
Bouroum Burkina Faso 13°37N 0°39W 263 C4
Bouse U.S.A. 33°56N 114°0W 307 M13
Boussac France 46°22N 2°13E 173 F9
Boussé Burkina Faso 12°39N 1°53W 263 C4
Boussens France 43°12N 0°58E 174 E4
Bousso Chad 10°34N 16°52E 259 F3
Boussouma Burkina Faso 12°52N 1°13W 263 C4
Bout, Pte. du Martinique 14°33N 61°3W 322 j
Bout Stable Bay Dominica 15°21N 61°15W 323 k
Boutilimit Mauritania 17°45N 14°40W 262 B2
Boutonne → France 45°54N 0°50W 174 C3
Bouvet I. = Bouvetøya Antarctica 54°26S 3°24E 152 M12
Bouvetøya Antarctica 54°26S 3°24E 152 M12
Bouviers France 48°46N 2°4E 134 B1
Bouxwiller France 48°49N 7°27E 173 D14
Bouza Niger 14°29N 6°2E 263 C6
Bouznika Morocco 33°46N 7°6W 260 B3
Bouzonville France 49°17N 6°32E 173 C13
Bova Marina Italy 37°56N 15°55E 201 E8
Bovalino Italy 38°10N 16°10E 201 D9
Bovec Slovenia 46°20N 13°33E 199 B10
Boven Kapuas, Pegunungan Malaysia 1°25N 113°15E 235 B4
Bovenkerk Neths. 52°18N 4°51E 112 B2
Bovenkerker Polder Neths. 52°16N 4°52E 112 B2
Bøverdal Norway 61°44N 8°20E 164 C5
Bøverfjorden Norway 63°1N 8°32E 164 A5
Bovill U.S.A. 46°51N 116°24W 304 C5
Bovino Italy 41°15N 15°20E 201 A8
Bovisa Italy 45°30N 9°10E 128 A2
Bovril Argentina 31°21S 59°26W 334 C4
Bow U.K. 51°31N 0°1W 125 A3
Bow → Canada 49°57N 111°41W 296 C6
Bow Island Canada 49°50N 111°23W 304 B8
Bowbells U.S.A. 48°48N 102°15W 308 A2
Bowdle U.S.A. 45°27N 99°39W 308 C4
Bowdon U.S.A. 33°32N 85°15W 316 B4
Bowdon Junction U.S.A. 33°40N 85°9W 316 B4
Bowelling Australia 33°25S 116°30E 279 F2
Bowen Argentina 35°0S 67°31W 334 D2
Bowen Queens., Australia 20°0S 148°16E 280 J6
Bowen Mts. Australia 37°0S 147°50E 283 D7
Bowers Basin Pac. Oc. 53°45N 176°0E 150 D16
Bowers Ridge Pac. Oc. 54°0N 180°0E 150 D17
Bowery New York, U.S.A. 132 e2
Bowie Ariz., U.S.A. 32°19N 109°29W 305 K9
Bowie Tex., U.S.A. 33°34N 97°51W 314 E6
Bowkān Iran 36°31N 46°12E 213 D12
Bowland, Forest of U.K. 54°0N 2°30W 168 D5
Bowling Green Fla., U.S.A. 27°38N 81°50W 317 H8
Bowling Green Ky., U.S.A. 36°59N 86°27W 308 G10
Bowling Green Mo., U.S.A. 39°21N 91°12W 310 E5
Bowling Green Ohio, U.S.A. 41°23N 83°39W 311 C13
Bowling Green, C. Australia 19°19S 147°25E 280 B4
Bowling Green Bay △ Australia 19°26S 146°57E 280 B4
Bowman N. Dak., U.S.A. 46°11N 103°24W 308 B2
Bowman S.C., U.S.A. 33°21N 80°41W 316 B9
Bowman I. Antarctica 65°0S 104°0E 151 C8
Bowmanville = Clarington Canada 43°55N 78°41W 312 C6
Bowmore U.K. 55°45N 6°17W 167 F2
Bowral Australia 34°26S 150°27E 283 C9
Bowraville Australia 30°37S 152°52E 281 E5
Bowron → Canada 54°3N 121°50W 296 C4
Bowron Lake ⌂ Canada 53°10N 121°5W 296 C4
Bowser L. Canada 56°30N 129°30W 296 B3
Bowsman Canada 52°14N 101°12W 297 C8
Bowutu Mts. Papua N. G. 7°45S 147°10E 286 D4
Bowwood Zambia 17°5S 26°20E 269 F2
Box Cr. → Australia 34°10S 143°50E 281 E3
Boxholm Sweden 58°12N 15°3E 163 F9
Boxmeer Neths. 51°38N 5°56E 170 C5
Boxtel Neths. 51°36N 5°20E 170 C5
Boyabat Turkey 41°28N 34°47E 212 B6
Boyabo Dem. Rep. of the Congo 3°43N 18°46E 264 B3
Boyacá □ Colombia 5°30N 73°20W 328 B3
Boyacıköy Turkey 41°5N 29°2E 122 B2
Boyalıca Turkey 40°29N 29°33E 203 F13
Boyang China 29°0N 116°38E 229 C11
Boyany Ukraine 48°17N 26°8E 183 B11
Boyasegese Dem. Rep. of the Congo 3°29N 20°33E 264 B4
Boyce U.S.A. 31°23N 92°40W 314 F8
Boyd U.S.A. 30°11N 83°37W 316 E7
Boyd Conservation Area Canada 43°49N 79°35W 141 A1
Boyd L. Canada 52°46N 76°42W 298 B4
Boyenge Dem. Rep. of the Congo 0°14N 18°55E 264 B3
Boyer, C. N. Cal. 21°37S 168°6E 288 d
Boyera Dem. Rep. of the Congo 0°40S 19°23E 264 C3
Boyle Alta., Canada 54°35N 112°49W 296 C6
Boyle Roscommon, Ireland 53°59N 8°18W 166 C3
Boyle Heights U.S.A. 34°1N 118°12W 126 B3
Boyne → Ireland 53°43N 6°15W 166 C5
Boyne City U.S.A. 45°13N 85°1W 309 C11
Boyne, Bend of the Ireland 53°41N 6°27W 166 C5
Boyni Qara Afghan. 36°20N 67°0E 240 A2
Boynitsa Bulgaria 43°58N 22°32E 202 C6
Boynton Beach U.S.A. 26°32N 80°4W 317 J9
Boyoma, Chutes Dem. Rep. of the Congo 0°35N 25°23E 264 B5
Boysen Res. U.S.A. 43°25N 108°11W 304 E9
Boyup Brook Australia 33°50S 116°23E 279 F2
Boz Burun Turkey 40°32N 28°46E 203 F12
Boz Dağ Turkey 37°18N 29°11E 205 D11
Boz Dağları Turkey 38°20N 28°0E 205 C10
Bozai Gumbaz Afghan. 37°8N 74°0E 240 A4
Bozburun Turkey 36°43N 28°4E 205 E10
Bozcaada Turkey 39°49N 26°3E 212 C2
Bozdağ Turkey 36°50N 36°22E 250 B7
Bozdoğan Turkey 37°40N 28°17E 205 D10
Boze Papua N. G. 9°3S 143°3E 286 E2
Bozeman U.S.A. 45°41N 111°2W 304 D8
Bozen = Bolzano Italy 46°31N 11°22E 199 B8
Bozene Dem. Rep. of the Congo 2°56N 19°12E 264 B3
Boževac Serbia 44°32N 21°24E 202 B5
Bozhou China 33°55N 115°41E 226 H8
Bozkır Turkey 37°11N 32°14E 212 D5
Bozkurt Turkey 37°50N 29°37E 205 D11
Bozouls France 44°28N 2°43E 174 D6
Bozoum C.A.R. 6°25N 16°35E 264 A3
Bozova Antalya, Turkey 37°13N 30°18E 205 D12
Bozova Sanliurfa, Turkey 37°21N 38°32E 213 D8
Bozovici Romania 44°56N 22°0E 182 F7
Bozüyük Turkey 39°54N 30°3E 205 B12
Bozyazı Turkey 36°6N 33°0E 250 B4
Bra Italy 44°42N 7°51E 198 D4
Braås Sweden 57°4N 15°3E 163 G9
Brabant □ Belgium 50°46N 4°30E 170 D4
Brabant L. Canada 55°58N 103°43W 297 B8
Brabrand Denmark 56°9N 10°7E 163 H4
Brač Croatia 43°20N 16°40E 199 E13
Bracadale, L. U.K. 57°20N 6°30W 167 D2
Bracciano Italy 42°6N 12°10E 199 F9
Bracciano, L. di Italy 42°7N 12°14E 199 F9
Bracebridge Canada 45°2N 79°19W 312 A5
Bracieux France 47°30N 1°30E 172 E8
Bräcke Sweden 62°45N 15°26E 162 B9
Brackettville U.S.A. 29°19N 100°25W 314 G4
Bracki Kanal Croatia 43°24N 16°40E 199 E13
Bracknell U.K. 51°25N 0°43W 169 F7
Bracknell Forest □ U.K. 51°25N 0°44W 169 F7
Brad Romania 46°10N 22°50E 182 D7
Brădano → Italy 40°23N 16°51E 201 B9
Bradbury Building Los Angeles, U.S.A. 127 b2
Bradenton U.S.A. 27°30N 82°34W 317 H7
Brades Montserrat 16°47N 62°13W 323 p
Bradford Ont., Canada 44°7N 79°34W 312 B5
Bradford W. Yorks., U.K. 53°47N 1°45W 168 D6
Bradford Ill., U.S.A. 41°11N 89°39W 310 C7
Bradford Ohio, U.S.A. 40°8N 84°27W 311 D12
Bradford Pa., U.S.A. 41°58N 78°38W 312 E6
Bradford Vt., U.S.A. 43°59N 72°9W 313 C12
Bradley Ark., U.S.A. 33°6N 93°39W 314 E8
Bradley Calif., U.S.A. 35°52N 120°48W 306 K6
Bradley Ill., U.S.A. 41°9N 87°52W 311 C9
Bradley Institute Zimbabwe 17°7S 31°25E 269 F3
Bradley Junction U.S.A. 27°48N 81°59W 317 H8
Bradner U.S.A. 41°20N 83°26W 311 C13
Brady U.S.A. 31°9N 99°20W 314 F5
Brædstrup Denmark 55°58N 9°37E 163 J3
Braemar Australia 33°12S 139°35E 282 B3
Braepark U.K. 55°58N 3°18W 121 B2
Braeside Canada 45°28N 76°24W 313 A8
Braeton Jamaica 17°57N 76°53W 320 a
Braga Portugal 41°35N 8°25W 194 D2
Braga □ Portugal 41°30N 8°30W 194 D2
Bragadiru Romania 43°46N 25°31E 183 G10
Bragado Argentina 35°2S 60°27W 334 D3
Bragança Brazil 1°0S 47°2W 332 B2
Bragança Portugal 41°48N 6°50W 194 D4
Bragança □ Portugal 41°30N 6°45W 194 D4
Bragança Paulista Brazil 22°55S 46°32W 335 A6
Bragg's Spur = West Memphis U.S.A. 35°8N 90°10W 315 D9
Brahestad = Raahe Finland 64°40N 24°28E 160 D21
Brahmakund India 27°52N 96°22E 241 B6
Brahmanbaria Bangla. 23°58N 91°15E 241 D3
Brahmani → India 20°39N 86°46E 244 D8
Brahmapur India 19°15N 84°54E 244 E7
Brahmaputra → Asia 23°40N 90°35E 241 D3
Braich-y-pwll U.K. 52°47N 4°46W 168 E3
Braid U.K. 55°55N 3°11W 121 B2
Braidwood Australia 35°27S 149°49E 283 C8
Brăila Romania 45°19N 27°59E 183 E12
Brăila □ Romania 45°5N 27°30E 183 E12
Brainerd U.S.A. 46°22N 94°12W 308 B6
Braintree Essex, U.K. 51°53N 0°34E 169 F8
Braintree Mass., U.S.A. 42°13N 71°0W 313 D14
Brak → S. Africa 29°35S 22°55E 270 C3
Brake Germany 53°20N 8°28E 178 B4
Brakel Germany 51°42N 9°11E 178 D5
Brakna □ Mauritania 17°0N 13°20W 262 B2
Bräkne-Hoby Sweden 56°14N 15°6E 163 H9
Brakwater Namibia 22°28S 17°3E 270 B2
Brålanda Sweden 58°34N 12°21E 163 F6
Bramberg Germany 50°6N 10°40E 179 E6
Bramdrupdam Denmark 55°31N 9°28E 163 J3
Bramhapuri India 20°36N 79°52E 244 D4
Bramley S. Africa 26°7S 28°4E 123 A2
Bramming Denmark 55°28N 8°42E 163 J2
Brämön Sweden 62°14N 17°40E 162 B11
Brampton Ont., Canada 43°45N 79°45W 312 C5
Brampton Cumb., U.K. 54°57N 2°44W 168 C5
Brampton I. Australia 20°49S 149°16E 280 b
Bramsche Germany 52°24N 7°59E 178 C3
Branchville U.S.A. 33°15N 80°49W 316 B9
Branco → Brazil 1°20S 61°50W 329 D5
Branco, C. Brazil 7°9S 34°47W 332 C5
Brandaris Bonaire 12°16N 68°23W 322 h
Brandberg Namibia 21°10S 14°33E 270 B1
Brandberg △ Namibia 21°10S 14°30E 270 B1
Brandbu Norway 60°26N 10°28E 164 D7
Brande Denmark 55°57N 9°8E 163 J3
Brandeis Univ. U.S.A. 42°21N 71°17W 116 A1
Brandenburg = Neubrandenburg Germany 53°33N 13°15E 178 B9
Brandenburg Brandenburg, Germany 52°25N 12°33E 178 C8
Brandenburg Ky., U.S.A. 38°0N 86°10W 310 G10
Brandenburg □ Germany 52°50N 13°0E 178 C9
Brandenburger Tor Germany 52°30N 13°21E 115 A3
Brandfort S. Africa 28°40S 26°30E 270 C4
Brando France 42°47N 9°27E 175 F13
Brandon Man., Canada 49°50N 99°57W 297 D9
Brandon Fla., U.S.A. 27°56N 82°17W 317 H7
Brandon Vt., U.S.A. 43°48N 73°6W 313 C11
Brandon B. Ireland 52°17N 10°8W 166 D1
Brandon Mt. Ireland 52°15N 10°15W 166 D1
Brandsen Argentina 35°10S 58°15W 334 D4
Brandvlei S. Africa 30°25S 20°30E 270 D3
Brandýs nad Labem Czech Rep. 50°10N 14°40E 180 A7
Brăneşti Romania 44°27N 26°20E 183 F11
Branford Conn., U.S.A. 41°17N 72°49W 313 E12
Branford Fla., U.S.A. 29°58N 82°56W 316 F7
Brani, Pulau Singapore 1°15N 103°50E 138 B3
Braniewo Poland 54°25N 19°50E 184 D6
Branik Czech Rep. 50°1N 14°25E 135 B2
Brännkyrka Sweden 59°17N 18°0E 139 B2
Bransfield Str. Antarctica 63°0S 59°0W 151 C18
Brańsk Poland 52°45N 22°50E 185 F9
Branson U.S.A. 36°39N 93°13W 308 G7
Brantford Canada 43°10N 80°15W 312 C4
Brantley U.S.A. 31°35N 86°16W 316 D3
Brantôme France 45°22N 0°39E 174 C4
Branxholme Australia 37°52S 141°49E 282 D4
Branxton Australia 32°38S 151°21E 283 B9
Branzi Italy 46°1N 9°46E 198 B6
Brás Amazonas, Brazil 2°5S 58°10W 329 D6
Brás São Paulo, Brazil 23°32S 46°36W 137 B2
Bras d'Or L. Canada 45°50N 60°50W 299 C7
Bras-Panon Réunion 20°59S 55°41E 272 f
Brasher Falls U.S.A. 44°49N 74°47W 313 B10
Brasil = Brazil ■ S. Amer. 12°0S 50°0W 327 E6
Brasil, Planalto Brazil 18°0S 46°30W 326 E6
Brasil Novo Brazil 3°19S 52°38W 329 D7
Brasilândia Brazil 23°28S 46°42W 137 A1
Brasiléia Brazil 11°0S 68°45W 330 C4
Brasília Distrito Federal, Brazil 15°47S 47°55W 333 E2
Brasília Minas Gerais, Brazil 16°12S 44°26W 333 E3
Brasília △ Brazil 15°41S 48°0W 333 E2
Brasília Legal Brazil 3°49S 55°36W 329 D6
Braskereidfoss Norway 60°44N 11°46E 164 D8
Braslaw Belarus 55°38N 27°0E 188 E4
Braslawskiya Azyory △ Belarus 55°36N 27°3E 188 E4
Braslovče Slovenia 46°21N 15°3E 199 B12
Braşov Romania 45°38N 25°35E 183 E10
Braşov □ Romania 45°45N 25°15E 183 E10
Brass Nigeria 4°35N 6°14E 263 E6
Brass → Nigeria 4°15N 6°13E 263 E6
Brassac-les-Mines France 45°24N 3°20E 174 C7
Brasschaat Belgium 51°19N 4°27E 170 C4
Brassey, Banjaran Malaysia 5°0N 117°15E 235 B5
Brassey Ra. Australia 25°8S 122°15E 279 E3
Brasso Seco Trin. & Tob. 10°45N 61°16W 323 t
Brasstown Bald U.S.A. 34°53N 83°49W 315 D13
Brastad Sweden 58°23N 11°30E 163 F5
Brastavăţu Romania 43°55N 24°24E 183 G9
Bratan = Morozov Bulgaria 42°30N 25°10E 203 D9
Brateş Romania 45°50N 26°4E 183 E11
Brateyevo Russia 55°39N 37°45E 129 C3
Bratislava Slovak Rep. 48°10N 17°7E 181 C10
Bratislava M.R. Štefánik ✕ (BTS) Slovak Rep. 48°11N 17°9E 181 C10
Bratislavský □ Slovak Rep. 48°15N 17°20E 181 C10
Bratsberg = Telemark □ Norway 59°25N 8°30E 164 E5
Bratsigovo Bulgaria 42°1N 24°22E 203 D8
Bratsk Russia 56°10N 101°30E 215 D11
Bratskoye Vdkhr. Russia 56°0N 101°40E 215 D11
Brattleboro U.S.A. 42°51N 72°34W 313 D12
Brattvåg Norway 62°37N 6°25E 164 B3
Bratunac Bos.-H. 44°13N 19°21E 182 F4
Braunau Austria 48°15N 13°3E 180 C6
Braunsberg = Braniewo Poland 54°25N 19°50E 184 D6
Braunschweig Germany 52°15N 10°31E 178 C6
Braunton U.K. 51°7N 4°10W 169 F3
Brava = Baraawe Somalia 1°20N 44°8E 267 D5
Brava C. Verde Is. 15°0N 24°40W 153 j
Brava, Costa Spain 41°30N 3°0E 196 D8
Bravicea Moldova 47°22N 28°27E 183 C13
Bråviken Sweden 58°38N 16°32E 163 F10
Bravo del Norte, Rio = Grande, Rio → N. Amer. 25°58N 97°9W 314 J6
Brawley U.S.A. 32°59N 115°31W 307 N11
Bray Ireland 53°13N 6°7W 166 C5
Bray, Mt. Australia 14°0S 134°30E 280 A1
Bray, Pays de France 49°46N 1°26E 173 C8
Bray-sur-Seine France 48°25N 3°14E 173 D10
Braybrook Australia 37°46S 144°51E 128 A1
Braymer U.S.A. 39°35N 93°48W 310 E3
Brázdim Czech Rep. 50°10N 14°35E 135 A3
Brazeau → Canada 52°55N 115°14W 296 C5
Brazil U.S.A. 39°32N 87°8W 311 E9
Brazil ■ S. Amer. 12°0S 50°0W 327 E6
Brazil Basin Atl. Oc. 15°0S 25°0W 152 H9
Brazilian Highlands = Brasil, Planalto Brazil 18°0S 46°30W 326 E6
Brazo Sur → S. Amer. 25°21S 57°42W 334 B4
Brazos → U.S.A. 28°53N 95°23W 314 G7
Brazzaville Congo 4°9S 15°12E 265 C3
Brčko Bos.-H. 44°54N 18°46E 182 F3
Brda → Poland 53°8N 18°8E 185 E5
Brdy Czech Rep. 49°43N 13°55E 180 B6
Bré = Bray Ireland 53°13N 6°7W 166 C5
Breach Candy Mumbai, India 130 a1
Breaden, L. Australia 25°51S 125°28E 279 E4
Breakheart Reservation U.S.A. 42°28N 71°0W 116 A2
Breaksea Sd. N.Z. 45°35S 166°35E 285 F1
Bream B. N.Z. 35°56S 174°28E 284 B3
Bream Hd. N.Z. 35°51S 174°36E 284 B3
Bream Tail N.Z. 36°3S 174°36E 284 C3
Breas Chile 25°29S 70°24W 334 B1
Breaza Romania 45°11N 25°40E 183 E10
Brebes Indonesia 6°52S 109°3E 235 D3
Brechin Ont., Canada 44°32N 79°10W 312 B5
Brechin Angus, U.K. 56°44N 2°39W 167 E6
Brecht Belgium 51°21N 4°38E 170 C4
Breckenridge Colo., U.S.A. 39°29N 106°3W 304 G10
Breckenridge Minn., U.S.A. 46°16N 96°35W 308 B5
Breckenridge Tex., U.S.A. 32°45N 98°54W 314 E5
Breckland U.K. 52°30N 0°40E 169 E8
Brecknock, Pen. Chile 54°35S 71°30W 336 D2
Břeclav Czech Rep. 48°46N 16°53E 181 C9
Brecon U.K. 51°57N 3°23W 169 F4
Brecon Beacons U.K. 51°53N 3°26W 169 F4
Brecon Beacons △ U.K. 51°50N 3°30W 169 F4
Breda Neths. 51°35N 4°45E 170 C4
Bredaryd Sweden 57°10N 13°45E 163 G7
Bredasdorp S. Africa 34°33S 20°2E 270 D3
Bredbo Australia 35°58S 149°10E 283 C8
Brede Denmark 55°47N 12°30E 118 A3
Bredebro Denmark 55°4N 8°50E 163 J2
Bredstedt Germany 54°37N 8°55E 178 A4
Bredy Russia 52°26N 60°21E 216 B6
Bree Belgium 51°8N 5°35E 170 C5
Breezy Point U.S.A. 40°33N 73°56W 132 C2
Brega = Marsá al Burayqah Libya 30°24N 19°32E 258 B3
Bregalnica → Macedonia 41°43N 22°9E 202 E6
Bregenz Austria 47°30N 9°45E 180 D2
Bregovo Bulgaria 44°9N 22°39E 202 B6
Bréhal France 48°53N 1°30W 172 D5
Bréhat, Î. de France 48°51N 3°0W 172 D4
Breiðafjörður Iceland 65°15N 23°15W 155 B3
Breiðdalsvík Iceland 64°44N 14°0W 155 D7
Breil-sur-Roya France 43°56N 7°31E 175 E11
Breim Norway 61°44N 6°25E 164 C3
Breisach Germany 48°1N 7°36E 179 G3
Breitenlee Austria 48°14N 16°30E 142 A3
Brejinho de Nazaré Brazil 11°1S 48°34W 332 D2
Brejo Brazil 3°31S 42°47W 332 B3
Brekke Norway 61°1N 5°26E 164 C2
Brekken Norway 62°40N 11°51E 164 B8
Brekkestø Norway 58°11N 8°22E 164 F5
Bremanger Norway 61°51N 4°58E 164 C1
Bremangerlandet Norway 61°51N 5°0E 164 C1
Bremen Bremen, Germany 53°4N 8°47E 178 B4
Bremen Ga., U.S.A. 33°43N 85°9W 316 B4
Bremen Ind., U.S.A. 41°27N 86°9W 311 C10
Bremen □ Germany 53°4N 8°47E 178 B4
Bremer Bay Australia 34°21S 119°20E 279 F2
Bremer I. Australia 12°5S 136°45E 280 A2
Bremerhaven Germany 53°33N 8°36E 178 B4
Bremersdorp = Manzini Swaziland 26°30S 31°25E 271 C5
Bremerton U.S.A. 47°34N 122°37W 306 C4
Bremervörde Germany 53°29N 9°8E 178 B5
Bremnes Norway 59°47N 5°8E 164 E2
Bremsnes Norway 63°6N 7°40E 164 A4
Breña Peru 12°3S 77°3W 124 B2
Brenes Spain 37°32N 5°54W 195 H5
Brenham U.S.A. 30°10N 96°24W 314 F6
Brenne France 46°44N 1°14E 174 B5
Brenne ⌂ France 46°40N 1°15E 174 B5
Brennerpass Austria 47°2N 11°30E 180 D4
Brennhaug Norway 61°54N 9°21E 164 C6
Breno Italy 45°57N 10°18E 198 C7
Brent U.S.A. 32°56N 87°10W 315 E11
Brent □ U.K. 51°33N 0°16W 125 A2
Brent Res. U.K. 51°34N 0°14W 125 A2
Brenta → Italy 45°11N 12°18E 199 C9
Brentford U.K. 51°28N 0°18W 125 B2
Brentwood Essex, U.K. 51°37N 0°19E 169 F8
Brentwood Calif., U.S.A. 34°3N 118°29W 126 B2
Brentwood Calif., U.S.A. 37°56N 121°42W 306 H5
Brentwood N.Y., U.S.A. 40°47N 73°15W 313 F11
Brentwood Park U.S.A. 34°3N 118°29W 126 B2
Brera Italy 45°28N 9°11E 128 B2
Brereton Barbados 13°7N 59°30W 323 r
Bréscia Italy 45°33N 10°15E 198 C7
Breskens Neths. 51°23N 3°33E 170 C3
Breslau = Wrocław Poland 51°5N 17°5E 185 G4
Bresle → France 50°4N 1°22E 172 B8
Bressanone Italy 46°43N 11°39E 199 B8
Bressay U.K. 60°9N 1°6W 167 A7
Bresse France 46°50N 5°10E 173 F12
Bresso Italy 45°32N 9°11E 128 A2
Bressuire France 46°51N 0°30W 172 F6
Brest Belarus 52°10N 23°40E 177 B12
Brest Finistère, France 48°24N 4°31W 172 D2
Brest □ Belarus 52°30N 26°10E 177 B13
Brest-Litovsk = Brest Belarus 52°10N 23°40E 177 B12
Bretagne □ France 48°10N 3°0W 172 D3
Bretanha, Pta. da Azores 37°54N 25°47W 153 d3
Bretçu Romania 46°7N 26°18E 183 D11
Bretenoux France 44°54N 1°51E 174 D5
Breteuil Eure, France 48°50N 0°57E 172 D7
Breteuil Oise, France 49°38N 2°18E 173 C9
Breton Canada 53°7N 114°28W 296 C6
Breton, Pertuis France 46°17N 1°25W 174 B2
Breton Sd. U.S.A. 29°35N 89°15W 315 G10
Brett, C. N.Z. 35°10S 174°20E 284 B3
Bretten Germany 49°2N 8°42E 179 F4
Breueh Indonesia 5°44N 95°3E 234 A1
Breuil-Cervinia Italy 45°56N 7°38E 198 C4
Brevard U.S.A. 35°14N 82°44W 315 D13
Breves Brazil 1°40S 50°29W 332 B1
Brevig Mission U.S.A. 65°20N 166°29W 303 D6
Brevik Telemark, Norway 59°4N 9°42E 164 E6
Brevik Stockholm, Sweden 59°20N 18°12E 139 A3
Břevnov Czech Rep. 50°4N 14°22E 135 B2
Brewarrina Australia 30°0S 146°51E 281 E4
Brewer U.S.A. 44°48N 68°46W 309 C19
Brewer, Mt. U.S.A. 36°44N 118°28W 306 J8
Brewerville Liberia 6°26N 10°47W 262 D2
Brewster N.Y., U.S.A. 41°24N 73°36W 313 E11
Brewster Ohio, U.S.A. 40°43N 81°36W 312 F3
Brewster Wash., U.S.A. 48°6N 119°47W 304 B4
Brewster, Kap = Kangikajik Greenland 70°7N 22°0W 154 C8
Brewton U.S.A. 31°7N 87°4W 315 F11
Breyten S. Africa 26°16S 30°0E 271 C5
Breza Bos.-H. 44°2N 18°16E 182 F3
Brežice Slovenia 45°54N 15°35E 199 C12
Brézina Algeria 33°4N 1°14E 261 B5
Březnice Czech Rep. 49°32N 13°57E 180 B6
Breznik Bulgaria 42°44N 22°55E 202 D6
Brezno Slovak Rep. 48°50N 19°40E 181 C12
Brezoi Romania 45°21N 24°15E 183 E9
Brezovicë Kosovo 42°15N 21°3E 202 D5
Brezovo Bulgaria 42°21N 25°5E 203 D9
Bria C.A.R. 6°30N 21°58E 264 A4
Briançon France 44°54N 6°39E 175 D10
Briare France 47°38N 2°45E 173 E9
Briars St. Helena 15°56S 5°43W 153 h
Briático Italy 38°43N 16°2E 201 D9
Bribie I. Australia 27°0S 153°10E 281 D5
Bribri Costa Rica 9°38N 82°50W 320 E3
Briceni Moldova 48°5N 27°5E 183 B12
Brickyard, The U.S.A. 41°55N 87°47W 119 B2
Bricquebec France 49°28N 1°38W 172 C5
Bridge City U.S.A. 29°55N 90°9W 131 B2
Bridge of Sighs = Sospiri, Ponte dei Venice, Italy 142 b3
Bridgehampton U.S.A. 40°56N 72°19W 313 F12
Bridgend U.K. 51°30N 3°34W 169 F4
Bridgend □ U.K. 51°36N 3°36W 169 F4
Bridgenorth Canada 44°23N 78°23W 312 B6
Bridgeport Calif., U.S.A. 38°15N 119°14W 306 G7
Bridgeport Conn., U.S.A. 41°11N 73°12W 313 E11
Bridgeport Ill., U.S.A. 41°50N 87°39W 119 B3
Bridgeport Ill., U.S.A. 38°43N 87°46W 311 F9
Bridgeport N.Y., U.S.A. 43°9N 75°58W 313 C9
Bridgeport Nebr., U.S.A. 41°40N 103°6W 308 E2
Bridgeport Tex., U.S.A. 33°13N 97°45W 314 E6
Bridger U.S.A. 45°18N 108°55W 304 D9
Bridgeton U.S.A. 39°26N 75°14W 309 F16
Bridgetown W. Austral., Australia 33°58S 116°7E 279 F2
Bridgetown Barbados 13°6N 59°37W 323 r
Bridgetown N.S., Canada 44°55N 65°18W 299 D6
Bridgetown Western Cape, S. Africa 33°58S 18°33E 118 A2
Bridgeview U.S.A. 41°45N 87°48W 119 C2
Bridgewater Tas., Australia 42°44S 147°14E 281 G4
Bridgewater Vic., Australia 36°36S 143°59E 282 D5
Bridgewater N.S., Canada 44°25N 64°31W 299 D7
Bridgewater Mass., U.S.A. 41°59N 70°58W 313 E14
Bridgewater N.Y., U.S.A. 42°53N 75°15W 313 D9
Bridgewater, C. Australia 38°23S 141°23E 282 E4
Bridgman U.S.A. 41°57N 86°33W 311 C10
Bridgnorth U.K. 52°32N 2°25W 169 E5
Bridgton U.S.A. 44°3N 70°42W 313 B14
Bridgwater U.K. 51°8N 2°59W 169 F5
Bridgwater B. U.K. 51°15N 3°15W 169 F4
Bridlington U.K. 54°5N 0°12W 168 C7
Bridlington B. U.K. 54°4N 0°10W 168 C7
Bridport Tas., Australia 40°59S 147°23E 281 G4
Bridport Dorset, U.K. 50°44N 2°45W 169 G5
Briec France 48°6N 4°0W 172 D2
Brieg = Brzeg Poland 50°52N 17°30E 185 H4
Brienne-le-Château France 48°24N 4°30E 173 D11
Brienon-sur-Armançon France 47°59N 3°38E 173 E10
Brienz Switz. 46°46N 8°2E 179 J4
Brienzersee Switz. 46°44N 7°53E 179 J3
Brier Cr. → U.S.A. 32°44N 81°26W 316 C8
Brière ⌂ France 47°22N 2°13W 172 E4
Brievengat Curaçao 12°9N 68°54W 322 g
Brig Switz. 46°18N 7°59E 179 J3
Brigg U.K. 53°34N 0°28W 168 D7
Brigham City U.S.A. 41°31N 112°1W 304 F7
Bright Australia 36°42S 146°56E 283 D7
Brighton S. Austral., Australia 35°5S 138°30E 282 C3
Brighton Vic., Australia 37°55S 144°59E 128 B1
Brighton Ont., Canada 44°2N 77°44W 312 B7
Brighton Trin. & Tob. 10°15N 61°39W 323 t
Brighton Brighton & Hove, U.K. 50°49N 0°7W 169 G7
Brighton Fla., U.S.A. 27°14N 81°6W 317 H8
Brighton Ill., U.S.A. 39°2N 90°8W 310 E6
Brighton Iowa, U.S.A. 41°10N 91°49W 310 C5
Brighton Mass., U.S.A. 42°21N 71°9W 116 A2
Brighton Mich., U.S.A. 42°32N 83°47W 311 B13
Brighton N.Y., U.S.A. 43°8N 77°34W 312 C7
Brighton Beach U.S.A. 40°34N 73°57W 132 C2
Brighton-Le-Sands Australia 33°57S 151°9E 139 B1
Brighton Park U.S.A. 41°48N 87°41W 119 C2
Brightside Canada 45°7N 76°29W 313 A8
Brightwater N.Z. 41°22S 173°9E 285 B8
Brightwood U.S.A. 38°57N 77°1W 143 B2
Brigittenau Austria 48°14N 16°22E 142 A2
Brignogan-Plage France 48°40N 4°20W 172 D2
Brignoles France 43°25N 6°5E 175 E10
Brihuega Spain 40°45N 2°52W 196 E2
Brikama Gambia 13°15N 16°45W 262 C1
Brilliant U.S.A. 40°15N 80°39W 312 F4
Brilon Germany 51°23N 8°35E 178 D4
Brim Australia 36°3S 142°27E 282 D5
Brimbank Park Australia 37°43S 144°50E 128 A1
Brimfield U.S.A. 40°50N 89°53W 310 D7
Brimstone Hill Fort St. Kitts & Nevis 17°20N 62°50W 322 d
Brindabella △ Australia 35°14S 148°52E 283 C8
Brindisi Italy 40°39N 17°55E 201 B10
Brinje Croatia 44°59N 15°9E 199 D12
Brinkley U.S.A. 34°53N 91°12W 314 D9
Brinkworth Australia 33°42S 138°26E 282 B3
Brinnon U.S.A. 47°41N 122°54W 306 C4
Brinson U.S.A. 30°59N 84°44W 316 E5
Brion, Î. Canada 47°46N 61°26W 299 C7
Brionne France 49°11N 0°43E 172 C7
Brionski Croatia 44°55N 13°45E 199 D10
Brioude France 45°18N 3°24E 174 C7
Briouze France 48°42N 0°23W 172 D6
Brisay Canada 54°26N 70°31W 299 B5
Brisbane Queens., Australia 27°25S 153°2E 281 D5
Brisbane Calif., U.S.A. 37°40N 122°23W 136 B2
Brisbane → Australia 27°24S 153°9E 281 D5
Brisbane Ranges △ Australia 37°47S 144°16E 282 D6
Brisbane Water △ Australia 33°26S 151°13E 283 B9
Brisighella Italy 44°13N 11°46E 199 D8
Bristol Bristol, U.K. 51°26N 2°35W 169 F5
Bristol Conn., U.S.A. 41°40N 72°57W 313 E12
Bristol Fla., U.S.A. 30°26N 84°59W 316 E5
Bristol Pa., U.S.A. 40°6N 74°51W 313 F10
Bristol R.I., U.S.A. 41°40N 71°16W 313 E13
Bristol Tenn., U.S.A. 36°36N 82°11W 315 C13
Bristol Vt., U.S.A. 44°8N 73°4W 313 B11
Bristol, City of □ U.K. 51°27N 2°36W 169 F5
Bristol B. U.S.A. 58°0N 160°0W 303 H8
Bristol Channel U.K. 51°18N 4°30W 169 F3
Bristol I. Antarctica 58°45S 28°0W 151 B1
Bristol L. U.S.A. 34°28N 115°41W 307 L11
Bristow U.S.A. 35°50N 96°23W 314 D6
Bristow I. Papua N. G. 9°8S 143°14E 286 E2
Britain = Great Britain Europe 54°0N 2°15W 158 E5
Britânia Brazil 15°14S 51°9W 331 D7
British Central Africa = Malawi ■ Africa 11°55S 34°0E 269 E3
British Columbia □ Canada 55°0N 125°15W 296 C3
British East Africa = Kenya ■ Africa 1°0N 38°0E 268 B4
British Guiana = Guyana ■ S. Amer. 5°0N 59°0W 329 C6
British Honduras = Belize ■ Cent. Amer. 17°0N 88°30W 320 C2
British Indian Ocean Terr. = Chagos Arch. ☑ Ind. Oc. 6°0S 72°0E 273 E6
British Isles Europe 54°0N 4°0W 165 D5
British Mts. N. Amer. 68°50N 140°0W 300 B12
British Museum London, U.K. 125 a3
British Virgin Is. ☑ W. Indies 18°30N 64°30W 321 C7
Brits S. Africa 25°37S 27°48E 271 C4
Britstown S. Africa 30°37S 23°30E 270 D3
Britt Ont., Canada 45°46N 80°34W 298 C3
Britt Iowa, U.S.A. 43°6N 93°48W 310 A3
Brittany = Bretagne □ France 48°10N 3°0W 172 D3
Britton U.S.A. 45°48N 97°45W 308 C5
Britz Germany 52°26N 13°27E 115 B3
Brive-la-Gaillarde France 45°10N 1°32E 174 C5
Briviesca Spain 42°32N 3°19W 194 C7
Brixen = Bressanone Italy 46°43N 11°39E 199 B8
Brixham U.K. 50°23N 3°31W 169 G4
Brixton U.K. 51°27N 0°8W 125 B3
Brnaze Croatia 43°41N 16°40E 199 E13
Brněnský □ Czech Rep. 49°10N 16°40E 181 B9
Brno Czech Rep. 49°10N 16°35E 181 B9
Broach = Bharuch India 21°47N 73°0E 244 D1
Broad → Ga., U.S.A. 33°59N 82°39W 316 B7
Broad → S.C., U.S.A. 34°1N 81°4W 315 D14
Broad Arrow Australia 30°23S 121°15E 279 F3
Broad B. U.K. 58°14N 6°18W 167 C2
Broad Haven Ireland 54°20N 9°55W 166 B2
Broad Law U.K. 55°30N 3°21W 167 F5
Broad Pk. = Faichan Kangri India 35°48N 76°34E 243 B7
Broad Sd. Australia 22°0S 149°45E 280 C4
Broadalbin U.S.A. 43°4N 74°12W 313 C10
Broadback → Canada 51°21N 78°52W 298 B4
Broadford Australia 37°14S 145°4E 283 D6
Broadhurst Ra. Australia 22°30S 122°30E 278 D3
Broadmeadows Australia 37°40S 144°55E 128 A1
Broadmoor U.S.A. 37°41N 122°29W 136 B2
Broads, The U.K. 52°45N 1°30E 168 E9
Broadus U.S.A. 45°27N 105°25W 304 D11
Broadview U.S.A. 41°51N 87°52W 119 B1
Broadview Park U.S.A. 26°5N 80°12W 129 B2
Broadway New York, U.S.A. 132 d2
Broager Denmark 54°53N 9°40E 163 K3
Broby Sweden 56°15N 14°4E 163 H8
Brocēni Latvia 56°42N 22°32E 184 B9
Brochet Canada 57°53N 101°40W 297 B8
Brochet, L. Canada 58°36N 101°35W 297 B8
Brock I. Canada 77°52N 114°19W 295 B9
Brocken Germany 51°47N 10°37E 178 D6
Brocklehurst Australia 32°9S 148°38E 283 B8
Brocklesby Australia 35°48S 146°40E 283 C7
Brockley U.K. 51°27N 0°2W 125 B3
Brockport U.S.A. 43°13N 77°56W 312 C7
Brockton U.S.A. 42°5N 71°1W 313 D13
Brockville Canada 44°35N 75°41W 313 B9
Brockway Mont., U.S.A. 47°18N 105°45W 304 C11
Brockway Pa., U.S.A. 41°15N 78°47W 312 E6
Brocton U.S.A. 42°23N 79°26W 312 D5

Brod *Macedonia* 41°32N 21°17E 202 E5
Brodarevo *Serbia* 43°14N 19°44E 202 C3
Brodeur Pen. *Canada* 72°30N 88°10W 295 C14
Brodhead *U.S.A.* 42°37N 89°22W 310 B7
Brodick *U.K.* 55°35N 5°9W 167 F3
Brodnica *Poland* 53°15N 19°25E 185 E6
Bródno *Poland* 52°17N 21°1E 143 B2
Bródnowski, Kanal *Poland* 52°17N 21°3E 143 B2
Brody *Ukraine* 50°5N 25°10E 177 C13
Broek *Neths.* 52°26N 5°0E 112 A2
Brogan *U.S.A.* 44°15N 117°31W 304 D5
Broglie *France* 49°2N 0°30E 172 C7
Brok *Poland* 52°43N 21°52E 185 F8
Broken Arrow *U.S.A.* 36°3N 95°48W 314 C7
Broken Bow *Nebr., U.S.A.* 41°24N 99°38W 308 E4
Broken Bow *Okla., U.S.A.* 34°2N 94°44W 314 D7
Broken Bow Lake *U.S.A.* 34°9N 94°40W 314 D7
Broken Hill = Kabwe *Zambia* 14°30S 28°29E 269 E2
Broken Hill *Australia* 31°58S 141°29E 282 A4
Broken River Ra. *Australia* 21°0S 148°22E 280 b
Brokind *Sweden* 58°13N 15°42E 163 F9
Brokopondo *Suriname* 5°3N 54°59W 329 B7
Bromberg = Bydgoszcz *Poland* 53°10N 18°0E 185 E5
Bromley □ *U.K.* 51°24N 0°2E 125 B4
Bromley Common *U.K.* 51°22N 0°2E 125 B4
Bromma *Sweden* 59°21N 17°55E 139 A1
Bromma ✕ (BMA) *Sweden* 59°21N 17°56E 139 A1
Bromo, Gunung *Indonesia* 7°56N 112°57E 231 H15
Bromo Tengger Semeru △ *Indonesia* 7°56S 112°57E 235 D4
Bromölla *Sweden* 56°5N 14°28E 163 H8
Brompton *London, U.K.* 125 c2
Bromsgrove *U.K.* 52°21N 2°2W 169 E5
Bronaugh *U.S.A.* 37°41N 94°28W 310 G2
Brøndby Strand *Denmark* 55°36N 12°25E 118 B2
Brøndbyøster *Denmark* 55°39N 12°26E 118 B2
Brøndbyvester *Denmark* 55°37N 12°23E 118 B2
Brønderslev *Denmark* 57°16N 9°57E 163 G3
Brondesbury *U.K.* 51°32N 0°12W 125 A2
Brong-Ahafo □ *Ghana* 7°50N 2°0W 262 D4
Broni *Italy* 45°4N 9°16E 198 C6
Bronkhorstspruit *S. Africa* 25°46S 28°45E 271 C4
Brønnøya *Norway* 59°51N 10°32E 133 A2
Brønnøysund *Norway* 65°28N 12°14E 160 D15
Brønshøj *Denmark* 55°41N 12°29E 118 A2
Bronson *Fla., U.S.A.* 29°27N 82°39W 317 F7
Bronson *Mich., U.S.A.* 41°52N 85°12W 311 C11
Bronte *Italy* 37°47N 14°50E 201 E7
Bronwood *U.S.A.* 31°50N 84°22W 316 D5
Bronxville *U.S.A.* 40°56N 73°49W 132 A3
Brook Park *U.S.A.* 41°23N 81°48W 312 E4
Brooke's Point *Phil.* 8°47N 117°50E 233 G1
Brookfield *Mo., U.S.A.* 39°47N 93°4W 310 E3
Brookfield *Wis., U.S.A.* 43°4N 88°9W 311 A8
Brookfield Zoo *U.S.A.* 41°50N 87°50W 119 B1
Brookhaven *Georgia, U.S.A.* 33°52N 84°19W 113 A2
Brookhaven *Miss., U.S.A.* 31°35N 90°26W 315 F9
Brookings *Oreg., U.S.A.* 42°3N 124°17W 304 E1
Brookings *S. Dak., U.S.A.* 44°19N 96°48W 308 C5
Brookland = West Columbia *U.S.A.* 33°59N 81°4W 316 B8
Brooklet *U.S.A.* 32°23N 81°40W 316 C8
Brooklin *Canada* 43°55N 78°55W 312 C6
Brookline *U.S.A.* 42°19N 71°8W 116 B2
Brooklyn *Western Cape, S. Africa* 33°54S 18°29E 118 A1
Brooklyn *Iowa, U.S.A.* 41°44N 92°27W 310 C4
Brooklyn *N.Y., U.S.A.* 40°37N 73°57W 132 C2
Brooklyn-Battery Tunnel *New York, U.S.A.* 132 f1
Brooklyn Bridge *New York, U.S.A.* 132 f2
Brooklyn Heights *New York, U.S.A.* 132 f2
Brooklyn Park *U.S.A.* 45°6N 93°23W 308 C7
Brookmont *U.S.A.* 38°57N 77°7W 143 B2
Brooks *Canada* 50°35N 111°55W 296 C6
Brooks Range *U.S.A.* 68°0N 152°0W 303 C9
Brookston *U.S.A.* 40°36N 86°52W 311 D10
Brooksville *Fla., U.S.A.* 28°33N 82°23W 317 G7
Brooksville *Ky., U.S.A.* 38°41N 84°4W 311 F12
Brookton *Australia* 32°22S 117°0E 279 F2
Brookville *Ind., U.S.A.* 39°25N 85°1W 311 E11
Brookville *Ohio, U.S.A.* 39°50N 84°24W 311 E12
Brookville *Pa., U.S.A.* 41°10N 79°5W 312 E5
Brookville L. *U.S.A.* 39°28N 85°0W 311 E11
Broom, L. *U.K.* 57°55N 5°15W 167 D3
Broome *Australia* 18°0S 122°15E 278 C3
Broons *France* 48°20N 2°16W 172 D4
Brora *U.K.* 58°0N 3°52W 167 C5
Brora ➜ *U.K.* 58°0N 3°51W 167 C5
Brørup *Denmark* 55°29N 9°1E 163 J2
Brösarp *Sweden* 55°43N 14°6E 163 J8
Brosna ➜ *Ireland* 53°14N 7°58W 166 C4
Brossard *Canada* 45°27N 73°28W 130 B2
Broşteni *Mehedinţi, Romania* 44°45N 22°59E 182 F7
Broşteni *Suceava, Romania* 47°14N 25°43E 183 C10
Brøsterud *Norway* 60°18N 8°34E 164 D5
Brotas de Macaúbas *Brazil* 12°0S 42°38W 333 D3
Brothers *U.S.A.* 43°49N 120°36W 304 E3
Brothers, The *Hong Kong, China* 22°20N 113°58E 122 A1
Brothers, The *Yemen* 12°8N 53°10E 249 D6
Brøttum *Norway* 61°2N 10°34E 164 C7
Brou *France* 48°13N 1°11E 172 D8
Brou-sur-Chantereine *France* 48°53N 2°37E 134 A4
Brouage *France* 45°52N 1°4W 174 C2
Brough *U.K.* 54°32N 2°18W 168 C5
Brough Hd. *U.K.* 59°8N 3°20W 167 B5
Broughton *U.S.A.* 37°56N 88°27W 311 G8
Broughton Island = Qikiqtarjuaq *Canada* 67°33N 63°0W 295 D19
Broumov *Czech Rep.* 50°35N 16°20E 181 A9
Brovary *Ukraine* 50°34N 30°48E 189 G6
Brovst *Denmark* 57°6N 9°31E 163 G3
Brown *Canada* 43°48N 79°14W 141 A3
Brown, L. *Australia* 31°5S 118°15E 279 F2
Brown, Mt. *Australia* 32°30S 138°0E 282 B3
Brown, Pt. *Australia* 32°32S 133°50E 281 E1
Brown City *U.S.A.* 43°13N 82°59W 312 C2
Brown Willy *U.K.* 50°35N 4°37W 169 G3
Brownfield *U.S.A.* 33°11N 102°17W 314 E3
Browning *Ill., U.S.A.* 40°8N 90°22W 310 D6
Browning *Mo., U.S.A.* 40°3N 93°12W 310 D3
Browning *Mont., U.S.A.* 48°34N 113°1W 304 B7
Browns Town *Jamaica* 18°24N 77°22W 320 a
Brownsburg *U.S.A.* 39°51N 86°24W 311 E10
Brownstown *U.S.A.* 38°53N 86°3W 311 F10
Brownsville *Fla., U.S.A.* 25°49N 80°15W 129 D1
Brownsville *Oreg., U.S.A.* 44°24N 122°59W 304 D2
Brownsville *Pa., U.S.A.* 40°1N 79°53W 312 F5
Brownsville *Tenn., U.S.A.* 35°36N 89°16W 315 D10
Brownsville *Tex., U.S.A.* 25°54N 97°30W 314 J6
Brownsweg *Suriname* 5°5N 55°15W 329 B6
Brownville *U.S.A.* 44°0N 75°59W 313 C9
Brownwood *U.S.A.* 31°43N 98°59W 314 F5
Browse I. *Australia* 14°7S 123°33E 278 B3
Broxton *U.S.A.* 31°38N 82°53W 316 D7
Bru *Norway* 61°32N 5°11E 164 C2
Bruas *Malaysia* 4°30N 100°47E 237 K3
Bruay-la-Buissière *France* 50°29N 2°33E 173 B9
Bruce *U.S.A.* 30°28N 85°58W 316 E4
Bruce, Mt. *Australia* 22°37S 118°8E 278 D2
Bruce B. *N.Z.* 43°35S 169°42E 285 D4
Bruce Pen. *Canada* 45°0N 81°30W 312 B3
Bruce Peninsula △ *Canada* 45°14N 81°36W 312 A3
Bruce Rock *Australia* 31°52S 118°8E 279 F2
Bruche ➜ *France* 48°34N 7°43E 173 D14
Bruchsal *Germany* 49°7N 8°35E 179 F4
Bruck an der Leitha *Austria* 48°1N 16°47E 181 C9
Bruck an der Mur *Austria* 47°24N 15°16E 180 D8
Brue ➜ *U.K.* 51°13N 2°59W 169 F5
Bruflat *Norway* 60°53N 9°37E 164 D6
Bruges = Brugge *Belgium* 51°13N 3°13E 170 C3
Brugg *Switz.* 47°29N 8°11E 179 H4
Brugge *Belgium* 51°13N 3°13E 170 C3
Brughério *Italy* 45°33N 9°17E 128 A2
Bruin *U.S.A.* 41°3N 79°43W 312 E5
Bruini *India* 29°10N 96°11E 241 A6
Bruit, Pulau *Malaysia* 2°35N 111°20E 235 B4
Brûk, W. el ➜ *Egypt* 30°15N 33°50E 251 H4
Bruksvallarna *Sweden* 62°38N 12°27E 162 B6
Brûlé *Canada* 53°15N 117°58W 296 C5
Brûlé, L. *Canada* 53°33N 64°4W 299 B7
Brûlon *France* 47°58N 0°15W 172 E6
Brumado *Brazil* 14°14S 41°40W 333 D3
Brumado ➜ *Brazil* 14°13S 41°40W 333 D3
Brumath *France* 48°43N 7°40E 173 D14
Brumunddal *Norway* 60°53N 10°56E 164 D7
Brundidge *U.S.A.* 31°43N 85°49W 316 D4
Bruneau *U.S.A.* 42°53N 115°48W 304 E6
Bruneau ➜ *U.S.A.* 42°56N 115°57W 304 E6
Bruneck = Brunico *Italy* 46°48N 11°56E 199 B8
Brunei = Bandar Seri Begawan *Brunei* 4°52N 115°0E 235 B4
Brunei ■ *Asia* 4°50N 115°0E 235 B4
Brunflo *Sweden* 63°5N 14°50E 162 A8
Brunico *Italy* 46°48N 11°56E 199 B8
Brünn = Brno *Czech Rep.* 49°10N 16°35E 181 B9
Brunnen *Switz.* 46°59N 8°37E 179 J4
Brunner, L. *N.Z.* 42°37S 171°27E 285 C6
Brunnhóll *Iceland* 64°17N 15°26W 155 C11
Brunnsberg *Sweden* 61°17N 13°56E 162 C8
Brunsbüttel *Germany* 53°53N 9°6E 178 B5
Brunssum *Neths.* 50°57N 5°59E 170 D5
Brunswick = Braunschweig *Germany* 52°15N 10°31E 178 C6
Brunswick *Vic., Australia* 37°45S 144°57E 128 A1
Brunswick *Ga., U.S.A.* 31°10N 81°30W 316 D8
Brunswick *Maine, U.S.A.* 43°55N 69°58W 309 D19
Brunswick *Md., U.S.A.* 39°19N 77°38W 309 F15
Brunswick *Mo., U.S.A.* 39°26N 93°8W 310 E3
Brunswick *Ohio, U.S.A.* 41°14N 81°51W 312 E3
Brunswick, Pen. de *Chile* 53°30S 71°30W 336 D2
Brunswick B. *Australia* 15°15S 124°50E 278 C3
Brunswick Junction *Australia* 33°15S 115°50E 279 F2
Brunt Ice Shelf *Antarctica* 75°30S 25°0W 151 D2
Bruntál *Czech Rep.* 49°59N 17°27E 181 B10
Brus Laguna *Honduras* 15°47N 84°35W 320 C3
Brusa = Bursa *Turkey* 40°15N 29°5E 203 F13
Brusartsi *Bulgaria* 43°40N 23°5E 202 C7
Brush *U.S.A.* 40°15N 103°37W 304 F12
Brushton *U.S.A.* 44°50N 74°31W 313 B10
Brusio *Switz.* 46°14N 10°8E 179 J6
Brusque *Brazil* 27°5S 49°0W 335 B6
Brussegem *Belgium* 50°56N 4°16E 116 A1
Brussel *Belgium* 50°51N 4°21E 116 A2
Brussel ✕ (BRU) *Belgium* 50°54N 4°29E 116 A2
Brussels = Brussel *Belgium* 50°51N 4°21E 116 A2
Brussels *Canada* 43°44N 81°15W 312 C3
Brusy *Poland* 53°53N 17°43E 184 E4
Bruthen *Australia* 37°42S 147°50E 283 D7
Bruvoll *Norway* 60°27N 11°29E 164 D8
Bruxelles = Brussel *Belgium* 50°51N 4°21E 116 A2
Bruyères *France* 48°10N 6°40E 173 D13
Bruz *France* 48°1N 1°46W 172 D5
Bruzzano *Italy* 45°31N 9°10E 128 A2
Brwinów *Poland* 52°9N 20°40E 185 F7
Bry-sur-Marne *France* 48°50N 2°32E 134 A4
Bryagovo *Bulgaria* 41°58N 25°8E 203 E9
Bryan *Ohio, U.S.A.* 41°28N 84°33W 311 C12
Bryan *Tex., U.S.A.* 30°40N 96°22W 314 F6
Bryan, L. *U.S.A.* 28°22N 81°29W 133 B2
Bryan, Mt. *Australia* 33°30S 139°0E 282 B3
Bryanka *Ukraine* 48°32N 38°45E 189 H10
Bryansk *Bryansk, Russia* 53°13N 34°25E 189 F8
Bryansk *Dagestan, Russia* 44°20N 47°10E 191 H8
Bryansk □ *Russia* 53°10N 33°10E 189 F7
Bryanston *S. Africa* 26°4S 28°0E 123 A1
Bryant Park *New York, U.S.A.* 132 c2
Bryce Canyon △ *U.S.A.* 37°30N 112°10W 305 H7
Bryne *Norway* 58°44N 5°38E 164 F2
Bryson City *U.S.A.* 35°26N 83°27W 315 D13
Bryukhovetskaya *Russia* 45°48N 39°0E 189 K10
Brza Palanka *Serbia* 44°28N 22°27E 202 B6
Brzeg *Poland* 50°52N 17°30E 185 H4
Brzeg Dolny *Poland* 51°16N 16°41E 185 G3
Brześć Kujawski *Poland* 52°36N 18°55E 185 F5
Brześć nad Bugiem = Brest *Belarus* 52°10N 23°40E 177 B12
Brzesko *Poland* 49°59N 20°34E 185 J7
Brzeziny *Łódzkie, Poland* 51°49N 19°42E 185 G6
Brzeziny *Warszawa, Poland* 52°19N 21°1E 143 B2
Brzozów *Poland* 49°41N 22°3E 185 J9
Bsharri *Lebanon* 34°15N 36°0E 250 D7
Bû al Ḥidân, W. ➜ *Libya* 27°25N 19°22E 258 C3
Bû Athlah *Libya* 30°9N 15°39E 258 B3
Bû Baqarah *U.A.E.* 25°35N 56°25E 247 E8
Bu Craa *W. Sahara* 26°45N 12°50W 260 C2
Bû Ḥasā *U.A.E.* 23°30N 53°20E 247 F7
Bû Tummayyim, W. ➜ *Libya* 26°56N 19°13E 258 C3
Bua *Fiji* 16°48S 178°37E 287 A2
Bua *Sweden* 57°14N 12°7E 163 G6
Bua ➜ *Malawi* 12°45S 34°16E 269 E3
Bua Yai *Thailand* 15°33N 102°26E 236 E4
Bu'aale *Somalia* 1°5N 42°35E 267 D5
Buad I. *Phil.* 11°40N 124°51E 233 F5
Buala *Solomon Is.* 8°10S 159°35E 287 M10
Buan *S. Korea* 35°44N 126°44E 224 E3
Buapinang *Indonesia* 4°40S 121°30E 231 E6
Buatan *Indonesia* 0°44N 101°49E 234 B2
Buayan = General Santos *Phil.* 6°5N 125°14E 233 H5
Buba *Guinea-Biss.* 11°40N 14°59W 262 C2
Bubali Bird Sanctuary *Aruba* 12°33N 70°2W 322 f
Bubanda *Dem. Rep. of the Congo* 4°14N 19°38E 264 B3
Bubanza *Burundi* 3°6S 29°23E 268 C2
Bubaque *Guinea-Biss.* 11°16N 15°51W 262 C1
Bube *Ethiopia* 8°46N 35°48E 257 F4
Bubeneč *Czech Rep.* 50°6N 14°24E 135 B2
Bubi ➜ *Zimbabwe* 22°20S 31°7E 271 B5
Būbiyān *Kuwait* 29°45N 48°15E 247 D6
Buc *France* 48°46N 2°7E 134 B1
Buca *Fiji* 16°38S 179°52E 287 A2
Buca *Turkey* 38°22N 27°11E 205 C9
Bucaco *Angola* 11°26S 20°10E 265 E4
Bucak *Turkey* 37°28N 30°36E 205 D12
Bucakkışla *Turkey* 36°57N 33°1E 250 B4
Bucaramanga *Colombia* 7°0N 73°0W 328 B3
Bucas Grande I. *Phil.* 9°40N 125°57E 233 G5
Bucasia *Australia* 21°2S 149°10E 280 b
Bucay *Phil.* 17°32N 120°43E 232 C3
Buccaneer Arch. *Australia* 16°7S 123°20E 278 C3
Buccino *Italy* 40°38N 15°22E 201 B8
Buccoo Reef *Trin. & Tob.* 11°10N 60°51W 323 s
Bucecea *Romania* 47°47N 26°28E 183 C11
Bucegi △ *Romania* 45°25N 25°25E 183 E10
Buchach *Ukraine* 49°5N 25°25E 177 D13
Buchan *Vic., Australia* 37°30S 148°12E 283 D8
Buchan *Aberds., U.K.* 57°32N 2°21W 167 D6
Buchan Ness *U.K.* 57°29N 1°46W 167 D7
Buchanan *Sask., Canada* 51°40N 102°45W 297 C8
Buchanan *Liberia* 5°57N 10°2W 262 D2
Buchanan *Ga., U.S.A.* 33°48N 85°11W 316 B4
Buchanan *Mich., U.S.A.* 41°50N 86°22W 311 C10
Buchanan, L. *Queens., Australia* 21°35S 145°52E 280 C4
Buchanan, L. *W. Austral., Australia* 25°33S 123°2E 279 E3
Buchanan, L. *Tex., U.S.A.* 30°45N 98°25W 314 F5
Buchanan Cr. ➜ *Australia* 19°13S 136°33E 280 B2
Buchans *Canada* 48°50N 56°52W 299 C8
Bucharest = Bucureşti *Romania* 44°27N 26°10E 183 F11
Buchen *Germany* 49°32N 9°20E 179 F5
Buchenhain *Germany* 48°1N 11°29E 131 B1
Bucheon *S. Korea* 37°28N 126°45E 224 D3
Buchholz *Berlin, Germany* 52°36N 13°25E 115 A3
Buchholz *Niedersachsen, Germany* 53°19N 9°52E 178 B5
Buchloe *Germany* 48°1N 10°44E 179 G6
Buchon, Pt. *U.S.A.* 35°15N 120°54W 306 K6
Buciumi *Romania* 47°3N 23°1E 182 C8
Buck Hill Falls *U.S.A.* 41°11N 75°16W 313 E9
Bückeburg *Germany* 52°16N 9°7E 178 C5
Buckeye Lake *U.S.A.* 39°55N 82°29W 312 G2
Buckhannon *U.S.A.* 39°0N 80°8W 309 F13
Buckhaven *U.K.* 56°11N 3°3W 167 E5
Buckhead *U.S.A.* 33°51N 84°24W 113 A2
Buckhorn L. *Canada* 44°29N 78°23W 312 B6
Buckie *U.K.* 57°41N 2°58W 167 D6
Buckingham *Qué., Canada* 45°37N 75°24W 298 C4
Buckingham *Bucks., U.K.* 51°59N 0°57W 169 F7
Buckingham B. *Australia* 12°10S 135°40E 280 A2
Buckingham Canal *India* 14°0N 80°5E 245 H5
Buckingham Fountain *Chicago, U.S.A.* 119 d2
Buckingham Palace *London, U.K.* 125 b3
Buckinghamshire □ *U.K.* 51°53N 0°55W 169 F7
Buckland *U.S.A.* 65°59N 161°8W 303 D7
Buckle Hd. *Australia* 14°26S 127°52E 278 B4
Buckleboo *Australia* 32°54S 136°12E 282 B2
Buckley *Flints., U.K.* 53°10N 3°5W 168 D4
Buckley *Ill., U.S.A.* 40°36N 88°2W 311 D8
Buckley ➜ *Australia* 20°10S 138°49E 280 C2
Bucklin *Kans., U.S.A.* 37°33N 99°38W 308 G4
Bucklin *Mo., U.S.A.* 39°47N 92°53W 310 E4
Buckow *Germany* 52°25N 13°26E 115 B3
Bucks L. *U.S.A.* 39°54N 121°12W 306 F5
Bucktown *U.S.A.* 30°1N 90°8W 131 A2
Buco Zau *Angola* 4°46S 12°33E 265 C2
Bucquoy *France* 50°9N 2°43E 173 B9
Bucureşti *Romania* 44°27N 26°10E 183 F11
Bucureşti Otopeni ✕ (OTP) *Romania* 44°30N 26°11E 183 F11
Bucyrus *U.S.A.* 40°48N 82°59W 311 D14
Bud *Norway* 62°55N 6°55E 164 B3
Bud Bud *Somalia* 4°11N 46°28E 267 D6
Buda *Hungary* 47°30N 19°2E 117 A2
Buda Castle = Budaváripalota *Budapest, Hungary* 117 b2
Budacu, Vf. *Romania* 47°7N 25°41E 183 C10
Budafok *Hungary* 47°25N 19°2E 117 B2
Budai = Putai *Taiwan* 23°23N 120°9E 225 C2
Budalin *Burma* 22°20N 95°10E 241 D5
Budaörs *Hungary* 47°27N 18°57E 117 B1
Budapest *Hungary* 47°29N 19°3E 117 B2
Budapest □ *Hungary* 47°29N 19°5E 182 C4
Budapest ✕ (BUD) *Hungary* 47°26N 19°14E 117 B3
Budatétény *Hungary* 47°25N 19°1E 117 B2
Budaun *India* 28°5N 79°10E 243 E8
Budaváripalota *Budapest, Hungary* 117 b2
Budawang △ *Australia* 35°10S 150°12E 283 C9
Budd Coast *Antarctica* 68°0S 112°0E 151 C8
Buddenbrock = Brodnica *Poland* 53°15N 19°25E 185 E6
Budderoo △ *Australia* 35°40S 150°41E 283 C9
Budding *Denmark* 55°44N 12°30E 118 A3
Buddusò *Italy* 40°35N 9°15E 200 B2
Bude *U.K.* 50°49N 4°34W 169 G3
Budennovsk *Russia* 44°50N 44°10E 191 H7
Budeşti *Romania* 44°13N 26°30E 183 F11
Budeyi *Ukraine* 48°3N 29°16E 183 B14
Budge Budge = Baj Baj *India* 22°30N 88°5E 243 H13
Budgewoi *Australia* 33°13S 151°34E 283 B9
Búðardalur *Iceland* 65°7N 21°46W 155 B3
Budia *Spain* 40°38N 2°46W 196 E2
Büdingen *Germany* 50°16N 9°7E 179 E5
Budjala *Dem. Rep. of the Congo* 2°50N 19°40E 264 B3
Budo-Sungai Padi △ *Thailand* 6°19N 101°42E 237 J3
Budokan *Tokyo, Japan* 140 a4
Budoni *Italy* 40°42N 9°43E 200 B2
Búdrio *Italy* 44°32N 11°32E 199 D8
Büdszentmihály = Tiszavasvári *Hungary* 47°58N 21°18E 182 C6
Budva *Montenegro* 42°17N 18°50E 202 D2
Budweis = České Budějovice *Czech Rep.* 48°55N 14°25E 180 C7
Budyonnovka = Novoazovsk *Ukraine* 47°15N 38°4E 189 J10
Budzyń *Poland* 52°54N 16°59E 185 F3
Bue *Norway* 58°40N 5°58E 164 F2
Buea *Cameroon* 4°10N 9°9E 263 E6
Buela *Angola* 5°54S 14°40E 265 D2
Buellton *U.S.A.* 34°37N 120°12W 307 L6
Buena Esperanza *Argentina* 34°45S 65°15W 334 C2
Buena Park *U.S.A.* 33°52N 117°59W 307 M9
Buena Vista *Bolivia* 17°27S 63°40W 331 D5
Buena Vista *Curaçao* 12°8N 68°57W 322 g
Buena Vista *Solomon Is.* 8°52S 160°3E 287 M11
Buena Vista *Colo., U.S.A.* 38°51N 106°8W 304 G10
Buena Vista *Ga., U.S.A.* 32°19N 84°31W 316 C5
Buena Vista *Va., U.S.A.* 37°44N 79°21W 309 G14
Buena Vista Lake Bed *U.S.A.* 35°12N 119°18W 307 K7
Buenaventura *Colombia* 3°53N 77°4W 328 C2
Buenaventura *Chihuahua, Mexico* 29°51N 107°29W 318 B3
Buenaventura, B. de *Colombia* 3°48N 77°17W 328 C2
Buenavista *Agusan del N., Phil.* 8°59N 125°24E 233 G5
Buenavista *Quezon, Phil.* 13°35N 122°34E 232 E4
Buendia, Embalse de *Spain* 40°25N 2°43W 196 E2
Buenópolis *Brazil* 17°54S 44°11W 333 E3
Buenos Aires *Argentina* 34°36S 58°22W 117 B2
Buenos Aires *Colombia* 1°36N 73°18W 328 C3
Buenos Aires *Costa Rica* 9°10N 83°20W 321 D3
Buenos Aires □ *Argentina* 36°30S 60°0W 334 D4
Buenos Aires, L. = General Carrera, L. *S. Amer.* 46°35S 72°0W 336 C2
Buenos Aires Ezeiza ✕ (EZE) *Argentina* 34°49S 58°32W 117 C1
Buenos Ayres *Trin. & Tob.* 10°6N 61°41W 323 t
Buesaco *Colombia* 1°23N 77°9W 328 C2
Bufalotta *Italy* 41°59N 12°33E 136 B2
Buff Bay *Jamaica* 18°14N 76°40W 320 a
Buffalo *Mo., U.S.A.* 37°39N 93°6W 310 G3
Buffalo *N.Y., U.S.A.* 42°53N 78°53W 312 D6
Buffalo *Okla., U.S.A.* 36°50N 99°38W 314 C5
Buffalo *S. Dak., U.S.A.* 45°35N 103°33W 308 C2
Buffalo *Wyo., U.S.A.* 44°21N 106°42W 304 D10
Buffalo ➜ *Alta., Canada* 60°5N 115°5W 296 A5
Buffalo ➜ *S. Africa* 28°43S 30°37E 271 C5
Buffalo △ *U.S.A.* 36°14N 92°36W 314 C8
Buffalo Head Hills *Canada* 57°25N 115°55W 296 B5
Buffalo L. *Alta., Canada* 52°27N 112°54W 296 C6
Buffalo L. *N.W.T., Canada* 60°12N 115°25W 296 A5
Buffalo Narrows *Canada* 55°51N 108°29W 297 B7
Buffalo Springs △ *Kenya* 0°32N 37°35E 268 B4
Buffels ➜ *S. Africa* 29°36S 17°3E 270 C2
Buford *U.S.A.* 34°7N 83°59W 316 A6
Bug = Buh ➜ *Ukraine* 46°59N 31°58E 189 J6
Bug ➜ *Poland* 52°31N 21°5E 185 F8
Buga *Colombia* 4°0N 76°15W 328 C2
Bugala I. *Uganda* 0°40S 32°20E 268 C3
Buganda *Uganda* 0°0 31°30E 268 C3
Buganga *Uganda* 0°3S 32°0E 268 C3
Bugasong *Phil.* 11°3N 122°4E 233 F4
Bugda Acable *Somalia* 4°4N 45°15E 267 D6
Bugeat *France* 45°36N 1°55E 174 C5
Bugel, Tanjung *Indonesia* 6°26S 111°3E 235 D4
Búger *Spain* 39°45N 2°59E 206 B3
Bugibba *Malta* 35°57N 14°25E 206 F7
Bugio *Portugal* 38°39N 9°18W 126 B1
Bugojno *Bos.-H.* 44°2N 17°25E 182 F2
Bugsuk I. *Phil.* 8°12N 117°18E 233 G1
Buguey *Phil.* 18°17N 121°50E 232 B3
Buguias *Phil.* 16°43N 120°50E 232 C3
Bugulma *Russia* 54°33N 52°48E 186 D9
Buguma *Nigeria* 4°42N 6°55E 263 E6
Bugungu △ *Uganda* 2°17N 31°50E 268 B3
Buguruslan *Russia* 53°39N 52°26E 186 D9
Buh ➜ *Ukraine* 46°59N 31°58E 189 J6
Buharkent *Turkey* 37°58N 28°44E 205 D10
Buheirat-Murrat-el-Kubra *Egypt* 30°18N 32°26E 256 H8
Buhera *Zimbabwe* 19°18S 31°29E 271 A5
Bühl *Baden-W., Germany* 48°40N 8°8E 179 G4
Buhl *Idaho, U.S.A.* 42°36N 114°46W 304 E6
Buhuşi *Romania* 46°41N 26°45E 183 D11
Bui △ *Ghana* 8°21N 2°21W 262 D4
Buikslooot *Neths.* 52°24N 4°55E 112 A2
Buila-Vanturariţa △ *Romania* 45°15N 24°0E 183 E8
Builth Wells *U.K.* 52°9N 3°25W 169 E4
Buin *Papua N. G.* 6°48S 155°42E 287 L8
Buinsk *Russia* 55°0N 48°18E 190 C9
Buíque *Brazil* 8°37S 37°9W 332 C4
Buir Nur *Mongolia* 47°50N 117°42E 219 B12
Buis-les-Baronnies *France* 44°17N 5°16E 175 D9
Buitenveldert *Neths.* 52°20N 4°53E 112 B2
Buitenzorg = Bogor *Indonesia* 6°36S 106°48E 234 D3
Buitrago del Lozoya *Spain* 40°58N 3°38W 194 E7
Buizingen *Belgium* 50°44N 4°15E 116 B1
Bujalance *Spain* 37°54N 4°23W 195 H6
Bujanovac *Serbia* 42°28N 21°44E 202 D5
Bujaraloz *Spain* 41°29N 0°10W 196 D4
Buje *Croatia* 45°24N 13°39E 199 C10
Buji *China* 22°37N 114°5E 219 a
Bujumbura *Burundi* 3°16S 29°18E 268 C2
Bük *Hungary* 47°22N 16°45E 182 C1
Buk *Poland* 52°21N 16°30E 185 F3
Buka I. *Papua N. G.* 5°10S 154°35E 286 C8
Bukachacha *Russia* 52°55N 116°50E 215 D12
Bukama *Dem. Rep. of the Congo* 9°10S 25°50E 269 D2
Bukavu *Dem. Rep. of the Congo* 2°20S 28°52E 268 C2
Bukene *Tanzania* 4°15S 32°48E 268 C3
Bukhansan *S. Korea* 37°38N 126°58E 137 B1
Bukhara = Buxoro *Uzbekistan* 39°48N 64°25E 216 E6
Bukhoro = Buxoro *Uzbekistan* 39°48N 64°25E 216 E6
Bukhtarma Res. = Zaysan Köli *Kazakhstan* 48°0N 83°0E 217 C10
Bukidnon □ *Phil.* 8°0N 125°0E 233 G5
Bukima *Tanzania* 1°50S 33°25E 268 C3
Bukit Baka Bukit Raya △ *Indonesia* 0°43S 112°40E 235 C4
Bukit Barisan Selatan △ *Indonesia* 5°8S 104°4E 234 D2
Bukit Bendera *Malaysia* 5°25N 100°15E 237 c
Bukit Duabelas △ *Indonesia* 2°3S 102°48E 234 C2
Bukit Mertajam *Malaysia* 5°22N 100°28E 237 c
Bukit Nil *Malaysia* 1°22N 104°12E 237 d
Bukit Panjang *Singapore* 1°23N 103°46E 138 A2
Bukit Panjang Nature Reserve *Singapore* 1°22N 103°45E 138 A2
Bukit Tengah *Malaysia* 5°22N 100°25E 237 c
Bukit Tigapuluh △ *Indonesia* 1°15S 102°25E 234 C2
Bukit Timah Nature Reserve *Singapore* 1°20N 103°47E 138 A2
Bukitkemuning *Indonesia* 4°51S 104°33E 234 C2
Bukittinggi *Indonesia* 0°20S 100°20E 234 C2
Bükk *Hungary* 48°0N 20°30E 182 B5
Bukkapatnam *India* 14°14N 77°46E 245 G3
Bükki △ *Hungary* 48°3N 20°30E 182 B5
Bukoba *Tanzania* 1°20S 31°49E 268 C3
Bukum, Pulau *Singapore* 1°14N 103°46E 138 B2
Bukuru *Nigeria* 9°42N 8°48E 263 D6
Bukuya *Uganda* 0°40N 31°52E 268 B3
Būl, Kuh-e *Iran* 30°48N 52°45E 247 D7
Bula *Guinea-Biss.* 12°7N 15°43W 262 C1
Bula *Indonesia* 3°6S 130°30E 231 E8
Bula *Camarines S., Phil.* 13°28N 123°16E 232 E4
Bula-Atumba *Angola* 8°41S 14°52E 265 D2
Bulabog-Putian △ *Phil.* 11°2N 122°4E 233 F4
Bulacan □ *Phil.* 15°0N 121°5E 232 D3
Bülach *Switz.* 47°31N 8°32E 179 H4
Bulaevo *Kazakhstan* 54°54N 70°26E 217 B8
Bulahdelah *Australia* 32°23S 152°13E 283 B10
Bulalacao *Phil.* 12°31N 121°26E 232 E3
Bulan *Phil.* 12°40N 123°52E 232 E4
Bulancak *Turkey* 40°56N 38°14E 213 B8
Búland *Iceland* 63°46N 18°30W 155 D8
Bulanık *Turkey* 39°4N 42°14E 213 C10
Bûlâq *El Khârga, Egypt* 25°10N 30°38E 256 B3
Bûlâq *El Qâhira, Egypt* 30°3N 31°14E 117 A2
Bulawayo *Zimbabwe* 20°7S 28°32E 269 G2
Buldan *Turkey* 38°2N 28°50E 205 C10
Buldana *India* 20°30N 76°18E 244 D3
Buldir I. *U.S.A.* 52°21N 175°56E 303 K1
Buldon *Phil.* 7°33N 124°25E 233 H5
Bule *Phil.* 14°26N 121°2E 127 C2
Bulenga *Ghana* 9°56N 2°12W 262 C4
Bulgan *Mongolia* 48°45N 103°34E 218 B9
Bulgar *Russia* 54°57N 49°4E 190 C9
Bulgaria ■ *Europe* 42°35N 25°30E 203 D9
Bulgheria, Monte *Italy* 40°4N 15°26E 201 B8
Bulgurca *Turkey* 38°9N 27°9E 205 C9
Bulhale *Somalia* 5°20N 46°29E 267 C6
Bulhar *Somalia* 10°25N 44°30E 267 B5
Buli, Teluk *Indonesia* 0°48N 128°25E 231 D7
Buliluyan, C. *Phil.* 8°20N 117°15E 233 G1
Bulki *Ethiopia* 6°11N 36°31E 257 F4
Bulkley ➜ *Canada* 55°15N 127°40W 296 B3
Bull Head *Jamaica* 18°10N 77°16W 320 a
Bull Savanna *Jamaica* 17°53N 77°35W 320 a
Bull Shoals L. *U.S.A.* 36°22N 92°35W 314 C8
Bullaque ➜ *Spain* 38°59N 4°17W 195 G6
Bullard *U.S.A.* 32°38N 83°30W 316 C6
Bullas *Spain* 38°2N 1°40W 197 G3
Bulle *Switz.* 46°37N 7°3E 179 J3
Bullen Park *Australia* 37°46S 145°4E 128 A2
Bullenbaai *Curaçao* 12°11N 69°2W 322 g
Buller ➜ *N.Z.* 41°44S 171°36E 285 B6
Buller, Mt. *Australia* 37°10S 146°28E 283 D7
Buller Gorge *N.Z.* 41°40S 172°10E 285 B7
Bulleringa △ *Australia* 17°39S 143°56E 280 B3
Bullhead City *U.S.A.* 35°8N 114°32W 307 K12
Bulli *Australia* 34°15S 150°57E 283 C9
Büllingen *Belgium* 50°25N 6°16E 170 D6
Bullock Creek *Australia* 17°43S 144°31E 280 B3
Bulloo ➜ *Australia* 28°43S 142°30E 281 D3
Bulloo L. *Australia* 28°43S 142°25E 281 D3
Bulls *N.Z.* 40°10S 175°24E 284 G4
Bully-les-Mines *France* 50°27N 2°44E 173 B9
Bulman *Australia* 13°39S 134°20E 280 A1
Bulnes *Chile* 36°42S 72°19W 334 D1
Bulo Ghedudo *Somalia* 2°52N 43°1E 267 D5
Bulolo *Papua N. G.* 7°10S 146°40E 286 D4
Bulongo *Dem. Rep. of the Congo* 4°45S 21°30E 265 C4
Bulqizë *Albania* 41°30N 20°21E 202 E4
Bulsar = Valsad *India* 20°40N 72°58E 244 D1
Bultfontein *S. Africa* 28°18S 26°10E 270 C4
Buluan *Phil.* 6°44N 124°47E 233 H5
Buluan, L. *Phil.* 6°40N 124°49E 233 H5
Bulukumba *Indonesia* 5°33S 120°11E 231 F6
Bulun *Russia* 70°37N 127°30E 215 B13
Bulungkol *China* 38°36N 74°58E 217 E8
Bulungu *Bandundu, Dem. Rep. of the Congo* 4°33S 18°36E 265 C3
Bulungu *Kasai-Occ., Dem. Rep. of the Congo* 6°4S 21°54E 265 D4
Bulusan *Phil.* 12°45N 124°8E 232 E5
Bulusan Vol. *Phil.* 12°46N 124°3E 232 E5
Bumba *Bandundu, Dem. Rep. of the Congo* 6°58S 19°19E 265 D3
Bumba *Équateur, Dem. Rep. of the Congo* 2°13N 22°30E 264 B4
Bumbah, Khalīj *Libya* 32°20N 23°15E 258 B4
Bumbeşti-Jiu *Romania* 45°10N 23°24E 183 E8
Bumbiri I. *Tanzania* 1°40S 31°55E 268 C3
Bumbuna *S. Leone* 9°2N 11°49W 262 D2
Bumhkang Bum *Burma* 26°51N 97°14E 241 B6
Bumhpa Bum *Burma* 26°51N 97°14E 241 B6
Bumi ➜ *Zimbabwe* 17°0S 28°20E 269 F2
Bumtang = Jakar Dzong *Bhutan* 27°33N 90°43E 241 B3
Bumtang ➜ *Bhutan* 26°56N 90°53E 241 B3
Buna *Dem. Rep. of the Congo* 3°14S 18°59E 264 C3
Buna *North Eastern, Kenya* 2°58N 39°30E 268 B4
Buna *Papua N. G.* 8°42S 148°27E 286 E5
Bunaken *Indonesia* 1°37N 124°46E 231 D6
Bunama *Papua N. G.* 10°9S 151°9E 286 F6
Bunawan *Phil.* 8°12N 125°57E 233 G5
Bunazi *Tanzania* 1°3S 31°23E 268 C3
Bunbury *Australia* 33°20S 115°35E 279 F2
Bunclody *Ireland* 52°39N 6°40W 166 D5
Buncrana *Ireland* 55°8N 7°27W 166 A4
Bund, The *China* 31°14N 121°30E 138 B1
Bunda *Dem. Rep. of the Congo* 4°58S 14°29E 265 C3
Bundaberg *Australia* 24°54S 152°22E 281 C5
Bundanoon *Australia* 34°40S 150°16E 283 C9
Bünde *Germany* 52°11N 8°35E 178 C4
Bundestag = Reichstag *Berlin, Germany* 115 a3
Bundey ➜ *Australia* 21°46S 135°37E 280 C2
Bundi *India* 25°30N 75°35E 242 G6
Bundjalung △ *Australia* 29°16S 153°21E 281 D5
Bundoora North *Australia* 37°41S 145°2E 128 A2
Bundoora Park *Australia* 37°42S 145°2E 128 A2
Bundoran *Ireland* 54°28N 8°18W 166 B3
Bundukia *South Sudan* 5°14N 30°55E 257 F3
Bundure *Australia* 35°10S 146°1E 283 C7
Bung Kan *Thailand* 18°23N 103°37E 236 C4
Bunga ➜ *Nigeria* 11°23N 9°56E 263 C6
Bungalaut, Selat *Indonesia* 2°0S 99°25E 234 C1
Bungay *U.K.* 52°27N 1°28E 169 E9
Bungendore *Australia* 35°14S 149°30E 283 C8
Bungil Cr. ➜ *Australia* 27°5S 149°5E 281 D4
Bungle Bungle = Purnululu △ *Australia* 17°20S 128°20E 278 C4
Bungo *Angola* 7°26S 15°33E 265 D3
Bungo, Gunung *Malaysia* 1°16N 110°9E 235 B4
Bungo-Suidō *Japan* 33°0N 132°15E 222 E4
Bungoma *Kenya* 0°34N 34°34E 268 B3
Bungotakada *Japan* 33°35N 131°25E 222 D3
Bungu *Tanzania* 7°35S 39°0E 268 D4
Bunia *Dem. Rep. of the Congo* 1°35N 30°20E 268 B3
Bunianga *Dem. Rep. of the Congo* 3°28S 20°11E 264 C4
Bunji *Pakistan* 35°45N 74°40E 243 B6
Bunker Hill *Ill., U.S.A.* 39°3N 89°57W 310 E7
Bunker Hill *Ind., U.S.A.* 40°40N 86°6W 311 D10
Bunker Hill Memorial *U.S.A.* 42°22N 71°4W 116 A2
Bunker I. *Pakistan* 24°48N 66°57E 123 B1
Bunkie *U.S.A.* 30°57N 92°11W 314 F8
Bunkyō *Japan* 35°42N 139°45E 140 A3
Bunnefjorden *Norway* 59°50N 10°44E 133 A3
Bunnell *U.S.A.* 29°28N 81°16W 317 F8
Bunnythorpe *N.Z.* 40°16S 175°39E 284 G4
Buñol *Spain* 39°25N 0°47W 197 F4
Bunsuru ➜ *Nigeria* 13°21N 6°23E 263 C5
Buntok *Indonesia* 1°40S 114°58E 235 C4
Bununu Dass *Nigeria* 10°5N 9°31E 263 C6
Bununu Kasa *Nigeria* 9°51N 9°32E 263 D6
Bunya Mts. △ *Australia* 26°51S 151°34E 281 D5
Bünyan *Turkey* 38°51N 35°51E 212 C6
Bunyola *Spain* 39°41N 2°42E 206 B3
Bunyu *Indonesia* 3°35N 117°50E 235 B5
Bunza *Nigeria* 12°8N 4°0E 263 C5
Bunzlau = Bolesławiec *Poland* 51°17N 15°37E 185 G2
Buol *Indonesia* 1°15N 121°32E 231 D6
Buon Brieng *Vietnam* 13°9N 108°12E 236 F7
Buon Ho *Vietnam* 12°57N 108°18E 236 F7
Buon Ma Thuot *Vietnam* 12°40N 108°3E 236 F7
Buona Vista Park *Singapore* 1°16N 103°47E 138 B2
Buong Long *Cambodia* 13°44N 106°59E 236 F6
Buorkhaya, Mys *Russia* 71°50N 132°40E 215 B14
Buqayq *Si. Arabia* 26°0N 49°45E 247 E6
Buqbuq *Egypt* 31°29N 25°29E 256 A2
Bur Acaba = Buurhakaba *Somalia* 3°12N 44°20E 267 D5
Bur Dubai *U.A.E.* 25°15N 55°17E 119 A2
Bûr Fuad *Egypt* 31°15N 32°20E 256 H8
Bûr Safâga *Egypt* 26°43N 33°57E 246 E2
Bûr Sa'îd *Egypt* 31°16N 32°18E 256 H8
Bûr Sûdân *Sudan* 19°32N 37°9E 256 D4
Bûr Taufiq *Egypt* 29°54N 32°32E 256 J8
Bura *Kenya* 1°4S 39°58E 268 C4
Buraan *Somalia* 10°14N 48°44E 267 B6
Burakin *Australia* 30°31S 117°10E 279 F2
Buram *Sudan* 10°51N 25°9E 257 E2
Buran = Buraan *Somalia* 10°14N 48°44E 267 B6
Burang *China* 30°15N 81°10E 218 C5
Burao = Burco *Somalia* 9°32N 45°32E 267 C6
Burāq *Syria* 33°11N 36°29E 250 E7
Burathum *Nepal* 28°4N 84°50E 243 E11
Burauen *Phil.* 10°58N 124°53E 233 F5
Buraydah *Si. Arabia* 26°20N 43°59E 246 E4
Burbank *Calif., U.S.A.* 34°12N 118°18W 126 A3
Burbank *Ill., U.S.A.* 41°44N 87°46W 119 C2
Burç *Turkey* 36°59N 37°8E 250 B8
Burcher *Australia* 33°30S 147°16E 283 B7
Burco *Somalia* 9°32N 45°32E 267 C6
Burda *India* 25°50N 77°35E 242 G7
Burdekin ➜ *Australia* 19°38S 147°25E 280 B4
Burden, L. *U.S.A.* 28°27N 81°33W 133 B1
Burdeos *Phil.* 14°50N 121°58E 232 D3
Burdeos B. *Phil.* 14°48N 122°6E 232 D4
Burdur *Turkey* 37°45N 30°17E 205 D12
Burdur □ *Turkey* 37°45N 30°0E 205 D12
Burdur Gölü *Turkey* 37°44N 30°10E 205 D12
Burdwan = Barddhaman *India* 23°14N 87°39E 243 H12
Burdwood Bank *Atl. Oc.* 54°0S 59°0W 152 M6
Bure *Gojam, Ethiopia* 10°40N 37°4E 257 E4
Bure *Ilubabor, Ethiopia* 8°19N 35°8E 257 F4
Bure ➜ *U.K.* 52°38N 1°43E 168 E9
Burela *Spain* 43°39N 7°24W 194 B3
Büren *Germany* 51°33N 8°35E 178 D4
Bureskoye Vdkhr. *Russia* 50°16N 130°20E 215 D14
Bureya ➜ *Russia* 49°27N 129°30E 215 E13
Burford *Canada* 43°7N 80°27W 312 C4
Burg *Germany* 52°16N 11°51E 178 C7
Burg auf Fehmarn *Germany* 54°28N 11°9E 178 A7
Burg el Arab *Egypt* 30°54N 29°32E 256 H6
Burg et Tuyur *Sudan* 20°55N 27°56E 256 C2
Burg Stargard *Germany* 53°29N 13°18E 178 B9
Burgas *Bulgaria* 42°33N 27°29E 203 D11
Burgas □ *Bulgaria* 42°30N 27°20E 203 D11
Burgaski Zaliv *Bulgaria* 42°30N 27°39E 203 D11
Burgdorf *Niedersachsen, Germany* 52°27N 10°1E 178 C6
Burgdorf *Switz.* 47°3N 7°37E 179 H3
Burgenland □ *Austria* 47°20N 16°20E 181 D9
Burgeo *Canada* 47°37N 57°38W 299 C8
Burgersdorp *S. Africa* 31°0S 26°20E 270 D4
Burgess, Mt. *Australia* 30°50S 121°5E 279 F3
Burghausen *Germany* 48°9N 12°49E 179 G8
Burghead *U.K.* 57°43N 3°30W 167 D5
Búrgio *Italy* 37°36N 13°17E 200 E6
Burglengenfeld *Germany* 49°12N 12°2E 179 F8
Burgohondo *Spain* 40°26N 4°47W 194 E6
Burgos *Ilocos N., Phil.* 18°31N 120°39E 232 B3
Burgos *Pangasinan, Phil.* 16°4N 119°52E 232 C2
Burgos *Spain* 42°21N 3°41W 194 C7
Burgos □ *Spain* 42°21N 3°42W 194 C7
Burgstädt *Germany* 50°54N 12°49E 178 E8
Burgsvik *Sweden* 57°3N 18°19E 163 G12
Burguillos del Cerro *Spain* 38°23N 6°35W 195 G4
Burgundy = Bourgogne □ *France* 47°0N 4°50E 173 F11
Burhaniye *Turkey* 39°30N 26°58E 205 B8
Burhanpur *India* 21°18N 76°14E 244 D3
Burhi Gandak ➜ *India* 25°20N 86°37E 243 G12
Burhner ➜ *India* 22°43N 80°31E 243 H9
Buri Pen. *Eritrea* 15°25N 39°55E 257 D4
Burias I. *Phil.* 12°55N 123°5E 232 E4
Burias Pass. *Phil.* 13°0N 123°15E 232 E4
Burica, Pta. *Costa Rica* 8°3N 82°51W 320 E3
Burien *U.S.A.* 47°28N 122°20W 306 C4
Burigi, L. *Tanzania* 2°2S 31°22E 268 C3
Burigi △ *Tanzania* 2°20S 31°6E 268 C3
Burim *Kosovo* 42°45N 20°24E 202 D4
Burin *Canada* 47°1N 55°14W 299 C8
Buriram *Thailand* 15°0N 103°0E 236 E4
Buriti Alegre *Brazil* 18°9S 49°3W 333 E2
Buriti Bravo *Brazil* 5°50S 43°50W 332 C3
Buriti dos Lopes *Brazil* 3°10S 41°52W 332 B3
Burj Al Arab *U.A.E.* 25°8N 55°11E 119 B2
Burj Khalifa *Dubai, U.A.E.* 25°12N 55°16E 119 B2
Burji *Ethiopia* 5°29N 37°51E 257 F4
Burkburnett *U.S.A.* 34°6N 98°34W 314 D5
Burke ➜ *Australia* 23°12S 139°33E 280 C2
Burke Chan. *Canada* 52°10N 127°30W 296 C3
Burketown *Australia* 17°45S 139°33E 280 B2
Burkina Faso ■ *Africa* 12°0N 1°0W 262 C4
Burk's Falls *Canada* 45°37N 79°24W 298 C4
Burlada *Spain* 42°49N 1°36W 196 C3
Burleigh Falls *Canada* 44°33N 78°12W 312 B6
Burley *U.S.A.* 42°32N 113°48W 304 E7
Burlingame *U.S.A.* 37°35N 122°21W 306 H4
Burlington *Ont., Canada* 43°18N 79°45W 312 C5
Burlington *Colo., U.S.A.* 39°18N 102°16W 304 G12
Burlington *Iowa, U.S.A.* 40°49N 91°14W 310 D5
Burlington *Kans., U.S.A.* 38°12N 95°45W 308 F6
Burlington *Ky., U.S.A.* 39°2N 84°43W 311 E12
Burlington *Mass., U.S.A.* 42°30N 71°13W 116 A1
Burlington *N.C., U.S.A.* 36°6N 79°26W 315 C15
Burlington *N.J., U.S.A.* 40°4N 74°51W 313 F10
Burlington *Vt., U.S.A.* 44°29N 73°12W 313 B11
Burlington *Wash., U.S.A.* 48°28N 122°20W 306 B4
Burlington *Wis., U.S.A.* 42°41N 88°17W 311 B8
Burma ■ *Asia* 21°0N 96°30E 241 E6
Burnaby I. *Canada* 52°25N 131°19W 296 C2
Burnet *U.S.A.* 30°45N 98°14W 314 F5
Burney *U.S.A.* 40°53N 121°40W 304 F3
Burnham *U.S.A.* 40°38N 77°34W 312 F7
Burnham-on-Sea *U.K.* 51°14N 3°0W 169 F5
Burnham Park *U.S.A.* 41°49N 87°35W 119 C3
Burnham Park Harbor *U.S.A.* 41°51N 87°36W 119 B3
Burnhamthorpe *Canada* 43°37N 79°35W 141 B1
Burnie *Australia* 41°4S 145°56E 281 G4
Burnley *U.K.* 53°47N 2°14W 168 D5
Burns *U.S.A.* 43°35N 119°3W 304 E4
Burns Junction *U.S.A.* 42°47N 117°51W 304 E5
Burns Lake *Canada* 54°14N 125°45W 296 C3
Burnside ➜ *Canada* 66°51N 108°4W 294 D10
Burnside, L. *Australia* 25°22S 123°0E 279 E3
Burnsville *U.S.A.* 44°47N 93°17W 308 C7
Burnt Oak *U.K.* 51°36N 0°15W 125 A2
Burnt Paw *U.S.A.* 66°54N 143°44W 303 C12
Burnt River *Canada* 44°41N 78°42W 312 B6
Burntisland *U.K.* 56°4N 3°13W 121 A2
Burntwood ➜ *Canada* 56°8N 96°34W 297 B9
Burntwood L. *Canada* 55°22N 100°26W 297 B8
Burnwynd *U.K.* 55°54N 3°23W 121 B1
Buronga *Australia* 34°18S 142°20E 282 C5
Burqa *West Bank* 31°54N 35°15E 251 D4
Burqān *Kuwait* 29°0N 47°57E 246 D5
Burqin *China* 47°43N 87°0E 217 C11
Burra *S. Austral., Australia* 33°40S 138°55E 282 B3
Burra *Nigeria* 11°0N 8°56E 263 C6
Burragorang, L. *Australia* 33°52S 150°37E 283 B9
Burray *U.K.* 58°51N 2°54W 167 C6
Burrel *Albania* 41°36N 20°1E 202 E4
Burren △ *Ireland* 53°9N 9°5W 166 C2
Burren Junction *Australia* 30°7S 148°58E 281 E4
Burrendong, L. *Australia* 32°45S 149°10E 283 B8
Burriana *Spain* 39°50N 0°4W 196 F4
Burrinjuck, L. *Australia* 35°0S 148°36E 283 C8
Burro, Serranías del *Mexico* 28°56N 102°5W 318 B4
Burrow Hd. *U.K.* 54°41N 4°24W 167 G4
Burrowa-Pine Mountain △ *Australia* 36°6S 147°45E 283 D7
Burrum Coast △ *Australia* 25°13S 152°36E 281 D5
Burruyacú *Argentina* 26°30S 64°40W 334 B3
Burry Port *U.K.* 51°41N 4°15W 169 F3
Bursa *Turkey* 40°15N 29°5E 203 F13
Bursa □ *Turkey* 40°10N 29°0E 212 B3
Burseryd *Sweden* 57°12N 13°17E 163 G7
Burstall *Canada* 50°39N 109°54W 297 C7
Burton *Mich., U.S.A.* 43°0N 83°40W 311 B13
Burton *Ohio, U.S.A.* 41°28N 81°8W 312 E3

Burton S.C., U.S.A. 32°26N 80°43W 316 C9
Burton, L. Canada 54°45N 78°20W 298 B4
Burton upon Trent U.K. 52°48N 1°38W 168 E6
Burtundy Australia 33°45S 142°15E 282 B5
Burtus Egypt 30°8N 31°8E 117 A1
Buru Indonesia 3°30S 126°30E 231 E7
Buruanga Phil. 11°51N 121°53E 233 F3
Burudvatn Norway 59°58N 10°35E 133 A2
Burullus, Bahra el Egypt 31°25N 31°0E 256 H7
Burûm Yemen 14°22N 48°59E 249 D5
Burûn, Râs Egypt 31°14N 33°7E 251 G4
Burundi ■ Africa 3°15S 30°0E 268 C3
Burunny = Tsagan Aman Russia 47°34N 46°43E 191 G8
Bururi Burundi 3°57S 29°37E 268 C2
Burutu Nigeria 5°20N 5°29E 263 D6
Burwell U.S.A. 41°47N 99°8W 308 E4
Burwick U.K. 58°45N 2°58W 167 C5
Burwood Australia 33°52S 151°5E 139 B1
Bury U.K. 53°35N 2°17W 168 D5
Bury St. Edmunds U.K. 52°15N 0°43E 169 E8
Buryatia □ Russia 53°0N 110°0E 215 D12
Bürylbaytal Kazakhstan 44°56N 74°0E 217 D8
Buryn Ukraine 51°13N 33°50E 189 G7
Burzenin Poland 51°28N 18°47E 185 G5
Busa, Mt. Phil. 6°8N 124°39E 233 H5
Busalla Italy 44°34N 8°57E 198 D5
Busan S. Korea 35°5N 129°0E 224 E4
Busanga Dem. Rep. of the Congo 0°53S 22°7E 264 C4
Busango Swamp Zambia 14°15S 25°45E 269 E2
Busaso = Boosaaso Somalia 11°12N 49°18E 267 B6
Buşayrah Syria 35°9N 40°26E 213 E9
Busca Italy 44°31N 7°29E 198 D4
Bûsh Egypt 29°9N 31°6E 251 J2
Bushat Albania 41°58N 19°34E 202 E3
Būshehr Iran 28°55N 50°55E 247 D6
Būshehr □ Iran 28°20N 51°45E 247 D6
Bushenyi Uganda 0°35S 30°10E 268 C3
Bushimaie → Dem. Rep. of the Congo 6°2S 23°45E 265 D4
Bushire = Būshehr Iran 28°55N 50°55E 247 D6
Bushiribana Aruba 12°33N 69°58W 322 f
Bushnell Fla., U.S.A. 28°40N 82°7W 317 G7
Bushnell Ill., U.S.A. 40°33N 90°31W 310 D6
Bushtyna Ukraine 48°3N 23°28E 183 B8
Bushwick U.S.A. 40°41N 73°54W 132 B2
Bushy Park U.K. 51°24N 0°20W 125 B1
Busie Ghana 10°29N 2°22W 262 C4
Business Bay U.A.E. 25°11N 55°16E 119 B2
Businga Dem. Rep. of the Congo 3°16N 20°59E 264 B4
Büsingen Germany 47°42N 8°41E 179 H4
Buskerud □ Norway 60°20N 9°0E 164 D5
Busko-Zdrój Poland 50°28N 20°42E 185 H7
Buslei Ethiopia 5°28N 44°25E 267 C5
Busovača Bos.-H. 44°6N 17°53E 182 F2
Buşra ash Shām Syria 32°30N 36°25E 251 F7
Busselton Australia 33°42S 115°15E 279 F2
Busseri → South Sudan 7°41N 28°3E 257 F2
Busseto Italy 44°59N 10°2E 198 D7
Bussière-Badil France 45°39N 0°36E 174 C4
Bussol, Proliv Russia 46°30N 151°0E 215 E16
Bussolengo Italy 45°28N 10°51E 198 C7
Bussum Neths. 52°16N 5°10E 170 B5
Bustamante, B. Argentina 45°5S 66°18W 336 C3
Buşteni Romania 45°24N 25°32E 183 E10
Busto, C. Spain 43°34N 6°28W 194 B4
Busto Arsizio Italy 45°37N 8°51E 198 C5
Busu Djanoa Dem. Rep. of the Congo 1°43N 21°23E 264 B4
Busu Kwanga Dem. Rep. of the Congo 1°48N 20°21E 264 B4
Busu Mandji Dem. Rep. of the Congo 2°52N 21°14E 264 B4
Busuanga Phil. 12°14N 119°52E 232 E2
Busuanga I. Phil. 12°10N 120°0E 232 E2
Büsum Germany 54°7N 8°51E 178 A4
Busungbiu Indonesia 8°16S 114°58E 231 J17
Busy Corner Trin. & Tob. 10°18N 61°17W 323 t
Buta Dem. Rep. of the Congo 2°50N 24°53E 264 B4
Butantã Brazil 23°34S 46°42W 137 B1
Butare Rwanda 2°31S 29°52E 268 C2
Butaritari Kiribati 3°30N 174°0E 288 G9
Butcher I. India 18°57N 72°53E 130 B2
Bute S. Austral., Australia 33°51S 138°0E 282 B3
Bute Scotland, U.K. 55°48N 5°2W 167 F3
Bute Inlet Canada 50°40N 124°53W 296 C4
Butemba Uganda 1°9N 31°37E 268 B3
Butembo Dem. Rep. of the Congo 0°9N 29°18E 268 B2
Buteni Romania 46°19N 22°7E 182 D7
Butera Italy 37°11N 14°11E 201 E7
Butere Kenya 0°13N 34°30E 268 B3
Butha-Buthe Lesotho 28°47S 28°14E 271 C4
Buthidaung Burma 20°52N 92°32E 241 E4
Butiaba Uganda 1°50N 31°20E 268 B3
Butler Ga., U.S.A. 32°33N 84°14W 316 C5
Butler Ind., U.S.A. 41°26N 84°52W 311 C12
Butler Ky., U.S.A. 38°47N 84°22W 311 F12
Butler Mo., U.S.A. 38°16N 94°20W 310 F2
Butler Pa., U.S.A. 40°52N 79°54W 312 F5
Butler, L. U.S.A. 28°29N 81°33W 133 B1
Buton Indonesia 5°0S 122°45E 231 E6
Bütow = Bytów Poland 54°10N 17°30E 184 D4
Butrint Albania 39°45N 20°1E 206 B10
Butrintit, L. e Albania 39°43N 20°5E 206 B10
Butte Mont., U.S.A. 46°0N 112°32W 304 C7
Butte Nebr., U.S.A. 42°58N 98°51W 308 D4
Butte Creek → U.S.A. 39°12N 121°56W 306 F5
Butterworth = Gcuwa S. Africa 32°20S 28°11E 271 D4
Butterworth Malaysia 5°24N 100°23E 237 c
Buttevant Ireland 52°14N 8°40W 166 D3
Buttfield, Mt. Australia 24°45S 128°9E 279 D4
Button B. Canada 58°45N 94°23W 297 B10
Buttonwillow U.S.A. 35°24N 119°28W 307 K7
Butty Hd. Australia 33°54S 121°39E 279 F3
Butuan Phil. 8°57N 125°33E 233 G5
Butuan B. Phil. 9°4N 125°21E 233 G5
Butuku-Luba Eq. Guin. 3°29N 8°33E 263 E6
Butung = Buton Indonesia 5°0S 122°45E 231 E6
Buturlinovka Russia 50°50N 40°35E 190 E5
Butwal Nepal 27°33N 83°31E 243 F10
Butzbach Germany 50°25N 8°40E 179 E4
Bützow Germany 53°50N 11°58E 178 B7
Buuhoodle Somalia 8°20N 46°25E 267 C6
Buulobarde Somalia 3°50N 45°33E 267 D6
Buur Gaabo Somalia 1°13S 41°51E 267 E5
Buurhakaba Somalia 3°12N 44°20E 267 D5
Buvika Norway 63°18N 10°11E 164 A7
Buxa Duar India 27°45N 89°35E 243 F13
Buxar India 25°34N 83°58E 243 G10
Buxoro Uzbekistan 39°48N 64°25E 216 E6
Buxtehude Germany 53°28N 9°39E 178 B5
Buxton U.K. 53°16N 1°54W 168 D6
Buxy France 46°44N 4°40E 173 F11
Buy Russia 58°28N 41°28E 190 A5
Buyant-Uhaa Mongolia 44°55N 110°11E 226 B6
Buynaksk Russia 42°48N 47°7E 191 J8
Buyo Ivory C. 6°21N 7°5W 262 D3
Buyo, L. de Ivory C. 6°16N 7°10W 262 D3
Büyük Menderes → Turkey 37°28N 27°11E 205 D9
Büyükçekmece Turkey 41°2N 28°35E 203 E12
Büyükdere Turkey 41°9N 29°2E 122 B2
Büyükeğri Dağı Turkey 36°45N 33°33E 250 B4
Büyükkarıştıran Turkey 41°18N 27°33E 203 E11
Büyükkemikli Burnu Turkey 40°18N 26°14E 203 F10
Büyükkonuk = Komi Cyprus 35°24N 34°0E 207 E9
Büyükorhan Turkey 39°46N 28°56E 205 B10
Büyükyoncalı Turkey 41°20N 27°55E 203 E11
Buyun Shan China 40°4N 122°43E 227 D12
Buzançais France 46°54N 1°25E 172 F8
Buzău Romania 45°10N 26°50E 183 E11
Buzău □ Romania 45°20N 26°30E 183 E11
Buzău → Romania 45°26N 27°44E 183 E12
Buzău, Pasul Romania 45°35N 26°12E 183 E11
Buzaymah Libya 24°55N 22°2E 258 D4
Buzen Japan 33°35N 131°5E 222 D3
Buzet Croatia 45°24N 13°58E 199 C10
Buzi → Mozam. 19°50S 34°43E 269 F3
Buziaş Romania 45°38N 21°36E 182 E6
Büzmeýin Turkmenistan 38°3N 58°12E 247 B8
Buzuluk Russia 52°48N 52°12E 186 D9
Buzuluk → Russia 50°15N 42°7E 190 E6
Buzzards Bay U.S.A. 41°45N 70°37W 313 E14
Bwagaoia Papua N. G. 10°40S 152°52E 286 F7
Bwana Mkubwa Zambia 13°8S 28°38E 269 E2
Bwasa Dem. Rep. of the Congo 3°55S 18°24E 264 C3
Bwatnapné Vanuatu 15°41S 168°9E 287 E6
Bwindi △ Uganda 1°2S 29°42E 268 C2
Byakar Dzong = Jakar Dzong Bhutan 27°33N 90°43E 241 B3
Byala Ruse, Bulgaria 43°28N 25°44E 203 C9
Byala Varna, Bulgaria 42°53N 27°55E 203 D11
Byala Slatina Bulgaria 43°26N 23°58E 202 C7
Byam Martin I. Canada 75°15N 104°15W 295 B11
Byarezina → Belarus 52°33N 30°14E 177 B16
Byaroza Belarus 52°31N 24°51E 177 B13
Byblos = Jubayl Lebanon 34°5N 35°39E 250 D6
Bychawa Poland 51°1N 22°36E 185 G9
Byculla India 18°58N 72°50E 130 B2
Byczyna Poland 51°7N 18°12E 185 G5
Bydgoszcz Poland 53°10N 18°0E 185 E5
Byelorussia = Belarus ■ Europe 53°30N 27°0E 177 B14
Byeonsan △ S. Korea 35°40N 126°30E 224 E3
Byers U.S.A. 39°43N 104°14W 304 G11
Byesville U.S.A. 39°58N 81°32W 312 G3
Byfield △ Australia 22°52S 150°45E 280 C5
Bygdin Norway 61°21N 8°32E 164 C5
Bygdøy Norway 59°54N 10°40E 133 A3
Bygland Norway 58°50N 7°48E 164 F4
Byglandsfjorden Norway 58°44N 7°50E 164 F4
Bygstad Norway 61°23N 5°40E 164 C2
Bykhaw Belarus 53°31N 30°14E 177 B16
Bykhov = Bykhaw Belarus 53°31N 30°14E 177 B16
Bykle Norway 59°20N 7°22E 164 E4
Bykovo Russia 49°50N 45°25E 190 F7
Bylas U.S.A. 33°8N 110°7W 305 K8
Bylot Canada 58°25N 94°8W 297 B10
Bylot I. Canada 73°13N 78°34W 295 C16
Byram U.S.A. 32°11N 90°15W 315 E9
Byrd, C. Antarctica 69°38S 76°7W 151 C17
Byrock Australia 30°40S 146°27E 283 A7
Byron Ga., U.S.A. 32°39N 83°46W 316 C6
Byron Ill., U.S.A. 42°8N 89°15W 310 B7
Byron, C. Australia 28°43S 153°38E 281 D5
Byron Bay Australia 28°43S 153°37E 281 D5
Byrranga, Gory Russia 75°0N 100°0E 215 B11
Byrranga Mts. = Byrranga, Gory Russia 75°0N 100°0E 215 B11
Byrum Denmark 57°16N 11°0E 163 G5
Byske Sweden 64°57N 21°11E 160 D19
Byskeälven → Sweden 64°57N 21°13E 160 D19
Bystrytsya Ukraine 48°27N 24°14E 183 B9
Bystrzyca → Dolnośląskie, Poland 51°12N 16°55E 185 G3
Bystrzyca → Lubelskie, Poland 51°21N 22°46E 185 G9
Bystrzyca Kłodzka Poland 50°19N 16°39E 185 H3
Bytča Slovak Rep. 49°13N 18°34E 181 B11
Bytkiv Ukraine 48°38N 24°28E 183 B9
Bytom Poland 50°25N 18°54E 185 H5
Bytom Odrzański Poland 51°44N 15°48E 185 G2
Bytów Poland 54°10N 17°30E 184 D4
Byumba Rwanda 1°35S 30°4E 268 C3
Bywater U.S.A. 29°58N 90°2W 131 B2
Byzantine Museum = Vizandino, Moussio Athens, Greece 112 b3
Bzenec Czech Rep. 48°58N 17°18E 181 C10
Bzura → Poland 52°25N 20°15E 185 F7

## C

C.B.S. Fox Studios U.S.A. 34°9N 118°24W 126 B2
C.N. Tower Toronto, Canada 141 c1
C.W. McConaughy, L. U.S.A. 41°14N 101°40W 308 E3
Ca → Vietnam 18°45N 105°45E 236 C5
Ca' da Mosto Venice, Italy 142 b3
Ca' d'Oro Venice, Italy 142 b2
Ca' Foscari Venice, Italy 142 b2
Ca Mau Vietnam 9°7N 105°8E 237 H5
Ca Mau, Mui Vietnam 8°38N 104°44E 237 H5
Ca Na Vietnam 11°20N 108°54E 237 G7
Ca' Pesaro Venice, Italy 142 b2
Ca' Rezzonico Venice, Italy 142 b2
Caacupé Paraguay 25°23S 57°5W 334 B4
Caaguazú △ Paraguay 26°5S 55°31W 335 B4
Caála Angola 12°46S 15°30E 265 E3
Caamaño Sd. Canada 52°55N 129°25W 296 C3
Caapiranga Brazil 3°18S 61°13W 329 D5
Caazapá Paraguay 26°8S 56°19W 334 B4
Caazapá □ Paraguay 26°10S 56°0W 335 B4
Cabaad, Ras Somalia 6°18N 49°4E 267 C6
Cabadbaran Phil. 9°10N 125°38E 233 G5
Cabagan Phil. 17°26N 121°46E 232 C3
Cabalete I. Phil. 14°16N 121°49E 232 D3
Cabalian = San Juan Phil. 10°16N 125°10E 233 F5
Caballito Argentina 34°37S 58°25W 117 B2
Cabana Peru 8°25S 78°5W 330 B2
Cabana de Bergantiños = A Carballa Spain 43°13N 8°54W 194 B2
Cabanaconde Peru 15°38S 71°58W 330 D3
Cabañaquinta Spain 43°10N 5°38W 194 B5
Cabanatuan Phil. 15°30N 120°58E 232 D3
Cabañeros △ Spain 39°18N 4°35W 195 F6
Cabanes Spain 40°9N 0°2E 196 E5
Cabangon Phil. 15°10N 120°3E 232 D3
Cabanilla Peru 15°29S 70°28W 330 D3
Cabano Canada 47°40N 68°56W 299 C6
Čabar Croatia 45°36N 14°39E 199 C11
Cabarroguis Phil. 16°50N 121°30E 232 C3
Cabarruyan I. Phil. 16°18N 119°59E 232 C2
Cabazon U.S.A. 33°55N 116°47W 307 M10
Cabedelo Brazil 7°0S 34°50W 333 C9
Cabeza del Buey Spain 38°44N 5°13W 195 G5
Cabezón de la Sal Spain 43°18N 4°14W 194 B6
Cabhán, An = Cavan Ireland 54°0N 7°22W 166 B4
Cabildo Chile 32°30S 71°5W 334 C1
Cabimas Venezuela 10°23N 71°25W 328 A3
Cabin John U.S.A. 38°58N 77°10W 143 B1
Cabin John Regional Park ⌂ U.S.A. 39°0N 77°10W 143 A1
Cabinda Angola 5°33S 12°11E 265 D2
Cabinda □ Angola 5°0S 12°30E 265 D2
Cabinet Mts. U.S.A. 48°10N 115°50W 304 B6
Cabinteely Ireland 53°16N 6°9W 120 B3
Cabiri Angola 8°52S 13°39E 265 D2
Cable Beach Bahamas 25°4N 77°24W 153 b
Cabo Blanco Argentina 47°15S 65°47W 336 C3
Cabo de Gata-Níjar △ Spain 36°51N 2°6W 197 J2
Cabo de Hornos △ Chile 55°42S 67°20W 336 E3
Cabo de Santo Agostinho Brazil 8°20S 34°55W 332 C5
Cabo Frio Brazil 22°51S 42°3W 333 F3
Cabo Pantoja Peru 1°0S 75°10W 328 D2
Cabo Raso Argentina 44°20S 65°15W 336 B3
Cabo Rojo Puerto Rico 18°5N 67°9W 321 b
Cabo San Lucas Mexico 22°53N 109°54W 318 C3
Cabo Verde = Cape Verde Is. ■ Atl. Oc. 16°0N 24°0W 153 j
Cabo Yubi = Tarfaya Morocco 27°55N 12°55W 260 C2
Cabonga, Réservoir Canada 47°20N 76°40W 298 C4
Cabool U.S.A. 37°7N 92°6W 308 G7
Caboolture Australia 27°5S 152°58E 281 D5
Cabora Bassa Dam = Cahora Bassa, Lago de Mozam. 15°20S 32°50E 269 F3
Caborca Mexico 30°37N 112°6W 318 A2
Cabot, Mt. U.S.A. 44°30N 71°25W 313 B13
Cabot Hd. Canada 45°14N 81°17W 312 A3
Cabot Str. Canada 47°15N 59°40W 299 C8
Cabourg France 49°17N 0°7W 172 C6
Cabra Dublin, Ireland 53°21N 6°18W 120 A2
Cabra Spain 37°30N 4°28W 195 H6
Cabra del Santo Cristo Spain 37°42N 3°16W 195 H7
Cabra I. India 7°18N 93°50E 245 L11
Cabra I. Phil. 13°53N 120°2E 232 E3
Cábras Italy 39°56N 8°32E 200 C1
Cabras I. Guam 13°27N 144°44E 302 d
Cabrera Spain 39°8N 2°57E 206 B3
Cabrera, Sierra de la Spain 42°12N 6°40W 194 C4
Cabrera △ Spain 39°13N 2°53E 197 F7
Cabri Canada 50°35N 108°25W 297 C7
Cabriel → Spain 39°14N 1°3W 197 F3
Cabrits, Î. Martinique 14°23N 60°52W 322 j
Cabrits △ Dominica 15°35N 61°26W 323 k
Cabruta Venezuela 7°50N 66°10W 328 B4
Cabuçú de Baixo → Brazil 23°30S 46°40W 137 A1
Cabuçú de Cima → Brazil 23°30S 46°33W 137 A2
Cabugao Phil. 17°48N 120°27E 232 C3
Cabulauan Is. Phil. 11°25N 120°8E 233 F3
Cabulo Angola 10°18S 16°22E 265 E3
Caburan = Jose Abad Santos Phil. 5°55N 125°39E 233 J5
Cabuta Angola 9°48S 14°58E 265 D2
Cabuyaro Colombia 4°18N 72°49W 328 C3
Cacabelos Spain 42°36N 6°44W 194 C4
Caçador Brazil 26°47S 51°0W 335 B5
Čačak Serbia 43°54N 20°20E 202 C4
Cacandee Settlement Trin. & Tob. 10°33N 61°26W 323 t
Cacao Fr. Guiana 4°33N 52°26W 329 C7
Caçapava do Sul Brazil 30°30S 53°30W 335 C5
Càccamo Italy 37°56N 13°40E 200 E6
Cacém Portugal 38°46N 9°18W 195 G1
Cáceres Brazil 16°5S 57°40W 331 D6
Cáceres Colombia 7°35N 75°20W 328 B2
Cáceres Spain 39°26N 6°23W 195 F4
Cáceres □ Spain 39°45N 6°0W 194 F5
Cachan France 48°47N 2°19E 134 B2
Cache Bay Canada 46°22N 80°0W 298 C4
Cache Cr. → U.S.A. 38°42N 121°42W 306 G5
Cache Creek Canada 50°48N 121°19W 296 C4
Cacheu Guinea-Biss. 12°14N 16°8W 262 C1
Cachi Argentina 25°5S 66°10W 334 B2
Cachimbo Brazil 8°57S 54°54W 331 B7
Cachimbo, Serra do Brazil 9°30S 55°30W 331 B6
Cachimo Angola 8°21S 21°24E 265 D4
Cachinal de la Sierra Chile 24°58S 69°32W 334 A2
Cachingues Angola 13°5S 16°43E 265 E3
Cachoeira = Solonópole Brazil 5°44S 39°1W 332 C4
Cachoeira Brazil 12°30S 39°0W 333 D4
Cachoeira, Rib. da → Brazil 23°38S 46°43W 137 B1
Cachoeira Alta Brazil 18°48S 50°58W 333 E1
Cachoeira do Sul Brazil 30°3S 52°53W 335 C5
Cachoeiro de Itapemirim Brazil 20°51S 41°7W 333 F3
Cachoeiro do Arari Brazil 1°1S 48°58W 332 B2
Cachopo Portugal 37°20N 7°49W 195 H3
Cachuela Esperanza Bolivia 10°32S 65°38W 331 C4
Cacilhas Portugal 38°41N 9°8W 126 A2
Cacine Guinea-Biss. 11°8N 14°57W 262 C1
Cacoal Brazil 11°32S 61°18W 331 C5
Cacólo Angola 10°9S 19°21E 265 E3
Caconda Angola 13°48S 15°8E 265 E3
Cacongo Angola 5°11S 12°5E 264 D2
Caçu Brazil 18°37S 51°4W 333 E1
Cacuaco Angola 8°47S 13°21E 265 D2
Cacuchi → Angola 14°26S 16°46E 265 E3
Cacula Angola 14°29S 14°10E 265 E2
Caculé Brazil 14°30S 42°13W 333 D3
Caculuvar → Angola 16°47S 14°56E 265 F2
Cacuso Angola 9°25S 15°45E 265 D3
Cadale Somalia 2°45N 46°19E 267 D6
Cadaqués Spain 42°17N 3°17E 196 C8
Čadca Slovak Rep. 49°26N 18°45E 181 B11
Caddo U.S.A. 34°7N 96°16W 314 D6
Cader Idris U.K. 52°42N 3°53W 169 E4
Cadereyta de Jiménez Mexico 25°36N 100°0W 318 B5
Cades U.S.A. 33°47N 79°47W 316 B10
Cadí, Serra del Spain 42°17N 1°42E 196 C6
Cadí-Moixeró △ Spain 42°17N 1°44E 196 C6
Cadibarrawirracanna, L. Australia 28°52S 135°27E 281 D2
Cadillac Gironde, France 44°38N 0°20W 174 D3
Cadillac Mich., U.S.A. 44°15N 85°24W 309 C11
Cadiz Phil. 10°57N 123°15E 233 F4
Cádiz Spain 36°30N 6°20W 195 J4
Cadiz Calif., U.S.A. 34°30N 115°28W 307 L11
Cadiz Ohio, U.S.A. 40°22N 81°0W 312 F4
Cádiz □ Spain 36°36N 5°45W 195 J5
Cádiz, G. de Spain 36°40N 7°0W 195 J3
Cadiz L. U.S.A. 34°18N 115°24W 307 L11
Cadley U.S.A. 33°32N 82°40W 316 B7
Cadney Park Australia 27°55S 134°3E 281 D1
Cadomin Canada 53°2N 117°20W 296 C5
Cadotte Lake Canada 56°26N 116°23W 296 B5
Cadours France 43°44N 1°2E 174 E5
Cadoux Australia 30°46S 117°7E 279 F2
Cadwell U.S.A. 32°20N 83°3W 316 C6
Caen France 49°10N 0°22W 172 C6
Caerdydd = Cardiff U.K. 51°29N 3°10W 169 F4
Caerfyrddin = Carmarthen U.K. 51°52N 4°19W 169 F3
Caergybi = Holyhead U.K. 53°18N 4°38W 168 D3
Caernarfon U.K. 53°8N 4°16W 168 D3
Caernarfon B. U.K. 53°4N 4°40W 168 D3
Caernarvon = Caernarfon U.K. 53°8N 4°16W 168 D3
Caerphilly U.K. 51°35N 3°13W 169 F4
Caerphilly □ U.K. 51°37N 3°12W 169 F4
Caesarea Israel 32°30N 34°53E 251 F5
Caeté Brazil 19°55S 43°40W 333 E3
Caetité Brazil 13°50S 42°32W 333 D3
Cafayate Argentina 26°2S 66°0W 334 B2
Cafu Angola 16°30S 15°8E 265 F3
Cagayan □ Phil. 18°0N 121°50E 232 C3
Cagayan → Phil. 18°25N 121°42E 232 B3
Cagayan de Oro Phil. 8°30N 124°40E 233 G5
Cagayan Is. Phil. 9°40N 121°16E 233 G4
Cagayan Sulu I. Phil. 7°1N 118°30E 233 H2
Cagli Italy 43°33N 12°39E 199 E9
Cágliari Italy 39°13N 9°7E 200 C2
Cágliari, G. di Italy 39°8N 9°11E 200 C2
Cagnano Varano Italy 41°49N 15°47E 199 G12
Cagnes-sur-Mer France 43°40N 7°9E 175 E11
Caguán → Colombia 0°8S 74°18W 328 D3
Caguas Puerto Rico 18°14N 66°2W 321 C6
Caha Mts. Ireland 51°45N 9°40W 166 E2
Cahama Angola 16°17S 14°19E 265 F2
Cahir Ireland 52°22N 7°56W 166 D4
Cahirciveen Ireland 51°56N 10°14W 166 E1
Cahora Bassa, Lago de Mozam. 15°20S 32°50E 269 F3
Cahore Pt. Ireland 52°33N 6°12W 166 D5
Cahors France 44°27N 1°27E 174 D5
Cahuapanas Peru 5°15S 77°0W 330 B2
Cahuenga Park U.S.A. 34°8N 118°19W 126 B3
Cahuinari → Colombia 1°21S 70°44W 328 D3
Cahuinari △ Colombia 1°20S 71°10W 328 D3
Cahul Moldova 45°50N 28°15E 183 E13
Cai Bau, Dao Vietnam 21°10N 107°27E 228 G6
Cai Be Vietnam 10°20N 106°2E 237 G6
Cai Nuoc Vietnam 8°56N 105°1E 237 H5
Caia Mozam. 17°51S 35°24E 269 F4
Caiabis, Serra dos Brazil 11°30S 56°30W 331 C6
Caianda Angola 11°2S 23°31E 265 E4
Caiapó, Serra do Brazil 17°0S 52°0W 331 D7
Caiapônia Brazil 16°57S 51°49W 331 D7
Caibarién Cuba 22°30N 79°30W 320 B4
Caibiran Phil. 11°34N 124°35E 233 F5
Caiçara = Alvarães Brazil 3°12S 64°50W 329 D5
Caicara Bolívar, Venezuela 7°38N 66°10W 328 B4
Caicara Monagas, Venezuela 9°52N 63°38W 329 B5
Caicó Brazil 6°20S 37°0W 332 C4
Caicos Is. Turks & Caicos 21°40N 71°40W 321 B5
Caicos Passage W. Indies 22°45N 72°45W 321 B5
Caidian China 30°35N 114°2E 229 B10
Caiguna Australia 32°16S 125°29E 279 F4
Caillandre, Morne St. Lucia 13°46N 60°57W 323 m
Caille I. Grenada 12°16N 61°34W 323 q
Cailloma Peru 15°9S 71°45W 330 D3
Cain, L. U.S.A. 28°28N 81°28W 133 B2
Căinari Moldova 46°41N 29°3E 183 D14
Cainde Angola 15°29S 13°24E 265 F2
Caine → Bolivia 18°23S 65°21W 331 D4
Caird Coast Antarctica 75°0S 25°0W 151 D1
Cairn Gorm U.K. 57°7N 3°39W 167 D5
Cairngorm Mts. U.K. 57°6N 3°42W 167 D5
Cairngorms △ U.K. 57°10N 3°50W 167 D5
Cairnryan U.K. 54°59N 5°1W 167 G3
Cairns Australia 16°57S 145°45E 280 B4
Cairns L. Canada 51°42N 94°30W 297 C10
Cairo = El Qâhira Egypt 30°2N 31°13E 117 A2
Cairo Ga., U.S.A. 30°52N 84°13W 316 E5
Cairo Ill., U.S.A. 37°0N 89°11W 308 G9
Cairo N.Y., U.S.A. 42°18N 74°0W 313 D10
Cairo Int. ✕ (CAI) Egypt 30°7N 31°24E 117 A3
Cairo Montenotte Italy 44°23N 8°16E 198 D5
Cairofa Angola 14°3S 12°54E 265 E2
Caiseal = Cashel Ireland 52°30N 7°53W 166 D4
Caisleán an Bharraigh = Castlebar Ireland 53°52N 9°18W 166 C2
Caithness U.K. 58°25N 3°35W 167 C5
Caithness, Ord of U.K. 58°8N 3°36W 167 C5
Caitou Angola 14°28S 13°7E 265 E2
Caiuás = Rio Brilhante Brazil 21°48S 54°33W 335 A5
Caiundo Angola 15°50S 17°28E 265 F3
Caiza Bolivia 20°2S 65°40W 331 E4
Caja de Muertos, I. Puerto Rico 17°54N 66°32W 321 b
Cajabamba Peru 7°38S 78°4W 330 B2
Cajamarca Peru 7°5S 78°28W 330 B2
Cajamarca □ Peru 6°15S 78°50W 330 B2
Cajamarquilla = Bolívar Peru 7°18S 77°48W 330 B2
Cajapió Brazil 2°58S 44°48W 332 B3
Cajarc France 44°29N 1°50E 174 D5
Cajas △ Ecuador 2°48S 79°15W 328 D2
Cajatambo Peru 10°30S 77°2W 330 C2
Cajazeiras Brazil 6°52S 38°30W 332 C4
Čajetina Serbia 43°47N 19°42E 202 C3
Cajidiocan Phil. 12°22N 122°41E 232 E4
Caju Brazil 22°52S 43°12W 135 B1
Çakırgol Turkey 40°33N 39°40E 213 B8
Çakırlar Turkey 36°52N 30°33E 205 E12
Čakovec Croatia 46°23N 16°26E 199 B13
Čakovice Czech Rep. 50°9N 14°31E 135 B3
Çal Turkey 38°4N 29°23E 205 C11
Cala Spain 37°59N 6°21W 195 H4
Cala → Spain 37°38N 6°5W 195 H4
Cala Cadolar, Punta de = Rotja, Pta. Spain 38°38N 1°35E 206 D2
Cala d'Or Spain 39°23N 3°14E 206 B4
Cala en Porter Spain 39°52N 4°8E 206 B5
Cala Figuera Spain 39°20N 3°10E 206 B4
Cala Figuera, C. de Spain 39°27N 2°31E 206 B3
Cala Forcat Spain 40°0N 3°47E 206 B4
Cala Major Spain 39°33N 2°37E 206 B3
Cala Mezquida = Sa Mesquida Spain 39°55N 4°16E 206 B5
Cala Millor Spain 39°35N 3°22E 206 B4
Cala Murada Spain 39°27N 3°17E 206 B4
Cala Ratjada Spain 39°43N 3°27E 206 B4
Cala Santa Galdana Spain 39°56N 3°58E 206 B4
Calabanga Phil. 13°42N 123°17E 232 E4
Calabar Nigeria 4°57N 8°20E 263 E6
Calabogie Canada 45°18N 76°43W 313 A8
Calabozo Venezuela 9°0N 67°28W 328 B4
Calábria □ Italy 39°0N 16°30E 201 C9
Calábria △ Italy 39°16N 16°35E 201 C9
Calaburras, Pta. de Spain 36°30N 4°38W 195 J6
Calaceite Spain 41°1N 0°11E 196 D5
Calacoto Bolivia 17°16S 68°38W 330 D4
Calacuccia France 42°21N 9°1E 175 F13
Calafat Romania 43°58N 22°59E 182 G7
Calafell Spain 41°11N 1°34E 196 D6
Calagnaan I. Phil. 11°29N 123°12E 233 F4
Calagua Is. Phil. 14°30N 122°55E 232 D4
Calahorra Spain 42°18N 1°59W 196 C3
Calai Angola 17°47S 19°41E 265 F3
Calais Pas-de-Calais, France 50°57N 1°56E 173 B8
Calais Maine, U.S.A. 45°11N 67°17W 309 C20
Calakmul △ Mexico 18°14N 89°48W 319 D7
Calalaste, Cord. de Argentina 25°0S 67°0W 334 B2
Calama Brazil 8°0S 62°50W 331 B5
Calama Chile 22°30S 68°55W 334 A2
Calamar Bolívar, Colombia 10°15N 74°55W 328 A3
Calamar Vaupés, Colombia 1°58N 72°32W 328 C3
Calamarca Bolivia 16°55S 68°9W 330 D4
Calamba Cavite, Phil. 14°12N 121°10E 232 D3
Calamba Mis. Occ., Phil. 8°35N 123°39E 233 G4
Calamian Group Phil. 11°50N 119°55E 233 F2
Calamocha Spain 40°50N 1°17W 196 E3
Calamonte Spain 38°53N 6°23W 195 G4
Călan Romania 45°44N 22°59E 182 E7
Calañas Spain 37°40N 6°53W 195 H4
Calanda Spain 40°56N 0°15W 196 E4
Calandagan I. Phil. 10°39N 120°15E 233 F3
Calandula Angola 9°6S 15°57E 265 D3
Calang Indonesia 4°37N 95°37E 234 B1
Calangiánus Italy 40°56N 9°11E 200 B2
Calanques △ France 43°14N 5°30E 175 E9
Calanscio, Sarīr Libya 27°30N 22°30E 258 C4
Calapan Phil. 13°25N 121°7E 232 E3
Călăraşi Moldova 47°16N 28°19E 183 C13
Călăraşi Romania 44°12N 27°20E 183 F12
Călăraşi □ Romania 44°10N 27°0E 183 F12
Calasparra Spain 38°14N 1°41W 197 G3
Calatafimi Italy 37°55N 12°52E 200 E5
Calatagan Phil. 13°50N 120°38E 232 E3
Calatayud Spain 41°20N 1°40W 196 D3
Călăţele Romania 46°46N 23°1E 182 D8
Calato = Kalathos Greece 36°9N 28°8E 206 E12
Calatrava Eq. Guin. 1°6N 9°25E 264 B1
Calatrava Phil. 10°35N 123°28E 233 F4
Calatrava, Ponte di Venice, Italy 142 b1
Calauag Phil. 13°55N 122°15E 232 E4
Calavà, C. Italy 38°11N 14°55E 201 D7
Calavite, C. Phil. 13°26N 120°20E 232 E3
Calavite Pass. Phil. 13°36N 120°25E 232 E3
Calayan Phil. 19°16N 121°28E 232 B3
Calayan I. Phil. 19°20N 121°27E 232 B3
Calbayog Phil. 12°4N 124°38E 232 E5
Calbiga Phil. 11°38N 125°0E 233 F5
Calca Peru 13°22S 72°0W 330 C3
Calcasieu L. U.S.A. 29°55N 93°18W 314 G8
Calcium U.S.A. 44°1N 75°50W 313 B9
Calcutta = Kolkata India 22°34N 88°21E 124 B2
Calcutta U.S.A. 40°40N 80°34W 312 F4
Caldaro Italy 46°25N 11°14E 199 B8
Caldas □ Colombia 5°15N 75°30W 328 B2
Caldas da Rainha Portugal 39°24N 9°8W 195 F1
Caldas de Reis Spain 42°36N 8°39W 194 C2
Caldas Novas Brazil 17°45S 48°38W 333 E2
Calder → U.K. 53°44N 1°22W 168 D6
Caldera Chile 27°5S 70°55W 334 B1
Caldera de Taburiente △ Canary Is. 28°43N 17°52W 153 e1
Caldwell Idaho, U.S.A. 43°40N 116°41W 304 E5
Caldwell Kans., U.S.A. 37°2N 97°37W 308 G5
Caldwell Tex., U.S.A. 30°32N 96°42W 314 F6
Caledon Ont., Canada 43°51N 79°51W 312 C5
Caledon Western Cape, S. Africa 34°14S 19°26E 270 D2
Caledon → S. Africa 30°31S 26°5E 270 D4
Caledon B. Australia 12°45S 137°0E 280 A2
Caledonia Ont., Canada 43°7N 79°58W 312 C5
Caledonia Mo., U.S.A. 37°45N 90°46W 310 G6
Caledonia N.Y., U.S.A. 42°58N 77°51W 312 D7
Calella Spain 41°37N 2°40E 196 D7
Calemba Angola 16°0S 15°44E 270 A2
Calen Australia 20°56S 148°48E 280 b
Calenzana France 42°31N 8°51E 175 F12
Caleta Olivia Argentina 46°25S 67°25W 336 C3
Caletones Chile 34°6S 70°27W 334 C1
Calexico U.S.A. 32°40N 115°30W 307 N11
Calf of Man I. of Man 54°3N 4°48W 168 C3
Calgary Canada 51°0N 114°10W 296 C6
Calheta Azores 38°36N 28°1W 153 d1
Calheta Madeira 32°44N 17°11W 153 c
Calheta de Nesquim Azores 38°24N 28°5W 153 d1
Calhoun U.S.A. 34°30N 84°57W 315 D12
Calhoun Falls U.S.A. 34°6N 82°36W 316 A7
Cali Colombia 3°25N 76°35W 328 C2
Calibishie Dominica 15°35N 61°21W 323 k
Calicoan I. Phil. 10°59N 125°48E 233 F5
Calicut = Kozhikode India 11°15N 75°43E 245 J2
Cálida, Costa Spain 37°30N 1°30W 197 H3
Caliente U.S.A. 37°37N 114°31W 305 H6
California Trin. & Tob. 10°24N 61°28W 323 t
California Mo., U.S.A. 38°38N 92°34W 310 F4
California Pa., U.S.A. 40°4N 79°54W 312 F5
California □ U.S.A. 37°30N 119°30W 306 H7
California, Baja, T.N. = Baja California □ Mexico 30°0N 115°0W 318 B2
California, Baja, T.S. = Baja California Sur □ Mexico 25°50N 111°50W 318 B2
California, G. de Mexico 27°0N 111°0W 318 B2
California City U.S.A. 35°10N 117°55W 307 K9
California Hot Springs U.S.A. 35°51N 118°41W 307 K8
California Institute of Technology Los Angeles, U.S.A. 34°8N 118°8W 126 B4
California Los Angeles, Univ. of U.S.A. 34°4N 118°27W 126 B2
California Plaza Los Angeles, U.S.A. 127 b1
California State Univ. U.S.A. 34°4N 118°10W 126 B3
Cälilabad Azerbaijan 39°12N 48°29E 213 C13
Calilegua △ Argentina 25°36S 64°50W 334 B3
Călimăneşti Romania 45°14N 24°20E 183 E9
Călimani, Munţii Romania 47°12N 25°0E 183 C10
Călimani △ Romania 47°5N 25°10E 183 C10
Calingasta Argentina 31°15S 69°30W 334 C2
Calinog Phil. 11°7N 122°32E 233 F4
Calintaan Phil. 12°35N 120°57E 232 E3
Calipatria U.S.A. 33°8N 115°31W 307 M11
Calistoga U.S.A. 38°35N 122°35W 306 G4
Calitri Italy 40°54N 15°26E 201 B8
Calitzdorp S. Africa 33°33S 21°42E 270 D3
Calivigny I. Grenada 12°0N 61°43W 323 q
Callabonna, L. Australia 29°40S 140°5E 281 D3
Callac France 48°25N 3°27W 172 D3
Callahan U.S.A. 30°34N 81°50W 316 E8
Callahan Tunnel Boston, U.S.A. 116 a3
Callan Ireland 52°32N 7°24W 166 D4
Callander U.K. 56°15N 4°13W 167 E4
Callang = San Manuel Phil. 16°4N 120°40E 232 C3
Callao Peru 12°3S 77°8W 124 B2
Callaway U.S.A. 30°8N 85°36W 316 E4
Calliaqua St. Vincent 13°8N 61°12W 323 n
Callicoon U.S.A. 41°46N 75°3W 313 E9
Calling Lake Canada 55°15N 113°12W 296 B6
Calliope Australia 24°0S 151°16E 280 C5
Callosa de Segura Spain 38°7N 0°53W 197 G4
Callosa d'En Sarrià Spain 38°40N 0°8W 197 G4
Calma, Costa de la Spain 39°28N 2°26E 206 B3
Calmar U.S.A. 43°11N 91°52W 310 A5
Calne U.K. 51°26N 2°0W 169 F6
Calola Angola 16°25S 17°48E 265 F3
Calolbon = San Andres Phil. 13°36N 124°6E 232 E5
Calonge Spain 41°52N 3°5E 196 D8
Caloocan Phil. 14°39N 120°58E 127 B1
Caloosahatchee → U.S.A. 26°31N 82°1W 317 J7
Calore → Italy 41°11N 14°28E 201 A7
Caloundra Australia 26°45S 153°10E 281 D5
Calpe Spain 38°39N 0°3E 197 G5
Calpella U.S.A. 39°14N 123°12W 306 F3
Calpine U.S.A. 39°40N 120°27W 306 F6
Calstock Canada 49°47N 84°9W 298 C3
Caltabellotta Italy 37°34N 13°13E 200 E6
Caltagirone Italy 37°14N 14°31E 201 E7
Caltanissetta Italy 37°29N 14°4E 201 E7
Çaltılıbük Turkey 39°57N 28°36E 203 G12
Caluango Angola 8°20S 19°39E 265 D3
Calubian Phil. 11°27N 124°26E 233 F5
Calucinga Angola 11°18S 16°12E 265 E3
Caluire-et-Cuire France 45°48N 4°52E 173 G11
Calulo Angola 10°1S 14°56E 265 E2
Calumet, L. U.S.A. 41°41N 87°35W 119 C3
Calumet City U.S.A. 41°37N 87°32W 119 D3
Calumet Park U.S.A. 41°40N 87°39W 119 C3
Calumet Sag Channel → U.S.A. 41°40N 87°40W 119 C2
Calunda Angola 12°7S 23°36E 265 E4
Caluquembe Angola 13°47S 14°44E 265 E2
Caluso Italy 45°18N 7°53E 198 C4
Caluula Somalia 11°50N 50°45E 267 B7
Caluya I. Phil. 11°55N 121°34E 233 F3
Calvados □ France 49°5N 0°15W 172 C6
Calvados Chain, The Papua N. G. 11°10S 152°45E 286 F7
Calvairate Italy 45°27N 9°13E 128 B2
Calvert → Australia 16°17S 137°44E 280 B2
Calvert I. Canada 51°30N 128°0W 296 C3
Calvert Ra. Australia 24°0S 122°30E 278 D3
Calvi France 42°34N 8°45E 175 F12
Calvià Spain 39°34N 2°31E 206 B3
Calvillo Mexico 21°51N 102°43W 318 C4
Calvinia S. Africa 31°28S 19°45E 270 D2
Calvo, Mte. Italy 41°44N 15°46E 199 G12
Calwa U.S.A. 36°42N 119°46W 306 J7
Calzada Almuradiel = Almuradiel Spain 38°32N 3°28W 195 G7
Calzada de Calatrava Spain 38°42N 3°46W 195 G7
Cam → U.K. 52°21N 0°16E 169 E8
Cam Lam = Ba Ngoi Vietnam 11°54N 109°10E 237 G7
Cam Pha Vietnam 21°7N 107°18E 228 G6
Cam Ranh Vietnam 11°54N 109°12E 237 G7
Cam Xuyen Vietnam 18°15N 106°0E 236 C6
Camabatela Angola 8°20S 15°26E 265 D3
Camacã Brazil 15°24S 39°30W 333 E4
Camaçari Brazil 12°41S 38°18W 333 D4
Camacha Madeira 32°41N 16°49W 153 c
Camacupa Angola 11°58S 17°22E 265 E3
Camaguán Venezuela 8°6N 67°36W 328 B4
Camagüey Cuba 21°20N 77°55W 320 B4
Camagüey, Arch. de Cuba 22°18N 78°0W 320 B4
Camaiore Italy 43°56N 10°18E 198 E7
Camamu Brazil 13°57S 39°7W 333 D4
Camaná Peru 16°30S 72°50W 330 D3
Camanche U.S.A. 41°47N 90°15W 310 C6
Camanche Res. U.S.A. 38°14N 121°1W 306 G6
Camapuã Brazil 19°30S 54°5W 331 D7
Camaquã Brazil 30°51S 51°49W 335 C5
Camaquã → Brazil 31°17S 51°47W 335 C5
Câmara de Lobos Madeira 32°39N 16°59W 153 c
Camararé → Brazil 12°15S 58°55W 331 C6
Camarat, C. France 43°12N 6°41E 175 E10
Camarate Portugal 38°48N 9°7W 126 A2
Çamardı Turkey 37°49N 34°58E 212 D6
Camarès France 43°49N 2°53E 174 E6
Camaret-sur-Mer France 48°16N 4°37W 172 D2
Camargo Bolivia 20°38S 65°15W 331 E4
Camargo Tamaulipas, Mexico 26°19N 98°50W 319 B5
Camargue France 43°34N 4°34E 175 E8
Camargue △ France 43°30N 4°40E 175 E8
Camarillo U.S.A. 34°13N 119°2W 307 L7
Camariñas Spain 43°8N 9°12W 194 B1
Camarines Norte □ Phil. 14°10N 122°45E 232 D4
Camarines Sur □ Phil. 13°40N 123°20E 232 E4
Camaroes Portugal 38°49N 9°14W 126 A1
Camarón, C. Honduras 16°0N 85°5W 320 C2
Camarones Argentina 44°50S 65°40W 336 B3
Camarones, B. Argentina 44°45S 65°35W 336 B3
Camas Spain 37°24N 6°2W 195 H4
Camas Wash., U.S.A. 45°35N 122°24W 306 E4
Camas Valley U.S.A. 43°2N 123°40W 304 E2
Camatambo Angola 6°31S 15°21E 265 D3
Camataquí = Villa Abecia Bolivia 21°0S 68°18W 334 A2
Camaxilo Angola 8°21S 18°56E 265 D3
Camba Cassai Angola 9°47S 19°9E 265 D3
Camballin Australia 17°59S 124°12E 278 C3
Cambamba Angola 8°53S 14°44E 265 D2
Cambará Brazil 23°2S 50°5W 335 A5
Cambay = Khambhat India 22°23N 72°33E 242 H5
Cambay, G. of = Khambhat, G. of India 20°45N 72°30E 239 E10
Camberwell Vic., Australia 37°50S 145°5E 128 B2
Camberwell London, U.K. 51°28N 0°5W 125 B3
Cambil Spain 37°40N 3°33W 195 H7
Cambo Angola 10°55S 20°6E 265 E4
Cambo-les-Bains France 43°22N 1°23W 174 E2
Cambodia ■ Asia 12°15N 105°0E 236 F5
Camborne U.K. 50°12N 5°19W 169 G2
Cambrai S. Austral., Australia 34°40S 139°16E 282 C3
Cambrai Nord, France 50°11N 3°14E 173 B10
Cambre Spain 43°17N 8°20W 194 B2
Cambria U.S.A. 35°34N 121°5W 306 K5
Cambrian Mts. U.K. 52°3N 3°57W 169 E4
Cambridge Ont., Canada 43°23N 80°15W 312 C4
Cambridge Jamaica 18°18N 77°54W 320 a
Cambridge N.Z. 37°54S 175°29E 284 D4
Cambridge Cambs., U.K. 52°12N 0°8E 169 E8
Cambridge Ill., U.S.A. 41°18N 90°12W 310 C6
Cambridge Iowa, U.S.A. 41°54N 93°32W 310 C3
Cambridge Mass., U.S.A. 42°23N 71°7W 116 A2
Cambridge Minn., U.S.A. 45°34N 93°13W 308 C7
Cambridge N.Y., U.S.A. 43°2N 73°22W 313 C11
Cambridge Nebr., U.S.A. 40°17N 100°10W 308 E3
Cambridge Ohio, U.S.A. 40°2N 81°35W 312 F3
Cambridge Bay Canada 69°10N 105°0W 294 D11
Cambridge City U.S.A. 39°49N 85°10W 311 E11
Cambridge G. Australia 14°55S 128°15E 278 B4
Cambridge Springs U.S.A. 41°48N 80°4W 312 E4
Cambridgeshire □ U.K. 52°25N 0°7W 169 E7
Cambrils Spain 41°8N 1°3E 196 D6
Cambuci Rio de J., Brazil 21°35S 41°55W 333 F3
Cambuci São Paulo, Brazil 23°33S 46°37W 137 B2
Cambulo Angola 7°49S 21°15E 265 D4
Cambundi-Catembo Angola 10°10S 17°35E 265 E3
Camdeboo △ S. Africa 32°28S 24°25E 270 D3
Camden N.S.W., Australia 34°1S 150°43E 283 C9
Camden Ala., U.S.A. 31°59N 87°17W 315 F11
Camden Ark., U.S.A. 33°35N 92°50W 314 E8
Camden Maine, U.S.A. 44°13N 69°4W 309 C19
Camden N.J., U.S.A. 39°55N 75°7W 313 G9
Camden N.Y., U.S.A. 43°20N 75°45W 313 C9
Camden Ohio, U.S.A. 39°38N 84°39W 311 E12
Camden S.C., U.S.A. 34°16N 80°36W 315 D14
Camden □ U.K. 51°32N 0°8W 125 A3
Camden Bay U.S.A. 70°10N 145°15W 303 A11
Camden Sd. Australia 15°27S 124°25E 278 C3
Camdenton U.S.A. 38°1N 92°45W 310 F4
Cameia △ Angola 12°5S 21°40E 265 E4
Camelford U.K. 50°37N 4°42W 169 G3
Çameli Turkey 37°5N 29°24E 205 D11
Camenca Moldova 48°3N 28°42E 183 B13
Camerino Italy 43°8N 13°4E 199 E10
Camerón Chile 53°38S 69°39W 336 D3
Cameron Ariz., U.S.A. 35°53N 111°25W 305 J8
Cameron La., U.S.A. 29°48N 93°20W 314 G8
Cameron Mo., U.S.A. 39°44N 94°14W 310 E2
Cameron S.C., U.S.A. 33°34N 80°43W 316 B9
Cameron Tex., U.S.A. 30°51N 96°59W 314 F6
Cameron Highlands Malaysia 4°27N 101°22E 237 K3
Cameron Hills Canada 59°48N 118°0W 296 B5
Cameron Mts. N.Z. 46°1S 167°0E 285 G2
Cameroon ■ Africa 6°0N 12°30E 264 A2
Camerota Italy 40°2N 15°22E 201 B8
Cameroun → Cameroon 4°0N 9°35E 263 E6
Cameroun, Mt. Cameroon 4°13N 9°10E 263 E6

Cametá Brazil 2°12S 49°30W 332 B2
Çamiçi Gölü Turkey 37°29N 27°28E 205 D9
Camiguin ☐ Phil. 9°11N 124°42E 233 G5
Camiguin I. Phil. 18°56N 121°55E 232 B3
Camiling Phil. 15°42N 120°24E 232 D3
Camilla U.S.A. 31°14N 84°12W 316 D5
Caminha Portugal 41°50N 8°50W 194 D2
Camino U.S.A. 38°44N 120°41W 306 G6
Camiranga Brazil 1°48S 46°17W 332 B2
Camiri Bolivia 20°3S 63°31W 331 E5
Camissombo Angola 8°7S 20°38E 265 D4
Camlıbel = Myrtou Cyprus 35°18N 33°4E 207 E9
Çamlıca Turkey 41°1N 29°3E 122 B2
Çamlıyayla Turkey 37°10N 34°36E 250 A5
Cammal U.S.A. 41°24N 77°28W 312 E7
Cammarata Italy 37°38N 13°38E 200 E6
Cammin = Kamień Pomorski Poland 53°57N 14°43E 184 E1
Camo Ethiopia 4°29N 38°24E 266 D4
Camocim Brazil 2°55S 40°50W 332 B3
Camonica, Val Italy 46°0N 10°20E 198 B7
Camooweal Australia 19°56S 138°7E 280 B2
Camooweal Caves △ Australia 20°1S 138°11E 280 C2
Camopi Fr. Guiana 3°12N 52°17W 329 C7
Camopi ➔ Fr. Guiana 3°10N 52°20W 329 C7
Camorta India 8°8N 93°30E 245 K11
Camotes Is. Phil. 10°40N 124°24E 233 F5
Camotes Sea Phil. 10°30N 124°15E 233 F5
Camp Coulter = Powell U.S.A. 44°45N 108°46W 304 D9
Camp Hill Ala., U.S.A. 32°48N 85°39W 316 C4
Camp Hill Pa., U.S.A. 40°14N 76°55W 312 F8
Camp Nelson U.S.A. 36°8N 118°39W 307 J8
Camp Nou F.C. Barcelona Spain 41°22N 2°7E 114 A1
Camp Pendleton U.S.A. 33°13N 117°24W 307 M9
Camp Point U.S.A. 40°3N 91°4W 310 D5
Camp Springs U.S.A. 38°48N 76°55W 143 C3
Camp Verde U.S.A. 34°34N 111°51W 305 J8
Camp Wood U.S.A. 29°40N 100°1W 314 G4
Campagna Italy 40°40N 15°6E 201 B8
Campamento Spain 40°23N 3°46W 127 B1
Campana Argentina 34°10S 58°55W 334 C4
Campana, I. Chile 48°20S 75°20W 336 C1
Campanário Madeira 32°39N 17°2W 153 c
Campanario Spain 38°52N 5°36W 195 G5
Campanet Spain 39°46N 2°58E 206 B3
Campánia ☐ Italy 41°0N 14°30E 201 B7
Campas del Tuyú △ Argentina 36°17S 56°50W 334 D4
Campbell Northern Cape, S. Africa 28°48S 23°44E 270 C3
Campbell Calif., U.S.A. 37°17N 121°57W 306 H5
Campbell Fla., U.S.A. 28°16N 81°27W 317 G8
Campbell Ohio, U.S.A. 41°5N 80°37W 312 E4
Campbell, C. N.Z. 41°47S 174°18E 285 B9
Campbell I. Pac. Oc. 52°30S 169°0E 288 N8
Campbell L. Canada 63°14N 106°55W 297 A7
Campbell Plateau S. Ocean 50°0S 170°0E 151 A11
Campbell River Canada 50°5N 125°20W 296 C3
Campbellfield Australia 37°41S 144°57E 128 A1
Campbellford Canada 44°18N 77°48W 312 B7
Campbellpur Pakistan 33°46N 72°26E 242 C5
Campbellsburg U.S.A. 38°39N 86°16W 311 F10
Campbellsville U.S.A. 37°21N 85°20W 309 G11
Campbellton N.B., Canada 47°57N 66°43W 299 C6
Campbellton Fla., U.S.A. 30°57N 85°24W 316 E4
Campbelltown = Bluff N.Z. 46°37S 168°20E 285 G3
Campbelltown Australia 34°4S 150°49E 283 C9
Campbeltown U.K. 55°26N 5°36W 167 F3
Campêche Guadeloupe 16°26N 61°26W 322 e
Campeche Campeche, Mexico 19°51N 90°32W 319 D6
Campeche ☐ Mexico 19°0N 90°30W 319 D6
Campeche, Banco Mexico 22°30N 88°0W 320 B2
Campeche, Golfo de Mexico 19°30N 93°0W 319 D6
Câmpeni Romania 46°22N 23°3E 182 D8
Camperdown N.S.W., Australia 33°53S 151°11E 139 B2
Camperdown Vic., Australia 38°14S 143°9E 282 E5
Camperville Canada 51°59N 100°9W 297 C8
Campi Salentina Italy 40°24N 18°1E 201 B11
Câmpia Turzii Romania 46°34N 23°53E 183 D8
Campidano Italy 39°30N 8°47E 200 C1
Campidoglio, Piazza de Rome, Italy 136 c3
Campíglia Maríttima Italy 43°4N 10°37E 198 E7
Campillo de Altobuey Spain 39°36N 1°49W 197 F3
Campillos Spain 37°4N 4°51W 195 H6
Câmpina Romania 45°10N 25°45E 183 E10
Campina Grande Brazil 7°20S 35°47W 332 C4
Campina Verde Brazil 19°31S 49°28W 333 E2
Campinas Brazil 22°50S 47°0W 335 A6
Campione Italy 45°58N 8°58E 175 C12
Campli Italy 42°43N 13°41E 199 F10
Campo = Ntem ➔ Cameroon 2°21N 9°49E 264 B2
Campo Cameroon 2°22N 9°50E 264 B1
Campo Spain 42°25N 0°24E 196 C5
Campo, Casa de Spain 40°25N 3°45W 127 B1
Campo ⌂ Cameroon 2°23N 10°5E 264 B2
Campo Belo Brazil 20°52S 45°16W 333 F2
Campo de Criptana Spain 39°24N 3°7W 195 F7
Campo de Diauarum Brazil 11°12S 53°14W 331 C7
Campo de Gibraltar Spain 36°15N 5°25W 195 J5
Campo de los Alisos △ Argentina 27°15S 66°0W 334 B2
Campo Florido Brazil 19°47S 48°35W 333 E2
Campo Formoso = Campo Florido Brazil 19°47S 48°35W 333 E2
Campo Formoso Brazil 10°30S 40°20W 332 D3
Campo Grande Brazil 20°25S 54°40W 331 E7
Campo Grande Portugal 38°45N 9°9W 126 A2
Campo Maior Brazil 4°50S 42°12W 332 B3
Campo Maior Portugal 39°2N 7°7W 195 F3
Campo Mourão Brazil 24°3S 52°22W 335 A5
Campo Pequeño Portugal 38°44N 9°8W 126 A2
Campo Santa Margherita Venice, Italy 142 b2
Campo Túres Italy 46°53N 11°55E 199 B8
Campoalegre Colombia 2°41N 75°20W 328 C2
Campobasso Italy 41°34N 14°39E 201 A7
Campobello di Licata Italy 37°15N 13°55E 200 E6
Campobello di Mazara Italy 37°38N 12°45E 200 E5
Campofelice di Roccella Italy 37°59N 13°53E 200 E6
Campolide Portugal 38°43N 9°9W 126 A2
Campomarino Italy 41°57N 15°2E 199 G12
Camporeale Italy 37°54N 13°6E 200 E6
Camporrobles Spain 39°39N 1°24W 196 F3
Campos Brazil 21°50S 41°20W 333 F3
Campos Spain 39°26N 3°1E 206 B4
Campos Altos Brazil 19°47S 46°10W 333 E2
Campos Belos Brazil 13°10S 47°3W 333 D2
Campos del Paraíso = Carrascosa del Campo Spain 40°2N 2°45W 196 E2
Campos Novos Brazil 27°21S 51°50W 335 B5
Campos Sales Brazil 7°4S 40°23W 332 C3
Camprodon Spain 42°19N 2°23E 196 C7
Camps Bay S. Africa 33°57S 18°23E 118 A1
Campton Fla., U.S.A. 30°53N 86°31W 317 E3
Campton Ga., U.S.A. 33°52N 83°43W 316 B6
Campton Ky., U.S.A. 37°44N 83°33W 311 G13
Camptonville U.S.A. 39°27N 121°3W 306 F5
Camptown U.S.A. 41°44N 76°14W 313 E8
Câmpulung Argeş, Romania 45°17N 25°3E 183 E10
Câmpulung Suceava, Romania 47°32N 25°30E 183 C10
Câmpuri Romania 46°0N 26°50E 183 D11
Campuya ➔ Peru 1°40S 73°30W 328 D3
Campville U.S.A. 29°40N 82°7W 316 F7
Camrose Canada 53°0N 112°50W 296 C6
Camsell Portage Canada 59°37N 109°15W 297 B7
Camucuio Angola 14°7S 13°15E 265 E2
Camuy Puerto Rico 18°29N 66°51W 321 b
Çamyuva Turkey 36°30N 30°30E 205 E12
Çan Turkey 40°2N 27°3E 203 F11
Can Clavo Spain 38°57N 1°27E 206 D1
Can Creu Spain 38°58N 1°28E 206 D1
Can Gio Vietnam 10°25N 106°58E 237 G6
Can Pastilla Spain 39°32N 2°42E 206 B3
C'an San Joan Spain 41°28N 2°11E 114 A2
Can Tho Vietnam 10°2N 105°46E 237 G5
Canaan Trin. & Tob. 11°9N 60°49W 323 s
Canaan Conn., U.S.A. 42°2N 73°20W 313 D11
Canaan Hill Jamaica 18°23N 77°14W 320 a
Cañacao B. Phil. 14°29N 120°54E 127 C1
Canacona India 15°1N 74°4E 245 G2
Canada ■ N. Amer. 60°0N 100°0W 294 G11
Canada Abyssal Plain Arctic 80°0N 140°0W 150 B18
Canada Basin Arctic 75°0N 145°0W 150 B18
Cañada de Gómez Argentina 32°40S 61°30W 334 C3
Canadian U.S.A. 35°55N 100°23W 314 D4
Canadian ➔ U.S.A. 35°28N 95°3W 314 D7
Canadian Shield Canada 53°0N 75°0W 292 D12
Canadys U.S.A. 33°3N 80°37W 316 B9
Canajoharie U.S.A. 42°54N 74°35W 313 D10
Çanakkale Turkey 40°8N 26°24E 203 F10
Çanakkale ☐ Turkey 40°10N 26°25E 203 F10
Çanakkale Boğazı Turkey 40°17N 26°32E 203 F10
Canal Flats Canada 50°10N 115°48W 296 C5
Canal Grande Venice, Italy 142 b2
Canal Point U.S.A. 26°52N 80°38W 317 J9
Canal Street New Orleans, U.S.A. 131 b2
Canala N. Cal. 21°32S 165°57E 288 d
Canalejas Argentina 35°15S 66°34W 334 D2
Canals Argentina 33°35S 62°53W 334 C3
Canals Spain 38°58N 0°35W 197 G4
Canandaigua U.S.A. 42°54N 77°17W 312 D7
Canandaigua L. U.S.A. 42°47N 77°19W 312 D7
Cananea Mexico 31°0N 110°18W 318 A2
Cañar Ecuador 2°33S 78°56W 328 D2
Cañar ☐ Ecuador 2°30S 79°0W 328 D2
Canarias, Is. Atl. Oc. 28°30N 16°0W 153 e1
Canaries St. Lucia 13°55N 61°4W 323 m
Canarreos, Arch. de los Cuba 21°35N 81°40W 320 B3
Canarsie U.S.A. 40°38N 73°53W 132 C2
Canary Is. = Canarias, Is. Atl. Oc. 28°30N 16°0W 153 e1
Canary Wharf U.K. 51°30N 0°1W 125 A3
Canaseraga U.S.A. 42°27N 77°45W 312 D7
Canastra, Serra da Brazil 20°0S 46°20W 333 F2
Canatlán Mexico 24°31N 104°47W 318 C4
Cañaveral Peru 3°56S 80°39W 328 D1
Cañaveral, C. U.S.A. 28°27N 80°32W 317 G9
Cañaveral ⌂ U.S.A. 28°28N 80°34W 317 G9
Cañaveruelas Spain 40°24N 2°38W 196 E2
Canavieiras Brazil 15°39S 39°0W 333 E4
Canbelego Australia 31°32S 146°18E 283 A7
Canberra Australia 35°15S 149°8E 283 C8
Canby Calif., U.S.A. 41°27N 120°52W 304 F3
Canby Minn., U.S.A. 44°43N 96°16W 308 C5
Canby Oreg., U.S.A. 45°16N 122°42W 306 E4
Cancale France 48°40N 1°50W 172 D5
Cancelleria, Palazzo dei Rome, Italy 136 c2
Canche ➔ France 50°31N 1°39E 173 B8
Canchungo = Teixeira Pinto Guinea-Biss. 12°3N 16°0W 262 C1
Canchungo Guinea-Biss. 12°26N 16°5W 262 C1
Canchyuaya, Cordillera de Peru 7°30S 74°0W 330 B3
Cancún Mexico 21°8N 86°44W 319 C7
Candanchú Spain 42°47N 0°32W 196 C4
Candarave Peru 17°15S 70°13W 330 D3
Çandarlı Turkey 38°56N 26°56E 205 C8
Çandarlı Körfezi Turkey 38°52N 26°55E 205 C8
Candás Spain 43°35N 5°45W 194 B5
Candé France 47°34N 1°2W 172 E5
Candeias ➔ Brazil 8°39S 63°31W 331 B5
Candela Italy 41°8N 15°31E 201 A8
Candelaria Argentina 27°29S 55°44W 335 B4
Candelaria Canary Is. 28°22N 16°22W 153 e1
Candelaria Phil. 13°56N 121°25E 232 E3
Candelario ⌂ Spain 40°20N 5°46W 194 E5
Candeleda Spain 40°10N 5°14W 194 E5
Candelo Australia 36°47S 149°43E 283 D8
Candi Dasa Indonesia 8°30S 115°34E 231 J18
Candia = Iraklio Greece 35°20N 25°12E 207 E6
Candia, Sea of = Crete, Sea of Greece 36°0N 25°0E 205 E7
Candiac Canada 45°23N 73°29W 130 B3
Cândido de Abreu Brazil 24°35S 51°20W 333 F1
Cândido Mendes Brazil 1°27S 45°43W 332 B2
Candle U.S.A. 65°55N 161°56W 303 D7
Candle L. Canada 53°50N 105°18W 297 C7
Candlemas I. Antarctica 57°3S 26°40W 151 B1
Cando U.S.A. 48°32N 99°12W 308 A4
Candon Phil. 17°12N 120°27E 232 C3
Canea = Chania Greece 35°30N 24°4E 207 E5
Caneças Portugal 38°48N 9°13W 126 A1
Canefield Dominica 15°20N 61°24W 323 k
Canela Brazil 10°15S 43°25W 332 D2
Canelles ➔ St. Lucia 13°47N 60°55W 323 m
Canelli Italy 44°43N 8°17E 198 D5
Canelones Uruguay 34°32S 56°17W 335 C4
Canet de Mar Spain 41°35N 2°35E 196 D7
Canet-Plage France 42°41N 3°2E 174 F7
Cañete Chile 37°50S 73°30W 334 D1
Cañete Spain 40°3N 1°54W 196 E3
Cañete de las Torres Spain 37°53N 4°19W 195 H6
Cangamba Angola 13°40S 19°54E 265 E3
Cangandala Angola 9°45S 16°33E 265 D3
Cangandala △ Angola 9°53S 16°42E 265 D3
Cangas Spain 42°16N 8°47W 194 C2
Cangas de Narcea Spain 43°10N 6°32W 194 B4
Cangas de Onís Spain 43°21N 5°8W 194 B5
Cangas de Tineo = Cangas del Narcea Spain 43°10N 6°32W 194 B4
Cangas del Narcea Spain 43°10N 6°32W 194 B4
Cangnan China 27°30N 120°23E 229 D13
Cangoa Angola 13°8S 18°30E 265 E3
Cangola Angola 7°58S 15°53E 265 D3
Cangolo Angola 15°0S 13°52E 265 E2
Cangombe Angola 14°24S 19°59E 265 E3
Cangongo Angola 9°24S 17°30E 265 D3
Cangshan China 34°50N 118°2E 227 G10
Canguaretama Brazil 6°20S 35°5W 332 C4
Canguçu Brazil 31°22S 52°43W 335 C5
Canguçu, Serra do Brazil 31°20S 52°40W 335 C5
Cangumbe Angola 11°58S 19°12E 265 E3
Cangxi China 31°47N 105°59E 228 B5
Cangyuan China 23°12N 99°14E 228 F2
Cangzhou China 38°19N 116°52E 226 E9
Canhoca Angola 9°15S 14°45E 265 D2
Cani, I. Tunisia 36°21N 10°5E 258 A2
Caniapiscau ➔ Canada 56°40N 69°30W 299 A6
Caniapiscau, L. Canada 54°10N 69°55W 299 B6
Caniçal Madeira 32°44N 16°43W 153 c
Canicattì Italy 37°21N 13°51E 200 E6
Canicattini Bagni Italy 37°2N 15°4E 201 E8
Canigao Channel Phil. 10°15N 124°42E 233 F5
Canigou France 42°31N 2°27E 174 F6
Canillas Spain 40°27N 3°38W 127 B2
Canillas Spain 40°26N 3°36W 127 B2
Canillejas Spain 40°26N 3°36W 127 B2
Canim Lake Canada 51°47N 120°54W 296 C4
Canindé Brazil 4°22S 39°19W 332 B4
Canindé ➔ Brazil 6°15S 42°52W 332 C3
Canindeyu ☐ Paraguay 24°10S 55°0W 335 A5
Canino Italy 42°28N 11°45E 199 F8
Canisteo U.S.A. 42°16N 77°36W 312 D7
Canisteo ➔ U.S.A. 42°7N 77°8W 312 D7
Cañitas de Felipe Pescador Mexico 23°36N 102°43W 318 C4
Cañizal Spain 41°12N 5°22W 194 D5
Canjáyar Spain 37°1N 2°44W 195 H8
Canjinge Angola 10°12S 21°17E 265 E4
Çankırı Turkey 40°40N 33°37E 212 B5
Çankırı ☐ Turkey 40°40N 33°40E 212 B5
Cankuzo Burundi 3°10S 30°31E 268 C3
Canlaon Phil. 10°22N 123°12E 233 F4
Canlaon Volcano Phil. 10°25N 123°8E 233 F4
Canmore Canada 51°7N 115°18W 296 C5
Cann River Australia 37°35S 149°7E 283 D8
Canna U.K. 57°3N 6°33W 167 D2
Cannanore = Kannur India 11°53N 75°27E 245 J2
Cannanore Is. India 10°30N 72°30E 245 J1
Cannaregio Venice, Italy 142 a2
Cannaregio, Canale di Venice, Italy 142 a2
Cannelton U.S.A. 37°55N 86°45W 311 G10
Cannery, The San Francisco, U.S.A. 136 a1
Cannes France 43°32N 7°1E 175 E11
Canning Town = Port Canning India 22°23N 88°40E 243 H13
Canning Town U.K. 51°30N 0°1E 125 A4
Cannington Canada 44°20N 79°2W 312 B5
Cannóbio Italy 46°4N 8°42E 198 B5
Cannock U.K. 52°41N 2°1W 169 E5
Cannonball ➔ U.S.A. 46°26N 100°35W 308 B3
Cannondale Mt. Australia 25°13S 148°57E 280 D4
Cannonsville Res. U.S.A. 42°4N 75°22W 313 D9
Cannonvale Australia 20°17S 148°43E 280 b
Caño Colorado Colombia 2°18N 68°22W 328 C4
Canoas Brazil 29°56S 51°11W 335 B5
Canoe L. Canada 55°10N 108°15W 297 B7
Cañon City U.S.A. 38°27N 105°14W 304 G11
Cañón del Río Blanco △ Mexico 18°43N 97°15W 319 D5
Cañón del Río Lobos ⌂ Spain 41°46N 3°28W 194 D7
Canonnier, Pte. du St.-Martin 18°4N 63°7W 322 a
Canonniers Pt. Mauritius 20°2S 57°32E 272 e
Canoochee ➔ U.S.A. 31°59N 81°19W 316 D8
Canopus Australia 33°29S 140°42E 282 B4
Canora Canada 51°40N 102°30W 297 C8
Canosa di Púglia Italy 41°13N 16°4E 201 A9
Canouan St. Vincent 12°43N 61°20W 323 n
Canowindra Australia 33°35S 148°38E 283 B8
Canso Canada 45°20N 61°0W 299 C7
Canso, Str. of Canada 45°37N 61°22W 299 C7
Canta Peru 11°29S 76°37W 330 C2
Cantabria ☐ Spain 43°10N 4°0W 194 B7
Cantabria, Sierra de Spain 42°40N 2°30W 196 C2
Cantabrian Mts. = Cantábrica, Cordillera Spain 43°0N 5°10W 194 C5
Cantábrica, Cordillera Spain 43°0N 5°10W 194 C5
Cantal ☐ France 45°5N 2°45E 174 C6
Cantal, Plomb du France 45°3N 2°45E 174 C6
Cantanhede Portugal 40°20N 8°36W 194 E2
Cantaura Venezuela 9°19N 64°21W 329 B5
Cantavieja Spain 40°31N 0°25W 196 E4
Čantavir Serbia 45°55N 19°46E 182 E4
Cantemir Moldova 46°17N 28°14E 183 D13
Canteras de Vallecas Spain 40°20N 3°37W 127 B2
Canterbury = Invermere Canada 50°30N 116°2W 296 C5
Canterbury N.S.W., Australia 33°55S 151°7E 139 B1
Canterbury Queens., Australia 25°23S 141°53E 280 D3
Canterbury Vic., Australia 37°49S 145°4E 128 A2
Canterbury Kent, U.K. 51°16N 1°6E 169 F9
Canterbury ☐ N.Z. 43°45S 171°19E 285 D6
Canterbury Bight N.Z. 44°16S 171°55E 285 E6
Canterbury Plains N.Z. 43°55S 171°22E 285 D6
Cantil U.S.A. 35°18N 117°58W 307 K9
Cantilan Phil. 9°20N 125°58E 233 G5
Cantillana Spain 37°36N 5°50W 195 H5
Canto do Buriti Brazil 8°7S 42°58W 332 C3
Canton = Guangzhou China 23°6N 113°13E 121 B2
Canton Ga., U.S.A. 34°14N 84°29W 315 D12
Canton Ill., U.S.A. 40°33N 90°2W 310 D6
Canton Miss., U.S.A. 32°37N 90°2W 315 E9
Canton Mo., U.S.A. 40°8N 91°32W 310 D5
Canton N.Y., U.S.A. 44°36N 75°10W 313 B9
Canton Ohio, U.S.A. 40°48N 81°23W 312 F3
Canton Pa., U.S.A. 41°39N 76°51W 312 E8
Canton S. Dak., U.S.A. 43°18N 96°35W 308 D5
Canton Tex., U.S.A. 32°33N 95°52W 315 E7
Canton L. U.S.A. 36°6N 98°35W 314 C5
Canton Tower China 23°6N 113°19E 121 B2
Cantonment U.S.A. 30°37N 87°20W 317 E2
Cantù Italy 45°44N 9°8E 198 C6
Cantwell U.S.A. 63°24N 148°57W 303 E10
Canudos Brazil 7°13S 58°5W 331 B6
Canumã Amazonas, Brazil 4°2S 59°4W 329 D6
Canumã Amazonas, Brazil 6°8S 60°10W 331 B5
Canumã ➔ Brazil 3°55S 59°10W 331 A6
Canunda △ Australia 37°42S 140°16E 282 D4
Canutama Brazil 6°30S 64°20W 331 B5
Canutillo U.S.A. 31°55N 106°36W 314 F1
Canvey U.K. 51°31N 0°37E 169 F8
Canyon U.S.A. 34°59N 101°55W 314 D4
Canyon De Chelly ⌂ U.S.A. 36°10N 109°20W 305 H9
Canyonlands △ U.S.A. 38°15N 110°0W 305 G9
Canyons of the Ancients ⌂ U.S.A. 37°30N 108°55W 305 H9
Canyonville U.S.A. 42°56N 123°17W 304 E2
Canzar Angola 7°35S 21°34E 265 D4
Cao Bang Vietnam 22°40N 106°15E 228 F6
Cao He ➔ China 40°10N 124°32E 227 D13
Cao Lanh Vietnam 10°27N 105°38E 237 G5
Cao Xian China 34°50N 115°35E 226 G8
Caofeidian China 38°56N 118°32E 227 E10
Caohejing China 31°10N 121°25E 138 B1
Caombo Angola 8°42S 16°33E 265 D3
Cáorle Italy 45°36N 12°53E 199 C9
Cap-aux-Meules Canada 47°23N 61°52W 299 C7
Cap-Chat Canada 49°6N 66°40W 299 C6
Cap-de-la-Madeleine Canada 46°22N 72°31W 298 C5
Cap-de-Ville Trin. & Tob. 10°9N 61°42W 323 t
Cap-Haïtien Haiti 19°40N 72°20W 321 C5
Cap I. Phil. 5°57N 120°6E 233 J3
Cap Pt. St. Lucia 14°7N 60°57W 323 m
Capac U.S.A. 43°1N 82°56W 312 C2
Capáccio Italy 40°25N 15°5E 201 B8
Capaci Italy 38°10N 13°14E 200 D6
Capaia Angola 8°27S 20°13E 265 D4
Capalonga Phil. 14°20N 122°30E 232 D4
Capanaparo ➔ Venezuela 7°1N 67°7W 328 B4
Capanema Brazil 1°12S 47°11W 332 B2
Capangombe Angola 15°6S 13°8E 265 F2
Capánnori Italy 43°50N 10°34E 198 E7
Capão Redondo Brazil 23°39S 46°45W 137 B1
Caparaó △ Brazil 20°25S 41°46W 333 F3
Caparica Portugal 38°40N 9°9W 126 A2
Caparica, Costa da Portugal 38°38N 9°15W 126 B1
Caparo ➔ Trin. & Tob. 10°31N 61°28W 323 t
Capas Phil. 15°38N 120°28E 232 D3
Capatárida Venezuela 11°11N 70°37W 328 A3
Capayas Phil. 10°28N 119°39E 233 F2
Capbreton France 43°39N 1°26W 174 E2
Capdenac France 44°34N 2°5E 174 D6
Capdepera Spain 39°42N 3°26E 206 B4
Cape ➔ Australia 20°59S 146°51E 280 C4
Cape Arid △ Australia 33°58S 123°13E 279 F3
Cape Barren I. Australia 40°25S 148°15E 281 G4
Cape Basin Atl. Oc. 34°0S 7°0E 152 K12
Cape Breton Highlands △ Canada 46°50N 60°40W 299 C7
Cape Breton I. Canada 46°0N 60°30W 299 C7
Cape Canaveral U.S.A. 28°24N 80°36W 317 G9
Cape Charles U.S.A. 37°16N 76°1W 309 G15
Cape Coast Ghana 5°5N 1°15W 263 D4
Cape Cod ⌂ U.S.A. 41°56N 70°6W 309 E18
Cape Coral U.S.A. 26°33N 81°57W 317 J8
Cape Crawford Australia 16°41S 135°43E 280 B2
Cape Dorset = Kinngait Canada 64°14N 76°32W 295 E16
Cape Fear ➔ U.S.A. 33°53N 78°1W 315 E15
Cape Flats S. Africa 34°3S 18°33E 118 B2
Cape Girardeau U.S.A. 37°19N 89°32W 308 G9
Cape Hatteras ⌂ U.S.A. 35°30N 75°28W 315 D17
Cape Hillsborough △ Australia 20°54S 149°2E 280 b
Cape Jervis Australia 35°40S 138°5E 282 C3
Cape Krusenstern ⌂ U.S.A. 67°30N 163°30W 303 C7
Cape Le Grand △ Australia 33°54S 122°26E 279 F3
Cape Lisburne = Wevok U.S.A. 68°53N 166°13W 303 B6
Cape Lookout ⌂ U.S.A. 35°45N 76°25W 315 D16
Cape May U.S.A. 38°56N 74°56W 309 F16
Cape May Point U.S.A. 38°56N 74°58W 309 F16
Cape Melville △ Australia 14°26S 144°28E 280 A3
Cape Mount △ Liberia 6°44N 11°24W 262 D2
Cape Pole U.S.A. 55°58N 133°48W 303 J14
Cape Range △ Australia 22°3S 114°0E 278 D1
Cape St. George Canada 48°28N 59°14W 299 C8
Cape Tormentine Canada 46°8N 63°47W 299 C7
Cape Town S. Africa 33°55S 18°22E 118 A1
Cape Town Int. ✕ (CPT) S. Africa 33°58S 18°35E 118 A2
Cape Upstart △ Australia 19°45S 147°48E 280 B4
Cape Verde Abyssal Plain Atl. Oc. 23°0N 26°0W 152 D9
Cape Verde Is. ■ Atl. Oc. 16°0N 24°0W 153 j
Cape Verde Plateau Atl. Oc. 18°0N 20°0W 152 E10
Cape Vincent U.S.A. 44°8N 76°20W 313 B8
Cape Yakataga U.S.A. 60°4N 142°26W 303 F12
Cape York Peninsula Australia 12°0S 142°30E 286 F2
Capela Brazil 10°30S 37°0W 332 D4
Capelas Azores 37°50N 25°41W 153 d3
Capele Angola 13°39S 14°53E 265 E2
Capelengue Angola 8°53S 19°42E 265 D3
Capelinha Brazil 17°42S 42°31W 333 E3
Capelinhos, Pta. dos Azores 38°36N 28°50W 153 d1
Capella Australia 23°2S 148°1E 280 C4
Capella, Mt. Papua N. G. 5°4S 141°8E 286 C1
Capelongo Angola 14°54S 15°8E 265 E3
Capenda Camulemba Angola 9°24S 18°27E 265 D3
Capendu France 43°11N 2°31E 174 E6
Capertree Australia 33°6S 149°58E 283 B8
Capestang France 43°20N 3°2E 174 E7
Capesterre, Grande Rivière de la ➔ Guadeloupe 16°3N 61°33W 322 e
Capesterre, Pte. de la Guadeloupe 16°3N 61°33W 322 e
Capesterre-Belle-Eau Guadeloupe 16°4N 61°36W 322 e
Capesterre-de-Marie-Galante Guadeloupe 15°53N 61°14W 322 e
Capim ➔ Brazil 1°40S 47°47W 332 B2
Capinópolis Brazil 18°41S 49°35W 333 E2
Capinota Bolivia 17°43S 66°14W 330 D4
Capira Panama 8°45N 79°53W 328 B2
Capistrello Italy 41°57N 13°23E 199 G10
Capitan U.S.A. 33°35N 105°35W 305 K11
Capitán Aracena, I. Chile 54°10S 71°20W 336 G2
Capitán Arturo Prat Antarctica 63°0S 61°0W 151 C17
Capitán Pastene Chile 38°13S 73°1W 336 A2
Capitão de Campos Brazil 4°40S 41°55W 332 B3
Capitol Heights U.S.A. 38°52N 76°55W 143 B3
Capitol Hill N. Marianas 15°13N 145°45E 302 e
Capitol Reef △ U.S.A. 38°15N 111°10W 305 G8
Capitola U.S.A. 36°59N 121°57W 306 J5
Capitolini, Musei Rome, Italy 136 c3
Capivara, Serra da Brazil 14°35S 45°0W 333 D3
Capiz ☐ Phil. 11°35N 122°30E 233 F4
Capizzi Italy 37°51N 14°29E 201 E7
Capoche ➔ Mozam. 15°35S 33°0E 269 F3
Capodichino, Nápoli ✕ (NAP) Italy 40°53N 14°16E 201 B7
Capodistria = Koper Slovenia 45°31N 13°44E 199 C10
Capoeira Brazil 5°37S 59°33W 331 B6
Capolo Angola 10°22S 14°7E 265 E2
Caporetto = Kobarid Slovenia 46°15N 13°30E 199 B10
Caporolo ➔ Angola 12°56S 12°58E 265 E2
Capot ➔ Martinique 14°50N 61°5W 322 j
Capoterra Italy 39°11N 8°58E 200 C1
Cappadocia Turkey 39°0N 35°0E 212 C6
Capps U.S.A. 30°24N 83°54W 316 E6
Capraia Italy 43°2N 9°50E 198 E6
Caprara, Pta. Italy 41°7N 8°19E 200 A1
Caprarola Italy 42°19N 12°14E 199 F9
Caprera Italy 41°12N 9°28E 200 A2
Capri Italy 40°33N 14°14E 201 B7
Capricorn Coast Australia 23°16S 150°49E 280 C5
Capricorn Group Australia 23°30S 151°55E 280 C5
Capricorn Ra. Australia 23°20S 116°50E 278 D2
Caprino Veronese Italy 45°36N 10°47E 198 C7
Caprivi ☐ Namibia 18°0S 23°0E 270 A3
Caprivi ⌂ Namibia 17°55S 22°37E 270 A3
Caprivi Strip Namibia 18°0S 23°0E 270 A3
Caps et Marais d'Opale ⌂ France 50°40N 2°0E 173 B9
Captain Cook U.S.A. 19°30N 155°55W 302 D6
Captain Cook Bridge Australia 34°0S 151°7E 139 C1
Captain Cook Landing Place Park Australia 34°1S 151°14E 139 C2
Captains Flat Australia 35°35S 149°27E 283 C8
Captieux France 44°18N 0°16W 174 D3
Captiva U.S.A. 26°31N 82°11W 317 J7
Capuçа Angola 17°22S 21°18E 265 F4
Capuchos Portugal 38°38N 9°16W 126 B1
Capucin Dominica 15°38N 61°28W 323 k
Capul I. Phil. 12°26N 124°10E 232 E5
Capulin Volcano ⌂ U.S.A. 36°47N 103°58W 314 C3
Capunda Angola 10°41S 17°23E 265 E3
Caquetá ☐ Colombia 1°0N 74°0W 328 C3
Caquetá ➔ Colombia 1°15S 69°15W 328 D4
Car Nicobar India 9°10N 92°47E 245 K11
Cara-Paraná ➔ Colombia 1°45S 73°13W 328 D3
Carabanchel Alto Spain 40°22N 3°44W 127 B1
Carabanchel Bajo Spain 40°23N 3°44W 127 B1
Carabao I. Phil. 12°4N 121°56E 232 E3
Carabobo ☐ Venezuela 10°10N 68°5W 328 A4
Caracal Romania 44°8N 24°22E 183 F9
Caracaraí Brazil 1°50N 61°8W 329 C5
Caracas Venezuela 10°30N 66°55W 328 A4
Caracol Belize 16°45N 89°6W 320 C2
Caracol Mato Grosso do Sul, Brazil 22°18S 57°1W 334 A4
Caracol Piauí, Brazil 9°15S 43°22W 332 C3
Caracoli, Pte. Martinique 14°45N 60°52W 322 j
Caracollo Bolivia 17°39S 67°10W 330 D4
Caraga Phil. 7°20N 126°34E 233 H6
Caraga ☐ Phil. 9°40N 125°30E 233 G6
Caragabal Australia 33°49S 147°45E 283 B7
Caráglio Italy 44°25N 7°26E 198 D4
Carahue Chile 38°43S 73°12W 336 A2
Caraí Brazil 17°12S 41°42W 333 E3
Caraïbes, Mts. Guadeloupe 16°1N 61°41W 322 e
Carajás Brazil 2°57S 51°22W 332 C1
Carajás, Serra dos Brazil 6°0S 51°30W 332 C1
Caral Peru 10°53S 77°31W 330 C2
Caramoan Phil. 13°46N 123°52E 232 E4
Caramoan Pen. Phil. 13°47N 123°44E 232 E4
Caramoran Phil. 14°0N 124°8E 232 D5
Caranapatuba Brazil 6°38S 62°34W 331 B5
Carandaiti Bolivia 20°45S 63°4W 331 E5
Carangola Brazil 20°44S 42°5W 333 F3
Caransebeş Romania 45°28N 22°18E 182 E7
Carantec France 48°40N 3°55W 172 D3
Carapachay Argentina 34°31S 58°32W 117 B1
Carapichaima Trin. & Tob. 10°28N 61°27W 323 t
Carapo ➔ Barinas, Venezuela 7°46N 70°23W 328 B3
Carapo ➔ Bolívar, Venezuela 7°30N 64°0W 329 B5
Carapuse B. Trin. & Tob. 11°14N 60°35W 323 s
Caraquet Canada 47°48N 64°57W 299 C6
Caraş Severin ☐ Romania 45°10N 22°10E 182 E7
Caraşova Romania 45°11N 21°51E 182 E6
Caratasca, L. de Honduras 15°20N 83°40W 320 C3
Caratinga Brazil 19°50S 42°10W 333 E3
Carauari Brazil 4°52S 66°54W 328 D4
Caraúbas Brazil 5°43S 37°33W 332 C4
Caravaca de la Cruz Spain 38°8N 1°52W 197 G3
Caravággio Italy 45°30N 9°38E 198 C6
Caravela Guinea-Biss. 11°30N 16°30W 262 C1
Caravelas Brazil 17°45S 39°15W 333 E4
Caraveli Peru 15°45S 73°25W 330 D3
Caravelle, Presqu'île de la Martinique 14°46N 60°48W 322 j
Caraz Peru 9°3S 77°47W 330 B2
Caraza Argentina 34°41S 58°25W 117 C2
Carazinho Brazil 28°16S 52°46W 335 B5
Carballino = O Carballiño Spain 42°26N 8°5W 194 C2
Carballo Spain 43°13N 8°41W 194 B2
Carberry Canada 49°50N 99°25W 297 D9
Carbet, Chutes du Guadeloupe 16°2N 61°38W 322 e
Carbet, Pitons du Martinique 14°42N 61°7W 322 j
Carbó Mexico 29°42N 110°58W 318 B2
Carbón, L. del Argentina 49°35S 68°21W 336 C3
Carbonara, C. Italy 39°6N 9°31E 200 C2
Carbondale Colo., U.S.A. 39°24N 107°13W 304 G10
Carbondale Ill., U.S.A. 37°44N 89°13W 310 G7
Carbondale Pa., U.S.A. 41°35N 75°30W 313 E9
Carbonear Canada 47°42N 53°13W 299 C9
Carboneras Spain 36°59N 1°53W 197 J3
Carboneras de Guadazón Spain 39°54N 1°50W 196 F3
Carbónia Italy 39°10N 8°30E 200 C1
Carbonne France 43°18N 1°13E 174 E5
Carcabuey Spain 37°27N 4°17W 195 H6
Carcagente = Carcaixent Spain 39°8N 0°28W 197 F4
Carcaixent Spain 39°8N 0°28W 197 F4
Carcajou Canada 57°47N 117°6W 296 B5
Carcar Phil. 10°3N 123°38E 233 F4
Carcarana ➔ Argentina 32°27S 60°48W 334 C3
Carcasse, C. Haiti 18°30N 74°28W 321 C5
Carcassonne France 43°13N 2°20E 174 E6
Carchi ☐ Ecuador 0°45N 78°0W 328 C2
Carcoar Australia 33°36S 149°8E 283 B8
Carcross Canada 60°13N 134°45W 296 A2
Çardak Çanakkale, Turkey 40°22N 26°43E 203 F10
Çardak Denizli, Turkey 37°49N 29°39E 205 D11
Cardamon Hills India 9°30N 77°15E 245 K3
Cardamon Mts. = Kravanh, Chuor Phnum Cambodia 12°0N 103°32E 237 G4
Cardeña Spain 38°16N 4°20W 195 G6
Cárdenas Cuba 23°0N 81°30W 320 B3
Cárdenas San Luis Potosí, Mexico 22°0N 99°38W 319 C5
Cárdenas Tabasco, Mexico 17°59N 93°22W 319 D6
Cardener ➔ Spain 41°41N 1°51E 196 D6
Cardenete Spain 39°46N 1°41W 196 F3
Cardiel, L. Argentina 48°55S 71°10W 336 C2
Cardiff U.K. 51°29N 3°10W 169 F4
Cardiff ☐ U.K. 51°31N 3°12W 169 F4
Cardiff-by-the-Sea U.S.A. 33°1N 117°17W 307 M9
Cardigan U.K. 52°5N 4°40W 169 E3
Cardigan B. U.K. 52°30N 4°30W 169 E3
Cardinal Canada 44°47N 75°23W 313 B9
Cardón, Punta Venezuela 11°37N 70°14W 328 A3
Cardona Spain 41°56N 1°40E 196 D6
Cardona Uruguay 33°53S 57°18W 334 C4
Cardoso, Ilha do Brazil 25°8S 47°58W 335 B5
Cardross Canada 49°50N 105°40W 297 D7
Cardstadt Canada 18°14S 146°2E 280 B4
Cardwell Australia 18°14S 146°2E 280 B4
Careen L. Canada 57°0N 108°11W 297 B7
Carei Romania 47°40N 22°29E 182 C7
Careiro Brazil 3°12S 59°45W 329 D6
Carenage Trin. & Tob. 10°41N 61°36W 323 t
Carentan France 49°19N 1°15W 172 C5
Carey Idaho, U.S.A. 43°19N 113°57W 304 E7
Carey Ohio, U.S.A. 40°57N 83°23W 311 D13
Carey, L. Australia 29°0S 122°15E 279 E3
Carey L. Canada 62°12N 102°55W 297 A8
Careysburg Liberia 6°34N 10°30W 262 D2
Cargèse France 42°7N 8°35E 175 F12
Carhaix-Plouguer France 48°18N 3°36W 172 D3
Carhuamayo Peru 10°51S 76°4W 330 C2
Carhuas Peru 9°15S 77°39W 330 B2
Carhué Argentina 37°10S 62°50W 334 D3
Caria Turkey 37°20N 28°10E 205 D10
Cariacica Brazil 20°16S 40°25W 333 F3
Cariaco Venezuela 10°29N 63°33W 329 A5
Cariango Angola 10°37S 15°20E 265 E3
Cariati Italy 39°30N 16°57E 201 C9
Caribbean Sea W. Indies 15°0N 75°0W 320 C4
Cariboo Mts. Canada 53°0N 121°0W 296 C4
Caribou U.S.A. 46°52N 68°1W 309 B19
Caribou ➔ Man., Canada 59°20N 94°44W 297 B10
Caribou ➔ N.W.T., Canada 61°27N 125°45W 296 A3
Caribou I. Canada 47°22N 85°49W 298 C2
Caribou Is. Canada 61°55N 113°15W 296 A6
Caribou L. Man., Canada 59°21N 96°10W 297 B9
Caribou L. Ont., Canada 50°25N 89°5W 298 B2
Caribou Mts. Canada 59°12N 115°40W 296 B5
Caribou River ⌂ Canada 59°35N 96°35W 297 B9
Caribrod = Dimitrovgrad Serbia 43°2N 22°48E 202 C6
Carichic Mexico 27°56N 107°3W 318 B3
Caridad Phil. 14°28N 120°53E 127 C1
Carigara Phil. 11°18N 124°41E 233 F5
Carigara B. Phil. 11°22N 124°37E 233 F5
Carignan France 49°38N 5°10E 173 C12
Carignano Italy 44°55N 7°40E 198 D4
Carinda Australia 30°28S 147°41E 283 A7
Cariñena Spain 41°20N 1°13W 196 D3
Carinhanha Brazil 14°15S 44°46W 333 D3
Carinhanha ➔ Brazil 14°20S 43°47W 333 D3
Carini Italy 38°8N 13°11E 200 D6
Cariño Spain 43°45N 7°52W 194 B3
Carínola Italy 41°11N 13°58E 200 A6
Carinthia = Kärnten ☐ Austria 46°52N 13°30E 180 E6
Carioca, Sa. da Brazil 22°57S 43°13W 135 B1
Caripito Venezuela 10°8N 63°6W 329 A5
Cariré Brazil 3°57S 40°27W 332 B3
Caritianas Brazil 9°20S 63°6W 331 B5
Carles Phil. 11°34N 123°8E 233 F4
Carlet Spain 39°14N 0°31W 197 F4
Carleton, Mt. Canada 47°23N 66°53W 299 C6
Carleton Place Canada 45°8N 76°9W 313 A8
Carletonville S. Africa 26°23S 27°22E 270 C4
Cărlibaba Romania 47°35N 25°8E 183 C10
Carlin U.S.A. 40°43N 116°7W 304 F5
Carlingford L. U.K. 54°3N 6°9W 166 B5
Carlinville U.S.A. 39°17N 89°53W 310 E7
Carlisle Cumb., U.K. 54°54N 2°56W 168 C5
Carlisle Ind., U.S.A. 38°58N 87°24W 311 F9
Carlisle Ky., U.S.A. 38°19N 84°1W 311 F12
Carlisle Pa., U.S.A. 40°12N 77°12W 312 F7
Carlisle I. Australia 20°49S 149°18E 280 b
Carlit, Pic France 42°35N 1°55E 174 F5
Carloforte Italy 39°8N 8°18E 200 C1
Carlos Casares Argentina 35°32S 61°20W 334 D3
Carlos Chagas Brazil 17°43S 40°45W 333 E3
Carlos Tejedor Argentina 35°25S 62°25W 334 D3
Carlota I. Phil. 13°1N 121°53E 232 E3
Carlow Ireland 52°50N 6°56W 166 D5
Carlow ☐ Ireland 52°43N 6°50W 166 D5
Carlsbad = Karlovy Vary Czech Rep. 50°13N 12°51E 180 A5
Carlsbad Calif., U.S.A. 33°10N 117°21W 307 M9
Carlsbad N. Mex., U.S.A. 32°25N 104°14W 305 K11
Carlsbad Caverns △ U.S.A. 32°10N 104°35W 305 K11
Carlsberg Ridge Ind. Oc. 1°0N 66°0E 273 D5
Carlstadt U.S.A. 40°50N 74°6W 132 A1
Carlton Australia 37°47S 144°57E 128 A1
Carlton Gardens Australia 37°48S 144°58E 128 A1
Carluke U.K. 55°45N 3°50W 167 F5
Carlyle Sask., Canada 49°40N 102°20W 297 D8
Carlyle Ill., U.S.A. 38°37N 89°22W 310 F7
Carlyle L. U.S.A. 38°37N 89°21W 310 F7
Carmacks Canada 62°5N 136°16W 294 E4
Carmagnola Italy 44°51N 7°43E 198 D4
Carman Canada 49°30N 98°0W 297 D9
Carmarthen U.K. 51°52N 4°19W 169 F3
Carmarthen B. U.K. 51°40N 4°30W 169 F3
Carmarthenshire ☐ U.K. 51°55N 4°13W 169 F3
Carmaux France 44°3N 2°10E 174 D6
Carmel Ind., U.S.A. 39°58N 86°7W 310 E10
Carmel N.Y., U.S.A. 41°26N 73°41W 313 E11
Carmel, Mt. = Ha Karmel, Har Israel 32°44N 35°3E 250 F5
Carmel-by-the-Sea U.S.A. 36°33N 121°55W 306 J5
Carmel Valley U.S.A. 36°29N 121°43W 306 J5
Carmelitane Scalze, Monastero Venice, Italy 142 a2
Carmelo Uruguay 34°0S 58°20W 334 C4
Carmen Bolivia 11°40S 67°51W 330 C4
Carmen Paraguay 27°13S 56°12W 335 B4
Carmen Bohol, Phil. 9°50N 124°12E 233 G5
Carmen Cebu, Phil. 10°35N 124°1E 233 F5
Carmen N. Cotabato, Phil. 7°13N 124°45E 233 H5
Carmen Venezuela 1°16N 66°52W 328 C4
Carmen, I. Mexico 25°57N 111°12W 318 B2
Carmen de Huechuraba Chile 33°20S 70°40W 137 B1
Carmen de la Legua -Reynosa Peru 12°3S 77°7W 124 B2
Carmen de Patagones Argentina 40°50S 63°0W 336 B4
Cármenes Spain 42°58N 5°34W 194 C5
Carmensa Argentina 35°15S 67°40W 334 D2
Carmi B.C., Canada 49°36N 119°8W 296 D5
Carmi Ill., U.S.A. 38°5N 88°10W 311 F8
Carmichael Village Bahamas 25°0N 77°26W 153 b
Carmila Australia 21°55S 149°24E 280 C4
Carmini, Scuola dei Venice, Italy 142 b2
Carmona Costa Rica 10°0N 85°15W 320 E2
Carmona Spain 37°28N 5°42W 195 H5
Carn Ban U.K. 57°7N 4°15W 167 D4
Carn Eige U.K. 57°17N 5°8W 167 D3
Carnac France 47°35N 3°6W 172 E3
Carnamah Australia 29°41S 115°53E 279 E2
Carnarvon W. Austral., Australia 24°51S 113°42E 279 D1
Carnarvon Ont., Canada 45°3N 78°41W 312 A6
Carnarvon Northern Cape, S. Africa 30°56S 22°8E 270 D3
Carnarvon △ Australia 24°54S 148°2E 280 C4
Carnarvon Ra. Queens., Australia 25°15S 148°30E 280 D4
Carnarvon Ra. W. Austral., Australia 25°20S 120°45E 279 E3
Carnatic India 12°0N 79°0E 245 H3
Carnation U.S.A. 47°39N 121°55W 306 C5
Carnaxide Portugal 38°43N 9°14W 126 A1
Carncastle U.K. 54°54N 5°53W 166 B6
Carndonagh Ireland 55°16N 7°15W 166 A4
Carnduff Canada 49°10N 101°50W 297 D8
Carnegie Vic., Australia 37°53S 145°3E 128 B2
Carnegie Pa., U.S.A. 40°24N 80°5W 312 F4
Carnegie, L. Australia 26°5S 122°30E 279 E3
Carnegie Hall New York, U.S.A. 132 c2
Carnegie Ridge Pac. Oc. 1°0S 87°0W 289 H19
Carney I. Antarctica 74°0S 121°0W 151 D14
Carnic Alps = Karnische Alpen Europe 46°36N 13°0E 180 E6
Carniche Alpi = Karnische Alpen Europe 46°36N 13°0E 180 E6
Carnide Portugal 38°45N 9°10W 126 A1
Carnot C.A.R. 4°59N 15°56E 264 B3
Carnot, C. Australia 34°57S 135°38E 281 E2
Carnot B. Australia 17°20S 122°15E 278 C3
Carnoustie U.K. 56°30N 2°42W 167 E6
Carnsore Pt. Ireland 52°10N 6°22W 166 D5
Caro U.S.A. 43°29N 83°24W 309 D12
Caroço São Tomé & Príncipe 1°32N 7°27E 265 a
Caroga Lake U.S.A. 43°8N 74°28W 313 C10
Carol City U.S.A. 25°56N 80°14W 317 K9
Carolina Brazil 7°10S 47°30W 332 C2
Carolina Puerto Rico 18°23N 65°58W 321 C6
Carolina Mpumalanga, S. Africa 26°5S 30°6E 271 C5
Carolinas Pt. N. Marianas 14°55N 145°38E 302 e
Caroline I. Kiribati 9°58S 150°13W 289 H12

**Caroline Is.** *Micronesia* 8°0N 150°0E **288** G6
**Caroline Pk.** *N.Z.* 45°57S 167°15E **285** F2
**Carollton** *U.S.A.* 29°57N 90°8W **131** B2
**Carondelet Reef** *Kiribati* 5°33S 173°50E **277** B16
**Caroni** *Trin. & Tob.* 10°34N 61°23W **323** t
**Caroni** → *Trin. & Tob.* 10°37N 61°30W **323** t
**Caroni** → *Venezuela* 8°21N 62°43W **329** B5
**Caroni Arena Res.**
*Trin. & Tob.* 10°33N 61°15W **323** t
**Caroni Bird Sanctuary**
*Trin. & Tob.* 10°36N 61°28W **323** t
**Caroni Swamp** *Trin. & Tob.* 10°36N 61°27W **323** t
**Caronie = Nébrodi, Monti**
*Italy* 37°54N 14°35E **201** E7
**Caroona** *Australia* 31°24S 150°26E **283** A9
**Carora** *Venezuela* 10°11N 70°5W **328** A4
**Carpathians** *Europe* 49°30N 21°0E **177** D11
**Carpaţii Meridionali**
*Romania* 45°30N 25°0E **183** E9
**Carpentaria, G. of** *Australia* 14°0S 139°0E **280** A2
**Carpentersville** *U.S.A.* 42°6N 88°17W **311** B8
**Carpentras** *France* 44°3N 5°2E **175** D9
**Carpi** *Italy* 44°47N 10°53E **198** D7
**Carpina** *Brazil* 7°51S 35°15W **332** C4
**Cărpineni** *Moldova* 46°46N 28°22E **183** D13
**Carpinteria** *U.S.A.* 34°24N 119°31W **307** L7
**Carpio** *Spain* 41°13N 5°7W **194** D5
**Carr Boyd Ra.** *Australia* 16°15S 128°35E **278** C4
**Carra, L.** *Ireland* 53°41N 9°14W **166** C2
**Carrabelle** *U.S.A.* 29°51N 84°40W **316** F5
**Carraig Mhachaire Rois =**
**Carrickmacross** *Ireland* 53°59N 6°43W **166** C5
**Carraig na Siúire = Carrick-on-Suir**
*Ireland* 52°21N 7°24W **166** D4
**Carral** *Spain* 43°14N 8°21W **194** B2
**Carranglan** *Phil.* 15°58N 121°4E **232** D3
**Carranya** ◎ *Australia* 19°13S 127°46E **278** C4
**Carrara** *Italy* 44°5N 10°6E **198** D7
**Carrascal** *Santiago, Chile* 33°25S 70°42W **137** B1
**Carrascal** *Phil.* 9°22N 125°56E **233** G5
**Carrasco** △ *Bolivia* 17°23S 64°59W **331** D5
**Carrascosa del Campo**
*Spain* 40°2N 2°45W **196** E2
**Carrauntoohill** *Ireland* 52°0N 9°45W **166** D2
**Carretas, Punta** *Peru* 14°12S 76°17W **330** C2
**Carriacou** *Grenada* 12°29N 61°26W **323** q
**Carrick-on-Shannon**
*Ireland* 53°57N 8°7W **166** C3
**Carrick-on-Suir** *Ireland* 52°21N 7°24W **166** D4
**Carrickfergus** *U.K.* 54°43N 5°49W **166** B6
**Carrickmacross** *Ireland* 53°59N 6°43W **166** C5
**Carrickmines** *Ireland* 53°15N 6°10W **120** B3
**Carrières-sous-Bois** *France* 48°55N 2°6E **134** A1
**Carrières-sous-Poissy**
*France* 48°56N 2°2E **134** A1
**Carrières-sur-Seine** *France* 48°55N 2°11E **134** A2
**Carrieton** *Australia* 32°25S 138°31E **282** B3
**Carrigaline** *Ireland* 51°48N 8°23W **166** E3
**Carrigeen B.** *Ireland* 53°24N 6°5W **120** A3
**Carrillo** *Mexico* 26°54N 103°55W **318** B4
**Carrington** *U.S.A.* 47°27N 99°8W **308** B4
**Carrión** → *Spain* 41°53N 4°32W **194** D6
**Carrión de los Condes**
*Spain* 42°20N 4°37W **194** C6
**Carrizal Bajo** *Chile* 28°5S 71°20W **334** B1
**Carrizalillo** *Chile* 29°5S 71°30W **334** B1
**Carrizo Cr.** → *U.S.A.* 36°55N 103°55W **305** H12
**Carrizo Plain** ⌂ *U.S.A.* 35°11N 119°47W **306** K7
**Carrizo Springs** *U.S.A.* 28°31N 99°52W **314** G5
**Carrizozo** *U.S.A.* 33°38N 105°53W **305** K11
**Carroll** *U.S.A.* 42°4N 94°52W **310** D2
**Carrollton** *Ga., U.S.A.* 33°35N 85°5W **316** B4
**Carrollton** *Ill., U.S.A.* 39°18N 90°24W **310** E6
**Carrollton** *Ky., U.S.A.* 38°41N 85°11W **311** F11
**Carrollton** *Mo., U.S.A.* 39°22N 93°30W **310** E3
**Carrollton** *Ohio, U.S.A.* 40°34N 81°5W **312** F3
**Carron** → *U.K.* 57°53N 4°22W **167** D4
**Carron, L.** *U.K.* 57°22N 5°35W **167** D3
**Carrot** → *Canada* 53°50N 101°17W **297** C8
**Carrot River** *Canada* 53°17N 103°35W **297** C8
**Carrouges** *France* 48°34N 0°10W **172** D6
**Carrù** *Italy* 44°29N 7°52E **198** D4
**Carruthers** *Canada* 52°52N 109°16W **297** C7
**Carsa Dek** *Ethiopia* 5°13N 39°50E **257** F4
**Çarşamba** *Turkey* 41°11N 36°44E **212** B7
**Carsòli** *Italy* 42°6N 13°5E **199** F10
**Carson** *Calif., U.S.A.* 33°49N 118°16W **307** M8
**Carson** *N. Dak., U.S.A.* 46°25N 101°34W **308** B3
**Carson** → *U.S.A.* 39°45N 118°40W **306** F8
**Carson City** *Mich.,*
*U.S.A.* 43°11N 84°51W **311** A12
**Carson City** *Nev., U.S.A.* 39°10N 119°46W **306** F7
**Carson Sink** *U.S.A.* 39°50N 118°25W **304** G4
**Carstensz Pyramid = Jaya, Puncak**
*Indonesia* 3°57S 137°17E **231** E9
**Cartagena** *Colombia* 10°25N 75°33W **328** A2
**Cartagena** *Spain* 37°38N 0°59W **197** H4
**Cartago** *Colombia* 4°45N 75°55W **328** C2
**Cartago** *Costa Rica* 9°50N 83°55W **320** E3
**Cártama** *Spain* 36°43N 4°39W **195** J6
**Cartaxo** *Portugal* 39°10N 8°47W **195** F2
**Cartaya** *Spain* 37°16N 7°9W **195** H3
**Carteret Is. = Kilinailau Is.**
*Papua N. G.* 4°45S 155°20E **286** C8
**Cartersville** *U.S.A.* 34°10N 84°48W **316** A5
**Carterton** *N.Z.* 41°2S 175°31E **284** H4
**Carterville** *U.S.A.* 37°46N 89°5W **310** G7
**Carthage** *Tunisia* 36°52N 10°20E **200** F3
**Carthage** *Ill., U.S.A.* 40°25N 91°8W **310** D5
**Carthage** *Mo., U.S.A.* 37°11N 94°19W **308** G6
**Carthage** *N.Y., U.S.A.* 43°59N 75°37W **313** C9
**Carthage** *Tex., U.S.A.* 32°9N 94°20W **314** E7
**Cartier I.** *Australia* 12°31S 123°29E **278** B3
**Cartierville** *Canada* 45°31N 73°42W **130** A1
**Cartwright** *Canada* 53°41N 56°58W **299** B8
**Caruaru** *Brazil* 8°15S 35°55W **332** C4
**Carúpano** *Venezuela* 10°39N 63°15W **329** A5
**Caruray** *Phil.* 10°20N 119°0E **233** F2
**Carutapera** *Brazil* 1°13S 46°1W **332** B2
**Caruthersville** *U.S.A.* 36°11N 89°39W **308** G9
**Carvalho** *Brazil* 2°16S 51°29W **329** D7
**Carvin** *France* 50°30N 2°57E **173** B9
**Carvoeiro** *Brazil* 1°30S 61°59W **329** D5
**Carvoeiro, C.** *Portugal* 39°21N 9°24W **195** F1
**Cary** *Ill., U.S.A.* 42°13N 88°14W **311** B8
**Cary** *N.C., U.S.A.* 35°47N 78°46W **315** D15
**Cas-gwent = Chepstow**
*U.K.* 51°38N 2°41W **169** F5
**Casa, Pas de la = Envalira, Port d'**
*Europe* 42°33N 1°43E **196** C6
**Casa Branca** *Brazil* 21°46S 47°4W **333** F2
**Casa Branca** *Portugal* 38°29N 8°12W **195** G2
**Casa de Piedra** *Argentina* 38°5S 67°28W **334** D2
**Casa de Piedra, Embalse**
*Argentina* 38°5S 67°32W **334** D2
**Casa Grande** *U.S.A.* 32°53N 111°45W **305** K8
**Casa Loma** *Canada* 43°41N 79°24W **141** A2
**Casa Nova** *Brazil* 9°25S 41°5W **332** C3
**Casa Verde** *Brazil* 23°29S 46°40W **137** A1
**Casablanca** *Chile* 33°20S 71°25W **334** C1
**Casablanca** *Morocco* 33°36N 7°36W **260** B3
**Casablanca** ☐ *Morocco* 33°38N 7°30W **260** B3
**Casacalenda** *Italy* 41°44N 14°51E **199** G11
**Casal da Mira** *Portugal* 38°47N 9°14W **126** A1
**Casàl Morena** *Italy* 41°49N 12°37E **136** C2
**Casalbordino** *Italy* 42°9N 14°35E **199** F11
**Casale Monferrato** *Italy* 45°8N 8°27E **198** C5
**Casalmaggiore** *Italy* 44°59N 10°26E **198** D7
**Casalotti** *Italy* 41°54N 12°22E **136** B1
**Casalpusterlengo** *Italy* 45°11N 9°39E **198** C6
**Casamance** → *Senegal* 12°33N 16°46W **262** C1
**Casanare** ☐ *Colombia* 5°30N 72°0W **328** B3
**Casanare** → *Colombia* 6°2N 69°51W **328** B4
**Casarano** *Italy* 40°0N 18°10E **201** B11
**Casares** *Spain* 36°27N 5°16W **195** J5
**Casas Ibáñez** *Spain* 39°17N 1°30W **197** F3
**Casasimarro** *Spain* 39°22N 2°3W **197** F2
**Casatejada** *Spain* 39°54N 5°40W **194** F5
**Casavieja** *Spain* 40°17N 4°46W **194** E6
**Cascada de Basaseachic** △
*Mexico* 28°9N 108°15W **318** B3
**Cascade** *Seychelles* 4°39S 55°29E **272** c
**Cascade** *Idaho, U.S.A.* 44°31N 116°2W **304** D5
**Cascade** *Iowa, U.S.A.* 42°18N 91°0W **310** B6
**Cascade** *Mont., U.S.A.* 47°16N 111°42W **304** C8
**Cascade Heights** *U.S.A.* 33°43N 84°26W **113** B2
**Cascade Locks** *U.S.A.* 45°40N 121°54W **306** E5
**Cascade Pt.** *N.Z.* 44°1S 168°20E **285** E3
**Cascade Ra.** *U.S.A.* 47°0N 121°30W **306** D5
**Cascade Res.** *U.S.A.* 44°32N 116°3W **304** D5
**Cascades, Pte. des** *Réunion* 21°9S 55°51E **272** f
**Cascais** *Portugal* 38°41N 9°25W **195** G1
**Cascavel** *Ceará, Brazil* 4°7S 38°14W **332** B4
**Cascavel** *Paraná, Brazil* 24°57S 53°28W **335** A5
**Cáscina** *Italy* 43°41N 10°33E **198** E7
**Casco B.** *U.S.A.* 43°45N 70°0W **309** D19
**Case Noyale** *Mauritius* 20°23S 57°22E **272** e
**Case-Pilote** *Martinique* 14°38N 61°9W **322** j
**Caselle Torinese** *Italy* 45°10N 7°39E **198** C4
**Caserta** *Italy* 41°4N 14°20E **201** A7
**Casey** *Antarctica* 66°0S 76°0E **151** C8
**Casey** *Ill., U.S.A.* 39°18N 87°59W **311** E9
**Caseyr, Raas = Asir, Ras**
*Somalia* 11°55N 51°10E **267** B7
**Cashel** *Ireland* 52°30N 7°53W **166** D4
**Casibare** → *Colombia* 3°48N 72°18W **328** C3
**Casiguran** *Phil.* 16°22N 122°7E **232** C4
**Casiguran Sound** *Phil.* 16°6N 121°58E **232** C3
**Casilda** *Argentina* 33°10S 61°10W **334** C3
**Casim = General Toshevo**
*Bulgaria* 43°42N 28°6E **203** C12
**Casimcea** *Romania* 44°45N 28°23E **183** F13
**Casino** *Australia* 28°52S 153°3E **281** D5
**Casiquiare** → *Venezuela* 2°1N 67°7W **328** C4
**Casitas** *Peru* 3°54S 80°39W **330** A1
**Čáslav** *Czech Rep.* 49°54N 15°22E **180** B8
**Casma** *Peru* 9°30S 78°20W **330** B2
**Casmalia** *U.S.A.* 34°50N 120°32W **307** L6
**Casnewydd = Newport**
*U.K.* 51°35N 3°0W **169** F5
**Cásola Valsénio** *Italy* 44°12N 11°40E **199** D8
**Cásoli** *Italy* 42°7N 14°18E **199** F11
**Caspe** *Spain* 41°14N 0°1W **196** D4
**Casper** *U.S.A.* 42°51N 106°19W **304** E10
**Caspian Depression** *Eurasia* 47°0N 48°0E **191** G9
**Caspian Sea** *Eurasia* 43°0N 50°0E **187** F9
**Cass City** *U.S.A.* 43°36N 83°10W **312** C1
**Cass Lake** *U.S.A.* 47°23N 94°37W **308** B6
**Cassà de la Selva** *Spain* 41°53N 2°52E **196** D7
**Cassadaga** *U.S.A.* 42°20N 79°19W **312** D5
**Cassai** *Angola* 10°33S 21°59E **265** E4
**Cassai** → *Angola* 3°2S 16°57E **265** E4
**Cassamba** *Angola* 13°6S 20°18E **265** E4
**Cassano allo Iónio** *Italy* 39°47N 16°20E **201** C9
**Casselberry** *U.S.A.* 28°41N 81°20W **317** G8
**Casselman** *Canada* 45°19N 75°5W **313** A9
**Casselton** *U.S.A.* 46°54N 97°13W **308** B5
**Cassiar Mts.** *Canada* 59°30N 130°30W **296** B2
**Cassilândia** *Brazil* 19°9S 51°45W **331** D7
**Cassilis** *Australia* 32°3S 149°58E **283** B8
**Cassinga** *Angola* 15°5S 16°4E **265** F3
**Cassino** *Italy* 41°30N 13°49E **200** A6
**Cassis** *France* 43°14N 5°32E **175** E9
**Cassoalala** *Angola* 9°30S 14°25E **265** D2
**Cassoango** *Angola* 13°42S 20°56E **265** E4
**Cassongue** *Angola* 11°53S 15°2E **265** E3
**Cassopolis** *U.S.A.* 41°55N 86°1W **311** C10
**Cassunda** *Angola* 10°57S 21°3E **265** E4
**Cassville** *Mo., U.S.A.* 36°41N 93°52W **308** G7
**Cassville** *Wis., U.S.A.* 42°43N 90°59W **310** B6
**Castagneto Carducci** *Italy* 43°9N 10°36E **198** E7
**Castaic** *U.S.A.* 34°30N 118°38W **307** L8
**Castalia** *U.S.A.* 41°24N 82°49W **312** E2
**Castanhal** *Brazil* 1°18S 47°55W **332** B2
**Castara** *Trin. & Tob.* 11°17N 60°42W **323** s
**Castara B.** *Trin. & Tob.* 11°17N 60°42W **323** s
**Casteddu = Cágliari** *Italy* 39°13N 9°7E **200** C2
**Castéggio** *Italy* 45°0N 9°7E **198** C6
**Castejón de Monegros**
*Spain* 41°37N 0°15W **196** D4
**Castel Guadeloupe** 16°15N 61°35W **322** e
**Castèl del Monte** *Italy* 41°5N 16°16E **201** A9
**Castèl di Leva** *Italy* 41°46N 12°33E **136** C2
**Castèl di Sangro** *Italy* 41°47N 14°6E **199** G11
**Castèl San Giovanni** *Italy* 45°4N 9°26E **198** C6
**Castèl San Pietro Terme**
*Italy* 44°24N 11°35E **199** D8
**Castèl Sant'Angelo** *Rome, Italy* **136** b1
**Castelbuono** *Italy* 37°56N 14°5E **201** E7
**Castelfidardo** *Italy* 43°28N 13°33E **199** E10
**Castelfiorentino** *Italy* 43°36N 10°58E **198** E7
**Castelfranco Véneto** *Italy* 45°40N 11°55E **199** C8
**Casteljaloux** *France* 44°19N 0°6E **174** D4
**Castell-Nedd = Neath** *U.K.* 51°39N 3°48W **169** F4
**Castellabate** *Italy* 40°17N 14°57E **201** B7
**Castellammare, G. di** *Italy* 38°8N 12°54E **200** D5
**Castellammare del Golfo**
*Italy* 38°1N 12°53E **200** D5
**Castellammare di Stábia**
*Italy* 40°42N 14°29E **201** B7
**Castellamonte** *Italy* 45°23N 7°42E **198** C4
**Castellane** *France* 43°50N 6°31E **175** E10
**Castellaneta** *Italy* 40°38N 16°56E **201** B9
**Castelli** *Argentina* 36°7S 57°47W **334** D4
**Castello** *Venice, Italy* **142** b4
**Castelló de la Plana** *Spain* 39°58N 0°3W **196** F4
**Castellón de la Plana** ☐
*Spain* 40°15N 0°5W **196** E4
**Castellote** *Spain* 40°48N 0°15W **196** E4
**Castelmáuro** *Italy* 41°50N 14°43E **199** G11
**Castelnau-de-Médoc** *France* 45°2N 0°48W **174** C3
**Castelnau-Magnoac**
*France* 43°17N 0°31E **174** E4
**Castelnaudary** *France* 43°20N 1°58E **174** E5
**Castelnovo ne' Monti**
*Italy* 44°26N 10°24E **198** D7
**Castelnuovo di Val di Cécina**
*Italy* 43°12N 10°59E **198** E7
**Castelo = Manuel Urbano**
*Brazil* 8°53S 69°18W **330** B4
**Castelo** *Brazil* 20°33S 41°14W **333** F3
**Castelo, Pta. do** *Azores* 36°56N 25°1W **153** d4
**Castelo Branco** *Azores* 38°31N 28°44W **153** d1
**Castelo Branco** *Portugal* 39°50N 7°31W **194** F3
**Castelo Branco** ☐ *Portugal* 39°52N 7°45W **194** F3
**Castelo de Paiva** *Portugal* 41°2N 8°16W **194** D2
**Castelo de Vide** *Portugal* 39°25N 7°27W **195** F3
**Castelo do Piauí** *Brazil* 5°20S 41°33W **332** C3
**Castelrosso = Megisti**
*Greece* 36°8N 29°34E **205** E11
**Castelsardo** *Italy* 40°55N 8°43E **200** B1
**Castelsarrasin** *France* 44°2N 1°7E **174** D5
**Casteltérmini** *Italy* 37°32N 13°39E **200** E6
**Castelvetrano** *Italy* 37°41N 12°47E **200** E5
**Castendo** *Angola* 8°39S 14°10E **265** D2
**Casterton** *Australia* 37°30S 141°30E **282** D4
**Castets** *France* 43°52N 1°6W **174** E2
**Castiglion Fiorentino** *Italy* 43°20N 11°55E **199** E8
**Castiglione = Bou Ismaïl**
*Algeria* 36°38N 2°42E **261** A5
**Castiglione del Lago** *Italy* 43°7N 12°3E **199** E9
**Castiglione della Pescáia**
*Italy* 42°46N 10°53E **198** F7
**Castiglione delle Stiviere**
*Italy* 45°23N 10°29E **198** C7
**Castilblanco** *Spain* 39°17N 5°5W **195** F5
**Castile** *U.S.A.* 42°38N 78°3W **312** D6
**Castilla** *Peru* 5°12S 80°38W **330** B1
**Castilla, Playa de** *Spain* 37°0N 6°33W **195** J4
**Castilla-La Mancha** ☐
*Spain* 39°30N 3°30W **195** F7
**Castilla y Leon** ☐ *Spain* 42°0N 5°0W **194** D6
**Castillo de Locubín** *Spain* 37°32N 3°56W **195** H7
**Castillo de San Marcos** ⌂
*U.S.A.* 29°54N 81°19W **316** F8
**Castillon-en-Couserans**
*France* 42°56N 1°1E **174** F5
**Castillonès** *France* 44°39N 0°37E **174** D4
**Castillos** *Uruguay* 34°12S 53°52W **335** C5
**Castle Bruce** *Dominica* 15°26N 61°16W **323** k
**Castle Dale** *U.S.A.* 39°13N 111°1W **304** G8
**Castle Douglas** *U.K.* 54°56N 3°56W **167** G5
**Castle Harbour** *Bermuda* 32°21N 64°40W **153** a
**Castle Mt.** *Jamaica* 18°8N 76°22W **320** a
**Castle of Good Hope** *Cape Town, S. Africa* **118** c3
**Castle Peak B.**
*Hong Kong, China* 22°23N 113°58E **122** A1
**Castle Pk.**
*Hong Kong, China* 22°23N 113°57E **122** A1
**Castle Roads** *Bermuda* 32°20N 64°40W **153** a
**Castle Rock** *Colo.,*
*U.S.A.* 39°22N 104°51W **304** G11
**Castle Rock** *Wash.,*
*U.S.A.* 46°17N 122°54W **306** D4
**Castle Rock Pt.** *St. Helena* 16°1S 5°45W **153** h
**Castlebar** *Ireland* 53°52N 9°18W **166** C2
**Castlebay** *U.K.* 56°57N 7°31W **167** E1
**Castleblayney** *Ireland* 54°7N 6°44W **166** B5
**Castlecliff** *N.Z.* 39°57S 175°5E **284** F4
**Castlecomer** *Ireland* 52°48N 7°14W **166** D4
**Castlederg** *U.K.* 54°42N 7°36W **166** B4
**Castleford** *U.K.* 53°43N 1°21W **168** D6
**Castlegar** *Canada* 49°20N 117°40W **296** D5
**Castleisland** *Ireland* 52°14N 9°28W **166** D2
**Castleknock** *Ireland* 53°22N 6°21W **120** A1
**Castlemaine** *Vic., Australia* 37°2S 144°12E **282** D6
**Castlemaine** *Kerry, Ireland* 52°10N 9°42W **166** D2
**Castlepoint** *N.Z.* 40°54S 176°15E **284** G5
**Castlepollard** *Ireland* 53°41N 7°19W **166** C4
**Castlerea** *Ireland* 53°46N 8°29W **166** C3
**Castlereagh** → *Australia* 30°12S 147°32E **283** A7
**Castlereagh B.** *Australia* 12°10S 135°10E **280** A2
**Castleton** *U.S.A.* 43°37N 73°11W **313** C11
**Castleton Corners** *U.S.A.* 40°36N 74°8W **132** C1
**Castleton-on-Hudson**
*U.S.A.* 42°31N 73°45W **313** D11
**Castletown** *I. of Man* 54°5N 4°38W **168** C3
**Castletown Bearhaven**
*Ireland* 51°39N 9°55W **166** E2
**Castor** *Canada* 52°15N 111°50W **296** C6
**Castor** → *Canada* 53°24N 78°58W **298** B4
**Castorland** *U.S.A.* 43°53N 75°31W **313** C9
**Castres** *France* 43°37N 2°13E **174** E6
**Castricum** *Neths.* 52°33N 4°40E **170** B4
**Castries** *St. Lucia* 14°2N 60°58W **323** m
**Castril** *Spain* 37°48N 2°46W **195** H8
**Castro** *Brazil* 24°45S 50°0W **335** A6
**Castro** *Chile* 42°30S 73°50W **336** B2
**Castro Alves** *Brazil* 12°46S 39°33W **333** D4
**Castro del Río** *Spain* 37°41N 4°29W **195** H6
**Castro-Urdiales** *Spain* 43°23N 3°11W **194** B7
**Castro Valley** *U.S.A.* 37°41N 122°5W **306** H4
**Castro Verde** *Portugal* 37°41N 8°4W **195** H2
**Castrogiovanni = Enna**
*Italy* 37°34N 14°16E **201** E7
**Castrojeriz** *Spain* 42°17N 4°9W **194** C6
**Castropol** *Spain* 43°32N 7°0W **194** B4
**Castroreale** *Italy* 38°6N 15°12E **201** D8
**Castrovillari** *Italy* 39°49N 16°12E **201** C9
**Castroville** *U.S.A.* 36°46N 121°45W **306** J5
**Castrovirreyna** *Peru* 13°20S 75°18W **330** C2
**Castuera** *Spain* 38°43N 5°37W **195** G5
**Caswell Sound** *N.Z.* 44°59S 167°8E **285** E2
**Çat** *Turkey* 39°40N 41°3E **213** C9
**Cat Ba, Dao** *Vietnam* 20°50N 107°0E **236** B6
**Cat Ba** △ *Vietnam* 20°47N 107°3E **236** B6
**Cat I.** *Bahamas* 24°30N 75°30W **321** B4
**Cat L.** *Canada* 51°40N 91°50W **298** B1
**Cat Lake** *Canada* 51°40N 91°50W **298** B1
**Cat Tien** △ *Vietnam* 11°25N 107°17E **237** G6
**Čata** *Slovak Rep.* 47°58N 18°38E **181** D11
**Catabola** *Angola* 12°9S 17°16E **265** E3
**Catacamas** *Honduras* 14°54N 85°56W **320** D2
**Catacaos** *Peru* 5°20S 80°45W **330** B1
**Cataguases** *Brazil* 21°23S 42°39W **333** F3
**Catagupan** *Phil.* 8°1N 116°58E **233** G1
**Cataingan** *Phil.* 12°0N 124°0E **232** E4
**Çatak** *Turkey* 38°1N 43°8E **213** C10
**Çatalağzı** *Turkey* 41°30N 31°59E **212** B4
**Catalão** *Brazil* 18°10S 47°57W **333** E2
**Çatalca** *Turkey* 41°8N 28°27E **203** E12
**Catalina** *Nfld. & L., Canada* 48°31N 53°4W **299** C9
**Catalina** *Chile* 25°13S 69°43W **334** B2
**Catalina** *Ariz., U.S.A.* 32°30N 110°50W **305** K8
**Catalonia = Cataluña** ☐
*Spain* 41°40N 1°15E **196** D6
**Cataluña** ☐ *Spain* 41°40N 1°15E **196** D6
**Çatalzeytin** *Turkey* 41°57N 34°12E **212** B6
**Catamarca** *Argentina* 28°30S 65°50W **334** B2
**Catamarca** ☐ *Argentina* 27°0S 65°50W **334** B2
**Catanauan** *Phil.* 13°36N 122°19E **232** E4
**Catanduanes** ☐ *Phil.* 13°50N 124°20E **232** E5
**Catanduva** *Brazil* 21°5S 48°58W **335** A6
**Catánia** *Italy* 37°30N 15°6E **201** E8
**Catánia, G. di** *Italy* 37°24N 15°9E **201** E8
**Cataño** *Puerto Rico* 18°27N 66°7W **321** b
**Catanzaro** *Italy* 38°54N 16°35E **201** D9
**Cataouatche, L.** *U.S.A.* 29°50N 90°14W **131** B1
**Catarman** *Camiguin, Phil.* 9°8N 124°40E **233** G5
**Catarman** *N. Samar, Phil.* 12°28N 124°35E **232** E5
**Catatumbo** → *Venezuela* 9°21N 71°45W **328** B3
**Catauala** *U.S.A.* 32°39N 84°52W **316** C5
**Catbalogan** *Phil.* 11°46N 124°53E **233** F5
**Catchacoma** *Canada* 44°44N 78°19W **312** B6
**Cateco Cangola** *Angola* 8°28S 15°51E **265** D3
**Cateel** *Phil.* 7°47N 126°24E **233** H6
**Cateel B.** *Phil.* 7°54N 126°25E **233** H6
**Catembe** *Mozam.* 26°0S 32°33E **271** C5
**Catende** *Angola* 11°14S 21°30E **265** E4
**Catende** *Brazil* 8°40S 35°43W **332** C4
**Caterham** *U.K.* 51°15N 0°4W **169** F7
**Catete** *Angola* 9°6S 13°43E **265** D2
**Catete** *Rio de J., Brazil* 22°54S 43°10W **135** B1
**Catford** *U.K.* 51°26N 0°1W **125** B3
**Cathair na Mart = Westport**
*Ireland* 53°48N 9°31W **166** C2
**Cathcart** *N.S.W.,*
*Australia* 36°52S 149°24E **283** D8
**Cathcart** *Eastern Cape,*
*S. Africa* 32°18S 27°10E **270** D4
**Cathedral City** *U.S.A.* 33°47N 116°28W **307** M10
**Cathedral Rock** △
*Australia* 30°24S 152°15E **283** A10
**Catherine, L.** *U.S.A.* 28°30N 81°24W **133** B2
**Cathlamet** *U.S.A.* 46°12N 123°23W **306** D3
**Catió** *Guinea-Biss.* 11°17N 15°15W **262** C1
**Catismiña** *Venezuela* 4°5N 63°40W **329** C5
**Catita** *Brazil* 9°31S 43°1W **332** C3
**Cativa** *Panama* 9°21N 79°49W **320** c
**Catlettsburg** *U.S.A.* 38°25N 82°36W **309** F12
**Catlin** *U.S.A.* 40°4N 87°42W **311** D9
**Catlins** *N.Z.* 46°22S 169°17E **285** G4
**Catma Dağı** *Turkey* 38°25N 29°50E **205** C11
**Catmon** *Phil.* 10°43N 124°1E **233** F5
**Catoche, C.** *Mexico* 21°35N 87°5W **319** C7
**Catolé do Rocha** *Brazil* 6°21S 37°45W **332** C4
**Catota** *Angola* 13°57S 17°20E **265** E3
**Cátria, Mte.** *Italy* 43°28N 12°42E **199** E9
**Catriló** *Argentina* 36°26S 63°24W **334** D3
**Catrimani** *Brazil* 0°27N 61°41W **329** C5
**Catrimani** → *Brazil* 0°28N 61°44W **329** C5
**Catskill** *U.S.A.* 42°14N 73°52W **313** D11
**Catskill** ⌂ *U.S.A.* 42°8N 74°39W **313** D10
**Catskill Mts.** *U.S.A.* 42°10N 74°25W **313** D10
**Catt, Mt.** *Australia* 13°49S 134°23E **280** A1
**Cattaraugus** *U.S.A.* 42°20N 78°52W **312** D6
**Cattaro = Kotor**
*Montenegro* 42°25N 18°47E **202** D2
**Catterick** *U.K.* 54°23N 1°37W **168** C6
**Cattólica** *Italy* 43°58N 12°44E **199** E9
**Cattólica Eraclea** *Italy* 37°26N 13°24E **200** E6
**Catu** *Brazil* 12°21S 38°23W **333** D4
**Catuala** *Angola* 16°25S 19°2E **265** F3
**Catuane** *Mozam.* 26°48S 32°18E **271** C5
**Catubig** *Phil.* 12°24N 125°3E **232** E5
**Catumbela** *Angola* 12°25S 13°34E **265** E2
**Catumbela** → *Angola* 12°29S 13°28E **265** E2
**Catur** *Mozam.* 13°45S 35°30E **269** E4
**Catwick Is. = Hon Hai**
*Vietnam* 10°0N 109°0E **237** H7
**Cauayan** *Isabela, Phil.* 16°56N 121°46E **232** C3
**Cauayan** *Neg. Occ., Phil.* 9°58N 122°37E **233** G4
**Caubvick, Mt. = Iberville, Mt. d'**
*Canada* 58°50N 63°50W **295** F19
**Cauca** ☐ *Colombia* 2°30N 76°50W **328** C2
**Cauca** → *Colombia* 8°54N 74°28W **328** B3
**Caucaia** *Brazil* 3°40S 38°35W **332** B4
**Caucasia** *Colombia* 8°0N 75°12W **328** B2
**Caucasus Mountains**
*Eurasia* 42°50N 44°0E **191** J7
**Caucete** *Argentina* 31°38S 68°20W **334** C2
**Caudete** *Spain* 38°42N 1°2W **197** G3
**Caudry** *France* 50°7N 3°22E **173** B10
**Caúese Mts.** *Mozam.* 15°14S 30°33E **269** F3
**Caulfield** *Australia* 37°52S 145°1E **128** B2
**Caulnes** *France* 48°18N 2°10W **172** D4
**Caulónia** *Italy* 38°23N 16°24E **201** D9
**Caungula** *Angola* 8°26S 18°38E **265** D3
**Cauquenes** *Chile* 36°0S 72°22W **334** D1
**Caura** → *Venezuela* 7°38N 64°53W **329** B5
**Caurés** → *Brazil* 1°21S 62°20W **329** D5
**Cauresi** → *Mozam.* 17°8S 33°0E **269** F3
**Căuşani** *Moldova* 46°38N 29°25E **183** D14
**Causapscal** *Canada* 48°19N 67°12W **299** C6
**Caussade** *France* 44°10N 1°33E **174** D5
**Causse-Méjean** *France* 44°18N 3°42E **174** D7
**Causses du Quercy** ⌂
*France* 44°35N 1°35E **174** D5
**Cauterets** *France* 42°52N 0°8W **174** F3
**Cauvery** → *India* 11°9N 78°52E **245** J4
**Caux, Pays de** *France* 49°38N 0°35E **172** C7
**Cava de' Tirreni** *Italy* 40°42N 14°42E **201** B7
**Cávado** → *Portugal* 41°32N 8°48W **194** D2
**Cavagrande del Cassibile** ⌂
*Italy* 36°58N 15°6E **201** F8
**Cavaillon** *France* 43°50N 5°2E **175** E9
**Cavalaire-sur-Mer** *France* 43°10N 6°33E **175** E10
**Cavalcante** *Brazil* 13°48S 47°30W **333** D2
**Cavalese** *Italy* 46°17N 11°27E **199** B8
**Cavalier** *U.S.A.* 48°48N 97°37W **308** A5
**Cavalla = Cavally** → *Africa* 4°22N 7°32W **262** E3
**Cavalla** △ *Liberia* 5°8N 7°20W **262** D3
**Cavalli, Palazzo** *Venice, Italy* **142** b2
**Cavalli Is.** *N.Z.* 35°0S 173°58E **284** B2
**Cavally** → *Africa* 4°22N 7°32W **262** E3
**Cavan** *Ireland* 54°0N 7°22W **166** B4
**Cavan** ☐ *Ireland* 54°1N 7°16W **166** C4
**Cavárzere** *Italy* 45°8N 12°5E **199** C9
**Cavazuccherina = Jésolo**
*Italy* 45°32N 12°38E **199** C9
**Çavdarhisar** *Turkey* 39°12N 29°37E **205** B11
**Çavdır** *Turkey* 37°10N 29°42E **205** D11
**Cave Creek** *U.S.A.* 33°50N 111°57W **305** K8
**Cave Run L.** *U.S.A.* 38°5N 83°25W **311** F13
**Cave Spring** *U.S.A.* 34°6N 85°20W **316** A4
**Cavelleria, C. de** *Spain* 40°5N 4°5E **206** A5
**Cavenagh Ra.** *Australia* 26°12S 127°55E **279** E4
**Cavendish** *Australia* 37°31S 142°2E **282** D5
**Caverna do Peruaçu** △
*Brazil* 15°0S 44°35W **333** E3
**Caviana, I.** *Brazil* 0°10N 50°10W **329** C7
**Cavili I.** *Phil.* 9°16N 120°49E **233** G3
**Cavite** *Phil.* 14°29N 120°54E **127** C1
**Cavite** ☐ *Phil.* 14°15N 120°50E **232** D3
**Caviúna = Rolândia**
*Brazil* 23°18S 51°23W **335** A5
**Cavnic** *Romania* 47°40N 23°52E **183** C8
**Cavour** *Italy* 44°47N 7°22E **198** D4
**Cavtat** *Croatia* 42°35N 18°13E **202** D2
**Cawayan** *Phil.* 11°56N 123°46E **233** F4
**Cawayanon = Vintar**
*Phil.* 18°14N 120°39E **232** B3
**Cawndilla L.** *Australia* 32°30S 142°15E **282** B5
**Cawnpore = Kanpur** *India* 26°28N 80°20E **243** F9
**Caxias** *Brazil* 4°55S 43°20W **332** B3
**Caxias** *Lisboa, Portugal* 38°42N 9°16W **126** A1
**Caxias do Sul** *Brazil* 29°10S 51°10W **335** B5
**Caxito** *Angola* 8°30S 13°30E **265** D2
**Caxopa** *Angola* 11°52S 20°29E **265** E4
**Çay** *Turkey* 38°35N 31°1E **212** C4
**Cay Pt.** *Bahamas* 24°59N 77°25W **153** b
**Cay Sal Bank** *Bahamas* 23°45N 80°0W **320** B4
**Cayambe** *Napo, Ecuador* 0°2N 77°59W **328** C2
**Cayambe** *Quito, Ecuador* 0°3N 78°8W **328** C2
**Cayce** *U.S.A.* 33°58N 81°4W **316** B8
**Çaycuma** *Turkey* 41°25N 32°4E **212** B5
**Çayeli** *Turkey* 41°5N 40°45E **213** B9
**Cayenne** *Fr. Guiana* 5°5N 52°18W **329** B7
**Cayenne** ☐ *Fr. Guiana* 5°0N 53°0W **329** C7
**Cayey** *Puerto Rico* 18°7N 66°10W **321** b
**Caygören Barajı** *Turkey* 39°15N 28°12E **205** B10
**Cayiralan** *Turkey* 39°17N 35°38E **212** C6
**Cayirova = Áyios Theodhoros**
*Cyprus* 35°22N 34°1E **207** E10
**Caylus** *France* 44°15N 1°47E **174** D5
**Cayman Brac** *Cayman Is.* 19°43N 79°49W **320** C4
**Cayman Is.** ☑ *W. Indies* 19°40N 80°30W **320** C3
**Cayman Trench** *Caribbean* 17°0N 83°0W **320** D3
**Caynabo** *Somalia* 9°0N 46°25E **267** C6
**Cayon** *St. Kitts & Nevis* 17°21N 62°52W **322** d
**Cayres** *France* 44°55N 3°48E **174** D7
**Cayuga** *Ont., Canada* 42°59N 79°50W **312** D5
**Cayuga** *Ind., U.S.A.* 39°57N 87°28W **311** E9
**Cayuga** *N.Y., U.S.A.* 42°54N 76°44W **313** D8
**Cayuga Heights** *U.S.A.* 42°27N 76°29W **313** D8
**Cayuga L.** *U.S.A.* 42°41N 76°41W **313** D8
**Cazage** *Angola* 11°2S 20°45E **265** E4
**Cazalla de la Sierra** *Spain* 37°56N 5°45W **195** H5
**Căzănești** *Romania* 44°36N 27°3E **183** F12
**Cazaubon** *France* 43°56N 0°4W **174** E3
**Cazaux et de Sanguinet, Étang de**
*France* 44°29N 1°10W **174** D2
**Cazenovia** *U.S.A.* 42°56N 75°51W **313** D9
**Cazères** *France* 43°13N 1°5E **174** E5
**Cazin** *Bos.-H.* 44°57N 15°57E **199** D12
**Čazma** *Croatia* 45°45N 16°39E **199** C13
**Cazombo** *Angola* 11°54S 22°56E **265** E4
**Cazorla** *Spain* 37°55N 3°2W **195** H7
**Cazorla, Sierra de** *Spain* 38°5N 2°55W **195** G8
**Cea** → *Spain* 42°0N 5°36W **194** C5
**Ceahlău** △ *Romania* 46°58N 25°55E **183** D10
**Ceamurlia de Jos**
*Romania* 44°43N 28°47E **183** F13
**Ceanannus Mor = Kells**
*Ireland* 53°44N 6°53W **166** C5
**Ceará = Fortaleza** *Brazil* 3°45S 38°35W **332** B4
**Ceará** ☐ *Brazil* 5°0S 40°0W **332** B4
**Ceara Abyssal Plain** *Atl. Oc.* 0°0 36°30W **152** F7
**Ceará-Mirim** *Brazil* 5°38S 35°25W **332** C4
**Ceara Rise** *Atl. Oc.* 4°30N 43°30W **152** F7
**Ceatharlach = Carlow**
*Ireland* 52°50N 6°56W **166** D5
**Ceauru, L.** *Romania* 44°58N 23°11E **183** F8
**Cébaco, I. de** *Panama* 7°33N 81°9W **320** E3
**Cebecci** *Turkey* 41°7N 28°52E **122** B1
**Cebollar** *Argentina* 29°10S 66°35W **334** B2
**Cebollera, Sierra** *Spain* 42°0N 2°30W **196** D2
**Cebreros** *Spain* 40°27N 4°28W **194** E6
**Cebu** *Phil.* 10°18N 123°54E **233** F4
**Cebu** ☐ *Phil.* 10°20N 123°40E **233** F4
**Čečava** *Bos.-H.* 44°42N 17°44E **182** F2
**Ceccano** *Italy* 41°34N 13°20E **200** A6
**Cecchignola** *Italy* 41°48N 12°29E **136** C2
**Cece** *Hungary* 46°46N 18°39E **182** D3
**Cechi** *Ivory C.* 6°15N 4°25W **262** D4
**Cecil Plains** *Australia* 27°30S 151°11E **281** D5
**Cecilienhof, Schloss**
*Germany* 52°35N 13°5E **115** B1
**Cécina** *Italy* 43°19N 10°31E **198** E7
**Cécina** → *Italy* 43°18N 10°29E **198** E7
**Ceclavín** *Spain* 39°50N 6°45W **194** F4
**Cedar** → *U.S.A.* 41°17N 91°21W **310** C5
**Cedar City** *U.S.A.* 37°41N 113°4W **305** H7
**Cedar Creek Res.** *U.S.A.* 32°11N 96°4W **314** E6
**Cedar Falls** *Iowa, U.S.A.* 42°32N 92°27W **310** B4
**Cedar Falls** *Wash.,*
*U.S.A.* 47°25N 121°45W **306** C5
**Cedar Grove** *Georgia,*
*U.S.A.* 33°40N 84°16W **113** C3
**Cedar Grove** *Ind., U.S.A.* 39°22N 84°56W **311** E12
**Cedar Key** *U.S.A.* 29°8N 83°2W **317** F6
**Cedar L.** *Canada* 53°10N 100°0W **297** C9
**Cedar Lake** *U.S.A.* 41°22N 87°26W **311** C9
**Cedar Park** *U.S.A.* 30°30N 97°49W **314** F6
**Cedar Point** *U.S.A.* 41°44N 83°21W **311** C13
**Cedar Rapids** *U.S.A.* 41°59N 91°40W **310** C5
**Cedar Tree Pt.** *Antigua & B.* 17°42N 61°53W **322** c
**Cedartown** *U.S.A.* 34°1N 85°15W **316** A4
**Cedarvale** *Canada* 55°1N 128°22W **296** B3
**Cedarvale Park** *Canada* 43°42N 79°26W **141** A2
**Cedarville** *KwaZulu Natal,*
*S. Africa* 30°23S 29°3E **271** D4
**Cedarville** *Ill., U.S.A.* 42°23N 89°38W **310** B7
**Cedarville** *Ohio, U.S.A.* 39°44N 83°49W **311** E13
**Cedeira** *Spain* 43°39N 8°2W **194** B2
**Cedral** *Mexico* 23°50N 100°45W **318** C4
**Cedrino** → *Italy* 40°11N 9°24E **200** B2
**Cedro** *Brazil* 6°34S 39°3W **332** C4
**Cedros** *Azores* 38°38N 28°42W **153** d1
**Cedros, I.** *Mexico* 28°12N 115°15W **318** B1
**Cedros B.** *Trin. & Tob.* 10°16N 61°54W **323** t
**Cedros Pt.** *Trin. & Tob.* 10°7N 61°49W **323** t
**Ceduna** *Australia* 32°7S 133°46E **281** E1
**Cedynia** *Poland* 52°53N 14°12E **185** F1
**Cée** *Spain* 42°57N 9°10W **194** C1
**Ceel Gaal** *Somalia* 10°58N 50°20E **267** B7
**Ceel Waaq** *Kenya* 2°49N 40°56E **267** D5
**Ceelbuur = El Bur** *Somalia* 4°40N 46°37E **267** D6
**Ceeldheere** *Galguduud,*
*Somalia* 3°50N 47°8E **267** D6
**Ceeldheere** *Galguduud,*
*Somalia* 5°22N 46°11E **267** C6
**Ceerigaabo** *Somalia* 10°35N 47°20E **267** B6
**Cefalù** *Italy* 38°2N 14°1E **201** D7
**Cega** → *Spain* 41°33N 4°46W **194** D6
**Cegléd** *Hungary* 47°11N 19°47E **182** C4
**Céglie Messápica** *Italy* 40°39N 17°31E **201** B10
**Cehegín** *Spain* 38°6N 1°48W **197** G3
**Ceheng** *China* 24°58N 105°48E **228** E5
**Cehu-Silvaniei** *Romania* 47°24N 23°9E **183** C8
**Ceiba** *Puerto Rico* 18°16N 65°39W **321** b
**Ceica** *Romania* 46°53N 22°10E **182** D7
**Ceira** → *Portugal* 40°13N 8°16W **194** E2
**Çekerek** *Turkey* 40°4N 35°29E **212** B6
**Cekik** *Indonesia* 8°12S 114°27E **231** J17
**Cela** *Angola* 11°25S 15°7E **265** E3
**Čelákovice** *Czech Rep.* 50°10N 14°46E **180** A7
**Celano** *Italy* 42°5N 13°33E **199** F10
**Celanova** *Spain* 42°9N 7°58W **194** C3
**Celaque** △ *Honduras* 14°30N 88°43W **320** D2
**Celaya** *Mexico* 20°31N 100°37W **318** C4
**Celbridge** *Ireland* 53°20N 6°32W **166** C5
**Celebes = Sulawesi** *Indonesia* 2°0S 120°0E **235** C5
**Celebes Sea** *Indonesia* 3°0N 123°0E **231** D6
**Celendín** *Peru* 6°52S 78°10W **330** B2
**Celestial Mts. = Tian Shan**
*Asia* 40°30N 76°0E **217** D9
**Čelić** *Bos.-H.* 44°43N 18°49E **182** F3
**Celica** *Ecuador* 4°7S 79°59W **328** D2
**Celina** *U.S.A.* 40°33N 84°35W **311** D12
**Celinac** *Bos.-H.* 44°44N 17°22E **182** F2
**Celje** *Slovenia* 46°16N 15°18E **199** B12
**Celldömölk** *Hungary* 47°16N 17°10E **182** C2
**Celle** *Germany* 52°37N 10°4E **178** C6
**Celorico da Beira** *Portugal* 40°38N 7°24W **194** E3
**Celtic Sea** *Atl. Oc.* 50°9N 9°34W **165** F2
**Çeltikçi** *Turkey* 37°32N 30°29E **205** D12
**Çemişgezek** *Turkey* 39°3N 38°56E **213** C8
**Cempaka Putih** *Indonesia* 6°10S 106°51E **122** B2
**Cempi, Teluk** *Indonesia* 8°44S 118°22E **235** D5
**Cenderawasih, Teluk**
*Indonesia* 3°0S 135°20E **231** E9
**Cenepa** → *Peru* 4°40S 78°10W **328** D2
**Çengelköy** *Turkey* 41°2N 29°3E **122** B2
**Cengkareng** *Indonesia* 6°9S 106°45E **122** A1
**Cengong** *China* 27°13N 108°44E **228** D7
**Ceno** → *Italy* 44°43N 10°5E **198** D7
**Centallo** *Italy* 44°30N 7°35E **198** D4
**Centelles** *Spain* 41°50N 2°14E **196** D7
**Centenário do Sul** *Brazil* 22°48S 51°36W **333** F1
**Centennial** *U.S.A.* 39°34N 104°52W **304** G11
**Centennial Olympic Park**
*Atlanta, U.S.A.* 33°46N 84°23W **113** B2
**Centennial Park**
*Sydney, Australia* 33°53S 151°14E **139** B2
**Center** *N. Dak., U.S.A.* 47°7N 101°18W **308** B3
**Center** *Tex., U.S.A.* 31°48N 94°11W **314** F7
**Center Hill** *Fla., U.S.A.* 28°38N 82°3W **317** G7
**Center Hill** *Georgia, U.S.A.* 33°46N 84°29W **113** B2
**Center Point** *U.S.A.* 42°12N 91°46W **310** B5
**Centerburg** *U.S.A.* 40°18N 82°42W **312** F2
**Centerville** *Calif., U.S.A.* 36°44N 119°30W **306** J7
**Centerville** *Iowa, U.S.A.* 40°44N 92°52W **310** D4
**Centerville** *Ohio, U.S.A.* 39°38N 84°8W **312** G1
**Centerville** *Pa., U.S.A.* 40°3N 79°59W **312** F5
**Centerville** *Tenn., U.S.A.* 35°47N 87°28W **315** D11
**Centerville** *Tex., U.S.A.* 31°16N 95°59W **314** F7
**Cento** *Italy* 44°43N 11°17E **199** D8
**Centocelle** *Italy* 41°52N 12°34E **136** B2
**Centraal Station** *Amsterdam, Neths.* **112** a3
**Central = Tsentralnyy** ☐
*Russia* 52°0N 40°0E **214** D4
**Central** *Brazil* 11°8S 42°8W **332** D3
**Central** *Alaska, U.S.A.* 65°35N 144°48W **303** D11
**Central** ☐ *Botswana* 22°0S 26°30E **270** B4
**Central** ☐ *Ghana* 5°30N 1°0W **263** D4
**Central** ☐ *Kenya* 0°30S 37°30E **268** C4
**Central** ☐ *Malawi* 13°30S 33°30E **269** E3
**Central** ☐ *Papua N. G.* 10°0S 148°0E **286** F5
**Central** ☐ *Zambia* 14°25S 28°50E **269** E2
**Central, Cordillera** *Bolivia* 18°30S 64°55W **331** D5
**Central, Cordillera** *Colombia* 5°0N 75°0W **328** C3
**Central, Cordillera**
*Costa Rica* 10°10N 84°5W **320** D3
**Central, Cordillera**
*Dom. Rep.* 19°15N 71°0W **321** C5
**Central, Cordillera** *Peru* 7°0S 77°30W **330** B2
**Central, Cordillera** *Phil.* 17°20N 120°57E **232** C3
**Central, Cordillera**
*Puerto Rico* 18°8N 66°35W **321** b
**Central, Gare** *Montréal, Canada* **130** c2
**Central African Empire = Central**
**African Rep.** ■ *Africa* 7°0N 20°0E **264** A4
**Central African Rep.** ■
*Africa* 7°0N 20°0E **264** A4
**Central America** *America* 12°0N 85°0W **292** H11
**Central Australia** ◎
*Australia* 22°30S 128°30E **278** D4
**Central Bedfordshire** ☐
*U.K.* 52°5N 0°20W **169** E7
**Central Butte** *Canada* 50°48N 106°31W **297** C7
**Central City** *Colo.,*
*U.S.A.* 39°48N 105°31W **304** G11
**Central City** *Iowa, U.S.A.* 42°12N 91°32W **310** B5
**Central City** *Ky., U.S.A.* 37°18N 87°7W **308** G10
**Central City** *Nebr., U.S.A.* 41°7N 98°0W **308** E4
**Central Desert** ◎
*Australia* 19°56S 130°46E **278** C5
**Central Equatoria** ☐
*South Sudan* 4°0N 31°0E **257** G3
**Central I.** *Kenya* 3°30N 36°0E **268** B4
**Central Island** △ *Kenya* 3°33N 36°1E **268** B4
**Central Japan Int.** ✕ **(NGO)**
*Japan* 34°53N 136°45E **223** C8
**Central Kalahari** ⌂
*Botswana* 22°36S 23°58E **270** B3
**Central Makran Range**
*Pakistan* 26°30N 64°15E **240** D2
**Central Pacific Basin**
*Pac. Oc.* 8°0N 175°0W **288** G10
**Central Park** *New York, U.S.A.* **132** a3
**Central Park Zoo** *New York, U.S.A.* **132** b2
**Central Patricia** *Canada* 51°30N 90°9W **298** B1
**Central Point** *U.S.A.* 42°23N 122°55W **304** E2
**Central Provinces = Madhya**
**Pradesh** ☐ *India* 22°50N 78°0E **242** J8
**Central Ra.** *Papua N. G.* 5°0S 143°0E **286** C2
**Central Ra.** *Trin. & Tob.* 10°25N 61°15W **323** t
**Central Range Wildlife Sanctuary** △
*Trin. & Tob.* 10°27N 61°14W **323** t
**Central Russian Uplands**
*Europe* 54°0N 36°0E **158** E13
**Central Siberian Plateau**
*Russia* 65°0N 105°0E **210** B12
**Central Square** *U.S.A.* 43°17N 76°9W **313** C8
**Central Village** *Jamaica* 17°59N 76°55W **320** a
**Centralia** *Ont., Canada* 43°17N 81°28W **312** C3
**Centralia** *Ill., U.S.A.* 38°32N 89°8W **310** F7
**Centralia** *Mo., U.S.A.* 39°13N 92°8W **310** E4
**Centralia** *Wash., U.S.A.* 46°43N 122°58W **306** D4
**Centre** *U.S.A.* 34°9N 85°41W **316** A4
**Centre** ☐ *Cameroon* 4°45N 12°0E **263** E7
**Centre de Flacq** *Mauritius* 20°12S 57°43E **272** e
**Centreville** *Mich., U.S.A.* 41°55N 85°32W **311** C11
**Centreville** *N.Y., U.S.A.* 42°28N 78°14W **312** D6
**Centreville** *Pa., U.S.A.* 41°44N 79°45W **312** E5
**Century** *U.S.A.* 30°58N 87°16W **317** E2
**Century City** *U.S.A.* 34°3N 118°25W **126** B2
**Cenxi** *China* 22°57N 110°57E **229** F8
**Čeotina** → *Bos.-H.* 43°36N 18°50E **202** C2
**Cephalonia = Kefalonia**
*Greece* 38°15N 20°30E **207** C2
**Čepin** *Croatia* 45°32N 18°34E **182** E3
**Ceprano** *Italy* 41°33N 13°31E **200** A6
**Ceptia** *Angola* 12°56S 17°35E **265** E3
**Ceptura** *Romania* 45°1N 26°21E **183** E11
**Cepu** *Indonesia* 7°9S 111°35E **235** D4
**Ceram = Seram** *Indonesia* 3°10S 129°0E **231** E7
**Ceram Sea = Seram Sea**
*Indonesia* 2°30S 128°30E **231** E7
**Cerbère** *France* 42°26N 3°10E **174** F7
**Cerbicales, Îs.** *France* 41°33N 9°22E **175** G13
**Cercal** *Portugal* 37°48N 8°40W **195** H2
**Cerdanya** *Spain* 42°22N 1°35E **196** C6
**Cerdanyola del Vallès** *Spain* 41°27N 2°8W **114** A1
**Cère** → *France* 44°55N 1°49E **174** D5
**Cerea** *Italy* 45°12N 11°13E **199** C8
**Ceredigion** ☐ *U.K.* 52°16N 4°15W **169** E3
**Ceres** *Argentina* 29°55S 61°55W **334** B3
**Ceres** *Brazil* 15°17S 49°35W **333** E2
**Ceres** *Western Cape,*
*S. Africa* 33°21S 19°18E **270** D2
**Ceres** *Calif., U.S.A.* 37°35N 120°57W **306** H6
**Ceresio, L. di = Lugano, L. di**
*Switz.* 46°0N 9°0E **198** C6
**Céret** *France* 42°30N 2°42E **174** F6
**Cereté** *Colombia* 8°53N 75°48W **328** B2
**Cerf** *Seychelles* 4°38S 55°40E **272** c
**Cerfs, Îs. aux** *Mauritius* 20°16S 57°47E **272** e
**Cergy** *France* 49°2N 2°4E **173** C9
**Cerignola** *Italy* 41°17N 15°53E **201** A8
**Cerigo = Kythira** *Greece* 36°8N 23°0E **204** E5
**Cerillos** *Chile* 33°29S 70°42W **137** B1
**Cérilly** *France* 46°37N 2°50E **173** F9
**Cerisiers** *France* 48°8N 3°30E **173** D10
**Cerizay** *France* 46°50N 0°40W **172** F6
**Çerkeş** *Turkey* 40°49N 32°52E **212** B5
**Çerkezköy** *Turkey* 41°17N 28°0E **203** E12
**Cerkníca** *Slovenia* 45°48N 14°21E **199** C11
**Cerkovica** *Bulgaria* 43°41N 24°50E **203** C8
**Cermenon** *Serbia* 43°35N 20°25E **202** C4
**Çermik** *Turkey* 38°8N 39°26E **213** C8
**Cerna** *Romania* 45°4N 28°17E **183** E13
**Cerna** → *Romania* 44°38N 23°58E **183** F8
**Cernauti = Chernivtsi**
*Ukraine* 48°15N 25°52E **183** B10
**Cernavodă** *Romania* 44°22N 28°3E **183** F13
**Cernay** *France* 47°44N 7°10E **173** E14
**Cernik** *Croatia* 45°17N 17°22E **182** E2
**Cerralvo, I.** *Mexico* 24°15N 109°55W **318** C3
**Cërrik** *Albania* 41°2N 19°58E **202** E3
**Cerritos** *Mexico* 22°25N 100°16W **318** C4
**Cerro Chato** *Uruguay* 33°6S 55°8W **335** C4
**Cerro Chovoreca** △
*Paraguay* 19°19S 59°7W **331** D6
**Cerro Cofre de Perote** △
*Mexico* 19°29N 97°8W **319** D5
**Cerro Corá** △ *Paraguay* 22°35S 56°2W **335** A4
**Cerro de la Estrella** △
*Mexico* 19°23N 99°5W **128** B2
**Cerro de los Angeles** *Spain* 40°18N 3°41W **127** C1
**Cerro de Pasco** *Peru* 10°45S 76°10W **330** C2
**Cerro El Copey** △ *Venezuela* 11°11N 63°54W **329** a
**Cerro Gordo** *U.S.A.* 39°53N 88°44W **311** E8
**Cerro Hoya** △ *Panama* 7°17N 80°45W **320** E3
**Cerro Navia** *Chile* 33°25S 70°42W **137** B1
**Cerro Saroche** △ *Venezuela* 10°8N 69°38W **328** A4
**Cerro Sombrero** *Chile* 52°45S 69°15W **336** D3

Cerros Colorados, Embalse Argentina 38°30S 68°50W 336 A3
Certaldo Italy 43°33N 11°2E 198 E8
Cervantes Phil. 17°0N 120°44E 232 C3
Cervaro → Italy 41°30N 15°52E 201 A8
Cervati, Monte Italy 40°17N 15°29E 201 B8
Cerventes Australia 30°31S 115°3E 279 F2
Cervera Spain 41°40N 1°16E 196 D6
Cervera de Pisuerga Spain 42°51N 4°30W 194 C6
Cervera del Río Alhama Spain 42°2N 1°58W 196 C3
Cerveteri Italy 42°0N 12°6E 199 F9
Cérvia Italy 44°15N 12°22E 199 D9
Cervignano del Friuli Italy 45°49N 13°20E 199 C10
Cervinara Italy 41°1N 14°37E 201 A7
Cervione France 42°20N 9°29E 175 F13
Cervo Spain 43°40N 7°24W 194 B3
Cesano Boscone Italy 45°26N 9°5E 128 B1
César □ Colombia 9°0N 73°30W 328 B3
Cesarò Italy 37°50N 14°38E 201 E7
Cesate Italy 45°35N 9°4E 128 A1
Cesena Italy 44°8N 12°15E 199 D9
Cesenático Italy 44°12N 12°24E 199 D9
Cēsis Latvia 57°18N 25°15E 188 D3
Česká Lípa Czech Rep. 50°45N 14°30E 180 A7
Česká Rep. = Czech Rep. ■ Europe 50°0N 15°0E 180 B8
Česká Třebová Czech Rep. 49°54N 16°27E 181 B9
České Budějovice Czech Rep. 48°55N 14°25E 180 C7
České Švýcarsko △ Czech Rep. 50°50N 14°15E 180 A7
České Velenice Czech Rep. 48°45N 14°57E 180 C7
Českobudějovický □ Czech Rep. 49°10N 14°30E 180 B7
Českomoravská Vrchovina Czech Rep. 49°30N 15°40E 180 B8
Český Brod Czech Rep. 50°4N 14°52E 180 A7
Český Krumlov Czech Rep. 48°43N 14°21E 180 C7
Český Těšín Czech Rep. 49°45N 18°39E 181 B11
Česma → Croatia 45°35N 16°29E 199 C13
Çeşme Turkey 38°20N 26°23E 205 C8
Cessnock Australia 32°50S 151°21E 283 B9
Cesson-Sévigné France 48°7N 1°36W 172 D5
Cestas France 44°44N 0°41W 174 D3
Cestos → Liberia 5°40N 9°10W 262 D3
Cestos Sehnkwehn △ Liberia 5°40N 9°10W 262 D3
Cetaceo, Mt. Phil. 17°42N 122°3E 232 C4
Cetate Romania 44°7N 23°2E 182 F8
Cetatea-Albă = Bilhorod-Dnistrovskyy Ukraine 46°11N 30°23E 189 J6
Cetin Grad Croatia 45°9N 15°45E 199 C12
Cetina → Croatia 43°26N 16°42E 199 E13
Cetinje Montenegro 42°23N 18°59E 202 D2
Çetmı Turkey 36°52N 32°38E 250 B3
Cetraro Italy 39°31N 15°55E 201 C8
Ceuta N. Afr. 35°52N 5°18W 260 A3
Ceva Italy 44°23N 8°2E 198 D5
Ceve-i-Ra Fiji 21°46S 174°31E 277 E13
Cévennes France 44°10N 3°50E 174 D7
Cévennes △ France 44°15N 3°45E 174 D7
Ceyhan Turkey 37°4N 35°47E 250 A6
Ceyhan → Turkey 36°38N 35°40E 250 B6
Ceylanpınar Turkey 36°50N 40°2E 213 D9
Ceylon = Sri Lanka ■ Asia 7°30N 80°50E 245 L5
Ceylon Plain Ind. Oc. 4°0S 82°0E 273 E7
Cèze → France 44°6N 4°43E 175 D8
Cha-am Thailand 12°48N 99°58E 236 F2
Cha Kwo Ling Hong Kong, China 22°18N 114°13E 122 B3
Chá Pungana Angola 13°44S 18°39E 265 E3
Chabanais France 45°52N 0°48E 174 C4
Chabeuil France 44°54N 5°3E 175 D9
Chablais France 46°20N 6°36E 173 F13
Chablis France 47°47N 3°48E 173 E10
Chabounia Algeria 35°20N 2°38E 261 A5
Chacabuco Argentina 34°40S 60°27W 334 C3
Chacachacare Venezuela 10°58N 64°9W 329 a
Chacachacare I. Trin. & Tob. 10°41N 61°45W 323 t
Chacao, Canal Chile 41°47S 73°42W 336 B2
Chacarrita Argentina 34°35S 58°27W 117 B2
Chachani, Nevado Peru 16°11S 71°31W 330 D3
Chachapoyas Peru 6°15S 77°50W 330 B2
Chachasp Peru 15°30S 72°15W 330 D3
Chachoengsao Thailand 13°42N 101°5E 236 F3
Chachran Pakistan 28°55N 70°30E 242 E4
Chachro Pakistan 25°5N 70°15E 242 G4
Chaco □ Argentina 26°30S 61°0W 334 B3
Chaco □ Paraguay 26°0S 60°0W 334 B4
Chaco → U.S.A. 36°46N 108°39W 305 H9
Chaco △ Argentina 27°0S 59°30W 334 B4
Chaco Culture △ U.S.A. 36°3N 107°58W 305 H10
Chacon, C. U.S.A. 54°42N 132°0W 296 C2
Chad ■ Africa 15°0N 17°15E 259 F3
Chad, L. = Tchad, L. Chad 13°30N 14°30E 259 F2
Chadileuvú → Argentina 37°46S 66°0W 334 D2
Chadiza Zambia 14°45S 32°27E 269 E3
Chadron U.S.A. 42°50N 103°0W 308 D2
Chadwell Heath U.K. 51°34N 0°8E 125 A4
Chadyr-Lunga = Ciadâr-Lunga Moldova 46°3N 28°51E 183 D13
Chae Hom Thailand 18°43N 99°35E 236 C2
Chae Son △ Thailand 18°42N 99°20E 236 C2
Chaem → Thailand 18°11N 98°38E 236 C2
Chaeryŏng N. Korea 38°24N 125°36E 224 C2
Chafe Nigeria 11°59N 6°50E 263 C6
Chagai Hills = Chāh Gay Hills Afghan. 29°30N 64°0E 240 C2
Chagang-do □ N. Korea 40°50N 126°30E 224 B3
Chagda Russia 58°45N 130°38E 215 D14
Chagdo Kangri China 34°15N 84°10E 217 F10
Chaghcharān Afghan. 34°31N 65°15E 240 B2
Chagne Ethiopia 10°57N 36°30E 266 B4
Chagny France 46°57N 4°45E 173 F11
Chagoda Russia 59°10N 35°15E 188 C8
Chagos Arch. ☑ Ind. Oc. 6°0S 72°0E 273 E6
Chagos-Laccadive Ridge Ind. Oc. 3°0N 73°0E 273 D6
Chagres → Panama 9°10N 79°40W 320 c
Chagres △ Panama 9°33N 79°37W 320 c
Chaguanas Trin. & Tob. 10°30N 61°26W 323 t
Chaguaramas Trin. & Tob. 10°41N 61°38W 323 t
Chāh Ākhvor Iran 32°41N 59°40E 247 C8
Chāh Bahar Iran 25°20N 60°40E 247 E9
Chāh-e Āb Afghan. 37°23N 69°48E 240 A3
Chāh-e Kavīr Iran 34°29N 56°52E 247 C8
Chāh Gay Hills Afghan. 29°30N 64°0E 240 C2
Chahār Borj Iran 37°6N 45°59E 213 D11
Chahār Borjak Afghan. 30°17N 62°3E 240 C1
Chahār Mahāll va Bakhtīarī □ Iran 32°0N 49°0E 247 C6
Chahtung Burma 26°41N 98°10E 241 B7
Chai Badan Thailand 15°12N 101°8E 236 E3
Chai Chee Singapore 1°19N 103°46E 138 B3
Chai Wan Hong Kong, China 22°16N 114°14E 122 B3
Chai Wan Kok Hong Kong, China 22°22N 114°6E 122 A2
Chaibasa India 22°42N 85°49E 243 H11
Chaidari Greece 38°2N 23°38E 112 A1
Chaillé-les-Marais France 46°25N 1°2W 174 B2
Chaillot, Palais de Paris, France 134 b2
Chaillu, Massif du Gabon 2°32S 11°10E 264 C2
Chain Ridge Ind. Oc. 6°0N 54°0E 273 D4
Chainat Thailand 15°11N 100°8E 236 E3
Chainpur Nepal 27°17N 87°19E 243 F12
Chaires U.S.A. 30°26N 84°7W 316 E5
Chaitén Chile 42°55S 72°43W 336 B2
Chaiya Thailand 9°23N 99°14E 237 H2
Chaiyaphum Thailand 15°43N 102°2E 236 E4
Chaj Doab Pakistan 32°15N 73°0E 242 C5
Chajari Argentina 30°42S 58°0W 334 C4
Chak Amru Pakistan 32°22N 75°11E 242 C6
Chaka South Sudan 4°49N 31°14E 257 G3
Chakar → Pakistan 29°29N 68°2E 242 E3
Chakari Zimbabwe 18°5S 29°51E 271 A4
Chakaria Bangla. 21°45N 92°5E 241 E4
Chakarnaba Chad 14°13N 20°51E 259 F4
Chakdaha India 22°26N 88°19E 124 C1
Chake Chake Tanzania 5°15S 39°45E 268 D4
Chakhānsūr Afghan. 31°10N 62°0E 240 C1
Chakonipau, L. Canada 56°18N 68°30W 299 A6
Chakradharpur India 22°45N 85°40E 243 H11
Chakrata India 30°42N 77°51E 242 D7
Chakwadam Burma 27°29N 98°31E 241 B7
Chakwal Pakistan 32°56N 72°53E 242 C5
Chala Peru 15°48S 74°20W 330 D3
Chalais France 45°16N 0°3E 174 C4
Chalakudi India 10°18N 76°20E 245 J3
Chalan Kanoa N. Marianas 15°8N 145°42E 302 e
Chalandri Greece 38°3N 23°48E 112 A2
Chalchihuites Mexico 23°29N 103°53W 318 C4
Chalcis = Chalkida Greece 38°27N 23°42E 204 C5
Châlette-sur-Loing France 48°1N 2°44E 173 D9
Chaleur B. Canada 47°55N 65°30W 299 C6
Chalfant U.S.A. 37°32N 118°21W 306 H8
Chalhuanca Peru 14°15S 73°15W 330 C3
Chaliki Greece 39°36N 22°30E 204 B4
Chalindrey France 47°43N 5°26E 173 E12
Chaling China 26°58N 113°30E 229 D9
Chalisgaon India 20°30N 75°10E 244 D2
Chalk River Canada 46°1N 77°27W 298 C4
Chalkar, Ozero = Shalkar Köli Kazakhstan 50°35N 51°47E 190 E10
Chalki Greece 36°17N 27°35E 205 E9
Chalkida Greece 38°27N 23°42E 204 C5
Chalkidiki Greece 40°25N 23°20E 202 F7
Chalky Inlet N.Z. 46°3S 166°31E 285 G1
Chalkyitsik U.S.A. 66°39N 143°43W 303 C12
Challakere India 14°19N 76°39E 245 G3
Challans France 46°50N 1°52W 172 F5
Challapata Bolivia 18°53S 66°50W 330 D4
Challawa Gorge Res. Nigeria 11°54N 8°25E 263 C6
Challenger Deep Pac. Oc. 11°30N 142°0E 288 F6
Challenger Fracture Zone Pac. Oc. 35°0S 105°0W 289 L17
Challis U.S.A. 44°30N 114°14W 304 D6
Chalmette U.S.A. 29°56N 89°57W 315 G10
Chaloem Rattanakosin △ Thailand 14°40N 99°17E 236 E2
Chalon-sur-Saône France 46°48N 4°50E 173 F11
Chalong Thailand 7°50N 98°22E 237 a
Chalonnes-sur-Loire France 47°20N 0°45W 172 E6
Châlons-en-Champagne France 48°58N 4°20E 173 D11
Chálten, Cerro = Fitz Roy, Cerro Argentina 49°17S 73°5W 336 C2
Châlus Haute-Vienne, France 45°39N 0°58E 174 C4
Chālūs Iran 36°38N 51°26E 247 B6
Cham Germany 49°13N 12°39E 179 F8
Cham, Cu Lao Vietnam 15°57N 108°30E 236 E7
Chama U.S.A. 36°54N 106°35W 305 H10
Chamah, Gunung Malaysia 5°13N 101°35E 234 A2
Chamaicó Argentina 35°3S 64°58W 334 D3
Chaman Pakistan 30°58N 66°25E 240 C2
Chamartín Spain 40°27N 3°40W 127 B1
Chamba India 32°35N 76°10E 242 C7
Chamba Tanzania 11°37S 37°0E 269 E4
Chambal → India 26°29N 79°15E 243 F8
Chamberi Spain 40°26N 3°42W 127 B1
Chamberlain U.S.A. 43°49N 99°20W 308 D4
Chamberlain → Australia 15°30S 127°54E 278 C4
Chamberlain L. U.S.A. 46°14N 69°19W 309 B19
Chambers U.S.A. 35°11N 109°26W 305 J9
Chambersburg U.S.A. 39°56N 77°40W 309 F15
Chambéry France 45°34N 5°55E 175 C9
Chambi, Jebel Tunisia 35°11N 8°39E 261 A6
Chamblee U.S.A. 33°53N 84°18W 316 B5
Chambly Canada 45°27N 73°17W 313 A11
Chambord Canada 48°25N 72°6W 299 C5
Chamboulive France 45°26N 1°42E 174 C5
Chambourcy France 48°54N 2°2E 134 A1
Chambri L. Papua N. G. 4°15S 143°10E 286 C2
Chamchamal Iraq 35°32N 44°50E 213 E11
Chamela Mexico 19°32N 105°5W 318 D3
Chamical Argentina 30°22S 66°27W 334 C2
Chamili Greece 35°50N 26°15E 205 F8
Chamkar Luong Cambodia 11°0N 103°45E 237 G4
Chamois U.S.A. 38°41N 91°46W 310 F5
Chamoli India 30°24N 79°21E 243 D8
Chamonix-Mont Blanc France 45°55N 6°51E 175 C10
Chamouchuane = Ashuapmushuan → Canada 48°37N 72°20W 298 C5
Champ de Mars, Parc du Paris, France 134 c2
Champa India 22°2N 82°43E 243 H10
Champagne Canada 60°49N 136°30W 296 A1
Champagne France 48°40N 4°20E 173 D11
Champagnole France 46°45N 5°55E 173 F12
Champaign U.S.A. 40°7N 88°15W 311 D8
Champaner India 22°29N 73°32E 242 H5
Champassak Laos 14°53N 105°52E 236 E5
Champaubert France 48°50N 3°45E 173 D10
Champawat India 29°20N 80°6E 243 E9
Champdeniers-St-Denis France 46°29N 0°25W 174 B3
Champdoré, L. Canada 55°55N 65°49W 299 A6
Champeix France 45°37N 3°8E 174 C7
Champhai India 23°28N 93°20E 241 D4
Champigny-sur-Marne France 48°49N 2°30E 134 B4
Champion U.S.A. 41°19N 80°51W 312 E4
Champlain U.S.A. 44°59N 73°27W 313 B11
Champlain, L. U.S.A. 44°40N 73°20W 313 B11
Champlain, Pont Canada 45°28N 73°31W 130 B2
Champlitte France 47°32N 5°31E 173 E12
Champotón Mexico 19°21N 90°43W 319 D6
Champs Elysées, Avenue des Paris, France 134 b2
Champs-sur-Marne France 48°50N 2°34E 134 A4
Champua India 22°5N 85°40E 243 H11
Chamrail India 22°38N 88°17E 124 B1
Chamrajnagar India 11°52N 76°52E 245 J3
Chamusca Portugal 39°21N 8°29W 195 F2
Chan Chan Peru 8°7S 73°0W 330 B2
Chana Thailand 6°55N 100°44E 237 J3
Chanakyapuri India 28°35N 77°11E 120 B2
Chañaral Chile 26°23S 70°40W 334 B1
Chanārān Iran 36°39N 59°6E 247 B8
Chanasma India 23°44N 72°5E 242 H5
Chancay Peru 11°32S 77°25W 330 C2
Chancel, Î. Martinique 14°41N 60°53W 322 j
Chanching = Zhanjiang China 21°15N 110°20E 229 G8
Chanco Chile 35°44S 72°32W 334 D1
Chand India 21°57N 79°7E 243 J8
Chandalar → U.S.A. 66°37N 146°0W 303 C11
Chandan Chauki India 28°33N 80°47E 243 E9
Chandannagar India 22°52N 88°24E 243 H13
Chandausi India 28°27N 78°49E 243 E8
Chandeleur Is. U.S.A. 29°55N 88°57W 315 G10
Chandeleur Sd. U.S.A. 29°55N 89°0W 315 G10
Chandigarh India 30°43N 76°47E 242 D7
Chandil India 22°58N 86°3E 243 H12
Chanditala India 22°41N 88°15E 124 A1
Chandler S. Austral., Australia 27°0S 133°19E 281 D1
Chandler Qué., Canada 48°18N 64°46W 299 C7
Chandler Ariz., U.S.A. 33°18N 111°50W 305 K8
Chandler Okla., U.S.A. 35°42N 96°53W 314 D6
Chandless → Brazil 9°8S 69°51W 330 B4
Chandod India 21°59N 73°28E 242 J5
Chandpur Bangla. 23°8N 90°45E 241 D3
Chandra Greece 35°3N 26°8E 205 F8
Chandragiri India 13°35N 79°19E 245 H4
Chandrapur India 19°57N 79°25E 244 E4
Chandrupatla India 18°33N 80°24E 244 E5
Chānf Iran 26°38N 60°29E 247 E9
Chang Pakistan 26°59N 68°30E 242 F3
Chang, Ko Thailand 12°0N 102°23E 237 G4
Chang, Ko Thailand 9°50N 98°27E 237 H2
Ch'ang Chiang = Chang Jiang → China 31°48N 121°10E 229 B13
Chang Jiang → China 31°48N 121°10E 229 B13
Chang-won S. Korea 35°16N 128°37E 224 E4
Changan = Xi'an China 34°15N 109°0E 226 G5
Changan China 22°48N 113°48E 219 a
Changanacheri India 9°25N 76°31E 245 K3
Changanassery = Changanacheri India 9°25N 76°31E 245 K3
Changane → Mozam. 24°30S 33°30E 271 B5
Changbai China 41°25N 128°5E 224 B4
Changbai Shan China 42°20N 129°0E 224 A4
Changchiak'ou = Zhangjiakou China 40°48N 114°55E 226 D8
Ch'angchih = Changzhi China 36°10N 113°6E 226 F7
Changchih Taiwan 22°41N 120°32E 225 D2
Ch'angchou = Changzhou China 31°47N 119°58E 229 B12
Changchow = Changzhou China 31°47N 119°58E 229 B12
Changchun China 43°57N 125°17E 227 C13
Changchunling China 45°18N 125°27E 227 B13
Changde China 29°4N 111°35E 229 C8
Changdo-ri N. Korea 38°30N 127°40E 224 C3
Changfeng China 32°28N 117°10E 229 A11
Changfeng Park China 31°14N 121°24E 138 B1
Changge China 34°13N 113°46E 226 G7
Changhai = Shanghai China 31°15N 121°26E 138 B2
Changhua Zhejiang, China 30°12N 119°12E 229 B12
Changhua Taiwan 24°2N 120°30E 225 B2
Changhua □ Taiwan 24°15N 120°55E 225 B2
Changhŭngni N. Korea 40°24N 128°19E 224 B4
Changi Singapore 1°23N 103°59E 138 A3
Changi, Singapore ✈ (SIN) Singapore 1°23N 103°59E 138 A3
Changji China 44°1N 87°19E 217 D11
Changjiang China 19°20N 108°55E 229 a
Changjiang Shuiku China 22°29N 113°27E 219 a
Changjin N. Korea 40°23N 127°15E 224 B3
Changjin-ho N. Korea 40°30N 127°15E 224 B3
Changle China 25°59N 119°27E 229 E12
Changli China 39°40N 119°13E 227 E10
Changling China 44°20N 123°58E 227 B12
Changlun Malaysia 6°25N 100°26E 237 J3
Changning Hunan, China 26°28N 112°22E 229 D9
Changning Shanghai, China 31°13N 121°24E 138 B1
Changning Sichuan, China 28°40N 104°56E 228 C5
Changning Yunnan, China 24°45N 99°30E 228 E2
Ch'angpin Taiwan 23°19N 121°27E 225 C3
Changping China 40°14N 116°12E 226 D9
Changsha China 28°12N 113°0E 229 C9
Changshan China 28°55N 118°27E 229 C12
Changshan Qundao China 39°11N 122°32E 227 E12
Changshou China 29°50N 107°4E 228 C6
Changshu China 31°38N 120°43E 229 B13
Changshun China 26°3N 106°25E 228 D6
Changtai China 24°35N 117°42E 229 E11
Changt'e = Chongde China 30°32N 120°26E 229 B13
Changting China 25°50N 116°22E 229 E11
Changtu China 42°46N 124°6E 227 C13
Changuinola Panama 9°26N 82°31W 320 E3
Changwu Guangxi Zhuangzu, China 23°25N 111°17E 229 F8
Changwu Shaanxi, China 35°10N 107°45E 226 G4
Changxing China 31°0N 119°55E 229 B12
Changyang China 30°30N 111°10E 229 B8
Changyi China 36°40N 119°30E 227 F10
Changyŏn N. Korea 38°15N 125°6E 224 C2
Changyuan Henan, China 35°15N 114°42E 226 G8
Changyuan Taiwan 23°25N 121°29E 225 C3
Changzhi = Changchih Taiwan 22°41N 120°32E 225 D2
Changzhi China 36°10N 113°6E 226 F7
Changzhou China 31°47N 119°58E 229 B12
Chanhanga Angola 16°0S 14°8E 265 F2
Chania Greece 35°30N 24°4E 207 E5
Chania ✈ (CHQ) Greece 35°30N 24°4E 207 E5
Chanion, Kolpos Greece 35°33N 23°55E 207 E4
Chanlar = Goygöl Azerbaijan 40°37N 46°12E 191 K8
Channagiri India 14°2N 75°56E 245 G2
Channapatna India 12°40N 77°15E 245 H3
Channel Is. U.K. 49°19N 2°24W 169 H5
Channel Is. Calif., U.S.A. 33°40N 119°15W 307 M7
Channel Islands △ U.S.A. 34°0N 119°24W 307 L7
Channel-Port aux Basques Canada 47°30N 59°9W 299 C8
Channel Tunnel Europe 51°0N 1°30E 169 F9
Channing U.S.A. 35°41N 102°20W 314 D3
Chantada Spain 42°36N 7°46W 194 C3
Chantereine France 48°53N 2°37E 134 A4
Chanthaburi Thailand 12°38N 102°12E 236 F4
Chantian China 23°12N 113°16E 121 A2
Chantilly France 49°12N 2°29E 173 C9
Chantonnay France 46°40N 1°3W 172 F5
Chantrey Inlet Canada 67°48N 96°20W 294 D12
Chanumla India 8°19N 93°5E 245 K11
Chanute U.S.A. 37°41N 95°27W 308 G6
Chany, Ozero Russia 54°49N 77°29E 217 B9
Chanza → Spain 37°32N 7°30W 195 H3
Chao Hu China 31°30N 117°30E 229 B11
Chao Phraya → Thailand 13°40N 100°31E 236 F3
Chao Phraya Lowlands Thailand 15°30N 100°0E 236 E3
Chaocheng China 36°4N 115°37E 226 F8
Ch'aochou Taiwan 22°33N 120°32E 225 D2
Chaohu China 31°38N 117°50E 229 B11
Chaouia-Ouardigha □ Morocco 33°0N 7°30W 260 B3
Chaoyang Beijing, China 39°53N 116°26E 114 B2
Chaoyang Guangdong, China 23°17N 116°30E 229 F11
Chaoyang Liaoning, China 41°35N 120°22E 227 D11
Chaoyangmen China 39°54N 116°23E 114 B2
Chaozhou = Ch'aochou Taiwan 22°33N 120°32E 225 D2
Chaozhou China 23°42N 116°32E 229 F11
Chapada Diamantina △ Brazil 12°52S 41°30W 333 D3
Chapada dos Guimarães Brazil 15°26S 55°45W 331 D6
Chapada dos Guimarães △ Brazil 15°18S 55°54W 331 D6
Chapada dos Veadeiros △ Brazil 14°0S 47°30W 333 D2
Chapaev Kazakhstan 50°25N 51°10E 190 E10
Chapais Canada 49°47N 74°51W 298 C5
Chapala Mozam. 15°50S 37°35E 269 F4
Chapala, L. de Mexico 20°15N 103°0W 318 C4
Chaparé → Bolivia 15°58S 64°42W 331 D5
Chaparmukh India 26°12N 92°31E 241 B4
Chaparral Colombia 3°43N 75°28W 328 C2
Chapayevsk Russia 53°0N 49°40E 190 D9
Chapecó Brazil 27°14S 52°41W 335 B5
Chapel Hill U.S.A. 35°55N 79°4W 315 D15
Chapelizod Ireland 53°21N 6°21W 120 A1
Chapelton Jamaica 18°5N 77°16W 320 a
Chapin = Edinburg U.S.A. 26°18N 98°10W 314 H5
Chapin U.S.A. 39°46N 90°24W 310 E6
Chapleau Canada 47°50N 83°24W 298 C3
Chaplin Canada 50°28N 106°40W 297 C7
Chaplin L. Canada 50°22N 106°36W 297 C7
Chaplino Ukraine 48°8N 36°15E 189 H9
Chaplygin Russia 53°15N 40°0E 188 F11
Chappell U.S.A. 41°6N 102°28W 308 E2
Chappells U.S.A. 34°11N 81°52W 316 A8
Chapra = Chhapra India 25°48N 84°44E 243 G11
Chapultepec, Bosque de Mexico 19°25N 99°11W 128 B1
Chapultepec, Castillo de Mexico 19°25N 99°10W 128 B1
Chaqābel Iran 33°16N 47°30E 213 F12
Châr Mauritania 21°32N 12°45W 260 D2
Chara Russia 56°54N 118°20E 215 D12
Charadai Argentina 27°35S 59°55W 334 B4
Charagato, Pta. Venezuela 10°50N 64°9W 329 a
Charagua Bolivia 19°45S 63°10W 331 D5
Charakas Greece 35°1N 25°7E 207 E6
Charalá Colombia 6°17N 73°10W 328 B3
Charambirá, Punta Colombia 4°16N 77°32W 328 C2
Charaña Bolivia 17°30S 69°25W 330 D4
Charantsavan Armenia 40°35N 44°41E 191 K7
Charanwala India 27°51N 72°10E 242 F5
Charapita Colombia 0°37S 74°21W 328 D3
Charata Argentina 27°13S 61°14W 334 B3
Charcas Mexico 23°8N 101°7W 318 C4
Charcot I. Antarctica 70°0S 70°0W 151 C17
Chard U.K. 50°52N 2°58W 169 G5
Chardon U.S.A. 41°35N 81°12W 312 E3
Charduar India 26°51N 92°46E 241 B4
Chardzhou = Türkmenabat Turkmenistan 39°6N 63°34E 247 B9
Charente □ France 45°50N 0°16E 174 C4
Charente → France 45°57N 1°5W 174 C2
Charente-Inférieure = Charente-Maritime □ France 45°45N 0°45W 174 C3
Charente-Maritime □ France 45°45N 0°45W 174 C3
Charenton-du-Cher France 46°44N 2°39E 173 F9
Charenton-le-Pont France 48°49N 2°25E 134 B3
Chari → Chad 12°58N 14°31E 259 F2
Chari-Baguirmi □ Chad 11°0N 17°0E 259 F3
Chārīkār Afghan. 35°0N 69°10E 240 B3
Charing U.S.A. 32°28N 84°22W 316 C5
Charing Cross London, U.K. 125 b4
Chariton U.S.A. 41°1N 93°19W 310 C3
Chariton → U.S.A. 39°19N 92°58W 310 E4
Charity Guyana 7°24N 58°36W 329 B6
Chärjew = Türkmenabat Turkmenistan 39°6N 63°34E 247 B9
Charkhari India 25°24N 79°45E 243 G8
Charkhi Dadri India 28°37N 76°17E 242 E7
Charleroi Belgium 50°24N 4°27E 170 D4
Charleroi Pa., U.S.A. 40°9N 79°57W 312 F5
Charleroi, Kanal de → Belgium 50°51N 4°19E 116 B1
Charles, C. U.S.A. 37°7N 75°58W 309 G16
Charles, I. = Santa María, I. Ecuador 1°17S 90°26W 330 a
Charles, Peak Australia 32°52S 121°11E 279 F3
Charles Bridge = Karlův most Prague, Czech Rep. 135 b1
Charles City U.S.A. 43°4N 92°41W 310 A4
Charles de Gaulle, Paris ✈ (CDG) France 49°0N 2°32E 173 D9
Charles Gates Dawes House U.S.A. 42°2N 87°40W 119 A2
Charles I. Canada 62°39N 74°15W 295 E17
Charles L. Canada 59°50N 110°33W 297 B6
Charles Sound N.Z. 45°2S 167°4E 285 F2
Charles Square = Karlovo náměstí Prague, Czech Rep. 135 c1
Charles Town U.S.A. 39°17N 77°52W 309 F15
Charlesbourg Canada 46°51N 71°16W 309 B18
Charleston Ill., U.S.A. 39°30N 88°10W 311 E8
Charleston Miss., U.S.A. 34°1N 90°4W 315 D9
Charleston Mo., U.S.A. 36°55N 89°21W 308 G9
Charleston S.C., U.S.A. 32°46N 79°56W 316 C10
Charleston W. Va., U.S.A. 38°21N 81°38W 309 F13
Charleston L. Canada 44°32N 76°0W 313 B9
Charleston Peak U.S.A. 36°16N 115°42W 307 J11
Charlestown Mayo, Ireland 53°58N 8°48W 166 C3
Charlestown St. Kitts & Nevis 17°8N 62°37W 322 d
Charlestown KwaZulu Natal, S. Africa 27°26S 29°53E 271 C4
Charlestown Ind., U.S.A. 38°27N 85°40W 311 F11
Charlestown Mass., U.S.A. 42°22N 71°4W 116 A2
Charlestown N.H., U.S.A. 43°14N 72°25W 313 C12
Charlestown Bridge Boston, U.S.A. 116 a2
Charlestown of Aberlour U.K. 57°28N 3°14W 167 D5
Charleville Queens., Australia 26°24S 146°15E 281 D4
Charleville Cork, Ireland 52°21N 8°40W 166 D3
Charleville-Mézières France 49°44N 4°40E 173 C11
Charlevoix U.S.A. 45°19N 85°16W 309 C11
Charlie Gibbs Fracture Zone Atl. Oc. 52°45N 35°30W 152 A8
Charlieu France 46°10N 4°10E 173 F11
Charlotte Dominica 15°17N 61°24W 323 k
Charlotte Mich., U.S.A. 42°34N 84°50W 311 B11
Charlotte N.C., U.S.A. 35°13N 80°50W 315 D14
Charlotte Vt., U.S.A. 44°19N 73°16W 313 B11
Charlotte Amalie U.S. Virgin Is. 18°21N 64°56W 321 C7
Charlotte Harbor U.S.A. 26°57N 82°4W 317 J7
Charlotte L. Canada 52°12N 125°19W 296 C3
Charlottenburg Sweden 59°54N 12°17E 162 E6
Charlottenburg Germany 52°31N 13°16E 115 A2
Charlottenburg, Schloss Germany 52°31N 13°18E 115 A2
Charlottenlund Denmark 55°44N 12°35E 118 A3
Charlottesville U.S.A. 38°2N 78°30W 309 F14
Charlottetown Nfld. & L., Canada 52°46N 56°7W 299 B8
Charlottetown P.E.I., Canada 46°14N 63°8W 299 C7
Charlotteville Trin. & Tob. 11°20N 60°33W 323 s
Charlton Vic., Australia 36°16S 143°24E 282 D5
Charlton London, U.K. 51°29N 0°1E 125 B4
Charlton I. Canada 52°0N 79°20W 298 B4
Charmes France 48°22N 6°17E 173 D13
Charneca Lisboa, Portugal 38°47N 9°8W 126 A2
Charneca Setúbal, Portugal 38°37N 9°12W 126 B1
Charny Canada 46°43N 71°15W 299 C5
Charnyany Belarus 51°59N 24°12E 185 G11
Charolles France 46°27N 4°16E 173 F11
Chârost France 47°0N 2°7E 173 F9
Charouine Algeria 29°0N 0°15W 261 C4
Charre Mozam. 17°13S 35°10E 269 F4
Charroux France 46°9N 0°25E 174 B4
Charsadda Pakistan 34°7N 71°45E 242 B4
Charshanga = Köytendag Turkmenistan 37°30N 66°1E 240 A2
Charters Towers Australia 20°5S 146°13E 280 C4
Chartres France 48°29N 1°30E 172 D8
Chartreuse △ France 45°22N 5°42E 175 C9
Charuma Trin. & Tob. 10°24N 61°9W 323 t
Charysh → Russia 52°22N 83°45E 217 B10
Chascomús Argentina 35°30S 58°0W 334 D4
Chase Canada 50°50N 119°41W 296 C5
Chase, L. U.S.A. 28°28N 81°31W 133 B1
Chasefu Zambia 11°55S 33°8E 269 E3
Chashma Barrage Pakistan 32°27N 71°20E 242 C4
Chaslands Mistake N.Z. 46°38S 169°22E 285 G4
Chasong N. Korea 41°27N 126°38E 224 B3
Chasseneuil-sur-Bonnieure France 45°52N 0°29E 174 C4
Chastanet, Anse St. Lucia 13°52N 61°5W 323 m
Chāt Iran 37°59N 55°16E 247 B7
Chatal Balkan = Udvoy Balkan Bulgaria 42°50N 26°50E 203 D10
Chatanika U.S.A. 65°7N 147°28W 303 D11
Château-Arnoux-St-Auban France 44°6N 6°0E 175 D10
Château-Chinon France 47°4N 3°56E 173 E10
Château-d'Olonne France 46°30N 1°44W 174 B2
Château-du-Loir France 47°40N 0°25E 172 E7
Château Dubuc Martinique 14°46N 60°55W 322 j
Château Gaillard Guadeloupe 16°18N 61°23W 322 e
Château-Gontier France 47°50N 0°48W 172 E6
Château-la-Vallière France 47°30N 0°20E 172 E7
Château-Landon France 48°8N 2°40E 173 D9
Château Murat Guadeloupe 15°52N 61°17W 322 e
Château-Renard France 47°56N 2°55E 173 E9
Château-Renault France 47°36N 0°56E 172 E7
Château-Salins France 48°50N 6°30E 173 D13
Château-Thierry France 49°3N 3°20E 173 C10
Châteaubelair St. Vincent 13°17N 61°15W 323 n
Châteaubourg France 48°7N 1°25W 172 D5
Châteaubriant France 47°43N 1°23W 172 E5
Châteaudun France 48°3N 1°20E 172 D8
Châteaufort France 48°44N 2°5E 134 B1
Chateaugay U.S.A. 44°56N 74°5W 313 B10
Châteaugiron France 48°3N 1°30W 172 D5
Châteauguay, L. Canada 56°26N 70°3W 299 A5
Châteaulin France 48°11N 4°8W 172 D2
Châteaumeillant France 46°35N 2°12E 173 F9
Châteauneuf-du-Faou France 48°11N 3°50W 172 D3
Châteauneuf-sur-Charente France 45°36N 0°3W 174 C3
Châteauneuf-sur-Cher France 46°52N 2°18E 173 F9
Châteauneuf-sur-Loire France 47°52N 2°13E 173 E9
Châteaurenard France 43°53N 4°51E 175 E8
Châteauroux France 46°50N 1°40E 173 F8
Châteauvillain France 48°2N 4°55E 173 D11
Châteaux, Pte. des Guadeloupe 16°15N 61°10W 322 e
Châtel-Guyon France 45°55N 3°4E 174 C7
Châtelaillon-Plage France 46°5N 1°5W 174 B2
Châtellerault France 46°50N 0°30E 172 F7
Châtelus-Malvaleix France 46°18N 2°1E 173 F9
Châtenay-Malabry France 48°46N 2°16E 134 B2
Chatham = Miramichi Canada 47°2N 65°28W 299 C6
Chatham Ont., Canada 42°24N 82°11W 312 D2
Chatham Medway, U.K. 51°22N 0°32E 169 F8
Chatham Ill., U.S.A. 41°45N 87°36W 119 C3
Chatham Ill., U.S.A. 39°40N 89°42W 310 E7
Chatham N.Y., U.S.A. 42°21N 73°36W 313 D11
Chatham, I. = San Cristóbal, I. Ecuador 0°50S 89°26W 330 a
Chatham, I. Chile 50°40S 74°25W 336 D2
Chatham I. N.Z. 43°50S 176°20W 285 a
Chatham Is. Pac. Oc. 44°0S 176°40W 285 a
Chatham Rise Pac. Oc. 43°30S 180°0E 288 M10
Châtillon Hauts-de-Seine, France 48°48N 2°17E 134 B2
Châtillon Italy 45°45N 7°37E 198 C4
Châtillon-Coligny France 47°50N 2°51E 173 E9
Châtillon-en-Diois France 44°41N 5°29E 175 D9
Châtillon-sur-Indre France 46°59N 1°10E 172 F8
Châtillon-sur-Loire France 47°35N 2°44E 173 E9
Châtillon-sur-Seine France 47°50N 4°33E 173 E11
Chatmohar Bangla. 24°15N 89°15E 243 G13
Chatou France 48°53N 2°9E 134 A1
Chatpur India 22°36N 88°22E 124 B2
Chatra India 24°12N 84°56E 243 G11
Chatrapur India 19°22N 85°2E 244 E7
Chats, L. des Canada 45°30N 76°20W 313 A8
Chatsu India 26°36N 75°57E 242 F6
Chatswood Australia 33°47S 151°11E 139 A2
Chatsworth Ont., Canada 44°27N 80°54W 312 B4
Chatsworth Ill., U.S.A. 40°45N 88°18W 311 D8
Chatsworth Zimbabwe 19°38S 31°13E 269 F3
Chatta-Hantō Japan 34°45N 136°55E 223 G8
Châttagâm = Chittagong Bangla. 22°19N 91°48E 241 D3
Chattahoochee U.S.A. 30°42N 84°51W 316 E5
Chattahoochee → U.S.A. 30°54N 84°57W 316 E5
Chattanooga U.S.A. 35°3N 85°19W 315 D12
Chatteris U.K. 52°28N 0°2E 169 E8
Chatturat Thailand 15°40N 101°51E 236 E3
Chatuchak Thailand 13°48N 100°33E 113 B2
Chatuchak Park Thailand 13°48N 100°32E 113 B2
Chau Doc Vietnam 10°42N 105°7E 237 G5
Chaubourg, Mt. St. Lucia 14°2N 60°59W 323 m
Chaudes-Aigues France 44°51N 3°1E 174 D7
Chauffailles France 46°13N 4°20E 173 F11
Chauk Burma 20°53N 94°49E 241 E5
Chaukan Pass Burma 27°8N 97°10E 241 B6
Chaukuli Pakistan 24°55N 66°55E 123 A1
Chaumont Haute-Marne, France 48°7N 5°8E 173 D12
Chaumont N.Y., U.S.A. 44°4N 76°8W 313 B8
Chaumont-en-Vexin France 49°16N 1°53E 173 C8
Chaumont-sur-Loire France 47°29N 1°11E 172 E8
Chaunay France 46°13N 0°9E 174 B4
Chaung-u Burma 21°57N 95°16E 241 E5
Chaunskaya G. Russia 69°0N 169°0E 215 C17
Chauny France 49°37N 3°12E 173 C10
Chaura India 8°27N 93°2E 245 K11
Chausey, Îs. France 48°52N 1°49W 172 D5
Chaussin France 46°59N 5°22E 173 F12
Chautara Nepal 27°46N 85°42E 243 F11
Chautauqua L. U.S.A. 42°10N 79°24W 312 D5
Chauvigny France 46°34N 0°39E 172 F7
Chauvin Canada 52°45N 110°10W 297 C6
Chavakachcheri Sri Lanka 9°39N 80°9E 245 K5
Chavanges France 48°30N 4°35E 173 D11
Chavantina Brazil 14°40S 52°21W 331 C7
Chavarria Peru 12°0S 77°7W 124 B2
Chavash Varmane △ Russia 54°50N 47°10E 190 C8
Chavdata Greece 38°12N 20°23E 207 C1
Chaves Brazil 0°15S 49°55W 332 B2
Chaves Portugal 41°45N 7°32W 194 D3
Chaville France 48°48N 2°11E 134 B2
Chavín Peru 9°35S 77°10W 330 B2
Chavuma Zambia 13°4S 22°40E 265 E4
Chawang Thailand 8°25N 99°30E 237 H2
Chayang S. Korea 37°32N 127°3E 137 B2
Chaykovskiy Russia 56°47N 54°9E 186 C9
Chazelles-sur-Lyon France 45°39N 4°22E 175 C8
Chazuta Peru 6°30S 76°0W 330 B2
Chazy U.S.A. 44°53N 73°26W 313 B11
Cheaha Mt. U.S.A. 33°29N 85°49W 316 B4
Cheb Czech Rep. 50°9N 12°28E 180 A5
Chebanse U.S.A. 41°0N 87°54W 311 D9
Chebbi, Erg Africa 31°12N 3°58W 260 B4
Cheboksarskoye Vdkhr. Russia 56°13N 46°58E 190 B8
Cheboksary Russia 56°8N 47°12E 190 B8
Cheboygan U.S.A. 45°39N 84°29W 309 C11
Chebsara Russia 59°10N 38°59E 188 C10
Chech, Erg Africa 25°0N 2°15W 260 D4
Chechelnyk Ukraine 48°13N 29°22E 183 B14
Chechen, Ostrov Russia 43°59N 47°40E 191 H8
Ch'ech'eng Taiwan 22°5N 120°42E 225 D2
Chechenia □ Russia 43°30N 45°29E 191 J7
Checheno-Ingush Republic = Chechenia □ Russia 43°30N 45°29E 191 J7
Chechnya = Chechenia □ Russia 43°30N 45°29E 191 J7
Chęciny Poland 50°46N 20°28E 185 H7
Checotah U.S.A. 35°28N 95°31W 314 D7
Chedabucto B. Canada 45°25N 61°8W 299 C7
Cheduba I. Burma 18°45N 93°40E 241 F4
Cheektowaga U.S.A. 42°54N 78°45W 312 D6
Cheepie Australia 26°33S 145°0E 281 D4
Cheeyou Trin. & Tob. 10°33N 61°8W 323 t
Chef-Boutonne France 46°7N 0°4W 174 B3
Chefchaouen Morocco 35°9N 5°15W 260 A3
Cheffadine Niger 19°57N 12°11E 259 D2
Chefoo = Yantai China 37°34N 121°22E 227 F11
Chefornak U.S.A. 60°13N 164°12W 303 F6
Chegdomyn Russia 51°7N 133°1E 215 D14
Chegga Mauritania 25°27N 5°40W 260 C3
Chegutu Zimbabwe 18°10S 30°14E 269 F3
Chehalis U.S.A. 46°40N 122°58W 306 D4
Chehalis → U.S.A. 46°57N 123°50W 306 D3
Cheile Bicazului-Hăşmaş △ Romania 46°55N 25°50E 183 D10
Cheile Nerei-Beusnita △ Romania 44°56N 21°52E 182 F6
Cheiron, Mt. du France 43°49N 6°58E 175 E10
Cheju = Jeju S. Korea 33°31N 126°32E 224 a
Cheju-do = Jeju-do S. Korea 33°29N 126°34E 224 a
Cheju Str. = Jeju Haehyop S. Korea 33°50N 126°30E 227 H14
Chek Lap Kok Hong Kong, China 22°18N 113°56E 122 B1
Chek Lap Kok ✈ (HKG) Hong Kong, China 22°19N 113°57E 122 B1
Chekalin Russia 54°10N 36°10E 188 E9
Chekhovo Russia 54°33N 20°43E 184 D7
Chekiang = Zhejiang □ China 29°0N 120°0E 229 C13
Chel = Kuru, Bahr el → South Sudan 8°10N 26°50E 257 F2
Chela, Sa. da Angola 16°20S 13°20E 265 F2
Chelan U.S.A. 47°51N 120°1W 304 C3
Chelan, L. U.S.A. 48°11N 120°30W 304 B3
Cheleken = Hazar Turkmenistan 39°34N 53°16E 187 G9
Cheleken Yarymadasy Turkmenistan 39°30N 53°15E 247 B7
Chelforó Argentina 39°0S 66°33W 336 A3
Chéliff, O. → Algeria 36°0N 0°8E 261 A5
Chelkar = Shalqar Kazakhstan 47°48N 59°39E 216 C5
Chella Ethiopia 5°0N 37°26E 257 F4
Chellala Dahrania Algeria 33°2N 0°1E 261 B5
Chelles France 48°53N 2°35E 134 A4
Chelles, Canal de France 48°51N 2°35E 134 A4
Chells-le-Pin ✈ France 48°53N 2°36E 134 A4
Chełm Poland 51°8N 23°30E 185 G10
Chełmno Poland 53°20N 18°30E 185 E5
Chelmsford U.K. 51°44N 0°29E 169 F8
Chełmża Poland 53°10N 18°39E 185 E5
Chelny = Naberezhnyye Chelny Russia 55°42N 52°19E 190 C11
Chelsea Vic., Australia 38°5S 145°8E 283 E6
Chelsea London, U.K. 51°29N 0°10W 125 B2
Chelsea Mass., U.S.A. 42°23N 71°1W 116 A2
Chelsea Mich., U.S.A. 42°19N 84°1W 311 B12
Chelsea New York, U.S.A. 132 c1
Chelsea Vt., U.S.A. 43°59N 72°27W 313 C12
Cheltenham U.K. 51°54N 2°4W 169 F5
Chelva Spain 39°45N 1°0W 196 F4
Chelyabinsk Russia 55°10N 61°24E 216 A6
Chelyakobi = Kopeysk Russia 55°7N 61°37E 216 A6
Chelyuskin, C. = Chelyuskin, Mys Russia 77°30N 103°0E 215 B11
Chelyuskin, Mys Russia 77°30N 103°0E 215 B11
Chemainus Canada 48°55N 123°42W 306 B3
Chembar = Belinskiy Russia 53°0N 43°25E 190 D6
Chembur India 19°3N 72°53E 130 A2
Chemchâm, Sebkhet Mauritania 21°2N 12°4W 260 D2
Chemillé France 47°14N 0°45W 172 E6
Chemin Grenier Mauritius 20°29S 57°28E 272 e
Chemnitz Germany 50°51N 12°54E 178 E8
Chemulpho = Incheon S. Korea 37°27N 126°40E 224 D3
Chemult U.S.A. 43°14N 121°47W 304 E3
Chen, Gora Russia 65°16N 141°50E 215 C15
Chenab → Pakistan 30°23N 71°2E 242 D4
Chenab Nagar Pakistan 31°45N 72°55E 242 D5
Chenachane Algeria 26°0N 4°15W 260 C4
Chenachane, O. → Algeria 25°20N 3°20W 260 C4
Chenango Forks U.S.A. 42°15N 75°51W 313 D9
Chencha Ethiopia 6°15N 37°32E 257 F4
Chenchiang = Zhenjiang China 32°11N 119°26E 229 A12
Cheney U.S.A. 47°30N 117°35W 304 C5
Cheng Xian China 33°43N 105°42E 226 H3
Chengalpattu India 12°42N 79°58E 245 H4
Chengbu China 26°18N 110°16E 229 D8
Chengcheng China 35°8N 109°56E 226 G5
Chengchou = Zhengzhou China 34°45N 113°34E 226 G7
Chengde China 40°59N 117°58E 227 D9
Chengdong Hu China 32°15N 116°20E 229 A11
Chengdu China 30°38N 104°2E 228 B5
Chengele India 28°47N 96°16E 241 A6
Chenggong = Ch'engkung Taiwan 23°6N 121°22E 225 C3
Chenggong China 24°52N 102°56E 228 E4
Chenggu China 33°10N 107°21E 228 A6
Chenghai China 23°30N 116°42E 229 F11
Chengjiang China 24°39N 103°0E 228 E4

Chengkou China 31°54N 108°31E 228 B7
Ch'engkung Taiwan 23°6N 121°22E 225 C3
Chengmai China 19°50N 109°58E 229 a
Chengnan Taiwan 23°3N 120°7E 225 C2
Chengshan Jiao China 37°25N 122°44E 227 F12
Chengshousi China 39°49N 116°24E 114 C2
Chengteh = Chengde China 40°59N 117°58E 227 D9
Ch'engtu = Chengdu China 30°38N 104°2E 228 B5
Chengwu China 34°58N 115°50E 226 G8
Chengxi Hu China 32°15N 116°10E 229 A11
Chengyang China 36°18N 120°21E 227 F11
Chenjiagang China 34°23N 119°47E 227 G10
Chenkaladi Sri Lanka 7°47N 81°35E 245 L5
Chennai India 13°8N 80°19E 245 H5
Chennevières-sur-Marne France 48°47N 2°31E 134 B4
Chenoa U.S.A. 40°45N 88°43W 311 D8
Chenôve France 47°16N 5°1E 173 E12
Chenxi China 28°2N 110°12E 229 C8
Chenzhou China 25°47N 113°1E 229 E9
Cheò, Eilean a' = Skye U.K. 57°15N 6°10W 167 D2
Cheo Reo Vietnam 13°20N 108°25E 236 F7
Cheom Ksan Cambodia 14°13N 104°56E 236 E5
Cheonan S. Korea 36°48N 127°9E 224 D3
Cheongdam S. Korea 37°31N 127°2E 137 B2
Cheongdo S. Korea 35°38N 128°42E 224 E4
Cheongju S. Korea 36°39N 127°27E 224 D3
Cheongsando S. Korea 34°11N 126°53E 224 E3
Cheongsong S. Korea 36°25N 129°3E 224 D4
Cheonho S. Korea 37°32N 127°6E 137 B2
Cheonsumman S. Korea 36°33N 126°25E 224 D3
Cheops Egypt 29°58N 31°8E 117 B1
Cheorwon S. Korea 38°15N 127°10E 224 C3
Chepelare Bulgaria 41°44N 24°40E 203 E8
Chepelarska ➔ Bulgaria 42°9N 24°54E 203 D8
Chepén Peru 7°15S 79°23W 330 B2
Chépénéhé N. Cal. 20°47S 167°9E 288 d
Chepes Argentina 31°20S 66°35W 334 C2
Chepo Panama 9°10N 79°6W 320 E4
Chepstow U.K. 51°38N 2°41W 169 F5
Chequamegon B. U.S.A. 46°39N 90°51W 308 B8
Cher □ France 47°10N 2°30E 173 E9
Cher ➔ France 47°21N 0°29E 172 E7
Chéradi Italy 40°27N 17°10E 201 B10
Cheran India 25°45N 90°44E 241 C3
Cherasco Italy 44°39N 7°51E 198 D4
Cherating Malaysia 3°35N 103°5E 234 B2
Cheraw U.S.A. 34°42N 79°53W 315 D15
Cherbourg-Octeville France 49°39N 1°40W 172 C5
Cherchell Algeria 36°35N 2°12E 261 A5
Cherdakly Russia 54°25N 48°50E 190 C9
Cherdyn Russia 60°24N 56°29E 186 B10
Cheremkhovo Russia 53°8N 103°1E 218 A9
Cherepanovo Russia 54°15N 83°30E 217 B10
Cherepovets Russia 59°5N 37°55E 188 C9
Chergui, Chott ech Algeria 34°21N 0°25E 261 B5
Chergui, Zahrez Algeria 35°11N 3°31E 261 A5
Cherial India 17°55N 78°59E 244 F4
Cheribon = Cirebon Indonesia 6°45S 108°32E 235 D3
Cherikov = Cherykaw Belarus 53°32N 31°20E 177 B16
Cheriyam I. India 10°9N 73°40E 245 J1
Cherkasy Ukraine 49°27N 32°4E 189 H7
Cherkasy □ Ukraine 48°55N 30°50E 189 H6
Cherkessk Russia 44°15N 42°5E 191 H6
Cherla India 18°5N 80°49E 244 E5
Cherlak Russia 54°15N 74°55E 217 B8
Chernaya Russia 70°30N 89°10E 215 B9
Chernelytsya Ukraine 48°49N 25°26E 183 B10
Cherni Bulgaria 42°35N 23°18E 202 D7
Chernigov = Chernihiv Ukraine 51°28N 31°20E 189 G6
Chernigovka Russia 44°19N 132°34E 220 B6
Chernihiv Ukraine 51°28N 31°20E 189 G6
Chernihiv □ Ukraine 51°10N 32°5E 189 G7
Chernivtsi Chernivtsi, Ukraine 48°15N 25°52E 183 B10
Chernivtsi Vinnyts'ka, Ukraine 48°32N 28°9E 183 B13
Chernivtsi □ Ukraine 48°5N 25°30E 183 B10
Chernobyl = Chornobyl Ukraine 51°20N 30°15E 177 C16
Chernogorsk Russia 53°49N 91°18E 217 B12
Chernomorskoye = Chornomorske Ukraine 45°31N 32°40E 189 K7
Chernorechye = Dzerzhinsk Russia 56°14N 43°30E 190 B6
Chernovtsy = Chernivtsi Ukraine 48°15N 25°52E 183 B10
Chernyakhovsk Russia 54°36N 21°48E 184 D8
Chernyanka Russia 50°56N 37°49E 189 G9
Chernysheyskiy Russia 63°0N 112°30E 215 C12
Chernyye Zemli Russia 46°10N 46°0E 191 H8
Cherokee Iowa, U.S.A. 42°45N 95°33W 308 D6
Cherokee Okla., U.S.A. 36°45N 98°21W 314 C5
Cherokee Village U.S.A. 36°18N 91°31W 314 C9
Cherokees, Grand Lake O' The U.S.A. 36°28N 94°55W 314 C7
Cherquenco Chile 38°35S 72°0W 336 A2
Cherrapunji India 25°17N 91°47E 241 C3
Cherry Valley U.S.A. 42°48N 74°45W 313 D10
Cherryville U.S.A. 37°51N 91°16W 310 G5
Cherskiy Russia 68°45N 161°18E 215 C17
Cherskogo Khrebet Russia 65°0N 143°0E 215 C15
Cherso Greece 41°5N 22°47E 202 E6
Chersonisos Akrotiri Greece 35°30N 24°10E 207 E5
Chertanovka ➔ Russia 55°38N 37°48E 129 C2
Chertanovo Russia 55°38N 37°36E 129 C2
Cherthala India 9°42N 76°20E 245 K3
Chertkov = Chortkiv Ukraine 49°2N 25°46E 177 D13
Chertkovo Russia 49°25N 40°19E 189 H11
Cherven Belarus 53°45N 28°28E 177 B15
Cherven-Bryag Bulgaria 43°17N 24°7E 203 C8
Chervonoarmiyske Ukraine 45°47N 28°44E 183 E13
Chervonohrad Ukraine 50°25N 24°10E 177 C13
Cherwell ➔ U.K. 51°44N 1°14W 169 F6
Cherykaw Belarus 53°32N 31°20E 177 B16
Cheryomushki Russia 55°40N 37°35E 129 B2
Chesapeake U.S.A. 36°49N 76°16W 309 G15
Chesapeake B. U.S.A. 38°0N 76°10W 309 F14
Cheshire East □ U.K. 53°15N 2°15W 168 D5
Cheshire West and Chester □ U.K. 53°15N 2°40W 168 D5
Cheshskaya Guba Russia 67°20N 47°0E 186 A8
Cheshunt U.K. 51°43N 0°1W 169 F7
Chesil Beach U.K. 50°37N 2°33W 169 G5
Chesley Canada 44°17N 81°5W 312 B3
Chesnokovka = Novoaltaysk Russia 53°30N 84°0E 217 B10
Cheste Spain 39°30N 0°41W 197 F4
Chester Ches., U.K. 53°12N 2°53W 168 D5
Chester Calif., U.S.A. 40°19N 121°14W 304 F3
Chester Ga., U.S.A. 32°24N 83°9W 316 C6
Chester Ill., U.S.A. 37°55N 89°49W 310 G7
Chester Mont., U.S.A. 48°31N 110°58W 304 B8
Chester Pa., U.S.A. 39°51N 75°22W 309 F16
Chester S.C., U.S.A. 34°43N 81°12W 315 D14
Chester Vt., U.S.A. 43°16N 72°36W 313 C12
Chester W. Va., U.S.A. 40°37N 80°34W 312 F4
Chester-le-Street U.K. 54°51N 1°34W 168 C6
Chesterfield Derby, U.K. 53°15N 1°25W 168 D6
Chesterfield Mo., U.S.A. 38°40N 90°35W 310 F6
Chesterfield, Îs. N. Cal. 19°52S 158°15E 277 D10
Chesterfield Inlet Canada 63°30N 90°45W 294 E13
Chesterton Ra. Australia 25°30S 147°27E 281 D4
Chesterton Range △ Australia 26°16S 147°22E 281 D4
Chestertown U.S.A. 43°40N 73°48W 313 C11
Chesterville Canada 45°6N 75°14W 313 A9
Chestnut Hill U.S.A. 42°19N 71°10W 116 B1
Chesuncook L. U.S.A. 46°0N 69°21W 309 C19
Chetamale India 10°43N 92°33E 245 J11
Chéticamp Canada 46°37N 60°59W 299 C7
Chetlat I. India 11°42N 72°42E 245 J1
Chetrosu Moldova 48°5N 27°54E 183 B12
Chetumal Mexico 18°30N 88°20W 319 D7
Chetumal, B. de Cent. Amer. 18°40N 88°10W 319 D7
Chetwynd Canada 55°45N 121°36W 296 B4
Cheung Chau Hong Kong, China 22°13N 114°1E 122 B2
Cheung Sha Hong Kong, China 22°14N 113°57E 122 B1
Cheung Sha Wan Hong Kong, China 22°20N 114°8E 122 B1
Cheung Shue Tan Hong Kong, China 22°26N 114°11E 122 A3
Chevak U.S.A. 61°32N 165°35W 303 B6
Chevalier, Î. de Martinique 14°25N 60°50W 322 j
Chevanceaux France 45°18N 0°14W 174 C3
Cheverly U.S.A. 38°55N 76°54W 143 B3
Chevilly-Larue France 48°46N 2°21E 134 B3
Cheviot U.S.A. 39°9N 84°36W 311 E12
Cheviot, The U.K. 55°29N 2°9W 168 B5
Cheviot Hills Northumberland, U.K. 55°20N 2°30W 168 B5
Cheviot Hills Calif., U.S.A. 34°2N 118°24W 126 B2
Cheviot Ra. Australia 25°20S 143°45E 280 D3
Chevreau, Île St. Barts 17°56N 62°51W 322 a
Chevy Chase U.S.A. 38°59N 77°4W 143 B2
Chew Bahir Ethiopia 4°40N 36°50E 257 G4
Chewelah U.S.A. 48°17N 117°43W 304 B5
Chewore ⌂ Zimbabwe 16°0S 29°52E 269 F2
Cheyenne Okla., U.S.A. 35°37N 99°40W 314 D5
Cheyenne Wyo., U.S.A. 41°8N 104°49W 304 F11
Cheyenne ➔ U.S.A. 44°41N 101°18W 308 C3
Cheyenne Wells U.S.A. 38°49N 102°21W 304 G12
Cheyne B. Australia 34°35S 118°50E 279 F2
Cheyur India 12°21N 80°0E 245 H5
Chhabra India 24°40N 76°54E 242 G7
Chhaktala India 22°6N 74°11E 242 H6
Chhapra India 25°48N 84°44E 243 G11
Chhata India 27°42N 77°30E 242 F7
Chhatak Bangla. 25°5N 91°37E 241 C3
Chhatarpur Jharkhand, India 24°23N 84°11E 243 G11
Chhatarpur Mad. P., India 24°55N 79°35E 243 G8
Chhati India 20°47N 81°40E 244 D5
Chhatrapati Shivaji, Mumbai ✈ (BOM) India 19°5N 72°51E 130 A2
Chhatrapati Shivaji Terminus India 18°56N 72°50E 130 B2
Chhattisgarh □ India 22°0N 82°0E 243 J10
Chhaygaon India 26°3N 91°24E 241 B3
Chhep Cambodia 13°45N 105°24E 236 F5
Chhindwara Mad. P., India 23°3N 79°29E 243 H8
Chhindwara Mad. P., India 22°2N 78°59E 243 H8
Chhinhdipada India 21°6N 84°52E 244 D7
Chhlong Cambodia 12°15N 105°58E 237 F5
Chhota Tawa ➔ India 22°14N 76°36E 242 H7
Chhoti Kali Sindh ➔ India 24°2N 75°31E 242 G6
Chhuikhadan India 21°32N 80°59E 243 J9
Chhuk Cambodia 10°46N 104°28E 237 G5
Chi ➔ Thailand 15°11N 104°43E 236 E5
Chi Ma Wan Pen. Hong Kong, China 22°14N 114°0E 122 B1
Chi Thanh Vietnam 13°17N 109°16E 236 F7
Chia Keng Singapore 1°21N 103°52E 138 A3
Chiahsien Taiwan 23°5N 120°35E 225 C2
Chiai Taiwan 23°29N 120°25E 225 C2
Chiai □ Taiwan 23°30N 120°30E 225 C2
Chiaksan △ S. Korea 37°15N 128°0E 224 D4
Chiali Taiwan 23°9N 120°10E 225 C2
Chialulantsun Taiwan 22°49N 121°11E 225 D3
Chiamboni Somalia 1°39S 41°35E 267 E5
Chiamussu = Jiamusi China 46°40N 130°26E 219 B15
Chian Taiwan 23°59N 121°33E 225 C3
Chianapu Taiwan 22°47N 120°36E 225 D2
Chianciano Terme Italy 43°2N 11°49E 199 E8
Chiang Dao Thailand 19°22N 98°58E 236 C2
Chiang Dao, Doi Thailand 19°23N 98°54E 236 C2
Chiang Kham Thailand 19°32N 100°18E 236 C3
Chiang Khan Thailand 17°52N 101°36E 236 D3
Chiang Khong Thailand 20°17N 100°24E 228 G3
Chiang Mai Thailand 18°47N 98°59E 236 C2
Chiang Rai Thailand 19°52N 99°50E 228 H2
Chiang Saen Thailand 20°16N 100°5E 228 G3
Chiangchun Taiwan 23°12N 120°9E 225 C2
Chiange Angola 15°35S 13°40E 265 F2
Chianti Italy 43°32N 11°25E 199 E8
Chiaohsi Taiwan 24°49N 121°46E 225 B3
Chiaotou Taiwan 22°45N 120°18E 225 D2
Chiapa ➔ Mexico 16°42N 93°0W 319 D6
Chiapa de Corzo Mexico 16°42N 93°0W 319 D6
Chiapas □ Mexico 16°30N 92°30W 319 D6
Chiapas, Sa. Madre de Mexico 15°40N 93°0W 319 D6
Chiaramonte Gulfi Italy 37°2N 14°42E 201 E7
Chiaravalle Italy 43°36N 13°19E 199 E10
Chiaravalle Centrale Italy 38°41N 16°25E 201 D9
Chiaravalle Milanese Italy 45°24N 9°16E 128 B2
Chiari Italy 45°32N 9°56E 198 C6
Chiatung Taiwan 22°25N 120°32E 225 D2
Chiatura Georgia 42°15N 43°17E 191 J6
Chiautla de Tapia Mexico 18°18N 98°36W 319 D5
Chiávari Italy 44°19N 9°19E 198 D6
Chiavenna Italy 46°19N 9°24E 198 B6
Chiayi = Chiai Taiwan 23°29N 120°25E 225 C2
Chiba Japan 35°30N 140°7E 223 B12
Chiba □ Japan 35°30N 140°20E 223 B12
Chibabava Mozam. 20°17S 33°35E 271 B5
Chibango Angola 13°38S 21°56E 265 E4
Chibemba Cunene, Angola 15°48S 14°8E 265 F2
Chibemba Huíla, Angola 16°20S 15°20E 265 F3
Chibi Zimbabwe 20°18S 30°25E 271 B5
Chibia Angola 15°10S 13°42E 265 F2
Chibizovka = Zherdevka Russia 51°56N 41°29E 190 E5
Chibougamau Canada 49°56N 74°24W 298 C5
Chibougamau, L. Canada 49°50N 74°20W 298 C5
Chibuk Nigeria 10°52N 12°50E 263 C7
Chibuto Mozam. 24°40S 33°33E 271 B5
Chibyu = Ukhta Russia 63°34N 53°41E 186 B9
Chic-Chocs, Mts. Canada 48°55N 66°0W 299 C6
Chicacole = Srikakulam India 18°14N 83°58E 244 E6
Chicago U.S.A. 41°52N 87°38W 119 B3
Chicago, Univ. of U.S.A. 41°47N 87°35W 119 C3
Chicago Harbor Chicago, U.S.A. 119 d3
Chicago Heights U.S.A. 41°30N 87°38W 311 C9
Chicago Lawn U.S.A. 41°47N 87°40W 119 C2
Chicago O'Hare Int. ✈ (ORD) U.S.A. 41°59N 87°54W 311 C9
Chicago Ridge U.S.A. 41°41N 87°46W 119 C2
Chicago River ➔ Chicago, U.S.A. 119 b3
Chicago River, North Branch ➔ U.S.A. 41°53N 87°42W 119 B2
Chicago Sanitary and Ship Canal U.S.A. 41°49N 87°45W 119 C2
Chicago State Univ. U.S.A. 41°43N 87°36W 119 C3
Chicapa ➔ Dem. Rep. of the Congo 6°25S 20°48E 265 D4
Chicha Chad 16°57N 18°34E 259 E3
Chichagof I. U.S.A. 57°30N 135°30W 303 H14
Chichaoua Morocco 31°32N 8°44W 260 B3
Chichawatni Pakistan 30°32N 72°42E 242 D5
Chichén-Itzá Mexico 20°37N 88°35W 319 C7
Chicheng China 40°55N 115°55E 226 D8
Chichester U.K. 50°50N 0°47W 169 G7
Chichester Ra. Australia 22°12S 119°15E 278 D2
Chichi Hualien, Taiwan 23°44N 121°33E 225 C3
Chichi Nant'ou, Taiwan 23°49N 120°47E 225 C2
Chichibu Japan 35°59N 139°10E 223 A11
Chichibu-Tama-Kai △ Japan 35°52N 138°42E 223 B10
Ch'ich'ihaerh = Qiqihar China 47°26N 124°0E 219 B13
Chicholi India 22°1N 77°40E 242 H8
Ch'ich'ou Taiwan 23°45N 120°33E 225 C2
Chickasaw ⌂ U.S.A. 34°26N 97°0W 314 D6
Chickasha U.S.A. 35°3N 97°58W 314 D6
Chicken U.S.A. 64°5N 141°56W 303 D12
Chiclana de la Frontera Spain 36°26N 6°9W 195 J4
Chiclayo Peru 6°42S 79°50W 330 B2
Chico U.S.A. 39°44N 121°50W 306 F5
Chico ➔ Chubut, Argentina 44°0S 67°0W 336 B3
Chico ➔ Santa Cruz, Argentina 50°0S 68°30W 336 D3
Chico ➔ Phil. 17°57N 121°36E 232 C3
Chicoa Mozam. 15°36S 32°20E 269 F3
Chicomba Angola 14°10S 14°52E 265 E2
Chicomo Mozam. 24°31S 34°6E 271 B5
Chicomostoc Mexico 22°28N 102°46W 318 C4
Chiconi Mayotte 12°50S 45°7E 272 b
Chicontepec Mexico 20°58N 98°10W 319 C5
Chicopee U.S.A. 42°9N 72°37W 313 D12
Chicoutimi Canada 48°28N 71°5W 299 C5
Chicualacuala Mozam. 22°6S 31°42E 271 B5
Chicuma Angola 13°26S 14°50E 265 E2
Chidambaram India 11°20N 79°45E 245 J4
Chidenguele Mozam. 24°55S 34°11E 271 B5
Chidley, C. Canada 60°23N 64°26W 295 E19
Chiducuane Mozam. 24°35S 34°25E 271 B5
Chiede Angola 17°15S 16°22E 265 F3
Chiefland U.S.A. 29°29N 82°52W 317 F7
Chiefs Pt. Canada 44°41N 81°18W 312 B3
Chiehting Taiwan 22°54N 120°11E 225 D2
Chiem Hoa Vietnam 22°12N 105°17E 236 A5
Chiemsee Germany 47°53N 12°28E 179 H8
Chienchen Taiwan 22°35N 120°18E 225 D2
Chiengi Zambia 8°45S 29°10E 269 D2
Chiengmai = Chiang Mai Thailand 18°47N 98°59E 236 C2
Chiengo Angola 13°20S 21°55E 265 E4
Chienti ➔ Italy 43°18N 13°45E 199 E10
Chienzui China 23°12N 113°22E 121 A3
Chieri Italy 45°1N 7°49E 198 C4
Chiers ➔ France 49°39N 4°59E 173 C11
Chiesa in Valmalenco Italy 46°16N 9°51E 198 B6
Chiese ➔ Italy 45°8N 10°25E 198 C7
Chieti Italy 42°21N 14°10E 199 F11
Chifeng China 42°18N 118°58E 227 C10
Chigasaki Japan 35°19N 139°24E 223 B11
Chigirin Ukraine 49°4N 32°38E 189 H7
Chignecto B. Canada 45°30N 64°40W 299 C7
Chignik U.S.A. 56°18N 158°24W 303 H8
Chigorodó Colombia 7°41N 76°42W 328 B2
Chiguana Bolivia 21°0S 67°58W 334 A2
Chigwell U.K. 51°37N 0°6E 169 F8
Chihli, G. of = Bo Hai China 39°0N 119°0E 227 E10
Ch'ihpen Taiwan 22°42N 121°2E 225 D3
Ch'ihshang Taiwan 23°7N 121°12E 225 C3
Chihsi = Jixi China 45°20N 130°50E 227 B16
Chihu Taiwan 23°54N 120°24E 225 C2
Chihuahua Mexico 28°38N 106°5W 318 B3
Chihuahua □ Mexico 28°30N 106°0W 318 B3
Chiili = Shīeli Kazakhstan 44°20N 66°15E 217 D7
Chik Bollapur India 13°25N 77°45E 245 H3
Chik Sha Hong Kong, China 22°17N 114°16E 122 B3
Chikalda India 21°24N 77°19E 244 D3
Chikhli Ahmadabad, India 20°45N 73°4E 244 D1
Chikhli Maharashtra, India 20°20N 76°18E 244 D3
Chikmagalur India 13°15N 75°45E 245 H2
Chiknayakanhalli India 13°26N 76°37E 245 H3
Chikodi India 16°26N 74°38E 245 F2
Chiku Taiwan 23°8N 120°7E 225 C2
Chikugo Japan 33°14N 130°28E 222 D2
Chikuma-Gawa ➔ Japan 36°59N 138°35E 223 A10
Chikura Japan 34°55N 139°57E 223 C11
Chikushino Japan 33°30N 130°30E 222 D2
Chikwawa Malawi 16°2S 34°50E 269 F3
Chila Angola 12°3S 14°29E 265 E2
Ch'ilaichu Shan Taiwan 24°5N 121°20E 225 B3
Chilanga Zambia 15°33S 28°16E 269 F2
Chilapa Mexico 17°36N 99°10W 319 D5
Chilas Pakistan 35°25N 74°5E 243 B6
Chilaw Sri Lanka 7°30N 79°50E 245 L4
Chilcotin ➔ Canada 51°44N 122°23W 296 C4
Childers Australia 25°15S 152°17E 281 D5
Childersburg U.S.A. 33°16N 86°21W 316 B3
Children's Museum Boston, U.S.A. 116 c3
Children's Palace Beijing, China 114 b2
Childress U.S.A. 34°25N 100°13W 314 D4
Child's Hill U.K. 51°33N 0°12W 125 A2
Chile ■ S. Amer. 35°0S 72°0W 327 G3
Chile, Univ. de Chile 33°26S 70°39W 137 B2
Chile Basin Pac. Oc. 33°0S 80°0W 289 L20
Chile Chico Chile 46°33S 71°44W 336 C2
Chile Rise Pac. Oc. 38°0S 92°0W 289 L18
Chilecito Argentina 29°10S 67°30W 334 B2
Chilengue, Serra do Angola 13°18S 15°22E 265 E2
Chilesso Angola 11°35S 16°34E 265 E3
Chilete Peru 7°10S 78°50W 330 B2
Chilhowee U.S.A. 38°36N 93°51W 310 F3
Chilia, Braţul ➔ Romania 45°14N 29°42E 183 E14
Chilibre Panama 9°9N 79°37W 320 c
Chilik = Shelek Kazakhstan 43°33N 78°17E 217 D9
Chililabombwe Zambia 12°18S 27°43E 269 E2
Chilim Pakistan 35°5N 75°5E 243 B6
Chilin = Jilin China 43°44N 126°30E 227 C14
Chiliomodi Greece 37°48N 22°51E 204 D4
Chilka L. India 19°40N 85°25E 244 E7
Chilko ➔ Canada 52°0N 123°40W 296 C4
Chilko L. Canada 51°20N 124°10W 296 C4
Chilla Saroda India 28°35N 77°18E 122 B3
Chillagoe Australia 17°7S 144°33E 280 B3
Chillán Chile 36°40S 72°10W 336 A2
Chillicothe Ill., U.S.A. 40°55N 89°29W 310 D7
Chillicothe Mo., U.S.A. 39°48N 93°33W 310 E3
Chillicothe Ohio, U.S.A. 39°20N 82°59W 309 F12
Chilliwack Canada 49°10N 121°54W 296 D4
Chillum U.S.A. 38°56N 76°58W 143 B3
Chilly-Mazarin France 48°42N 2°17E 134 B3
Chilmari Bangla. 25°33N 89°43E 241 C2
Chilo India 27°25N 73°32E 242 F5
Chiloane, I. Mozam. 20°40S 34°55E 271 B5
Chiloé, I. de Chile 42°30S 73°50W 336 B2
Chiloé △ Chile 42°11S 73°59W 336 B2
Chilonda Angola 11°19S 16°12E 265 E3
Chilongo Angola 13°55S 16°35E 265 E3
Chilpancingo Mexico 17°33N 99°30W 319 D5
Chiltern Australia 36°10S 146°36E 283 D7
Chiltern Hills U.K. 51°40N 0°53W 169 F7
Chilton U.S.A. 44°2N 88°10W 308 C9
Chiluage Angola 9°30S 21°50E 265 D4
Chilubi Zambia 11°5S 29°58E 269 E2
Chilubula Zambia 10°14S 30°51E 269 E3
Chilumba Malawi 10°28S 34°12E 269 E3
Chilung Taiwan 25°3N 121°45E 225 A3
Chilwa, L. Malawi 15°15S 35°40E 269 F4
Chimakela Angola 15°24S 16°58E 265 F3
Chimakudi India 25°47N 93°48E 241 C4
Chimaltitán Mexico 21°35N 103°50W 318 C4
Chimán Panama 8°45N 78°40W 320 E4
Chimanimani Zimbabwe 19°48S 32°52E 271 A5
Chimanimani △ Zimbabwe 19°48S 33°0E 271 A5
Chimay Belgium 50°3N 4°20E 170 D4
Chimayo U.S.A. 36°0N 105°56W 305 J11
Chimba Zambia 9°54S 31°28E 269 D3
Chimborazo Ecuador 1°29S 78°55W 328 D2
Chimborazo □ Ecuador 1°0S 78°40W 328 D2
Chimbote Peru 9°0S 78°35W 330 B2
Chimboy Uzbekistan 42°57N 59°47E 216 D5
Chimbu □ Papua N. G. 6°15S 144°50E 286 D3
Ch'imei Taiwan 23°12N 119°25E 225 C1
Ch'imei Yü Taiwan 23°13N 119°26E 225 C1
Chimichagua Colombia 9°15N 73°49W 328 B3
Chimkent = Shymkent Kazakhstan 42°18N 69°36E 217 D7
Chimoio Mozam. 19°4S 33°30E 269 F3
Chimpembe Zambia 9°31S 29°33E 269 D2
Chimur India 20°30N 79°23E 244 D4
Chin □ Burma 22°0N 93°0E 241 E4
Chin Hills Burma 22°30N 93°30E 241 D4
Chin Ling Shan = Qinling Shandi China 33°50N 108°10E 226 H5
China Mexico 25°42N 99°14W 319 B5
China ■ Asia 30°0N 110°0E 219 E11
China, Great Plain of Asia 35°0N 115°0E 210 E13
China Basin San Francisco, U.S.A. 136 c3
China Lake U.S.A. 35°44N 117°37W 307 K9
China Town Toronto, Canada 141 b1
Chinacota Colombia 7°37N 72°36W 328 B3
Chinan = Jinan China 36°38N 117°1E 226 F9
Chinandega Nic. 12°35N 87°12W 320 D2
Chinati Peak U.S.A. 29°57N 104°29W 314 G2
Chinatown Singapore 138 c2
Chinatown Boston, U.S.A. 116 c2
Chinatown Los Angeles, U.S.A. 127 a3
Chinatown New York, U.S.A. 132 e2
Chinatown San Francisco, U.S.A. 136 b2
Chincha Alta Peru 13°25S 76°7W 330 C2
Chinchaga ➔ Canada 58°53N 118°20W 296 B5
Chincheros Peru 13°30S 73°44W 330 C3
Chinchilla Australia 26°45S 150°38E 281 D5
Chinchilla de Monte Aragón Spain 38°53N 1°40W 197 G3
Chincholi India 17°28N 77°26E 244 E3
Chinchorro, Banco Mexico 18°35N 87°22W 319 D7
Chinchou = Jinzhou China 41°5N 121°3E 227 D11
Chinchoua Gabon 0°1N 9°48E 264 B1
Chincoteague U.S.A. 37°56N 75°23W 309 G16
Chinde Mozam. 18°35S 36°30E 269 F4
Chindwin ➔ Burma 21°26N 95°15E 241 E5
Chineni India 33°2N 75°15E 243 C6
Chinese Theatre Los Angeles, U.S.A. 34°6N 118°20W 126 B2
Chinga Mozam. 15°13S 38°35E 269 F4
Chingaza △ Colombia 4°30N 73°40W 328 C3
Chingola Zambia 12°31S 27°53E 269 E2
Chingole Malawi 13°4S 34°17E 269 E3
Chingoni Mayotte 12°48S 45°8E 272 b
Chingpu Taiwan 23°28N 121°29E 225 C3
Ch'ingshui Changhua, Taiwan 24°16N 120°34E 225 B2
Chingshui Hualien, Taiwan 24°13N 121°41E 225 B3
Chingshui Ilan, Taiwan 24°39N 121°35E 225 B3
Ch'ingtao = Qingdao China 36°5N 120°20E 227 F11
Chinguar Angola 12°25S 16°45E 265 E3
Chinguetti Mauritania 20°25N 12°24W 260 D2
Chingune Mozam. 20°33S 34°58E 271 B5
Chingupota India 22°29N 88°14E 124 C1
Chinhanguanine Mozam. 25°21S 32°30E 271 C5
Chinhoyi Zimbabwe 17°20S 30°8E 269 F3
Chinhsien = Jinxian China 28°26N 116°17E 229 C11
Chiniot Pakistan 31°45N 73°0E 242 D5
Chínipas Mexico 27°23N 108°32W 318 B3
Chinji Pakistan 32°42N 72°22E 242 C5
Chinju = Jinju S. Korea 35°12N 128°2E 224 E4
Chinkai Afghan. 31°57N 67°26E 240 C2
Chinkapook Australia 35°11S 142°57E 282 C5
Chinkiang = Zhenjiang China 32°11N 119°26E 229 A12
Chinko ➔ C.A.R. 4°50N 23°53E 264 B4
Chinle U.S.A. 36°9N 109°33W 305 H9
Ch'inlun Taiwan 22°32N 120°57E 225 D2
Chinmen Taiwan 24°26N 118°19E 225 a
Chinmen Tao Taiwan 24°26N 118°22E 225 a
Chinna Cr. ➔ Pakistan 24°50N 67°0E 123 B2
Chinnamanur India 9°50N 77°24E 245 K3
Chinnampo = Namp'o N. Korea 38°52N 125°10E 224 C2
Chino Japan 35°59N 138°9E 223 B10
Chino Calif., U.S.A. 34°1N 117°41W 307 L9
Chino Valley U.S.A. 34°45N 112°27W 305 J7
Chinois, Quartier Montréal, Canada 130 b2
Chinon France 47°10N 0°15E 172 E7
Chinook U.S.A. 48°35N 109°14W 304 B9
Chinook Trough Pac. Oc. 44°0N 175°0W 288 C10
Chinoya Zambia 13°55S 23°16E 265 E4
Chinsali Zambia 10°30S 32°2E 269 E3
Chinshan Taiwan 25°13N 121°38E 225 A3
Chinsura = Chunchura India 22°53N 88°27E 243 H13
Chintalapudi India 17°4N 80°59E 244 F5
Chintamani India 13°26N 78°3E 245 H4
Chinwangtao = Qinhúangdao China 39°56N 119°30E 227 E10
Chióggia Italy 45°13N 12°17E 199 C9
Chios Greece 38°27N 26°9E 205 C8
Chipata Zambia 13°38S 32°28E 269 E3
Chipei Tao Taiwan 23°45N 119°37E 225 C1
Chiperceni Moldova 47°31N 28°50E 183 C13
Chipindo Angola 13°49S 15°48E 265 E3
Chipinge Zimbabwe 20°13S 32°28E 269 G3
Chipinge ⌂ Zimbabwe 20°14S 33°0E 269 G3
Chipiona Spain 36°44N 6°26W 195 J4
Chipley U.S.A. 30°47N 85°32W 316 E4
Chiplun India 17°31N 73°34E 244 F1
Chipman Canada 46°6N 65°53W 299 C6
Chipoka Malawi 13°57S 34°28E 269 E3
Chippenham U.K. 51°27N 2°6W 169 F5
Chippewa ➔ U.S.A. 44°25N 92°5W 308 C7
Chippewa Falls U.S.A. 44°56N 91°24W 308 C8
Chipping Norton U.K. 51°56N 1°32W 169 F6
Chiprovtsi Bulgaria 43°24N 22°52E 202 C6
Chiputneticook Lakes N. Amer. 45°35N 67°35W 309 C20
Chiputo = Vila Vasco da Gama Mozam. 14°54S 32°14E 269 E3
Chipwi Burma 25°53N 98°8E 241 C7
Chiquelequele Angola 16°44S 19°5E 265 F3
Chiquián Peru 10°10S 77°0W 330 C2
Chiquibul △ Belize 16°49N 88°52W 320 C2
Chiquihuite, Cerro Mexico 19°32N 99°8W 128 A2
Chiquimula Guatemala 14°51N 89°37W 320 D2
Chiquinquira Colombia 5°37N 73°50W 328 B3
Chiquitos, Llanos de Bolivia 18°0S 61°30W 331 D5
Chir ➔ Russia 48°30N 43°0E 191 F6
Chira ➔ Peru 4°54S 81°8W 328 D1
Chirala India 15°50N 80°26E 245 G5
Chiramba Mozam. 16°55S 34°39E 269 F3
Chirawa India 28°14N 75°42E 242 E6
Chirchiq Uzbekistan 41°29N 69°35E 217 D7
Chiredzi Zimbabwe 21°0S 31°38E 271 B5
Chirfa Niger 20°55N 12°22E 259 D2
Chirgua ➔ Venezuela 8°54N 67°58W 328 B4
Chiribiquete △ Colombia 0°31N 72°50W 328 C3
Chiricahua ⌂ U.S.A. 32°0N 109°20W 305 K9
Chiricahua Peak U.S.A. 31°51N 109°18W 305 L9
Chirikof I. U.S.A. 55°50N 155°40W 300 D8
Chiriquí, G. de Panama 8°0N 82°10W 320 E3
Chiriquí, L. de Panama 9°10N 82°0W 320 E3
Chirisa ⌂ Zimbabwe 17°53S 28°15E 269 F2
Chirivira Falls Zimbabwe 21°10S 32°12E 269 G3
Chirmiri India 23°15N 82°20E 243 H10
Chirnogi Romania 44°7N 26°32E 183 F11
Chirongui Mayotte 12°55S 45°9E 272 b
Chirpan Bulgaria 42°10N 25°19E 203 D9
Chirripó Grande, Cerro Costa Rica 9°29N 83°29W 320 E3
Chirundu Zimbabwe 16°3S 28°50E 271 A4
Chisamba Zambia 14°55S 28°20E 269 E2
Chisapani Nepal 28°37N 81°16E 243 E9
Chisasa Zambia 12°6S 25°30E 265 E5
Chisasibi Canada 53°50N 79°0W 298 B4
Ch'ishan Taiwan 22°44N 120°31E 225 D2
Ch'ishan Hsi ➔ Taiwan 22°51N 120°28E 225 C2
Chisholm Alta., Canada 54°55N 114°10W 296 C6
Chisholm Minn., U.S.A. 47°29N 92°53W 308 B7
Chishtian Mandi Pakistan 29°50N 72°55E 242 E5
Chishui China 28°30N 105°42E 228 C5
Chishui He ➔ China 28°49N 105°50E 228 C5
Chisimaio = Kismaayo Somalia 0°22S 42°32E 267 E5
Chisimba Falls Zambia 10°12S 30°56E 269 E3
Chişinău Moldova 47°2N 28°50E 183 C13
Chişinău ✈ (KIV) Moldova 47°3N 28°46E 183 C13
Chişineu Criş Romania 46°32N 21°37E 182 D6
Chislehurst U.K. 51°24N 0°6E 125 B4
Chisone ➔ Italy 44°49N 7°25E 198 D4
Chisos Mts. U.S.A. 29°5N 103°15W 314 G3
Chissengue Angola 9°13S 20°34E 265 D4
Chissilo Angola 13°48S 16°31E 265 E3
Chistochina U.S.A. 62°34N 144°40W 303 E11
Chistopol Russia 55°25N 50°38E 190 C10
Chiswick U.K. 51°29N 0°16W 125 B2
Chiswick House U.K. 51°28N 0°15W 125 B2
Chita Colombia 6°11N 72°28W 328 B3
Chita Russia 52°0N 113°35E 219 A11
Chitado Angola 17°10S 14°8E 265 F2
Chitaldrug = Chitradurga India 14°14N 76°24E 245 G3
Chitan Taiwan 24°35N 121°29E 225 B3
Chitanda ➔ Angola 16°1S 15°12E 265 F3
Chitapur India 17°10N 77°5E 244 F3
Chitembo Angola 13°30S 16°50E 265 E3
Chitina U.S.A. 61°31N 144°26W 303 F11
Chitipa Malawi 9°41S 33°19E 269 D3
Chitose Hokkaidō, Japan 42°49N 141°39E 220 C10
Chitose Kanagawa, Japan 35°33N 139°37E 140 B2
Chitradurga India 14°14N 76°24E 245 G3
Chitrakot India 19°10N 81°40E 244 E5
Chitral Pakistan 35°50N 71°56E 240 B3
Chitralada Palace Thailand 13°45N 100°31E 113 B2
Chitravati ➔ India 14°45N 78°15E 245 G4
Chitré Panama 7°59N 80°27W 320 E3
Chittagong Bangla. 22°19N 91°48E 241 D3
Chittagong □ Bangla. 24°5N 91°0E 241 C3
Chittaurgarh India 24°52N 74°38E 242 G6
Chittoor India 13°15N 79°5E 245 H4
Chittur India 10°40N 76°45E 245 J3
Chitungwiza Zimbabwe 18°0S 31°6E 269 F3
Chiuju Taiwan 22°44N 120°29E 225 D2
Chiumbe ➔ Dem. Rep. of the Congo 6°59S 21°12E 265 D4
Chiumbo Angola 12°29S 16°8E 265 E3
Chiume Angola 15°3S 21°14E 265 F4
Chiusi Italy 43°1N 11°57E 199 E8
Chiva Spain 39°27N 0°41W 197 F4
Chivacoa Venezuela 10°10N 68°54W 328 A4
Chivasso Italy 45°11N 7°53E 198 C4
Chivay Peru 15°40S 71°35W 330 D3
Chive Bolivia 12°23S 68°35W 330 C4
Chivhu Zimbabwe 19°2S 30°52E 269 F3
Chivilcoy Argentina 34°55S 60°0W 334 C4
Chiwanda Tanzania 11°23S 34°55E 269 E3
Chixi China 22°0N 112°58E 229 G9
Chiyoda Tokyo, Japan 140 b4
Chizarira Zimbabwe 17°36S 27°45E 269 F2
Chizarira △ Zimbabwe 17°44S 27°52E 269 F2
Chizela Zambia 13°8S 25°0E 265 E4
Chizu Japan 35°16N 134°14E 222 B6
Chkalov = Orenburg Russia 51°45N 55°6E 186 D10
Chkolovsk Russia 56°50N 43°10E 190 B6
Chloride U.S.A. 35°25N 114°12W 307 K12
Chlumec nad Cidlinou Czech Rep. 50°9N 15°29E 180 A8
Chmielnik Poland 50°37N 20°43E 185 H7
Cho-do N. Korea 38°30N 124°40E 224 C2
Cho Phuoc Hai Vietnam 10°26N 107°18E 237 G6
Choa Chu Kang Singapore 1°22N 103°41E 138 A2
Choba Kenya 2°30N 38°5E 266 D4
Chobe △ Botswana 18°37S 24°23E 270 A4
Choc B. St. Lucia 14°3N 60°59W 323 m
Choch'i Taiwan 23°20N 121°16E 225 C3
Chocianów Poland 51°27N 15°55E 185 G2
Chociwel Poland 53°29N 15°21E 184 E2
Chocó □ Colombia 6°0N 77°0W 328 B2
Chocolate Hills Phil. 9°55N 124°10E 233 G5
Chocolate Mts. U.S.A. 33°15N 115°15W 307 M11
Chocontá Colombia 5°9N 73°41W 328 B3
Choctawhatchee ➔ U.S.A. 30°25N 86°8W 316 E3
Choctawhatchee B. U.S.A. 30°20N 86°20W 317 E3
Chodavaram Andhra Pradesh, India 17°50N 82°57E 244 F6
Chodavaram Andhra Pradesh, India 17°27N 81°46E 244 F5
Chodecz Poland 52°24N 19°2E 185 F6
Chodov Czech Rep. 50°15N 12°45E 180 A5
Chodov u Prahy Czech Rep. 50°1N 14°30E 135 B3
Chodziez Poland 52°58N 16°58E 185 F3
Choele Choel Argentina 39°11S 65°40W 336 A3
Chōfu Japan 35°38N 139°32E 140 B2
Choghā Zanbīl Iran 32°1N 48°32E 247 C6
Choirokoitia Cyprus 34°47N 33°20E 207 F9
Choiseul St. Lucia 13°47N 61°3W 323 m
Choiseul Solomon Is. 7°0S 156°40E 287 L9
Choisy-le-Roi France 48°46N 2°24E 134 B3
Choix Mexico 26°43N 108°17W 318 B3
Chojna Poland 52°58N 14°25E 185 F1
Chojnice Poland 53°42N 17°32E 184 E4
Chojnów Poland 51°18N 15°58E 185 G2
Chok Chai Thailand 14°44N 102°10E 236 E4
Chōkai-San Japan 39°6N 140°3E 220 E10
Choke Canyon Res. U.S.A. 28°30N 98°20W 314 G5
Choke Mts. Ethiopia 11°18N 37°15E 257 E4
Chokurdakh Russia 70°38N 147°55E 215 B15
Chokwé Mozam. 24°32S 32°59E 271 B5
Cholame U.S.A. 35°44N 120°18W 306 K6
Cholan Taiwan 24°18N 120°49E 225 B2
Cholargos Greece 37°59N 23°48E 112 B2
Cholet France 47°4N 0°52W 172 E6
Cholguan Chile 37°10S 72°3W 334 D1
Choloma Honduras 15°37N 87°57W 320 C2
Cholpon-Ata Kyrgyzstan 42°40N 77°6E 217 D9
Cholupice Czech Rep. 49°59N 14°27E 135 C2
Choluteca Honduras 13°20N 87°14W 320 D2
Choluteca ➔ Honduras 13°0N 87°20W 320 D2
Chom Bung Thailand 13°37N 99°36E 236 F2
Chom Thong Bangkok, Thailand 13°41N 100°29E 113 B1
Chom Thong Chiang Mai, Thailand 18°25N 98°41E 236 C2
Choma Zambia 16°48S 26°59E 269 F2
Chomo Lhari Asia 27°49N 89°16E 241 B2
Chomolungma = Everest, Mt. Nepal 28°5N 86°58E 243 E12
Chomun India 27°15N 75°40E 242 F6
Chomutov Czech Rep. 50°28N 13°23E 180 A6
Chon Buri Thailand 13°21N 101°1E 236 F3
Chon Thanh Vietnam 11°24N 106°36E 237 G6
Chone Ecuador 0°40S 80°0W 328 D2
Chong Kai Cambodia 13°57N 103°35E 236 F4
Chong Mek Thailand 15°10N 105°27E 236 E5
Chong Pang Singapore 1°26N 103°49E 138 A2
Chong Phangan Thailand 9°39N 100°0E 237 b
Chong Samui Thailand 9°21N 99°50E 237 b
Chongde China 30°32N 120°26E 229 B13
Ch'ŏngjin N. Korea 41°47N 129°50E 224 B4
Chŏngju N. Korea 39°40N 125°5E 224 C2
Chongli China 40°58N 115°15E 226 D8
Chongming China 31°38N 121°23E 229 B13
Chongming Dao China 31°40N 121°30E 229 B13
Chongoni Rock Art Malawi 14°17S 34°16E 269 E3
Chongoroi Angola 13°37S 14°1E 265 E2
Chongoyape Peru 6°35S 79°25W 330 B2
Chŏngp'yŏng N. Korea 39°47N 127°23E 224 C3
Chongqing Chongqing, China 29°35N 106°25E 228 C6
Chongqing Sichuan, China 30°38N 103°40E 228 B4
Chongqing Shi □ China 30°0N 108°0E 228 C6
Chongren China 27°46N 116°3E 229 D11
Chonguene Mozam. 25°3S 33°49E 271 C5
Chongwe Zambia 15°21S 28°42E 269 F2
Chongwen Beijing, China 114 c2
Chongyi China 25°45N 114°29E 229 E10
Chongzuo China 22°23N 107°20E 228 F6
Chonogol Mongolia 45°54N 115°22E 226 B8
Chonos, Arch. de los Chile 45°0S 75°0W 336 C2
Chop Ukraine 48°26N 22°12E 182 B7
Chopda India 21°20N 75°15E 244 D2
Chopim ➔ Brazil 25°35S 53°5W 335 B5
Chopin Museum Warsaw, Poland 143 b2
Chor Pakistan 25°31N 69°46E 242 G3
Chora Greece 37°3N 21°42E 204 D3
Chora Sfakion Greece 35°15N 24°9E 207 E5
Chorbat La India 34°42N 76°37E 243 B7
Chorley U.K. 53°39N 2°38W 168 D5
Chorna Ukraine 47°36N 29°20E 183 C14
Chornobyl Ukraine 51°20N 30°15E 177 C16
Chornomorske Ukraine 45°31N 32°40E 189 K7
Chorolque, Cerro Bolivia 20°59S 66°5W 334 A2
Choroszcz Poland 53°10N 22°59E 185 E9
Chorregon Australia 22°40S 143°32E 280 C3
Chorrillos Peru 12°10S 77°1W 124 C2
Chortkiv Ukraine 49°2N 25°46E 177 D13
Chorzele Poland 53°15N 20°55E 185 E7
Chorzów Poland 50°18N 18°57E 185 H5
Chos-Malal Argentina 37°20S 70°15W 334 D1
Ch'osan N. Korea 40°50N 125°47E 224 B2
Chosheta Shan Taiwan 23°50N 121°6E 225 C3
Chōshi Japan 35°45N 140°51E 223 B12
Choshui Hsi ➔ Taiwan 23°50N 120°15E 225 C2
Choszczno Poland 53°7N 15°25E 185 E2
Chota Peru 6°33S 78°39W 330 B2
Choteau U.S.A. 47°49N 112°11W 304 C7
Chotěboř Czech Rep. 49°43N 15°40E 180 B8
Chotila India 22°23N 71°15E 242 H4
Chotta Udepur India 22°19N 74°1E 242 H6
Choûm Mauritania 21°11N 13°3W 260 D2
Choungui Mayotte 12°57S 45°8E 272 b
Chowchilla U.S.A. 37°7N 120°16W 306 H6
Chowpatty Beach Mumbai, India 130 b1
Choybalsan Mongolia 48°4N 114°30E 219 B11
Choyr Mongolia 46°24N 108°30E 219 B10
Chrisman U.S.A. 39°48N 87°41W 311 E9
Chrisoupoli Greece 40°58N 24°42E 203 F8
Christ Church Cathedral Montréal, Canada 130 c2
Christburg = Dzierzgoń Poland 53°58N 19°20E 184 E6
Christchurch N.Z. 43°33S 172°47E 285 D7
Christchurch Dorset, U.K. 50°44N 1°47W 169 G6
Christian I. Canada 44°50N 80°12W 312 B4
Christian Quarter Jerusalem 123 b3
Christian Sd. U.S.A. 55°56N 134°40W 303 J14
Christiana Greece 36°14N 25°13E 205 E7
Christiana Jamaica 18°10N 77°29W 320 a
Christiana North West, S. Africa 27°52S 25°8E 270 C4
Christiansborg Slot Copenhagen, Denmark 118 c2
Christiansfeld Denmark 55°21N 9°29E 163 J3
Christianshåb = Qasigiannguit Greenland 68°50N 51°18W 154 D5
Christianshavn Denmark 55°40N 12°35E 118 A3
Christiansted U.S. Virgin Is. 17°45N 64°42W 321 C7
Christie B. Canada 62°32N 111°10W 297 A6
Christina ➔ Canada 56°40N 111°3W 297 B6
Christmas Cr. ➔ Australia 18°29S 125°23E 278 C4
Christmas I. = Kiritimati Kiribati 1°58N 157°27W 289 G12
Christmas I. Ind. Oc. 10°30S 105°40E 273 F9
Christoffel △ Curaçao 12°21N 69°8W 322 g
Christopher U.S.A. 37°59N 89°3W 310 G7
Christopher, L. Australia 24°49S 127°42E 279 D4
Christyakovo = Thorez Ukraine 48°4N 38°34E 189 H10
Chrudim Czech Rep. 49°58N 15°43E 180 B8
Chrysler Building New York, U.S.A. 132 c2
Chrzanów Małopolskie, Poland 50°10N 19°21E 185 H6
Chrzanów Warszawa, Poland 52°13N 20°53E 143 B1
Chtapodia Greece 37°24N 25°34E 205 D7
Chtimba Malawi 10°35S 34°13E 269 E3
Chū = Shū Kazakhstan 43°36N 73°42E 217 D8
Chū = Shū ➔ Kazakhstan 45°0N 67°44E 217 D7
Chu ➔ Vietnam 19°53N 105°45E 236 C5
Chu Lai Vietnam 15°28N 108°45E 236 E7
Chu Mom Ray △ Vietnam 14°29N 107°38E 236 E6
Chu Se Vietnam 13°40N 108°8E 236 F7
Chuadanga Bangla. 23°38N 88°51E 241 D2
Chuak, Ko Thailand 9°28N 99°41E 237 b

**Ch'uanchou** = Quanzhou
*China* 24°55N 118°34E **229** E12
**Chüanchow** = Quanzhou
*China* 24°55N 118°34E **229** E12
**Chuangwei** *Taiwan* 24°45N 121°47E **225** B3
**Chuankou** *China* 34°20N 110°59E **226** G6
**Chuathbaluk** *U.S.A.* 61°40N 159°15W **303** E8
**Chubarovka** = Pology
*Ukraine* 47°29N 36°15E **189** J9
**Chubbuck** *U.S.A.* 42°55N 112°28W **304** E7
**Chūbu** □ *Japan* 36°45N 137°30E **223** A9
**Chūbu-Sangaku** △ *Japan* 36°30N 137°40E **223** A9
**Chubut** □ *Argentina* 43°30S 69°00W **336** B3
**Chubut** ➔ *Argentina* 43°20S 65°5W **336** B3
**Chuch'i** *Taiwan* 23°31N 120°33E **225** C2
**Chuchi L.** *Canada* 55°12N 124°30W **296** B4
**Chuchow** = Zhuzhou
*China* 27°49N 113°12E **229** D9
**Chuda** *India* 22°29N 71°41E **242** H4
**Chudovo** *Russia* 59°10N 31°41E **188** C6
**Chudskoye, Ozero** *Russia* 58°13N 27°30E **188** C4
**Chuen Lung**
*Hong Kong, China* 22°23N 114°6E **122** A2
**Chugach Mts.** *U.S.A.* 60°45N 147°0W **303** F11
**Chuginadak I.** *U.S.A.* 52°50N 169°45W **303** K5
**Chūgoku** □ *Japan* 35°0N 133°0E **222** C5
**Chūgoku-Sanchi** *Japan* 35°0N 133°0E **222** B5
**Chuguyev** = Chuhuiv
*Ukraine* 49°55N 36°45E **189** H9
**Chugwater** *U.S.A.* 41°46N 104°50W **304** F11
**Chuhuiv** *Ukraine* 49°55N 36°45E **189** H9
**Chuk Kok**
*Hong Kong, China* 22°20N 114°15E **122** A3
**Chuka** *Kenya* 0°20S 37°39E **268** C4
**Chukchi Plateau** *Arctic* 78°0N 165°0W **150** B17
**Chukchi Sea** *Russia* 68°0N 175°0W **215** C19
**Chukotskiy Mys** *Russia* 64°14N 173°8W **300** C5
**Chukotskiy Poluostrov**
*Russia* 66°0N 174°0W **300** B5
**Chukotskoye Nagorye**
*Russia* 68°0N 175°0E **215** C18
**Chula** *U.S.A.* 31°33N 83°32W **316** D6
**Chula Vista** *U.S.A.* 32°38N 117°5W **307** N9
**Chulalongkom Univ.**
*Thailand* 13°44N 100°31E **113** B2
**Chulband** ➔ *India* 20°40N 79°54E **244** D4
**Ch'ulin** *Taiwan* 22°8N 120°42E **225** D2
**Chulucanas** *Peru* 5°8S 80°10W **330** B1
**Chulumani** *Bolivia* 16°24S 67°31W **330** D4
**Chulym** ➔ *Russia* 57°43N 83°51E **214** D9
**Chum Phae** *Thailand* 16°40N 102°6E **236** D4
**Chum Saeng** *Thailand* 15°55N 100°15E **236** E3
**Chuma** *Bolivia* 15°24S 68°56W **330** D4
**Chumar** *India* 32°40N 78°35E **243** C8
**Chumbicha** *Argentina* 29°0S 66°10W **334** B2
**Chumerna** *Bulgaria* 42°45N 25°55E **203** D9
**Chumikan** *Russia* 54°40N 135°10E **215** D14
**Chumphon** *Thailand* 10°35N 99°14E **237** G2
**Chumpi** *Peru* 15°4S 73°46W **330** D3
**Chumuare** *Mozam.* 14°31S 31°50E **269** E3
**Chuna** ➔ *Russia* 57°47N 94°37E **215** D10
**Chun'an** *Zhejiang, China* 29°35N 119°3E **229** C12
**Chunan** *Taiwan* 24°41N 120°52E **225** B2
**Chuncheon** *S. Korea* 37°58N 127°44E **224** D3
**Chunchura** *India* 22°53N 88°27E **243** H13
**Chung Hau**
*Hong Kong, China* 22°14N 114°0E **122** B2
**Chunga** *Zambia* 15°0S 26°2E **269** F2
**Chungcheongbuk-do** □
*S. Korea* 36°45N 128°0E **224** D4
**Chungcheonnam-do** □
*S. Korea* 36°30N 127°0E **224** D3
**Ch'ungch'ing** = Chongqing
*China* 29°35N 106°25E **228** C6
**Chunggang-ŭp** *N. Korea* 41°48N 126°48E **224** B3
**Chungho** *Taiwan* 25°0N 121°28E **225** A3
**Chunghwa** *N. Korea* 38°52N 125°47E **224** C2
**Chungju** *S. Korea* 36°58N 127°58E **224** D3
**Chungjubo** *S. Korea* 36°57N 128°3E **224** D4
**Chungking** = Chongqing
*China* 29°35N 106°25E **228** C6
**Chungli** *Taiwan* 24°57N 121°13E **225** B3
**Chungpu** *Taiwan* 23°26N 120°31E **225** C2
**Chungt'iaoshan** = Zhongtiao Shan
*China* 35°0N 111°10E **226** G6
**Chungtungwan** *Taiwan* 24°31N 120°40E **225** B2
**Chungyang Shanmo**
*Taiwan* 23°10N 121°0E **225** C3
**Chunian** *Pakistan* 30°57N 74°0E **242** D6
**Chunya** *Tanzania* 8°30S 33°27E **269** D3
**Chunyang** *China* 43°38N 129°23E **227** C15
**Chuō** *Tokyo, Japan* **140** b5
**Chupara B.** *Trin. & Tob.* 10°48N 61°22W **323** t
**Chupara Pt.** *Trin. & Tob.* 10°49N 61°22W **323** t
**Chupei** *Taiwan* 24°50N 121°0E **225** B3
**Chuquibamba** *Peru* 15°47S 72°44W **330** D3
**Chuquibambilla** *Peru* 14°7S 72°41W **330** C3
**Chuquicamata** *Chile* 22°15S 69°0W **334** A2
**Chuquisaca** □ *Bolivia* 20°30S 63°30W **331** E5
**Chur** *Switz.* 46°52N 9°32E **179** J5
**Churachandpur** *India* 24°20N 93°40E **241** C4
**Church End** *U.K.* 51°35N 0°11W **125** A2
**Church of our Lady** = Frauenkirche
*Munich, Germany* **131** b2
**Church Stretton** *U.K.* 52°32N 2°48W **169** E5
**Churchill** *Vic., Australia* 38°19S 146°25E **283** E7
**Churchill** *Man., Canada* 58°47N 94°11W **297** B10
**Churchill** ➔ *Man., Canada* 58°47N 94°12W **297** B10
**Churchill** ➔ *Nfld. & L., Canada* 53°19N 60°10W **299** B7
**Churchill, C.** *Canada* 58°46N 93°12W **297** B10
**Churchill Falls** *Canada* 53°36N 64°19W **299** B7
**Churchill L.** *Canada* 55°55N 108°20W **297** B7
**Churchill Pk.** *Canada* 58°10N 125°10W **296** B3
**Churchtown** *Ireland* 53°18N 6°16W **120** B2
**Churdan** *U.S.A.* 42°9N 94°29W **310** D2
**Churki** *India* 23°50N 83°12E **243** H10
**Churu** *India* 28°20N 74°50E **242** E6
**Churubusco** *U.S.A.* 41°14N 85°19W **311** C11
**Churún Merú** = Angel Falls
*Venezuela* 5°57N 62°30W **329** B5
**Chushal** *India* 33°40N 78°40E **243** C8
**Chushan** *Taiwan* 23°45N 120°40E **225** C2
**Chuska Mts.** *U.S.A.* 36°15N 108°50W **305** H9
**Chusovoy** *Russia* 58°22N 57°50E **186** C10
**Chusovskoy Zavod** = Chusovoy
*Russia* 58°22N 57°50E **186** C10
**Chuspipata** *Bolivia* 16°18S 67°48W **330** D4
**Chust** = Khust *Ukraine* 48°10N 23°18E **183** B8
**Chust** *Uzbekistan* 41°0N 71°13E **217** D8
**Chute-aux-Outardes**
*Canada* 49°7N 68°24W **299** C6
**Chutung** *Taiwan* 24°44N 121°5E **225** B3
**Chuuk** = Truk
*Micronesia* 7°25N 151°46E **287** T17
**Chuuk Lagoon**
*Micronesia* 7°24N 151°45E **287** T18
**Chuvash Republic** = Chuvashia □
*Russia* 55°30N 47°0E **190** C8
**Chuvashia** □ *Russia* 55°30N 47°0E **190** C8
**Chuwārtah** *Iraq* 35°43N 45°34E **213** E11
**Chuwei** *Taiwan* 25°6N 121°14E **225** A3
**Chuxiong** *China* 25°2N 101°28E **228** E3
**Chüy** *Kyrgyzstan* 42°55N 75°15E **217** D9
**Chuy** *Uruguay* 33°41S 53°27W **335** C5
**Chüy** □ *Kyrgyzstan* 42°25N 75°16E **217** D9
**Chuzenji-Ko** *Japan* 36°44N 139°27E **223** A11
**Chuzhou** *China* 32°19N 118°20E **229** A12
**Chynadiyeve** *Ukraine* 48°29N 22°50E **182** B7
**Ci Xian** *China* 36°20N 114°25E **226** F8
**Ciacova** *Romania* 45°35N 21°10E **182** E6
**Ciadâr-Lunga** *Moldova* 46°3N 28°51E **183** D13
**Ciales** *Puerto Rico* 18°20N 66°28W **321** b
**Ciamis** *Indonesia* 7°20S 108°21E **235** D3
**Ciampino** *Italy* 41°47N 12°36E **136** C2
**Ciampino** ✕ (CIA) *Italy* 41°47N 12°35E **136** C2
**Cianjur** *Indonesia* 6°49S 107°8E **234** D3
**Cianorte** *Brazil* 23°37S 52°37W **335** A5
**Cibola** *U.S.A.* 33°17N 114°42W **307** M12
**Çiçekdağı** *Turkey* 39°36N 34°24E **212** C6
**Cicero** *U.S.A.* 41°51N 87°44W **119** B2
**Cicero Dantas** *Brazil* 10°36S 38°23W **332** D4
**Ciceron** *St. Lucia* 13°59N 61°1W **323** m
**Cicia** *Fiji* 17°45S 179°18W **287** A3
**Cicilia** *Turkey* 36°50N 34°0E **212** D5
**Cidacos** ➔ *Spain* 42°21N 1°38W **196** C3
**Cidade de Minas** = Belo Horizonte
*Brazil* 19°55S 43°56W **333** E3
**Cide** *Turkey* 41°53N 33°1E **212** B5
**Cidra** *Puerto Rico* 18°11N 66°10W **321** b
**Ciechanów** *Poland* 52°52N 20°38E **185** F7
**Ciechanowiec** *Poland* 52°40N 22°31E **185** F9
**Ciechocinek** *Poland* 52°53N 18°45E **185** F5
**Ciego de Ávila** *Cuba* 21°50N 78°50W **320** B4
**Ciénaga** *Colombia* 11°1N 74°15W **328** A3
**Ciénaga de Oro** *Colombia* 8°53N 75°37W **328** B2
**Ciénagas del Catatumbo** △
*Venezuela* 9°26N 72°8W **328** B3
**Cienfuegos** *Cuba* 22°10N 80°30W **320** B3
**Cierp-Gaud** *France* 42°55N 0°40E **174** F4
**Cíes, Is.** *Spain* 42°12N 8°55W **194** C2
**Cieszanów** *Poland* 50°14N 23°8E **185** H10
**Cieszyn** *Poland* 49°45N 18°35E **185** J5
**Cieza** *Spain* 38°17N 1°23W **197** G3
**Çifteler** *Turkey* 39°22N 31°2E **212** C4
**Cifuentes** *Spain* 40°47N 2°37W **196** E2
**Cihanbeyli** *Turkey* 38°40N 32°55E **212** C5
**Cihuatlán** *Mexico* 19°14N 104°35W **318** D4
**Cijara, Embalse de** *Spain* 39°18N 4°52W **195** F6
**Cijara** △ *Spain* 39°18N 4°35W **195** F6
**Cijulang** *Indonesia* 7°42S 108°27E **235** D3
**Cilacap** *Indonesia* 7°43S 109°0E **235** D3
**Cilandak** *Indonesia* 6°17S 106°47E **122** B1
**Cilao, Cirque de** *Réunion* 21°7S 55°28E **272** f
**Cilaos** *Réunion* 21°8S 55°27E **272** f
**Çıldır** *Turkey* 41°7N 43°8E **213** B10
**Çıldır Gölü** *Turkey* 41°5N 43°15E **213** B10
**Cilento e Vallo di Diano** △
*Italy* 40°15N 15°20E **201** B8
**Cili** *China* 29°30N 111°8E **229** C8
**Cilibia** *Romania* 45°4N 27°4E **183** E12
**Cilicia** *Turkey* 36°30N 35°0E **250** B5
**Cilincing** *Indonesia* 6°6S 106°54E **122** A2
**Ciliwung** ➔ *Indonesia* 6°6S 106°47E **122** B2
**Cill Airne** = Killarney
*Ireland* 52°4N 9°30W **166** D2
**Cill Chainnigh** = Kilkenny
*Ireland* 52°39N 7°15W **166** D4
**Cill Dara** = Kildare *Ireland* 53°9N 6°55W **166** C5
**Cill Droichid** = Celbridge
*Ireland* 53°20N 6°32W **166** C5
**Cill Mhantáin** = Wicklow
*Ireland* 52°59N 6°3W **166** D5
**Cilo Dağı** *Turkey* 37°28N 43°55E **213** D10
**Cima** *U.S.A.* 35°14N 115°30W **307** K11
**Cimarron** *Kans., U.S.A.* 37°48N 100°21W **308** G3
**Cimarron** *N. Mex., U.S.A.* 36°31N 104°55W **305** H11
**Cimarron** ➔ *U.S.A.* 36°10N 96°16W **314** C6
**Čimice** *Czech Rep.* 50°8N 14°25E **135** B2
**Cimişlia** *Moldova* 46°34N 28°44E **183** D13
**Cimone, Mte.** *Italy* 44°12N 10°42E **198** D7
**Cina, Tanjung** *Indonesia* 5°55S 104°45E **234** D2
**Çinar** *Turkey* 37°46N 40°19E **213** D9
**Çınarcık** *Turkey* 40°38N 29°5E **203** F13
**Cinaruco-Capanaparo** △
*Venezuela* 6°51N 67°32W **328** B4
**Cinca** ➔ *Spain* 41°26N 0°21E **196** D5
**Cincar** *Bos.-H.* 43°55N 17°5E **182** G2
**Cincinnati** *Iowa, U.S.A.* 40°38N 92°56W **310** D4
**Cincinnati** *Ohio, U.S.A.* 39°9N 84°27W **311** E12
**Cincinnati-Northern Kentucky Int.** ✕ (CVG) *U.S.A.* 39°3N 84°40W **311** E12
**Cincinnatus** *U.S.A.* 42°33N 75°54W **313** D9
**Çine** *Turkey* 37°37N 28°2E **205** D10
**Cinecittà** *Italy* 41°51N 12°34E **136** B2
**Ciney** *Belgium* 50°18N 5°5E **170** D5
**Cingoli** *Italy* 43°23N 13°10E **199** E10
**Cinigiano** *Italy* 42°53N 11°24E **199** F8
**Cinisello Bálsamo** *Italy* 45°33N 9°13E **128** A2
**Cinkota** *Hungary* 47°31N 19°14E **117** A3
**Cinque I.** *India* 11°16N 92°42E **245** J11
**Cinque Terre** △ *Italy* 44°10N 9°45E **198** D6
**Cinto, Mte.** *France* 42°24N 8°54E **175** F12
**Cintra, G. de** *W. Sahara* 23°0N 16°15W **260** D1
**Cintruénigo** *Spain* 42°5N 1°49W **196** C3
**Ciocile** *Romania* 44°49N 27°14E **183** F12
**Ciolăneşti din Deal**
*Romania* 44°19N 25°5E **183** F10
**Ciorani** *Romania* 44°45N 26°25E **183** F11
**Čiovo** *Croatia* 43°30N 16°17E **199** E13
**Cipero** ➔ *Trin. & Tob.* 10°16N 61°28W **323** t
**Cipete** *Indonesia* 6°15S 106°47E **122** B1
**Cipó** *Brazil* 11°6S 38°31W **332** D4
**Cipolletti** *Argentina* 38°56S 67°59W **336** A3
**Circeo, Mte.** *Italy* 41°14N 13°3E **200** A6
**Çirçir** *Turkey* 40°3N 36°47E **212** C7
**Circle** *Alaska, U.S.A.* 65°50N 144°4W **303** D11
**Circle** *Mont., U.S.A.* 47°25N 105°35W **304** C11
**Circleville** *U.S.A.* 39°36N 82°57W **309** F12
**Circular Reef** *Papua N. G.* 3°25S 147°47E **286** B4
**Cirebon** *Indonesia* 6°45S 108°32E **235** D3
**Cirencester** *U.K.* 51°43N 1°57W **169** F6
**Cireşu** *Romania* 44°47N 22°31E **182** F7
**Cirey-sur-Vezouze** *France* 48°35N 6°57E **173** D13
**Ciriè** *Italy* 45°14N 7°36E **198** C4
**Cirium** *Cyprus* 34°40N 32°53E **207** F8
**Cirò** *Italy* 39°23N 17°4E **201** C10
**Cirò Marina** *Italy* 39°22N 17°8E **201** C10
**Ciron** ➔ *France* 44°36N 0°18W **174** D3
**Cisco** *U.S.A.* 32°23N 98°59W **314** E5
**Cislău** *Romania* 45°14N 26°20E **183** E11
**Cisna** *Poland* 49°12N 22°20E **185** J9
**Cisnădie** *Romania* 45°42N 24°9E **183** E9
**Cisne** *U.S.A.* 38°31N 88°26W **311** F8
**Cisneros** *Colombia* 6°33N 75°4W **328** B2
**Cissna Park** *U.S.A.* 40°34N 87°54W **311** D9
**Cisterna di Latina** *Italy* 41°35N 12°49E **200** A5
**Cisternino** *Italy* 40°44N 17°25E **201** B10
**Cistierna** *Spain* 42°48N 5°7W **194** C5
**Citadel** = Kastellet *Copenhagen, Denmark* **118** a3
**Citadel** *Budapest, Hungary* **117** c2
**Citaré** ➔ *Brazil* 1°11N 54°41W **329** C7
**Citeli-Ckaro** = Dedopolis Tsqaro
*Georgia* 41°33N 46°0E **191** K8
**Citi Performing Arts Center**
*Boston, U.S.A.* **116** c2
**Citlaltépetl** = Orizaba, Pico de
*Mexico* 18°58N 97°15W **319** D5
**Citra** *U.S.A.* 29°25N 82°7W **317** F7
**Citron** *Fr. Guiana* 4°44N 53°57W **329** C7
**Citrus Heights** *U.S.A.* 38°42N 121°17W **306** G5
**Citrus Springs** *U.S.A.* 29°2N 82°27W **317** F7
**Citrusdal** *S. Africa* 32°35S 19°0E **270** D2
**Città degli Studi** *Italy* 45°28N 9°12E **128** B2
**Città del Vaticano** = Vatican City ■
*Europe* 41°54N 12°27E **136** B1
**Città della Pieve** *Italy* 42°57N 12°1E **199** F9
**Città di Castello** *Italy* 43°27N 12°14E **199** E9
**Città Sant' Angelo** *Italy* 42°32N 14°5E **199** F11
**Cittadella** *Italy* 45°39N 11°47E **199** C8
**Cittaducale** *Italy* 42°23N 12°57E **199** F9
**Cittanova** *Italy* 38°21N 16°5E **201** D9
**City, The** *U.K.* 51°30N 0°6W **125** A3
**City Hall** = Rådhus *Oslo, Norway* **133** b1
**City Hall** = Stadshuset
*Stockholm, Sweden* **139** b1
**City of the Dead** *Egypt* 30°0N 31°15E **117** A2
**City Park** *U.S.A.* 30°0N 90°5W **131** A2
**City Terrace** *U.S.A.* 34°3N 118°11W **126** B3
**Ciuc, Munţii** *Romania* 46°25N 26°5E **183** D11
**Ciucaş, Vf.** *Romania* 45°31N 25°56E **183** E10
**Ciucea** *Romania* 46°57N 22°49E **182** D7
**Ciucileia** *Moldova* 47°40N 27°29E **183** C12
**Ciuciuleni** *Moldova* 47°2N 28°25E **183** C13
**Ciudad Acuña** *Mexico* 29°18N 100°55W **318** B4
**Ciudad Altamirano**
*Mexico* 18°20N 100°40W **318** D4
**Ciudad Anáhuac** *Mexico* 27°14N 100°7W **318** B4
**Ciudad Bolívar** *Venezuela* 8°5N 63°36W **329** B5
**Ciudad Bolivia** *Venezuela* 8°21N 70°34W **328** B3
**Ciudad Camargo** *Mexico* 27°40N 105°10W **318** B3
**Ciudad Cortés** *Costa Rica* 8°55N 84°0W **320** E3
**Ciudad de México** *Mexico* 19°24N 99°9W **128** B2
**Ciudad de Nutrias** *Venezuela* 8°5N 69°18W **328** B4
**Ciudad del Carmen**
*Mexico* 18°38N 91°50W **319** D6
**Ciudad del Este** *Paraguay* 25°30S 54°50W **335** B5
**Ciudad Delicias** = Delicias
*Mexico* 28°13N 105°28W **318** B3
**Ciudad Deportiva** *Mexico* 19°24N 99°5W **128** B2
**Ciudad Fin de Semana**
*Spain* 40°26N 3°34W **127** B2
**Ciudad Frontera** *Mexico* 26°56N 101°27W **318** B4
**Ciudad General Belgrano**
*Argentina* 34°43S 58°33W **117** C1
**Ciudad Guayana** *Venezuela* 8°0N 62°30W **329** B5
**Ciudad Guerrero** *Mexico* 28°33N 107°30W **318** B3
**Ciudad Guzmán** *Mexico* 19°41N 103°29W **318** D4
**Ciudad Juárez** *Mexico* 31°44N 106°29W **318** A3
**Ciudad Lerdo** *Mexico* 25°32N 103°32W **318** B4
**Ciudad Lineál** *Spain* 40°26N 3°38W **127** B2
**Ciudad Madero** *Mexico* 22°19N 97°50W **319** C5
**Ciudad Mante** *Mexico* 22°44N 98°59W **319** C5
**Ciudad Obregón** *Mexico* 27°29N 109°56W **318** B3
**Ciudad Ojeda** *Venezuela* 10°12N 71°19W **328** A3
**Ciudad Piar** *Venezuela* 7°27N 63°19W **329** B5
**Ciudad Porfirio Díaz** = Piedras Negras *Mexico* 28°42N 100°31W **318** B4
**Ciudad Real** *Spain* 38°59N 3°55W **195** G7
**Ciudad Real** □ *Spain* 38°50N 4°0W **195** G7
**Ciudad Rodrigo** *Spain* 40°35N 6°32W **194** E4
**Ciudad Satélite** *Mexico* 19°30N 99°13W **128** A1
**Ciudad Trujillo** = Santo Domingo
*Dom. Rep.* 18°30N 69°59W **321** C6
**Ciudad Universitaria** *B. Aires, Argentina* 34°33S 58°27W **117** B2
**Ciudad Universitaria** *México, Mexico* 19°20N 99°11W **128** C1
**Ciudad Valles** *Mexico* 21°59N 99°1W **319** C5
**Ciudad Victoria** *Mexico* 23°44N 99°8W **319** C5
**Ciudadela** *Spain* 40°0N 3°50E **206** B4
**Ciulniţa** *Romania* 44°26N 27°22E **183** F12
**Ciumeghiu** *Romania* 46°44N 21°35E **182** D6
**Ciuperceni** *Romania* 44°54N 23°4E **182** F8
**Ciutadella, Parc de la** *Barcelona, Spain* **114** b3
**Civa Burnu** *Turkey* 41°21N 36°38E **212** B7
**Civic Center** *Los Angeles, U.S.A.* **127** b2
**Civico Correr, Museo** *Venice, Italy* **142** b3
**Cividale del Friuli** *Italy* 46°6N 13°25E **199** B10
**Civita Castellana** *Italy* 42°18N 12°24E **199** F9
**Civitanova Marche** *Italy* 43°18N 13°44E **199** E10
**Civitavécchia** *Italy* 42°6N 11°48E **199** F8
**Civray** *France* 46°10N 0°17E **174** B4
**Çivril** *Turkey* 38°20N 29°43E **205** C11
**Cixerri** ➔ *Italy* 39°17N 8°59E **200** C1
**Cixi** *China* 30°17N 121°9E **229** B13
**Cizre** *Turkey* 37°19N 42°10E **213** D10
**Clackmannanshire** □
*U.K.* 56°10N 3°43W **167** E5
**Clacton-on-Sea** *U.K.* 51°47N 1°11E **169** F9
**Clain** ➔ *France* 46°47N 0°33E **172** F7
**Claire, L.** *Canada* 58°35N 112°5W **296** B6
**Claireville Res.** *Canada* 43°45N 79°39W **141** A1
**Clairton** *U.S.A.* 40°18N 79°53W **312** F5
**Clairvaux-les-Lacs** *France* 46°35N 5°45E **173** F12
**Claise** ➔ *France* 46°56N 0°42E **174** B5
**Clallam Bay** *U.S.A.* 48°15N 124°16W **306** B2
**Clam Gulch** *U.S.A.* 60°15N 151°23W **303** F10
**Clamart** *France* 48°48N 2°15E **134** B2
**Clamecy** *France* 47°28N 3°30E **173** E10
**Clanton** *U.S.A.* 32°51N 86°38W **315** E11
**Clanwilliam** *S. Africa* 32°11S 18°52E **270** D2
**Clapham** *U.K.* 51°27N 0°8W **125** B3
**Clapton** *U.K.* 51°33N 0°3W **125** A3
**Clara** *Ireland* 53°21N 7°37W **166** C4
**Claraville** *U.S.A.* 35°24N 118°20W **307** K8
**Clare** *S. Austral., Australia* 33°50S 138°37E **282** B3
**Clare** *Mich., U.S.A.* 43°49N 84°46W **309** D11
**Clare** □ *Ireland* 52°45N 9°0W **166** D3
**Clare** ➔ *Ireland* 53°20N 9°2W **166** C2
**Clare I.** *Ireland* 53°47N 10°0W **166** C1
**Claremont** *Jamaica* 18°19N 77°11W **320** a
**Claremont** *Western Cape, S. Africa* 34°8S 18°28E **118** A1
**Claremont** *Calif., U.S.A.* 34°6N 117°43W **307** L9
**Claremont** *N.H., U.S.A.* 43°23N 72°20W **313** C12
**Claremont Pt.** *Australia* 14°1S 143°41E **280** A3
**Claremore** *U.S.A.* 36°19N 95°36W **314** C7
**Claremorris** *Ireland* 53°45N 9°0W **166** C3
**Clarence** *U.S.A.* 39°45N 92°16W **310** E4
**Clarence** ➔ *N.S.W., Australia* 29°25S 153°22E **281** D5
**Clarence** ➔ *N.Z.* 42°10S 173°56E **285** E4
**Clarence, I.** *Chile* 54°0S 72°0W **336** D2
**Clarence, Port** *U.S.A.* 65°15N 166°40W **303** D6
**Clarence B.** *Ascension I.* 7°55S 14°25W **153** g
**Clarence I.** *Antarctica* 61°10S 54°0W **151** C18
**Clarence Str.** *Australia* 12°0S 131°0E **278** B5
**Clarence Town** *Bahamas* 23°6N 74°59W **321** B5
**Clarendon** *Pa., U.S.A.* 41°47N 79°6W **312** E5
**Clarendon** *Tex., U.S.A.* 34°56N 100°53W **314** D4
**Clarenville** *Canada* 48°10N 54°1W **299** C9
**Claresholm** *Canada* 50°2N 113°33W **296** D6
**Clarie Coast** *Antarctica* 68°0S 135°0E **151** C10
**Clarinda** *U.S.A.* 40°44N 95°2W **308** E6
**Clarington** *Canada* 43°55N 78°41W **312** C6
**Clarion** *Iowa, U.S.A.* 42°44N 93°44W **310** B3
**Clarion** *Pa., U.S.A.* 41°13N 79°23W **312** E5
**Clarion** ➔ *U.S.A.* 41°7N 79°41W **312** E5
**Clarion Fracture Zone**
*Pac. Oc.* 20°0N 120°0W **292** H7
**Clark** *Mo., U.S.A.* 39°17N 92°21W **310** E4
**Clark** *S. Dak., U.S.A.* 44°53N 97°44W **308** C5
**Clark, Pt.** *Canada* 44°4N 81°45W **312** B3
**Clark Fork** *U.S.A.* 48°9N 116°11W **304** B5
**Clark Fork** ➔ *U.S.A.* 48°9N 116°15W **304** B5
**Clarkdale** *U.S.A.* 34°46N 112°3W **305** J7
**Clarke City** *Canada* 50°12N 66°38W **299** B6
**Clarke I.** *Australia* 40°32S 148°10E **281** G4
**Clarke Ra.** *Australia* 20°40S 148°30E **280** b
**Clarks Fork Yellowstone** ➔
*U.S.A.* 45°32N 108°50W **304** D9
**Clark's Harbour** *Canada* 43°25N 65°38W **299** D6
**Clarks Hill L.** = J. Strom Thurmond L. *U.S.A.* 33°40N 82°12W **316** B7
**Clarks Point** *U.S.A.* 58°51N 158°33W **303** G8
**Clarks Summit** *U.S.A.* 41°30N 75°42W **313** E9
**Clarks Town** *Jamaica* 18°25N 77°33W **320** a
**Clarksburg** *U.S.A.* 39°17N 80°30W **309** F13
**Clarksdale** *U.S.A.* 34°12N 90°35W **315** D9
**Clarkston** *U.S.A.* 46°25N 117°3W **304** C5
**Clarksville** *Ark., U.S.A.* 35°28N 93°28W **314** D8
**Clarksville** *Ind., U.S.A.* 38°17N 85°45W **311** F11
**Clarksville** *Iowa, U.S.A.* 42°47N 92°40W **310** B4
**Clarksville** *Mo., U.S.A.* 39°22N 90°54W **310** E6
**Clarksville** *Tenn., U.S.A.* 36°32N 87°21W **315** C11
**Clarksville** *Tex., U.S.A.* 33°37N 95°3W **314** E7
**Claro** ➔ *Brazil* 19°8S 50°40W **333** E1
**Clatskanie** *U.S.A.* 46°6N 123°12W **306** D3
**Claude** *U.S.A.* 35°7N 101°22W **314** D4
**Claveria** *Cagayan, Phil.* 18°37N 121°4E **232** B3
**Claveria** *Masbate, Phil.* 12°54N 123°15E **232** E4
**Claveria** *Mis. Or., Phil.* 8°38N 124°55E **233** G5
**Clavering Ø** *Greenland* 74°15N 21°0W **154** C8
**Claxton** *U.S.A.* 32°10N 81°55W **316** C8
**Claxton B.** *Trin. & Tob.* 10°21N 61°28W **323** t
**Claxton Bay** *Trin. & Tob.* 10°21N 61°28W **323** t
**Clay** *U.S.A.* 38°17N 121°10W **306** G5
**Clay Center** *U.S.A.* 39°23N 97°8W **308** F5
**Clay City** *Ind., U.S.A.* 39°17N 87°7W **311** E9
**Clay City** *Ky., U.S.A.* 37°52N 83°55W **311** G13
**Clayhall** *U.K.* 51°35N 0°3E **125** A4
**Claypool** *U.S.A.* 33°25N 110°51W **305** K8
**Claysburg** *U.S.A.* 40°17N 78°27W **312** F6
**Claysville** *U.S.A.* 40°7N 80°25W **312** F4
**Clayton** *Ont., Canada* 45°11N 76°19W **313** A8
**Clayton** *Ala., U.S.A.* 31°53N 85°27W **316** D4
**Clayton** *Ind., U.S.A.* 39°41N 86°31W **311** E10
**Clayton** *N. Mex., U.S.A.* 36°27N 103°11W **305** H12
**Clayton** *N.Y., U.S.A.* 44°14N 76°5W **313** B8
**Clear, C.** *Ireland* 51°25N 9°32W **166** E2
**Clear, L.** *Ont., Canada* 45°26N 77°12W **312** A7
**Clear, L.** *Fla., U.S.A.* 28°31N 81°24W **133** A2
**Clear Hills** *Canada* 56°40N 119°30W **296** B5
**Clear I.** *Ireland* 51°26N 9°30W **166** E2
**Clear L.** *U.S.A.* 39°2N 122°47W **306** F4
**Clear Lake** *Iowa, U.S.A.* 43°8N 93°23W **310** A3
**Clear Lake** *S. Dak., U.S.A.* 44°45N 96°41W **308** C5
**Clear Lake Res.** *U.S.A.* 41°56N 121°5W **304** F3
**Clear Water B.**
*Hong Kong, China* 22°17N 114°18E **122** B3
**Clearfield** *Pa., U.S.A.* 41°2N 78°27W **312** E6
**Clearfield** *Utah, U.S.A.* 41°7N 112°2W **304** F7
**Clearlake** *U.S.A.* 38°57N 122°38W **306** G4
**Clearwater** *B.C., Canada* 51°38N 120°2W **296** C4
**Clearwater** *Fla., U.S.A.* 27°59N 82°48W **317** H7
**Clearwater** ➔ *Alta., Canada* 52°22N 114°57W **296** C6
**Clearwater** ➔ *Alta., Canada* 56°44N 111°23W **297** B6
**Clearwater L.** *Canada* 53°34N 99°49W **297** C9
**Clearwater Lake** △ *Canada* 54°0N 101°0W **297** C8
**Clearwater Mts.** *U.S.A.* 46°5N 115°20W **304** C6
**Clearwater River** △
*Canada* 56°55N 109°10W **297** B7
**Cleburne** *U.S.A.* 32°21N 97°23W **314** E6
**Clee Hills** *U.K.* 52°26N 2°35W **169** E5
**Cleethorpes** *U.K.* 53°33N 0°3W **168** D7
**Cleeve Cloud** *U.K.* 51°56N 2°0W **169** F6
**Clelles** *France* 44°50N 5°38E **175** D9
**Clemson** *U.S.A.* 34°41N 82°50W **315** D13
**Cleopatra Needle** *Phil.* 10°7N 118°58E **233** F2
**Clerke Reef** *Australia* 17°22S 119°20E **278** C2
**Clerkenwell** *London, U.K.* **125** a4
**Clermiston** *U.K.* 55°57N 3°17W **121** B2
**Clermont** *Queens., Australia* 22°49S 147°39E **280** C4
**Clermont** *Oise, France* 49°23N 2°24E **173** C9
**Clermont** *Fla., U.S.A.* 28°33N 81°46W **317** G8
**Clermont-en-Argonne**
*France* 49°5N 5°4E **173** C12
**Clermont-Ferrand** *France* 45°46N 3°4E **174** C7
**Clermont-l'Hérault** *France* 43°38N 3°26E **174** E7
**Clerval** *France* 47°25N 6°30E **173** E13
**Clervaux** *Lux.* 50°4N 6°2E **170** D6
**Cles** *Italy* 46°22N 11°2E **198** B8
**Cleve** *Australia* 33°43S 136°30E **282** B2
**Clevedon** *U.K.* 51°26N 2°52W **169** F5
**Cleveland** *Miss., U.S.A.* 33°45N 90°43W **315** E9
**Cleveland** *Ohio, U.S.A.* 41°29N 81°41W **312** E3
**Cleveland** *Okla., U.S.A.* 36°19N 96°28W **314** C6
**Cleveland** *Tenn., U.S.A.* 35°10N 84°53W **315** D12
**Cleveland** *Tex., U.S.A.* 30°21N 95°5W **314** F7
**Cleveland, C.** *Australia* 19°11S 147°1E **280** B4
**Cleveland, Mt.** *U.S.A.* 48°56N 113°51W **304** B7
**Cleveland Heights** *U.S.A.* 41°31N 81°33W **312** E3
**Clevelândia** *Brazil* 26°24S 52°23W **335** B5
**Clevelândia do Norte**
*Brazil* 3°49N 51°52W **329** C7
**Cleves** *U.S.A.* 39°10N 84°45W **311** E12
**Clew B.** *Ireland* 53°50N 9°49W **166** C2
**Clewiston** *U.S.A.* 26°45N 80°56W **317** J9
**Clichy** *France* 48°54N 2°18E **134** A2
**Clichy-sous-Bois** *France* 48°54N 2°32E **134** A4
**Clifden** *Galway, Ireland* 53°29N 10°1W **166** C1
**Clifden** *N.Z.* 46°1S 167°42E **285** G2
**Cliffdell** *U.S.A.* 46°56N 121°5W **306** D5
**Cliffside** *Canada* 43°44N 79°14W **141** A3
**Cliffside Park** *U.S.A.* 40°49N 73°59W **132** B2
**Cliffy Hd.** *Australia* 35°1S 116°29E **279** G2
**Clifton** *Queens., Australia* 27°59S 151°53E **281** D5
**Clifton** *Sindh, Pakistan* 24°48N 67°1E **123** B2
**Clifton** *Western Cape, S. Africa* 33°56S 18°22E **118** A1
**Clifton** *Ariz., U.S.A.* 33°3N 109°18W **305** K9
**Clifton** *Colo., U.S.A.* 39°7N 108°25W **304** G9
**Clifton** *Ill., U.S.A.* 40°56N 87°56W **311** D9
**Clifton** *N.J., U.S.A.* 40°37N 74°9W **132** C1
**Clifton** *Tex., U.S.A.* 31°47N 97°35W **314** F6
**Clifton Beach** *Queens., Australia* 16°46S 145°39E **280** B4
**Clifton Beach** *Sindh, Pakistan* 24°48N 67°2E **123** B2
**Clifton Pt.** *Bahamas* 25°2N 77°34W **153** b
**Cliftondale** *U.S.A.* 42°26N 71°0W **116** A2
**Climax** *U.S.A.* 30°53N 84°26W **316** E5
**Clinch** ➔ *U.S.A.* 35°53N 84°29W **315** D12
**Clingmans Dome** *U.S.A.* 35°34N 83°30W **315** D13
**Clint** *U.S.A.* 31°35N 106°14W **314** F1
**Clinton** *B.C., Canada* 51°6N 121°35W **296** C4
**Clinton** *Ont., Canada* 43°37N 81°32W **312** C3
**Clinton** *N.Z.* 46°12S 169°23E **285** G4
**Clinton** *Ark., U.S.A.* 35°36N 92°28W **314** D8
**Clinton** *Conn., U.S.A.* 41°17N 72°32W **313** E12
**Clinton** *Ill., U.S.A.* 40°9N 88°57W **310** D8
**Clinton** *Ind., U.S.A.* 39°40N 87°24W **311** E9
**Clinton** *Iowa, U.S.A.* 41°51N 90°12W **310** C6
**Clinton** *Mass., U.S.A.* 42°25N 71°41W **313** D13
**Clinton** *Mich., U.S.A.* 42°4N 83°58W **311** C12
**Clinton** *Miss., U.S.A.* 32°20N 90°20W **315** E9
**Clinton** *Mo., U.S.A.* 38°22N 93°46W **310** F3
**Clinton** *N.C., U.S.A.* 35°0N 78°22W **315** D15
**Clinton** *Okla., U.S.A.* 35°31N 98°58W **314** D5
**Clinton** *S.C., U.S.A.* 34°29N 81°53W **315** D14
**Clinton** *Tenn., U.S.A.* 36°6N 84°8W **315** C12
**Clinton** *Wash., U.S.A.* 47°59N 122°21W **306** C4
**Clinton** *Wis., U.S.A.* 42°34N 88°52W **311** B8
**Clinton, C.** *Australia* 22°30S 150°45E **280** C5
**Clinton, L.** *U.S.A.* 40°15N 88°45W **311** D8
**Clinton Colden L.**
*Canada* 63°58N 107°27W **294** E10
**Clio** *U.S.A.* 31°43N 85°37W **316** D4
**Clipperton, Î.** *Pac. Oc.* 10°18N 109°13W **289** F17
**Clipperton Fracture Zone**
*Pac. Oc.* 19°0N 122°0W **289** G16
**Clisham** *U.K.* 57°58N 6°49W **167** D2
**Clisson** *France* 47°5N 1°16W **172** E5
**Clitheroe** *U.K.* 53°53N 2°22W **168** D5
**Clive** *N.Z.* 39°36S 176°58E **284** F5
**Clive** *Iowa, U.S.A.* 41°36N 93°43W **310** C3
**Cliza** *Bolivia* 17°36S 65°56W **331** D4
**Clo-oose** *Canada* 48°39N 124°49W **306** B2
**Cloates, Pt.** *Australia* 22°43S 113°40E **278** D1
**Clocolan** *S. Africa* 28°55S 27°34E **271** C4
**Clodomira** *Argentina* 27°35S 64°14W **334** B3
**Cloghaneely** *Ireland* 55°8N 8°5W **166** A3
**Clogher Hd.** *Ireland* 53°48N 6°14W **166** C5
**Cloghran** *Ireland* 53°27N 6°14W **120** A2
**Clonakilty** *Ireland* 51°37N 8°53W **166** E3
**Clonakilty B.** *Ireland* 51°35N 8°51W **166** E3
**Cloncurry** *Queens., Australia* 20°40S 140°28E **280** C3
**Cloncurry** *Kildare, Ireland* 53°25N 6°48W **166** C5
**Cloncurry** ➔ *Australia* 18°37S 140°40E **280** B3
**Clondalkin** *Ireland* 53°19N 6°25W **166** C5
**Clones** *Ireland* 54°11N 7°15W **166** B4
**Clonmel** *Ireland* 52°21N 7°42W **166** D4
**Clonskeagh** *Ireland* 53°19N 6°14W **120** B2
**Clontarf** *N.S.W., Australia* 33°48S 151°16E **139** A2
**Clontarf** *Dublin, Ireland* 53°22N 6°11W **120** A2
**Cloppenburg** *Germany* 52°51N 8°1E **178** C4
**Cloquet** *U.S.A.* 46°43N 92°28W **308** B7
**Clorinda** *Argentina* 25°16S 57°45W **334** B4
**Cloud Peak** *U.S.A.* 44°23N 107°11W **304** D10
**Cloudcroft** *U.S.A.* 32°58N 105°45W **305** K11
**Cloudy B.** *N.Z.* 41°25S 174°10E **285** B9
**Clovelly** *Australia* 33°54S 151°15E **139** B2
**Cloverdale** *Calif., U.S.A.* 38°48N 123°1W **306** G4
**Cloverdale** *Ind., U.S.A.* 39°31N 86°48W **311** E10
**Cloverport** *U.S.A.* 37°50N 86°38W **311** G10
**Clovis** *Calif., U.S.A.* 36°49N 119°42W **306** J7
**Clovis** *N. Mex., U.S.A.* 34°24N 103°12W **305** J12
**Cloyes-sur-le-Loir** *France* 48°0N 1°14E **172** E8
**Cloyne** *Canada* 44°49N 77°11W **312** B7
**Cluain Meala** = Clonmel
*Ireland* 52°21N 7°42W **166** D4
**Club Terrace** *Australia* 37°35S 148°58E **283** D8
**Cluj** □ *Romania* 46°45N 23°30E **183** D8
**Cluj-Napoca** *Romania* 46°47N 23°38E **183** D8
**Clunes** *Australia* 37°20S 143°45E **282** D5
**Cluny** *France* 46°26N 4°38E **173** F11
**Cluses** *France* 46°5N 6°35E **173** F13
**Clusone** *Italy* 45°53N 9°57E **198** C6
**Clutha** ➔ *N.Z.* 46°20S 169°49E **285** G4
**Clwyd** ➔ *U.K.* 53°19N 3°31W **168** D4
**Clyattville** *U.S.A.* 30°42N 83°19W **316** E6
**Clyde** *Alta., Canada* 54°9N 113°39W **296** C6
**Clyde** *N.Z.* 45°12S 169°20E **285** F4
**Clyde** *N.Y., U.S.A.* 43°5N 76°52W **312** C8
**Clyde** *Ohio, U.S.A.* 41°18N 82°59W **311** C14
**Clyde** ➔ *U.K.* 55°55N 4°30W **167** F4
**Clyde, Firth of** *U.K.* 55°22N 5°1W **167** F3
**Clyde River** *Canada* 70°30N 68°30W **295** C18
**Clydebank** *U.K.* 55°54N 4°23W **167** F4
**Clymer** *N.Y., U.S.A.* 42°1N 79°37W **312** D5
**Clymer** *Pa., U.S.A.* 40°40N 79°1W **312** D5
**Clyo** *U.S.A.* 32°29N 81°16W **316** C8
**Ćmielów** *Poland* 50°53N 21°31E **185** H8
**CNN Center** *U.S.A.* 33°45N 84°23W **113** B2
**Côa** ➔ *Portugal* 41°5N 7°6W **194** D3
**Coachella** *U.S.A.* 33°41N 116°10W **307** M10
**Coachella Canal** *U.S.A.* 32°43N 114°57W **307** N12
**Coahoma** *U.S.A.* 32°18N 101°18W **314** E4
**Coahuayana** ➔ *Mexico* 18°41N 103°45W **318** D4
**Coahuila** □ *Mexico* 27°20N 102°0W **318** B4
**Coal** ➔ *Canada* 59°39N 126°57W **296** B3
**Coal City** *U.S.A.* 41°17N 88°17W **311** C8
**Coal I.** *N.Z.* 46°8S 166°40E **285** G1
**Coalane** *Mozam.* 17°48S 37°2E **269** F4
**Coalcomán** *Mexico* 18°47N 103°9W **318** D4
**Coaldale** *Canada* 49°45N 112°35W **296** D6
**Coalgate** *U.S.A.* 34°32N 96°13W **314** D6
**Coalinga** *U.S.A.* 36°9N 120°21W **306** J6
**Coalisland** *U.K.* 54°33N 6°42W **166** B5
**Coalville** *Leics., U.K.* 52°44N 1°23W **168** E6
**Coalville** *Utah, U.S.A.* 40°55N 111°24W **304** F8
**Coamo** *Puerto Rico* 18°5N 66°22W **321** b
**Coaraci** *Brazil* 14°38S 39°32W **333** D4
**Coari** *Brazil* 4°8S 63°7W **329** D5
**Coari** ➔ *Brazil* 4°30S 63°33W **329** D5
**Coari, L.** *Brazil* 4°15S 63°22W **329** D5
**Coast** □ *Kenya* 2°40S 39°45E **268** C4
**Coast Mts.** *Canada* 55°0N 129°20W **296** C3
**Coast Ranges** *U.S.A.* 39°0N 123°0W **306** G4
**Coatbridge** *U.K.* 55°52N 4°6W **167** F4
**Coatepec** *Mexico* 19°27N 96°58W **319** D5
**Coatepeque** *Guatemala* 14°46N 91°55W **320** D1
**Coatesville** *U.S.A.* 39°59N 75°50W **309** F16
**Coaticook** *Canada* 45°10N 71°46W **313** A13
**Coats I.** *Canada* 62°30N 83°0W **295** E15
**Coats Land** *Antarctica* 77°0S 25°0W **151** D1
**Coatzacoalcos** *Mexico* 18°7N 94°25W **319** D6
**Cobá** *Mexico* 20°31N 87°45W **319** C7
**Cobadin** *Romania* 44°5N 28°13E **183** F13
**Cobalt** *Canada* 47°25N 79°42W **298** C4
**Cobán** *Guatemala* 15°30N 90°21W **320** C1
**Çobanlar** *Turkey* 38°41N 30°47E **205** C12
**Cobar** *Australia* 31°27S 145°48E **283** A6
**Cobargo** *Australia* 36°20S 149°55E **283** D8
**Cobbannah** *Australia* 37°37S 147°12E **283** D7
**Cobberas, Mt.** *Australia* 36°53S 148°12E **283** D8
**Cobden** *Australia* 38°20S 143°3E **282** E5
**Cobh** *Ireland* 51°51N 8°17W **166** E3
**Cobh, An** = Cobh *Ireland* 51°51N 8°17W **166** E3
**Cobija** *Bolivia* 11°0S 68°50W **330** C4
**Cobleskill** *U.S.A.* 42°41N 74°29W **313** D10
**Coboconk** *Canada* 44°39N 78°48W **312** B6
**Cobourg** *Canada* 43°58N 78°10W **312** C6
**Cobourg Pen.** *Australia* 11°20S 132°15E **278** B5
**Cobram** *Australia* 35°54S 145°40E **283** C6
**Cobras, I. das** *Brazil* 22°53S 43°9W **135** B2
**Cóbué** *Mozam.* 12°0S 34°58E **269** E3
**Coburg** *Vic., Australia* 37°44S 144°56E **128** A1
**Coburg** *Bayern, Germany* 50°15N 10°58E **179** E6
**Coburg I.** *Canada* 75°57N 79°26W **295** B16
**Coca** *Spain* 41°13N 4°32W **194** D6
**Coca** ➔ *Ecuador* 0°29S 76°58W **328** D2
**Cocachacra** *Peru* 17°5S 71°45W **330** D3
**Cocal** *Brazil* 3°28S 41°34W **332** B3
**Cocanada** = Kakinada
*India* 16°57N 82°11E **244** F6
**Cocentaina** *Spain* 38°45N 0°27W **197** G4
**Cochabamba** *Bolivia* 17°26S 66°10W **330** D4
**Coche, I.** *Venezuela* 10°47N 63°56W **329** a
**Cochem** *Germany* 50°8N 7°9E **179** E3
**Cochemane** *Mozam.* 17°0S 32°54E **269** F3
**Cochin** = Kochi *India* 9°58N 76°20E **245** K3
**Cochin China** = Nam-Phan
*Vietnam* 10°30N 106°0E **237** G6
**Cochran** *U.S.A.* 32°23N 83°21W **316** C6
**Cochrane** *Alta., Canada* 51°11N 114°30W **296** C6
**Cochrane** *Ont., Canada* 49°0N 81°0W **298** C3
**Cochrane** *Chile* 47°15S 72°33W **336** C2
**Cochrane** ➔ *Canada* 59°0N 103°40W **297** B8
**Cochrane, L.** *Chile* 47°10S 72°0W **336** C2
**Cochranton** *U.S.A.* 41°31N 80°3W **312** E4
**Cockburn** *Australia* 32°5S 141°0E **282** B4
**Cockburn, Canal** *Chile* 54°30S 72°0W **336** D2
**Cockburn I.** *Canada* 45°55N 83°22W **298** C3
**Cockburn Ra.** *Australia* 15°46S 128°0E **278** C4
**Cockermouth** *U.K.* 54°40N 3°22W **168** C4
**Cocklebiddy** *Australia* 32°0S 126°3E **279** F4
**Cockpit** *Jamaica* 18°16N 77°39W **320** a
**Cockpit Country, The**
*Jamaica* 18°15N 77°45W **320** a
**Côco** ➔ *Brazil* 9°27S 50°2W **332** C2
**Coco** ➔ *Cent. Amer.* 15°0N 83°8W **320** D3
**Coco, I. del** *Pac. Oc.* 5°25N 87°55W **289** G19
**Coco, Pta.** *Colombia* 2°58N 77°43W **328** C2
**Coco Channel** *Asia* 13°45N 93°10E **245** H11
**Cocoa** *U.S.A.* 28°21N 80°44W **317** G9
**Cocoa Beach** *U.S.A.* 28°19N 80°37W **317** G9
**Cocoa Point** *Antigua & B.* 17°33N 61°46W **322** c
**Cocobeach** *Gabon* 0°59N 9°34E **264** B1
**Coconut Grove** *U.S.A.* 25°42N 80°15W **129** D2
**Coconara** △ *Australia* 34°10S 146°12E **283** C7
**Cocora** *Romania* 44°45N 27°3E **183** F12
**Côcos** *Brazil* 14°10S 44°33W **333** D3
**Côcos** ➔ *Brazil* 12°44S 44°48W **333** D3
**Cocos B.** *Trin. & Tob.* 10°24N 61°2W **323** t
**Cocos Basin** *Ind. Oc.* 1°0N 94°0E **273** D8
**Cocos I.** = Coco, I. del
*Pac. Oc.* 5°25N 87°55W **289** G19
**Cocos I.** *Guam* 13°14N 144°39E **302** d
**Cocos Is.** *Ind. Oc.* 12°10S 96°55E **273** F8
**Cocos Ridge** *Pac. Oc.* 4°0N 88°0W **289** G19
**Cocotá** *Brazil* 22°48S 43°11W **135** A1
**Cod, C.** *U.S.A.* 42°5N 70°10W **309** D18
**Codajás** *Brazil* 3°55S 62°0W **329** D5
**Codera, C.** *Venezuela* 10°35N 66°4W **328** A4
**Codfish I.** *N.Z.* 46°47S 167°38E **285** G2
**Codigoro** *Italy* 44°49N 12°8E **199** D9
**Codlea** *Romania* 45°42N 25°27E **183** E10
**Codó** *Brazil* 4°30S 43°55W **332** B3
**Codogno** *Italy* 45°9N 9°42E **198** C6
**Codpa** *Chile* 18°50S 69°44W **330** D4
**Codrington** *Antigua & B.* 17°38N 61°50W **322** c
**Codrington Lagoon**
*Antigua & B.* 17°39N 61°50W **322** c
**Codróipo** *Italy* 45°58N 13°0E **199** C10
**Codru, Munţii** *Romania* 46°30N 22°15E **182** D7
**Cody** *U.S.A.* 44°32N 109°3W **304** D9
**Coe Hill** *Canada* 44°52N 77°50W **312** B7
**Coelemu** *Chile* 36°30S 72°48W **334** D1
**Coelho Neto** *Brazil* 4°15S 43°0W **332** B3
**Coen** *Australia* 13°52S 143°12E **280** A3
**Coeroeni** *Suriname* 3°22N 57°21W **329** C6
**Coeroeni** ➔ *Suriname* 3°21N 57°31W **329** C6
**Coesfeld** *Germany* 51°56N 7°10E **178** D3
**Coetivy I.** *Seychelles* 7°8S 56°16E **273** E4
**Cœuilly** *France* 48°48N 2°32E **134** B4
**Coeur d'Alene** *U.S.A.* 47°41N 116°46W **304** C5
**Coeur d'Alene L.** *U.S.A.* 47°32N 116°49W **304** C5
**Coevorden** *Neths.* 52°40N 6°44E **170** B6
**Cofete** *Canary Is.* 28°6N 14°23W **153** e2
**Coffeyville** *U.S.A.* 37°2N 95°37W **308** G6
**Coffin B.** *Australia* 34°38S 135°28E **281** E2
**Coffin Bay** *Australia* 34°37S 135°29E **281** E2
**Coffin Bay** △ *Australia* 34°34S 135°19E **281** E2
**Coffin Bay Peninsula**
*Australia* 34°32S 135°15E **281** E2
**Coffs Harbour** *Australia* 30°16S 153°5E **283** A10
**Cofrentes** *Spain* 39°13N 1°5W **197** F3
**Cogalnic** = Kohylnyk ➔
*Ukraine* 45°49N 29°40E **183** E14
**Cogealac** *Romania* 44°36N 28°36E **183** F13
**Coghinas** ➔ *Italy* 40°55N 8°48E **200** B1
**Coghinas, L. del** *Italy* 40°46N 9°3E **200** B2
**Cognac** *France* 45°41N 0°20W **174** C3
**Cogne** *Italy* 45°37N 7°21E **198** C4
**Cogolin** *France* 43°15N 6°32E **175** E10
**Cogolludo** *Spain* 40°59N 3°10W **196** E1
**Cohocton** *U.S.A.* 42°30N 77°30W **312** D7
**Cohocton** ➔ *U.S.A.* 42°9N 77°6W **312** D7
**Cohoes** *U.S.A.* 42°46N 73°42W **313** D11
**Cohuna** *Australia* 35°45S 144°15E **282** C6
**Coiba, I. de** *Panama* 7°30N 81°40W **320** E3
**Coig** ➔ *Argentina* 51°0S 69°10W **336** D3
**Coigeach, Rubha** *U.K.* 58°6N 5°26W **167** C3
**Coihaique** *Chile* 45°30S 71°45W **336** C2
**Coimbatore** *India* 11°2N 76°59E **245** J3
**Coimbra** *Mato Grosso, Brazil* 19°55S 57°48W **331** D6
**Coimbra** *Portugal* 40°15N 8°27W **194** E2
**Coimbra** □ *Portugal* 40°12N 8°25W **194** E2
**Coín** *Spain* 36°40N 4°48W **195** J6
**Coina** *Portugal* 38°39N 9°5W **126** B2
**Coipasa, L. de** *Bolivia* 19°12S 68°7W **330** D4
**Coipasa, Salar de** *Bolivia* 19°26S 68°9W **330** D4
**Coit Tower** *San Francisco, U.S.A.* **136** a2
**Cojata** *Peru* 15°2S 69°25W **330** D4
**Cojedes** □ *Venezuela* 9°20N 68°20W **328** B4
**Cojedes** ➔ *Venezuela* 8°34N 68°5W **328** B4
**Cojimies** *Ecuador* 0°20N 80°0W **328** C1
**Cojocna** *Romania* 46°45N 23°50E **183** D8
**Cojutepeque** *El Salv.* 13°41N 88°54W **320** D2
**Čoka** *Serbia* 45°57N 20°12E **182** E5
**Coker** *Nigeria* 6°28N 3°20E **124** B2
**Cokeville** *U.S.A.* 42°5N 110°57W **304** E8
**Colaba** *India* 18°53N 72°48E **130** B1
**Colaba Pt.** *India* 18°53N 72°48E **130** B1
**Colac** *Australia* 38°21S 143°35E **282** E5
**Colachel** = Kolachel *India* 8°10N 77°15E **245** K3
**Colán** *Peru* 5°0S 81°0W **330** B1
**Colatina** *Brazil* 19°32S 40°37W **333** E3
**Colbeck, C.** *Antarctica* 77°6S 157°48W **151** D13
**Colbert** *U.S.A.* 34°2N 83°13W **316** A6
**Colborne** *Canada* 44°0N 77°53W **312** C7
**Colby** *U.S.A.* 39°24N 101°3W **308** F3
**Colca** = Majes ➔ *Peru* 16°40S 72°44W **330** D3
**Colca, Cañón del** *Peru* 15°50S 72°20W **330** D3
**Colchester** *Essex, U.K.* 51°54N 0°55E **169** F8
**Colchester** *Conn., U.S.A.* 41°35N 72°20W **313** E12
**Cold Bay** *U.S.A.* 55°12N 162°42W **303** J7
**Cold L.** *Canada* 54°33N 110°5W **297** C7
**Cold Lake** *Canada* 54°27N 110°10W **297** C6
**Coldstream** *B.C., Canada* 50°13N 119°11W **296** C5
**Coldstream** *Borders, U.K.* 55°39N 2°15W **167** F6
**Coldwater** *Ont., Canada* 44°42N 79°40W **312** B5
**Coldwater** *Kans., U.S.A.* 37°16N 99°20W **308** G4
**Coldwater** *Mich., U.S.A.* 41°57N 85°0W **311** C11
**Coldwater** *Ohio, U.S.A.* 40°29N 84°38W **311** D12
**Coldwater, L.** *U.S.A.* 41°48N 84°59W **311** C12
**Cole Camp** *U.S.A.* 38°28N 93°12W **310** F3
**Coleambally** *Australia* 34°49S 145°52E **283** C6
**Colebrook** *U.S.A.* 44°54N 71°30W **313** B13
**Colegiales** *Argentina* 34°34S 58°27W **117** B2
**Coleman** *Alta., Canada* 49°40N 114°30W **296** D6
**Coleman** *Fla., U.S.A.* 28°48N 82°4W **317** G7
**Coleman** *Tex., U.S.A.* 31°50N 99°26W **314** F5
**Coleman** ➔ *Australia* 15°6S 141°38E **280** B3
**Colenso** *S. Africa* 28°44S 29°50E **271** C4
**Coleraine** *Vic., Australia* 37°36S 141°40E **282** D4
**Coleraine** *L'derry., U.K.* 55°8N 6°41W **166** A5
**Coleridge, L.** *N.Z.* 43°17S 171°30E **285** D3
**Coleroon** ➔ *India* 11°25N 79°50E **245** J4
**Colesberg** *S. Africa* 30°45S 25°5E **270** D4
**Coleville** *U.S.A.* 38°34N 119°30W **306** G7
**Colfax** *Calif., U.S.A.* 39°6N 120°57W **306** F6
**Colfax** *Ill., U.S.A.* 40°34N 88°37W **311** D8
**Colfax** *Ind., U.S.A.* 40°12N 86°40W **311** D10
**Colfax** *Iowa, U.S.A.* 41°41N 93°14W **310** C3
**Colfax** *La., U.S.A.* 31°31N 92°42W **314** F8
**Colfax** *Wash., U.S.A.* 46°53N 117°22W **304** C5
**Colhué Huapi, L.** *Argentina* 45°30S 69°0W **336** C3
**Colibaşi** = Mioveni
*Romania* 44°56N 24°54E **183** F9

Colibași Moldova 45°43N 28°11E 183 E13
Colibris, Pte. des Guadeloupe 16°17N 61°5W 322 e
Cólico Italy 46°8N 9°22E 198 B6
Colider Brazil 10°45S 55°25W 331 C6
Coligny Ain, France 46°23N 5°21E 173 F12
Coligny North West, S. Africa 26°17S 26°15E 271 C4
Colihaut Dominica 15°29N 61°29W 323 k
Colima Mexico 19°14N 103°43W 318 D4
Colima □ Mexico 19°10N 104°0W 318 D4
Colima, Nevado de Mexico 19°33N 103°38W 318 D4
Colina Chile 33°13S 70°45W 334 C1
Colina do Norte Guinea-Biss. 12°28N 15°0W 262 C2
Colinas Goiás, Brazil 14°15S 48°2W 333 D2
Colinas Maranhão, Brazil 6°0S 44°10W 332 C3
Colindale U.K. 51°35N 0°15W 125 A2
Colindres Spain 43°24N 3°27W 194 B7
Colinton U.K. 55°55N 3°14W 121 B2
Coll U.K. 56°39N 6°34W 167 E2
Collahuasi Chile 21°5S 68°45W 334 A2
Collarada, Peña Spain 42°43N 0°29W 196 C4
Collarenebri Australia 29°33S 148°34E 281 D4
Colle di Val d'Elsa Italy 43°25N 11°7E 198 E8
Collécchio Italy 44°45N 10°13E 198 D7
Colleen Bawn Zimbabwe 21°0S 29°12E 269 G2
College U.S.A. 64°52N 147°49W 303 D11
College Park Ga., U.S.A. 33°39N 84°27W 113 C2
College Park Md., U.S.A. 38°59N 76°55W 143 B3
College Point U.S.A. 40°47N 73°50W 132 B2
College Station U.S.A. 30°37N 96°21W 314 F6
Collégien France 48°50N 2°41E 134 A4
Collesalvetti Italy 43°34N 10°27E 198 E7
Colli Euganei ⌓ Italy 45°18N 11°43E 199 C8
Collie N.S.W., Australia 31°41S 148°18E 283 A8
Collie W. Austral., Australia 33°22S 116°8E 279 F2
Collier B. Australia 16°10S 124°15E 278 C3
Collier Ra. Australia 24°45S 119°10E 279 D2
Collier Range △ Australia 24°39S 119°7E 279 D2
Collier Row U.K. 51°35N 0°9E 125 A4
Colliers Wood U.K. 51°24N 0°10W 125 B2
Colliersville U.S.A. 35°3N 89°40W 315 D10
Collina, Passo di Italy 44°2N 10°56E 198 D7
Collingwood Ont., Canada 44°29N 80°13W 312 B4
Collingwood N.Z. 40°41S 172°40E 285 A7
Collins Ont., Canada 50°17N 89°27W 298 B2
Collins Ga., U.S.A. 32°11N 82°7W 316 C7
Collins Mo., U.S.A. 37°54N 93°37W 310 G3
Collins Bay Canada 44°14N 76°36W 313 B8
Collinson Pen. Canada 69°58N 101°24W 294 D11
Collinsville Queens., Australia 20°30S 147°56E 280 C4
Collinsville Ill., U.S.A. 38°40N 89°59W 310 F7
Collipulli Chile 37°55S 72°30W 334 D1
Collo Algeria 36°58N 6°37E 261 A6
Collooney Ireland 54°11N 8°29W 166 B3
Colma U.S.A. 37°40N 122°27W 136 B2
Colmar France 48°5N 7°20E 173 D14
Colmars France 44°11N 6°39E 175 D10
Colmenar Spain 36°54N 4°20W 195 J6
Colmenar de Oreja Spain 40°6N 3°25W 194 E7
Colmenar Viejo Spain 40°39N 3°47W 194 E7
Colney Hatch U.K. 51°36N 0°9W 125 A3
Colo → Australia 33°25S 150°52E 283 B9
Cologne = Köln Germany 50°56N 6°57E 178 E2
Cologno Monzese Italy 45°31N 9°16E 128 A2
Colom, I. d'en Spain 39°58N 4°16E 206 B5
Coloma Calif., U.S.A. 38°48N 120°53W 306 G6
Coloma Mich., U.S.A. 42°11N 86°19W 311 B10
Colomb-Béchar = Béchar Algeria 31°38N 2°18W 261 B4
Colombes France 48°55N 2°15E 134 A2
Colombey-les-Belles France 48°32N 5°54E 173 D12
Colombey-les-Deux-Églises France 48°13N 4°50E 173 D11
Colômbia Brazil 20°10S 48°40W 333 F2
Colombia ■ S. Amer. 3°45N 73°0W 328 C3
Colombian Basin Caribbean 14°0N 76°0W 321 D5
Colombier St.-Martin 18°5N 63°4W 322 a
Colombo Sri Lanka 6°56N 79°58E 245 L4
Colomiers France 43°36N 1°21E 174 E5
Colón B. Aires, Argentina 33°53S 61°7W 334 C3
Colón Entre Ríos, Argentina 32°12S 58°10W 334 C4
Colón Cuba 22°42N 80°54W 320 B3
Colón Panama 9°20N 79°54W 320 c
Colón, Arch. de Ecuador 0°0 91°0W 330 a
Colón, Monumente a Barcelona, Spain 114 c3
Colón, Plaza de Madrid, Spain 127 a3
Colón Ridge Pac. Oc. 2°0N 96°0W 289 G18
Colonarie St. Vincent 13°14N 61°8W 323 n
Colonia Micronesia 9°30N 138°10E 287 R16
Colonia 25 de Mayo Argentina 37°48S 67°41W 336 A3
Colònia de Sant Jordi Spain 39°19N 2°59E 206 B3
Colonia del Sacramento Uruguay 34°25S 57°50W 334 C4
Colonia Dora Argentina 28°34S 62°59W 334 B3
Colonia Güell Spain 41°21N 2°2E 114 A1
Colonial Beach U.S.A. 38°15N 76°58W 309 F15
Colonie U.S.A. 42°43N 73°50W 313 D11
Colonna, C. Italy 39°2N 17°12E 201 C10
Colonsay Sask., Canada 51°59N 105°52W 297 C7
Colonsay Argyll & Bute, U.K. 56°5N 6°12W 167 E2
Colorado □ U.S.A. 39°30N 105°30W 304 G11
Colorado → Argentina 39°50S 62°8W 336 A4
Colorado → N. Amer. 31°45N 114°40W 305 L6
Colorado → Tex., U.S.A. 28°36N 95°59W 314 G7
Colorado City U.S.A. 32°24N 100°52W 314 E4
Colorado Plateau U.S.A. 37°0N 111°0W 305 H8
Colorado River Aqueduct U.S.A. 33°50N 117°23W 307 L12
Colorado Springs U.S.A. 38°50N 104°49W 304 G11
Colorno Italy 44°56N 10°23E 198 D7
Colosseo Rome, Italy 136 c3
Colosseum = Colosseo Rome, Italy 136 c3
Colotlán Mexico 22°6N 103°16W 318 C4
Colquechaca Bolivia 18°40S 66°1W 331 D4
Colquitt U.S.A. 31°10N 84°44W 316 D5
Colstrip U.S.A. 45°53N 106°38W 304 D10
Colton U.S.A. 44°33N 74°56W 313 B10
Columbia Ala., U.S.A. 31°18N 85°7W 316 D4
Columbia Ill., U.S.A. 38°27N 90°12W 310 F6
Columbia Ky., U.S.A. 37°6N 85°18W 309 G11
Columbia La., U.S.A. 32°6N 92°5W 314 E8
Columbia Miss., U.S.A. 31°15N 89°50W 315 F10
Columbia Mo., U.S.A. 38°57N 92°20W 310 F4
Columbia Pa., U.S.A. 40°2N 76°30W 313 F8
Columbia S.C., U.S.A. 34°0N 81°2W 316 A8
Columbia Tenn., U.S.A. 35°37N 87°2W 315 D11
Columbia → N. Amer. 46°15N 124°5W 306 D2
Columbia, C. Canada 83°6N 69°57W 295 A18
Columbia, District of □ U.S.A. 38°55N 77°0W 309 F15
Columbia, Mt. Canada 52°8N 117°20W 296 C5
Columbia Basin U.S.A. 46°45N 119°5W 304 C4
Columbia City U.S.A. 41°10N 85°29W 311 C11
Columbia Falls U.S.A. 48°23N 114°11W 304 B6
Columbia Mts. Canada 52°0N 119°0W 296 C5
Columbia Plateau U.S.A. 44°0N 117°30W 304 E5
Columbiana U.S.A. 40°53N 80°42W 312 F4
Columbretes, Is. Spain 39°50N 0°50E 196 F5
Columbus Ga., U.S.A. 32°28N 84°59W 316 C5
Columbus Ind., U.S.A. 39°13N 85°55W 311 E11
Columbus Kans., U.S.A. 37°10N 94°50W 308 G6
Columbus Miss., U.S.A. 33°30N 88°25W 315 E10
Columbus Mont., U.S.A. 45°38N 109°15W 304 D9
Columbus N. Mex., U.S.A. 31°50N 107°38W 305 L10
Columbus Nebr., U.S.A. 41°26N 97°22W 308 E5
Columbus Ohio, U.S.A. 39°58N 83°0W 311 E13
Columbus Tex., U.S.A. 29°42N 96°33W 314 G6
Columbus Circle Washington, D.C., U.S.A. 143 b3
Columbus Circle New York, U.S.A. 132 b2
Columbus Grove U.S.A. 40°55N 84°4W 311 D12
Columbus Junction U.S.A. 41°17N 91°22W 310 C5
Columbus Monument = Colón, Monumente a Barcelona, Spain 114 c3
Columbus Park Jamaica 18°28N 77°25W 320 a
Columbus Park Boston, U.S.A. 116 b3
Colunga Spain 43°29N 5°16W 194 B5
Colusa U.S.A. 39°13N 122°1W 306 F4
Colville U.S.A. 48°33N 117°54W 304 B5
Colville → U.S.A. 70°25N 150°30W 303 A10
Colville, C. N.Z. 36°29S 175°21E 284 C4
Colville Channel N.Z. 36°25S 175°27E 284 C4
Colville Ridge Pac. Oc. 30°0S 180°0E 277 G15
Colwood Canada 48°26N 123°29W 306 B3
Colwyn Bay U.K. 53°18N 3°44W 168 D4
Coma Ethiopia 8°29N 36°53E 257 F4
Comácchio Italy 44°42N 12°11E 199 D9
Comalcalco Mexico 18°16N 93°13W 319 D6
Comallo Argentina 41°0S 70°5W 336 B2
Comana Romania 44°10N 26°10E 183 F11
Comanche U.S.A. 31°54N 98°36W 314 F5
Comandante Arbues = Mirandópolis Brazil 21°9S 51°6W 335 A5
Comandante Ferraz Antarctica 62°30S 58°0W 151 C18
Comandante Luis Piedrabuena Argentina 49°59S 68°54W 336 C3
Comănești Romania 46°25N 26°26E 183 D11
Comarapa Bolivia 17°54S 64°29W 331 D5
Comarnic Romania 45°15N 25°38E 183 E10
Comayagua Honduras 14°25N 87°37W 320 D2
Combahee → U.S.A. 32°31N 80°31W 316 C9
Combarbalá Chile 31°11S 71°2W 334 C1
Combault France 48°48N 2°37E 134 B4
Combe Martin U.K. 51°12N 4°3W 169 F3
Combeaufontaine France 47°38N 5°54E 173 E12
Comber Ont., Canada 42°14N 82°33W 312 D2
Comber Down, U.K. 54°33N 5°45W 166 B6
Combermere Canada 45°22N 77°37W 312 A7
Combermere Bay Burma 19°37N 93°34E 241 F4
Comblain-au-Pont Belgium 50°29N 5°35E 170 D5
Combourg France 48°25N 1°46W 172 D5
Comboyne Australia 31°34S 152°27E 283 A10
Combrailles France 46°8N 2°8E 173 F9
Combronde France 45°58N 3°5E 174 C7
Comer Ala., U.S.A. 32°2N 85°23W 316 C4
Comer Ga., U.S.A. 34°4N 83°8W 316 A6
Comeragh Mts. Ireland 52°18N 7°34W 166 D4
Comércio, Praça do Portugal 38°41N 9°9W 126 A2
Comerio Puerto Rico 18°12N 66°12W 321 b
Comet Australia 23°36S 148°38E 280 C4
Comilla Bangla. 23°28N 91°10E 241 D3
Comino Malta 36°1N 14°20E 206 E7
Comino, C. Italy 40°32N 9°49E 200 B2
Cómiso Italy 36°56N 14°36E 201 F7
Comitán de Domínguez Mexico 16°15N 92°8W 319 D6
Commentry France 46°20N 2°46E 173 F9
Commerce Calif., U.S.A. 34°0N 118°9W 126 B4
Commerce Ga., U.S.A. 34°12N 83°28W 316 A6
Commerce Tex., U.S.A. 33°15N 95°54W 314 E7
Commercy France 48°43N 5°34E 173 D12
Commissioner's Pt. Bermuda 32°19N 64°49W 153 a
Committee B. Canada 68°30N 86°30W 295 D14
Commodore, C. Canada 44°47N 80°54W 312 B4
Commonwealth B. Antarctica 67°0S 144°0E 151 C10
Commoron Cr. → Australia 28°22S 150°8E 281 D5
Communism Pk. = imeni Ismail Samani, Pik Tajikistan 39°0N 72°2E 217 E8
Como Italy 45°47N 9°5E 198 C6
Como, L. di Italy 46°0N 9°11E 198 B6
Comodoro Rivadavia Argentina 45°50S 67°40W 336 C3
Comoé → Ivory C. 5°12N 3°44W 262 D4
Comoé △ Ivory C. 9°0N 3°35W 262 D4
Comoràște Romania 45°10N 21°35E 182 E6
Comorin, C. = Kannyakumari India 8°3N 77°40E 245 K3
Comoros ■ Ind. Oc. 12°10S 44°15E 272 a
Comox Canada 49°42N 124°55W 296 D4
Company's Gardens Cape Town, S. Africa 118 c2
Compass Lake U.S.A. 30°36N 85°24W 316 E4
Compiègne France 49°24N 2°50E 173 C9
Comporta Portugal 38°22N 8°46W 195 G2
Compostela Nayarit, Mexico 21°14N 104°55W 318 C4
Compostela Phil. 7°40N 126°2E 233 H6
Comprida, I. Brazil 24°50S 47°42W 335 A6
Compton Qué., Canada 45°14N 71°49W 313 A13
Compton Calif., U.S.A. 33°53N 118°13W 307 M8
Comrat Moldova 46°18N 28°40E 183 D13
Comunidad Peru 13°59S 69°20W 330 C4
Con Cuong Vietnam 19°2N 104°54E 236 C5
Con Dao △ Vietnam 8°42N 106°35E 237 H6
Con Son, Dao Vietnam 8°41N 106°37E 237 H6
Cona Niyeu Argentina 41°58S 67°0W 336 B3
Conakry Guinea 9°29N 13°49W 262 D2
Conara Australia 41°50S 147°26E 281 G4
Conargo Australia 35°16S 145°10E 283 C6
Concarneau France 47°52N 3°56W 172 E3
Conceição Paraíba, Brazil 7°33S 38°31W 332 C4
Conceição Mozam. 18°47S 36°7E 269 F4
Conceição, I. da Brazil 22°52S 43°6W 135 B2
Conceição da Barra Brazil 18°35S 39°45W 333 E4
Conceição do Araguaia Brazil 8°0S 49°2W 332 C2
Conceição do Canindé Brazil 7°54S 41°34W 332 C3
Conceição do Maú Brazil 3°35N 59°53W 329 C6
Conceição do Paraíba = Capela Brazil 10°30S 37°0W 332 D4
Concepción Argentina 27°20S 65°35W 334 B2
Concepción Bolivia 16°15S 62°8W 331 D5
Concepción Chile 36°50S 73°0W 334 D1
Concepción Paraguay 23°22S 57°26W 334 A4
Concepción Peru 11°54S 75°19W 330 C2
Concepcion Tarlac, Phil. 15°27N 120°47E 232 D3
Concepción □ Chile 37°0S 72°30W 334 D1
Concepción, Est. de Chile 50°30S 74°55W 336 D2
Concepción, L. Bolivia 17°20S 61°20W 331 D5
Concepción, Pta. Mexico 26°53N 111°50W 318 B2
Concepción del Oro Mexico 24°38N 101°25W 318 C4
Concepción del Uruguay Argentina 32°35S 58°20W 334 C4
Conception, Pt. U.S.A. 34°27N 120°28W 307 L6
Conception B. Nfld. & L., Canada 47°45N 53°0W 299 C9
Conception B. Namibia 23°55S 14°22E 270 B1
Conception I. Bahamas 23°52N 75°9W 321 B4
Concession Zimbabwe 17°27S 30°56E 269 F3
Conchali Chile 33°22S 70°39W 137 B2
Conchas Dam U.S.A. 35°22N 104°11W 305 J11
Conches-en-Ouche France 48°58N 0°56E 172 D7
Concho U.S.A. 34°28N 109°36W 305 J9
Concho → U.S.A. 31°34N 99°43W 314 F5
Conchos → Chihuahua, Mexico 29°35N 104°25W 318 B4
Conchos → Tamaulipas, Mexico 24°55N 97°38W 319 B5
Concord N.S.W., Australia 33°52S 151°6E 139 B1
Concord Ont., Canada 43°48N 79°29W 141 A2
Concord Grenada 12°7N 61°44W 323 q
Concord Calif., U.S.A. 37°59N 122°2W 306 H4
Concord Ga., U.S.A. 33°5N 84°27W 316 B5
Concord Mich., U.S.A. 42°11N 84°38W 311 B12
Concord Mo., U.S.A. 38°32N 90°23W 310 F6
Concord N.C., U.S.A. 35°25N 80°35W 315 D14
Concord N.H., U.S.A. 43°12N 71°32W 313 C13
Concorde, Place de la Paris, France 134 b3
Concordia Antarctica 75°6S 123°23E 151 D9
Concordia Argentina 31°20S 58°2W 334 C4
Concórdia Amazonas, Brazil 4°36S 66°36W 328 D4
Concórdia Sta. Catarina, Brazil 27°14S 52°1W 335 B5
Concordia Sinaloa, Mexico 23°17N 106°4W 318 C3
Concordia Kans., U.S.A. 39°34N 97°40W 308 F5
Concordia Mo., U.S.A. 38°59N 93°34W 310 F3
Concordia Univ. Montréal, Canada 130 c1
Concorezzo Italy 45°35N 9°19E 128 A2
Concrete U.S.A. 48°32N 121°45W 304 B3
Conda Angola 11°9S 14°20E 265 E2
Condah Australia 37°57S 141°44E 282 D4
Condamine Australia 26°56S 150°9E 281 D5
Condat France 45°21N 2°46E 174 C6
Condé Angola 10°50S 14°37E 265 E2
Conde Brazil 11°49S 37°37W 333 D4
Conde S. Dak., U.S.A. 45°9N 98°6W 308 C4
Condé-sur-Noireau France 48°51N 0°33W 172 D6
Condet Indonesia 6°17S 106°51E 122 A2
Condeúba Brazil 14°52S 42°0W 333 D3
Condobolin Australia 33°4S 147°6E 283 B7
Condom France 43°57N 0°22E 174 E4
Condon U.S.A. 45°14N 120°11W 304 D3
Conegliano Italy 45°53N 12°18E 199 C9
Conejera, I. = Conills, I. des Spain 39°11N 2°58E 206 B3
Conejos Mexico 26°14N 103°53W 318 B4
Conemaugh → U.S.A. 40°28N 79°19W 312 F5
Conero ⌓ Italy 43°32N 13°35E 199 E10
Coney I. = Serangoon, Pulau Singapore 1°23N 103°55E 138 A3
Coney Island U.S.A. 40°34N 74°0W 132 C2
Conflict Group Papua N. G. 10°47S 151°45E 286 F6
Confolens France 46°2N 0°40E 174 B4
Confuso → Paraguay 25°9S 57°34W 334 B4
Congaree → U.S.A. 33°44N 80°38W 316 B9
Congaree △ U.S.A. 33°47N 80°47W 316 B9
Congaz Moldova 46°7N 28°36E 183 D13
Congerville U.S.A. 40°38N 89°11W 310 D7
Conghua China 23°36N 113°31E 229 F9
Congjiang China 25°43N 108°52E 228 E7
Congleton U.K. 53°10N 2°13W 168 D5
Congo Brazil 7°48S 36°40W 332 C4
Congo (Brazzaville) = Congo ■ Africa 1°0S 16°0E 264 C3
Congo (Kinshasa) = Congo, Dem. Rep. of the ■ Africa 3°0S 23°0E 265 C4
Congo ■ Africa 1°0S 16°0E 264 C3
Congo → Africa 6°4S 12°24E 265 D2
Congo, Dem. Rep. of the ■ Africa 3°0S 23°0E 265 C4
Congo Basin Africa 0°10S 24°30E 254 G6
Congo Free State = Congo, Dem. Rep. of the ■ Africa 3°0S 23°0E 265 C4
Congonhas Brazil 20°30S 43°52W 333 F3
Congonhas São Paulo ✈ (CGH) Brazil 23°38S 46°39W 137 B2
Congress U.S.A. 34°9N 112°51W 305 J7
Conguillio △ Chile 38°40S 71°42W 336 A2
Conil de la Frontera Spain 36°17N 6°10W 195 J4
Conills, I. des Spain 39°11N 2°58E 206 B3
Coniston Canada 46°29N 80°51W 298 C3
Conjeeveram = Kanchipuram India 12°52N 79°45E 245 H4
Conklin Alta., Canada 55°38N 111°5W 297 B6
Conklin N.Y., U.S.A. 42°2N 75°49W 313 D9
Conkouati ⌓ Congo 3°50S 11°28E 264 C2
Conlea Australia 30°7S 144°35E 283 A5
Conlendas, Pta. das Azores 38°38N 27°14W 153 d1
Conn, L. Ireland 54°3N 9°15W 166 B2
Connaught □ Ireland 53°43N 9°12W 166 C2
Connaught Place Delhi, India 120 b2
Conneaut U.S.A. 41°57N 80°34W 312 E4
Conneautville U.S.A. 41°45N 80°22W 312 E4
Connecticut □ U.S.A. 41°30N 72°45W 313 E12
Connecticut → U.S.A. 41°16N 72°20W 313 E12
Connell U.S.A. 46°40N 118°52W 304 C4
Connellsville U.S.A. 40°1N 79°35W 312 F5
Connemara Ireland 53°29N 9°45W 166 C2
Connemara △ Ireland 53°32N 9°52W 166 C2
Conner Phil. 17°48N 121°19E 232 C3
Connerré France 48°3N 0°30E 172 D7
Connersville U.S.A. 39°39N 85°8W 311 E11
Connors Ra. Australia 21°40S 149°10E 280 C4
Conoble Australia 32°55S 144°33E 283 B6
Conococheague → U.S.A. 39°38N 77°49W 312 G7
Conocoto Ecuador 0°16S 78°29W 328 D2
Conon Bridge U.K. 57°33N 4°25W 167 D4
Conoocheague → U.S.A. 41°14N 81°32W 312 E3
Conquest Canada 51°32N 107°14W 297 C7
Conques France 44°36N 2°23E 174 D6
Conquista = Vitória da Conquista Brazil 14°51S 40°51W 333 D3
Conrad Iowa, U.S.A. 42°14N 92°52W 310 B4
Conrad Mont., U.S.A. 48°10N 111°57W 304 B8
Conrad Rise S. Ocean 53°0S 41°0E 151 B5
Conran, C. Australia 37°49S 148°44E 283 D8
Conroe U.S.A. 30°19N 95°27W 314 F7
Consecon Canada 44°0N 77°31W 312 C7
Conselheiro Lafaiete Brazil 20°40S 43°48W 333 F3
Conselheiro Pena Brazil 19°10S 41°30W 333 E3
Consell Spain 39°40N 2°49E 206 B3
Conselve Italy 45°14N 11°52E 199 C8
Conservatori, Palazzo dei Rome, Italy 136 c3
Consett U.K. 54°51N 1°50W 168 C6
Consolação Brazil 23°32S 46°38W 137 B2
Consort Canada 52°1N 110°46W 297 C6
Constance = Konstanz Germany 47°40N 9°10E 179 H5
Constance, L. = Bodensee Europe 47°35N 9°25E 179 H5
Constanța Romania 44°14N 28°38E 183 F13
Constanța □ Romania 44°15N 28°15E 183 F13
Constantia S. Africa 34°2S 18°26E 118 B1
Constantina Spain 37°51N 5°40W 195 H5
Constantine Algeria 36°25N 6°42E 261 A6
Constantine Mich., U.S.A. 41°50N 85°40W 311 C11
Constantine □ Algeria 36°30N 6°40E 261 A6
Constantine, Arch of = Costantino, Arco di Rome, Italy 136 c3
Constantine, C. U.S.A. 58°24N 158°54W 303 G8
Constantinople = İstanbul Turkey 41°0N 28°58E 122 C1
Constitución B. Aires, Argentina 34°38S 58°23W 117 B2
Constitución Chile 35°20S 72°30W 334 D1
Constitución Uruguay 31°0S 57°50W 334 C4
Constitución de 1857 △ Mexico 32°4N 115°55W 318 A1
Constitution U.S.A. 33°42N 84°20W 113 B2
Constitution Avenue Washington, D.C., U.S.A. 143 b2
Constitution Square = Syntagma Square Athens, Greece 112 b2
Consuegra Spain 39°28N 3°36W 195 F7
Consul Canada 49°20N 109°30W 297 D7
Contact U.S.A. 41°46N 114°45W 304 F6
Contagem Brazil 19°55S 44°6W 333 E3
Contai India 21°54N 87°46E 243 J12
Contamana Peru 7°19S 74°55W 330 B3
Contarini Dal Zaffo, Palazzo Venice, Italy 142 c2
Contas → Brazil 14°17S 39°1W 333 D4
Contes France 43°49N 7°19E 175 E11
Continental U.S.A. 41°6N 84°16W 311 C12
Contoocook U.S.A. 43°13N 71°45W 313 C13
Contra Costa Mozam. 25°9S 33°30E 271 C5
Contres France 47°24N 1°26E 172 E8
Contrexéville France 48°10N 5°53E 173 D12
Controller B. U.S.A. 60°7N 144°15W 303 F11
Contumaza Peru 7°23S 78°57W 330 B2
Contwoyto L. Canada 65°42N 110°50W 294 D9
Convención Colombia 8°28N 73°21W 328 B3
Conversano Italy 40°58N 17°7E 201 B10
Converse U.S.A. 40°35N 85°52W 311 D11
Convoy U.S.A. 40°55N 84°43W 311 D12
Conway = Conwy U.K. 53°17N 3°50W 168 D4
Conway = Conwy → U.K. 53°17N 3°50W 168 D4
Conway Australia 20°24S 148°41E 280 b
Conway Ont., Canada 44°6N 76°54W 312 B8
Conway Ark., U.S.A. 35°5N 92°26W 314 D8
Conway Fla., U.S.A. 28°30N 81°19W 133 B2
Conway N.H., U.S.A. 43°59N 71°7W 313 C13
Conway S.C., U.S.A. 33°51N 79°3W 315 E15
Conway, C. Australia 20°34S 148°46E 280 b
Conway, L. S. Austral., Australia 28°17S 135°35E 281 D2
Conway, L. Fla., U.S.A. 28°28N 81°21W 133 B2
Conwy U.K. 53°17N 3°50W 168 D4
Conwy □ U.K. 53°10N 3°44W 168 D4
Conwy → U.K. 53°17N 3°50W 168 D4
Conyers U.S.A. 33°40N 84°1W 316 B5
Coober Pedy Australia 29°1S 134°43E 281 D1
Cooch Behar = Koch Bihar India 26°22N 89°29E 241 B2
Coogee Australia 33°55S 151°16E 139 B2
Cooinda Australia 13°15S 130°5E 278 B5
Cook S. Austral., Australia 30°37S 130°25E 279 F5
Cook Minn., U.S.A. 47°51N 92°41W 308 B7
Cook, B. Chile 55°10S 70°0W 336 E3
Cook, C. Canada 50°8N 127°55W 296 C3
Cook, Mt. = Aoraki Mount Cook N.Z. 43°36S 170°9E 285 D5
Cook, Récif de N. Cal. 19°25S 163°50E 288 d
Cook B. Vanuatu 18°46S 169°15E 287 H7
Cook Inlet U.S.A. 60°0N 152°0W 303 G10
Cook Is. ☑ Pac. Oc. 17°0S 160°0W 289 J12
Cook Strait N.Z. 41°15S 174°29E 284 H3
Cooke Plains Australia 35°23S 139°34E 282 C3
Cookeville U.S.A. 36°10N 85°30W 315 C12
Cookhouse S. Africa 32°44S 25°47E 270 D4
Cooks Hammock U.S.A. 29°56N 83°17W 316 F6
Cooks Harbour Canada 51°36N 55°52W 299 B8
Cookshire Canada 45°25N 71°38W 313 A13
Cookstown Ont., Canada 44°11N 79°42W 312 B5
Cookstown Tyrone, U.K. 54°38N 6°45W 166 B5
Cooksville Canada 43°35N 79°38W 141 B1
Cooktown Australia 15°30S 145°16E 280 B4
Coolabah Australia 31°1S 146°43E 283 A7
Cooladdi Australia 26°37S 145°23E 281 D4
Coolah Australia 31°48S 149°41E 283 A8
Coolah Tops △ Australia 31°52S 150°0E 283 A9
Coolamon Australia 34°46S 147°8E 283 C7
Coolgardie Australia 30°55S 121°8E 279 F3
Coolidge Ariz., U.S.A. 32°59N 111°31W 305 K8
Coolidge Ga., U.S.A. 31°1N 83°52W 316 D6
Coolidge Dam U.S.A. 33°10N 110°32W 305 K8
Coolock Ireland 53°22N 6°12W 120 A2
Cooma Australia 36°12S 149°8E 283 D8
Coon Rapids Iowa, U.S.A. 41°53N 94°41W 310 C2
Coon Rapids Minn., U.S.A. 45°9N 93°19W 308 C7
Coonabarabran Australia 31°14S 149°18E 283 A8
Coonalpyn Australia 35°43S 139°52E 282 C3
Coonamble Australia 30°56S 148°27E 283 A8
Coonana Australia 31°0S 123°0E 279 F3
Coonana ✪ Australia 30°51S 122°53E 279 F3
Coondapoor India 13°42N 74°40E 245 H2
Cooninnie, L. Australia 26°4S 139°59E 281 D2
Coonoor India 11°21N 76°45E 245 J3
Cooper U.S.A. 33°23N 95°42W 314 E7
Cooper → U.S.A. 32°50N 79°56W 316 C10
Cooper City U.S.A. 26°3N 80°16W 129 B1
Cooper Cr. → Australia 28°29S 137°46E 281 D2
Cooper Ridge Pac. Oc. 10°0N 150°30W 289 G12
Cooper's Hill Jamaica 18°4N 76°51W 320 a
Cooperstown N. Dak., U.S.A. 47°27N 98°8W 308 B4
Cooperstown N.Y., U.S.A. 42°42N 74°56W 313 D10
Coopersville U.S.A. 43°4N 85°57W 311 A11
Coopracambra △ Australia 37°20S 149°20E 283 D8
Coora → Trin. & Tob. 10°10N 61°28W 323 t
Coorabie Australia 31°54S 132°18E 279 F5
Coorong, The Australia 35°50S 139°20E 282 C3
Coorong △ Australia 36°0S 139°29E 282 D3
Coorow Australia 29°53S 116°2E 279 E2
Cooroy Australia 26°22S 152°54E 281 D5
Coos Bay U.S.A. 43°22N 124°13W 304 E1
Coosa → U.S.A. 32°30N 86°16W 315 E11
Cootamundra Australia 34°36S 148°1E 283 C8
Cootehill Ireland 54°4N 7°5W 166 B4
Copacabana Brazil 22°58S 43°11W 135 B1
Copahue Paso Argentina 37°49S 71°8W 334 D1
Copainalá Mexico 17°4N 93°18W 319 D6
Copake U.S.A. 42°7N 73°31W 313 D11
Copalnic Mănăștur Romania 47°30N 23°41E 183 C8
Copán Honduras 14°50N 89°9W 320 D2
Copatana Brazil 2°48S 67°4W 328 D4
Cope Colo., U.S.A. 39°40N 102°51W 304 G12
Cope S.C., U.S.A. 33°23N 81°0W 316 B8
Cope, C. Spain 37°26N 1°28W 197 H3
Copeland U.S.A. 25°57N 81°22W 317 K8
Copenhagen = København Denmark 55°40N 12°26E 118 A2
Copenhagen U.S.A. 43°54N 75°41W 313 C9
Copertino Italy 40°16N 18°3E 201 B11
Copiapó Chile 27°30S 70°20W 334 B1
Copiapó → Chile 27°19S 70°56W 334 B1
Coplay U.S.A. 40°44N 75°29W 313 F9
Copley Australia 30°36S 138°26E 282 A3
Copo △ Argentina 25°53S 61°41W 334 B3
Copp L. Canada 60°14N 114°40W 296 A6
Copparo Italy 44°54N 11°49E 199 D8
Coppename → Suriname 5°48N 55°55W 329 B6
Copper → U.S.A. 60°18N 145°3W 303 F11
Copper Canyon = Barranca del Cobre △ Mexico 27°18N 107°40W 318 B3
Copper Center U.S.A. 61°58N 145°18W 303 F11
Copper City = Invermere Canada 50°30N 116°2W 296 C5
Copper Harbor U.S.A. 47°28N 87°53W 308 B10
Copper Queen Zimbabwe 17°29S 29°18E 269 F2
Copperas Cove U.S.A. 31°8N 97°54W 314 F6
Copperbelt □ Zambia 13°15S 27°30E 269 E2
Coppermine = Kugluktuk Canada 67°50N 115°5W 294 D8
Coppermine → Canada 67°49N 116°4W 294 D8
Copperopolis U.S.A. 37°58N 120°38W 306 H6
Copșa Mică Romania 46°7N 24°15E 183 D9
Coquet → U.K. 55°20N 1°32W 168 B6
Coquilhatville = Mbandaka Dem. Rep. of the Congo 0°1N 18°18E 264 B3
Coquille U.S.A. 43°11N 124°11W 304 E1
Coquimbo Chile 30°0S 71°20W 334 C1
Coquimbo □ Chile 31°0S 71°0W 334 C1
Coquitlam Canada 49°17N 122°45W 296 D4
Corabia Romania 43°48N 24°30E 183 G9
Coração de Jesus Brazil 16°43S 44°22W 333 E3
Coracora Peru 15°5S 73°45W 330 D3
Coraki Australia 28°59S 153°17E 281 D5
Coral U.S.A. 40°29N 79°10W 312 F5
Coral B. Phil. 8°25N 117°20E 233 G1
Coral Bay Australia 23°8S 113°46E 278 D1
Coral Gables U.S.A. 25°43N 80°16W 129 D1
Coral Harbour Bahamas 24°58N 77°28W 153 b
Coral Harbour Nunavut, Canada 64°8N 83°10W 295 E15
Coral Heights Bahamas 25°0N 77°27W 153 b
Coral Hills U.S.A. 38°51N 76°55W 143 B3
Coral Sea Pac. Oc. 15°0S 150°0E 276 C9
Coral Sea Basin Pac. Oc. 14°0S 152°0E 288 J7
Coral Sea Islands Terr. □ Australia 20°0S 155°0E 276 D9
Coral Springs U.S.A. 26°16N 80°16W 317 J9
Corales del Rosario △ Colombia 10°8N 75°46W 328 A2
Coralville U.S.A. 41°40N 91°35W 310 C5
Coralville L. U.S.A. 41°42N 91°33W 310 C5
Corangamite, L. Australia 38°5S 143°30E 282 E5
Corantijn = Courantyne → S. Amer. 5°50N 57°8W 329 B6
Coraopolis U.S.A. 40°31N 80°10W 312 F4
Corato Italy 41°9N 16°25E 201 A9
Corbeil-Essonnes France 48°36N 2°26E 173 D9
Corbeiro, C. W. Sahara 21°50N 17°0W 260 D1
Corbett △ India 29°20N 79°0E 243 E8
Corbie France 49°54N 2°30E 173 C9
Corbières France 42°55N 2°35E 174 F6
Corbigny France 47°16N 3°40E 173 E10
Corbin U.S.A. 36°57N 84°6W 309 G11
Corbones → Spain 37°36N 5°39W 195 H5
Corbu Romania 44°25N 28°39E 183 F13
Corby U.K. 52°30N 0°41W 169 E7
Corcaigh = Cork Ireland 51°54N 8°29W 166 E3
Corcoran U.S.A. 36°6N 119°33W 306 J7
Corcovado, Cristo Redentor Brazil 22°57S 43°12W 135 B1
Corcovado △ Chile 43°25S 72°45W 336 B2
Corcovado △ Costa Rica 8°33N 83°35W 320 E3
Cordele U.S.A. 31°58N 83°47W 316 D6
Cordell U.S.A. 35°17N 98°59W 314 D5
Cordenòns Italy 45°59N 12°42E 199 C9
Cordes-sur-Ciel France 44°5N 1°57E 174 D5
Cordillera Azul △ Peru 7°30S 76°30W 330 B2
Cordillera de los Picachos △ Colombia 2°39N 74°30W 328 C3
Cordisburgo Brazil 19°7S 44°21W 333 E3
Córdoba Argentina 31°20S 64°10W 334 C3
Córdoba Veracruz, Mexico 18°53N 96°56W 319 D5
Córdoba Spain 37°50N 4°50W 195 H6
Córdoba □ Argentina 31°22S 64°15W 334 C3
Córdoba □ Colombia 8°20N 75°40W 328 B2
Córdoba □ Spain 38°5N 5°0W 195 G6
Córdoba, Sierra de Argentina 31°10S 64°25W 334 C3
Cordon Phil. 16°42N 121°32E 232 C3
Cordova U.S.A. 60°33N 145°45W 303 F11
Corduff Ireland 53°23N 6°21W 120 A1
Corella Spain 42°7N 1°48W 196 C3
Corella → Australia 19°34S 140°47E 280 B3
Coremas Brazil 7°1S 37°58W 332 C4
Corentyne = Courantyne → S. Amer. 5°50N 57°8W 329 B6
Corfield Australia 21°40S 143°21E 280 C3
Corfu = Kerkyra Greece 39°38N 19°50E 206 B9
Corfu U.S.A. 42°57N 78°24W 312 D6
Corfu ✈ (CFU) Greece 39°35N 19°54E 204 B1
Corfu, Str. of = Kerkyras, Notio Steno Greece 39°34N 20°0E 206 B10
Corgo = O Corgo Spain 42°56N 7°25W 194 C3
Corguinho Brazil 19°53S 54°52W 331 D7
Cori Italy 41°39N 12°55E 200 A5
Coria Spain 39°58N 6°33W 194 F4
Coria del Río Spain 37°16N 6°3W 195 H4
Coricudgy Australia 32°51S 150°24E 283 B9
Corigliano Cálabro Italy 39°36N 16°31E 201 C9
Corimba, Barra de Angola 8°52S 13°9E 265 D2
Coringa Is. Australia 16°58S 149°58E 280 B4
Corinth = Korinthos Greece 37°56N 22°55E 204 D4
Corinth Grenada 12°2N 61°40W 323 q
Corinth Ky., U.S.A. 38°30N 84°34W 311 F12
Corinth Miss., U.S.A. 34°56N 88°31W 315 D10
Corinth N.Y., U.S.A. 43°15N 73°49W 313 C11
Corinth, G. of = Korinthiakos Kolpos Greece 38°16N 22°30E 204 C4
Corinth Canal Greece 37°58N 23°0E 204 D4
Corinto Brazil 18°20S 44°30W 333 E3
Corinto Nic. 12°30N 87°10W 320 D2
Coriole Somalia 1°47N 44°32E 267 D5
Corisco Eq. Guin. 0°55N 9°18E 264 B1
Cork Ireland 51°54N 8°29W 166 E3
Cork □ Ireland 51°57N 8°40W 166 E3
Cork Harbour Ireland 51°47N 8°16W 166 E3
Corlay France 48°20N 3°5W 172 D3
Corleone Italy 37°49N 13°18E 200 E6
Corleto Perticara Italy 40°23N 16°2E 201 B9
Çorlu Turkey 41°11N 27°49E 203 E11
Cormack L. Canada 60°56N 121°37W 296 A4
Cormano Italy 45°32N 9°10E 128 A2
Cormòns Italy 45°58N 13°28E 199 C10
Cormorant Canada 54°14N 100°35W 297 C8
Cormorant L. Canada 54°15N 100°50W 297 C8
Corn Is. = Maíz, Is. del Nic. 12°15N 83°4W 320 D3
Cornalvo ⌓ Spain 39°1N 6°13W 195 F4
Cornaredo Italy 45°30N 9°1E 128 A1
Cornélio Procópio Brazil 23°7S 50°40W 335 A5
Cornell U.S.A. 41°0N 88°44W 311 D8
Corner Brook Canada 48°57N 57°58W 299 C8
Corner della Regina, Palazzo Venice, Italy 142 b2
Corner Inlet Australia 38°45S 146°20E 283 E7
Corner Seamounts Atl. Oc. 35°0N 52°0W 152 C6
Corner Spinelli, Palazzo Venice, Italy 142 b2
Cornești Moldova 47°21N 28°1E 183 C13
Corneto = Tarquinia Italy 42°15N 11°45E 199 F8
Corniglio Italy 44°29N 10°5E 198 D7
Corning Ark., U.S.A. 36°25N 90°35W 315 C9
Corning Calif., U.S.A. 39°56N 122°11W 304 G2
Corning Iowa, U.S.A. 40°59N 94°44W 310 D2
Corning N.Y., U.S.A. 42°9N 77°3W 312 D7
Corno Grande Italy 42°28N 13°34E 199 F10
Cornwall Ont., Canada 45°2N 74°44W 313 A10
Cornwall Pa., U.S.A. 40°17N 76°25W 313 F8
Cornwall □ Jamaica 18°15N 77°54W 320 a
Cornwall □ U.K. 50°26N 4°40W 169 G3
Cornwall I. Canada 77°37N 94°38W 295 B13
Cornwallis I. Canada 75°8N 95°0W 295 B13
Cornwell U.S.A. 27°23N 81°6W 317 H8
Coro Pt. Australia 34°55S 137°0E 282 C2
Coro Venezuela 11°25N 69°41W 328 A4
Coroaci Brazil 18°35S 42°17W 333 E3
Coroatá Brazil 4°8S 44°0W 332 B3
Corocoro Bolivia 17°15S 68°28W 330 D4
Corocoro, I. Venezuela 8°30N 60°10W 329 B5
Coroico Bolivia 16°0S 67°50W 330 D4
Coromandel Brazil 18°28S 47°13W 333 E2
Coromandel N.Z. 36°45S 175°31E 284 C4
Coromandel Coast India 12°30N 81°0E 245 H5
Coromandel Pen. N.Z. 37°0S 175°45E 284 D4
Coromandel Ra. N.Z. 37°0S 175°40E 284 D4
Coron Phil. 12°1N 120°12E 232 E3
Coron B. Phil. 11°54N 120°8E 233 F3
Coron I. Phil. 11°55N 120°14E 233 F3
Corona Calif., U.S.A. 33°53N 117°34W 307 M9
Corona N. Mex., U.S.A. 34°15N 105°36W 305 J11
Coronado U.S.A. 32°41N 117°10W 307 N9
Coronado, B. de Costa Rica 9°0N 83°40W 320 E3
Coronados, G. de los Chile 41°40S 74°0W 336 B2
Coronados, Is. Los Mexico 32°26N 117°19W 307 N9
Coronation Canada 52°5N 111°27W 296 C6
Coronation Gulf Canada 68°25N 110°0W 294 D10
Coronation I. Antarctica 60°45S 46°0W 151 C18
Coronation Is. Australia 14°57S 124°55E 278 B3
Coronda Argentina 31°58S 60°56W 334 C3
Coronel Chile 37°0S 73°10W 334 D1
Coronel Bogado Paraguay 27°11S 56°18W 334 B4
Coronel Dorrego Argentina 38°40S 61°10W 334 D3
Coronel Fabriciano Brazil 19°31S 42°38W 333 E3
Coronel Murta Brazil 16°37S 42°11W 333 E3
Coronel Oviedo Paraguay 25°24S 56°30W 334 B4
Coronel Ponce Brazil 15°34S 55°1W 331 D6
Coronel Pringles Argentina 38°0S 61°30W 334 D3
Coronel Suárez Argentina 37°30S 61°52W 334 D3
Coronel Vidal Argentina 37°28S 57°45W 334 D4
Corongo Peru 8°30S 77°53W 330 B2
Coropuna, Nevado Peru 15°30S 72°41W 330 D3
Corossol St. Barts 17°54N 62°51W 322 a
Çorovodë Albania 40°31N 20°14E 202 F4
Corowa Australia 35°58S 146°21E 283 C7
Corozal Colombia 9°19N 75°18W 328 B2
Corozal □ Belize 18°23N 88°23W 319 D7
Corozal Pt. Trin. & Tob. 10°45N 61°37W 323 t
Corps France 44°50N 5°56E 175 D9
Corpus Argentina 27°10S 55°30W 335 B4
Corpus Christi U.S.A. 27°47N 97°24W 314 H6
Corpus Christi, L. U.S.A. 28°2N 97°52W 314 G6
Corque Bolivia 18°20S 67°41W 330 D4
Corral Chile 39°52S 73°26W 336 A2
Corral de Almaguer Spain 39°45N 3°10W 194 F7
Corralejo Canary Is. 28°43N 13°53W 153 e2
Corraun Pen. Ireland 53°54N 9°54W 166 C2
Corrèggio Italy 44°46N 10°47E 198 D7
Corregidor Phil. 14°23N 120°35E 232 D3
Corrente Brazil 10°27S 45°10W 332 D2
Corrente → Brazil 13°8S 43°28W 333 D3
Correntes → Brazil 17°38S 55°8W 331 D6
Correntes, C. das Mozam. 24°6S 35°34E 271 B6
Correntina Brazil 13°20S 44°39W 333 D3
Corrèze □ France 45°20N 1°45E 174 C5
Corrèze → France 45°10N 1°28E 174 C5
Corrib, L. Ireland 53°27N 9°16W 166 C2
Corridónia Italy 43°15N 13°30E 199 E10
Corrientes Argentina 27°30S 58°45W 334 B4
Corrientes □ Argentina 28°0S 57°0W 334 B4
Corrientes → Argentina 30°42S 59°38W 334 C4
Corrientes → Peru 3°43S 74°35W 328 D3
Corrientes, C. Colombia 5°30N 77°34W 328 B2
Corrientes, C. Cuba 21°43N 84°30W 320 B3
Corrientes, C. Jalisco, Mexico 20°25N 105°42W 318 C3
Corrigan U.S.A. 31°0N 94°52W 314 F7
Corrigin Australia 32°20S 117°53E 279 F2
Corriverton Guyana 5°55N 57°20W 329 B6
Corry U.S.A. 41°55N 79°39W 312 E5
Corryong Australia 36°12S 147°53E 283 D7
Corse □ France 42°0N 9°0E 175 G13
Corse, C. France 43°1N 9°25E 175 E13
Corse ⌓ France 42°14N 9°10E 175 F13
Corse-du-Sud □ France 41°45N 9°0E 175 G13
Corsica = Corse □ France 42°0N 9°0E 175 G13
Corsicana U.S.A. 32°6N 96°28W 314 E6
Corsico Italy 45°25N 9°6E 128 B1
Corsini, Palazzo Rome, Italy 136 c1
Corstorphine U.K. 55°56N 3°17W 121 B2
Corte France 42°19N 9°11E 175 F13
Corte Pinto Portugal 37°42N 7°29W 195 H3
Cortegana Spain 37°52N 6°49W 195 H4
Cortes Phil. 9°17N 126°11E 233 G6
Cortés, Mar de = California, G. de Mexico 27°0N 111°0W 318 B2
Cortez U.S.A. 37°21N 108°35W 305 H9
Córthaidh, Inis = Enniscorthy Ireland 52°30N 6°34W 166 D5
Cortina d'Ampezzo Italy 46°32N 12°8E 199 B9
Cortland N.Y., U.S.A. 42°36N 76°11W 313 D8
Cortland Ohio, U.S.A. 41°20N 80°44W 312 E4
Cortona Italy 43°16N 11°59E 199 E8
Corubal → Guinea-Biss. 11°57N 15°5W 262 C2
Coruche Portugal 38°57N 8°30W 195 G2
Çoruh → Turkey 41°38N 41°38E 191 K5
Çorum Turkey 40°30N 34°57E 212 B6
Çorum □ Turkey 40°40N 35°0E 212 B6
Corumbá Brazil 19°0S 57°30W 331 D6
Corumbá de Goiás Brazil 16°0S 48°50W 333 E2
Corumbaíba Brazil 18°9S 48°34W 333 E2
Corund Romania 46°30N 25°13E 183 D10
Corunna = A Coruña Spain 43°20N 8°25W 194 B2
Corunna U.S.A. 42°59N 84°7W 311 B12
Corvallis U.S.A. 44°34N 123°16W 304 D2
Corvette, L. de la Canada 53°25N 74°3W 298 B5
Corviale Italy 41°51N 12°25E 136 B1
Corvo Azores 39°42N 31°6W 153 d2
Coryal Trin. & Tob. 10°30N 61°11W 323 t
Corydon Ind., U.S.A. 38°13N 86°7W 311 F10
Corydon Iowa, U.S.A. 40°46N 93°19W 310 D3
Corydon Ky., U.S.A. 37°44N 87°43W 311 G9
Cosalá Mexico 24°23N 106°41W 318 C3
Cosamaloapan de Carpio Mexico 18°22N 95°48W 319 D5
Cosenza Italy 39°18N 16°15E 201 C9
Coșereni Romania 44°38N 26°35E 183 F11
Coshocton U.S.A. 40°16N 81°51W 312 F3
Coslada Spain 40°25N 3°35W 127 B2
Cosmo Newberry Australia 28°0S 122°54E 279 E3
Cosmo Newberry ✪ Australia 27°59S 122°53E 279 E3
Cosmonaut Sea S. Ocean 66°30S 40°0E 151 C5
Cosne-Cours-sur-Loire France 47°24N 2°54E 173 E9
Coso Junction U.S.A. 36°3N 117°57W 307 J9
Coso Pk. U.S.A. 36°13N 117°44W 307 J9
Cospeito = A Feira do Monte Spain 43°12N 7°34W 194 B3
Cosquín Argentina 31°15S 64°30W 334 C3
Cossato Italy 45°34N 8°10E 198 C5
Cossé-le-Vivien France 47°57N 0°54W 172 E6
Cossigny France 48°43N 2°38E 134 B4
Cosson → France 47°30N 1°15E 172 E8
Costa Calma Canary Is. 28°8N 14°16W 153 e2
Costa dels Pins Spain 39°38N 3°26E 206 B4
Costa Mesa U.S.A. 33°38N 117°55W 307 M9

Costa Rica ■ *Cent. Amer.* 10°0N 84°0W **320** E3
Costa Teguise *Canary Is.* 29°0N 13°31W **153** e2
Costantino, Arco di *Rome, Italy* **136** c3
Costermansville = Bukavu
*Dem. Rep. of the Congo* 2°20S 28°52E **268** C2
Costeşti *Romania* 44°40N 24°53E **183** F9
Costigliole d'Asti *Italy* 44°47N 8°11E **198** D5
Cosumnes → *U.S.A.* 38°16N 121°26W **306** G5
Coswig *Sachsen, Germany* 51°7N 13°34E **178** D9
Coswig *Sachsen-Anhalt, Germany* 51°53N 12°27E **178** D8
Cotabato *Phil.* 7°14N 124°15E **233** H5
Cotacajes → *Bolivia* 16°0S 67°1W **330** D4
Cotagaita *Bolivia* 20°45S 65°40W **334** A2
Cotahuasi *Peru* 15°12S 72°50W **330** D3
Cotao *Portugal* 38°45N 9°17W **126** A1
Côte-d'Ivoire = Ivory Coast ■
*Africa* 7°30N 5°0W **262** D4
Côte-d'Or □ *France* 47°30N 4°50E **173** E11
Côte-St-Luc *Canada* 45°28N 73°39W **130** B2
Coteau des Prairies
*U.S.A.* 45°20N 97°50W **308** C5
Coteau du Missouri *U.S.A.* 47°0N 100°0W **308** B4
Cotegipe *Brazil* 12°2S 44°15W **333** D3
Cotentin *France* 49°15N 1°30W **172** C5
Côtes-d'Armor □ *France* 48°25N 2°40W **172** D4
Côtes de Meuse *France* 49°15N 5°22E **173** C12
Côtes-du-Nord = Côtes-d'Armor □
*France* 48°25N 2°40W **172** D4
Cotiella *Spain* 42°31N 0°19E **196** C5
Cotiujeni *Moldova* 47°51N 28°33E **183** C13
Cotoca *Bolivia* 17°49S 63°3W **331** D5
Cotonou *Benin* 6°20N 2°25E **263** D5
Cotopaxi *Ecuador* 0°40S 78°30W **328** D2
Cotopaxi □ *Ecuador* 0°5S 78°55W **328** D2
Cotopaxi △ *Ecuador* 0°39S 78°24W **328** D2
Cotronei *Italy* 39°9N 16°47E **201** C9
Cotswold Hills *U.K.* 51°42N 2°10W **169** F5
Cottage Grove *U.S.A.* 43°48N 123°3W **304** E2
Cottageville *U.S.A.* 32°56N 80°29W **316** C9
Cottam *Canada* 42°8N 82°45W **312** D2
Cottbus *Germany* 51°45N 14°20E **178** D10
Cotton Ground
*St. Kitts & Nevis* 17°11N 62°36W **322** d
Cottondale *U.S.A.* 30°48N 85°23W **316** E4
Cottonwood *Ala., U.S.A.* 31°3N 85°18W **316** D4
Cottonwood *Ariz., U.S.A.* 34°45N 112°1W **305** J7
Cotulla *U.S.A.* 28°26N 99°14W **314** G5
Cotunduba, I. de *Brazil* 22°57S 43°8W **135** B2
Coubre, Pte. de la *France* 45°42N 1°15W **174** C2
Coubron *France* 48°54N 2°34E **134** A4
Couches *France* 46°53N 4°30E **173** F11
Couço *Portugal* 38°59N 8°17W **195** G2
Coudersport *U.S.A.* 41°46N 78°1W **312** E6
Couedic, C. du *Australia* 36°5S 136°40E **282** D2
Couëron *France* 47°13N 1°44W **172** E5
Couesnon → *France* 48°38N 1°32W **172** D5
Couhé *France* 46°17N 0°11E **174** B4
Coulanges-sur-Yonne
*France* 47°31N 3°33E **173** E10
Coulee City *U.S.A.* 47°37N 119°17W **304** C4
Coulee Dam Nat. Recr. Area = Lake
Roosevelt ⌂ *U.S.A.* 48°5N 118°14W **304** B4
Coulibistrie *Dominica* 15°27N 61°28W **323** k
Coulman I. *Antarctica* 73°35S 170°0E **351** D11
Coulommiers *France* 48°50N 3°3E **173** D10
Coulon → *France* 43°51N 5°6E **175** E9
Coulonge → *Canada* 45°52N 76°46W **298** C4
Coulonges-sur-l'Autize
*France* 46°29N 0°36W **174** B3
Coulounieix-Chamiers
*France* 45°11N 0°42E **174** C4
Coulterville *Calif., U.S.A.* 37°43N 120°12W **306** H6
Coulterville *Ill., U.S.A.* 38°11N 89°36W **310** F7
Council *Alaska, U.S.A.* 64°53N 163°41W **303** D7
Council *Ga., U.S.A.* 30°37N 82°31W **316** E7
Council *Idaho, U.S.A.* 44°44N 116°26W **304** D5
Council Bluffs *U.S.A.* 41°16N 95°52W **308** E6
Council Grove *U.S.A.* 38°40N 96°29W **308** F5
Coupeville *U.S.A.* 48°13N 122°41W **306** B4
Courantyne → *S. Amer.* 5°50N 57°8W **329** B6
Courbevoie *France* 48°53N 2°14E **134** A2
Courcelles *Belgium* 50°28N 4°22E **170** D4
Courchevel *France* 45°25N 6°36E **175** C10
Courçon *France* 46°15N 0°50W **174** B3
Courland → *Trin. & Tob.* 11°13N 60°47W **323** s
Courmayeur *Italy* 45°47N 6°58E **198** C3
Couronne, C. *France* 43°19N 5°3E **175** E9
Cours-la-Ville *France* 46°7N 4°19E **173** F11
Coursan *France* 43°14N 3°4E **174** E7
Courseulles-sur-Mer
*France* 49°20N 0°29W **172** C6
Courtenay *B.C., Canada* 49°45N 125°0W **296** D4
Courtenay *Loiret, France* 48°2N 3°3E **173** D10
Courtland *Ont., Canada* 42°51N 80°38W **312** D4
Courtland *Calif., U.S.A.* 38°20N 121°34W **306** G5
Courtrai = Kortrijk
*Belgium* 50°50N 3°17E **170** D3
Courtright *Canada* 42°49N 82°28W **312** D2
Courtry *France* 48°55N 2°35E **134** A4
Coushatta *U.S.A.* 32°1N 93°21W **314** E8
Coutances *France* 49°3N 1°28W **172** C5
Coutras *France* 45°3N 0°8W **174** C3
Coutts Crossing *Australia* 29°49S 152°55E **281** D5
Couva *Trin. & Tob.* 10°25N 61°27W **323** t
Couva □ *Trin. & Tob.* 10°25N 61°27W **323** t
Couvin *Belgium* 50°3N 4°29E **170** D4
Covarrubias *Spain* 42°4N 3°31W **194** C7
Covasna *Romania* 45°50N 26°10E **183** E11
Covasna □ *Romania* 45°50N 26°10E **183** E10
Cove I. *Canada* 45°17N 81°44W **312** A3
Coveñas *Colombia* 9°24N 75°44W **328** B2
Covent Garden *London, U.K.* **125** b4
Coventry *U.K.* 52°25N 1°28W **169** E6
Coverdale *U.S.A.* 31°38N 83°58W **316** D6
Covilhã *Portugal* 40°17N 7°31W **194** E3
Covington *Ga., U.S.A.* 33°36N 83°51W **316** B6
Covington *Ind., U.S.A.* 40°9N 87°24W **311** D9
Covington *Ky., U.S.A.* 39°5N 84°30W **311** E12
Covington *Ohio, U.S.A.* 40°7N 84°21W **311** D12
Covington *Tenn., U.S.A.* 35°34N 89°39W **315** D10
Covington *Va., U.S.A.* 37°47N 79°59W **309** G14
Cowal, L. *Australia* 33°40S 147°25E **283** B7
Cowan, Cerro *Ecuador* 0°12S 90°48W **330** a
Cowan, L. *Australia* 31°45S 121°45E **279** F3
Cowan L. *Canada* 54°0N 107°15W **297** C7
Cowangie *Australia* 35°12S 141°26E **282** C4
Cowansville *Canada* 45°14N 72°46W **313** A12
Coward Springs *Australia* 29°24S 136°49E **281** D2
Cowcowing Lakes
*Australia* 30°55S 117°20E **279** F2
Cowden *U.S.A.* 39°15N 88°52W **311** E8
Cowdenbeath *U.K.* 56°7N 3°21W **167** E5
Cowell *Australia* 33°39S 136°56E **282** B2
Cowes *Vic., Australia* 38°28S 145°14E **283** E6
Cowes *I. of W., U.K.* 50°45N 1°18W **169** G6
Cowgate *Edinburgh, U.K.* **121** b3
Cowichan L. *Canada* 48°53N 124°17W **306** B2
Cowley *U.K.* 51°31N 0°28W **125** A1
Cowlitz → *U.S.A.* 46°6N 122°55W **306** D4
Cowra *Australia* 33°49S 148°42E **283** B8
Cox *Spain* 38°8N 0°53W **197** G4
Coxilha Grande *Brazil* 28°18S 51°30W **335** B5
Coxim *Brazil* 18°30S 54°55W **331** D7
Coxim → *Brazil* 18°34S 54°46W **331** D7
Cox's Bazar *Bangla.* 21°26N 91°59E **241** E3
Coyah *Guinea* 9°42N 13°22W **262** D2
Coyoacán *Mexico* 19°21N 99°9W **128** B2
Coyote Wells *U.S.A.* 32°44N 115°58W **307** N11
Coyuca de Benítez *Mexico* 17°2N 100°4W **319** D4
Coyuca de Catalán
*Mexico* 18°20N 100°39W **318** D4
Cozad *U.S.A.* 40°52N 99°59W **308** E4
Cozes *France* 45°34N 0°49W **174** C3
Cozia △ *Romania* 45°25N 24°16E **183** E9
Cozumel *Mexico* 20°31N 86°55W **319** C7
Cozumel, Isla *Mexico* 20°30N 86°40W **319** C7
Crab Hill *Barbados* 13°19N 59°38W **323** r
Crabs Pen. *Antigua & B.* 17°7N 61°45W **322** b
Crac des Chevaliers *Syria* 34°47N 36°18E **250** D7
Cracow = Kraków *Poland* 50°4N 19°57E **185** H6
Cracow *Australia* 25°17S 150°17E **281** D5
Craddock Channel *N.Z.* 36°10S 175°13E **284** C4
Cradle Mt.-Lake St. Clair △
*Australia* 41°49S 147°56E **281** G4
Cradock *S. Austral., Australia* 32°6S 138°31E **281** E2
Cradock *Eastern Cape, S. Africa* 32°8S 25°36E **270** D4
Crafers *Australia* 35°0S 138°42E **282** C3
Craig *Alaska, U.S.A.* 55°29N 133°9W **303** J14
Craig *Colo., U.S.A.* 40°31N 107°33W **304** F10
Craigavon *U.K.* 54°27N 6°23W **166** B5
Craighall Park *S. Africa* 26°7S 28°1E **123** A2
Craigieburn *Australia* 37°36S 144°56E **283** D6
Craiglockhart *U.K.* 55°55N 3°14W **121** B2
Craigmillar *U.K.* 55°56N 3°9W **121** B3
Craigmore *Zimbabwe* 20°28S 32°50E **269** G3
Craik *Canada* 51°3N 105°49W **297** C7
Crailsheim *Germany* 49°8N 10°5E **179** F6
Craiova *Romania* 44°21N 23°48E **183** F8
Cramond *U.K.* 55°58N 3°18W **121** B2
Cramond Bridge *U.K.* 55°57N 3°19W **121** B1
Cramond I. *U.K.* 55°59N 3°17W **121** B2
Cramsie *Australia* 23°20S 144°15E **280** C3
Cranberry L. *U.S.A.* 44°11N 74°50W **313** B10
Cranberry Portage
*Canada* 54°35N 101°23W **297** C8
Cranbrook *W. Austral., Australia* 34°18S 117°33E **279** F2
Cranbrook *B.C., Canada* 49°30N 115°46W **296** D5
Crandon *U.S.A.* 45°34N 88°54W **308** C9
Crandon Park *U.S.A.* 25°42N 80°9W **129** D3
Crane *Oreg., U.S.A.* 43°25N 118°35W **304** E4
Crane *Tex., U.S.A.* 31°24N 102°21W **314** F3
Crane, The *Barbados* 13°6N 59°27W **323** r
Cranford *U.K.* 51°29N 0°25W **125** B1
Cranganore *India* 10°13N 76°13E **245** J3
Cranston *U.S.A.* 41°47N 71°26W **313** E13
Craon *France* 47°50N 0°58W **172** E6
Craonne *France* 49°27N 3°46E **173** C10
Craponne-sur-Arzon
*France* 45°19N 3°51E **174** C7
Crasna *Romania* 46°32N 27°51E **183** D12
Crasna → *Romania* 47°44N 22°35E **182** C7
Crasnei, Munţii *Romania* 47°0N 23°20E **183** C8
Crater L. *St. Vincent* 13°17N 61°13W **323** n
Crater L. *Oreg., U.S.A.* 42°56N 122°6W **304** E2
Crater Lake △ *U.S.A.* 42°55N 122°10W **304** E2
Crater Mt. *Papua N. G.* 6°37S 145°7E **286** D3
Crater Pt. *Papua N. G.* 5°25S 152°9E **286** C7
Craters of the Moon ⌂
*U.S.A.* 43°25N 113°30W **304** E7
Crateús *Brazil* 5°10S 40°39W **332** C3
Crati → *Italy* 39°43N 16°31E **201** C9
Crato *Brazil* 7°10S 39°25W **332** C4
Crato *Portugal* 39°16N 7°39W **195** F3
Craven, L. *Canada* 54°20N 76°56W **298** B4
Cravo Norte *Colombia* 6°18N 70°12W **328** B3
Cravo Norte → *Colombia* 6°18N 70°12W **328** B3
Crawford *Western Cape, S. Africa* 33°59S 18°30E **118** A2
Crawford *Ala., U.S.A.* 32°27N 85°11W **316** C4
Crawford *Nebr., U.S.A.* 42°41N 103°25W **308** D2
Crawfordsville *Ind., U.S.A.* 40°2N 86°54W **311** D10
Crawfordsville *Iowa, U.S.A.* 41°12N 91°32W **310** C5
Crawfordville *Fla., U.S.A.* 30°11N 84°23W **316** E5
Crawfordville *Ga., U.S.A.* 33°33N 82°54W **316** B7
Crawley *U.K.* 51°7N 0°11W **169** F7
Crayford *U.K.* 51°27N 0°11E **125** B5
Crazy Mts. *U.S.A.* 46°12N 110°20W **304** C8
Crean L. *Canada* 54°5N 106°9W **297** C7
Crécy-en-Ponthieu *France* 50°15N 1°53E **173** B8
Crediton *Ont., Canada* 43°17N 81°33W **312** C3
Crediton *Devon, U.K.* 50°47N 3°40W **169** G4
Cree → *Sask., Canada* 58°57N 105°47W **297** B7
Cree → *Dumf. & Gall., U.K.* 54°55N 4°25W **167** G4
Cree L. *Canada* 57°30N 106°30W **297** B7
Creede *U.S.A.* 37°51N 106°56W **305** H10
Creekmouth *U.K.* 51°30N 0°6E **125** A4
Creekside *U.S.A.* 40°40N 79°11W **312** F5
Creel *Mexico* 27°45N 107°38W **318** B3
Creemore *Canada* 44°19N 80°6W **312** B4
Creighton *Sask., Canada* 54°45N 101°54W **297** C8
Creighton *Nebr., U.S.A.* 42°28N 97°54W **308** D5
Creil *France* 49°15N 2°29E **173** C9
Crema *Italy* 45°22N 9°41E **198** C6
Cremona *Italy* 45°7N 10°2E **198** C7
Crepaja *Serbia* 45°1N 20°38E **182** E5
Crepori → *Brazil* 5°42S 57°8W **331** B6
Crépy *France* 49°35N 3°32E **173** C10
Crépy-en-Valois *France* 49°14N 2°54E **173** C9
Cres *Croatia* 44°58N 14°25E **199** D11
Crescent, L. *U.S.A.* 28°30N 81°33W **133** A1
Crescent Beach *U.S.A.* 29°46N 81°15W **316** F8
Crescent City *Calif., U.S.A.* 41°45N 124°12W **304** F1
Crescent City *Fla., U.S.A.* 29°26N 81°31W **317** F8
Crescent Group
*S. China Sea* 16°30N 111°40E **230** A4
Crescent Hd. *Australia* 31°11S 152°59E **283** A10
Crescent L. *U.S.A.* 29°28N 81°30W **317** F8
Crescentino *Italy* 45°11N 8°6E **198** C5
Crescenzago *Italy* 45°30N 9°14E **128** A2
Crespi d'Adda *Italy* 45°35N 9°32E **198** C6
Crespo *Argentina* 32°2S 60°19W **334** C3
Cressely *France* 48°44N 2°6E **134** B1
Cresskill *U.S.A.* 40°56N 73°57W **132** A2
Cresson *U.S.A.* 40°28N 78°36W **312** F6
Cressy *Australia* 38°2S 143°40E **282** E5
Crest *France* 44°44N 5°2E **175** D9
Cresta, Mt. *Phil.* 17°17N 122°6E **232** C4
Crestline *Calif., U.S.A.* 34°14N 117°18W **307** L9
Crestline *Ohio, U.S.A.* 40°47N 82°44W **312** F2
Creston *B.C., Canada* 49°10N 116°31W **296** D5
Creston *Calif., U.S.A.* 35°32N 120°33W **306** K6
Creston *Iowa, U.S.A.* 41°4N 94°22W **310** C2
Crestview *Calif., U.S.A.* 37°46N 118°58W **306** H8
Crestview *Fla., U.S.A.* 30°46N 86°34W **317** E3
Crestwood *U.S.A.* 41°38N 87°46W **119** D2
Creswick *Australia* 37°25S 143°58E **282** D5
Crêt de la Neige *France* 46°16N 5°58E **175** B9
Crete = Kriti *Greece* 35°15N 25°0E **207** E6
Crete *Ill., U.S.A.* 41°27N 87°38W **311** C9
Crete *Nebr., U.S.A.* 40°38N 96°58W **308** E5
Crete, Sea of *Greece* 36°0N 25°0E **205** E7
Créteil *France* 48°47N 2°27E **134** B3
Cretin, C. *Papua N. G.* 6°40S 147°53E **286** D4
Creus, C. de *Spain* 42°20N 3°19E **196** C8
Creuse □ *France* 46°10N 2°0E **173** F9
Creuse → *France* 47°0N 0°34E **174** B4
Creutzwald *France* 49°12N 6°42E **173** C13
Creuzburg *Germany* 51°3N 10°14E **178** D6
Crèvecœur-le-Grand *France* 49°37N 2°5E **173** C9
Crevillent *Spain* 38°12N 0°48W **197** G4
Crewe *U.K.* 53°6N 2°26W **168** D5
Crewkerne *U.K.* 50°53N 2°48W **169** G5
Crianlarich *U.K.* 56°24N 4°37W **167** E4
Criciúma *Brazil* 28°40S 49°23W **335** B6
Cricklewood *U.K.* 51°33N 0°13W **125** A2
Cricova *Moldova* 47°8N 28°52E **183** C13
Cridersville *U.S.A.* 40°39N 84°9W **311** D12
Crieff *U.K.* 56°22N 3°50W **167** E5
Crikvenica *Croatia* 45°11N 14°40E **199** C11
Crimea □ *Ukraine* 45°30N 33°10E **189** K8
Crimean Pen. = Krymskyy Pivostriv
*Ukraine* 45°0N 34°0E **189** K8
Crimmitschau *Germany* 50°48N 12°24E **178** E8
Cristal, Mts. de *Gabon* 0°30N 10°30E **264** B2
Cristalândia *Brazil* 10°36S 49°11W **332** D2
Cristino Castro *Brazil* 8°49S 44°13W **332** C3
Cristo Redentor, Corcovado
*Brazil* 22°56S 43°12W **135** B1
Cristóbal *Panama* 9°19N 79°54W **320** c
Cristóbal, Pta. *Ecuador* 0°54S 91°31W **330** a
Cristuru Secuiesc
*Romania* 46°17N 25°2E **183** D10
Crişul Alb → *Romania* 46°42N 21°17E **182** D6
Crişul Negru → *Romania* 46°42N 21°16E **182** D6
Crişul Repede → *Romania* 46°55N 20°59E **182** D5
Crittenden *U.S.A.* 38°47N 84°36W **311** F12
Criuleni *Moldova* 47°13N 29°10E **183** C14
Crivitz *Germany* 53°34N 11°39E **178** B7
Crixás *Brazil* 14°27S 49°58W **333** D2
Crna → *Macedonia* 41°33N 21°59E **202** E5
Crna Gora = Montenegro ■
*Europe* 42°40N 19°20E **202** D3
Crna Gora *Macedonia* 42°10N 21°30E **202** D5
Crna Reka = Crna →
*Macedonia* 41°33N 21°59E **202** E5
Crna Trava *Serbia* 42°49N 22°19E **202** D6
Crni Drim → *Macedonia* 41°17N 20°40E **202** E4
Crni Timok → *Serbia* 43°53N 22°15E **202** C6
Crnoljeva Planina = Zhar, Mali
*Kosovo* 42°20N 21°0E **202** D5
Črnomelj *Slovenia* 45°33N 15°10E **199** C12
Croagh Patrick *Ireland* 53°46N 9°40W **166** C2
Croajingolong △
*Australia* 37°45S 149°26E **283** D8
Croatia ■ *Europe* 45°20N 16°0E **199** C13
Croce, Ex Chiesa della *Venice, Italy* **142** c3
Crockenhill *U.K.* 51°22N 0°9E **125** B4
Crocker *U.S.A.* 37°57N 92°16W **310** G4
Crocker, Banjaran
*Malaysia* 5°40N 116°30E **235** A5
Crocker, Cerro *Ecuador* 0°36S 90°21W **330** a
Crocker Range △ *Malaysia* 5°33N 116°8E **235** A5
Crockett *U.S.A.* 31°19N 95°27W **314** F7
Crocodile = Umgwenya →
*Mozam.* 25°14S 32°18E **271** C5
Crocodile → *S. Africa* 24°12S 26°53E **270** B4
Crocodile Is. *Australia* 12°3S 134°58E **280** A1
Crocq *France* 45°52N 2°21E **174** C6
Crocus B. *Anguilla* 18°13N 63°5W **322** a
Crohy Hd. *Ireland* 54°55N 8°26W **166** B3
Croisette, C. *France* 43°14N 5°22E **175** E9
Croisic, Pte. du *France* 47°19N 2°31W **172** E4
Croissy-Beaubourg *France* 48°49N 2°39E **134** B4
Croissy-sur-Seine *France* 48°52N 2°8E **134** A1
Croix, L. la *Canada* 48°20N 92°15W **298** C1
Croke Park *Dublin, Ireland* 53°21N 6°15W **120** A2
Croker, C. *N. Terr., Australia* 10°58S 132°35E **278** B5
Croker, C. *Ont., Canada* 44°58N 80°59W **312** B4
Croker I. *Australia* 11°12S 132°32E **278** B5
Croker Islands Seas ✪
*Australia* 11°20S 132°30E **278** B5
Cromarty *U.K.* 57°40N 4°2W **167** D4
Cromer *U.K.* 52°56N 1°17E **168** E9
Crompton Pt. *Dominica* 15°35N 61°19W **323** k
Cromwell *N.Z.* 45°3S 169°14E **285** F4
Cromwell *Conn., U.S.A.* 41°36N 72°39W **313** E12
Cronat *France* 46°43N 3°40E **173** F10
Crook *U.K.* 54°43N 1°45W **168** C6
Crooked → *B.C., Canada* 54°50N 122°54W **296** C4
Crooked → *Oreg., U.S.A.* 44°32N 121°16W **304** D3
Crooked Creek *U.S.A.* 61°52N 158°7W **303** F8
Crooked I. *Bahamas* 22°50N 74°10W **321** B5
Crooked Island Passage
*Bahamas* 22°55N 74°35W **321** B5
Crookston *Minn., U.S.A.* 47°47N 96°37W **308** B5
Crookston *Nebr., U.S.A.* 42°56N 100°45W **308** D3
Crookwell *Australia* 34°28S 149°24E **283** C8
Cropane-Micone ⌂ *Italy* 38°31N 16°18E **201** D9
Crosby *Gauteng, S. Africa* 26°11S 27°59E **123** B1
Crosby *Mersey., U.K.* 53°30N 3°3W **168** D4
Crosby *N. Dak., U.S.A.* 48°55N 103°18W **308** A2
Crosby *Pa., U.S.A.* 41°45N 78°23W **312** E6
Crosbyton *U.S.A.* 33°40N 101°14W **314** E4
Crosia *Italy* 39°35N 16°45E **201** C9
Crosne *France* 48°43N 2°27E **134** B3
Cross → *Nigeria* 4°42N 8°21E **263** E6
Cross City *U.S.A.* 29°38N 83°7W **317** F6
Cross Fell *U.K.* 54°43N 2°28W **168** C5
Cross I. *India* 18°56N 72°51E **130** B2
Cross L. *Canada* 54°45N 97°30W **297** C9
Cross Lake *Canada* 54°37N 97°47W **297** C9
Cross River □ *Nigeria* 6°0N 8°0E **263** D6
Cross River △ *Nigeria* 5°50N 9°50E **263** D6
Cross Sound *U.S.A.* 58°0N 135°0W **303** G14
Cross Timbers *U.S.A.* 38°1N 93°14W **310** F3
Crossen = Krosno Odrzańskie
*Poland* 52°3N 15°7E **185** F2
Crossett *U.S.A.* 33°8N 91°58W **314** E9
Crosshaven *Ireland* 51°47N 8°17W **166** E3
Crossley, Mt. *N.Z.* 42°50S 172°5E **285** E4
Crossmaglen *U.K.* 54°5N 6°36W **166** B5
Crossmolina *Ireland* 54°6N 9°20W **166** B2
Crossville *Ill., U.S.A.* 38°10N 88°4W **311** F8
Crossville *Tenn., U.S.A.* 35°57N 85°2W **315** D12
Croswell *U.S.A.* 43°16N 82°37W **312** C2
Croton-on-Hudson
*U.S.A.* 41°12N 73°55W **313** E11
Crotone *Italy* 39°5N 17°8E **201** C10
Crouch End *U.K.* 51°34N 0°7W **125** A3
Crow → *Canada* 59°41N 124°20W **296** B4
Crow Agency *U.S.A.* 45°36N 107°28W **304** D10
Crow Hd. *Ireland* 51°35N 10°9W **166** E1
Crowdy Bay △ *Australia* 31°45S 152°45E **283** A10
Crowell *U.S.A.* 33°59N 99°43W **314** E5
Crowl Cr. → *Australia* 32°0S 145°30E **283** B6
Crowley *U.S.A.* 30°13N 92°22W **314** F8
Crowley, L. *U.S.A.* 37°35N 118°42W **306** H8
Crown I. *Papua N. G.* 5°7S 146°58E **286** C4
Crown Mine *S. Africa* 26°12S 27°57E **123** B1
Crown Point *Ind., U.S.A.* 41°25N 87°22W **311** C9
Crown Point *N.Y., U.S.A.* 43°57N 73°26W **313** C11
Crown Point ✕ (TAB)
*Trin. & Tob.* 11°9N 60°50W **323** s
Crown Pt. *Trin. & Tob.* 11°18N 60°51W **323** s
Crownpoint *U.S.A.* 35°41N 108°9W **305** J9
Crows Landing *U.S.A.* 37°23N 121°6W **306** H5
Crows Nest *N.S.W., Australia* 33°49S 151°12E **139** A2
Crows Nest *Queens., Australia* 27°16S 152°4E **281** D5
Crowsnest Pass *Canada* 49°40N 114°40W **296** D6
Croydon *Queens., Australia* 18°13S 142°14E **280** B3
Croydon *London, U.K.* 51°22N 0°5W **125** B3
Croydon □ *U.K.* 51°22N 0°5W **169** F7
Croydon Park *Australia* 33°55S 151°7E **139** B1
Crozet, Îs. *Ind. Oc.* 46°27S 52°0E **273** J4
Crozet Basin *Ind. Oc.* 39°0S 60°0E **273** H5
Crozon *France* 48°15N 4°30W **172** D2
Cruagh Mt. *Ireland* 53°14N 6°17W **120** B2
Cruce de Sardina
*Canary Is.* 27°52N 15°22W **153** e1
Cruces, Punta *Colombia* 6°39N 77°32W **328** B2
Crumlin *Ireland* 53°19N 6°19W **120** B2
Crusheen *Ireland* 52°57N 8°53W **166** D3
Cruz, C. *Cuba* 19°50N 77°50W **320** C4
Cruz Alta *Brazil* 28°45S 53°40W **335** B5
Cruz Bay *U.S. Virgin Is.* 18°20N 64°48W **321** b
Cruz das Almas *Brazil* 12°0S 39°6W **333** D4
Cruz de Pau *Portugal* 38°37N 9°7W **126** B2
Cruz del Eje *Argentina* 30°45S 64°50W **334** C3
Cruzeiro *Brazil* 22°33S 45°0W **333** F3
Cruzeiro do Oeste *Brazil* 23°46S 53°4W **335** A5
Cruzeiro do Sul = Joaçaba
*Brazil* 27°5S 51°31W **335** B5
Cruzeiro do Sul *Brazil* 7°35S 72°35W **330** B3
Cry L. *Canada* 58°45N 129°0W **296** B3
Crystal B. *U.S.A.* 28°50N 82°45W **317** G7
Crystal Bay *U.S.A.* 39°15N 120°0W **306** F7
Crystal Brook *Australia* 33°21S 138°12E **282** B3
Crystal City *Mo., U.S.A.* 38°13N 90°23W **310** F6
Crystal City *Tex., U.S.A.* 28°41N 99°50W **314** G5
Crystal Falls *U.S.A.* 46°5N 88°20W **308** B9
Crystal Lake *Fla., U.S.A.* 30°26N 85°42W **316** E4
Crystal Lake *Ill., U.S.A.* 42°14N 88°19W **311** B8
Crystal Palace *U.K.* 51°25N 0°4W **125** B3
Crystal River *U.S.A.* 28°54N 82°35W **317** G7
Crystal Springs *U.S.A.* 31°59N 90°21W **315** F9
Csenger *Hungary* 47°50N 22°41E **182** C7
Csepel *Hungary* 47°25N 19°4E **117** B2
Csepelsziget *Hungary* 47°25N 19°4E **117** B2
Csillaghegy *Hungary* 47°35N 19°2E **117** A2
Csillagtelep *Hungary* 47°24N 19°5E **117** B2
Csömör *Hungary* 47°33N 19°14E **117** A3
Csömöri-patak → *Hungary* 47°35N 19°5E **117** A3
Csongrád *Hungary* 46°43N 20°12E **182** D5
Csongrád □ *Hungary* 46°32N 20°15E **182** D5
Csorna *Hungary* 47°38N 17°18E **182** C2
Csurgo *Hungary* 46°16N 17°9E **182** D2
Cu Lao Hon *Vietnam* 10°54N 108°18E **237** G7
Cua Rao *Vietnam* 19°16N 104°27E **236** C5
Cuácua → *Mozam.* 17°54S 37°0E **269** F4
Cuále *Angola* 8°22S 16°10E **265** D3
Cuále → *Angola* 8°29S 15°1E **265** D3
Cuamato *Angola* 17°2S 15°7E **265** F3
Cuamba *Mozam.* 14°45S 36°22E **269** E4
Cuando *Angola* 14°34S 19°1E **265** E3
Cuando → *Angola* 17°30S 23°15E **265** F4
Cuando Cubango □ *Angola* 16°25S 20°0E **265** F4
Cuangar *Angola* 17°36S 18°39E **265** F3
Cuango = Kwango →
*Dem. Rep. of the Congo* 3°14S 17°22E **264** C3
Cuango *Lunda Norte, Angola* 9°8S 18°3E **265** D3
Cuango *Mexico, Angola* 14°30S 19°0E **265** E3
Cuango *Uige, Angola* 6°15S 16°42E **265** D3
Cuanza → *Angola* 9°21S 13°9E **265** D2
Cuanza Norte □ *Angola* 8°50S 14°30E **265** D2
Cuanza Sul □ *Angola* 10°50S 14°50E **265** E2
Cuao → *Venezuela* 4°55N 67°40W **328** C4
Cuare → *Trin. & Tob.* 10°36N 61°6W **323** t
Cuarto → *Argentina* 33°25S 63°2W **334** C3
Cuatir → *Angola* 17°1S 18°9E **265** F3
Cuatro Vientos *Spain* 40°22N 3°47W **127** B1
Cuatrociénegas *Mexico* 26°59N 102°5W **318** B4
Cuauhtémoc *Chihuahua, Mexico* 28°25N 106°52W **318** B3
Cuauhtémoc *México, Mexico* 19°25N 99°9W **128** B2
Cuba *Portugal* 38°10N 7°54W **195** G3
Cuba *Mo., U.S.A.* 38°4N 91°24W **310** F5
Cuba *N. Mex., U.S.A.* 36°1N 107°4W **305** H10
Cuba *N.Y., U.S.A.* 42°13N 78°17W **312** D6
Cuba ■ *W. Indies* 22°0N 79°0W **320** B4
Cuba City *U.S.A.* 42°36N 90°26W **310** B6
Cubagua, I. *Venezuela* 10°49N 64°11W **329** a
Cubal *Angola* 12°26S 14°3E **265** E2
Cubal → *Angola* 15°9S 12°9E **265** F2
Cubango → *Africa* 18°50S 22°25E **265** F4
Cubanja *Angola* 14°49S 21°20E **265** E4
Cubao *Phil.* 14°37N 121°3E **127** B2
Cubia *Angola* 15°58S 21°42E **265** F4
Çubuk *Turkey* 40°14N 33°3E **212** B5
Çubuklu *Turkey* 41°5N 29°4E **122** B2
Cuc Phuong △ *Vietnam* 20°17N 105°38E **236** B5
Cuche *Trin. & Tob.* 10°22N 61°10W **323** t
Cuchi *Angola* 14°37S 16°58E **265** E3
Cuchi → *Angola* 15°13S 17°20E **265** F3
Cuchillo-Co *Argentina* 38°20S 64°37W **336** A4
Cuchivero → *Venezuela* 7°40N 65°57W **328** B4
Cuchumatanes, Sierra de los
*Guatemala* 15°35N 91°25W **320** C1
Cuckfield *U.K.* 51°1N 0°8W **169** F7
Cucuí *Brazil* 1°12N 66°50W **328** C4
Cucumbi *Angola* 10°17S 19°5E **265** E3
Cucurpé *Mexico* 30°20N 110°43W **318** A2
Cucurrupí *Colombia* 4°23N 76°56W **328** C2
Cúcuta *Colombia* 7°54N 72°31W **328** B3
Cudahy *Calif., U.S.A.* 33°57N 118°11W **126** C3
Cudahy *Wis., U.S.A.* 42°57N 87°51W **311** B9
Cudalbi *Romania* 45°46N 27°41E **183** E12
Cudarebe = Kudarebe
*Aruba* 12°37N 70°4W **322** f
Cuddalore *India* 11°46N 79°45E **245** J4
Cuddapah = Kadapa
*India* 14°30N 78°47E **245** G4
Cuddapan, L. *Australia* 25°45S 141°26E **280** D3
Cudgewa *Australia* 36°10S 147°42E **283** D7
Cudillero *Spain* 43°33N 6°9W **194** B4
Cudjoehead *Montserrat* 16°47N 62°12W **323** p
Cue *Australia* 27°25S 117°54E **279** E2
Cuebe → *Angola* 15°46S 17°32E **265** F3
Cuéllar *Spain* 41°23N 4°21W **194** D6
Cuemba *Angola* 11°50S 17°42E **265** E3
Cuenca *Ecuador* 2°50S 79°9W **328** D2
Cuenca *Spain* 40°5N 2°10W **196** E2
Cuenca □ *Spain* 40°0N 2°0W **196** F3
Cuenca, Serranía de *Spain* 39°55N 1°50W **196** F3
Cuenca Alta del Manzanares ⌂
*Spain* 40°40N 3°55W **194** E7
Cuerda del Pozo, Embalse de la
*Spain* 41°51N 2°44W **196** D2
Cuernavaca *Mexico* 18°55N 99°15W **319** D5
Cuero *U.S.A.* 29°6N 97°17W **314** G6
Cuers *France* 43°14N 6°5E **175** E10
Cueva de la Quebrada del Toro △
*Venezuela* 10°46N 69°3W **328** A4
Cueva de los Guácharos △
*Colombia* 1°35N 76°1W **328** C2
Cuevas, Cerro *Bolivia* 22°0S 65°12W **331** E4
Cuevas de Vera = Cuevas del
Almanzora *Spain* 37°18N 1°58W **197** H3
Cuevas del Almanzora
*Spain* 37°18N 1°58W **197** H3
Cuevo *Bolivia* 20°15S 63°30W **331** E5
Cugir *Romania* 45°48N 23°25E **183** E8
Cuglieri *Italy* 40°11N 8°34E **200** B1
Cugnaux *France* 43°32N 1°20E **174** E5
Cuhai-Bakony →
*Hungary* 47°35N 17°54E **182** C2
Cuiabá *Brazil* 15°30S 56°0W **331** D6
Cuiabá → *Brazil* 17°5S 56°36W **331** D6
Cuicuilco, Pirámide de
*Mexico* 19°18N 99°11W **128** C1
Cuihangcun *China* 22°27N 113°32E **219** a
Cuijk *Neths.* 51°44N 5°50E **170** C5
Cuilco *Guatemala* 15°24N 91°58W **320** C1
Cuillin Hills *U.K.* 57°13N 6°15W **167** D2
Cuillin Sd. *U.K.* 57°4N 6°20W **167** D2
Cuilo = Kwilu →
*Dem. Rep. of the Congo* 3°22S 17°22E **265** C3
Cuilo *Angola* 8°12S 19°28E **265** D3
Cuilo-Futa *Angola* 6°28S 15°51E **265** D3
Cuima *Angola* 13°25S 15°45E **265** E3
Cuimba *Angola* 6°10S 14°41E **265** D2
Cuiseaux *France* 46°30N 5°22E **173** F12
Cuité *Brazil* 6°29S 36°9W **332** C4
Cuito → *Angola* 18°1S 20°48E **265** F4
Cuito Cuanavale *Angola* 15°10S 19°10E **265** F3
Cuitzeo, L. de *Mexico* 19°55N 101°5W **318** D4
Cuiuni → *Brazil* 0°45S 63°7W **329** D5
Cuivre → *U.S.A.* 38°56N 90°41W **310** F6
Cujmir *Romania* 44°13N 22°57E **182** F7
Cukai *Malaysia* 4°13N 103°25E **237** K4
Çukurca *Turkey* 37°14N 43°36E **213** D10
Çukurova = Cilicia *Turkey* 36°30N 34°0E **212** D5
Cul-de-Sac *St.-Maarten* 18°2N 63°4W **322** a
Cul de Sac *St.-Martin* 18°6N 63°2W **322** a
Culasi *Phil.* 11°26N 122°3E **233** F4
Culbertson *U.S.A.* 48°9N 104°31W **304** B11
Culburra *N.S.W., Australia* 34°56S 150°46E **283** C9
Culburra *S. Austral., Australia* 35°50S 139°58E **282** C3
Culcairn *Australia* 35°41S 147°3E **283** C7
Culebra *Puerto Rico* 18°19N 65°18W **321** b
Culebra, Sierra de la *Spain* 41°55N 6°20W **194** D4
Culfa *Azerbaijan* 38°57N 45°38E **213** C11
Culgoa *Australia* 35°44S 143°6E **282** C5
Culgoa → *Australia* 29°56S 146°20E **281** D4
Culgoa Flood Plain △
*Australia* 28°58S 147°5E **281** D4
Culiacán *Mexico* 24°50N 107°23W **318** C3
Culiacán → *Mexico* 24°30N 107°42W **318** C3
Culik *Indonesia* 8°21S 115°37E **231** J18
Culion *Phil.* 11°54N 119°58E **233** F3
Culion I. *Phil.* 11°50N 120°0E **233** F3
Culiseu → *Brazil* 12°14S 53°17W **331** C7
Cúllar *Spain* 37°35N 2°34W **195** H8
Cullarin Ra. *Australia* 34°30S 149°30E **283** C8
Cullen *U.K.* 57°42N 2°49W **167** D6
Cullen Bullen *Australia* 33°18S 150°2E **283** B9
Cullen Pt. *Australia* 11°57S 141°54E **286** F1
Cullera *Spain* 39°9N 0°17W **197** F4
Cullman *U.S.A.* 34°11N 86°51W **315** D11
Culloden *U.S.A.* 32°52N 84°6W **316** C5
Cullom *U.S.A.* 40°53N 88°16W **311** D8
Cullompton *U.K.* 50°51N 3°24W **169** G4
Culmore *U.S.A.* 38°51N 77°8W **143** B2
Culo → *Angola* 6°13S 15°34E **265** D3
Culoz *France* 45°47N 5°46E **175** C9
Culpeper *U.S.A.* 38°30N 78°0W **309** F14
Culuene → *Brazil* 12°56S 52°51W **331** C7
Culver *U.S.A.* 41°13N 86°25W **311** C10
Culver, Pt. *Australia* 32°54S 124°43E **279** F3
Culver City *U.S.A.* 34°1N 118°24W **126** B2
Culverden *N.Z.* 42°47S 172°49E **285** E4
Culverton *U.S.A.* 33°19N 82°54W **316** B7
Cuma *Angola* 12°52S 15°5E **265** E3
Cumaná *Venezuela* 10°30N 64°5W **329** A5
Cumana B. *Trin. & Tob.* 10°48N 60°56W **323** t
Cumaovası *Turkey* 38°15N 27°9E **205** C9
Cumari *Brazil* 18°16S 48°11W **333** E2
Cumballa Hill *Mumbai, India* **130** a1
Cumbe = Euclides da Cunha
*Brazil* 10°31S 39°1W **332** D4
Cumberland *B.C., Canada* 49°40N 125°0W **296** D4
Cumberland *Ont., Canada* 45°29N 75°24W **313** A9
Cumberland *St. Vincent* 13°16N 61°16W **323** n
Cumberland *Iowa, U.S.A.* 41°16N 94°52W **310** C2
Cumberland *Md., U.S.A.* 39°39N 78°46W **309** F14
Cumberland → *U.S.A.* 37°9N 88°25W **308** G9
Cumberland, B. *Chile* 33°37S 78°49W **330** c
Cumberland, C. *Vanuatu* 14°39S 166°37E **287** D4
Cumberland, L. *U.S.A.* 36°52N 85°9W **309** G11
Cumberland Gap ⌂
*U.S.A.* 36°36N 83°40W **309** G12
Cumberland I. *U.S.A.* 30°50N 81°25W **316** E8
Cumberland Is. *Australia* 20°35S 149°10E **280** b
Cumberland Island ⌂
*U.S.A.* 30°12N 81°24W **316** E8
Cumberland L. *Canada* 54°3N 102°18W **297** C8
Cumberland Pen. *Canada* 67°0N 64°0W **295** D19
Cumberland Plateau
*U.S.A.* 36°0N 85°0W **315** D12
Cumberland Sd. *Canada* 65°30N 66°0W **295** D18
Cumbernauld *U.K.* 55°57N 3°58W **167** F5
Cumbira *Angola* 12°11S 15°8E **265** E3
Cumborah *Australia* 29°40S 147°45E **281** D4
Cumbres de Majalca △
*Mexico* 28°48N 106°30W **318** B3
Cumbres de Monterrey △
*Mexico* 25°26N 100°25W **318** B4
Cumbres Mayores *Spain* 38°4N 6°39W **195** G4
Cumbria □ *U.K.* 54°42N 2°52W **168** C5
Cumbrian Mts. *U.K.* 54°30N 3°0W **168** C5
Cumbum *India* 15°40N 79°10E **245** G4
Cuminá *Brazil* 1°57S 56°0W **329** D6
Cuminá → *Brazil* 1°30S 56°0W **329** D6
Cuminapanema → *Brazil* 1°9S 54°54W **329** D7
Cumming, C. *Chile* 27°6S 109°14W **330** b
Cummings Mt. *U.S.A.* 35°2N 118°34W **307** K8
Cummins *Australia* 34°16S 135°43E **281** E2
Cumnock *N.S.W., Australia* 32°59S 148°46E **283** B8
Cumnock *E. Ayrs., U.K.* 55°28N 4°17W **167** F4
Cumpas *Mexico* 30°2N 109°48W **318** B3
Cumplida, Pta. *Canary Is.* 28°50N 17°48W **153** e1
Çumra *Turkey* 37°34N 32°45E **212** D5
Cumuto *Trin. & Tob.* 10°35N 61°12W **323** t
Cunapo → *Trin. & Tob.* 10°35N 61°8W **323** t
Cuñare *Colombia* 0°49N 72°32W **328** C3
Cunaripa *Trin. & Tob.* 10°33N 61°10W **323** t
Cuncumén *Chile* 31°53S 70°38W **334** C1
Cundeelee ✪ *Australia* 30°43S 123°25E **279** F3
Cunderdin *Australia* 31°37S 117°12E **279** F2
Cundinamarca □ *Colombia* 5°0N 74°0W **328** C3
Cunene □ *Angola* 16°30S 15°0E **265** F3
Cunene → *Angola* 17°20S 11°50E **265** F2
Cúneo *Italy* 44°23N 7°32E **198** D4
Cung Son *Vietnam* 13°2N 108°58E **236** F7
Çüngüş *Turkey* 38°13N 39°17E **246** B3
Cunhinga *Angola* 12°11S 16°47E **265** E3
Cunhinga → *Angola* 10°42S 16°41E **265** E3
Cunillera, I. = Sa Conillera
*Spain* 38°59N 1°13E **206** D1
Cunjamba *Angola* 15°27S 20°10E **265** E4
Cunlhat *France* 45°38N 3°32E **174** C7
Cunnamulla *Australia* 28°2S 145°38E **281** D4
Cunningham *Bahamas* 25°5N 77°26W **153** b
Cunupia *Trin. & Tob.* 10°32N 61°22W **323** t
Cuorgnè *Italy* 45°23N 7°39E **198** C4
Cupar *Sask., Canada* 50°57N 104°10W **297** C8
Cupar *Fife, U.K.* 56°19N 3°1W **167** E5
Cupcini *Moldova* 48°6N 27°23E **183** B12
Cupecé → *Brazil* 23°39S 46°40W **137** B1
Cupertino *U.S.A.* 37°19N 122°2W **306** H4
Cupica, G. de *Colombia* 6°25N 77°30W **328** B2
Ćuprija *Serbia* 43°57N 21°26E **202** C5
Curaçá *Brazil* 8°59S 39°54W **332** C4
Curaçao *W. Indies* 12°10N 69°0W **322** g
Curaçao Int. ✕ (CUR)
*Curaçao* 12°11N 68°57W **322** g
Curacautín *Chile* 38°26S 71°53W **336** A2
Curador = Presidente Dutra
*Brazil* 5°15S 44°30W **332** C3
Curahuara de Carangas
*Bolivia* 17°52S 68°26W **330** D4
Curalhinho = Coelho Neto
*Brazil* 4°15S 43°0W **332** B3
Curamata → *Trin. & Tob.* 10°11N 61°28W **323** t
Curanilahue *Chile* 37°29S 73°28W **334** D1
Curaray → *Peru* 2°20S 74°5W **328** D3
Curatabaca *Venezuela* 6°19N 62°51W **329** B5
Cure → *France* 47°40N 3°41E **173** E10
Curepipe *Mauritius* 20°19S 57°31E **272** e
Curepipe Point *Mauritius* 20°21S 57°31E **272** e
Curepto *Chile* 35°8S 72°1W **334** D1
Curia *Portugal* 40°22N 8°22W **194** E2
Curiapo *Venezuela* 8°33N 61°5W **329** B5
Curicó *Chile* 34°55S 71°20W **334** C1
Curicuriari → *Brazil* 0°14S 66°48W **328** D4
Curieuse *Seychelles* 4°15S 55°44E **272** c
Curimatá *Brazil* 10°2S 44°17W **332** D3
Curinga *Italy* 38°49N 16°19E **201** D9
Curiplaya *Colombia* 0°16N 74°52W **328** C3
Curitiba *Brazil* 25°20S 49°10W **335** B6
Curitibanos *Brazil* 27°18S 50°36W **335** B5
Curlewis *Australia* 31°7S 150°16E **283** A9
Curoca → *Angola* 15°43S 11°55E **265** F2
Curonian Lagoon = Kurshskiy Zaliv
*Russia* 55°9N 21°6E **184** C8
Curonian Spit *Europe* 55°20N 20°55E **184** C7
Currabubula *Australia* 31°16S 150°44E **283** A9
Currais Novos *Brazil* 6°13S 36°30W **332** C4
Curral Velho *C. Verde Is.* 16°8N 22°48W **153** j
Curralinho *Brazil* 1°45S 49°46W **332** B2
Currane, L. *Ireland* 51°49N 10°4W **166** E1
Currant *U.S.A.* 38°44N 115°28W **304** G6
Curraweena *Australia* 30°47S 145°54E **283** A6
Currawinya △ *Australia* 28°55S 144°27E **281** D3
Current → *U.S.A.* 36°15N 90°55W **310** C9
Currie *Tas., Australia* 39°56S 143°53E **281** F3
Currie *Edinburgh, U.K.* 55°54N 3°17W **121** B2
Currie *Nev., U.S.A.* 40°16N 114°45W **304** F6
Curt-Bunar = Tervel
*Bulgaria* 43°45N 27°28E **203** C11
Curtea de Argeș *Romania* 45°12N 24°42E **183** E9
Curtici *Romania* 46°21N 21°18E **182** D6
Curtin Springs *Australia* 25°20S 131°45E **279** E5
Curtis *U.S.A.* 40°38N 100°31W **308** E3
Curtis Group *Australia* 39°30S 146°37E **281** F4
Curtis I. *Queens., Australia* 23°35S 151°10E **280** C5
Curtis I. *Pac. Oc.* 30°30S 178°34W **277** G15
Curuá → *Pará, Brazil* 2°24S 54°5W **329** D7
Curuá → *Pará, Brazil* 5°23S 54°22W **331** B7
Curuá, I. *Brazil* 0°48N 50°10W **332** A1
Curuaés → *Brazil* 7°30S 54°45W **331** B7
Curuai *Brazil* 2°17S 55°29W **329** D6
Curuápanema → *Brazil* 2°25S 55°2W **329** D6
Curuçá *Brazil* 0°43S 47°50W **332** B2
Curuçá → *Brazil* 4°27S 71°23W **330** A3
Çürüksu Çayi = Büyük
Menderes → *Turkey* 37°28N 27°11E **205** D9
Curup *Indonesia* 3°26S 102°13E **234** C2
Curupira, Serra *S. Amer.* 1°25N 64°30W **329** C5
Cururu → *Brazil* 7°12S 58°3W **331** B6
Cururupu *Brazil* 1°50S 44°50W **332** B3
Curuzú Cuatiá *Argentina* 29°50S 58°5W **334** B4
Curvelo *Brazil* 18°45S 44°27W **333** E3
Cusago *Italy* 45°26N 9°1E **128** B1
Cusano Milanino *Italy* 45°33N 9°11E **128** A2
Cusco *Peru* 13°32S 72°0W **330** C3
Cusco □ *Peru* 13°31S 71°59W **330** C3
Cushendall *U.K.* 55°5N 6°4W **166** A5
Cushing *U.S.A.* 35°59N 96°46W **314** D6
Cushing, Mt. *Canada* 57°35N 126°57W **296** B3
Cusihuiriáchic *Mexico* 28°14N 106°50W **318** B3
Cusna, Mte. *Italy* 44°17N 10°23E **198** D7
Cussabat = Al Qaşabāt
*Libya* 32°39N 14°1E **258** B2
Cusset *France* 46°8N 3°28E **173** F10
Cusseta *U.S.A.* 32°18N 84°47W **316** C5
Cusso, Sa. do *Angola* 6°30S 14°58E **265** D2
Custer *U.S.A.* 43°46N 103°36W **308** D2
Custom House *Dublin, Ireland* **120** b3
Cut Bank *U.S.A.* 48°38N 112°20W **304** B7
Cutchogue *U.S.A.* 41°1N 72°30W **313** E12
Cutervo *Peru* 6°25S 78°55W **330** B2
Cuthbert *U.S.A.* 31°46N 84°48W **316** D5
Cutler *U.S.A.* 36°31N 119°17W **306** J7
Cutler Park *U.S.A.* 42°17N 71°12W **116** B1
Cutler Ridge *U.S.A.* 25°35N 80°20W **317** K9
Cutlerville *U.S.A.* 42°50N 85°40W **311** B11
Cutral-Có *Argentina* 38°58S 69°15W **336** A3
Cutro *Italy* 39°2N 16°59E **201** C9
Cuttaburra → *Australia* 29°43S 144°22E **281** D3
Cuttack *India* 20°25N 85°57E **244** D7
Cuva → *Angola* 11°42S 14°52E **265** E2
Cuvelai *Angola* 15°44S 15°50E **265** F3
Cuvette □ *Congo* 0°30S 16°0E **264** C3
Cuvette-Ouest □ *Congo* 0°10N 14°30E **264** B2
Cuvier, C. *Australia* 23°14S 113°22E **279** D1
Cuvier I. *N.Z.* 36°27S 175°50E **284** C4
Çuvuşabaşı → *Turkey* 40°58N 28°51E **122** B1
Cuwei *China* 39°54N 116°15E **114** B1
Cuxhaven *Germany* 53°51N 8°41E **178** B4
Cuyabeno *Ecuador* 0°16S 75°53W **328** D2
Cuyahoga Falls *U.S.A.* 41°8N 81°29W **312** E3
Cuyahoga Valley △
*U.S.A.* 41°24N 81°33W **312** E3
Cuyapo *Phil.* 15°46N 120°40E **232** D3
Cuyo *Phil.* 10°51N 121°2E **233** F3
Cuyo East Pass. *Phil.* 11°0N 121°28E **233** F3
Cuyo Islands *Phil.* 11°4N 120°57E **233** F3
Cuyo West Pass. *Phil.* 11°0N 120°30E **233** F3
Cuyuni → *Guyana* 6°23N 58°41W **329** B6
Cuzco = Cusco *Peru* 13°32S 72°0W **330** C3
Čvrsnica *Bos.-H.* 43°36N 17°35E **182** G2
Cwmbran *U.K.* 51°39N 3°2W **169** F4
Cyangugu *Rwanda* 2°29S 28°54E **268** C2
Cybinka *Poland* 52°12N 14°46E **185** F1
Cyclades = Kyklades
*Greece* 37°0N 24°30E **204** E6
Cygnet *Australia* 43°8S 147°1E **281** G4
Cynthiana *U.S.A.* 38°23N 84°18W **311** F12
Cypress Hills *Sask., Canada* 49°40N 109°30W **297** D7
Cypress Hills *N.Y., U.S.A.* 40°41N 73°53W **132** B2
Cypress Hills ⌂ *Canada* 49°40N 109°30W **297** D7
Cypress Park *U.S.A.* 34°6N 118°13W **126** B3
Cyprus ■ *Asia* 35°0N 33°0E **207** F9
Cyrenaica = Barqa *Libya* 27°0N 23°0E **258** B4
Cyrene *Libya* 32°53N 21°52E **258** B4
Czaplinek *Poland* 53°34N 16°14E **184** E3
Czar *Canada* 52°27N 110°50W **297** C6
Czarna → *Łódzkie, Poland* 51°18N 19°55E **185** G6
Czarna → *Świętokrzyskie, Poland* 50°28N 21°21E **185** H8
Czarna Białostocka
*Poland* 53°18N 23°17E **185** E10
Czarna Woda *Poland* 53°51N 18°6E **184** E5
Czarne *Poland* 53°42N 16°58E **184** E3
Czarnków *Poland* 52°55N 16°38E **185** F3
Czaslau = Čáslav
*Czech Rep.* 49°54N 15°22E **180** B8
Czech Rep. ■ *Europe* 50°0N 15°0E **180** B8
Czechowice-Dziedzice
*Poland* 49°54N 18°59E **185** J5
Czempiń *Poland* 52°9N 16°43E **185** F3

Czeremcha Poland 52°31N 23°21E 185 F10
Czerniejewo Poland 52°26N 17°30E 185 F4
Czernowitz = Chernivtsi Ukraine 48°15N 25°52E 183 B10
Czerniaków Poland 52°11N 21°3E 143 B2
Czersk Poland 53°46N 17°58E 184 E4
Czerwieńsk Poland 52°1N 15°23E 185 F2
Czerwionka-Leszczyny Poland 50°7N 18°37E 185 H5
Częstochowa Poland 50°49N 19°7E 185 H6
Człopa Poland 53°6N 16°6E 185 E3
Człuchów Poland 53°41N 17°22E 184 E4
Czortów = Chortkiv Ukraine 49°2N 25°46E 177 D13
Czyste Poland 52°13N 20°57E 143 B1
Czyżew-Osada Poland 52°48N 22°19E 185 F9

# D

D.C. War Memorial Washington, D.C., U.S.A. 143 b1
D.H.A. Phase VIII Pakistan 24°47N 67°2E 123 B2
Da → Vietnam 21°15N 105°20E 228 G5
Da Hinggan Ling China 48°0N 121°0E 219 B13
Da Lat Vietnam 11°56N 108°25E 237 G7
Da Moóca → Brazil 23°35S 46°35W 137 B2
Da Nang Vietnam 16°4N 108°13E 236 D7
Da Qaidam China 37°50N 95°15E 218 D8
Da Yunhe → Hopei, China 39°10N 117°10E 227 E9
Da Yunhe → Jiangsu, China 34°25N 120°5E 227 H10
Da'an China 45°30N 124°7E 227 B13
Daan Viljoen △ Namibia 22°2S 16°45E 270 B2
Daanbantayan Phil. 11°17N 124°2E 233 F5
Dab'a, Ras el Egypt 31°3N 28°31E 256 H6
Daba Shan China 32°0N 109°0E 228 B7
Dabai Nigeria 11°25N 5°15E 263 C6
Dabajuro Venezuela 11°2N 70°40W 328 A3
Dabakala Ivory C. 8°15N 4°20W 262 D4
Dabaka India 26°7N 92°52E 241 B4
Dabaro Somalia 6°21N 48°43E 267 C6
Dabas Hungary 47°11N 19°19E 182 C4
Dabat Ethiopia 12°58N 37°41E 257 E4
Dabbagh, Jabal Si. Arabia 27°52N 35°45E 246 E2
Dabeiba Colombia 7°1N 76°16W 328 B2
Daber = Dobra Poland 53°34N 15°20E 184 E2
Dabhoi India 22°10N 73°20E 242 H5
Dąbie Poland 52°5N 18°50E 185 F5
Dabie Shan China 31°20N 115°20E 229 B10
Dabilda Cameroon 12°45N 14°35E 259 F2
Dabl, W. → Si. Arabia 29°5N 36°16E 251 J7
Ďáblice Czech Rep. 50°8N 14°29E 135 B2
Dabnou Niger 14°10N 5°22E 263 C6
Dabo Indonesia 0°30S 104°33E 234 C2
Dabola Guinea 10°50N 11°5W 262 C2
Dabou Ivory C. 5°20N 4°23W 262 D4
Daboya Ghana 9°30N 1°20W 263 D4
Dabravolya Belarus 52°55N 23°59E 185 F10
Dąbrowa Poland 52°19N 20°52E 143 B1
Dąbrowa Białostocka Poland 53°40N 23°21E 184 E10
Dąbrowa Górnicza Poland 50°15N 19°10E 185 H6
Dąbrowa Tarnowska Poland 50°10N 20°59E 185 H7
Dabu China 24°22N 116°41E 229 E11
Dabugam India 19°27N 82°26E 244 E6
Dabung Malaysia 5°23N 102°1E 237 K4
Dabus → Ethiopia 10°48N 35°10E 257 E4
Dacato → Ethiopia 7°25N 42°40E 257 F5
Dacca = Dhaka Bangla. 23°43N 90°26E 241 D3
Dachang Jiangsu, China 32°13N 118°45E 229 A12
Dachang Shanghai, China 31°17N 121°24E 138 B1
Dachang ✈ China 31°18N 121°25E 138 B1
Dachaoshan Dam China 24°1N 100°22E 228 E3
Dachau Germany 48°15N 11°26E 131 A1
Dachau-Ost Germany 48°15N 11°27E 131 A1
Dachauer Moos Germany 48°13N 11°27E 131 A1
Dacheng = Tacheng Taiwan 23°51N 120°19E 225 C2
Dachigam △ India 34°10N 75°0E 242 B6
Dachstein, Hoher Austria 47°28N 13°35E 180 D6
Dačice Czech Rep. 49°5N 15°26E 180 B8
Dacre Canada 45°22N 76°57W 312 A8
Dacula U.S.A. 33°59N 83°54W 316 B6
Dadanawa Guyana 2°50N 59°30W 329 C6
Dadar India 19°0N 72°49E 130 A1
Daday Turkey 41°28N 33°27E 212 B5
Dade City U.S.A. 28°22N 82°11W 317 G7
Dadès, Oued → Morocco 30°58N 6°44W 260 B3
Dadeville U.S.A. 32°50N 85°46W 316 C4
Dadhar Pakistan 29°28N 67°39E 242 E2
Dadiya Nigeria 9°35N 11°24E 263 D7
Dadnah U.A.E. 25°32N 56°22E 247 E8
Dadohae △ S. Korea 34°0N 126°0E 224 E3
Dadra = Achalpur India 21°22N 77°32E 244 D3
Dadra & Nagar Haveli □ India 20°5N 73°0E 244 D1
Dadri = Charkhi Dadri India 28°37N 76°17E 242 E7
Dadu Pakistan 26°45N 67°45E 242 F2
Dadu He → China 29°31N 103°46E 228 C4
Daebang S. Korea 37°30N 126°55E 137 B1
Daebudo S. Korea 37°14N 126°35E 224 D3
Daecheongdo S. Korea 37°49N 124°42E 224 D2
Daechi S. Korea 37°30N 127°2E 137 B2
Daegu S. Korea 35°50N 128°37E 224 E4
Daejeon S. Korea 36°20N 127°28E 224 D3
Daejeon □ S. Korea 36°20N 127°25E 224 D3
Daejeong S. Korea 33°8N 126°17E 224 a
Daemodo S. Korea 34°11N 126°45E 224 E3
Daet Phil. 14°2N 122°55E 232 D4
Daeyeonpyeong = Yeonpyeongdo S. Korea 37°40N 125°45E 224 D2
Dafang China 27°9N 105°39E 228 D5
Dafdaf, J. Si. Arabia 28°16N 35°35E 251 K6
Dafeng China 33°3N 120°45E 227 H11
Dafnes Greece 35°13N 25°3E 207 E6
Dafni Athina, Greece 37°55N 23°44E 112 B2
Dafni Peloponnese, Greece 37°48N 22°1E 204 D4
Dafnoudi, Akra Greece 38°28N 20°32E 207 C2
Dağ Turkey 37°12N 30°31E 205 D12
Daga Post South Sudan 9°13N 33°58E 266 C3
Dagali Norway 60°25N 8°28E 164 D5
Dagana Senegal 16°30N 15°35W 262 B1
Dagash Sudan 19°19N 33°25E 256 D3
Dagenham U.K. 51°32N 0°8E 125 A4
Dagestan □ Russia 42°30N 47°0E 191 J8
Dagestanskiye Ogni Russia 42°6N 48°12E 191 J9
Dagg Sd. N.Z. 45°23S 166°45E 285 F1
Daggett U.S.A. 34°52N 116°52W 307 L10
Daghestan Republic = Dagestan □ Russia 42°30N 47°0E 191 J8
Daghfeli Sudan 19°18N 32°40E 256 D3
Daglfing Germany 48°8N 11°39E 131 B2
Dağlıq Qarabağ = Nagorno-Karabakh □ Azerbaijan 39°55N 46°45E 213 C12
Dagö = Hiiumaa Estonia 58°50N 22°45E 188 C2
Dagu China 38°59N 117°40E 227 E9
Dagua Papua N. G. 3°27S 143°20E 286 B2
Daguan China 27°43N 103°56E 228 D4
D'Aguilar Pen. Hong Kong, China 22°13N 114°5E 122 B2
Dagupan Phil. 16°3N 120°20E 232 C3
Daguragu Australia 17°33S 130°30E 278 C5
Daguragu ◎ Australia 17°24S 130°48E 278 C5
Dahab Egypt 28°31N 34°31E 251 K5
Dahab, Gezîret el Egypt 29°59N 31°13E 117 B2
Dahanu India 19°58N 72°44E 244 E1
Daheisha West Bank 31°42N 35°11E 123 B2
Dahivadi India 17°43N 74°33E 244 F2
Dahlak Kebir Eritrea 15°50N 40°10E 257 D5
Dahlak Marine △ Eritrea 15°35N 40°1E 257 D5
Dahlem Germany 52°27N 13°16E 115 B2
Dahlenburg Germany 53°11N 10°44E 178 B6
Dahlonega U.S.A. 34°32N 83°59W 315 D13
Dahlwitz-Hoppegarten Germany 52°30N 13°41E 115 A5
Dahme Germany 51°52N 13°25E 178 D9
Dahod India 22°50N 74°15E 242 H6
Dahomey = Benin ■ Africa 10°0N 2°0E 263 D5
Dahong Shan China 31°25N 113°0E 229 B9
Dahongliutan China 35°45N 79°20E 243 B8
Dahongmen China 39°48N 116°21E 124 C2
Dahra Libya 29°30N 17°50E 258 C3
Dahra Senegal 15°22N 15°30W 262 B1
Dahra, Massif de Algeria 36°7N 1°21E 261 A5
Dahshûr Egypt 29°45N 31°14E 256 J7
Dahu = Tahu Taiwan 24°26N 120°52E 225 B2
Dahūk Iraq 36°50N 43°1E 213 D10
Dahūk □ Iraq 36°50N 42°50E 213 D10
Dahuofan Shuiku China 41°52N 124°12E 224 B2
Dahy, Nafūd ad Si. Arabia 22°0N 45°25E 248 B4
Dai Solomon Is. 7°54S 160°40E 287 L11
Dai Hao Vietnam 18°1N 106°25E 236 C6
Dai-Sen Japan 35°22N 133°32E 222 B5
Dai Shan China 30°25N 122°10E 229 B14
Dai Xian China 39°4N 112°58E 226 E7
Daiba = Odaiba Japan 35°38N 139°47E 140 B3
Daicheng China 38°42N 116°38E 226 E9
Daigo Japan 36°46N 140°21E 223 A12
Daik-u Burma 17°47N 96°40E 241 G6
Daikondi = Dāykondī □ Afghan. 34°0N 66°0E 240 B2
Dailekh Nepal 28°50N 81°44E 243 E9
Daimanji-San Japan 36°14N 133°20E 222 A5
Daimiel Spain 39°5N 3°35W 195 F7
Daingean Ireland 53°18N 7°17W 166 C4
Daingean, An = Dingle Ireland 52°9N 10°17W 166 D1
Daingkog China 32°30N 97°58E 228 A1
Daintree Australia 16°20S 145°20E 280 B4
Daintree △ Australia 16°8S 145°2E 280 B4
Daiō-Misaki Japan 34°15N 136°45E 223 C8
Dair, J. ed Sudan 12°27N 30°42E 257 E3
Dairen = Dalian China 38°50N 121°40E 227 E11
Dairût Egypt 27°34N 30°43E 256 B3
Daisen Japan 39°27N 140°29E 220 E10
Daisen-Oki △ Japan 35°23N 133°34E 222 B5
Daisetsu-Zan Japan 43°30N 142°57E 220 C11
Daisetsu-Zan △ Japan 43°30N 142°55E 220 C11
Daitari India 21°10N 85°46E 244 D7
Daitō Japan 35°19N 132°58E 222 B4
Daiyun Shan China 25°50N 118°15E 229 E12
Dajarra Australia 21°42S 139°30E 280 C2
Dajia = Tachia Taiwan 24°25N 120°28E 225 B2
Dajiaoting China 39°51N 116°27E 114 B2
Dajing China 28°25N 121°5E 229 C13
Dajin Chuan → China 31°16N 101°59E 228 B3
Dak Dam Cambodia 12°20N 107°21E 236 F6
Dak Nhe Vietnam 15°28N 107°48E 236 E6
Dak Pek Vietnam 15°4N 107°44E 236 E6
Dak Song Vietnam 12°19N 107°35E 237 F6
Dak Sui Vietnam 14°55N 107°43E 236 E6
Dakar Senegal 14°34N 17°29W 262 C1
Dakar ✈ Senegal 14°45N 17°20W 262 C1
Dakhal, W. el → Egypt 28°48N 32°47E 251 K3
Dakhin Bangla. 22°30N 90°45E 241 D3
Dakhla W. Sahara 23°50N 15°53W 260 D1
Dakhla, El Wâhât el Egypt 25°30N 28°50E 256 B2
Dakhnoye Russia 59°49N 30°15E 137 C1
Dakingari Nigeria 11°37N 4°1E 263 C5
Dakoank India 7°2N 93°43E 245 L11
Dakor India 22°45N 73°11E 242 H5
Dakoro Niger 14°31N 6°46E 263 C6
Dakota City Iowa, U.S.A. 42°43N 94°12W 310 B2
Dakota City Nebr., U.S.A. 42°25N 96°25W 308 D5
Đakovica = Gjakovë Kosovo 42°22N 20°26E 202 D4
Đakovo Croatia 45°19N 18°24E 182 E3
Dal Norway 59°53N 8°40E 164 E5
Dala Lunda Sul, Angola 11°3S 20°17E 265 E4
Dala Uíge, Angola 8°5S 15°49E 265 D3
Dala Solomon Is. 8°30S 160°41E 287 M11
Dala-Cachibo Angola 10°30S 14°41E 265 E2
Dala-Järna Sweden 60°33N 14°26E 162 D8
Dalaba Guinea 10°47N 12°12W 262 C2
Dalachi China 36°48N 105°0E 226 F3
Dalagan = San Antonio Phil. 14°57N 120°5E 232 D3
Dalaguete Phil. 9°46N 123°32E 233 G4
Dalai Nur China 43°20N 116°45E 226 C9
Dālakī Iran 29°26N 51°17E 247 D6
Dalälven → Sweden 60°12N 16°43E 162 D10
Dalaman Turkey 36°48N 28°47E 205 E10
Dalaman → Turkey 36°41N 28°43E 205 E10
Dalandzadgad Mongolia 43°27N 104°30E 226 C3
Dalanganem Is. Phil. 10°40N 120°17E 233 F3
Dalap-Uliga-Darrit = Majuro Marshall Is. 7°9N 171°12E 288 G9
Dalarna Sweden 61°0N 14°0E 162 D8
Dalarnas län □ Sweden 61°0N 14°15E 162 D8
Dalasýsla Iceland 65°15N 22°0W 155 B4
Dalat Malaysia 2°44N 111°56E 235 B4
Dalay Mongolia 43°28N 103°30E 226 C2
Dālbandīn Pakistan 29°0N 64°23E 240 C2
Dalbeattie U.K. 54°56N 3°50W 167 G5
Dalbeg Australia 20°16S 147°18E 280 C4
Dalbosjön Sweden 58°40N 12°45E 163 F6
Dalby Queens., Australia 27°10S 151°17E 281 D5
Dalby Skåne, Sweden 55°40N 13°22E 163 J7
Dalby Söderskog △ Sweden 55°41N 13°21E 163 J7
Dale Sogn og Fjordane, Norway 61°22N 5°23E 164 C2
Dale Ind., U.S.A. 38°10N 86°59W 311 F10
Dale City U.S.A. 38°38N 77°19W 309 F15
Dale Hollow L. U.S.A. 36°32N 85°27W 315 C12
Dalejsky potok → Czech Rep. 50°2N 14°24E 135 B2
Dalen Norway 59°26N 8°0E 164 E4
Dalet Burma 19°59N 93°51E 241 F4
Daletme Burma 21°36N 92°46E 241 E4
Daleville Ala., U.S.A. 31°19N 85°43W 316 D4
Daleville Ind., U.S.A. 40°7N 85°33W 311 D11
Dalga Egypt 27°39N 30°41E 256 B3
Dalgān Iran 27°31N 59°19E 247 E8
Dalgety Bay U.K. 56°2N 3°20W 121 A1
Dalhart U.S.A. 36°4N 102°31W 314 C3
Dalhousie N.B., Canada 48°5N 66°26W 299 C6
Dalhousie India 32°38N 75°58E 242 C6
Dali Shaanxi, China 34°48N 109°58E 226 G5
Dali Yunnan, China 25°40N 100°10E 228 E3
Dalian China 38°50N 121°40E 227 E11
Daliang Shan China 28°0N 102°45E 228 D4
Daliao = Taliao Taiwan 22°36N 120°23E 225 D2
Dalin = Talin Taiwan 23°36N 120°27E 225 C2
Daling He → China 40°55N 121°40E 227 D11
Dalj Croatia 45°29N 18°59E 182 E3
Dalkeith Midloth., U.K. 55°54N 3°4W 121 B3
Dalkeith Fla., U.S.A. 30°0N 85°9W 316 E4
Dalkey Ireland 53°16N 6°6W 120 B3
Dalkey I. Ireland 53°17N 6°5W 120 B3
Dallas Ga., U.S.A. 33°55N 84°51W 316 B5
Dallas Oreg., U.S.A. 44°55N 123°19W 304 D2
Dallas Tex., U.S.A. 32°47N 96°48W 314 E6
Dallas City U.S.A. 40°38N 91°10W 310 D5
Dalle = Yirga Alem Ethiopia 6°48N 38°22E 257 F4
Dalles, The U.S.A. 45°36N 121°10W 304 D3
Dallgow Germany 52°32N 13°3E 115 A1
Dallol Ethiopia 14°14N 40°17E 257 E5
Dalmā U.A.E. 24°30N 52°20E 247 E7
Dalmacija Croatia 43°20N 17°0E 199 E13
Dalmas, L. Canada 53°30N 71°50W 299 B5
Dalmatia = Dalmacija Croatia 43°20N 17°0E 199 E13
Dalmau India 26°4N 81°2E 243 F9
Dalmellington U.K. 55°19N 4°23W 167 F4
Dalmeny N.S.W., Australia 36°10S 150°8E 283 D9
Dalmeny Edinburgh, U.K. 55°59N 3°22W 121 B1
Dalnegorsk Russia 44°32N 135°33E 220 B7
Dalnerechensk Russia 45°50N 133°40E 220 B6
Dalnevostochnyy □ Russia 67°0N 140°0E 215 C14
Dalny = Dalian China 38°50N 121°40E 227 E11
Daloa Ivory C. 7°0N 6°30W 262 D3
Dalou Shan China 28°15N 107°0E 228 C6
Dalry U.K. 55°42N 4°43W 167 F4
Dalrymple, L. Australia 20°40S 147°0E 280 C4
Dalrymple, Mt. Australia 21°1S 148°39E 280 b
Dals Långed Sweden 58°56N 12°18E 163 F6
Dalsætra Norway 61°28N 9°26E 164 C6
Dalsjöfors Sweden 57°46N 13°5E 163 G7
Dalsland Sweden 58°50N 12°15E 163 F6
Dalsmynni Iceland 64°48N 21°29W 155 C5
Dalston U.K. 51°32N 0°4W 125 A3
Daltenganj India 24°0N 84°4E 243 H11
Dalton Ga., U.S.A. 34°46N 84°58W 315 D12
Dalton Mass., U.S.A. 42°28N 73°11W 313 D11
Dalton Nebr., U.S.A. 41°25N 102°58W 308 E2
Dalton, Kap Greenland 69°25N 24°3W 154 D8
Dalton-in-Furness U.K. 54°10N 3°11W 168 C4
Daludalu Indonesia 1°4N 100°15E 234 B2
Dalupiri I. Cagayan, Phil. 19°5N 121°12E 232 B3
Dalupiri I. N. Samar, Phil. 12°25N 124°16E 232 E5
Dalvík Iceland 65°58N 18°32W 155 B8
Dálvvadis = Jokkmokk Sweden 66°35N 19°50E 160 C18
Dalwallinu Australia 30°17S 116°40E 279 F2
Daly → Australia 13°35S 130°19E 278 B5
Daly City U.S.A. 37°42N 122°27W 136 B2
Daly L. Canada 56°32N 105°39W 297 B7
Daly River Australia 13°46S 130°42E 278 B5
Daly River-Port Keats ◎ Australia 14°13S 129°36E 278 B4
Daly Waters Australia 16°15S 133°24E 280 B1
Dalyan Turkey 36°50N 28°39E 205 E10
Dam Amsterdam, Neths. 112 a2
Dam Doi Vietnam 8°50N 105°12E 237 H5
Dam Ha Vietnam 21°21N 107°36E 236 B6
Damachova Belarus 51°45N 23°36E 185 G10
Damaia Portugal 38°44N 9°12W 126 A1
Daman India 20°25N 72°57E 244 D1
Daman & Diu □ India 20°25N 72°58E 244 D1
Dāmaneh Iran 33°1N 50°29E 247 C6
Damanganga → India 20°25N 72°56E 244 D1
Damanhûr Egypt 31°0N 30°30E 256 H7
Damant L. Canada 61°45N 105°5W 297 A7
Damaq Iran 35°25N 48°49E 213 E13
Damar Indonesia 7°7S 128°40E 231 F7
Damara C.A.R. 4°58N 18°42E 264 B3
Damarakia Greece 37°58N 23°39E 112 B1
Damaraland Namibia 20°0S 15°0E 270 B2
Damascus = Dimashq Syria 33°30N 36°18E 250 E7
Damascus U.S.A. 31°18N 84°43W 316 D5
Damasi Greece 39°43N 22°11E 204 B4
Damaturu Nigeria 11°45N 11°55E 263 C7
Damāvand Iran 35°47N 52°0E 247 C7
Damāvand, Qolleh-ye Iran 35°56N 52°10E 247 C7
Damba Angola 6°44S 15°20E 265 D3
Damboa Nigeria 11°15N 12°55E 259 F2
Dâmboviţa □ Romania 45°0N 25°30E 183 F10
Dâmboviţa → Romania 44°12N 26°26E 183 F11
Dâmbovnic → Romania 44°28N 25°18E 183 F10
Dambrowica = Dubrovytsya Ukraine 51°31N 26°35E 177 C14
Dambulla Sri Lanka 7°51N 80°39E 245 L5
Dame Marie Haiti 18°34N 74°26W 321 C5
Dämeritzsee Germany 52°34N 13°43E 115 B5
Dāmghān Iran 36°10N 54°17E 247 B7
Dămienesti Romania 46°44N 26°59E 183 D11
Damietta = Dumyât Egypt 31°24N 31°48E 251 G2
Daming China 36°15N 115°6E 226 F8
Damīr Qābū Syria 36°58N 41°51E 246 B4
Dammai I. Phil. 5°47N 120°25E 233 J3
Dammam = Ad Dammām Si. Arabia 26°20N 50°5E 247 E6
Dammarie-les-Lys France 48°31N 2°39E 173 D9
Dammartin-en-Goële France 49°3N 2°41E 173 C9
Damme Germany 52°32N 8°11E 178 C4
Damodar → India 23°17N 87°35E 243 H12
Damoh India 23°50N 79°28E 243 H8
Damous Algeria 36°31N 1°42E 261 A5
Dampier Australia 20°41S 116°42E 278 D2
Dampier, Selat Indonesia 0°40S 131°0E 231 E8
Dampier Arch. Australia 20°38S 116°32E 278 D2
Dampier Str. Papua N. G. 5°50S 148°0E 286 C5
Damqawt Yemen 16°34N 52°50E 249 C6
Damrak Amsterdam, Neths. 112 a2
Damrani Algeria 27°45N 2°56W 260 C4
Damrei, Chuor Phnum Cambodia 11°30N 103°0E 237 G4
Damroh India 28°26N 95°14E 241 A5
Damvillers France 49°20N 5°21E 173 C12
Damyang S. Korea 35°19N 126°59E 224 E3
Dan Gorayo Somalia 8°43N 49°20E 267 C6
Dan-Gulbi Nigeria 11°40N 6°15E 263 C6
Dan Ryan Woods U.S.A. 41°44N 87°40W 119 C2
Dan-Sadau Nigeria 11°17N 6°29E 263 C6
Dana Indonesia 11°0S 121°15E 231 F6
Dana Jordan 30°41N 35°37E 250 H6
Dana Nepal 28°32N 83°37E 243 E10
Dana, L. Canada 50°53N 77°20W 298 B4
Dana, Mt. U.S.A. 37°54N 119°12W 306 H7
Danakil Depression Ethiopia 13°10N 41°0E 257 E5
Danakil Desert Ethiopia 12°45N 41°0E 257 E5
Danan Ethiopia 6°31N 43°30E 267 C5
Danané Ivory C. 7°16N 8°9W 262 D3
Danao Phil. 10°31N 124°1E 233 F5
Danau Sentarum △ Indonesia 0°51N 112°6E 235 B4
Danba China 30°54N 101°48E 228 B3
Danbury U.S.A. 41°24N 73°28W 313 E11
Danby L. U.S.A. 34°13N 115°5W 307 L12
Dand Afghan. 31°28N 65°32E 242 D1
Dande → Angola 8°28S 13°21E 265 D2
Dande △ Zimbabwe 15°56S 30°16E 269 F3
Dandeldhura Nepal 29°20N 80°35E 243 E9
Dandeli India 15°5N 74°30E 245 G2
Dandenong Australia 38°0S 145°15E 283 E6
Danderhall U.K. 55°55N 3°7W 121 B3
Danderyd Sweden 59°24N 18°1E 139 A2
Dandī Iran 36°32N 47°37E 213 D12
Dandîl Egypt 29°10N 31°2E 256 J7
Dandong China 40°10N 124°20E 224 B2
Daneborg Greenland 74°18N 20°14W 154 C8
Danfeng China 33°45N 110°25E 226 H6
Danforth Canada 43°43N 79°16W 141 A3
Dangan Liedao China 22°2N 114°8E 229 F10
Dangcagan Phil. 7°36N 125°0E 233 H5
Dange Angola 7°56S 15°3E 265 D3
Dangé-St-Romain France 46°56N 0°36E 174 B4
Dângeni Romania 47°51N 26°58E 183 C11
Danger Is. = Pukapuka Cook Is. 10°53S 165°49W 289 J11
Danger Pt. S. Africa 34°40S 19°17E 270 D2
Dangjin S. Korea 36°53N 126°37E 224 D3
Dangla Ethiopia 11°18N 36°56E 257 E4
Dangla Shan = Tanggula Shan China 32°40N 92°10E 218 E7
Dangora Nigeria 11°30N 8°7E 263 C6
Dangouadougou Burkina Faso 10°9N 4°56W 262 D4
Dangrek, Mts. = Dangrek, Phnom Thailand 14°20N 104°0E 236 E5
Dangrek, Phnom Thailand 14°20N 104°0E 236 E5
Dangriga Belize 17°0N 88°13W 320 C2
Dangshan China 34°27N 116°22E 226 G9
Dangtu China 31°32N 118°25E 229 B12
Dangyang China 30°52N 111°44E 229 B8
Dania Beach U.S.A. 26°3N 80°8W 129 B3
Daniel U.S.A. 42°52N 110°4W 304 E8
Daniel's Harbour Canada 50°13N 57°35W 299 B8
Danielskuil S. Africa 28°11S 23°33E 270 C3
Danielson U.S.A. 41°48N 71°53W 313 E13
Danielsville U.S.A. 34°8N 83°13W 316 A6
Danilov Russia 58°16N 40°13E 188 C11
Danilovgrad Montenegro 42°38N 19°4E 202 D3
Danilovka Russia 50°25N 44°12E 190 E7
Daning China 36°28N 110°45E 226 F6
Danish West Indies = Virgin Is. (U.S.) ☒ W. Indies 18°20N 65°0W 321 C7
Danissa Kenya 3°17N 40°59E 267 D5
Danja Nigeria 11°21N 7°30E 263 C6
Danje-la-Menha Angola 9°32S 14°39E 265 D2
Danjiangkou China 32°31N 111°30E 229 A8
Danjiangkou Shuiku China 32°37N 111°30E 229 A8
Ḑank Oman 23°33N 56°16E 247 F8
Dankalwa Nigeria 11°52N 12°12E 263 C7
Dankama Nigeria 13°20N 7°44E 263 C6
Dankhar Gompa India 32°10N 78°10E 242 C8
Dankov Russia 53°20N 39°5E 188 F10
Danleng China 30°1N 103°31E 228 B4
Danli Honduras 14°4N 86°35W 320 D2
Danmark = Denmark ■ Europe 55°45N 10°0E 163 J3
Danmark Fjord Greenland 81°30N 22°0W 154 A8
Danmarkshavn Greenland 76°45N 18°50W 154 B9
Dannemora U.S.A. 44°43N 73°44W 313 B11
Dannenberg Germany 53°6N 11°5E 178 B7
Dannevirke N.Z. 40°12S 176°8E 284 G5
Dannhauser S. Africa 28°0S 30°3E 271 C5
Danot Ethiopia 7°33N 45°17E 267 C6
Dansalan = Marawi City Phil. 8°0N 124°21E 233 G5
Danshuei = Tanshui Taiwan 25°10N 121°28E 225 A3
Dansville U.S.A. 42°34N 77°42W 312 D7
Danta India 24°11N 72°46E 242 G5
Dantan India 21°57N 87°20E 243 J12
Dante = Xaafuun Somalia 10°25N 51°16E 267 B7
Dantewara India 18°54N 81°21E 244 E5
Danube = Dunărea → Europe 45°20N 29°40E 183 E14
Danubyu Burma 17°15N 95°35E 241 G5
Danvers U.S.A. 42°34N 70°56W 313 D14
Danville Ga., U.S.A. 32°37N 83°15W 316 C6
Danville Ill., U.S.A. 40°8N 87°37W 311 D9
Danville Ind., U.S.A. 39°46N 86°32W 311 E10
Danville Ky., U.S.A. 37°39N 84°46W 311 G12
Danville Pa., U.S.A. 40°58N 76°37W 313 F8
Danville Va., U.S.A. 36°36N 79°23W 309 G14
Danville Vt., U.S.A. 44°25N 72°9W 313 B12
Danyang China 32°0N 119°31E 229 B12
Danzhai China 26°11N 107°48E 228 D6
Danzhou China 19°31N 109°33E 229 a
Danzig = Gdańsk Poland 54°22N 18°40E 184 D5
Dao Antique, Phil. 10°30N 121°57E 233 F3
Dao Capiz, Phil. 11°24N 122°41E 233 F4
Dao Xian China 25°36N 111°31E 229 E8
Daocheng China 29°0N 100°10E 228 C3
Daora W. Sahara 27°5N 12°59W 260 C2
Daoud = Aïn Beïda Algeria 35°50N 7°29E 261 A6
Daoukro Ivory C. 7°10N 3°58W 262 D4
Dapa Phil. 9°46N 126°3E 233 G6
Dapaong Togo 10°55N 0°16E 263 C5
Dapchi Nigeria 12°32N 11°31E 263 C7
Dapiak, Mt. Phil. 8°15N 123°28E 233 G4
Dapitan Phil. 8°39N 123°25E 233 G4
Dapoli India 17°46N 73°11E 244 F1
Daporijo India 27°59N 94°13E 241 B5
Daqahlîya □ Egypt 30°55N 31°30E 251 H2
Daqing China 46°35N 125°0E 219 B13
Daqing Shan China 40°40N 111°0E 226 D6
Daqq-e Sorkh, Kavīr Iran 33°45N 52°50E 247 C7
Daqu Shan China 30°25N 122°20E 229 B14
Dar Banda Africa 8°0N 23°0E 254 F6
Dar el Beida = Casablanca Morocco 33°36N 7°36W 260 B3
Dar es Salaam Tanzania 6°50S 39°12E 268 D4
Dar Mazār Iran 29°14N 57°20E 247 D8
Dar Rounga C.A.R. 0°45N 22°20E 264 A4
Dār Ta'izzah Syria 36°20N 36°52E 250 B7
Dar'ā Syria 32°36N 36°7E 250 F7
Dar'ā □ Syria 32°55N 36°10E 250 F7
Dara Dere = Zlatograd Bulgaria 41°22N 25°7E 203 E9
Dārāb Iran 28°50N 54°30E 247 D7
Daraban Pakistan 31°44N 70°20E 242 D4
Darabani Romania 48°10N 26°39E 183 B11
Darai Hills Papua N. G. 7°8S 143°33E 286 D2
Daraina Madag. 13°12S 49°40E 272 A2
Daraj Libya 30°10N 10°28E 258 B2
Darakeh Iran 35°49N 51°22E 141 A2
Daram Phil. 11°38N 124°48E 233 F5
Dārān Iran 32°59N 50°24E 247 C6
Daravica = Gjeravicë Kosovo 42°32N 20°8E 202 D4
Darawa Egypt 24°22N 32°51E 256 C3
Dārayyā Syria 33°28N 36°15E 250 E7
Darazo Nigeria 11°1N 10°24E 263 C7
Darband Tehrān, Iran 35°49N 51°27E 141 A2
Darband Pakistan 34°20N 72°50E 242 B5
Darband, Kūh-e Iran 31°34N 57°8E 247 D8
Darbhanga India 26°15N 85°55E 243 F11
Darburruk Somalia 9°44N 44°31E 267 C5
Darby, C. U.S.A. 64°19N 162°47W 303 D7
D'Arcy Canada 50°33N 122°29W 296 C4
Darda Croatia 45°40N 18°41E 182 E3
Dardanë Kosovo 42°35N 21°35E 202 D5
Dardanelle Ark., U.S.A. 35°13N 93°9W 314 D8
Dardanelle Calif., U.S.A. 38°20N 119°50W 306 G7
Dardanelles = Çanakkale Boğazı Turkey 40°17N 26°32E 203 F10
Dare → Ethiopia 7°20N 42°11E 257 F5
Darende Turkey 38°31N 37°30E 212 C7
Darent → U.K. 51°28N 0°13E 125 B5
Darfield N.Z. 43°29S 172°7E 285 D7
Darfo-Boario Terme Italy 45°53N 10°11E 198 C7
Dârfûr Sudan 13°40N 24°0E 259 F4
Dargai Pakistan 34°25N 71°55E 242 B4
Dargaville N.Z. 35°57S 173°52E 284 B2
Dargol Niger 13°54N 1°22E 263 C5
Darhan Mongolia 49°37N 106°21E 218 B10
Darhan Muminggan China 41°40N 110°28E 226 D6
Dari South Sudan 5°48N 30°26E 257 F3
Darıca Turkey 40°45N 29°23E 212 B3
Darien U.S.A. 31°23N 81°26W 316 D8
Darién, G. del Colombia 9°0N 77°0W 320 E4
Darién, Serranía del Colombia 8°30N 77°30W 320 E4
Darién △ Panama 7°36N 77°57W 320 E4
Dariganga = Ovoot Mongolia 45°21N 113°45E 226 B7
Daringbadi India 19°54N 84°8E 244 E7
Dario, Palazzo Venice, Italy 142 c2
Darjeeling = Darjiling India 27°3N 88°18E 241 B2
Darjiling India 27°3N 88°18E 241 B2
Darkan Australia 33°20S 116°43E 279 F2
Darke Peak Australia 33°27S 136°12E 282 B2
Darkhana Pakistan 30°39N 72°11E 242 D5
Darkhazīneh Iran 31°54N 48°39E 247 D6
Darkot Pass Pakistan 36°45N 73°26E 243 A5
Darling → Australia 34°4S 141°54E 282 C4
Darling Downs Australia 27°30S 150°30E 281 D5
Darling Harbour Sydney, Australia 139 b1
Darling Point Australia 33°52S 151°15E 139 B2
Darling Ra. Australia 32°30S 116°20E 279 F2
Darlington Durham, U.K. 54°32N 1°33W 168 C6
Darlington Fla., U.S.A. 30°57N 86°3W 316 E3
Darlington S.C., U.S.A. 34°18N 79°52W 315 D15
Darlington Wis., U.S.A. 42°41N 90°7W 310 B6
Darlington □ U.K. 54°32N 1°33W 168 C6
Darlington, L. S. Africa 33°10S 25°9E 270 D4
Darlington Point Australia 34°37S 146°1E 283 C7
Darlot, L. Australia 27°48S 121°35E 279 E3
Darłowo Poland 54°25N 16°25E 184 D3
Dărmăneşti Bacău, Romania 46°21N 26°33E 183 D11
Dărmăneşti Suceava, Romania 47°44N 26°9E 183 C11
Darmstadt Germany 49°51N 8°39E 179 F4
Darnah Libya 32°45N 22°45E 258 B4
Darnah □ Libya 31°0N 23°40E 258 B4
Darnall S. Africa 29°23S 31°18E 271 C5
Darndale Ireland 53°23N 6°12W 120 A2
Darney France 48°5N 6°2E 173 D13
Darnick Australia 32°48S 143°38E 282 B5
Darnley Australia 9°35S 143°46E 280 a
Darnley, C. Antarctica 68°0S 69°0E 151 C6
Darnley B. Canada 69°30N 123°30W 294 D7
Daroca Spain 41°9N 1°25W 196 D3
Daror Ethiopia 8°14N 44°52E 267 C5
Darou-Mousti Senegal 15°3N 16°3W 262 B1
Darr → Australia 23°39S 143°50E 280 C3
Darra Pezu Pakistan 32°19N 70°44E 242 C4
Darran Mts. N.Z. 44°37S 167°59E 285 E2
Darreh Shahr Iran 33°7N 47°22E 213 F12
Darrequeira Argentina 37°42S 63°10W 334 D3
Darrington U.S.A. 48°15N 121°36W 304 B3
Darrūs Iran 35°46N 51°27E 141 A2
Darsah Yemen 12°6N 53°16E 249 D6
Darsana Bangla. 23°35N 88°48E 241 D2
Darsi India 15°46N 79°44E 245 G4
Darsser Ort Germany 54°28N 12°32E 178 A8
Dart → U.K. 50°24N 3°39W 169 G4
Dartford U.K. 51°26N 0°13E 125 B5
Dartmoor Vic., Australia 37°56S 141°19E 282 D4
Dartmoor Devon, U.K. 50°38N 3°57W 169 G4
Dartmoor △ U.K. 50°37N 3°59W 169 G4
Dartmouth N.S., Canada 44°40N 63°30W 299 D7
Dartmouth Devon, U.K. 50°21N 3°36W 169 G4
Dartmouth, L. Queens., Australia 26°4S 145°18E 281 D4
Dartmouth, L. Vic., Australia 36°34S 147°32E 283 D7
Dartuch, C. = Artrutx, C. de Spain 39°55N 3°49E 206 B4
Daru Papua N. G. 9°3S 143°13E 286 E2
Daruvar Croatia 45°35N 17°14E 182 E2
Darvaza = Içoguz Turkmenistan 40°11N 58°24E 216 D5
Darvel, Teluk = Lahad Datu, Telok Malaysia 4°50N 118°20E 235 B5
Darvi Mongolia 46°27N 94°7E 217 C12
Darwen U.K. 53°42N 2°29W 168 D5
Darwendale Zimbabwe 17°41S 30°33E 271 A5
Darwha India 20°15N 77°45E 244 D3
Darwin N. Terr., Australia 12°25S 130°51E 278 B5
Darwin Calif., U.S.A. 36°15N 117°35W 307 J9
Darwin, Mt. Chile 54°47S 69°55W 336 D3
Darwin, Volcán Ecuador 0°10S 91°18W 330 a
Darya Ganj Delhi, India 120 a3
Darya Khan Pakistan 31°48N 71°6E 242 D4
Daryapur India 20°55N 77°20E 244 D3
Daryoi Amu = Amudarya → Uzbekistan 43°58N 59°34E 216 D5
Dās U.A.E. 25°20N 53°30E 247 E7
Dashahe China 42°44N 128°10E 224 A4
Dashen, Ras Ethiopia 13°8N 38°26E 257 E4
Dasher U.S.A. 30°45N 83°13W 316 E6
Dashetai China 41°0N 109°5E 226 D5
Dashi China 23°1N 113°17E 121 B2
Dashiqiao China 40°38N 122°30E 227 D12
Dashkesan = Daşkäsän Azerbaijan 40°25N 46°0E 191 K7
Dashköpri Turkmenistan 36°16N 62°8E 247 B9
Dasht → Pakistan 25°10N 61°40E 240 D1
Dasht-i-Tahlab Pakistan 28°40N 62°25E 240 C1
Dashu = Tashu Taiwan 22°41N 120°25E 225 D2
Daska Pakistan 32°20N 74°20E 242 C6
Daşkäsän Azerbaijan 40°25N 46°0E 191 K7
Dasmariñas Phil. 14°20N 120°56E 232 D3
Daşoguz Turkmenistan 41°49N 59°58E 216 D5
Dasol B. Phil. 15°52N 119°50E 232 C3
Dassa Benin 7°46N 2°14E 263 D5
Dasuya India 31°49N 75°38E 242 D6
Datadian Indonesia 2°1N 115°13E 235 B5
Datansha China 23°8N 113°12E 121 B2
Datça Turkey 36°46N 27°40E 205 E9
Date Japan 42°28N 140°52E 220 C10
Datia India 25°39N 78°27E 243 G8
Datian China 25°40N 117°50E 229 E11
Datong Anhui, China 30°48N 117°44E 229 B11
Datong Qinghai, China 36°20N 102°50E 218 D9
Datong Shanxi, China 40°6N 113°18E 226 D7
Dattakhel Pakistan 32°54N 69°46E 242 C3
Dattapur = Dhamangaon India 20°48N 78°9E 244 D4
Datteln Germany 51°39N 7°21E 178 D3
Datu, Tanjung Indonesia 2°5N 109°39E 235 B3
Datu Piang Phil. 7°2N 124°30E 233 H5
Datuk, Tanjong = Datu, Tanjung Indonesia 2°5N 109°39E 235 B3
Datun China 40°0N 116°23E 114 B2
Daua = Dawa → Africa 4°11N 42°6E 257 G5
Daud Khel Pakistan 32°53N 71°34E 242 C4
Daudnagar India 25°2N 84°24E 243 G11
Daugava → Latvia 57°4N 24°3E 188 C3
Daugavpils Latvia 55°53N 26°32E 188 E4
Daulatabad India 19°57N 75°15E 244 E2
Daulatpur India 28°44N 77°6E 120 A1
Daule Ecuador 1°56S 79°56W 328 D2
Daule → Ecuador 2°10S 79°52W 328 D2
Daule-Peripa, Presa Ecuador 1°0S 79°35W 328 D2
Daulpur India 26°45N 77°59E 242 F7
Daun Germany 50°11N 6°49E 179 E2
Daund India 18°26N 74°40E 244 E2
Daung Kyun Burma 12°13N 98°4E 237 F1
Dauphin Man., Canada 51°9N 100°5W 297 C8
Dauphin Pa., U.S.A. 40°22N 76°56W 312 F8
Dauphin L. Canada 51°20N 99°45W 297 C9
Dauphiné France 45°15N 5°25E 175 C9
Daura Borno, Nigeria 11°31N 11°24E 263 C7
Daura Katsina, Nigeria 13°2N 8°21E 263 C6
Daurada, Costa Spain 41°12N 1°15E 196 D6
Dausa India 26°52N 76°20E 242 F7
Dăvăçi Azerbaijan 41°15N 48°57E 191 K9
Davangere India 14°25N 75°55E 245 G2
Davao Phil. 7°0N 125°40E 233 H5
Davao □ Phil. 7°0N 125°55E 233 H5
Davao del Sur □ Phil. 6°30N 125°25E 233 H5
Davao G. Phil. 6°30N 125°48E 233 H6
Davao Oriental □ Phil. 7°10N 126°30E 233 H6
Dāvar Panāh = Sarāvān Iran 27°25N 62°15E 247 E9
Davenport Calif., U.S.A. 37°1N 122°12W 306 H4
Davenport Fla., U.S.A. 28°10N 81°36W 317 G8
Davenport Iowa, U.S.A. 41°32N 90°35W 310 C6
Davenport Wash., U.S.A. 47°39N 118°9W 304 C4
Davenport Ra. Australia 20°28S 134°0E 280 C1
Davenport Range △ Australia 20°36S 134°22E 280 C1
Daventry U.K. 52°16N 1°10W 169 E6
David Panama 8°30N 82°30W 320 E3
David City U.S.A. 41°15N 97°8W 308 E5
David Glacier Antarctica 75°20S 162°0E 151 D11
David Gorodok = Davyd Haradok Belarus 52°4N 27°8E 177 B14
David's Citadel Jerusalem 123 b3
David's Tomb Jerusalem 123 b3
Davidson Canada 51°16N 105°59W 297 C7
Davidson, Mt. U.S.A. 37°44N 122°27W 136 B2
Davidson Mts. U.S.A. 68°41N 142°22W 303 B12
Davidson's Mains U.K. 55°58N 3°16W 121 B2
Davie U.S.A. 26°3N 80°14W 129 B2
Davis Antarctica 68°34S 77°55E 151 C6
Davis Calif., U.S.A. 38°33N 121°44W 306 G5
Davis Dam U.S.A. 35°12N 114°34W 307 K12
Davis Inlet Canada 55°50N 60°59W 299 A7
Davis Mts. U.S.A. 30°50N 103°55W 314 F3
Davis Sea Antarctica 66°0S 92°0E 151 C7
Davis Str. N. Amer. 65°0N 58°0W 295 D19
Davisboro U.S.A. 32°59N 82°36W 316 C7
Davison U.S.A. 43°2N 83°31W 311 A13
Davlos Cyprus 35°25N 33°54E 207 E9
Davo → Ivory C. 5°0N 6°10W 262 D3
Davos Switz. 46°48N 9°49E 179 J5
Dāvūdīyeh Iran 35°45N 51°25E 141 A2
Davutlar Turkey 37°43N 27°17E 205 D9
Davy L. Canada 58°53N 108°18W 297 B7
Davyd Haradok Belarus 52°4N 27°8E 177 B14
Davydkovo Russia 55°43N 37°29E 129 B1
Dawa → Africa 4°11N 42°6E 257 G5
Dawaki Bauchi, Nigeria 9°25N 9°33E 263 D6
Dawaki Kano, Nigeria 12°5N 8°23E 263 C6
Dawei = Tavoy Burma 14°2N 98°12E 236 E2
Dawes Ra. Australia 24°40S 150°40E 280 C5
Dawidy Poland 52°8N 20°58E 143 C1
Dawkah Oman 18°39N 54°5E 249 C6
Dawley = Telford U.K. 52°40N 2°27W 169 E5
Dawlish U.K. 50°35N 3°28W 169 G4
Dawna Ra. Burma 16°30N 98°30E 236 D2
Dawnyein Burma 15°54N 95°36E 241 G5
Dawqah Si. Arabia 19°36N 40°54E 248 C3
Dawrān Yemen 14°45N 44°12E 248 D4
Dawros Hd. Ireland 54°50N 8°33W 166 B3
Dawson U.S.A. 31°46N 84°27W 316 D5
Dawson, I. Chile 53°50S 70°50W 336 D2
Dawson B. Canada 52°53N 100°49W 297 C8
Dawson City Canada 64°10N 139°30W 294 E4
Dawson Creek Canada 55°45N 120°15W 296 B4
Dawson Inlet Canada 61°50N 93°25W 297 A10
Dawson Ra. Australia 24°30S 149°48E 280 C4
Dawu Hubei, China 31°34N 114°7E 229 B10
Dawu Sichuan, China 30°55N 101°10E 228 B3
Dawwah Oman 20°38N 58°54E 249 B7
Dawwara, Ras id- Malta 35°52N 14°21E 206 F7
Dax France 43°44N 1°3W 174 E2
Daxi = Tach'i Taiwan 24°53N 121°17E 225 B3
Daxian China 31°15N 107°23E 228 B6
Daxin China 22°50N 107°11E 228 F6
Daxindian China 37°30N 120°50E 227 F11
Daxing China 39°47N 116°24E 114 C2
Daxinggou China 43°25N 129°40E 227 C15
Daxue Shan Sichuan, China 30°30N 101°30E 228 B3
Daxue Shan Yunnan, China 23°42N 99°48E 228 F2
Day U.S.A. 30°12N 83°17W 316 E6
Daya el Khadra Mauritania 25°14N 6°2W 260 C3
Dayang He → China 39°51N 123°38E 224 C1
Dayao China 25°43N 101°20E 228 E3
Daye China 30°6N 114°58E 229 B10
Dayet en Naharat Mali 17°39N 3°10W 262 B4
Dayi China 30°41N 103°29E 228 B4
Dāykondī □ Afghan. 34°0N 66°0E 240 B2
Daylesford Australia 37°21S 144°9E 282 D6
Dayong China 29°11N 110°30E 229 C8
Dayr az Zawr Syria 35°20N 40°5E 213 E9
Dayr az Zawr □ Syria 34°50N 40°10E 213 E9
Daysland Canada 52°50N 112°20W 296 C6
Dayton Iowa, U.S.A. 42°16N 94°4W 310 B2
Dayton Nev., U.S.A. 39°14N 119°36W 306 F7
Dayton Ohio, U.S.A. 39°45N 84°12W 311 E12
Dayton Pa., U.S.A. 40°53N 79°15W 312 F5
Dayton Tenn., U.S.A. 35°30N 85°1W 315 D12
Dayton Wash., U.S.A. 46°19N 117°59W 304 C5
Dayton Wyo., U.S.A. 44°53N 107°16W 304 D10
Daytona Beach U.S.A. 29°13N 81°1W 317 F8
Dayu China 25°24N 114°22E 229 E10
Dayuan = Tayuan Taiwan 25°3N 121°11E 225 A3
Dayville U.S.A. 44°28N 119°32W 304 D4
Dazaifu Japan 33°32N 130°32E 222 D2
Dazhu China 30°41N 107°15E 228 B6
Dazkırı Turkey 37°57N 29°52E 205 D11
Dazu China 29°40N 105°42E 228 C5
De Aar S. Africa 30°39S 24°0E 270 D3
De Armanville U.S.A. 33°38N 85°45W 316 B4
De Bary U.S.A. 28°54N 81°18W 317 G8
De Forest U.S.A. 43°15N 89°20W 310 A7
De Funiak Springs U.S.A. 30°43N 86°7W 316 E3
De Grey → Australia 20°12S 119°13E 278 D2
De Haan Belgium 51°16N 3°2E 170 C3
De Hoop △ S. Africa 34°30S 20°28E 270 D3
De Kalb Junction U.S.A. 44°30N 75°16W 313 B9
De Land U.S.A. 29°2N 81°18W 317 F8
De Leon U.S.A. 32°7N 98°32W 314 E5
De Leon Springs U.S.A. 29°7N 81°21W 317 F8
De Long Mts. U.S.A. 68°10N 163°30W 303 B7
De Panne Belgium 51°6N 2°34E 170 C2
De Pere U.S.A. 44°27N 88°4W 308 C9
De Queen U.S.A. 34°2N 94°21W 314 D7
De Quincy U.S.A. 30°27N 93°26W 314 F8
De Ruyters U.S.A. 42°45N 75°53W 313 D9
De Smet U.S.A. 44°23N 97°33W 308 C5
De Soto U.S.A. 38°8N 90°34W 310 F6
De Soto City U.S.A. 27°27N 81°24W 317 H8
De Tour Village U.S.A. 46°0N 83°56W 309 B12
De Witt Ark., U.S.A. 34°18N 91°20W 314 D9
De Witt Iowa, U.S.A. 41°49N 90°33W 310 C6
De Witt Mich., U.S.A. 42°51N 84°34W 311 B12
Dead L. U.S.A. 30°10N 85°10W 316 E4
Dead Sea Asia 31°30N 35°30E 251 G6

**Deadhorse** *U.S.A.* 70°11N 148°27W **303** A10
**Deadman B.** *U.S.A.* 29°30N 83°30W **317** F6
**Deadwood** *U.S.A.* 44°23N 103°44W **308** C2
**Deadwood L.** *Canada* 59°10N 128°30W **296** B3
**Deal** *U.K.* 51°13N 1°25E **169** F9
**Deal I.** *Australia* 39°30S 147°20E **281** F4
**Dealesville** *S. Africa* 28°41S 25°44E **270** C4
**De'an** *China* 29°21N 115°46E **229** C10
**Dean** → *Canada* 52°49N 126°58W **296** C3
**Dean, Forest of** *U.K.* 51°45N 2°33W **169** F5
**Dean Chan.** *Canada* 52°30N 127°15W **296** C3
**Deán Funes** *Argentina* 30°20S 64°20W **334** C3
**Dearborn** *Mich., U.S.A.* 42°19N 83°10W **311** B13
**Dearborn** *Mo., U.S.A.* 39°32N 94°46W **310** E2
**Dease** → *Canada* 59°56N 128°32W **296** B3
**Dease Inlet** *U.S.A.* 71°2N 155°26W **303** A9
**Dease L.** *Canada* 58°40N 130°5W **296** B2
**Dease Lake** *Canada* 58°25N 130°6W **296** B2
**Death Valley** *U.S.A.* 36°15N 116°50W **307** J10
**Death Valley** △ *U.S.A.* 36°29N 117°6W **307** J9
**Death Valley Junction**
*U.S.A.* 36°20N 116°25W **307** J10
**Deatnu = Tana** →
*Norway* 70°30N 28°14E **160** A23
**Deauville** *France* 49°23N 0°2E **172** C7
**Deba** *Spain* 43°18N 2°21W **196** B2
**Deba Habe** *Nigeria* 10°14N 11°20E **263** C7
**Debagram** *India* 23°41N 88°18E **243** H13
**Debak** *Malaysia* 1°34N 111°25E **235** B4
**Debaltsevo** *Ukraine* 48°22N 38°26E **189** H10
**Debao** *China* 23°21N 106°46E **228** F6
**Debar** *Macedonia* 41°31N 20°30E **202** E4
**Debark** *Ethiopia* 13°1N 37°48E **257** E4
**Debden** *Canada* 53°30N 106°50W **297** C7
**Debdou** *Morocco* 33°59N 3°0W **261** B4
**Debe** *Trin. & Tob.* 10°12N 61°27W **323** t
**Dębica** *Poland* 50°2N 21°25E **185** H8
**Dęblin** *Poland* 51°34N 21°50E **185** G8
**Dębno** *Poland* 52°44N 14°41E **185** F1
**Débo, L.** *Mali* 15°14N 4°15W **262** B4
**DeBolt** *Canada* 55°12N 118°1W **296** B5
**Deborah East, L.**
*Australia* 30°45S 119°30E **279** F2
**Deborah West, L.**
*Australia* 30°45S 119°5E **279** F2
**Deboyne Is.** *Papua N. G.* 10°43S 152°22E **286** F7
**Debrc** *Serbia* 44°38N 19°53E **202** B3
**Debre Birhan** *Ethiopia* 9°41N 39°31E **257** F4
**Debre Markos** *Ethiopia* 10°20N 37°40E **257** E4
**Debre May** *Ethiopia* 11°20N 37°25E **257** E4
**Debre Sina** *Ethiopia* 9°51N 39°50E **257** F4
**Debre Tabor** *Ethiopia* 11°50N 38°26E **257** E4
**Debre Zebit** *Ethiopia* 11°48N 38°30E **257** E4
**Debre Zeyit** *Ethiopia* 8°50N 39°0E **257** F4
**Debrecen** *Hungary* 47°33N 21°42E **182** C6
**Debrzno** *Poland* 53°31N 17°14E **184** E4
**Deçan** *Kosovo* 42°30N 20°18E **202** D4
**Decatur** *Ala., U.S.A.* 34°36N 86°59W **315** D11
**Decatur** *Ga., U.S.A.* 33°46N 84°16W **113** B3
**Decatur** *Ill., U.S.A.* 39°51N 88°57W **310** E8
**Decatur** *Ind., U.S.A.* 40°50N 84°56W **311** D12
**Decatur** *Mich., U.S.A.* 42°7N 85°58W **311** B11
**Decatur** *Tex., U.S.A.* 33°14N 97°35W **314** E6
**Decazeville** *France* 44°34N 2°15E **174** D6
**Deccan** *India* 18°0N 79°0E **244** F4
**Deception, Mt.** *Australia* 30°42S 138°16E **282** A3
**Deception B.** *Papua N. G.* 7°45S 144°40E **286** D3
**Deception Bay** *Australia* 27°10S 153°5E **281** D5
**Deception I.** *Antarctica* 63°0S 60°15W **151** C17
**Deception L.** *Canada* 56°33N 104°13W **297** B8
**Dechang** *China* 27°25N 102°11E **228** D4
**Dechhu** *India* 26°46N 72°20E **242** F5
**Decimomannu** *Italy* 39°19N 8°58E **200** C1
**Děčín** *Czech Rep.* 50°47N 14°12E **180** A7
**Decize** *France* 46°50N 3°28E **173** F10
**Deckerville** *U.S.A.* 43°32N 82°44W **312** C2
**Decollatura** *Italy* 39°3N 16°21E **201** C9
**Decorah** *U.S.A.* 43°18N 91°48W **308** D8
**Deda** *Romania* 46°56N 24°50E **183** D9
**Dedaye** *Burma* 16°24N 95°53E **241** G5
**Dedéagach = Alexandroupoli**
*Greece* 40°50N 25°54E **203** F9
**Dededo** *Guam* 13°31N 144°50E **302** d
**Deder** *Ethiopia* 9°19N 41°27E **257** F5
**Dedham** *U.S.A.* 42°15N 71°10W **116** B1
**Dedoplis Tsqaro** *Georgia* 41°33N 46°0E **191** K8
**Dédougou** *Burkina Faso* 12°30N 3°25W **262** C4
**Dedovichi** *Russia* 57°32N 29°56E **188** D5
**Dedza** *Malawi* 14°20S 34°20E **269** E3
**Dee** → *Aberds., U.K.* 57°9N 2°5W **167** D6
**Dee** → *Dumf. & Gall., U.K.* 54°51N 4°3W **167** G4
**Dee** → *Wales, U.K.* 53°22N 3°17W **168** D4
**Deep B.** *Canada* 61°15N 116°35W **296** A5
**Deep Bay = Chilumba**
*Malawi* 10°28S 34°12E **269** E3
**Deep Bay = Shenzhen Wan**
*China* 22°27N 113°55E **219** a
**Deep Lead** *Australia* 37°0S 142°43E **282** D5
**Deep Water B.**
*Hong Kong, China* 22°14N 114°11E **122** B3
**Deepwater** *N.S.W., Australia* 29°25S 151°51E **281** D5
**Deepwater** *Mo., U.S.A.* 38°16N 93°47W **310** F3
**Deer** → *Canada* 58°23N 94°13W **297** B10
**Deer I.** *U.S.A.* 54°55N 162°18W **303** J7
**Deer L.** *Canada* 52°40N 94°20W **297** C10
**Deer Lake** *Nfld. & L., Canada* 49°11N 57°27W **299** C8
**Deer Lake** *Ont., Canada* 52°36N 94°20W **297** C10
**Deer Lodge** *U.S.A.* 46°24N 112°44W **304** C7
**Deer Park** *Fla., U.S.A.* 28°6N 80°54W **317** G9
**Deer Park** *Ohio, U.S.A.* 39°12N 84°23W **311** E12
**Deer Park** *Wash., U.S.A.* 47°57N 117°28W **304** C5
**Deer River** *U.S.A.* 47°20N 93°48W **308** B7
**Deeragun** *Australia* 19°16S 146°33E **280** B4
**Deerfield** *Ill., U.S.A.* 42°10N 87°51W **311** B9
**Deerfield** *Mo., U.S.A.* 37°50N 94°30W **310** G2
**Deerfield Beach** *U.S.A.* 26°19N 80°6W **317** J9
**Deering** *U.S.A.* 66°4N 162°42W **303** C7
**Defensores del Chaco** △
*Paraguay* 20°13S 60°27W **331** E5
**Defiance** *U.S.A.* 41°17N 84°22W **311** C12
**Dega Medo** *Ethiopia* 7°59N 43°1E **267** C5
**Degana** *India* 26°50N 74°20E **242** F6
**Dêgê** *China* 31°44N 98°39E **228** B2
**Degebe** → *Portugal* 38°13N 7°29W **195** G3
**Degeberga** *Sweden* 55°51N 14°5E **163** J8
**Degeh Bur** *Ethiopia* 8°11N 43°31E **267** C5
**Dégelis** *Canada* 47°30N 68°35W **299** C6
**Degema** *Nigeria* 4°50N 6°48E **263** E6
**Degerfors** *Sweden* 59°15N 14°27E **162** E8
**Degerhamn** *Sweden* 56°20N 16°24E **163** H10
**Deggendorf** *Germany* 48°50N 12°57E **179** G8
**Degh** → *Pakistan* 31°3N 73°21E **242** D5
**Değirmendere** *Turkey* 40°42N 29°47E **203** F13
**Degirmenlik = Kythréa**
*Cyprus* 35°15N 33°29E **207** E9
**Degunino** *Russia* 55°52N 37°33E **129** A2
**Deh Bīd** *Iran* 30°39N 53°11E **247** D7
**Deh Dasht** *Iran* 30°47N 50°33E **247** D6
**Deh-e Shīr** *Iran* 31°29N 53°45E **247** D7
**Deh Nugaled = Nugaaleed, Dooxo**
*Somalia* 8°35N 48°35E **267** C6
**Dehaj** *Iran* 30°42N 54°53E **247** D7
**Dehak** *Iran* 27°11N 62°37E **240** D1
**Déhane** *Cameroon* 3°30N 10°5E **264** B2
**Dehdez** *Iran* 31°43N 50°17E **247** D6
**Dehej** *India* 21°44N 72°40E **242** J5
**Dehestān** *Iran* 28°30N 55°35E **247** D7
**Dehgolān** *Iran* 35°17N 47°25E **213** E12
**Dehibat** *Tunisia* 32°0N 10°47E **258** B2
**Dehiwala** *Sri Lanka* 6°50N 79°51E **245** L4
**Dehlorān** *Iran* 32°41N 47°16E **213** F12
**Dehnow-e Kūhestān** *Iran* 27°58N 58°32E **247** E8
**Dehra Dun** *India* 30°20N 78°4E **242** D8
**Dehri** *India* 24°50N 84°15E **243** G11
**Dehua** *China* 25°26N 118°14E **229** E12
**Dehui** *China* 44°30N 125°40E **227** B13
**Deim Zubeir** *South Sudan* 7°49N 26°16E **257** F2
**Deinze** *Belgium* 50°59N 3°32E **170** D3
**Deir al Balah** *Gaza Strip* 31°25N 34°21E **251** G5
**Deir Dibwan** *West Bank* 31°55N 35°16E **123** A2
**Deir Ibzi'e** *West Bank* 31°55N 35°7E **123** A1
**Deira** *U.A.E.* 25°16N 55°18E **119** A2
**Dej** *Romania* 47°10N 23°52E **183** C8
**Deje** *Sweden* 59°35N 13°29E **162** E7
**Dejiang** *China* 28°18N 108°7E **228** C7
**Dejvice** *Czech Rep.* 50°6N 14°23E **135** B2
**Deka** → *Zimbabwe* 18°4S 26°42E **270** A4
**Dekabristov, Ostrov**
*Russia* 59°56N 30°15E **137** B1
**DeKalb** *U.S.A.* 41°56N 88°46W **311** C8
**Dekemhare** *Eritrea* 15°6N 39°0E **257** D4
**Dekese**
*Dem. Rep. of the Congo* 3°24S 21°24E **264** C4
**Dekoa** *C.A.R.* 6°19N 19°4E **264** A3
**Del Caño Rise** *Ind. Oc.* 45°15S 44°15E **273** J3
**Del Carmen** *Phil.* 9°50N 126°0E **233** G6
**Del Mar** *U.S.A.* 32°58N 117°16W **307** N9
**Del Norte** *U.S.A.* 37°41N 106°21W **305** H10
**Del Rey** *U.S.A.* 33°59N 118°25W **126** C2
**Del Rio** *U.S.A.* 29°22N 100°54W **314** G4
**Delai** *Sudan* 17°21N 36°6E **256** D4
**Delambre I.** *Australia* 20°26S 117°5E **278** D2
**Delami** *Sudan* 11°38N 30°23E **257** E3
**Delano** *U.S.A.* 35°46N 119°15W **307** K7
**Delano Peak** *U.S.A.* 38°22N 112°22W **304** G7
**Delārām** *Afghan.* 32°9N 63°25E **240** B1
**Delareyville** *S. Africa* 26°41S 25°26E **270** C4
**Delaronde L.** *Canada* 54°3N 107°3W **297** C7
**Delavan** *Ill., U.S.A.* 40°22N 89°33W **310** D7
**Delavan** *Wis., U.S.A.* 42°38N 88°39W **311** B8
**Delaware** *U.S.A.* 40°18N 83°4W **311** D13
**Delaware** □ *U.S.A.* 39°0N 75°20W **309** F16
**Delaware B.** *U.S.A.* 39°0N 75°10W **309** F16
**Delaware Water Gap** ⌓
*U.S.A.* 41°10N 74°55W **313** E10
**Delay** → *Canada* 56°56N 71°28W **299** A5
**Delbrück** *Germany* 51°46N 8°34E **178** D4
**Delčevo** *Macedonia* 41°58N 22°46E **202** E6
**Delegate** *Australia* 37°4S 148°56E **283** D8
**Delémont** *Switz.* 47°22N 7°20E **179** H3
**Delevan** *U.S.A.* 42°29N 78°29W **312** D6
**Delft** *Neths.* 52°1N 4°22E **170** B4
**Delft I.** *Sri Lanka* 9°30N 79°40E **245** K4
**Delfzijl** *Neths.* 53°20N 6°55E **170** A6
**Delgada, Punta** *Chile* 52°28S 69°32W **336** D3
**Delgado, C.** *Mozam.* 10°45S 40°40E **269** E5
**Delgerhet** *Mongolia* 45°50N 110°30E **226** B6
**Delgo** *Sudan* 20°6N 30°40E **256** C3
**Delhi** *Ont., Canada* 42°51N 80°30W **312** D4
**Delhi** *India* 28°39N 77°13E **120** B2
**Delhi** *La., U.S.A.* 32°28N 91°30W **314** E9
**Delhi** *N.Y., U.S.A.* 42°17N 74°55W **313** D10
**Delhi Gate** *Delhi, India* **120** b3
**Delhi Indira Gandhi Int.** ✈ **(DEL)**
*India* 28°34N 77°5E **120** B1
**Deli Jovan** *Serbia* 44°13N 22°9E **202** B6
**Delia** *Canada* 51°38N 112°23W **296** C6
**Delice** *Turkey* 39°54N 34°2E **212** C6
**Delice** → *Turkey* 40°45N 34°15E **212** B6
**Délices** *Dominica* 15°17N 61°17W **323** k
**Delicias** *Mexico* 28°13N 105°28W **318** B3
**Delījān** *Iran* 33°59N 50°40E **247** C6
**Delimara Point** *Malta* 35°49N 14°34E **206** F8
**Déline** *Canada* 65°11N 123°25W **294** D7
**Delingha** *China* 37°23N 97°23E **218** D8
**Delisle** *Canada* 51°55N 107°8W **297** C7
**Delitzsch** *Germany* 51°31N 12°20E **178** D8
**Deliverance I.** *Australia* 9°31S 141°34E **280** a
**Dell City** *U.S.A.* 31°56N 105°12W **314** F2
**Dell Rapids** *U.S.A.* 43°50N 96°43W **308** D5
**Delle** *France* 47°30N 7°2E **173** E14
**Dellys** *Algeria* 36°57N 3°57E **261** A5
**Delmar** *Iowa, U.S.A.* 42°0N 90°37W **310** C6
**Delmar** *N.Y., U.S.A.* 42°37N 73°47W **313** D11
**Delmenhorst** *Germany* 53°3N 8°37E **178** B4
**Delmiro Gouveia** *Brazil* 9°24S 38°6W **332** C4
**Delnice** *Croatia* 45°23N 14°50E **199** C11
**Delonga, Ostrova**
*Russia* 76°40N 149°20E **215** B15
**Deloraine** *Tas., Australia* 41°30S 146°40E **281** G4
**Deloraine** *Man., Canada* 49°15N 100°29W **297** D8
**Delos = Dilos** *Greece* 37°23N 25°15E **205** D7
**Delphi** *Greece* 38°28N 22°30E **204** C4
**Delphi** *Ind., U.S.A.* 40°36N 86°41W **311** D10
**Delphos** *U.S.A.* 40°51N 84°21W **311** D12
**Delportshoop** *S. Africa* 28°22S 24°20E **270** C3
**Delray Beach** *U.S.A.* 26°28N 80°4W **317** J9
**Delsbo** *Sweden* 61°48N 16°32E **162** C10
**Delta** *Ala., U.S.A.* 33°26N 85°42W **316** B4
**Delta** *Colo., U.S.A.* 38°44N 108°4W **304** G9
**Delta** *Utah, U.S.A.* 39°21N 112°35W **304** G7
**Delta** □ *Nigeria* 5°30N 6°0E **263** D6
**Delta Amacuro** □
*Venezuela* 8°30N 61°30W **329** B5
**Delta del Ebre** ⌓ *Spain* 40°43N 0°43E **196** E5
**Delta del Po** ⌓ *Italy* 44°50N 12°15E **199** D9
**Delta du Saloum** △
*Senegal* 13°42N 16°43W **262** C1
**Delta Dunărea** ⌓
*Romania* 45°15N 29°25E **183** E14
**Delta Junction** *U.S.A.* 64°2N 145°44W **303** D11
**Deltebre** *Spain* 40°43N 0°43E **196** E5
**Deltona** *U.S.A.* 28°54N 81°16W **317** G8
**Delungra** *Australia* 29°39S 150°51E **281** D5
**Delvada** *India* 20°46N 71°2E **242** J4
**Delvinaki** *Greece* 39°57N 20°32E **204** B2
**Delvinë** *Albania* 39°59N 20°6E **202** G4
**Delyatyn** *Ukraine* 48°32N 24°38E **183** B9
**Demagiri** *India* 22°55N 92°28E **241** D4
**Demak** *Indonesia* 6°53S 110°38E **235** D4
**Demanda, Sierra de la**
*Spain* 42°15N 3°0W **196** C2
**Demarcation Pt.** *U.S.A.* 69°41N 141°18W **303** B12
**Demarest** *U.S.A.* 40°57N 73°57W **132** A2
**Demavend = Damāvand, Qolleh-ye**
*Iran* 35°56N 52°10E **247** C7
**Demba**
*Dem. Rep. of the Congo* 5°28S 22°15E **265** D4
**Demba Chio** *Angola* 9°41S 13°41E **265** D2
**Dembecha** *Ethiopia* 10°32N 37°30E **257** E4
**Dembéni** *Comoros Is.* 11°52S 43°23E **272** a
**Dembéni** *Mayotte* 12°50S 45°11E **272** b
**Dembi** *Ethiopia* 8°5N 36°25E **257** F4
**Dembia** *C.A.R.* 4°56N 23°53E **264** B4
**Dembia**
*Dem. Rep. of the Congo* 3°33N 25°48E **268** B2
**Dembica = Dębica** *Poland* 50°2N 21°25E **185** H8
**Dembidolo** *Ethiopia* 8°34N 34°50E **257** F3
**Demchok** *India* 32°42N 79°29E **243** C8
**Demer** → *Belgium* 50°57N 4°42E **170** D4
**Demerara Abyssal Plain**
*Atl. Oc.* 10°0N 48°0W **152** F7
**Demetrias** *Greece* 39°22N 23°1E **204** B5
**Demidov** *Russia* 55°16N 31°30E **188** E6
**Deming** *N. Mex., U.S.A.* 32°16N 107°46W **305** K10
**Deming** *Wash., U.S.A.* 48°50N 122°13W **306** B4
**Demini** → *Brazil* 0°46S 62°56W **329** D5
**Demirci** *Turkey* 39°2N 28°38E **205** B10
**Demirköprü Barajı**
*Turkey* 38°42N 28°25E **205** C10
**Demirköy** *Turkey* 41°49N 27°45E **203** E11
**Demirtas** *Turkey* 36°25N 32°11E **250** B3
**Demmin** *Germany* 53°54N 13°2E **178** B9
**Demnate** *Morocco* 31°44N 6°59W **260** B3
**Democracia** *Brazil* 5°48S 61°26W **331** B5
**Demonte** *Italy* 44°19N 7°17E **198** D4
**Demopolis** *U.S.A.* 32°31N 87°50W **315** E11
**Dempo** *Indonesia* 4°2S 103°15E **234** C2
**Demyansk** *Russia* 57°40N 32°27E **188** D7
**Den Bosch = 's-Hertogenbosch**
*Neths.* 51°42N 5°17E **170** C5
**Den Burg** *Neths.* 53°3N 4°47E **170** A4
**Den Chai** *Thailand* 17°59N 100°4E **236** D3
**Den Haag = 's-Gravenhage**
*Neths.* 52°7N 4°17E **170** B4
**Den Helder** *Neths.* 52°57N 4°45E **170** B4
**Den Ilp** *Neths.* 52°27N 4°55E **112** A2
**Den Lille Havfrue** *Copenhagen, Denmark* **118** a3
**Den Oever** *Neths.* 52°56N 5°2E **170** B5
**Denain** *France* 50°20N 3°22E **173** B10
**Denair** *U.S.A.* 37°32N 120°48W **306** H6
**Denali = McKinley, Mt.**
*U.S.A.* 63°4N 151°0W **303** E10
**Denali** △ *U.S.A.* 63°30N 152°0W **303** E10
**Denau = Denov**
*Uzbekistan* 38°16N 67°54E **217** E7
**Denbigh** *Ont., Canada* 45°8N 77°15W **312** A7
**Denbigh** *Denbs., U.K.* 53°12N 3°25W **168** D4
**Denbigh, C.** *U.S.A.* 64°23N 161°32W **303** D7
**Denbighshire** □ *U.K.* 53°8N 3°22W **168** D4
**Dendang** *Indonesia* 3°7S 107°56E **235** C3
**Dendé = Ndindi** *Gabon* 3°46S 11°9E **264** C2
**Dendermonde** *Belgium* 51°2N 4°5E **170** C4
**Deneba** *Ethiopia* 9°47N 39°10E **257** F4
**Deng Deng** *Cameroon* 5°12N 13°31E **264** A2
**Dengchuan** *China* 25°59N 100°3E **228** E3
**Denge** *Nigeria* 12°52N 5°21E **263** C6
**Dengfeng** *China* 34°25N 113°2E **226** G7
**Dengi** *Nigeria* 9°25N 9°55E **263** D6
**Dengkou** *China* 40°18N 106°55E **226** D4
**Denguélé** □ *Ivory C.* 9°45N 7°30W **262** D3
**Dengzhou** *China* 32°34N 112°4E **229** A9
**Denham** *Australia* 25°56S 113°31E **279** E1
**Denham, Mt.** *Jamaica* 18°13N 77°32W **320** a
**Denham Ra.** *Australia* 21°55S 147°46E **280** C4
**Denham Sd.** *Australia* 25°45S 113°15E **279** E1
**Denholm** *Canada* 52°39N 108°1W **297** C7
**Denia** *Spain* 38°49N 0°8E **197** G5
**Denial B.** *Australia* 32°14S 133°32E **281** E1
**Deniliquin** *Australia* 35°30S 144°58E **283** C6
**Denimoo = Fort Resolution**
*Canada* 61°10N 113°40W **296** A6
**Denis** *Gabon* 0°19N 9°22E **264** B1
**Denison** *Iowa, U.S.A.* 42°1N 95°21W **308** D6
**Denison** *Tex., U.S.A.* 33°45N 96°33W **314** E6
**Denison Plains** *Australia* 18°35S 128°0E **278** C4
**Denīsovka** *Kazakhstan* 52°27N 61°39E **216** B6
**Denistone Heights**
*Australia* 33°48S 151°8E **139** A1
**Deniyaya** *Sri Lanka* 6°21N 80°33E **245** L5
**Denizli** *Turkey* 37°42N 29°2E **205** D11
**Denizli** □ *Turkey* 37°45N 29°5E **205** D11
**Denman** *Australia* 32°24S 150°42E **283** B9
**Denman Glacier**
*Antarctica* 66°45S 100°0E **151** C8
**Denmark** *W. Austral., Australia* 34°59S 117°25E **279** F2
**Denmark** *S.C., U.S.A.* 33°19N 81°9W **316** B8
**Denmark** ■ *Europe* 55°45N 10°0E **163** J3
**Denmark Str.** *Atl. Oc.* 66°0N 30°0W **154** D8
**Dennery** *St. Lucia* 13°55N 60°54W **323** m
**Dennison** *U.S.A.* 40°24N 81°19W **312** F3
**Denny** *U.K.* 56°1N 3°55W **167** E5
**Denov** *Uzbekistan* 38°16N 67°54E **217** E7
**Denpasar** *Indonesia* 8°39S 115°13E **231** K18
**Denpasar** ✈ **(DPS)**
*Indonesia* 8°44S 115°10E **231** K18
**Denton** *Ga., U.S.A.* 31°44N 82°42W **316** D7
**Denton** *Mont., U.S.A.* 47°19N 109°57W **304** C9
**Denton** *Tex., U.S.A.* 33°13N 97°8W **314** E6
**Dentonia Park** *Canada* 43°42N 79°17W **141** A3
**D'Entrecasteaux, Îs.**
*N. Cal.* 18°0S 163°0E **277** D11
**D'Entrecasteaux, Pt.**
*Australia* 34°50S 115°57E **279** F2
**D'Entrecasteaux** △
*Australia* 34°20S 115°33E **279** F2
**D'Entrecasteaux Is.**
*Papua N. G.* 9°0S 151°0E **286** E6
**Dentsville** *U.S.A.* 34°4N 80°58W **316** A9
**Denu** *Ghana* 6°4N 1°8E **263** D5
**Denver** *Colo., U.S.A.* 39°42N 104°59W **304** G11
**Denver** *Ind., U.S.A.* 40°52N 86°5W **311** D10
**Denver** *Iowa, U.S.A.* 42°40N 92°20W **310** B4
**Denver** *Pa., U.S.A.* 40°14N 76°8W **313** F8
**Denver City** *U.S.A.* 32°58N 102°50W **314** E3
**Denwood = Wainwright**
*Canada* 52°50N 110°50W **297** C6
**Deoband** *India* 29°42N 77°43E **242** E7
**Deobhog** *India* 19°53N 82°44E **244** E6
**Deodrug** *India* 16°26N 76°55E **245** F3
**Deogarh** *Odisha, India* 21°32N 84°45E **244** D7
**Deogarh** *Raj., India* 25°32N 73°54E **242** G5
**Deoghar** *India* 24°30N 86°42E **243** G12
**Deogyusan** △ *S. Korea* 35°45N 127°40E **224** E3
**Deokjeokdo** *S. Korea* 37°13N 126°7E **224** D3
**Deolali** *India* 19°58N 73°50E **244** E1
**Deoli = Devli** *India* 25°50N 75°20E **242** G6
**Déols** *France* 46°50N 1°43E **173** F8
**Deora** *India* 26°22N 70°55E **242** F4
**Deorha = Jubbal** *India* 31°5N 77°40E **242** D7
**Deori** *India* 23°24N 79°1E **243** H8
**Deoria** *India* 26°31N 83°48E **243** F10
**Deosai Mts.** *Pakistan* 35°40N 75°0E **243** B6
**Deosri** *India* 26°46N 90°29E **241** B3
**Depalpur** *India* 22°51N 75°33E **242** H6
**DePaul Univ.** *U.S.A.* 41°55N 87°39W **119** B3
**Deposit** *U.S.A.* 42°4N 75°25W **313** D9
**Deptford** *U.K.* 51°28N 0°1W **125** B3
**Depuch I.** *Australia* 20°37S 117°44E **278** D2
**Deputati, Camera dei** *Rome, Italy* **136** b2
**Deputatskiy** *Russia* 69°18N 139°54E **215** C14
**Dêqên** *China* 28°34N 98°51E **228** C2
**Deqing** *China* 23°8N 111°42E **229** F8
**Der-Chantecoq, L. du**
*France* 48°35N 4°40E **173** D11
**Dera, Lach** → *Somalia* 0°15N 42°17E **267** D5
**Dera Ghazi Khan** *Pakistan* 30°5N 70°43E **242** D4
**Dera Ismail Khan**
*Pakistan* 31°50N 70°50E **242** D4
**Derabugti** *Pakistan* 29°2N 69°9E **242** E3
**Derawar Fort** *Pakistan* 28°46N 71°20E **242** E4
**Derbent** *Russia* 42°5N 48°15E **191** J9
**Derbent** *Turkey* 38°11N 28°33E **205** C10
**Derby** *W. Austral., Australia* 17°18S 123°38E **278** C3
**Derby** *Derby City, U.K.* 52°56N 1°28W **168** E6
**Derby** *Conn., U.S.A.* 41°19N 73°5W **313** E11
**Derby** *Kans., U.S.A.* 37°33N 97°16W **308** G5
**Derby** *N.Y., U.S.A.* 42°41N 78°58W **312** D6
**Derby City** □ *U.K.* 52°56N 1°28W **168** E6
**Derby Line** *U.S.A.* 45°0N 72°6W **313** B12
**Derbyshire** □ *U.K.* 53°11N 1°38W **168** D6
**Đerdap** △ *Serbia* 44°40N 22°23E **202** B6
**Derdepoort** *S. Africa* 24°38S 26°24E **270** B4
**Derecske** *Hungary* 47°20N 21°33E **182** C6
**Dereham** *U.K.* 52°41N 0°57E **169** E8
**Dereköy** *Turkey* 41°55N 27°21E **203** E11
**Dereli** *Turkey* 40°44N 38°26E **213** B8
**Derg** → *U.K.* 54°44N 7°26W **166** B4
**Derg, L.** *Ireland* 53°0N 8°20W **166** D3
**Dergachi = Derhaci**
*Ukraine* 50°9N 36°11E **189** G9
**Derhaci** *Ukraine* 50°9N 36°11E **189** G9
**Deridder** *U.S.A.* 30°51N 93°17W **314** F8
**Derik** *Turkey* 37°21N 40°18E **213** D9
**Derinkuyu** *Turkey* 38°22N 34°45E **212** C6
**Dermantsi** *Bulgaria* 43°8N 24°17E **203** C8
**Dermott** *U.S.A.* 33°32N 91°26W **314** E9
**Dernière Rivière** *St. Lucia* 13°57N 60°55W **323** m
**Dêrong** *China* 28°44N 99°9E **228** C2
**Derri** *Somalia* 4°20N 46°37E **267** D6
**Derrinallum** *Australia* 37°57S 143°15E **282** D5
**Derry = Londonderry** *U.K.* 55°0N 7°20W **166** B4
**Derry = Londonderry** □
*U.K.* 55°0N 7°20W **166** B4
**Derry** *N.H., U.S.A.* 42°53N 71°19W **313** D13
**Derry** *Pa., U.S.A.* 40°20N 79°18W **312** F5
**Derryveagh Mts.** *Ireland* 54°56N 8°11W **166** B3
**Derudub** *Sudan* 17°31N 36°7E **256** D4
**Derval** *France* 47°40N 1°41W **172** E5
**Derveni** *Greece* 38°8N 22°25E **204** C4
**Derventa** *Bos.-H.* 44°59N 17°55E **182** F2
**Derwent** → *Cumb., U.K.* 54°39N 3°33W **168** C4
**Derwent** → *Derby, U.K.* 52°57N 1°28W **168** E6
**Derwent** → *N. Yorks., U.K.* 53°45N 0°58W **168** D7
**Derwent Water** *U.K.* 54°35N 3°9W **168** C4
**Derzhavīnsk** *Kazakhstan* 51°6N 66°19E **217** B7
**Des Moines** *Iowa, U.S.A.* 41°35N 93°37W **310** C3
**Des Moines** *N. Mex., U.S.A.* 36°46N 103°50W **305** H12
**Des Moines** *Wash., U.S.A.* 47°24N 122°19W **306** C4
**Des Moines** → *U.S.A.* 40°23N 91°25W **310** D5
**Des Moines** ✈ **(DSM)**
*U.S.A.* 41°32N 93°40W **310** C3
**Des Plaines** *U.S.A.* 42°2N 87°54W **311** B9
**Des Plaines** → *U.S.A.* 41°23N 88°15W **311** C8
**Desa** *Romania* 43°52N 23°2E **182** G8
**Desaguadero** *Peru* 16°34S 69°3W **330** D4
**Desaguadero** →
*Argentina* 34°30S 66°46W **334** C2
**Desaguadero** → *Bolivia* 16°35S 69°5W **330** D4
**Desantne** *Ukraine* 45°34N 29°32E **183** E14
**Désappointement, Is. du**
*French Polynesia* 14°10S 141°20W **289** f
**Desaru** *Malaysia* 1°31N 104°17E **237** d
**Descanso, Pta.** *Mexico* 32°21N 117°3W **307** N9
**Descartes** *France* 46°59N 0°42E **174** B4
**Deschaillons-sur-St-Laurent**
*Canada* 46°32N 72°7W **299** C5
**Deschambault L.** *Canada* 54°50N 103°30W **297** C8
**Deschutes** → *U.S.A.* 45°38N 120°55W **304** D3
**Descobrimento** △ *Brazil* 16°53S 39°21W **333** E4
**Dese** *Ethiopia* 11°5N 39°40E **257** E4
**Deseado, C.** *Chile* 52°45S 74°42W **336** D2
**Desenzano del Garda**
*Italy* 45°28N 10°32E **198** C7
**Deseronto** *Canada* 44°12N 77°3W **312** B7
**Desert Center** *U.S.A.* 33°43N 115°24W **307** M11
**Desert Hot Springs**
*U.S.A.* 33°58N 116°30W **307** M10
**Desert Wetlands Park**
*U.S.A.* 36°7N 115°2W **124** B2
**Desertas, Ilhas** *Madeira* 32°30N 16°30W **260** B1
**Deset** *Norway* 61°20N 11°26E **164** C8
**Desfina** *Greece* 38°25N 22°31E **204** C4
**Deshaies** *Guadeloupe* 16°18N 61°47W **322** e
**Deshauteur** *Guadeloupe* 16°15N 61°25W **322** e
**Deshnok** *India* 27°48N 73°21E **242** F5
**Desierto Central de Baja**
**California** ⌓ *Mexico* 29°40N 114°50W **318** B2
**Desjardins, Complexe** *Montréal, Canada* **130** b2
**Deskati** *Greece* 39°55N 21°49E **202** G5
**Desna** → *Ukraine* 50°33N 30°32E **177** C16
**Desnătui** → *Romania* 43°53N 23°35E **183** G8
**Desolación, I.** *Chile* 53°0S 74°0W **336** D2
**Despeñaperros, Paso**
*Spain* 38°24N 3°30W **195** G7
**Despeñaperros** ⌓ *Spain* 38°23N 3°32W **195** G7
**Despotiko** *Greece* 36°57N 24°58E **204** E6
**Despotovac** *Serbia* 44°6N 21°30E **202** B5
**Dessau** *Germany* 51°51N 12°14E **178** D8
**Dessye = Dese** *Ethiopia* 11°5N 39°40E **257** E4
**Destin** *U.S.A.* 30°24N 86°30W **317** E3
**D'Estrees B.** *Australia* 35°55S 137°45E **282** C2
**Desuri** *India* 25°18N 73°35E **242** G5
**Desvres** *France* 50°40N 1°48E **173** B8
**Det Udom** *Thailand* 14°54N 105°5E **236** E5
**Deta** *Romania* 45°24N 21°13E **182** E6
**Dete** *Zimbabwe* 18°38S 26°50E **270** A4
**Đetinja** → *Serbia* 43°51N 20°5E **202** C4
**Detmold** *Germany* 51°56N 8°52E **178** D4
**Detour, Pt.** *U.S.A.* 45°40N 86°40W **308** C10
**Detroit** *U.S.A.* 42°19N 83°12W **312** D1
**Detroit Lakes** *U.S.A.* 46°49N 95°51W **308** B6
**Detroit Metropolitan Wayne**
**County** ✈ **(DTW)**
*U.S.A.* 42°13N 83°21W **311** B13
**Detskoye Selo = Pushkin**
*Russia* 59°45N 30°25E **188** C6
**Dettifoss** *Iceland* 65°48N 16°24W **155** B10
**Detva** *Slovak Rep.* 48°34N 19°25E **181** C12
**Deua** △ *Australia* 35°32S 149°46E **283** C8
**Deurne** *Neths.* 51°27N 5°49E **170** C5
**Deutsch = Przemyśl**
*Poland* 49°50N 22°45E **185** J9
**Deutsch Brod = Havlíčkův Brod**
*Czech Rep.* 49°36N 15°33E **180** B8
**Deutsch-Eylau = Iława**
*Poland* 53°36N 19°34E **184** E6
**Deutsch Krone = Wałcz**
*Poland* 53°17N 16°27E **185** E3
**Deutsch-Luxemburgischer** ⌓
*Germany* 49°58N 6°12E **179** F2
**Deutsche Bucht** *Germany* 54°15N 8°0E **178** A4
**Deutsche Oper** *Germany* 52°30N 13°19E **115** A2
**Deutsches Museum**
*Germany* 48°7N 11°35E **131** B2
**Deutschland = Germany** ■
*Europe* 51°0N 10°0E **178** E6
**Deutschlandsberg** *Austria* 46°49N 15°14E **180** E8
**Deux-Sèvres** □ *France* 46°35N 0°20W **172** F6
**Deva** *Romania* 45°53N 22°55E **182** E7
**Devakottai** *India* 9°55N 78°45E **245** K4
**Devaprayag** *India* 30°13N 78°35E **243** D8
**Devarkonda** *India* 16°42N 78°56E **244** F4
**Dévaványa** *Hungary* 47°2N 20°59E **182** C5
**Deveci Dağları** *Turkey* 40°6N 36°15E **212** B7
**Devecikonağı** *Turkey* 39°55N 28°34E **203** G12
**Devecser** *Hungary* 47°6N 17°26E **182** C2
**Develi** *Turkey* 38°23N 35°29E **212** C6
**Deventer** *Neths.* 52°15N 6°10E **170** B6
**Devereux** *U.S.A.* 33°13N 83°5W **316** B6
**Deveron** → *U.K.* 57°41N 2°32W **167** D6
**Devesel** *Romania* 44°28N 22°41E **182** F7
**Devgad I.** *India* 14°48N 74°5E **245** G2
**Devgadh Bariya** *India* 22°40N 73°55E **242** H5
**Devgarh** *India* 16°23N 73°23E **245** F1
**Devi** → *India* 19°59N 86°24E **244** E8
**Devikot** *India* 26°42N 71°12E **242** F4
**Devil River Pk.** *N.Z.* 40°56S 172°37E **285** A7
**Devil's Bridge** *Antigua & B.* 17°6N 61°41W **322** b
**Devils Den** *U.S.A.* 35°46N 119°58W **306** K7
**Devils Hole = Death Valley** △
*U.S.A.* 36°29N 117°6W **307** J9
**Devils Island, I. = Diable, Île du**
*Fr. Guiana* 5°16N 52°34W **329** B7
**Devils Lake** *U.S.A.* 48°7N 98°52W **308** A4
**Devils Paw** *Canada* 58°47N 134°0W **296** B2
**Devil's Peak** *S. Africa* 33°57S 18°27E **118** A1
**Devils Postpile** ⌓ *U.S.A.* 37°37N 119°5W **306** H7
**Devil's Pt.** *Sri Lanka* 9°26N 80°6E **245** K5
**Devils Tower** *U.S.A.* 44°35N 104°42W **304** D11
**Devils Tower** △ *U.S.A.* 44°48N 104°55W **304** D11
**Devil's Woodyard Mud Volcano**
*Trin. & Tob.* 10°16N 61°22W **323** t
**Devin** *Bulgaria* 41°44N 24°24E **203** E8
**Devine** *U.S.A.* 29°8N 98°54W **314** G5
**Devipattinam** *India* 9°29N 78°54E **245** K4
**Devizes** *U.K.* 51°22N 1°58W **169** F6
**Devli** *India* 25°50N 75°20E **242** G6
**Devnya** *Bulgaria* 43°13N 27°33E **203** C11
**Devoll** → *Albania* 40°57N 20°15E **202** F4
**Devon** *Canada* 53°24N 113°44W **296** C6
**Devon** □ *U.K.* 50°50N 3°40W **169** G4
**Devon I.** *Canada* 75°10N 85°0W **295** B15
**Devonport** *Australia* 41°10S 146°22E **281** G4
**Devrek** *Turkey* 41°13N 31°57E **212** B4
**Devrekâni** *Turkey* 41°36N 33°50E **212** B5
**Devrez** → *Turkey* 41°6N 34°25E **212** B6
**Devrukh** *India* 17°3N 73°37E **244** F1
**Dewas** *India* 22°59N 76°3E **242** H7
**Dewetsdorp** *S. Africa* 29°33S 26°39E **270** C4
**Dewey** *Puerto Rico* 18°18N 65°18W **321** b
**Dexing** *China* 28°46N 117°30E **229** C11
**Dexter** *Maine, U.S.A.* 45°1N 69°18W **309** C19
**Dexter** *Mich., U.S.A.* 42°20N 83°53W **311** B13
**Dexter** *Mo., U.S.A.* 36°48N 89°57W **308** G9
**Dexter** *N. Mex., U.S.A.* 33°12N 104°22W **305** K11
**Dey-Dey, L.** *Australia* 29°12S 131°4E **279** E5
**Deyang** *China* 31°3N 104°27E **228** B5
**Deyhūk** *Iran* 33°15N 57°30E **247** C8
**Deyyer** *Iran* 27°55N 51°55E **247** E6
**Dez** → *Iran* 31°39N 48°52E **213** F13
**Dezadeash L.** *Canada* 60°28N 136°58W **296** A1
**Dezfūl** *Iran* 32°20N 48°30E **213** F13
**Dezhneva, Mys** *Russia* 66°5N 169°40W **215** C19
**Dezhou** *China* 37°26N 116°18E **226** F9
**Dhadhar** → *India* 24°56N 85°24E **243** G11
**Dhahabān** *Si. Arabia* 21°58N 39°3E **248** B2
**Dhahiriya = Az̧ Z̧āhirīyah**
*West Bank* 31°25N 34°58E **251** G5
**Dhahran = Az̧ Z̧ahrān**
*Si. Arabia* 26°10N 50°7E **247** E6
**Dhak** *Pakistan* 32°25N 72°33E **242** C5
**Dhaka** *Bangla.* 23°43N 90°26E **241** D3
**Dhaka** □ *Bangla.* 24°25N 90°25E **241** C3
**Dhakuria** *India* 22°30N 88°22E **124** B2
**Dhali** *Cyprus* 35°1N 33°25E **207** E9
**Dhamangaon** *India* 20°48N 78°9E **244** D4
**Dhamār** *Yemen* 14°30N 44°20E **248** D4
**Dhamār** □ *Yemen* 14°30N 44°20E **248** D4
**Dhampur** *India* 29°19N 78°33E **243** E8
**Dhamra** → *India* 20°47N 86°58E **244** D8
**Dhamtari** *India* 20°42N 81°35E **244** D5
**Dhanbad** *India* 23°50N 86°30E **243** H12
**Dhangarhi** *Nepal* 28°55N 80°40E **243** E9
**Dhankuta** *Nepal* 26°55N 87°40E **243** F12
**Dhanora** *India* 20°20N 80°22E **244** D5
**Dhanpuri** *India* 23°13N 81°30E **244** C5
**Dhanushkodi** *India* 9°11N 79°24E **245** K4
**Dhar** *India* 22°35N 75°26E **242** H6
**Dharampur** *India* 22°13N 75°18E **242** H6
**Dharamsala = Dharmsala**
*India* 32°16N 76°23E **242** C7
**Dharan** *Nepal* 26°49N 87°17E **243** F12
**Dharangaon** *India* 21°1N 75°16E **244** D2
**Dharapuram** *India* 10°45N 77°34E **245** J3
**Dharavi** *India* 19°1N 72°51E **130** A2
**Dhari** *India* 21°42N 71°2E **242** J4
**Dhariwal** *India* 31°57N 75°19E **242** D6
**Dharla** → *Bangla.* 25°46N 89°42E **243** G13
**Dharmanagar** *India* 24°22N 92°10E **241** C4
**Dharmapuri** *India* 12°10N 78°10E **245** H4
**Dharmavaram** *India* 14°29N 77°44E **245** G3
**Dharmjaygarh** *India* 22°28N 83°13E **243** H10
**Dharmsala** *India* 32°16N 76°23E **242** C7
**Dharni** *India* 21°33N 76°53E **242** J7
**Dharug** △ *Australia* 33°20S 151°2E **283** B9
**Dharur** *India* 18°3N 76°8E **244** E3
**Dharwad** *India* 15°30N 75°4E **245** G2
**Dhasan** → *India* 25°48N 79°24E **243** G8
**Dhaulagiri** *Nepal* 28°39N 83°28E **243** E10
**Dhebar, L.** *India* 24°10N 74°0E **242** G6
**Dheftera** *Cyprus* 35°5N 33°16E **207** E9
**Dhemaji** *India* 27°29N 94°35E **241** B5
**Dhenkanal** *India* 20°45N 85°35E **244** D7
**Dherinia** *Cyprus* 35°3N 33°57E **207** E9
**Dheskáti = Deskati**
*Greece* 39°55N 21°49E **202** G5
**Dhī Qār** □ *Iraq* 31°0N 46°15E **246** D5
**Dhiarrizos** → *Cyprus* 34°41N 32°34E **207** F8
**Dhībān** *Jordan* 31°30N 35°46E **251** G6
**Dhilwan** *India* 31°31N 75°21E **242** D6
**Dhimarkhera** *India* 23°28N 80°22E **243** H9
**Dholka** *India* 22°44N 72°29E **242** H5
**Dhomokós = Domokos**
*Greece* 39°10N 22°18E **204** B4
**Dhond = Daund** *India* 18°26N 74°40E **244** E2
**Dhone** *India* 15°25N 77°53E **245** E3
**Dhoraji** *India* 21°45N 70°37E **242** J4
**Dhorpatan** *Nepal* 28°29N 83°4E **243** E10
**Dhragonísi = Tragonhsi**
*Greece* 37°27N 25°29E **205** D7
**Dhrangadhra** *India* 22°59N 71°31E **242** H4
**Dhrol** *India* 22°33N 70°25E **242** H4
**Dhubāb** *Yemen* 12°56N 43°25E **248** D3
**Dhuburi** *India* 26°2N 89°59E **241** B2
**Dhulasar** *Bangla.* 21°52N 90°14E **241** E3
**Dhule** *India* 20°58N 74°50E **244** D2
**Dhupdhara** *India* 26°10N 91°4E **241** B3
**Dhurbo** *Somalia* 11°37N 50°20E **267** B7
**Dhuusamarreeb** *Somalia* 5°30N 46°15E **267** C6
**Di-ib, W.** → *Sudan* 22°38N 36°6E **256** C4
**Di Linh** *Vietnam* 11°35N 108°4E **237** G7
**Di Linh, Cao Nguyen**
*Vietnam* 11°30N 108°0E **237** G7
**Dia** *Greece* 35°28N 25°14E **207** E6
**Dia Deva = Butcher I.**
*India* 18°57N 72°53E **130** B2
**Diabakania** *Guinea* 10°38N 10°58W **262** C2
**Diable, Île du** *Fr. Guiana* 5°16N 52°34W **329** B7
**Diable, Pte. du** *Martinique* 14°46N 60°53W **322** j
**Diables, Morne aux**
*Dominica* 15°37N 61°27W **323** k
**Diablo Pt.** *N. Marianas* 15°0N 145°35E **302** e
**Diablo Range** *U.S.A.* 37°20N 121°25W **306** J5
**Diablotins, Morne**
*Dominica* 15°30N 61°24W **323** k
**Diadema** *Brazil* 23°41S 46°37W **137** C2
**Diafarabé** *Mali* 14°9N 4°57W **262** C4
**Diala** *Mali* 14°10N 9°58W **262** C3
**Dialakoro** *Mali* 12°18N 7°54W **262** C3
**Dialakoto** *Senegal* 13°21N 13°19W **262** C2
**Diallassagou** *Mali* 13°47N 3°41W **262** C4
**Diamant, Pte. du** *Martinique* 14°27N 61°3W **322** j
**Diamant, Rocher du**
*Martinique* 14°27N 61°2W **322** j
**Diamante** *Argentina* 32°5S 60°40W **334** C3
**Diamante** *Italy* 39°41N 15°49E **201** C8
**Diamante** → *Argentina* 34°30S 66°46W **334** C2
**Diamantina** *Brazil* 18°17S 43°40W **333** E3
**Diamantina** → *Australia* 26°45S 139°10E **281** D2
**Diamantina** △ *Australia* 23°33S 141°23E **280** C3
**Diamantino** *Brazil* 14°30S 56°30W **331** C6
**Diamond Bar** *U.S.A.* 34°1N 117°48W **307** L9
**Diamond Harbour** *India* 22°11N 88°14E **243** H13
**Diamond Head** *U.S.A.* 21°16N 157°49W **302** K14
**Diamond I.** *Grenada* 12°20N 61°35W **323** q
**Diamond Is.** *Australia* 17°25S 151°5E **280** B5
**Diamond Mts.** *U.S.A.* 39°40N 115°50W **304** G6
**Diamond Springs** *U.S.A.* 38°42N 120°49W **306** G6
**Diamou** *Mali* 14°5N 11°16W **262** C2
**Dian Chi** *China* 24°50N 102°43E **228** E4
**Dianalund** *Denmark* 55°32N 11°30E **163** J5
**Diana's Peak** *St. Helena* 15°58S 5°42W **153** h
**Dianbai** *China* 21°33N 111°0E **229** G8
**Diancheng** *China* 21°30N 111°4E **229** G8
**Dianjiang** *China* 30°24N 107°20E **228** B6
**Diano Marina** *Italy* 43°54N 8°5E **198** E5
**Dianópolis** *Brazil* 11°38S 46°50W **333** D2
**Dianra** *Ivory C.* 8°45N 6°14W **262** D3
**Diaoyu Dao = Senkaku-Shotō**
*E. China Sea* 25°45N 123°30E **221** M1
**Diaoyu Tai = Senkaku-Shotō**
*E. China Sea* 25°45N 123°30E **221** M1
**Diapaga** *Burkina Faso* 12°5N 1°46E **263** C5
**Diapangou** *Burkina Faso* 12°5N 0°10E **263** C5
**Diariguila** *Guinea* 10°35N 10°2W **262** C2
**Diavolo, Mt.** *India* 12°40N 92°56E **245** H11
**Diba = Dibbā al Ḩişn**
*U.A.E.* 25°45N 56°16E **247** E8
**Dibagah** *Iraq* 35°52N 43°48E **213** E10
**Dibai** *India* 28°13N 78°15E **242** E8
**Dibaya**
*Dem. Rep. of the Congo* 6°30S 22°57E **265** D4
**Dibaya-Lubue**
*Dem. Rep. of the Congo* 4°12S 19°54E **265** C3
**Dibbā al Ḩişn** *U.A.E.* 25°45N 56°16E **247** E8
**Dibbeen** △ *Jordan* 32°20N 35°45E **251** F6
**Dibella** *Niger* 17°32N 13°6E **259** E2
**D'Iberville, Lac** *Canada* 55°55N 73°15W **298** A5
**Dibete** *Botswana* 23°45S 26°32E **270** B4
**Dibi** *Cameroon* 7°8N 13°43E **264** A2
**Dibru-Saikhowa** △ *India* 27°40N 95°25E **241** B5
**Dibrugarh** *India* 27°29N 94°55E **241** B5
**Diciosânmartin = Târnăveni**
*Romania* 46°19N 24°13E **183** D9
**Dickens** *U.S.A.* 33°37N 100°50W **314** E4
**Dickeyville** *U.S.A.* 42°38N 90°36W **310** B6
**Dickinson** *U.S.A.* 46°53N 102°47W **308** B2
**Dickinson B.** *Antigua & B.* 17°10N 61°51W **322** b
**Dick's Pt.** *Bahamas* 25°4N 77°18W **153** b
**Dickson = Dikson** *Russia* 73°40N 80°5E **214** B9
**Dickson** *U.S.A.* 36°5N 87°23W **315** C11
**Dickson City** *U.S.A.* 41°28N 75°36W **313** E9
**Dicle Barajı** *Turkey* 38°20N 40°11E **213** C9
**Dicle Nehri** → *Turkey* 37°44N 41°10E **213** D9
**Dicomano** *Italy* 43°53N 11°31E **199** E8
**Didesa, W.** → *Ethiopia* 10°2N 35°32E **257** E4
**Didiéni** *Mali* 13°53N 8°6W **262** C3
**Didim** *Turkey* 37°22N 27°16E **205** D9
**Didimbo** *Angola* 17°30S 21°45E **265** F4
**Didimoticho** *Greece* 41°22N 26°29E **203** E10
**Didsbury** *Canada* 51°35N 114°10W **296** C6
**Didwana** *India* 27°23N 74°36E **242** F6
**Die** *France* 44°47N 5°22E **175** D9
**Diébougou** *Burkina Faso* 11°0N 3°15W **262** C4
**Diecke** *Guinea* 7°27N 8°54W **262** D3
**Diedenhofen = Thionville**
*France* 49°20N 6°10E **173** C13
**Diefenbaker, L.** *Canada* 51°0N 106°55W **297** C7
**Diegen** *Belgium* 50°53N 4°26E **116** A2
**Diego de Almagro** *Chile* 26°22S 70°3W **334** B1
**Diego Garcia** *Ind. Oc.* 7°50S 72°50E **273** E6
**Diego Martin** *Trin. & Tob.* 10°43N 61°34W **323** t
**Diego Ramírez, Islas** *Chile* 56°30S 68°44W **336** E3
**Diego Suarez = Antsiranana**
*Madag.* 12°25S 49°20E **272** A2
**Diekirch** *Lux.* 49°52N 6°10E **170** E6
**Diéma** *Mali* 14°32N 9°12W **262** C3
**Diembéring** *Senegal* 12°29N 16°47W **262** C1
**Diemelsee** ⌓ *Germany* 51°20N 8°40E **178** D4
**Diemen** *Neths.* 52°21N 4°58E **112** A2
**Dien Ban** *Vietnam* 15°53N 108°16E **236** E7
**Dien Bien Phu** *Vietnam* 21°20N 103°0E **228** G4
**Dien Chau, Vinh** *Vietnam* 19°0N 105°55E **236** C5
**Dien Khanh** *Vietnam* 12°15N 109°6E **237** F7
**Diepholz** *Germany* 52°37N 8°22E **178** C4
**Diepkloof** *S. Africa* 26°14S 27°57E **123** B1
**Dieppe** *France* 49°54N 1°4E **172** C8
**Dieppe Bay Town**
*St. Kitts & Nevis* 17°25N 62°48W **322** d
**Dieprivier** *S. Africa* 34°2S 18°27E **118** B1
**Dierks** *U.S.A.* 34°7N 94°1W **314** D7
**Diest** *Belgium* 50°58N 5°4E **170** D5
**Dieterich** *U.S.A.* 39°4N 88°23W **311** E8
**Dietikon** *Switz.* 47°24N 8°24E **179** H4
**Dieulefit** *France* 44°32N 5°4E **175** D9
**Dieuze** *France* 48°49N 6°43E **173** D13
**Dievenow = Dziwnów**
*Poland* 54°2N 14°45E **184** D1
**Dif** *Somalia* 0°59N 40°58E **267** D5
**Diffa** *Niger* 13°18N 12°36E **263** C7
**Diffa** □ *Niger* 14°0N 12°30E **263** C7
**Differdange** *Lux.* 49°31N 5°54E **170** E5
**Diffun** *Phil.* 16°36N 121°33E **232** C3
**Dig** *India* 27°28N 77°20E **242** F7
**Digba** *Dem. Rep. of the Congo* 4°25N 25°48E **268** B2
**Digboi** *India* 27°23N 95°38E **241** B5
**Digby** *Canada* 44°38N 65°50W **299** D6
**Digges Is.** *Canada* 62°40N 77°50W **295** E16
**Diggi** *India* 26°22N 75°26E **242** F6
**Dighinala** *Bangla.* 23°15N 92°5E **241** D4
**Dighton** *U.S.A.* 38°29N 100°28W **308** F3
**Digity Mud Volcanoes**
*Trin. & Tob.* 10°12N 61°25W **323** t
**Diglur** *India* 18°34N 77°33E **244** E3
**Digna** *Mali* 14°48N 8°10W **262** C3
**Digne-les-Bains** *France* 44°5N 6°12E **175** D10
**Digoin** *France* 46°29N 4°1E **173** F11
**Digor** *Turkey* 40°22N 43°25E **213** B10
**Digos** *Phil.* 6°45N 125°20E **233** H5
**Digranes** *Iceland* 66°4N 14°44W **155** A12
**Digras** *India* 20°6N 77°45E **244** D3
**Digul** → *Indonesia* 7°7S 138°42E **231** F9
**Digya** △ *Ghana* 7°15N 0°5E **263** D5
**Dihang = Brahmaputra** →
*Asia* 23°40N 90°35E **241** D3
**Diinsoor** *Somalia* 2°24N 42°59E **267** D5
**Dijlah, Nahr** → *Asia* 31°0N 47°25E **246** D5
**Dijon** *France* 47°20N 5°3E **173** E12
**Dikhil** *Djibouti* 11°8N 42°20E **257** E5
**Dikili** *Turkey* 39°4N 26°53E **205** B8
**Dikirnis** *Egypt* 31°6N 31°35E **256** H7
**Dikkil = Dikhil** *Djibouti* 11°8N 42°20E **257** E5
**Dikodougou** *Ivory C.* 9°4N 5°45W **262** D3
**Diksmuide** *Belgium* 51°2N 2°52E **170** C2
**Dikson** *Russia* 73°40N 80°5E **214** B9
**Dikti Oros** *Greece* 35°8N 25°30E **207** E6
**Dikwa** *Nigeria* 12°4N 13°30E **263** C7
**Dila** *Ethiopia* 6°21N 38°22E **257** F4
**Dilasag** *Phil.* 16°25N 122°11E **232** C4
**Dilbeek** *Belgium* 50°51N 4°17E **116** A1
**Dilek Yarimadisi** △
*Turkey* 37°40N 27°10E **205** D9
**Dili** *E. Timor* 8°39S 125°34E **231** F7

Diligent Strait India 12°11N 92°57E 245 H11
Dilijan Armenia 40°46N 44°57E 191 K7
Dilinata Greece 38°13N 20°31E 207 C2
Dilj Croatia 45°29N 18°1E 182 E3
Dillenburg Germany 50°43N 8°17E 178 E4
Dilley U.S.A. 28°40N 99°10W 314 G5
Dilli = Delhi India 28°39N 77°13E 120 B2
Dilli Mali 15°1N 7°40W 262 C3
Dillia → Niger 14°9N 12°50E 259 F2
Dilling Sudan 12°3N 29°35E 257 E2
Dillingen Bayern, Germany 48°36N 10°30E 179 G6
Dillingen Saarland, Germany 49°22N 6°43E 179 F2
Dillingham U.S.A. 59°3N 158°28W 303 G8
Dillon Sask., Canada 55°56N 108°35W 297 B7
Dillon Mont., U.S.A. 45°13N 112°38W 304 D7
Dillon S.C., U.S.A. 34°25N 79°22W 315 D15
Dillon → Canada 55°56N 108°56W 297 B7
Dillsboro U.S.A. 39°1N 85°4W 311 E11
Dillsburg U.S.A. 40°7N 77°2W 312 F7
Dilolo Dem. Rep. of the Congo 10°28S 22°18E 265 E4
Dilos Greece 37°23N 25°15E 205 D7
Dilove Ukraine 47°56N 24°11E 183 C9
Dimapur India 25°54N 93°45E 241 C4
Dimas Mexico 23°43N 106°47W 318 C3
Dimasalang Phil. 12°12N 123°51E 232 E4
Dimashq Syria 33°30N 36°18E 250 E7
Dimashq □ Syria 33°30N 36°30E 250 E7
Dimbaza S. Africa 32°50S 27°14E 271 D4
Dimbelenge Dem. Rep. of the Congo 5°33S 23°7E 265 D4
Dimbokro Ivory C. 6°45N 4°46W 262 D4
Dimboola Australia 36°28S 142°7E 282 D5
Dîmbovița = Dâmbovița → Romania 44°12N 26°26E 183 F11
Dimbulah Australia 17°8S 145°4E 280 B4
Dimitrovgrad Bulgaria 42°5N 25°35E 203 D9
Dimitrovgrad Russia 54°14N 49°39E 190 C9
Dimitrovgrad Serbia 43°2N 22°48E 202 C6
Dimitrovo = Pernik Bulgaria 42°35N 23°2E 202 D7
Dimitsana Greece 37°36N 22°3E 204 D4
Dimmitt U.S.A. 34°33N 102°19W 314 D3
Dimo South Sudan 5°19N 29°10E 257 F2
Dimona Israel 31°2N 35°1E 251 G6
Dimonika ⌓ Congo 4°13S 12°21E 264 C2
Dimovo Bulgaria 43°43N 22°50E 202 C6
Dinagat □ Phil. 10°0N 125°35E 233 F5
Dinagat I. Phil. 10°10N 125°40E 233 F5
Dinaig Phil. 7°11N 124°10E 233 H5
Dinajpur Bangla. 25°33N 88°43E 241 C2
Dinalupihan Phil. 14°52N 120°28E 232 D3
Dinan France 48°28N 2°2W 172 D4
Dīnān Āb Iran 32°4N 56°49E 247 C8
Dinant Belgium 50°16N 4°55E 170 D4
Dinapur India 25°38N 85°5E 243 G11
Dinar Turkey 38°5N 30°10E 205 C12
Dīnār, Kūh-e Iran 30°42N 51°46E 247 D6
Dinara Planina Croatia 44°0N 16°30E 199 D13
Dinard France 48°38N 2°6W 172 D4
Dinaric Alps = Dinara Planina Croatia 44°0N 16°30E 199 D13
Dinas Phil. 7°38N 123°20E 233 H4
Dinbych-y-Pysgod = Tenby U.K. 51°40N 4°42W 169 F3
Dindanko Mali 14°8N 9°30W 262 C3
Dinde Angola 14°17S 13°42E 265 E2
Dinder, Nahr ed → Sudan 14°6N 33°40E 257 E3
Dinder △ Sudan 12°30N 35°10E 257 E4
Dindi → India 16°24N 78°15E 245 F4
Dindigul India 10°25N 78°0E 245 J4
Dindori India 22°57N 81°5E 243 H9
Ding Xian = Dingzhou China 38°30N 114°59E 226 E8
Dinga Dem. Rep. of the Congo 5°17S 16°42E 265 D3
Dinga Pakistan 25°26N 67°10E 242 G2
Dingalan Phil. 15°18N 121°25E 232 D3
Dingalan B. Phil. 15°18N 121°25E 232 D3
Ding'an China 19°42N 110°19E 229 a
Dingbian China 37°35N 107°32E 226 F4
Dingelstädt Germany 51°18N 10°19E 178 D6
Dingle Kerry, Ireland 52°9N 10°17W 166 D1
Dingle Sweden 58°32N 11°35E 163 F5
Dingle B. Ireland 52°3N 10°20W 166 D1
Dingle Pen. Ireland 52°12N 10°5W 166 D1
Dingli Malta 35°52N 14°23E 206 F7
Dingmans Ferry U.S.A. 41°13N 74°55W 313 E10
Dingnan China 24°45N 115°0E 229 E10
Dingo Australia 23°38S 149°19E 280 C4
Dingolfing Germany 48°37N 12°30E 179 G8
Dingras Phil. 18°6N 120°42E 232 B3
Dingtao China 35°5N 115°35E 226 G8
Dinguiraye Guinea 11°18N 10°49W 262 C2
Dingwall U.K. 57°36N 4°26W 167 D4
Dingxi China 35°30N 104°33E 226 G3
Dingxiang China 38°30N 112°58E 226 E7
Dingyuan China 32°32N 117°41E 229 A11
Dingzhou China 38°30N 114°59E 226 E8
Dinh, Mui Vietnam 11°22N 109°1E 237 G7
Dinh Lap Vietnam 21°33N 107°6E 228 G6
Dinhata India 26°8N 89°27E 241 B2
Dinin → Ireland 52°43N 7°18W 166 D4
Dinira △ Venezuela 9°57N 70°6W 328 B3
Dinokwe Botswana 23°29S 26°37E 270 B4
Dinorwic Canada 49°41N 92°30W 297 D10
Dinosaur ⌓ Alta., Canada 50°47N 111°30W 296 C6
Dinosaur ⌓ Colo., U.S.A. 40°30N 108°45W 304 F9
Dinuba U.S.A. 36°32N 119°23W 306 J7
Diö Sweden 56°37N 14°15E 163 H8
Dioïla Mali 12°23N 6°50W 262 C3
Dioka Mali 14°57N 10°4W 262 C2
Diomede U.S.A. 65°47N 169°0W 303 D5
Diona Chad 17°51N 22°36E 259 E4
Diongoï Mali 14°38N 8°34W 262 C3
Dionisades Greece 35°20N 26°10E 207 E7
Dionysos, Theatro Athens, Greece 112 c2
Diósgyör Hungary 48°7N 20°43E 182 B5
Diosig Romania 47°18N 22°2E 182 C7
Diougani Mali 14°19N 2°44W 262 C4
Diouloulou Senegal 13°5N 16°38W 262 C1
Dioura Mali 14°59N 5°12W 262 C3
Diourbel Senegal 14°39N 16°12W 262 C1
Diourbel □ Senegal 14°45N 16°15W 262 C1
Dipaculao Phil. 15°51N 121°32E 232 D3
Dipalpur Pakistan 30°40N 73°39E 242 D5
Diphu India 25°50N 93°26E 241 C4
Dipkarpaz = Rizokarpaso Cyprus 35°36N 34°23E 207 E10
Diplo Pakistan 24°35N 69°35E 242 G3
Dipolog Phil. 8°36N 123°20E 233 G4
Dipperu △ Australia 21°56S 148°42E 280 C4
Dipton N.Z. 45°54S 168°22E 285 F3
Dir Pakistan 35°8N 71°59E 240 B3
Diré Mali 16°20N 3°25W 262 B4
Dire Dawa Ethiopia 9°35N 41°45E 257 F5
Dirfis Oros Greece 38°40N 23°54E 204 C5
Diriamba Nic. 11°51N 86°19W 320 D2
Dirico Angola 17°50S 20°42E 265 F4
Dirk Hartog I. Australia 25°50S 113°5E 279 E1
Dirkou Niger 19°1N 12°53E 259 E2
Dirnismaning Germany 48°13N 11°38E 131 A2
Dirranbandi Australia 28°33S 148°17E 281 D4
Dirs Si. Arabia 18°32N 42°5E 248 C3
Dirschau = Tczew Poland 54°8N 18°50E 184 D5
Disa India 24°18N 72°10E 242 G5
Disa Sudan 12°5N 34°15E 257 E3
Disappointment, C. U.S.A. 46°18N 124°5W 306 D2
Disappointment, L. Australia 23°20S 122°40E 278 D3
Disaster B. Australia 37°15S 149°58E 283 D8
Discovery B. Vic., Australia 38°10S 140°40E 282 E4
Discovery B. Hong Kong, China 22°18N 114°1E 122 B2
Discovery Bay △ Australia 38°9S 141°16E 282 E4
Discovery Seamount Atl. Oc. 42°0S 0°10E 152 L12
Disentis Muster Switz. 46°42N 8°50E 179 J4
Dishna Egypt 26°9N 32°32E 256 B3
Disina Nigeria 11°35N 9°50E 263 C6
Disko = Qeqertarsuaq Greenland 69°45N 53°30W 154 D5
Disko Bugt Greenland 69°10N 52°0W 154 D5
Disna = Dzisna → Belarus 55°34N 28°12E 188 E5
Disney-M.G.M. Studios U.S.A. 28°21N 81°33W 133 B1
Disney Reef Tonga 19°17S 174°7W 287 P13
Disney Studios U.S.A. 34°9N 118°19W 126 B3
Disneyland Hong Kong China 22°19N 114°2E 122 B2
Disneyland Tōkyō Tokyo, Japan 35°37N 139°53E 140 B4
Dispur India 26°3N 91°52E 241 B3
Diss U.K. 52°23N 1°7E 169 E9
Disteghil Sar Pakistan 36°20N 75°12E 243 A6
District of Columbia □ U.S.A. 38°55N 77°0W 309 F15
Distrito Federal □ Brazil 15°45S 47°45W 333 E2
Distrito Federal □ Mexico 19°15N 99°10W 319 D5
Distrito Federal □ Venezuela 10°30N 66°55W 328 A4
Disûq Egypt 31°8N 30°35E 256 H7
Ditan Park Beijing, China 114 a2
Diu India 20°45N 70°58E 242 J4
Diuata Mts. Phil. 9°0N 125°50E 233 G5
Dīvāndarreh Iran 35°55N 47°2E 213 E12
Divarata Greece 38°20N 20°33E 207 C2
Divenié Congo 2°43S 12°1E 264 C2
Dives → France 49°18N 0°7W 172 C6
Dives-sur-Mer France 49°18N 0°8W 172 C6
Divi Pt. India 15°59N 81°9E 245 G5
Divichi = Däväçi Azerbaijan 41°15N 48°57E 191 K9
Divide U.S.A. 45°45N 112°45W 304 D7
Dividing Ra. Australia 27°45S 116°0E 279 E2
Divilican B. Phil. 17°21N 122°19E 232 C4
Divinópolis Brazil 20°10S 44°54W 333 F3
Divisões, Serra dos Brazil 17°0S 51°0W 333 E1
Divjake Albania 41°0N 19°32E 202 F3
Divnoye Russia 45°55N 43°21E 191 H6
Divo Ivory C. 5°48N 5°15W 262 D3
Divriği Turkey 39°22N 38°7E 213 C8
Dīwāl Kol Afghan. 34°23N 67°52E 242 B2
Dix → U.S.A. 37°49N 84°43W 311 G12
Dix-Huit Montagnes □ Ivory C. 7°30N 7°40W 262 D3
Dixie Mt. U.S.A. 39°55N 120°16W 306 F6
Dixie Union U.S.A. 31°20N 82°28W 316 D7
Dixmoor U.S.A. 41°37N 87°41W 119 D2
Dixon Calif., U.S.A. 38°27N 121°49W 306 G5
Dixon Ill., U.S.A. 41°50N 89°29W 310 C7
Dixon Mo., U.S.A. 37°59N 92°6W 310 G4
Dixon Entrance U.S.A. 54°30N 132°0W 303 J14
Dixville Canada 45°4N 71°46W 313 A13
Diyadin Turkey 39°33N 43°40E 213 C10
Diyālá □ Iraq 33°45N 44°50E 246 C5
Diyālá → Iraq 33°13N 44°30E 213 F11
Diyarb Nigm Egypt 30°45N 31°26E 251 H2
Diyarbakır Turkey 37°55N 40°18E 213 D9
Diyarbakır □ Turkey 38°0N 40°10E 213 D9
Diyodar India 24°8N 71°50E 242 G4
Dizangué Cameroon 3°46N 9°59E 264 B1
Dja ⌓ Cameroon 3°10N 12°58E 264 B2
Djadié → Gabon 0°46N 12°58E 264 B2
Djado Niger 21°4N 12°14E 259 D2
Djado, Plateau du Niger 21°29N 12°21E 259 D2
Djakarta = Jakarta Indonesia 6°9S 106°52E 122 A2
Djalma Dutra = Miguel Calmon Brazil 11°26S 40°36W 332 D3
Djalma Dutra = Poções Brazil 14°31S 40°21W 333 D3
Djamâa Algeria 33°32N 5°59E 261 B6
Djamba Angola 16°45S 13°58E 265 F2
Djambala Congo 2°32S 14°30E 264 C2
Djanet Algeria 24°35N 9°32E 261 D6
Djaul I. Papua N. G. 2°58S 150°57E 286 B6
Djawa = Jawa Indonesia 7°0S 110°0E 235 D4
Djebel Tazzeka △ Morocco 34°6N 4°11W 260 B4
Djebiniana Tunisia 35°1N 11°0E 258 A2
Djédaa Chad 13°31N 18°34E 259 F3
Djelfa Algeria 34°40N 3°15E 261 B5
Djelfa □ Algeria 34°20N 3°40E 261 B5
Djema C.A.R. 6°3N 25°15E 264 A5
Djember Chad 10°25N 17°50E 259 F3
Djembo Dem. Rep. of the Congo 9°54S 22°18E 265 D4
Djémila Algeria 36°19N 5°44E 261 A6
Djendel Algeria 36°15N 2°25E 261 A5
Djenné Mali 14°0N 4°30W 262 C4
Djenoun, Garet el Algeria 25°4N 5°31E 261 C6
Djerba Tunisia 33°48N 10°54E 258 B2
Djerba, Î. de Tunisia 33°50N 10°48E 258 B2
Djeréme → Cameroon 5°20N 13°24E 264 A2
Djerid, Chott Tunisia 33°42N 8°30E 258 B1
Djermaya Chad 12°24N 15°3E 259 F3
Djibo Burkina Faso 14°9N 1°35W 263 C4
Djibouti Djibouti 11°30N 43°5E 257 E5
Djibouti ■ Africa 12°0N 43°0E 257 E5
Djohong Cameroon 6°47N 14°20E 264 A2
Djolu Dem. Rep. of the Congo 0°35N 22°5E 264 B4
Djouab → Gabon 1°13N 13°12E 264 B2
Djoudj △ Senegal 16°24N 16°14W 262 B1
Djougou Benin 9°40N 1°45E 263 D5
Djoum Cameroon 2°41N 12°35E 264 B2
Djouna Chad 10°27N 20°4E 259 F4
Djugu Dem. Rep. of the Congo 1°55N 30°35E 268 B3
Djukbinj △ Australia 12°11S 131°2E 278 B5
Djúpavík Iceland 65°57N 21°34W 155 B5
Djúpivogur Iceland 64°39N 14°17W 155 C12
Djupvasshytta Norway 62°2N 7°16E 164 B4
Djurås Sweden 60°34N 15°8E 162 D9
Djurdjura △ Algeria 36°20N 4°15E 261 A5
Djurö △ Sweden 58°52N 13°28E 163 F7
Djursholm Sweden 59°24N 18°5E 139 A2
Djursland Denmark 56°27N 10°45E 163 H4
Dmitriya Lapteva, Proliv Russia 73°0N 140°0E 215 B15
Dmitriyev Lgovskiy Russia 52°10N 35°0E 189 F8
Dmitriyevsk = Makiyivka Ukraine 48°0N 38°0E 189 H9
Dmitriyevskoye = Talas Kyrgyzstan 42°30N 72°13E 217 D8
Dmitrov Russia 56°25N 37°32E 188 D9
Dmitrovsk-Orlovskiy Russia 52°29N 35°10E 189 F8
Dnepr = Dnipro → Ukraine 46°30N 32°18E 189 J7
Dneprodzerzhinsk = Dniprodzerzhynsk Ukraine 48°32N 34°37E 189 H8
Dneprodzerzhinskoye Vdkhr. = Dniprodzerzhynske Vdskh. Ukraine 48°49N 34°8E 189 H8
Dnepropetrovsk = Dnipropetrovsk Ukraine 48°30N 35°0E 189 H8
Dneprorudnoye = Dniprorudne Ukraine 47°21N 34°58E 189 J8
Dnestr = Dnister → Europe 46°18N 30°17E 177 E16
Dnestrovski = Belgorod Russia 50°35N 36°35E 189 G9
Dnieper = Dnipro → Ukraine 46°30N 32°18E 189 J7
Dniester = Dnister → Europe 46°18N 30°17E 177 E16
Dnipro → Ukraine 46°30N 32°18E 189 J7
Dniprodzerzhynsk Ukraine 48°32N 34°37E 189 H8
Dniprodzerzhynske Vdskh. Ukraine 48°49N 34°8E 189 H8
Dnipropetrovsk Ukraine 48°30N 35°0E 189 H8
Dnipropetrovsk □ Ukraine 48°15N 34°50E 189 H8
Dniprorudne Ukraine 47°21N 34°58E 189 J8
Dnister → Europe 46°18N 30°17E 177 E16
Dnistrovskyy Lyman Ukraine 46°15N 30°17E 189 J6
Dno Russia 57°50N 29°58E 188 D5
Dnyapro = Dnipro → Ukraine 46°30N 32°18E 189 J7
Do Gonbadān = Gachsārān Iran 30°15N 50°45E 247 D6
Doabi Afghan. 36°1N 69°32E 240 A3
Doaktown Canada 46°33N 66°8W 299 C6
Doan Hung Vietnam 21°30N 105°10E 228 G5
Doany Madag. 14°21S 49°30E 272 A2
Doba Chad 8°40N 16°50E 259 G3
Dobandi Pakistan 31°13N 66°50E 242 D2
Dobbiaco Italy 46°44N 12°14E 199 B9
Dobbyn Australia 19°44S 140°2E 280 B3
Dobczyce Poland 49°52N 20°5E 185 J7
Dobele Latvia 56°37N 23°16E 184 B10
Dobele □ Latvia 56°35N 23°5E 184 B10
Döbeln Germany 51°6N 13°7E 178 D9
Doberai, Jazirah Indonesia 1°25S 133°0E 231 E8
Döberitz Germany 52°32N 13°3E 115 A1
Dobiegniew Poland 52°59N 15°45E 185 F2
Doblas Argentina 37°5S 64°0W 334 D3
Döbling Austria 48°14N 16°20E 142 A2
Dobo Dem. Rep. of the Congo 2°20N 22°11E 264 B4
Dobo Indonesia 5°45S 134°15E 231 F8
Doboj Bos.-H. 44°46N 18°4E 182 F3
Dobong S. Korea 37°39N 127°2E 137 B2
Dobongsan S. Korea 37°40N 127°0E 137 A2
Dobra Wielkopolskie, Poland 51°55N 18°37E 185 G5
Dobra Zachodnio-Pomorskie, Poland 53°34N 15°20E 184 E2
Dobra Dâmbovita, Romania 44°52N 25°40E 183 F10
Dobra Hunedoara, Romania 45°54N 22°36E 182 E7
Dobre Miasto Poland 53°58N 20°26E 184 E7
Dobreşti Romania 46°51N 22°18E 182 D7
Dobrich Bulgaria 43°37N 27°49E 203 C11
Dobrich □ Bulgaria 43°37N 27°49E 203 C11
Dobrinishta Bulgaria 41°49N 23°34E 202 E7
Dobříš Czech Rep. 49°46N 14°10E 180 B7
Dobrodzień Poland 50°45N 18°25E 185 H5
Dobromyl Ukraine 49°34N 22°46E 185 J9
Dobron Ukraine 48°25N 22°23E 182 B7
Dobropole Ukraine 48°25N 37°2E 189 H9
Dobrovolsk Russia 54°46N 22°31E 184 D9
Dobruja Europe 44°30N 28°15E 183 F13
Dobrush Belarus 52°25N 31°22E 177 B16
Dobrzany Poland 53°22N 15°25E 184 E2
Dobrzyń nad Wisłą Poland 52°39N 19°22E 185 F6
Doc, Mui Vietnam 17°58N 106°30E 236 D6
Doc Can I. Phil. 5°55N 119°56E 233 J2
Doce → Brazil 19°37S 39°49W 333 E4
Docker River = Kaltukatjara Australia 24°52S 129°5E 279 D4
Docklands U.K. 51°30N 0°1W 125 A3
Docksta Sweden 63°3N 18°18E 162 A12
Doctor Arroyo Mexico 23°40N 100°11W 318 C4
Doctor Pedro P. Peña Paraguay 22°27S 62°21W 331 E5
Doctor Phillips U.S.A. 28°26N 81°29W 133 B2
Doctors Inlet U.S.A. 30°6N 81°47W 316 E8
Doda India 33°10N 75°34E 243 C6
Doda, L. Canada 49°25N 75°13W 298 C4
Doda Betta India 11°24N 76°44E 245 J3
Dodballapur India 13°18N 77°32E 245 H3
Dodder → Ireland 53°20N 6°13W 120 B1
Dodecanese = Dodekanisa Greece 36°35N 27°0E 205 E8
Dodekanisa Greece 36°35N 27°0E 205 E8
Dodge City U.S.A. 37°45N 100°1W 308 G3
Dodge L. Canada 59°50N 105°36W 297 B7
Dodger Stadium U.S.A. 34°4N 118°14W 126 B3
Dodgeville U.S.A. 42°58N 90°8W 310 B6
Dodo Cameroon 7°30N 12°3E 263 D7
Dodo South Sudan 5°10N 29°57E 257 F2
Dodola Ethiopia 6°59N 39°11E 257 F4
Dodoma Tanzania 6°8S 35°45E 268 D4
Dodoma □ Tanzania 6°0S 36°0E 268 D4
Dodoni Greece 39°40N 20°46E 204 B2
Dodori ⌓ Kenya 1°55S 41°7E 268 C5
Dodsland Canada 51°50N 108°45W 297 C7
Dodson U.S.A. 48°24N 108°15W 304 B9
Dodurga Turkey 39°49N 29°57E 205 B11
Doerun U.S.A. 31°19N 83°55W 316 D6
Doesburg Neths. 52°1N 6°9E 170 B6
Doetinchem Neths. 51°59N 6°18E 170 C6
Dog Creek Canada 51°35N 122°14W 296 C4
Dog I. U.S.A. 29°48N 84°36W 316 F5
Dog L. Man., Canada 51°2N 98°31W 297 C9
Dog L. Ont., Canada 48°48N 89°30W 298 C2
Dogana di Mare, Palazzo Venice, Italy 142 c3
Doğankent Turkey 36°52N 35°18E 250 B6
Doğanşehir Turkey 38°5N 37°53E 212 C7
Dogliani Italy 44°32N 7°56E 198 D4
Dōgo Japan 36°15N 133°16E 222 A5
Dōgo-San Japan 35°2N 133°13E 222 B5
Dogondoutchi Niger 13°38N 4°2E 263 C5
Dogran Pakistan 31°48N 73°35E 242 D5
Dogs, Isle of U.K. 51°29N 0°1W 125 B3
Doğubayazıt Turkey 39°31N 44°5E 213 C11
Doguéraoua Niger 14°0N 5°31E 263 C6
Dogura Papua N. G. 10°6S 150°5E 286 F6
Doha = Ad Dawḩah Qatar 25°15N 51°35E 247 E6
Dohazari Bangla. 22°10N 92°5E 241 D4
Dohinog = Manukan Phil. 8°32N 123°12E 233 G4
Dohrighat India 26°16N 83°31E 243 F10
Doi Indonesia 2°14N 127°49E 231 D7
Doi Inthanon Thailand 18°35N 98°29E 236 C2
Doi Inthanon △ Thailand 18°33N 98°34E 236 C2
Doi Khuntan △ Thailand 18°33N 99°14E 236 C2
Doi Luang Thailand 18°30N 101°0E 236 C3
Doi Luang △ Thailand 19°22N 99°35E 236 C2
Doi Phukha △ Thailand 19°8N 101°9E 236 C3
Doi Saket Thailand 18°52N 99°9E 236 C2
Doi Suthep Pui △ Thailand 18°49N 98°53E 236 C2
Doi Toa Thailand 17°55N 98°30E 236 D2
Dois Irmãos, Sa. Brazil 9°0S 42°30W 332 C3
Dojransko Jezero Macedonia 41°13N 22°44E 202 E6
Doka Sudan 13°31N 35°46E 257 E4
Dokdo = Liancourt Rocks Asia 37°15N 131°52E 221 F5
Dokka Norway 60°49N 10°7E 164 D7
Dokka → Norway 60°49N 10°7E 164 D7
Dokkum Neths. 53°20N 5°59E 170 A5
Dokos Greece 37°20N 23°20E 204 D5
Dokri Pakistan 27°25N 68°7E 242 F3
Dokshukino = Nartkala Russia 43°33N 43°51E 191 J6
Dokuchayevsk Ukraine 47°44N 37°40E 189 J9
Dol-de-Bretagne France 48°34N 1°47W 172 D5
Dolak, Pulau Indonesia 8°0S 138°30E 231 F9
Dolban = Liman Russia 45°45N 47°12E 191 H8
Dolbeau-Mistassini Canada 48°53N 72°14W 299 C5
Dole France 47°7N 5°31E 173 E12
Doleib, Wadi → Sudan 12°10N 33°15E 257 E3
Dolenji Logatec = Logatec Slovenia 45°56N 14°15E 199 C11
Dolgellau U.K. 52°45N 3°53W 168 E4
Dolgelley = Dolgellau U.K. 52°45N 3°53W 168 E4
Dolgoe Ozero Russia 60°0N 30°15E 137 A1
Dolhasca Romania 47°26N 26°36E 183 C11
Doliana Greece 39°54N 20°32E 204 B2
Dolianova Italy 39°22N 9°10E 200 C2
Dolinsk Russia 47°21N 142°48E 215 E15
Dolinskaya = Dolynska Ukraine 48°6N 32°46E 189 H7
Dolj □ Romania 44°10N 23°30E 183 F8
Doll Museum Delhi, India 120 b3
Dollard Neths. 53°20N 7°10E 170 A7
Dollis Hill U.K. 51°33N 0°13W 125 A2
Dollymount Ireland 53°22N 6°11W 120 A2
Dolna Banya Bulgaria 42°18N 23°44E 202 D7
Dolni Czech Rep. 50°3N 14°33E 135 B3
Dolni Chabry Czech Rep. 50°8N 14°26E 135 B2
Dolni Chiflik Bulgaria 42°59N 27°43E 203 D11
Dolni Dŭbnik Bulgaria 43°24N 24°26E 203 C8
Dolni Počernice Czech Rep. 50°5N 14°34E 135 B3
Dolnośląskie □ Poland 51°10N 16°30E 185 G3
Dolný Kubín Slovak Rep. 49°12N 19°18E 181 B12
Dolo Ethiopia 4°11N 42°3E 257 G5
Dolo Italy 45°25N 12°5E 199 C9
Dolomites = Dolomiti Italy 46°23N 11°51E 199 B8
Dolomiti Italy 46°23N 11°51E 199 B8
Dolomiti Bellunesi △ Italy 46°10N 12°5E 199 B9
Dolores Argentina 36°20S 57°40W 334 D4
Dolores Phil. 12°2N 125°29E 232 E5
Dolores Uruguay 33°34S 58°15W 334 C4
Dolores Colo., U.S.A. 37°28N 108°30W 305 H9
Dolores → U.S.A. 38°49N 109°17W 304 G9
Dolovo Serbia 44°55N 20°52E 182 F5
Dolphin, C. Falk. Is. 51°10S 59°0W 153 f
Dolphin and Union Str. Canada 69°5N 114°45W 294 D9
Dolphin Head Jamaica 18°22N 78°10W 320 a
Dolphin I. Jamaica 17°48N 77°10W 320 a
Dolphins Barn Ireland 53°20N 6°17W 120 B2
Dolsk Poland 51°59N 17°3E 185 G4
Dolton U.S.A. 41°38N 87°36W 119 D3
Dolungmukh India 27°30N 94°18E 241 B5
Dolyna Ukraine 48°58N 24°1E 183 B9
Dolynska Ukraine 48°6N 32°46E 189 H7
Dolynske Ukraine 47°32N 29°55E 183 C14
Dolzhanskaya Russia 46°37N 37°48E 189 J9
Dom Joaquim Brazil 18°57S 43°16W 333 E3
Dom Pedrito Brazil 31°0S 54°40W 335 C5
Dom Pedro Brazil 4°59S 44°27W 332 B3
Dom Pedro II, Parque Brazil 23°33S 46°36W 137 B2
Doma = Gombe Nigeria 10°19N 11°2E 263 C7
Doma Nigeria 8°25N 8°18E 263 D6
Doma ⌓ Zimbabwe 16°28S 30°12E 269 F3
Domadare Somalia 1°52N 41°15E 267 D5
Domain, The Sydney, Australia 139 b2
Domaniç Turkey 39°48N 29°36E 205 B11
Domar, Enneri → Chad 18°11N 18°4E 259 E3
Domariaganj → India 26°17N 83°44E 243 F10
Domasi Malawi 15°15S 35°22E 269 F4
Domažlice Czech Rep. 49°28N 12°58E 180 B5
Dombarovka = Dombarovskiy Russia 50°46N 59°32E 214 D6
Dombarovskiy Russia 50°46N 59°32E 214 D6
Dombås Norway 62°4N 9°8E 164 B6
Dombasle-sur-Meurthe France 48°38N 6°21E 173 D13
Dombe Grande Angola 12°57S 13°6E 265 E2
Dombes France 45°58N 5°0E 175 C9
Dombóvár Hungary 46°21N 18°9E 182 D3
Dombrád Hungary 48°13N 21°54E 182 B6
Dombrova = Dąbrowa Górnicza Poland 50°15N 19°10E 185 H6
Dombrowitsa = Dubrovytsya Ukraine 51°31N 26°35E 177 C14
Dome Argus Antarctica 80°50S 76°30E 151 E6
Dome C. Antarctica 75°12S 123°37E 151 D9
Dome Fuji Antarctica 77°20S 39°45E 151 D5
Dome of the Rock Jerusalem 123 b3
Domel I. = Letsôk-aw Kyun Burma 11°30N 98°25E 237 G2
Domérat France 46°21N 2°32E 173 F9
Domett N.Z. 42°53S 173°12E 285 C8
Domeyko Chile 29°0S 71°0W 334 B1
Domeyko, Cordillera Chile 24°30S 69°0W 334 A2
Domfront France 48°37N 0°40W 172 D6
Dominador Chile 24°21S 69°20W 334 A2
Dominica ■ W. Indies 15°20N 61°20W 323 k
Dominica Passage W. Indies 15°10N 61°20W 321 C7
Dominican Rep. ■ W. Indies 19°0N 70°30W 321 C5
Dominion Centre Toronto, Canada 141 b2
Domiongo Dem. Rep. of the Congo 4°37S 21°15E 265 C4
Dömitz Germany 53°8N 11°15E 178 B7
Domme France 44°48N 1°12E 174 D5
Domneşti Romania 45°12N 24°50E 183 E9
Domo Ethiopia 7°50N 47°10E 267 C6
Domodóssola Italy 46°7N 8°17E 198 B5
Domogled-Valea Cernei △ Romania 44°52N 22°27E 182 F7
Domokos Greece 39°10N 22°18E 204 B4
Domoni Comoros Is. 12°15S 44°32E 272 a
Dompaire France 48°14N 6°14E 173 D13
Dompierre-sur-Besbre France 46°31N 3°41E 173 F10
Dompim Ghana 5°10N 2°5W 262 D4
Dompu Indonesia 8°32S 118°28E 235 D5
Domrémy-la-Pucelle France 48°26N 5°40E 173 D12
Domvena Greece 38°15N 22°59E 204 C4
Domville, Mt. Australia 28°1S 151°15E 281 D5
Domžale Slovenia 46°9N 14°35E 199 B11
Don → India 16°20N 76°15E 245 F3
Don → Russia 47°4N 39°18E 189 J10
Don → Aberds., U.K. 57°11N 2°5W 167 D6
Don → S. Yorks., U.K. 53°41N 0°52W 168 D7
Don, C. Australia 11°18S 131°46E 278 B5
Don Benito Spain 38°53N 5°51W 195 G5
Don Figuereroa Mts. Jamaica 18°5N 77°36W 320 a
Don Mills Canada 43°44N 79°21W 141 A2
Don Muang Int. ✈ (BKK) Thailand 13°53N 100°36E 113 A2
Don Sak Thailand 9°18N 99°41E 237 b
Dona Ana = Nhamaabué Mozam. 17°25S 35°5E 269 F4
Doña Mencía Spain 37°33N 4°21W 195 H6
Donaghadee U.K. 54°39N 5°33W 166 B6
Donaghmede Ireland 53°23N 6°9W 120 A3
Donaghmore Ireland 52°52N 7°36W 166 D4
Donald Australia 36°23S 143°0E 282 D5
Donaldsonville U.S.A. 30°6N 90°59W 314 F9
Donalsonville U.S.A. 31°3N 84°53W 316 D5
Doñana △ Spain 36°59N 6°23W 195 J4
Donau = Dunărea → Europe 45°20N 29°40E 183 E14
Donau → Austria 48°10N 17°0E 181 C10
Donau Auen △ Austria 48°8N 16°44E 181 C9
Donau-Oder Kanal Austria 48°12N 16°32E 142 A3
Donaueschingen Germany 47°56N 8°29E 179 H4
Donaufeld Austria 48°15N 16°24E 142 A2
Donaupark Austria 48°14N 16°24E 142 A2
Donaustadt Austria 48°13N 16°29E 142 A2
Donauwörth Germany 48°43N 10°47E 179 G6
Doncaster U.K. 53°32N 1°6W 168 D6
Dondo Angola 9°45S 14°25E 265 D2
Dondo Dem. Rep. of the Congo 4°11N 21°39E 264 B4
Dondo Mozam. 19°33S 34°46E 269 F3
Dondo, Teluk Indonesia 0°50N 120°30E 231 D6
Dondra Head Sri Lanka 5°55N 80°40E 245 M5
Donduşeni Moldova 48°14N 27°36E 183 B12
Donegal Ireland 54°39N 8°5W 166 B3
Donegal □ Ireland 54°53N 8°0W 166 B4
Donegal B. Ireland 54°31N 8°49W 166 B3
Donets → Russia 47°33N 40°55E 191 G5
Donets Basin Ukraine 49°0N 38°0E 158 F13
Donetsk Ukraine 48°0N 37°45E 189 J9
Donetsk □ Ukraine 47°30N 37°50E 189 J9
Dong Ba Thin Vietnam 12°8N 109°13E 237 F7
Dong Dang Vietnam 21°54N 106°42E 228 G6
Dong Giam Vietnam 19°25N 105°31E 236 C5
Dong Ha Vietnam 16°55N 107°8E 236 D6
Dong Hene Laos 16°40N 105°18E 236 D5
Dong Hoi Vietnam 17°29N 106°36E 236 D6
Dong Jiang → China 23°6N 114°0E 229 F10
Dong Khe Vietnam 22°26N 106°27E 236 A6
Dong Phayayen Thailand 14°20N 101°22E 236 E3
Dong Ujimqin Qi China 45°32N 116°55E 226 B9
Dong Van Vietnam 23°16N 105°22E 236 A5
Dong Xoai Vietnam 11°32N 106°55E 237 G6
Donga Nigeria 7°45N 10°2E 263 D7
Donga → Nigeria 8°20N 9°58E 263 D7
Dong'an China 26°23N 111°12E 229 D8
Dongan Hills U.S.A. 40°35N 74°5W 132 C1
Dongara Australia 29°14S 114°57E 279 E1
Dongargarh India 21°10N 80°40E 244 D5
Dongbei China 45°0N 125°0E 227 D13
Dongcheng Beijing, China 114 b2
Dongchuan China 26°8N 103°1E 228 D4
Dongdaemung S. Korea 37°34N 127°2E 137 B2
Dongducheon S. Korea 37°54N 127°3E 224 D3
Donges France 47°18N 2°4W 172 E4
Dongfang China 18°50N 108°33E 229 a
Dongfeng China 42°40N 125°34E 224 A2
Donggala Indonesia 0°30S 119°40E 235 C5
Donggan China 23°22N 105°9E 228 F5
Donggang = Tungkang Taiwan 22°27N 120°26E 225 D2
Donggang China 39°52N 124°10E 224 C2
Donggou China 31°17N 121°33E 138 B2
Dongguan China 22°58N 113°44E 229 F9
Dongguang China 37°50N 116°30E 226 F9
Donghae S. Korea 37°29N 129°7E 224 D4
Donghai Dao China 21°0N 110°15E 229 G8
Dongjak S. Korea 37°30N 126°56E 137 B1
Dongjiao China 23°5N 113°12E 121 B2
Dongjingcheng China 44°5N 129°10E 227 B15
Dongkou China 27°6N 110°35E 229 D8
Donglan China 24°30N 107°21E 228 E6
Dongliao He → China 42°58N 123°32E 227 C12
Dongliu China 30°13N 116°55E 229 B11
Dongmen China 22°20N 107°48E 228 F6
Dongnae S. Korea 35°12N 129°5E 224 E4
Dongning China 44°2N 131°5E 227 B16
Dongnyi China 28°3N 100°15E 228 C3
Dongo Angola 14°36S 15°48E 265 E3
Dongobe Dem. Rep. of the Congo 4°35N 23°13E 264 B4
Dongola Sudan 19°9N 30°22E 256 D3
Dongou Congo 2°0N 18°5E 264 B3
Dongping China 35°55N 116°20E 226 G9
Dongri India 18°53N 72°57E 130 B2
Dongsha Dao S. China Sea 20°45N 116°43E 219 G12
Dongshan = Tungshan Taiwan 24°38N 121°47E 225 B3
Dongshan China 23°43N 117°30E 229 F11
Dongshanhu Park China 23°7N 113°17E 121 B2
Dongsheng China 39°50N 110°0E 226 E6
Dongshi = Tungshih Changhua, Taiwan 24°12N 120°43E 225 B2
Dongshi = Tungshih Chiai, Taiwan 23°27N 120°8E 225 C2
Dongsi Mosque Beijing, China 114 b2
Dongtai China 32°51N 120°21E 229 A13
Dongting Hu China 29°18N 112°45E 229 C9
Dongtou China 27°51N 121°10E 229 D13
Dongwe → Zambia 13°59S 23°53E 265 E4
Dongxiang China 28°11N 116°34E 229 C11
Dongxing China 21°34N 108°0E 228 G7
Dongyang China 29°13N 120°15E 229 C13
Dongying China 37°37N 118°37E 227 F10
Dongyinggang China 37°55N 118°58E 227 F10
Dongzhi China 30°9N 117°0E 229 B11
Dongzhimen China 39°55N 116°24E 114 B2
Donington, C. Australia 34°45S 136°0E 282 C2
Doniphan U.S.A. 36°37N 90°50W 308 G8
Donja Stubica Croatia 45°59N 15°59E 199 C12
Donji Dušnik Serbia 43°12N 22°5E 202 C6
Donji Miholjac Croatia 45°45N 18°10E 182 E3
Donji Milanovac Serbia 44°28N 22°6E 202 B6
Donji Vakuf Bos.-H. 44°8N 17°24E 182 F2
Dønna Nordland, Norway 66°6N 12°30E 160 C15
Donna Tex., U.S.A. 26°9N 98°4W 314 H5
Donnacona Canada 46°41N 71°41W 299 C5
Donnelly's Crossing N.Z. 35°42S 173°38E 284 B2
Donner Pass U.S.A. 39°19N 120°20W 306 F6
Donnybrook W. Austral., Australia 33°34S 115°48E 279 F2
Donnybrook Dublin, Ireland 53°19N 6°14W 120 B2
Donnybrook KwaZulu Natal, S. Africa 29°59S 29°48E 271 C4
Donora U.S.A. 40°11N 79°52W 312 F5
Donostia = Donostia-San Sebastián Spain 43°17N 1°58W 196 B3
Donostia-San Sebastián Spain 43°17N 1°58W 196 B3
Donousa Greece 37°8N 25°48E 205 D7
Donovan U.S.A. 40°53N 87°37W 311 D9
Donque Angola 15°28S 14°6E 265 F2
Donskoy Russia 53°55N 38°15E 188 F10
Donsol Phil. 12°54N 123°36E 232 E4
Donwood Canada 44°19N 78°16W 312 B6
Donzère France 44°28N 4°43E 175 D8
Donzy France 47°20N 3°6E 173 E10
Dookie Australia 36°20S 145°41E 283 D6
Doomadgee Australia 17°56S 138°49E 280 B2
Doomadgee ✿ Australia 17°56S 138°49E 280 B2
Doon → U.K. 55°27N 4°39W 167 F4
Doon Doon ✿ Australia 16°18S 128°14E 278 C4
Doornfontein S. Africa 26°11S 28°3E 123 B2
Doornik = Tournai Belgium 50°35N 3°25E 170 D3
Dora, L. Australia 22°0S 123°0E 278 D3
Dora Báltea → Italy 45°11N 8°3E 198 C5
Dora Ripária → Italy 45°5N 7°44E 198 C4
Doran L. Canada 61°13N 108°6W 297 A7
Doraville U.S.A. 33°54N 84°17W 316 B5
Dorchester Dorset, U.K. 50°42N 2°27W 169 G5
Dorchester Mass., U.S.A. 42°17N 71°4W 116 B2
Dorchester, C. Canada 65°27N 77°27W 295 D16
Dorchester B. U.S.A. 42°18N 71°1W 116 B2
Dorchester Heights Nat. Historical Site ⌓ U.S.A. 42°20N 71°2W 116 B2
Dordabis Namibia 22°52S 17°38E 270 B2
Dordogne □ France 45°5N 0°40E 174 C4
Dordogne → France 45°2N 0°36W 174 C3
Dordrecht Neths. 51°48N 4°39E 170 C4
Dordrecht Eastern Cape, S. Africa 31°20S 27°3E 270 D4
Dore → France 45°50N 3°35E 174 C7
Dore, Mts. France 45°32N 2°50E 174 C6
Doré L. Canada 54°46N 107°17W 297 C7
Dorée → St. Lucia 13°46N 61°3W 323 m
Dores da Boa Esperança = Boa Esperança Brazil 3°21N 61°23W 329 C5
Dores do Indaiá Brazil 19°27S 45°36W 333 E2
Dorfen Germany 48°15N 12°8E 179 G8
Dorgali Italy 40°17N 9°35E 200 B2
Dori Burkina Faso 14°3N 0°2W 263 C4
Doring → S. Africa 31°54S 18°39E 270 D2
Doringbos S. Africa 31°59S 19°16E 270 D2
Dorking U.K. 51°14N 0°19W 169 F7
Dormaa-Ahenkro Ghana 7°15N 2°52W 262 D4
Dormans France 49°4N 3°38E 173 C10
Dormo, Ras Eritrea 13°14N 42°35E 257 E5
Dornach Germany 48°9N 11°41E 131 B3
Dornakal India 17°27N 80°10E 244 F5
Dornbirn Austria 47°25N 9°45E 180 D2
Dornes France 46°48N 3°18E 173 F10
Dorneşti Romania 47°52N 26°1E 183 C11
Dornie U.K. 57°17N 5°31W 167 D3
Dornoch Ont., Canada 44°18N 80°51W 312 B4
Dornoch Highl., U.K. 57°53N 4°2W 167 D4
Dornoch Firth U.K. 57°51N 4°4W 167 D4
Dornogovĭ □ Mongolia 44°0N 110°0E 226 C6
Doro Mali 16°9N 0°51W 263 B4
Doro, Kavo Greece 38°9N 24°38E 204 C6
Dorog Hungary 47°42N 18°45E 182 C3
Dorogobuzh Russia 54°50N 33°18E 188 E7
Dorohoi Romania 47°56N 26°23E 183 C11
Döröö Nuur Mongolia 48°0N 93°0E 217 C12
Dorpat = Tartu Estonia 58°20N 26°44E 188 C4
Dorr Iran 33°17N 50°38E 247 C6
Dorre I. Australia 25°13S 113°12E 279 E1
Dorrigo Australia 30°20S 152°44E 283 A10
Dorrigo △ Australia 30°22S 152°47E 283 A10
Dorris U.S.A. 41°58N 121°55W 304 F3
Dorset Ont., Canada 45°14N 78°54W 312 A6
Dorset Ohio, U.S.A. 41°40N 80°40W 312 E4
Dorset Vt., U.S.A. 43°15N 73°5W 313 C11
Dorset □ U.K. 50°45N 2°26W 169 G5
Dorsoduro Venice, Italy 142 b1
Dorsten Germany 51°40N 6°58E 178 D2
Dortmund Germany 51°30N 7°28E 178 D3
Dortmund-Ems-Kanal → Germany 51°50N 7°26E 178 D3
Dörtyol Turkey 36°50N 36°13E 250 B7
Doruk Turkey 36°53N 35°45E 250 B6
Dorum Germany 53°41N 8°34E 178 B4
Doruma Dem. Rep. of the Congo 4°42N 27°33E 268 B2
Dorūneh Iran 35°10N 57°18E 247 C8
Dorval Int., Montréal ✈ (YUL) Canada 45°28N 73°44W 130 B1
Dos Bahías, C. Argentina 44°58S 65°32W 336 B3
Dos d'Âne Réunion 20°58S 55°23E 272 f
Dos Hermanas Spain 37°16N 5°55W 195 H5
Dos Moninos → Brazil 23°40S 46°33W 137 B2
Dos Palos U.S.A. 36°59N 120°37W 306 J6
Döşemealtı Turkey 37°4N 30°36E 205 D12
Dosso Niger 13°0N 3°13E 263 C5
Dosso □ Niger 13°30N 3°30E 263 C5
Dosso ⌓ Niger 12°36N 2°36E 263 C5
Dostyq Kazakhstan 45°15N 82°29E 217 C10
Dot Lake U.S.A. 63°40N 144°4W 303 E11
Dothan U.S.A. 31°13N 85°24W 316 D4
Doty U.S.A. 46°38N 123°17W 306 D3
Douai France 50°21N 3°4E 173 B10
Douako Guinea 9°45N 10°8W 262 D2
Douala Cameroon 4°0N 9°45E 263 E6
Douala-Édéa ⌓ Cameroon 3°20N 9°41E 264 B1
Douamoungo, C. Mayotte 12°38S 45°8E 272 b
Douaouir Mali 20°45N 3°0W 260 D4
Douarnenez France 48°6N 4°21W 172 D2
Doubabougou Mali 14°13N 7°59W 262 C3
Double Cone N.Z. 45°4S 168°49E 285 F3
Double Island Pt. Australia 25°56S 153°11E 281 D5
Double Mountain Fork → U.S.A. 33°16N 100°0W 314 E4
Doubrava → Czech Rep. 50°2N 15°20E 180 A8
Doubs □ France 47°10N 6°20E 173 E13
Doubs → France 46°53N 5°1E 173 F12
Doubtful Sd. N.Z. 45°20S 166°49E 285 F1
Doubtless B. N.Z. 34°55S 173°26E 284 A2
Doudeville France 49°43N 0°47E 172 C7
Doué-la-Fontaine France 47°11N 0°16W 172 E6
Douentza Mali 14°58N 2°48W 262 C4
Douentza ⌓ Mali 15°40N 2°25W 262 B4
Dougga Tunisia 36°25N 9°13E 258 A1
Doughboy B. N.Z. 47°2S 167°40E 285 H2
Douglas Ont., Canada 45°31N 76°56W 312 A8
Douglas I. of Man 54°10N 4°28W 168 C3
Douglas Northern Cape, S. Africa 29°4S 23°46E 270 C3
Douglas Alaska, U.S.A. 58°17N 134°24W 303 G14
Douglas Ariz., U.S.A. 31°21N 109°33W 305 L9
Douglas Ga., U.S.A. 31°31N 82°51W 316 D7
Douglas Mich., U.S.A. 42°39N 86°14W 311 B10
Douglas Wyo., U.S.A. 42°45N 105°24W 304 E11
Douglas Apsley △ Australia 41°45S 148°11E 281 G4
Douglas B. Dominica 15°36N 61°29W 323 k
Douglas C. U.S.A. 58°51N 153°15W 303 G9
Douglas Chan. Canada 53°40N 129°20W 296 C3
Douglas Park U.S.A. 41°51N 87°42W 119 B2
Douglas Pt. Canada 44°19N 81°37W 312 B3
Douglasville U.S.A. 33°45N 84°45W 316 B5
Douirat Morocco 33°2N 4°11W 260 B4
Doukaton, Akra Greece 38°34N 20°33E 207 B2
Doukkala-Abda □ Morocco 32°10N 8°50W 260 B3
Doukoula Cameroon 10°10N 15°0E 259 F2
Doulevant-le-Château France 48°23N 4°55E 173 D11
Douliou = Touliu Taiwan 23°42N 120°31E 225 C2
Doullens France 50°10N 2°20E 173 B9
Doumé Cameroon 4°15N 13°25E 264 B2
Doumen China 22°10N 113°18E 229 F9
Douna Mali 13°13N 6°0W 262 C3
Dounan = Tounan Taiwan 23°41N 120°28E 225 C2
Dounreay U.K. 58°35N 3°44W 167 C5
Dourada, Serra Brazil 13°10S 48°45W 333 D2
Dourados Brazil 22°9S 54°50W 335 A5
Dourados → Brazil 21°58S 54°18W 335 A5
Dourados, Serra dos Brazil 23°30S 53°30W 335 A5
Dourbali Chad 11°49N 15°52E 259 F3
Dourdan France 48°30N 2°1E 173 D9

Douro → Europe 41°8N 8°40W 194 D2
Douvaine France 46°19N 6°16E 173 F13
Douville Guadeloupe 16°15N 61°22W 322 e
Douz Tunisia 33°25N 9°0E 258 B1
Douze → France 43°54N 0°30W 174 E3
Dove → U.K. 52°51N 1°36W 168 E6
Dove Creek U.S.A. 37°46N 108°54W 305 H9
Dover Tas., Australia 43°18S 147°2E 281 G4
Dover Kent, U.K. 51°7N 1°19E 169 F9
Dover Del., U.S.A. 39°10N 75°32W 309 F16
Dover Ky., U.S.A. 38°43N 83°52W 311 F13
Dover N.H., U.S.A. 43°12N 70°56W 313 C14
Dover N.J., U.S.A. 40°53N 74°34W 313 F10
Dover Ohio, U.S.A. 40°32N 81°29W 312 F3
Dover, Pt. Australia 32°32S 125°32E 279 F4
Dover, Str. of Europe 51°0N 1°30E 169 G9
Dover-Foxcroft U.S.A. 45°11N 69°13W 309 C19
Dover Heights Australia 33°52S 151°16E 139 B2
Dover Plains U.S.A. 41°43N 73°35W 313 E11
Dovey = Dyfi → U.K. 52°32N 4°3W 169 E3
Dovhe Ukraine 48°22N 23°17E 183 B8
Dovlen = Devin Bulgaria 41°44N 24°24E 203 E8
Dovre Norway 61°58N 9°15E 164 C6
Dovre △ Norway 62°10N 9°30E 164 B6
Dovrefjell Norway 62°15N 9°33E 164 B6
Dovrefjell-Sunndalsfjella △ Norway 62°23N 9°11E 164 B6
Dow Rūd Iran 33°28N 49°4E 247 C6
Dowa Malawi 13°38S 33°58E 269 E3
Dowagiac U.S.A. 41°59N 86°6W 311 C10
Dowerin Australia 31°12S 117°2E 279 F2
Dowgha'i Iran 36°54N 58°32E 247 B8
Dowlat Yār Afghan. 34°30N 65°45E 240 B2
Dowlatābād Farāh, Afghan. 32°47N 62°40E 240 B1
Dowlatābād Fāryāb, Afghan. 36°26N 64°55E 240 A2
Dowlatābād Kermān, Iran 28°20N 56°40E 247 D8
Dowlatābād Khorāsān, Iran 35°16N 59°29E 247 C8
Dowlatābād Tehrān, Iran 35°38N 51°27E 141 B2
Dowling Park U.S.A. 30°15N 83°15W 316 E6
Down □ U.K. 54°23N 6°2W 166 B5
Down, L. U.S.A. 28°30N 81°31W 133 A1
Downers Grove U.S.A. 41°48N 88°1W 311 C8
Downey Calif., U.S.A. 33°56N 118°9W 126 C4
Downey Idaho, U.S.A. 42°26N 112°7W 304 E7
Downham Market U.K. 52°37N 0°23E 169 E8
Downieville U.S.A. 39°34N 120°50W 306 F6
Downing U.S.A. 40°29N 92°22W 310 D4
Downpatrick U.K. 54°20N 5°43W 166 B6
Downpatrick Hd. Ireland 54°20N 9°21W 166 B2
Downsview Canada 43°43N 79°30W 141 A2
Downsview Park Canada 43°45N 79°29W 141 A2
Downsville U.S.A. 42°5N 75°0W 313 D10
Downton, Mt. Canada 52°42N 124°52W 296 C4
Dowsārī Iran 28°25N 57°59E 247 D8
Dowshī Afghan. 35°35N 68°43E 240 B3
Doxato Greece 41°9N 24°16E 203 E8
Doyle U.S.A. 40°2N 120°6W 306 E6
Doylestown U.S.A. 40°21N 75°10W 313 F9
Dōzen Japan 36°5N 133°2E 222 A5
Dozois, Rés. Canada 47°30N 77°5W 298 C4
Dra Khel Pakistan 27°58N 66°45E 242 F2
Drâa, C. Morocco 28°47N 11°0W 260 C2
Drâa, Hamada du Algeria 28°0N 7°0W 260 C3
Drâa, Oued → Morocco 28°40N 11°10W 260 C2
Drac → France 45°12N 5°42E 175 C9
Drac, Coves del Spain 39°31N 3°19E 206 B4
Dračevo Macedonia 41°56N 21°31E 202 E5
Drachten Neths. 53°7N 6°5E 170 A6
Drăgănești Moldova 47°43N 28°15E 183 C13
Drăgănești-Olt Romania 44°9N 24°32E 183 F9
Drăgănești-Vlașca Romania 44°5N 25°33E 183 F10
Dragaš = Sharr Kosovo 42°5N 20°41E 202 D4
Drăgășani Romania 44°39N 24°17E 183 F9
Dragichyn Belarus 52°15N 25°8E 177 B13
Dragocvet Serbia 43°58N 21°15E 202 C5
Dragon's Mouths Trin. & Tob. 11°0N 61°50W 323 t
Dragør Denmark 55°35N 12°38E 118 B3
Dragovishtitsa Bulgaria 42°22N 22°39E 202 D6
Draguignan France 43°32N 6°27E 175 E10
Drahove Ukraine 48°14N 23°33E 183 B8
Drain U.S.A. 43°40N 123°19W 304 E2
Drake U.S.A. 47°55N 100°23W 308 B3
Drake Passage S. Ocean 58°0S 68°0W 151 B17
Drakensberg S. Africa 31°0S 28°0E 271 D4
Drama Greece 41°9N 24°10E 203 E8
Dramburg = Drawsko Pomorskie Poland 53°35N 15°50E 184 E2
Drammen Norway 59°42N 10°12E 164 E7
Drancy France 48°55N 2°26E 134 A3
Drangajökull Iceland 66°9N 22°15W 155 A4
Drangedal Norway 59°6N 9°3E 164 E6
Drangsnes Iceland 65°41N 21°27W 155 B5
Dranov, Ostrov Romania 44°55N 29°30E 183 F14
Drapetsona Greece 37°56N 23°37E 112 B1
Dras India 34°25N 75°48E 243 B6
Drastis, Akra Greece 39°48N 19°40E 206 B9
Drau = Drava → Croatia 45°33N 18°55E 182 E3
Drava → Croatia 45°33N 18°55E 182 E3
Dravograd Slovenia 46°36N 15°5E 199 B12
Drawa → Poland 52°52N 15°59E 185 F2
Drawieński △ Poland 53°6N 15°58E 185 E2
Drawno Poland 53°13N 15°46E 185 E2
Drawsko Pomorskie Poland 53°35N 15°50E 184 E2
Drayton Canada 43°46N 80°40W 312 C4
Drayton Plains U.S.A. 42°41N 83°23W 311 B13
Drayton Valley Canada 53°12N 114°58W 296 C6
Dreieich Germany 50°1N 8°41E 179 E4
Dreikikir Papua N. G. 3°35S 142°46E 286 B2
Dreilinden Germany 52°24N 13°10E 115 B2
Drenthe □ Neths. 52°52N 6°40E 170 B6
Drepano, Akra Greece 35°28N 24°14E 207 E5
Drepanum, C. Cyprus 34°54N 32°19E 207 F8
Dresden Canada 42°35N 82°11W 312 D2
Dresden Sachsen, Germany 51°3N 13°44E 178 D9
Dresden N.Y., U.S.A. 42°41N 76°57W 312 D8
Dreux France 48°44N 1°23E 172 D8
Drevsjø Norway 61°53N 12°1E 164 C9
Drewnica Poland 52°18N 21°6E 143 B2
Drexel U.S.A. 39°45N 84°18W 311 E12
Drezdenko Poland 52°50N 15°49E 185 F2
Driesen = Drezdenko Poland 52°50N 15°49E 185 F2
Driffield U.K. 54°0N 0°26W 168 C7
Driftwood U.S.A. 41°20N 78°8W 312 E6
Driggs U.S.A. 43°44N 111°6W 304 E8
Drigh Road Pakistan 24°52N 67°7E 123 A2
Drimnagh Ireland 53°19N 6°19W 120 B2
Drin → Albania 42°1N 19°38E 202 D3
Drin i Zi → Albania 41°37N 20°28E 202 E4
Drina → Bos.-H. 44°53N 19°21E 202 B3
Drincea → Romania 44°20N 22°55E 182 F7
Drinjača → Bos.-H. 44°15N 19°8E 182 F4
Driopida Greece 37°25N 24°26E 204 D6
Drissa = Vyerkhnyadzvinsk Belarus 55°45N 27°58E 188 E4
Driva → Norway 62°41N 9°31E 164 B6
Drivstoggo Norway 62°26N 9°47E 164 B6
Drniš Croatia 43°51N 16°10E 199 E13
Drøbak Norway 59°39N 10°39E 164 E7
Drobeta-Turnu Severin Romania 44°39N 22°41E 182 F7
Drobin Poland 52°42N 19°58E 185 F6
Drochia Moldova 48°2N 27°48E 183 B12
Drogenbos Belgium 50°47N 4°19E 116 B1
Drogheda Ireland 53°43N 6°22W 166 C5
Drogichin = Dragichyn Belarus 52°15N 25°8E 177 B13
Drogobych = Drohobych Ukraine 49°20N 23°30E 185 J10
Drohiczyn Poland 52°24N 22°39E 185 F9
Drohobych Ukraine 49°20N 23°30E 185 J10
Droichead Átha = Drogheda Ireland 53°43N 6°22W 166 C5
Droichead na Bandan = Bandon Ireland 51°44N 8°44W 166 E3
Droichead Nua = Newbridge Ireland 53°11N 6°48W 166 C5
Droitwich U.K. 52°16N 2°8W 169 E5
Drôme □ France 44°38N 5°15E 175 D9
Drôme → France 44°46N 4°46E 175 D8
Dromedary, C. Australia 36°17S 150°10E 283 D9
Drömling △ Germany 52°29N 11°5E 178 C7
Dromore Down, U.K. 54°25N 6°9W 166 B5
Dromore Tyrone, U.K. 54°31N 7°28W 166 B4
Dromore West Ireland 54°15N 8°52W 166 B3
Dronero Italy 44°28N 7°22E 198 D4
Dronfield U.K. 53°19N 1°27W 168 D6
Dronne → France 45°2N 0°9W 174 C3
Dronning Ingrid Land Greenland 64°25N 52°5W 154 E5
Dronning Maud Land Antarctica 72°30S 12°0E 151 D3
Dronninglund Denmark 57°10N 10°19E 163 G4
Dronten Neths. 52°32N 5°43E 170 B5
Dropt → France 44°35N 0°6W 174 D3
Drosendorf Austria 48°52N 15°37E 180 C8
Drosh Pakistan 35°33N 71°48E 240 B3
Drottningholm Sweden 59°19N 17°53E 139 B1
Droué France 48°3N 1°6E 172 D8
Drouin Australia 38°10S 145°53E 283 E6
Druid Hills U.S.A. 33°47N 84°21W 113 B2
Drujba Uzbekistan 41°13N 61°18E 216 D6
Druk Yul = Bhutan ■ Asia 27°25N 90°30E 241 B3
Drum Tower Beijing, China 114 a3
Drumbo Canada 43°16N 80°35W 312 C4
Drumcliff Ireland 54°20N 8°29W 166 B3
Drumcondra Ireland 53°21N 6°16W 120 A2
Drumheller Canada 51°25N 112°40W 296 C6
Drummond U.S.A. 46°40N 113°9W 304 C7
Drummond I. U.S.A. 46°1N 83°39W 309 B12
Drummond Pt. Australia 34°9S 135°16E 281 E2
Drummond Ra. Australia 23°45S 147°10E 280 C4
Drummondville Canada 45°55N 72°25W 298 C5
Drummoyne Australia 33°51S 151°8E 139 B1
Drumright U.S.A. 35°59N 96°36W 314 D6
Druskeniki = Druskininkai Lithuania 54°3N 23°58E 188 E2
Druskininkai Lithuania 54°3N 23°58E 188 E2
Drut → Belarus 53°8N 30°5E 177 B16
Druya Belarus 55°45N 27°28E 188 E4
Druzhba Bulgaria 43°15N 28°1E 203 C12
Druzhina Russia 68°14N 145°18E 215 C15
Drvar Bos.-H. 44°21N 16°23E 199 D13
Drvenik Croatia 43°27N 16°3E 199 E13
Drwęca → Poland 53°0N 18°42E 185 E5
Dry Harbour Mts. Jamaica 18°19N 77°24W 320 a
Dry Tortugas U.S.A. 24°38N 82°55W 315 J13
Dryander △ Australia 20°13S 148°34E 280 b
Dryanovo Bulgaria 42°59N 25°28E 203 D9
Dryden Ont., Canada 49°47N 92°50W 297 D10
Dryden N.Y., U.S.A. 42°30N 76°18W 313 D8
Drygalski I. Antarctica 66°0S 92°0E 151 C7
Drygalski Ice Tongue Antarctica 75°24S 163°30E 151 D11
Drylaw U.K. 55°58N 3°15W 121 B2
Drysdale → Australia 13°59S 126°51E 278 B4
Drysdale I. Australia 11°41S 136°0E 280 A2
Drysdale River △ Australia 14°56S 127°2E 278 B4
Drzewica Poland 51°27N 20°29E 185 G7
Drzewiczka → Poland 51°36N 20°36E 185 G7
Dschang Cameroon 5°32N 10°3E 263 D7
Du Gué → Canada 57°21N 70°45W 298 A5
Du He → China 32°48N 110°40E 229 A8
Du Quoin U.S.A. 38°1N 89°14W 310 G7
Du'an China 23°59N 108°3E 228 F7
Duanesburg U.S.A. 42°45N 74°11W 313 D10
Duaringa Australia 23°42S 149°42E 280 C4
Duarte, Pico Dom. Rep. 19°2N 70°59W 321 C5
Dubai = Dubayy U.A.E. 25°18N 55°20E 119 A2
Dubai Creek U.A.E. 25°15N 55°19E 119 A2
Dubai Int. ✈ (DXB) U.A.E. 25°15N 55°21E 119 A2
Dubai Int. Financial Centre U.A.E. 25°12N 55°17E 119 B2
Dubai Internet City U.A.E. 25°11N 55°10E 119 B1
Dubai Marina U.A.E. 25°11N 55°10E 119 B1
Dubai Maritime City U.A.E. 25°16N 55°16E 119 A2
Dubăsari Moldova 47°15N 29°10E 183 C14
Dubăsari Vdkhr. Moldova 47°30N 29°0E 183 C13
Dubawnt → Canada 64°33N 100°6W 297 A8
Dubawnt L. Canada 63°8N 101°28W 297 A8
Dubayy U.A.E. 25°18N 55°20E 119 A2
Dubbo Australia 32°11S 148°35E 283 B8
Dube → Liberia 5°16N 7°29W 262 D3
Dubeč Czech Rep. 50°3N 14°35E 135 B3
Dubele Dem. Rep. of the Congo 2°56N 29°35E 268 B2
Dübendorf Switz. 47°24N 8°37E 179 H4
Dubica Croatia 45°11N 16°48E 199 C13
Dublanc Dominica 15°31N 61°28W 323 k
Dublin Ireland 53°21N 6°15W 120 A2
Dublin Ga., U.S.A. 32°32N 82°54W 316 C7
Dublin Ohio, U.S.A. 40°5N 83°7W 311 D13
Dublin Tex., U.S.A. 32°5N 98°21W 314 E5
Dublin □ Ireland 53°24N 6°20W 166 C5
Dublin ✈ (DUB) Ireland 53°26N 6°15W 120 A2
Dublin B. Ireland 53°19N 6°7W 120 B3
Dublin Castle Dublin, Ireland 120 c2
Dublin Harbour Ireland 53°21N 6°11W 120 A2
Dubna Russia 56°44N 37°10E 188 D9
Dubnica nad Váhom Slovak Rep. 48°58N 18°11E 181 C11
Dubno Ukraine 50°25N 25°45E 177 C13
Dubois Idaho, U.S.A. 44°10N 112°14W 304 D7
Dubois Ind., U.S.A. 38°27N 86°48W 311 F10
DuBois Pa., U.S.A. 41°7N 78°46W 312 E6
Dubossary = Dubăsari Moldova 47°15N 29°10E 183 C14
Dubove Ukraine 48°10N 23°53E 183 B8
Dubovka Russia 49°5N 44°50E 191 F7
Dubovskoye Russia 47°28N 42°46E 191 G6
Dubrajpur India 23°48N 87°25E 243 H12
Dubréka Guinea 9°46N 13°31W 262 D2
Dubrovitsa = Dubrovytsya Ukraine 51°31N 26°35E 177 C14
Dubrovnik Croatia 42°39N 18°6E 202 D2
Dubrovytsya Ukraine 51°31N 26°35E 177 C14
Dubulu Dem. Rep. of the Congo 4°18N 20°16E 264 B4
Dubuque U.S.A. 42°30N 90°41W 310 B6
Dubysa → Lithuania 55°5N 23°26E 184 C10
Duc de Gloucester, Îs. French Polynesia 20°38S 143°20W 289 f
Duc Tho Vietnam 18°32N 105°35E 236 C5
Ducale, Palazzo Venice, Italy 142 b3
Ducassous, Pte. Martinique 14°32N 60°50W 322 j
Duchang China 29°18N 116°12E 229 C11
Duchesne U.S.A. 40°10N 110°24W 304 F8
Duchess Australia 21°20S 139°50E 280 C2
Ducie I. Pac. Oc. 24°40S 124°48W 289 K15
Duck → U.S.A. 36°2N 87°52W 315 C11
Duck Cr. → Australia 22°37S 116°53E 278 D2
Duck Lake Canada 52°50N 106°16W 297 C7
Duck Mountain △ Canada 51°45N 101°0W 297 C8
Duckwall, Mt. U.S.A. 37°58N 120°7W 306 H6
Ducos Martinique 14°33N 60°59W 322 j
Duda → Colombia 2°34N 74°3W 328 C3
Duddington U.K. 55°56N 3°8W 121 B3
Duderstadt Germany 51°31N 10°15E 178 D6
Dudhi India 24°15N 83°10E 243 G10
Dudhnoi India 25°59N 90°47E 241 C3
Dudinka Russia 69°30N 86°13E 215 C9
Dudley W. Mids., U.K. 52°31N 2°5W 169 E5
Dudley Ga., U.S.A. 32°32N 83°5W 316 C6
Dudna → India 19°17N 76°54E 244 E3
Dudo Somalia 9°20N 50°12E 267 C7
Dudo, W. → Somalia 9°14N 50°40E 267 C7
Dudub Ethiopia 6°55N 46°43E 267 C6
Dudwa India 28°30N 80°41E 243 E9
Dudwa △ India 28°30N 80°40E 243 E9
Duékoué Ivory C. 6°40N 7°15W 262 D3
Duenas Phil. 11°4N 122°37E 233 F4
Dueñas Spain 41°52N 4°33W 194 D6
Duerê Brazil 11°20S 49°17W 333 D2
Duero = Douro → Europe 41°8N 8°40W 194 D2
Duff Is. Pac. Oc. 9°50S 167°10E 277 B12
Dufftown U.K. 57°27N 3°8W 167 D5
Dufourspitz Switz. 45°56N 7°52E 179 K3
Dugger U.S.A. 39°4N 87°18W 311 E9
Dugi Otok Croatia 44°0N 15°3E 199 D11
Duguima Somalia 1°15N 42°34E 267 D5
Dugnano Italy 45°33N 9°11E 128 A2
Dugo Selo Croatia 45°51N 16°18E 199 C13
Duida-Marahuaca △ Venezuela 3°33N 65°33W 328 C4
Duisburg Germany 51°26N 6°45E 178 D2
Duitama Colombia 5°50N 73°2W 328 B3
Duivendrecht Neths. 52°20N 4°55E 112 B2
Duiwelskloof = Modjadjiskloof S. Africa 23°42S 30°10E 271 B5
Dujiangyan China 31°2N 103°38E 228 B4
Duk Fadiat South Sudan 7°45N 31°25E 257 F3
Duk Faiwil South Sudan 7°30N 31°29E 257 F3
Dukat Albania 40°16N 19°32E 202 F3
Dūkdamīn Iran 35°59N 57°43E 247 C8
Dukelský Průsmyk Slovak Rep. 49°25N 21°42E 181 B14
Dukhān Qatar 25°25N 50°50E 247 E6
Dukhovshchina Russia 55°15N 32°27E 188 E7
Duki Pakistan 30°14N 68°25E 240 D3
Dukla Poland 49°30N 21°35E 185 J8
Duku Bauchi, Nigeria 10°43N 10°43E 263 C7
Duku Sokoto, Nigeria 11°11N 4°55E 263 C5
Dula Dem. Rep. of the Congo 4°40N 20°21E 264 B4
Dūlāb Iran 35°39N 51°27E 141 B2
Dulag Phil. 10°57N 125°2E 233 F5
Dulan China 36°0N 97°11E 218 D8
Dulawan = Datu Piang Phil. 7°2N 124°30E 233 H5
Dulce U.S.A. 36°56N 107°0W 305 H10
Dulce → Argentina 30°32S 62°33W 334 C3
Dulce, G. Costa Rica 8°40N 83°20W 320 E3
Dulcina Antigua & B. 17°35N 61°49W 322 c
Dulf Iraq 35°7N 45°51E 246 C5
Dŭlgopol Bulgaria 43°3N 27°22E 203 C11
Duliu China 39°2N 116°55E 226 E9
Dullabchara India 24°30N 92°26E 241 C4
Dullewala Pakistan 31°50N 71°25E 242 D4
Dullstroom S. Africa 25°27S 30°7E 271 C5
Dülmen Germany 51°49N 7°17E 178 D3
Dulovo Bulgaria 43°48N 27°9E 203 C11
Dulpetorpet Norway 60°34N 12°19E 164 D9
Dulq Maghār Syria 36°22N 38°39E 213 D8
Duluth Ga., U.S.A. 34°0N 84°9W 316 A5
Duluth Minn., U.S.A. 46°47N 92°6W 308 B7
Dulwich U.K. 51°27N 0°5W 125 B3
Dum Dum India 22°39N 88°26E 124 B2
Dum Duma India 27°40N 95°40E 241 B5
Dūmā Syria 33°34N 36°24E 250 E7
Dumaguete Phil. 9°17N 123°15E 233 G4
Dumai Indonesia 1°35N 101°28E 234 B2
Dumalinao Phil. 7°49N 123°23E 233 H4
Dumanjug Phil. 10°4N 123°26E 233 F4
Dumanquilas B. Phil. 7°34N 123°4E 233 H4
Dumaran Phil. 10°33N 119°50E 233 F2
Dumaran I. Phil. 10°33N 119°51E 233 F2
Dumarao Phil. 11°16N 122°41E 233 F4
Dumas Ark., U.S.A. 33°53N 91°29W 314 E9
Dumas Tex., U.S.A. 35°52N 101°58W 314 D4
Ḍumayr Syria 33°39N 36°42E 250 E7
Dumbarton U.K. 55°57N 4°33W 167 F4
Dumbéa N. Cal. 22°10S 166°27E 288 d
Ďumbier Slovak Rep. 48°56N 19°38E 181 C12
Dumbleyung Australia 33°17S 117°42E 279 F2
Dumbo Angola 14°6S 17°24E 265 E3
Dumbrăveni Romania 46°14N 24°34E 183 D9
Dumfries U.K. 55°4N 3°37W 167 F5
Dumfries & Galloway □ U.K. 55°9N 3°58W 167 F5
Dumingag Phil. 8°20N 123°20E 233 G4
Dumitrești Romania 45°33N 26°55E 183 E11
Dumka India 24°12N 87°15E 243 G12
Dumlupınar Turkey 38°53N 30°0E 205 C12
Dümmer Germany 52°31N 8°20E 178 C4
Dümmer △ Germany 52°31N 8°21E 178 C4
Dumoine → Canada 46°13N 77°51W 298 C4
Dumoine, L. Canada 46°55N 77°55W 298 C4
Dumont U.S.A. 40°56N 73°59W 132 A2
Dumont d'Urville Antarctica 66°40S 140°0E 151 C10
Dumont d'Urville Sea S. Ocean 63°30S 138°0E 151 C9
Dumoulin Is. Papua N. G. 10°54S 150°46E 286 F6
Dumpu Papua N. G. 5°53S 145°44E 286 C3
Dumyât Egypt 31°24N 31°48E 251 G2
Dumyât, Far → Egypt 31°32N 31°51E 251 G2
Dumyât, Masabb Egypt 31°28N 31°51E 251 G2
Dún Dealgan = Dundalk Ireland 54°1N 6°24W 166 B5
Dún Garbhán = Dungarvan Ireland 52°5N 7°37W 166 D4
Dún Laoghaire Ireland 53°17N 6°8W 120 B3
Dun-le-Palestel France 46°18N 1°39E 173 F8
Dun-sur-Auron France 46°53N 2°33E 173 F9
Dun-sur-Meuse France 49°23N 5°11E 173 C12
Duna = Dunărea → Europe 45°20N 29°40E 183 E14
Duna-Drava △ Hungary 46°15N 18°50E 182 D3
Duna Dzong Bhutan 27°2N 89°24E 241 B2
Duna-völgyi-főcsatorna Hungary 46°40N 19°14E 182 D4
Dünaburg = Daugavpils Latvia 55°53N 26°32E 188 E4
Dunaföldvár Hungary 46°50N 18°57E 182 D3
Dunagiri India 30°31N 79°52E 243 D8
Dunaj = Dunărea → Europe 45°20N 29°40E 183 E14
Dunajec → Poland 50°15N 20°44E 185 H7
Dunajská Streda Slovak Rep. 48°0N 17°37E 181 C10
Dunakeszi Hungary 47°37N 19°8E 182 C4
Dunapataj Hungary 46°39N 19°4E 182 D4
Dunărea → Europe 45°20N 29°40E 183 E14
Dunaszekcső Hungary 46°6N 18°45E 182 D3
Dunaújváros Hungary 46°58N 18°57E 182 D3
Dunav = Dunărea → Europe 45°20N 29°40E 183 E14
Dunavațu de Jos Romania 44°59N 29°13E 183 F14
Dunavtsi Bulgaria 43°57N 22°53E 202 C6
Dunay Russia 42°52N 132°22E 220 C6
Dunayivtsi Ukraine 48°54N 26°50E 183 B11
Dunback N.Z. 45°23S 170°36E 285 F5
Dunbar U.K. 56°0N 2°31W 167 E6
Dunblane U.K. 56°11N 3°58W 167 E5
Duncan B.C., Canada 48°45N 123°40W 306 B3
Duncan Ariz., U.S.A. 32°43N 109°6W 305 K9
Duncan Okla., U.S.A. 34°30N 97°57W 314 D6
Duncan, L. Canada 53°29N 77°58W 298 B4
Duncan Dock Cape Town, S. Africa 118 a3
Duncan L. Canada 62°51N 113°58W 296 A6
Duncan Passage India 11°0N 92°0E 245 J11
Duncan Town Bahamas 22°15N 75°45W 320 B4
Duncannon U.S.A. 40°23N 77°2W 312 F7
Duncans Jamaica 18°27N 77°32W 320 a
Duncansby Head U.K. 58°38N 3°1W 167 C5
Duncansville U.S.A. 40°25N 78°26W 312 F6
Dund-Us Mongolia 48°1N 91°38E 217 C12
Dundaga Latvia 57°31N 22°21E 184 A9
Dundalk Ont., Canada 44°10N 80°24W 312 B4
Dundalk Louth, Ireland 54°1N 6°24W 166 B5
Dundalk Md., U.S.A. 39°15N 76°31W 309 F15
Dundalk Bay Ireland 53°55N 6°15W 166 C5
Dundas = Uummannaq Greenland 77°33N 68°52W 154 B4
Dundas Canada 43°17N 79°59W 312 C5
Dundas, L. Australia 32°35S 121°50E 279 F3
Dundas I. Canada 54°30N 130°50W 296 C2
Dundas Str. Australia 11°15S 131°35E 278 B5
Dundee KwaZulu Natal, S. Africa 28°11S 30°15E 271 C5
Dundee Dundee C., U.K. 56°28N 2°59W 167 E6
Dundee Mich., U.S.A. 41°57N 83°40W 311 C13
Dundee N.Y., U.S.A. 42°32N 76°59W 312 D8
Dundee City □ U.K. 56°30N 2°58W 167 E6
Dundgovĭ □ Mongolia 45°10N 106°0E 226 B4
Dundrum Dublin, Ireland 53°18N 6°14W 120 B2
Dundrum Down, U.K. 54°16N 5°52W 166 B6
Dundrum B. U.K. 54°13N 5°47W 166 B6
Dunearn Singapore 1°19N 103°49E 138 B2
Dunedin N.Z. 45°50S 170°33E 285 F5
Dunedin Fla., U.S.A. 28°1N 82°46W 317 G7
Dunedoo Australia 32°0S 149°25E 283 A8
Dunfanaghy Ireland 55°11N 7°58W 166 A4
Dunfermline U.K. 56°5N 3°27W 167 E5
Dungannon Ont., Canada 43°51N 81°36W 312 C3
Dungannon Tyrone, U.K. 54°31N 6°46W 166 B5
Dungarpur India 23°52N 73°45E 242 H5
Dungarvan Ireland 52°5N 7°37W 166 D4
Dungarvan Harbour Ireland 52°4N 7°35W 166 D4
Dungeness U.K. 50°54N 0°59E 169 G8
Dungiven U.K. 54°56N 6°56W 166 B5
Dunglow Ireland 54°57N 8°21W 166 B3
Dungo, L. do Angola 17°15S 19°0E 265 F3
Dungog Australia 32°22S 151°46E 283 B9
Dungu Dem. Rep. of the Congo 3°40N 28°32E 268 B2
Dungun Malaysia 4°45N 103°25E 237 K4
Dungunâb Sudan 21°10N 37°9E 256 C4
Dungunâb, Khalîg Sudan 21°5N 37°12E 256 C4
Dunhua China 43°20N 128°14E 227 C15
Dunhuang China 40°8N 94°36E 218 C7
Dunk I. Australia 17°59S 146°29E 280 B4
Dunkassa Benin 10°21N 3°10E 263 C5
Dunkeld Queens., Australia 33°25S 149°29E 281 E4
Dunkeld Vic., Australia 37°40S 142°22E 282 D5
Dunkeld Perth & Kinr., U.K. 56°34N 3°35W 167 E5
Dunkerque France 51°2N 2°20E 173 A9
Dunkery Beacon U.K. 51°9N 3°36W 169 F4
Dunkirk = Dunkerque France 51°2N 2°20E 173 A9
Dunkirk U.S.A. 42°29N 79°20W 312 D5
Dunkuj Sudan 12°50N 32°49E 257 E3
Dunkwa Central, Ghana 6°0N 1°47W 262 D4
Dunkwa Central, Ghana 5°30N 1°0W 263 D4
Dunleary = Dún Laoghaire Ireland 53°17N 6°8W 120 B3
Dunleer Ireland 53°50N 6°24W 166 C5
Dunmanus B. Ireland 51°31N 9°50W 166 E2
Dunmanway Ireland 51°43N 9°6W 166 E2
Dunmarra Australia 16°42S 133°25E 280 B1
Dunmore U.S.A. 41°25N 75°38W 313 E9
Dunmore East Ireland 52°9N 7°0W 166 D5
Dunmore Town Bahamas 25°30N 76°39W 320 A4
Dunn U.S.A. 35°19N 78°37W 315 D15
Dunnellon U.S.A. 29°3N 82°28W 317 F7
Dunnet Hd. U.K. 58°40N 3°21W 167 C5
Dunning Ill., U.S.A. 41°56N 87°48W 119 B2
Dunning Nebr., U.S.A. 41°50N 100°6W 308 E3
Dunn's River Falls Jamaica 18°25N 77°8W 320 a
Dunnville Canada 42°54N 79°36W 312 D5
Dunolly Australia 36°51S 143°44E 282 D5
Dunoon U.K. 55°57N 4°56W 167 F4
Dunqul Egypt 23°26N 31°37E 256 C3
Duns U.K. 55°47N 2°20W 167 F6
Dunseith U.S.A. 48°50N 100°3W 308 A3
Dunshaughlin Ireland 53°31N 6°33W 166 C5
Dunsmuir U.S.A. 41°13N 122°16W 304 F2
Dunstable U.K. 51°53N 0°32W 169 F7
Dunstan Mts. N.Z. 44°53S 169°35E 285 E4
Dunster Canada 53°8N 119°50W 296 C5
Duntroon N.Z. 44°51S 170°40E 285 E5
Dunvegan Gauteng, S. Africa 26°9S 28°8E 123 A2
Dunvegan Highl., U.K. 57°27N 6°35W 167 D2
Dunvegan L. Canada 60°8N 107°10W 297 A7
Duolun China 42°12N 116°28E 226 C9
Duomo Italy 45°28N 9°11E 128 B2
Duomula China 34°8N 82°29E 217 F10
Duong Dong Vietnam 10°13N 103°58E 237 G4
Dupax del Norte Phil. 16°17N 121°5E 232 C3
Dupree U.S.A. 45°4N 101°35W 308 C3
Dupuyer U.S.A. 48°13N 112°30W 304 B7
Duque de Caxias Brazil 22°46S 43°18W 135 A1
Duque de York, I. Chile 50°37S 75°25W 336 D1
Durack → Australia 15°33S 127°52E 278 C4
Durack Ra. Australia 16°50S 127°40E 278 C4
Durack River Australia 15°32S 127°39E 278 C4
Durağan Turkey 41°25N 35°3E 212 B6
Durak Turkey 39°42N 28°17E 205 B10
Durakovac = Gjurakoc Kosovo 42°43N 20°29E 202 D4
Durance → France 43°55N 4°45E 175 E8
Durand Ga., U.S.A. 32°55N 84°46W 316 C5
Durand Ill., U.S.A. 42°26N 89°20W 310 B7
Durand Mich., U.S.A. 42°55N 83°59W 311 B13
Durand Wis., U.S.A. 44°38N 91°58W 308 C8
Durandeau St. Lucia 13°56N 60°59W 323 m
Durango Mexico 24°3N 104°39W 318 C4
Durango Colo., U.S.A. 37°16N 107°53W 305 H10
Durango □ Mexico 24°50N 105°20W 318 C4
Durankulak Bulgaria 43°41N 28°32E 203 C12
Durant Miss., U.S.A. 33°4N 89°51W 315 E10
Durant Okla., U.S.A. 33°59N 96°25W 314 E6
Duratón → Spain 41°37N 4°7W 194 D6
Durazno Uruguay 33°25S 56°31W 334 C4
Durazzo = Durrës Albania 41°19N 19°28E 202 E3
Durban Aude, France 42°59N 2°49E 174 F6
Durban KwaZulu Natal, S. Africa 29°49S 31°1E 271 C5
Durban ✈ (DIA) S. Africa 29°37S 31°7E 271 C5
Durbuy Belgium 50°21N 5°28E 170 D5
Dúrcal Spain 36°59N 3°34W 195 J7
Đurđevac Croatia 46°2N 17°3E 182 D2
Düren Germany 50°48N 6°29E 178 E2
Duren Sawit Indonesia 6°13S 106°54E 122 B2
Durg = Bhilainagar-Durg India 21°13N 81°26E 244 D5
Durgapur India 23°30N 87°20E 243 H12
Durham Ont., Canada 44°10N 80°49W 312 B4
Durham Darlington, U.K. 54°47N 1°34W 168 C6
Durham Calif., U.S.A. 39°39N 121°48W 306 F5
Durham N.C., U.S.A. 35°59N 78°54W 315 D15
Durham N.H., U.S.A. 43°8N 70°56W 313 C14
Durham □ U.K. 54°42N 1°45W 168 C6
Duri Indonesia 1°27N 101°15E 234 B2
Durlas = Thurles Ireland 52°41N 7°49W 166 D4
Durlești Moldova 47°1N 28°46E 183 C13
Ḍurmā Si. Arabia 24°37N 46°8E 246 E5
Durmitor Montenegro 43°10N 19°0E 202 C2
Durmitor △ Montenegro 43°15N 19°5E 202 C3
Durness U.K. 58°34N 4°45W 167 C4
Durnford, Pta. W. Sahara 23°37N 16°0W 260 D1
Durrës Albania 41°19N 19°28E 202 E3
Durrow Ireland 52°51N 7°24W 166 D4
Dursey I. Ireland 51°36N 10°12W 166 E1
Dursley U.K. 51°40N 2°21W 169 F5
Dursunbey Turkey 39°35N 28°37E 205 B10
Durtal France 47°40N 0°18W 172 E6
Duru Dem. Rep. of the Congo 4°14N 28°50E 268 B2
Duru Gölü Turkey 41°20N 28°35E 203 E12
Durukhsi Ethiopia 8°31N 45°28E 267 C6
Durusu Turkey 41°17N 28°41E 203 E12
Durūz, Jabal ad Jordan 32°35N 36°40E 250 F7
D'Urville, Tanjung Indonesia 1°28S 137°54E 231 E9
D'Urville I. N.Z. 40°50S 173°55E 285 A8
Duryea U.S.A. 41°20N 75°45W 313 E9
Dusa Mareb = Dhuusamarreeb Somalia 5°30N 46°15E 267 C6
Dûsh Egypt 24°35N 30°41E 256 C3
Dushak Turkmenistan 37°13N 60°1E 247 B9
Dushan China 25°48N 107°30E 228 E6
Dushanbe Tajikistan 38°33N 68°48E 217 E7
Dusheti Georgia 42°10N 44°42E 191 J7
Dushore U.S.A. 41°31N 76°24W 313 E8
Dusit Bangkok, Thailand 113 a2
Dusit Zoo Bangkok, Thailand 113 a2
Dusky Sd. N.Z. 45°47S 166°30E 285 F1
Dussejour, C. Australia 14°45S 128°13E 278 B4
Düsseldorf Germany 51°14N 6°47E 178 D2
Düsseldorf Rhein-Ruhr ✈ (DUS) Germany 51°17N 6°46E 178 D2
Dusti Tajikistan 37°20N 68°40E 217 E7
Duszniki-Zdrój Poland 50°24N 16°24E 185 H3
Dutch East Indies = Indonesia ■ Asia 5°0S 115°0E 235 C4
Dutch Guiana = Suriname ■ S. Amer. 4°0N 56°0W 329 C6
Dutch Harbor U.S.A. 53°53N 166°32W 303 K6
Dutlwe Botswana 23°58S 23°46E 270 B3
Dutsan Wai Nigeria 10°50N 8°10E 263 C6
Dutse Nigeria 11°46N 9°20E 263 C6
Dutton Canada 42°39N 81°30W 312 D3
Dutton → Australia 20°44S 143°10E 280 C3
Dutywa S. Africa 32°8S 28°18E 271 D4
Duved Sweden 63°23N 12°55E 162 A6
Düvertepe Turkey 39°14N 28°27E 205 B10
Dúvida = Roosevelt → Brazil 7°35S 60°20W 331 B5
Duwayhin, Khawr U.A.E. 24°20N 51°25E 247 E6
Duyfken Pt. Australia 12°33S 141°38E 280 A3
Duyun China 26°18N 107°29E 228 D6
Düzağaç Turkey 38°48N 30°10E 205 C12
Duzce = Akhna Cyprus 35°3N 33°47E 207 E9
Düzce Turkey 40°50N 31°10E 212 B4
Düzce □ Turkey 40°50N 31°10E 212 B4
Duzdab = Zāhedān Iran 29°30N 60°50E 247 D9
Duzer Guadeloupe 16°20N 61°44W 322 e
Düziçi Turkey 37°15N 36°28E 212 D7
Dve Mogili Bulgaria 43°35N 25°55E 203 C9
Dvigatelstroy = Kaspiysk Russia 42°52N 47°40E 191 J8
Dvina, Severnaya → Russia 64°32N 40°30E 186 B7
Dvinsk = Daugavpils Latvia 55°53N 26°32E 188 E4
Dvinskaya Guba Russia 65°0N 39°0E 186 B6
Dvor Croatia 45°4N 16°22E 199 C13
Dvůr Králové nad Labem Czech Rep. 50°27N 15°50E 180 A8
Dwarka India 22°18N 69°8E 242 H3
Dwellingup Australia 32°43S 116°4E 279 F2
Dwight Ont., Canada 45°20N 79°1W 312 A5
Dwight Ill., U.S.A. 41°5N 88°26W 311 C8
Dworp Belgium 50°44N 4°18E 116 B1
Dyakove Ukraine 48°1N 23°0E 182 B7
Dyakovo Russia 55°40N 37°39E 129 B2
Dyatkovo Russia 53°40N 34°27E 188 F8
Dyatlovo = Dzyatlava Belarus 53°28N 25°28E 177 B13
Dyce U.K. 57°13N 2°12W 167 D6
Dyer, C. Canada 66°37N 61°16W 295 D19
Dyer Bay Canada 45°10N 81°20W 312 A3
Dyer Plateau Antarctica 70°45S 65°30W 151 D17
Dyersburg U.S.A. 36°3N 89°23W 315 C10
Dyersville U.S.A. 42°29N 91°8W 310 B5
Dyfi → U.K. 52°32N 4°3W 169 E3
Dyhernfurth = Brzeg Dolny Poland 51°16N 16°41E 185 G3
Dyje → Czech Rep. 48°37N 16°56E 181 C9
Dyke Ackland B. Papua N. G. 9°0S 148°45E 286 E5
Dyker Beach Park U.S.A. 40°36N 74°1W 132 C1
Dykh Tau Russia 43°3N 43°8E 191 J6
Dymer Ukraine 50°47N 30°18E 177 C16
Dynów Poland 49°50N 22°11E 185 J9
Dyranut Norway 60°22N 7°31E 164 D4
Dyrhólaey Iceland 63°24N 19°8W 155 D7
Dyrnes Norway 63°25N 7°52E 164 A4
Dysart Queens., Australia 22°32S 148°23E 280 C4
Dysart Iowa, U.S.A. 42°10N 92°18W 310 B4
Dytiki Ellas □ Greece 38°20N 21°30E 204 C3
Dyushambe = Dushanbe Tajikistan 38°33N 68°48E 217 E7
Dyviziya Ukraine 45°55N 29°53E 183 E14
Dzamin Üüd = Borhoyn Tal Mongolia 43°50N 111°58E 226 C6
Dzaoudzi Mayotte 12°47S 45°16E 272 b
Dzaoudzi ✈ (DZA) Mayotte 12°48S 45°18E 272 b
Dzaudzhikau = Vladikavkaz Russia 43°0N 44°35E 191 J7
Dzavhan □ Mongolia 48°0N 96°0E 217 C13
Dzavhan Gol → Mongolia 48°54N 93°23E 218 B7
Dzerzhinsk Russia 56°14N 43°30E 190 B6
Dzerzhinskiy Russia 55°37N 37°50E 129 B2
Dzerzhinskiy Park Russia 55°50N 37°37E 129 B2
Dzhalal-Abad = Jalal-Abad Kyrgyzstan 40°56N 73°0E 217 D8
Dzhalal-Ogly = Stepanavan Armenia 41°1N 44°23E 191 K7
Dzhalinda Russia 53°26N 124°0E 215 D13
Dzhambeyty = Zhympīty Kazakhstan 50°16N 52°35E 216 B4
Dzhambul = Taraz Kazakhstan 42°54N 71°22E 217 D8
Dzhankoy Ukraine 45°40N 34°20E 189 K8
Dzhanybek = Zhänibek Kazakhstan 49°25N 46°50E 190 F8
Dzhargalantu = Hovd □ Mongolia 48°2N 91°37E 217 C12
Dzharkent = Zharkent Kazakhstan 44°10N 80°0E 217 D10
Dzharylhach, Ostriv Ukraine 46°2N 32°55E 189 J7
Dzhezkazgan = Zhezqazghan Kazakhstan 47°44N 67°40E 217 C7
Dzhibkhalantu = Uliastay Mongolia 47°56N 97°28E 218 B8
Dzhizak = Jizzax Uzbekistan 40°6N 67°50E 217 D7
Dzhugdzur, Khrebet Russia 57°30N 138°0E 215 D14
Dzhulynk Ukraine 48°26N 29°45E 183 B14
Dzhumgoltau, Khrebet Kyrgyzstan 42°15N 74°30E 217 D8
Dzhungarskiye Vorota = Dzungarian Gate Asia 45°10N 82°0E 217 C10
Dzhuryn Ukraine 48°41N 28°18E 183 B13
Dzhvari = Jvari Georgia 42°42N 42°4E 191 J6
Działdowo Poland 53°15N 20°15E 185 E7
Działoszyce Poland 50°22N 20°20E 185 H7
Działoszyn Poland 51°6N 18°50E 185 G5
Dzibilchaltún Mexico 21°10N 89°35W 319 C7
Dzierzgoń Poland 53°58N 19°20E 184 E6
Dzierżoniów Poland 50°45N 16°39E 185 H3
Dzilam de Bravo Mexico 21°24N 88°53W 319 C7
Dzioua Algeria 33°14N 5°14E 261 B6
Dzisna Belarus 55°34N 28°12E 188 E5
Dzisna → Belarus 55°34N 28°12E 188 E5
Dziwnów Poland 54°2N 14°45E 184 D1
Dzūkija △ Lithuania 54°10N 24°30E 161 J21
Dzungarian Basin = Junggar Pendi China 44°30N 86°0E 217 D11
Dzungarian Gate Asia 45°10N 82°0E 217 C10
Dzur Mongolia 49°39N 95°46E 217 C13
Dzüünbayan Mongolia 44°29N 110°2E 226 B6
Dzüünharaa Mongolia 48°52N 106°28E 218 B10
Dzüünmod Mongolia 47°45N 106°58E 218 B10
Dzyarzhynsk Belarus 53°40N 27°1E 177 B14
Dzyatlava Belarus 53°28N 25°28E 177 B13


# E


E.C. Manning △ Canada 49°5N 120°45W 296 D4
E.T. Joshua ✈ (SVD) St. Vincent 13°8N 61°13W 323 n
E.U.R. = Esposizione Universale di Roma Italy 41°49N 12°28E 136 C1
Eabamet L. Canada 51°30N 87°46W 298 B2
Eabametoong Canada 51°30N 88°0W 298 B2
Éadan Doire = Edenderry Ireland 53°21N 7°4W 166 C4
Eads U.S.A. 38°29N 102°47W 304 G12
Eagar U.S.A. 34°6N 109°17W 305 J9
Eagle Alaska, U.S.A. 64°47N 141°12W 303 D12
Eagle Colo., U.S.A. 39°39N 106°50W 304 G10
Eagle → Canada 53°36N 57°26W 299 B8
Eagle, Mt. U.S. Virgin Is. 17°46N 64°49W 321 b
Eagle Beach Aruba 12°32N 70°3W 322 f
Eagle Butte U.S.A. 45°0N 101°10W 308 C3
Eagle Cr. → U.S.A. 38°36N 85°4W 311 F11
Eagle Grove U.S.A. 42°40N 93°54W 310 B3
Eagle L. Ont., Canada 49°42N 93°13W 297 D10
Eagle L. Calif., U.S.A. 40°39N 120°45W 304 F3
Eagle L. Maine, U.S.A. 46°20N 69°22W 309 B19
Eagle Lake Ont., Canada 45°8N 78°29W 312 A6
Eagle Lake Maine, U.S.A. 47°3N 68°36W 309 B19
Eagle Lake Tex., U.S.A. 29°35N 96°20W 314 G6
Eagle Mountain U.S.A. 33°49N 115°27W 307 M11
Eagle Nest U.S.A. 36°33N 105°16W 305 H11
Eagle Pass U.S.A. 28°43N 100°30W 314 G4
Eagle Pk. U.S.A. 38°10N 119°25W 306 G7
Eagle Pt. Australia 16°11S 124°23E 278 C3
Eagle River Mich., U.S.A. 47°25N 88°18W 308 B9
Eagle River Wis., U.S.A. 45°55N 89°15W 308 C9
Eagle Rock U.S.A. 34°8N 118°12W 126 B3
Eaglehawk Australia 36°44S 144°15E 282 D6
Eagles Mere U.S.A. 41°25N 76°33W 313 E8
Eagleville U.S.A. 40°28N 93°59W 310 D3
Ealing □ U.K. 51°31N 0°20W 125 A2
Ear Falls Canada 50°38N 93°13W 297 C10
Earlimart U.S.A. 35°53N 119°16W 307 K7
Earl's Court London, U.K. 125 c1
Earlsfield U.K. 51°26N 0°10W 125 B2
Earlville Ill., U.S.A. 41°35N 88°55W 311 C8
Earlville N.Y., U.S.A. 42°44N 75°32W 313 D9
Earlwood Australia 33°55S 151°8E 139 B1
Early Branch U.S.A. 32°45N 80°55W 316 C9
Earn → U.K. 56°21N 3°18W 167 E5
Earn, L. U.K. 56°23N 4°13W 167 E4
Earnslaw, Mt. N.Z. 44°32S 168°27E 285 E3
Earth U.S.A. 34°14N 102°24W 314 D3
Eas Vanuatu 16°20S 168°15E 287 F6
Easley U.S.A. 34°50N 82°36W 315 D13
East Anglia U.K. 52°50N 1°0E 168 E9
East Angus Canada 45°30N 71°40W 299 C5
East Antarctica Antarctica 80°0S 90°0E 151 D7
East Arlington Mass., U.S.A. 42°24N 71°8W 116 A2
East Arlington Va., U.S.A. 38°51N 77°4W 143 B2
East Aurora U.S.A. 42°46N 78°37W 312 D6
East Ayrshire □ U.K. 55°26N 4°11W 167 F4
East Bedfont U.K. 51°26N 0°28W 125 B1
East Beskids = Vychodné Beskydy Europe 49°20N 22°0E 181 B15
East Boston U.S.A. 42°22N 71°1W 116 A2
East Brady U.S.A. 40°59N 79°37W 312 F5
East Branch Clarion River L. U.S.A. 41°35N 78°35W 312 E6
East C. = Dezhneva, Mys Russia 66°5N 169°40W 215 C19
East C. N.Z. 37°42S 178°35E 284 D7
East C. Papua N. G. 10°13S 150°53E 286 F6
East Caroline Basin Pac. Oc. 4°0N 146°45E 288 G6
East Chicago U.S.A. 41°38N 87°27W 311 C9
East China Sea Asia 30°0N 126°0E 219 F14
East Coulee Canada 51°23N 112°27W 296 C6
East Dereham = Dereham U.K. 52°41N 0°57E 169 E8
East Don → Canada 43°48N 79°25W 141 A2
East Don Parkland Canada 43°47N 79°22W 141 A2
East Dublin U.S.A. 32°32N 82°52W 316 C7
East Dubuque U.S.A. 42°30N 90°39W 310 B6
East Dunbartonshire □ U.K. 55°57N 4°13W 167 F4
East Elmhurst U.S.A. 40°45N 73°52W 132 B2
East End Pt. Bahamas 25°3N 77°16W 153 b
East Falkland Falk. Is. 51°30S 58°30W 153 f
East Finchley U.K. 51°35N 0°10W 125 A2
East Flatbush U.S.A. 40°39N 73°55W 132 B2
East Fork White → U.S.A. 38°33N 87°14W 311 F9
East Grand Forks U.S.A. 47°56N 97°1W 308 B5
East Grand Rapids U.S.A. 42°58N 85°37W 311 B11
East Greenwich U.S.A. 41°40N 71°27W 313 E13
East Grinstead U.K. 51°7N 0°0 169 F8
East Ham U.K. 51°32N 0°3E 125 A4
East Hartford U.S.A. 41°46N 72°39W 313 E12
East Haydon Australia 18°0S 141°30E 280 B3
East Helena U.S.A. 46°35N 111°56W 304 C8

East Humber → Canada 43°47N 79°35W 141 A1
East Indies Asia 0°0 120°0E 210 J14
East Kilbride U.K. 55°47N 4°11W 167 F4
East Lamma Channel
Hong Kong, China 22°14N 114°9E 122 B2
East Lansing U.S.A. 42°44N 84°29W 311 B12
East Las Vegas = Whitney
U.S.A. 36°4N 115°5W 124 B2
East Lexington U.S.A. 42°25N 71°12W 116 A1
East Livermore = Livermore Falls
U.S.A. 44°29N 70°11W 309 C18
East Liverpool U.S.A. 40°37N 80°35W 312 F4
East London S. Africa 33°0S 27°55E 271 D4
East Los Angeles U.S.A. 34°1N 118°10W 126 B3
East Lothian □ U.K. 55°58N 2°44W 167 F6
East Main = Eastmain
Canada 52°10N 78°30W 298 B4
East Mariana Basin
Pac. Oc. 12°0N 153°0E 288 F7
East Milwaukee = Shorewood
U.S.A. 43°5N 87°53W 311 A9
East Molesey U.K. 51°24N 0°21W 125 B1
East Moline U.S.A. 41°32N 90°26W 310 C6
East Naples U.S.A. 26°8N 81°46W 317 J8
East New Britain □
Papua N. G. 6°30S 152°30E 286 D7
East New York U.S.A. 40°40N 73°53W 132 B2
East Northport U.S.A. 40°53N 73°20W 313 F11
East Orange U.S.A. 40°46N 74°12W 313 F10
East Pacific Rise Pac. Oc. 15°0S 110°0W 289 J17
East Pakistan = Bangladesh ■
Asia 24°0N 90°0E 241 D3
East Palatka U.S.A. 29°39N 81°36W 316 F8
East Palestine U.S.A. 40°50N 80°33W 312 F4
East Peoria U.S.A. 40°40N 89°34W 310 D7
East Pine Canada 55°48N 120°12W 296 B4
East Pines U.S.A. 38°57N 76°54W 143 B3
East Point U.S.A. 33°41N 84°25W 113 B2
East Potomac Park
Washington, D.C., U.S.A. 143 c1
East Providence U.S.A. 41°49N 71°23W 313 E13
East Pt. Br. Virgin Is. 18°40N 64°18W 321 b
East Pt. N.S., Canada 46°27N 61°58W 299 C7
East Pt. U.S. Virgin Is. 17°45N 64°34W 321 b
East Renfrewshire □ U.K. 55°46N 4°21W 167 F4
East Retford = Retford
U.K. 53°19N 0°56W 168 D7
East Riding of Yorkshire □
U.K. 53°55N 0°30W 168 D7
East River → New York, U.S.A. 132 e3
East Rochester U.S.A. 43°7N 77°29W 312 C7
East Rutherford U.S.A. 40°50N 74°5W 132 A1
East St. Louis U.S.A. 38°37N 90°9W 310 F6
East Schelde = Oosterschelde →
Neths. 51°33N 4°0E 170 C4
East Sea = Japan, Sea of
Asia 40°0N 135°0E 220 E7
East Sepik □ Papua N. G. 4°0S 143°45E 286 C2
East Sheen U.K. 51°27N 0°16W 125 B2
East Siberian Sea Russia 73°0N 160°0E 215 B17
East Stroudsburg U.S.A. 41°1N 75°11W 313 E9
East Sussex □ U.K. 50°56N 0°19E 169 G8
East Talpiyot West Bank 31°45N 35°13E 123 B2
East Tasman Plateau
Pac. Oc. 43°30S 152°0E 288 M7
East Tawas U.S.A. 44°17N 83°29W 309 C12
East Timor ■ Asia 8°50S 126°0E 231 F7
East Toorale Australia 30°27S 145°28E 281 E4
East Troy U.S.A. 42°47N 88°24W 311 B8
East Village New York, U.S.A. 132 e2
East Walker → U.S.A. 38°52N 119°10W 306 G7
East Wickham U.K. 51°28N 0°5E 125 B4
East Windsor U.S.A. 40°17N 74°34W 313 F10
East York Canada 43°40N 79°22W 141 A2
East Youngstown = Campbell
U.S.A. 41°5N 80°37W 312 E4
Eastbourne N.Z. 41°19S 174°55E 284 H3
Eastbourne E. Sussex, U.K. 50°46N 0°18E 169 G8
Eastcote U.K. 51°34N 0°23W 125 A1
Eastend Canada 49°32N 108°50W 297 D7
Easter Fracture Zone
Pac. Oc. 25°0S 115°0W 289 K16
Easter Howgate U.K. 55°52N 3°12W 121 B2
Easter I. = Pascua, I. de
Chile 27°7S 109°23W 330 b
Eastern □ Ghana 6°30N 0°30W 263 D4
Eastern □ Kenya 0°0 38°30E 268 C4
Eastern □ S. Leone 8°15N 11°0W 262 D2
Eastern Cape □ S. Africa 32°0S 26°0E 270 D4
Eastern Cr. → Australia 20°40S 141°35E 280 C3
Eastern Desert = Es Sahrâ' Esh
Sharqîya Egypt 27°30N 32°30E 256 B3
Eastern Equatoria □
South Sudan 5°0N 33°0E 257 G3
Eastern Ghats India 14°0N 78°50E 245 H4
Eastern Group = Lau Group
Fiji 17°0S 178°30W 287 A3
Eastern Group Australia 33°30S 124°30E 279 F3
Eastern Guruma ⊙
Australia 22°0S 117°30E 278 D2
Eastern Highlands □
Papua N. G. 6°30S 145°35E 286 D3
Eastern I. Midway Is. 28°12N 177°19W 302 c
Eastern Samar □ Phil. 11°40N 125°40E 233 F5
Eastern Transvaal =
Mpumalanga □ S. Africa 26°0S 30°0E 271 C5
Easterville Canada 53°8N 99°49W 297 C9
Easthampton U.S.A. 42°16N 72°40W 313 D12
Eastlake U.S.A. 41°40N 81°26W 312 E3
Eastland U.S.A. 32°24N 98°49W 314 E5
Eastleigh U.K. 50°58N 1°21W 169 G6
Eastmain Canada 52°10N 78°30W 298 B4
Eastmain → Canada 52°27N 78°26W 298 B4
Eastman Qué., Canada 45°18N 72°19W 313 A12
Eastman Ga., U.S.A. 32°12N 83°11W 316 C6
Eastman Wis., U.S.A. 43°10N 91°1W 310 A5
Easton Md., U.S.A. 38°47N 76°5W 309 F15
Easton Pa., U.S.A. 40°41N 75°13W 313 F9
Easton Wash., U.S.A. 47°14N 121°11W 306 C5
Eastover U.S.A. 33°52N 80°41W 316 B9
Eastpoint U.S.A. 29°44N 84°53W 316 F5
Eastpoint Park Canada 43°46N 79°10W 141 A4
Eastport U.S.A. 44°56N 67°0W 309 C20
Eastsound U.S.A. 48°42N 122°55W 306 B4
Eastwood Australia 33°47S 151°4E 139 A1
Eaton Colo., U.S.A. 40°32N 104°42W 304 F11
Eaton Ohio, U.S.A. 39°45N 84°38W 311 E12
Eaton Canyon Park
U.S.A. 34°10N 118°7W 126 A4
Eaton Centre Toronto, Canada 141 a2
Eaton Rapids U.S.A. 42°31N 84°39W 311 B12
Eatonia Canada 51°13N 109°25W 297 C7
Eatonton U.S.A. 33°20N 83°23W 316 B6
Eatontown U.S.A. 40°19N 74°4W 313 F10
Eatonville U.S.A. 46°52N 122°16W 306 D4
Eau Claire Fr. Guiana 3°30N 53°40W 329 C7
Eau Claire Wis., U.S.A. 44°49N 91°30W 308 C8
Eau Claire, L. à l' Canada 56°10N 74°25W 298 A5
Eauripik Rise Pac. Oc. 2°0N 142°0E 288 G6
Eauze France 43°53N 0°7E 174 E4
Eban Nigeria 9°40N 4°50E 263 D5
Ebanga Angola 12°45S 14°45E 265 E2
Ebangalakata
Dem. Rep. of the Congo 0°29S 21°29E 264 C4
Ebano Mexico 22°13N 98°24W 319 C5
Ebara Japan 35°35N 139°42E 140 B3
Ebbegebirge ⌂ Germany 51°10N 7°55E 178 D3
Ebbw Vale U.K. 51°46N 3°12W 169 F4
Ebebiyín Eq. Guin. 2°9N 11°20E 264 B2
Ebel Gabon 0°7N 11°5E 264 B2
Ebeltoft Denmark 56°12N 10°41E 163 H4
Ebeltoft Vig Denmark 56°10N 10°35E 163 H4
Ebensburg U.S.A. 40°29N 78°44W 312 F6
Ebensee Austria 47°48N 13°46E 180 D6
Eber Gölü Turkey 38°38N 31°11E 212 C4
Eberbach Germany 49°28N 8°59E 179 F4
Eberswalde-Finow
Germany 52°50N 13°49E 178 C9
Ebetsu Japan 43°7N 141°34E 220 C10
Ebey's Landing ⌂ U.S.A. 48°12N 122°41W 306 B4
Ebian China 29°11N 103°13E 228 C4
Ebingen Germany 48°13N 9°1E 179 G5
Ebino Japan 32°2N 130°48E 222 E2
Ebinur Hu China 44°55N 82°55E 217 D10
Ebisu Japan 35°38N 139°42E 140 B3
Ebla Syria 35°50N 36°48E 250 C7
Ebo Angola 11°40S 14°40E 265 E2
Ebola →
Dem. Rep. of the Congo 3°20N 20°57E 264 B4
Éboli Italy 40°39N 15°2E 201 B8
Ebolowa Cameroon 2°55N 11°10E 263 E7
Ebonda
Dem. Rep. of the Congo 2°12N 22°21E 264 B4
Ebonyi □ Nigeria 6°20N 8°0E 263 D6
Eboy Dem. Rep. of the Congo 2°50N 23°11E 264 B4
Ebrach Germany 49°51N 10°29E 179 F6
Ebre = Ebro → Spain 40°43N 0°54E 196 E5
Ébrié, Lagune Ivory C. 5°12N 4°26W 262 D4
Ebro → Spain 40°43N 0°54E 196 E5
Ebro, Embalse del Spain 43°0N 3°58W 194 C7
Ebstorf Germany 53°2N 10°24E 178 B6
Ebute-Metta Nigeria 6°28N 3°23E 124 B2
Ecatepec de Morelos
Mexico 19°36N 99°3W 319 D5
Ecbatana = Hamadān
Iran 34°52N 48°32E 213 E13
Ecclesville Trin. & Tob. 10°19N 61°8W 323 f
Eceabat Turkey 40°11N 26°21E 203 F10
Ech Chéliff Algeria 36°10N 1°20E 261 A5
Ech Chéliff □ Algeria 36°15N 1°30E 261 A5
Echague Phil. 16°42N 121°38E 232 C3
Echechonnee → U.S.A. 32°39N 83°36W 316 C6
Echigo-Sammyaku Japan 36°50N 139°50E 221 F9
Echinades Greece 38°25N 21°2E 207 C3
Echinos Greece 41°16N 25°1E 203 E9
Échirolles France 45°8N 5°44E 175 C9
Echizen Japan 35°50N 136°10E 223 B8
Echizen-Misaki Japan 35°59N 135°57E 223 B7
Echmiadzin = Ejmiatsin
Armenia 40°12N 44°19E 191 K7
Echo U.S.A. 31°29N 85°28W 316 D4
Echo Bay N.W.T., Canada 66°5N 117°55W 294 D8
Echo Bay Ont., Canada 46°29N 84°4W 298 C3
Echo Park Los Angeles, U.S.A. 127 a1
Echoing → Canada 55°51N 92°5W 298 B1
Echterdingen, Stuttgart ✕ (STR)
Germany 48°42N 9°11E 179 G5
Echternach Lux. 49°49N 6°25E 170 E6
Echuca Australia 36°10S 144°45E 283 D6
Écija Spain 37°30N 5°10W 195 H5
Eckental Germany 49°35N 11°12E 179 F7
Eckernförde Germany 54°28N 9°50E 178 A5
Eclectic U.S.A. 32°38N 86°2W 316 C3
Eclipse I. Australia 35°5S 117°58E 279 G2
Eclipse Is. Australia 13°54S 126°19E 278 B4
Eclipse Sd. Canada 72°38N 79°0W 295 C16
Écommoy France 47°50N 0°17E 172 E7
Economy = Ambridge
U.S.A. 40°36N 80°14W 312 F4
Ecoporanga Brazil 18°23S 40°50W 333 E3
Écouché France 48°42N 0°10W 172 D6
Ecrins △ France 44°54N 6°18E 175 D10
Ecuador ■ S. Amer. 2°0S 78°0W 328 D2
Ecuador, Volcán Ecuador 1°1S 91°32W 330 a
Écueillé France 47°5N 1°21E 172 E8
Ed Sweden 58°55N 11°55E 163 F5
Ed Dabbura Sudan 17°40N 34°15E 256 D3
Ed Da'ein Sudan 11°26N 26°9E 257 E2
Ed Damazin Sudan 11°46N 34°21E 266 B3
Ed Dâmer Sudan 17°27N 34°0E 256 D3
Ed Dar el Beida = Casablanca
Morocco 33°36N 7°36W 260 B3
Ed Debba Sudan 18°0N 30°51E 256 D3
Ed Déffa Egypt 30°40N 26°30E 256 A2
Ed Deim Sudan 10°10N 28°20E 257 E2
Ed Dibeikir Sudan 10°23N 29°9E 266 B2
Ed Dueim Sudan 14°0N 32°10E 257 E3
Eda Japan 35°33N 139°33E 140 B2
Edam Sask., Canada 53°11N 108°46W 297 C7
Edam Neths. 52°31N 5°3E 170 B5
Edane Sweden 59°38N 12°49E 162 E6
Edapally India 11°19N 78°3E 245 J4
Eday U.K. 59°11N 2°47W 167 B6
Edchera W. Sahara 27°2N 13°4W 260 C2
Edd Eritrea 14°0N 41°38E 257 E5
Eddrachillis B. U.K. 58°17N 5°14W 167 C3
Eddystone U.K. 50°11N 4°16W 169 G3
Eddystone Pt. Australia 40°59S 148°20E 281 G4
Eddyville U.S.A. 41°9N 92°38W 310 C4
Ede Neths. 52°4N 5°40E 170 B5
Ede Nigeria 7°45N 4°29E 263 D5
Édéa Cameroon 3°51N 10°9E 263 E7
Edebäck Sweden 60°4N 13°32E 162 D7
Edehon L. Canada 60°25N 97°15W 297 A9
Edelény Hungary 48°18N 20°44E 182 B5
Eden = Bar Harbor
U.S.A. 44°23N 68°13W 309 C19
Eden N.S.W., Australia 37°3S 149°55E 283 D8
Eden N.C., U.S.A. 36°29N 79°53W 315 C15
Eden N.Y., U.S.A. 42°39N 78°55W 312 D6
Eden Tex., U.S.A. 31°13N 99°51W 314 F5
Eden → U.K. 54°57N 3°1W 168 C4
Eden Gardens
Kolkata, India 22°34N 88°20E 124 B2
Edenburg S. Africa 29°43S 25°58E 270 C4
Edendale N.Z. 46°19S 168°48E 285 G3
Edendale Gauteng, S. Africa 26°8S 28°9E 123 A2
Edendale KwaZulu Natal,
S. Africa 29°39S 30°18E 271 C5
Edenderry Ireland 53°21N 7°4W 166 C4
Edenhope Australia 37°4S 141°19E 282 D4
Edenmore Ireland 53°22N 6°11W 120 A2
Edenton U.S.A. 36°4N 76°39W 315 C16
Edenville S. Africa 27°37S 27°34E 271 C4
Eder → Germany 51°12N 9°28E 178 D5
Eder-Stausee Germany 51°10N 8°57E 178 D4
Edessa Greece 40°48N 22°5E 202 F6
Edewecht Germany 53°8N 7°58E 178 B3
Edfu = Idfû Egypt 24°55N 32°49E 256 C3
Edgar U.S.A. 40°22N 97°58W 308 E5
Edgars Cr. → Australia 37°43S 144°58E 128 A1
Edgartown U.S.A. 41°23N 70°31W 313 E14
Edge Hill U.K. 52°8N 1°26W 169 E6
Edgecumbe N.Z. 37°59S 176°47E 284 D5
Edgefield U.S.A. 33°47N 81°56W 316 B8
Edgeley Ont., Canada 43°47N 79°31W 141 A1
Edgeley N. Dak., U.S.A. 46°22N 98°43W 308 B4
Edgemere U.S.A. 37°39N 122°29W 136 C2
Edgemont U.S.A. 43°18N 103°50W 308 D2
Edgeøya Svalbard 77°45N 22°30E 150 B9
Edgerton Ohio, U.S.A. 41°27N 84°45W 311 C12
Edgerton Wis., U.S.A. 42°50N 89°4W 310 B7
Edgewater Fla., U.S.A. 28°59N 80°54W 317 G9
Edgewater N.J., U.S.A. 40°49N 73°58W 132 B2
Edgewood Fla., U.S.A. 28°29N 81°22W 133 B2
Edgewood Ill., U.S.A. 38°55N 88°40W 311 F8
Édhessa = Edessa Greece 40°48N 22°5E 202 F6
Edievale N.Z. 45°49S 169°22E 285 F4
Edina Liberia 6°0N 10°10W 262 D2
Edina Mo., U.S.A. 40°10N 92°11W 310 D4
Edinboro U.S.A. 41°52N 80°8W 312 E4
Edinburg Ill., U.S.A. 39°39N 89°23W 310 E7
Edinburg Tex., U.S.A. 26°18N 98°10W 314 H5
Edinburgh Edinburgh, U.K. 55°57N 3°13W 121 B2
Edinburgh Ind., U.S.A. 39°21N 85°58W 311 E11
Edinburgh ✕ (EDI) U.K. 55°54N 3°22W 121 B1
Edinburgh, City of □ U.K. 55°57N 3°17W 167 F5
Edinburgh Castle Edinburgh, U.K. 121 b2
Edineţ Moldova 48°9N 27°18E 183 B12
Edirne Turkey 41°40N 26°34E 203 E10
Edirne □ Turkey 41°12N 26°30E 203 E10
Edison Ga., U.S.A. 31°34N 84°44W 316 D5
Edison Wash., U.S.A. 48°33N 122°27W 306 B4
Edison Park U.S.A. 42°1N 87°48W 119 A2
Edisto → U.S.A. 32°29N 80°21W 316 C9
Edisto Beach U.S.A. 32°29N 80°20W 316 C9
Edisto I. U.S.A. 32°35N 80°20W 316 C9
Edithburgh Australia 35°5S 137°43E 282 C2
Edjeleh Algeria 28°38N 9°50E 261 C6
Edmeston U.S.A. 42°42N 75°15W 313 D9
Edmond U.S.A. 35°39N 97°29W 314 D6
Edmonds U.S.A. 47°48N 122°22W 306 C4
Edmondston U.S.A. 38°56N 76°54W 143 B3
Edmondstown Ireland 53°17N 6°18W 120 B2
Edmonton Queens.,
Australia 17°2S 145°46E 280 B4
Edmonton Alta., Canada 53°30N 113°30W 296 C6
Edmund L. Canada 54°45N 93°17W 298 B1
Edmundston Canada 47°23N 68°20W 299 C6
Edna U.S.A. 28°59N 96°39W 314 G6
Edo □ Nigeria 6°30N 6°0E 263 D6
Edo → Japan 35°38N 139°52E 140 B4
Edogawa Japan 35°43N 139°52E 140 A4
Edolo Italy 46°10N 10°21E 198 B7
Edøya Norway 63°18N 8°10E 164 A5
Edremit Turkey 39°34N 27°0E 205 B9
Edremit Körfezi Turkey 39°30N 26°45E 205 B8
Edsberg Sweden 59°26N 17°57E 139 A1
Edsbro Sweden 59°54N 18°29E 162 E12
Edsbruk Sweden 58°1N 16°29E 163 F10
Edsbyn Sweden 61°23N 15°49E 162 C9
Edson Canada 53°35N 116°28W 296 C5
Eduardo Castex Argentina 35°50S 64°18W 334 D3
Eduardo Frei Antarctica 62°30S 58°0W 151 C18
Edward → Australia 35°5S 143°30E 282 C5
Edward, L. Africa 0°25S 29°40E 268 C2
Edward VII Land
Antarctica 80°0S 150°0W 151 E13
Edwardesabad = Bannu
Pakistan 33°0N 70°18E 240 B3
Edwards Calif., U.S.A. 34°50N 117°40W 307 L9
Edwards N.Y., U.S.A. 44°20N 75°15W 313 B9
Edwards → U.S.A. 41°9N 90°59W 310 C6
Edwards I. Australia 37°42S 144°59E 128 A1
Edwards Plateau U.S.A. 30°45N 101°20W 314 F4
Edwardsburg U.S.A. 41°48N 86°6W 311 C10
Edwardsville Ill., U.S.A. 38°49N 89°58W 310 F7
Edwardsville Pa., U.S.A. 41°15N 75°56W 313 E9
Edzná Mexico 19°39N 90°19W 319 D6
Edzo = Behchoko Canada 62°49N 116°4W 296 A5
Eek U.S.A. 60°14N 162°2W 303 F7
Eeklo Belgium 51°11N 3°33E 170 C3
Eel → Ind., U.S.A. 39°7N 86°57W 311 E10
Eel → Ind., U.S.A. 40°45N 86°22W 311 D10
Eenhana Namibia 17°30S 16°23E 270 A2
Eesti = Estonia ■ Europe 58°30N 25°30E 188 C3
Efate, I. Vanuatu 17°40S 168°25E 287 G6
Eferding Austria 48°18N 14°1E 180 C7
Effigy Mounds ⌂ U.S.A. 43°5N 91°11W 310 A5
Effingham U.S.A. 39°7N 88°33W 311 E8
Eforie Romania 44°1N 28°37E 183 F13
Efoulen Cameroon 2°46N 10°43E 264 B2
Eftelot Norway 59°33N 9°49E 164 E6
Efxinoupoli Greece 39°12N 22°44E 204 B4
Efzonos Greece 37°55N 23°49E 112 B2
Ega → Spain 42°19N 1°55W 196 C3
Egadi, Ísole Italy 37°55N 12°16E 200 E5
Egaleo Greece 37°59N 23°40E 112 B2
Egaleo, Oros Greece 38°0N 23°36E 112 B1
Egan Range U.S.A. 39°35N 114°55W 304 G6
Eganville Canada 45°32N 77°5W 312 A7
Egedesminde = Aasiaat
Greenland 68°43N 52°56W 154 D5
Egegik U.S.A. 58°13N 157°22W 303 G8
Eger = Cheb Czech Rep. 50°9N 12°28E 180 A5
Eger Hungary 47°53N 20°27E 182 C5
Eger → Hungary 47°38N 20°50E 182 C5
Egersund Norway 58°26N 6°1E 164 F3
Egg L. Canada 55°5N 105°30W 297 B7
Egg I. St. Helena 15°58S 5°47W 153 h
Eggedal Norway 60°14N 9°22E 164 D6
Eggegebirge Südlicher Teutoburger
Wald ⌂ Germany 51°40N 8°59E 178 D4
Eggenburg Austria 48°38N 15°50E 180 C8
Eggenfelden Germany 48°23N 12°46E 179 G8
Egherta Somalia 2°4N 43°11E 267 D5
Eghezée Belgium 50°35N 4°55E 170 D4
Egholo Solomon Is. 8°25S 157°25E 287 M9
Egilsstaðir Iceland 65°16N 14°25W 155 B12
Egina Greece 37°45N 23°26E 204 D5
Eginio Greece 40°28N 22°28E 202 F6
Egio Greece 38°15N 22°5E 204 C4
Egito Angola 12°4S 13°58E 265 E2
Egletons France 45°24N 2°3E 174 C6
Eglinton I. Canada 75°48N 118°30W 295 B8
Egmont Canada 49°45N 123°56W 296 D4
Egmont, C. N.Z. 39°16S 173°45E 284 F2
Egmont, Mt. = Taranaki, Mt.
N.Z. 39°17S 174°5E 284 F3
Egmont △ N.Z. 39°17S 174°4E 284 F3
Egra India 21°54N 87°32E 243 J12
Eğridir Turkey 37°52N 30°51E 212 D4
Eğridir Gölü Turkey 37°53N 30°50E 212 D4
Egtved Denmark 55°38N 9°18E 163 J3
Éguas → Brazil 13°26S 44°14W 333 D3
Egum Atoll Papua N. G. 9°25S 152°0E 286 E7
Éguzon-Chantôme France 46°27N 1°33E 173 F8
Egvekinot Russia 66°19N 179°50W 215 C19
Egyek Hungary 47°39N 20°52E 182 C5
Egypt ■ Africa 28°0N 31°0E 256 B3
Eha Amufu Nigeria 6°30N 7°46E 263 D6
Eheli Algeria 22°26N 4°40E 261 D5
Ehime □ Japan 33°30N 132°40E 222 D4
Ehingen Germany 48°16N 9°43E 179 G5
Ehrenberg U.S.A. 33°36N 114°31W 307 M12
Ehrhardt U.S.A. 33°6N 81°1W 316 B8
Ehrwald Austria 47°24N 10°56E 180 D3
Eiao French Polynesia 8°0S 140°40W 289 f
Eibar Spain 43°11N 2°28W 196 B2
Eibenschitz = Ivančice
Czech Rep. 49°6N 16°23E 181 B9
Eiche Germany 52°33N 13°35E 115 A4
Eiche Süd Germany 52°33N 13°35E 115 A4
Eichstätt Germany 48°54N 11°11E 179 G7
Eide Hordaland, Norway 60°31N 6°44E 164 D3
Eide Møre og Romsdal,
Norway 62°55N 7°27E 164 B4
Eider → Germany 54°19N 8°57E 178 A4
Eidsbugarden Norway 61°23N 8°16E 164 C5
Eidsbygda Norway 62°36N 7°33E 164 B4
Eidsdalen Norway 62°16N 7°10E 164 B4
Eidsvåg Norway 62°46N 8°2E 164 B5
Eidsvold Australia 25°25S 151°12E 281 D5
Eidsvoll Norway 60°19N 11°14E 164 D8
Eielson U.S.A. 64°40N 147°4W 303 D11
Eifel Germany 50°15N 6°50E 179 E2
Eiffel, Tour Paris, France 134 c2
Eiffel Flats Zimbabwe 18°20S 30°0E 269 F3
Eiger Switz. 46°34N 8°1E 198 B5
Eigg U.K. 56°54N 6°10W 167 E2
Eighty Mile Beach
Australia 19°30S 120°40E 278 C3
Eikefjord Norway 61°35N 5°27E 164 C2
Eikelandsosen Norway 60°15N 5°43E 164 D2
Eiken Norway 58°29N 7°14E 164 F4
Eikeren Norway 59°38N 9°58E 164 E6
Eikesdalen Norway 62°28N 8°12E 164 B5
Eil, L. U.K. 56°51N 5°16W 167 E3
Eil Malk Palau 7°10N 134°23E 288 c
Eilat = Elat Israel 29°30N 34°56E 251 J5
Eildon Australia 37°14S 145°55E 283 D6
Eildon, L. Australia 37°10S 146°0E 283 D7
Eilean Siar □ U.K. 57°30N 7°10W 167 D1
Eilenburg Germany 51°27N 12°36E 178 D8
Ein Arik West Bank 31°54N 35°8E 123 A1
Ein el Luweiqa Sudan 14°5N 33°50E 257 E3
Ein Naquba Israel 31°47N 35°7E 123 B1
Ein Rafa Israel 31°47N 35°7E 123 B1
Eina Norway 60°38N 10°35E 164 D7
Einarsstaðir Iceland 65°44N 17°24W 155 B9
Einasleigh Australia 18°32S 144°5E 280 B3
Einasleigh → Australia 17°30S 142°17E 280 B3
Einbeck Germany 51°49N 9°53E 178 D5
Eindhoven Neths. 51°26N 5°28E 170 C5
Einsiedeln Switz. 47°7N 8°46E 179 H4
Eire = Ireland ■ Europe 53°50N 7°52W 166 C4
Eiríksjökull Iceland 64°46N 20°24W 155 C6
Eiriksstaðir Iceland 65°7N 15°25W 155 B11
Eiriosgaigh = Eriskay U.K. 57°4N 7°18W 167 D1
Eirunepé Brazil 6°35S 69°53W 330 B4
Eiseb → Namibia 20°33S 20°59E 270 B2
Eisenach Germany 50°58N 10°19E 178 E6
Eisenberg Germany 50°58N 11°54E 178 E7
Eisenerz Austria 47°32N 14°54E 180 D7
Eisenhüttenstadt Germany 52°9N 14°38E 178 C10
Eisenkappel Austria 46°29N 14°36E 180 E7
Eisenstadt Austria 47°51N 16°31E 181 D9
Eisenstein = Železná Ruda
Czech Rep. 49°8N 13°15E 180 B6
Eisfeld Germany 50°25N 10°54E 179 E6
Eisleben Germany 51°32N 11°32E 178 D7
Eislingen Germany 48°41N 9°42E 179 G5
Eivindvik Norway 60°59N 5°5E 164 D2
Eivissa Spain 38°54N 1°26E 206 D1
Eixe, Serra do Spain 42°24N 6°54W 194 C4
Eizariya West Bank 31°46N 35°16E 123 B2
Ejby Denmark 55°41N 12°24E 118 A2
Ejea de los Caballeros Spain 42°7N 1°9W 196 C3
Ejeda Madag. 24°20S 44°31E 272 C1
Ejigbo Nigeria 6°33N 3°18E 124 A1
Ejmiatsin Armenia 40°12N 44°19E 191 K7
Ejura Ghana 7°23N 1°15W 263 D4
Ejutla Mexico 16°34N 96°44W 319 D5
Ekalaka U.S.A. 45°53N 104°33W 304 D11
Ekalla Gabon 1°27S 14°0E 264 C2
Ekanga
Dem. Rep. of the Congo 2°23S 23°14E 264 C4
Ekaterinburg = Yekaterinburg
Russia 56°50N 60°30E 214 D7
Ekeberg Norway 59°53N 10°46E 133 A3
Ekenäs = Raasepori
Finland 60°0N 23°26E 188 B2
Ekenässjön Sweden 57°28N 15°1E 163 G9
Ekerö Sweden 59°16N 17°45E 162 E11
Eket Nigeria 4°38N 7°56E 263 E6
Eketahuna N.Z. 40°38S 175°43E 284 G4
Ekibastuz Kazakhstan 51°50N 75°10E 217 B9
Ekiti □ Nigeria 7°25N 5°20E 263 D6
Eklutna U.S.A. 61°27N 149°22W 303 F10
Eknäs Sweden 59°18N 18°13E 139 B3
Ekoli Dem. Rep. of the Congo 0°23S 24°13E 264 C4
Ekoln Sweden 59°45N 17°37E 162 E11
Ekouamou Congo 0°8N 16°31E 264 B3
Ekoungounou Congo 1°10S 15°52E 264 C3
Ekshärad Sweden 60°10N 13°30E 162 D7
Eksjö Sweden 57°40N 14°58E 163 G8
Ekukola
Dem. Rep. of the Congo 0°31S 18°56E 264 C3
Ekuku
Dem. Rep. of the Congo 0°41S 21°42E 264 C4
Ekukula
Dem. Rep. of the Congo 0°15N 21°30E 264 B4
Ekuma → Namibia 18°40S 16°2E 270 A2
Ekuta Dem. Rep. of the Congo 3°0N 18°50E 264 B3
Ekwan → Canada 53°12N 82°15W 298 B3
Ekwan Pt. Canada 53°16N 82°7W 298 B3
Ekwok U.S.A. 59°22N 157°30W 303 G8
El Aaiún W. Sahara 27°9N 13°12W 260 C2
El Aargub Mauritania 23°37N 15°52W 260 D1
El Abanico Chile 37°20S 71°31W 334 D1
El 'Abbasiya El Qâhira,
Egypt 30°3N 31°16E 117 A2
El Abbasiya Sudan 12°10N 31°18E 257 E3
El Abiodh-Sidi-Cheikh
Algeria 32°53N 0°31E 261 B5
El Adde Somalia 2°35N 46°9E 267 D6
El Adeb Larache Algeria 27°22N 8°52E 261 C6
El 'Agrûd Egypt 30°14N 34°24E 251 H5
El Agua Venezuela 11°8N 63°52W 329 a
El Agustino Peru 12°2S 77°0W 124 B2
El Agustino, Cerro Peru 12°3S 76°59W 124 B3
El Aïoun Morocco 34°33N 2°30W 261 B4
El Ait Sudan 12°22N 27°27E 257 E2
El 'Aiyat Egypt 29°36N 31°15E 256 J7
El Alamein Egypt 30°48N 28°58E 256 A2
El Alto Peru 4°15S 81°14W 330 A1
El Aouj Mauritania 22°53N 12°49W 260 D2
El 'Aqaba, W. → Egypt 30°7N 33°54E 251 H4
El 'Arag Egypt 28°40N 26°20E 256 B2
El Aricha Algeria 34°13N 1°10W 261 B4
El Arîḥâ West Bank 31°52N 35°27E 251 G4
El 'Arîsh Egypt 31°8N 33°50E 251 G4
El 'Arîsh, W. → Egypt 31°8N 33°47E 251 G4
El Arrouch Algeria 36°37N 6°53E 261 A6
El Asnam = Ech Chéliff
Algeria 36°10N 1°20E 261 A5
El Astillero Spain 43°24N 3°49W 194 B7
El Avagi Somalia 3°36N 46°57E 267 D6
El Badâri Egypt 27°4N 31°25E 256 B3
El Badrshein Egypt 29°51N 31°16E 251 J2
El Bagur Egypt 30°25N 31°2E 251 H2
El Bahrein Egypt 28°30N 26°25E 256 B2
El Ballâs Egypt 26°2N 32°43E 256 B3
El Balyana Egypt 26°10N 32°3E 256 B3
El Banco Colombia 9°0N 73°58W 328 B3
El Baqeir Sudan 18°40N 33°40E 256 D3
El Baragil Egypt 30°4N 31°9E 117 A1
El Barco de Ávila Spain 40°21N 5°31W 194 E5
El Barco de Valdeorras = O Barco
Spain 42°23N 6°58W 194 C4
El Basâlîn Egypt 29°58N 31°16E 117 B2
El Bauga Sudan 18°18N 33°52E 256 D3
El Baúl Venezuela 8°57N 68°17W 328 B4
El Bawiti Egypt 28°25N 28°45E 256 B2
El Bayadh Algeria 33°40N 1°1E 261 B5
El Bayadh □ Algeria 32°30N 1°10E 261 B5
El Bichar Venezuela 10°46N 63°58W 329 a
El Bierzo Spain 42°45N 6°30W 194 C4
El Bira West Bank 31°54N 35°13E 123 A2
El Bluff Nic. 11°59N 83°40W 320 D3
El Bolsón Argentina 41°55S 71°30W 336 B2
El Bonillo Spain 38°57N 2°35W 197 G2
El Bosque Chile 33°32S 70°40W 137 C2
El Buheirat = Lakes □
South Sudan 7°0N 30°0E 257 F3
El Bur Somalia 4°40N 46°37E 267 D6
El Burgo de Osma Spain 41°35N 3°4W 196 D1
El Cain Argentina 41°38S 68°19W 336 B3
El Cajon U.S.A. 32°48N 116°58W 307 N10
El Calafate Argentina 50°19S 72°15W 336 D2
El Callao Venezuela 7°18N 61°50W 329 B5
El Campello Spain 38°26N 0°24W 197 G4
El Campo U.S.A. 29°12N 96°16W 314 G6
El Capitan U.S.A. 37°44N 119°38W 306 H7
El Carbón Honduras 15°25N 85°32W 320 C2
El Cardón Venezuela 11°6N 63°51W 329 a
El Carmen Bolivia 13°40S 63°55W 331 C5
El Carmen Santiago, Chile 33°22S 70°43W 137 B1
El Carmen Colombia 9°43N 75°8W 328 B2
El Centro U.S.A. 32°48N 115°34W 307 N11
El Cerro Bolivia 17°30S 61°40W 331 D5
El Cerro de Andévalo
Spain 37°45N 6°57W 195 H4
El Cocuy Colombia 6°25N 72°27W 328 B3
El Cocuy △ Colombia 6°33N 72°5W 328 B3
El Compadre Mexico 32°20N 116°14W 307 N10
El Copey, Cerro Venezuela 11°11N 63°55W 329 a
El Corcovado Argentina 43°25S 71°35W 336 B2
El Coronil Spain 37°5N 5°38W 195 H5
El Cortijo Chile 33°22S 70°42W 137 B1
El Cotillo Canary Is. 28°41N 14°1W 153 e2
El Cristo, Vaso Regulador
Mexico 19°30N 99°5W 128 B1
El Cuy Argentina 39°55S 68°25W 336 A3
El Cuyo Mexico 21°31N 87°41W 319 C7
El Dab'a Egypt 31°0N 28°27E 256 H6
El Daheir Egypt 31°13N 34°10E 251 G5
El Dambahaddo Somalia 3°17N 46°40E 267 D6
El Deir Egypt 25°25N 32°20E 256 B3
El Dere = Ceeldheere
Somalia 5°22N 46°11E 267 C6
El Dere Ethiopia 5°6N 43°5E 267 C5
El Descanso Mexico 32°12N 116°58W 307 N10
El Desemboque Mexico 30°33N 113°1W 318 A2
El Dilingat Egypt 30°50N 30°31E 256 H7
El Diviso Colombia 1°22N 78°14W 328 C2
El Djouf Mauritania 21°25N 6°40W 260 D3
El Dorado Sinaloa,
Mexico 24°17N 107°21W 318 C3
El Dorado Ark., U.S.A. 33°12N 92°40W 314 E8
El Dorado Kans., U.S.A. 37°49N 96°52W 308 G5
El Dorado Venezuela 6°55N 61°37W 329 B5
El Dorado Springs U.S.A. 37°52N 94°1W 310 G2
El Duqqi Egypt 30°1N 31°12E 117 A2
El Eglab Algeria 26°20N 4°30W 260 C4
El 'Ein Sudan 16°35N 29°22E 257 D2
El Ejido Spain 36°47N 2°49W 195 J8
El Encinar de los Reyes
Spain 40°30N 3°39W 127 A2
El Escorial Spain 40°35N 4°7W 194 E6
El Espinal Venezuela 10°58N 63°59W 329 a
El Espinar Spain 41°43N 4°15W 194 D6
El Eulma Algeria 36°9N 5°42E 261 A6
El Faiyûm Egypt 29°19N 30°50E 256 J7
El Faourar Tunisia 33°22N 8°45E 258 B1
El Fâsher Sudan 13°33N 25°26E 257 E2
El Fashn Egypt 28°50N 30°54E 256 J7
El Ferrol = Ferrol Spain 43°29N 8°15W 194 B2
El Fifi Sudan 10°4N 25°0E 257 E2
El Fud Ethiopia 7°15N 42°52E 267 C5
El Fuerte Mexico 26°25N 108°39W 318 B3
El Ga'a Sudan 14°16N 29°59E 257 E2
El Gamâlîya Egypt 31°10N 31°52E 251 G2
El Garef Sudan 12°3N 34°19E 257 E3
El Gebir Sudan 13°40N 29°40E 257 E2
El Gedida Egypt 25°40N 28°30E 256 B2
El Geneina = Al Junaynah
Sudan 13°27N 22°45E 259 F4
El Geteina Sudan 14°50N 32°27E 257 E3
El Gezira Egypt 30°2N 31°13E 117 A2
El Gezira □ Sudan 15°0N 33°0E 257 E3
El Gharbîya □ Egypt 30°50N 31°0E 251 H2
El Ghurîya Egypt 30°2N 31°15E 117 A2
El Gir Sudan 19°50N 28°18E 256 D2
El Gîza Egypt 30°0N 31°12E 117 A2
El Gogorrón △ Mexico 21°49N 100°57W 318 C4
El Goléa Algeria 30°30N 2°50E 261 B5
El Gouna Egypt 27°5N 33°47E 256 B3
El Guamache Nueva Esparta,
Venezuela 10°44N 63°54W 329 a
El Guamache Nueva Esparta,
Venezuela 10°54N 64°3W 329 a
El Hadjira Algeria 32°36N 5°30E 261 B6
El Hagiz Sudan 15°15N 35°50E 257 D4
El Hâi Egypt 29°39N 31°18E 256 J7
El Hajeb Morocco 33°43N 5°13W 260 B3
El Hamma Tunisia 33°54N 9°48E 258 B1
El Hammam Egypt 30°52N 29°25E 256 A2
El Hammâmi Mauritania 23°3N 11°30W 260 D2
El Hâmûl Egypt 31°18N 31°9E 251 G2
El Hamurre Somalia 7°13N 48°54E 267 C6
El Hank Mauritania 24°30N 7°0W 260 D3
El Hasian W. Sahara 26°20N 14°0W 260 C2
El Hawata Sudan 13°25N 34°42E 257 E3
El Hideib Sudan 13°0N 32°50E 257 E3
El Hilla Sudan 13°24N 27°2E 257 E2
El Homr Algeria 29°43N 1°45E 261 C5
El 'Idisât Egypt 25°30N 32°35E 256 B3
El Iskandarîya Egypt 31°13N 29°58E 256 H6
El Jadida Morocco 33°11N 8°17W 260 B3
El Jardal Honduras 14°54N 88°50W 320 D2
El Jebelein Sudan 12°40N 32°55E 257 E3
El Jebha Morocco 35°11N 4°43W 260 A4
El Jem Tunisia 35°19N 10°41E 258 A2
El Kab Sudan 19°27N 32°46E 256 D3
El Kafr el Sharqi Egypt 31°16N 31°10E 256 H7
El Kala Algeria 36°53N 8°26E 261 A6
El Kamlin Sudan 15°3N 33°11E 257 D3
El Kantara Algeria 35°14N 5°45E 261 A6
El Kantara Tunisia 33°45N 10°58E 258 B2
El Karaba Sudan 18°32N 33°41E 256 D3
El Kef Tunisia 36°12N 8°47E 258 A1
El Kef □ Tunisia 36°0N 9°0E 261 A6
El Kelaâ de Srahna Morocco 32°4N 7°27W 260 B3
El Kelaâ M'Gouna Morocco 31°14N 6°7W 260 B3
El Kere Ethiopia 5°50N 42°5E 257 F5
El Khadr West Bank 31°42N 35°10E 123 B1
El Khalîfa Egypt 30°1N 31°15E 117 B2
El Khandaq Sudan 18°30N 30°30E 256 D3
El Khârga Egypt 25°30N 30°33E 256 B3
El Khartûm Sudan 15°31N 32°35E 257 D3
El Khartûm □ Sudan 16°0N 33°0E 257 D3
El Khartûm Bahrî Sudan 15°40N 32°31E 257 D3
El Khroub Algeria 36°10N 6°55E 261 A6
El Kôm el Ahmar Egypt 30°6N 31°10E 117 A2
El Kseur Algeria 36°46N 4°49E 261 A5
El Ksiba Morocco 32°45N 6°1W 260 B3
El Kuntilla Egypt 30°1N 34°45E 251 H5
El Laqâwa Sudan 11°25N 29°1E 257 E2
El Leh Ethiopia 3°46N 39°13E 257 G4
El Leiya Sudan 16°15N 35°28E 257 D4
El Leoncito △ Argentina 31°58S 69°10W 334 C2
El Limón Panama 9°15N 79°49W 320 c
El Lucero Mexico 30°37N 106°31W 318 A3
El Ma'âdi Egypt 29°57N 31°15E 117 B2
El Maestrazgo Spain 40°30N 0°25W 196 E4
El Mafâza Sudan 13°38N 34°30E 257 E3
El Maghra Egypt 30°15N 28°55E 256 A2
El Mahalla el Kubra Egypt 31°0N 31°0E 256 H7
El Mahârîq Egypt 25°35N 30°35E 256 B3
El Maîmûn Egypt 29°14N 31°12E 256 J7
El Maitén Argentina 42°3S 71°10W 336 B2
El Maiz Algeria 28°19N 0°9W 261 C4
El Maks el Bahari Egypt 24°30N 30°40E 256 C3
El Malpais ⌂ U.S.A. 34°53N 108°0W 305 J10
El Manshâh Egypt 26°26N 31°50E 256 B3
El Mansour Algeria 27°47N 0°14W 261 C4
El Mansûra Egypt 31°0N 31°19E 256 H7
El Manteco Venezuela 7°38N 62°45W 329 B5
El Manzala Egypt 31°10N 31°50E 256 H7
El Marâgha Egypt 26°35N 31°10E 256 B3
El Masid Sudan 15°15N 33°0E 257 D3
El Masnou Spain 41°28N 2°20E 196 D7
El Matariya El Mansûra,
Egypt 31°15N 32°0E 256 H8
El Matarîya El Qâhira, Egypt 30°7N 31°18E 117 A2
El Meda Ethiopia 5°39N 41°47E 257 F5
El Medano Canary Is. 28°3N 16°32W 153 e1
El Meghaier Algeria 33°55N 5°58E 261 B6
El Ménia = El Goléa Algeria 30°30N 2°50E 261 B5
El Meraguen Algeria 28°0N 0°7W 261 C4
El Metemma Sudan 16°50N 33°10E 257 D3
El Miamo Venezuela 7°39N 61°46W 329 B5
El Milagro Argentina 30°59S 65°59W 334 C2
El Milia Algeria 36°51N 6°13E 261 A6
El Minufîya □ Egypt 30°30N 31°0E 251 H2
El Minyâ Egypt 28°7N 30°33E 256 B3
El Mohandessin Egypt 30°2N 31°11E 117 A2
El Monte U.S.A. 34°4N 118°1W 126 B4
El Montseny Spain 41°55N 2°25E 196 D7
El Mreiti Mauritania 23°29N 7°51W 260 D3
El Mreyye Mauritania 18°0N 6°0W 262 B3
El Muqattam Egypt 30°1N 31°17E 117 A2
El Mûskî Egypt 30°3N 31°15E 117 A2
El Nido Phil. 11°10N 119°25E 233 F2
El Niybo Ethiopia 4°40N 39°55E 257 G4
El Obeid Sudan 13°8N 30°10E 257 E3
El Odaiya Sudan 12°8N 28°12E 257 E2
El Oro Mexico 19°51N 100°7W 319 D4
El Oro □ Ecuador 3°30S 79°50W 328 D2
El Oued Algeria 33°20N 6°58E 261 B6
El Oued □ Algeria 33°10N 7°15E 261 B6
El Palmar Bolivia 17°50S 63°9W 331 D5
El Palmar Venezuela 7°58N 61°53W 329 B5
El Palmar △ Argentina 32°10S 58°31W 334 C4
El Pardo Spain 40°30N 3°46W 127 A1
El Paso = Derby U.S.A. 37°33N 97°16W 308 G5
El Paso Ill., U.S.A. 40°44N 89°1W 310 D7
El Paso Tex., U.S.A. 31°45N 106°29W 314 F1
El Paso de Robles = Paso Robles
U.S.A. 35°38N 120°41W 306 K6
El Pedernoso Spain 39°29N 2°45W 197 F2
El Pedroso Spain 37°51N 5°45W 195 H5
El Pilar Venezuela 10°32N 63°9W 329 A5
El Pinacate y Gran Desierto de
Altar = Gran Desierto del
Pinacate ⌂ Mexico 31°51N 113°32W 318 A2
El Pobleneu Spain 41°23N 2°11E 114 A2
El Pobo de Dueñas Spain 40°46N 1°39W 196 E3
El Portal Calif., U.S.A. 37°41N 119°47W 306 H7
El Portal Fla., U.S.A. 25°51N 80°11W 129 C2
El Porvenir Mexico 31°15N 105°51W 318 A3
El Prat Barcelona ✕ (BCN)
Spain 41°18N 2°5E 114 B1
El Prat de Llobregat Spain 41°19N 2°5E 114 B1
El Progreso Galápagos Is.,
Ecuador 0°54S 89°33W 330 a
El Progreso Honduras 15°26N 87°51W 320 C2
El Pueblo Canary Is. 28°36N 17°47W 153 e1
El Pueblo de Los Angeles Historic
Park Los Angeles, U.S.A. 127 b2
El Puente del Arzobispo
Spain 39°48N 5°10W 194 F5
El Puerto de Santa María
Spain 36°36N 6°13W 195 J4
El Qâhira Egypt 30°2N 31°13E 117 A2
El Qanâyat Egypt 30°37N 31°27E 251 H2
El Qantara Egypt 30°51N 32°20E 251 H3
El Qasr Egypt 25°44N 28°42E 256 B2
El Qassâsîn Egypt 30°33N 31°55E 251 H2
El Qubâbât Egypt 29°28N 31°16E 256 J7
El Qubba Egypt 30°4N 31°16E 117 A2
El Quseima Egypt 30°40N 34°15E 251 H5
El Qusîya Egypt 27°29N 30°44E 256 B3
El Râshda Egypt 25°36N 28°57E 256 B2
El Reloj Mexico 19°19N 99°9W 128 C2
El Reno U.S.A. 35°32N 97°57W 301 H20
El Retiro Spain 40°25N 3°41W 127 B1
El Rey △ Argentina 24°40S 64°34W 334 A3
El Rîdisiya Egypt 24°56N 32°51E 256 C3
El Rio U.S.A. 34°14N 119°10W 307 L7
El Ronquillo Spain 37°44N 6°10W 195 H4
El Roque, Pta. Canary Is. 28°10N 15°25W 153 e1
El Rosario Mexico 30°1N 115°45W 318 A1
El Rubio Spain 37°22N 5°0W 195 H5
El Saff Egypt 29°34N 31°16E 256 J7
El Salto Santiago, Chile 33°22S 70°38W 137 B2
El Salto Durango, Mexico 23°47N 105°22W 318 C3
El Salvador ■ Cent. Amer. 13°50N 89°0W 320 D2
El Sauce Nic. 13°0N 86°40W 320 D2
El Saucejo Spain 37°4N 5°6W 195 H5
El Sereno U.S.A. 34°4N 118°10W 126 B3
El Shallal Egypt 24°0N 32°53E 256 C3
El Simbillawein Egypt 30°48N 31°13E 256 H7
El Sombrero Venezuela 9°23N 67°3W 328 B4
El Suweis Egypt 29°58N 32°31E 256 B3
El Suweis □ Egypt 29°30N 32°15E 251 J3
El Tabbîn Egypt 29°47N 31°18E 256 J7
El Talibîya Egypt 29°59N 31°10E 117 B2
El Tamà △ S. Amer. 7°25N 72°25W 328 B3
El Tamarâni, W. → Egypt 30°7N 34°43E 251 H5
El Tarf Algeria 36°46N 8°19E 261 A6
El Tarf □ Algeria 36°45N 8°10E 261 A6
El Thamad Egypt 29°40N 34°28E 251 J5
El Tigre Venezuela 8°44N 64°15W 329 B5
El Tîh, Gebel Egypt 29°40N 33°50E 251 J4
El Tîna Egypt 31°3N 32°22E 256 H8
El Tirano Puerte Fermín
Venezuela 11°7N 63°51W 329 a
El Tocuyo Venezuela 9°47N 69°48W 328 B4
El Tofo Chile 29°22S 71°18W 334 B1
El Tránsito Chile 28°52S 70°17W 334 B1
El Tucuche Trin. & Tob. 10°43N 61°25W 323 f
El Tuey Venezuela 11°1N 63°57W 329 a
El Tunal Venezuela 11°3N 63°58W 329 a
El Tuparro △ Colombia 5°19N 68°28W 328 B4
El Tûr Egypt 28°14N 33°36E 251 K4
El Turbio Argentina 51°45S 72°5W 336 D2
El Uarre Somalia 3°4N 45°20E 267 D6
El Uqsur Egypt 25°41N 32°38E 256 B3
El Valle △ Spain 37°56N 1°6W 197 H3
El Valle del Espíritu Santo
Venezuela 10°49N 63°53W 329 a
El Vendrell Spain 41°10N 1°30E 196 D6
El Vergel Chihuahua,
Mexico 26°28N 106°22W 318 B3
El Vergel Distrito Federal,
Mexico 19°18N 99°5W 128 C2
El Vigía Venezuela 8°38N 71°39W 328 B3
El Viso del Alcor Spain 37°23N 5°43W 195 H5
El Wabeira Egypt 29°34N 33°6E 251 J4
El Wâhli Egypt 30°3N 31°16E 117 A2
El Wak Somalia 2°49N 41°1E 267 D5
El Weguet Ethiopia 5°28N 42°17E 257 F5
El Wuz Sudan 15°5N 30°7E 257 D3
El Yaque Venezuela 10°54N 63°57W 329 a
El Yunque, Cerro Chile 33°39S 78°50W 330 c

El Yunque Puerto Rico 18°19N 65°48W 321 b
El Zamâlik Egypt 30°3N 31°12E 117 A2
El Zeitûn Egypt 30°6N 31°18E 117 A2
Elafonisos Greece 36°29N 22°56E 204 E4
Elamanchili India 17°33N 82°50E 244 F6
Élancourt France 48°47N 1°58E 173 D8
Elands Australia 31°37S 152°20E 283 A10
Elandsfontein Junc. = Germiston S. Africa 26°13S 28°10E 123 B2
Elasa Greece 35°18N 26°21E 205 F8
Elassona Greece 39°53N 22°12E 204 B4
Elat Israel 29°30N 34°56E 251 J5
Elati Oros Greece 38°43N 20°39E 207 B2
Elatia Greece 38°37N 22°46E 204 C4
Elâzığ Turkey 38°37N 39°14E 213 C8
Elâzığ □ Turkey 38°40N 39°15E 213 C8
Elba Italy 42°46N 10°17E 198 F7
Elba Ala., U.S.A. 31°25N 86°4W 316 D3
Elbasan Albania 41°9N 20°9E 202 E4
Elbe U.S.A. 46°45N 122°10W 306 D4
Elbe → Europe 53°50N 9°0E 178 B4
Elbe-Seitenkanal Germany 52°45N 10°32E 178 C6
Elberfeld U.S.A. 38°10N 87°27W 311 F9
Elbert, Mt. U.S.A. 39°7N 106°27W 304 G10
Elberton U.S.A. 34°7N 82°52W 316 A7
Elbeuf France 49°17N 1°2E 172 C8
Elbeyli Turkey 36°40N 37°27E 250 B8
Elbing = Elbląg Poland 54°10N 19°25E 184 D6
Elbistan Turkey 38°13N 37°15E 212 C7
Elbląg Poland 54°10N 19°25E 184 D6
Elbow Canada 51°7N 106°35W 297 C7
Elbrus Russia 43°21N 42°30E 191 J6
Elbufer-Drawehn ⌓ Germany 53°8N 10°58E 178 B6
Elburn U.S.A. 41°54N 88°28W 311 C8
Elburz Mts. = Alborz, Reshteh-ye Kūhhā-ye Iran 36°0N 52°0E 247 C7
Elche Spain 38°15N 0°42W 197 G4
Elche de la Sierra Spain 38°27N 2°3W 197 G2
Elcho I. Australia 11°55S 135°45E 280 A2
Elda Spain 38°29N 0°47W 197 G4
Eldama Ravine Kenya 0°3N 35°43E 268 B4
Elde → Germany 53°7N 11°15E 178 B7
Eldey Iceland 63°45N 22°55W 155 D4
Eldon Iowa, U.S.A. 40°55N 92°13W 310 D4
Eldon Mo., U.S.A. 38°21N 92°35W 310 F4
Eldon Wash., U.S.A. 47°33N 123°3W 306 C3
Eldora U.S.A. 42°22N 93°5W 310 B3
Eldorado = Echo Bay Canada 66°5N 117°55W 294 D8
Eldorado Argentina 26°28S 54°43W 335 B5
Eldorado Ont., Canada 44°35N 77°31W 312 B7
Eldorado Ill., U.S.A. 37°49N 88°26W 311 G8
Eldorado Tex., U.S.A. 30°52N 100°36W 314 F4
Eldorendo U.S.A. 31°3N 84°39W 316 D5
Eldoret Kenya 0°30N 35°17E 268 B4
Eldred U.S.A. 41°58N 78°23W 312 E6
Eldridge U.S.A. 41°39N 90°35W 310 C6
Elea, C. Cyprus 35°19N 34°4E 207 E10
Eleanora, Pk. Australia 32°57S 121°9E 279 F3
Eleao U.S.A. 21°27N 157°52W 302 K14
Elefantes → Africa 24°10S 32°40E 271 B5
Elefantes, B. das Angola 13°13S 12°44E 265 E2
Elefantes, G. Chile 46°28S 73°49W 336 C2
Elefsina Greece 38°4N 23°26E 204 C5
Eleftherios Venizelos ✈ (ATH) Greece 37°56N 23°56E 112 A3
Elektrogorsk Russia 55°56N 38°50E 188 E10
Elektroperedacha = Elektrogorsk Russia 55°56N 38°50E 188 E10
Elektrostal Russia 55°41N 38°32E 188 E10
Elektrovoz = Stupino Russia 54°57N 38°2E 188 E10
Elele Nigeria 5°5N 6°50E 263 D6
Elemi Triangle = Ilemi Triangle Africa 5°0N 35°20E 257 G4
Elena Bulgaria 42°55N 25°53E 203 D9
Elephant Butte Res. U.S.A. 33°9N 107°11W 305 K10
Elephant I. Antarctica 61°0S 55°0W 151 C18
Elephant Pass Sri Lanka 9°35N 80°25E 245 K5
Elephanta Caves India 18°57N 72°57E 130 B2
Elephanta I. India 18°57N 72°56E 130 B2
Elesbão Veloso Brazil 6°13S 42°8W 332 C3
Eleshnitsa Bulgaria 41°52N 23°36E 202 E7
Eleşkirt Turkey 39°50N 42°50E 213 C10
Eleuthera I. Bahamas 25°0N 76°20W 320 B4
Eleutheroupoli Greece 40°52N 24°20E 203 F8
Elfin Cove U.S.A. 58°12N 136°22W 303 G13
Elgå Norway 62°10N 11°56E 164 B8
Elgin Ont., Canada 44°36N 76°13W 313 B8
Elgin Moray, U.K. 57°39N 3°19W 167 D5
Elgin Ill., U.S.A. 42°2N 88°17W 311 B8
Elgin N. Dak., U.S.A. 46°24N 101°51W 308 B3
Elgin Oreg., U.S.A. 45°34N 117°55W 304 D5
Elgin S.C., U.S.A. 34°10N 80°48W 316 A9
Elgin Tex., U.S.A. 30°21N 97°22W 314 F6
Elgoibar Spain 43°13N 2°24W 196 B2
Elgon, Mt. Africa 1°10N 34°30E 268 B3
Elgspiggen Norway 62°10N 11°21E 164 B8
Eliase Indonesia 8°21S 130°48E 231 F8
Elikonos Oros Greece 38°18N 22°45E 204 C4
Elim Namibia 17°48S 15°31E 270 A2
Elim Western Cape, S. Africa 34°35S 19°45E 270 D2
Elim Alaska, U.S.A. 64°37N 162°15W 303 D7
Elin Pelin Bulgaria 42°40N 23°36E 202 D7
Elingampangu Dem. Rep. of the Congo 2°0S 24°4E 264 C4
Elipa Dem. Rep. of the Congo 1°3S 24°20E 264 C4
Elis = Ilia Greece 37°45N 21°35E 204 D3
Eliseu Martins Brazil 8°13S 43°42W 332 C3
Elista Russia 46°16N 44°14E 191 G7
Eliza, L. Australia 37°15S 139°50E 282 D3
Elizabeth S. Austral., Australia 34°42S 138°41E 282 C3
Elizabeth Ill., U.S.A. 42°19N 90°13W 310 B6
Elizabeth N.J., U.S.A. 40°39N 74°12W 313 F10
Elizabeth, B. Ecuador 0°36S 91°12W 330 a
Elizabeth City U.S.A. 36°18N 76°14W 315 C16
Elizabethton U.S.A. 36°21N 82°13W 315 C13
Elizabethtown Ky., U.S.A. 37°42N 85°52W 311 G11
Elizabethtown N.Y., U.S.A. 44°13N 73°36W 313 B11
Elizabethtown Pa., U.S.A. 40°9N 76°36W 313 F8
Elizabethville = Lubumbashi Dem. Rep. of the Congo 11°40S 27°28E 269 E2
Elizondo Spain 43°12N 1°30W 196 B3
Elk Poland 53°50N 22°21E 184 E9
Elk → B.C., Canada 49°11N 115°14W 296 C5
Elk → Poland 53°41N 22°28E 184 E9
Elk → Ala., U.S.A. 34°46N 87°16W 315 D11
Elk City U.S.A. 35°25N 99°25W 314 D5
Elk Creek U.S.A. 39°36N 122°32W 306 F4
Elk Grove U.S.A. 38°25N 121°22W 306 G5
Elk Island △ Canada 53°35N 112°59W 296 C6
Elk Lake Canada 47°40N 80°25W 298 C3
Elk Point Canada 53°54N 110°55W 297 C6
Elk River Idaho, U.S.A. 46°47N 116°11W 304 C5
Elk River Minn., U.S.A. 45°18N 93°35W 308 C7
Elkader U.S.A. 42°51N 91°24W 310 B5
Elkedra → Australia 21°8S 136°22E 280 C2
Elkhart Ind., U.S.A. 41°41N 85°58W 311 C11
Elkhart Kans., U.S.A. 37°0N 101°54W 308 G3
Elkhart → U.S.A. 41°41N 85°58W 311 C11
Elkhorn Man., Canada 49°59N 101°14W 297 D8
Elkhorn Wis., U.S.A. 42°40N 88°33W 311 B8
Elkhorn → U.S.A. 41°8N 96°19W 308 E5
Elkhovo Bulgaria 42°10N 26°35E 203 D10
Elkin U.S.A. 36°15N 80°51W 315 C14
Elkins U.S.A. 38°55N 79°51W 309 F14
Elkland U.S.A. 41°59N 77°19W 312 E7
Elko B.C., Canada 49°20N 115°10W 296 D5
Elko Nev., U.S.A. 40°50N 115°46W 304 F6
Elkton U.S.A. 43°49N 83°11W 312 C1
Ellas = Greece ■ Europe 40°0N 23°0E 204 B3
Ellaville Fla., U.S.A. 30°23N 83°10W 316 E6
Ellaville Ga., U.S.A. 32°14N 84°19W 316 C5
Ellboda Sweden 59°24N 18°15E 139 A3
Ellef Ringnes I. Canada 78°30N 102°2W 295 B11
Ellen, Mt. U.S.A. 44°9N 72°56W 313 B12
Ellenburg U.S.A. 44°54N 73°48W 313 B11
Ellendale U.S.A. 46°0N 98°32W 308 B4
Ellenor, L. U.S.A. 28°28N 81°25W 133 B2
Ellensburg U.S.A. 46°59N 120°34W 304 C3
Ellenville U.S.A. 41°43N 74°24W 313 E10
Ellerton Barbados 13°7N 59°33W 323 r
Ellery, Mt. Australia 37°28S 148°47E 283 D8
Ellesmere = Scottsdale Australia 41°9S 147°31E 281 G4
Ellesmere, L. N.Z. 43°47S 172°28E 285 D7
Ellesmere I. Canada 79°30N 80°0W 295 B16
Ellesmere Island = Quttinirpaaq △ Canada 82°13N 72°13W 295 A17
Ellesmere Port U.K. 53°17N 2°54W 168 D5
Ellettsville U.S.A. 39°14N 86°38W 311 E10
Ellice Is. = Tuvalu ■ Pac. Oc. 8°0S 178°0E 277 B14
Ellicottville U.S.A. 42°17N 78°40W 312 D6
Ellington U.S.A. 42°13N 79°6W 312 D5
Elliniko Olympic Complex Greece 37°50N 23°45E 112 B2
Elliot N. Terr., Australia 17°33S 133°32E 280 B1
Elliot Eastern Cape, S. Africa 31°22S 27°48E 271 D4
Elliot Lake Canada 46°25N 82°35W 298 C3
Elliotdale = Xhora S. Africa 31°55S 28°38E 271 D4
Elliott U.S.A. 34°6N 80°10W 316 A9
Elliott Key U.S.A. 25°27N 80°12W 317 K9
Ellipse, The Washington, D.C., U.S.A. 143 b1
Ellis U.S.A. 38°56N 99°34W 308 F4
Ellis I. U.S.A. 40°41N 74°2W 132 B1
Elliston Australia 33°39S 134°53E 281 E1
Ellisville U.S.A. 31°36N 89°12W 315 F10
Ellon U.K. 57°22N 2°4W 167 D6
Ellora India 20°1N 75°10E 244 D2
Ellore = Eluru India 16°48N 81°8E 244 F5
Elloree U.S.A. 33°32N 80°34W 316 B9
Ellsworth Kans., U.S.A. 38°44N 98°14W 308 F4
Ellsworth Maine, U.S.A. 44°33N 68°25W 309 C19
Ellsworth Land Antarctica 76°0S 89°0W 151 D16
Ellsworth Mts. Antarctica 78°30S 85°0W 151 D16
Ellwangen Germany 48°57N 10°8E 179 G6
Ellwood City U.S.A. 40°52N 80°17W 312 F4
Ellzey U.S.A. 29°19N 82°48W 317 F7
Elm Switz. 46°54N 9°10E 179 J5
Elm-Lappwald ⌓ Germany 52°15N 10°50E 178 C6
Elma Man., Canada 49°52N 95°55W 297 D9
Elma Wash., U.S.A. 47°0N 123°25W 306 D3
Elmadağ Turkey 39°55N 33°14E 212 C5
Elmalı Turkey 36°44N 29°56E 205 E11
Elmers End U.K. 51°23N 0°2W 125 B3
Elmhurst Ill., U.S.A. 41°53N 87°56W 311 C9
Elmhurst N.Y., U.S.A. 40°44N 73°53W 132 B2
Elmina Ghana 5°5N 1°21W 263 D4
Elmira Ont., Canada 43°36N 80°33W 312 C4
Elmira N.Y., U.S.A. 42°6N 76°48W 312 D8
Elmira Heights U.S.A. 42°8N 76°50W 312 D8
Elmodel U.S.A. 31°21N 84°29W 316 D5
Elmore Vic., Australia 36°30S 144°37E 282 D6
Elmore Ala., U.S.A. 32°32N 86°19W 316 C3
Elmore Ohio, U.S.A. 41°29N 83°18W 311 C13
Elmshorn Germany 53°43N 9°40E 178 B5
Elmstead U.K. 51°24N 0°2E 125 B4
Elmvale Canada 44°35N 79°52W 312 B5
Elmwood Ill., U.S.A. 40°47N 89°58W 310 D7
Elmwood La., U.S.A. 29°57N 90°11W 131 B1
Elmwood Park Ill., U.S.A. 41°55N 87°48W 119 B2
Elmwood Park N.J., U.S.A. 40°54N 74°7W 132 A1
Elne France 42°36N 2°58E 174 F6
Elnesvågen Norway 62°52N 7°10E 164 B4
Elnora U.S.A. 38°53N 87°5W 311 F9
Eloaua I. Papua N. G. 1°38S 149°40E 286 A5
Elobey, Is. Eq. Guin. 1°1N 9°29E 264 B1
Elongo Dem. Rep. of the Congo 0°19S 21°39E 264 C4
Elora Canada 43°41N 80°26W 312 C4
Elorza Venezuela 7°3N 69°31W 328 B4
Elos Greece 36°46N 22°43E 204 E4
Elounda Greece 35°16N 25°42E 207 E6
Eloy U.S.A. 32°45N 111°33W 305 K8
Éloyes France 48°6N 6°36E 173 D13
Elphin Canada 44°55N 76°37W 313 B8
Elpitiya Sri Lanka 6°17N 80°10E 245 L5
Elrose Canada 51°12N 108°0W 297 C7
Elsberry U.S.A. 39°10N 90°47W 310 E6
Elsby △ Australia 14°55S 133°10E 278 B5
Elsdorf Germany 50°55N 6°34E 178 E2
Elsie Mich., U.S.A. 43°5N 84°23W 311 A12
Elsie Oreg., U.S.A. 45°52N 123°36W 306 E3
Elsiesrivier S. Africa 33°55S 18°35E 118 A2
Elsinore = Helsingør Denmark 56°2N 12°35E 163 H6
Elster → Germany 51°25N 11°57E 178 D7
Elsternwick Australia 37°52S 145°0E 128 B2
Elsterwerda Germany 51°27N 13°31E 178 D9
Eltanin Fracture Zone System S. Ocean 54°0S 130°0W 151 B14
Eltham N.Z. 39°26S 174°19E 284 F3
Eltham London, U.K. 51°27N 0°3E 125 B4
Elton Russia 49°5N 46°52E 191 F8
Elton, Ozero Russia 49°5N 46°42E 191 F8
Eltville Germany 50°2N 8°7E 179 E4
Eluanbi = Oluanpi Taiwan 21°54N 120°51E 225 E2
Eluru India 16°48N 81°8E 244 F5
Elvas Portugal 38°50N 7°10W 195 G3
Elven France 47°44N 2°36W 172 E4
Elverum Norway 60°53N 11°34E 164 D8
Elvire → Australia 17°51S 128°11E 278 C4
Elvire, Mt. Australia 29°22S 119°36E 279 E2
Elvo → Italy 45°23N 8°21E 198 C5
Elwell, L. = Tiber Res. U.S.A. 48°19N 111°6W 304 B8
Elwood Vic., Australia 37°53S 144°59E 128 B1
Elwood Ill., U.S.A. 41°24N 88°7W 311 C8
Elwood Ind., U.S.A. 40°17N 85°50W 311 D11
Elwood Nebr., U.S.A. 40°36N 99°52W 308 E4
Elx = Elche Spain 38°15N 0°42W 197 G4
Ely Cambs., U.K. 52°24N 0°16E 169 E8
Ely Minn., U.S.A. 47°55N 91°51W 308 B8
Ely Nev., U.S.A. 39°15N 114°54W 304 G6
Elyria U.S.A. 41°22N 82°7W 312 E2
Elyros Greece 35°15N 23°45E 204 F5
Élysée France 48°52N 2°19E 134 A2
Elysian Park Los Angeles, U.S.A. 127 a3
Elz → Germany 48°18N 7°44E 179 G3
Émaé Vanuatu 17°4S 168°24E 287 G6
Emajõgi → Estonia 58°25N 27°20E 188 C4
eMakhazeni S. Africa 25°42S 30°2E 271 C5
eMalahleni S. Africa 25°51S 29°14E 271 C4
Emāmrūd Iran 36°30N 55°0E 247 B7
Emāmzādeh Sāleh Iran 35°48N 51°26E 141 A2
Emån → Sweden 57°8N 16°30E 163 G10
Emao Vanuatu 17°29S 168°30E 287 G6
Emas △ Brazil 18°2S 52°50W 331 D7
Emateloa Dem. Rep. of the Congo 1°16N 18°42E 264 B3
Embajadores Madrid, Spain 127 c2
eMbalenhle S. Africa 26°32S 29°4E 271 C4
Embarcación Argentina 23°10S 64°0W 334 A3
Embarcadero, The San Francisco, U.S.A. 136 b3
Embarras → U.S.A. 38°39N 87°37W 311 F9
Embetsu Japan 44°44N 141°47E 220 B10
Embi Kazakhstan 48°50N 58°8E 216 C5
Embi → Kazakhstan 46°55N 53°28E 187 E9
Embonas Greece 36°13N 27°51E 206 E11
Embro Canada 43°9N 80°54W 312 C4
Embrun France 44°34N 6°30E 175 D10
Embu Kenya 0°32S 37°38E 268 C4
Emden Germany 53°21N 7°12E 178 B3
Emecik Turkey 36°46N 27°49E 205 E9
Emei Shan China 29°32N 103°46E 228 C4
Emeishan China 29°31N 103°23E 228 C4
Emek Refa'im Jerusalem 123 c2
Émerainville France 48°48N 2°37E 134 B4
Emerald Queens., Australia 23°32S 148°10E 280 C4
Emerald Vic., Australia 37°56S 145°29E 276 E8
Emerald Buddha = Phra Kaeo Bangkok, Thailand 113 b1
Emerald I. Canada 76°48N 114°10W 295 B9
Émeraude, Côte d' France 48°45N 2°40W 172 D4
Emerson Man., Canada 49°0N 97°10W 297 D9
Emerson Ga., U.S.A. 34°8N 84°45W 316 A5
Emeryville U.S.A. 37°49N 122°17W 136 A3
Emet Turkey 39°20N 29°15E 205 B11
Emeti Papua N. G. 7°53S 143°15E 286 D2
Emgwenya S. Africa 25°40S 30°18E 271 C5
Emi Koussi Chad 19°45N 18°55E 259 E3
Emília-Romagna □ Italy 44°45N 11°0E 198 D8
Emilius, Mte. Italy 45°45N 7°20E 198 C4
Emin China 46°34N 83°36E 217 C10
Eminabad Pakistan 32°2N 74°8E 242 C6
Emine, Nos Bulgaria 42°40N 27°56E 203 D11
Eminence U.S.A. 38°22N 85°11W 311 F11
Eminönü Turkey 41°0N 28°57E 122 B1
Emirates, Mall of the U.A.E. 25°7N 55°12E 119 B1
Emirau I. Papua N. G. 1°40S 150°0E 286 A6
Emirdağ Turkey 39°2N 31°8E 212 C4
Emirgan Turkey 41°6N 29°2E 122 B2
Emissi, Tarso Chad 21°27N 18°36E 259 D3
Emlenton U.S.A. 41°11N 79°43W 312 E5
Emlichheim Germany 52°37N 6°51E 178 C2
Emmaboda Sweden 56°37N 15°32E 163 H9
Emmalane U.S.A. 32°46N 82°0W 316 C7
Emmarentia S. Africa 26°9S 28°0E 123 A2
Emmastad Curaçao 12°8N 68°55W 322 g
Emmaus S. Africa 29°2S 25°15E 270 C4
Emmaus Pa., U.S.A. 40°32N 75°30W 313 F9
Emme → Switz. 47°14N 7°32E 179 H3
Emmeloord Neths. 52°44N 5°46E 170 B5
Emmen Neths. 52°48N 6°57E 170 B6
Emmen Switz. 47°5N 8°18E 179 H4
Emmendingen Germany 48°6N 7°51E 179 G3
Emmental Switz. 46°55N 7°40E 179 J3
Emmerich Germany 51°50N 6°14E 178 D2
Emmet Australia 24°45S 144°30E 280 C3
Emmetsburg U.S.A. 43°7N 94°41W 310 A2
Emmett Idaho, U.S.A. 43°52N 116°30W 304 E5
Emmett Mich., U.S.A. 42°59N 82°46W 312 D2
Emmiganuru = Yemmiganur India 15°44N 77°29E 245 G3
Emmonak U.S.A. 62°47N 164°31W 303 E6
Emo Canada 48°38N 93°50W 297 D10
Emőd Hungary 47°57N 20°47E 182 C5
Emona Bulgaria 42°43N 27°53E 203 D11
Empalme Mexico 27°58N 110°51W 318 B2
Empangeni S. Africa 28°50S 31°52E 271 C5
Empedrado Argentina 28°0S 58°46W 334 B4
Emperor Seamount Chain Pac. Oc. 40°0N 170°0E 288 D9
Emperor Trough Pac. Oc. 43°0N 175°30E 288 C9
Empingham Res. = Rutland Water U.K. 52°39N 0°38W 169 E7
Empire U.S.A. 32°21N 83°18W 316 C6
Empire State Building New York, U.S.A. 132 c2
Empoli Italy 43°43N 10°57E 198 E7
Emporia Kans., U.S.A. 38°25N 96°11W 308 F5
Emporia Va., U.S.A. 36°42N 77°32W 309 G15
Emporium U.S.A. 41°31N 78°14W 312 E6
Empress Canada 50°57N 110°0W 297 C7
Empty Quarter = Rub' al Khālī Si. Arabia 19°0N 48°0E 249 C5
Ems → Germany 53°20N 7°12E 178 B3
Emsdale Canada 45°32N 79°19W 312 A5
Emsdetten Germany 52°10N 7°32E 178 C3
Emu China 43°40N 128°6E 227 C15
Emu Park Australia 23°13S 150°50E 280 C5
eMuziwezinto S. Africa 30°15S 30°45E 271 D5
'En 'Avrona Israel 29°43N 35°0E 251 J6
'En Boqeq Israel 31°12N 35°21E 251 G6
En Gannim = Ramat Gan Israel 32°4N 34°48E 251 F5
'En Gedi Israel 31°28N 35°25E 251 G6
En Na'am Sudan 10°21N 27°58E 266 B2
En Nahrat Mali 22°55N 3°36W 260 D4
En Nahud Sudan 12°45N 28°25E 257 E2
En Nofalab Sudan 15°52N 32°32E 257 D3
En Nuqra Sudan 10°4N 28°10E 266 B2
Ena Japan 35°25N 137°25E 223 B9
Ena-San Japan 35°26N 137°36E 223 B9
Enambú Colombia 1°1N 70°17W 328 C3
Enånger Sweden 61°30N 17°9E 162 C11
Enard B. U.K. 58°5N 5°20W 167 C3
Enare träsk = Inarijärvi Finland 69°0N 28°0E 160 B23
Enarotali Indonesia 3°55S 136°21E 231 E9
Encampment U.S.A. 41°12N 106°47W 304 F10
Encantadas, Serra Brazil 30°40S 53°0W 335 C5
Encantado Brazil 22°53S 43°19W 135 B1
Encarnación Paraguay 27°15S 55°50W 335 B4
Encarnación de Díaz Mexico 21°31N 102°14W 318 C4
Enchi Ghana 5°53N 2°48W 262 D4
Encinitas U.S.A. 33°3N 117°17W 307 M9
Encino Calif., U.S.A. 34°9N 118°28W 126 B2
Encino N. Mex., U.S.A. 34°39N 105°28W 305 J11
Encino Res. U.S.A. 34°8N 118°30W 126 B1
Encontrados Venezuela 9°3N 72°14W 328 B3
Encounter B. Australia 35°45S 138°45E 282 C3
Encruzilhada Brazil 15°31S 40°54W 333 E3
Encs Hungary 48°20N 21°8E 182 B6
Endako Canada 54°6N 125°2W 296 C3
Endau Kenya 1°18S 38°31E 268 C4
Endau Rompin △ Malaysia 2°27N 103°45E 237 L4
Ende Indonesia 8°45S 121°40E 231 F6
Endeavour Str. Australia 10°45S 142°0E 286 F2
Endelave Denmark 55°46N 10°18E 163 J4
Enden Norway 61°47N 10°15E 164 C7
Enderbury Kiribati 3°8S 171°5W 277 A16
Enderby Canada 50°35N 119°10W 296 C5
Enderby Abyssal Plain S. Ocean 60°0S 40°0E 151 C5
Enderby I. Australia 20°35S 116°30E 278 D2
Enderby Land Antarctica 66°0S 53°0E 151 C5
Enderlin U.S.A. 46°38N 97°36W 308 B5
Enderrocat, C. Spain 39°28N 2°43E 206 B3
Endicott U.S.A. 42°6N 76°4W 313 D8
Endicott Mts. U.S.A. 68°0N 152°0W 303 C9
Endimari → Brazil 8°46S 66°7W 330 B4
Endwell U.S.A. 42°6N 76°2W 313 D8
Endyalgout I. Australia 11°40S 132°35E 278 B5
Ené → Peru 11°10S 74°18W 330 C3
Eneabba Australia 29°49S 115°16E 279 E2
Enebyberg Sweden 59°25N 17°59E 139 A1
Enerhodar Ukraine 47°30N 34°28E 189 J8
Enewetak Atoll Marshall Is. 11°30N 162°15E 288 F8
Enez Turkey 40°45N 26°5E 203 F10
Enfer, Pte. d' Martinique 14°22N 60°54W 322 j
Enfield N.S.W., Australia 33°53S 151°6E 139 B1
Enfield N.S., Canada 44°56N 63°32W 299 D7
Enfield Conn., U.S.A. 41°58N 72°36W 313 E12
Enfield Ill., U.S.A. 38°6N 88°20W 311 F8
Enfield N.C., U.S.A. 36°11N 77°41W 315 C16
Enfield N.H., U.S.A. 43°39N 72°9W 313 C12
Enga □ Papua N. G. 5°30S 143°30E 286 C2
Engadin Switz. 46°45N 10°10E 179 J6
Engan Norway 63°8N 8°31E 164 A5
Engaño, C. Dom. Rep. 18°30N 68°20W 321 C6
Engaño, C. Phil. 18°35N 122°23E 232 B4
Engaru Japan 44°3N 143°31E 220 B11
Engcobo = Ngcobo S. Africa 31°37S 28°0E 271 D4
Engelberg Switz. 46°48N 8°26E 179 J4
Engels Russia 51°28N 46°6E 190 E8
Engelsberg = Ängelsberg Sweden 59°58N 16°0E 162 E10
Engemann L. Canada 58°0N 106°55W 297 B7
Engenho, I. do Brazil 22°50S 43°6W 135 B2
Engerdal Norway 61°45N 11°58E 164 C8
Engershatu Eritrea 16°7N 38°34E 257 D4
Enggano Indonesia 5°20S 102°40E 234 D2
Engineer Group Papua N. G. 10°35S 151°20E 286 F6
Engkilili Malaysia 1°3N 111°42E 235 B4
England U.S.A. 34°33N 91°58W 314 D9
England □ U.K. 53°0N 2°0W 169 E5
Englee Canada 50°45N 56°5W 299 B8
Englehart Canada 47°49N 79°52W 298 C4
Englewood Fla., U.S.A. 26°58N 82°21W 317 J7
Englewood Ill., U.S.A. 41°46N 87°38W 119 C3
Englewood N.J., U.S.A. 40°54N 73°58W 132 A2
Englewood Ohio, U.S.A. 39°53N 84°18W 311 E12
Englewood Cliffs U.S.A. 40°53N 73°59W 132 A2
English U.S.A. 38°20N 86°28W 311 F10
English → Ont., Canada 49°12N 91°5W 297 C10
English → Iowa, U.S.A. 41°29N 91°32W 310 C5
English B. Ascension I. 7°54S 14°23W 153 g
English Bazar = Ingraj Bazar India 24°58N 88°10E 243 G13
English Channel Europe 50°0N 2°0W 169 G6
English Company's Is., The Australia 11°50S 136°32E 280 A2
English Harbour Town Antigua & B. 17°1N 61°46W 322 b
English River Canada 49°14N 91°0W 298 C1
Engures ezers Latvia 57°16N 23°6E 184 A10
Enguri → Georgia 42°27N 41°38E 191 J5
Enid U.S.A. 36°24N 97°53W 314 C6
Enipeas → Greece 39°22N 22°17E 204 B4
Eniwa Japan 43°0N 141°30E 220 C10
Enkhuizen Neths. 52°42N 5°17E 170 B5
Enköping Sweden 59°37N 17°4E 162 E11
Enle China 24°0N 101°9E 228 F3
Enmore Australia 33°54S 151°10E 139 B2
Enna Italy 37°34N 14°16E 201 E7
Ennadai L. Canada 60°58N 101°20W 297 A8
Enné, O. → Chad 14°24N 18°45E 259 F4
Ennedi Chad 17°15N 22°0E 259 E4
Enneri Achelouma → Niger 21°55N 13°35E 261 D7
Enngonia Australia 29°21S 145°50E 281 D4
Ennigerloh Germany 51°50N 8°2E 178 D4
Ennis Clare, Ireland 52°51N 8°59W 166 D3
Ennis Mont., U.S.A. 45°21N 111°44W 304 D8
Ennis Tex., U.S.A. 32°20N 96°38W 314 E6
Enniscorthy Ireland 52°30N 6°34W 166 D5
Enniskillen U.K. 54°21N 7°39W 166 B4
Ennistimon Ireland 52°57N 9°17W 166 D2
Enns Austria 48°12N 14°28E 180 C7
Enns → Austria 48°14N 14°32E 180 C7
Eno Finland 62°47N 30°10E 160 E24
Enosburg Falls U.S.A. 44°55N 72°48W 313 B12
Enping China 22°16N 112°21E 229 F9
Enrekang Indonesia 3°34S 119°47E 235 C5
Enrile Phil. 17°34N 121°42E 232 C3
Enriquillo, L. Dom. Rep. 18°20N 71°40W 321 C5
Enschede Neths. 52°13N 6°53E 170 B6
Ensenada Argentina 34°55S 57°55W 334 C4
Ensenada Chile 41°12S 72°33W 336 B2
Ensenada Baja Calif., Mexico 31°52N 116°37W 318 A1
Ensenada de los Muertos Mexico 23°59N 109°51W 318 C2
Ensenada La Guardia Venezuela 11°2N 64°5W 329 a
Enshi China 30°18N 109°29E 228 B7
Enshū-Nada Japan 34°27N 137°38E 223 C9
Ensiola, Pta. de n' Spain 39°7N 2°55E 206 B3
Ensisheim France 47°50N 7°20E 173 E14
Enskede Sweden 59°17N 18°4E 139 B2
Ensley U.S.A. 30°31N 87°16W 317 E2
Entebbe Uganda 0°4N 32°28E 268 B3
Enterprise N.W.T., Canada 60°47N 115°45W 296 A5
Enterprise Ala., U.S.A. 31°19N 85°51W 316 D4
Enterprise Nev., U.S.A. 36°13N 115°14W 124 B1
Enterprise Oreg., U.S.A. 45°25N 117°17W 304 D5
Entorno de Doñana ⌓ Spain 37°0N 6°26W 195 J4
Entrance, The Australia 33°21S 151°30E 283 B9
Entraygues-sur-Truyère France 44°38N 2°35E 174 D6
Entre-Deux Réunion 21°14S 55°28E 272 f
Entre Rios = Rio Brilhante Brazil 21°48S 54°33W 335 A5
Entre Rios = Três Rios Brazil 22°6S 43°15W 333 F3
Entre Ríos Bolivia 21°30S 64°25W 334 A3
Entre Rios Bahia, Brazil 11°56S 38°5W 333 D4
Entre Rios Pará, Brazil 5°24S 54°21W 331 B7
Entre Ríos □ Argentina 30°30S 58°30W 334 C4
Entrepeñas, Embalse de Spain 40°34N 2°42W 196 E2
Entrevias Spain 40°22N 3°40W 127 B1
Entroncamento Portugal 39°28N 8°28W 195 F2
Enugu Nigeria 6°30N 7°30E 263 D6
Enugu □ Nigeria 6°30N 7°45E 263 D6
Enugu Ezike Nigeria 7°0N 7°29E 263 D6
Enumclaw U.S.A. 47°12N 121°59W 306 C5
Envalira, Port d' Europe 42°33N 1°43E 196 C6
Envermeu France 49°53N 1°15E 172 C8
Envigado Colombia 6°10N 75°35W 328 B2
Enviken Sweden 60°49N 15°46E 162 D9
Envira Brazil 7°18S 70°13W 330 B3
Envira → Brazil 7°19S 70°15W 330 B3
Enying Hungary 46°56N 18°15E 182 D3
Enyonga Gabon 0°59S 9°22E 264 C1
Enza → Italy 44°54N 10°31E 198 D7
Enzan = Kōshū Japan 35°42N 138°44E 223 B10
Eochaill = Youghal Ireland 51°56N 7°52W 166 E4
Éolie, Ís. Italy 38°30N 14°57E 201 D7
Eot I. Micronesia 7°23N 151°44E 287 T17
Epanomi Greece 40°25N 22°59E 202 F6
Epcot U.S.A. 28°21N 81°32W 133 B1
Epe Neths. 52°21N 5°59E 170 B5
Epe Nigeria 6°36N 3°59E 263 D5
Epéna Congo 1°22N 17°29E 264 B3
Épernay France 49°3N 3°56E 173 C10
Épernon France 48°35N 1°40E 173 D8
Ephesus Turkey 37°55N 27°22E 205 D9
Ephraim U.S.A. 39°22N 111°35W 304 G8
Ephrata Pa., U.S.A. 40°11N 76°11W 313 F8
Ephrata Wash., U.S.A. 47°19N 119°33W 304 C4
Epi Vanuatu 16°43S 168°15E 287 F6
Epidaurus = Epidavros Greece 37°40N 23°7E 204 D5
Epidavros Greece 37°40N 23°7E 204 D5
Epidavros Limira Greece 36°46N 23°0E 204 E5
Épila Spain 41°36N 1°17W 196 D3
Épinac France 46°59N 4°31E 173 F11
Épinal France 48°10N 6°27E 173 D13
Epira Guyana 5°5N 57°20W 329 B6
Epiros □ Greece 39°30N 20°30E 204 B2
Episkopi Cyprus 34°40N 32°54E 207 F8
Episkopi Kriti, Greece 35°20N 24°20E 207 E5
Episkopi Bay Cyprus 34°35N 32°50E 207 F8
Epitalio Greece 37°37N 21°30E 204 D3
Eppalock, L. Australia 36°52S 144°34E 282 D6
Eppan = Appiano Italy 46°28N 11°15E 199 B8
Epping Australia 33°46S 151°5E 139 A1
Eppingen Germany 49°8N 8°53E 179 F4
Epsom U.K. 51°19N 0°16W 169 F7
Epukiro Namibia 21°40S 19°9E 270 B2
Equality U.S.A. 37°44N 88°20W 311 G8
Équateur □ Dem. Rep. of the Congo 2°0N 21°0E 264 B4
Equatorial Channel Maldives 0°0 73°10E 272 d
Equatorial Guinea ■ Africa 2°0N 8°0E 264 B1
Equeipa Venezuela 5°22N 62°43W 329 B5
Er Hai China 25°48N 100°11E 228 E3
Er Rachidia Morocco 31°58N 4°20W 260 B4
Er Rahad Sudan 12°45N 30°32E 257 E3
Er Rif Morocco 35°1N 4°1W 261 A4
Er Rogel Sudan 18°10N 35°25E 256 D4
Er Roseires Sudan 11°55N 34°30E 257 E3
Er Rua'at Sudan 12°21N 32°17E 257 E3
Eraclea Italy 45°35N 12°40E 199 C9
Eran Phil. 9°4N 117°42E 233 G1
Eran B. Phil. 9°5N 117°43E 233 G1
Erandol India 20°56N 75°20E 244 D2
Eranga Dem. Rep. of the Congo 1°52S 18°56E 264 C3
Erap Papua N. G. 6°37S 146°51E 286 D4
Erasmus = Bronkhorstspruit S. Africa 25°46S 28°45E 271 C4
Erave Papua N. G. 6°39S 144°0E 286 D2
Erave → Papua N. G. 6°54S 144°47E 286 D3
Erāwadī Myit = Irrawaddy → Burma 15°50N 95°6E 241 G5
Erāwadī Myitwanya = Irrawaddy, Mouths of the Burma 15°30N 95°0E 241 H5
Erawan △ Thailand 14°25N 98°58E 236 E2
Erba Italy 45°48N 9°15E 198 C6
Erba Sudan 19°5N 36°51E 256 D4
Erba, J. Sudan 20°48N 36°47E 256 C4
Erbaa Turkey 40°42N 36°36E 212 B7
Erbeng Shan China 42°50N 84°59E 217 D10
Erbeskopf Germany 49°44N 7°2E 179 F3
Erbil = Arbīl Iraq 36°15N 44°5E 213 D11
Erbu Ethiopia 6°44N 34°53E 257 E3
Ercan, Nicosia ✈ (ECN) Cyprus 35°10N 33°30E 207 E9
Erçek Turkey 38°39N 43°36E 246 B4
Erçis Turkey 39°2N 43°21E 213 C10
Erciyaş Dağı Turkey 38°30N 35°30E 246 B2
Érd Hungary 47°22N 18°56E 182 C3
Erdao Jiang → China 42°37N 128°0E 224 A3
Erdek Turkey 40°23N 27°47E 203 F11
Erdély = Transilvania Romania 46°30N 24°0E 183 D9
Erdemli Turkey 36°36N 34°19E 250 B5
Erdene = Ulaan-Uul Mongolia 46°4N 100°49E 218 B9
Erdenet Mongolia 49°2N 104°5E 218 B9
Erdenetsogt Mongolia 42°55N 106°5E 226 C4
Erding Germany 48°18N 11°54E 179 G7
Erdre → France 47°13N 1°32W 172 E5
Erebato → Venezuela 5°54N 64°16W 329 B5
Erebus, Mt. Antarctica 77°35S 167°0E 151 D11
Erechim Brazil 27°35S 52°15W 335 B5
Ereğli Konya, Turkey 37°31N 34°4E 212 D6
Ereğli Zonguldak, Turkey 41°15N 31°24E 212 B4
Erei, Monti Italy 37°20N 14°20E 201 E7
Erenhot China 43°48N 112°2E 226 C7
Erenköy = Kokkina Cyprus 35°11N 32°36E 207 E8
Erenköy Turkey 40°58N 29°3E 122 C2
Eresfjord Norway 62°40N 8°8E 164 B5
Eresma → Spain 41°26N 4°45W 194 D6
Eresos Greece 39°11N 25°57E 205 B7
Ereymentaū Kazakhstan 51°37N 73°6E 217 B8
Erfelek Turkey 41°53N 34°55E 212 B6
Erfenisdam S. Africa 28°30S 26°50E 270 C4
Erfjord Norway 59°20N 6°14E 164 E3
Erfoud Morocco 31°30N 4°15W 260 B4
Erfstadt Germany 50°50N 6°50E 178 E2
Erft → Germany 51°11N 6°44E 178 D2
Erfurt Germany 50°58N 11°2E 178 E7
Ergani Turkey 38°17N 39°49E 213 C8
Ergel Mongolia 43°8N 109°5E 226 C5
Ergene → Turkey 41°1N 26°22E 203 E10
Ergeni Vozvyshennost Russia 47°0N 44°0E 191 G7
Ērgli Latvia 56°54N 25°38E 188 D3
Ergun He = Argun → Russia 53°20N 121°28E 219 A13
Ergun Youqi China 50°15N 120°11E 219 A13
Erhlin Taiwan 23°54N 120°22E 225 C2
Erhshui Taiwan 23°45N 120°37E 225 C2
Eria → Spain 42°3N 5°44W 194 C5
Eriba Sudan 16°40N 36°10E 257 D4
Eriboll, L. U.K. 58°30N 4°42W 167 C4
Érice Italy 38°2N 12°35E 200 D5
Eridu U.S.A. 30°18N 83°45W 316 E6
Erie Mich., U.S.A. 41°47N 83°31W 311 C13
Erie Pa., U.S.A. 42°8N 80°5W 312 D4
Erie, L. N. Amer. 42°15N 81°0W 312 D4
Erie Canal U.S.A. 43°5N 78°43W 312 C7
Erieau Canada 42°16N 81°57W 312 D3
Erigavo = Ceerigaabo Somalia 10°35N 47°20E 267 B6
Erikoussa Greece 39°53N 19°34E 206 B9
Eriksdale Canada 50°52N 98°7W 297 C9
Erimanthos Greece 37°57N 21°50E 204 D3
Erimo-Misaki Japan 41°50N 143°15E 220 D11
Erin Ont., Canada 43°45N 80°7W 312 C4
Erin Trin. & Tob. 10°5N 61°39W 323 t
Erin B. Trin. & Tob. 10°4N 61°43W 323 t
Erin Pt. Trin. & Tob. 10°3N 61°39W 323 t
Erinpura India 25°9N 73°3E 242 G5
Eriskay U.K. 57°4N 7°18W 167 D1
Erith U.K. 51°28N 0°11E 125 B5
Erithres Greece 38°13N 23°20E 204 C5
Eritrea ■ Africa 14°0N 38°30E 257 E4
Erivan = Yerevan Armenia 40°10N 44°31E 191 K7
Erjas → Portugal 39°40N 7°1W 194 F3
Erkech-Tam Pass Asia 39°46N 74°2E 217 E8
Erkelenz Germany 51°4N 6°19E 178 D2
Erkner Germany 52°25N 13°44E 178 C9
Erlaa Austria 48°9N 16°19E 142 B1
Erlangen Germany 49°36N 11°0E 179 F6
Erlanger U.S.A. 39°1N 84°36W 311 E12
Erldunda Australia 25°14S 133°12E 280 D1
Erlin = Erhlin Taiwan 23°54N 120°22E 225 C2
Ermelo Neths. 52°18N 5°35E 170 B5
Ermelo Mpumalanga, S. Africa 26°31S 29°59E 271 C4
Ermenek Turkey 36°38N 33°0E 250 B4
Ermenek → Turkey 36°35N 33°23E 250 B4
Ermil Sudan 13°35N 27°40E 257 E2
Ermington Australia 33°48S 151°4E 139 A1
Ermioni Greece 37°23N 23°15E 204 D5
Ermita Phil. 14°35N 120°59E 127 B1
Ermones Greece 39°37N 19°46E 206 B9
Ermoupoli Greece 37°28N 24°57E 204 D6
Ernakulam India 9°59N 76°22E 245 K3
Erne → Ireland 54°30N 8°16W 166 B3
Erne, Lower L. U.K. 54°28N 7°47W 166 B4
Erne, Upper L. U.K. 54°14N 7°32W 166 B4
Ernée France 48°18N 0°56W 172 D6
Ernest Giles Ra. Australia 27°0S 123°45E 279 E3
Ernest N. Morial Convention Center New Orleans, U.S.A. 131 c3
Ernstberg Germany 50°13N 6°47E 179 E2
Erode India 11°24N 77°45E 245 J3
Eromanga Australia 26°40S 143°11E 281 D3
Erongo Namibia 21°39S 15°58E 270 B2
Erongo □ Namibia 22°20S 15°0E 270 B2
Erquy France 48°38N 2°29W 172 D4
Erramala Hills India 15°30N 78°15E 245 G4
Errentería Spain 43°19N 1°54W 196 B3
Errer → Ethiopia 7°32N 42°35E 257 F5
Errigal Ireland 55°2N 8°6W 166 A3
Errinundra △ Australia 37°20S 148°47E 283 D8
Erris Hd. Ireland 54°17N 10°0W 166 B1
Erromango Vanuatu 18°45S 169°5E 287 H7
Ersekë Albania 40°22N 20°40E 202 F4
Ersekújvár = Nové Zámky Slovak Rep. 48°2N 18°8E 181 C11
Ershatou China 23°6N 113°18E 121 B2
Erskine U.S.A. 47°40N 96°0W 308 B6
Erskineville Australia 33°54S 151°12E 139 B2
Erstein France 48°25N 7°38E 173 D14
Ertai China 46°3N 90°5E 217 C12
Ertan Shuiku China 27°5N 101°52E 228 D3
Ertholmene Denmark 55°19N 15°11E 163 J9
Ertil Russia 51°55N 40°50E 190 E5
Ertis = Irtysh → Russia 61°4N 68°52E 214 C7
Ertis Kazakhstan 53°20N 75°27E 217 B9
Ertis → Kazakhstan 47°52N 84°16E 217 C10
Ertvågøy Norway 63°13N 8°26E 164 A5
Eruh Turkey 37°46N 42°13E 213 D10
Erunkan Nigeria 6°36N 3°23E 124 A2
Ervy-le-Châtel France 48°2N 3°55E 173 D10
Erwin U.S.A. 36°9N 82°25W 315 C13
Eryuan China 26°7N 99°57E 228 D2
Erzgebirge Germany 50°27N 12°55E 178 E8
Erzin Russia 50°15N 95°10E 217 B13
Erzin Turkey 36°57N 36°11E 250 B7
Erzincan Turkey 39°46N 39°30E 213 C8
Erzincan □ Turkey 39°45N 39°30E 213 C8
Erzsébet-Telep Hungary 47°27N 19°10E 117 B3
Erzurum Turkey 39°57N 41°15E 213 C9
Erzurum □ Turkey 39°55N 41°15E 213 C9
Es Caló Spain 38°40N 1°30E 206 D2
Es Canar Spain 39°2N 1°36E 206 C2
Es Mercadal Spain 39°59N 4°5E 206 B5
Es Migjorn Gran Spain 39°57N 4°3E 206 B5
Es Safiya Sudan 15°31N 30°7E 257 D3
Es Sahrâ al Beida Egypt 27°50N 28°45E 256 B2
Es Sahrâ' Esh Sharqîya Egypt 27°30N 32°30E 256 B3
Es Sînâ' Egypt 29°0N 34°0E 246 D2
Es Sûkî Sudan 13°20N 33°58E 257 E3
Es Vedrà Spain 38°52N 1°12E 206 D1
Esa'ala Papua N. G. 9°45S 150°49E 286 E6
Esambo Dem. Rep. of the Congo 3°48S 23°30E 264 C4
Esan-Misaki Japan 41°40N 141°10E 220 D10
Esashi Hokkaidō, Japan 44°56N 142°35E 220 B11
Esashi Hokkaidō, Japan 41°52N 140°7E 220 D10
Esbjerg Denmark 55°29N 8°29E 163 J2
Esbo = Espoo Finland 60°12N 24°40E 188 B3
Escada Brazil 8°22S 35°8W 332 C4
Escalante Phil. 10°50N 123°33E 233 F4
Escalante Utah, U.S.A. 37°47N 111°36W 305 H8
Escalante → U.S.A. 37°24N 110°57W 305 H8
Escalón Mexico 26°45N 104°20W 318 B4
Escambia → U.S.A. 30°32N 87°11W 317 E2
Escanaba U.S.A. 45°45N 87°4W 308 C10
Escárcega Mexico 18°37N 90°43W 319 D6
Escarparda Pt. Phil. 18°31N 122°13E 232 B4
Escarpé, C. N. Cal. 20°41S 167°13E 288 d
Escaut = Schelde → Belgium 51°15N 4°16E 170 C4
Esch-sur-Alzette Lux. 49°32N 6°0E 170 E6
Eschede Germany 52°44N 10°14E 178 C6
Eschenried Germany 48°13N 11°24E 131 A1
Eschwege Germany 51°11N 10°2E 178 D6
Eschweiler Germany 50°49N 6°15E 178 E2
Escobal Panama 9°6N 80°1W 320 c
Escoma Bolivia 15°40S 69°8W 330 D4
Escondido U.S.A. 33°7N 117°5W 307 M9
Escravos → Nigeria 5°35N 5°10E 263 D6
Escuinapa de Hidalgo Mexico 22°50N 105°50W 318 C3
Escuintla Guatemala 14°20N 90°48W 320 D1
Eséka Cameroon 3°41N 10°44E 263 E7
Eşen → Turkey 36°27N 29°16E 205 E11
Esenguly Turkmenistan 37°37N 53°59E 216 E4
Esenler Turkey 41°1N 28°52E 122 B1
Esens Germany 53°38N 7°36E 178 B3
Esentepe = Áyios Amvrósios Cyprus 35°20N 33°35E 207 E9
Esenyurt Turkey 41°3N 28°48E 203 E12
Esera → Spain 42°6N 0°15E 196 C5
Eşfahān Iran 32°39N 51°43E 247 C6
Eşfahān □ Iran 32°50N 51°50E 247 C6
Esfarāyen Iran 37°4N 57°30E 247 B8
Esfideh Iran 33°39N 59°46E 247 C8
Esgueva → Spain 41°40N 4°43W 194 D6
Esh Sham = Dimashq Syria 33°30N 36°18E 250 E7
Esh Shamâlîya □ Sudan 19°0N 29°0E 256 D2
Esha Ness U.K. 60°29N 1°38W 167 A7
Eshan China 24°11N 102°24E 228 E4
Esher U.K. 51°21N 0°20W 125 B1
Eshkāshem = Ishkashim Tajikistan 36°44N 71°37E 217 E8
Eshkol △ Israel 31°20N 34°30E 251 G5
Eshowe S. Africa 28°50S 31°30E 271 C5
Esiama Ghana 4°56N 2°25W 262 E4
Esigodini Zimbabwe 20°18S 28°56E 271 B4
Esil = Ishim → Russia 57°45N 71°10E 214 D8
Esil Kazakhstan 51°57N 66°24E 217 B7
Esino → Italy 43°39N 13°22E 199 E10
Esira Madag. 24°20S 46°42E 272 C2
Esk → Dumf. & Gall., U.K. 54°58N 3°2W 167 G5
Esk → N. Yorks., U.K. 54°30N 0°37W 168 C7
Eskān Iran 26°48N 63°9E 240 D1
Eskbank U.K. 55°52N 3°4W 121 B3
Esker Siding Canada 53°53N 66°25W 299 B6
Eskifjörður Iceland 65°3N 13°55W 155 B13
Eskije = Xanthi Greece 41°10N 24°58E 203 E8
Eskilsäter Sweden 58°57N 13°10E 163 F7
Eskilstuna Sweden 59°22N 16°32E 162 E10
Eskimalatya Turkey 38°24N 38°22E 213 C8
Eskimo Point = Arviat Canada 61°6N 93°59W 297 A10
Eskişehir Turkey 39°50N 30°30E 205 B12
Eskişehir □ Turkey 39°40N 31°0E 205 B12
Esla → Spain 41°29N 6°3W 194 D4
Eslāmābād-e Gharb Iran 34°10N 46°30E 213 E12

Eslāmshahr Iran 35°40N 51°10E 247 C6
Eslöv Sweden 55°50N 13°20E 163 J7
Eşme Turkey 38°23N 28°58E 205 C10
Esmeralda, I. Chile 48°55S 75°25W 336 C1
Esmeraldas Ecuador 1°0N 79°40W 328 C2
Esmeraldas □ Ecuador 0°40N 79°30W 328 C2
Esmeraldas ➜ Ecuador 0°58N 79°38W 328 C2
Esna = Isna Egypt 25°17N 32°30E 256 B3
Esnagi L. Canada 48°36N 84°33W 298 C3
Esom Hill U.S.A. 33°57N 85°23W 316 B4
Espa Norway 60°34N 11°16E 164 D8
Espada, Pta. Colombia 12°5N 71°7W 328 A3
Espalion France 44°32N 2°47E 174 D6
España = Spain ■ Europe 39°0N 4°0W 192 D3
Espanola Ont., Canada 46°15N 81°46W 298 C3
Espanola N. Mex., U.S.A. 35°59N 106°5W 305 J10
Española, I. Ecuador 1°23S 89°39W 330 a
Espanya, Plaça d' Barcelona, Spain 114 c1
Esparreguera Spain 41°33N 1°52E 196 D6
Esparza Costa Rica 9°59N 84°40W 320 E3
Espeland Norway 60°23N 5°28E 164 D2
Espelkamp Germany 52°24N 8°36E 178 C4
Espenberg, C. U.S.A. 66°33N 163°36W 303 C7
Esperança Amazonas, Brazil 4°24S 69°52W 328 D4
Esperança Paraíba, Brazil 7°1S 35°51W 332 C4
Esperance Australia 33°45S 121°55E 279 F3
Esperance, C. Solomon Is. 9°15S 159°43E 287 M10
Esperance B. Australia 33°48S 121°55E 279 F3
Esperantinópolis Brazil 4°53S 44°53W 332 B3
Esperanza Antarctica 65°0S 55°0W 151 C18
Esperanza Santa Cruz, Argentina 51°1S 70°49W 336 D2
Esperanza Santa Fe, Argentina 31°29S 61°3W 334 C3
Esperanza Mexico City, Mexico 128 c3
Esperanza Agusan del S., Phil. 8°43N 125°36E 233 G5
Esperanza Masbate, Phil. 11°45N 124°3E 233 F5
Esperanza Puerto Rico 18°6N 65°28W 321 b
Espéraza France 42°56N 2°14E 174 F6
Espevær Norway 59°35N 5°7E 164 E2
Espichel, C. Portugal 38°22N 9°16W 195 G1
Espiel Spain 38°11N 5°1W 195 G5
Espigão, Serra do Brazil 26°35S 50°30W 335 B5
Espinal Colombia 4°9N 74°53W 328 C3
Espinar Peru 14°51S 71°24W 330 C3
Espinazo, Sierra del = Espinhaço, Serra do Brazil 17°30S 43°30W 333 E3
Espinhaço, Serra do Brazil 17°30S 43°30W 333 E3
Espinho Portugal 41°1N 8°38W 194 D2
Espinilho, Serra do Brazil 28°30S 55°0W 335 B5
Espinosa de los Monteros Spain 43°5N 3°34W 194 B7
Espírito Santo □ Brazil 20°0S 40°45W 333 F3
Espírito Santo do Pinhal Brazil 22°10S 46°46W 335 A6
Espíritu Santo Vanuatu 15°15S 166°50E 287 E4
Espíritu Santo, B. del Mexico 19°20N 87°35W 319 D7
Espíritu Santo, I. Mexico 24°30N 110°22W 318 C2
Espita Mexico 21°1N 88°19W 319 C7
Espiye Turkey 40°56N 38°43E 213 B8
Esplanada Brazil 11°47S 37°57W 333 D4
Esplanade Singapore 138 c3
Esplugas Spain 41°22N 2°5E 114 A1
Espoo Finland 60°12N 24°40E 188 B3
Esposizione Universale di Roma Italy 41°49N 12°28E 136 C1
Espuña, Sierra de Spain 37°51N 1°35W 197 H3
Espungabera Mozam. 20°29S 32°45E 271 B5
Esquel Argentina 42°55S 71°20W 336 B2
Esquimalt Canada 48°26N 123°25W 306 B3
Esquina Argentina 30°0S 59°30W 334 C4
Essandsjøen Norway 63°0N 12°0E 164 A8
Essaouira Morocco 31°32N 9°42W 260 B3
Essen Belgium 51°28N 4°28E 170 C4
Essen Nordrhein-Westfalen, Germany 51°28N 7°2E 178 D3
Essendon Australia 37°44S 144°55E 128 A1
Essendon ✈ (MEB) Australia 37°43S 144°54E 128 A1
Essendon, Mt. Australia 25°0S 120°29E 279 E3
Essequibo ➜ Guyana 6°50N 58°30W 329 B6
Essex Ont., Canada 42°10N 82°49W 312 D2
Essex Calif., U.S.A. 34°44N 115°15W 307 L11
Essex N.Y., U.S.A. 44°19N 73°21W 313 B11
Essex □ U.K. 51°54N 0°27E 169 F8
Essex Junction U.S.A. 44°29N 73°7W 313 B11
Essingen Sweden 59°19N 17°59E 139 B1
Essling Austria 48°12N 16°30E 142 A3
Esslingen Germany 48°44N 9°18E 179 G5
Essonne □ France 48°30N 2°20E 173 D9
Est, Gare de l' Paris, France 134 a5
Estaca de Bares, C. de Spain 43°46N 7°42W 194 B3
Estación Camacho Mexico 24°25N 102°18W 318 C4
Estación Simón Mexico 24°42N 102°35W 318 C4
Estadilla Spain 42°4N 0°16E 196 C5
Estado, Parque do Brazil 23°38S 46°38W 137 B2
Estados, I. de Los Argentina 54°40S 64°30W 336 D4
Estagel France 42°47N 2°40E 174 F6
Estagno Pt. Phil. 17°20N 122°24E 232 C4
Eşţahbānāt Iran 29°8N 54°4E 247 D7
Estância Brazil 11°16S 37°26W 332 D4
Estancia N. Mex., U.S.A. 34°46N 106°4W 305 J10
Estancia Monte León Argentina 50°14S 68°55W 336 D3
Estārm Iran 28°21N 58°21E 247 D8
Estarreja Portugal 40°45N 8°35W 194 E2
Estats, Pic d' Spain 42°40N 1°24E 196 C6
Estcourt S. Africa 29°0S 29°53E 271 C4
Este Italy 45°14N 11°39E 199 C8
Este △ Dom. Rep. 18°14N 68°42W 321 C6
Estefânia Lisbon, Portugal 126 a2
Estelí Nic. 13°9N 86°22W 320 D2
Estella Spain 42°40N 2°2W 196 C2
Estelle U.S.A. 29°50N 90°6W 131 B2
Estellencs Spain 39°39N 2°29E 206 B3
Estena ➜ Spain 39°23N 4°44W 195 F6
Estepa Spain 37°17N 4°52W 195 H6
Estepona Spain 36°24N 5°7W 195 J5
Esterhazy Canada 50°37N 102°5W 297 C8
Esterias, C. Gabon 0°40N 9°20E 264 B1
Esternay France 48°44N 3°33E 173 D10
Esterri d'Aneu Spain 42°38N 1°5E 196 C6
Estevan Canada 49°10N 102°59W 297 D8
Estevan Group Canada 53°3N 129°38W 296 C3
Estherville U.S.A. 43°24N 94°50W 308 D6
Estill U.S.A. 32°45N 81°15W 316 C8
Estissac France 48°16N 3°48E 173 D10
Eston Canada 51°8N 108°40W 297 C7
Estonia ■ Europe 58°30N 25°30E 188 C3
Estoril Portugal 38°42N 9°23W 195 G1
Estouk Mali 18°14N 1°2E 263 B5
Estreito Brazil 6°34S 47°27W 332 C2
Estrela, Basilica da Portugal 38°42N 9°9W 126 A2
Estrela, Serra da Portugal 40°10N 7°45W 194 E3
Estrella Spain 38°25N 3°35W 195 G7
Estremoz Portugal 38°51N 7°39W 195 G3
Estrondo, Serra do Brazil 7°20S 48°0W 332 C2
Estuaire □ Gabon 0°30N 9°30E 264 B1
Esutoru = Uglegorsk Russia 49°5N 142°2E 215 E15
Esztergom Hungary 47°47N 18°44E 182 C3
Et Tîdra Mauritania 19°45N 16°20W 262 B1
Etah India 27°35N 78°40E 243 F8
Étain France 49°13N 5°38E 173 C12
Étampes France 48°26N 2°10E 173 D9
Étang-Salé-les-Bains Réunion 21°15S 55°20E 272 f
Etanga Namibia 17°55S 13°0E 270 A1
Étaples France 50°30N 1°39E 173 B8
Etawah India 26°48N 79°6E 243 F8
Etawney L. Canada 57°50N 96°50W 297 B9
Etchojoa Mexico 26°55N 109°38W 318 B3
Ete Nigeria 7°2N 7°28E 263 D6
Etéké Gabon 1°29S 11°35E 264 C2
eThekwini = Durban S. Africa 29°49S 31°1E 271 C5
Ethel U.S.A. 46°32N 122°46W 306 D4
Ethelbert Canada 51°32N 100°25W 297 C8
Ethiopia ■ Africa 8°0N 40°0E 267 C4
Ethiopian Highlands Ethiopia 10°0N 37°0E 254 E7
Etili Turkey 39°59N 26°54E 203 G10
Etive, L. U.K. 56°29N 5°10W 167 E3
Etna Italy 37°50N 14°55E 201 E7
Etna ➜ Norway 60°49N 10°7E 164 C6
Etne Norway 59°40N 5°58E 164 E2
Etobicoke Canada 43°39N 79°34W 141 B1
Etobicoke Cr. ➜ Canada 43°35N 79°32W 141 B1
Etoile Dem. Rep. of the Congo 11°33S 27°30E 269 E2
Etoliko Greece 38°26N 21°21E 204 C3
Etolin Strait U.S.A. 60°20N 165°15W 303 F6
Etoloakarnania Greece 38°45N 21°18E 204 C3
Etosha △ Namibia 19°0S 16°0E 270 A2
Etosha Pan Namibia 18°40S 16°30E 270 A2
Etoumbi Congo 0°1S 14°57E 264 C2
Etowah U.S.A. 35°20N 84°32W 315 D12
Étréchy France 48°30N 2°12E 173 D9
Etrek Turkmenistan 37°36N 54°46E 247 B7
Étrépagny France 49°18N 1°36E 173 C8
Étretat France 49°42N 0°12E 172 C7
Etropole Bulgaria 42°50N 24°0E 203 D8
Ettelbruck Lux. 49°51N 6°5E 170 E6
Etterbeek Belgium 50°50N 4°23E 116 B2
Ettlingen Germany 48°56N 8°25E 179 G4
Ettrick Water ➜ U.K. 55°31N 2°55W 167 F6
Etuku Dem. Rep. of the Congo 3°42S 25°45E 264 C5
Etulia Moldova 45°32N 28°27E 183 E13
Etzná-Tixmucuy = Edzná Mexico 19°39N 90°19W 319 D6
Eu France 50°3N 1°26E 172 B8
Eua Tonga 21°22S 174°56W 287 Q13
Euboea = Evia Greece 38°30N 24°0E 204 C6
Eucaliptus = Tomás Barrón Bolivia 17°35S 67°31W 330 D4
Euchareena Australia 32°57S 149°6E 283 B8
Eucla Australia 31°41S 128°52E 279 F4
Euclid U.S.A. 41°34N 81°32W 312 E3
Euclides da Cunha Brazil 10°31S 39°1W 332 D4
Eucumbene, L. Australia 36°2S 148°40E 283 D8
Eudora U.S.A. 33°7N 91°16W 314 E9
Eudunda Australia 34°12S 139°7E 282 C3
Eufaula Ala., U.S.A. 31°54N 85°9W 316 D4
Eufaula Okla., U.S.A. 35°17N 95°35W 314 D7
Eufaula L. U.S.A. 35°18N 95°21W 314 D7
Eugene U.S.A. 44°5N 123°4W 304 D2
Eugowra Australia 33°22S 148°24E 283 B8
Eulo Australia 28°10S 145°3E 281 D4
Eulonia U.S.A. 31°32N 81°26W 316 D8
Eumungerie Australia 31°56S 148°36E 283 A8
Eung-am S. Korea 37°34N 126°55E 137 B1
Eungella △ Australia 20°57S 148°40E 280 b
Eunice La., U.S.A. 30°30N 92°25W 314 F8
Eunice N. Mex., U.S.A. 32°26N 103°10W 305 K12
Eunpyeong S. Korea 37°36N 126°56E 137 B1
Eupen Belgium 50°37N 6°3E 170 D6
Euphrates = Furāt, Nahr al ➜ Asia 31°0N 47°25E 246 D5
Eure □ France 49°10N 1°0E 172 C8
Eure ➜ France 49°18N 1°12E 172 C8
Eure-et-Loir □ France 48°22N 1°30E 172 D8
Eureka Nunavut, Canada 80°0N 85°56W 295 B14
Eureka Calif., U.S.A. 40°47N 124°9W 304 F1
Eureka Ill., U.S.A. 40°43N 89°16W 310 D7
Eureka Kans., U.S.A. 37°49N 96°17W 308 G5
Eureka Mo., U.S.A. 38°30N 90°38W 310 F6
Eureka Mont., U.S.A. 48°53N 115°3W 304 B6
Eureka Nev., U.S.A. 39°31N 115°58W 304 G6
Eureka S.C., U.S.A. 33°42N 81°46W 316 B8
Eureka S. Dak., U.S.A. 45°46N 99°38W 308 C4
Eureka, Mt. Australia 26°35S 121°35E 279 E3
Eureka Sd. Canada 79°0N 85°0W 295 B15
Eurelia Australia 32°33S 138°35E 282 B3
Eurinilla Cr. ➜ Australia 30°53S 140°11E 282 A4
Euroa Australia 36°44S 145°35E 283 D6
Euroairport ✈ (EAP) France 47°36N 7°33E 173 E14
Europa, Île Ind. Oc. 22°20S 40°22E 271 B7
Europa, Picos de Spain 43°10N 4°49W 194 B6
Europa, Pt. Gib. 36°3N 5°21W 195 J5
Europe 50°0N 20°0E 158 E10
Europoort Neths. 51°57N 4°10E 170 C4
Euskadi = País Vasco □ Spain 42°50N 2°45W 196 C2
Euskirchen Germany 50°39N 6°48E 178 E2
Eustis U.S.A. 28°51N 81°41W 317 G8
Euston N.S.W., Australia 34°30S 142°46E 282 C5
Euston London, U.K. 125 a3
Eutawville U.S.A. 33°24N 80°21W 316 B9
Eutin Germany 54°8N 10°36E 178 A6
Eutsuk L. Canada 53°20N 126°45W 296 C3
Eva Perón = La Pampa □ Argentina 36°50S 66°0W 334 D2
Eva Perón = La Plata Argentina 35°0S 57°55W 334 C4
Evale Angola 16°33S 15°44E 265 F3
Evanger Norway 60°39N 6°7E 164 D3
Evanlı Turkey 36°46N 34°26E 250 B5
Evans U.S.A. 40°23N 104°41W 304 F11
Evans, L. Canada 50°50N 77°0W 298 B4
Evans City U.S.A. 40°46N 80°4W 312 F4
Evans Head Australia 29°7S 153°27E 281 D5
Evansburg Canada 53°36N 114°59W 296 C5
Evansdale U.S.A. 42°30N 92°17W 310 B4
Evanston Ill., U.S.A. 42°3N 87°40W 119 A2
Evanston Wyo., U.S.A. 41°16N 110°58W 304 F8
Evansville Ill., U.S.A. 38°5N 89°56W 310 F7
Evansville Ind., U.S.A. 37°58N 87°35W 311 G9
Evansville Wis., U.S.A. 42°47N 89°18W 310 B7
Évaux-les-Bains France 46°12N 2°29E 173 F9
Evaz Iran 27°46N 53°59E 247 E7
Evciler Afyon, Turkey 38°4N 29°54E 205 C11
Evciler Çanakkale, Turkey 39°47N 26°44E 205 B8
Eveleth U.S.A. 47°28N 92°32W 308 B7
Even Sapir Israel 31°46N 35°8E 123 B1
Evensk Russia 62°12N 159°30E 215 C16
Evenstad Norway 61°25N 11°7E 164 C8
Everard, L. Australia 31°30S 135°0E 281 E2
Everard Ranges Australia 27°5S 132°28E 279 E5
Evere Belgium 50°52N 4°25E 116 A2
Everest, Mt. Nepal 28°5N 86°58E 243 E12
Everett Ga., U.S.A. 31°24N 81°38W 316 D8
Everett Mass., U.S.A. 42°24N 71°3W 116 A2
Everett Pa., U.S.A. 40°1N 78°23W 312 F6
Everett Wash., U.S.A. 47°59N 122°12W 306 C4
Everglades, The U.S.A. 25°50N 81°0W 317 K9
Everglades △ U.S.A. 25°30N 81°0W 317 K9
Everglades City U.S.A. 25°52N 81°23W 317 K8
Evergreen Ala., U.S.A. 31°26N 86°57W 315 F11
Evergreen Mont., U.S.A. 48°14N 114°17W 304 B6
Evergreen Park U.S.A. 41°43N 87°42W 119 C2
Everöd Sweden 55°53N 14°5E 163 J8
Everton Australia 36°25S 146°33E 283 D7
Evertsberg Sweden 61°8N 13°58E 162 C7
Evesham U.K. 52°6N 1°56W 169 E6
Evia Greece 38°30N 24°0E 204 C6
Évian-les-Bains France 46°24N 6°35E 173 F13
Evīn Iran 35°47N 51°23E 141 A2
Evinayong Eq. Guin. 1°26N 10°35E 264 B2
Evinos ➜ Greece 38°27N 21°40E 204 C3
Évisa France 42°15N 8°48E 175 F12
Evje Norway 58°36N 7°51E 164 F4
Évora Portugal 38°33N 7°57W 195 G3
Évora □ Portugal 38°33N 7°50W 195 G3
Evowghlī Iran 38°43N 45°13E 213 C11
Évreux France 49°3N 1°8E 172 C8
Evritania Greece 39°5N 21°30E 204 B3
Évron France 48°10N 0°24W 172 D6
Evros ➜ Greece 41°40N 26°34E 203 F10
Evrotas ➜ Greece 36°50N 22°40E 204 E4
Évry France 48°38N 2°27E 173 D9
Évvoia = Evia Greece 38°30N 24°0E 204 C6
'Ewa Beach U.S.A. 21°19N 158°1W 302 K13
'Ewa District U.S.A. 21°25N 158°0W 302 K14
'Ewa Villages U.S.A. 21°20N 158°3W 302 K13
Ewarton Jamaica 18°11N 77°6W 320 a
Ewasse Papua N. G. 5°19S 151°1E 286 C6
Ewe, L. U.K. 57°49N 5°38W 167 D3
Ewing Mo., U.S.A. 40°6N 91°43W 310 E5
Ewing Nebr., U.S.A. 42°16N 98°21W 308 D4
Ewo Congo 0°48S 14°45E 264 C2
Ewu Nigeria 6°33N 3°19E 124 A1
Exaltación Bolivia 13°10S 65°20W 331 C4
Excelsior Springs U.S.A. 39°20N 94°13W 310 E2
Excideuil France 45°20N 1°4E 174 C5
Exe ➜ U.K. 50°41N 3°29W 169 G4
Exeter Ont., Canada 43°21N 81°29W 312 C3
Exeter Devon, U.K. 50°43N 3°31W 169 G4
Exeter Calif., U.S.A. 36°18N 119°9W 306 J7
Exeter N.H., U.S.A. 42°59N 70°57W 313 D14
Exhibition Place Canada 43°38N 79°25W 141 B2
Exira U.S.A. 41°35N 94°52W 310 C2
Exmoor U.K. 51°12N 3°45W 169 F4
Exmoor △ U.K. 51°8N 3°42W 169 F4
Exmouth W. Austral., Australia 21°54S 114°10E 278 D1
Exmouth Devon, U.K. 50°37N 3°25W 169 G4
Exmouth G. Australia 22°15S 114°15E 278 D1
Exmouth Plateau Ind. Oc. 19°0S 114°0E 288 J3
Expedition △ Australia 25°41S 149°7E 281 D4
Expedition Ra. Australia 24°30S 149°12E 280 C4
Experiment = Highland Mills U.S.A. 33°17N 84°17W 316 B5
Expo Centre Shanghai, China 31°11N 121°29E 138 B1
Exposições, Palácio das Brazil 22°53S 43°13W 135 B1
Extremadura □ Spain 39°30N 6°5W 195 F4
Extrême-Nord □ Cameroon 11°0N 14°30E 259 F2
Exuma Sound Bahamas 24°30N 76°20W 320 B4
Eyak U.S.A. 60°32N 145°36W 303 F11
Eyasi, L. Tanzania 3°30S 35°0E 268 C4
Eydehavn Norway 58°30N 8°53E 164 F5
Eydhafushi Maldives 5°7N 73°2E 272 d
Eye Pen. U.K. 58°13N 6°10W 167 C2
Eyemouth U.K. 55°52N 2°5W 167 F6
Eygues = Aigues ➜ France 44°7N 4°43E 175 D8
Eygurande France 45°40N 2°26E 173 G9
Eyjafjallajökull Iceland 63°38N 19°36W 155 D7
Eyjafjarðarsýsla Iceland 65°30N 18°30W 155 B8
Eyjafjörður Iceland 66°15N 18°30W 155 A8
Eyl Somalia 8°0N 49°50E 267 C6
Eymet France 44°40N 0°25E 174 D4
Eymoutiers France 45°40N 1°45E 174 C5
Eynesil Turkey 41°4N 39°9E 213 B8
Eyrarbakki Iceland 63°52N 21°9W 155 D5
Eyre (North), L. Australia 28°30S 137°20E 281 D2
Eyre (South), L. Australia 29°18S 137°25E 281 D2
Eyre ➜ France 44°39N 1°1W 174 D2
Eyre, L. Australia 29°30S 137°26E 276 F6
Eyre Mts. N.Z. 45°25S 168°25E 285 F3
Eyre Pen. Australia 33°30S 136°17E 282 C1
Eysturoy Færoe Is. 62°13N 6°54W 160 E9
Eyüp Turkey 41°2N 28°55E 122 B1
Eyvān = Jūy Zar Iran 33°50N 46°18E 213 F12
Eyvānkī Iran 35°24N 51°56E 247 C6
Ez Zeidab Sudan 17°25N 33°55E 256 D3
Ezcaray Spain 42°19N 3°0W 196 C1
Ezeiza ✈ (EZE) Argentina 34°49S 58°32W 117 C1
Ežerėlis Lithuania 54°53N 23°37E 184 D10
Ezhou China 30°23N 114°50E 229 B10
Ezhva Russia 61°48N 50°35E 186 B9
Ezine Turkey 39°48N 26°20E 205 B8
Ezouza ➜ Cyprus 34°44N 32°27E 207 F8

F

F.Y.R.O.M. = Macedonia ■ Europe 41°53N 21°40E 202 E5
Faaa Tahiti 17°34S 149°35W 289 e
Faaborg Denmark 55°6N 10°15E 163 J4
Faaone Tahiti 17°40S 149°21W 289 e
Fabala Guinea 9°44N 9°5W 262 D3
Fabbriche Nuove Venice, Italy 142 b2
Fabens U.S.A. 31°30N 106°10W 314 F1
Faber, Mt. Singapore 1°16N 103°49E 138 B2
Fåberg Norway 61°10N 10°25E 164 C7
Fabero Spain 42°46N 6°37W 194 C4
Fabius U.S.A. 42°50N 75°59W 313 D9
Fabriano Italy 43°20N 12°54E 199 E9
Făcăeni Romania 44°32N 27°53E 183 F12
Facatativá Colombia 4°49N 74°22W 328 C3
Faceville U.S.A. 30°45N 84°38W 316 E5
Fachi Niger 18°6N 11°34E 259 E2
Facundo Argentina 45°18S 69°58W 336 C3
Fada Chad 17°13N 21°34E 259 E4
Fada-n-Gourma Burkina Faso 12°10N 0°30E 263 C5
Fadd Hungary 46°28N 18°49E 182 D3
Faddeyevskiy, Ostrov Russia 76°0N 144°0E 215 B15
Faddor South Sudan 8°7N 32°17E 257 F3
Fadghāmī Syria 35°53N 40°52E 213 E9
Fadiffolu Atoll Maldives 5°23N 73°29E 272 d
Fadlab Sudan 17°42N 34°2E 256 D3
Fadwel South Sudan 8°11N 29°20E 266 C2
Fælledparken Denmark 55°42N 12°34E 118 A3
Faenza Italy 44°17N 11°53E 199 D8
Færingehavn = Kangerluarsoruseq Greenland 63°45N 51°27W 154 E5
Færoe Is. = Føroyar ⊘ Atl. Oc. 62°0N 7°0W 160 F9
Fafa Mali 15°22N 0°48E 263 B5
Fafe Portugal 41°27N 8°11W 194 D2
Fafen ➜ Ethiopia 5°59N 44°25E 267 C5
Fagam Nigeria 11°1N 10°1E 263 C7
Fagamalo Amer. Samoa 14°18S 170°48W 302 f
Făgăras Romania 45°48N 24°58E 183 E9
Făgăras, Munţii Romania 45°40N 24°40E 183 E9
Fagasa Amer. Samoa 14°17S 170°43W 302 f
Fagatele Bay △ Amer. Samoa 14°22S 170°46W 302 f
Fagatogo Amer. Samoa 14°16S 170°41W 302 f
Fågelfors Sweden 57°12N 15°51E 163 H9
Fågelmara Sweden 56°16N 15°58E 163 H9
Fågelön Sweden 59°18N 17°55E 139 B1
Fagerheim Norway 60°26N 7°46E 164 D4
Fagerhult Sweden 57°8N 15°40E 163 G9
Fagernes Norway 60°59N 9°14E 164 D6
Fagersjö Sweden 59°14N 18°4E 139 B2
Fagersta Sweden 60°1N 15°46E 162 D9
Făget Romania 45°52N 22°10E 182 E7
Făget, Munţii Romania 47°40N 23°10E 183 C8
Faggo Nigeria 11°21N 9°57E 263 C6
Faghmah Yemen 16°9N 49°26E 249 C5
Fagnano, L. Argentina 54°30S 68°0W 336 D3
Fagnières France 48°58N 4°20E 173 D11
Faguibine, L. Mali 16°45N 4°0W 262 B4
Fahlīān Iran 30°11N 51°28E 247 D6
Fahraj Kermān, Iran 29°0N 59°0E 247 D8
Fahraj Yazd, Iran 31°46N 54°36E 247 D7
Fai Tsi Long Vietnam 21°0N 107°30E 228 G6
Faial Azores 38°34N 28°42W 153 d1
Faial Madeira 32°47N 16°53W 153 c
Faial, Canal do Azores 38°33N 28°35W 153 d1
Faichan Kangri India 35°48N 76°34E 243 B7
Faichuk Micronesia 7°21N 151°38E 287 T17
Fair Haven N.Y., U.S.A. 43°18N 76°42W 313 C8
Fair Haven Vt., U.S.A. 43°36N 73°16W 313 C11
Fair Hd. U.K. 55°14N 6°9W 166 A5
Fair Isle U.K. 59°32N 1°38W 165 B6
Fair Oaks U.S.A. 38°39N 121°16W 306 G5
Fairbank U.S.A. 42°38N 92°3W 310 B4
Fairbanks Alaska, U.S.A. 64°51N 147°43W 303 D11
Fairbanks Fla., U.S.A. 29°44N 82°16W 316 F7
Fairborn U.S.A. 39°49N 84°2W 311 E12
Fairburn U.S.A. 33°34N 84°35W 316 B5
Fairbury Ill., U.S.A. 40°45N 88°31W 311 D8
Fairbury Nebr., U.S.A. 40°8N 97°11W 308 E5
Fairfax Ohio, U.S.A. 39°5N 83°37W 311 E13
Fairfax S.C., U.S.A. 32°59N 81°15W 316 C8
Fairfax Vt., U.S.A. 44°40N 73°1W 313 B11
Fairfield N.S.W., Australia 33°53S 150°57E 283 B9
Fairfield Calif., U.S.A. 38°15N 122°3W 306 G4
Fairfield Conn., U.S.A. 41°9N 73°16W 313 E11
Fairfield Idaho, U.S.A. 43°21N 114°44W 304 E6
Fairfield Ill., U.S.A. 38°23N 88°22W 311 F8
Fairfield Iowa, U.S.A. 40°56N 91°57W 310 D5
Fairfield Ohio, U.S.A. 39°20N 84°34W 311 E12
Fairfield Tex., U.S.A. 31°44N 96°10W 314 F6
Fairford Canada 51°37N 98°38W 297 C9
Fairhope U.S.A. 30°31N 87°54W 315 F11
Fairland S. Africa 26°8S 27°57E 123 A1
Fairlie N.Z. 44°5S 170°49E 285 E5
Fairmead U.S.A. 37°5N 120°10W 306 H6
Fairmilehead U.K. 55°54N 3°11W 121 B2
Fairmont Minn., U.S.A. 43°39N 94°28W 308 D6
Fairmont W. Va., U.S.A. 39°29N 80°9W 309 F13
Fairmount Calif., U.S.A. 34°45N 118°26W 307 L8
Fairmount N.Y., U.S.A. 43°5N 76°12W 313 C8
Fairplay U.S.A. 39°15N 106°2W 304 G10
Fairport Ont., Canada 43°49N 79°4W 141 A4
Fairport N.Y., U.S.A. 43°6N 77°27W 312 C7
Fairport Harbor U.S.A. 41°45N 81°17W 312 E3
Fairview Alta., Canada 56°5N 118°25W 296 B5
Fairview Mont., U.S.A. 47°51N 104°3W 304 C11
Fairview N.J., U.S.A. 40°48N 73°59W 132 B2
Fairview Okla., U.S.A. 36°16N 98°29W 314 C5
Fairview, L. U.S.A. 28°35N 81°24W 133 A2
Fairweather, Mt. U.S.A. 58°55N 137°32W 296 B1
Faisalabad Pakistan 31°30N 73°5E 242 D5
Faith U.S.A. 45°2N 102°2W 308 C2
Faizabad India 26°45N 82°10E 243 F10
Faizpur India 21°14N 75°49E 244 D2
Fajã Grande Azores 39°27N 31°16W 153 d2
Fajardo Puerto Rico 18°20N 65°39W 321 C6
Fajou, Îlet à Guadeloupe 16°21N 61°35W 322 e
Fajr, W. ➜ Si. Arabia 29°10N 38°10E 246 D3
Fakaofo Pac. Oc. 9°23S 171°15W 277 B16
Fakarava French Polynesia 16°20S 145°37W 289 f
Fakenham U.K. 52°51N 0°51E 168 E8
Fåker Sweden 63°0N 14°34E 162 A8
Fakfak Indonesia 2°55S 132°18E 231 E8
Fakiya Bulgaria 42°10N 27°6E 203 D11
Fakobli Ivory C. 7°23N 7°23W 262 D3
Fakse Denmark 55°15N 12°8E 163 J6
Fakse Bugt Denmark 55°11N 12°15E 163 J6
Fakse Ladeplads Denmark 55°11N 12°9E 163 J6
Faku China 42°32N 123°21E 224 A1
Fala Beguets I. Micronesia 7°21N 151°41E 287 U17
Falaba S. Leone 9°54N 11°22W 262 D2
Falaise France 48°54N 0°12W 172 D6
Falakro Oros Greece 41°15N 23°58E 202 E7
Falam Burma 23°0N 93°45E 241 D4
Falas I. Micronesia 7°31N 151°44E 287 T18
Fălciu Romania 46°17N 28°7E 183 D13
Falcó, C. des Spain 38°50N 1°23E 206 D1
Falcón □ Venezuela 11°0N 69°50W 328 A4
Falcon, C. Algeria 35°50N 0°50W 261 A4
Falcón, Presa Mexico 26°35N 99°10W 319 B5
Falcon Lake Canada 49°42N 95°15W 297 D9
Falcon Res. U.S.A. 26°34N 99°10W 314 H5
Falconara Maríttima Italy 43°37N 13°24E 199 E10
Falcone, C. del Italy 40°58N 8°12E 200 B1
Falconer U.S.A. 42°7N 79°12W 312 D5
Faléa Mali 12°16N 11°17W 262 C2
Falefa Samoa 13°54S 171°31W 287 V20
Falelatai Samoa 13°55S 171°59W 287 V20
Falelima Samoa 13°32S 172°41W 287 V19
Falémé ➜ Senegal 14°46N 12°14W 262 C2
Faleniu Amer. Samoa 14°19S 170°44W 302 f
Falenty Poland 52°8N 20°55E 143 C1
Falerum Sweden 58°8N 16°13E 163 F10
Faleshty = Făleşti Moldova 47°32N 27°44E 183 C12
Făleşti Moldova 47°32N 27°44E 183 C12
Falfurrias U.S.A. 27°14N 98°9W 314 H5
Falher Canada 55°44N 117°15W 296 B5
Faliraki Greece 36°22N 28°12E 206 E12
Faliro Greece 37°55N 23°39E 112 B1
Faliro, Ormos Greece 37°54N 23°40E 112 B2
Falkenberg Brandenburg, Germany 51°35N 13°14E 178 D9
Falkenberg Sweden 56°54N 12°30E 163 H6
Falkenburg = Niemodlin Poland 50°38N 17°38E 185 H4
Falkenburg Germany 52°34N 13°32E 115 A4
Falkenhagen Germany 52°34N 13°5E 115 A1
Falkensee Germany 52°34N 13°4E 115 A1
Falkirk U.K. 56°0N 3°47W 167 F5
Falkirk □ U.K. 55°58N 3°49W 167 F5
Falkland U.K. 56°16N 3°12W 167 E5
Falkland, East, I. Falk. Is. 51°40S 58°30W 336 D5
Falkland, West, I. Falk. Is. 51°40S 60°0W 336 D5
Falkland Is. ⊘ Atl. Oc. 51°30S 59°0W 153 f
Falkland Plateau Atl. Oc. 51°0S 50°0W 152 M7
Falkland Ridge Atl. Oc. 49°20S 40°0W 152 L8
Falkland Sd. Falk. Is. 52°0S 60°0W 153 f
Falknov nad Ohří = Sokolov Czech Rep. 50°12N 12°40E 180 A5
Falkonera Greece 36°50N 23°52E 204 E5
Falköping Sweden 58°12N 13°33E 163 F7
Fall River U.S.A. 41°43N 71°10W 313 E13
Fallbrook U.S.A. 33°23N 117°15W 307 M9
Fallon U.S.A. 39°28N 118°47W 304 G4
Falls City U.S.A. 40°3N 95°36W 308 E6
Falls Creek U.S.A. 41°9N 78°48W 312 E6
Falmouth Jamaica 18°30N 77°40W 320 a
Falmouth Corn., U.K. 50°9N 5°5W 169 G2
Falmouth Ky., U.S.A. 38°41N 84°20W 311 F12
Falmouth Mass., U.S.A. 41°33N 70°37W 313 E14
Falo I. Micronesia 7°28N 151°52E 287 T18
Falomo Nigeria 6°26N 3°26E 124 B2
Falsa, Pta. Mexico 27°51N 115°3W 318 B1
False B. S. Africa 34°15S 18°40E 270 D2
False Bay S. Africa 34°6S 18°33E 118 B2
False Divi Pt. India 15°43N 80°50E 245 G5
False Pass U.S.A. 54°51N 163°25W 303 J7
False Pt. India 20°18N 86°48E 244 D8
Falso, C. Honduras 15°12N 83°21W 320 C3
Falster Denmark 54°45N 11°55E 163 K5
Fălticeni Romania 47°21N 26°20E 183 C11
Falun Sweden 60°37N 15°37E 162 D9
Famagusta Cyprus 35°8N 33°55E 207 E9
Famagusta Bay Cyprus 35°15N 34°0E 207 E10
Famatina, Sierra de Argentina 27°30S 68°0W 334 B2
Famenin Iran 35°5N 48°58E 213 E13
Family L. Canada 51°54N 95°27W 297 C9
Famões Portugal 38°47N 9°13W 126 A1
Famoso U.S.A. 35°37N 119°12W 307 K7
Fan Lau Hong Kong, China 22°12N 113°51E 122 B1
Fan Xian China 35°55N 115°38E 226 G8
Fana Mali 13°0N 6°56W 262 C3
Fanad Hd. Ireland 55°17N 7°38W 166 A4
Fanahammaren Norway 60°16N 5°20E 164 D2
Fanari Greece 39°24N 21°47E 204 B3
Fandriana Madag. 20°14S 47°21E 272 C2
Fánes-Sénnes-Braies ⌓ Italy 46°38N 12°4E 199 B9
Faneuil Hall Marketplace Boston, U.S.A. 116 b3
Fang Thailand 19°55N 99°13E 236 C2
Fang Xian China 32°3N 110°40E 229 A8
Fangaga Sudan 17°40N 37°50E 256 D4
Fangak South Sudan 9°4N 30°53E 257 F3
Fangatau French Polynesia 15°22S 138°45W 289 f
Fangataufa French Polynesia 15°50S 140°52W 289 f
Fangchang China 31°5N 118°4E 229 B12
Fangcheng China 33°18N 112°59E 226 H7
Fangchenggang China 21°42N 108°21E 228 G7
Fangcun China 23°6N 113°13E 121 B2
Fangliao Taiwan 22°22N 120°38E 225 D2
Fangshan Beijing, China 39°41N 116°0E 226 E9
Fangshan Shanxi, China 38°3N 111°25E 226 E6
Fangshan Taiwan 22°15N 120°39E 225 D2
Fangyüan Taiwan 23°56N 120°19E 225 C2
Fangzi China 36°33N 119°10E 227 F10
Fani i Madh ➜ Albania 41°56N 20°16E 202 E4
Fanjakana Madag. 21°10S 46°53E 272 C2
Fanjiatun China 43°40N 125°15E 227 C13
Fanling China 22°30N 114°8E 219 a
Fannich, L. U.K. 57°38N 4°59W 167 D4
Fannrem Norway 63°16N 9°50E 164 A6
Fannūj Iran 26°35N 59°38E 247 E8
Fanø Denmark 55°25N 8°25E 163 J2
Fano Italy 43°50N 13°1E 199 E10
Fanshi China 39°12N 113°20E 226 E7
Fantzuliao Hsi ➜ Taiwan 22°42N 120°28E 225 D2
Fanuet I. Micronesia 7°32N 151°48E 287 T18
Fao = Al Fāw Iraq 30°0N 48°30E 247 D6
Faqirwali Pakistan 29°27N 73°0E 242 E5
Fâqûs Egypt 30°44N 31°47E 256 H7
Far East = Dalnevostochnyy □ Russia 67°0N 140°0E 215 C14
Far East Asia 40°0N 130°0E 210 E14
Fara in Sabina Italy 42°12N 12°43E 199 F9
Faradje Dem. Rep. of the Congo 3°50N 29°45E 268 B2
Farafangana Madag. 22°49S 47°50E 272 C2
Farafenni Gambia 13°34N 15°36W 262 C1
Farâfra, El Wâhât el Egypt 27°15N 28°20E 256 B2
Farāh Afghan. 32°20N 62°7E 240 B1
Farāh □ Afghan. 32°25N 62°10E 240 B1
Farāh ➜ Afghan. 31°27N 61°28E 240 C1
Faraḩābād Iran 35°41N 51°30E 141 A2
Farahalana Madag. 14°26S 50°10E 272 A3
Faraid, Gebel Egypt 23°33N 35°19E 256 C4
Farako Ivory C. 10°45N 6°50W 262 D4
Farallon de Medinilla N. Marianas 16°1N 146°4E 302 a
Farallon de Pajaros N. Marianas 20°32N 144°54E 302 a
Farallones de Cali △ Colombia 3°13N 76°46W 328 C2
Faramana Burkina Faso 11°56N 4°45W 262 C4
Faranah Guinea 10°3N 10°45W 262 C2
Farap Turkmenistan 39°9N 63°36E 216 E6
Fararah Oman 17°55N 55°38E 249 C6
Farasān, Jazā'ir Si. Arabia 16°45N 41°55E 248 C3
Farasan Is. = Farasān, Jazā'ir Si. Arabia 16°45N 41°55E 248 C3
Faratsiho Madag. 19°24S 46°57E 272 B2
Farbaraki Somalia 2°30N 45°30E 267 D6
Fardes ➜ Spain 37°35N 3°0W 195 H7
Fareham U.K. 50°51N 1°11W 169 G6
Farewell U.S.A. 62°31N 153°54W 303 E9
Farewell, C. N.Z. 40°29S 172°43E 285 A7
Farewell C. = Nunap Isua Greenland 59°48N 43°55W 154 F6
Farewell Spit N.Z. 40°35S 173°0E 285 A8
Farforovskaya Russia 59°52N 30°27E 137 B2
Färgelanda Sweden 58°34N 12°0E 163 F5
Farghona Uzbekistan 40°23N 71°19E 217 D8
Farghona □ Uzbekistan 40°30N 71°15E 217 D8
Farghona Vodiysi Asia 40°46N 71°30E 217 D8
Fargo Ga., U.S.A. 30°41N 82°34W 316 E7
Fargo N. Dak., U.S.A. 46°53N 96°48W 308 B5
Fār'iah, W. al ➜ West Bank 32°12N 35°27E 251 F6
Faribault U.S.A. 44°18N 93°16W 308 C7
Faridabad India 28°26N 77°19E 242 E6
Faridkot India 30°44N 74°45E 242 D6
Faridpur Bangla. 23°15N 89°55E 241 D2
Faridpur India 28°13N 79°33E 243 E8
Färigh, W. al ➜ Libya 30°28N 20°44E 258 B3
Färila Sweden 61°48N 15°50E 162 C9
Farim Guinea-Biss. 12°27N 15°9W 262 C1
Farīmān Iran 35°40N 59°49E 247 C8
Farinha ➜ Brazil 6°51S 47°30W 332 C2
Fariones, Pta. Canary Is. 29°13N 13°28W 153 e2
Fâriskûr Egypt 31°20N 31°43E 256 H7
Färjestaden Sweden 56°39N 16°27E 163 H10
Farkadona Greece 39°36N 22°4E 204 B4
Farleigh Australia 21°4S 149°8E 280 b
Farley U.S.A. 42°27N 91°0W 310 B6
Farmakonisi Greece 37°17N 27°5E 205 D9
Farmer City U.S.A. 40°15N 88°39W 311 D8
Farmersburg U.S.A. 39°15N 87°23W 311 E9
Farmerville U.S.A. 32°47N 92°24W 314 E8
Farmingdale U.S.A. 40°12N 74°10W 313 F10
Farmington B.C., Canada 55°54N 120°30W 296 B4
Farmington Calif., U.S.A. 37°55N 120°59W 306 H6
Farmington Ga., U.S.A. 33°47N 83°26W 316 B6
Farmington Ill., U.S.A. 40°42N 90°0W 310 D7
Farmington Iowa, U.S.A. 40°38N 91°44W 310 D5
Farmington Maine, U.S.A. 44°40N 70°9W 309 C18
Farmington Mo., U.S.A. 37°47N 90°25W 310 G6
Farmington N.H., U.S.A. 43°24N 71°4W 313 C13
Farmington N. Mex., U.S.A. 36°44N 108°12W 305 H9
Farmington Utah, U.S.A. 40°59N 111°53W 304 F8
Farmington ➜ U.S.A. 41°51N 72°38W 313 E12
Farmland U.S.A. 40°15N 85°5W 311 D11
Farmville U.S.A. 37°18N 78°24W 309 G14
Färnäs Sweden 61°0N 14°39E 162 D8
Farne Is. U.K. 55°38N 1°37W 168 B6
Färnebofjärden △ Sweden 60°10N 16°48E 162 D10
Farnham Canada 45°17N 72°59W 313 A12
Farnham, Mt. Canada 50°29N 116°30W 296 C5
Farningham U.K. 51°23N 0°12E 125 B5
Faro Brazil 2°10S 56°39W 329 D6
Faro Yukon, Canada 62°11N 133°22W 294 E5
Faro Portugal 37°2N 7°55W 195 H3
Fårö Gotland, Sweden 57°55N 19°5E 163 G13
Faro □ Portugal 37°12N 8°10W 195 H2
Faro ✈ (FAO) Portugal 37°2N 7°57W 195 H3
Faro ⌓ Cameroon 8°15N 12°37E 264 A2
Fårösund Sweden 57°52N 19°2E 163 G13
Farquhar, C. Australia 23°50S 113°36E 279 D1
Farquhar Is. Seychelles 11°0S 52°0E 273 F4
Farrars Cr. ➜ Australia 25°35S 140°43E 280 D3
Farrāshband Iran 28°57N 52°5E 247 D7
Farrell U.S.A. 41°13N 80°30W 312 E4
Farrell Flat Australia 33°48S 138°48E 282 B3
Farrokhī Iran 33°50N 59°31E 247 C8
Farruch, C. = Ferrutx, C. de Spain 39°47N 3°21E 206 B4
Farrukhabad India 27°24N 79°34E 244 A4
Fārs □ Iran 29°30N 55°0E 247 D7
Farsala Greece 39°17N 22°23E 204 B4
Fārsī Afghan. 33°47N 63°15E 240 B1
Fārsī Iran 27°58N 50°11E 247 E6
Farsø Denmark 56°46N 9°19E 163 H3
Farson U.S.A. 42°7N 109°26W 304 E9
Farsta Sweden 59°14N 18°5E 139 B2
Farsund Norway 58°5N 6°55E 164 F3
Fartak, Râs Si. Arabia 28°5N 34°34E 246 D2
Fartak, Ra's Yemen 15°38N 52°15E 249 D6
Fârţăneşti Romania 45°49N 27°59E 183 E12
Fartura, Serra da Brazil 26°21S 52°52W 335 B5
Faru Nigeria 12°48N 6°12E 263 C6
Fārūj Iran 37°14N 58°14E 247 B8
Fårup Denmark 56°33N 9°51E 163 H3
Farvel, Kap = Nunap Isua Greenland 59°48N 43°55W 154 F6
Farwell U.S.A. 34°23N 103°2W 314 D3
Fāryāb □ Afghan. 36°0N 65°0E 240 B2
Fasā Iran 29°0N 53°39E 247 D7
Fasanerie-Nord Germany 48°11N 11°32E 131 A2
Fasangarten Germany 48°5N 11°36E 131 B2
Fasano Italy 40°50N 17°22E 201 B10
Fashoda South Sudan 9°50N 32°2E 257 F3
Fasil Ghebbi Ethiopia 12°36N 37°28E 266 B4
Fáskrúðsfjörður Iceland 64°56N 14°1W 155 C12
Fassa Mali 13°26N 8°15W 262 C3
Fastiv Ukraine 50°7N 29°57E 177 C15
Fastnet Rock Ireland 51°22N 9°37W 166 E2
Fastov = Fastiv Ukraine 50°7N 29°57E 177 C15
Fatagartuting, Tanjung Indonesia 2°46S 131°57E 231 E8
Fataka Solomon Is. 11°55S 170°12E 277 C12
Fatatsu Ne Iwo Jima 24°45N 141°18E 288 b
Fatehabad Haryana, India 29°31N 75°27E 242 E6
Fatehabad Ut. P., India 27°1N 78°19E 242 F8
Fatehgarh India 27°25N 79°35E 243 F8
Fatehpur Bihar, India 24°38N 85°14E 243 G11
Fatehpur Raj., India 28°0N 74°40E 242 F6
Fatehpur Ut. P., India 25°56N 81°13E 243 G9
Fatehpur Ut. P., India 27°10N 81°13E 243 F9
Fatehpur Sikri India 27°6N 77°40E 242 F6
Fatesh Russia 52°8N 35°57E 189 F8
Fathai South Sudan 8°5N 31°48E 257 F3
Fathom Five ⌓ Canada 45°17N 81°40W 312 A3
Fatick Senegal 14°19N 16°27W 262 C1
Fatick □ Senegal 14°15N 16°30W 262 C1
Fatih Turkey 41°0N 28°56E 122 B1
Fatima Qué., Canada 47°24N 61°53W 299 C7
Fátima Portugal 39°37N 8°39W 195 F2
Fatoya Guinea 11°37N 9°10W 262 C3
Fatsa Turkey 41°2N 37°31E 212 B7
Fatshan = Foshan China 23°3N 113°9E 121 B1
Faucille, Col de la France 46°22N 6°2E 173 F13
Faulkton U.S.A. 45°2N 99°8W 308 C4
Faulquemont France 49°3N 6°36E 173 C13
Faure I. Australia 25°52S 113°50E 279 E1
Făurei Romania 45°6N 27°19E 183 E12
Fauresmith S. Africa 29°44S 25°17E 270 C4
Fauro Solomon Is. 6°55S 156°7E 287 L9
Fauske Norway 67°17N 15°25E 160 C16
Fåvang Norway 61°27N 10°11E 164 C7
Favânia Brazil 3°7S 51°48W 329 D7
Favara Italy 37°19N 13°39E 200 E6
Faváritx, C. de Spain 40°0N 4°15E 206 B5
Faverges France 45°45N 6°17E 175 C10
Favignana Italy 37°56N 12°20E 200 E5
Favignana, I. Italy 37°56N 12°19E 200 E5
Favoriten Austria 48°9N 16°23E 142 B2
Fawcett, Pt. Australia 11°46S 130°2E 278 B5
Fawkner Australia 37°42S 144°56E 128 A1
Fawkner Park Australia 37°50S 144°58E 128 B1
Fawn ➜ Canada 55°20N 87°35W 298 A2
Fawnskin U.S.A. 34°16N 116°56W 307 L10
Faxaflói Iceland 64°29N 23°0W 155 C3
Faxälven ➜ Sweden 63°13N 17°13E 162 A10
Faya-Largeau Chad 17°58N 19°6E 259 E3
Fayaoué N. Cal. 20°38S 166°33E 288 d
Fayd Si. Arabia 27°1N 42°52E 246 E4
Fayence France 43°38N 6°42E 175 E10
Fayette Ala., U.S.A. 33°41N 87°50W 315 E11
Fayette Iowa, U.S.A. 42°51N 91°48W 310 B5
Fayette Mo., U.S.A. 39°9N 92°41W 310 E4
Fayette N.Y., U.S.A. 42°48N 76°48W 313 D8
Fayette Ohio, U.S.A. 41°40N 84°20W 311 C12
Fayetteville Ark., U.S.A. 36°4N 94°10W 314 C7
Fayetteville Ga., U.S.A. 33°27N 84°27W 316 B5
Fayetteville N.C., U.S.A. 35°3N 78°53W 315 D15
Fayetteville N.Y., U.S.A. 43°1N 76°0W 313 C9
Fayetteville Tenn., U.S.A. 35°9N 86°34W 315 D11
Fayied Egypt 30°18N 32°16E 256 H8
Faylakah Kuwait 29°27N 48°20E 247 D6
Fayón Spain 41°15N 0°20E 196 D5
Fazao-Malfakassa △ Togo 8°45N 0°50E 263 D5
Fazenda Libongo Angola 8°24S 13°24E 265 D2
Fazenda Nova Brazil 16°11S 50°48W 333 E1
Fazilka India 30°27N 74°2E 242 D6
Fazilpur Pakistan 29°18N 70°29E 242 E4
Fdérik Mauritania 22°40N 12°45W 260 D2
Feakle Ireland 52°56N 8°40W 166 D3
Feale ➜ Ireland 52°27N 9°37W 166 D2
Fear, C. U.S.A. 33°50N 77°58W 315 E16
Feather ➜ U.S.A. 38°47N 121°36W 306 G5
Feather Falls U.S.A. 39°36N 121°16W 306 F5
Featherston N.Z. 41°6S 175°20E 284 H4
Featherstone Zimbabwe 18°42S 30°55E 269 F3
Fécamp France 49°45N 0°22E 172 C7
Feda Norway 58°17N 6°50E 164 F3
Fedala = Mohammedia Morocco 33°44N 7°21W 260 B3
Federación Argentina 31°0S 57°55W 334 C4
Féderal Argentina 30°57S 58°48W 334 C4
Federal Capital Terr. □ Nigeria 9°0N 7°10E 263 D6
Federal Way U.S.A. 47°18N 122°19W 306 C4
Fedeshkūh Iran 28°49N 53°50E 247 D7
Fedje Norway 60°47N 4°43E 164 D1
Fedorovka Kazakhstan 53°37N 62°42E 216 B6
Fefan I. Pac. Oc. 7°21N 151°51E 287 T18
Fehérgyarmat Hungary 47°58N 22°30E 182 C7
Fehmarn Germany 54°27N 11°7E 178 A7
Fehmarn Bælt Europe 54°35N 11°20E 163 K5
Fehmarn Belt = Fehmarn Bælt Europe 54°35N 11°20E 163 K5
Fei Xian China 35°18N 117°59E 227 G9
Feicheng China 36°14N 116°45E 226 F9
Feidong China 32°0N 117°35E 229 B11

Feijó Brazil 8°9S 70°21W 330 B3
Feilding N.Z. 40°13S 175°35E 284 G4
Feira de Santana Brazil 12°15S 38°57W 333 D4
Feirân, W. → Egypt 28°39N 33°12E 251 K4
Feirâni, G. Egypt 28°31N 34°19E 251 K5
Feiring Norway 60°30N 11°10E 164 D8
Feixi China 31°43N 117°59E 229 B11
Feixiang China 36°30N 114°45E 226 F8
Fejaj, Chott el Tunisia 33°52N 9°14E 258 B1
Fejér □ Hungary 47°9N 18°30E 182 C3
Fejø Denmark 54°55N 11°30E 163 K5
Feke Turkey 37°48N 35°56E 212 D6
Fekete → Hungary 45°47N 18°15E 182 E3
Felanitx Spain 39°28N 3°9E 206 B4
Felda U.S.A. 26°34N 81°26W 317 J8
Feldbach Austria 46°57N 15°52E 180 E8
Feldberg Baden-W., Germany 47°52N 8°0E 179 H3
Feldberg Mecklenburg-Vorpommern, Germany 53°20N 13°25E 178 B9
Feldkirch Austria 47°15N 9°37E 180 D2
Feldkirchen Austria 46°44N 14°6E 180 E7
Feldkirchen Oberbayern, Germany 48°8N 11°43E 131 B3
Feldmoching Germany 48°14N 11°32E 131 A2
Félicité Seychelles 4°19S 55°52E 272 c
Felicity U.S.A. 38°51N 84°6W 311 F12
Felidhoo Maldives 3°29N 73°32E 272 d
Felidu Atoll Maldives 3°29N 73°29E 272 d
Felipe Carrillo Puerto Mexico 19°38N 88°3W 319 D7
Felixburg Zimbabwe 19°29S 30°51E 271 A5
Felixlândia Brazil 18°47S 44°55W 333 E3
Felixstowe U.K. 51°58N 1°23E 169 F9
Felletin France 45°53N 2°11E 174 C6
Fellingsbro Sweden 59°26N 15°37E 162 E9
Fellsmere U.S.A. 27°46N 80°36W 317 H9
Felshtin = Gvardeyskoye Ukraine 45°7N 34°1E 189 K8
Felsogalla = Tatabánya Hungary 47°32N 18°25E 182 C3
Feltham U.K. 51°26N 0°24W 125 B1
Felton U.S.A. 37°3N 122°4W 306 H4
Feltre Italy 46°1N 11°54E 199 B8
Femer Bælt = Fehmarn Bælt Europe 54°35N 11°20E 163 K5
Femø Denmark 54°58N 11°35E 163 K5
Femunden Norway 62°10N 11°53E 164 B8
Femundsmarka △ Norway 62°18N 12°6E 164 B9
Fen He → China 35°36N 110°42E 226 G6
Fenchih Taiwan 23°30N 120°40E 225 C2
Fene Spain 43°27N 8°9W 194 B2
Fenelon Falls Canada 44°32N 78°45W 312 B6
Fener Turkey 41°1N 28°56E 122 B1
Fener Burnu Turkey 36°58N 27°18E 205 E9
Fenerbahçe Turkey 40°58N 29°2E 122 C2
Feneroa Ethiopia 13°5N 39°3E 257 E4
Feng Xian Jiangsu, China 34°43N 116°35E 226 G9
Feng Xian Shaanxi, China 33°54N 106°40E 226 H4
Fengari Greece 40°25N 25°32E 203 F9
Fengcheng Jiangxi, China 28°12N 115°48E 229 C10
Fengcheng Liaoning, China 40°28N 124°5E 224 B2
Fengdu China 29°55N 107°48E 228 C6
Fengfeng China 36°28N 114°8E 226 F8
Fenggang China 27°57N 107°47E 228 D6
Fenghua China 29°40N 121°25E 229 C13
Fenghuang China 27°57N 109°29E 228 D7
Fengjie China 31°3N 109°31E 228 B7
Fengkai China 23°24N 111°30E 229 F8
Fengkang Taiwan 22°12N 120°41E 225 D2
Fengle China 31°29N 112°29E 229 B9
Fenglin Taiwan 23°45N 121°26E 225 C3
Fengning China 41°10N 116°33E 226 D9
Fengpin Taiwan 23°36N 121°31E 225 C3
Fengqing China 24°38N 99°55E 228 E2
Fengqiu China 35°2N 114°25E 226 G8
Fengrun China 39°48N 118°8E 227 E10
Fengshan Guangxi Zhuangzu, China 24°39N 109°15E 228 E7
Fengshan Guangxi Zhuangzu, China 24°31N 107°3E 228 E6
Fengshan Taiwan 22°38N 120°21E 225 D2
Fengshun China 23°46N 116°10E 229 F11
Fengtai Anhui, China 32°50N 116°40E 229 A11
Fengtai Beijing, China 39°49N 116°14E 114 C1
Fengtai Stadium China 39°51N 116°15E 114 B1
Fengtongzhai △ China 30°32N 102°54E 228 B4
Fengxiang China 34°29N 107°25E 226 G4
Fengxin China 28°41N 115°18E 229 C10
Fengyang China 32°51N 117°29E 229 A11
Fengyi China 25°37N 100°20E 228 E3
Fengyüan Taiwan 24°15N 120°35E 225 B2
Fengzhen China 40°25N 113°2E 226 D7
Feni Bangla. 22°55N 91°32E 241 D3
Feni Is. Papua N. G. 4°0S 153°40E 286 C7
Fennimore U.S.A. 42°59N 90°39W 310 B6
Feno, C. de France 41°58N 8°33E 175 G12
Fenoarivo Fianarantsoa, Madag. 21°43S 46°24E 272 C2
Fenoarivo Fianarantsoa, Madag. 20°52S 46°53E 272 C2
Fenoarivo Afovoany Madag. 18°26S 46°34E 272 B2
Fenoarivo Atsinanana Madag. 17°22S 49°25E 272 B2
Fens, The U.K. 52°38N 0°2W 168 E7
Fensmark Denmark 55°17N 11°48E 163 J5
Fenton U.S.A. 42°48N 83°42W 311 B13
Fenxi China 36°40N 111°31E 226 F6
Fenyang China 37°18N 111°48E 226 F6
Fenyi China 27°45N 114°47E 229 D10
Fenyuan Taiwan 24°1N 120°37E 225 B2
Feodosiya Ukraine 45°2N 35°16E 189 K8
Fer, C. de Algeria 37°3N 7°10E 261 A6
Fera Solomon Is. 8°6S 159°37E 287 M10
Ferbane Ireland 53°16N 7°50W 166 C4
Ferdows Iran 33°58N 58°2E 247 C8
Fère-Champenoise France 48°45N 3°59E 173 D10
Fère-en-Tardenois France 49°10N 3°30E 173 C10
Ferencváros Hungary 47°29N 19°5E 117 B2
Ferentino Italy 41°42N 13°15E 199 G10
Feres Greece 40°53N 26°10E 203 F10
Ferfer Somalia 5°4N 45°9E 267 C6
Fergana = Farghona Uzbekistan 40°23N 71°19E 217 D8
Fergana Range Asia 41°0N 73°50E 217 D8
Fergus Canada 43°43N 80°24W 312 C4
Fergus Falls U.S.A. 46°17N 96°4W 308 B5
Ferguson U.S.A. 38°44N 90°18W 310 F6
Fergusson I. Papua N. G. 9°30S 150°45E 286 E6
Fériana Tunisia 34°59N 8°33E 258 B1
Feričanci Croatia 45°32N 18°0E 182 E2
Ferihegy, Budapest ✕ (BUD) Hungary 47°26N 19°14E 117 B3
Ferizaj Kosovo 42°23N 21°10E 202 D5
Ferkane Algeria 34°37N 7°26E 261 B6
Ferkéssédougou Ivory C. 9°35N 5°6W 262 D3
Ferlach Austria 46°32N 14°18E 180 E7
Ferland Canada 50°19N 88°27W 298 B2
Ferlo, Vallée du Senegal 15°15N 14°15W 262 B2
Ferlo-Nord ⌓ Senegal 15°43N 14°0W 262 B2
Ferlo-Sud ⌓ Senegal 15°43N 14°0W 262 B2
Fermanagh □ U.K. 54°21N 7°40W 166 B4
Fermo Italy 43°9N 13°43E 199 E10
Fermont Canada 52°47N 67°5W 299 B6
Fermoselle Spain 41°19N 6°27W 194 D4
Fermoy Ireland 52°9N 8°16W 166 D3
Fern Creek U.S.A. 38°9N 85°36W 311 G11
Fern Gully Jamaica 18°22N 77°5W 320 a
Fernán Núñez Spain 37°40N 4°44W 195 H6
Fernández Argentina 27°55S 63°50W 334 B3
Fernandina, I. Ecuador 0°25S 91°30W 330 a
Fernandina Beach U.S.A. 30°40N 81°27W 316 E8
Fernando de Noronha Brazil 4°0S 33°10W 152 G8
Fernando Póo = Bioko Eq. Guin. 3°30N 8°40E 263 E6
Fernandópolis Brazil 20°16S 50°14W 333 F1
Ferndale Ont., Canada 44°58N 81°17W 312 B3
Ferndale Gauteng, S. Africa 26°5S 28°0E 123 A2
Ferndale Wash., U.S.A. 48°51N 122°36W 306 B4
Fernie Canada 49°30N 115°5W 296 D5
Fernlees Australia 23°51S 148°7E 280 C4
Fernley U.S.A. 39°36N 119°15W 304 G4
Fernwood U.S.A. 43°16N 73°38W 313 C11
Feroke India 11°9N 75°46E 245 J2
Feroz Shah Kotla Cricket Stadium Delhi, India 120 b3
Ferozepore = Firozpur India 30°55N 74°40E 242 D6
Ferrandina Italy 40°29N 16°27E 201 B9
Ferrara Italy 44°50N 11°35E 199 D8
Ferrato, C. Italy 39°18N 9°38E 200 C2
Ferré, C. Martinique 14°27N 60°49W 322 j
Ferreira do Alentejo Portugal 38°4N 8°6W 195 G2
Ferreira Gomes Brazil 0°48N 51°8W 329 C7
Ferreñafe Peru 6°42S 79°50W 330 B2
Ferrerías Spain 39°59N 4°1E 206 B5
Ferret, C. France 44°38N 1°15W 174 D2
Ferrette France 47°30N 7°20E 173 E14
Ferriday U.S.A. 31°38N 91°33W 314 F9
Ferriere Italy 44°40N 9°30E 198 D6
Ferrières France 48°5N 2°48E 173 D9
Ferro, Capo Italy 41°9N 9°31E 200 A2
Ferrol Spain 43°29N 8°15W 194 B2
Ferrol, Pen. de Peru 9°10S 78°35W 330 B2
Ferron U.S.A. 39°5N 111°8W 304 G8
Ferros Brazil 19°14S 43°2W 333 E3
Ferrutx, C. de Spain 39°47N 3°21E 206 B4
Ferry Pass U.S.A. 30°31N 87°13W 317 E2
Ferryland Canada 47°2N 52°53W 299 C9
Ferrysburg U.S.A. 43°5N 86°13W 311 A10
Ferryville = Menzel-Bourguiba Tunisia 37°9N 9°49E 258 A1
Fertile U.S.A. 47°32N 96°17W 308 B5
Fertő-Hanság △ Hungary 47°25N 16°50E 182 C1
Fertőszentmiklós Hungary 47°35N 16°53E 182 C1
Fès Morocco 34°0N 5°0W 260 B4
Fès □ Morocco 34°1N 5°0W 260 B4
Feshi Dem. Rep. of the Congo 6°8S 18°10E 265 D3
Fessenden U.S.A. 47°39N 99°38W 308 B4
Festenberg = Twardogóra Poland 51°23N 17°28E 185 G4
Festøya Norway 62°22N 6°19E 164 B3
Festus U.S.A. 38°13N 90°24W 310 F6
Feté Bowé Senegal 14°56N 13°30W 262 C2
Feteşti Romania 44°22N 27°51E 183 F12
Fethiye Turkey 36°36N 29°6E 205 E11
Fethiye Körfezi Turkey 36°40N 28°50E 205 E10
Fetlar U.K. 60°36N 0°52W 167 A8
Fetsund Norway 59°56N 11°10E 164 E8
Feuilles → Canada 58°47N 70°4W 295 F17
Feurs France 45°45N 4°13E 175 C8
Fevik Norway 58°22N 8°39E 164 F5
Fevzipaşa Turkey 37°6N 36°37E 250 A7
Feyzābād Badākhshān, Afghan. 37°7N 70°33E 240 A3
Feyzābād Fāryāb, Afghan. 36°17N 64°52E 240 A2
Fez = Fès Morocco 34°0N 5°0W 260 B4
Fezzan Libya 27°0N 13°0E 258 C2
Fia Congo 3°25S 14°49E 264 C2
Fiambalá Argentina 27°45S 67°37W 334 B2
Fianarantsoa Madag. 21°26S 47°5E 272 C2
Fianarantsoa □ Madag. 22°30S 47°0E 272 B2
Fianga Cameroon 9°55N 15°9E 259 G3
Fiche Ethiopia 9°50N 38°46E 257 F4
Fichtelgebirge Germany 50°2N 11°55E 179 E7
Fichtelgebirge ⌓ Germany 50°8N 12°0E 179 E8
Fichtenau Germany 52°27N 13°42E 115 B5
Ficksburg S. Africa 28°51S 27°53E 271 C4
Fidenza Italy 44°52N 10°3E 198 D7
Fiditi Nigeria 7°45N 3°53E 263 D5
Fidjeland Norway 58°57N 6°56E 164 F3
Field → Australia 23°48S 138°0E 280 C2
Field I. Australia 12°5S 132°23E 278 B5
Field Museum of Natural History Chicago, U.S.A. 41°51N 87°37W 119 B3
Fields Corner U.S.A. 42°18N 71°3W 116 B2
Fieni Romania 45°8N 25°25E 183 E10
Fier Albania 40°43N 19°33E 202 F3
Fiera Camp Italy 45°28N 9°9E 128 B1
Fierzë Albania 42°15N 20°1E 202 D4
Fife □ U.K. 56°16N 3°1W 167 E5
Fife Ness U.K. 56°17N 2°35W 167 E6
Fifth Cataract Sudan 18°22N 33°50E 256 D3
Fig Tree St. Kitts & Nevis 17°8N 62°35W 322 d
Figari France 41°29N 9°7E 175 G13
Figeac France 44°37N 2°2E 174 D6
Figeholm Sweden 57°22N 16°33E 163 G10
Figino Italy 45°29N 9°4E 128 B1
Figline Valdarno Italy 43°37N 11°28E 199 E8
Figtree Zimbabwe 20°22S 28°20E 269 G2
Figueira = Governador Valadares Brazil 18°15S 41°57W 333 E3
Figueira Castelo Rodrigo Portugal 40°57N 6°58W 194 E4
Figueira da Foz Portugal 40°7N 8°54W 194 E2
Figueiró dos Vinhos Portugal 39°55N 8°16W 194 F2
Figueres Spain 42°18N 2°58E 196 C7
Figuig Morocco 32°5N 1°11W 261 B4
Fihaonana Madag. 18°36S 47°12E 272 B2
Fiherenana Madag. 18°29S 48°24E 272 B2
Fiherenana → Madag. 23°19S 43°37E 272 C1
Fiji ■ Pac. Oc. 17°20S 179°0E 287 A2
Fijir Iraq 33°21N 44°21E 113 A2
Fik Ethiopia 8°10N 42°19E 257 F5
Fika Nigeria 11°15N 11°13E 263 C7
Filabres, Sierra de los Spain 37°13N 2°20W 195 H8
Filabus Zimbabwe 20°34S 29°20E 271 B4
Filadelfia Bolivia 11°20S 68°46W 330 C4
Filadélfia Brazil 7°21S 47°30W 332 C2
Filadelfia Athina, Greece 38°2N 23°43E 112 A2
Filadélfia Italy 38°47N 16°17E 201 D9
Filadelfia Paraguay 22°21S 60°2W 334 A3
Fil'akovo Slovak Rep. 48°17N 19°50E 181 C12
Filchner Ice Shelf Antarctica 79°0S 40°0W 151 D1
Filefjell Norway 61°8N 8°10E 164 C5
Filey U.K. 54°12N 0°18W 168 C7
Filey B. U.K. 54°12N 0°15W 168 C7
Filfla Malta 35°47N 14°24E 206 F7
Fili-Mazilovo Russia 55°44N 37°29E 129 B1
Filiaşi Romania 44°32N 23°31E 183 F8
Filiates Greece 39°38N 20°16E 206 B10
Filiatra Greece 37°9N 21°35E 204 D3
Filicudi Italy 38°35N 14°33E 201 D7
Filim Oman 20°37N 58°12E 249 B7
Filingué Niger 14°21N 3°22E 263 C5
Filiourí = Lissos → Greece 41°15N 25°40E 203 E9
Filipada Greece 39°12N 20°53E 204 B2
Filipstad Sweden 59°43N 14°9E 162 E8
Filisur Switz. 46°41N 9°40E 179 J5
Filitosa France 41°45N 8°52E 175 G12
Fillmore Calif., U.S.A. 34°24N 118°55W 307 L8
Fillmore Utah, U.S.A. 38°58N 112°20W 304 G7
Filothei Greece 38°2N 23°46E 112 A2
Filotio Greece 37°3N 25°30E 205 D7
Filottrano Italy 43°26N 13°21E 199 E10
Filtu Ethiopia 5°8N 40°35E 257 F5
Filyos Çayı → Turkey 41°35N 32°10E 212 B5
Fimbul Ice Shelf S. Ocean 69°30S 1°0W 151 C2
Fimi → Dem. Rep. of the Congo 3°1S 16°58E 264 C3
Fina ⌓ Mali 13°15N 8°46W 262 C3
Finale Emília Italy 44°50N 11°18E 199 D8
Finale Lígure Italy 44°10N 8°20E 198 D5
Finalmarina = Finale Lígure Italy 44°10N 8°20E 198 D5
Fiñana Spain 37°10N 2°50W 195 H8
Financial District San Francisco, U.S.A. 136 b3
Finch Canada 45°11N 75°7W 313 A9
Finch Hatton Australia 20°25S 148°39E 280 b
Finchaa, L. Ethiopia 9°35N 37°20E 266 C4
Finchley U.K. 51°36N 0°11W 125 A2
Findhorn → U.K. 57°38N 3°38W 167 D5
Fındıklı Turkey 41°16N 41°9E 213 B9
Findlay U.S.A. 41°2N 83°39W 311 C13
Fine U.S.A. 44°14N 75°8W 313 B9
Fine Art, Museum of = Kunsthistorischesmuseum Vienna, Austria 142 b1
Fine Arts, Museum of Boston, U.S.A. 42°20N 71°5W 116 A2
Finger L. Canada 53°33N 93°30W 298 B1
Finger Lakes U.S.A. 42°40N 76°30W 313 D8
Finglas Ireland 53°23N 6°19W 120 A2
Fíngoè Mozam. 15°55S 31°50E 269 F3
Finike Turkey 36°21N 30°10E 205 E12
Finike Körfezi Turkey 36°17N 30°16E 205 E12
Finiq Albania 39°54N 20°3E 202 G4
Finistère □ France 48°20N 4°0W 172 D3
Finisterre = Fisterra Spain 42°54N 9°16W 194 C1
Finisterre, C. = Fisterra, C. Spain 42°50N 9°19W 194 C1
Finisterre Ra. Papua N. G. 6°0S 146°30E 286 D4
Finke Australia 25°34S 134°35E 280 D1
Finke Gorge △ Australia 24°8S 132°49E 278 D5
Finland ■ Europe 63°0N 27°0E 160 E22
Finland, G. of Europe 60°0N 26°0E 188 C3
Finlay → Canada 57°0N 125°10W 296 B3
Finley N.S.W., Australia 35°38S 145°35E 283 C6
Finley N. Dak., U.S.A. 47°31N 97°50W 308 B5
Finn → Ireland 54°51N 7°28W 166 B4
Finnerödja Sweden 58°57N 14°24E 163 F8
Finnigan, Mt. Australia 15°49S 145°17E 280 B4
Finniss, C. Australia 33°8S 134°51E 281 E1
Finnmark Norway 69°37N 23°57E 160 B20
Finnsnes Norway 69°14N 18°0E 160 B18
Finsbury U.K. 51°31N 0°6W 125 A3
Finsbury Park U.K. 51°34N 0°6W 125 A3
Finschhafen Papua N. G. 6°33S 147°50E 286 D4
Finse Norway 60°36N 7°30E 164 D4
Finspång Sweden 58°43N 15°47E 163 F9
Finsteraarhorn Switz. 46°31N 8°10E 179 J4
Finsterwalde Germany 51°37N 13°42E 178 D9
Fiora → Italy 42°20N 11°34E 199 F8
Fiordland △ N.Z. 45°46S 167°0E 285 F2
Fiorenzuola d'Arda Italy 44°56N 9°55E 198 D6
Fiorito Argentina 34°42S 58°26W 117 C2
Fīq Syria 32°46N 35°41E 250 F6
Firat = Furāt, Nahr al → Asia 31°0N 47°25E 246 D5
Fire Island ⌓ U.S.A. 40°38N 73°8W 313 F11
Firebag → Canada 57°45N 111°21W 297 B6
Firebaugh U.S.A. 36°52N 120°27W 306 J6
Firedrake L. Canada 61°25N 104°30W 297 A8
Firenze Italy 43°46N 11°15E 199 E8
Firenze Amerigo Vespucci ✕ (FLR) Italy 43°49N 11°13E 199 E8
Firenze Pisa ✕ (PSA) Italy 43°40N 10°22E 198 E7
Firenzuola Italy 44°7N 11°23E 199 D8
Firhouse Ireland 53°17N 6°20W 120 B2
Firk, Sha'ib → Iraq 30°59N 44°34E 246 D5
Firkachi Niger 15°40N 14°20E 259 E2
Firmi France 44°33N 2°19E 174 D6
Firminy France 45°23N 4°18E 175 C8
Firozabad India 27°10N 78°25E 243 F8
Firozpur India 30°55N 74°40E 242 D6
Firozpur-Jhirka India 27°48N 76°57E 242 F7
Fīrūzābād Iran 28°52N 52°35E 247 D7
Fīrūzkūh Iran 35°50N 52°50E 247 C7
Firvale Canada 52°27N 126°13W 296 C3
Fischerhäuser Germany 48°14N 11°41E 131 A3
Fish → Namibia 28°7S 17°10E 270 C2
Fish → Northern Cape, S. Africa 31°30S 20°16E 270 D3
Fish River Canyon Namibia 27°40S 17°35E 270 C2
Fisheating Cr. → U.S.A. 26°57N 81°7W 317 J8
Fisher B. Canada 51°35N 97°13W 297 C9
Fisher I. U.S.A. 25°45N 80°8W 129 D3
Fishermans Bend Australia 37°49S 144°55E 128 A1
Fisherman's Village U.S.A. 33°58N 118°27W 126 C2
Fisherman's Wharf San Francisco, U.S.A. 136 a1
Fishers U.S.A. 39°57N 86°0W 311 E11
Fishers I. U.S.A. 41°15N 72°0W 313 E13
Fisherville Canada 43°46N 79°28W 141 A2
Fishguard U.K. 52°0N 4°58W 169 E3
Fishing L. Canada 52°10N 95°24W 297 C9
Fishkill U.S.A. 41°32N 73°54W 313 E11
Fiskardo Greece 38°28N 20°35E 207 C2
Fiskenæsset = Qeqertarsuatsiaat Greenland 63°5N 50°45W 154 E5
Fisksätra Sweden 59°17N 18°13E 139 B3
Fismes France 49°20N 3°40E 173 C10
Fisterra Spain 42°54N 9°16W 194 C1
Fisterra, C. Spain 42°50N 9°19W 194 C1
Fitchburg Mass., U.S.A. 42°35N 71°48W 313 D13
Fitchburg Wis., U.S.A. 42°58N 89°28W 310 B7
Fitjar Iceland 64°28N 21°18W 155 C5
Fitjar Hordaland, Norway 59°55N 5°17E 164 E2
Fitri, L. Chad 12°50N 17°28E 259 F3
Fitz Roy Argentina 47°0S 67°0W 336 C3
Fitz Roy, Cerro Argentina 49°17S 73°5W 336 C2
Fitzgerald Alta., Canada 59°51N 111°36W 296 B6
Fitzgerald Ga., U.S.A. 31°43N 83°15W 316 D6
Fitzgerald River △ Australia 33°53S 119°55E 279 F3
Fitzmaurice → Australia 14°45S 130°5E 278 B5
Fitzroy → Queens., Australia 23°32S 150°52E 280 C5
Fitzroy → W. Austral., Australia 17°31S 123°35E 278 C3
Fitzroy Crossing Australia 18°9S 125°38E 278 C4
Fitzroy Gardens Australia 37°48S 144°58E 128 A1
Fitzwilliam I. Canada 45°30N 81°45W 312 A3
Fiuggi Italy 41°48N 13°13E 199 G10
Fiume = Rijeka Croatia 45°20N 14°21E 199 C11
Fiumicino, Roma ✕ (FCO) Italy 41°48N 12°15E 199 G9
Five Cowrie Cr. → Nigeria 6°26N 3°24E 124 B2
Five Dock Australia 33°52S 151°8E 139 B1
Five Island Harbour Antigua & B. 17°6N 61°54W 322 b
Five Points U.S.A. 36°26N 120°6W 306 J6
Fivizzano Italy 44°14N 10°8E 198 D7
Fizi Dem. Rep. of the Congo 4°17S 28°55E 268 C2
Fjæra Norway 59°52N 6°22E 164 E3
Fjærland Norway 61°24N 6°43E 164 C3
Fjærlandsfjorden Norway 61°17N 6°40E 164 C3
Fjällbacka Sweden 58°36N 11°17E 163 F5
Fjällnäs Sweden 62°36N 12°11E 162 B6
Fjärdhundra Sweden 59°47N 16°56E 162 E10
Fjellerup Denmark 56°29N 10°34E 163 H4
Fjellstrand Norway 59°47N 10°36E 133 B2
Fjerritslev Denmark 57°5N 9°15E 163 G3
Fjugesta Sweden 59°11N 14°52E 162 E8
Fkih ben Salah Morocco 32°32N 6°45W 260 B3
Flå Norway 60°25N 9°28E 164 D6
Flacq Plain Mauritius 20°13S 57°43E 272 e
Flagler Beach U.S.A. 29°29N 81°8W 317 F8
Flagstaff U.S.A. 35°12N 111°39W 305 J8
Flagstaff B. St. Helena 15°54S 5°41W 153 h
Flagstaff L. U.S.A. 45°12N 70°18W 313 A14
Flaherty I. Canada 56°15N 79°15W 298 A4
Flåm Norway 60°50N 7°7E 164 D4
Flamands St. Barts 17°55N 62°51W 322 a
Flambeau → U.S.A. 45°18N 91°14W 308 C8
Flamborough Hd. U.K. 54°7N 0°5W 168 C7
Flamengo Brazil 22°56S 43°11W 135 B1
Flamengos Azores 38°33N 28°39W 153 d1
Fläming Germany 52°6N 12°23E 178 C8
Flaming Gorge ⌓ U.S.A. 41°10N 109°25W 304 F9
Flaming Gorge Res. U.S.A. 41°10N 109°25W 304 F9
Flamingo Fla., U.S.A. 28°22N 81°22W 133 B2
Flamingo Fla., U.S.A. 25°8N 80°57W 317 K9
Flamingo, Teluk Indonesia 5°30S 138°0E 231 F9
Flaminio Italy 41°55N 12°28E 136 B1
Flanagan U.S.A. 40°53N 88°52W 311 D8
Flanagin Town Trin. & Tob. 10°25N 61°19W 323 t
Flanders = Flandre Europe 50°50N 2°30E 173 B9
Flandre Europe 50°50N 2°30E 173 B9
Flandre-Occidentale = West-Vlaanderen □ Belgium 51°0N 3°0E 170 D2
Flandre-Orientale = Oost-Vlaanderen □ Belgium 51°5N 3°50E 170 C3
Flandreau U.S.A. 44°3N 96°36W 308 C5
Flanigan U.S.A. 40°10N 119°53W 306 E7
Flannan Is. U.K. 58°9N 7°52W 167 C1
Flåsjön Sweden 64°5N 15°40E 160 D16
Flaskebekk Norway 59°51N 10°39E 133 A2
Flat U.S.A. 62°28N 158°1W 303 E8
Flat → N.W.T., Canada 61°33N 125°18W 296 A3
Flat → Mich., U.S.A. 42°56N 85°20W 311 B11
Flat I. S. China Sea 10°49N 115°49E 230 B5
Flat Pt. N.Z. 41°14S 175°57E 284 H4
Flat Rock U.S.A. 42°6N 83°17W 311 B13
Flatbush U.S.A. 40°39N 73°56W 132 C2
Flateby Norway 59°50N 11°10E 164 E8
Flaten Sweden 59°15N 18°9E 139 B2
Flatey Iceland 66°10N 17°52W 155 A9
Flateyri Iceland 66°3N 23°31W 155 A3
Flathead L. U.S.A. 47°51N 114°8W 304 C6
Flatiron Building New York, U.S.A. 132 d2
Flatlands U.S.A. 40°37N 73°56W 132 C2
Flatow = Złotów Poland 53°22N 17°2E 184 E4
Flatrock → U.S.A. 39°12N 85°56W 311 F10
Flattery, C. Queens., Australia 14°58S 145°21E 280 A4
Flattery, C. Wash., U.S.A. 48°23N 124°29W 306 B2
Flatts Village Bermuda 32°18N 64°43W 153 a
Flatwoods U.S.A. 38°31N 82°43W 309 F12
Flecha Pt. Phil. 7°22N 123°24E 233 H4
Flechas Pt. Phil. 10°22N 119°34E 233 F2
Fleetwood Lancs., U.K. 53°55N 3°1W 168 D4
Fleetwood Pa., U.S.A. 40°27N 75°49W 313 F9
Flekke Norway 61°19N 5°20E 164 C2
Flekkefjord Norway 58°18N 6°39E 164 F3
Flemingsburg U.S.A. 38°25N 83°45W 311 F13
Flemington U.S.A. 41°7N 77°28W 312 E7
Flemington Racecourse Australia 37°47S 144°54E 128 A1
Flemish Cap Atl. Oc. 47°0N 45°0W 152 B7
Flen Sweden 59°4N 16°35E 162 E10
Flensburg Germany 54°47N 9°27E 178 A5
Flers France 48°47N 0°33W 172 D6
Flesberg Norway 59°51N 9°27E 164 E6
Flesherton Canada 44°16N 80°33W 312 B4
Flesko, Tanjung Indonesia 0°29N 124°30E 231 D6
Fletcher = Aurora U.S.A. 39°43N 104°49W 304 G11
Fleurance France 43°52N 0°40E 174 E4
Fleurie, Côte France 49°25N 0°40W 172 C6
Fleurier Switz. 46°54N 6°35E 179 J2
Fleurieu Pen. Australia 35°40S 138°5E 282 C3
Flevoland □ Neths. 52°30N 5°30E 170 B5
Flin Flon Canada 54°46N 101°53W 297 C8
Flinders → Australia 17°36S 140°36E 280 B3
Flinders B. Australia 34°19S 115°19E 279 F2
Flinders Chase △ Australia 35°50S 136°42E 282 C2
Flinders Group Australia 14°11S 144°15E 280 A3
Flinders I. S. Austral., Australia 33°44S 134°41E 281 E1
Flinders I. Tas., Australia 40°0S 148°0E 281 G4
Flinders Ranges Australia 31°30S 138°30E 282 A3
Flinders Ranges △ Australia 31°30S 138°40E 282 A3
Flinders Reefs Australia 17°37S 148°31E 280 B4
Flint Flints., U.K. 53°15N 3°8W 168 D4
Flint Mich., U.S.A. 43°1N 83°41W 311 A13
Flint → U.S.A. 30°57N 84°34W 316 E5
Flint I. Kiribati 11°26S 151°48W 289 f
Flint Pk. U.S.A. 34°9N 118°11W 126 B3
Flintshire □ U.K. 53°17N 3°17W 168 D4
Flipper Pt. Wake I. 19°18N 166°37E 302 b
Flisa Norway 60°37N 12°0E 164 D9
Flisa → Norway 60°37N 12°0E 164 D9
Fliseryd Sweden 57°6N 16°15E 163 G10
Flix Spain 41°14N 0°32E 196 D5
Flixecourt France 50°1N 2°5E 173 B9
Floby Sweden 58°8N 13°20E 163 F7
Floda Sweden 57°49N 12°22E 163 G6
Flodden U.K. 55°37N 2°8W 168 B5
Flogny-la-Chapelle France 47°57N 3°57E 173 E10
Floodplains △ Sri Lanka 8°10N 81°10E 245 K5
Floodwood U.S.A. 46°56N 92°55W 308 B7
Flora Apayao, Phil. 18°14N 121°5E 232 B3
Flora Ill., U.S.A. 38°40N 88°29W 311 F8
Flora Ind., U.S.A. 40°33N 86°31W 311 D10
Florac France 44°20N 3°37E 174 D7
Florahome U.S.A. 29°44N 81°54W 316 F8
Floral City U.S.A. 28°45N 82°17W 317 G7
Florala U.S.A. 31°0N 86°20W 315 F11
Florânia Brazil 6°8S 36°49W 332 C4
Floreana, I. = Santa María, I. Ecuador 1°17S 90°26W 330 a
Florence = Firenze Italy 43°46N 11°15E 199 E8
Florence Ala., U.S.A. 34°48N 87°41W 315 D11
Florence Ariz., U.S.A. 33°2N 111°23W 305 K8
Florence Calif., U.S.A. 33°57N 118°13W 126 C3
Florence Colo., U.S.A. 38°23N 105°8W 304 G11
Florence Oreg., U.S.A. 43°58N 124°7W 304 D1
Florence S.C., U.S.A. 34°12N 79°46W 315 D15
Florence, L. Australia 28°53S 138°9E 281 D2
Florence Bay = Chtimba Malawi 10°35S 34°13E 269 E3
Florence Bloom Bird Sanctuary ⌓ S. Africa 26°7S 28°0E 123 A2
Florencia Colombia 1°36N 75°36W 328 C2
Florennes Belgium 50°15N 4°35E 170 D4
Florensac France 43°23N 3°28E 174 E7
Florentia S. Africa 26°16S 28°8E 123 B2
Florenville Belgium 49°40N 5°19E 170 E5
Flores = Florânia Brazil 6°8S 36°49W 332 C4
Flores = Timon Brazil 5°8S 42°52W 332 C3
Flores B. Aires, Argentina 34°38S 58°27W 117 B2
Flores Azores 39°26N 31°13W 153 d2
Flores Brazil 7°51S 37°59W 332 C4
Flores Guatemala 16°59N 89°50W 320 C2
Flores Indonesia 8°35S 121°0E 231 F6
Flores, Mercado de Mexico 19°19N 99°5W 128 C2
Flores I. Canada 49°20N 126°10W 296 D3
Flores Sea Indonesia 6°30S 120°0E 231 F6
Floresta B. Aires, Argentina 34°37S 58°27W 117 B2
Floresta Brazil 8°40S 37°26W 332 C4
Floreşti Moldova 47°53N 28°17E 183 C13
Floresville U.S.A. 29°8N 98°10W 314 G5
Floriano Brazil 6°50S 43°0W 332 C3
Florianópolis Brazil 27°30S 48°30W 335 B6
Florida B. Aires, Argentina 34°31S 58°28W 117 B2
Florida Cuba 21°32N 78°14W 320 B4
Florida Puerto Rico 18°22N 66°34W 321 b
Florida Gauteng, S. Africa 26°10S 27°55E 123 B1
Florida Uruguay 34°7S 56°10W 335 C4
Florida □ U.S.A. 28°0N 82°0W 317 H8
Florida, Straits of U.S.A. 25°0N 80°0W 320 B4
Florida B. U.S.A. 25°0N 80°45W 320 B3
Florida City U.S.A. 25°27N 80°29W 317 K9
Florida Is. Solomon Is. 9°55S 160°15E 287 M11
Florida Keys U.S.A. 24°40N 81°0W 317 L8
Floridablanca Phil. 14°59N 120°31E 232 D3
Floridia Italy 37°5N 15°9E 201 E8
Floridsdorf Austria 48°15N 16°26E 142 A2
Florin U.S.A. 38°30N 121°24W 306 G5
Florina Greece 40°48N 21°26E 202 F5
Florissant U.S.A. 38°47N 90°19W 310 F6
Florø Norway 61°35N 5°1E 164 C2
Flotte, C. de N. Cal. 21°10S 167°25E 288 d
Flower Station Canada 45°10N 76°41W 313 A8
Flowerpot I. Canada 45°18N 81°38W 312 A3
Floydada U.S.A. 33°59N 101°20W 314 E4
Fludir Iceland 64°7N 20°6W 155 C6
Flugumyri Iceland 65°34N 19°19W 155 B7
Fluk Indonesia 1°42S 127°44E 231 E7
Flúmen → Spain 41°43N 0°9W 196 D4
Flumendosa → Italy 39°26N 9°37E 200 C2
Fluminimaggiore Italy 39°26N 8°30E 200 C1
Flushing = Vlissingen Neths. 51°26N 3°34E 170 C3
Flushing Mich., U.S.A. 43°4N 83°51W 311 A13
Flushing N.Y., U.S.A. 40°45N 73°49W 132 B3
Flushing Meadows Corona Park U.S.A. 40°44N 73°50W 132 B2
Fluvià → Spain 42°12N 3°7E 196 C8
Fly → Papua N. G. 8°25S 143°0E 286 E2
Flying Fish, C. Antarctica 72°6S 102°29W 151 D15
Flysta Sweden 59°22N 17°54E 139 A1
Fo Tan Hong Kong, China 22°23N 114°11E 122 A3
Foa Tonga 19°45S 174°18W 287 P13
Foam Lake Canada 51°40N 103°32W 297 C8
Foča Bos.-H. 43°31N 18°47E 202 C2
Foça Turkey 38°39N 26°46E 205 C8
Fochabers U.K. 57°37N 3°6W 167 D5
Focşani Romania 45°41N 27°15E 183 E12
Fodé C.A.R. 5°29N 23°18E 264 A4
Fodécontéa Guinea 10°50N 14°22W 262 C2
Fogang China 23°52N 113°30E 229 F9
Foggaret el Arab Algeria 27°13N 2°49E 261 C5
Foggaret ez Zoua Algeria 27°20N 2°53E 261 C5
Fóggia Italy 41°27N 15°34E 201 A8
Foggy Bottom U.S.A. 38°54N 77°3W 143 B2
Foglia → Italy 43°55N 12°54E 199 E9
Fogo Nfld & L., Canada 49°43N 54°17W 299 C9
Fogo C. Verde Is. 15°5N 24°20W 153 j
Fogo I. Canada 49°40N 54°5W 299 C9
Fohnsdorf Austria 47°12N 14°40E 180 D7
Föhr Germany 54°43N 8°30E 178 A4
Föhrenhain Austria 48°19N 16°26E 142 A2
Fóia Portugal 37°19N 8°37W 195 H2
Foix France 42°58N 1°38E 174 E5
Fojnica Bos.-H. 43°59N 17°51E 182 G2
Fokida Greece 38°30N 22°15E 204 C4
Fokino Russia 53°30N 34°22E 188 F8
Fokku Nigeria 11°36N 4°32E 263 C5
Fokstugu Norway 62°7N 9°17E 164 B6
Folda Nord-Trøndelag, Norway 64°32N 10°30E 160 D14
Folda Nordland, Norway 67°38N 14°50E 160 C16
Földeák Hungary 46°19N 20°30E 182 D5
Folegandros Greece 36°40N 24°55E 204 E6
Foley Botswana 21°34S 27°21E 270 B4
Foley Ala., U.S.A. 30°24N 87°41W 315 F11
Foley Fla., U.S.A. 30°4N 83°32W 316 E6
Foleyet Canada 48°15N 82°25W 298 C3
Folgefonna Norway 60°3N 6°23E 164 D3
Folgefonna △ Norway 60°5N 6°15E 164 D3
Foligno Italy 42°57N 12°42E 199 F9
Folkestad Norway 62°7N 6°1E 164 B3
Folkestone U.K. 51°5N 1°12E 169 F9
Folkestone Marine Park △ Barbados 13°11N 59°38W 323 r
Folkston U.S.A. 30°50N 82°0W 316 E7
Folla → Norway 62°7N 10°37E 164 B7
Follansbee U.S.A. 40°19N 80°35W 312 F4
Folldal Norway 62°8N 10°0E 164 B6
Folle Anse, Pte. de Guadeloupe 15°56N 61°19W 322 e
Follebu Norway 61°13N 10°16E 164 C7
Follónica Italy 42°55N 10°45E 198 F7
Follónica, G. di Italy 42°54N 10°43E 198 F7
Folsom U.S.A. 38°40N 121°9W 306 G5
Folsom L. U.S.A. 38°42N 121°9W 306 G5
Folteşti Romania 45°45N 28°3E 183 E13
Fomboni Comoros Is. 12°18S 43°46E 272 a
Fomm ir-Rih Bay Malta 35°54N 14°20E 206 F7
Fond-du-Lac Sask., Canada 59°19N 107°12W 297 B7
Fond du Lac Wis., U.S.A. 43°47N 88°27W 308 D9
Fond-du-Lac → Canada 59°17N 106°0W 297 B7
Fond Rousseau Martinique 14°38N 61°6W 322 j
Fond St. Jacques St. Lucia 13°50N 61°1W 323 m
Fonda Iowa, U.S.A. 42°35N 94°51W 310 B2
Fonda N.Y., U.S.A. 42°57N 74°22W 313 D10
Fondamenta Nuove Venice, Italy 142 a3
Fondi Italy 41°21N 13°25E 200 A6
Fonds-St-Denis Martinique 14°44N 61°8W 322 j
Fonfría Spain 41°37N 6°9W 194 D4
Fongafale Tuvalu 8°31S 179°13E 277 B14
Fongen Norway 63°11N 11°38E 164 A8
Fongshan = Fengshan Taiwan 22°38N 120°21E 225 D2
Fongyuan = Fengyüan Taiwan 24°15N 120°35E 225 B2
Fonni Italy 40°7N 9°15E 200 B2
Fonsagrada = A Fonsagrada Spain 43°8N 7°4W 194 B3
Fonseca, G. de Cent. Amer. 13°10N 87°40W 320 D2
Font-Romeu-Odeillo-Via France 42°31N 2°3E 174 F5
Fontaine-Française France 47°32N 5°21E 173 E12
Fontainebleau Seine-et-Marne, France 48°24N 2°40E 173 D9
Fontainebleau Gauteng, S. Africa 26°6S 27°57E 123 A1
Fontana U.S.A. 34°6N 117°26W 307 L9
Fontana, L. Argentina 44°55S 71°30W 336 B2
Fontas → Canada 58°14N 121°48W 296 B4
Fonte Boa Brazil 2°33S 66°0W 328 D4
Fontem Cameroon 5°32N 9°52E 263 D6
Fontenay-aux-Roses France 48°47N 2°17E 134 B2
Fontenay-le-Comte France 46°28N 0°48W 174 B3
Fontenay-le-Fleury France 48°48N 2°2E 134 B1
Fontenay-sous-Bois France 48°51N 2°28E 134 A3
Fontenelle Res. U.S.A. 42°1N 110°3W 304 E8
Fontur Iceland 66°23N 14°32W 155 A12
Fonuafo'ou Tonga 20°19S 175°25W 287 Q13
Fonuakula Cook Is. 19°2S 169°55W 289 g
Fonualei Tonga 18°1S 174°19W 287 P13
Fonyód Hungary 46°44N 17°33E 182 D2
Foochow = Fuzhou China 26°5N 119°16E 229 D12
Foots Cray U.K. 51°24N 0°7E 125 B4
Footscray Australia 37°48S 144°56E 128 A1
Foping China 33°41N 108°0E 226 H5
Foraker, Mt. U.S.A. 62°58N 151°24W 303 E10
Forari Vanuatu 17°40S 168°31E 287 G6
Forbach France 49°10N 6°52E 173 C13
Forbes Australia 33°22S 148°5E 283 B8
Forbesganj India 26°17N 87°18E 243 F12
Forbidden City = Imperial Palace Museum Beijing, China 114 b3
Forcados Nigeria 5°26N 5°26E 263 D6
Forcados → Nigeria 5°25N 5°19E 263 D6
Forcalquier France 43°58N 5°47E 175 E9
Forchheim Germany 49°43N 11°2E 179 F7
Ford City Calif., U.S.A. 35°9N 119°27W 307 K7
Ford City Pa., U.S.A. 40°46N 79°32W 312 F5
Ford d'Or B. St. Lucia 13°56N 60°54W 323 m
Ford I. U.S.A. 21°22N 157°58W 302 K14
Forda → Norway 62°57N 10°40E 164 B7
Førde Hordaland, Norway 59°36N 5°27E 164 E2
Førde Rogaland, Norway 59°26N 5°23E 164 E2
Førde Sogn og Fjordane, Norway 61°27N 5°53E 164 C2
Førdefjorden Norway 61°29N 5°18E 164 C2
Fords Bridge Australia 29°41S 145°29E 281 D4
Ford's Theater Washington, D.C., U.S.A. 143 b2
Fordyce U.S.A. 33°49N 92°25W 314 E8
Forécariah Guinea 9°28N 13°10W 262 D2
Forel, Mt. Greenland 66°52N 36°55W 154 D7
Foremost Canada 49°26N 111°34W 296 D6
Foreshore Cape Town, S. Africa 118 a3
Forest Belgium 50°49N 4°20E 116 B1
Forest Ont., Canada 43°6N 82°0W 312 C3
Forest Miss., U.S.A. 32°22N 89°29W 315 E10
Forest Acres U.S.A. 34°1N 80°58W 316 A9
Forest City Iowa, U.S.A. 43°16N 93°39W 308 D7
Forest City N.C., U.S.A. 35°20N 81°52W 315 D14
Forest City Pa., U.S.A. 41°39N 75°28W 313 E9
Forest Gate U.K. 51°32N 0°1E 125 A4
Forest Grove U.S.A. 45°31N 123°7W 306 E3
Forest Heights U.S.A. 38°48N 77°0W 143 C2
Forest Hill Ont., Canada 43°41N 79°25W 141 A2
Forest Hill London, U.K. 51°26N 0°2W 125 B3
Forest Hills U.S.A. 40°42N 73°51W 132 B2
Forest Park Ga., U.S.A. 33°37N 84°22W 316 B5
Forest Park Ill., U.S.A. 41°51N 87°47W 119 B2
Forest Park N.Y., U.S.A. 40°42N 73°51W 132 B2
Forest Park Ohio, U.S.A. 39°17N 84°30W 311 E12
Forest View U.S.A. 41°48N 87°47W 119 C2
Forestburg Canada 52°35N 112°1W 296 C6
Foreste Casentinesi-Monte Falterona-Campigna △ Italy 43°50N 11°48E 199 E8
Foresthill U.S.A. 39°1N 120°49W 306 F6
Forestier Pen. Australia 43°0S 148°0E 281 G4
Forestville Qué., Canada 48°48N 69°2W 299 C6
Forestville Calif., U.S.A. 38°28N 122°54W 306 G4
Forestville N.Y., U.S.A. 42°28N 79°10W 312 D5
Forêt d'Orient ⌓ France 48°16N 4°25E 173 D11
Forêt du Day △ Djibouti 11°56N 42°40E 267 B5
Forez, Mts. du France 45°40N 3°50E 174 C7
Forfar U.K. 56°39N 2°53W 167 E6
Forillon △ Canada 48°46N 64°12W 299 C7
Forks U.S.A. 47°57N 124°23W 306 C2
Forks, The = Merritt Canada 50°10N 120°45W 296 C4
Forksville U.S.A. 41°29N 76°35W 313 E8
Forlì Italy 44°13N 12°3E 199 D9
Forlí-Cesena □ Italy 44°10N 12°20E 199 D9
Forman U.S.A. 46°7N 97°38W 308 B5
Formazza Italy 46°22N 8°26E 198 B5
Formby Pt. U.K. 53°33N 3°6W 168 D4
Formentera Spain 38°43N 1°27E 206 D1
Formentor, C. de Spain 39°58N 3°13E 206 B4
Formentor, Pen. de Spain 39°56N 3°11E 206 B4
Former Yugoslav Republic of Macedonia = Macedonia ■ Europe 41°53N 21°40E 202 E5
Fórmia Italy 41°15N 13°37E 200 A6
Formiga Brazil 20°27S 45°25W 333 F2
Formígine Italy 44°37N 10°51E 198 D7
Formosa = Taiwan ■ Asia 23°30N 121°0E 225 C3
Formosa Argentina 26°15S 58°10W 334 B4
Formosa Brazil 15°32S 47°20W 333 E2
Formosa □ Argentina 25°0S 60°0W 334 B4
Formosa, Serra Brazil 12°0S 55°0W 331 C7
Formosa B. = Ungwana B. Kenya 2°45S 40°20E 268 C5
Formosa do Rio Prêto Brazil 11°2S 45°3W 332 D2
Formosa Strait = Taiwan Strait Asia 24°40N 120°0E 229 E12
Formoso → Brazil 10°34S 49°56W 333 D2
Fornebu Norway 59°53N 10°36E 133 A2
Fornells Spain 40°3N 4°7E 206 A5
Fornos de Algodres Portugal 40°38N 7°32W 194 E3
Fornovo di Taro Italy 44°42N 10°6E 198 D7
Foro Romano Rome, Italy 136 c3
Forollhogna △ Norway 62°39N 10°41E 164 B7
Føroyar ☑ Atl. Oc. 62°0N 7°0W 160 F9
Forres U.K. 57°37N 3°37W 167 D5
Forrest Vic., Australia 38°33S 143°47E 282 E5
Forrest W. Austral., Australia 30°51S 128°6E 279 F4
Forrest, Mt. Australia 24°48S 127°45E 279 D4
Forrest City U.S.A. 35°1N 90°47W 315 D9
Forreston U.S.A. 42°8N 89°35W 310 B7
Fors Sweden 60°14N 16°20E 162 D10
Forsand Norway 58°54N 6°5E 164 F3
Forsayth Australia 18°33S 143°34E 280 B3
Forserum Sweden 57°42N 14°30E 163 G8
Forshaga Sweden 59°33N 13°29E 162 E7
Förslöv Sweden 56°21N 12°48E 163 H6
Forsmo Sweden 63°16N 17°11E 162 A11
Forssa Finland 60°49N 23°38E 188 B2
Forst Germany 51°45N 14°37E 178 D10
Forstenried Germany 48°5N 11°29E 131 B1
Forstenrieder Park Germany 48°3N 11°27E 131 B1
Forster Australia 32°12S 152°31E 283 B10
Forsvik Sweden 58°35N 14°26E 163 F8
Forsyth Ga., U.S.A. 33°2N 83°56W 316 B6
Forsyth Mont., U.S.A. 46°16N 106°41W 304 C10
Forsyth I. N.Z. 40°58S 174°5E 285 A9
Fort Mumbai, India 130 c2
Fort Abbas Pakistan 29°12N 72°52E 242 E5
Fort Albany Canada 52°15N 81°35W 298 B3
Fort-Aleksandrovsky = Fort Shevchenko Kazakhstan 44°35N 50°23E 191 H10
Fort Archambault = Sarh Chad 9°5N 18°23E 259 G3
Fort Assiniboine Canada 54°20N 114°45W 296 C6
Fort Atkinson U.S.A. 42°56N 88°50W 311 B8
Fort Augustus U.K. 57°9N 4°42W 167 D4

Fort Bay *Saba* 17°37N 63°15W **322** a
Fort Bayard = Zhanjiang *China* 21°15N 110°20E **229** G8
Fort Beaufort *S. Africa* 32°46S 26°40E **270** D4
Fort Benton *U.S.A.* 47°49N 110°40W **304** C8
Fort Bragg *U.S.A.* 39°26N 123°48W **304** G2
Fort Bridger *U.S.A.* 41°19N 110°23W **304** F8
Fort Canning Park *Singapore* **138** b2
Fort Caroline ⌂ *U.S.A.* 30°23N 81°30W **316** E8
Fort Charles *Jamaica* 17°55N 76°50W **320** a
Fort Charlotte *St. Lucia* 13°59N 61°0W **323** m
Fort Chipewyan *Canada* 58°42N 111°8W **297** B6
Fort Clatsop = Lewis and Clark ⌂ *U.S.A.* 46°8N 123°53W **306** D3
Fort Collins *U.S.A.* 40°35N 105°5W **304** F11
Fort-Coulonge *Canada* 45°50N 76°45W **298** C4
Fort Covington *U.S.A.* 44°59N 74°29W **313** B10
Fort Dauphin = Taolanaro *Madag.* 25°2S 47°0E **272** D2
Fort Davis *Ala., U.S.A.* 32°15N 85°43W **316** C4
Fort Davis *Tex., U.S.A.* 30°35N 103°54W **314** F3
Fort-de-France *Martinique* 14°36N 61°5W **322** j
Fort-de-France, B. de *Martinique* 14°34N 61°4W **322** j
Fort de Kock = Bukittinggi *Indonesia* 0°20S 100°20E **234** C2
Fort de Polignac = Illizi *Algeria* 26°31N 8°32E **261** C6
Fort de Possel = Possel *C.A.R.* 5°5N 19°10E **264** A3
Fort Defiance *U.S.A.* 35°45N 109°5W **305** J9
Fort Dodge *U.S.A.* 42°30N 94°11W **310** B2
Fort Drum *U.S.A.* 27°32N 80°48W **317** H9
Fort Dupont Park *U.S.A.* 38°52N 76°56W **143** B3
Fort Edward *U.S.A.* 43°16N 73°35W **313** C11
Fort Erie *Canada* 42°54N 78°56W **312** D6
Fort Fairfield *U.S.A.* 46°46N 67°50W **309** B20
Fort Flatters = Bordj Omar Driss *Algeria* 28°10N 6°40E **261** C6
Fort Foote Village *U.S.A.* 38°46N 77°1W **143** C2
Fort Foureau = Kousseri *Cameroon* 12°0N 14°55E **259** F2
Fort Frances *Canada* 48°36N 93°24W **297** D10
Fort Franklin = Déline *Canada* 65°11N 123°25W **294** D7
Fort Frederica ⌂ *U.S.A.* 31°13N 81°23W **316** D8
Fort Gaines *U.S.A.* 31°36N 85°3W **316** D4
Fort Garland *U.S.A.* 37°26N 105°26W **305** H11
Fort George = Chisasibi *Canada* 53°50N 79°0W **298** B4
Fort George = Prince George *Canada* 53°55N 122°50W **296** C4
Fort George *Grenada* 12°3N 61°45W **323** q
Fort Good Hope *Canada* 66°14N 128°40W **294** D6
Fort Gouraud = Fdérik *Mauritania* 22°40N 12°45W **260** D2
Fort Hancock *U.S.A.* 31°18N 105°51W **314** F2
Fort Hertz = Putao *Burma* 27°28N 97°30E **241** B6
Fort Hill = Chitipa *Malawi* 9°41S 33°19E **269** D3
Fort Hope = Eabametoong *Canada* 51°30N 88°0W **298** B2
Fort Irwin *U.S.A.* 35°16N 116°41W **307** K10
Fort Jameson = Chipata *Zambia* 13°38S 32°28E **269** E3
Fort Jeudy, Pt. of *Grenada* 11°59N 61°42W **323** q
Fort Johnston = Mangoche *Malawi* 14°25S 35°16E **269** E4
Fort Kent *U.S.A.* 47°15N 68°36W **309** B19
Fort Klamath *U.S.A.* 42°42N 122°0W **304** D3
Fort Lamy = Ndjamena *Chad* 12°10N 15°0E **259** F3
Fort-Laperrine = Tamanrasset *Algeria* 22°50N 5°30E **261** D6
Fort Laramie *U.S.A.* 42°13N 104°31W **304** E11
Fort Lauderdale *U.S.A.* 26°7N 80°8W **129** B3
Fort Lauderdale Executive ✈ (FXE) *U.S.A.* 26°11N 80°10W **129** A2
Fort Lauderdale-Hollywood Int. ✈ (FLL) *U.S.A.* 26°4N 80°10W **129** B3
Fort Lee *U.S.A.* 40°50N 73°58W **132** A2
Fort Liard *Canada* 60°14N 123°30W **296** A4
Fort Liberté *Haiti* 19°42N 71°51W **321** C5
Fort Lupton *U.S.A.* 40°5N 104°49W **304** F11
Fort MacKay *Canada* 57°12N 111°41W **296** B6
Fort Macleod *Canada* 49°45N 113°30W **296** D6
Fort MacMahon = El Homr *Algeria* 29°43N 1°45E **261** C5
Fort McMurray *Canada* 56°44N 111°7W **296** B6
Fort McPherson *Canada* 67°30N 134°55W **294** D5
Fort Madison *U.S.A.* 40°38N 91°27W **310** D5
Fort Manning = Mchinji *Malawi* 13°47S 32°58E **269** E3
Fort Marlborough *Indonesia* 3°48S 102°15E **234** C2
Fort Mason Center *San Francisco, U.S.A.* **136** a1
Fort Matanzas ⌂ *U.S.A.* 29°43N 81°14W **316** F8
Fort Meade *U.S.A.* 27°45N 81°48W **317** H8
Fort Mitchell *U.S.A.* 32°20N 85°1W **316** C4
Fort Morgan *U.S.A.* 40°15N 103°48W **304** F12
Fort Myers *U.S.A.* 26°39N 81°52W **317** J8
Fort Myers Beach *U.S.A.* 26°26N 81°52W **317** J8
Fort Myers Villas *U.S.A.* 26°33N 81°52W **317** J8
Fort Napoléon *Guadeloupe* 15°52N 61°35W **322** e
Fort Nelson *Canada* 58°50N 122°44W **296** B4
Fort Nelson → *Canada* 59°32N 124°0W **296** B4
Fort Norman = Tulita *Canada* 64°57N 125°30W **294** E6
Fort Ogden *U.S.A.* 27°5N 81°57W **317** H8
Fort Payne *U.S.A.* 34°26N 85°43W **315** D12
Fort Peck *U.S.A.* 48°1N 106°27W **304** B10
Fort Peck Dam *U.S.A.* 48°0N 106°26W **304** C10
Fort Peck L. *U.S.A.* 48°0N 106°26W **304** C10
Fort Pierce *U.S.A.* 27°27N 80°20W **317** H9
Fort Pierre *U.S.A.* 44°21N 100°22W **308** C3
Fort Pierre Bordes = Ti-n-Zaouatene *Algeria* 19°55N 2°55E **261** E5
Fort Plain *U.S.A.* 42°56N 74°37W **313** D10
Fort Portal *Uganda* 0°40N 30°20E **268** B3
Fort Providence *Canada* 61°3N 117°40W **296** A5
Fort Pulaski ⌂ *U.S.A.* 32°2N 80°56W **316** C9
Fort Qu'Appelle *Canada* 50°45N 103°50W **297** C8
Fort Recovery *U.S.A.* 40°25N 84°47W **311** D12
Fort Resolution *Canada* 61°10N 113°40W **296** A6
Fort Rixon *Zimbabwe* 20°2S 29°17E **269** G2
Fort Rosebery = Mansa *Zambia* 11°13S 28°55E **269** E2
Fort Ross *U.S.A.* 38°32N 123°13W **306** G3
Fort-Rousset = Owando *Congo* 0°29S 15°55E **264** C3
Fort Rupert = Waskaganish *Canada* 51°30N 78°40W **298** B4
Fort St. James *Canada* 54°30N 124°10W **296** C4
Fort St. John *Canada* 56°15N 120°50W **296** B4
Fort Sandeman = Zhob *Pakistan* 31°20N 69°31E **242** D3
Fort Saskatchewan *Canada* 53°40N 113°15W **296** C6
Fort Scott *U.S.A.* 37°50N 94°42W **308** G6
Fort Severn *Canada* 56°0N 87°40W **298** A2
Fort Shevchenko *Kazakhstan* 44°35N 50°23E **191** H10
Fort Simpson *Canada* 61°45N 121°15W **296** A4
Fort Smith *Alta., Canada* 60°0N 111°51W **296** B6
Fort Smith *Ark., U.S.A.* 35°23N 94°25W **314** D7
Fort Stockton *U.S.A.* 30°53N 102°53W **314** F3
Fort Sumner *U.S.A.* 34°28N 104°15W **305** J11
Fort Thomas *U.S.A.* 39°4N 84°26W **311** E12
Fort Thompson *U.S.A.* 44°3N 99°26W **308** C4
Fort Trinquet = Bîr Mogreïn *Mauritania* 25°10N 11°25W **260** C2
Fort Union ⌂ *U.S.A.* 35°54N 105°1W **305** J11
Fort Uritskogo = Fort Shevchenko *Kazakhstan* 44°35N 50°23E **191** H10
Fort Valley *U.S.A.* 32°33N 83°53W **316** C6
Fort Vermilion *Canada* 58°24N 116°0W **296** B5
Fort Walton Beach *U.S.A.* 30°25N 86°36W **317** E3
Fort Ware *Canada* 57°26N 125°41W **296** B3
Fort Wayne *U.S.A.* 41°4N 85°9W **311** C11
Fort White *U.S.A.* 29°55N 82°43W **316** F7
Fort William *U.K.* 56°49N 5°7W **167** E3
Fort Worth *U.S.A.* 32°43N 97°19W **314** E6
Fort Yates *U.S.A.* 46°5N 100°38W **308** B3
Fort Yukon *U.S.A.* 66°34N 145°16W **303** C11
Fortaleza = Pedra Azul *Brazil* 16°2S 41°17W **333** E3
Fortaleza *Bolivia* 12°6S 66°49W **330** C4
Fortaleza *Brazil* 3°45S 38°35W **332** B4
Forteau *Canada* 51°28N 56°58W **299** B8
Fortescue → *Australia* 21°0S 116°4E **278** D2
Fortescue River Roadhouse *Australia* 21°17S 116°8E **278** D2
Forth → *U.K.* 56°9N 3°50W **167** E5
Forth, Firth of *U.K.* 56°5N 2°55W **121** A3
Forth Rail Bridge *U.K.* 56°0N 3°23W **121** A1
Forth Road Bridge *U.K.* 56°0N 3°24W **121** A1
Forthassa Rharbia *Algeria* 32°52N 1°18W **261** B4
Fortín General Pando *Paraguay* 19°45S 59°47W **331** D6
Fortín Madrejón *Paraguay* 20°45S 59°52W **331** E6
Fortín Teniente Primero Ramiro Espínola *Paraguay* 21°27S 61°30W **331** E5
Fortín Uno *Argentina* 38°50S 65°18W **336** A3
Fortore → *Italy* 41°55N 15°17E **199** G12
Fortrose *N.Z.* 46°38S 168°45E **285** G3
Fortrose *Highl., U.K.* 57°35N 4°9W **167** D4
Fortuna *Spain* 38°11N 1°7W **197** G3
Fortuna *Calif., U.S.A.* 40°36N 124°9W **304** F1
Fortuna *N. Dak., U.S.A.* 48°55N 103°47W **308** A2
Fortuna Ledge = Marshall *U.S.A.* 61°53N 162°5W **303** F7
Fortune *Canada* 47°4N 55°50W **299** C8
Fortune B. *Canada* 47°30N 55°22W **299** C8
Forūr *Iran* 26°17N 54°32E **247** E7
Fos-sur-Mer *France* 43°26N 4°56E **175** E8
Fosen *Norway* 63°50N 10°20E **160** E14
Foshan *China* 23°3N 113°9E **121** B1
Fosnavåg *Norway* 62°22N 5°38E **164** B2
Foso *Ghana* 5°43N 1°15W **263** D4
Foss *Iceland* 63°51N 17°52W **155** D9
Fossano *Italy* 44°33N 7°43E **198** D4
Fossil *U.S.A.* 45°0N 120°9W **304** D3
Fossil Butte ⌂ *U.S.A.* 41°50N 110°27W **304** F8
Fossombrone *Italy* 43°41N 12°48E **199** E9
Fossvellir *Iceland* 65°27N 14°37W **155** B12
Foster *Vic., Australia* 38°40S 146°15E **283** E7
Foster *Qué., Canada* 45°17N 72°30W **313** A12
Foster *Ky., U.S.A.* 38°48N 84°13W **311** F12
Foster → *Canada* 55°47N 105°49W **297** B7
Foster Village *U.S.A.* 21°21N 157°55W **302** K14
Fosters Ra. *Australia* 21°35S 133°48E **280** C1
Fostoria *U.S.A.* 41°10N 83°25W **311** C13
Fót *Hungary* 47°35N 19°11E **117** A3
Fotadrevo *Madag.* 24°3S 45°1E **272** C2
Fouesnant *France* 47°53N 4°1W **172** E2
Fougamou *Gabon* 1°16S 10°30E **264** C2
Fougères *France* 48°21N 1°14W **172** D5
Foul Pt. *Sri Lanka* 8°35N 81°18E **245** K5
Foula *U.K.* 60°10N 2°5W **167** A6
Foulalaba *Mali* 10°40N 7°20W **262** C3
Foulness I. *U.K.* 51°36N 0°55E **169** F8
Foulpointe *Madag.* 17°41S 49°31E **272** B2
Foulwind, C. *N.Z.* 41°45S 171°28E **285** B6
Foum Assaka *Morocco* 29°8N 10°24W **260** C2
Foum Zguid *Morocco* 30°2N 6°59W **260** B3
Foumban *Cameroon* 5°45N 10°50E **263** D7
Foumbot *Cameroon* 5°31N 10°28E **263** D7
Foumbouni *Comoros Is.* 11°51S 43°29E **272** a
Foumirate *Algeria* 27°30N 3°12W **260** C4
Foundiougne *Senegal* 14°5N 16°32W **262** C1
Fountain *Colo., U.S.A.* 38°41N 104°42W **304** G11
Fountain *Fla., U.S.A.* 30°29N 85°25W **316** E4
Fountain Hills *U.S.A.* 33°37N 111°43W **305** K8
Fountain Springs *U.S.A.* 35°54N 118°51W **307** K8
Four Mountains, Is. of *U.S.A.* 53°0N 170°0W **303** K5
Four Roads *Trin. & Tob.* 10°41N 61°33W **323** t
Fourchambault *France* 47°2N 3°3E **173** E10
Fourchue, Île *St. Barts* 17°58N 62°54W **322** a
Fouriesburg *S. Africa* 28°38S 28°14E **271** C4
Fourmies *France* 50°1N 4°2E **173** B11
Fourna *Greece* 39°3N 21°52E **204** B3
Fournaise, Piton de la *Réunion* 21°14S 55°43E **272** f
Fourni *Greece* 37°36N 26°32E **205** D8
Fourqueux *France* 48°53N 2°3E **134** A1
Fours *France* 46°50N 3°42E **173** F10
Fous, Pte. des *Dominica* 15°12N 61°20W **323** k
Fousinshin = Fuxin *China* 42°5N 121°48E **227** C11
Fouta Djallon *Guinea* 11°20N 12°10W **262** C2
Foux, Cap-à- *Haiti* 19°43N 73°27W **321** C5
Foveaux Str. *N.Z.* 46°42S 168°10E **285** G3
Fowey *U.K.* 50°20N 4°39W **169** G3
Fowler *Calif., U.S.A.* 36°38N 119°41W **306** J7
Fowler *Colo., U.S.A.* 38°8N 104°2W **304** G11
Fowler *Ind., U.S.A.* 40°37N 87°19W **311** D9
Fowler *Mich., U.S.A.* 43°0N 84°45W **311** B12
Fowler, Pt. *Australia* 32°2S 132°3E **279** F5
Fowlers B. *Australia* 31°59S 132°34E **279** F5
Fowlerville *U.S.A.* 42°40N 84°4W **311** B12
Fowman *Iran* 37°13N 49°19E **213** D13
Fox → *Canada* 56°3N 93°18W **297** B10
Fox Creek *Canada* 54°24N 116°48W **296** C5
Fox Is. *U.S.A.* 53°0N 168°0W **303** K6
Fox Lake *Alta., Canada* 58°28N 114°31W **296** B6
Fox Lake *Ill., U.S.A.* 42°24N 88°11W **311** B8
Fox Studios *Australia* 33°55S 151°13E **139** B2
Fox Valley *Canada* 50°30N 109°25W **297** C7
Foxboro *Ont., Canada* 44°14N 77°26W **312** B7
Foxboro *Mass., U.S.A.* 42°4N 71°16W **313** D13
Foxdale *Australia* 20°22S 148°35E **280** b
Foxe Basin *Canada* 66°0N 77°0W **295** D16
Foxe Chan. *Canada* 65°0N 80°0W **295** E16
Foxe Pen. *Canada* 65°0N 76°0W **295** E16
Foxen *Sweden* 59°25N 11°55E **162** E5
Foxford *Ireland* 53°59N 9°7W **166** C2
Foxrock *Ireland* 53°17N 6°11W **120** B2
Foxton *N.Z.* 40°29S 175°18E **284** G4
Foyle, Lough *U.K.* 55°7N 7°4W **166** A4
Foynes *Ireland* 52°37N 9°7W **166** D2
Foz *Spain* 43°33N 7°20W **194** B3
Foz do Copeá *Brazil* 3°52S 63°19W **329** D5
Foz do Cunene *Angola* 17°15S 11°48E **265** F2
Foz do Gregório *Brazil* 6°47S 70°44W **330** B3
Foz do Iguaçu *Brazil* 25°30S 54°30W **335** B5
Foz do Mamoriá *Brazil* 2°27S 66°32W **328** D4
Frackville *U.S.A.* 40°47N 76°14W **313** F8
Fraga *Spain* 41°32N 0°21E **196** D5
Fraile Muerto *Uruguay* 32°31S 54°32W **335** C5
Framingham *U.S.A.* 42°18N 71°24W **313** D13
Framnes *Iceland* 66°1N 20°26W **155** A6
Frampol *Poland* 50°41N 22°40E **185** H9
Franca *Brazil* 20°33S 47°30W **333** F2
Francavilla al Mare *Italy* 42°25N 14°17E **199** F11
Francavilla Fontana *Italy* 40°32N 17°35E **201** B10
France ■ *Europe* 47°0N 3°0E **171** C5
Frances *Australia* 36°41S 140°55E **282** D4
Frances → *Canada* 60°16N 129°10W **296** A3
Frances L. *Canada* 61°23N 129°30W **296** A3
Francesville *U.S.A.* 40°59N 86°53W **311** D10
Franceville *Gabon* 1°40S 13°32E **264** C2
Franche-Comté □ *France* 46°50N 5°55E **173** F12
Francis Case, L. *U.S.A.* 43°4N 98°34W **308** D4
Francisco Beltrão *Brazil* 26°5S 53°4W **335** B5
Francisco de Orellana *Ecuador* 0°28S 76°58W **328** D2
Francisco Ignacio Madero *Coahuila, Mexico* 25°48N 103°18W **318** B4
Francisco Ignacio Madero *Durango, Mexico* 24°26N 104°18W **318** C4
Francisco Ignacio Madero, Presa *Mexico* 28°10N 105°37W **318** B3
Francisco Sá *Brazil* 16°28S 43°30W **333** E3
Francistown *Botswana* 21°7S 27°33E **271** B4
Francofonte *Italy* 37°14N 14°53E **201** E7
François *Canada* 47°35N 56°45W **299** C8
François, B. du *Martinique* 14°38N 60°54W **322** j
François-Joseph, Chutes *Dem. Rep. of the Congo* 7°37S 17°17E **265** D3
François L. *Canada* 54°0N 125°30W **296** C3
Francois Peron △ *Australia* 25°42S 113°33E **279** E1
Franconia *U.S.A.* 38°47N 77°7W **143** C2
Francs Pk. *U.S.A.* 43°58N 109°20W **304** E9
Franeker *Neths.* 53°12N 5°33E **170** A5
Frank Hann △ *Australia* 32°52S 120°19E **279** F3
Frank Lloyd Wright Home *Chicago, U.S.A.* 41°53N 87°47W **119** B2
Frankel *Singapore* 1°18N 103°55E **138** B3
Frankenberg *Germany* 51°3N 8°48E **178** D4
Frankenhöhe ⌂ *Germany* 49°20N 10°25E **179** F6
Frankenstein = Ząbkowice Śląskie *Poland* 50°35N 16°50E **185** H3
Frankenwald *Germany* 50°20N 11°30E **179** E7
Frankenwald ⌂ *Germany* 50°15N 11°30E **179** E7
Frankfield *Jamaica* 18°8N 77°22W **320** a
Frankford *Ont., Canada* 44°12N 77°36W **312** B7
Frankford *Mo., U.S.A.* 39°29N 91°19W **310** E5
Frankfort *Free State, S. Africa* 27°17S 28°30E **271** C4
Frankfort *Ind., U.S.A.* 40°17N 86°31W **311** D10
Frankfort *Kans., U.S.A.* 39°42N 96°25W **308** F5
Frankfort *Ky., U.S.A.* 38°12N 84°52W **311** F12
Frankfort *N.Y., U.S.A.* 43°2N 75°4W **313** C9
Frankfort *Ohio, U.S.A.* 39°24N 83°11W **311** E13
Frankfurt *Brandenburg, Germany* 52°20N 14°32E **178** C10
Frankfurt *Hessen, Germany* 50°7N 8°41E **179** E4
Frankfurt ✈ (FRA) *Germany* 50°1N 8°34E **179** E4
Fränkische Alb *Germany* 49°10N 11°23E **179** F7
Fränkische Rezat → *Germany* 49°11N 11°1E **179** F7
Fränkische Saale → *Germany* 50°3N 9°42E **179** E5
Fränkische Schweiz *Germany* 49°50N 11°16E **179** F7
Fränkische Schweiz-Veldensteiner Forst ⌂ *Germany* 49°45N 11°22E **179** F7
Frankland → *Australia* 35°0S 116°48E **279** G2
Franklin *Ga., U.S.A.* 33°17N 85°6W **316** B4
Franklin *Ind., U.S.A.* 39°29N 86°3W **311** E10
Franklin *Ky., U.S.A.* 36°43N 86°35W **308** G10
Franklin *La., U.S.A.* 29°48N 91°30W **314** G9
Franklin *Mass., U.S.A.* 42°5N 71°24W **313** D13
Franklin *N.H., U.S.A.* 43°27N 71°39W **313** C13
Franklin *N.Y., U.S.A.* 42°20N 75°9W **313** D9
Franklin *Nebr., U.S.A.* 40°6N 98°57W **308** E4
Franklin *Ohio, U.S.A.* 39°34N 84°18W **311** E12
Franklin *Pa., U.S.A.* 41°24N 79°50W **312** E5
Franklin *Va., U.S.A.* 36°41N 76°56W **309** G15
Franklin *W. Va., U.S.A.* 38°39N 79°20W **309** F14
Franklin, Pt. *U.S.A.* 70°55N 158°48W **303** A8
Franklin B. *Canada* 69°45N 126°0W **294** D6
Franklin D. Roosevelt L. *U.S.A.* 48°18N 118°9W **304** B4
Franklin-Gordon Wild Rivers △ *Australia* 42°19S 145°51E **281** G4
Franklin Harb. *Australia* 33°43S 136°55E **282** B2
Franklin I. *Antarctica* 76°10S 168°30E **151** D11
Franklin I. *Ont., Canada* 45°24N 80°20W **312** A4
Franklin L. *U.S.A.* 40°25N 115°22W **304** F6
Franklin Mts. *N.W.T., Canada* 65°0N 125°0W **294** D6
Franklin Mts. *N.Z.* 44°55S 167°45E **285** E2
Franklin Park *Mass., U.S.A.* 42°18N 71°5W **116** B2
Franklin Park *Va., U.S.A.* 38°55N 77°9W **143** B2
Franklin Res. *U.S.A.* 34°5N 118°24W **126** B2
Franklin Str. *Canada* 72°0N 96°0W **294** C12
Franklinton *U.S.A.* 30°51N 90°9W **315** F9
Franklinville *U.S.A.* 42°20N 78°27W **312** D6
Franklyn Mt. *N.Z.* 42°4S 172°42E **285** C7
Frankston *Australia* 38°8S 145°8E **283** E6
Frånö *Sweden* 62°55N 17°50E **162** B11
Fransfontein *Namibia* 20°12S 15°1E **270** B2
Fränsta *Sweden* 62°30N 16°11E **162** B10
Frantsa Iosifa, Zemlya *Arctic* 82°0N 55°0E **214** A6
Franz *Canada* 48°25N 84°30W **298** C3
Franz Josef Land = Frantsa Iosifa, Zemlya *Arctic* 82°0N 55°0E **214** A6
Franz Josef Strauss ✈ (MUC) *Germany* 48°21N 11°47E **131** A2
Franzburg *Germany* 54°11N 12°51E **178** A8
Frascati *Italy* 41°48N 12°41E **199** G9
Fraser *U.S.A.* 42°32N 82°57W **312** D2
Fraser → *B.C., Canada* 49°7N 123°11W **306** A3
Fraser → *Nfld. & L., Canada* 56°39N 62°10W **299** A7
Fraser, Mt. *Australia* 25°35S 118°20E **279** E2
Fraser I. *Australia* 25°15S 153°10E **281** D5
Fraser Lake *Canada* 54°0N 124°50W **296** C4
Fraserburg *S. Africa* 31°55S 21°30E **270** D3
Fraserburg Road = Leeu Gamka *S. Africa* 32°47S 21°59E **270** D3
Fraserburgh *U.K.* 57°42N 2°1W **167** D6
Fraserdale *Canada* 49°55N 81°37W **298** C3
Fraserpet = Kushalnagar *India* 12°14N 75°57E **245** H2
Frasertown *N.Z.* 38°58S 177°28E **284** E6
Fraserville = Rivière-du-Loup *Canada* 47°50N 69°30W **299** C6
Frashër *Albania* 40°23N 20°30E **202** F4
Frasne *France* 46°50N 6°10E **173** F13
Frăteşti *Romania* 43°58N 25°58E **183** G10
Frauenfeld *Switz.* 47°34N 8°54E **179** H4
Frauenkirche *Munich, Germany* **131** b2
Frauenstadt = Wadowice *Poland* 49°52N 19°30E **185** J6
Fraustadt = Wschowa *Poland* 51°48N 16°20E **185** G3
Fray Bentos *Uruguay* 33°10S 58°15W **334** C4
Fray Jorge △ *Chile* 30°42S 71°40W **334** C1
Frazier Downs ☼ *Australia* 18°48S 121°42E **278** C3
Frechilla *Spain* 42°8N 4°50W **194** C6
Fredericia *Denmark* 55°34N 9°45E **163** J3
Frederick *Md., U.S.A.* 39°25N 77°25W **309** F15
Frederick *Okla., U.S.A.* 34°23N 99°1W **314** D5
Frederick *S. Dak., U.S.A.* 45°50N 98°31W **308** C4
Frederick E. Hyde Fjord *Greenland* 83°25N 29°0W **154** A8
Fredericksburg *Pa., U.S.A.* 40°27N 76°26W **313** F8
Fredericksburg *Tex., U.S.A.* 30°16N 98°52W **314** F5
Fredericksburg *Va., U.S.A.* 38°18N 77°28W **309** F15
Fredericktown *Mo., U.S.A.* 37°34N 90°18W **308** G8
Fredericktown *Ohio, U.S.A.* 40°29N 82°33W **312** F2
Frederico Westphalen *Brazil* 27°22S 53°24W **335** B5
Fredericton *Canada* 45°57N 66°40W **299** C6
Fredericton Junction *Canada* 45°41N 66°40W **299** C6
Frederiksberg *Denmark* 55°40N 12°33E **118** A3
Frederiksdal *Denmark* 55°46N 12°25E **118** A2
Frederikshåb = Paamiut *Greenland* 62°0N 49°43W **154** E6
Frederikshald = Halden *Norway* 59°9N 11°23E **164** E8
Frederikshamn = Hamina *Finland* 60°34N 27°12E **188** B4
Frederikshavn *Denmark* 57°28N 10°31E **163** G4
Frederikssund *Denmark* 55°50N 12°3E **163** J6
Frederiksted *U.S. Virgin Is.* 17°43N 64°53W **321** C7
Frederiksværk *Denmark* 55°58N 12°4E **163** J6
Fredersdorf *Germany* 52°31N 13°45E **115** A5
Fredonia *Ariz., U.S.A.* 36°57N 112°32W **305** H7
Fredonia *Kans., U.S.A.* 37°32N 95°49W **308** G6
Fredonia *N.Y., U.S.A.* 42°26N 79°20W **312** D5
Fredriksberg *Sweden* 60°8N 14°23E **162** D8
Fredrikstad *Norway* 59°13N 10°57E **164** E7
Fredriksvern = Stavern *Norway* 59°0N 10°1E **164** F7
Free State □ *S. Africa* 28°30S 27°0E **270** C4
Freeburg *U.S.A.* 38°19N 91°56W **310** F5
Freehold *U.S.A.* 40°16N 74°17W **313** F10
Freeland *U.S.A.* 41°1N 75°54W **313** E9
Freels, C. *Nfld. & L., Canada* 49°15N 53°30W **299** C9
Freels, C. *Nfld. & L., Canada* 46°37N 53°32W **299** C9
Freeman *Calif., U.S.A.* 35°35N 117°53W **307** K9
Freeman *Mo., U.S.A.* 38°37N 94°30W **310** F2
Freeman *S. Dak., U.S.A.* 43°21N 97°26W **308** D5
Freeport *Bahamas* 26°30N 78°47W **320** A4
Freeport *Trin. & Tob.* 10°27N 61°25W **323** t
Freeport *Fla., U.S.A.* 30°30N 86°8W **316** E3
Freeport *Ill., U.S.A.* 42°17N 89°36W **310** B7
Freeport *N.Y., U.S.A.* 40°39N 73°35W **313** F11
Freeport *Ohio, U.S.A.* 40°12N 81°15W **312** F3
Freeport *Pa., U.S.A.* 40°41N 79°41W **312** F5
Freeport *Tex., U.S.A.* 28°57N 95°21W **314** G7
Freetown *Antigua & B.* 17°3N 61°42W **322** b
Freetown *S. Leone* 8°30N 13°17W **262** D2
Freeville *U.S.A.* 42°30N 76°20W **313** D8
Frégate, L. de la *Canada* 53°15N 74°45W **298** B5
Fregate Island Nature Reserve *St. Lucia* 13°52N 60°53W **323** m
Fregenal de la Sierra *Spain* 38°10N 6°39W **195** G4
Fregene *Italy* 41°51N 12°12E **199** G9
Fregon *Australia* 26°45S 132°1E **279** E5
Freguesia *Brazil* 22°48S 43°10W **135** A1
Fréhel, C. *France* 48°40N 2°20W **172** D4
Freiberg *Germany* 50°55N 13°20E **178** E9
Freibourg = Fribourg *Switz.* 46°49N 7°9E **179** J3
Freiburg *Baden-W., Germany* 47°59N 7°51E **179** H3
Freiburg *Niedersachsen, Germany* 53°49N 9°16E **178** B5
Freiburg in Schlesien = Świebodzice *Poland* 50°51N 16°20E **185** H3
Freidrichshain, Volkspark *Germany* 52°31N 13°25E **115** A3
Freienwalde = Chociwel *Poland* 53°29N 15°21E **184** E2
Freiham *Germany* 48°8N 11°25E **131** B1
Freilassing *Germany* 47°50N 12°58E **179** H8
Freimann *Germany* 48°11N 11°37E **131** A2
Freire *Chile* 38°54S 72°38W **336** A2
Freirina *Chile* 28°30S 71°10W **334** B1
Freising *Germany* 48°24N 11°45E **179** G7
Freistadt *Austria* 48°30N 14°30E **180** C7
Freital *Germany* 51°1N 13°39E **178** D9
Freiwaldau = Jeseník *Czech Rep.* 50°14N 17°8E **181** A10
Fréjus *France* 43°25N 6°44E **175** E10
Fremantle *Australia* 32°7S 115°47E **279** F2
Fremont *Calif., U.S.A.* 37°32N 121°57W **306** H4
Fremont *Ind., U.S.A.* 41°44N 84°56W **311** C12
Fremont *Iowa, U.S.A.* 41°13N 92°26W **310** C4
Fremont *Mich., U.S.A.* 43°28N 85°57W **309** D11
Fremont *Nebr., U.S.A.* 41°26N 96°30W **308** E5
Fremont *Ohio, U.S.A.* 41°21N 83°7W **311** C13
Fremont → *U.S.A.* 38°24N 110°42W **304** G8
French Camp *U.S.A.* 37°53N 121°16W **306** H5
French Cays = Plana Cays *Bahamas* 22°38N 73°30W **321** B5
French Creek → *U.S.A.* 41°24N 79°50W **312** E5
French Frigate Shoals *U.S.A.* 23°45N 166°10W **302** G10
French Guiana ◩ *S. Amer.* 4°0N 53°0W **329** C7
French Guinea = Guinea ■ *W. Afr.* 10°20N 11°30W **262** C2
French I. *Australia* 38°20S 145°22E **283** E6
French Island △ *Australia* 38°20S 145°22E **283** E6
French Lick *U.S.A.* 38°33N 86°37W **311** F10
French Market *New Orleans, U.S.A.* **131** a3
French Pass *N.Z.* 40°55S 173°55E **285** A8
French Polynesia ◩ *Pac. Oc.* 20°0S 145°0W **289** f
French Quarter *New Orleans, U.S.A.* **131** a2
French Riviera = Azur, Côte d' *France* 43°25N 7°10E **175** E11
French Sudan = Mali ■ *Africa* 17°0N 3°0W **262** B4
French Territory of the Afars and Issas = Djibouti ■ *Africa* 12°0N 43°0E **257** E5
French Togoland = Togo ■ *W. Afr.* 8°30N 1°35E **263** D5
Frenchburg *U.S.A.* 37°57N 83°38W **311** G13
Frenchman Cr. → *N. Amer.* 48°31N 107°10W **304** B10
Frenchman Cr. → *Nebr., U.S.A.* 40°14N 100°50W **308** E3
Frenda *Algeria* 35°2N 1°1E **261** A5
Frenštát pod Radhoštěm *Czech Rep.* 49°33N 18°13E **181** B11
Fresco *Ivory C.* 5°3N 5°31W **262** D3
Fresco → *Brazil* 7°15S 51°30W **331** B7
Fresh Pond *U.S.A.* 42°22N 71°8W **116** A2
Freshfield, C. *Antarctica* 68°25S 151°10E **151** C10
Fresnay-sur-Sarthe *France* 48°17N 0°1E **172** D7
Fresnes *France* 48°45N 2°18E **134** B2
Fresnillo *Mexico* 23°10N 102°53W **318** C4
Fresno *U.S.A.* 36°44N 119°47W **306** J7
Fresno Alhándiga *Spain* 40°42N 5°37W **194** E5
Fresno Res. *U.S.A.* 48°36N 109°57W **304** B9
Fresvik *Norway* 61°4N 6°55E **164** C3
Freudenau *Austria* 48°11N 16°25E **142** A2
Freudenstadt *Germany* 48°27N 8°24E **179** G4
Freudenthal = Bruntál *Czech Rep.* 49°59N 17°27E **181** B10
Frévent *France* 50°15N 2°17E **173** B9
Frew → *Australia* 20°0S 135°38E **280** C2
Frewsburg *U.S.A.* 42°3N 79°10W **312** D5
Freycinet △ *Australia* 42°11S 148°19E **281** G4
Freycinet Pen. *Australia* 42°10S 148°25E **281** G4
Freyming-Merlebach *France* 49°8N 6°48E **173** C13
Freystadt = Kisielice *Poland* 53°36N 19°16E **184** E6
Freystadt = Kożuchów *Poland* 51°45N 15°31E **185** G2
Freyung *Germany* 48°48N 13°31E **179** G9
Fria *Guinea* 10°27N 13°38W **262** C2
Fria, C. *Namibia* 18°0S 12°0E **270** A1
Friant *U.S.A.* 36°59N 119°43W **306** J7
Friar's B. *St. Kitts & Nevis* 17°16N 62°40W **322** d
Friarstown *Ireland* 53°15N 6°21W **120** B1
Frías *Argentina* 28°40S 65°5W **334** B2
Fribourg *Switz.* 46°49N 7°9E **179** J3
Fribourg □ *Switz.* 46°40N 7°0E **179** J3
Frick Collection *New York, U.S.A.* **132** b3
Fridafors *Sweden* 56°25N 14°39E **163** H8
Friday Harbor *U.S.A.* 48°32N 123°1W **306** B3
Friedberg *Bayern, Germany* 48°21N 10°59E **179** G6
Friedberg *Hessen, Germany* 50°19N 8°45E **179** E4
Friedeberg = Mirsk *Poland* 50°58N 15°23E **185** H2
Friedeberg in Neumark = Strzelce Krajeńskie *Poland* 52°52N 15°33E **185** F2
Friedenau *Germany* 52°28N 13°22E **115** B3
Friedens *U.S.A.* 40°3N 78°59W **312** F6
Friedland = Mieroszów *Poland* 50°40N 16°11E **185** H3
Friedland = Pravdinsk *Russia* 56°29N 43°28E **190** B6
Friedland *Germany* 53°40N 13°33E **178** B9
Friedrichsfelde *Germany* 52°29N 13°33E **115** B4
Friedrichshafen *Germany* 47°39N 9°30E **179** H5
Friedrichshagen *Germany* 52°27N 13°37E **115** B4
Friedrichshain *Germany* 52°31N 13°25E **115** A3
Friedrichskoog *Germany* 54°1N 8°53E **178** A4
Friedrichslust *Germany* 52°33N 13°43E **115** A5
Friedrichstadt *Germany* 54°23N 9°6E **178** A5
Friendly Is. = Tonga ■ *Pac. Oc.* 19°50S 174°30W **287** P13
Friends Arena *Stockholm, Sweden* 59°53N 18°0E **139** A2
Friendship *U.S.A.* 42°12N 78°8W **312** D6
Friesach *Austria* 46°57N 14°24E **180** E7
Friesack *Germany* 52°44N 12°34E **178** C8
Friesland □ *Neths.* 53°5N 5°50E **170** A5
Friesoythe *Germany* 53°1N 7°51E **178** B3
Frigate *Seychelles* 4°35S 55°56E **272** c
Frigate Bay *St. Kitts & Nevis* 17°16N 62°41W **322** d
Frigate I. *Grenada* 12°25N 61°29W **323** q
Friggesund *Sweden* 61°54N 16°33E **162** C10
Friherrs *Finland* 60°16N 24°49E **121** B1
Frillesås *Sweden* 57°20N 12°12E **163** G6
Frilufts Museum *Finland* 60°11N 24°52E **121** B2
Frinnaryd *Sweden* 57°55N 14°50E **163** G8
Frio → *U.S.A.* 28°26N 98°11W **314** G5
Frio, C. *Brazil* 22°50S 41°50W **326** F6
Friol *Spain* 43°2N 7°47W **194** B3
Friona *U.S.A.* 34°38N 102°43W **314** D3
Frisches Haff = Zalew Wiślany *Poland* 54°20N 19°50E **184** D6
Frisco *U.S.A.* 33°8N 96°49W **314** E6
Fristad *Sweden* 57°50N 13°0E **163** G6
Fritch *U.S.A.* 35°38N 101°36W **314** D4
Fritsla *Sweden* 57°33N 12°47E **163** G6
Fritzlar *Germany* 51°7N 9°16E **178** D5
Friuli-Venézia Giulia □ *Italy* 46°0N 13°0E **199** B9
Friza, Proliv *Russia* 45°30N 149°0E **215** E15
Frobisher B. *Canada* 62°30N 66°0W **295** E18
Frobisher Bay = Iqaluit *Canada* 63°44N 68°31W **295** E18
Frobisher L. *Canada* 56°20N 108°15W **297** B7
Frohavet *Norway* 64°0N 9°30E **160** E13
Frohenbruck = Veselí nad Lužnicí *Czech Rep.* 49°12N 14°43E **180** B7
Frohnleiten *Austria* 47°16N 15°19E **180** D8
Frolovo *Russia* 49°45N 43°40E **190** F6
Fromager □ *Ivory C.* 7°0N 6°15W **262** D3
Frombork *Poland* 54°21N 19°41E **184** D6
Frome *U.K.* 51°14N 2°19W **169** F5
Frome → *U.K.* 50°41N 2°6W **169** G5
Frome, L. *Australia* 30°45S 139°45E **282** A3
Frome Downs *Australia* 31°13S 139°45E **282** A3
Frómista *Spain* 42°16N 4°25W **194** C6
Front Range *U.S.A.* 40°25N 105°45W **304** F11
Front Royal *U.S.A.* 38°55N 78°12W **309** F14
Fronteira *Portugal* 39°3N 7°39W **195** F3
Fronteiras *Brazil* 7°5S 40°37W **332** C3
Frontenac ⌂ *Canada* 44°32N 76°30W **313** B8
Frontera *Canary Is.* 27°47N 17°59W **153** e1
Frontera *Tabasco, Mexico* 18°32N 92°38W **319** D6
Fronteras *Mexico* 30°56N 109°31W **318** A3
Frontignan *France* 43°27N 3°45E **174** E7
Frontón, I. *Peru* 12°7S 77°11W **124** B1
Frosinone *Italy* 41°38N 13°19E **200** A6
Frostburg *U.S.A.* 39°39N 78°56W **309** F14
Frostisen *Norway* 68°14N 17°10E **160** B17
Frostproof *U.S.A.* 27°45N 81°32W **317** H8
Frouard *France* 48°47N 6°8E **173** D13
Frövi *Sweden* 59°28N 15°24E **162** E9
Frøya *Norway* 63°43N 8°40E **160** E13
Fruita *U.S.A.* 39°9N 108°44W **304** G9
Fruithurst *U.S.A.* 33°44N 85°26W **316** B4
Fruitland Park *U.S.A.* 28°51N 81°54W **317** G8
Frumoasa *Romania* 46°28N 25°48E **183** D10
Frunze = Bishkek *Kyrgyzstan* 42°54N 74°46E **217** D8
Frunze *Russia* 55°47N 37°33E **129** B2
Frunzivka *Ukraine* 47°20N 29°45E **183** C14
Fruška Gora *Serbia* 45°7N 19°30E **182** E4
Fruška Gora △ *Serbia* 45°8N 19°40E **202** A3
Frutal *Brazil* 20°0S 49°0W **333** F2
Frutigen *Switz.* 46°35N 7°38E **179** J3
Frýdek-Místek *Czech Rep.* 49°40N 18°20E **181** B11
Frýdlant *Czech Rep.* 50°56N 15°9E **180** A8
Fryeburg *U.S.A.* 44°1N 70°59W **313** B14
Fryvaldov = Jeseník *Czech Rep.* 50°14N 17°8E **181** A10
Fthiotida *Greece* 38°50N 22°25E **204** C4
Fu Jiang → *China* 30°0N 106°16E **228** C6
Fu Xian = Wafangdian *China* 39°38N 121°58E **227** E11
Fu Xian *China* 36°0N 109°20E **226** G5
Fua Mulaku *Maldives* 0°17S 73°26E **272** d
Fu'an *China* 27°11N 119°36E **229** D12
Fubian *China* 31°17N 102°22E **228** B4
Fucécchio *Italy* 43°44N 10°48E **198** E7
Fucheng *China* 37°50N 116°10E **226** F9
Fuchou = Fuzhou *China* 26°5N 119°16E **229** D12
Fuchū *Hiroshima, Japan* 34°34N 133°14E **222** C5
Fuchū *Tōkyō, Japan* 35°40N 139°29E **140** A1
Fuchuan *China* 24°50N 111°5E **229** E8
Fuchun Jiang → *China* 30°5N 120°5E **229** B13
Fúcino, Piana del *Italy* 42°1N 13°31E **199** F10
Fuding *China* 27°20N 120°12E **229** D13
Fuencaliente *Canary Is.* 28°28N 17°50W **153** e1
Fuencaliente *Spain* 38°25N 4°18W **195** G6
Fuencaliente, Pta. *Canary Is.* 28°27N 17°51W **153** e1
Fuencarral *Spain* 40°29N 3°42W **127** B1
Fuengirola *Spain* 36°32N 4°41W **195** J6
Fuenlabrada *Spain* 40°17N 3°48W **127** C1
Fuensalida *Spain* 40°3N 4°12W **194** E6
Fuente-Álamo *Spain* 38°44N 1°24W **197** G3
Fuente Álamo de Murcia *Spain* 37°42N 1°6W **197** H3
Fuente de Cantos *Spain* 38°15N 6°18W **195** G4
Fuente del Maestre *Spain* 38°31N 6°28W **195** G4
Fuente el Fresno *Spain* 39°14N 3°46W **195** F7
Fuente Obejuna *Spain* 38°15N 5°25W **195** G5
Fuente Palmera *Spain* 37°42N 5°6W **195** H5
Fuentes de Andalucía *Spain* 37°28N 5°20W **195** H5
Fuentes de Ebro *Spain* 41°31N 0°38W **196** D4
Fuentes de León *Spain* 38°5N 6°32W **195** G4
Fuentes de Oñoro *Spain* 40°33N 6°52W **194** E4
Fuentesaúco *Spain* 41°15N 5°30W **194** D5
Fuerte → *Mexico* 25°54N 109°22W **318** B3
Fuerte Olimpo *Paraguay* 21°0S 57°51W **334** A4
Fuerteventura *Canary Is.* 28°30N 14°0W **153** e2
Fuerteventura ✈ (FUE) *Canary Is.* 28°24N 13°52W **153** e2
Fufeng *China* 34°22N 108°0E **226** G5
Fuga I. *Phil.* 18°52N 121°20E **232** B3
Fugong *China* 27°5N 98°47E **228** D2
Fugou *China* 34°3N 114°25E **226** G8
Fugu *China* 39°2N 111°3E **226** E6
Fuhai *China* 47°2N 87°25E **217** C11
Fuḩaymī *Iraq* 34°16N 42°10E **213** E10
Fuhlsbüttel, Hamburg ✈ (HAM) *Germany* 53°35N 9°59E **178** B5
Fuhsien = Fu Xian *China* 36°0N 109°20E **226** G5
Fuhsing *Changhua, Taiwan* 24°3N 120°25E **225** B2
Fuhsing *Kaohsung, Taiwan* 23°13N 120°48E **225** C2
Fuhsing *Taoyüan, Taiwan* 24°49N 121°21E **225** B3
Fuidhaigh = Wiay *U.K.* 57°24N 7°13W **167** D1
Fuji *Japan* 35°9N 138°39E **223** B10
Fuji-Hakone-Izu △ *Japan* 35°15N 138°45E **223** B10
Fuji-San *Japan* 35°22N 138°44E **223** B10
Fuji-Yoshida *Japan* 35°30N 138°46E **223** B10
Fujian □ *China* 26°0N 118°0E **229** E12
Fujieda *Japan* 34°52N 138°16E **223** C10
Fujin *China* 47°16N 132°1E **219** B15
Fujinomiya *Japan* 35°10N 138°40E **223** B10
Fujioka *Japan* 36°15N 139°5E **223** A11
Fujisawa *Japan* 35°22N 139°29E **223** B11
Fujiyama, Mt. = Fuji-San *Japan* 35°22N 138°44E **223** B10
Fukagawa *Hokkaidō, Japan* 43°43N 142°2E **220** C11
Fukagawa *Tōkyō, Japan* 35°39N 139°48E **140** B3
Fukang *China* 44°10N 87°59E **217** D11
Fukaya *Japan* 36°12N 139°12E **223** A11
Fukiage *Japan* 31°27N 130°17E **222** F2
Fukiage Imperial Garden *Tokyo, Japan* **140** a4
Fukien = Fujian □ *China* 26°0N 118°0E **229** E12
Fukuchiyama *Japan* 35°19N 135°9E **223** B7
Fukue *Japan* 32°41N 128°51E **221** H4
Fukue-Shima *Japan* 32°40N 128°45E **221** H4
Fukuei Chiao *Taiwan* 25°17N 121°32E **225** A3
Fukui *Japan* 36°5N 136°10E **223** A8
Fukui □ *Japan* 36°0N 136°12E **223** B8
Fukuma *Japan* 33°46N 130°28E **222** D2
Fukuoka *Japan* 33°39N 130°21E **222** D2
Fukuoka □ *Japan* 33°30N 131°0E **222** D3
Fukuoka Int. ✈ (FUK) *Japan* 33°34N 130°28E **222** D2
Fukuroi *Japan* 34°45N 137°55E **223** C9
Fukushima *Fukushima, Japan* 37°44N 140°28E **220** F10
Fukushima *Ōsaka, Japan* 34°41N 135°28E **133** A1
Fukushima □ *Japan* 37°30N 140°15E **220** F10
Fukuyama *Japan* 34°35N 133°20E **222** C5
Ful Bura *South Sudan* 7°50N 31°50E **257** F3
Fulacunda *Guinea-Biss.* 11°44N 15°3W **262** C1
Fulaga *Fiji* 19°8S 178°33W **287** B3
Fulan → *Sweden* 61°18N 13°4E **162** C7
Fulda *Germany* 50°32N 9°40E **178** E5
Fulda → *Germany* 51°25N 9°39E **178** D5
Fulford = North Miami Beach *U.S.A.* 25°55N 80°9W **129** C2
Fulford Harbour *Canada* 48°47N 123°27W **306** B3
Fulham *U.K.* 51°28N 0°12W **125** B2
Fuli *Taiwan* 23°11N 121°14E **225** C3
Fuliang *China* 29°23N 117°14E **229** C11
Fuling *China* 29°39N 107°17E **228** C6
Fullarton *Trin. & Tob.* 10°5N 61°54W **323** t
Fullerton *Calif., U.S.A.* 33°53N 117°56W **307** M9
Fullerton *Nebr., U.S.A.* 41°22N 97°58W **308** E5
Fulongquan *China* 44°20N 124°42E **227** B13
Fülöpszállás *Hungary* 46°49N 19°15E **182** D4
Fulton *Ill., U.S.A.* 41°52N 90°11W **310** C6
Fulton *Ind., U.S.A.* 40°57N 86°16W **311** D10
Fulton *Mo., U.S.A.* 38°52N 91°57W **310** F5
Fulton *N.Y., U.S.A.* 43°19N 76°25W **313** C8
Fulufjället *Sweden* 61°32N 12°41E **162** C6
Fumay *France* 49°58N 4°40E **173** C11
Fumel *France* 44°30N 0°58E **174** D4
Fumin *China* 25°10N 102°20E **228** E4
Funabashi *Japan* 35°45N 140°0E **223** B12
Funabori *Japan* 35°41N 139°52E **140** A4
Funafuti = Fongafale *Tuvalu* 8°31S 179°13E **277** B14
Funafuti *Pac. Oc.* 8°31S 179°13E **277** B14
Funan *China* 32°39N 115°42E **229** A10
Funäsdalen *Sweden* 62°33N 12°32E **162** B6
Funchal *Madeira* 32°38N 16°54W **153** c
Funchal ✈ (FNC) *Madeira* 32°42N 16°45W **153** c
Fundación *Colombia* 10°31N 74°11W **328** A3
Fundão *Brazil* 19°55S 40°24W **333** E3
Fundão *Portugal* 40°8N 7°30W **194** E3
Fundão, I. do *Brazil* 22°51S 43°13W **135** B1
Fundong *Cameroon* 6°15N 10°16E **264** A2
Fundu Moldovei *Romania* 47°32N 25°24E **183** C10
Fundulea *Romania* 44°28N 26°31E **183** F11
Fundy, B. of *Canada* 45°0N 66°0W **299** D6
Fundy △ *Canada* 45°35N 65°10W **299** C6
Fünfhaus *Austria* 48°11N 16°20E **142** A2
Fünfkirchen = Pécs *Hungary* 46°5N 18°15E **182** D3
Funhalouro *Mozam.* 23°3S 34°25E **271** B5
Funing *Hebei, China* 39°53N 119°12E **227** E10
Funing *Jiangsu, China* 33°45N 119°50E **227** H10
Funing *Yunnan, China* 23°35N 105°45E **228** F5
Funiu Shan *China* 33°30N 112°20E **226** H7
Funsi *Ghana* 10°21N 1°54W **262** C4
Funtua *Nigeria* 11°30N 7°18E **263** C6
Fuping *Hebei, China* 38°48N 114°12E **226** E8
Fuping *Shaanxi, China* 34°42N 109°10E **226** G5
Fuqing *China* 25°41N 119°21E **229** E12
Fuquan *China* 26°40N 107°27E **228** D6
Furano *Japan* 43°21N 142°23E **220** C11
Furāt, Nahr al → *Asia* 31°0N 47°25E **246** D5
Furesø *Denmark* 55°47N 12°25E **118** A2
Fūrg *Iran* 28°18N 55°13E **247** D7
Furkating *India* 26°28N 93°59E **241** B4
Furman *U.S.A.* 32°41N 81°11W **316** C8
Furmanov *Russia* 57°10N 41°9E **190** B5
Furnas *Azores* 37°46N 25°19W **153** d3
Furnás *Spain* 39°3N 1°32E **206** C2
Furnas, Represa de *Brazil* 20°50S 45°30W **333** F2
Furneaux Group *Australia* 40°10S 147°50E **281** G4
Furqlus *Syria* 34°36N 37°8E **250** D8
Fürstenau *Germany* 52°31N 7°40E **178** C3
Fürstenberg = Eisenhüttenstadt *Germany* 52°9N 14°38E **178** C10
Fürstenberg *Germany* 53°10N 13°8E **178** B9
Fürstenfeld *Austria* 47°3N 16°3E **180** D9

Fürstenfeldbruck Germany 48°11N 11°15E 179 G7
Fürstenwalde Germany 52°22N 14°3E 178 C10
Fürth Mittelfranken, Germany 49°28N 10°59E 179 F6
Fürth Oberbayern, Germany 48°12N 11°35E 131 B2
Fürth im Wald Germany 49°18N 12°50E 179 F8
Furtwangen Germany 48°2N 8°12E 179 G4
Furudal Sweden 61°10N 15°11E 162 C9
Furukawa = Hida Japan 36°14N 137°11E 223 A9
Furukawa = Ōsaki Japan 38°34N 140°58E 220 E10
Furulund Sweden 55°46N 13°6E 163 J7
Furuvik Sweden 61°38N 17°20E 162 D11
Fury and Hecla Str. Canada 69°56N 84°0W 295 D15
Fusagasugá Colombia 4°21N 74°22W 328 C3
Fuscaldo Italy 39°25N 16°2E 201 C9
Fushan Shandong, China 37°30N 121°15E 227 F11
Fushan Shanxi, China 35°58N 111°51E 226 G6
Fushë Arrëz Albania 42°4N 20°2E 202 D4
Fushë Kosovë Kosovo 42°40N 21°5E 202 D5
Fushë Krujë Albania 41°29N 19°43E 202 E3
Fushun Liaoning, China 41°50N 123°56E 224 B1
Fushun Sichuan, China 29°13N 104°52E 228 C5
Fusong China 42°20N 127°15E 224 A3
Füssen Germany 47°34N 10°42E 179 H6
Fusui China 22°40N 107°56E 228 F6
Futago-tamagawaen Japan 35°36N 139°39E 140 B2
Futago-Yama Japan 33°35N 131°36E 222 D3
Futian China 22°32N 114°4E 219 a
Futiga Amer. Samoa 14°21S 170°45W 302 f
Futog Serbia 45°15N 19°42E 182 E4
Futrono Chile 40°8S 72°24W 336 B2
Futtsu Japan 35°13N 139°49E 223 B11
Fuwa Egypt 31°12N 30°33E 256 H7
Fuxian Hu China 24°30N 102°53E 228 E4
Fuxin China 42°5N 121°48E 227 C11
Fuxing Dao China 31°16N 121°33E 138 B2
Fuxing Park China 31°13N 121°27E 138 B2
Fuxinglu China 39°52N 116°16E 114 B1
Fuyang Anhui, China 33°0N 115°48E 229 A10
Fuyang Zhejiang, China 30°5N 119°57E 229 B12
Fuyang He → China 38°12N 117°0E 226 E9
Fuying Dao China 26°34N 120°9E 229 D13
Fuyong China 22°40N 113°49E 219 a
Fuyot Springs △ Phil. 17°1N 121°58E 232 C3
Fuyu Heilongjiang, China 47°49N 124°27E 219 B13
Fuyu Jilin, China 45°12N 124°43E 227 B13
Fuyuan China 25°40N 104°16E 228 E5
Fuyun China 47°0N 89°28E 217 C11
Füzesgyarmat Hungary 47°6N 21°14E 182 C6
Fuzhou = Linchuan China 27°57N 116°15E 229 D11
Fuzhou China 26°5N 119°16E 229 D12
Füzuli Azerbaijan 39°36N 47°8E 213 C12
Fyn Denmark 55°20N 10°30E 163 J4
Fyne, L. U.K. 55°59N 5°23W 167 F3
Fynshav Denmark 54°59N 9°59E 163 K3
Fyresdal Norway 59°11N 8°5E 164 E5
Fyresvatn Norway 59°6N 8°10E 164 E5
Fyzabad = Faizabad India 26°45N 82°10E 243 F10
Fyzabad Trin. & Tob. 10°12N 61°33W 323 t

G

G. Ross Lord Park Canada 43°47N 79°28W 141 A2
Ga Ghana 9°47N 2°30W 262 D4
Ga-eun S. Korea 36°38N 128°5E 224 D4
Gaa Faru Atoll Maldives 4°45N 73°26E 272 d
Gaalkacyo Somalia 6°30N 47°30E 267 C6
Gaanda Nigeria 10°10N 12°27E 263 C7
Gabaldon Phil. 15°37N 121°20E 232 D3
Gabas → France 43°46N 0°42W 174 E3
Gabba Australia 9°45S 142°38E 280 a
Gabela Angola 11°0S 14°24E 265 E2
Gaberones = Gaborone Botswana 24°45S 25°57E 270 B4
Gabès Tunisia 33°53N 10°2E 258 B2
Gabès □ Tunisia 33°35N 9°30E 261 B6
Gabès, G. de Tunisia 34°0N 10°30E 258 B2
Gabgaba, W. → Egypt 22°10N 33°5E 256 C3
Gabia Dem. Rep. of the Congo 4°37S 17°14E 265 C3
Gabia la Grande Spain 37°8N 3°40W 195 H7
Gąbin Poland 52°23N 19°41E 185 F6
Gablonz = Jablonec nad Nisou Czech Rep. 50°43N 15°10E 180 A8
Gabon ■ Africa 0°10S 10°0E 264 C2
Gabon → Gabon 0°25N 9°20E 264 B1
Gaborone Botswana 24°45S 25°57E 270 B4
Gabrat Sai'd Sudan 16°6N 31°50E 266 A3
Gabriels U.S.A. 44°26N 74°12W 313 B10
Gābrīk Iran 25°44N 58°28E 247 E8
Gabro Ethiopia 6°18N 43°16E 267 C5
Gabrovo Bulgaria 42°52N 25°19E 203 D9
Gabú = Nova Lamego Guinea-Biss. 12°19N 14°11W 262 C2
Gacé France 48°49N 0°20E 172 D7
Gāch Sār Iran 36°7N 51°19E 247 B6
Gachsārān Iran 30°15N 50°45E 247 D6
Gacko Bos.-H. 43°10N 18°33E 202 C2
Gad Hinglaj India 16°14N 74°21E 245 F2
Gadag India 15°30N 75°45E 245 G2
Gadaisu Papua N. G. 10°22S 149°46E 286 F5
Gadamai Sudan 17°11N 36°10E 257 D4
Gadap Pakistan 25°5N 67°28E 242 G2
Gadarwara India 22°50N 78°50E 243 H8
Gadebusch Germany 53°42N 11°7E 178 B7
Gadein South Sudan 8°10N 28°45E 257 F2
Gadhada India 22°0N 71°35E 242 J4
Gadis → Indonesia 1°2N 98°55E 234 B1
Gádor, Sierra de Spain 36°57N 2°45W 195 J8
Gadra Pakistan 25°40N 70°38E 242 G4
Gadsden Ala., U.S.A. 34°1N 86°1W 316 A3
Gadsden S.C., U.S.A. 33°51N 80°46W 316 B9
Gadwal India 16°10N 77°50E 245 F3
Gadyach = Hadyach Ukraine 50°21N 34°0E 189 G8
Gadzi C.A.R. 4°47N 16°42E 264 B3
Gaebong S. Korea 37°29N 126°52E 137 C1
Găeşti Romania 44°48N 25°19E 183 F10
Gaeta Italy 41°12N 13°35E 200 A6
Gaeta, G. di Italy 41°6N 13°30E 200 A6
Gaffney U.S.A. 35°5N 81°39W 315 D14
Gafsa Tunisia 34°24N 8°43E 258 B1
Gafsa □ Tunisia 34°30N 8°48E 261 B6
Gagarawa Nigeria 12°25N 9°32E 263 C6
Gagaria India 25°43N 70°46E 242 G4
Gagarin Russia 55°38N 35°0E 188 E8
Găgăuzia □ Moldova 46°10N 28°40E 183 D13
Gage Park U.S.A. 41°47N 87°42W 119 C2
Gaggenau Germany 48°48N 8°18E 179 G4
Gaghamni Sudan 11°41N 28°19E 257 E2
Gagil-Tomil, I. Pac. Oc. 9°31N 138°12E 287 R16
Gagino Russia 55°15N 45°1E 190 C7
Gagliano del Capo Italy 39°50N 18°22E 201 C11
Gagnef Sweden 60°36N 15°56E 162 D9
Gagnoa Ivory C. 6°56N 6°16W 262 D3
Gagnon Canada 51°50N 68°5W 299 B6
Gagnon, L. Canada 62°3N 110°27W 297 A6
Gagny France 48°53N 2°32E 134 A4
Gago Coutinho São Tomé & Príncipe 0°1S 6°32E 265 a
Gagra Georgia 43°20N 40°10E 191 J5
Gahini Rwanda 1°50S 30°30E 268 C3
Gahmar India 25°27N 83°49E 243 G10
Gai Xian = Gaizhou China 40°22N 122°20E 224 B1
Gaibandha Bangla. 25°20N 89°36E 241 C2
Gaidouronisi Greece 34°53N 25°41E 207 F6
Gail U.S.A. 32°46N 101°27W 314 E4
Gail → Austria 46°36N 13°53E 180 E6
Gaillac France 43°54N 1°54E 174 E5
Gaillard Cut Panama 9°3N 79°40W 320 c
Gaillimh = Galway Ireland 53°17N 9°3W 166 C2
Gaillon France 49°10N 1°20E 172 C8
Gaimán Argentina 43°10S 65°25W 336 B3
Gaines U.S.A. 41°46N 77°35W 312 E7
Gainesville Fla., U.S.A. 29°40N 82°20W 317 F7
Gainesville Ga., U.S.A. 34°18N 83°50W 315 D13
Gainesville Mo., U.S.A. 36°36N 92°26W 308 G7
Gainesville Tex., U.S.A. 33°38N 97°8W 314 E6
Gainsborough U.K. 53°24N 0°46W 168 D7
Gairdner, L. Australia 31°30S 136°0E 282 A2
Gairloch U.K. 57°43N 5°41W 167 D3
Gairloch, L. U.K. 57°43N 5°45W 167 D3
Gaizhou China 40°22N 122°20E 224 B1
Gaj Croatia 45°28N 17°3E 182 E2
Gaj → Pakistan 26°26N 67°21E 242 F2
Gajendragarh India 15°44N 75°59E 245 G2
Gakona U.S.A. 62°18N 145°18W 303 E11
Gakuch Pakistan 36°7N 73°45E 243 A5
Gal Oya △ Sri Lanka 7°0N 81°20E 245 L5
Gal Oya Res. Sri Lanka 7°5N 81°30E 245 L5
Gal Tardo Somalia 3°34N 45°58E 267 D6
Galachipa Bangla. 22°8N 90°26E 241 D3
Galâla, Gebel el Egypt 29°21N 32°22E 256 J8
Galâla el Bahariya, G. el Egypt 29°22N 32°23E 251 J3
Galâla el Qiblîya, G. el Egypt 28°42N 32°22E 251 K3
Galán, Cerro Argentina 25°55S 66°52W 334 B2
Galana → Kenya 3°9S 40°8E 268 C5
Galangue Angola 13°42S 16°9E 265 E3
Galangue, Serra Angola 14°18S 15°52E 265 E3
Galanta Slovak Rep. 48°11N 17°45E 181 C10
Galapagar Spain 40°36N 3°58W 194 E7
Galápagos = Colón, Arch. de Ecuador 0°0 91°0W 330 a
Galapagos Fracture Zone Pac. Oc. 3°0N 110°0W 289 G17
Galapagos Rise Pac. Oc. 15°0S 95°0W 289 J18
Galashiels U.K. 55°37N 2°49W 167 F6
Galata Turkey 41°1N 28°58E 122 B1
Galata Tower Turkey 41°1N 28°59E 122 B1
Galatas Greece 37°30N 23°26E 204 D5
Galatea N.Z. 38°24S 176°45E 284 E5
Galateia Cyprus 35°25N 34°4E 207 E10
Galaţi Romania 45°27N 28°2E 183 E13
Galaţi □ Romania 45°45N 27°30E 183 E12
Galatia Turkey 39°30N 33°0E 212 C5
Galatina Italy 40°10N 18°10E 201 B11
Galátone Italy 40°9N 18°4E 201 B11
Galatsi Greece 38°1N 23°45E 112 A2
Galax U.S.A. 36°40N 80°56W 309 G13
Galaxidi Greece 38°22N 22°23E 204 C4
Galbīn Govĭ Mongolia 43°0N 107°0E 226 C4
Galcaio = Gaalkacyo Somalia 6°30N 47°30E 267 C6
Gáldar Canary Is. 28°9N 15°39W 153 e1
Galdhøpiggen Norway 61°38N 8°18E 164 C5
Galeana Chihuahua, Mexico 30°7N 107°38W 318 A3
Galeana Nuevo León, Mexico 24°50N 100°4W 318 A3
Galeão, Int. de ✕ (GIG) Brazil 22°49S 43°15W 135 A1
Galegu Sudan 12°36N 35°2E 257 E4
Galela Indonesia 1°50N 127°49E 231 D7
Galena Alaska, U.S.A. 64°44N 156°56W 303 D8
Galena Ill., U.S.A. 42°25N 90°26W 310 B6
Galeota Pt. Trin. & Tob. 10°8N 60°59W 323 t
Galera Spain 37°45N 2°33W 197 H2
Galera, Pta. Chile 39°59S 73°43W 336 A2
Galera, Pta. de Azores 37°42N 25°30W 153 d3
Galera Pt. Trin. & Tob. 10°49N 60°54W 323 t
Galeras Colombia 1°13N 77°20W 328 C2
Galesburg Ill., U.S.A. 40°57N 90°22W 310 D6
Galesburg Mich., U.S.A. 42°17N 85°26W 311 B11
Galestan △ Iran 37°30N 56°0E 247 B8
Galeton U.S.A. 41°44N 77°39W 312 E7
Galets → Réunion 20°56S 55°17E 272 f
Galga Ethiopia 6°39N 37°47E 257 F4
Galgasc Somalia 0°11N 41°38E 267 D5
Galguduud □ Somalia 5°0N 47°0E 267 D6
Galheirão → Brazil 12°23S 45°5W 333 D2
Gali Georgia 42°37N 41°46E 191 J5
Galicea Mare Romania 44°4N 23°19E 183 F8
Galich Russia 58°22N 42°24E 190 A6
Galiche Bulgaria 43°34N 23°53E 202 C7
Galicia □ Spain 42°43N 7°45W 194 C3
Galičica △ Macedonia 41°2N 20°55E 202 E4
Galien U.S.A. 41°48N 86°30W 311 C10
Galilee = Hagalil Israel 32°53N 35°18E 250 F6
Galilee, L. Australia 22°20S 145°50E 280 C4
Galilee, Sea of = Yam Kinneret Israel 32°45N 35°35E 250 F6
Galim Cameroon 7°6N 12°25E 263 D7
Galina Pt. Jamaica 18°24N 76°58W 320 a
Galinoporni Cyprus 35°31N 34°18E 207 E10
Galion U.S.A. 40°44N 82°47W 312 F2
Galion, B. du Martinique 14°44N 60°56W 322 j
Galite, Îs. de la Tunisia 37°30N 8°59E 261 A6
Galiuro Mts. U.S.A. 32°30N 110°20W 305 K8
Galiwinku Australia 12°2S 135°34E 280 A2
Gallâbât Sudan 12°58N 36°11E 257 E4
Gallan Hd. U.K. 58°15N 7°2W 167 C1
Gallarate Italy 45°40N 8°48E 198 C5
Gallatin Mo., U.S.A. 39°55N 93°58W 310 E3
Gallatin Tenn., U.S.A. 36°24N 86°27W 315 C11
Galle Sri Lanka 6°5N 80°10E 245 L5
Gállego → Spain 41°39N 0°51W 196 D4
Gallegos → Argentina 51°35S 69°0W 336 D3
Gallery of Inuit Art = Dominion Centre Toronto, Canada 141 b2
Galletti → Ethiopia 8°46N 41°10E 257 F5
Galley Hd. Ireland 51°32N 8°55W 166 E3
Galliate Italy 45°29N 8°42E 198 C5
Gallinas, Pta. Colombia 12°28N 71°40W 328 A3
Gallipoli = Gelibolu Turkey 40°28N 26°43E 203 F10
Gallípoli Italy 40°3N 17°58E 201 B10
Gallipolis U.S.A. 38°49N 82°12W 309 F12
Gällivare Sweden 67°9N 20°40E 160 C19
Gallneukirchen Austria 48°21N 14°25E 180 C7
Gällö Sweden 62°55N 15°13E 162 B9
Gallo, C. Italy 38°13N 13°19E 200 D6
Gallocanta, L. de Spain 40°58N 1°30W 196 E3
Galloo I. U.S.A. 43°55N 76°25W 313 C8
Galloway U.K. 55°1N 4°29W 167 F4
Galloway, Mull of U.K. 54°39N 4°52W 167 G4
Gallup U.S.A. 35°32N 108°45W 305 J9
Gallur Spain 41°52N 1°19W 196 D3
Galluro Italy 41°59N 9°20E 200 A2
Galma Galla Kenya 1°11S 40°47E 267 E5
Galmudug Somalia 6°30N 48°0E 267 C6
Galong Australia 34°37S 148°34E 283 C8
Galoya Sri Lanka 8°10N 80°55E 245 K5
Galt Calif., U.S.A. 38°15N 121°18W 306 G5
Galt Mo., U.S.A. 40°8N 93°23W 310 D3
Galten Denmark 56°9N 9°54E 163 H3
Galtür Austria 46°58N 10°11E 180 E3
Galty Mts. Ireland 52°22N 8°10W 166 D3
Galtymore Ireland 52°21N 8°11W 166 D3
Galugāh Iran 36°43N 53°48E 247 B7
Galva U.S.A. 41°10N 90°3W 310 C6
Galvarino Chile 38°24S 72°47W 336 A2
Galve de Sorbe Spain 41°13N 3°10W 196 D1
Galveston Ind., U.S.A. 40°35N 86°11W 311 D10
Galveston Tex., U.S.A. 29°18N 94°48W 314 G7
Galveston B. U.S.A. 29°36N 94°50W 314 G7
Gálvez Argentina 32°0S 61°14W 334 C3
Galway Ireland 53°17N 9°3W 166 C2
Galway □ Ireland 53°22N 9°1W 166 C2
Galway B. Ireland 53°13N 9°10W 166 C2
Galyanovo Russia 55°48N 37°47E 129 B3
Gam → Vietnam 21°55N 105°12E 236 B5
Gamagōri Japan 34°50N 137°14E 223 C9
Gamari, L. Ethiopia 11°32N 41°40E 257 E5
Gamawa Nigeria 12°10N 10°31E 263 C7
Gamay Phil. 12°23N 125°18E 232 E5
Gamay B. Phil. 12°21N 125°21E 232 E5
Gamba Angola 11°42S 17°21E 265 E3
Gambaga Ghana 10°30N 0°28W 263 C4
Gambat Pakistan 27°17N 68°26E 242 F3
Gambela Ethiopia 8°14N 34°38E 257 F3
Gambela △ Ethiopia 8°0N 34°0E 257 F3
Gambela Hizboch □ Ethiopia 8°0N 34°0E 257 F3
Gambell U.S.A. 63°47N 171°45W 303 E5
Gambhir → India 26°58N 77°27E 242 F6
Gambia ■ W. Afr. 13°25N 16°0W 262 C1
Gambia → W. Afr. 13°28N 16°34W 262 C1
Gambier U.S.A. 40°22N 82°23W 312 F2
Gambier, C. Australia 11°56S 130°57E 278 D5
Gambier, Îs. French Polynesia 23°8S 134°58W 289 f
Gambier Is. Australia 35°3S 136°30E 282 C2
Gambier Village Bahamas 25°4N 77°30W 153 e1
Gambir Indonesia 6°9S 106°48E 122 A1
Gambo C.A.R. 4°39N 22°16E 264 B4
Gambo Canada 48°47N 54°13W 299 C9
Gamboa Rio de J., Brazil 22°53S 43°11W 135 B1
Gamboa Panama 9°7N 79°42W 320 c
Gamboli Pakistan 29°53N 68°24E 242 E3
Gambolòita Italy 45°26N 9°13E 128 B2
Gamboma Congo 1°55S 15°52E 264 C3
Gamboula C.A.R. 4°8N 15°9E 264 B3
Gamka → S. Africa 33°18S 21°39E 270 D3
Gamkab → Namibia 28°4S 17°54E 270 C2
Gamla Stan Stockholm, Sweden 139 c2
Gamla Uppsala Sweden 59°54N 17°40E 162 E11
Gamlakarleby = Kokkola Finland 63°50N 23°8E 160 E20
Gamleby Sweden 57°54N 16°24E 163 G10
Gamlebyen Norway 59°54N 10°46E 133 A3
Gammon → Canada 51°24N 95°44W 297 C9
Gammon Ranges △ Australia 30°38S 139°8E 281 E2
Gamo-Gofa Ethiopia 5°40N 36°40E 257 F4
Gamoda-Saki Japan 33°50N 134°45E 222 D6
Gamou Niger 14°20N 9°55E 259 F1
Gampaha Sri Lanka 7°5N 79°59E 245 L4
Gampo S. Korea 35°48N 129°31E 224 E4
Gampola Sri Lanka 7°10N 80°34E 245 L5
Gamtoos → S. Africa 33°58S 25°1E 270 D4
Gamzigrad-Romuliana Serbia 43°53N 22°11E 202 C6
Gan France 43°12N 0°27W 174 E3
Gan ✕ (GAN) Maldives 0°41S 73°1E 272 d
Gan Gan Argentina 42°30S 68°10W 336 B3
Gan Goriama, Mts. Cameroon 7°44N 12°45E 263 D7
Gan Jiang → China 29°15N 116°0E 229 C11
Ganado U.S.A. 35°43N 109°33W 305 J9
Gananita Sudan 18°22N 33°50E 256 D3
Gananoque Canada 44°20N 76°10W 313 B8
Ganassi Phil. 7°49N 124°6E 233 H5
Ganāveh Iran 29°35N 50°35E 247 D6
Gäncä Azerbaijan 40°45N 46°20E 191 K8
Gancheng China 18°51N 108°37E 229 a
Gand = Gent Belgium 51°2N 3°42E 170 C3
Ganda Angola 13°3S 14°35E 265 E2
Gandajika Dem. Rep. of the Congo 6°46S 23°58E 265 D4
Gandak → India 25°39N 85°13E 243 G11
Gandara Phil. 12°1N 124°49E 232 E5
Gandava Pakistan 28°32N 67°32E 242 E2
Gander Canada 48°58N 54°35W 299 C9
Gander L. Canada 48°58N 54°35W 299 C9
Ganderkesee Germany 53°2N 8°32E 178 B4
Ganderowe Falls Zimbabwe 17°20S 29°10E 269 F2
Gandesa Spain 41°3N 0°26E 196 D5
Gandhi Sagar India 24°40N 75°40E 242 G6
Gandhinagar India 23°15N 72°45E 242 H5
Gandi Nigeria 12°55N 5°49E 263 C6
Gandia Spain 38°58N 0°9W 197 G4
Gandino Italy 45°49N 9°54E 198 C6
Gando, Pta. Canary Is. 27°55N 15°22W 153 e1
Gandole Nigeria 8°28N 11°35E 263 D7
Gandou Congo 2°25N 17°25E 264 B3
Gandu Brazil 13°45S 39°30W 333 D4
Gâneb Mauritania 18°29N 10°8W 262 B2
Ganedidalem = Gani Indonesia 0°48S 128°14E 231 E7
Ganga → India 23°20N 90°30E 243 H14
Ganga Sagar India 21°38N 88°5E 243 J13
Gangafani Mali 14°20N 2°20W 262 C4
Gangakher India 18°57N 76°45E 244 E3
Gangan → India 28°38N 78°58E 243 E8
Ganganagar India 29°56N 73°56E 242 E5
Gangapur Maharashtra, India 19°41N 75°1E 244 E2
Gangapur Raj., India 26°32N 76°49E 242 F7
Gangara Niger 14°35N 8°29E 259 F1
Gangaw Burma 22°5N 94°5E 241 D5
Gangaw Taungdan Burma 24°55N 96°35E 241 C6
Gangawati India 15°30N 76°36E 245 G3
Gangdisê Shan China 31°20N 81°0E 243 D9
Gangdong S. Korea 37°30N 127°5E 137 B2
Ganges = Ganga → India 23°20N 90°30E 243 H14
Ganges Canada 48°51N 123°31W 296 D4
Ganges Hérault, France 43°56N 3°42E 174 E7
Ganges, Mouths of the India 21°30N 90°0E 241 E3
Ganggyeong S. Korea 36°10N 127°0E 224 D3
Gånghester Sweden 57°42N 13°1E 163 G7
Ganghwa S. Korea 37°45N 126°30E 224 D3
Gangi Italy 37°48N 14°12E 201 E7
Gângiova Romania 43°54N 23°50E 183 G8
Gangnam S. Korea 37°30N 126°59E 137 B1
Gangneung S. Korea 37°45N 128°54E 224 D4
Gangoh India 29°46N 77°18E 242 E7
Gangotri India 30°50N 79°10E 243 D8
Gangotri △ India 30°50N 79°10E 243 D8
Gangseo S. Korea 37°32N 126°51E 137 B1
Gangseong S. Korea 38°24N 128°30E 224 C4
Gangshan = Kangshan Taiwan 22°48N 120°17E 225 D2
Gangtok India 27°20N 88°37E 241 B2
Gangtou China 23°12N 113°8E 121 A1
Gangu China 34°40N 105°15E 226 G3
Gangwa Dem. Rep. of the Congo 3°30S 20°54E 264 C4
Gangwei China 23°4N 113°16E 121 B2
Gangwon-do □ S. Korea 37°45N 128°15E 224 D4
Gangyao China 44°12N 126°37E 227 B14
Ganj India 27°45N 78°57E 243 F8
Ganjam India 19°23N 85°4E 244 E7
Ganjiakou China 39°54N 116°16E 114 B1
Ganluo China 28°58N 102°59E 228 C4
Ganmain Australia 34°47S 147°1E 283 C7
Ganna South Sudan 7°30N 28°0E 266 C2
Gannat France 46°7N 3°11E 173 F10
Gannett Peak U.S.A. 43°11N 109°39W 304 E9
Ganquan China 36°20N 109°20E 226 F5
Gänserdorf Austria 48°20N 16°43E 181 C9
Ganshoren Belgium 50°52N 4°18E 116 A1
Ganshui China 28°40N 106°40E 228 C6
Gansu □ China 36°0N 104°0E 226 G3
Ganta Liberia 7°15N 8°59W 262 D3
Gantheaume, C. Australia 36°4S 137°32E 282 D2
Gantheaume B. Australia 27°40S 114°10E 279 E1
Gants Hill U.K. 51°34N 0°4E 125 A4
Gantsevichi = Hantsavichy Belarus 52°49N 26°30E 177 B14
Gantung Indonesia 2°58S 108°9E 235 C3
Ganye Nigeria 8°25N 12°4E 263 D7
Ganyem = Genyem Indonesia 2°46S 140°12E 231 E10
Ganyu China 34°50N 119°8E 227 G10
Ganyushkino Kazakhstan 46°35N 49°20E 191 G9
Ganzhou China 25°51N 114°56E 229 E10
Gao Mali 16°15N 0°5W 263 B4
Gao Xian China 28°21N 104°32E 228 C5
Gao'an China 28°26N 115°17E 229 C10
Gaobeidian China 39°19N 115°51E 226 E8
Gaocheng China 38°2N 114°49E 226 E8
Gaochun China 31°20N 118°49E 229 B12
Gaohang China 31°20N 121°36E 138 B2
Gaohebu China 30°43N 116°49E 229 B11
Gaokeng China 27°40N 113°58E 229 D9
Gaolan Dao China 21°55N 113°10E 229 G9
Gaoligong Shan China 24°45N 98°45E 228 E2
Gaomi China 36°20N 119°42E 227 F10
Gaoping China 35°45N 112°55E 226 G7
Gaoqiao China 31°21N 121°34E 138 A2
Gaoshu = Kaoshu Taiwan 22°49N 120°36E 225 D2
Gaotang China 36°50N 116°15E 226 F9
Gaoua Burkina Faso 10°20N 3°8W 262 C4
Gaoual Guinea 11°45N 13°25W 262 C2
Gaoxiong = Kaohsiung Taiwan 22°35N 120°16E 225 D2
Gaoyang China 38°40N 115°45E 226 E8
Gaoyao China 23°3N 112°27E 229 F9
Gaoyou China 32°47N 119°26E 229 A12
Gaoyou Hu China 32°45N 119°20E 229 A12
Gaoyuan China 37°8N 117°58E 227 F9
Gaozhou China 21°58N 110°50E 229 G8
Gap France 44°33N 6°5E 175 D10
Gapan Phil. 15°19N 120°57E 232 D3
Gapat → India 24°30N 82°28E 243 G10
Gapuwiyak Australia 12°25S 135°43E 280 A2
Gar China 32°10N 79°58E 218 E4
Gara, L. Ireland 53°57N 8°26W 166 C3
Garāb Iran 33°27N 47°16E 213 F12
Garabogazköl Aylagy Turkmenistan 41°0N 53°30E 187 F9
Garacad Somalia 6°57N 49°24E 267 C6
Garachico Canary Is. 28°22N 16°46W 153 e1
Garachiné Panama 8°0N 78°12W 320 E4
Garafia Canary Is. 28°48N 17°57W 153 e1
Garagum Turkmenistan 39°30N 60°0E 247 B8
Garah Australia 29°5S 149°38E 281 D4
Garaina Papua N. G. 7°53S 147°8E 286 D4
Garajonay Canary Is. 28°7N 17°14W 153 e1
Garajonay △ Canary Is. 28°7N 17°14W 153 e1
Garamba △ Dem. Rep. of the Congo 4°10N 29°40E 268 B2
Garango Burkina Faso 11°48N 0°34W 263 C4
Garanhuns Brazil 8°50S 36°30W 332 C4
Garapan N. Marianas 15°12N 145°43E 302 e
Garautha India 25°34N 79°18E 243 G8
Garawa ⊙ Australia 16°43S 136°51E 280 B2
Garawe Liberia 4°35N 8°0W 262 E3
Garba Harre = Garbahaarrey Somalia 3°19N 42°13E 267 D5
Garba Tula Kenya 0°30N 38°32E 268 B4
Garbagnate Milanese Italy 45°34N 9°4E 128 A1
Garbaguddu Ethiopia 6°12N 43°50E 267 C5
Garbahaarrey → Somalia 3°19N 42°13E 267 D5
Garbatella Italy 41°51N 12°30E 136 B2
Garberville U.S.A. 40°6N 123°48W 304 F2
Garbiyang India 30°8N 80°54E 243 D9
Garbsen Germany 52°26N 9°31E 178 C5
Garça Brazil 22°14S 49°37W 333 F2
Garças → Mato Grosso, Brazil 15°54S 52°16W 331 D7
Garças → Pernambuco, Brazil 8°43S 39°41W 332 C4
Garches France 48°50N 2°11E 134 A2
Garching Germany 48°14N 11°39E 131 A3
Garchitorena Phil. 13°52N 123°40E 232 E4
Garcia Hernandez Phil. 9°37N 124°18E 233 G5
Garcias Brazil 20°34S 52°13W 331 E7
Gard □ France 44°2N 4°10E 175 D8
Gard → France 43°51N 4°37E 175 E8
Garda, L. di Italy 45°40N 10°41E 198 C7
Gardabani Georgia 41°27N 45°5E 191 K7
Gardanne France 43°27N 5°27E 175 E9
Gårdby Sweden 56°36N 16°38E 163 H10
Garde L. Canada 62°50N 106°13W 297 A7
Gardelegen Germany 52°32N 11°23E 178 C7
Garden City El Qâhira, Egypt 30°2N 31°14E 117 A2
Garden City Ga., U.S.A. 32°6N 81°9W 316 C8
Garden City Kans., U.S.A. 37°58N 100°53W 308 G3
Garden City Mo., U.S.A. 38°34N 94°12W 310 F2
Garden City Tex., U.S.A. 31°52N 101°29W 314 F4
Garden District U.S.A. 29°56N 90°5W 132 B2
Garden Grove U.S.A. 33°47N 117°55W 307 M9
Garden Reach India 22°33N 88°15E 124 B1
Gardens of Stone △ Australia 33°14S 150°11E 283 B9
Garder Norway 59°45N 10°38E 133 B2
Gardez Afghan. 33°37N 69°9E 242 C3
Garðabær Iceland 64°5N 21°55W 155 C5
Garðskagi Iceland 64°5N 22°43W 155 C4
Garður Iceland 66°4N 16°46W 155 A10
Gardiki Greece 38°50N 21°55E 204 C3
Gardiner Maine, U.S.A. 44°14N 69°47W 309 C19
Gardiner Mont., U.S.A. 45°2N 110°22W 304 D8
Gardiners I. U.S.A. 41°6N 72°6W 313 E12
Gardner Fla., U.S.A. 27°21N 81°48W 317 H8
Gardner Ill., U.S.A. 41°12N 88°17W 311 C8
Gardner Mass., U.S.A. 42°34N 71°59W 313 D13
Gardner Canal Canada 53°27N 128°8W 296 C3
Gardner Pinnacles U.S.A. 25°0N 167°55W 302 F10
Gardnerville U.S.A. 38°56N 119°45W 306 G7
Gardno, Jezioro Poland 54°40N 17°7E 184 D4
Gardo = Qardho Somalia 9°30N 49°6E 267 C6
Gardone Riviera Italy 45°37N 10°34E 198 C7
Gardone Val Trómpia Italy 45°41N 10°11E 198 C7
Gárdony Hungary 47°12N 18°39E 182 C3
Gare Tigre Fr. Guiana 4°58N 53°9W 329 C7
Gareloi I. U.S.A. 51°48N 178°48W 303 L3
Gares = Puente la Reina Spain 42°40N 1°49W 196 C3
Garešnica Croatia 45°36N 16°56E 199 C13
Garéssio Italy 44°12N 8°2E 198 D5
Garey U.S.A. 34°53N 120°19W 307 L6
Garfield N.J., U.S.A. 40°52N 74°7W 132 A1
Garfield Wash., U.S.A. 47°1N 117°9W 304 C5
Garfield Park U.S.A. 41°52N 87°42W 119 B2
Garforth U.K. 53°47N 1°24W 168 D6
Gargaliani Greece 37°4N 21°38E 204 D3
Gargan, Mt. France 45°37N 1°39E 174 C5
Gargano △ Italy 41°43N 15°52E 199 G12
Gargantua, C. Canada 47°36N 85°2W 309 B11
Gargareta Greece 37°57N 23°43E 112 B2
Gargett Australia 21°9S 148°46E 280 b
Gargouna Mali 15°56N 0°13E 263 B5
Gargždai Lithuania 55°43N 21°24E 184 C8
Garhchiroli India 20°10N 80°0E 244 D5
Garibaldi ⌓ Canada 49°50N 122°40W 296 D4
Garibong S. Korea 37°29N 126°54E 137 C1
Gariep, L. S. Africa 30°40S 25°40E 270 D4
Garies S. Africa 30°32S 17°59E 270 D2
Garig Gunak Barlu △ Australia 11°26S 131°58E 278 B5
Garigliano → Italy 41°13N 13°45E 200 A6
Garissa Kenya 0°25S 39°40E 268 C4
Garkida Nigeria 10°27N 12°36E 263 C7
Garko Nigeria 11°45N 8°35E 263 C6
Garland Tex., U.S.A. 32°54N 96°38W 314 E6
Garland Utah, U.S.A. 41°45N 112°10W 304 F7
Garlasco Italy 45°12N 8°55E 198 C5
Garliava Lithuania 54°49N 23°52E 184 D10
Garlin France 43°33N 0°16W 174 E3
Garmāb Semnān, Iran 35°25N 56°45E 247 C8
Garmāb Zanjān, Iran 35°50N 48°11E 213 E13
Garmisch-Partenkirchen Germany 47°30N 11°6E 179 H7
Garmo, Qullai = imeni Ismail Samani, Pik Tajikistan 39°0N 72°2E 217 E8
Garmsār Iran 35°20N 52°25E 247 C7
Garner U.S.A. 43°6N 93°36W 310 A3
Garnett U.S.A. 38°17N 95°14W 308 F6
Garnpung, L. Australia 33°25S 143°10E 282 B5
Garo Hills India 25°30N 90°30E 241 C3
Garoe = Garoowe Somalia 8°25N 48°33E 267 C6
Garonne → France 45°2N 0°36W 173 C6
Garonne, Canal Latéral à la France 44°15N 0°18E 174 D4
Garoowe Somalia 8°25N 48°33E 267 C6
Garorimman S. Korea 36°54N 126°21E 224 D3
Garot India 24°19N 75°41E 242 G6
Garou, L. Mali 16°2N 2°45W 262 B4
Garoua Cameroon 9°19N 13°21E 263 D7
Garoua Boulaï Cameroon 5°53N 14°33E 264 A2
Garove I. Papua N. G. 4°42S 149°30E 286 C5
Garpenberg Sweden 60°19N 16°12E 162 D10
Garphyttan Sweden 59°18N 14°56E 162 E8
Garrauli India 25°5N 79°22E 243 G8
Garrel Germany 52°57N 8°1E 178 C4
Garreru Palau 7°19N 134°32E 288 c
Garrett U.S.A. 41°21N 85°8W 311 C11
Garrison Ky., U.S.A. 38°36N 83°10W 311 F13
Garrison Mont., U.S.A. 46°31N 112°49W 304 C7
Garrison N. Dak., U.S.A. 47°40N 101°25W 308 B3
Garrison Res. = Sakakawea, L. U.S.A. 47°30N 101°25W 308 B3
Garron Pt. U.K. 55°3N 5°59W 166 A6
Garrovillas de Alconétar Spain 39°40N 6°33W 195 F4
Garrucha Spain 37°11N 1°49W 197 H3
Garry → U.K. 56°44N 3°47W 167 E5
Garry, L. Canada 65°58N 100°18W 294 D11
Garrygala Turkmenistan 38°31N 56°29E 247 B8
Garsen Kenya 2°20S 40°5E 268 C5
Gärsnäs Sweden 55°32N 14°10E 163 J8
Garson L. Canada 56°19N 110°2W 297 B6
Garstang U.K. 53°55N 2°46W 168 D5
Gartempe → France 46°47N 0°49E 174 B4
Gartz Germany 53°13N 14°22E 178 B10
Garu Ghana 10°55N 0°11W 263 C4
Garu India 23°40N 84°14E 243 H11
Garub Namibia 26°37S 16°0E 270 C2
Garusuun Palau 7°21N 134°34E 288 c
Garut Indonesia 7°14S 107°53E 235 D3
Garvanza U.S.A. 34°6N 118°11W 126 B3
Garvão Portugal 37°42N 8°21W 195 H2
Garvie Mts. N.Z. 45°30S 168°50E 285 F3
Garwa = Garoua Cameroon 9°19N 13°21E 263 D7
Garwa India 24°11N 83°47E 243 G10
Garwolin Poland 51°55N 21°38E 185 G8
Gary U.S.A. 41°36N 87°20W 311 C9
Garz Germany 54°19N 13°20E 178 A9
Garzê China 31°38N 100°1E 228 B3
Garzón Colombia 2°10N 75°40W 328 C2
Gas City U.S.A. 40°29N 85°37W 311 D11
Gas-San Japan 38°32N 140°1E 220 E10
Gasa Bhutan 27°55N 89°44E 241 B2
Gasan Phil. 13°19N 121°51E 232 E3
Gasan Kuli = Esenguly Turkmenistan 37°37N 53°59E 216 E4
Gascogne France 43°45N 0°20E 174 E4
Gascogne, G. de Europe 44°0N 2°0W 196 B2
Gasconade U.S.A. 38°40N 91°34W 310 F5
Gasconade → U.S.A. 38°41N 91°33W 310 F5
Gascony = Gascogne France 43°45N 0°20E 174 E4
Gascoyne → Australia 24°52S 113°37E 279 D1
Gascoyne Junction Australia 25°2S 115°17E 279 E2
Gascueña Spain 40°18N 2°31W 196 E2
Gash, Wadi → Africa 16°48N 35°51E 257 D4
Gash Setit ⌓ Eritrea 15°12N 36°58E 257 D4
Gåshaga Sweden 59°21N 18°13E 139 A3
Gashagar Nigeria 13°22N 12°47E 263 C7
Gashaka Nigeria 7°20N 11°29E 263 D7
Gashaka-Gumti △ Nigeria 7°23N 11°34E 263 D7
Gasherbrum Pakistan 35°40N 76°40E 243 B7
Gashua Nigeria 12°54N 11°0E 263 C7
Gasmata Papua N. G. 6°17S 150°20E 286 D6
Gaspar Grande Trin. & Tob. 10°40N 61°39W 323 t
Gaspar Str. = Gelasa, Selat Indonesia 2°50S 107°0E 235 C3
Gasparilla I. U.S.A. 26°46N 82°16W 317 J7
Gasparillo Trin. & Tob. 10°18N 61°26W 323 t
Gasparito Curaçao 12°8N 68°56W 322 g
Gaspé Canada 48°52N 64°30W 299 C7
Gaspé, C. de Canada 48°48N 64°7W 299 C7
Gaspé Pen. = Gaspésie, Pén. de la Canada 48°45N 65°40W 299 C6
Gaspésie, Pén. de la Canada 48°45N 65°40W 299 C6
Gaspésie ⌓ Canada 48°55N 66°10W 299 C6
Gassan Burkina Faso 12°49N 3°12W 262 C4
Gassen = Jasień Poland 51°46N 15°0E 185 G2
Gassol Nigeria 8°34N 10°25E 263 D7
Gasteiz = Vitoria-Gasteiz Spain 42°50N 2°41W 196 C2
Gaston U.S.A. 33°49N 81°5W 316 B8
Gastonia U.S.A. 35°16N 81°11W 315 D14
Gastouni Greece 37°51N 21°15E 204 D3
Gastouri Greece 39°34N 19°54E 206 B1
Gastre Argentina 42°20S 69°15W 336 B3
Gästrikland Sweden 60°45N 16°40E 162 D10
Gata, C. Cyprus 34°34N 33°2E 207 F9
Gata, C. de Spain 36°41N 2°13W 197 J2
Gata, Sierra de Spain 40°20N 6°45W 194 E4
Gataga → Canada 58°35N 126°59W 296 B3
Gătaia Romania 45°26N 21°30E 182 E6
Gatchina Russia 59°35N 30°9E 188 C6
Gatehouse of Fleet U.K. 54°53N 4°12W 167 G4
Gates U.S.A. 43°9N 77°42W 312 C7
Gates of the Arctic ⌓ U.S.A. 67°45N 153°15W 303 C9
Gateshead U.K. 54°57N 1°35W 168 C6
Gateshead I. Canada 70°36N 100°26W 294 C11
Gatesville U.S.A. 31°26N 97°45W 314 F6
Gateway ⌓ U.S.A. 40°38N 73°51W 132 C2
Gateway of India India 18°55N 72°50E 130 B2
Gaths Zimbabwe 20°2S 30°32E 269 G3
Gâtinais France 48°5N 2°40E 173 D9
Gâtine, Hauteurs de France 46°35N 0°45W 174 B3
Gatineau Canada 45°29N 75°39W 313 A9
Gatineau → Canada 45°27N 75°42W 298 C4
Gatineau △ Canada 45°40N 76°0W 298 C4
Gatow Germany 52°29N 13°11E 115 B1
Gattaran Phil. 18°4N 121°38E 232 B3
Gattinara Italy 45°37N 8°22E 198 C5
Gatton Australia 27°32S 152°17E 281 D5
Gatún, L. Panama 9°7N 79°56W 320 c
Gatún Dam Panama 9°16N 79°55W 320 c
Gatún Locks Panama 9°16N 79°55W 320 c
Gatwick, London ✕ (LGW) U.K. 51°10N 0°11W 169 F7
Gatyana S. Africa 32°16S 28°31E 271 D4
Gau Fiji 18°2S 179°18E 287 B2
Gaua Vanuatu 14°15S 167°30E 287 D5
Gaucín Spain 36°31N 5°19W 195 J5
Gauer L. Canada 57°0N 97°50W 297 B9
Gauhati = Guwahati India 26°10N 91°45E 241 B3
Gauja → Latvia 57°10N 24°16E 188 D3
Gaujas △ Latvia 57°10N 24°50E 161 H21
Gaula → Norway 63°21N 10°14E 164 A7
Gaupne Norway 61°25N 7°18E 164 C4
Gaurdak = Gowurdak Turkmenistan 37°50N 66°4E 217 E7
Gauri Phanta India 28°41N 80°36E 243 E9
Gauribidanur India 13°37N 77°32E 245 H3
Gaustatoppen Norway 59°48N 8°40E 164 E5
Gauteng □ S. Africa 26°0S 28°0E 271 C4
Gāv Koshī Iran 28°38N 57°12E 247 D8
Gavà Spain 41°18N 2°1W 114 B1
Gāvakān Iran 29°37N 53°10E 247 D7
Gavamar Spain 41°15N 2°1E 114 B1
Gavarnie France 42°44N 0°1W 174 F3
Gaväter Iran 25°10N 61°31E 247 E9
Gāvbandī Iran 27°12N 53°4E 247 E7
Gavdopoula Greece 34°56N 24°0E 207 F5
Gavdos Greece 34°50N 24°5E 207 F5
Gávea Brazil 22°58S 43°13W 135 B1
Gávea, Pedra da Brazil 22°59S 43°18W 135 B1
Gavi Italy 44°41N 8°49E 198 D5
Gavião Portugal 39°28N 7°56W 195 F3
Gaviota U.S.A. 34°29N 120°13W 307 L6
Gāvkhūnī, Bāţlāq-e Iran 32°6N 52°52E 247 C7
Gävle Sweden 60°40N 17°9E 162 D11
Gävleborgs län □ Sweden 61°30N 16°15E 162 C10
Gävlebukten Sweden 60°40N 17°20E 162 D11
Gavorrano Italy 42°55N 10°54E 198 F7
Gavray France 48°55N 1°20W 172 D5
Gavrilov Yam Russia 57°18N 39°49E 188 D10
Gavrio Greece 37°54N 24°44E 204 D6
Gawachab Namibia 27°4S 17°55E 270 C2
Gawai Burma 27°56N 97°30E 241 B6
Gawilgarh Hills India 21°15N 76°45E 244 D3
Gawler Australia 34°30S 138°42E 282 C3
Gawler Ranges Australia 32°30S 135°45E 282 B2
Gawu Nigeria 9°14N 6°52E 263 D6
Gaxun Nur China 42°22N 100°30E 218 C9
Gay Russia 51°27N 58°27E 186 D10
Gay Ga., U.S.A. 33°6N 84°35W 316 B5
Gaya India 24°47N 85°4E 243 G11
Gaya Niger 11°52N 3°28E 263 C5
Gaya Nigeria 11°57N 9°0E 263 C6
Gayasan △ S. Korea 35°45N 128°10E 224 E4
Gayéri Burkina Faso 12°39N 0°29E 263 C5
Gaylord U.S.A. 45°2N 84°41W 309 C11
Gayndah Australia 25°35S 151°32E 281 D5
Gaysin = Haysyn Ukraine 48°57N 29°25E 183 B14
Gayvoron = Hayvoron Ukraine 48°22N 29°52E 183 B14
Gaza Gaza Strip 31°30N 34°28E 251 G5
Gaza □ Mozam. 23°10S 32°45E 271 B5
Gaza Strip ■ Asia 31°29N 34°25E 251 G5
Gazanjyk = Bereket Turkmenistan 39°16N 55°32E 247 B7
Gazaoua Niger 13°32N 7°55E 263 C6
Gāzbor Iran 28°5N 58°51E 247 D8
Gazdagrét Hungary 47°29N 19°0E 117 B1
Gazelle Pen. Papua N. G. 4°40S 152°0E 286 C7
Gazi Dem. Rep. of the Congo 1°3N 24°30E 264 B4
Gaziantep Turkey 37°6N 37°23E 250 A8
Gaziantep □ Turkey 37°0N 37°0E 250 B8
Gazimağusa = Famagusta Cyprus 35°8N 33°55E 207 E9
Gaziosmanpaşa Turkey 41°5N 28°50E 122 B1
Gazipaşa Turkey 36°16N 32°18E 250 B3
Gazipur Bangla. 23°48N 90°39E 241 D3
Gazli Uzbekistan 40°8N 63°27E 216 D6
Gbadolite Dem. Rep. of the Congo 4°17N 21°1E 264 B4
Gbarnga Liberia 7°19N 9°13W 262 D3
Gboko Nigeria 7°17N 9°4E 263 D6
Gcoverega Botswana 19°8S 24°18E 270 A3
Gcuwa S. Africa 32°20S 28°11E 271 D4
Gdańsk Poland 54°22N 18°40E 184 D5
Gdańsk ✕ (GDN) Poland 54°22N 18°30E 184 D5
Gdańska, Zatoka Poland 54°30N 19°20E 184 D6
Gdingen = Gdynia Poland 54°35N 18°33E 184 D5
Gdov Russia 58°48N 27°55E 188 C4
Gdynia Poland 54°35N 18°33E 184 D5
Geba → Guinea-Biss. 11°46N 15°36W 262 C1
Gebe Indonesia 0°5N 129°25E 231 D7
Gebeciler Turkey 38°46N 30°46E 205 C12
Gebeit Mine Sudan 21°3N 36°29E 256 C4
Gebel Abyad Sudan 19°0N 28°0E 256 D2
Gebel el Ahmar Egypt 30°2N 31°21E 117 A2
Gebel el Muqattam Egypt 30°1N 31°17E 117 A2
Gebel el Tura Egypt 29°56N 31°15E 117 B2
Gebel Iweibid Egypt 30°2N 31°32E 256 H8
Gebiley Somalia 9°42N 43°37E 267 C5
Gebze Turkey 40°47N 29°25E 203 F13
Gecha Ethiopia 7°30N 35°18E 257 F4
Geçitkale = Lefkoniko Cyprus 35°18N 33°44E 207 D12
Gedaref Sudan 14°2N 35°28E 257 E4
Gedaref □ Sudan 14°0N 35°0E 257 E4
Gede, Tanjung Indonesia 6°46S 105°12E 234 D3
Gediz Turkey 39°1N 29°24E 205 B11
Gediz → Turkey 38°35N 26°48E 205 C8
Gedo Ethiopia 9°2N 37°25E 257 F4
Gedo □ Somalia 3°15N 42°10E 267 D5
Gèdre France 42°47N 0°2E 174 F4
Gedser Denmark 54°35N 11°55E 163 K5
Gedung, Pulau Malaysia 5°17N 100°23E 237 c
Geegully Cr. → Australia 18°32S 123°41E 278 C3
Geel Belgium 51°10N 4°59E 170 C4
Geelong Australia 38°10S 144°22E 282 E6
Geelvink B. = Cenderawasih, Teluk Indonesia 3°0S 135°20E 231 E9
Geelvink Chan. Australia 28°30S 114°0E 279 E1
Geesthacht Germany 53°26N 10°22E 178 B6
Geidam Nigeria 12°57N 11°57E 263 C7
Geikie → Canada 57°45N 103°52W 297 B8
Geikie Gorge △ Australia 18°3S 125°41E 278 C4
Geilenkirchen Germany 50°57N 6°8E 178 E2
Geili Sudan 16°1N 32°37E 257 D3
Geilo Norway 60°32N 8°14E 164 D5
Geiranger Norway 62°7N 7°10E 164 B4
Geirangerfjorden Norway 62°5N 7°0E 164 B4
Geiselgasteig Germany 48°3N 11°33E 131 B2
Geisingen Germany 47°54N 8°38E 179 H4

Geislingen Germany 48°37N 9°50E 179 G5
Geistown U.S.A. 40°18N 78°52W 312 F6
Geita Tanzania 2°48S 32°12E 268 C3
Geitastrand Norway 63°22N 9°56E 164 A6
Geithus Norway 59°57N 9°59E 164 E6
Gejiu China 23°20N 103°10E 228 F4
Gel → South Sudan 7°5N 29°10E 257 F2
Gel, Meydān-e Iran 29°4N 54°50E 247 D7
Gel River South Sudan 7°5N 29°10E 257 F2
Gela Italy 37°4N 14°15E 201 F7
Gela, G. di Italy 37°0N 14°20E 201 F7
Geladi Ethiopia 6°59N 46°30E 267 C6
Gelahun Liberia 7°55N 10°28W 262 D2
Gelam Indonesia 2°54S 110°11E 235 C4
Gelang Patah Malaysia 1°27N 103°35E 237 d
Gelasa, Selat Indonesia 2°50S 107°0E 235 C3
Gelderland □ Neths. 52°5N 6°10E 170 B6
Geldern Germany 51°31N 6°20E 178 D2
Geldrop Neths. 51°25N 5°32E 170 C5
Geleen Neths. 50°57N 5°49E 170 D5
Gelehun S. Leone 8°20N 11°40W 262 D2
Gelembe Turkey 39°10N 27°50E 205 B9
Gelemso Ethiopia 8°49N 40°31E 257 F5
Gelendost Turkey 38°7N 31°1E 212 C4
Gelendzhik Russia 44°33N 38°10E 189 K10
Gelib = Jilib Somalia 0°29N 42°46E 267 D5
Gelibolu Turkey 40°28N 26°43E 203 F10
Gelibolu Yarımadası Turkey 40°20N 26°30E 203 F10
Gelidonya Burnu Turkey 36°12N 30°24E 212 D4
Gellinsoor Somalia 6°28N 46°39E 267 C6
Gelnhausen Germany 50°11N 9°11E 179 E5
Gelnica Slovak Rep. 48°51N 20°55E 181 C13
Gelora Bung Karno Stadium Jakarta, Indonesia 6°13S 106°47E 122 B1
Gelsenkirchen Germany 51°32N 7°6E 178 D3
Gelting Germany 54°45N 9°53E 178 A5
Gelugur Malaysia 5°22N 100°18E 237 c
Gemas Malaysia 2°37N 102°36E 237 L4
Gembloux Belgium 50°34N 4°43E 170 D4
Gembu Nigeria 6°42N 11°10E 263 D7
Gemena Dem. Rep. of the Congo 3°13N 19°48E 264 B3
Gemerek Turkey 39°15N 36°10E 212 C7
Gemikonağı = Karavostasi Cyprus 35°8N 32°50E 207 E8
Gemla Sweden 56°52N 14°39E 163 H8
Gemlik Turkey 40°26N 29°9E 203 F13
Gemlik Körfezi Turkey 40°25N 28°55E 203 F12
Gemona del Friuli Italy 46°16N 13°9E 199 B10
Gemsa Egypt 27°39N 33°35E 256 B3
Gemsbok △ Botswana 25°5S 21°1E 270 C3
Gemünden Germany 50°3N 9°42E 179 E5
Genadi Greece 36°2N 27°56E 206 E11
Genale → Ethiopia 6°2N 39°1E 257 F4
Genç Turkey 38°44N 40°34E 213 C9
Gençay France 46°23N 0°23E 174 B4
General Acha Argentina 37°20S 64°38W 334 D3
General Alvear B. Aires, Argentina 36°0S 60°0W 334 D4
General Alvear Mendoza, Argentina 35°0S 67°40W 334 D2
General Artigas Paraguay 26°52S 56°16W 334 B4
General Belgrano Argentina 36°35S 58°47W 334 D4
General Bernardo O'Higgins Antarctica 63°0S 58°3W 151 C18
General Cabrera Argentina 32°53S 63°52W 334 C3
General Carrera, L. S. Amer. 46°35S 72°0W 336 C2
General Cepeda Mexico 25°21N 101°22W 318 B4
General Conesa Argentina 40°6S 64°25W 336 B4
General Eugenio A. Garay Paraguay 20°31S 62°8W 331 E5
General Germán Busch = Villa Abecia Bolivia 21°0S 68°18W 334 A2
General Guido Argentina 36°40S 57°50W 334 D4
General Juan Madariaga Argentina 37°0S 57°0W 334 D4
General La Madrid Argentina 37°17S 61°20W 334 D3
General Lorenzo Vintter Argentina 40°45S 64°26W 336 B4
General Luna Phil. 13°41N 122°10E 232 E4
General MacArthur Phil. 11°18N 125°28E 233 F5
General Martin Miguel de Güemes Argentina 24°50S 65°0W 334 A3
General Pico Argentina 35°45S 63°50W 334 D3
General Pinedo Argentina 27°15S 61°20W 334 B3
General Pinto Argentina 34°45S 61°50W 334 C3
General Roca Argentina 39°2S 67°35W 336 A3
General Sampaio Brazil 4°2S 39°29W 332 B4
General San Martín Argentina 34°35S 58°32W 117 B1
General Santos Phil. 6°5N 125°14E 233 H5
General Tinio Phil. 15°39N 121°10E 232 D3
General Toshevo Bulgaria 43°42N 28°6E 203 C12
General Treviño Mexico 26°14N 99°29W 319 B5
General Trías Mexico 28°21N 106°22W 318 B3
General Uriburu = Zárate Argentina 34°7S 59°0W 334 C4
General Viamonte Argentina 35°1S 61°3W 334 D3
General Villegas Argentina 35°5S 63°0W 334 D3
General Vintter, L. Argentina 43°55S 71°40W 336 B2
Generoso Ponce = Jaci-Paraná Brazil 9°15S 64°23W 331 B5
Genesee Idaho, U.S.A. 46°33N 116°56W 304 C5
Genesee Pa., U.S.A. 41°59N 77°54W 312 E7
Genesee → U.S.A. 43°16N 77°36W 312 C7
Geneseo Ill., U.S.A. 41°27N 90°9W 310 C6
Geneseo N.Y., U.S.A. 42°48N 77°49W 312 D7
Geneva = Genève Switz. 46°12N 6°9E 179 J2
Geneva Ala., U.S.A. 31°2N 85°52W 316 D4
Geneva Ga., U.S.A. 32°35N 84°33W 316 C5
Geneva Ill., U.S.A. 41°53N 88°18W 311 D8
Geneva Ind., U.S.A. 40°36N 84°58W 311 D12
Geneva N.Y., U.S.A. 42°52N 76°59W 312 D8
Geneva Nebr., U.S.A. 40°32N 97°36W 308 E5
Geneva Ohio, U.S.A. 41°48N 80°57W 312 E4
Geneva, L. = Léman, L. Europe 46°26N 6°30E 173 F13
Geneva, L. U.S.A. 42°38N 88°30W 311 B8
Genève Switz. 46°12N 6°9E 179 J2
Geng Afghan. 31°22N 61°28E 240 C1
Gengenbach Germany 48°24N 8°1E 179 G4
Gengma China 23°32N 99°20E 228 F2
Genhe China 50°47N 121°31E 219 A13
Genichesk = Henichesk Ukraine 46°12N 34°50E 189 J8
Genil → Spain 37°42N 5°19W 195 H5
Génipa, B. de Martinique 14°33N 61°0W 322 j
Genisea Greece 41°1N 24°57E 203 E8
Genk Belgium 50°58N 5°32E 170 D5
Genkai-Nada Japan 34°0N 130°0E 222 D2
Genlis France 47°11N 5°12E 173 E12
Gennargentu, Mti. del Italy 40°1N 9°19E 200 B2
Gennes France 47°20N 0°17W 172 E6
Gennevilliers France 48°56N 2°17E 134 A2
Genoa = Génova Italy 44°25N 8°57E 198 D5
Genoa Vic., Australia 37°29S 149°35E 283 D8
Genoa Ill., U.S.A. 42°6N 88°42W 311 B8
Genoa N.Y., U.S.A. 42°40N 76°32W 313 D8
Genoa Nebr., U.S.A. 41°27N 97°44W 308 E5
Genoa Nev., U.S.A. 39°2N 119°50W 306 F7
Genoa → Argentina 44°55S 70°5W 336 B2
Genoa City U.S.A. 42°30N 88°20W 311 B8
Génova Italy 44°25N 8°57E 198 D5
Génova ✈ (GOA) Italy 44°25N 8°56E 198 D5
Génova, G. di Italy 44°0N 9°0E 198 E6
Genovesa, I. Ecuador 0°20N 89°58W 330 a
Genriyetty, Ostrov Russia 77°6N 156°30E 215 B16
Gent Belgium 51°2N 3°42E 170 C3
Genteng Jawa Barat, Indonesia 7°22S 106°24E 234 D3
Genteng Jawa Timur, Indonesia 8°22S 114°9E 231 J17
Genthin Germany 52°25N 12°9E 178 C8
Gentilly Val-de-Marne, France 48°48N 2°21E 134 B3
Gentilly La., U.S.A. 30°0N 90°2W 131 A2
Gentio do Ouro Brazil 11°25S 42°30W 332 D3
Gentofte Denmark 55°44N 12°32E 118 A3
Gentryville U.S.A. 38°6N 87°2W 311 F9
Genval Belgium 50°43N 4°29E 116 B2
Genyem Indonesia 2°46S 140°12E 231 E10
Genzano di Lucánia Italy 40°51N 16°2E 201 B9
Genzano di Roma Italy 41°42N 12°41E 199 G9
Geoagiu Romania 45°55N 23°12E 183 E8
Geochang S. Korea 35°41N 127°55E 224 E3
Geogeumdo S. Korea 34°27N 127°10E 224 E3
Geographe B. Australia 33°30S 115°15E 279 F2
Geographe Chan. Australia 24°30S 113°0E 279 D1
Geographical Society Ø Greenland 72°57N 23°15W 154 C8
Geoje S. Korea 34°51N 128°35E 224 E4
Geojedo S. Korea 34°51N 128°38E 224 E4
Geokchay = Göyçay Azerbaijan 40°42N 47°43E 191 K8
Georga, Zemlya Russia 80°30N 49°0E 214 A5
George S. Africa 33°58S 22°29E 270 D3
George → Canada 58°49N 66°10W 299 A6
George, L. N.S.W., Australia 35°10S 149°25E 283 C8
George, L. S. Austral., Australia 37°25S 140°0E 282 D4
George, L. W. Austral., Australia 22°45S 123°40E 278 D3
George, L. Uganda 0°5N 30°10E 268 B3
George, L. Fla., U.S.A. 29°17N 81°36W 317 F8
George, L. N.Y., U.S.A. 43°37N 73°33W 313 C11
George Gill Ra. Australia 24°22S 131°45E 278 D5
George I. Hong Kong, China 22°13N 114°7E 122 B2
George I. St. Helena 15°58S 5°38W 153 h
George Pt. Australia 20°6S 148°36E 280 b
George River = Kangiqsualujjuaq Canada 58°30N 65°59W 295 F18
George Rogers Clark Nat. Memorial ⌂ U.S.A. 38°41N 87°32W 311 F9
George Sound N.Z. 44°52S 167°25E 285 E2
George Town Tas., Australia 41°6S 146°49E 281 G4
George Town Bahamas 23°33N 75°47W 320 B4
George Town Cayman Is. 19°20N 81°24W 320 C3
George Town Malaysia 5°25N 100°20E 237 c
George V Land Antarctica 69°0S 148°0E 151 C10
George VI Sound Antarctica 71°0S 68°0W 151 D17
George West U.S.A. 28°20N 98°7W 314 G5
Georges River Bridge Australia 34°0S 151°6E 139 C1
Georgetown = Janjanbureh Gambia 13°30N 14°47W 262 C2
Georgetown Ascension I. 7°56S 14°25W 153 g
Georgetown Queens., Australia 18°17S 143°33E 280 B3
Georgetown Ont., Canada 43°40N 79°56W 312 C5
Georgetown P.E.I., Canada 46°13N 62°24W 299 C7
Georgetown Guyana 6°50N 58°12W 329 B6
Georgetown St. Vincent 13°16N 61°7W 323 n
Georgetown Calif., U.S.A. 38°54N 120°50W 306 G6
Georgetown Colo., U.S.A. 39°42N 105°42W 304 G11
Georgetown D.C., U.S.A. 38°54N 77°3W 143 B2
Georgetown Fla., U.S.A. 29°23N 81°38W 317 F8
Georgetown Ga., U.S.A. 31°53N 85°6W 316 D4
Georgetown Ill., U.S.A. 39°59N 87°38W 311 E9
Georgetown Ky., U.S.A. 38°13N 84°33W 311 F12
Georgetown N.Y., U.S.A. 42°46N 75°44W 313 D9
Georgetown Ohio, U.S.A. 38°52N 83°54W 311 F13
Georgetown S.C., U.S.A. 33°23N 79°17W 315 E15
Georgetown Tex., U.S.A. 30°38N 97°41W 314 F6
Georgia □ U.S.A. 32°50N 83°15W 316 C6
Georgia ■ Asia 42°0N 43°0E 191 J6
Georgia, Str. of N. Amer. 49°25N 124°0W 306 A3
Georgia Aquarium Atlanta, U.S.A. 33°46N 84°23W 113 B2
Georgia Basin S. Ocean 50°45S 35°30W 151 B1
Georgia Dome U.S.A. 33°45N 84°23W 113 B2
Georgian B. Canada 45°15N 81°0W 312 A4
Georgian Bay Islands △ Canada 44°53N 79°52W 312 B5
Georgievka Kazakhstan 49°19N 84°34E 217 C10
Georgina → Australia 23°30S 139°47E 280 C2
Georgina I. Canada 44°22N 79°17W 312 B5
Georgioupoli Greece 35°20N 24°15E 207 E5
Georgiu-Dezh = Liski Russia 51°3N 39°30E 189 G10
Georgiyevsk Russia 44°12N 43°28E 191 H6
Georgsmarienhütte Germany 52°13N 8°3E 178 C4
Gera Germany 50°53N 12°4E 178 E8
Geraardsbergen Belgium 50°45N 3°53E 170 D3
Geraki Greece 37°0N 22°42E 204 D4
Geraki, Akra Greece 37°42N 20°59E 207 D2
Geral, Serra Bahia, Brazil 14°0S 41°0W 333 D3
Geral, Serra Goiás, Brazil 11°15S 46°30W 332 D2
Geral, Serra Sta. Catarina, Brazil 26°25S 50°0W 335 B6
Geral de Goiás, Serra Brazil 12°0S 46°0W 332 D2
Geral do Paraná, Serra Brazil 15°0S 47°30W 333 E2
Gerald U.S.A. 38°24N 91°20W 310 F5
Geraldine N.Z. 44°5S 171°15E 285 E6
Geraldine Mont., U.S.A. 47°36N 110°16W 304 C8
Geraldton = Innisfail Australia 17°33S 146°5E 280 B4
Geraldton W. Austral., Australia 28°48S 114°32E 279 E1
Geraldton Ont., Canada 49°44N 87°10W 298 C2
Geranium Australia 35°23S 140°11E 282 C4
Gérardmer France 48°3N 6°50E 173 D13
Gerasdorf bei Wien Austria 48°17N 16°28E 142 A2
Gerberau Germany 48°12N 11°27E 131 A1
Gercüş Turkey 37°34N 41°23E 213 D9
Gerdine, Mt. U.S.A. 61°35N 152°27W 303 F9
Gerede Turkey 40°45N 32°10E 212 B5
Gerês, Sierra do Portugal 41°48N 8°0W 194 D3
Gereshk Afghan. 31°47N 64°35E 240 C2
Geretsried Germany 47°51N 11°28E 179 H7
Gérgal Spain 37°7N 2°31W 197 H2
Gerik Malaysia 5°50N 101°15E 237 K3
Gering U.S.A. 41°50N 103°40W 308 E2
Geriş Turkey 36°57N 31°43E 250 B2
Gerlach U.S.A. 40°39N 119°21W 304 F4
Gerlachovský štít Slovak Rep. 49°11N 20°7E 181 B13
Gerli Argentina 34°41S 58°22W 117 C2
Gerlogubi Ethiopia 6°53N 45°3E 267 C6
German Bight = Deutsche Bucht Germany 54°15N 8°0E 178 A4
German East Africa = Tanzania ■ Africa 6°0S 34°0E 268 D3
German Planina Macedonia 42°20N 22°0E 202 D6
German South West Africa = Namibia ■ Africa 22°0S 18°9E 270 B2
Germania Land Greenland 77°5N 19°30W 154 B9
Germansen Landing Canada 55°43N 124°40W 296 B4
Germantown Ohio, U.S.A. 39°38N 84°22W 311 E12
Germantown Tenn., U.S.A. 35°5N 89°49W 315 D10
Germantown Wis., U.S.A. 43°14N 88°6W 311 A8
Germany ■ Europe 51°0N 10°0E 178 E6
Germencik Turkey 37°52N 27°37E 205 D9
Germering Germany 48°8N 11°22E 179 G7
Germersheim Germany 49°12N 8°22E 179 F4
Germī Iran 39°1N 48°3E 213 C13
Germiston S. Africa 26°13S 28°10E 123 B2
Gern Germany 48°10N 11°32E 131 B2
Gernene Algeria 21°40N 2°24E 261 D5
Gernika-Lumo Spain 43°19N 2°40W 196 B2
Gernsheim Germany 49°45N 8°30E 179 F4
Gero Japan 35°48N 137°14E 223 B9
Gerogery Australia 35°50S 147°0E 283 C7
Gerokgak Indonesia 8°11S 114°27E 231 J17
Gerolzhofen Germany 49°54N 10°21E 179 F6
Gerona = Girona Spain 41°58N 2°46E 196 D7
Gerona Phil. 15°36N 120°36E 232 D3
Geropotamos → Greece 35°3N 24°50E 207 E5
Gerrard Canada 50°30N 117°17W 296 C5
Gerringong Australia 34°46S 150°47E 283 C9
Gers □ France 43°35N 0°30E 174 E4
Gers → France 44°9N 0°39E 174 D4
Gersfeld Germany 50°27N 9°56E 178 E5
Gersoppa Falls India 14°12N 74°46E 245 G2
Gersthofen Germany 48°25N 10°53E 179 G6
Gertak Sanggul Malaysia 5°17N 100°12E 237 c
Gertak Sanggul, Tanjung Malaysia 5°16N 100°11E 237 c
Gerung Indonesia 8°43S 116°7E 231 K19
Géryville = El Bayadh Algeria 33°40N 1°1E 261 B5
Gerzat France 45°48N 3°8E 174 C7
Gerze Turkey 41°48N 35°12E 212 B6
Geseke Germany 51°38N 8°31E 178 D4
Geser Indonesia 3°50S 130°54E 231 E8
Gesira △ Somalia 1°58N 44°59E 267 D5
Gesso → Italy 44°24N 7°33E 198 D4
Gestro, Wabi → Ethiopia 4°12N 42°2E 257 G5
Gesuit, Ex Convento dei Venice, Italy 142 a3
Getafe Spain 40°18N 3°43W 127 C1
Getinge Sweden 56°49N 12°44E 163 H6
Getty Center, The U.S.A. 34°4N 118°29W 126 B2
Gettysburg Pa., U.S.A. 39°50N 77°14W 309 F15
Gettysburg S. Dak., U.S.A. 45°1N 99°57W 308 C4
Getxo = Algorta Spain 43°21N 2°59W 196 B2
Getz Ice Shelf Antarctica 75°0S 130°0W 151 D14
Geumdo S. Korea 34°31N 127°45E 224 E3
Geumpang Indonesia 4°52N 96°6E 234 B1
Geunjeong S. Korea 37°28N 126°54E 137 C1
Geureudong, Gunung Indonesia 4°13N 96°42E 234 B1
Geurie Australia 32°22S 148°50E 283 B8
Geva Binyamin West Bank 31°51N 35°17E 123 A2
Gevaş Turkey 38°15N 43°6E 213 C10
Gévaudan France 44°40N 3°40E 174 D7
Gevgelija Macedonia 41°9N 22°30E 202 E6
Gévora → Spain 38°53N 6°57W 195 G4
Gevrai India 19°16N 75°45E 244 E2
Gewani Ethiopia 10°12N 40°40E 257 E5
Gex France 46°21N 6°3E 173 F13
Geyikli Turkey 39°48N 26°12E 205 B8
Geylang Serai Singapore 1°19N 103°53E 138 B3
Geyser U.S.A. 47°16N 110°30W 304 C8
Geyserville U.S.A. 38°42N 122°54W 306 G4
Geysir Iceland 64°19N 20°18W 155 C6
Geyve Turkey 40°30N 30°18E 212 B4
Gezhouba Dam China 30°40N 111°20E 229 B8
Ghâbat el Arab = Wang Kai South Sudan 9°3N 29°23E 257 F2
Ghabeish Sudan 12°9N 27°21E 257 E2
Ghadāf, W. al → Iraq 32°56N 43°30E 213 F10
Ghadāmis Libya 30°11N 9°29E 258 B1
Ghaddūwah Libya 26°26N 14°19E 258 C2
Ghaggar → India 29°30N 74°53E 242 E6
Ghaghara → India 25°45N 84°40E 243 G11
Ghaghat → Bangla. 25°19N 89°38E 241 C2
Ghaghe Solomon Is. 7°24S 158°15E 287 L10
Ghagra India 23°17N 84°33E 243 H11
Ghagra → India 27°29N 81°9E 243 F9
Ghajn Tuffieha Bay Malta 35°56N 14°21E 206 F7
Ghajnsielem Malta 36°2N 14°17E 206 F7
Ghalla, Wadi el → Sudan 10°25N 27°32E 257 E2
Ghallamane Mauritania 23°15N 10°0W 260 D3
Ghallamane, Sebkhet Mauritania 23°41N 9°50W 260 D3
Ghamid az Zenad Si. Arabia 19°35N 41°24E 248 C3
Ghana ■ W. Afr. 8°0N 1°0W 263 D4
Ghanpokhara Nepal 28°17N 84°14E 243 E11
Ghansor India 22°39N 80°1E 243 H9
Ghanzi Botswana 21°50S 21°34E 270 B3
Ghanzi □ Botswana 22°30S 22°30E 270 B3
Gharapuri = Elephanta I. India 18°57N 72°56E 130 B2
Gharapuri India 18°57N 72°57E 130 B2
Gharb = Shahrak-e Qods Iran 35°47N 51°22E 141 A2
Gharb Malta 36°4N 14°13E 206 E6
Gharb Bahr el Ghazâl = Western Bahr el Ghazâl □ South Sudan 7°30N 25°30E 257 F2
Gharb-Chrarda-Beni Hssen □ Morocco 35°35N 6°0W 260 A3
Gharb Dârfûr □ Sudan 13°0N 23°0E 259 F4
Gharb el Istiwa'iya = Western Equatoria □ South Sudan 5°0N 30°0E 257 G3
Gharb Kordofân □ Sudan 12°0N 28°0E 257 E2
Gharbîya, Es Sahrâ el Egypt 27°40N 26°30E 256 B2
Ghardaïa Algeria 32°20N 3°37E 261 B5
Ghardaïa □ Algeria 31°5N 3°10E 261 B5
Ghârib, G. Egypt 28°6N 32°54E 256 B3
Gharig Sudan 10°47N 27°33E 257 E2
Gharm Tajikistan 39°0N 70°20E 214 F8
Gharm, W. → Oman 19°57N 57°38E 249 C7
Gharyān Libya 32°10N 13°0E 258 B2
Ghāt Libya 24°59N 10°11E 258 D2
Ghāt □ Libya 25°35N 10°15E 258 C2
Ghatal India 22°40N 87°46E 243 H12
Ghatampur India 26°8N 80°13E 243 F9
Ghatgaon India 21°24N 85°53E 244 D7
Ghatkopar India 19°4N 72°54E 130 A2
Ghatprabha → India 16°15N 75°20E 245 F2
Ghats, Eastern India 14°0N 78°50E 245 H4
Ghats, Western India 14°0N 75°0E 245 H2
Ghatsila India 22°36N 86°29E 243 H12
Ghaţţī Si. Arabia 31°16N 37°31E 246 D3
Ghawdex = Gozo Malta 36°3N 14°15E 206 F6
Ghayl Si. Arabia 21°40N 46°20E 248 B4
Ghayl Bā Wazīr Yemen 14°46N 49°22E 249 D5
Ghazal, Bahr el → Chad 13°0N 15°47E 259 F3
Ghazal, Bahr el → South Sudan 9°31N 30°25E 257 F3
Ghazaouet Algeria 35°8N 1°50W 261 A4
Ghaziabad India 28°42N 77°26E 242 E7
Ghazipur Delhi, India 28°37N 77°19E 120 B2
Ghazipur Ut. P., India 25°38N 83°35E 243 G10
Ghaznī Afghan. 33°30N 68°28E 242 C3
Ghaznī □ Afghan. 32°10N 68°20E 240 B3
Ghedi Italy 45°24N 10°16E 198 C7
Ghelari Romania 45°38N 22°45E 182 E7
Ghent = Gent Belgium 51°2N 3°42E 170 C3
Gheorghe Gheorghiu-Dej = Onești Romania 46°17N 26°47E 183 D11
Gheorgheni Romania 46°43N 25°41E 183 D10
Gherla Romania 47°2N 23°57E 183 C8
Ghidigeni Romania 46°3N 27°30E 183 D12
Ghilarza Italy 40°7N 8°50E 200 B1
Ghimeș-Făget Romania 46°35N 26°2E 183 D11
Ghīnah, Wādī al → Si. Arabia 30°27N 38°14E 246 D3
Ghirān, W. → Si. Arabia 20°52N 47°10E 248 B4
Ghirardelli Square San Francisco, U.S.A. 136 a1
Ghisonaccia France 42°1N 9°26E 175 F13
Ghisoni France 42°7N 9°12E 175 F13
Ghizar → Pakistan 36°15N 73°43E 243 A5
Ghizri Pakistan 24°49N 67°2E 123 B2
Ghizri Cr. → Pakistan 24°47N 67°5E 123 B2
Ghod → India 18°30N 74°35E 244 E2
Ghogha India 21°40N 72°20E 244 D1
Ghonda India 28°41N 77°16E 120 A2
Ghot Ogrein Egypt 31°10N 25°20E 256 A2
Ghotaru India 27°20N 70°1E 242 F4
Ghotki Pakistan 28°5N 69°21E 242 E3
Ghowr □ Afghan. 34°0N 64°20E 240 B2
Ghubbet el Bûs Egypt 29°35N 32°21E 251 J3
Ghughri India 22°39N 80°41E 243 H9
Ghugus India 19°58N 79°12E 244 E4
Ghulam Mohammad Barrage Pakistan 25°30N 68°20E 242 G3
Ghurayrah Si. Arabia 18°37N 42°41E 248 C3
Ghūriān Afghan. 34°17N 61°25E 240 B1
Ghusuri India 22°37N 88°21E 124 B2
Ghuzayyil, Sabkhat Libya 29°30N 19°30E 258 C3
Gia Dinh Vietnam 10°49N 106°42E 237 G6
Gia Lai = Plei Ku Vietnam 13°57N 108°0E 236 F7
Gia Nghia Vietnam 11°58N 107°42E 237 G6
Gia Ngoc Vietnam 14°50N 108°58E 236 E7
Gia Vuc Vietnam 14°42N 108°34E 236 E7
Giali Greece 36°41N 27°11E 205 E9
Gialtra Greece 38°51N 22°59E 204 C4
Giamama = Jamaame Somalia 0°4N 42°44E 267 D5
Gian Phil. 5°49N 125°12E 233 J5
Gianicolense Italy 41°53N 12°28E 136 B1
Gianicolense, Parco Rome, Italy 136 c1
Gianitsa Greece 40°46N 22°24E 202 F6
Giannutri Italy 42°15N 11°6E 198 F8
Giant Forest U.S.A. 36°36N 118°43W 306 J8
Giant Mts. = Krkonoše Czech Rep. 50°50N 15°35E 180 A8
Giant Sequoia ⌂ U.S.A. 36°10N 118°35W 306 K8
Giant Wheel = Riesenrad Austria 48°14N 16°23E 142 A2
Giants Causeway U.K. 55°16N 6°29W 166 A5
Giant's Tank Sri Lanka 8°51N 80°2E 245 K5
Gianyar Indonesia 8°32S 115°20E 231 K18
Giarabub = Al Jaghbūb Libya 29°42N 24°38E 258 C4
Giaros Greece 37°32N 24°40E 204 D6
Giarre Italy 37°43N 15°11E 201 E8
Giaveno Italy 45°2N 7°21E 198 C4
Gibara Cuba 21°9N 76°11W 320 B4
Gibbon U.S.A. 40°45N 98°51W 308 E4
Gibe → Ethiopia 7°20N 37°36E 257 F4
Gibe I Ethiopia 8°7N 37°0E 257 F4
Gibe II Ethiopia 8°0N 37°30E 257 F4
Gibe III Ethiopia 7°0N 37°30E 257 F4
Gibellina Nuova Italy 37°47N 12°58E 200 E5
Gibeon Namibia 25°9S 17°43E 270 C2
Gibraleón Spain 37°23N 6°58W 195 H4
Gibraltar ☑ Europe 36°7N 5°22W 195 J5
Gibraltar, Str. of Medit. S. 35°55N 5°40W 195 K5
Gibraltar Pt. Canada 43°36N 79°23W 141 B2
Gibraltar Range △ Australia 29°31S 152°19E 281 D5
Gibson U.S.A. 33°14N 82°36W 316 B7
Gibson City U.S.A. 40°28N 88°22W 311 D8
Gibson Desert Australia 24°0S 126°0E 278 D4
Gibsonburg U.S.A. 41°23N 83°19W 311 C13
Gibsons Canada 49°24N 123°32W 296 D4
Gibsonton U.S.A. 27°51N 82°23W 317 H7
Gibsonville U.S.A. 39°46N 120°54W 306 F6
Gidami Ethiopia 8°59N 34°37E 266 C3
Giddalur India 15°20N 78°57E 245 G4
Giddings U.S.A. 30°11N 96°56W 314 F6
Gidea Park U.K. 51°35N 0°11E 125 A5
Gidole Ethiopia 5°40N 37°25E 257 F4
Giebnegáisi = Kebnekaise Sweden 67°53N 18°33E 160 C18
Gien France 47°40N 2°36E 173 E9
Giengen Germany 48°37N 10°14E 179 G6
Giesing Germany 48°6N 11°35E 131 B2
Giessen Germany 50°34N 8°41E 178 E4
Gīfān Iran 37°54N 57°28E 247 B8
Gifatin, Geziret Egypt 27°10N 33°50E 256 B3
Gifford U.S.A. 27°40N 80°25W 317 H9
Gifhorn Germany 52°30N 10°33E 178 C6
Gift Lake Canada 55°53N 115°49W 296 B5
Gifu Japan 35°30N 136°45E 223 B8
Gifu □ Japan 35°40N 137°0E 223 B9
Gigant Russia 46°28N 41°20E 191 G5
Giganta, Sa. de la Mexico 26°0N 111°39W 318 B2
Gigen Bulgaria 43°40N 24°28E 203 C8
Gigha U.K. 55°42N 5°44W 167 F3
Giglio Italy 42°20N 10°52E 198 F7
Gignac France 43°39N 3°32E 174 E7
Gigüela → Spain 39°8N 3°44W 195 F7
Gijang S. Korea 35°14N 129°12E 224 E4
Gijón Spain 43°32N 5°42W 194 B5
Gikongoro Rwanda 2°28S 29°34E 268 C2
Gil I. Canada 53°12N 129°15W 296 C3
Gila → U.S.A. 32°43N 114°33W 305 K6
Gila Bend U.S.A. 32°57N 112°43W 305 K7
Gila Bend Mts. U.S.A. 33°10N 113°0W 305 K7
Gila Cliff Dwellings ⌂ U.S.A. 33°12N 108°16W 305 K9
Gīlān □ Iran 37°0N 50°0E 247 B6
Gīlān-e Gharb Iran 34°8N 45°55E 213 E11
Gilău Romania 46°45N 23°23E 183 D8
Gilbert → Australia 16°35S 141°15E 280 B3
Gilbert Is. Kiribati 1°0N 172°0E 277 A10
Gilbert River Australia 18°9S 142°52E 280 B3
Gilbert Seamounts Pac. Oc. 52°50N 150°10W 150 D18
Gilbués Brazil 9°50S 45°21W 332 C2
Gilead U.S.A. 44°24N 70°59W 313 B14
Gilf el Kebîr, Hadabat el Egypt 23°50N 25°50E 256 C2
Gilford I. Canada 50°40N 126°30W 296 C3
Gilgandra Australia 31°43S 148°39E 283 A8
Gilgil Kenya 0°30S 36°20E 268 C4
Gilgit India 35°50N 74°15E 243 B6
Gilgit → Pakistan 35°44N 74°37E 243 B6
Gilgit-Baltistan □ Pakistan 36°30N 73°0E 243 A5
Gilgunnia Australia 32°26S 146°2E 283 B7
Gili, Pulau 10°0S 115°0E 235 D5
Gili △ Mozam. 16°39S 38°27E 269 F4
Gilimanuk Indonesia 8°10S 114°26E 231 J17
Giljeva Planina Europe 43°9N 20°0E 202 C3
Gill Pt. St. Helena 15°58S 5°38W 153 h
Gillam Canada 56°20N 94°40W 297 B10
Gilleleje Denmark 56°8N 12°19E 163 H6
Gillen, L. Australia 26°11S 124°38E 279 E3
Gilles, L. Australia 32°50S 136°45E 282 B2
Gillespie U.S.A. 39°8N 89°49W 310 E7
Gillespies Pt. N.Z. 43°24S 169°49E 285 D4
Gillette U.S.A. 44°18N 105°30W 304 D11
Gilliat Australia 20°40S 141°28E 280 C3
Gillingham U.K. 51°23N 0°33E 169 F8
Gilman U.S.A. 40°46N 88°0W 311 D9
Gilman City U.S.A. 40°8N 93°53W 310 D3
Gilmer U.S.A. 32°44N 94°57W 314 E7
Gilmerton U.K. 55°54N 3°7W 121 B3
Gilmore, L. Australia 32°29S 121°37E 279 F3
Gilmour Canada 44°48N 77°37W 312 B7
Gilo West Bank 31°44N 35°11E 123 B2
Gilo → Ethiopia 8°10N 33°15E 257 F3
Gilort → Romania 44°38N 23°32E 183 F8
Gilroy U.S.A. 37°1N 121°34W 306 H5
Gilwe, Mt. Papua N. G. 6°8S 143°52E 286 D2
Gimbi Ethiopia 9°3N 35°42E 257 F4
Gimcheon S. Korea 36°11N 128°4E 224 D4
Gimhae S. Korea 35°14N 128°53E 224 E4
Gimhwa S. Korea 38°17N 127°28E 224 C3
Gimie, Mt. St. Lucia 13°54N 61°0W 323 m
Gimje S. Korea 35°48N 126°45E 224 E3
Gimli Canada 50°40N 97°0W 297 C9
Gimmersta Sweden 59°14N 18°14E 139 B3
Gimo Sweden 60°11N 18°12E 162 D12
Gimone → France 44°0N 1°6E 174 E5
Gimont France 43°38N 0°52E 174 E4
Gin → Sri Lanka 6°5N 80°7E 245 L5
Gin Gin Australia 25°0S 151°58E 281 D5
Ginâh Egypt 25°21N 30°30E 256 B3
Ginatilan Phil. 9°34N 123°19E 233 G4
Gineifa Egypt 30°12N 32°25E 256 H8
Gingee India 12°15N 79°25E 245 H4
Gingin Australia 31°22S 115°54E 279 F2
Gingindlovu S. Africa 29°2S 31°30E 271 C5
Gingoog Phil. 8°50N 125°7E 233 G5
Gingoog B. Phil. 8°54N 125°7E 233 G5
Ginir Ethiopia 7°6N 40°40E 257 F5
Ginosa Italy 40°35N 16°45E 201 B9
Ginowan Japan 26°15N 127°45E 288 a
Ginza Tokyo, Japan 140 b5
Ginzo de Limia = Xinzo de Limia Spain 42°3N 7°47W 194 C3
Giofyros → Greece 35°20N 25°6E 207 E6
Giohar = Jawhar Somalia 2°48N 45°30E 267 D6
Gióia, G. di Italy 38°30N 15°45E 201 D8
Gióia del Colle Italy 40°48N 16°55E 201 B9
Gióia Táuro Italy 38°25N 15°54E 201 D8
Gioiosa Iónica Italy 38°20N 16°18E 201 D9
Gioiosa Marea Italy 38°10N 14°54E 201 D7
Giona, Oros Greece 38°38N 22°14E 204 C4
Giovi, Passo dei Italy 44°33N 8°57E 198 D5
Giovinazzo Italy 41°11N 16°40E 201 A9
Gippsland Australia 37°52S 147°0E 283 D7
Gir △ India 21°0N 71°0E 242 J4
Gir Hills India 21°0N 71°0E 242 J4
Girab India 26°2N 70°38E 242 F4
Girâfi, W. → Egypt 29°58N 34°39E 251 J5
Giraltovce Slovak Rep. 49°7N 21°32E 181 B14
Girapetra, Akra Greece 38°51N 20°41E 207 B2
Girard St. Lucia 13°59N 60°57W 323 m
Girard Ga., U.S.A. 33°3N 81°43W 316 B8
Girard Ill., U.S.A. 39°27N 89°47W 310 E7
Girard Kans., U.S.A. 37°31N 94°51W 308 G6
Girard Ohio, U.S.A. 41°9N 80°42W 312 E4
Girard Pa., U.S.A. 42°0N 80°19W 312 E4
Girardot Colombia 4°18N 74°48W 328 C3
Giraud, Pte. Dominica 15°20N 61°15W 323 k
Girdle Ness U.K. 57°9N 2°3W 167 D6
Giresun Turkey 40°55N 38°30E 213 B8
Giresun □ Turkey 40°30N 38°30E 213 B8
Girga Egypt 26°17N 31°55E 256 B3
Girgaum Mumbai, India 130 b2
Girgenti = Agrigento Italy 37°19N 13°34E 200 E6
Girgir, C. Papua N. G. 3°50S 144°35E 286 B3
Giri → Dem. Rep. of the Congo 0°28N 17°59E 264 B3
Giri → India 30°28N 77°41E 242 D7
Giridih India 24°10N 86°21E 243 G12
Girifalco Italy 38°49N 16°25E 201 D9
Giriftu Kenya 1°59N 39°46E 268 B4
Girilambone Australia 31°16S 146°57E 283 A7
Girne = Kyrenia Cyprus 35°20N 33°20E 207 E9
Giro Nigeria 11°7N 4°42E 263 C5
Giromagny France 47°45N 6°50E 173 E13
Giron = Kiruna Sweden 67°52N 20°15E 160 C19
Girona Spain 41°58N 2°46E 196 D7
Girona □ Spain 42°11N 2°30E 196 C7
Gironde □ France 44°45N 0°30W 174 D3
Gironde → France 45°32N 1°7W 174 C2
Gironella Spain 42°2N 1°53E 196 C6
Girraween △ Australia 28°46S 151°54E 281 D5
Girringun △ Australia 18°15S 145°32E 280 B4
Giru Australia 19°30S 147°5E 280 B4
Girvan U.K. 55°14N 4°51W 167 F4
Gisborne Vic., Australia 37°29S 144°36E 282 D6
Gisborne N.Z. 38°39S 178°5E 284 E7
Gisborne □ N.Z. 38°30S 178°0E 284 E7
Gisenyi Rwanda 1°41S 29°15E 268 C2
Gislaved Sweden 57°19N 13°32E 163 G7
Gisors France 49°15N 1°47E 173 C8
Gitarama Rwanda 2°4S 29°45E 268 C2
Gitega Burundi 3°26S 29°56E 268 C2
Githio Greece 36°46N 22°34E 204 E4
Gitschin = Jičín Czech Rep. 50°25N 15°28E 180 A8
Giuba = Juba → Somalia 1°30N 42°35E 267 D5
Giudecca, Canale della Venice, Italy 142 c2
Giugliano in Campania Italy 40°56N 14°12E 201 B7
Giulianova Italy 42°45N 13°57E 199 F10
Giura Greece 39°23N 24°10E 204 B6
Giurgeni Romania 44°45N 27°48E 183 F12
Giurgiu Romania 43°52N 25°57E 183 G10
Giurgiu □ Romania 44°20N 26°0E 183 F10
Giurgiulești Moldova 45°29N 28°12E 183 E13
Giustinian, Palazzo Venice, Italy 142 b3
Giv'at Ram Israel 31°47N 35°12E 123 B2
Giv'at Ye'arim Israel 31°47N 35°5E 123 B1
Giv'at Ze'ev West Bank 31°52N 35°10E 123 A2
Give Denmark 55°51N 9°13E 163 J3
Givet France 50°8N 4°49E 173 B11
Giv'on West Bank 31°51N 35°10E 123 A1
Givors France 45°35N 4°45E 175 C8
Givry France 46°41N 4°46E 173 F11
Giyani S. Africa 23°19S 30°43E 271 B5
Giyon Ethiopia 8°33N 38°1E 257 F4
Giza = El Giza Egypt 30°0N 31°12E 256 H7
Giza Pyramids Egypt 29°58N 31°9E 117 B1
Gizab Afghan. 33°22N 66°17E 242 C1
Gizhiga Russia 62°3N 160°30E 215 C17
Gizhiginskaya Guba Russia 61°0N 158°0E 215 C16
Gizo Solomon Is. 8°7S 156°50E 287 M9
Giżycko Poland 54°2N 21°48E 184 D8
Gizzeria Italy 38°59N 16°12E 201 D9
Gjakovë Kosovo 42°22N 20°26E 202 D4
Gjalicë e Lumës, Mal. Albania 42°2N 20°25E 202 D4
Ggantija Malta 36°2N 14°16E 206 F7
Gjegjan Albania 41°58N 20°3E 202 E4
Gjendesheim Norway 61°30N 8°48E 164 C5
Gjeravicë Kosovo 42°32N 20°8E 202 D4
Gjermundshamn Norway 60°40N 5°55E 164 D2
Gjersjøen Norway 59°47N 10°47E 153 B3
Gjerstad Norway 58°54N 9°1E 164 F6
Gjevillvatnet Norway 62°43N 9°23E 164 B6
Gjilan Kosovo 42°28N 21°29E 202 D5
Gjirokastër Albania 40°7N 20°10E 202 F4
Gjoa Haven Canada 68°38N 95°53W 294 D12
Gjøra Norway 62°33N 9°8E 164 B6
Gjøvik Norway 60°47N 10°43E 164 D7
Gjuhës, Kep i Albania 40°28N 19°15E 202 F3
Gjurakoc Kosovo 42°43N 20°29E 202 D4
Glace Bay Canada 46°11N 59°58W 299 C8
Glacier △ B.C., Canada 51°15N 117°30W 296 C5
Glacier △ Mont., U.S.A. 48°42N 113°48W 304 B7
Glacier Bay U.S.A. 58°40N 136°0W 303 G14
Glacier Bay ⌂ U.S.A. 58°45N 136°30W 296 B1
Glacier Peak U.S.A. 48°7N 121°7W 304 B3
Gladesville Australia 33°50S 151°8E 139 B1
Gladewater U.S.A. 32°33N 94°56W 314 E7
Gladsakse Denmark 55°45N 12°25E 118 A2
Gladstone Queens., Australia 23°52S 151°16E 280 C5
Gladstone S. Austral., Australia 33°15S 138°22E 282 B3
Gladstone Man., Canada 50°13N 98°57W 297 C9
Gladstone Ill., U.S.A. 40°52N 90°57W 310 D6
Gladstone Mich., U.S.A. 45°51N 87°1W 308 C10
Gladstone Mo., U.S.A. 39°13N 94°35W 310 E2
Gladwin U.S.A. 43°59N 84°29W 309 D11
Glafsfjorden Sweden 59°30N 12°37E 162 E6
Glagah Indonesia 8°13S 114°18E 231 J17
Głogów Małapolski Poland 50°10N 21°56E 185 H8
Glåma = Glomma → Norway 59°12N 10°57E 164 E7
Gláma Iceland 65°48N 23°0W 155 B4
Glamis U.S.A. 32°55N 115°5W 307 N11
Glamoč Bos.-H. 44°3N 16°51E 199 D13
Glamorgan, Vale of □ U.K. 51°28N 3°25W 169 F4
Glåmos Norway 62°41N 11°25E 164 B8
Glamsbjerg Denmark 55°17N 10°6E 163 J4
Glanvillia Dominica 15°34N 61°28W 323 k
Glarus Switz. 47°3N 9°4E 179 H5
Glarus □ Switz. 47°0N 9°5E 179 J5
Glasco Kans., U.S.A. 39°22N 97°50W 308 F5
Glasco N.Y., U.S.A. 42°3N 73°57W 313 D11
Glasgow C. of Glasg., U.K. 55°51N 4°15W 167 F4
Glasgow Ky., U.S.A. 37°0N 85°55W 309 G11
Glasgow Mo., U.S.A. 39°14N 92°51W 310 E4
Glasgow Mont., U.S.A. 48°12N 106°38W 304 B10
Glasgow, City of □ U.K. 55°51N 4°12W 167 F4
Glasgow Int. ✈ (GLA) U.K. 55°51N 4°21W 167 F4
Glaslyn Canada 53°22N 108°21W 297 C7
Glasnevin Ireland 53°22N 6°15W 120 A2
Glassmanor U.S.A. 38°49N 77°0W 143 C3
Glasthule Ireland 53°17N 6°7W 120 B3
Glastonbury U.K. 51°9N 2°43W 169 F5
Glastonbury Conn., U.S.A. 41°43N 72°37W 313 E12
Glatz = Kłodzko Poland 50°28N 16°38E 185 H3
Glauchau Germany 50°49N 12°31E 178 E8
Glava Sweden 59°33N 12°35E 162 E6
Glavice Croatia 43°43N 16°41E 199 E13
Glazov Russia 58°9N 52°40E 190 A11
Gleichen Canada 50°52N 113°3W 296 C6
Gleisdorf Austria 47°6N 15°44E 180 D8
Gleiwitz = Gliwice Poland 50°22N 18°41E 185 H5
Glen U.S.A. 44°7N 71°11W 313 B13
Glen Affric U.K. 57°17N 5°1W 167 D3
Glen Afton N.Z. 37°37S 175°4E 284 D4
Glen Canyon U.S.A. 37°30N 110°40W 305 H8
Glen Canyon ⌂ U.S.A. 37°15N 111°0W 305 H8
Glen Canyon Dam U.S.A. 36°57N 111°29W 305 H8
Glen Coe U.K. 56°40N 5°0W 167 E3
Glen Cove U.S.A. 40°52N 73°38W 313 F11
Glen Garry U.K. 57°3N 5°7W 167 D3
Glen Innes Australia 29°44S 151°44E 281 D5
Glen Iris Australia 37°51S 145°3E 128 B2
Glen Lyon U.S.A. 41°10N 76°5W 313 E8
Glen Mar Park U.S.A. 38°57N 77°7W 143 B2
Glen Massey N.Z. 37°38S 175°2E 284 D4
Glen Mor U.K. 57°9N 4°37W 167 D4
Glen Moriston U.K. 57°11N 4°52W 167 D4
Glen Robertson Canada 45°22N 74°30W 313 A10
Glen Rouge Park Canada 43°49N 79°10W 141 A4
Glen Spean U.K. 56°53N 4°40W 167 E4
Glen Ullin U.S.A. 46°49N 101°50W 308 B3
Glénan, Îs. de France 47°42N 4°0W 172 E3
Glenasmole Reservoirs Ireland 53°15N 6°21W 120 B1
Glenavy N.Z. 44°54S 171°7E 285 E6
Glenbeigh Ireland 52°3N 9°58W 166 D2
Glenburn Australia 37°27S 145°26E 283 D6
Glencoe Ont., Canada 42°45N 81°43W 312 D3
Glencoe KwaZulu Natal, S. Africa 28°11S 30°11E 271 C5
Glencoe Ala., U.S.A. 33°57N 85°56W 316 B4
Glencoe Ill., U.S.A. 42°8N 87°45W 119 A2
Glencoe Minn., U.S.A. 44°46N 94°9W 308 C6
Glencolumbkille Ireland 54°43N 8°42W 166 B3
Glencorse Res. U.K. 55°51N 3°15W 121 B2
Glencullen Ireland 53°14N 6°12W 120 B2
Glendale Ariz., U.S.A. 33°32N 112°11W 305 K7
Glendale Calif., U.S.A. 34°9N 118°15W 126 B3
Glendale Fla., U.S.A. 30°52N 86°7W 316 E3
Glendale Zimbabwe 17°22S 31°5E 269 F3
Glendive U.S.A. 47°7N 104°43W 304 C11
Glendo U.S.A. 42°30N 105°2W 304 E11
Glendoo Mt. Ireland 53°14N 6°16W 120 B2
Glenelg Australia 34°58S 138°31E 282 C3
Glenelg → Australia 38°4S 140°59E 282 E4
Glenfield U.S.A. 43°43N 75°24W 313 C9
Glengad Hd. Ireland 55°20N 7°10W 166 A4
Glengarriff Ireland 51°45N 9°34W 166 E2
Glengoffe Jamaica 18°10N 76°53W 320 a
Glenham N.Z. 46°26S 168°52E 285 G3
Glenhope N.Z. 41°40S 172°39E 285 B7
Glenhuntly Australia 37°52S 145°1E 128 B2
Glenmary, Mt. N.Z. 43°55S 169°55E 285 D4
Glenmont U.S.A. 40°31N 82°6W 312 F2
Glenmorgan Australia 27°14S 149°42E 281 D4
Glenn U.S.A. 39°31N 122°1W 306 F4
Glennallen U.S.A. 62°7N 145°33W 303 E11
Glennamaddy Ireland 53°37N 8°33W 166 C3
Glenns Ferry U.S.A. 42°57N 115°18W 304 E6
Glennville U.S.A. 31°56N 81°56W 316 D8
Glenora Canada 44°2N 77°3W 312 B7
Glenorchy Tas., Australia 42°49S 147°18E 281 G4
Glenorchy Vic., Australia 36°55S 142°41E 282 D5
Glenorchy N.Z. 44°51S 168°24E 285 E3
Glenore Australia 17°50S 141°12E 280 B3
Glenreagh Australia 30°2S 153°1E 281 E5
Glenrock U.S.A. 42°52N 105°52W 304 E11
Glenrothes U.K. 56°12N 3°10W 167 E5
Glenrowan Australia 36°29S 146°13E 283 D7
Glens Falls U.S.A. 43°19N 73°39W 313 C11
Glenside U.S.A. 40°6N 75°9W 313 F9
Glenthompson Australia 37°38S 142°38E 282 D5
Glenties Ireland 54°48N 8°17W 166 B3
Glenveagh △ Ireland 55°3N 8°1W 166 A3
Glenview U.S.A. 42°3N 87°48W 119 A2
Glenview Countryside U.S.A. 42°3N 87°49W 119 A2
Glenville U.S.A. 38°56N 80°50W 309 F13
Glenvista S. Africa 26°17S 28°3E 123 B2
Glenwood Nfld. & L., Canada 49°0N 54°58W 299 C9
Glenwood Ark., U.S.A. 34°20N 93°33W 314 D8

Glenwood *Ga., U.S.A.* 32°11N 82°40W **316** C7
Glenwood *Hawai'i, U.S.A.* 19°29N 155°9W **302** D6
Glenwood *Iowa, U.S.A.* 41°3N 95°45W **308** E6
Glenwood *Minn., U.S.A.* 45°39N 95°23W **308** C6
Glenwood *Wash., U.S.A.* 46°1N 121°17W **306** D5
Glenwood Springs *U.S.A.* 39°33N 107°19W **304** G10
Glettinganes *Iceland* 65°30N 13°37W **155** B13
Glidden *U.S.A.* 42°4N 94°44W **310** B2
Glifada *Athens, Greece* 37°52N 23°45E **112** B2
Glimåkra *Sweden* 56°19N 14°7E **163** H8
Glin *Ireland* 52°34N 9°17W **166** D2
Glina *Croatia* 45°20N 16°6E **199** C13
Glinojeck *Poland* 52°49N 20°21E **185** F7
Glittertind *Norway* 61°40N 8°32E **164** C5
Gliwice *Poland* 50°22N 18°41E **185** H5
Globe *U.S.A.* 33°24N 110°47W **305** K8
Glodeanu Siliştea *Romania* 44°50N 26°48E **183** F11
Glodeni *Moldova* 47°45N 27°31E **183** C12
Glödnitz *Austria* 46°53N 14°7E **180** E7
Glogau = Głogów *Poland* 51°37N 16°5E **185** G3
Gloggnitz *Austria* 47°41N 15°56E **180** D8
Głogów *Poland* 51°37N 16°5E **185** G3
Głogówek *Poland* 50°21N 17°53E **185** H4
Glomma ➝ *Norway* 59°12N 10°57E **164** E7
Gloria *Phil.* 12°59N 121°30E **232** E3
Glorieuses, Îs. *Ind. Oc.* 11°30S 47°20E **272** A2
Glosa *Greece* 39°10N 23°45E **204** B5
Glossop *U.K.* 53°27N 1°56W **168** D6
Glostrup *Denmark* 55°39N 12°23E **118** B2
Gloucester *N.S.W., Australia* 32°0S 151°59E **283** B9
Gloucester *Papua N. G.* 5°31S 148°31E **286** C5
Gloucester *Gloucs., U.K.* 51°53N 2°15W **169** F5
Gloucester *Mass., U.S.A.* 42°37N 70°40W **313** D14
Gloucester, C. *Papua N. G.* 5°26S 148°21E **286** C5
Gloucester I. *Australia* 20°0S 148°30E **280** b
Gloucester Island △ *Australia* 20°2S 148°30E **280** b
Gloucester Point *U.S.A.* 37°15N 76°30W **309** G15
Gloucestershire □ *U.K.* 51°46N 2°15W **169** F5
Glover I. *Grenada* 11°59N 61°47W **323** q
Gloversville *U.S.A.* 43°3N 74°21W **313** C10
Glovertown *Canada* 48°40N 54°3W **299** C9
Gloverville = Warrenville *U.S.A.* 33°33N 81°48W **316** B8
Głowno *Poland* 51°59N 19°42E **185** G6
Głubczyce *Poland* 50°13N 17°52E **185** H4
Glubokiy *Russia* 48°35N 40°25E **191** F5
Glubokoe *Kazakhstan* 50°8N 82°18E **217** B10
Glubokoye = Hlybokaye *Belarus* 55°10N 27°45E **188** E4
Głuchołazy *Poland* 50°19N 17°24E **185** H4
Glücksburg *Germany* 54°50N 9°33E **178** A5
Glückstadt *Germany* 53°45N 9°25E **178** B5
Glukhov = Hlukhiv *Ukraine* 51°40N 33°58E **189** G7
Glusk *Belarus* 52°53N 28°41E **177** B15
Głuszyca *Poland* 50°41N 16°23E **185** H3
Glyfada = Glifada *Athens, Greece* 37°52N 23°45E **112** B2
Glyn Ebwy = Ebbw Vale *U.K.* 51°46N 3°12W **169** F4
Glyngøre *Denmark* 56°46N 8°52E **163** H2
Gmünd *Kärnten, Austria* 46°54N 13°31E **180** E6
Gmünd *Niederösterreich, Austria* 48°45N 15°0E **180** C8
Gmunden *Austria* 47°55N 13°48E **180** D6
Gnali *Gabon* 2°34S 11°18E **262** D2
Gnarp *Sweden* 62°3N 17°16E **162** B11
Gnesen = Gniezno *Poland* 52°30N 17°35E **185** F4
Gnesta *Sweden* 59°3N 17°17E **162** E11
Gniew *Poland* 53°50N 18°50E **184** E5
Gniewkowo *Poland* 52°54N 18°25E **185** F5
Gniezno *Poland* 52°30N 17°35E **185** F4
Gnjilane = Gjilan *Kosovo* 42°28N 21°29E **202** D5
Gnoien *Germany* 53°58N 12°41E **178** B8
Gnosjö *Sweden* 57°22N 13°43E **163** G7
Gnowangerup *Australia* 33°58S 117°59E **279** F2
Go Cong *Vietnam* 10°22N 106°40E **237** G6
Gō-Gawa ➝ *Japan* 35°2N 132°13E **222** B4
Gō-no-ura *Japan* 33°44N 129°40E **222** D1
Goa *India* 15°33N 73°59E **245** G1
Goa *Phil.* 13°42N 123°29E **232** E4
Goa □ *India* 15°33N 73°59E **245** G1
Goalen Hd. *Australia* 36°33S 150°4E **283** D9
Goalpara *India* 26°10N 90°40E **241** B3
Goaltor *India* 22°43N 87°10E **243** H12
Goalundo Ghat *Bangla.* 23°50N 89°47E **243** H13
Goaso *Ghana* 6°48N 2°30W **262** D4
Goat Fell *U.K.* 55°38N 5°11W **167** F3
Goat I. *Antigua & B.* 17°43N 61°51W **322** c
Goat Pt. *Antigua & B.* 17°44N 61°51W **322** c
Goba *Ethiopia* 7°1N 39°59E **257** F4
Goba *Mozam.* 26°15S 32°13E **271** C5
Gobabis *Namibia* 22°30S 19°0E **270** B2
Gobe *Papua N. G.* 9°4S 149°0E **286** E5
Göbel *Turkey* 40°0N 28°9E **203** F12
Gobernador Gregores *Argentina* 48°46S 70°15W **336** C2
Gobi *Asia* 44°0N 110°0E **226** C6
Gobichettipalayam *India* 11°31N 77°21E **245** J3
Gobles *U.S.A.* 42°22N 85°53W **311** B11
Gobō *Japan* 33°53N 135°10E **223** D7
Gobo *South Sudan* 5°40N 31°10E **257** F3
Gobustan *Azerbaijan* 40°7N 49°22E **213** B13
Göçbeyli *Turkey* 39°13N 27°25E **205** B9
Goch *Germany* 51°41N 6°9E **178** D2
Gochang *S. Korea* 35°26N 126°42E **224** E3
Gochas *Namibia* 24°59S 18°55E **270** B2
God Dere *Ethiopia* 5°12N 44°1E **267** C5
Godalming *U.K.* 51°11N 0°36W **169** F7
Godavari ➝ *India* 16°25N 82°18E **244** F6
Godavari Pt. *India* 17°0N 82°20E **244** F6
Godbout *Canada* 49°20N 67°38W **299** C6
Godda *India* 24°50N 87°13E **243** G12
Gode *Ethiopia* 5°53N 43°35E **267** C5
Godech *Bulgaria* 43°1N 23°4E **202** C7
Goderich *Canada* 43°45N 81°41W **312** C3
Goderville *France* 49°38N 0°22E **172** C7
Godfrey *U.S.A.* 38°58N 90°11W **310** F6
Godfrey Ra. *Australia* 24°0S 117°0E **279** D2
Godhavn = Qeqertarsuaq *Greenland* 69°15N 53°38W **154** D5
Gōdalir *Iceland* 65°20N 19°6W **155** B7
Godhra *India* 22°49N 73°40E **242** H5
Godinlabe *Somalia* 5°54N 46°38E **267** C6
Gödöllő *Hungary* 47°38N 19°25E **182** C4
Godoy Cruz *Argentina* 32°56S 68°52W **334** C2
Gods ➝ *Canada* 56°22N 92°51W **298** A1
Gods L. *Canada* 54°40N 94°15W **298** B1
Gods River *Canada* 54°50N 94°5W **297** C10
Godthåb = Nuuk *Greenland* 64°10N 51°35W **154** E5
Godwin Austen = K2 *Pakistan* 35°58N 76°32E **243** B7
Goeie Hoop, Kaap die = Good Hope, C. of *S. Africa* 34°24S 18°30E **270** D2
Goéland, L. au *Canada* 49°50N 76°48W **298** C4
Goélands, L. aux *Canada* 55°27N 64°17W **299** A7
Goeree *Neths.* 51°50N 4°0E **170** C3
Goes *Neths.* 51°30N 3°55E **170** C3
Gofca ➝ *Somalia* 1°10N 43°43E **267** D5
Goffstown *U.S.A.* 43°1N 71°36W **313** C13
Gogama *Canada* 47°35N 81°43W **298** C3
Gogar *U.K.* 55°56N 3°20W **121** B2
Gogebic, L. *U.S.A.* 46°30N 89°35W **308** B9
Goggetti *Ethiopia* 8°11N 38°35E **257** F4
Gogolin *Poland* 50°30N 18°0E **185** H5
Gogonou *Benin* 10°50N 2°50E **263** C5
Gogra = Ghaghara ➝ *India* 25°45N 84°40E **243** G11
Gogrial *South Sudan* 8°30N 28°8E **257** F2
Gogti *Ethiopia* 10°7N 42°51E **257** E5
Gogui *Mali* 15°32N 9°25W **262** B3
Gohana *India* 29°8N 76°42E **242** E7
Goharganj *India* 23°1N 77°41E **242** H7
Goheung *S. Korea* 34°36N 127°17E **224** E3
Goi ➝ *India* 22°4N 74°46E **242** H6
Goiana *Brazil* 7°33S 34°59W **332** C5
Goianésia *Brazil* 15°18S 49°7W **333** E2
Goiânia *Brazil* 16°43S 49°20W **333** E2
Goiás *Brazil* 15°55S 50°10W **333** E1
Goiás □ *Brazil* 12°10S 48°0W **332** D2
Goiatins *Brazil* 7°42S 47°10W **332** C2
Goiatuba *Brazil* 18°1S 49°23W **333** E2
Goidu Atoll *Maldives* 4°53N 72°54E **272** d
Goio-Erê *Brazil* 24°12S 53°1W **335** A5
Góis *Portugal* 40°10N 8°6W **194** E2
Gojam *Ethiopia* 10°55N 36°30E **257** E4
Gojeb, Wabi ➝ *Ethiopia* 7°12N 36°40E **257** F4
Gojō *Japan* 34°21N 135°42E **223** C7
Gojra *Pakistan* 31°10N 72°40E **242** D5
Gokak *India* 16°11N 74°52E **245** F2
Gokarn *India* 14°33N 74°17E **245** G2
Gökçe = Sevana Lich *Armenia* 40°30N 45°20E **191** K7
Gökçe *Turkey* 40°10N 25°55E **203** F9
Gökçeada *Turkey* 40°10N 25°50E **203** F9
Gökçedağ *Turkey* 39°33N 28°56E **205** B10
Gökçen *Turkey* 38°7N 27°53E **205** C9
Gökçeören *Turkey* 38°37N 28°35E **205** C10
Gökçeyazı *Turkey* 39°40N 27°40E **205** B9
Gökırmak ➝ *Turkey* 41°25N 35°8E **212** B6
Gökova *Turkey* 37°1N 28°17E **205** D10
Gökova Körfezi *Turkey* 36°55N 27°50E **205** E9
Göksu ➝ *Turkey* 36°19N 34°5E **250** B5
Göksun *Turkey* 38°2N 36°30E **212** C7
Gokteik *Burma* 22°26N 97°0E **241** D6
Göktepe *Karaman, Turkey* 36°37N 32°37E **250** B3
Göktepe *Muğla, Turkey* 37°25N 28°34E **205** D10
Göktürk *Turkey* 41°10N 28°53E **122** A1
Gokurt *Pakistan* 29°40N 67°26E **242** E2
Gokwe *Zimbabwe* 18°7S 28°58E **271** A4
Gol *Norway* 60°42N 8°55E **164** D5
Gol Gol *Australia* 34°12S 142°14E **282** C5
Gola *India* 28°3N 80°32E **243** E9
Golabari *India* 22°35N 88°20E **124** B2
Golabki *Poland* 52°12N 20°52E **143** B1
Golaghat *India* 26°30N 94°0E **241** B5
Golakganj *India* 26°8N 89°52E **241** B2
Golan Heights = Hagolan *Syria* 33°0N 35°45E **250** F6
Gołańcz *Poland* 52°57N 17°18E **185** F4
Goläshkerd *Iran* 27°59N 57°16E **247** E8
Golaya Pristen = Hola Prystan *Ukraine* 46°29N 32°32E **189** J7
Gölbaşı *Adiyaman, Turkey* 37°43N 37°25E **212** D7
Gölbaşı *Ankara, Turkey* 39°47N 32°49E **212** C5
Golconda *India* 17°24N 78°23E **244** F4
Golconda *Nev., U.S.A.* 40°58N 117°30W **304** F5
Gölcük *Kocaeli, Turkey* 40°42N 29°48E **203** F13
Gölcük *Niğde, Turkey* 38°14N 34°47E **212** C6
Gold *U.S.A.* 41°52N 77°50W **312** E7
Gold Beach *U.S.A.* 42°25N 124°25W **304** E1
Gold Coast = Ghana ■ *W. Afr.* 8°0N 1°0W **263** D4
Gold Coast *Queens., Australia* 28°0S 153°25E **276** F9
Gold Coast *Chicago, U.S.A.* **119** a2
Gold Coast *W. Afr.* 4°0N 1°40W **263** E4
Gold Creek *U.S.A.* 62°46N 149°41W **303** E10
Gold Hill *U.S.A.* 42°26N 123°3W **304** E2
Gold River *Canada* 49°46N 126°3W **296** D3
Goldap *Poland* 54°19N 22°18E **184** D9
Goldberg = Złotoryja *Poland* 51°8N 15°55E **185** G2
Goldberg *Germany* 53°35N 12°4E **178** B8
Golden *B.C., Canada* 51°20N 116°59W **296** C5
Golden *Ill., U.S.A.* 40°7N 91°1W **310** D5
Golden B. *N.Z.* 40°40S 172°50E **285** A7
Golden Beach *U.S.A.* 25°57N 80°7W **129** C3
Golden Buddha = Traimit *Bangkok, Thailand* **113** c2
Golden Gate *U.S.A.* 37°48N 122°29W **136** B2
Golden Gate △ *U.S.A.* 37°49N 122°31W **136** A2
Golden Gate Bridge *U.S.A.* 37°49N 122°28W **136** B2
Golden Gate Highlands △ *S. Africa* 28°40S 28°40E **271** C4
Golden Gate Park *U.S.A.* 37°46N 122°28W **136** B2
Golden Grove *Middlesex, Jamaica* 18°19N 77°9W **320** a
Golden Grove *Surrey, Jamaica* 17°55N 76°16W **320** a
Golden Hinde *Canada* 49°40N 125°44W **296** D3
Golden Horn = Haliç *Turkey* 41°1N 28°57E **122** B1
Golden Lake *Canada* 45°34N 77°21W **312** A7
Golden Rock *India* 10°45N 78°48E **245** J4
Golden Spike △ *U.S.A.* 41°37N 112°33W **304** F7
Golden Vale *Ireland* 52°33N 8°17W **166** D3
Goldendale *U.S.A.* 45°49N 120°50W **304** D3
Golders Green *U.K.* 51°34N 0°11W **125** A2
Goldfield *U.S.A.* 37°42N 117°14W **305** H5
Goldingen = Kuldīga *Latvia* 56°58N 21°59E **184** B8
Goldoni, Casa *Venice, Italy* **142** b2
Goldoni, Teatro *Venice, Italy* **142** b3
Goldpines *Canada* 50°45N 93°5W **297** C10 
Goldsand L. *Canada* 57°2N 101°8W **297** B8
Goldsboro *U.S.A.* 35°23N 77°59W **315** D16
Goldsmith *U.S.A.* 31°59N 102°37W **314** F3
Goldthwaite *U.S.A.* 31°27N 98°34W **314** F5
Golegã *Portugal* 39°24N 8°29W **195** F2
Goleniów *Poland* 53°35N 14°50E **184** E1
Golestān □ *Iran* 37°20N 55°25E **247** B7
Golestan Palace *Iran* 35°41N 51°25E **141** A2
Golestānak *Iran* 30°36N 54°14E **247** D7
Goleta *U.S.A.* 34°27N 119°50W **307** L7
Golf *U.S.A.* 42°3N 87°46W **119** A2
Golfito *Costa Rica* 8°41N 83°5W **320** E3
Golfo Aranci *Italy* 40°59N 9°38E **200** B2
Golfo de Santa Clara *Mexico* 31°42N 114°30W **318** A2
Golfo di Orosei e del Gennargentu △ *Italy* 40°15N 9°15E **200** B2
Gölhisar *Turkey* 37°8N 29°31E **205** D11
Goliad *U.S.A.* 28°40N 97°23W **314** G6
Golija *Montenegro* 43°5N 18°45E **202** C2
Golija *Serbia* 43°22N 20°15E **202** C4
Golina *Poland* 52°15N 18°4E **185** F5
Golitsyno *Russia* 55°36N 36°58E **190** C1
Golija Bratan = Morozov *Bulgaria* 42°30N 25°10E **203** D9
Gölköy *Turkey* 40°41N 37°37E **212** B7
Gollel = Lavumisa *Swaziland* 27°20S 31°55E **271** C5
Göllersdorf *Austria* 48°29N 16°7E **180** C9
Gollnow = Goleniów *Poland* 53°35N 14°50E **184** E1
Gölmarmara *Turkey* 38°42N 27°55E **205** C9
Golmud *China* 36°25N 94°53E **218** D7
Golo ➝ *France* 42°31N 9°32E **175** F13
Golo I. *Phil.* 13°39N 120°22E **232** E3
Gölova *Turkey* 36°48N 30°5E **205** E12
Golovin *U.S.A.* 64°33N 163°2W **303** D7
Golpāyegān *Iran* 33°27N 50°18E **247** C6
Gölpazarı *Turkey* 40°16N 30°18E **212** B4
Golra *Pakistan* 33°37N 72°56E **242** C5
Golspie *U.K.* 57°58N 3°59W **167** D5
Golub-Dobrzyń *Poland* 53°7N 19°2E **185** E6
Golubac *Serbia* 44°38N 21°38E **202** B5
Golungo Alto *Angola* 9°8S 14°46E **265** D2
Golyam Perelik *Bulgaria* 41°36N 24°33E **203** E8
Golyama Kamchiya ➝ *Bulgaria* 43°10N 27°55E **203** C11
Golyshi = Vetluzhskiy *Russia* 58°23N 45°26E **190** A7
Goma *Dem. Rep. of the Congo* 1°37S 29°10E **268** C2
Gomal Pass *Pakistan* 31°56N 69°20E **242** D3
Gomantong Caves *Malaysia* 5°40N 118°6E **235** A5
Gomati ➝ *India* 25°32N 83°11E **243** G10
Gombari *Dem. Rep. of the Congo* 2°45N 29°3E **268** B2
Gombe *Dem. Rep. of the Congo* 0°45S 17°36E **264** C3
Gombe *Nigeria* 10°19N 11°2E **263** C7
Gömbe *Turkey* 36°33N 29°38E **205** E11
Gombe □ *Nigeria* 10°0N 11°10E **263** C7
Gombe ➝ *Tanzania* 4°38S 31°40E **268** C3
Gombe Stream △ *Tanzania* 4°42S 29°37E **268** C2
Gombi *Nigeria* 10°12N 12°30E **263** C7
Gomel = Homyel *Belarus* 52°28N 31°0E **177** B16
Gomera *Canary Is.* 28°7N 17°14W **153** e1
Gómez Palacio *Mexico* 25°34N 103°30W **318** B4
Gomfi *Greece* 39°26N 21°36E **204** B3
Gomīshān *Iran* 37°4N 54°6E **247** B7
Gommern *Germany* 52°4N 11°50E **178** C7
Gomogomo *Indonesia* 6°39S 134°43E **231** F8
Gomoh *India* 23°52N 86°10E **243** H12
Gomotartsi *Bulgaria* 44°6N 22°57E **202** B6
Gompa = Ganta *Liberia* 7°15N 8°59W **262** D3
Gonābād *Iran* 34°15N 58°45E **247** C8
Gonaïves *Haiti* 19°20N 72°42W **321** C5
Gonâve, G. de la *Haiti* 19°29N 72°42W **321** C5
Gonâve, Île de la *Haiti* 18°51N 73°3W **321** C5
Gonbad-e Kāvūs *Iran* 37°20N 55°25E **247** B7
Gönc *Hungary* 48°28N 21°14E **182** B6
Gonda *India* 27°9N 81°58E **243** F9
Gondal *India* 21°58N 70°52E **242** J4
Gonder *Ethiopia* 12°39N 37°30E **257** E4
Gondia *India* 21°23N 80°10E **244** D5
Gondola *Mozam.* 19°10S 33°37E **269** F3
Gondomar *Portugal* 41°10N 8°35W **194** D2
Gondrecourt-le-Château *France* 48°31N 5°30E **173** D12
Gonen *Israel* 33°12N 35°40E ... 
Gönen *Balıkesir, Turkey* 40°6N 27°39E **203** F11
Gönen *Isparta, Turkey* 37°57N 30°31E **205** D12
Gönen ➝ *Turkey* 40°6N 27°39E **203** F11
Gong Xian *China* 28°23N 104°47E **228** C5
Gong'an *China* 30°7N 112°12E **229** B9
Gongbei *China* 22°12N 113°32E **219** a
Gongchangling *China* 41°7N 123°27E **224** B1
Gongcheng *China* 24°50N 110°49E **229** E8
Gongga Shan *China* 29°40N 101°55E **228** C3
Gonggar *China* 29°23N 91°7E **218** F7
Gongguan = Kungkuan *Taiwan* 24°35N 120°44E **225** B2
Gongguan *China* 21°48N 109°36E **228** G7
Gonghe *China* 36°18N 100°32E **218** D9
Gongju *S. Korea* 36°27N 127°7E **224** D3
Gongliu *China* 43°28N 82°8E **217** D10
Gongming *China* 22°47N 113°53E **219** a
Gongneung *S. Korea* 37°36N 127°3E **137** B2
Gongo Yembe *Dem. Rep. of the Congo* 1°58S 18°40E **264** C3
Gongola ➝ *Nigeria* 9°30N 12°4E **263** D7
Gongolgon *Australia* 30°21S 146°54E **281** E4
Gongoué *Gabon* 0°31S 9°13E **264** C1
Gongshan *China* 27°43N 98°29E **228** D2
Gongtan *China* 28°55N 108°20E **228** C7
Gongyi *China* 34°45N 112°58E **226** G7
Gongzhuling *China* 43°30N 124°40E **227** C13
Goni *Greece* 39°52N 22°29E **204** B4
Goniadz *Poland* 53°30N 22°44E **184** E9
Goniri *Nigeria* 11°30N 12°15E **263** C7
Gonjo *China* 30°52N 98°17E **228** B2
Gonnesa *Italy* 39°16N 8°28E **200** C1
Gonnosfanàdiga *Italy* 39°29N 8°39E **200** C1
Gonzaga *Phil.* 18°16N 122°0E **232** B4
Gonzales *Calif., U.S.A.* 36°30N 121°26W **306** J5
Gonzales *Tex., U.S.A.* 29°30N 97°27W **314** G6
González *Mexico* 22°48N 98°25W **319** C5
Goobang △ *Australia* 33°0S 148°32E **283** B8
Good Hope, C. of *S. Africa* 34°24S 18°30E **270** D2
Good Hope Lake *Canada* 59°16N 129°18W **296** B3
Good Hope Plantation *Jamaica* 18°25N 77°41W **320** a
Goodenough I. *Papua N. G.* 9°20S 150°15E **286** E6
Gooderham *Canada* 44°54N 78°21W **312** B6
Goodhouse *S. Africa* 28°57S 18°13E **270** C2
Gooding *U.S.A.* 42°56N 114°43W **304** E6
Goodland *U.S.A.* 39°21N 101°43W **308** F3
Goodlands *Mauritius* 20°2S 57°39E **272** e
Goodlow *Canada* 56°20N 120°8W **296** B4
Goodmayes *U.K.* 51°33N 0°6E **125** A4
Goodnews Bay *U.S.A.* 59°7N 161°35W **303** G7
Goodooga *Australia* 29°3S 147°28E **281** D4
Goodsprings *U.S.A.* 35°49N 115°27W **307** K11
Goodwater *U.S.A.* 33°4N 86°3W **316** B3
Goodwood *S. Africa* 33°55S 18°32E **118** A2
Goole *U.K.* 53°42N 0°53W **168** D7
Goolgowi *Australia* 33°58S 145°41E **283** B6
Goolwa *Australia* 35°30S 138°47E **282** C3
Goomalling *Australia* 31°15S 116°49E **279** F2
Goomeri *Australia* 26°12S 152°6E **281** D5
Goonda *Mozam.* 19°48S 33°57E **269** F3
Goondiwindi *Australia* 28°30S 150°21E **281** D5
Goongarrie, L. *Australia* 30°3S 121°9E **279** F3
Goongarrie △ *Australia* 30°7S 121°30E **279** F3
Goonyella *Australia* 21°47S 147°58E **280** C4
Goose ➝ *Canada* 53°20N 60°35W **299** B7
Goose Creek *U.S.A.* 32°59N 80°2W **316** C9
Goose L. *Calif., U.S.A.* 41°56N 120°26W **304** F3
Goose L. *Ill., U.S.A.* 40°55N 89°27W **310** C10
Gooty *India* 15°7N 77°41E **245** G3
Gop *India* 22°5N 69°50E **242** H3
Gopalganj *Bangla.* 23°1N 89°50E **241** D2
Gopalganj *India* 26°28N 84°30E **243** F11
Gopalpur *India* 22°38N 88°26E **124** B2
Göppingen *Germany* 48°42N 9°39E **179** G5
Goqên *China* 31°2N 92°6E **218** E7
Gor *Spain* 37°23N 2°58W **195** H8
Góra *Dolnośląskie, Poland* 51°40N 16°31E **185** G3
Góra *Mazowieckie, Poland* 52°39N 20°6E **185** F7
Góra Kalwaria *Poland* 51°59N 21°14E **185** G8
Gorakhpur *India* 26°47N 83°23E **243** F10
Goražde *Bos.-H.* 43°38N 18°58E **202** C3
Gorbatov *Russia* 56°12N 43°2E **190** B6
Gorbea *Spain* 43°1N 2°50W **196** B2
Górce *Poland* 52°15N 20°55E **143** B1
Gorczański △ *Poland* 49°30N 20°10E **185** J7
Gorda, Banco *Caribbean* 15°40N 80°27W **320** C3
Gorda, Pta. *Canary Is.* 28°45N 18°0W **153** e1
Gorda, Pta. *Nic.* 14°20N 83°10W **320** D3
Gordan B. *Australia* 11°35S 130°10E **278** B5
Gördes *Turkey* 38°54N 28°17E **205** C10
Gordon *Ga., U.S.A.* 32°54N 83°20W **316** C6
Gordon *Nebr., U.S.A.* 42°48N 102°12W **308** D2
Gordon ➝ *Australia* 42°27S 145°30E **281** G4
Gordon, I. *Chile* 54°55S 69°30W **336** D3
Gordon Bay *Canada* 45°12N 79°47W **312** A5
Gordon L. *Alta., Canada* 56°30N 110°25W **297** B6
Gordon L. *N.W.T., Canada* 63°5N 113°11W **296** A6
Gordonvale *Australia* 17°5S 145°50E **280** B4
Goré *Chad* 7°59N 16°31E **259** G3
Gore *Ethiopia* 8°12N 35°32E **257** F4
Gore *N.Z.* 46°5S 168°58E **285** G3
Gore Bay *Canada* 45°57N 82°28W **298** C3
Gore Hill *Australia* 33°49S 151°10E **139** A2
Gorée, Île de *Senegal* 14°40N 17°23W **262** C1
Görele *Turkey* 41°2N 39°0E **213** B8
Gorelyy ➝ *Russia* 60°1N 30°30E **137** A3
Göreme *Turkey* 38°35N 34°52E **212** C6
Gorey *Ireland* 52°41N 6°18W **166** D5
Gorg *Iran* 29°29N 59°43E **247** D8
Gorgān *Iran* 36°55N 54°30E **247** B7
Gorgie *U.K.* 55°56N 3°14W **121** B2
Gorgol □ *Mauritania* 15°45N 13°0W **262** B2
Gorgona *Italy* 43°26N 9°54E **198** E6
Gorgora *Ethiopia* 12°15N 37°17E **257** E4
Gorgoram *Nigeria* 12°40N 10°45E **263** C7
Gorham *U.S.A.* 44°23N 71°10W **313** B13
Gori *Georgia* 42°0N 44°7E **191** J7
Goribidnur = Gauribidanur *India* 13°37N 77°32E **245** H3
Goriganga ➝ *India* 29°45N 80°23E **243** E9
Gorinchem *Neths.* 51°50N 4°59E **170** C4
Goris *Armenia* 39°31N 46°22E **213** C12
Goritsy *Russia* 57°4N 36°43E **188** D9
Gorizia *Italy* 45°56N 13°37E **199** C10
Gorj □ *Romania* 45°5N 23°25E **183** E8
Gorki = Horki *Belarus* 54°17N 30°59E **188** E6
Gorkiy = Nizhniy Novgorod *Russia* 56°20N 44°0E **190** B7
Gorkovskoye Vdkhr. *Russia* 57°2N 43°4E **190** B6
Gorky Park *Russia* 55°43N 37°36E **129** B2
Gorleston *U.K.* 52°35N 1°44E **169** E9
Gorlice *Poland* 49°35N 21°11E **185** J8
Görlitz *Germany* 51°9N 14°58E **178** D10
Gorlovka = Horlivka *Ukraine* 48°19N 38°5E **189** H10
Gorman *U.S.A.* 34°47N 118°51W **307** L8
Gorna Djumaya = Blagoevgrad *Bulgaria* 42°2N 23°5E **202** D7
Gorna Dzhumayo = Blagoevgrad *Bulgaria* 42°2N 23°5E **202** D7
Gorna Oryakhovitsa *Bulgaria* 43°7N 25°40E **203** C9
Gornja Radgona *Slovenia* 46°40N 16°2E **199** B13
Gornja Tuzla *Bos.-H.* 44°35N 18°46E **182** F3
Gornji Grad *Slovenia* 46°20N 14°52E **199** B11
Gornji Milanovac *Serbia* 44°3N 20°29E **202** B4
Gornji Vakuf *Bos.-H.* 43°57N 17°34E **182** G2
Gorno Ablanovo *Bulgaria* 43°37N 25°43E **203** C9
Gorno-Altay □ *Russia* 51°0N 86°0E **217** B11
Gorno-Altaysk *Russia* 51°50N 86°5E **217** B11
Gorno-Badakhshan = Kŭhiston-Badakhshon □ *Tajikistan* 38°30N 73°0E **217** E8
Gornozavodsk *Russia* 46°33N 141°50E **215** E15
Gornyak *Russia* 50°59N 81°27E **217** B10
Gornyatski *Russia* 67°32N 64°3E **186** A11
Gornyatskiy *Russia* 48°18N 40°56E **191** F5
Gornyy *Primorsk, Russia* 44°57N 133°59E **220** B6
Gornyy *Saratov, Russia* 51°50N 48°30E **190** E9
Goro ➝ *C.A.R.* 9°14N 21°16E **264** A4
Gorodenka = Horodenka *Ukraine* 48°41N 25°29E **183** B10
Gorodets *Russia* 56°38N 43°28E **190** B6
Gorodishche = Horodyshche *Ukraine* 49°17N 31°27E **189** H6
Gorodishche *Russia* 53°13N 45°40E **190** D7
Gorodnya = Horodnya *Ukraine* 51°55N 31°33E **189** G6
Gorodok = Haradok *Belarus* 55°30N 30°3E **188** E6
Gorodok = Horodok *Ukraine* 49°46N 23°32E **177** D12
Gorodok = Zakamensk *Russia* 50°23N 103°17E **215** D11
Gorodovikovsk *Russia* 46°8N 41°58E **191** G5
Goroka *Papua N. G.* 6°7S 145°25E **286** D3
Goroke *Australia* 36°43S 141°29E **282** D4
Gorokhov = Horokhiv *Ukraine* 50°30N 24°45E **177** C13
Gorokhovets *Russia* 56°13N 42°39E **190** B6
Gorom Gorom *Burkina Faso* 14°26N 0°14W **263** C4
Goromonzi *Zimbabwe* 17°52S 31°22E **269** F3
Gorong, Kepulauan *Indonesia* 3°59S 131°25E **231** E8
Gorongose ➝ *Mozam.* 20°30S 34°40E **271** B5
Gorongoza *Mozam.* 18°44S 34°2E **269** F3
Gorongoza, Sa. da *Mozam.* 18°27S 34°2E **269** F3
Gorongoza △ *Mozam.* 18°50S 34°29E **271** A5
Gorontalo *Indonesia* 0°35N 123°5E **231** D6
Gorontalo □ *Indonesia* 0°50N 122°20E **231** D6
Goronyo *Nigeria* 13°29N 5°39E **263** C6
Górowo Iławeckie *Poland* 54°17N 20°30E **184** D7
Gorron *France* 48°25N 0°50W **172** D6
Gorror *Micronesia* 9°26N 138°4E **287** S16
Gorshechnoye *Russia* 51°31N 38°2E **189** G10
Gort *Ireland* 53°3N 8°49W **166** C3
Gortis *Greece* 35°4N 24°58E **207** E5
Gorumahisani *India* 22°20N 86°24E **244** C8
Gorumara △ *India* 26°42N 88°55E **241** B2
Góry Bystrzyckie *Poland* 50°16N 16°33E **185** H3
Goryachiy Klyuch *Russia* 44°38N 39°8E **191** H4
Goryeong *S. Korea* 35°44N 128°15E **224** E4
Gorzkowice *Poland* 51°13N 19°36E **185** G6
Górzno *Poland* 53°12N 19°38E **185** E6
Gorzów Śląski *Poland* 51°3N 18°22E **185** G5
Gorzów Wielkopolski *Poland* 52°43N 15°15E **185** F2
Gose *Japan* 34°27N 135°44E **223** C7
Gosen *Germany* 52°23N 13°43E **115** B5
Gosener kanal *Germany* 52°24N 13°42E **115** B5
Goseong *S. Korea* 34°58N 128°19E **224** E4
Gosford *Australia* 33°23S 151°18E **283** B9
Goshen *Calif., U.S.A.* 36°21N 119°25W **306** J7
Goshen *Ind., U.S.A.* 41°35N 85°50W **311** C11
Goshen *N.Y., U.S.A.* 41°24N 74°20W **313** E10
Goshogawara *Japan* 40°48N 140°27E **220** D10
Goshquduq Qum = Tosquduq Qumlari *Uzbekistan* 42°25N 65°24E ...
Goskopi = Kopeysk *Russia* 55°7N 61°37E **216** A6
Goslar *Germany* 51°54N 10°25E **178** D6
Gospel Oak *U.K.* 51°32N 0°9W **125** A3
Gospič *Croatia* 44°35N 15°23E **199** D12
Gosport *Hants., U.K.* 50°48N 1°9W **169** G6
Gosport *Ind., U.S.A.* 39°21N 86°40W **311** E10
Gosse ➝ *Australia* 19°32S 134°37E **280** B1
Gossas *Senegal* 14°28N 16°0W **262** C1
Gosselies *Belgium* 50°29N 4°26E ...
Gossi *Mali* 15°48N 1°20W **263** B4
Gossinga *South Sudan* 8°36N 25°59E **257** F2
Gostingen = Gostyń *Poland* 51°50N 17°3E **185** G4
Gostinopolye = Volkhov *Russia* 59°55N 32°15E **188** C7
Gostivar *Macedonia* 41°48N 20°57E **202** E4
Gostyń *Poland* 51°50N 17°3E **185** G4
Gostynin *Poland* 52°26N 19°29E **185** F6
Göta älv ➝ *Sweden* 57°42N 11°54E **163** G5
Göta kanal *Sweden* 58°30N 15°58E **163** F10
Götaland *Sweden* 57°30N 14°30E **163** G8
Gotanda *Japan* 35°37N 139°43E **140** B3
Göteborg *Sweden* 57°43N 11°59E **163** G5
Gotemba *Japan* 35°18N 138°56E **223** B10
Götene *Sweden* 58°32N 13°30E **163** F7
Gotenhafen = Gdynia *Poland* 54°35N 18°33E **184** D5
Goteşti *Moldova* 46°9N 28°10E **183** D13
Goth Goli Mar *Pakistan* 24°53N 67°1E **123** A2
Goth Sher Shah *Pakistan* 24°53N 66°59E **123** A1
Gotha *Thüringen, Germany* 50°56N 10°42E **178** E6
Gotha *Fla., U.S.A.* 28°31N 81°31W **133** A1
Gothenburg = Göteborg *Sweden* 57°43N 11°59E **163** G5
Gothenburg *U.S.A.* 40°56N 100°10W **308** E3
Gothèye *Niger* 13°52N 1°34E **263** C5
Gotland *Sweden* 57°30N 18°33E **163** G12
Gotlands län □ *Sweden* 57°15N 18°30E **163** G12
Gotō = Fukue *Japan* 32°41N 128°51E **221** H4
Goto Meer *Bonaire* 12°14N 68°22W **322** h
Gotō-Rettō *Japan* 32°55N 129°5E **221** H4
Gotse Delchev *Bulgaria* 41°36N 23°46E **202** E7
Gotska Sandön *Sweden* 58°24N 19°15E **163** F13
Gōtsu *Japan* 35°0N 132°14E **222** C4
Göttero, Monte *Italy* 44°22N 9°42E **198** D6
Gottesberg = Boguszów-Gorce *Poland* 50°45N 16°12E **185** H3
Göttingen *Germany* 51°31N 9°55E **178** D5
Gottschee = Kočevje *Slovenia* 45°39N 14°50E **199** C11
Gottskär *Sweden* 57°25N 12°2E **163** G6
Gottwald = Zmiyev *Ukraine* 49°39N 36°27E **189** H9
Gottwaldov = Zlín *Czech Rep.* 49°14N 17°40E **181** B10
Goubangzi *China* 41°20N 121°52E **227** D11
Gouda *Neths.* 52°1N 4°42E **170** B4
Goudiri *Senegal* 14°15N 12°45W **262** C2
Goudoumaria *Niger* 13°40N 11°10E **259** F2
Goudouras, Akra *Greece* 34°59N 26°6E **207** F7
Gouéké *Guinea* 8°2N 8°43W **262** D3
Gough I. *Atl. Oc.* 40°10S 9°45W **152** L11
Gouin, Rés. *Canada* 48°35N 74°40W **298** C5
Gouitafla *Ivory C.* 7°30N 5°53W **262** D3
Goulburn *Australia* 34°44S 149°44E **283** C8
Goulburn Is. *Australia* 11°40S 133°20E **280** A1
Goulburn River △ *Australia* 32°19S 150°10E **283** B9
Goulds *U.S.A.* 25°33N 80°23W **317** K9
Goulia *Ivory C.* 10°1N 7°11W **262** C3
Goulimine *Morocco* 28°56N 10°0W **260** C3
Goulimine □ *Morocco* 28°0N 11°0W **260** C3
Goulmima *Morocco* 31°41N 4°57W **260** B4
Goumbou *Mali* 15°2N 7°25W **262** B3
Goumenissa *Greece* 40°56N 22°37E **202** F6
Gounatolo *Solomon Is.* 8°25S 160°52E **287** M11
Goundam *Mali* 16°27N 3°40W **262** B4
Goundi *Chad* 9°22N 17°21E **259** G3
Gounou-Gaya *Chad* 9°38N 15°31E **259** G3
Goura *Greece* 37°56N 22°20E **204** D4
Gouraya *Algeria* 36°31N 1°56E **261** A5
Gourbassi *Mali* 13°24N 11°38W **262** C2
Gourbeyre *Guadeloupe* 16°0N 61°41W **322** b
Gourdon, Pt. *Trin. & Tob.* 10°40N 61°38W **323** t
Gourdon *France* 44°44N 1°23E **174** D5
Gouré *Niger* 14°0N 10°10E **259** F2
Gouri *Chad* 18°50N 16°49E **259** E3
Gourin *France* 48°8N 3°37W **172** D3
Gourits ➝ *S. Africa* 34°21S 21°52E **270** D3
Gourma-Rharous *Mali* 16°55N 1°50W **263** B4
Gournay-en-Bray *France* 49°29N 1°44E **173** C8
Gournay-sur-Marne *France* 48°51N 2°34E **134** A4
Gournes *Greece* 35°19N 25°16E **207** E6
Gouro *Chad* 19°36N 19°36E **259** E3
Gourock *U.K.* 55°57N 4°49W **167** F4
Gourock Ra. *Australia* 36°0S 149°25E **283** D8
Goursi *Burkina Faso* 12°42N 2°37W **262** C4
Gouvea *Brazil* 18°27S 43°44W **333** E3
Gouverneur *U.S.A.* 44°20N 75°28W **313** B9
Gouvia *Greece* 39°39N 19°50E **206** B9
Gouyave *Grenada* 12°10N 61°44W **323** q
Gouzon *France* 46°12N 2°14E **173** F9
Gove, Barragem do *Angola* 13°26S 15°53E **265** E3
Gove Peninsula *Australia* 12°17S 136°49E **280** A2
Governador, I. do *Brazil* 22°48S 43°13W **135** A1
Governador Valadares *Brazil* 18°15S 41°57W **333** E3
Governor Generoso *Phil.* 6°39N 126°5E **233** H6
Governor's Harbour *Bahamas* 25°10N 76°14W **320** A4
Governors I. *New York, U.S.A.* **132** f1
Govialtay □ *Mongolia* 45°30N 96°0E **217** C13
Govindgarh *India* 24°23N 81°18E **243** G9
Gowan Ra. *Australia* 25°0S 145°0E **280** D4
Gowanda *U.S.A.* 42°28N 78°56W **312** D6
Gower *U.K.* 51°35N 4°10W **169** F3
Gowers Corner *U.S.A.* 28°20N 82°30W **317** G7
Gowna, L. *Ireland* 53°51N 7°34W **166** C4
Gowrie *U.S.A.* 42°17N 94°17W **310** B2
Gowurdak *Turkmenistan* 37°50N 66°4E **217** E7
Goya *Argentina* 29°10S 59°10W **334** B4
Goyang *S. Korea* 37°39N 126°50E **224** D3
Goyave *Guadeloupe* 16°8N 61°34W **322** b
Goyaves, Grande Rivière ➝ *Guadeloupe* 16°18N 61°36W **322** b
Göyçay *Azerbaijan* 40°42N 47°43E **191** K8
Goyder Lagoon *Australia* 27°3S 138°58E **281** D2
Goygöl *Azerbaijan* 40°37N 46°12E **191** K8
Goyllarisquizga *Peru* 10°31S 76°24W **330** C2
Göynük *Antalya, Turkey* 36°41N 30°33E **205** E12
Göynük *Bolu, Turkey* 40°24N 30°48E **212** B4
Goz Beïda *Chad* 12°10N 21°20E **259** F4
Goz Regeb *Sudan* 16°3N 35°33E **257** D4
Gozdnica *Poland* 51°28N 15°4E **185** G2
Gözneköy *Turkey* 36°58N 34°33E **250** B5
Gozo *Malta* 36°3N 14°15E **206** E7
Graaff-Reinet *S. Africa* 32°13S 24°32E **270** D3
Graben *Vienna, Austria* **142** b2
Grabill *U.S.A.* 41°13N 84°57W **311** C12
Grabo *Ivory C.* 4°57N 7°30W **262** D3
Grabow *Mecklenburg-Vorpommern, Germany* 53°17N 11°34E **178** B7
Grabów *Warszawa, Poland* 52°8N 20°59E **143** C1
Grabów nad Prosną *Poland* 51°31N 18°7E **185** G5
Graça *Lisbon, Portugal* **126** b3
Gračac *Croatia* 44°18N 15°57E **199** D12
Gračanica *Bos.-H.* 44°43N 18°18E **182** F3
Graçay *France* 47°10N 1°50E **173** E8
Grace Cathedral *San Francisco, U.S.A.* **136** b2
Graceville *U.S.A.* 30°58N 85°31W **316** E4
Gracewood *U.S.A.* 33°22N 82°2W **316** B7
Gràcia *Spain* 41°24N 2°10E **114** A2
Gracias a Dios, C. *Honduras* 15°0N 83°10W **320** D3
Graciosa *Azores* 39°4N 28°0W **153** d1
Graciosa, I. *Canary Is.* 29°15N 13°32W **153** e2
Grad Sofiya □ *Bulgaria* 42°35N 23°20E **202** D7
Gradac *Montenegro* 43°23N 19°9E **202** C3
Gradačac *Bos.-H.* 44°52N 18°26E **182** F3
Gradaús *Brazil* 7°43S 51°11W **332** C1
Gradaús, Serra dos *Brazil* 8°0S 50°45W **332** C1
Gradeška Planina *Macedonia* 41°30N 22°15E **202** E6
Gradets *Bulgaria* 42°46N 26°30E **203** D10
Gradišće *Slovenia* 46°37N 15°50E **199** B12
Grădiştea de Munte *Romania* 45°37N 23°13E **183** E8
Grado *Italy* 45°40N 13°23E **199** C10
Grado *Spain* 43°23N 6°4W **194** B4
Grady *U.S.A.* 34°49N 103°19W **305** J12
Graeca, Lacul *Romania* 44°5N 26°10E **183** F11
Grafarnes *Iceland* 64°55N 23°16W **155** C3
Gräfelfing *Germany* 48°7N 11°25E **131** B1
Grafenau *Germany* 48°51N 13°22E **179** G9
Gräfenberg *Germany* 49°39N 11°14E **179** F7
Grafham Water *U.K.* 52°19N 0°18W **169** E7
Grafton *N.S.W., Australia* 29°38S 152°58E **281** D5
Grafton *Ill., U.S.A.* 38°58N 90°26W **310** F6
Grafton *N. Dak., U.S.A.* 48°25N 97°25W **308** A5
Grafton *W. Va., U.S.A.* 39°21N 80°2W **309** F13
Grafton Caledonia Wildlife Estate *Trin. & Tob.* 11°11N 60°47W **323** s
Grafton's Pt. *Anguilla* 18°20N 62°54W **322** a
Gragoatá *Brazil* 22°53S 43°8W **135** B2
Graham *Ont., Canada* 49°20N 90°30W **298** C1
Graham *Ga., U.S.A.* 31°50N 82°30W **316** D7
Graham *Tex., U.S.A.* 33°6N 98°35W **314** E5
Graham, Mt. *U.S.A.* 32°42N 109°52W **305** K9
Graham Bell, Ostrov = Greem-Bell, Ostrov *Russia* 81°0N 62°0E **214** A7
Graham I. *B.C., Canada* 53°40N 132°30W **296** C2
Graham I. *Nunavut, Canada* 77°25N 90°30W **295** B13
Graham Land *Antarctica* 65°0S 64°0W **151** C17
Grahamstown *S. Africa* 33°19S 26°31E **270** D4
Grahamsville *U.S.A.* 41°51N 74°33W **313** E10
Grahovo *Montenegro* 42°40N 18°40E **202** D2
Graïba *Tunisia* 34°30N 10°13E **258** B2
Graie, Alpi *Europe* 45°30N 7°10E **175** C11
Grain Coast *W. Afr.* 4°20N 10°0W **262** E3
Grajagan *Indonesia* 8°35S 114°13E **231** K17
Grajaú *Brazil* 5°50S 46°4W **332** C2
Grajaú ➝ *Brazil* 3°41S 44°48W **332** B3
Grajewo *Poland* 53°39N 22°30E **184** E9
Gramada *Bulgaria* 43°49N 22°39E **202** C6
Gramat *France* 44°48N 1°43E **174** D5
Grammichele *Italy* 37°13N 14°38E **201** E7
Grámmos, Óros *Greece* 40°18N 20°47E **202** F4
Grampian *U.S.A.* 40°58N 78°37W **312** F6
Grampian Highlands = Grampian Mts. *U.K.* 56°50N 4°0W **167** E5
Grampian Mts. *U.K.* 56°50N 4°0W **167** E5
Grampians, The *Australia* 37°15S 142°20E **282** D5
Grampians △ *Australia* 37°15S 142°28E **282** D5
Gramsh *Albania* 40°52N 20°12E **202** F4
Gran *Norway* 60°23N 10°31E **164** D7
Gran ➝ *Suriname* 4°1N 55°30W **329** C6
Gran Altiplanicie Central *Argentina* 49°0S 69°30W **336** C3
Gran Canaria *Canary Is.* 27°55N 15°35W **153** e1
Gran Chaco *S. Amer.* 25°0S 61°0W **334** B3
Gran Couva *Trin. & Tob.* 10°24N 61°22W **323** t
Gran Desierto del Pinacate △ *Mexico* 31°51N 113°32W **318** A2
Gran Laguna Salada *Argentina* 44°24S 67°23W **336** B3
Gran Pajonal *Peru* 10°45S 74°30W **330** C3
Gran Paradiso *Italy* 45°33N 7°17E **198** C4
Gran Sasso d'Itália *Italy* 42°27N 13°42E **199** F10
Gran Sasso e Monti Della Laga △ *Italy* 42°32N 13°22E **199** F10
Gran Tarajal *Canary Is.* 28°13N 14°1W **153** e2
Granada *Nic.* 11°58N 86°0W **320** D2
Granada *Spain* 37°10N 3°35W **195** H7
Granada *Colo., U.S.A.* 38°4N 102°19W **304** G12
Granada □ *Spain* 37°18N 3°0W **195** H7
Granadilla de Abona *Canary Is.* 28°7N 16°33W **153** e1
Granard *Ireland* 53°47N 7°30W **166** C4
Granbury *U.S.A.* 32°27N 97°47W **314** E6
Granby *Qué., Canada* 45°25N 72°45W **313** A12
Granby *Colo., U.S.A.* 40°5N 105°56W **304** F11
Grand ➝ *Ont., Canada* 42°51N 79°34W **312** D5
Grand ➝ *Mich., U.S.A.* 43°4N 86°15W **311** A10
Grand ➝ *Mo., U.S.A.* 39°23N 93°7W **310** E3
Grand ➝ *S. Dak., U.S.A.* 45°40N 100°45W **308** C3
Grand Abaque, Pte.du *Guadeloupe* 16°21N 61°0W **322** e
Grand-Anse = Portsmouth *Dominica* 15°34N 61°27W **323** k
Grand Anse *Grenada* 12°1N 61°45W **323** q
Grand Anse B. *Grenada* 12°2N 61°45W **323** q
Grand B. *Dominica* 15°14N 61°18W **323** k
Grand Bahama I. *Bahamas* 26°40N 78°30W **320** A4
Grand Baie *Mauritius* 20°0S 57°35E **272** e
Grand Bank *Canada* 47°6N 55°48W **299** C8
Grand Banks *Atl. Oc.* 45°0N 52°0W **152** B6
Grand Bassam *Ivory C.* 5°10N 3°49W **262** D4
Grand Bassin *Réunion* 21°10S 55°32E **272** f
Grand Batanga *Cameroon* 2°50N 9°55E **264** B1
Grand Bazaar = Kapali Carsi *Turkey* 41°1N 28°58E **122** B1
Grand Bénare *Réunion* 21°6S 55°25E **272** f
Grand Bend *Canada* 43°18N 81°45W **312** C3
Grand Béréby *Ivory C.* 4°38N 6°55W **262** E3
Grand Blanc *U.S.A.* 42°56N 83°38W **311** B13
Grand Bois *Mauritius* 20°25S 57°32E **272** e
Grand-Bourg *Guadeloupe* 15°53N 61°19W **322** e
Grand Canal = Canal Grande *Venice, Italy* **142** b2
Grand Canal = Da Yunhe ➝ *China* 39°10N 117°10E **227** E9
Grand Canyon *U.S.A.* 36°3N 112°9W **305** H7
Grand Canyon △ *U.S.A.* 36°15N 112°30W **305** H7
Grand Canyon-Parashant △ *U.S.A.* 36°30N 113°45W **305** H7
Grand Case *St.-Martin* 18°6N 63°4W **322** a
Grand Cayman *Cayman Is.* 19°20N 81°20W **320** C3
Grand Central Station *New York, U.S.A.* **132** c2
Grand Cess *Liberia* 4°40N 8°12W **262** E3
Grand Coulee *U.S.A.* 47°57N 119°0W **304** C4
Grand Coulee Dam *U.S.A.* 47°57N 118°59W **304** C4
Grand Cul-de-Sac Marin *Guadeloupe* 16°20N 61°35W **322** e
Grand Étang △ *Grenada* 12°5N 61°42W **323** q
Grand Falls *Canada* 47°3N 67°44W **299** C6
Grand Falls-Windsor *Canada* 48°56N 55°40W **299** C8
Grand Fond *St. Barts* 17°53N 62°48W **322** a
Grand Forks *B.C., Canada* 49°0N 118°30W **296** D5
Grand Forks *N. Dak., U.S.A.* 47°55N 97°3W **308** B5
Grand Galet *Réunion* 21°17S 55°38E **272** f
Grand Gaube *Mauritius* 20°0S 57°39E **272** e
Grand Gorge *U.S.A.* 42°21N 74°29W **313** D10
Grand Haven *U.S.A.* 43°4N 86°13W **311** A10
Grand I. *Mich., U.S.A.* 46°31N 86°40W **308** B10
Grand I. *N.Y., U.S.A.* 43°0N 78°58W **312** D6
Grand Îlet *Guadeloupe* 15°50N 61°35W **322** e
Grand Îlet *Réunion* 21°1S 55°29E **272** f
Grand Island *U.S.A.* 40°55N 98°21W **308** E4
Grand Isle *La., U.S.A.* 29°14N 90°0W **315** G9
Grand Isle *Vt., U.S.A.* 44°43N 73°18W **313** B11
Grand Junction *Colo., U.S.A.* 39°4N 108°33W **304** G9
Grand Junction *Iowa, U.S.A.* 42°2N 94°14W **310** B2
Grand L. *N.B., Canada* 45°57N 66°7W **299** C6
Grand L. *Nfld. & L., Canada* 49°0N 57°30W **299** C8
Grand L. *Nfld. & L., Canada* 53°40N 60°30W **299** B7
Grand L. *La., U.S.A.* 29°55N 92°47W **314** G8
Grand L. *Ohio, U.S.A.* 40°32N 84°25W **311** D12
Grand Lahou *Ivory C.* 5°10N 5°5W **262** D3
Grand Lake *U.S.A.* 40°15N 105°49W **304** F11

Grand Ledge U.S.A. 42°45N 84°45W 311 B12
Grand-Lieu, L. de France 47°6N 1°40W 172 E5
Grand Mal B. Grenada 12°4N 61°45W 323 q
Grand Manan I. Canada 44°45N 66°52W 299 D6
Grand Marais Mich., U.S.A. 46°40N 85°59W 309 B11
Grand Marais Minn., U.S.A. 47°45N 90°25W 298 C1
Grand Marigot B. Dominica 15°25N 61°16W 323 k
Grand-Mère Canada 46°36N 72°40W 298 C5
Grand Palace Bangkok, Thailand 113 b1
Grand Place Belgium 50°50N 4°21E 116 A2
Grand Popo Benin 6°15N 1°57E 263 D5
Grand Portage U.S.A. 47°58N 89°41W 308 B9
Grand Prairie U.S.A. 32°44N 96°59W 314 E6
Grand Rapids = Wisconsin Rapids U.S.A. 44°23N 89°49W 308 C9
Grand Rapids Man., Canada 53°12N 99°19W 297 C9
Grand Rapids Mich., U.S.A. 42°58N 85°40W 311 B10
Grand Rapids Minn., U.S.A. 47°14N 93°31W 308 B7
Grand Rapids ✕ (GRR) U.S.A. 42°53N 85°31W 311 B11
Grand Récif Sud N. Cal. 22°47S 166°55E 288 d
Grand Ridge U.S.A. 30°43N 85°1W 316 E4
Grand River U.S.A. 40°49N 93°58W 310 D3
Grand River Bay Mauritius 20°9S 57°27E 272 e
Grand River South East → Mauritius 20°17S 57°46E 272 e
Grand' Rivière Martinique 14°52N 61°11W 322 j
Grand Roy Grenada 12°8N 61°45W 323 q
Grand St-Bernard, Col du Europe 45°50N 7°10E 179 K3
Grand Santi Fr. Guiana 4°20N 54°24W 329 C7
Grand Staircase-Escalante ⌂ U.S.A. 37°25N 111°33W 305 H8
Grand Teton U.S.A. 43°54N 110°50W 304 E8
Grand Teton △ U.S.A. 43°50N 110°50W 304 E8
Grand Union Canal U.K. 52°7N 0°53W 169 E7
Grandas Spain 43°13N 6°53W 194 B4
Grande → Jujuy, Argentina 24°20S 65°2W 334 A2
Grande → Mendoza, Argentina 36°52S 69°45W 334 D2
Grande → Bolivia 15°51S 64°39W 331 D5
Grande → Bahia, Brazil 11°30S 44°30W 332 D3
Grande → Minas Gerais, Brazil 20°6S 51°4W 333 F1
Grande → Venezuela 8°36N 61°39W 329 B5
Grande, B. Argentina 50°30S 68°20W 336 D3
Grande, Darsena Venice, Italy 142 b4
Grande, I. Brazil 23°9S 44°14W 333 F3
Grande, Rio → N. Amer. 25°58N 97°9W 314 J6
Grande, Serra Piauí, Brazil 8°0S 45°10W 332 C2
Grande, Serra Tocantins, Brazil 11°15S 46°30W 332 D2
Grande Anse = Beauséjour Guadeloupe 16°18N 61°4W 322 e
Grande Anse Guadeloupe 16°19N 61°47W 322 e
Grande Anse Martinique 14°30N 61°5W 322 j
Grande Anse St. Lucia 14°1N 60°54W 323 m
Grande Anse Seychelles 4°18S 55°45E 272 c
Grande Baleine → Canada 55°16N 77°47W 298 A4
Grande Cache Canada 53°53N 119°8W 296 C5
Grande Casse, Pte. de la France 45°24N 6°49E 175 C10
Grande Comore Comoros Is. 11°35S 43°20E 272 a
Grande Cul de Sac B St. Lucia 13°59N 61°2W 323 m
Grande-Entrée Canada 47°30N 61°40W 299 C7
Grande Matelot Pt. Trin. & Tob. 10°49N 61°9W 323 t
Grande Place Brussels, Belgium 116 b2
Grande Prairie Canada 55°10N 118°50W 296 B5
Grande Pte. Guadeloupe 15°58N 61°37W 322 e
Grande-Rivière Qué., Canada 48°26N 64°30W 299 C7
Grande Riviere Trin. & Tob. 10°50N 61°3W 323 t
Grande Rivière, Pte. de la Guadeloupe 16°18N 61°36W 322 e
Grande Rivière Noire Mauritius 20°21S 57°21E 272 e
Grande Rivière Sud Est Mauritius 20°17S 57°46E 272 e
Grande Sertão Veredas △ Brazil 15°10S 45°40W 333 E2
Grande-Terre Guadeloupe 16°20N 61°25W 322 e
Grande Terre Mayotte 12°46S 45°7E 272 b
Grande-Vallée Canada 49°14N 65°8W 299 C6
Grande Vigie, Pte. de la Guadeloupe 16°32N 61°27W 322 e
Grandfalls U.S.A. 31°20N 102°51W 314 F3
Grândola Portugal 38°12N 8°35W 195 G2
Grandpré France 49°20N 4°50E 173 C11
Grands Causses ⌂ France 44°5N 2°58E 174 D6
Grands-Jardins ⌂ Canada 47°41N 70°51W 299 C5
Grandview Man., Canada 51°10N 100°42W 297 C8
Grandview Mo., U.S.A. 38°53N 94°32W 310 F2
Grandview Wash., U.S.A. 46°15N 119°54W 304 C4
Grandview Heights U.S.A. 39°58N 83°2W 311 E13
Grandvilliers France 49°40N 1°57E 173 C8
Graneros Chile 34°5S 70°45W 334 C1
Grange Hill Jamaica 18°18N 78°11W 320 a
Grangemouth U.K. 56°1N 3°42W 167 E5
Granger U.S.A. 41°35N 109°58W 304 F9
Grängesberg Sweden 60°6N 15°1E 162 D9
Grangeville U.S.A. 45°56N 116°7W 304 D5
Granisle Canada 54°53N 126°13W 296 C3
Granit Rose, Côte France 48°50N 4°10W 172 D2
Granite City U.S.A. 38°42N 90°8W 310 F6
Granite Falls U.S.A. 44°49N 95°33W 308 C6
Granite L. Canada 48°8N 57°5W 299 C8
Granite Mt. U.S.A. 33°5N 116°28W 307 M10
Granite Pk. U.S.A. 45°10N 109°48W 304 D9
Graniteville S.C., U.S.A. 33°34N 81°49W 316 B8
Graniteville Vt., U.S.A. 44°8N 72°29W 313 B12
Granitola, C. Italy 37°34N 12°39E 200 E5
Granity N.Z. 41°39S 171°51E 285 B6
Granja Brazil 3°7S 40°50W 332 B3
Granja de Moreruela Spain 41°48N 5°44W 194 D5
Granja de Torrehermosa Spain 38°19N 5°35W 195 G5
Grankulla = Kauniainen Finland 60°13N 24°44E 121 B1
Gränna Sweden 58°1N 14°28E 163 F8
Granollers Spain 41°39N 2°18E 196 D7
Gransee Germany 53°1N 13°8E 178 B9
Grant Fla., U.S.A. 27°56N 80°32W 317 H9
Grant Nebr., U.S.A. 40°53N 101°43W 308 E3
Grant, Mt. U.S.A. 38°34N 118°48W 304 G4
Grant City U.S.A. 40°29N 94°25W 310 D2
Grant I. Australia 11°10S 132°52E 278 B5
Grant Park Chicago, U.S.A. 119 c2
Grant Range U.S.A. 38°30N 115°25W 304 G6
Grantham U.K. 52°55N 0°38W 168 E7
Grantley Adams Int. ✕ (BGI) Barbados 13°5N 59°29W 323 r
Granton U.K. 55°58N 3°14W 121 B2
Grantown-on-Spey U.K. 57°20N 3°36W 167 D5
Grants U.S.A. 35°9N 107°52W 305 J10
Grants Pass U.S.A. 42°26N 123°19W 304 E2
Grantsville U.S.A. 40°36N 112°28W 304 F7
Grantville U.S.A. 33°14N 84°50W 316 B5
Granville Manche, France 48°50N 1°35W 172 D5
Granville Trin. & Tob. 10°7N 61°48W 323 t
Granville Ill., U.S.A. 41°16N 89°14W 310 C7
Granville N. Dak., U.S.A. 48°16N 100°47W 308 A3
Granville N.Y., U.S.A. 43°24N 73°16W 313 C11
Granville Ohio, U.S.A. 40°4N 82°31W 312 F2
Granville L. Canada 56°18N 100°30W 297 B8
Granvin Norway 60°33N 6°45E 164 D3
Graskop S. Africa 24°56S 30°49E 271 B5
Gräsö Sweden 60°28N 18°35E 162 D12
Grass → Canada 56°3N 96°33W 297 B9
Grass Range U.S.A. 47°2N 108°48W 304 C9
Grass River ⌂ Canada 54°40N 100°50W 297 C8
Grass Valley Calif., U.S.A. 39°13N 121°4W 306 F6
Grass Valley Oreg., U.S.A. 45°22N 120°47W 304 D3
Grassano Italy 40°38N 16°17E 201 B9
Grasse France 43°38N 6°56E 175 E10
Grassflat U.S.A. 41°0N 78°6W 312 E6
Grassi, Palazzo Venice, Italy 142 b2
Grasslands △ Canada 49°11N 107°38W 297 D7
Grassy Australia 40°3S 144°5E 281 G3
Grassy Park S. Africa 34°3S 18°30E 118 B2
Gråsten Denmark 54°55N 9°35E 163 K3
Grästorp Sweden 58°20N 12°40E 163 F6
Gratis U.S.A. 39°38N 84°32W 311 E12
Gratkorn Austria 47°8N 15°21E 180 D8
Gratosóglio Italy 45°24N 9°1E 128 B2
Gratz U.S.A. 38°28N 84°57W 311 F12
Gratzwalde Germany 52°28N 13°42E 115 B5
Graubünden □ Switz. 46°45N 9°30E 179 J5
Graudenz = Grudziądz Poland 53°30N 18°47E 184 E5
Graulhet France 43°45N 1°59E 174 E5
Graus Spain 42°11N 0°20E 196 C5
Gravberget Norway 60°53N 12°14E 164 D9
Grave, Pte. de France 45°34N 1°4W 174 C2
Gravelbourg Canada 49°50N 106°35W 297 D7
Gravelines France 51°1N 2°10E 173 A9
's-Gravenhage Neths. 52°7N 4°17E 170 B4
Gravenhurst Canada 44°52N 79°20W 312 B5
Gravesend N.S.W., Australia 29°35S 150°20E 281 D5
Gravesend Kent, U.K. 51°26N 0°22E 169 F8
Gravesend N.Y., U.S.A. 40°36N 73°56W 132 C2
Gravina in Púglia Italy 40°49N 16°25E 201 B9
Gravois, Pointe-à- Haiti 18°2N 73°56W 321 C5
Gravona → France 41°58N 8°45E 175 G12
Gray Haute-Saône, France 47°22N 5°35E 173 E12
Gray Ga., U.S.A. 33°1N 83°32W 316 B6
Grayling Alaska, U.S.A. 62°57N 160°3W 303 E7
Grayling Mich., U.S.A. 44°40N 84°43W 309 C11
Grays U.K. 51°28N 0°21E 169 F8
Grays Harbor U.S.A. 46°59N 124°1W 306 D2
Grays L. U.S.A. 43°4N 111°26W 304 E8
Grays River U.S.A. 46°21N 123°37W 306 D3
Grayville U.S.A. 38°16N 88°0W 311 F9
Grayvoron Russia 50°29N 35°41E 189 G8
Graz Austria 47°4N 15°27E 180 D8
Grazhdanka Russia 59°59N 30°24E 137 B2
Grdelica Serbia 42°55N 22°3E 202 D6
Greåker Norway 59°16N 11°12E 164 E8
Greasy L. Canada 62°55N 122°12W 296 A4
Great Abaco I. = Abaco I. Bahamas 26°25N 77°10W 320 A4
Great Artesian Basin Australia 23°0S 144°0E 280 C3
Great Australian Bight Australia 33°30S 130°0E 279 F5
Great Bacolet Bay Grenada 12°4N 61°37W 323 q
Great Bahama Bank Bahamas 23°15N 78°0W 320 B4
Great Barrier I. N.Z. 36°11S 175°25E 284 C4
Great Barrier Reef Australia 18°0S 146°50E 280 B4
Great Barrier Reef ⌂ Australia 20°0S 150°0E 280 B4
Great Barrington U.S.A. 42°12N 73°22W 313 D11
Great Basalt Wall △ Australia 19°52S 145°43E 280 B4
Great Basin U.S.A. 40°0N 117°0W 304 G5
Great Basin △ U.S.A. 38°56N 114°15W 304 G6
Great Basses Sri Lanka 6°11N 81°29E 245 L5
Great Bear → Canada 65°0N 126°0W 294 E7
Great Bear L. Canada 65°30N 120°0W 294 D8
Great Belt = Store Bælt Denmark 55°20N 11°0E 163 J4
Great Bend Kans., U.S.A. 38°22N 98°46W 308 F4
Great Bend Pa., U.S.A. 41°58N 75°45W 313 E9
Great Blasket I. Ireland 52°6N 10°32W 166 D1
Great Britain Europe 54°0N 2°15W 158 E5
Great Camanoe Br. Virgin Is. 18°30N 64°35W 321 b
Great Channel Asia 6°0N 94°0E 245 L11
Great Coco I. = Koko Kyunzu Burma 14°7N 93°22E 245 G11
Great Codroy Canada 47°51N 59°16W 299 C8
Great Divide, The = Great Dividing Ra. Australia 23°0S 146°0E 280 C4
Great Divide Basin U.S.A. 42°0N 108°0W 304 E9
Great Dividing Ra. Australia 23°0S 146°0E 280 C4
Great Driffield = Driffield U.K. 54°0N 0°26W 168 C7
Great Exuma I. Bahamas 23°30N 75°50W 320 B4
Great Falls Guyana 5°35N 61°0W 329 B5
Great Falls Mont., U.S.A. 47°30N 111°17W 304 C8
Great Fish = Groot-Vis → S. Africa 33°28S 27°5E 270 D4
Great Goat I. Jamaica 17°52N 77°3W 320 a
Great Guana Cay Bahamas 24°0N 76°20W 320 B4
Great Hall of the People Beijing, China 114 c3
Great Himalayan △ India 31°30N 77°30E 242 D7
Great Inagua I. Bahamas 21°0N 73°20W 321 B5
Great Indian Desert = Thar Desert India 28°0N 72°0E 242 F5
Great Karoo S. Africa 31°55S 21°0E 270 D3
Great Khingan Mts. = Da Hinggan Ling China 48°0N 121°0E 219 B13
Great Lake Australia 41°50S 146°40E 281 G4
Great Lakes N. Amer. 46°0N 84°0W 292 E11
Great Limpopo Transfrontier △ Africa 23°0S 31°45E 271 B5
Great Malvern U.K. 52°7N 2°18W 169 E5
Great Miami → U.S.A. 39°7N 84°49W 311 E12
Great Nicobar India 7°0N 93°50E 245 L11
Great Ormes Head U.K. 53°20N 3°52W 168 D4
Great Otway △ Australia 38°50S 143°50E 282 E5
Great Ouse → U.K. 52°48N 0°21E 168 E8
Great Palm I. Australia 18°45S 146°40E 280 B4
Great Pedro Bluff Jamaica 17°51N 77°44W 320 a
Great Pee Dee → U.S.A. 33°21N 79°10W 315 E15
Great Plains N. Amer. 47°0N 105°0W 292 E9
Great Ruaha → Tanzania 7°56S 37°52E 268 D4
Great Sacandaga L. U.S.A. 43°6N 74°16W 313 C10
Great Saint Bernard Pass = Grand St-Bernard, Col du Europe 45°50N 7°10E 179 K3
Great Salt Desert = Kavīr, Dasht-e Iran 34°30N 55°0E 247 C7
Great Salt L. U.S.A. 41°15N 112°40W 304 F7
Great Salt Lake Desert U.S.A. 40°50N 113°30W 304 F7
Great Salt Plains L. U.S.A. 36°45N 98°8W 314 C5
Great Salt Pond St. Kitts & Nevis 17°14N 62°40W 322 d
Great Sand Dunes ⌂ U.S.A. 37°48N 105°45W 305 H11
Great Sand Sea N. Afr. 29°0N 24°0E 258 C4
Great Sandy △ Australia 26°13S 153°2E 281 D5
Great Sandy Desert Australia 21°0S 124°0E 278 D3
Great Sangi = Sangihe, Pulau Indonesia 3°35N 125°30E 231 D7
Great Scarcies → S. Leone 9°0N 13°0W 262 D2
Great Sd. Bermuda 32°17N 64°51W 153 a
Great Sea Reef Fiji 16°15S 179°0E 287 A2
Great Sitkin I. U.S.A. 52°3N 176°6W 303 K3
Great Skellig Ireland 51°47N 10°33W 166 E1
Great Slave L. Canada 61°23N 115°38W 296 A5
Great Smoky Mts. △ U.S.A. 35°40N 83°40W 315 D13
Great Stour = Stour → U.K. 51°18N 1°22E 169 F9
Great Victoria Desert Australia 29°30S 126°30E 279 E4
Great Wall Antarctica 62°30S 58°0W 151 C18
Great Wall China 38°30N 109°30E 226 E5
Great Western Forum U.S.A. 33°57N 118°20W 126 C2
Great Whale River = Kuujjuarapik Canada 55°20N 77°35W 298 A4
Great Whernside U.K. 54°10N 1°58W 168 C6
Great Yarmouth U.K. 52°37N 1°44E 169 E9
Great Zab = Zāb al Kabīr → Iraq 36°1N 43°24E 213 D10
Great Zimbabwe Zimbabwe 20°16S 30°54E 269 G3
Greater Antilles W. Indies 17°40N 74°0W 321 C5
Greater London □ U.K. 51°31N 0°6W 169 F7
Greater Manchester □ U.K. 53°30N 2°15W 168 D5
Greater Sunda Is. Indonesia 7°0S 112°0E 230 F4
Grebbestad Sweden 58°42N 11°15E 163 F5
Grebenka = Hrebenka Ukraine 50°9N 32°22E 189 G7
Greco Italy 45°30N 9°12E 128 A2
Greco, C. Cyprus 34°57N 34°5E 207 F10
Greco, Mte. Italy 41°48N 13°58E 199 G10
Gredos, Sierra de Spain 40°20N 5°0W 194 E6
Greece U.S.A. 43°13N 77°41W 312 C7
Greece ■ Europe 40°0N 23°0E 204 B3
Greeley Colo., U.S.A. 40°25N 104°42W 304 F11
Greeley Nebr., U.S.A. 41°33N 98°32W 308 E4
Greeleyville U.S.A. 33°40N 79°59W 316 B10
Greely Fd. Canada 80°30N 85°0W 295 A15
Greem-Bell, Ostrov Russia 81°0N 62°0E 214 A7
Green → Ky., U.S.A. 37°54N 87°30W 308 G10
Green → Utah, U.S.A. 38°11N 109°53W 304 G9
Green B. U.S.A. 45°0N 87°30W 308 C10
Green Bay U.S.A. 44°31N 88°0W 308 C9
Green C. Australia 37°13S 150°1E 283 D9
Green City U.S.A. 40°16N 92°57W 310 D4
Green Cove Springs U.S.A. 29°59N 81°42W 316 F8
Green I. = Lütao Taiwan 22°40N 121°30E 225 D3
Green I. Antigua & B. 17°2N 61°40W 322 b
Green I. Hong Kong, China 22°17N 114°6E 122 B2
Green I. Grenada 12°13N 61°35W 323 q
Green Is. Papua N. G. 4°35S 154°10E 286 C8
Green Island Jamaica 18°23N 78°17W 320 a
Green Island B. Phil. 10°12N 119°22E 233 F2
Green Lake Canada 54°17N 107°47W 297 C7
Green Mt. = Peak, The Ascension I. 7°57S 14°20W 153 g
Green Mts. U.S.A. 43°45N 72°45W 313 C12
Green Point S. Africa 33°54S 18°25E 118 A1
Green Pond U.S.A. 32°44N 80°37W 316 C9
Green River Papua N. G. 3°54S 141°11E 286 B1
Green River Utah, U.S.A. 38°59N 110°10W 304 G8
Green River Wyo., U.S.A. 41°32N 109°28W 304 F9
Green Valley U.S.A. 31°52N 110°56W 305 L8
Greenacres U.S.A. 26°38N 80°7W 317 J9
Greenbank U.S.A. 48°6N 122°34W 306 B4
Greenbush Mich., U.S.A. 44°35N 83°19W 312 B1
Greenbush Minn., U.S.A. 48°42N 96°11W 308 A5
Greencastle U.S.A. 39°38N 86°52W 311 E10
Greene Iowa, U.S.A. 42°54N 92°48W 310 B4
Greene N.Y., U.S.A. 42°20N 75°46W 313 D9
Greeneville U.S.A. 36°10N 82°50W 315 C13
Greenfield Calif., U.S.A. 36°19N 121°15W 306 J5
Greenfield Calif., U.S.A. 35°15N 119°0W 307 K8
Greenfield Ill., U.S.A. 39°21N 90°12W 310 E6
Greenfield Ind., U.S.A. 39°47N 85°46W 311 E11
Greenfield Iowa, U.S.A. 41°18N 94°28W 310 C2
Greenfield Mass., U.S.A. 42°35N 72°36W 313 D12
Greenfield Mo., U.S.A. 37°25N 93°51W 308 G7
Greenfield Ohio, U.S.A. 39°21N 83°23W 311 E13
Greenfield Park Canada 45°29N 73°28W 130 B3
Greenford U.K. 51°31N 0°21W 125 A1
Greenhill U.K. 51°34N 0°18W 125 A2
Greenhills Ireland 53°18N 6°20W 120 B1
Greenland ☒ N. Amer. 66°0N 45°0W 154 D6
Greenland Sea Arctic 73°0N 10°0W 154 B10
Greenmarket Square Cape Town, S. Africa 118 c2
Greenock U.K. 55°57N 4°46W 167 F4
Greenore Ireland 54°1N 6°9W 166 B5
Greenore Pt. Ireland 52°14N 6°19W 166 D5
Greenough Australia 28°58S 114°43E 279 E1
Greenough → Australia 28°51S 114°38E 279 E1
Greenough Pt. Canada 44°58N 81°26W 312 B3
Greenpoint New York, U.S.A. 132 e1
Greenport U.S.A. 41°6N 72°22W 313 E12
Greensboro Fla., U.S.A. 30°34N 84°45W 316 E5
Greensboro Ga., U.S.A. 33°35N 83°11W 316 B6
Greensboro N.C., U.S.A. 36°4N 79°48W 315 C15
Greensboro Vt., U.S.A. 44°36N 72°18W 313 B12
Greensburg Ind., U.S.A. 39°20N 85°29W 311 E11
Greensburg Kans., U.S.A. 37°36N 99°18W 308 G4
Greensburg Pa., U.S.A. 40°18N 79°33W 312 F5
Greenstone = Geraldton Canada 49°44N 87°10W 298 C2
Greenstone Pt. U.K. 57°55N 5°37W 167 D3
Greentown U.S.A. 40°29N 85°58W 311 D11
Greenup U.S.A. 39°15N 88°10W 311 E8
Greenvale Australia 18°59S 145°7E 280 B4
Greenville Liberia 5°1N 9°6W 262 D3
Greenville Ala., U.S.A. 31°50N 86°38W 315 F11
Greenville Calif., U.S.A. 40°8N 120°57W 306 E6
Greenville Fla., U.S.A. 30°28N 83°38W 316 E6
Greenville Ga., U.S.A. 33°2N 84°43W 316 B5
Greenville Ill., U.S.A. 38°53N 89°25W 310 F7
Greenville Ind., U.S.A. 38°22N 85°59W 311 F11
Greenville Maine, U.S.A. 45°28N 69°35W 309 C19
Greenville Mich., U.S.A. 43°11N 85°15W 311 A11
Greenville Miss., U.S.A. 33°24N 91°4W 315 E9
Greenville Mo., U.S.A. 37°8N 90°27W 308 G8
Greenville N.C., U.S.A. 35°37N 77°23W 315 D16
Greenville N.H., U.S.A. 42°46N 71°49W 313 D13
Greenville N.Y., U.S.A. 42°25N 74°1W 313 D10
Greenville Ohio, U.S.A. 40°6N 84°38W 311 D12
Greenville Pa., U.S.A. 41°24N 80°23W 312 E4
Greenville S.C., U.S.A. 34°51N 82°24W 315 D13
Greenville Tex., U.S.A. 33°8N 96°7W 314 E6
Greenwater Lake ⌂ Canada 52°32N 103°30W 297 C8
Greenwich Conn., U.S.A. 41°2N 73°38W 313 E11
Greenwich N.Y., U.S.A. 43°5N 73°30W 313 C11
Greenwich Ohio, U.S.A. 41°2N 82°31W 312 E2
Greenwich □ U.K. 51°29N 0°1E 125 B3
Greenwich Observatory U.K. 51°28N 0°0 125 B3
Greenwich Village New York, U.S.A. 132 d1
Greenwood B.C., Canada 49°10N 118°40W 296 D5
Greenwood Ark., U.S.A. 35°13N 94°16W 314 D7
Greenwood Fla., U.S.A. 30°52N 85°10W 316 E4
Greenwood Ind., U.S.A. 39°37N 86°7W 311 E10
Greenwood Mass., U.S.A. 42°29N 71°2W 116 A2
Greenwood Miss., U.S.A. 33°31N 90°11W 315 E9
Greenwood S.C., U.S.A. 34°12N 82°10W 316 A7
Greenwood, Mt. Australia 13°48S 130°4E 278 B5
Greenwood Great House Jamaica 18°29N 77°44W 320 a
Grefsen Norway 59°56N 10°47E 133 A3
Gregbe Ivory C. 6°48N 6°43W 262 D3
Gregório → Brazil 6°50S 70°46W 330 B3
Gregory U.S.A. 43°14N 99°26W 308 D4
Gregory → Australia 17°53S 139°17E 280 B2
Gregory, L. S. Austral., Australia 28°55S 139°0E 281 D2
Gregory, L. W. Austral., Australia 20°0S 127°40E 278 D4
Gregory, L. W. Austral., Australia 25°38S 119°58E 279 E2
Gregory △ Australia 15°38S 131°15E 278 C5
Gregory Downs Australia 18°35S 138°45E 280 B2
Gregory Ra. Queens., Australia 19°30S 143°40E 280 B3
Gregory Ra. W. Austral., Australia 21°20S 121°12E 278 D3
Greifenberg = Gryfice Poland 53°55N 15°13E 184 E2
Greifenhagen = Gryfino Poland 53°16N 14°29E 185 E1
Greiffenberg = Gryfów Śląski Poland 51°2N 15°24E 185 G2
Greiffenberg Germany 53°5N 13°57E 178 B9
Greifswald Germany 54°5N 13°23E 178 A9
Greifswalder Bodden Germany 54°12N 13°35E 178 A9
Grein Austria 48°14N 14°51E 180 C7
Greiz Germany 50°39N 12°10E 178 E8
Gremikha Russia 67°59N 39°47E 186 A6
Grenaa Denmark 56°25N 10°53E 163 H4
Grenada U.S.A. 33°47N 89°49W 315 E10
Grenada ■ W. Indies 12°10N 61°40W 323 q
Grenade France 43°47N 1°17E 174 E5
Grenadier I. U.S.A. 44°3N 76°22W 313 B8
Grenadines, The St. Vincent 12°40N 61°20W 323 n
Grenchen Switz. 47°12N 7°24E 179 H3
Grenen Denmark 57°44N 10°40E 163 G4
Grenfell N.S.W., Australia 33°52S 148°8E 283 B8
Grenfell Sask., Canada 50°30N 102°56W 297 C8
Grenivík Iceland 65°57N 18°11W 155 B8
Grenjaðarstaður Iceland 65°49N 17°21W 155 B9
Grenoble France 45°12N 5°42E 175 C9
Grenville Grenada 12°7N 61°37W 323 q
Grenville, C. Australia 12°0S 143°13E 286 F2
Grenville Chan. Canada 53°40N 129°46W 296 C3
Gréoux-les-Bains France 43°45N 5°52E 175 E9
Gresham U.S.A. 45°30N 122°25W 306 E4
Gresham Park U.S.A. 33°43N 84°20W 113 B2
Gresik Indonesia 7°13S 112°38E 235 D4
Gretna Dumf. & Gall., U.K. 55°0N 3°3W 167 F5
Gretna Fla., U.S.A. 30°37N 84°40W 316 E5
Gretna La., U.S.A. 29°54N 90°3W 131 B2
Gretna City Park U.S.A. 29°54N 90°3W 131 B2
Greve Strand Denmark 55°34N 12°18E 118 B1
Greven Germany 52°6N 7°37E 178 C3
Grevena Greece 40°4N 21°25E 202 F5
Grevenbroich Germany 51°5N 6°35E 178 D2
Grevenmacher Lux. 49°41N 6°26E 170 E6
Grevesmühlen Germany 53°52N 11°12E 178 B7
Grey → Nfld. & L., Canada 47°34N 57°6W 299 C8
Grey → N.Z. 42°27S 171°12E 285 C6
Grey, C. Australia 13°0S 136°35E 280 A2
Grey Is. Canada 50°50N 55°35W 295 G20
Grey Ra. Australia 27°0S 143°30E 281 D3
Greybull U.S.A. 44°30N 108°3W 304 D9
Greyfriars Kirk Edinburgh, U.K. 121 c3
Greymouth N.Z. 42°29S 171°13E 285 C6
Greynolds Park U.S.A. 25°56N 80°9W 129 C3
Greystones Ireland 53°9N 6°5W 166 C5
Greytown N.Z. 41°5S 175°29E 284 F4
Greytown KwaZulu Natal, S. Africa 29°1S 30°36E 271 C5
Gribanovskiy Russia 51°28N 41°50E 190 E5
Gribbell I. Canada 53°23N 129°0W 296 C3
Gribës, Mal i Albania 40°17N 19°45E 202 F3
Gribingui → C.A.R. 8°33N 19°5E 264 A3
Gribingui-Bamingui ⌂ C.A.R. 7°45N 19°17E 264 A3
Gridley U.S.A. 39°22N 121°42W 306 F5
Griebeg, Ras il- Malta 35°58N 14°23E 206 F7
Griebnitzsee Germany 52°23N 13°8E 115 B1
Griekwastad S. Africa 28°49S 23°15E 270 C3
Griesheim Germany 49°51N 8°33E 179 F4
Grieskirchen Austria 48°16N 13°48E 180 C6
Griffin U.S.A. 33°15N 84°16W 316 B5
Griffin, L. U.S.A. 28°52N 81°51W 317 G8
Griffith N.S.W., Australia 34°18S 146°2E 283 C7
Griffith Ont., Canada 45°15N 77°10W 312 A7
Griffith I. Canada 44°50N 80°55W 312 B4
Griffith Park U.S.A. 34°8N 118°17W 126 B3
Griggsville U.S.A. 39°43N 90°43W 310 E6
Grignols France 44°23N 0°2W 174 D3
Grigoriopol Moldova 47°9N 29°18E 183 C14
Grimari C.A.R. 5°43N 20°6E 264 A4
Grimaylov = Hrymayliv Ukraine 49°20N 26°5E 177 D14
Grimbergen Belgium 50°56N 4°22E 116 A2
Grimes U.S.A. 39°4N 121°54W 306 F5
Grimm = Kamenskiy Russia 50°48N 45°25E 190 E7
Grimma Germany 51°14N 12°43E 178 D8
Grimmen Germany 54°7N 13°2E 178 A9
Grimsay U.K. 57°29N 7°14W 167 D1
Grimsby Ont., Canada 43°12N 79°34W 312 C5
Grimsby N.E. Lincs., U.K. 53°34N 0°5W 168 D7
Grímsey Iceland 66°33N 17°58W 155 A9
Grimshaw Canada 56°10N 117°40W 296 B5
Grimslöv Sweden 56°44N 14°34E 163 H8
Grímsstaðir Iceland 65°39N 16°7W 155 B10
Grimstad Norway 58°20N 8°35E 164 F5
Grímsvötn Iceland 64°26N 17°22W 155 D9
Grindavík Iceland 63°50N 22°26W 155 D4
Grindelwald Switz. 46°38N 8°2E 179 J4
Grindsted Denmark 55°46N 8°55E 163 J2
Grindstone I. U.S.A. 44°17N 76°27W 313 B8
Grindu Romania 44°44N 26°50E 183 F11
Grinnell U.S.A. 41°45N 92°43W 310 C4
Grinnell Pen. Canada 76°40N 95°0W 295 B13
Grintavec Slovenia 46°22N 14°32E 199 B11
Grinzing Austria 48°15N 16°20E 142 A2
Griomasaigh = Grimsay U.K. 57°29N 7°14W 167 D1
Gris-Nez, C. France 50°52N 1°35E 173 B8
Grise Fiord Canada 76°25N 82°57W 295 B15
Grishino = Krasnoarmeisk Ukraine 48°18N 37°11E 189 H9
Grisolles France 43°49N 1°19E 174 E5
Grisons = Graubünden □ Switz. 46°45N 9°30E 179 J5
Grisslehamn Sweden 60°5N 18°49E 162 D12
Grmeč Planina Bos.-H. 44°43N 16°16E 199 D13
Groais I. Canada 50°55N 55°35W 299 B8
Gröbenried Germany 48°13N 11°25E 121 A1
Grobiņa Latvia 56°33N 21°10E 184 B8
Groblersdal S. Africa 25°15S 29°25E 271 C4
Grobming Austria 47°27N 13°54E 180 D6
Grochów Poland 52°15N 21°5E 143 B2
Grocka Serbia 44°40N 20°42E 202 B4
Gródek Poland 53°6N 23°40E 185 E10
Gródek Jagielloński = Horodok Ukraine 49°46N 23°32E 177 D12
Grodekovo = Pogranichnyy Russia 44°25N 131°24E 220 B5
Grodków Poland 50°43N 17°21E 185 H4
Grodno = Hrodna Belarus 53°42N 23°52E 184 E10
Grodzisk Poland 52°19N 21°4E 143 B2
Grodzisk Mazowiecki Poland 52°7N 20°37E 185 F7
Grodzisk Wielkopolski Poland 52°15N 16°22E 185 F3
Grodzyanka = Hrodzyanka Belarus 53°31N 28°42E 177 B15
Groenendaal Belgium 50°46N 4°26E 116 B2
Groesbeck U.S.A. 31°31N 96°32W 314 F6
Grogol Petamburin Indonesia 6°9S 106°46E 122 A1
Groix France 47°38N 3°29W 172 E3
Groix, Î. de France 47°38N 3°28W 172 E3
Grójec Poland 51°50N 20°58E 185 G7
Gronau Niedersachsen, Germany 52°5N 9°47E 178 C5
Gronau Nordrhein-Westfalen, Germany 52°12N 7°2E 178 C3
Grong Norway 64°25N 12°8E 160 D15
Grönhögen Sweden 56°16N 16°24E 163 H10
Groningen Neths. 53°15N 6°35E 170 A6
Groningen Suriname 5°48N 55°28W 329 B6
Groningen □ Neths. 53°16N 6°40E 170 A6
Grønlands △ Greenland 75°0N 35°0W 154 C7
Grønnedal = Kangilinnguit Greenland 61°20N 47°57W 154 E6
Gronsdorf Germany 48°7N 11°42E 131 B3
Groom U.S.A. 35°12N 101°6W 314 D4
Groot → S. Africa 33°45S 24°36E 270 D3
Groot-Berg → S. Africa 32°47S 18°8E 270 D2
Groot-Brakrivier S. Africa 34°2S 22°18E 270 D3
Groot Karasberge Namibia 27°20S 18°40E 270 C2
Groot-Kei → S. Africa 32°41S 28°22E 271 D4
Groot-Vis → S. Africa 33°28S 27°5E 270 D4
Grootdrink S. Africa 28°33S 21°42E 270 C3
Groote Eylandt Australia 14°0S 136°40E 280 A2
Groote Peel △ Neths. 51°22N 5°49E 170 C5
Grootfontein Namibia 19°31S 18°6E 270 A2
Grootlaagte → Africa 20°55S 21°27E 270 B3
Grootvloer → S. Africa 30°0S 20°40E 270 D3
Grorud Norway 59°57N 10°52E 133 A4
Gros C. Canada 61°59N 113°32W 296 A6
Gros Cap Guadeloupe 16°24N 61°25W 322 e
Gros Islet St. Lucia 14°5N 60°58W 323 m
Gros-Morne Martinique 14°43N 61°2W 322 j
Gros Morne △ Canada 49°40N 57°50W 299 C8
Gros Piton St. Lucia 13°49N 61°5W 323 m
Grósio Italy 46°18N 10°16E 198 B7
Grosne → France 46°42N 4°56E 173 F11
Gross Glienicke Berlin, Germany 52°28N 13°6E 115 B1
Gross-Hadern Germany 48°6N 11°29E 131 B1
Gross-Lappen Germany 48°12N 11°35E 131 A2
Gross-Meseritsch = Velké Meziříčí Czech Rep. 49°21N 16°1E 180 B9
Gross-Strehlitz = Strzelce Opolskie Poland 50°31N 18°18E 185 H5
Gross Wartenberg = Syców Poland 51°19N 17°40E 185 G4
Grossa, Pta. Spain 39°6N 1°36E 206 C2
Grosse I. U.S.A. 42°8N 83°9W 311 B13
Grosse Krampe Germany 52°23N 13°40E 115 B5
Grosse Müggelsee Germany 52°26N 13°38E 115 B4
Grosse Point U.S.A. 42°23N 82°54W 312 D2
Grosse Point Lighthouse U.S.A. 42°2N 87°41W 119 A2
Grosse Pte. Guadeloupe 16°1N 61°17W 322 e
Grossenbrode Germany 54°21N 11°4E 178 A7
Grossenhain Germany 51°17N 13°32E 178 D9
Grossenzersdorf Austria 48°12N 16°33E 142 A3
Grossenzersdorfer Arm → Austria 48°12N 16°31E 142 A3
Grosser Arber Germany 49°6N 13°8E 179 F9
Grosser Biberhaufen Austria 48°12N 16°28E 142 A2
Grosser Plöner See Germany 54°10N 10°22E 178 A6
Grosser Wannsee Germany 52°25N 13°10E 115 B2
Grosseto Italy 42°46N 11°8E 199 F8
Grossfeld-Siedlung Austria 48°16N 16°26E 142 A2
Grossgerungs Austria 48°34N 14°57E 180 C7
Grossglockner Austria 47°5N 12°40E 180 D5
Grosshesselohe Germany 48°3N 11°32E 131 B2
Grossjedlersdorf Austria 48°16N 16°23E 142 A2
Grosswardein = Oradea Romania 47°2N 21°58E 182 C6
Grossziethen Germany 52°23N 13°26E 115 B3
Groswater B. Canada 54°20N 57°40W 299 B8
Grotli Norway 62°2N 7°42E 164 B4
Groton Conn., U.S.A. 41°21N 72°5W 313 E12
Groton N.Y., U.S.A. 42°36N 76°22W 313 D8
Groton S. Dak., U.S.A. 45°27N 98°6W 308 C4
Grottáglie Italy 40°32N 17°26E 201 B10
Grottaminarda Italy 41°4N 15°2E 201 A8
Grottammare Italy 42°59N 13°52E 199 F10
Grottkau = Grodków Poland 50°43N 17°21E 185 H4
Grouard Mission Canada 55°33N 116°9W 296 B5
Grouin, Pte. du France 48°43N 1°51W 172 D5
Ground Zero = National September 11 Memorial and Museum New York, U.S.A. 132 e1
Groundhog → Canada 48°45N 82°58W 298 C3
Grouw Neths. 53°5N 5°51E 170 A5
Grove City Fla., U.S.A. 26°56N 82°19W 317 J7
Grove City Ohio, U.S.A. 39°53N 83°6W 311 E13
Grove City Pa., U.S.A. 41°10N 80°5W 312 E4
Grove Hall U.S.A. 42°18N 71°4W 116 B2
Grove Hill U.S.A. 31°42N 87°47W 315 F11
Grove Park Hounslow, U.K. 51°28N 0°15W 125 B2
Grove Park Lewisham, U.K. 51°25N 0°1E 125 B4
Grove Park Georgia, U.S.A. 33°46N 84°26W 113 B2
Groveland Calif., U.S.A. 37°50N 120°14W 306 H6
Groveland Fla., U.S.A. 28°34N 81°51W 317 G8
Grover = Tiltonsville U.S.A. 40°10N 80°41W 312 F4
Grover Beach U.S.A. 35°7N 120°37W 307 K6
Groves U.S.A. 29°57N 93°54W 314 G8
Groveton N.H., U.S.A. 44°36N 71°31W 313 B13
Groveton Va., U.S.A. 38°46N 77°6W 143 C2
Grovetown U.S.A. 33°27N 82°12W 316 B7
Grožnjan Croatia 45°22N 13°43E 199 C10
Groznyy Russia 43°20N 45°45E 191 J7
Grua Norway 60°16N 10°40E 164 D7
Grubišno Polje Croatia 45°44N 17°12E 182 E2
Grudovo Bulgaria 42°21N 27°10E 203 D11
Grudusk Poland 53°3N 20°38E 185 E7
Grudziądz Poland 53°30N 18°47E 184 E5
Gruinard B. U.K. 57°56N 5°35W 167 D3
Gruissan France 43°8N 3°7E 174 E7
Grumo Áppula Italy 41°1N 16°42E 201 A9
Grums Sweden 59°22N 13°5E 162 E7
Grünau Germany 52°25N 13°34E 115 B4
Grünberg Germany 50°35N 8°58E 178 E4
Grünberg in Schlesien = Zielona Góra Poland 51°57N 15°31E 185 G2
Grund Iceland 65°31N 18°9W 155 B8
Gründau Germany 50°10N 9°9E 179 E5
Grundy Center U.S.A. 42°22N 92°47W 310 B4
Grunewald Germany 52°28N 13°15E 115 B2
Grungedal Norway 59°44N 7°43E 164 E4
Grünstadt Germany 49°34N 8°9E 179 F4
Grünwald Germany 48°2N 11°31E 131 B2
Grünwalder Forst Germany 48°2N 11°33E 131 B2
Gruppo di Tessa ⌂ Italy 46°47N 11°0E 198 B8
Gruvberget Sweden 61°6N 16°10E 162 C10
Gruver U.S.A. 36°16N 101°24W 314 C4
Gruyères Switz. 46°35N 7°4E 179 J3
Gruža Serbia 43°54N 20°46E 202 C4
Gryazi Russia 52°30N 39°58E 189 F10
Gryazliv = Borovichi Russia 58°25N 33°55E 188 C7
Gryazovets Russia 58°50N 40°10E 188 C11
Grybów Poland 49°36N 20°55E 185 J7
Grycksbo Sweden 60°40N 15°29E 162 D9
Gryfice Poland 53°55N 15°13E 184 E2
Gryfino Poland 53°16N 14°29E 185 E1
Gryfów Śląski Poland 51°2N 15°24E 185 G2
Grymes Hill U.S.A. 40°36N 74°6W 132 C1
Gryt Sweden 58°12N 16°48E 163 F10
Grythyttan Sweden 59°41N 14°32E 162 E8
Grytviken S. Georgia 54°19S 36°33W 152 M8
Gstaad Switz. 46°28N 7°18E 179 J3
Gua India 22°18N 85°20E 243 H11
Gua Musang Malaysia 4°53N 101°58E 237 K3
Guabún, Pta. Chile 41°48S 74°2W 336 B2
Guacanayabo, G. de Cuba 20°40N 77°20W 320 B4
Guacara Venezuela 10°14N 67°53W 328 A4
Guachipas → Argentina 25°40S 65°30W 334 B2
Guadajoz → Spain 37°50N 4°51W 195 H6
Guadalajara Jalisco, Mexico 20°40N 103°20W 318 C4
Guadalajara Spain 40°37N 3°12W 196 E1
Guadalajara □ Spain 40°47N 2°30W 196 E2
Guadalaviar = Turia → Spain 39°27N 0°19W 197 F4
Guadalcanal Solomon Is. 9°32S 160°12E 287 M11
Guadalcanal Spain 38°5N 5°52W 195 G5
Guadalén → Spain 38°5N 3°32W 195 G7
Guadales Argentina 34°30S 67°55W 334 C2
Guadalete → Spain 36°35N 6°13W 195 J4
Guadalimar → Spain 38°5N 3°28W 195 G7
Guadalmena → Spain 38°19N 2°56W 195 G8
Guadalmez → Spain 38°46N 5°4W 195 G5
Guadalope → Spain 41°15N 0°3W 196 D4
Guadalquivir → Spain 36°47N 6°22W 195 J4
Guadalupe = Guadeloupe ☒ W. Indies 16°15N 61°40W 322 e
Guadalupe Brazil 6°44S 43°47W 332 C3
Guadalupe Zacatecas, Mexico 22°45N 102°31W 318 C4
Guadalupe Manila, Phil. 14°34N 121°2E 127 B2
Guadalupe Spain 39°27N 5°17W 195 F5
Guadalupe Calif., U.S.A. 34°58N 120°34W 307 L6
Guadalupe → U.S.A. 28°27N 96°47W 314 G6
Guadalupe, Basilica de Mexico 19°29N 99°7W 128 B2
Guadalupe, Sierra de Spain 39°28N 5°30W 195 F5
Guadalupe de Bravo Mexico 31°23N 106°7W 318 A3
Guadalupe I. Pac. Oc. 29°0N 118°50W 292 G8
Guadalupe Mts. △ U.S.A. 31°40N 104°30W 314 F2
Guadalupe Peak U.S.A. 31°50N 104°52W 314 F2
Guadalupe y Calvo Mexico 26°6N 106°58W 318 B3
Guadarrama, Sierra de Spain 41°0N 4°0W 194 E7
Guadeloupe ☒ W. Indies 16°15N 61°40W 322 e
Guadeloupe △ Guadeloupe 16°10N 61°40W 322 e
Guadeloupe Passage W. Indies 16°50N 62°15W 322 e
Guadalupe Peru 7°15S 79°29W 330 B2
Guadiamar → Spain 36°55N 6°24W 195 J4
Guadiana → Portugal 37°14N 7°22W 195 H3
Guadiana Menor → Spain 37°56N 3°15W 195 H7
Guadiaro → Spain 36°17N 5°17W 195 J5
Guadiato → Spain 37°48N 5°5W 195 H5
Guadiela → Spain 40°22N 2°49W 196 E2
Guadix Spain 37°18N 3°11W 195 H7
Guafo, Boca del Chile 43°35S 74°0W 336 B2
Guafo, I. Chile 43°35S 74°50W 336 B2
Guåhån = Guam ☒ Pac. Oc. 13°27N 144°45E 302 d
Guaico Trin. & Tob. 10°35N 61°9W 323 t
Guainía □ Colombia 2°30N 69°0W 328 C4
Guainía → Colombia 2°1N 67°7W 328 C4
Guaíra Brazil 24°5S 54°10W 335 A5
Guairá □ Paraguay 25°45S 56°30W 334 B4
Guaire = Gorey Ireland 52°41N 6°18W 166 D5
Guaitecas, Is. Chile 44°0S 74°30W 336 B2
Guajará-Mirim Brazil 10°50S 65°20W 331 C4
Guajira □ Colombia 11°30N 72°30W 328 A3
Guajira, Pen. de la Colombia 12°0N 72°0W 328 A3
Gualaceo Ecuador 2°54S 78°47W 328 D2
Gualán Guatemala 15°8N 89°22W 320 C2
Gualdo Tadino Italy 43°14N 12°47E 199 E9
Gualeguay Argentina 33°10S 59°14W 334 C4
Gualeguaychú Argentina 33°3S 59°31W 334 C4
Gualequay → Argentina 33°19S 59°39W 334 C4
Gualicho, Salina Argentina 40°25S 65°20W 336 B3
Gualjaina Argentina 42°45S 70°30W 336 B2
Guam ☒ Pac. Oc. 13°27N 144°45E 302 d
Guamblin, I. Chile 44°50S 75°0W 336 B2
Guamini Argentina 37°1S 62°28W 334 D3
Guamote Ecuador 1°56S 78°43W 328 D2
Guampí, Sierra de Venezuela 6°0N 65°35W 329 B4
Guamúchil Mexico 25°28N 108°6W 318 B3
Guana I. Br. Virgin Is. 18°30N 64°30W 321 b
Guanabacoa Cuba 23°8N 82°18W 320 B3
Guanabara, B. de Brazil 22°52S 43°10W 135 B1
Guanabara, Jardim Brazil 22°48S 43°11W 135 A1
Guanabara, Palácio da Brazil 22°56S 43°11W 135 B1
Guanacaste, Cordillera de Costa Rica 10°40N 85°4W 320 D2
Guanacaste △ Costa Rica 10°57N 85°30W 320 D2
Guanaceví Mexico 25°56N 105°57W 318 B3
Guanahani = San Salvador I. Bahamas 24°0N 74°30W 321 B5
Guanajay Cuba 22°56N 82°42W 320 B3
Guanajuato Mexico 21°1N 101°15W 318 C4
Guanajuato □ Mexico 21°0N 101°0W 318 C4
Guanambi Brazil 14°13S 42°47W 333 D3
Guanapo Trin. & Tob. 10°36N 61°15W 323 t
Guanare Venezuela 8°42N 69°12W 328 B4
Guanare → Venezuela 8°13N 67°46W 328 B4
Guandacol Argentina 29°30S 68°40W 334 B2
Guandi Shan China 37°53N 111°29E 226 F6
Guane Cuba 22°10N 84°7W 320 B3
Guang'an China 30°28N 106°35E 228 B6
Guang'anmen China 39°51N 116°18E 114 B1
Guangchang China 26°50N 116°21E 229 D11
Guangde China 30°54N 119°25E 229 B12
Guangdong □ China 23°0N 113°0E 229 F9
Guangdong Olympic Stadium Guangzhou, China 23°9N 113°22E 121 B3
Guangfeng China 28°20N 118°15E 229 C12
Guangfu = Kuangfu Taiwan 23°40N 121°25E 225 C3
Guanghan China 30°58N 104°17E 228 B5
Guangling China 39°47N 114°22E 226 E8

Guangnan China 24°5N 105°4E 228 E5
Guangning China 23°40N 112°22E 229 F9
Guangqumen China 39°52N 116°25E 114 B2
Guangrao China 37°5N 118°25E 227 F10
Guangshui China 31°37N 114°0E 229 B10
Guangshun China 26°8N 106°21E 228 D6
Guangwu China 37°48N 105°57E 226 F3
Guangxi Zhuangzu Zizhiqu □ China 24°0N 109°0E 228 F7
Guangyuan China 32°26N 105°51E 226 H3
Guangze China 27°30N 117°12E 229 D11
Guangzhou China 23°6N 113°13E 121 B2
Guanhães Brazil 18°47S 42°57W 333 E3
Guanica Puerto Rico 17°58N 66°55W 321 b
Guanipa → Venezuela 9°56N 62°26W 329 B5
Guanling China 25°56N 105°35E 228 E5
Guanmiao = Kuanmiao Taiwan 22°58N 120°19E 225 D2
Guannan China 34°8N 119°21E 227 G10
Guanshuo China 23°4N 113°22E 121 B3
Guanta Venezuela 10°14N 64°36W 329 A5
Guantánamo Cuba 20°10N 75°14W 321 B4
Guantánamo B. Cuba 19°59N 75°10W 321 C4
Guantao China 36°42N 115°25E 226 F8
Guanting Shuiku China 40°14N 115°35E 226 D8
Guanxi = Kuanhsi Taiwan 24°48N 121°10E 225 B3
Guanyang China 25°30N 111°8E 229 E8
Guanyin = Kuanyin Taiwan 25°2N 121°4E 225 A3
Guanyun China 34°20N 119°18E 227 G10
Guapay = Grande → Bolivia 15°51S 64°39W 331 D5
Guapí Colombia 2°36N 77°54W 328 C2
Guápiles Costa Rica 10°10N 83°46W 320 D3
Guapo → Trin. & Tob. 10°11N 61°40W 323 t
Guapo B. Trin. & Tob. 10°12N 61°41W 323 t
Guaporé = Rondônia Brazil 10°52S 61°57W 331 C5
Guaporé Brazil 28°51S 51°54W 335 B5
Guaporé → Brazil 11°55S 65°4W 331 C4
Guaqui Bolivia 16°41S 68°54W 330 D4
Guara, Sierra de Spain 42°19N 0°15W 196 C4
Guarabira Brazil 6°51S 35°29W 332 C4
Guaracara → Trin. & Tob. 10°18N 61°28W 323 t
Guarachirá → Colombia 5°27N 70°36W 328 B3
Guaranda Ecuador 1°36S 79°0W 328 D2
Guarani = Pacajus Brazil 4°10S 38°31W 332 B4
Guarapari Brazil 20°40S 40°30W 333 F3
Guarapuava Brazil 25°20S 51°30W 333 G1
Guaratinguetá Brazil 22°49S 45°9W 335 A6
Guaratuba Brazil 25°53S 48°38W 335 B6
Guarda Portugal 40°32N 7°20W 194 E3
Guarda □ Portugal 40°40N 7°20W 194 E3
Guardafui, C. = Asir, Ras Somalia 11°55N 51°10E 267 B7
Guardamar del Segura Spain 38°5N 0°39W 197 G4
Guardavalle Italy 38°30N 16°30E 201 D9
Guárdia Sanframondi Italy 41°15N 14°36E 201 A7
Guardiagrele Italy 42°11N 14°13E 199 F11
Guardo Spain 42°47N 4°50W 194 C6
Guareña Spain 38°51N 6°6W 195 G4
Guareña → Spain 41°29N 5°23W 194 D5
Guari Papua N. G. 8°3S 146°52E 286 E4
Guárico □ Venezuela 8°40N 66°35W 328 B4
Guarrojo → Colombia 4°6N 70°42W 328 C3
Guarujá Brazil 24°2S 46°25W 335 A6
Guarulhos Brazil 23°29S 46°33W 335 A6
Guasave Mexico 25°34N 108°27W 318 B3
Guascama, Pta. Colombia 2°32N 78°24W 328 C2
Guasdualito Venezuela 7°15N 70°44W 328 B3
Guasipati Venezuela 7°28N 61°54W 329 B5
Guasopa Papua N. G. 9°12S 152°56E 286 E7
Guastalla Italy 44°55N 10°39E 198 D7
Guatemala Guatemala 14°40N 90°22W 320 D1
Guatemala ■ Cent. Amer. 15°40N 90°30W 320 C1
Guatemala Basin Pac. Oc. 11°0N 95°0W 289 F18
Guatemala Trench Pac. Oc. 14°0N 95°0W 292 H10
Guatire Venezuela 10°28N 66°32W 328 A4
Guatopo △ Venezuela 10°5N 66°30W 328 A4
Guatuaro Pt. Trin. & Tob. 10°19N 60°59W 323 t
Guavi → Papua N. G. 7°48S 143°16E 286 D2
Guaviare □ Colombia 2°0N 72°30W 328 C3
Guaviare → Colombia 4°3N 67°44W 328 C4
Guaxupé Brazil 21°10S 47°5W 335 A6
Guayabero → Colombia 2°36N 72°47W 328 C3
Guayacán Venezuela 11°8N 63°55W 329 a
Guayacancito Venezuela 10°56N 64°13W 329 a
Guayaguayare Trin. & Tob. 10°8N 61°2W 323 t
Guayaguayare B. Trin. & Tob. 10°7N 61°2W 323 t
Guayama Puerto Rico 17°59N 66°7W 321 C6
Guayamuri, Cerro Venezuela 11°4N 63°51W 329 a
Guayaneco, Arch. Chile 47°45S 75°10W 336 C1
Guayanilla Puerto Rico 18°1N 66°47W 321 b
Guayaquil Ecuador 2°15S 79°52W 328 D2
Guayaquil Baja Calif., Mexico 29°59N 115°4W 318 B1
Guayaquil, G. de Ecuador 3°10S 81°0W 328 D1
Guayaramerín Bolivia 10°48S 65°23W 331 C4
Guayas → Ecuador 2°36S 79°52W 328 D2
Guaymas Mexico 27°56N 110°54W 318 B2
Guaynabo Puerto Rico 18°22N 66°7W 321 b
Guba Dem. Rep. of the Congo 10°38S 26°27E 269 E2
Guba Ethiopia 11°17N 35°20E 257 E4
Gûbâl, Madîq Egypt 27°30N 34°0E 251 L4
Gubam Papua N. G. 8°39S 141°53E 286 E1
Guban Somalia 10°30N 44°0E 267 B5
Gubat Phil. 12°55N 124°7E 232 E5
Gubbi India 13°19N 76°56E 245 H3
Gúbbio Italy 43°21N 12°35E 199 E9
Guben Germany 51°57N 14°42E 178 D10
Gubin Poland 51°57N 14°43E 185 G1
Gubio Nigeria 12°30N 12°42E 263 C7
Gubkin Russia 51°17N 37°32E 189 G9
Gubkinskiy Russia 64°27N 76°36E 214 C8
Guča Serbia 43°46N 20°15E 202 C4
Gucheng China 32°20N 111°30E 229 A8
Gucun China 31°21N 121°22E 138 A1
Gudå Norway 63°27N 11°36E 164 A8
Gudalur India 11°30N 76°29E 245 J3
Gudauta Georgia 43°7N 40°32E 191 J5
Gudbrandsdalen Norway 61°33N 10°10E 164 C7
Guddu Barrage Pakistan 28°30N 69°50E 242 E3
Gudenå → Denmark 56°29N 10°13E 163 H4
Gudermes Russia 43°24N 46°5E 191 J8
Gudhjem Denmark 55°12N 14°58E 163 J8
Gudivada India 16°30N 81°3E 245 F5
Gudiyattam India 12°57N 78°55E 245 H4
Gudö Sweden 59°12N 18°12E 139 B3
Gudur India 14°12N 79°55E 245 G4
Gudvangen Norway 60°52N 6°49E 164 D3
Guebwiller France 47°55N 7°12E 173 E14
Guecho = Algorta Spain 43°21N 2°59W 196 B2
Guékédou Guinea 8°40N 10°5W 262 D2
Guelb er Rîchât Mauritania 21°7N 11°24W 260 D2
Guéle Mendouka Cameroon 4°23N 12°55E 263 E7
Guélengdeng Chad 10°55N 15°31E 259 F3
Güell, Parque de Spain 41°24N 2°10E 114 A2
Guelma Algeria 36°25N 7°29E 261 A6
Guelma □ Algeria 36°25N 7°25E 261 A6
Guelmine = Goulimine Morocco 28°56N 10°0W 260 C3
Guelph Canada 43°35N 80°20W 312 C4
Guelta Zemmur W. Sahara 25°8N 12°22W 260 C2
Guemar Algeria 33°30N 6°49E 261 B6
Guéméné-Penfao France 47°38N 1°50W 172 E5
Guéméné-sur-Scorff France 48°4N 3°13W 172 D3
Guéné Benin 11°44N 3°16E 263 C5
Güeppí Peru 0°7S 75°15W 328 D2
Guer France 47°54N 2°8W 172 E4
Güer Aike Argentina 51°39S 69°35W 336 D3
Guera Chad 11°55N 18°12E 259 F3
Guéra □ Chad 11°30N 18°30E 259 F3
Guérande France 47°20N 2°26W 172 E4
Guerara Algeria 32°51N 4°22E 261 B5
Guercif Morocco 34°14N 3°21W 261 B4
Guéréda Chad 14°31N 22°5E 259 F4
Guéret France 46°11N 1°51E 173 F8
Guérigny France 47°6N 3°10E 173 E10
Guerneville U.S.A. 38°30N 123°0W 306 G4
Guernica = Gernika-Lumo Spain 43°19N 2°40W 196 B2
Guernsey Chan. Is., U.K. 49°26N 2°35W 169 H5
Guernsey Wyo., U.S.A. 42°16N 104°45W 304 E11
Guerrara Algeria 28°5N 0°8W 261 C4
Guerrero Mexico City, Mexico 128 a1
Guerrero □ Mexico 17°40N 100°0W 319 D5
Guerzim Algeria 29°39N 1°40W 261 C4
Guessou-Sud Benin 10°3N 2°38E 263 C5
Gueugnon France 46°36N 4°4E 173 F11
Guéyo Ivory C. 5°25N 6°5W 262 D3
Gufuðalur Iceland 65°34N 22°25W 155 B4
Guggenheim Museum New York, U.S.A. 132 b3
Gughe Ethiopia 6°12N 37°30E 257 F4
Gūgher Iran 29°28N 56°27E 247 D8
Guglionesi Italy 41°55N 14°55E 199 G11
Guguan N. Marianas 17°18N 145°51E 302 a
Guhrau = Góra Poland 51°40N 16°31E 185 G3
Gui Jiang → China 23°30N 111°15E 229 F8
Guia Canary Is. 28°8N 15°38W 153 e1
Guia de Isora Canary Is. 28°12N 16°46W 153 e1
Guia Lopes da Laguna Brazil 21°26S 56°7W 335 A4
Guiana Venezuela 5°9N 63°36W 329 B5
Guiana Highlands S. Amer. 5°10N 60°40W 326 C4
Guiana I. Antigua & B. 17°6N 61°44W 322 b
Guibéroua Ivory C. 6°14N 6°10W 262 D3
Guichen B. Australia 37°10S 139°45E 282 D3
Guichi China 30°39N 117°27E 229 B11
Guider Cameroon 9°56N 13°57E 263 D7
Guidiguir Niger 13°40N 9°50E 259 F1
Guidimaka □ Mauritania 15°20N 12°0W 262 B2
Guidimouni Niger 13°42N 9°31E 259 F1
Guiding China 26°34N 107°11E 228 D6
Guidong China 26°7N 113°57E 229 D9
Guidónia-Montecélio Italy 42°1N 12°45E 199 F9
Guiers, L. de Senegal 16°10N 15°50W 262 B1
Guigang China 23°8N 109°35E 228 F7
Guiglo Ivory C. 6°45N 7°30W 262 D3
Guihulngan Phil. 10°7N 123°16E 233 F4
Guijá Mozam. 24°27S 33°0E 271 B5
Guijuelo Spain 40°33N 5°40W 194 E5
Guildford U.K. 51°14N 0°34W 169 F7
Guilford U.S.A. 41°17N 72°41W 313 E12
Guilin China 25°18N 110°15E 229 E8
Guillaume-Delisle, L. Canada 56°15N 76°17W 298 A4
Guillaumes France 44°5N 6°52E 175 D10
Guillestre France 44°39N 6°40E 175 D10
Guilvinec France 47°48N 4°17W 172 E2
Güimar Canary Is. 28°18N 16°24W 153 e1
Guimarães Brazil 2°9S 44°42W 332 B3
Guimarães Portugal 41°28N 8°24W 194 D2
Guimaras □ Phil. 10°35N 122°37E 233 F4
Guimaras Str. Phil. 10°38N 122°48E 233 F4
Guimba Phil. 15°40N 120°46E 232 D3
Guinardó Spain 41°24N 2°10E 114 A2
Guinayangan Phil. 13°54N 122°27E 232 E4
Guinda U.S.A. 38°50N 122°12W 306 G4
Guindulman Phil. 9°46N 124°29E 233 G5
Guinea Africa 8°0N 8°0E 254 F4
Guinea ■ W. Afr. 10°20N 11°30W 262 C2
Guinea, Gulf of Atl. Oc. 3°0N 2°30E 263 E5
Guinea Basin Atl. Oc. 0°0 5°0W 152 G11
Guinea-Bissau ■ Africa 12°0N 15°0W 262 C2
Güines Cuba 22°50N 82°0W 320 B3
Guingamp France 48°34N 3°10W 172 D3
Guinguinéo Senegal 14°20N 15°57W 262 C1
Güinima Venezuela 10°44N 63°55W 329 a
Guinobatan Phil. 13°11N 123°36E 232 E4
Guipavas France 48°26N 4°29W 172 D2
Guiping China 23°21N 110°2E 229 F8
Guipúzcoa □ Spain 43°12N 2°15W 196 B2
Guir Mali 18°52N 2°52W 262 B4
Guir, O. → Algeria 31°29N 2°17W 261 B4
Guiratinga Brazil 16°21S 53°45W 331 D7
Guirel Mauritania 15°30N 7°3W 262 B3
Güiria Venezuela 10°32N 62°18W 329 F8
Guiscard France 49°40N 3°1E 173 C10
Guise France 49°52N 3°35E 173 C10
Guishan Dao = Kueishan Tao Taiwan 24°51N 121°57E 225 B3
Guissona Spain 41°47N 1°17E 196 D6
Guita-Koulouba C.A.R. 5°58N 23°21E 264 A4
Guitiriz Spain 43°11N 7°50W 194 B3
Guitri Ivory C. 5°30N 5°14W 262 D3
Guiuan Phil. 11°5N 125°55E 233 F5
Guixi China 28°16N 117°15E 229 C11
Guiyang Guizhou, China 26°32N 106°40E 228 D6
Guiyang Hunan, China 25°46N 112°42E 229 E9
Guizhou □ China 27°0N 107°0E 228 D6
Gujan-Mestras France 44°38N 1°4W 174 D2
Gujar Khan Pakistan 33°16N 73°19E 242 C5
Gujarat □ India 23°20N 71°0E 242 H4
Gujiang China 27°11N 114°47E 229 D10
Gujiao China 37°54N 112°8E 226 F7
Gujō Japan 35°45N 136°57E 223 B8
Gujranwala Pakistan 32°10N 74°12E 242 C6
Gujrat Pakistan 32°40N 74°2E 242 C6
Gukovo Russia 48°1N 39°58E 191 F5
Gulargambone Australia 31°20S 148°30E 283 A8
Gulbai Pakistan 24°52N 66°58E 123 A1
Gulbarga India 17°20N 76°50E 244 F3
Gulbene Latvia 57°8N 26°52E 188 D4
Gülchö Kyrgyzstan 40°19N 73°26E 217 D8
Guledagudda India 16°3N 75°48E 245 F2
Gülek Turkey 37°12N 34°48E 250 A5
Gulf □ Papua N. G. 8°0S 145°0E 286 D3
Gulf, The = Persian Gulf Asia 27°0N 50°0E 247 E6
Gulf Breeze U.S.A. 30°21N 87°9W 317 E2
Gulf Hammock U.S.A. 29°15N 82°43W 317 F7
Gulf Islands ⌓ U.S.A. 30°10N 87°10W 317 K2
Gulfport Fla., U.S.A. 27°44N 82°42W 317 H7
Gulfport Miss., U.S.A. 30°22N 89°6W 315 F10
Gulgong Australia 32°20S 149°49E 283 B8
Gulian China 52°56N 122°21E 219 A13
Gulin China 28°1N 105°50E 228 C5
Gulistan Pakistan 30°30N 66°35E 242 D2
Guliston Uzbekistan 40°29N 68°46E 217 D7
Gulja = Yining China 43°58N 81°10E 217 D10
Gulkana U.S.A. 62°16N 145°23W 303 E11
Gull Lake Canada 50°10N 108°29W 297 C7
Gullbrå Norway 60°50N 6°17E 164 D3
Gullbrandstorp Sweden 56°42N 12°43E 163 H6
Gullbringusýsla Iceland 64°0N 22°0W 155 D4
Gullfoss Iceland 64°20N 20°8W 155 C6
Gullhaug Norway 59°30N 10°15E 164 E7
Gullivan B. U.S.A. 25°45N 81°40W 317 K8
Gullspång Sweden 58°59N 14°6E 163 F8
Gullstein Norway 63°13N 8°9E 164 A5
Güllük Turkey 37°14N 27°35E 205 D9
Güllük Dağı △ Turkey 37°0N 30°30E 205 E12
Güllük Korfezi Turkey 37°12N 27°30E 205 D9
Gulma Nigeria 12°40N 4°23E 263 C5
Gulmarg India 34°3N 74°25E 243 B6
Gülnar Turkey 36°19N 33°24E 250 B4
Gulnare Australia 33°27S 138°27E 282 B3
Gülpınar Turkey 39°32N 26°7E 205 B8
Gülşehir Turkey 38°44N 34°37E 212 C6
Gulshan-e Iqbal Pakistan 24°54N 67°5E 123 A2
Gülshat Kazakhstan 46°38N 74°21E 217 C8
Gulsvik Norway 60°24N 9°38E 164 D6
Gulu Uganda 2°48N 32°17E 268 B3
Gŭlŭbovo Bulgaria 42°8N 25°55E 203 D9
Gulud, J. Sudan 11°41N 29°31E 257 E2
Gulwe Tanzania 6°30S 36°25E 268 D4
Gulyaypole = Hulyaypole Ukraine 47°45N 36°21E 189 J9
Gum Lake Australia 32°42S 143°9E 282 B5
Gumaca Phil. 13°55N 122°6E 232 E4
Gumal → Pakistan 31°40N 71°50E 242 D4
Gumbaz Pakistan 30°2N 69°0E 242 D3
Gumbinnen = Gusev Russia 54°35N 22°10E 184 D9
Gumdag Turkmenistan 39°9N 54°56E 216 E4
Gumel Nigeria 12°39N 9°22E 263 C6
Gumi S. Korea 36°10N 128°12E 224 D4
Gumiel de Izán Spain 41°46N 3°41W 194 D7
Gumla India 23°3N 84°33E 243 H11
Gumlu Australia 19°53S 147°41E 280 B4
Gummersbach Germany 51°1N 7°34E 178 D3
Gummi Nigeria 12°4N 5°9E 263 C6
Gümüldür Turkey 38°6N 27°0E 205 C9
Gumuljina = Komotini Greece 41°9N 25°26E 203 E9
Gümüşçay Turkey 40°16N 27°17E 203 F11
Gümüşhacıköy Turkey 40°50N 35°18E 212 B6
Gümüşhane Turkey 40°30N 39°30E 213 B8
Gümüşsu Turkey 38°14N 29°1E 205 C11
Gumzai Indonesia 5°28S 134°42E 231 F8
Gun Hill Tower Barbados 13°8N 59°33W 323 r
Gun Pt. Grenada 12°32N 61°37W 323 q
Guna Amara, Ethiopia 11°43N 38°14E 266 B4
Guna Oromiya, Ethiopia 8°18N 39°52E 257 F4
Guna India 24°40N 77°19E 242 G7
Gunbalanya Australia 12°20S 133°4E 278 B5
Gundabooka △ Australia 30°30S 145°20E 281 E4
Gundagai Australia 35°3S 148°6E 283 C8
Gundarehi India 20°57N 81°17E 244 D5
Gundelfingen Germany 48°34N 10°22E 179 G6
Gundji Dem. Rep. of the Congo 2°5N 21°27E 264 B4
Gundlakamma → India 15°30N 80°15E 245 G5
Gundlupet India 11°48N 76°41E 245 J3
Gündoğmuş Turkey 36°48N 32°0E 250 B3
Gunebang Australia 33°1S 146°38E 283 B7
Güney Burdur, Turkey 37°29N 29°34E 205 D11
Güney Denizli, Turkey 38°9N 29°4E 205 C11
Güneydoğu Toroslar Turkey 38°20N 40°30E 213 C9
Gungal Australia 32°17S 150°32E 283 B9
Gungo Angola 10°58S 15°30E 265 E2
Güngören Turkey 41°1N 28°52E 122 B1
Gungu Dem. Rep. of the Congo 5°43S 19°20E 265 D3
Gunisao → Canada 53°56N 97°53W 297 C9
Gunisao L. Canada 53°33N 96°15W 297 C9
Gunjur Gambia 13°12N 16°44W 262 C1
Gunjyal Pakistan 32°20N 71°55E 242 C4
Günlüce Turkey 36°50N 28°20E 205 E10
Gunma □ Japan 36°30N 138°20E 223 A10
Gunnarskog Sweden 59°49N 12°34E 162 E6
Gunnbjørn Fjeld Greenland 68°55N 29°47W 154 D8
Gunnebo Sweden 57°44N 16°32E 163 G10
Gunnedah Australia 30°59S 150°15E 283 A9
Gunnersbury U.K. 51°29N 0°17W 125 B2
Gunnewin Australia 25°59S 148°33E 281 D4
Gunningbar Cr. → Australia 31°14S 147°6E 283 A7
Gunnison Colo., U.S.A. 38°33N 106°56W 304 G10
Gunnison Utah, U.S.A. 39°9N 111°49W 304 G8
Gunnison → U.S.A. 39°4N 108°35W 304 G9
Gunsan S. Korea 35°59N 126°45E 224 E3
Guntakal India 15°11N 77°27E 245 G3
Gunter Canada 44°52N 77°32W 312 B7
Guntersville U.S.A. 34°21N 86°18W 315 D11
Guntong Malaysia 4°36N 101°3E 237 K3
Guntur India 16°23N 80°30E 245 F5
Gunung Buda △ Malaysia 4°12N 114°57E 235 B4
Gunung Ciremay △ Indonesia 6°53S 108°24E 235 D3
Gunung Gading △ Malaysia 2°2N 109°52E 235 B3
Gunung Leuser △ Indonesia 3°39N 97°32E 234 B1
Gunung Mulu △ Malaysia 4°6N 114°53E 235 B4
Gunung Palung △ Indonesia 1°9S 110°13E 235 C4
Gunungapi Indonesia 6°45S 126°30E 231 F7
Gunungsitoli Indonesia 1°15N 97°30E 234 B1
Gunungtua Indonesia 1°30N 99°37E 234 B1
Gunupur India 19°5N 83°50E 244 E6
Günz → Germany 48°27N 10°16E 179 G6
Gunza Angola 10°50S 13°50E 265 E2
Günzburg Germany 48°26N 10°17E 179 G6
Gunzenhausen Germany 49°7N 10°44E 179 F6
Guo He → China 32°59N 117°10E 229 A11
Guomao China 39°54N 116°26E 114 B2
Guoxing = Kuohsing Taiwan 24°2N 120°51E 225 B2
Guoyang China 33°32N 116°12E 226 H9
Gupis Pakistan 36°15N 73°20E 243 A5
Gura Humorului Romania 47°35N 25°53E 183 C10
Gura-Teghii Romania 45°30N 26°25E 183 E11
Gurabo Puerto Rico 18°16N 65°58W 321 b
Gurag Ethiopia 8°20N 38°20E 257 F4
Gurahonț Romania 46°16N 22°21E 182 D7
Gurbantünggüt Shamo China 45°8N 87°20E 217 C11
Gurdaspur India 32°5N 75°31E 242 C6
Gurdon U.S.A. 33°55N 93°9W 314 E8
Güre Balıkesir, Turkey 39°36N 26°54E 205 B8
Güre Uşak, Turkey 38°39N 29°10E 205 C11
Gurgaon India 28°27N 77°1E 242 E7
Gürgentepe Turkey 40°51N 37°50E 212 B7
Gurghiu, Munții Romania 46°41N 25°15E 183 D10
Gurgueia → Brazil 6°50S 43°24W 332 C3
Gurha India 25°12N 71°39E 242 G4
Guri, Embalse de Venezuela 7°50N 62°52W 329 B5
Gurimatu Papua N. G. 6°45S 144°45E 286 D3
Gurin Nigeria 9°5N 12°54E 263 D7
Gurinhatã Brazil 19°14S 49°48W 333 E2
Gurjaani Georgia 41°43N 45°52E 191 K7
Gurk → Austria 46°35N 14°31E 180 E7
Gurkfeld = Krško Slovenia 45°57N 15°30E 199 C12
Gurkha Nepal 28°5N 84°40E 243 E11
Gurla Mandhata = Naimona'nyi Feng China 30°26N 81°18E 243 D9
Gurley Australia 29°45S 149°48E 281 D4
Gurnee U.S.A. 42°22N 87°55W 311 B9
Gurnet Point U.S.A. 42°1N 70°34W 313 D14
Guro Mozam. 17°26S 32°30E 269 F3
Gürpınar İstanbul, Turkey 40°59N 28°37E 203 F12
Gürpınar Van, Turkey 38°18N 43°25E 213 C10
Gürsu Turkey 40°13N 29°11E 203 F13
Gurué Mozam. 15°25S 36°58E 269 F4
Gurueragu Ethiopia 6°23N 45°31E 267 C6
Gurun Malaysia 5°49N 100°27E 237 K3
Gürün Turkey 38°43N 37°15E 212 C7
Gurupá Brazil 1°25S 51°35W 329 D7
Gurupá, I. Grande de Brazil 1°25S 51°45W 329 D7
Gurupi Brazil 11°43S 49°4W 333 D2
Gurupi → Brazil 1°13S 46°6W 332 B2
Gurupi, Serra do Brazil 5°0S 47°50W 332 C2
Guruwe Zimbabwe 16°40S 30°42E 271 A5
Gurvan Sayhan Uul Mongolia 43°50N 104°0E 226 C3
Guryev = Atyraū Kazakhstan 47°5N 52°0E 187 E9
Guryevsk Russia 54°47N 20°38E 184 D7
Gus-Khrustalnyy Russia 55°42N 40°44E 190 C5
Gusau Nigeria 12°12N 6°40E 263 C6
Gusev Russia 54°35N 22°10E 184 D9
Gushan China 39°50N 123°35E 224 C1
Gushgy = Serhetabat Turkmenistan 35°20N 62°18E 247 C9
Gushi China 32°11N 115°41E 229 A10
Gushiago Ghana 9°55N 0°15W 263 D4
Gushikami Japan 26°7N 127°44E 288 a
Gushikawa = Uruma Japan 26°21N 127°52E 288 a
Gusinje Montenegro 42°35N 19°50E 202 D3
Gusinoozersk Russia 51°16N 106°27E 215 D11
Gúspini Italy 39°32N 8°37E 200 C1
Güssing Austria 47°3N 16°20E 181 D9
Gustav Holm, Kap Greenland 66°36N 34°15W 154 D7
Gustavia St. Barts 17°53N 62°51W 322 a
Gustavo A. Madero Mexico 19°29N 99°8W 128 B2
Gustavus U.S.A. 58°25N 135°44W 296 B1
Gustine U.S.A. 37°16N 121°0W 306 H6
Güstrow Germany 53°47N 12°10E 178 B8
Gusum Sweden 58°16N 16°30E 163 F10
Guta = Kolárovo Slovak Rep. 47°54N 18°0E 181 D10
Gütersloh Germany 51°54N 8°24E 178 D4
Gutha Australia 28°58S 115°55E 279 E2
Guthalungra Australia 19°52S 147°50E 280 B4
Guthrie Ont., Canada 44°28N 79°32W 312 B5
Guthrie Okla., U.S.A. 35°53N 97°25W 314 D6
Guthrie Tex., U.S.A. 33°37N 100°19W 314 E4
Guthrie Center U.S.A. 41°41N 94°30W 310 C2
Gutian China 26°32N 118°43E 229 D12
Gutiérrez Bolivia 19°25S 63°34W 331 D5
Guttenberg Iowa, U.S.A. 42°47N 91°6W 310 B5
Guttenberg New York, U.S.A. 132 a1
Guttentag = Dobrodzień Poland 50°45N 18°25E 185 H5
Guttstadt = Dobre Miasto Poland 53°58N 20°26E 184 E7
Gutu Zimbabwe 19°41S 31°9E 271 A5
Gutulia △ Norway 62°2N 12°11E 164 B9
Gutuyevskiy, Ostrov Russia 59°53N 30°15E 137 B1
Guwahati India 26°10N 91°45E 241 B3
Guy Fawkes River △ Australia 30°0S 152°20E 281 D5
Guy-Fayreau, Complexe Montréal, Canada 130 b2
Guyana ■ S. Amer. 5°0N 59°0W 329 C6
Guyancourt France 48°46N 2°4E 134 B1
Guyane française = French Guiana ☒ S. Amer. 4°0N 53°0W 329 C7
Guyang China 41°0N 110°5E 226 D6
Guyenne France 44°30N 0°40E 174 D4
Guymon U.S.A. 36°41N 101°29W 314 C4
Guyotville = Aïn Benian Algeria 36°48N 2°55E 261 A5
Guyra Australia 30°15S 151°40E 281 E5
Guyton U.S.A. 32°20N 81°24W 316 C8
Guyuan Hebei, China 41°37N 115°40E 226 D8
Guyuan Ningxia Huizu, China 36°0N 106°20E 226 F4
Guzar Uzbekistan 38°36N 66°15E 217 E7
Güzelbağ Turkey 36°44N 31°53E 250 B2
Güzelbahçe Turkey 38°21N 26°54E 205 C8
Güzeloluk Turkey 36°47N 34°4E 250 B5
Güzelsu Turkey 36°53N 31°51E 250 B2
Güzelyurt = Morphou Cyprus 35°12N 32°59E 207 E8
Guzhang China 28°42N 109°58E 228 C7
Guzhen China 33°22N 117°18E 227 H9
Guzmán, L. de Mexico 31°20N 107°30W 318 A3
Gvardeysk Russia 54°39N 21°5E 184 D8
Gvardeyskoye Ukraine 45°7N 34°1E 189 K8
Gvarv Norway 59°23N 9°9E 164 E6
Gwa Burma 17°36N 94°34E 241 G5
Gwaai Zimbabwe 19°15S 27°45E 269 F2
Gwaai → Zimbabwe 17°59S 26°52E 269 F2
Gwabegar Australia 30°37S 148°59E 283 A8
Gwadabawa Nigeria 13°28N 5°15E 263 C6
Gwādar Pakistan 25°10N 62°18E 240 D1
Gwagwada Nigeria 10°15N 7°15E 263 C6
Gwaii Haanas △ Canada 52°21N 131°26W 296 C2
Gwalior India 26°12N 78°10E 242 F8
Gwanak S. Korea 37°29N 126°57E 137 C1
Gwanaksan S. Korea 37°27N 126°58E 137 C1
Gwanara Nigeria 8°55N 3°9E 263 D5
Gwanda Zimbabwe 20°55S 29°0E 269 G2
Gwandu Nigeria 12°30N 4°41E 263 C5
Gwane Dem. Rep. of the Congo 4°45N 25°48E 268 B2
Gwang-yang S. Korea 34°58N 127°35E 224 E3
Gwangju S. Korea 35°9N 126°54E 224 E3
Gwangju □ S. Korea 35°10N 126°45E 224 E3
Gwangyang S. Korea 34°56N 127°41E 227 G14
Gwanju = Gwangju S. Korea 35°9N 126°54E 224 E3
Gwaram Nigeria 10°15N 10°25E 263 C7
Gwarzo Nigeria 12°20N 8°55E 263 C6
Gwasero Nigeria 9°29N 3°30E 263 D5
Gwda → Poland 53°3N 16°44E 185 E3
Gweebarra B. Ireland 54°51N 8°23W 166 B3
Gweedore Ireland 55°3N 8°14W 166 A3
Gweru Zimbabwe 19°28S 29°45E 269 F2
Gwi Nigeria 9°0N 7°10E 263 D6
Gwinn U.S.A. 46°19N 87°27W 308 B10
Gwio Kura Nigeria 12°40N 11°2E 263 C7
Gwoza Nigeria 11°5N 13°40E 263 C7
Gwydir → Australia 29°27S 149°48E 281 D4
Gwynedd □ U.K. 52°52N 4°10W 168 E3
Gyál Hungary 47°23N 19°13E 117 B3
Gyáli-patak → Hungary 47°23N 19°7E 117 B2
Gyandzha = Gäncä Azerbaijan 40°45N 46°20E 191 K8
Gyangzê China 29°5N 89°47E 218 F6
Gyaring Hu China 34°50N 97°40E 218 E8
Gydanskiy Poluostrov Russia 70°0N 78°0E 214 C8
Gyeonggi-do □ S. Korea 36°37N 127°15E 224 D3
Gyeonggi-man S. Korea 37°0N 125°30E 227 F13
Gyeongju S. Korea 35°51N 129°14E 224 E4
Gyeongsan S. Korea 35°49N 128°44E 224 E4
Gyeongsangbuk-do □ S. Korea 36°20N 128°45E 224 D4
Gyeongsangnam-do □ S. Korea 35°15N 128°15E 224 E4
Gyeryongsan △ S. Korea 36°20N 127°15E 224 D3
Gyigang China 28°40N 97°31E 241 A6
Gyl Norway 62°57N 8°7E 164 B5
Gyldenløve Fjord Greenland 64°15N 40°30W 154 E6
Gympie Australia 26°11S 152°38E 281 D5
Gyobingauk Burma 18°13N 95°39E 241 F5
Gyōda Japan 36°10N 139°30E 223 A11
Gyodongdo S. Korea 37°47N 126°15E 224 D3
Gyomaendrőd Hungary 46°56N 20°50E 182 D5
Gyöngyös Hungary 47°48N 19°56E 182 C4
Győr Hungary 47°41N 17°40E 182 C2
Győr-Moson-Sopron □ Hungary 47°40N 17°20E 182 C2
Gypsum Pt. Canada 61°53N 114°35W 296 A6
Gypsumville Canada 51°45N 98°40W 297 C9
Gyueshevo Bulgaria 42°14N 22°28E 202 D6
Gyula Hungary 46°38N 21°17E 182 D6
Gyumri Armenia 40°47N 43°50E 191 K6
Gyzylarbat = Serdar Turkmenistan 39°4N 56°23E 247 B8
Gyzyletrek = Etrek Turkmenistan 37°36N 54°46E 247 B7
Gzhatsk = Gagarin Russia 55°38N 35°0E 188 E8
Gzira Malta 35°54N 14°29E 206 F7


# H


H. Neely Henry L. U.S.A. 33°55N 86°2W 316 B3
Ha 'Arava → Israel 30°50N 35°20E 251 H6
Ha Coi Vietnam 21°26N 107°46E 228 G6
Ha Dong Vietnam 20°58N 105°46E 228 G5
Ha Giang Vietnam 22°50N 104°59E 228 F5
Ha Karmel, Har Israel 32°44N 35°3E 250 F5
Ha Karmel △ Israel 32°45N 35°5E 250 F6
Ha Long = Hong Gai Vietnam 20°57N 107°5E 228 G6
Ha Long, Vinh Vietnam 20°56N 107°3E 236 B6
Ha Tien Vietnam 10°23N 104°29E 237 G5
Ha Tinh Vietnam 18°20N 105°54E 236 C5
Ha Trung Vietnam 19°58N 105°50E 236 C5
Haaga Finland 60°13N 24°53E 121 B2
Haakon VII Topp = Beerenberg Norway 71°0N 8°20W 154 C10
Haaksbergen Neths. 52°9N 6°45E 170 B6
Ha'ano Tonga 19°41S 174°18W 287 P13
Ha'apai Group Tonga 19°47S 174°27W 287 P13
Haapiti Moorea 17°34S 149°52W 289 e
Haapsalu Estonia 58°56N 23°30E 188 C2
Haar Germany 48°6N 11°43E 131 B3
Haarby Denmark 55°13N 10°7E 163 J4
Haarlem Neths. 52°23N 4°39E 170 B4
Haas-Lilienthal House San Francisco, U.S.A. 136 b1
Haast N.Z. 43°51S 169°1E 285 D4
Haast → N.Z. 43°50S 169°2E 285 D4
Haast Pass N.Z. 44°6S 169°21E 285 E4
Haasts Bluff Australia 23°22S 132°0E 278 D5
Haasts Bluff ☼ Australia 23°39S 130°34E 278 D5
Hab → Pakistan 24°53N 66°41E 242 G3
Hab Nadi Chauki Pakistan 25°0N 66°50E 242 G2
Habahe China 48°3N 86°23E 217 C11
Ḩabarūt Yemen 17°18N 52°44E 249 C6
Habaswein Kenya 1°2N 39°30E 268 B4
Ḩabawnah, W. → Si. Arabia 17°57N 44°58E 248 C4
Habay Alta., Canada 58°50N 118°44W 296 B5
Habay Manila, Phil. 14°27N 120°56E 127 C1
Ḩabbān Yemen 14°21N 47°5E 248 D4
Ḩabbānīyah Iraq 33°17N 43°29E 213 F10
Ḩabbānīyah, Hawr al Iraq 33°17N 43°29E 213 F10
Habelschwerdt = Bystrzyca Kłodzka Poland 50°19N 16°39E 185 H3
Habibas, Îles Algeria 35°44N 1°8W 197 K3
Habichtswald ⌓ Germany 51°15N 9°15E 178 D5
Habiganj Bangla. 24°24N 91°30E 241 C3
Habirag China 42°17N 115°42E 226 C8
Habisa Sudan 15°38N 31°18E 266 A3
Habo Sweden 57°55N 14°6E 163 G8
Haboro Japan 44°22N 141°42E 220 B10
Ḩabshān U.A.E. 23°50N 53°37E 247 F7
Hachenburg Germany 50°40N 7°49E 178 E3
Hachi India 27°48N 94°2E 241 B5
Hachijō-Jima Japan 33°5N 139°45E 223 D11
Hachiman = Gujō Japan 35°45N 136°57E 223 B8
Hachinohe Japan 40°30N 141°29E 220 D10
Hachiōji Japan 35°40N 139°20E 223 B11
Hacı Zeynalabdin Azerbaijan 40°37N 49°33E 191 K9
Hacıbektaş Turkey 38°56N 34°33E 212 C6
Hacılar Turkey 38°38N 35°26E 212 C6
Hack, Mt. Australia 30°45S 138°55E 282 A3
Hackås Sweden 62°56N 14°30E 162 B8
Hackbridge U.K. 51°23N 0°9W 125 B3
Hackensack U.S.A. 40°52N 74°4W 132 A1
Hackensack → U.S.A. 40°42N 74°7W 132 B1
Hackettstown U.S.A. 40°51N 74°50W 313 F10
Hackney □ U.K. 51°33N 0°3W 125 A3
Hackney Wick U.K. 51°32N 0°1W 125 A3
Håckrenmagasinet Sweden 63°15N 13°30E 162 C7
Haco Angola 10°15S 15°44E 265 E3
Hadali Pakistan 32°16N 72°11E 242 C5
Hadano Japan 35°22N 139°14E 223 B11
Hadarba, Ras Sudan 22°4N 36°51E 256 C4
Hadarom □ Israel 31°0N 35°0E 251 H6
Ḩadbaram Oman 17°27N 55°15E 249 C6
Ḩadd, Ra's al Oman 22°35N 59°50E 249 B7
Ḩaddā Si. Arabia 21°27N 39°34E 248 B2
Haddington U.K. 55°57N 2°47W 167 F6
Haddock U.S.A. 33°2N 83°26W 316 B6
Haddummati Atoll Maldives 2°0N 73°30E 272 d
Hadejia Nigeria 12°30N 10°5E 263 C7
Hadejia → Nigeria 12°50N 10°51E 263 C7
Hadera Israel 32°27N 34°55E 251 F5
Hadersleben = Haderslev Denmark 55°15N 9°30E 163 J3
Haderslev Denmark 55°15N 9°30E 163 J3
Hadgaon India 19°30N 77°40E 244 E3
Hadhramaut = Ḩaḑramawt □ Yemen 15°30N 49°30E 249 D5
Hadīboh Yemen 12°39N 54°2E 249 D6
Hadilik China 37°56N 86°6E 217 E11
Hadım Turkey 36°58N 32°26E 250 B3
Hadithah Si. Arabia 31°27N 37°9E 251 G8
Hadjadj, O. el → Algeria 28°18N 5°20E 261 C6
Hadjeb el Aïoun Tunisia 35°21N 9°32E 258 A1
Hadjer Kamaran Chad 12°41N 21°46E 259 F4
Hadjer-Lamis □ Chad 12°55N 16°0E 259 F3
Hadjer Mornou Chad 17°12N 23°8E 259 E4
Hadlaskar Norway 60°15N 7°9E 164 D4
Hadley B. Canada 72°31N 108°12W 294 C10
Hadong S. Korea 35°5N 127°44E 224 E3
Hadr, Warrâq el Egypt 30°5N 31°12E 117 A2
Ḩaḑramawt □ Yemen 15°30N 49°30E 249 D5
Ḩaḑramawt, W. → Yemen 15°10N 51°8E 249 D5
Ḩadrānīyah Iraq 35°38N 43°14E 246 C4
Hadrian's Wall U.K. 55°0N 2°30W 168 B5
Hadsten Denmark 56°19N 10°3E 163 H4
Hadsund Denmark 56°44N 10°8E 163 H4
Hadyach Ukraine 50°21N 34°0E 189 G8
Hae, Ko Thailand 7°44N 98°22E 237 a
Hægeland Norway 58°22N 7°45E 164 F4
Haeinsa △ S. Korea 35°47N 128°5E 224 E4
Haeju N. Korea 38°3N 125°45E 224 C2
Haeju-man N. Korea 37°54N 125°45E 224 D2
Hä'ena U.S.A. 22°14N 159°34W 302 A2
Haenam S. Korea 34°34N 126°35E 224 E3
Haenertsburg S. Africa 24°0S 29°50E 271 B4
Haerhpin = Harbin China 45°48N 126°40E 227 B14
Hafar al Bāţin Si. Arabia 28°32N 45°52E 246 D5
Hafik Turkey 39°51N 37°23E 212 C7
Ḩafīrat al 'Aydā Si. Arabia 26°26N 39°12E 246 E3
Ḩafit Oman 23°59N 55°49E 247 F7
Hafizabad Pakistan 32°5N 73°40E 242 C5
Haflong India 25°10N 93°5E 241 C4
Hafnarfjörður Iceland 64°4N 21°57W 155 C5
Hafnir Iceland 63°56N 22°41W 155 D4
Hafslo Norway 61°19N 7°10E 164 C4
Haft Gel Iran 31°30N 49°32E 247 D6
Haga Sweden 59°21N 18°1E 139 A2
Hagalil Israel 32°53N 35°18E 250 F6
Hagari → India 15°40N 77°0E 245 G3
Hagåtña Guam 13°28N 144°45E 302 d
Hagby Sweden 56°34N 16°11E 163 H10
Hagemeister I. U.S.A. 58°39N 160°54W 303 G7
Hagen Germany 51°21N 7°27E 178 D3
Hagenbrunn Austria 48°19N 16°27E 142 A2
Hagenow Germany 53°26N 11°12E 178 B7
Hagere Hiywet Ethiopia 8°59N 37°51E 266 C4
Hagerman U.S.A. 33°7N 104°20W 305 K11
Hagerman Fossil Beds ⌓ U.S.A. 42°48N 114°57W 304 E6
Hägersten Sweden 59°18N 17°59E 139 B1
Hagerstown Ind., U.S.A. 39°55N 85°10W 311 E11
Hagerstown Md., U.S.A. 39°39N 77°43W 309 F15
Hagersville Canada 42°58N 80°3W 312 D4
Hagetmau France 43°39N 0°37W 174 E3
Hagfors Sweden 60°3N 13°45E 162 D7
Häggvik Sweden 59°26N 17°56E 139 A1
Hagi Iceland 65°28N 23°25W 155 B3
Hagi Japan 34°30N 131°22E 222 C3
Hagolan Syria 33°0N 35°45E 250 F6
Hagondange France 49°16N 6°11E 173 C13
Hágöngulón Iceland 64°35N 18°8W 155 C8
Hagonoy Bulacan, Phil. 14°50N 120°44E 232 D3
Hagonoy Manila, Phil. 14°31N 121°3E 127 B2
Hags Hd. Ireland 52°57N 9°28W 166 D2
Hague, C. de la France 49°44N 1°56W 172 C5
Hague, The = 's-Gravenhage Neths. 52°7N 4°17E 170 B4
Hague Park Canada 43°45N 79°14W 141 A3
Haguenau France 48°49N 7°47E 173 D14
Hagunía W. Sahara 27°26N 12°24W 260 C2
Hahira U.S.A. 30°59N 83°22W 316 E6
Hai Duong Vietnam 20°56N 106°19E 228 G6
Hai'an Guangdong, China 20°18N 110°11E 229 a
Hai'an Jiangsu, China 32°37N 120°27E 229 A13
Haian Shanmo Taiwan 23°25N 121°25E 225 C3
Haicheng China 40°50N 122°45E 224 B1
Haida Gwaii Canada 53°20N 132°10W 296 C2
Haidar Khel Afghan. 33°58N 68°38E 242 C3
Haidarâbâd = Hyderabad India 17°22N 78°29E 244 F4
Haidargarh India 26°37N 81°22E 243 F9
Haidari = Chaidari Greece 38°2N 23°38E 112 A1
Haidarpur India 28°43N 77°8E 120 A1
Haidhausen Germany 48°7N 11°36E 131 B2
Haidian China 39°59N 116°16E 114 B1
Haifa = Ḩefa Israel 32°46N 35°0E 250 F6
Haifeng China 22°58N 115°10E 229 F10
Haiger Germany 50°43N 8°12E 178 E4
Haight-Ashbury U.S.A. 37°46N 122°26W 136 B2
Haikou China 20°1N 110°16E 229 a
Haiku-Pauwela U.S.A. 20°56N 156°19W 302 C5
Ḩā'il Si. Arabia 27°28N 41°45E 246 E4
Ḩā'il □ Si. Arabia 26°40N 41°40E 246 E4
Hailakandi India 24°42N 92°34E 241 C4
Hailar China 49°10N 119°38E 219 B12
Hailey U.S.A. 43°31N 114°19W 304 E6
Haileybury Canada 47°30N 79°38W 298 C4
Hailin China 44°37N 129°30E 227 B15
Hailing Dao China 21°35N 111°47E 229 G8
Hailun China 47°28N 126°50E 219 B14
Hailuoto Finland 65°3N 24°45E 160 D21
Haimen Guangdong, China 23°15N 116°38E 229 F11
Haimen Jiangsu, China 31°52N 121°10E 229 B13
Hainan □ China 19°0N 109°30E 229 a
Hainan Dao China 19°0N 109°30E 229 a
Hainan Str. = Qiongzhou Haixia China 20°10N 110°15E 229 a
Hainault U.K. 51°36N 0°6E 125 A4
Hainaut □ Belgium 50°30N 4°0E 170 D4
Hainburg Austria 48°9N 16°56E 181 C9
Haines Alaska, U.S.A. 59°14N 135°26W 296 B1
Haines Oreg., U.S.A. 44°55N 117°56W 304 D5
Haines City U.S.A. 28°7N 81°38W 317 G8
Haines Junction Canada 60°45N 137°30W 296 A1
Hainfeld Austria 48°3N 15°48E 180 C8
Haining China 30°28N 120°40E 229 B13
Haiphong Vietnam 20°47N 106°41E 228 G6
Haitan Dao China 25°30N 119°45E 229 E12
Haiti ■ W. Indies 19°0N 72°30W 321 C5
Haiya Sudan 18°20N 36°21E 256 D4
Haiyan Qinghai, China 36°53N 100°59E 218 D9
Haiyan Zhejiang, China 30°28N 120°58E 229 B13
Haiyang China 36°47N 121°9E 227 F11
Haiyang Dao China 39°2N 123°10E 224 C1
Haiyuan Guangxi Zhuangzu, China 22°8N 107°35E 228 F6
Haiyuan Ningxia Huizu, China 36°35N 105°52E 226 F3
Haizhou Guangdong, China 23°5N 113°18E 121 B2
Haizhou Jiangsu, China 34°37N 119°7E 227 G10
Haizhou Wan China 34°50N 119°20E 227 G10
Haizhu Guangchang China 23°6N 113°14E 121 B2
Haj Ali Qoli, Kavīr Iran 35°55N 54°50E 247 C7
Hajar Bangar Sudan 10°40N 22°45E 259 F4
Hajdú-Bihar □ Hungary 47°30N 21°30E 182 C6
Hajdúböszörmény Hungary 47°40N 21°30E 182 C6
Hajdúdorog Hungary 47°48N 21°30E 182 C6
Hajdúhadház Hungary 47°40N 21°40E 182 C6
Hajdúnánás Hungary 47°50N 21°26E 182 C6
Hajdúsámson Hungary 47°37N 21°42E 182 C6
Hajdúszoboszló Hungary 47°27N 21°22E 182 C6
Haji Ibrahim Iraq 36°40N 44°30E 213 D11
Hājīābād Iran 33°37N 60°0E 247 C9
Hajipur India 25°45N 85°13E 243 G11
Ḩajjah Yemen 15°42N 43°36E 248 D3
Ḩajjah □ Yemen 15°42N 43°36E 248 D3
Ḩājjīābād Iran 28°19N 55°55E 247 D7
Ḩājjīābād-e Zarrīn Iran 33°9N 54°51E 247 C7
Hajnówka Poland 52°47N 23°35E 185 F10
Hajo India 26°15N 91°32E 241 B3
Hajodo S. Korea 34°17N 126°3E 224 E3
Ḩajrah Si. Arabia 20°14N 41°3E 248 B3
Haka Burma 22°39N 93°37E 241 D4
Hakansson, Mts. Dem. Rep. of the Congo 8°40S 25°45E 265 D5
Hakataramea N.Z. 44°43S 170°30E 285 E5
Hakkâri Turkey 37°34N 43°44E 213 D10
Hakkâri □ Turkey 37°30N 44°0E 213 D10
Hakkâri Dağları Turkey 38°2N 42°58E 213 C10
Hakken-Zan Japan 34°10N 135°54E 223 C7
Hakkōda San Japan 40°50N 141°0E 220 D10
Hakodate Japan 41°45N 140°44E 220 D10
Hakos Namibia 23°13S 16°21E 270 B2
Hakota Japan 36°5N 140°30E 223 A12
Håksberg Sweden 60°11N 15°12E 162 D9
Hakskeenpan S. Africa 26°48S 20°13E 270 C3
Haku-San Japan 36°9N 136°46E 223 A8
Haku-San △ Japan 36°15N 136°45E 223 A8
Hakuba Japan 36°42N 137°51E 223 A9
Hakui Japan 36°53N 136°47E 221 F8
Hakun Burma 26°46N 95°42E 241 B5

Hakunila Finland 60°16N 25°6E 121 B3
Hakupu Cook Is. 19°6S 169°50W 289 g
Hakusan Japan 36°31N 136°34E 223 A8
Hal Saflieni Malta 35°52N 14°30E 206 F8
Hala Pakistan 25°43N 68°20E 240 D3
Ḥalab Syria 36°10N 37°15E 250 B8
Ḥalab □ Syria 36°10N 37°10E 250 B8
Ḥalaban Si. Arabia 23°29N 44°23E 248 B4
Ḥalabjah Iraq 35°10N 45°58E 213 E11
Halaib Sudan 22°12N 36°30E 256 C4
Halaib Triangle Africa 22°30N 35°20E 256 C4
Halandri = Chalandri Greece 38°3N 23°48E 112 A2
Halangingie Pt. Cook Is. 19°2S 169°58W 289 g
Halasa Sudan 14°26N 30°39E 257 E3
Halásztelek Hungary 47°22N 19°0E 117 B1
Hālat 'Ammār Si. Arabia 29°10N 36°4E 251 J7
Hālawa, C. U.S.A. 21°10N 156°43W 302 B5
Hālawa Heights U.S.A. 21°23N 157°55W 302 K14
Halbā Lebanon 34°34N 36°6E 250 D7
Halberstadt Germany 51°54N 11°3E 178 D7
Halcombe N.Z. 40°8S 175°30E 284 G4
Halcon, Mt. Phil. 13°16N 121°0E 232 E3
Halde Fjäll = Haltiatunturi Finland 69°17N 21°18E 160 B19
Halden Norway 59°9N 11°23E 164 E8
Haldensleben Germany 52°17N 11°24E 178 C7
Haldia Bangla. 22°1N 88°3E 243 H13
Haldwani India 29°31N 79°30E 243 E8
Hale U.S.A. 39°36N 93°20W 310 E3
Hale → Australia 24°56S 135°53E 280 C2
Haleakalā △ U.S.A. 20°40N 156°15W 302 C5
Hale'iwa U.S.A. 21°36N 158°6W 302 J13
Halesowen U.K. 52°27N 2°3W 169 E5
Halesworth U.K. 52°20N 1°31E 169 E9
Haleyville U.S.A. 34°14N 87°37W 315 D11
Half Assini Ghana 5°1N 2°50W 262 D4
Half Dome U.S.A. 37°44N 119°32E 306 H7
Half Tree Hollow St. Helena 15°56S 5°42W 153 h
Half Way Tree Jamaica 18°0N 76°48W 320 a
Halfa al Jadidah Sudan 15°20N 35°35E 266 A4
Halfeti Turkey 37°15N 37°52E 212 D7
Halfmoon Bay N.Z. 46°50S 168°5E 285 G3
Halfway → Canada 56°12N 121°32W 296 B4
Halia India 24°50N 82°19E 243 G10
Haliburton Canada 45°3N 78°30W 312 A6
Haliç Turkey 41°1N 28°57E 122 B1
Halifax Queens., Australia 18°32S 146°22E 280 B4
Halifax N.S., Canada 44°38N 63°35W 299 D7
Halifax W. Yorks., U.K. 53°43N 1°52W 168 D6
Halifax Pa., U.S.A. 40°25N 76°55W 312 F8
Halifax B. Australia 18°50S 147°0E 280 B4
Halifax Harbour Grenada 12°6N 61°45W 323 q
Halifax I. Namibia 26°38S 15°4E 270 C2
Halik Shan China 42°20N 81°22E 217 D10
Halīl → Iran 27°40N 58°30E 247 E8
Halim Perdana Kusuma Int. ✕ (HLP) Indonesia 6°16S 106°53E 122 B2
Halimun △ Indonesia 6°42S 106°26E 234 D3
Halkett, C. U.S.A. 70°48N 152°11W 303 A9
Halki = Chalki Greece 36°17N 27°35E 205 E9
Halkida = Chalkida Greece 38°27N 23°42E 204 C5
Halkidiki = Chalkidiki Greece 40°25N 23°20E 202 F7
Halkirk U.K. 58°30N 3°29W 167 C5
Hall Beach Canada 68°46N 81°12W 295 D15
Hall I. U.S.A. 60°40N 173°6W 303 F4
Hall in Tirol Austria 47°17N 11°30E 180 D4
Hall Pen. Canada 63°30N 66°0W 295 E18
Hall Pt. Australia 15°40S 124°23E 278 C3
Hallabro Sweden 56°22N 15°5E 163 H9
Halland Sweden 57°8N 12°47E 161 H15
Hallandale Beach U.S.A. 25°58N 80°8W 129 C3
Hallands län □ Sweden 57°0N 12°40E 163 H6
Hallands Väderö Sweden 56°27N 12°34E 163 H6
Hallandsås Sweden 56°22N 13°0E 163 H7
Ḥallāniyat, Ghubbat al Oman 17°40N 55°45E 249 C6
Ḥallāniyat, Jazā'ir al Oman 17°30N 55°58E 249 C6
Hallasan S. Korea 33°22N 126°32E 224 a
Hallasan △ S. Korea 33°20N 126°30E 224 a
Hällbybrunn Sweden 59°24N 16°25E 162 E10
Halle Belgium 50°44N 4°13E 116 B1
Halle Nordrhein-Westfalen, Germany 52°3N 8°22E 178 C4
Halle Sachsen-Anhalt, Germany 51°30N 11°56E 178 D7
Hällefors Sweden 59°47N 14°31E 162 E8
Hälleforsnäs Sweden 59°10N 16°30E 162 E10
Hallein Austria 47°40N 13°5E 180 D6
Hällekis Sweden 58°38N 13°27E 163 F7
Hallen Sweden 63°11N 14°4E 162 A8
Hallett Australia 33°25S 138°55E 282 B3
Hallettsville U.S.A. 29°27N 96°57W 314 G6
Halley Antarctica 75°35S 26°39W 151 D1
Hallia → India 16°55N 79°20E 244 F4
Hallim S. Korea 33°24N 126°15E 224 a
Hallingby Norway 60°7N 10°10E 164 D7
Hallingdal Norway 60°34N 9°12E 164 D6
Hallingdalselva → Norway 60°23N 9°35E 164 D6
Hallingskarvet Norway 60°36N 7°47E 164 D4
Hallingskarvet △ Norway 60°37N 7°45E 164 D4
Hallingskeid Norway 60°40N 7°17E 164 D4
Hallock U.S.A. 48°47N 96°57W 308 A5
Hallormsstaður Iceland 65°6N 14°45W 155 B12
Halls Creek Australia 18°16S 127°38E 278 C4
Halls Gap Australia 37°8S 142°34E 281 F3
Halls Lake Canada 45°7N 78°45W 312 A6
Hallsberg Sweden 59°5N 15°7E 162 E9
Hallstahammar Sweden 59°38N 16°15E 162 E10
Hallstatt Austria 47°33N 13°38E 180 D6
Hallstavik Sweden 60°5N 18°37E 162 D12
Hallstead U.S.A. 41°58N 75°45W 313 E9
Hallyeo △ S. Korea 34°45N 128°25E 224 E4
Halmahera Indonesia 0°40N 128°0E 231 D7
Halmahera Sea Indonesia 2°0N 130°0E 231 D7
Halmeu Romania 47°57N 23°2E 182 C8
Halmstad Sweden 56°41N 12°52E 163 H6
Halong Bay = Ha Long, Vinh Vietnam 20°56N 107°3E 236 B6
Halq el Oued = La Goulette Tunisia 36°53N 10°18E 200 F3
Hals Denmark 57°0N 10°18E 163 H4
Halsa Norway 63°3N 8°14E 164 A5
Halsafjorden Norway 63°5N 8°10E 164 A5
Hälsingborg = Helsingborg Sweden 56°3N 12°42E 163 H6
Hälsingland Sweden 61°40N 16°5E 162 C10
Halstead U.K. 51°57N 0°40E 169 F8
Haltdalen Norway 62°56N 11°8E 164 B8
Haltern Germany 51°44N 7°11E 178 D3
Haltiala Finland 60°16N 24°57E 121 B2
Haltiatunturi Finland 69°17N 21°18E 160 B19
Haltiavuori Finland 60°16N 24°56E 121 B2
Halton □ U.K. 53°22N 2°45W 168 D5
Haltwhistle U.K. 54°58N 2°26W 168 C5
Ḥālūl Qatar 25°40N 52°40E 247 E7
Halvad India 23°1N 71°11E 242 H4
Ḥalvān Iran 33°57N 56°15E 247 C8
Halve Dag, Pt. Curaçao 12°14N 69°7W 322 g
Ham Chad 10°1N 15°35E 259 F3
Ham Somme, France 49°45N 3°4E 173 C10
Ham London, U.K. 51°25N 0°18W 125 B2
Hamab Namibia 28°7S 19°16E 270 C2
Hamad Sudan 15°20N 33°32E 257 D3
Hamada Japan 34°56N 132°4E 222 C4
Hamadān Iran 34°52N 48°32E 213 E13
Hamadān □ Iran 35°0N 49°0E 247 C6
Hamadia Algeria 35°28N 1°57E 261 A5
Ḥamāh Syria 35°5N 36°40E 250 C7
Ḥamāh □ Syria 35°10N 37°0E 250 C8
Hamakita Japan 34°45N 137°47E 223 C9
Hamamatsu Japan 34°45N 137°45E 223 C9
Haman S. Korea 35°14N 128°28E 224 E4
Hamar Norway 60°48N 11°7E 164 D8
Hamâta, Gebel Egypt 24°17N 35°0E 246 E2
Hamatonbetsu Japan 45°10N 142°20E 220 B11
Hambantota Sri Lanka 6°10N 81°10E 245 L5
Hamber △ Canada 52°20N 118°0W 296 C5
Hamburg Hamburg, Germany 53°33N 9°59E 178 B5
Hamburg Ark., U.S.A. 33°14N 91°48W 314 E9
Hamburg N.Y., U.S.A. 42°43N 78°50W 312 D6
Hamburg Pa., U.S.A. 40°33N 75°59W 313 F9
Hamburg □ Germany 53°30N 10°0E 178 B5
Hamburg Fuhlsbüttel ✕ (HAM) Germany 53°35N 9°59E 178 B5
Ḥamḍ, W. al → Si. Arabia 24°55N 36°20E 246 E3
Ḥamḍah Si. Arabia 19°2N 43°36E 248 C3
Ḥamdānah Si. Arabia 19°59N 40°34E 248 C3
Hamden U.S.A. 41°23N 72°54W 313 E12
Hamdibey Turkey 39°50N 27°15E 205 B9
Häme Finland 61°38N 25°10E 160 F21
Hämeenkylä Finland 60°16N 24°48E 121 B1
Hämeenlinna Finland 61°0N 24°28E 188 B3
Hamélé Ghana 10°56N 2°45W 262 C4
Hamelin Pool Australia 26°22S 114°20E 279 E1
Hameln Germany 52°6N 9°21E 178 C5
Hamerkaz □ Israel 32°15N 34°55E 251 F5
Hamero Hadad Ethiopia 7°27N 42°14E 267 C5
Hamersley Ra. Australia 22°0S 117°45E 278 D2
Hamgyong-sanmaek N. Korea 41°35N 129°15E 224 B4
Hamgyŏngbuk-do □ N. Korea 41°50N 129°25E 224 B4
Hamgyŏngnam-do □ N. Korea 40°0N 127°30E 224 C3
Hamhŭng N. Korea 39°54N 127°30E 224 C3
Hamhŭng-man N. Korea 39°48N 127°37E 224 C3
Hami China 42°55N 93°25E 218 C7
Hamilton = Churchill → Canada 53°19N 60°10W 299 B7
Hamilton Vic., Australia 37°45S 142°2E 282 D5
Hamilton Bermuda 32°17N 64°47W 153 a
Hamilton Ont., Canada 43°15N 79°50W 312 C5
Hamilton N.Z. 37°47S 175°19E 284 D4
Hamilton S. Lanarks., U.K. 55°46N 4°2W 167 F4
Hamilton Ala., U.S.A. 34°9N 87°59W 315 D11
Hamilton Alaska, U.S.A. 62°54N 163°53W 303 E7
Hamilton Ga., U.S.A. 32°45N 84°53W 316 C5
Hamilton Ill., U.S.A. 40°24N 91°21W 310 D5
Hamilton Ind., U.S.A. 41°33N 84°56W 311 C12
Hamilton Mo., U.S.A. 39°45N 94°0W 310 E2
Hamilton Mont., U.S.A. 46°15N 114°10W 304 C6
Hamilton N.Y., U.S.A. 42°50N 75°33W 313 D9
Hamilton Ohio, U.S.A. 39°24N 84°34W 311 E12
Hamilton Tex., U.S.A. 31°42N 98°7W 314 F5
Hamilton → Queens., Australia 23°30S 139°47E 280 C2
Hamilton → S. Austral., Australia 26°40S 135°19E 281 D2
Hamilton City U.S.A. 39°45N 122°1W 306 F4
Hamilton I. Australia 20°21S 148°56E 280 b
Hamilton Inlet Canada 54°0N 57°30W 299 B8
Hamilton Mt. U.S.A. 43°25N 74°22W 313 C10
Hamina Finland 60°34N 27°12E 188 B4
Hamirpur H.P., India 31°41N 76°31E 242 D7
Hamirpur Ut. P., India 25°57N 80°9E 243 G9
Hamitabat Turkey 41°30N 27°17E 203 E11
Hamju N. Korea 39°51N 127°26E 224 C3
Hamlet U.S.A. 34°53N 79°42W 315 D15
Hamley Bridge Australia 34°17S 138°35E 282 C3
Hamlin = Hameln Germany 52°6N 9°21E 178 C5
Hamlin N.Y., U.S.A. 43°17N 77°55W 312 C7
Hamlin Tex., U.S.A. 32°53N 100°8W 314 E4
Hamm Germany 51°40N 7°50E 178 D3
Ḥammām al 'Alīl Iraq 36°9N 43°15E 213 D10
Hammam Bouhadjar Algeria 35°23N 0°58W 261 A4
Ḥammām Damt Yemen 14°5N 44°40E 248 D4
Hammamet Tunisia 36°24N 10°38E 258 A2
Hammamet, G. de Tunisia 36°10N 10°48E 258 A2
Ḥammār, Hawr al Iraq 30°50N 47°10E 246 D5
Hammarby Sweden 59°17N 18°5E 139 B2
Hammarstrand Sweden 63°7N 16°20E 162 A10
Hamme Belgium 50°55N 4°17E 116 A1
Hammelburg Germany 50°6N 9°53E 179 E5
Hammeren Denmark 55°18N 14°47E 163 J8
Hammerfest Norway 70°39N 23°41E 160 A20
Hammersmith U.K. 51°29N 0°14W 125 B2
Hammerstein = Czarne Poland 53°42N 16°58E 184 E3
Hammerum Denmark 56°8N 9°3E 163 H3
Hamminkeln Germany 51°43N 6°35E 178 D2
Hammond Ind., U.S.A. 41°38N 87°30W 311 C9
Hammond La., U.S.A. 30°30N 90°28W 315 F9
Hammond N.Y., U.S.A. 44°27N 75°42W 313 B9
Hammondsport U.S.A. 42°25N 77°13W 312 D7
Hammonton U.S.A. 39°39N 74°48W 309 F16
Hamoyet, Jebel Sudan 17°33N 38°2E 256 D4
Hampden N.Z. 45°18S 170°50E 285 F5
Hampi India 15°18N 76°28E 245 G3
Hampshire □ U.K. 51°7N 1°23W 169 F6
Hampshire Downs U.K. 51°15N 1°10W 169 F6
Hampstead Qué., Canada 45°28N 73°37W 130 B2
Hampstead Dominica 15°36N 61°23W 323 k
Hampstead London, U.K. 51°33N 0°10W 125 A2
Hampstead Garden Suburb U.K. 51°34N 0°11W 125 A2
Hampstead Heath U.K. 51°33N 0°10W 125 A2
Hampton N.B., Canada 45°32N 65°51W 299 C6
Hampton Ont., Canada 43°58N 78°45W 312 C6
Hampton London, U.K. 51°24N 0°21W 125 B1
Hampton Ark., U.S.A. 33°32N 92°28W 314 E8
Hampton Ga., U.S.A. 33°23N 84°17W 316 B5
Hampton Iowa, U.S.A. 42°45N 93°13W 310 B3
Hampton N.H., U.S.A. 42°57N 70°50W 313 D14
Hampton S.C., U.S.A. 32°52N 81°7W 316 C8
Hampton Va., U.S.A. 37°2N 76°21W 309 G15
Hampton Bays U.S.A. 40°53N 72°30W 313 F12
Hampton Court Palace U.K. 51°24N 0°20W 125 B1
Hampton Springs U.S.A. 30°5N 83°40W 316 E6
Hampton Tableland Australia 32°0S 127°0E 279 F4
Hampton Wick U.K. 51°24N 0°18W 125 B2
Hampyeong S. Korea 35°3N 126°31E 224 E3
Hampyeongman S. Korea 35°6N 126°23E 224 E3
Ḥamrā' Baghdād, Iraq 33°18N 44°18E 113 B1
Hamra Gävleborg, Sweden 61°39N 14°59E 162 C8
Ḥamra → Chad 12°52N 21°15E 259 F4
Hamrat esh Sheykh Sudan 14°38N 27°55E 257 E2
Ḥamrin, Jabal Iraq 34°30N 44°30E 213 E11
Hamrun Malta 35°53N 14°29E 206 F8
Hamtic Phil. 10°42N 121°59E 233 F3
Hamur Turkey 39°37N 43°2E 213 C10
Hamyang S. Korea 35°32N 127°42E 224 E3
Hamzalar Turkey 37°7N 32°33E 250 A3
Han i Hotit Albania 42°19N 19°27E 202 D3
Han Jiang → China 23°25N 116°40E 229 F11
Han Shui → China 30°34N 114°17E 229 B10
Hāna U.S.A. 20°45N 155°59W 302 C6
Hanahan U.S.A. 32°55N 80°0W 316 C10
Hanak Si. Arabia 25°32N 37°0E 246 E3
Hanak Turkey 41°14N 42°50E 213 B10
Hanala Finland 60°20N 25°12E 121 A3
Hanalei U.S.A. 22°12N 159°30W 302 A2
Hanamaki Japan 39°23N 141°7E 220 E10
Hanamaulu U.S.A. 21°59N 159°22W 302 B2
Hanang Tanzania 4°30S 35°25E 268 C4
Hanapēpē U.S.A. 21°55N 159°35W 302 B2
Hanare Iwa Iwo Jima 24°48N 141°21E 288 b
Hanau Germany 50°7N 8°56E 179 E4
Hanauma B. U.S.A. 21°15N 157°40W 302 K14
Hanbogd = Ihbulag Mongolia 43°11N 107°10E 226 C4
Hançalar Turkey 38°8N 29°24E 205 C11
Hâncești Moldova 46°50N 28°36E 183 D13
Hancheng China 35°31N 110°25E 226 G6
Hanchuan China 30°40N 113°50E 229 B9
Hanchung = Hanzhong China 33°10N 107°1E 228 A6
Hancock Mich., U.S.A. 47°8N 88°35W 308 B9
Hancock N.Y., U.S.A. 41°57N 75°17W 313 E9
Hancock Vt., U.S.A. 43°55N 72°50W 313 C12
Handa Japan 34°53N 136°55E 223 C8
Handa I. U.K. 58°23N 5°11W 167 C3
Handan China 36°35N 114°28E 226 F8
Handeni Tanzania 5°25S 38°2E 268 D4
Handlová Slovak Rep. 48°45N 18°35E 181 C11
Handub Sudan 19°15N 37°16E 256 D4
Handwara India 34°21N 74°20E 243 B6
Haneda Japan 35°32N 139°44E 140 B3
Haneda, Tōkyō ✕ (HND) Japan 35°33N 139°46E 140 B3
Hanegev Israel 30°50N 35°0E 251 H6
Hanford U.S.A. 36°20N 119°39W 306 J7
Hanford Reach △ U.S.A. 46°40N 119°30W 304 C4
Hang Chat Thailand 18°20N 99°21E 236 C2
Hang Hau Hong Kong, China 22°19N 114°16E 122 B3
Hanga Roa Chile 27°8S 109°26W 330 b
Hangang → S. Korea 37°50N 126°30E 227 F14
Hangayn Nuruu Mongolia 47°30N 99°0E 218 B8
Hangchou = Hangzhou China 30°18N 120°11E 229 B13
Hanger Sweden 57°6N 13°58E 163 G7
Hanggin Houqi China 40°58N 107°4E 226 D4
Hanggin Qi China 39°52N 108°50E 226 E5
Hanging Gardens Mumbai, India 130 b1
Hangkow = Wuhan China 30°31N 114°18E 229 B10
Hangku = Hangu China 39°18N 117°53E 227 E9
Hangu China 39°18N 117°53E 227 E9
Hangzhou China 30°18N 120°11E 229 B13
Hangzhou Wan China 30°15N 120°45E 229 B13
Hanh Mongolia 51°32N 100°35E 218 A9
Hanhöhiy Uul Mongolia 49°30N 94°30E 217 C12
Hanhongor Mongolia 43°55N 104°28E 226 C3
Hani Turkey 38°24N 40°23E 213 C9
Hania = Chania Greece 35°30N 24°4E 207 E5
Ḥanīdh Si. Arabia 26°35N 48°38E 247 E6
Ḥanīsh Yemen 13°45N 42°46E 248 D3
Haniska Slovak Rep. 48°37N 21°15E 181 C14
Hanjiang China 25°26N 119°6E 229 E12
Hankinson U.S.A. 46°4N 96°54W 308 B5
Hanko Finland 59°50N 22°57E 188 C2
Hankou China 30°35N 114°30E 229 B10
Hanksville U.S.A. 38°22N 110°43W 304 G8
Hanle India 32°42N 79°4E 243 C8
Hanlon Canada 43°38N 79°39W 141 B1
Hanmer Springs N.Z. 42°32S 172°50E 285 C7
Hann → Australia 17°26S 126°17E 278 C4
Hann, Mt. Australia 15°45S 126°0E 278 C4
Hanna Alta., Canada 51°40N 111°54W 296 C6
Hanna Wyo., U.S.A. 41°52N 106°34W 304 F10
Hannah B. Canada 51°40N 80°0W 298 B4
Hannibal Mo., U.S.A. 39°42N 91°22W 310 E5
Hannibal N.Y., U.S.A. 43°19N 76°35W 313 C8
Hannik Sudan 18°12N 32°20E 256 D3
Hannover Germany 52°22N 9°46E 178 C5
Hanö Sweden 56°1N 14°50E 163 H8
Hanöbukten Sweden 55°35N 14°30E 163 J8
Hanoi Vietnam 21°5N 105°55E 228 G5
Hanover = Hannover Germany 52°22N 9°46E 178 C5
Hanover Ont., Canada 44°9N 81°2W 312 B3
Hanover Northern Cape, S. Africa 31°4S 24°29E 270 D3
Hanover N.H., U.S.A. 43°42N 72°17W 313 C12
Hanover Ohio, U.S.A. 40°4N 82°16W 312 F2
Hanover Pa., U.S.A. 39°48N 76°59W 309 F15
Hanover, I. Chile 51°0S 74°50W 336 D2
Hanpan, C. Papua N. G. 5°0S 154°35E 286 C8
Hans Lollik I. U.S. Virgin Is. 18°24N 64°53W 321 b
Hans Meyer Ra. Papua N. G. 4°20S 152°55E 286 C7
Hansdiha India 24°36N 87°5E 243 G12
Hanshou China 28°56N 111°50E 229 C8
Hansi H.P., India 32°27N 77°50E 242 C7
Hansi Haryana, India 29°10N 75°57E 242 E6
Hanson, L. Australia 31°0S 136°15E 282 A2
Hanstholm Denmark 57°7N 8°36E 163 G2
Hantan = Handan China 36°35N 114°28E 226 F8
Hanting China 36°46N 119°12E 227 F10
Hantsavichy Belarus 52°49N 26°30E 177 B14
Hanumangarh India 29°35N 74°19E 242 E6
Hanwell U.K. 51°30N 0°20W 125 B1
Hanworth U.K. 51°26N 0°23W 125 B1
Hanyin China 32°54N 108°28E 226 H5
Hanyū Japan 36°10N 139°32E 223 A11
Hanyuan China 29°21N 102°40E 228 C4
Hanzhong China 33°10N 107°1E 228 A6
Hanzhuang China 34°33N 117°23E 227 G9
Hao French Polynesia 18°15S 140°54W 289 f
Haora India 22°34N 88°18E 124 B1
Haouach, O. → Chad 16°45N 19°35E 259 E4
Haoxue China 30°3N 112°24E 229 B9
Haparanda Sweden 65°52N 24°8E 160 D21
Haparanda Skärgård △ Sweden 65°35N 23°44E 160 D20
Hapdeok S. Korea 36°48N 126°46E 224 D3
Hapeville U.S.A. 33°39N 84°24W 113 C2
Happy U.S.A. 34°45N 101°52W 314 D4
Happy Camp U.S.A. 41°48N 123°23W 304 F2
Happy Valley Hong Kong, China 22°16N 114°10E 122 B3
Happy Valley-Goose Bay Canada 53°15N 60°20W 299 B7
Hapsu N. Korea 41°13N 128°51E 224 B4
Hapur India 28°45N 77°45E 242 E7
Ḥaql Si. Arabia 29°10N 34°58E 251 J5
Haquira Peru 14°14S 72°12W 330 C3
Har Indonesia 5°16S 133°14E 231 F8
Har Adar West Bank 31°49N 35°8E 123 B1
Har-Ayrag Mongolia 45°47N 109°16E 226 B5
Har Gilo West Bank 31°43N 35°10E 123 B2
Har Homa West Bank 31°44N 35°12E 123 B2
Har Hu China 38°20N 97°38E 218 D8
Har Nof Israel 31°47N 35°11E 123 B2
Har Tsiyon Jerusalem 123 b3
Har Us Nuur Mongolia 48°0N 92°0E 217 C12
Har Yehuda Israel 31°35N 34°57E 251 G5
Ḥaraḍ Si. Arabia 24°22N 49°0E 249 A5
Ḥaraḍ Yemen 16°26N 43°5E 248 C3
Haradok Belarus 55°30N 30°3E 188 E6
Häradsbäck Sweden 56°32N 14°26E 163 H8
Harahan U.S.A. 29°56N 90°12W 131 B1
Haraiki French Polynesia 17°38S 143°27W 289 f
Haramosh Pakistan 35°50N 74°54E 243 B6
Haranomachi = Minamisōma Japan 37°38N 140°58E 220 F10
Harar = Harer Ethiopia 9°20N 42°8E 257 F5
Harare Zimbabwe 17°43S 31°2E 269 F3
Ḥarāsīs, Jiddat al Oman 19°30N 56°0E 249 C7
Harat Eritrea 16°5N 39°26E 257 D4
Harau Indonesia 0°7S 100°35E 234 C2
Haraz-Djombo Chad 14°20N 19°12E 259 F3
Harazé Chad 9°57N 20°48E 259 G4
Harbel Liberia 6°16N 10°20W 262 D2
Harbhanga India 20°38N 84°36E 244 D7
Harbin China 45°48N 126°40E 227 B14
Harbiye Turkey 36°10N 36°8E 250 B7
Harbo Sweden 60°7N 17°12E 162 D11
Harboøre Denmark 56°38N 8°10E 163 H2
Harbor Beach U.S.A. 43°51N 82°39W 312 C2
Harborcreek U.S.A. 42°9N 79°57W 312 D5
Harbour Breton Canada 47°29N 55°50W 299 C8
Harbour Deep Canada 50°25N 56°32W 299 B8
Harbour Front Centre Singapore 1°16N 103°49E 138 B2
Harbour View Jamaica 17°59N 76°50W 320 a
Harburg Germany 53°27N 9°58E 178 B5
Harburger Berge △ Germany 53°26N 9°51E 178 B5
Harda India 22°27N 77°5E 242 H7
Hardangerfjorden Norway 60°5N 6°0E 164 D3
Hardangerjøkulen Norway 60°30N 7°27E 164 D4
Hardangervidda Norway 60°7N 7°20E 164 D4
Hardangervidda △ Norway 60°10N 7°25E 164 D4
Hardap □ Namibia 24°0S 17°0E 270 B2
Hardap △ Namibia 24°29S 17°45E 270 B2
Hardap Dam Namibia 24°32S 17°50E 270 B2
Hardeeville U.S.A. 32°17N 81°5W 316 C8
Harden Australia 34°32S 148°24E 283 C8
Hardenberg Neths. 52°34N 6°37E 170 B6
Harderwijk Neths. 52°21N 5°38E 170 B5
Hardey → Australia 22°45S 116°8E 278 D2
Hardin Ill., U.S.A. 39°10N 90°37W 310 E6
Hardin Mont., U.S.A. 45°44N 107°37W 304 D10
Harding S. Africa 30°35S 29°55E 271 D4
Harding, L. U.S.A. 32°40N 85°5W 316 C4
Harding Ra. Australia 16°17S 124°55E 278 C3
Hardinsburg U.S.A. 37°47N 86°28W 311 G10
Hardisty Canada 52°40N 111°18W 296 C6
Hardoi India 27°26N 80°6E 243 F9
Hardwar = Haridwar India 29°58N 78°9E 242 E8
Hardwick Ga., U.S.A. 33°4N 83°14W 316 B6
Hardwick Vt., U.S.A. 44°30N 72°22W 313 B12
Hardwicke B. Australia 34°55S 137°20E 282 C2
Hardwood Lake Canada 45°12N 77°26W 312 A7
Hardy, Pen. Chile 55°30S 68°20W 336 E3
Hardy, Pte. St. Lucia 14°6N 60°56W 323 m
Hare B. Canada 51°15N 55°45W 299 B8
Hareid Norway 62°22N 6°1E 164 B3
Haren Brussels, Belgium 50°53N 4°25E 116 A2
Haren Niedersachsen, Germany 52°47N 7°13E 178 C3
Harer Ethiopia 9°20N 42°8E 257 F5
Harerge Ethiopia 7°12N 42°0E 257 F5
Hareskovby Denmark 55°45N 12°23E 118 A2
Harestua Norway 60°11N 10°44E 164 D7
Hareto Ethiopia 9°23N 37°6E 257 F4
Harfleur France 49°30N 0°10E 172 C7
Hargeisa Somalia 9°30N 44°2E 267 C5
Hargeisa △ Somalia 10°2N 44°2E 267 B5
Harghita □ Romania 46°30N 25°30E 183 D10
Harghita, Munţii Romania 46°25N 25°35E 183 D10
Hargshamn Sweden 60°12N 18°30E 162 D12
Hari → Indonesia 1°16S 104°5E 234 C2
Ḥarīb Yemen 14°56N 45°30E 248 D4
Haricha, Hamada el Mali 22°40N 3°15W 260 D4
Haridwar India 29°58N 78°9E 242 E8
Harihar India 14°32N 75°44E 245 G2
Harihari N.Z. 43°9S 170°33E 285 D5
Hariharpur Garhi Nepal 27°19N 85°29E 243 F11
Ḥārim Syria 36°14N 36°29E 250 B7
Harim, Jabal al Oman 25°58N 56°14E 247 E8
Harima-Nada Japan 34°30N 134°35E 222 C6
Haringey □ U.K. 51°34N 0°5W 125 A3
Haringhata → Bangla. 22°0N 89°58E 241 E2
Haripad India 9°14N 76°28E 245 K3
Harīr, W. al → Syria 32°44N 35°59E 250 F6
Harīrūd → Asia 37°24N 60°38E 240 A1
Härjedalen Sweden 62°22N 13°5E 162 B7
Harjusuo Finland 60°19N 25°0E 121 B3
Harlaching Germany 48°5N 11°33E 131 B2
Harlan Iowa, U.S.A. 41°39N 95°19W 308 E6
Harlan Ky., U.S.A. 36°51N 83°19W 309 G12
Hârlău Romania 47°23N 26°55E 183 C12
Harlaw Res. U.K. 55°52N 3°18W 121 B2
Harlech U.K. 52°52N 4°6W 168 E3
Harlem Ga., U.S.A. 33°25N 82°19W 316 B7
Harlem Mont., U.S.A. 48°32N 108°47W 304 B9
Harlem New York, U.S.A. 132 a3
Harlesden U.K. 51°32N 0°14W 125 A2
Hårlev Denmark 55°21N 12°14E 163 J6
Harleyville U.S.A. 33°13N 80°27W 316 B9
Harlingen Neths. 53°11N 5°25E 170 A5
Harlingen Tex., U.S.A. 26°12N 97°42W 314 H6
Harlington U.K. 51°29N 0°25W 125 B1
Harlow U.K. 51°46N 0°8E 169 F8
Harlowton U.S.A. 46°26N 109°50W 304 C9
Harmaja Finland 60°6N 24°58E 121 C2
Harmancık Turkey 39°41N 29°9E 205 B11
Harmånger Sweden 61°55N 17°20E 162 C11
Harmashatar hegy Hungary 47°33N 19°0E 117 A2
Harmil Eritrea 16°30N 40°10E 257 D5
Harnai India 17°48N 73°6E 244 F1
Harnai Pakistan 30°6N 67°56E 242 D2
Harney, L. U.S.A. 28°45N 81°3W 317 G8
Harney Basin U.S.A. 43°0N 119°30W 304 E4
Harney L. U.S.A. 43°14N 119°8W 304 E4
Harney Peak U.S.A. 43°52N 103°32W 308 D2
Härnön Sweden 62°36N 18°0E 162 B12
Härnösand Sweden 62°38N 17°55E 162 B11
Haro Spain 42°35N 2°55W 196 C2
Harold U.S.A. 30°40N 86°53W 317 E3
Harold Pond Bahamas 25°2N 77°22W 153 b
Harolds Cross Ireland 53°19N 6°16W 120 B2
Haroldswick U.K. 60°48N 0°50W 167 A8
Háros Hungary 47°23N 19°2E 117 B2
Harp L. Canada 55°5N 61°50W 299 A7
Harpanahalli India 14°47N 76°2E 245 G3
Harper = Costa Mesa U.S.A. 33°38N 117°55W 307 M9
Harper Liberia 4°25N 7°43W 262 E3
Harper, Mt. U.S.A. 64°14N 143°51W 303 D12
Harperrig Res. U.K. 55°50N 3°26W 121 B1
Harplinge Sweden 56°45N 12°45E 163 H6
Harrah's Casino New Orleans, U.S.A. 131 b2
Harrai India 22°37N 79°13E 243 H8
Harrand Pakistan 29°28N 70°3E 242 E4
Harricana → Canada 50°56N 79°32W 298 B4
Harriman U.S.A. 35°56N 84°33W 315 D12
Harrington Australia 31°52S 152°42E 283 A10
Harrington Harbour Canada 50°31N 59°30W 299 B8
Harrington Sd. Bermuda 32°20N 64°44W 153 a
Harris Montserrat 16°44N 62°11W 323 p
Harris W. Isles, U.K. 57°50N 6°55W 167 D2
Harris, L. S. Austral., Australia 31°10S 135°10E 281 E2
Harris, L. Fla., U.S.A. 28°47N 81°49W 317 G8
Harris, Sd. of U.K. 57°44N 7°6W 167 D1
Harris Mts. N.Z. 44°49S 168°49E 285 E3
Harris Pt. Canada 43°6N 82°9W 312 C2
Harrisburg Ill., U.S.A. 37°44N 88°32W 311 G8
Harrisburg Nebr., U.S.A. 41°33N 103°44W 308 E2
Harrisburg Pa., U.S.A. 40°16N 76°53W 312 F8
Harrismith S. Africa 28°15S 29°8E 271 C4
Harrison Ark., U.S.A. 36°14N 93°7W 314 C8
Harrison Maine, U.S.A. 44°7N 70°39W 313 B14
Harrison Nebr., U.S.A. 42°41N 103°53W 308 D2
Harrison, C. Canada 54°55N 57°55W 299 B8
Harrison Bay U.S.A. 70°40N 151°0W 303 A10
Harrison L. Canada 49°33N 121°50W 296 D4
Harrisonburg U.S.A. 38°27N 78°52W 309 F14
Harrison's Cave Barbados 13°11N 59°34W 323 r
Harrisonville U.S.A. 38°39N 94°21W 310 F2
Harriston Canada 43°57N 80°53W 312 C4
Harrisville Mich., U.S.A. 44°39N 83°17W 312 B1
Harrisville N.Y., U.S.A. 44°9N 75°19W 313 B9
Harrisville Pa., U.S.A. 41°8N 80°0W 312 E5
Harrodsburg Ind., U.S.A. 39°1N 86°33W 311 E10
Harrodsburg Ky., U.S.A. 37°46N 84°51W 311 G12
Harrogate U.K. 54°0N 1°33W 168 C6
Harrow Vic., Australia 37°9S 141°35E 282 D4
Harrow Ont., Canada 42°2N 82°55W 312 D2
Harrow □ U.K. 51°35N 0°21W 125 A1
Harrow on the Hill U.K. 51°34N 0°21W 125 A1
Harrow School U.K. 51°34N 0°20W 125 A1
Harrow Weald U.K. 51°36N 0°20W 125 A1
Harrowsmith Canada 44°24N 76°40W 313 B8
Harry S. Truman Res. U.S.A. 38°16N 93°24W 310 F3
Harsefeld Germany 53°27N 9°30E 178 B5
Harsewinkel Germany 51°56N 8°14E 178 D4
Harsīn Iran 34°18N 47°33E 213 E12
Hârşova Romania 44°40N 27°59E 183 F12
Harstad Norway 68°48N 16°30E 160 B17
Harsud India 22°6N 76°44E 242 H7
Hart U.S.A. 43°42N 86°22W 308 D10
Hart, L. Australia 31°10S 136°25E 282 A2
Hartbees → S. Africa 28°45S 20°32E 270 C3
Hartberg Austria 47°17N 15°58E 180 D8
Hårteigen Norway 60°11N 7°3E 164 D4
Hartford Ala., U.S.A. 31°6N 85°42W 316 D4
Hartford Conn., U.S.A. 41°46N 72°41W 313 E12
Hartford Ky., U.S.A. 37°27N 86°55W 308 G10
Hartford Mich., U.S.A. 42°13N 86°10W 311 B10
Hartford S. Dak., U.S.A. 43°38N 96°57W 308 D5
Hartford Vt., U.S.A. 43°40N 72°20W 313 C12
Hartford Wis., U.S.A. 43°19N 88°22W 308 D9
Hartford City U.S.A. 40°27N 85°22W 311 D11
Hartingsburg = Bela Bela S. Africa 24°51S 28°19E 271 B4
Hartland N.B., Canada 46°20N 67°32W 299 C6
Hartland Wis., U.S.A. 43°6N 88°21W 311 A8
Hartland Pt. U.K. 51°1N 4°32W 169 F3
Hartlepool U.K. 54°42N 1°13W 168 C6
Hartlepool □ U.K. 54°42N 1°17W 168 C6
Hartley Bay Canada 53°25N 129°15W 296 C3
Hartmannberge Namibia 17°0S 13°0E 270 A1
Hartney Canada 49°30N 100°35W 297 D8
Hârtop Moldova 46°39N 28°40E 183 D13
Harts → S. Africa 28°24S 24°17E 270 C3
Harts Range Australia 23°6S 134°55E 280 C1
Hartselle U.S.A. 34°27N 86°56W 315 D11
Hartsfield-Jackson Atlanta Int. ✕ (ATL) U.S.A. 33°38N 84°26W 113 C2
Hartshorne U.S.A. 34°51N 95°34W 314 D7
Hartstown U.S.A. 41°33N 80°23W 312 E4
Hartsville U.S.A. 34°23N 80°4W 315 D14
Hartswater S. Africa 27°34S 24°43E 270 C3
Hartwell U.S.A. 34°21N 82°56W 315 D13
Harumi Tokyo, Japan 140 c5
Harunabad Pakistan 29°35N 73°8E 242 E5
Harur India 12°3N 78°29E 245 H4
Harūt → Afghan. 31°29N 61°24E 240 C1
Harvand Iran 28°25N 55°43E 247 D7
Harvard U.S.A. 42°25N 88°37W 311 B8
Harvard Univ. U.S.A. 42°22N 71°7W 116 A2
Harvey W. Austral., Australia 33°5S 115°54E 279 F2
Harvey Ill., U.S.A. 41°36N 87°50W 119 D3
Harvey La., U.S.A. 29°54N 90°4W 131 B2
Harvey N. Dak., U.S.A. 47°47N 99°56W 308 B4
Harwich U.K. 51°56N 1°17E 169 F9
Harwood Heights U.S.A. 41°57N 87°46W 119 B2
Haryana □ India 29°0N 76°10E 242 E7
Haryn → Belarus 52°7N 27°17E 177 B14
Harz Germany 51°38N 10°44E 178 D6
Harz △ Germany 51°40N 10°48E 178 D6
Harzgerode Germany 51°38N 11°8E 178 D7
Hasa Si. Arabia 25°50N 49°0E 247 E6
Ḥasā, W. al → Jordan 31°4N 35°29E 251 G6
Hasaheisa Sudan 14°44N 33°20E 257 E3
Ḥasanābād Eşfahan, Iran 32°8N 52°44E 247 C7
Ḥasanābād Tehrān, Iran 35°44N 51°16E 141 A1
Hasankeyf Turkey 37°42N 41°24E 213 D9
Hasanparti India 18°4N 79°32E 244 E4
Hasawinah, Jabal al Libya 28°15N 14°0E 258 C2
Ḥasb, W. → Iraq 31°45N 44°17E 246 D5
Hasbrouck Heights U.S.A. 40°51N 74°6W 132 A1
Hasdo → India 21°44N 82°44E 243 J10
Haselhorst Germany 52°33N 13°14E 115 A2
Haselünne Germany 52°40N 7°29E 178 C3
Hashima Japan 35°20N 136°40E 223 B8
Hashimoto Japan 34°19N 135°37E 223 C7
Hashtjerd Iran 35°52N 50°40E 247 C6
Hashtpur = Tālesh Iran 37°58N 48°58E 213 D13
Hashtrud Iran 37°28N 47°4E 213 D12
Hasi Nueifed W. Sahara 24°54N 14°49W 260 C2
Ḥāsik Oman 17°22N 55°17E 249 C6
Haskell U.S.A. 33°10N 99°44W 314 E5
Haskovo = Khaskovo Bulgaria 41°56N 25°30E 203 E9
Hasköy Edirne, Turkey 41°38N 26°52E 203 E10
Hasköy İstanbul, Turkey 41°2N 28°57E 122 B1
Haslach Germany 48°16N 8°5E 179 G4
Hasle Denmark 55°11N 14°44E 163 J8
Hasle Oslo, Norway 59°46N 10°38E 133 B2
Haslemere U.K. 51°5N 0°43W 169 F7
Haslev Denmark 55°18N 11°57E 163 J5
Haslum Norway 59°55N 10°34E 133 A2
Hasparren France 43°24N 1°18W 174 E2
Hassa Turkey 36°48N 36°29E 250 B7
Hassan India 13°0N 76°5E 245 H3
Hassberge △ Germany 50°8N 10°45E 179 E6
Hassela Sweden 62°7N 16°42E 162 B10
Hasselt Belgium 50°56N 5°21E 170 D5
Hassfurt Germany 50°2N 10°30E 179 E6
Hassi bel Guebbour Algeria 28°30N 6°41E 261 C6
Hassi bou Khelala Algeria 30°17N 0°18W 261 B4
Hassi Bourarchet Algeria 27°26N 9°19E 261 C6
Hassi Djafou Algeria 30°55N 3°35E 261 B5
Hassi el Hadjar Algeria 31°28N 4°45E 261 B5
Hassi Imoulaye Algeria 29°54N 9°10E 261 C6
Hassi Inifeg Algeria 28°15N 1°30E 261 C4
Hassi Inifel Algeria 29°50N 3°41E 261 C5
Hassi Mana Algeria 28°48N 2°37W 261 C4
Hassi Marroket Algeria 30°10N 3°0E 261 B5
Hassi Mengoub Algeria 29°49N 5°26W 260 C3
Hassi Messaoud Algeria 31°51N 6°1E 261 B6
Hassi Sougoued Algeria 26°50N 9°28E 261 C6
Hassi Tartrat Algeria 30°5N 6°28E 261 B6
Hassi Zerzour Morocco 30°51N 3°56W 260 B4
Hassi Zguilma Morocco 30°19N 6°10W 260 B3
Hässleholm Sweden 56°10N 13°46E 163 H7
Hasslö Sweden 56°7N 15°28E 163 H9
Hassloch Germany 49°22N 8°16E 179 F4
Hästhagen Sweden 59°18N 18°9E 139 B2
Hästholmen Sweden 58°17N 14°38E 163 F8
Hastings Vic., Australia 38°18S 145°12E 283 E6
Hastings Barbados 13°4N 59°36W 323 r
Hastings N.Z. 39°39S 176°52E 284 F5
Hastings E. Sussex, U.K. 50°51N 0°35E 169 G8
Hastings Fla., U.S.A. 29°43N 81°31W 316 F8
Hastings Mich., U.S.A. 42°39N 85°17W 311 B11
Hastings Minn., U.S.A. 44°44N 92°51W 308 C7
Hastings Nebr., U.S.A. 40°35N 98°23W 308 E4
Hastings Ra. Australia 31°15S 152°14E 283 A10
Hästveda Sweden 56°17N 13°55E 163 H7
Ḥaşwayn Yemen 15°35N 52°6E 249 D6
Hat Ukraine 48°19N 22°38E 182 B7
Hat Head △ Australia 31°3S 153°1E 283 A10
Hat Lot Vietnam 21°15N 104°7E 236 B5
Hat Yai Thailand 7°1N 100°27E 237 J3
Hatanbulag = Ergel Mongolia 43°8N 109°5E 226 C5
Hatay Turkey 36°14N 36°10E 250 B7
Hatay □ Turkey 36°25N 36°15E 250 B7
Hatch U.S.A. 32°40N 107°9W 305 K10
Hatch End U.K. 51°36N 0°22W 125 A1
Hatchet L. Canada 58°36N 103°40W 297 B8
Haţeg Romania 45°36N 22°55E 182 E7
Hateruma-Shima Japan 24°3N 123°47E 221 M1
Hatfield Australia 33°54S 143°49E 282 B5
Hatgal Mongolia 50°26N 100°9E 218 A9
Hathras India 27°36N 78°6E 242 F8
Hatia Bangla. 22°30N 91°5E 241 D3
Hatia Nepal 27°43N 87°21E 243 F12
Hatia Is. Bangla. 22°30N 91°0E 241 D3
Hatiara India 22°36N 88°26E 124 B2
Ḥāṭībah, Ra's Si. Arabia 21°55N 38°57E 256 C4
Hatid India 17°17N 75°3E 244 F2
Hatillo Puerto Rico 18°29N 66°50W 321 b
Hato Bonaire 12°11N 68°17W 322 h
Hato Curaçao 12°11N 68°57W 322 g
Hato Caves Curaçao 12°11N 68°57W 322 g
Hato Corozal Colombia 6°11N 71°45W 328 B3
Hato Mayor Dom. Rep. 18°46N 69°15W 321 C6
Hatra = Al Ḥaḍr Iraq 35°35N 42°44E 213 E10
Hatsukaichi Japan 34°22N 132°22E 222 C4
Hatta India 24°7N 79°36E 243 G8
Hatta U.A.E. 24°45N 56°4E 247 E8
Hattah Australia 34°48S 142°17E 282 C5
Hattah Kulkyne △ Australia 34°16S 142°33E 282 C5
Hatteras, C. U.S.A. 35°14N 75°32W 315 D17
Hatteras Abyssal Plain Atl. Oc. 28°0N 72°0W 152 D4
Hattiesburg U.S.A. 31°20N 89°17W 315 F10
Hattusa Turkey 40°0N 34°37E 212 B6
Hatutu French Polynesia 7°56S 140°38W 289 f
Hatvan Hungary 47°40N 19°45E 182 C4
Hau → Vietnam 9°30N 106°13E 237 H6
Haubstadt U.S.A. 38°12N 87°34W 311 F9
Haud Ethiopia 8°0N 45°0E 267 C6
Hauganes Iceland 65°56N 18°17W 155 B8
Haugastøl Norway 60°30N 7°50E 164 D4
Hauge Norway 58°20N 6°15E 164 F3
Haugesund Norway 59°23N 5°13E 164 E2
Hauhui Solomon Is. 9°10S 160°59E 287 M11
Hauhungaroa Ra. N.Z. 38°42S 175°40E 284 E4
Haukeligrend Norway 59°44N 7°33E 164 E4
Hauketo Norway 59°50N 10°48E 133 A3
Haukipudas Finland 65°12N 25°20E 160 D21
Haultain → Canada 55°51N 106°46W 297 B7
Haungpa Burma 25°29N 96°7E 241 C6
Hauraha Solomon Is. 10°46S 161°59E 287 N11
Hauraki G. N.Z. 36°35S 175°5E 284 C4
Hauroko L. N.Z. 45°59S 167°21E 285 F2
Hausruck Austria 48°6N 13°30E 180 C6
Haut Atlas Morocco 32°30N 5°0W 260 B4
Haut de la Montagne Guadeloupe 16°26N 61°28W 322 e
Haut-Jura △ France 46°23N 2°23E 173 F9
Haut-Kotto □ C.A.R. 8°0N 23°30E 264 A4
Haut-Languedoc △ France 43°30N 2°43E 174 E6
Haut-Mbomou □ C.A.R. 5°30N 25°30E 264 A5
Haut-Niger △ Guinea 10°20N 10°20W 262 C2
Haut-Ogooué □ Gabon 2°0S 14°0E 264 C2
Haut-Rhin □ France 48°0N 7°15E 173 E14
Haut-Sassandra □ Ivory C. 7°0N 6°30W 262 D3
Haut-Zaïre = Orientale □ Dem. Rep. of the Congo 2°20N 26°0E 268 B2
Haute-Corse □ France 42°30N 9°30E 175 F13
Haute-Garonne □ France 43°30N 1°30E 174 E5
Haute-Loire □ France 45°5N 3°50E 174 C7
Haute-Marne □ France 48°10N 5°20E 173 D12
Haute-Normandie □ France 49°20N 1°0E 172 C7
Haute-Saône □ France 47°45N 6°10E 173 E13
Haute-Savoie □ France 46°0N 6°20E 175 C10
Haute-Vienne □ France 45°50N 1°10E 174 C5
Hautes-Alpes □ France 44°42N 6°20E 175 D10
Hautes Fagnes = Hohes Venn Belgium 50°30N 6°5E 170 D6
Hautes-Pyrénées □ France 43°0N 0°10E 174 F4
Hauteville-Lompnès France 45°58N 5°36E 175 C9
Hautmont France 50°15N 3°55E 173 B10
Hauts-de-Seine □ France 48°52N 2°15E 173 D9
Hauts Plateaux Algeria 35°0N 1°0E 261 B5
Hau'ula U.S.A. 21°37N 157°55W 302 J14
Hauz Khas India 28°33N 77°11E 120 B2
Hauzenberg Germany 48°40N 13°37E 179 G9
Havana = La Habana Cuba 23°8N 82°22W 320 B3
Havana Fla., U.S.A. 30°37N 84°25W 316 E5
Havana Ill., U.S.A. 40°18N 90°4W 310 D6
Havant U.K. 50°51N 0°58W 169 G7
Havârna Romania 48°4N 26°43E 183 B11
Havasor = Kığzı Turkey 38°18N 43°25E 246 B4
Havasu, L. U.S.A. 34°18N 114°28W 307 L12
Havdhem Sweden 57°10N 18°20E 163 G12
Havel → Germany 52°50N 12°3E 115 A2
Havelian Pakistan 34°2N 73°10E 242 B5
Havelkanal Germany 52°36N 13°10E 115 A2
Havelock Ont., Canada 44°26N 77°53W 312 B7
Havelock N.Z. 41°17S 173°48E 285 B8
Havelock N.C., U.S.A. 34°53N 76°54W 315 D16
Havelock I. India 11°58N 93°0E 245 J11
Havelock North N.Z. 39°40S 176°53E 284 F5
Haverfordwest U.K. 51°48N 4°58W 169 F3
Haverhill Suffolk, U.K. 52°5N 0°28E 169 E8
Haverhill Fla., U.S.A. 26°42N 80°7W 317 J9
Haverhill Mass., U.S.A. 42°47N 71°5W 313 D13
Haveri India 14°53N 75°24E 245 G2
Havering □ U.K. 51°34N 0°13E 125 A5
Havering-atte-Bower U.K. 51°37N 0°11E 125 A5
Havern Sweden 62°18N 15°7E 162 B9
Haverstraw U.S.A. 41°12N 73°58W 313 E11
Håverud Sweden 58°50N 12°28E 163 F6
Havirga Mongolia 45°41N 113°5E 226 B7
Havířov Czech Rep. 49°46N 18°20E 181 B11
Havlíčkův Brod Czech Rep. 49°36N 15°33E 180 B8
Havneby Denmark 55°5N 8°34E 163 J2
Havran Turkey 39°33N 27°6E 205 B9
Havre U.S.A. 48°33N 109°41W 304 B9
Havre-Aubert Canada 47°12N 61°56W 299 C7
Havre-St.-Pierre Canada 50°18N 63°33W 299 B7
Havsa Turkey 41°31N 26°48E 203 E10
Havza Turkey 41°0N 35°35E 212 B6
Haw → U.S.A. 35°36N 79°3W 315 D15
Hawadax U.S.A. 51°48N 178°15E 303 L2
Hawai'i U.S.A. 19°30N 156°30W 302 D5
Hawai'i □ U.S.A. 19°30N 156°30W 302 D5
Hawai'i County U.S.A. 19°30N 155°30W 302 D6

Hawai'i Kai U.S.A. 21°16N 157°42W 302 K14
Hawai'i Volcanoes △ U.S.A. 19°25N 155°18W 302 D6
Hawaiian Is. Pac. Oc. 20°30N 156°0W 302 G12
Hawaiian Ridge Pac. Oc. 24°0N 165°0W 289 E11
Hawarden U.S.A. 43°0N 96°29W 308 D5
Hawashîyah, W. Egypt 28°31N 32°58E 251 K3
Hawea, L. N.Z. 44°28S 169°19E 285 E4
Hawea Flat N.Z. 44°40S 169°19E 285 E4
Hawera N.Z. 39°35S 174°19E 284 F3
Hawesville U.S.A. 37°54N 86°45W 311 G10
Ḩawf Yemen 16°38N 53°2E 249 C6
Hawi U.S.A. 20°14N 155°50W 302 C6
Hawick U.K. 55°26N 2°47W 167 F6
Hawk Junction Canada 48°5N 84°38W 298 C3
Hawk Point U.S.A. 38°58N 91°8W 310 F5
Hawkdun Ra. N.Z. 44°53S 170°5E 285 E5
Hawke B. N.Z. 39°25S 177°20E 284 F6
Hawker Australia 31°59S 138°22E 282 A3
Hawke's Bay Canada 50°36N 57°10W 299 B8
Hawke's Bay □ N.Z. 39°45S 176°35E 284 F5
Hawkesbury Canada 45°37N 74°37W 298 C5
Hawkesbury I. Canada 53°37N 129°3W 296 C3
Hawkesbury Pt. Australia 11°55S 134°5E 280 A1
Hawkinsville U.S.A. 32°17N 83°28W 316 C6
Hawks Nest Australia 32°41S 152°11E 283 B10
Hawley Minn., U.S.A. 46°53N 96°19W 308 B5
Hawley Pa., U.S.A. 41°28N 75°11W 313 E9
Haworth U.S.A. 40°57N 73°59W 132 A2
Ḩawrā' Yemen 15°42N 48°16E 249 D5
Ḩawrān, W. → Iraq 33°58N 42°34E 213 F10
Hawsh Mūssá Lebanon 33°45N 35°55E 250 E6
Hawthorne Fla., U.S.A. 29°36N 82°5W 317 F7
Hawthorne Nev., U.S.A. 38°32N 118°38W 304 G4
Hawthorne Racecourse U.S.A. 41°49N 87°44W 119 C2
Hay Australia 34°30S 144°51E 283 C6
Hay → N. Terr., Australia 24°50S 138°0E 280 C2
Hay → Alta., Canada 60°50N 116°26W 296 A5
Hay, C. Australia 14°5S 129°29E 278 B4
Hay I. Canada 44°53N 80°58W 312 B4
Hay L. Canada 58°50N 118°50W 296 B5
Hay-on-Wye U.K. 52°5N 3°8W 169 E4
Hay Point Australia 21°18S 149°17E 280 C4
Hay River Canada 60°51N 115°44W 296 A5
Hay Springs U.S.A. 42°41N 102°41W 308 D2
Hayachine-San Japan 39°34N 141°29E 220 E10
Hayange France 49°20N 6°2E 173 C13
Hayastan = Armenia ■ Asia 40°20N 45°0E 191 K7
Hayato Japan 31°40N 130°43E 222 F2
Haydān, W. al → Jordan 31°29N 35°34E 251 G6
Haydarlı Turkey 38°16N 30°23E 205 C12
Hayden U.S.A. 40°30N 107°16W 304 F10
Hayes Jamaica 17°52N 77°14W 320 a
Hayes Kent, U.K. 51°22N 0°0 125 B4
Hayes Middlesex, U.K. 51°30N 0°25W 125 A1
Hayes S. Dak., U.S.A. 44°23N 101°1W 308 C3
Hayes → Canada 57°3N 92°12W 298 A1
Hayes, Mt. U.S.A. 63°37N 146°43W 303 E11
Hayes Creek Australia 13°43S 131°22E 278 B5
Hayes End U.K. 51°31N 0°25W 125 A1
Hayford U.S.A. 41°45N 87°42W 119 C2
Hayle U.K. 50°11N 5°26W 169 G2
Hayling I. U.K. 50°48N 0°59W 169 G7
Haymā' Oman 19°56N 56°19E 249 C7
Hayman I. Australia 20°4S 148°53E 280 b
Haymana Turkey 39°26N 32°31E 212 C5
Haynan Yemen 15°50N 48°18E 249 D5
Haynau = Chojnów Poland 51°18N 15°58E 185 G2
Hayneville U.S.A. 32°23N 83°37W 316 C6
Hayrabolu Turkey 41°12N 27°5E 203 E11
Hays Alta., Canada 50°6N 111°48W 296 C6
Hays Kans., U.S.A. 38°53N 99°20W 308 F4
Ḩays Yemen 13°56N 43°29E 248 D3
Haysville U.S.A. 38°28N 86°55W 311 F10
Haysyn Ukraine 48°57N 29°25E 183 B14
Hayvoron Ukraine 48°22N 29°52E 183 B14
Hayward Calif., U.S.A. 37°40N 122°4W 306 H4
Hayward Wis., U.S.A. 46°1N 91°29W 308 B8
Haywards Heath U.K. 51°0N 0°5W 169 G7
Hazafon □ Israel 32°40N 35°20E 250 F6
Hazar Turkmenistan 39°34N 53°16E 187 G9
Hazārān, Kūh-e Iran 29°35N 57°20E 247 D8
Hazard U.S.A. 37°15N 83°12W 309 G12
Hazaribag India 23°58N 85°26E 243 H11
Hazaribag Road India 24°12N 85°57E 243 G11
Hazebrouck France 50°42N 2°31E 173 B9
Hazelton B.C., Canada 55°20N 127°42W 296 B3
Hazelton N. Dak., U.S.A. 46°29N 100°17W 308 B3
Hazen U.S.A. 47°18N 101°38W 308 B3
Hazen, L. Canada 81°47N 71°1W 154 A3
Hazlehurst Ga., U.S.A. 31°52N 82°36W 316 D7
Hazlehurst Miss., U.S.A. 31°52N 90°24W 315 F9
Hazlet U.S.A. 40°25N 74°12W 313 F10
Hazleton Ind., U.S.A. 38°29N 87°33W 311 F9
Hazleton Pa., U.S.A. 40°57N 75°59W 313 F9
Hazlett, L. Australia 21°30S 128°48E 278 D4
Hazro Turkey 38°15N 40°47E 246 B4
He Xian = Hezhou China 24°27N 111°30E 229 E8
He Xian China 31°45N 118°20E 229 B12
Head of Bight Australia 31°30S 131°25E 279 F5
Head-Smashed-In Buffalo Jump Canada 49°44N 113°37W 296 D6
Headland U.S.A. 31°21N 85°21W 316 D4
Headlands Zimbabwe 18°15S 32°2E 269 F3
Healdsburg U.S.A. 38°37N 122°52W 306 G4
Healdton U.S.A. 34°14N 97°29W 314 D6
Healesville Australia 37°35S 145°30E 283 D6
Healy U.S.A. 63°52N 148°58W 303 E10
Heany Junction Zimbabwe 20°6S 28°54E 271 B4
Heanza-shima Japan 26°20N 127°57E 288 a
Heard I. Ind. Oc. 53°6S 72°36E 273 K6
Hearne U.S.A. 30°53N 96°36W 314 F6
Hearst Canada 49°40N 83°41W 298 C3
Heart → U.S.A. 46°46N 100°50W 308 B3
Heart's Content Canada 47°54N 53°27W 299 C9
Heath → Bolivia 12°31S 68°38W 330 C4
Heath, Pte. Canada 49°8N 61°40W 299 C7
Heath Mts. N.Z. 45°39S 167°9E 285 F2
Heathcote Australia 36°56S 144°45E 283 D6
Heatherwood = Edson Canada 53°35N 116°28W 296 C5
Heathfield S. Africa 34°3S 18°27E 118 B1
Heathrow, London ✈ (LHR) U.K. 51°28N 0°27W 125 B1
Heavener U.S.A. 34°53N 94°36W 314 D7
Hebbronville U.S.A. 27°18N 98°41W 314 H5
Hebe Haven Hong Kong, China 22°21N 114°15E 122 A3
Hebei □ China 39°0N 116°0E 226 E9
Hebel Australia 28°58S 147°47E 281 D4
Heber U.S.A. 32°44N 115°32W 307 N11
Heber Springs U.S.A. 35°30N 92°2W 314 D8
Hebgen L. U.S.A. 44°52N 111°20W 304 D8
Hebi China 35°57N 114°7E 226 G8
Hebrides U.K. 57°30N 7°0W 158 D4
Hebrides, Sea of the U.K. 57°5N 7°0W 167 D2
Hebron = Al Khalīl West Bank 31°32N 35°6E 251 G6
Hebron Nfld. & L., Canada 58°5N 62°30W 295 F19
Hebron N. Dak., U.S.A. 46°54N 102°3W 308 B2
Hebron Nebr., U.S.A. 40°10N 97°35W 308 E5
Heby Sweden 59°56N 16°53E 162 E10
Hecate Str. Canada 53°10N 130°30W 296 C2
Heceta I. U.S.A. 55°46N 133°40W 296 B2
Hechi China 24°40N 108°2E 228 E7
Hechingen Germany 48°21N 8°57E 179 G4
Hechuan China 30°2N 106°12E 228 B6
Hecla U.S.A. 45°53N 98°9W 308 C4
Hecla I. Canada 51°10N 96°43W 297 C9
Hedal Norway 60°37N 9°41E 162 D3
Heddal Norway 59°36N 9°9E 164 E6
Hédé Ille-et-Vilaine, France 48°18N 1°49W 172 D5
Hede Jämtland, Sweden 62°23N 13°30E 162 B7
Hedemora Sweden 60°18N 15°58E 162 D9
Hedensted Denmark 55°46N 9°42E 163 J3
Hedesunda Sweden 60°24N 17°0E 162 D10
Hedgehope N.Z. 46°12S 168°34E 285 G3
Hedmark □ Norway 61°17N 11°40E 164 C8
Hedo Japan 26°52N 128°15E 288 a
Hedo-misaki Japan 26°52N 128°16E 288 a
Hedong China 23°5N 113°14E 121 B2
Hedrick U.S.A. 41°11N 92°19W 310 C4
He'eia U.S.A. 21°25N 157°48W 302 K14
Heel Pt. Wake I. 19°18N 166°38E 302 b
Heerde Neths. 52°24N 6°2E 170 B6
Heerenveen Neths. 52°57N 5°55E 170 B5
Heerhugowaard Neths. 52°40N 4°51E 170 B4
Heerlen Neths. 50°55N 5°58E 170 D5
Heerwegen = Polkowice Poland 51°29N 16°3E 185 G3
Ḩefa Israel 32°46N 35°0E 250 F6
Ḩefa □ Israel 32°40N 35°0E 250 F6
Hefei China 31°52N 117°18E 229 B11
Hefeng China 29°55N 109°52E 228 C7
Heflin U.S.A. 33°39N 85°35W 316 B4
Hegalig Sudan 14°36N 31°54E 257 E3
Hegang China 47°20N 130°19E 219 B15
Heggenes Norway 61°9N 9°4E 164 C6
Heglig Sudan 10°0N 29°24E 257 F2
Hegra Norway 63°27N 11°8E 164 A8
Hei Ling Chau Hong Kong, China 22°15N 114°2E 122 B2
Heiban Sudan 11°13N 30°31E 257 E3
Heichengzhen China 36°24N 106°3E 226 F4
Heidal Norway 61°45N 9°19E 164 C6
Heide Germany 54°11N 9°6E 178 A5
Heidelberg Baden-W., Germany 49°24N 8°42E 179 F4
Heidelberg Western Cape, S. Africa 34°6S 20°59E 270 D3
Heidelberg Heights Australia 37°45S 145°4E 128 A2
Heidelberg West Australia 37°43S 145°2E 128 A2
Heidelburg S. Africa 26°30S 28°21E 271 C4
Heidemühle Germany 52°29N 13°40E 115 B5
Heidenau Germany 50°57N 13°52E 178 E9
Heidenheim Germany 48°41N 10°9E 179 G6
Heideveld S. Africa 33°58S 18°32E 118 A2
Heigun-Tō Japan 33°47N 132°14E 222 D4
Heihe China 50°10N 127°30E 219 A14
Heijing China 25°22N 101°44E 228 E3
Heijo = P'yŏngyang N. Korea 39°0N 125°30E 224 C2
Heilbad Heiligenstadt Germany 51°22N 10°8E 178 D6
Heilbron S. Africa 27°16S 27°59E 271 C4
Heilbronn Germany 49°9N 9°13E 179 F5
Heiligenblut Austria 47°2N 12°51E 180 D5
Heiligenhafen Germany 54°22N 10°59E 178 A6
Heiligensee Germany 52°36N 13°13E 115 A2
Heiligenstadt Austria 48°14N 16°21E 142 A2
Heilongjiang □ China 48°0N 126°0E 219 B14
Heilprin Land Greenland 82°5N 33°0W 154 A7
Heilsberg = Lidzbark Warmiński Poland 54°7N 20°34E 184 D7
Heilunkiang = Heilongjiang □ China 48°0N 126°0E 219 B14
Heim Norway 63°26N 9°5E 164 A6
Heimaey Iceland 63°26N 20°17W 155 D6
Heimdal Norway 63°21N 10°22E 164 A7
Heineken Experience Amsterdam, Neths. 112 c2
Heinersdorf Germany 52°34N 13°26E 115 A3
Heinola Finland 61°13N 26°2E 188 B4
Heinsberg Germany 51°3N 6°5E 178 D2
Heinsun Burma 25°52N 95°35E 241 C5
Heinze Chaung Burma 14°42N 97°52E 236 E1
Heinze Kyun Burma 14°25N 97°45E 236 E1
Heirnkut Burma 25°14N 94°44E 241 C5
Heishan China 41°40N 122°5E 227 D12
Heishui Liaoning, China 42°8N 119°30E 227 C10
Heishui Sichuan, China 32°4N 103°2E 228 A4
Hejaz = Ḩijāz Si. Arabia 24°0N 40°0E 246 E3
Hejian China 38°25N 116°5E 226 E9
Hejiang China 28°43N 105°46E 228 C5
Hejin China 35°35N 110°42E 226 G6
Hejing China 42°18N 86°22E 217 D11
Hekımhan Turkey 38°50N 37°55E 212 C7
Hekinan Japan 34°52N 137°0E 223 C9
Hekla Iceland 63°56N 19°35W 155 D7
Hekou Gansu, China 36°10N 103°26E 226 F2
Hekou Guangdong, China 23°13N 112°45E 229 F9
Hekou Yunnan, China 22°30N 103°59E 228 F4
Hel Poland 54°37N 18°47E 184 D5
Helagsfjället Sweden 62°54N 12°25E 162 B6
Helan Shan China 38°30N 105°55E 226 E3
Heldenplatz Vienna, Austria 142 b1
Helden's Pt. St. Kitts & Nevis 17°25N 62°51W 322 d
Helechosa de los Montes Spain 39°22N 4°53W 195 F6
Helemano → U.S.A. 21°35N 158°7W 302 J13
Helen Atoll Palau 2°40N 132°0E 231 D8
Helena Ga., U.S.A. 32°5N 82°55W 316 C7
Helena Mont., U.S.A. 46°36N 112°2W 304 C7
Helena -West Helena U.S.A. 34°32N 90°36W 315 D9
Helendale U.S.A. 34°44N 117°19W 307 L9
Hélène de Champlain, Parc ⌂ Canada 45°31N 73°32W 130 A2
Helenelund Sweden 59°24N 17°58E 139 A1
Helensburgh N.S.W., Australia 34°11S 151°1E 283 C9
Helensburgh Argyll & Bute, U.K. 56°1N 4°43W 167 E4
Helensville N.Z. 36°41S 174°29E 284 C3
Helenvale Australia 15°43S 145°14E 280 B4
Helgasjön Sweden 56°55N 14°50E 163 H8
Helgeland Norway 66°7N 13°29E 160 C15
Helgoland Germany 54°10N 7°53E 178 A3
Helheim Gletscher Greenland 66°24N 38°12W 154 D7
Heligoland = Helgoland Germany 54°10N 7°53E 178 A3
Heligoland B. = Deutsche Bucht Germany 54°15N 8°0E 178 A4
Heliopolis = Masr el Gedida Egypt 30°5N 31°21E 117 A2
Hell Norway 63°26N 10°54E 164 A7
Hell-Bourg Réunion 21°3S 55°32E 272 f
Hell Hole Gorge △ Australia 25°31S 144°12E 280 D3
Hella Iceland 63°50N 20°24W 155 D6
Hellas = Greece ■ Europe 40°0N 23°0E 204 B3
Helleland Norway 58°33N 6°7E 164 F3
Hellersdorf Germany 52°32N 13°35E 115 A4
Hellertown U.S.A. 40°35N 75°21W 313 F9
Hellerup Denmark 55°44N 12°33E 118 A3
Hellespont = Çanakkale Boğazı Turkey 40°17N 26°32E 203 F10
Hellesylt Norway 62°6N 6°51E 164 B3
Hellevoetsluis Neths. 51°50N 4°8E 170 C4
Hellín Spain 38°31N 1°40W 197 G3
Hellissandur Iceland 64°55N 23°54W 155 C3
Hells Canyon ⌂ U.S.A. 45°30N 117°45W 304 D5
Hells Gate Saba 17°39N 63°14W 322 a
Hell's Gate △ Kenya 0°54S 36°19E 268 C4
Hellvik Norway 58°29N 5°52E 164 F2
Helmand □ Afghan. 31°20N 64°0E 240 C2
Helmand → Afghan. 31°12N 61°34E 240 C1
Helme → Germany 51°20N 11°21E 178 D7
Helmeringhausen Namibia 25°54S 16°57E 270 C2
Helmond Neths. 51°29N 5°41E 170 C5
Helmsdale U.K. 58°7N 3°39W 167 C5
Helmsdale → U.K. 58°8N 3°43W 167 C5
Helmstedt Germany 52°12N 11°0E 178 C7
Helong China 42°40N 129°0E 224 A4
Helper U.S.A. 39°41N 110°51W 304 G8
Helsingborg Sweden 56°3N 12°42E 163 H6
Helsinge Denmark 56°2N 12°12E 163 H6
Helsingfors = Helsinki Finland 60°10N 24°55E 121 B2
Helsingør Denmark 56°2N 12°35E 163 H6
Helsinki Finland 60°10N 24°55E 121 B2
Helsinki-Vantaa ✈ (HEL) Finland 60°18N 24°58E 121 B2
Helska, Mierzeja Poland 54°45N 18°40E 184 D5
Helston U.K. 50°6N 5°17W 169 G2
Helvellyn U.K. 54°32N 3°1W 168 C4
Helvetinjärvi △ Finland 62°5N 23°47E 160 E20
Helwân Egypt 29°50N 31°20E 256 J7
Helwân □ Egypt 29°30N 31°30E 251 J2
Hemavati → India 12°30N 76°20E 245 H3
Hemei = Homei Taiwan 24°7N 120°29E 225 B2
Hemel Hempstead U.K. 51°44N 0°28W 169 F7
Hemet U.S.A. 33°45N 116°58W 307 M10
Hemingford U.S.A. 42°19N 103°4W 308 D2
Hemis △ India 34°10N 77°15E 242 B7
Hemmingford Canada 45°3N 73°35W 313 A11
Hempe Dem. Rep. of the Congo 1°54N 22°42E 264 B4
Hempstead N.Y., U.S.A. 40°42N 73°37W 313 F11
Hempstead Tex., U.S.A. 30°6N 96°5W 314 F6
Hemse Sweden 57°15N 18°22E 163 G12
Hemsedal Norway 60°53N 8°30E 164 D5
Hemsön Sweden 62°42N 18°5E 162 B12
Hen Norway 60°13N 10°14E 164 D7
Hen and Chicken B. Australia 33°50S 151°7E 139 B1
Hen and Chickens Is. N.Z. 35°58S 174°45E 284 B3
Henån Sweden 58°14N 11°40E 163 F5
Henan □ China 34°0N 114°0E 226 H8
Henares → Spain 40°24N 3°30W 194 E7
Henashi-Misaki Japan 40°37N 139°51E 220 D9
Hendaye France 43°23N 1°47W 174 E2
Hendek Turkey 40°48N 30°44E 212 B4
Henderson Argentina 36°18S 61°43W 334 D3
Henderson Ga., U.S.A. 32°21N 83°47W 316 C6
Henderson Ky., U.S.A. 37°50N 87°35W 311 G9
Henderson N.C., U.S.A. 36°20N 78°25W 315 C15
Henderson N.Y., U.S.A. 43°50N 76°10W 313 C8
Henderson Nev., U.S.A. 36°2N 114°58W 124 B2
Henderson Tenn., U.S.A. 35°26N 88°38W 315 D10
Henderson Tex., U.S.A. 32°9N 94°48W 314 E7
Henderson I. Pac. Oc. 24°22S 128°19W 289 K15
Hendersonville N.C., U.S.A. 35°19N 82°28W 315 D13
Hendersonville Tenn., U.S.A. 36°18N 86°37W 315 C11
Hendījān Iran 30°14N 49°43E 247 D6
Hendon U.K. 51°35N 0°14W 125 A2
Hendorābī Iran 26°40N 53°37E 247 E7
Heng Jiang → China 28°40N 104°25E 228 C5
Heng Xian China 22°40N 109°17E 228 F7
Hengām Iran 26°38N 55°53E 249 A6
Henganofi Papua N. G. 6°15S 145°38E 286 D3
Hengcheng China 38°18N 106°28E 226 E4
Hëngch'un Taiwan 22°0N 120°44E 225 D2
Hengdaohezi China 44°52N 129°0E 227 B15
Hengduan Shan China 28°30N 98°50E 228 C2
Hengelo Neths. 52°16N 6°48E 170 B6
Henggang China 22°39N 114°12E 219 a
Hengmen China 22°33N 113°35E 219 a
Hengsha China 23°9N 113°12E 121 B2
Hengshan Hunan, China 27°16N 112°45E 229 D9
Hengshan Shaanxi, China 37°58N 109°5E 226 F5
Hengshui China 37°41N 115°40E 226 F8
Hengyang China 26°59N 112°22E 229 D9
Henichesk Ukraine 46°12N 34°50E 189 J8
Henima India 25°22N 93°36E 241 C4
Hénin-Beaumont France 50°25N 2°58E 173 B9
Hénin-Liétard = Hénin-Beaumont France 50°25N 2°58E 173 B9
Henley-on-Thames U.K. 51°32N 0°54W 169 F7
Henlopen, C. U.S.A. 38°48N 75°6W 309 F16
Henna Japan 26°19N 127°53E 288 a
Hennan Sweden 62°2N 15°54E 162 B9
Hennebont France 47°49N 3°19W 172 E3
Hennenman S. Africa 27°59S 27°1E 270 C4
Hennepin U.S.A. 41°15N 89°21W 310 C7
Hennessey U.S.A. 36°6N 97°54W 314 C6
Hennigsdorf Germany 52°38N 13°12E 115 A2
Henrietta N.Y., U.S.A. 43°4N 77°37W 312 C7
Henrietta Tex., U.S.A. 33°49N 98°12W 314 E5
Henrietta, Ostrov = Genriyetty, Ostrov Russia 77°6N 156°30E 215 B16
Henrietta Maria, C. Canada 55°9N 82°20W 298 A3
Henry U.S.A. 41°7N 89°22W 310 C7
Henry Ice Rise Antarctica 80°35S 62°0W 151 E17
Henry Lawrence I. India 12°9N 93°5E 245 H11
Henryetta U.S.A. 35°27N 95°59W 314 D7
Henryków Poland 52°19N 20°58E 143 B1
Henryville Canada 45°8N 73°11W 313 A11
Hensall Canada 43°26N 81°30W 312 C3
Henson Cr. → U.S.A. 38°47N 76°58W 143 C3
Henstedt-Ulzburg Germany 53°47N 10°0E 178 B6
Hentiesbaai Namibia 22°8S 14°18E 270 B1
Hentiyn Nuruu Mongolia 48°30N 108°30E 219 B10
Henttaa Finland 60°11N 24°45E 121 B1
Henty Australia 35°30S 147°3E 283 C7
Henzada Burma 17°38N 95°26E 241 G5
Hephaestia Greece 39°55N 25°14E 205 B7
Hephzibah U.S.A. 33°19N 82°6W 316 B7
Heping China 24°29N 115°0E 229 E10
Heping Park China 31°16N 121°30E 138 B2
Hepingli China 39°57N 116°23E 114 B2
Heppner U.S.A. 45°21N 119°33W 304 D4
Hepu China 21°40N 109°12E 228 G7
Hepworth Canada 44°37N 81°9W 312 B3
Heqing China 26°37N 100°11E 228 D3
Hequ China 39°20N 111°15E 226 E6
Héraðsflói Iceland 65°42N 14°12W 155 B12
Héraðsvötn → Iceland 65°45N 19°25W 155 B7
Heradsbygd Norway 60°49N 11°39E 164 D8
Heraklion = Iraklio Greece 35°20N 25°12E 207 E6
Herald Cays Australia 16°58S 149°9E 280 B4
Herand Norway 60°20N 6°22E 164 D3
Herangi Ra. N.Z. 38°33S 174°48E 284 E3
Herāt Afghan. 34°20N 62°7E 240 B1
Herāt □ Afghan. 35°0N 62°0E 240 B1
Hérault □ France 43°34N 3°15E 174 E7
Hérault → France 43°17N 3°26E 174 E7
Herbault France 47°36N 1°8E 172 E8
Herbert Canada 50°30N 107°10W 297 C7
Herbert → Australia 18°31S 146°17E 280 B4
Herbert Hoover Nat. Historic Site ⌂ U.S.A. 41°40N 91°21W 310 C5
Herbert I. U.S.A. 52°45N 170°7W 303 K5
Herbertabad India 11°43N 92°37E 245 J11
Herberton Australia 17°20S 145°25E 280 B4
Herbertsdale S. Africa 34°1S 21°46E 270 D3
Herbertville N.Z. 40°30S 176°33E 284 G5
Herbignac France 47°27N 2°18W 172 E4
Herborn Germany 50°40N 8°18E 178 E4
Herby Poland 50°45N 18°50E 185 H5
Herceg-Novi Montenegro 42°30N 18°33E 202 D2
Hercegfalva = Mezőfalva Hungary 46°55N 18°49E 182 D3
Herchmer Canada 57°22N 94°10W 297 B10
Herculânia = Coxim Brazil 18°30S 54°55W 331 D7
Herðubreið Iceland 65°11N 16°21W 155 B10
Hereford Hereford, U.K. 52°4N 2°43W 169 E5
Hereford Tex., U.S.A. 34°49N 102°24W 314 D3
Herefordshire □ U.K. 52°8N 2°40W 169 E5
Herefoss Norway 58°32N 8°23E 164 F5
Héréhérétué French Polynesia 19°45S 144°58W 289 f
Herehogna Sweden 61°44N 12°8E 164 C9
Herekino N.Z. 35°18S 173°11E 284 B2
Herencia Spain 39°21N 3°22W 195 F7
Herentals Belgium 51°12N 4°51E 170 C4
Herford Germany 52°7N 8°39E 178 C4
Héricourt France 47°32N 6°45E 173 E13
Herington U.S.A. 38°40N 96°57W 308 F5
Heris Iran 38°14N 47°6E 213 C12
Herisau Switz. 47°22N 9°17E 179 H5
Hérisson France 46°32N 2°42E 173 F9
Herkimer U.S.A. 43°2N 74°59W 313 D10
Herlen → Asia 48°48N 117°0E 219 B12
Herlev Denmark 55°43N 12°27E 118 A2
Herlong U.S.A. 40°8N 120°8W 306 E6
Herm U.K. 49°30N 2°28W 169 H5
Hermakivka Ukraine 48°42N 26°11E 183 B11
Herman Eckstein Park S. Africa 26°9S 28°1E 123 A2
Hermana Mayor I. Phil. 15°47N 119°47E 232 D2
Hermann U.S.A. 38°42N 91°27W 310 F5
Hermannsbad = Ciechocinek Poland 52°53N 18°45E 185 F5
Hermannsburg N. Terr., Australia 23°57S 132°45E 278 D5
Hermannsburg Niedersachsen, Germany 52°50N 10°5E 178 C6
Hermannskogel Austria 48°16N 16°17E 142 A1
Hermannstadt = Sibiu Romania 45°45N 24°9E 183 E9
Hermansverk Norway 61°11N 6°52E 164 C3
Hermanus S. Africa 34°27S 19°12E 270 D2
Herment France 45°45N 2°24E 174 C6
Hermidale Australia 31°30S 146°42E 283 A7
Hermiston Edinburgh, U.K. 55°55N 3°19W 121 B2
Hermiston Oreg., U.S.A. 45°51N 119°17W 304 D4
Hermit Is. Papua N. G. 1°32S 145°5E 286 A3
Hermitage Grenada 12°27N 61°28W 323 q
Hermitage Mo., U.S.A. 37°56N 93°19W 310 G3
Hermitage and Winter Palace Russia 59°55N 30°19E 137 B2
Hermon Ont., Canada 45°6N 77°37W 312 A7
Hermon N.Y., U.S.A. 44°28N 75°14W 313 B9
Hermon, Mt. = Shaykh, J. ash Lebanon 33°25N 35°50E 250 E6
Hermosillo Mexico 29°10N 111°0W 318 B2
Hermsdorf Germany 52°37N 13°18E 115 A2
Hernád → Hungary 47°56N 21°8E 182 C6
Hernals Austria 48°13N 16°20E 142 A2
Hernandarias Paraguay 25°20S 54°40W 335 B5
Hernandez U.S.A. 36°24N 120°46W 306 J6
Hernando Argentina 32°28S 63°40W 334 C3
Hernando Fla., U.S.A. 28°54N 82°23W 317 G7
Hernando Miss., U.S.A. 34°50N 90°0W 315 D10
Hernando de Magallanes △ Chile 54°0S 72°40W 336 D2
Hernani Spain 43°16N 1°58W 196 B3
Herndon U.S.A. 40°43N 76°51W 312 F8
Herne Germany 51°32N 7°14E 178 D3
Herne Bay U.K. 51°21N 1°8E 169 F9
Herne Hill U.K. 51°27N 0°6W 125 B3
Herning Denmark 56°8N 8°58E 163 H2
Herod U.S.A. 31°42N 84°26W 316 D5
Héroes de Churubusco Mexico 19°21N 99°6W 128 B2
Heroica Caborca = Caborca Mexico 30°37N 112°6W 318 A2
Heroica Nogales = Nogales Mexico 31°19N 110°56W 318 A2
Heron Bay Canada 48°40N 86°25W 298 C2
Heron I. Australia 23°27S 151°55E 280 C5
Herons, Î. aux Canada 45°25N 73°34W 130 B2
Herradura, Pta. de la Canary Is. 28°26N 14°8W 153 e2
Herre Norway 59°6N 9°34E 164 E6
Herreid U.S.A. 45°50N 100°4W 308 C3
Herrenberg Germany 48°35N 8°52E 179 G4
Herrera Spain 37°26N 4°55W 195 H6
Herrera de Alcántara Spain 39°39N 7°25W 195 F3
Herrera de Pisuerga Spain 42°35N 4°20W 194 C6
Herrera del Duque Spain 39°10N 5°3W 195 F5
Herrestad Sweden 58°21N 11°50E 163 F5
Herrin U.S.A. 37°48N 89°2W 310 G7
Herriot Canada 56°22N 101°16W 297 B8
Herrljunga Sweden 58°5N 13°1E 163 F7
Hersbruck Germany 49°30N 11°26E 179 F7
Herschel I. Canada 69°35N 139°5W 150 C1
Hershey U.S.A. 40°17N 76°39W 313 F8
Herso = Cherso Greece 41°5N 22°47E 202 E6
Herstal Belgium 50°40N 5°38E 170 D5
Herstedøster Denmark 55°40N 12°22E 118 A2
Hertford U.K. 51°48N 0°4W 169 F7
Hertfordshire □ U.K. 51°51N 0°5W 169 F7
's-Hertogenbosch Neths. 51°42N 5°17E 170 C5
Hertsa Ukraine 48°9N 26°15E 183 B11
Herttoniemi Finland 60°12N 25°2E 121 B3
Hertzogville S. Africa 28°9S 25°30E 270 C4
Hervás Spain 40°16N 5°52W 194 E5
Hervey B. Australia 25°0S 152°52E 280 C5
Herzberg Brandenburg, Germany 51°41N 13°14E 178 D9
Herzberg Niedersachsen, Germany 51°38N 10°20E 178 D6
Herzliyya Israel 32°10N 34°50E 251 F5
Herzogenburg Austria 48°17N 15°41E 180 C8
Ḩeşār Fārs, Iran 29°52N 50°16E 247 D6
Ḩeşār Markazī, Iran 35°50N 49°12E 247 C6
Ḩeşārak Iran 35°47N 51°18E 141 A1
Hesdin France 50°21N 2°2E 173 B9
Heshan Guangdong, China 22°34N 113°4E 229 F9
Heshan Guangxi Zhuangzu, China 23°50N 108°53E 228 F7
Heshui China 35°48N 108°0E 226 G5
Heshun China 37°22N 113°32E 226 F7
Heskestad Norway 58°28N 6°22E 164 F3
Hesperia U.S.A. 34°25N 117°18W 307 L9
Hessdalen Norway 62°48N 11°10E 164 B8
Hesse = Hessen □ Germany 50°30N 9°0E 178 E4
Hessen □ Germany 50°30N 9°0E 178 E4
Hessenreuther und Manteler Wald ⌂ Germany 49°45N 12°1E 179 F8
Hesso Australia 32°8S 137°27E 282 B2
Hesteyri Iceland 66°20N 22°53W 155 A4
Heston U.K. 51°28N 0°22W 125 B1
Hestra Sweden 57°26N 13°35E 163 G7
Hetauda Nepal 27°25N 85°2E 243 F11
Hetch Hetchy Aqueduct U.S.A. 37°29N 122°19W 306 H5
Hetta Enontekiö Finland 68°23N 23°37E 160 B20
Hettinger U.S.A. 46°0N 102°42W 308 B2
Hettstedt Germany 51°39N 11°31E 178 D7
Hetzendorf Austria 48°9N 16°17E 142 B1
Heuksando S. Korea 34°40N 125°30E 224 E2
Heunghae S. Korea 36°12N 129°21E 224 D4
Heuvelton U.S.A. 44°37N 75°25W 313 B9
Hevelândia Brazil 5°12S 61°50W 329 E5
Heves Hungary 47°36N 20°17E 182 C5
Heves □ Hungary 47°50N 20°0E 182 C5
Hewitt U.S.A. 31°28N 97°12W 314 F6
Hexham U.K. 54°58N 2°4W 168 C5
Hexi Yunnan, China 24°9N 102°38E 228 E4
Hexi Zhejiang, China 27°58N 119°38E 229 D12
Hexigten Qi China 43°18N 117°30E 227 C9
Hextable U.K. 51°24N 0°10E 125 B5
Ḩeydarābād Iran 30°33N 55°38E 247 D7
Heydebreck = Kędzierzyn-Koźle Poland 50°20N 18°12E 185 H5
Heyfield Australia 37°59S 146°47E 283 D7
Heysham U.K. 54°3N 2°53W 168 C5
Heyuan China 23°39N 114°40E 229 F10
Heywood Australia 38°8S 141°37E 282 E4
Heyworth U.S.A. 40°19N 88°59W 310 D8
Heze China 35°14N 115°20E 226 G8
Hezhang China 27°8N 104°41E 228 D5
Hezhou China 24°27N 111°30E 229 E8
Hi-no-Misaki Japan 35°26N 132°38E 222 B4
Hi Vista U.S.A. 34°45N 117°46W 307 L9
Hialeah U.S.A. 25°51N 80°16W 129 C1
Hialeah Race Track U.S.A. 25°51N 80°16W 129 C1
Hiawassa, L. U.S.A. 28°33N 81°28W 133 A2
Hiawatha U.S.A. 39°51N 95°32W 308 F6
Hibbing U.S.A. 47°25N 92°56W 308 B7
Hibernia Reef Australia 12°0S 123°23E 278 B3
Hibiki-Nada Japan 34°0N 130°0E 222 D2
Hibok-Hibok, Mt. Phil. 9°12N 124°40E 233 G5
Hickam Housing U.S.A. 21°21N 157°57W 302 K14
Hickman U.S.A. 36°34N 89°11W 308 G9
Hickory U.S.A. 35°44N 81°21W 315 D14
Hickory Hills U.S.A. 41°43N 87°49W 119 C2
Hicks, Pt. Australia 37°49S 149°17E 283 D8
Hicks Bay N.Z. 37°34S 178°21E 284 D7
Hicks L. Canada 61°25N 100°0W 297 A9
Hicksville N.Y., U.S.A. 40°46N 73°32W 313 F11
Hicksville Ohio, U.S.A. 41°18N 84°46W 311 C12
Hicpochee, L. U.S.A. 26°48N 81°9W 317 J8
Hida Gifu, Japan 36°14N 137°11E 223 A9
Hida Romania 47°10N 23°19E 183 C8
Hida-Gawa → Japan 35°26N 137°3E 223 B9
Hida-Sammyaku Japan 36°30N 137°40E 223 A9
Hida-Sanchi Japan 36°10N 137°0E 223 A9
Hidaka Hokkaidō, Japan 42°30N 142°10E 220 C11
Hidaka Hyōgo, Japan 35°30N 134°44E 222 B6
Hidaka-Sammyaku Japan 42°35N 142°45E 220 C11
Hidalgo □ Mexico 20°30N 99°0W 319 C5
Hidalgo del Parral Mexico 26°56N 105°40W 318 B3
Hiddensee Germany 54°32N 13°6E 178 A9
Hidrolândia Brazil 17°0S 49°15W 333 E2
Hieflau Austria 47°36N 14°46E 180 D7
Hiekkaharju Finland 60°18N 25°2E 121 B3
Hiendelaencina Spain 41°5N 3°0W 196 D2
Hienghène N. Cal. 20°41S 164°56E 288 d
Hierapolis-Pamukkale Turkey 37°55N 29°7E 205 D11
Hierro Canary Is. 27°44N 18°0W 153 e1
Hietaniemi Finland 60°10N 24°54E 121 B2
Hietzing Austria 48°10N 16°17E 142 A1
Higashi Japan 34°41N 135°30E 133 A2
Higashi-Hiroshima Japan 34°25N 132°45E 222 C4
Higashi-Matsuyama Japan 36°2N 139°25E 223 A11
Higashi-Suidō Japan 34°0N 129°30E 222 D1
Higashiajima-San Japan 37°40N 140°10E 220 F10
Higashikagawa Japan 34°13N 134°24E 222 C6
Higashimurayama Japan 35°45N 139°26E 140 A1
Higashinari Japan 34°40N 135°32E 133 A2
Higashiōsaka Japan 34°39N 135°37E 223 C7
Higashisumiyoshi Japan 34°37N 135°31E 133 B2
Higashiyodogawa Japan 34°44N 135°28E 133 A1
Higbee U.S.A. 39°19N 92°31W 310 E4
Higgins U.S.A. 36°7N 100°2W 314 C4
Higgins Corner U.S.A. 39°2N 121°5W 306 F5
Higginsville U.S.A. 39°4N 93°43W 310 E3
High Bridge U.S.A. 40°40N 74°54W 313 F10
High Desert U.S.A. 43°40N 120°20W 304 E3
High Island Res. China 22°22N 114°21E 219 a
High Junk Pk. Hong Kong, China 22°18N 114°17E 122 B3
High Level Canada 58°31N 117°8W 296 B5
High Park Canada 43°38N 79°27W 141 B2
High Peak Phil. 15°29N 120°7E 232 D3
High Pk. St. Helena 15°58S 5°44W 153 h
High Point U.S.A. 35°57N 80°0W 315 D15
High Prairie Canada 55°30N 116°30W 296 B5
High River Canada 50°30N 113°50W 296 C6
High Springs U.S.A. 29°50N 82°36W 316 F7
High Tatra = Tatry Slovak Rep. 49°20N 20°0E 181 B13
High Veld Africa 27°0S 27°0E 254 J6
High Wycombe U.K. 51°37N 0°45W 169 F7
Highbank N.Z. 43°37S 171°45E 285 D6
Highbury U.K. 51°33N 0°6W 125 A3
Highgate Jamaica 18°16N 76°57W 320 a
Highgate London, U.K. 51°34N 0°8W 125 A3
Highland Ill., U.S.A. 38°44N 89°41W 310 F7
Highland Ind., U.S.A. 41°33N 87°28W 311 C9
Highland Wis., U.S.A. 43°5N 90°22W 310 A6
Highland □ U.K. 57°17N 4°21W 167 D4
Highland City U.S.A. 27°58N 81°53W 317 H8
Highland Cr. → Canada 43°45N 79°13W 141 A3
Highland Creek Canada 43°46N 79°8W 141 A3
Highland Home U.S.A. 31°57N 86°19W 316 D3
Highland Mills U.S.A. 33°17N 84°17W 316 B5
Highland Park Calif., U.S.A. 34°7N 118°13W 126 B3
Highland Park Ill., U.S.A. 42°11N 87°48W 311 B9
Highland View U.S.A. 29°50N 85°19W 316 F4
Highlands = Fort Thomas U.S.A. 39°4N 84°26W 311 E12
Highlands, The Antigua & B. 17°38N 61°47W 322 c
Highlands North S. Africa 26°8S 28°5E 123 A2
Highmore U.S.A. 44°31N 99°27W 308 C4
Highrock L. Canada 55°45N 100°30W 297 B8
Higuero, Pta. Puerto Rico 18°22N 67°16W 321 b
Higüey Dom. Rep. 18°37N 68°42W 321 C6
Hihya Egypt 30°40N 31°36E 256 H7
Hiidenportti △ Finland 63°53N 29°0E 160 E23
Hiiraan □ Somalia 4°0N 45°30E 267 D6
Hiiumaa Estonia 58°50N 22°45E 188 C2
Híjar Spain 41°10N 0°27W 196 D4
Ḩijārah, Şaḩrā' al Iraq 30°25N 44°30E 246 D5
Ḩijāz Si. Arabia 24°0N 40°0E 246 E3
Hiji Japan 33°22N 131°32E 222 D3
Hijo = Tagum Phil. 7°33N 125°53E 233 H5
Hikari Japan 33°58N 131°58E 222 D3
Hiketa = Higashikagawa Japan 34°13N 134°24E 222 C6
Hikkaduwa Sri Lanka 6°8N 80°6E 245 L5
Hikmak, Ras el Egypt 31°15N 27°51E 256 A2
Hiko U.S.A. 37°32N 115°14W 306 H11
Hikone Japan 35°15N 136°10E 223 B8
Hikurangi Gisborne, N.Z. 37°55S 178°4E 284 D7
Hikurangi Northland, N.Z. 35°36S 174°17E 284 B3
Hikutavake Niue 18°56S 169°53W 289 g
Hiland Park U.S.A. 30°12N 85°33W 316 E4
Hilawng Burma 21°23N 93°48E 241 E4
Hildburghausen Germany 50°25N 10°42E 178 E6
Hildesheim Germany 52°9N 9°56E 178 C5
Hilðarendi Iceland 63°44N 19°57W 155 D7
Hill → Australia 30°23S 115°3E 279 F2
Hill City Idaho, U.S.A. 43°18N 115°3W 304 E6
Hill City Kans., U.S.A. 39°22N 99°51W 308 F4
Hill City Minn., U.S.A. 46°59N 93°36W 308 B7
Hill City S. Dak., U.S.A. 43°56N 103°35W 308 D2
Hill Island L. Canada 60°30N 109°50W 297 A7
Hillaby, Mt. Barbados 13°12N 59°35W 323 r
Hillared Sweden 57°37N 13°10E 163 G7
Hillbrow Tower Johannesburg, S. Africa 26°11S 28°3E 123 B2
Hillcrest Heights U.S.A. 38°49N 76°57W 143 C3
Hillegom Neths. 52°18N 4°35E 170 B4
Hillend U.K. 56°2N 3°22W 121 A1
Hillerød Denmark 55°56N 12°19E 163 J6
Hillerstorp Sweden 57°20N 13°52E 163 G7
Hilli Bangla. 25°17N 89°1E 241 C2
Hilliard U.S.A. 30°41N 81°55W 316 E8
Hillingdon □ U.K. 51°32N 0°27W 125 A1
Hillsboro = Deerfield Beach U.S.A. 26°19N 80°6W 317 J9
Hillsboro Ga., U.S.A. 33°11N 83°38W 316 B6
Hillsboro Ill., U.S.A. 39°9N 89°29W 310 E7
Hillsboro Kans., U.S.A. 38°21N 97°12W 308 F5
Hillsboro Mo., U.S.A. 38°14N 90°34W 310 F6
Hillsboro N. Dak., U.S.A. 47°26N 97°3W 308 B5
Hillsboro Ohio, U.S.A. 39°12N 83°37W 311 E13
Hillsboro Oreg., U.S.A. 45°31N 122°59W 306 E4
Hillsboro Tex., U.S.A. 32°1N 97°8W 314 E6
Hillsboro Canal U.S.A. 26°30N 80°15W 317 J9
Hillsborough Grenada 12°28N 61°28W 323 q
Hillsborough N.H., U.S.A. 43°7N 71°54W 313 C13
Hillsborough Channel Australia 20°56S 149°15E 280 b
Hillsborough Dam Trin. & Tob. 11°13N 60°40W 323 s
Hillsborough Land = Belle Glade U.S.A. 26°41N 80°40W 317 J9
Hillsdale Mich., U.S.A. 41°56N 84°38W 311 C12
Hillsdale N.Y., U.S.A. 42°11N 73°32W 313 D11
Hillsport Canada 49°27N 85°34W 298 C2
Hillston Australia 33°30S 145°31E 283 B6
Hilltonia U.S.A. 32°53N 81°40W 316 C8
Hillwood U.S.A. 38°52N 77°9W 143 B2
Hilmîya Egypt 30°6N 31°19E 117 A2
Hilo U.S.A. 19°44N 155°5W 302 D6
Hilo ✈ (ITO) U.S.A. 19°43N 155°2W 302 D6
Hilo B. U.S.A. 19°45N 155°5W 302 D6
Hilongos Phil. 10°22N 124°44E 233 F5
Hilton U.S.A. 43°17N 77°48W 312 C7
Hilton Head Island U.S.A. 32°13N 80°45W 316 C9
Hilvan Turkey 37°34N 38°58E 213 D8
Hilversum Neths. 52°14N 5°10E 170 B5
Himachal Pradesh □ India 31°30N 77°0E 242 D7
Himalaya Asia 29°0N 84°0E 243 E11
Himalchuli Nepal 28°27N 84°38E 243 E11
Himamaylan Phil. 10°6N 122°52E 233 F4
Himarë Albania 40°8N 19°43E 202 F3
Himatnagar India 23°37N 72°57E 242 H5
Himchari △ Bangla. 21°28N 92°5E 241 E4
Hime-Jima Japan 33°43N 131°40E 222 D3
Himeji Japan 34°50N 134°40E 222 C6
Himi Japan 36°50N 136°55E 223 A8
Himmerland Denmark 56°45N 9°30E 163 H3
Ḩimş Syria 34°40N 36°45E 250 D7
Ḩimş □ Syria 34°30N 37°0E 250 D8
Hin Keng Hong Kong, China 22°22N 114°10E 122 A3
Hin Khom, Laem Thailand 9°25N 99°56E 237 b
Hinatuan Phil. 8°23N 126°20E 233 G6
Hinatuan Passage Phil. 9°45N 125°47E 233 G5
Hinche Haiti 19°9N 72°1W 321 C5
Hinchinbrook I. Australia 18°20S 146°15E 280 B4
Hinchinbrook Island △ Australia 18°14S 146°6E 280 B4
Hinckley Leics., U.K. 52°33N 1°22W 169 E6
Hinckley Minn., U.S.A. 46°1N 92°56W 308 B7
Hindaun India 26°44N 77°5E 242 F7
Hindenburg = Zabrze Poland 50°18N 18°50E 185 H5
Hindmarsh, L. Australia 36°5S 141°55E 282 D4
Hindol India 20°40N 85°10E 244 D7
Hinds N.Z. 43°59S 171°36E 285 D6
Hindsholm Denmark 55°30N 10°40E 163 J4
Hindu Bagh Pakistan 30°56N 67°50E 242 D2
Hindu Kush Asia 36°0N 71°0E 240 B3
Hindupur India 13°49N 77°32E 245 H3
Hines Creek Canada 56°20N 118°40W 296 B5
Hinesville U.S.A. 31°51N 81°36W 316 D8
Hinganghat India 20°30N 78°52E 244 D4
Hingham U.S.A. 48°33N 110°25W 304 B8
Hinghwa = Xinghua China 32°58N 119°48E 229 A12
Hingir India 21°57N 83°41E 243 J10
Hingoli India 19°41N 77°15E 244 E3
Hinigaran Phil. 10°16N 122°50E 233 F4
Hinis Turkey 39°22N 41°43E 213 C9
Hinna = Imi Ethiopia 6°28N 42°10E 257 F5
Hinna Nigeria 10°25N 11°35E 263 C7
Hinnerup Denmark 56°16N 10°4E 163 H4
Hinnøya Norway 68°35N 15°50E 160 B16
Hino Japan 35°0N 136°15E 223 C8
Hinoba-an Phil. 9°35N 122°28E 233 G4
Hinojosa del Duque Spain 38°30N 5°9W 195 G5
Hinokage Japan 32°39N 131°24E 222 E3
Hinsdale U.S.A. 42°47N 72°29W 313 D12
Hinterrhein → Switz. 46°40N 9°25E 179 J5
Hinthada = Henzada Burma 17°38N 95°26E 241 G5
Hinton Alta., Canada 53°26N 117°34W 296 C5
Hinton W. Va., U.S.A. 37°40N 80°54W 309 G13
Hinubuan = Antipolo Phil. 14°35N 121°10E 232 D3
Hinunangan Phil. 10°25N 125°12E 233 F5
Hios = Chios Greece 38°27N 26°9E 205 C8
Hirado Japan 33°22N 129°33E 222 D1
Hirado-Shima Japan 33°20N 129°30E 222 D1
Hirakata Japan 34°48N 135°38E 223 C7
Hirakud Dam India 21°32N 83°45E 244 D6
Hiran → India 23°6N 79°21E 243 H8
Hirapur India 24°22N 79°13E 243 G8
Hirara = Miyakojima Japan 24°48N 125°17E 221 M2
Hirata Japan 35°24N 132°49E 222 B4
Hiratsuka Japan 35°19N 139°21E 223 B11
Hirekerur India 14°28N 75°23E 245 G2
Hirfanlı Barajı Turkey 39°18N 33°31E 212 C5
Hirhafok Algeria 23°49N 5°45E 261 D6
Hiromi = Kihoku Japan 33°13N 132°36E 222 D4
Hiroo Japan 42°17N 143°19E 220 C11
Hirosaki Japan 40°34N 140°28E 220 D10
Hiroshima Japan 34°24N 132°30E 222 C4
Hiroshima □ Japan 34°50N 133°0E 222 C5
Hiroshima-Wan Japan 34°5N 132°20E 222 C4
Hirota Japan 34°45N 135°20E 133 A1
Hirschberg = Jelenia Góra Poland 50°50N 15°45E 185 H2
Hirschstetten Austria 48°14N 16°27E 142 A2
Hirson France 49°55N 4°4E 173 C11
Hirtshals Denmark 57°36N 9°57E 163 G3

Hisai Japan 34°40N 136°28E 223 C8
Hisar India 29°12N 75°45E 242 E6
Hisarcık Turkey 39°15N 29°14E 205 B11
Hisaria Bulgaria 42°30N 24°44E 203 D8
Hisb, Sha'ib = Ḩasb, W. ➝
Iraq 31°45N 44°17E 246 D5
Ḩismá Si. Arabia 28°30N 36°0E 251 K7
Ḩişn al 'Abr Yemen 16°8N 47°14E 248 C4
Hispaniola W. Indies 19°0N 71°0W 321 C5
Hīt Iraq 33°38N 42°49E 213 F10
Hita Japan 33°20N 130°58E 222 D2
Hitachi Japan 36°36N 140°39E 223 A12
Hitachi-Ōta Japan 36°30N 140°30E 223 A12
Hitan, W. el Egypt 29°19N 30°10E 256 J7
Hitchin U.K. 51°58N 0°16W 169 F7
Hithadhoo Maldives 0°36S 73°5E 272 d
Hither Green U.K. 51°26N 0°0 125 B3
Hitiaa Tahiti 17°36S 149°18W 289 e
Hitoyoshi Japan 32°13N 130°45E 222 E2
Hitra Norway 63°30N 8°45E 164 A5
Hitzacker Germany 53°9N 11°2E 178 B7
Hiu Vanuatu 13°10S 166°35E 287 C4
Hiuchi-Nada Japan 34°5N 133°20E 222 C5
Hiva Oa French Polynesia 9°45S 139°0W 289 f
Hixon Canada 53°25N 122°35W 296 C4
Hiyoshi Japan 35°32N 139°38E 140 B2
Ḩiyyon, N. ➝ Israel 30°25N 35°10E 251 H6
Hizma West Bank 31°50N 35°16E 123 B2
Hjalmar L. Canada 61°33N 109°25W 297 A7
Hjälmaren Sweden 59°18N 15°40E 162 E9
Hjältevad Sweden 57°38N 15°20E 163 G9
Hjalteyri Iceland 65°55N 18°18W 155 B8
Hjartdal Norway 59°37N 8°41E 164 E5
Hjelmelandsvågen Norway 59°14N 6°10E 164 E3
Hjelset Norway 62°48N 7°30E 164 B4
Hjerkinn Norway 62°13N 9°33E 164 B6
Hjo Sweden 58°22N 14°17E 163 F8
Hjørring Denmark 57°29N 9°59E 163 G3
Hjörsey Iceland 64°32N 22°21W 155 C4
Hjort Trench S. Ocean 58°0S 157°30E 151 B10
Hjortekær Denmark 55°47N 12°32E 118 A3
Hjortespring Denmark 55°44N 12°25E 118 A2
Hjortkvarn Sweden 58°54N 15°26E 163 F9
Hjukse Norway 59°31N 9°19E 164 E6
Hkakabo Razi Burma 28°25N 97°23E 228 C1
Hkakabo Razi △ Burma 28°0N 97°55E 241 A6
Hkamti Burma 26°0N 95°39E 241 C5
Hko-lam Burma 21°7N 98°5E 241 E7
Hko-ut Burma 20°58N 98°2E 241 E7
Hkyenhpa Burma 27°43N 97°25E 241 B6
Hlaingbwe Burma 17°8N 97°50E 241 G6
Hlinsko Czech Rep. 49°45N 15°54E 180 B8
Hlobane S. Africa 27°42S 31°0E 271 C5
Hlohovec Slovak Rep. 48°26N 17°49E 181 C10
Hluboćepy Czech Rep. 50°2N 14°23E 135 B2
Hlučín Czech Rep. 49°54N 18°11E 181 B11
Hluhluwe S. Africa 28°1S 32°15E 271 C5
Hluhluwe ⌓ S. Africa 22°10S 32°5E 271 B5
Hlukhiv Ukraine 51°40N 33°58E 189 G7
Hlwaze Burma 18°54N 96°37E 241 F6
Hlyboka Ukraine 48°5N 25°56E 183 B10
Hlybokaye Belarus 55°10N 27°45E 188 E4
Hnappadalssýsla Iceland 64°50N 22°30W 155 C4
Hnífsdalur Iceland 66°7N 23°8W 155 A3
Hnúšťa Slovak Rep. 48°35N 19°58E 181 C12
Ho Ghana 6°37N 0°27E 263 D5
Ho Chi Minh City = Thanh Pho Ho
Chi Minh Vietnam 10°58N 106°40E 237 G6
Ho Chung
Hong Kong, China 22°21N 114°14E 122 A3
Ho Hoa Binh Vietnam 20°50N 105°0E 228 G5
Ho Thac Ba Vietnam 21°42N 105°1E 236 A5
Ho Thuong Vietnam 19°32N 105°48E 236 C5
Hoa Binh Vietnam 20°50N 105°20E 228 G5
Hoa Hiep Vietnam 11°34N 105°51E 237 G5
Hoai Nhon Vietnam 14°28N 109°1E 236 E7
Hoang Lien △ Vietnam 21°30N 105°32E 236 B5
Hoang Lien Son Vietnam 22°0N 104°0E 228 F4
Hoang Sa, Dao = Paracel Is.
S. China Sea 15°50N 112°0E 230 A4
Hoanib ➝ Namibia 19°27S 12°46E 270 A2
Hoare B. Canada 65°17N 62°30W 295 D19
Hoarusib ➝ Namibia 19°3S 12°36E 270 A2
Hobart Tas., Australia 42°50S 147°21E 281 G4
Hobart Ind., U.S.A. 41°32N 87°15W 311 C9
Hobart Okla., U.S.A. 35°1N 99°6W 314 D5
Hobbs U.S.A. 32°42N 103°8W 305 K12
Hobbs Coast Antarctica 74°50S 131°0W 151 D14
Hobe Sound U.S.A. 27°4N 80°8W 317 H9
Hobo Colombia 2°35N 75°30W 328 C2
Hoboken Ga., U.S.A. 31°11N 82°8W 316 D7
Hoboken New York, U.S.A. 132 d1
Hobro Denmark 56°39N 9°46E 163 H3
Hobsons B. Australia 37°51S 144°55E 128 B1
Hoburgen Sweden 56°55N 18°7E 163 H12
Hobyo Somalia 5°25N 48°30E 267 C6
Hocalar Turkey 38°36N 30°0E 205 C11
Hochbrück Germany 48°14N 11°37E 131 A2
Hochelaga Canada 45°32N 73°33W 130 A2
Hochfeld Namibia 21°28S 17°58E 270 B2
Hochharz △ Germany 51°48N 10°38E 178 D6
Hochschwab Austria 47°35N 15°0E 180 D8
Höchstadt Germany 49°42N 10°47E 179 F6
Hochtaunus ⌓ Germany 50°20N 8°30E 179 E4
Hoch'uan = Hechuan
China 30°2N 106°12E 228 B6
Hochwan = Hechuan
China 30°2N 106°12E 228 B6
Hockenheim Germany 49°19N 8°32E 179 F4
Hockley = Levelland
U.S.A. 33°35N 102°23W 314 E3
Hodaka-Dake Japan 36°17N 137°39E 223 A9
Hodeida = Al Ḩudaydah
Yemen 14°50N 43°0E 248 D3
Hodgeville Canada 50°7N 106°58W 297 C7
Hodgson Canada 51°13N 97°36W 297 C9
Hodh El Gharbi □
Mauritania 16°30N 10°0W 262 B3
Hódmezővásárhely
Hungary 46°28N 20°22E 182 D5
Hodna, Chott el Algeria 35°26N 4°43E 261 A5
Hodo-dan N. Korea 39°23N 127°32E 224 C3
Hodonín Czech Rep. 48°50N 17°10E 181 C10
Hœdic, Î. de France 47°20N 2°53W 172 E4
Hoegi S. Korea 37°35N 127°3E 137 B2
Hoeilaart Belgium 50°46N 4°28E 116 B2
Hoek van Holland Neths. 52°0N 4°7E 170 C4
Hoengseong S. Korea 37°29N 127°59E 224 D3
Hoeryong N. Korea 42°30N 129°45E 224 A4
Hoeyang N. Korea 38°43N 127°36E 224 C3
Hof Bayern, Germany 50°19N 11°55E 179 E7
Hof Austurland Iceland 65°39N 15°0W 155 B11
Hof Austurland Iceland 64°33N 14°40W 155 C12
Hof Vestfold, Norway 59°32N 10°5E 164 E7
Hofburg Vienna, Austria 142 b1
Hofei = Hefei China 31°52N 117°18E 229 B11
Hoffell Iceland 64°23N 15°20W 155 C11
Hoffman I. U.S.A. 40°34N 74°3W 132 C1
Hofgarten Munich, Germany 131 a3
Hofgeismar Germany 51°29N 9°23E 178 D5
Hofheim Germany 50°5N 8°26E 179 E4
Hofmeyr S. Africa 31°39S 25°50E 270 D4
Höfn Iceland 64°15N 15°13W 155 C11
Hofors Sweden 60°31N 16°15E 162 D10
Hofsjökull Iceland 64°49N 18°48W 155 C8
Hofsós Iceland 65°53N 19°26W 155 B7
Hōfu Japan 34°3N 131°34E 222 C3
Hog Harbour Vanuatu 15°8S 167°6E 287 E5
Hog I. = Paradise I.
Bahamas 25°6N 77°19W 153 b
Hog I. Grenada 12°0N 61°44W 323 q
Hog Pt. Antigua & B. 17°41N 61°47W 322 c
Hogan Group Australia 39°13S 147°1E 281 F4
Höganäs Sweden 56°12N 12°33E 163 H6
Hogansville U.S.A. 33°10N 84°55W 316 B5
Hogarth, Mt. Australia 21°48S 136°58E 280 C2
Hoge Kempen △ Belgium 51°6N 5°35E 170 C5
Hoge Veluwe △ Neths. 52°5N 5°46E 170 B5
Høgeloft Norway 61°3N 8°12E 164 C5
Hogenakai Falls India 12°6N 77°50E 245 H3
Hoggar = Ahaggar Algeria 23°0N 6°30E 261 D6
Högsäter Sweden 58°38N 12°5E 163 F6
Högsby Sweden 57°10N 16°1E 163 G10
Högsjö Sweden 59°4N 15°44E 162 E9
Hogsty Reef Bahamas 21°41N 73°48W 321 B5
Hoh ➝ U.S.A. 47°45N 124°29W 306 C2
Hoh Xil Shan China 36°30N 89°0E 218 D6
Hohd ech Chargui □
Mauritania 19°0N 7°15W 260 E3
Hohe Acht Germany 50°22N 7°0E 179 E3
Hohe Tauern Austria 47°11N 12°40E 180 D5
Hohe Tauern △ Austria 47°5N 12°20E 180 D5
Hohenau Austria 48°36N 16°55E 181 C9
Hohenbrunn Germany 48°2N 11°42E 131 B3
Hohenelbe = Vrchlabí
Czech Rep. 50°38N 15°37E 180 A8
Hohenems Austria 47°22N 9°42E 180 D2
Hohenloher Ebene
Germany 49°14N 9°36E 179 F5
Hohenmauth = Vysoké Mýto
Czech Rep. 49°58N 16°10E 181 B9
Hohensalza = Inowrocław
Poland 52°50N 18°12E 185 F5
Hohensalzburg = Lunino
Russia 53°38N 45°18E 190 D7
Hohenschönhausen
Germany 52°33N 13°30E 115 A4
Hohenstadt = Zábřeh
Czech Rep. 49°53N 16°52E 181 B9
Hohenstein = Olsztynek
Poland 53°34N 20°19E 184 E7
Hohenwald U.S.A. 35°33N 87°33W 315 D11
Hohenwestedt Germany 54°5N 9°40E 178 A5
Hoher Rhön = Rhön
Germany 50°24N 9°58E 178 E5
Hoher Vogelsberg ⌓
Germany 51°45N 9°35E 178 D5
Hohes Venn Belgium 50°30N 6°5E 170 D6
Hohes Venn-Eifel ⌓ Europe 50°30N 6°10E 178 E2
Hohhot China 40°52N 111°40E 226 D6
Hohoe Ghana 7°8N 0°32E 263 D5
Hoi An Vietnam 15°53N 108°19E 236 E7
Hoi Xuan Vietnam 20°25N 105°9E 228 G5
Hoihow = Haikou China 20°1N 110°16E 229 a
Hoisington U.S.A. 38°31N 98°47W 308 F4
Hojai India 26°2N 92°54E 241 B4
Hojambaz Turkmenistan 38°7N 65°0E 216 E6
Højer Denmark 54°58N 8°42E 163 K2
Hōjō Japan 33°58N 132°46E 222 D4
Hok Sweden 57°31N 14°16E 163 G8
Hok Tsui
Hong Kong, China 22°12N 114°14E 122 B3
Hokang = Hegang
China 47°20N 130°19E 219 B15
Hökensås Sweden 58°0N 14°5E 163 G8
Hökerum Sweden 57°51N 13°16E 163 G7
Hokianga Harbour N.Z. 35°31S 173°22E 284 B2
Hokitika N.Z. 42°42S 171°0E 285 C6
Hokkaidō □ Japan 43°30N 143°0E 220 C11
Hokksund Norway 59°48N 9°54E 164 E6
Hokuto Japan 41°49N 140°39E 220 D10
Hol-Hol Djibouti 11°20N 42°50E 257 E5
Hola Kenya 1°29S 40°2E 268 B4
Hola Prystan Ukraine 46°29N 32°32E 189 J7
Holakas Greece 35°57N 27°53E 206 F11
Holalkere India 14°2N 76°11E 245 G3
Hólar Iceland 65°44N 19°8W 155 B7
Holargos = Cholargos
Greece 37°59N 23°48E 112 B2
Holašovice Czech Rep. 48°57N 14°15E 180 C7
Holbæk Denmark 55°43N 11°43E 163 J5
Holborn London, U.K. 125 a4
Holbrook N.S.W.,
Australia 35°42S 147°18E 283 C7
Holbrook Ariz., U.S.A. 34°54N 110°10W 305 J8
Holbrook Idaho, U.S.A. 42°10N 112°39W 306 E7
Holcomb U.S.A. 42°54N 77°25W 312 D7
Holden Mo., U.S.A. 38°43N 94°0W 310 F3
Holden Utah, U.S.A. 39°6N 112°16W 304 G7
Holden, L. U.S.A. 28°30N 81°23W 133 B2
Holdenville U.S.A. 35°5N 96°24W 314 D6
Holdich Argentina 45°57S 68°13W 336 C3
Holdrege U.S.A. 40°26N 99°23W 308 E4
Hole-Narsipur India 12°48N 76°16E 245 H3
Holešov Czech Rep. 49°20N 17°35E 181 B10
Holešovice Czech Rep. 50°6N 14°28E 135 B2
Holetown Barbados 13°11N 59°38W 323 r
Holgate U.S.A. 41°15N 84°8W 311 C12
Holguín Cuba 20°50N 76°20W 320 B4
Holíč Slovak Rep. 48°49N 17°10E 181 C10
Holice Czech Rep. 50°5N 16°0E 180 A8
Holiday U.S.A. 28°11N 82°44W 317 G7
Holiday Park U.S.A. 26°8N 80°7W 129 B3
Höljes Sweden 60°50N 12°35E 162 D6
Hollabrunn Austria 48°34N 16°5E 180 C9
Hollams Bird I. Namibia 24°40S 14°30E 270 B1
Holland = Netherlands ■
Europe 52°0N 5°30E 170 C5
Holland Mich., U.S.A. 42°47N 86°7W 311 B10
Holland N.Y., U.S.A. 42°38N 78°32W 312 D6
Holland B. Jamaica 17°57N 76°13W 320 a
Holland Centre Canada 44°23N 80°47W 312 B4
Holland Patent U.S.A. 43°14N 75°15W 313 C9
Holland Tunnel New York, U.S.A. 132 d1
Holland Village Singapore 1°18N 103°47E 138 B2
Hollandale U.S.A. 33°10N 90°51W 315 E9
Hollandia = Jayapura
Indonesia 2°28S 140°38E 231 E10
Holley U.S.A. 43°14N 78°2W 312 C6
Hollfeld Germany 49°56N 11°18E 179 F7
Hollidaysburg U.S.A. 40°26N 78°24W 312 F6
Hollis U.S.A. 34°41N 99°55W 314 D5
Hollis Reservoir
Trin. & Tob. 10°40N 61°10W 323 t
Hollister Calif., U.S.A. 36°51N 121°24W 306 J5
Hollister Idaho, U.S.A. 42°21N 114°35W 306 E6
Höllriegelskreuth Germany 48°2N 11°30E 131 B1
Höllviken Sweden 55°26N 12°58E 163 J6
Höllviksnäs = Höllviken
Sweden 55°26N 12°58E 163 J6
Holly U.S.A. 42°48N 83°38W 311 B13
Holly Hill Fla., U.S.A. 29°16N 81°3W 317 F8
Holly Hill S.C., U.S.A. 33°19N 80°25W 316 B9
Holly Springs Ga., U.S.A. 34°10N 84°30W 316 A5
Holly Springs Miss.,
U.S.A. 34°46N 89°27W 315 D10
Hollywood Wicklow, Ireland 53°6N 6°35W 166 B6
Hollywood Calif., U.S.A. 34°5N 118°19W 126 B2
Hollywood Fla., U.S.A. 26°0N 80°8W 129 B3
Hollywood Bowl U.S.A. 34°7N 118°20W 126 B2
Holman Canada 70°44N 117°44W 294 C8
Hólmavík Iceland 65°42N 21°40W 155 B5
Holmen Oppland, Norway 60°40N 10°22E 164 D7
Holmen Wis., U.S.A. 43°58N 91°15W 308 D8
Holmenkollen Norway 59°57N 10°41E 133 A3
Holmes Beach U.S.A. 27°31N 82°43W 317 H7
Holmes Cr. ➝ U.S.A. 30°30N 85°50W 316 E4
Holmes Reefs Australia 16°27S 148°0E 280 B4
Holmestrand Norway 59°31N 10°14E 164 E7
Holmgård Sweden 59°14N 18°0E 139 B1
Holmlia Norway 59°49N 10°46E 133 B3
Holmsjö Sweden 56°25N 15°32E 163 H9
Holmsjön Västernorrland,
Sweden 62°41N 16°33E 162 B10
Holmsjön Västernorrland,
Sweden 62°26N 15°20E 162 B9
Holmsland Klit Denmark 56°0N 8°5E 163 J2
Holmsund Sweden 63°41N 20°20E 160 E19
Holocaust Memorial
Jerusalem 31°47N 35°11E 123 B2
Holocaust Memorial Park
Boston, U.S.A. 116 b2
Holod Romania 46°49N 22°8E 182 D7
Holon Israel 32°0N 34°46E 251 G5
Holopaw U.S.A. 28°8N 81°5W 317 G8
Holovne Ukraine 51°20N 24°5E 185 G11
Holøydal Norway 62°12N 11°27E 164 B8
Holozubyntsi Ukraine 48°50N 26°55E 183 B11
Holroyd ➝ Australia 14°10S 141°36E 280 A3
Holstebro Denmark 56°22N 8°37E 163 H2
Holsteinische Schweiz ⌓
Germany 54°8N 10°30E 178 A6
Holsteinsborg = Sisimiut
Greenland 66°40N 53°30W 154 D5
Holsworthy U.K. 50°48N 4°22W 169 G3
Holt Iceland 63°33N 19°48W 155 D7
Holt Fla., U.S.A. 30°43N 86°45W 317 E3
Holt Mich., U.S.A. 42°39N 84°31W 311 B12
Holton Nfld. & L., Canada 54°31N 57°12W 299 B8
Holton Kans., U.S.A. 39°28N 95°44W 308 F6
Holts Summit U.S.A. 38°38N 92°7W 310 F4
Holtville U.S.A. 32°49N 115°23W 307 N11
Holualoa U.S.A. 19°37N 155°57W 302 D6
Holum Norway 58°6N 7°32E 164 F4
Holwerd Neths. 53°22N 5°54E 170 A5
Holy Cross U.S.A. 62°12N 159°46W 303 E8
Holy I. Anglesey, U.K. 53°17N 4°37W 168 D3
Holy I. Northumberland,
U.K. 55°40N 1°47W 168 B6
Holyhead U.K. 53°18N 4°38W 168 D3
Holyoke Colo., U.S.A. 40°35N 102°18W 304 F12
Holyoke Mass., U.S.A. 42°12N 72°37W 313 D12
Holyrood Canada 47°27N 53°8W 299 C9
Holyrood House, Palace of
U.K. 55°57N 3°10W 121 B3
Holysloot Neths. 52°25N 5°2E 112 A3
Holzkirchen Germany 47°52N 11°42E 179 H7
Holzminden Germany 51°50N 9°28E 178 D5
Homa Bay Kenya 0°36S 34°30E 268 C3
Homalin Burma 24°55N 95°0E 241 C5
Homand Iran 32°28N 59°37E 247 C8
Homathko ➝ Canada 51°0N 124°56W 296 C4
Homberg Germany 51°2N 9°25E 178 D5
Hombori Mali 15°20N 1°38W 263 B4
Hombori Tondo Mali 15°16N 1°40W 263 B4
Homburg Germany 49°28N 7°18E 179 F3
Home B. Canada 68°40N 67°10W 295 D18
Home Hill Australia 19°43S 147°25E 280 B4
Home Reef Tonga 18°59S 174°47W 287 P13
Homedale U.S.A. 43°37N 116°56W 304 E5
Homei Taiwan 24°7N 120°29E 225 B2
Homeland U.S.A. 30°51N 82°1W 316 E7
Homer Alaska, U.S.A. 59°39N 151°33W 303 G10
Homer Ill., U.S.A. 40°4N 87°57W 311 D9
Homer La., U.S.A. 32°48N 93°4W 314 E8
Homer Mich., U.S.A. 42°9N 84°49W 311 B12
Homer N.Y., U.S.A. 42°38N 76°10W 313 D8
Homer City U.S.A. 40°32N 79°10W 312 F5
Homert ⌓ Germany 51°15N 8°0E 178 D4
Homerton U.K. 51°32N 0°2W 125 A3
Homerville U.S.A. 31°2N 82°45W 316 D7
Homestead Queens.,
Australia 20°20S 145°40E 280 C4
Homestead Fla., U.S.A. 25°28N 80°29W 317 K9
Homestead △ U.S.A. 40°17N 96°50W 308 E5
Hometown U.S.A. 41°44N 87°42W 119 C2
Homewood U.S.A. 41°34N 87°40W 311 C9
Hommelvik Norway 63°25N 10°48E 164 A7
Hommersåk Norway 58°56N 5°50E 164 F2
Homnabad India 17°45N 77°11E 244 F3
Homoine Mozam. 23°55S 35°8E 271 B6
Homoljske Planina Serbia 44°10N 21°45E 202 B5
Homonhon I. Phil. 10°44N 125°43E 233 F5
Homorod Romania 46°5N 25°15E 183 D10
Homosassa Springs
U.S.A. 28°48N 82°35W 317 G7
Homs = Al Khums Libya 32°40N 14°17E 258 B2
Homs = Ḩimş Syria 34°40N 36°45E 250 D7
Homyel Belarus 52°28N 31°0E 177 B16
Homyel □ Belarus 52°40N 30°10E 189 F6
Hon Chong Vietnam 10°25N 104°30E 237 G5
Hon Hai Vietnam 10°0N 109°0E 237 H7
Hon Me Vietnam 19°23N 105°56E 236 C5
Honan = Henan □ China 34°0N 114°0E 226 H8
Hōnanchō Japan 35°40N 139°39E 140 A2
Hōnaunau U.S.A. 19°26N 155°55W 302 D6
Honavar India 14°17N 74°27E 245 G2
Honaz Turkey 37°46N 29°18E 205 D11
Honbetsu Japan 43°7N 143°37E 220 C11
Honcho Japan 35°40N 139°41E 140 A3
Honcut U.S.A. 39°20N 121°32W 306 F5
Honda Colombia 5°12N 74°45W 328 B3
Honda Bay Phil. 9°53N 118°49E 233 G2
Hondarribia Spain 43°22N 1°47W 196 B3
Hondeklipbaai S. Africa 30°19S 17°17E 270 D2
Honden Japan 35°43N 139°50E 140 A4
Hondo Japan 32°27N 130°12E 222 E2
Hondo Tex., U.S.A. 29°21N 99°9W 314 G5
Hondo, Rio ➝ Belize 18°25N 88°21W 319 D7
Hondo, Rio ➝ Calif.,
U.S.A. 34°2N 118°9W 126 B4
Honduras ■ Cent. Amer. 14°40N 86°30W 320 D2
Honduras, G. de Caribbean 16°50N 87°0W 320 C2
Hønefoss Norway 60°10N 10°18E 164 D7
Honesdale U.S.A. 41°34N 75°16W 313 E9
Honey Harbour Canada 44°52N 79°49W 312 B5
Honey L. U.S.A. 40°15N 120°19W 306 E6
Honfleur France 49°25N 0°13E 172 C7
Høng Denmark 55°31N 11°18E 163 J5
Hong ➝ Vietnam 20°16N 106°34E 236 B5
Hong Gai Vietnam 20°57N 107°5E 228 G6
Hong He ➝ China 32°25N 115°35E 229 A10
Hong Hu China 29°54N 113°24E 229 C9
Hong Kong □ China 22°11N 114°14E 219 a
Hong Kong I. China 22°16N 114°12E 122 B3
Hong Kong Int. ✈ (HKG)
Hong Kong, China 22°19N 113°57E 122 B1
Hong Kong Univ.
Hong Kong, China 22°16N 114°8E 122 B2
Honga Angola 15°9S 15°12E 265 F3
Hong'an China 31°20N 114°40E 229 B10
Hongcheon S. Korea 37°44N 127°53E 224 D3
Hongdo S. Korea 34°41N 125°12E 224 E2
Honghai Wan China 22°40N 115°0E 229 F10
Honghe China 23°25N 102°25E 228 F4
Honghu China 29°50N 113°30E 229 C9
Hongje S. Korea 37°35N 126°56E 137 B1
Hongjiang China 27°7N 109°59E 228 D7
Hongjimun Tunnel
S. Korea 37°37N 126°58E 137 B1
Hongkou China 31°16N 121°29E 138 B1
Hongliu He ➝ China 38°0N 109°50E 226 F5
Hongor Mongolia 45°45N 112°50E 226 B7
Hongqiao China 31°11N 121°22E 138 B1
Hongseong S. Korea 36°37N 126°38E 224 D3
Hongshan China 36°38N 117°58E 227 F9
Hongshui He ➝ China 23°48N 109°30E 228 F7
Hongtong China 36°16N 111°40E 226 F6
Honguedo, Détroit d'
Canada 49°15N 64°0W 299 C7
Hongwon N. Korea 40°0N 127°56E 224 C3
Hongya China 29°57N 103°22E 228 C4
Hongyuan China 32°51N 102°40E 228 A4
Hongze Hu China 33°15N 118°35E 227 H10
Honiara Solomon Is. 9°27S 159°57E 287 M10
Honiton U.K. 50°47N 3°11W 169 G4
Honjō = Yurihonjō Japan 39°23N 140°3E 220 E10
Honjō Japan 36°14N 139°11E 223 A11
Honjyo Japan 35°41N 139°48E 140 A3
Honkawane Japan 35°5N 138°5E 223 B10
Honkorâb, Ras Egypt 24°35N 35°10E 256 C4
Honnali India 14°15N 75°40E 245 G2
Honningsvåg Norway 70°59N 25°59E 160 A21
Hönö Sweden 57°41N 11°39E 163 G5
Honoka'a U.S.A. 20°5N 155°28W 302 C6
Honokai Hale U.S.A. 21°20N 158°6W 302 K13
Honolulu U.S.A. 21°19N 157°52W 302 K14
Honolulu District
U.S.A. 21°19N 157°46W 302 K14
Honolulu Int. ✈ (HNL)
U.S.A. 21°19N 157°55W 302 K14
Honomu U.S.A. 19°52N 155°7W 302 D6
Honoré Mercier, Pont
Canada 45°24N 73°39W 130 B1
Honouliuli U.S.A. 21°22N 158°2W 302 K13
Hönow Germany 52°32N 13°38E 115 A4
Honshū Japan 36°0N 138°0E 223 A8
Hontoria del Pinar Spain 41°50N 3°10W 196 D1
Honu'apo B. U.S.A. 19°5N 155°33W 302 D6
Hood, I. = Española, I.
Ecuador 1°23S 89°39W 330 a
Hood, Mt. U.S.A. 45°23N 121°42W 304 D3
Hood, Pt. Australia 34°23S 119°34E 279 F2
Hood Pt. Papua N. G. 10°4S 147°45E 286 F4
Hood River U.S.A. 45°43N 121°31W 304 D3
Hoodsport U.S.A. 47°24N 123°9W 306 C3
Hooge Germany 54°34N 8°33E 178 A4
Hoogeveen Neths. 52°44N 6°28E 170 B6
Hoogezand-Sappemeer
Neths. 53°9N 6°45E 170 A6
Hooghly = Hugli ➝ India 21°56N 88°4E 243 J13
Hooghly-Chinsura = Chunchura
India 22°53N 88°27E 243 H13
Hook U.K. 51°22N 0°17W 125 B2
Hook Hd. Ireland 52°7N 6°56W 166 D5
Hook I. Australia 20°4S 149°0E 280 b
Hook of Holland = Hoek van
Holland Neths. 52°0N 4°7E 170 C4
Hooker U.S.A. 36°52N 101°13W 314 C4
Hooker Creek = Lajamanu
Australia 18°23S 130°38E 278 C5
Hooker Creek ✪ Australia 18°6S 130°23E 278 C5
Ho'olehua U.S.A. 21°10N 157°5W 302 B4
Hoonah U.S.A. 58°7N 135°27W 296 B1
Hoop Bonaire 12°7N 68°17W 322 h
Hooper Bay U.S.A. 61°32N 166°6W 303 F6
Hoopeston U.S.A. 40°28N 87°40W 311 D9
Hoopstad S. Africa 27°50S 25°55E 270 C4
Höör Sweden 55°56N 13°33E 163 J7
Hoorn Neths. 52°38N 5°4E 170 B5
Hoover U.S.A. 33°24N 86°49W 315 E11
Hoover Dam U.S.A. 36°1N 114°44W 307 K12
Hooversville U.S.A. 40°9N 78°55W 312 F6
Hop Bottom U.S.A. 41°42N 75°46W 313 E9
Hopa Turkey 41°28N 41°30E 213 B9
Hope B.C., Canada 49°25N 121°25W 296 D4
Hope Ariz., U.S.A. 33°43N 113°42W 307 M13
Hope Ark., U.S.A. 33°40N 93°36W 314 E8
Hope Ind., U.S.A. 39°18N 85°46W 311 E11
Hope, L. S. Austral.,
Australia 28°24S 139°18E 281 D2
Hope, L. W. Austral.,
Australia 32°35S 120°15E 279 F3
Hope, Pt. U.S.A. 68°21N 166°47W 303 B6
Hope Bay Jamaica 18°12N 76°34W 320 a
Hope I. Canada 44°55N 80°11W 312 B4
Hope Town Bahamas 26°35N 76°57W 320 A4
Hope Vale Australia 15°16S 145°20E 280 B4
Hope Vale ✪ Australia 15°8S 145°15E 280 B4
Hopedale Nfld. & L.,
Canada 55°28N 60°13W 299 A7
Hopedale Mass., U.S.A. 42°8N 71°33W 313 D13
Hopefield S. Africa 33°3S 18°22E 270 D2
Hopei = Hebei □ China 39°0N 116°0E 226 E9
Hopelchén Mexico 19°46N 89°51W 319 D7
Hopetoun Vic., Australia 35°42S 142°22E 282 C5
Hopetoun W. Austral.,
Australia 33°57S 120°7E 279 F3
Hopetown S. Africa 29°34S 24°3E 270 C3
Hopewell U.S.A. 37°18N 77°17W 309 G15
Hopfgarten Austria 47°27N 12°10E 180 D5
Hopin Burma 24°58N 96°30E 241 C6
Hoping Changhua, Taiwan 24°10N 120°56E 225 B2
Hoping T'aitung, Taiwan 23°4N 121°20E 225 C3
Hopkins U.S.A. 40°33N 94°49W 310 D2
Hopkins, L. Australia 24°15S 128°35E 278 D4
Hopkinsville U.S.A. 36°52N 87°29W 308 G10
Hopland U.S.A. 38°58N 123°7W 306 G3
Hopong Burma 20°47N 97°11E 241 E6
Hopwood's Ferry = Echuca
Australia 36°10S 144°45E 283 D6
Hoque Angola 14°40S 13°55E 265 E2
Hoquiam U.S.A. 46°59N 123°53W 306 D3
Hora Hoverla Ukraine 48°7N 24°41E 183 B9
Hora Sfakion = Chora Sfakion
Greece 35°15N 24°9E 207 E5
Hōrai Japan 34°58N 137°32E 223 C9
Horana Sri Lanka 6°43N 80°4E 245 L5
Horasan Turkey 40°3N 42°11E 213 B10
Horažďovice Czech Rep. 49°19N 13°42E 180 B6
Horb Germany 48°26N 8°47E 179 G4
Hörby Sweden 55°51N 13°40E 163 J7
Horcajo de Santiago Spain 39°50N 3°1W 196 F1
Hordabø Norway 60°42N 4°54E 164 D1
Hordaland □ Norway 60°25N 6°15E 164 D3
Hordern Hills Australia 20°15S 130°0E 278 D5
Horezu Romania 45°6N 24°0E 183 E8
Horgen Switz. 47°15N 8°35E 179 H4
Horgoš Serbia 46°10N 20°0E 182 D4
Hořice Czech Rep. 50°21N 15°39E 180 A8
Horikiri Japan 35°44N 139°50E 140 A4
Horinchove Ukraine 48°16N 23°26E 183 B8
Horinger China 40°28N 111°48E 226 D6
Horizontina Brazil 27°37S 54°19W 335 B5
Horki Belarus 54°17N 30°59E 188 E6
Horlick Mts. Antarctica 84°0S 102°0W 151 E15
Horlivka Ukraine 48°19N 38°5E 189 H10
Hormak Iran 29°58N 60°51E 247 D9
Hormigueros Puerto Rico 18°8N 67°8W 321 b
Hormoz Iran 27°35N 55°0E 247 E7
Hormoz, Jaz.-ye Iran 27°8N 56°28E 247 E8
Hormozgān □ Iran 27°30N 56°0E 247 E8
Hormuz, Kūh-e Iran 27°27N 55°10E 247 E7
Hormuz, Str. of The Gulf 26°30N 56°30E 247 E8
Horn Austria 48°39N 15°40E 180 C8
Horn Vestfirðir Iceland 66°28N 22°25W 155 A4
Horn Sweden 57°54N 15°51E 163 G9
Horn ➝ Canada 61°30N 118°1W 296 A5
Horn, Cape = Hornos, C. de
Chile 55°50S 67°30W 336 E3
Horn, Is. Wall. & F. Is. 14°16S 178°6W 287 E8
Horn Head Ireland 55°14N 8°0W 166 A3
Horn I. Australia 10°37S 142°17E 286 F2
Horn Plateau Canada 62°15N 119°15W 296 A5
Horn Pond U.S.A. 42°28N 71°9W 116 A1
Hornachuelos Spain 37°50N 5°14W 195 H5
Hornavan Sweden 66°15N 17°30E 160 C17
Hornbeck U.S.A. 31°20N 93°24W 314 F8
Hornbrook U.S.A. 41°55N 122°33W 304 F2
Hornburg Germany 52°2N 10°37E 178 C6
Hornby N.Z. 43°33S 172°33E 285 D7
Horncastle U.K. 53°13N 0°7W 168 D7
Hornchurch U.K. 51°33N 0°12E 125 A5
Horndal Sweden 60°18N 16°23E 162 D10
Hornell U.S.A. 42°20N 77°40W 312 D7
Hornell L. Canada 62°20N 119°25W 296 A5
Hornepayne Canada 49°14N 84°48W 298 C3
Horni Czech Rep. 50°2N 14°33E 135 B3
Horní Planá Czech Rep. 48°46N 14°2E 180 C7
Horní Počernice Czech Rep. 50°6N 14°36E 135 B3
Hornindal Norway 61°58N 6°30E 164 C3
Hornings Mills Canada 44°9N 80°12W 312 B4
Hornitos U.S.A. 37°30N 120°14W 306 H6
Hornopirén △ Chile 41°58S 72°17W 336 B2
Hornos, C. de Chile 55°50S 67°30W 336 E3
Hornos Is. Papua N. G. 2°12S 147°45E 286 B4
Hornoy-le-Bourg France 49°50N 1°54E 173 C8
Hornsby Australia 33°42S 151°2E 283 B9
Hornsea U.K. 53°55N 0°11W 168 D7
Hornsey U.K. 51°35N 0°7W 125 A3
Hornsjø Norway 61°19N 10°38E 164 C7
Hornslandet Sweden 61°35N 17°37E 162 C11
Hörnum Germany 54°45N 8°17E 178 A4
Horobetsu = Noboribetsu
Japan 42°24N 141°6E 220 C10
Horodenka Ukraine 48°41N 25°29E 183 B10
Horodnya Ukraine 51°55N 31°33E 189 G6
Horodok Khmelnytskyy,
Ukraine 49°10N 26°34E 177 D14
Horodok Lviv, Ukraine 49°46N 23°32E 177 D12
Horodyshche Ukraine 49°17N 31°27E 189 H6
Horokhiv Ukraine 50°30N 24°45E 177 C13
Horoměřice Czech Rep. 50°8N 14°20E 135 B1
Hořovice Czech Rep. 49°48N 13°53E 180 B6
Horqin Youyi Qianqi
China 46°5N 122°3E 227 A12
Horqin Zuoyi Zhongqi
China 44°8N 123°18E 227 B12
Horqueta Paraguay 23°15S 56°55W 334 A4
Horred Sweden 57°22N 12°28E 163 G6
Horse Cr. ➝ U.S.A. 41°57N 103°58W 304 F12
Horse I. Canada 53°20N 99°6W 297 C9
Horse Is. Canada 50°15N 55°50W 299 B8
Horsefly L. Canada 52°25N 121°0W 296 C4
Horseheads U.S.A. 42°10N 76°49W 312 D8
Horsens Denmark 55°52N 9°51E 163 J3
Horseshoe Bend △ U.S.A. 32°59N 85°44W 316 C4
Horseshoe Lake Canada 45°17N 79°51W 312 A5
Horsham Vic., Australia 36°44S 142°13E 282 D5
Horsham W. Susx., U.K. 51°4N 0°20W 169 F7
Horšovský Týn Czech Rep. 49°31N 12°58E 180 B5
Horta Azores 38°32N 28°38W 153 d1
Hortaleza Spain 40°28N 3°38W 127 B2
Horten Norway 59°25N 10°32E 164 E7
Hortense U.S.A. 31°20N 81°57W 316 D8
Horti India 17°7N 75°47E 244 F2
Hortobágy ➝ Hungary 47°30N 21°6E 182 C6
Hortobágyi △ Hungary 47°36N 21°10E 182 C6
Horton U.K. 51°29N 0°32W 125 B1
Horton Kans., U.S.A. 39°40N 95°32W 308 F6
Horton Mo., U.S.A. 37°58N 94°22W 310 G2
Horton ➝ Canada 69°56N 126°52W 294 D6
Hortus Botanicus Amsterdam, Neths. 112 b3
Horwood L. Canada 48°5N 82°20W 298 C3
Hosaina Ethiopia 7°30N 37°47E 257 F4
Hosapete = Hospet India 15°15N 76°20E 245 G3
Hosdrug = Kanhangad
India 12°21N 74°58E 245 H2
Hosdurga India 13°49N 76°17E 245 H3
Hosenofu Libya 23°41N 21°4E 258 D4
Ḩoseynābād Khuzestān,
Iran 32°45N 48°20E 247 C6
Ḩoseynābād Kordestān,
Iran 35°33N 47°8E 213 E12
Hosford U.S.A. 30°23N 84°48W 316 E5
Hôsh 'Îsa Egypt 30°55N 30°17E 256 H7
Hoshangabad India 22°45N 77°45E 242 H7
Hoshiarpur India 31°30N 75°58E 242 D6
Hoskins Papua N. G. 5°29S 150°27E 286 C6
Hoskote India 13°4N 77°48E 245 H3
Hosoyama Japan 35°36N 139°31E 140 B2
Hospet India 15°15N 76°20E 245 G3
Hossegor France 43°39N 1°25W 174 E2
Hostafrancs Spain 41°21N 2°8E 114 A1
Hoste, I. Chile 55°0S 69°0W 336 E3
Hostens France 44°30N 0°40W 174 D3
Hostivař Czech Rep. 50°3N 14°31E 135 B3
Hosur India 12°43N 77°49E 245 H3
Hot Thailand 18°8N 98°29E 236 C2
Hot Creek Range U.S.A. 38°40N 116°20W 304 G5
Hot Springs = Truth or
Consequences U.S.A. 33°8N 107°15W 305 K10
Hot Springs Ark., U.S.A. 34°31N 93°3W 314 D8
Hot Springs S. Dak.,
U.S.A. 43°26N 103°29W 308 D2
Hot Springs △ U.S.A. 34°31N 93°3W 314 D8
Hotagen Sweden 63°59N 14°12E 160 E16
Hotan China 37°25N 79°55E 217 E9
Hotan He ➝ China 40°22N 80°56E 217 D10
Hotazel S. Africa 27°17S 22°58E 270 C3
Hotchkiss U.S.A. 38°48N 107°43W 304 G10
Hôtel des Invalides Paris, France 134 c2
Hotham, C. Australia 12°2S 131°18E 278 B5
Hoting Sweden 64°8N 16°15E 160 D17
Hotolisht Albania 41°10N 20°25E 202 E4
Hotspur Seamount
Atl. Oc. 17°55S 35°55W 152 H8
Hotte, Massif de la Haiti 18°30N 73°45W 321 C5
Hottentotsbaai Namibia 26°8S 14°59E 270 C1
Hou Hai China 22°32N 113°56E 219 a
Houailou N. Cal. 21°17S 165°38E 288 d
Houat, Î. de France 47°24N 2°58W 172 E4
Houbětín Czech Rep. 50°6N 14°33E 135 B3
Houbi = Houpi Taiwan 23°22N 120°21E 225 C2
Houdan France 48°48N 1°35E 173 D8
Houei Sai Laos 20°18N 100°26E 228 G3
Houeillès France 44°12N 0°2E 174 D4
Houffalize Belgium 50°8N 5°48E 170 D5
Hougang Singapore 1°21N 103°53E 138 A3
Houghton Gauteng, S. Africa 26°10S 28°3E 123 B2
Houghton Mich., U.S.A. 47°7N 88°34W 308 B9
Houghton N.Y., U.S.A. 42°25N 78°10W 312 D6
Houghton L. U.S.A. 44°21N 84°44W 309 C11
Houghton-le-Spring U.K. 54°51N 1°28W 168 C6
Houhora Heads N.Z. 34°49S 173°9E 284 A2
Houilles France 48°56N 2°11E 134 A2
Houli Taiwan 24°19N 120°44E 225 B2
Houlton U.S.A. 46°8N 67°51W 309 B20
Houlung Taiwan 24°37N 120°47E 225 B2
Houma China 35°36N 111°20E 226 G6
Houma La., U.S.A. 29°36N 90°43W 315 G9
Houmt Souk = Djerba
Tunisia 33°48N 10°54E 258 B2
Houndé Burkina Faso 11°34N 3°31W 262 C4
Hounslow □ U.K. 51°28N 0°21W 125 B1
Houpi Taiwan 23°22N 120°21E 225 C2
Hourtin France 45°11N 1°4W 174 C2
Hourtin-Carcans, L. d'
France 45°10N 1°6W 174 C2
Housatonic ➝ U.S.A. 41°10N 73°7W 313 E11
House of Nobility = Riddarhuset
Stockholm, Sweden 139 c2
House of Parliament =
Riksdagshuset Stockholm, Sweden 139 b2
Houses of Parliament London, U.K. 125 c3
Houston B.C., Canada 54°25N 126°39W 296 C3
Houston Fla., U.S.A. 30°15N 82°54W 316 E7
Houston Mo., U.S.A. 37°22N 91°58W 308 G8
Houston Tex., U.S.A. 29°45N 95°21W 314 G7
Hout = Mogwadi ➝
S. Africa 23°4S 29°36E 271 B4
Hout Bay S. Africa 34°2S 18°23E 118 B1
Houtkraal S. Africa 30°23S 24°5E 270 D3
Houtman Abrolhos
Australia 28°43S 113°48E 279 E1
Hov Norway 60°42N 10°20E 164 D7
Hovd = Dund-Us
Mongolia 48°1N 91°38E 217 C12
Hovd □ Mongolia 48°2N 91°37E 217 C12
Hovda Norway 60°53N 9°11E 164 D6
Hovden Aust-Agder, Norway 59°33N 7°22E 164 E4
Hovden Sogn og Fjordane,
Norway 61°41N 4°52E 164 C1
Hove U.K. 50°50N 0°10W 169 G7
Hove Å ➝ Denmark 55°36N 12°23E 118 B2
Hovedøya Norway 59°53N 10°43E 133 A3
Hovedstaden □ Denmark 56°0N 10°0E 163 J6
Hovenweep △ U.S.A. 37°20N 109°0W 305 H9
Hovet Norway 60°38N 8°2E 164 D5
Hoveyzeh Iran 31°27N 48°4E 247 D6
Hovgaard Ø Greenland 79°55N 18°50W 154 B9
Høvik Norway 59°54N 10°34E 133 A2
Hovin Norway 59°51N 9°0E 164 E6
Hovmantorp Sweden 56°47N 15°7E 163 H9
Hovorčovice Czech Rep. 50°10N 14°31E 135 A3
Hövsgöl Mongolia 43°37N 109°39E 226 C5
Hövsgöl Nuur Mongolia 51°0N 100°30E 218 A9
Hovsta Sweden 59°22N 15°15E 162 E9
Howakil Eritrea 15°10N 40°16E 257 D5
Howar, Wadi ➝ Sudan 17°30N 27°8E 257 D2
Howard Queens., Australia 25°16S 152°32E 281 D5
Howard Pa., U.S.A. 41°1N 77°40W 312 F7
Howard S. Dak., U.S.A. 44°1N 97°32W 308 C5
Howard Beach U.S.A. 40°39N 73°50W 132 C2
Howe U.S.A. 43°48N 113°0W 304 E7
Howe, C. Australia 37°30S 150°0E 283 D9
Howe, West Cape
Australia 35°8S 117°36E 279 G2
Howe I. Canada 44°16N 76°17W 313 B8
Howell U.S.A. 42°36N 83°56W 311 B13
Howick Qué., Canada 45°11N 73°51W 313 A11
Howick N.Z. 36°54S 174°56E 284 C3
Howick KwaZulu Natal,
S. Africa 29°28S 30°14E 271 C5
Howick Group Australia 14°20S 145°30E 280 A4
Howitt, L. Australia 27°40S 138°40E 281 D2
Howland I. Pac. Oc. 0°48N 176°38W 288 G10
Howlong Australia 35°59S 146°38E 283 C7
Howrah = Haora India 22°34N 88°18E 124 B1
Howth Ireland 53°23N 6°7W 120 A3
Howth Hd. Ireland 53°22N 6°4W 120 A3
Höxter Germany 51°46N 9°22E 178 D5
Hoxtolgay China 46°35N 85°59E 217 C11
Hoxton London, U.K. 125 a5
Hoxud China 42°15N 86°51E 217 D11
Hoy U.K. 58°50N 3°15W 167 C5
Hoya Niedersachsen, Germany 52°49N 9°8E 178 C5
Hōya Tōkyō, Japan 35°44N 139°34E 140 A2
Høyanger Norway 61°13N 6°4E 164 C3
Hoyerswerda Germany 51°26N 14°14E 178 D10
Hoylake U.K. 53°24N 3°10W 168 D4
Hōyo-Kaikyō Japan 33°20N 131°58E 222 D3
Hoyos Spain 40°9N 6°45W 194 E4
Hpa-an = Pa-an Burma 16°51N 97°40E 241 G6
Hpawlum Burma 27°12N 98°12E 241 B7
Hpettintha Burma 24°14N 95°23E 241 C5
Hpizow Burma 26°57N 98°24E 241 B7
Hpunan Pass Asia 27°30N 96°55E 241 A6
Hpyu = Pyu Burma 18°30N 96°28E 241 F6
Hradčany Czech Rep. 50°5N 14°24E 135 B2
Hradec Králové Czech Rep. 50°15N 15°50E 180 A8
Hrádek Czech Rep. 48°46N 16°16E 181 C9
Hrafnseyri Iceland 65°46N 23°28W 155 B3
Hranice Czech Rep. 49°34N 17°45E 181 B10
Hrazdan Armenia 40°30N 44°46E 191 K7
Hrebenka Ukraine 50°9N 32°22E 189 G7
Hrífunes Iceland 63°38N 18°30W 155 D8
Hrísey Iceland 66°0N 18°23W 155 B8
Hrisoupoli = Chrisoupoli
Greece 40°58N 24°42E 203 F8
Hrodna Belarus 53°42N 23°52E 184 E10
Hrodna □ Belarus 53°20N 24°45E 188 F3
Hrodzyanka Belarus 53°31N 28°42E 177 B15
Hron ➝ Slovak Rep. 47°49N 18°45E 181 D11
Hrubieszów Poland 50°49N 23°51E 185 H10
Hrubý Jeseník Czech Rep. 50°5N 17°10E 181 A10
Hrvatska = Croatia ■
Europe 45°20N 16°0E 199 C13
Hrymayliv Ukraine 49°20N 26°5E 177 D14
Hrynyava Ukraine 47°59N 24°53E 183 C9
Hsa-paw Burma 19°1N 97°30E 241 F6
Hsenwi Burma 23°22N 97°55E 241 D6
Hsi-hkip Burma 20°25N 96°42E 241 E6
Hsiafu Taiwan 25°7N 121°17E 225 A3
Hsiamen = Xiamen
China 24°25N 118°4E 229 E12
Hsian = Xi'an China 34°15N 109°0E 226 G5
Hsiangshan Taiwan 24°48N 120°54E 225 B2
Hsiaochinmen Tao
Taiwan 24°26N 118°14E 225 a
Hsiaohungt'ou Hsü
Taiwan 21°57N 121°36E 225 E3
Hsiaokang Taiwan 22°34N 120°20E 225 D2
Hsiatahsi Taiwan 22°28N 120°56E 225 D2
Hsiaying Taiwan 23°14N 120°15E 225 C2
Hsichih Taiwan 25°4N 121°39E 225 A3
Hsikang Taiwan 23°7N 120°12E 225 C2
Hsilo Taiwan 23°48N 120°27E 225 C2
Hsinche Taiwan 24°10N 120°50E 225 B2
Hsinch'eng Taiwan 24°8N 121°39E 225 B3
Hsinchu Taiwan 24°48N 120°58E 225 B2
Hsinchu □ Taiwan 24°45N 121°10E 225 B3
Hsinchuang Kaohsiung,
Taiwan 22°34N 120°29E 225 D2
Hsinchuang T'aipei,
Taiwan 25°2N 121°27E 225 A3
Hsinfa Taiwan 23°8N 120°48E 225 C2
Hsinfeng Taiwan 24°54N 120°59E 225 B2
Hsinhailien = Lianyungang
China 34°40N 119°11E 227 G10
Hsinhua Taiwan 23°2N 120°18E 225 C2
Hsini Taiwan 23°41N 120°51E 225 C2
Hsinkai = Bhamo Burma 24°15N 97°15E 241 C6
Hsinking = Changchun
China 43°57N 125°17E 227 C13
Hsinpi Taiwan 22°28N 120°33E 225 D2
Hsinshih Taiwan 23°4N 120°17E 225 C2
Hsintien Taiwan 24°57N 121°32E 225 B3
Hsinwu Taiwan 24°59N 121°6E 225 B3
Hsinying Taiwan 23°18N 120°17E 225 C2
Hsinyuan Taiwan 22°32N 120°27E 225 D2
Hsipaw Burma 22°37N 97°18E 241 D6
Hsiukuluan Hsi ➝
Taiwan 23°28N 121°30E 225 C3
Hsiushui Taiwan 24°3N 120°30E 225 B2
Hsiyu Taiwan 23°36N 119°30E 225 C1
Hsopket Burma 23°11N 98°26E 228 F2
Hsüchou = Xuzhou
China 34°18N 117°10E 227 G9
Hsüeh Shan China 24°24N 121°12E 225 B3

Hsüehchia Taiwan 23°14N 120°10E 225 C2
Hsühaitsun Taiwan 22°12N 120°52E 225 D2
Htawei = Tavoy Burma 14°2N 98°12E 236 E2
Hu Xian China 34°8N 108°42E 226 G5
Hua Hin Thailand 12°34N 99°58E 236 F2
Hua Lamphong Railway Station Bangkok, Thailand 113 c2
Hua Muang Laos 20°13N 103°52E 236 B4
Hua Shan China 34°28N 110°4E 226 G6
Hua Xian Henan, China 35°30N 114°30E 226 G8
Hua Xian Shaanxi, China 34°30N 109°48E 226 G5
Hua Yü Taiwan 23°24N 119°19E 225 C1
Hua'an China 25°1N 117°32E 229 E11
Huab → Namibia 20°52S 13°25E 270 A2
Huacaya Bolivia 20°45S 63°43W 331 E5
Huachacalla Bolivia 18°45S 68°17W 330 D4
Huacheng China 24°4N 115°37E 229 E10
Huachinera Mexico 30°9N 108°55W 318 A3
Huacho Peru 11°10S 77°35W 330 C2
Huachón Peru 10°35S 76°0W 330 C2
Huade China 41°55N 113°59E 226 D7
Huadian China 43°0N 126°40E 227 C14
Huadu China 23°22N 113°12E 229 F9
Huahine, Î. French Polynesia 16°46S 150°58W 289 f
Huai Hat △ Thailand 16°52N 104°17E 236 D5
Huai He → China 33°0N 118°30E 229 A12
Huai Kha Khaeng ⌓ Thailand 15°20N 98°55E 236 E2
Huai Nam Dang △ Thailand 19°30N 98°30E 236 C2
Huai Yot Thailand 7°45N 99°37E 237 J2
Huai'an Hebei, China 40°30N 114°20E 226 D8
Huai'an Jiangsu, China 33°30N 119°10E 227 H10
Huaibei China 34°0N 116°48E 226 G9
Huaibin China 32°32N 115°27E 229 A10
Huaicho = Puerto Acosta Bolivia 15°32S 69°15W 330 D4
Huaide = Gongzhuling China 43°30N 124°40E 227 C13
Huaidezhen China 43°48N 124°50E 227 C13
Huaihua China 27°32N 109°57E 228 D7
Huaiji China 23°55N 112°12E 229 F9
Huainan China 32°38N 116°58E 229 A11
Huaining China 30°24N 116°40E 229 B11
Huairen China 39°48N 113°20E 226 E7
Huairou China 40°20N 116°35E 226 D9
Huaiyang China 33°40N 114°52E 226 H8
Huaiyin China 33°30N 119°2E 227 H10
Huaiyuan Anhui, China 32°55N 117°10E 229 A11
Huaiyuan Guangxi Zhuangzu, China 24°31N 108°22E 228 E7
Huajuapán de León Mexico 17°48N 97°46W 319 D5
Hualälai U.S.A. 19°42N 155°52W 302 D6
Hualapai Peak U.S.A. 35°5N 113°54W 307 K13
Hualien Taiwan 23°59N 121°36E 225 C3
Hualien □ Taiwan 23°45N 121°25E 225 C3
Huallaga → Peru 5°15S 75°30W 330 B2
Huallanca Peru 8°50S 77°56W 330 B2
Huamachuco Peru 7°50S 78°5W 330 B2
Huambo Angola 12°42S 15°54E 265 E3
Huambo □ Angola 13°0S 16°0E 265 E3
Huan Jiang → China 34°28N 109°0E 226 G5
Huan Xian China 36°33N 107°7E 226 F4
Huancabamba Peru 5°10S 79°15W 330 B2
Huancane Peru 15°10S 69°44W 330 D4
Huancapi Peru 13°40S 74°0W 330 C3
Huancavelica Peru 12°50S 75°5W 330 C2
Huancavelica □ Peru 13°0S 75°0W 330 C3
Huancayo Peru 12°5S 75°12W 330 C2
Huanchaca Bolivia 20°15S 66°40W 330 E4
Huanchaca, Serranía de Bolivia 14°30S 60°39W 331 C5
Huang Hai = Yellow Sea China 35°0N 123°0E 227 G12
Huang He → China 37°55N 118°50E 227 F10
Huang Xian China 37°38N 120°30E 227 F11
Huangchuan China 32°15N 115°10E 229 A10
Huangdao China 36°0N 120°7E 227 G11
Huanggang China 30°29N 114°52E 229 B10
Huangguoshu China 26°0N 105°40E 228 E5
Huanghua China 38°22N 117°20E 227 E9
Huanghuagang China 38°20N 117°54E 227 E9
Huanghuagang Mausoleum China 23°9N 113°17E 121 B2
Huangling China 35°34N 109°15E 226 G5
Huanglong China 35°30N 109°59E 226 G5
Huanglong ⌓ China 32°44N 103°50E 228 A4
Huanglongtan China 32°40N 110°33E 229 A8
Huangmei China 30°5N 115°56E 229 B10
Huangpi China 30°50N 114°22E 229 B10
Huangping China 26°52N 107°54E 228 D6
Huangpu China 31°14N 121°30E 138 B2
Huangpu Jiang → China 31°11N 121°29E 138 B1
Huangshan Anhui, China 30°8N 118°9E 229 B12
Huangshan Anhui, China 29°42N 118°25E 229 C12
Huangshi China 30°10N 115°3E 229 B10
Huangsongdian China 43°45N 127°25E 227 C14
Huangtugang China 39°49N 116°15E 114 C1
Huangyan China 28°38N 121°19E 229 C13
Huangyangsi China 26°33N 111°39E 229 D8
Huaning China 24°17N 102°56E 228 E4
Huanjiang China 24°50N 108°18E 228 E7
Huanren China 41°23N 125°20E 224 B2
Huanren Shuiku China 41°17N 125°34E 224 B2
Huanta Peru 12°55S 74°20W 330 C3
Huantai China 36°58N 117°56E 227 F9
Huánuco Peru 9°55S 76°15W 330 B2
Huánuco □ Peru 9°55S 76°14W 330 B2
Huanuni Bolivia 18°16S 66°51W 330 D4
Huanzo, Cordillera de Peru 14°35S 73°20W 330 C3
Huaping China 26°46N 101°25E 228 D3
Huara Chile 19°59S 69°47W 330 D4
Huaral Peru 11°32S 77°13W 330 C2
Huaraz Peru 9°30S 77°32W 330 B2
Huari Peru 9°14S 77°14W 330 B2
Huarmey Peru 10°5S 78°5W 330 C2
Huarochiri Peru 12°9S 76°15W 330 C2
Huarocondo Peru 13°26S 72°14W 330 C3
Huarong China 29°29N 112°30E 229 C9
Huascar Peru 11°59S 77°1W 124 A2
Huascarán, Nevado Peru 9°7S 77°37W 330 B2
Huasco Chile 28°30S 71°15W 334 B1
Huasco → Chile 28°27S 71°13W 334 B1
Huasna U.S.A. 35°6N 120°24W 307 K6
Huatabampo Mexico 26°50N 109°38W 318 B3
Huauchinango Mexico 20°12N 98°3W 319 C5
Huautla de Jiménez Mexico 18°8N 96°51W 319 D5
Huaxi China 26°25N 106°40E 228 D6
Huay Khwang Thailand 13°47N 100°33E 113 B2
Huayhuash, Cordillera Peru 10°30S 76°45W 330 B2
Huayin China 34°35N 110°5E 226 G6
Huaying China 30°8N 106°44E 228 B6
Huayllay Peru 11°3S 76°21W 330 C2
Huayuan China 28°37N 109°29E 228 C7
Huazhou China 21°33N 110°33E 229 G8
Hubballi = Hubli India 15°22N 75°15E 245 G2
Hubbard Iowa, U.S.A. 42°18N 93°18W 310 B3
Hubbard Ohio, U.S.A. 41°9N 80°34W 312 E4
Hubbard Tex., U.S.A. 31°51N 96°48W 314 F6
Hubbard, Mt. N. Amer. 60°19N 139°4W 303 F13
Hubbard Glacier Canada 60°18N 139°22W 294 E4
Hubbart Pt. Canada 59°21N 94°41W 297 B10
Hubei □ China 31°0N 112°0E 229 B9
Hubli India 15°22N 75°15E 245 G2
Huch'ang N. Korea 41°25N 127°2E 224 B3
Huchow = Huzhou China 30°51N 120°8E 229 B13
Hucknall U.K. 53°3N 1°13W 168 D6
Huddersfield U.K. 53°39N 1°47W 168 D6
Huddinge Sweden 59°14N 18°0E 139 B2
Hude Germany 53°7N 8°26E 178 B4
Hudi Sudan 17°43N 34°18E 256 D3
Hudiksvall Sweden 61°43N 17°10E 162 C11
Hudson Ont., Canada 50°6N 92°9W 298 B1
Hudson Fla., U.S.A. 28°22N 82°42W 317 G7
Hudson Mass., U.S.A. 42°23N 71°34W 313 D13
Hudson Mich., U.S.A. 41°51N 84°21W 311 C12
Hudson N.Y., U.S.A. 42°15N 73°46W 313 D11
Hudson Wis., U.S.A. 44°58N 92°45W 308 C7
Hudson Wyo., U.S.A. 42°54N 108°35W 304 E9
Hudson → U.S.A. 40°42N 74°2W 313 F10
Hudson, C. Antarctica 68°21S 153°45E 151 C10
Hudson, Vol. Chile 46°4S 72°55W 336 C2
Hudson Bay Nunavut, Canada 60°0N 86°0W 295 F14
Hudson Bay Sask., Canada 52°51N 102°23W 297 C8
Hudson Falls U.S.A. 43°18N 73°35W 313 C11
Hudson Mts. Antarctica 74°32S 99°20W 151 D16
Hudson River Park New York, U.S.A. 132 e1
Hudson Str. Canada 62°0N 70°0W 295 E18
Hudson's Hope Canada 56°0N 121°54W 296 B4
Hudsonville U.S.A. 42°52N 85°52W 311 B11
Hue Vietnam 16°30N 107°35E 236 D6
Huebra → Spain 41°2N 6°48W 194 D4
Huechuraba Chile 33°22S 70°39W 137 B1
Huedin Romania 46°52N 23°2E 182 D8
Huehuetenango Guatemala 15°20N 91°28W 320 C1
Huejúcar Mexico 22°21N 103°13W 318 C4
Huélamo Spain 40°17N 1°48W 196 E3
Huelgoat France 48°22N 3°46W 172 D3
Huelma Spain 37°39N 3°28W 195 H7
Huelva Spain 37°18N 6°57W 195 H4
Huelva □ Spain 37°40N 7°0W 195 H4
Huelva → Spain 37°27N 6°0W 195 H5
Hueneme = Port Hueneme U.S.A. 34°7N 119°12W 307 L7
Huentelauquén Chile 31°38S 71°33W 334 C1
Huércal-Overa Spain 37°23N 1°57W 197 H3
Huerquehue △ Chile 39°6S 71°42W 336 A2
Huerta, Sa. de la Argentina 31°10S 67°30W 334 C2
Huertas, C. de las Spain 38°21N 0°24W 197 G4
Huerva → Spain 41°39N 0°52W 196 D4
Huesca Spain 42°8N 0°25W 196 C4
Huesca □ Spain 42°20N 0°1E 196 C5
Huéscar Spain 37°44N 2°35W 197 H2
Hueso Ballena, Pta. Chile 33°40S 78°46W 330 c
Huetamo Mexico 18°35N 100°53W 318 D4
Huete Spain 40°10N 2°43W 196 E2
Huevos I. Trin. & Tob. 10°42N 61°43W 323 t
Huger U.S.A. 33°6N 79°48W 316 B10
Hugh → Australia 25°1S 134°1E 280 D1
Hugh Taylor Birch State Recr. Area ⌓ U.S.A. 26°8N 80°6W 129 B3
Hughenden Australia 20°52S 144°10E 280 C3
Hughes U.S.A. 66°3N 154°15W 303 C9
Hughesville U.S.A. 41°14N 76°44W 313 E8
Hugli → India 21°56N 88°4E 243 J13
Hugo Colo., U.S.A. 39°8N 103°28W 304 G12
Hugo Okla., U.S.A. 34°1N 95°31W 314 D7
Hugoton U.S.A. 37°11N 101°21W 308 G3
Huguang Opera Museum Beijing, China 114 c2
Huhehaote = Hohhot China 40°52N 111°40E 226 D6
Huhsi Taiwan 23°35N 119°39E 225 C1
Hui Xian = Huixian China 35°27N 113°12E 226 G7
Hui Xian China 33°50N 106°4E 226 H4
Hui'an China 25°1N 118°43E 229 E12
Hui'anbu China 37°28N 106°38E 226 F4
Huiarau Ra. N.Z. 38°45S 176°55E 284 E5
Huichang China 25°32N 115°45E 229 E10
Huichapan Mexico 20°23N 99°39W 319 C5
Huichon N. Korea 40°10N 126°16E 224 B3
Huidong Guangdong, China 22°58N 114°43E 229 F10
Huidong Sichuan, China 26°34N 102°35E 228 D4
Huifa He → China 43°0N 127°50E 227 C14
Huíla Angola 15°4S 13°32E 265 F2
Huíla □ Angola 14°0S 15°0E 265 E2
Huila □ Colombia 2°30N 75°45W 328 C2
Huila, Nevado del Colombia 3°0N 76°0W 328 C2
Huilai China 23°0N 116°18E 229 F11
Huili China 26°35N 102°17E 228 D4
Huimin China 37°27N 117°28E 227 F9
Huinan China 42°40N 126°2E 224 A3
Huinca Renancó Argentina 34°51S 64°22W 334 C3
Huining China 35°38N 105°0E 226 G3
Huinong China 39°5N 106°35E 226 E4
Huiroa N.Z. 39°15S 174°30E 284 F3
Huishui China 26°7N 106°38E 228 D6
Huisne → France 47°59N 0°11E 172 E7
Huiting China 34°5N 116°5E 226 G9
Huitong China 26°51N 109°45E 228 D7
Huixian China 35°27N 113°12E 226 G7
Huixtla Mexico 15°9N 92°28W 319 D6
Huize China 26°24N 103°15E 228 D4
Huizhou China 23°0N 114°23E 229 F10
Huizingen Belgium 50°45N 4°17E 116 B1
Hukawng Valley Burma 26°30N 96°30E 241 B6
Hukeri India 16°14N 74°36E 245 F2
Hukou Jiangxi, China 29°45N 116°21E 229 C11
Huk'ou Taiwan 24°54N 121°2E 225 B3
Hukuntsi Botswana 23°58S 21°45E 270 B3
Hula Papua N. G. 10°5S 147°43E 286 F4
Ḩulayfā' Si. Arabia 25°58N 40°45E 246 E4
Huld = Ulaanjirem Mongolia 45°5N 105°30E 226 B3
Hulin China 45°48N 132°59E 219 B15
Hulin He → China 45°0N 122°10E 227 B12
Hull = Kingston upon Hull U.K. 53°45N 0°21W 168 D7
Hull Canada 45°26N 75°43W 313 A9
Hull → U.K. 53°44N 0°20W 168 D7
Hulst Neths. 51°17N 4°2E 170 C4
Hultschin = Hlučín Czech Rep. 49°54N 18°11E 181 B11
Hultsfred Sweden 57°30N 15°52E 163 G9
Huludao China 40°45N 120°50E 227 D11
Hulun = Hailar China 49°10N 119°38E 219 B12
Hulun Nur China 49°0N 117°30E 219 B12
Hulunbuir = Hailar China 49°10N 119°38E 219 B12
Hulyaypole Ukraine 47°45N 36°21E 189 J9
Huma, Tanjung Malaysia 5°29N 100°16E 237 c
Humacao Puerto Rico 18°9N 65°50W 321 b
Humahuaca Argentina 23°10S 65°25W 334 A2
Humaitá = Porto Walter Brazil 8°15S 72°40W 330 B3
Humaitá Brazil 7°35S 63°1W 331 B5
Humaitá Paraguay 27°2S 58°31W 334 B4
Humansdorp S. Africa 34°2S 24°46E 270 D3
Humansville U.S.A. 37°48N 93°35W 310 G3
Humara, J. Sudan 16°16N 30°59E 257 D3
Humayun's Tomb India 28°35N 77°15E 120 B2
Humbe Angola 16°40S 14°55E 265 F2
Humbe, Serra do Angola 12°10S 15°25E 265 E2
Humber → Ont., Canada 43°47N 79°38W 141 A1
Humber → England, U.K. 53°42N 0°27W 168 D7
Humber B. Canada 43°37N 79°27W 141 B2
Humber Bay Canada 43°38N 79°29W 141 B2
Humber Bay Park Canada 43°37N 79°28W 141 B2
Humber College Canada 43°35N 79°30W 141 B1
Humber Summit Canada 43°45N 79°32W 141 A1
Humber Valley Village Canada 43°40N 79°31W 141 A1
Humberlea Canada 43°43N 79°31W 141 A1
Humberwood Park Canada 43°44N 79°37W 141 A1
Humboldt Sask., Canada 52°15N 105°9W 297 C7
Humboldt Iowa, U.S.A. 42°44N 94°13W 310 B2
Humboldt Tenn., U.S.A. 35°50N 88°55W 315 D10
Humboldt → U.S.A. 39°59N 118°36W 304 G4
Humboldt Gletscher = Sermersuaq Greenland 79°30N 62°0W 154 B4
Humboldt Mts. N.Z. 44°30S 168°15E 285 E3
Humboldt Park U.S.A. 41°54N 87°42W 119 B2
Humbolt, Mt. N. Cal. 21°53S 166°25E 288 d
Hume U.S.A. 36°48N 118°54W 306 J8
Hume, L. Australia 36°0S 147°5E 283 D7
Humen China 22°50N 113°40E 219 a
Humenné Slovak Rep. 48°55N 21°50E 181 C14
Humera Spain 40°25N 3°46W 127 B1
Humeston U.S.A. 40°52N 93°30W 310 D3
Hummelsta Sweden 59°34N 16°58E 162 E10
Hummelvika Norway 63°29N 8°19E 164 A5
Hummingbird Centre Toronto, Canada 141 b3
Hummock Hill = Whyalla Australia 33°2S 137°30E 282 B2
Humpata Angola 15°2S 13°24E 265 F2
Humphreys, Mt. U.S.A. 37°17N 118°40W 306 H8
Humphreys Peak U.S.A. 35°21N 111°41W 305 J8
Humpolec Czech Rep. 49°31N 15°20E 180 B8
Humptulips U.S.A. 47°14N 123°57W 306 C3
Humula Australia 35°30S 147°46E 283 C7
Hūn Libya 29°2N 16°0E 258 C3
Hun He → China 40°41N 122°8E 224 B1
Hun Jiang → China 40°50N 125°38E 227 D13
Húnaflói Iceland 65°50N 20°50W 155 B6
Hunan □ China 27°30N 112°0E 229 D9
Húnavatnssýsla Iceland 65°30N 20°25W 155 B6
Hunaydī Iraq 33°18N 44°29E 113 B2
Hunchun China 42°52N 130°28E 227 C16
Hundested Denmark 55°58N 11°52E 163 J5
Hundewali Pakistan 31°55N 72°38E 242 D5
Hundige Denmark 55°35N 12°18E 118 B1
Hundige Strand Denmark 55°35N 12°20E 118 B2
Hundorp Norway 61°33N 9°59E 164 C7
Hundred Islands △ Phil. 16°10N 120°2E 232 C3
Hundred Mile House Canada 51°38N 121°18W 296 C4
Hundvåg Norway 59°0N 5°43E 164 E2
Hunedoara Romania 45°40N 22°50E 182 E7
Hunedoara □ Romania 45°50N 22°54E 182 E7
Hunei Taiwan 22°53N 120°14E 225 D2
Hünfeld Germany 50°39N 9°46E 178 E5
Hung Hom Hong Kong, China 22°18N 114°11E 122 B3
Hung Yen Vietnam 20°39N 106°4E 228 G6
Hunga Ha'apai Tonga 20°41S 175°7W 287 Q13
Hungary ■ Europe 47°20N 19°20E 181 D12
Hungary, Plain of Europe 47°0N 20°0E 158 F10
Hungerford Australia 28°58S 144°24E 281 D3
Hŭngnam N. Korea 39°49N 127°45E 224 C3
Hungt'ou Hsü = Lan Yü Taiwan 22°4N 121°25E 225 D3
Huni Valley Ghana 5°33N 1°56W 262 D4
Hunjiang China 41°54N 126°26E 224 B3
Hunneberg Sweden 58°18N 12°30E 163 F6
Hunnebostrand Sweden 58°27N 11°18E 163 F5
Hunsberge Namibia 27°45S 17°12E 270 C2
Hunsrück Germany 49°56N 7°27E 179 F3
Hunstanton U.K. 52°56N 0°29E 168 E8
Hunsur India 12°16N 76°16E 245 H3
Hunte → Germany 53°14N 8°28E 178 B4
Hunter N.Z. 44°36S 171°2E 285 E6
Hunter N.Y., U.S.A. 42°13N 74°13W 313 D10
Hunter → N.S.W., Australia 32°52S 151°46E 283 B9
Hunter → N.Z. 44°21S 169°27E 285 E4
Hunter, C. Solomon Is. 9°48S 159°50E 287 M10
Hunter Hills, The N.Z. 44°26S 170°46E 285 E5
Hunter I. Tas., Australia 40°30S 144°45E 281 G3
Hunter I. B.C., Canada 51°55N 128°0W 296 C3
Hunter Mts. N.Z. 45°43S 167°25E 285 F2
Hunter Ra. Australia 32°45S 150°15E 283 B9
Hunters Hill Australia 33°50S 151°9E 139 B1
Hunters Pt. U.S.A. 37°43N 122°21W 136 B2
Hunters Road Zimbabwe 19°9S 29°49E 269 F2
Hunterville N.Z. 39°56S 175°35E 284 F4
Huntingburg U.S.A. 38°18N 86°57W 311 F10
Huntingdon Cambs., U.K. 52°20N 0°11W 169 E7
Huntingdon Pa., U.S.A. 40°30N 78°1W 312 F6
Huntington = Shelton U.S.A. 41°19N 73°5W 313 E11
Huntington Ind., U.S.A. 40°53N 85°30W 311 D11
Huntington N.Y., U.S.A. 40°52N 73°26W 313 F11
Huntington Oreg., U.S.A. 44°21N 117°16W 304 D5
Huntington Utah, U.S.A. 39°20N 110°58W 304 G8
Huntington Va., U.S.A. 38°47N 77°4W 143 C2
Huntington W. Va., U.S.A. 38°25N 82°27W 309 F12
Huntington Beach U.S.A. 33°40N 118°5W 307 M9
Huntington Park U.S.A. 33°58N 118°13W 126 C3
Huntley Jamaica 18°4N 77°35W 320 a
Huntley Ill., U.S.A. 42°10N 88°26W 311 B8
Huntly N.Z. 37°34S 175°11E 284 D4
Huntly Aberds., U.K. 57°27N 2°47W 167 D6
Huntsville Ont., Canada 45°20N 79°14W 312 A5
Huntsville Ala., U.S.A. 34°44N 86°35W 315 D11
Huntsville Mo., U.S.A. 39°26N 92°33W 310 E4
Huntsville Tex., U.S.A. 30°43N 95°33W 314 F7
Hunyani → Zimbabwe 15°57S 30°39E 269 F3
Hunyuan China 39°42N 113°42E 226 E7
Hunza → India 35°54N 74°20E 243 B6
Huo Shan China 36°26N 111°52E 226 F6
Huo Xian = Huozhou China 36°36N 111°42E 226 F6
Huocheng China 44°0N 80°48E 217 D10
Huolin Gol China 45°32N 119°38E 227 B10
Huon G. Papua N. G. 7°0S 147°30E 286 D4
Huon Pen. Papua N. G. 6°20S 147°30E 286 D4
Huong Khe Vietnam 18°13N 105°41E 236 C5
Huonville Australia 43°0S 147°5E 281 G4
Huoqiu China 32°20N 116°12E 229 A11
Huoshan China 31°25N 116°20E 229 B11
Huoshao Dao = Lütao Taiwan 22°40N 121°30E 225 D3
Huozhou China 36°36N 111°42E 226 F6
Hupeh = Hubei □ China 31°0N 112°0E 229 B9
Ḩūr Iran 30°50N 57°7E 247 D8
Hurānd Iran 38°51N 47°22E 213 C12
Ḩuraymīla Si. Arabia 25°8N 46°8E 246 E5
Hurbanovo Slovak Rep. 47°51N 18°11E 181 D11
Hurd, C. Canada 45°13N 81°44W 312 A3
Hurdiyo Somalia 10°33N 51°6E 267 B7
Hure Qi China 42°45N 121°45E 227 C11
Hurezani Romania 44°49N 23°40E 183 F8
Hurghada Egypt 27°15N 33°50E 256 B3
Hurīya Iraq 33°21N 44°19E 113 A1
Hurley N. Mex., U.S.A. 32°42N 108°8W 305 K9
Hurley Wis., U.S.A. 46°27N 90°11W 308 B8
Huron Calif., U.S.A. 36°12N 120°6W 306 J6
Huron Ohio, U.S.A. 41°24N 82°33W 312 E2
Huron S. Dak., U.S.A. 44°22N 98°13W 308 C4
Huron, L. U.S.A. 44°30N 82°40W 312 B2
Huron East Canada 43°37N 81°18W 312 C3
Hurricane U.S.A. 37°11N 113°17W 305 H7
Hurso Ethiopia 9°35N 41°33E 257 F5
Hurstville Australia 33°57S 151°6E 139 B1
Hurtsboro U.S.A. 32°15N 85°25W 316 C4
Hurungwe ⌓ Zimbabwe 16°7S 29°5E 269 F2
Hurunui → N.Z. 42°54S 173°18E 285 C8
Hurup Denmark 56°46N 8°25E 163 H2
Húsafell Iceland 64°42N 20°53W 155 C6
Husan West Bank 31°42N 35°8E 123 B1
Húsavík Iceland 66°3N 17°21W 155 A9
Husby Sweden 59°24N 17°56E 139 A1
Huşi Romania 46°41N 28°7E 183 D13
Huskisson Australia 35°2S 150°41E 283 C9
Huskvarna Sweden 57°47N 14°15E 163 G8
Huslia U.S.A. 65°41N 156°24W 303 D8
Husnes Norway 59°52N 5°45E 164 E2
Hustad Norway 62°57N 7°6E 164 B4
Hustadvika Norway 63°0N 7°0E 164 A3
Hustontown U.S.A. 40°3N 78°2W 312 F6
Hustopeče Czech Rep. 48°57N 16°43E 181 C9
Husum København, Denmark 55°42N 12°27E 118 A2
Husum Schleswig-Holstein, Germany 54°28N 9°4E 178 A5
Husum Sweden 63°21N 19°12E 162 A13
Huszt = Khust Ukraine 48°10N 23°18E 183 B8
Hutanopan Indonesia 0°40N 99°42E 234 B1
Hutchinson Kans., U.S.A. 38°5N 97°56W 308 F5
Hutchinson Minn., U.S.A. 44°54N 94°22W 308 C6
Ḩūth Yemen 16°14N 43°58E 248 C3
Hutiao Xia China 27°13N 100°9E 228 D3
Hutjena Papua N. G. 5°23S 154°42E 286 C8
Hutsonville U.S.A. 39°7N 87°40W 311 E9
Hutte Sauvage, L. de la Canada 56°15N 64°45W 299 A7
Hütteldorf Austria 48°12N 16°15E 142 A1
Hüttenberg Austria 46°56N 14°33E 180 E7
Hüttener Berge ⌓ Germany 54°24N 9°40E 178 A5
Hutton, Mt. Australia 25°51S 148°20E 281 D4
Huvadu Atoll Maldives 0°30N 73°15E 272 d
Hüvösvölgy Hungary 47°32N 19°0E 117 A2
Huwaki Indonesia 7°55S 126°30E 231 F7
Huwei Taiwan 23°42N 120°26E 225 C2
Huwei Hsi → Taiwan 23°37N 120°22E 225 C2
Huwon Secret Garden S. Korea 37°34N 126°59E 137 B1
Huwun Ethiopia 4°23N 40°6E 257 G5
Huy Belgium 50°31N 5°15E 170 D5
Huzhou China 30°51N 120°8E 229 B13
Huzurabad India 18°12N 79°25E 244 E4
Huzurnagar India 16°54N 79°53E 244 F4
Hvalfjörður Iceland 64°20N 21°40W 155 C5
Hvalpsund Denmark 56°42N 9°11E 163 H3
Hvalstad Norway 59°51N 10°27E 133 A1
Hvalstrand Norway 59°50N 10°30E 133 A2
Hvammsfjörður Iceland 65°4N 22°5W 155 B4
Hvammstangi Iceland 65°24N 20°57W 155 B6
Hvammur Norðurland Vestra, Iceland 65°53N 19°51W 155 B7
Hvammur Vesturland, Iceland 64°50N 21°21W 155 C5
Hvannadalshnúkur Iceland 64°1N 16°41W 155 C10
Hvanneyri Iceland 64°34N 21°36W 155 C5
Hvar Croatia 43°11N 16°28E 199 E13
Hvarski Kanal Croatia 43°15N 16°35E 199 E13
Hveragerði Iceland 64°0N 21°12W 155 C5
Hvidovre Denmark 55°38N 12°27E 118 B2
Hvítá → Iceland 64°30N 21°58W 155 C5
Hvítárvatn Iceland 64°37N 19°50W 155 C7
Hvittingfoss Norway 59°29N 10°0E 164 E7
Hvizdets Ukraine 48°35N 25°17E 183 B10
Hvolsvöllur Iceland 63°45N 20°14W 155 D6
Hwacheon-Cheosuji S. Korea 38°5N 127°50E 224 C3
Hwagok S. Korea 37°32N 126°51E 137 B1
Hwainan = Huainan China 32°38N 116°58E 229 A11
Hwaiyin = Huaiyin China 33°30N 119°2E 227 H10
Hwang Ho = Huang He → China 37°55N 118°50E 227 F10
Hwange Zimbabwe 18°18S 26°30E 269 F2
Hwange △ Zimbabwe 19°0S 26°30E 270 A4
Hwanghaebuk-do □ N. Korea 38°30N 126°25E 224 C3
Hwanghaenam-do □ N. Korea 38°15N 125°30E 224 C2
Hwangju N. Korea 38°40N 125°46E 224 C2
Hwangshih = Huangshi China 30°10N 115°3E 229 B10
Hwaseong S. Korea 37°12N 126°48E 224 D3
Hwasun S. Korea 35°3N 126°59E 224 E3
Hwekum Burma 26°7N 95°22E 241 B5
Hwlffordd = Haverfordwest U.K. 51°48N 4°58W 169 F3
Hyaing Burma 22°39N 94°44E 241 D5
Hyannis Mass., U.S.A. 41°39N 70°17W 309 E18
Hyannis Nebr., U.S.A. 42°0N 101°46W 308 E3
Hyargas Nuur Mongolia 49°0N 93°0E 217 C12
Hyattsville U.S.A. 38°57N 76°57W 143 B3
Hybo Sweden 61°49N 16°15E 162 C10
Hydaburg U.S.A. 55°15N 132°50W 296 B2
Hyde N.Z. 45°18S 170°16E 285 F5
Hyde Park Sydney, Australia 139 b2
Hyde Park Guyana 6°30N 58°16W 329 B6
Hyde Park Gauteng, S. Africa 26°6S 28°2E 123 A2
Hyde Park London, U.K. 51°30N 0°10W 125 A2
Hyde Park Calif., U.S.A. 33°58N 118°19W 126 C3
Hyde Park Ill., U.S.A. 41°47N 87°35W 119 C3
Hyde Park Mass., U.S.A. 42°15N 71°7W 116 B2
Hyde Park N.Y., U.S.A. 41°47N 73°56W 313 E11
Hyden Australia 32°24S 118°53E 279 F2
Hyder U.S.A. 55°55N 130°5W 296 B2
Hyderabad India 17°22N 78°29E 244 F4
Hyderabad Pakistan 25°23N 68°24E 242 G3
Hydra Greece 37°20N 23°28E 204 D5
Hyen Norway 61°44N 5°56E 164 C2
Hyères France 43°8N 6°9E 175 E10
Hyères, Îs. d' France 43°0N 6°20E 175 F10
Hyesan N. Korea 41°20N 128°10E 224 B4
Hyland → Canada 59°52N 128°12W 296 B3
Hylestad Norway 59°6N 7°29E 164 E4
Hyllestad Norway 61°10N 5°17E 164 C2
Hyltebruk Sweden 56°59N 13°15E 163 H7
Hyndman Peak U.S.A. 43°45N 114°8W 304 E6
Hynnekleiv Norway 58°36N 8°25E 164 F5
Hyōgo □ Japan 35°15N 134°50E 222 B6
Hyrra Banda C.A.R. 5°58N 22°1E 264 A4
Hyrum U.S.A. 41°38N 111°51W 304 F8
Hysham U.S.A. 46°18N 107°14W 304 C10
Hythe U.K. 51°4N 1°5E 169 F9
Hyūga Japan 32°25N 131°35E 222 E3
Hyvinge = Hyvinkää Finland 60°38N 24°50E 188 B3
Hyvinkää Finland 60°38N 24°50E 188 B3


# I


I-n-Akhmed Mali 19°49N 0°56W 261 E4
I-n-Azaoua Illizi, Algeria 25°42N 6°54E 261 C6
I-n-Azaoua Tamanrasset, Algeria 20°46N 7°32E 261 D6
I-n-Échaï Mali 20°10N 2°5W 260 D4
I-n-Ezzane Algeria 23°29N 11°15E 261 D7
I-n-Gall Niger 16°51N 7°1E 263 B6
I-n-Kelemet Algeria 26°57N 5°47E 261 C6
I-n-Oudad Algeria 20°17N 4°38E 261 D5
I-n-Ouzzal Algeria 20°41N 2°34E 261 D5
I-n-Tadreft Niger 19°5N 6°38E 263 B6
Iabès, Erg Algeria 27°30N 2°2W 261 C4
Iablaniţa Romania 44°57N 22°19E 182 F7
Iaco → Brazil 9°3S 68°34W 330 B4
Iacobeni Romania 47°25N 25°20E 183 C10
Iaçu Brazil 12°45S 40°13W 333 D3
Iakora Madag. 23°6S 46°40E 272 C2
Ialibu Papua N. G. 6°17S 143°59E 286 D2
Ialissos Greece 36°24N 28°10E 206 E12
Ialomiţa □ Romania 44°30N 27°30E 183 F12
Ialomiţa → Romania 44°42N 27°51E 183 F12
Ialoveni Moldova 46°56N 28°47E 183 D13
Ialpug → Moldova 45°41N 28°35E 183 E13
Iamonia L. U.S.A. 30°38N 84°14W 316 E5
Ianca Romania 45°6N 27°29E 183 E12
Iara Romania 46°31N 23°35E 183 D8
Iarda Ethiopia 11°9N 35°53E 257 E4
Iargara Moldova 46°24N 28°23E 183 D13
Iaşi Romania 47°10N 27°40E 183 C12
Iaşi □ Romania 47°20N 27°0E 183 C12
Iasmos Greece 41°8N 25°11E 203 E9
Iauaretê Colombia 0°36N 69°12W 328 C4
Ib → India 21°34N 83°48E 243 J10
Iba Phil. 15°22N 120°0E 232 D2
Ibadan Nigeria 7°22N 3°58E 263 D5
Ibagué Colombia 4°20N 75°20W 328 C2
Ibaiti Brazil 23°50S 50°10W 333 F1
Ibajay Phil. 11°49N 122°10E 233 F4
Iballë Albania 42°12N 20°2E 202 D4
Ibăneşti Botoşani, Romania 48°4N 26°22E 183 B11
Ibăneşti Mureş, Romania 46°45N 24°57E 183 D9
Ibanshe Dem. Rep. of the Congo 4°58S 21°30E 265 C4
Ibar → Serbia 43°43N 20°45E 202 C4
Ibara Japan 34°36N 133°28E 222 C5
Ibaraki Ibaraki, Japan 36°20N 140°30E 223 A12
Ibaraki Ōsaka, Japan 34°49N 135°34E 223 C7
Ibaraki □ Japan 36°10N 140°10E 223 A12
Ibarra Ecuador 0°21N 78°7W 328 C2
Ibb Yemen 14°2N 44°10E 248 D4
Ibb □ Yemen 14°2N 44°10E 248 D4
Ibba South Sudan 4°49N 29°2E 257 G2
Ibba, Bahr el → South Sudan 5°30N 28°55E 257 F2
Ibbenbüren Germany 52°16N 7°43E 178 C3
Ibeke Gembo Dem. Rep. of the Congo 1°24S 18°51E 264 C3
Ibembo Dem. Rep. of the Congo 2°35N 23°35E 264 B4
Ibenga → Congo 2°19N 18°9E 264 B3
Ibera, L. Argentina 28°30S 57°9W 334 B4
Iberia Peru 11°21S 69°35W 330 C4
Iberia Mo., U.S.A. 38°5N 92°18W 310 F4
Iberian Peninsula Europe 40°0N 5°0W 158 H5
Iberville Canada 45°19N 73°17W 313 A11
Iberville, Mt. d' Canada 58°50N 63°50W 295 F19
Ibese Nigeria 6°33N 3°28E 124 A2
Ibeto Nigeria 10°29N 5°8E 263 C6
Ibi Nigeria 8°15N 9°44E 263 D6
Ibi Spain 38°38N 0°34W 197 G4
Ibiá Brazil 19°30S 46°30W 333 E2
Ibiapaba, Sa. da Brazil 4°0S 41°30W 332 B3
Ibicaraí Brazil 14°51S 39°36W 333 D4
Ibicuí Brazil 14°51S 39°59W 333 D4
Ibicuí → Brazil 29°25S 56°47W 335 B4
Ibicuy Argentina 33°55S 59°10W 334 C4
Ibirapuera Brazil 23°36S 46°40W 137 B1
Ibirapuera, Parque do Brazil 23°35S 46°38W 137 B2
Ibitiara Brazil 12°39S 42°13W 333 D3
Ibiza = Eivissa Spain 38°54N 1°26E 206 D1
Ibiza ✕ (IBZ) Spain 38°53N 1°22E 197 G6
Íblei, Monti Italy 37°15N 14°45E 201 E7
Ibn Hānī', Ra's Syria 35°35N 35°43E 250 C6
Ibo Mozam. 12°22S 40°40E 269 E5
Ibonma Indonesia 3°29S 133°31E 231 E8
Ibotirama Brazil 12°13S 43°12W 333 D3
Iboundji Gabon 1°0S 11°51E 264 C2
Ibrā' Oman 22°41N 58°33E 249 B7
İbradı Turkey 37°4N 31°35E 250 A2
Ibrāhīm → Lebanon 34°4N 35°38E 250 D6
'Ibrī Oman 23°14N 56°30E 249 B7
İbriktepe Turkey 41°0N 26°30E 203 E10
Ibshawâi Egypt 29°21N 30°40E 256 J7
Ibu Indonesia 1°35N 127°33E 231 D7
Ibuki-Sanchi Japan 35°25N 136°18E 223 B8
Ibusuki Japan 31°12N 130°40E 222 F2
Ica Peru 14°0S 75°48W 330 C2
Ica □ Peru 14°20S 75°30W 330 C2
Iça → Brazil 2°55S 67°58W 330 A4
Icabarú Venezuela 4°20N 61°45W 329 C5
Icabarú → Venezuela 4°45N 62°15W 329 C5
Icacos Trin. & Tob. 10°3N 61°54W 323 t
Icacos Pt. Trin. & Tob. 10°3N 61°57W 323 t
Içana Brazil 0°21N 67°19W 328 C4
Içana → Brazil 0°26N 67°19W 328 C4
Icarai Brazil 22°54S 43°6W 135 B2
Icatu Brazil 2°46S 44°4W 332 B3
Icaturama = Santa Rosa de Viterbo Colombia 5°53N 72°59W 328 B3
İçel Turkey 36°51N 34°36E 250 B5
İcel □ Turkey 36°45N 34°0E 250 B5
Iceland ■ Europe 64°45N 19°0W 155 C8
Iceland Basin Atl. Oc. 61°0N 19°0W 150 C7
Icelandic Plateau Arctic 64°0N 10°0W 150 C7
Içerenköy Turkey 40°58N 29°6E 122 C2
İçeriçumra Turkey 37°34N 32°39E 212 D5
Ichalkaranji India 16°40N 74°33E 244 F2
Ich'ang = Yichang China 30°40N 111°20E 229 B8
Ichchapuram India 19°10N 84°40E 244 E7
Icheon S. Korea 37°17N 127°27E 224 D3
Ichgao Japan 35°32N 139°32E 140 B2
Ichhawar India 23°1N 77°1E 242 H7
Ichigat Muja-Cordillera del Condor ⌓ Peru 4°20S 77°30W 330 A2
Ichigaya Tokyo, Japan 140 a3
Ichihara Japan 35°28N 140°5E 223 B12
Ichikawa Japan 35°43N 139°54E 140 A4
Ichilo → Bolivia 15°57S 64°50W 331 D5
Ichinohe Japan 40°13N 141°17E 220 D10
Ichinomiya Gifu, Japan 35°18N 136°48E 223 B8
Ichinomiya Kumamoto, Japan 32°58N 131°5E 222 E3
Ichinoseki Japan 38°55N 141°8E 220 E10
Ichkeul △ Tunisia 37°5N 9°37E 258 A1
Ichnya Ukraine 50°52N 32°24E 189 G7
Icht Morocco 29°6N 8°54W 260 C3
Ichu Taiwan 23°20N 120°14E 225 C2
Ichun = Yichun China 47°44N 128°52E 219 B14
Ickenham U.K. 51°33N 0°26W 125 A1
Icó Brazil 6°24S 38°51W 332 C4
Icoca Angola 6°12S 16°20E 265 D3
Icod Canary Is. 28°22N 16°43W 153 e1
Içoguz Turkmenistan 40°11N 58°24E 216 D5
Iconi Comoros Is. 12°21S 43°51E 272 a
Icy C. U.S.A. 70°20N 161°52W 303 A7
Ida Grove U.S.A. 42°21N 95°28W 308 D6
Idaan Somalia 6°10N 48°55E 267 C6
Idabel U.S.A. 33°54N 94°50W 314 E7
Idaga Hamus Ethiopia 14°13N 39°48E 257 E4
Idah Nigeria 7°5N 6°40E 263 D6
Idaho □ U.S.A. 45°0N 115°0W 304 D6
Idaho City U.S.A. 43°50N 115°50W 304 E6
Idaho Falls U.S.A. 43°30N 112°2W 304 E7
Idalia △ Australia 24°49S 144°36E 280 C3
Idanha-a-Nova Portugal 39°50N 7°15W 194 F3
Idar-Oberstein Germany 49°43N 7°16E 179 F3
Iday Niger 14°54N 11°33E 259 F2
'Idd el Ghanam Sudan 11°30N 24°19E 259 F4
Iddo Nigeria 6°28N 3°22E 124 B2
Idelès Algeria 23°50N 5°53E 261 D6
Idensalmi = Iisalmi Finland 63°32N 27°10E 160 E22
Idfû Egypt 24°55N 32°49E 256 C3
Ídhra = Hydra Greece 37°20N 23°28E 204 D5
Idi Indonesia 5°2N 97°37E 234 A1
Idi, Oros = Psiloritis, Oros Greece 35°15N 24°45E 207 E5
Idi Amin Dada, L. = Edward, L. Africa 0°25S 29°40E 268 C2
Idi-Oro Nigeria 6°31N 3°21E 124 A2
İdil Turkey 37°20N 41°53E 213 D9
Idiofa Dem. Rep. of the Congo 4°55S 19°42E 265 C3
Idjil = Fdérik Mauritania 22°40N 12°45W 260 D2
Idkerberget Sweden 60°22N 15°15E 162 D9
Idku Egypt 31°18N 30°17E 256 H7
Idku, Bahra el Egypt 31°18N 30°18E 256 H7
Idlib Syria 35°55N 36°36E 250 C7
Idlib □ Syria 35°45N 36°45E 250 C7
Idre Sweden 61°52N 12°42E 162 C6
Idria U.S.A. 36°25N 120°41W 306 J6
Idrija Slovenia 46°0N 14°5E 199 C11
Idritsa Russia 56°17N 28°53E 188 D5
Idutywa = Dutywa S. Africa 32°8S 28°18E 271 D4
Ie Shima Japan 26°43N 127°48E 288 a
Ie Suido Japan 26°42N 127°51E 288 a
Ieper Belgium 50°51N 2°53E 170 D2
Ierapetra Greece 35°1N 25°44E 207 F6
Ierissos Greece 40°22N 23°52E 202 F7
Ierissos Kolpos Greece 40°27N 23°57E 202 F7
Iernut Romania 46°27N 24°15E 183 D9
Ieshima-Shotō Japan 34°40N 134°32E 222 C6
Iesi Italy 43°31N 13°14E 199 E10
Iet Ethiopia 4°33N 43°1E 267 D5
Ifac, Penyal d' Spain 38°38N 0°5E 197 G5
'Ifāl, W. al → Si. Arabia 28°7N 35°3E 251 K6
Ifanadiana Madag. 21°19S 47°39E 272 C2
Ife Nigeria 7°30N 4°31E 263 D5
Iférouâne Niger 19°5N 8°24E 259 E1
Ifetesene Algeria 25°30N 4°33E 261 C5
Iffley Australia 18°53S 141°12E 280 B3
Ifon Nigeria 6°58N 5°40E 263 D6
Iforas, Adrar des Africa 19°40N 1°40E 261 D5
Ifould, L. Australia 30°52S 132°6E 279 F5
Ifrane Morocco 33°33N 5°7W 260 B3
Ifugao □ Phil. 16°40N 121°10E 232 C3
Iga Japan 34°45N 136°10E 223 C8
Igalo Montenegro 42°28N 18°30E 202 D2
Iganga Uganda 0°37N 33°28E 268 B3
Iganmu Nigeria 6°28N 3°22E 124 B2
Igara-Paraná → Colombia 2°9S 71°47W 328 D3
Igarapava Brazil 20°3S 47°47W 333 F2
Igarapé-Açu Brazil 1°4S 47°33W 332 B2
Igarapé-Miri Brazil 1°59S 48°58W 332 B2
Igarka Russia 67°30N 86°33E 214 C9
Igatpuri India 19°40N 73°35E 244 E1
Igbetti Nigeria 8°44N 4°8E 263 D5
Igbo-Ora Nigeria 7°29N 3°15E 263 D5
Igbobi Nigeria 6°31N 3°22E 124 A2
Igboho Nigeria 8°53N 3°50E 263 D5
Igbologun Nigeria 6°24N 3°19E 124 B1
Igbor Nigeria 7°27N 8°34E 263 D6
Iğdır Turkey 39°55N 44°2E 213 C11
Igelfors Sweden 58°52N 15°41E 163 F9
Iggesund Sweden 61°39N 17°10E 162 C11
Ighil Izane = Relizane Algeria 35°44N 0°31E 261 A5
Igiugig U.S.A. 59°20N 155°55W 303 G9
Iglau = Jihlava Czech Rep. 49°28N 15°35E 180 B8
Iglésias Italy 39°19N 8°32E 200 C1
Igli Algeria 30°25N 2°19W 261 B4
Igloolik = Iglulik Canada 69°20N 81°49W 295 D15
Igluligaarjuk = Chesterfield Inlet Canada 63°30N 90°45W 294 E13
Iglulik Canada 69°20N 81°49W 295 D15
'Igma, G. el Egypt 29°10N 34°0E 251 J5
Ignace Canada 49°30N 91°40W 298 C1
İğneada Turkey 41°52N 27°59E 203 E11
İğneada Burnu Turkey 41°53N 28°2E 203 E12
Igny France 48°44N 2°13E 134 B2
Igoumenitsa Greece 39°32N 20°18E 206 B10
Igrim Russia 63°12N 64°30E 214 C7
Iguaçu → Brazil 25°36S 54°36W 335 B5
Iguaçu, Cat. del Brazil 25°41S 54°26W 335 B5
Iguaçu △ Brazil 25°30S 54°0W 335 B5
Iguaçu Falls = Iguaçu, Cat. del Brazil 25°41S 54°26W 335 B5
Iguala Mexico 18°21N 99°32W 319 D5
Igualada Spain 41°37N 1°37E 196 D6
Iguape Brazil 24°43S 47°33W 333 F2
Iguaratinga = São Francisco do Maranhão Brazil 6°15S 42°52W 332 C3
Iguassu = Iguaçu → Brazil 25°36S 54°36W 335 B5
Iguatu Brazil 6°20S 39°18W 332 C4
Iguazú △ Argentina 25°42S 54°22W 335 B5
Iguéla Gabon 2°0S 9°16E 264 C1
Iguéla, Lagune Gabon 1°48S 9°16E 264 C2
Iguidi, Erg Africa 27°0N 6°0W 260 C3
Iguig Phil. 17°45N 121°44E 232 C3
Igumen = Cherven Belarus 53°45N 28°28E 177 B15
Iharana Madag. 13°25S 50°0E 272 A3
Ihavandiffulu Atoll Maldives 7°0N 72°50E 272 d
Ihbulag Mongolia 43°11N 107°10E 226 C4
Iheya-Shima Japan 27°4N 127°58E 221 L3
Ihiala Nigeria 5°51N 6°55E 263 D6
Ihirene, O. → Algeria 20°28N 4°37E 261 D5
Ihosy Madag. 22°24S 46°8E 272 C2
Ihotry, Farihy Madag. 21°56S 43°41E 272 C1
Ihu Papua N. G. 7°55S 145°24E 286 D3
Ihugh Nigeria 7°2N 9°0E 263 D6
Ii Finland 65°19N 25°22E 160 D21
Ii-Shima Japan 26°43N 127°47E 221 L3
Iida Japan 35°35N 137°50E 223 B9
Iijoki → Finland 65°20N 25°20E 160 D21
Iisalmi Finland 63°32N 27°10E 160 E22
Iiyama Japan 36°51N 138°22E 221 F9
Iizuka Japan 33°38N 130°42E 222 D2
IJ, Het → Neths. 52°23N 4°54E 112 A2
IJ-meer Neths. 52°23N 4°54E 112 A3
Ijâfene Mauritania 20°40N 8°0W 260 D3
IJberg Amsterdam, Neths. 52°22N 5°0E 112 A3
Ijebu-Igbo Nigeria 6°56N 4°1E 263 D5
Ijebu-Ode Nigeria 6°47N 3°58E 263 D5
Ijesa-Tedo Nigeria 6°29N 3°19E 124 B1
Ijevan Armenia 40°52N 45°8E 191 K7
Ijill, Sebkhet Mauritania 22°47N 12°53W 260 D2
IJmuiden Neths. 52°28N 4°35E 170 B4
Ijo älv = Iijoki → Finland 65°20N 25°20E 160 D21
Ijora Nigeria 6°27N 3°22E 124 B2
IJssel → Neths. 52°35N 5°50E 170 B5
IJsselmeer Neths. 52°45N 5°20E 170 B5
Ijuí Brazil 28°23S 53°55W 335 B5
Ijuí → Brazil 27°58S 55°20W 335 B4
Ijūin Japan 31°37N 130°24E 222 F2
Ikalamavony Madag. 21°9S 46°35E 272 C2
Ikali Dem. Rep. of the Congo 2°2S 21°4E 264 C4
Ikamatua N.Z. 42°16S 171°41E 285 C6
Ikang Nigeria 4°49N 8°30E 263 E6

Ikanga *Kenya* 1°42S 38°4E **268** C4
Ikara *Nigeria* 11°12N 8°15E **263** C6
Ikare *Nigeria* 7°32N 5°40E **263** D6
Ikaria *Greece* 37°35N 26°10E **205** D8
Ikast *Denmark* 56°8N 9°10E **163** H3
Ikebe *Japan* 35°31N 139°34E **140** B2
Ikebukuro *Japan* 35°43N 139°42E **140** A3
Ikeda *Japan* 34°1N 133°48E **222** C5
Ikegami *Japan* 35°33N 139°42E **140** B3
Ikei-shima *Japan* 26°23N 127°59E **288** a
Ikeja *Nigeria* 6°35N 3°20E **124** A2
Ikela *Dem. Rep. of the Congo* 1°6S 23°6E **264** C4
Ikélemba *Congo* 1°12N 16°38E **264** B3
Ikélemba →
*Dem. Rep. of the Congo* 0°7N 18°17E **264** B3
Ikengo *Dem. Rep. of the Congo* 0°8S 18°8E **264** C3
Ikere *Nigeria* 7°25N 5°19E **263** D6
Ikeuchi *Japan* 34°35N 135°32E **133** B2
Ikhtiman *Bulgaria* 42°27N 23°48E **202** D7
Iki *Japan* 33°45N 129°42E **222** D1
Iki-Kaikyō *Japan* 33°40N 129°45E **222** D1
Ikimba L. *Tanzania* 1°30S 31°20E **268** C3
Ikire *Nigeria* 7°23N 4°15E **263** D5
Ikitsuki-Shima *Japan* 33°23N 129°26E **222** D1
İkizdere *Turkey* 40°46N 40°32E **213** B9
Iko *Congo* 0°35S 16°0E **264** C3
Ikom *Nigeria* 6°0N 8°42E **263** D6
Ikoma *Japan* 34°30N 135°40E **223** C7
Ikomu
*Dem. Rep. of the Congo* 1°54S 19°40E **264** C3
Ikongo *Madag.* 21°52S 47°27E **272** C2
Ikopa → *Madag.* 16°45S 46°40E **272** B2
Ikorodu *Nigeria* 6°37N 3°29E **124** A2
Ikorongo ⌓ *Tanzania* 1°50S 34°53E **268** C3
Ikot Ekpene *Nigeria* 5°12N 7°40E **263** D6
Ikoyi *Nigeria* 6°27N 3°26E **124** B2
Ikparjuk = Arctic Bay
*Canada* 73°1N 85°7W **295** C14
Iksan *S. Korea* 35°59N 127°0E **224** E3
Ikuata *Nigeria* 6°24N 3°21E **124** B2
Ikungu *Tanzania* 1°33S 33°42E **268** C3
Ikuno *Hyōgo, Japan* 35°10N 134°48E **222** B6
Ikuno *Ōsaka, Japan* 34°40N 135°30E **133** A2
Ikuntji = Haasts Bluff
*Australia* 23°22S 132°0E **278** D5
Ikurun *Nigeria* 7°54N 4°40E **263** D5
Ikuta *Japan* 35°36N 139°32E **140** B2
Il-Kullana *Malta* 35°50N 14°24E **206** F7
Il-Munxar *Malta* 35°51N 14°34E **206** F8
Ila *Dem. Rep. of the Congo* 2°53S 21°7E **264** C4
Ila *Nigeria* 8°0N 4°39E **263** D5
Ilaflo *Oslo, Norway* 59°57N 10°35E **133** A2
Ilafer *Algeria* 21°40N 1°58E **261** D5
Ilagan *Phil.* 17°7N 121°53E **232** C3
Ilaka *Madag.* 19°33S 48°52E **272** B2
Īlām *Iran* 33°36N 46°36E **213** F12
Ilam *Nepal* 26°58N 87°58E **243** F12
Īlām □ *Iran* 33°0N 47°0E **246** C5
Ilan *Taiwan* 24°45N 121°44E **225** B3
Ilan □ *Taiwan* 24°30N 121°35E **225** B3
Ilan, Mt. *Phil.* 10°26N 119°33E **233** F2
Ilanskiy *Russia* 56°14N 96°3E **215** D10
Ilaro *Nigeria* 6°53N 3°3E **263** D5
Ilatane *Niger* 16°30N 4°45E **263** B5
Ilave *Peru* 16°5S 69°40W **330** D4
Iława *Poland* 53°36N 19°34E **184** E6
Ilayangudi *India* 9°34N 78°37E **245** K4
Ile → *Kazakhstan* 45°53N 77°10E **217** C9
Île-à-la-Crosse *Canada* 55°27N 107°53W **297** B7
Île-à-la-Crosse, Lac
*Canada* 55°40N 107°45W **297** B7
Ile-Ala Tau △ *Kazakhstan* 43°5N 77°5E **217** D9
Île-de-France □ *France* 49°0N 2°20E **173** D9
Ileanda *Romania* 47°20N 23°38E **183** C8
Ilebo *Dem. Rep. of the Congo* 4°17S 20°55E **265** C4
Ilek *Russia* 51°32N 53°21E **216** B4
Ilek → *Russia* 51°30N 53°22E **186** D9
Ilemi Triangle *Africa* 5°0N 35°20E **257** G4
Iler, O. → *Algeria* 20°59N 3°14E **261** D5
Ilero *Nigeria* 8°0N 3°20E **263** D5
Ilesha *Kwara, Nigeria* 8°57N 3°28E **263** D5
Ilesha *Oyo, Nigeria* 7°37N 4°40E **263** D5
Ilet = Krasnogorskiy
*Russia* 56°10N 48°28E **190** B9
Iletskaya = Sol Iletsk
*Russia* 51°10N 55°0E **186** D10
Iletsky Gorodok = Ilek
*Russia* 51°32N 53°21E **216** B4
Ilford *Man., Canada* 56°4N 95°35W **297** B9
Ilford *London, U.K.* 51°33N 0°4E **125** A4
Ilfracombe *Queens., Australia* 23°30S 144°30E **280** C3
Ilfracombe *Devon, U.K.* 51°12N 4°8W **169** F3
Ilgaz *Turkey* 40°55N 33°37E **212** B5
Ilgaz Dağları *Turkey* 41°10N 33°50E **212** B5
Ilgın *Turkey* 38°16N 31°55E **212** C4
Ilha, Pta. da *Azores* 38°25N 28°3W **153** d1
Ilha Grande *Brazil* 0°27S 65°2W **329** D4
Ilha Grande, B. da *Brazil* 23°9S 44°30W **333** F3
Ilha Grande, Represa
*Brazil* 23°10S 53°5W **335** A5
Ilha Grande △ *Brazil* 23°10S 53°20W **335** A5
Ílhavo *Portugal* 40°33N 8°43W **194** E2
Ilhéus *Brazil* 14°49S 39°2W **333** D4
Ili = Ile → *Kazakhstan* 45°53N 77°10E **217** C9
Ilia *Greece* 37°45N 21°35E **204** D3
Ilia *Romania* 45°57N 22°40E **182** E7
Iliamna *U.S.A.* 59°45N 154°55W **303** G9
Iliamna L. *U.S.A.* 59°30N 155°0W **303** G9
Ilias, Profitis *Greece* 36°17N 27°56E **206** E11
Iliç *Turkey* 39°27N 38°33E **213** C8
Ilıca *Turkey* 39°52N 27°46E **205** B9
Ilig, Ras *Somalia* 7°47N 49°50E **267** C6
Iligan *Phil.* 8°12N 124°13E **233** G5
Iligan B. *Phil.* 8°25N 124°5E **233** G5
Iligan Pt. *Phil.* 18°25N 122°25E **232** B4
Ilin I. *Phil.* 12°14N 121°5E **232** E3
'Īlio Pt. *U.S.A.* 21°13N 157°16W **302** B4
Ilion *U.S.A.* 43°1N 75°2W **313** D9
Ilioupoli *Greece* 37°54N 23°47E **112** B2
Ilirska-Bistrica *Slovenia* 45°34N 14°14E **199** C11
Iliwa = Rewa → *Guyana* 3°19N 58°42W **329** C6
Iliysk = Qapshaghay
*Kazakhstan* 43°51N 77°14E **217** D9
Ilkal *India* 15°57N 76°8E **245** G3
Ilkenau = Olkusz *Poland* 50°18N 19°33E **185** H6
Ilkeston *U.K.* 52°58N 1°19W **168** E6
Ilkley *U.K.* 53°56N 1°48W **168** D6
Illampu = Ancohuma, Nevado
*Bolivia* 16°0S 68°50W **330** D4
Illana B. *Phil.* 7°35N 123°45E **233** H4
Illapel *Chile* 32°0S 71°10W **334** C1
Ille-et-Vilaine □ *France* 48°10N 1°30W **172** D5
Ille-sur-Têt *France* 42°40N 2°38E **174** F6
Illéla *Niger* 14°32N 5°20E **263** C6
Iller → *Germany* 48°23N 9°58E **179** G5
Illertissen *Germany* 48°12N 10°7E **179** G6
Illes Balears = Baleares, Is.
*Spain* 39°30N 3°0E **206** B4
Illescas *Spain* 40°8N 3°51W **194** E7
Illetas *Spain* 39°32N 2°35E **206** B3
Illichivsk *Ukraine* 46°20N 30°35E **189** J6
Illiers-Combray *France* 48°18N 1°15E **172** D8
Illimani, Nevado *Bolivia* 16°30S 67°50W **330** D4
Illinois □ *U.S.A.* 40°15N 89°30W **310** D7
Illinois → *U.S.A.* 38°58N 90°28W **310** F6
Illinois at Chicago, Univ. of
*U.S.A.* 41°52N 87°38W **119** B3
Illinois Institute of Technology
*U.S.A.* 41°50N 87°37W **119** B3
Illiopolis *U.S.A.* 39°51N 89°15W **310** E7
Illium = Troy *Turkey* 39°57N 26°12E **205** B8
Illizi *Algeria* 26°31N 8°32E **261** C6
Illizi □ *Algeria* 26°50N 8°10E **261** C6
Illkirch-Graffenstaden
*France* 48°34N 7°42E **173** D14
Íllora *Spain* 37°17N 3°53W **195** H7
Ilm → *Germany* 51°6N 11°40E **178** D7
Ilma, L. *Australia* 29°13S 127°46E **279** E4
Ilmajoki *Finland* 62°44N 22°34E **160** E20
Ilmen, Ozero *Russia* 58°15N 31°10E **188** C6
Ilmenau = Jordanów
*Poland* 49°41N 19°49E **185** J6
Ilmenau = Limanowa
*Poland* 49°42N 20°22E **185** J7
Ilmenau *Germany* 50°41N 10°54E **178** E6
Ilnytsya *Ukraine* 48°21N 23°5E **182** B8
Ilo *Peru* 17°40S 71°20W **330** D3
Ilobu *Nigeria* 7°45N 4°25E **263** D5
Iloc I. *Phil.* 11°17N 119°40E **233** F2
Ilocos Norte □ *Phil.* 18°10N 120°45E **232** B3
Ilocos Sur □ *Phil.* 17°20N 120°35E **232** C3
Iloilo *Phil.* 10°45N 122°33E **233** F4
Iloilo □ *Phil.* 11°0N 122°40E **233** F4
Ilomantsi *Finland* 62°38N 30°57E **160** E24
Ilora *Nigeria* 7°45N 3°50E **263** D5
Ilorin *Nigeria* 8°30N 4°35E **263** D5
Ilovatka *Russia* 50°30N 45°50E **190** E7
Ilovlya *Russia* 49°15N 44°2E **191** F7
Ilovlya → *Russia* 49°14N 44°0E **191** F7
Iłowa *Poland* 51°30N 15°10E **182** D5
Ilpendam *Neths.* 52°28N 4°57E **112** A2
Ilsos → *Greece* 37°55N 23°41E **112** B2
Ilubabor *Ethiopia* 7°25N 35°0E **257** F4
Ilulissat *Greenland* 69°12N 51°10W **154** D5
Ilva Mică *Romania* 47°17N 24°40E **183** C9
Ilwaco *U.S.A.* 46°19N 124°3W **306** D2
Ilyichevsk = Illichivsk
*Ukraine* 46°20N 30°35E **189** J6
Iłża *Poland* 51°10N 21°15E **185** G8
Iłżanka → *Poland* 51°14N 21°48E **185** G8
Imabari *Japan* 34°4N 133°0E **222** C5
Imagem e do Som, Museu da
*Rio de J., Brazil* **135** b3
Imaichi *Japan* 36°43N 139°46E **223** A11
Imaloto → *Madag.* 23°27S 45°13E **272** C2
İmamoğlu *Turkey* 37°15N 35°38E **212** D6
Iman = Dalnerechensk
*Russia* 45°50N 133°40E **220** B6
Imandra, Ozero *Russia* 67°30N 33°0E **160** C25
Imanombo *Madag.* 24°26S 45°49E **272** C2
Imari *Japan* 33°15N 129°52E **222** D1
Imasa *Sudan* 18°0N 36°12E **256** D4
Imatra *Finland* 61°12N 28°48E **188** B5
Imbâbah *Egypt* 30°3N 31°12E **117** A2
Imbabura □ *Ecuador* 0°30N 78°45W **328** C2
Imbaimadai *Guyana* 5°44N 60°17W **329** B5
Imbiah Lookout *Singapore* 1°16N 103°49E **138** B2
Imbonga
*Dem. Rep. of the Congo* 0°43S 19°44E **264** C3
Iménas *Mali* 16°20N 0°40E **263** B5
imeni 26 Bakinskikh Komissarov =
Neftçala *Azerbaijan* 39°19N 49°12E **213** C13
imeni 26 Bakinskikh Komissarov
*Turkmenistan* 39°22N 54°10E **247** B7
imeni Dvadtsati Shesti Bakinskikh
Komissarov = Neftçala
*Azerbaijan* 39°19N 49°12E **213** C13
imeni Dzerzhinskogo =
Naryan-Mar *Russia* 67°42N 53°12E **186** A9
imeni Ismail Samani, Pik
*Tajikistan* 39°0N 72°2E **217** E8
imeni Karl Libknekhta
*Russia* 51°40N 35°35E **189** G8
imeni Mikoyana = Kara-Balta
*Kyrgyzstan* 42°50N 73°49E **217** D8
imeni Petrovskogo G.I. =
Horodyshche *Ukraine* 49°17N 31°27E **189** H6
imeni Sverdlova = Sverdlovsk
*Ukraine* 48°5N 39°47E **189** H10
imeni Tovarishcha Khateyevicha =
Synelnykove *Ukraine* 48°25N 35°30E **189** H8
imeni Tretyego Internatsionala =
Novoshakhtinsk
*Russia* 47°46N 39°58E **189** J10
Imeri, Serra *Brazil* 0°50N 65°25W **328** C4
Imerimandroso *Madag.* 17°26S 48°35E **272** B2
Imese *Dem. Rep. of the Congo* 2°6N 18°9E **264** B3
Imfolozi ⌓ *S. Africa* 28°18S 31°50E **271** C5
Imi *Ethiopia* 6°28N 42°10E **257** F5
Imielin *Poland* 52°9N 21°0E **143** C2
Imirim *Brazil* 23°29S 46°39W **137** A2
İmişli *Azerbaijan* 39°55N 48°4E **191** L9
Imitek *Morocco* 29°43N 8°10W **260** C3
Imitos *Greece* 37°55N 23°45E **112** B2
Imitos, Oros *Greece* 37°53N 23°48E **112** B2
Imizu *Japan* 36°47N 137°4E **223** A9
Imjado *S. Korea* 35°5N 126°5E **224** E3
Imjin-gang → *N. Korea* 37°47N 126°39E **224** D3
Imlay *U.S.A.* 40°40N 118°9W **304** F4
Imlay City *U.S.A.* 43°2N 83°5W **312** D1
Immaseri *Sudan* 15°40N 25°31E **257** D2
Immenstadt *Germany* 47°33N 10°13E **179** H6
Immingham *U.K.* 53°37N 0°13W **168** D7
Immokalee *U.S.A.* 26°25N 81°25W **317** J8
Imo □ *Nigeria* 5°30N 7°10E **263** D6
Imo → *Nigeria* 4°36N 7°35E **263** E6
İmola *Italy* 44°20N 11°42E **199** D8
Imotski *Croatia* 43°27N 17°12E **199** E14
Impé *Congo* 2°45S 15°16E **264** C3
Imperatorskaya Gavan = Vanino
*Russia* 48°50N 140°5E **215** E15
Imperatriz *Amazonas, Brazil* 5°18S 67°11W **330** B4
Imperatriz *Maranhão,*
*Brazil* 5°30S 47°29W **332** C2
Impéria *Italy* 43°53N 8°3E **198** E5
Imperial *Sask., Canada* 51°21N 105°28W **297** C7
Imperial *Peru* 13°4S 76°21W **330** C2
Imperial *Calif., U.S.A.* 32°51N 115°34W **307** N11
Imperial *Nebr., U.S.A.* 40°31N 101°39W **308** E3
Imperial Beach *U.S.A.* 32°35N 117°6W **307** N9
Imperial Dam *U.S.A.* 32°55N 114°25W **307** N12
Imperial Palace = Paço Imperial
*Rio de J., Brazil* **135** a2
Imperial Palace Museum *Beijing, China* **114** b3
Imperial Res. *U.S.A.* 32°53N 114°28W **307** N12
Imperial Valley *U.S.A.* 33°0N 115°30W **307** N11
Imperieuse Reef *Australia* 17°36S 118°50E **278** C2
Impfondo *Congo* 1°40N 18°0E **264** B3
Imphal *India* 24°48N 93°56E **241** C4
Imphy *France* 46°55N 3°16E **173** F10
Impulo *Angola* 13°51S 13°39E **265** E2
İmranlı *Turkey* 39°54N 38°7E **213** C8
İmroz = Gökçeada *Turkey* 40°10N 25°50E **203** F9
Imst *Austria* 47°15N 10°44E **180** D3
Imuris *Mexico* 30°47N 110°52W **318** A2
Imuruan B. *Phil.* 10°40N 119°10E **233** F2
Imus *Phil.* 14°26N 120°56E **232** D3
In Aleï *Mali* 17°42N 2°30W **262** B4
In Amenas *Algeria* 28°5N 9°33E **261** C6
In Amguel *Algeria* 23°41N 5°9E **261** D6
In Atei *Algeria* 20°33N 6°4E **261** D6
In Belbel *Algeria* 27°55N 1°12E **261** C5
In Delimane *Mali* 15°52N 1°31E **263** B5
In Ghar *Algeria* 27°10N 1°59E **261** C5
In Guezzam *Algeria* 19°37N 5°52E **261** E6
In Koufi *Mali* 19°11N 1°25E **263** B5
In Salah *Algeria* 27°10N 2°32E **261** C5
In Tallak *Mali* 16°19N 3°15E **263** B5
In Tebezas *Mali* 17°49N 1°53E **263** B5
Ina *Japan* 35°50N 137°55E **223** B9
Ina Ill., *U.S.A.* 38°9N 88°54W **311** F8
Ina-Bonchi *Japan* 35°45N 137°58E **223** B9
Inabanga *Phil.* 10°2N 124°4E **233** F5
Inaccessible I. *Atl. Oc.* 37°18S 12°40W **152** K10
Inabaan *Phil.* 9°33N 118°39E **233** G2
Inagi *Japan* 35°38N 139°31E **140** B2
Inajá *Brazil* 8°54S 37°49W **332** C4
Inambari → *Peru* 12°41S 69°44W **330** C4
Inangahua *N.Z.* 41°52S 171°59E **285** B6
Inanwatan *Indonesia* 2°8S 132°10E **231** E8
Iñapari *Peru* 11°0S 69°40W **330** C4
Inarajan *Guam* 13°16N 144°45E **302** d
Inari *Finland* 68°54N 27°1E **160** B22
Inarijärvi *Finland* 69°0N 28°0E **160** B23
Inawashiro-Ko *Japan* 37°29N 140°6E **220** F10
Inazawa *Japan* 35°15N 136°47E **223** B8
tInbhear Mór, An = Arklow
*Ireland* 52°48N 6°10W **166** D5
Inbin *Burma* 18°6N 95°16E **241** F5
Inca *Spain* 39°43N 2°54E **206** B3
Inca de Oro *Chile* 26°45S 69°54W **334** B2
Incahuasi *Argentina* 27°2S 68°18W **334** B2
Incahuasi *Chile* 29°12S 71°5W **334** B1
İnce Burun *Turkey* 42°7N 34°56E **212** A6
İncekum Burnu *Turkey* 36°13N 33°57E **250** B4
İncesu *Turkey* 38°38N 35°11E **212** C6
Inchcolm *U.K.* 56°2N 3°18W **121** A2
Incheon *S. Korea* 37°27N 126°40E **224** D3
Inchicore *Ireland* 53°20N 6°20W **120** A1
Inchiri □ *Mauritania* 20°0N 15°0W **260** E2
Inchkeith *U.K.* 56°2N 3°8W **121** A3
Inchmickery *U.K.* 56°0N 3°16W **121** A2
Incio = A Cruz do Incio
*Spain* 42°39N 7°21W **194** C3
Incirano *Italy* 45°34N 9°9E **128** A1
İncirliova *Turkey* 37°50N 27°41E **205** D9
Incline Village *U.S.A.* 39°10N 119°58W **306** F7
Incomáti → *Mozam.* 25°46S 32°43E **271** C5
Incudine, Mte. *France* 41°50N 9°12E **175** G13
Inda Silase *Ethiopia* 14°10N 38°15E **257** E4
Indal *Sweden* 62°35N 17°5E **162** B11
Indalsälven → *Sweden* 62°36N 17°30E **162** B11
Indaw *Burma* 24°15N 96°5E **241** C6
Indawgyi In *Burma* 25°8N 96°20E **241** C6
Indbir *Ethiopia* 8°7N 37°52E **257** F4
Indefatigable, I. = Santa Cruz, I.
*Ecuador* 0°38S 90°23W **330** a
Independence *Calif.,*
*U.S.A.* 36°48N 118°12W **306** J8
Independence *Iowa,*
*U.S.A.* 42°28N 91°54W **310** B5
Independence *Kans.,*
*U.S.A.* 37°14N 95°42W **308** G6
Independence *Ky.,*
*U.S.A.* 38°57N 84°33W **311** F12
Independence *Mo., U.S.A.* 39°6N 94°25W **310** E2
Independence Avenue
*Washington, D.C., U.S.A.* **143** c2
Independence Fjord
*Greenland* 82°10N 29°0W **154** A8
Independence Mts.
*U.S.A.* 41°20N 116°0W **304** F5
Independência *Brazil* 5°23S 40°19W **332** C3
Independencia *Santiago,*
*Chile* 33°25S 70°39W **137** B2
Independencia *Lima, Peru* 11°59S 77°3W **124** A2
Independencia, I. *Peru* 14°16S 76°12W **330** C2
Independenţa *Romania* 45°25N 27°42E **183** E12
Inderbor *Kazakhstan* 48°33N 51°47E **216** C4
Index *U.S.A.* 47°50N 121°33W **306** C5
Indi *India* 17°10N 75°58E **244** F2
India ■ *Asia* 20°0N 78°0E **239** F11
India Gate *Delhi, India* **120** c2
Indialantic *U.S.A.* 28°6N 80°34W **317** G9
Indian → *U.S.A.* 27°59N 80°34W **317** G9
Indian Cabins *Canada* 59°52N 117°40W **296** B5
Indian Creek Village
*U.S.A.* 25°52N 80°8W **129** C3
Indian Harbour *Canada* 54°27N 57°13W **299** B8
Indian Harbour Beach
*U.S.A.* 28°10N 80°35W **317** G9
Indian Head *Canada* 50°30N 103°41W **297** C8
Indian L. *U.S.A.* 43°46N 74°16W **313** C10
Indian Lake *U.S.A.* 43°47N 74°16W **313** C10
Indian Ocean 5°0S 75°0E **273** E6
Indian Rocks Beach
*U.S.A.* 27°52N 82°51W **317** H7
Indian Springs *U.S.A.* 36°35N 115°40W **307** J11
Indian Town Pt.
*Antigua & B.* 17°6N 61°40W **322** b
Indian Walk *Trin. & Tob.* 10°16N 61°20W **323** t
Indiana *U.S.A.* 40°37N 79°9W **312** F5
Indiana □ *U.S.A.* 40°0N 86°0W **311** E11
Indiana Dunes ⌓ *U.S.A.* 41°40N 87°0W **311** C9
Indianapolis *U.S.A.* 39°46N 86°9W **311** E10
Indianapolis Int. ✕ (IND)
*U.S.A.* 39°43N 86°17W **311** E10
Indianola *Iowa, U.S.A.* 41°22N 93°34W **310** C3
Indianola *Miss., U.S.A.* 33°27N 90°39W **315** E9
Indianópolis *Brazil* 23°35S 46°38W **137** B2
Indiantown *U.S.A.* 27°1N 80°28W **317** H9
Indiapora *Brazil* 19°57S 50°17W **333** E1
Indiga *Russia* 67°38N 49°9E **186** A8
Indigirka → *Russia* 70°48N 148°54E **215** B15
Inđija *Serbia* 45°6N 20°7E **182** E5
Indio *U.S.A.* 33°43N 116°13W **307** M10
Indira Gandhi Canal *India* 28°0N 72°0E **242** F5
Indira Gandhi Int. ✕ (DEL)
*India* 28°34N 77°5E **120** B1
Indira Pt. *India* 6°44N 93°49E **245** L11
Indira Sagar *India* 22°15N 76°40E **242** H7
Indispensable Str.
*Solomon Is.* 9°0S 160°30E **287** M11
Indo-China *Asia* 15°0N 102°0E **210** G12
Indonesia ■ *Asia* 5°0S 115°0E **235** C4
Indore *India* 22°42N 75°53E **242** H6
Indramayu *Indonesia* 6°20S 108°19E **235** D3
Indrapura = Kerinci
*Indonesia* 1°40S 101°15E **234** C2
Indravati → *India* 19°20N 80°20E **244** E5
Indre □ *France* 46°50N 1°39E **173** F8
Indre → *France* 47°16N 0°11E **172** E7
Indre Ålvik *Norway* 60°26N 6°26E **164** D3
Indre Arna *Norway* 60°26N 5°30E **164** D2
Indre-et-Loire □ *France* 47°20N 0°40E **172** E7
Indrio *U.S.A.* 27°31N 80°21W **317** H9
Indulkana *Australia* 26°58S 133°5E **281** D1
Indungo *Angola* 14°48S 16°17E **265** E3
Indura *Belarus* 53°26N 23°53E **184** E10
Indus → *Pakistan* 24°20N 67°47E **242** G2
Indus, Mouths of the
*Pakistan* 24°0N 68°0E **242** H3
Industria *S. Africa* 26°11S 27°58E **123** B1
Industrial Canal *U.S.A.* 30°4N 90°4W **131** A2
Industry *U.S.A.* 40°20N 90°36W **310** D6
İnebolu *Turkey* 41°55N 33°40E **212** B5
İnecik *Turkey* 40°56N 27°16E **203** F11
İnegöl *Turkey* 40°5N 29°31E **203** F13
Inés, Mt. *Argentina* 48°30S 69°40W **336** C3
Ineu *Romania* 46°26N 21°51E **182** D6
Inezgane *Morocco* 30°25N 9°29W **260** B3
Infanta *Phil.* 14°45N 121°39E **232** D3
Infantes = Villanueva de los
Infantes *Spain* 38°43N 3°1W **195** G7
Infiernillo, Presa del
*Mexico* 18°35N 101°50W **318** D4
Infiesto *Spain* 43°21N 5°21W **194** B5
Inga, Barrage d'
*Dem. Rep. of the Congo* 5°39S 13°39E **265** D2
Ingabu *Burma* 17°37N 95°20E **241** G5
Inganda
*Dem. Rep. of the Congo* 0°5S 20°57E **264** C4
Ingapirca *Ecuador* 2°38S 78°56W **328** D2
Ingaro *Sweden* 59°12N 18°45E **162** E12
Ingelstad *Sweden* 56°45N 14°56E **163** H8
Ingende
*Dem. Rep. of the Congo* 0°12S 18°57E **264** C3
Ingeniero Jacobacci
*Argentina* 41°20S 69°36W **336** B3
Ingenio *Canary Is.* 27°55N 15°26W **153** e1
Ingenio Santa Ana
*Argentina* 27°25S 65°40W **334** B2
Ingersoll *Canada* 43°4N 80°55W **312** C4
Ingham *Australia* 18°43S 146°10E **280** B4
Ingierstrand *Norway* 59°49N 10°46E **133** B3
Ingleborough *U.K.* 54°10N 2°22W **168** C5
Inglefield Land *Greenland* 78°30N 70°0W **154** B4
Inglewood *Queens.,*
*Australia* 28°25S 151°2E **281** D5
Inglewood *Vic., Australia* 36°29S 143°53E **282** D5
Inglewood *N.Z.* 39°9S 174°14E **284** F3
Inglewood *Calif., U.S.A.* 33°58N 118°21W **126** C3
Inglis *U.S.A.* 29°2N 82°40W **317** F7
Ingliston *U.K.* 55°56N 3°23W **121** B1
Ingolf Fjord *Greenland* 80°35N 17°30W **154** A9
Ingólfshöfði *Iceland* 63°48N 16°39W **155** D10
Ingolstadt *Germany* 48°46N 11°26E **179** G7
Ingomar *U.S.A.* 46°35N 107°23W **304** C10
Ingonish *Canada* 46°42N 60°18W **299** C7
Ingore *Guinea-Biss.* 12°24N 15°48W **262** C1
Ingraj Bazar *India* 24°58N 88°10E **243** G13
Ingrid Christensen Coast
*Antarctica* 69°30S 76°0E **151** C6
Ingul = Inhul → *Ukraine* 46°50N 32°0E **189** J7
Ingulec = Inhulec *Ukraine* 47°42N 33°14E **189** J7
Ingulets = Inhulets →
*Ukraine* 46°46N 32°47E **189** J7
Inguri = Enguri →
*Georgia* 42°27N 41°38E **191** J5
Ingushetia □ *Russia* 43°20N 44°50E **191** J7
Ingwavuma *S. Africa* 27°9S 31°59E **271** C5
Inhaca *Mozam.* 26°1S 32°57E **271** C5
Inhaca Pen. *Mozam.* 26°13S 32°55E **271** C5
Inhafenga *Mozam.* 20°36S 33°53E **271** B5
Inhambane *Mozam.* 23°54S 35°30E **271** B6
Inhambane □ *Mozam.* 22°30S 34°20E **271** B5
Inhambupe *Brazil* 11°47S 38°21W **333** D4
Inhaminga *Mozam.* 18°26S 35°0E **269** F4
Inharrime *Mozam.* 24°30S 35°0E **271** B6
Inharrime → *Mozam.* 24°30S 35°0E **271** B6
Inhaúma *Brazil* 22°51S 43°17W **135** B1
Inhisar *Turkey* 40°3N 30°23E **205** A12
Inhul → *Ukraine* 46°50N 32°0E **189** J7
Inhulec *Ukraine* 47°42N 33°14E **189** J7
Inhulets → *Ukraine* 46°46N 32°47E **189** J7
Inhuma *Brazil* 6°40S 41°42W **332** C3
Inhumas *Brazil* 16°22S 49°30W **333** E2
Iniesta *Spain* 39°27N 1°45W **197** F3
Ining = Yining *China* 43°58N 81°10E **217** D10
Inini □ *Fr. Guiana* 4°0N 53°0W **329** C7
Inirida → *Colombia* 3°55N 67°52W **328** C4
Inis = Ennis *Ireland* 52°51N 8°59W **166** D3
Inishbofin *Ireland* 53°37N 10°13W **166** C1
Inisheer *Ireland* 53°3N 9°32W **166** C2
Inishfree B. *Ireland* 55°4N 8°23W **166** A3
Inishkea North *Ireland* 54°9N 10°11W **166** B1
Inishkea South *Ireland* 54°7N 10°12W **166** B1
Inishmaan *Ireland* 53°5N 9°35W **166** C2
Inishmore *Ireland* 53°8N 9°45W **166** C2
Inishmurray *Ireland* 54°26N 8°39W **166** B3
Inishowen Pen. *Ireland* 55°14N 7°15W **166** A4
Inishshark *Ireland* 53°37N 10°16W **166** C1
Inishturk *Ireland* 53°42N 10°7W **166** C1
Inishvickillane *Ireland* 52°3N 10°37W **166** D1
Initao *Phil.* 8°56N 124°20E **233** G5
Injāna *Iraq* 34°29N 44°38E **213** E11
Injibara *Ethiopia* 10°59N 37°0E **257** E4
Injinoo ✪ *Australia* 10°56S 142°15E **280** A3
Injune *Australia* 25°53S 148°32E **281** D4
Inkisi →
*Dem. Rep. of the Congo* 4°46S 14°52E **265** D3
Inklin → *N. Amer.* 58°50N 133°10W **296** B2
Inland Kaikoura Ra.
*N.Z.* 41°59S 173°41E **285** B8
Inland Sea = Setonaikai
*Japan* 34°20N 133°30E **222** C5
Inle L. *Burma* 20°30N 96°58E **241** E6
Inlet *U.S.A.* 43°45N 74°48W **313** C10
Inn → *Austria* 48°35N 13°28E **180** C6
Innamincka *Australia* 27°44S 140°46E **281** D3
Innbygda *Norway* 61°19N 12°17E **164** C9
Inner Hebrides *U.K.* 57°0N 6°30W **167** E2
Inner Mongolia = Nei Mongol
Zizhiqu □ *China* 42°0N 112°0E **226** D7
Inner Port Shelter
*Hong Kong, China* 22°22N 114°17E **122** A3
Inner Sound *U.K.* 57°30N 5°55W **167** D3
Innerkip *Canada* 43°13N 80°42W **312** C4
Innes △ *Australia* 35°52S 136°53E **282** C2
Innetalling I. *Canada* 56°0N 79°0W **298** A4
Innisfail *Queens., Australia* 17°33S 146°5E **280** B4
Innisfail *Alta., Canada* 52°2N 113°57W **296** C6
Innoko Nat. Wildlife Refuge ⌓
*U.S.A.* 63°20N 158°25W **303** E8
In'noshima *Japan* 34°19N 133°10E **222** C5
Innsbruck *Austria* 47°16N 11°23E **180** D4
Innviertel *Austria* 48°15N 13°15E **180** C6
Innvik *Norway* 61°51N 6°37E **164** C3
Inny → *Ireland* 53°30N 7°50W **166** C4
Ino *Japan* 33°33N 133°26E **222** D5
Inocência *Brazil* 19°47S 51°48W **333** E1
Inongo
*Dem. Rep. of the Congo* 1°55S 18°30E **264** C3
Inoni *Congo* 3°4S 15°39E **264** C3
İnönü *Turkey* 39°48N 30°9E **205** B12
Inoucdjouac = Inukjuak
*Canada* 58°25N 78°15W **295** F16
Inousses *Greece* 38°33N 26°14E **205** C8
Inowrocław *Poland* 52°50N 18°12E **185** F5
Inquisivi *Bolivia* 16°50S 67°10W **330** D4
Inscription, C. *Australia* 25°29S 112°59E **279** E1
Insein *Burma* 16°50N 96°5E **241** G6
Insjön *Sweden* 60°41N 15°6E **162** D9
Ińsko *Poland* 53°25N 15°32E **184** E2
Insterburg = Chernyakhovsk
*Russia* 54°36N 21°48E **184** D8
Însurăței *Romania* 44°50N 27°40E **183** F12
Inta *Russia* 66°5N 60°8E **186** A11
Intendente Alvear
*Argentina* 35°12S 63°32W **334** D3
İntepe *Turkey* 40°1N 26°20E **205** A8
Interlachen *U.S.A.* 29°37N 81°53W **317** F8
Interlagos *Brazil* 23°41S 46°42W **137** C1
Interlaken *Switz.* 46°41N 7°50E **179** J3
Interlaken *N.Y., U.S.A.* 42°37N 76°44W **313** D8
International Falls *U.S.A.* 48°36N 93°25W **308** A7
Interview I. *India* 12°55N 92°43E **245** H11
Intiyaco *Argentina* 28°43S 60°5W **334** B3
Întorsura Buzăului
*Romania* 45°41N 26°2E **183** E11
Intramuros *Phil.* 14°35N 120°57E **127** B1
Intrepid Air and Space Museum
*New York, U.S.A.* **132** b1
Intutu *Peru* 3°32S 74°48W **328** D3
Inubō-Zaki *Japan* 35°42N 140°52E **223** B12
Inukjuak *Canada* 58°25N 78°15W **295** F16
Inútil, B. *Chile* 53°30S 70°15W **336** D2
Inuvik *Canada* 68°16N 133°40W **294** D5
Inuyama *Japan* 35°23N 136°56E **223** B8
Invalides *France* 48°51N 2°18E **134** A2
Inveraray *U.K.* 56°14N 5°5W **167** E3
Inverbervie *U.K.* 56°51N 2°17W **167** E6
Invercargill *N.Z.* 46°24S 168°24E **285** G3
Inverclyde □ *U.K.* 55°55N 4°49W **167** F4
Inverell *Australia* 29°45S 151°8E **281** D5
Invergordon *U.K.* 57°41N 4°10W **167** D4
Inverkeithing *U.K.* 56°2N 3°24W **121** A1
Inverleigh *Australia* 38°6S 144°3E **282** E6
Inverloch *Australia* 38°38S 145°45E **281** F4
Invermere *Canada* 50°30N 116°2W **296** C5
Inverness *N.S., Canada* 46°15N 61°19W **299** C7
Inverness *Highl., U.K.* 57°29N 4°13W **167** D4
Inverness *Ala., U.S.A.* 32°1N 85°45W **316** C4
Inverness *Fla., U.S.A.* 28°50N 82°20W **317** G7
Inverurie *U.K.* 57°17N 2°23W **167** D6
Investigator Group
*Australia* 34°45S 134°20E **281** E1
Investigator Ridge *Ind. Oc.* 11°30S 98°10E **273** F8
Investigator Str. *Australia* 35°30S 137°0E **282** C2
Inya *Russia* 50°28N 86°37E **217** B11
Inyanga *Zimbabwe* 18°12S 32°40E **269** F3
Inyangani *Zimbabwe* 18°5S 32°50E **269** F3
Inyantue *Zimbabwe* 18°33S 26°39E **270** A4
Inyo Mts. *U.S.A.* 36°40N 118°0W **306** J9
Inyokern *U.S.A.* 35°39N 117°49W **307** K9
Inyonga *Tanzania* 6°45S 32°5E **268** D3
Inywa *Burma* 23°56N 96°17E **241** D6
Inza *Russia* 53°55N 46°25E **190** D8
Inzersdorf *Austria* 48°8N 16°21E **142** B2
Inzhavino *Russia* 52°22N 42°30E **190** D6
Inzia →
*Dem. Rep. of the Congo* 3°45S 17°57E **265** C3
Iō-Jima *Japan* 30°48N 130°18E **221** J5
Ioannina *Greece* 39°42N 20°47E **204** B2
Iokea *Papua N. G.* 8°25S 146°16E **286** E4
Iola *U.S.A.* 37°55N 95°24W **308** G6
Iolani Palace *U.S.A.* 21°18N 157°51W **302** K14
Ioma *Papua N. G.* 8°19S 147°52E **286** E4
Ion Corvin *Romania* 44°7N 27°50E **183** F12
Iona *Angola* 16°54S 12°34E **265** F2
Iona *Argyll & Bute, U.K.* 56°20N 6°25W **167** E2
Iona △ *Angola* 16°47S 12°20E **265** F2
Ione *U.S.A.* 38°21N 120°56W **306** G6
Iongo *Angola* 9°11S 17°45E **265** D3
Ionia *U.S.A.* 42°59N 85°4W **311** B11
Ionian Is. = Ionioi Nisoi
*Greece* 38°40N 20°0E **204** C2
Ionian Sea *Medit. S.* 37°30N 17°30E **193** D7
Ionioi Nisoi *Greece* 38°40N 20°0E **204** C2
Ionioi Nisoi □ *Greece* 38°40N 20°0E **207** B2
Iony, Ostrov *Russia* 56°24N 143°22E **215** D15
Ios *Greece* 36°41N 25°20E **205** E7
Iowa □ *U.S.A.* 42°18N 93°30W **310** C3
Iowa → *U.S.A.* 41°10N 91°1W **310** C5
Iowa City *U.S.A.* 41°40N 91°32W **310** C5
Iowa Falls *U.S.A.* 42°31N 93°16W **310** B3
Iowa Park *U.S.A.* 33°57N 98°40W **314** E5
Ipala *Tanzania* 4°30S 32°52E **268** C3
Ipameri *Brazil* 17°44S 48°9W **333** E2
Ipanema *Minas Gerais,*
*Brazil* 19°47S 41°44W **333** E3
Ipanema *Rio de J., Brazil* 22°59S 43°12W **135** B1
Iparia *Peru* 9°17S 74°29W **330** B3
Ipati *Greece* 38°52N 22°14E **204** C4
Ipatinga *Brazil* 19°32S 42°30W **333** E3
Ipatovo *Russia* 45°45N 42°50E **191** H6
Ipek = Pejë *Kosovo* 42°40N 20°17E **202** D4
Ipel' → *Europe* 47°48N 18°53E **181** D11
Ipiales *Colombia* 0°50N 77°37W **328** C2
Ipiaú *Brazil* 14°8S 39°44W **333** D4
Ipil *Phil.* 7°47N 122°35E **233** H4
Ipin = Yibin *China* 28°45N 104°32E **228** C5
Ipirá *Brazil* 12°10S 39°44W **333** D4
Ipiranga *Brazil* 23°35S 46°36W **137** B2
Ipiranga → *Brazil* 23°37S 46°37W **137** B2
Ipixuna *Brazil* 7°0S 71°40W **330** B3
Ipixuna → *Amazonas,*
*Brazil* 7°11S 71°51W **330** B3
Ipixuna → *Amazonas, Brazil* 5°45S 63°2W **331** B5
Ipoh *Malaysia* 4°35N 101°5E **237** K3
Iponri *Nigeria* 6°28N 3°22E **124** B2
Iporá *Brazil* 16°28S 51°7W **331** D7
Ipota *Vanuatu* 18°52S 169°20E **287** H7
Ippy *C.A.R.* 6°5N 21°7E **264** A4
İpsala *Turkey* 40°55N 26°23E **203** F10
Ipsario, Oros *Greece* 40°40N 24°40E **203** F8
Ipsos *Greece* 39°43N 19°48E **206** B9
Ipswich *Queens., Australia* 27°35S 152°40E **281** D5
Ipswich *Suffolk, U.K.* 52°4N 1°10E **169** E9
Ipswich *Mass., U.S.A.* 42°41N 70°50W **313** D14
Ipswich *S. Dak., U.S.A.* 45°27N 99°2W **308** C4
Ipu *Brazil* 4°23S 40°44W **332** B3
Ipueiras *Brazil* 4°33S 40°43W **332** B3
Ipuh *Indonesia* 3°0S 101°30E **234** C2
Ipupiara *Brazil* 11°49S 42°37W **333** D3
Iqaluit *Canada* 63°44N 68°31W **295** E18
Iqaluktuutiaq = Cambridge Bay
*Canada* 69°10N 105°0W **294** D11
Iquique *Chile* 20°19S 70°5W **330** E3
Iquitos *Peru* 3°45S 73°10W **328** D3
Ir Gannim = Bat Yam
*Israel* 32°2N 34°44E **251** F5
Irabu-Jima *Japan* 24°50N 125°10E **221** M2
Iracoubo *Fr. Guiana* 5°30N 53°10W **329** B7
Īrafshān *Iran* 26°42N 61°56E **247** E9
Irago-Suidō *Japan* 34°25N 137°0E **223** C8
Irahuan *Phil.* 9°48N 118°41E **233** G2
Iraklia *Cyclades, Greece* 36°50N 25°28E **205** E7
Iraklia *Serres, Greece* 41°10N 23°16E **202** E7
Iraklio *Greece* 35°20N 25°12E **207** E6
Iraklio ✕ (HER) *Greece* 35°20N 25°12E **207** E6
Iráklion = Iraklio *Greece* 35°20N 25°12E **207** E6
Irakliou, Kolpos *Greece* 35°23N 25°8E **207** E6
Irako-Zaki *Japan* 34°35N 137°1E **223** C9
Irala *Paraguay* 25°55S 54°35W **335** B5
Iran ■ *Asia* 33°0N 53°0E **247** C7
Iran, Pegunungan
*Malaysia* 2°20N 114°50E **235** B4
Iran Ra. = Iran, Pegunungan
*Malaysia* 2°20N 114°50E **235** B4
Iranamadu Tank *Sri Lanka* 9°23N 80°29E **245** K5
Īrānshahr *Iran* 27°15N 60°40E **247** E9
Irapa *Venezuela* 10°34N 62°35W **329** A5
Irapuato *Mexico* 20°41N 101°28W **318** C4
Iraq ■ *Asia* 33°0N 44°0E **213** F10
Irarrar, O. → *Mali* 20°0N 1°30E **261** E5
Irati *Brazil* 25°25S 50°38W **335** B5
Irazú, Volcan *Costa Rica* 10°28N 84°42W **320** D3
Irbes saurums *Latvia* 57°45N 22°5E **184** A9
Irbid *Jordan* 32°35N 35°48E **251** F6
Irbid □ *Jordan* 32°30N 35°50E **250** F6
Irebu *Dem. Rep. of the Congo* 0°40S 17°46E **264** C3
Irecê *Brazil* 11°18S 41°52W **332** D3
Iregua → *Spain* 42°27N 2°24E **196** C7
Ireland ■ *Europe* 53°50N 7°52W **166** C4
Ireland I. *Bermuda* 32°19N 64°50W **153** a
Ireland Island *Bermuda* 32°19N 64°50W **153** a
Ireland's Eye *Ireland* 53°24N 6°4W **120** A3
Irele *Nigeria* 7°40N 5°40E **263** D6
Ireng → *Brazil* 3°33N 59°51W **329** C6
Irerrer, O. → *Algeria* 19°25N 5°47E **261** E6
Irgiz = Yrghyz *Kazakhstan* 48°37N 61°16E **216** C6
Irgiz = Yrghyz →
*Kazakhstan* 48°6N 62°30E **216** C6
Irgiz, Bolshaya → *Russia* 52°10N 49°10E **190** D9
Irharrhar, O. → *Algeria* 28°3N 6°15E **261** C6
Irherm *Morocco* 30°7N 8°18W **260** B3
Irhil M'Goun *Morocco* 31°30N 6°28W **260** B3
Iri = Iksan *S. Korea* 35°59N 127°0E **224** E3
Irian Barat = Papua □
*Indonesia* 4°0S 137°0E **231** E9
Irian Jaya = Papua □
*Indonesia* 4°0S 137°0E **231** E9
Irian Jaya Barat □
*Indonesia* 2°5S 132°50E **231** E8
Iriba *Chad* 15°7N 22°15E **259** E4
Irié *Guinea* 8°15N 9°10W **262** D3
Iriga *Phil.* 13°25N 123°25E **232** E4
Iriklinskoye Vdkhr. *Russia* 52°0N 59°0E **216** B5
Iringa *Tanzania* 7°48S 35°43E **268** D4
Iringa □ *Tanzania* 7°48S 35°43E **268** D4
Irinjalakuda *India* 10°21N 76°14E **245** J3
Iriomote △ *Japan* 24°29N 123°53E **221** M1
Iriomote-Jima *Japan* 24°19N 123°48E **221** M1
Iriona *Honduras* 15°57N 85°11W **320** C2
Iriri → *Brazil* 3°52S 52°37W **329** D7
Iriri Novo → *Brazil* 8°46S 53°22W **331** B7
Irish Sea *Europe* 53°38N 4°48W **168** D3
Irkeshtam Pass = Erkech-Tam Pass
*Asia* 39°46N 74°2E **217** E8
Irkutsk *Russia* 52°18N 104°20E **218** A9
Irlığanlı *Turkey* 37°53N 29°12E **205** D11
Irma *Canada* 52°55N 111°14W **297** C6
Irō-Zaki *Japan* 34°36N 138°51E **223** C10
Irois B. *Trin. & Tob.* 10°9N 61°45W **323** t
Iroise, Mer d' *France* 48°15N 4°45W **172** D2
Iron Baron *Australia* 32°58S 137°11E **282** B2
Iron Gate = Portile de Fier
*Europe* 44°44N 22°30E **182** F7
Iron Knob *Australia* 32°46S 137°8E **282** B2
Iron Mountain *U.S.A.* 45°49N 88°4W **308** C9
Iron Range △ *Australia* 12°34S 143°18E **280** A3
Iron River *U.S.A.* 46°6N 88°39W **308** B9
Irondequoit *U.S.A.* 43°13N 77°35W **312** C7
Ironton *Mo., U.S.A.* 37°36N 90°38W **308** G8
Ironton *Ohio, U.S.A.* 38°32N 82°41W **309** F12
Ironwood *U.S.A.* 46°27N 90°9W **308** B8
Ironwood Forest ⌓
*U.S.A.* 32°32N 111°28W **305** K8
Iroquois *Canada* 44°51N 75°19W **313** B9
Iroquois → *U.S.A.* 41°5N 87°49W **311** C9
Iroquois Falls *Canada* 48°46N 80°41W **298** C3
Iroquois Point *U.S.A.* 21°19N 157°58W **302** K14
Irosin *Phil.* 12°42N 124°2E **232** E5
Irpin *Ukraine* 50°30N 30°15E **177** C16
Irqieqa, Ras I- *Malta* 35°56N 14°29E **206** F7
Irrara Cr. → *Australia* 29°35S 145°31E **281** D4
Irrawaddy □ *Burma* 17°0N 95°0E **241** G5
Irrawaddy → *Burma* 15°50N 95°6E **241** G5
Irrawaddy, Mouths of the
*Burma* 15°30N 95°0E **241** H5
Irricana *Canada* 51°19N 113°37W **296** C6
Irrunytju *Australia* 26°3S 128°56E **279** E4
Irshava *Ukraine* 48°19N 23°3E **182** B8
Irsina *Italy* 40°45N 16°14E **201** B9
Irtysh → *Russia* 61°4N 68°52E **214** C7
Irumu *Dem. Rep. of the Congo* 1°32N 29°53E **268** B2
Irún *Spain* 43°20N 1°52W **196** B3
Iruñea = Pamplona-Iruña
*Spain* 42°48N 1°38W **196** C3
Irurzun *Spain* 42°55N 1°50W **196** C3
Irvine *Alta., Canada* 49°57N 110°16W **297** D6
Irvine *N. Ayrs., U.K.* 55°37N 4°41W **167** F4
Irvine *Calif., U.S.A.* 33°41N 117°46W **307** M9
Irvine *Ky., U.S.A.* 37°42N 83°58W **311** G13
Irvinestown *U.K.* 54°28N 7°39W **166** B4
Irving *U.S.A.* 32°48N 96°56W **314** E6
Irving Park *U.S.A.* 41°57N 87°42W **119** B2
Irvington *U.S.A.* 37°53N 86°17W **311** G10
Irvona *U.S.A.* 40°46N 78°33W **312** F6
Irwin → *Australia* 29°15S 114°54E **279** E1
Irwinton *U.S.A.* 32°49N 83°10W **316** C6
Irwinville *U.S.A.* 31°39N 83°23W **316** D6
Irymple *Australia* 34°14S 142°8E **282** C5
Is, Jebel *Sudan* 22°3N 35°28E **256** C4
Is-sur-Tille *France* 47°30N 5°8E **173** E12
Isa *Nigeria* 13°14N 6°24E **263** C6
Isa Khel *Pakistan* 32°41N 71°17E **242** C4
Isaac → *Australia* 22°55S 149°20E **280** C4
Isabel *Rio de J., Brazil* 22°55S 43°14W **135** B1
Isabel *S. Dak., U.S.A.* 45°24N 101°26W **308** C3
Isabel, I. *Mexico* 21°51N 105°55W **318** C3
Isabel Segunda *Puerto Rico* 18°9N 65°27W **321** b
Isabela *Basilan, Phil.* 6°40N 121°59E **233** H3
Isabela *Negros, Phil.* 10°12N 122°59E **233** F4
Isabela *Puerto Rico* 18°30N 67°2W **321** b
Isabela □ *Phil.* 17°0N 122°0E **232** C4
Isabela, Canal *Ecuador* 0°20S 90°55W **330** a
Isabela, I. *Ecuador* 0°30S 91°4W **330** a
Isabela, Cord. *Nic.* 13°30N 85°25W **320** D2
Isabella Ra. *Australia* 21°0S 121°4E **278** D3
Isaccea *Romania* 45°16N 28°28E **183** E13
Isachsen, C. *Canada* 79°20N 105°28W **295** B10
Isachsen Mt. *Antarctica* 72°8S 26°5E **151** D4
Ísafjarðardjúp *Iceland* 66°10N 23°0W **155** A3
Ísafjarðarsýsla *Iceland* 66°0N 23°0W **155** B3
Ísafjörður *Iceland* 66°5N 23°9W **155** A3
Isagarh *India* 24°48N 77°51E **242** G7
Isagatedo *Nigeria* 6°31N 3°19E **124** A1
Isahaya *Japan* 32°52N 130°2E **222** E2
Isaka *Dem. Rep. of the Congo* 2°33S 18°54E **264** C3
Isaka *Tanzania* 3°56S 32°59E **268** C3
Işalniţa *Romania* 44°24N 23°44E **183** F8
Isalo, Tangorombohitr'
*Madag.* 22°45S 45°15E **272** C2
Isalo △ *Madag.* 22°23S 45°20E **272** C2
Isan → *India* 26°51N 80°7E **243** F9
Isana = Içana → *Brazil* 0°26N 67°19W **328** C4
Isandja
*Dem. Rep. of the Congo* 2°59S 21°59E **264** C4
Isangano ⌓ *Zambia* 11°8S 30°35E **269** E3
Isangi *Dem. Rep. of the Congo* 0°52N 24°10E **264** B4
Isanlu Makutu *Nigeria* 8°20N 5°50E **263** D6
Isar → *Bayern, Germany* 48°48N 12°57E **179** G8
Isar → *Oberbayern,*
*Germany* 48°15N 11°41E **131** A3
Isarco → *Italy* 46°27N 11°18E **199** B8
Isaris *Greece* 37°22N 22°0E **204** D3
Isarog, Mt. *Phil.* 13°39N 123°23E **232** E4
Isawa *Japan* 35°40N 138°35E **223** B10
Isbergues *France* 50°37N 2°24E **173** B9
Iscar *Spain* 41°22N 4°32W **194** D6
Iscayachi *Bolivia* 21°31S 65°3W **331** E4
İscehisar *Turkey* 38°51N 30°45E **205** C12
Ischia *Italy* 40°44N 13°57E **200** B6
Ischigualasto △ *Argentina* 30°0S 68°0W **334** B2
Iscuandé *Colombia* 2°28N 77°59W **328** C2
Isdell → *Australia* 16°27S 124°51E **278** C3
Ise *Japan* 34°25N 136°45E **223** C8
Ise-Shima △ *Japan* 34°25N 136°48E **223** C8
Ise-Wan *Japan* 34°43N 136°43E **223** C8
Iseffjord *Denmark* 55°53N 11°50E **163** J5
Isel → *Austria* 46°50N 12°47E **180** E5
Iseo *Italy* 45°39N 10°3E **198** C7
Iseo, L. d' *Italy* 45°43N 10°4E **198** C7
Iseramagazi *Tanzania* 4°37S 32°10E **268** C3
Isère □ *France* 45°15N 5°40E **175** C9
Isère → *France* 44°59N 4°51E **175** D8
Iserlohn *Germany* 51°22N 7°41E **178** D3
Isérnia *Italy* 41°36N 14°14E **201** A7

**Isesaki** *Japan* 36°19N 139°12E **223** A11
**Iseyin** *Nigeria* 8°0N 3°36E **263** D5
**Isfahan = Eşfahān** *Iran* 32°39N 51°43E **247** C6
**Isfjorden** *Norway* 62°35N 7°49E **164** B4
**Ishbīlīya** *Iraq* 33°21N 44°26E **113** A2
**Ishëm** *Albania* 41°33N 19°34E **202** E3
**Ishenga Oshwe** *Dem. Rep. of the Congo* 3°57S 22°33E **264** C4
**Isherton** *Guyana* 2°20N 59°25W **329** C6
**Ishigaki** *Japan* 24°26N 124°10E **221** M2
**Ishigaki-Shima** *Japan* 24°20N 124°10E **221** M2
**Ishikari** *Japan* 43°20N 141°15E **220** C10
**Ishikari-Gawa** → *Japan* 43°15N 141°23E **220** C10
**Ishikari-Sammyaku** *Japan* 43°30N 143°0E **220** C11
**Ishikari-Wan** *Japan* 43°25N 141°1E **220** C10
**Ishikawa** *Japan* 26°25N 127°49E **288** a
**Ishikawa** □ *Japan* 36°30N 136°30E **223** A8
**Ishim** *Russia* 56°10N 69°30E **214** D7
**Ishim** → *Russia* 57°45N 71°10E **214** D8
**Ishimbay** *Russia* 53°28N 56°2E **216** B5
**Ishinomaki** *Japan* 38°32N 141°20E **220** E10
**Ishioka** *Japan* 36°11N 140°16E **223** A12
**Ishizuchi-Yama** *Japan* 33°45N 133°6E **222** D5
**Ishkashim** *Tajikistan* 36°44N 71°37E **217** E8
**Ishkoman** *Pakistan* 36°30N 73°50E **243** A5
**Ishøj Strand** *Denmark* 55°36N 12°20E **118** B2
**Ishpeming** *U.S.A.* 46°29N 87°40W **308** B10
**Ishurdi** *Bangla.* 24°9N 89°3E **241** C2
**Isiboro Sécure** △ *Bolivia* 16°15S 65°50W **331** D4
**Isigny-sur-Mer** *France* 49°19N 1°6W **172** C5
**Isıklar Dağı** *Turkey* 40°45N 27°15E **203** F11
**Işıklı** *Turkey* 38°19N 29°51E **205** C11
**Isil Kul** *Russia* 54°55N 71°16E **217** B8
**Ísili** *Italy* 39°44N 9°6E **200** C2
**iSimangaliso** ⌓ *S. Africa* 27°50S 32°32E **271** C5
**Isiolo** *Kenya* 0°24N 37°33E **268** B4
**Isiro** *Dem. Rep. of the Congo* 2°53N 27°40E **268** B2
**Isisford** *Australia* 24°15S 144°21E **280** C3
**İskele = Trikomo** *Cyprus* 35°17N 33°52E **207** E9
**İskenderun** *Turkey* 36°32N 36°10E **250** B7
**İskenderun Körfezi** *Turkey* 36°40N 35°50E **250** B6
**İskilip** *Turkey* 40°45N 34°29E **212** B6
**Iskitim** *Russia* 54°38N 83°18E **217** B10
**Iskŭr** → *Bulgaria* 43°45N 24°25E **203** C8
**Iskŭr, Yazovir** *Bulgaria* 42°23N 23°30E **202** D7
**Iskushuban** *Somalia* 10°18N 50°12E **267** B7
**Iskut** → *Canada* 56°45N 131°49W **296** B2
**Isla** → *U.K.* 56°32N 3°20W **167** E5
**Isla Coiba** △ *Panama* 7°33N 81°36W **320** E4
**Isla Cristina** *Spain* 37°13N 7°17W **195** H3
**Isla de Salamanca** △ *Colombia* 10°59N 74°40W **328** A3
**Isla Gorge** △ *Australia* 25°10S 149°57E **280** D4
**Isla Gorgona** △ *Colombia* 2°59N 78°10W **328** C2
**Isla Guamblin** △ *Chile* 44°50S 75°4W **336** B1
**Isla Isabel** △ *Mexico* 21°54N 105°58W **318** C3
**Isla Magdalena** △ *Chile* 44°20S 73°13W **336** B2
**Isla Tiburón y San Estebán** ⌓ *Mexico* 29°0N 112°27W **318** B2
**Isla Vista** *U.S.A.* 34°25N 119°53W **307** L7
**İslahiye** *Turkey* 37°0N 36°35E **250** B7
**Islam Headworks** *Pakistan* 29°49N 72°33E **242** E5
**Islamabad** *Pakistan* 33°40N 73°10E **242** C5
**Islamgarh** *Pakistan* 27°51N 70°48E **242** F4
**Islamkot** *Pakistan* 24°42N 70°13E **242** G4
**Islamorada** *U.S.A.* 24°56N 80°37W **317** L9
**Islampur** *Bihar, India* 25°9N 85°12E **243** G11
**Islampur** *Maharashtra, India* 17°2N 74°20E **244** F2
**Islampur** *Paschimbanga, India* 26°16N 88°12E **243** F13
**Island = Iceland** ■ *Europe* 64°45N 19°0W **155** C8
**Island B.** *Phil.* 9°6N 118°10E **233** G2
**Island Harbour** *Anguilla* 18°12N 63°0W **322** a
**Island L.** *Canada* 53°47N 94°25W **297** C10
**Island Lagoon** *Australia* 31°30S 136°40E **282** A2
**Island Park** *Canada* 43°37N 79°22W **141** B2
**Island Pond** *U.S.A.* 44°49N 71°53W **313** B13
**Islands, B. of** *Nfld. & L., Canada* 49°11N 58°15W **299** C8
**Islands, B. of** *N.Z.* 35°15S 174°6E **284** B3
**Islas Atlánticas de Galicia** △ *Spain* 42°23N 8°55W **194** C2
**Islay** *U.K.* 55°46N 6°10W **167** F2
**Isle** → *France* 44°55N 0°15W **174** D3
**Isle aux Morts** *Canada* 47°35N 59°0W **299** C8
**Isle of Hope** *U.S.A.* 31°58N 81°5W **316** D8
**Isle of Wight** □ *U.K.* 50°41N 1°17W **169** G6
**Isle Royale** △ *U.S.A.* 48°0N 88°55W **308** B9
**Isleton** *U.S.A.* 38°10N 121°37W **306** G5
**Islev** *Denmark* 55°41N 12°27E **118** A2
**Isleworth** *U.K.* 51°28N 0°19W **125** B2
**Islington** *Canada* 43°38N 79°30W **141** B1
**Islington** □ *U.K.* 51°33N 0°5W **125** A3
**Islote Pt.** *Trin. & Tob.* 10°4N 61°47W **323** t
**Ismail = Izmayil** *Ukraine* 45°22N 28°46E **183** E13
**Ismâ'ilîya** *Egypt* 30°37N 32°18E **251** H3
**Ismâ'ilîya** □ *Egypt* 30°35N 32°16E **251** H3
**Ismâ'ilîya, Qanâ el** *Egypt* 30°7N 31°17E **117** A2
**Ismâ'ilîya, Tir'at el** → *Egypt* 30°4N 31°16E **251** H2
**Ismaning** *Germany* 48°13N 11°40E **131** A3
**Ismayloskiy Park** *Russia* 55°46N 37°46E **129** B3
**Isna** *Egypt* 25°17N 32°30E **256** B3
**Isoanala** *Madag.* 23°50S 45°44E **272** C2
**Isojärvi** △ *Finland* 61°40N 25°0E **160** F21
**Ísola del Liri** *Italy* 41°41N 13°34E **199** G10
**Ísola della Scala** *Italy* 45°16N 11°0E **198** C7
**Ísola di Capo Rizzuto** *Italy* 38°58N 17°6E **201** D10
**Isolo** *Nigeria* 6°31N 3°19E **124** A1
**Isparta** *Turkey* 37°47N 30°30E **205** D12
**Isparta** □ *Turkey* 38°0N 31°0E **212** D4
**Isperikh** *Bulgaria* 43°43N 26°50E **203** C10
**Íspica** *Italy* 36°47N 14°55E **201** F7
**İspir** *Turkey* 40°28N 40°59E **213** B9
**Israel** ■ *Asia* 32°0N 34°50E **251** G5
**Isratu** *Eritrea* 16°20N 39°53E **257** D4
**Issakly** *Russia* 54°8N 51°32E **190** C10
**Issano** *Guyana* 5°49N 59°26W **329** B6
**Issaouane, Erg** *Algeria* 26°58N 8°42E **258** C1
**Issia** *Ivory C.* 6°33N 6°33W **262** D3
**Issoire** *France* 45°32N 3°15E **174** C7
**Issoudun** *France* 46°57N 1°59E **173** F8
**Issy-les-Moulineaux** *France* 48°49N 2°15E **134** B2
**Issyk-Kul = Balykchy** *Kyrgyzstan* 42°26N 76°12E **217** D9
**Issyk-Kul, Ozero = Ysyk-Köl** *Kyrgyzstan* 42°25N 77°15E **217** D9
**Ist** *Croatia* 44°17N 14°47E **199** D11
**Istállós-kő** *Hungary* 48°4N 20°26E **182** B5
**İstanbul** *Turkey* 41°0N 28°58E **122** C1
**İstanbul** □ *Turkey* 41°0N 29°0E **203** E12
**İstanbul** ✕ **(IST)** *Turkey* 40°59N 28°49E **203** F12
**İstanbul Boğazı** *Turkey* 41°5N 29°3E **122** B2
**Istaravshān** *Tajikistan* 39°55N 69°1E **217** E7
**Isteren** *Norway* 61°58N 11°47E **164** B8
**Istiea** *Greece* 38°57N 23°9E **204** C5
**İstinye** *Turkey* 41°6N 29°3E **122** B2
**Istmina** *Colombia* 5°10N 76°39W **328** B2
**Isto, Mt.** *U.S.A.* 69°12N 143°48W **303** B12
**Istok = Burim** *Kosovo* 42°45N 20°24E **202** D4
**Istokpoga, L.** *U.S.A.* 27°23N 81°17W **317** H8
**Istra** *Croatia* 45°10N 14°0E **199** C10
**Istres** *France* 43°31N 4°59E **175** E8
**Istria = Istra** *Croatia* 45°10N 14°0E **199** C10
**Isugod** *Phil.* 9°19N 118°5E **233** G2
**Isulan** *Phil.* 6°30N 124°29E **233** H5
**Isumrud Str.** *Papua N. G.* 4°50S 145°50E **286** D3
**Itá** *Paraguay* 25°29S 57°21W **334** B4
**Itä Hakkila** *Finland* 60°17N 25°7E **121** B3
**Itabaiana** *Paraíba, Brazil* 7°18S 35°19W **332** C4
**Itabaiana** *Sergipe, Brazil* 10°41S 37°37W **332** D4
**Itabaianinha** *Brazil* 11°16S 37°47W **332** D4
**Itaberaba** *Brazil* 12°32S 40°18W **333** D3
**Itaberaí** *Brazil* 16°2S 49°48W **333** E2
**Itabira** *Brazil* 19°37S 43°13W **333** E3
**Itabirito** *Brazil* 20°15S 43°48W **333** F3
**Itaboca** *Brazil* 4°50S 62°40W **329** D5
**Itabuna** *Brazil* 14°48S 39°16W **333** D4
**Itacajá** *Brazil* 8°19S 47°46W **332** C2
**Itacaunas** → *Brazil* 5°21S 49°8W **332** C2
**Itacoatiara** *Brazil* 2°58S 58°30W **329** D6
**Itaewon** *S. Korea* 37°32N 126°58E **137** B1
**Itaguari** → *Brazil* 14°11S 44°40W **333** D3
**Itaguatins** *Brazil* 5°47S 47°29W **332** C2
**Itaim** → *Brazil* 7°2S 42°2W **332** C3
**Itainópolis** *Brazil* 7°24S 41°31W **332** C3
**Itaipú, Represa de** *Brazil* 25°30S 54°30W **335** B5
**Itäisen Suomenlahti** △ *Finland* 60°25N 27°15E **160** F22
**Itaituba** *Brazil* 4°10S 55°50W **329** D6
**Itajaí** *Brazil* 27°50S 48°39W **335** B6
**Itajany do Sul = Rio do Sul** *Brazil* 27°13S 49°37W **335** B6
**Itajubá** *Brazil* 22°24S 45°30W **333** F2
**Itajuípe** *Brazil* 14°41S 39°22W **333** D4
**Itaka** *Tanzania* 8°50S 32°49E **269** D3
**Itako** *Japan* 35°56N 140°33E **223** B12
**Itala** ⌓ *S. Africa* 27°30S 31°7E **271** C5
**Italy** ■ *Europe* 42°0N 13°0E **192** C6
**Itamaraju** *Brazil* 17°4S 39°32W **333** E4
**Itamarati** *Brazil* 6°24S 68°15W **330** B4
**Itamataré** *Brazil* 2°16S 46°24W **332** B2
**Itambacuri** *Brazil* 18°1S 41°42W **333** E3
**Itambé** *Brazil* 15°15S 40°37W **333** E3
**Itami** *Japan* 34°46N 135°24E **133** A1
**Itampolo** *Madag.* 24°41S 43°57E **272** C1
**Itanagar** *India* 27°6N 93°37E **241** B4
**Itandrano** *Madag.* 21°47S 45°17E **272** C2
**Itanhaém** *Brazil* 24°11S 46°47W **333** F2
**Itanhanga** *Brazil* 22°59S 43°19W **135** B1
**Itanhauã** → *Brazil* 4°45S 63°48W **329** D5
**Itanhém** *Brazil* 17°9S 40°20W **333** E3
**Itano** *Japan* 34°7N 134°28E **222** C6
**Itapaci** *Brazil* 14°57S 49°34W **333** D2
**Itapagé** *Brazil* 3°41S 39°34W **332** B4
**Itaparica = Petrolândia** *Brazil* 9°5S 38°20W **332** C4
**Itaparica, I. de** *Brazil* 12°54S 38°42W **333** D4
**Itaparica, Represa de** *Brazil* 11°3S 42°47W **332** D3
**Itapebi** *Brazil* 15°56S 39°32W **333** E4
**Itapecuru Mirim** *Brazil* 3°24S 44°20W **332** B3
**Itaperuna** *Brazil* 21°10S 41°54W **333** F3
**Itapetinga** *Brazil* 15°15S 40°15W **333** E3
**Itapetininga** *Brazil* 23°36S 48°7W **335** A6
**Itapeva** *Brazil* 23°59S 48°59W **335** A6
**Itapicuru** → *Bahia, Brazil* 11°47S 37°32W **332** D4
**Itapicuru** → *Maranhão, Brazil* 2°52S 44°12W **332** B3
**Itapipoca** *Brazil* 3°30S 39°35W **332** B4
**Itapira = Ubaitaba** *Brazil* 14°18S 39°20W **333** D4
**Itapiranga** *Brazil* 2°45S 58°1W **329** D6
**Itapiúna** *Brazil* 4°33S 38°57W **332** B4
**Itaporanga** *Paraíba, Brazil* 7°18S 38°0W **332** C4
**Itaporanga** *São Paulo, Brazil* 23°42S 49°29W **333** F2
**Itapuá** □ *Paraguay* 26°40S 55°40W **335** B4
**Itapuranga** *Brazil* 15°40S 49°59W **333** E2
**Itaquai** → *Brazil* 4°20S 70°12W **330** A3
**Itaquí** *Maranhão, Brazil* 2°34S 44°22W **332** B3
**Itaquí** *Rio Grande do S., Brazil* 29°8S 56°30W **334** B4
**Itararé** *Brazil* 24°6S 49°23W **335** A6
**Itarsi** *India* 22°36N 77°51E **242** H7
**Itarumã** *Brazil* 18°42S 51°25W **333** E1
**Itatí** *Argentina* 27°16S 58°15W **334** B4
**Itatiaia** △ *Brazil* 22°22S 44°38W **335** A7
**Itatira** *Brazil* 4°30S 39°37W **332** B4
**Itatuba** *Brazil* 5°46S 63°20W **331** B5
**Itatupã** *Brazil* 0°37S 51°12W **329** D7
**Itaueira** *Brazil* 7°36S 43°2W **332** C3
**Itaueira** → *Brazil* 6°41S 42°55W **332** C3
**Itaúna** *Brazil* 20°4S 44°34W **333** F3
**Itbayat** *Phil.* 20°47N 121°51E **232** A3
**Itbayat I.** *Phil.* 20°45N 121°50E **232** A3
**Itchen** → *U.K.* 50°55N 1°22W **169** G6
**Itchouma** *Niger* 20°14N 13°32E **261** D7
**Ite** *Peru* 17°55S 70°57W **330** D3
**Itea** *Greece* 38°25N 22°25E **204** C4
**Itezhi Tezhi, L.** *Zambia* 15°30S 25°30E **269** F2
**Ithaca = Ithaki** *Greece* 38°25N 20°40E **207** C2
**Ithaca** *U.S.A.* 42°27N 76°30W **313** D8
**Ithaki** *Greece* 38°25N 20°40E **207** C2
**Ithakis, Stenon** *Greece* 38°22N 20°39E **207** C2
**Iti** △ *Greece* 38°50N 22°15E **204** C4
**Itimbiri** → *Dem. Rep. of the Congo* 2°2N 22°44E **264** B4
**Itinga** *Brazil* 16°36S 41°47W **333** E3
**Itiquira** *Brazil* 17°12S 54°7W **331** D7
**Itiquira** → *Brazil* 17°18S 56°44W **331** D6
**Itiruçu** *Brazil* 13°31S 40°9W **333** D3
**Itiúba** *Brazil* 10°43S 39°51W **332** D4
**Itiyuro** → *Argentina* 22°40S 63°50W **334** A3
**Itkilik** → *U.S.A.* 70°9N 150°56W **303** A10
**Itō** *Japan* 34°58N 139°5E **223** C11
**Itogon** *Phil.* 16°22N 120°41E **232** C3
**Itoigawa** *Japan* 37°2N 137°51E **221** F8
**Itoko** *Dem. Rep. of the Congo* 1°0S 21°48E **264** C4
**Itoman** *Japan* 26°7N 127°40E **288** a
**Iton** → *France* 49°9N 1°12E **172** C8
**Itonamas** → *Bolivia* 12°28S 64°24W **331** C5
**Itri** *Italy* 41°17N 13°32E **200** A6
**Itsa** *Egypt* 29°15N 30°47E **256** J7
**Itsamia** *Comoros Is.* 12°21S 43°52E **272** a
**Itsandra** *Comoros Is.* 11°40S 43°15E **272** a
**Itsuki** *Japan* 32°24N 130°50E **222** E2
**Itsukushima Shrine** *Japan* 34°17N 132°19E **222** C4
**Íttiri** *Italy* 40°36N 8°34E **200** B1
**Ittoqqortoormiit** *Greenland* 70°20N 23°0W **154** C8
**Itu** *Brazil* 23°17S 47°15W **335** A6
**Itu** *Nigeria* 5°10N 7°58E **263** D6
**Itu Aba I.** *S. China Sea* 10°23N 114°21E **230** B4
**Ituaçu** *Brazil* 13°50S 41°18W **333** D3
**Ituango** *Colombia* 7°4N 75°45W **328** B2
**Ituí** → *Brazil* 4°38S 70°19W **328** D3
**Ituiutaba** *Brazil* 19°0S 49°25W **333** E2
**Itumbiara** *Brazil* 18°20S 49°10W **333** E2
**Ituna** *Canada* 51°10N 103°24W **297** C8
**Itunge Port** *Tanzania* 9°40S 33°55E **269** D3
**Ituni** *Guyana* 5°28N 58°15W **329** B6
**Itupiranga** *Brazil* 5°9S 49°20W **332** C2
**Iturama** *Brazil* 19°44S 50°11W **333** E1
**Iturbe** *Argentina* 23°0S 65°25W **334** A2
**Ituri** → *Dem. Rep. of the Congo* 1°40N 27°1E **268** B2
**Iturup, Ostrov** *Russia* 45°0N 148°0E **215** E15
**Ituverava** *Brazil* 20°20S 47°47W **333** F2
**Ituxi** → *Brazil* 7°18S 64°51W **331** B5
**Itzehoe** *Germany* 53°55N 9°31E **178** B5
**Iuka** *U.S.A.* 38°37N 88°47W **311** F8
**Iungsdalshytta** *Norway* 60°49N 7°55E **164** D4
**Ivahona** *Madag.* 23°27S 46°10E **272** C2
**Ivaí** → *Brazil* 23°18S 53°42W **335** A5
**Ivalo** *Finland* 68°38N 27°35E **160** B22
**Ivalojoki** → *Finland* 68°40N 27°40E **160** B22
**Ivanava** *Belarus* 52°7N 25°29E **177** B13
**Ivančice** *Czech Rep.* 49°6N 16°23E **181** B9
**Ivane-Puste** *Ukraine* 48°39N 26°10E **183** B11
**Ivăneşti** *Romania* 46°39N 27°27E **183** D12
**Ivangorod = Dęblin** *Poland* 51°34N 21°50E **185** G8
**Ivangorod** *Russia* 59°27N 28°13E **188** C5
**Ivanhoe** *N.S.W., Australia* 32°56S 144°20E **282** B6
**Ivanhoe** *Vic., Australia* 37°45S 145°3E **128** A2
**Ivanhoe** *Ont., Canada* 44°23N 77°28W **312** B7
**Ivanhoe** *Calif., U.S.A.* 36°23N 119°13W **306** J7
**Ivanhoe** *Minn., U.S.A.* 44°28N 96°15W **308** C5
**Ivanhorod** *Ukraine* 48°48N 29°50E **183** B14
**Ivanić Grad** *Croatia* 45°41N 16°25E **199** C13
**Ivanjica** *Serbia* 43°35N 20°12E **202** C4
**Ivanjska** *Bos.-H.* 44°55N 17°4E **182** F2
**Ivankoyskoye Vdkhr.** *Russia* 56°37N 36°32E **188** D9
**Ivano-Frankivsk** *Ukraine* 48°40N 24°40E **183** B9
**Ivano-Frankivsk** □ *Ukraine* 48°45N 24°30E **183** B9
**Ivanof Bay** *U.S.A.* 55°54N 159°29W **303** J8
**Ivanovo = Ivanava** *Belarus* 52°7N 25°29E **177** B13
**Ivanovo** *Bulgaria* 43°43N 25°58E **203** C9
**Ivanovo** *Russia* 57°5N 41°0E **188** D11
**Ivanovo** □ *Russia* 57°10N 41°50E **190** B5
**Ivanšćica** *Croatia* 46°12N 16°13E **199** B13
**Ivashchenkovo = Chapayevsk** *Russia* 53°0N 49°40E **190** D9
**Ivato** *Madag.* 20°37S 47°10E **272** C2
**Ivatsevichy** *Belarus* 52°43N 25°21E **177** B13
**Ivaylovgrad** *Bulgaria* 41°32N 26°8E **203** E10
**Ivdel** *Russia* 60°42N 60°24E **186** B11
**Iveragh Pen.** *Ireland* 51°52N 10°15W **166** E1
**Ives Estates** *U.S.A.* 25°58N 80°10W **129** C2
**Ivgres = Komsomolsk** *Russia* 57°2N 40°20E **188** D11
**Ivindo** → *Gabon* 0°9S 12°9E **264** C2
**Ivinheima** → *Brazil* 23°14S 53°42W **335** A5
**Ivinhema** *Brazil* 22°10S 53°37W **335** A5
**Ivittuut** *Greenland* 61°14N 48°12W **154** E6
**Iviza = Eivissa** *Spain* 38°54N 1°26E **206** D1
**Ivohibe** *Madag.* 22°31S 46°57E **272** C2
**Ivolândia** *Brazil* 16°34S 50°51W **333** E1
**Ivory Coast** *W. Afr.* 4°20N 5°0W **262** E4
**Ivory Coast** ■ *Africa* 7°30N 5°0W **262** D4
**Ivösjön** *Sweden* 56°8N 14°25E **163** H8
**Ivrea** *Italy* 45°28N 7°52E **198** C4
**İvrindi** *Turkey* 39°34N 27°30E **205** B9
**Ivry-sur-Seine** *France* 48°49N 2°22E **134** B3
**Ivujivik** *Canada* 62°24N 77°55W **295** E16
**Ivvavik** △ *Canada* 69°6N 139°30W **294** D4
**Ivybridge** *U.K.* 50°23N 3°56W **169** G4
**Iwa** *Japan* 36°5N 139°52E **223** A11
**Iwai-Jima** *Japan* 33°47N 131°58E **222** D3
**Iwaizumi** *Japan* 39°50N 141°45E **220** E10
**Iwaki** *Japan* 37°3N 140°55E **221** F10
**Iwakuni** *Japan* 34°15N 132°8E **222** C4
**Iwami** *Japan* 35°32N 134°15E **222** B6
**Iwami Ginzan** *Japan* 35°6N 132°26E **222** B4
**Iwamizawa** *Japan* 43°12N 141°46E **220** C10
**Iwanai** *Japan* 42°58N 140°30E **220** C10
**Iwase** *Japan* 36°21N 140°6E **223** A12
**Iwata** *Japan* 34°42N 137°51E **223** C9
**Iwate** □ *Japan* 39°30N 141°30E **220** E10
**Iwate-San** *Japan* 39°51N 141°0E **220** E10
**Iwo** *Nigeria* 7°39N 4°9E **263** D5
**Iwo Jima** *Pac. Oc.* 24°47N 141°20E **288** b
**Iwŏn** *N. Korea* 40°19N 128°39E **224** B4
**Iwonicz-Zdrój** *Poland* 49°37N 21°47E **185** J8
**Iwungu** *Dem. Rep. of the Congo* 5°16S 19°17E **265** D3
**Ixelles** *Belgium* 50°50N 4°22E **116** B2
**Ixiamas** *Bolivia* 13°50S 68°5W **330** C4
**Ixopo** *S. Africa* 30°11S 30°5E **271** D5
**Ixtepec** *Mexico* 16°34N 95°6W **319** D5
**Ixtlán del Río** *Mexico* 21°2N 104°22W **318** C4
**Iyal Bakhit** *Sudan* 13°20N 28°39E **257** E2
**Iyo** *Japan* 33°45N 132°45E **222** D4
**Iyo-Mishima** *Japan* 33°58N 133°30E **222** D5
**Iyo-Nada** *Japan* 33°40N 132°20E **222** D4
**Izabal, L. de** *Guatemala* 15°30N 89°10W **320** C2
**Izamal** *Mexico* 20°56N 89°1W **319** C7
**Izberbash** *Russia* 42°35N 47°52E **191** J8
**Izbica** *Poland* 50°53N 23°10E **185** H10
**Izbica Kujawska** *Poland* 52°25N 18°40E **185** F5
**Izbiceni** *Romania* 43°45N 24°40E **183** G9
**Izembek Nat. Wildlife Refuge** ⌓ *U.S.A.* 55°15N 162°45W **303** J7
**Izena-Shima** *Japan* 26°56N 127°56E **221** L3
**Izgrev** *Bulgaria* 43°36N 26°58E **203** C10
**Izhevsk** *Russia* 56°51N 53°14E **186** C9
**Izhma = Sosnogorsk** *Russia* 63°37N 53°51E **186** B9
**Izhma** → *Russia* 65°19N 52°54E **186** A9
**Izileg** *Algeria* 20°20N 6°4E **261** D6
**Izkī** *Oman* 22°56N 57°46E **249** B7
**Izmayil** *Ukraine* 45°22N 28°46E **183** E13
**Izmaylovo** *Russia* 55°47N 37°47E **129** B3
**İzmir** *Turkey* 38°25N 27°8E **205** C9
**İzmir** □ *Turkey* 38°15N 27°40E **205** C9
**İzmir Adnan Menderes** ✕ **(ADB)** *Turkey* 38°23N 27°6E **205** C9
**İzmir Körfezi** *Turkey* 38°30N 26°50E **205** C8
**İzmit = Kocaeli** *Turkey* 40°45N 29°50E **203** F13
**Iznájar** *Spain* 37°15N 4°19W **195** H6
**Iznalloz** *Spain* 37°24N 3°30W **195** H7
**İznik** *Turkey* 40°23N 29°46E **212** B3
**İznik Gölü** *Turkey* 40°27N 29°30E **203** F13
**Izobilno-Tishchenskoye = Izobil'nyy** *Russia* 45°25N 41°44E **191** H5
**Izobil'nyy** *Russia* 45°25N 41°44E **191** H5
**Izola** *Slovenia* 45°32N 13°39E **199** C10
**Izozog, Bañados de** *Bolivia* 18°48S 62°10W **331** D5
**Izra** *Syria* 32°51N 36°15E **250** F7
**Iztacalco** *Mexico* 19°23N 99°5W **128** B2
**Iztapalapa** *Mexico* 19°21N 99°6W **128** B2
**Iztochni Rodopi** *Bulgaria* 41°45N 25°30E **203** E9
**Izu** *Japan* 34°58N 138°56E **223** C10
**Izu-Hantō** *Japan* 34°45N 139°0E **223** C11
**Izu-Shotō** *Japan* 34°30N 140°0E **221** G10
**Izúcar de Matamoros** *Mexico* 18°36N 98°28W **319** D5
**Izuhara** *Japan* 34°12N 129°17E **222** C1
**Izumi** *Kagoshima, Japan* 32°5N 130°22E **222** E2
**Izumi** *Ōsaka, Japan* 34°28N 135°24E **223** C7
**Izumi-Sano** *Japan* 34°23N 135°18E **223** C7
**Izumo** *Japan* 35°20N 132°46E **222** B4
**Izunokuni** *Japan* 35°2N 138°55E **223** B10
**Izyaslav** *Ukraine* 50°5N 26°50E **177** C14
**Izyum** *Ukraine* 49°12N 37°19E **189** H9


# J


**J.F.K. Int.** ✕ **(JFK)** *U.S.A.* 40°38N 73°47W **313** F11
**J.F. Rodrigues** *Brazil* 2°55S 50°20W **332** B1
**J.P. Koch Fjord** *Greenland* 82°45N 44°0W **154** A6
**J. Strom Thurmond L.** *U.S.A.* 33°40N 82°12W **316** B7
**Ja-ela** *Sri Lanka* 7°5N 79°53E **245** L4
**Ja-eundo** *S. Korea* 34°53N 126°2E **224** E3
**Ja'ār** *Yemen* 13°13N 45°18E **248** D4
**Jaba** *Ethiopia* 6°20N 35°7E **257** F4
**Jaba** *West Bank* 31°51N 35°16E **123** A2
**Jabal al Awliya'** *Sudan* 15°14N 32°29E **266** A3
**Jabal as Sirāj** *Afghan.* 35°7N 69°16E **240** B3
**Jabalón** → *Spain* 38°53N 4°5W **195** G6
**Jabalpur** *India* 23°9N 79°58E **243** H8
**Jabālya** *Gaza Strip* 31°32N 34°29E **251** G5
**Jabbūl** *Syria* 36°4N 37°30E **246** B3
**Jabiru** *Australia* 12°40S 132°53E **278** B5
**Jablah** *Syria* 35°20N 36°0E **250** C7
**Jablanac** *Croatia* 44°42N 14°56E **199** D11
**Jablanica** *Bos.-H.* 43°40N 17°45E **182** G2
**Jablonec nad Nisou** *Czech Rep.* 50°43N 15°10E **180** A8
**Jablonica** *Slovak Rep.* 48°37N 17°26E **181** C10
**Jabłonowo Pomorskie** *Poland* 53°23N 19°10E **184** E6
**Jablunkov** *Czech Rep.* 49°35N 18°46E **181** B11
**Jaboatão** *Brazil* 8°7S 35°1W **332** C4
**Jabonga** *Phil.* 9°20N 125°32E **233** G5
**Jabotabek = Jakarta** *Indonesia* 6°9S 106°52E **122** A2
**Jaboticabal** *Brazil* 21°15S 48°17W **335** A6
**Jabukovac** *Serbia* 44°22N 22°21E **202** B6
**Jaburu** *Brazil* 5°30S 64°0W **331** B5
**Jaca** *Spain* 42°35N 0°33W **196** C4
**Jacaré** *Brazil* 22°53S 43°14W **135** B1
**Jacaré** → *Brazil* 10°3S 42°13W **332** D3
**Jacareí** *Brazil* 23°20S 46°0W **335** A6
**Jacarèzinho** *Brazil* 23°5S 49°58W **335** A6
**Jaci-Paraná** *Brazil* 9°15S 64°23W **331** B5
**Jaciara** *Brazil* 15°59S 54°57W **331** D7
**Jacinto** *Brazil* 16°10S 40°17W **333** E3
**Jack River** △ *Australia* 14°58S 144°19E **280** A3
**Jackman** *U.S.A.* 45°37N 70°15W **309** C18
**Jacksboro** *U.S.A.* 33°13N 98°10W **314** E5
**Jackson** *Barbados* 13°7N 59°36W **323** r
**Jackson** *Ala., U.S.A.* 31°31N 87°53W **315** F11
**Jackson** *Calif., U.S.A.* 38°21N 120°46W **306** G6
**Jackson** *Ga., U.S.A.* 33°20N 83°57W **316** B6
**Jackson** *Ky., U.S.A.* 37°33N 83°23W **309** G12
**Jackson** *Mich., U.S.A.* 42°15N 84°24W **311** B12
**Jackson** *Minn., U.S.A.* 43°37N 95°1W **308** D6
**Jackson** *Miss., U.S.A.* 32°18N 90°12W **315** E9
**Jackson** *Mo., U.S.A.* 37°23N 89°40W **308** G9
**Jackson** *N.H., U.S.A.* 44°10N 71°11W **313** B13
**Jackson** *Ohio, U.S.A.* 39°3N 82°39W **309** F12
**Jackson** *S.C., U.S.A.* 33°20N 81°47W **316** B8
**Jackson** *Tenn., U.S.A.* 35°37N 88°49W **315** D10
**Jackson** *Wyo., U.S.A.* 43°29N 110°46W **304** E8
**Jackson, C.** *N.Z.* 40°59S 174°20E **285** A9
**Jackson B.** *N.Z.* 43°58S 168°42E **285** D3
**Jackson Center** *U.S.A.* 40°27N 84°4W **311** D12
**Jackson Hd.** *N.Z.* 43°58S 168°37E **285** D3
**Jackson Heights** *U.S.A.* 40°44N 73°53W **132** B2
**Jackson L.** *Fla., U.S.A.* 30°30N 84°17W **316** E5
**Jackson L.** *Ga., U.S.A.* 33°19N 83°50W **316** B6
**Jackson L.** *Wyo., U.S.A.* 43°52N 110°36W **304** E8
**Jackson Park** *U.S.A.* 41°46N 87°34W **119** C3
**Jacksons** *N.Z.* 42°46S 171°32E **285** C6
**Jackson's Arm** *Canada* 49°52N 56°47W **299** C8
**Jacksonville** *Ala., U.S.A.* 33°49N 85°46W **316** B4
**Jacksonville** *Ark., U.S.A.* 34°52N 92°7W **314** D8
**Jacksonville** *Calif., U.S.A.* 37°52N 120°24W **306** H6
**Jacksonville** *Fla., U.S.A.* 30°20N 81°39W **316** E8
**Jacksonville** *Ga., U.S.A.* 31°49N 82°59W **316** D7
**Jacksonville** *Ill., U.S.A.* 39°44N 90°14W **310** E6
**Jacksonville** *N.C., U.S.A.* 34°45N 77°26W **315** D16
**Jacksonville** *Tex., U.S.A.* 31°58N 95°17W **314** F7
**Jacksonville Beach** *U.S.A.* 30°17N 81°24W **316** E8
**Jacksonville Int.** ✕ **(JAX)** *U.S.A.* 30°30N 81°41W **316** E8
**Jacmel** *Haiti* 18°14N 72°32W **321** C5
**Jaco, Pte.** *Dominica* 15°39N 61°24W **323** k
**Jacob Lake** *U.S.A.* 36°43N 112°13W **305** H7
**Jacobabad** *Pakistan* 28°20N 68°29E **242** E3
**Jacobina** *Brazil* 11°11S 40°30W **332** D3
**Jacobshagen = Dobrzany** *Poland* 53°22N 15°25E **184** E2
**Jacon Javits Convention Center** *New York, U.S.A.* **132** c1
**Jacotet, B.** *Mauritius* 20°30S 57°26E **272** e
**Jacqueline Kennedy Onassis Res.** *New York, U.S.A.* **132** a3
**Jacques-Cartier** *Canada* 45°31N 73°27W **130** A3
**Jacques-Cartier, Dét. de** *Canada* 50°0N 63°30W **299** C7
**Jacques-Cartier, Mt.** *Canada* 48°57N 66°0W **299** C6
**Jacques-Cartier, Pont** *Canada* 45°31N 73°32W **130** A2
**Jacques-Cartier** ⌓ *Canada* 47°15N 71°33W **299** C5
**Jacqueville** *Ivory C.* 5°12N 4°25W **262** D4
**Jacuí** → *Brazil* 30°2S 51°15W **335** C5
**Jacumba** *U.S.A.* 32°37N 116°11W **307** N10
**Jacundá** → *Brazil* 1°57S 50°26W **332** B1
**Jadavpur** *India* 22°28N 88°22E **124** C2
**Jadcherla** *India* 16°46N 78°9E **244** F4
**Jade** *Germany* 53°20N 8°14E **178** B4
**Jade, Côte de** *France* 46°40N 2°0W **172** F4
**Jade Buddha Temple** *China* 31°15N 121°25E **138** B1
**Jade City** *Canada* 59°15N 129°37W **296** B3
**Jade Dragon Snow Mt. = Yulong Xueshan** *China* 27°6N 100°10E **228** D3
**Jade Island** *Beijing, China* **114** b2
**Jade Mt. = Yü Shan** *Taiwan* 23°25N 120°52E **225** C2
**Jadebusen** *Germany* 53°29N 8°12E **178** B4
**Jadotville = Likasi** *Dem. Rep. of the Congo* 10°55S 26°48E **269** E2
**Jadovnik** *Serbia* 43°20N 19°45E **202** C3
**Jadraque** *Spain* 40°55N 2°55W **196** E2
**Jādū** *Libya* 32°0N 12°0E **258** B2
**Jægersborg** *Denmark* 55°45N 12°31E **118** A3
**Jægersborg Dyrehave** *Denmark* 55°46N 12°33E **118** A3
**Jaén** *Peru* 5°25S 78°40W **330** B2
**Jaén** *Spain* 37°44N 3°43W **195** H7
**Jaén** □ *Spain* 37°50N 3°30W **195** H7
**Jæren** *Norway* 58°42N 5°47E **164** F2
**Jærens Rev** *Norway* 58°45N 5°45E **164** F2
**Jafarabad** *India* 20°52N 71°22E **242** J4
**Jaffa = Tel Aviv-Yafo** *Israel* 32°4N 34°48E **251** F5
**Jaffa, C.** *Australia* 36°58S 139°40E **282** D3
**Jaffna** *Sri Lanka* 9°45N 80°2E **245** K5
**Jaffrey** *U.S.A.* 42°49N 72°2W **313** D12
**Jagadhri** *India* 30°10N 77°20E **242** D7
**Jagadishpur** *Bihar, India* 25°30N 84°21E **243** G11
**Jagadishpur** *Paschimbanga, India* 22°39N 88°17E **124** B1
**Jagat** *Nepal* 28°19N 84°53E **243** E11
**Jagatpur** *India* 28°44N 77°13E **120** A2
**Jagdalpur** *India* 19°3N 82°0E **244** E6
**Jagdaqi** *China* 50°25N 124°7E **219** A13
**Jagersfontein** *S. Africa* 29°44S 25°27E **270** C4
**Jaghīn** → *Iran* 27°17N 57°13E **247** E8
**Jagna** *Phil.* 9°39N 124°22E **233** G5
**Jagodina** *Serbia* 44°5N 21°15E **202** B5
**Jagraon** *India* 30°50N 75°25E **242** D6
**Jagst** → *Germany* 49°14N 9°10E **179** F5
**Jagtial** *India* 18°50N 79°0E **244** E4
**Jaguaquara** *Brazil* 13°32S 39°58W **333** D4
**Jaguaré, Rib. do** → *Brazil* 23°32S 46°45W **137** B1
**Jaguariaíva** *Brazil* 24°10S 49°50W **335** A6
**Jaguaribe** *Brazil* 5°53S 38°37W **332** C4
**Jaguaribe** → *Brazil* 4°25S 37°45W **332** B4
**Jaguaruana** *Brazil* 4°50S 37°47W **332** B4
**Jagüey Grande** *Cuba* 22°35N 81°7W **320** B3
**Jagungal, Mt.** *Australia* 36°8S 148°22E **283** D8
**Jahanabad** *India* 25°13N 84°59E **243** G11
**Jahangirpur** *India* 28°43N 77°12E **120** A2
**Jahazpur** *India* 25°37N 75°17E **242** G6
**Jahrom** *Iran* 28°30N 53°31E **247** D7
**Jaicós** *Brazil* 7°21S 41°8W **332** C3
**Jaigarh** *India* 17°17N 73°13E **244** F1
**Jaijon** *India* 31°21N 76°9E **242** D7
**Jailolo** *Indonesia* 1°5N 127°30E **231** D7
**Jailolo, Selat** *Indonesia* 0°5N 129°5E **231** D7
**Jaintiapur** *Bangla.* 25°8N 92°7E **241** C4
**Jaipur** *Assam, India* 27°16N 95°24E **241** B5
**Jaipur** *Raj., India* 27°0N 75°50E **242** F6
**Jais** *India* 26°15N 81°32E **243** F9
**Jaisalmer** *India* 26°55N 70°54E **242** F4
**Jaisinghnagar** *India* 23°38N 78°34E **243** H8
**Jaitaran** *India* 26°12N 73°56E **242** F5
**Jaithari** *India* 23°14N 78°37E **243** H8
**Jajarkot** *Nepal* 28°42N 82°14E **243** E10
**Jājarm** *Iran* 36°58N 56°27E **247** B8
**Jajce** *Bos.-H.* 44°19N 17°17E **182** F2
**Jajpur** *India* 20°53N 86°22E **244** D8
**Jakam** → *India* 23°54N 74°13E **242** H6
**Jakar Dzong** *Bhutan* 27°33N 90°43E **241** B3
**Jakarta** *Indonesia* 6°9S 106°52E **122** A2
**Jakarta, Teluk** *Indonesia* 6°5S 106°50E **122** A1
**Jakarta Halim Perdana Kusuma Int.** ✕ **(HLP)** *Indonesia* 6°16S 106°53E **122** B2
**Jakhal** *India* 29°48N 75°50E **242** E6
**Jakharrah** *Libya* 29°13N 21°34E **258** C4
**Jakhau** *India* 23°13N 68°43E **242** H3
**Jakobshavn = Ilulissat** *Greenland* 69°12N 51°10W **154** D5
**Jakobstad = Pietarsaari** *Finland* 63°40N 22°43E **160** E20
**Jakupica** *Macedonia* 41°45N 21°22E **202** E5
**Jal** *U.S.A.* 32°7N 103°12W **305** K12
**Jalaihai Pt.** *Guam* 13°18N 144°46E **302** d
**Jalājil** *Si. Arabia* 25°40N 45°27E **246** E5
**Jalal-Abad** *Kyrgyzstan* 40°56N 73°0E **217** D8
**Jalal-Abad** □ *Kyrgyzstan* 41°30N 72°30E **217** D8
**Jalālābād** *Afghan.* 34°30N 70°29E **242** B4
**Jalalabad** *India* 27°41N 79°42E **243** F8
**Jalalpur Jattan** *Pakistan* 32°38N 74°11E **242** C6
**Jalama** *U.S.A.* 34°29N 120°29W **307** L6
**Jalan Kayu** *Singapore* 1°24N 103°52E **138** A3
**Jalandhar = Jullundur** *India* 31°20N 75°40E **242** D6
**Jalapa** *Guatemala* 14°39N 89°59W **320** D2
**Jalapa Enríquez = Xalapa** *Mexico* 19°32N 96°55W **319** D5
**Jalasjärvi** *Finland* 62°29N 22°47E **160** E20
**Jalaun** *India* 26°8N 79°25E **243** F8
**Jalāzin** *Afghan.* 37°2N 64°49E **240** A2
**Jaldak** *Afghan.* 31°58N 66°43E **240** C2
**Jaldhaka** → *Bangla.* 26°16N 89°16E **241** B2
**Jales** *Brazil* 20°10S 50°33W **333** F1
**Jalesar** *India* 27°29N 78°19E **242** F8
**Jaleswar** *Nepal* 26°38N 85°48E **243** F11
**Jalgaon** *India* 21°0N 75°42E **244** D2
**Jalībah** *Iraq* 30°35N 46°32E **246** D5
**Jalingo** *Nigeria* 8°55N 11°25E **263** D7
**Jalisco** □ *Mexico* 20°20N 103°40W **318** D4
**Jalkot** *Pakistan* 35°14N 73°24E **243** B5
**Jalna** *India* 19°48N 75°38E **244** E2
**Jalón** → *Spain* 41°47N 1°4W **196** D3
**Jalor** *India* 25°21N 72°37E **242** G5
**Jalpa** *Mexico* 21°38N 102°58W **318** C4
**Jalpaiguri** *India* 26°32N 88°46E **241** B2
**Jalpan** *Mexico* 21°14N 99°29W **319** C5
**Jālq** *Iran* 27°35N 62°46E **240** D1
**Jālū** *Libya* 29°2N 21°33E **258** C4
**Jaluit I.** *Marshall Is.* 6°0N 169°30E **288** G8
**Jalūlā** *Iraq* 34°16N 45°10E **213** E11
**Jam, Minaret of** *Afghan.* 34°23N 64°30E **240** B2
**Jamaame** *Somalia* 0°4N 42°44E **267** D5
**Jamaari** *Nigeria* 11°44N 9°53E **263** C6
**Jamaica** ■ *W. Indies* 18°10N 77°30W **320** a
**Jamaica B.** *U.S.A.* 40°36N 73°50W **132** C3
**Jamaica Channel** *Jamaica* 17°0N 76°0W **321** C4
**Jamaica Plain** *U.S.A.* 42°18N 71°6W **116** B2
**Jamakpuri** *India* 28°37N 77°5E **120** B1
**Jamalpur** *Bangla.* 24°52N 89°56E **241** C2
**Jamalpur** *India* 25°18N 86°28E **243** G12
**Jamalpurganj** *India* 23°2N 87°59E **243** H13
**Jamanota** *Aruba* 12°29N 69°57W **322** f
**Jamanxim** → *Brazil* 4°43S 56°18W **331** A6
**Jamari** *Brazil* 8°45S 63°27W **331** B5
**Jamari** → *Brazil* 8°27S 63°30W **331** B5
**Jamba** *Angola* 14°40S 16°2E **265** E3
**Jambewangi** *Indonesia* 8°17S 114°7E **231** J17
**Jambi** *Indonesia* 1°38S 103°30E **234** C2
**Jambi** □ *Indonesia* 1°30S 102°30E **234** C2
**Jambongan, Pulau** *Malaysia* 6°45N 117°20E **235** A5
**Jambusar** *India* 22°3N 72°51E **242** H5
**James** *U.S.A.* 32°58N 83°29W **316** C6
**James** → *S. Dak., U.S.A.* 42°52N 97°18W **308** D5
**James** → *Va., U.S.A.* 36°56N 76°27W **309** G15
**James, I. = San Salvador, I.** *Ecuador* 0°16S 90°42W **330** a
**James B.** *Canada* 54°0N 80°0W **298** B3
**James I.** *Gambia* 13°19N 16°21W **262** C1
**James Island** *U.S.A.* 32°45N 79°55W **316** C10
**James Ranges** *Australia* 24°10S 132°30E **278** D5
**James Ross I.** *Antarctica* 63°58S 57°50W **151** C18
**James Ross Str.** *Canada* 69°40N 96°10W **294** D12
**Jamesabad** *Pakistan* 25°17N 69°15E **242** G3
**Jameson Land** *Greenland* 71°0N 23°30W **154** C8
**Jamesport** *U.S.A.* 39°58N 93°48W **310** E3
**Jamestown = Wawa** *Canada* 47°59N 84°47W **298** C3
**Jamestown** *S. Austral., Australia* 33°10S 138°32E **282** B3
**Jamestown** *St. Helena* 15°55S 5°43W **153** h
**Jamestown** *Eastern Cape, S. Africa* 31°6S 26°45E **270** D4
**Jamestown** *Ind., U.S.A.* 39°56N 86°38W **311** E10
**Jamestown** *Mo., U.S.A.* 38°48N 92°30W **310** F4
**Jamestown** *N. Dak., U.S.A.* 46°54N 98°42W **308** B4
**Jamestown** *N.Y., U.S.A.* 42°6N 79°14W **312** D5
**Jamestown** *Ohio, U.S.A.* 39°39N 83°33W **311** E13
**Jamestown** *Pa., U.S.A.* 41°29N 80°27W **312** E4
**Jamestown** *S.C., U.S.A.* 33°17N 79°42W **316** B10
**Jamīlābād** *Iran* 34°24N 48°28E **247** C6
**Jamira** → *India* 21°35N 88°28E **243** J13
**Jämjö** *Sweden* 56°12N 15°49E **163** H9
**Jamkhandi** *India* 16°30N 75°15E **244** F2
**Jamkhed** *India* 18°43N 75°19E **244** E2
**Jammalamadugu** *India* 14°51N 78°25E **245** G4
**Jammerbugten** *Denmark* 57°15N 9°20E **163** G3
**Jammu** *India* 32°43N 74°54E **242** C6
**Jammu & Kashmir** □ *India* 34°25N 77°0E **243** B7
**Jamnagar** *India* 22°30N 70°6E **242** H4
**Jamner** *India* 20°45N 75°52E **244** D2
**Jamni** → *India* 25°13N 78°35E **243** G8
**Jampur** *Pakistan* 29°39N 70°40E **242** E4
**Jamrud** *Pakistan* 33°59N 71°24E **242** C4
**Jämsä** *Finland* 61°53N 25°10E **188** B3
**Jamshedpur** *India* 22°44N 86°12E **243** H12
**Jamshīdīyeh** *Iran* 35°42N 51°22E **141** A2
**Jamsil** *S. Korea* 37°30N 127°4E **137** B2
**Jamtara** *India* 23°59N 86°49E **243** H12
**Jämtland** *Sweden* 63°31N 14°0E **160** E16
**Jämtlands län** □ *Sweden* 63°0N 14°40E **162** B7
**Jamuna** → *Bangla.* 23°51N 89°45E **241** D2
**Jamurki** *Bangla.* 24°9N 90°2E **241** C3
**Jamwon** *S. Korea* 37°30N 127°0E **137** B2
**Jan L.** *Canada* 54°56N 102°55W **297** C8
**Jan Mayen** *Arctic* 71°0N 9°0W **150** B7
**Janakkala** *Finland* 60°54N 24°36E **188** B3
**Janakpur** *Nepal* 26°42N 85°55E **244** A7
**Janaúba** *Brazil* 15°48S 43°19W **333** E3
**Janaucu, I.** *Brazil* 0°30N 50°10W **332** A1
**Jand** *Pakistan* 33°30N 72°6E **242** C5
**Jandaia** *Brazil* 17°6S 50°7W **333** E1
**Jandanku** ☼ *Australia* 16°20S 135°45E **280** B2
**Jandaq** *Iran* 34°3N 54°22E **247** C7
**Jandía** *Canary Is.* 28°6N 14°21W **153** e2
**Jandía, Pta. de** *Canary Is.* 28°3N 14°31W **153** e2
**Jandía** △ *Canary Is.* 28°4N 14°19W **153** e2
**Jandiatuba** → *Brazil* 3°28S 68°42W **328** D4
**Jandola** *Pakistan* 32°20N 70°9E **242** C4
**Jandowae** *Australia* 26°45S 151°7E **281** D5
**Jándula** → *Spain* 38°3N 4°6W **195** G6
**Jane Pk.** *N.Z.* 45°15S 168°20E **285** F3
**Janesville** *U.S.A.* 42°41N 89°1W **310** B7
**Janga** *Ghana* 10°5N 1°0W **263** C4
**Jangamo** *Mozam.* 24°6S 35°21E **271** B6
**Janghai** *India* 25°33N 82°19E **243** G10
**Jangheung** *S. Korea* 34°41N 126°52E **224** E3
**Janghowon** *S. Korea* 37°7N 127°37E **224** D3
**Jangipur** *India* 24°28N 88°4E **243** G12
**Jangoon** *India* 17°44N 79°5E **244** F4
**Jangsu** *S. Korea* 35°38N 127°31E **224** E3
**Janhtang Ga** *Burma* 26°32N 96°38E **241** B6
**Jani Khel** *Afghan.* 32°46N 68°24E **240** B3
**Janikowo** *Poland* 52°45N 18°7E **185** F5
**Janiuay** *Phil.* 10°58N 122°30E **233** F4
**Janja** *Bos.-H.* 44°40N 19°14E **182** F4
**Janjanbureh** *Gambia* 13°30N 14°47W **262** C2
**Janjevë** *Kosovo* 42°35N 21°19E **202** D5
**Janjgir** *India* 22°1N 82°34E **243** J10
**Janjina** *Croatia* 42°58N 17°25E **199** F14
**Janjina** *Madag.* 20°30S 45°50E **272** C2
**Jankau = Janikowo** *Poland* 52°45N 18°7E **185** F5
**Janki** *Poland* 52°8N 20°52E **143** C1
**Jannaale** *Somalia* 1°48N 44°42E **267** D5
**Janos** *Mexico* 30°54N 108°10W **318** A3
**Jánoshalma** *Hungary* 46°18N 19°21E **182** D4
**Jánosháza** *Hungary* 47°8N 17°12E **182** C2
**Jánossomorja** *Hungary* 47°47N 17°11E **182** C2
**Janów** *Poland* 50°44N 19°27E **185** H6
**Janów Lubelski** *Poland* 50°48N 22°23E **185** H9
**Janów Podlaski** *Poland* 52°11N 23°11E **185** F10
**Janowiec Wielkopolski** *Poland* 52°45N 17°30E **185** F4
**Jantho** *Indonesia* 5°17N 95°38E **234** A1
**Januária** *Brazil* 15°25S 44°25W **333** E3
**Janub = Southern** △ *South Sudan* 6°50N 28°45E **257** F2
**Janub Dârfûr** □ *Sudan* 11°0N 25°0E **257** E2
**Janub Kordofân** □ *Sudan* 12°0N 30°0E **257** E3
**Janûb Sînî** □ *Egypt* 29°30N 33°50E **251** J4
**Janubio** *Canary Is.* 28°56N 13°50W **153** e2
**Janville** *France* 48°10N 1°50E **173** D8
**Janwada** *India* 18°0N 77°29E **244** E3
**Janzé** *France* 47°55N 1°28W **172** E5
**Jaora** *India* 23°40N 75°10E **242** H6
**Japan** ■ *Asia* 36°0N 136°0E **221** G8
**Japan, Sea of** *Asia* 40°0N 135°0E **220** E7
**Japan Center** *San Francisco, U.S.A.* **136** c1
**Japan Trench** *Pac. Oc.* 32°0N 142°0E **288** D6
**Japen = Yapen** *Indonesia* 1°50S 136°0E **231** E9
**Japiim** *Brazil* 7°37S 72°54W **330** B3
**Japla** *India* 24°33N 84°1E **243** G11
**Japurá** *Brazil* 1°48S 66°34W **328** D4
**Japura** *Indonesia* 0°19S 102°21E **234** C2
**Japurá** → *Brazil* 3°8S 65°46W **328** D4
**Jaquarão** *Brazil* 32°34S 53°23W **335** C5
**Jaqué** *Panama* 7°27N 78°8W **320** E4
**Jarābulus** *Syria* 36°49N 38°1E **213** D8
**Jaraguá** *Goiás, Brazil* 15°45S 49°20W **333** E2
**Jaraguá** *São Paulo, Brazil* 23°27S 46°44W **137** A1
**Jaraguá, Pico de** *Brazil* 23°27S 46°46W **137** A1
**Jaraguá do Sul** *Brazil* 26°29S 49°4W **335** B6
**Jaraguari** *Brazil* 20°9S 54°35W **331** E7
**Jaraicejo** *Spain* 39°40N 5°49W **195** F5
**Jaraíz de la Vera** *Spain* 40°4N 5°45W **194** E5
**Jarama** → *Spain* 40°24N 3°32W **194** E7
**Jaramānah** *Syria* 33°29N 36°21E **250** E7
**Jaramillo** *Argentina* 47°10S 67°7W **336** C3
**Jarandilla de la Vera** *Spain* 40°8N 5°39W **194** E5
**Jaranwala** *Pakistan* 31°15N 73°26E **242** D5
**Jarash** *Jordan* 32°17N 35°54E **251** F6
**Jarash** □ *Jordan* 32°17N 35°54E **251** F6
**Jarauçu** → *Brazil* 1°48S 52°22W **329** D7
**Järbo** *Sweden* 60°43N 16°36E **162** D10
**Jarboesville = Lexington Park** *U.S.A.* 38°16N 76°27W **309** F15
**Jardas al 'Abīd** *Libya* 32°18N 20°59E **258** B4
**Jardim** *Brazil* 21°28S 56°2W **334** A4
**Jardim Paulista** *Brazil* 23°34S 46°41W **137** B1
**Jardín** → *Spain* 38°50N 2°10W **197** G2
**Jardín América** *Argentina* 27°3S 55°14W **335** B4
**Jardin Botanique** *Brussels, Belgium* **116** a3
**Jardine River** △ *Australia* 11°9S 142°21E **280** A3
**Jardines de la Reina, Arch. de los** *Cuba* 20°50N 78°50W **320** B4
**Jargalang** *China* 43°5N 122°55E **227** C12
**Jargalant = Hovd** □ *Mongolia* 48°2N 91°37E **217** C12
**Jari** → *Brazil* 1°9S 51°54W **329** D7
**Jaria Janjail** *Bangla.* 25°0N 90°40E **241** C3
**Jarīr, W. al** → *Si. Arabia* 25°38N 42°30E **246** E4
**Järlåsa** *Sweden* 59°53N 17°12E **162** E11
**Jarlsberg og Larvik = Vestfold** □ *Norway* 59°15N 10°0E **164** E7
**Jarmen** *Germany* 53°54N 13°20E **178** B9
**Järna** *Sweden* 59°6N 17°34E **162** E11
**Jarnac** *France* 45°40N 0°11W **174** C3
**Jarny** *France* 49°9N 5°53E **173** C12
**Jaro** *Phil.* 11°11N 124°47E **233** F5
**Jarocin** *Poland* 51°59N 17°29E **185** G4
**Jaroměř** *Czech Rep.* 50°22N 15°52E **180** A8
**Jarosław** *Poland* 50°2N 22°42E **185** H9
**Järpås** *Sweden* 58°23N 12°57E **163** F6
**Järpen** *Sweden* 63°21N 13°26E **162** A7
**Jarrahdale** *Australia* 32°24S 116°5E **279** F2
**Jarrahi** → *Iran* 30°49N 48°48E **247** D6
**Jarso** *Ethiopia* 5°15N 37°30E **257** F4
**Jartai** *China* 39°45N 105°48E **226** E3
**Jaru** *Brazil* 10°26S 62°27W **331** C5
**Jaru** → *Brazil* 10°5S 61°59W **331** C5
**Jarud Qi** *China* 44°28N 120°50E **227** B11
**Järvatältet** *Sweden* 59°25N 17°54E **139** A1
**Järvenpää** *Finland* 60°29N 25°5E **188** B3
**Jarvis** *Canada* 42°53N 80°6W **312** D4
**Jarvis I.** *Pac. Oc.* 0°15S 160°5W **289** H12
**Jarvorník** *Czech Rep.* 50°23N 17°2E **181** A10
**Järvsö** *Sweden* 61°43N 16°10E **162** C10
**Jarwa** *India* 27°38N 82°30E **243** F10
**Jaša Tomić** *Serbia* 45°26N 20°50E **182** E5
**Jasaan** *Phil.* 8°39N 124°45E **233** G5
**Jasdan** *India* 22°2N 71°12E **242** H4
**Jashpurnagar** *India* 22°54N 84°9E **243** H11
**Jasidih** *India* 24°31N 86°39E **243** G12
**Jasień** *Poland* 51°46N 15°0E **185** G2
**Jāsimīyah** *Iraq* 33°45N 44°41E **213** F11
**Jasin** *Malaysia* 2°20N 102°26E **237** L4
**Jāsk** *Iran* 25°38N 57°45E **247** E8

**Jaskhar** *India* 18°54N 72°58E **130** B2
**Jasło** *Poland* 49°45N 21°30E **185** J8
**Jasmund** *Germany* 54°32N 13°35E **178** A9
**Jasmund △** *Germany* 54°31N 13°38E **178** A9
**Jaso** *India* 24°30N 80°29E **243** G9
**Jason Is.** *Falk. Is.* 51°0S 61°0W **153** f
**Jasonville** *U.S.A.* 39°10N 87°12W **311** E9
**Jasper** *Alta., Canada* 52°55N 118°5W **296** C5
**Jasper** *Ont., Canada* 44°52N 75°57W **313** B9
**Jasper** *Ala., U.S.A.* 33°50N 87°17W **315** E11
**Jasper** *Fla., U.S.A.* 30°31N 82°57W **316** E7
**Jasper** *Ind., U.S.A.* 38°24N 86°56W **311** F10
**Jasper** *Tex., U.S.A.* 30°56N 94°1W **314** F7
**Jasper △** *Canada* 52°50N 118°8W **296** C5
**Jasrasar** *India* 27°43N 73°49E **242** F5
**Jassān** *Iraq* 32°58N 45°52E **213** G11
**Jassey = Iaşi** *Romania* 47°10N 27°40E **183** C12
**Jastarnia** *Poland* 54°42N 18°40E **184** D5
**Jastrebarsko** *Croatia* 45°41N 15°39E **199** C12
**Jastrow = Jastrowie** *Poland* 53°26N 16°49E **184** E3
**Jastrowie** *Poland* 53°26N 16°49E **184** E3
**Jastrzębie Zdrój** *Poland* 49°57N 18°35E **185** J5
**Jász-Nagykun-Szolnok □** *Hungary* 47°15N 20°30E **182** C5
**Jászapáti** *Hungary* 47°32N 20°10E **182** C5
**Jászárokszállás** *Hungary* 47°39N 19°58E **182** C4
**Jászberény** *Hungary* 47°30N 19°55E **182** C4
**Jászkisér** *Hungary* 47°27N 20°20E **182** C5
**Jászladány** *Hungary* 47°23N 20°10E **182** C5
**Jataí** *Brazil* 17°58S 51°48W **333** E1
**Jatapu →** *Brazil* 2°13S 58°17W **329** D6
**Jath** *India* 17°3N 75°13E **244** F2
**Jati** *Pakistan* 24°20N 68°19E **242** G3
**Jatibarang** *Indonesia* 6°28S 108°18E **235** D3
**Jatiluwih** *Indonesia* 8°23S 115°8E **231** J18
**Jatinegara** *Indonesia* 6°13S 106°52E **122** B2
**Játiva = Xátiva** *Spain* 38°59N 0°32W **197** G4
**Jatobá = Petrolândia** *Brazil* 9°5S 38°20W **332** C4
**Jättendal** *Sweden* 61°58N 17°15E **162** C11
**Jaú** *Angola* 15°12S 13°31E **265** F2
**Jaú** *Brazil* 22°10S 48°30W **335** A6
**Jaú →** *Brazil* 1°54S 61°26W **329** D5
**Jauaperi →** *Brazil* 1°26S 61°35W **329** D5
**Jauer = Jawor** *Poland* 51°4N 16°11E **185** G3
**Jauja** *Peru* 11°45S 75°15W **330** C2
**Jaunpur** *India* 25°46N 82°44E **243** G10
**Jauru →** *Brazil* 16°22S 57°46W **331** D6
**Java = Jawa** *Indonesia* 7°0S 110°0E **235** D4
**Java Sea** *Indonesia* 4°35S 107°15E **235** C3
**Java Trench** *Ind. Oc.* 9°0S 105°0E **234** D2
**Javadi Hills** *India* 12°40N 78°40E **245** H4
**Javādīyeh** *Iran* 35°39N 51°22E **141** B2
**Javalambre, Sa. de** *Spain* 40°6N 1°0W **196** E4
**Javānrud** *Iran* 34°47N 46°31E **213** E12
**Jávea** *Spain* 38°48N 0°10E **197** G5
**Javhlant = Uliastay** *Mongolia* 47°56N 97°28E **218** B8
**Javier, I.** *Chile* 47°5S 74°25W **336** C2
**Javla** *India* 17°18N 75°9E **244** F2
**Jawa** *Indonesia* 7°0S 110°0E **235** D4
**Jawa Barat □** *Indonesia* 7°0S 107°0E **231** G12
**Jawa Tengah □** *Indonesia* 7°0S 110°0E **235** D3
**Jawa Timur □** *Indonesia* 8°0S 113°0E **235** D4
**Jawad** *India* 24°36N 74°51E **242** G6
**Jawaharlal Nehru Port = Nhava Sheva** *India* 18°58N 72°55E **130** B2
**Jawf, W. al →** *Yemen* 15°50N 45°30E **248** D4
**Jawhar** *India* 19°55N 73°14E **244** E1
**Jawhar** *Somalia* 2°48N 45°30E **267** D6
**Jawor** *Poland* 51°4N 16°11E **185** G3
**Jaworowa** *Poland* 52°9N 20°56E **143** C1
**Jaworzno** *Poland* 50°13N 19°11E **185** H6
**Jaworzyna Śląska** *Poland* 50°55N 16°28E **185** H3
**Jawoyn ◎** *Australia* 14°16S 132°28E **278** B5
**Jay** *U.S.A.* 30°57N 87°9W **317** E2
**Jay Peak** *U.S.A.* 44°55N 72°32W **313** B12
**Jaya, Puncak** *Indonesia* 3°57S 137°17E **231** E9
**Jayanca** *Peru* 6°24S 79°50W **330** B2
**Jayanti** *India* 26°45N 89°40E **241** B2
**Jayapura** *Indonesia* 2°28S 140°38E **231** E10
**Jayawijaya, Pegunungan** *Indonesia* 5°0S 139°0E **231** F9
**Jaynagar** *India* 26°43N 86°9E **243** F12
**Jaypur = Jeypore** *India* 18°50N 82°38E **244** E6
**Jayrūd** *Syria* 33°49N 36°44E **250** E7
**Jayton** *U.S.A.* 33°15N 100°34W **314** E4
**Jāz Mūrīān, Hāmūn-e** *Iran* 27°20N 58°55E **247** E8
**Jazīreh-ye Shīf** *Iran* 29°4N 50°54E **247** D6
**Jazminal** *Mexico* 24°52N 101°24W **318** C4
**Jazzīn** *Lebanon* 33°31N 35°35E **250** E6
**Jean** *U.S.A.* 35°47N 115°20W **307** K11
**Jean Lafitte Nat. Historical Park ⌂** *U.S.A.* 29°51N 90°9W **131** B1
**Jean Marie River** *Canada* 61°32N 120°38W **296** A4
**Jean-Rabel** *Haiti* 19°50N 73°5W **321** C5
**Jeanerette** *U.S.A.* 29°55N 91°40W **314** G9
**Jeanette, Ostrov = Zhannetty, Ostrov** *Russia* 76°43N 158°0E **215** B16
**Jeanne-Mance, Parc** *Montréal, Canada* **130** b1
**Jeanneton, Morne** *Guadeloupe* 16°14N 61°43W **322** e
**Jeannette** *U.S.A.* 40°20N 79°36W **312** F5
**Jebāl Bārez, Kūh-e** *Iran* 28°30N 58°20E **247** D8
**Jebba** *Nigeria* 9°9N 4°48E **263** D5
**Jebel, Bahr el →** *South Sudan* 9°30N 30°25E **257** F3
**Jebel Ali = Minā' Jabal 'Alī** *U.A.E.* 25°2N 55°8E **247** E7
**Jebel Dud** *Sudan* 13°25N 33°9E **257** E3
**Jebel Elba △** *Egypt* 22°11N 36°22E **256** C4
**Jebel Qerri** *Sudan* 16°16N 32°50E **257** D3
**Jeberos** *Peru* 5°15S 76°10W **330** B2
**Jebus** *Indonesia* 1°43S 105°28E **234** C3
**Jecheon** *S. Korea* 37°8N 128°12E **224** D4
**Jedburgh** *U.K.* 55°29N 2°33W **167** F6
**Jedda = Jiddah** *Si. Arabia* 21°29N 39°10E **248** B2
**Jeddore L.** *Canada* 48°3N 55°55W **299** C8
**Jedlesee** *Austria* 48°15N 16°23E **142** A2
**Jedlicze** *Poland* 49°43N 21°40E **185** J8
**Jędrzejów** *Poland* 50°35N 20°15E **185** H7
**Jedwabne** *Poland* 53°17N 22°18E **185** E9
**Jeetzel →** *Germany* 53°9N 11°3E **178** B7
**Jefferson** *Ga., U.S.A.* 34°7N 83°35W **316** A6
**Jefferson** *Iowa, U.S.A.* 42°1N 94°23W **310** B2
**Jefferson** *La., U.S.A.* 29°57N 90°9W **131** B2
**Jefferson** *Ohio, U.S.A.* 41°44N 80°46W **312** E4
**Jefferson** *Tex., U.S.A.* 32°46N 94°21W **314** E7
**Jefferson** *Wis., U.S.A.* 43°0N 88°48W **311** B8
**Jefferson, Mt.** *Nev., U.S.A.* 38°47N 116°56W **304** G5
**Jefferson, Mt.** *Oreg., U.S.A.* 44°41N 121°48W **304** D3
**Jefferson City** *Mo., U.S.A.* 38°34N 92°10W **310** F4
**Jefferson City** *Tenn., U.S.A.* 36°7N 83°30W **315** C13
**Jefferson Memorial** *Washington, D.C., U.S.A.* **143** c1
**Jefferson Park** *Calif., U.S.A.* 34°2N 118°19W **126** B3
**Jefferson Park** *Ill., U.S.A.* 41°58N 87°46W **119** B2
**Jeffersontown** *U.S.A.* 38°12N 85°35W **311** F11
**Jeffersonville** *Ga., U.S.A.* 32°41N 83°20W **316** C6
**Jeffersonville** *Ind., U.S.A.* 38°17N 85°44W **311** F11
**Jeffersonville** *Ohio, U.S.A.* 39°39N 83°34W **311** E13
**Jeffrey City** *U.S.A.* 42°30N 107°49W **304** E10
**Jega** *Nigeria* 12°15N 4°23E **263** C5
**Jegi** *S. Korea* 37°34N 127°1E **137** B2
**Jejevo** *Solomon Is.* 8°6S 159°8E **287** M10
**Jeju** *S. Korea* 33°31N 126°32E **224** a
**Jeju-do** *S. Korea* 33°29N 126°34E **224** a
**Jeju-do □** *S. Korea* 33°25N 126°30E **224** a
**Jeju Haehyop** *S. Korea* 33°50N 126°30E **227** H14
**Jēkabpils** *Latvia* 56°29N 25°57E **188** D3
**Jekyll I.** *U.S.A.* 31°4N 81°25W **316** D8
**Jelambar** *Indonesia* 6°9S 106°47E **122** A1
**Jelcz-Laskowice** *Poland* 51°2N 17°19E **185** G4
**Jelenia Góra** *Poland* 50°50N 15°45E **185** H2
**Jelgava** *Latvia* 56°41N 23°49E **184** B10
**Jelgava □** *Latvia* 56°35N 23°45E **184** B10
**Jelica** *Serbia* 43°50N 20°17E **202** C4
**Jelli** *South Sudan* 5°25N 31°45E **257** F3
**Jelonki** *Poland* 52°14N 20°54E **143** B1
**Jelšava** *Slovak Rep.* 48°37N 20°15E **181** C13
**Jema'a Mallam = Kafanchan** *Nigeria* 9°40N 8°20E **263** D6
**Jemaja** *Indonesia* 3°5N 105°45E **234** B3
**Jemaluang** *Malaysia* 2°16N 103°52E **237** L4
**Jember** *Indonesia* 8°11S 113°41E **235** D4
**Jempang, Danau** *Indonesia* 0°25S 116°12E **235** C5
**Jena** *Thüringen, Germany* 50°54N 11°35E **178** E7
**Jena** *La., U.S.A.* 31°41N 92°8W **314** F8
**Jenai** *Taiwan* 24°2N 121°8E **225** B3
**Jenbach** *Austria* 47°24N 11°47E **180** D4
**Jendouba** *Tunisia* 36°29N 8°47E **258** A1
**Jendouba □** *Tunisia* 36°34N 8°52E **261** A6
**Jeneponto** *Indonesia* 5°40S 119°44E **235** D5
**Jengish Chokoso = Pobedy, Pik** *Kyrgyzstan* 42°0N 79°58E **217** D9
**Jenho** *Taiwan* 23°54N 121°36E **225** C3
**Jenīn** *West Bank* 32°28N 35°18E **251** F6
**Jenison** *U.S.A.* 42°54N 85°47W **311** B11
**Jenkins** *U.S.A.* 37°10N 82°38W **309** G12
**Jenner** *U.S.A.* 38°27N 123°7W **306** G3
**Jennings** *Fla., U.S.A.* 30°36N 83°6W **316** E6
**Jennings** *La., U.S.A.* 30°13N 92°40W **314** F8
**Jennings** *Mo., U.S.A.* 38°43N 90°15W **310** F6
**Jenny Pt.** *Dominica* 15°28N 61°15W **323** k
**Jensen Beach** *U.S.A.* 27°15N 80°14W **317** H9
**Jente** *Taiwan* 22°58N 120°16E **225** D2
**Jenwu** *Taiwan* 22°42N 120°20E **225** D2
**Jeollabuk-do □** *S. Korea* 35°45N 127°15E **224** E3
**Jeollanam-do □** *S. Korea* 34°45N 127°0E **224** E3
**Jeong-eup** *S. Korea* 35°35N 126°50E **224** E3
**Jeongseon** *S. Korea* 37°20N 128°45E **227** F15
**Jeonju** *S. Korea* 35°50N 127°4E **224** E3
**Jepara** *Indonesia* 7°40S 109°14E **235** D3
**Jeparit** *Australia* 36°8S 142°1E **282** D5
**Jequié** *Brazil* 13°51S 40°5W **333** D3
**Jequitaí →** *Brazil* 17°4S 44°50W **333** E3
**Jequitinhonha** *Brazil* 16°30S 41°0W **333** E3
**Jequitinhonha →** *Brazil* 15°51S 38°53W **333** E4
**Jerada** *Morocco* 34°17N 2°10W **261** B4
**Jerantut** *Malaysia* 3°56N 102°22E **237** L4
**Jerejak, Pulau** *Malaysia* 5°19N 100°19E **237** c
**Jérémie** *Haiti* 18°40N 74°10W **321** C5
**Jeremoabo** *Brazil* 10°4S 38°21W **332** D4
**Jerez, Pta.** *Mexico* 22°58N 97°40W **319** C5
**Jerez de García Salinas** *Mexico* 22°39N 103°0W **318** C4
**Jerez de la Frontera** *Spain* 36°41N 6°7W **195** J4
**Jerez de los Caballeros** *Spain* 38°20N 6°45W **195** G4
**Jericho = El Arīḥā** *West Bank* 31°52N 35°27E **251** G6
**Jericho** *Australia* 23°38S 146°6E **280** C4
**Jerichow** *Germany* 52°30N 12°1E **178** C8
**Jerico Springs** *U.S.A.* 37°37N 94°1W **310** G2
**Jerid, Chott el = Djerid, Chott** *Tunisia* 33°42N 8°30E **258** B1
**Jerilderie** *Australia* 35°20S 145°41E **283** C6
**Jermyn** *U.S.A.* 41°32N 75°33W **313** E9
**Jerningham Junction** *Trin. & Tob.* 10°33N 61°23W **323** t
**Jerome** *U.S.A.* 42°44N 114°31W **304** E6
**Jerónimos, Mosteiro dos** *Portugal* 38°41N 9°11W **126** A1
**Jerramungup** *Australia* 33°55S 118°55E **279** F2
**Jersey** *U.K.* 49°11N 2°7W **169** H5
**Jersey City** *U.S.A.* 40°42N 74°4W **132** B1
**Jersey Shore** *U.S.A.* 41°12N 77°15W **312** E7
**Jerseyville** *U.S.A.* 39°7N 90°20W **310** E6
**Jerumenha** *Brazil* 7°5S 43°30W **332** C3
**Jerusalem** *Israel/West Bank* 31°47N 35°10E **123** B2
**Jervis B.** *Australia* 35°8S 150°46E **283** C9
**Jervis Bay △** *Australia* 35°9S 150°40E **283** C9
**Jervis Inlet** *Canada* 50°0N 123°57W **296** C4
**Jerzu** *Italy* 39°47N 9°31E **200** C2
**Jesenice** *Slovenia* 46°28N 14°3E **199** B11
**Jeseník** *Czech Rep.* 50°14N 17°8E **181** A10
**Jesenké** *Slovak Rep.* 48°20N 20°10E **181** C13
**Jesi = Iesi** *Italy* 43°31N 13°14E **199** E10
**Jésolo** *Italy* 45°32N 12°38E **199** C9
**Jessamine, L.** *U.S.A.* 28°28N 81°23W **133** B2
**Jessel = Jasło** *Poland* 49°45N 21°30E **185** J8
**Jesselton = Kota Kinabalu** *Malaysia* 6°0N 116°4E **235** A5
**Jessheim** *Norway* 60°9N 11°10E **164** D8
**Jessnitz** *Germany* 51°40N 12°18E **178** D8
**Jessore** *Bangla.* 23°10N 89°10E **241** D2
**Jesup** *Ga., U.S.A.* 31°36N 81°53W **316** D8
**Jesup** *Iowa, U.S.A.* 42°29N 92°4W **310** B4
**Jesup, L.** *U.S.A.* 28°43N 81°14W **317** G8
**Jesús** *Peru* 7°15S 78°25W **330** B2
**Jésus, Î.** *Canada* 45°36N 73°44W **130** A1
**Jesús Carranza** *Mexico* 17°26N 95°2W **319** D5
**Jesús María** *Argentina* 30°59S 64°5W **334** C3
**Jesús Maria** *Lima, Peru* 12°4S 77°3W **124** B2
**Jetmore** *U.S.A.* 38°4N 99°54W **308** F4
**Jetpur** *India* 21°45N 70°10E **242** J4
**Jette** *Belgium* 50°53N 4°20E **116** A1
**Jeumont** *France* 50°18N 4°6E **173** B11
**Jeungdo** *S. Korea* 34°56N 126°9E **224** E3
**Jeungpyeong** *S. Korea* 36°47N 127°34E **224** D3
**Jevnaker** *Norway* 60°15N 10°26E **164** D7
**Jewell** *U.S.A.* 42°20N 93°39W **310** B3
**Jewett** *U.S.A.* 40°22N 81°2W **312** F3
**Jewett City** *U.S.A.* 41°36N 71°59W **313** E13
**Jewish Quarter** *Jerusalem* **123** b3
**Jey** *Iran* 35°41N 51°20E **141** B2
**Jeyḥūnābād** *Iran* 34°58N 48°59E **247** C6
**Jeypore** *India* 18°50N 82°38E **244** E6
**Jeziorak, Jezioro** *Poland* 53°40N 19°35E **184** E6
**Jeziorany** *Poland* 53°58N 20°46E **184** E7
**Jeziorka →** *Poland* 52°8N 21°9E **185** F8
**Jha Jha** *India* 24°46N 86°22E **243** G12
**Jhaarkand = Jharkhand □** *India* 24°0N 85°50E **243** H11
**Jhabua** *India* 22°46N 74°36E **242** H6
**Jhajjar** *India* 28°37N 76°42E **242** E7
**Jhal** *Pakistan* 28°17N 67°27E **242** E2
**Jhal Jhao** *Pakistan* 26°20N 65°35E **240** D2
**Jhalakati** *Bangla.* 22°39N 90°12E **241** D3
**Jhalawar** *India* 24°40N 76°10E **242** G7
**Jhalida** *India* 23°22N 85°58E **243** H11
**Jhalrapatan** *India* 24°33N 76°10E **242** G7
**Jhang Maghiana** *Pakistan* 31°15N 72°22E **242** D5
**Jhang Sadr = Jhang Maghiana** *Pakistan* 31°15N 72°22E **242** D5
**Jhansi** *India* 25°30N 78°36E **243** G8
**Jhargram** *India* 22°27N 86°59E **243** H12
**Jharia** *India* 23°45N 86°26E **243** H12
**Jharkhand □** *India* 24°0N 85°50E **243** H11
**Jharsuguda** *India* 21°56N 84°5E **244** D7
**Jhelum** *Pakistan* 33°0N 73°45E **242** C5
**Jhelum →** *Pakistan* 31°20N 72°10E **242** D5
**Jhenaidah** *Bangla.* 23°33N 89°10E **241** D2
**Jhilmilli** *India* 23°24N 82°51E **243** H10
**Jhudo** *Pakistan* 24°58N 69°18E **242** G3
**Jhunjhunun** *India* 28°10N 75°30E **242** E6
**Ji-Paraná** *Brazil* 10°50S 61°58W **331** C5
**Ji Xian** *China* 36°7N 110°40E **226** F6
**Jia Xian** *Henan, China* 33°59N 113°12E **226** H7
**Jia Xian** *Shaanxi, China* 38°12N 110°28E **226** E6
**Jiading = Chiehting** *Taiwan* 22°54N 120°11E **225** D2
**Jiadong = Chiatung** *Taiwan* 22°25N 120°32E **225** D2
**Jiahe** *China* 25°38N 112°19E **229** E9
**Jiaji = Qionghai** *China* 19°15N 110°26E **229** a
**Jiali = Chiali** *Taiwan* 23°9N 120°10E **225** C2
**Jialing Jiang →** *China* 29°30N 106°20E **228** C6
**Jiamusi** *China* 46°40N 130°26E **219** B15
**Jian = Chian** *Taiwan* 23°59N 121°33E **225** C3
**Ji'an** *Jiangxi, China* 27°6N 114°59E **229** D10
**Ji'an** *Jilin, China* 41°5N 126°10E **227** D14
**Jianchang** *China* 40°55N 120°35E **227** D11
**Jianchuan** *China* 26°38N 99°55E **228** D2
**Jiande** *China* 29°23N 119°15E **229** C12
**Jiang'an** *China* 28°40N 105°3E **228** C5
**Jiangbei** *China* 29°40N 106°34E **228** C6
**Jiangcheng** *China* 22°36N 101°52E **228** F3
**Jiangchuan** *China* 24°8N 102°39E **228** E4
**Jiangdi** *China* 26°57N 103°37E **228** D4
**Jiangdu** *China* 32°27N 119°36E **229** A12
**Jiange** *China* 32°4N 105°32E **228** A5
**Jianggao** *China* 23°13N 113°13E **121** A2
**Jianghua** *China* 25°0N 111°47E **229** E8
**Jiangjin** *China* 29°14N 106°14E **228** C6
**Jiangjun = Chiangchun** *Taiwan* 23°12N 120°9E **225** C2
**Jiangkou** *China* 27°40N 108°49E **228** D7
**Jiangle** *China* 26°42N 117°23E **229** D11
**Jiangmen** *China* 22°32N 113°0E **229** F9
**Jiangning** *China* 31°55N 118°50E **229** B12
**Jiangshan** *China* 28°40N 118°37E **229** C12
**Jiangsu □** *China* 33°0N 120°0E **227** H11
**Jiangwan** *China* 31°18N 121°28E **138** B1
**Jiangxi □** *China* 27°30N 116°0E **229** D11
**Jiangyan** *China* 32°30N 120°7E **229** A13
**Jiangyin** *China* 31°54N 120°17E **229** B13
**Jiangyong** *China* 25°20N 111°22E **229** E8
**Jiangyou** *China* 31°44N 104°43E **228** B5
**Jiangyuan** *China* 42°2N 126°34E **227** C14
**Jianhe** *China* 26°37N 108°31E **228** D7
**Jianli** *China* 29°46N 112°56E **229** C9
**Jianning** *China* 26°50N 116°50E **229** D11
**Jian'ou** *China* 27°3N 118°17E **229** D12
**Jianping** *China* 41°53N 119°42E **227** D10
**Jianshi** *China* 30°37N 109°38E **228** B7
**Jianshui** *China* 23°36N 102°43E **228** F4
**Jianyang** *Fujian, China* 27°20N 118°5E **229** D12
**Jianyang** *Sichuan, China* 30°24N 104°33E **228** B5
**Jiao Xian = Jiaozhou** *China* 36°18N 120°1E **227** F11
**Jiaohe** *Hebei, China* 38°2N 116°20E **226** E9
**Jiaohe** *Jilin, China* 43°40N 127°22E **227** C14
**Jiaoling** *China* 24°41N 116°12E **229** E11
**Jiaonan** *China* 35°52N 119°58E **227** G10
**Jiaoxi = Chiaohsi** *Taiwan* 24°49N 121°46E **225** B3
**Jiaozhou** *China* 36°18N 120°1E **227** F11
**Jiaozhou Wan** *China* 36°5N 120°10E **227** F11
**Jiaozuo** *China* 35°16N 113°12E **226** G7
**Jiawang** *China* 34°28N 117°26E **227** G9
**Jiaxiang** *China* 35°25N 116°20E **226** G9
**Jiaxing** *China* 30°49N 120°45E **229** B13
**Jiayi = Chiai** *Taiwan* 23°29N 120°25E **225** C2
**Jiayu** *China* 29°55N 113°55E **229** C9
**Jiayuguan** *China* 39°49N 98°18E **218** D8
**Jib** *West Bank* 31°51N 35°11E **123** A2
**Jibão, Serra do** *Brazil* 14°48S 45°0W **333** D3
**Jibeiyu = Chipei Tao** *Taiwan* 23°45N 119°37E **225** C1
**Jibiya** *Nigeria* 13°5N 7°12E **263** C6
**Jiblah** *Yemen* 13°55N 44°9E **248** D4
**Jibou** *Romania* 47°15N 23°17E **183** C8
**Jibuti = Djibouti ■** *Africa* 12°0N 43°0E **257** E5
**Jicarón, I.** *Panama* 7°10N 81°50W **320** E3
**Jičín** *Czech Rep.* 50°25N 15°28E **180** A8
**Jiddah** *Si. Arabia* 21°29N 39°10E **248** B2
**Jido** *India* 29°2N 94°58E **241** A5
**Jido** *S. Korea* 35°4N 126°14E **224** E3
**Jieshou** *China* 33°18N 115°22E **226** H8
**Jiexiu** *China* 37°2N 111°55E **226** F6
**Jieyang** *China* 23°35N 116°21E **229** F11
**Jigalong** *Australia* 23°21S 120°47E **278** D3
**Jigalong ◎** *Australia* 23°21S 120°46E **278** D3
**Jigawa □** *Nigeria* 12°0N 9°45E **263** C6
**Jigme Dorje △** *Bhutan* 28°0N 89°40E **241** B2
**Jigme Singye Wangchuck** *Bhutan* 27°20N 90°25E **241** B3
**Jigni** *India* 25°45N 79°25E **243** G8
**Jihād** *Iraq* 33°17N 44°19E **113** B1
**Jihlava** *Czech Rep.* 49°28N 15°35E **180** B8
**Jihlava →** *Czech Rep.* 48°55N 16°36E **181** C9
**Jihlavský □** *Czech Rep.* 49°30N 15°30E **180** B8
**Jihnan** *Taiwan* 24°22N 120°39E **225** B2
**Jihočeský □** *Czech Rep.* 49°8N 14°35E **180** B7
**Jihomoravský □** *Czech Rep.* 49°5N 16°30E **181** B9
**Jihu = Chihu** *Taiwan* 23°54N 120°24E **225** C2
**Jiigley** *Somalia* 5°25N 45°20E **267** C6
**Jijel** *Algeria* 36°52N 5°50E **261** A6
**Jijel □** *Algeria* 36°45N 6°0E **261** A6
**Jijiga** *Ethiopia* 9°20N 42°50E **267** C5
**Jikamshi** *Nigeria* 12°12N 7°45E **263** C6
**Jikau** *South Sudan* 8°28N 33°47E **257** F3
**Jilib** *Somalia* 0°29N 42°46E **267** D5
**Jilin** *China* 43°44N 126°30E **227** C14
**Jilin □** *China* 44°0N 127°0E **227** C14
**Jiloca →** *Spain* 41°21N 1°39W **196** D3
**Jilong = Chilung** *Taiwan* 25°3N 121°45E **225** A3
**Jim Thompson's House** *Bangkok, Thailand* **113** b3
**Jim Thorpe** *U.S.A.* 40°52N 75°44W **313** F9
**Jima** *Ethiopia* 7°40N 36°47E **257** F4
**Jimbaran, Teluk** *Indonesia* 8°46S 115°9E **231** K18
**Jimbōchō** *Tokyo, Japan* **140** a4
**Jimbolia** *Romania* 45°47N 20°43E **182** E5
**Jimena de la Frontera** *Spain* 36°27N 5°24W **195** J5
**Jiménez** *Chihuahua, Mexico* 27°8N 104°54W **318** B4
**Jimenez** *Phil.* 8°20N 123°50E **233** G4
**Jimeta** *Nigeria* 9°17N 12°28E **263** D7
**Jimo** *China* 36°23N 120°30E **227** F11
**Jimsar** *China* 43°59N 89°4E **217** D11
**Jin Jiang →** *China* 28°24N 115°48E **229** C10
**Jin Xian = Jinzhou** *China* 38°55N 121°42E **227** E11
**Jinan** *China* 36°38N 117°1E **226** F9
**Jinchang** *China* 38°30N 102°10E **218** D9
**Jincheng** *China* 35°29N 112°50E **226** G7
**Jinchuan** *China* 31°30N 102°3E **228** B4
**Jind** *India* 29°19N 76°22E **242** E7
**Jindabyne** *Australia* 36°25S 148°35E **283** D8
**Jinding** *China* 22°22N 113°33E **219** a
**Jindo** *S. Korea* 34°28N 126°15E **224** E3
**Jindřichův Hradec** *Czech Rep.* 49°10N 15°2E **180** B8
**Jing He →** *China* 34°27N 109°4E **226** G5
**Jing Shan** *China* 31°20N 111°35E **229** B8
**Jing Xian** *China* 30°38N 118°25E **229** B12
**Jing'an** *Jiangxi, China* 28°50N 115°17E **229** C10
**Jingan** *Shanghai, China* 31°14N 121°25E **138** B1
**Jingbian** *China* 37°20N 108°30E **226** F5
**Jingchuan** *China* 35°20N 107°20E **226** G4
**Jingde** *China* 30°15N 118°27E **229** B12
**Jingdezhen** *China* 29°20N 117°11E **229** C11
**Jingdong** *China* 24°23N 100°47E **228** E3
**Jinggangshan** *China* 26°58N 114°15E **229** D10
**Jinggu** *China* 23°35N 100°41E **228** F3
**Jinghai** *Guangdong, China* 22°59N 116°31E **229** F11
**Jinghai** *Tianjin, China* 38°55N 116°55E **226** E9
**Jinghong** *China* 22°0N 100°45E **228** G3
**Jinghong Dam** *China* 22°10N 100°46E **228** F3
**Jingjiang** *China* 32°2N 120°16E **229** A13
**Jingle** *China* 38°20N 111°55E **226** E6
**Jingmen** *China* 31°0N 112°10E **229** B9
**Jingning** *China* 35°30N 105°43E **226** G3
**Jingpo Hu** *China* 43°55N 128°55E **227** C15
**Jingshan** *China* 31°1N 113°7E **229** B9
**Jingtai** *China* 37°10N 104°6E **226** F3
**Jingtang** *China* 39°10N 119°5E **227** E10
**Jingu Outer Garden** *Tokyo, Japan* **140** b2
**Jingxi** *China* 23°8N 106°27E **228** F6
**Jingyang** *China* 34°30N 108°50E **226** G5
**Jingyu** *China* 42°25N 126°45E **224** A3
**Jingyuan** *China* 36°30N 104°40E **226** F3
**Jingzhou** *Hubei, China* 30°21N 112°11E **229** B9
**Jingzhou** *Hunan, China* 26°33N 109°40E **228** D7
**Jingziguan** *China* 33°15N 111°0E **226** H6
**Jinhua** *China* 29°8N 119°38E **229** C12
**Jining** *Nei Monggol Zizhiqu, China* 41°5N 113°0E **226** D7
**Jining** *Shandong, China* 35°22N 116°34E **226** G9
**Jinja** *Uganda* 0°25N 33°12E **268** B3
**Jinjang** *Malaysia* 3°13N 101°39E **237** L3
**Jinji** *China* 37°58N 106°8E **226** F4
**Jinjiang** *Fujian, China* 24°43N 118°33E **229** E12
**Jinjiang** *Yunnan, China* 26°14N 100°34E **228** D3
**Jinjini** *Ghana* 7°26N 2°42W **262** D4
**Jinju** *S. Korea* 35°12N 128°2E **224** E4
**Jinkou** *China* 30°20N 114°8E **229** B10
**Jinkouhe** *China* 29°18N 103°4E **228** C4
**Jinmu Jiao** *China* 18°9N 109°34E **229** a
**Jinnah Barrage** *Pakistan* 32°58N 71°33E **242** C4
**Jinnah Int. ✈ (KHI)** *Karachi, Pakistan* 24°53N 67°9E **123** A2
**Jinning** *China* 24°38N 102°38E **228** E4
**Jinočany** *Czech Rep.* 50°2N 14°16E **135** B1
**Jinonice** *Czech Rep.* 50°3N 14°22E **135** B2
**Jinotega** *Nic.* 13°6N 85°59W **320** D2
**Jinotepe** *Nic.* 11°50N 86°10W **320** D2
**Jinping** *Guizhou, China* 26°41N 109°10E **228** D7
**Jinping** *Yunnan, China* 22°45N 103°18E **228** F4
**Jinqiao** *China* 31°15N 121°36E **138** B2
**Jinsha** *China* 27°29N 106°12E **228** D6
**Jinsha Jiang →** *China* 28°50N 104°36E **228** C5
**Jinshi** *China* 29°40N 111°50E **229** C8
**Jintan** *China* 31°42N 119°36E **229** B12
**Jintotolo Channel** *Phil.* 11°48N 123°5E **233** F4
**Jintotolo I.** *Phil.* 11°51N 123°7E **233** F4
**Jintur** *India* 19°37N 76°42E **244** E3
**Jinxi** *Jiangxi, China* 27°56N 116°45E **229** D11
**Jinxi** *Liaoning, China* 40°52N 120°50E **227** D11
**Jinxian** *China* 28°26N 116°17E **229** C11
**Jinxiang** *China* 35°5N 116°22E **226** G9
**Jinyang** *China* 27°28N 103°5E **228** D4
**Jinyun** *China* 28°35N 120°5E **229** C13
**Jinzhai** *China* 31°40N 115°53E **229** B10
**Jinzhong** *China* 37°42N 112°46E **226** F7
**Jinzhou** *Liaoning, China* 38°55N 121°42E **227** E11
**Jinzhou** *Liaoning, China* 41°5N 121°3E **227** D11
**Jiparaná →** *Brazil* 8°3S 62°52W **331** B5
**Jipijapa** *Ecuador* 1°0S 80°40W **328** D1
**Jiquilpan** *Mexico* 19°59N 102°43W **318** D4
**Jirisan** *S. Korea* 35°20N 127°44E **224** E3
**Jirisan △** *S. Korea* 35°15N 127°30E **224** E3
**Jiroft** *Iran* 28°45N 57°50E **247** D8
**Jishan** *China* 35°34N 110°58E **226** G6
**Jishou** *China* 28°21N 109°43E **228** C7
**Jishui** *China* 27°12N 115°8E **229** D10
**Jisr ash Shughūr** *Syria* 35°49N 36°18E **250** C7
**Jitarning** *Australia* 32°48S 117°57E **279** F2
**Jitra** *Malaysia* 6°16N 100°25E **237** J3
**Jiu →** *Romania* 43°47N 23°48E **183** G8
**Jiudengkou** *China* 39°56N 106°40E **226** E4
**Jiujiang** *Guangdong, China* 22°50N 113°0E **229** F9
**Jiujiang** *Jiangxi, China* 29°42N 115°58E **229** C10
**Jiuling Shan** *China* 28°40N 114°40E **229** C10
**Jiulong = Kowloon** *Hong Kong, China* 22°19N 114°11E **122** B3
**Jiulong** *China* 28°57N 101°31E **228** C3
**Jiuquan** *China* 39°50N 98°20E **218** D8
**Jiutai** *China* 44°10N 125°50E **227** B13
**Jiuxincheng** *China* 39°17N 115°59E **226** E8
**Jiuzhaigou ⌂** *China* 33°8N 103°52E **228** A4
**Jiwani** *Pakistan* 25°1N 61°44E **240** D1
**Jiwani, Ras** *Pakistan* 25°1N 61°44E **240** D1
**Jixi** *Anhui, China* 30°5N 118°34E **229** B12
**Jixi** *Heilongjiang, China* 45°20N 130°50E **227** B16
**Jiyang** *China* 37°0N 117°12E **227** F9
**Jiyuan** *China* 35°7N 112°57E **226** G7
**Jiyūgaoka** *Japan* 35°35N 139°40E **140** B3
**Jiz', W. →** *Yemen* 16°12N 52°14E **249** C6
**Jizā'ir** *Iraq* 33°15N 44°23E **113** B2
**Jīzān** *Si. Arabia* 17°0N 42°20E **248** C3
**Jize** *China* 36°54N 114°56E **226** F8
**Jizera →** *Czech Rep.* 50°10N 14°43E **180** A7
**Jizhou** *China* 37°35N 115°30E **226** F8
**Jizīra** *Iraq* 33°15N 44°25E **113** B2
**Jizl, Wādī al →** *Si. Arabia* 25°39N 38°25E **246** E3
**Jizō-Zaki** *Japan* 35°34N 133°20E **222** B5
**Jizzax** *Uzbekistan* 40°6N 67°50E **217** D7
**Jizzax □** *Uzbekistan* 40°20N 67°40E **217** D7
**Joaçaba** *Brazil* 27°5S 51°31W **335** B5
**Joaíma** *Brazil* 16°39S 41°2W **333** E3
**Joal Fadiout** *Senegal* 14°9N 16°50W **262** C1
**João Amaro** *Brazil* 12°46S 40°22W **333** D3
**João Belo = Xai-Xai** *Mozam.* 25°6S 33°31E **271** C5
**João Câmara** *Brazil* 5°32S 35°48W **332** C4
**João Neiva** *Brazil* 19°45S 40°24W **333** E3
**João Pessoa = Eirunepé** *Brazil* 6°35S 69°53W **330** B4
**João Pessoa = Porto** *Brazil* 3°54S 42°42W **332** B3
**João Pessoa** *Brazil* 7°10S 34°52W **332** C5
**João Pinheiro** *Brazil* 17°45S 46°10W **333** E2
**Joaquín V. González** *Argentina* 25°10S 64°0W **334** B3
**Jobat** *India* 22°25N 74°34E **242** H6
**Jobourg, Nez de** *France* 49°41N 1°57W **172** C5
**Jódar** *Spain* 37°50N 3°21W **195** H7
**Jodhpur** *India* 26°23N 73°8E **242** F5
**Jodiya** *India* 22°42N 70°18E **242** H4
**Joensuu** *Finland* 62°37N 29°49E **160** E23
**Jōetsu** *Japan* 37°12N 138°10E **221** F9
**Jœuf** *France* 49°12N 6°0E **173** C12
**Jofane** *Mozam.* 21°15S 34°18E **271** B5
**Joffre, Morne = Moustique, Morne** *Guadeloupe* 16°7N 61°44W **322** e
**Jog Falls = Gersoppa Falls** *India* 14°12N 74°46E **245** G2
**Jogbani** *India* 26°25N 87°15E **243** F12
**Jõgeva** *Estonia* 58°45N 26°24E **188** C4
**Jogjakarta = Yogyakarta** *Indonesia* 7°49S 110°22E **235** D4
**Joglo** *Indonesia* 6°13S 106°45E **122** B1
**Jōhana** *Japan* 36°30N 136°57E **223** A8
**Johannesburg** *Gauteng, S. Africa* 26°11S 28°2E **123** B2
**Johannesburg** *Calif., U.S.A.* 35°22N 117°38W **307** K9
**Johannesburg, Univ. of** *S. Africa* 26°11S 28°0E **123** B2
**Johanneskirchen** *Germany* 48°10N 11°38E **131** A2
**Johannesstift** *Germany* 52°34N 13°12E **115** A2
**Johannisburg = Pisz** *Poland* 53°38N 21°49E **184** E8
**Johannisthal** *Germany* 52°26N 13°30E **115** B4
**Johansfors** *Sweden* 56°42N 15°32E **163** H9
**Johilla →** *India* 23°37N 81°14E **243** H9
**John Crow Mts.** *Jamaica* 18°5N 76°25W **320** a
**John Day** *U.S.A.* 44°25N 118°57W **304** D4
**John Day →** *U.S.A.* 45°44N 120°39W **304** D3
**John Day Fossil Beds ⌂** *U.S.A.* 44°33N 119°38W **304** D4
**John D'or Prairie** *Canada* 58°30N 115°8W **296** B5
**John F. Kennedy Nat. Historic Site ⌂** *U.S.A.* 42°20N 71°7W **116** A2
**John F. Kennedy Space Center** *U.S.A.* 28°40N 80°42W **317** G9
**John H. Kerr Res.** *U.S.A.* 36°36N 78°18W **315** C15
**John Hancock Center** *Chicago, U.S.A.* **119** a2
**John McLaren Park** *U.S.A.* 37°43N 122°24W **136** B2
**John o' Groats** *U.K.* 58°38N 3°4W **167** C5
**John U. Lloyd Beach ⌂** *U.S.A.* 26°4N 80°6W **129** B3
**Johnnie** *U.S.A.* 36°25N 116°5W **307** J10
**Johns Creek** *U.S.A.* 34°2N 84°12W **316** A5
**Johns I.** *U.S.A.* 32°47N 80°7W **316** C9
**John's Ra.** *Australia* 21°55S 133°23E **280** C1
**Johnson** *U.S.A.* 44°38N 72°41W **313** B12
**Johnson City** *Kans., U.S.A.* 37°34N 101°45W **308** G3
**Johnson City** *N.Y., U.S.A.* 42°7N 75°58W **313** D9
**Johnson City** *Tenn., U.S.A.* 36°19N 82°21W **315** C13
**Johnson City** *Tex., U.S.A.* 30°17N 98°25W **314** F5
**Johnsonburg** *U.S.A.* 41°29N 78°41W **312** E6
**Johnsondale** *U.S.A.* 35°58N 118°32W **307** K8
**Johnsons Crossing** *Canada* 60°29N 133°18W **296** A2
**Johnsons Pt.** *Antigua & B.* 17°2N 61°53W **322** b
**Johnsonville** *N.Z.* 41°13S 174°48E **284** H3
**Johnston** *Iowa, U.S.A.* 41°40N 93°42W **310** C3
**Johnston** *S.C., U.S.A.* 33°50N 81°48W **316** B8
**Johnston, L.** *Australia* 32°25S 120°30E **279** F3
**Johnston City** *U.S.A.* 37°49N 88°56W **310** G8
**Johnston Falls = Mambilima Falls** *Zambia* 10°31S 28°45E **269** E2
**Johnston I.** *Pac. Oc.* 17°10N 169°8W **289** F11
**Johnstone Str.** *Canada* 50°28N 126°0W **296** C3
**Johnstown** *Kilkenny, Ireland* 52°45N 7°33W **166** D4
**Johnstown** *N.Y., U.S.A.* 43°0N 74°22W **313** C10
**Johnstown** *Ohio, U.S.A.* 40°9N 82°41W **312** F2
**Johnstown** *Pa., U.S.A.* 40°20N 78°55W **312** F6
**Johor □** *Malaysia* 2°5N 103°20E **237** M4
**Johor, Selat** *Asia* 1°28N 103°47E **237** d
**Johor Bahru** *Malaysia* 1°28N 103°46E **237** d
**Jõhvi** *Estonia* 59°22N 27°27E **188** C4
**Joigny** *France* 47°58N 3°20E **173** E10
**Joinville** *Brazil* 26°15S 48°55W **335** B6
**Joinville** *Haute-Marne, France* 48°27N 5°10E **173** D12
**Joinville I.** *Antarctica* 65°0S 55°30W **151** C18
**Joinville-le-Pont** *France* 48°49N 2°27E **134** B3
**Jojutla** *Mexico* 18°37N 99°11W **319** D5
**Jøkelbugten** *Greenland* 78°25N 20°20W **154** B9
**Jokkmokk** *Sweden* 66°35N 19°50E **160** C18
**Jökulsá á Bru →** *Iceland* 65°40N 14°16W **155** B12
**Jökulsá á Fjöllum →** *Iceland* 66°10N 16°30W **155** A10
**Jökulsárgljúfur △** *Iceland* 65°56N 16°31W **155** B10
**Jolfā** *Āzarbājān-e Sharqī, Iran* 38°57N 45°38E **213** C11
**Jolfā** *Eşfahan, Iran* 32°58N 51°37E **247** C6
**Joli-Bois** *Belgium* 50°42N 4°24E **116** B2
**Joliet** *U.S.A.* 41°32N 88°5W **311** C8
**Joliette** *Canada* 46°3N 73°24W **298** C5
**Jollas** *Finland* 60°10N 25°5E **121** B3
**Jolo** *Phil.* 6°0N 121°0E **233** H3
**Jolo Group** *Phil.* 6°0N 121°9E **233** J3
**Jolon** *U.S.A.* 35°58N 121°9W **306** K5
**Jølstravatnet** *Norway* 61°32N 6°23E **164** C3
**Jomalig I.** *Phil.* 14°42N 122°22E **232** D4
**Jombang** *Indonesia* 7°33S 112°14E **235** D4
**Jomda** *China* 31°28N 98°12E **228** B2
**Jonåker** *Sweden* 58°45N 16°45E **163** F10
**Jonava** *Lithuania* 55°8N 24°12E **188** E3
**Jondal** *Norway* 60°16N 6°15E **164** D3
**Jones** *Phil.* 16°33N 121°42E **232** C3
**Jones Sound** *Canada* 76°0N 85°0W **295** B15
**Jonesboro** *Ark., U.S.A.* 35°50N 90°42W **315** D9
**Jonesboro** *Ga., U.S.A.* 33°31N 84°22W **316** B5
**Jonesboro** *La., U.S.A.* 32°15N 92°43W **314** E8
**Jonesburg** *U.S.A.* 38°51N 91°18W **310** F5
**Jonesville** *Ind., U.S.A.* 39°5N 85°54W **311** E11
**Jonesville** *Mich., U.S.A.* 41°59N 84°40W **311** C12
**Jong →** *S. Leone* 7°32N 12°23W **262** D2
**Jonglei** *South Sudan* 6°25N 31°30E **257** F3
**Jonglei □** *South Sudan* 7°30N 32°30E **257** F3
**Jonglei Canal** *South Sudan* 9°20N 31°39E **266** C3
**Jongmyo Royal Shrine** *S. Korea* 37°34N 126°59E **137** B1
**Jongno** *S. Korea* 37°35N 126°59E **137** B1
**Joniškis** *Lithuania* 56°13N 23°35E **184** B10
**Jönköping** *Sweden* 57°45N 14°8E **163** G8
**Jönköpings län □** *Sweden* 57°30N 14°30E **163** G8
**Jonquière** *Canada* 48°27N 71°14W **299** C5
**Jonsered** *Sweden* 57°45N 12°10E **163** G6
**Jonstrup** *Denmark* 55°45N 12°20E **118** A2
**Jonzac** *France* 45°27N 0°28W **174** C3
**Joplin** *U.S.A.* 37°6N 94°31W **308** G6
**Joppa** *U.K.* 55°57N 3°6W **121** B3
**Jora** *India* 26°20N 77°49E **242** F6
**Jordan** *Guimaras, Phil.* 10°40N 122°35E **233** F4
**Jordan** *Mont., U.S.A.* 47°19N 106°55W **304** C10
**Jordan** *N.Y., U.S.A.* 43°4N 76°29W **313** C8
**Jordan ■** *Asia* 31°0N 36°0E **251** H7
**Jordan →** *Asia* 31°48N 35°32E **251** G6
**Jordan Valley** *U.S.A.* 42°59N 117°3W **304** E5
**Jordânia** *Brazil* 15°55S 40°11W **333** E3
**Jordanów** *Poland* 49°41N 19°49E **185** J6
**Jordet** *Norway* 61°25N 12°8E **164** C9
**Jorge, C.** *Chile* 51°40S 75°35W **336** D1
**Jorge Chavez Int. ✈ (LIM)** *Lima, Peru* 12°2S 77°8W **124** B2
**Jorge Newbery ✈ (AEP)** *Argentina* 34°34S 58°25W **117** B2
**Jorgen Brønlund Fjord** *Greenland* 82°30N 31°0W **154** A7
**Jorhat** *India* 26°45N 94°12E **241** B5
**Jori →** *Norway* 62°4N 9°5E **162** B3
**Jorm** *Afghan.* 36°50N 70°52E **240** A3
**Jörn** *Sweden* 65°4N 20°1E **160** D19
**Jorong** *Indonesia* 3°58S 114°56E **235** C4
**Jørpeland** *Norway* 59°3N 6°1E **164** E3
**Jorquera →** *Chile* 28°3S 69°58W **334** B2
**Joru** *S. Leone* 7°41N 11°3W **262** D2
**Jos** *Nigeria* 9°53N 8°51E **263** D6
**Jos Plateau** *Nigeria* 9°55N 9°0E **263** D6
**Jošanička Banja** *Serbia* 43°24N 20°47E **202** C4
**Jose Abad Santos** *Phil.* 5°55N 125°39E **233** J5
**José Batlle y Ordóñez** *Uruguay* 33°20S 55°10W **335** C4
**José Bonifácio = Erechim** *Brazil* 27°35S 52°15W **335** B5
**José de San Martín** *Argentina* 44°4S 70°26W **336** B2
**Jose Panganiban** *Phil.* 14°17N 122°41E **232** D4
**Józefa Piłsudskiego Park** *Poland* 52°15N 21°2E **143** B1
**Joseni** *Romania* 46°42N 25°29E **183** D10
**Joseph, L.** *Canada* 45°10N 79°44W **312** A5
**Joseph Banks Group** *Australia* 34°36S 136°16E **282** C2
**Joseph Bonaparte G.** *Australia* 14°35S 128°50E **278** B4
**Joseph L.** *Canada* 52°45N 65°18W **299** B6
**Joshinath** *India* 30°34N 79°34E **243** D8
**Joshinetsu-Kōgen △** *Japan* 36°42N 138°32E **223** A10
**Joshua Tree** *U.S.A.* 34°8N 116°19W **307** L10
**Joshua Tree △** *U.S.A.* 33°55N 116°0W **307** M10
**Joss House B.** *Hong Kong, China* 22°16N 114°17E **122** B3
**Josselin** *France* 47°57N 2°33W **172** E4
**Jost Van Dyke I.** *Br. Virgin Is.* 18°29N 64°47W **321** b
**Jostedal** *Norway* 61°35N 7°15E **164** C4
**Jostedalsbreen** *Norway* 61°40N 6°59E **164** C3
**Jōtō** *Japan* 34°42N 135°33E **133** A2
**Jotunheimen** *Norway* 61°35N 8°25E **164** C5
**Jotunheimen △** *Norway* 61°32N 8°25E **164** C5
**Joubertberge** *Namibia* 18°30S 14°0E **270** A1
**Joué-lès-Tours** *France* 47°21N 0°40E **172** E7
**Jourdanton** *U.S.A.* 28°55N 98°33W **314** G5
**Joutseno** *Finland* 61°7N 28°31E **188** B5
**Jouy-en-Josas** *France* 48°46N 2°10E **134** B2
**Jovellanos** *Cuba* 22°40N 81°10W **320** B3
**Jovellar** *Phil.* 13°4N 123°36E **232** E4
**Jowai** *India* 25°26N 92°12E **241** C4
**Jowkār** *Iran* 34°25N 48°40E **213** E13
**Jowzjān □** *Afghan.* 36°10N 66°0E **240** A2
**Joya de Cerén** *El Salv.* 13°49N 89°22W **320** D2
**Joyeuse** *France* 44°29N 4°16E **175** D8
**Jōyō** *Japan* 34°50N 135°47E **223** C7
**Józefów** *Lubelskie, Poland* 50°28N 23°2E **185** H10
**Józefów** *Mazowieckie, Poland* 52°10N 21°11E **185** F8
**Ju Xian** *China* 36°35N 118°20E **227** F10
**Juan Aldama** *Mexico* 24°19N 103°21W **318** C4
**Juan Anchorena** *Argentina* 34°30S 58°29W **117** A2
**Juan Bautista Alberdi** *Argentina* 34°26S 61°48W **334** C3
**Juan de Bolas** *Jamaica* 18°5N 77°9W **320** a
**Juan de Fuca, Str of.** *N. Amer.* 48°15N 124°0W **306** B3
**Juan de Nova** *Ind. Oc.* 17°3S 43°45E **271** A7
**Juan Fernández, Arch. de** *Pac. Oc.* 33°50S 80°0W **326** G2
**Juan Fernández △** *Chile* 33°38S 78°52W **330** c
**Juan González Romero** *Mexico* 19°30N 99°3W **128** A2
**Juan José Castelli** *Argentina* 25°27S 60°57W **334** B3
**Juan L. Lacaze** *Uruguay* 34°26S 57°25W **334** C4
**Juana Días** *Puerto Rico* 18°3N 66°31W **321** b
**Juangriego** *Venezuela* 11°5N 63°58W **329** a
**Juangriego, B. de** *Venezuela* 11°5N 63°59W **329** a
**Juanjuí** *Peru* 7°10S 76°45W **330** B2
**Juankoski** *Finland* 63°3N 28°19E **160** E23
**Juara** *Brazil* 11°20S 57°25W **331** C6
**Juárez** *Mexico* 27°37N 100°44W **318** B4
**Juárez, Sa. de** *Mexico* 32°0N 115°50W **318** A1
**Juárez Int. ✈ (MEX)** *Mexico* 19°25N 99°5W **128** B2
**Juatinga, Pta. da** *Brazil* 23°17S 44°30W **333** F3
**Juàzeiro** *Brazil* 9°30S 40°30W **332** C3
**Juàzeiro do Norte** *Brazil* 7°10S 39°18W **332** C4
**Juazohn** *Liberia* 5°22N 8°50W **262** D3
**Juba** *South Sudan* 4°50N 31°35E **257** G3
**Juba →** *Somalia* 1°30N 42°35E **267** D5
**Jubail = Al Jubayl** *Si. Arabia* 27°0N 49°50E **247** E6
**Jubany** *Antarctica* 62°30S 58°0W **151** C18
**Jubayl** *Lebanon* 34°5N 35°39E **250** D6
**Jubbada Dhexe □** *Somalia* 2°0N 41°30E **267** D5
**Jubbada Hoose □** *Somalia* 0°0 42°0E **267** E5
**Jubbah** *Si. Arabia* 28°2N 40°56E **246** D4
**Jubbal** *India* 31°5N 77°40E **242** D7
**Jubbulpore = Jabalpur** *India* 23°9N 79°58E **243** H8
**Jübek** *Germany* 54°33N 9°22E **178** A5
**Jubga** *Russia* 44°19N 38°48E **191** H4
**Jubilee L.** *Australia* 29°0S 126°50E **279** E4
**Juby, C.** *Morocco* 28°0N 12°59W **260** C2
**Júcar = Xúquer →** *Spain* 39°5N 0°10W **197** F4
**Júcaro** *Cuba* 21°37N 78°51W **320** B4
**Juchitán de Zaragoza** *Mexico* 16°26N 95°1W **319** D5
**Judaberg** *Norway* 59°10N 5°51E **164** E2
**Judea = Har Yehuda** *Israel* 31°35N 34°57E **251** G5
**Judeira** *West Bank* 31°52N 35°12E **123** A2
**Judenburg** *Austria* 47°12N 14°38E **180** D7
**Judith →** *U.S.A.* 47°44N 109°39W **304** C9
**Judith, Pt.** *U.S.A.* 41°22N 71°29W **313** E13
**Judith Gap** *U.S.A.* 46°41N 109°45W **304** C9
**Juelsminde** *Denmark* 55°43N 10°1E **163** J4
**Jufari →** *Brazil* 1°13S 62°0W **329** D5
**Juhdum** *West Bank* 31°42N 35°15E **123** B2
**Juhu** *India* 19°5N 73°0E **130** A2
**Juifang** *Taiwan* 25°7N 121°48E **225** A3
**Juigalpa** *Nic.* 12°6N 85°26W **320** D2
**Juillac** *France* 45°20N 1°19E **174** C5
**Juist** *Germany* 53°40N 6°59E **178** B2
**Juisui** *Taiwan* 23°30N 121°22E **225** C3
**Juiz de Fora** *Brazil* 21°43S 43°19W **333** F3
**Jūjā** *Japan* 35°45N 139°43E **140** A3
**Jujuy □** *Argentina* 23°20S 65°40W **334** A2
**Jukao = Rugao** *China* 32°23N 120°31E **229** A13
**Jukskeirivier →** *S. Africa* 26°5S 28°6E **123** A2
**Julesburg** *U.S.A.* 40°59N 102°16W **304** F12
**Juli** *Peru* 16°10S 69°25W **330** D4
**Julia Cr. →** *Australia* 20°0S 141°11E **280** C3
**Julia Creek** *Australia* 20°39S 141°44E **280** C3
**Juliaca** *Peru* 15°25S 70°10W **330** D3
**Julian** *U.S.A.* 33°4N 116°38W **307** M10
**Julian, L.** *Canada* 54°25N 77°57W **298** B4
**Julian Alps = Julijske Alpe** *Slovenia* 46°15N 14°1E **199** B11
**Juliana Top = Mandala, Puncak** *Indonesia* 4°44S 140°20E **231** E10
**Julianadorp** *Curaçao* 12°9N 68°57W **322** g
**Julianatop** *Suriname* 3°40N 56°30W **329** C6
**Julianehåb = Qaqortoq** *Greenland* 60°43N 46°0W **154** E6
**Julianów** *Poland* 52°10N 21°9E **143** B2
**Jülich** *Germany* 50°55N 6°22E **178** E2
**Juliette, L.** *U.S.A.* 33°2N 83°50W **316** B6
**Julijske Alpe** *Slovenia* 46°15N 14°1E **199** B11
**Julimes** *Mexico* 28°25N 105°27W **318** B3
**Jullundur** *India* 31°20N 75°40E **242** D6
**Julu** *China* 37°15N 115°2E **226** F8
**Jumbo** *Zimbabwe* 17°30S 30°58E **269** F3
**Jumbo Pk.** *U.S.A.* 36°12N 114°11W **307** J12
**Jumeirah** *U.A.E.* 25°11N 55°14E **119** B1
**Jumentos Cays** *Bahamas* 23°0N 75°40W **320** B4
**Jumilla** *Spain* 38°28N 1°19W **197** G3
**Jumla** *Nepal* 29°15N 82°13E **243** E10
**Jumna = Yamuna →** *India* 25°30N 81°53E **243** G9

Jumunjin S. Korea 37°55N 128°54E 224 D4
Junagadh India 21°30N 70°30E 242 J4
Junan China 35°12N 118°53E 227 G10
Juncos Puerto Rico 18°14N 65°55W 321 b
Junction Tex., U.S.A. 30°29N 99°46W 314 F5
Junction Utah, U.S.A. 38°14N 112°13W 305 G7
Junction B. Australia 11°52S 133°55E 280 A1
Junction City Ga., U.S.A. 32°36N 84°28W 316 C5
Junction City Kans., U.S.A. 39°2N 96°50W 308 F5
Junction City Oreg., U.S.A. 44°13N 123°12W 304 D2
Junction Pt. Australia 11°45S 133°50E 280 A1
Jundah Australia 24°46S 143°2E 280 C3
Jundiaí Brazil 24°30S 47°0W 335 A6
Juneau U.S.A. 58°18N 134°25W 296 B2
Junee Australia 34°53S 147°35E 283 C7
Jung S. Korea 37°33N 126°59E 137 B1
Jungar Qi China 39°49N 110°57E 226 E6
Jungbunzlau = Mladá Boleslav Czech Rep. 50°27N 14°53E 180 A7
Jungfernheide, Volkspark Germany 52°32N 13°18E 115 A2
Jungfernsee Germany 52°25N 13°6E 115 B1
Jungfrau Switz. 46°32N 7°58E 179 J3
Junggar Pendi China 44°30N 86°0E 217 D11
Junghans, Teatro Venice, Italy 142 c2
Junghwa S. Korea 37°35N 127°3E 137 B2
Jungkat Indonesia 0°4N 109°13E 235 B3
Jungnang S. Korea 37°36N 127°5E 137 B2
Jungnangcheon → S. Korea 37°32N 126°55E 137 B1
Jungsdalshytta = Iungsdalshytta Norway 60°49N 7°55E 164 D4
Jungshahi Pakistan 24°52N 67°44E 242 G2
Juniata → U.S.A. 40°24N 77°1W 312 F7
Junín Argentina 34°33S 60°57W 334 C3
Junín Peru 11°12S 76°0W 330 C2
Junín □ Peru 11°30S 75°0W 330 C3
Junín, L. de Peru 11°2S 76°6W 330 C2
Junín de los Andes Argentina 39°45S 71°0W 336 A2
Juniper Green U.K. 55°54N 3°16W 121 B2
Jūniyah Lebanon 33°59N 35°38E 250 E6
Junk B. Hong Kong, China 22°17N 114°15E 122 B3
Junkerdal △ Norway 66°50N 15°50E 160 C16
Junlian China 28°8N 104°29E 228 C5
Junnar India 19°12N 73°58E 244 E1
Juno Beach U.S.A. 26°52N 80°3W 317 J9
Juntas Chile 28°24S 69°58W 334 B2
Juntura U.S.A. 43°45N 118°5W 304 E4
Juparanã, L. Brazil 19°16S 40°8W 333 E3
Jupiter U.S.A. 26°57N 80°6W 317 J9
Juquiá Brazil 24°19S 47°38W 333 F2
Jur → South Sudan 8°45N 29°15E 257 F2
Jura = Jura, Mts. du Europe 46°40N 6°5E 173 F13
Jura = Schwäbische Alb Germany 48°20N 9°30E 179 G5
Jura U.K. 56°0N 5°50W 167 F3
Jura □ France 46°47N 5°45E 173 F12
Jura □ Switz. 47°20N 7°20E 179 H3
Jūra → Lithuania 55°3N 22°9E 184 C9
Jura, Mts. du Europe 46°40N 6°5E 173 F13
Jura, Sd. of U.K. 55°57N 5°45W 167 F3
Juradó Colombia 7°7N 77°46W 328 B2
Jurassic Coast U.K. 50°42N 2°50W 169 G5
Jurbarkas Lithuania 55°4N 22°46E 184 C9
Jurien Bay Australia 30°18S 115°2E 279 F2
Jurilovca Romania 44°46N 28°52E 183 F13
Jūrmala Latvia 56°58N 23°34E 184 B10
Jurong Jiangsu, China 31°57N 119°9E 229 B12
Jurong Singapore 1°19N 103°42E 138 B2
Jurong, Selat Singapore 1°17N 103°42E 138 B2
Jurong Industrial Estate Singapore 1°19N 103°40E 138 B1
Juruá Brazil 3°27S 66°3W 328 D4
Juruá → Brazil 2°37S 65°44W 328 D4
Juruena Brazil 13°0S 58°10W 331 C6
Juruena → Brazil 7°20S 58°3W 331 B6
Jurujuba, Enseada de Brazil 22°54S 43°6W 135 B2
Juruti Brazil 2°9S 56°4W 329 D6
Jūsō Japan 34°42N 135°27E 133 A1
Jussey France 47°50N 5°55E 173 E12
Justice U.S.A. 41°44N 87°49W 119 C2
Justicia Madrid, Spain 127 a3
Justo Daract Argentina 33°52S 65°12W 334 C2
Jutaí Amazonas, Brazil 2°44S 66°57W 328 D4
Jutaí Amazonas, Brazil 5°11S 68°54W 330 B4
Jutaí → Brazil 2°43S 66°57W 328 D4
Jüterbog Germany 51°59N 13°5E 178 D9
Juticalpa Honduras 14°40N 86°12W 320 D2
Jutland = Jylland Denmark 56°25N 9°30E 163 H3
Juuka Finland 63°13N 29°17E 160 E23
Juventud, I. de la Cuba 21°40N 82°40W 320 B3
Juvigny-sous-Andaine France 48°32N 0°30W 172 D6
Juwangsan △ S. Korea 36°20N 129°15E 224 D4
Jūy Zar Iran 33°50N 46°18E 213 F12
Juye China 35°22N 116°5E 226 G9
Juzennecourt France 48°10N 4°58E 173 D11
Južni Brod = Brod Macedonia 41°32N 21°17E 202 E5
Jvari Georgia 42°42N 42°4E 191 J6
Jwalahari India 28°40N 77°6E 120 B1
Jyderup Denmark 55°40N 11°26E 163 J5
Jylland Denmark 56°25N 9°30E 163 H3
Jyväskylä Finland 62°14N 25°50E 188 A3

## K

K2 Pakistan 35°58N 76°32E 243 B7
Ka → Nigeria 11°40N 4°10E 263 C5
Kaa-Iya △ Bolivia 18°35S 61°40W 331 D5
Ka'a'awa U.S.A. 21°33N 157°51W 302 J14
Kaakha = Kaka Turkmenistan 37°21N 59°36E 247 B8
Ka'ala U.S.A. 21°31N 158°9W 302 J13
Kaala-Gomén N. Cal. 20°40S 164°25E 288 d
Ka'alu'alu B. U.S.A. 18°58N 155°37W 302 E6
Kaap Plateau S. Africa 28°30S 24°0E 270 C3
Kaapkruis Namibia 21°55S 13°57E 270 B1
Kaapstad = Cape Town S. Africa 33°55S 18°22E 118 A1
Kaashidhoo Atoll Maldives 4°58N 73°28E 272 d
Kaashidhoo Channel Maldives 5°1N 73°28E 272 d
Kaataon, Mt. Phil. 8°10N 124°52E 233 G5
Kaba Guinea 10°9N 11°40W 262 C2
Kabacan Phil. 7°8N 124°49E 233 H5
Kabachishche = Zelenodolsk Russia 55°55N 48°30E 190 C9
Kabaena Indonesia 5°15S 122°0E 231 F6
Kabala S. Leone 9°38N 11°37W 262 D2
Kabale Uganda 1°15S 30°0E 268 C3
Kabalo Dem. Rep. of the Congo 6°0S 27°0E 265 D5
Kabambare Dem. Rep. of the Congo 4°41S 27°39E 268 C2
Kabango Dem. Rep. of the Congo 8°35S 28°30E 269 D2
Kabanjahe Indonesia 3°6N 98°30E 234 B1
Kabankalan Phil. 9°59N 122°49E 233 G4
Kabara Fiji 18°59S 178°56W 287 B3
Kabara Mali 16°40N 2°50W 262 B4
Kabardinka Russia 44°40N 37°57E 189 K10
Kabardino-Balkaria □ Russia 43°30N 43°30E 191 J6
Kabarega Falls = Murchison Falls Uganda 2°15N 31°30E 268 B3
Kabarnet Kenya 0°30N 35°45E 268 B4
Kabasalan Phil. 7°47N 122°44E 233 H4
Kabat Indonesia 8°16S 114°19E 231 J17
Kabaty Poland 52°8N 21°4E 143 C2
Kabba Nigeria 7°50N 6°3E 263 D6
Kabbani → India 12°13N 76°54E 245 H3
Kabi Niger 13°30N 12°35E 259 F2
Kabin Buri Thailand 13°57N 101°43E 236 F3
Kabinakagami L. Canada 48°54N 84°25W 298 C3
Kabinda Dem. Rep. of the Congo 6°10S 24°29E 265 D4
Kabkabīyah Sudan 13°50N 24°0E 259 F4
Kablungu, C. Papua N. G. 6°20S 150°1E 286 D6
Kabna Sudan 19°6N 32°40E 256 D3
Kabo C.A.R. 7°35N 18°38E 264 A3
Kabompo Zambia 13°36S 24°14E 265 E4
Kabompo → Zambia 14°11S 23°11E 265 E4
Kabondo Dem. Rep. of the Congo 8°58S 25°40E 265 D5
Kabongo Dem. Rep. of the Congo 7°22S 25°33E 265 D5
Kabot Guinea 10°48N 14°57W 262 C2
Kabou Togo 9°28N 0°55E 263 D5
Kaboudia, Rass Tunisia 35°13N 11°10E 258 A2
Kabr Sudan 10°54N 26°50E 257 E2
Kabrît, G. el Egypt 29°42N 33°16E 251 J4
Kabrousse Senegal 12°25N 16°45W 262 C1
Kabubu Dem. Rep. of the Congo 9°42S 24°40E 265 D4
Kabūd Gonbad Iran 37°5N 59°45E 247 B8
Kabudar Ahang Iran 35°11N 48°43E 213 E13
Kabugao Phil. 18°2N 121°11E 232 B3
Kābul Afghan. 34°28N 69°11E 242 B3
Kābul □ Afghan. 34°30N 69°0E 240 B3
Kābul → Pakistan 33°55N 72°14E 242 C5
Kabuli Papua N. G. 2°7S 146°40E 286 B4
Kabunga Dem. Rep. of the Congo 1°38S 28°3E 268 C2
Kaburuang Indonesia 3°50N 126°30E 231 D7
Kabushiya Sudan 16°54N 33°41E 257 D3
Kabwanga Dem. Rep. of the Congo 7°2S 22°36E 265 D4
Kabwe Zambia 14°30S 28°29E 269 E2
Kabwum Papua N. G. 6°11S 147°15E 286 D4
Kaçanik Kosovo 42°13N 21°12E 202 D5
Kačerginė Lithuania 54°56N 23°42E 184 D10
Kachar Kazakhstan 53°23N 62°55E 216 B6
Kachchh, Gulf of India 22°50N 69°15E 242 H3
Kachchh, Rann of India 24°0N 70°0E 242 H4
Kachchhidhana India 21°44N 78°46E 243 J8
Kachebera Zambia 13°50S 32°50E 269 E3
Kachia Nigeria 9°50N 7°55E 263 D6
Kachikau Botswana 18°8S 24°26E 270 A3
Kachin □ Burma 26°0N 97°30E 228 D1
Kachira, L. Uganda 0°40S 31°7E 268 C3
Kachīry Kazakhstan 53°10N 75°50E 217 B9
Kachisi Ethiopia 9°40N 37°50E 257 F4
Kachnara India 23°50N 75°6E 242 H6
Kachot Cambodia 11°30N 103°3E 237 G4
Kaçkar Turkey 40°45N 41°10E 213 B9
Kada Chad 19°20N 19°39E 259 E3
Kadaingti Burma 17°37N 97°32E 241 G6
Kadaiyanallur India 9°3N 77°22E 245 K3
Kadam, Mt. Uganda 1°45N 34°45E 268 B3
Kadan Czech Rep. 50°23N 13°16E 180 A6
Kadan Kyun Burma 12°30N 98°20E 236 F2
Kadanai → Afghan. 31°22N 65°45E 242 D1
Kadapa India 14°30N 78°47E 245 G4
Kadarkút Hungary 46°13N 17°39E 182 D2
Kadavu Fiji 19°0S 178°15E 287 B2
Kadavu Passage Fiji 18°45S 178°0E 287 B2
Kade Ghana 6°7N 0°56W 263 D4
Kadei → C.A.R. 3°31N 16°3E 264 B3
Kademlija = Triglav Slovenia 46°21N 13°50E 199 B10
Kadena Japan 26°22N 127°45E 288 a
Kadhimain = Al Kāẓimīyah Iraq 33°22N 44°18E 213 F11
Kadi India 23°18N 72°23E 242 H5
Kadiak I. = Kodiak I. U.S.A. 57°30N 152°45W 303 H9
Kadiana Mali 10°45N 6°30W 262 C3
Kadıköy Turkey 40°59N 29°1E 122 C2
Kadina Australia 33°55S 137°43E 282 B2
Kadınhanı Turkey 38°14N 32°13E 212 C5
Kadiolo Mali 10°35N 7°41W 262 C3
Kadipur India 26°10N 82°23E 243 F10
Kadirabad India 19°51N 75°54E 244 E2
Kadiri India 14°12N 78°13E 245 G4
Kadirli Turkey 37°23N 36°5E 212 D7
Kadiyevka = Stakhanov Ukraine 48°35N 38°40E 189 H10
Kadja, O. → Chad 12°2N 22°28E 259 F4
Kadmat I. India 11°14N 72°47E 245 J1
Kadodo Sudan 11°4N 29°31E 257 E2
Kadoka U.S.A. 43°50N 101°31W 308 D3
Kadom Russia 54°37N 42°30E 190 C6
Kadoma Ōsaka, Japan 34°44N 135°35E 133 A2
Kadoma Zimbabwe 18°20S 29°52E 269 F2
Kâdugli Sudan 11°0N 29°45E 257 E2
Kaduna Nigeria 10°30N 7°21E 263 C6
Kaduna □ Nigeria 11°0N 7°30E 263 C6
Kaduna → Nigeria 8°45N 5°48E 263 D6
Kadur India 13°34N 76°1E 245 H3
Kaduy Russia 59°12N 37°9E 188 C9
Kaédi Mauritania 16°9N 13°28W 262 B2
Kaélé Cameroon 10°7N 14°27E 259 F2
Ka'ena U.S.A. 21°34N 158°14W 302 J13
Ka'ena Pt. U.S.A. 21°35N 158°17W 302 J13
Kaeng Khoi Thailand 14°35N 101°0E 236 E3
Kaeng Krachan △ Thailand 12°57N 99°23E 236 F2
Kaeng Krung △ Thailand 9°30N 98°50E 237 H2
Kaeng Tana △ Thailand 15°25N 105°32E 236 E5
Kaeo N.Z. 35°6S 173°49E 284 B2
Kaesŏng N. Korea 37°58N 126°35E 224 D3
Kaesŏng □ N. Korea 38°0N 126°37E 224 D3
Kāf Si. Arabia 31°25N 37°29E 246 D3
Kafakumba Dem. Rep. of the Congo 9°38S 23°46E 265 D4
Kafan = Kapan Armenia 39°18N 46°27E 213 C12
Kafanchan Nigeria 9°40N 8°20E 263 D6
Kafareti Nigeria 10°25N 11°12E 263 C7
Kaffrine Senegal 14°8N 15°36W 262 C1
Kafia Kingi Sudan 9°20N 24°25E 264 A4
Kafin Nigeria 9°30N 7°4E 263 D6
Kafin Madaki Nigeria 10°41N 9°46E 263 C6
Kafinda Zambia 12°32S 30°20E 269 E3
Kafireos, Stenon Greece 37°55N 24°35E 204 D6
Kafr 'Aqab West Bank 31°52N 35°13E 123 A2
Kafr el Battikh Egypt 31°25N 31°44E 256 H7
Kafr el Dauwâr Egypt 31°8N 30°8E 256 H7
Kafr el Sheikh Egypt 31°15N 30°50E 251 G1
Kafr el Sheikh □ Egypt 31°15N 30°55E 251 G1
Kafr el Zaiyāt Egypt 30°49N 30°48E 256 H7
Kafue Zambia 15°46S 28°9E 269 F2
Kafue △ Zambia 15°12S 25°38E 269 F2
Kafue Flats Zambia 15°40S 27°25E 269 F2
Kafulwe Zambia 9°0S 29°1E 269 D2
Kafumba Dem. Rep. of the Congo 5°23S 18°55E 265 D3
Kaga Afghan. 34°14N 70°10E 242 B4
Kaga Japan 36°16N 136°15E 223 A8
Kaga Bandoro C.A.R. 7°0N 19°10E 264 A3
Kagamil I. U.S.A. 53°0N 169°43W 303 K5
Kaganovich = Tovarkovskiy Russia 53°40N 38°14E 188 F10
Kagarko Nigeria 9°28N 7°36E 263 D6
Kagawa □ Japan 34°15N 134°0E 222 C6
Kagera □ Tanzania 2°0S 31°30E 268 C3
Kagera → Uganda 0°57S 31°47E 268 C3
Kâğıthane Turkey 41°4N 28°58E 122 B1
Kâğıthane → Turkey 41°9N 28°56E 122 B1
Kağızman Turkey 40°5N 43°10E 213 B10
Kagmar Sudan 14°24N 30°25E 257 E3
Kagologolo Indonesia 1°9S 98°37E 234 C1
Kagopal Chad 8°16N 16°23E 259 G3
Kagoro Nigeria 9°36N 8°23E 263 D6
Kagoshima Japan 31°35N 130°33E 222 F2
Kagoshima □ Japan 31°30N 130°30E 222 F2
Kagoshima-Wan Japan 31°25N 130°40E 222 F2
Kagran Austria 48°14N 16°26E 142 A2
Kagua Papua N. G. 6°26S 143°48E 286 D2
Kagul = Cahul Moldova 45°50N 28°15E 183 E13
Kahak Iran 36°6N 49°46E 247 B6
Kāhala U.S.A. 21°16N 157°47W 302 K14
Kahalu'u U.S.A. 21°27N 157°50W 302 K14
Kahama Tanzania 4°8S 32°30E 268 C3
Kahan Pakistan 29°18N 68°54E 242 E3
Kahana U.S.A. 21°34N 157°53W 302 J14
Kahana B. U.S.A. 21°35N 157°50W 302 J14
Kahana Valley State Park ⌓ U.S.A. 21°32N 157°53W 302 J14
Kahang Malaysia 2°12N 103°32E 237 L4
Kahayan → Indonesia 3°40S 114°0E 235 C4
Kahe Tanzania 3°30S 37°25E 268 C4
Kahemba Dem. Rep. of the Congo 7°18S 18°55E 265 D3
Kaherekoau Mts. N.Z. 45°45S 167°15E 285 F2
Kahil, Djebel bou Algeria 34°26N 4°0E 261 B5
Kahnawake Canada 45°24N 73°40W 130 B1
Kahnūj Iran 27°55N 57°40E 247 E8
Kahoka U.S.A. 40°25N 91°44W 310 D5
Kaho'olawe U.S.A. 20°33N 156°37W 302 C5
Kahouanne Guadeloupe 16°15N 61°12W 322 e
Kahouanne, Îlet à Guadeloupe 16°22N 61°46W 322 e
Kahramanmaraş Turkey 37°37N 36°53E 212 D7
Kahramanmaraş □ Turkey 37°35N 36°33E 212 D7
Kâhta Turkey 37°46N 38°36E 213 D8
Kahuku U.S.A. 21°41N 157°57W 302 J14
Kahuku Pt. U.S.A. 21°43N 157°59W 302 J14
Kahul, Ozero Ukraine 45°24N 28°24E 183 E13
Kahului U.S.A. 20°54N 156°28W 302 C5
Kahului ✈ (OGG) U.S.A. 20°54N 156°26W 302 C5
Kahurangi △ N.Z. 41°10S 172°32E 285 B7
Kahurangi Pt. N.Z. 40°50S 172°10E 285 A7
Kahuta Pakistan 33°35N 73°24E 242 C5
Kahuzi-Biega △ Dem. Rep. of the Congo 1°50S 27°55E 268 C2
Kai Japan 35°42N 138°30E 223 B10
Kai, Kepulauan Indonesia 5°55S 132°45E 231 F8
Kai Besar Indonesia 5°35S 133°0E 231 F8
Kai Is. = Kai, Kepulauan Indonesia 5°55S 132°45E 231 F8
Kai Kecil Indonesia 5°45S 132°40E 231 F8
Kai Xian China 31°11N 108°21E 228 B7
Kaiama Nigeria 9°36N 4°1E 263 D5
Kaiapit Papua N. G. 6°18S 146°18E 286 D4
Kaiapoi N.Z. 43°24S 172°40E 285 D7
Kaidu He → China 41°46N 86°31E 218 C6
Kaieteur Falls Guyana 5°1N 59°10W 329 B6
Kaifeng China 34°48N 114°21E 226 G8
Kaihua China 29°12N 118°20E 229 C12
Kaijiang China 31°7N 107°55E 228 B6
Kaikohe N.Z. 35°25S 173°49E 284 B2
Kaikoura N.Z. 42°25S 173°43E 285 C8
Kaikoura Pen. N.Z. 42°25S 173°43E 285 C8
Kailahun S. Leone 8°18N 10°39W 262 D2
Kailash = Kangrinboqe Feng China 31°0N 81°25E 243 D9
Kailashahar India 24°19N 92°0E 241 C4
Kaileuna I. Papua N. G. 8°32S 150°57E 286 E6
Kaili China 26°33N 107°59E 228 D6
Kailu China 43°38N 121°18E 227 C11
Kailua U.S.A. 21°24N 157°44W 302 K14
Kailua B. U.S.A. 21°25N 157°40W 302 K14
Kailua Kona U.S.A. 19°39N 155°59W 302 D6
Kaim → Papua N. G. 6°55S 141°33E 286 D1
Kaimaktsalan Oros = Voras Oros Greece 40°57N 21°45E 202 F5
Kaimana Indonesia 3°39S 133°45E 231 E8
Kaimanawa Mts. N.Z. 39°15S 175°56E 284 F4
Kaimata N.Z. 42°34S 171°28E 285 C6
Kaimes U.K. 55°54N 3°10W 121 B2
Kaimganj India 27°33N 79°24E 243 F8
Kaimon-Dake Japan 31°11N 130°32E 222 F2
Kaimur Hills India 24°30N 82°0E 243 G10
Kainab → Namibia 28°32S 19°34E 270 C2
Kainan Japan 34°9N 135°12E 223 C7
Kainantu Papua N. G. 6°18S 145°52E 286 D3
Kainji Dam Nigeria 9°55N 4°35E 263 D5
Kainji Lake △ Nigeria 10°5N 4°6E 263 C5
Kainji Res. Nigeria 10°1N 4°40E 263 C5
Kainsk = Samara Russia 53°8N 50°6E 190 D10
Kainuu □ Finland 64°30N 29°7E 160 D23
Kaipara Harbour N.Z. 36°25S 174°14E 284 C3
Kaiping China 22°23N 112°42E 229 F9
Kaipokok B. Canada 54°54N 59°47W 299 B8
Kaira India 22°45N 72°50E 242 H5
Kairana India 29°24N 77°15E 242 E7
Kairiru I. Papua N. G. 3°21S 143°34E 286 B2
Kaironi Indonesia 0°47S 133°40E 231 E8
Kairouan Tunisia 35°45N 10°5E 258 A2
Kairouan □ Tunisia 35°30N 9°46E 261 A6
Kairuku Papua N. G. 8°51S 146°35E 286 E4
Kaiser Wilhelm Gedächtniskirche Berlin, Germany 115 b2
Kaiser Wilhelm Kanal = Nord-Ostsee-Kanal Germany 54°12N 9°32E 178 A5
Kaiser-Wilhelmsland = Papua □ Indonesia 4°0S 137°0E 231 E9
Kaiserebersdorf Austria 48°9N 16°26E 142 B2
Kaiserslautern Germany 49°26N 7°45E 179 F3
Kaiserstuhl Germany 48°4N 7°40E 179 G3
Kaita Japan 34°22N 132°32E 222 C4
Kaitaia N.Z. 35°8S 173°17E 284 B2
Kaitangata N.Z. 46°17S 169°51E 285 G4
Kaithal India 29°48N 76°26E 242 E7
Kaitu → Pakistan 33°10N 70°30E 242 C4
Kaivoksela Finland 60°15N 24°53E 121 B2
Kaiwi Channel U.S.A. 21°15N 157°30W 302 K14
Kaiyang China 27°4N 106°59E 228 D6
Kaiyuan Liaoning, China 42°28N 124°1E 224 A2
Kaiyuan Yunnan, China 23°40N 103°12E 228 F4
Kaiyuh Mts. U.S.A. 64°30N 158°0W 303 D8
Kajaani Finland 64°17N 27°46E 160 D22
Kajabbi Australia 20°0S 140°1E 280 C3
Kajaki Afghan. 32°18N 65°5E 240 B2
Kajana = Kajaani Finland 64°17N 27°46E 160 D22
Kajang Malaysia 2°59N 101°48E 237 L3
Kajaran Armenia 39°10N 46°7E 213 C12
Kajiado Kenya 1°53S 36°48E 268 C4
Kajo Kaji South Sudan 3°58N 31°40E 257 G3
Kajok South Sudan 8°19N 28°0E 257 F2
Kajuru Nigeria 10°15N 7°34E 263 C6
Kaka South Sudan 10°38N 32°10E 257 E3
Kaka Turkmenistan 37°21N 59°36E 247 B8
Kakabeka Falls Canada 48°24N 89°37W 298 C2
Kakadu △ Australia 12°0S 132°3E 278 B5
Kakamas S. Africa 28°45S 20°33E 270 C3
Kakamega Kenya 0°20N 34°46E 268 B3
Kakamigahara Japan 35°28N 136°48E 223 B8
Kakana India 9°7N 92°48E 245 K11
Kakanj Bos.-H. 44°4N 18°4E 182 F3
Kakanui Mts. N.Z. 45°10S 170°30E 285 F5
Kakata Liberia 6°35N 10°20W 262 D2
Kakching India 24°29N 94°0E 241 C5
Kakdwip India 21°53N 88°11E 243 J13
Kake = Akiōta Japan 34°36N 132°19E 222 C4
Kake U.S.A. 56°59N 133°57W 296 B2
Kakegawa Japan 34°45N 138°1E 223 C10
Kakeroma-Jima Japan 28°8N 129°14E 221 K4
Kākhak Iran 34°9N 58°38E 247 C8
Kakhib Russia 42°28N 46°34E 191 J8
Kakhonak U.S.A. 59°26N 154°51W 303 G9
Kakhovka Ukraine 46°45N 33°30E 189 J7
Kakhovske Vdskh. Ukraine 47°5N 34°0E 189 J7
Kakinada India 16°57N 82°11E 244 F6
Kakisa Canada 60°56N 117°25W 296 A5
Kakisa → Canada 61°3N 118°10W 296 A5
Kakisa L. Canada 60°56N 117°43W 296 A5
Käkisalmi = Priozersk Russia 61°2N 30°7E 188 B6
Kakogawa Japan 34°46N 134°51E 222 C6
Kaktovik U.S.A. 70°8N 143°38W 303 A12
Kakum △ Ghana 5°24N 1°20W 263 D4
Kakuma Kenya 3°43N 34°52E 268 B3
Kakwa → Canada 54°37N 118°28W 296 C5
Kāl Gūsheh Iran 30°59N 58°12E 247 D8
Kal Sefid Iran 34°52N 47°23E 213 E12
Kala Nigeria 12°2N 14°40E 263 C7
Kala Oya → Sri Lanka 8°20N 79°45E 245 K4
Kalaa-Kebira Tunisia 35°59N 10°32E 258 A2
Kalaallit Nunaat = Greenland ⧄ N. Amer. 66°0N 45°0W 154 D6
Kalabagh Pakistan 33°0N 71°28E 242 C4
Kalabahi Indonesia 8°13S 124°31E 231 F6
Kalabak = Radomir Bulgaria 42°37N 22°59E 202 D6
Kalabakan Malaysia 4°25N 117°29E 235 B5
Kalabana Mali 14°10N 8°35W 262 C3
Kalabo Zambia 14°58S 22°40E 265 E4
Kalach Russia 50°22N 41°0E 190 E5
Kalach na Donu Russia 48°43N 43°32E 191 F6
Kalachinsk Russia 55°3N 74°33E 217 A8
Kaladan → Burma 20°20N 93°5E 241 E4
Kaladar Canada 44°37N 77°5W 312 B7
Kalae U.S.A. 18°55N 155°41W 302 E6
Kalahari Africa 24°0S 21°30E 270 B3
Kalahari Gemsbok △ S. Africa 25°30S 20°30E 270 C3
Kalaheo U.S.A. 21°56N 159°32W 302 B2
Kalaikhum Tajikistan 38°28N 70°46E 217 E8
Kalajoki Finland 64°12N 24°10E 160 D21
Kalakamati Botswana 20°40S 27°25E 271 B4
Kalakan Russia 55°15N 116°45E 215 D12
Kalakol Kenya 3°33N 35°54E 266 D4
K'alak'unlun Shank'ou = Karakoram Pass Asia 35°33N 77°50E 243 B7
Kalam Pakistan 35°34N 72°30E 243 B5
Kalama Dem. Rep. of the Congo 2°52S 28°35E 268 C2
Kalama Wash., U.S.A. 46°1N 122°51W 306 E4
Kalamaki Greece 37°52N 23°43E 112 B2
Kalamaloué △ Cameroon 12°9N 14°58E 259 F2
Kalamansig Phil. 6°33N 124°3E 233 H5
Kalamaria Greece 40°33N 22°55E 202 F6
Kalamata Greece 37°3N 22°10E 204 D4
Kalamazoo U.S.A. 42°17N 85°35W 311 B11
Kalamazoo → U.S.A. 42°40N 86°10W 311 B10
Kalamb India 18°3N 74°48E 244 E2
Kalambaka Greece 39°42N 21°39E 204 B3
Kalambo Falls Tanzania 8°37S 31°35E 269 D3
Kalamitsi Greece 38°45N 20°36E 207 B2
Kalamnuri India 19°40N 77°20E 244 E3
Kalamos Attiki, Greece 38°17N 23°52E 204 C5
Kalamos Lefkada, Greece 38°37N 20°55E 207 B2
Kalan Turkey 39°7N 39°32E 246 B3
Kalangadoo Australia 37°34S 140°41E 282 D4
Kalankalan Guinea 10°7N 8°54W 262 C3
Kalannie Australia 30°22S 117°5E 279 F2
Kalāntarī Iran 32°10N 54°8E 247 C7
Kalao Indonesia 7°21S 121°0E 231 F6
Kalaoa U.S.A. 19°43N 155°58W 302 D6
Kalaotoa Indonesia 7°20S 121°50E 231 F6
Kalapana U.S.A. 19°21N 154°59W 302 D7
Kälarne Sweden 62°59N 16°5E 162 B10
Kalasin Thailand 16°26N 103°30E 236 D4
Kālat Iran 25°29N 59°22E 247 E8
Kalat Pakistan 29°8N 66°31E 240 C2
Kalāteh Iran 36°33N 55°41E 247 B7
Kalāteh-ye Ganj Iran 27°31N 57°55E 247 E8
Kalathos Greece 36°9N 28°8E 206 E12
Kalatungan, Mt. Phil. 7°54N 124°50E 233 H5
Kalaupapa U.S.A. 21°12N 156°59W 302 B5
Kalaupapa ⌓ U.S.A. 21°10N 156°59W 302 B5
Kalaus → Russia 45°40N 44°7E 191 H7
Kalavrita Greece 38°3N 22°8E 204 C4
Kalaw Burma 20°38N 96°34E 241 E6
Kalawao County U.S.A. 21°11N 156°58W 302 B5
Kalbā U.A.E. 25°5N 56°22E 247 E8
Kalbadevi Mumbai, India 130 b2
Kalbān Oman 20°18N 58°38E 249 B7
Kalbarri Australia 27°40S 114°10E 279 E1
Kalbarri △ Australia 27°51S 114°30E 279 E1
Kalburgi = Gulbarga India 17°20N 76°50E 244 F3
Kalce Slovenia 45°54N 14°13E 176 F8
Kaldrananes Iceland 65°45N 21°25W 155 B5
Kale Antalya, Turkey 36°14N 30°0E 205 E12
Kale Denizli, Turkey 37°27N 28°49E 205 D10
Kaleburnu = Galinoporni Cyprus 35°31N 34°18E 207 E10
Kalecik Turkey 40°4N 33°26E 212 B5
Kalegauk Kyun Burma 15°33N 97°35E 236 E1
Kalehe Dem. Rep. of the Congo 2°6S 28°50E 268 C2
Kalema Tanzania 1°12S 31°55E 268 C3
Kalemie Dem. Rep. of the Congo 5°55S 29°9E 268 D2
Kalemyo Burma 23°11N 94°4E 241 D5
Kalety Poland 50°35N 18°52E 185 H5
Kalewa Burma 23°10N 94°15E 241 D5
Kaleybar Iran 38°47N 47°2E 213 C12
Kálfafell Iceland 63°57N 17°41W 155 D9
Kalgan = Zhangjiakou China 40°48N 114°55E 226 D8
Kalghatgi India 15°11N 74°58E 245 G2
Kalgoorlie-Boulder Australia 30°40S 121°22E 279 F3
Kalhovd Norway 60°4N 8°21E 164 D5
Kali → India 27°6N 79°55E 243 F8
Kali Sindh → India 25°32N 76°17E 242 G6
Kaliakra, Nos Bulgaria 43°21N 28°30E 203 C12
Kalianda Indonesia 5°50S 105°45E 234 D3
Kalibo Phil. 11°43N 122°22E 233 F4
Kaliganj Bangla. 22°25N 89°8E 241 D2
Kalihi U.S.A. 21°20N 157°53W 302 K14
Kalihi Valley U.S.A. 21°20N 157°52W 302 K14
Kalima Dem. Rep. of the Congo 2°33S 26°32E 268 C2
Kalimantan Indonesia 0°0 114°0E 235 C4
Kalimantan Barat □ Indonesia 0°0 110°30E 235 C4
Kalimantan Selatan □ Indonesia 2°30S 115°30E 235 C5
Kalimantan Tengah □ Indonesia 2°0S 113°30E 235 C4
Kalimantan Timur □ Indonesia 1°30N 116°30E 235 B5
Kálimnos Greece 37°0N 27°0E 205 D8
Kalimpong India 27°4N 88°35E 241 B2
Kalinadi → India 14°50N 74°7E 245 G2
Kalinga □ Phil. 17°30N 121°20E 232 C3
Kalinikinsk Russia 51°29N 44°28E 216 B2
Kalinin = Tver Russia 56°55N 35°59E 188 D8
Kaliningrad Russia 54°42N 20°32E 184 D7
Kaliningrad ✈ (KGD) Russia 54°45N 20°33E 184 D7
Kalininsk = Petrozavodsk Russia 61°41N 34°20E 188 B8
Kalininsk Russia 51°30N 44°40E 190 E7
Kalinkavichy Belarus 52°12N 29°20E 177 B15
Kalinkovichi = Kalinkavichy Belarus 52°12N 29°20E 177 B15
Kalinovik Bos.-H. 43°31N 18°25E 202 C2
Kalipetrovo Bulgaria 44°5N 27°14E 203 B11
Kalipur India 22°40N 88°17E 124 A1
Kalirachi Greece 40°40N 24°35E 203 F8
Kaliro Uganda 0°56N 33°30E 268 B3
Kalispell U.S.A. 48°12N 114°19W 304 B6
Kalisz Poland 51°45N 18°8E 185 G5
Kalisz Pomorski Poland 53°17N 15°55E 185 E2
Kalithea Greece 37°56N 23°43E 112 B2
Kaliua Tanzania 5°5S 31°48E 268 D3
Kaliveli Tank India 12°5N 79°50E 245 H4
Kalivia Thorikou Greece 37°50N 23°55E 204 D5
Kalix Sweden 65°53N 23°12E 160 D20
Kalixälven → Sweden 65°50N 23°11E 160 D20
Kalka India 30°46N 76°57E 242 D7
Kalkaji India 28°32N 77°12E 120 B2
Kalkali Ghat India 24°36N 92°20E 241 C4
Kalkan Turkey 36°15N 29°23E 205 E11
Kalkarindji Australia 17°30S 130°47E 278 C5
Kalkaska U.S.A. 44°44N 85°11W 309 C11
Kalkfeld Namibia 20°57S 16°14E 270 B2
Kalkfontein Botswana 22°4S 20°57E 270 B3
Kalkım Turkey 39°48N 27°13E 205 B9
Kalkrand Namibia 24°1S 17°35E 270 B2
Kallakkurichchi India 11°44N 79°1E 245 J4
Kallam India 18°36N 76°2E 244 E3
Kållandsö Sweden 58°40N 13°5E 163 F7
Kallavesi Finland 62°58N 27°30E 160 E22
Källby Sweden 58°30N 13°8E 163 F7
Kållered Sweden 57°32N 12°4E 163 G6
Kallidaikurichi India 8°38N 77°31E 245 K3
Kallies = Kalisz Pomorski Poland 53°17N 15°55E 185 E2
Kallimasia Greece 38°18N 26°6E 205 C8
Kallinge Sweden 56°15N 15°18E 163 H9
Kallmet Albania 41°51N 19°41E 202 E3
Kallsjön Sweden 63°38N 13°0E 160 E15
Kalmalo Nigeria 13°40N 5°20E 263 C6
Kalmanstunga Iceland 64°44N 20°48W 155 C6
Kalmar Sweden 56°40N 16°20E 163 H10
Kalmar län □ Sweden 57°25N 16°0E 163 G10
Kalmar sund Sweden 56°40N 16°25E 163 H10
Kalmunai Sri Lanka 7°25N 81°49E 245 L5
Kalmykia □ Russia 46°5N 46°1E 191 G8
Kalna India 23°13N 88°25E 243 H13
Kalnai India 22°46N 83°30E 243 H10
Kalni → Bangla. 24°21N 91°13E 241 C3
Kalo Papua N. G. 10°1S 147°48E 286 F4
Kalo Nero Greece 37°20N 21°38E 204 D3
Kalocsa Hungary 46°32N 19°0E 182 D4
Kalofer Bulgaria 42°37N 24°59E 203 D8
Kalohi Channel U.S.A. 21°0N 157°0W 302 C5
Kalokhorio Cyprus 34°51N 33°2E 207 F9
Kaloko Dem. Rep. of the Congo 6°47S 25°48E 265 D5
Kaloko-Honokōhau ⌓ U.S.A. 19°40N 156°1W 302 D5
Kalol Gujarat, India 22°37N 73°31E 242 H5
Kalol Gujarat, India 23°15N 72°33E 242 H5
Kalolimnos Greece 37°4N 27°5E 205 D9
Kalomo Zambia 17°0S 26°30E 269 F2
Kalona U.S.A. 41°29N 91°43W 310 C5
Kaloni Greece 39°14N 26°12E 205 B8
Kaloni, Kolpos Greece 39°10N 26°10E 205 B8
Kalookan = Caloocan Phil. 14°39N 120°58E 127 B1
Kalpeni I. India 10°5N 73°38E 245 J1
Kalpi India 26°8N 79°47E 243 F8
Kalpitiya Sri Lanka 8°14N 79°46E 245 K4
Kalputhi I. India 10°49N 72°10E 245 J1
Kalrayan Hills India 11°45N 78°40E 245 J4
Kalsubai India 19°35N 73°45E 244 E1
Kaltag U.S.A. 64°20N 158°43W 303 D8
Kaltern = Caldaro Italy 46°25N 11°14E 199 B8
Kaltukatjara Australia 24°52S 129°5E 279 D4
Kaltungo Nigeria 9°48N 11°19E 263 D7
Kalu Pakistan 25°5N 67°39E 242 G2
Kaluga Russia 54°35N 36°10E 188 E9
Kaluga □ Russia 54°15N 34°50E 188 E8
Kalulong, Bukit Malaysia 3°14N 114°39E 235 B4
Kalulushi Zambia 12°50S 28°3E 269 E2
Kalumburu Australia 13°55S 126°35E 278 B4
Kalumburu ✲ Australia 14°17S 126°38E 278 B4
Kalundborg Denmark 55°41N 11°5E 163 J5
Kalush Ukraine 49°3N 24°23E 177 D13
Kałuszyn Poland 52°13N 21°52E 185 F8
Kalutara Sri Lanka 6°35N 80°0E 245 L5
Kalvåg Norway 61°46N 4°51E 164 C1
Kalvarija Lithuania 54°24N 23°14E 184 D10
Kalvebod Fælled Denmark 55°35N 12°33E 118 B3
Kalveboderne Denmark 55°37N 12°31E 118 B3
Kalwakurti India 16°41N 78°30E 244 F4
Kalya Russia 60°15N 59°59E 186 B10
Kalyan Maharashtra, India 20°30N 74°3E 244 D2
Kalyan Maharashtra, India 19°15N 73°9E 244 E1
Kalyandurg India 14°33N 77°6E 245 G3
Kalyani India 17°52N 76°57E 244 F3
Kalyansingapuram India 19°30N 83°19E 244 E6
Kalyazin Russia 57°15N 37°55E 188 D9
Kam Albania 42°17N 20°18E 202 D4
Kam → Nigeria 8°15N 1°10E 263 D7
Kam Shan Country Park ⌓ Hong Kong, China 22°21N 114°9E 122 A2
Kama Burma 19°1N 95°4E 241 F5
Kama Dem. Rep. of the Congo 3°30S 27°5E 268 C2
Kama Fukuoka, Japan 33°33N 130°49E 222 D2
Kama → Russia 55°45N 52°0E 186 C9
Kama Iwa Iwo Jima 24°47N 141°17E 288 b
Kamachumu Tanzania 1°37S 31°37E 268 C3
Kamae Japan 32°48N 131°56E 222 E3
Kamaing Burma 25°26N 96°35E 241 C6
Kamaishi Japan 39°16N 141°53E 220 E10
Kamakou U.S.A. 21°7N 156°52W 302 B5
Kamakura Japan 35°19N 139°33E 223 B11
Kamalapurum India 14°35N 78°39E 245 G4
Kamaléte Gabon 0°43S 11°49E 264 C2
Kamalia Pakistan 30°44N 72°42E 242 D5
Kamamaung Burma 17°21N 97°40E 241 G6
Kaman India 27°39N 77°16E 242 F6
Kaman Turkey 39°22N 33°44E 212 C5
Kamana Dem. Rep. of the Congo 5°59S 24°58E 265 D4
Kamananui → U.S.A. 21°38N 158°4W 302 J13
Kamanjab Namibia 19°35S 14°51E 270 A2
Kamapanda Zambia 12°5S 24°0E 269 E1
Kamara Mali 14°38N 9°23W 262 C3
Kamarān Yemen 15°21N 42°35E 248 D3
Kamareddi India 18°19N 78°21E 244 E4
Kamarhati India 22°40N 88°23E 124 A2
Kamata Japan 35°33N 139°43E 140 B3
Kamativi Zimbabwe 18°20S 27°6E 270 A4
Kamba Dem. Rep. of the Congo 4°0S 22°22E 265 C4
Kamba Nigeria 11°50N 3°45E 263 C5
Kambalda West Australia 31°10S 121°37E 279 F3
Kambam India 9°45N 77°16E 245 K3
Kambangan, Nusa Indonesia 7°40S 108°10E 235 D3
Kambar Pakistan 27°37N 68°1E 242 F3
Kambarka Russia 56°15N 54°11E 186 C9
Kambia S. Leone 9°3N 12°53W 262 D2
Kambolé Togo 8°43N 1°39E 263 D5
Kambolé Zambia 8°47S 30°48E 269 D3
Kambos Cyprus 35°2N 32°44E 207 E8
Kambove Dem. Rep. of the Congo 10°51S 26°33E 269 E2
Kambuie Dem. Rep. of the Congo 6°59S 22°19E 265 D4
Kambwata Zambia 14°3S 23°43E 265 E4
Kamchatka, Poluostrov Russia 57°0N 160°0E 215 D17
Kamchatka Pen. = Kamchatka, Poluostrov Russia 57°0N 160°0E 215 D17
Kamchiya → Bulgaria 43°4N 27°44E 203 C11
Kame Ruins Zimbabwe 20°7S 28°25E 269 G2
Kameari Japan 35°45N 139°50E 140 A4
Kameda-Hantō Japan 41°50N 141°0E 220 D10
Kameido Japan 35°42N 139°50E 140 A4
Kamen Russia 53°50N 81°30E 217 B10
Kamen-Rybolov Russia 44°46N 132°2E 220 B5
Kamende Dem. Rep. of the Congo 6°26S 24°35E 265 D4
Kamenica Serbia 43°27N 22°27E 202 C6
Kamenica Serbia 44°25N 19°45E 202 B3
Kamenice nad Lipou Czech Rep. 49°18N 15°2E 180 B8
Kamenjak, Rt Croatia 44°47N 13°55E 199 D10
Kamenka = Kamyanka Ukraine 49°3N 32°6E 189 H7
Kamenka Kazakhstan 51°7N 50°19E 190 E10
Kamenka Arkhangelsk, Russia 65°58N 44°0E 186 A7
Kamenka Penza, Russia 53°10N 44°5E 190 D6
Kamenka Voronezh, Russia 50°47N 39°20E 189 G10
Kamenka Bugskaya = Kamyanka-Buzka Ukraine 50°8N 24°16E 177 C13
Kamenka Dneprovskaya = Kamyanka-Dniprovska Ukraine 47°29N 34°28E 189 J8
Kamenka-Shevchenkovskaya = Kamyanka-Buzka Ukraine 50°8N 24°16E 177 C13
Kamennomostskiy Russia 44°18N 40°13E 191 H5
Kameno Bulgaria 42°34N 27°18E 203 D11
Kamenolomini Russia 47°40N 40°14E 191 G5
Kamensk-Shakhtinskiy Russia 48°23N 40°20E 191 F5
Kamensk Uralskiy Russia 56°25N 62°2E 214 D7
Kamenskaya = Kamensk-Shakhtinskiy Russia 48°23N 40°20E 191 F5
Kamenskiy Russia 50°48N 45°25E 190 E7
Kamenskoye = Dniprodzerzhynsk Ukraine 48°32N 34°37E 189 H8
Kamenskoye Russia 62°45N 165°30E 215 C17
Kamenyak Bulgaria 43°24N 26°57E 203 C10
Kamenz Germany 51°15N 14°5E 178 D10
Kameoka Japan 35°0N 135°35E 223 C7
Kamet India 30°55N 79°35E 243 D8
Kameyama Japan 34°51N 136°27E 223 C8
Kami Japan 33°36N 133°38E 222 D5
Kami-Itabashi Japan 35°45N 139°40E 140 A3
Kami-Jima Japan 32°27N 130°20E 222 E2
Kami-Koshiki-Jima Japan 31°50N 129°52E 222 F1
Kamiagata Japan 34°47N 129°24E 222 C1
Kamiah U.S.A. 46°14N 116°2W 304 C5
Kamień Krajeński Poland 53°32N 17°32E 184 E4
Kamień Pomorski Poland 53°57N 14°43E 184 E1
Kamienna → Poland 51°6N 21°47E 185 G8
Kamienna Góra Poland 50°47N 16°2E 185 H3
Kamieńsk Poland 51°12N 19°29E 185 G6
Kamieskroon S. Africa 30°9S 17°56E 270 D2
Kamikitazawa Japan 35°39N 139°36E 140 B2
Kamilukuak L. Canada 62°22N 101°40W 297 A8
Kamin-Kashyrskyy Ukraine 51°39N 24°56E 177 C13
Kamina Dem. Rep. of the Congo 8°45S 25°0E 265 D5
Kaminak L. Canada 62°10N 95°0W 297 A10
Kaminoyama Japan 38°9N 140°17E 220 E10
Kamioka Japan 36°25N 137°15E 223 A9
Kamiros Greece 36°20N 27°56E 206 E11
Kamishak Bay U.S.A. 59°15N 153°45W 303 G9
Kamisu Japan 35°50N 140°45E 223 B12
Kamitsuruma Japan 35°30N 139°26E 140 B1
Kamitsushima Japan 34°50N 129°28E 222 C1
Kamituga Dem. Rep. of the Congo 3°2S 28°10E 268 C2
Kamla → India 25°35N 86°36E 243 G12
Kamloops Canada 50°40N 120°20W 296 C4
Kamnik Slovenia 46°14N 14°37E 199 B11
Kamo Armenia 40°21N 45°7E 191 K7
Kamo Japan 37°39N 139°3E 220 F9
Kamo N.Z. 35°42S 174°20E 284 B3
Kamoa Mts. Guyana 1°30N 59°0W 329 C6
Kamogawa Japan 35°5N 140°5E 223 B12
Kamojima = Yoshinogawa Japan 34°4N 134°21E 222 C6
Kamoke Pakistan 32°4N 74°4E 242 C6
Kamo'oloa U.S.A. 21°34N 158°7W 302 J13
Kamoshida Japan 35°33N 139°31E 140 B2
Kamp → Austria 48°23N 15°42E 180 C8
Kampala Uganda 0°20N 32°32E 268 B3
Kampar Malaysia 4°18N 101°9E 237 K3
Kampar → Indonesia 0°30N 103°8E 234 B2
Kampen Neths. 52°33N 5°53E 170 B5
Kamphaeng Phet Thailand 16°28N 99°30E 236 D2
Kampinoski △ Poland 52°21N 20°40E 185 F7
Kampolombo, L. Zambia 11°37S 29°42E 269 E2
Kampong Cham Cambodia 12°0N 105°30E 237 G5
Kampong Chhnang Cambodia 12°20N 104°35E 237 F5
Kampong Landang Singapore 1°20N 103°55E 138 A3
Kampong Pengerang Malaysia 1°22N 104°7E 237 d
Kampong Punggai Malaysia 1°27N 104°18E 237 d
Kampong Saom Cambodia 10°38N 103°30E 237 G4
Kampong Saom, Chaak Cambodia 10°50N 103°32E 237 G4
Kampong Tanjong Langsat Malaysia 1°28N 104°1E 237 d
Kampong Tanjong Penjuru Singapore 1°18N 103°45E 138 B2
Kampong Telok Ramunia Malaysia 1°22N 104°15E 237 d
Kampot Cambodia 10°36N 104°10E 237 G5
Kampsville U.S.A. 39°18N 90°37W 310 E6
Kampti Burkina Faso 10°7N 3°25W 262 C4
Kampuchea = Cambodia ■ Asia 12°15N 105°0E 236 F5
Kampung Air Putih Malaysia 4°15N 103°10E 237 K4
Kampung Bali Indonesia 6°11S 106°48E 122 B1
Kampung Jerangau Malaysia 4°50N 103°10E 237 K4
Kampung Raja Malaysia 5°45N 102°35E 237 K4
Kampungbaru = Tolitoli Indonesia 1°5N 120°50E 231 D6

Kamrau, Teluk Indonesia 3°30S 133°36E 231 E8
Kamsack Canada 51°34N 101°54W 297 C8
Kamsar Guinea 10°40N 14°36W 262 C2
Kamskoye Ustye Russia 55°10N 49°20E 190 C9
Kamskoye Vdkhr. Russia 58°41N 56°7E 186 C10
Kamsuuma Somalia 0°15N 42°46E 267 D5
Kamthi India 21°9N 79°19E 244 D4
Kamuchawie L. Canada 56°18N 101°59W 297 B8
Kamuela U.S.A. 20°1N 155°41W 302 C6
Kamui-Misaki Japan 43°20N 140°21E 220 C10
Kamyanets-Podilskyy Ukraine 48°45N 26°40E 183 B11
Kamyanka Ukraine 49°3N 32°6E 189 H7
Kamyanka-Buzka Ukraine 50°8N 24°16E 177 C13
Kamyanka-Dniprovska Ukraine 47°29N 34°28E 189 J8
Kamyanyets Belarus 52°23N 23°49E 185 F10
Kamyanyuki Belarus 52°32N 23°49E 185 F10
Kāmyārān Iran 34°47N 46°56E 213 E12
Kamyshin Russia 50°10N 45°24E 190 E7
Kamyzyak Russia 46°4N 48°10E 191 G9
Kan = Gan Jiang → China 29°15N 116°0E 229 C11
Kan Burma 22°25N 94°5E 241 D5
Kan South Sudan 9°1N 31°47E 257 F3
Kanaaupscow → Canada 54°2N 76°30W 298 B4
Kanab U.S.A. 37°3N 112°32W 305 H7
Kanab Cr. → U.S.A. 36°24N 112°38W 305 H7
Kanacea Lau Group, Fiji 17°15S 179°6W 287 A3
Kanacea Taveuni, Fiji 16°59S 179°56E 287 A2
Kanaga I. U.S.A. 51°45N 177°22W 303 L3
Kanagawa □ Japan 35°20N 139°20E 223 B11
Kanagi Japan 40°54N 140°27E 220 D10
Kanairiktok → Canada 55°2N 60°18W 299 A7
Kanakanak U.S.A. 59°0N 158°32W 303 G8
Kanakapura India 12°33N 77°28E 245 H3
Kanalia Greece 39°30N 22°53E 204 B4
Kanamori Japan 35°31N 139°27E 140 B1
Kananga Dem. Rep. of the Congo 5°55S 22°18E 265 D4
Kanangra-Boyd △ Australia 33°57S 150°15E 283 B9
Kanash Russia 55°30N 47°32E 190 C8
Kanaskat U.S.A. 47°19N 121°54W 306 C5
Kanastraion, Ákra = Paliouri, Ákra Greece 39°57N 23°45E 202 G7
Kanawha → U.S.A. 38°50N 82°9W 309 F12
Kanazawa Japan 36°30N 136°38E 223 A8
Kanbalu Burma 23°12N 95°31E 241 D5
Kanchanaburi Thailand 14°2N 99°31E 236 E2
Kanchenjunga Nepal 27°50N 88°10E 243 F13
Kanchenjunga △ India 27°42N 88°8E 241 B2
Kanchipuram India 12°52N 79°45E 245 H4
Kanchow = Ganzhou China 25°51N 114°56E 229 E10
Kańczuga Poland 49°59N 22°25E 185 J9
Kanda Tokyo, Japan 140 a5
Kanda Kanda Dem. Rep. of the Congo 6°52S 23°48E 265 D4
Kandagach = Qandyaghash Kazakhstan 49°28N 57°25E 187 E10
Kandaghat India 30°59N 77°7E 242 D7
Kandahār Kandahār, Afghan. 31°32N 65°43E 240 C2
Kandahar India 18°52N 77°12E 244 E3
Kandahār □ Afghan. 31°0N 65°0E 240 C2
Kandala Dem. Rep. of the Congo 6°20S 19°40E 265 D3
Kandalaksha Russia 67°9N 32°30E 160 C25
Kandalakshskiy Zaliv Russia 66°0N 35°0E 186 A6
Kandang Indonesia 3°3N 97°19E 234 B1
Kandangan Indonesia 2°50S 115°20E 235 C5
Kandanos Greece 35°19N 23°44E 207 E4
Kandava Latvia 57°2N 22°46E 184 A9
Kadavu = Kadavu Fiji 19°0S 178°15E 287 B2
Kandavu Passage = Kadavu Passage Fiji 18°45S 178°0E 287 B2
Kandé = Kanté Togo 9°57N 1°3E 263 D5
Kandep Papua N. G. 5°54S 143°32E 286 C2
Kandhkot Pakistan 28°16N 69°8E 242 E3
Kandhla India 29°18N 77°19E 242 E7
Kandi Benin 11°7N 2°55E 263 C5
Kandi India 23°58N 88°5E 243 H13
Kandiaro Pakistan 27°4N 68°13E 242 F3
Kandila Arkadia, Greece 37°46N 22°22E 204 D4
Kandila Etoloakarnania, Greece 38°42N 20°56E 207 B2
Kandilli Turkey 41°4N 29°3E 122 B2
Kandıra Turkey 41°4N 30°9E 212 B4
Kandla India 23°0N 70°10E 242 H4
Kandor, O. → Chad 17°13N 20°52E 259 E4
Kandos Australia 32°45S 149°58E 283 B8
Kandreho Madag. 17°29S 46°6E 272 B2
Kandrian Papua N. G. 6°14S 149°37E 286 D5
Kandy Sri Lanka 7°18N 80°43E 245 L5
Kane U.S.A. 41°40N 78°49W 312 E6
Kane Basin Greenland 79°1N 70°0W 154 B4
Kaneilio Pt. U.S.A. 21°27N 158°12W 302 K13
Kanel Senegal 15°30N 13°18W 262 B2
Kanem □ Chad 15°0N 15°20E 259 E3
Kāne'ohe U.S.A. 21°25N 157°48W 302 K14
Kāne'ohe B. U.S.A. 21°30N 157°50W 302 K14
Kaneohe Station U.S.A. 21°27N 157°46W 302 K14
Kanevskaya Russia 46°3N 38°57E 191 G4
Kanfanar Croatia 45°7N 13°50E 199 C10
Kang Botswana 23°41S 22°50E 270 B3
Kangaamiut Greenland 65°50N 53°20W 154 D5
Kangaatsiaq Greenland 68°18N 53°28W 154 D5
Kangaba Mali 11°56N 8°25W 262 C3
Kangal Turkey 39°14N 37°23E 212 C7
Kangān Fārs, Iran 27°50N 52°3E 247 E7
Kangān Hormozgān, Iran 25°48N 57°28E 247 E8
Kangar Malaysia 6°27N 100°12E 237 J3
Kangaré Mali 11°36N 8°4W 262 C3
Kangaroo I. Australia 35°45S 137°0E 282 C2
Kangaroo Mts. Australia 23°29S 141°51E 280 C3
Kangasala Finland 61°28N 24°4E 188 B3
Kangāvar Iran 34°40N 48°0E 213 E12
Kangding China 30°2N 101°57E 228 B3
Kangdong N. Korea 39°9N 126°5E 224 C3
Kangean, Kepulauan Indonesia 6°55S 115°23E 235 D5
Kangean Is. = Kangean, Kepulauan Indonesia 6°55S 115°23E 235 D5
Kangen → South Sudan 6°47N 33°9E 257 F3
Kangerdlugssuak Greenland 68°10N 32°20W 154 D7
Kangerluarsoruseq Greenland 63°45N 51°27W 154 E5
Kangerluarsoruset = Kangerluarsoruseq Greenland 63°45N 51°27W 154 E5
Kangerlussuaq Greenland 66°59N 50°40W 154 D5
Kangertittivaq = Scoresby Sund Greenland 70°28N 21°46W 154 C8
Kanggye N. Korea 41°0N 126°35E 224 B3
Kanghsi Taiwan 23°34N 120°8E 225 C2
Kangikajik Greenland 70°7N 22°0W 154 C8
Kangilinnguit Greenland 61°20N 47°57W 154 E6
Kangiqliniq = Rankin Inlet Canada 62°30N 93°0W 294 E13
Kangiqsualujjuaq Canada 58°30N 65°59W 295 F18
Kangiqsujuaq Canada 61°30N 72°0W 295 E17
Kangiqtugaapik = Clyde River Canada 70°30N 68°30W 295 C18
Kangirsuk Canada 60°0N 70°0W 295 F18
Kangkar Chemaran Malaysia 1°34N 104°12E 237 d
Kangkar Sungai Tiram Malaysia 1°35N 103°55E 237 d
Kangkar Teberau Malaysia 1°32N 103°51E 237 d
Kango Gabon 0°11N 10°5E 264 B2
Kangoku Iwa Iwo Jima 24°48N 141°17E 288 b
Kangoya Dem. Rep. of the Congo 9°55S 22°48E 265 D4
Kangping China 42°43N 123°18E 227 C12
Kangpokpi India 25°8N 93°58E 241 C4
Kangra India 32°6N 76°16E 242 C7
Kangrinboqe Feng China 31°0N 81°25E 243 D9
Kangshan Taiwan 22°48N 120°17E 225 D2
Kangto China 27°50N 92°35E 241 B4
Kangtzu Taiwan 22°8N 120°52E 225 D2
Kangwon-do □ N. Korea 38°47N 127°35E 224 C3
Kangyidaung Burma 16°56N 94°54E 241 G5
Kanha △ India 22°15N 80°40E 243 H9
Kanhan → India 21°4N 79°34E 244 D4
Kanhangad India 12°21N 74°58E 245 H2
Kanhar → India 24°28N 83°8E 243 G10
Kani Sagaing, Burma 23°52N 95°22E 241 D5
Kani Sagaing, Burma 22°26N 94°51E 241 D5
Kani Ivory C. 8°29N 6°36W 262 D3
Kani Japan 35°25N 137°7E 223 B9
Kani-Keli Mayotte 12°57S 45°6E 272 b
Kaniama Dem. Rep. of the Congo 7°30S 24°12E 265 D4
Kaniapiskau = Caniapiscau → Canada 56°40N 69°30W 299 A6
Kaniapiskau, L. = Caniapiscau, L. Canada 54°10N 69°55W 299 B6
Kaniere, L. N.Z. 42°50S 171°10E 285 C6
Kanif Micronesia 9°31N 138°5E 287 R16
Kanigiri India 15°24N 79°31E 245 G4
Kanin, Poluostrov Russia 68°0N 45°0E 186 A8
Kanin Nos, Mys Russia 68°39N 43°32E 186 A7
Kanin Pen. = Kanin, Poluostrov Russia 68°0N 45°0E 186 A8
Kaninë Albania 40°23N 19°30E 202 F3
Kaniva Australia 36°22S 141°18E 282 D4
Kanjiža Serbia 46°3N 20°4E 182 D5
Kanjut Sar Pakistan 36°7N 75°25E 243 A6
Kankaanpää Finland 61°44N 22°50E 188 B2
Kankakee U.S.A. 41°7N 87°52W 311 C9
Kankakee → U.S.A. 41°23N 88°15W 311 C8
Kankan Guinea 10°23N 9°15W 262 C3
Kankendy = Xankändi Azerbaijan 39°52N 46°49E 213 C12
Kanker India 20°10N 81°40E 244 D5
Kankesanturai Sri Lanka 9°49N 80°2E 245 K5
Kankossa Mauritania 15°54N 11°31W 262 B2
Kankroli India 25°4N 73°53E 242 G5
Kankurgachi India 22°34N 88°23E 124 B2
Kanlıca Turkey 41°5N 29°3E 122 B2
Kanmaw Kyun Burma 11°40N 98°28E 237 G2
Kanmuri-Yama Japan 34°30N 132°4E 222 C4
Kannabe Japan 34°32N 133°23E 222 C5
Kannapolis U.S.A. 35°30N 80°37W 315 D14
Kannauj India 27°3N 79°56E 243 F8
Kanniyakumari India 8°5N 77°34E 245 K3
Kannur India 11°53N 75°27E 245 J2
Kannyakumari India 8°3N 77°40E 245 K3
Kano Nigeria 12°2N 8°30E 263 C6
Kano □ Nigeria 11°30N 8°30E 263 C6
Kanonerskiy, Ostrov Russia 59°53N 30°13E 137 B1
Kan'onji Japan 34°7N 133°39E 222 C5
Kanoroba Ivory C. 9°7N 6°8W 262 D3
Kanowha U.S.A. 42°57N 93°47W 310 B3
Kanowit Malaysia 2°14N 112°20E 235 B4
Kanoya Japan 31°25N 130°50E 222 F2
Kanpetlet Burma 21°10N 93°59E 241 E4
Kanpur India 26°28N 80°20E 243 F9
Kansai Int. ✕ (KIX) Japan 34°27N 135°12E 133 B2
Kansas U.S.A. 39°33N 87°56W 311 E9
Kansas □ U.S.A. 38°30N 99°0W 308 F4
Kansas → U.S.A. 39°7N 94°37W 308 F6
Kansas City Kans., U.S.A. 39°7N 94°38W 310 E2
Kansas City Mo., U.S.A. 39°6N 94°35W 310 E2
Kansas City Int. ✕ (MCI) U.S.A. 39°18N 94°43W 310 E2
Kansenia Dem. Rep. of the Congo 10°20S 26°0E 269 E2
Kansk Russia 56°20N 95°37E 215 D10
Kansu = Gansu □ China 36°0N 104°0E 226 G3
Kantaphor India 22°35N 76°34E 242 H7
Kantchari Burkina Faso 12°37N 1°37E 263 C5
Kantché Niger 13°31N 8°30E 259 F1
Kanté Togo 9°57N 1°3E 263 D5
Kantemirovka Russia 49°43N 39°55E 189 H10
Kantharalak Thailand 14°39N 104°39E 236 E5
Kanthi = Contai India 21°54N 87°46E 243 J12
Kantishna U.S.A. 63°31N 150°57W 303 E10
Kantishna → U.S.A. 64°45N 149°58W 303 D10
Kantli → India 28°20N 75°30E 242 E6
Kantō □ Japan 36°15N 139°30E 223 A11
Kantō-Sanchi Japan 35°59N 138°50E 223 B10
Kantu-long Burma 19°57N 97°36E 241 F6
Kanturk Ireland 52°11N 8°54W 166 D3
Kanuma Japan 36°34N 139°42E 223 A11
Kanus Namibia 27°50S 18°39E 270 C2
Kanuti Nat. Wildlife Refuge ⌂ U.S.A. 66°25N 151°50W 303 C10
Kanye Botswana 24°55S 25°28E 270 B4
Kanzaki → Japan 34°41N 135°24E 133 A1
Kanzenze Dem. Rep. of the Congo 10°30S 25°12E 265 E5
Kanzi, Ras Tanzania 7°1S 39°33E 268 D4
Kanzoni, Chissioua Comoros Is. 12°23S 43°40E 272 a
Kao Tonga 19°40S 175°1W 287 P13
Kao Phara Thailand 8°3N 98°22E 237 a
Kaohsiung Taiwan 22°35N 120°16E 225 D2
Kaohsung □ Taiwan 23°0N 120°35E 225 D2
Kaoka Solomon Is. 9°42S 160°43E 287 M11
Kaokaona = Kirakira Solomon Is. 10°27S 161°56E 287 N11
Kaokoveld Namibia 19°15S 14°30E 270 A1
Kaolack Senegal 14°5N 16°8W 262 C1
Kaolack □ Senegal 14°0N 15°15W 262 C1
Kaolan = Lanzhou China 36°1N 103°52E 226 F2
Kaolo Solomon Is. 8°24S 159°38E 287 M10
Kaoma Zambia 14°47S 24°48E 265 E4
Kaoshan China 44°38N 124°50E 227 B13
Kaoshu Taiwan 22°49N 120°36E 225 D2
Kaouar Niger 19°5N 12°52E 259 E2
Kaoyao = Zhaoqing China 23°0N 112°20E 229 F9
Kapa'a U.S.A. 22°5N 159°19W 302 K12
Kapadvanj India 23°5N 73°0E 242 H5
Kapagere Papua N. G. 9°46S 147°42E 286 E4
Kapahulu U.S.A. 21°16N 157°49W 302 K14
Kapaklı Turkey 41°19N 27°59E 203 E11
Kapali Carsi Turkey 41°1N 28°58E 122 B1
Kapalua U.S.A. 20°59N 156°39W 302 C5
Kapan Armenia 39°18N 46°27E 213 C12
Kapanga Bandundu, Dem. Rep. of the Congo 5°4S 16°58E 265 D3
Kapanga Katanga, Dem. Rep. of the Congo 8°30S 22°40E 265 D4
Kapapa I. U.S.A. 21°29N 157°48W 302 K14
Kapatagan Phil. 7°52N 123°44E 233 H4
Kapchagai = Qapshaghay Kazakhstan 43°51N 77°14E 217 D9
Kapchagaiskoye Vdkhr. = Qapshaghay Bögeni Kazakhstan 43°45N 77°50E 217 D9
Kapedo Kenya 1°10N 36°6E 268 B4
Kapela = Velika Kapela Croatia 45°10N 15°5E 199 C12
Kapellerfeld Austria 48°18N 16°29E 142 A2
Kapellskär Sweden 59°44N 19°2E 162 E13
Kapelo, Akra Greece 36°9N 23°3E 204 E5
Kapema Dem. Rep. of the Congo 10°45S 28°22E 269 E2
Kapenguria Kenya 1°14N 35°7E 268 B4
Kapfenberg Austria 47°26N 15°18E 180 D8
Kapı Dağı Turkey 40°28N 27°50E 203 F11
Kapia Dem. Rep. of the Congo 4°17S 19°46E 265 C3
Kapiri Mposhi Zambia 13°59S 28°43E 269 E2
Kāpīsā □ Afghan. 35°0N 69°20E 240 B3
Kapiskau → Canada 52°47N 81°55W 298 B3
Kapit Malaysia 2°0N 112°55E 235 B4
Kapiti I. N.Z. 40°50S 174°56E 284 G3
Kapka, Massif du Chad 15°7N 21°45E 259 E4
Kaplan U.S.A. 30°0N 92°17W 314 F8
Kaplica = Davlos Cyprus 35°25N 33°54E 207 E9
Kaplice Czech Rep. 48°42N 14°30E 180 C7
Kapoe Thailand 9°34N 98°32E 237 H2
Kapoeta South Sudan 4°50N 33°35E 257 G3
Kapoho U.S.A. 19°30N 154°50W 302 D7
Kapolei U.S.A. 21°19N 158°5W 302 K13
Kápolnásnyék Hungary 47°16N 18°41E 182 C3
Kapombo Dem. Rep. of the Congo 10°40S 23°30E 265 E4
Kaponga N.Z. 39°29S 174°9E 284 F3
Kapos → Hungary 46°44N 18°30E 182 D3
Kaposvár Hungary 46°25N 17°47E 182 D2
Káposztásmegyer Hungary 47°35N 19°6E 117 A2
Kapotnya Russia 55°39N 37°48E 129 C3
Kapowsin U.S.A. 46°59N 122°13W 306 D4
Kapp Norway 60°43N 10°52E 164 D7
Käppala Sweden 59°21N 18°13E 139 A3
Kappeln Germany 54°40N 9°55E 178 A5
Kappelshamn Sweden 57°52N 18°47E 163 G12
Kapps Namibia 22°32S 17°18E 270 B2
Kaprije Croatia 43°42N 15°43E 199 E12
Kapsabet Kenya 0°12N 35°6E 268 B4
Kapsan N. Korea 41°4N 128°19E 224 B4
Kapsukas = Marijampolė Lithuania 54°33N 23°19E 184 D10
Kaptai Bangla. 22°21N 92°17E 241 D4
Kaptai L. Bangla. 22°40N 92°20E 241 D4
Kapuas → Kalimantan Barat, Indonesia 0°25S 109°20E 235 C3
Kapuas → Kalimantan Tengah, Indonesia 3°1S 114°19E 235 C4
Kapuas Hulu, Pegunungan Malaysia 1°30N 113°30E 235 B4
Kapuas Hulu Ra. = Kapuas Hulu, Pegunungan Malaysia 1°30N 113°30E 235 B4
Kapuk Indonesia 6°7S 106°44E 122 A1
Kapulo Dem. Rep. of the Congo 8°18S 29°15E 269 D2
Kapunda Australia 34°20S 138°56E 282 C3
Kapuni N.Z. 39°29S 174°8E 284 F3
Kapurthala India 31°23N 75°25E 242 D6
Kapuskasing Canada 49°25N 82°30W 298 C3
Kapuskasing → Canada 49°49N 82°0W 298 C3
Kapustin Yar Russia 48°37N 45°40E 191 F7
Kaputar, Mt. Australia 30°15S 150°10E 281 E5
Kaputir Kenya 2°5N 35°28E 268 B4
Kapuvár Hungary 47°36N 17°1E 182 C2
Käpylä Finland 60°13N 24°57E 121 B2
Kara Russia 69°10N 65°0E 214 C7
Karā, W. → Si. Arabia 20°45N 41°42E 256 C5
Kara Ada Turkey 36°58N 27°28E 205 E9
Kara-Balta Kyrgyzstan 42°50N 73°49E 217 D8
Kara Bogaz Gol, Zaliv = Garabogazköl Aylagy Turkmenistan 41°0N 53°30E 187 F9
Kara Burun Turkey 36°32N 27°58E 205 E9
Kara-Kala = Garrygala Turkmenistan 38°31N 56°29E 247 B8
Kara Kalpak Republic = Qoraqalpoghistan □ Uzbekistan 43°0N 58°0E 216 D5
Kara-Köl Kyrgyzstan 41°40N 72°43E 217 D8
Kara Kum = Garagum Turkmenistan 39°30N 60°0E 247 B8
Kara-Saki Japan 34°41N 129°30E 222 C1
Kara Sea Russia 75°0N 70°0E 214 B8
Karaadilli Turkey 38°18N 30°37E 205 C12
Karabiğa Turkey 40°23N 27°17E 203 F11
Karabük Turkey 41°12N 32°37E 212 B5
Karabük □ Turkey 41°10N 32°30E 212 B5
Karaburun Albania 40°25N 19°20E 202 F3
Karaburun Turkey 38°41N 26°28E 205 C8
Karabutak = Qarabutaq Kazakhstan 50°0N 60°14E 216 C6
Karacabey Turkey 40°12N 28°21E 203 F12
Karacakılavuz Turkey 41°8N 27°21E 203 E11
Karacaköy Turkey 41°24N 28°22E 203 E12
Karaçal Tepesi Turkey 36°21N 32°38E 250 B3
Karacasu Turkey 37°43N 28°35E 205 D10
Karachala = Qaraçala Azerbaijan 39°45N 48°53E 191 L9
Karachayevsk Russia 43°50N 41°55E 191 J5
Karachev Russia 53°10N 35°5E 189 F8
Karachey-Cherkessia □ Russia 43°40N 41°30E 191 J5
Karachi Pakistan 24°50N 67°0E 123 A2
Karad India 17°15N 74°10E 244 F2
Karadirek Turkey 38°34N 30°11E 205 C12
Karaga Ghana 9°58N 0°28W 263 D4
Karaganda = Qaraghandy Kazakhstan 49°50N 73°10E 217 C8
Karagayly = Qaraghayly Kazakhstan 49°26N 76°0E 214 E8
Karaginskiy, Ostrov Russia 58°45N 164°0E 215 D17
Karagiye, Vpadina Kazakhstan 43°27N 51°45E 187 F9
Karagiye Depression = Karagiye, Vpadina Kazakhstan 43°27N 51°45E 187 F9
Karagola Road India 25°29N 87°23E 243 G12
Karagüney Dağları Turkey 40°30N 34°40E 212 B6
Karahallı Turkey 38°21N 29°32E 205 C11
Kárahnjúkar Iceland 64°57N 15°46W 155 C11
Karaikal India 10°59N 79°50E 245 J4
Karaikkudi India 10°5N 78°45E 245 J4
Karaisali Turkey 37°16N 35°2E 212 D6
Karaiskakis Greece 38°35N 21°47E 207 B3
Karaitivu I. Sri Lanka 9°45N 79°52E 245 K4
Karaj Iran 35°48N 51°0E 247 C6
Karajarri ✪ Australia 19°0S 122°30E 278 C3
Karak Malaysia 3°25N 102°2E 237 L4
Karakalpakstan = Qoraqalpoghistan □ Uzbekistan 43°0N 58°0E 216 D5
Karakaya Barajı Turkey 38°31N 38°23E 213 C8
Karakelong Indonesia 4°35N 126°50E 231 D7
Karakitang Indonesia 3°14N 125°28E 231 D7
Karaklis = Vanadzor Armenia 40°48N 44°30E 191 K7
Karakoçan Turkey 38°57N 40°2E 213 C9
Karakol Kyrgyzstan 42°30N 78°20E 217 D9
Karakoram Pass Asia 35°33N 77°50E 243 B7
Karakoram Ra. Pakistan 35°30N 77°0E 243 B7
Karakul = Qarakol Uzbekistan 39°32N 63°50E 216 E6
Karakul Tajikistan 39°2N 73°33E 217 E8
Karakul, Ozero Tajikistan 39°5N 73°25E 217 E8
Karakurt Turkey 40°10N 42°37E 213 B10
Karakuwisa Namibia 18°56S 19°40E 270 A2
Karal Chad 12°50N 14°46E 259 F2
Karalon Russia 57°5N 115°50E 215 D12
Karama Jordan 31°57N 35°35E 251 G6
Karaman Balıkesir, Turkey 39°39N 28°0E 205 B9
Karaman Konya, Turkey 37°14N 33°13E 212 D5
Karaman □ Turkey 37°5N 33°15E 250 A4
Karamanlı Turkey 37°23N 29°47E 205 D11
Karamay China 45°30N 84°58E 226 C10
Karambu Indonesia 3°53S 116°6E 235 C5
Karamea N.Z. 41°14S 172°6E 285 B7
Karamea → N.Z. 41°13S 172°26E 285 B7
Karamea Bight N.Z. 41°22S 171°40E 285 B6
Karamian Indonesia 5°5S 114°40E 235 D4
Karamnasa → India 25°31N 83°52E 243 G10
Karamürsel Turkey 40°41N 29°36E 203 F13
Karān Si. Arabia 27°43N 49°49E 247 E6
Karand Iran 34°16N 46°15E 213 E12
Karangana Mali 12°15N 5°4W 262 C3
Karanganyar Indonesia 7°38S 109°37E 235 D3
Karangasem = Amlapura Indonesia 8°27S 115°37E 231 J18
Karanja Maharashtra, India 21°11N 78°24E 244 D4
Karanja Maharashtra, India 20°29N 77°31E 244 D3
Karanjia India 21°47N 85°58E 243 J11
Karankasso Burkina Faso 10°50N 3°53W 262 C4
Karaova Turkey 37°5N 27°40E 205 D9
Karapınar Turkey 37°41N 33°30E 212 D5
Karapiro N.Z. 37°53S 175°32E 284 D4
Karas □ Namibia 27°0S 17°30E 270 C2
Karasburg Namibia 28°0S 18°44E 270 C2
Karasino Russia 66°50N 86°50E 214 C9
Karasjok Norway 69°27N 25°30E 160 B21
Karasu Turkey 41°4N 30°46E 212 B4
Karasu → Antalya, Turkey 36°18N 30°10E 205 E12
Karasu → Hatay, Turkey 36°20N 36°20E 250 B7
Karasubazar = Bilohirsk Ukraine 45°3N 34°35E 189 K8
Karasuk Russia 53°44N 78°2E 217 B9
Karasuyama Japan 36°39N 140°9E 223 A12
Karataş Adana, Turkey 36°32N 35°21E 250 B6
Karataş Manisa, Turkey 38°35N 28°16E 205 C10
Karataş Burnu Turkey 36°31N 35°24E 250 B6
Karatau, Khrebet = Qarataū Kazakhstan 43°30N 69°30E 217 D7
Karatax Shan China 35°57N 81°0E 217 E10
Karateki Shan China 40°40N 77°50E 217 D9
Karativu Sri Lanka 8°22N 79°47E 245 K4
Karatoprak Turkey 37°2N 27°15E 205 D9
Karatoya → India 24°7N 89°36E 241 C2
Karatsu Japan 33°26N 129°58E 222 D1
Karaul Russia 70°6N 82°15E 214 B9
Karauli India 26°30N 77°4E 242 F7
Karavastasë, L. e Albania 40°55N 19°30E 202 F3
Karavia Greece 36°49N 23°37E 204 E5
Karavostasi Cyprus 35°8N 32°50E 207 E8
Karawa Dem. Rep. of the Congo 3°18N 20°17E 264 B4
Karawang Indonesia 6°30S 107°15E 235 D3
Karawanken Europe 46°30N 14°40E 180 E7
Karayazı Turkey 39°41N 42°9E 213 C10
Karazhal = Qarazhal Kazakhstan 48°2N 70°49E 214 E8
Karbalā' Iraq 32°36N 44°3E 213 F11
Karbalā' □ Iraq 32°30N 43°50E 213 F10
Kårböle Sweden 61°59N 15°22E 162 C9
Karcag Hungary 47°19N 20°57E 182 C5
Karcha → Pakistan 34°45N 76°10E 243 B7
Karchana India 25°17N 81°56E 243 G9
Karczew Poland 52°5N 21°15E 185 F8
Kardakata Greece 38°17N 20°28E 207 C1
Kardam Bulgaria 43°45N 28°6E 203 C12
Kardamila Greece 38°35N 26°5E 205 C8
Kardamili Greece 36°53N 22°13E 204 E4
Kardeljovo = Ploče Croatia 43°4N 17°26E 199 E14
Karditsa Greece 39°23N 21°54E 204 B3
Kärdla Estonia 59°0N 22°45E 188 C2
Kardzhali = Kŭrdzhali Bulgaria 41°38N 25°21E 203 E9
Kareeberge S. Africa 30°59S 21°50E 270 D3
Kareha → India 25°44N 86°21E 243 G12
Kareima Sudan 18°30N 31°49E 256 D3
Karelia □ Russia 65°30N 32°30E 186 A5
Karelian Republic = Karelia □ Russia 65°30N 32°30E 186 A5
Karelo-Finnish S.S.R. = Karelia □ Russia 65°30N 32°30E 186 A5
Karema Papua N. G. 9°12S 147°18E 286 E4
Karen = Kayin □ Burma 18°0N 97°30E 241 G6
Karenni = Kayah □ Burma 19°15N 97°15E 241 F6
Karera India 25°32N 78°9E 242 G8
Karēvāndar Iran 27°53N 60°44E 247 E9
Kargasok Russia 59°3N 80°53E 214 D9
Kargat Russia 55°10N 80°15E 214 D9
Kargi Eastern, Kenya 2°31N 37°34E 268 B4
Kargı Turkey 41°11N 34°30E 212 B6
Kargil India 34°32N 76°12E 243 B7
Kargopol Russia 61°30N 38°58E 188 B10
Kargowa Poland 52°5N 15°51E 185 F2
Karguéri Niger 13°27N 10°30E 259 F2
Karia Greece 38°45N 20°39E 207 B2
Karia ba Mohammed Morocco 34°22N 5°12W 260 B3
Karīān Iran 26°57N 57°14E 247 E8
Karianga Madag. 22°25S 47°22E 272 C2
Kariba Zimbabwe 16°28S 28°50E 269 F2
Kariba, L. Zimbabwe 16°40S 28°25E 269 F2
Kariba Dam Zimbabwe 16°30S 28°35E 269 F2
Kariba Gorge Zambia 16°30S 28°50E 269 F2
Karibib Namibia 22°0S 15°56E 270 B2
Karies Greece 40°14N 24°19E 203 F8
Karijini △ Australia 23°8S 118°15E 278 D2
Karikari, C. N.Z. 34°46S 173°24E 284 A2
Karimata, Kepulauan Indonesia 1°25S 109°0E 235 C3
Karimata, Selat Indonesia 2°0S 108°40E 235 C3
Karimata Is. = Karimata, Kepulauan Indonesia 1°25S 109°0E 235 C3
Karimganj India 24°52N 92°20E 241 C4
Karimnagar India 18°26N 79°10E 244 E4
Karimun, Pulau Indonesia 1°3N 103°22E 237 d
Karimun Kecil, Pulau Indonesia 1°8N 103°22E 237 d
Karimunjawa, Kepulauan Indonesia 5°50S 110°30E 235 D4
Karin Bari, Somalia 10°50N 45°52E 267 B6
Karin Woqooyi Galbeed, Somalia 10°59N 49°13E 267 B6
Karistos Greece 38°1N 24°29E 204 C6
Karīt Iran 33°29N 56°55E 247 C8
Kariya Japan 34°58N 137°1E 223 C9
Kariyangwe Zimbabwe 18°0S 27°38E 271 A4
Karjaa Finland 62°0N 30°25E 188 A5
Karjat India 18°33N 75°0E 244 E2
Karkal India 13°15N 74°56E 245 H2
Karkar Papua N. G. 4°32S 145°57E 286 C3
Karkar I. Papua N. G. 4°40S 146°0E 286 C4
Karkaralinsk = Qarqaraly Kazakhstan 49°26N 75°30E 217 C9
Karkh Iraq 33°20N 44°22E 113 A2
Karkheh → Iran 31°2N 47°29E 246 D5
Karki Azerbaijan 39°47N 44°57E 213 C11
Karkinitska Zatoka Ukraine 45°56N 33°0E 189 K7
Karkinitskiy Zaliv = Karkinitska Zatoka Ukraine 45°56N 33°0E 189 K7
Karkuk = Kirkūk Iraq 35°30N 44°21E 213 E11
Karkur Tohl Egypt 22°5N 25°5E 256 C2
Karl Liebknecht = imeni Karl Libknekhta Russia 51°40N 35°35E 189 G8
Karl-Marx-Stadt = Chemnitz Germany 50°51N 12°54E 178 E8
Karla, L. = Volvi, L. Greece 40°40N 23°34E 202 F7
Karlantijpa North ✪ Australia 19°27S 133°33E 278 C5
Karlantijpa South ✪ Australia 20°31S 133°9E 278 D5
Karleby = Kokkola Finland 63°50N 23°8E 160 E20
Karlholmsbruk Sweden 60°31N 17°37E 162 D11
Karlin Czech Rep. 50°5N 14°26E 135 B2
Karlino Poland 54°3N 15°53E 184 D2
Karlıova Turkey 39°17N 41°0E 213 C9
Karlivka Ukraine 49°29N 35°8E 189 H8
Karlobag Croatia 44°32N 15°5E 199 D12
Karlovac Croatia 45°31N 15°36E 199 C12
Karlovarský □ Czech Rep. 50°10N 12°50E 180 A5
Karlovasi Greece 37°45N 26°42E 205 D8
Karlovka = Karlivka Ukraine 49°29N 35°8E 189 H8
Karlovo Bulgaria 42°38N 24°47E 203 D8
Karlovo náměstí Prague, Czech Rep. 135 c1
Karlovy Vary Czech Rep. 50°13N 12°51E 180 A5
Karlowitz = Sremski Karlovci Serbia 45°12N 19°56E 182 E4
Karlowitz = Velké Karlovice Czech Rep. 49°20N 18°17E 181 B11
Karlsbad = Karlovy Vary Czech Rep. 50°13N 12°51E 180 A5
Karlsborg Sweden 58°33N 14°33E 163 F8
Karlsburg = Alba-Iulia Romania 46°8N 23°39E 183 D8
Karlsena, Mys Russia 77°0N 67°42E 214 B7
Karlsfeld Germany 48°13N 11°28E 131 A1
Karlshamn Sweden 56°10N 14°51E 163 H8
Karlshorst Germany 52°29N 13°31E 115 B4
Karlshus Norway 59°21N 10°52E 164 E7
Karlskoga Sweden 59°28N 14°33E 162 E8
Karlskrona Sweden 56°10N 15°35E 163 H9
Karlsplatz Munich, Germany 131 b1
Karlsruhe Germany 49°0N 8°23E 179 F4
Karlstad = Karlovac Croatia 45°31N 15°36E 199 C12
Karlstad Sweden 59°23N 13°30E 162 E7
Karlstad Minn., U.S.A. 48°35N 96°31W 308 A5
Karlstadt Germany 49°57N 9°47E 179 F5
Karluk U.S.A. 57°34N 154°28W 303 H9
Karlův most Prague, Czech Rep. 135 b1
Karma Niger 13°38N 1°52E 263 C5
Karmala India 18°25N 75°12E 244 E2
Karmi'el Israel 32°55N 35°18E 250 F6
Karmoy Norway 59°15N 5°15E 164 E2
Karnak Egypt 25°43N 32°39E 256 B3
Karnal India 29°42N 77°2E 242 E7
Karnali → Nepal 28°45N 81°16E 243 E9
Karnaphuli Res. = Kaptai L. Bangla. 22°40N 92°20E 241 D4
Karnaprayag India 30°16N 79°15E 243 D8
Karnataka □ India 13°15N 77°0E 245 H3
Karnes City U.S.A. 28°53N 97°54W 314 G6
Karnische Alpen Europe 46°36N 13°0E 180 E6
Karnobat Bulgaria 42°39N 26°59E 203 D10
Kärnten □ Austria 46°52N 13°30E 180 E6
Karntner Strasse Vienna, Austria 142 b2
Karo Mali 12°16N 3°18W 262 C4
Karoi Zimbabwe 16°48S 29°45E 269 F2
Karol Bagh India 28°39N 77°11E 120 B2
Karolinenhof Germany 52°23N 13°38E 115 B4
Karon, Ao Thailand 7°51N 98°17E 237 a
Karonga Malawi 9°57S 33°55E 269 D3
Karoo △ S. Africa 32°18S 22°27E 270 D3
Karoonda Australia 35°1S 139°59E 282 C3
Karor Pakistan 31°15N 70°59E 242 D4
Karora Sudan 17°44N 38°15E 256 D4
Karosa Indonesia 1°48S 119°20E 235 C5
Karounga Mali 15°20N 7°35W 262 B3
Karousades Greece 39°47N 19°45E 206 B9
Karow Germany 52°36N 13°29E 115 A3
Karpacz Poland 50°46N 15°46E 185 H2
Karpasia Cyprus 35°32N 34°15E 207 E10
Karpathos Greece 35°37N 27°10E 205 F9
Karpathos, Stenon Greece 36°0N 27°30E 205 F9
Karpatsky △ Ukraine 48°20N 24°35E 183 B9
Karpenisi Greece 38°55N 21°40E 204 C3
Karpilovka = Aktsyabrski Belarus 52°38N 28°53E 177 B15
Karpinsk Russia 59°45N 60°1E 186 C11
Karpogory Russia 64°0N 44°27E 186 B7
Karpuz Burnu = Apostolos Andreas, C. Cyprus 35°42N 34°35E 207 E10
Karpuzlu Turkey 37°33N 27°51E 205 D9
Karrādah Iraq 33°17N 44°23E 113 B2
Karratha Australia 20°44S 116°52E 278 D2
Kars Turkey 40°40N 43°5E 213 B10
Kars □ Turkey 40°40N 43°0E 213 B10
Karsakpay Kazakhstan 47°55N 66°40E 217 C7
Karsha Kazakhstan 49°45N 51°35E 190 F10
Karshi = Qarshi Uzbekistan 38°53N 65°48E 217 E7
Karsiyang India 26°56N 88°18E 241 B2
Karsog India 31°23N 77°12E 242 D7
Kärsön Sweden 59°19N 17°54E 139 B1
Karst = Kras Croatia 45°35N 14°0E 199 C10
Kartal Turkey 40°53N 29°11E 203 F13
Kartal Dağları Turkey 37°4N 36°55E 250 A7
Kartala Comoros Is. 11°45S 43°21E 272 a
Kartaly Russia 53°3N 60°40E 216 B6
Kartapur India 31°27N 75°32E 242 D6
Karthaus U.S.A. 41°8N 78°9W 312 E6
Kartuzy Poland 54°22N 18°10E 184 D5
Karuah Australia 32°37S 151°56E 283 B9
Karufa Indonesia 3°50S 133°20E 231 E8
Karula △ Estonia 57°43N 26°30E 188 D4
Karuma △ Uganda 2°5N 32°15E 268 B3
Karumba Australia 17°31S 140°50E 280 B3
Karumo Tanzania 2°25S 32°50E 268 C3
Karumwa Tanzania 3°12S 32°38E 268 C3
Kārūn → Iran 30°26N 48°10E 247 D6
Karungu Kenya 0°50S 34°10E 268 C3
Karup Denmark 56°19N 9°10E 163 H3
Karur India 10°59N 78°2E 245 J4
Karviná Czech Rep. 49°53N 18°31E 181 B11
Karwan → India 27°26N 78°4E 242 F8
Karwar India 14°55N 74°13E 245 G2
Karwendel △ Austria 47°25N 11°30E 180 D4
Karwi India 25°12N 80°57E 243 G9
Karymskoye Russia 51°36N 114°21E 215 D12
Kas Sudan 12°30N 24°17E 259 F4
Kaş Turkey 36°11N 29°37E 205 E11
Kasaan U.S.A. 55°32N 132°24W 303 J14
Kasaba Turkey 36°18N 29°44E 205 E11
Kasabi Zambia 14°52S 23°45E 265 E4
Kasache Malawi 13°25S 34°20E 269 E3
Kasai Hyōgo, Japan 34°55N 134°52E 222 C6
Kasai Tōkyō, Japan 35°39N 139°52E 140 B4
Kasai → Dem. Rep. of the Congo 3°30S 16°10E 265 C3
Kasai-Occidental □ Dem. Rep. of the Congo 6°0S 22°0E 265 D4
Kasai-Oriental □ Dem. Rep. of the Congo 5°0S 24°30E 265 D4
Kasaji Dem. Rep. of the Congo 10°25S 23°27E 265 E4
Kasama Japan 36°23N 140°16E 223 A12
Kasama Zambia 10°16S 31°9E 269 E3
Kasan-dong N. Korea 41°18N 126°55E 224 B3
Kasandra Greece 40°0N 23°30E 202 F7
Kasandra Kolpos Greece 40°5N 23°30E 202 F7
Kasandras, Akra Greece 39°57N 23°30E 202 G7
Kasane Namibia 17°34S 24°50E 270 A3
Kasanga Tanzania 8°30S 31°10E 269 D3
Kasangaie Dem. Rep. of the Congo 6°20S 22°42E 265 D4
Kasangulu Dem. Rep. of the Congo 4°33S 15°15E 265 C3
Kasanka △ Zambia 11°34S 30°15E 269 E3
Kasaoka Japan 34°30N 133°30E 222 C5
Kasar, Ras Sudan 18°2N 38°35E 256 D4
Kasaragod India 12°30N 74°58E 245 H2
Kasat Burma 15°56N 98°13E 241 G7
Kasba L. Canada 60°20N 102°10W 297 A8
Kasba Tadla Morocco 32°36N 6°17W 260 B3
Kaschau = Košice Slovak Rep. 48°42N 21°15E 181 C14
Kaseda Japan 31°25N 130°19E 222 F2
Kāseh Garān Iran 34°5N 46°2E 246 C5
Kasempa Zambia 13°30S 25°44E 269 E2
Kasenga Dem. Rep. of the Congo 10°20S 28°45E 269 E2
Kasese Uganda 0°13N 30°3E 268 B3
Kasganj India 27°48N 78°42E 243 F8
Kashabowie Canada 48°40N 90°26W 298 C1
Kashaf Iran 35°58N 61°7E 247 C9
Kāshān Iran 34°5N 51°30E 247 C6
Kashechewan Canada 52°18N 81°37W 298 B3
Kashgar → Iran 33°5N 47°31E 213 F12
Kashgar = Kashi China 39°30N 76°2E 217 E9
Kashi China 39°30N 76°2E 217 E9
Kashihara Japan 34°27N 135°46E 223 C7
Kashiji Plain Zambia 13°12S 22°20E 265 E4
Kashima Ibaraki, Japan 35°58N 140°38E 223 B12
Kashima Saga, Japan 33°7N 130°6E 222 D2
Kashima-Nada Japan 36°0N 140°45E 223 B12
Kashimbo Dem. Rep. of the Congo 11°12S 26°19E 269 E2
Kashin Russia 57°20N 37°36E 188 D9
Kashing = Jiaxing China 30°49N 120°45E 229 B13
Kashipur Odisha, India 19°16N 83°3E 244 E6
Kashipur Uttarakhand, India 29°15N 79°0E 243 E8
Kashira Russia 54°45N 38°10E 188 E10
Kashiwa Japan 35°52N 139°59E 223 B11
Kashiwabara = Severo-Kurilsk Russia 50°40N 156°8E 215 D16
Kashiwazaki Japan 37°22N 138°33E 221 F9
Kashk-e Kohneh Afghan. 34°55N 62°30E 240 B1
Kashksaray Iran 38°27N 45°34E 213 C11
Kashkū'iyeh Iran 30°31N 55°40E 247 D7
Kāshmar Iran 35°16N 58°26E 247 C8
Kashmir Asia 34°0N 76°0E 243 C7
Kashmor Pakistan 28°28N 69°32E 242 E3
Kashpirovka Russia 53°0N 48°30E 190 D9
Kashun Noerh = Gaxun Nur China 42°22N 100°30E 218 C9
Kasiari India 22°8N 87°14E 243 H12
Kasilof U.S.A. 60°23N 151°18W 303 F10
Kasimov Russia 54°55N 41°20E 190 C5
Kasinge Dem. Rep. of the Congo 6°15S 26°58E 268 D2
Kasipur India 22°37N 88°22E 124 B2
Kasiruta Indonesia 0°25S 127°12E 231 E7
Kaskaskia → U.S.A. 37°58N 89°57W 310 G7
Kaskattama → Canada 57°3N 90°4W 297 B10
Kaskazini Mashariki = North Eastern □ Kenya 1°30N 40°0E 268 B5
Kaskinen Finland 62°22N 21°15E 160 E19
Kaskö = Kaskinen Finland 62°22N 21°15E 160 E19
Kaslo Canada 49°55N 116°55W 296 D5
Kasmere L. Canada 59°34N 101°10W 297 B8
Kasongan Indonesia 2°0S 113°23E 235 C4
Kasongo Dem. Rep. of the Congo 4°30S 26°33E 268 C2
Kasongo Lunda Dem. Rep. of the Congo 6°35S 16°49E 265 D3
Kasos Greece 35°20N 26°55E 205 F8
Kasou, Stenon Greece 35°30N 26°30E 205 F8
Kaspi Georgia 41°59N 44°26E 191 K7
Kaspichan Bulgaria 43°18N 27°11E 203 C11
Kaspiysk Russia 42°52N 47°40E 191 J8
Kaspiyskiy Russia 45°22N 47°23E 191 H8
Kassab Syria 35°55N 35°59E 250 C6
Kassab ed Doleib Sudan 13°30N 33°35E 257 E3
Kassaba Egypt 22°40N 29°55E 256 C2
Kassalâ Sudan 15°30N 36°0E 257 D4
Kassalâ □ Sudan 15°20N 36°26E 257 D4
Kassandrino Greece 40°1N 23°27E 202 F7
Kassel Germany 51°18N 9°26E 178 D5
Kasserine Tunisia 35°10N 8°50E 258 A1
Kasserine □ Tunisia 35°15N 9°0E 258 A1
Kassinger Sudan 18°46N 31°51E 256 D3
Kassiopi Greece 39°48N 19°53E 206 B9
Kasson U.S.A. 44°2N 92°45W 308 C7
Kastamonu Turkey 41°25N 33°43E 212 B5
Kastamonu □ Turkey 41°20N 34°0E 212 B5
Kastav Croatia 45°22N 14°20E 199 C11
Kasteli Greece 35°29N 23°38E 207 E4
Kastellet Copenhagen, Denmark 118 a3
Kastelli Greece 35°12N 25°20E 207 E6
Kastellorizo = Megisti Greece 36°8N 29°34E 205 E11
Kastelo, Akra Greece 35°30N 27°20E 205 F9
Kasterlee Belgium 51°15N 4°59E 170 C4
Kastlösa Sweden 56°26N 16°25E 163 H10
Kastoria Greece 40°30N 21°19E 202 F5
Kastorias, L. Greece 40°30N 21°20E 202 F5
Kastorio Greece 37°10N 22°17E 204 D4
Kastornoye Russia 51°55N 38°2E 189 G10
Kastos Greece 38°35N 20°55E 207 B2
Kastrom Mefa'a = Umm al Rasas Jordan 31°30N 35°55E 251 G6
Kastrosikia Greece 39°6N 20°38E 207 A2
Kastrup Denmark 55°38N 12°39E 118 B3
Kastrup, København ✕ (CPH) Denmark 55°37N 12°39E 118 B3
Kastsyukovichy Belarus 53°20N 32°4E 189 F7
Kasubi Tombs Uganda 0°20N 32°30E 268 B3
Kasuga Fukuoka, Japan 33°32N 130°26E 222 D2
Kasuga Tōkyō, Japan 35°45N 139°38E 140 A2
Kasugai Japan 35°12N 136°59E 223 B8
Kasuge Japan 35°45N 139°49E 140 A3
Kasukabe Japan 35°58N 139°49E 223 B11
Kasulu Tanzania 4°37S 30°5E 268 C3
Kasumi Japan 35°38N 134°38E 222 B6
Kasumiga-Ura Japan 36°0N 140°25E 223 B12
Kasumigaseki Tokyo, Japan 140 b4
Kasumkent Russia 41°47N 48°15E 191 K9
Kasungu Malawi 13°0S 33°29E 269 E3
Kasungu △ Malawi 12°53S 33°9E 269 E3
Kasur Pakistan 31°5N 74°25E 242 D6
Kata, Ao Thailand 7°48N 98°18E 237 J2
Kata Archanes Greece 35°15N 25°10E 207 E6
Kata Tjuta Australia 25°20S 130°50E 279 E5
Kataba Zambia 16°5S 25°10E 269 F2
Katagum Nigeria 12°18N 10°21E 263 C7
Katahdin, Mt. U.S.A. 45°54N 68°56W 309 C19
Kataka = Cuttack India 20°25N 85°57E 244 D7

Katako Kombe Dem. Rep. of the Congo 3°25S 24°20E 264 C4
Katakolo Greece 37°38N 21°19E 204 D3
Katale Tanzania 4°52S 31°7E 268 C3
Katalla U.S.A. 60°12N 144°31W 303 F11
Katamatite Australia 36°6S 145°41E 283 D6
Katanda Katanga, Dem. Rep. of the Congo 7°52S 24°13E 265 D4
Katanda Nord-Kivu, Dem. Rep. of the Congo 0°55S 29°21E 268 C2
Katanga □ Dem. Rep. of the Congo 8°0S 25°0E 268 D2
Katangi India 21°56N 79°50E 244 D4
Katanning Australia 33°40S 117°33E 279 F2
Katapakishi Dem. Rep. of the Congo 8°15S 22°49E 265 D4
Katastari Greece 37°50N 20°45E 207 D2
Katavi △ Tanzania 6°51S 31°3E 268 D3
Katavi Swamp Tanzania 6°50S 31°10E 268 D3
Katchall India 7°57N 93°22E 245 L11
Katchiungo Angola 12°35S 16°13E 265 E3
Katerini Greece 40°18N 22°37E 202 F6
Katghora India 22°30N 82°33E 243 H10
Katha Burma 24°10N 96°30E 241 C6
Katherîna, Gebel Egypt 28°30N 33°57E 251 K4
Katherine Australia 14°27S 132°20E 278 B5
Katherine Gorge = Nitmiluk △ Australia 14°6S 132°15E 278 B5
Kathi India 21°47N 74°3E 242 J6
Kathiawar India 22°20N 71°0E 242 H4
Kathikas Cyprus 34°55N 32°25E 207 F8
Kathleen U.S.A. 28°7N 82°2W 317 G7
Kathmandu Nepal 27°45N 85°20E 243 F11
Kathua India 32°23N 75°34E 242 C6
Kati = Central □ Kenya 0°30S 37°30E 268 C4
Kati Mali 12°41N 8°4W 262 C3
Katihar India 25°34N 87°36E 243 G12
Katikati N.Z. 37°32S 175°57E 284 D4
Katima Mulilo Namibia 17°28S 24°13E 270 A3
Katimbira Malawi 12°40S 34°0E 269 E3
Katingan = Mendawai → Indonesia 3°30S 113°0E 235 C4
Katiola Ivory C. 8°10N 5°10W 262 D3
Katipunan Phil. 8°31N 123°17E 233 G4
Katiti ✪ Australia 25°1S 131°11E 279 E5
Katla Iceland 63°36N 19°7W 155 D7
Katlabukh, Ozero Ukraine 45°28N 29°0E 183 E14
Katlanovo Macedonia 41°52N 21°40E 202 E5
Katmai △ U.S.A. 58°20N 155°0W 303 G9
Katmandu = Kathmandu Nepal 27°45N 85°20E 243 F11
Katni India 23°51N 80°24E 243 H9
Kato Achaia Greece 38°8N 21°33E 204 C3
Kato Chorio Greece 35°3N 25°47E 207 E6
Kato Korakiana Greece 39°42N 19°45E 206 B9
Kato Pyrgos Cyprus 35°11N 32°41E 207 E8
Katochi Greece 38°26N 21°15E 204 C3
Katol India 21°17N 78°38E 244 D4
Katompe Dem. Rep. of the Congo 6°2S 26°23E 265 D5
Katong Singapore 1°18N 103°53E 138 B3
Katonga → Uganda 0°34N 31°50E 268 B3
Katoomba Australia 33°41S 150°19E 283 B9
Katouna Greece 38°47N 21°7E 204 C3
Katowice Poland 50°17N 19°5E 185 H6
Katrancı Dağı Turkey 37°27N 30°25E 205 D12
Katrine, L. U.K. 56°15N 4°30W 167 E4
Katrineholm Sweden 59°0N 16°12E 162 E10
Katsepe Madag. 15°45S 46°15E 272 B2
Katsina Nigeria 13°0N 7°32E 263 C6
Katsina □ Nigeria 12°30N 7°30E 263 C6
Katsina Ala Nigeria 7°10N 9°30E 263 D6
Katsina Ala → Nigeria 7°10N 9°20E 263 D6
Katsumoto Japan 33°51N 129°42E 222 D1
Katsushika Japan 35°44N 139°51E 140 A4
Katsuta Japan 36°25N 140°31E 223 A12
Katsuura Japan 35°10N 140°20E 223 B12
Katsuyama Fukui, Japan 36°3N 136°30E 223 A8
Katsuyama Okayama, Japan 35°5N 133°41E 222 B5
Kattaqŭrghon Uzbekistan 39°55N 66°15E 217 E7
Kattavia Greece 35°57N 27°46E 206 F11
Kattegat Denmark 56°40N 11°20E 163 H5
Katthammarsvik Sweden 57°26N 18°51E 163 G12
Kattowitz = Katowice Poland 50°17N 19°5E 185 H6
Katul, J. Sudan 14°12N 29°25E 257 E2
Katumba Dem. Rep. of the Congo 7°40S 25°17E 265 D5
Katun → Russia 52°25N 85°1E 217 B11
Katwa India 23°30N 88°5E 243 H13
Katwijk Neths. 52°12N 4°24E 170 B4
Kąty Wrocławskie Poland 51°2N 16°45E 185 G3
Ka'ū Desert U.S.A. 19°21N 155°19W 302 D6
Kau Pai Chau Hong Kong, China 22°12N 114°15E 122 B3
Kau Sai Chau Hong Kong, China 22°22N 114°19E 122 A3
Kau-Ye Kyun Burma 11°1N 98°32E 237 G2
Kau Yi Chau Hong Kong, China 22°17N 114°4E 122 B2
Kaua'i U.S.A. 22°3N 159°30W 302 A2
Kauai Channel U.S.A. 21°45N 158°50W 302 B3
Kauai Island Lihue Municipal ✈ (LIH) U.S.A. 21°58N 159°20W 302 B2
Kaub Germany 50°5N 7°46E 179 E3
Kaudom ⌓ Namibia 18°45S 20°51E 270 A3
Kauehi French Polynesia 15°49S 145°10W 289 f
Kaufbeuren Germany 47°53N 10°37E 179 H6
Kaufman U.S.A. 32°35N 96°19W 314 E6
Kauhajoki Finland 62°25N 22°10E 160 E20
Kauhaneva-Pohjankangas △ Finland 62°13N 22°20E 160 E20
Kaukauna U.S.A. 44°17N 88°17W 308 C9
Kaukauveld Namibia 20°0S 20°15E 270 B3
Kaukonahua → U.S.A. 21°35N 158°7W 302 J13
Ka'ula I. U.S.A. 21°40N 160°33W 302 B1
Kaulakahi Channel U.S.A. 22°0N 159°55W 302 B2
Kaulsdorf Germany 52°29N 13°34E 115 B4
Kaunā Pt. U.S.A. 19°2N 155°53W 302 D6
Kaunakakai U.S.A. 21°6N 157°1W 302 B4
Kaunas Lithuania 54°54N 23°54E 184 D10
Kaunas ✈ (KUN) Lithuania 54°57N 24°3E 184 D11
Kaunchi = Yangiyul Uzbekistan 41°0N 69°3E 217 D7
Kaunghein Burma 25°41N 95°26E 241 C5
Kaunia Bangla. 25°46N 89°26E 241 C2
Kauniainen Finland 60°13N 24°44E 121 B1
Kaunos Turkey 36°49N 28°39E 205 E10
Kaupangur Iceland 65°38N 18°2W 155 B8
Kaura Namoda Nigeria 12°37N 6°33E 263 C6
Kauru Nigeria 10°33N 8°12E 263 C6
Kautokeino Norway 69°0N 23°4E 160 B20
Kauwapur India 27°31N 82°18E 243 F10
Kavacha Russia 60°16N 169°51E 215 C17
Kavadarci Macedonia 41°26N 22°3E 202 E6
Kavajë Albania 41°11N 19°33E 202 E3
Kavak Turkey 41°4N 36°3E 212 B7
Kavak Dağı Turkey 37°10N 28°2E 205 D10
Kavaklı Turkey 41°39N 27°10E 203 E11
Kavaklıdere Turkey 37°27N 28°21E 205 D10
Kavaklii = Topolovgrad Bulgaria 42°5N 26°20E 203 D10
Kavala Greece 40°57N 24°28E 203 F8
Kavala Kolpos Greece 40°50N 24°25E 203 F8
Kavalerovo Russia 44°15N 135°4E 220 B7
Kavali India 14°55N 80°1E 245 G5
Kavār Iran 29°11N 52°44E 247 D7
Kavaratti India 10°34N 72°37E 245 J1
Kavaratti I. India 10°33N 72°38E 245 J1
Kavarna Bulgaria 43°26N 28°22E 203 C12
Kavava Dem. Rep. of the Congo 8°52S 22°19E 265 D4
Kavi India 22°12N 72°38E 242 H5
Kavieng Papua N. G. 2°36S 150°51E 286 B6
Kavimba Botswana 18°2S 24°38E 270 A3
Kavīr, Dasht-e Iran 34°30N 55°0E 247 C7
Kavīr △ Iran 34°40N 52°0E 247 C7
Kavirondo G. = Winam G. Kenya 0°20S 34°15E 268 C3
Kavkaz Russia 45°20N 36°40E 189 K9
Kävlinge Sweden 55°47N 13°9E 163 J7
Kavos Greece 39°23N 20°3E 206 C10
Kavousi Greece 35°7N 25°51E 207 E6
Kavungo Angola 11°31S 23°3E 265 E4
Kaw Fr. Guiana 4°30N 52°15W 329 C7
Kawa Sudan 13°42N 32°34E 257 E3
Kawachi-Nagano Japan 34°28N 135°31E 223 C7
Kawagama L. Canada 45°18N 78°45W 312 A6
Kawagoe Japan 35°55N 139°29E 223 B11
Kawaguchi Japan 35°52N 139°45E 223 B11
Kawah Ijen △ Indonesia 8°3S 114°14E 235 D4
Kawaihae B. U.S.A. 20°0N 155°50W 302 C6
Kawaihoa Pt. U.S.A. 21°47N 160°12W 302 B1
Kawaikini U.S.A. 22°5N 159°29W 302 A2
Kawailoa U.S.A. 21°36N 158°3W 302 J13
Kawailoa Beach U.S.A. 21°37N 158°5W 302 J13
Kawakawa N.Z. 35°23S 174°6E 284 B3
Kawambwa Zambia 9°48S 29°3E 269 D2
Kawana Zambia 13°5S 25°58E 265 E5
Kawanabe Japan 31°23N 130°24E 222 F2
Kawanoe = Shikokochūō Japan 34°1N 133°34E 222 C5
Kawardha India 22°0N 81°17E 243 J9
Kawasaki Japan 35°31N 139°43E 140 B3
Kawasi Indonesia 1°38S 127°28E 231 E7
Kawau I. N.Z. 36°25S 174°52E 284 C3
Kawawa Japan 35°31N 139°33E 140 B2
Kawawachikamach Canada 54°48N 66°50W 299 B6
Kawęczyn Poland 52°16N 21°5E 143 B2
Kaweka Ra. N.Z. 39°17S 176°19E 284 F5
Kawela U.S.A. 21°42N 158°1W 302 J13
Kawerau N.Z. 38°7S 176°42E 284 E5
Kawhia N.Z. 38°4S 174°49E 284 E3
Kawhia Harbour N.Z. 38°5S 174°51E 284 E3
Kawio, Kepulauan Indonesia 4°30N 125°30E 231 D7
Kawkareik Burma 16°33N 98°14E 241 G7
Kawlin Burma 23°47N 95°41E 241 D5
Kawthaung Burma 10°5N 98°36E 237 H2
Kawthoolei = Kayin □ Burma 18°0N 97°30E 241 G6
Kawthule = Kayin □ Burma 18°0N 97°30E 241 G6
Kawya Burma 24°50N 94°58E 241 C5
Kaxgar He → China 39°45N 78°24E 217 E9
Kaxholmen Sweden 57°51N 14°19E 163 G8
Kaya Burkina Faso 13°4N 1°10W 263 C4
Kayah □ Burma 19°15N 97°15E 241 F6
Kayak I. U.S.A. 59°56N 144°23W 303 G11
Kayalıköy Barajı Turkey 41°50N 27°5E 203 E11
Kayamkulam India 9°10N 76°33E 245 K3
Kayan Burma 16°54N 96°34E 241 G6
Kayan → Indonesia 2°55N 117°35E 235 B5
Kayan Mentarang △ Indonesia 2°25N 115°30E 235 B5
Kaycee U.S.A. 43°43N 106°38W 304 E10
Kayeli Indonesia 3°20S 127°10E 231 E7
Kayenda Dem. Rep. of the Congo 10°48S 23°6E 265 E4
Kayenta U.S.A. 36°44N 110°15W 305 H8
Kayes Congo 4°25S 11°41E 265 C2
Kayes Mali 14°25N 11°30W 262 C2
Kayes □ Mali 14°0N 11°0W 262 C2
Kayı Turkey 39°12N 30°46E 205 B12
Kayima S. Leone 8°54N 11°15W 262 D2
Kayin □ Burma 18°0N 97°30E 241 G6
Kaymakçı Turkey 38°10N 28°8E 205 C10
Kayoa Indonesia 0°1N 127°28E 231 D7
Kayomba Zambia 13°11S 24°2E 269 E1
Kayombo Zambia 13°3S 23°51E 265 E4
Kaysatskoye Russia 49°47N 46°49E 190 F8
Kayseri Turkey 38°45N 35°30E 212 C6
Kayseri □ Turkey 38°40N 36°0E 212 C7
Kaysville U.S.A. 41°2N 111°56W 304 F8
Kayts Sri Lanka 9°42N 79°51E 245 K4
Kayu Putih Indonesia 6°10S 106°53E 122 B2
Kayuagung Indonesia 3°24S 104°50E 234 C2
Kaz Dağı Turkey 39°42N 26°50E 205 B8
Kazachye Russia 70°52N 135°58E 215 B14
Kazakhstan ■ Asia 50°0N 70°0E 217 C8
Kazaly = Qazaly Kazakhstan 45°45N 62°6E 216 C6
Kazan Russia 55°50N 49°10E 190 C9
Kazan → Canada 64°2N 95°29W 297 A9
Kazan-Rettō Pac. Oc. 25°0N 141°0E 288 E6
Kazancı Turkey 36°29N 32°51E 250 B3
Kazanlăk Bulgaria 42°38N 25°20E 203 D9
Kazanlı Turkey 36°49N 34°43E 250 B5
Kazanskaya Russia 49°50N 41°10E 190 F5
Kazatin = Kozyatyn Ukraine 49°45N 28°50E 177 D15
Kazaure Nigeria 12°42N 8°28E 263 C6
Kazbek Russia 42°42N 44°30E 191 J7
Kāzerūn Iran 29°38N 51°40E 247 D6
Kazi Magomed = Qazımämmäd Azerbaijan 40°3N 49°0E 191 K9
Kazimierz Dolny Poland 51°19N 21°57E 185 G8
Kazimierza Wielka Poland 50°15N 20°30E 185 H7
Kazincbarcika Hungary 48°17N 20°36E 182 B5
Kazipet India 17°58N 79°30E 244 F4
Kaziranga △ India 26°40N 93°30E 241 B4
Kaziza Dem. Rep. of the Congo 10°42S 23°52E 265 E4
Kazlų Rūda Lithuania 54°46N 23°30E 184 D10
Kazo Japan 36°7N 139°36E 223 A11
Kaztalovka Kazakhstan 49°47N 48°43E 190 F9
Kazu Burma 25°27N 97°46E 241 C6
Kazuma Pan △ Zimbabwe 18°20S 25°48E 269 F2
Kazumba Dem. Rep. of the Congo 6°25S 22°5E 265 D4
Kazungula Zambia 17°35S 25°15E 265 F5
Kazuno Japan 40°10N 140°45E 220 D10
Kazym → Russia 63°54N 65°50E 214 C7
Kbely Czech Rep. 50°8N 14°32E 135 B3
Kcynia Poland 53°0N 17°30E 185 F4
Ke-hsi Mansam Burma 21°56N 97°50E 241 E6
Ké-Macina Mali 13°58N 5°22W 262 C3
Kea Greece 37°35N 24°22E 204 D6
Kea'au U.S.A. 19°37N 155°2W 302 D6
Keady U.K. 54°15N 6°42W 166 B5
Keahi Pt. U.S.A. 21°19N 157°59W 302 K14
Keahole Pt. U.S.A. 19°44N 156°4W 302 D5
Kealaikahiki Channel U.S.A. 20°35N 156°50W 302 C5
Kealakekua U.S.A. 19°31N 155°55W 302 D6
Kearney Mo., U.S.A. 39°22N 94°22W 310 E2
Kearney Nebr., U.S.A. 40°42N 99°5W 308 E4
Kearney ✪ Australia 20°10S 128°4E 278 D4
Kearny U.S.A. 33°3N 110°55W 305 K8
Kearsarge, Mt. U.S.A. 43°22N 71°50W 313 C13
Keban Turkey 38°50N 38°50E 213 C8
Keban Barajı Turkey 38°41N 38°33E 213 C8
Kebara Congo 2°27S 14°25E 264 C2
Kebayoran Baru Indonesia 6°14S 106°47E 122 B1
Kebayoran Lama Indonesia 6°13S 106°46E 122 B1
Kebbi □ Nigeria 11°35N 4°0E 263 C5
Kébémèr Senegal 15°23N 16°34W 262 B1
Kébi Ivory C. 9°18N 6°37W 262 D3
Kebi, Mayo → Cameroon 9°18N 13°33E 264 A2
Kebili Tunisia 33°47N 9°0E 258 B1
Kebili □ Tunisia 33°30N 8°50E 261 B6
Kebnekaise Sweden 67°53N 18°33E 160 C18
Kebon Jeruk Indonesia 6°11S 106°46E 122 B1
Kebri Dehar Ethiopia 6°45N 44°17E 267 C5
Kebumen Indonesia 7°42S 109°40E 235 D3
Kecel Hungary 46°31N 19°16E 182 D4
Kechika → Canada 59°41N 127°12W 296 B3
Keçiborlu Turkey 37°57N 30°18E 205 D12
Kecskemét Hungary 46°57N 19°42E 182 D4
Kedada Ethiopia 5°25N 35°58E 257 F4
Kedah □ Malaysia 5°50N 100°40E 237 K3
Kėdainiai Lithuania 55°15N 24°2E 184 C11
Kedar West Bank 31°44N 35°18E 123 B2
Kedarnath India 30°44N 79°4E 243 D8
Kedgwick Canada 47°40N 67°20W 299 C6
Kediet Ijill Mauritania 22°38N 12°33W 260 D2
Kediri Indonesia 7°51S 112°1E 235 D4
Kedja Dem. Rep. of the Congo 4°50N 19°16E 264 B3
Kedjebi Ghana 8°12N 0°25E 263 D5
Kédougou Senegal 12°35N 12°10W 262 C2
Kedoya Indonesia 6°10S 106°45E 122 B1
Kedros Oros Greece 35°11N 24°37E 207 E5
Kędzierzyn-Koźle Poland 50°20N 18°12E 185 H5
Ke'ehi Lagoon U.S.A. 21°20N 157°54W 302 K14
Keeler U.S.A. 36°29N 117°52W 306 J9
Keeley L. Canada 54°54N 108°8W 297 C7
Keeling Is. = Cocos Is. Ind. Oc. 12°10S 96°55E 273 F8
Keelung = Chilung Taiwan 25°3N 121°45E 225 A3
Keenapusan Phil. 6°50N 118°50E 233 H2
Keene Ont., Canada 44°15N 78°10W 312 B6
Keene Calif., U.S.A. 35°13N 118°33W 307 K8
Keene N.H., U.S.A. 42°56N 72°17W 313 D12
Keene N.Y., U.S.A. 44°16N 73°46W 313 B11
Keep River △ Australia 15°49S 129°8E 278 C4
Keeper Hill Ireland 52°45N 8°16W 166 D3
Keepit, L. Australia 30°50S 150°30E 283 A9
Keerweer, C. Australia 14°0S 141°32E 280 A3
Keeseville U.S.A. 44°29N 73°30W 313 B11
Keetmanshoop Namibia 26°35S 18°8E 270 C2
Keewatin Canada 49°46N 94°34W 297 D10
Keewatin → Canada 56°29N 100°46W 297 B8
Kefa Ethiopia 6°55N 36°30E 257 F4
Kefalonia Greece 38°15N 20°30E 207 C2
Kefalonia ✈ (EFL) Greece 38°10N 20°30E 207 C1
Kefalos Greece 36°45N 26°59E 205 E8
Kefamenanu Indonesia 9°28S 124°29E 231 F6
Kefar Sava Israel 32°11N 34°54E 251 F5
Keffi Nigeria 8°55N 7°43E 263 D6
Keffin Hausa Nigeria 12°13N 9°59E 263 C6
Keflavík Iceland 64°2N 22°35W 155 C4
Keflavík ✈ (KEF) Iceland 64°0N 22°45W 155 C4
Keftya Ethiopia 13°54N 37°7E 257 E4
Keg River Canada 57°54N 117°55W 296 B5
Kegalla Sri Lanka 7°15N 80°21E 245 L5
Kegaska Canada 50°9N 61°18W 299 B7
Kehancha Kenya 1°11S 34°37E 268 C3
Keheili Sudan 19°25N 32°50E 256 D3
Kehena U.S.A. 19°23N 154°55W 302 D7
Kehl Germany 48°34N 7°50E 179 G3
Kei Ling Ha Hong Kong, China 22°25N 114°16E 122 A3
Keibul Lamjao △ India 24°30N 93°55E 241 C4
Keighley U.K. 53°52N 1°54W 168 D6
Keijo = Seoul S. Korea 37°31N 126°58E 137 B2
Keila Estonia 59°18N 24°25E 188 C3
Keilor Australia 37°42S 144°50E 128 A1
Keilor North Australia 37°44S 144°51E 128 A1
Keimoes S. Africa 28°41S 20°59E 270 C3
Keimola Finland 60°20N 24°49E 121 A1
Keita Niger 14°46N 5°56E 263 C6
Keïta, B. → Chad 9°14N 18°21E 259 G3
Keitele Finland 63°10N 26°20E 160 E22
Keith S. Austral., Australia 36°6S 140°20E 282 D4
Keith Moray, U.K. 57°32N 2°57W 167 D6
Keithsburg U.S.A. 41°6N 90°56W 310 C6
Keiyasi Fiji 17°53S 177°46E 287 A1
Keizer U.S.A. 44°57N 123°1W 304 D2
Kejimkujik △ Canada 44°25N 65°25W 299 D6
Kejserr Franz Joseph Fd. Greenland 73°30N 24°30W 154 C8
Kekaha U.S.A. 21°58N 159°43W 302 B2
Kekri India 26°0N 75°10E 242 G6
Keksgolm = Priozersk Russia 61°2N 30°7E 188 B6
Kelafo Ethiopia 5°37N 44°8E 267 C5
Kelam Ethiopia 4°48N 35°58E 257 G4
Kelamet Eritrea 16°0N 38°30E 257 D4
Kelan China 38°43N 111°31E 226 E6
Kelang = Klang Malaysia 3°2N 101°26E 237 L3
Kelani Ganga → Sri Lanka 6°58N 79°50E 245 L4
Kelantan □ Malaysia 5°10N 102°0E 237 K3
Kelantan → Malaysia 6°13N 102°14E 237 J4
Kelapa Gading Indonesia 6°9S 106°52E 122 A2
Këlcyrë Albania 40°20N 20°12E 202 F4
Kelekçi Turkey 37°15N 29°20E 205 D11
Kelenföld Hungary 47°27N 19°2E 117 B2
Keles Turkey 39°54N 29°14E 203 G13
Keleti-főcsatorna Hungary 47°45N 21°20E 182 C6
Kelheim Germany 48°54N 11°52E 179 G7
Kelibia Tunisia 36°50N 11°3E 258 A2
Kelkit Turkey 40°7N 39°16E 213 B8
Kelkit → Turkey 40°45N 36°32E 212 B7
Kellé Congo 0°8S 14°38E 264 C2
Kellé Niger 14°16N 10°7E 263 C7
Keller U.S.A. 31°50N 81°15W 316 D8
Kellerberrin Australia 31°36S 117°38E 279 F2
Kellett, C. Canada 72°0N 126°0W 150 B1
Kelleys I. U.S.A. 41°36N 82°42W 312 E2
Kellogg U.S.A. 47°32N 116°7W 304 C5
Kells Ireland 53°44N 6°53W 166 C5
Kelmė Lithuania 55°38N 22°56E 184 C9
Kelmentsi Ukraine 48°28N 26°50E 183 B11
Kélo Chad 9°10N 15°45E 259 G3
Kelokedhara Cyprus 34°48N 32°39E 207 F8
Kelowna Canada 49°50N 119°25W 296 D5
Kelsey Creek Australia 20°26S 148°31E 280 b
Kelseyville U.S.A. 38°59N 122°50W 306 G4
Kelso N.Z. 45°54S 169°15E 285 F4
Kelso Borders, U.K. 55°36N 2°26W 167 F6
Kelso Wash., U.S.A. 46°9N 122°54W 306 D4
Keluang = Kluang Malaysia 2°3N 103°18E 237 L4
Kelud Indonesia 7°56N 112°18E 231 H15
Kelvin S. Africa 26°4S 28°5E 123 A2
Kelvington Canada 52°10N 103°30W 297 C8
Kem Russia 65°0N 34°38E 186 B5
Kem → Russia 64°57N 34°41E 186 B5
Kem-Kem Morocco 30°40N 4°30W 260 B4
Kema Indonesia 1°22N 125°8E 231 D7
Kemah Turkey 39°32N 39°5E 213 C8
Kemaliye Erzincan, Turkey 39°16N 38°29E 213 C8
Kemaliye Manisa, Turkey 38°27N 28°25E 205 C10
Kemalpaşa Turkey 38°25N 27°27E 205 C9
Kemaman Malaysia 4°12N 103°18E 237 K4
Kemang Indonesia 6°15S 106°48E 122 B1
Kemano Canada 53°35N 128°0W 296 C3
Kemapyu Burma 18°49N 97°19E 241 F6
Kemasik Malaysia 4°25N 103°27E 237 K4
Kemayoran Indonesia 6°10S 106°51E 122 B2
Kembé C.A.R. 4°36N 21°54E 264 B4
Kembolcha Ethiopia 11°2N 39°42E 257 E4
Kemer Antalya, Turkey 36°36N 30°34E 205 E12
Kemer Burdur, Turkey 37°21N 30°4E 205 D12
Kemer Muğla, Turkey 36°40N 29°22E 205 E11
Kemer Barajı Turkey 37°30N 28°37E 205 D10
Kemerburgaz Turkey 41°9N 28°54E 122 B1
Kemerovo Russia 55°20N 86°5E 214 D9
Kemerovo □ Russia 55°0N 86°0E 217 B11
Ķemeru △ Latvia 56°58N 23°25E 184 B10
Kemi Finland 65°44N 24°34E 160 D21
Kemi älv = Kemijoki → Finland 65°47N 24°32E 160 D21
Kemi träsk = Kemijärvi Finland 66°43N 27°22E 160 C22
Kemijärvi Finland 66°43N 27°22E 160 C22
Kemijoki → Finland 65°47N 24°32E 160 D21
Kemmerer U.S.A. 41°48N 110°32W 304 F8
Kemmuna = Comino Malta 36°1N 14°20E 206 E7
Kémo □ C.A.R. 6°0N 19°0E 264 A3
Kemp, L. U.S.A. 33°46N 99°9W 314 E5
Kemp Land Antarctica 69°0S 55°0E 151 C5
Kempas Malaysia 1°33N 103°42E 237 d
Kempen = Kępno Poland 51°18N 17°58E 185 G4
Kempsey Australia 31°1S 152°50E 283 A10
Kempt, L. Canada 47°25N 74°22W 298 C5
Kempten Germany 47°45N 10°17E 179 H6
Kempton Tas., Australia 42°31S 147°12E 281 G4
Kempton Ind., U.S.A. 40°17N 86°14W 311 D10
Kempton Park Races U.K. 51°24N 0°23W 125 B1
Kemptville Canada 45°0N 75°38W 313 B9
Ken → India 25°13N 80°27E 243 G9
Kenadsa Algeria 31°48N 2°26W 261 B4
Kenai U.S.A. 60°33N 151°16W 303 F10
Kenai Fjords △ U.S.A. 59°40N 149°50W 303 G10
Kenai Mts. U.S.A. 60°0N 150°0W 303 G10
Kenai Nat. Wildlife Refuge ⌓ U.S.A. 60°20N 150°30W 303 F10
Kenamuke Swamp South Sudan 5°55N 33°48E 257 F3
Kenansville U.S.A. 27°53N 80°59W 317 H9
Kendai India 22°45N 82°37E 243 H10
Kendal Indonesia 6°56S 110°14E 235 D4
Kendal Cumb., U.K. 54°20N 2°44W 168 C5
Kendall N.S.W., Australia 31°35S 152°44E 283 A10
Kendall Fla., U.S.A. 25°40N 80°19W 129 D1
Kendall → Australia 14°4S 141°35E 280 A3
Kendallville U.S.A. 41°27N 85°16W 311 C11
Kendari Indonesia 3°50S 122°30E 231 E6
Kendawangan Indonesia 2°32S 110°17E 235 C4
Kende Nigeria 11°30N 4°12E 263 C5
Kendégué Chad 10°0N 18°36E 259 F3
Kendi, Pulau Malaysia 5°13N 100°11E 237 c
Kendrapara India 20°35N 86°30E 244 D8
Këndrevicës, Maja e Albania 40°15N 19°52E 202 F3
Kendrew S. Africa 32°32S 24°30E 270 D3
Kendrick U.S.A. 29°15N 82°10W 317 F7
Kene Thao Laos 17°44N 101°10E 236 D3
Kenedy U.S.A. 28°49N 97°51W 314 G6
Kenema S. Leone 7°50N 11°14W 262 D2
Keng Kok Laos 16°26N 105°12E 236 D5
Keng Tawng Burma 20°45N 98°18E 241 E7
Keng Tung Burma 21°18N 99°39E 236 B2
Kengani Dem. Rep. of the Congo 2°59S 17°36E 264 C3
Kenge Dem. Rep. of the Congo 4°50S 17°4E 265 C3
Kengeja Tanzania 5°26S 39°45E 268 D4
Kenhardt S. Africa 29°19S 21°12E 270 C3
Kéniéba Mali 12°54N 11°17W 262 C2
Kenilworth Western Cape, S. Africa 33°59S 18°27E 118 A1
Kenilworth Ill., U.S.A. 42°5N 87°43W 119 A2
Keningau Malaysia 5°20N 116°10E 235 A5
Kenitra Morocco 34°15N 6°40W 260 B3
Kenli China 37°30N 118°20E 227 F10
Kenmare Kerry, Ireland 51°53N 9°36W 166 E2
Kenmare N. Dak., U.S.A. 48°41N 102°5W 308 A2
Kenmare River → Ireland 51°48N 9°51W 166 E2
Kennebago Lake U.S.A. 45°4N 70°40W 313 A14
Kennebec U.S.A. 43°54N 99°52W 308 D4
Kennebec → U.S.A. 43°45N 69°46W 309 D19
Kennebunk U.S.A. 43°23N 70°33W 313 C14
Kennedy Zimbabwe 18°52S 27°10E 270 A4
Kennedy, C. = Canaveral, C. U.S.A. 28°27N 80°32W 317 G9
Kennedy Channel Arctic 80°50N 66°0W 154 A4
Kennedy Entrance U.S.A. 59°1N 152°0W 303 G10
Kennedy Ra. Australia 24°45S 115°10E 279 D2
Kennedy Range △ Australia 24°34S 115°2E 279 D2
Kennedy Space Center U.S.A. 28°40N 80°42W 317 G9
Kennedy Town Hong Kong, China 22°16N 114°6E 122 B2
Kennemerduinen △ Neths. 52°27N 4°33E 170 B4
Kenner U.S.A. 29°59N 90°14W 131 A1
Kennesaw U.S.A. 34°1N 84°37W 316 A5
Kennet → U.K. 51°27N 0°57W 169 F7
Kenneth Hahn State Recreation Area Los Angeles, U.S.A. 34°1N 118°21W 126 B2
Kenneth Ra. Australia 23°50S 117°8E 279 D2
Kennett U.S.A. 36°14N 90°3W 308 G8
Kennewick U.S.A. 46°12N 119°7W 304 C4
Kennington London, U.K. 125 c4
Kennisis Lake Canada 45°13N 78°36W 312 A6
Kenogami → Canada 51°6N 84°28W 298 B3
Kenora Canada 49°47N 94°29W 297 D10
Kenosha U.S.A. 42°35N 87°49W 311 B9
Kenozersky △ Russia 62°5N 38°10E 214 C1
Kensal Green U.K. 51°32N 0°13W 125 A2
Kensal Rise London, U.K. 125 a1
Kensington N.S.W., Australia 33°54S 151°13E 139 B2
Kensington P.E.I., Canada 46°28N 63°34W 299 C7
Kensington Gauteng, S. Africa 26°11S 28°6E 123 B2
Kensington London, U.K. 51°29N 0°10W 125 B2
Kensington N.Y., U.S.A. 40°38N 73°57W 132 C2
Kensington Palace U.K. 51°30N 0°11W 125 A2
Kent Ohio, U.S.A. 41°9N 81°22W 312 E3
Kent Tex., U.S.A. 31°4N 104°13W 314 F2
Kent Wash., U.S.A. 47°22N 122°14W 306 C4
Kent □ U.K. 51°12N 0°40E 169 F8
Kent Group Australia 39°30S 147°20E 281 F4
Kent Pen. Canada 68°30N 107°0W 294 D10
Kentaū Kazakhstan 43°32N 68°36E 217 D7
K'enting △ Taiwan 21°57N 120°48E 225 E2
Kentish Town U.K. 51°32N 0°8W 125 A3
Kentland U.S.A. 40°46N 87°27W 311 D9
Kenton London, U.K. 51°34N 0°17W 125 A2
Kenton Ohio, U.S.A. 40°39N 83°37W 311 D13
Kentucky □ U.S.A. 37°0N 84°0W 309 G11
Kentucky → U.S.A. 38°41N 85°11W 311 F11
Kentucky L. U.S.A. 37°1N 88°16W 308 G9
Kentville Canada 45°6N 64°29W 299 C7
Kentwood La., U.S.A. 30°56N 90°31W 315 F9
Kentwood Mich., U.S.A. 42°52N 85°39W 311 B11
Kenwood House U.K. 51°34N 0°9W 125 A3
Kenya ■ Africa 1°0N 38°0E 268 B4
Kenya, Mt. Kenya 0°10S 37°18E 268 C4
Kenyir, Tasik Malaysia 5°1N 102°54E 237 K4
Kenzou Cameroon 4°10N 15°2E 264 B3
Keo Neua, Deo Vietnam 18°23N 105°10E 236 C5
Keokuk U.S.A. 40°24N 91°24W 310 D5
Keoladeo △ India 27°0N 77°20E 242 F7
Keonjhargarh India 21°28N 85°35E 243 J11
Keosauqua U.S.A. 40°44N 91°58W 310 D5
Keota U.S.A. 41°22N 91°57W 310 C5
Kep Cambodia 10°29N 104°19E 237 G5
Kep Vietnam 21°24N 106°16E 236 B6
Kep △ Cambodia 10°30N 104°18E 237 G5
Kepa Poland 52°13N 21°3E 143 B2
Kepala Batas Malaysia 5°31N 100°26E 237 c
Kepez Turkey 40°5N 26°24E 203 F10
Kepi Indonesia 6°32S 139°19E 231 F9
Kępice Poland 54°16N 16°51E 184 D3
Kepler Mts. N.Z. 45°25S 167°20E 285 F2
Kępno Poland 51°18N 17°58E 185 G4
Keppel Harbour Singapore 1°15N 103°49E 138 B2
Keppel Pt. Papua N. G. 10°10S 147°58E 286 F4
Kepsut Turkey 39°40N 28°9E 205 B10
Kepuhi Pt. U.S.A. 21°29N 158°14W 302 K13
Kepulauan Karimunjawa △ Indonesia 5°50S 110°25E 235 D4
Kerala □ India 11°0N 76°15E 245 J3
Keram → Papua N. G. 4°7S 144°5E 286 C3
Kerama-Rettō Japan 26°5N 127°15E 221 L3
Keramikos Athens, Greece 112 b1
Keran Pakistan 34°35N 73°59E 243 B5
Keran △ Togo 10°9N 0°41E 263 C5
Kerang Vic., Australia 35°40S 143°55E 282 C5
Kerang Indonesia 2°15S 116°3E 235 C5
Keranyo Ethiopia 5°3N 38°18E 257 F4
Kerao → South Sudan 11°0N 32°41E 257 E3
Keratea Greece 37°48N 23°58E 204 D5
Keraudren, C. Australia 19°58S 119°45E 278 C2
Kerava Finland 60°25N 25°5E 188 B3
Keravat Papua N. G. 4°17S 152°2E 286 C7
Kerch Ukraine 45°20N 36°20E 189 K9
Kerchenskiy Proliv Black Sea 45°10N 36°30E 189 K9
Kerchoual Mali 17°12N 0°20E 263 B5
Kerema Papua N. G. 7°58S 145°50E 286 D3
Kerempe Burnu Turkey 42°2N 33°20E 212 A5
Keren Eritrea 15°45N 38°28E 257 D4
Kerepakupai-Meru = Angel Falls Venezuela 5°57N 62°30W 329 B5
Kerewan Gambia 13°29N 16°10W 262 C1
Kerguelen Ind. Oc. 49°15S 69°10E 273 J5
Kerguelen Plateau S. Ocean 55°0S 75°0E 273 K6
Keri Greece 37°40N 20°49E 207 D2
Keri Kera Sudan 12°21N 32°42E 257 E3
Kerian, Kuala Malaysia 5°10N 100°25E 237 c
Kericho Kenya 0°22S 35°15E 268 C4
Kerikeri N.Z. 35°12S 173°59E 284 B2
Kerinci Indonesia 1°40S 101°15E 234 C2
Kerinci Seblat △ Indonesia 2°30S 101°30E 234 C1
Kerintji = Kerinci Indonesia 1°40S 101°15E 234 C2
Keriya He → China 38°30N 82°10E 217 E10
Kerkenna, Îs. Tunisia 34°48N 11°11E 258 B2
Kerki = Atamyrat Turkmenistan 37°50N 65°12E 217 E7
Kerkini, L. Greece 41°12N 23°10E 202 E7
Kerkouane Tunisia 36°58N 11°2E 200 F4
Kerkrade Neths. 50°53N 6°4E 170 D6
Kerkyra Greece 39°38N 19°50E 206 B9
Kerkyra ✈ (CFU) Greece 39°35N 19°54E 204 B1
Kerkyras, Notio Steno Greece 39°34N 20°0E 206 B10
Kerma Sudan 19°33N 30°32E 256 D3
Kermadec Is. Pac. Oc. 30°0S 178°15W 277 G15
Kermadec Trench Pac. Oc. 30°30S 176°0W 277 G15
Kermān Iran 30°15N 57°1E 247 D8
Kerman Calif., U.S.A. 36°43N 120°4W 306 J6
Kermān □ Iran 30°0N 57°0E 247 D8
Kermān, Bīābān-e Iran 28°45N 59°45E 247 D8
Kermānshāh Iran 34°23N 47°0E 213 E12
Kermānshāh □ Iran 34°0N 46°30E 246 C5
Kermen Bulgaria 42°30N 26°16E 203 D10
Kermine = Navoi Uzbekistan 40°9N 65°22E 216 D7
Kermit U.S.A. 31°52N 103°6W 314 F3
Kern → U.S.A. 35°16N 119°18W 307 K7
Kernavė Lithuania 54°53N 24°49E 188 E3
Kernhof Austria 47°49N 15°32E 180 D8
Kernow = Cornwall □ U.K. 50°26N 4°40W 169 G3
Kernville U.S.A. 35°45N 118°26W 307 K8
Keroh Malaysia 5°43N 101°1E 237 K3
Keros Greece 36°54N 25°40E 205 E7
Kérou Benin 10°50N 2°5E 263 C5
Kérouane Guinea 9°15N 9°0W 262 D3
Kerowagi Papua N. G. 5°51S 144°51E 286 C3
Kerpen Germany 50°51N 6°41E 178 E2
Kerrera U.K. 56°24N 5°33W 167 E3
Kerrobert Canada 51°56N 109°8W 297 C7
Kerrville U.S.A. 30°3N 99°8W 314 F5
Kerry □ Ireland 52°7N 9°35W 166 D2
Kerry Hd. Ireland 52°25N 9°56W 166 D2
Kersa Ethiopia 9°28N 41°48E 257 F5
Kertosono Indonesia 7°38S 112°9E 235 D4
Kerulen = Herlen → Asia 48°48N 117°0E 219 B12
Kervo = Kerava Finland 60°25N 25°5E 188 B3
Kerzaz Algeria 29°29N 1°37W 261 C4
Kesagami → Canada 51°40N 79°45W 298 B4
Kesagami L. Canada 50°23N 80°15W 298 B3
Keşan Turkey 40°49N 26°38E 203 F10
Kesariani Greece 37°57N 23°46E 112 B2
Kesennuma Japan 38°54N 141°35E 220 E10
Keshāvar Iran 36°50N 46°22E 213 D12
Keshit Iran 29°43N 58°17E 247 D8
Kesigi = Kosgi India 15°51N 77°16E 245 G3
Keşiş Dağ Turkey 39°47N 39°46E 213 C8
Keskal India 20°5N 81°35E 244 D5
Keskin Turkey 39°40N 33°36E 212 C5
Kestenga Russia 65°50N 31°45E 160 D24
Keswick U.K. 54°36N 3°8W 168 C4
Keszthely Hungary 46°50N 17°15E 182 D2
Ket → Russia 58°55N 81°32E 214 D9
Keta Ghana 5°49N 1°0E 263 D5
Keta Lagoon Ghana 5°55N 1°0E 263 D5
Ketapang Jawa Timur, Indonesia 8°9S 114°23E 231 J17
Ketapang Kalimantan Barat, Indonesia 1°55S 110°0E 235 C4
Ketchenery Russia 47°18N 44°32E 191 G7
Ketchikan U.S.A. 55°21N 131°39W 296 B2
Ketchum U.S.A. 43°41N 114°22W 304 E6
Kete Krachi Ghana 7°46N 0°1W 263 D4
Ketef, Khalîg Umm el Egypt 23°40N 35°35E 246 F2
Keti Bandar Pakistan 24°8N 67°27E 242 G2
Kétou Benin 7°25N 2°45E 263 D5
Ketri India 28°1N 75°50E 242 E6
Kętrzyn Poland 54°7N 21°22E 184 D8
Ketta Congo 1°28N 15°54E 264 B3
Kettering Northants., U.K. 52°24N 0°43W 169 E7
Kettering Ohio, U.S.A. 39°41N 84°10W 311 E12
Kettle → Canada 56°40N 89°34W 297 B11
Kettle Falls U.S.A. 48°37N 118°3W 304 B4
Kettle Point Canada 43°10N 82°1W 312 C2
Kettle Pt. Canada 43°13N 82°1W 312 C2
Kettleman City U.S.A. 36°1N 119°58W 306 J7
Kęty Poland 49°51N 19°16E 185 J6
Keuka L. U.S.A. 42°30N 77°9W 312 D7
Keung Shan Hong Kong, China 22°15N 113°53E 122 B1
Keuruu Finland 62°16N 24°41E 188 A3
Kevelaer Germany 51°36N 6°15E 178 D2
Kew Vic., Australia 37°48S 145°2E 128 A2
Kew London, U.K. 51°28N 0°17W 125 B2
Kew Gardens Ont., Canada 43°39N 79°18W 141 A3
Kew Gardens London, U.K. 51°28N 0°17W 125 B2
Kewanee U.S.A. 41°14N 89°56W 310 C7
Kewanna U.S.A. 41°1N 86°25W 311 C10
Keware Nepal 27°57N 83°47E 243 F10
Kewaunee U.S.A. 44°27N 87°31W 308 C10
Keweenaw B. U.S.A. 47°0N 88°15W 308 B9
Keweenaw Pen. U.S.A. 47°15N 88°15W 308 B9
Keweenaw Pt. U.S.A. 47°25N 87°43W 308 B10
Kexholm = Priozersk Russia 61°2N 30°7E 188 B6
Key, L. Ireland 54°0N 8°15W 166 C3
Key Biscayne U.S.A. 25°41N 80°9W 129 D3
Key Colony Beach U.S.A. 24°45N 80°57W 317 L9
Key Lake Mine Canada 57°5N 105°32W 297 B7
Key Largo U.S.A. 25°5N 80°27W 317 K9
Key West U.S.A. 24°33N 81°48W 317 L8
Keyala South Sudan 4°27N 32°52E 257 G3
Keynsham U.K. 51°24N 2°29W 169 F5
Keyser U.S.A. 39°26N 78°59W 309 F14
Keystone Heights U.S.A. 29°47N 82°2W 316 F7
Keytesville U.S.A. 39°26N 92°56W 310 E4
Kezhma Russia 58°59N 101°9E 215 D11
Kezi Zimbabwe 20°58S 28°32E 271 B4
Kežmarok Slovak Rep. 49°10N 20°28E 181 B13
Kgalagadi □ Botswana 24°30S 22°0E 270 B3
Kgalagadi Transfrontier ⌓ Africa 25°10S 21°0E 270 C3
Khabarovsk Russia 48°30N 135°5E 219 B16
Khabr △ Iran 28°51N 56°22E 247 D8
Khābūr → Syria 35°17N 40°35E 213 E9
Khachmas = Xaçmaz Azerbaijan 41°31N 48°42E 191 K9
Khachrod India 23°25N 75°20E 242 H6
Khadari, W. el → Sudan 10°29N 27°15E 257 E2
Khadro Pakistan 26°11N 68°50E 242 F3
Khadyzhensk Russia 44°26N 39°32E 191 H4
Khadzhilyangar = Dahongliutan China 35°45N 79°20E 243 B8
Khaga India 25°47N 81°7E 243 G9
Khagaria India 25°30N 86°32E 243 G12
Khagrachari Bangla. 23°6N 91°58E 241 D3
Khaipur Pakistan 29°34N 72°17E 242 E5
Khair India 27°57N 77°46E 242 F7
Khairabad India 27°33N 80°47E 243 F9
Khairagarh India 21°27N 81°2E 243 J9
Khairpur Pakistan 27°32N 68°49E 242 F3
Khairpur Nathan Shah Pakistan 27°6N 67°44E 242 F2
Khairwara India 23°58N 73°38E 242 H5
Khaisor → Pakistan 31°17N 68°59E 242 D3
Khajuraho India 24°51N 79°55E 243 G8
Khajuri Kach Pakistan 32°4N 69°51E 242 C3
Khāk Dow Afghan. 34°57N 67°16E 240 B2
Khakassia □ Russia 53°0N 90°0E 217 B12
Khakhea Botswana 24°48S 23°22E 270 B3
Khalafābād Iran 30°54N 49°24E 247 D6
Khalīj Iraq 33°18N 44°28E 113 B2
Khalilabad India 26°48N 83°5E 243 F10
Khalīlī Iran 27°38N 53°17E 247 E7
Khalkhāl Iran 37°37N 48°32E 213 D13
Khalkís = Chalkida Greece 38°27N 23°42E 204 C5
Khalmer-Sede = Tazovskiy Russia 67°30N 78°44E 214 C8
Khalmer Yu Russia 67°58N 65°1E 214 C7
Khalturin Russia 58°40N 48°50E 186 C8
Kham Keut Laos 18°15N 104°43E 236 C5
Khamaria India 23°5N 80°48E 243 H9
Khambhaliya India 22°14N 69°41E 242 H3
Khambhat India 22°23N 72°33E 242 H5
Khambhat, G. of India 20°45N 72°30E 239 E10
Khamgaon India 20°42N 76°37E 244 D3
Khami Ruins = Kame Ruins Zimbabwe 20°7S 28°25E 269 G2
Khamīr Iran 26°57N 55°36E 247 E7
Khamir Yemen 16°2N 44°0E 248 C4
Khamīs Mushayţ Si. Arabia 18°18N 42°44E 248 C3
Khammam India 17°11N 80°6E 244 F5
Khamsa Egypt 30°27N 32°23E 251 H3
Khan → Namibia 22°37S 14°56E 270 B2
Khān Abū Shāmat Syria 33°39N 36°53E 250 E7
Khān al Baghdādī Iraq 33°51N 42°32E 213 G10
Khān al Ḩammād Iraq 32°19N 44°16E 213 G11
Khān Azād Iraq 33°7N 44°22E 246 C5
Khān Mujiddah Iraq 32°21N 43°48E 246 C4
Khān Shaykhūn Syria 35°26N 36°38E 212 E7
Khan Tengri, Pik Asia 42°12N 80°10E 217 D10
Khān Yūnis Gaza Strip 31°21N 34°18E 251 G5
Khānābād Afghan. 36°45N 69°5E 240 A3
Khanai Pakistan 30°30N 67°8E 242 D2
Khānaqīn Iraq 34°23N 45°25E 213 E11
Khanāşir Syria 35°45N 37°30E 250 C8
Khānbāghī Iran 36°10N 55°25E 247 B7
Khandwa India 21°49N 76°22E 244 D3
Khandyga Russia 62°42N 135°35E 215 C14
Khanewal Pakistan 30°20N 71°55E 242 D4
Khangah Dogran Pakistan 31°50N 73°37E 242 D5
Khangchendzonga = Kanchenjunga △ India 27°42N 88°8E 241 B2
Khanh Duong Vietnam 12°44N 108°44E 236 F7
Khaniá = Chania Greece 35°30N 24°4E 207 E5
Khaniadhana India 25°1N 78°8E 242 G8
Khanka, L. Asia 45°0N 132°24E 220 B6
Khankendy = Xankändi Azerbaijan 39°52N 46°49E 213 C12
Khanna India 30°42N 76°16E 242 D7
Khanozai Pakistan 30°37N 67°19E 242 D2
Khanpur Pakistan 28°42N 70°35E 242 E4
Khansā' Iraq 33°21N 44°28E 113 A2
Khanty-Mansiysk Russia 61°0N 69°0E 214 C7
Khanzira, Ras Somalia 10°52N 45°48E 267 B6
Khao Khitchakut △ Thailand 12°50N 102°10E 236 F4
Khao Laem △ Thailand 14°56N 98°31E 236 E2
Khao Laem Res. Thailand 14°50N 98°30E 236 E2
Khao Lak △ Malaysia 8°38N 98°18E 237 H2
Khao Luang △ Thailand 8°34N 99°42E 237 H2
Khao Nam Khang △ Thailand 6°32N 100°35E 237 J3
Khao Phlu Thailand 9°29N 99°59E 237 b
Khao Pu -Khao Ya △ Thailand 7°26N 99°57E 237 J2
Khao Sam Roi Yot △ Thailand 12°13N 99°57E 237 F2
Khao Sok △ Thailand 8°55N 98°38E 237 H2
Khao Yai △ Thailand 14°21N 101°29E 236 E3
Khaoen Si Nakarin △ Thailand 14°47N 99°0E 236 E2
Khapalu Pakistan 35°10N 76°20E 243 B7
Khapcheranga Russia 49°42N 112°24E 215 E12
Khaptao △ Nepal 29°20N 81°10E 243 E9
Kharabali Russia 47°25N 47°15E 191 G8
Kharagauli Georgia 42°1N 43°12E 191 J6
Kharaghoda India 23°11N 71°46E 242 H4
Kharagpur India 22°20N 87°25E 243 H12
Kharan Kalat Pakistan 28°34N 65°21E 240 C2
Kharānaq Iran 32°20N 54°45E 247 C7
Kharavli India 18°54N 72°55E 130 B2
Kharda India 18°40N 75°34E 244 E2
Khardung La India 34°20N 77°43E 243 B7
Kharg = Khārk, Jazīreh-ye Iran 29°15N 50°28E 247 D6

Khârga, El Wâhât el Egypt 25°10N 30°35E 256 B3
Khargon India 21°45N 75°40E 244 D2
Khari → India 25°54N 74°31E 242 G6
Kharian Pakistan 32°49N 73°52E 242 C5
Khariar India 20°17N 82°46E 244 D6
Kharit, Wadi el → Egypt 24°26N 33°3E 256 C3
Khārk, Jazīreh-ye Iran 29°15N 50°28E 247 D6
Kharkiv Ukraine 49°58N 36°20E 189 H9
Kharkiv □ Ukraine 48°20N 36°20E 189 H9
Kharkov = Kharkiv Ukraine 49°58N 36°20E 189 H9
Kharmanli Bulgaria 41°55N 25°55E 203 E9
Kharovsk Russia 59°56N 40°13E 188 C11
Kharsawangarh India 22°48N 85°50E 243 H11
Kharta Turkey 40°55N 29°7E 212 B3
Khartoum = El Khartûm Sudan 15°31N 32°35E 257 D3
Khartum Canada 45°15N 77°5W 312 A7
Khasan Russia 42°25N 130°40E 220 C5
Khasavyurt Russia 43°16N 46°40E 191 J8
Khāsh Iran 28°15N 61°15E 240 C1
Khāsh, Dasht-e Afghan. 31°50N 62°30E 240 C1
Khashm el Girba Sudan 14°59N 35°58E 257 E4
Khashum Sudan 12°27N 28°2E 257 E2
Khashuri Georgia 42°3N 43°35E 191 J6
Khasi Hills India 25°30N 91°30E 241 C3
Khaskovo Bulgaria 41°56N 25°30E 203 E9
Khaskovo □ Bulgaria 42°0N 25°40E 203 E9
Khat, Laem Thailand 8°6N 98°26E 237 a
Khatanga Russia 72°0N 102°20E 215 B11
Khatanga → Russia 72°55N 106°0E 215 B11
Khatauli India 29°17N 77°43E 242 E7
Khatlon □ Tajikistan 37°50N 69°0E 217 E7
Khatra India 22°59N 86°51E 243 H12
Khātūnābād Iran 30°1N 55°25E 247 D7
Khatyrka Russia 62°3N 175°15E 215 C18
Khavda India 23°51N 69°43E 242 H3
Khawlaf, Ra's Yemen 12°40N 54°7E 249 D6
Khawr Fakkān U.A.E. 25°21N 56°22E 247 E8
Khay' Si. Arabia 18°45N 41°24E 248 C3
Khaybar, Ḩarrat Si. Arabia 25°30N 39°45E 246 E4
Khāzimiyah Iraq 34°46N 43°37E 246 C4
Khazzān Jabal al Awliyā Sudan 15°24N 32°20E 257 D3
Khe Bo Vietnam 19°8N 104°41E 236 C5
Khe Long Vietnam 21°29N 104°46E 236 B5
Khe Sanh Vietnam 16°37N 106°45E 236 D6
Khed Maharashtra, India 17°43N 73°27E 244 F1
Khed Maharashtra, India 18°51N 73°56E 244 E1
Khed Brahma India 24°7N 73°5E 242 G5
Khefren Egypt 29°58N 31°8E 117 B1
Khekra India 28°52N 77°20E 242 E7
Khem-Beldyr = Kyzyl Russia 51°50N 94°30E 217 B12
Khemarak Phouminville = Krong Kaoh Kong Cambodia 11°37N 102°59E 237 G4
Khemisset Morocco 33°50N 6°1W 260 B3
Khemmarat Thailand 16°10N 105°15E 236 D5
Khenāmān Iran 30°27N 56°29E 247 D8
Khenchela Algeria 35°28N 7°11E 261 A6
Khenchela □ Algeria 35°0N 7°0E 261 B6
Khenifra Morocco 32°58N 5°46W 260 B3
Kherrata Algeria 36°27N 5°13E 261 A6
Khersān → Iran 31°33N 50°22E 247 D6
Kherson Ukraine 46°35N 32°35E 189 J7
Kherson □ Ukraine 46°15N 33°10E 189 J7
Kheta → Russia 71°54N 102°6E 215 B11
Khewari Pakistan 26°36N 68°52E 242 F3
Khibinogorsk = Kirovsk Russia 67°32N 33°41E 186 A5
Khichripur India 28°37N 77°18E 120 B2
Khidirpur India 22°32N 88°19E 124 B1
Khilchipur India 24°2N 76°34E 242 G7
Khilok Russia 51°30N 110°45E 215 D12
Khimki Russia 55°50N 37°20E 188 E9
Khimki-Khovrino Russia 55°51N 37°31E 129 A2
Khíos = Chios Greece 38°27N 26°9E 205 C8
Khirbet Batin Abu Lihyah West Bank 31°50N 35°6E 123 A1
Khirbet el-Misbah West Bank 31°53N 35°4E 123 A1
Khirbet Jub e-Rum West Bank 31°44N 35°16E 123 B2
Khirsadoh India 22°11N 78°47E 243 H8
Khiuma = Hiiumaa Estonia 58°50N 22°45E 188 C2
Khiva = Xiva Uzbekistan 41°30N 60°18E 216 D6
Khlebarovo Bulgaria 43°37N 26°15E 203 C10
Khlong Khlung Thailand 16°12N 99°43E 236 D2
Khlong Lan △ Thailand 16°12N 99°13E 236 D2
Khlong Phanom △ Thailand 8°45N 98°38E 237 H2
Khlong San Thailand 13°43N 100°29E 113 B2
Khlong Toey Thailand 13°43N 100°36E 113 B2
Khmelnik Ukraine 49°33N 27°58E 177 D14
Khmelnytskyy Ukraine 49°23N 27°0E 177 D14
Khmelnytskyy □ Ukraine 49°50N 26°40E 177 D14
Khmer Rep. = Cambodia ■ Asia 12°15N 105°0E 236 F5
Khoai, Hon Vietnam 8°26N 104°50E 237 H5
Khobar = Al Khubar Si. Arabia 26°17N 50°12E 247 E6
Khodoriv Ukraine 49°24N 24°19E 177 D13
Khodzent = Khŭjand Tajikistan 40°17N 69°37E 217 D7
Khojak Pass Afghan. 30°51N 66°34E 242 D2
Khojayli = Xo'jayli Uzbekistan 42°29N 59°31E 216 D5
Khok Kloi Thailand 8°17N 98°19E 237 a
Khok Pho Thailand 6°43N 101°6E 237 J3
Khok Samrong Thailand 15°3N 100°43E 236 E3
Khokhropār Pakistan 25°42N 70°12E 240 D3
Kholm Afghan. 36°45N 67°40E 240 A2
Kholm Russia 57°10N 31°15E 188 D6
Kholmsk Russia 47°40N 142°5E 215 E15
Khomārlu Iran 39°6N 47°3E 213 C12
Khomas □ Namibia 23°30S 17°0E 270 B2
Khomas Hochland Namibia 22°40S 16°0E 270 B2
Khombole Senegal 14°43N 16°42W 262 C1
Khomeyn Iran 33°40N 50°7E 247 C6
Khomeynī Shahr Iran 32°41N 51°31E 247 C6
Khomodino Botswana 22°46S 23°52E 270 B3
Khon Kaen Thailand 16°30N 102°47E 236 D4
Khong → Cambodia 13°32N 105°58E 236 F5
Khong Sedone Laos 15°34N 105°49E 236 E5
Khonsa India 26°57N 95°33E 241 B5
Khonuu Russia 66°30N 143°12E 215 C15
Khoper → Russia 49°30N 42°20E 190 F6
Khor el 'Atash Sudan 13°20N 34°15E 257 E3
Khorāsān-e Janūb □ Iran 32°0N 59°0E 247 C8
Khorāsān-e Razavī □ Iran 35°0N 59°0E 247 C8
Khorāsān-e Shemālī □ Iran 37°0N 57°0E 247 B8
Khorat = Nakhon Ratchasima Thailand 14°59N 102°12E 236 E4
Khorat, Cao Nguyen Thailand 15°30N 102°50E 236 E4
Khorazm = Xorazm □ Uzbekistan 43°0N 60°0E 216 D6
Khorb el Ethel Algeria 28°30N 6°17W 260 C3
Khorel India 22°41N 88°18E 124 A1
Khorixas Namibia 20°16S 14°59E 270 B1
Khorol Ukraine 49°48N 33°15E 189 H7
Khorosovo Russia 55°46N 37°27E 129 B1
Khorramābād Khorāsān, Iran 35°6N 57°57E 247 C8
Khorramābād Lorestān, Iran 33°30N 48°25E 213 F13
Khorramdarreh Iran 36°11N 49°11E 213 D13
Khorramshahr Iran 30°29N 48°15E 247 D6
Khorugh Tajikistan 37°30N 71°36E 240 A3
Khosravī Iran 30°48N 51°28E 247 D6
Khosrowābād Khuzestān, Iran 30°10N 48°25E 247 D6
Khosrowābād Kordestān, Iran 35°31N 47°38E 213 E12
Khost Pakistan 30°13N 67°35E 242 D2
Khosūyeh Iran 28°32N 54°26E 247 D7
Khotan = Hotan China 37°25N 79°55E 217 E9
Khotang Nepal 27°1N 86°51E 243 F12
Khotyn Ukraine 48°31N 26°27E 183 B11
Khouribga Morocco 32°58N 6°57W 260 B3
Khowai Bangla. 24°5N 91°40E 241 C3
Khowst Afghan. 33°22N 69°58E 242 C3
Khowst □ Afghan. 33°20N 70°0E 240 B3
Khoyniki Belarus 51°54N 29°55E 177 C15
Khram, Ko Thailand 12°42N 100°47E 236 F3
Khrami → Georgia 41°25N 45°0E 191 K7
Khrenovoye Russia 51°4N 40°16E 190 E5
Khromtaū Kazakhstan 50°17N 58°27E 216 B5
Khrysokhou B. Cyprus 35°6N 32°25E 207 E8
Khuan Wa Thailand 7°53N 98°17E 237 a
Khudrah, W. → Yemen 18°10N 50°20E 249 C5
Khudzhand = Khŭjand Tajikistan 40°17N 69°37E 217 D7
Khuff Si. Arabia 24°55N 44°53E 246 E5
Khūgīānī Afghan. 31°34N 66°32E 242 D2
Khuis Botswana 26°40S 21°49E 270 C3
Khuiyala India 27°9N 70°25E 242 F4
Khŭjand Tajikistan 40°17N 69°37E 217 D7
Khujner India 23°47N 76°36E 242 H7
Khukhan Thailand 14°42N 104°12E 236 E5
Khulayş Si. Arabia 22°9N 39°19E 248 B2
Khulna Bangla. 22°45N 89°34E 241 D2
Khulna □ Bangla. 22°25N 89°35E 241 D2
Khulo Georgia 41°33N 42°19E 191 K6
Khumago Botswana 20°26S 24°32E 270 B3
Khumrah Si. Arabia 21°22N 39°13E 248 B2
Khunjerab △ Pakistan 36°40N 75°30E 243 A6
Khunjerab Pass = Kinjirap Daban Asia 36°40N 75°25E 240 A4
Khūnsorkh Iran 27°9N 56°7E 247 E8
Khunti India 23°5N 85°17E 243 H11
Khūr Iran 32°55N 58°18E 247 C8
Khurai India 24°3N 78°23E 242 G8
Khuraydah Yemen 15°33N 48°18E 249 D5
Khurayş Si. Arabia 25°6N 48°2E 247 E6
Khurda India 20°11N 85°37E 244 D7
Khureit Sudan 13°59N 26°3E 257 E2
Khurja India 28°15N 77°58E 242 E7
Khūrmāl Iraq 35°18N 46°2E 213 E12
Khurr, Wādī al Iraq 32°3N 43°52E 246 C4
Khūsf Iran 32°46N 58°53E 247 C8
Khushab Pakistan 32°20N 72°20E 242 C5
Khust Ukraine 48°10N 23°18E 183 B8
Khutse ⌓ Botswana 23°31S 24°12E 270 B3
Khuwei Sudan 13°5N 29°14E 257 E2
Khuzdar Pakistan 27°52N 66°30E 242 F2
Khūzestān □ Iran 31°0N 49°0E 247 D6
Khvāf Iran 34°33N 60°8E 247 C9
Khvājeh Iran 38°9N 46°35E 246 B5
Khvājeh Moḩammad, Kūh-e Afghan. 36°22N 70°17E 240 A3
Khvalynsk Russia 52°30N 48°2E 190 D9
Khvalynsky △ Russia 52°30N 48°0E 190 D9
Khvānsār Iran 29°56N 54°8E 247 D7
Khvatovka Russia 52°24N 46°32E 190 D8
Khvor Iran 33°45N 55°0E 247 C7
Khvorgū Iran 27°34N 56°27E 247 E8
Khvormūj Iran 28°40N 51°30E 247 D6
Khvoy Iran 38°35N 45°0E 213 C11
Khvoynaya Russia 58°58N 34°28E 188 C8
Khwae Noi → Thailand 14°1N 99°32E 236 E2
Khyber Pakhtunkhwa □ Pakistan 34°0N 72°0E 242 C4
Khyber Pass Afghan. 34°10N 71°8E 242 B4
Khyriv Ukraine 49°32N 22°50E 185 J9
Kia Fiji 16°16S 179°8E 287 A2
Kia Solomon Is. 7°32S 158°26E 287 L10
Kiabukwa Dem. Rep. of the Congo 8°40S 24°48E 265 D4
Kiadho → India 19°37N 77°40E 244 E3
Kiama N.S.W., Australia 34°40S 150°50E 283 C9
Kiama Dem. Rep. of the Congo 7°19S 17°49E 265 D3
Kiamari Pakistan 24°49N 66°58E 123 B1
Kiamba Phil. 6°2N 124°46E 233 H5
Kiambi Dem. Rep. of the Congo 7°15S 28°0E 268 D2
Kiamusze = Jiamusi China 46°40N 130°26E 219 B15
Kian = Ji'an China 41°5N 126°10E 227 D14
Kiana U.S.A. 66°58N 160°26W 303 C7
Kiang West △ Gambia 13°25N 15°50W 262 C1
Kiangara Madag. 17°58S 47°2E 272 B2
Kiangsi = Jiangxi □ China 27°30N 116°0E 229 D11
Kiangsu = Jiangsu □ China 33°0N 120°0E 227 H11
Kiato Greece 38°1N 22°45E 204 C4
Kibæk Denmark 56°2N 8°51E 163 H2
Kibale △ Uganda 0°16N 30°18E 268 B3
Kibanga Port Uganda 0°10N 32°58E 268 B3
Kibangou Congo 3°26S 12°22E 264 C2
Kibara Tanzania 2°8S 33°30E 268 C3
Kibare, Mts. Dem. Rep. of the Congo 8°25S 27°10E 268 D2
Kibawe Phil. 7°34N 125°0E 233 H5
Kibenga Dem. Rep. of the Congo 7°56S 17°30E 265 D3
Kibira △ Burundi 3°6S 30°24E 268 C3
Kiboga Uganda 0°58N 31°45E 268 B3
Kibombo Dem. Rep. of the Congo 3°57S 25°53E 265 C5
Kibondo Tanzania 3°35S 30°45E 268 C3
Kibre Mengist Ethiopia 5°54N 38°59E 257 F4
Kıbrıs = Cyprus ■ Asia 35°0N 33°0E 207 F9
Kibumbu Burundi 3°32S 29°45E 268 C2
Kibungo Rwanda 2°10S 30°32E 268 C3
Kibuye Burundi 3°39S 29°59E 268 C2
Kibuye Rwanda 2°3S 29°21E 268 C2
Kibwesa Tanzania 6°30S 29°58E 268 D2
Kibwezi Kenya 2°27S 37°57E 268 C4
Kicasalih Turkey 41°23N 26°48E 203 E10
Kičevo Macedonia 41°34N 20°59E 202 E4
Kichha → India 28°41N 79°18E 243 E8
Kichmengskiy Gorodok Russia 59°59N 45°48E 186 B8
Kicking Horse Pass Canada 51°28N 116°16W 296 C5
Kîd, W. → Egypt 28°9N 34°27E 251 K5
Kid I. Antigua & B. 17°42N 61°49W 322 c
Kidal Mali 18°26N 1°22E 263 B5
Kidal □ Mali 19°55N 1°5E 261 E5
Kidapawan Phil. 7°1N 125°3E 233 H5
Kidderminster U.K. 52°24N 2°15W 169 E5
Kidepo Valley △ Uganda 3°52N 33°50E 268 B3
Kidete Tanzania 6°25S 37°17E 268 D4
Kidira Senegal 14°28N 12°13W 262 C2
Kidnappers, C. N.Z. 39°38S 177°5E 284 F6
Kidsgrove U.K. 53°5N 2°14W 168 D5
Kidston Australia 18°52S 144°8E 280 B3
Kidugallo Tanzania 6°49S 38°15E 268 D4
Kidurong, Tanjong Malaysia 3°16N 113°3E 235 B4
Kiel Germany 54°19N 10°8E 178 A6
Kiel Canal = Nord-Ostsee-Kanal Germany 54°12N 9°32E 178 A5
Kiel-Kanal = Nord-Ostsee-Kanal Germany 54°12N 9°32E 178 A5
Kielce Poland 50°52N 20°42E 185 H7
Kielder Water U.K. 55°11N 2°31W 168 B5
Kieler Bucht Germany 54°35N 10°25E 178 A6
Kiembara Burkina Faso 13°15N 2°44W 262 C4
Kienge Dem. Rep. of the Congo 10°30S 27°30E 269 E2
Kierling Austria 48°18N 16°16E 142 A1
Kierlingbach → Austria 48°18N 16°19E 142 A1
Kiessé Niger 13°29N 4°1E 263 C5
Kieta Papua N. G. 6°12S 155°36E 286 D8
Kiev = Kyyiv Ukraine 50°30N 30°28E 177 C16
Kifaya Guinea 12°10N 13°4W 262 C2
Kiffa Mauritania 16°37N 11°24W 262 B2
Kifisos → Athina, Greece 37°58N 23°42E 112 B2
Kifisos → Voiotia, Greece 38°35N 23°20E 204 C5
Kifissia Greece 38°4N 23°49E 204 C5
Kifrī Iraq 34°45N 45°0E 213 E11
Kigali Rwanda 1°59S 30°4E 268 C3
Kigarama Tanzania 1°1S 31°50E 268 C3
Kigelle South Sudan 8°40N 34°2E 257 F3
Kigezi ⌓ Uganda 0°34S 29°55E 268 C2
Kiğı Turkey 39°18N 40°21E 213 C9
Kigoma □ Tanzania 5°0S 30°0E 268 D3
Kigoma-Ujiji Tanzania 4°55S 29°36E 268 C2
Kigomasha, Ras Tanzania 4°58S 38°58E 268 C4
Kigosi ⌓ Tanzania 4°10S 31°45E 268 C3
Kığzı Turkey 38°18N 43°25E 246 B4
Kīhei U.S.A. 20°47N 156°28W 302 C5
Kihikihi N.Z. 38°2S 175°22E 284 E4
Kihnu Estonia 58°9N 24°1E 188 C3
Kihoku Japan 33°13N 132°36E 222 D4
Kīholo B. U.S.A. 19°50N 155°55W 302 D6
Kii-Hantō Japan 34°0N 135°45E 223 D7
Kii-Nagashima Japan 34°12N 136°20E 223 C8
Kii-Sanchi Japan 34°20N 136°0E 223 C8
Kii-Suidō Japan 33°40N 134°45E 222 D6
Kiira Dam Uganda 0°25N 33°0E 268 B3
Kiire Japan 31°22N 130°33E 222 F2
Kijik U.S.A. 60°20N 154°20W 303 F9
Kikaiga-Shima Japan 28°19N 129°59E 221 K4
Kikiak = Rigolet Canada 54°10N 58°23W 299 B8
Kikinda Serbia 45°50N 20°30E 182 E5
Kikládhes = Kyklades Greece 37°0N 24°30E 204 E6
Kikoira Australia 33°39S 146°40E 283 B7
Kikombo Bandundu, Dem. Rep. of the Congo 5°37S 18°50E 265 D3
Kikombo Bandundu, Dem. Rep. of the Congo 5°49S 17°45E 265 D3
Kikongo Dem. Rep. of the Congo 4°16S 17°17E 265 C3
Kikori Papua N. G. 7°25S 144°15E 286 D3
Kikori → Papua N. G. 7°38S 144°20E 286 D3
Kikuchi Japan 32°59N 130°47E 222 E2
Kikuna Japan 35°30N 139°37E 140 B2
Kikuyu Kenya 1°15S 36°40E 268 C4
Kikwit Dem. Rep. of the Congo 5°0S 18°45E 265 D3
Kil Sweden 59°30N 13°20E 162 E7
Kilafors Sweden 61°14N 16°36E 162 C10
Kilakkarai India 9°12N 78°47E 245 K4
Kilar India 33°6N 76°25E 242 C7
Kilauea U.S.A. 22°13N 159°25W 302 A2
Kīlauea Caldera U.S.A. 19°25N 155°17W 302 D6
Kilbarrack Ireland 53°23N 6°9W 120 A3
Kilbeggan Ireland 53°22N 7°30W 166 C4
Kilbrannan Sd. U.K. 55°37N 5°26W 167 F3
Kilbuck Mts. U.S.A. 60°36N 159°53W 303 F8
Kilburn U.K. 51°32N 0°11W 125 A2
Kilchu N. Korea 40°57N 129°25E 224 B4
Kilcoy Australia 26°59S 152°30E 281 D5
Kildare Ireland 53°9N 6°55W 166 C5
Kildare □ Ireland 53°10N 6°50W 166 C5
Kildinstroy Russia 68°48N 33°6E 160 B25
Kileikli Sudan 11°25N 25°31E 257 E2
Kilembe Dem. Rep. of the Congo 5°42S 19°55E 265 D3
Kilen Norway 59°20N 8°49E 164 E5
Kilfinnane Ireland 52°21N 8°28W 166 D3
Kilgarvan Ireland 51°54N 9°27W 166 E2
Kilgore U.S.A. 32°23N 94°53W 314 E7
Kilgoris Kenya 1°0S 34°53E 268 C3
Kilibo Benin 8°32N 2°38E 263 D5
Kilifi Kenya 3°40S 39°48E 268 C4
Kilimanjaro Tanzania 3°7S 37°20E 268 C4
Kilimanjaro □ Tanzania 4°0S 38°0E 268 C4
Kilimanjaro △ Tanzania 3°2S 37°19E 268 C4
Kilimli Turkey 41°28N 31°50E 212 B4
Kilinailau Is. Papua N. G. 4°45S 155°20E 286 C8
Kilindini Kenya 4°4S 39°40E 268 C4
Kilinochchi Sri Lanka 9°24N 80°25E 245 K5
Kilis Turkey 36°42N 37°6E 250 B8
Kilis □ Turkey 36°50N 37°10E 212 D7
Kiliya Ukraine 45°28N 29°16E 183 E14
Kilkee Ireland 52°41N 9°39W 166 D2
Kilkeel U.K. 54°7N 5°55W 166 B5
Kilkenny Ireland 52°39N 7°15W 166 D4
Kilkenny □ Ireland 52°35N 7°15W 166 D4
Kilkieran B. Ireland 53°20N 9°41W 166 C2
Kilkis Greece 40°58N 22°57E 202 F6
Killakee Ireland 53°15N 6°19W 120 B2
Killala Ireland 54°13N 9°13W 166 B2
Killala B. Ireland 54°16N 9°8W 166 B2
Killaloe Ont., Canada 45°33N 77°25W 312 A7
Killaloe Clare, Ireland 52°48N 8°28W 166 D3
Killarney Queens., Australia 28°20S 152°18E 281 D5
Killarney Man., Canada 49°10N 99°40W 297 D9
Killarney Kerry, Ireland 52°4N 9°30W 166 D2
Killarney, L. Bahamas 25°3N 77°27W 153 b
Killarney △ Ireland 52°0N 9°33W 166 D2
Killary Harbour Ireland 53°38N 9°52W 166 C2
Killdeer U.S.A. 47°22N 102°45W 308 B2
Killeberg Sweden 56°29N 14°5E 163 H8
Killeen U.S.A. 31°7N 97°44W 314 F6
Killester Ireland 53°22N 6°11W 120 A2
Killin U.K. 56°28N 4°19W 167 E4
Killiney Ireland 53°15N 6°7W 120 B3
Killiney B. Ireland 53°16N 6°5W 120 B3
Killington Pk. U.S.A. 43°36N 72°49W 313 C12
Killíni = Kyllini Greece 37°55N 21°8E 207 D3
Killini Greece 37°54N 22°25E 204 D4
Killiniq I. Canada 60°24N 64°37W 295 E19
Killorglin Ireland 52°6N 9°47W 166 D2
Killybegs Ireland 54°38N 8°26W 166 B3
Kilmacud Ireland 53°17N 6°13W 120 B2
Kilmainham Ireland 53°20N 6°17W 120 A2
Kilmainham Gaol Ireland 53°21N 6°19W 120 A2
Kilmarnock U.K. 55°37N 4°29W 167 F4
Kilmashogue Mt. Ireland 53°15N 6°15W 120 B2
Kilmez Russia 56°58N 50°55E 190 B10
Kilmez → Russia 56°58N 50°28E 190 B10
Kilmore Vic., Australia 37°25S 144°53E 283 D6
Kilmore Dublin, Ireland 53°23N 6°13W 120 A2
Kilmore Quay Ireland 52°10N 6°36W 166 D5
Kilnamanagh Ireland 53°18N 6°22W 120 B1
Kilo Finland 60°13N 24°47E 121 B1
Kilokri India 28°34N 77°15E 120 B2
Kilómetro 1082 = Joaquín V. González Argentina 25°10S 64°0W 334 B3
Kilondo Tanzania 9°45S 34°20E 269 D3
Kilosa Tanzania 6°48S 37°0E 268 D4
Kilrush Ireland 52°38N 9°29W 166 D2
Kiltan I. India 11°29N 73°0E 245 J1
Kiltiernan Ireland 53°15N 6°11W 120 B2
Kilwa Kisiwani Tanzania 8°58S 39°32E 269 D4
Kilwa Kivinje Tanzania 8°45S 39°25E 269 D4
Kilwa Masoko Tanzania 8°55S 39°30E 269 D4
Kilwinning U.K. 55°39N 4°43W 167 F4
Kim U.S.A. 37°15N 103°21W 305 H12
Kim → Cameroon 5°28N 11°7E 263 D7
Kimaam Indonesia 7°58S 138°53E 231 F9
Kimamba Tanzania 6°45S 37°10E 268 D4
Kimba Australia 33°8S 136°23E 282 B2
Kimball Nebr., U.S.A. 41°14N 103°40W 308 E2
Kimball S. Dak., U.S.A. 43°45N 98°57W 308 D4
Kimbanda Dem. Rep. of the Congo 4°16S 18°30E 265 C3
Kimbe Papua N. G. 5°33S 150°11E 286 C6
Kimbe B. Papua N. G. 5°15S 150°30E 286 C6
Kimberley W. Austral., Australia 16°20S 127°0E 278 C4
Kimberley B.C., Canada 49°40N 115°59W 296 D5
Kimberley Ont., Canada 44°23N 80°32W 312 B4
Kimberley Northern Cape, S. Africa 28°43S 24°46E 270 C3
Kimberly U.S.A. 42°32N 114°22W 304 E6
Kimbongo Dem. Rep. of the Congo 6°8S 18°1E 265 D3
Kimch'aek N. Korea 40°40N 129°10E 224 B4
Kimhae = Gimhae S. Korea 35°14N 128°53E 224 E4
Kimhwa N. Korea 38°25N 127°36E 224 C3
Kimi Greece 38°38N 24°6E 204 C6
Kimitsu Japan 35°19N 139°54E 223 B11
Kimjŏngsugŭp N. Korea 41°24N 127°45E 224 B3
Kimmage Ireland 53°18N 6°17W 120 B2
Kimmirut Canada 62°50N 69°50W 295 E18
Kimolos Greece 36°48N 24°37E 204 E6
Kimongo Congo 4°27S 12°53E 265 C2
Kimovsk Moskva, Russia 55°21N 37°28E 188 E9
Kimovsk Tula, Russia 54°0N 38°29E 188 E10
Kimpangu Dem. Rep. of the Congo 5°52S 15°3E 265 D3
Kimparana Mali 12°48N 5°0W 262 C4
Kimpese Congo 5°33S 14°26E 265 D2
Kimpese Dem. Rep. of the Congo 5°35S 14°26E 265 D2
Kimry Russia 56°55N 37°15E 188 D9
Kimstad Sweden 58°35N 15°58E 163 F9
Kimvula Dem. Rep. of the Congo 5°44S 15°58E 265 D3
Kin Burma 22°46N 94°42E 241 D5
Kin-u Burma 22°46N 95°37E 241 D5
Kin-wan Japan 26°23N 127°55E 288 a
Kinabalian, Mt. Phil. 8°12N 125°26E 233 G5
Kinabalu, Gunung Malaysia 6°3N 116°14E 235 A5
Kinabalu △ Malaysia 6°0N 116°30E 235 A5
Kinango Kenya 4°8S 39°19E 268 C4
Kinard U.S.A. 30°16N 85°15W 316 E4
Kinaros Greece 36°59N 26°15E 205 E8
Kinaskan L. Canada 57°38N 130°8W 296 B2
Kinbasket L. Canada 52°0N 118°10W 296 C5
Kincaid U.S.A. 39°35N 89°25W 310 E7
Kincardine Canada 44°10N 81°40W 312 B3
Kinchafoonee Cr. → U.S.A. 31°38N 84°10W 316 D5
Kinchega △ Australia 32°27S 142°15E 282 B5
Kincolith Canada 55°0N 129°57W 296 C3
Kincsem Park Budapest, Hungary 47°30N 19°8E 117 B2
Kinda Kasai-Or., Dem. Rep. of the Congo 9°18S 25°4E 265 D5
Kinda Katanga, Dem. Rep. of the Congo 4°47S 21°48E 265 C4
Kindambi Dem. Rep. of the Congo 5°6S 18°14E 265 D4
Kindberg Austria 47°30N 15°27E 180 D8
Kinde U.S.A. 43°56N 83°0W 312 C2
Kindele Dem. Rep. of the Congo 8°39S 24°10E 265 D4
Kinder Scout U.K. 53°24N 1°52W 168 D6
Kinderhook U.S.A. 39°42N 91°10W 310 E5
Kindersley Canada 51°30N 109°10W 297 C7
Kindi Iraq 33°18N 44°22E 113 B2
Kindia Guinea 10°0N 12°52W 262 D2
Kindongo Dem. Rep. of the Congo 3°58S 17°30E 264 C3
Kindu Dem. Rep. of the Congo 2°55S 25°50E 264 C5
Kinel Russia 53°15N 50°40E 190 D10
Kineshma Russia 57°30N 42°5E 190 B6
Kinesi Tanzania 1°25S 33°50E 268 C3
King, L. Australia 33°10S 119°35E 279 F2
King, Mt. Australia 25°10S 147°30E 280 D4
King Christian I. Canada 77°48N 101°40W 295 B11
King City Calif., U.S.A. 36°13N 121°8W 306 J5
King City Mo., U.S.A. 40°3N 94°31W 310 D2
King Cove U.S.A. 55°3N 162°19W 303 J7
King Cr. → Australia 24°35S 139°30E 280 C2
King Edward → Australia 14°14S 126°35E 278 B4
King Edward Point S. Georgia 54°17S 36°30W 151 B1
King Frederick VI Land = Kong Frederik VI.s Kyst Greenland 63°0N 43°0W 154 E6
King George B. Falk. Is. 51°30S 60°30W 153 f
King George I. Antarctica 60°0S 60°0W 151 C18
King George Is. Canada 57°20N 80°30W 295 F15
King George Sd. Australia 35°5S 118°0E 279 G2
King George VI Falls Guyana 5°42N 61°5W 329 B5
King I. = Kadan Kyun Burma 12°30N 98°20E 236 F2
King I. Tas., Australia 39°50S 144°0E 281 F3
King I. B.C., Canada 52°10N 127°40W 296 C3
King Khalid Military City = Madinat al Malik Khālid al Askarīyah Si. Arabia 27°54N 45°31E 246 E5
King Leopold Ranges Australia 17°30S 125°45E 278 C4
King of Prussia U.S.A. 40°5N 75°23W 313 F9
King Salmon U.S.A. 58°42N 156°40W 303 G8
King Sd. Australia 16°50S 123°20E 278 C3
King Sejong Antarctica 62°30S 58°0W 151 C18
King Shaka = Durban ✈ (DIA) S. Africa 29°37S 31°7E 271 C5
King William I. Canada 69°10N 97°25W 294 D12
King William's Town S. Africa 32°51S 27°22E 270 D4
Kingaok = Bathurst Inlet Canada 66°50N 108°1W 294 D10
Kingaroy Australia 26°32S 151°51E 281 D5
Kingdom City U.S.A. 38°56N 91°56W 310 F5
Kingfisher U.S.A. 35°52N 97°56W 314 D6
Kinghorn U.K. 56°5N 3°10W 121 A2
Kingirbān Iraq 34°40N 44°54E 246 C5
Kingisepp = Kuressaare Estonia 58°15N 22°30E 188 C2
Kingisepp Russia 59°25N 28°40E 188 C5
Kingking = Pantukan Phil. 7°9N 125°54E 233 H5
Kinglake △ Australia 37°30S 145°22E 283 D6
Kingman Ariz., U.S.A. 35°12N 114°4W 307 K12
Kingman Ind., U.S.A. 39°58N 87°18W 311 E9
Kingman Kans., U.S.A. 37°39N 98°7W 308 G4
Kingoonya Australia 30°55S 135°19E 281 E2
Kingri Pakistan 30°27N 69°49E 242 D3
Kings → U.S.A. 36°3N 119°50W 306 J7
Kings Canyon Australia 24°15S 131°34E 278 D5
Kings Canyon △ U.S.A. 36°50N 118°40W 306 J8
Kings County = Offaly □ Ireland 53°15N 7°30W 166 C4
Kings Cross Sydney, Australia 139 c3
King's Cross London, U.K. 125 a4
Kings Domain Australia 37°49S 144°58E 128 A1
Kings Forest = Kongelunden Denmark 55°34N 12°34E 118 B3
King's Lynn U.K. 52°45N 0°24E 168 E8
Kings Park U.S.A. 40°53N 73°16W 313 F11
Kings Peak U.S.A. 40°46N 110°23W 304 F8
King's Trough Atl. Oc. 43°48N 22°0W 152 B9
Kingsbridge U.K. 50°17N 3°47W 169 G4
Kingsburg U.S.A. 36°31N 119°33W 306 J7
Kingsbury Vic., Australia 37°43S 145°2E 128 A2
Kingsbury London, U.K. 51°34N 0°15W 125 A2
Kingscote Australia 35°40S 137°38E 282 C2
Kingscourt Ireland 53°54N 6°48W 166 C5
Kingsford N.S.W., Australia 33°56S 151°14E 139 B2
Kingsford Mich., U.S.A. 45°48N 88°4W 308 C9
Kingsford Smith, Sydney ✈ (SYD) Australia 33°57S 151°11E 139 B2
Kingsland U.S.A. 30°48N 81°41W 316 E8
Kingsport U.S.A. 36°33N 82°33W 315 C13
Kingston Ont., Canada 44°14N 76°30W 313 B8
Kingston Jamaica 17°55N 76°50W 320 a
Kingston N.Z. 45°20S 168°43E 285 F3
Kingston N.H., U.S.A. 42°56N 71°3W 313 D13
Kingston N.Y., U.S.A. 41°56N 73°59W 313 E11
Kingston Pa., U.S.A. 41°16N 75°54W 313 E9
Kingston R.I., U.S.A. 41°29N 71°30W 313 E13
Kingston Pk. U.S.A. 35°44N 115°55W 307 K11
Kingston South East Australia 36°51S 139°55E 282 D3
Kingston upon Hull U.K. 53°45N 0°21W 168 D7
Kingston upon Hull □ U.K. 53°45N 0°21W 168 D7
Kingston-upon-Thames □ U.K. 51°24N 0°17W 125 B2
Kingston Vale U.K. 51°25N 0°25W 125 B2
Kingstown = Dún Laoghaire Ireland 53°17N 6°8W 120 B3
Kingstown N.S.W., Australia 30°29S 151°6E 283 A9
Kingstown St. Vincent 13°10N 61°10W 323 n
Kingstree U.S.A. 33°40N 79°50W 316 B10
Kingsville Ont., Canada 42°2N 82°45W 312 D2
Kingsville Tex., U.S.A. 27°31N 97°52W 314 H6
Kingsway Canada 43°38N 79°32W 141 B1
Kingtechen = Jingdezhen China 29°20N 117°11E 229 C11
Kingunda Dem. Rep. of the Congo 6°36S 16°58E 265 D3
Kingussie U.K. 57°6N 4°2W 167 D4
Kingwood U.S.A. 30°2N 95°16W 314 F7
Kinhwa = Jinhua China 29°8N 119°38E 229 C12
Kınık Antalya, Turkey 36°20N 29°20E 205 E11
Kınık İzmir, Turkey 39°6N 27°24E 205 B9
Kinistino Canada 52°57N 105°2W 297 C7
Kinjirap Daban Asia 36°40N 75°25E 240 A4
Kinkala Congo 4°18S 14°49E 265 C2
Kinki □ Japan 33°45N 136°0E 223 D8
Kinkony, Farihin' Madag. 16°8S 45°50E 272 B2
Kinleith N.Z. 38°20S 175°56E 284 E4
Kinlochleven U.K. 56°43N 5°0W 167 E4
Kinmen = Chinmen Taiwan 24°26N 118°19E 225 a
Kinmount Canada 44°48N 78°45W 312 B6
Kinmundy U.S.A. 38°46N 88°51W 311 F8
Kinn Norway 61°34N 4°45E 164 C1
Kinna Sweden 57°32N 12°42E 163 G6
Kinnairds Hd. U.K. 57°43N 2°1W 167 D6
Kinnared Sweden 57°2N 13°7E 163 G7
Kinnarodden = Nordkinn Norway 71°8N 27°40E 160 A22
Kinnarp Sweden 58°5N 13°32E 163 F7
Kinneviken Sweden 58°35N 13°15E 163 F7
Kinngait Canada 64°14N 76°32W 295 E16
Kinniyai Sri Lanka 8°29N 81°11E 245 K5
Kino Nuevo Mexico 28°52N 112°3W 318 B2
Kinogitan Phil. 9°0N 124°48E 233 G5
Kinoje → Canada 52°8N 81°25W 298 B3
Kinokawa Japan 34°15N 135°20E 223 C7
Kinomoto Japan 35°30N 136°13E 223 B8
Kinoni Uganda 0°41S 30°28E 268 C3
Kinoosao Canada 57°5N 102°1W 297 B8
Kinross U.K. 56°13N 3°25W 167 E5
Kinsale Cork, Ireland 51°42N 8°31W 166 E3
Kinsale Montserrat 16°42N 62°13W 323 p
Kinsale, Old Hd. of Ireland 51°37N 8°33W 166 E3
Kinsaley Ireland 53°24N 6°11W 120 A2
Kinsarvik Norway 60°22N 6°43E 164 D3
Kinsha = Chang Jiang → China 31°48N 121°10E 229 B13
Kinshasa Dem. Rep. of the Congo 4°20S 15°15E 265 C3
Kinsley U.S.A. 37°55N 99°25W 308 G4
Kinsman U.S.A. 41°26N 80°35W 312 E4
Kinston Ala., U.S.A. 31°13N 86°10W 316 D3
Kinston N.C., U.S.A. 35°16N 77°35W 315 D16
Kintamani Indonesia 8°14S 115°19E 231 J18
Kintampo Ghana 8°5N 1°41W 263 D4
Kintap Indonesia 3°51S 115°13E 235 C5
Kintore U.K. 57°14N 2°20W 167 D6
Kintore Ra. Australia 23°15S 128°47E 278 D4
Kintshua Dem. Rep. of the Congo 4°27S 19°38E 265 C3
Kintyre U.K. 55°30N 5°35W 167 F3
Kintyre, Mull of U.K. 55°17N 5°47W 167 F3
Kinu-Gawa → Japan 35°36N 139°57E 223 B11
Kinushseo → Canada 55°15N 83°45W 298 A3
Kinuso Canada 55°20N 115°25W 296 B5
Kinvarra Ireland 53°8N 8°56W 166 C3
Kinwat India 19°38N 78°12E 244 E4
Kinyangiri Tanzania 4°25S 34°37E 268 C3
Kinyeti South Sudan 3°57N 32°54E 257 G3
Kinzia Dem. Rep. of the Congo 3°36S 18°26E 264 C3
Kinzig → Germany 48°36N 7°49E 179 G3
Kinzua U.S.A. 41°52N 78°58W 312 E6
Kioni Greece 38°27N 20°41E 207 C2
Kiosk Canada 46°6N 78°53W 298 C4
Kiowa Kans., U.S.A. 37°1N 98°29W 308 G4
Kiowa Okla., U.S.A. 34°43N 95°54W 314 D7
Kipahigan L. Canada 55°20N 101°55W 297 B8
Kipanga Tanzania 6°15S 35°20E 268 D4
Kipapa → U.S.A. 21°24N 158°1W 302 K13
Kiparissia Greece 37°15N 21°40E 204 D3
Kiparissiakos Kolpos Greece 37°25N 21°25E 204 D3
Kipawa, L. Canada 46°50N 79°0W 298 C4
Kipembawe Tanzania 7°38S 33°27E 268 D3
Kipengere Ra. Tanzania 9°12S 34°15E 269 D3
Kipili Tanzania 7°28S 30°32E 268 D3
Kipini Kenya 2°30S 40°32E 268 C5
Kipling Canada 50°6N 102°38W 297 C8
Kipling Heights Canada 43°43N 79°34W 141 A1
Kipnuk U.S.A. 59°56N 164°3W 303 G6
Kippure Ireland 53°11N 6°21W 166 C5
Kipseli Athens, Greece 112 a3
Kipushi Dem. Rep. of the Congo 11°48S 27°12E 269 E2
Kira Uganda 0°24N 32°38E 268 B3
Kira Panagia Greece 39°17N 24°4E 204 B6
Kirakira Solomon Is. 10°27S 161°56E 287 N11
Kirandul India 18°33N 81°10E 244 E5
Kirane Mali 15°20N 10°20W 262 B2
Kiranomena Madag. 18°17S 46°2E 272 B2
Kiraz Turkey 38°14N 28°13E 205 C10
Kirazlı Turkey 40°2N 26°41E 203 F10
Kirchhain Germany 50°47N 8°56E 178 E4
Kirchheim Germany 48°39N 9°27E 179 G5
Kirchheimbolanden Germany 49°40N 8°0E 179 F3
Kirchschlag Austria 47°30N 16°19E 181 D9
Kirchstockbach Germany 48°1N 11°40E 131 B3
Kirchtrudering Germany 48°7N 11°40E 131 B3
Kirdâsa Egypt 30°2N 31°6E 251 H2
Kirdimi Chad 18°11N 18°31E 259 E3
Kireç Turkey 39°33N 28°22E 205 B10
Kirensk Russia 57°50N 107°55E 215 D11
Kirghiz Range Asia 42°40N 73°40E 217 D8
Kirghizia = Kyrgyzstan ■ Asia 42°0N 75°0E 217 D9
Kirgiz-Kulak = Chirchiq Uzbekistan 41°29N 69°35E 217 D7
Kirgiziya Steppe Eurasia 50°0N 55°0E 187 E10
Kiri Dem. Rep. of the Congo 1°29S 19°0E 264 C3
Kiri Buru India 22°0N 85°0E 244 D7
Kiribati ■ Pac. Oc. 3°0S 180°0E 277 A15
Kırıkhan Turkey 36°31N 36°21E 250 B7
Kirikiri Nigeria 6°26N 3°18E 124 B1
Kırıkkale Turkey 39°51N 33°32E 212 C5
Kirikopuni N.Z. 35°50S 174°1E 284 B3
Kirillov Russia 59°49N 38°24E 188 C10
Kirin = Jilin China 43°44N 126°30E 227 C14
Kirindi Oya → Sri Lanka 6°15N 81°20E 245 L5
Kirinyaga = Kenya, Mt. Kenya 0°10S 37°18E 268 C4
Kirirom △ Cambodia 11°18N 104°5E 237 G5
Kirishi Russia 59°28N 32°0E 188 C7
Kirishima Japan 31°44N 130°46E 222 F2
Kirishima Yaku △ Japan 31°24N 130°50E 221 J5
Kirishima-Yama Japan 31°58N 130°55E 222 F2
Kiritimati Kiribati 1°58N 157°27W 289 G12
Kiriwina I. Papua N. G. 8°40S 151°6E 286 E6
Kırka Turkey 39°17N 30°33E 205 B12
Kırkağaç Turkey 39°8N 27°40E 205 B9
Kirkby U.K. 53°30N 2°54W 168 D5
Kirkby-in-Ashfield U.K. 53°6N 1°14W 168 D6
Kirkby Lonsdale U.K. 54°12N 2°36W 168 C5
Kirkby Stephen U.K. 54°29N 2°21W 168 C5
Kirkcaldy U.K. 56°7N 3°9W 167 E5
Kirkcudbright U.K. 54°50N 4°2W 167 G4
Kirke Værløse Denmark 55°47N 12°19E 118 A1
Kirkehamn Norway 58°14N 6°31E 164 F3
Kirkenær Norway 60°27N 12°3E 164 D9
Kirkenes Norway 69°40N 30°5E 160 B24
Kirkfield Canada 44°34N 78°59W 312 B6
Kirkhill U.K. 55°50N 3°13W 121 B2
Kirkintilloch U.K. 55°56N 4°8W 167 F4
Kirkjubæjarklaustur Iceland 63°47N 18°4W 155 D8
Kirkkonummi Finland 60°8N 24°26E 188 B3
Kirkland Ill., U.S.A. 42°6N 88°51W 311 B8
Kirkland Wash., U.S.A. 47°40N 122°12W 306 C4
Kirkland Lake Canada 48°9N 80°2W 298 C3
Kırklareli Turkey 41°44N 27°15E 203 E11
Kırklareli □ Turkey 41°45N 27°15E 203 E11
Kirklin U.S.A. 40°12N 86°22W 311 D10
Kirkliston U.K. 55°57N 3°24W 121 B1
Kirkliston Ra. N.Z. 44°25S 170°34E 285 E5
Kirknewton U.K. 55°53N 3°25W 121 B1
Kirknitz = Cerknica Slovenia 45°48N 14°21E 199 C11
Kirkpatrick, Mt. Antarctica 84°20S 166°25E 151 E11
Kirksville U.S.A. 40°12N 92°35W 310 D4
Kirkūk Iraq 35°30N 44°21E 213 E11
Kirkwall U.K. 58°59N 2°58W 167 C6
Kirkwood Eastern Cape, S. Africa 33°22S 25°15E 270 D4
Kirkwood Mo., U.S.A. 38°35N 90°24W 310 F6
Kirlampudi India 17°12N 82°12E 244 F6
Kirmasti = Mustafakemalpaşa Turkey 40°2N 28°24E 203 F12
Kirn Germany 49°47N 7°26E 179 F3
Kirobası Turkey 36°43N 33°52E 250 B4
Kirov Kaluga, Russia 54°3N 34°20E 188 E8
Kirov Kirov, Russia 58°35N 49°40E 186 C8
Kirov Palace of Culture Russia 59°55N 30°16E 137 B1
Kirovabad = Gäncä Azerbaijan 40°45N 46°20E 191 K8
Kirovakan = Vanadzor Armenia 40°48N 44°30E 191 K7
Kirovo = Kirovohrad Ukraine 48°35N 32°20E 189 H7
Kirovo-Chepetsk Russia 58°28N 50°0E 186 C9
Kirovograd = Kirovohrad Ukraine 48°35N 32°20E 189 H7
Kirovohrad Ukraine 48°35N 32°20E 189 H7
Kirovohrad □ Ukraine 48°30N 31°30E 189 H6
Kirovsk Russia 67°32N 33°41E 186 A5
Kirovskiy = Balpyq Bī Kazakhstan 44°52N 78°12E 217 D9
Kirovskiy Astrakhan, Russia 45°51N 48°11E 191 H9
Kirovskiy Kamchatka, Russia 54°27N 155°42E 215 D16
Kirovskiy Primorsk, Russia 45°7N 133°30E 220 B6
Kirriemuir U.K. 56°41N 3°1W 167 E5
Kirsanov Russia 52°35N 42°40E 190 D6
Kırşehir Turkey 39°14N 34°5E 212 C6
Kirtachi Niger 12°52N 2°30E 263 C5
Kīrteh Afghan. 32°15N 63°0E 240 B1
Kirthar △ Pakistan 25°45N 67°30E 242 F2
Kirthar Range Pakistan 27°0N 67°0E 242 F2
Kirtland U.S.A. 36°44N 108°21W 305 H9
Kiruna Sweden 67°52N 20°15E 160 C19
Kirundu Dem. Rep. of the Congo 0°50S 25°35E 264 C5
Kirya Russia 55°8N 46°55E 190 C8
Kiryat Anavim Israel 31°49N 35°6E 123 B1
Kiryat Ha Yovel Israel 31°46N 35°10E 123 B1
Kiryū Japan 36°24N 139°20E 223 A11
Kisa Sweden 58°0N 15°39E 163 G9
Kisaga Tanzania 4°30S 34°23E 268 C3
Kisalföld Hungary 47°30N 17°0E 182 C2
Kisambo Dem. Rep. of the Congo 6°25S 18°14E 265 D3
Kisandji Dem. Rep. of the Congo 6°18S 19°16E 265 D3
Kisanga Dem. Rep. of the Congo 2°30N 26°35E 268 B2
Kisangani Dem. Rep. of the Congo 0°35N 25°15E 268 B2
Kisantu Dem. Rep. of the Congo 5°7S 15°5E 265 D3
Kisar Indonesia 8°5S 127°10E 231 F7
Kisaran Indonesia 3°0N 99°37E 234 B1
Kisarawe Tanzania 6°53S 39°0E 268 D4
Kisarazu Japan 35°23N 139°55E 223 B11
Kisbér Hungary 47°30N 18°2E 182 C3
Kiselevsk Russia 54°5N 86°39E 217 B11
Kish = Qeys Iran 26°32N 53°58E 249 A6
Kishanganga → Pakistan 34°18N 73°28E 243 B5
Kishanganj India 26°3N 88°14E 241 B2
Kishangarh Raj., India 26°34N 74°52E 242 F6
Kishangarh Raj., India 27°50N 70°30E 242 F4
Kishb, Ḩarrat al Si. Arabia 22°30N 40°15E 248 B3
Kishi Nigeria 9°1N 3°52E 263 D5
Kishinev = Chişinău Moldova 47°2N 28°50E 183 C13
Kishiwada Japan 34°28N 135°22E 223 C7
Kishkareny = Lazo Moldova 47°33N 28°2E 183 C13

Kishkeneköl Kazakhstan 53°38N 72°20E 217 B8
Kishorganj Bangla. 24°26N 90°40E 241 C3
Kishtwar India 33°20N 75°48E 242 C6
Kishwaukee → U.S.A. 42°12N 89°8W 310 B7
Kisielice Poland 53°36N 19°16E 184 E6
Kisigo △ Tanzania 6°27S 34°17E 268 D3
Kisii Kenya 0°40S 34°45E 268 C3
Kisiju Tanzania 7°23S 39°19E 268 D4
Kısıklı Turkey 41°1N 29°2E 122 B2
Kisir Turkey 41°0N 43°5E 213 B10
Kisizi Uganda 1°0S 29°58E 268 C2
Kiska I. U.S.A. 51°59N 177°30E 303 L2
Kiskomárom = Zalakomár Hungary 46°33N 17°10E 182 D2
Kiskőrei-víztároló Hungary 47°31N 20°36E 182 C5
Kiskőrös Hungary 46°37N 19°20E 182 D4
Kiskundorozsma Hungary 46°16N 20°5E 182 D5
Kiskunfélegyháza Hungary 46°42N 19°53E 182 D4
Kiskunhalas Hungary 46°28N 19°37E 182 D4
Kiskunmajsa Hungary 46°30N 19°48E 182 D4
Kiskunsági △ Hungary 46°39N 19°30E 182 D4
Kislovodsk Russia 43°50N 42°45E 191 J6
Kismaayo Somalia 0°22S 42°32E 267 E5
Kismayu △ Somalia 1°25N 41°30E 267 D5
Kiso-Gawa → Japan 35°20N 136°45E 223 B8
Kiso-Sammyaku Japan 35°45N 137°45E 223 B9
Kisofukushima Japan 35°52N 137°43E 223 B9
Kisoro Uganda 1°17S 29°48E 268 C2
Kispest Hungary 47°27N 19°8E 117 B2
Kissamos = Kasteli Greece 35°29N 23°38E 207 E4
Kissamos, Kolpos Greece 35°30N 23°38E 207 E4
Kissidougou Guinea 9°5N 10°5W 262 D2
Kissimmee U.S.A. 28°18N 81°24W 317 G8
Kissimmee → U.S.A. 27°9N 80°52W 317 H8
Kissimmee, L. U.S.A. 27°55N 81°17W 317 H8
Kississing L. Canada 55°10N 101°20W 297 B8
Kissónerga Cyprus 34°49N 32°24E 207 F8
Kissu, J. Sudan 21°37N 25°10E 256 C2
Kista Sweden 59°24N 17°57E 139 A1
Kistanje Croatia 43°58N 15°55E 199 E12
Kistna = Krishna → India 15°57N 80°59E 245 G5
Kisújszállás Hungary 47°12N 20°50E 182 C5
Kisuki Japan 35°17N 132°54E 222 B4
Kisumu Kenya 0°3S 34°45E 268 C3
Kisvárda Hungary 48°14N 22°4E 182 B7
Kiswani Tanzania 4°5S 37°57E 268 C4
Kiswere Tanzania 9°27S 39°30E 269 D4
Kit Carson U.S.A. 38°46N 102°48W 304 G12
Kita Ōsaka, Japan 34°41N 135°30E 133 A2
Kita Tōkyō, Japan 35°44N 139°44E 140 A3
Kita Mali 13°5N 9°25W 262 C3
Kita-Ura Japan 36°0N 140°34E 223 B12
Kitaibaraki Japan 36°50N 140°45E 221 F10
Kitakami Japan 39°20N 141°10E 220 E10
Kitakami-Gawa → Japan 38°25N 141°19E 220 E10
Kitakami-Sammyaku Japan 39°30N 141°30E 220 E10
Kitakata Japan 37°39N 139°52E 220 F9
Kitakyūshū Japan 33°50N 130°50E 222 D2
Kitale Kenya 1°0N 35°0E 268 B4
Kitami Japan 43°48N 143°54E 220 C11
Kitami-Sammyaku Japan 44°22N 142°43E 220 B11
Kitangiri, L. Tanzania 4°5S 34°20E 268 C3
Kitanglad △ Phil. 8°57N 124°21E 233 G5
Kitano Hana Iwo Jima 24°49N 141°20E 288 b
Kitano-Kaikyō Japan 34°17N 134°58E 222 C6
Kitaotao Phil. 7°40N 125°1E 233 H5
Kitava I. Papua N. G. 8°40S 151°20E 286 E6
Kitaya Tanzania 10°38S 40°8E 269 E5
Kitazawa Japan 35°39N 139°40E 140 B3
Kitcharao Phil. 9°27N 125°36E 233 G5
Kitchener Canada 43°27N 80°29W 312 C4
Kitee Finland 62°5N 30°8E 188 A6
Kitega = Gitega Burundi 3°26S 29°56E 268 C2
Kitengo Dem. Rep. of the Congo 7°26S 24°8E 265 D4
Kitgum Uganda 3°17N 32°52E 268 B3
Kíthira = Kythira Greece 36°8N 23°0E 204 E5
Kíthnos = Kythnos Greece 37°26N 24°27E 204 D6
Kiti Cyprus 34°50N 33°34E 207 F9
Kiti, C. Cyprus 34°48N 33°36E 207 F9
Kitimat Canada 54°3N 128°38W 296 C3
Kitinen → Finland 67°14N 27°27E 160 C22
Kitiyab Sudan 17°13N 33°35E 257 D3
Kitombe Dem. Rep. of the Congo 5°22S 18°59E 265 D3
Kitridge Pt. Barbados 13°9N 59°25W 323 r
Kítros Greece 40°22N 22°34E 202 F6
Kitsman Ukraine 48°26N 25°46E 183 B10
Kitsuki Japan 33°25N 131°37E 222 D3
Kittakittaooloo, L. Australia 28°3S 138°14E 281 D2
Kittanning U.S.A. 40°49N 79°31W 312 F5
Kittatinny Mt. U.S.A. 41°19N 74°39W 313 F10
Kittery U.S.A. 43°5N 70°45W 313 C14
Kittilä Finland 67°40N 24°51E 160 C21
Kitui Kenya 1°17S 38°0E 268 C4
Kitwanga Canada 55°6N 128°4W 296 B3
Kitwe Zambia 12°54S 28°13E 269 E2
Kityang = Jieyang China 23°35N 116°21E 229 F11
Kitzbühel Austria 47°27N 12°24E 180 D5
Kitzbühler Alpen Austria 47°20N 12°20E 180 D5
Kitzingen Germany 49°44N 10°9E 179 F6
Kiukiang = Jiujiang China 29°42N 115°58E 229 C10
Kiunga Papua N. G. 6°7S 141°18E 286 D1
Kiunga Marine △ Kenya 2°1S 41°14E 268 C5
Kivalina U.S.A. 67°44N 164°33W 303 C6
Kivarli India 24°33N 72°46E 242 G5
Kivertsi Ukraine 50°50N 25°28E 177 C13
Kividhes Cyprus 34°46N 32°51E 207 F8
Kivik Sweden 55°41N 14°13E 163 J8
Kivistö Finland 60°18N 24°50E 121 B2
Kivotos Greece 40°13N 21°26E 202 F5
Kivu, L. Dem. Rep. of the Congo 1°48S 29°0E 268 C2
Kiwai I. Papua N. G. 8°35S 143°30E 286 E2
Kiwirrkurra Australia 22°49S 127°45E 278 D4
Kiwirrkurra © Australia 22°49S 127°45E 278 D4
Kiyev = Kyyiv Ukraine 50°30N 30°28E 177 C16
Kiyevskoye Vdkhr. = Kyyivske Vdskh. Ukraine 51°0N 30°25E 177 C16
Kıyıköy Turkey 41°38N 28°5E 203 E12
Kiza → Japan 34°37N 135°27E 133 B1
Kizel Russia 59°3N 57°40E 186 C10
Kizhi, Ostrov Russia 62°4N 35°13E 188 B8
Kiziba-Baluba △ Congo 11°50S 28°0E 269 E2
Kizinga Rwanda 1°46S 30°23E 268 C3
Kızıl Adalar Turkey 40°52N 29°5E 203 F13
Kızıl Dağ Turkey 36°19N 35°57E 250 B6
Kızıl Irmak → Turkey 41°44N 35°58E 212 B6
Kizil Jilga China 35°26N 78°50E 243 B8
Kizil Yurt Russia 43°13N 46°54E 191 J8
Kızılcabölük Turkey 37°37N 29°1E 205 D11
Kızılcadağ Turkey 37°1N 29°58E 205 D11
Kızılcahamam Turkey 40°30N 32°30E 212 B5
Kızıldağ △ Turkey 38°5N 31°20E 246 B1
Kızılhisar Turkey 37°32N 29°17E 212 D3
Kızılırmak Turkey 40°21N 33°59E 212 B5
Kızılkaya Turkey 37°18N 30°27E 205 D12
Kızılören Turkey 38°15N 30°10E 205 C12
Kızıltepe Turkey 37°12N 40°35E 213 D9
Kızıltoprak Turkey 40°58N 29°3E 122 C2
Kizimkazi Tanzania 6°28S 39°30E 268 D4
Kizlyar Russia 43°51N 46°40E 191 J8
Kizuri Japan 34°38N 135°34E 133 B2
Kizyl-Arvat = Serdar Turkmenistan 39°4N 56°23E 247 B8
Kjellerup Denmark 56°17N 9°25E 163 H3
Kjellmyra Norway 60°39N 12°1E 164 D9
Kjelsås Norway 59°57N 10°47E 133 A3
Kjølen Norway 62°3N 8°45E 164 C5
Kjölur Iceland 64°50N 19°25W 155 C7
Kjósarsýsla Iceland 64°15N 21°30W 155 C5
Kladanj Bos.-H. 44°14N 18°42E 182 F3
Kladnica Serbia 43°23N 20°2E 202 C4
Kladno Czech Rep. 50°10N 14°7E 180 A7
Kladovo Serbia 44°36N 22°33E 202 B6
Kladow Germany 52°27N 13°9E 115 B1
Klæbu Norway 63°18N 10°29E 164 A7
Klaeng Thailand 12°47N 101°39E 236 F3
Klagan Malaysia 5°58N 117°27E 235 A5
Klagenfurt Austria 46°38N 14°20E 180 E7
Klaipėda Lithuania 55°43N 21°10E 184 C8
Klaipėda □ Lithuania 55°43N 21°7E 184 C8
Klaksvík Færoe Is. 62°14N 6°35W 160 E9
Klamath U.S.A. 41°33N 124°5W 304 F1
Klamath Falls U.S.A. 42°13N 121°46W 304 E3
Klamath Mts. U.S.A. 41°50N 123°20W 304 F2
Klamono Indonesia 1°8S 131°30E 231 E8
Klampenborg Denmark 55°46N 12°35E 112 B3
Klampo Indonesia 0°7N 116°58E 235 B5
Klang Malaysia 3°2N 101°26E 237 L3
Klangklang Burma 22°41N 93°26E 241 D4
Klanjec Croatia 46°3N 15°45E 199 B12
Klappan → Canada 58°0N 129°43W 296 B3
Klara = Trysilelva → Norway 61°2N 12°35E 164 C9
Klarälven → Sweden 59°23N 13°32E 162 E7
Klässbol Sweden 59°33N 12°45E 162 E6
Klaten Indonesia 7°43S 110°36E 235 D4
Klatovy Czech Rep. 49°23N 13°18E 180 B6
Klausenburg = Cluj-Napoca Romania 46°47N 23°38E 183 D8
Klawer S. Africa 31°44S 18°36E 270 D2
Klawock U.S.A. 55°33N 133°6W 303 J14
Klazienaveen Neths. 52°44N 7°0E 170 B6
Klé Mali 12°0N 6°28W 262 C3
Klečany Czech Rep. 50°10N 14°24E 135 A2
Klecko Poland 52°38N 17°25E 185 F4
Kleczew Poland 52°22N 18°9E 185 F5
Kledering Austria 48°8N 16°26E 142 B2
Kleena Kleene Canada 52°0N 124°59W 296 C4
Klein Bonaire Bonaire 12°9N 68°18W 322 h
Klein Jukskei → S. Africa 26°5S 27°57E 123 A1
Klein-Karas Namibia 27°33S 18°7E 270 C2
Klein-Schlatten = Zlatna Romania 46°8N 23°11E 183 D8
Kleinbegin S. Africa 28°54S 21°40E 270 C3
Kleinmachnow Germany 52°24N 13°14E 115 B2
Kleinschönebeck Germany 52°29N 13°42E 115 B5
Klekovača Bos.-H. 44°25N 16°32E 199 D13
Klembivka Ukraine 48°23N 28°25E 183 B13
Klemetsrud Norway 59°50N 10°51E 133 A4
Klender Indonesia 6°12S 106°54E 122 B2
Klenoec Macedonia 41°32N 20°49E 202 E4
Klenovec Slovak Rep. 48°36N 19°54E 181 C12
Klerksdorp S. Africa 26°53S 26°38E 270 C4
Kleszczele Poland 52°35N 23°19E 185 F10
Kletnya Russia 53°23N 33°12E 188 F7
Kletsk = Klyetsk Belarus 53°5N 26°45E 177 B14
Kletskiy Russia 49°16N 43°11E 191 F6
Kleve Germany 51°47N 6°7E 178 D2
Kličany Czech Rep. 50°11N 14°25E 135 A2
Klickitat U.S.A. 45°49N 121°9W 304 D3
Klickitat → U.S.A. 45°42N 121°17W 306 E5
Klidhes Cyprus 35°42N 34°36E 207 E10
Klimovichi Belarus 53°36N 32°0E 188 F6
Klin Russia 56°20N 36°48E 188 D9
Klinaklini → Canada 51°21N 125°40W 296 C3
Klinë Kosovo 42°37N 20°35E 202 D4
Klintehamn Sweden 57°24N 18°12E 163 G12
Klintsy Russia 52°50N 32°10E 189 F7
Klip → S. Africa 27°3S 29°3E 271 C4
Klipdale S. Africa 34°19S 19°57E 270 D2
Klippan Sweden 56°8N 13°10E 163 H7
Klipplaat S. Africa 33°1S 24°22E 270 D3
Klipriviersberg Nature Reserve S. Africa 26°16S 28°2E 123 B2
Klishkivtsi Ukraine 48°26N 26°16E 183 B11
Klisura Bulgaria 42°40N 24°28E 203 D8
Kljajićevo Serbia 45°45N 19°17E 182 E4
Ključ Bos.-H. 44°32N 16°48E 199 D13
Kłobuck Poland 50°55N 18°55E 185 H5
Klockestrand Sweden 62°53N 17°55E 162 B11
Kłodawa Poland 52°15N 18°55E 185 F5
Kłodzko Poland 50°28N 16°38E 185 H3
Klofta Norway 60°4N 11°10E 164 D8
Klondike Canada 64°0N 139°26W 294 E4
Klondike Goldrush △ U.S.A. 59°27N 135°19W 303 G14
Klong Wang Chao △ Thailand 16°20N 99°9E 236 D2
Klos Albania 41°28N 20°10E 202 E4
Klosterneuburg Austria 48°18N 16°19E 142 A1
Klosters Switz. 46°52N 9°52E 179 J5
Klötze Germany 52°37N 11°10E 178 C7
Klouto Togo 6°57N 0°44E 263 D5
Klövsjö Sweden 62°32N 14°11E 162 B8
Kluane △ Canada 60°45N 139°30W 296 A1
Kluane L. Canada 61°15N 138°40W 294 E4
Kluang Malaysia 2°3N 103°18E 237 L4
Kluczbork Poland 50°58N 18°12E 185 H5
Klukhori = Karachayevsk Russia 43°50N 41°55E 191 J5
Klukwan U.S.A. 59°24N 135°54W 296 B1
Klungkung Indonesia 8°32S 115°24E 231 K18
Klyetsk Belarus 53°5N 26°45E 177 B14
Klyuchevskaya, Sopka Russia 55°50N 160°30E 215 D17
Klyuchi Russia 56°18N 160°51E 215 D17
Knaben Norway 58°40N 7°4E 164 F4
Knappavellir Iceland 63°54N 16°36W 155 D10
Knäred Sweden 56°31N 13°19E 163 H7
Knaresborough U.K. 54°1N 1°28W 168 C6
Knarvik Norway 60°32N 5°19E 164 D2
Knee L. Man., Canada 55°3N 94°45W 298 A1
Knee L. Sask., Canada 55°51N 107°0W 297 B7
Kneïss, Îs. Tunisia 34°22N 10°18E 258 B2
Knesset Jerusalem 123 b1
Knezha Bulgaria 43°30N 24°5E 203 C8
Knight I. U.S.A. 60°21N 147°45W 303 F11
Knight Inlet Canada 50°45N 125°40W 296 C3
Knighton U.K. 52°21N 3°3W 169 E4
Knights Ferry U.S.A. 37°50N 120°40W 306 H6
Knights Landing U.S.A. 38°48N 121°43W 306 G5
Knightsbridge London, U.K. 125 c2
Knightstown U.S.A. 39°48N 85°32W 311 E11
Knin Croatia 44°3N 16°17E 199 D13
Knislinge Sweden 56°12N 14°5E 163 H8
Knittelfeld Austria 47°13N 14°51E 180 D7
Knivsta Sweden 59°43N 17°48E 162 E11
Knjaževac Serbia 43°35N 22°18E 202 C6
Knob, C. Australia 34°32S 119°16E 279 F2
Knob Lake = Kawawachikamach Canada 54°48N 66°50W 299 B6
Knob Noster U.S.A. 38°46N 93°33W 310 F3
Knock Ireland 53°48N 8°55W 166 C3
Knockmealdown Mts. Ireland 52°14N 7°56W 166 D4
Knokke-Heist Belgium 51°21N 3°17E 170 C3
Knossos Greece 35°16N 25°10E 207 D6
Knowlton Canada 45°13N 72°31W 313 A12
Knox U.S.A. 41°18N 86°37W 311 C10
Knox Coast Antarctica 66°30S 108°0E 151 C8
Knoxville Ga., U.S.A. 32°47N 83°59W 316 C6
Knoxville Ill., U.S.A. 40°55N 90°17W 310 D6
Knoxville Iowa, U.S.A. 41°19N 93°6W 310 C4
Knoxville Pa., U.S.A. 41°57N 77°27W 312 E7
Knoxville Tenn., U.S.A. 35°58N 83°55W 315 D13
Knud Rasmussen Land Greenland 78°0N 60°0W 154 B4
Knysna S. Africa 34°2S 23°2E 270 D3
Knyszyn Poland 53°20N 22°56E 184 E9
Ko Kha Thailand 18°11N 99°24E 236 C2
Kō-Saki Japan 34°5N 129°13E 222 C1
Ko Tarutao △ Thailand 6°31N 99°26E 237 J2
Ko Yao Thailand 8°7N 98°35E 237 a
Koartac = Quaqtaq Canada 60°55N 69°40W 295 E18
Koba Aru, Indonesia 6°37S 134°37E 231 F8
Koba Bangka, Indonesia 2°26S 106°14E 234 C3
Kőbánya Hungary 47°28N 19°9E 117 B2
Kobarid Slovenia 46°15N 13°30E 199 B10
Kobayashi Japan 31°56N 130°59E 222 F2
Kobbegem Belgium 50°55N 4°15E 116 A1
Kobdo = Hovd □ Mongolia 48°2N 91°37E 217 C12
Kōbe Japan 34°41N 135°13E 223 C7
Kobelyaky Ukraine 49°11N 34°9E 189 H8
København Denmark 55°40N 12°26E 118 A2
København ✈ (CPH) Denmark 55°37N 12°39E 118 B3
Kobenni Mauritania 15°58N 9°24W 262 B3
Kōbi-Sho E. China Sea 25°56N 123°41E 221 M1
Koblenz Germany 50°21N 7°36E 179 E3
Kobo Dem. Rep. of the Congo 4°54S 17°9E 265 C3
Kobo Ethiopia 12°2N 39°56E 257 E4
Kobryn Belarus 52°15N 24°22E 177 B13
Kobuchizawa Japan 35°52N 138°19E 223 B10
Kobuk U.S.A. 66°55N 156°52W 303 C8
Kobuk → U.S.A. 66°54N 160°38W 303 C7
Kobuk Valley △ U.S.A. 67°0N 160°0W 303 C7
Kobuleti Georgia 41°55N 41°45E 191 K5
Kobyletska Polyana Ukraine 48°3N 24°4E 183 B9
Kobylin Poland 51°43N 17°12E 185 G4
Kobylisy Czech Rep. 50°7N 14°26E 135 B2
Kobyłka Poland 52°20N 21°10E 143 A3
Kobylkino Russia 54°8N 43°56E 190 C6
Koca → Turkey 40°8N 27°57E 203 F11
Kocabaş Turkey 37°49N 29°20E 205 D11
Kocaeli Turkey 40°45N 29°50E 203 F13
Kocaeli □ Turkey 40°45N 29°55E 203 F13
Kočane Serbia 43°12N 21°52E 202 C5
Kočani Macedonia 41°55N 22°25E 202 E6
Koçarlı Turkey 37°45N 27°43E 205 D9
Koceljevo Serbia 44°28N 19°50E 202 B3
Kočevje Slovenia 45°39N 14°50E 199 C11
Kocgiri = Zara Turkey 39°58N 37°43E 212 C7
Koch Bihar India 26°22N 89°29E 241 B2
Kochas India 25°15N 83°56E 243 G10
Kocher → Germany 49°13N 9°12E 179 F5
Kochi India 9°58N 76°20E 245 K3
Kōchi Japan 33°30N 133°35E 222 D5
Kōchi □ Japan 33°40N 133°30E 222 D5
Kochiu = Gejiu China 23°20N 103°10E 228 F4
Kochkor Kyrgyzstan 42°13N 75°46E 217 D9
Kochubey Russia 44°23N 46°32E 191 H8
Kock Poland 51°38N 22°27E 185 G9
Kodaira Japan 35°43N 139°28E 140 A1
Kodala India 19°38N 84°57E 244 E7
Kodanaka Japan 35°34N 139°37E 140 B2
Kodarma India 24°28N 85°36E 243 G11
Koddiyar B. Sri Lanka 8°33N 81°15E 245 K5
Kode Sweden 57°57N 11°51E 163 G5
Kodenmacho Tokyo, Japan 140 a5
Kodi Dem. Rep. of the Congo 3°34S 22°12E 264 C4
Kodiak U.S.A. 57°47N 152°24W 303 H9
Kodiak I. U.S.A. 57°30N 152°45W 303 H9
Kodikkarai = Point Calimere India 10°17N 79°49E 245 J4
Kodinar India 20°46N 70°46E 242 J4
Kodinsk Russia 58°40N 99°10E 215 D10
Kodlipet India 12°48N 75°53E 245 H2
Kodok South Sudan 9°53N 32°7E 257 F3
Kodori → Georgia 42°47N 41°10E 191 J5
Kodoro Dem. Rep. of the Congo 1°16N 20°6E 264 B4
Kodungallur = Cranganore India 10°13N 76°13E 245 J3
Kodyma Ukraine 48°6N 29°7E 183 B14
Koedoesberge S. Africa 32°40S 20°11E 270 D3
Koekelberg Belgium 50°52N 4°20E 116 A1
Koes Namibia 26°0S 19°15E 270 C2
Kofarnihon Tajikistan 38°33N 69°1E 217 E7
Kofçaz Turkey 41°58N 27°12E 203 E11
Koffiefontein S. Africa 29°30S 25°0E 270 C4
Kofiau Indonesia 1°11S 129°50E 231 E7
Köflach Austria 47°4N 15°5E 180 D8
Koforidua Ghana 6°3N 0°17W 263 D4
Kōfu Japan 35°40N 138°30E 223 B10
Koga Fukuoka, Japan 33°45N 130°25E 222 D2
Koga Ibaraki, Japan 36°11N 139°43E 223 A11
Kogaluc → Canada 56°12N 61°44W 299 A7
Kogan Australia 27°2S 150°40E 281 D5
Koganei Japan 35°42N 139°31E 140 A2
Kogarah Australia 33°57S 151°8E 139 B1
Køge Denmark 55°27N 12°11E 163 J6
Køge Bugt Denmark 55°34N 12°24E 163 J6
Kogi □ Nigeria 7°45N 6°45E 263 D6
Kogin Baba Nigeria 7°55N 11°35E 263 D7
Koh Eq. Guin. 1°5N 9°42E 264 B1
Kogon Uzbekistan 39°43N 64°33E 216 E6
Koh-i-Khurd Afghan. 33°30N 65°59E 242 C1
Koh-i-Maran Pakistan 29°18N 66°50E 242 E2
Koh Ker Cambodia 13°47N 104°32E 236 F5
Koh Wai Thailand 11°54N 102°25E 237 H4
Kohala Mts. U.S.A. 20°5N 155°45W 302 C6
Kohat Pakistan 33°40N 71°29E 242 C4
Kohima India 25°35N 94°10E 241 C5
Kohkīluyeh va Būyer Aḩmadi □ Iran 31°30N 50°30E 247 D6
Kohler Ra. Antarctica 77°0S 110°0W 151 D15
Kohlfurt = Węgliniec Poland 51°18N 15°10E 185 G2
Kohlu Pakistan 29°54N 69°15E 242 E3
Kohtla-Järve Estonia 59°20N 27°20E 188 C4
Kohukohu N.Z. 35°22S 173°38E 284 B2
Kohylnyk → Ukraine 45°49N 29°40E 183 E14
Koi Sanjaq Iraq 36°5N 44°38E 213 D11
Koidu S. Leone 8°38N 10°59W 262 D2
Koihoa India 8°12N 93°29E 245 K11
Koilkuntla India 15°14N 78°19E 245 G4
Koillismaa Finland 65°44N 28°36E 160 D23
Koimbani Comoros Is. 11°37S 43°21E 272 a
Koin N. Korea 40°28N 126°18E 224 D14
Koinare Bulgaria 43°21N 24°8E 203 C8
Koindu S. Leone 8°26N 10°19W 262 D2
Koivisto = Primorsk Russia 60°22N 28°37E 188 B5
Koivupää Finland 60°18N 24°53E 121 B2
Koja Indonesia 6°8S 106°52E 122 A2
Koja Utara Indonesia 6°5S 106°53E 122 A2
Kojetín Czech Rep. 49°21N 17°20E 181 B10
Kojō N. Korea 38°58N 127°58E 224 C3
Kojonup Australia 33°48S 117°10E 279 F2
Kojūr Iran 36°23N 51°43E 247 B6
Kokand = Qŭqon Uzbekistan 40°31N 70°56E 217 D8
Kokang Burma 23°45N 98°30E 228 F2
Kokas Indonesia 2°42S 132°26E 231 E8
Kokava Slovak Rep. 48°35N 19°50E 181 C12
Kokcha → Afghan. 37°9N 69°24E 240 A3
Kokchetav = Kökshetaū Kazakhstan 53°20N 69°25E 217 B7
Köke'e State Park △ U.S.A. 22°6N 159°40W 302 A2
Kokemäenjoki → Finland 61°32N 21°44E 188 B1
Kokerite Guyana 7°12N 59°35W 329 B6
Kokhav Ya'akov West Bank 31°53N 35°14E 123 A2
Kokhma Russia 56°57N 41°8E 190 B5
Koki Senegal 15°30N 15°59W 262 B1
Kokiu = Gejiu China 23°20N 103°10E 228 F4
Kokkilai Sri Lanka 9°0N 80°57E 245 K5
Kokkina Cyprus 35°11N 32°36E 207 E8
Kokkola Finland 63°50N 23°8E 160 E20
Koko Nigeria 11°28N 4°29E 263 C5
Koko Head U.S.A. 21°16N 157°43W 302 K14
Koko Kyunzu Burma 14°7N 93°22E 245 G11
Koko Nur = Qinghai Hu China 36°40N 100°10E 218 D9
Kokobunji Japan 35°42N 139°27E 140 A1
Kokobunji-Temple Japan 35°44N 139°55E 140 A4
Kokoda Papua N. G. 8°54S 147°47E 286 E4
Kokologo Burkina Faso 12°11N 1°53W 262 C4
Kokolopozo Ivory C. 5°8N 6°5W 262 D3
Kokomo U.S.A. 40°29N 86°8W 311 D10
Kokopo Papua N. G. 4°22S 152°19E 286 C7
Kokoro Niger 14°12N 0°55E 263 C5
Koksan N. Korea 38°46N 126°40E 224 C3
Kökshetaū Kazakhstan 53°20N 69°25E 217 B7
Koksoak → Canada 58°30N 68°10W 295 F18
Kokstad S. Africa 30°32S 29°29E 271 D4
Köktal Kazakhstan 44°8N 79°48E 217 D9
Kokubu = Kirishima Japan 31°44N 130°46E 222 F2
Kokyar China 37°23N 77°10E 217 E9
Kola Indonesia 5°35S 134°30E 231 F8
Kola Russia 68°45N 33°8E 160 B25
Kola Pen. = Kolskiy Poluostrov Russia 67°30N 38°0E 186 A6
Kolachel India 8°10N 77°15E 245 K3
Kolachi → Pakistan 27°8N 67°2E 242 F2
Kolahoi India 34°12N 75°22E 243 B6
Kolahun Liberia 8°15N 10°4W 262 D2
Kolaka Indonesia 4°3S 121°46E 231 E6
Kolar India 13°12N 78°15E 245 H4
Kolar Gold Fields India 12°58N 78°16E 245 H4
Kolarängen Sweden 59°16N 18°10E 139 B3
Kolaras India 25°14N 77°36E 242 G6
Kolari Finland 67°20N 23°48E 160 C20
Kolarovgrad = Shumen Bulgaria 43°18N 26°55E 203 C10
Kolárovo Slovak Rep. 47°54N 18°0E 181 D10
Kolasib India 24°15N 92°45E 241 C4
Kolašin Montenegro 42°50N 19°31E 202 D3
Kolayat India 27°50N 72°50E 242 F5
Kolbäck Sweden 59°34N 16°15E 162 E10
Kolbäcksån → Sweden 59°36N 16°16E 162 E10
Kolbeinsstaðir Iceland 64°59N 22°16W 155 C4
Kolberg = Kołobrzeg Poland 54°10N 15°35E 184 D2
Kolbermoor Germany 47°51N 12°4E 179 H8
Kolbio Kenya 1°8S 41°12E 267 E5
Kolbotn Norway 59°48N 10°48E 133 B3
Kolbu Norway 60°39N 10°45E 164 D7
Kolbuszowa Poland 50°15N 21°46E 185 H8
Kolchugino = Leninsk-Kuznetskiy Russia 54°44N 86°10E 217 B11
Kolchugino Russia 56°17N 39°22E 188 D10
Kolda Senegal 12°55N 14°57W 262 C2
Kolda □ Senegal 13°5N 14°50W 262 C2
Koldegi Sudan 12°30N 30°16E 257 E3
Kolding Denmark 55°30N 9°29E 163 J3
Kole Dem. Rep. of the Congo 3°16S 22°42E 264 C4
Koléa Algeria 36°38N 2°46E 261 A5
Kolepom = Dolak, Pulau Indonesia 8°0S 138°30E 231 F9
Kolguyev, Ostrov Russia 69°20N 48°30E 186 A8
Kolhapur India 16°43N 74°15E 244 F2
Kolia Ivory C. 9°46N 6°28W 262 D3
Koliganek U.S.A. 59°48N 157°25W 303 G8
Kolimbia Greece 36°15N 28°10E 206 E12
Kolín Czech Rep. 50°2N 15°9E 180 A8
Kolind Denmark 56°21N 10°34E 163 H4
Kolkas rags Latvia 57°46N 22°37E 184 A9
Kolkata India 22°34N 88°21E 124 B2
Kolkata Maidan India 22°33N 88°21E 124 B1
Kolkata Netaji Subhash Chandra Bose Int. ✈ (CCU) India 22°38N 88°26E 124 B2
Kollam India 8°50N 76°38E 245 K3
Kölleda Germany 51°11N 11°15E 178 D7
Kollegal India 12°9N 77°9E 245 H3
Kolleru L. India 16°40N 81°10E 244 F5
Kollum Neths. 53°17N 6°10E 170 A6
Kolmanskop Namibia 26°45S 15°14E 270 C2
Köln Germany 50°56N 6°57E 178 E2
Kolno Poland 53°25N 21°56E 184 E8
Koło Warszawa, Poland 52°14N 20°56E 143 B1
Koło Wielkopolskie, Poland 52°14N 18°40E 185 F5
Kołobrzeg Poland 54°10N 15°35E 184 D2
Kolochava Ukraine 48°26N 23°41E 183 B8
Kologi Sudan 10°51N 30°58E 257 E3
Kolokani Mali 13°35N 7°45W 262 C3
Kolokinthou Greece 38°0N 23°42E 112 B2
Koloko Burkina Faso 11°5N 5°19W 262 C3
Kololo Ethiopia 7°29N 41°58E 257 F5
Kolombangara Solomon Is. 8°0S 157°5E 287 M9
Kolomna Russia 55°8N 38°45E 188 E10
Kolomyagi Russia 60°0N 30°19E 137 A1
Kolomyya Ukraine 48°31N 25°2E 183 B10
Kolondiéba Mali 11°5N 6°54W 262 C3
Kolonodale Indonesia 2°0S 121°19E 231 E6
Kolonos Greece 37°59N 23°43E 112 B2
Kolonowskie Poland 50°39N 18°22E 185 H5
Kolpashevo Russia 58°20N 83°5E 214 D9
Kolpino Russia 59°44N 30°39E 188 C6
Kolpny Russia 52°17N 37°1E 189 F9
Kolsås Norway 59°55N 10°30E 133 A2
Kolskiy Poluostrov Russia 67°30N 38°0E 186 A6
Kolskiy Zaliv Russia 69°23N 34°0E 160 B26
Kolsva Sweden 59°36N 15°51E 162 E9
Kolubara → Serbia 44°35N 20°15E 202 B4
Kolumadulu Atoll Maldives 2°22N 73°7E 272 d
Koluszki Poland 51°45N 19°46E 185 G6
Kolwezi Dem. Rep. of the Congo 10°40S 25°25E 269 E2
Kolyma → Russia 69°30N 161°0E 215 C17
Kolymskoye Nagorye Russia 63°0N 157°0E 215 C16
Kôm Hamâda Egypt 30°46N 30°41E 256 H7
Kôm Ombo Egypt 24°25N 32°52E 256 C3
Koma Tou Yialou Cyprus 35°25N 34°8E 207 E10
Komadugu Gana → Nigeria 13°5N 12°24E 263 C7
Komae Japan 35°37N 139°34E 140 B2
Komagane Japan 35°43N 137°58E 223 B9
Komagome Japan 35°43N 139°45E 140 A3
Komaki Japan 35°17N 136°55E 223 B8
Komandorskiye Is. = Komandorskiye Ostrova Russia 55°0N 167°0E 215 D17
Komandorskiye Ostrova Russia 55°0N 167°0E 215 D17
Komárno Slovak Rep. 47°49N 18°5E 181 D11
Komarnyky Ukraine 48°59N 23°3E 182 B8
Komárom Hungary 47°43N 18°7E 182 C3
Komárom-Esztergom □ Hungary 47°35N 18°20E 182 C3
Komáromújváros = Komárom Hungary 47°43N 18°7E 182 C3
Komatipoort S. Africa 25°25S 31°55E 271 C5
Komatsu Japan 36°25N 136°30E 223 A8
Komatsushima Japan 34°0N 134°35E 222 D6
Komavangard = Sobinka Russia 56°0N 40°0E 188 E11
Komazawa Japan 35°37N 139°40E 140 B3
Komba Dem. Rep. of the Congo 2°52N 24°3E 264 B4
Kombissiri Burkina Faso 12°4N 1°20W 263 C4
Kombo Gabon 0°20S 12°22E 264 C2
Kombong India 28°7N 94°51E 241 A5
Kombori Burkina Faso 13°26N 3°56W 262 C4
Komboti Greece 39°6N 21°5E 204 B3
Kome Channel Uganda 0°10S 32°35E 268 C3
Komebail Lagoon Palau 7°25N 134°29E 288 c
Komen Slovenia 45°49N 13°45E 199 C10
Komenda Ghana 5°4N 1°28W 263 D4
Komi Cyprus 35°24N 34°0E 207 E9
Komi □ Russia 64°0N 55°0E 186 B10
Kominter = Novoshakhtinsk Russia 47°46N 39°58E 189 J10
Komintern = Marhanets Ukraine 47°40N 34°40E 189 J8
Komiža Croatia 43°3N 16°11E 199 E13
Komló Hungary 46°15N 18°16E 182 D3
Kommamur Canal India 16°0N 80°25E 245 G5
Kommunarsk = Alchevsk Ukraine 48°30N 38°45E 189 H10
Kommunizma, Pik = imeni Ismail Samani, Pik Tajikistan 39°0N 72°2E 217 E8
Komodo Indonesia 8°37S 119°20E 235 D5
Komodo △ Indonesia 8°36S 119°34E 235 D5
Komono Congo 3°10S 13°20E 264 C2
Komoran, Pulau Indonesia 8°18S 138°45E 231 F9
Komoro Japan 36°19N 138°26E 223 A10
Komotau = Chomutov Czech Rep. 50°28N 13°23E 180 A6
Komotini Greece 41°9N 25°26E 203 E9
Komovi Montenegro 42°41N 19°39E 202 D3
Kompasberg S. Africa 31°45S 24°32E 270 D3
Kompong Chhnang = Kampong Chhnang Cambodia 12°20N 104°35E 237 F5
Kompong Chikreng Cambodia 13°5N 104°18E 236 F5
Kompong Kleang Cambodia 13°6N 104°8E 236 F5
Kompong Luong Cambodia 11°49N 104°48E 237 G5
Kompong Pranak Cambodia 13°35N 104°55E 236 F5
Kompong Som = Kampong Saom Cambodia 10°38N 103°30E 237 G4
Kompong Som, Chhung = Kampong Saom, Chaak Cambodia 10°50N 103°32E 237 G4
Kompong Speu Cambodia 11°26N 104°32E 237 G5
Kompong Sralau Cambodia 14°5N 105°46E 236 E5
Kompong Thom Cambodia 12°35N 104°51E 236 F5
Kompong Trabeck Cambodia 13°6N 105°14E 236 F5
Kompong Trach Cambodia 11°25N 105°48E 237 G5
Kompong Tralach Cambodia 11°54N 104°47E 237 G5
Komrat = Comrat Moldova 46°18N 28°40E 183 D13
Komsberg S. Africa 32°40S 20°45E 270 D3
Komsomolets = Qarabalyq Kazakhstan 53°45N 62°2E 216 B6
Komsomolets, Ostrov Russia 80°30N 95°0E 215 A10
Komsomolsk Ivanovo, Russia 57°2N 40°20E 188 D11
Komsomolsk Ukraine 49°1N 33°38E 189 H7
Komsomolsk-na-Amur Russia 50°30N 137°0E 219 A16
Komsomolskiy Russia 54°27N 45°33E 190 C7
Komsomolskoe Kazakhstan 50°25N 60°5E 216 B6
Komsomolsky = Chirchiq Uzbekistan 41°29N 69°35E 217 D7
Kömür Burnu Turkey 38°39N 26°12E 205 C8
Kon Ka Kinh △ Vietnam 14°19N 107°23E 236 E6
Kon Tum Vietnam 14°24N 108°0E 236 E7
Kon Tum, Plateau du Vietnam 14°30N 108°30E 236 E7
Kona Paschimbanga, India 22°37N 88°18E 124 B1
Kona Mali 14°57N 3°53W 262 C4
Kona Nigeria 8°57N 11°21E 263 D7
Kona ✈ (KOA) U.S.A. 19°44N 156°3W 302 D5
Konāhuanui U.S.A. 21°21N 157°47W 302 K14
Konakovo Russia 56°40N 36°51E 188 D9
Konala Finland 60°14N 24°52E 121 B2
Konar □ Afghan. 34°30N 71°3E 240 B3
Konarak India 19°54N 86°7E 244 E8
Konārī Iran 28°13N 51°36E 247 D6
Konch India 26°0N 79°10E 243 G8
Kondagaon India 19°35N 81°35E 244 E5
Konde Tanzania 4°57S 39°45E 268 C4
Kondias Greece 39°49N 25°10E 205 B7
Kondinin Australia 32°34S 118°8E 279 F2
Kondli India 28°36N 77°19E 120 B2
Kondo Dem. Rep. of the Congo 5°35S 13°0E 265 D2
Kondoa Tanzania 4°55S 35°50E 268 C4
Kondopoga Russia 62°12N 34°17E 188 A8
Kondoz Afghan. 36°50N 68°50E 240 A3
Kondoz → Afghan. 37°0N 68°16E 240 A3
Kondratyevo Russia 57°22N 98°15E 215 D10
Kondrovo Russia 54°48N 35°56E 188 E8
Konduga Nigeria 11°35N 13°26E 263 C7
Kondukur India 15°12N 79°57E 245 G4
Kondūz Afghan. 36°50N 68°50E 240 A3
Kondūz □ Afghan. 36°50N 68°50E 240 A3
Koné Cameroon 8°50N 13°37E 263 D7
Koné N. Cal. 21°4S 164°52E 288 d
Köneürgench Turkmenistan 42°19N 59°10E 216 D5
Konevo Russia 62°8N 39°20E 188 A10
Kong = Khong → Cambodia 13°32N 105°58E 236 F5
Kong Ivory C. 8°54N 4°36W 262 D4
Kong, Koh Cambodia 11°20N 103°0E 237 G4
Kong Christian IX.s Land Greenland 68°0N 36°0W 154 D7
Kong Christian X.s Land Greenland 74°0N 29°0W 154 C8
Kong Frederik IX.s Land Greenland 67°0N 52°0W 154 D5
Kong Frederik VI.s Kyst Greenland 63°0N 43°0W 154 E6
Kong Frederik VIII.s Land Greenland 78°30N 26°0W 154 B8
Kong Karls Land Svalbard 79°0N 28°0E 154 B13
Kong Oscar Fjord Greenland 72°20N 24°0W 154 C8
Kongauru I. Palau 7°3N 134°16E 288 c
Kongbo C.A.R. 4°44N 21°23E 264 B4
Kongeå → Denmark 55°23N 8°39E 163 J2
Kongelunden Denmark 55°34N 12°34E 118 B3
Kongens Lyngby Denmark 55°46N 12°30E 118 A3
Kongens Nordsjælland △ Denmark 56°5N 12°15E 163 H6
Kongerslev Denmark 56°54N 10°6E 163 H4
Kongkemul Indonesia 1°52N 116°10E 235 B5
Konglu Burma 27°13N 97°57E 241 B6
Kongmoon = Jiangmen China 22°32N 113°0E 229 F9
Kongo Finland 60°20N 24°47E 121 A1
Kongola Namibia 17°45S 23°20E 270 A3
Kongolo Kasai-Or., Dem. Rep. of the Congo 5°26S 24°49E 265 D4
Kongolo Katanga, Dem. Rep. of the Congo 5°22S 27°0E 268 D2
Kongor South Sudan 7°1N 31°27E 257 F3
Kongossambougou △ Mali 14°0N 8°30W 262 C3
Kongoulou Cameroon 2°59N 11°7E 264 B2
Kongoussi Burkina Faso 13°19N 1°32W 263 C4
Kongsberg Norway 59°39N 9°39E 164 E6
Kongsvinger Norway 60°12N 12°2E 164 D9
Kongur Shan China 38°34N 75°18E 217 E9
Kongwa Tanzania 6°11S 36°26E 268 D4
Koni Dem. Rep. of the Congo 10°40S 27°11E 269 E2
Koniakari Mali 14°35N 10°53W 262 C2
Koniecpol Poland 50°46N 19°40E 185 H6
Königgrätz = Hradec Králové Czech Rep. 50°15N 15°50E 180 A8
Königs Wusterhausen Germany 52°19N 13°38E 178 C9
Königsberg = Chojna Poland 52°58N 14°25E 185 F1
Königsberg = Kaliningrad Russia 54°42N 20°32E 184 D7
Königsbrunn Germany 48°16N 10°54E 179 G6
Königshütte = Chorzów Poland 50°18N 18°57E 185 H5
Königslutter Germany 52°15N 10°49E 178 C6
Konin Poland 52°12N 18°15E 185 F5
Königinhof an der Elbe = Dvůr Králové nad Labem Czech Rep. 50°27N 15°50E 180 A8
Koninklijk Paleis Amsterdam, Neths. 112 a2
Konispol Albania 39°42N 20°10E 206 B10
Konitsa Greece 40°5N 20°48E 204 A2
Konjic Bos.-H. 43°42N 17°58E 182 G2
Konkiep Namibia 26°49S 17°15E 270 C2
Konkō Japan 34°33N 133°36E 222 C4
Konkouré → Guinea 9°50N 13°42W 262 D2
Konnagar India 22°42N 88°21E 124 A2
Könnern Germany 51°41N 11°47E 178 D7
Konnur India 16°14N 74°49E 245 F2
Kono S. Leone 8°30N 11°5W 262 D2
Konogogo Papua N. G. 3°29S 152°10E 286 B7
Konohana Japan 34°40N 135°26E 133 A1
Kononogo Ghana 6°40N 1°15W 263 D4
Konos Papua N. G. 3°10S 151°44E 286 B6
Konosha Russia 61°0N 40°5E 188 B11
Kōnosu Japan 36°3N 139°31E 223 A11
Konotop Ukraine 51°12N 33°7E 189 G7
Konqi He → China 41°0N 86°0E 217 D11
Konradshof = Skawina Poland 49°59N 19°50E 185 J6
Konradshöhe Germany 52°35N 13°13E 115 A2
Konrei Palau 7°43N 134°36E 288 c
Konsankoro Guinea 9°2N 9°0W 262 D3
Końskie Poland 51°15N 20°23E 185 G7
Konsmo Norway 58°16N 7°23E 164 F4
Konstadt = Wołczyn Poland 51°1N 18°3E 185 G5
Konstancin-Jeziorna Poland 52°5N 21°7E 185 F8
Konstantinograd = Krasnohrad Ukraine 49°27N 35°27E 189 H8
Konstantinovka = Kostyantynivka Ukraine 48°32N 37°39E 189 H9
Konstantinovsk Russia 47°33N 41°10E 191 G5
Konstantynów Łódzki Poland 51°45N 19°20E 185 G6
Konstanz Germany 47°40N 9°10E 179 H5
Kont Iran 26°55N 61°50E 247 E9
Konta India 17°48N 81°23E 244 F5
Kontagora Nigeria 10°23N 5°27E 263 C6
Kontcha Cameroon 7°59N 12°15E 263 D7
Kontiolahti Finland 62°46N 29°50E 160 E23
Kontokali Greece 39°38N 19°51E 206 B9
Konya Turkey 37°52N 32°35E 212 D5
Konya □ Turkey 37°46N 32°20E 212 D5
Konya Ovası Turkey 38°30N 33°5E 212 C5
Konyin Burma 22°58N 94°42E 241 D5
Konz Germany 49°42N 6°34E 179 F2
Konza Kenya 1°45S 37°7E 268 C4
Koo-wee-rup Australia 38°13S 145°28E 283 E6
Koocanusa, L. Canada 49°20N 115°15W 304 B6
Kookynie Australia 29°17S 121°22E 279 E3
Ko'olau Range U.S.A. 21°35N 157°50W 302 J14
Ko'olauloa District U.S.A. 21°35N 157°55W 302 J14
Ko'olaupoko District U.S.A. 21°25N 157°50W 302 K14
Kō'Ōlina U.S.A. 21°19N 158°7W 302 K13
Koolyanobbing Australia 30°48S 119°36E 279 F2
Koondrook Australia 35°33S 144°8E 282 C6
Koonibba Australia 31°54S 133°25E 281 E1
Koorawatha Australia 34°2S 148°33E 283 C8
Koorda Australia 30°48S 117°35E 279 F2
Kooskia U.S.A. 46°9N 115°59W 304 C6
Kootenay → U.S.A. 49°19N 117°39W 296 D5
Kootenay △ Canada 51°0N 116°0W 296 C5
Kootenay L. Canada 49°45N 116°50W 304 B5
Kootingal Australia 31°3S 151°4E 283 A9
Kootjieskolk S. Africa 31°15S 20°21E 270 D3
Kopanina Czech Rep. 50°3N 14°17E 135 B1
Kopanovka Russia 47°28N 46°50E 191 G8
Kopaonik Serbia 43°10N 20°50E 202 C4
Kopaonik △ Serbia 43°20N 20°50E 202 C4
Kopargaon India 19°51N 74°28E 244 E2
Koparkhairna India 19°6N 72°59E 130 A2
Kópasker Iceland 66°18N 16°27W 155 A10
Kópavogur Iceland 64°6N 21°55W 155 C5
Kopayhorod Ukraine 48°52N 27°53E 183 B12
Köpenick Germany 52°26N 13°35E 115 B4
Koper Slovenia 45°31N 13°44E 199 C10
Kopervik Norway 59°17N 5°17E 164 E2
Kopet Dagh Asia 38°0N 58°0E 247 B8
Kopeysk Russia 55°7N 61°37E 216 A6
Kopi Australia 33°24S 135°40E 281 E2
Köping Sweden 59°31N 16°3E 162 E10
Köpingsvik Sweden 56°53N 16°43E 163 H10
Kopište Croatia 42°48N 16°42E 199 F13
Koplik Albania 42°15N 19°25E 202 D3
Köpmanholmen Sweden 63°10N 18°35E 162 A12
Koppa India 13°33N 75°21E 245 H2
Koppal India 15°23N 76°5E 245 G3
Koppang Norway 61°34N 11°3E 164 C8
Kopparberg Sweden 59°52N 15°0E 162 E9
Koppeh Dāgh = Kopet Dagh Asia 38°0N 58°0E 247 B8
Kopperå Norway 63°24N 11°50E 164 A8
Koppies S. Africa 27°20S 27°30E 271 C4
Koppom Sweden 59°43N 12°10E 162 E6
Koprivlen Bulgaria 41°31N 23°53E 202 E7
Koprivnica Croatia 46°12N 16°45E 199 B13
Kopřivnice Czech Rep. 49°36N 18°9E 181 B11
Koprivshtitsa Bulgaria 42°40N 24°19E 203 D8
Köprü → Turkey 36°48N 31°11E 250 B2
Köprübaşı Turkey 38°43N 28°23E 205 C10
Köprülü Turkey 36°43N 32°10E 250 B3
Köprülü △ Turkey 37°20N 31°5E 246 B1
Kopychyntsi Ukraine 49°7N 25°58E 177 D13
Kor Aban Somalia 3°58N 42°44E 267 D5
Kora △ Kenya 0°14S 38°44E 268 C4
Koraa Shiir Somalia 3°16N 46°16E 267 D6
Korab Macedonia 41°44N 20°40E 202 E4
Korahe Ethiopia 6°39N 44°35E 267 C5
Koral India 21°50N 73°12E 242 J5
Korangal India 17°6N 77°38E 244 E3

Korangi Pakistan 24°47N 67°8E 123 B2
Koraput India 18°50N 82°40E 244 E6
Korarou, L. Mali 15°15N 3°15W 262 B4
Korba India 22°20N 82°45E 243 H10
Korbach Germany 51°16N 8°52E 178 D4
Korbu, Gunung Malaysia 4°41N 101°18E 237 K3
Korçë Albania 40°37N 20°50E 202 F4
Korčula Croatia 42°56N 16°57E 199 F13
Korčulanski Kanal Croatia 43°3N 16°40E 199 E13
Kord Küy Iran 36°48N 54°7E 247 B7
Kord Sheykh Iran 28°31N 52°53E 247 D7
Kordestan = Kurdistan Asia 37°20N 43°30E 213 D10
Kordestān □ Iran 36°0N 47°0E 246 C5
Kordié Burkina Faso 12°36N 2°22W 262 C4
Koré Mayroua Niger 13°18N 3°55E 263 C5
Korea, North ■ Asia 40°0N 127°0E 224 C3
Korea, South ■ Asia 36°0N 128°0E 224 D4
Korea Bay Korea 39°0N 124°0E 224 C2
Korea Strait Asia 34°0N 129°30E 227 H15
Koregaon India 17°40N 74°10E 244 F2
Korem Ethiopia 12°30N 39°32E 257 E4
Korenevo Russia 51°27N 34°55E 189 G8
Korenica = Titova Korenica Croatia 44°45N 15°41E 199 D12
Korenovsk Russia 45°30N 39°22E 191 H4
Korets Ukraine 50°40N 27°5E 177 C14
Korfantów Poland 50°29N 17°36E 185 H4
Körfez Turkey 40°47N 29°44E 203 F13
Korff Ice Rise Antarctica 79°0S 69°30W 151 D17
Korgalzhyn = Qorghalzhyn Kazakhstan 50°25N 69°11E 217 B7
Korgan Turkey 40°44N 37°13E 212 B7
Korgus Sudan 19°16N 33°29E 256 D3
Korhogo Ivory C. 9°29N 5°28W 262 D3
Koribundu S. Leone 7°41N 11°46W 262 D2
Koridalos Greece 37°59N 23°39E 112 B1
Korienzé Mali 15°22N 3°50W 262 B4
Korinthiakos Kolpos Greece 38°16N 22°30E 204 C4
Korinthos Greece 37°56N 22°55E 204 D4
Korioumé Mali 16°35N 3°0W 262 B4
Korissia, L. Greece 39°27N 19°53E 206 C9
Korithi Greece 37°55N 20°42E 207 D2
Kōriyama Japan 37°24N 140°23E 220 F10
Korkino Russia 54°54N 61°23E 216 B6
Korkuteli Turkey 37°4N 30°13E 205 D12
Korla China 41°45N 86°4E 217 D11
Kormakiti, C. Cyprus 35°23N 32°56E 207 E8
Körmend Hungary 47°5N 16°35E 182 C1
Kormor Iraq 35°8N 44°50E 213 E11
Kornat Croatia 43°50N 15°20E 199 E12
Kornat △ Croatia 43°50N 15°12E 199 E12
Korneshty = Corneşti Moldova 47°21N 28°1E 183 C13
Korneuburg Austria 48°20N 16°20E 181 C9
Kórnik Poland 52°15N 17°6E 185 F4
Kornsjø Norway 58°57N 11°39E 164 F8
Koro Fiji 17°19S 179°23E 287 A2
Koro Ivory C. 8°32N 7°30W 262 D3
Koro Mali 14°1N 2°58W 262 C4
Koro Sea Fiji 17°30S 179°45W 287 A3
Koro Toro Chad 16°5N 18°30E 259 E3
Koroba Papua N. G. 5°44S 142°47E 286 C2
Korobkovo = Gubkin Russia 51°17N 37°32E 189 G9
Korocha Russia 50°54N 37°19E 189 G9
Köroğlu Dağları Turkey 40°38N 33°0E 212 B5
Korogwe Tanzania 5°5S 38°25E 268 D4
Koroit Australia 38°18S 142°24E 282 E5
Koroleve Ukraine 48°9N 23°8E 183 B8
Korolevu Fiji 18°12S 177°46E 287 B1
Koromiri Cook Is. 21°15S 159°43W 289 h
Korona U.S.A. 29°25N 81°12W 317 F8
Koronadal Phil. 6°12N 124°51E 233 H5
Korong Vale Australia 36°22S 143°45E 282 D5
Koroni Greece 36°48N 21°57E 204 E3
Koronia, L. Greece 40°47N 23°10E 202 F7
Koronos Greece 37°12N 25°35E 205 D7
Koronowo Poland 53°19N 17°55E 185 E4
Koropelé C.A.R. 4°44N 17°11E 264 B3
Koropets Ukraine 48°56N 25°10E 183 B10
Koror Palau 7°20N 134°28E 288 c
Körös → Hungary 46°43N 20°12E 182 D5
Körös Maros △ Hungary 47°8N 20°52E 182 C5
Köröstarcsa Hungary 46°53N 21°3E 182 D6
Korosten Ukraine 50°54N 28°36E 177 C15
Korostyshev Ukraine 50°19N 29°4E 177 C15
Korotoyak Russia 51°1N 39°2E 189 G10
Korovou Fiji 17°47S 178°32E 287 A2
Koroyanitu △ Fiji 17°40S 177°35E 287 A1
Korraraika, Helodranon' i Madag. 17°45S 43°57E 272 B1
Korror I. Palau 7°20N 134°29E 288 c
Korsakov Russia 46°36N 142°42E 215 E15
Korsberga Sweden 57°19N 15°7E 163 G9
Korshiv Ukraine 48°39N 25°1E 183 B10
Korshunovo Russia 58°37N 110°10E 215 D12
Korsør Denmark 55°20N 11°9E 163 J5
Korsun Shevchenkovskiy Ukraine 49°26N 31°16E 189 H6
Korsze Poland 54°11N 21°9E 184 D8
Korti Sudan 18°6N 31°33E 256 D3
Kortrijk Belgium 50°50N 3°17E 170 D3
Korucu Turkey 39°28N 27°22E 205 B9
Korumburra Australia 38°26S 145°50E 283 E6
Korup △ Cameroon 5°15N 9°2E 264 A1
Korwai India 24°7N 78°5E 242 G8
Koryakskoye Nagorye Russia 61°0N 171°0E 215 C18
Koryukovka Ukraine 51°46N 32°16E 189 G7
Kos Greece 36°50N 27°15E 205 E9
Kosa Ethiopia 7°50N 36°50E 257 F4
Kosai Japan 34°42N 137°32E 223 C9
Kosan N. Korea 38°52N 127°25E 224 C3
Kosaya Gora Russia 54°10N 37°30E 188 E9
Kościan Poland 52°5N 16°40E 185 F3
Kościerzyna Poland 54°8N 17°59E 184 D4
Kosciusko U.S.A. 33°4N 89°35W 315 E10
Kosciuszko, Mt. Australia 36°27S 148°16E 283 D8
Kosciuszko △ Australia 36°30S 148°20E 283 D8
Kösély → Hungary 47°25N 21°5E 182 C6
Kosgi Andhra Pradesh, India 16°58N 77°43E 244 F3
Kosgi Andhra Pradesh, India 15°51N 77°16E 245 G3
Kosha Sudan 20°50N 30°30E 256 C3
Koshava Bulgaria 44°4N 23°2E 202 B7
Kōshi Japan 32°53N 130°48E 222 E2
Koshigaya Japan 35°54N 139°48E 223 B11
K'oshih = Kashi China 39°30N 76°2E 217 E9
Koshiki-Kaikyō Japan 31°30N 130°0E 222 F1
Koshiki-Rettō Japan 31°45N 129°49E 222 F1
Koshim → Kazakhstan 49°20N 50°30E 190 F10
Koshkonong L. U.S.A. 42°52N 88°58W 311 B8
Kōshoku Japan 36°38N 138°6E 223 A10
Kōshū Japan 35°42N 138°44E 223 B10
Koshu-Kavak = Krumovgrad Bulgaria 41°29N 25°38E 203 E9
Kosi India 27°48N 77°29E 242 F7
Kosi → India 28°41N 78°57E 243 E8
Košice Slovak Rep. 48°42N 21°15E 181 C14
Košický □ Slovak Rep. 48°45N 21°0E 181 C14
Kosino Russia 55°43N 37°50E 129 B4
Kosiv Ukraine 48°19N 25°6E 183 B10
Kosjerić Serbia 44°0N 19°55E 202 B3
Köşk Turkey 37°50N 28°3E 205 D10
Koskinou Greece 36°23N 28°13E 206 E12
Koslan Russia 63°34N 49°14E 186 B8
Köslin = Koszalin Poland 54°11N 16°8E 184 D3
Kosmach Ukraine 48°20N 24°50E 183 B9
Kosŏng N. Korea 38°40N 128°22E 224 C4
Kosovo ■ Europe 42°30N 21°0E 202 D4
Kosovo Polje = Fushë Kosovë Kosovo 42°40N 21°5E 202 D5
Kosovska Kamenica = Dardanë Kosovo 42°35N 21°35E 202 D5
Kosovska Mitrovica = Mitrovicë Kosovo 42°54N 20°52E 202 D4
Kossou, L. de Ivory C. 6°59N 5°31W 262 D3
Kosta Sweden 56°50N 15°24E 163 H9
Kostajnica Croatia 45°17N 16°30E 199 C13
Kostanjevica Slovenia 45°51N 15°27E 199 C12
Kostenets = Pernik Bulgaria 42°35N 23°2E 202 D7
Kostenets Bulgaria 42°15N 23°52E 202 D7
Koster S. Africa 25°52S 26°54E 270 C4
Kôstî Sudan 13°8N 32°43E 257 E3
Kostinbrod Bulgaria 42°49N 23°13E 202 D7
Kostolac Serbia 44°37N 21°15E 202 B5
Kostopil Ukraine 50°51N 26°22E 177 C14
Kostroma Russia 57°50N 40°58E 188 D11
Kostroma □ Russia 58°10N 42°50E 190 A6
Kostromskoye Vdkhr. Russia 57°52N 40°49E 188 D11
Kostryzhivka Ukraine 48°39N 25°43E 183 B10
Kostrzyn Lubuskie, Poland 52°35N 14°39E 185 F1
Kostrzyn Wielkopolskie, Poland 52°24N 17°14E 185 F4
Kostyantynivka Ukraine 48°32N 37°39E 189 H9
Kostyukovichi = Kastsyukovichy Belarus 53°20N 32°4E 189 F7
Kosugi Japan 35°34N 139°39E 140 B2
Koszalin Poland 54°11N 16°8E 184 D3
Kőszeg Hungary 47°23N 16°33E 182 C1
Kot Addu Pakistan 30°30N 71°0E 242 D4
Kot Kapura India 30°35N 74°50E 242 D6
Kot Moman Pakistan 32°13N 73°0E 242 C5
Kot Sultan Pakistan 30°46N 70°56E 242 D4
Kota India 25°14N 75°49E 242 G6
Kota Jakarta, Indonesia 6°7S 106°48E 122 A1
Kota Barrage India 25°6N 75°51E 242 G6
Kota Belud Malaysia 6°21N 116°26E 235 A5
Kota Bharu Malaysia 6°7N 102°14E 237 J4
Kota I. = Loaita I. S. China Sea 10°41N 114°25E 230 B4
Kota Kinabalu Malaysia 6°0N 116°4E 235 A5
Kota Tinggi Malaysia 1°44N 103°53E 237 M4
Kotaagung Indonesia 5°38S 104°29E 234 D2
Kotabaru Kalimantan Barat, Indonesia 0°49S 111°31E 235 C4
Kotabaru Kalimantan Selatan, Indonesia 3°20S 116°20E 235 C5
Kotabaru Sumatera Barat, Indonesia 1°7S 101°43E 234 C2
Kotabesi Indonesia 2°24S 112°58E 235 C4
Kotabumi Indonesia 4°49S 104°54E 234 C2
Kotajawa Indonesia 5°37S 104°19E 234 D2
Kotamobagu Indonesia 0°57N 124°31E 231 D6
Kotapad India 19°9N 82°21E 244 E6
Kotapinang Indonesia 1°53N 100°5E 237 M3
Kotawaringin Indonesia 2°28S 111°27E 235 C4
Kotcho L. Canada 59°7N 121°12W 296 B4
Kotdwara India 29°45N 78°32E 243 E8
Kotel Bulgaria 42°52N 26°26E 203 D10
Kotelnich Russia 58°22N 48°24E 190 A9
Kotelnikovo Russia 47°38N 43°8E 191 G6
Kotelnyy, Ostrov Russia 75°10N 139°0E 215 B14
Kothapet India 19°21N 79°28E 244 E4
Kothari → India 25°20N 75°4E 242 G6
Köthen Germany 51°45N 11°59E 178 D7
Kothi Chhattisgarh, India 23°21N 82°3E 243 H10
Kothi Mad. P., India 24°45N 80°40E 243 G9
Kotiro Pakistan 26°17N 67°13E 242 F2
Kotka Finland 60°28N 26°58E 188 B4
Kotlas Russia 61°17N 46°43E 186 B8
Kotlenska Planina Bulgaria 42°56N 26°30E 203 D10
Kotli Pakistan 33°30N 73°55E 242 C5
Kotlik U.S.A. 63°2N 163°33W 303 E7
Kotma India 23°12N 81°58E 243 H9
Kōtō Japan 35°40N 139°48E 140 A3
Kotohira Japan 34°11N 133°49E 222 C5
Koton-Karifi Nigeria 8°0N 6°48E 263 D6
Kotonkoro Nigeria 11°3N 5°58E 263 C6
Kotor Montenegro 42°25N 18°47E 202 D2
Kotor Varoš Bos.-H. 44°38N 17°22E 182 F2
Kotoriba Croatia 46°23N 16°48E 199 B13
Kotovo Russia 50°22N 44°45E 190 E7
Kotovsk Russia 52°36N 41°32E 190 D5
Kotovsk Ukraine 47°45N 29°35E 177 E15
Kotputli India 27°43N 76°12E 242 F7
Kotri Pakistan 25°22N 68°22E 242 G3
Kotri → India 19°15N 80°35E 244 E5
Kotronas Greece 36°38N 22°29E 204 E4
Kotrung India 22°41N 88°20E 124 A2
Kötschach-Mauthen Austria 46°41N 13°1E 180 E6
Kottagudem India 17°30N 80°40E 244 F5
Kottayam India 9°35N 76°33E 245 K3
Kotto C.A.R. 4°14N 22°2E 264 B4
Kotto → C.A.R. 4°14N 22°2E 264 B4
Kottur India 10°34N 76°56E 245 J3
Kotturu India 14°45N 76°10E 245 G3
Kotu Group Tonga 20°0S 174°45W 287 Q13
Kotuy → Russia 71°54N 102°6E 215 B11
Kotyuzhany Ukraine 48°48N 27°42E 183 B12
Kotzebue U.S.A. 66°53N 162°39W 303 C7
Kotzebue Sound U.S.A. 66°20N 163°0W 303 C7
Kotzenau = Chocianów Poland 51°27N 15°55E 185 G2
Kouango C.A.R. 5°0N 20°10E 264 B4
Kouchibouguac △ Canada 46°50N 65°0W 299 C6
Koudougou Burkina Faso 12°10N 2°20W 262 C4
Koufey Niger 13°57N 7°56E 259 F1
Koufonisi Iraklio, Greece 34°56N 26°8E 207 F7
Koufonisi Notio Aigaio, Greece 36°57N 25°35E 205 E7
Kougaberge S. Africa 33°48S 23°50E 270 D3
K'ouhu Taiwan 23°35N 120°11E 225 C2
Kouibli Ivory C. 7°15N 7°14W 262 D3
Kouilou □ Congo 4°30S 12°0E 264 C2
Kouilou → Congo 4°10S 12°5E 265 C2
Koukdjuak → Canada 66°43N 73°0W 295 D17
Kouki C.A.R. 7°22N 17°3E 264 A3
Koukoulé, Mt. Comoros Is. 12°18S 43°41E 272 a
Koukourou C.A.R. 7°12N 20°2E 264 A4
Koula Greece 41°23N 24°44E 203 E8
Koula Moutou Gabon 1°15S 12°25E 264 C2
Koulen = Kulen Cambodia 13°50N 104°40E 236 F5
Koulikoro Mali 12°40N 7°50W 262 C3
Koulikoro □ Mali 14°0N 7°45W 262 C3
Kouloura Greece 39°42N 19°54E 206 B9
Koumac N. Cal. 20°33S 164°17E 288 d
Koumala Australia 21°38S 149°15E 280 C4
Koumameyong Gabon 0°11N 11°51E 264 B2
Koumankou Mali 11°58N 6°6W 262 C3
Koumbia Burkina Faso 11°10N 3°50W 262 C4
Koumbia Guinea 11°48N 13°29W 262 C2
Koumboum Guinea 10°25N 13°0W 262 C2
Koumpenntoum Senegal 13°59N 14°34W 262 C2
Koumra Chad 8°50N 17°35E 259 G3
Koun-Fao Ivory C. 7°30N 3°15W 262 D4
Koundara Guinea 12°29N 13°18W 262 C2
Koundé C.A.R. 6°7N 14°38E 264 A2
Koungheul Senegal 14°0N 14°50W 262 C2
Koungou Mayotte 12°43S 45°12E 272 b
Koungoulou Congo 3°31S 13°20E 264 C2
Kountze U.S.A. 30°22N 94°19W 314 F7
Koupéla Burkina Faso 12°11N 0°21W 263 C4
Kouponia Greece 37°57N 23°47E 112 B2
Kourémalé Mali 11°59N 8°42W 262 C3
Kouri-shima Japan 26°42N 128°1E 288 a
Kouris → Cyprus 34°38N 32°54E 207 F8
Kourizo, P. de Chad 22°28N 15°27E 258 D3
Kourou Fr. Guiana 5°9N 52°39W 329 B7
Kourouba Mali 13°22N 10°57W 262 C2
Koûroudjél Mauritania 16°12N 11°30W 262 B2
Kouroukoto Mali 12°35N 10°5W 262 C2
Kourouma Burkina Faso 11°35N 4°50W 262 C4
Kourouninkoto Mali 13°52N 9°35W 262 C3
Kouroussa Guinea 10°45N 9°45W 262 C3
Koussanar Senegal 13°52N 14°5W 262 C2
Koussané Mali 14°53N 11°14W 262 C2
Koussané Senegal 14°10N 12°20W 262 C2
Kousseri Cameroon 12°0N 14°55E 259 F2
Koutiala Mali 12°25N 5°23W 262 C3
Kouto Ivory C. 9°53N 6°25W 262 D3
Kouts U.S.A. 41°19N 87°2W 311 C9
Kouvé Togo 6°25N 1°25E 263 D5
Kouvola Finland 60°52N 26°43E 188 B4
Kouyi Congo 2°29S 12°25E 264 C2
Kouyou → Congo 0°44S 16°38E 264 C3
Kovačica Serbia 45°5N 20°38E 182 E5
Kovdor Russia 67°34N 30°24E 160 C24
Kovel Ukraine 51°11N 24°38E 177 C13
Kovilpatti India 9°10N 77°50E 245 K3
Kovin Serbia 44°44N 20°59E 182 F5
Kovno = Kaunas Lithuania 54°54N 23°54E 184 D10
Kovrov Russia 56°25N 41°25E 190 B5
Kovur Andhra Pradesh, India 17°3N 81°39E 244 F5
Kovur Andhra Pradesh, India 14°30N 80°1E 245 G5
Kowal Poland 52°32N 19°7E 185 F6
Kowalewo Pomorskie Poland 53°10N 18°52E 185 E5
Kowanyama Australia 15°29S 141°44E 280 B3
Kowanyama ✪ Australia 15°20S 141°47E 280 B3
Kowlīnī Afghan. 37°39N 65°58E 240 A2
Kowloon Hong Kong, China 22°19N 114°11E 122 B3
Kowloon Peak Hong Kong, China 22°20N 114°13E 122 A3
Kowloon Tong Hong Kong, China 22°20N 114°10E 122 B3
Kowŏn N. Korea 39°26N 127°14E 224 C3
Kōyama Japan 31°20N 130°56E 222 F2
Koyampattur = Coimbatore India 11°2N 76°59E 245 J3
Köyceğiz Turkey 36°57N 28°40E 205 E10
Köyceğiz Gölü Turkey 36°56N 28°42E 205 E10
Köytendag Turkmenistan 37°30N 66°1E 240 A2
Koyuk U.S.A. 64°56N 161°9W 303 D7
Koyukuk U.S.A. 64°53N 157°42W 303 D8
Koyukuk → U.S.A. 64°55N 157°32W 303 D8
Koyukuk Nat. Wildlife Refuge △ U.S.A. 65°35N 156°30W 303 D8
Koyulhisar Turkey 40°20N 37°52E 212 B7
Koyunyeri Turkey 40°50N 26°26E 203 F10
Koza = Okinawa Japan 26°19N 127°46E 288 a
Kozak Turkey 39°15N 27°6E 205 B9
Kozaklı Turkey 39°13N 34°49E 212 C6
Kozan Turkey 37°26N 35°50E 212 D6
Kozani Greece 40°19N 21°47E 202 F5
Kozara Bos.-H. 45°0N 17°0E 199 D14
Kozara △ Bos.-H. 45°0N 17°0E 182 F2
Kozarac Bos.-H. 44°58N 16°48E 199 D13
Kozelets Ukraine 50°55N 31°7E 189 G6
Kozelsk Russia 54°2N 35°48E 188 E8
Kozhikode India 11°15N 75°43E 245 J2
Kozhva Russia 65°10N 57°0E 186 A10
Koziegłowy Poland 50°37N 19°8E 185 H6
Kozienice Poland 51°35N 21°34E 185 G8
Kozje Slovenia 46°5N 15°35E 199 B12
Kozloduy Bulgaria 43°45N 23°42E 202 C7
Kozlov = Michurinsk Russia 52°58N 40°27E 190 D5
Kozlovets Bulgaria 43°30N 25°20E 203 C9
Kozlovka Russia 55°52N 48°14E 190 C9
Kozlu Turkey 41°26N 31°45E 212 B4
Kozluk Turkey 38°11N 41°31E 213 C9
Koźmin Poland 51°48N 17°27E 185 G4
Kozmodemyansk Russia 56°20N 46°36E 190 B8
Kōzu-Shima Japan 34°13N 139°10E 223 C11
Kożuchów Poland 51°45N 15°31E 185 G2
Kozyatyn Ukraine 49°45N 28°50E 177 D15
Kozyrevsk Russia 56°3N 159°51E 215 D16
Kpabia Ghana 9°10N 0°20W 263 D4
Kpalimé Togo 6°57N 0°44E 263 D5
Kpandae Ghana 8°30N 0°2W 263 D4
Kpessi Togo 8°4N 1°16E 263 D5
Kra, Isthmus of = Kra, Kho Khot Thailand 10°15N 99°30E 237 G2
Kra, Kho Khot Thailand 10°15N 99°30E 237 G2
Kra Buri Thailand 10°22N 98°46E 237 G2
Kraai → S. Africa 30°40S 26°45E 270 D4
Kraainem Belgium 50°52N 4°28E 116 A2
Krabi Thailand 8°4N 98°55E 237 H2
Kracheh = Kratie Cambodia 12°32N 106°10E 236 F6
Kragan Indonesia 6°43S 111°38E 235 D4
Kragerø Norway 58°52N 9°25E 164 F6
Kragujevac Serbia 44°2N 20°56E 202 B4
Krailling Germany 48°5N 11°25E 131 B1
Krainburg = Kranj Slovenia 46°16N 14°22E 199 B11
Krajenka Poland 53°18N 16°59E 185 E3
Krak Castle = Crac des Chevaliers Syria 34°47N 36°18E 250 D7
Krakatau = Rakata, Pulau Indonesia 6°10S 105°20E 234 D3
Krakatoa = Rakata, Pulau Indonesia 6°10S 105°20E 234 D3
Krakau = Kraków Poland 50°4N 19°57E 185 H6
Krakor Cambodia 12°32N 104°12E 236 F5
Kraków Poland 50°4N 19°57E 185 H6
Kraków ✕ (KRK) Poland 50°5N 19°52E 185 H6
Kraksaan Indonesia 7°43S 113°23E 235 D4
Kralanh Cambodia 13°35N 103°25E 236 F4
Kralendijk Bonaire 12°9N 68°16W 322 h
Králiky Czech Rep. 50°6N 16°45E 181 A9
Kraljevo Serbia 43°44N 20°41E 202 C4
Královéhradecký □ Czech Rep. 50°25N 15°50E 180 A8
Královský Chlmec Slovak Rep. 48°27N 22°0E 181 C14
Kralupy nad Vltavou Czech Rep. 50°13N 14°20E 180 A7
Kramatorsk Ukraine 48°50N 37°30E 189 H9
Kramfors Sweden 62°55N 17°48E 162 B11
Kramis, C. Algeria 36°26N 0°45E 261 A5
Krampnitz Germany 52°27N 13°3E 115 B1
Krampnitzsee Germany 52°27N 13°3E 115 B1
Krania Greece 39°53N 21°18E 202 G5
Krania Elasonas Greece 39°57N 22°2E 204 B4
Kranidi Greece 37°20N 23°10E 204 D5
Kranj Slovenia 46°16N 14°22E 199 B11
Kranji Industrial Estate Singapore 1°26N 103°45E 138 A2
Kranji Res. Singapore 1°25N 103°44E 138 A2
Kranjska Gora Slovenia 46°29N 13°48E 199 B10
Krankskop S. Africa 28°0S 30°47E 271 C5
Kranz = Zelenogradsk Russia 54°53N 20°29E 184 D7
Krapina Croatia 46°10N 15°52E 199 B12
Krapina → Croatia 45°50N 15°50E 199 C12
Krapkowice Poland 50°29N 17°56E 185 H4
Krappitz = Krapkowice Poland 50°29N 17°56E 185 H4
Kras Croatia 45°35N 14°0E 199 C10
Krasavino Russia 60°58N 46°29E 186 B8
Krasieo Res. Thailand 14°49N 99°30E 236 E2
Kraskino Russia 42°44N 130°48E 220 C5
Krāslava Latvia 55°54N 27°10E 188 E4
Kraslice Czech Rep. 50°19N 12°31E 180 A5
Krasnaya Gorbatka Russia 55°52N 41°45E 190 C5
Krasnaya Polyana Russia 43°40N 40°13E 191 J5
Krasnaya Sloboda = Krasnoslobodsk Russia 48°42N 44°33E 191 F7
Krasne Ukraine 46°7N 29°15E 183 D14
Krasni Okny Ukraine 47°32N 29°27E 183 C14
Kraśnik Poland 50°55N 22°15E 185 H9
Krasno-Presnenskaya Russia 55°45N 37°32E 129 B2
Krasnoarmeisk Ukraine 48°18N 37°11E 189 H9
Krasnoarmeysk = Tayynsha Kazakhstan 53°50N 69°45E 217 B7
Krasnoarmeysk Russia 51°0N 45°42E 190 E7
Krasnoarmeyskiy Russia 47°0N 42°12E 191 G6
Krasnoarmeyskiy Rudnik = Dobropole Ukraine 48°25N 37°2E 189 H9
Krasnobrod Poland 50°33N 23°12E 185 H10
Krasnodar Russia 45°5N 39°0E 191 H4
Krasnodar □ Russia 46°30N 39°30E 191 G4
Krasnodarskoye Vdkhr. Russia 45°1N 39°23E 191 H4
Krasnodon Ukraine 48°17N 39°44E 189 H10
Krasnogorskiy Russia 56°10N 48°28E 190 B9
Krasnograd = Krasnohrad Ukraine 49°27N 35°27E 189 H8
Krasnogvardeysk = Gatchina Russia 59°35N 30°9E 188 C6
Krasnogvardeysk Ukraine 45°32N 34°16E 189 K8
Krasnogvardeyskoye Russia 45°52N 41°33E 191 H5
Krasnohrad Ukraine 49°27N 35°27E 189 H8
Krasnokamensk Russia 50°3N 118°0E 215 D12
Krasnokamsk Russia 58°4N 55°48E 186 C10
Krasnokokshaysk = Yoshkar Ola Russia 56°38N 47°55E 190 B8
Krasnokutsk Ukraine 50°10N 34°50E 189 G8
Krasnolesnyy Russia 51°53N 39°35E 189 G10
Krasnoperekopsk Ukraine 46°0N 33°54E 189 J7
Krasnorechenskiy Russia 44°41N 135°14E 220 B7
Krasnoselkup Russia 65°20N 82°10E 214 C9
Krasnoslobodsk Mordvinia, Russia 54°25N 43°45E 190 C6
Krasnoslobodsk Volgograd, Russia 48°42N 44°33E 191 F7
Krasnoturinsk Russia 59°46N 60°12E 186 C11
Krasnoufimsk Russia 56°36N 57°38E 186 C10
Krasnouralsk Russia 58°21N 60°3E 186 C11
Krasnovishersk Russia 60°23N 57°3E 186 B10
Krasnovodsk = Türkmenbashi Turkmenistan 40°5N 53°5E 247 A7
Krasnoyarsk Russia 56°8N 93°0E 215 D10
Krasnoyarskoye Russia 54°31N 21°56E 184 D8
Krasnoyarskoye Vdkhr. Russia 56°0N 92°30E 215 D10
Krasnoye = Krasnyy Russia 54°25N 31°30E 188 E6
Krasnoye = Ulan Erge Russia 46°19N 44°53E 191 G7
Krasnoyilsk Ukraine 47°59N 25°38E 183 C10
Krasnozavodsk Russia 56°27N 38°25E 188 D10
Krasnoznamensk Russia 54°57N 22°30E 184 D9
Krasny = Kyzyl Russia 51°50N 94°30E 217 B12
Krasny = Mozhga Russia 56°26N 52°15E 190 B11
Krasny Boyevik = Kotovsk Russia 52°36N 41°32E 190 D5
Krasny Sulin Russia 47°52N 40°8E 191 G5
Krasnystaw Poland 50°57N 23°5E 185 H10
Krasnyy Russia 54°25N 31°30E 188 E6
Krasnyy Kholm Russia 58°10N 37°10E 188 C9
Krasnyy Kut Russia 50°50N 47°0E 190 E8
Krasnyy Liman Ukraine 48°58N 37°50E 189 H9
Krasnyy Luch Ukraine 48°13N 39°0E 189 H10
Krasnyy Profintern Russia 57°45N 40°27E 188 D11
Krasnyy Yar Astrakhan, Russia 46°43N 48°23E 191 G9
Krasnyy Yar Samara, Russia 53°30N 50°22E 190 D10
Krasnyy Yar Volgograd, Russia 50°42N 44°45E 190 E7
Krasnyye Baki Russia 57°8N 45°10E 190 B7
Krasnyyoskolske Vdskh. Ukraine 49°27N 37°40E 189 H9
Kraszna → Hungary 48°4N 22°20E 182 B7
Kratie Cambodia 12°32N 106°10E 236 F6
Kratke Ra. Papua N. G. 6°45S 146°0E 286 D4
Kratovo Macedonia 42°6N 22°10E 202 D6
Krau Indonesia 3°19S 140°5E 231 E10
Kraulshavn = Nuussauq Greenland 74°8N 57°3W 154 C5
Kravanh, Chuor Phnum Cambodia 12°0N 103°32E 237 G4
Krč Czech Rep. 50°2N 14°26E 135 B2
Krefeld Germany 51°20N 6°33E 178 D2
Kremaston, L. Greece 38°52N 21°30E 204 C3
Kremen Croatia 44°28N 15°53E 199 D12
Kremenchuk Ukraine 49°5N 33°25E 189 H7
Kremenchuksk Vdskh. Ukraine 49°20N 32°30E 189 H7
Kremenets Ukraine 50°8N 25°43E 177 C13
Kremennaya Ukraine 49°1N 38°10E 189 H10
Kremges = Svitlovodsk Ukraine 49°2N 33°13E 189 H7
Kremlin Moscow, Russia 129 c2
Kremmen Germany 52°45N 13°1E 178 C9
Kremmling U.S.A. 40°4N 106°24W 304 F10
Kremnica Slovak Rep. 48°45N 18°50E 181 C11
Krems Austria 48°25N 15°36E 180 C8
Kremsmünster Austria 48°3N 14°8E 180 C7
Krenau = Chrzanów Poland 50°10N 19°21E 185 H6
Krestena Greece 37°35N 21°37E 204 D3
Krestovskiye, Ostrov Russia 59°57N 30°14E 137 B1
Kretinga Lithuania 55°53N 21°15E 184 C8
Krettamia Algeria 28°47N 3°27W 260 C4
Krettsy Russia 58°15N 32°30E 188 C7
Kreuzberg Bayern, Germany 50°22N 9°58E 179 E5
Kreuzberg Berlin, Germany 52°30N 13°24E 115 A3
Kreuzburg = Kluczbork Poland 50°58N 18°12E 185 H5
Kreuztal Germany 50°57N 8°0E 178 E4
Kria Vrisi Greece 40°41N 22°18E 202 F6
Kribi Cameroon 2°57N 9°56E 263 E6
Krichem Bulgaria 42°8N 24°28E 203 D8
Krichev = Krychaw Belarus 53°40N 31°41E 177 B16
Kril'on, Mys Russia 45°53N 142°5E 220 B11
Krim Slovenia 45°53N 14°30E 199 C11
Krim-Krim Chad 9°0N 15°24E 259 G3
Krindachyovka = Krasnyy Luch Ukraine 48°13N 39°0E 189 H10
Krios, Akra Greece 35°13N 23°34E 207 E4
Krishna → India 15°57N 80°59E 245 G5
Krishnagiri India 12°32N 78°16E 245 H4
Krishnanagar India 23°24N 88°33E 243 H13
Krishnaraja Sagar India 12°20N 76°30E 245 H3
Kristdala Sweden 57°24N 16°13E 163 G10
Kristians = Oppland □ Norway 61°15N 9°40E 164 C6
Kristiansand Norway 58°8N 8°1E 164 F5
Kristianstad Sweden 56°2N 14°9E 163 H8
Kristiansund Norway 63°7N 7°45E 164 A4
Kristiinankaupunki Finland 62°16N 21°21E 160 E19
Kristinehamn Sweden 59°18N 14°7E 162 E8
Kristinestad = Kristiinankaupunki Finland 62°16N 21°21E 160 E19
Kristinopol = Chervonohrad Ukraine 50°25N 24°10E 177 C13
Krithoti, Akra Greece 38°30N 21°2E 207 B3
Kriti Greece 35°15N 25°0E 207 E6
Kritsa Greece 35°10N 25°41E 207 E6
Kritzendorf Austria 48°19N 16°18E 142 A1
Kriva → Macedonia 42°5N 21°47E 202 D5
Kriva Palanka Macedonia 42°11N 22°19E 202 D6
Krivaja → Bos.-H. 44°27N 18°9E 182 F3
Krivelj Serbia 44°10N 22°5E 202 B6
Křivoklátsko △ Czech Rep. 50°1N 13°51E 180 A6
Krivoy Rog = Kryvyy Rih Ukraine 47°51N 33°20E 189 J7
Križevci Croatia 46°3N 16°32E 199 B13
Krk Croatia 45°8N 14°40E 199 C11
Krka → Slovenia 45°50N 15°30E 199 C12
Krka △ Croatia 43°53N 15°56E 199 E12
Krkonoše Czech Rep. 50°50N 15°35E 180 A8
Krkonoše △ Czech Rep. 50°43N 15°39E 180 A8
Krnjaja = Kljajićevo Serbia 45°45N 19°17E 182 E4
Krnov Czech Rep. 50°5N 17°40E 181 A10
Krobia Poland 51°47N 16°59E 185 G3
Krøderen Norway 60°9N 9°49E 164 D6
Krokees Greece 36°53N 22°32E 204 E4
Krokek Sweden 58°40N 16°24E 163 F10
Krokodil = Umgwenya → Mozam. 25°14S 32°18E 271 C5
Krokom Sweden 63°20N 14°30E 162 A8
Krokowa Poland 54°47N 18°9E 184 D5
Króksfjarðarnes Iceland 65°27N 21°56W 155 B5
Krokstadelva Norway 59°56N 10°1E 164 E7
Krolevets Ukraine 51°35N 33°20E 189 G7
Królewska Huta = Chorzów Poland 50°18N 18°57E 185 H5
Kroměříž Czech Rep. 49°18N 17°21E 181 B10
Krompachy Slovak Rep. 48°54N 20°52E 181 C13
Kromy Russia 52°48N 35°48E 189 F8
Kronach Germany 50°14N 11°19E 179 E7
Kronau = Kranjska Gora Slovenia 46°29N 13°48E 199 B10
Krong Kaoh Kong Cambodia 11°37N 102°59E 237 G4
Kronobergs län □ Sweden 56°45N 14°30E 163 H8
Kronprins Christian Land Greenland 80°30N 22°0W 154 A8
Kronprins Frederik Land Greenland 81°0N 45°0W 154 A6
Kronprins Olav Kyst Antarctica 69°0S 42°0E 151 C5
Kronprinsesse Märtha Kyst Antarctica 73°30S 10°0W 151 D2
Kronshtadt Russia 59°57N 29°51E 188 C5
Kronstadt = Brașov Romania 45°38N 25°35E 183 E10
Kroonstad S. Africa 27°43S 27°19E 270 C4
Kröpelin Germany 54°4N 11°47E 178 A7
Kropotkin Russia 45°28N 40°28E 191 H5
Kropp Germany 54°24N 9°31E 178 A5
Krosna Lithuania 54°23N 23°33E 184 D10
Krośniewice Poland 52°15N 19°11E 185 F6
Krosno Poland 49°42N 21°46E 185 J8
Krosno Odrzańskie Poland 52°3N 15°7E 185 F2
Krotoszyn Poland 51°42N 17°23E 185 G4
Krotovka Russia 53°18N 51°10E 190 D10
Krousonas Greece 35°13N 24°59E 207 E5
Krrabë Albania 41°13N 20°0E 202 E3
Krško Slovenia 45°57N 15°30E 199 C12
Krstača Serbia 42°57N 20°8E 202 D4
Kruger △ S. Africa 24°50S 26°10E 271 B4
Krugersdorp S. Africa 26°5S 27°46E 271 C4
Krui Indonesia 5°10S 103°55E 234 D2
Kruisfontein S. Africa 33°59S 24°43E 270 D3
Krujë Albania 41°32N 19°46E 202 E3
Krulevshchina = Krulyewshchyna Belarus 55°5N 27°45E 188 E4
Krulyewshchyna Belarus 55°5N 27°45E 188 E4
Krumbach Germany 48°13N 10°22E 179 G6
Krumë Albania 42°14N 20°28E 202 D4
Krummau = Český Krumlov Czech Rep. 48°43N 14°21E 180 C7
Krumme Lanke Germany 52°27N 13°14E 115 B2
Krummensee Germany 52°35N 13°41E 115 A5
Krummhübel = Karpacz Poland 50°46N 15°46E 185 H2
Krumovgrad Bulgaria 41°29N 25°38E 203 E9
Krung Thep = Bangkok Thailand 13°45N 100°35E 113 B2
Krupanj Serbia 44°25N 19°22E 202 B3
Krupina Slovak Rep. 48°22N 19°5E 181 C12
Krupinica → Slovak Rep. 48°4N 18°25E 181 C11
Krupki Belarus 54°19N 29°8E 177 A15
Krusboda Sweden 59°13N 18°14E 139 B3
Krusenstern, C. U.S.A. 67°8N 163°45W 303 C7
Kruševac Serbia 43°35N 21°28E 202 C5
Kruševo Macedonia 41°23N 21°19E 202 E5
Krushchyov = Svitlovodsk Ukraine 49°2N 33°13E 189 H7
Krushë e Madhe Kosovo 42°19N 20°39E 202 D4
Krushelnytsya Ukraine 49°7N 23°29E 185 J10
Kruszwica Poland 52°40N 18°20E 185 F5
Kruzenshterna, Proliv Russia 48°0N 154°0E 215 E16
Krychaw Belarus 53°40N 31°41E 177 B16
Krymsk Russia 44°50N 38°0E 189 K10
Krymskiy Poluostrov = Krymskyy Pivostriv Ukraine 45°0N 34°0E 189 K8
Krymskyy Pivostriv Ukraine 45°0N 34°0E 189 K8
Krynica Poland 49°25N 20°57E 185 J7
Krynica Morska Poland 54°23N 19°28E 184 D6
Krynki Poland 53°17N 23°43E 185 E10
Krynychne Ukraine 45°32N 28°40E 183 E13
Kryvyy Rih Ukraine 47°51N 33°20E 189 J7
Kryzhopil Ukraine 48°23N 28°53E 183 B13
Krzemieniec = Kremenets Ukraine 50°8N 25°43E 177 C13
Krzepice Poland 50°58N 18°50E 185 H5
Krzeszów Poland 50°24N 22°21E 185 H9
Krzna → Poland 52°8N 23°32E 185 F10
Krzywiń Poland 51°58N 16°50E 185 G3
Krzyż Wielkopolski Poland 52°52N 16°0E 185 F2
Ksabi Morocco 32°51N 4°13W 260 B4
Ksar Chellala Algeria 35°13N 2°19E 261 A5
Ksar el Boukhari Algeria 35°51N 2°52E 261 A5
Ksar el Kebir Morocco 35°0N 6°0W 260 B3
Ksar es Souk = Er Rachidia Morocco 31°58N 4°20W 260 B4
Ksar Rhilane Tunisia 33°0N 9°39E 258 B1
Książ Wielkopolski Poland 52°4N 17°14E 185 F4
Ksour, Mts. des Algeria 32°45N 0°30W 261 B4
Kstovo Russia 56°12N 44°13E 190 B7
Ku, W. el → Sudan 13°37N 25°15E 257 E2
Ku-Ring-Gai Chase △ Australia 33°39S 151°14E 283 B9
Ku Tree Res. U.S.A. 21°30N 157°59W 302 J14
Kuah Malaysia 6°19N 99°51E 237 J2
Kuala Indonesia 2°55N 105°47E 234 B3
Kuala Belait Malaysia 4°35N 114°11E 235 B4
Kuala Berang Malaysia 5°5N 103°1E 237 K4
Kuala Dungun = Dungun Malaysia 4°45N 103°25E 237 K4
Kuala Kangsar Malaysia 4°46N 100°56E 237 K3
Kuala Kelawang Malaysia 2°56N 102°5E 237 L4
Kuala Kerai Malaysia 5°30N 102°12E 237 K4
Kuala Kubu Bharu Malaysia 3°34N 101°39E 237 L3
Kuala Lipis Malaysia 4°10N 102°3E 237 K4
Kuala Lumpur Malaysia 3°9N 101°41E 237 L3
Kuala Nerang Malaysia 6°16N 100°37E 237 J3
Kuala Pilah Malaysia 2°45N 102°15E 237 L4
Kuala Rompin Malaysia 2°49N 103°29E 237 L4
Kuala Selangor Malaysia 3°20N 101°15E 237 L3
Kuala Sepetang Malaysia 4°49N 100°28E 237 K3
Kuala Terengganu Malaysia 5°20N 103°8E 237 K4
Kualajelai Indonesia 2°58S 110°46E 235 C4
Kualakapuas Indonesia 2°55S 114°20E 235 C4
Kualakurun Indonesia 1°10S 113°50E 235 C4
Kualapembuang Indonesia 3°14S 112°38E 235 C4
Kualapesaguan Indonesia 2°1S 110°7E 235 C4
Kualapu'u U.S.A. 21°9N 157°2W 302 B4
Kualasimpang Indonesia 4°17N 98°3E 234 B1
Kualatungkal Indonesia 0°49S 103°28E 234 C2
Kualoa Pt. U.S.A. 21°31N 157°50W 302 J14
Kuamat Malaysia 5°13N 117°30E 235 A5
Kuan Shan Taiwan 23°14N 120°54E 225 C2
Kuanao Taiwan 24°31N 118°24E 225 a
Kuancheng China 40°37N 118°30E 227 D10
Kuandang Indonesia 0°56N 123°1E 231 D6
Kuandian China 40°45N 124°45E 224 B2
Kuangchou = Guangzhou China 23°6N 113°13E 121 B2
Kuangfu Taiwan 23°40N 121°25E 225 C3
Kuanhsi Taiwan 24°48N 121°10E 225 B3
Kuanmiao Taiwan 22°58N 120°19E 225 D2
Kuanshan Taiwan 23°3N 121°9E 225 D3
Kuantan Malaysia 3°49N 103°20E 237 L4
Kuanyin Ilan, Taiwan 24°23N 121°46E 225 B3
Kuanyin Taoyüan, Taiwan 25°2N 121°4E 225 A3
Kuapā Pond U.S.A. 21°17N 157°43W 302 K14
Kuapnit Balinsasayao △ Phil. 10°53N 124°55E 233 F5
Kuba = Quba Azerbaijan 41°21N 48°32E 191 K9
Kubah △ Malaysia 1°35N 110°9E 235 B4
Kuban → Russia 45°20N 37°30E 189 K9
Kuban Depression = Prikubanskaya Nizmennost Russia 45°39N 38°33E 191 H4
Kubaysah Iraq 33°35N 42°37E 213 G10
Kubenskoye, Ozero Russia 59°40N 39°25E 188 C10
Kuberle = Krasnoarmeyskiy Russia 47°0N 42°12E 191 G6
Kubokawa = Shimanto Japan 33°12N 133°8E 222 D5
Kubor, Mt. Papua N. G. 6°10S 144°44E 286 D3
Kubrat Bulgaria 43°49N 26°31E 203 C10
Kubu Indonesia 8°16S 115°35E 231 J18
Kubumesaai Indonesia 1°31N 115°6E 235 B5
Kubutambahan Indonesia 8°5S 115°10E 231 J18
Kucar, Tanjung Indonesia 8°39S 114°34E 231 K18
Kučevo Serbia 44°30N 21°40E 202 B5
Kuchaman India 27°13N 74°47E 242 F6
Kuchchaveli Sri Lanka 8°49N 81°6E 245 K5
Kuchenspitze Austria 47°7N 10°12E 180 D3
Kuchinda India 21°44N 84°21E 243 J11
Kuching Malaysia 1°33N 110°25E 235 B4
Kuchino-eruba-Jima Japan 30°28N 130°12E 221 J5
Kuchino-Shima Japan 29°57N 129°55E 221 K4
Kuchinotsu Japan 32°36N 130°11E 222 E2
Kuchl Austria 47°37N 13°9E 180 D6
Kūchnay Darvīshān Afghan. 30°59N 64°10E 240 C2
Kuchurhan → Ukraine 46°33N 29°57E 183 D14
Kucing = Kuching Malaysia 1°33N 110°25E 235 B4
Kuçovë Albania 40°47N 19°57E 202 F3
Küçükbahçe Turkey 38°33N 26°24E 205 C8
Küçükköy Balıkesir, Turkey 39°16N 26°42E 205 B8
Küçükköy İstanbul, Turkey 41°3N 28°52E 122 B1
Küçükkuyu Turkey 39°32N 26°36E 205 B8
Küçükmenderes → Turkey 37°57N 27°16E 205 D9
Küçüksu Turkey 41°5N 29°5E 122 B2
Kud → Pakistan 26°5N 66°20E 242 F2
Kuda India 23°10N 71°15E 242 H4
Kuda Indonesia 1°1N 112°58E 235 B4
Kudahuvadhoo Maldives 2°40N 72°54E 272 d
Kudahuvadhoo Channel Maldives 2°40N 73°0E 272 d
Kudaka-shima Japan 26°9N 127°53E 288 a
Kudal India 16°2N 73°41E 245 F1
Kudalier → India 18°35N 79°48E 244 E4
Kudamatsu Japan 34°0N 131°52E 222 D3
Kudankita Tokyo, Japan 140 a3
Kudarebe Aruba 12°37N 70°4W 322 f
Kudat Malaysia 6°55N 116°55E 235 A5
Kudirkos Naumiestis Lithuania 54°46N 22°53E 184 D9
Kudowa-Zdrój Poland 50°27N 16°15E 185 H3
Kudremukh India 13°15N 75°20E 245 H2
Kudrovo Russia 59°54N 30°30E 137 B3
Kudus Indonesia 6°48S 110°51E 235 D4
Kudymkar Russia 59°1N 54°39E 186 C9
Kueishan Tao Taiwan 24°51N 121°57E 225 B3
Kueiyang = Guiyang China 26°32N 106°40E 228 D6
Kufra Oasis = Al Kufrah Libya 24°17N 23°15E 258 D4
Kufstein Austria 47°35N 12°11E 180 D5
Kugaaruk = Pelly Bay Canada 68°38N 89°50W 295 D14
Kugluktuk Canada 67°50N 115°5W 294 D8
Kugong I. Canada 56°18N 79°50W 298 A4
Kūh Dasht Iran 33°32N 47°36E 213 F12
Kūh-e Sorkh Iran 35°30N 58°45E 216 E5
Kūhak Iran 27°12N 63°10E 240 D1
Kuhan Pakistan 28°19N 67°14E 242 E2
Kūhbonān Iran 31°23N 56°19E 247 D8
Kūhestak Iran 26°47N 57°2E 247 E8
Kūhestān Afghan. 34°39N 61°12E 240 B1
Kuhin Iran 36°22N 49°40E 247 B6
Kūhīrī Iran 26°55N 61°2E 247 E9
Kühiston-Badakhshon □ Tajikistan 38°30N 73°0E 217 E8
Kuhmo Finland 64°7N 29°31E 160 D23
Kuhn Chae △ Thailand 19°8N 99°24E 236 C2
Kuhnsdorf Austria 46°37N 14°38E 180 E7
Kūhpāyeh Eşfahan, Iran 32°44N 52°20E 247 C7
Kūhpāyeh Kermān, Iran 30°35N 57°15E 247 D8
Kūhrān, Kūh-e Iran 26°46N 58°12E 247 E8
Kui Buri Thailand 12°3N 99°52E 237 F2
Kuiburi △ Thailand 12°10N 99°37E 237 F2
Kuichong China 22°38N 114°25E 219 a
Kuiseb → Namibia 22°59S 14°31E 270 B1
Kuito Angola 12°22S 16°55E 265 E3
Kuiu I. U.S.A. 57°45N 134°10W 296 B2
Kujalleq □ Greenland 61°0N 44°0W 154 E6
Kujang N. Korea 39°57N 126°1E 224 C3

Kujawsko-Pomorskie □ Poland 53°20N 18°30E 184 E5
Kuji Japan 40°11N 141°46E 220 D10
Kujū-San Japan 33°5N 131°15E 222 D3
Kuk Papua N. G. 5°47S 144°19E 286 C3
Kukarka = Sovetsk Russia 57°38N 48°53E 190 B9
Kukava Ukraine 48°37N 27°43E 183 B12
Kukavica Serbia 42°48N 21°57E 202 D5
Kukawa Nigeria 12°58N 13°27E 263 C7
Kuk'eng Taiwan 23°38N 120°33E 225 C2
Kukës Albania 42°5N 20°27E 202 D4
Kuki Japan 36°4N 139°40E 223 A11
Kukipi Papua N. G. 8°10S 146°6E 286 E4
Kukmor Russia 56°11N 50°54E 190 B10
Kükong = Shaoguan China 24°48N 113°35E 229 E9
Kuku Pt. Wake I. 19°18N 166°34E 302 b
Kukuan Taiwan 24°17N 121°2E 225 B3
Kukuihaele U.S.A. 20°5N 155°35W 302 C6
Kukup Malaysia 1°20N 103°27E 237 d
Kukup, Pulau Malaysia 1°18N 103°25E 237 d
Kukvidze Russia 50°40N 43°0E 190 E6
Kula Bulgaria 43°52N 22°36E 202 C6
Kula Serbia 45°37N 19°32E 182 E4
Kula Turkey 38°32N 28°40E 205 C10
Kula Gulf Solomon Is. 8°5S 157°18E 287 M9
K'ula Kangri Asia 28°14N 90°36E 241 A3
K'ula Shan Bhutan 28°14N 90°36E 241 A3
Kulachi Pakistan 31°56N 70°27E 242 D4
Kulai Malaysia 1°44N 103°35E 237 M4
Kulal, Mt. Kenya 2°43N 36°56E 266 D4
Kulaly Aral Kazakhstan 45°0N 50°5E 191 H10
Kulasekarappattinam India 8°20N 78°5E 245 K4
Kulassein I. Phil. 6°25N 120°41E 233 H3
Kulaura Bangla. 24°32N 92°3E 241 C4
Kulautuva Lithuania 54°56N 23°36E 184 D10
Kuldiga Latvia 56°58N 21°59E 184 B8
Kuldiga □ Latvia 56°55N 22°0E 184 B8
Kuldja = Yining China 43°58N 81°10E 217 D10
Kuldu Sudan 12°50N 28°30E 257 E2
Kulebaki Russia 55°22N 42°25E 190 C6
Kulen Cambodia 13°50N 104°40E 236 F5
Kulen Vakuf Bos.-H. 44°35N 16°2E 199 D13
Kulgam India 33°36N 75°2E 243 C6
Kulgera Australia 25°50S 133°18E 280 D1
Kulhudhuffushi Maldives 6°37N 73°3E 272 d
Kulim Malaysia 5°22N 100°34E 237 K3
Kulin Australia 32°40S 118°2E 279 F2
Kulittalai India 10°55N 78°25E 245 J4
Kulkayu = Hartley Bay Canada 53°25N 129°15W 296 C3
Kullen Sweden 56°18N 12°26E 163 H6
Kullu India 31°58N 77°6E 242 D7
Kulmbach Germany 50°6N 11°26E 179 E7
Kŭlob Tajikistan 37°55N 69°50E 217 E7
Kulosaari Finland 60°11N 25°0E 121 B3
Kulp Turkey 38°29N 41°2E 213 C9
Kulpawn ➜ Ghana 10°20N 1°5W 263 D4
Kulsary = Qulsary Kazakhstan 46°59N 54°1E 187 E9
Kulti India 23°43N 86°50E 243 H12
Kulu Turkey 39°5N 33°4E 212 C5
Kulumadau Papua N. G. 9°3S 152°43E 286 E7
Kulunda Russia 52°35N 78°57E 217 B9
Kulundinskoye, Ozero Russia 53°0N 79°36E 217 B9
Kulungar Afghan. 34°0N 69°2E 242 C3
Külvand Iran 31°21N 54°35E 247 D7
Kulwin Australia 35°2S 142°42E 282 C5
Kulyab = Kŭlob Tajikistan 37°55N 69°50E 217 E7
Kuma Japan 33°39N 132°54E 222 D4
Kuma ➜ Russia 44°55N 47°0E 191 H8
Kumafşarı Turkey 37°19N 29°32E 205 D11
Kumaganum Nigeria 13°8N 10°38E 263 C7
Kumagaya Japan 36°9N 139°22E 223 A11
Kumai Indonesia 2°44S 111°43E 235 C4
Kumai, Teluk Indonesia 3°0S 111°43E 235 C4
Kumalar Dağı Turkey 38°15N 30°20E 205 C12
Kumamba, Kepulauan Indonesia 1°36S 138°45E 231 E9
Kumamoto Japan 32°45N 130°45E 222 E2
Kumamoto □ Japan 32°55N 130°55E 222 E2
Kumano Japan 33°54N 136°5E 223 D8
Kumano-Nada Japan 33°47N 136°20E 223 D8
Kumanovo Macedonia 42°9N 21°42E 202 D5
Kumar ➜ Afghan. 34°30N 70°28E 240 B3
Kumara N.Z. 42°37S 171°12E 285 C6
Kumarina Roadhouse Australia 24°41S 119°32E 279 D2
Kumarkhali Bangla. 23°51N 89°15E 241 D2
Kumasi Ghana 6°41N 1°38W 262 D4
Kumba Cameroon 4°36N 9°24E 263 E6
Kumbağ Turkey 40°51N 27°27E 203 F11
Kumbakonam India 10°58N 79°25E 245 J4
Kumbarilla Australia 27°15S 150°55E 281 D5
Kumbatine △ Australia 31°8S 152°35E 283 A10
Kumbhraj India 24°22N 77°3E 242 G7
Kumbia Australia 26°41S 151°39E 281 D5
Kumbo Cameroon 6°15N 10°36E 263 D7
Kumbukkan Oya ➜ Sri Lanka 6°35N 81°40E 245 L5
Kŭmch'on N. Korea 38°10N 126°29E 224 C3
Kumdah Si. Arabia 20°23N 45°5E 248 B4
Kume-Shima Japan 26°20N 126°47E 221 L3
Kumeny Russia 58°10N 49°47E 190 A9
Kumertau Russia 52°45N 55°57E 186 D10
Kumharsain India 31°19N 77°27E 242 D7
Kumi Uganda 1°30N 33°58E 268 B3
Kumkale Turkey 39°59N 26°11E 203 G10
Kumla Örebro, Sweden 59°8N 15°10E 162 E9
Kumla Stockholm, Sweden 59°13N 18°11E 139 B3
Kumlu Turkey 36°21N 36°27E 250 B7
Kumluca Turkey 36°22N 30°20E 205 E12
Kummerower See Germany 53°49N 12°51E 178 B8
Kumo Nigeria 10°1N 11°12E 263 C7
Kumo älv = Kokemäenjoki ➜ Finland 61°32N 21°44E 188 B1
Kumon Bum Burma 26°30N 97°15E 241 B6
Kumotori-Yama Japan 35°51N 138°57E 223 B10
Kumta India 14°29N 74°25E 245 G2
Kumtag Shamo China 39°40N 92°0E 218 D7
Kumukahi, C. U.S.A. 19°31N 154°49W 302 D7
Kumusi ➜ Papua N. G. 8°16S 148°13E 286 E5
Kumyalı = Koma Tou Yialou Cyprus 35°25N 34°8E 207 E10
Kumylzhenskaya Russia 49°51N 42°38E 190 E6
Kuna U.S.A. 43°30N 116°25W 304 E5
Kunágota Hungary 46°26N 21°3E 182 D6
Kunak Malaysia 4°41N 118°15E 235 B5
Kunashir, Ostrov Russia 44°0N 146°0E 215 E15
Kunchaung Burma 23°50N 96°35E 241 D6
Kunchha Nepal 28°8N 84°20E 243 E11
Kunda Estonia 59°30N 26°34E 188 C4
Kunda India 25°43N 81°31E 243 G9
Kundar ➜ Pakistan 31°56N 69°19E 242 D3
Kundelungu △ Dem. Rep. of the Congo 10°30S 27°40E 269 E2
Kundelungu Ouest △ Dem. Rep. of the Congo 9°55S 27°17E 269 D2
Kundian Pakistan 32°27N 71°28E 242 C4
Kundiawa Papua N. G. 6°2S 145°1E 286 D3
Kundla India 21°21N 71°25E 242 J4
Kundur Indonesia 0°45N 103°25E 234 B2
Kunene □ Namibia 20°0S 14°0E 270 A1
Kung, Ao Thailand 8°5N 98°24E 237 a
Kunga ➜ Bangla. 21°46N 89°30E 241 E2
Kungälv Sweden 57°53N 11°59E 163 G5
Kungens kurva Sweden 59°15N 17°53E 139 B1
Kunghit I. Canada 52°6N 131°3W 296 C2
Kungkuan Taiwan 24°35N 120°44E 225 B2
Kungliao Taiwan 25°1N 121°54E 225 A3
Kungliga Slottet Stockholm, Sweden 139 b2
Kungrad = Qŭnghirot Uzbekistan 43°2N 58°50E 216 D5
Kungsängen Sweden 59°29N 17°45E 162 E11
Kungsbacka Sweden 57°30N 12°5E 163 G6
Kungsgården Sweden 60°37N 16°35E 162 D10
Kungshamn Sweden 58°22N 11°15E 163 F5
Kungshatt Sweden 59°17N 17°53E 139 B1
Kungsholmen Sweden 59°20N 18°2E 139 A2
Kungsör Sweden 59°25N 16°5E 162 E10
Kungssuliao Taiwan 24°37N 120°45E 225 B2
Kungu Dem. Rep. of the Congo 2°47N 19°12E 264 B3
Kungur Russia 57°25N 56°57E 186 C10
Kungurri Australia 21°4S 148°45E 280 b
Kungyangon Burma 16°27N 96°20E 241 G6
Kunhar ➜ Pakistan 34°20N 73°30E 243 B5
Kunhegyes Hungary 47°22N 20°36E 182 C5
Kunia U.S.A. 21°28N 158°4W 302 K13
Kunigami Japan 26°46N 128°12E 288 a
Kunimi-Dake Japan 32°33N 131°1E 222 E3
Kuningan Jakarta, Indonesia 6°13S 106°49E 122 B1
Kuningan Jawa Barat, Indonesia 6°59S 108°29E 235 D3
Kunisaki Japan 33°33N 131°45E 222 D3
Kunitachi Japan 35°41N 139°27E 140 A1
Kunjirap Daban Pakistan 36°52N 75°27E 240 A4
Kunlara Australia 34°54S 139°55E 282 C3
Kunlong Burma 23°20N 98°50E 228 F2
Kunlun Shan Asia 36°0N 86°30E 217 E11
Kunlun Shankou China 35°38N 94°4E 218 D7
Kunmadaras Hungary 47°28N 20°45E 182 C5
Kunming China 25°1N 102°41E 228 E4
Kunming Hu China 39°59N 116°13E 114 B1
Kunmunya ✪ Australia 15°26S 124°42E 278 C3
Kunnamkulam India 10°38N 76°7E 245 J3
Kunów Poland 50°57N 21°17E 185 H8
Kunratice Czech Rep. 50°0N 14°28E 135 B2
Kunshan China 31°22N 120°58E 229 B13
Kunsthistorisches Museum Vienna, Austria 142 b1
Kunszentmárton Hungary 46°50N 20°20E 182 D5
Kunszentmiklós Hungary 47°2N 19°8E 182 C4
Kuntaur Senegal 13°40N 14°48W 262 C2
Kunua Papua N. G. 5°46S 154°43E 286 C8
Kununurra Australia 15°40S 128°50E 278 C4
Kunwari ➜ India 26°26N 79°11E 243 F8
Kunya-Urgench = Köneürgench Turkmenistan 42°19N 59°10E 216 D5
Künzelsau Germany 49°17N 9°42E 179 F5
Kunzulu Dem. Rep. of the Congo 3°28S 16°12E 264 C3
Kuohsing Taiwan 24°2N 120°51E 225 B2
Kuopio Finland 62°53N 27°35E 160 E22
Kupa ➜ Croatia 45°28N 16°24E 199 C13
Kupang Indonesia 10°19S 123°39E 231 F6
Kupchino Russia 59°50N 30°23E 137 B2
Kupiano Papua N. G. 10°4S 148°14E 286 F5
Kūpikipiki'ō Pt. U.S.A. 21°15N 157°47W 302 K14
Kupino Russia 54°21N 77°16E 217 B9
Kupreanof I. U.S.A. 56°50N 133°30W 296 B2
Kupres Bos.-H. 43°56N 17°15E 182 G2
Kupyansk Ukraine 49°52N 37°35E 189 H9
Kupyansk-Uzlovoi Ukraine 49°40N 37°43E 189 H9
Kuqa China 41°35N 82°30E 217 D10
Kür ➜ Azerbaijan 39°29N 49°15E 213 C13
Kur ➜ Bhutan 26°50N 91°0E 241 B3
Kür Dili Azerbaijan 39°3N 49°13E 213 C13
Kura = Kür ➜ Azerbaijan 39°29N 49°15E 213 C13
Kurahashi-Jima Japan 34°8N 132°31E 222 C4
Kuramo Waters Nigeria 6°25N 3°26E 124 B2
Kuranda Australia 16°48S 145°35E 280 B4
Kuranga India 22°4N 69°10E 242 H3
Kurashiki Japan 34°40N 133°50E 222 C5
Kurayn Si. Arabia 27°39N 49°50E 247 E6
Kurayoshi Japan 35°26N 133°50E 222 B5
Kurbağalı ➜ Turkey 40°58N 29°1E 122 C2
Kūrchatov Kazakhstan 50°45N 78°32E 217 B9
Kürdämir Azerbaijan 40°25N 48°3E 191 K9
Kurdistan Asia 37°20N 43°30E 213 D10
Kurduvadi India 18°8N 75°29E 244 E2
Kŭrdzhali Bulgaria 41°38N 25°21E 203 E9
Kŭrdzhali □ Bulgaria 41°38N 25°21E 203 E9
Kure Japan 34°14N 132°32E 222 C4
Küre Turkey 41°48N 33°43E 212 B5
Küre Dağları Turkey 41°50N 34°10E 212 B6
Kure I. U.S.A. 28°25N 178°25W 302 F8
Kuressaare Estonia 58°15N 22°30E 188 C2
Kurgan Russia 55°26N 65°18E 216 A7
Kurgan-Tyube = Qŭrghonteppa Tajikistan 37°50N 68°47E 217 E7
Kurganinsk Russia 44°54N 40°34E 191 H5
Kurgannaya = Kurganinsk Russia 44°54N 40°34E 191 H5
Kuri India 26°37N 70°43E 242 F4
Kuria Maria Is. = Ḩallāniyat, Jazā'ir al Oman 17°30N 55°58E 249 C6
Kurichchi India 11°36N 77°35E 245 J3
Kuridala Australia 21°16S 140°29E 280 C3
Kurigram Bangla. 25°49N 89°39E 241 C2
Kurihara Japan 35°45N 139°34E 140 A2
Kurikka Finland 62°36N 22°24E 160 E20
Kuril Basin Pac. Oc. 47°0N 150°0E 150 E15
Kuril Is. = Kurilskiye Ostrova Russia 45°0N 150°0E 215 E16
Kuril-Kamchatka Trench Pac. Oc. 44°0N 153°0E 288 C7
Kurilsk Russia 45°14N 147°53E 215 E15
Kurilskiye Ostrova Russia 45°0N 150°0E 215 E16
Kurino Japan 31°57N 130°43E 222 F2
Kurinskaya Kosa = Kür Dili Azerbaijan 39°3N 49°13E 213 C13
Kurisches Haff = Kurshskiy Zaliv Russia 55°9N 21°6E 184 C8
Kürkçü Turkey 36°34N 33°39E 250 B4
Kurkheda India 20°37N 80°12E 244 D5
Kurkur Egypt 23°50N 32°0E 256 C3
Kurla India 19°4N 72°52E 130 A2
Kurlkuta ✪ Australia 24°0S 127°5E 278 D4
Kurlovskiy Russia 55°25N 40°40E 190 C5
Kurmuk Sudan 10°33N 34°21E 257 E3
Kurmuri India 19°4N 72°53E 130 A2
Kurnool India 15°45N 78°0E 245 G4
Kuro-Shima Kagoshima, Japan 30°50N 129°57E 221 J4
Kuro-Shima Okinawa, Japan 24°14N 124°1E 221 M2
Kurobe-Gawe ➜ Japan 36°55N 137°25E 223 A9
Kurogi Japan 33°12N 130°40E 222 D2
Kuror, J. Sudan 20°27N 31°30E 256 C3
Kurow N.Z. 44°44S 170°29E 285 E5
Kurów Poland 51°23N 22°12E 185 G9
Kurrajong Australia 33°33S 150°42E 283 B9
Kurram ➜ Pakistan 32°36N 71°20E 242 C4
Kurri Kurri Australia 32°50S 151°28E 283 B9
Kurrimine Australia 17°47S 146°6E 280 B4
Kursavka Russia 44°29N 42°32E 191 H6
Kurse Korhi India 20°14N 80°46E 244 D5
Kurseong = Karsiyang India 26°56N 88°18E 241 B2
Kürshim Kazakhstan 48°34N 83°39E 217 C10
Kurshskaya Kosa ⌂ Russia 55°7N 20°45E 184 C7
Kurshskiy Zaliv Russia 55°9N 21°6E 184 C8
Kuršių Nerijos △ Lithuania 55°30N 21°6E 184 C8
Kursk Russia 51°42N 36°11E 189 G9
Kursk □ Russia 51°50N 36°10E 189 G9
Kursu = Salla Finland 66°50N 28°49E 160 C23
Kuršumlija Serbia 43°9N 21°19E 202 C5
Kuršumlijska Banja Serbia 43°3N 21°11E 202 C5
Kurşunlu Bursa, Turkey 40°3N 29°40E 203 F13
Kurşunlu Çankırı, Turkey 40°51N 33°15E 212 B5
Kurtalan Turkey 37°56N 41°44E 213 D9
Kurtbey Turkey 41°9N 26°35E 203 E10
Kurtistown U.S.A. 19°36N 155°4W 302 D6
Kuru South Sudan 7°43N 26°31E 257 F2
Kuru, Bahr el ➜ South Sudan 8°10N 26°50E 257 F2
Kurucaşile Turkey 41°49N 32°42E 212 B5
Kuruçay Turkey 39°39N 38°29E 246 B3
Kurukshetra = Thanesar India 30°1N 76°52E 242 D7
Kuruktag China 41°0N 89°0E 217 D11
Kuruman S. Africa 27°28S 23°28E 270 C3
Kuruman ➜ S. Africa 26°56S 20°39E 270 C3
Kurume Fukuoka, Japan 33°15N 130°30E 222 D2
Kurume Tōkyō, Japan 35°45N 139°31E 140 A2
Kurun ➜ South Sudan 5°30N 34°17E 257 F3
Kurunegala Sri Lanka 7°30N 80°23E 245 L5
Kurupukari Guyana 4°43N 58°37W 329 C6
Kurya Russia 61°42N 57°9E 186 B10
Kuryanovo Russia 55°39N 37°42E 129 C3
Kus Gölü Turkey 40°10N 27°55E 203 F11
Kuşadası Turkey 37°52N 27°15E 212 D2
Kuşadası Körfezi Turkey 37°56N 27°0E 205 D8
Kusamba Indonesia 8°34S 115°27E 231 K18
Kusatsu Gumma, Japan 36°37N 138°36E 223 A10
Kusatsu Shiga, Japan 34°58N 135°57E 223 C7
Kusawa L. Canada 60°20N 136°13W 296 A1
Kusel Germany 49°32N 7°24E 179 F3
Kushaka Nigeria 10°32N 6°48E 263 C6
Kushalgarh India 23°10N 74°27E 242 H6
Kushalnagar India 12°14N 75°57E 245 H2
Kushchevskaya Russia 46°33N 39°35E 191 G4
Kusheriki Nigeria 10°33N 6°28E 263 C6
Kushikino Japan 31°44N 130°16E 222 F2
Kushima Japan 31°29N 131°14E 222 F3
Kushimoto Japan 33°28N 135°47E 223 D7
Kushiro Japan 43°0N 144°25E 220 C12
Kushiro-Gawa ➜ Japan 42°59N 144°23E 220 C12
Kushiro Shitsugen △ Japan 43°9N 144°26E 220 C12
Kūshk Iran 28°46N 56°51E 247 D8
Kushka = Serhetabat Turkmenistan 35°20N 62°18E 247 C9
Kushmurun = Qusmuryn Kazakhstan 52°27N 64°36E 216 B6
Kushnytsya Ukraine 48°27N 23°15E 183 B8
Kushol India 33°40N 76°36E 243 C7
Kushtia Bangla. 23°55N 89°5E 241 D2
Kushva Russia 58°18N 59°45E 186 C10
Kuskan Turkey 36°29N 33°17E 250 B4
Kuskokwim ➜ U.S.A. 60°5N 162°25W 303 F7
Kuskokwim B. U.S.A. 59°45N 162°25W 303 G7
Kuskokwim Mts. U.S.A. 62°30N 156°0W 303 E9
Kuskovo Russia 55°44N 37°48E 129 B3
Kusmi India 23°17N 83°55E 243 H10
Kusŏng N. Korea 39°59N 125°15E 224 C2
Kussharo-Ko Japan 43°38N 144°21E 220 C12
Kustanay = Qostanay Kazakhstan 53°10N 63°35E 216 B6
Küstenje = Constanța Romania 44°14N 28°38E 183 F13
Kustia India 22°31N 88°23E 124 B2
Küstrin = Kostrzyn Poland 52°35N 14°39E 185 F1
Kusu Japan 33°16N 131°9E 222 D3
Kut, Ko Thailand 11°40N 102°35E 237 G4
Kuta Indonesia 8°43S 115°11E 231 K18
Kutacane Indonesia 3°50N 97°50E 234 B1
Kütahya Turkey 39°30N 30°2E 205 B12
Kütahya □ Turkey 39°10N 29°30E 205 B11
Kutai △ Indonesia 0°23N 117°16E 235 B5
Kutaisi Georgia 42°19N 42°40E 191 J6
Kutaraja = Banda Aceh Indonesia 5°35N 95°20E 234 A1
Kutch, Gulf of = Kachchh, Gulf of India 22°50N 69°15E 242 H3
Kutch, Rann of = Kachchh, Rann of India 24°0N 70°0E 242 H4
Kutina Croatia 45°29N 16°48E 199 C13
Kutiyana India 21°36N 70°2E 242 J4
Kutjevo Croatia 45°23N 17°55E 182 E2
Kutkai Burma 23°27N 97°56E 241 D6
Kutkashen = Qäbälä Azerbaijan 40°58N 47°47E 191 K8
Kutná Hora Czech Rep. 49°57N 15°16E 180 B8
Kutno Poland 52°15N 19°23E 185 F6
Kutru India 19°5N 80°46E 244 E5
Kutse Botswana 21°7S 22°16E 270 B3
Kuttabul Australia 21°1S 148°54E 280 b
Kutu Dem. Rep. of the Congo 2°40S 18°11E 264 C3
Kutu Moke Dem. Rep. of the Congo 3°12S 17°21E 264 C3
Kutum Sudan 14°10N 24°40E 257 E1
Kúty Slovak Rep. 48°40N 17°3E 181 C10
Kuty Ukraine 48°16N 25°11E 183 B10
Kuujjuaq Canada 58°6N 68°15W 295 F18
Kuujjuarapik Canada 55°20N 77°35W 295 F16
Kuusamo Finland 65°57N 29°8E 160 D23
Kuusankoski Finland 60°55N 26°38E 188 B4
Kuvango Angola 14°28S 16°20E 265 E3
Kuvshinovo Russia 57°2N 34°11E 188 D8
Kuwait = Al Kuwayt Kuwait 29°30N 48°0E 246 D5
Kuwait ■ Asia 29°30N 47°30E 246 D5
Kuwana Japan 35°5N 136°43E 223 B8
Kuwana ➜ India 26°25N 83°15E 243 F10
Kuwol-san N. Korea 38°30N 125°15E 224 C2
Kuybyshev = Samara Russia 53°8N 50°6E 190 D10
Kuybyshev Russia 55°27N 78°19E 214 D8
Kuybyshevka-Vostochnaya = Belogorsk Russia 51°0N 128°20E 215 D13
Kuybyshevo Ukraine 47°25N 36°40E 189 J9
Kuybyshevskoye Vdkhr. Russia 55°2N 49°30E 190 C9
Kuye He ➜ China 38°23N 110°46E 226 E6
Kūyeh Iran 38°45N 47°57E 246 B5
Kuyto, Ozero Russia 65°6N 31°20E 160 D24
Kuytun China 44°25N 85°0E 217 D11
Kuyucak Turkey 37°55N 28°28E 205 D10
Kuyumba Russia 60°58N 96°59E 215 C10
Kuzey Anadolu Dağları Turkey 41°0N 36°45E 212 B7
Kuzguncuk Turkey 41°2N 29°2E 122 B2
Kuzhitturai India 8°18N 77°11E 245 K3
Kuzitrin ➜ U.S.A. 65°10N 165°25W 303 D6
Kuzmin Serbia 45°2N 19°25E 182 E4
Kuznetsk Russia 53°12N 46°40E 190 D8
Kuznetsovo = Konakovo Russia 56°40N 36°51E 188 D9
Kuzomen Russia 66°22N 36°50E 186 A6
Kuzucubelen Turkey 36°51N 34°27E 250 B5
Kuzyminki Russia 55°42N 37°46E 129 B3
Kværnangen Norway 70°5N 21°15E 160 A19
Kværndrup Denmark 55°10N 10°31E 163 J4
Kvaløya Norway 69°40N 18°30E 160 B18
Kvam Norway 61°40N 9°42E 164 C6
Kvänum Sweden 58°18N 13°11E 163 F7
Kvareli = Qvareli Georgia 41°57N 45°47E 191 K7
Kvarner Croatia 44°50N 14°10E 199 D11
Kvarnerič Croatia 44°43N 14°37E 199 D11
Kvås Norway 58°16N 7°14E 164 F4
Kvernaland Norway 58°47N 5°45E 164 F2
Kvichak B. U.S.A. 58°48N 157°30W 303 G8
Kvicksund Sweden 59°27N 16°19E 162 E10
Kvikne Norway 62°35N 10°16E 164 B7
Kvillsfors Sweden 57°24N 15°29E 163 G9
Kvinesdal Norway 58°19N 6°55E 164 F3
Kvina ➜ Norway 58°17N 6°56E 164 F3
Kvinlog Norway 58°31N 6°55E 164 F3
Kvirily = Zestaponi Georgia 42°6N 43°0E 191 J6
Kvismare kanal Sweden 59°11N 15°35E 162 E9
Kvissleby Sweden 62°18N 17°22E 162 B11
Kviteseid Norway 59°24N 8°29E 164 E5
Kvitøya Svalbard 80°8N 32°35E 154 A14
Kwabhaca S. Africa 30°51S 29°0E 271 D4
Kwai = Khwae Noi ➜ Thailand 14°1N 99°32E 236 E2
Kwai Chung Hong Kong, China 22°22N 114°7E 122 A2
Kwajalein Marshall Is. 9°5N 167°20E 288 G8
Kwakhanai Botswana 21°39S 21°16E 270 B3
Kwakoegron Suriname 5°12N 55°25W 329 B6
Kwale Coast, Kenya 4°15S 39°31E 268 C4
Kwale Nigeria 5°46N 6°26E 263 D6
Kwamalasamutu Suriname 2°20N 56°47W 329 C6
KwaMashu S. Africa 29°45S 30°58E 271 C5
Kwamouth Dem. Rep. of the Congo 3°9S 16°12E 264 C3
Kwando ➜ Africa 18°27S 23°32E 265 F4
Kwangchow = Guangzhou China 23°6N 113°13E 121 B2
Kwangdaeri N. Korea 40°34N 127°33E 227 D14
Kwango ➜ Dem. Rep. of the Congo 3°14S 17°22E 264 C3
Kwangsi-Chuang = Guangxi Zhuangzu Zizhiqu □ China 24°0N 109°0E 228 F7
Kwangtung = Guangdong □ China 23°0N 113°0E 229 F9
Kwara □ Nigeria 8°45N 4°30E 263 D6
Kwataboahegan ➜ Canada 51°9N 80°50W 298 B3
Kwatisore Indonesia 3°18S 134°50E 231 E8
KwaZulu Natal □ S. Africa 29°0S 30°0E 271 C5
Kweichow = Guizhou □ China 27°0N 107°0E 228 D6
Kweilin = Guilin China 25°18N 110°15E 229 E8
Kweisui = Hohhot China 40°52N 111°40E 226 D6
Kweiyang = Guiyang China 26°32N 106°40E 228 D6
Kwekwe Zimbabwe 18°58S 29°48E 269 F2
Kweneng □ Botswana 24°0S 25°0E 270 B3
Kwenge ➜ Dem. Rep. of the Congo 4°50S 18°42E 265 C3
Kwethluk U.S.A. 60°49N 161°26W 303 F7
Kwidzyn Poland 53°44N 18°55E 184 E5
Kwigillingok U.S.A. 59°51N 163°8W 303 G7
Kwiha Ethiopia 13°29N 39°32E 257 E4
Kwikila Papua N. G. 9°49S 147°38E 286 E4
Kwilu ➜ Dem. Rep. of the Congo 3°22S 17°22E 265 C3
Kwinana Australia 32°15S 115°47E 279 F2
Kwinbet Burma 16°20N 94°14E 241 G5
Kwisa ➜ Poland 51°34N 15°24E 185 G2
Kwoka Indonesia 0°31S 132°27E 231 E8
Kwolla Nigeria 9°0N 9°15E 263 D6
Kwun Tong Hong Kong, China 22°19N 114°13E 122 B3
Kya-in-Seikkyi Burma 16°2N 98°8E 241 G7
Kyabé Chad 9°30N 19°0E 259 G3
Kyabra Cr. ➜ Australia 25°36S 142°55E 281 D3
Kyabram Australia 36°19S 145°4E 283 D6
Kyaikkami Burma 16°4N 97°34E 241 G6
Kyaiklat Burma 16°25N 95°40E 241 G5
Kyaikmaraw Burma 16°23N 97°44E 241 G6
Kyaikthin Burma 23°32N 95°40E 241 D5
Kyaikto Burma 17°20N 97°3E 236 D1
Kyaing Tong = Keng Tung Burma 21°18N 99°39E 236 B2
Kyakhta Russia 50°30N 106°25E 215 D11
Kyambura ⌂ Uganda 0°7S 30°9E 268 C3
Kyan-zaki Japan 26°5N 127°39E 288 a
Kyancutta Australia 33°8S 135°33E 281 E2
Kyangin Burma 18°20N 95°20E 241 F5
Kyaukhnyat Burma 18°15N 97°31E 241 F6
Kyaukki Burma 18°27N 96°56E 241 F6
Kyaukkyi Burma 18°15N 94°29E 241 F5
Kyaukme Burma 22°32N 97°2E 241 D6
Kyaukpadaung Burma 20°52N 95°8E 241 E5
Kyaukpyu Burma 19°28N 93°30E 241 F4
Kyaukse Burma 21°36N 96°10E 241 E6
Kyauktaga Burma 18°10N 96°37E 241 F6
Kyauktan Burma 16°38N 96°19E 241 G6
Kyauktaw Burma 20°51N 92°59E 241 E4
Kyaunggon Burma 17°6N 95°11E 241 G5
Kyawkku Burma 21°48N 96°56E 241 E6
Kybartai Lithuania 54°39N 22°45E 184 D9
Kyburz U.S.A. 38°47N 120°18W 306 G6
Kyeintali Burma 18°0N 94°29E 241 G5
Kyelang India 32°35N 77°2E 242 C7
Kyenjojo Uganda 0°40N 30°37E 268 B3
Kyidaunggan Burma 19°53N 96°12E 241 F6
Kyje Czech Rep. 50°6N 14°33E 135 B3
Kyjov Czech Rep. 49°1N 17°7E 181 B10
Kyklades Greece 37°0N 24°30E 204 E6
Kyle Sask., Canada 50°50N 108°2W 297 C7
Kyle Tex., U.S.A. 29°59N 97°53W 314 F6
Kyle Dam Zimbabwe 20°15S 31°0E 269 G3
Kyle of Lochalsh U.K. 57°17N 5°44W 167 D3
Kyll ➜ Germany 49°48N 6°41E 179 F2
Kyllburg Germany 50°2N 6°34E 179 E2
Kyllini Greece 37°55N 21°8E 207 D3
Kyllini, Akra Greece 37°57N 21°8E 207 D3
Kymijoki ➜ Finland 60°30N 26°55E 188 B4
Kymmene älv = Kymijoki ➜ Finland 60°30N 26°55E 188 B4
Kyneton Australia 37°10S 144°29E 282 D6
Kynuna Australia 21°37S 141°55E 280 C3
Kyō-ga-Saki Japan 35°45N 135°15E 223 B7
Kyoga, L. Uganda 1°35N 33°0E 268 B3
Kyogle Australia 28°40S 153°0E 281 D5
Kyom ➜ South Sudan 8°58N 28°13E 257 F2
Kyŏngju = Gyeongju S. Korea 35°51N 129°14E 224 E4
Kyŏngsŏng N. Korea 41°35N 129°36E 224 B4
Kyōtamba Japan 35°6N 135°17E 223 B7
Kyōto Japan 35°0N 135°45E 223 C7
Kyōto □ Japan 35°15N 135°45E 223 B7
Kyparissovouno Cyprus 35°19N 33°10E 207 E9
Kyperounda Cyprus 34°56N 32°58E 207 F8
Kypros = Cyprus ■ Asia 35°0N 33°0E 207 F9
Kyrenia Cyprus 35°20N 33°20E 207 E9
Kyrgyzstan ■ Asia 42°0N 75°0E 217 D9
Kyritz Germany 52°56N 12°24E 178 C8
Kyrkhult Sweden 56°22N 14°34E 163 H8
Kyrksæterøra Norway 63°18N 9°5E 164 A6
Kyrnasivka Ukraine 48°35N 28°58E 183 B13
Kyrnychky Ukraine 45°42N 29°4E 183 E14
Kyro älv = Kyrönjoki ➜ Finland 63°14N 21°45E 160 E19
Kyrönjoki ➜ Finland 63°14N 21°45E 160 E19
Kystatyam Russia 67°20N 123°10E 215 C13
Kysucké Nové Mesto Slovak Rep. 49°18N 18°47E 181 B11
Kytay, Ozero Ukraine 45°40N 29°13E 183 E14
Kythira Greece 36°8N 23°0E 204 E5
Kythnos Greece 37°26N 24°27E 204 D6
Kythréa Cyprus 35°15N 33°29E 207 E9
Kyu-hkok Burma 24°4N 98°4E 241 C7
Kyūhōji Japan 34°38N 135°33E 133 B2
Kyunhla Burma 23°25N 95°15E 241 D5
Kyunquot Sound Canada 50°2N 127°22W 296 D3
Kyurdamir = Kürdämir Azerbaijan 40°25N 48°3E 191 K9
Kyūshū Japan 33°0N 131°0E 222 E3
Kyūshū □ Japan 33°0N 131°0E 222 E3
Kyūshū-Palau Ridge Pac. Oc. 20°0N 136°0E 288 E5
Kyūshū-Sanchi Japan 32°35N 131°17E 222 E3
Kyūshū Trench Japan 31°35N 134°10E 222 F6
Kyustendil Bulgaria 42°16N 22°41E 202 D6
Kyustendil □ Bulgaria 42°16N 22°41E 202 D6
Kyusyur Russia 70°19N 127°30E 215 B13
Kywong Australia 34°58S 146°44E 283 C7
Kyyiv Ukraine 50°30N 30°28E 177 C16
Kyyiv □ Ukraine 50°5N 30°45E 189 G6
Kyyivske Vdskh. Ukraine 51°0N 30°25E 177 C16
Kyzyl Russia 51°50N 94°30E 217 B12
Kyzyl-Adyr Kyrgyzstan 42°39N 71°35E 217 D8
Kyzyl-Burun = Siyäzän Azerbaijan 41°3N 49°10E 191 K9
Kyzyl-Khoto = Kyzyl Russia 51°50N 94°30E 217 B12
Kyzyl Kum Uzbekistan 42°30N 65°0E 217 D7
Kyzyl-Kyya Kyrgyzstan 40°16N 72°8E 217 D8
Kyzyl Orda = Qyzylorda Kazakhstan 44°48N 65°28E 216 D7
Kyzyl-Suu Kyrgyzstan 42°20N 78°0E 217 D9


# L


L.A. County Art Museum U.S.A. 34°4N 118°21W 126 B2
La Albuera Spain 38°45N 6°49W 195 G4
La Alcarria Spain 40°31N 2°45W 196 E2
La Almarcha Spain 39°41N 2°24W 196 F2
La Almunia de Doña Godina Spain 41°29N 1°23W 196 D3
La Amistad △ Cent. Amer. 9°28N 83°18W 320 E3
La Asunción Venezuela 11°2N 63°51W 329 a
La Baie Canada 48°19N 70°53W 299 C5
La Banda Argentina 27°45S 64°10W 334 B3
La Bañeza Spain 42°17N 5°54W 194 C5
La Barca Mexico 20°17N 102°34W 318 C4
La Barceloneta Spain 41°22N 2°11E 114 A2
La Barge U.S.A. 42°16N 110°12W 304 E8
La Barra Nic. 12°54N 83°33W 320 D3
La Bastide-Puylaurent France 44°35N 3°55E 174 D7
La Baule France 47°17N 2°24W 172 E4
La Belle Fla., U.S.A. 26°46N 81°26W 317 J8
La Belle Mo., U.S.A. 40°7N 91°55W 310 D5
La Biche ➜ Canada 59°57N 123°50W 296 B4
La Biche, L. Canada 54°50N 112°3W 296 C6
La Bisbal d'Empordà Spain 41°58N 3°2E 196 D8
La Blanca Chile 33°30S 70°40W 137 C2
La Boca Argentina 34°38S 58°22W 117 B2
La Brea Peru 4°40S 81°7W 330 A1
La Brea Trin. & Tob. 10°15N 61°37W 323 t
La Brède France 44°41N 0°32W 174 D3
La Bresse France 48°2N 6°53E 173 D13
La Bretèche France 48°51N 2°1E 134 A1
La Bureba Spain 42°36N 3°24W 194 C7
La Cal ➜ Bolivia 17°27S 58°15W 331 D6
La Calera Chile 32°50S 71°10W 334 C1
La Calle = El Kala Algeria 36°53N 8°26E 261 A6
La Campana △ Chile 32°58S 71°14W 334 C1
La Campiña Lima, Peru 12°11S 77°0W 124 C2
La Campiña Spain 37°45N 4°45W 195 H6
La Canal = Sa Canal Spain 38°51N 1°23E 206 D1
La Cañiza = A Cañiza Spain 42°13N 8°16W 194 C2
La Canourgue France 44°26N 3°13E 174 D7
La Capelle France 49°59N 3°50E 173 C10
La Carlota Argentina 33°30S 63°20W 334 C3
La Carlota Phil. 10°25N 122°55E 233 F4
La Carlota Spain 37°40N 4°56W 195 H6
La Carolina Spain 38°17N 3°38W 195 G7
La Castellana Phil. 10°20N 123°3E 233 F4
La Cavalerie France 44°1N 3°10E 174 D7
La Ceiba Honduras 15°40N 86°50W 320 C2
La Ceiba Venezuela 9°28N 71°4W 328 B3
La Celle-St-Cloud France 48°50N 2°9E 134 A1
La Certosa, Isole Venice, Italy 142 b5
La Chaise-Dieu France 45°18N 3°42E 174 C7
La Chapelle d'Angillon France 47°21N 2°25E 173 E9
La Chapelle-St-Luc France 48°20N 4°3E 173 D11
La Chapelle-sur-Erdre France 47°18N 1°34W 172 E5
La Charité-sur-Loire France 47°10N 3°1E 173 E10
La Chartre-sur-le-Loir France 47°44N 0°34E 172 E7
La Châtaigneraie France 46°39N 0°44W 174 B3
La Châtre France 46°35N 2°0E 173 F9
La Chaux ➜ Mauritius 20°23S 57°41E 272 e
La Chaux-de-Fonds Switz. 47°7N 6°50E 179 H2
La Chorrera Colombia 0°44S 73°1W 328 D3
La Chorrera Panama 8°53N 79°47W 320 c
La Ciotat France 43°10N 5°37E 175 E9
La Cisterna Chile 33°32S 70°39W 137 C2
La Ciudadela Mexico City, Mexico 128 c2
La Clayette France 46°17N 4°19E 173 F11
La Cocha Argentina 27°50S 65°40W 334 B2
La Concepción = Ri-Aba Eq. Guin. 3°28N 8°40E 263 E6
La Concepción Panama 8°31N 82°37W 320 E3
La Concepción Venezuela 10°30N 71°50W 328 A3
La Concordia Mexico 16°5N 92°38W 319 D6
La Constitución, Plaza de = Zócalo Mexico City, Mexico 128 b3
La Coruña = A Coruña Spain 43°20N 8°25W 194 B2
La Côte-St-André France 45°24N 5°15E 175 C9
La Courneuve France 48°55N 2°22E 134 A3
La Courtine France 45°41N 2°15E 174 C6
La Crau Bouches-du-Rhône, France 43°32N 4°40E 175 E8
La Crau Var, France 43°9N 6°4E 175 E10
La Crescent U.S.A. 43°50N 91°18W 308 D8
La Crete Canada 58°11N 116°24W 296 B5
La Crosse Fla., U.S.A. 29°51N 82°24W 316 F7
La Crosse Kans., U.S.A. 38°32N 99°18W 308 F4
La Crosse Wis., U.S.A. 43°48N 91°15W 308 D8
La Cruz Costa Rica 11°4N 85°39W 320 D2
La Cruz Sinaloa, Mexico 23°55N 106°54W 318 C3
La Cumbre, Volcán Ecuador 0°21S 91°30W 330 a
La Dehesa Chile 33°21S 70°33W 137 B2
La Désirade Guadeloupe 16°18N 61°3W 322 b
La Digue Seychelles 4°20S 55°51E 272 c
La Dorada Colombia 5°30N 74°40W 328 B3
La Encantada Peru 12°13S 77°1W 124 C2
La Esperanza Argentina 40°26S 68°32W 336 B3
La Esperanza Cuba 22°46N 83°44W 320 B3
La Esperanza Honduras 14°15N 88°10W 320 D2
La Estación Spain 40°27N 3°48W 127 B1
La Estrada = A Estrada Spain 42°43N 8°27W 194 C2
La Falaise, Gorges de Martinique 14°49N 61°10W 322 j
La Faouët France 48°2N 3°30W 172 D3
La Fayette U.S.A. 34°42N 85°17W 315 D12
La Fé Cuba 22°2N 84°15W 320 B3
La Fenice, Teatro Venice, Italy 142 b2
La Fère France 49°39N 3°21E 173 C10
La Ferté-Bernard France 48°10N 0°40E 172 D7
La Ferté-Gaucher France 48°47N 3°19E 173 D10
La Ferté-Macé France 48°35N 0°22W 172 D6
La Ferté-St-Aubin France 47°42N 1°57E 173 E8
La Ferté-sous-Jouarre France 48°56N 3°8E 173 D10
La Ferté-Vidame France 48°37N 0°53E 172 D7
La Flèche France 47°42N 0°4W 172 E6
La Floresta Spain 41°26N 2°3E 114 A1
La Florida Chile 33°33S 70°34W 137 C2
La Foa N. Cal. 21°43S 165°50E 288 d
La Follette U.S.A. 36°23N 84°7W 315 C12
La Fontaine U.S.A. 40°40N 85°43W 311 D11
La Fortuna Spain 40°21N 3°46W 127 B1
La França Spain 41°22N 2°9E 114 A1
La Fregeneda Spain 40°58N 6°54W 194 E4
La Fria Venezuela 8°13N 72°15W 328 B3
La Fuente Venezuela 11°4N 63°52W 329 a
La Fuente de San Esteban Spain 40°49N 6°15W 194 E4
La Gacilly France 47°45N 2°8W 172 E4
La Garenne-Colombes France 48°54N 2°15E 134 A2
La Gi Vietnam 10°40N 107°45E 237 G6
La Gineta Spain 39°8N 2°1W 197 F2
La Giudecca Venice, Italy 142 c2
La Giustiniana Italy 41°59N 12°24E 136 B1
La Glória Colombia 8°37N 73°48W 328 B3
La Goulette Tunisia 36°53N 10°18E 200 F3
La Gran Sabana Venezuela 5°30N 61°30W 329 B5
La Grand'Combe France 44°13N 4°2E 175 D8
La Grande U.S.A. 45°20N 118°5W 304 D4
La Grande ➜ Canada 53°50N 79°0W 298 B5
La Grande 3, Rés. Canada 53°40N 75°10W 298 B4
La Grande 4, Rés. Canada 54°0N 73°15W 298 B5
La Grande-Motte France 43°23N 4°5E 175 E8
La Grange Calif., U.S.A. 37°42N 120°27W 306 H6
La Grange Ga., U.S.A. 33°2N 85°2W 316 B4
La Grange Ky., U.S.A. 38°24N 85°22W 311 F11
La Grange Mo., U.S.A. 40°3N 91°35W 310 D5
La Grange Tex., U.S.A. 29°54N 96°52W 314 G6
La Granja Chile 33°31S 70°38W 137 C2
La Grave France 45°3N 6°18E 175 C10
La Grazia, Isola Venice, Italy 142 c3
La Grita Venezuela 8°8N 71°59W 328 B3
La Guaira Venezuela 10°36N 66°56W 328 A4
La Guardia = A Guarda Spain 41°56N 8°52W 194 D2
La Guardia Venezuela 11°0N 64°1W 329 a
La Guardia, New York ✈ (LGA) U.S.A. 40°46N 73°52W 132 B2
La Gudiña = A Gudiña Spain 42°4N 7°8W 194 C3
La Güera Mauritania 20°51N 17°0W 260 D1
La Guerche-de-Bretagne France 47°57N 1°16W 172 E5
La Guerche-sur-l'Aubois France 46°58N 2°56E 173 F9
La Habana Cuba 23°8N 82°22W 320 B3
La Harpe U.S.A. 40°35N 90°58W 310 D6
La Haute Vallée de Chevreuse ⌂ France 48°35N 1°58E 173 D8
La Haye-du-Puits France 49°17N 1°33W 172 C5
La Horqueta Venezuela 7°55N 60°20W 329 B5
La Horra Spain 41°44N 3°53W 194 D7
La Hulpe Belgium 50°43N 4°30E 116 B2
La Independencia Mexico 16°15N 92°1W 319 D6
La Isabela Dom. Rep. 19°58N 71°2W 321 C5
La Isleta Venezuela 10°54N 63°56W 329 a
La Jonquera Spain 42°25N 2°53E 196 C7
La Joya Peru 16°43S 71°52W 330 D3
La Junta U.S.A. 37°59N 103°33W 304 H12
La Laguna = San Cristóbal de la Laguna Canary Is. 28°28N 16°18W 153 e1
La Lézarde ➜ Martinique 14°35N 61°1W 322 j
La Libertad = Puerto Libertad Mexico 29°55N 112°43W 318 B2
La Libertad Guatemala 16°47N 90°7W 320 C1
La Libertad □ Peru 8°0S 78°30W 330 B2
La Ligua Chile 32°30S 71°16W 334 C1
La Línea de la Concepción Spain 36°15N 5°23W 195 J5
La Llacuna Spain 41°24N 2°12E 114 A2
La Loche Canada 56°29N 109°26W 297 B7
La Loma Mexico 19°31N 99°11W 128 A1
La Londe-les-Maures France 43°8N 6°14E 175 E10
La Lora Spain 42°45N 4°0W 194 C7
La Loupe France 48°29N 1°0E 172 D8
La Louvière Belgium 50°27N 4°10E 170 D4
La Lucila Argentina 34°30S 58°29W 117 B2
La Lune Trin. & Tob. 10°3N 61°22W 323 t
La Machine France 46°54N 3°27E 173 F10
La Maddalena Italy 41°13N 9°24E 200 A2
La Maladrerie France 48°54N 2°1E 134 A1
La Malbaie Canada 47°40N 70°10W 299 C5
La Malinche △ Mexico 19°15N 98°3W 319 D5
La Mancha Spain 39°10N 2°54W 197 F2
La Manche ➜ Martinique 14°33N 61°0W 322 j
La Mariña Spain 43°30N 7°40W 194 B3
La Martre, L. Canada 63°15N 117°55W 296 A5
La Merced Peru 11°3S 75°19W 330 C2
La Mercy = Durban ✈ (DIA) S. Africa 29°37S 31°7E 271 C5
La Mesa Baja Calif., Mexico 32°30N 116°57W 307 N10
La Mesa Calif., U.S.A. 32°46N 117°1W 307 N9
La Mesilla U.S.A. 32°16N 106°48W 305 K10
La Milla, Cerro Peru 12°2S 77°5W 124 B2
La Moille U.S.A. 41°32N 89°17W 310 C7
La Moine ➜ U.S.A. 39°59N 90°31W 310 E6
La Monachina Italy 41°53N 12°21E 136 B1
La Montagne Réunion 20°53S 55°26E 272 f
La Monte U.S.A. 38°46N 93°26W 310 F3
La Moraleja Spain 40°30N 3°38W 127 A2
La Motte-Achard France 46°37N 1°40W 172 F5
La Motte-Chalançon France 44°30N 5°21E 175 D9
La Motte-du-Caire France 44°20N 6°3E 175 D10
La Motte-Servolex France 45°35N 5°53E 175 C9
La Moure U.S.A. 46°21N 98°18W 308 B4
La Moustique ➜ Guadeloupe 16°10N 61°34W 322 e
La Muela Spain 41°36N 1°7W 196 D3
La Mure France 44°55N 5°48E 175 D9
La Negra Chile 23°46S 70°18W 334 A1
La Nopalera Mexico 19°18N 99°5W 128 C2
La Oliva Canary Is. 28°36N 13°57W 153 e2
La Oraya Peru 11°32S 75°54W 330 C2
La Orotava Canary Is. 28°22N 16°31W 153 e1
La Oroya Peru 11°32S 75°54W 330 C2
La Pacaudière France 46°11N 3°52E 173 F10
La Pagerie Martinique 14°32N 61°3W 322 j
La Palma Canary Is. 28°40N 17°50W 153 e1
La Palma Panama 8°15N 78°0W 320 E4
La Palma del Condado Spain 37°21N 6°38W 195 H4
La Palmyre France 45°43N 1°9W 174 C2
La Paloma Chile 30°35S 71°0W 334 C1
La Pampa □ Argentina 36°50S 66°0W 334 D2
La Paragua Venezuela 6°50N 63°20W 329 B5
La Pastora Trin. & Tob. 10°42N 61°19W 323 t
La Paternal Argentina 34°35S 58°26W 117 B2
La Paya △ Colombia 0°0 75°55W 328 C2
La Paz Entre Ríos, Argentina 30°50S 59°45W 334 C4

La Paz *San Luis, Argentina* 33°30S 67°20W 334 C2
La Paz *Bolivia* 16°20S 68°10W 330 D4
La Paz *Honduras* 14°20N 87°47W 320 D2
La Paz *Baja Calif. S., Mexico* 24°10N 110°18W 318 C2
La Paz *Abra, Phil.* 17°40N 120°41E 232 C3
La Paz *Tarlac, Phil.* 15°26N 120°45E 232 D3
La Paz ☐ *Bolivia* 15°30S 68°0W 330 D4
La Paz Centro *Nic.* 12°20N 86°41W 320 D2
La Pedrera *Colombia* 1°18S 69°43W 328 D4
La Pérade *Canada* 46°35N 72°12W 299 C5
La Perla *Chihuahua, Mexico* 28°18N 104°32W 318 B4
La Perla *Lima, Peru* 12°4S 77°7W 124 B2
La Perouse *Australia* 33°59S 151°14E 139 B2
La Perouse, Bahía *Chile* 27°5S 109°18W 330 b
La Perouse Str. *Asia* 45°40N 142°0E 220 B11
La Pesca *Mexico* 23°46N 97°47W 319 C5
La Piedad *Mexico* 20°21N 102°0W 318 C4
La Pine *U.S.A.* 43°40N 121°30W 304 E3
La Pisana *Italy* 41°51N 12°23E 136 B1
La Plaine *Dominica* 15°20N 61°15W 323 k
La Plaine des Cafres *Réunion* 21°13S 55°33E 272 f
La Plaine des Palmistes *Réunion* 21°7S 55°38E 272 f
La Plata *Argentina* 35°0S 57°55W 334 C4
La Plata *Colombia* 2°23N 75°53W 328 C2
La Plata *Mo., U.S.A.* 40°2N 92°29W 310 D4
La Plata, L. *Argentina* 44°55S 71°50W 336 B2
La Playa, Pta. *Venezuela* 10°48N 64°0W 329 a
La Plaza *Venezuela* 11°6N 63°52W 329 a
La Pobla de Lillet *Spain* 42°16N 1°59E 196 C6
La Pobla de Segur *Spain* 42°15N 0°58E 196 C5
La Pocatière *Canada* 47°22N 70°2W 299 C5
La Pola de Gordón *Spain* 42°51N 5°41W 194 C5
La Porta *France* 42°25N 9°21E 175 F13
La Porte *U.S.A.* 29°40N 95°1W 314 G7
La Porte City *U.S.A.* 42°19N 92°12W 310 B4
La Possession *Réunion* 20°55S 55°21E 272 f
La Prairie *Canada* 45°25N 73°29W 130 B3
La Presanella *Italy* 46°13N 10°40E 198 B7
La Puebla = Sa Pobla *Spain* 39°46N 3°1E 206 B4
La Puebla de Cazalla *Spain* 37°10N 5°20W 195 H5
La Puebla de los Infantes *Spain* 37°47N 5°24W 195 H5
La Puebla de Montalbán *Spain* 39°52N 4°22W 194 F6
La Puebla del Río *Spain* 37°16N 6°3W 195 H4
La Puerta de Segura *Spain* 38°22N 2°45W 195 G8
La Punta *Peru* 12°4S 77°10W 124 B1
La Puntigala *Spain* 41°27N 2°13E 114 A2
La Purísima *Mexico* 26°10N 112°4W 318 B2
La Push *U.S.A.* 47°55N 124°38W 306 C2
La Queue-en-Brie *France* 48°47N 2°34E 134 B4
La Quiaca *Argentina* 22°5S 65°35W 334 A2
La Rambla *Barcelona, Spain* 114 b2
La Reina *Chile* 33°26S 70°33W 137 B2
La Réole *France* 44°35N 0°1W 174 D3
La Republica, Plaza de *Mexico City, Mexico* 128 b1
La Restinga *Canary Is.* 27°38N 17°59W 153 e1
La Ribera *Spain* 41°21N 2°4E 114 A1
La Rinconada *Peru* 14°38S 69°27W 330 C4
La Rioja *Argentina* 29°20S 67°0W 334 B2
La Rioja ☐ *Argentina* 29°30S 67°0W 334 B2
La Rioja ☐ *Spain* 42°20N 2°20W 196 C2
La Rivière des Pluies *Réunion* 20°54S 55°31E 272 f
La Robla *Spain* 42°50N 5°41W 194 C5
La Roche *N. Cal.* 21°26S 168°2E 288 d
La Roche-Bernard *France* 47°31N 2°19W 172 E4
La Roche-Canillac *France* 45°12N 1°57E 174 C5
La Roche-en-Ardenne *Belgium* 50°11N 5°35E 170 D5
La Roche-sur-Foron *France* 46°4N 6°19E 173 F13
La Roche-sur-Yon *France* 46°40N 1°25W 172 F5
La Rochefoucauld *France* 45°44N 0°24E 174 C4
La Rochelle *France* 46°10N 1°9W 174 B2
La Roda *Spain* 39°13N 2°15W 197 F2
La Roda de Andalucía *Spain* 37°12N 4°46W 195 H6
La Romaine *Canada* 50°13N 60°40W 299 B7
La Romana *Dom. Rep.* 18°27N 68°57W 321 C6
La Ronge *Canada* 55°5N 105°20W 297 B7
La Rue *U.S.A.* 40°35N 83°23W 311 D13
La Rumorosa *Mexico* 32°34N 116°6W 307 N10
La Sabina = Sa Savina *Spain* 38°44N 1°25E 206 D1
La Sagra *Spain* 37°57N 2°35W 197 H2
La Sagrera *Spain* 41°25N 2°11E 114 A2
La Salada *Argentina* 34°43S 58°28W 117 C2
La Saline *Réunion* 21°4S 55°16E 272 f
La Salle *U.S.A.* 41°20N 89°6W 310 C7
La Sanabria *Spain* 42°0N 6°30W 194 C4
La Santa *Canary Is.* 29°5N 13°40W 153 e2
La Sarre *Canada* 48°45N 79°15W 298 C4
La Scala *Italy* 45°28N 9°11E 128 B2
La Scie *Canada* 49°57N 55°36W 299 C8
La Selva *Spain* 42°0N 2°45E 196 C7
La Selva Beach *U.S.A.* 36°56N 121°51W 306 J5
La Selva del Camp *Spain* 41°13N 1°8E 196 D6
La Serena *Chile* 29°55S 71°10W 334 B1
La Serena *Spain* 38°45N 5°40W 195 G5
La Seu d'Urgell *Spain* 42°22N 1°23E 196 C6
La Seyne-sur-Mer *France* 43°7N 5°52E 175 E9
La Sila *Italy* 39°15N 16°35E 201 C9
La Solana *Spain* 38°59N 3°14W 195 G7
La Soufrière *St. Vincent* 13°20N 61°11W 323 n
La Souterraine *France* 46°15N 1°30E 173 F8
La Spézia *Italy* 44°7N 9°50E 198 D6
La Storta *Italy* 41°59N 12°20E 136 A1
La Suze-sur-Sarthe *France* 47°53N 0°2E 172 E7
La Tagua *Colombia* 0°3N 74°40W 328 C3
La Taxonera *Spain* 41°25N 2°10E 114 A2
La Teste-de-Buch *France* 44°37N 1°8W 174 D2
La Tortuga, I. *Venezuela* 11°0N 65°22W 321 D6
La Tour-du-Pin *France* 45°33N 5°27E 175 C9
La Tranche-sur-Mer *France* 46°20N 1°27W 172 F5
La Tremblade *France* 45°46N 1°8W 174 C2
La Trinidad *Phil.* 16°28N 120°35E 232 C3
La Trinité *Martinique* 14°45N 60°58W 322 j
La Tuque *Canada* 47°30N 72°50W 298 C5
La Unión *Chile* 40°10S 73°0W 336 B2
La Unión *Colombia* 1°35N 77°5W 328 C2
La Unión *El Salv.* 13°20N 87°50W 320 D2
La Unión *Guerrero, Mexico* 17°58N 101°49W 318 D4
La Unión *Peru* 9°43S 76°45W 330 B2
La Unión *Spain* 37°38N 0°53W 197 H4
La Unión ☐ *Phil.* 16°30N 120°25E 232 C3
La Urbana *Venezuela* 7°8N 66°56W 328 B4
La Vache B. *Trin. & Tob.* 10°45N 61°29W 323 t
La Vache Pt. *Trin. & Tob.* 10°47N 61°28W 323 t
La Vall d'Uixó *Spain* 39°49N 0°15W 196 F4
La Vecilla *Spain* 42°51N 5°27W 194 C5
La Vecindad *Venezuela* 11°4N 63°56W 329 a
La Vega *Dom. Rep.* 19°20N 70°30W 321 C5
La Vega *Peru* 10°41S 77°44W 330 C2
La Vela de Coro *Venezuela* 11°27N 69°34W 328 A4
La Veleta *Spain* 37°1N 3°22W 195 H7
La Venta *Mexico* 18°5N 94°3W 319 D6
La Venturosa *Colombia* 6°8N 68°48W 328 B4
La Vergne *U.S.A.* 36°1N 86°35W 315 C11
La Veronica *Trin. & Tob.* 10°42N 61°21W 323 t
La Victoria *Lima, Peru* 12°3S 77°2W 124 B2
La Victoria *Venezuela* 10°14N 67°20W 328 A4
La Villa Joiosa = Villajoyosa *Spain* 38°30N 0°12W 197 G4
La Vista *U.S.A.* 33°48N 84°21W 113 B2
La Voulte-sur-Rhône *France* 44°48N 4°46E 175 D8
Laa an der Thaya *Austria* 48°43N 16°23E 181 C9
Laaber, Grosse ➛ *Germany* 48°55N 12°30E 179 G8
Laage *Germany* 53°55N 12°21E 178 B8
Laajalahti *Finland* 60°11N 24°48E 121 B1
Laajasalo *Finland* 60°10N 25°1E 121 B3
Laaksolahti *Finland* 60°14N 24°45E 121 B1
Laas Dawaco *Somalia* 10°28N 49°0E 267 B6
Laascaanood = Las Anod *Somalia* 8°26N 47°19E 267 C6
Laasqoray *Somalia* 11°10N 48°20E 267 B6
Laatzen *Germany* 52°19N 9°48E 178 C5
Lā'au Pt. *U.S.A.* 21°6N 157°19W 302 B4
Laba ➛ *Russia* 45°11N 39°42E 191 H4
Labagou Nat. Forest Park *China* 40°1N 116°22E 114 A2
Laban *Burma* 25°52N 96°40E 241 C6
Labasa *Fiji* 16°30S 179°27E 287 A2
Labason *Phil.* 8°4N 122°31E 233 G4
Labastide-Murat *France* 44°39N 1°33E 174 D5
Labastide-Rouairoux *France* 43°28N 2°39E 174 E6
Labbézenga *Mali* 15°2N 0°48E 263 B5
Labdah = Leptis Magna *Libya* 32°40N 14°12E 258 B2
Labe = Elbe ➛ *Europe* 53°50N 9°0E 178 B4
Labé *Guinea* 11°24N 12°16W 262 C2
Laberge, L. *Canada* 61°11N 135°12W 296 A1
Labes = Lobez *Poland* 53°38N 15°39E 184 E2
Labia, Palazzo *Venice, Italy* 142 a2
Labian, Tanjong *Malaysia* 5°9N 119°13E 235 A5
Labiau = Polessk *Russia* 54°50N 21°8E 184 D8
Labig Pt. = Iligan Pt. *Phil.* 18°25N 122°25E 232 B4
Labin *Croatia* 45°5N 14°8E 199 C11
Labinsk *Russia* 44°40N 40°48E 191 H5
Labis *Malaysia* 2°22N 103°2E 237 L4
Łabiszyn *Poland* 52°57N 17°54E 185 F4
Lablâba, W. el ➛ *Egypt* 30°1N 31°19E 117 A2
Labo *Phil.* 14°9N 122°51E 232 D4
Laboe *Germany* 54°24N 10°13E 178 A6
Laborec ➛ *Slovak Rep.* 48°37N 21°58E 181 C14
Laborie *St. Lucia* 13°45N 61°2W 323 m
Labouheyre *France* 44°13N 0°55W 174 D3
Laboulaye *Argentina* 34°10S 63°30W 334 C3
Labrador *Canada* 53°20N 61°0W 299 B7
Labrador City *Canada* 52°57N 66°55W 299 B6
Labrador Sea *Atl. Oc.* 57°0N 54°0W 295 F21
Lábrea *Brazil* 7°15S 64°51W 331 B5
Labruguière *France* 43°31N 2°16E 174 E6
Labuan ☐ *Malaysia* 5°20N 115°12E 235 A5
Labuan, Pulau *Malaysia* 5°21N 115°13E 235 A5
Labuha *Indonesia* 0°30S 127°30E 231 E7
Labuhan *Indonesia* 6°22S 105°50E 234 D3
Labuhanbajo *Indonesia* 8°28S 119°54E 235 D5
Labuhanbilik *Indonesia* 2°31N 100°10E 237 L3
Labuk, Telok *Malaysia* 6°10N 117°50E 235 A5
Labutta *Burma* 16°9N 94°46E 241 G5
Labyrinth, L. *Australia* 30°40S 135°11E 281 E2
Labytnangi *Russia* 66°39N 66°21E 186 A12
Laç *Albania* 41°38N 19°43E 202 E3
Lac ☐ *Chad* 13°30N 14°30E 259 F2
Lac Bay *Bonaire* 12°6N 68°13W 322 h
Lac-Bouchette *Canada* 48°16N 72°11W 299 C5
Lac-Édouard *Canada* 47°40N 72°16W 299 C5
Lac La Biche *Canada* 54°45N 111°58W 296 C6
Lac la Martre = Wha Ti *Canada* 63°8N 117°16W 294 E8
Lac La Ronge ⌂ *Canada* 55°9N 104°41W 297 B7
Lac-Mégantic *Canada* 45°35N 70°53W 299 C5
Lac Thien *Vietnam* 12°25N 108°11E 236 F7
Lacanau *France* 44°58N 1°5W 174 D2
Lacanau, L. de *France* 44°58N 1°7W 174 D2
Lacantún ➛ *Mexico* 16°36N 90°39W 319 D6
Lácara ➛ *Spain* 38°55N 6°25W 195 G4
Lacaune *France* 43°43N 2°40E 174 E6
Lacaune, Mts. de *France* 43°43N 2°50E 174 E6
Laccadive Is. = Lakshadweep Is. *India* 10°0N 72°30E 245 J1
Lacepede B. *Australia* 36°40S 139°40E 282 D3
Lacepede Is. *Australia* 16°55S 122°0E 278 C3
Lacerdónia *Mozam.* 18°3S 35°35E 269 F4
Lacey *U.S.A.* 47°7N 122°49W 306 C4
Lachania *Greece* 35°58N 27°54E 206 F11
Lachay, Pta. *Peru* 11°17S 77°44W 330 C2
Lachen *India* 27°46N 88°36E 241 B2
Lachhmangarh *India* 27°50N 75°4E 242 F6
Lachi *Pakistan* 33°25N 71°20E 242 C4
Lachia *Taiwan* 22°43N 120°53E 225 D2
Lachine *Canada* 45°26N 73°42W 130 B1
Lachine, Canal de *Canada* 45°26N 73°38W 130 B2
Lachlan ➛ *Australia* 34°22S 143°55E 282 C5
Lachoc *Peru* 12°50S 75°6W 330 C2
Lachute *Canada* 45°39N 74°21W 298 C5
Laçın *Azerbaijan* 39°38N 46°33E 213 C12
Lackagh Hills *Ireland* 54°16N 8°10W 166 B3
Lackawanna *U.S.A.* 42°50N 78°50W 312 D6
Lackawaxen *U.S.A.* 41°29N 74°59W 313 E10
Lacolle *Canada* 45°5N 73°22W 313 A11
Lacombe *Canada* 52°30N 113°44W 296 C6
Lacon *U.S.A.* 41°2N 89°24W 310 C7
Lacona *Iowa, U.S.A.* 41°12N 93°23W 310 C3
Lacona *N.Y., U.S.A.* 43°39N 76°10W 313 C8
Láconi *Italy* 39°54N 9°4E 200 C2
Laconia = Lakonia *Greece* 36°55N 22°30E 204 E4
Laconia *U.S.A.* 43°32N 71°28W 313 C13
Lacoochee *U.S.A.* 28°28N 82°11W 317 G7
Lacq *France* 43°25N 0°35W 174 E3
Lacre Punt *Bonaire* 12°1N 68°14W 322 h
Lacs ☐ *Ivory C.* 6°50N 5°0W 262 D3
Lad Phrao *Thailand* 13°47N 100°35E 113 B2
Ladakh Ra. *India* 34°0N 78°0E 243 C8
Ladário *Brazil* 19°1S 57°35W 331 D6
Ladd *U.S.A.* 41°23N 89°13W 310 C7
Laddonia *U.S.A.* 39°15N 91°39W 310 E5
Lądek-Zdrój *Poland* 50°21N 16°53E 185 H3
Ladera Heights *U.S.A.* 33°59N 118°22W 126 C2
Lâdik *Turkey* 40°57N 35°58E 212 B6
Ladismith *S. Africa* 33°28S 21°15E 270 D3
Ladíspoli *Italy* 41°56N 12°5E 199 G9
Lādīz *Iran* 28°55N 61°15E 247 D9
Ladnun *India* 27°38N 74°25E 242 F6
Ladoga, L. = Ladozhskoye Ozero *Russia* 61°15N 30°30E 188 B6
Ladonas ➛ *Greece* 37°40N 21°50E 204 D3
Ladozhskoye Ozero *Russia* 61°15N 30°30E 188 B6
Ladrillero, G. *Chile* 49°20S 75°35W 336 C1
Ladson *U.S.A.* 32°59N 80°6W 316 C9
Ladushkin *Russia* 54°34N 20°10E 184 D7
Ladví *Czech Rep.* 50°8N 14°27E 135 B2
Lady *Poland* 52°8N 20°57E 143 C1
Lady Elliott I. *Australia* 24°7S 152°42E 280 C5
Lady Frere *S. Africa* 31°42S 27°14E 270 D4
Lady Grey *S. Africa* 30°43S 27°13E 270 D4
Lady Lake *U.S.A.* 28°55N 81°55W 317 G8
Ladybrand *S. Africa* 29°9S 27°29E 270 C4
Ladysmith *B.C., Canada* 49°0N 123°49W 306 B3
Ladysmith *KwaZulu Natal, S. Africa* 28°32S 29°46E 271 C4
Ladysmith *Wis., U.S.A.* 45°28N 91°12W 308 C8
Ladyznyn *Ukraine* 48°40N 29°15E 183 B14
Lae *Papua N. G.* 6°40S 147°2E 286 D4
Lae 'o Kealaikahiki *U.S.A.* 20°32N 156°42W 302 C5
Laem Ngop *Thailand* 12°10N 102°26E 237 F4
Laem Son △ *Thailand* 9°29N 98°24E 237 H2
Lærdalsøyri *Norway* 61°6N 7°28E 164 C4
Laerma *Greece* 36°9N 27°57E 206 E11
Læsø *Denmark* 57°15N 11°5E 163 G5
Læsø Rende *Denmark* 57°20N 10°45E 163 G4
Lafayette *Ala., U.S.A.* 32°54N 85°24W 316 C4
Lafayette *Ind., U.S.A.* 40°25N 86°54W 311 D10
Lafayette *La., U.S.A.* 30°14N 92°1W 314 F8
Lafayette *Tenn., U.S.A.* 36°31N 86°2W 315 C11
Lafayette Park *San Francisco, U.S.A.* 136 b1
Lafayette Square *New Orleans, U.S.A.* 131 b2
Laferte ➛ *Canada* 61°53N 117°44W 296 A5
Lafia *Nigeria* 8°30N 8°34E 263 D6
Lafiagi *Nigeria* 8°52N 5°20E 263 D6
Lafkos *Greece* 39°9N 23°14E 204 B5
Lafleche *Canada* 49°45N 106°40W 297 D7
Lafon *South Sudan* 5°5N 32°29E 257 F3
Lafontaine *Montréal, Canada* 130 a1
Lafontaine, Parc *Canada* 45°33N 73°34W 130 A2
Laful *India* 7°10N 93°52E 245 L11
Lagaip ➛ *Papua N. G.* 5°4S 142°52E 286 C2
Lagan = Kaspiyskiy *Russia* 45°22N 47°23E 191 H8
Lagan *Sweden* 56°56N 13°58E 163 H7
Lagan ➛ *Sweden* 56°30N 12°58E 163 H6
Lagan ➛ *Antrim, U.K.* 54°36N 5°55W 166 B6
Lagana, Kolpas *Greece* 37°42N 20°53E 207 D2
Laganas *Greece* 37°44N 20°53E 207 D2
Lagangilang *Phil.* 17°37N 120°44E 232 C3
Lagarfljót ➛ *Iceland* 65°40N 14°18W 155 B12
Lagarto *Brazil* 10°54S 37°41W 332 D4
Lagawe *Phil.* 16°49N 121°6E 232 C3
Lagdo *Cameroon* 9°3N 13°44E 259 G2
Lagdo, L. de *Cameroon* 8°40N 14°0E 264 A2
Lage *Germany* 51°59N 8°48E 178 D4
Lågen ➛ *Oppland, Norway* 61°8N 10°25E 164 C7
Lågen ➛ *Vestfold, Norway* 59°3N 10°3E 164 E7
Lägerdorf *Germany* 53°53N 9°34E 178 B5
Lages *Brazil* 27°48S 50°20W 335 B5
Laggan = Lake Louise *Canada* 51°30N 116°10W 296 C5
Lagh Badana △ *Somalia* 1°16S 41°49E 267 E5
Laghmān ☐ *Afghan.* 34°20N 70°0E 240 B3
Laghouat *Algeria* 33°50N 2°59E 261 B5
Laghouat ☐ *Algeria* 33°35N 2°40E 261 B5
Lagnieu *France* 45°55N 5°20E 175 C9
Lagny-sur-Marne *France* 48°52N 2°44E 173 D9
Lago = Niassa ☐ *Mozam.* 13°30S 36°0E 269 E4
Lago *Italy* 39°10N 16°9E 201 C9
Lago Agrio *Ecuador* 0°5N 76°52W 328 C2
Lago de Sanabria y Entorno ⌂ *Spain* 42°9N 6°45W 194 C4
Lago Posadas *Argentina* 47°30S 71°40W 336 C2
Lago Puelo △ *Argentina* 42°30S 71°55W 336 B2
Lago Ranco *Chile* 40°19S 72°30W 336 B2
Lagoa *Azores* 37°45N 25°20W 153 d3
Lagoa *Rio de J., Brazil* 22°58S 43°11W 135 B1
Lagôa *Portugal* 37°8N 8°27W 195 H2
Lagoa do Peixe △ *Brazil* 31°12S 50°55W 335 C5
Lagoa Vermelha *Brazil* 28°13S 51°32W 335 B5
Lagoaça *Portugal* 41°11N 6°44W 194 D4
Lagodekhi *Georgia* 41°50N 46°22E 191 K8
Lagona = Laguna Beach *U.S.A.* 33°33N 117°47W 307 M9
Lagónegro *Italy* 40°8N 15°45E 201 B8
Lagonoy G. *Phil.* 13°35N 123°50E 232 E4
Lagos *Angola* 16°3S 16°35E 265 F3
Lagos *Greece* 41°1N 25°6E 203 E9
Lagos *Nigeria* 6°25N 3°27E 124 B2
Lagos *Portugal* 37°5N 8°41W 195 H2
Lagos ☐ *Nigeria* 6°28N 3°25E 263 D5
Lagos de Moreno *Mexico* 21°21N 101°55W 318 C4
Lagos Harbour *Nigeria* 6°26N 3°23E 124 B2
Lagos-Ikeja ✈ (LOS) *Nigeria* 6°34N 3°19E 124 A1
Lagos Island *Nigeria* 6°26N 3°23E 124 B2
Lagos Lagoon *Nigeria* 6°30N 3°28E 124 B2
Lagrange = Bidyadanga *Australia* 18°45S 121°43E 278 C3
Lagrange *U.S.A.* 41°39N 85°25W 311 C11
Lagrange B. *Australia* 18°38S 121°42E 278 C3
Laguardia *Spain* 42°33N 2°35W 196 C2
Laguépie *France* 44°8N 1°57E 174 D5
Lagún *Curaçao* 12°19N 69°10W 322 g
Laguna = Padilla *Bolivia* 19°19S 64°20W 331 D5
Laguna *Brazil* 28°30S 48°50W 335 B6
Laguna *N. Mex., U.S.A.* 35°2N 107°25W 305 J10
Laguna *Phil.* 14°10N 121°20E 232 D3
Laguna, Sa. de la *Mexico* 23°35N 109°55W 318 C3
Laguna Beach *U.S.A.* 33°33N 117°47W 307 M9
Laguna Blanca △ *Argentina* 39°0S 70°5W 336 A2
Laguna de B. *Phil.* 14°29N 121°6E 127 C2
Laguna de Duero *Spain* 41°35N 4°43W 194 D6
Laguna de la Restinga △ *Venezuela* 11°0N 64°10W 329 a
Laguna de Lachuá △ *Guatemala* 15°55N 90°40W 320 C1
Laguna de Raya *Venezuela* 10°56N 64°7W 329 a
Laguna del Laja △ *Chile* 37°27S 71°20W 334 D1
Laguna del Tigre △ *Guatemala* 17°32N 90°56W 320 C1
Laguna Limpia *Argentina* 26°32S 59°45W 334 B4
Laguna San Rafael △ *Chile* 46°54S 73°31W 336 C2
Lagunas *Chile* 21°0S 69°45W 334 A2
Lagunas *Peru* 5°10S 75°35W 330 B2
Lagunas de Chacahua △ *Mexico* 16°0N 97°43W 319 D5
Lagunas de Montebello △ *Mexico* 16°4N 91°42W 319 D6
Lagunas de Ruidera ⌂ *Spain* 38°57N 2°52W 197 G2
Lagunes ☐ *Ivory C.* 5°30N 4°0W 262 D4
Lagunillas *Bolivia* 19°38S 63°43W 331 D5
Lahad Datu *Malaysia* 5°0N 118°20E 235 A5
Lahad Datu, Telok *Malaysia* 4°50N 118°20E 235 B5
Lahaina *U.S.A.* 20°53N 156°41W 302 C5
Lahan Sai *Thailand* 14°25N 102°52E 236 E4
Lahanam *Laos* 16°16N 105°16E 236 D5
Lahar *India* 26°12N 78°57E 243 F8
Laharpur *India* 27°43N 80°56E 243 F9
Lahat *Indonesia* 3°45S 103°30E 234 C2
Lahe *Burma* 26°20N 95°26E 241 B5
Lahewa *Indonesia* 1°22N 97°12E 234 B1
Laḥij *Yemen* 13°4N 44°53E 248 D4
Laḥij ☐ *Yemen* 13°10N 44°30E 248 D4
Lāhījān *Iran* 37°10N 50°6E 247 B6
Lahilahi Pt. *U.S.A.* 21°28N 158°13W 302 K13
Lähn = Wleń *Poland* 51°2N 15°39E 185 G2
Lahn ➛ *Germany* 50°19N 7°37E 179 E3
Lahnstein *Germany* 50°19N 7°37E 179 E3
Laholm *Sweden* 56°30N 13°2E 163 H7
Laholmsbukten *Sweden* 56°30N 12°45E 163 H6
Lahore *Pakistan* 31°32N 74°22E 242 D6
Lahpongsel *Burma* 27°7N 98°25E 241 B7
Lahr *Germany* 48°20N 7°53E 179 G3
Lahri *Pakistan* 29°11N 68°13E 242 E3
Lāhrūd *Iran* 38°30N 47°52E 213 C12
Lahti *Finland* 60°58N 25°40E 188 B3
Lahtis = Lahti *Finland* 60°58N 25°40E 188 B3
Lahugala Kitulana △ *Sri Lanka* 6°50N 81°40E 245 L5
Laï *Chad* 9°25N 16°18E 259 G3
Lai Chau *Vietnam* 22°5N 103°3E 228 F4
Lai Chi Wo *Hong Kong, China* 22°32N 114°15E 122
Lai-hka *Burma* 21°16N 97°40E 241 E6
Laiagam *Papua N. G.* 5°33S 143°30E 286 C2
Lai'an *China* 32°28N 118°30E 229 A12
Laibach = Ljubljana *Slovenia* 46°4N 14°33E 199 B11
Laibin *China* 23°42N 109°14E 228 F7
Lā'ie *U.S.A.* 21°39N 157°56W 302 J14
Laifeng *China* 29°27N 109°20E 228 C7
L'Aigle *France* 48°46N 0°38E 172 D7
Laignes *France* 47°50N 4°20E 173 E11
L'Aiguillon-sur-Mer *France* 46°20N 1°18W 174 B2
Laila = Layla *Si. Arabia* 22°10N 46°40E 248 B4
Laim *Germany* 48°7N 11°30E 131 B2
Lainate *Italy* 45°34N 9°1E 128 A1
Laingsburg *S. Africa* 33°9S 20°52E 270 D3
Lainioälven ➛ *Sweden* 67°35N 22°40E 160 C20
Lainz *Austria* 48°10N 16°16E 142 B1
Lairg *U.K.* 58°2N 4°24W 167 C4
Laïri, B. de *Chad* 12°28N 16°45E 259 F3
Lais *Indonesia* 3°31S 102°3E 234 C2
Lais *Phil.* 6°20N 125°39E 233 H5
Laisamis *Kenya* 1°36N 37°48E 268 B4
Laissac *France* 44°23N 2°50E 174 D6
Láives *Italy* 46°26N 11°20E 199 B8
Laiwu *China* 36°15N 117°40E 227 F9
Laixi *China* 36°50N 120°31E 227 F11
Laiyang *China* 36°59N 120°45E 227 F11
Laiyuan *China* 39°20N 114°40E 226 E8
Laizhou *China* 37°8N 119°57E 227 F10
Laizhou Wan *China* 37°30N 119°30E 227 F10
Lajamanu *Australia* 18°23S 130°38E 278 C5
Lajeado = Guiratinga *Brazil* 16°21S 53°45W 331 D7
Lajedo *Azores* 39°23N 31°15W 153 d2
Lajere *Nigeria* 12°10N 11°25E 263 C7
Lajes *Azores* 38°46N 27°6W 153 d1
Lajes *Rio Grande do N., Brazil* 5°41S 36°14W 332 C4
Lajes das Flores *Azores* 39°23N 31°10W 153 d2
Lajes do Pico *Azores* 38°23N 28°16W 153 d1
Lajinha *Brazil* 20°9S 41°37W 333 F3
Lajkovac *Serbia* 44°27N 20°14E 202 B4
Lajosmizse *Hungary* 47°3N 19°32E 182 C4
Lak Sao *Laos* 18°11N 104°59E 236 C5
Lakaband *Pakistan* 31°2N 69°15E 242 D3
Lakamané *Mali* 14°35N 9°44W 262 C3
Lakatoro *Vanuatu* 16°6S 167°25E 287 F5
Lake *U.S.A.* 44°33N 110°24W 304 D8
Lake Alfred *U.S.A.* 28°6N 81°44W 317 G8
Lake Alpine *U.S.A.* 38°29N 120°0W 306 G7
Lake Andes *U.S.A.* 43°9N 98°32W 308 D4
Lake Arthur *U.S.A.* 30°5N 92°41W 314 F8
Lake Bindegolly △ *Australia* 28°0S 144°12E 281 D3
Lake Boga *Australia* 35°26S 143°38E 282 C5
Lake Buena Vista *U.S.A.* 28°23N 81°32W 133 B1
Lake Butig △ *Phil.* 7°45N 124°16E 233 H5
Lake Butler *U.S.A.* 30°1N 82°21W 316 E7
Lake Cain Hills *U.S.A.* 28°29N 81°28W 133 B2
Lake Cargelligo *Australia* 33°15S 146°22E 283 B7
Lake Charles *U.S.A.* 30°14N 93°13W 314 F8
Lake City *Colo., U.S.A.* 38°2N 107°19W 304 G10
Lake City *Fla., U.S.A.* 30°11N 82°38W 316 E7
Lake City *Iowa, U.S.A.* 42°16N 94°44W 310 B2
Lake City *Mich., U.S.A.* 44°20N 85°13W 309 C11
Lake City *Minn., U.S.A.* 44°27N 92°16W 308 C7
Lake City *Pa., U.S.A.* 42°1N 80°21W 312 D4
Lake City *S.C., U.S.A.* 33°52N 79°45W 316 B10
Lake Clark △ *U.S.A.* 61°0N 154°0W 303 F9
Lake Coleridge *N.Z.* 43°17S 171°30E 285 D6
Lake Cowichan *Canada* 48°49N 124°3W 296 D4
Lake District △ *U.K.* 54°30N 3°21W 168 C4
Lake Eildon ⌂ *Australia* 37°10S 145°56E 283 D6
Lake Elsinore *U.S.A.* 33°38N 117°20W 307 M9
Lake Eyre △ *Australia* 28°40S 137°31E 281 D2
Lake Forest *U.S.A.* 42°15N 87°50W 311 B9
Lake Gairdner △ *Australia* 31°41S 135°51E 281 E2
Lake Geneva *U.S.A.* 42°36N 88°26W 311 B8
Lake George *U.S.A.* 43°26N 73°43W 313 C11
Lake Grace *Australia* 33°7S 118°28E 279 F2
Lake Gregory ✪ *Australia* 20°12S 127°27E 278 D4
Lake Harbor *U.S.A.* 26°42N 80°48W 317 J9
Lake Harbour = Kimmirut *Canada* 62°50N 69°50W 295 E18
Lake Havasu City *U.S.A.* 34°27N 114°22W 307 L12
Lake Helen *U.S.A.* 28°59N 81°14W 317 G8
Lake Hughes *U.S.A.* 34°41N 118°26W 307 L8
Lake Isabella *U.S.A.* 35°38N 118°28W 307 K8
Lake Jackson *U.S.A.* 29°3N 95°27W 314 G7
Lake King *Australia* 33°5S 119°45E 279 F2
Lake Kopiago *Papua N. G.* 5°23S 142°31E 286 C2
Lake Kutubu *Papua N. G.* 6°20S 143°18E 286 D2
Lake Lenore *Canada* 52°24N 104°59W 297 C8
Lake Louise *Canada* 51°30N 116°10W 296 C5
Lake Mackay ✪ *Australia* 21°48S 129°46E 278 D4
Lake Mburo △ *Uganda* 0°33S 30°56E 268 C3
Lake Mead ⌂ *U.S.A.* 36°30N 114°22W 307 K12
Lake Meredith ⌂ *U.S.A.* 35°50N 101°50W 314 D4
Lake Mills *Iowa, U.S.A.* 43°25N 93°32W 308 D7
Lake Mills *Wis., U.S.A.* 43°5N 88°55W 311 A8
Lake Murray *Papua N. G.* 6°48S 141°29E 286 D1
Lake Nakura △ *Kenya* 0°21S 36°8E 268 C4
Lake Odessa *U.S.A.* 42°47N 85°8W 311 B11
Lake Orion *U.S.A.* 42°47N 83°14W 311 B13
Lake Park *Fla., U.S.A.* 26°48N 80°3W 317 J9
Lake Park *Ga., U.S.A.* 30°41N 83°11W 316 E6
Lake Placid *Fla., U.S.A.* 27°18N 81°22W 317 H8
Lake Placid *N.Y., U.S.A.* 44°17N 73°59W 313 B11
Lake Pleasant *U.S.A.* 43°28N 74°25W 313 C10
Lake Point Tower *Chicago, U.S.A.* 119 b3
Lake Providence *U.S.A.* 32°48N 91°10W 314 E9
Lake Pukaki *N.Z.* 44°11S 170°8E 285 E5
Lake Roosevelt ⌂ *U.S.A.* 48°5N 118°14W 304 B4
Lake St. Peter *Canada* 45°18N 78°2W 312 A6
Lake Shore Drive *Chicago, U.S.A.* 119 a2
Lake Shore Park *Chicago, U.S.A.* 119 a2
Lake Stevens *U.S.A.* 48°1N 122°4W 306 B4
Lake Superior ⌂ *Canada* 47°45N 84°45W 298 C3
Lake Tekapo *N.Z.* 44°0S 170°30E 285 E5
Lake Torrens △ *Australia* 30°55S 137°40E 281 E2
Lake View *U.S.A.* 42°18N 95°3W 310 B1
Lake Village *U.S.A.* 33°20N 91°17W 314 E9
Lake Wales *U.S.A.* 27°54N 81°35W 317 H8
Lake Worth *U.S.A.* 26°37N 80°3W 317 J9
Lake Zurich *U.S.A.* 42°12N 88°5W 311 B8
Lakeba *Fiji* 18°13S 178°47W 287 B3
Lakeba Passage *Fiji* 18°0S 178°45W 287 B3
Lakefield *Canada* 44°25N 78°16W 312 B6
Lakefield △ *Australia* 15°24S 144°26E 280 B3
Lakehurst *U.S.A.* 40°1N 74°19W 313 F10
Lakeland *Queens., Australia* 15°49S 144°57E 280 B3
Lakeland *Fla., U.S.A.* 28°3N 81°57W 317 G8
Lakeland *Ga., U.S.A.* 31°2N 83°4W 316 D6
Lakemba = Lakeba *Fiji* 18°13S 178°47W 287 B3
Lakemba *Australia* 33°55S 151°5E 139 B1
Lakepa *Cook Is.* 18°59S 169°48W 289 g
Lakeport *Calif., U.S.A.* 39°3N 122°55W 306 F4
Lakeport *Mich., U.S.A.* 43°7N 82°30W 312 C2
Lakes ☐ *South Sudan* 7°0N 30°0E 257 F3
Lakes Entrance *Australia* 37°50S 148°0E 283 D8
Lakeside *Gauteng, S. Africa* 26°5S 28°8E 123 A2
Lakeside *Western Cape, S. Africa* 34°5S 18°27E 118 B1
Lakeside *Calif., U.S.A.* 32°52N 116°55W 307 N10
Lakeside *Nebr., U.S.A.* 42°3N 102°26W 308 D2
Lakeview *Ill., U.S.A.* 41°56N 87°38W 119 B3
Lakeview *La., U.S.A.* 30°0N 90°6W 131 A2
Lakeview *Oreg., U.S.A.* 42°11N 120°21W 304 E3
Lakeville *U.S.A.* 44°39N 93°14W 308 C7
Lakewood *Colo., U.S.A.* 39°42N 105°4W 304 G11
Lakewood *N.J., U.S.A.* 40°6N 74°13W 313 F10
Lakewood *N.Y., U.S.A.* 42°6N 79°19W 312 D5
Lakewood *Ohio, U.S.A.* 41°28N 81°47W 312 E3
Lakewood *Wash., U.S.A.* 47°11N 122°32W 306 C4
Lakewood Park *Fla., U.S.A.* 27°33N 80°24W 317 H9
Lakewood Park *Georgia, U.S.A.* 33°43N 84°24W 113 B2
Lakha *India* 26°9N 70°54E 242 F4
Lakhimpur *India* 27°57N 80°46E 243 F9
Lakhipur *Assam, India* 24°48N 93°0E 241 C4
Lakhipur *Assam, India* 26°2N 90°18E 241 B3
Lakhisarai *India* 25°11N 86°5E 243 G12
Lakhnadon *India* 22°36N 79°36E 243 H8
Lakhnau = Lucknow *India* 26°50N 81°0E 243 F9
Lakhonpheng *Laos* 15°54N 105°34E 236 E5
Lakhpat *India* 23°48N 68°47E 242 H3
Lakhtinskiy *Russia* 59°59N 30°9E 137 B1
Lakhtinskiy Razliv, Oz. *Russia* 59°59N 30°12E 137 B1
Läki *Azerbaijan* 40°34N 47°22E 191 K8
Laki *Iceland* 64°4N 18°14W 155 C8
Lakin *U.S.A.* 37°57N 101°15W 308 G3
Lakitusaki ➛ *Canada* 54°21N 82°25W 298 B3
Lakka *Greece* 39°17N 20°9E 206 C10
Lakki *Greece* 35°24N 23°57E 207 E4
Lakki *Pakistan* 32°36N 70°55E 242 C4
Lakonia *Greece* 36°55N 22°30E 204 E4
Lakonikos Kolpos *Greece* 36°40N 22°40E 204 E4
Lakor *Indonesia* 8°15S 128°17E 231 F7
Lakota *Ivory C.* 5°50N 5°30W 262 D3
Lakota *N. Dak., U.S.A.* 48°2N 98°21W 308 A4
Laksar *India* 29°46N 78°3E 242 E8
Laksefjorden *Norway* 70°45N 26°50E 160 A22
Lakselv *Norway* 70°2N 25°0E 160 A21
Laksettipet *India* 18°52N 79°13E 244 E4
Lakshadweep ☐ *India* 10°0N 72°30E 245 J1
Lakshadweep Is. *India* 10°0N 72°30E 245 J1
Laksham *Bangla.* 23°14N 91°8E 241 D3
Lakshmipur *Bangla.* 22°58N 90°50E 241 D3
Lakshmanpur *Chhattisgarh, India* 22°58N 83°3E 243 H10
Lakshmanpur *Paschimbanga, India* 22°38N 88°16E 124 B1
Lakshmeshwar *India* 15°9N 75°28E 245 G2
Lakshmikantapur *India* 22°5N 88°20E 243 H13
Laksi *Thailand* 13°53N 100°35E 113 A2
Lakuramau *Papua N. G.* 2°54S 151°15E 286 B6
Lal-lo *Phil.* 18°12N 121°40E 232 B3
Lal Qila *Delhi, India* 120 a3
Lala *Dem. Rep. of the Congo* 4°10S 20°30E 265 C4
Lala *Phil.* 7°59N 123°46E 233 H4
Lala Musa *Pakistan* 32°40N 73°57E 242 C5
Lalaghat *India* 24°30N 92°40E 241 C4
Lalago *Tanzania* 3°28S 33°58E 268 C3
Lalang ➛ *Indonesia* 2°24S 104°39E 234 C2
Lalapanzi *Zimbabwe* 19°20S 30°15E 269 F3
Lalapaşa *Turkey* 41°49N 26°44E 203 E10
Lalara *Gabon* 0°19N 11°32E 264 B2
Lalbenque *France* 44°19N 1°34E 174 D5
Lalbert *Australia* 35°38S 143°20E 282 C5
L'Albufera *Spain* 39°20N 0°27W 197 F4
L'Alcora *Spain* 40°5N 0°14W 196 E4
L'Alfàs del Pi *Spain* 38°35N 0°5W 197 G4
Lalganj *India* 25°52N 85°13E 243 G11
Lalgola *India* 24°25N 88°15E 243 G13
Lālī *Iran* 32°21N 49°6E 247 C6
Lalibela *Ethiopia* 12°3N 39°2E 257 E4
Lalin *Heilongjiang, China* 45°12N 127°0E 227 B14
Lalín *Spain* 42°40N 8°5W 194 C2
Lalin He ➛ *China* 45°32N 125°40E 227 B13
Lalinde *France* 44°50N 0°44E 174 D4
Lalitpur *India* 24°42N 78°28E 243 G8
Lalitpur *Nepal* 27°40N 85°20E 243 F11
Lalkua *India* 29°5N 79°31E 243 E8
Lalm *Norway* 61°50N 9°17E 164 C6
Lalmanir Hat *Bangla.* 25°54N 89°27E 241 C2
Lalsot *India* 26°34N 76°20E 242 F7
Lam Nam Nan △ *Thailand* 17°55N 100°28E 236 D3
Lam Pao Res. *Thailand* 16°50N 103°15E 236 D4
Lam Tin *Hong Kong, China* 22°18N 114°14E 122 B3
Lama Kara *Togo* 9°30N 1°15E 263 D5
Lamae *Thailand* 9°51N 99°5E 237 H2
Lamag *Malaysia* 5°29N 117°49E 235 A5
Lamaing *Burma* 15°25N 97°53E 236 E1
Lamaipum *Burma* 25°40N 97°57E 241 C6
Lamap *Vanuatu* 16°26S 167°43E 287 F5
Lamar *Colo., U.S.A.* 38°5N 102°37W 304 G12
Lamar *Mo., U.S.A.* 37°30N 94°16W 308 G6
Lamarque *Argentina* 39°24S 65°40W 336 A3
Lamas *Peru* 6°28S 76°31W 330 B2
Lamastre *France* 44°59N 4°35E 175 D8
Lamayuru *India* 34°25N 76°56E 243 B7
Lambach *Austria* 48°6N 13°51E 180 C6
Lamballe *France* 48°29N 2°31W 172 D4
Lambaréné *Gabon* 0°41S 10°12E 264 C2
Lambasa = Labasa *Fiji* 16°30S 179°27E 287 A2
Lambay I. *Ireland* 53°29N 6°1W 166 C5
Lambayeque ☐ *Peru* 6°45S 80°0W 330 B2
Lambert *Norway* 59°52N 10°48E 133 A3
Lambert, C. *Papua N. G.* 4°11S 151°31E 286 C6
Lambert-St. Louis Int. ✈ (STL) *U.S.A.* 38°45N 90°22W 310 F6
Lambert's Bay *S. Africa* 32°5S 18°17E 270 D2
Lambertville *U.S.A.* 41°46N 83°35W 311 C13
Lambesc *France* 43°39N 5°16E 175 E9
Lambèse = Tazoult *Algeria* 35°29N 6°11E 261 A6
Lambeth *Canada* 42°54N 81°18W 312 D3
Lambeth ☐ *U.K.* 51°28N 0°6W 125 B3
Lambi *Solomon Is.* 9°22S 159°39E 287 M10
Lambia *Greece* 37°52N 21°53E 204 D3
Lambir Hills △ *Malaysia* 4°12N 114°1E 235 B4
Lambomakondro *Madag.* 22°41S 44°44E 272 C1
Lambon *Papua N. G.* 4°45S 152°48E 286 C7
Lambrate *Italy* 45°28N 9°16E 128 B2
Lambro ➛ *Italy* 45°8N 9°32E 198 C6
Lambro, Parco *Italy* 45°29N 9°15E 128 B2
Lambton Mills *Canada* 43°39N 79°30W 141 B1
Lambu *Papua N. G.* 3°18S 151°43E 286 B6
Lambunao *Phil.* 11°3N 122°29E 233 F4
Lamé *Chad* 9°15N 14°32E 259 G2
Lame *Nigeria* 10°30N 9°20E 263 C6
Lame Deer *U.S.A.* 45°37N 106°40W 304 D10
Lamego *Portugal* 41°5N 7°52W 194 D3
Lamentin *Guadeloupe* 16°16N 61°38W 322 e
Lamèque *Canada* 47°45N 64°38W 299 C7
Lameroo *Australia* 35°19S 140°33E 282 C4
Lamesa *U.S.A.* 32°44N 101°58W 314 E4
L'Ametlla de Mar *Spain* 40°53N 0°48E 196 E5
Lamezia Terme *Italy* 38°55N 16°16E 201 D9
Lami *Fiji* 18°7S 178°25E 287 B2
Lamia *Greece* 38°55N 22°26E 204 C4
Lamigan Pt. *Phil.* 6°48N 126°21E 233 H6
Lamine ➛ *U.S.A.* 38°59N 92°51W 310 F4
Lamington △ *Australia* 28°13S 153°12E 281 D5
Lamitan *Phil.* 6°39N 122°8E 233 H4
Lamlam, Mt. *Guam* 13°22N 144°41E 302 d
Lamma I. *Hong Kong, China* 22°12N 114°7E 122 B2
Lammermuir Hills *U.K.* 55°50N 2°40W 167 F6
Lammeulo *Indonesia* 5°14N 95°56E 234 A1
Lammhult *Sweden* 57°10N 14°35E 163 G8
Lamoille ➛ *U.S.A.* 44°38N 73°13W 313 B11
Lamon B. *Phil.* 14°30N 122°20E 232 D4
Lamongan *Indonesia* 7°7S 112°25E 235 D4
Lamoni *U.S.A.* 40°37N 93°56W 310 D3
Lamont *Alta., Canada* 53°46N 112°50W 296 C6
Lamont *Calif., U.S.A.* 35°15N 118°55W 307 K8
Lamont *Fla., U.S.A.* 30°23N 83°49W 316 E6
Lamont *Iowa, U.S.A.* 42°36N 91°39W 310 B5
Lamont *Wyo., U.S.A.* 42°13N 107°29W 304 E10
Lamotte-Beuvron *France* 47°36N 2°2E 173 E9
Lampa *Peru* 15°22S 70°22W 330 D3
Lampang *Thailand* 18°16N 99°32E 236 C2
Lampasas *U.S.A.* 31°4N 98°11W 314 F5
Lampazos de Naranjo *Mexico* 27°1N 100°31W 318 B4
Lampedusa *Medit. S.* 35°36N 12°40E 258 A2
Lampertheim *Germany* 49°35N 8°27E 179 F4
Lampeter *U.K.* 52°7N 4°4W 169 E3
Lamphun *Thailand* 18°40N 99°2E 236 C2
Lampione *Medit. S.* 35°33N 12°20E 258 A2
Lampman *Canada* 49°25N 102°50W 297 D8
Lamprechtshausen *Austria* 48°0N 12°58E 180 D5
Lampung ☐ *Indonesia* 5°30S 104°30E 234 D2
Lampung, Teluk *Indonesia* 5°40S 105°20E 234 D3
Lamta *India* 22°8N 80°7E 243 H9
Lamu *Burma* 19°14N 94°10E 241 F5
Lamu *Coast, Kenya* 2°16S 40°55E 268 C5
Lamud *Peru* 6°10S 77°57W 330 B2
Lamy *U.S.A.* 35°29N 105°53W 305 J11
Lan Xian *China* 38°15N 111°35E 226 E6
Lan Yü *Taiwan* 22°4N 121°25E 225 D3
Lāna'i *U.S.A.* 20°50N 156°55W 302 C5
Lāna'i City *U.S.A.* 20°50N 156°55W 302 C5
Lāna'ihale *U.S.A.* 20°49N 156°53W 302 C5
Lanak La *China* 34°27N 79°32E 243 B8
Lanak'o Shank'ou = Lanak La *China* 34°27N 79°32E 243 B8
Lanao, L. *Phil.* 7°52N 124°15E 233 H5
Lanao del Norte ☐ *Phil.* 8°0N 124°10E 233 H5
Lanao del Sur ☐ *Phil.* 7°40N 124°15E 233 H5
Lanark *Ont., Canada* 45°1N 76°22W 313 A8
Lanark *S. Lanarks., U.K.* 55°40N 3°47W 167 F5
Lanark *Ill., U.S.A.* 42°6N 89°50W 310 B7
Lanbi Kyun *Burma* 10°50N 98°20E 237 G2
Lancang *China* 22°36N 99°58E 228 F2
Lancang Jiang ➛ *China* 21°40N 101°10E 228 G3
Lancashire ☐ *U.K.* 53°50N 2°48W 168 D5
Lancaster *Ont., Canada* 45°10N 74°30W 313 A10
Lancaster *Lancs., U.K.* 54°3N 2°48W 168 C5
Lancaster *Calif., U.S.A.* 34°42N 118°8W 307 L8
Lancaster *Ky., U.S.A.* 37°37N 84°35W 309 G11
Lancaster *Mo., U.S.A.* 40°31N 92°32W 310 D4
Lancaster *N.H., U.S.A.* 44°29N 71°34W 313 B13
Lancaster *Ohio, U.S.A.* 39°43N 82°36W 309 F12
Lancaster *Pa., U.S.A.* 40°2N 76°19W 313 F8
Lancaster *S.C., U.S.A.* 34°43N 80°46W 315 D14
Lancaster *Wis., U.S.A.* 42°51N 90°43W 310 B6
Lancaster, Récif = Neilson, Récif *Pac. Oc.* 27°1S 146°2W 289 f
Lancaster Sd. *Canada* 74°13N 84°0W 295 C15
Lancelin *Australia* 31°0S 115°18E 279 F2
Lanchow = Lanzhou *China* 36°1N 103°52E 226 F2
Lanchyn *Ukraine* 48°33N 24°45E 183 B9
Lanciano *Italy* 42°14N 14°23E 199 F11
Lanco *Chile* 39°24S 72°46W 336 A2
Lancones *Peru* 4°30S 80°30W 330 A1
Lancun *China* 36°25N 120°10E 227 F11
Łańcut *Poland* 50°10N 22°13E 185 H9
Land Between the Lakes ⌂ *U.S.A.* 36°25N 88°0W 315 C11
Landau *Bayern, Germany* 48°40N 12°41E 179 G8
Landau *Rhld-Pfz., Germany* 49°12N 8°6E 179 F4
Landay *Afghan.* 30°31N 63°47E 240 C1
Landeck *Austria* 47°9N 10°34E 180 D3
Lander *U.S.A.* 42°50N 108°44W 304 E9
Lander ➛ *Australia* 22°0S 132°0E 278 D5
Landerneau *France* 48°28N 4°17W 172 D2
Landeryd *Sweden* 57°7N 13°15E 163 G7
Landes *France* 44°0N 1°0W 174 D2
Landes ☐ *France* 43°57N 0°48W 174 E3
Landes de Gascogne ⌂ *France* 44°23N 0°50W 174 D3
Landeshut = Kamienna Góra *Poland* 50°47N 16°2E 185 H3
Landete *Spain* 39°56N 1°25W 196 F3
Landfall I. *India* 13°40N 93°2E 245 H11
Landi Kotal *Pakistan* 34°7N 71°6E 242 B4
Landianchang *China* 39°56N 116°17E 114 B1
Landisburg *U.S.A.* 40°21N 77°19W 312 F7
Landivisiau *France* 48°31N 4°6W 172 D2
Landmannalaugar *Iceland* 63°59N 19°4W 155 D7
Landquart *Switz.* 46°58N 9°32E 179 J5
Landrecies *France* 50°7N 3°40E 173 B10
Land's End *U.K.* 50°4N 5°44W 169 G2
Landsberg = Gorówo Iławeckie *Poland* 54°17N 20°30E 184 D7
Landsberg *Germany* 48°2N 10°53E 179 G6
Landsberg an der Warthe = Gorzów Wielkopolski *Poland* 52°43N 15°15E 185 F2
Landsberg in Oberschlesien = Gorzów Śląski *Poland* 51°3N 18°22E 185 G5
Landsborough Cr. ➛ *Australia* 22°28S 144°35E 280 C3
Landsbro *Sweden* 57°24N 14°56E 163 G8
Landshut *Germany* 48°34N 12°8E 179 G8
Landskrona *Sweden* 55°53N 12°50E 163 J6
Landsmeer *Neths.* 52°26N 4°55E 112 A2
Landstrasse *Austria* 48°12N 16°23E 142 A2
Landstuhl *Germany* 49°24N 7°33E 179 F3
Landvetter *Sweden* 57°41N 12°17E 163 G6
Landwehr kanal *Germany* 52°29N 13°24E 115 B3
Lane *U.S.A.* 33°32N 79°53W 316 B10
Lane Cove *Australia* 33°48S 151°9E 139 A1
Lane Cove Nat. Park △ *Australia* 33°47S 151°8E 139 A1
Lanesboro *U.S.A.* 41°57N 75°34W 313 E9
Lanester *France* 47°46N 3°22W 172 E3
Lanett *U.S.A.* 32°52N 85°12W 316 C4
Lang Shan *China* 41°0N 106°30E 226 D4
Lang Son *Vietnam* 21°52N 106°42E 228 G6
Lang Suan *Thailand* 9°57N 99°4E 237 H2
Langå *Midtjylland, Denmark* 56°23N 9°54E 163 H3
Langa *Western Cape, S. Africa* 33°57S 18°31E 118 A2
La'nga Co *China* 30°45N 81°15E 243 D9
Langa-Langa *Dem. Rep. of the Congo* 3°50S 15°59E 264 C3
Langadas *Greece* 40°46N 23°2E 202 F7
Langadia *Greece* 37°43N 22°1E 204 D4
Långan ➛ *Sweden* 63°19N 14°44E 162 A8
Langanes *Iceland* 66°20N 14°53W 155 A12
Langano, L. *Ethiopia* 7°36N 38°43E 257 F4
Langar *Afghan.* 37°2N 73°47E 240 A4
Langar *Iran* 35°23N 60°25E 247 C9
Langara I. *Canada* 54°14N 133°1W 296 C2
Langarūd *Iran* 37°11N 50°8E 247 B6
Långås *Sweden* 56°58N 12°26E 163 H6
Langatabbetje *Suriname* 4°59N 54°28W 329 C7
Langdai *China* 26°6N 105°21E 228 D5
Langdon *U.S.A.* 48°45N 98°22W 308 A4
Långe Jan = Ölands södra udde *Sweden* 56°12N 16°23E 163 H10

Langeac France 45°7N 3°29E 174 C7
Langeais France 47°20N 0°24E 172 E7
Langeb Baraka → Sudan 17°28N 36°50E 256 D4
Langeberg S. Africa 33°55S 21°0E 270 D3
Langeberge S. Africa 28°15S 22°33E 270 C3
Langeland Denmark 54°56N 10°48E 163 K4
Langelands Bælt Denmark 54°50N 10°55E 163 K4
Langen Hessen, Germany 49°59N 8°40E 179 F4
Langen Niedersachsen, Germany 53°36N 8°36E 178 B4
Langenbielau = Bielawa Poland 50°43N 16°37E 185 H3
Langenburg Canada 50°51N 101°43W 297 C8
Langeneß Germany 54°38N 8°36E 178 A4
Langenlois Austria 48°29N 15°40E 180 C8
Langenzersdorf Austria 48°18N 16°21E 142 A2
Langeoog Germany 53°45N 7°32E 178 B3
Langer See Germany 52°24N 13°37E 115 B4
Langeskov Denmark 55°22N 10°35E 163 J4
Langesund Norway 59°0N 9°45E 164 F6
Langevåg Norway 62°26N 6°13E 164 B3
Langfang China 39°30N 116°41E 226 E9
Langgapayung Indonesia 1°43N 99°58E 234 B1
Långhem Sweden 57°36N 13°14E 163 G7
Langhirano Italy 44°37N 10°16E 198 D7
Langholm U.K. 55°9N 3°0W 167 F5
Langisjór Iceland 64°11N 18°15W 155 C8
Langjökull Iceland 64°39N 20°12W 155 C6
Langkawi, Pulau Malaysia 6°25N 99°45E 237 J2
Langklip S. Africa 28°12S 20°20E 270 C3
Langkon Malaysia 6°30N 116°40E 235 A5
Langley B.C., Canada 49°7N 122°39W 306 A4
Langley Va., U.S.A. 38°57N 77°11W 143 B1
Langley Park U.S.A. 38°59N 76°58W 143 B3
Langnau Switz. 46°56N 7°47E 179 J3
Langogne France 44°43N 3°50E 174 D7
Langon France 44°33N 0°16W 174 D3
Langøya Norway 68°45N 14°50E 160 B16
Langreo Spain 43°18N 5°40W 194 B5
Langres France 47°52N 5°20E 173 E12
Langres, Plateau de France 47°45N 5°3E 173 E12
Langsa Indonesia 4°30N 97°57E 234 B1
Långsele Sweden 63°12N 17°4E 162 A11
Långshyttan Sweden 60°27N 16°2E 162 D10
Langtang △ Nepal 28°10N 85°30E 243 E11
Langtao Burma 27°15N 97°34E 241 B6
Langting India 25°31N 93°7E 241 C4
Langtou China 40°1N 124°19E 227 D13
Langtry U.S.A. 29°49N 101°34W 314 G4
Langu Thailand 6°53N 99°47E 237 J2
Langue de Barbarie △ Senegal 14°54N 16°30W 262 C1
Languedoc France 43°58N 3°55E 174 E7
Languedoc-Roussillon □ France 43°25N 3°0E 174 E6
Langwald Germany 48°10N 11°25E 131 A1
Langwang China 22°38N 113°27E 219 a
Langxi China 31°10N 119°12E 229 B12
Langzhong China 31°38N 105°58E 228 B5
Lanigan Canada 51°51N 105°2W 297 C7
Lanikai U.S.A. 21°23N 157°42W 302 K14
Lanín △ Argentina 40°0S 71°58W 336 A2
Lanjigarh India 19°43N 83°23E 244 E6
Lanjin China 34°48N 114°50E 226 G8
Länkäran Azerbaijan 38°48N 48°52E 213 C13
Lankwitz Germany 52°25N 13°21E 115 B3
Lanmeur France 48°39N 3°43W 172 D3
Lannemezan France 43°8N 0°23E 174 E4
Lannilis France 48°35N 4°32W 172 D2
Lannion France 48°46N 3°29W 172 D3
L'Annonciation Canada 46°25N 74°55W 298 C5
L'Annunziatella Italy 41°49N 12°33E 136 C2
Lanouaille France 45°24N 1°9E 174 C5
Lanping China 26°28N 99°15E 228 D2
Lansang △ Thailand 16°45N 99°0E 236 D2
Lansdale U.S.A. 40°14N 75°17W 313 F9
Lansdowne N.S.W., Australia 31°48S 152°30E 283 A10
Lansdowne Ont., Canada 44°24N 76°1W 313 B8
Lansdowne India 29°50N 78°41E 243 E8
Lansdowne Western Cape, S. Africa 33°59S 18°30E 118 A2
Lansdowne House = Neskantaga Canada 52°14N 87°53W 298 B2
L'Anse U.S.A. 46°45N 88°27W 308 B9
L'Anse à l'Âne Martinique 14°32N 61°4W 322 j
L'Anse au Loup Canada 51°32N 56°50W 299 B8
L'Anse aux Epines Grenada 11°59N 61°45W 323 q
L'Anse aux Meadows Canada 51°36N 55°32W 299 B8
L'Anse Mitan Martinique 14°32N 61°3W 322 j
Lansford U.S.A. 40°50N 75°53W 313 F9
Lanshan China 25°24N 112°10E 229 E9
Lanshantou China 35°5N 119°20E 227 G10
Länsi-Turunmaa Finland 60°18N 22°18E 188 B2
Lansing Ont., Canada 43°45N 79°24W 141 A2
Lansing Mich., U.S.A. 42°44N 84°33W 311 B12
Lanslebourg-Mont-Cenis France 45°17N 6°52E 175 C10
Lanta, Ko Thailand 7°35N 99°3E 237 J2
Lantana U.S.A. 26°35N 80°3W 317 J9
Lantau I. Hong Kong, China 22°15N 113°56E 122 B1
Lantau Pk. Hong Kong, China 22°15N 113°55E 122 B1
Lantewa Nigeria 12°16N 11°44E 263 C7
Lantian China 34°11N 109°20E 226 G5
Lanus Argentina 34°42S 58°23W 117 C2
Lanusei Italy 39°52N 9°34E 200 C2
Lanuza Phil. 9°14N 126°4E 233 G6
Lanxi China 29°13N 119°28E 229 C12
Lanyang Hsi → Taiwan 24°43N 121°49E 225 B3
Lanyü Taiwan 22°2N 121°33E 225 D3
Lanzarote Canary Is. 29°0N 13°40W 153 e2
Lanzarote ✕ (ACE) Canary Is. 28°57N 13°40W 153 e2
Lanzhou China 36°1N 103°52E 226 F2
Lanzo Torinese Italy 45°16N 7°28E 198 C4
Lao → Italy 39°47N 15°48E 201 C8
Lao Cai Vietnam 22°30N 103°57E 228 F4
Laoag Phil. 18°7N 120°34E 232 B3
Laoang Phil. 12°32N 125°8E 232 E5
Laoha He → China 43°25N 120°35E 227 C11
Laohekou China 32°22N 111°38E 229 A8
Laois □ Ireland 52°57N 7°27W 166 D4
Laon France 49°33N 3°35E 173 C10
Laona U.S.A. 45°34N 88°40W 308 C9
Laonung Hsi → Taiwan 22°47N 120°27E 225 D2
Laos ■ Asia 17°45N 105°0E 236 D5
Lapa Paraná, Brazil 25°46S 49°44W 335 B6
Lapa Rio de J., Brazil 22°54S 43°10W 135 B1
Lapac I. Phil. 5°32N 120°47E 233 J3
Lapai Nigeria 9°5N 6°32E 263 D6
Lapalisse France 46°15N 3°38E 173 F10
Laparan I. Phil. 5°57N 120°0E 233 J2
Lapeer U.S.A. 43°3N 83°19W 311 A13
Lapeyrade France 44°4N 0°3W 174 D3
Lapithos Cyprus 35°21N 33°11E 207 E9
Lapland = Lappland Europe 68°7N 24°0E 160 B21
LaPorte Ind., U.S.A. 41°36N 86°43W 311 C10
Laporte Pa., U.S.A. 41°25N 76°30W 313 E8
Lapovo Serbia 44°10N 21°7E 202 B5
Lappeenranta Finland 61°3N 28°12E 188 B5
Lappland Europe 68°7N 24°0E 160 B21
Lappo = Lapua Finland 62°58N 23°0E 160 E20
Laprida Argentina 37°34S 60°45W 334 D3
Lâpseki Turkey 40°20N 26°41E 203 F10
Lapta = Lapithos Cyprus 35°21N 33°11E 207 E9
Laptev Sea Russia 76°0N 125°0E 215 B13
Lapu-Lapu Phil. 10°20N 123°55E 233 F4
Lapua Finland 62°58N 23°0E 160 E20
Lăpuş → Romania 47°25N 23°40E 183 C8
Lăpuş, Munţii Romania 47°20N 23°50E 183 C8
Lăpuşna Moldova 46°53N 28°25E 183 D13
Łapy Poland 52°59N 22°52E 185 F9
Laqiya Arba'in Sudan 20°1N 28°1E 256 C2
Laqiya Umran Sudan 19°55N 28°18E 256 D2
L'Àquila Italy 42°22N 13°22E 199 F10
Lār Iran 27°40N 54°14E 247 E7
Lara Australia 38°2S 144°26E 282 E6
Lara □ Venezuela 10°10N 69°50W 328 A4
Larabanga Ghana 9°16N 1°56W 262 D4
Larache Morocco 35°10N 6°5W 260 A3
Laragaran = Plaridel Phil. 8°37N 123°43E 233 G4
Laragne-Montéglin France 44°18N 5°49E 175 D9
Lārak Iran 26°51N 56°21E 249 A7
Laramie U.S.A. 41°19N 105°35W 304 F11
Laramie Mts. U.S.A. 42°0N 105°30W 304 F11
Laranda = Karaman Turkey 37°14N 33°13E 212 D5
Laranjal do Jari Brazil 0°51S 52°32W 329 D7
Laranjeiras Brazil 22°55S 43°10W 135 B1
Laranjeiras do Sul Brazil 25°23S 52°23W 335 B5
Larantuka Indonesia 8°21S 122°55E 231 F6
Larat Indonesia 7°0S 132°0E 231 F8
L'Arbresle France 45°50N 4°36E 175 C8
Lärbro Sweden 57°47N 18°50E 163 G12
Lårdal Norway 59°25N 8°10E 164 E5
Larde Mozam. 16°28S 39°43E 269 F4
Larder Lake Canada 48°5N 79°40W 298 C4
Lardos Greece 36°6N 28°1E 206 E12
Lardos, Akra = Lindos, Akra Greece 36°4N 28°10E 206 E12
Lardos, Ormos Greece 36°4N 28°2E 206 E12
Lare Kenya 0°20N 37°56E 268 C4
Laredo Spain 43°26N 3°28W 194 B7
Laredo Tex., U.S.A. 27°30N 99°30W 314 H5
Laredo Sd. Canada 52°30N 128°53W 296 C3
Larena Phil. 9°15N 123°35E 233 G4
Lares Puerto Rico 18°18N 66°53W 321 b
Large I. Grenada 12°24N 61°30W 323 q
Largentière France 44°34N 4°18E 175 D8
L'Argentière-la-Bessée France 44°47N 6°33E 175 D10
Largo U.S.A. 27°54N 82°47W 317 H7
Largo, Key U.S.A. 25°15N 80°15W 317 K9
Largs U.K. 55°47N 4°52W 167 F4
Lari Italy 43°34N 10°35E 198 E7
Lariang Indonesia 1°26S 119°17E 235 C5
Larimore U.S.A. 47°54N 97°38W 308 B5
Larino Italy 41°48N 14°54E 199 G11
Lario, Il = Como, L. di Italy 46°0N 9°11E 198 B6
Larisa Greece 39°36N 22°27E 204 B4
Larisis Station Athens, Greece 112 a1
Larissa = Larisa Greece 39°36N 22°27E 204 B4
Larkana Pakistan 27°32N 68°18E 242 F3
Larkins = South Miami U.S.A. 25°42N 80°17W 129 D1
Larnaca Cyprus 34°55N 33°38E 207 F9
Larnaca ✕ (LCA) Cyprus 34°50N 33°34E 207 F9
Larnaca Bay Cyprus 34°53N 33°45E 207 F9
Larnare, Pte. Martinique 14°47N 61°13W 322 j
Larne U.K. 54°51N 5°51W 166 B6
Larned U.S.A. 38°11N 99°6W 308 F4
Laroquebrou France 44°58N 2°12E 174 D6
Larose U.S.A. 29°34N 90°23W 315 G9
Larose, Pte. Martinique 14°39N 60°53W 322 j
Larrimah Australia 15°35S 133°12E 278 C5
Larsen Bay U.S.A. 57°32N 153°59W 303 H9
Larsen Ice Shelf Antarctica 67°0S 62°0W 151 C17
Laruns France 43°0N 0°26W 174 F3
Larvik Norway 59°4N 10°2E 164 E7
Larzac, Causse du France 43°50N 3°17E 174 E7
Las Poland 52°13N 21°6E 143 B2
Las Alpujarras Spain 36°55N 3°20W 197 J1
Las Animas U.S.A. 38°4N 103°13W 304 G12
Las Anod Somalia 8°26N 47°19E 267 C6
Las Arenas Spain 43°17N 4°50W 194 B6
Las Batuecas ⌂ Spain 40°32N 6°5W 194 E4
Las Bermúdez Venezuela 10°56N 64°1W 329 a
Las Bonitas Venezuela 7°52N 65°40W 328 B4
Las Breñas Argentina 27°5S 61°7W 334 B3
Las Cabezas de San Juan Spain 36°57N 5°58W 195 J5
Las Cabreras Venezuela 11°3N 63°58W 329 a
Las Cañadas del Teide △ Canary Is. 28°15N 16°37W 153 e1
Las Cejas Argentina 26°53S 64°44W 334 B3
Las Chimeneas Mexico 32°8N 116°5W 307 N10
Las Coloradas Argentina 39°34S 70°36W 336 A2
Las Corts Spain 41°23N 2°9E 114 A1
Las Cruces U.S.A. 32°19N 106°47W 305 K10
Las Flores Argentina 36°10S 59°7W 334 D4
Las Gabias = Gabia la Grande Spain 37°8N 3°40W 195 H7
Las Heras Mendoza, Argentina 32°51S 68°49W 334 C2
Las Heras Santa Cruz, Argentina 46°33S 68°57W 336 C3
Las Hermosas △ Colombia 3°48N 75°51W 328 C2
Las Horquetas Argentina 48°14S 71°11W 336 C2
Las Kabacki Poland 52°7N 21°2E 143 C2
Las Khoreh = Laasqoray Somalia 11°10N 48°20E 267 B6
Las Lajas Argentina 38°30S 70°25W 336 A2
Las Lomas Peru 4°40S 80°10W 330 A1
Las Lomitas Argentina 24°43S 60°35W 334 A3
Las Manos, Cueva de Argentina 47°9S 70°40W 336 C2
Las Marismas Spain 37°5N 6°20W 195 H4
Las Médulas Spain 42°28N 6°46W 194 C4
Las Mercedes Venezuela 9°7N 66°24W 328 B4
Las Minas Spain 38°20N 1°41W 197 G3
Las Navas de la Concepción Spain 37°56N 5°30W 195 H5
Las Navas del Marqués Spain 40°36N 4°20W 194 E6
Las Nieves Phil. 8°46N 125°34E 233 G5
Las Orquideas △ Colombia 6°36N 76°16W 328 B2
Las Palmas Argentina 27°8S 58°45W 334 B4
Las Palmas → Mexico 32°31N 116°58W 307 N10
Las Palmas ✕ (LPA) Canary Is. 27°55N 15°25W 153 e1
Las Palmas de Gran Canaria Canary Is. 28°7N 15°26W 153 e1
Las Pedroñeras Spain 39°26N 2°40W 197 F2
Las Piedras Puerto Rico 18°11N 65°52W 321 b
Las Piedras Uruguay 34°44S 56°14W 335 C4
Las Pinas Phil. 14°29N 120°58E 127 C1
Las Pipinas Argentina 35°30S 57°19W 334 D4
Las Plumas Argentina 43°40S 67°15W 336 B3
Las Ramblas = La Rambla Barcelona, Spain 114 b2
Las Rejas Chile 33°27S 70°42W 137 B1
Las Rosas Argentina 32°30S 61°35W 334 C3
Las Rozas Spain 40°29N 3°52W 194 E7
Las Tablas Panama 7°49N 80°14W 320 E3
Las Toscas Argentina 28°21S 59°18W 334 B4
Las Tunas Cuba 20°58N 76°59W 320 B4
Las Varillas Argentina 31°50S 62°50W 334 C3
Las Vegas N. Mex., U.S.A. 35°36N 105°13W 305 J11
Las Vegas Nev., U.S.A. 36°10N 115°8W 124 A2
Las Vegas McCarran Int. ✕ (LAS) U.S.A. 36°5N 115°9W 124 B2
Lasa = Lhasa China 29°25N 90°58E 218 F7
LaSalle Canada 45°26N 73°38W 130 B2
LaSalle Street Chicago, U.S.A. 119 a1
LaSalle Street Station Chicago, U.S.A. 119 d1
Lasanga I. Papua N. G. 7°25S 147°15E 286 D4
Lasarte-Oria Spain 43°16N 2°1W 196 B2
Lascano Uruguay 33°35S 54°12W 335 C5
Lascelles Australia 35°34S 142°34E 282 C5
Lasek Bielański Poland 52°17N 20°57E 143 B1
Lasek Na Kole Poland 52°15N 20°56E 143 B1
Lash-e Joveyn Afghan. 31°45N 61°30E 240 C1
Lashburn Canada 53°10N 109°40W 297 C7
Lashio Burma 22°56N 97°45E 241 D6
Lashkar India 26°10N 78°10E 242 F8
Lashkar Gāh Afghan. 31°35N 64°21E 240 C2
Lasin Poland 53°30N 19°2E 184 E6
Lasithi Greece 35°11N 25°31E 207 E6
Lāsjerd Iran 35°24N 53°4E 247 C7
Lask Poland 51°34N 19°8E 185 G6
Laskarzew Poland 51°48N 21°36E 185 G8
Laško Slovenia 46°10N 15°16E 199 B12
Lassance Brazil 17°54S 44°34W 333 E3
Lassay-les-Châteaux France 48°27N 0°30W 172 D6
Lassen Pk. U.S.A. 40°29N 121°30W 304 F3
Lassen Volcanic △ U.S.A. 40°30N 121°20W 304 F3
Lassongo Angola 12°55S 22°46E 265 E4
Last Mountain L. Canada 51°5N 105°14W 297 C7
Lastchance Cr. → U.S.A. 40°2N 121°15W 306 E5
Lastoursville Gabon 0°55S 12°38E 264 C2
Lastovo Croatia 42°46N 16°55E 199 F13
Lastovski Kanal Croatia 42°50N 17°0E 199 F14
Lat Yao Thailand 15°45N 99°48E 236 E2
Lata Mt. Amer. Samoa 14°14S 169°27W 302 f
Latacunga Ecuador 0°50S 78°35W 328 D2
Latady I. Antarctica 70°45S 74°35W 151 D17
Latakia = Al Lādhiqīyah Syria 35°30N 35°45E 250 C6
Latchford Canada 47°20N 79°50W 298 C4
Late Tonga 18°48S 174°39W 287 P13
Latehar India 23°45N 84°30E 243 H11
Laterza Italy 40°37N 16°48E 201 B9
Latham Australia 29°44S 116°20E 279 E2
Lathen Germany 52°52N 7°19E 178 C3
Lathi India 27°43N 71°23E 242 F4
Lathi Vanuatu 14°57S 167°8E 287 D5
Lathrop U.S.A. 39°33N 94°20W 310 E2
Lathrop Wells U.S.A. 36°39N 116°24W 307 J10
Latiano Italy 40°33N 17°43E 201 B10
Latin, Quartier Montréal, Canada 130 b2
Latina Italy 41°28N 12°52E 200 A5
Latina Madrid, Spain 40°24N 3°44W 127 B1
Latisana Italy 45°47N 13°0E 199 C10
Latium = Lazio □ Italy 42°10N 12°30E 199 F9
Laton U.S.A. 36°26N 119°41W 306 J7
Latorytsya → Slovak Rep. 48°28N 21°50E 181 C14
Latouche Treville, C. Australia 18°27S 121°49E 278 C3
Latouma Niger 22°10N 14°50E 259 D2
Látrar Iceland 66°24N 23°2W 155 A3
Latrobe Tas., Australia 41°14S 146°30E 281 G4
Latrobe Pa., U.S.A. 40°19N 79°23W 312 F5
Latrónico Italy 40°5N 16°1E 201 B9
Latur India 18°25N 76°40E 244 E3
Latvia ■ Europe 56°50N 24°0E 188 D2
Lau Nigeria 9°11N 11°19E 263 D7
Lau Basin Pac. Oc. 20°0S 177°0W 277 E15
Lau Group Fiji 17°0S 178°30W 287 A3
Lau Ridge Pac. Oc. 21°0S 178°30W 277 E15
Lauban = Lubań Poland 51°5N 15°15E 185 G2
Lauca → Bolivia 19°9S 68°10W 330 D4
Lauchhammer Germany 51°29N 13°47E 178 D9
Lauda-Königshofen Germany 49°33N 9°42E 179 F5
Laudal Norway 58°15N 7°30E 164 F4
Laudat Dominica 15°20N 61°21W 323 k
Lauderdale Lakes U.S.A. 26°9N 80°12W 129 B1
Lauderhill U.S.A. 26°8N 80°12W 129 B2
Laudio = Llodio Spain 43°9N 2°58W 196 B2
Lauenburg = Lębork Poland 54°33N 17°46E 184 D4
Lauenburg Germany 53°22N 10°32E 178 B6
Lauenburgische Seen ⌂ Germany 53°38N 10°45E 178 B6
Lauf Germany 49°30N 11°16E 179 F7
Laufás Iceland 65°53N 18°4W 155 B8
Laugar Iceland 65°15N 21°48W 155 B5
Laugarás Iceland 64°7N 20°30W 155 C6
Laugarbakki Iceland 65°20N 20°55W 155 B6
Laugarvatn Iceland 64°13N 20°44W 155 C6
Lauge Koch Kyst Greenland 75°45N 57°45W 295 B20
Laughlin U.S.A. 35°10N 114°34W 307 K12
Lauhanvuori △ Finland 62°8N 22°4E 160 E20
Laujar de Andarax Spain 37°0N 2°54W 197 H2
Laukaa Finland 62°24N 25°56E 160 E21
Laukkaing Burma 23°52N 98°38E 241 D7
Laulau, Bahia N. Marianas 15°8N 145°45E 302 e
Launceston Tas., Australia 41°24S 147°8E 281 G4
Launceston Corn., U.K. 50°38N 4°22W 169 G3
Laune → Ireland 52°7N 9°47W 166 D2
Launglon Bok Burma 13°50N 97°54E 236 F1
Laupheim Germany 48°14N 9°52E 179 G5
Laura Queens., Australia 15°32S 144°32E 280 B3
Laura S. Austral., Australia 33°10S 138°18E 282 B3
Laureana di Borrello Italy 38°30N 16°5E 201 D9
Laurel Fla., U.S.A. 27°8N 82°27W 317 H7
Laurel Ind., U.S.A. 39°30N 85°11W 311 E11
Laurel Miss., U.S.A. 31°41N 89°8W 315 F10
Laurel Mont., U.S.A. 45°40N 108°46W 304 D9
Laurel Bay U.S.A. 32°27N 80°47W 316 C9
Laurel Hill U.S.A. 40°14N 79°6W 312 F5
Laurencekirk U.K. 56°50N 2°28W 167 E6
Laurens Iowa, U.S.A. 42°51N 94°52W 310 B2
Laurens S.C., U.S.A. 34°30N 82°1W 315 D13
Laurentian Plateau Canada 52°0N 70°0W 299 B6
Lauria Italy 40°2N 15°50E 201 B8
Laurie L. Canada 56°35N 101°57W 297 B8
Laurinburg U.S.A. 34°47N 79°28W 315 D15
Laurium U.S.A. 47°14N 88°27W 308 B9
Lausanne Switz. 46°32N 6°38E 179 J2
Laut Indonesia 4°45N 108°0E 235 B3
Laut, Pulau Indonesia 3°40S 116°10E 235 C5
Laut Kecil, Kepulauan Indonesia 4°45S 115°40E 235 C5
Lautaro Chile 38°31S 72°27W 336 A2
Lauterbach Germany 50°37N 9°24E 178 E5
Lauterecken Germany 49°38N 7°35E 179 F3
Lautoka Fiji 17°37S 177°27E 287 A1
L'Autre Bord Guadeloupe 16°20N 61°20W 322 e
Lauttasaari Finland 60°9N 24°53E 121 C2
Lauwersmeer △ Neths. 53°22N 6°11E 170 A6
Lauzès France 44°34N 1°35E 174 D5
Lava → Russia 54°37N 21°14E 184 D8
Lava, Nosy Madag. 14°33S 47°36E 272 A2
Lava Beds ⌂ U.S.A. 41°40N 121°30W 304 F3
Lavagh More Ireland 54°46N 8°6W 166 B3
Lavagna Italy 44°18N 9°20E 198 D6
Laval France 48°4N 0°48W 172 D6
Laval-des-Rapides Canada 45°33N 73°42W 130 A1
Lavalle Argentina 28°15S 65°15W 334 B2
Lāvān Iran 26°48N 53°22E 247 E7
Lavanggu Solomon Is. 11°36S 160°16E 287 N11
Lavant Canada 45°3N 76°42W 313 A8
Lāvar Meydān Iran 30°20N 54°30E 247 D7
Lavara Greece 41°19N 26°22E 203 E10
Lavardac France 44°12N 0°20E 174 D4
Lavaur France 43°40N 1°49E 174 E5
Lavelanet France 42°57N 1°51E 174 F5
Lavello Italy 41°3N 15°48E 201 A8
Laventille □ Trin. & Tob. 10°39N 61°30W 323 t
L'Averdy, C. Papua N. G. 5°33S 155°4E 286 C8
Lavers Hill Australia 38°40S 143°25E 282 E5
Laverton Australia 28°44S 122°29E 279 E3
Lavezzi, Îs. France 41°22N 9°16E 175 G13
Lavik Norway 61°6N 5°25E 164 C2
Lavis Italy 46°8N 11°7E 198 B8
Lavīzān Iran 35°47N 51°30E 141 A2
Lavos Portugal 40°6N 8°49W 194 E2
Lavoutte, Anse St. Lucia 14°5N 60°55W 323 m
Lavradio Portugal 38°40N 9°2W 126 A2
Lavras Brazil 21°20S 45°0W 333 F3
Lavre Portugal 38°46N 8°22W 195 G2
Lavrio Greece 37°40N 24°4E 204 D6
Lavris Greece 35°25N 24°40E 207 E5
Lavumisa Swaziland 27°20S 31°55E 271 C5
Lavushi Manda △ Zambia 12°46S 31°0E 269 E3
Law Phil. 6°12N 125°41E 233 H5
Lawa-an Phil. 11°51N 125°5E 233 F5
Lawachara △ Bangla. 24°20N 91°43E 241 C3
Lawak I. = Nanshan I. S. China Sea 10°45N 115°49E 230 B5
Lawaki Fiji 17°40S 178°35E 287 A2
Lawas Malaysia 4°55N 115°25E 235 B5
Lawdar Yemen 13°53N 45°52E 248 D4
Lawele Indonesia 5°13S 122°57E 231 F6
Lawit Indonesia 1°23N 112°55E 235 B4
Lawksawk Burma 21°15N 96°52E 241 E6
Lawn Hill = Boodjamulla △ Australia 18°15S 138°6E 280 B2
Lawndale U.S.A. 41°50N 87°42W 119 B2
Lawne L. U.S.A. 28°33N 81°26W 133 A2
Lawqah Si. Arabia 29°49N 42°45E 246 D4
Lawra Ghana 10°39N 2°51W 262 C4
Lawrence N.Z. 45°55S 169°41E 285 F4
Lawrence Ind., U.S.A. 39°50N 86°2W 311 E10
Lawrence Kans., U.S.A. 38°58N 95°14W 308 F6
Lawrence Mass., U.S.A. 42°43N 71°10W 313 D13
Lawrence Heights Canada 43°43N 79°25W 141 A2
Lawrenceburg Ind., U.S.A. 39°6N 84°52W 311 E12
Lawrenceburg Ky., U.S.A. 38°2N 84°54W 311 F12
Lawrenceburg Tenn., U.S.A. 35°14N 87°20W 315 D11
Lawrenceville Ga., U.S.A. 33°57N 83°59W 316 B6
Lawrenceville Ill., U.S.A. 38°44N 87°41W 311 F9
Lawrenceville Pa., U.S.A. 41°59N 77°8W 312 E7
Laws U.S.A. 37°24N 118°20W 306 H8
Lawson U.S.A. 39°26N 94°12W 310 E2
Lawtey U.S.A. 30°3N 82°5W 316 E7
Lawton Mich., U.S.A. 42°10N 85°50W 311 B11
Lawton Okla., U.S.A. 34°37N 98°25W 314 D5
Lawu Indonesia 7°40S 111°13E 235 D4
Lawz, J. al Si. Arabia 28°39N 35°18E 251 K6
Laxå Sweden 58°59N 14°37E 163 F8
Laxamýri Iceland 65°58N 17°24W 155 B9
Laxford, L. U.K. 58°24N 5°6W 167 C3
Laxiwa Dam China 36°4N 101°11E 218 D9
Laxou France 48°41N 6°8E 173 D13
Lay → France 46°18N 1°17W 174 B2
Layari Pakistan 24°52N 67°0E 123 A2
Layari → Pakistan 24°52N 66°58E 123 A1
Layla Si. Arabia 22°10N 46°40E 248 B4
Laylān Iraq 35°18N 44°31E 246 C5
Layon → France 47°20N 0°45W 172 E6
Layou St. Vincent 13°12N 61°17W 323 n
Layou → Dominica 15°23N 61°21W 323 k
Laysan I. U.S.A. 25°50N 171°50W 302 F9
Layton Fla., U.S.A. 24°50N 80°47W 317 L9
Layton Utah, U.S.A. 41°4N 111°58W 304 F8
Laytonville U.S.A. 39°41N 123°29W 304 G2
Laza Burma 26°30N 97°38E 241 B6
Lazarata Greece 38°47N 20°40E 207 B2
Lazarev Russia 52°13N 141°30E 215 D15
Lazarev Sea S. Ocean 67°30S 3°0W 151 C2
Lazarevac Serbia 44°23N 20°17E 202 B4
Lazarevskoye Russia 43°55N 39°21E 191 J4
Lazarivo Madag. 23°54S 44°59E 272 C1
Lázaro Cárdenas Mexico 17°55N 102°11W 318 D4
Lazdijai Lithuania 54°14N 23°31E 184 D10
Lazhuglung China 34°52N 81°24E 217 F10
Lazi Phil. 9°8N 123°38E 233 G4
Lazienki Palace Warsaw, Poland 143 c3
Łazienkowski Park Poland 52°13N 21°1E 143 B2
Lazio □ Italy 42°10N 12°30E 199 F9
Lazo Moldova 47°33N 28°2E 183 C13
Lazo Russia 43°25N 133°55E 220 C6
Lazy Lake U.S.A. 26°9N 80°8W 129 B3
Lbishchensk = Chapaev Kazakhstan 50°25N 51°10E 190 E10
Le Beausset France 43°12N 5°48E 175 E9
Le Bélier Réunion 21°2S 55°28E 272 f
Le Bic Canada 48°20N 68°41W 299 C6
Le Blanc France 46°37N 1°3E 174 B5
Le Blanc-Mesnil France 48°56N 2°27E 134 A3
Le Bleymard France 44°30N 3°42E 174 D7
Le Bourget France 48°56N 2°25E 134 A3
Le Bourgneuf-la-Forêt France 48°10N 0°59W 172 D6
Le Bugue France 44°55N 0°56E 174 D4
Le Carbet Martinique 14°42N 61°11W 322 j
Le Cateau Cambrésis France 50°7N 3°32E 173 B10
Le Caylar France 43°51N 3°19E 174 E7
Le Chambon-Feugerolles France 45°24N 4°19E 175 C8
Le Chameau Guadeloupe 15°51N 61°35W 322 e
Le Châtelet France 46°38N 2°16E 173 F9
Le Chenoi Belgium 50°41N 4°18E 116 B2
Le Chesnay France 48°49N 2°8E 134 B1
Le Chesne France 49°30N 4°45E 173 C11
Le Cheylard France 44°55N 4°25E 175 D8
Le Christ de Saclay France 48°43N 1°59E 134 B2
Le Claire U.S.A. 41°36N 90°21W 310 C6
Le Conquet France 48°21N 4°46W 172 D2
Le Creusot France 46°48N 4°24E 173 F11
Le Croisic France 47°18N 2°30W 172 E4
Le Diamant Martinique 14°28N 61°2W 322 j
Le Donjon France 46°22N 3°48E 173 F10
Le Dorat France 46°14N 1°5E 174 B5
Le François Martinique 14°38N 60°57W 322 j
Le Gosier Guadeloupe 16°14N 61°29W 322 e
Le Grand Brûlé Réunion 21°14S 55°47E 272 f
Le Grand-Lucé France 47°52N 0°28E 172 E7
Le Grand-Pressigny France 46°55N 0°48E 172 F7
Le Grand-Quevilly France 49°24N 1°3E 172 C8
Le Gris Gris Mauritius 20°31S 57°32E 272 e
Le Gros Morne Réunion 21°5S 55°28E 272 f
Le Havre France 49°30N 0°5E 172 C7
Le Kremlin-Bicêtre France 48°48N 2°21E 134 B3
Le Lamentin Martinique 14°35N 61°2W 322 j
Le Lavandou France 43°8N 6°22E 175 E10
Le Lion-d'Angers France 47°37N 0°43W 172 E6
Le Lorrain Martinique 14°48N 61°3W 322 j
Le Louroux-Béconnais France 47°30N 0°55W 172 E6
Le Luc France 43°23N 6°21E 175 E10
Le Lude France 47°39N 0°9E 172 E7
Le Maire, Estr. de Argentina 54°50S 65°0W 336 D4
Le Mans France 48°0N 0°10E 172 E7
Le Marigot Martinique 14°50N 61°1W 322 j
Le Marin Martinique 14°27N 60°55W 322 j
Le Mars U.S.A. 42°47N 96°10W 308 D5
Le Mayet-de-Montagne France 46°4N 3°40E 173 F10
Le Mêle-sur-Sarthe France 48°31N 0°22E 172 D7
Le Mesnil-le-Roi France 48°56N 2°7E 134 A1
Le Monastier-sur-Gazeille France 44°57N 3°59E 174 D7
Le Monêtier-les-Bains France 44°58N 6°30E 175 D10
Le Mont-Dore France 45°35N 2°49E 174 C6
Le Mont-St-Michel France 48°40N 1°30W 172 D5
Le Morne Brabant Mauritius 20°27S 57°19E 272 e
Le Morne Rouge Martinique 14°47N 61°8W 322 j
Le Morne-Vert Martinique 14°42N 61°8W 322 j
Le Moule Guadeloupe 16°20N 61°22W 322 e
Le Moyne, L. Canada 56°45N 68°47W 299 A6
Le Muy France 43°28N 6°34E 175 E10
Le Palais France 47°20N 3°10W 172 E3
Le Pecq France 48°53N 2°6E 134 A1
Le Perreux France 48°50N 2°29E 134 A3
Le Perthus France 42°30N 2°53E 174 F6
Le Pin France 48°54N 2°37E 134 A4
Le Plessis-Robinson France 48°47N 2°15E 134 B2
Le Plessis-Trévise France 48°48N 2°34E 134 B4
Le Port Réunion 20°56S 55°18E 272 f
Le Port-Marly France 48°52N 2°6E 134 A1
Le Pré-St-Gervais France 48°53N 2°23E 134 A3
Le Prêcheur Martinique 14°50N 61°12W 322 j
Le Puy-en-Velay France 45°3N 3°52E 174 C7
Le Raincy France 48°53N 2°31E 134 A4
Le Raysville U.S.A. 41°50N 76°10W 313 E8
Le Robert Martinique 14°40N 60°56W 322 j
Le Roy Ill., U.S.A. 40°21N 88°46W 311 D8
Le Roy N.Y., U.S.A. 42°58N 77°59W 312 D7
Le St-Esprit Martinique 14°34N 60°56W 322 j
Le Souffleur Guadeloupe 16°19N 61°2W 322 e
Le Sueur U.S.A. 44°28N 93°55W 308 C7
Le Tampon Réunion 21°16S 55°32E 272 f
Le Teil France 44°33N 4°40E 175 D8
Le Teilleul France 48°32N 0°53W 172 D6
Le Theil France 48°16N 0°42E 172 D7
Le Thillot France 47°53N 6°46E 173 E13
Le Thuy Vietnam 17°14N 106°49E 236 D6
Le Touquet-Paris-Plage France 50°30N 1°36E 173 B8
Le Tréport France 50°3N 1°20E 172 B8
Le Trou à Diable Guadeloupe 15°57N 61°14W 322 e
Le Val-André France 48°35N 2°32W 172 D4
Le Val-d'Ajol France 47°55N 6°30E 173 E13
Le Val Nature Park Mauritius 20°22S 57°37E 272 e
Le Vauclin Martinique 14°33N 60°52W 322 j
Le Verdon-sur-Mer France 45°33N 1°4W 174 C2
Le Vésinet France 48°54N 2°8E 134 A1
Le Vigan France 43°59N 3°36E 174 E7
Le Vignoble, Isola Venice, Italy 142 a4
Lea → U.K. 51°31N 0°1E 169 F8
Lea Bridge U.K. 51°33N 0°2W 125 A3
Lea Lea Papua N. G. 9°17S 146°59E 286 E4
Leach Cambodia 12°21N 103°46E 237 F4
Lead U.S.A. 44°21N 103°46W 308 C2
Leader Canada 50°50N 109°30W 297 C7
Leadville U.S.A. 39°15N 106°18W 304 G10
Leaf → U.S.A. 30°59N 88°44W 315 F10
Leaf Rapids Canada 56°30N 99°59W 297 B9
Leaghur, L. Australia 33°35S 143°3E 282 B5
League City U.S.A. 29°31N 95°6W 314 C7
Leaksville = Eden U.S.A. 36°29N 79°53W 315 C15
Lealui Zambia 15°10S 23°2E 265 F4
Leamington Ont., Canada 42°3N 82°36W 312 D2
Leamington N.Z. 37°55S 175°30E 284 D4
Leamington Utah, U.S.A. 39°32N 112°17W 304 G7
Leamington Spa = Royal Leamington Spa U.K. 52°18N 1°31W 169 E6
Le'an China 27°22N 115°48E 229 D10
Leander U.S.A. 30°34N 97°52W 314 F5
Leandro Norte Alem Argentina 27°34S 55°15W 335 B4
Leane, L. Ireland 52°2N 9°32W 166 D2
Learmonth Australia 22°13S 114°10E 278 D1
Leary U.S.A. 31°29N 84°31W 316 D5
Leaside Canada 43°42N 79°22W 141 A2
Leask Canada 53°5N 106°45W 297 C7
Leatherhead U.K. 51°18N 0°20W 169 F7
Leavdnja = Lakselv Norway 70°2N 25°0E 160 A21
Leavenworth Ind., U.S.A. 38°12N 86°21W 311 F10
Leavenworth Kans., U.S.A. 39°19N 94°55W 308 F6
Leavenworth Wash., U.S.A. 47°36N 120°40W 304 C3
Leawood U.S.A. 38°58N 94°37W 310 F2
Leba Poland 54°45N 17°32E 184 D4
Leba → Poland 54°46N 17°33E 184 D4
Lebach Germany 49°25N 6°54E 179 F2
Lebak Phil. 6°32N 124°5E 233 H5
Lebam U.S.A. 46°34N 123°33W 306 D3
Lebane Serbia 42°56N 21°44E 202 D5
Lebango Congo 0°39N 14°21E 264 B2
Lebango → Congo 0°2N 14°52E 264 B2
Lebanon Fla., U.S.A. 29°10N 82°37W 317 F7
Lebanon Ill., U.S.A. 38°38N 89°49W 310 F7
Lebanon Ind., U.S.A. 40°3N 86°28W 311 D10
Lebanon Kans., U.S.A. 39°49N 98°33W 308 F4
Lebanon Ky., U.S.A. 37°34N 85°15W 309 G11
Lebanon Mo., U.S.A. 37°41N 92°40W 310 G4
Lebanon N.H., U.S.A. 43°39N 72°15W 313 C12
Lebanon Ohio, U.S.A. 39°26N 84°13W 311 E12
Lebanon Oreg., U.S.A. 44°32N 122°55W 304 D2
Lebanon Pa., U.S.A. 40°20N 76°26W 313 F8
Lebanon Tenn., U.S.A. 36°12N 86°18W 315 C11
Lebanon ■ Asia 34°0N 36°0E 250 E7
Lebanon Junction U.S.A. 37°50N 85°44W 311 G11
Lebap □ Turkmenistan 40°0N 63°0E 216 D6
Lebec U.S.A. 34°51N 118°52W 307 L8
Lebedyan Russia 53°0N 39°10E 189 F10
Lebedyn Ukraine 50°35N 34°30E 189 G8
Lebel-sur-Quévillon Canada 49°3N 76°59W 298 C4
Leblon Brazil 22°59S 43°14W 135 B1
Lebo Dem. Rep. of the Congo 4°30N 23°58E 264 B4
Lebomboberge S. Africa 24°30S 32°0E 271 B5
Lębork Poland 54°33N 17°46E 184 D4
Lebowakgomo S. Africa 24°12S 29°30E 271 B4
Lebrija Spain 36°53N 6°5W 195 J4
Łebsko, Jezioro Poland 54°40N 17°25E 184 D4
Lebu Chile 37°40S 73°47W 334 D1
Leça da Palmeira Portugal 41°12N 8°42W 194 D2
Lecce Italy 40°23N 18°11E 201 B11
Lecco Italy 45°51N 9°23E 198 C6
Lecco, L. di Italy 45°51N 9°19E 198 C6
Lécera Spain 41°13N 0°43W 196 D4
Lech Austria 47°13N 10°9E 180 D3
Lech → Germany 48°43N 10°56E 179 G6
Lechang China 25°10N 113°20E 229 E9
Lechena Greece 37°57N 21°16E 204 D3
Lechtaler Alpen Austria 47°15N 10°30E 180 D3
Lecontes Mills U.S.A. 41°5N 78°17W 312 E6
Lectoure France 43°56N 0°38E 174 E4
Łęczna Poland 51°18N 22°53E 185 G9
Łęczyca Poland 52°5N 19°15E 185 F6
Ledang, Gunung Malaysia 2°22N 102°37E 237 L4
Ledesma Spain 41°6N 5°59W 194 D5
Lediba Dem. Rep. of the Congo 3°15S 16°34E 264 C3
Lednice Czech Rep. 48°46N 16°46E 181 C9
Ledo India 27°18N 95°44E 241 B5
Lédo, Cabo Angola 9°43S 13°12E 265 D2
Ledong China 18°41N 109°5E 229 a
Leduc Canada 53°15N 113°30W 296 C6
Lee London, U.K. 51°27N 0°0 125 B4
Lee Fla., U.S.A. 30°25N 83°18W 316 E6
Lee Mass., U.S.A. 42°19N 73°15W 313 D11
Lee → Ireland 51°53N 8°56W 166 E3
Lee Vining U.S.A. 37°58N 119°7W 306 H7
Leech L. U.S.A. 47°10N 94°24W 308 B6
Leechburg U.S.A. 40°37N 79°36W 312 F5
Leeds U.K. 53°48N 1°33W 168 D6
Leeds Ala., U.S.A. 33°33N 86°33W 315 E11
Leek Neths. 53°10N 6°24E 170 A6
Leek Staffs., U.K. 53°7N 2°1W 168 D5
Leeman Australia 29°57S 114°58E 279 E1
Leeper U.S.A. 41°22N 79°18W 312 E5
Leer Germany 53°13N 7°26E 178 B3
Lee's Summit U.S.A. 38°55N 94°23W 310 F2
Leesburg Fla., U.S.A. 28°49N 81°53W 317 G8
Leesburg Ga., U.S.A. 31°44N 84°10W 316 D5
Leesburg Ohio, U.S.A. 39°21N 83°33W 311 E13
Leeston N.Z. 43°45S 172°19E 285 D7
Leesville U.S.A. 31°8N 93°16W 314 F8
Leeton Australia 34°33S 146°23E 283 C7
Leetonia U.S.A. 40°53N 80°45W 312 F4
Leeu Gamka S. Africa 32°47S 21°59E 270 D3
Leeuwarden Neths. 53°15N 5°48E 170 A5
Leeuwin, C. Australia 34°20S 115°9E 279 F2
Leeuwin Naturaliste △ Australia 34°6S 115°3E 279 F2
Leeward Is. Atl. Oc. 16°30N 63°30W 321 C7
Léfini Congo 2°55S 15°39E 264 C3
Léfini → Congo 2°56S 16°9E 264 C3
Léfini ⌂ Congo 2°55S 15°20E 264 C3
Lefka Cyprus 35°6N 32°51E 207 E8
Lefkada Greece 38°40N 20°43E 207 B2
Lefkimi Greece 39°25N 20°3E 206 C10
Lefkimis, Akra Greece 39°29N 20°4E 206 C10
Lefkoniko Cyprus 35°18N 33°44E 207 E9
Lefkosia = Nicosia Cyprus 35°10N 33°25E 207 E9
Lefroy Canada 44°16N 79°34W 312 B5
Lefroy, L. Australia 31°21S 121°40E 279 F3
Łeg → Poland 50°42N 21°50E 185 H8
Leganés Spain 40°19N 3°45W 127 C1
Legazpi Phil. 13°10N 123°45E 232 E4
Legazpi Madrid, Spain 40°23N 3°41W 127 B1
Lège-Cap-Ferret France 44°48N 1°9W 174 D2
Lege Hida Ethiopia 7°56N 41°4E 257 F5
Legendre I. Australia 20°22S 116°55E 278 D2
Leghorn = Livorno Italy 43°33N 10°19E 198 F7
Legian Indonesia 8°42S 115°10E 231 K18
Legionowo Poland 52°25N 20°50E 185 F7
Legnago Italy 45°11N 11°18E 199 C8
Legnano Italy 45°36N 8°54E 198 C5
Legnica Poland 51°12N 16°10E 185 G3
Legrad Croatia 46°17N 16°51E 199 B13
Leh India 34°9N 77°35E 243 B7
Lehigh Acres U.S.A. 26°36N 81°39W 317 J8
Lehighton U.S.A. 40°50N 75°43W 313 F9
Lehliu Romania 44°29N 26°50E 183 F11
Leho South Sudan 7°7N 33°52E 257 F3
Lehrte Germany 52°22N 9°58E 178 C5
Lehtisaari Finland 60°10N 24°51E 121 B2
Lehua I. U.S.A. 22°1N 160°6W 302 A1
Lehututu Botswana 23°54S 21°55E 270 B3
Lei Shui → China 26°55N 112°35E 229 D9
Lei Yue Mun Hong Kong, China 22°17N 114°14E 122 B3
Leiah Pakistan 30°58N 70°58E 242 D4
Leião Portugal 38°43N 9°17W 126 A1
Leibnitz Austria 46°47N 15°34E 180 E8
Leibo China 28°11N 103°34E 228 C4
Leicester U.K. 52°38N 1°8W 169 E6
Leicester City □ U.K. 52°38N 1°8W 169 E6
Leicester Square London, U.K. 125 b3
Leicestershire □ U.K. 52°41N 1°17W 169 E6
Leichhardt Australia 33°53S 151°9E 139 B1
Leichhardt → Australia 17°35S 139°48E 280 B2
Leichhardt Ra. Australia 20°46S 147°40E 280 C4
Leiden Neths. 52°9N 4°30E 170 B4
Leie → Belgium 51°2N 3°45E 170 C3
Leifers = Láives Italy 46°26N 11°20E 199 B8
Leigh → Australia 38°18S 144°30E 282 E6
Leigh Creek Australia 30°38S 138°26E 282 A3
Leikang Norway 62°15N 5°47E 164 B2
Leikanger Sogn og Fjordane, Norway 62°8N 5°18E 164 B2
Leikanger Sogn og Fjordane, Norway 61°10N 6°51E 164 C3
Leiktho Burma 19°13N 96°35E 241 F6
Leimen Germany 49°21N 8°41E 179 F4
Leimus Nic. 14°40N 84°3W 320 D3
Leine → Germany 52°43N 9°36E 178 C5
Leinefelde Germany 51°23N 10°19E 178 D6
Leinster Australia 27°51S 120°36E 279 E3
Leinster □ Ireland 53°3N 7°8W 166 C4
Leinster, Mt. Ireland 52°37N 6°46W 166 D5
Leipalingis Lithuania 54°5N 23°51E 184 D10
Leipe = Lipno Poland 52°49N 19°15E 185 F6
Leipzig Germany 51°18N 12°22E 178 D8
Leira Norway 60°58N 9°17E 164 D6
Leiria Portugal 39°46N 8°53W 194 F2
Leiria □ Portugal 39°46N 8°53W 194 F2
Leirvassbu Norway 61°33N 8°13E 164 C5
Leirvik Norway 59°47N 5°28E 164 E2
Leishan China 26°15N 108°20E 228 D7
Leisler, Mt. Australia 23°23S 129°20E 278 D4
Leisure City U.S.A. 25°30N 80°27W 317 K9
Leith U.K. 55°59N 3°11W 167 F5
Leith Hill U.K. 51°11N 0°22W 169 F7
Leitha → Europe 47°50N 17°15E 181 D10
Leitir Ceanainn = Letterkenny Ireland 54°57N 7°45W 166 B4
Leitrim Ireland 54°0N 8°5W 166 B3
Leitrim □ Ireland 54°8N 8°0W 166 B4
Leitza Spain 43°5N 1°55W 196 B3
Leixlip Ireland 53°22N 6°30W 166 C5
Leiyang China 26°27N 112°45E 229 D9
Leizhou China 20°52N 110°8E 229 G8
Leizhou Bandao China 21°0N 110°0E 228 G7
Leizhou Wan China 20°50N 110°20E 229 G8
Lek → Neths. 51°54N 4°35E 170 C4
Leka Norway 65°5N 11°35E 160 D14
Lekani Greece 41°10N 24°35E 203 E8
Lekbibaj Albania 42°17N 19°56E 202 D3
Lekeitio Spain 43°20N 2°32W 196 B2
Lékéti, Mt. Congo 2°34S 14°17E 264 C2
Lekki Nigeria 6°26N 3°28E 124 B2
Lekki Lagoon Nigeria 6°30N 4°7E 263 D5
Lekki Peninsula Nigeria 6°26N 3°29E 124 B2
Léko Mali 13°37N 9°2W 262 C3
Lékoli-Pandaka ⌂ Congo 0°41N 14°50E 264 B2
Lékoni Gabon 1°35S 14°14E 264 C2
Lékoni → Gabon 1°11S 13°16E 264 C2
Lekoui Burkina Faso 12°37N 3°40W 262 C4
Lékoumou □ Congo 2°0S 13°0E 264 C2
Leksand Sweden 60°44N 15°1E 162 D9
Leksura = Lentekhi Georgia 42°47N 42°45E 191 J6
Leland Mich., U.S.A. 45°1N 85°45W 309 C11
Leland Miss., U.S.A. 33°24N 90°54W 315 E9
Lelång Sweden 59°10N 12°5E 162 E6
Lelepa Vanuatu 17°35S 168°13E 287 G6
Leleque Argentina 42°28S 71°0W 336 B2
Leli Solomon Is. 8°42S 161°4E 287 M11
Leling China 37°44N 117°13E 227 F9
Lélouma Guinea 11°11N 12°56W 262 C2

**Lelu** *Burma* 19°4N 95°30E **241** F5
**Lelydorp** *Suriname* 5°42N 55°14W **329** B6
**Lelystad** *Neths.* 52°30N 5°25E **170** B5
**Lem** *Denmark* 56°1N 8°24E **163** H2
**Lema** *Nigeria* 12°58N 4°13E **263** C5
**Lema Shilindi** *Ethiopia* 4°50N 42°6E **257** G5
**Léman, L.** *Europe* 46°26N 6°30E **173** F13
**Lemankoa** *Papua N. G.* 5°3S 154°34E **286** C8
**Lembar** *Indonesia* 8°45S 116°4E **231** K19
**Lemberg = Lviv** *Ukraine* 49°50N 24°0E **177** D13
**Lembongan, Nusa** *Indonesia* 8°40S 115°27E **231** K18
**Lembuak** *Indonesia* 8°36S 116°11E **231** K19
**Leme** *Brazil* 22°58S 43°10W **135** B1
**Lemera** *Dem. Rep. of the Congo* 3°0S 28°55E **268** C2
**Lemery** *Phil.* 13°51N 120°56E **232** E3
**Lemesós = Limassol** *Cyprus* 34°42N 33°1E **207** F9
**Lemfu** *Dem. Rep. of the Congo* 5°18S 15°13E **265** D3
**Lemhi Ra.** *U.S.A.* 44°0N 113°0W **304** D7
**Lemmenjoki** △ *Finland* 68°40N 25°30E **160** B21
**Lemmer** *Neths.* 52°51N 5°43E **170** B5
**Lemmon** *U.S.A.* 45°57N 102°10W **308** C2
**Lemon Grove** *U.S.A.* 32°44N 117°1W **307** N9
**Lemoore** *U.S.A.* 36°18N 119°46W **306** J7
**Lemotol B.** *Micronesia* 7°21N 151°35E **287** T17
**Lemoyne** *Canada* 45°29N 73°29W **130** B3
**Lempdes-sur-Allagnon** *France* 45°22N 3°17E **174** C7
**Lemsid** *W. Sahara* 26°33N 13°51W **260** C2
**Lemukutan** *Indonesia* 0°45N 108°43E **235** B3
**Lemvig** *Denmark* 56°33N 8°20E **163** H2
**Lemyethna** *Burma* 17°36N 95°9E **241** G5
**Lena** *U.S.A.* 42°23N 89°49W **310** B7
**Lena** → *Russia* 72°52N 126°40E **215** B13
**Lena Pillars = Lenskiy Stolby** *Russia* 60°55N 126°0E **215** C13
**Lenadoon Pt.** *Ireland* 54°18N 9°3W **166** B2
**Lenakel** *Vanuatu* 19°38S 169°16E **287** J7
**Lenart** *Slovenia* 46°36N 15°48E **199** B12
**Lenartovce** *Slovak Rep.* 48°18N 20°19E **181** C13
**Lencloître** *France* 46°50N 0°20E **172** F7
**Lençóis** *Brazil* 12°35S 41°24W **333** D3
**Lençóis Maranhenses** △ *Brazil* 2°30S 43°0W **332** B3
**Lendava** *Slovenia* 46°35N 16°25E **199** B13
**Lendinara** *Italy* 45°5N 11°36E **199** C8
**Lenger** *Kazakhstan* 42°12N 69°54E **217** D7
**Lengerich** *Germany* 52°11N 7°52E **178** C3
**Lenggong** *Malaysia* 5°6N 100°58E **237** K3
**Lenggries** *Germany* 47°41N 11°35E **179** H7
**Léngoué** *Congo* 1°15N 15°38E **264** B3
**Lengshuijiang** *China* 27°40N 111°26E **229** D8
**Lengshuitan** *China* 26°27N 111°35E **229** D8
**Lengua de Vaca, Pta.** *Chile* 30°14S 71°38W **334** C1
**Lengwe** △ *Malawi* 16°14S 34°45E **269** F3
**Lengwethen = Lunino** *Russia* 53°38N 45°18E **190** D7
**Lengyeltóti** *Hungary* 46°40N 17°40E **182** D2
**Lengyeltóthács = Lengyeltóti** *Hungary* 46°40N 17°40E **182** D2
**Lenhovda** *Sweden* 57°0N 15°16E **163** G9
**Lenin Mausoleum** *Moscow, Russia* **129** b2
**Lenina, Kanal** → *Russia* 43°44N 45°17E **191** J7
**Leninabad = Khŭjand** *Tajikistan* 40°17N 69°37E **217** D7
**Leninakan = Gyumri** *Armenia* 40°47N 43°50E **191** K6
**Lenine** *Ukraine* 45°17N 35°46E **189** K8
**Leningrad = Sankt-Peterburg** *Russia* 59°55N 30°20E **137** B1
**Leningrad** □ *Russia* 59°40N 32°0E **188** C7
**Lenino = Leninsk-Kuznetskiy** *Russia* 54°44N 86°10E **217** B11
**Lenino** *Russia* 55°38N 37°39E **129** C2
**Leninogorsk = Ridder** *Kazakhstan* 50°20N 83°30E **217** B10
**Leninogorsk** *Russia* 54°36N 52°30E **216** B4
**Leninsk = Petrodvorets** *Russia* 59°52N 29°54E **188** C5
**Leninsk** *Russia* 48°40N 45°15E **191** F7
**Leninsk-Kuznetskiy** *Russia* 54°44N 86°10E **217** B11
**Leninsk-Turkmensky = Türkmenabat** *Turkmenistan* 39°6N 63°34E **247** B9
**Leninskiye Gory** *Russia* 55°41N 37°32E **129** B2
**Leninskoye** *Russia* 58°23N 47°3E **190** A8
**Lenk** *Switz.* 46°27N 7°28E **179** J3
**Lenkoran = Länkäran** *Azerbaijan* 38°48N 48°52E **213** C13
**Lenmalu** *Indonesia* 1°45S 130°15E **231** E8
**Lennartsfors** *Sweden* 59°20N 11°55E **162** E5
**Lenne** → *Germany* 51°25N 7°29E **178** D3
**Lennestadt** *Germany* 51°8N 8°2E **178** D4
**Lennox** *Calif., U.S.A.* 33°56N 118°20W **126** C2
**Lennox** *S. Dak., U.S.A.* 43°21N 96°53W **308** D5
**Lennox, I.** *Chile* 55°18S 66°50W **336** E3
**Lennoxville** *Canada* 45°22N 71°51W **313** A13
**Leno** *Italy* 45°22N 10°13E **198** C7
**Lenoir** *U.S.A.* 35°55N 81°32W **315** D14
**Lenoir City** *U.S.A.* 35°48N 84°16W **315** D12
**Lenore L.** *Canada* 52°30N 104°59W **297** C8
**Lenox** *Ga., U.S.A.* 31°16N 83°28W **316** D6
**Lenox** *Iowa, U.S.A.* 40°53N 94°34W **310** D2
**Lenox** *Mass., U.S.A.* 42°22N 73°17W **313** D11
**Lens** *France* 50°26N 2°50E **173** B9
**Lensahn** *Germany* 54°13N 10°53E **178** A6
**Lensk** *Russia* 60°48N 114°55E **215** C12
**Lenskiy Stolby** *Russia* 60°55N 126°0E **215** C13
**Lensvik** *Norway* 63°31N 9°48E **164** A6
**Lentas** *Greece* 34°56N 24°56E **207** F5
**Lentekhi** *Georgia* 42°47N 42°45E **191** J6
**Lenti** *Hungary* 46°37N 16°33E **182** D1
**Lentini** *Italy* 37°17N 15°0E **201** E8
**Lentschütz = Łęczyca** *Poland* 52°5N 19°15E **185** F6
**Lenwood** *U.S.A.* 34°53N 117°7W **307** L9
**Lenya** *Burma* 11°33N 98°57E **237** G2
**Lenzen** *Germany* 53°5N 11°29E **178** B7
**Léo** *Burkina Faso* 11°3N 2°2W **262** C4
**Leoben** *Austria* 47°22N 15°5E **180** D8
**Leobschütz = Głubczyce** *Poland* 50°13N 17°52E **185** H4
**Leodhais = Lewis** *U.K.* 58°9N 6°40W **167** C2
**Leola** *U.S.A.* 45°43N 98°56W **308** C4
**Leominster** *Hereford, U.K.* 52°14N 2°43W **169** E5
**Leominster** *Mass., U.S.A.* 42°32N 71°46W **313** D13
**León = Cotopaxi** □ *Ecuador* 0°5S 78°55W **328** D2
**Léon** *Landes, France* 43°53N 1°18W **174** E2
**León** *Guanajuato, Mexico* 21°6N 101°41W **318** C4
**León** *Nic.* 12°27N 86°51W **320** D2
**León** *Spain* 42°38N 5°34W **194** C5
**Leon** *Iowa, U.S.A.* 40°44N 93°45W **310** D3
**León** □ *Spain* 42°40N 5°55W **194** C5
**Leon** → *U.S.A.* 31°14N 97°28W **314** F6
**León, Montes de** *Spain* 42°30N 6°18W **194** C4
**Leonardo da Vinci, Roma** ✕ **(FCO)** *Italy* 41°48N 12°15E **199** G9
**Leonardtown** *U.S.A.* 38°17N 76°38W **309** F15
**Leonardville** *Namibia* 23°29S 18°49E **270** B2
**Leonárisso** *Cyprus* 35°28N 34°8E **207** E10
**Leonberg** *Germany* 48°48N 9°1E **179** G5
**Leonding** *Austria* 48°16N 14°15E **180** C7
**Leone** *Amer. Samoa* 14°23S 170°48W **302** f
**Leonessa** *Italy* 42°34N 12°58E **199** F9
**Leonforte** *Italy* 37°38N 14°23E **201** E7
**Leongatha** *Australia* 38°30S 145°58E **283** E6
**Leonia** *Fla., U.S.A.* 30°55N 86°1W **316** E3
**Leonia** *N.J., U.S.A.* 40°51N 73°59W **132** A2
**Leonídio** *Greece* 37°9N 22°52E **204** D4
**Leonora** *Australia* 28°49S 121°19E **279** E3
**Leopardstown** *Ireland* 53°16N 6°11W **120** B2
**Leopold II, L. = Mai-Ndombe, L.** *Dem. Rep. of the Congo* 2°0S 18°20E **264** C3
**Leopoldau** *Austria* 48°15N 16°26E **142** A2
**Leopoldina = Aruanã** *Brazil* 14°54S 51°10W **333** D1
**Leopoldina = Parnamirim** *Brazil* 8°5S 39°34W **332** C4
**Leopoldina** *Brazil* 21°28S 42°40W **333** F3
**Leopoldo Bulhões** *Brazil* 16°37S 48°46W **333** E2
**Leopoldsburg** *Belgium* 51°7N 5°13E **170** C5
**Leopoldsdorf** *Austria* 48°7N 16°23E **142** B2
**Leopoldstadt** *Austria* 48°13N 16°22E **142** B2
**Leopoldville = Kinshasa** *Dem. Rep. of the Congo* 4°20S 15°15E **265** C3
**Leoti** *U.S.A.* 38°29N 101°21W **308** F3
**Leova** *Moldova* 46°28N 28°15E **183** D13
**Leoville** *Canada* 53°39N 107°33W **297** C7
**Lepar** *Indonesia* 2°57S 106°49E **234** C3
**Lepe** *Spain* 37°15N 7°12W **195** H3
**Lepel = Lyepyel** *Belarus* 54°50N 28°40E **188** E5
**Lepenou** *Greece* 38°42N 21°17E **204** C3
**Leping** *China* 28°47N 117°7E **229** C11
**Lépo, L. do** *Angola* 17°0S 19°0E **265** F3
**Lepontine, Alpi** *Italy* 46°22N 8°27E **198** B5
**Leportovo** *Russia* 55°46N 37°43E **129** B3
**Leposavić** *Kosovo* 43°6N 20°48E **202** C4
**Leppävaara** *Finland* 60°13N 24°49E **121** B1
**Leppävirta** *Finland* 62°29N 27°46E **160** E22
**Lepsény** *Hungary* 47°0N 18°15E **182** D3
**Leptis Magna** *Libya* 32°40N 14°12E **258** B2
**Lequeitio = Lekeitio** *Spain* 43°20N 2°32W **196** B2
**Lercara Friddi** *Italy* 37°45N 13°36E **200** E6
**Léré** *C.A.R.* 6°46N 17°25E **264** A3
**Léré** *Chad* 9°39N 14°13E **259** G2
**Léré** *Mali* 15°45N 4°55W **262** B4
**Lere** *Bauchi, Nigeria* 9°43N 9°18E **263** D6
**Lere** *Kaduna, Nigeria* 10°23N 8°35E **263** C6
**Leribe** *Lesotho* 28°51S 28°3E **271** D4
**Lérici** *Italy* 44°4N 9°55E **198** D6
**Lérida = Lleida** *Spain* 41°37N 0°39E **196** D5
**Lérins, Îs. de** *France* 43°31N 7°3E **175** E11
**Lerma** *Spain* 42°0N 3°47W **194** C7
**Leros** *Greece* 37°10N 26°50E **205** D8
**Lérouville** *France* 48°44N 5°30E **173** D12
**Lerum** *Sweden* 57°46N 12°16E **163** G6
**Lerwick** *U.K.* 60°9N 1°9W **167** A7
**Leş** *Romania* 46°58N 21°50E **182** D6
**Les Abrets** *France* 45°32N 5°35E **175** C9
**Les Abymes** *Guadeloupe* 16°17N 61°32W **322** e
**Les Andelys** *France* 49°15N 1°25E **172** C8
**Les Anses-d'Arlets** *Martinique* 14°28N 61°5W **322** j
**Les Avirons** *Réunion* 21°14S 55°20E **272** f
**Les Borges Blanques** *Spain* 41°31N 0°52E **196** D5
**Les Cayes** *Haiti* 18°15N 73°46W **321** C5
**Les Coteaux** *Canada* 45°15N 74°13W **313** A10
**Les Escoumins** *Canada* 48°21N 69°24W **299** C6
**Les Essarts** *France* 46°47N 1°12W **172** F5
**Les Grands Fonds** *Guadeloupe* 16°16N 61°26W **322** e
**Les Herbiers** *France* 46°52N 1°1W **172** F5
**Les Lilas** *France* 48°52N 2°25E **134** A3
**Les Loges-en-Josas** *France* 48°45N 2°8E **134** B1
**Les Mangles** *Guadeloupe* 16°23N 61°27W **322** e
**Les Minquiers, Plateau des** *Chan. Is.* 48°58N 2°8W **172** D4
**Les Moroubas** *C.A.R.* 6°11N 20°13E **264** A4
**Les Pavillons-sous-Bois** *France* 48°54N 2°30E **134** A4
**Les Pieux** *France* 49°30N 1°48W **172** C5
**Les Ponts-de-Cé** *France* 47°25N 0°30W **172** E6
**Les Riceys** *France* 47°59N 4°22E **173** E11
**Les Sables-d'Olonne** *France* 46°30N 1°45W **174** B2
**Les Tantes** *Grenada* 12°19N 61°33W **323** q
**Les Trois-Bassins** *Réunion* 21°5S 55°18E **272** f
**Les Trois-Îlets** *Martinique* 14°32N 61°2W **322** j
**Les Vans** *France* 44°25N 4°7E **175** D8
**Lesbos** *Greece* 39°10N 26°20E **205** B8
**L'Escala** *Spain* 42°7N 3°8E **196** C8
**L'Escalier** *Mauritius* 20°28S 57°36E **272** e
**Leschnitz = Leśnica** *Poland* 50°26N 18°11E **185** H5
**Leshan** *China* 29°33N 103°41E **228** C4
**Leshukonskoye** *Russia* 64°54N 45°46E **186** B8
**Leshwe** ⌓ *Dem. Rep. of the Congo* 12°45S 29°30E **269** E2
**Lésigny** *France* 48°44N 2°37E **134** B4
**Lésina** *Italy* 41°52N 15°21E **199** G12
**Lésina, L. di** *Italy* 41°53N 15°26E **199** G12
**Lesjaskog** *Norway* 62°14N 8°22E **164** B5
**Lesjaverk** *Norway* 62°12N 8°34E **164** B5
**Lesjöfors** *Sweden* 59°58N 14°11E **162** E8
**Leskhimstroy = Syeverodonetsk** *Ukraine* 48°58N 38°35E **189** H10
**Lesko** *Poland* 49°30N 22°23E **185** J9
**Leskov I.** *Antarctica* 56°0S 28°0W **151** B1
**Leskovac** *Serbia* 43°0N 21°58E **202** C5
**Leskovik** *Albania* 40°10N 20°34E **202** F4
**Leslau = Włocławek** *Poland* 52°40N 19°3E **185** F6
**Leslie** *Ga., U.S.A.* 31°57N 84°5W **316** D5
**Leslie** *Mich., U.S.A.* 42°27N 84°26W **311** B12
**Leśna** *Poland* 51°1N 15°15E **185** G2
**Lesneven** *France* 48°35N 4°20W **172** D2
**Leśnica** *Poland* 50°26N 18°11E **185** H5
**Lešnica** *Serbia* 44°39N 19°20E **202** B3
**Lesnoi = Umba** *Russia* 66°42N 34°11E **186** A5
**Lesnoye** *Russia* 58°15N 35°18E **188** C8
**Lesnozavodskaya** *Russia* 59°51N 30°29E **137** B2
**Lesopilnoye** *Russia* 46°44N 134°20E **220** A7
**Lesotho** ■ *Africa* 29°40S 28°0E **271** C4
**Lesozavodsk** *Russia* 45°30N 133°29E **220** B6
**Lesparre-Médoc** *France* 45°18N 0°57W **174** C3
**L'Espluga de Francolí** *Spain* 41°24N 1°7E **196** D6
**Lessay** *France* 49°14N 1°30W **172** C5
**Lesse** → *Belgium* 50°15N 4°54E **170** D4
**Lesse et Lomme** ⌓ *Belgium* 50°8N 5°9E **170** D5
**Lessebo** *Sweden* 56°45N 15°16E **163** H9
**Lesser Antilles** *W. Indies* 15°0N 61°0W **321** D7
**Lesser Slave L.** *Canada* 55°30N 115°25W **296** B5
**Lesser Sunda Is.** *Indonesia* 8°0S 120°0E **235** D5
**Lessines** *Belgium* 50°42N 3°50E **170** D3
**Lester B. Pearson Int., Toronto** ✕ **(YYZ)** *Canada* 43°46N 79°35W **141** A1
**L'Esterre** *Grenada* 12°28N 61°29W **323** q
**Lestershire = Johnson City** *U.S.A.* 42°7N 75°58W **313** D9
**Lestock** *Canada* 51°19N 103°59W **297** C8
**Lesueur I.** *Australia* 13°50S 127°17E **278** B4
**Lesueur** △ *Australia* 30°11S 115°10E **279** F2
**Lesung** *Indonesia* 0°42N 114°42E **235** B4
**Lésvos = Lesbos** *Greece* 39°10N 26°20E **205** B8
**Leszno** *Poland* 51°50N 16°30E **185** G3
**Letaba** *S. Africa* 23°59S 31°50E **271** B5
**Letälven** → *Sweden* 59°5N 14°20E **162** E8
**L'Étang-la-Ville** *France* 48°52N 2°4E **134** A1
**L'Étang-Salé** *Réunion* 21°15S 55°23E **272** f
**Létavértes** *Hungary* 47°23N 21°55E **182** C6
**Letchworth** *U.K.* 51°59N 0°13W **169** F7
**Letea, Ostrov** *Romania* 45°18N 29°20E **183** E14
**Lethbridge** *Canada* 49°45N 112°45W **296** D6
**Lethem** *Guyana* 3°20N 59°50W **329** C6
**Leti, Kepulauan** *Indonesia* 8°10S 128°0E **231** F7
**Leti Is. = Leti, Kepulauan** *Indonesia* 8°10S 128°0E **231** F7
**Letiahau** → *Botswana* 21°16S 24°0E **270** B3
**Leticia** *Colombia* 4°9S 70°0W **328** D4
**Leting** *China* 39°23N 118°55E **227** E10
**Letjiesbos** *S. Africa* 32°34S 22°16E **270** D3
**Letlhakane** *Botswana* 21°27S 25°30E **270** B4
**Letlhakeng** *Botswana* 24°0S 24°59E **270** B3
**Letná** *Prague, Czech Rep.* **135** a2
**Letňany** *Czech Rep.* 50°8N 14°30E **135** B3
**Letopolis = Ausîm** *Egypt* 30°7N 31°8E **117** A1
**Letpadan** *Burma* 17°45N 95°45E **241** G5
**Letpan** *Burma* 19°28N 94°10E **241** F5
**Letsôk-aw Kyun** *Burma* 11°30N 98°25E **237** G2
**Letterkenny** *Ireland* 54°57N 7°45W **166** B4
**Leu** *Romania* 44°10N 24°0E **183** F9
**Léua** *Angola* 11°34S 20°32E **265** E4
**Leucadia** *U.S.A.* 33°4N 117°18W **307** M9
**Leucate** *France* 42°56N 3°3E **174** F7
**Leucate, Étang de** *France* 42°50N 3°0E **174** F7
**Leuchars** *U.K.* 56°24N 2°53W **167** E6
**Leuk** *Switz.* 46°19N 7°37E **179** J3
**Leuşeni** *Moldova* 46°49N 28°12E **183** D13
**Leuser, Gunung** *Indonesia* 3°46N 97°12E **234** B1
**Leusoalii** *Amer. Samoa* 14°14S 169°25W **302** f
**Leutkirch** *Germany* 47°49N 10°1E **179** H6
**Leutschau = Levoča** *Slovak Rep.* 49°2N 20°35E **181** B13
**Leuven** *Belgium* 50°52N 4°42E **170** D4
**Leuze-en-Hainaut** *Belgium* 50°36N 3°37E **170** D3
**Lev Tolstoy** *Russia* 53°13N 39°29E **188** F10
**Levallois-Perret** *France* 48°53N 2°16E **134** A2
**Levan** *Albania* 40°40N 19°28E **202** F3
**Levanger** *Norway* 63°45N 11°19E **160** E14
**Levant, Î. du** *France* 43°3N 6°28E **175** E10
**Lévanto** *Italy* 44°10N 9°38E **198** D6
**Lévanzo** *Italy* 38°0N 12°20E **200** D5
**Leveld** *Norway* 60°44N 8°33E **164** D5
**Levelland** *U.S.A.* 33°35N 102°23W **314** E3
**Levelock** *U.S.A.* 59°7N 156°51W **303** G8
**Leven** *U.K.* 56°12N 3°0W **167** E6
**Leven, L.** *U.K.* 56°12N 3°22W **167** E5
**Leven, Toraka** *Madag.* 12°30S 47°45E **272** A2
**Levent** *Turkey* 41°5N 29°0E **122** B2
**Leveque C.** *Australia* 16°20S 123°0E **278** C3
**Levera** △ *Grenada* 12°13N 61°38W **323** q
**Leverano** *Italy* 40°17N 18°0E **201** B10
**Leverger = Santo Antônio do Leverger** *Brazil* 15°52S 56°5W **331** D6
**Leverkusen** *Germany* 51°1N 7°1E **178** D3
**Levice** *Slovak Rep.* 48°13N 18°35E **181** C11
**Lévico Terme** *Italy* 46°0N 11°18E **199** C8
**Levie** *France* 41°40N 9°7E **175** G13
**Levier** *France* 46°58N 6°8E **173** F13
**Levin** *N.Z.* 40°37S 175°18E **284** G4
**Lévis** *Canada* 46°48N 71°9W **299** C5
**Levis, L.** *Canada* 62°37N 117°58W **296** A5
**Levitha** *Greece* 37°0N 26°28E **205** D8
**Levittown** *N.Y., U.S.A.* 40°44N 73°31W **313** F11
**Levittown** *Pa., U.S.A.* 40°9N 74°51W **313** F10
**Levka** *Bulgaria* 41°52N 26°15E **203** E10
**Levka Oros** *Greece* 35°18N 24°3E **207** E5
**Levkás = Lefkada** *Greece* 38°40N 20°43E **207** B2
**Levoča** *Slovak Rep.* 49°2N 20°35E **181** B13
**Levroux** *France* 46°59N 1°38E **173** F8
**Levski** *Bulgaria* 43°21N 25°10E **203** C9
**Levskigrad = Karlovo** *Bulgaria* 42°38N 24°47E **203** D8
**Levuka** *Fiji* 17°34S 179°0E **287** A2
**Lewe** *Burma* 19°38N 96°7E **241** F6
**Lewes** *E. Sussex, U.K.* 50°52N 0°1E **169** G8
**Lewes** *Del., U.S.A.* 38°46N 75°9W **309** F16
**Lewin Brzeski** *Poland* 50°45N 17°37E **185** H4
**Lewis** *U.K.* 58°9N 6°40W **167** C2
**Lewis** → *U.S.A.* 45°51N 122°48W **306** E4
**Lewis, Butt of** *U.K.* 58°31N 6°16W **167** C2
**Lewis and Clark** ⌓ *U.S.A.* 46°8N 123°53W **306** D3
**Lewis Pass** *N.Z.* 42°31S 172°11E **285** C7
**Lewis Ra.** *Australia* 20°3S 128°50E **278** D4
**Lewis Range** *U.S.A.* 48°5N 113°5W **304** B7
**Lewis Run** *U.S.A.* 41°52N 78°40W **312** E6
**Lewisburg** *Ohio, U.S.A.* 39°51N 84°33W **311** E12
**Lewisburg** *Pa., U.S.A.* 40°58N 76°54W **312** F8
**Lewisburg** *Tenn., U.S.A.* 35°27N 86°48W **315** D11
**Lewisburg** *W. Va., U.S.A.* 37°48N 80°27W **309** G13
**Lewisdale** *U.S.A.* 38°58N 76°59W **143** B3
**Lewisham** □ *U.K.* 51°27N 0°1W **125** B3
**Lewisporte** *Canada* 49°15N 55°3W **299** C8
**Lewiston** *Idaho, U.S.A.* 46°25N 117°1W **304** C5
**Lewiston** *Maine, U.S.A.* 44°6N 70°13W **309** C18
**Lewiston** *N.Y., U.S.A.* 43°11N 79°3W **312** C5
**Lewistown** *Ill., U.S.A.* 40°24N 90°9W **310** D6
**Lewistown** *Mo., U.S.A.* 40°5N 91°49W **310** D5
**Lewistown** *Mont., U.S.A.* 47°4N 109°26W **304** C9
**Lewistown** *Pa., U.S.A.* 40°36N 77°34W **312** F7
**Lexington** *Ga., U.S.A.* 33°52N 83°7W **316** B6
**Lexington** *Ill., U.S.A.* 40°39N 88°47W **311** D8
**Lexington** *Ky., U.S.A.* 38°3N 84°30W **311** F12
**Lexington** *Mass., U.S.A.* 42°25N 71°12W **116** A1
**Lexington** *Mich., U.S.A.* 43°16N 82°32W **312** C2
**Lexington** *Mo., U.S.A.* 39°11N 93°52W **310** E3
**Lexington** *N.C., U.S.A.* 35°49N 80°15W **315** D14
**Lexington** *N.Y., U.S.A.* 42°15N 74°22W **313** D10
**Lexington** *Nebr., U.S.A.* 40°47N 99°45W **308** E4
**Lexington** *Ohio, U.S.A.* 40°41N 82°35W **312** F2
**Lexington** *S.C., U.S.A.* 33°59N 81°11W **316** B8
**Lexington** *Tenn., U.S.A.* 35°39N 88°24W **315** D10
**Lexington** *Va., U.S.A.* 37°47N 79°27W **309** G14
**Lexington Park** *U.S.A.* 38°16N 76°27W **309** F15
**Leyburn** *U.K.* 54°19N 1°48W **168** C6
**Leye** *China* 24°48N 106°29E **228** E6
**Leyeh** *Taiwan* 23°28N 120°42E **225** C2
**Leyland** *U.K.* 53°42N 2°43W **168** D5
**Leyte** *Phil.* 10°30N 125°0E **233** F5
**Leyte** □ *Phil.* 11°0N 125°0E **233** F5
**Leyte Gulf** *Phil.* 10°50N 125°25E **233** F5
**Leyton** *U.K.* 51°33N 0°1W **125** A3
**Leytonstone** *U.K.* 51°34N 0°0 **125** A4
**Leżajsk** *Poland* 50°16N 22°25E **185** H9
**Lezay** *France* 46°15N 0°1W **174** B3
**Lezhë** *Albania* 41°47N 19°39E **202** E3
**Lezhi** *China* 30°19N 104°58E **228** B5
**Lézignan-Corbières** *France* 43°13N 2°43E **174** E6
**Lezoux** *France* 45°49N 3°21E **174** C7
**Lgov** *Russia* 51°42N 35°16E **189** G8
**Lhasa** *China* 29°25N 90°58E **218** F7
**L'Haÿ-les-Roses** *France* 48°46N 2°20E **134** B3
**Lhazê** *China* 29°5N 87°38E **218** F6
**L'Hermite, I.** *Chile* 55°50S 68°0W **336** E3
**Lhokkruet** *Indonesia* 4°55N 95°24E **234** B1
**Lhokseumawe** *Indonesia* 5°10N 97°10E **234** A1
**Lhoksukon** *Indonesia* 5°2N 97°19E **234** A1
**L'Hospitalet de Llobregat** *Spain* 41°21N 2°6E **114** A1
**Lhotka** *Czech Rep.* 50°1N 14°26E **135** B2
**Lhuntsi Dzong** *Bhutan* 27°39N 91°10E **241** B3
**Lhut, W.** → *Somalia* 10°17N 50°9E **267** B7
**Li** *Thailand* 17°48N 98°57E **236** D2
**Li Jiang** → *China* 24°40N 110°40E **229** E8
**Li Jiang** △ *China* 24°38N 110°38E **229** E8
**Li Shan** *China* 35°30N 111°56E **226** G6
**Li Shui** → *China* 29°24N 112°1E **229** C9
**Li Xian** *Gansu, China* 34°10N 105°5E **226** G3
**Li Xian** *Hebei, China* 38°30N 115°35E **226** E8
**Li Xian** *Hunan, China* 29°36N 111°42E **229** C8
**Li Yuba** *South Sudan* 5°23N 27°25E **266** C2
**Lia-Moya** *C.A.R.* 6°54N 16°17E **264** A3
**Liadi** *Greece* 36°50N 26°11E **205** E8
**Liamuiga, Mt.** *St. Kitts & Nevis* 17°22N 62°48W **322** d
**Lian** *Phil.* 14°3N 120°39E **232** D3
**Liancheng** *China* 25°42N 116°40E **229** E11
**Liancourt Rocks** *Asia* 37°15N 131°52E **221** F5
**Liang Tao** *Taiwan* 26°23N 128°28E **225** b
**Lianga** *Phil.* 8°38N 126°6E **233** G6
**Lianga B.** *Phil.* 8°37N 126°12E **233** G6
**Liangcheng** *Nei Monggol Zizhiqu, China* 40°28N 112°25E **226** D7
**Liangcheng** *Shandong, China* 35°32N 119°37E **227** G10
**Liangdang** *China* 33°56N 106°18E **226** H4
**Lianghe** *China* 24°50N 98°20E **228** E2
**Lianghekou** *China* 29°11N 108°44E **228** C7
**Liangping** *China* 30°38N 107°47E **228** B6
**Liangpran** *Indonesia* 1°4N 114°23E **235** B4
**Liangshui He** → *China* 39°48N 116°23E **114** C2
**Lianhua** *China* 27°3N 113°54E **229** D9
**Lianhua Chi** *China* 39°52N 116°16E **114** B1
**Lianhua He** → *China* 39°52N 116°13E **114** B1
**Lianhua Shan** *China* 23°40N 115°48E **229** F10
**Lianjiang** *Fujian, China* 26°12N 119°27E **229** D12
**Lianjiang** *Guangdong, China* 21°40N 110°20E **229** G8
**Lianping** *China* 24°26N 114°30E **229** E10
**Lianshan** *China* 24°38N 112°8E **229** E9
**Lianshanguan** *China* 40°53N 123°43E **224** B1
**Lianshui** *China* 33°42N 119°20E **227** H10
**Lianyuan** *China* 27°40N 111°38E **229** D8
**Lianyungang** *China* 34°40N 119°11E **227** G10
**Lianzhou** *China* 24°51N 112°22E **229** E9
**Liao He** → *China* 41°0N 121°50E **227** D11
**Liaocheng** *China* 36°28N 115°58E **226** F8
**Liaodong Bandao** *China* 40°0N 122°30E **227** E12
**Liaodong Wan** *China* 40°20N 121°10E **227** D11
**Liaoning** □ *China* 41°40N 122°30E **224** B1
**Liaotung, G. of = Liaodong Wan** *China* 40°20N 121°10E **227** D11
**Liaoyang** *China* 41°15N 122°58E **224** B1
**Liaoyuan** *China* 42°58N 125°2E **227** C13
**Liaozhong** *China* 41°23N 122°50E **224** B1
**Liapades** *Greece* 39°42N 19°40E **206** B9
**Liard** → *Canada* 61°51N 121°18W **296** A4
**Liard River** *Canada* 59°25N 126°5W **296** B3
**Liari** *Pakistan* 25°37N 66°30E **242** G2
**Liat** *Indonesia* 2°53S 107°5E **234** C3
**Libanggaon** *Nepal* 28°18N 82°38E **243** E10
**Líbano** *Colombia* 4°55N 75°4W **328** C2
**Libau = Liepāja** *Latvia* 56°30N 21°0E **184** B8
**Libby** *U.S.A.* 48°23N 115°33W **304** B6
**Libčice nad Vitavou** *Czech Rep.* 50°11N 14°22E **135** A2
**Libeň** *Czech Rep.* 50°6N 14°27E **135** B2
**Libenge** *Dem. Rep. of the Congo* 3°40N 18°55E **264** B3
**Liberal** *U.S.A.* 37°3N 100°55W **308** G3
**Liberdade** *Acre, Brazil* 10°5S 70°20W **330** C3
**Liberdade** *São Paulo, Brazil* 23°33S 46°37W **137** B2
**Liberdade** → *Brazil* 9°40S 52°17W **331** B7
**Liberdade, Avenida da** *Lisbon, Portugal* **126** b1
**Liberec** *Czech Rep.* 50°47N 15°7E **180** A8
**Liberecký** □ *Czech Rep.* 50°45N 15°0E **180** A8
**Liberia** *Costa Rica* 10°40N 85°30W **320** D2
**Liberia** ■ *W. Afr.* 6°30N 9°30W **262** D3
**Libertà, Ponte della** *Venice, Italy* **142** a1
**Libertad** *Antique, Phil.* 11°46N 121°55E **233** F3
**Libertad** *Venezuela* 8°20N 69°37W **328** B4
**Libertador** □ *Chile* 34°15S 70°45W **334** C1
**Liberton** *U.K.* 55°54N 3°9W **121** B3
**Liberty** *Ind., U.S.A.* 39°38N 84°56W **311** E12
**Liberty** *Mo., U.S.A.* 39°15N 94°25W **310** E2
**Liberty** *N.Y., U.S.A.* 41°48N 74°45W **313** E10
**Liberty** *Pa., U.S.A.* 41°34N 77°6W **312** E7
**Liberty** *Tex., U.S.A.* 30°3N 94°48W **314** F7
**Liberty Center** *U.S.A.* 41°27N 84°1W **311** C12
**Liberty I.** *U.S.A.* 40°41N 74°2W **132** B1
**Liberty-Newark Int.** ✕ **(EWR)** *U.S.A.* 40°42N 74°10W **313** F10
**Liberty Ōsaka Museum** *Japan* 34°38N 135°29E **133** B1
**Liberty State Park** ⌓ *U.S.A.* 40°42N 74°2W **132** B1
**Libertyville** *U.S.A.* 42°18N 87°57W **311** B9
**Libeznice** *Czech Rep.* 50°11N 14°29E **135** A2
**Libiąż** *Poland* 50°7N 19°21E **185** H6
**Libibi** *Angola* 14°42S 17°44E **265** E3
**Lîbîya, Sahrâ'** *Africa* 25°0N 25°0E **258** C4
**Libjo** *Phil.* 10°12N 125°32E **233** F5
**Libmanan** *Phil.* 13°42N 123°4E **232** E4
**Libo** *China* 25°22N 107°53E **228** E6
**Libobo, Tanjung** *Indonesia* 0°54S 128°28E **231** E7
**Libode** *S. Africa* 31°33S 29°2E **271** D4
**Libohovë** *Albania* 40°3N 20°10E **202** F4
**Liboi** *Kenya* 0°24N 40°57E **267** D5
**Libona** *Phil.* 8°20N 124°44E **233** G5
**Libonda** *Zambia* 14°28S 23°12E **265** E4
**Libong, Ko** *Thailand* 7°15N 99°23E **237** J2
**Libourne** *France* 44°55N 0°14W **174** D3
**Libramont** *Belgium* 49°55N 5°23E **170** E5
**Library of Congress** *Washington, D.C., U.S.A.* **143** b3
**Librazhd** *Albania* 41°12N 20°22E **202** E4
**Libreville** *Gabon* 0°25N 9°26E **264** B1
**Libro Pt.** *Phil.* 11°25N 119°28E **233** F2
**Libuš** *Czech Rep.* 50°0N 14°27E **135** B2
**Libya** ■ *N. Afr.* 27°0N 17°0E **258** C3
**Libyan Desert = Lîbîya, Sahrâ'** *Africa* 25°0N 25°0E **258** C4
**Libyan Plateau = Ed Déffa** *Egypt* 30°40N 26°30E **256** A2
**Licantén** *Chile* 35°55S 72°0W **334** D1
**Licata** *Italy* 37°6N 13°56E **200** E6
**Lice** *Turkey* 38°27N 40°39E **213** C9
**Licheng** *China* 36°28N 113°20E **226** F7
**Lichfield** *U.K.* 52°41N 1°49W **169** E6
**Lichia** *Taiwan* 22°47N 121°3E **225** D3
**Lichiao** *China* 23°3N 113°18E **121** B2
**Lichinga** *Mozam.* 13°13S 35°11E **269** E4
**Lichtenburg** *Berlin, Germany* 52°31N 13°30E **115** A4
**Lichtenburg** *North West, S. Africa* 26°8S 26°8E **270** C4
**Lichtenfels** *Germany* 50°8N 11°4E **179** E7
**Lichterfelde** *Germany* 52°25N 13°19E **115** B2
**Lichuan** *Hubei, China* 30°18N 108°57E **228** B7
**Lichuan** *Jiangxi, China* 27°18N 116°55E **229** D11
**Licking** → *U.S.A.* 39°6N 84°30W **311** F12
**Licosa, Punta** *Italy* 40°15N 14°54E **201** B7
**Licungo** → *Mozam.* 17°40S 37°15E **269** F4
**Lida** *Belarus* 53°53N 25°15E **177** B13
**Liden** *Sweden* 62°42N 16°48E **162** B10
**Lidhult** *Sweden* 56°50N 13°27E **163** H7
**Lidingö** *Sweden* 59°21N 18°8E **139** A2
**Lidköping** *Sweden* 58°31N 13°7E **163** F7
**Lido** *Niger* 12°54N 3°44E **263** C5
**Lido di Roma = Óstia, Lido di** *Italy* 41°43N 12°17E **199** G9
**Lidoriki** *Greece* 38°32N 22°12E **204** C4
**Lidzbark** *Poland* 53°15N 19°49E **185** E6
**Lidzbark Warmiński** *Poland* 54°7N 20°34E **184** D7
**Liebenthal = Lubomierz** *Poland* 51°1N 15°31E **185** G2
**Liebenwalde** *Germany* 52°52N 13°24E **178** C9
**Lieberose** *Germany* 51°59N 14°17E **178** D10
**Liebig, Mt.** *Australia* 23°18S 131°22E **278** D5
**Liebling** *Romania* 45°36N 21°20E **182** E6
**Liechtenstein** ■ *Europe* 47°8N 9°35E **179** H5
**Liège** *Belgium* 50°38N 5°35E **170** D5
**Liège** □ *Belgium* 50°32N 5°35E **170** D5
**Liegnitz = Legnica** *Poland* 51°12N 16°10E **185** G3
**Lieksa** *Finland* 63°18N 30°2E **160** E24
**Lienart** *Dem. Rep. of the Congo* 3°3N 25°31E **268** B2
**Lienyünchiangshih = Lianyungang** *China* 34°40N 119°11E **227** G10
**Lienz** *Austria* 46°50N 12°46E **180** E5
**Liepāja** *Latvia* 56°30N 21°0E **184** B8
**Liepāja** □ *Latvia* 56°30N 21°30E **184** B8
**Liepājas ezers** *Latvia* 56°27N 21°3E **184** B8
**Lier** *Belgium* 51°7N 4°34E **170** C4
**Liernais** *France* 47°13N 4°16E **173** E11
**Lierne** △ *Norway* 64°20N 13°50E **160** D15
**Lieshi Lingyuan** *China* 23°7N 113°16E **121** B2
**Liesing** *Austria* 48°8N 16°17E **142** B1
**Liesing** → *Austria* 48°8N 16°28E **142** B2
**Lieşti** *Romania* 45°38N 27°34E **183** E12
**Lietuva = Lithuania** ■ *Europe* 55°30N 24°0E **188** E2
**Liévin** *France* 50°24N 2°47E **173** B9
**Lièvre** → *Canada* 45°31N 75°26W **298** C4
**Liezen** *Austria* 47°34N 14°15E **180** D7
**Liffey** → *Ireland* 53°21N 6°13W **166** C5
**Lifford** *Ireland* 54°51N 7°29W **166** B4
**Liffré** *France* 48°12N 1°30W **172** D5
**Lifjell** *Norway* 59°27N 8°45E **164** E5
**Lifou, Î.** *N. Cal.* 20°53S 167°13E **288** d
**Lifudzin** *Russia* 44°21N 134°58E **220** B7
**Lifuka** *Tonga* 19°48S 174°21W **287** P13
**Ligang = Likang** *Taiwan* 22°47N 120°29E **225** D2
**Ligao** *Phil.* 13°14N 123°32E **232** E4
**Ligasa** *Dem. Rep. of the Congo* 0°44N 23°49E **264** B4
**Lighthouse Point** *U.S.A.* 26°15N 80°7W **317** J9
**Lighthouse Pt.** *U.S.A.* 29°54N 84°21W **316** F5
**Lightning Ridge** *Australia* 29°22S 148°0E **281** D4
**Lignano Sabbiadoro** *Italy* 45°42N 13°9E **199** C10
**Ligny-en-Barrois** *France* 48°36N 5°20E **173** D12
**Ligonha** → *Mozam.* 16°54S 39°9E **269** F4
**Ligonier** *Ind., U.S.A.* 41°28N 85°35W **311** C11
**Ligonier** *Pa., U.S.A.* 40°15N 79°14W **312** F5
**Ligourio** *Greece* 37°37N 23°4E **204** D5
**Ligovo** *Russia* 59°49N 30°10E **137** C1
**Ligueil** *France* 47°2N 0°49E **172** E7
**Liguria** □ *Italy* 44°30N 8°50E **198** D5
**Ligurian Sea** *Medit. S.* 43°20N 9°0E **198** E5
**Lihir Group** *Papua N. G.* 3°0S 152°35E **286** B7
**Lihir I.** *Papua N. G.* 3°5S 152°35E **286** B7
**Lihou Reefs and Cays** *Australia* 17°25S 151°40E **280** B5
**Lihu'e** *U.S.A.* 21°59N 159°23W **302** B2
**Lihué Calel** △ *Argentina* 38°0S 65°10W **334** D2
**Lijiang** *China* 26°55N 100°20E **228** D3
**Lijordet** *Norway* 59°56N 10°36E **133** A2
**Lik** → *Laos* 18°31N 102°30E **236** C4
**Likala** *Dem. Rep. of the Congo* 0°9N 19°12E **264** B3
**Likang** *Taiwan* 22°47N 120°29E **225** D2
**Likasi** *Dem. Rep. of the Congo* 10°55S 26°48E **269** E2
**Likati** *Dem. Rep. of the Congo* 3°20N 24°0E **264** B4
**Likati** → *Dem. Rep. of the Congo* 2°53N 24°3E **264** B4
**Likenäs** *Sweden* 60°37N 13°3E **162** D7
**Likete** *Dem. Rep. of the Congo* 0°48S 21°31E **264** C4
**Likhaya = Likhovskoy** *Russia* 48°10N 40°10E **191** F5
**Likhoborka** → *Russia* 55°50N 37°37E **129** A2
**Likhoslavl** *Russia* 57°12N 35°30E **188** D8
**Likhovskoy** *Russia* 48°10N 40°10E **191** F5
**Likhvin = Chekalin** *Russia* 54°10N 36°10E **188** E9
**Likimi** *Dem. Rep. of the Congo* 2°44N 20°47E **264** B4
**Likita** *Dem. Rep. of the Congo* 4°15N 23°36E **264** B4
**Liknes** *Norway* 58°19N 6°59E **164** F3
**Likokou** *Gabon* 0°12S 12°48E **264** C2
**Likoma I.** *Malawi* 12°3S 34°45E **269** E3
**Likouala** □ *Congo* 2°0N 17°30E **264** B3
**Likouala** → *Congo* 0°2N 14°53E **264** C3
**Likouala aux Herbes** → *Congo* 0°52S 17°8E **264** C3
**Liku** *Cook Is.* 19°2S 168°47W **289** g
**Likumburu** *Tanzania* 9°43S 35°8E **269** D4
**Lilanga** *Dem. Rep. of the Congo* 0°34S 23°56E **264** C4
**L'Île-Bouchard** *France* 47°7N 0°26E **172** E7
**L'Île-Rousse** *France* 42°38N 8°57E **175** F12
**Lilenga** *Dem. Rep. of the Congo* 1°4N 22°2E **264** B4
**Liling** *China* 27°42N 113°29E **229** D9
**Lilla Edet** *Sweden* 58°9N 12°8E **163** F6
**Lilla Värtan** *Sweden* 59°20N 18°11E **139** A3
**Lille** *France* 50°38N 3°3E **173** B10
**Lille Bælt** *Denmark* 55°20N 9°45E **163** J3
**Lille Værløse** *Denmark* 55°47N 12°22E **118** A2
**Lillebonne** *France* 49°30N 0°32E **172** C7
**Lillehammer** *Norway* 61°8N 10°30E **164** C7
**Lillesand** *Norway* 58°15N 8°23E **164** F5
**Lillestrøm** *Norway* 59°58N 11°5E **164** E8
**Lillhärdal** *Sweden* 61°51N 14°5E **162** C8
**Lillian Pt.** *Australia* 27°40S 126°6E **279** E4
**Lillo** *Spain* 39°45N 3°20W **194** F7
**Lillooet** *Canada* 50°44N 121°57W **296** C4
**Lillooet** → *Canada* 49°15N 121°57W **296** D4
**Lilongwe** *Malawi* 14°0S 33°48E **269** E3
**Liloy** *Phil.* 8°4N 122°39E **233** G4
**Liluah** *India* 22°37N 88°19E **124** B1
**Lim** → *Europe* 43°45N 19°15E **202** C3
**Lim Chu Kang** *Singapore* 1°26N 103°43E **138** A2
**Lima** *Brazil* 4°36S 63°40W **329** D5
**Lima** *Indonesia* 3°39S 127°58E **231** E7
**Lima** *Peru* 12°3S 77°2W **124** B2
**Lima** *Ill., U.S.A.* 40°11N 91°23W **310** D5
**Lima** *Mont., U.S.A.* 44°38N 112°36W **304** D7
**Lima** *N.Y., U.S.A.* 42°54N 77°36W **312** D7
**Lima** *Ohio, U.S.A.* 40°44N 84°6W **311** D12
**Lima** □ *Peru* 12°3S 77°3W **330** C2
**Lima** → *Portugal* 41°41N 8°50W **194** D2
**Lima Jorge Chavez Int.** ✕ **(LIM)** *Lima, Peru* 12°2S 77°8W **124** B2
**Liman = Krasnyy Liman** *Ukraine* 48°58N 37°50E **189** H9
**Liman** *Russia* 45°45N 47°12E **191** H8
**Limanowa** *Poland* 49°42N 20°22E **185** J7
**Limassol** *Cyprus* 34°42N 33°1E **207** F9
**Limavady** *U.K.* 55°3N 6°56W **166** A5
**Limay** → *Argentina* 39°0S 68°0W **336** A3
**Limay Mahuida** *Argentina* 37°10S 66°45W **334** D2
**Limbach-Oberfrohna** *Germany* 50°52N 12°43E **178** E8
**Limbang** *Malaysia* 4°42N 115°6E **235** B5
**Limbara, Mte.** *Italy* 40°51N 9°10E **200** B2
**Limbaži** *Latvia* 57°31N 24°42E **188** D3
**Limbdi** *India* 22°34N 71°51E **242** H4
**Limbe** *Cameroon* 4°1N 9°10E **263** E6
**Limbiate** *Italy* 45°35N 9°7E **128** A1
**Limbueta** *Angola* 12°30S 18°42E **265** E3
**Limbuhan = Pio V. Corpuz** *Phil.* 11°55N 124°2E **233** F5
**Limburg** *Germany* 50°22N 8°4E **179** E4
**Limburg** □ *Belgium* 51°2N 5°25E **170** C5
**Limburg** □ *Neths.* 51°20N 5°55E **170** C5
**Lime Village** *U.S.A.* 61°21N 155°28W **303** F9
**Limedsforsen** *Sweden* 60°52N 13°25E **162** D7
**Limehouse** *U.K.* 51°30N 0°1W **125** A3
**Limeil-Brévannes** *France* 48°44N 2°29E **134** B3
**Limeira = Joaçaba** *Brazil* 27°5S 51°31W **335** B5
**Limeira** *Brazil* 22°35S 47°28W **335** A6
**Limenaria** *Greece* 40°38N 24°32E **203** F8
**Limenas Chersonisou** *Greece* 35°18N 25°21E **207** E6
**Limerick** *Limerick, Ireland* 52°40N 8°37W **166** D3
**Limerick** *Maine, U.S.A.* 43°41N 70°48W **313** C14
**Limerick** □ *Ireland* 52°30N 8°50W **166** D3
**Limestone** *U.S.A.* 42°2N 78°38W **312** D6
**Limestone** → *Canada* 56°31N 94°7W **297** B10
**Limestone Hill = Lackawanna** *U.S.A.* 42°50N 78°50W **312** D6
**Limfjorden** *Denmark* 56°55N 9°0E **163** H3
**Limia = Lima** → *Portugal* 41°41N 8°50W **194** D2
**Limingen** *Norway* 64°48N 13°35E **160** D15
**Limmared** *Sweden* 57°34N 13°20E **163** G7
**Limmen** ✿ *Australia* 15°15S 135°30E **280** B2
**Limmen Bight** *Australia* 14°40S 135°35E **280** A2
**Limmen Bight** → *Australia* 15°7S 135°44E **280** B2
**Limni** *Greece* 38°43N 23°18E **204** C5
**Limnos** *Greece* 39°50N 25°5E **205** B7
**Limoeiro** *Brazil* 7°52S 35°27W **332** C4
**Limoeiro do Norte** *Brazil* 5°5S 38°0W **332** C4
**Limoges** *Ont., Canada* 45°20N 75°16W **313** A9
**Limoges** *Haute-Vienne, France* 45°50N 1°15E **174** C5
**Limón** *Costa Rica* 10°0N 83°2W **320** E3
**Limon** *Colo., U.S.A.* 39°16N 103°41W **304** G12
**Limone** *Italy* 45°48N 10°47E **198** C7
**Limone Piemonte** *Italy* 44°12N 7°34E **198** D4
**Limonlu** *Turkey* 36°34N 34°15E **250** B5
**Limousin** □ *France* 45°30N 1°30E **174** C5
**Limousin, Plateaux du** *France* 45°45N 1°15E **174** C5
**Limoux** *France* 43°4N 2°12E **174** E6
**Limpopo** □ *S. Africa* 24°5S 29°0E **271** B4
**Limpopo** → *Africa* 25°5S 33°30E **271** C5
**Lin Xian** *China* 37°57N 110°58E **226** F6
**Lin'an** *China* 30°15N 119°42E **229** B12
**Linao Pt.** *Phil.* 6°46N 123°58E **233** H4
**Linapacan** *Phil.* 11°30N 119°52E **233** F2
**Linapacan I.** *Phil.* 11°27N 119°49E **233** F2
**Linapacan Str.** *Phil.* 11°37N 119°56E **233** F2
**Linares** *Chile* 35°50S 71°40W **334** D1
**Linares** *Colombia* 1°23N 77°31W **328** C2
**Linares** *Nuevo León, Mexico* 24°52N 99°34W **319** C5
**Linares** *Spain* 38°10N 3°40W **195** G7
**Linaria** *Greece* 38°52N 24°31E **204** C6
**Linaro, Capo** *Italy* 42°2N 11°50E **199** F8
**Línas Mte.** *Italy* 39°25N 8°38E **200** C1
**Linate, Milano** ✕ **(LIN)** *Italy* 45°27N 9°16E **128** B2
**Linbian = Linpien** *Taiwan* 22°26N 120°30E **225** D2
**Linbropark** *S. Africa* 26°5S 28°7E **123** A2
**Lincang** *China* 23°58N 100°1E **228** F3
**Lincheng** *China* 37°25N 114°30E **226** F8
**Linchuan** *China* 27°57N 116°15E **229** D11
**Lincoln = Beamsville** *Canada* 43°12N 79°28W **312** C5
**Lincoln** *Argentina* 34°55S 61°30W **334** C3
**Lincoln** *N.Z.* 43°38S 172°30E **285** D7
**Lincoln** *Lincs., U.K.* 53°14N 0°32W **168** D7
**Lincoln** *Calif., U.S.A.* 38°54N 121°17W **306** G5
**Lincoln** *Ill., U.S.A.* 40°9N 89°22W **310** D7
**Lincoln** *Kans., U.S.A.* 39°3N 98°9W **308** F4
**Lincoln** *Maine, U.S.A.* 45°22N 68°30W **309** C19
**Lincoln** *N.H., U.S.A.* 44°3N 71°40W **313** B13
**Lincoln** *N. Mex., U.S.A.* 33°30N 105°23W **305** K11
**Lincoln** *Nebr., U.S.A.* 40°49N 96°41W **308** E5
**Lincoln Boyhood** ⌓ *U.S.A.* 38°7N 86°59W **311** F10
**Lincoln Center for Performing Arts** *New York, U.S.A.* **132** b2
**Lincoln City** *U.S.A.* 44°57N 124°1W **304** D1
**Lincoln Hav = Lincoln Sea** *Arctic* 84°0N 55°0W **154** A5
**Lincoln Heights** *U.S.A.* 34°4N 118°12W **126** B3
**Lincoln Memorial** *U.S.A.* 38°52N 77°4W **143** B2
**Lincoln Park** *Calif., U.S.A.* 37°47N 122°30W **136** B1
**Lincoln Park** *Ga., U.S.A.* 32°52N 84°20W **316** C5
**Lincoln Park** *Ill., U.S.A.* 41°57N 87°38W **119** B3
**Lincoln Park** *Mich., U.S.A.* 42°15N 83°11W **311** B13
**Lincoln Park** *N.J., U.S.A.* 40°55N 74°18W **132** B1
**Lincoln Park Zoo** *U.S.A.* 41°55N 87°38W **119** B3
**Lincoln Sea** *Arctic* 84°0N 55°0W **154** A5
**Lincoln Tunnel** *New York, U.S.A.* **132** c1
**Lincolnshire** □ *U.K.* 53°14N 0°32W **168** D7
**Lincolnshire Wolds** *U.K.* 53°26N 0°13W **168** D7
**Lincolnton** *Ga., U.S.A.* 33°48N 82°29W **316** B7
**Lincolnton** *N.C., U.S.A.* 35°29N 81°16W **315** D14
**Lincolnwood** *U.S.A.* 42°1N 87°43W **119** A2
**Lind** *U.S.A.* 46°58N 118°37W **304** C4
**Linda** *U.S.A.* 39°8N 121°34W **306** F5
**Linda-a-Pastora** *Portugal* 38°42N 9°15W **126** A1
**Lindale** *U.S.A.* 34°11N 85°11W **316** A4
**Lindås** *Norway* 60°44N 5°9E **164** D2
**Lindau** *Germany* 47°33N 9°42E **179** H5
**Lindeman I.** *Australia* 20°27S 149°3E **280** b
**Lindeman Islands** △ *Australia* 20°28S 149°5E **280** b
**Linden = Gladstone** *U.S.A.* 39°13N 94°35W **310** E2
**Linden** *Guyana* 6°0N 58°10W **329** B6
**Linden** *Gauteng, S. Africa* 26°8S 28°0E **123** A2
**Linden** *Ala., U.S.A.* 32°18N 87°48W **315** E11
**Linden** *Calif., U.S.A.* 38°1N 121°5W **306** G5
**Linden** *Ind., U.S.A.* 40°11N 86°54W **311** D10
**Linden** *Mich., U.S.A.* 42°49N 83°47W **311** B13
**Linden** *Tex., U.S.A.* 33°1N 94°22W **314** E7
**Lindenberg** *Germany* 52°36N 13°31E **115** A4
**Lindenhurst** *U.S.A.* 40°41N 73°23W **313** F11
**Lindenow Fjord** *Greenland* 60°30N 43°25W **154** E6
**Lindesberg** *Sweden* 59°36N 15°15E **162** E9
**Lindesnes** *Norway* 57°58N 7°3E **164** G4
**Lindi** *Tanzania* 9°58S 39°38E **269** D4
**Lindi** □ *Tanzania* 9°40S 38°30E **269** D4
**Lindi** → *Dem. Rep. of the Congo* 0°33N 25°5E **268** B2
**Lindley** *U.S.A.* 42°1N 77°8W **312** D7
**Lindö** *Sweden* 58°37N 16°15E **163** F10
**Lindome** *Sweden* 57°35N 12°5E **163** G6
**Lindos** *Greece* 36°6N 28°4E **206** E12
**Lindos, Akra** *Greece* 36°4N 28°10E **206** E12
**Lindoso** *Portugal* 41°52N 8°11W **194** D2
**Lindow** *Germany* 52°58N 12°59E **178** C8
**Lindøya** *Norway* 59°53N 10°42E **133** A3
**Lindsay** *Ont., Canada* 44°22N 78°43W **312** B6
**Lindsay** *Calif., U.S.A.* 36°12N 119°5W **306** J7
**Lindsay** *Okla., U.S.A.* 34°50N 97°38W **314** D6
**Lindsborg** *U.S.A.* 38°35N 97°40W **308** F5
**Lindsdal** *Sweden* 56°44N 16°18E **163** H10
**Line Islands** *Pac. Oc.* 7°0N 160°0W **289** H12
**Linesville** *U.S.A.* 41°39N 80°26W **312** E4
**Lineville** *Ala., U.S.A.* 33°19N 85°45W **316** B4
**Lineville** *Iowa, U.S.A.* 40°35N 93°32W **310** D3
**Linfen** *China* 36°3N 111°30E **226** F6
**Ling Xian** *Hunan, China* 26°29N 113°48E **229** D9
**Ling Xian** *Shandong, China* 37°22N 116°30E **226** F9
**Lingal** *India* 16°17N 78°31E **245** F4
**Linganamakki Res.** *India* 14°6N 74°52E **245** G2

Lingao China 19°56N 109°42E 229 a
Lingayen Phil. 16°1N 120°14E 232 C3
Lingayen G. Phil. 16°10N 120°15E 232 C3
Lingbao China 34°31N 110°51E 226 G6
Lingbi China 33°33N 117°33E 227 H9
Lingbo Sweden 61°3N 16°41E 162 C10
Lingchuan Guangxi Zhuangzu, China 25°26N 110°21E 229 E8
Lingchuan Shanxi, China 35°45N 113°12E 226 G7
Lingding Yang China 22°25N 113°44E 219 a
Lingen Germany 52°31N 7°19E 178 C3
Lingga Indonesia 0°12S 104°37E 234 C2
Lingga, Kepulauan Indonesia 0°10S 104°30E 234 C2
Lingga Arch. = Lingga, Kepulauan Indonesia 0°10S 104°30E 234 C2
Linghai China 41°11N 121°22E 227 D11
Linghed Sweden 60°48N 15°55E 162 D9
Linghem Sweden 58°26N 15°47E 163 F9
Lingig Phil. 8°2N 126°24E 233 G6
Lingle U.S.A. 42°8N 104°21W 304 E11
Lingomo Dem. Rep. of the Congo 0°38N 22°3E 264 B4
Lingqiu China 39°28N 114°22E 226 E8
Lingshan China 22°25N 109°18E 228 F7
Lingshi China 36°48N 111°48E 226 F6
Lingshou China 38°20N 114°20E 226 E8
Lingshui China 18°27N 110°0E 229 a
Lingsugur India 16°10N 76°31E 245 F3
Lingtai China 35°0N 107°40E 226 G4
Linguère Senegal 15°25N 15°5W 262 B1
Lingui China 25°12N 110°2E 229 E8
Lingunda Dem. Rep. of the Congo 0°49N 21°8E 264 C3
Lingwu China 38°6N 106°20E 226 E4
Lingyuan China 41°10N 119°15E 227 D10
Lingyun China 25°2N 106°35E 228 E6
Linhai China 28°50N 121°8E 229 C13
Linhares Brazil 19°25S 40°4W 333 E3
Linhe China 40°48N 107°20E 226 D4
Liniers Argentina 34°39S 58°30W 117 B1
Linjiang China 41°50N 127°0E 224 B3
Linkebeek Belgium 50°46N 4°20E 116 B2
Linköping Sweden 58°28N 15°36E 163 F9
Linkou China 45°15N 130°18E 227 B16
Linksfield S. Africa 26°9S 28°6E 123 A2
Linli China 29°27N 111°30E 229 C8
Linlithgow = West Lothian □ U.K. 55°54N 3°36W 167 F5
Linmeyer S. Africa 26°15S 28°4E 123 B2
Linn U.S.A. 38°29N 91°51W 310 F5
Linnanmaa Finland 60°20N 24°50E 121 A2
Linnansaari △ Finland 62°3N 28°40E 160 E23
Linnei Taiwan 23°45N 120°36E 225 C2
Linneus U.S.A. 39°53N 93°11W 310 E3
Linnhe, L. U.K. 56°36N 5°25W 167 E3
Linosa Medit. S. 35°51N 12°50E 258 A2
Linpien Taiwan 22°26N 120°30E 225 D2
Linqi China 35°45N 113°52E 226 G7
Linqing China 36°50N 115°42E 226 F8
Linqu China 36°25N 118°30E 227 F10
Linquan China 33°5N 115°17E 229 A10
Lins Brazil 21°40S 49°44W 335 A6
Linshu China 34°53N 118°38E 227 G10
Linshui China 30°21N 106°57E 228 B6
Linsia = Linxia China 35°36N 103°10E 218 D9
Linstead Jamaica 18°8N 77°2W 320 a
Linta → Madag. 25°2S 44°5E 272 D1
Lintao China 35°26N 103°58E 226 G2
Linth → Switz. 47°7N 9°7E 179 H5
Linthal Switz. 46°54N 9°0E 179 J5
Linton Ind., U.S.A. 39°2N 87°10W 311 F9
Linton N. Dak., U.S.A. 46°16N 100°14W 308 B3
Lintong China 34°20N 109°10E 226 G5
Lintuvaara Finland 60°14N 24°49E 121 B1
Linwood Canada 43°35N 80°43W 312 C4
Linwu China 25°19N 112°31E 229 E9
Linxi Hebei, China 39°42N 118°26E 227 E10
Linxi Liaoning, China 43°36N 118°2E 227 C10
Linxia China 35°36N 103°10E 218 D9
Linxiang China 29°28N 113°23E 229 C9
Linyanti → Africa 17°50S 25°5E 270 A4
Linyi Shandong, China 37°13N 116°54E 226 F9
Linyi Shandong, China 35°5N 118°21E 227 G10
Linying China 33°48N 113°56E 226 H7
Linyuan Taiwan 22°30N 120°23E 225 D2
Linz Austria 48°18N 14°18E 180 C7
Linz Rhld-Pfz., Germany 50°34N 7°17E 178 E3
Linzhenzhen China 36°30N 109°59E 226 F5
Linzhou China 36°4N 113°49E 226 F7
Linzi China 36°50N 118°20E 227 F10
Lioko Équateur, Dem. Rep. of the Congo 0°2N 22°4E 264 B4
Lioko Orientale, Dem. Rep. of the Congo 1°25N 23°7E 264 B4
Liomsheter Norway 61°15N 9°35E 164 C6
Lion, G. du France 43°10N 4°0E 174 E7
Lion Rock Country Park △ Hong Kong, China 22°21N 114°11E 122 A3
Lionel Town Jamaica 17°50N 77°15W 320 a
Lions, G. of = Lion, G. du France 43°10N 4°0E 174 E7
Lion's Den Zimbabwe 17°15S 30°5E 269 F3
Lion's Head Ont., Canada 44°58N 81°15W 312 B3
Lion's Head Western Cape, S. Africa 33°56S 18°23E 118 A1
Liouesso Congo 1°2N 15°43E 264 B3
Lioumi Greece 38°0N 23°40E 112 B2
Liozno = Lyozna Belarus 55°0N 30°50E 188 E6
Lipa Phil. 13°57N 121°10E 232 E3
Lipali Mozam. 15°50S 35°50E 269 F4
Lipany Slovak Rep. 49°9N 20°58E 181 B13
Lipari Italy 38°26N 14°58E 201 D7
Lipari, I. Italy 38°29N 14°56E 201 D7
Lipari, Is. = Eólie, Ís. Italy 38°30N 14°57E 201 D7
Lipatkain Indonesia 0°1N 101°12E 234 B2
Lipcani Moldova 48°14N 26°48E 183 B11
Liperi Finland 62°31N 29°24E 160 E23
Lipetsk Russia 52°37N 39°35E 189 F10
Lipetsk □ Russia 52°50N 38°50E 190 D4
Lipiany Poland 53°2N 14°58E 185 E1
Liping China 26°15N 109°7E 228 D7
Lipsi Greece 37°19N 26°50E 205 D8
Lipjan Kosovo 42°31N 21°7E 202 D5
Lipkany = Lipcani Moldova 48°14N 26°48E 183 B11
Lipník nad Bečvou Czech Rep. 49°32N 17°36E 181 B10
Lipno Poland 52°49N 19°15E 185 F6
Lipova Romania 46°8N 21°42E 182 D6
Lipovets Ukraine 49°12N 29°1E 177 D15
Lippe → Germany 51°39N 6°36E 178 D2
Lippehne = Lipiany Poland 53°2N 14°58E 185 E1
Lippstadt Germany 51°41N 8°22E 178 D4
Lipscomb U.S.A. 36°14N 100°16W 314 C4
Lipsk Poland 53°44N 23°24E 184 E10
Lipsko Poland 51°9N 21°40E 185 G8
Liptovský Hrádok Slovak Rep. 49°2N 19°44E 181 B12
Liptovský Milkuláš Slovak Rep. 49°6N 19°35E 181 B12
Liptrap, C. Australia 38°50S 145°55E 283 E6
Lipu China 24°30N 110°22E 229 E8
Lira Uganda 2°17N 32°57E 268 B3
Liranga Congo 0°43S 17°32E 264 C3
Liri → Italy 41°25N 13°52E 200 A6
Liria = Lliria Spain 39°37N 0°35W 197 F4
Lisakovsk Kazakhstan 52°33N 62°37E 216 B6
Lisala Dem. Rep. of the Congo 2°12N 21°38E 264 B4
Lisboa Portugal 38°42N 9°8W 126 A2
Lisboa □ Portugal 39°0N 9°12W 195 F1
Lisboa ✕ (LIS) Portugal 38°46N 9°8W 126 A2
Lisbon = Lisboa Portugal 38°42N 9°8W 126 A2
Lisbon N. Dak., U.S.A. 46°27N 97°41W 308 B5
Lisbon N.H., U.S.A. 44°13N 71°55W 313 B13
Lisbon N.Y., U.S.A. 44°43N 75°19W 313 B9
Lisbon Ohio, U.S.A. 40°46N 80°46W 312 F4
Lisbon Falls U.S.A. 44°0N 70°4W 309 D18
Lisburn U.K. 54°31N 6°3W 166 B5
Lisburn, C. Vanuatu 15°39S 166°46E 287 E4
Lisburne, C. U.S.A. 68°53N 166°13W 303 B6
Liscannor B. Ireland 52°55N 9°24W 166 D2
Liscia → Italy 41°11N 9°9E 200 A2
Lisdoonvarna Ireland 53°2N 9°18W 166 C2
Lishan Taiwan 24°16N 121°14E 225 B3
Lishe Jiang → China 24°15N 101°35E 228 E3
Lishi China 37°31N 111°8E 226 F6
Lishu China 43°20N 124°18E 227 C13
Lishui Guangdong, China 23°12N 113°9E 121 A1
Lishui Jiangsu, China 31°38N 119°2E 229 B12
Lishui Zhejiang, China 28°28N 119°54E 229 C12
Lisianski I. U.S.A. 26°2N 174°0W 302 F9
Lisichansk = Lysychansk Ukraine 48°55N 38°30E 189 H10
Lisieux France 49°10N 0°12E 172 C7
Liski Russia 51°3N 39°30E 189 G10
L'Isle-Jourdain Gers, France 43°36N 1°5E 174 E5
L'Isle-Jourdain Vienne, France 46°13N 0°31E 174 B4
L'Isle-sur-la-Sorgue France 43°54N 5°2E 175 E9
Lisle-sur-Tarn France 43°52N 1°49E 174 E5
Lismore N.S.W., Australia 28°44S 153°21E 281 D5
Lismore Waterford, Ireland 52°8N 7°55W 166 D4
Lissa = Leszno Poland 51°50N 16°30E 185 G3
Lissos → Greece 41°15N 25°40E 203 E9
Lista Norway 58°7N 6°39E 164 F3
Lister, Mt. Antarctica 78°0S 162°0E 151 D11
Lister og Mandals = Vest-Agder □ Norway 58°30N 7°15E 164 F4
Liston Australia 28°39S 152°6E 281 D5
Listowel Ont., Canada 43°44N 80°58W 312 C4
Listowel Kerry, Ireland 52°27N 9°29W 166 D2
Lit Sweden 63°19N 14°51E 162 A8
Lit-et-Mixe France 44°2N 1°15W 174 D2
Litang Guangxi Zhuangzu, China 23°12N 109°8E 228 F7
Litang Sichuan, China 30°1N 100°17E 228 B3
Litang Malaysia 5°27N 118°31E 235 A5
Litang Qu → China 28°4N 101°32E 228 C3
Litani → Lebanon 33°20N 35°15E 250 E6
Litchfield Vic., Australia 36°18S 142°52E 282 D5
Litchfield Calif., U.S.A. 40°24N 120°23W 306 E6
Litchfield Conn., U.S.A. 41°45N 73°11W 313 E11
Litchfield Ill., U.S.A. 39°11N 89°39W 310 E7
Litchfield Minn., U.S.A. 45°8N 94°32W 308 C6
Litchfield △ Australia 13°14S 131°1E 278 B5
Liteni Romania 47°32N 26°32E 183 C11
Lithakia Greece 37°43N 20°50E 207 D2
Lithgow Australia 33°25S 150°8E 283 B9
Lithino, Akra Greece 34°55N 24°44E 207 F5
Lithuania ■ Europe 55°30N 24°0E 188 E2
Litija Slovenia 46°3N 14°50E 199 B11
Lititz U.S.A. 40°9N 76°18W 313 F8
Litochoro Greece 40°8N 22°34E 202 F6
Litoko Dem. Rep. of the Congo 1°13S 24°47E 264 C4
Litoměřice Czech Rep. 50°33N 14°10E 180 A7
Litomyšl Czech Rep. 49°52N 16°20E 181 B9
Litschau Austria 48°58N 15°4E 180 C8
Little Abaco Bahamas 26°50N 77°30W 320 A4
Little Andaman I. India 10°45N 92°30E 245 J11
Little Aral Sea = Northern Aral Sea Kazakhstan 46°20N 60°30E 216 C6
Little B. N.S.W., Australia 33°58S 151°15E 139 B2
Little B. Montserrat 16°43N 62°11W 323 p
Little Barrier I. N.Z. 36°12S 175°8E 284 C4
Little Basses Sri Lanka 6°24N 81°43E 245 L5
Little Belt Mts. U.S.A. 46°40N 110°45W 304 C8
Little Bighorn Battlefield △ U.S.A. 45°34N 107°25W 304 D10
Little Blue → U.S.A. 39°42N 96°41W 308 F5
Little Buffalo → Canada 61°0N 113°46W 296 A6
Little Calumet → U.S.A. 41°39N 87°34W 119 D3
Little Cayman Cayman Is. 19°41N 80°3W 320 C3
Little Churchill → Canada 57°30N 95°22W 297 B9
Little Coco I. Burma 14°0N 93°13E 245 H11
Little Colorado → U.S.A. 36°12N 111°48W 305 H8
Little Current Canada 45°55N 82°0W 298 C3
Little Current → Canada 50°57N 84°36W 298 B3
Little Desert △ Australia 37°25S 141°30E 282 D4
Little Diomede I. U.S.A. 65°45N 168°56W 303 D5
Little Falls Minn., U.S.A. 45°59N 94°22W 308 C6
Little Falls N.Y., U.S.A. 43°3N 74°51W 313 C10
Little Ferry U.S.A. 40°50N 74°2W 132 A1
Little Fork → U.S.A. 48°31N 93°35W 308 A7
Little Grand Rapids Canada 52°0N 95°29W 297 C9
Little Haiti U.S.A. 25°50N 80°11W 129 C2
Little Havana U.S.A. 25°47N 80°15W 129 D1
Little Humboldt → U.S.A. 41°1N 117°43W 304 F5
Little Inagua I. Bahamas 21°40N 73°50W 321 B5
Little India Singapore 138 a2
Little Italy New York, U.S.A. 132 e2
Little Karoo S. Africa 33°45S 21°0E 270 D3
Little Khingan Mts. = Xiao Hinggan Ling China 49°0N 127°0E 219 B14
Little Lake U.S.A. 35°56N 117°55W 307 K9
Little Lake Conway U.S.A. 28°29N 81°21W 133 B2
Little Laut Is. = Laut Kecil, Kepulauan Indonesia 4°45S 115°40E 235 C5
Little London Jamaica 18°15N 78°13W 320 a
Little Mecatina = Petit-Mécatina → Canada 50°40N 59°30W 299 B8
Little Mermaid = Den Lille Havfrue Copenhagen, Denmark 118 a3
Little Minch U.K. 57°35N 6°45W 167 D2
Little Missouri → U.S.A. 47°36N 102°25W 308 B2
Little Nicobar India 7°20N 93°40E 245 L11
Little Ouse → U.K. 52°22N 1°12E 169 E9
Little Rann India 23°25N 71°25E 242 H4
Little Red → U.S.A. 35°11N 91°27W 314 D9
Little River N.Z. 43°45S 172°49E 285 D7
Little Rock U.S.A. 34°45N 92°17W 314 D8
Little Rouge → Canada 43°49N 79°11W 141 A4
Little Ruaha → Tanzania 7°57S 37°53E 268 D4
Little Sable Pt. U.S.A. 43°38N 86°33W 308 D10
Little Scarcies → S. Leone 8°50N 13°10W 262 D2
Little Sioux → U.S.A. 41°48N 96°4W 308 E5
Little Sitkin I. U.S.A. 51°57N 178°31E 303 L2
Little Smoky → Canada 54°44N 117°11W 296 C5
Little Snake → U.S.A. 40°27N 108°26W 304 F9
Little Sound Bermuda 32°15N 64°50W 153 a
Little Tokyo Los Angeles, U.S.A. 127 c2
Little Valley U.S.A. 42°15N 78°48W 312 D6
Little Wabash → U.S.A. 37°55N 88°5W 311 G8
Little White → U.S.A. 43°40N 100°40W 308 D3
Little York U.S.A. 41°1N 90°45W 310 C6
Little Zab = Zāb aş Şaghīr → Iraq 35°17N 43°29E 213 E10
Littlefield U.S.A. 33°55N 102°20W 314 E3
Littlehampton U.K. 50°49N 0°32W 169 G7
Littleton U.S.A. 44°18N 71°46W 313 B13
Littoral □ Cameroon 4°0N 10°0E 263 E7
Littoria = Latina Italy 41°28N 12°52E 200 A5
Litunga Angola 13°19S 16°48E 265 E3
Litvinov Czech Rep. 50°36N 13°37E 180 A6
Liu He → Jilin, China 42°46N 126°13E 224 A3
Liu He → Liaoning, China 40°55N 121°35E 227 D11
Liu Jiang → China 23°55N 109°30E 228 F7
Liuba China 33°38N 106°55E 228 A6
Liucheng China 24°38N 109°14E 228 E7
Liuchia Taiwan 23°13N 120°21E 225 C2
Liuch'iu Taiwan 22°21N 120°23E 225 D2
Liuch'iu Yü Taiwan 22°21N 120°22E 225 D2
Liugou China 40°57N 118°15E 227 D10
Liuhang China 31°21N 121°21E 138 A1
Liuhe China 42°17N 125°43E 224 A2
Liuheng Dao China 29°40N 122°5E 229 C14
Liujiang China 24°26N 109°11E 228 E7
Liukang Tenggaja = Sabalana, Kepulauan Indonesia 6°45S 118°50E 231 F5
Liuli Tanzania 11°3S 34°38E 269 E3
Liupan Shan China 35°39N 106°12E 226 G4
Liupanshui China 26°38N 104°48E 228 D5
Liuqiu = Liuch'iu Taiwan 22°21N 120°23E 225 D2
Liurong Temple China 23°8N 113°15E 121 B2
Liuwa Plain Zambia 14°20S 22°30E 265 E4
Liuwa Plain △ Zambia 14°45S 22°35E 265 E4
Liuyang China 28°10N 113°37E 229 C9
Liuying Taiwan 23°17N 120°18E 225 C2
Liuzhou China 24°22N 109°22E 228 E7
Liuzhuang China 33°12N 120°18E 227 H11
Livada Romania 47°52N 23°5E 182 C8
Livadero Greece 40°2N 21°57E 202 F5
Livadhia Cyprus 34°57N 33°38E 207 E12
Livadhje Albania 39°47N 20°7E 206 B10
Livadi Greece 40°8N 22°9E 204 A4
Livadia Greece 38°27N 22°54E 204 C4
Livarot France 48°58N 0°9E 172 D7
Live Oak Calif., U.S.A. 39°17N 121°40W 306 F5
Live Oak Fla., U.S.A. 30°18N 82°59W 316 E7
Live Oak Manor U.S.A. 29°57N 90°14W 131 B1
Lively Canada 46°26N 81°9W 309 B13
Livengood U.S.A. 65°32N 148°33W 303 D10
Liveras Cyprus 35°23N 32°57E 207 E8
Livermore U.S.A. 37°41N 121°47W 306 H5
Livermore, Mt. U.S.A. 30°38N 104°11W 314 F2
Livermore Falls U.S.A. 44°29N 70°11W 309 C18
Liverpool N.S.W., Australia 33°54S 150°58E 283 B9
Liverpool N.S., Canada 44°5N 64°41W 299 D7
Liverpool Mersey., U.K. 53°25N 3°0W 168 D4
Liverpool N.Y., U.S.A. 43°6N 76°13W 313 C8
Liverpool Bay U.K. 53°30N 3°20W 168 D4
Liverpool Plains Australia 31°15S 150°15E 283 A9
Liverpool Ra. Australia 31°50S 150°30E 283 A9
Liverpool Street London, U.K. 125 a5
Livigno Italy 46°35N 10°10E 198 B7
Livingston Guatemala 15°50N 88°50W 320 C2
Livingston W. Loth., U.K. 55°54N 3°30W 167 F5
Livingston Ala., U.S.A. 32°35N 88°11W 315 E10
Livingston Calif., U.S.A. 37°23N 120°43W 306 H6
Livingston Mont., U.S.A. 45°40N 110°34W 304 D8
Livingston S.C., U.S.A. 33°38N 81°7W 316 B8
Livingston Tenn., U.S.A. 36°23N 85°19W 315 C12
Livingston Tex., U.S.A. 30°43N 94°56W 314 F7
Livingston Wis., U.S.A. 42°54N 90°26W 310 B6
Livingston, L. U.S.A. 30°50N 95°10W 314 F7
Livingston Manor U.S.A. 41°54N 74°50W 313 E10
Livingstone Zambia 17°46S 25°52E 269 F2
Livingstone △ Australia 35°22S 147°22E 283 C7
Livingstone Mts. N.Z. 45°15S 168°9E 285 F3
Livingstone Mts. Tanzania 9°40S 34°20E 269 D3
Livingstonia Malawi 10°38S 34°5E 269 E3
Livno Bos.-H. 43°50N 17°1E 182 G2
Livny Russia 52°30N 37°30E 189 F9
Livonia Mich., U.S.A. 42°23N 83°23W 311 B13
Livonia N.Y., U.S.A. 42°49N 77°40W 312 D7
Livorno Italy 43°33N 10°19E 198 E7
Livradois-Forez △ France 44°0N 3°0E 174 E7
Livramento = Nossa Senhora do Livramento Brazil 15°48S 56°22W 331 D6
Livramento Brazil 30°55S 55°30W 335 C4
Livramento do Brumado Brazil 13°39S 41°50W 333 D3
Livron-sur-Drôme France 44°46N 4°51E 175 D8
Livry-Gargan France 48°55N 2°31E 134 A4
Livyntsi Ukraine 48°25N 26°37E 183 B11
Liwā' U.A.E. 23°0N 54°10E 249 B6
Liwale Tanzania 9°48S 37°58E 269 D4
Liwan China 23°13N 113°12E 121 B1
Liwiec → Poland 52°36N 21°34E 185 F8
Liwonde Malawi 15°4S 35°13E 269 F4
Liwonde △ Malawi 14°48S 35°20E 269 E4
Lixi China 26°23N 101°59E 228 D3
Lixian China 31°23N 103°13E 228 B4
Lixin China 33°8N 116°13E 229 A11
Lixouri Greece 38°12N 20°26E 207 C2
Liyang China 31°26N 119°28E 229 B12
Lizard → Trin. & Tob. 10°9N 61°1W 323 t
Lizard I. Australia 14°42S 145°30E 280 A4
Lizard Pt. U.K. 49°57N 5°13W 169 H2
Lizarda Brazil 9°36S 46°41W 332 C2
Lizarra = Estella Spain 42°40N 2°2W 196 C2
Lizella U.S.A. 32°48N 83°49W 316 C6
Lizzano Italy 40°23N 17°27E 201 B10
Ljan Norway 59°50N 10°46E 133 A3
Ljig Serbia 44°13N 20°18E 202 B4
Ljøra → Norway 61°24N 12°36E 164 C9
Ljørdalen Norway 61°23N 12°41E 164 C9
Ljosland Norway 58°47N 7°22E 164 F4
Ljubija Bos.-H. 44°55N 16°35E 199 D13
Ljubinje Bos.-H. 42°58N 18°5E 202 D2
Ljubišnja Europe 43°18N 19°6E 202 C3
Ljubljana Slovenia 46°4N 14°33E 199 B11
Ljubljana ✕ (LJU) Slovenia 46°14N 14°33E 199 B11
Ljubno Slovenia 46°25N 14°46E 199 B11
Ljubovija Serbia 44°11N 19°22E 202 B3
Ljugarn Sweden 57°20N 18°43E 163 G12
Ljung Sweden 57°59N 13°3E 163 G7
Ljungan → Sweden 62°18N 17°23E 162 B11
Ljungaverk Sweden 62°30N 16°5E 162 B10
Ljungby Sweden 56°49N 13°55E 163 H7
Ljungbyholm Sweden 56°39N 16°5E 163 H10
Ljungdalen Sweden 62°51N 12°47E 162 B6
Ljungsbro Sweden 58°31N 15°30E 163 F9
Ljungskile Sweden 58°14N 11°55E 163 F5
Ljusdal Sweden 61°46N 16°3E 162 C10
Ljusfallshammar Sweden 58°48N 15°30E 163 F9
Ljusnan → Sweden 61°12N 17°8E 162 C11
Ljusne Sweden 61°13N 17°7E 162 C11
Ljusterö Sweden 59°31N 18°37E 162 E12
Ljustorp Sweden 62°38N 17°19E 162 B11
Ljutomer Slovenia 46°31N 16°11E 199 B13
Llagostera Spain 41°50N 2°54E 196 D7
Llamellin Peru 9°0S 76°54W 330 B2
Llançà Spain 42°22N 3°9E 196 C8
Llancanelo, Salina Argentina 35°40S 69°8W 334 D2
Llandeilo U.K. 51°53N 3°59W 169 F4
Llandovery U.K. 51°59N 3°48W 169 F4
Llandrindod Wells U.K. 52°14N 3°22W 169 E4
Llandudno U.K. 53°19N 3°50W 168 D4
Llanelli U.K. 51°41N 4°10W 169 F3
Llanes Spain 43°25N 4°50W 194 B6
Llanfair-ym-Muallt = Builth Wells U.K. 52°9N 3°25W 169 E4
Llanganates △ Ecuador 0°51S 72°20W 328 D3
Llangollen U.K. 52°58N 3°11W 168 E4
Llanidloes U.K. 52°27N 3°31W 169 E4
Llano U.S.A. 30°45N 98°41W 314 F5
Llano → U.S.A. 30°39N 98°26W 314 F5
Llano de Can Gineu Spain 41°27N 2°10E 114 A2
Llano Estacado U.S.A. 33°30N 103°0W 314 E3
Llanos S. Amer. 5°0N 71°35W 326 C3
Llanos de Challe △ Chile 28°8S 71°1W 334 B1
Llanquihue, L. Chile 41°10S 72°50W 336 B1
Llanwrtyd Wells U.K. 52°7N 3°38W 169 E4
Llata Peru 9°25S 76°47W 330 B2
Llebeig, C. des Spain 39°33N 2°18E 206 B3
Lleida Spain 41°37N 0°39E 196 D5
Lleida □ Spain 42°6N 1°0E 196 C6
Llentrisca, C. Spain 38°52N 1°15E 206 D1
Llera de Canales Mexico 23°19N 99°1W 319 C5
Llerena Spain 38°17N 6°0W 195 G5
Llevant, Sa. de Spain 39°35N 3°17E 206 B4
Lleyn Peninsula U.K. 52°51N 4°36W 168 E3
Llica Bolivia 19°52S 68°16W 330 D4
Llico Chile 34°46S 72°5W 334 C1
Lliria Spain 39°37N 0°35W 197 F4
Llivia Spain 42°28N 1°59E 174 F5
Llobregat → Spain 41°19N 2°5E 196 D7
Llodio Spain 43°9N 2°58W 196 B2
Llorente Phil. 11°25N 125°33E 233 F5
Lloret de Mar Spain 41°41N 2°53E 196 D7
Lloseta Spain 39°43N 2°52E 206 B3
Lloyd B. Australia 12°45S 143°27E 280 A3
Lloyd L. Canada 57°22N 108°57W 297 B7
Lloydminster Canada 53°17N 110°0W 297 C7
Llubi Spain 39°42N 3°0E 206 B4
Llucena del Cid Spain 40°9N 0°17W 196 E4
Llucmajor Spain 39°29N 2°53E 206 B3
Lluidas Vale Jamaica 18°6N 77°5W 320 a
Llullaillaco, Volcán S. Amer. 24°43S 68°30W 334 A2
Llullaillaco △ Chile 24°50S 68°51W 334 A2
Lo → Vietnam 21°18N 105°25E 236 B5
Lo Aranguiz Chile 33°23S 70°40W 137 B2
Lo Boza Chile 33°23S 70°43W 137 B1
Lo Espejo Chile 33°31S 70°42W 137 C1
Lo Hermida Chile 33°28S 70°33W 137 B2
Lo Prado Chile 33°26S 70°42W 137 B1
Lo So Shing Hong Kong, China 22°12N 114°7E 122 B2
Lo Wai Hong Kong, China 22°22N 114°8E 122 A2
Loa U.S.A. 38°24N 111°39W 304 G8
Loa → Chile 21°26S 70°41W 334 A1
Loagan Bunut △ Malaysia 3°32N 114°40E 235 B4
Loaita I. S. China Sea 10°41N 114°25E 230 B4
Loakulu Indonesia 0°31S 117°1E 235 C5
Loange → Dem. Rep. of the Congo 4°17S 20°2E 265 C4
Loango Congo 4°38S 11°50E 265 C2
Loanhead U.K. 55°53N 3°9W 121 B3
Loano Italy 44°8N 8°15E 198 D5
Loay Phil. 9°36N 124°1E 233 G5
Lobamba Swaziland 26°28S 31°12E 271 C5
Lobatse Botswana 25°12S 25°40E 270 C4
Lobau Wien, Austria 48°10N 16°31E 142 A3
Löbau Sachsen, Germany 51°5N 14°40E 178 D10
Lobaye □ C.A.R. 4°0N 17°30E 264 B3
Lobaye → C.A.R. 3°41N 18°35E 264 B3
Loben = Lubliniec Poland 50°43N 18°45E 185 H5
Lobenstein Germany 50°25N 11°39E 178 E7
Loberia Argentina 38°10S 58°40W 334 D4
Löberöd Sweden 55°47N 13°31E 163 J7
Lobez Poland 53°38N 15°39E 184 E2
Lobito Angola 12°18S 13°35E 265 E2
Lobo Phil. 13°39N 121°13E 232 E3
Lobo → Ivory C. 6°2N 6°45W 262 D3
Lobos Argentina 35°10S 59°0W 334 D4
Lobos, I. Mexico 27°20N 110°36W 318 B2
Lobos, I. de Canary Is. 28°45N 13°50W 153 e2
Lobos, Pt. U.S.A. 37°46N 122°30W 136 B1
Lobos de Afuera, Islas Peru 6°57S 80°42W 330 B1
Lobos de Tierra, I. Peru 6°27S 80°52W 330 B1
Lobżenica Poland 53°18N 17°15E 185 E4
Loc Binh Vietnam 21°46N 106°54E 236 B6
Loc Ninh Vietnam 11°50N 106°34E 237 G6
Locarno Switz. 46°10N 8°47E 179 J4
Loch Garman = Wexford Ireland 52°20N 6°28W 166 D5
Loch Lomond and the Trossachs △ U.K. 56°10N 4°40W 167 E4
Lochaber U.K. 56°59N 5°1W 167 E3
Locham Germany 48°7N 11°26E 131 B1
Locharbriggs U.K. 55°7N 3°35W 167 F5
Lochboisdale U.K. 57°9N 7°20W 167 D1
Loche, L. La Canada 56°30N 109°30W 297 B7
Lochem Neths. 52°9N 6°26E 170 B6
Loches France 47°7N 1°0E 172 E7
Lochgilphead U.K. 56°2N 5°26W 167 E3
Lochinvar △ Zambia 15°55S 27°15E 269 F2
Lochinver U.K. 58°9N 5°14W 167 C3
Lochkov Czech Rep. 50°0N 14°21E 135 B2
Lochloosa L. U.S.A. 29°30N 82°7W 317 F7
Lochmaddy U.K. 57°36N 7°10W 167 D1
Lochnagar Queens., Australia 23°33S 145°38E 280 C4
Lochnagar Aberds., U.K. 56°57N 3°15W 167 E5
Łochów Poland 52°33N 21°42E 185 F8
Lochy, L. U.K. 57°0N 4°53W 167 E4
Lock Australia 33°34S 135°46E 281 E2
Lock Haven U.S.A. 41°8N 77°28W 312 E7
Lockeford U.S.A. 38°10N 121°9W 306 G5
Lockeport Canada 43°47N 65°4W 299 D6
Lockerbie U.K. 55°7N 3°21W 167 F5
Lockhart N.S.W., Australia 35°14S 146°40E 283 C7
Lockhart Tex., U.S.A. 29°53N 97°40W 314 G6
Lockhart, L. Australia 33°15S 119°3E 279 F2
Lockhart River Australia 12°58S 143°30E 280 A3
Lockhart River ✪ Australia 12°47S 143°20E 280 A3
Lockhausen Germany 48°10N 11°24E 131 A1
Lockney U.S.A. 34°7N 101°27W 314 D4
Lockport Ill., U.S.A. 41°35N 88°3W 311 C8
Lockport N.Y., U.S.A. 43°10N 78°42W 312 C6
Locminé France 47°54N 2°51W 172 E4
Locri Italy 38°14N 16°16E 201 D9
Locronan France 48°7N 4°15W 172 D2
Locust Cr. → U.S.A. 39°40N 93°17W 310 E3
Locust Grove U.S.A. 33°21N 84°7W 316 B5
Lod Israel 31°57N 34°54E 251 G5
Lodalskåpa Norway 61°47N 7°13E 164 C4
Lodeinoye Pole Russia 60°44N 33°33E 188 B7
Lodève France 43°44N 3°19E 174 E7
Lodge Bay Canada 52°14N 55°51W 299 B8
Lodge Grass U.S.A. 45°19N 107°22W 304 D10
Lodhran Pakistan 29°32N 71°30E 242 E4
Lodi Italy 45°19N 9°30E 198 C6
Lodi Calif., U.S.A. 38°8N 121°16W 306 G5
Lodi N.J., U.S.A. 40°52N 74°5W 132 A1
Lodi Ohio, U.S.A. 41°2N 82°1W 312 E3
Lodi Estate India 28°36N 77°15E 120 B2
Lodja Dem. Rep. of the Congo 3°30S 23°23E 264 C4
Lodosa Spain 42°25N 2°4W 196 C2
Lödöse Sweden 58°2N 12°9E 163 F6
Lodwar Kenya 3°7N 35°36E 268 B4
Łódź Poland 51°45N 19°27E 185 G6
Łódzkie □ Poland 51°30N 19°30E 185 G6
Loei Thailand 17°29N 101°35E 236 D3
Loengo Dem. Rep. of the Congo 4°48S 26°30E 265 C5
Loeriesfontein S. Africa 31°0S 19°26E 270 D2
Lofa → Liberia 6°35N 11°8W 262 D2
Lofa Mano △ Liberia 7°55N 10°25W 262 D2
Lofer Austria 47°35N 12°41E 180 D5
Lofoten Norway 68°30N 13°59E 160 B16
Lofsdalen Sweden 62°10N 13°20E 162 B7
Lofsen → Sweden 62°7N 13°57E 162 B7
Loftahammar Sweden 57°54N 16°41E 163 G10
Loga Niger 13°40N 3°15E 263 C5
Logan Iowa, U.S.A. 41°39N 95°47W 308 E6
Logan Ohio, U.S.A. 39°32N 82°25W 309 F12
Logan Utah, U.S.A. 41°44N 111°50W 304 F8
Logan W. Va., U.S.A. 37°51N 81°59W 309 G13
Logan, Mt. Canada 60°34N 140°23W 294 E3
Logan Int., Boston ✕ (BOS) U.S.A. 42°22N 71°1W 116 A2
Logan Martin L. U.S.A. 33°26N 86°20W 316 B3
Logan Square U.S.A. 41°55N 87°42W 119 B2
Logandale U.S.A. 36°36N 114°29W 307 J12
Logansport Ind., U.S.A. 40°45N 86°22W 311 D10
Logansport La., U.S.A. 31°58N 94°0W 314 F8
Loganville U.S.A. 33°50N 83°54W 316 B6
Logatec Slovenia 45°56N 14°15E 199 C11
Logirim South Sudan 4°43N 33°14E 257 G3
Lognes-Émerainville ✕ (XLG) France 48°49N 2°37E 134 B4
Logo South Sudan 5°20N 30°18E 257 F3
Logodoro Italy 40°35N 8°45E 200 B1
Logone → Chad 12°6N 15°2E 259 F3
Logone Gana Chad 11°36N 15°4E 259 F3
Logone Occidental □ Chad 8°30N 16°0E 259 G3
Logone Occidental → Chad 8°50N 16°0E 259 G3
Logone Oriental □ Chad 8°30N 16°30E 259 G3
Logone Oriental → Chad 9°7N 16°26E 259 G3
Logroño Spain 42°28N 2°27W 196 C2
Logrosán Spain 39°20N 5°32W 195 F5
Løgstør Denmark 56°58N 9°14E 163 H3
Logtak L. India 24°33N 93°50E 241 C4
Løgumkloster Denmark 55°4N 8°57E 163 J2
Loh Vanuatu 13°21S 166°38E 287 C4
Lohals Denmark 55°8N 10°55E 163 J4
Lohardaga India 23°27N 84°45E 243 H11
Loharia India 23°45N 74°14E 242 H6
Loharu India 28°27N 75°49E 242 E6
Lohja Finland 60°12N 24°5E 188 B3
Löhme Germany 52°37N 13°40E 115 A5
Löhne Germany 52°11N 8°40E 178 C4
Lohoo = Luohe China 33°32N 114°2E 226 H8
Lohr Germany 49°59N 9°35E 179 F5
Lohri Wah → Pakistan 27°27N 67°37E 242 F2
Loi-lem Burma 20°52N 97°28E 241 F6
Loikaw Burma 19°40N 97°17E 241 F6
Loimaa Finland 60°50N 23°5E 188 B2
Loir → France 47°33N 0°32W 172 E6
Loir-et-Cher □ France 47°40N 1°20E 172 E8
Loire □ France 45°40N 4°5E 175 C8
Loire → France 47°16N 2°10W 172 E4
Loire-Anjou-Touraine △ France 47°14N 0°5W 172 E6
Loire-Atlantique □ France 47°25N 1°40W 172 E5
Loire Inférieure = Loire-Atlantique □ France 47°25N 1°40W 172 E5
Loiret □ France 47°55N 2°30E 173 E9
Loitz Germany 53°58N 13°8E 178 B9
Loja Ecuador 3°59S 79°16W 330 A2
Loja Spain 37°10N 4°10W 195 H6
Loja □ Ecuador 4°0S 79°13W 328 D2
Loje → Angola 7°49S 13°6E 265 D2
Loji = Kawasi Indonesia 1°38S 127°28E 231 E7
Lojo = Lohja Finland 60°12N 24°5E 188 B3
Løjt Kirkeby Denmark 55°7N 9°26E 163 J3
Lojung China 24°27N 109°36E 228 E7
Loka Dem. Rep. of the Congo 0°22N 18°2E 264 B3
Loka South Sudan 4°13N 31°0E 257 G3
Lokako Dem. Rep. of the Congo 0°57S 18°55E 264 C3
Lokandu Dem. Rep. of the Congo 2°30S 25°45E 264 C5
Lokaw Dem. Rep. of the Congo 2°40S 20°12E 264 C4
Løken Norway 59°48N 11°29E 164 E8
Lokeren Belgium 51°6N 3°59E 170 C3
Lokgwabe Botswana 24°10S 21°50E 270 B3
Lokhvytsya Ukraine 50°25N 33°18E 189 G7
Lokichar Kenya 2°23N 35°39E 268 B4
Lokichokio Kenya 4°19N 34°13E 268 B3
Lokitaung Kenya 4°12N 35°48E 268 B4
Lokkan tekojärvi Finland 67°55N 27°35E 160 C22
Løkken Denmark 57°22N 9°41E 163 G3
Løkken Sør-Trøndelag, Norway 63°9N 9°41E 164 A6
Loknya Russia 56°49N 30°4E 188 D6
Loko C.A.R. 3°38N 18°2E 264 B3
Loko Nigeria 8°1N 7°53E 263 D6
Lokoja Nigeria 7°47N 6°45E 263 D6
Lokolama Dem. Rep. of the Congo 2°35S 19°50E 264 C3
Lokolenge Dem. Rep. of the Congo 1°12N 22°38E 264 B4
Lokolo → Dem. Rep. of the Congo 1°43S 18°23E 264 C3
Lokot Russia 52°34N 34°36E 189 F8
Loktak L. = Logtak L. India 24°33N 93°50E 241 C4
Lokuru Solomon Is. 8°20S 157°0E 287 M9
Lol South Sudan 6°26N 29°37E 257 F2
Lol → South Sudan 9°13N 26°30E 257 F2
Lola Angola 14°19S 13°37E 265 E2
Lola Guinea 7°52N 8°29W 262 D3
Lola, Mt. U.S.A. 39°26N 120°22W 306 F6
Lolgorien Kenya 1°14S 34°48E 268 C3
Lolibai, Gebel South Sudan 3°50N 33°0E 257 G3
Lolimi South Sudan 4°35N 34°0E 257 G3
Loliondo Tanzania 2°2S 35°39E 268 C4
Lolland Denmark 54°45N 11°30E 163 K5
Lollar Germany 50°37N 8°43E 178 E4
Lolo U.S.A. 46°45N 114°5W 304 C6
Lolo → Eq. Guin. 1°36N 9°37E 264 B1
Lolo → Gabon 0°18S 12°18E 264 C2
Lolobau I. Papua N. G. 4°55S 151°10E 286 C6
Lolodorf Cameroon 3°16N 10°49E 263 E7
Lolokhet Pakistan 24°54N 67°2E 123 A2
Loloma Zambia 13°24S 24°21E 265 E4
Loltong Vanuatu 15°32S 168°10E 287 E6
Lom Bulgaria 43°48N 23°12E 202 C7
Lom Oppland, Norway 61°50N 8°34E 164 C5
Lom → Bulgaria 43°45N 23°15E 202 C7
Lom → Cameroon 5°20N 13°24E 264 A2
Lom Kao Thailand 16°53N 101°14E 236 D3
Lom Sak Thailand 16°47N 101°15E 236 D3
Loma U.S.A. 47°56N 110°30W 304 C8
Loma Linda U.S.A. 34°3N 117°16W 307 L9
Loma Mansa S. Leone 9°13N 11°7W 262 D2
Loma Mts. S. Leone 9°10N 11°7W 262 D2
Lomako → Dem. Rep. of the Congo 0°50N 20°50E 264 B4
Lomaloma Fiji 17°17S 178°59W 287 A3
Lomami → Dem. Rep. of the Congo 0°46N 24°16E 264 B4
Lomas Chapultepec Mexico 19°25N 99°12W 128 B1
Lomas de San Angel Inn Mexico 19°20N 99°13W 128 B1
Lomas de Zamora Argentina 34°45S 58°24W 334 C4
Lombadina Australia 16°31S 122°54E 278 C3
Lombard U.S.A. 41°53N 88°1W 311 C8
Lombárdia □ Italy 45°40N 9°30E 198 C6
Lombardy = Lombárdia □ Italy 45°40N 9°30E 198 C6
Lombardy East S. Africa 26°6S 28°7E 123 A2
Lombe Angola 9°27S 16°13E 265 D3
Lombez France 43°29N 0°55E 174 E4
Lomblen Indonesia 8°30S 123°32E 231 F6
Lombok Indonesia 8°45S 116°30E 235 D5
Lombok, Selat Indonesia 8°30S 115°50E 231 K18
Lomé Togo 6°9N 1°20E 263 D5
Lomela Dem. Rep. of the Congo 2°19S 23°15E 264 C4
Lomela → Dem. Rep. of the Congo 0°15S 20°40E 264 C4
Lomianki Poland 52°21N 20°54E 143 A1
Lomié Cameroon 3°13N 13°38E 264 B2
Lomma Sweden 55°43N 13°6E 163 J7
Lommel Belgium 51°14N 5°19E 170 C5
Lomond Canada 50°24N 112°36W 296 C6
Lomond, L. U.K. 56°8N 4°38W 167 E4
Lomonosov Ridge Arctic 88°0N 140°0E 150 A
Lomphat Cambodia 13°30N 106°59E 236 F6
Lompobatang Indonesia 5°24S 119°56E 231 F5
Lompoc U.S.A. 34°38N 120°28W 307 L6
Lomsegga Norway 61°49N 8°21E 164 C5
Lomus Reforma Mexico 19°24N 99°14W 128 B1
Łomża Poland 53°10N 22°2E 185 E9
Lon, Ko Thailand 7°47N 98°23E 237 a
Lonavale India 18°46N 73°29E 244 E1
Loncoche Chile 39°20S 72°50W 336 A2
Loncopué Argentina 38°4S 70°37W 336 A2
Londa India 15°30N 74°30E 245 G2
Londiani Kenya 0°10S 35°33E 268 C4
Londinières France 49°50N 1°25E 172 C8
London Ont., Canada 42°59N 81°15W 312 D3
London London, U.K. 51°30N 0°3W 125 B3
London Ky., U.S.A. 37°8N 84°5W 309 G11
London Ohio, U.S.A. 39°53N 83°27W 311 E13
London, Greater □ U.K. 51°36N 0°5W 169 F7
London Avenue Canal U.S.A. 30°3N 90°6W 131 A2
London Bridge Grenada 12°15N 61°35W 323 q
London Bridge London, U.K. 125 b5
London City ✕ (LCY) U.K. 51°30N 0°3E 125 A4
London Gatwick ✕ (LGW) U.K. 51°10N 0°11W 169 F7
London Heathrow ✕ (LHR) U.K. 51°28N 0°27W 125 B1
London Mills U.S.A. 40°43N 90°11W 310 D6
London Stansted ✕ (STN) U.K. 51°54N 0°14E 169 F8
London Zoo U.K. 51°31N 0°9W 125 A3
Londonderry U.K. 55°0N 7°20W 166 B4
Londonderry □ U.K. 55°0N 7°20W 166 B4
Londonderry, C. Australia 13°45S 126°55E 278 B4
Londonderry, I. Chile 55°0S 71°0W 336 E2
Londres Argentina 27°46S 67°7W 334 B2
Londrina Brazil 23°18S 51°10W 335 A5
Londuimbale Angola 12°15S 15°19E 265 E3
Lone Pine U.S.A. 36°36N 118°4W 306 J8
Lonely Mine Zimbabwe 19°30S 28°49E 271 A4
Long, Î. Martinique 14°36N 60°51W 322 j
Long Akah Malaysia 3°19N 114°47E 235 B4
Long B. N.S.W., Australia 33°59S 151°15E 139 B2
Long B. Cornwall, Jamaica 18°20N 78°20W 320 a
Long B. S.C., U.S.A. 33°35N 78°45W 315 E15
Long Beach Calif., U.S.A. 33°46N 118°11W 307 M8
Long Beach N.Y., U.S.A. 40°35N 73°39W 313 F11
Long Beach Wash., U.S.A. 46°21N 124°3W 306 D2
Long Branch Ont., Canada 43°35N 79°31W 141 B1
Long Branch N.J., U.S.A. 40°18N 74°0W 313 F11
Long Cay Bahamas 25°6N 77°22W 153 b
Long Creek U.S.A. 44°43N 119°6W 304 D4
Long Ditton U.K. 51°22N 0°19W 125 B2
Long Eaton U.K. 52°53N 1°15W 168 E6
Long I. Antigua & B. 17°8N 61°45W 322 b
Long I. Queens., Australia 20°22S 148°51E 280 b
Long I. Bahamas 23°20N 75°10W 321 B4
Long I. Nunavut, Canada 54°50N 79°20W 298 B4
Long I. Cork, Ireland 51°30N 9°34W 166 E2
Long I. Papua N. G. 5°20S 147°5E 286 C4
Long I. N.Y., U.S.A. 40°45N 73°30W 313 F11
Long Island City U.S.A. 40°45N 73°56W 132 B2
Long Island Sd. U.S.A. 41°10N 73°0W 313 E12
Long L. Ont., Canada 49°30N 86°50W 298 C2
Long L. N.Y., U.S.A. 44°0N 74°23W 313 C10
Long Lake U.S.A. 43°58N 74°25W 313 C10
Long Mountain Mauritius 20°8S 57°33E 272 e
Long Point Canada 42°34N 80°25W 312 D4
Long Point B. Canada 42°40N 80°10W 312 D4
Long Prairie U.S.A. 45°59N 94°52W 308 C6
Long Prairie → U.S.A. 46°20N 94°36W 308 B6
Long Pt. Bahamas 25°1N 77°20W 153 b
Long Pt. Ont., Canada 42°35N 80°2W 312 D4
Long Pt. Ont., Canada 43°56N 76°53W 313 C8
Long Pt. Otago, N.Z. 46°34S 169°36E 285 G4
Long Range Mts. Canada 49°30N 57°30W 299 C8
Long Reef Australia 14°1S 125°48E 278 B4
Long Sault Canada 45°2N 74°53W 313 A10
Long Str. = Longa, Proliv Russia 70°0N 175°0E 215 C18
Long Street Cape Town, S. Africa 118 c2
Long Thanh Vietnam 10°47N 106°57E 237 G6
Long Xian China 34°55N 106°55E 226 G4
Long Xuyen Vietnam 10°19N 105°28E 237 G5
Longa Angola 14°42S 18°32E 265 E3
Longa Greece 36°53N 21°55E 204 E3
Longa → Angola 10°14S 13°29E 265 E2
Longa, Proliv Russia 70°0N 175°0E 215 C18
Longa Mavinga △ Angola 16°20S 20°15E 265 F4
Longagung Indonesia 2°16N 115°16E 235 B5
Long'an China 23°10N 107°40E 228 F6
Longana Vanuatu 15°18S 168°0E 287 E5
Longarone Italy 46°16N 12°18E 199 B9
Longbenton U.K. 55°1N 1°31W 168 B6
Longberang Indonesia 3°43N 116°7E 235 B5
Longbia Indonesia 2°37N 116°42E 235 B5
Longboat Key U.S.A. 27°23N 82°39W 317 H7
Longboh Indonesia 0°52N 115°1E 235 B5
Longburn N.Z. 40°23S 175°35E 284 G4
Longchamp, Hippodrome de France 48°51N 2°13E 134 A2
Longchang China 29°18N 105°15E 228 C5
Longchuan Guangdong, China 24°5N 115°17E 229 E10
Longchuan Yunnan, China 24°23N 97°58E 228 E1
Longde China 35°30N 106°20E 226 G4
Longdenville Trin. & Tob. 10°31N 61°23W 323 t
Longeau-Percey France 47°47N 5°20E 173 E12
Longford Tas., Australia 41°32S 147°3E 281 G4
Longford Longf., Ireland 53°43N 7°49W 166 C4
Longford □ Ireland 53°42N 7°45W 166 C4
Longfort, An = Longford Ireland 53°43N 7°49W 166 C4
Longgan Shan China 42°19N 126°30E 224 A3
Longhai China 24°25N 117°46E 229 E11
Longhua Guangdong, China 22°39N 114°0E 219 a
Longhua Hebei, China 41°18N 117°45E 227 D9
Longhua Pagoda China 31°10N 121°26E 138 B1
Longhua Park China 31°10N 121°26E 138 B1
Longhui China 27°7N 111°2E 229 D8
Longido Tanzania 2°43S 36°42E 268 C4
Longiram Indonesia 0°5S 115°45E 235 C5
Longjela Indonesia 2°28N 115°28E 235 B5
Longjing China 42°46N 129°25E 227 C15
Longkou Jiangxi, China 26°8N 115°10E 229 D10

Longkou Shandong, China 37°40N 120°18E 227 F11
Longlac Canada 49°45N 86°25W 298 C2
Longli China 26°25N 106°58E 228 D6
Longlin China 24°47N 105°20E 228 E5
Longling China 24°37N 98°39E 228 E2
Longmeadow U.S.A. 42°3N 72°34W 313 D12
Longmen China 23°40N 114°18E 229 F10
Longmen Shiku China 34°28N 112°28E 226 G7
Longming China 22°59N 107°7E 228 F6
Longmont U.S.A. 40°10N 105°6W 304 F11
Longnan China 24°55N 114°47E 229 E10
Longnawan Indonesia 1°51N 114°55E 235 B4
Longobucco Italy 39°27N 16°37E 201 C9
Longoni, B. de Mayotte 12°41S 45°8E 272 b
Longonot △ Kenya 0°55S 36°28E 266 E4
Longos Greece 39°16N 20°7E 206 C10
Longquan China 28°7N 119°10E 229 C12
Longreach Australia 23°28S 144°14E 280 C3
Longshan China 29°29N 109°25E 228 C7
Longsheng China 25°48N 110°0E 229 E8
Longtan = Lung'tan Taiwan 24°52N 121°12E 225 B3
Longtan Dam China 25°0N 107°0E 228 E6
Longtan Hu ➔ China 39°51N 116°24E 114 B2
Longué-Jumelles France 47°22N 0°8W 172 E6
Longue-Pointe Canada 45°35N 73°31W 130 A2
Longueau France 49°52N 2°21E 173 C9
Longueuil Canada 45°31N 73°29W 130 A3
Longuy Cameroon 3°5N 9°58E 264 B1
Longuyon France 49°27N 5°35E 173 C12
Longvic France 47°17N 5°4E 173 E12
Longview Tex., U.S.A. 32°30N 94°44W 314 E7
Longview Wash., U.S.A. 46°8N 122°57W 306 D4
Longwood St. Helena 15°57S 5°41W 153 h
Longwood Fla., U.S.A. 28°42N 81°21W 317 G8
Longwy France 49°30N 5°46E 173 C12
Longxi China 34°53N 104°40E 226 G3
Longxue Dao China 22°41N 113°38E 219 a
Longyan China 25°10N 117°0E 229 E11
Longyearbyen Svalbard 78°13N 15°40E 150 B8
Longyou China 29°1N 119°8E 229 C12
Longzhou China 22°22N 106°50E 228 F6
Loni India 28°45N 77°17E 120 A2
Lonigo Italy 45°23N 11°23E 199 C8
Löningen Germany 52°44N 7°46E 178 C3
Lonja ➔ Croatia 45°22N 16°40E 199 C13
Lonkala Dem. Rep. of the Congo 4°37S 23°14E 265 C4
Lonkin Burma 25°39N 96°22E 241 C6
Lonoke U.S.A. 34°47N 91°54W 314 D9
Lonquimay Chile 38°26S 71°14W 336 A2
Lons-le-Saunier France 46°40N 5°31E 173 F12
Lönsboda Sweden 56°24N 14°20E 163 H8
Lønset Norway 62°46N 7°24E 164 B4
Lonton Burma 25°6N 96°17E 241 C6
Looc Phil. 12°15N 121°59E 232 E3
Looe U.K. 50°22N 4°28W 169 G3
Loogootee U.S.A. 38°41N 86°55W 311 F10
Lookout, C. Canada 55°18N 83°56W 298 A3
Lookout, C. N.C., U.S.A. 34°35N 76°32W 315 D16
Loolmalasin Tanzania 3°0S 35°53E 268 C4
Loon ➔ Alta., Canada 57°8N 115°3W 296 B5
Loon ➔ Man., Canada 55°53N 101°59W 297 B8
Loon Lake Canada 54°2N 109°10W 297 C7
Loongana Australia 30°52S 127°5E 279 F4
Loop, The Chicago, U.S.A. 119 c1
Loop Hd. Ireland 52°34N 9°56W 166 D2
Lop China 37°3N 80°11E 217 E10
Lop Nor = Lop Nur China 40°20N 90°10E 217 D12
Lop Nur China 40°20N 90°10E 217 D12
Lopare Bos.-H. 44°39N 18°46E 182 F3
Lopatin Russia 43°50N 47°35E 191 J8
Lopatina, Gora Russia 50°47N 143°10E 215 D15
Lopatino = Volzhsk Russia 55°57N 48°23E 190 C9
Lopatka, Mys Russia 50°52N 156°40E 215 D16
Lopaye South Sudan 6°37N 33°40E 257 F3
Lopburi Thailand 14°48N 100°37E 236 E3
Lopé-Okanda △ Gabon 0°45S 11°34E 264 C2
Lopevi Vanuatu 16°30S 168°21E 287 F6
Lopez Phil. 13°53N 122°15E 232 E4
Lopez Pa., U.S.A. 41°27N 76°20W 313 E8
Lopez, C. Gabon 0°47S 8°40E 264 C1
López de Filippis = Mariscal Estigarribia Paraguay 22°3S 60°40W 334 A3
Lopinot Trin. & Tob. 10°41N 61°19W 323 t
Lopori ➔ Dem. Rep. of the Congo 1°14N 19°49E 264 B3
Lopphavet Norway 70°27N 21°15E 160 A19
Lora Norway 62°8N 8°45E 164 B5
Lora ➔ Afghan. 31°35N 66°32E 240 C2
Lora ➔ Oppland, Norway 62°8N 8°42E 164 B5
Lora, Hāmūn-i- Pakistan 29°38N 64°58E 240 C2
Lora Cr. ➔ Australia 28°10S 135°22E 281 D2
Lora del Río Spain 37°39N 5°33W 195 H5
Lorain U.S.A. 41°28N 82°11W 312 E2
Loraine U.S.A. 40°9N 91°13W 310 D5
Loralai Pakistan 30°20N 68°41E 242 D3
Lorca Spain 37°41N 1°42W 197 H3
Lord Howe I. Pac. Oc. 31°33S 159°6E 277 G10
Lord Howe Rise Pac. Oc. 30°0S 162°30E 277 H12
Lord Howe Seamount Chain Pac. Oc. 28°0S 159°0E 277 F10
Lord Loughborough I. Burma 10°25N 97°54E 237 G1
Lord's Cricket Ground U.K. 51°31N 0°10W 125 A2
Lordsburg U.S.A. 32°21N 108°43W 305 K9
Lorengau Papua N. G. 2°1S 147°15E 286 B4
Lorestān □ Iran 33°30N 48°40E 247 C6
Loreto Bolivia 15°13S 64°40W 331 D5
Loreto Brazil 7°5S 45°10W 332 C2
Loreto Marche, Italy 43°26N 13°36E 199 E10
Loreto Piemonte, Italy 45°29N 9°12E 128 B2
Loreto Baja Calif. S., Mexico 26°0N 111°21W 318 B2
Loreto Surigao N., Phil. 10°21N 125°34E 233 F5
Loreto □ Peru 5°0S 75°0W 328 E3
Lorgues France 43°28N 6°22E 175 E10
Lorhosso = Loropéni Burkina Faso 10°17N 3°38W 262 C4
Lorian Swamp Kenya 0°40N 39°35E 267 D4
Lorica Colombia 9°14N 75°49W 328 B2
Lorient Morbihan, France 47°45N 3°23W 172 E3
Lorient St. Barts 17°54N 62°49W 322 a
Lorimor U.S.A. 41°8N 94°3W 310 C2
Lőrinci Hungary 47°44N 19°41E 182 C4
Lormi India 22°17N 81°41E 243 H9
Lorn U.K. 56°26N 5°10W 167 E3
Lorn, Firth of U.K. 56°20N 5°40W 167 E3
Lorne Australia 38°33S 143°59E 282 E5
Loronyo South Sudan 4°38N 32°38E 257 G3
Loropéni Burkina Faso 10°17N 3°38W 262 C4
Lorovouno Cyprus 35°8N 32°36E 207 E8
Lörrach Germany 47°36N 7°40E 179 H3
Lorrain ➔ Martinique 14°50N 61°3W 322 j
Lorraine = Baker U.S.A. 46°22N 104°17W 304 C11
Lorraine □ France 48°53N 6°0E 173 D13
Lorraine ⌂ France 48°55N 5°50E 173 D12
Los Sweden 61°45N 15°10E 162 C9
Los, Îles de Guinea 9°30N 13°50W 262 D2
Los Alamos Calif., U.S.A. 34°44N 120°17W 307 L6
Los Alamos N. Mex., U.S.A. 35°53N 106°19W 305 J10
Los Alcornocales ⌂ Spain 36°21N 5°32W 195 J5
Los Alerces △ Argentina 42°55S 71°55W 336 B2
Los Altos U.S.A. 37°23N 122°7W 306 H4
Los Andes Chile 32°50S 70°40W 334 C1
Los Angeles Chile 37°28S 72°23W 334 D1
Los Angeles Calif., U.S.A. 34°4N 118°15W 126 B3
Los Angeles Aqueduct U.S.A. 35°22N 118°5W 307 K9
Los Angeles Int. ✈ (LAX) U.S.A. 33°57N 118°25W 126 C2
Los Antiguos Argentina 46°35S 71°40W 336 C2
Los Bagres Venezuela 10°57N 63°58W 329 a
Los Banos U.S.A. 37°4N 120°51W 306 H6
Los Barrios Spain 36°11N 5°30W 195 J5
Los Blancos Argentina 23°40S 62°30W 334 A3
Los Cabos Int. ✈ (SJD) Mexico 23°9N 109°43W 318 C3
Los Cardones △ Argentina 25°8S 65°55W 334 B2
Los Cerrillos ✈ (ULC) Chile 33°29S 70°42W 137 B1
Los Chiles Costa Rica 11°2N 84°43W 320 D3
Los Corrales de Buelna Spain 43°16N 4°4W 194 B6
Los Cristianos Canary Is. 28°3N 16°42W 153 e1
Los Frailes, I. Venezuela 11°11N 63°44W 329 a
Los Gallardos Spain 37°10N 1°57W 197 H3
Los Gallos Pt. Trin. & Tob. 10°5N 61°55W 323 t
Los Gatos U.S.A. 37°14N 121°59W 306 H5
Los Glaciares △ Argentina 50°0S 73°55W 336 C2
Los Gómez Venezuela 10°57N 64°4W 329 a
Los Haitises △ Dom. Rep. 19°4N 69°36W 321 C6
Los Hermanos, Is. Venezuela 11°45N 64°25W 321 D7
Los Huemules △ Chile 46°10S 73°23W 336 C2
Los Islotes Canary Is. 29°4N 13°44W 153 e2
Los Katíos △ Colombia 7°50N 77°10W 328 B2
Los Lagos Chile 39°51S 72°50W 336 A2
Los Llanos de Aridane Canary Is. 28°38N 17°54W 153 e1
Los Loros Chile 27°50S 70°6W 334 B1
Los Lunas U.S.A. 34°48N 106°44W 305 J10
Los Menucos Argentina 40°50S 68°10W 336 B3
Los Mochis Mexico 25°45N 108°57W 318 B3
Los Monegros Spain 41°29N 0°13W 196 D4
Los Monos Argentina 46°1S 69°36W 336 C3
Los Muermos Chile 41°24S 73°29W 336 B2
Los Nevados △ Colombia 4°41N 75°21W 328 C2
Los Nietos Spain 37°39N 0°47W 197 H4
Los Nietos Calif., U.S.A. 33°57N 118°4W 126 C4
Los Olivos Lima, Peru 11°59S 77°5W 124 A2
Los Olivos Calif., U.S.A. 34°40N 120°7W 307 L6
Los Palacios Cuba 22°35N 83°15W 320 B3
Los Palacios y Villafranca Spain 37°10N 5°55W 195 H5
Los Queñes Chile 35°1S 70°48W 334 D1
Los Remedios △ Mexico 19°28N 99°17W 128 B1
Los Reyes Mexico 19°21N 99°1W 128 B2
Los Reyes de Salgado Mexico 19°35N 102°29W 318 D4
Los Ríos □ Ecuador 1°30S 79°25W 328 D2
Los Roques, Is. Venezuela 11°50N 66°45W 321 D6
Los Santos de Maimona Spain 38°27N 6°22W 195 G4
Los Teques Venezuela 10°21N 67°2W 328 A4
Los Testigos, Is. Venezuela 11°23N 63°6W 329 A5
Los Vilos Chile 32°10S 71°30W 334 C1
Los Yébenes Spain 39°36N 3°55W 195 F7
Loshan = Leshan China 29°33N 103°41E 228 C4
Losice Poland 52°13N 22°43E 185 F9
Lošinj Croatia 44°30N 14°30E 199 D11
Losinyy Ostrov △ Russia 55°50N 37°45E 129 A3
Loskop Dam S. Africa 25°23S 29°20E 271 C4
Løsning Denmark 55°48N 9°42E 163 J3
Losombo Dem. Rep. of the Congo 1°2N 19°4E 264 B3
Lossiemouth U.K. 57°42N 3°17W 167 D5
Lossnen Sweden 62°26N 12°45E 162 B6
Lostwithiel U.K. 50°24N 4°41W 169 G3
Losuia Papua N. G. 8°30S 151°4E 286 E6
Lot Belgium 50°46N 4°16E 116 B1
Lot □ France 44°39N 1°40E 174 D5
Lot ➔ France 44°18N 0°20E 174 D4
Lot-et-Garonne □ France 44°22N 0°30E 174 D4
Lota Chile 37°5S 73°10W 334 D1
Lotagipi Swamp Kenya 4°36N 34°55E 257 G3
Løten Norway 60°51N 11°21E 164 D8
Lotfābād Iran 37°32N 59°20E 247 B8
Lothair S. Africa 26°22S 30°27E 271 C5
Loto Dem. Rep. of the Congo 2°48S 22°30E 264 C4
Lotoi ➔ Dem. Rep. of the Congo 1°35S 18°30E 264 C3
Lotorp Sweden 58°44N 15°50E 163 F9
Lötschbergtunnel Switz. 46°26N 7°43E 179 J3
Lotta ➔ Europe 68°42N 31°6E 160 B24
Lottefors Sweden 61°25N 16°24E 162 C10
Löttorp Sweden 57°10N 17°0E 163 G11
Lotung Taiwan 24°41N 121°46E 225 B3
Lotus River S. Africa 34°4S 18°31E 118 B2
Lotus Temple India 28°33N 77°15E 120 B2
Lötzen = Giżycko Poland 54°2N 21°48E 184 D8
Lou I. Papua N. G. 2°25S 147°22E 286 B4
Loubière Dominica 15°16N 61°3W 323 k
Loubomo Congo 4°9S 12°47E 264 C2
Loudéac France 48°11N 2°47W 172 D4
Loudi China 27°42N 111°59E 229 D8
Loudima Congo 4°6S 13°5E 264 C2
Loudonville U.S.A. 40°38N 82°14W 312 F2
Loudun France 47°3N 0°5E 172 E7
Loue ➔ France 47°1N 5°28E 173 E12
Louga Senegal 15°45N 16°5W 262 B1
Louga □ Senegal 15°20N 15°35W 262 B1
Loughborough U.K. 52°47N 1°11W 168 E6
Lougheed I. Canada 77°26N 105°6W 295 B10
Loughlinstown Ireland 53°15N 6°7W 120 B3
Loughman U.S.A. 28°14N 81°34W 317 G8
Loughrea Ireland 53°12N 8°33W 166 C3
Loughros More B. Ireland 54°48N 8°32W 166 B3
Louhans France 46°38N 5°12E 173 F12
Louis Armstrong New Orleans Int. ✈ (MSY) U.S.A. 30°0N 90°15W 131 B1
Louis Armstrong Park New Orleans, U.S.A. 131 a2
Louis-Gentil = Youssoufia Morocco 32°16N 8°31W 260 B3
Louis Trichardt S. Africa 23°1S 29°43E 271 B4
Louis XIV, Pte. Canada 54°37N 79°45W 298 B4
Louisa U.S.A. 38°7N 82°36W 309 F12
Louisbourg Canada 45°55N 60°0W 299 C8
Louisburg U.S.A. 38°37N 94°41W 310 F2
Louisburgh Ireland 53°46N 9°49W 166 C2
Louise, L. U.S.A. 28°28N 81°32W 133 B1
Louise I. Canada 52°55N 131°50W 296 C2
Louiseville Canada 46°20N 72°56W 298 C5
Louisiade Arch. Papua N. G. 11°10S 153°0E 286 F7
Louisiana U.S.A. 39°27N 91°3W 310 E8
Louisiana □ U.S.A. 30°50N 92°0W 314 F9
Louisiana Superdome = Mercedes-Benz Superdome New Orleans, U.S.A. 131 b1
Louisville Ala., U.S.A. 31°47N 85°33W 316 D4
Louisville Ga., U.S.A. 33°0N 82°25W 316 B7
Louisville Ill., U.S.A. 38°46N 88°30W 311 F8
Louisville Ky., U.S.A. 38°15N 85°46W 311 F11
Louisville Miss., U.S.A. 33°7N 89°3W 315 E10
Louisville Ohio, U.S.A. 40°50N 81°16W 312 F3
Louisville Ridge Pac. Oc. 31°0S 172°30W 288 L10
Loukoléla Congo 1°4S 17°10E 264 C3
Loukouo Congo 3°38S 14°39E 264 C2
Loulay France 46°3N 0°30W 174 B3
Loulé Portugal 37°9N 8°0W 195 H3
Loulouni Mali 10°54N 5°36W 262 C3
Loum Cameroon 4°42N 9°44E 264 B1
Louny Czech Rep. 50°20N 13°48E 180 A6
Loup City U.S.A. 41°17N 98°58W 308 E4
Loups Marins, Lacs des Canada 56°30N 73°45W 298 A5
Lourdes France 43°6N 0°3W 174 E3
Lourdes-de-Blanc-Sablon Canada 51°24N 57°12W 299 B8
Lourenço Brazil 2°30N 51°40W 329 C7
Lourenço Marques = Maputo Mozam. 25°58S 32°32E 271 C5
Loures Portugal 38°49N 9°10W 126 A1
Lourinhã Portugal 39°14N 9°17W 195 F1
Louros Greece 39°3N 20°47E 207 A2
Louroujina Cyprus 35°0N 33°28E 207 F9
Lousã Portugal 40°7N 8°14W 194 E2
Louta Burkina Faso 13°30N 3°10W 262 C4
Louth N.S.W., Australia 30°30S 145°8E 283 A6
Louth Louth, Ireland 53°58N 6°32W 166 C5
Louth Lincs., U.K. 53°22N 0°1W 168 D7
Louth □ Ireland 53°56N 6°34W 166 C5
Louth B. Australia 34°33S 135°56E 282 C1
Loutra Edipsou Greece 38°54N 23°2E 204 C5
Loutra Kyllinis Greece 37°52N 21°7E 207 D3
Loutraki Greece 37°58N 22°57E 204 D4
Loutropoli Thermis Greece 39°11N 26°29E 205 B8
Louvain = Leuven Belgium 50°52N 4°42E 170 D4
Louvale U.S.A. 32°10N 84°50W 316 C5
Louveciennes France 48°51N 2°8E 134 A1
Louviers France 49°12N 1°10E 172 C8
Louvre, Musée du Paris, France 134 b4
Louvre, Palais du Paris, France 134 b4
Louwsburg S. Africa 27°37S 31°7E 271 C5
Lovat ➔ Russia 58°14N 31°28E 188 C6
Lovćen Montenegro 42°23N 18°51E 202 D2
Lovćen △ Montenegro 42°20N 18°50E 202 D2
Lovech Bulgaria 43°8N 24°42E 203 C8
Lovech □ Bulgaria 43°0N 24°45E 203 D8
Loveland Colo., U.S.A. 40°24N 105°5W 304 F11
Loveland Ohio, U.S.A. 39°16N 84°16W 311 E12
Lovell U.S.A. 44°50N 108°24W 304 D9
Lovelock U.S.A. 40°11N 118°28W 304 F4
Lóvere Italy 45°49N 10°4E 198 C7
Lovers Leap Jamaica 17°52N 77°39W 320 a
Loves Park U.S.A. 42°19N 89°3W 310 B7
Lövestad Sweden 55°40N 13°54E 163 J7
Loviisa Finland 60°28N 26°12E 188 B4
Lovilia U.S.A. 41°8N 92°55W 310 C3
Lovina Indonesia 8°9S 115°1E 231 J18
Loving U.S.A. 32°17N 104°6W 305 K11
Lovington Ill., U.S.A. 39°43N 88°38W 311 E8
Lovington N. Mex., U.S.A. 32°57N 103°21W 305 K12
Lovisa = Loviisa Finland 60°28N 26°12E 188 B4
Lovosice Czech Rep. 50°30N 14°2E 180 A7
Lovran Croatia 45°18N 14°15E 199 C11
Lovrin Romania 45°58N 20°48E 182 E5
Lövstabruk Sweden 60°25N 17°53E 162 D11
Lövstabukten Sweden 60°35N 17°45E 162 D11
Lóvua Lunda Norte, Angola 7°19S 20°12E 265 D4
Lóvua Moxico, Angola 11°33S 23°35E 265 E4
Lóvua ➔ Dem. Rep. of the Congo 6°6S 20°37E 265 D4
Low, L. Canada 52°29N 76°17W 298 B4
Low B. Antigua & B. 17°39N 61°51W 322 b
Low Pt. Australia 32°25S 127°25E 279 F4
Low Tatra = Nízké Tatry Slovak Rep. 48°55N 19°30E 181 C12
Lowa Dem. Rep. of the Congo 1°25S 25°47E 268 C2
Lowa ➔ Dem. Rep. of the Congo 1°24S 25°51E 268 C2
Lowden U.S.A. 41°52N 90°56W 310 C6
Lowell Ind., U.S.A. 41°18N 87°25W 311 C9
Lowell Mass., U.S.A. 42°38N 71°19W 313 D13
Lowell Mich., U.S.A. 42°56N 85°20W 311 B11
Lowellville U.S.A. 41°2N 80°32W 312 E4
Löwen = Lewin Brzeski Poland 50°45N 17°37E 185 H4
Löwen ➔ Namibia 26°51S 18°17E 270 C2
Löwenberg = Lwówek Śląski Poland 51°7N 15°38E 185 G2
Löwenstadt = Brzeziny Poland 51°49N 19°42E 185 G6
Lower Alkali L. U.S.A. 41°16N 120°2W 304 F3
Lower Arrow L. Canada 49°40N 118°5W 296 D5
Lower Austria = Niederösterreich □ Austria 48°25N 15°40E 180 C8
Lower B. U.S.A. 40°32N 74°5W 132 C1
Lower California = Baja California Mexico 31°10N 115°12W 318 A1
Lower East Side New York, U.S.A. 132 e2
Lower Glenelg △ Australia 38°4S 141°41E 282 E4
Lower Hutt N.Z. 41°10S 174°55E 284 H3
Lower Kalskag U.S.A. 61°31N 160°22W 303 F7
Lower Lake U.S.A. 38°55N 122°37W 306 G4
Lower Manhattan New York, U.S.A. 132 e1
Lower Manitou L. Canada 49°15N 93°0W 297 D10
Lower Manzanilla Trin. & Tob. 10°31N 61°3W 323 t
Lower New York B. = Lower B. U.S.A. 40°32N 74°5W 132 C1
Lower Paia U.S.A. 20°55N 156°23W 302 C5
Lower Peirce Res. Singapore 1°22N 103°49E 138 A2
Lower Post Canada 59°58N 128°30W 296 B3
Lower Red L. U.S.A. 47°58N 95°0W 308 B6
Lower Saxony = Niedersachsen □ Germany 52°50N 9°0E 178 C4
Lower Tunguska = Tunguska, Nizhnyaya ➔ Russia 65°48N 88°4E 215 C9
Lower Zambezi △ Zambia 15°25S 29°40E 269 F2
Lowestoft U.K. 52°29N 1°45E 169 E9
Lowgar □ Afghan. 34°0N 69°0E 240 B3
Łowicz Poland 52°6N 19°55E 185 F6
Lowly, Pt. Australia 33°0S 137°46E 282 B2
Lowry City U.S.A. 38°8N 93°44W 310 F3
Lowther I. Canada 74°33N 97°30W 295 C12
Lowville U.S.A. 43°47N 75°29W 313 C9
Loxton S. Austral., Australia 34°28S 140°31E 282 C4
Loxton Northern Cape, S. Africa 31°30S 22°22E 270 D3
Loyalton U.S.A. 39°41N 120°14W 306 F6
Loyalty Is. = Loyauté, Îs. N. Cal. 20°50S 166°30E 288 d
Loyang = Luoyang China 34°40N 112°26E 226 G7
Loyauté, Îs. N. Cal. 20°50S 166°30E 288 d
Loyev = Loyew Belarus 51°56N 30°46E 177 C16
Loyew Belarus 51°56N 30°46E 177 C16
Loyola Univ. U.S.A. 42°0N 87°39W 119 B3
Loyoro Uganda 3°22N 34°14E 268 B3
Lož Slovenia 45°43N 14°30E 199 C11
Lozère □ France 44°35N 3°30E 174 D7
Loznica Serbia 44°32N 19°12E 202 B3
Lozova Ukraine 49°0N 36°20E 189 H9
Ltalaltuma ⊙ Australia 23°57S 132°25E 278 D5
Lu India 26°58N 95°14E 241 B5
Lü Shan China 29°30N 115°55E 229 C10
Lü Shan △ China 29°26N 115°52E 229 C10
Lu Verne U.S.A. 42°55N 94°5W 310 B2
Lu Wo China 22°33N 114°6E 219 a
Lu Xun, Tomb of China 31°17N 121°29E 138 B1
Lu Xun Museum Beijing, China 114 b1
Lu Xun Park China 31°17N 121°28E 138 B1
Lua ➔ Dem. Rep. of the Congo 2°46N 18°26E 264 B3
Lua Makiki U.S.A. 20°33N 156°37W 302 C5
Luachimo Angola 7°23S 20°48E 265 D4
Luacano Angola 11°15S 21°37E 265 E4
Luakan = India 24°44N 85°1E 243 G11
Lualaba ➔ Dem. Rep. of the Congo 0°26N 25°20E 264 B4
Luale Dem. Rep. of the Congo 1°9N 23°5E 264 B4
Luambe △ Zambia 12°30S 32°15E 269 E3
Luampa Zambia 15°4S 24°20E 265 F4
Lu'an China 31°45N 116°29E 229 B11
Luan Chau Vietnam 21°38N 103°24E 228 G4
Luan He ➔ China 39°20N 119°5E 227 E10
Luan Xian China 39°40N 118°40E 227 E10
Luancheng Guangxi Zhuangzu, China 22°48N 108°55E 228 F7
Luancheng Hebei, China 37°53N 114°40E 226 F8
Luanco Spain 43°37N 5°48W 194 B5
Luanda Angola 8°50S 13°15E 265 D2
Luando ➔ Angola 10°21S 16°27E 265 E3
Luando ⌂ Angola 11°0S 17°32E 265 E3
Luang, Doi Thailand 18°30N 101°15E 236 C3
Luang, Thale Thailand 7°30N 100°15E 237 J3
Luang Nam Tha Laos 20°58N 101°30E 228 G3
Luang Prabang Laos 19°52N 102°10E 228 H4
Luanginga ➔ Zambia 15°11S 22°56E 265 F4
Luangwa Zambia 15°35S 30°16E 269 F3
Luangwa ➔ Zambia 14°25S 30°25E 269 E3
Luangwa Valley Zambia 13°30S 31°30E 269 E3
Luangwe = Loange ➔ Dem. Rep. of the Congo 4°17S 20°2E 265 C4
Luania-Bubi Dem. Rep. of the Congo 7°28S 24°49E 265 D4
Luanne China 40°55N 117°40E 227 D9
Luanping China 40°53N 117°23E 227 D9
Luanshya Zambia 13°3S 28°28E 269 E2
Luapula □ Zambia 11°0S 29°0E 269 E2
Luapula ➔ Africa 9°26S 28°33E 269 D2
Luar, Danau Indonesia 0°55N 112°15E 235 B4
Luarca Spain 43°32N 6°32W 194 B4
Luashi Dem. Rep. of the Congo 10°50S 23°36E 265 E4
Luatamba Angola 12°6S 20°19E 265 E4
Luatira Angola 12°52S 17°14E 265 E3
Luau Angola 10°40S 22°10E 265 E4
Luba Phil. 17°19N 120°42E 232 C3
Lubaczów Poland 50°10N 23°8E 185 H10
Lubalo Angola 9°10S 19°15E 265 D3
Lubamiti Dem. Rep. of the Congo 2°28S 17°47E 264 C3
Lubań Poland 51°5N 15°15E 185 G2
Lubana, Ozero = Lubānas Ezers Latvia 56°45N 27°0E 188 D4
Lubānas Ezers Latvia 56°45N 27°0E 188 D4
Lubang Phil. 13°52N 120°7E 232 E3
Lubang Is. Phil. 13°50N 120°12E 232 E3
Lubango Angola 14°55S 13°30E 265 E2
Lubao Dem. Rep. of the Congo 5°17S 25°42E 265 D5
Lubao Phil. 14°56N 120°36E 232 D3
Lübars Germany 52°37N 13°21E 115 A3
Lubartów Poland 51°28N 22°42E 185 G9
Lubawa Poland 53°30N 19°48E 184 E6
Lübbecke Germany 52°18N 8°37E 178 C4
Lübben Germany 51°56N 13°54E 178 D9
Lübbenau Germany 51°52N 13°57E 178 D9
Lubbock U.S.A. 33°35N 101°51W 314 E4
Lübeck Germany 53°52N 10°40E 178 B6
Lübecker Bucht Germany 54°3N 10°54E 178 A6
Lubefu Dem. Rep. of the Congo 4°47S 24°27E 265 C4
Lubefu ➔ Dem. Rep. of the Congo 4°10S 23°0E 265 C4
Lubelskie □ Poland 51°20N 22°50E 185 G9
Lüben = Lubin Poland 51°24N 16°11E 185 G3
Lubero = Luofu Dem. Rep. of the Congo 0°10S 29°15E 268 C2
Luberon ⌂ France 43°52N 5°25E 175 E9
Lubersac France 45°26N 1°23E 174 C5
Lubicon L. Canada 56°23N 115°56W 296 B5
Lubień Kujawski Poland 52°23N 19°9E 185 F6
Lubilash ➔ Dem. Rep. of the Congo 6°2S 23°45E 265 D4
Lubin Poland 51°24N 16°11E 185 G3
Lublin Poland 51°12N 22°38E 185 G9
Lubliniec Poland 50°43N 18°45E 185 H5
Lubnān = Lebanon ■ Asia 34°0N 36°0E 250 E7
Lubnān, Jabal Lebanon 33°45N 35°40E 250 E6
Lubniewice Poland 52°31N 15°15E 185 F2
Lubny Ukraine 50°3N 32°58E 189 G7
Lubomierz Poland 51°1N 15°31E 185 G2
Luboń Poland 52°21N 16°51E 185 F3
Lubondaie Dem. Rep. of the Congo 8°1S 26°32E 265 D5
Lubongola Dem. Rep. of the Congo 2°35S 27°50E 268 C2
L'ubotín Slovak Rep. 49°17N 20°53E 181 B13
Lubraniec Poland 52°33N 18°50E 185 F5
Lubsko Poland 51°45N 14°57E 185 G1
Lübtheen Germany 53°18N 11°5E 178 B7
Lubuagan Phil. 17°21N 121°10E 232 C3
Lubudi Dem. Rep. of the Congo 6°51S 21°18E 265 D4
Lubudi ➔ Kasai-Occ., Dem. Rep. of the Congo 4°19S 20°23E 265 C4
Lubudi ➔ Katanga, Dem. Rep. of the Congo 9°0S 25°35E 265 D5
Lubuklinggau Indonesia 3°15S 102°55E 234 C2
Lubukpakam Indonesia 3°33N 98°52E 234 B1
Lubuksikaping Indonesia 0°10N 100°15E 234 B2
Lubumbashi Dem. Rep. of the Congo 11°40S 27°28E 269 E2
Lubunda Dem. Rep. of the Congo 5°12S 26°41E 265 D5
Lubungu Zambia 14°35S 26°24E 269 E2
Lubuskie □ Poland 52°10N 15°20E 185 F2
Lubutu Dem. Rep. of the Congo 0°45S 26°30E 268 C2
Luc-en-Diois France 44°36N 5°28E 175 D9
Lucala Angola 9°7S 15°58E 265 D3
Lucala ➔ Angola 9°38S 14°14E 265 D3
Lucan Ont., Canada 43°11N 81°24W 312 C3
Lucan Dublin, Ireland 53°22N 6°28W 166 C5
Lucania, Mt. Canada 61°1N 140°27W 294 E3
Lucapa Angola 8°25S 20°45E 265 D4
Lucas U.S.A. 41°2N 93°29W 310 C3
Lucas Channel = Main Channel Canada 45°21N 81°45W 312 A3
Lucban Phil. 14°6N 121°33E 232 D3
Lucca Italy 43°50N 10°29E 198 E7
Lucé France 48°26N 1°27E 172 D8
Luce Bay U.K. 54°45N 4°48W 167 G4
Lucea Jamaica 18°27N 78°10W 320 a
Lucedale U.S.A. 30°56N 88°35W 315 F10
Lucena Phil. 13°56N 121°37E 232 E3
Lucena Spain 37°27N 4°31W 195 H6
Lučenec Slovak Rep. 48°18N 19°42E 181 C12
Lucera Italy 41°30N 15°20E 201 A8
Lucerne = Lake Worth U.S.A. 26°37N 80°3W 317 J9
Lucerne = Luzern Switz. 47°3N 8°18E 179 H4
Lucerne U.S.A. 39°6N 122°48W 306 F4
Lucerne Valley U.S.A. 34°27N 116°57W 307 L10
Luchena ➔ Spain 37°44N 1°50W 197 H3
Lucheng China 36°20N 113°11E 226 F7
Lucheringo ➔ Mozam. 11°43S 36°17E 269 E4
Luchow = Luzhou China 28°52N 105°20E 228 C5
Lüchow Germany 52°58N 11°8E 178 C7
Luchu Taiwan 22°52N 120°15E 225 D2
Luchuan China 22°21N 110°12E 229 F8
Lucia U.S.A. 36°2N 121°33W 306 J5
Luciara Brazil 10°45S 50°34W 333 D1
Lucie ➔ Suriname 3°35N 57°38W 329 C6
Lucinda Australia 18°32S 146°20E 280 B4
Lucindale Australia 36°58S 140°26E 282 D4
Lucira Angola 14°0S 12°35E 265 E2
Luciras, B. das Angola 13°52S 12°31E 265 E2
Luckau Germany 51°50N 13°42E 178 D9
Luckenwalde Germany 52°5N 13°10E 178 C9
Luckey U.S.A. 41°27N 83°29W 311 C13
Luckhoff S. Africa 29°44S 24°43E 270 C3
Lucknow Ont., Canada 43°57N 81°31W 312 C3
Lucknow India 26°50N 81°0E 243 F9
Luçon France 46°28N 1°10W 174 B2
Lucusse Angola 12°32S 20°48E 265 E4
Lucy, L. U.S.A. 28°34N 81°29W 133 A2
Lüda = Dalian China 38°50N 121°40E 227 E11
Luda Kamchiya ➔ Bulgaria 43°3N 27°29E 203 C11
Ludbreg Croatia 46°15N 16°38E 199 B13
Lüdenscheid Germany 51°13N 7°37E 178 D3
Lüderitz Namibia 26°41S 15°8E 270 C2
Lüderitzbaai Namibia 26°36S 15°8E 270 C2
Ludhiana India 30°57N 75°56E 242 D6
Ludian China 27°10N 103°33E 228 D4
Luding Qiao China 29°53N 102°12E 228 C4
Lüdinghausen Germany 51°46N 7°26E 178 D3
Ludington U.S.A. 43°57N 86°27W 308 D10
Ludlow Shrops., U.K. 52°22N 2°42W 169 E5
Ludlow Calif., U.S.A. 34°43N 116°10W 307 L10
Ludlow Pa., U.S.A. 41°43N 78°56W 312 E6
Ludlow Vt., U.S.A. 43°24N 72°42W 313 C12
Ludowici U.S.A. 31°43N 81°45W 316 D8
Ludus Romania 46°29N 24°5E 183 D9
Ludvika Sweden 60°8N 15°14E 162 D9
Ludwigsburg Germany 48°53N 9°11E 179 G5
Ludwigsfeld Germany 48°12N 11°27E 131 A1
Ludwigsfelde Germany 52°17N 13°17E 178 C9
Ludwigshafen Germany 49°29N 8°26E 179 F4
Ludwigslust Germany 53°19N 11°30E 178 B7
Ludza Latvia 56°32N 27°43E 188 D4
Lue Australia 32°38S 149°50E 283 B8
Luebo Dem. Rep. of the Congo 5°21S 21°23E 265 D4
Lueki Dem. Rep. of the Congo 3°20S 25°48E 264 C5
Luena Angola 12°13S 19°51E 265 E3
Luena Dem. Rep. of the Congo 9°28S 25°43E 269 D2
Luena Zambia 10°40S 30°25E 269 E3
Luena ➔ Angola 12°30S 22°34E 265 E4
Luena ➔ Zambia 14°46S 23°20E 265 E4
Luena Flats Zambia 14°47S 23°17E 265 E4
Luengué ⌂ Angola 16°55S 19°55E 265 F3
Luenha = Ruenya ➔ Africa 16°24S 33°48E 269 F3
Luepa Venezuela 5°43N 61°31W 329 B5
Lueta ➔ Dem. Rep. of the Congo 7°4S 21°40E 265 D4
Luete ➔ Zambia 15°46S 23°10E 265 F4
Lüeyang China 33°22N 106°10E 228 A6
Lufeng Guangdong, China 22°57N 115°38E 229 F10
Lufeng Yunnan, China 25°0N 102°5E 228 E4
Lufico Angola 6°24S 13°23E 265 D2
Lufira ➔ Dem. Rep. of the Congo 9°30S 27°0E 269 D2
Lufkin U.S.A. 31°21N 94°44W 314 F7
Lufupa Dem. Rep. of the Congo 10°37S 24°56E 265 E4
Luga Russia 58°40N 29°55E 188 C5
Luga ➔ Russia 59°40N 28°18E 188 C5
Lugang = Lukang Taiwan 24°1N 120°22E 225 B2
Lugano Switz. 46°1N 8°57E 179 J4
Lugano, L. di Switz. 46°0N 9°0E 198 C6
Lugansk = Luhansk Ukraine 48°38N 39°15E 189 H10
Luganville Vanuatu 15°27S 167°10E 287 E5
Lugard's Falls Kenya 3°6S 38°41E 268 C4
Lugela Mozam. 16°25S 36°43E 269 F4
Lugenda ➔ Mozam. 11°25S 38°33E 269 E4
Lugh = Luuq Somalia 3°48N 42°34E 267 D5
Lugnaquilla Ireland 52°58N 6°28W 166 D5
Lugnvik Sweden 62°56N 17°55E 162 B11
Lugo Italy 44°25N 11°54E 199 D8
Lugo Spain 43°2N 7°35W 194 B3
Lugo □ Spain 43°0N 7°30W 194 C3
Lugoj Romania 45°42N 21°57E 182 E6
Lugovoy = Qulan Kazakhstan 42°55N 72°43E 214 E8
Lugu = Luku Taiwan 23°44N 120°45E 225 C2
Lugus I. Phil. 5°41N 120°50E 233 J3
Luhansk Ukraine 48°38N 39°15E 189 H10
Luhansk □ Ukraine 49°10N 38°40E 189 H10
Luhe China 32°19N 118°50E 229 A12
Luhe ➔ Germany 53°23N 10°12E 178 B6
Luhit ➔ India 27°48N 95°28E 241 B5
Luhu China 23°9N 113°16E 121 B2
Luhuo China 31°21N 100°48E 228 B3
Lui ➔ Angola 8°21S 17°33E 265 D3
Lui ➔ Zambia 16°18S 23°17E 265 F4
Luia Angola 8°10S 21°32E 265 D4
Luia ➔ Angola 8°32S 21°47E 265 D4
Luiana Angola 17°25S 22°59E 265 F4
Luiana ➔ Angola 17°24S 23°3E 265 F4
Luiana ⌂ Angola 16°55S 22°20E 265 F4
Luichow = Liuzhou China 24°22N 109°22E 228 E7
Luichow Pen. = Leizhou Bandao China 21°0N 110°0E 228 G7
Luikuei Taiwan 23°0N 120°38E 225 D2
Luilaka ➔ Dem. Rep. of the Congo 0°52S 20°12E 264 C4
Luimneach = Limerick Ireland 52°40N 8°37W 166 D3
Luing U.K. 56°14N 5°39W 167 E3
Luino Italy 45°59N 8°44E 198 C5
Luio ➔ Angola 13°17S 21°37E 265 E4
Luis Correia Brazil 3°0S 41°35W 332 B3
Luís Gonçalves Brazil 5°37S 50°25W 332 C1
Luitpold Coast Antarctica 78°30S 32°0W 151 D1
Luiza Dem. Rep. of the Congo 7°40S 22°30E 265 D4
Luizi Dem. Rep. of the Congo 6°0S 27°25E 268 D2
Luján Argentina 34°45S 59°5W 334 C4
Lujiang China 31°20N 117°15E 229 B11
Luk Chau = George I. Hong Kong, China 22°13N 114°7E 122 B2
Lukala Dem. Rep. of the Congo 5°31S 14°32E 265 D2
Lukang Taiwan 24°1N 120°22E 225 B2
Lukanga Bandundu, Dem. Rep. of the Congo 1°41S 18°9E 264 C3
Lukanga Équateur, Dem. Rep. of the Congo 1°0S 18°8E 264 C3
Lukanga Swamp Zambia 14°30S 27°40E 269 E2
Lukavac Bos.-H. 44°33N 18°32E 182 F3
Lukenie ➔ Dem. Rep. of the Congo 3°0S 18°50E 264 C3
Lŭki Bulgaria 41°50N 24°43E 203 E8
Lukk Libya 32°1N 24°26E 258 B4
Lukla Nepal 27°42N 86°43E 243 F12
Lukolela Équateur, Dem. Rep. of the Congo 1°10S 17°12E 264 C3
Lukolela Kasai-Or., Dem. Rep. of the Congo 5°23S 24°32E 265 D4
Lukosi Zimbabwe 18°30S 26°30E 269 F2
Lukovë Albania 39°59N 19°54E 202 G3
Lukovit Bulgaria 43°13N 24°11E 203 C8
Łuków Poland 51°55N 22°23E 185 G9
Lukoyanov Russia 55°2N 44°29E 190 C7
Luksefjell Norway 59°23N 9°34E 164 E6
Luku Taiwan 23°44N 120°45E 225 C2
Lukulu Zambia 14°23S 23°15E 265 E4
Lukuni Dem. Rep. of the Congo 5°50S 17°16E 265 D3
Lukusuzi △ Zambia 12°43S 32°36E 269 E3
Lula Dem. Rep. of the Congo 5°22S 16°2E 265 D3
Lulang Shan China 38°0N 111°55E 226 F6
Luleå Sweden 65°35N 22°10E 160 D20
Luleälven ➔ Sweden 65°35N 22°10E 160 D20
Lüleburgaz Turkey 41°23N 27°22E 203 E11
Luliang China 25°0N 103°40E 228 E4
Lulima Dem. Rep. of the Congo 4°12S 25°36E 268 C2
Luling U.S.A. 29°41N 97°39W 314 G6
Lulong China 39°53N 118°51E 227 E10
Lulonga ➔ Dem. Rep. of the Congo 1°0N 18°10E 264 B3
Lulu U.S.A. 30°7N 82°29W 316 E7
Lulu ➔ Dem. Rep. of the Congo 1°18N 23°42E 264 B4
Lulua ➔ Dem. Rep. of the Congo 4°30S 20°30E 265 C4
Luluaburg = Kananga Dem. Rep. of the Congo 5°55S 22°18E 265 D4
Luma Amer. Samoa 14°16S 169°33W 302 f
Lumai Angola 13°13S 21°25E 265 E4
Lumajang Indonesia 8°8S 113°13E 235 D4
Lumaku, Gunong Malaysia 4°52N 115°38E 235 B5
Lumār Iran 33°33N 46°49E 213 F12
Lumbala ➔ Angola 12°39S 22°35E 265 E4
Lumbala Kaquengue Angola 12°39S 22°34E 265 E4
Lumbala N'guimbo Angola 14°18S 21°18E 265 E4
Lumbe ➔ Zambia 16°44S 23°41E 265 F4
Lumber City U.S.A. 31°56N 82°41W 316 D7
Lumberton N.C., U.S.A. 34°37N 79°0W 315 D15
Lumberton Tex., U.S.A. 30°16N 94°12W 314 F7
Lumbis Indonesia 4°18N 116°15E 235 B5
Lumding India 25°46N 93°10E 241 C4
Lumi Papua N. G. 3°30S 142°2E 286 B2
Lumiar Portugal 38°46N 9°10W 126 A2
Lumière, Côte de France 46°50N 2°10W 172 F4
Lumpkin U.S.A. 32°3N 84°48W 316 C5
Lumsden Sask., Canada 50°39N 104°52W 297 C8
Lumsden N.Z. 45°44S 168°27E 285 F3
Lumut Malaysia 4°13N 100°37E 237 K3
Lumut, Tanjung Indonesia 3°50S 105°58E 234 C3
Lumwana Zambia 11°50S 25°8E 269 E2
Luna India 23°43N 69°16E 242 H3
Luna Apayao, Phil. 18°18N 121°21E 232 B3
Lunan China 24°40N 103°18E 228 E4
Lunavada India 23°8N 73°37E 242 H5
Lunbei = Lunpei Taiwan 24°45N 120°21E 225 C2
Lunca Romania 47°22N 25°1E 183 C10
Lunca Corbului Romania 44°42N 24°45E 183 F9
Lund Sweden 55°44N 13°12E 163 J7
Lunda Norte □ Angola 8°0S 20°0E 265 D4
Lunda Sul □ Angola 10°0S 20°0E 265 E4
Lundamo Norway 63°9N 10°19E 164 A7
Lundazi Zambia 12°20S 33°7E 269 E3
Lunde Sweden 62°53N 17°51E 162 B11
Lundenburg = Břeclav Czech Rep. 48°46N 16°53E 181 C9
Lunderskov Denmark 55°29N 9°19E 163 J3
Lundi ➔ Zimbabwe 21°43S 32°34E 269 G3
Lundtofte Denmark 55°47N 12°32E 118 A3
Lundu Malaysia 1°40N 109°50E 235 B3
Lundy U.K. 51°10N 4°41W 169 F3
Lune ➔ U.K. 54°0N 2°51W 168 C5
Lüneburg Germany 53°15N 10°24E 178 B6
Lüneburg Heath = Lüneburger Heide Germany 53°10N 10°12E 178 B6
Lüneburger Heide Germany 53°10N 10°12E 178 B6
Lunel France 43°39N 4°9E 175 E8
Lünen Germany 51°37N 7°32E 178 D3
Lunenburg Canada 44°22N 64°18W 299 D7
Lunéville France 48°36N 6°30E 173 D13
Lung Kwu Chau Hong Kong, China 22°23N 113°53E 122 A1
Lung Kwu Tan Hong Kong, China 22°23N 113°55E 122 A1
Lung Mei Hong Kong, China 22°23N 114°15E 122 A3
Lunga Dem. Rep. of the Congo 5°46S 12°14E 265 C4
Lunga ➔ Zambia 14°34S 26°25E 269 E2
Lunga Lunga Kenya 4°33S 39°7E 268 C4
Lungchin Taiwan 24°12N 120°31E 225 B2
Lunge Angola 12°13S 16°7E 265 E3
Lungga Solomon Is. 9°25S 160°3E 287 M11
Lungi S. Leone 8°40N 13°17W 262 D2
Lunglei India 22°55N 92°45E 241 D4
Lungngo Burma 21°57N 93°36E 241 E4
Lung'tan Taiwan 24°52N 121°12E 225 B3
Lungwebungu ➔ Zambia 14°19S 23°14E 265 E4
Luni India 26°0N 73°6E 242 G5
Luni ➔ India 24°41N 71°14E 242 G4
Luninets = Luninyets Belarus 52°15N 26°50E 177 B14
Luning U.S.A. 38°30N 118°11W 304 G4
Lunino Russia 53°38N 45°18E 190 D7
Luninyets Belarus 52°15N 26°50E 177 B14
Lunkaransar India 28°29N 73°44E 242 E5
Lunner Norway 60°19N 10°35E 164 D7
Lunpei Taiwan 24°45N 120°21E 225 C2
Lunsar S. Leone 8°41N 12°32W 262 D2
Lunsemfwa ➔ Zambia 14°54S 30°12E 269 E3
Lunsemfwa Falls Zambia 14°30S 29°6E 269 E2
Luntai China 41°46N 84°14E 217 D10
Luo He ➔ China 34°35N 110°20E 226 G6
Luocheng China 24°48N 108°53E 228 E7
Luochuan China 35°45N 109°26E 226 G5
Luoci China 25°19N 102°18E 228 E4
Luodian China 25°24N 106°43E 228 E6
Luoding China 22°45N 111°40E 229 F8
Luodong = Lotung Taiwan 24°41N 121°46E 225 B3
Luofu Dem. Rep. of the Congo 0°10S 29°15E 268 C2
Luohe China 33°32N 114°2E 226 H8
Luojiang Guangdong, China 23°5N 113°17E 121 B2
Luojiang Sichuan, China 31°18N 104°33E 228 B5
Luonan China 34°5N 110°10E 226 G6
Luoning China 34°35N 111°40E 226 G6
Luoshan China 32°13N 114°30E 229 A10
Luotian China 30°46N 115°22E 229 B10
Luoxiao Shan China 26°30N 114°1E 229 D10
Luoyang China 34°40N 112°26E 226 G7
Luoyuan China 26°28N 119°30E 229 D12
Luozi Dem. Rep. of the Congo 4°54S 14°0E 265 C2
Luozigou China 43°42N 130°18E 227 C16
Lupanshui China 26°38N 104°48E 228 D5
Lupeni Romania 45°21N 23°13E 183 E8
Lupilichi Mozam. 11°47S 35°13E 269 E4
Lupire Angola 14°36S 19°29E 265 E3
Lupków Poland 49°15N 22°4E 185 J9
Lupoing China 24°53N 104°21E 228 E5
Lupon Phil. 6°54N 126°0E 233 H6
Luputa Dem. Rep. of the Congo 7°7S 23°43E 265 D4
Luqa Malta 35°52N 14°29E 206 F7
Luquan Hebei, China 38°4N 114°17E 226 E8
Luquan Yunnan, China 25°35N 102°25E 228 E4
Luque Paraguay 25°19S 57°25W 334 B4
Luquembo Angola 10°44S 17°43E 265 E3
Luquillo, Sierra de Puerto Rico 18°20N 65°47W 321 b
Lūras Italy 40°56N 9°10E 200 B2
Luray U.S.A. 38°40N 78°28W 309 F14

Lure France 47°40N 6°30E 173 E13
Luremo Angola 8°30S 17°50E 265 D3
Lurgan U.K. 54°27N 6°20W 166 B5
Luribay Bolivia 17°6S 67°39W 330 D4
Lurin Peru 12°17S 76°52W 330 C2
Lúrio Mozam. 13°32S 40°30E 269 E5
Lusaka Zambia 15°28S 28°16E 269 F2
Lusaka □ Zambia 15°30S 29°0E 269 F2
Lusambo Dem. Rep. of the Congo 4°58S 23°28E 265 C4
Lusancay Is. and Reefs Papua N. G. 8°30S 150°30E 286 E6
Lusangaye Dem. Rep. of the Congo 4°54S 26°0E 265 C5
Luseland Canada 52°5N 109°24W 297 C7
Lusenga Plain △ Zambia 9°22S 29°14E 269 D2
Lusengo Dem. Rep. of the Congo 1°47N 19°31E 264 B3
Lushan Henan, China 33°45N 112°55E 226 H7
Lushan Sichuan, China 30°12N 102°52E 228 B4
Lushi China 34°3N 111°3E 226 G6
Lushnjë Albania 40°55N 19°41E 202 F3
Lushoto Tanzania 4°47S 38°20E 268 C4
Lushui China 25°58N 98°44E 228 E2
Lushuihe China 42°31N 127°47E 224 A3
Lüshun China 38°45N 121°15E 227 E11
Lusignan France 46°26N 0°8E 174 B4
Lusigny-sur-Barse France 48°16N 4°15E 173 D11
Lusiye Zambia 15°30S 23°57E 265 F4
Lusk U.S.A. 42°46N 104°27W 304 E11
Luso Portugal 40°23N 8°23W 194 E2
Lussac-les-Châteaux France 46°24N 0°43E 174 B4
Lustenau Austria 47°26N 9°39E 180 D2
Lustheim Germany 48°14N 11°34E 131 A2
Lustrafjorden Norway 61°23N 7°25E 164 C4
Lūt, Dasht-e Iran 31°30N 58°0E 247 D8
Luta = Dalian China 38°50N 121°40E 227 E11
Lütao Taiwan 22°40N 121°30E 225 D3
Lutembo Angola 13°26S 21°16E 265 E4
Lutherstadt Wittenberg Germany 51°53N 12°39E 178 D8
Luthersville U.S.A. 33°13N 84°45W 316 B5
Luti Solomon Is. 7°14S 157°0E 287 L9
Luton U.K. 51°53N 0°24W 169 F7
Luton □ U.K. 51°53N 0°24W 169 F7
Lutong Malaysia 4°28N 114°0E 235 B4
Łutsel K'e Canada 62°24N 110°44W 297 A6
Lutshima → Dem. Rep. of the Congo 5°22S 18°59E 265 D3
Lutsk Ukraine 50°50N 25°15E 177 C13
Luttenberg = Ljutomer Slovenia 46°31N 16°11E 199 B13
Lutto = Lotta → Europe 68°42N 31°6E 160 B24
Lutuai Angola 12°41S 20°7E 265 E4
Lutz U.S.A. 28°9N 82°28W 317 G7
Lützow Holmbukta Antarctica 69°10S 37°30E 151 C4
Lutzputs S. Africa 28°3S 20°40E 270 C3
Luuk Phil. 5°58N 121°18E 233 J3
Luuq Somalia 3°48N 42°34E 267 D5
Luverne Ala., U.S.A. 31°43N 86°16W 316 D3
Luverne Minn., U.S.A. 43°39N 96°13W 308 D5
Luvo Angola 5°51S 14°5E 265 D2
Luvua Dem. Rep. of the Congo 8°48S 25°17E 265 D5
Luvua → Dem. Rep. of the Congo 6°50S 27°30E 268 D2
Luvuvhu → S. Africa 22°25S 31°18E 271 B5
Luwan China 31°12N 121°27E 138 B1
Luwegu → Tanzania 8°31S 37°23E 269 D4
Luwero Uganda 0°50N 32°28E 268 B3
Luwuk Indonesia 0°56S 122°47E 231 E6
Luxembourg Lux. 49°37N 6°9E 170 E6
Luxembourg □ Belgium 49°58N 5°30E 170 E5
Luxembourg ■ Europe 49°45N 6°0E 170 E5
Luxembourg ✕ (LUX) Lux. 49°37N 6°10E 170 E6
Luxembourg, Palais du Paris, France 134 c4
Luxemburg U.S.A. 42°36N 91°5W 310 B5
Luxeuil-les-Bains France 47°49N 6°24E 173 E13
Luxi Hunan, China 28°20N 110°7E 229 C8
Luxi Yunnan, China 24°40N 103°55E 228 E4
Luxi Yunnan, China 24°27N 98°36E 228 E2
Luxian China 29°9N 105°24E 228 C5
Luxor = El Uqsur Egypt 25°41N 32°38E 256 B3
Luy-de-Béarn → France 43°39N 0°48W 174 E3
Luy-de-France → France 43°39N 0°48W 174 E3
Luyeh Hualien, Taiwan 23°35N 121°32E 225 C3
Luyeh T'aitung, Taiwan 22°55N 121°8E 225 D3
Luyi China 33°50N 115°35E 226 H8
Luykau = Loikaw Burma 19°40N 97°17E 241 F6
Luz Azores 39°1N 28°0W 153 d1
Luz, Estádio da Lisbon, Portugal 38°45N 9°11W 126 A1
Luz-St-Sauveur France 42°53N 0°0 174 F4
Luza Russia 60°39N 47°10E 186 B8
Luzern Switz. 47°3N 8°18E 179 H4
Luzern □ Switz. 47°2N 7°55E 179 H3
Luzhai China 24°29N 109°42E 228 E7
Luzhany Ukraine 48°22N 25°47E 183 B10
Luzhi China 26°21N 105°16E 228 D5
Luzhniki Sports Centre Russia 55°43N 37°31E 129 B2
Luzhou China 28°52N 105°20E 228 C5
Luzhu = Luchu Taiwan 22°52N 120°15E 225 D2
Luziânia Brazil 16°20S 48°0W 333 E2
Luzilândia Brazil 3°28S 42°22W 332 B3
Lužnice → Czech Rep. 49°14N 14°23E 180 B7
Luzon Phil. 16°0N 121°0E 232 C3
Luzon Strait Asia 21°0N 120°40E 229 G13
Luzy France 46°47N 3°58E 173 F10
Luzzi Italy 39°27N 16°17E 201 C9
Lviv Ukraine 49°50N 24°0E 177 D13
Lviv □ Ukraine 49°30N 23°45E 177 D12
Lvov = Lviv Ukraine 49°50N 24°0E 177 D13
Lwówek Poland 52°28N 16°10E 185 F3
Lwówek Śląski Poland 51°7N 15°38E 185 G2
Lyakhavichy Belarus 53°2N 26°32E 177 B14
Lyakhovskiye, Ostrova Russia 73°40N 141°0E 215 B15
Lyaki = Läki Azerbaijan 40°34N 47°22E 191 K8
Lyal I. Canada 44°57N 81°24W 312 B3
Lyall Mt. N.Z. 45°16S 167°32E 285 F2
Lyallpur = Faisalabad Pakistan 31°30N 73°5E 242 D5
Lyaskovets Bulgaria 43°6N 25°44E 203 C9
Lyasnaya → Belarus 52°9N 23°31E 185 F10
Lybster U.K. 58°18N 3°15W 167 C5
Lycabettus Athens, Greece 112 b3
Lycaonia Turkey 38°0N 33°0E 212 D5
Lychen Germany 53°12N 13°18E 178 B9
Lychkova Russia 57°55N 32°24E 188 D7
Lycia Turkey 36°30N 29°30E 205 E11
Lyck = Ełk Poland 53°50N 22°21E 184 E9
Lyckebyån → Sweden 56°12N 15°39E 163 H9
Lycksele Sweden 64°38N 18°40E 160 D18
Lycosura Greece 37°20N 22°3E 204 D4
Lydda = Lod Israel 31°57N 34°54E 251 D3
Lyddan I. Antarctica 74°0S 21°0W 151 D2
Lydenburg S. Africa 25°10S 30°29E 271 C5
Lydia Turkey 38°48N 28°19E 205 C10
Lydynia → Poland 52°43N 20°26E 185 F7
Lyell N.Z. 41°48S 172°4E 285 B7
Lyell I. Canada 52°40N 131°35W 296 C2
Lyepyel Belarus 54°50N 28°40E 188 E5
Lyford Cay Bahamas 25°2N 77°33W 153 b
Lygnern Sweden 57°30N 12°15E 163 G6
Lykavittos Hill = Lycabettus Athens, Greece 112 b3
Lykens U.S.A. 40°34N 76°42W 313 F8
Lyman Ukraine 45°41N 29°45E 183 E14
Lyman Wyo., U.S.A. 41°20N 110°18W 304 F8
Lymanske Ukraine 46°40N 29°58E 183 D14
Lyme B. U.K. 50°42N 2°53W 169 G4
Lyme Regis U.K. 50°43N 2°57W 169 G5
Lymington U.K. 50°45N 1°32W 169 G6
Lyna → Poland 54°37N 21°14E 184 D8
Lynchburg Ohio, U.S.A. 39°15N 83°48W 311 E13
Lynchburg S.C., U.S.A. 34°3N 80°4W 316 A9
Lynchburg Va., U.S.A. 37°25N 79°9W 309 G14
Lynd → Australia 16°28S 143°18E 280 B3
Lynd Ra. Australia 25°30S 149°20E 281 D4
Lynden Ont., Canada 43°14N 80°9W 312 C4
Lynden Wash., U.S.A. 48°57N 122°27W 306 B4
Lyndhurst S. Austral., Australia 30°15S 138°18E 281 E2
Lyndhurst N.J., U.S.A. 40°49N 74°7W 132 B1
Lyndon → Australia 23°29S 114°6E 279 D1
Lyndonville N.Y., U.S.A. 43°20N 78°23W 312 C6
Lyndonville Vt., U.S.A. 44°31N 72°1W 313 B12
Lyngdal Buskerud, Norway 59°54N 9°32E 164 E6
Lyngdal Vest-Agder, Norway 58°8N 7°7E 164 F4
Lyngen Norway 69°45N 20°30E 160 B19
Lyngør Norway 58°38N 9°8E 164 F6
Lynher Reef Australia 15°27S 121°55E 278 C3
Lynn Ind., U.S.A. 40°3N 84°56W 311 D12
Lynn Mass., U.S.A. 42°28N 70°57W 313 D14
Lynn Canal U.S.A. 58°50N 135°15W 303 G14
Lynn Haven U.S.A. 30°15N 85°39W 316 E4
Lynn Lake Canada 56°51N 101°3W 297 B8
Lynn Woods Res. U.S.A. 42°29N 71°0W 116 A2
Lynne U.S.A. 29°12N 81°55W 317 F8
Lynnville U.S.A. 38°12N 87°18W 311 F9
Lynnwood U.S.A. 47°49N 122°18W 306 C4
Lynton U.K. 51°13N 3°50W 169 F4
Lyntupy Belarus 55°4N 26°23E 188 E4
Lynx L. Canada 62°25N 106°15W 297 A7
Lyon France 45°46N 4°50E 175 C8
Lyon, Gare de Paris, France 134 c5
Lyon St-Exupery ✕ (LYS) France 45°44N 5°2E 175 C9
Lyonnais France 45°45N 4°15E 175 C8
Lyons = Lyon France 45°46N 4°50E 175 C8
Lyons Ga., U.S.A. 32°12N 82°19W 316 C7
Lyons Ill., U.S.A. 41°48N 87°49W 119 C2
Lyons Kans., U.S.A. 38°21N 98°12W 308 F4
Lyons N.Y., U.S.A. 43°5N 77°0W 312 C8
Lyons → Australia 25°2S 115°9E 279 E2
Lyons Falls U.S.A. 43°37N 75°22W 313 C9
Lyozna Belarus 55°0N 30°50E 188 E6
Lyra Reef Papua N. G. 1°50S 153°35E 286 A7
Lys = Leie → Belgium 51°2N 3°45E 170 C3
Lysá nad Labem Czech Rep. 50°11N 14°51E 180 A7
Lysaker Norway 59°54N 10°38E 133 A2
Lysakerselva → Norway 59°54N 10°38E 133 A2
Lysebotn Norway 59°3N 6°37E 164 E3
Lysefjorden Norway 59°0N 6°23E 164 E3
Lysekil Sweden 58°17N 11°26E 163 F5
Lysi Cyprus 35°6N 33°41E 207 E9
Lyskovo Russia 56°0N 45°3E 190 B7
Lysolaje Czech Rep. 50°8N 14°22E 135 B2
Lystrup Denmark 56°14N 10°14E 163 H4
Lysva Russia 58°7N 57°49E 186 C10
Lysvik Sweden 60°1N 13°9E 162 D7
Lysychansk Ukraine 48°55N 38°30E 189 H10
Lytham St. Anne's U.K. 53°45N 3°0W 168 D4
Lyttelton N.Z. 43°35S 172°44E 285 D7
Lytton Canada 50°13N 121°31W 296 C4
Lyuban Russia 59°16N 31°18E 188 C6
Lyubertsy Russia 55°40N 37°51E 188 E9
Lyubim Russia 58°20N 40°39E 188 C11
Lyubimets Bulgaria 41°50N 26°5E 203 E10
Lyublino Russia 55°41N 37°44E 129 B3
Lyuboml Ukraine 51°11N 24°4E 185 G11
Lyubotyn Ukraine 50°0N 36°0E 189 H8
Lyubytino Russia 58°50N 33°16E 188 C7
Lyudao = Lütao Taiwan 22°40N 121°30E 225 D3
Lyudinovo Russia 53°52N 34°28E 188 F8

# M

M.R. Štefánik, Bratislava ✕ (BTS) Slovak Rep. 48°11N 17°9E 181 C10
Ma → Vietnam 19°47N 105°56E 228 H5
Ma, O. el → Algeria 27°45N 7°52W 260 C3
Ma Nam Wat Hong Kong, China 22°21N 114°16E 122 A3
Ma On Shan Hong Kong, China 22°23N 114°12E 122 A3
Ma On Shan Country Park ⌂ Hong Kong, China 22°22N 114°14E 122 A3
Ma Wan Hong Kong, China 22°21N 114°3E 122 A2
Ma Wan Channel Hong Kong, China 22°21N 114°4E 122 A2
Ma'adaba Jordan 31°43N 35°47E 251 H6
Maafushi Maldives 3°59N 73°27E 272 d
Maakhir Somalia 10°30N 47°30E 267 B6
Ma'ale Adumim West Bank 31°49N 35°17E 123 B2
Ma'ale Ha Khamisha Israel 31°49N 35°7E 123 B1
Ma'ale Mikhmas West Bank 31°52N 35°18E 123 A2
Ma'alot-Tarshiha Israel 33°1N 35°17E 250 E6
Maamba Zambia 17°17S 26°28E 270 A4
Ma'ān Jordan 30°12N 35°44E 251 H6
Ma'ān □ Jordan 30°0N 36°0E 251 J7
Maana'oba Solomon Is. 8°17S 160°50E 287 M11
Maanselkä Finland 63°52N 28°32E 160 C23
Ma'anshan China 31°44N 118°29E 229 B12
Maantiekylä Finland 60°20N 25°0E 121 A3
Maarianhamina = Mariehamn Finland 60°5N 19°55E 161 F18
Maarifa Iraq 33°15N 44°21E 113 B2
Maarmorilik Greenland 71°3N 51°0W 154 C5
Ma'arrat an Nu'mān Syria 35°43N 36°43E 250 C7
Maas → Neths. 51°45N 4°32E 170 C4
Maaseik Belgium 51°6N 5°45E 170 C5
Maasim Phil. 5°52N 125°0E 233 J5
Maasin Phil. 10°8N 124°50E 233 F5
Maastricht Neths. 50°50N 5°40E 170 D5
Maasupa Solomon Is. 9°16S 161°17E 287 M11
Maave Mozam. 21°4S 34°47E 271 B5
Mababe Depression Botswana 18°50S 24°15E 270 A3
Mabaia Angola 7°12S 14°2E 265 D2
Mabalane Mozam. 23°37S 32°31E 271 B5
Mabanga Dem. Rep. of the Congo 1°30N 19°6E 264 B3
Ma'bar Yemen 14°48N 44°17E 248 D4
Mabaruma Guyana 8°10N 59°50W 329 B6
Mabato Pt. Phil. 14°29N 121°3E 127 C2
Mabein Burma 23°29N 96°37E 241 D6
Mabel, L. U.S.A. 28°25N 81°32W 133 B1
Mabel L. Canada 50°35N 118°43W 296 C5
Mabenga Dem. Rep. of the Congo 3°39S 18°40E 264 C3
Mabenge Dem. Rep. of the Congo 4°15N 24°12E 264 B4
Maberly Canada 44°50N 76°32W 313 B8
Mabesi, L. S. Leone 7°10N 11°42W 262 D2
Mabian China 28°47N 103°37E 228 C4
Mabil Ethiopia 10°26N 36°52E 257 E4
Mabinay Phil. 9°48N 122°54E 233 G4
Mabirou Congo 1°3S 15°42E 264 C3
Mablethorpe U.K. 53°20N 0°15E 168 D8
Mableton U.S.A. 33°49N 84°35W 316 B5
Mably France 46°5N 4°4E 173 F11
Maboma Dem. Rep. of the Congo 2°30N 28°10E 268 B2
Mabonto S. Leone 8°53N 11°50W 262 D2
Maboukou Congo 3°39S 12°31E 264 C2
Mabouya I. Grenada 12°29N 61°30W 323 q
Mabroûk Mali 19°29N 1°15W 261 E4
Mabrous Niger 21°14N 13°35E 259 D2
Mabuasehube ⌂ Botswana 25°5S 21°10E 270 C3
Mabudis Phil. 20°55N 121°55E 232 A3
Mabuiag Australia 9°57S 142°11E 280 a
Mac Bac Vietnam 9°46N 106°7E 237 H6
Macachín Argentina 37°10S 63°43W 334 D3
Macaco, Morro do Brazil 22°56S 43°6W 135 B2
Macaé Brazil 22°20S 41°43W 333 F3
Macael Spain 37°20N 2°18W 197 H2
Macaíba Brazil 5°51S 35°21W 332 C4
Macajalar B. Phil. 8°55N 124°39E 233 G5
Macajuba Brazil 12°9S 40°22W 333 D3
McAlester U.S.A. 34°56N 95°46W 314 D7
McAllen U.S.A. 26°12N 98°14W 314 H5
McAlpin U.S.A. 30°8N 82°57W 316 E7
McAlpine L. Canada 66°32N 102°45W 294 D11
Macamic Canada 48°45N 79°0W 298 C4
Macanao, B. de Venezuela 11°2N 64°23W 329 a
Macanao, Pen. de Venezuela 11°0N 64°18W 329 a
Macao = Macau China 22°12N 113°33E 229 F9
Macão Portugal 39°35N 7°59W 195 F3
Macapá Brazil 0°5N 51°4W 329 C7
Macaque, Morne Dominica 15°20N 61°20W 323 k
Macará Ecuador 4°23S 79°57W 328 D2
Macarani Brazil 15°33S 40°24W 333 E3
Macarena, Serranía de la Colombia 2°45N 73°55W 328 C3
Macareo, Caño → Venezuela 9°47N 61°36W 329 B5
Macarthur Australia 38°5S 142°0E 282 E5
McArthur → Australia 15°54S 136°40E 280 B2
McArthur, Port Australia 16°4S 136°23E 280 B2
Macas Ecuador 2°19S 78°7W 328 D2
Macate Peru 8°48S 78°7W 330 B2
Macau Brazil 5°15S 36°40W 332 C4
Macau China 22°12N 113°33E 229 F9
Macaúbas Brazil 13°2S 42°42W 333 D3
Macauley I. Pac. Oc. 30°12S 178°28W 277 G15
Macaya → Colombia 0°59N 72°20W 328 C3
McBride Canada 53°20N 120°19W 296 C4
McCall U.S.A. 44°55N 116°6W 304 D5
McCamey U.S.A. 31°8N 102°14W 314 F3
McCammon U.S.A. 42°39N 112°12W 304 E7
McCarran Int., Las Vegas ✕ (LAS) U.S.A. 36°5N 115°9W 124 B2
McCarthy U.S.A. 61°26N 142°56W 303 F12
McCauley I. Canada 53°40N 130°15W 296 C2
McCleary U.S.A. 47°3N 123°16W 306 C3
Macclenny U.S.A. 30°17N 82°7W 316 E7
Macclesfield U.K. 53°15N 2°8W 168 D5
Macclesfield Bank S. China Sea 16°0N 114°30E 230 A4
M'Clintock Chan. Canada 72°0N 102°0W 294 C11
McClintock Ra. Australia 18°44S 127°38E 278 C4
McCloud U.S.A. 41°15N 122°8W 304 F2
McCluer I. Australia 11°5S 133°0E 278 B5
McClure U.S.A. 40°42N 77°19W 312 F7
McClure, L. U.S.A. 37°35N 120°16W 306 H6
M'Clure Str. Canada 75°0N 119°0W 295 B8
McClusky U.S.A. 47°29N 100°27W 308 B3
McComb U.S.A. 31°15N 90°27W 315 F9
McCook Ill., U.S.A. 41°47N 87°49W 119 C2
McCook Nebr., U.S.A. 40°12N 100°38W 308 E3
McCormick U.S.A. 33°55N 82°17W 316 B7
McCreary Canada 50°47N 99°29W 297 C9
McCullough Mt. U.S.A. 35°35N 115°13W 307 K11
McCusker → Canada 55°32N 108°39W 297 B7
McDavid U.S.A. 30°52N 87°19W 317 E2
McDermitt U.S.A. 41°59N 117°43W 304 F5
McDonald U.S.A. 40°22N 80°14W 312 F4
Macdonald, L. Australia 23°30S 129°0E 278 D4
Macdonald, Mt. Vanuatu 17°36S 168°23E 287 G6
McDonald Is. Ind. Oc. 53°0S 73°0E 273 K6
MacDonnell Ranges Australia 23°40S 133°0E 278 D5
McDonough U.S.A. 33°27N 84°9W 316 B5
McDougalls Well Australia 31°8S 141°15E 282 A4
MacDowell L. Canada 52°15N 92°45W 298 B1
Macduff U.K. 57°40N 2°31W 167 D6
Maceda Spain 42°16N 7°39W 194 C3
Macedonia U.S.A. 41°19N 81°31W 312 E3
Macedonia ■ Europe 41°53N 21°40E 202 E5
Maceió Brazil 9°40S 35°41W 332 C4
Maceira Portugal 39°41N 8°55W 194 F2
Macenta Guinea 8°35N 9°32W 262 D3
Macerata Italy 43°18N 13°27E 199 E10
McFarland U.S.A. 35°41N 119°14W 307 K7
McFarlane → Canada 59°12N 107°58W 297 B7
Macfarlane, L. Australia 32°0S 136°40E 282 B2
McGehee U.S.A. 33°38N 91°24W 314 E9
McGill U.S.A. 39°23N 114°47W 304 G6
McGill Univ. Montréal, Canada 130 b1
Macgillycuddy's Reeks Ireland 51°58N 9°45W 166 E2
McGrath U.S.A. 62°58N 155°36W 303 E9
McGraw U.S.A. 42°36N 76°8W 313 D8
McGregor U.S.A. 43°1N 91°11W 310 A5
McGregor Ra. Australia 27°0S 142°45E 281 D3
McGuire, Mt. Australia 20°18S 148°23E 280 b
Mach Pakistan 29°50N 67°20E 242 E2
Māch Kowr Iran 25°48N 61°28E 247 E9
Machacalis Brazil 17°5S 40°45W 333 E3
Machado = Jiparaná → Brazil 8°3S 62°52W 331 B5
Machagai Argentina 26°56S 60°2W 334 B3
Machakos Kenya 1°30S 37°15E 268 C4
Machala Ecuador 3°20S 79°57W 328 D2
Machalilla △ Ecuador 1°24S 80°42W 328 D1
Machanbaw Burma 27°16N 97°36E 241 B6
Machanga Mozam. 20°59S 35°0E 271 B6
Machattie, L. Australia 24°50S 139°48E 280 C2
Machault France 49°21N 4°29E 173 C11
Machava Mozam. 25°54S 32°28E 271 C5
Machecoul France 47°0N 1°49W 172 F5
Macheke Zimbabwe 18°5S 31°51E 271 A5
Machelen Belgium 50°55N 4°26E 116 A2
Macheng China 31°12N 115°2E 229 B10
McHenry U.S.A. 42°21N 88°16W 311 B8
Macherado Greece 37°46N 20°49E 204 D2
Macherla India 16°29N 79°26E 244 F4
Machero Spain 39°21N 4°20W 195 F6
Machgaon India 20°5N 86°17E 244 D8
Machhu → India 23°6N 70°46E 242 H4
Machiara △ Pakistan 34°40N 73°30E 242 B5
Machias Maine, U.S.A. 44°43N 67°28W 309 C20
Machias N.Y., U.S.A. 42°25N 78°29W 312 D6
Machichi → Canada 57°3N 92°6W 297 B10
Machico Madeira 32°43N 16°44W 153 c
Machida Japan 35°32N 139°26E 140 B1
Machilipatnam India 16°12N 81°8E 245 F5
Machiques Venezuela 10°4N 72°34W 328 A3
Machu Picchu Peru 13°8S 72°30W 330 C3
Machynlleth U.K. 52°35N 3°50W 169 E4
Macia Mozam. 25°2S 33°8E 271 C5
Macias Nguema Biyoga = Bioko Eq. Guin. 3°30N 8°40E 263 E6
Maciejowice Poland 51°36N 21°26E 185 G8
McIlwraith Ra. Australia 13°50S 143°20E 280 A3
Măcin Romania 45°16N 28°8E 183 E13
Macina Mali 14°50N 5°0W 262 C4
McInnes L. Canada 52°13N 93°45W 297 C10
McIntosh U.S.A. 45°55N 101°21W 308 C3
McIntosh L. Canada 55°45N 105°0W 297 B8
Macintosh Ra. Australia 27°39S 125°32E 279 E4
Macintyre → Australia 28°37S 150°47E 281 D5
Maciolki Poland 52°19N 21°9E 143 B2
Macizo Galaico Spain 42°30N 7°30W 194 C3
Maçka Turkey 40°49N 39°36E 213 B8
Mackay Queens., Australia 21°8S 149°11E 280 K7
Mackay Idaho, U.S.A. 43°55N 113°37W 304 E7
MacKay → Canada 57°10N 111°38W 296 B6
Mackay, L. Australia 22°30S 129°0E 278 D4
McKay Ra. Australia 23°0S 122°30E 278 D3
McKean Kiribati 3°36S 174°8W 277 A16
McKeesport U.S.A. 40°20N 79°51W 312 F5
McKellar Canada 45°30N 79°55W 312 A5
McKenna U.S.A. 46°56N 122°33W 306 D4
Mackenzie = Linden Guyana 6°0N 58°10W 329 B6
Mackenzie Canada 55°20N 123°5W 296 B4
McKenzie U.S.A. 36°8N 88°31W 315 C10
Mackenzie → Queens., Australia 23°38S 149°46E 280 C4
Mackenzie → N.W.T., Canada 69°10N 134°20W 294 D5
McKenzie → U.S.A. 44°7N 123°6W 304 D2
Mackenzie Bay Canada 69°0N 137°30W 292 C6
Mackenzie King I. Canada 77°45N 111°0W 295 B9
Mackenzie Mts. Canada 64°0N 130°0W 292 C6
Mackenzie Plains N.Z. 44°10S 170°25E 285 E5
McKerrow, L. N.Z. 44°25S 168°5E 285 E3
Mackheim = Maków Mazowiecki Poland 52°52N 21°6E 185 F8
Mackinac, Straits of U.S.A. 45°50N 84°40W 309 C11
Mackinaw U.S.A. 40°32N 89°21W 310 D7
Mackinaw → U.S.A. 40°33N 89°44W 310 D7
Mackinaw City U.S.A. 45°47N 84°44W 309 C11
McKinlay Australia 21°16S 141°18E 280 C3
McKinlay → Australia 20°50S 141°28E 280 C3
McKinley, Mt. U.S.A. 63°4N 151°0W 303 E10
McKinley Park Alaska, U.S.A. 63°44N 148°55W 303 E10
McKinley Park Ill., U.S.A. 41°49N 87°40W 119 C2
McKinley Sea Arctic 82°0N 0°0 154 A11
McKinney U.S.A. 33°12N 96°37W 314 E6
Mackinnon Road Kenya 3°40S 39°1E 268 C4
McKittrick Calif., U.S.A. 35°18N 119°37W 307 K7
McKittrick Mo., U.S.A. 38°44N 91°27W 310 F5
Macklin Canada 52°20N 109°56W 297 C7
Macksville Australia 30°40S 152°56E 283 A10
McLaren Vale Australia 35°13S 138°31E 282 C3
McLaughlin U.S.A. 45°49N 100°49W 308 C3
Maclean Australia 29°26S 153°16E 281 D5
McLean Ill., U.S.A. 40°19N 89°10W 310 D7
McLean Tex., U.S.A. 35°14N 100°36W 314 D4
McLean Va., U.S.A. 38°56N 77°10W 143 B1
McLeansboro U.S.A. 38°6N 88°32W 311 F8
Maclear S. Africa 31°2S 28°23E 271 D4
Maclear, C. Malawi 13°58S 34°49E 269 E3
Macleay → Australia 30°56S 153°0E 283 A10
McLennan Canada 55°42N 116°50W 296 B5
MacLeod = Fort Macleod Canada 49°45N 113°30W 296 D6
McLeod → Canada 54°9N 115°44W 296 C5
MacLeod, L. Australia 24°9S 113°47E 279 D1
McLeod B. Canada 62°53N 110°0W 297 A7
McLeod Lake Canada 54°58N 123°0W 296 C4
McLoughlin, Mt. U.S.A. 42°27N 122°19W 304 E2
MacMahon = Aïn Touta Algeria 35°26N 5°54E 261 A6
McMechen U.S.A. 39°57N 80°44W 312 G4
McMinnville Oreg., U.S.A. 45°13N 123°12W 304 D2
McMinnville Tenn., U.S.A. 35°41N 85°46W 315 D12
McMurdo Antarctica 77°51S 166°37E 151 D11
McMurdo Sd. Antarctica 77°0S 170°0E 151 D11
McMurray = Fort McMurray Canada 56°44N 111°7W 296 B6
McMurray U.S.A. 48°19N 122°14W 306 B4
Maco Phil. 7°20N 125°50E 233 H5
Maçobere Mozam. 21°13S 32°47E 269 G3
Macocolo Angola 6°47S 16°8E 265 D3
Macodoene Mozam. 23°32S 35°5E 271 B6
Macolo Angola 7°5S 16°42E 265 D3
Macomb U.S.A. 40°27N 90°40W 310 D6
Macomer Italy 40°16N 8°47E 200 B1
Mâcon Saône-et-Loire, France 46°19N 4°50E 173 F11
Macon Ga., U.S.A. 32°51N 83°38W 316 C6
Macon Ill., U.S.A. 39°43N 89°0W 310 E8
Macon Miss., U.S.A. 33°7N 88°34W 315 E10
Macon Mo., U.S.A. 39°44N 92°28W 310 E4
Macondo Angola 12°37S 23°46E 265 E4
Macopocho → Chile 33°24S 70°40W 137 B1
Macossa Mozam. 17°55S 33°56E 269 F3
Macou → Dominica 15°25N 61°27W 323 e
Macou, Pte. Guadeloupe 16°21N 61°31W 322 e
Macouba Martinique 14°52N 61°9W 322 j
Macoun L. Canada 56°32N 103°40W 297 B8
Macoupin Cr. → U.S.A. 39°11N 90°38W 310 E6
Macovane Mozam. 21°30S 35°2E 271 B6
MacPherson = Kapuskasing Canada 49°25N 82°30W 298 C3
McPherson U.S.A. 38°22N 97°40W 308 F5
McPherson Pk. U.S.A. 34°53N 119°53W 307 L7
McPherson Ra. Australia 28°15S 153°15E 281 D5
Macquarie → Australia 30°7S 147°24E 283 A7
Macquarie Harbour Australia 42°15S 145°23E 281 G4
Macquarie I. Pac. Oc. 54°36S 158°55E 288 N7
Macquarie Ridge S. Ocean 57°0S 159°0E 151 B10
Macqueripe B. Trin. & Tob. 10°44N 61°37W 323 t
McRae U.S.A. 32°4N 82°54W 316 C7
MacRitchie Res. Singapore 1°20N 103°49E 138 A2
MacRobertson Land Antarctica 71°0S 64°0E 151 D6
Macrohon Phil. 10°4N 124°56E 233 F5
Macroom Ireland 51°54N 8°57W 166 E3
MacTier Canada 45°8N 79°47W 312 A5
Macubela Mozam. 16°53S 37°49E 269 F4
Macugnaga Italy 45°58N 7°58E 198 C4
Macuira △ Colombia 12°9N 71°21W 328 A3
Macuje Colombia 0°24N 73°10W 328 C3
Macul Chile 33°30S 70°35W 137 C2
Macumba → Australia 27°52S 137°12E 281 D2
Macuro Venezuela 10°42N 61°55W 329 F9
Macusani Peru 14°4S 70°29W 330 C3
Macuse Mozam. 17°45S 37°10E 269 F4
Macuspana Mexico 17°46N 92°36W 319 D6
Macusse Angola 17°48S 20°23E 265 F4
Macy's on State Street Chicago, U.S.A. 119 c2
Mada → Nigeria 7°59N 7°55E 263 D6
Ma'dabā □ Jordan 31°43N 35°47E 251 G6
Madadeni S. Africa 27°43S 30°3E 271 C5
Madadi Chad 18°28N 20°45E 259 E4
Madagali Nigeria 10°56N 13°33E 263 C7
Madagascar ■ Africa 20°0S 47°0E 272 B2
Madagoi → Somalia 0°49N 42°58E 267 D5
Madā'in Sālih Si. Arabia 26°46N 37°57E 246 E3
Madakasira India 13°56N 77°16E 245 H3
Madalena Azores 38°32N 28°32W 153 d1
Madama Niger 22°0N 13°40E 259 D2
Madame, I. Canada 45°30N 60°58W 299 C7
Madame Tussaud's London, U.K. 125 a3
Madan Bulgaria 41°30N 24°57E 203 E8
Madanapalle India 13°33N 78°28E 245 H4
Madang Papua N. G. 5°12S 145°49E 286 C3
Madang □ Papua N. G. 5°0S 145°30E 286 C3
Madaoua Niger 14°5N 6°27E 263 C6
Madara Bulgaria 43°17N 27°8E 203 C11
Madara Nigeria 11°45N 10°35E 263 C7
Madaripur Bangla. 23°19N 90°15E 241 D3
Madau I. Papua N. G. 8°58S 152°28E 286 E7
Madauk Burma 17°56N 96°52E 241 G6
Madawaska Canada 45°30N 78°0W 312 A7
Madawaska → Canada 45°27N 76°21W 312 A7
Madaxmaroodi Somalia 2°39N 44°36E 267 D5
Madaya Burma 22°12N 96°10E 241 D6
Madbar South Sudan 6°17N 30°45E 257 F3
Maddalena Italy 41°16N 9°23E 200 A2
Maddalena, Ex Monastero della Venice, Italy 142 c2
Maddaloni Italy 41°2N 14°23E 201 A7
Maddela Phil. 16°21N 121°41E 232 C3
Maddur India 12°36N 77°4E 245 H3
Madeira Atl. Oc. 32°50N 17°0W 153 c
Madeira Ohio, U.S.A. 39°11N 84°21W 311 E12
Madeira → Brazil 3°22S 58°45W 329 D6
Madeleine, Îs. de la Canada 47°30N 61°40W 299 C7
Maden Turkey 38°23N 39°40E 213 C8
Madera Chihuahua, Mexico 29°12N 108°7W 318 B3
Madera Calif., U.S.A. 36°57N 120°3W 306 J6
Madera Pa., U.S.A. 40°49N 78°26W 312 F6
Madgaon India 15°12N 73°58E 245 G1
Madha India 18°0N 75°30E 244 F2
Madhavpur India 21°15N 69°58E 242 J3
Madhepura India 26°11N 86°23E 243 F12
Madhira India 16°55N 80°22E 244 F5
Madhubani India 26°21N 86°7E 243 F12
Madhudaha India 22°30N 88°24E 124 B2
Madhugiri India 13°40N 77°12E 245 H3
Madhumati → Bangla. 22°53N 89°52E 241 D2
Madhupur Bangla. 24°37N 90°2E 241 C3
Madhupur India 24°16N 86°39E 243 G12
Madhupur △ Bangla. 24°43N 90°4E 241 C3
Madhya Pradesh □ India 22°50N 78°0E 242 J8
Madhyamgram India 22°41N 88°26E 124 A2
Madidi → Bolivia 12°32S 66°52W 330 C4
Madikeri India 12°30N 75°45E 245 H2
Madikwe ⌂ S. Africa 27°38S 32°15E 271 C5
Madill U.S.A. 34°6N 96°46W 314 D6
Madimba Angola 6°36S 14°23E 265 D2
Madimba Dem. Rep. of the Congo 4°58S 15°5E 265 C3
Madin Mexico, Mexico 19°32N 99°16W 128 A1
Ma'din Syria 35°45N 39°36E 213 E8
Madin, L. Mexico 19°31N 99°16W 128 A1
Madina Mali 13°25N 8°50W 262 C3
Madīnah Al Mansūr Iraq 33°19N 44°20E 113 B2
Madinani Ivory C. 9°37N 6°57W 262 D3
Madīnat al Malik Khālid al Askarīyah Si. Arabia 27°54N 45°31E 246 E5
Madīnat ash Sha'b Yemen 12°50N 45°0E 248 D4
Madīnat ath Thawrah Syria 35°50N 38°32E 213 E8
Madīnat Masdar U.A.E. 24°26N 54°37E 247 E7
Mâdinet Nasr Egypt 30°4N 31°18E 117 A2
Madingo Congo 4°5S 11°24E 264 C2
Madingou Congo 4°10S 13°33E 264 C2
Madirovalo Madag. 16°26S 46°32E 272 B2
Madison Calif., U.S.A. 38°41N 121°59W 306 G5
Madison Fla., U.S.A. 30°28N 83°25W 316 E6
Madison Ga., U.S.A. 33°36N 83°28W 316 B6
Madison Ind., U.S.A. 38°44N 85°23W 311 F11
Madison Mo., U.S.A. 39°28N 92°13W 310 E4
Madison Nebr., U.S.A. 41°50N 97°27W 308 E5
Madison Ohio, U.S.A. 41°46N 81°3W 312 E3
Madison S. Dak., U.S.A. 44°0N 97°7W 308 C5
Madison Wis., U.S.A. 43°4N 89°24W 310 A7
Madison → U.S.A. 45°56N 111°31W 304 D8
Madison Avenue New York, U.S.A. 132 c2
Madison Heights U.S.A. 37°25N 79°8W 309 G14
Madison Square New York, U.S.A. 132 d2
Madison Square Garden New York, U.S.A. 132 c2
Madisonville Ky., U.S.A. 37°20N 87°30W 308 G10
Madisonville Tex., U.S.A. 30°57N 95°55W 314 F7
Madista Botswana 21°15S 25°6E 270 B4
Madiun Indonesia 7°38S 111°32E 235 D4
Madjingo Gabon 1°20N 14°4E 264 B2
Mado Gashi Kenya 0°44N 39°10E 268 B4
Madoc Canada 44°30N 77°28W 312 B7
Madoi China 34°46N 98°18E 218 E8
Madon → France 48°36N 6°6E 173 D13
Madona Latvia 56°53N 26°5E 188 D4
Madonie Italy 37°50N 13°50E 200 E6
Madonna dell' Orto Venice, Italy 142 a2
Madonna di Campiglio Italy 46°14N 10°49E 198 B7
Madou = Matou Taiwan 23°11N 120°15E 225 C2
Madra Dağı Turkey 39°23N 27°12E 205 B9
Madrakah, Ra's al Oman 19°0N 57°50E 249 C7
Madras = Chennai India 13°8N 80°19E 245 H5
Madras = Tamil Nadu □ India 11°0N 77°0E 245 J3
Madras U.S.A. 44°38N 121°8W 304 D3
Madre, L. U.S.A. 26°50N 97°30W 314 J6
Madre, Sierra Phil. 17°0N 122°0E 232 C4
Madre de Dios □ Peru 12°0S 70°15W 330 C3
Madre de Dios → Bolivia 10°59S 66°8W 330 C4
Madre de Dios, I. Chile 50°20S 75°10W 336 D1
Madre del Sur, Sierra Mexico 17°30N 100°0W 319 D5
Madre Occidental, Sierra Mexico 27°0N 107°0W 318 B3
Madre Oriental, Sierra Mexico 25°0N 100°0W 318 C5
Madri India 24°16N 73°32E 242 G5
Madrid Spain 40°24N 3°42W 127 B1
Madrid Ala., U.S.A. 31°2N 85°24W 316 D4
Madrid Iowa, U.S.A. 41°53N 93°49W 310 C3
Madrid N.Y., U.S.A. 44°45N 75°8W 313 B9
Madrid □ Spain 40°30N 3°45W 194 E7
Madrid Barajas ✕ (MAD) Spain 40°26N 3°34W 127 B2
Madridejos Spain 39°28N 3°33W 195 F7
Madrigal de las Altas Torres Spain 41°5N 5°0W 194 D6
Madrona, Sierra Spain 38°27N 4°16W 195 G6
Madroñera Spain 39°26N 5°42W 195 F5
Madrusah Libya 24°48N 14°58E 258 D2
Madu Sudan 14°37N 26°4E 257 E2
Madula Dem. Rep. of the Congo 0°27N 25°22E 264 B5
Maduo Dem. Rep. of the Congo 1°24S 20°44E 264 C4
Madupi Burma 19°30N 93°8E 241 E4
Madura W. Austral., Australia 31°55S 127°0E 279 F4
Madura Indonesia 7°30S 114°0E 231 G15
Madura, Selat Indonesia 7°30S 113°20E 235 D4
Madura Oya △ Sri Lanka 7°20N 81°10E 245 L5
Madurai India 9°55N 78°10E 245 K4
Madurantakam India 12°30N 79°50E 245 H4
Madzhalis Russia 42°9N 47°47E 191 J8
Mae Chan Thailand 20°9N 99°52E 236 B2
Mae Charim △ Thailand 18°17N 100°59E 236 C3
Mae Hong Son Thailand 19°16N 97°56E 236 C2
Mae Khlong → Thailand 13°24N 100°0E 236 F3
Mae Moei △ Thailand 17°26N 98°7E 236 D2
Mae Phang △ Thailand 19°7N 99°13E 236 C2
Mae Phrik Thailand 17°27N 99°7E 236 D2
Mae Ping △ Thailand 17°37N 98°51E 236 D2
Mae Ramat Thailand 16°58N 98°31E 236 D2
Mae Rim Thailand 18°54N 98°57E 236 C2
Mae Sai Thailand 20°20N 99°55E 228 G2
Mae Sot Thailand 16°43N 98°34E 236 D2
Mae Suai Thailand 19°39N 99°33E 228 H2
Mae Tha Thailand 18°28N 99°8E 236 C2
Mae Tup Res. Thailand 17°52N 98°45E 236 D2
Mae Wa △ Thailand 17°23N 99°16E 236 D2
Mae Wong △ Thailand 15°54N 99°12E 236 E2
Mae Yom △ Thailand 18°43N 100°15E 236 C3
Maebaru Japan 33°33N 130°12E 222 D2
Maebashi Japan 36°24N 139°4E 223 A11
Maella Spain 41°8N 0°7E 196 D5
Maelpaeg L. Canada 48°20N 56°30W 299 C8
Maesawa Japan 35°44N 139°31E 140 A2
Maesteg U.K. 51°36N 3°40W 169 F4
Maestra, Sierra Cuba 20°15N 77°0W 320 B4
Maestre de Campo I. Phil. 12°56N 121°42E 232 E3
Maetambe, Mt. Solomon Is. 7°3S 157°1E 287 L9
Maevatanana Madag. 16°56S 46°49E 272 B2
Maéwo Vanuatu 15°10S 168°10E 287 E6
Mafadi S. Africa 29°12S 29°21E 271 C4
Mafate, Cirque de Réunion 21°3S 55°25E 272 f
Mafeking = Mafikeng S. Africa 25°50S 25°38E 270 C4
Mafeking Canada 52°40N 101°10W 297 C8
Maféré Ivory C. 5°30N 3°2W 262 D4
Mafeteng Lesotho 29°51S 27°15E 270 C4
Maffra Australia 37°53S 146°58E 283 D7
Mafia I. Tanzania 7°45S 39°50E 268 D4
Mafikeng S. Africa 25°50S 25°38E 270 C4
Mafra Brazil 26°10S 49°55W 335 B6
Mafra Portugal 38°55N 9°20W 195 G1
Mafungabusi Plateau Zimbabwe 18°30S 29°8E 269 F2
Magadan Russia 59°38N 150°50E 215 D16
Magadi India 12°58N 77°14E 245 H3
Magadi Rift Valley, Kenya 1°54S 36°19E 268 C4
Magadi, L. Kenya 1°54S 36°19E 268 C4
Magaliesburg S. Africa 26°0S 27°32E 271 C4
Magallanes = Punta Arenas Chile 53°10S 71°0W 336 D2
Magallanes □ Chile 52°0S 72°0W 336 D2
Magallanes, Estrecho de Chile 52°30S 75°0W 336 D2
Magallanes y Antártica Chilena □ Chile 12°50N 123°50E 232 E4
Magaluf Spain 39°29N 2°32E 206 B3
Magangué Colombia 9°14N 74°45W 328 B3
Maganoy Phil. 6°51N 124°31E 233 H5
Magaria Niger 13°4N 9°5E 259 F1
Magarida Papua N. G. 10°18S 149°20E 286 F5
Magburaka S. Leone 8°47N 12°0W 262 D2
Magdagachi Russia 53°27N 125°48E 215 D13
Magdalen Is. = Madeleine, Îs. de la Canada 47°30N 61°40W 299 C7
Magdalena Argentina 35°5S 57°30W 334 D4
Magdalena Bolivia 13°13S 63°57W 331 C5
Magdalena Lima, Peru 12°5S 77°5W 124 B2
Magdalena N. Mex., U.S.A. 34°7N 107°15W 305 J10
Magdalena □ Colombia 10°0N 74°0W 328 B3
Magdalena → Colombia 11°6N 74°51W 328 A3
Magdalena, B. Mexico 24°35N 112°0W 318 C2
Magdalena, I. Chile 44°40S 73°0W 336 B2
Magdalena, I. Mexico 24°40N 112°15W 318 C2
Magdalena, Llano de Mexico 25°0N 111°25W 318 C2
Magdalena Contreras Mexico 19°20N 99°13W 128 C1
Magdalena de Kino Mexico 30°38N 110°57W 318 A2
Magdeburg Germany 52°7N 11°38E 178 C7
Magdelaine Cays Australia 16°33S 150°18E 280 B5
Magdub Sudan 13°42N 25°5E 257 E2
Magee U.S.A. 31°52N 89°44W 315 F10
Magelang Indonesia 7°29S 110°13E 235 D4
Magellan's Str. = Magallanes, Estrecho de Chile 52°30S 75°0W 336 D2
Magelungen Sweden 59°13N 18°4E 139 B2
Magenta Italy 45°28N 8°53E 198 C5
Magenta, L. Australia 33°30S 119°2E 279 F2
Magerøya Norway 71°3N 25°40E 160 A21
Maggea Australia 34°28S 140°2E 282 C4
Maggia → Switz. 46°18N 8°36E 179 J4
Maggiorasca, Mte. Italy 44°33N 9°29E 198 D6
Maggiore, L. Italy 45°57N 8°39E 198 B5
Maggotty Jamaica 18°9N 77°46W 320 a
Maghâgha Egypt 28°38N 30°50E 256 B3
Maghama Mauritania 15°32N 12°57W 262 B2
Magharibi = Western □ Kenya 0°30N 34°30E 268 B3
Maghera U.K. 54°51N 6°41W 166 B5
Magherafelt U.K. 54°45N 6°37W 166 B5
Maghnia Algeria 34°50N 1°43W 261 B4
Maghreb Baghdād, Iraq 33°23N 44°22E 113 A2
Maghreb N. Afr. 32°0N 4°0W 254 C3
Maginu Japan 35°34N 139°34E 140 B2
Magione Italy 43°8N 12°12E 199 E9
Magistralnyy Russia 56°16N 107°36E 215 D11
Maglaj Bos.-H. 44°33N 18°7E 182 F3
Magliana Italy 41°50N 12°26E 136 B1
Magliano in Toscana Italy 42°36N 11°17E 199 F8
Máglie Italy 40°7N 18°18E 201 B11
Magnac-Laval France 46°13N 1°11E 174 B5
Magnesia = Magnisia Greece 39°15N 23°0E 204 B5
Magnetic Pole (North) Arctic 85°6N 134°0W 150 A1
Magnetic Pole (South) Antarctica 64°24S 137°12E 151 C9
Magnisia Greece 39°15N 23°0E 204 B5
Magnitogorsk Russia 53°27N 59°4E 186 D10
Magnolia Ark., U.S.A. 33°16N 93°14W 315 E8
Magnolia Miss., U.S.A. 31°9N 90°28W 315 F9
Magnor Norway 59°56N 12°15E 164 E9
Magny-en-Vexin France 49°9N 1°47E 173 C8
Magny-les-Hameaux France 48°44N 2°3E 134 B1
Mago Fiji 17°26S 179°8W 287 A3
Mago △ Ethiopia 5°40N 36°18E 257 F4
Magog Canada 45°18N 72°9W 313 A12
Magong = Makung Taiwan 23°34N 119°34E 225 C1
Magoro Uganda 1°45N 34°12E 268 B3
Magoye Zambia 16°1S 27°30E 269 F2
Magpet Phil. 7°6N 125°6E 233 H5
Magpie, L. Canada 51°0N 64°41W 299 B7
Magrath Canada 49°25N 112°50W 296 D6
Magre → Spain 39°11N 0°15W 197 F4
Magrur Sudan 14°1N 30°27E 257 E3
Magrur, Wadi → Sudan 16°5N 26°30E 257 D2
Magsingal Phil. 17°41N 120°25E 232 C3
Magta Lahjar Mauritania 17°28N 13°17W 262 B2
Magu Tanzania 2°30S 33°30E 268 C3
Maguan China 23°0N 104°21E 228 F5
Maguarinho, C. Brazil 0°15S 48°30W 332 B2
Magude Mozam. 25°2S 32°40E 271 C5

Maguindanao □ Phil. 7°5N 124°40E 233 H5
Magura Bangla. 23°26N 89°26E 241 D2
Magurski △ Poland 49°30N 21°30E 185 J8
Mağusa = Famagusta Cyprus 35°8N 33°55E 207 E9
Maguse L. Canada 61°37N 95°10W 297 A9
Maguse Pt. Canada 61°20N 93°50W 297 A10
Magvana India 23°13N 69°22E 242 H3
Magwe Burma 20°10N 95°0E 241 E5
Magwe South Sudan 4°8N 32°17E 257 G3
Magwe □ Burma 20°0N 95°0E 241 F5
Magyarorszag = Hungary ■ Europe 47°20N 19°20E 181 D12
Maha Oya Sri Lanka 7°31N 81°22E 245 L5
Maha Sarakham Thailand 16°12N 103°16E 236 D4
Mahābād Iran 36°50N 45°45E 213 D11
Mahabaleshwar India 17°58N 73°43E 244 F1
Mahabalipuram India 12°37N 80°11E 245 H5
Mahabharat Lekh Nepal 28°30N 82°0E 243 E10
Mahabo Madag. 20°23S 44°40E 272 C1
Mahad India 18°6N 73°29E 244 E1
Mahaddayweyne Somalia 2°58N 45°32E 267 D6
Mahadeo Hills India 22°20N 78°30E 243 H8
Mahadeopur India 18°48N 80°0E 244 E5
Mahaffey U.S.A. 40°53N 78°44W 312 F6
Mahagi Dem. Rep. of the Congo 2°20N 31°0E 268 B3
Mahagnao Volcano △ Phil. 10°52N 124°51E 233 F5
Mahaicony Guyana 6°36N 57°48W 329 B6
Mahajamba → Madag. 15°33S 47°8E 272 B2
Mahajamba, Helodranon' i Madag. 15°24S 47°5E 272 B2
Mahajan India 28°48N 73°56E 242 E5
Mahajanga Madag. 15°40S 46°25E 272 B2
Mahajanga □ Madag. 17°0S 47°0E 272 B2
Mahajilo → Madag. 19°42S 45°22E 272 B2
Mahakam → Indonesia 0°35S 117°17E 235 C5
Mahalapye Botswana 23°1S 26°51E 270 B4
Mahalaxmi Mumbai, India 130 a1
Mahalchhar Bangla. 22°55N 92°2E 241 D4
Mahale Mts. Tanzania 6°20S 30°0E 268 D3
Mahale Mts. △ Tanzania 6°10S 29°50E 268 D2
Maḩallāt Iran 33°55N 50°30E 247 C6
Māhān Iran 30°5N 57°18E 247 D8
Mahan → India 23°30N 82°50E 243 H10
Mahanadi → India 20°20N 86°25E 244 D8
Mahananda → India 25°12N 87°52E 243 G12
Mahanoro Madag. 19°54S 48°48E 272 B2
Mahanoy City U.S.A. 40°49N 76°9W 313 F8
Mahaplag Phil. 10°35N 124°57E 233 F5
Mahar, L. U.S.A. 25°46N 80°18W 129 D1
Maharashtra □ India 20°30N 75°30E 244 D2
Maharès Tunisia 34°32N 10°29E 258 B2
Maharivo → Madag. 20°26S 44°10E 272 C1
Mahasamund India 21°6N 82°6E 244 D6
Mahasham, W. → Egypt 30°15N 34°10E 251 H5
Mahasoa Madag. 22°12S 46°6E 272 C2
Mahasolo Madag. 19°7S 46°22E 272 B2
Mahattat ash Shīdīyah Jordan 29°55N 35°55E 251 J6
Mahattat 'Unayzah Jordan 30°30N 35°47E 251 H6
Mahaut Dominica 15°21N 61°24W 323 k
Mahaut Guadeloupe 16°11N 61°46W 322 e
Mahavavy → Madag. 15°57S 45°54E 272 B2
Mahaweli Ganga → Sri Lanka 8°27N 81°13E 245 K5
Mahaxay Laos 17°22N 105°12E 236 D5
Mahbubabad India 17°42N 80°2E 244 F5
Mahbubnagar India 16°45N 77°59E 244 F3
Mahd adh Dhahab Si. Arabia 23°30N 40°52E 248 B3
Mahda U.A.E. 25°20N 56°15E 247 E8
Maḩḑah Oman 24°24N 55°59E 247 E7
Mahdia Guyana 5°13N 59°8W 329 B6
Mahdia Tunisia 35°28N 11°0E 258 A2
Mahdia □ Tunisia 35°20N 10°35E 261 A7
Mahe Jammu & Kashmir, India 33°10N 78°32E 243 C8
Mahé Pondicherry, India 11°42N 75°34E 245 J2
Mahé Seychelles 5°0S 55°30E 272 c
Mahé ✈ (SEZ) Seychelles 4°40S 55°31E 272 c
Mahébourg Mauritius 20°24S 57°42E 272 e
Mahendra Giri India 8°20N 77°30E 245 K3
Mahendragarh India 28°17N 76°14E 242 E7
Mahendranagar Nepal 28°55N 80°20E 243 E9
Mahenge Tanzania 8°45S 36°41E 269 D4
Maheno N.Z. 45°10S 170°50E 285 F5
Mahesana India 23°39N 72°26E 242 H5
Maheshtala India 22°29N 88°15E 124 C1
Maheshwar India 22°11N 75°35E 242 H6
Maheskhali I. Bangla. 21°36N 91°56E 241 E3
Mahgawan India 26°29N 78°37E 243 F8
Mahi → India 22°15N 72°55E 242 H5
Mahia Pen. N.Z. 39°9S 177°55E 284 F6
Mahibadhoo Maldives 3°47N 72°58E 272 d
Mahighe Solomon Is. 8°30S 159°58E 287 M10
Mahikeng = Mafikeng S. Africa 25°50S 25°38E 270 C4
Mahilyow Belarus 53°55N 30°18E 177 B16
Mahilyow □ Belarus 54°10N 30°50E 188 E6
Mahim Maharashtra, India 19°2N 72°50E 130 A2
Mahim Maharashtra, India 19°39N 72°44E 244 E1
Mahim B. India 19°2N 72°49E 130 A1
Mahina Tahiti 17°30S 149°27W 289 e
Mahipalpur India 28°32N 77°7E 120 B1
Mahirija Morocco 34°0N 3°16W 261 B4
Mahlaing Burma 21°6N 95°39E 241 E5
Mahlsdorf Germany 52°30N 13°37E 115 A4
Mahmiya Sudan 17°12N 33°43E 257 D3
Mahmoodabad Pakistan 24°51N 67°4E 123 A2
Mahmud Kot Pakistan 30°16N 71°0E 242 D4
Mahmudia Romania 45°5N 29°5E 183 E14
Mahmudiye Turkey 39°48N 30°15E 205 B12
Mahmutbey Turkey 41°3N 28°49E 203 E12
Mahmutlar Turkey 36°29N 32°5E 250 B3
Māhneshān Iran 36°44N 47°39E 213 D12
Mahnomen U.S.A. 47°19N 95°58W 308 B6
Maho Sri Lanka 7°49N 80°16E 245 L5
Mahoba India 25°15N 79°55E 243 G8
Mahomet U.S.A. 40°12N 88°24W 311 D8
Mahón = Maó Spain 39°53N 4°16E 206 B5
Mahon, Menorca ✈ (MAH) Spain 39°50N 4°16E 196 F9
Mahone Bay Canada 44°27N 64°23W 299 D7
Mahongo ⌂ Namibia 18°0S 23°15E 270 B3
Mahopac U.S.A. 41°22N 73°45W 313 E11
Mahoua Chad 11°49N 18°26E 259 F3
Mahrāt, Jabal Yemen 17°0N 51°0E 249 C5
Mahrauli India 28°31N 77°10E 120 B2
Mährisch-Budwitz = Moravské Budějovice Czech Rep. 49°4N 15°49E 180 B8
Mährisch-Schönberg = Šumperk Czech Rep. 49°59N 16°59E 181 B9
Mährisch-Trubau = Moravská Třebová Czech Rep. 49°45N 16°40E 181 B9
Mahul India 19°0N 72°53E 130 A2
Mahuta Nigeria 11°32N 4°58E 263 C5
Mahuva India 21°5N 71°48E 242 J4
Mahya Daği Turkey 41°47N 27°36E 203 E11
Mai-Ndombe, L. Dem. Rep. of the Congo 2°0S 18°20E 264 C3
Mai Thon, Ko Thailand 7°40N 98°28E 237 a
Maia Amer. Samoa 14°13S 169°25W 302 g
Maia Azores 36°56N 25°1W 153 d4
Maia Portugal 41°14N 8°37W 194 D2
Maials Spain 41°22N 0°30E 196 D5
Maibong India 25°18N 93°10E 241 C4
Maicao Colombia 11°23N 72°13W 328 A3
Maîche France 47°16N 6°48E 173 E13
Maici → Brazil 6°30S 61°43W 331 B5
Maicuru → Brazil 2°14S 54°17W 329 D7
Máida Italy 38°51N 16°22E 201 D9
Maida Vale London, U.K. 125 a1
Maidan Khula Afghan. 33°36N 69°50E 242 C3
Maidenhead U.K. 51°31N 0°42W 169 F7
Maidstone Vic., Australia 37°47S 144°52E 128 A1
Maidstone Sask., Canada 53°5N 109°20W 297 C7
Maidstone Kent, U.K. 51°16N 0°32E 169 F8
Maiduguri Nigeria 12°0N 13°20E 263 C7
Maiella △ Italy 42°5N 14°5E 199 F11
Măieruş Romania 45°53N 25°31E 183 E10
Maigatari Nigeria 12°46N 9°27E 263 C6
Maigh Nuad = Maynooth Ireland 53°23N 6°34W 166 C5
Maignelay Montigny France 49°32N 2°30E 173 C9
Maigo Phil. 8°10N 123°57E 233 G4
Maigualida, Sierra Venezuela 5°30N 65°10W 329 B4
Maigudo Ethiopia 7°30N 37°8E 257 F4
Maihar India 24°16N 80°45E 243 G9
Maihara Japan 35°19N 136°17E 223 B8
Maikala Ra. India 22°0N 81°0E 244 D5
Maiko △ Dem. Rep. of the Congo 0°30S 27°50E 268 C2
Mailani India 28°17N 80°21E 243 E9
Mä'ili U.S.A. 21°25N 158°11W 302 K13
Mä'ili Pt. U.S.A. 21°24N 158°11W 302 K13
Mailiao Taiwan 23°48N 120°13E 225 C2
Maillezais France 46°22N 0°45W 174 B3
Mailsi Pakistan 29°48N 72°15E 242 E5
Maimbung Phil. 5°56N 121°2E 233 J3
Main → Bayern, Germany 50°0N 8°18E 179 F4
Main → Antrim, U.K. 54°48N 6°18W 166 B5
Main Channel Canada 45°21N 81°45W 312 A3
Main Range △ Australia 28°11S 152°27E 281 D5
Main Ridge Trin. & Tob. 11°16N 60°40W 323 s
Mainburg Germany 48°38N 11°47E 179 G7
Maindargi India 17°28N 76°18E 244 F3
Maine France 48°20N 0°15W 172 D6
Maine □ U.S.A. 45°20N 69°0W 309 C19
Maine → Ireland 52°9N 9°45W 166 D2
Maine, G. of U.S.A. 43°0N 68°30W 301 G26
Maine-et-Loire □ France 47°31N 0°30W 172 E6
Maïne-Soroa Niger 13°13N 12°2E 263 C7
Maingkaing Burma 24°48N 95°16E 241 C5
Maingkwan Burma 26°15N 96°37E 241 B6
Mainistir na Corann = Midleton Ireland 51°55N 8°10W 166 E3
Mainit Phil. 9°32N 125°32E 233 G5
Mainit, L. Phil. 9°31N 125°30E 233 G5
Mainland Orkney, U.K. 58°59N 3°8W 167 C5
Mainland Shet., U.K. 60°15N 1°22W 167 A7
Mainpuri India 27°18N 79°4E 243 F8
Maintal Germany 50°7N 8°52E 179 E4
Maintenon France 48°35N 1°35E 173 D8
Maintirano Madag. 18°3S 44°1E 272 B1
Mainz Germany 50°1N 8°14E 179 E4
Maio C. Verde Is. 15°10N 23°10W 153 j
Maipú Argentina 36°52S 57°50W 334 D4
Maipú Santiago, Chile 33°30S 70°45W 137 C1
Maiquetía Venezuela 10°36N 66°57W 328 A4
Máira → Italy 44°49N 7°38E 198 D4
Mairabari India 26°30N 92°22E 241 B4
Mairena del Aljarafe Spain 37°20N 6°6W 195 H4
Mairipotaba Brazil 17°18S 49°28W 333 E2
Maisi Cuba 20°17N 74°9W 321 B5
Maisi, Pta. de Cuba 20°10N 74°10W 321 B5
Maiskhal I. Bangla. 21°36N 91°56E 241 E3
Maison Coloniale Guadeloupe 16°18N 61°16W 322 e
Maisonneuve, Parc Canada 45°32N 73°33W 130 A2
Maisons-Alfort France 48°48N 2°26E 134 B3
Maisons-Laffitte France 48°57N 2°8E 134 A1
Maissoneuve Canada 45°32N 73°33W 130 A2
Maitland N.S.W., Australia 32°33S 151°36E 283 B9
Maitland S. Austral., Australia 34°23S 137°40E 282 C2
Maitland Western Cape, S. Africa 33°53S 18°29E 118 A1
Maitland → Canada 43°45N 81°43W 312 C3
Maitland, Banjaran Malaysia 4°55N 116°37E 235 B5
Maitri Antarctica 70°0S 3°0W 151 D3
Maitum Phil. 6°2N 124°30E 233 H5
Maiyema Nigeria 12°5N 4°25E 263 C5
Maiyuan China 25°34N 117°28E 229 E11
Maíz, Is. del Nic. 12°15N 83°4W 320 D3
Maizuru Japan 35°25N 135°22E 223 B7
Majagual Colombia 8°33N 74°38W 328 B3
Majalengka Indonesia 6°50S 108°13E 235 D3
Majanji Uganda 0°16N 34°0E 268 B3
Majari → Brazil 3°29N 60°58W 329 C5
Majdūl Libya 25°51N 15°7E 258 C3
Majella = Maiella △ Italy 42°5N 14°5E 199 F11
Majene Indonesia 3°38S 118°57E 235 C5
Majes → Peru 16°40S 72°44W 330 D3
Majete ⌂ Malawi 15°54S 34°34E 269 F3
Majevica Bos.-H. 44°45N 18°50E 182 F3
Maji Ethiopia 6°12N 35°30E 257 F4
Majiang China 26°28N 107°32E 228 D6
Majorca = Mallorca Spain 39°30N 3°0E 206 B4
Majors Creek Australia 35°33S 149°45E 283 C8
Majuli I. India 26°58N 94°14E 241 B5
Majuriã Brazil 7°30S 64°55W 331 B5
Majuro Marshall Is. 7°9N 171°12E 288 G9
Mak, Ko Thailand 11°49N 102°29E 237 G4
Maka Senegal 13°40N 14°10W 262 C2
Mäkaha Hawai'i, U.S.A. 21°29N 158°13W 302 K13
Makaha Zimbabwe 17°20S 32°39E 271 A5
Makahoa Pt. U.S.A. 21°41N 157°56W 302 J14
Makak Cameroon 3°36N 11°0E 263 E7
Makaka Congo 3°45S 13°39E 264 C2
Makakilo City U.S.A. 21°22N 158°5W 302 K13
Makakou Gabon 0°11S 12°12E 264 C2
Makalamabedi Botswana 20°19S 23°51E 270 B3
Makale Indonesia 3°6S 119°51E 235 C5
Makalu Asia 27°55N 87°8E 243 F12
Makalu-Barun △ Nepal 27°45N 87°10E 243 F12
Makamba Burundi 4°8S 29°49E 268 C2
Makapu'u Pt. U.S.A. 21°19N 157°39W 302 K14
Makarewa Junction N.Z. 46°20S 168°21E 285 G3
Makari Cameroon 12°35N 10°27E 259 F2
Makarikari = Makgadikgadi Salt Pans Botswana 20°40S 25°45E 270 B4
Makarov Basin Arctic 87°0N 150°0W 150 A
Makarovo Russia 57°40N 107°45E 215 D11
Makarska Croatia 43°20N 17°2E 199 E14
Makaryev Russia 57°52N 43°50E 190 B6
Makasar Indonesia 6°17S 106°52E 122 A2
Makassar Indonesia 5°10S 119°20E 235 D5
Makassar, Selat Indonesia 1°0S 118°20E 235 C5
Makassar, Str. of = Makassar, Selat Indonesia 1°0S 118°20E 235 C5
Makat = Maqat Kazakhstan 47°39N 53°19E 187 E9
Makati Phil. 14°33N 121°7E 127 B2
Makaw Dem. Rep. of the Congo 3°29S 18°20E 264 C3
Makawao U.S.A. 20°52N 156°17W 302 C5
Makaya Dem. Rep. of the Congo 3°21S 18°1E 264 C3
Makedonija = Macedonia ■ Europe 41°53N 21°40E 202 E5
Makefu Cook Is. 18°59S 169°55W 289 g
Makemo French Polynesia 16°35S 143°40W 289 f
Makeni S. Leone 8°55N 12°5W 262 D2
Makeyevka = Makiyivka Ukraine 48°0N 38°0E 189 H9
Makgadikgadi △ Botswana 20°27S 24°47E 270 B3
Makgadikgadi Salt Pans Botswana 20°40S 25°45E 270 B4
Makhachkala Russia 43°0N 47°30E 191 J8
Makhado = Louis Trichardt S. Africa 23°1S 29°43E 271 B4
Makham, Ao Thailand 7°51N 98°25E 237 a
Makharadze = Ozurgeti Georgia 41°55N 42°0E 191 K5
Makhfar al Buşayyah Iraq 30°0N 46°10E 246 D5
Makhmūr Iraq 35°46N 43°35E 213 E10
Makhtal India 16°30N 77°31E 245 E3
Makhyah, W. → Yemen 17°40N 49°1E 249 C5
Makian Indonesia 0°20N 127°20E 231 D7
Makina Solomon Is. 9°50S 160°50E 287 M11
Makindu Kenya 2°18S 37°50E 268 C4
Mäkiniitty Finland 60°20N 24°58E 121 A2
Makinka = Makīnsk Kazakhstan 52°37N 70°26E 217 B8
Makīnsk Kazakhstan 52°37N 70°26E 217 B8
Makira = San Cristóbal Solomon Is. 10°30S 161°0E 287 N11
Makiyivka Ukraine 48°0N 38°0E 189 H9
Makkah Si. Arabia 21°30N 39°54E 248 B2
Makkah □ Si. Arabia 21°30N 42°30E 248 B3
Makkovik Canada 55°10N 59°10W 299 A8
Makó Hungary 46°14N 20°33E 182 D5
Mako Senegal 12°52N 12°20W 262 C2
Makogai Fiji 17°28S 179°0E 287 A2
Makok Gabon 0°1S 9°35E 264 C1
Makokou Gabon 0°40N 12°50E 264 B2
Makongo Dem. Rep. of the Congo 3°25N 26°17E 268 B2
Makoro Dem. Rep. of the Congo 3°10N 29°59E 268 B2
Makoua Congo 0°5S 15°50E 264 C3
Maków Mazowiecki Poland 52°52N 21°6E 185 F8
Maków Podhalański Poland 49°43N 19°45E 185 J6
Makra Greece 36°15N 25°54E 205 E7
Makrai India 22°2N 77°0E 242 H7
Makran Asia 26°13N 61°30E 240 D1
Makran Coast Range Pakistan 25°40N 64°0E 240 D2
Makrana India 27°2N 74°46E 242 F6
Makrany Belarus 51°48N 24°17E 185 G11
Makri Greece 40°52N 25°40E 203 F9
Makri India 19°46N 81°55E 244 E5
Makrigialos Greece 35°2N 25°59E 207 E6
Makthar Tunisia 35°48N 9°12E 258 A1
Mākū Iran 39°15N 44°31E 213 C11
Mäkua U.S.A. 21°32N 158°13W 302 J13
Makum India 27°30N 95°23E 241 B5
Makumbi Dem. Rep. of the Congo 5°50S 20°43E 265 D4
Makunda Botswana 22°30S 20°7E 270 B3
Makung Taiwan 23°34N 119°34E 225 C1
Makungo Somalia 0°49N 42°35E 267 D5
Makunudu Atoll Maldives 6°20N 72°35E 272 d
Makunza Dem. Rep. of the Congo 8°52S 24°19E 265 D4
Makurazaki Japan 31°15N 130°20E 222 F2
Makurdi Nigeria 7°43N 8°35E 263 D6
Makushin Volcano U.S.A. 53°53N 166°55W 303 K6
Makūyeh Iran 28°7N 53°9E 247 D7
Makwassie S. Africa 27°17S 26°0E 270 C4
Makwiro Zimbabwe 17°58S 30°25E 271 A5
Mal India 26°51N 88°45E 241 B2
Mâl Mauritania 16°58N 13°23W 262 B2
Mal B. Ireland 52°50N 9°30W 166 D2
Mala = Mallow Ireland 52°8N 8°39W 166 D3
Mala Peru 12°40S 76°38W 330 C2
Mala ⊛ Australia 21°39S 130°45E 278 D5
Mala, Pta. Panama 7°28N 80°2W 320 E3
Mala Belozërka Ukraine 47°12N 34°56E 189 J8
Malá Fatra △ Slovak Rep. 49°10N 19°0E 181 B12
Mala Kapela Croatia 44°45N 15°30E 199 D12
Mała Panew → Poland 50°43N 17°54E 185 H4
Malá Strana Czech Rep. 50°4N 14°24E 135 B2
Mala Vyska Ukraine 48°39N 31°36E 189 H6
Malabang Phil. 7°36N 124°3E 233 H5
Malabar N.S.W., Australia 33°58S 151°14E 139 B2
Malabar Fla., U.S.A. 28°0N 80°34W 317 H9
Malabar Coast India 11°0N 75°0E 245 J2
Malabar Hill India 18°57N 72°48E 130 B1
Malabar Pt. India 18°56N 72°48E 130 B1
Malabo = Rey Malabo Eq. Guin. 3°45N 8°50E 263 E6
Malabon Phil. 14°39N 120°56E 127 B1
Malabrigo = Puerto Chicama Peru 7°45S 79°20W 330 B2
Malabrigo Pt. Phil. 13°36N 121°15E 232 E3
Malabu Nigeria 9°32N 12°48E 263 D7
Malabuñgan Phil. 9°3N 117°38E 233 G1
Malacañang Palace Phil. 14°35N 120°59E 127 B1
Malacca, Straits of Indonesia 3°0N 101°0E 237 L3
Malacky Slovak Rep. 48°27N 17°0E 181 C10
Malad City U.S.A. 42°12N 112°15W 304 E7
Maladeta Spain 42°39N 0°39E 196 C5
Maladzyechna Belarus 54°20N 26°50E 177 A14
Málaga Colombia 6°42N 72°44W 328 B3
Málaga Spain 36°43N 4°23W 195 J6
Málaga □ Spain 36°38N 4°58W 195 J6
Malagarasi Tanzania 5°5S 30°50E 268 D3
Malagarasi → Tanzania 5°12S 29°47E 268 D2
Malagasy Rep. = Madagascar ■ Africa 20°0S 47°0E 272 B2
Malagón Spain 39°11N 3°52W 195 F7
Malagón → Spain 37°35N 7°29W 195 H3
Malah Syria 32°33N 36°54E 251 F7
Malahide Ireland 53°26N 6°9W 120 A3
Malaimbandy Madag. 20°20S 45°36E 272 C2
Malaita Solomon Is. 9°0S 161°0E 287 M11
Malakal South Sudan 9°33N 31°40E 257 F3
Malakal Harb. Palau 7°19N 134°27E 288 c
Malakanagiri India 18°21N 81°54E 244 E5
Malakand Pakistan 34°40N 71°55E 242 B4
Malakoff France 48°49N 2°18E 134 B2
Malakula Vanuatu 16°15S 167°30E 287 F5
Malakwal Pakistan 32°34N 73°13E 242 C5
Malalag Phil. 6°36N 125°24E 233 H5
Malalaua Papua N. G. 8°4S 146°10E 286 E4
Malam Chad 11°27N 20°59E 259 F4
Malamala Indonesia 3°21S 120°55E 231 E6
Malanda Australia 17°22S 145°35E 280 B4
Malang Indonesia 7°59S 112°45E 235 D4
Malanga Mozam. 13°28S 36°7E 269 E4
Malangas Phil. 7°37N 123°1E 233 H4
Malange □ Angola 9°30S 16°0E 265 D3
Malangen Norway 69°24N 18°37E 160 B18
Malangwa Nepal 26°52N 85°34E 243 F11
Malanje Angola 9°36S 16°17E 265 D3
Malanut B. Phil. 9°15N 117°59E 233 G1
Malapatan Phil. 5°59N 125°18E 233 J5
Malappuram India 11°7N 76°11E 245 J3
Mälaren Sweden 59°30N 17°10E 162 E11
Malargüe Argentina 35°32S 69°30W 334 D2
Mälarhöjaen Sweden 59°18N 17°58E 139 B1
Malartic Canada 48°9N 78°9W 298 C4
Malaryta Belarus 51°50N 24°3E 185 G11
Malasiqui Phil. 15°55N 120°24E 232 D3
Malaspina Glacier U.S.A. 59°50N 140°30W 303 G12
Malate Phil. 14°34N 120°59E 127 B1
Malatya Turkey 38°25N 38°20E 213 C8
Malatya □ Turkey 38°15N 38°0E 212 C7
Malawali, Pulau Malaysia 7°3N 117°18E 235 A5
Malawi ■ Africa 11°55S 34°0E 269 E3
Malawi, L. Africa 12°30S 34°30E 269 E3
Malay Phil. 11°54N 121°55E 233 F3
Malay Pen. Asia 7°25N 100°0E 237 J3
Malay Quarter Cape Town, S. Africa 118 c2
Malaya Belozërka = Mala Belozërka Ukraine 47°12N 34°56E 189 J8
Malaya Neva Russia 59°56N 30°16E 137 B1
Malaya Okhta Russia 59°55N 30°25E 137 B2
Malaya Vishera Russia 58°55N 32°25E 188 C7
Malaya Viska = Mala Vyska Ukraine 48°39N 31°36E 189 H6
Malaybalay Phil. 8°5N 125°7E 233 G5
Malāyer Iran 34°19N 48°51E 213 E13
Malaysia ■ Asia 5°0N 110°0E 235 B4
Malazgirt Turkey 39°10N 42°33E 213 C10
Malbaza Niger 13°59N 5°38E 263 C6
Malbon Australia 21°5S 140°17E 280 C3
Malbooma Australia 30°41S 134°11E 281 E1
Malbork Poland 54°3N 19°1E 184 D6
Malca Dube Ethiopia 6°47N 42°4E 267 C5
Malcésine Italy 45°46N 10°48E 198 C7
Malchin Germany 53°44N 12°44E 178 B8
Malchow Berlin, Germany 52°34N 13°29E 115 A3
Malchow Mecklenburg-Vorpommern, Germany 53°28N 12°25E 178 B8
Malcolm Australia 28°51S 121°25E 279 E3
Malcolm, Pt. Australia 33°48S 123°45E 279 F3
Malczyce Poland 51°14N 16°29E 185 G3
Maldah India 25°2N 88°9E 243 G13
Maldegem Belgium 51°14N 3°26E 170 C3
Malden London, U.K. 51°23N 0°15W 125 B2
Malden Mass., U.S.A. 42°26N 71°3W 116 A2
Malden Mo., U.S.A. 36°34N 89°57W 308 G9
Malden I. Kiribati 4°3S 155°1W 289 H12
Maldives ■ Ind. Oc. 5°0N 73°0E 272 d
Maldon Vic., Australia 37°0S 144°6E 282 D6
Maldon Essex, U.K. 51°44N 0°42E 169 F8
Maldonado Uruguay 34°59S 55°0W 335 C5
Maldonado, Pta. Mexico 16°20N 98°33W 319 D5
Malè Italy 46°21N 10°55E 198 B7
Malé Maldives 4°10N 73°28E 272 d
Malé ✈ (MLE) Maldives 4°11N 73°28E 272 d
Malé Atoll Maldives 4°45N 73°15E 272 d
Malé Karpaty Slovak Rep. 48°30N 17°20E 181 C10
Maleas, Akra Greece 36°28N 23°7E 204 E5
Malebo, Pool Africa 4°17S 15°20E 265 C3
Malegaon India 20°30N 74°38E 244 D2
Malei Mozam. 17°12S 36°58E 269 F4
Maleizen Belgium 50°45N 4°31E 116 B3
Malek South Sudan 6°4N 31°36E 257 F3
Malek Kandī Iran 37°9N 46°6E 213 D12
Malela Bas-Congo, Dem. Rep. of the Congo 5°59S 12°37E 265 D2
Malela Maniema, Dem. Rep. of the Congo 4°22S 26°8E 265 C5
Malema Mozam. 14°57S 37°20E 269 E4
Maleme Greece 35°31N 23°49E 207 E4
Malendok I. Papua N. G. 3°28S 153°13E 286 B7
Maler Kotla India 30°32N 75°58E 242 D6
Måleräs Sweden 56°54N 15°34E 163 H9
Males Greece 35°6N 25°35E 207 E6
Malesherbes France 48°15N 2°24E 173 D9
Maleshevska Planina Europe 41°38N 23°7E 202 E7
Malešice Czech Rep. 50°5N 14°30E 135 B3
Malesina Greece 38°37N 23°14E 204 C5
Malestroit France 47°49N 2°25W 172 E4
Malfa Italy 38°35N 14°50E 201 D7
Malgobek Russia 43°30N 44°34E 191 J7
Malgomaj Sweden 64°40N 16°30E 160 D17
Malgrat de Mar Spain 41°39N 2°46E 196 D7
Malha Sudan 15°8N 25°10E 257 D2
Malhada Brazil 14°21S 43°47W 333 D3
Malhargarh India 24°17N 74°59E 242 G6
Malheur → U.S.A. 44°4N 116°59W 304 D5
Malheur L. U.S.A. 43°20N 118°48W 304 E4
Mali Guinea 12°10N 12°20W 262 C2
Mali ■ Africa 17°0N 3°0W 262 B4
Mali → Burma 25°42N 97°30E 241 C6
Mali Kanal Serbia 45°36N 19°24E 182 E4
Mali Kyun Burma 13°0N 98°20E 236 F2
Malia Greece 35°17N 25°32E 207 E6
Malia, Kolpos Greece 35°19N 25°27E 207 E6
Malibran, Teatro Venice, Italy 142 b3
Malibu U.S.A. 34°2N 118°41W 307 L8
Maligaya = Gloria Phil. 12°59N 121°30E 232 E3
Maliku = Minicoy I. India 8°17N 73°2E 245 K1
Maliku Indonesia 0°39S 123°16E 231 E6
Malili Indonesia 2°42S 121°6E 231 E6
Målilla Sweden 57°23N 15°48E 163 G9
Malimba, Mts. Dem. Rep. of the Congo 7°30S 29°30E 268 D2
Malin Hd. Ireland 55°23N 7°23W 166 A4
Malin Pen. Ireland 55°20N 7°17W 166 A4
Malindang, Mt. Phil. 8°13N 123°38E 233 G4
Malindi Kenya 3°12S 40°5E 268 C5
Malindi Marine ⌂ Kenya 3°15S 40°7E 268 C5
Malines = Mechelen Belgium 51°2N 4°29E 170 C4
Malino Indonesia 1°0N 121°0E 231 D6
Malinyi Tanzania 8°56S 36°0E 269 D4
Malipo China 23°7N 104°42E 228 F5
Maliq Albania 40°45N 20°48E 202 F4
Malir → Pakistan 24°49N 67°4E 123 B2
Malita Phil. 6°19N 125°39E 233 H5
Maliwun Burma 10°17N 98°40E 237 G2
Maliya India 23°5N 70°46E 242 H4
Maljenik Serbia 43°54N 21°43E 202 C5
Malka Mari △ Kenya 4°11N 40°46E 268 B5
Malkapur India 20°53N 76°12E 244 D3
Malkara Turkey 40°53N 26°53E 203 F10
Malkhangiri = Malakanagiri India 18°21N 81°54E 244 E5
Malkinia Górna Poland 52°42N 22°5E 185 F9
Malko Tŭrnovo Bulgaria 41°59N 27°31E 203 E11
Mall, The Washington, D.C., U.S.A. 143 b2
Mallacoota Australia 37°40S 149°40E 283 D8
Mallacoota Inlet Australia 37°34S 149°40E 283 D8
Mallaig U.K. 57°0N 5°50W 167 D3
Mallala Australia 34°26S 138°30E 282 C3
Mallaoua Niger 13°2N 9°36E 263 C6
Mallard U.S.A. 42°56N 94°41W 310 B2
Mallawan India 27°4N 80°12E 243 F9
Mallawi Egypt 27°44N 30°44E 256 B3
Mallee Cliffs △ Australia 34°16S 142°32E 282 C5
Mallembe Gabon 3°34S 10°53E 264 C2
Mallemort France 43°43N 5°11E 175 E9
Malleny Mills U.K. 55°52N 3°20W 121 B2
Málles Venosta Italy 46°41N 10°32E 198 B7
Mallicolo = Malakula Vanuatu 16°15S 167°30E 287 F5
Mallorca Spain 39°30N 3°0E 206 B4
Mallorytown Canada 44°29N 75°53W 313 B9
Mallow Ireland 52°8N 8°39W 166 D3
Malmbäck Sweden 57°34N 14°28E 163 G8
Malmberget Sweden 67°11N 20°40E 160 C19
Malmédy Belgium 50°25N 6°2E 170 D6
Malmesbury S. Africa 33°28S 18°41E 270 D2
Malmi Finland 60°15N 24°59E 121 B2
Malmivaara = Malmberget Sweden 67°11N 20°40E 160 C19
Malmköping Sweden 59°8N 16°44E 162 E10
Malmö Sweden 55°36N 12°59E 163 J7
Malmok Aruba 12°36N 70°4W 322 f
Malmøya Norway 59°52N 10°45E 133 A3
Malmslätt Sweden 58°27N 15°33E 163 F9
Malmyzh Russia 56°31N 50°41E 190 B10
Malnaş Romania 46°2N 25°49E 183 D10
Malo Vanuatu 15°40S 167°11E 287 E5
Malo Konare Bulgaria 42°12N 24°24E 203 D8
Maloarkhangelsk Russia 52°28N 36°30E 189 F9
Maloca Brazil 0°43N 55°57W 329 C6
Malolo Fiji 17°45S 177°11E 287 A1
Malolos Phil. 14°50N 120°49E 232 D3
Malolotja ⌂ Swaziland 26°4S 31°6E 271 C5
Malombe L. Malawi 14°40S 35°15E 269 E4
Małomice Poland 51°34N 15°29E 185 G2
Malomir Bulgaria 42°16N 26°32E 203 D10
Malone Fla., U.S.A. 30°57N 85°10W 316 E4
Malone N.Y., U.S.A. 44°51N 74°18W 313 B10
Malong China 25°24N 103°34E 228 E4
Malonga Dem. Rep. of the Congo 10°24S 23°10E 265 E4
Małopolskie □ Poland 49°50N 20°20E 185 J7
Malorad Bulgaria 43°28N 23°41E 202 C7
Måløv Denmark 55°44N 12°20E 118 A1
Måløy Norway 61°57N 5°6E 164 C2
Maloyaroslovets Russia 55°2N 36°20E 188 E9
Malpartida de Cáceres Spain 39°26N 6°30W 195 F4
Malpaso Canary Is. 27°43N 18°3W 153 e1
Malpaso, Presa = Netzahualcóyotl, Presa Mexico 17°8N 93°35W 319 D6
Malpelo, I. de Colombia 4°3N 81°35W 289 G19
Malpense, Milano ✈ (MXP) = Milano Malpense ✈ (MXP) Italy 45°38N 8°43E 128 A1
Malpica de Bergantiños Spain 43°19N 8°50W 194 B2
Malprabha → India 16°20N 76°5E 245 F3
Malpur India 23°21N 73°27E 242 H5
Malpura India 26°17N 75°23E 242 F6
Mals = Málles Venosta Italy 46°41N 10°32E 198 B7
Malsiras India 17°52N 74°55E 244 F2
Malta Brazil 6°54S 37°31W 332 C4
Malta Idaho, U.S.A. 42°18N 113°22W 304 E7
Malta Mont., U.S.A. 48°21N 107°52W 304 B10
Malta ■ Europe 35°55N 14°26E 206 F7
Malta ✈ (MLA) Malta 35°52N 14°29E 206 F7
Maltahöhe Namibia 24°55S 17°0E 270 B2
Maltepe Turkey 40°55N 29°8E 203 F13
Malton Ont., Canada 43°42N 79°38W 141 A1
Malton N. Yorks., U.K. 54°8N 0°49W 168 C7
Malu'a Solomon Is. 8°20S 160°38E 287 M11
Maludam △ Malaysia 1°39N 111°2E 235 B4
Maluko = Manolo Fortich Phil. 8°28N 124°50E 233 G5
Maluku Indonesia 1°0S 127°0E 231 E7
Maluku □ Indonesia 3°0S 128°0E 231 E7
Maluku Sea = Molucca Sea Indonesia 0°0 125°0E 231 E6
Malumfashi Nigeria 11°48N 7°39E 263 C6
Malunda Indonesia 3°0S 118°50E 235 C5
Malundo Angola 14°51S 22°0E 265 E4
Malung Sweden 60°42N 13°44E 162 D7
Malungon Phil. 6°16N 125°14E 233 H5
Malungsfors Sweden 60°44N 13°33E 162 D7
Malur India 13°0N 77°55E 245 H3
Maluso Phil. 6°33N 121°53E 233 H3
Maluwe Ghana 8°40N 2°17W 262 D4
Malvalli India 12°28N 77°8E 245 H3
Malvan India 16°2N 73°30E 245 F1
Malvern Vic., Australia 37°50S 145°2E 128 B2
Malvern Ont., Canada 43°47N 79°13W 141 A3
Malvern Gauteng, S. Africa 26°11S 28°5E 123 B2
Malvern Ark., U.S.A. 34°22N 92°49W 314 D8
Malvern Hills U.K. 52°0N 2°19W 169 E5
Malvik Norway 63°25N 10°40E 164 A7
Malvinas, Is. = Falkland Is. ☒ Atl. Oc. 51°30S 59°0W 153 f
Malwal South Sudan 9°19N 31°35E 257 F3
Malý Dunaj → Slovak Rep. 47°45N 18°9E 181 D11
Malya Tanzania 3°5S 33°38E 268 C3
Malye Derbety Russia 47°57N 44°42E 191 G7
Malyn Ukraine 50°46N 29°3E 177 C15
Malyy Lyakhovskiy, Ostrov Russia 74°7N 140°36E 215 B15
Malyy Taymyr, Ostrov Russia 78°6N 107°15E 215 B11
Mama Russia 58°18N 112°54E 215 D12
Mamaku N.Z. 38°5S 176°8E 284 E5
Mämala B. U.S.A. 21°15N 157°55W 302 K14
Mamanguape Brazil 6°50S 35°4W 332 C4
Mamanuca Group Fiji 17°35S 177°5E 287 A1
Mamarr Mitlā Egypt 30°2N 32°54E 251 H3
Mamasa Indonesia 2°55S 119°20E 235 C5
Mambajao Phil. 9°15N 124°43E 233 G5
Mambasa Dem. Rep. of the Congo 1°22N 29°3E 268 B2
Mamberamo → Indonesia 2°0S 137°50E 231 E9
Mambéré → C.A.R. 3°31N 16°3E 264 B3
Mambéré-Kadéï □ C.A.R. 4°30N 15°30E 264 B3
Mambili → Congo 0°6N 16°5E 264 B3
Mambilima Falls Zambia 10°31S 28°45E 269 E2
Mambirima Dem. Rep. of the Congo 11°25S 27°33E 269 E2
Mambo Tanzania 4°52S 38°22E 268 C4
Mambrui Kenya 3°5S 40°5E 268 C5
Mamburao Phil. 13°13N 120°39E 232 E3
Mamedkala Russia 42°10N 48°7E 191 J9
Mameigwess L. Canada 52°35N 87°50W 298 B2
Mamers France 48°21N 0°22E 172 D7
Mamfé Cameroon 5°50N 9°15E 263 D6
Māmī, Ra's Yemen 12°32N 54°30E 249 D6
Mamili △ Namibia 18°2S 24°1E 270 A3
Mamiña Chile 20°5S 69°14W 330 E4
Mamlyutka Kazakhstan 54°56N 68°32E 217 B7
Mammoth U.S.A. 32°43N 110°39W 305 K8
Mammoth Cave △ U.S.A. 37°8N 86°13W 308 G10
Mammoth Lakes U.S.A. 37°39N 118°59W 306 H8
Mamonovo Russia 54°28N 19°55E 184 D6
Mamoré → Bolivia 10°23S 65°53W 331 C4
Mamou Guinea 10°15N 12°0W 262 C2
Mamoudzou Mayotte 12°48S 45°14E 272 b
Mampang Prapatan Indonesia 6°15S 106°49E 122 B1
Mampikony Madag. 16°6S 47°38E 272 B2
Mampoko Dem. Rep. of the Congo 0°51N 18°42E 264 B3
Mampong Ghana 7°6N 1°26W 263 D4
Mampukuji Japan 35°36N 139°31E 140 B2
Mamry, Jezioro Poland 54°5N 21°50E 184 D8
Mamuil Malal, Paso S. Amer. 39°35S 71°28W 336 A2
Mamuju Indonesia 2°41S 118°50E 235 C5
Ma'mūl Oman 18°8N 55°16E 249 C6
Mamuno Botswana 22°16S 20°1E 270 B3
Mamuras Albania 41°34N 19°41E 202 E3
Man Ivory C. 7°30N 7°40W 262 D3
Man → India 17°31N 75°32E 244 F2
Man, I. of India 8°28N 93°36E 245 K11
Man, I. of U.K. 54°15N 4°30W 168 C3
Man-Bazar India 23°4N 86°39E 243 H12
Man Budrukh India 19°2N 72°55E 130 A2
Man Kat Burma 22°5N 98°1E 241 D7
Man Khurd India 19°3N 72°55E 130 A2
Man Na Burma 23°27N 97°19E 241 D6
Man of War B. Trin. & Tob. 11°19N 60°34W 323 s
Mana Fr. Guiana 5°45N 53°55W 329 B7
Mänä Hawai'i, U.S.A. 22°2N 159°47W 302 A2
Mana → Fr. Guiana 5°45N 53°55W 329 B7
Mana Pools △ Zimbabwe 15°56S 29°25E 269 F2
Manaar, G. of = Mannar, G. of Asia 8°30N 79°0E 245 K4
Manabí □ Ecuador 0°40S 80°5W 328 D1
Manacacías → Colombia 4°23N 72°4W 328 C3
Manacapuru Brazil 3°16S 60°37W 329 D5
Manacapuru → Brazil 3°18S 60°37W 329 D5
Manacor Spain 39°34N 3°13E 206 B4
Manadas Azores 38°38N 28°6W 153 d1
Manado Indonesia 1°29N 124°51E 231 D6
Managua Nic. 12°6N 86°20W 320 D2
Managua, L. de Nic. 12°20N 86°30W 320 D2
Manaia N.Z. 39°33S 174°8E 284 F3
Manakara Madag. 22°8S 48°1E 272 C2
Manakau N.Z. 42°15S 173°42E 285 C8
Manākhah Yemen 15°5N 43°44E 248 D3
Manakhat Israel 31°45N 35°11E 123 B2
Manali India 32°16N 77°10E 242 C7
Manam I. Papua N. G. 4°5S 145°0E 286 C3
Manama = Al Manāmah Bahrain 26°10N 50°30E 247 E6
Manambao → Madag. 17°35S 44°0E 272 B1
Manambato Madag. 13°43S 49°7E 272 A2
Manambolo → Madag. 19°18S 44°22E 272 B1
Manambolosy Madag. 16°2S 49°40E 272 B2
Mánamo, Caño → Venezuela 9°55N 62°16W 329 B5
Mänana I. U.S.A. 21°20N 157°40W 302 K14
Mananara Madag. 16°10S 49°46E 272 B2
Mananara → Madag. 23°21S 47°42E 272 C2
Mananara ⌂ Madag. 16°14S 49°45E 272 B2
Manangatang Australia 35°5S 142°54E 282 C5
Mananjary Madag. 21°13S 48°20E 272 C2
Manankoro Mali 10°28N 7°25W 262 C3
Manantali, L. de Mali 13°12N 10°28W 262 C2
Manantavadi India 11°49N 76°1E 245 J3
Manantenina Madag. 24°17S 47°19E 272 C2
Manaos = Manaus Brazil 3°0S 60°0W 329 D6
Manapire → Venezuela 7°42N 66°7W 328 B4
Manapla Phil. 10°58N 123°5E 233 F4
Manapouri N.Z. 45°34S 167°39E 285 F2
Manapouri, L. N.Z. 45°32S 167°32E 285 F2
Manapparai India 10°36N 78°25E 245 J4
Manaqil Sudan 14°15N 32°59E 257 E3
Manar → India 18°50N 77°20E 244 E3
Manār, Jabal Yemen 14°2N 44°17E 248 D4
Manaravolo Madag. 23°59S 45°39E 272 C2
Manas Xinjiang Uygur, China 44°17N 86°10E 217 D11
Manas Somalia 2°57N 43°28E 267 D5
Manas → India 26°12N 90°40E 241 B3
Manas ⌂ India 26°40N 91°0E 241 B3
Manas He → China 45°38N 85°12E 218 B6
Manas Hu China 45°45N 85°55E 217 C11
Manaslu Nepal 28°33N 84°33E 243 E11
Manasquan U.S.A. 40°8N 74°3W 313 F10
Manassa U.S.A. 37°11N 105°56W 305 H11
Manatí Puerto Rico 18°26N 66°29W 321 b
Manati B. St. Helena 16°0S 5°46W 153 h
Manau Papua N. G. 8°4S 148°0E 286 E4
Manaus Brazil 3°0S 60°0W 329 D6
Manavgat Turkey 36°47N 31°26E 250 B2
Manavgat → Turkey 36°43N 31°27E 250 B2
Manawan = Rizal Phil. 17°51N 121°21E 232 C3
Manawan L. Canada 55°24N 103°14W 297 B8
Manawatu → N.Z. 40°28S 175°12E 284 G4
Manawatu-Wanganui □ N.Z. 39°50S 175°30E 284 F4
Manay Phil. 7°17N 126°33E 233 H6
Manbij Syria 36°31N 37°57E 212 D7
Mancha Real Spain 37°48N 3°39W 195 H7
Manche □ France 49°10N 1°20W 172 C5
Manchegorsk Russia 67°54N 32°58E 214 C4
Manchester Gt. Man., U.K. 53°29N 2°12W 168 D5
Manchester Calif., U.S.A. 38°58N 123°41W 306 G3
Manchester Conn., U.S.A. 41°47N 72°31W 313 E12
Manchester Ga., U.S.A. 32°51N 84°37W 316 C5
Manchester Iowa, U.S.A. 42°29N 91°27W 310 B5
Manchester Ky., U.S.A. 37°9N 83°46W 309 G12
Manchester Mich., U.S.A. 42°9N 84°2W 311 B12
Manchester N.H., U.S.A. 42°59N 71°28W 313 D13
Manchester N.Y., U.S.A. 42°56N 77°16W 312 D7
Manchester Ohio, U.S.A. 38°41N 83°36W 311 F13
Manchester Pa., U.S.A. 40°4N 76°43W 313 F8
Manchester Tenn., U.S.A. 35°29N 86°5W 315 D11
Manchester Vt., U.S.A. 43°10N 73°5W 313 C11
Manchester Int. ✈ (MAN) U.K. 53°21N 2°17W 168 D5
Manchester L. Canada 61°28N 107°29W 297 A7
Manchhar L. Pakistan 26°25N 67°39E 242 F2
Manchineel Bay Grenada 12°26N 61°29W 323 q
Manchou Taiwan 22°1N 120°50E 225 D2
Manchuria = Dongbei China 45°0N 125°0E 227 D13
Manchurian Plain China 47°0N 124°0E 210 D14
Manciano Italy 42°35N 11°31E 199 F8
Mancifa Ethiopia 6°53N 41°50E 257 F5
Máncora Peru 4°9S 81°1W 330 A1
Mand → India 21°42N 83°15E 243 J10
Mand → Iran 28°20N 52°30E 247 D7
Manda Ludewe, Tanzania 10°30S 34°40E 269 E3
Manda Mbeya, Tanzania 7°58S 32°29E 268 D3
Manda Mbeya, Tanzania 8°30S 32°49E 269 D3
Manda △ Chad 9°45N 17°52E 259 G3
Mandabé Madag. 21°0S 44°55E 272 C1
Mandaguari Brazil 23°32S 51°42W 335 A5
Mandah = Töhöm Mongolia 44°27N 108°2E 226 B5
Mandai Singapore 1°24N 103°45E 138 A2
Mandal Norway 58°2N 7°25E 164 F4
Mandala, Puncak Indonesia 4°44S 140°20E 231 E10
Mandalay Burma 22°0N 96°4E 241 E6
Mandalay □ Burma 22°0N 96°5E 241 E5
Mandale = Mandalay Burma 22°0N 96°4E 241 E6
Mandalgarh India 25°12N 75°6E 242 G6
Mandalgovĭ Mongolia 45°45N 106°10E 226 B4
Mandalī Iraq 33°43N 45°28E 213 F11
Mandalselva → Norway 58°2N 7°28E 164 F4
Mandaluyong Phil. 14°35N 121°1E 127 B2
Mandan U.S.A. 46°50N 100°54W 308 B3
Mandaoli India 28°37N 77°17E 120 B2
Mandaon Phil. 12°13N 123°17E 232 E4
Mandaqui → Brazil 23°30S 46°40W 137 A2
Mandar, Teluk Indonesia 3°32S 119°21E 235 C5
Mandara Mts. Nigeria 10°40N 13°40E 259 F2
Mándas Italy 39°40N 9°8E 200 C2
Mandasor = Mandsaur India 24°3N 75°8E 242 G6
Mandaue Phil. 10°20N 123°56E 233 F4
Mandel Afghan. 33°17N 61°53E 240 B1
Mandelieu-la-Napoule France 43°34N 6°57E 175 E10
Mandera Kenya 3°55N 41°53E 268 B5
Mandeville Jamaica 18°2N 77°31W 320 a
Mandi India 31°39N 76°58E 242 D7

Mandi Burewala Pakistan 30°9N 72°41E 242 D5
Mandi Dabwali India 29°58N 74°42E 242 E6
Mandiana Guinea 10°37N 8°39W 262 C3
Mandigos = Manica Mozam. 18°58S 32°59E 271 A5
Mandimba Mozam. 14°20S 35°40E 269 E4
Mandioli Indonesia 0°40S 127°20E 231 E7
Mandioré, L. S. Amer. 18°8S 57°33W 331 D6
Mandla India 22°39N 80°30E 243 H9
Mandø Denmark 55°18N 8°33E 163 J2
Mandoli India 28°41N 77°18E 120 A2
Mandorah Australia 12°32S 130°42E 278 B5
Mandoto Madag. 19°34S 46°17E 272 B2
Mandoudi Greece 38°48N 23°29E 204 C5
Mandoul Chad 9°40N 15°30E 259 G3
Mandra Greece 38°4N 23°30E 204 C5
Mandra Pakistan 33°23N 73°12E 242 C5
Mandraki Greece 36°36N 27°11E 205 E9
Mandrare → Madag. 25°10S 46°30E 272 D2
Mandritsara Madag. 15°50S 48°49E 272 B2
Mandronarivo Madag. 21°7S 45°38E 272 C2
Mandsaur India 24°3N 75°8E 242 G6
Mandurah Australia 32°36S 115°48E 279 F2
Mandúria Italy 40°24N 17°38E 201 B10
Mandvi Gujarat, India 22°51N 69°22E 242 H3
Mandvi Maharashtra, India 18°56N 72°50E 130 B2
Mandya India 12°30N 77°0E 245 H3
Mandzai Pakistan 30°55N 67°6E 242 D2
Mané Burkina Faso 12°59N 1°21W 263 C4
Maneh Iran 37°39N 57°7E 247 B8
Manenberg S. Africa 33°58S 18°33E 118 A2
Manengouba, Mts. Cameroon 5°0N 9°50E 263 E6
Maner → India 18°30N 79°40E 244 E4
Manera Madag. 22°55S 44°20E 272 C1
Manérbio Italy 45°21N 10°8E 198 C7
Maneroo Cr. → Australia 23°21S 143°53E 280 C3
Manfalût Egypt 27°20N 30°52E 256 B3
Manfred Australia 33°19S 143°45E 282 B5
Manfredónia Italy 41°38N 15°55E 199 G12
Manfredónia, G. di Italy 41°35N 16°5E 199 G13
Mang Kung Uk Hong Kong, China 22°18N 114°16E 122 B3
Mang-won S. Korea 37°33N 126°55E 137 B1
Manga Brazil 14°46S 43°56W 333 D3
Manga Burkina Faso 11°40N 1°4W 263 C4
Manga Congo 0°13S 16°5E 264 C3
Manga Niger 15°0N 14°0E 259 F2
Mangabeiras, Chapada das Brazil 10°0S 46°30W 332 D2
Mangai Dem. Rep. of the Congo 4°2S 19°33E 265 C3
Mangaia Cook Is. 21°55S 157°55W 289 K12
Mangakino N.Z. 38°22S 175°47E 284 E4
Mangal Phil. 6°25N 121°58E 233 H3
Mangalagiri India 16°26N 80°36E 245 F5
Mangaldai India 26°26N 92°2E 241 B4
Mangaldan Phil. 16°4N 120°24E 232 C3
Mangalia Romania 43°50N 28°35E 183 G13
Mangalmé Chad 12°26N 19°37E 259 F3
Mangalore India 12°55N 74°47E 245 H2
Mangaluru = Mangalore India 12°55N 74°47E 245 H2
Mangalvedha India 17°31N 75°28E 244 F2
Mangan India 27°31N 88°32E 241 B2
Mangaon India 18°15N 73°20E 244 E1
Mangarrayi ☼ Australia 15°5S 133°10E 280 B1
Mangawan India 24°41N 81°33E 243 G9
Mangaweka N.Z. 39°48S 175°47E 284 F4
Mangaweka, Mt. N.Z. 39°49S 176°5E 284 F5
Mange Dem. Rep. of the Congo 0°54N 20°30E 264 B4
Manger Norway 60°38N 5°3E 164 D2
Manggar Indonesia 2°50S 108°10E 235 C3
Manggawitu Indonesia 4°8S 133°32E 231 E8
Mangghystaū Kazakhstan 43°40N 51°13E 216 D4
Mangghystaū □ Kazakhstan 45°0N 53°0E 216 D4
Mangghystaū Tübegi Kazakhstan 44°30N 52°30E 216 D4
Manggis Indonesia 8°29S 115°31E 231 J18
Mangin Taungdan Burma 24°15N 95°45E 241 C5
Mangindrano Madag. 14°17S 48°58E 272 A2
Mangkalihat, Tanjung Indonesia 1°2N 118°59E 235 B5
Mangkururrpa ☼ Australia 20°35S 129°43E 278 D4
Mangla Pakistan 33°7N 73°39E 242 C5
Mangla Dam Pakistan 33°9N 73°44E 243 C5
Manglares, C. Colombia 1°36N 79°2W 328 C2
Manglaur India 29°44N 77°49E 242 E7
Mangle, B. de Venezuela 10°57N 64°10W 329 a
Mangle, Pta. Venezuela 10°52N 64°3W 329 a
Manglillo Venezuela 10°57N 64°19W 329 a
Manglisi Georgia 41°41N 44°22E 191 K7
Mangnai China 37°52N 91°43E 218 D7
Mangnai Zhen China 38°24N 90°14E 217 E12
Mango Togo 10°20N 0°30E 263 C5
Mango Tonga 20°17S 174°29W 287 Q13
Mangoche Malawi 14°25S 35°16E 269 E4
Mangoky → Madag. 21°29S 43°41E 272 C1
Mangole Indonesia 1°50S 125°55E 231 E6
Mangolpuri India 28°41N 77°6E 120 A1
Mangombe Dem. Rep. of the Congo 1°20S 26°48E 268 C2
Mangonui N.Z. 35°1S 173°32E 284 B2
Mangoro → Madag. 20°0S 48°45E 272 C2
Mangrol Mad. P., India 21°7N 70°7E 242 J4
Mangrol Raj., India 25°20N 76°31E 242 G6
Mangrul Pir India 20°19N 77°21E 244 D3
Manguaba = Pilar Brazil 9°36S 35°56W 332 C4
Mangualde Portugal 40°38N 7°48W 194 E3
Mangueigne Chad 10°30N 21°15E 259 F4
Mangueira, L. da Brazil 33°0S 52°50W 335 C5
Manguéni, Hamada Niger 22°35N 12°40E 258 D2
Manguinhos ✕ Brazil 22°52S 43°14W 135 B1
Mangum U.S.A. 34°53N 99°30W 314 D5
Mangungu Dem. Rep. of the Congo 5°16S 19°36E 265 D3
Manguri Australia 28°58S 134°22E 281 A1
Mangyshlak, Poluostrov = Mangghystaū Tübegi Kazakhstan 44°30N 52°30E 216 D4
Manhattan Kans., U.S.A. 39°11N 96°35W 308 F5
Manhattan New York, U.S.A. 132 d2
Manhattan Beach U.S.A. 40°34N 73°56W 132 C2
Manhattan Bridge New York, U.S.A. 132 f2
Manhatten U.S.A. 41°26N 87°59W 311 C9
Manhiça Mozam. 25°23S 32°49E 271 C5
Manhuaçu Brazil 20°15S 42°2W 333 F3
Manhumirim Brazil 20°22S 41°57W 333 F3
Maní Colombia 4°49N 72°17W 328 C3
Mania → Madag. 19°42S 45°22E 272 B2
Maniago Italy 46°10N 12°43E 199 B9
Manica Mozam. 18°58S 32°59E 271 A5
Manica □ Mozam. 19°10S 33°45E 271 A5
Manicahan Phil. 7°1N 122°12E 233 H4
Manicaland □ Zimbabwe 19°0S 32°30E 269 F3
Manicoré Brazil 5°48S 61°16W 331 B5
Manicoré → Brazil 5°51S 61°19W 331 B5
Manicouagan → Canada 49°30N 68°30W 299 C6
Manicouagan, Rés. Canada 51°5N 68°40W 299 B6
Maniema □ Dem. Rep. of the Congo 3°0S 26°0E 268 C2
Manīfah Si. Arabia 27°44N 49°0E 247 E6
Manifold, C. Australia 22°41S 150°50E 280 C5
Maniganggo China 31°56N 99°10E 228 B2
Manigotagan Canada 51°6N 96°18W 297 C9
Manigotagan → Canada 51°7N 96°20W 297 C9
Manihari India 25°21N 87°38E 243 G12
Manihi French Polynesia 14°24S 145°56W 289 f
Manihiki Cook Is. 10°24S 161°1W 289 J11
Manihiki Plateau Pac. Oc. 11°0S 164°0W 289 J11
Maniitsoq Greenland 65°26N 52°55W 154 D5
Manika, Plateau de la Dem. Rep. of the Congo 10°0S 25°5E 269 E2
Manikchhari Bangla. 22°51N 91°50E 241 D3
Manikganj Bangla. 23°52N 90°0E 241 D3
Manikpur India 25°4N 81°7E 243 G9
Manila Phil. 14°35N 120°58E 127 B1
Manila Utah, U.S.A. 40°59N 109°43W 304 F9
Manila B. Phil. 14°40N 120°35E 232 D3
Manila Ninoy Aquino Int. ✕ (MNL) Phil. 14°31N 121°0E 127 B2
Manildra Australia 33°11S 148°41E 283 B8
Manilla Australia 30°45S 150°43E 283 A9
Manilva Spain 36°23N 5°15W 195 J5
Manimpé Mali 14°11N 5°28W 262 C3
Maningrida Australia 12°3S 134°13E 280 A1
Maninian Ivory C. 10°3N 7°52W 262 C3
Maninjau, Danau Indonesia 0°19S 100°11E 234 C2
Manipa, Selat Indonesia 3°20S 127°25E 231 E7
Manipur □ India 25°0N 94°0E 241 C5
Manipur → Burma 23°45N 94°20E 241 D5
Manisa Turkey 38°38N 27°30E 205 C9
Manisa □ Turkey 38°40N 28°0E 205 C9
Manistee U.S.A. 44°15N 86°19W 308 C10
Manistee → U.S.A. 44°15N 86°21W 308 C10
Manistique U.S.A. 45°57N 86°15W 308 C10
Manito U.S.A. 40°26N 89°47W 310 D7
Manitoba □ Canada 53°30N 97°0W 297 B9
Manitoba, L. Canada 51°0N 98°45W 297 C9
Manitou Canada 49°15N 98°32W 297 D9
Manitou, L. Canada 50°55N 65°17W 299 B6
Manitou Beach U.S.A. 41°58N 84°19W 311 C12
Manitou Is. U.S.A. 45°8N 86°0W 308 C10
Manitou L. Canada 52°43N 109°43W 297 C7
Manitou Springs U.S.A. 38°52N 104°55W 304 G11
Manitoulin I. Canada 45°40N 82°30W 298 C3
Manitouwadge Canada 49°8N 85°48W 298 C2
Manitowoc U.S.A. 44°5N 87°40W 308 C10
Manitsauá-Missu → Brazil 10°58S 53°20W 331 C7
Maniyachi India 8°51N 77°55E 245 K3
Manizales Colombia 5°5N 75°32W 328 B2
Manja Madag. 21°26S 44°20E 272 C1
Manjacaze Mozam. 24°45S 34°0E 271 B5
Manjakandriana Madag. 18°55S 47°47E 272 B2
Manjhand Pakistan 25°50N 68°10E 242 G3
Manjiang China 41°56N 127°35E 224 B3
Manjimup Australia 34°15S 116°6E 279 F2
Manjlegaon India 19°9N 76°14E 244 E3
Manjo Cameroon 4°50N 9°49E 264 B1
Manjra → India 18°49N 77°52E 244 E3
Mankato Kans., U.S.A. 39°47N 98°13W 308 F4
Mankato Minn., U.S.A. 44°10N 94°0W 308 C6
Mankayan Phil. 16°52N 120°47E 232 C3
Mankayane Swaziland 26°40S 31°4E 271 C5
Mankera Pakistan 31°23N 71°26E 242 D4
Mankim Cameroon 5°6N 12°3E 263 D7
Mankkaa Finland 60°11N 24°47E 121 B1
Mankono Ivory C. 8°1N 6°10W 262 D3
Mankota Canada 49°25N 107°5W 297 D7
Mankulam Sri Lanka 9°8N 80°26E 245 K5
Manlay = Üydzin Mongolia 44°9N 107°0E 226 B4
Manleluag △ Phil. 15°4N 120°17E 232 D3
Manley Hot Springs U.S.A. 65°0N 150°38W 303 D10
Manlleu Spain 42°2N 2°17E 196 C7
Manly Australia 33°47S 151°17E 139 A2
Manmad India 20°18N 74°28E 244 D2
Mann, L. U.S.A. 28°32N 81°35W 133 A2
Mann Ranges Australia 26°6S 130°5E 279 E5
Manna Indonesia 4°25S 102°55E 234 C2
Mannahill Australia 32°25S 140°0E 282 B4
Mannar Sri Lanka 9°1N 79°54E 245 K4
Mannar, G. of Asia 8°30N 79°0E 245 K4
Mannar I. Sri Lanka 9°5N 79°45E 245 K4
Mannargudi India 10°45N 79°51E 245 J4
Mannheim Germany 49°29N 8°29E 179 F4
Manning Alta., Canada 56°53N 117°39W 296 B5
Manning Oreg., U.S.A. 45°45N 123°13W 306 E3
Manning S.C., U.S.A. 33°42N 80°13W 316 B9
Manning → Australia 31°52S 152°43E 283 A10
Manning Str. Solomon Is. 7°30S 158°0E 287 L10
Mannswörth Austria 48°8N 16°30E 142 B3
Mannu → Italy 39°16N 9°0E 200 C2
Mannu, C. Italy 40°3N 8°21E 200 B1
Mannum Australia 34°50S 139°20E 282 C3
Mano S. Leone 8°3N 12°2W 262 D2
Mano → Liberia 6°56N 11°30W 262 D2
Mano River Liberia 7°20N 11°6W 262 D2
Manoa Bolivia 9°40S 65°27W 331 B4
Manoharpur India 22°23N 85°12E 243 H11
Manokotak U.S.A. 58°58N 159°3W 303 G8
Manokwari Indonesia 0°54S 134°0E 231 E8
Manolada Greece 38°4N 21°21E 204 C3
Manolo Fortich Phil. 8°28N 124°50E 233 G5
Manombo Madag. 22°57S 43°28E 272 C1
Manono Dem. Rep. of the Congo 7°15S 27°25E 268 D2
Manono Samoa 13°50S 172°5W 287 V19
Manoppello Italy 42°15N 14°3E 199 F11
Manor Park U.K. 51°32N 0°1E 125 A4
Manora Pakistan 24°47N 66°58E 123 B1
Manora Pt. Pakistan 24°47N 66°58E 123 B1
Manorhamilton Ireland 54°18N 8°11W 166 B3
Manosque France 43°49N 5°47E 175 E9
Manotick Canada 45°13N 75°41W 313 A9
Manouane → Canada 49°30N 71°10W 299 C5
Manouane, L. Canada 50°45N 70°45W 299 B5
Manovo-Gounda Saint Floris △ C.A.R. 9°30N 21°25E 264 A4
Manp'o N. Korea 41°6N 126°24E 224 B3
Manpojin = Manp'o N. Korea 41°6N 126°24E 224 B3
Manpur Chhattisgarh, India 23°17N 83°35E 243 H10
Manpur Chhattisgarh, India 20°22N 80°43E 244 D5
Manpur Mad. P., India 22°26N 75°37E 242 H6
Manquehue, Cerro Chile 33°21S 70°35W 137 B2
Manra Kiribati 4°27S 171°15W 277 A16
Manresa Spain 41°48N 1°50E 196 D6
Mansa Gujarat, India 23°27N 72°45E 242 H5
Mansa Punjab, India 30°0N 75°27E 242 E6
Mansa Zambia 11°13S 28°55E 269 E2
Mansa Konko Gambia 13°28N 15°33W 262 C1
Mansalay Phil. 12°31N 121°26E 232 E3
Månsåsen Sweden 63°5N 14°18E 162 A8
Mansehra Pakistan 34°20N 73°15E 242 B5
Mansel I. Canada 62°0N 80°0W 295 E15
Mansfield Vic., Australia 37°4S 146°6E 283 D7
Mansfield Notts., U.K. 53°9N 1°11W 168 D6
Mansfield Ga., U.S.A. 33°31N 83°44W 316 B6
Mansfield La., U.S.A. 32°2N 93°43W 314 E8
Mansfield Mass., U.S.A. 42°2N 71°13W 313 D13
Mansfield Ohio, U.S.A. 40°45N 82°31W 312 F2
Mansfield Pa., U.S.A. 41°48N 77°5W 312 E7
Mansfield Tex., U.S.A. 32°33N 97°8W 314 E6
Mansfield, Mt. U.S.A. 44°33N 72°49W 313 B12
Mansi Burma 24°48N 95°52E 241 C5
Mansidão Brazil 10°43S 44°2W 332 D3
Mansilla de las Mulas Spain 42°30N 5°25W 194 C5
Mansle France 45°52N 0°12E 174 C4
Manso → Brazil 13°50S 47°0W 333 D2
Mansôa Guinea-Biss. 12°0N 15°20W 262 C1
Manson U.S.A. 42°32N 94°32W 310 B2
Manson Creek Canada 55°37N 124°32W 296 B4
Mansoura Algeria 36°1N 4°31E 261 A5
Manta Ecuador 1°0S 80°40W 328 D1
Manta, B. de Ecuador 0°54S 80°44W 328 D1
Mantalingajan, Mt. Phil. 8°55N 117°45E 233 G1
Mantantale Dem. Rep. of the Congo 2°10S 20°11E 264 C4
Mantare Tanzania 2°42S 33°13E 268 C3
Mantaro → Peru 12°16S 73°57W 330 C3
Manteca U.S.A. 37°48N 121°13W 306 H5
Mantecal Venezuela 7°34N 69°17W 328 B4
Mantena Brazil 18°47S 40°59W 333 E3
Manteno U.S.A. 41°15N 87°50W 311 C9
Manteo U.S.A. 35°55N 75°40W 315 D17
Mantes-la-Jolie France 48°58N 1°41E 173 D8
Mantha India 19°40N 76°23E 244 E3
Manthani India 18°40N 79°35E 244 E4
Manti U.S.A. 39°16N 111°38W 304 G8
Mantiqueira, Serra da Brazil 22°0S 44°0W 333 F3
Manton U.S.A. 44°25N 85°24W 309 C11
Mantorp Sweden 58°21N 15°20E 163 F9
Mántova Italy 45°9N 10°48E 198 C7
Mänttä Vilppula Finland 62°3N 24°40E 188 A3
Mantua = Mántova Italy 45°9N 10°48E 198 C7
Mantung Australia 34°35S 140°3E 282 C4
Manturovo Russia 58°23N 44°45E 190 A7
Manú Peru 12°10S 70°51W 330 C3
Manú → Peru 12°16S 70°55W 330 C3
Manu'a Is. Amer. Samoa 14°13S 169°35W 302 g
Manuel Alves → Brazil 11°19S 48°28W 333 D2
Manuel Alves Grande → Brazil 7°27S 47°35W 332 C2
Manuel Urbano Brazil 8°53S 69°18W 330 B4
Manui Indonesia 3°35S 123°5E 231 E6
Manukan Phil. 8°32N 123°12E 233 G4
Manukau N.Z. 37°0S 174°52E 284 D3
Manukau Harbour N.Z. 37°3S 174°45E 284 D3
Manunui N.Z. 38°54S 175°21E 284 E4
Manuoha N.Z. 38°39S 177°7E 284 E6
Manuripi → Bolivia 11°6S 67°36W 330 C4
Manus □ Papua N. G. 2°0S 147°0E 286 B4
Manus I. Papua N. G. 2°0S 147°0E 286 B4
Manvi India 15°57N 76°59E 245 G3
Manwan Dam China 24°44N 100°20E 228 E3
Manwath India 19°19N 76°32E 244 E3
Many U.S.A. 31°34N 93°29W 314 F8
Manyallaluk ☼ Australia 14°16S 132°49E 278 B5
Manyani Kenya 3°5S 38°30E 268 C4
Manyara □ Tanzania 4°30S 37°10E 268 C4
Manyara, L. Tanzania 3°40S 35°50E 268 C4
Manyara △ Tanzania 3°35S 35°50E 268 C4
Manyas Turkey 40°2N 27°59E 203 F11
Manyas Gölü = Kus Gölü Turkey 40°10N 27°55E 203 F11
Manyava Ukraine 48°39N 24°21E 183 B9
Manych → Russia 47°13N 40°40E 191 G5
Manych-Gudilo, Ozero Russia 46°24N 42°38E 191 G6
Manyonga → Tanzania 4°10S 34°15E 268 C3
Manyoni Tanzania 5°45S 34°55E 268 D3
Manzai Pakistan 32°12N 70°15E 242 C4
Manzala, Bahra el Egypt 31°10N 31°56E 256 H7
Manzanar ⌂ U.S.A. 36°44N 118°9W 306 J7
Manzanares Spain 39°2N 3°22W 195 F7
Manzanares, Canal de Spain 40°19N 3°38W 127 C2
Manzaneda Spain 42°12N 7°15W 194 C3
Manzanilla Pt. Trin. & Tob. 10°31N 61°1W 323 t
Manzanillo Cuba 20°20N 77°31W 320 B4
Manzanillo Colima, Mexico 19°3N 104°20W 318 D4
Manzanillo Venezuela 11°9N 63°54W 329 a
Manzanillo, Pta. Panama 9°30N 79°40W 320 E4
Manzano Mts. U.S.A. 34°40N 106°20W 305 J10
Manzarīyeh Iran 34°53N 50°50E 247 C6
Manzhouli China 49°35N 117°25E 219 B12
Manzini Swaziland 26°30S 31°25E 271 C5
Manzouli = Manzhouli China 49°35N 117°25E 219 B12
Manzur Vadisi △ Turkey 39°10N 39°30E 246 B3
Mao Chad 14°4N 15°19E 259 F3
Maó Spain 39°53N 4°16E 206 B5
Mao Mausoleum Beijing, China 114 c3
Maoka = Kholmsk Russia 47°40N 142°5E 215 E15
Maoke, Pegunungan Indonesia 3°40S 137°30E 231 E9
Maolin China 43°58N 123°30E 227 C12
Maoming China 21°50N 110°54E 229 G8
Maopi T'ou China 21°56N 120°43E 225 E2
Maouri, Dallol → Niger 12°5N 3°30E 263 C5
Maoxian China 31°41N 103°49E 228 B4
Maoxing China 45°28N 124°40E 227 B13
Map Micronesia 9°35N 138°10E 287 R16
Mapalma Dem. Rep. of the Congo 2°3N 24°30E 264 B4
Mapam Yumco China 30°45N 81°28E 243 D9
Mapastepec Mexico 15°26N 92°54W 319 D6
Mapfongui Gabon 1°15S 12°59E 264 C2
Maphrao, Ko Thailand 7°56N 98°26E 237 a
Mapia, Kepulauan Indonesia 0°50N 134°20E 231 D8
Mapimí Mexico 25°49N 103°51W 318 B4
Mapimí, Bolsón de Mexico 27°0N 104°15W 318 B4
Maping China 31°34N 113°32E 229 B9
Mapinga Tanzania 6°40S 39°12E 268 D4
Mapinhane Mozam. 22°20S 35°0E 271 B6
Mapire Venezuela 7°45N 64°42W 329 B5
Maple → U.S.A. 42°59N 84°57W 311 B12
Maple Creek Canada 49°55N 109°29W 297 D7
Maple Valley U.S.A. 47°25N 122°3W 306 C4
Mapleton U.S.A. 44°2N 123°52W 304 D2
Mapo S. Korea 37°32N 126°56E 137 B1
Mapoon ☼ Australia 11°44S 142°8E 280 A3
Mapourika, L. N.Z. 43°16S 170°12E 285 D5
Maprik Papua N. G. 3°44S 143°3E 286 B2
Mapuca India 15°36N 73°46E 245 G1
Mapuera → Brazil 1°5S 57°2W 329 D6
Mapulanguene Mozam. 24°29S 32°6E 271 B5
Mapungubwe △ S. Africa 22°12S 29°22E 271 B4
Maputo Mozam. 25°58S 32°32E 271 C5
Maputo □ Mozam. 26°0S 32°25E 271 C5
Maputo, B. de Mozam. 25°50S 32°45E 271 C5
Maputo ⌂ Mozam. 26°23S 32°48E 271 C5
Maqanshy Kazakhstan 46°47N 82°1E 217 C10
Maqat Kazakhstan 47°39N 53°19E 187 E9
Maqên China 34°24N 100°6E 218 E9
Maqên Gangri China 34°55N 99°18E 218 E8
Maqiaohe China 44°40N 130°30E 227 B16
Maqnā Si. Arabia 28°25N 34°50E 251 K5
Maqran, W. → Si. Arabia 20°55N 47°12E 248 B4
Maqteïr Mauritania 21°50N 11°40W 260 D2
Maqu China 33°52N 101°42E 218 E9
Maquan He = Brahmaputra → Asia 23°40N 90°35E 241 D3
Maqueda Spain 40°4N 4°22W 194 E6
Maqueda Channel Phil. 13°42N 124°1E 232 E5
Maquela do Zombo Angola 6°0S 15°15E 265 D3
Maquinchao Argentina 41°15S 68°50W 336 B3
Maquoketa U.S.A. 42°4N 90°40W 310 B6
Mar Canada 44°49N 81°12W 312 B3
Mar, Serra do Brazil 25°30S 49°0W 335 B6
Mar Chiquita, L. Argentina 30°40S 62°50W 334 C3
Mar del Plata Argentina 38°0S 57°30W 334 D4
Mar Menor Spain 37°40N 0°45W 197 H4
Mar Vista U.S.A. 34°0N 118°25W 126 B2
Mara Guyana 6°0N 57°36W 329 B6
Mara India 28°11N 94°14E 241 A5
Mara Tanzania 1°30S 34°32E 268 C3
Mara □ Tanzania 1°45S 34°20E 268 C3
Mara Rosa Brazil 13°58S 49°9W 333 D2
Maraã Brazil 1°52S 65°25W 328 D4
Maraa Tahiti 17°46S 149°34W 289 e
Marabá Brazil 5°20S 49°5W 332 C2
Marabahan Indonesia 3°0S 114°45E 235 C4
Maraboon, L. Australia 23°41S 148°0E 280 C4
Maracá, I. de Brazil 2°10N 50°30W 329 C7
Maracaibo Venezuela 10°40N 71°37W 328 A3
Maracaibo, L. de Venezuela 9°40N 71°30W 328 B3
Maracaju Brazil 21°38S 55°9W 335 A4
Maracajú, Serra de Brazil 20°57S 55°1W 331 E6
Maracanã Brazil 0°46S 47°27W 332 B2
Maracanã, Estádio Rio de J., Brazil 22°54S 43°13W 135 B1
Maracanaú Brazil 3°52S 38°38W 332 B4
Maracás Brazil 13°26S 40°18W 333 D3
Maracas Trin. & Tob. 10°41N 61°24W 323 t
Maracas → Trin. & Tob. 10°34N 61°25W 323 t
Maracas B. Trin. & Tob. 10°45N 61°26W 323 t
Maracas Bay Village Trin. & Tob. 10°46N 61°28W 323 t
Maracas Falls Trin. & Tob. 10°44N 61°24W 323 t
Maracay Venezuela 10°15N 67°28W 328 A4
Maracena Spain 37°12N 3°38W 195 H7
Marādah Libya 29°15N 19°15E 258 C3
Maradi Niger 13°29N 7°20E 263 C6
Maradi □ Niger 14°15N 7°15E 263 C6
Marāgheh Iran 37°30N 46°12E 213 D12
Maragogipe Brazil 12°46S 38°55W 333 D4
Marāh Si. Arabia 25°0N 45°35E 246 E5
Marahoué □ Ivory C. 7°0N 5°45W 262 D3
Marahoué △ Ivory C. 8°0N 7°8W 262 D3
Marais du Cotentin et du Bessin ⌂ France 49°10N 1°30W 172 C5
Marais Poitevin, Val de Sèvre et Vendée ⌂ France 46°18N 0°35W 174 B3
Maraisburg = Hofmeyr S. Africa 31°39S 25°50E 270 D4
Marajó, B. de Brazil 1°0S 48°30W 332 B2
Marajo, I. de Brazil 1°0S 49°30W 332 B2
Marākand Iran 38°51N 45°16E 246 B5
Marakele △ S. Africa 24°30S 25°30E 271 D4
Maralal Kenya 1°0N 36°38E 268 B4
Maralinga Australia 30°13S 131°32E 279 F5
Maralinga Tjarutja ☼ Australia 29°30S 131°0E 279 E5
Maram India 25°25N 94°6E 241 C5
Marama Australia 35°10S 140°10E 282 C4
Maramag Phil. 7°46N 125°0E 233 H5
Maramaraereğlisi Turkey 40°57N 27°57E 203 F11
Maramasike Solomon Is. 9°30S 161°25E 287 M11
Marambio Antarctica 64°0S 56°0W 151 C18
Maramureş □ Romania 47°45N 24°0E 183 C9
Maran Malaysia 3°35N 102°45E 237 L4
Marana U.S.A. 32°27N 111°13W 305 K8
Maranboy Australia 14°40S 132°39E 278 B5
Maranchón Spain 41°6N 2°15W 196 D2
Marand Iran 38°30N 45°45E 213 C11
Marandochori Greece 38°38N 20°39E 207 B2
Maranello Italy 44°32N 10°52E 198 D7
Marang Malaysia 5°12N 103°13E 237 K4
Maranguape Brazil 3°55S 38°50W 332 B4
Maranhão = São Luís Brazil 2°39S 44°15W 332 B3
Maranhão □ Brazil 5°0S 46°0W 332 B2
Marano, L. di Italy 45°44N 13°10E 199 C10
Maranoa → Australia 27°50S 148°37E 281 D4
Marañón → Peru 4°30S 73°35W 330 A3
Marão Mozam. 24°18S 34°2E 271 B5
Maraoli India 19°2N 72°53E 130 A2
Marapi → Brazil 0°37N 55°58W 329 C6
Marari Brazil 5°43S 67°47W 330 B4
Maraş = Kahramanmaraş Turkey 37°37N 36°53E 212 D7
Mărăşeşti Romania 45°52N 27°14E 183 E12
Maratea Italy 39°59N 15°43E 201 C8
Marateca Portugal 38°34N 8°40W 195 G2
Marathasa Cyprus 34°59N 32°51E 207 F8
Marathia, Akra Greece 37°39N 20°50E 207 D2
Marathokambos Greece 37°43N 26°42E 205 D8
Marathon Queens., Australia 20°51S 143°32E 280 C3
Marathon Ont., Canada 48°44N 86°23W 298 C2
Marathon Fla., U.S.A. 24°43N 81°5W 317 L8
Marathon N.Y., U.S.A. 42°27N 76°2W 313 D8
Marathon Tex., U.S.A. 30°12N 103°15W 314 F3
Marathonas Greece 38°11N 23°58E 204 C5
Marathóvounos Cyprus 35°13N 33°37E 207 E9
Maratua Indonesia 2°10N 118°35E 235 B5
Maraú Brazil 14°6S 39°0W 333 D4
Marau Indonesia 2°9S 110°42E 235 C4
Marau Solomon Is. 10°31S 161°31E 287 N11
Maraval Trin. & Tob. 10°42N 61°31W 323 t
Maraval → Trin. & Tob. 10°39N 61°32W 323 t
Maravari Solomon Is. 7°50S 156°42E 287 L9
Maravatío Mexico 19°54N 100°27W 318 D4
Marawi City Phil. 8°0N 124°21E 233 G5
Marāwih U.A.E. 24°18N 53°18E 247 E7
Marazliyivka Ukraine 46°8N 30°3E 183 D15
Marbella Spain 36°30N 4°57W 195 J6
Marble Bar Australia 21°9S 119°44E 278 D2
Marblehead Mass., U.S.A. 42°29N 70°51W 313 D14
Marblehead Ohio, U.S.A. 41°32N 82°44W 312 E2
Mårbu Norway 60°11N 8°9E 164 D5
Marburg = Maribor Slovenia 46°36N 15°40E 199 B12
Marburg Germany 50°47N 8°46E 178 E4
Marca, Pta. do Angola 16°31S 11°43E 265 F2
Marcal → Hungary 47°41N 17°40E 182 C2
Marcali Hungary 46°35N 17°25E 182 D2
Marcapata Peru 13°31S 70°52W 330 C3
Marcaria Italy 45°7N 10°32E 198 C7
Mărcăuţi Moldova 48°20N 27°14E 183 B12
Marcelin Poland 52°19N 20°59E 143 B1
Marceline U.S.A. 39°43N 92°57W 310 E4
March U.K. 52°33N 0°5E 169 E8
Marchal Dem. Rep. of the Congo 5°16S 14°58E 265 D2
Marchand = Rommani Morocco 33°31N 6°40W 260 B3
Marche France 46°5N 1°20E 174 B5
Marche □ Italy 43°30N 13°15E 199 E10
Marché Bonsecours Montréal, Canada 130 b3
Marche-en-Famenne Belgium 50°14N 5°19E 170 D5
Marchena Spain 37°18N 5°23W 195 H5
Marchena, Canal de Ecuador 0°19N 90°12W 330 a
Marchena, I. Ecuador 0°19N 90°29W 330 a
Marches = Marche □ Italy 43°30N 13°15E 199 E10
Marchesale ⌂ Italy 38°32N 16°13E 201 D9
Marciana Marina Italy 42°48N 10°12E 198 F7
Marcianise Italy 41°2N 14°17E 201 A7
Marcigny France 46°17N 4°2E 173 F11
Marcillat-en-Combraille France 46°12N 2°38E 173 F9
Marck France 50°57N 1°57E 173 B8
Marckolsheim France 48°10N 7°30E 173 D14
Marco Island U.S.A. 25°58N 81°44W 317 K8
Marco Rondon Brazil 12°0S 60°56W 331 C5
Marcona Peru 15°10S 75°0W 330 D3
Marcos Juárez Argentina 32°42S 62°5W 334 C3
Mărculeşti Moldova 47°52N 28°14E 183 C13
Marcus Baker, Mt. U.S.A. 61°26N 147°45W 303 F11
Marcus I. = Minami-Tori-Shima Pac. Oc. 24°20N 153°58E 288 E7
Marcy, Mt. U.S.A. 44°7N 73°56W 313 B11
Mardan Pakistan 34°20N 72°0E 242 B5
Mardarivka Ukraine 47°32N 29°44E 183 C14
Mardie Australia 21°12S 115°59E 278 D2
Mardin Turkey 37°20N 40°43E 213 D9
Mårdsjö Sweden 63°18N 15°35E 162 A9
Maré, Î. N. Cal. 21°30S 168°0E 277 E12
Marécchia → Italy 44°4N 12°34E 199 D9
Marechal Deodoro Brazil 9°43S 35°54W 332 C4
Marechal Floriano = Piranhas Brazil 9°27S 37°46W 332 C4
Maree, L. U.K. 57°40N 5°26W 167 D3
Mareeba Australia 16°59S 145°28E 280 B4
Mareeg Somalia 3°46N 47°18E 267 D6
Mareetsane S. Africa 26°9S 25°25E 270 C4
Mareil-Marly France 48°52N 2°4E 134 A1
Maremma Italy 42°30N 11°30E 199 F8
Maremma ⌂ Italy 42°35N 11°8E 198 F8
Maréna Kayes, Mali 14°36N 10°45W 262 C2
Maréna Koulikouro, Mali 13°55N 7°20W 262 C3
Marengo Ind., U.S.A. 38°22N 86°21W 311 F10
Marengo Iowa, U.S.A. 41°48N 92°4W 310 C4
Marennes France 45°49N 1°7W 174 C2
Marerano Madag. 21°23S 44°52E 272 C1
Maréttimo Italy 37°58N 12°4E 200 E5
Mareuil France 45°26N 0°29E 174 C4
Marfa U.S.A. 30°19N 104°1W 314 F2
Marganets = Marhanets Ukraine 47°40N 34°40E 189 J8
Margao = Madgaon India 15°12N 73°58E 245 G1
Margaret → Australia 18°9S 125°41E 278 C4
Margaret Bay Canada 51°20N 127°35W 296 C3
Margaret I. = Margitsziget Hungary 117 A2
Margaret L. Canada 58°56N 115°25W 296 B5
Margaret River Australia 33°57S 115°4E 279 F2
Margareten Austria 48°11N 16°20E 142 A2
Margarita, I. de Venezuela 11°0N 64°0W 329 a
Margariti Greece 39°22N 20°26E 204 B2
Margaritovo Russia 43°25N 134°45E 220 C7
Margate KwaZulu Natal, S. Africa 30°50S 30°20E 271 D5
Margate Kent, U.K. 51°23N 1°23E 169 F9
Margate Fla., U.S.A. 26°15N 80°12W 317 J9
Margeride, Mts. de la France 44°43N 3°38E 174 D7
Marggrabowa = Olecko Poland 54°2N 22°31E 184 D9
Margherita India 27°16N 95°40E 241 B5
Margherita di Savóia Italy 41°22N 16°9E 201 A9
Margherita Pk. Uganda 0°22N 29°51E 268 B3
Marghilon Uzbekistan 40°27N 71°42E 217 D8
Marghita Romania 47°22N 22°22E 182 C7
Margitsziget Hungary 117 A2
Margonin Poland 52°58N 17°5E 185 F4
Margosatubig Phil. 7°34N 123°10E 233 H4
Māřgow, Dasht-e Afghan. 30°40N 62°30E 240 C1
Marguerite Canada 52°30N 122°25W 296 C4
Marhanets Ukraine 47°40N 34°40E 189 J8
Marhoum Algeria 34°27N 0°11W 261 B4
Mari Papua N. G. 9°11S 141°42E 286 E1
Mārī' Syria 36°29N 37°10E 250 B8
Mari El □ Russia 56°30N 48°0E 190 B8
Mari Indus Pakistan 32°57N 71°34E 242 C4
Mari Republic = Mari El □ Russia 56°30N 48°0E 190 B8
Maria Austria 48°11N 16°21E 142 A2
Maria, Îs. French Polynesia 21°48S 154°41W 289 f
María, Sa. de Spain 37°39N 2°14W 197 H2
Maria Aurora Phil. 15°48N 121°28E 232 D3
María de la Salut Spain 39°40N 3°5E 206 B4
María Elena Chile 22°18S 69°40W 334 A2
María Grande Argentina 31°45S 59°55W 334 C4
Maria I. N. Terr., Australia 14°52S 135°45E 280 A2
Maria I. Tas., Australia 42°35S 148°0E 281 G4
Maria Is. St. Lucia 13°44N 60°56W 323 m
Maria Island △ Australia 42°38S 148°5E 281 G4
Maria Pereira = Mombaça Brazil 5°43S 39°45W 332 C4
Maria Theresiopel = Subotica Serbia 46°6N 19°39E 182 D4
Maria van Diemen, C. N.Z. 34°29S 172°40E 284 A1
Mariager Denmark 56°40N 9°59E 163 H3
Mariager Fjord Denmark 56°42N 10°19E 163 H4
Mariahilferstrasse Vienna, Austria 142 b1
Mariakani Kenya 3°50S 39°27E 268 C4
Mariala △ Australia 25°57S 145°2E 281 D4
Marian Australia 21°9S 148°57E 280 b
Marian L. Canada 63°0N 116°15W 296 A5
Mariana Islands Pac. Oc. 15°15N 145°48E 302 a
Mariana Trench Pac. Oc. 13°0N 145°0E 302 a
Mariani India 26°39N 94°19E 241 B5
Marianica, Cord. = Morena, Sierra Spain 38°20N 4°0W 195 G7
Marianna Ark., U.S.A. 34°46N 90°46W 315 D9
Marianna Fla., U.S.A. 30°46N 85°14W 316 E4
Mariannelund Sweden 57°37N 15°35E 163 G9
Mariánské Lázně Czech Rep. 49°58N 12°41E 180 B5
Marias → U.S.A. 47°56N 110°30W 304 C8
Marías, Is. Mexico 21°25N 106°28W 318 C3
Mariato, Punta Panama 7°12N 80°52W 320 E3
Mariazell Austria 47°47N 15°19E 180 D8
Ma'rib Yemen 15°25N 45°21E 248 D4
Ma'rib □ Yemen 15°25N 45°21E 248 D4
Maribo Denmark 54°48N 11°30E 163 K5
Maribor Slovenia 46°36N 15°40E 199 B12
Maricaban I. Phil. 13°39N 120°53E 232 E3
Maricao Puerto Rico 18°11N 66°59W 321 b
Marico → Africa 23°35S 26°57E 270 B4
Maricopa Ariz., U.S.A. 33°4N 112°3W 305 K7
Maricopa Calif., U.S.A. 35°4N 119°24W 307 K7
Maridalen Norway 59°59N 10°45E 133 A3
Maridalsvatnet Norway 59°59N 10°46E 133 A3
Maridi South Sudan 4°55N 29°25E 257 G2
Maridi, Wadi → South Sudan 6°15N 29°21E 257 F2
Marié → Brazil 0°27S 66°26W 328 D4
Marie Byrd Land Antarctica 79°30S 125°0W 151 D14
Marie-Galante Guadeloupe 15°56N 61°16W 322 e
Marie-Galante, Canal de Guadeloupe 16°0N 61°25W 322 e
Mariecourt = Kangiqsujuaq Canada 61°30N 72°0W 295 E17
Mariefred Sweden 59°15N 17°12E 162 E11
Mariehamn Finland 60°5N 19°55E 161 F18
Marieholm Sweden 55°53N 13°10E 163 J7
Mariembourg Belgium 50°6N 4°31E 170 D4
Marienbad = Mariánské Lázně Czech Rep. 49°58N 12°41E 180 B5
Marienberg Germany 50°39N 13°9E 178 E9
Marienburg = Malbork Poland 54°3N 19°1E 184 D6
Mariendorf Germany 52°26N 13°23E 115 B3
Marienfelde Germany 52°24N 13°23E 115 B3
Marienplatz Munich, Germany 131 b2
Mariental Namibia 24°36S 18°0E 270 B2
Marienville U.S.A. 41°28N 79°8W 312 E5
Mariestad Sweden 58°43N 13°50E 163 F7
Marietta Ga., U.S.A. 33°57N 84°33W 316 B5
Marietta Ohio, U.S.A. 39°25N 81°27W 309 F13
Marieville Canada 45°26N 73°10W 313 A11
Mariga → Nigeria 9°40N 5°55E 263 C6
Marignane France 43°25N 5°13E 175 E9
Marigot Dominica 15°33N 61°18W 323 k
Marigot Guadeloupe 16°5N 61°46W 322 e
Marigot St.-Martin 18°4N 63°5W 322 a
Marigot Bay St. Lucia 13°58N 61°1W 323 m
Marihatag Phil. 8°48N 126°18E 233 G6
Mariinsk Russia 56°10N 87°20E 214 D9
Mariinsk Water = Volgo-Baltiyskiy Kanal Russia 60°0N 38°0E 188 B9
Mariinskiy Posad Russia 56°10N 47°45E 190 B8
Marijampolė Lithuania 54°33N 23°19E 184 D10
Marijampolė □ Lithuania 54°34N 23°21E 184 D10
Marikina Phil. 14°37N 121°5E 127 B2
Marikina → Phil. 14°33N 121°3E 127 B2
Marília Brazil 22°13S 50°0W 335 A6
Marimba Angola 8°28S 17°8E 265 D3
Marín Spain 42°23N 8°42W 194 C2
Marin, Cul-de-Sac du Martinique 14°27N 60°53W 322 j
Marin City U.S.A. 37°52N 122°30W 136 A1
Marin Pen. U.S.A. 37°50N 122°30W 136 A1
Marina U.S.A. 36°41N 121°48W 306 J5
Marina Bay Sands Singapore 1°17N 103°51E 138 B3
Marina del Rey U.S.A. 33°58N 118°27W 126 C2
Marinduque Phil. 13°25N 122°0E 231 B6
Marinduque □ Phil. 13°18N 122°0E 232 E4
Marine City U.S.A. 42°43N 82°30W 312 D2
Marine Drive Mumbai, India 130 b1
Marineland U.S.A. 29°40N 81°13W 316 F8
Marineo Italy 37°57N 13°25E 200 E6
Marinette U.S.A. 45°6N 87°38W 308 C10
Maringá Brazil 23°26S 52°2W 335 A5
Maringa → Dem. Rep. of the Congo 1°14N 19°48E 264 B3
Marinha Grande Portugal 39°45N 8°56W 194 F2
Marinho dos Abrolhos △ Brazil 17°50S 39°0W 333 E4
Marino Dublin, Ireland 53°22N 6°14W 120 A2
Marino Italy 41°46N 12°39E 199 G9
Marino di Campo Italy 42°46N 10°11E 198 F7
Marion Ala., U.S.A. 32°38N 87°19W 315 E11
Marion Ark., U.S.A. 35°13N 90°12W 308 H8
Marion Ill., U.S.A. 37°44N 88°56W 310 G8
Marion Ind., U.S.A. 40°32N 85°40W 311 D11
Marion Iowa, U.S.A. 42°2N 91°36W 310 B5
Marion Kans., U.S.A. 38°21N 97°1W 308 F5
Marion N.C., U.S.A. 35°41N 82°1W 315 D13
Marion Ohio, U.S.A. 40°35N 83°8W 311 D13
Marion S.C., U.S.A. 34°11N 79°24W 315 D15
Marion Va., U.S.A. 36°50N 81°31W 309 G13
Marion, L. U.S.A. 33°28N 80°10W 316 B9
Marion Bay Australia 35°12S 136°59E 282 C2
Marion I. Ind. Oc. 47°0S 38°0E 273 J2
Maripa Venezuela 7°26N 65°9W 329 B4
Maripasoula Fr. Guiana 3°40N 54°4W 329 C7
Maripipi I. Phil. 11°47N 124°19E 233 F5
Mariposa U.S.A. 37°29N 119°58W 306 H7
Mariscal Estigarribia Paraguay 22°3S 60°40W 334 A3
Marisco, Ponta do Brazil 23°1S 43°18W 135 C1
Maritas, Laguna de las Venezuela 10°55N 63°56W 329 a
Maritime Alps = Maritimes, Alpes Europe 44°10N 7°10E 175 D11
Maritimes, Alpes Europe 44°10N 7°10E 175 D11
Maritsa = Evros → Greece 41°40N 26°34E 203 F10
Maritsa Greece 36°22N 28°8E 206 E12
Marittima, Stazione Venice, Italy 142 b1
Mariupol Ukraine 47°5N 37°31E 189 J9
Marīvān Iran 35°30N 46°25E 213 E12
Mariveles Phil. 14°26N 120°29E 232 D3
Mariy Chodra △ Russia 56°10N 48°30E 190 B9
Marj 'Uyūn Lebanon 33°21N 35°34E 250 E6
Marjan = Wazikhwah Afghan. 32°11N 68°21E 240 B3
Mark Twain L. U.S.A. 39°28N 91°55W 310 E5
Marka Si. Arabia 18°14N 41°19E 256 D5
Marka Somalia 1°48N 44°50E 267 D5
Markam China 29°42N 98°38E 228 C2
Markapur India 15°44N 79°19E 245 G4
Markaryd Sweden 56°28N 13°35E 163 H7
Markat Albania 39°44N 20°12E 206 B10
Markazī □ Iran 34°0N 49°30E 247 C6
Markdale Canada 44°19N 80°39W 312 B4
Marked Tree U.S.A. 35°32N 90°25W 315 D9
Markelsdorfer Huk Germany 54°33N 11°4E 178 A7
Market Drayton U.K. 52°54N 2°29W 168 E5
Market Harborough U.K. 52°29N 0°55W 169 E7
Market Rasen U.K. 53°24N 0°20W 168 D7
Markham Ont., Canada 43°52N 79°16W 141 A2
Markham Ill., U.S.A. 41°36N 87°42W 119 D2
Markham → Papua N. G. 6°41S 147°2E 286 D4
Markham, Mt. Antarctica 83°0S 164°0E 151 E11
Marki Poland 52°19N 21°6E 143 B2
Märkisch Friedland = Mirosławiec Poland 53°20N 16°5E 184 E3
Märkische Schweiz ⌂ Germany 52°34N 14°2E 178 C10
Markit China 38°54N 77°40E 217 E9
Markkleeberg Germany 51°16N 12°23E 178 D8
Markland Wood Canada 43°38N 79°34W 141 B1
Markleeville U.S.A. 38°42N 119°47W 306 G7
Markopoulo Greece 37°53N 23°57E 204 D5
Markounda C.A.R. 7°39N 16°55E 264 A3
Markovac Serbia 44°14N 21°7E 202 B5
Markovo Russia 64°40N 170°24E 215 C17
Markoye Burkina Faso 14°39N 0°2E 263 C5
Marks Russia 51°45N 46°50E 190 E8
Marksshtadt = Marks Russia 51°45N 46°50E 190 E8
Marksville U.S.A. 31°8N 92°4W 314 F8
Markt Schwaben Germany 48°11N 11°52E 179 G7
Marktoberdorf Germany 47°45N 10°37E 179 H6
Marktredwitz Germany 50°1N 12°6E 179 E8
Marl Germany 51°39N 7°4E 178 D3
Marla Australia 27°19S 133°33E 281 D1
Marlbank Canada 44°26N 77°6W 312 B7
Marlboro U.S.A. 41°36N 73°59W 313 E11
Marlborough Queens., Australia 22°46S 149°52E 280 C4
Marlborough Wilts., U.K. 51°25N 1°43W 169 F6
Marlborough Mass., U.S.A. 42°21N 71°33W 313 D13
Marlborough □ N.Z. 41°40S 173°50E 285 B8
Marlborough Downs U.K. 51°27N 1°53W 169 F6
Marle France 49°43N 3°47E 173 C10
Marlin U.S.A. 31°18N 96°54W 314 F6
Marlow Mecklenburg-Vorpommern, Germany 54°9N 12°33E 178 A8
Marlow Bucks., U.K. 51°34N 0°46W 169 F7
Marlow Okla., U.S.A. 34°39N 97°58W 314 D6
Marly, Forêt de France 48°52N 2°2E 134 A1
Marly-le-Roi France 48°52N 2°5E 134 A1
Marmagao India 15°25N 73°56E 245 G1
Marmande France 44°30N 0°10E 174 D4
Marmara Turkey 40°35N 27°34E 203 F11
Marmara, Sea of = Marmara Denizi Turkey 40°45N 28°15E 203 F12

Marmara Denizi *Turkey* 40°45N 28°15E **203** F12
Marmara Gölü *Turkey* 38°37N 28°2E **205** C10
Marmaris *Turkey* 36°50N 28°14E **205** E10
Marmaris Limanı *Turkey* 36°50N 28°19E **205** E10
Marmelos → *Brazil* 6°6S 61°46W **331** B5
Marmion, Mt. *Australia* 29°16S 119°50E **279** E2
Marmion L. *Canada* 48°55N 91°20W **298** C1
Marmolada, Mte. *Italy* 46°26N 11°51E **199** B8
Marmolejo *Spain* 38°3N 4°13W **195** G6
Marmora *Canada* 44°28N 77°41W **312** B7
Mármora, La *Italy* 39°59N 9°20E **200** C2
Marnay *France* 47°16N 5°48E **173** E12
Marne *Germany* 53°56N 9°2E **178** B5
Marne □ *France* 48°50N 4°10E **173** D11
Marne → *France* 48°47N 2°29E **173** D9
Marne-la-Vallée *France* 48°50N 2°37E **134** A4
Marneuli *Georgia* 41°30N 44°48E **191** K7
Marnia = Maghnia *Algeria* 34°50N 1°43W **261** B4
Marnoo *Australia* 36°40S 142°52E **282** D5
Maro *Chad* 8°30N 19°0E **259** G3
Maro Reef *U.S.A.* 25°25N 170°35W **302** F9
Maroa *Ill., U.S.A.* 40°2N 88°57W **310** D8
Maroa *Venezuela* 2°43N 67°33W **328** C4
Maroala *Madag.* 15°23S 47°59E **272** B2
Maroantsetra *Madag.* 15°26S 49°44E **272** B2
Maroelaboom *Namibia* 19°15S 18°53E **270** A2
Marofandilia *Madag.* 20°7S 44°34E **272** C1
Marojejy ⌓ *Madag.* 14°26S 49°21E **272** A2
Marokau *French Polynesia* 18°2S 142°17W **289** f
Marolambo *Madag.* 20°2S 48°7E **272** C2
Marolles-en-Brie *France* 48°44N 2°33E **134** B4
Maromandia *Madag.* 14°13S 48°5E **272** A2
Maromokotro *Madag.* 14°0S 49°0E **272** A2
Marondera *Zimbabwe* 18°5S 31°42E **269** F3
Maroni → *Fr. Guiana* 5°30N 54°0W **329** B7
Maronia *Greece* 40°53N 25°30E **203** F9
Maronne → *France* 45°5N 1°56E **174** C5
Maroochydore *Australia* 26°29S 153°5E **281** D5
Maroon Town *Jamaica* 18°22N 77°48W **320** a
Maroona *Australia* 37°27S 142°54E **282** D5
Maros *Indonesia* 5°0S 119°34E **235** C5
Maros → *Hungary* 46°15N 20°13E **182** D5
Marosakoa *Madag.* 15°26S 46°38E **272** B2
Maroseranana *Madag.* 18°32S 48°51E **272** B2
Maróstica *Italy* 45°44N 11°40E **199** C8
Marotandrano *Madag.* 16°10S 48°50E **272** B2
Marotiri, Îs. = Bass, Îs. de *French Polynesia* 27°55S 143°26W **289** f
Maroua *Cameroon* 10°40N 14°20E **259** F2
Maroubra *Australia* 33°56S 151°16E **139** B2
Marovato *Madag.* 15°48S 48°5E **272** B2
Marovoay *Madag.* 16°6S 46°39E **272** B2
Marowijne □ *Suriname* 4°0N 55°0W **329** C7
Marowijne → *Suriname* 5°45N 53°58W **329** B7
Marqaköl *Kazakhstan* 48°45N 85°45E **217** C11
Marquard *S. Africa* 28°40S 27°28E **270** C4
Marquesas Fracture Zone *Pac. Oc.* 9°0S 125°0W **289** H15
Marquesas Is. = Marquises, Îs. *French Polynesia* 9°30S 140°0W **289** f
Marquesas Keys *U.S.A.* 24°35N 82°10W **317** L7
Marquette *U.S.A.* 46°33N 87°24W **308** B10
Marquette Park *U.S.A.* 41°46N 87°42W **119** C2
Marquis *St. Lucia* 14°2N 60°54W **323** m
Marquis, C. *St. Lucia* 14°3N 60°54W **323** m
Marquis I. *Grenada* 12°5N 61°37W **323** q
Marquise *France* 50°50N 1°40E **173** B8
Marquises, Îs. *French Polynesia* 9°30S 140°0W **289** f
Marra, Gebel *South Sudan* 7°20N 27°35E **257** F2
Marra, Pta. da *Angola* 16°31S 11°43E **265** F2
Marra Cr. → *Australia* 30°8S 147°15E **283** A7
Marra-Marra △ *Australia* 33°30S 151°4E **283** B9
Marracuene *Mozam.* 25°45S 32°35E **271** C5
Marradi *Italy* 44°4N 11°37E **199** D8
Marrakech *Morocco* 31°9N 8°0W **260** B3
Marratxí *Spain* 39°39N 2°48E **206** B3
Marrawah *Australia* 40°55S 144°42E **281** G3
Marrecas, Serra das *Brazil* 9°0S 41°0W **332** C3
Marree *Australia* 29°39S 138°1E **281** D2
Marrero *U.S.A.* 29°53N 90°6W **131** B2
Marrickville *Australia* 33°54S 151°9E **139** B1
Marrimane *Mozam.* 22°58S 33°34E **271** B5
Marromeu *Mozam.* 18°15S 36°25E **271** A6
Marromeu ⌓ *Mozam.* 19°0S 36°0E **271** A6
Marroquí, Punta *Spain* 36°0N 5°37W **195** K5
Marrowie Cr. → *Australia* 33°23S 145°40E **283** B6
Marruás = Porto *Brazil* 3°54S 42°42W **332** B3
Marrubane *Mozam.* 18°0S 37°0E **269** F4
Marrúbiu *Italy* 39°40N 8°35E **200** C1
Marrupa *Mozam.* 13°8S 37°30E **269** E4
Mars B. *Ascension I.* 7°59S 14°24W **153** g
Mars Hill *U.S.A.* 46°31N 67°52W **309** B20
Marsá al Burayqah *Libya* 30°24N 19°37E **258** B3
Marsá ʻAlam *Egypt* 25°5N 34°54E **256** B3
Marsá Matrûh *Egypt* 31°19N 27°9E **256** A2
Marsá Sha'b *Sudan* 22°52N 35°47E **256** C4
Marsabit *Kenya* 2°18N 38°0E **268** B4
Marsabit △ *Kenya* 2°23N 37°56E **268** B4
Marsala *Italy* 37°48N 12°26E **200** E5
Marsalforn *Malta* 36°4N 14°16E **206** E7
Mârşani *Romania* 44°1N 24°1E **183** F9
Marsaskala *Malta* 35°52N 14°34E **206** F8
Marsaxlokk *Malta* 35°51N 14°33E **206** F8
Marsaxlokk Bay *Malta* 35°49N 14°33E **206** F8
Marsberg *Germany* 51°28N 8°52E **178** D4
Marsciano *Italy* 42°54N 12°20E **199** F9
Marsden *Australia* 33°47S 147°32E **283** B7
Marsden Point *N.Z.* 35°50S 174°31E **284** B3
Marseillan *France* 43°23N 3°31E **174** E7
Marseille *France* 43°18N 5°23E **175** E9
Marseille-Marignane ✈ (MRS) *France* 43°26N 5°14E **175** E9
Marseilles = Marseille *France* 43°18N 5°23E **175** E9
Marseilles *U.S.A.* 41°20N 88°43W **311** C8
Marsfield *Australia* 33°46S 151°7E **139** A1
Marsh I. *U.S.A.* 29°34N 91°53W **314** G9
Marsha, L. *U.S.A.* 28°29N 81°29W **133** B2
Marshall *Liberia* 6°8N 10°22W **262** D2
Marshall *Alaska, U.S.A.* 61°53N 162°5W **303** F7
Marshall *Ark., U.S.A.* 35°55N 92°38W **314** D8
Marshall *Ill., U.S.A.* 39°23N 87°42W **311** E9
Marshall *Mich., U.S.A.* 42°16N 84°58W **311** B12
Marshall *Minn., U.S.A.* 44°27N 95°47W **308** C6
Marshall *Mo., U.S.A.* 39°7N 93°12W **310** E3
Marshall *Tex., U.S.A.* 32°33N 94°23W **314** E7
Marshall → *Australia* 22°59S 136°59E **280** C2
Marshall, C. *Ecuador* 0°1S 91°12W **330** a
Marshall Bennett Is. *Papua N. G.* 8°50S 151°55E **286** E6
Marshall Is. ■ *Pac. Oc.* 9°0N 171°0E **288** G9
Marshalltown *U.S.A.* 42°3N 92°55W **310** B4
Marshallville = Lewisporte *Canada* 49°15N 55°3W **299** C8
Marshallville *U.S.A.* 32°27N 83°56W **316** C6
Marshbrook *Zimbabwe* 18°33S 31°9E **271** A5
Marshfield = Coos Bay *U.S.A.* 43°22N 124°13W **304** E1
Marshfield *Mo., U.S.A.* 37°15N 92°54W **308** G7
Marshfield *Vt., U.S.A.* 44°20N 72°20W **313** B12
Marshfield *Wis., U.S.A.* 44°40N 90°10W **308** C8
Marshūn *Iran* 36°19N 49°23E **247** B6
Mársico Nuovo *Italy* 40°25N 15°44E **201** B8
Marsouins, R. des → *Réunion* 21°1S 55°44E **272** f
Märsta *Sweden* 59°37N 17°52E **162** E11
Marstal *Denmark* 54°51N 10°30E **163** K4
Marstrand *Sweden* 57°53N 11°35E **163** G5
Mart *U.S.A.* 31°33N 96°50W **314** F6
Marta → *Italy* 42°14N 11°42E **199** F8
Martaban *Burma* 16°30N 97°35E **241** G6
Martaban, G. of *Burma* 16°5N 96°30E **241** G6
Martano *Italy* 40°12N 18°18E **201** B11
Martapura *Kalimantan Selatan, Indonesia* 3°22S 114°47E **235** C4
Martapura *Sumatera Selatan, Indonesia* 4°19S 104°22E **234** C2
Marte *Nigeria* 12°23N 13°46E **263** C7
Marte, Campo de *Brazil* 23°30S 46°38W **137** B2
Marte R. Gómez, Presa *Mexico* 26°10N 99°0W **319** B5
Martel *France* 44°57N 1°37E **174** D5
Martelange *Belgium* 49°49N 5°43E **170** E5
Martellago *Italy* 45°33N 12°9E **199** C9
Martés, Sierra *Spain* 39°20N 1°0W **197** F4
Martesana, Navíglio della *Italy* 45°31N 9°17E **128** A2
Martfű *Hungary* 47°1N 20°17E **182** C5
Marthaguy Cr. → *Australia* 30°16S 147°35E **283** A7
Marthapal *India* 19°24N 81°37E **244** E5
Martha's Vineyard *U.S.A.* 41°25N 70°38W **313** E14
Martigné-Ferchaud *France* 47°50N 1°20W **172** E5
Martigny *Switz.* 46°6N 7°3E **179** J3
Martigues *France* 43°24N 5°4E **175** E9
Martil *Morocco* 35°36N 5°15W **260** A3
Martin *Slovak Rep.* 49°6N 18°58E **181** B11
Martin *S. Dak., U.S.A.* 43°11N 101°44W **308** D3
Martin *Tenn., U.S.A.* 36°21N 88°51W **315** C10
Martín → *Spain* 41°18N 0°19W **196** D4
Martin L. *U.S.A.* 32°41N 85°55W **316** C4
Martin Luther King Nat. Historic Site ⌓ *U.S.A.* 33°45N 84°22W **113** B2
Martin Pt. *U.S.A.* 70°8N 143°16W **303** A12
Martin Vaz *Atl. Oc.* 20°30S 28°51W **152** J9
Martina Franca *Italy* 40°42N 17°20E **201** B10
Martinborough *N.Z.* 41°14S 175°29E **284** H4
Martinez *B. Aires, Argentina* 34°29S 58°31W **117** A1
Martinez *Calif., U.S.A.* 38°1N 122°8W **306** G4
Martinez *Ga., U.S.A.* 33°31N 82°5W **316** B7
Martinho Campos *Brazil* 19°20S 45°13W **333** E2
Martinique ☒ *W. Indies* 14°40N 61°0W **322** j
Martinique Channel *St. Vincent* 12°34N 61°25W **323** n
Martinique Passage *W. Indies* 15°15N 61°0W **321** C7
Martinkylä *Finland* 60°17N 24°51E **121** B2
Martino *Greece* 38°35N 23°12E **204** C5
Martinópolis *Brazil* 22°11S 51°12W **335** A5
Martins Ferry *U.S.A.* 40°6N 80°44W **312** F4
Martinsberg *Austria* 48°22N 15°9E **180** C8
Martinsburg *Pa., U.S.A.* 40°19N 78°20W **312** F6
Martinsburg *W. Va., U.S.A.* 39°27N 77°58W **309** F15
Martinsicuro *Italy* 42°54N 13°54E **199** F10
Martinsried *Germany* 48°6N 11°27E **131** B1
Martinsville *Ill., U.S.A.* 39°20N 87°53W **311** E9
Martinsville *Ind., U.S.A.* 39°26N 86°25W **311** E10
Martinsville *Va., U.S.A.* 36°41N 79°52W **309** G14
Marton *N.Z.* 40°4S 175°23E **284** G4
Martorell *Spain* 41°28N 1°56E **196** D6
Martos *Spain* 37°44N 3°58W **195** H7
Martu ✺ *Australia* 22°30S 122°30E **278** D3
Martūbah *Libya* 32°35N 22°46E **258** B4
Martuni *Armenia* 40°8N 45°20E **191** K7
Maru *Nigeria* 12°22N 6°22E **263** C6
Marudi *Malaysia* 4°11N 114°19E **235** B4
Maruf *Afghan.* 31°30N 67°6E **240** C2
Marugame *Japan* 34°15N 133°40E **222** C5
Marui = Pagwi *Papua N. G.* 4°4S 143°2E **286** C2
Maruia → *N.Z.* 41°47S 172°13E **285** B7
Maruim *Brazil* 10°45S 37°5W **332** D4
Maruko *Japan* 35°33N 139°40E **140** B3
Marulan *Australia* 34°43S 150°3E **283** C9
Marum, Mt. *Vanuatu* 16°15S 168°7E **287** F6
Marunga *Angola* 17°28S 20°2E **265** F4
Marungu, Mts. *Dem. Rep. of the Congo* 7°30S 30°0E **268** D3
Marunouchi *Tokyo, Japan* **140** b4
Maruoka = Sakai *Japan* 36°9N 136°16E **223** A8
Maruwa ✺ *Australia* 22°30S 127°30E **278** D4
Marv Dasht *Iran* 29°50N 52°40E **247** D7
Marvão = Castelo do Piauí *Brazil* 5°20S 41°33W **332** C3
Marvão *Portugal* 39°24N 7°20W **195** F3
Marvast *Iran* 30°30N 54°15E **247** D7
Marvejols *France* 44°33N 3°19E **174** D7
Marvel Loch *Australia* 31°28S 119°29E **279** F2
Marwar *India* 25°43N 73°45E **242** G5
Mary *Turkmenistan* 37°40N 61°50E **247** B9
Mary Esther *U.S.A.* 30°25N 86°40W **317** E3
Maryborough = Portlaoise *Ireland* 53°2N 7°18W **166** C4
Maryborough *Queens., Australia* 25°31S 152°37E **281** D5
Maryborough *Vic., Australia* 37°3S 143°44E **282** D5
Maryfield *Canada* 49°50N 101°35W **297** D8
Maryino = Pristen *Russia* 51°15N 36°44E **189** G9
Maryino *Russia* 55°40N 37°45E **129** B3
Maryland *Singapore* 1°19N 103°47E **138** B2
Maryland □ *U.S.A.* 39°0N 76°30W **309** F15
Maryland Junction *Zimbabwe* 17°45S 30°31E **269** F3
Marylebone *London, U.K.* **125** a2
Marymont *Poland* 52°16N 20°58E **143** B1
Maryport *U.K.* 54°44N 3°28W **168** C4
Mary's Harbour *Canada* 52°18N 55°51W **299** B8
Marysin Wawerski *Poland* 52°14N 21°9E **143** B2
Marystown *Canada* 47°10N 55°10W **299** C8
Marysville *Calif., U.S.A.* 39°9N 121°35W **306** F5
Marysville *Kans., U.S.A.* 39°51N 96°39W **308** F5
Marysville *Mich., U.S.A.* 42°54N 82°29W **312** D2
Marysville *Ohio, U.S.A.* 40°14N 83°22W **311** D13
Marysville *Wash., U.S.A.* 48°3N 122°11W **306** B4
Maryville *Mo., U.S.A.* 40°21N 94°52W **310** D2
Maryville *Tenn., U.S.A.* 35°46N 83°58W **315** D13
Marzahn *Germany* 52°32N 13°34E **115** A4
Marzo, Punta *Colombia* 6°50N 77°42W **328** B2
Masada *Israel* 31°18N 35°21E **251** G6
Mas'ada *Syria* 33°13N 35°45E **250** E6
Masahunga *Tanzania* 2°6S 33°18E **268** C3
Masai *Malaysia* 1°29N 103°55E **237** d
Masai Mara △ *Kenya* 1°25S 35°5E **268** C4
Masai Steppe *Tanzania* 4°30S 36°30E **268** C4
Masaka *Uganda* 0°21S 31°45E **268** C3
Māsāl *Iran* 37°23N 49°8E **213** D12
Masalembo, Kepulauan *Indonesia* 5°35S 114°30E **235** D4
Masalima, Kepulauan *Indonesia* 5°4S 117°5E **235** D5
Masallı *Azerbaijan* 39°3N 48°40E **213** C13
Masalog Pt. *N. Marianas* 15°1N 145°40E **302** e
Masamba *Indonesia* 2°30S 120°15E **231** E6
Masan *S. Korea* 35°11N 128°32E **224** E4
Masandam, Ra's *Oman* 26°30N 56°30E **247** E8
Masasi *Tanzania* 10°45S 38°52E **269** E4
Masaya *Nic.* 12°0N 86°7W **320** D2
Masba *Nigeria* 11°35N 13°1E **263** C7
Masbate *Phil.* 12°21N 123°36E **232** E4
Masbate □ *Phil.* 12°20N 123°30E **232** E4
Masbate Pass. *Phil.* 12°30N 123°35E **232** E4
Máscali *Italy* 37°45N 15°12E **201** E8
Mascara *Algeria* 35°26N 0°6E **261** A5
Mascara □ *Algeria* 35°25N 0°10E **261** A5
Mascarene Is. *Ind. Oc.* 22°0S 55°0E **254** J9
Mascot *Australia* 33°55S 151°12E **139** B2
Mascota *Mexico* 20°32N 104°49W **318** C4
Mascoutah *U.S.A.* 38°29N 89°48W **310** F7
Masdar City = Madīnat Masdar *U.A.E.* 24°26N 54°37E **247** E7
Masefau B. *Amer. Samoa* 14°15S 170°37W **302** f
Masein *Burma* 23°22N 94°21E **241** D5
Masela *Indonesia* 8°9S 129°51E **231** F7
Maseru *Lesotho* 29°18S 27°30E **270** C4
Masfjorden *Norway* 60°48N 5°18E **164** D2
Mashaba *Zimbabwe* 20°2S 30°29E **269** G3
Mashābih *Si. Arabia* 25°35N 36°30E **246** E3
Mashan *China* 23°40N 108°11E **228** F7
Mashang *China* 36°48N 117°57E **227** F9
Mashar *South Sudan* 9°16N 26°51E **257** F2
Mashariki = Eastern □ *Kenya* 0°0 38°30E **268** C4
Mashatu ⌓ *Botswana* 22°45S 29°5E **271** B4
Mashegu *Nigeria* 10°0N 5°35E **263** D6
Masherbrum *Pakistan* 35°38N 76°18E **243** B7
Mashhad *Iran* 36°20N 59°35E **247** B8
Mashi *Nigeria* 13°0N 7°54E **263** C6
Mashiki *Japan* 32°51N 130°53E **222** E2
Mashīz *Iran* 29°56N 56°37E **247** D8
Mashkal → *Pakistan* 26°2N 65°19E **240** D2
Māshkel, Hāmūn-i- *Pakistan* 28°20N 62°56E **240** C1
Mashki Chāh *Pakistan* 29°5N 62°30E **240** C1
Mashonaland Central □ *Zimbabwe* 17°30S 31°0E **271** A5
Mashonaland East □ *Zimbabwe* 18°0S 32°0E **271** A5
Mashonaland West □ *Zimbabwe* 17°30S 29°30E **271** A4
Mashrakh *India* 26°7N 84°48E **243** F11
Masi Manimba *Dem. Rep. of the Congo* 4°40S 17°54E **265** C3
Masibi *Angola* 11°6S 22°41E **265** E4
Masig *Australia* 9°45S 143°24E **280** a
Masindi *Uganda* 1°40N 31°43E **268** B3
Masindi Port *Uganda* 1°43N 32°2E **268** B3
Masinga Res. *Kenya* 0°58S 37°38E **268** C4
Masinloc *Phil.* 15°32N 119°57E **232** D2
Maşīrah, Jazīrat *Oman* 21°0N 58°50E **249** B7
Maşīrah, Khalīj *Oman* 20°10N 58°10E **249** B7
Maşīrah, Tur'at *Oman* 20°30N 58°40E **249** B7
Masisea *Peru* 8°35S 74°22W **330** B3
Masisi *Dem. Rep. of the Congo* 1°23S 28°49E **268** C2
Masjed Soleyman *Iran* 31°55N 49°18E **247** D6
Mask, L. *Ireland* 53°36N 9°22W **166** C2
Maskelyne Is. *Vanuatu* 16°32S 167°49E **287** F5
Maski *India* 15°56N 76°46E **245** G3
Maskin *Oman* 23°44N 56°52E **247** F8
Maslen Nos *Bulgaria* 42°18N 27°48E **203** D11
Maslinica *Croatia* 43°24N 16°13E **199** E13
Masmo *Sweden* 59°15N 17°53E **139** B1
Maşna'ah *Yemen* 14°27N 48°17E **249** D5
Masnou = El Masnou *Spain* 41°28N 2°20E **196** D7
Masoala, Saikanosy *Madag.* 15°45S 50°10E **272** B3
Masoala, Tanjon' i *Madag.* 15°59S 50°13E **272** B3
Masoala △ *Madag.* 15°30S 50°12E **272** B3
Masoarivo *Madag.* 19°3S 44°19E **272** B1
Masohi = Amahai *Indonesia* 3°20S 128°55E **231** E7
Masomeloka *Madag.* 20°17S 48°37E **272** C2
Mason *Mich., U.S.A.* 42°35N 84°27W **311** B12
Mason *Nev., U.S.A.* 38°56N 119°8W **306** G7
Mason *Ohio, U.S.A.* 39°22N 84°19W **311** E12
Mason *Tex., U.S.A.* 30°45N 99°14W **314** F5
Mason B. *N.Z.* 46°55S 167°45E **285** G2
Mason City *Ill., U.S.A.* 40°12N 89°42W **310** D7
Mason City *Iowa, U.S.A.* 43°9N 93°12W **310** A3
Mason Hall *Trin. & Tob.* 11°13N 60°43W **323** s
Maspalomas *Canary Is.* 27°46N 15°35W **153** e1
Maspalomas, Pta. *Canary Is.* 27°43N 15°36W **153** e1
Maspeth *U.S.A.* 40°43N 73°55W **132** B2
Masqat *Oman* 23°37N 58°36E **249** B7
Masr el Gedida *Egypt* 30°5N 31°21E **117** A2
Masr el Qadîma *Egypt* 30°0N 31°14E **117** A2
Massa *Congo* 3°45S 15°29E **264** C3
Massa *Italy* 44°1N 10°9E **198** D7
Massa, O. → *Morocco* 30°2N 9°40W **260** B3
Massa e Carrara □ *Italy* 44°10N 10°10E **198** D7
Massa Maríttima *Italy* 43°3N 10°52E **198** E7
Massachusetts □ *U.S.A.* 42°30N 72°0W **313** D13
Massachusetts Avenue *Washington, D.C., U.S.A.* **143** a2
Massachusetts B. *U.S.A.* 42°25N 70°50W **313** D14
Massachusetts Inst. of Tech. *Boston, U.S.A.* 42°21N 71°5W **116** A2
Massacre *Dominica* 15°20N 61°25W **323** k
Massafra *Italy* 40°35N 17°7E **201** B10
Massaguet *Chad* 12°28N 15°26E **259** F3
Massakory *Chad* 13°0N 15°49E **259** F3
Massamá *Portugal* 38°45N 9°16W **126** A1
Massamba *Mozam.* 15°58S 33°31E **269** F3
Massanella *Spain* 39°48N 2°51E **206** B3
Massangano *Angola* 9°40S 14°13E **265** D2
Massangena *Mozam.* 21°34S 33°0E **271** B5
Massango *Angola* 8°1S 16°10E **265** D3
Massapê *Brazil* 3°31S 40°19W **332** B3
Massat *France* 42°53N 1°21E **174** F5
Massawa = Mitsiwa *Eritrea* 15°35N 39°25E **257** D4
Massena *U.S.A.* 44°56N 74°54W **313** B10
Massenya *Chad* 11°21N 16°9E **259** F3
Masset *Canada* 54°2N 132°10W **296** C2
Masseube *France* 43°25N 0°34E **174** E4
Massey → *Canada* 43°42N 79°19W **141** A3
Massey Hall *Toronto, Canada* **141** a3
Massiac *France* 45°15N 3°11E **174** C7
Massif Central *France* 44°55N 3°0E **174** D7
Massif des Bauges ⌓ *France* 45°40N 6°10E **173** G13
Massigui *Mali* 11°48N 6°50W **262** C3
Massillon *U.S.A.* 40°48N 81°32W **312** F3
Massima *Gabon* 1°27S 11°33E **264** C2
Massine, O. → *Algeria* 36°13N 2°12E **261** A5
Massinga *Mozam.* 23°15S 35°22E **271** B6
Massingir *Mozam.* 23°51S 32°4E **271** B5
Masson-Angers *Canada* 45°32N 75°25W **313** A9
Masson I. *Antarctica* 66°10S 93°20E **151** C7
Massouka *Gabon* 1°37S 9°56E **264** C1
Massow = Maszewo *Poland* 53°29N 15°3E **184** E2
Massy *France* 48°43N 2°16E **134** B2
Mastābah *Si. Arabia* 20°49N 39°26E **248** B2
Maştağa *Azerbaijan* 40°35N 50°1E **191** K10
Mastanli = Momchilgrad *Bulgaria* 41°33N 25°23E **203** E9
Masterton *N.Z.* 40°56S 175°39E **284** G4
Mastic *U.S.A.* 40°47N 72°54W **313** F12
Mastuj *Pakistan* 36°20N 72°36E **243** A5
Mastung *Pakistan* 29°50N 66°56E **240** C2
Mastūrah *Si. Arabia* 23°7N 38°52E **248** B2
Masty *Belarus* 53°27N 24°38E **177** B13
Masuda *Japan* 34°40N 131°51E **222** C3
Masuika *Dem. Rep. of the Congo* 7°37S 22°32E **265** D4
Masuku = Franceville *Gabon* 1°40S 13°32E **264** C2
Masurai *Indonesia* 2°30S 101°51E **234** C2
Masurian Lakes = Mazurski, Pojezierze *Poland* 53°50N 21°0E **184** E7
Masvingo *Zimbabwe* 20°8S 30°49E **269** G3
Masvingo □ *Zimbabwe* 21°0S 31°30E **269** G3
Maswa ⌓ *Tanzania* 2°58S 34°19E **268** C3
Maşyāf *Syria* 35°4N 36°20E **250** C7
Maszewo *Poland* 53°29N 15°3E **184** E2
Mat → *Albania* 41°40N 19°35E **202** E3
Mât → *Réunion* 20°57S 55°42E **272** f
Mata *Israel* 31°43N 35°4E **123** B1
Mata-au = Clutha → *N.Z.* 46°20S 169°49E **285** G4
Mata de São João *Brazil* 12°31S 38°17W **333** D4
Mata Redonda *Venezuela* 10°57N 64°7W **329** a
Mata-Utu *Wall. & F. Is.* 13°17S 176°8W **277** C15
Matabele Plain *Zambia* 16°20S 23°10E **265** F4
Matabeleland North □ *Zimbabwe* 19°0S 28°0E **269** F2
Matabeleland South □ *Zimbabwe* 21°0S 29°0E **269** G2
Matachel → *Spain* 38°50N 6°17W **195** G4
Matachewan *Canada* 47°56N 80°39W **298** C3
Matacuni → *Venezuela* 3°2N 65°16W **329** C4
Matadi *Dem. Rep. of the Congo* 5°52S 13°31E **265** D2
Matafao, Mt. *Amer. Samoa* 14°17S 170°42W **302** f
Matagalpa *Nic.* 13°0N 85°58W **320** D2
Matagami *Canada* 49°45N 77°34W **298** C4
Matagami, L. *Canada* 49°50N 77°40W **298** C4
Matagorda B. *U.S.A.* 28°40N 96°12W **314** G6
Matagorda I. *U.S.A.* 28°15N 96°30W **314** G6
Matahiva *French Polynesia* 17°32S 149°20W **289** f
Mataiea *Tahiti* 17°46S 149°25W **289** e
Matak *Indonesia* 3°18N 106°16E **234** B3
Matakana *N.S.W., Australia* 32°59S 145°54E **283** B6
Matakana *N.Z.* 36°21S 174°43E **284** C3
Matala *Angola* 14°46S 15°4E **265** E3
Matala *Kriti, Greece* 34°59N 24°45E **207** F5
Matalam *Phil.* 7°5N 124°54E **233** H5
Matalaque *Peru* 16°26S 70°49W **330** D3
Matale *Sri Lanka* 7°30N 80°37E **245** L5
Matam *Senegal* 15°34N 13°17W **262** B2
Matam □ *Senegal* 15°37N 13°19W **262** B2
Matamata *N.Z.* 37°48S 175°47E **284** D4
Matameye *Niger* 13°26N 8°28E **259** F1
Matamoros *Coahuila, Mexico* 25°32N 103°15W **318** B4
Matamoros *Tamaulipas, Mexico* 25°53N 97°30W **319** B5
Ma'ţan as Sarra *Libya* 21°45N 22°0E **259** D4
Ma'ţan Bishārah *Libya* 23°0N 22°32E **258** D4
Matandu → *Tanzania* 8°45S 34°19E **269** D3
Matane *Canada* 48°50N 67°33W **299** C6
Matang *China* 23°30N 104°7E **228** F5
Matankari *Niger* 13°46N 4°1E **263** C5
Matanomadh *India* 23°33N 68°57E **242** H3
Matanzas *Cuba* 23°0N 81°40W **320** B3
Matapa *Botswana* 23°11S 24°39E **270** B3
Matapan, C. = Tenaro, Akra *Greece* 36°22N 22°27E **204** E4
Matapédia *Canada* 48°0N 66°59W **299** C6
Matapo △ *Zimbabwe* 20°30S 29°40E **269** G2
Mataporquera *Spain* 42°52N 4°10W **194** C6
Matara *Sri Lanka* 5°58N 80°30E **245** M5
Mataram *Indonesia* 8°35S 116°7E **231** K19
Matarani *Peru* 17°0S 72°10W **330** D3
Mataranka *Australia* 14°55S 133°4E **278** B5
Matarinao B. *Phil.* 11°12N 125°33E **233** F5
Matarma, Râs *Egypt* 30°27N 32°44E **251** H3
Mataró *Spain* 41°32N 2°29E **196** D7
Matarraña → *Spain* 41°14N 0°22E **196** D5
Mataruška Banja *Serbia* 43°40N 20°40E **202** C4
Matasiete, Cerro *Venezuela* 11°3N 63°51W **329** a
Mataso *Vanuatu* 17°14S 168°26E **287** G6
Matata *N.Z.* 37°54S 176°48E **284** D5
Matatiele *S. Africa* 30°20S 28°49E **271** D4
Matatila Dam *India* 25°0N 78°22E **244** B4
Matatula, C. *Amer. Samoa* 14°15S 170°33W **302** f
Mataura *N.Z.* 46°11S 168°51E **285** G3
Mataura → *N.Z.* 46°34S 168°44E **285** G3
Matavai, B. de *Tahiti* 17°30S 149°23W **289** e
Matavera *Cook Is.* 21°13S 159°44W **289** h
Mataveri *Chile* 27°9S 109°27W **330** b
Mategua *Bolivia* 13°1S 62°48W **331** C5
Matehuala *Mexico* 23°39N 100°39W **318** C4
Mateke *Dem. Rep. of the Congo* 4°52S 24°25E **264** C3
Mateke Hills *Zimbabwe* 21°48S 31°0E **269** G3
Matelot *Trin. & Tob.* 10°50N 61°7W **323** t
Matera *Italy* 40°40N 16°36E **201** B9
Matese, Monti del *Italy* 41°27N 14°22E **201** A7
Matese ⌓ *Italy* 41°24N 14°23E **201** A7
Mátészalka *Hungary* 47°58N 22°20E **182** C7
Matetsi *Zimbabwe* 18°12S 26°0E **269** F2
Mateur *Tunisia* 37°0N 9°40E **258** A1
Matfors *Sweden* 62°21N 17°2E **162** B11
Matha *France* 45°52N 0°20W **174** C3
Matheniko ⌓ *Uganda* 2°49N 34°27E **268** B3
Mathis *U.S.A.* 28°6N 97°50W **314** G6
Mathoura *Australia* 35°50S 144°55E **283** C6
Mathraki *Greece* 39°48N 19°31E **206** B9
Mathura *India* 27°30N 77°40E **242** F7
Mati *Phil.* 6°55N 126°15E **233** H6
Matiakoali *Burkina Faso* 12°28N 1°2E **263** C5
Matiali *India* 26°56N 88°49E **243** F13
Matías Romero *Mexico* 16°53N 95°2W **319** D5
Matibane *Mozam.* 14°49S 40°45E **269** E5
Matinha *Portugal* 38°45N 9°5W **126** A2
Matinhos *Brazil* 25°49S 48°32W **333** G2
Matiri Ra. *N.Z.* 41°38S 172°20E **285** B7
Matjiesfontein *S. Africa* 33°14S 20°35E **270** D3
Matla → *India* 21°40N 88°40E **243** J13
Matlab Bazar *Bangla.* 23°20N 90°43E **241** D3
Matlamanyane *Botswana* 19°33S 25°57E **270** A4
Matli *Pakistan* 25°2N 68°39E **242** G3
Matlock *U.K.* 53°9N 1°33W **168** D6
Matmata *Tunisia* 33°37N 9°59E **258** B1
Matna *Sudan* 13°49N 35°10E **257** E4
Matnog *Phil.* 12°35N 124°5E **232** E5
Mato *Dem. Rep. of the Congo* 8°1S 24°24E **265** D4
Mato → *Venezuela* 7°9N 65°7W **329** B4
Mato, Serrania de *Venezuela* 6°25N 65°25W **328** B4
Mato Grosso □ *Brazil* 14°0S 55°0W **331** C7
Mato Grosso, Planalto do *Brazil* 15°0S 55°0W **331** D7
Mato Grosso do Sul □ *Brazil* 18°0S 55°0W **331** D7
Matobo = Matapo △ *Zimbabwe* 20°30S 29°40E **269** G2
Matochkin Shar, Proliv *Russia* 73°23N 55°12E **214** B6
Matola *Mozam.* 25°57S 32°27E **271** C5
Matong *Papua N. G.* 5°36S 151°50E **286** C6
Matopo Hills *Zimbabwe* 20°36S 28°20E **269** G2
Matopos *Zimbabwe* 20°20S 28°29E **269** G2
Matosinhos *Portugal* 41°11N 8°42W **194** D2
Matou *Taiwan* 23°11N 120°15E **225** C2
Matouba *Guadeloupe* 16°2N 61°41W **322** e
Matour *France* 46°19N 4°29E **173** F11
Matramam *Indonesia* 6°12S 106°51E **122** B2
Matroosberg *S. Africa* 33°23S 19°40E **270** D2
Maţruḩ *Oman* 23°37N 58°30E **249** B7
Matsalu △ *Estonia* 58°45N 23°36E **188** C2
Matsena *Nigeria* 13°5N 10°5E **263** C7
Matsesta *Russia* 43°34N 39°51E **191** J4
Matsu Tao *Taiwan* 26°8N 119°56E **225** b
Matsubara = Takahagi *Japan* 36°43N 140°45E **221** F10
Matsubara *Japan* 34°34N 135°33E **133** B2
Matsubase *Japan* 32°40N 130°40E **222** E2
Matsudo *Japan* 35°47N 139°54E **223** B11
Matsue *Japan* 35°25N 133°10E **222** B5
Matsum, Ko *Thailand* 9°22N 99°59E **237** b
Matsumae *Japan* 41°26N 140°7E **220** D10
Matsumae-Hantō *Japan* 41°30N 140°15E **220** D10
Matsumoto *Japan* 36°15N 138°0E **223** A10
Matsusaka *Japan* 34°34N 136°32E **223** C8
Matsushima *Kumamoto, Japan* 32°30N 130°25E **222** E2
Matsushima *Miyagi, Japan* 38°20N 141°10E **220** E10
Matsuura *Japan* 33°20N 129°49E **222** D1
Matsuyama *Japan* 33°45N 132°45E **222** D4
Matsuzaki *Japan* 34°43N 138°50E **223** C10
Mattagami → *Canada* 50°43N 81°29W **298** B3
Mattancheri *India* 9°50N 76°15E **245** K3
Mattapan *U.S.A.* 42°16N 71°6W **116** B2
Mattawa *Canada* 46°20N 78°45W **298** C4
Matterhorn *Switz.* 45°58N 7°39E **179** K3
Mattersburg *Austria* 47°44N 16°24E **181** D9
Matteson *U.S.A.* 41°30N 87°42W **311** C9
Matthew, Î. *N. Cal.* 22°29S 171°15E **277** E13
Matthew Town *Bahamas* 20°57N 73°40W **321** B5
Matthews *U.S.A.* 40°23N 85°30W **311** D11
Matthews Ridge *Guyana* 7°37N 60°10W **329** B5
Mattias Church *Budapest, Hungary* **117** b1
Mattice *Canada* 49°40N 83°20W **298** C3
Mattili *India* 18°33N 82°12E **244** E6
Mattituck *U.S.A.* 40°59N 72°32W **313** F12
Mattō = Hakusan *Japan* 36°31N 136°34E **223** A8
Mattoon *U.S.A.* 39°29N 88°23W **311** E8
Matuba *Mozam.* 24°28S 32°49E **271** B5
Matucana *Peru* 11°55S 76°25W **330** C2
Matugama *Sri Lanka* 6°31N 80°7E **245** L5
Matuguinao *Phil.* 12°5N 124°55E **232** E5
Matuka *Papua N. G.* 4°54S 145°47E **286** C3
Matuku *Fiji* 19°10S 179°44E **287** B2
Matūn = Khowst *Afghan.* 33°22N 69°58E **242** C3
Matura *Trin. & Tob.* 10°40N 61°4W **323** t
Matura B. *Trin. & Tob.* 10°39N 61°1W **323** t
Maturín *Venezuela* 9°45N 63°11W **329** B5
Matusadona △ *Zimbabwe* 16°58S 28°42E **269** F2
Matutum, Mt. *Phil.* 6°22N 125°5E **233** H5
Matveyev Kurgan *Russia* 47°35N 38°57E **189** J10
Matxitxako, C. *Spain* 43°28N 2°47W **196** B2
Mátyásföld *Hungary* 47°30N 19°12E **117** A3
Mau *Mad. P., India* 26°17N 78°41E **243** F8
Mau *Ut. P., India* 25°56N 83°33E **243** G10
Mau *Ut. P., India* 25°17N 81°23E **243** G9
Mau Escarpment *Kenya* 0°40S 36°0E **268** C4
Mau Ranipur *India* 25°16N 79°8E **243** G8
Mau Tso Ngam *Hong Kong, China* 22°22N 114°13E **122** A3
Maua *Eastern, Kenya* 0°14N 37°56E **268** C4
Maua *Mozam.* 13°53S 37°10E **269** E4
Mauban *Phil.* 14°12N 121°44E **232** D3
Maubeuge *France* 50°17N 3°57E **173** B10
Maubin *Burma* 16°44N 95°39E **241** G5
Maubourguet *France* 43°29N 0°1E **174** E4
Maud, Pt. *Australia* 23°6S 113°45E **278** D1
Maud Rise *S. Ocean* 66°0S 3°0E **151** C3
Maude *Australia* 34°29S 144°18E **282** C6
Maudin Sun *Burma* 16°0N 94°30E **241** G5
Mauer *Austria* 48°9N 16°16E **142** B1
Maués *Brazil* 3°20S 57°45W **329** D6
Maués-Acu → *Brazil* 3°22S 57°44W **329** D6
Maug Is. *N. Marianas* 20°1N 145°13E **302** a
Mauganj *India* 24°50N 81°55E **243** G9
Maughold Hd. *I. of Man* 54°18N 4°18W **168** C3
Mauguio *France* 43°37N 4°1E **174** E7
Maui *U.S.A.* 20°48N 156°20W **302** C5
Maulamyaing = Moulmein *Burma* 16°30N 97°40E **241** G6
Maule □ *Chile* 36°5S 72°30W **334** D1
Mauléon-Licharre *France* 43°14N 0°54W **174** E3
Maullín *Chile* 41°38S 73°37W **336** B2
Maulvi Bazar *Bangla.* 24°29N 91°42E **241** C3
Maumee *U.S.A.* 41°34N 83°39W **311** C13
Maumee → *U.S.A.* 41°42N 83°28W **311** C13
Maumere *Indonesia* 8°38S 122°13E **231** F6
Maumusson, Pertuis de *France* 45°48N 1°14W **174** C2
Maun *Botswana* 20°0S 23°26E **270** B3
Mauna Kea *U.S.A.* 19°50N 155°28W **302** D6
Mauna Loa *U.S.A.* 19°30N 155°35W **302** D6
Mauna Loa Forest Reserve *U.S.A.* 19°35N 155°33W **302** D6
Maunabo *Puerto Rico* 18°1N 65°54W **321** b
Maunaloa *U.S.A.* 21°8N 157°13W **302** B4
Maunalua B. *U.S.A.* 21°15N 157°45W **302** K14
Maunath Bhanjan = Mau *India* 25°56N 83°33E **243** G10
Maunawili *U.S.A.* 21°23N 157°46W **302** K14
Maunga Orito *Chile* 27°10S 109°25W **330** b
Maunga Puakatiki *Chile* 27°6S 109°15W **330** b
Maunga Terevaka *Chile* 27°5S 109°23W **330** b
Maungaroa *Cook Is.* 21°13S 159°48W **289** h
Maungatongaiti *Cook Is.* 21°14S 159°48W **289** h
Maungaturoto *N.Z.* 36°6S 174°23E **284** C3
Maungdaw *Burma* 20°50N 92°21E **241** E4
Maungmagan Kyunzu *Burma* 14°0N 97°48E **236** E1
Maungu *Kenya* 3°33S 38°45E **268** C4
Maupihaa *French Polynesia* 16°50S 153°55W **289** f
Maupin *U.S.A.* 45°11N 121°5W **304** D3
Maupiti *French Polynesia* 16°27S 152°15W **289** f
Maure-de-Bretagne *France* 47°59N 1°58W **172** E5
Maurepas, L. *U.S.A.* 30°15N 90°30W **315** F9
Maures *France* 43°15N 6°15E **175** E10
Mauriac *France* 45°13N 2°19E **174** C6
Maurice, L. *Australia* 29°30S 131°0E **279** E5
Mauriceville *N.Z.* 40°45S 175°42E **284** G4
Mauricie △ *Canada* 46°45N 73°0W **298** C5
Maurienne *France* 45°13N 6°30E **175** C10
Mauripur *Pakistan* 24°52N 66°55E **123** A1
Mauritania ■ *Africa* 20°50N 10°0W **260** D3
Mauritius ■ *Ind. Oc.* 20°0S 57°0E **272** e
Mauritius ✈ (MRU) *Mauritius* 20°25S 57°40E **272** e
Mauron *France* 48°9N 2°18W **172** D4
Maurs *France* 44°43N 2°12E **174** D6
Mauston *U.S.A.* 43°48N 90°5W **308** D8
Mauterndorf *Austria* 47°9N 13°40E **180** D6
Mauthen *Austria* 46°40N 13°0E **180** E6
Mauvezin *France* 43°44N 0°53E **174** E4
Mauzé-sur-le-Mignon *France* 46°12N 0°41W **174** B3
Mavaca → *Venezuela* 2°31N 65°11W **329** C4
Mavinga *Angola* 15°50S 20°21E **265** F4
Mavli *India* 24°45N 73°55E **242** G5
Mavoko = Athi River *Kenya* 1°28S 36°58E **268** C4
Mavrata *Greece* 38°4N 20°44E **207** C2
Mavrovë *Albania* 40°26N 19°32E **202** F3
Mavrovo △ *Macedonia* 41°36N 20°45E **202** E4
Mavuradonha Mts. *Zimbabwe* 16°30S 31°30E **269** F3
Mawa *Dem. Rep. of the Congo* 2°45N 26°40E **268** B2
Mawai *India* 22°30N 81°4E **243** H9
Mawana *India* 29°6N 77°58E **242** E7
Mawand *Pakistan* 29°33N 68°38E **242** E3
Mawat *Iraq* 35°54N 45°24E **213** E11
Mawjib, W. al → *Jordan* 31°28N 35°36E **251** G6
Mawkmai *Burma* 20°14N 97°37E **241** E6
Mawlaik *Burma* 23°40N 94°26E **241** D5
Mawlamyine = Moulmein *Burma* 16°30N 97°40E **241** G6
Mawlamyinegyun *Burma* 16°23N 95°16E **241** G5
Mawlawkho *Burma* 17°50N 97°38E **241** G6
Mawqaq *Si. Arabia* 27°25N 41°8E **246** E4
Mawson *Antarctica* 67°30S 62°53E **151** C6
Mawson Coast *Antarctica* 68°30S 63°0E **151** C6
Mawson Pk. *Heard I.* 53°6S 73°31E **273** K6
Mawsynram *India* 25°15N 91°30E **241** C3
Mawzaʻ *Yemen* 13°16N 43°30E **248** D3
Max *U.S.A.* 47°49N 101°18W **308** B3
Maxambamba = Nova Iguaçu *Brazil* 22°45S 43°28W **333** F3
Maxcanú *Mexico* 20°35N 90°0W **319** C6
Maxesibeni *S. Africa* 30°49S 29°23E **271** D4
Maxeys *U.S.A.* 33°45N 83°11W **316** B6
Maxhamish L. *Canada* 59°50N 123°17W **296** B4
Maxhof *Germany* 48°4N 11°29E **131** B1
Maxixe *Mozam.* 23°54S 35°17E **271** B6
Maxville *Canada* 45°17N 74°51W **313** A10
Maxwell *N.Z.* 39°51S 174°49E **284** F3
Maxwell *Calif., U.S.A.* 39°17N 122°11W **306** F4
Maxwelton *Australia* 20°43S 142°41E **280** C3
May, C. *U.S.A.* 38°56N 74°58W **309** F16
May Jirgui *Niger* 13°44N 8°8E **259** F1
May Pen *Jamaica* 17°58N 77°15W **320** a
May River *Papua N. G.* 4°19S 141°58E **286** C1
Maya *Indonesia* 1°10S 109°35E **235** C3
Maya → *Russia* 60°28N 134°28E **215** D14
Maya, Costa *Mexico* 18°44N 87°42W **319** D7
Maya Mts. *Belize* 16°30N 89°0W **320** C2
Mayabandar *India* 12°56N 92°56E **245** H11
Mayaguana I. *Bahamas* 22°30N 72°44W **321** B5
Mayagüez *Puerto Rico* 18°12N 67°9W **321** C6
Mayahi *Niger* 13°58N 7°40E **263** C6
Mayaky *Ukraine* 47°26N 29°33E **183** C14
Mayals = Maials *Spain* 41°22N 0°30E **196** D5
Mayama *Congo* 3°51S 14°54E **264** C2
Mayāmey *Iran* 36°24N 55°42E **247** B7
Mayang *China* 27°53N 109°49E **228** D7
Mayanup *Australia* 33°57S 116°27E **279** F2
Mayapán *Mexico* 20°29N 89°11W **319** C7
Mayarí *Cuba* 20°40N 75°41W **321** B4
Mayaro *Trin. & Tob.* 10°17N 61°1W **323** t
Mayaro □ *Trin. & Tob.* 10°10N 61°5W **323** t
Mayaro B. *Trin. & Tob.* 10°14N 60°59W **323** t
Mayavaram = Mayiladuthurai *India* 11°3N 79°42E **245** J4
Maybell *U.S.A.* 40°31N 108°5W **304** F9
Maybio *Phil.* 5°50N 125°35E **233** J5
Maybole *U.K.* 55°21N 4°42W **167** F4
Maychew *Ethiopia* 12°50N 39°31E **257** E4
Maydān *Iraq* 34°55N 45°37E **213** E11
Maydan *Ukraine* 48°36N 23°29E **183** B8
Mayen *Germany* 50°19N 7°13E **179** E3
Mayenne *France* 48°20N 0°38W **172** D6
Mayenne □ *France* 48°10N 0°40W **172** D6
Mayenne → *France* 47°30N 0°32W **172** E6
Mayer *U.S.A.* 34°24N 112°14W **305** J7
Mayerthorpe *Canada* 53°57N 115°8W **296** C5
Mayesville *U.S.A.* 34°0N 80°12W **316** A9
Mayfair *Gauteng, S. Africa* 26°11S 28°0E **123** B2
Mayfair *London, U.K.* **125** b3
Mayfield *Ky., U.S.A.* 36°44N 88°38W **308** G9
Mayfield *N.Y., U.S.A.* 43°6N 74°16W **313** C10
Mayhill *U.S.A.* 32°53N 105°29W **305** K11
Mayiladuthurai *India* 11°3N 79°42E **245** J4
Maykop *Russia* 44°35N 40°10E **191** H5
Mayma *Russia* 52°3N 85°55E **217** B11
Maymyo *Burma* 22°2N 96°28E **236** A1
Maynard *Mass., U.S.A.* 42°26N 71°27W **313** D13
Maynard *Wash., U.S.A.* 47°59N 122°55W **306** C4
Maynard Hills *Australia* 28°28S 119°49E **279** E2
Mayne → *Australia* 23°40S 141°55E **280** C3
Maynooth *Ont., Canada* 45°13N 77°56W **312** A7
Maynooth *Kildare, Ireland* 53°23N 6°34W **166** C5
Mayo *Yukon, Canada* 63°38N 135°57W **294** E4
Mayo *Trin. & Tob.* 10°21N 61°23W **323** t
Mayo *Fla., U.S.A.* 30°3N 83°10W **316** E6
Mayo □ *Ireland* 53°53N 9°3W **166** C2
Mayo → *Argentina* 45°45S 69°45W **336** C3
Mayo → *Peru* 6°38S 76°15W **330** B2
Mayo B. *Phil.* 6°56N 126°22E **233** H6
Mayo Daga *Nigeria* 6°59N 11°25E **263** D7
Mayo Faran *Nigeria* 8°57N 12°4E **263** D7
Mayo-Kébbi Est □ *Chad* 10°20N 15°30E **259** F3
Mayo-Kébbi Ouest □ *Chad* 9°40N 17°50E **259** G3
Mayoko *Congo* 2°18S 12°49E **264** C2
Mayoko *Dem. Rep. of the Congo* 1°6S 23°50E **264** C4
Mayon Volcano *Phil.* 13°15N 123°41E **232** E4
Mayor Buratovich *Argentina* 39°15S 62°37W **336** A4
Mayor I. *N.Z.* 37°16S 176°17E **284** D5
Mayor Pablo Lagerenza *Paraguay* 19°55S 60°47W **331** D5
Mayorga *Spain* 42°10N 5°16W **194** C5
Mayotte ☒ *Ind. Oc.* 12°50S 45°10E **272** b
Mayoyao *Phil.* 16°59N 121°14E **232** C3
Mayqayyng *Kazakhstan* 51°27N 75°47E **217** B9
Mayraira Pt. *Phil.* 18°39N 120°51E **232** B3
Mayreau *St. Vincent* 12°39N 61°23W **323** n
Maysān □ *Iraq* 31°55N 47°15E **246** D5
Mayskiy *Russia* 43°47N 44°2E **191** J7
Maysville *Ky., U.S.A.* 38°39N 83°46W **311** F13
Maysville *Mo., U.S.A.* 39°53N 94°22W **310** E2
Maytiguid I. *Phil.* 11°3N 119°36E **233** F2
Mayu *Indonesia* 1°30N 126°30E **231** D7
Mayumba *Gabon* 3°25S 10°39E **264** C2
Mayuram = Mayiladuthurai *India* 11°3N 79°42E **245** J4
Mayville *N. Dak., U.S.A.* 47°30N 97°20W **308** B5
Mayville *N.Y., U.S.A.* 42°15N 79°30W **312** D5
Maywood *Calif., U.S.A.* 33°59N 118°12W **126** C3
Maywood *Ill., U.S.A.* 41°52N 87°51W **119** B1
Maywood *N.J., U.S.A.* 40°53N 74°3W **132** A1
Maywood Park Race Track *U.S.A.* 41°54N 87°50W **119** B1
Mazabuka *Zambia* 15°52S 27°44E **269** F2
Mazagán = El Jadida *Morocco* 33°11N 8°17W **260** B3
Mazagão *Brazil* 0°7S 51°16W **329** D7
Mazagaon *Mumbai, India* **130** a2
Mazamet *France* 43°30N 2°20E **174** E6
Mazán *Peru* 3°30S 73°0W **328** D3
Māzandarān □ *Iran* 36°30N 52°0E **247** B7
Mazapil *Mexico* 24°39N 101°34W **318** C4
Mazar *China* 36°32N 77°1E **217** E9
Mazar, O. → *Algeria* 31°50N 1°36E **261** B5
Mazār-e Sharīf *Afghan.* 36°41N 67°0E **240** A2
Mazara del Vallo *Italy* 37°39N 12°35E **200** E5
Mazarredo *Argentina* 47°10S 66°50W **336** C3
Mazarrón *Spain* 37°38N 1°19W **197** H3
Mazarrón, G. de *Spain* 37°27N 1°19W **197** H3
Mazaruni → *Guyana* 6°25N 58°35W **329** B6
Mazatán *Mexico* 29°0N 110°8W **318** B2
Mazatenango *Guatemala* 14°35N 91°30W **320** D1
Mazatlán *Mexico* 23°13N 106°25W **318** C3
Mažeikiai *Lithuania* 56°20N 22°20E **184** B9
Mazhafa, J. *Si. Arabia* 28°52N 35°5E **251** K6
Māzhān *Iran* 32°30N 59°0E **247** C8
Mazıdağı *Turkey* 37°28N 40°29E **213** D9
Mazīnān *Iran* 36°19N 56°56E **247** B8
Mazo Cruz *Peru* 16°45S 69°44W **330** D4
Mazoe *Mozam.* 16°42S 33°7E **269** F3

Mazoe → Mozam. 16°20S 33°30E 269 F3
Mazomanie U.S.A. 43°11N 89°48W 310 A7
Mazon U.S.A. 41°14N 88°25W 311 C8
Mazowe Zimbabwe 17°28S 30°58E 269 F3
Mazowieckie □ Poland 52°40N 21°0E 185 F8
Mazrûb Sudan 14°0N 29°20E 257 E2
Mazurski, Pojezierze Poland 53°50N 21°0E 184 E7
Mazyr Belarus 51°59N 29°15E 177 B15
Mba Fiji 17°33S 177°41E 287 A1
Mbaba Senegal 14°59N 16°44W 262 C1
Mbabane Swaziland 26°18S 31°6E 271 C5
Mbaéré → C.A.R. 3°47N 17°31E 264 B3
Mbagne Mauritania 16°6N 14°47W 262 B2
M'bahiakro Ivory C. 7°33N 4°19W 262 D4
Mbaïki C.A.R. 3°53N 18°1E 264 B3
Mbakana, Mt. de Cameroon 7°57N 15°6E 264 A3
Mbala Zambia 8°46S 31°24E 269 D3
Mbalabala Zimbabwe 20°27S 29°3E 271 B4
Mbalam Cameroon 2°13N 13°49E 264 B2
Mbale Uganda 1°8N 34°12E 268 B3
Mbali → C.A.R. 4°27N 18°20E 264 B3
Mbalmayo Cameroon 3°33N 11°33E 263 E7
Mbam → Cameroon 4°24N 11°17E 263 E7
Mbamba Bay Tanzania 11°13S 34°49E 269 E3
Mbandaka Dem. Rep. of the Congo 0°1N 18°18E 264 B3
Mbandjok Cameroon 4°27N 11°54E 264 B2
Mbanga Cameroon 4°30N 9°33E 263 E6
Mbanika Solomon Is. 9°3S 159°13E 287 M10
M'Banio, Lagune Gabon 3°35S 11°0E 264 C2
Mbanza Congo Angola 6°18S 14°16E 265 D2
Mbanza Ngungu Dem. Rep. of the Congo 5°12S 14°53E 265 D2
Mbarangandu Tanzania 10°11S 36°48E 269 D4
Mbarara Uganda 0°35S 30°40E 268 C3
Mbari → C.A.R. 4°34N 22°43E 264 B4
Mbatto Ivory C. 6°28N 4°22W 262 D4
Mbava Solomon Is. 7°47S 156°33E 287 L9
Mbé Congo 3°14S 15°50E 264 C3
Mbe Eq. Guin. 1°47N 9°56E 264 B1
Mbengga = Beqa Fiji 18°23S 178°8E 287 B2
Mbengué Gabon 2°2S 11°7E 264 C2
Mbengui Gabon 2°3S 10°4E 264 C2
Mbéni Comoros Is. 11°30S 43°22E 272 a
Mbenkuru → Tanzania 9°25S 39°50E 269 D4
Mbéré → Cameroon 7°45N 15°36E 264 A3
Mberengwa Zimbabwe 20°29S 29°57E 269 G2
Mberengwa, Mt. Zimbabwe 20°37S 29°55E 269 G2
Mberubu Nigeria 6°10N 7°38E 263 D6
Mbesuma Zambia 10°0S 32°2E 269 E3
Mbeya Tanzania 8°54S 33°29E 269 D3
Mbeya □ Tanzania 8°15S 33°30E 268 D3
Mbhashe → S. Africa 32°15S 28°54E 271 D4
Mbigou Gabon 1°53S 11°56E 264 C2
M'bili South Sudan 7°35N 28°15E 257 F2
Mbinga Tanzania 10°50S 35°0E 269 E4
Mbini = Río Muni □ Eq. Guin. 1°30N 10°0E 264 B2
Mbini Eq. Guin. 1°35N 9°37E 264 B1
Mbizi Zimbabwe 21°23S 31°1E 269 G3
Mboi Dem. Rep. of the Congo 6°57S 21°54E 265 D4
Mboki C.A.R. 5°19N 25°58E 257 F2
Mbokonimbeti Solomon Is. 8°57S 160°7E 287 M11
Mboli Dem. Rep. of the Congo 4°8N 23°9E 264 B4
Mbombela S. Africa 25°29S 30°59E 271 C5
Mbomo Congo 0°25N 14°42E 264 B2
Mbomou = Bomu → C.A.R. 4°40N 22°30E 264 B4
Mbomou □ C.A.R. 5°30N 23°30E 264 A4
M'bonge Cameroon 4°33N 9°5E 263 E6
Mboro Senegal 15°9N 16°54W 262 B1
Mboua Cameroon 4°25N 14°16E 264 A2
Mbouda Cameroon 5°38N 10°15E 264 A2
M'boukou, L. de Cameroon 6°23N 12°50E 263 D7
Mboune Senegal 14°42N 13°34W 262 C2
Mbouoma Congo 0°52S 15°4E 264 C3
Mbour Senegal 14°22N 16°54W 262 C1
Mbout Mauritania 16°1N 12°38W 262 B2
Mbrés C.A.R. 6°40N 19°48E 264 A3
M'Bridge → Angola 7°12S 12°51E 265 D2
Mbuji-Mayi Dem. Rep. of the Congo 6°9S 23°40E 265 D4
Mbulu Tanzania 3°45S 35°30E 268 C4
Mbuma Dem. Rep. of the Congo 3°32N 24°50E 264 B4
Mbuma Solomon Is. 8°59S 160°46E 287 M11
Mburucuyá Argentina 28°1S 58°14W 334 B4
Mburucuyá △ Argentina 28°1S 58°12W 334 B4
M'bwat Cameroon 6°29N 10°45E 264 A2
Mcherrah Algeria 27°0N 4°30W 260 C4
Mchinga Tanzania 9°44S 39°45E 269 D4
Mchinji Malawi 13°47S 32°58E 269 E3
Mdantsane S. Africa 32°56S 27°46E 271 D4
Mdennah Mauritania 24°37N 6°0W 260 D3
Me'a She' Arim Jerusalem 123 a2
Mead, L. U.S.A. 36°0N 114°44W 307 J12
Meade = Atqasuk → U.S.A. 70°52N 155°55W 303 A9
Meade U.S.A. 37°17N 100°20W 308 G3
Meade River = Atqasuk U.S.A. 70°28N 157°24W 303 A8
Meadow Lake Canada 54°10N 108°26W 297 C7
Meadow Lake ⌂ Canada 54°27N 109°0W 297 C7
Meadow Valley Wash → U.S.A. 36°40N 114°34W 307 J12
Meadowbank Park Australia 33°49S 151°6E 139 A1
Meadowlands Sports Complex New York, U.S.A. 40°49N 74°5W 132 B1
Meadville Mo., U.S.A. 39°47N 93°18W 310 E3
Meadville Pa., U.S.A. 41°39N 80°9W 312 E4
Meaford Canada 44°36N 80°35W 312 B4
Meakan Dake Japan 45°15N 144°0E 220 C11
Mealhada Portugal 40°22N 8°27W 194 E2
Mealy Mts. Canada 53°10N 58°0W 299 B8
Meander River Canada 59°2N 117°42W 296 B5
Meares, C. U.S.A. 45°37N 124°0W 304 D1
Mearim → Brazil 3°4S 44°35W 332 B3
Meath □ Ireland 53°40N 6°57W 166 C5
Meath Park Canada 53°27N 105°22W 297 C7
Meaulne France 46°36N 2°36E 173 F9
Meaux France 48°58N 2°50E 173 D9
Mebechi-Gawa → Japan 40°31N 141°31E 220 D10
Mebonden Norway 63°13N 11°2E 164 A8
Mebulu, Tanjung Indonesia 8°50S 115°5E 231 K18
Mecanhelas Mozam. 15°12S 35°54E 269 F4
Mecaya → Colombia 0°29N 75°11W 328 C2
Mecca = Makkah Si. Arabia 21°30N 39°54E 248 B2
Mecca U.S.A. 33°34N 116°5W 307 M10
Mechanicsburg Ohio, U.S.A. 40°4N 83°33W 311 D13
Mechanicsburg Pa., U.S.A. 40°13N 77°1W 312 F8
Mechanicsville U.S.A. 41°54N 91°16W 310 C5
Mechanicville U.S.A. 42°54N 73°41W 313 D11
Mechara Ethiopia 8°36N 40°20E 257 F5
Mechelen Belgium 51°2N 4°29E 170 C4
Mecherchar = Eil Malk Palau 7°10N 134°23E 288 c
Mecheria Algeria 33°35N 0°18W 261 B4
Mechernich Germany 50°35N 6°39E 178 E2
Mechetinskaya Russia 46°45N 40°32E 191 G5
Mechol Micronesia 9°37N 138°9E 287 R16
Měcholupy Czech Rep. 50°3N 14°32E 135 B3
Mechra Bel Ksiri Morocco 34°34N 5°57W 260 B3
Mechra Benâbbou Morocco 32°39N 7°48W 260 B3
Měčice Czech Rep. 50°11N 14°31E 135 A3
Mecidiye Turkey 40°38N 26°32E 203 F10
Mecidiyeköy Turkey 41°4N 29°0E 122 B2
Mecitözü Turkey 40°32N 35°17E 212 B6
Mecklenburg Germany 53°33N 11°40E 176 B7
Mecklenburg-Vorpommern □ Germany 53°45N 12°15E 178 B8
Mecklenburger Bucht Germany 54°20N 11°40E 178 A7
Meconta Mozam. 14°59S 39°50E 269 E4
Mecsek Hungary 46°10N 18°18E 182 D3
Mecubúri Mozam. 14°39S 38°54E 269 E4
Mecubúri → Mozam. 14°10S 40°30E 269 E5
Mecúfi Mozam. 13°20S 40°32E 269 E5
Mêda Portugal 40°57N 7°18W 194 E3
Medak India 18°1N 78°15E 244 E4
Medan Indonesia 3°40N 98°38E 234 B1
Medang Indonesia 8°9S 117°22E 235 D5
Médanos Argentina 38°50S 62°42W 336 A4
Médanos de Coro △ Venezuela 11°35N 69°44W 328 A4
Medanosa, Pta. Argentina 48°8S 66°0W 336 C3
Medart U.S.A. 30°5N 84°23W 316 E5
Medaryville U.S.A. 41°5N 86°55W 311 C10
Medawachchiya Sri Lanka 8°30N 80°30E 245 K5
Medchal India 17°37N 78°29E 244 F4
Mede Italy 45°6N 8°44E 198 C5
Médéa Algeria 36°12N 2°50E 261 A5
Médéa □ Algeria 36°0N 3°0E 261 A5
Mededa Bos.-H. 43°44N 19°10E 182 G4
Médégué Gabon 0°37N 10°8E 264 B2
Medeiros Neto Brazil 17°20S 40°14W 333 E3
Medellín Colombia 6°15N 75°35W 328 B2
Medelpad Sweden 62°33N 16°30E 162 B10
Medemblik Neths. 52°46N 5°8E 170 B5
Médenine Tunisia 33°21N 10°30E 258 B2
Médenine □ Tunisia 32°20N 10°0E 261 B7
Mederdra Mauritania 17°0N 15°38W 262 B1
Medford Mass., U.S.A. 42°25N 71°7W 116 A2
Medford Oreg., U.S.A. 42°19N 122°52W 304 E2
Medford Wis., U.S.A. 45°9N 90°20W 308 C8
Medgidia Romania 44°15N 28°19E 183 F13
Medi South Sudan 5°4N 30°42E 257 F3
Media Agua Argentina 31°58S 68°25W 334 C2
Media Luna Argentina 34°45S 66°44W 334 C2
Medianeira Brazil 25°17S 54°5W 335 B5
Mediapolis U.S.A. 41°0N 91°10W 310 D5
Mediaş Romania 46°9N 24°22E 183 D9
Medicilândia Brazil 3°33S 53°8W 329 D7
Medicina Italy 44°28N 11°38E 199 D8
Medicine Bow U.S.A. 41°54N 106°12W 304 F10
Medicine Bow Mts. U.S.A. 40°40N 106°0W 304 F10
Medicine Hat Canada 50°0N 110°45W 297 D6
Medicine Lake U.S.A. 48°30N 104°30W 304 B11
Medicine Lodge U.S.A. 37°17N 98°35W 308 G4
Medina = Al Madīnah Si. Arabia 24°35N 39°52E 246 E3
Medina Brazil 16°15S 41°29W 333 E3
Medina Colombia 4°30N 73°21W 328 C3
Medina Mis. Or., Phil. 8°55N 125°0E 233 G5
Medina N. Dak., U.S.A. 46°54N 99°18W 308 B4
Medina N.Y., U.S.A. 43°13N 78°23W 312 C6
Medina Ohio, U.S.A. 41°8N 81°52W 312 E3
Medina → U.S.A. 29°16N 98°29W 314 G5
Medina de Pomar Spain 42°56N 3°29W 194 C7
Medina de Rioseco Spain 41°53N 5°3W 194 D5
Medina del Campo Spain 41°18N 4°55W 194 D6
Médina Gounas Senegal 13°8N 13°45W 262 C2
Medina L. U.S.A. 29°32N 98°56W 314 G5
Medina Sidonia Spain 36°28N 5°57W 195 J5
Medinaceli Spain 41°12N 2°30W 196 D2
Medinipur India 22°25N 87°21E 243 H12
Medio-Campidano □ Italy 39°35N 8°30E 200 C1
Mediodia Spain 40°22N 3°39W 127 B2
Mediterranean Sea Europe 35°0N 15°0E 193 E8
Medjerda, O. → Tunisia 37°7N 10°13E 258 A2
Mednogorsk Russia 51°24N 57°37E 216 B5
Medny = Mednogorsk Russia 51°24N 57°37E 216 B5
Médoc France 45°10N 0°50W 174 C3
Medog China 29°19N 95°19E 241 A5
Medora U.S.A. 38°49N 86°10W 311 F10
Médouneu Gabon 0°57N 10°47E 264 B2
Medulin Croatia 44°49N 13°55E 199 D10
Medveđa Serbia 42°50N 21°32E 202 D5
Medvedevo Russia 56°37N 47°47E 190 B8
Medveditsa → Tver, Russia 57°5N 37°30E 188 D9
Medveditsa → Volgograd, Russia 49°35N 42°41E 190 F6
Medvedok Russia 57°20N 50°1E 190 B10
Medvezhi, Ostrava Russia 71°0N 161°0E 215 B17
Medvezhye = Krasnogvardeyskoye Russia 45°52N 41°33E 191 H5
Medvezhyegorsk Russia 63°0N 34°25E 186 B5
Medway □ U.K. 51°25N 0°32E 169 F8
Medway → U.K. 51°27N 0°46E 169 F8
Medzev Slovak Rep. 48°43N 20°55E 181 C13
Medzilaborce Slovak Rep. 49°17N 21°52E 181 B14
Medžitlija Macedonia 40°56N 21°26E 202 F5
Meekatharra Australia 26°32S 118°29E 279 E2
Meeker U.S.A. 40°2N 107°55W 304 F10
Meeniyan Australia 38°35S 146°3E 283 E7
Meersburg Germany 47°41N 9°16E 179 H5
Meerut India 29°1N 77°42E 242 E7
Meeteetse U.S.A. 44°9N 108°52W 304 D9
Mega Ethiopia 3°57N 38°19E 257 G4
Mega Sumatera Barat, Indonesia 4°0S 101°2E 234 C2
Megalo Ethiopia 6°51N 40°47E 267 C5
Megalo Chorio Greece 36°27N 27°24E 205 E9
Megalonisos Greece 38°0N 24°15E 204 D6
Megalopoli Greece 37°25N 22°7E 204 D4
Meganisi Greece 38°38N 20°46E 207 B2
Megara Greece 37°58N 23°22E 204 D5
Megasini India 21°38N 86°21E 243 J12
Megdovas = Tavropos → Greece 39°10N 21°45E 204 B3
Megève France 45°51N 6°37E 175 C10
Meghalaya □ India 25°50N 91°0E 241 C3
Meghezez Ethiopia 9°18N 39°26E 257 F4
Meghna → Bangla. 22°50N 90°50E 241 D3
Megion Russia 61°3N 76°6E 214 C8
Mégiscane, L. Canada 48°35N 75°55W 298 C4
Megisti Greece 36°8N 29°34E 205 E11
Megra Russia 60°11N 37°14E 188 B9
Meguro Japan 35°37N 139°42E 140 B3
Meguro → Japan 35°37N 139°45E 140 B3
Mehadia Romania 44°56N 22°23E 182 F7
Mehaïguene, O. → Algeria 32°15N 2°59E 261 B5
Meharry, Mt. Australia 22°59S 118°35E 278 D2
Mehedeby Sweden 60°27N 17°25E 162 D11
Mehedinţi □ Romania 44°40N 22°45E 182 F7
Meheisa Sudan 19°38N 32°57E 256 D3
Mehekar India 20°9N 76°34E 244 D3
Méhétia French Polynesia 17°52S 148°3W 289 f
Mehlville U.S.A. 38°31N 90°19W 308 F8
Mehmetçik = Galateia Cyprus 35°25N 34°4E 207 E10
Mehndawal India 26°58N 83°5E 243 F10
Mehr Jān Iran 33°50N 55°6E 247 C7
Mehrābād Iran 36°53N 47°55E 213 D12
Mehrābād ✕ (THR) Iran 35°41N 51°18E 141 A1
Mehrābān Iran 38°4N 47°7E 213 C12
Mehram Nagar India 28°34N 77°8E 120 B1
Mehrān Iran 33°7N 46°10E 213 F12
Mehrān → Iran 26°45N 55°26E 247 E7
Mehrgarh Pakistan 29°30N 67°30E 242 E2
Mehrīz Iran 31°35N 54°28E 247 D7
Mehrow Germany 52°34N 13°37E 115 A4
Mehtar Lam Afghan. 34°39N 70°11E 240 B3
Mehun-sur-Yèvre France 47°10N 2°13E 173 E9
Mei Jiang → China 24°25N 116°35E 229 E11
Mei Lanfang, Pantheon of Beijing, China 114 a2
Mei Xian China 34°18N 107°55E 226 G4
Meia Ponte → Brazil 18°32S 49°36W 333 E2
Meicheng China 29°29N 119°16E 229 C12
Meichengzhen China 28°9N 111°40E 229 C8
Meichuan China 30°8N 115°31E 229 B10
Meidling Austria 48°10N 16°20E 142 A2
Meidougou Cameroon 6°25N 14°13E 264 A2
Méier Brazil 22°52S 43°15W 135 B1
Meiganga Cameroon 6°30N 14°25E 264 A2
Meighen I. Canada 80°0N 99°30W 295 B12
Meigs U.S.A. 31°4N 84°6W 316 D5
Meigu China 28°16N 103°20E 228 C4
Meihekou China 42°32N 125°40E 224 A2
Meiji Shrine Tokyo, Japan 140 b1
Meiktila Burma 20°53N 95°54E 241 E5
Meili Xue Shan China 28°30N 98°39E 228 C2
Meimyu = Maymyo Burma 22°2N 96°28E 236 A1
Meinerzhagen Germany 51°6N 7°38E 178 D3
Meiningen Germany 50°34N 10°25E 178 E6
Meinung Taiwan 22°54N 120°32E 225 D2
Meio → Brazil 13°36S 44°7W 333 D3
Meira, Serra de Spain 43°15N 7°15W 194 B3
Meiringen Switz. 46°43N 8°12E 179 J4
Meise Belgium 50°56N 4°20E 116 A1
Meishan Sichuan, China 30°3N 103°23E 228 B4
Meishan Taiwan 23°35N 120°33E 225 C2
Meissen Germany 51°9N 13°29E 178 D9
Meissner Germany 51°14N 9°50E 178 D5
Meissner-Kaufunger Wald ⌂ Germany 51°16N 9°45E 178 D5
Meitan China 27°45N 107°29E 228 D6
Meizhou China 24°16N 116°6E 229 E11
Meja India 25°9N 82°7E 243 G10
Mejillones Chile 23°10S 70°30W 334 A1
Mejiro Japan 35°43N 139°43E 140 A3
Mékambo Gabon 1°2N 13°50E 264 B2
Mekdela Ethiopia 11°24N 39°10E 257 E4
Mekele Ethiopia 13°33N 39°30E 257 E4
Mekerghene, Sebkra Algeria 26°21N 1°30E 261 C5
Mékhé Senegal 15°7N 16°38W 262 B1
Mekhomiya = Razlog Bulgaria 41°53N 23°28E 202 E7
Mekhtar Pakistan 30°30N 69°15E 240 C3
Meknès Morocco 33°57N 5°33W 260 B3
Meknès-Tafilalet □ Morocco 33°3N 5°35W 260 B3
Meko Nigeria 7°27N 2°52E 263 D5
Mekong → Asia 9°30N 106°15E 237 H6
Mekongga Indonesia 3°39S 121°15E 231 E6
Mekoryuk U.S.A. 60°23N 166°11W 303 F6
Mekrou → Benin 12°25N 2°50E 263 C5
Mekvari = Kür → Azerbaijan 39°29N 49°15E 213 C13
Mel Italy 46°4N 12°5E 199 B9
Melagiri Hills India 12°20N 77°30E 245 H3
Melah, Oued el → Algeria 32°20N 2°28E 261 B5
Melaka Malaysia 2°15N 102°15E 237 L4
Melaka □ Malaysia 2°15N 102°15E 237 L4
Melambes Greece 35°8N 24°40E 207 E5
Melanesia Pac. Oc. 4°0S 155°0E 277 A10
Melanesian Basin Pac. Oc. 0°5N 160°35E 288 G8
Melapalaiyam India 8°39N 77°44E 245 K3
Melawi → Indonesia 0°5N 111°29E 235 B4
Melaya Indonesia 8°17S 114°30E 231 J17
Melbourne Vic., Australia 37°48S 144°58E 128 A1
Melbourne Fla., U.S.A. 28°5N 80°37W 317 G9
Melbourne Iowa, U.S.A. 41°57N 93°6W 310 C3
Melbourne ✕ (MEL) Australia 37°40S 144°50E 128 A1
Melcher-Dallas U.S.A. 41°14N 93°15W 310 C3
Melchor Múzquiz Mexico 27°53N 101°31W 318 B4
Melchor Ocampo Mexico 24°51N 101°39W 318 C4
Meldal Norway 63°3N 9°44E 164 A6
Méldola Italy 44°7N 12°5E 199 D9
Meldorf Germany 54°5N 9°5E 178 A5
Mélé C.A.R. 9°46N 21°33E 264 A4
Mele B. Vanuatu 17°44S 168°14E 287 G6
Meleden Somalia 10°25N 49°51E 267 B6
Melegnano Italy 45°21N 9°19E 198 C6
Meleizem Mauritania 22°19N 11°24W 260 D2
Melekeok Palau 7°27N 134°38E 288 c
Melekess = Dimitrovgrad Russia 54°14N 49°39E 190 C9
Melenci Serbia 45°32N 20°20E 182 E5
Melenki Russia 55°20N 41°37E 190 C5
Meleuz Russia 52°58N 55°55E 216 B5
Mélèzes → Canada 57°40N 69°29W 298 A5
Melfi Chad 11°0N 17°59E 259 F3
Melfi Italy 41°0N 15°39E 201 B8
Melfort Sask., Canada 52°50N 104°37W 297 C8
Melfort Zimbabwe 18°0S 31°25E 269 F3
Melgaço Portugal 42°7N 8°15W 194 C2
Melgar de Fernamental Spain 42°27N 4°17W 194 C6
Melgraseyri Iceland 66°1N 22°27W 155 A4
Melhus Norway 63°17N 10°18E 164 A7
Melide Spain 42°55N 8°1W 194 C2
Meligales Greece 37°15N 21°59E 204 D3
Melilla N. Afr. 35°21N 2°57W 261 A4
Melilli Italy 37°11N 15°7E 201 E8
Melintang, Danau Indonesia 0°18S 116°20E 235 C5
Melipilla Chile 33°42S 71°15W 334 C1
Melissa Canada 45°24N 79°14W 312 A5
Melissa, Akra Greece 35°6N 24°33E 207 E5
Melissa Oros Greece 37°32N 26°4E 205 D8
Melissani Cave Greece 38°15N 20°38E 207 C2
Melita Canada 49°15N 101°0W 297 D8
Mélito di Porto Salvo Italy 37°55N 15°47E 201 E8
Melitopol Ukraine 46°50N 35°22E 189 J8
Melk Austria 48°13N 15°20E 180 C8
Melkki Finland 60°8N 24°53E 121 C2
Mellan Fryken Sweden 59°45N 13°10E 162 E7
Mellansel Sweden 63°26N 18°19E 160 E18
Mellbystrand Sweden 56°30N 12°56E 163 H6
Melle Deux-Sèvres, France 46°14N 0°10W 174 B3
Melle Niedersachsen, Germany 52°12N 8°20E 178 C4
Mellègue, O. → Tunisia 36°36N 9°14E 258 A1
Mellen U.S.A. 46°20N 90°40W 308 B8
Mellerud Sweden 58°41N 12°28E 163 F6
Mellette U.S.A. 45°9N 98°30W 308 C4
Mellid = Melide Spain 42°55N 8°1W 194 C2
Mellieha Malta 35°57N 14°22E 206 F7
Mellieha Bay Malta 35°59N 14°22E 206 F7
Mellit Sudan 14°7N 25°34E 257 E2
Mellizo Sur, Cerro Chile 48°33S 73°10W 336 C2
Mellrichstadt Germany 50°25N 10°17E 178 E6
Mellunkylä Finland 60°14N 25°5E 121 B3
Mellunmäki Finland 60°14N 25°6E 121 B3
Melnik Bulgaria 41°30N 23°25E 202 E7
Mělník Czech Rep. 50°22N 14°23E 180 A7
Melnytsya Podilska Ukraine 48°37N 26°10E 183 B11
Melo Uruguay 32°20S 54°10W 335 C5
Melolo Indonesia 9°53S 120°40E 231 F6
Melouprey Cambodia 13°48N 105°16E 236 F5
Melrhir, Chott Algeria 34°13N 6°30E 261 B6
Melrose N.S.W., Australia 32°42S 146°57E 283 B7
Melrose Borders, U.K. 55°36N 2°43W 167 F6
Melrose Mass., U.S.A. 42°27N 71°2W 116 A2
Melrose Minn., U.S.A. 45°40N 94°49W 308 C6
Melrose N. Mex., U.S.A. 34°26N 103°38W 305 J12
Melrose N.Y., U.S.A. 40°49N 73°55W 132 B2
Melrose Park U.S.A. 26°6N 80°11W 129 B3
Melsbroek Belgium 50°55N 4°29E 116 A2
Melsisi Vanuatu 15°46S 168°10E 287 E6
Melstone U.S.A. 46°36N 107°52W 304 C10
Melsungen Germany 51°7N 9°32E 178 D5
Melton Australia 37°41S 144°35E 282 D6
Melton Mowbray U.K. 52°47N 0°54W 168 E7
Melun France 48°32N 2°39E 173 D9
Melung Nepal 27°31N 86°3E 243 F12
Melur India 10°2N 78°23E 245 J4
Melut South Sudan 10°30N 32°13E 257 E3
Melville Sask., Canada 50°55N 102°50W 297 C8
Melville Gauteng, S. Africa 26°11S 28°1E 123 B2
Melville, C. Queens., Australia 14°11S 144°30E 280 A3
Melville, C. Phil. 7°49N 117°0E 233 H1
Melville, L. Canada 53°30N 60°0W 299 B8
Melville B. N. Terr., Australia 12°0S 136°45E 280 A2
Melville B. Greenland 75°30N 63°0W 154 B4
Melville I. N. Terr., Australia 11°30S 131°0E 278 B5
Melville I. Canada 75°30N 112°0W 295 B9
Melville Pen. Canada 68°0N 84°0W 295 D15
Melvin, Lough Ireland 54°26N 8°10W 166 B3
Mélykút Hungary 46°11N 19°25E 182 D4
Memaliaj Albania 40°25N 19°56E 202 F3
Memba Mozam. 14°11S 40°30E 269 E5
Membalong Indonesia 3°9S 107°37E 235 C3
Memboro Indonesia 9°30S 119°30E 278 A2
Membrilla Spain 38°59N 3°21W 195 G7
Memel = Klaipėda Lithuania 55°43N 21°10E 184 C8
Memel S. Africa 27°38S 29°36E 271 C4
Memmingen Germany 47°58N 10°10E 179 H6
Mempawah Indonesia 0°30N 109°5E 235 B3
Memphis Egypt 29°52N 31°12E 256 J7
Memphis Mich., U.S.A. 42°54N 82°46W 312 D2
Memphis Mo., U.S.A. 40°28N 92°10W 310 D4
Memphis Tenn., U.S.A. 35°8N 90°2W 315 D9
Memphis Tex., U.S.A. 34°44N 100°33W 314 D4
Memphrémagog, L. N. Amer. 45°8N 72°17W 313 B12
Mena Ukraine 51°31N 32°13E 189 G7
Mena Ark., U.S.A. 34°35N 94°15W 314 D7
Mena → Ethiopia 5°40N 40°50E 257 F5
Menado = Manado Indonesia 1°29N 124°51E 231 D6
Menai Strait U.K. 53°11N 4°13W 168 D3
Ménaka Mali 15°59N 2°18E 263 B5
Menan = Chao Phraya → Thailand 13°40N 100°31E 236 F3
Menarandra → Madag. 25°17S 44°30E 272 D1
Menard U.S.A. 30°55N 99°47W 314 F5
Menard Fracture Zone Pac. Oc. 43°0S 97°0W 289 M18
Menate Indonesia 0°12S 113°3E 235 C4
Menawashei Sudan 12°41N 24°59E 257 E1
Mendaña Fracture Zone Pac. Oc. 16°0S 91°0W 289 J18
Mendawai → Indonesia 3°30S 113°0E 235 C4
Mende France 44°31N 3°30E 174 D7
Mendebo Mts. Ethiopia 7°0N 39°22E 257 F4
Mendeleyev Ridge Arctic 80°0N 178°0W 150 B17
Menden Germany 51°26N 7°47E 178 D3
Mendenhall, C. U.S.A. 59°45N 166°10W 303 G6
Menderes Turkey 38°14N 27°8E 205 C9
Mendhar India 33°35N 74°10E 243 C6
Mendi Ethiopia 9°47N 35°4E 257 F4
Mendi Papua N. G. 6°11S 143°39E 286 D2
Mendip Hills U.K. 51°17N 2°40W 169 F5
Mendocino U.S.A. 39°19N 123°48W 304 G2
Mendocino, C. U.S.A. 40°26N 124°25W 304 F1
Mendocino Fracture Zone Pac. Oc. 40°0N 142°0W 289 D13
Mendol Indonesia 0°36N 103°13E 234 B2
Mendon U.S.A. 42°0N 85°27W 311 B11
Mendooran Australia 31°50S 149°6E 283 A8
Mendota Calif., U.S.A. 36°45N 120°23W 306 J6
Mendota Ill., U.S.A. 41°33N 89°7W 310 C7
Mendoyo Indonesia 8°23S 114°42E 231 J17
Mendoza Argentina 32°50S 68°52W 334 C2
Mendoza □ Argentina 33°0S 69°0W 334 C2
Mene Grande Venezuela 9°49N 70°56W 328 B3
Menemen Turkey 38°34N 27°3E 205 C9
Menen Belgium 50°47N 3°7E 170 D3
Menéndez, L. Argentina 42°40S 71°51W 336 B2
Menfi Italy 37°36N 12°58E 200 E5
Mengcheng China 33°12N 116°36E 226 H9
Mengdingjie China 23°31N 98°58E 228 F2
Mengeš Slovenia 46°10N 14°35E 199 B11
Menggala Indonesia 4°30S 105°15E 234 C3
Menghai China 21°49N 100°55E 228 G3
Mengíbar Spain 37°58N 3°48W 195 H7
Mengjin China 34°55N 112°45E 226 G7
Mengla China 21°20N 101°25E 228 G3
Menglian China 22°21N 99°27E 228 F2
Mengong Cameroon 2°56N 11°25E 264 B2
Mengshan China 24°14N 110°55E 229 E8
Mengyin China 35°40N 117°58E 227 G9
Mengzhe China 22°2N 100°15E 228 F3
Mengzi China 23°20N 103°22E 228 F4
Menifee U.S.A. 33°41N 117°10W 307 M9
Menihek Canada 54°28N 56°36W 299 B6
Menihek L. Canada 54°0N 67°0W 299 B6
Menin = Menen Belgium 50°47N 3°7E 170 D3
Menindee Australia 32°20S 142°25E 282 B5
Menindee L. Australia 32°20S 142°25E 282 B5
Meningie Australia 35°50S 139°18E 282 C3
Menjangan, Pulau Indonesia 8°7S 114°31E 231 J17
Menkrour Algeria 26°27N 8°9E 261 C6
Menlo Park U.S.A. 37°27N 122°12W 306 H4
Menngen ۞ Australia 15°21S 131°16E 278 C5
Menominee U.S.A. 45°6N 87°37W 308 C10
Menominee → U.S.A. 45°6N 87°35W 308 C10
Menomonee Falls U.S.A. 43°10N 88°7W 311 A8
Menomonie U.S.A. 44°53N 91°55W 308 C8
Menongue Angola 14°48S 17°52E 265 E3
Menorca Spain 40°0N 4°0E 206 B5
Menorca ✕ (MAH) Spain 39°50N 4°16E 196 F9
Mentakab Malaysia 3°29N 102°21E 237 L4
Mentasta Lake U.S.A. 62°55N 143°45W 303 E12
Mentawai, Kepulauan Indonesia 2°0S 99°0E 234 C1
Mentawai, Selat Indonesia 1°45S 100°0E 234 C2
Menteng Indonesia 6°11S 106°49E 122 B1
Menton France 43°50N 7°29E 175 E11
Mentone U.S.A. 41°10N 86°2W 311 C10
Mentor U.S.A. 41°40N 81°21W 312 E3
Menyamya Papua N. G. 7°10S 145°59E 286 D3
Menyapa Indonesia 1°4N 116°4E 235 B5
Menzel-Bourguiba Tunisia 37°9N 9°49E 258 A1
Menzel-Chaker Tunisia 35°0N 10°26E 258 B2
Menzel-Temime Tunisia 36°46N 11°0E 258 A2
Menzelinsk Russia 55°47N 53°11E 186 C9
Menzies Australia 29°40S 121°2E 279 E3
Meob B. Namibia 24°25S 14°34E 270 B1
Meoqui Mexico 28°17N 105°29W 318 B3
Mepaco Mozam. 15°57S 30°48E 269 F3
Meppel Neths. 52°42N 6°12E 170 B6
Meppen Germany 52°42N 7°17E 178 C3
Mequinenza Spain 41°22N 0°17E 196 D5
Mequinenza, Embalse de Spain 41°25N 0°15E 196 D5
Mequon U.S.A. 43°14N 87°59W 311 A9
Mer France 47°42N 1°30E 172 E8
Merai Papua N. G. 4°52S 152°19E 286 C7
Merak Indonesia 6°10N 106°26E 231 F12
Meråker Norway 63°25N 11°46E 164 A8
Meramangye, L. Australia 28°25S 132°13E 279 E5
Meramec → U.S.A. 38°24N 90°21W 310 F6
Meran = Merano Italy 46°40N 11°9E 199 B8
Merano Italy 46°40N 11°9E 199 B8
Mérantaise → France 48°42N 2°8E 134 B1
Merapi Indonesia 7°32S 110°26E 235 D4
Merate Italy 45°42N 9°25E 198 C6
Meratus, Pegunungan Indonesia 2°45S 115°40E 235 C5
Merauke Indonesia 8°29S 140°24E 231 F10
Merbein Australia 34°10S 142°2E 282 C5
Merca = Marka Somalia 1°48N 44°50E 267 D5
Mercamadrid Spain 40°21N 3°39W 127 B2
Mercantour △ France 44°16N 6°43E 175 D10
Mercato Saraceno Italy 43°57N 12°12E 199 E9
Merced U.S.A. 37°18N 120°29W 306 H6
Merced → U.S.A. 37°21N 120°59W 306 H6
Merced, L. U.S.A. 37°43N 122°29W 136 B2
Merced Pk. U.S.A. 37°36N 119°24W 306 H7
Mercedes B. Aires, Argentina 34°40S 59°30W 334 C4
Mercedes Corrientes, Argentina 29°10S 58°5W 334 B4
Mercedes San Luis, Argentina 33°40S 65°21W 334 C2
Mercedes Camarines N., Phil. 14°7N 123°1E 232 D4
Mercedes Uruguay 33°12S 58°0W 334 C4
Mercedes-Benz Superdome New Orleans, U.S.A. 131 b1
Merceditas Chile 28°20S 70°35W 334 B1
Mercer N.Z. 37°16S 175°5E 284 D4
Mercer Mo., U.S.A. 40°31N 93°32W 310 D3
Mercer Pa., U.S.A. 41°14N 80°15W 312 E4
Mercer Island U.S.A. 47°34N 122°13W 306 C4
Merchandise Mart Chicago, U.S.A. 119 b1
Mercier Bolivia 10°42S 68°5W 330 C4
Mercury U.S.A. 36°40N 115°59W 307 J11
Mercury B. N.Z. 36°48S 175°45E 284 C4
Mercury Is. N.Z. 36°37S 175°52E 284 C4
Mercy, C. Canada 65°0N 63°30W 295 E19
Merdrignac France 48°11N 2°27W 172 D4
Mere U.K. 51°6N 2°16W 169 F5
Mere Lava Vanuatu 14°25S 168°3E 287 D6
Merebuk, Gunung Indonesia 8°13S 114°39E 231 J17
Meredale S. Africa 26°16S 27°58E 123 B1
Meredith Australia 37°49S 144°5E 282 D6
Meredith, C. Falk. Is. 52°15S 60°40W 153 f
Meredith, L. U.S.A. 35°43N 101°33W 314 D4
Meredosia U.S.A. 39°50N 90°34W 310 E6
Merefa Ukraine 49°48N 36°3E 189 H9
Merei Romania 45°7N 26°43E 183 E11
Merga = Nukheila Sudan 19°1N 26°21E 256 D2
Mergui Burma 12°26N 98°34E 236 F2
Mergui Arch. = Myeik Kyunzu Burma 11°30N 97°30E 237 G1
Meribah Australia 34°43S 140°51E 282 C4
Méribel-les-Allues France 45°25N 6°34E 175 C10
Meriç Turkey 41°11N 26°25E 203 E10
Meriç → Turkey 40°52N 26°12E 203 F10
Mérida Yucatán, Mexico 20°58N 89°37W 319 C7
Merida Phil. 10°55N 124°32E 233 F5
Mérida Spain 38°55N 6°25W 195 G4
Mérida Venezuela 8°24N 71°8W 328 B3
Mérida □ Venezuela 8°30N 71°10W 328 B3
Mérida, Cord. de Venezuela 9°0N 71°0W 328 B3
Meriden W. Mids., U.K. 52°26N 1°38W 169 E6
Meriden Conn., U.S.A. 41°32N 72°48W 313 E12
Meridian Calif., U.S.A. 39°9N 121°55W 306 F5
Meridian Ga., U.S.A. 31°27N 81°23W 316 D8
Meridian Idaho, U.S.A. 43°37N 116°24W 304 E5
Meridian Miss., U.S.A. 32°22N 88°42W 315 E10
Mérignac France 44°51N 0°39W 174 D3
Merimbula Australia 36°53S 149°54E 283 D8
Merin Gubai Somalia 1°26N 44°20E 267 D5
Merinda Australia 20°2S 148°11E 280 C4
Mering Germany 48°16N 10°59E 179 G6
Meringa Nigeria 10°44N 12°9E 263 C7
Meringur Australia 34°20S 141°19E 282 C4
Merir Palau 4°10N 132°30E 231 D8
Merirumã Brazil 1°15N 54°50W 329 C7
Merizo Guam 13°16N 144°40E 302 d
Merkel U.S.A. 32°28N 100°1W 314 E4
Merlimau, Pulau Singapore 1°17N 103°42E 138 B2
Mermaid Reef Australia 17°6S 119°36E 278 C2
Mero Dominica 15°25N 61°26W 323 k
Meroe India 7°33N 93°33E 245 L11
Merowe Sudan 18°29N 31°46E 256 D3
Merowe Dam Sudan 18°35N 31°56E 256 D3
Merredin Australia 31°28S 118°18E 279 F2
Merri Cr. → Australia 37°47S 144°59E 128 A1
Merrick U.K. 55°8N 4°28W 167 F4
Merrickville Canada 44°55N 75°50W 313 B9
Merrill Oreg., U.S.A. 42°1N 121°36W 304 E3
Merrill Wis., U.S.A. 45°11N 89°41W 308 C9
Merrillville U.S.A. 41°29N 87°20W 311 C9
Merrimack → U.S.A. 42°49N 70°49W 313 D14
Merriman U.S.A. 42°55N 101°42W 308 D3
Merrion Ireland 53°19N 6°12W 120 B2
Merrionette Park U.S.A. 41°41N 87°40W 119 C2
Merritt Canada 50°10N 120°45W 296 C4
Merritt Island U.S.A. 28°21N 80°42W 317 G9
Merriwa Australia 32°6S 150°22E 283 B9
Merriwagga Australia 33°47S 145°43E 283 B6
Merry I. Canada 55°29N 77°31W 298 A4
Merrygoen Australia 31°51S 149°12E 283 A8
Merryville U.S.A. 30°45N 93°33W 314 F8
Mersa Fatma Eritrea 14°57N 40°17E 257 E5
Mersch Lux. 49°44N 6°7E 170 E6
Merse → Italy 43°5N 11°22E 199 E8
Mersea I. U.K. 51°47N 0°58E 169 F8
Merseburg Germany 51°22N 11°59E 178 D7
Mersey → U.K. 53°25N 3°1W 168 D4
Merseyside □ U.K. 53°31N 3°2W 168 D4
Mersin = İçel Turkey 36°51N 34°36E 250 B5
Mersing Malaysia 2°25N 103°50E 237 L4
Merta India 26°39N 74°4E 242 F6
Merta Road India 26°43N 73°55E 242 F5
Merthyr Tydfil U.K. 51°45N 3°22W 169 F4
Merthyr Tydfil □ U.K. 51°46N 3°21W 169 F4
Merti Kenya 1°4N 38°40E 268 B4
Mértola Portugal 37°40N 7°40W 195 H3
Merton □ U.K. 51°25N 0°11W 125 B2
Mertz Glacier Antarctica 67°30S 144°45E 151 C10
Mertzon U.S.A. 31°16N 100°49W 314 F4
Méru Oise, France 49°13N 2°8E 173 C9
Meru Eastern, Kenya 0°3N 37°40E 268 B4
Meru Tanzania 3°15S 36°46E 268 C4
Meru △ Kenya 0°5N 38°10E 268 B4
Meru Betiri △ Indonesia 8°27S 113°51E 235 D4
Merv = Mary Turkmenistan 37°40N 61°50E 247 B9
Merville France 50°38N 2°38E 173 B9
Méry-sur-Seine France 48°31N 3°54E 173 D10
Merzifon Turkey 40°53N 35°32E 212 B6
Merzig Germany 49°26N 6°38E 179 F2
Merzouga, Erg Tin Algeria 24°0N 11°4E 261 D7
Mesa U.S.A. 33°25N 111°50W 305 K8
Mesa Verde △ U.S.A. 37°11N 108°29W 305 H9
Mesach Mellet Libya 24°30N 11°30E 258 D2
Mesada = Masada Israel 31°18N 35°21E 251 G6
Mesagne Italy 40°34N 17°48E 201 B10
Mesanagros Greece 36°1N 27°49E 206 E11
Mesaoría Cyprus 35°12N 33°14E 207 E9
Meschede Germany 51°20N 8°18E 178 D4
Mescit Turkey 40°21N 41°11E 213 B9
Mesemvriya = Nesebŭr Bulgaria 42°41N 27°46E 203 D11
Mesfinto Ethiopia 13°20N 37°22E 257 E4
Mesgarābād Iran 35°27N 51°30E 141 B3
Mesgouez, L. Canada 51°20N 75°0W 298 B5
Meshchovsk Russia 54°22N 35°17E 188 E8
Meshchyora △ Russia 55°30N 40°20E 190 C5
Meshchyorsky △ Russia 54°50N 41°0E 190 C5
Meshed = Mashhad Iran 36°20N 59°35E 247 B8
Meshgīn Shahr Iran 38°30N 47°45E 213 C12
Meshkede-Ser = Bābol Sar Iran 36°45N 52°45E 247 B7
Meshoppen U.S.A. 41°36N 76°3W 313 E8
Meshra er Req South Sudan 8°25N 29°18E 257 F2
Mesilinka → Canada 56°6N 124°30W 296 B4
Meslay-du-Maine France 47°58N 0°33W 172 E6
Mesocco Switz. 46°23N 9°12E 179 J5
Mesolongi Greece 38°21N 21°28E 204 C3
Mesongi Greece 39°29N 19°56E 206 C9
Mesopotamia = Al Jazirah Iraq 33°30N 44°0E 213 E10
Mesopotamia U.S.A. 41°27N 80°57W 312 E4
Mesopotamo Greece 39°14N 20°32E 204 B2
Mesoraca Italy 39°5N 16°48E 201 C9
Mésou Volímais = Volimes Greece 37°52N 20°39E 207 D2
Mesquite U.S.A. 36°48N 114°4W 305 H6
Messaad Algeria 34°8N 3°30E 261 B5
Messac France 47°49N 1°50W 172 E5
Messalo → Mozam. 12°25S 39°15E 269 E4
Messaména Cameroon 3°48N 12°49E 264 B2
Messara, Kolpos Greece 35°6N 24°47E 207 E5
Messe Austria 48°13N 16°24E 142 A2
Messier, Canal Chile 48°20S 74°33W 336 C2
Messina = Musina S. Africa 22°20S 30°5E 271 B5
Messina Italy 38°11N 15°34E 201 D8
Messina, Str. di Italy 38°15N 15°35E 201 D8
Messini Greece 37°4N 22°1E 204 D4
Messiniakos Kolpos Greece 36°45N 22°5E 204 E4
Messkirch Germany 47°59N 9°7E 179 H5
Messlingen Sweden 62°40N 12°50E 162 B6
Mesta = Nestos → Europe 40°54N 24°49E 203 F8
Mesta, Akra Greece 38°16N 25°53E 205 C7
Mestanza Spain 38°35N 4°4W 195 G6
Mestersvig Greenland 72°10N 23°40W 154 C8
Mestre Italy 45°29N 12°15E 199 C9
Mestre, Espigão Brazil 12°30S 46°10W 333 D2
Mesudiye Turkey 40°28N 37°46E 212 B7
Meta U.S.A. 38°19N 92°10W 310 F4
Meta □ Colombia 3°30N 73°0W 328 C3
Meta → S. Amer. 6°12N 67°28W 328 B4
Meta Incognita Pen. Canada 62°45N 68°30W 295 E18
Metabetchouan Canada 48°26N 71°52W 299 C5
Metairie U.S.A. 29°59N 90°9W 131 A2
Metalici, Munţii Romania 46°15N 22°50E 182 D7
Metaline Falls U.S.A. 48°52N 117°22W 304 B5
Metallifere, Colline Italy 43°10N 11°0E 198 E8
Metamora U.S.A. 40°47N 89°22W 310 D7
Metán Argentina 25°30S 65°0W 334 B3
Metangula Mozam. 12°40S 34°50E 269 E3
Metanópoli Italy 45°24N 9°15E 128 B2
Metauro → Italy 43°50N 13°3E 199 E10
Metcalf U.S.A. 30°43N 83°59W 316 E6
Metcalfe Canada 45°14N 75°28W 313 A9
Metema Ethiopia 12°58N 36°12E 257 E4
Metengobalame Mozam. 14°49S 34°30E 269 E3
Meteora Greece 39°43N 21°37E 204 B3
Methana Greece 37°35N 23°23E 204 D5
Methoni Greece 36°49N 21°42E 204 E3
Methven N.Z. 43°38S 171°40E 285 D6
Metil Mozam. 16°24S 39°0E 269 F4
Metkovets Bulgaria 43°37N 23°10E 202 C7
Metković Croatia 43°6N 17°39E 199 E14
Metlakatla U.S.A. 55°8N 131°35W 303 J15
Metlaoui Tunisia 34°24N 8°24E 258 B1
MetLife Stadium New York, U.S.A. 40°48N 74°5W 132 B1
Metlik Papua N. G. 4°46S 152°55E 286 C7
Metlika Slovenia 45°40N 15°20E 199 C12
Metlili Chaamba Algeria 32°16N 3°38E 261 B5
Metro Indonesia 5°5S 105°20E 234 D3
Metro Toronto Zoo Canada 43°48N 79°10W 141 A3
Metropolis U.S.A. 37°9N 88°44W 308 G9
Metropolitan Museum of Art New York, U.S.A. 132 b3
Metropolitana □ Chile 33°30S 70°50W 334 C1
Metsovo Greece 39°48N 21°12E 204 B3
Metter U.S.A. 32°24N 82°3W 316 C7
Mettuppalaiyam India 11°18N 76°59E 245 J3
Mettur India 11°48N 77°47E 245 J3
Metu Ethiopia 8°18N 35°35E 257 F4
Metz France 49°8N 6°10E 173 C13
Metzingen Germany 48°31N 9°17E 179 G5
Meudon France 48°48N 2°14E 134 B2
Meulaboh Indonesia 4°11N 96°3E 234 B1
Meung-sur-Loire France 47°50N 1°40E 173 E8
Meureudu Indonesia 5°19N 96°10E 234 A1
Meurthe → France 48°47N 6°9E 173 D13
Meurthe-et-Moselle □ France 48°52N 6°0E 173 D13
Meuse □ France 49°8N 5°25E 173 C12
Meuse → Europe 50°45N 5°41E 170 D5
Meuselwitz Germany 51°2N 12°17E 178 D8
Meutapok, Mt. Malaysia 5°40N 117°0E 235 A5
Mevaseret Zion Israel 31°48N 35°9E 123 B1
Mevo Beitar Israel 31°43N 35°6E 123 B1
Mexia U.S.A. 31°41N 96°29W 314 F6
Mexiana, I. Brazil 0°0 49°30W 332 B2
Mexicali Mexico 32°40N 115°30W 307 N11
Mexican Plateau Mexico 25°0N 104°0W 292 G9
Mexican Water U.S.A. 36°57N 109°32W 305 H9
Mexico Maine, U.S.A. 44°34N 70°33W 313 B14
Mexico Mo., U.S.A. 39°10N 91°53W 310 E5
Mexico N.Y., U.S.A. 43°28N 76°14W 313 C8
México □ Mexico 19°20N 99°30W 319 D5
Mexico ■ Cent. Amer. 25°0N 105°0W 318 C4
México, Ciudad de Mexico 19°24N 99°9W 128 B2
Mexico, G. of Cent. Amer. 25°0N 90°0W 319 C7
Mexico B. U.S.A. 43°35N 76°20W 313 C8
Mexico Beach U.S.A. 29°57N 85°25W 316 F4
Mexico City Int. ✕ (MEX) Mexico 19°25N 99°5W 128 B2
Meydān-e Naftūn Iran 31°56N 49°18E 247 D6
Meydani, Ra's-e Iran 25°24N 59°6E 247 E8
Meyenburg Germany 53°18N 12°14E 178 B8
Meyers Chuck U.S.A. 55°45N 132°15W 296 B2
Meyersdal S. Africa 26°17S 28°5E 123 B2
Meymac France 45°32N 2°10E 174 C6
Meymaneh Afghan. 35°53N 64°38E 240 B2
Meyo Cameroon 2°50N 11°1E 264 B2
Meyrueis France 44°12N 3°27E 174 D7
Meyssac France 45°3N 1°40E 174 C5
Meyzieu France 45°46N 4°59E 175 C8

Mezdra Bulgaria 43°12N 23°42E 202 C7
Mèze France 43°27N 3°36E 174 E7
Mezen Russia 65°50N 44°20E 186 A7
Mezen → Russia 65°44N 44°22E 186 A7
Mézenc, Mt. France 44°54N 4°11E 175 D8
Mezeş, Munţii Romania 47°5N 23°5E 182 C8
Mezha → Russia 55°44N 31°33E 188 E6
Mezhdurechensk Russia 53°41N 88°3E 217 B11
Mezhdurechenskiy Russia 59°36N 65°56E 214 D7
Mezhdurechye = Shali Russia 43°9N 45°55E 191 J7
Mezhevaya Utka = Sinegorskiy Russia 47°55N 40°52E 191 G5
Mézidon-Canon France 49°5N 0°1W 172 C6
Mézières-en-Brenne France 46°49N 1°13E 174 B5
Mézilhac France 44°49N 4°21E 175 D8
Mézin France 44°4N 0°16E 174 D4
Mezitli Turkey 36°45N 34°29E 250 B5
Mezőberény Hungary 46°49N 21°3E 182 D6
Mezőfalva Hungary 46°55N 18°49E 182 D3
Mezőhegyes Hungary 46°19N 20°49E 182 D5
Mezőkövácsháza Hungary 46°25N 20°57E 182 D5
Mezőkövesd Hungary 47°49N 20°35E 182 C5
Mézos France 44°5N 1°10W 174 D2
Mezőtúr Hungary 47°1N 20°41E 182 C5
Mezquital Mexico 23°29N 104°23W 318 C4
Mezzate Italy 45°26N 9°17E 128 B2
Mezzolombardo Italy 46°13N 11°5E 198 B8
Mfolozi → S. Africa 28°25S 32°26E 271 C5
Mgarr Malta 35°55N 14°22E 206 F7
Mgarr Gozo, Malta 36°2N 14°18E 206 E7
Mgeta Tanzania 8°22S 36°6E 269 D4
Mglin Russia 53°2N 32°50E 189 F7
Mhamid Morocco 29°49N 5°43W 260 C3
Mhlaba Hills Zimbabwe 18°30S 30°30E 269 F3
Mhow India 22°33N 75°50E 242 H6
Mi-Shima Japan 34°46N 131°9E 222 C3
Miadong S. Korea 37°36N 127°0E 137 B2
Miagao Phil. 10°39N 122°14E 233 F4
Miahuatlán Mexico 16°20N 96°36W 319 D5
Miaich South Sudan 9°30N 30°30E 257 F3
Miajadas Spain 39°9N 5°54W 195 F5
Miami Fla., U.S.A. 25°46N 80°11W 129 D2
Miami Okla., U.S.A. 36°53N 94°53W 314 C7
Miami Tex., U.S.A. 35°42N 100°38W 314 D4
Miami → U.S.A. 25°46N 80°11W 129 D1
Miami Beach U.S.A. 25°47N 80°7W 129 D3
Miami Canal U.S.A. 25°45N 80°12W 317 K9
Miami Gardens U.S.A. 25°56N 80°15W 129 C1
Miami Int. ✈ (MIA) U.S.A. 25°48N 80°17W 129 D1
Miami Lakes U.S.A. 25°54N 80°18W 129 C1
Miami Shores U.S.A. 25°51N 80°11W 129 C2
Miami Springs U.S.A. 25°49N 80°17W 129 D1
Miamisburg U.S.A. 39°38N 84°17W 311 E12
Mian Xian China 33°10N 106°32E 228 A6
Mianchi China 34°48N 111°48E 226 G6
Mīāndarreh Iran 35°37N 53°39E 247 C7
Mīāndowāb Iran 37°0N 46°5E 213 D12
Miandrivazo Madag. 19°31S 45°29E 272 B2
Mīāneh Iran 37°30N 47°40E 213 D12
Mianning China 28°32N 102°9E 228 C4
Mianwali Pakistan 32°38N 71°28E 242 C4
Mianyang China 31°22N 104°47E 228 B5
Mianzhu China 31°22N 104°7E 228 B5
Miao Ling China 26°5N 107°30E 228 D6
Miaodao Qundao China 38°10N 120°45E 227 E11
Miaoli Taiwan 24°37N 120°49E 225 B2
Miaoli □ Taiwan 24°30N 120°55E 225 B2
Miarinarivo Antananarivo, Madag. 18°57S 46°55E 272 B2
Miarinarivo Toamasina, Madag. 16°38S 48°15E 272 B2
Miariravaratra Madag. 20°13S 47°31E 272 C2
Miass Russia 54°59N 60°6E 186 D11
Miasteczko Krajeńskie Poland 53°7N 17°1E 185 E4
Miastko Poland 54°0N 16°58E 184 E3
Miasto Poland 52°15N 21°0E 143 B2
Mica S. Africa 24°10S 30°48E 271 B5
Micanopy U.S.A. 29°30N 82°17W 317 F7
Micăsasa Romania 46°7N 24°7E 183 D9
Micco U.S.A. 27°53N 80°30W 317 H9
Miccosukee U.S.A. 30°36N 84°3W 316 E5
Miccosukee, L. U.S.A. 30°33N 83°53W 316 E6
Michael, Mt. Papua N. G. 6°27S 145°22E 286 D3
Michalovce Slovak Rep. 48°47N 21°58E 181 C14
Michałowice Poland 52°10N 20°52E 143 B1
Michigan □ U.S.A. 44°0N 85°0W 309 C11
Michigan, L. U.S.A. 44°0N 87°0W 308 D10
Michigan Avenue Chicago, U.S.A. 119 b2
Michigan Center U.S.A. 42°14N 84°20W 311 B12
Michigan City U.S.A. 41°43N 86°54W 311 C10
Michika Nigeria 10°36N 13°23E 263 C7
Michipicoten I. Canada 47°40N 85°40W 298 C2
Michle Czech Rep. 50°3N 14°28E 135 B2
Michoacán □ Mexico 19°10N 101°50W 318 D4
Michurin Bulgaria 42°9N 27°51E 203 D11
Michurinsk Russia 52°58N 40°27E 190 D5
Miconje Angola 4°26S 12°48E 265 C2
Micoud St. Lucia 13°49N 60°54W 323 m
Micronesia Pac. Oc. 11°0N 160°0E 288 G7
Micronesia, Federated States of ■ Pac. Oc. 9°0N 150°0E 288 G7
Mid-Atlantic Ridge Atl. Oc. 0°0 20°0W 152 J10
Mid-City Calif., U.S.A. 34°4N 118°20W 126 B2
Mid City La., U.S.A. 29°58N 90°6W 131 B2
Mid-Indian Ocean Basin Ind. Oc. 10°0S 80°0E 273 F7
Mid-Indian Ridge Ind. Oc. 30°0S 75°0E 273 H6
Mid-Pacific Seamounts Pac. Oc. 18°0N 177°0W 288 F10
Midai Indonesia 3°0N 107°47E 235 B3
Midale Canada 49°25N 103°20W 297 D8
Middelburg Neths. 51°30N 3°36E 170 C3
Middelburg Eastern Cape, S. Africa 31°30S 25°0E 270 D4
Middelburg Mpumalanga, S. Africa 25°49S 29°28E 271 C4
Middelfart Denmark 55°30N 9°43E 163 J3
Middelpos S. Africa 31°55S 20°13E 270 D3
Middelwit S. Africa 24°51S 27°3E 270 B4
Middle → U.S.A. 41°26N 93°30W 310 C3
Middle Alkali L. U.S.A. 41°27N 120°5W 304 F3
Middle America Trench = Guatemala Trench Pac. Oc. 14°0N 95°0W 292 H10
Middle Andaman I. India 12°30N 92°50E 245 H11
Middle Bass I. U.S.A. 41°41N 82°48W 312 E2
Middle East Asia 35°0N 40°0E 210 E5
Middle Fork Feather → U.S.A. 38°33N 121°30W 306 F5
Middle Ground Midway Is. 28°14N 177°24W 302 c
Middle Harbour Australia 33°47S 151°14E 139 A2
Middle Hd. Australia 33°49S 151°16E 139 A2
Middle I. Australia 34°6S 123°11E 279 F3
Middle Island St. Kitts & Nevis 17°20N 62°48W 322 d
Middle Loup → U.S.A. 41°17N 98°24W 308 E4
Middle Park Australia 37°50S 144°57E 128 B1
Middle Raccoon → U.S.A. 41°35N 93°35W 310 C3
Middle Village U.S.A. 40°43N 73°52W 132 B2
Middleboro U.S.A. 41°54N 70°55W 313 E14
Middleburg Fla., U.S.A. 30°4N 81°52W 316 E8
Middleburg Pa., U.S.A. 40°47N 77°3W 312 F7
Middleburgh U.S.A. 42°36N 74°20W 313 D10
Middlebury Ind., U.S.A. 41°41N 85°42W 311 C11
Middlebury Vt., U.S.A. 44°1N 73°10W 313 B11
Middlefield U.S.A. 41°27N 81°4W 312 E3
Middlemarch N.Z. 45°30S 170°9E 285 F5
Middlemount Australia 22°50S 148°40E 280 C4
Middleport N.Y., U.S.A. 43°13N 78°29W 312 C6
Middleport Ohio, U.S.A. 39°0N 82°3W 309 F12
Middlesboro U.S.A. 36°36N 83°43W 309 G12
Middlesbrough U.K. 54°35N 1°13W 168 C6
Middlesbrough □ U.K. 54°28N 1°13W 168 C6
Middlesex Belize 17°2N 88°31W 320 C2
Middlesex N.J., U.S.A. 40°36N 74°30W 313 F10
Middlesex N.Y., U.S.A. 42°42N 77°16W 312 D7
Middlesex □ Jamaica 18°10N 77°5W 320 a
Middlesex Fells Reservation U.S.A. 42°27N 71°6W 116 A2
Middleton Queens., Australia 22°22S 141°32E 280 C3
Middleton N.S., Canada 44°57N 65°4W 299 D6
Middleton Wis., U.S.A. 43°6N 89°30W 310 A7
Middleton Cr. → Australia 22°35S 141°51E 280 C3
Middleton I. U.S.A. 59°26N 146°20W 303 G11
Middletown Armagh, U.K. 54°17N 6°51W 166 B5
Middletown Calif., U.S.A. 38°45N 122°37W 306 G4
Middletown Conn., U.S.A. 41°34N 72°39W 313 E12
Middletown Ky., U.S.A. 38°14N 85°32W 311 F11
Middletown N.Y., U.S.A. 41°27N 74°25W 313 E10
Middletown Ohio, U.S.A. 39°31N 84°24W 311 E12
Middletown Pa., U.S.A. 40°12N 76°44W 313 F8
Middleville U.S.A. 42°43N 85°28W 311 B11
Midelt Morocco 32°46N 4°44W 260 B4
Midge Point Australia 20°39S 148°43E 280 b
Midhirst N.Z. 39°17S 174°18E 284 F3
Miðsandur Iceland 64°24N 21°28W 155 C5
Midhurst Ont., Canada 44°26N 79°43W 312 B5
Midhurst W. Susx., U.K. 50°59N 0°44W 169 G7
Mīdī Yemen 16°19N 42°48E 248 C3
Midi, Canal du → France 43°45N 1°21E 174 E5
Midi, Gare du Brussels, Belgium 116 c1
Midi d'Ossau, Pic du France 42°50N 0°26W 174 F3
Midi-Pyrénées □ France 43°55N 1°45E 174 E5
Midland W. Austral., Australia 31°54S 116°1E 279 F2
Midland Ont., Canada 44°45N 79°50W 312 B5
Midland Calif., U.S.A. 33°52N 114°48W 307 M12
Midland Mich., U.S.A. 43°37N 84°14W 309 D11
Midland Pa., U.S.A. 40°39N 80°27W 312 F4
Midland Tex., U.S.A. 32°0N 102°3W 314 F3
Midland Beach U.S.A. 40°34N 74°6W 132 C1
Midlands □ Zimbabwe 19°40S 29°0E 269 F2
Midleton Ireland 51°55N 8°10W 166 E3
Midlothian U.S.A. 41°37N 87°45W 119 D2
Midlothian □ U.K. 55°51N 3°5W 167 F5
Midnapore = Medinipur India 22°25N 87°21E 243 H12
Midongy, Tangorombohitr' i Madag. 23°30S 47°0E 272 C2
Midongy Atsimo Madag. 23°35S 47°1E 272 C2
Midori Japan 36°30N 139°15E 223 A11
Midou → France 43°54N 0°30W 174 E3
Midouze → France 43°48N 0°51W 174 E3
Midsayap Phil. 7°12N 124°32E 233 H5
Midsund Norway 62°41N 6°40E 164 B3
Midtgulen Norway 61°44N 5°11E 164 C2
Midtjylland □ Denmark 56°30N 9°0E 163 H2
Midu China 25°18N 100°30E 228 E3
Midville U.S.A. 32°49N 82°14W 316 C7
Midway Ala., U.S.A. 32°5N 85°31W 316 C4
Midway Fla., U.S.A. 30°30N 84°27W 316 E5
Midway Is. Pac. Oc. 28°13N 177°22W 302 c
Midway Wells U.S.A. 32°41N 115°7W 307 N11
Midwest U.S.A. 42°0N 90°0W 301 G22
Midwest Wyo., U.S.A. 43°25N 106°16W 304 E10
Midwest City U.S.A. 35°27N 97°24W 314 D6
Midwood U.S.A. 40°37N 73°57W 132 C2
Midyat Turkey 37°25N 41°23E 213 D9
Midzŏr Bulgaria 43°24N 22°40E 202 C6
Mie Japan 32°58N 131°35E 222 E3
Mie □ Japan 34°30N 136°10E 223 C8
Miechów Poland 50°21N 20°5E 185 H7
Miedwie, Jezioro Poland 53°17N 14°54E 185 E1
Miedzeszyn Poland 52°10N 21°11E 143 B3
Międzybórz Poland 51°25N 17°34E 185 G4
Międzychód Poland 52°35N 15°53E 185 F2
Międzylesie Dolnośląskie, Poland 50°8N 16°40E 185 H3
Międzylesie Warszawa, Poland 52°12N 21°10E 143 B3
Międzyrzec Podlaski Poland 51°58N 22°45E 185 G9
Międzyrzecz Poland 52°26N 15°35E 185 F2
Międzyzdroje Poland 53°56N 14°26E 184 E1
Miejska Górka Poland 51°39N 16°58E 185 G3
Miélan France 43°27N 0°19E 174 E4
Mielau = Mława Poland 53°9N 20°25E 185 E7
Mielec Poland 50°15N 21°25E 185 H8
Mienga Angola 17°12S 19°48E 265 F3
Miercurea-Ciuc Romania 46°21N 25°48E 183 D10
Miercurea Sibiului Romania 45°53N 23°48E 183 E8
Mieres Spain 43°18N 5°48W 194 B5
Mieroszów Poland 50°40N 16°11E 185 H3
Mies = Stříbro Czech Rep. 49°44N 13°0E 180 A6
Mieso Ethiopia 9°15N 40°43E 257 F5
Miessaari Finland 60°8N 24°47E 121 C1
Mieszkowice Poland 52°47N 14°30E 185 F1
Mifflintown U.S.A. 40°34N 77°24W 312 F7
Mifraz Hefa Israel 32°52N 35°0E 250 F6
Migang Shan China 35°32N 106°13E 226 G4
Migennes France 47°58N 3°31E 173 E10
Migliarino Italy 44°46N 11°56E 199 D8
Migliarino-San Rossore-Massaciuccoli ⌓ Italy 43°44N 10°20E 198 E7
Migori Kenya 1°4S 34°28E 268 C3
Miguasha △ Canada 48°5N 66°26W 299 C6
Miguel Alemán, Presa Mexico 18°15N 96°32W 319 D5
Miguel Alves Brazil 4°11S 42°55W 332 B3
Miguel Calmon Brazil 11°26S 40°36W 332 D3
Miguel Hidalgo Mexico 19°25N 99°12W 128 B1
Miguel Hidalgo, Presa Mexico 26°30N 108°34W 318 B3
Miguelturra Spain 38°58N 3°53W 195 G7
Mihăileni Romania 47°58N 26°9E 183 C11
Mihăileşti Romania 44°20N 25°54E 183 F10
Mihailovca Moldova 46°33N 28°56E 183 D13
Mihalgazi Turkey 40°2N 30°34E 205 A12
Mihaliççık Turkey 39°53N 31°30E 212 C4
Mihara Japan 34°24N 133°5E 222 C5
Mihara-Yama Japan 34°43N 139°23E 223 C11
Miheşu de Cîmpie Romania 46°41N 24°9E 183 D9
Mijas Spain 36°36N 4°40W 195 J6
Mikawa-Wan Japan 34°44N 137°13E 223 C9
Mikese Tanzania 6°48S 37°55E 268 D4
Mikha-Tskhakaya = Senaki Georgia 42°15N 42°1E 191 J6
Mikhailovka = Mykhaylivka Ukraine 47°12N 35°15E 189 J8
Mikhaylov Russia 54°14N 39°0E 188 E10
Mikhaylovgrad = Montana Bulgaria 43°27N 23°16E 202 C7
Mikhaylovka = Kimovsk Russia 54°0N 38°29E 188 E10
Mikhaylovka Russia 50°3N 43°5E 190 E6
Mikhnevo Russia 55°4N 37°59E 188 E9
Miki Hyōgo, Japan 34°48N 134°59E 222 C6
Miki Kagawa, Japan 34°12N 134°7E 222 C6
Mikines Greece 37°43N 22°46E 204 D4
Mikir Hills India 26°10N 93°30E 241 B4
Mikkeli Finland 61°43N 27°15E 188 B4
Mikkwa → Canada 58°25N 114°46W 296 B6
Mikniya Sudan 17°0N 33°45E 257 D3
Mikołajki Poland 53°49N 21°37E 184 E8
Míkonos = Mykonos Greece 37°30N 25°25E 205 D7
Mikope Dem. Rep. of the Congo 4°58S 20°43E 265 C4
Mikoyan-Shakhar = Karachayevsk Russia 43°50N 41°55E 191 J5
Mikri Prespa, L. Greece 40°47N 21°3E 202 F5
Mikro Derio Greece 41°19N 26°6E 203 E10
Mikstat Poland 51°32N 17°59E 185 G4
Mikulov Czech Rep. 48°48N 16°39E 181 C9
Mikumi Tanzania 7°26S 37°0E 268 D4
Mikumi △ Tanzania 7°35S 37°15E 268 D4
Mikun Russia 62°20N 50°0E 186 B9
Mikuni Japan 36°13N 136°9E 223 A8
Mikuni-Tōge Japan 36°50N 138°50E 223 A10
Mikura-Jima Japan 33°52N 139°36E 223 D11
Mila Algeria 36°27N 6°15E 261 A6
Mila □ Algeria 36°25N 6°10E 261 A6
Milaca U.S.A. 45°45N 93°39W 308 C7
Miladummadulu Atoll Maldives 5°50N 73°30E 272 d
Milagro Ecuador 2°11S 79°36W 328 D2
Milagros Phil. 12°13N 123°30E 232 E4
Milan = Milano Italy 45°28N 9°10E 128 B1
Milan Ga., U.S.A. 32°1N 83°4W 316 C6
Milan Ill., U.S.A. 41°27N 90°34W 310 C6
Milan Mich., U.S.A. 42°5N 83°41W 311 B13
Milan Mo., U.S.A. 40°12N 93°7W 310 D3
Milan Tenn., U.S.A. 35°55N 88°46W 315 D10
Miland Norway 59°54N 8°45E 164 E5
Milando Angola 8°45S 17°36E 265 D3
Milando ⌓ Angola 8°45S 17°10E 265 D3
Milanese, Parco Regionale ⌓ Italy 45°35N 9°5E 128 A1
Milang Australia 35°24S 138°58E 282 C3
Milange Mozam. 16°3S 35°45E 269 F4
Milano Italy 45°28N 9°10E 128 B1
Milano Due Italy 45°29N 9°16E 128 B2
Milano Linate ✈ (LIN) Italy 45°27N 9°16E 128 B2
Milano Malpense ✈ (MXP) Italy 45°38N 8°43E 128 A1
Milano San Felice Italy 45°28N 9°18E 128 B2
Milanoa Madag. 13°35S 49°47E 272 A2
Milâs Turkey 37°20N 27°50E 205 D9
Milatos Greece 35°18N 25°34E 207 E6
Milazzo Italy 38°13N 15°15E 201 D8
Milbank U.S.A. 45°13N 96°38W 308 C5
Milbanke Sd. Canada 52°19N 128°33W 296 C3
Milbertshofen Germany 48°10N 11°34E 131 A2
Milden Canada 51°29N 107°32W 297 C7
Mildenhall U.K. 52°21N 0°32E 169 E8
Mildmay Canada 44°3N 81°7W 312 B3
Mildura Australia 34°13S 142°9E 282 C5
Mile China 24°28N 103°20E 228 E4
Mile and a Quarter Barbados 13°16N 59°37W 323 r
Miles Australia 26°40S 150°9E 281 D5
Miles City U.S.A. 46°25N 105°51W 304 C11
Mileşti Moldova 47°13N 28°3E 183 C13
Milestone Canada 49°59N 104°31W 297 D8
Mileto Italy 38°36N 16°4E 201 D9
Miletto, Mte. Italy 41°27N 14°22E 201 A7
Miletus Turkey 37°30N 27°18E 205 D9
Milevsko Czech Rep. 49°27N 14°21E 180 B7
Milford Calif., U.S.A. 40°10N 120°22W 306 E6
Milford Conn., U.S.A. 41°14N 73°3W 313 E11
Milford Del., U.S.A. 38°55N 75°26W 309 F16
Milford Ill., U.S.A. 40°38N 87°42W 311 D9
Milford Mass., U.S.A. 42°8N 71°31W 313 D13
Milford Mich., U.S.A. 42°35N 83°36W 311 B13
Milford N.H., U.S.A. 42°50N 71°39W 313 D13
Milford N.Y., U.S.A. 42°35N 74°56W 313 D10
Milford Pa., U.S.A. 41°19N 74°48W 313 E10
Milford Utah, U.S.A. 38°24N 113°1W 304 G7
Milford Haven U.K. 51°42N 5°7W 169 F2
Milford Sd. N.Z. 44°41S 167°47E 285 E2
Milḩ, Baḩr al = Razāzah, Buḩayrat ar Iraq 32°40N 43°35E 213 F10
Miliana Aïn Salah, Algeria 27°20N 2°32E 261 C5
Miliana Médéa, Algeria 36°20N 2°15E 261 A5
Milicz Poland 51°31N 17°19E 185 G4
Milies Greece 39°20N 23°9E 204 B5
Milikapiti Australia 11°26S 130°40E 278 B5
Mililani Town U.S.A. 21°28N 158°1W 302 K13
Miling Australia 30°30S 116°17E 279 F2
Militello in Val di Catánia Italy 37°16N 14°48E 201 E7
Militsch = Milicz Poland 51°31N 17°19E 185 G4
Milk, Wadi el → Sudan 17°55N 30°20E 256 D3
Milk River Canada 49°10N 112°5W 296 D6
Milk River Spa Jamaica 17°50N 77°22W 320 a
Mill → U.S.A. 42°57N 83°23W 312 D1
Mill Hill U.K. 51°37N 0°14W 125 A2
Mill I. Antarctica 66°0S 101°30E 151 C8
Mill I. Nunavut, Canada 63°58N 77°47W 295 E16
Mill Shoals U.S.A. 38°15N 88°21W 311 F8
Mill Valley U.S.A. 37°54N 122°32W 306 H4
Millárs → Spain 39°55N 0°1W 196 F4
Millau France 44°8N 3°4E 174 D7
Millbridge Canada 44°41N 77°36W 312 B7
Millbrook Ont., Canada 44°10N 78°29W 312 B6
Millbrook Ala., U.S.A. 32°29N 86°22W 315 E11
Millbrook N.Y., U.S.A. 41°47N 73°42W 313 E11
Mille Lacs, L. des Canada 48°45N 90°35W 298 C1
Mille Lacs L. U.S.A. 46°15N 93°39W 308 B7
Milledgeville Ga., U.S.A. 33°5N 83°14W 316 B6
Milledgeville Ill., U.S.A. 41°58N 89°46W 310 C7
Millen U.S.A. 32°48N 81°57W 316 C8
Millennium Dome U.K. 51°30N 0°0 125 A4
Millennium I. = Caroline I. Kiribati 9°58S 150°13W 289 H12
Millennium Park Chicago, U.S.A. 119 c2
Miller U.S.A. 44°31N 98°59W 308 C4
Miller Lake Canada 45°6N 81°26W 312 A3
Miller Meadow U.S.A. 41°51N 87°49W 119 B2
Millerhill U.K. 55°55N 3°5W 121 B3
Millerovo Russia 48°57N 40°28E 191 F5
Miller's Flat N.Z. 45°39S 169°23E 285 F4
Millers Point Sydney, Australia 139 a1
Millersburg Ind., U.S.A. 41°32N 85°42W 311 C11
Millersburg Ohio, U.S.A. 40°33N 81°55W 312 F3
Millersburg Pa., U.S.A. 40°32N 76°58W 312 F8
Millerton N.Z. 41°39S 171°54E 285 B6
Millerton N.Y., U.S.A. 41°57N 73°31W 313 E11
Millerton L. U.S.A. 37°1N 119°41W 306 J7
Millet St. Lucia 13°55N 60°59W 323 m
Millevaches, Plateau de France 45°45N 2°0E 174 C6
Millheim U.S.A. 40°54N 77°29W 312 F7
Millicent Australia 37°34S 140°21E 282 D4
Milligan U.S.A. 30°45N 86°38W 317 E3
Millington U.S.A. 35°20N 89°53W 315 D10
Millinocket U.S.A. 45°39N 68°43W 309 C19
Millmerran Australia 27°53S 151°16E 281 D5
Millom U.K. 54°13N 3°16W 168 C4
Mills L. Canada 61°30N 118°20W 296 A5
Millsboro U.S.A. 40°0N 80°0W 312 G5
Millstream Chichester △ Australia 21°35S 117°6E 278 D2
Millstreet Ireland 52°4N 9°4W 166 D2
Millthorpe Australia 33°26S 149°12E 283 B8
Milltown Ireland 53°19N 6°14W 120 B2
Milltown Malbay Ireland 52°52N 9°24W 166 D2
Millville N.J., U.S.A. 39°24N 75°2W 309 F16
Millville Pa., U.S.A. 41°7N 76°32W 313 E8
Millwood L. U.S.A. 33°42N 93°58W 314 E8
Milna Croatia 43°20N 16°28E 199 E13
Milne → Australia 21°10S 137°33E 280 C2
Milne Bay □ Papua N. G. 10°0S 152°30E 286 E7
Milne Land Greenland 70°40N 26°30W 154 C8
Milnerton S. Africa 33°53S 18°29E 118 A1
Milo U.S.A. 45°15N 68°59W 309 C19
Milo → Guinea 8°52N 9°0W 262 D3
Miloli'i U.S.A. 19°11N 155°55W 302 D6
Milon, Akra Greece 36°15N 28°11E 206 E12
Milon-la-Chapelle France 48°43N 2°3E 134 B1
Milos Greece 36°44N 24°25E 204 E6
Miłosław Poland 52°12N 17°32E 185 F4
Milot Albania 41°41N 19°43E 202 E3
Milparinka Australia 29°46S 141°57E 281 D3
Milpitas U.S.A. 37°26N 121°55W 306 H5
Milroy U.S.A. 39°30N 85°28W 311 E11
Miltenberg Germany 49°41N 9°16E 179 F5
Milton N.S.W., Australia 35°20S 150°27E 283 C9
Milton N.S., Canada 44°4N 64°45W 299 D7
Milton Ont., Canada 43°31N 79°53W 312 C5
Milton N.Z. 46°7S 169°59E 285 G4
Milton Calif., U.S.A. 38°3N 120°51W 306 G6
Milton Fla., U.S.A. 30°38N 87°3W 317 E2
Milton Iowa, U.S.A. 40°41N 92°10W 310 D4
Milton Mass., U.S.A. 42°14N 71°2W 116 B2
Milton Pa., U.S.A. 41°1N 76°51W 312 F8
Milton Vt., U.S.A. 44°38N 73°7W 313 B11
Milton Wis., U.S.A. 42°47N 88°56W 311 B8
Milton Bridge U.K. 55°51N 3°11W 121 B2
Milton-Freewater U.S.A. 45°56N 118°23W 304 D4
Milton Keynes U.K. 52°1N 0°44W 169 E7
Milton Keynes □ U.K. 52°1N 0°44W 169 E7
Milton Park Montréal, Canada 130 b1
Miltou Chad 10°14N 17°26E 259 F3
Miluo China 29°0N 112°59E 229 C9
Milverton Canada 43°34N 80°55W 312 C4
Milwaukee U.S.A. 43°2N 87°54W 311 A9
Milwaukee Deep Atl. Oc. 19°50N 68°0W 321 C6
Milwaukie U.S.A. 45°26N 122°38W 306 E4
Mim Ghana 6°57N 2°33W 262 D4
Mima Japan 34°4N 134°9E 222 C6
Mimico Canada 43°36N 79°29W 141 B2
Mimico Creek → Canada 43°37N 79°28W 141 B1
Mimili Australia 27°0S 132°42E 279 E5
Mimizan France 44°12N 1°13W 174 D2
Mimoň Czech Rep. 50°38N 14°43E 180 A7
Mimongo Gabon 1°11S 11°36E 264 C2
Mimoso Brazil 15°10S 48°5W 333 E2
Mims U.S.A. 28°40N 80°51W 317 G9
Min Jiang → Fujian, China 26°0N 119°35E 229 E12
Min Jiang → Sichuan, China 28°45N 104°40E 228 C5
Min Xian China 34°25N 104°5E 226 G3
Mīnā' al Aḩmadī Kuwait 29°5N 48°10E 247 D6
Mīnā' Jabal 'Alī U.A.E. 25°2N 55°8E 247 E7
Mina Pirquitas Argentina 22°40S 66°30W 334 A2
Mina Raysūt = Raysūt Oman 16°56N 53°59E 249 C6
Mīnā Su'ud Si. Arabia 28°45N 48°28E 247 D6
Minago → Canada 54°33N 98°59W 297 C9
Minakami Japan 36°49N 138°59E 223 A10
Minaki Canada 49°59N 94°40W 297 D10
Minakuchi Japan 34°58N 136°10E 223 C8
Minalungao △ Phil. 15°2N 121°8E 232 D3
Minamata Japan 32°10N 130°30E 222 E2
Minami Japan 34°40N 135°30E 133 A2
Minami-Arapusa △ Japan 35°30N 138°9E 223 B10
Minami-Tori-Shima Pac. Oc. 24°20N 153°58E 288 E7
Minamiaizu Japan 37°12N 139°46E 221 F9
Minamiawaji Japan 34°10N 134°42E 222 C6
Minamisōma Japan 37°38N 140°58E 220 F10
Minamitsunashima Japan 35°32N 139°37E 140 B2
Minas Indonesia 0°50N 101°26E 234 B2
Minas Uruguay 34°20S 55°10W 335 C4
Minas, Sierra de las Guatemala 15°9N 89°31W 320 C2
Minas Basin Canada 45°20N 64°12W 299 C7
Minas de Riotinto Spain 37°42N 6°35W 195 H4
Minas Gerais □ Brazil 18°50S 46°0W 333 E2
Minas Novas Brazil 17°15S 42°36W 333 E3
Minatitlán Mexico 17°59N 94°31W 319 D6
Minato Ōsaka, Japan 34°39N 135°25E 133 B1
Minato Tokyo, Japan 140 c3
Minbu Burma 20°10N 94°52E 241 E5
Minbya Burma 20°22N 93°16E 241 E4
Minchinabad Pakistan 30°10N 73°34E 242 D5
Mincio → Italy 45°4N 10°59E 198 C7
Minčol Slovak Rep. 49°15N 20°58E 181 B13
Mindanao Phil. 8°0N 125°0E 233 H5
Mindanao Sea = Bohol Sea Phil. 9°0N 124°0E 233 G5
Mindanao Trench Pac. Oc. 12°0N 126°6E 232 E5
Mindel → Germany 48°31N 10°23E 179 G6
Mindelheim Germany 48°2N 10°29E 179 G6
Mindelo C. Verde Is. 16°24N 25°0W 153 j
Minden Ont., Canada 44°55N 78°43W 312 B6
Minden Nordrhein-Westfalen, Germany 52°17N 8°55E 178 C4
Minden La., U.S.A. 32°37N 93°17W 314 E8
Minden Nev., U.S.A. 38°57N 119°46W 306 G7
Mindibungu = Billiluna Australia 19°37S 127°41E 278 C4
Mindiptana Indonesia 5°55S 140°22E 231 F10
Mindon Burma 19°21N 94°44E 241 F5
Mindona L. Australia 33°6S 142°6E 282 B5
Mindoro Phil. 13°0N 121°0E 232 E3
Mindoro Occidental □ Phil. 13°0N 120°55E 232 E3
Mindoro Oriental □ Phil. 13°0N 121°5E 232 E3
Mindoro Str. Phil. 12°30N 120°30E 232 E3
Mindouli Congo 4°12S 14°28E 265 C2
Mindourou Cameroon 3°29N 13°26E 264 B2
Mine Japan 34°12N 131°7E 222 C3
Minehead U.K. 51°12N 3°29W 169 F4
Mineiros Brazil 17°34S 52°34W 331 D7
Mineola N.Y., U.S.A. 40°44N 73°38W 313 F11
Mineola Tex., U.S.A. 32°40N 95°29W 314 E7
Mineral Bath Jamaica 17°58N 76°22W 320 a
Mineral King U.S.A. 36°27N 118°36W 306 J8
Mineral Point U.S.A. 42°52N 90°11W 310 B6
Mineral Wells U.S.A. 32°48N 98°7W 314 E5
Mineralnyye Vody Russia 44°15N 43°8E 191 H6
Miners Bay Canada 44°49N 78°46W 312 B6
Minersville U.S.A. 40°41N 76°16W 313 F8
Minerva N.Y., U.S.A. 43°47N 73°59W 313 C11
Minerva Ohio, U.S.A. 40°44N 81°6W 312 F3
Minervino Murge Italy 41°5N 16°5E 201 A9
Minetto U.S.A. 43°24N 76°28W 313 C8
Minfeng China 37°4N 82°46E 217 E10
Ming-Kush Kyrgyzstan 41°40N 74°28E 217 D8
Mingäçevir Azerbaijan 40°45N 47°0E 191 K8
Mingäçevir Su Anbarı Azerbaijan 40°57N 46°50E 191 K8
Mingala C.A.R. 5°6N 21°49E 264 A4
Mingan Canada 50°20N 64°0W 299 B7
Mingary Australia 32°8S 140°45E 282 B4
Mingchien Taiwan 23°50N 120°42E 225 C2
Mingechaur = Mingäçevir Azerbaijan 40°45N 47°0E 191 K8
Mingechaurskoye Vdkhr. = Mingäçevir Su Anbarı Azerbaijan 40°57N 46°50E 191 K8
Mingela Australia 19°52S 146°38E 280 B4
Mingenew Australia 29°12S 115°21E 279 E2
Mingera Cr. → Australia 20°38S 137°45E 280 C2
Minggang China 32°24N 114°3E 229 A10
Mingguang China 32°46N 117°59E 229 A11
Mingin Burma 22°50N 94°30E 241 D5
Mingir Moldova 46°40N 28°20E 183 D13
Minglanilla Spain 39°34N 1°38W 197 F3
Minglun China 25°10N 108°21E 228 E7
Mingo Congo 1°55S 15°1E 264 C3
Mingo Junction U.S.A. 40°19N 80°37W 312 F4
Mingora Pakistan 34°48N 72°22E 243 B5
Mingorría Spain 40°45N 4°40W 194 E6
Mingshan China 30°6N 103°10E 228 B4
Mingteke Daban = Mintaka Pass Pakistan 37°0N 74°58E 243 A6
Mingxi China 26°18N 117°12E 229 D11
Mingyuegue China 43°2N 128°50E 227 C15
Minhe China 36°9N 102°45E 218 D9
Minhla Magwe, Burma 19°58N 95°3E 241 F5
Minhla Pegu, Burma 17°59N 95°43E 241 G5
Minho = Miño → Spain 41°52N 8°40W 194 D2
Minhou China 26°0N 119°15E 229 E12
Minhsiung Taiwan 23°33N 120°35E 225 C2
Minićevo Serbia 43°42N 22°18E 182 G7
Minicoy I. India 8°17N 73°2E 245 K1
Minidoka U.S.A. 42°45N 113°29W 304 E7
Minier U.S.A. 40°26N 89°19W 310 D7
Minigwal, L. Australia 29°31S 123°14E 279 E3
Minilya → Australia 23°45S 114°0E 279 D1
Minilya Roadhouse Australia 23°55S 114°0E 279 D1
Mininera Australia 37°37S 142°58E 282 D5
Minipi L. Canada 52°25N 60°45W 299 B7
Minj Papua N. G. 5°54S 144°37E 286 C3
Minjilang Australia 11°8S 132°33E 278 B5
Mink L. Canada 61°54N 117°40W 296 A5
Minkammen South Sudan 6°3N 31°32E 257 F3
Minkebé Gabon 1°45N 12°45E 264 B2
Minlaton Australia 34°45S 137°35E 282 C2
Minna Nigeria 9°37N 6°30E 263 D6
Minna-shima Japan 26°39N 127°49E 288 a
Minneapolis Kans., U.S.A. 39°8N 97°42W 308 F5
Minneapolis Minn., U.S.A. 44°57N 93°16W 308 C7
Minnedosa Canada 50°14N 99°50W 297 C9
Minnesota □ U.S.A. 46°0N 94°15W 308 B6
Minnesota → U.S.A. 44°54N 93°9W 308 C7
Minnesund Norway 60°23N 11°14E 164 D8
Minnewaukan U.S.A. 48°4N 99°15W 308 A4
Minnipa Australia 32°51S 135°9E 281 E2
Minnitaki L. Canada 49°57N 92°10W 298 C1
Miño = A Carreira Spain 43°21N 8°12W 194 B2
Mino Japan 35°32N 136°55E 223 B8
Miño → Spain 41°52N 8°40W 194 D2
Mino-Kamo Japan 35°23N 137°2E 223 B9
Mino-Mikawa-Kōgen Japan 35°10N 137°23E 223 B9
Minoa Greece 35°6N 25°45E 207 E6
Minobu Japan 35°22N 138°26E 223 B10
Minobu-Sanchi Japan 35°14N 138°20E 223 B10
Minonk U.S.A. 40°54N 89°2W 310 D7
Minooka U.S.A. 41°27N 88°16W 311 C8
Minorca = Menorca Spain 40°0N 4°0E 206 B5
Minore Australia 32°14S 148°27E 283 B8
Minot U.S.A. 48°14N 101°18W 308 A3
Minqin China 38°38N 103°20E 226 E2
Minqing China 26°15N 118°50E 229 D12
Minsen Germany 53°41N 7°58E 178 B3
Minshât el Bekkarî Egypt 30°0N 31°8E 117 A1
Minsk Belarus 53°52N 27°30E 177 B14
Minsk □ Belarus 53°15N 27°30E 188 F4
Mińsk Mazowiecki Poland 52°10N 21°33E 185 F8
Minster U.S.A. 40°24N 84°23W 311 D12
Mintabie Australia 27°15S 133°7E 281 D1
Mintaka Pass Pakistan 37°0N 74°58E 243 A6
Minthami Burma 23°55N 94°16E 241 D5
Minto N.B., Canada 46°5N 66°5W 299 C6
Minto Alaska, U.S.A. 64°53N 149°10W 303 D10
Minto, L. Canada 57°13N 75°0W 298 A5
Minton Canada 49°10N 104°35W 297 D8
Mintoum Gabon 0°27N 12°16E 264 B2
Minturn U.S.A. 39°35N 106°26W 304 G10
Minturno Italy 41°15N 13°45E 200 A6
Minudasht Iran 37°17N 56°7E 247 B8
Minûf Egypt 30°26N 30°52E 256 H7
Minusinsk Russia 53°43N 91°20E 217 B12
Minutang India 28°15N 96°30E 241 A6
Minvoul Gabon 2°9N 12°8E 264 B2
Minwakh Yemen 16°48N 48°6E 249 C5
Minxiong = Minhsiung Taiwan 23°33N 120°35E 225 C2
Minya el Qamh Egypt 30°31N 31°21E 256 H7
Minya Konka = Gongga Shan China 29°40N 101°55E 228 C3
Minyip Australia 36°29S 142°36E 282 D5
Minzhong China 22°37N 113°30E 219 a
Mionica Bos.-H. 44°51N 18°29E 182 F3
Mionica Serbia 44°14N 20°6E 202 B4
Mioveni Romania 44°56N 24°54E 183 F9
Miquan China 43°58N 87°42E 217 D11
Miquelon Qué., Canada 49°25N 76°27W 298 C4
Miquelon St-P. & M. 47°8N 56°22W 299 C8
Mir Belarus 53°27N 26°28E 177 B14
Mir Niger 14°5N 11°59E 259 F2
Mīr Kūh Iran 26°22N 58°55E 247 E8
Mīr Shahdād Iran 26°15N 58°29E 247 E8
Mira Italy 45°26N 12°8E 199 C9
Mira Portugal 40°26N 8°44W 194 E2
Mira → Colombia 1°36N 79°1W 328 C2
Mira → Portugal 37°43N 8°47W 195 H2
Mira por vos Cay Bahamas 22°9N 74°30W 321 B5
Mīrābād Afghan. 30°25N 61°50E 240 C1
Mirabella Eclano Italy 41°2N 14°59E 201 A7
Mirabello, Kolpos Greece 35°10N 25°50E 207 E6
Miracema do Norte Brazil 9°33S 48°24W 332 C2
Mirador Brazil 6°22S 44°22W 332 C3
Mirador-Río Azul △ Guatemala 17°45N 89°50W 320 C1
Miraflores = Rovìra Colombia 4°15N 75°20W 328 C2
Miraflores Colombia 1°25N 72°13W 328 C3
Miraflores Lima, Peru 12°7S 77°2W 124 B2
Miraflores, L. Panama 9°1N 79°36W 320 c
Miraflores Locks Panama 9°0N 79°36W 320 c
Miraj India 16°50N 74°45E 244 F2
Miram Shah Pakistan 33°0N 70°2E 242 C4
Miramar Argentina 38°15S 57°50W 334 D4
Miramar Mozam. 23°50S 35°35E 271 B6
Miramar Fla., U.S.A. 25°59N 80°13W 129 C1
Miramas France 43°33N 4°59E 175 E8
Mirambeau France 45°23N 0°35W 174 C3
Miramichi Canada 47°2N 65°28W 299 C6
Miramichi B. Canada 47°15N 65°0W 299 C7
Miramont-de-Guyenne France 44°37N 0°21E 174 D4
Miranda Brazil 20°10S 56°15W 331 E6
Miranda □ Venezuela 10°15N 66°25W 328 A4
Miranda → Brazil 19°25S 57°20W 331 D6
Miranda de Ebro Spain 42°41N 2°57W 196 C2
Miranda do Corvo Portugal 40°6N 8°20W 194 E2
Miranda do Douro Portugal 41°30N 6°16W 194 D4
Mirande France 43°31N 0°25E 174 E4
Mirandela Portugal 41°32N 7°10W 194 D3
Mirándola Italy 44°53N 11°4E 198 D8
Mirandópolis Brazil 21°9S 51°6W 335 A5
Mirango Malawi 13°32S 34°58E 269 E3
Mirani Australia 21°8S 148°53E 280 b
Mirano Italy 45°30N 12°7E 199 C9
Miras Albania 40°30N 20°56E 202 F4
Mirassol Brazil 20°46S 49°28W 335 A6
Mirbāţ Oman 17°0N 54°45E 249 C6
Mirboo North Australia 38°24S 146°10E 283 E7
Mirear Egypt 23°15N 35°41E 256 C4
Mirebeau France 46°49N 0°10E 172 F7
Mirebeau-sur-Bèze France 47°25N 5°20E 173 E12
Mirecourt France 48°20N 6°10E 173 D13
Mires Greece 35°4N 24°56E 207 E5
Mirgorod = Myrhorod Ukraine 49°58N 33°37E 189 H7
Miri Malaysia 4°23N 113°59E 235 B4
Mirialguda India 16°52N 79°35E 244 F4
Miriam Vale Australia 24°20S 151°33E 280 C5
Miribel France 45°50N 4°57E 173 G11
Mirigama Sri Lanka 7°15N 80°8E 245 L5
Mirim, L. S. Amer. 32°45S 52°50W 335 C5
Mirimire Venezuela 11°10N 68°43W 328 A4
Miringoni Comoros Is. 12°17S 43°38E 272 a
Miriti Brazil 6°15S 59°0W 331 B6
Miriuwung Gajerrong ☼ Australia 15°0S 128°45E 278 C4
Mīrjāveh Iran 29°1N 61°30E 247 D9
Mirnyy Antarctica 66°50S 92°30E 151 C14
Mirnyy Russia 62°33N 113°53E 215 C12
Miroč Serbia 44°32N 22°16E 202 B6
Mirokhan Pakistan 27°46N 68°6E 242 F3
Mirond L. Canada 55°6N 102°47W 297 B8
Mirosławiec Poland 53°20N 16°5E 184 E3
Mirpur Pakistan 33°32N 73°56E 243 C5
Mirpur Batoro Pakistan 24°44N 68°16E 242 G3
Mirpur Bibiwari Pakistan 28°33N 67°44E 242 E2
Mirpur Khas Pakistan 25°30N 69°0E 242 G3
Mirpur Sakro Pakistan 24°33N 67°41E 242 G2
Mirria Niger 13°43N 9°7E 259 F1
Mirrool Australia 34°19S 147°10E 283 C7
Mirs Bay = Tai Pang Wan China 22°33N 114°24E 219 a
Mirsale Somalia 5°57N 47°59E 267 C6
Mirsk Poland 50°58N 15°23E 185 H2
Mirtağ Turkey 38°23N 41°56E 246 B4
Mirtoo Sea Greece 37°0N 23°20E 204 D5
Mirtou, Kolpos Greece 38°20N 20°27E 207 C1
Miryang S. Korea 35°31N 128°44E 224 E4
Mirzaani Georgia 41°24N 46°5E 191 K8
Mirzachul = Guliston Uzbekistan 40°29N 68°46E 217 D7
Mirzapur India 25°10N 82°34E 243 G10
Mirzapur-cum-Vindhyachal = Mirzapur India 25°10N 82°34E 243 G10
Mirzoyan = Taraz Kazakhstan 42°54N 71°22E 217 D8
Misaki Japan 34°18N 135°9E 223 C7
Misamis = Ozamiz Phil. 8°15N 123°50E 233 G4
Misamis Occidental □ Phil. 8°20N 123°42E 233 G4
Misamis Oriental □ Phil. 8°45N 125°0E 233 G5
Misantla Mexico 19°56N 96°50W 319 D5
Misawa Japan 40°41N 141°24E 220 D10
Miscou I. Canada 47°57N 64°31W 299 C7
Misdroy = Międzyzdroje Poland 53°56N 14°26E 184 E1
Misericordia = Itaporanga Brazil 7°18S 38°0W 332 C4
Misericordia, Sa. da Brazil 22°51S 43°17W 135 B1
Misha India 7°59N 93°20E 245 L10
Mish'āb, Ra's al Si. Arabia 28°15N 48°43E 247 D6
Mishagua → Peru 11°12S 72°58W 330 C3
Mishamo Tanzania 5°41S 30°41E 268 D3
Mishan China 45°37N 131°48E 220 B5
Mishawaka U.S.A. 41°40N 86°11W 311 C10
Mishbih, Gebel Egypt 22°38N 34°44E 256 C3
Mishima Japan 35°10N 138°52E 223 B10
Mishmi Hills India 29°0N 96°0E 241 A6
Mishō Japan 32°57N 132°35E 222 E4
Misima I. Papua N. G. 10°40S 152°45E 286 F7
Misión Mexico 32°6N 116°53W 307 N10
Misión Fagnano Argentina 54°32S 67°17W 336 D3
Misiones □ Argentina 27°0S 55°0W 335 B5
Misiones □ Paraguay 27°0S 56°0W 334 B4
Miskah Si. Arabia 24°49N 42°56E 246 E4
Miski, E. → Chad 20°0N 17°55E 259 E3
Miskitos, Cayos Nic. 14°26N 82°50W 320 D3
Miskolc Hungary 48°7N 20°50E 182 B5
Misoke Dem. Rep. of the Congo 0°42S 28°2E 268 C2
Misool Indonesia 1°52S 130°10E 231 E8
Mişr = Egypt ■ Africa 28°0N 31°0E 256 B3
Mişrātah Libya 32°24N 15°3E 258 B3
Mişrātah □ Libya 33°30N 15°0E 258 C3
Missanabie Canada 48°20N 84°6W 298 C3
Missão Catrimani Brazil 2°48N 62°18W 329 C5
Missão Velha Brazil 7°15S 39°10W 332 C4
Missinaibi → Canada 50°43N 81°29W 298 B3
Missinaibi L. Canada 48°23N 83°40W 298 C3
Mission B.C., Canada 49°10N 122°15W 296 D4
Mission Calif., U.S.A. 37°44N 122°25W 136 B2
Mission S. Dak., U.S.A. 43°18N 100°39W 308 D3
Mission Tex., U.S.A. 26°13N 98°20W 314 H5
Mission Beach Australia 17°53S 146°6E 280 B4
Mission Viejo U.S.A. 33°36N 117°40W 307 M9
Missirah Senegal 13°40N 16°30W 262 C1
Missisa L. Canada 52°20N 85°7W 298 B2
Missisicabi → Canada 51°14N 79°31W 298 B4
Mississagi → Canada 46°15N 83°9W 298 C3
Mississauga Canada 43°32N 79°35W 141 B1
Mississinewa L. U.S.A. 40°42N 85°52W 311 D10
Mississippi □ U.S.A. 33°0N 90°0W 315 E10
Mississippi → U.S.A. 29°9N 89°15W 315 G10
Mississippi L. Canada 45°5N 76°10W 313 A8
Mississippi River Delta U.S.A. 29°10N 89°15W 315 G10
Mississippi Sd. U.S.A. 30°20N 89°0W 315 F10
Missoula U.S.A. 46°52N 114°1W 304 C6
Missour Morocco 33°3N 4°0W 260 B4
Missouri □ U.S.A. 38°25N 92°30W 310 E3
Missouri → U.S.A. 38°49N 90°7W 310 F6
Missouri City U.S.A. 29°37N 95°32W 314 G7
Missouri Valley U.S.A. 41°34N 95°53W 308 E6
Mist U.S.A. 45°59N 123°15W 306 E3
Mistassibi → Canada 48°53N 72°13W 299 B5
Mistassini Canada 48°53N 72°12W 299 C5
Mistassini → Canada 48°42N 72°20W 299 C5
Mistassini, L. Canada 51°0N 73°30W 298 B5
Mistastin L. Canada 55°57N 63°20W 299 A7
Mistelbach Austria 48°34N 16°34E 181 C9
Misterbianco Italy 37°31N 15°1E 201 E8
Misteriosa Bank Caribbean 18°50N 83°50W 320 C3
Misti, Volcán Peru 16°18S 71°24W 330 D3
Mistinibi, L. Canada 55°56N 64°17W 299 A7
Mistissini Canada 48°53N 72°12W 299 C5
Mistras = Mystras Greece 37°4N 22°22E 204 D4
Mistretta Italy 37°56N 14°22E 201 E7
Misty Fjords Nat. Monument ⌓ U.S.A. 55°40N 130°40W 303 J15
Misty L. Canada 58°53N 101°40W 297 B8

**Misugi** *Japan* 34°31N 136°16E **223** C8
**Misumi** *Japan* 32°37N 130°27E **222** E2
**Misurata = Mişrātah** *Libya* 32°24N 15°3E **258** B3
**Mît Ghamr** *Egypt* 30°42N 31°12E **256** H7
**Mitaka** *Japan* 35°41N 139°34E **140** A2
**Mitande** *Mozam.* 14°6S 35°58E **269** E4
**Mitatib** *Sudan* 15°59N 36°12E **257** D4
**Mitau = Jelgava** *Latvia* 56°41N 23°49E **184** B10
**Mitava = Jelgava** *Latvia* 56°41N 23°49E **184** B10
**Mitcham** *U.K.* 51°23N 0°10W **125** B2
**Mitcham Common** *U.K.* 51°23N 0°8W **125** B3
**Mitchell** *Queens., Australia* 26°29S 147°58E **281** D4
**Mitchell** *Ont., Canada* 43°28N 81°12W **312** C3
**Mitchell** *Ga., U.S.A.* 33°13N 82°42W **316** B7
**Mitchell** *Ind., U.S.A.* 38°44N 86°28W **311** F10
**Mitchell** *Nebr., U.S.A.* 41°57N 103°49W **308** E2
**Mitchell** *Oreg., U.S.A.* 44°34N 120°9W **304** D3
**Mitchell** *S. Dak., U.S.A.* 43°43N 98°2W **308** D4
**Mitchell** → *Australia* 15°12S 141°35E **280** B3
**Mitchell, Mt.** *U.S.A.* 35°46N 82°16W **315** D13
**Mitchell-Alice Rivers** △ *Australia* 15°28S 142°5E **280** B3
**Mitchell Museum of the American Indian** *Chicago, U.S.A.* 42°4N 87°43W **119** A2
**Mitchell Ra.** *Australia* 12°49S 135°36E **280** A2
**Mitchell River** △ *Australia* 37°37S 147°22E **283** D7
**Mitchell's Plain** *S. Africa* 34°4S 18°35E **118** B2
**Mitchelstown** *Ireland* 52°15N 8°16W **166** D3
**Mitha Tiwana** *Pakistan* 32°13N 72°6E **242** C5
**Mithi** *Pakistan* 24°44N 69°48E **242** G3
**Mithimna** *Greece* 39°20N 26°12E **205** B8
**Mithrao** *Pakistan* 27°28N 69°40E **242** F3
**Mitiamo** *Australia* 36°12S 144°15E **282** D6
**Mitikas** *Etoloakarnania, Greece* 38°40N 20°56E **207** B2
**Mitikas** *Preveza, Greece* 39°0N 20°42E **207** B2
**Mitilini** *Greece* 39°6N 26°35E **205** B8
**Mitilinii** *Greece* 37°42N 26°56E **205** D8
**Mitla Pass = Mamarr Mitlā** *Egypt* 30°2N 32°54E **251** H3
**Mito** *Japan* 36°20N 140°30E **223** A12
**Mitra, Mt.** *Eq. Guin.* 1°23N 9°19E **264** B1
**Mitre, Mt.** *N.Z.* 40°50S 175°30E **284** G4
**Mitrofanovka** *Russia* 49°58N 39°42E **189** H10
**Mitrovicë** *Kosovo* 42°54N 20°52E **202** D4
**Mitrowitz = Sremska Mitrovica** *Serbia* 44°59N 19°38E **182** F4
**Mitsamiouli** *Comoros Is.* 11°20S 43°16E **272** a
**Mitsang** *Gabon* 0°42N 12°33E **264** B2
**Mitsinjo** *Madag.* 16°1S 45°52E **272** B2
**Mitsio, Nosy** *Madag.* 12°54S 48°36E **272** A2
**Mitsiwa** *Eritrea* 15°35N 39°25E **257** D4
**Mitsiwa Channel** *Eritrea* 15°30N 40°0E **257** D5
**Mitsoudjé** *Comoros Is.* 11°48S 43°16E **272** a
**Mitsukaidō** *Japan* 36°1N 139°59E **223** A11
**Mitsushima** *Japan* 34°15N 129°20E **222** C1
**Mittagong** *Australia* 34°28S 150°29E **283** C9
**Mitte** *Germany* 52°32N 13°24E **115** A3
**Mittel Isarkanal** → *Germany* 48°12N 11°40E **131** A3
**Mittel Schreiberhau = Szklarska Poreba** *Poland* 50°50N 15°33E **185** H2
**Mittelberg** *Austria* 47°20N 10°10E **180** D3
**Mittelfranken** □ *Germany* 49°25N 10°40E **179** F6
**Mittellandkanal** → *Germany* 52°20N 8°28E **178** C4
**Mittelwalde = Międzylesie** *Poland* 50°8N 16°40E **185** H3
**Mittenwalde** *Germany* 52°15N 13°31E **178** C9
**Mittersill** *Austria* 47°16N 12°29E **180** D5
**Mitterteich** *Germany* 49°57N 12°14E **179** F8
**Mittimatalik = Pond Inlet** *Canada* 72°40N 77°0W **295** C16
**Mittweida** *Germany* 50°59N 12°59E **178** E8
**Mitú** *Colombia* 1°15N 70°13W **328** C3
**Mituas** *Colombia* 3°52N 68°49W **328** C4
**Mitumba** *Tanzania* 7°8S 31°2E **268** D3
**Mitumba, Mts.** *Dem. Rep. of the Congo* 7°0S 27°30E **268** D2
**Mitwaba** *Dem. Rep. of the Congo* 8°2S 27°17E **269** D2
**Mityana** *Uganda* 0°23N 32°2E **268** B3
**Mitzic** *Gabon* 0°45N 11°40E **264** B2
**Miura** *Japan* 35°12N 139°40E **223** B11
**Mixcoac** *Mexico* 19°23N 99°11W **128** B1
**Mixteco** → *Mexico* 18°11N 98°30W **319** D5
**Miyagi** □ *Japan* 38°15N 140°45E **220** E10
**Miyāh, W. el** → *Egypt* 25°0N 33°23E **256** C3
**Miyāh, W. el** → *Syria* 34°44N 39°57E **246** C3
**Miyake-Jima** *Japan* 34°5N 139°30E **223** C11
**Miyako** *Japan* 39°40N 141°59E **220** E10
**Miyako-Jima** *Japan* 24°45N 125°20E **221** M2
**Miyako-Rettō** *Japan* 24°24N 125°0E **221** M2
**Miyakojima** *Okinawa, Japan* 24°48N 125°17E **221** M2
**Miyakojima** *Ōsaka, Japan* 34°42N 135°31E **133** A2
**Miyakonojō** *Japan* 31°40N 131°5E **222** F3
**Miyān Rahan** *Iran* 34°34N 47°26E **213** E12
**Miyani** *India* 21°50N 69°26E **242** J3
**Miyanojō** *Japan* 31°54N 130°27E **222** F2
**Miyanoura-Dake** *Japan* 30°20N 130°31E **221** J5
**Miyata** *Japan* 33°49N 130°42E **222** D2
**Miyazaki** *Japan* 31°56N 131°30E **222** F3
**Miyazaki** □ *Japan* 32°30N 131°30E **222** E3
**Miyazu** *Japan* 35°35N 135°10E **223** B7
**Miyet, Bahr el = Dead Sea** *Asia* 31°30N 35°30E **251** G6
**Miyi** *China* 26°47N 102°9E **228** D4
**Miyoshi** *Japan* 34°48N 132°51E **222** C4
**Miyun** *China* 40°28N 116°50E **226** D9
**Miyun Shuiku** *China* 40°30N 117°0E **227** D9
**Mizan Teferi** *Ethiopia* 6°57N 35°3E **257** F4
**Mizdah** *Libya* 31°30N 13°0E **258** B2
**Mizen Hd.** *Cork, Ireland* 51°27N 9°50W **166** E2
**Mizen Hd.** *Wicklow, Ireland* 52°51N 6°4W **166** D5
**Mizhhirya** *Ukraine* 48°32N 23°30E **183** B8
**Mizhi** *China* 37°47N 110°12E **226** F6
**Mizil** *Romania* 44°59N 26°29E **183** F11
**Mizo Hills = Mizoram** □ *India* 23°30N 92°40E **241** D4
**Mizonokuchi** *Japan* 35°35N 139°34E **140** B2
**Mizoram** □ *India* 23°30N 92°40E **241** D4
**Mizpe Ramon** *Israel* 30°34N 34°49E **251** H5
**Mizue** *Japan* 35°41N 139°54E **140** A4
**Mizuho = Kyōtamba** *Japan* 35°6N 135°17E **223** B7
**Mizuho** *Antarctica* 70°30S 41°0E **151** D5
**Mizunami** *Japan* 35°22N 137°15E **223** B9
**Mizusawa = Ōshū** *Japan* 39°8N 141°8E **220** E10
**Mjällby** *Sweden* 56°3N 14°40E **163** H8
**Mjöbäck** *Sweden* 57°28N 12°53E **163** G6
**Mjölby** *Sweden* 58°20N 15°10E **163** F9
**Mjølfjell** *Norway* 60°41N 6°55E **164** D3
**Mjømna** *Norway* 60°55N 4°55E **164** D1
**Mjörn** *Sweden* 57°55N 12°25E **163** G6
**Mjøsa** *Norway* 60°40N 11°0E **164** D8
**Mkata** *Tanzania* 5°45S 38°20E **268** D4
**Mkhaya** ⌓ *Swaziland* 26°34S 31°45E **271** C5
**Mkhuze** ⌓ *S. Africa* 29°27S 29°30E **271** C4
**Mkokotoni** *Tanzania* 5°55S 39°15E **268** D4
**Mkomazi** *Tanzania* 4°40S 38°7E **268** C4
**Mkomazi** → *S. Africa* 30°12S 30°50E **271** D5
**Mkomazi** ⌓ *Tanzania* 4°4S 30°2E **268** C3
**Mkulwe** *Tanzania* 8°37S 32°20E **269** D3
**Mkumbi, Ras** *Tanzania* 7°38S 39°55E **268** D4
**Mkushi** *Zambia* 14°25S 29°15E **269** E2
**Mkushi River** *Zambia* 13°32S 29°45E **269** E2
**Mkuze** *S. Africa* 27°10S 32°0E **271** C5
**Mladá Boleslav** *Czech Rep.* 50°27N 14°53E **180** A7
**Mladenovac** *Serbia* 44°28N 20°44E **202** B4
**Mlala Hills** *Tanzania* 6°50S 31°40E **268** D3
**M'lang** *Phil.* 6°56N 124°52E **233** H5
**Mlange = Mulanje, Mt.** *Malawi* 16°2S 35°33E **269** F4
**Mlava** → *Serbia* 44°45N 21°13E **202** B5
**Mława** *Poland* 53°9N 20°25E **185** E7
**Mlawula** ⌓ *Swaziland* 26°12S 32°2E **271** C5
**Mlinište** *Bos.-H.* 44°15N 16°50E **199** D13
**Mljet** *Croatia* 42°43N 17°30E **199** F14
**Mljet** △ *Croatia* 42°45N 17°25E **199** F14
**Mljetski Kanal** *Croatia* 42°48N 17°35E **199** F14
**Młocinski, Park** *Poland* 52°19N 20°57E **143** B1
**Młociny** *Poland* 52°18N 20°55E **143** B1
**Młynary** *Poland* 54°12N 19°46E **184** D6
**Mmabatho** *S. Africa* 25°49S 25°30E **270** C4
**Mme** *Cameroon* 6°18N 10°14E **263** D7
**Mnevniki** *Russia* 55°45N 37°28E **129** B1
**Mnichovo Hradiště** *Czech Rep.* 50°32N 14°59E **180** A7
**Mo** *Hordaland, Norway* 60°49N 5°48E **164** D2
**Mo** *Møre og Romsdal, Norway* 63°0N 8°59E **164** A5
**Mo** *Telemark, Norway* 59°28N 7°50E **164** E4
**Mo i Rana** *Norway* 66°20N 14°7E **160** C16
**Moa** *Queens., Australia* 10°11S 142°16E **280** a
**Moa** *Cuba* 20°40N 74°56W **321** B4
**Moa** *Indonesia* 8°0S 128°0E **231** F7
**Moa** → *S. Leone* 6°59N 11°36W **262** D2
**Moab** *U.S.A.* 38°35N 109°33W **304** G9
**Moabi** *Gabon* 2°24S 10°59E **264** C2
**Moaco** → *Brazil* 7°41S 68°18W **330** B4
**Moala** *Fiji* 18°36S 179°53E **287** B2
**Moama** *Australia* 36°7S 144°46E **281** F3
**Moamba** *Mozam.* 25°36S 32°15E **271** C5
**Moapa** *U.S.A.* 36°40N 114°37W **307** J12
**Moate** *Ireland* 53°24N 7°44W **166** C4
**Moba** *Dem. Rep. of the Congo* 7°0S 29°48E **268** D2
**Moba** *Lagos, Nigeria* 6°26N 3°28E **124** B2
**Mobara** *Japan* 35°25N 140°18E **223** B12
**Mobārakābād** *Iran* 28°24N 53°20E **247** D7
**Mobaye** *C.A.R.* 4°25N 21°5E **264** B4
**Mobayi** *Dem. Rep. of the Congo* 4°15N 21°8E **264** B4
**Mobeka** *Dem. Rep. of the Congo* 1°52N 19°49E **264** B3
**Mobenzélé** *Congo* 0°56N 17°50E **264** B3
**Moberly** *U.S.A.* 39°25N 92°26W **310** E4
**Moberly Lake** *Canada* 55°50N 121°44W **296** B4
**Mobile** *U.S.A.* 30°41N 88°3W **315** F10
**Mobile B.** *U.S.A.* 30°30N 88°0W **315** F11
**Mobridge** *U.S.A.* 45°32N 100°26W **308** C3
**Mobutu Sese Seko, L. = Albert, L.** *Africa* 1°30N 31°0E **268** B3
**Moc Chau** *Vietnam* 20°50N 104°38E **236** B5
**Moc Hoa** *Vietnam* 10°46N 105°56E **237** G5
**Moca** *Puerto Rico* 18°24N 67°10W **321** b
**Mocabe Kasari** *Dem. Rep. of the Congo* 9°58S 26°12E **269** D2
**Mocajuba** *Brazil* 2°35S 49°30W **332** B2
**Moçambique = Mozambique** ■ *Africa* 19°0S 35°0E **269** F4
**Moçambique** *Mozam.* 15°3S 40°42E **269** F5
**Moçâmedes = Namibe** *Angola* 15°7S 12°11E **265** F2
**Mocanaqua** *U.S.A.* 41°9N 76°8W **313** E8
**Mocapra** → *Venezuela* 7°56N 66°46W **328** B4
**Mocco, Morro de** *Angola* 12°28S 15°11E **265** E3
**Moce** *Fiji* 18°40S 178°29W **287** B3
**Mocenigo, Palazzo** *Venice, Italy* **142** b2
**Mocha = Al Mukhā** *Yemen* 13°18N 43°15E **248** D3
**Mocha, I.** *Chile* 38°22S 73°56W **336** A2
**Mochos** *Greece* 35°16N 25°27E **207** E6
**Mochudi** *Botswana* 24°27S 26°7E **270** B4
**Mocimboa da Praia** *Mozam.* 11°25S 40°20E **269** E5
**Mociu** *Romania* 46°46N 24°3E **183** D9
**Möckeln** *Sweden* 56°40N 14°15E **163** H8
**Mockfjärd** *Sweden* 60°30N 14°57E **162** D8
**Moclips** *U.S.A.* 47°14N 124°13W **306** C2
**Mocoa** *Colombia* 1°7N 76°35W **328** C2
**Mococa** *Brazil* 21°28S 47°0W **335** A6
**Mocorito** *Mexico* 25°29N 107°55W **318** B3
**Moctezuma** *Mexico* 29°48N 109°42W **318** B3
**Moctezuma** → *Mexico* 21°59N 98°34W **319** C5
**Mocuba** *Mozam.* 16°54S 36°57E **269** F4
**Moczydło** *Poland* 52°8N 21°2E **143** C2
**Moda** *Burma* 24°22N 96°29E **241** C6
**Modane** *France* 45°12N 6°40E **175** C10
**Modasa** *India* 23°30N 73°21E **242** H5
**Modder** → *S. Africa* 29°2S 24°37E **270** C3
**Modderfontein = Niekerkshoop** *S. Africa* 29°19S 22°51E **270** C3
**Modderfontein** *S. Africa* 26°5S 28°10E **123** A2
**Modderrivier** *S. Africa* 29°2S 24°38E **270** C3
**Módena** *Italy* 44°40N 10°55E **198** D7
**Modena** *Utah, U.S.A.* 37°48N 113°56W **305** H7
**Modernamuseet** *Stockholm, Sweden* **139** b3
**Modesto** *U.S.A.* 37°39N 121°0W **306** H6
**Möðrudalur** *Iceland* 65°22N 15°53W **155** B11
**Möðruvellir** *Iceland* 65°46N 18°15W **155** B8
**Módica** *Italy* 36°52N 14°46E **201** F7
**Modimolle** *S. Africa* 24°42S 28°22E **271** B4
**Modjadjiskloof** *S. Africa* 23°42S 30°10E **271** B5
**Modjamboli** *Dem. Rep. of the Congo* 2°28N 22°6E **264** B4
**Mödling** *Austria* 48°5N 16°17E **181** C9
**Modo** *South Sudan* 5°31N 30°33E **257** F3
**Modoc** *U.S.A.* 33°44N 82°13W **316** B7
**Modra** *Slovak Rep.* 48°19N 17°20E **181** C10
**Modřany** *Czech Rep.* 50°0N 14°24E **135** B2
**Modriča** *Bos.-H.* 44°57N 18°17E **182** F3
**Moe** *Australia* 38°12S 146°19E **283** E7
**Moebase** *Mozam.* 17°3S 38°41E **269** F4
**Moëlan-sur-Mer** *France* 47°49N 3°38W **172** E3
**Moelv** *Norway* 60°56N 10°43E **164** D7
**Moen I. = Weno** *Pac. Oc.* 7°27N 151°52E **287** T18
**Moengo** *Suriname* 5°45N 54°20W **329** B7
**Moenjodaro = Mohenjodaro** *Pakistan* 27°19N 68°7E **242** F3
**Moerewa** *N.Z.* 35°8S 174°1E **284** B3
**Moffat** *U.K.* 55°21N 3°27W **167** F5
**Moga** *India* 30°48N 75°8E **242** D6
**Mogadishu = Muqdisho** *Somalia* 2°2N 45°25E **267** D6
**Mogador = Essaouira** *Morocco* 31°32N 9°42W **260** B3
**Mogadouro** *Portugal* 41°22N 6°47W **194** D4
**Mogalakwena** → *S. Africa* 22°38S 28°40E **271** B4
**Mogami-Gawa** → *Japan* 38°45N 140°0E **220** E10
**Mogán** *Canary Is.* 27°53N 15°43W **153** e1
**Mogandjo** *Dem. Rep. of the Congo* 1°23N 24°15E **264** B4
**Mogaung** *Burma* 25°20N 97°0E **241** C6
**Mogen** *Norway* 60°2N 7°52E **164** D4
**Mogente = Moixent** *Spain* 38°52N 0°45W **197** G4
**Mogho** *Ethiopia* 4°54N 40°16E **257** G5
**Mogielnica** *Poland* 51°42N 20°41E **185** G7
**Mogige** *Ethiopia* 5°24N 36°14E **257** F4
**Mogilev = Mahilyow** *Belarus* 53°55N 30°18E **177** B16
**Mogilev-Podolskiy = Mohyliv-Podilskyy** *Ukraine* 48°26N 27°48E **183** B12
**Mogilno** *Poland* 52°39N 17°55E **185** F4
**Mogincual** *Mozam.* 15°35S 40°25E **269** F5
**Mogliano Véneto** *Italy* 45°33N 12°14E **199** C9
**Mogocha** *Russia* 53°40N 119°50E **215** D12
**Mogoditshane** *Botswana* 24°37S 25°51E **270** B4
**Mogok** *Burma* 23°0N 96°40E **241** D6
**Mogollon Rim** *U.S.A.* 34°10N 110°50W **305** J8
**Mógoro** *Italy* 39°41N 8°47E **200** C1
**Mograt** *Sudan* 19°28N 33°16E **256** D3
**Mogroum** *Chad* 11°6N 15°25E **259** F3
**Moguer** *Spain* 37°15N 6°52W **195** H4
**Mogumber** *Australia* 31°2S 116°3E **279** F2
**Mogwadi** → *S. Africa* 23°4S 29°36E **271** B4
**Mogyoród** *Hungary* 47°35N 19°14E **117** A3
**Mohács** *Hungary* 45°58N 18°41E **182** E3
**Mohaka** → *N.Z.* 39°7S 177°12E **284** F6
**Mohala** *India* 20°35N 80°44E **244** D5
**Mohales Hoek** *Lesotho* 30°7S 27°26E **270** D4
**Mohali** *Congo* 0°15N 15°29E **264** B3
**Mohali** *Punjab, India* 30°47N 76°41E **242** D7
**Mohall** *U.S.A.* 48°46N 101°31W **308** A3
**Moḩammadābād** *Iran* 37°52N 59°5E **247** B8
**Mohammadia** *Algeria* 35°33N 0°3E **261** A5
**Mohammedia** *Morocco* 33°44N 7°21W **260** B3
**Mohammerah = Khorramshahr** *Iran* 30°29N 48°15E **247** D6
**Mohana** *India* 19°27N 84°16E **244** E7
**Mohana** → *India* 24°43N 85°0E **243** G11
**Mohanganj** *Bangla.* 24°54N 90°59E **241** C3
**Mohanlalganj** *India* 26°41N 80°58E **243** F9
**Mohave, L.** *U.S.A.* 35°12N 114°34W **307** K12
**Mohawk** → *U.S.A.* 42°47N 73°41W **313** D11
**Moheda** *Sweden* 57°1N 14°35E **163** G8
**Mohéli** *Comoros Is.* 12°20S 43°40E **272** a
**Mohéli** ✈ **(NWA)** *Comoros Is.* 12°19S 43°47E **272** a
**Mohenjodaro** *Pakistan* 27°19N 68°7E **242** F3
**Moher, Cliffs of** *Ireland* 52°58N 9°27W **166** D2
**Mohican, C.** *U.S.A.* 60°12N 167°25W **303** F6
**Mohicanville Res.** *U.S.A.* 40°45N 82°9W **312** F2
**Möhne** → *Germany* 51°29N 7°57E **178** D3
**Mohns Ridge** *Arctic* 72°30N 5°0W **150** B7
**Mohnyin** *Burma* 24°47N 96°22E **241** C6
**Mohoro** *Tanzania* 8°6S 39°8E **268** D4
**Mohrin = Moryń** *Poland* 52°51N 14°22E **185** F1
**Mohsenābād** *Iran* 36°40N 59°35E **247** B8
**Mohyliv-Podilskyy** *Ukraine* 48°26N 27°48E **183** B12
**Moi** *Norway* 58°27N 6°32E **164** F3
**Moia** *South Sudan* 5°3N 28°2E **257** F2
**Moidart, L.** *U.K.* 56°47N 5°52W **167** E3
**Moinabad** *India* 17°44N 77°16E **244** F3
**Moinești** *Romania* 46°28N 26°31E **183** D11
**Moinho Velho, Cor.** → *Brazil* 23°35S 46°35W **137** B2
**Moira** → *Canada* 44°21N 77°24W **312** B7
**Moirang** *India* 24°30N 93°46E **241** C4
**Moirans** *France* 45°20N 5°33E **175** C9
**Moirans-en-Montagne** *France* 46°26N 5°43E **173** F12
**Moisaküla** *Estonia* 58°3N 25°12E **188** C3
**Moisie** *Canada* 50°12N 66°1W **299** B6
**Moisie** → *Canada* 50°14N 66°5W **299** B6
**Moissac** *France* 44°7N 1°5E **174** D5
**Moïssala** *Chad* 8°21N 17°46E **259** G3
**Moita** *Portugal* 38°38N 8°58W **195** G2
**Moixent** *Spain* 38°52N 0°45W **197** G4
**Möja** *Sweden* 59°26N 18°55E **162** E12
**Mojácar** *Spain* 37°6N 1°55W **197** H3
**Mojados** *Spain* 41°26N 4°40W **194** D6
**Mojave** *U.S.A.* 35°3N 118°10W **307** K8
**Mojave** ⌓ *U.S.A.* 35°7N 115°32W **307** K11
**Mojave Desert** *U.S.A.* 35°0N 116°30W **307** L10
**Moji das Cruzes** *Brazil* 23°31S 46°11W **335** A6
**Moji-Guaçu** *Brazil* 22°22S 46°57W **333** F2
**Moji-Guaçu** → *Brazil* 20°53S 48°10W **335** A6
**Mojiang** *China* 23°37N 101°35E **228** F3
**Mojjo** → *Ethiopia* 7°55N 42°0E **257** F5
**Mojkovac** *Montenegro* 42°58N 19°35E **202** D3
**Mojo** *Bolivia* 21°48S 65°33W **334** A2
**Mojo** *Ethiopia* 8°35N 39°5E **257** F4
**Mojokerto** *Indonesia* 7°28S 112°26E **235** D4
**Mojos, Llanos de** *Bolivia* 15°10S 65°0W **331** D5
**Moju** *Brazil* 1°53S 48°46W **332** B2
**Moju** → *Brazil* 1°40S 48°25W **332** B2
**Mok** *S. Korea* 37°32N 126°52E **137** B1
**Moka** *Mauritius* 20°13S 57°29E **272** e
**Mokai** *N.Z.* 38°32S 175°56E **284** E4
**Mokala** △ *S. Africa* 29°10S 24°10E **270** C3
**Mokambo** *Dem. Rep. of the Congo* 12°25S 28°20E **269** E2
**Mokameh** *India* 25°24N 85°55E **243** G11
**Mokane** *U.S.A.* 38°41N 91°53W **310** F5
**Mōkapu Peninsula** *U.S.A.* 21°25N 157°45W **302** K14
**Mokau** *N.Z.* 38°42S 174°39E **284** E3
**Mokau** → *N.Z.* 38°35S 174°35E **284** E3
**Mokelumne** → *U.S.A.* 38°13N 121°28W **306** G5
**Mokelumne Hill** *U.S.A.* 38°18N 120°43W **306** G6
**Mokhotlong** *Lesotho* 29°22S 29°2E **271** C4
**Mokihinui** → *N.Z.* 41°33S 171°58E **285** B6
**Möklinta** *Sweden* 60°4N 16°33E **162** D10
**Moknine** *Tunisia* 35°35N 10°58E **258** A2
**Mokoan, L.** *Australia* 36°27S 146°5E **283** D7
**Mokokchung** *India* 26°15N 94°30E **241** B5
**Mökölea Rock** *U.S.A.* 21°27N 157°44W **302** K14
**Mokolo** *Cameroon* 10°49N 13°54E **259** F2
**Mokolo** *Dem. Rep. of the Congo* 1°55N 18°6E **264** B3
**Mokolo** → *S. Africa* 23°14S 27°43E **271** B4
**Mokombe** *Dem. Rep. of the Congo* 0°14S 23°48E **264** C4
**Mokopane** *S. Africa* 24°10S 28°55E **271** B4
**Mokotów** *Poland* 52°12N 21°0E **143** B2
**Mokpalin** *Burma* 17°26N 96°53E **241** G6
**Mokpo** *S. Korea* 34°50N 126°25E **224** E3
**Mokra Gora** *Europe* 42°50N 20°30E **202** D4
**Mokronog** *Slovenia* 45°57N 15°9E **199** C12
**Moksha** → *Russia* 54°45N 41°53E **190** C6
**Mokshan** *Russia* 53°25N 44°35E **190** D7
**Mokuauia I.** *U.S.A.* 21°40N 157°56W **302** J14
**Mokulē'ia** *U.S.A.* 21°35N 158°9W **302** J13
**Mokulua Is.** *U.S.A.* 21°24N 157°42W **302** K14
**Mokumanu** *U.S.A.* 21°28N 157°43W **302** K14
**Mokwa** *Nigeria* 9°19N 5°0E **263** D6
**Mol** *Belgium* 51°11N 5°5E **170** C5
**Mola di Bari** *Italy* 41°4N 17°5E **201** A10
**Molai** *Greece* 36°49N 22°56E **204** E4
**Molakalmuru** *India* 14°55N 76°50E **245** G3
**Molale** *Ethiopia* 10°10N 39°41E **257** E4
**Molaly** *Kazakhstan* 45°27N 78°18E **217** C9
**Molanda** *Dem. Rep. of the Congo* 2°28N 20°48E **264** B4
**Molara** *Italy* 40°52N 9°43E **200** B2
**Molat** *Croatia* 44°15N 14°50E **199** D11
**Molave** *Phil.* 8°5N 123°30E **233** G4
**Molchanovo** *Russia* 57°40N 83°50E **214** D9
**Mold** *U.K.* 53°9N 3°8W **168** D4
**Moldava nad Bodvou** *Slovak Rep.* 48°38N 21°0E **181** C14
**Moldavia = Moldova** ■ *Europe* 47°0N 28°0E **183** C13
**Moldavia** *Romania* 46°30N 27°0E **183** D12
**Molde** *Norway* 62°45N 7°9E **164** B4
**Moldova** ■ *Europe* 47°0N 28°0E **183** C13
**Moldova Nouă** *Romania* 44°45N 21°41E **182** F6
**Moldoveanu, Vf.** *Romania* 45°36N 24°45E **183** E9
**Moldovița** *Romania* 47°41N 25°32E **183** C10
**Mole** → *U.K.* 51°24N 0°21W **169** F7
**Mole** △ *Ghana* 9°43N 1°44W **263** D4
**Molegbwe** *Dem. Rep. of the Congo* 4°12N 20°53E **264** B4
**Molenbeek-St-Jean** *Belgium* 50°51N 4°19E **116** A1
**Molepolole** *Botswana* 24°28S 25°28E **270** B4
**Molesworth** *N.Z.* 42°5S 173°16E **285** C8
**Molfetta** *Italy* 41°12N 16°36E **201** A9
**Mōli'i Pond** *U.S.A.* 21°31N 157°51W **302** J14
**Molina de Aragón** *Spain* 40°46N 1°52W **196** E3
**Molina de Segura** *Spain* 38°3N 1°12W **197** G3
**Moline** *U.S.A.* 41°30N 90°31W **310** C6
**Molinella** *Italy* 44°37N 11°40E **199** D8
**Molino** *U.S.A.* 30°43N 87°20W **317** E2
**Molino de Rosas** *Mexico* 19°21N 99°14W **128** B1
**Molinos** *Argentina* 25°28S 66°15W **334** B2
**Moliro** *Dem. Rep. of the Congo* 8°12S 30°30E **268** D3
**Moliterno** *Italy* 40°14N 15°52E **201** B8
**Molkom** *Sweden* 59°37N 13°44E **162** E7
**Mölle** *Sweden* 56°17N 12°31E **163** H6
**Molledo** *Spain* 43°8N 4°6W **194** B6
**Mollem** *Belgium* 50°56N 4°13E **116** A1
**Mollendo** *Peru* 17°0S 72°0W **330** D3
**Mollerin, L.** *Australia* 30°30S 117°35E **279** F2
**Mollerussa** *Spain* 41°37N 0°54E **196** D5
**Mollina** *Spain* 37°8N 4°38W **195** H6
**Mollins de Rey** *Spain* 41°24N 2°1E **114** A1
**Mölln** *Germany* 53°39N 10°32E **178** B6
**Mölltorp** *Sweden* 58°30N 14°26E **163** F8
**Mölndal** *Sweden* 57°40N 12°3E **163** G5
**Mölnlycke** *Sweden* 57°40N 12°8E **163** G6
**Molo** *Burma* 23°22N 96°53E **241** D6
**Molo** *Rift Valley, Kenya* 0°15S 35°44E **268** C4
**Molochansk** *Ukraine* 47°15N 35°35E **189** J8
**Molochnoye, Ozero** *Ukraine* 46°30N 35°20E **189** J8
**Molodechno = Maladzyechna** *Belarus* 54°20N 26°50E **177** A14
**Molodezhnaya** *Antarctica* 67°40S 45°51E **151** C9
**Molodove** *Ukraine* 46°13N 29°39E **183** D14
**Moloka'i** *U.S.A.* 21°8N 157°0W **302** B4
**Molokai Fracture Zone** *Pac. Oc.* 28°0N 125°0W **289** E15
**Molokini I.** *U.S.A.* 20°38N 156°30W **302** C5
**Molong** *Australia* 33°5S 148°54E **283** B8
**Molopo** → *Africa* 28°30S 20°12E **270** C3
**Molos** *Greece* 38°47N 22°37E **204** C4
**Molotov = Perm** *Russia* 58°0N 56°10E **186** C10
**Molotov, Mys = Arkticheskiy, Mys** *Russia* 81°10N 95°0E **215** A10
**Molotovsk = Nolinsk** *Russia* 57°28N 49°57E **190** B9
**Molotovsk = Severodvinsk** *Russia* 64°27N 39°58E **186** B6
**Molotovskoye = Krasnogvardeyskoye** *Russia* 45°52N 41°33E **191** H5
**Moloundou** *Cameroon* 2°8N 15°15E **264** B3
**Molowaie** *Dem. Rep. of the Congo* 5°47S 23°18E **265** D4
**Molsheim** *France* 48°33N 7°29E **173** D14
**Molson L.** *Canada* 54°22N 96°40W **297** C9
**Molteno** *S. Africa* 31°22S 26°22E **270** D4
**Molu** *Indonesia* 6°45S 131°40E **231** F8
**Molucca Sea** *Indonesia* 0°0 125°0E **231** E6
**Moluccas = Maluku** *Indonesia* 1°0S 127°0E **231** E7
**Molundo** *Phil.* 7°57N 124°23E **233** H5
**Moma** *Dem. Rep. of the Congo* 1°35S 23°52E **264** C4
**Moma** *Mozam.* 16°47S 39°4E **269** F4
**Momba** *Australia* 30°58S 143°30E **282** A5
**Mombaça** *Brazil* 5°43S 39°45W **332** C4
**Mombango** *Dem. Rep. of the Congo* 1°45N 24°26E **264** B4
**Mombasa** *Kenya* 4°3S 39°40E **268** C4
**Mombetsu** *Japan* 44°21N 143°22E **220** B11
**Mombil** *Burma* 27°46N 98°6E **241** B7
**Momboyo** → *Dem. Rep. of the Congo* 0°16S 19°0E **264** C3
**Mombuey** *Spain* 42°3N 6°20W **194** C4
**Momchilgrad** *Bulgaria* 41°33N 25°23E **203** E9
**Momence** *U.S.A.* 41°10N 87°40W **311** C9
**Momi** *Dem. Rep. of the Congo* 1°42S 27°0E **268** C2
**Momote** *Papua N. G.* 2°4S 147°27E **286** B4
**Mompog Pass.** *Phil.* 13°34N 122°13E **232** E4
**Mompós** *Colombia* 9°14N 74°26W **328** B3
**Møn** *Denmark* 54°57N 12°20E **163** K6
**Mon** *India* 26°45N 95°6E **241** B5
**Møn** *Hordaland, Norway* 60°37N 6°31E **164** D3
**Mon** □ *Burma* 16°0N 97°30E **241** G6
**Mona, Canal de la = Mona Passage** *W. Indies* 18°30N 67°45W **321** C6
**Mona, Isla** *Puerto Rico* 18°5N 67°54W **321** C6
**Mona, Pta.** *Costa Rica* 9°37N 82°36W **320** E3
**Mona Passage** *W. Indies* 18°30N 67°45W **321** C6
**Mona Quimbundo** *Angola* 9°55S 19°58E **265** D3
**Monaca** *U.S.A.* 40°41N 80°17W **312** F4
**Monaco** ■ *Europe* 43°46N 7°23E **175** E11
**Monadhliath Mts.** *U.K.* 57°10N 4°4W **167** D4
**Monadnock, Mt.** *U.S.A.* 42°52N 72°7W **313** D12
**Monagas** □ *Venezuela* 9°20N 63°0W **329** B5
**Monaghan** *Ireland* 54°15N 6°57W **166** B5
**Monaghan** □ *Ireland* 54°11N 6°56W **166** B5
**Monahans** *U.S.A.* 31°36N 102°54W **314** F3
**Monapo** *Mozam.* 14°56S 40°19E **269** E5
**Monar, L.** *U.K.* 57°26N 5°8W **167** D3
**Monaragala** *Sri Lanka* 6°52N 81°22E **245** L5
**Monarch Mt.** *Canada* 51°55N 125°57W **296** C3
**Monashee Mts.** *Canada* 51°0N 118°43W **296** C5
**Monasterevin** *Ireland* 53°8N 7°4W **166** C4
**Monastir = Bitola** *Macedonia* 41°1N 21°20E **202** E5
**Monastir** *Tunisia* 35°50N 10°49E **258** A2
**Monastir** □ *Tunisia* 35°37N 10°45E **261** A7
**Monbetsu = Hidaka** *Japan* 42°30N 142°10E **220** C11
**Moncalieri** *Italy* 45°0N 7°41E **198** D4
**Moncalvo** *Italy* 45°3N 8°16E **198** C5
**Monção** *Portugal* 42°4N 8°27W **194** C2
**Moncarapacho** *Portugal* 37°5N 7°46W **195** H3
**Moncayo, Sierra del** *Spain* 41°48N 1°50W **196** D3
**Moncha-Guba = Monchegorsk** *Russia* 67°54N 32°58E **160** C25
**Monchegorsk** *Russia* 67°54N 32°58E **160** C25
**Mönchengladbach** *Germany* 51°11N 6°27E **178** D2
**Monchique** *Portugal* 37°19N 8°38W **195** H2
**Moncks Corner** *U.S.A.* 33°12N 80°1W **316** B9
**Monclova** *Mexico* 26°54N 101°25W **318** B4
**Moncontour** *France* 48°22N 2°38W **172** D4
**Moncton** *Canada* 46°7N 64°51W **299** C7
**Mondariz** *Spain* 42°14N 8°27W **194** C2
**Mondego** → *Portugal* 40°9N 8°52W **194** E2
**Mondego, C.** *Portugal* 40°11N 8°54W **194** E2
**Mondeodo** *Indonesia* 3°34S 122°9E **231** E6
**Mondeor** *S. Africa* 26°16S 28°0E **123** B2
**Mondeville** *France* 49°10N 0°18W **172** C6
**Mondimbi** *Dem. Rep. of the Congo* 1°48N 22°46E **264** B4
**Mondjuku** *Dem. Rep. of the Congo* 1°41S 21°12E **264** C4
**Mondlo** *S. Africa* 27°59S 30°43E **271** C5
**Mondo** *Chad* 13°47N 15°32E **259** F3
**Mondolfo** *Italy* 43°45N 13°6E **199** E10
**Mondoñedo** *Spain* 43°25N 7°23W **194** B3
**Mondovì** *Italy* 44°23N 7°49E **198** D4
**Mondragó** *Spain* 39°21N 3°12E **206** B4
**Mondragon = Arrasate** *Spain* 43°4N 2°30W **196** B2
**Mondragon** *Phil.* 12°31N 124°45E **232** E5
**Mondragone** *Italy* 41°7N 13°53E **200** A6
**Mondrain I.** *Australia* 34°9S 122°14E **279** F3
**Moneague** *Jamaica* 18°16N 77°7W **320** a
**Moneda, Palacio de la** *Chile* 33°26S 70°39W **137** B2
**Monemvasia** *Greece* 36°41N 23°3E **204** E5
**Moneró** *Brazil* 22°48S 43°11W **135** A1
**Moneron, Ostrov** *Russia* 46°15N 141°16E **220** A10
**Monessen** *U.S.A.* 40°9N 79°54W **312** F5
**Monesterio** *Spain* 38°6N 6°15W **195** G4
**Monestier-de-Clermont** *France* 44°55N 5°38E **175** D9
**Monett** *U.S.A.* 36°55N 93°55W **308** G7
**Moneymore** *U.K.* 54°41N 6°40W **166** B5
**Monfalcone** *Italy* 45°49N 13°32E **199** C10
**Monflanquin** *France* 44°32N 0°47E **174** D4
**Monforte** *Portugal* 39°6N 7°25W **195** F3
**Monforte de Lemos** *Spain* 42°31N 7°33W **194** C3
**Monfragüe** ⌓ *Spain* 39°48N 5°52W **194** F5
**Mong Hpayak** *Burma* 20°52N 99°55E **236** B2
**Mong Hsat** *Shan, Burma* 21°54N 98°30E **228** G2
**Mong Hsat** *Shan, Burma* 20°31N 99°15E **236** B2
**Mong Hta** *Burma* 19°50N 98°35E **241** F7
**Mong Ket** *Burma* 23°8N 98°22E **241** D7
**Mong Kok** *Hong Kong, China* 22°19N 114°10E **122** B3
**Mong Kung** *Burma* 21°35N 97°35E **241** E6
**Mong Kyawt** *Burma* 19°56N 98°45E **241** F7
**Mong Long** *Burma* 22°47N 96°37E **241** D6
**Mong Mit** *Burma* 23°7N 96°41E **241** D6
**Mong Nai** *Burma* 20°32N 97°46E **241** E6
**Mong Pan** *Burma* 20°19N 98°22E **241** E7
**Mong Ping** *Burma* 21°22N 99°2E **228** G2
**Mong Pu** *Burma* 20°55N 98°44E **241** E7
**Mong Tai = Shan** □ *Burma* 21°30N 98°30E **241** E7
**Mong Ton** *Burma* 20°17N 98°45E **241** E7
**Mong Tung** *Burma* 22°2N 97°41E **241** D6
**Mong Yai** *Burma* 22°21N 98°3E **241** D7
**Mong Yang** *Burma* 21°50N 99°41E **236** B2
**Mong Yu** *Burma* 23°30N 97°47E **241** D6
**Monga** *Dem. Rep. of the Congo* 4°12N 22°49E **264** B4
**Mongala** → *Dem. Rep. of the Congo* 1°53N 19°46E **264** B3
**Mongalla** *South Sudan* 5°8N 31°42E **257** F3
**Mongandia** *Congo* 0°45N 17°11E **264** B3
**Mongers, L.** *Australia* 29°25S 117°5E **279** E2
**Mongga** *Solomon Is.* 7°52S 157°0E **287** L9
**Monghyr = Munger** *India* 25°23N 86°30E **243** G12
**Mongibello = Etna** *Italy* 37°50N 14°55E **201** E7
**Mongla** *Bangla.* 22°8N 89°35E **241** D2
**Mongmong** *Guam* 13°28N 144°45E **302** d
**Mongngaw** *Burma* 22°47N 96°59E **241** D6
**Mongo** *Chad* 12°14N 18°43E **259** F3
**Mongó** *Eq. Guin.* 1°52N 10°10E **264** B2
**Mongo** → *S. Leone* 9°35N 12°10W **262** D2
**Mongolia** ■ *Asia* 47°0N 103°0E **218** B9
**Mongolia, Plateau of** *Asia* 45°0N 105°0E **210** D12
**Mongomo** *Eq. Guin.* 1°38N 11°19E **264** B2
**Mongonu** *Nigeria* 12°40N 13°32E **263** C7
**Mongororo** *Chad* 12°3N 22°26E **259** F4
**Mongstad** *Norway* 60°49N 5°2E **164** D2
**Mongu** *Zambia* 15°16S 23°12E **265** F4
**Môngua** *Angola* 16°43S 15°20E **265** F3
**Moniac** *U.S.A.* 30°31N 82°14W **316** E7
**Monifieth** *U.K.* 56°30N 2°48W **167** E6
**Monistrol-sur-Loire** *France* 45°17N 4°11E **175** C8
**Monkayo** *Phil.* 7°50N 126°5E **233** H6
**Monkey Bay** *Malawi* 14°7S 35°1E **269** E4
**Monkey Mia** *Australia* 25°48S 113°43E **279** E1
**Monkey River** *Belize* 16°22N 88°29W **320** C2
**Monkey Town** *Trin. & Tob.* 10°12N 61°25W **323** t
**Mońki** *Poland* 53°23N 22°48E **184** E9
**Monkland** *Canada* 45°11N 74°52W **313** A10
**Monkoto** *Dem. Rep. of the Congo* 1°38S 20°35E **264** C4
**Monkstown** *Ireland* 53°18N 6°10W **120** B3
**Monkton** *Canada* 43°35N 81°5W **312** C3
**Monmouth** *Monmouths., U.K.* 51°48N 2°42W **169** F5
**Monmouth** *Ill., U.S.A.* 40°55N 90°39W **310** D6
**Monmouth** *Oreg., U.S.A.* 44°51N 123°14W **304** D2
**Monmouthshire** □ *U.K.* 51°48N 2°54W **169** F5
**Monnickendam** *Neths.* 52°28N 5°2E **112** A3
**Mono** *Solomon Is.* 7°20S 155°35E **287** L8
**Mono** → *Togo* 6°17N 1°51E **263** D5
**Mono, Pta.** *Nic.* 12°0N 83°30W **320** D3
**Mono L.** *U.S.A.* 38°1N 119°1W **306** H7
**Monolith** *U.S.A.* 35°7N 118°22W **307** K8
**Monolithos** *Greece* 36°7N 27°45E **206** E11
**Monon** *U.S.A.* 40°52N 86°53W **311** D10
**Monona** *Iowa, U.S.A.* 43°3N 91°23W **310** A5
**Monona** *Wis., U.S.A.* 43°4N 89°20W **310** A7
**Monongahela** *U.S.A.* 40°12N 79°56W **312** F5
**Monópoli** *Italy* 40°57N 17°13E **201** B10
**Monor** *Hungary* 47°21N 19°27E **182** C4
**Monos I.** *Trin. & Tob.* 10°42N 61°44W **323** t
**Monóvar** *Spain* 38°28N 0°53W **197** G4
**Monowai** *N.Z.* 45°53S 167°31E **285** F2
**Monowai, L.** *N.Z.* 45°53S 167°25E **285** F2
**Monqoumba** *C.A.R.* 3°33N 18°40E **264** B3
**Monreal del Campo** *Spain* 40°47N 1°20W **196** E3
**Monreale** *Italy* 38°5N 13°17E **200** D6
**Monroe** *Ga., U.S.A.* 33°47N 83°43W **316** B6
**Monroe** *Iowa, U.S.A.* 41°31N 93°6W **310** C3
**Monroe** *La., U.S.A.* 32°30N 92°7W **314** E8
**Monroe** *Mich., U.S.A.* 41°55N 83°24W **311** C13
**Monroe** *N.C., U.S.A.* 34°59N 80°33W **315** D14
**Monroe** *N.Y., U.S.A.* 41°20N 74°11W **313** E10
**Monroe** *Ohio, U.S.A.* 39°27N 84°22W **311** E12
**Monroe** *Utah, U.S.A.* 38°38N 112°7W **304** G7
**Monroe** *Wash., U.S.A.* 47°51N 121°58W **306** C5
**Monroe** *Wis., U.S.A.* 42°36N 89°38W **310** B7
**Monroe, L.** *U.S.A.* 28°50N 81°19W **317** G8
**Monroe City** *Ind., U.S.A.* 38°37N 87°20W **311** F9
**Monroe City** *Mo., U.S.A.* 39°39N 91°44W **310** E5
**Monroe L.** *U.S.A.* 39°1N 86°31W **311** E10
**Monroeton** *U.S.A.* 41°43N 76°29W **313** E8
**Monroeville** *Ala., U.S.A.* 31°31N 87°20W **315** F11
**Monroeville** *Ind., U.S.A.* 40°59N 84°52W **311** D12
**Monroeville** *Pa., U.S.A.* 40°26N 79°45W **312** F5
**Monrovia** *Liberia* 6°18N 10°47W **262** D2
**Monrovia** *Calif., U.S.A.* 34°9N 118°1W **126** B4
**Mons** *Belgium* 50°27N 3°58E **170** D3
**Møns Klint** *Denmark* 54°57N 12°33E **163** K6
**Monsanto** *Portugal* 38°44N 9°12W **126** A1
**Monsanto, Parque Florestal de** *Portugal* 38°43N 9°11W **126** A1
**Monsaraz** *Portugal* 38°28N 7°22W **195** G3
**Monse** *Indonesia* 4°7S 123°15E **231** E6
**Monsefú** *Peru* 6°52S 79°52W **330** B2
**Monségur** *France* 44°38N 0°4E **174** D4
**Monsélice** *Italy* 45°14N 11°45E **199** C8
**Mönsterås** *Sweden* 57°3N 16°26E **163** G10
**Mont Cenis, Col du** *France* 45°15N 6°55E **175** C10
**Mont-de-Marsan** *France* 43°54N 0°31W **174** E3
**Mont-Dore** *N. Cal.* 22°16S 166°34E **288** d
**Mont Fouari** ⌓ *Congo* 2°52S 11°32E **264** C2
**Mont-Joli** *Canada* 48°37N 68°10W **299** C6
**Mont-Laurier** *Canada* 46°35N 75°30W **298** C4
**Mont-Louis** *Canada* 49°15N 65°44W **299** C6
**Mont Peko** △ *Ivory C.* 9°5N 7°15W **262** D3
**Mont-roig del Camp** *Spain* 41°5N 0°58E **196** D5
**Mont-Royal** *Canada* 45°30N 73°38W **130** A2
**Mont-Royal, Parc** *Canada* 45°30N 73°36W **130** A2
**Mont-St-Michel, Le** *France* 48°40N 1°30W **172** D5
**Mont Sangbé** △ *Ivory C.* 8°0N 7°10W **262** D3
**Mont-Tremblant** ⌓ *Canada* 46°30N 74°30W **298** C5
**Montabaur** *Germany* 50°25N 7°50E **178** E3
**Montagnac = Remchi** *Algeria* 35°2N 1°26W **261** A4
**Montagnac** *France* 43°29N 3°28E **174** E7
**Montagnana** *Italy* 45°14N 11°28E **199** C8
**Montagne Blanche** *Mauritius* 20°16S 57°39E **272** e
**Montagne d'Ambre** △ *Madag.* 12°37S 49°8E **272** A2
**Montagne de Reims** ⌓ *France* 49°8N 4°0E **173** C11
**Montagu** *S. Africa* 33°45S 20°8E **270** D3
**Montagu I.** *Antarctica* 58°25S 26°20W **151** B1
**Montague** *Canada* 46°10N 62°39W **299** C7
**Montague, I.** *Mexico* 31°45N 114°48W **318** A2
**Montague I.** *N.S.W., Australia* 36°16S 150°13E **283** D9
**Montague I.** *Alaska, U.S.A.* 60°0N 147°30W **303** G11
**Montague Ra.** *Australia* 27°15S 119°30E **279** E2
**Montague Sd.** *Australia* 14°28S 125°20E **278** B4
**Montaigu** *France* 46°59N 1°18W **172** F5
**Montalbán** *Spain* 40°50N 0°45W **196** E4
**Montalbano Iónico** *Italy* 40°17N 16°34E **201** B9
**Montalbo** *Spain* 39°53N 2°42W **196** F2
**Montalcino** *Italy* 43°3N 11°29E **199** E8
**Montalegre** *Angola* 8°45S 17°4E **265** D3
**Montalegre** *Portugal* 41°49N 7°47W **194** D3
**Montalto** *Italy* 38°10N 15°55E **201** D8
**Montalto di Castro** *Italy* 42°21N 11°37E **199** F8
**Montalto Uffugo** *Italy* 39°24N 16°9E **201** C9
**Montalvo** *U.S.A.* 34°15N 119°12W **307** L7
**Montamarta** *Spain* 41°39N 5°49W **194** D5
**Montana** *Bulgaria* 43°27N 23°16E **202** C7
**Montaña** *Peru* 6°0S 73°0W **330** B3
**Montana** □ *Bulgaria* 43°30N 23°10E **202** C7
**Montana** □ *U.S.A.* 47°0N 110°0W **304** C9
**Montaña Clara, I.** *Canary Is.* 29°17N 13°33W **153** e2
**Montañas de Malaga** ⌓ *Spain* 36°48N 4°32W **195** J6
**Montánchez** *Spain* 39°15N 6°8W **195** F4
**Montanhas do Tumucumaque** △ *Brazil* 2°5N 53°0W **329** C7
**Montañita** *Colombia* 1°22N 75°28W **328** C2
**Montargil** *Portugal* 39°5N 8°10W **195** F2
**Montargis** *France* 47°59N 2°43E **173** E9
**Montauban** *France* 44°2N 1°21E **174** D5
**Montauk** *U.S.A.* 41°3N 71°57W **313** E13
**Montauk Pt.** *U.S.A.* 41°4N 71°51W **313** E13
**Montbard** *France* 47°38N 4°20E **173** E11
**Montbarrey** *France* 47°1N 5°39E **173** E12
**Montbéliard** *France* 47°31N 6°48E **173** E13
**Montblanc** *Spain* 41°23N 1°4E **196** D6
**Montbrison** *France* 45°36N 4°3E **175** C8
**Montcada i Reixac** *Spain* 41°29N 2°12W **114** A2
**Montcalm, Pic de** *France* 42°40N 1°25E **174** F5
**Montceau-les-Mines** *France* 46°40N 4°23E **173** F11
**Montcenis** *France* 46°47N 4°23E **175** B8
**Montchanin** *France* 46°45N 4°28E **175** B8
**Montclair** *U.S.A.* 40°49N 74°12W **313** F10
**Montcornet** *France* 49°40N 4°1E **173** C11
**Montcuq** *France* 44°21N 1°13E **174** D5
**Montdidier** *France* 49°38N 2°35E **173** C9
**Monte Albán** *Mexico* 17°2N 96°46W **319** D5
**Monte Alegre** *Brazil* 2°0S 54°0W **329** D7
**Monte Alegre de Goiás** *Brazil* 13°14S 47°10W **333** D2
**Monte Alegre de Minas** *Brazil* 18°52S 48°52W **333** E2
**Monte Alegre do Piauí** *Brazil* 9°46S 45°18W **332** C2
**Monte Azul** *Brazil* 15°9S 42°53W **333** E3
**Monte-Carlo** *Monaco* 43°44N 7°25E **175** E11
**Monte Carmelo** *Brazil* 18°43S 47°29W **333** E2
**Monte Caseros** *Argentina* 30°10S 57°50W **334** C4
**Monte Chingolo** *Argentina* 34°43S 58°22W **117** C2
**Monte Comán** *Argentina* 34°40S 67°53W **334** C2
**Monte Crísti** *Dom. Rep.* 19°52N 71°39W **321** C5
**Monte Cucco** ⌓ *Italy* 43°22N 12°43E **199** E9
**Monte Dinero** *Argentina* 52°18S 68°33W **336** D3
**Monte Dourado** *Brazil* 0°52S 52°31W **329** D7
**Monte Léon** *Argentina* 50°15S 69°0W **336** D3
**Monte Lindo** → *Paraguay* 23°56S 57°12W **334** A4
**Monte Palatino** *Rome, Italy* **136** c3
**Monte Pascoal** △ *Brazil* 16°51S 39°21W **333** E4
**Monte Patria** *Chile* 30°42S 70°58W **334** C1
**Monte Quemado** *Argentina* 25°53S 62°41W **334** B3
**Monte Redondo** *Portugal* 39°53N 8°50W **194** F2
**Monte Rio** *U.S.A.* 38°28N 123°0W **306** G4
**Monte San Giovanni Campano** *Italy* 41°38N 13°31E **200** A6
**Monte San Giuliano = Érice** *Italy* 38°2N 12°35E **200** D5
**Monte San Savino** *Italy* 43°20N 11°43E **199** E8
**Monte Sant' Ángelo** *Italy* 41°42N 15°59E **199** G12
**Monte Santu, C. di** *Italy* 40°5N 9°44E **200** B2
**Monte Subasio** ⌓ *Italy* 43°5N 12°40E **199** E9
**Monte Vista** *U.S.A.* 37°35N 106°9W **305** H10
**Monteagudo** *Argentina* 27°14S 54°8W **335** B5
**Monteagudo** *Bolivia* 19°49S 63°59W **331** D5
**Montealegre del Castillo** *Spain* 38°48N 1°17W **197** G3
**Montebello** *Qué., Canada* 45°40N 74°55W **298** C5
**Montebello** *Guadeloupe* 16°10N 61°36W **322** e
**Montebello** *Calif., U.S.A.* 34°1N 118°8W **126** B4
**Montebello Iónico** *Italy* 37°59N 15°45E **201** E8
**Montebello Is.** *Australia* 20°30S 115°45E **278** D2
**Montebelluna** *Italy* 45°47N 12°3E **199** C9
**Montebourg** *France* 49°30N 1°20W **172** C5
**Montecarlo** *Argentina* 26°34S 54°47W **335** B5
**Montecastrilli** *Italy* 42°39N 12°29E **199** F9
**Montecatini Terme** *Italy* 43°53N 10°46E **198** E7
**Montecito** *U.S.A.* 34°26N 119°40W **307** L7
**Montecristi** *Ecuador* 1°0S 80°40W **328** D1
**Montecristo** *Italy* 42°20N 10°19E **198** F7
**Montefalco** *Italy* 42°54N 12°39E **199** F9
**Montefiascone** *Italy* 42°32N 12°2E **199** F9
**Montefrío** *Spain* 37°20N 4°0W **195** H7
**Montegiórgio** *Italy* 43°6N 13°33E **199** E10
**Montego B.** *Jamaica* 18°28N 77°56W **320** a
**Montego Bay** *Jamaica* 18°28N 77°55W **320** a
**Montehermoso** *Spain* 40°5N 6°21W **194** E4
**Monteiro** *Brazil* 7°48S 37°2W **332** C4
**Montejícar** *Spain* 37°33N 3°30W **195** H7
**Montelbaanstoren** *Amsterdam, Neths.* **112** b3
**Monteleone di Calabria = Vibo Valéntia** *Italy* 38°40N 16°6E **201** D9
**Montelíbano** *Colombia* 8°5N 75°29W **328** B2
**Montélimar** *France* 44°33N 4°45E **175** D8
**Montella** *Italy* 40°51N 15°1E **201** B8
**Montellano** *Spain* 36°59N 5°29W **195** J5
**Montello** *U.S.A.* 43°48N 89°20W **308** D9
**Montemayor, Meseta de** *Argentina* 44°20S 66°10W **336** B3
**Montemor** *Portugal* 38°49N 9°12W **126** A1
**Montemor-o-Novo** *Portugal* 38°40N 8°12W **195** G2

Montemor-o-Velho *Portugal* 40°11N 8°40W 194 E2
Montemorelos *Mexico* 25°12N 99°49W 319 B5
Montendre *France* 45°16N 0°26W 174 C3
Montenegro *Brazil* 29°39S 51°29W 335 B5
Montenegro ■ *Europe* 42°40N 19°20E 202 D3
Montenero di Bisáccia *Italy* 41°57N 14°47E 199 G11
Montepuez *Mozam.* 13°8S 38°59E 269 E4
Montepuez → *Mozam.* 12°32S 40°27E 269 E5
Montepulciano *Italy* 43°5N 11°47E 199 E8
Montereale *Italy* 42°31N 13°15E 199 F10
Montereau-Faut-Yonne *France* 48°22N 2°57E 173 D9
Monterey *Calif., U.S.A.* 36°37N 121°55W 306 J5
Monterey *Ind., U.S.A.* 41°11N 86°30W 311 C10
Monterey B. *U.S.A.* 36°45N 122°0W 306 J5
Monterey Hills *U.S.A.* 34°6N 118°10W 126 B3
Monterey Park *U.S.A.* 34°3N 118°7W 126 B4
Montería *Colombia* 8°46N 75°53W 328 B2
Montero *Bolivia* 17°20S 63°15W 331 D5
Monteros *Argentina* 27°11S 65°30W 334 B2
Monterotondo *Italy* 42°3N 12°37E 199 F9
Monterrey *Mexico* 25°40N 100°19W 318 B4
Montes Altos *Brazil* 5°50S 47°4W 332 C2
Montes Azules △ *Mexico* 16°21N 91°3W 319 D6
Montes Claros *Brazil* 16°30S 43°50W 333 E3
Montesano *U.S.A.* 46°59N 123°36W 306 D3
Montesano sulla Marcellana *Italy* 40°16N 15°42E 201 B8
Montesárchio *Italy* 41°4N 14°38E 201 A7
Montescaglioso *Italy* 40°33N 16°40E 201 B9
Montesilvano *Italy* 42°29N 14°8E 199 F11
Montesinho △ *Portugal* 41°54N 6°52W 194 D4
Montespaccato *Italy* 41°54N 12°23E 136 B1
Montesson *France* 48°54N 2°8E 134 A1
Montevarchi *Italy* 43°31N 11°34E 199 E8
Monteverde Nuovo *Italy* 41°52N 12°26E 136 B1
Montevideo *Uruguay* 34°50S 56°11W 335 C4
Montevideo *Minn., U.S.A.* 44°57N 95°43W 308 C6
Montezuma *Ga., U.S.A.* 32°18N 84°2W 316 C5
Montezuma *Ind., U.S.A.* 39°48N 87°22W 311 E9
Montezuma *Iowa, U.S.A.* 41°35N 92°32W 310 C4
Montezuma Castle △ *U.S.A.* 34°39N 111°45W 305 J8
Montfaucon *France* 47°6N 1°7W 172 E5
Montfaucon-d'Argonne *France* 49°16N 5°8E 173 C12
Montfaucon-en-Velay *France* 45°11N 4°20E 175 C8
Montfermeil *France* 48°54N 2°33E 134 A4
Montfort-le-Gesnois *France* 48°3N 0°25E 172 D7
Montfort-sur-Meu *France* 48°9N 1°58W 172 D5
Montgenèvre *France* 44°56N 6°43E 175 D10
Montgó △ *Spain* 38°48N 0°7W 197 G5
Montgomery = Sahiwal *Pakistan* 30°45N 73°8E 242 D5
Montgomery *Powys, U.K.* 52°34N 3°8W 169 E4
Montgomery *Ala., U.S.A.* 32°23N 86°19W 316 C3
Montgomery *Ill., U.S.A.* 41°44N 88°21W 311 C8
Montgomery *Pa., U.S.A.* 41°10N 76°53W 312 E8
Montgomery *W. Va., U.S.A.* 38°11N 81°19W 309 F13
Montgomery City *U.S.A.* 38°59N 91°30W 310 F5
Montguyon *France* 45°12N 0°12W 174 C3
Monthermé *France* 49°52N 4°42E 173 C11
Monthey *Switz.* 46°15N 6°56E 179 J2
Monthois *France* 49°19N 4°43E 173 C11
Monti *Italy* 40°49N 9°19E 200 B2
Monti Lucrétili △ *Italy* 42°5N 12°50E 199 F9
Monti Picentini △ *Italy* 40°45N 15°2E 201 B8
Monti Sibillini △ *Italy* 42°55N 13°15E 199 F10
Monti Simbruini △ *Italy* 41°55N 13°12E 199 G10
Monticelli d'Ongina *Italy* 45°5N 9°56E 198 C6
Monticello *Ark., U.S.A.* 33°38N 91°47W 314 E9
Monticello *Fla., U.S.A.* 30°33N 83°52W 316 E6
Monticello *Ga., U.S.A.* 33°18N 83°40W 316 B6
Monticello *Ill., U.S.A.* 40°1N 88°34W 311 D8
Monticello *Ind., U.S.A.* 40°45N 86°46W 311 D10
Monticello *Iowa, U.S.A.* 42°15N 91°12W 310 B5
Monticello *Ky., U.S.A.* 36°50N 84°51W 309 G11
Monticello *Minn., U.S.A.* 45°18N 93°48W 308 C7
Monticello *Miss., U.S.A.* 31°33N 90°7W 315 F9
Monticello *Mo., U.S.A.* 40°7N 91°43W 310 D5
Monticello *N.Y., U.S.A.* 41°39N 74°42W 313 E10
Monticello *Utah, U.S.A.* 37°52N 109°21W 305 H9
Montichiari *Italy* 45°25N 10°23E 198 C7
Montier-en-Der *France* 48°30N 4°45E 173 D11
Montignac *France* 45°4N 1°10E 174 C5
Montigny-le-Bretonneux *France* 48°46N 2°1E 134 B1
Montigny-les-Metz *France* 49°7N 6°10E 173 C13
Montigny-sur-Aube *France* 47°57N 4°45E 173 E11
Montijo *Portugal* 38°41N 8°54W 195 G2
Montijo *Spain* 38°52N 6°39W 195 G4
Montilla *Spain* 37°36N 4°40W 195 H6
Montivilliers *France* 49°33N 0°12E 172 C7
Montjay-la-Tour *France* 48°54N 2°40E 134 A4
Montjuïc *Spain* 41°22N 2°10E 114 A2
Montjuïc, Parc de *Barcelona, Spain* 114 c1
Montluçon *France* 46°22N 2°36E 173 F9
Montmagny *Canada* 46°58N 70°34W 299 C5
Montmarault *France* 46°19N 2°57E 173 F9
Montmartre *Canada* 50°14N 103°27W 297 C8
Montmédy *France* 49°30N 5°20E 173 C12
Montmélian *France* 45°30N 6°4E 175 C10
Montmirail *France* 48°51N 3°30E 173 D10
Montmoreau-St-Cybard *France* 45°23N 0°8E 174 C4
Montmorillon *France* 46°26N 0°50E 174 B4
Montmort-Lucy *France* 48°55N 3°49E 173 D10
Monto *Australia* 24°52S 151°6E 280 C5
Montoire-sur-le-Loir *France* 47°45N 0°52E 172 E7
Montongbuwoh *Indonesia* 8°33S 116°4E 231 K19
Montório al Vomano *Italy* 42°35N 13°38E 199 F10
Montoro *Spain* 38°1N 4°27W 195 G6
Montour Falls *U.S.A.* 42°21N 76°51W 312 D8
Montoursville *U.S.A.* 41°15N 76°55W 312 E8
Montparnasse, Gare *Paris, France* 48°50N 2°19E 134 A2
Montpelier *Idaho, U.S.A.* 42°19N 111°18W 304 E8
Montpelier *Ind., U.S.A.* 40°33N 85°17W 311 D11
Montpelier *Ohio, U.S.A.* 41°35N 84°37W 311 C12
Montpelier *Vt., U.S.A.* 44°16N 72°35W 313 B12
Montpellier *France* 43°37N 3°52E 174 E7
Montpezat-de-Quercy *France* 44°15N 1°30E 174 D5
Montpon-Ménestérol *France* 45°0N 0°11E 174 D4
Montréal *Qué., Canada* 45°30N 73°33W 130 A2
Montréal *Aude, France* 43°13N 2°8E 174 E6
Montréal *Gers, France* 43°56N 0°11E 174 E4
Montreal → *Canada* 47°14N 84°39W 298 C3
Montréal, Î. de *Canada* 45°30N 73°40W 130 A2
Montréal, Univ. de *Canada* 45°29N 73°37W 130 B2
Montréal Est *Canada* 45°37N 73°31W 130 A2
Montréal L. *Canada* 54°20N 105°45W 297 C7
Montreal Lake *Canada* 54°3N 105°46W 297 C7
Montréal Nord *Canada* 45°36N 73°36W 130 A2
Montréal Ouest *Canada* 45°27N 73°39W 130 B1
Montréal Trudeau Int. ✕ (YUL) *Canada* 45°28N 73°44W 130 B1
Montredon-Labessonnié *France* 43°45N 2°18E 174 E6
Montrésor *France* 47°10N 1°10E 172 E8
Montret *France* 46°40N 5°7E 173 F12
Montreuil *Pas-de-Calais, France* 50°27N 1°45E 173 B8
Montreuil *Seine-St-Denis, France* 48°51N 2°27E 134 A3
Montreuil-Bellay *France* 47°8N 0°9W 172 E6
Montreux *Switz.* 46°26N 6°55E 179 J2
Montrevel-en-Bresse *France* 46°21N 5°8E 173 F12
Montrichard *France* 47°20N 1°10E 172 E8
Montrose *Angus, U.K.* 56°44N 2°27W 167 E6
Montrose *Colo., U.S.A.* 38°29N 107°53W 304 G10
Montrose *Pa., U.S.A.* 41°50N 75°53W 313 E9
Montrose, L. *U.S.A.* 38°18N 93°50W 310 F3
Montrouge *France* 48°48N 2°18E 134 B2
Monts, Pte. des *Canada* 49°20N 67°12W 299 C6
Montsalvy *France* 44°41N 2°30E 174 D6
Montsant, Serra de *Spain* 41°17N 1°0E 196 D6
Montsauche-les-Settons *France* 47°13N 4°2E 173 E11
Montsec, Serra del *Spain* 42°5N 0°45E 196 C5
Montseny △ *Spain* 41°43N 2°22W 196 D7
Montserrat *B. Aires, Argentina* 34°37S 58°24W 117 B2
Montserrat *Spain* 41°36N 1°49E 196 D6
Montserrat ☒ *W. Indies* 16°40N 62°10W 323 p
Montserrat Hills *Trin. & Tob.* 10°23N 61°21W 323 t
Montuenga *Spain* 41°3N 4°38W 194 D6
Montuiri *Spain* 39°34N 2°59E 206 B3
Montvert-les-Bas *Réunion* 21°19S 55°32E 272 f
Monveda *Dem. Rep. of the Congo* 2°52N 21°30E 264 B4
Monyo *Burma* 17°59N 95°30E 241 L19
Monywa *Burma* 22°7N 95°11E 241 D5
Monza *Italy* 45°35N 9°16E 128 A2
Monze *Zambia* 16°17S 27°29E 269 F2
Monze, C. *Pakistan* 24°47N 66°37E 242 G2
Monzón *Spain* 41°52N 0°10E 196 D5
Monzoro *Italy* 45°27N 9°2E 128 B1
Moóca *Brazil* 23°33S 46°35W 137 B2
Moodyville = North Vancouver *Canada* 49°19N 123°4W 306 A3
Mooers *U.S.A.* 44°58N 73°35W 313 B11
Mooi → *S. Africa* 28°45S 30°34E 271 C5
Mooi River *S. Africa* 29°13S 29°50E 271 C4
Mo'oka *Japan* 36°26N 140°1E 223 A12
Mookgopong *S. Africa* 24°31S 28°44E 271 B4
Moomba *Australia* 28°6S 140°12E 281 A3
Moonachie *U.S.A.* 40°50N 74°2W 132 B1
Moonah → *Australia* 22°3S 138°33E 280 C2
Moonda, L. *Australia* 25°52S 140°25E 280 D3
Moonee Ponds *Australia* 37°45S 144°53E 128 A1
Moonee Valley Racecourse *Australia* 37°45S 144°55E 128 A1
Moonie *Australia* 27°46S 150°20E 281 D5
Moonie → *Australia* 29°19S 148°43E 281 D4
Moonta *Australia* 34°6S 137°32E 282 C2
Moora *Australia* 30°37S 115°58E 279 F2
Moorcroft *U.S.A.* 44°16N 104°57W 304 D11
Moore → *Australia* 31°22S 115°30E 279 F2
Moore, L. *Australia* 29°50S 117°35E 279 E2
Moore Falls *Canada* 44°48N 78°48W 312 B6
Moore Haven *U.S.A.* 26°50N 81°6W 317 J8
Moore Park *Australia* 24°43S 152°17E 280 C5
Moore Res. *U.S.A.* 44°20N 71°53W 313 B13
Moore River △ *Australia* 31°7S 115°39E 279 F2
Moorea *French Polynesia* 17°30S 149°50W 289 e
Moorefield *U.S.A.* 39°4N 78°58W 309 F14
Mooresville *U.S.A.* 39°37N 86°22W 311 E10
Moorfoot Hills *U.K.* 55°44N 3°8W 167 F5
Moorhead *U.S.A.* 46°53N 96°45W 308 B5
Moorland *U.S.A.* 42°26N 94°18W 310 B2
Moormerland *Germany* 53°20N 7°20E 178 B3
Moornanyah L. *Australia* 33°15S 143°42E 282 B5
Mooroopna *Australia* 36°25S 145°22E 283 D6
Moorpark *U.S.A.* 34°17N 118°53W 307 L8
Moorreesburg *S. Africa* 33°6S 18°38E 270 D2
Moorrinya △ *Australia* 21°42S 144°58E 280 C3
Moosach *Germany* 48°10N 11°30E 131 A2
Moosburg *Germany* 48°27N 11°56E 179 G7
Moose → *Ont., Canada* 51°20N 80°25W 298 B3
Moose → *N.Y., U.S.A.* 43°38N 75°24W 313 C9
Moose Creek *Canada* 45°15N 74°58W 313 A10
Moose Factory *Canada* 51°16N 80°32W 298 B3
Moose Jaw *Canada* 50°24N 105°30W 297 C7
Moose Jaw → *Canada* 50°34N 105°18W 297 C7
Moose Lake *Man., Canada* 53°46N 100°8W 297 C8
Moose Lake *Minn., U.S.A.* 46°27N 92°46W 308 B7
Moose Mountain △ *Canada* 49°48N 102°25W 297 D8
Moose Pass *U.S.A.* 60°29N 149°22W 303 F10
Moosehead L. *U.S.A.* 45°38N 69°40W 309 C19
Mooselookmeguntic L. *U.S.A.* 44°55N 70°49W 313 B14
Moosilauke, Mt. *U.S.A.* 44°3N 71°40W 313 B13
Moosomin *Canada* 50°9N 101°40W 297 C8
Moosonee *Canada* 51°17N 80°39W 298 B3
Moosup *U.S.A.* 41°43N 71°53W 313 E13
Mootwingee △ *Australia* 31°10S 142°30E 282 A5
Mopane *S. Africa* 22°37S 29°52E 271 B4
Mopeia Velha *Mozam.* 17°30S 35°40E 269 F4
Mopipi *Botswana* 21°6S 24°55E 270 B3
Mopoi *C.A.R.* 5°6N 26°54E 268 A2
Mopti *Mali* 14°30N 4°0W 262 C4
Mopti □ *Mali* 14°40N 4°0W 262 C4
Moqatta *Sudan* 14°38N 35°50E 257 E4
Moqor *Afghan.* 32°50N 67°42E 242 C2
Moquegua *Peru* 17°15S 70°46W 330 D3
Moquegua □ *Peru* 16°50S 70°55W 330 D3
Mór *Hungary* 47°25N 18°12E 182 C3
Mora *Cameroon* 11°2N 14°7E 259 F2
Mora *Maharashtra, India* 18°54N 72°55E 130 B2
Móra *Portugal* 38°55N 8°10W 195 G2
Mora *Spain* 39°41N 3°46W 195 F7
Mora *Sweden* 61°2N 14°38E 162 C8
Mora *Minn., U.S.A.* 45°53N 93°18W 308 C7
Mora *N. Mex., U.S.A.* 35°58N 105°20W 305 J11
Móra de Rubielos *Spain* 40°15N 0°45W 196 E4
Móra d'Ebre *Spain* 41°6N 0°38E 196 D5
Móra la Nova *Spain* 41°7N 0°39E 196 D5
Morača → *Montenegro* 42°20N 19°9E 202 D3
Morada Nova *Brazil* 5°7S 38°23W 332 C4
Morada Nova de Minas *Brazil* 18°37S 45°22W 333 E2
Moradabad *India* 28°50N 78°50E 243 E8
Morafenobe *Madag.* 17°50S 44°53E 272 B1
Morąg *Poland* 53°55N 19°56E 184 E6
Moral de Calatrava *Spain* 38°51N 3°33W 195 G7
Moraleda, Canal *Chile* 44°30S 73°30W 336 B2
Moraleja *Spain* 40°6N 6°43W 194 E4
Morales *Bolivar, Colombia* 8°16N 73°51W 328 B3
Morales *Cauca, Colombia* 2°45N 76°38W 328 C2
Moramanga *Madag.* 18°56S 48°12E 272 B2
Moran *Kans., U.S.A.* 37°55N 95°10W 308 G6
Moran *Wyo., U.S.A.* 43°50N 110°31W 304 E8
Moranbah *Australia* 22°1S 148°6E 280 C4
Morané *French Polynesia* 23°10S 137°7W 289 f
Morang = Biratnagar *Nepal* 26°27N 87°17E 243 F12
Moranhat *India* 27°10N 94°50E 241 B5
Morano Cálabro *Italy* 39°50N 16°8E 201 C9
Morant Bay *Jamaica* 17°53N 76°25W 320 a
Morant Cays *Jamaica* 17°22N 76°0W 320 C4
Morant Pt. *Jamaica* 17°55N 76°12W 320 a
Morar *India* 26°14N 78°14E 242 F8
Morar, L. *U.K.* 56°57N 5°40W 167 E3
Moratalaz *Spain* 40°24N 3°39W 127 B2
Moratalla *Spain* 38°14N 1°49W 197 G3
Moratuwa *Sri Lanka* 6°45N 79°55E 245 L4
Morava → *Slovak Rep.* 48°10N 16°59E 181 C9
Moravia *Iowa, U.S.A.* 40°53N 92°49W 310 D4
Moravia *N.Y., U.S.A.* 42°43N 76°25W 313 D8
Moravian Hts. = Českomoravská Vrchovina *Czech Rep.* 49°30N 15°40E 180 B8
Moravica → *Serbia* 43°52N 20°8E 202 C4
Moraviţa *Romania* 45°17N 21°14E 182 E6
Moravská Třebová *Czech Rep.* 49°45N 16°40E 181 B9
Moravské Budějovice *Czech Rep.* 49°4N 15°49E 180 B8
Morawa *Australia* 29°13S 116°0E 279 E2
Morawhanna *Guyana* 8°30N 59°40W 329 B6
Moray □ *U.K.* 57°31N 3°18W 167 D5
Moray Firth *U.K.* 57°40N 3°52W 167 D5
Morbach *Germany* 49°48N 7°6E 179 F3
Morbegno *Italy* 46°8N 9°34E 198 B6
Morbi *India* 22°50N 70°42E 242 H4
Morbihan □ *France* 47°55N 2°50W 172 E4
Mörby *Sweden* 59°23N 18°3E 139 A2
Mörbylånga *Sweden* 56°32N 16°22E 163 H10
Morcenx *France* 44°3N 0°55W 174 D3
Morcone *Italy* 41°20N 14°40E 201 A7
Mordelles *France* 48°5N 1°52W 172 D5
Morden *Man., Canada* 49°15N 98°10W 297 D9
Morden *London, U.K.* 51°24N 0°13W 125 B2
Mordoğan *Turkey* 38°30N 26°37E 205 C8
Mordovian Republic = Mordvinia □ *Russia* 54°20N 44°30E 190 C7
Mordovo *Russia* 52°6N 40°50E 190 D5
Mordvinia □ *Russia* 54°20N 44°30E 190 C7
Mordy *Poland* 52°13N 22°31E 185 F9
Møre og Romsdal □ *Norway* 62°30N 8°0E 164 B4
Moreau → *U.S.A.* 45°18N 100°43W 308 C3
Morebeng *S. Africa* 23°30S 29°55E 271 B4
Morecambe *U.K.* 54°5N 2°52W 168 C5
Morecambe B. *U.K.* 54°7N 3°0W 168 C5
Moree *Australia* 29°28S 149°54E 281 D4
Morée → *France* 48°57N 2°25E 134 A3
Morehead *Papua N. G.* 8°41S 141°41E 286 E1
Morehead *Ky., U.S.A.* 38°11N 83°26W 311 F13
Morehead City *U.S.A.* 34°43N 76°43W 315 D16
Morel → *India* 26°13N 76°36E 242 F7
Moreland *U.S.A.* 33°17N 84°46W 316 B5
Morelia *Mexico* 19°42N 101°7W 318 D4
Morella *Queens., Australia* 23°0S 143°52E 280 C3
Morella *Spain* 40°35N 0°5W 196 E4
Morelos *Mexico* 26°42N 107°40W 318 B3
Morelos □ *Mexico* 18°45N 99°0W 319 D5
Moremi △ *Botswana* 19°18S 23°10E 270 A3
Morena *India* 26°30N 78°4E 242 F8
Morena, Sierra *Spain* 38°20N 4°0W 195 G7
Morenci *U.S.A.* 41°43N 84°13W 311 C12
Moreni *Romania* 44°59N 25°36E 183 F10
Moreno *Bolivia* 11°9S 66°15W 330 C4
Moreno Valley *U.S.A.* 33°56N 117°14W 307 M10
Moreru → *Brazil* 10°10S 59°15W 331 C6
Moresby I. *Canada* 52°30N 131°40W 296 C2
Morestel *France* 45°40N 5°28E 175 C9
Moreton I. *Australia* 27°10S 153°25E 281 D5
Moreton Island △ *Australia* 27°2S 153°24E 281 D5
Moreuil *France* 49°46N 2°30E 173 C9
Morez *France* 46°31N 6°2E 173 F13
Morgan *S. Austral., Australia* 34°2S 139°35E 282 C3
Morgan *Ga., U.S.A.* 31°32N 84°36W 316 D5
Morgan *Utah, U.S.A.* 41°2N 111°41W 304 F8
Morgan City *U.S.A.* 29°42N 91°12W 314 G9
Morgan Hill *U.S.A.* 37°8N 121°39W 306 H5
Morgan Park *U.S.A.* 41°41N 87°38W 119 C3
Morganfield *U.S.A.* 37°41N 87°55W 308 G10
Morganton *U.S.A.* 35°45N 81°41W 315 D14
Morgantown *Ind., U.S.A.* 39°22N 86°16W 311 E10
Morgantown *W. Va., U.S.A.* 39°38N 79°57W 309 F14
Morgenzon *S. Africa* 26°45S 29°36E 271 C4
Morges *Switz.* 46°31N 6°29E 179 J2
Morghak *Iran* 29°7N 57°54E 247 D8
Morgongåva *Sweden* 59°57N 16°58E 162 E10
Morhange *France* 48°55N 6°38E 173 D13
Morhar → *India* 25°29N 85°11E 243 G11
Mori *China* 43°49N 90°11E 217 D12
Mori *Japan* 42°6N 140°35E 220 C10
Moriah *Trin. & Tob.* 11°15N 60°43W 323 s
Moriarty *U.S.A.* 34°59N 106°3W 305 J10
Moribaya *Guinea* 9°53N 9°32W 262 D3
Morice L. *Canada* 53°50N 127°40W 296 C3
Morichal Largo → *Venezuela* 9°27N 62°25W 329 B5
Morichal Viejo *Colombia* 2°13N 70°2W 328 C3
Moriguchi *Japan* 34°43N 135°34E 133 A2
Moriki *Nigeria* 12°52N 6°30E 263 C6
Morinville *Canada* 53°49N 113°41W 296 C6
Morioka *Japan* 39°45N 141°8E 220 E10
Moris *Mexico* 28°10N 108°32W 318 B3
Morisset *Australia* 33°6S 151°30E 283 B9
Morivione *Italy* 45°26N 9°12E 128 B2
Moriyama *Japan* 35°4N 135°59E 223 B7
Morlaàs *France* 43°21N 0°18W 174 E3
Morlaix *France* 48°36N 3°52W 172 D3
Mörlunda *Sweden* 57°19N 15°52E 163 G9
Mormanno *Italy* 39°53N 15°59E 201 C8
Mormant *France* 48°37N 2°52E 173 D9
Mormugao = Marmagao *India* 15°25N 73°56E 245 G1
Morne-à-l'Eau *Guadeloupe* 16°20N 61°27W 322 e
Morne des Esses *Martinique* 14°44N 61°1W 322 j
Morne Diablotins *Dominica* 15°30N 61°24W 323 k
Morne Fendue *Grenada* 12°12N 61°38W 323 q
Morne Raquette *Dominica* 15°27N 61°27W 323 k
Morne Trois Pitons △ *Dominica* 15°22N 61°20W 323 k
Morningside *Gauteng, S. Africa* 26°4S 28°3E 123 A2
Morningside *Edinburgh, U.K.* 55°56N 3°12W 121 B2
Morningside Park *Ont., Canada* 43°47N 79°12W 141 A3
Morningside Park *Fla., U.S.A.* 28°26N 81°24W 133 B2
Mornington *Australia* 38°15S 145°5E 283 E6
Mornington, I. *Chile* 49°50S 75°30W 336 C1
Mornington I. *Australia* 16°30S 139°30E 280 B2
Mornington Peninsula △ *Australia* 38°28S 144°53E 283 E6
Mornos → *Greece* 38°25N 21°50E 204 C3
Moro *Pakistan* 26°40N 68°0E 242 F2
Moro *Sudan* 10°50N 30°9E 257 E3
Moro → *Pakistan* 29°42N 67°22E 242 E2
Moro G. *Phil.* 6°30N 123°0E 233 H4
Morobe *Papua N. G.* 7°49S 147°38E 286 D4
Morobe □ *Papua N. G.* 7°0S 147°0E 286 D4
Morocco *U.S.A.* 40°57N 87°27W 311 D9
Morocco ■ *N. Afr.* 32°0N 5°50W 260 B3
Morococha *Peru* 11°40S 76°5W 330 C2
Morogoro *Tanzania* 6°50S 37°40E 268 D4
Morogoro □ *Tanzania* 8°0S 37°0E 268 D4
Moroleón *Mexico* 20°8N 101°12W 318 C4
Morombe *Madag.* 21°45S 43°22E 272 C1
Moron = Mörong *Phil.* 14°41N 120°16E 232 D3
Morón *Argentina* 34°39S 58°37W 334 C4
Morón *Cuba* 22°8N 78°39W 320 B4
Mörön *Mongolia* 49°38N 100°9E 218 B9
Morón de Almazán *Spain* 41°29N 2°27W 196 D2
Morón de la Frontera *Spain* 37°6N 5°28W 195 H5
Morona → *Peru* 4°40S 77°10W 328 D2
Morona-Santiago □ *Ecuador* 2°30S 78°0W 328 D2
Morondava *Madag.* 20°17S 44°17E 272 C1
Morondo *Ivory C.* 8°57N 6°47W 262 D3
Morong *Phil.* 14°41N 120°16E 232 D3
Morongo Valley *U.S.A.* 34°3N 116°37W 307 L10
Moroni *Comoros Is.* 11°40S 43°16E 272 a
Moroni *Utah, U.S.A.* 39°32N 111°35W 304 G8
Moroni Iconi ✕ (YVA) *Comoros Is.* 11°32S 43°15E 272 a
Moronou *Ivory C.* 6°16N 4°59W 262 D4
Morotai *Indonesia* 2°10N 128°30E 231 D7
Moroto *Uganda* 2°28N 34°42E 268 B3
Moroto, Mt. *Uganda* 2°30N 34°43E 268 B3
Morozov *Bulgaria* 42°30N 25°10E 203 D9
Morozovsk *Russia* 48°25N 41°50E 191 F5
Morpeth *Ont., Canada* 42°23N 81°50W 312 D3
Morpeth *Northumberland, U.K.* 55°10N 1°41W 168 B6
Morphou *Cyprus* 35°12N 32°59E 207 E8
Morphou Bay *Cyprus* 35°15N 32°50E 207 E8
Morrelganj *Bangla.* 22°28N 89°51E 241 D2
Morrilton *U.S.A.* 35°9N 92°44W 314 D8
Morrinhos *Ceará, Brazil* 3°14S 40°7W 332 B3
Morrinhos *Minas Gerais, Brazil* 17°45S 49°10W 333 E2
Morrinsville *N.Z.* 37°40S 175°32E 284 D4
Morris *Man., Canada* 49°25N 97°22W 297 D9
Morris *Ill., U.S.A.* 41°22N 88°26W 311 C8
Morris *Minn., U.S.A.* 45°35N 95°55W 308 C6
Morris *N.Y., U.S.A.* 42°33N 75°15W 313 D9
Morris *Pa., U.S.A.* 41°35N 77°17W 312 E7
Morris, Mt. *Australia* 26°9S 131°4E 279 E5
Morris Jesup, Kap *Greenland* 83°40N 34°0W 154 A7
Morrisburg *Canada* 44°55N 75°7W 313 B9
Morrison *U.S.A.* 41°49N 89°58W 310 C7
Morrisonville *U.S.A.* 39°25N 89°27W 310 E7
Morristown *Ariz., U.S.A.* 33°51N 112°37W 305 K7
Morristown *Ind., U.S.A.* 39°40N 85°42W 311 E11
Morristown *N.J., U.S.A.* 40°48N 74°29W 313 F10
Morristown *N.Y., U.S.A.* 44°35N 75°39W 313 B9
Morristown *Tenn., U.S.A.* 36°13N 83°18W 315 C13
Morrisville *N.Y., U.S.A.* 42°53N 75°35W 313 D9
Morrisville *Pa., U.S.A.* 40°13N 74°47W 313 F10
Morrisville *Vt., U.S.A.* 44°34N 72°36W 313 B12
Morro, Pta. *Chile* 27°6S 71°0W 334 B1
Morro Bay *U.S.A.* 35°22N 120°51W 306 K6
Morro Chico *Chile* 52°2S 71°26W 336 D2
Morro del Jable *Canary Is.* 28°3N 14°23W 153 e2
Morro do Chapéu *Brazil* 11°33S 41°9W 333 D3
Morro do Chapéu = Barão de Cocais *Brazil* 19°56S 43°28W 333 E3
Morro Jable, Pta. de *Canary Is.* 28°2N 14°20W 153 e2
Morro Solar, Cerro *Peru* 12°11S 77°1W 124 C2
Morrocoy △ *Venezuela* 10°48N 68°13W 328 A4
Morros *Brazil* 2°52S 44°3W 332 B3
Morrosquillo, G. de *Colombia* 9°35N 75°40W 320 E4
Morrow *U.S.A.* 39°21N 84°8W 311 E12
Mörrum *Sweden* 56°12N 14°45E 163 H8
Morrumbene *Mozam.* 23°31S 35°16E 271 B6
Mörrumsån → *Sweden* 56°10N 14°45E 163 H8
Mors *Denmark* 56°50N 8°45E 163 H2
Morshansk *Russia* 53°28N 41°50E 190 D5
Morsi *India* 21°21N 78°0E 244 D4
Mörsil *Sweden* 63°19N 13°40E 162 A7
Mortagne → *France* 48°33N 6°27E 173 D13
Mortagne-au-Perche *France* 48°31N 0°33E 172 D7
Mortagne-sur-Gironde *France* 45°28N 0°47W 174 C3
Mortagne-sur-Sèvre *France* 47°0N 0°59W 172 F6
Mortain *France* 48°40N 0°57W 172 D6
Mortara *Italy* 45°15N 8°44E 198 C5
Morteau *France* 47°3N 6°35E 173 E13
Morteros *Argentina* 30°50S 62°0W 334 C3
Mortes, R. das → *Brazil* 11°45S 50°44W 333 D1
Mortlach *Canada* 50°27N 106°4W 297 C7
Mortlake *N.S.W., Australia* 33°50S 151°6E 139 B1
Mortlake *Vic., Australia* 38°5S 142°50E 282 E5
Mortlake *London, U.K.* 51°27N 0°15W 125 B2
Morton *Ill., U.S.A.* 40°37N 89°28W 310 D7
Morton *Tex., U.S.A.* 33°44N 102°46W 314 E3
Morton *Wash., U.S.A.* 46°34N 122°17W 306 D4
Morton △ *Australia* 35°0S 150°12E 283 C9
Morton Grove *U.S.A.* 42°2N 87°46W 119 A2
Moruga *Trin. & Tob.* 10°4N 61°16W 323 t
Moruga → *Trin. & Tob.* 10°5N 61°16W 323 t
Morumbi *Brazil* 23°35S 46°42W 137 B1
Morundah *Australia* 34°57S 146°19E 283 C7
Morung *Sudan* 10°32N 31°3E 266 B3
Moruya *Australia* 35°58S 150°3E 283 C9
Morvan *France* 47°5N 4°3E 173 E11
Morvan △ *France* 47°12N 4°3E 173 E11
Morvant *Trin. & Tob.* 10°40N 61°29W 323 t
Morven *Queens., Australia* 26°22S 147°5E 281 D4
Morven *N.Z.* 44°50S 171°6E 285 E6
Morven *Ga., U.S.A.* 30°57N 83°30W 316 E6
Morvern *U.K.* 56°38N 5°44W 167 E3
Morwell *Australia* 38°10S 146°22E 283 E7
Morwell △ *Australia* 38°14S 146°23E 283 E7
Moryń *Poland* 52°51N 14°22E 185 F1
Morzhovets, Ostrov *Russia* 66°44N 42°35E 186 A7
Morzine *France* 46°11N 6°42E 173 F13
Mosakahiken = Moose Lake *Canada* 53°46N 100°8W 297 C8
Mosalsk *Russia* 54°30N 34°55E 188 E8
Mosbach *Germany* 49°21N 9°9E 179 F5
Mosby *Norway* 58°12N 7°55E 164 F4
Moscavide *Portugal* 38°47N 9°6W 126 A2
Mošćenice *Croatia* 45°17N 14°16E 199 C11
Moschato *Greece* 37°55N 23°40E 112 B2
Mosciano Sant' Ángelo *Italy* 42°42N 13°52E 199 F10
Moscone Convention Center *San Francisco, U.S.A.* 136 c2
Moscos Is. *Burma* 14°0N 97°30E 236 F1
Moscow = Moskva *Russia* 55°45N 37°37E 129 B2
Moscow *Idaho, U.S.A.* 46°44N 117°0W 304 C5
Moscow *Mich., U.S.A.* 42°3N 84°30W 311 B11
Moscow *Pa., U.S.A.* 41°20N 75°31W 313 E9
Moscow Mills *U.S.A.* 38°57N 90°55W 310 F6
Mosel → *Europe* 50°22N 7°36E 173 B14
Moselle = Mosel → *Europe* 50°22N 7°36E 173 B14
Moselle □ *France* 48°59N 6°33E 173 D13
Moses Lake *U.S.A.* 47°8N 119°17W 304 C4
Mosgiel *N.Z.* 45°53S 170°21E 285 F5
Moshaweng → *S. Africa* 26°35S 22°50E 270 C3
Moshchnyy, Ostrov *Russia* 60°1N 27°50E 163 D19
Moshi *Tanzania* 3°22S 37°18E 268 C4
Moshi → *Nigeria* 9°18N 4°38E 263 D5
Moshupa *Botswana* 24°46S 25°29E 270 B4
Mosi-oa-Tunya = Victoria Falls *Zimbabwe* 17°58S 25°52E 269 F2
Mosina *Poland* 52°15N 16°50E 185 F3
Mosite *Dem. Rep. of the Congo* 0°53N 23°40E 264 B4
Mosjøen *Norway* 65°51N 13°12E 160 D15
Moskenesøya *Norway* 67°58N 13°0E 160 C15
Moskenstraumen *Norway* 67°47N 12°45E 160 C15
Moskog *Norway* 61°26N 6°0E 164 C2
Moskva *Russia* 55°45N 37°37E 129 B2
Moskva □ *Russia* 56°20N 37°20E 188 D9
Moskva → *Russia* 55°5N 38°51E 188 E10
Moskvoretskiy *Russia* 55°42N 37°37E 129 B2
Moslavačka Gora *Croatia* 45°40N 16°37E 199 C13
Mosman *Australia* 33°49S 151°15E 139 B2
Moso *Vanuatu* 17°30S 168°15E 287 G6
Mosomane *Botswana* 24°2S 26°19E 270 B4
Mosonmagyaróvár *Hungary* 47°52N 17°18E 182 C2
Mošorin *Serbia* 45°19N 20°4E 182 E5
Mospyne *Ukraine* 47°52N 38°0E 189 J9
Mosqueiro *Brazil* 1°10S 48°28W 332 B2
Mosquera *Colombia* 2°35N 78°24W 328 C2
Mosquero *U.S.A.* 35°47N 103°58W 305 J12
Mosqueruela *Spain* 40°21N 0°27W 196 E4
Mosquitia *Honduras* 15°20N 84°10W 320 C3
Mosquito, Pta. *Venezuela* 10°53N 63°53W 329 a
Mosquito Creek L. *U.S.A.* 41°18N 80°46W 312 E4
Mosquito L. *Canada* 62°35N 103°20W 297 A8
Mosquitos, G. de los *Panama* 9°15N 81°10W 320 E3
Moss *Norway* 59°27N 10°40E 164 F7
Moss Vale *Australia* 34°32S 150°25E 283 C9
Mossaka *Congo* 1°15S 16°45E 264 C3
Mossâmedes *Brazil* 16°7S 50°11W 333 E1
Mossbank *Canada* 49°56N 105°56W 297 D7
Mossburn *N.Z.* 45°41S 168°15E 285 F3
Mosselbaai *S. Africa* 34°11S 22°8E 270 D3
Mossendjo *Congo* 2°55S 12°42E 264 C2
Mossfellsbær *Iceland* 64°11N 21°45W 155 C5
Mossgiel *Australia* 33°15S 144°5E 282 B6
Mossingen *Germany* 48°24N 9°4E 179 G5
Mossman *Australia* 16°21S 145°15E 280 B4
Mossoró *Brazil* 5°10S 37°15W 332 C4
Mossuril *Mozam.* 14°58S 40°42E 269 E5
Mossy Head *U.S.A.* 30°45N 86°19W 317 E3
Mossy Point *Australia* 35°50S 150°11E 283 C9
Most *Czech Rep.* 50°31N 13°38E 180 A6
Mosta *Malta* 35°55N 14°26E 206 F7
Mostaganem *Algeria* 35°54N 0°5E 261 A5
Mostaganem □ *Algeria* 35°40N 0°15E 261 A5
Mostar *Bos.-H.* 43°22N 17°50E 182 G2
Mostardas *Brazil* 31°2S 50°51W 335 C5
Mostefa, Rass *Tunisia* 36°55N 11°3E 258 A2
Mosteiros *Azores* 37°53N 25°49W 153 d3
Mosterhamn *Norway* 59°42N 5°21E 164 E2
Mostiska = Mostyska *Ukraine* 49°48N 23°4E 185 J10
Móstoles *Spain* 40°19N 3°53W 194 E7
Mosty = Masty *Belarus* 53°27N 24°38E 177 B13
Mostyska *Ukraine* 49°48N 23°4E 185 J10
Mosul = Al Mawşil *Iraq* 36°15N 43°5E 213 D10
Mosvatnet *Norway* 59°52N 8°5E 164 E5
Mota *Ethiopia* 11°5N 37°52E 257 E4
Mota *Vanuatu* 13°49S 167°42E 287 C5
Mota del Cuervo *Spain* 39°30N 2°52W 197 F2
Mota del Marqués *Spain* 41°38N 5°11W 194 D5
Mota Lava *Vanuatu* 13°40S 167°40E 287 C5
Motaba *Congo* 2°6N 18°2E 264 B3
Motagua → *Guatemala* 15°44N 88°14W 320 C2
Motala *Sweden* 58°32N 15°1E 163 F9
Motaze *Mozam.* 24°48S 32°52E 271 B5
Moţca *Romania* 47°15N 26°37E 183 C11
Motegi *Japan* 36°32N 140°11E 223 A12
Moth *India* 25°43N 78°57E 243 G8
Motherwell *U.K.* 55°47N 3°58W 167 F5
Moti Bagh *India* 28°33N 77°10E 120 B2
Motihari *India* 26°30N 84°55E 243 F11
Motilla del Palancar *Spain* 39°34N 1°55W 197 F3
Motiti I. *N.Z.* 37°38S 176°25E 284 D5
Motnik *Slovenia* 46°14N 14°54E 199 B11
Motobu *Japan* 26°39N 127°53E 288 a
Motocurunya *Venezuela* 4°24N 64°5W 329 C5
Motol *Czech Rep.* 50°3N 14°21E 135 B2
Motovun *Croatia* 45°20N 13°50E 199 C10
Motozintla de Mendoza *Mexico* 15°22N 92°14W 319 D6
Motril *Spain* 36°31N 3°37W 195 J7
Motru *Romania* 44°48N 22°59E 182 F7
Motru → *Romania* 44°32N 23°31E 183 F8
Motsa *Israel* 31°47N 35°9E 123 B2
Motsa Ilit *Israel* 31°48N 35°9E 123 B1
Motspur Park *U.K.* 51°23N 0°14W 125 B2
Mott *U.S.A.* 46°23N 102°20W 308 B2
Mottingham *U.K.* 51°26N 0°1E 125 B4
Möttling = Metlika *Slovenia* 45°40N 15°20E 199 C12
Móttola *Italy* 40°38N 17°2E 201 B10
Motu → *N.Z.* 37°52S 177°36E 284 D6
Motu Nui *Chile* 27°12S 109°28W 330 b
Motu Tapu *Cook Is.* 21°14S 159°43W 289 h
Motuba *Dem. Rep. of the Congo* 2°20N 18°34E 264 B3
Motueka *N.Z.* 41°7S 173°1E 285 B8
Motueka → *N.Z.* 41°5S 173°1E 285 B8
Motul *Mexico* 21°6N 89°17W 319 C7
Motupena Pt. *Papua N. G.* 6°30S 155°10E 286 D8
Mou *N. Cal.* 21°5S 167°26E 288 d
Mouanda *Gabon* 1°28S 13°7E 264 C2
Mouchalagane → *Canada* 50°56N 68°41W 299 B6
Mouchoir Bank *W. Indies* 20°57N 70°47W 321 B5
Mouding *China* 25°20N 101°28E 222 E3
Moudjeria *Mauritania* 17°50N 12°28W 262 B2
Moudon *Switz.* 46°40N 6°49E 179 J2
Moudros *Greece* 39°50N 25°18E 205 B7
Mougins *France* 43°36N 7°0E 175 E10
Mougoundou *Congo* 2°40S 12°41E 264 C2
Mouhoun = Black Volta → *Africa* 8°41N 1°33W 262 D4
Mouila *Gabon* 1°50S 11°0E 264 C2
Mouka *C.A.R.* 7°16N 21°52E 264 A4
Moukalaba △ *Gabon* 2°50S 10°35E 264 C2
Moukambo *Gabon* 3°5S 11°28E 264 C2
Moul *Niger* 15°5N 13°11E 259 F2
Moulamein *Australia* 35°3S 144°1E 282 C6
Moule à Chique, C. *St. Lucia* 13°43N 60°57W 323 m
Moulhoulé *Djibouti* 12°35N 43°5E 267 B5
Mouliana *Greece* 35°10N 25°59E 207 E6
Moulin Rouge *Paris, France* 134 a3
Moulins *France* 46°35N 3°19E 173 F10
Moulmein *Burma* 16°30N 97°40E 241 G6
Moulouya, O. → *Morocco* 35°5N 2°25W 261 A4
Moulton *U.S.A.* 40°41N 92°41W 310 D4
Moultrie *U.S.A.* 31°11N 83°47W 316 D6
Moultrie, L. *U.S.A.* 33°20N 80°5W 316 B9
Mounana *Gabon* 1°18S 13°13E 264 C2
Mound City *Mo., U.S.A.* 40°7N 95°14W 310 D1
Mound City *S. Dak., U.S.A.* 45°44N 100°4W 308 C3
Moundou *Chad* 8°40N 16°10E 259 G3
Moundsville *U.S.A.* 39°55N 80°44W 312 G4
Mounembé *Congo* 3°20S 12°32E 264 C2
Moung *Cambodia* 12°46N 103°27E 236 F4
Moungoudi *Congo* 2°45S 11°46E 264 C2
Mount Airy *U.S.A.* 36°31N 80°37W 315 C14
Mount Albert *Canada* 44°8N 79°19W 312 B5
Mount Apo △ *Phil.* 7°0N 125°10E 233 H5
Mount Arayat △ *Phil.* 15°39N 120°44E 232 D3
Mount Aspiring △ *N.Z.* 44°19S 168°47E 285 E3
Mount Ayliff = Maxesibeni *S. Africa* 30°49S 29°23E 271 D4
Mount Ayr *U.S.A.* 40°43N 94°14W 310 D2
Mount Barker *S. Austral., Australia* 35°5S 138°52E 282 C3
Mount Barker *W. Austral., Australia* 34°38S 117°40E 279 F2
Mount Barnett Roadhouse *Australia* 16°39S 125°57E 278 C4
Mount Beauty *Australia* 36°47S 147°10E 283 D7
Mount Brydges *Canada* 42°54N 81°29W 312 D3
Mount Buffalo △ *Australia* 36°43S 146°46E 283 D7
Mount Burr *Australia* 37°34S 140°26E 281 F3
Mount Carmel = Ha Karmel △ *Israel* 32°45N 35°5E 250 F6
Mount Carmel *Ill., U.S.A.* 38°25N 87°46W 311 F9
Mount Carmel *Pa., U.S.A.* 40°47N 76°26W 313 F8
Mount Carroll *U.S.A.* 42°6N 89°59W 310 B7
Mount Clemens *U.S.A.* 42°35N 82°53W 312 D2
Mount Cook *N.Z.* 43°44S 170°5E 285 D5
Mount Cook △ *N.Z.* 43°35S 170°15E 285 D5
Mount Coolon *Australia* 21°25S 147°25E 280 C4
Mount Darwin *Zimbabwe* 16°47S 31°38E 269 F3
Mount Dennis *Canada* 43°40N 79°28W 141 A2
Mount Desert I. *U.S.A.* 44°21N 68°20W 309 C19
Mount Dora *U.S.A.* 28°48N 81°38W 317 G8
Mount Ebenezer *Australia* 25°6S 132°34E 279 E5
Mount Eccles △ *Australia* 38°5S 141°54E 282 E4
Mount Eden *U.S.A.* 38°3N 85°9W 311 F11
Mount Edziza △ *Canada* 57°30N 130°45W 296 B2
Mount Elgon △ *E. Afr.* 1°4N 34°42E 268 B3
Mount Field △ *Australia* 42°39S 146°35E 281 G4
Mount Fletcher *S. Africa* 30°40S 28°30E 271 D4
Mount Forest *Canada* 43°59N 80°43W 312 C4
Mount Frankland △ *Australia* 31°47S 116°37E 279 F2
Mount Frederick ✪ *Australia* 19°39S 129°18E 278 C4
Mount Frere = Kwabhaca *S. Africa* 30°51S 29°0E 271 D4
Mount Gambier *Australia* 37°50S 140°46E 282 D4
Mount Garnet *Australia* 17°37S 145°6E 280 B4
Mount Greenwood *U.S.A.* 41°42N 87°42W 119 C2
Mount Hagen *Papua N. G.* 5°52S 144°16E 286 C3
Mount Hamiguitan △ *Phil.* 6°44N 126°10E 233 H6
Mount Holly *U.S.A.* 39°59N 74°47W 313 G10
Mount Holly Springs *U.S.A.* 40°7N 77°12W 312 F7
Mount Hood Memorial Park △ *U.S.A.* 42°26N 71°1W 116 A2
Mount Hope *N.S.W., Australia* 32°51S 145°51E 283 B6
Mount Hope *S. Austral., Australia* 34°7S 135°23E 281 E2
Mount Horeb *U.S.A.* 43°1N 89°44W 310 B7
Mount Iglit-Mount Baco △ *Phil.* 12°45N 121°8E 232 E3
Mount Isa *Australia* 20°42S 139°26E 280 C2
Mount Isarog △ *Phil.* 13°38N 123°24E 232 E4
Mount James ✪ *Australia* 24°51S 116°54E 279 D2
Mount Jewett *U.S.A.* 41°44N 78°39W 312 E6
Mount Ka'ala Nat. Area Reserve △ *U.S.A.* 21°31N 158°7W 302 J13
Mount Kaputar △ *Australia* 30°16S 150°10E 281 E5
Mount Kenya △ *Kenya* 0°7S 37°21E 268 C4
Mount Kisco *U.S.A.* 41°12N 73°44W 313 E11
Mount Laguna *U.S.A.* 32°52N 116°25W 307 N10
Mount Larcom *Australia* 23°48S 150°59E 280 C5
Mount Lofty Ranges *Australia* 34°35S 139°5E 282 C3
Mount McKinley = Denali △ *U.S.A.* 63°30N 152°0W 303 E10
Mount Magnet *Australia* 28°2S 117°47E 279 E2
Mount Malindang △ *Phil.* 8°17N 123°32E 233 G4
Mount Manara *Australia* 32°29S 143°58E 282 B5
Mount Maunganui *N.Z.* 37°40S 176°14E 284 D5
Mount Merrion *Ireland* 53°18N 6°12W 120 B2
Mount Molloy *Australia* 16°42S 145°20E 280 B4
Mount Morgan *Australia* 23°40S 150°25E 280 C5
Mount Morris *Mich., U.S.A.* 43°7N 83°42W 311 A13
Mount Morris *N.Y., U.S.A.* 42°44N 77°52W 312 D7
Mount Olive *U.S.A.* 39°4N 89°44W 310 E7
Mount Olivet *U.S.A.* 38°32N 84°2W 311 F12
Mount Olympus *U.S.A.* 34°7N 118°21W 126 B2
Mount Orab *U.S.A.* 39°2N 83°55W 311 E13
Mount Pearl *Canada* 47°31N 52°47W 299 C9
Mount Penn *U.S.A.* 40°20N 75°54W 313 F9
Mount Perry *Australia* 25°13S 151°42E 281 D5
Mount Pleasant *Iowa, U.S.A.* 40°58N 91°33W 310 D5
Mount Pleasant *Mich., U.S.A.* 43°36N 84°46W 309 D11
Mount Pleasant *Pa., U.S.A.* 40°9N 79°33W 312 F5
Mount Pleasant *S.C., U.S.A.* 32°47N 79°52W 316 C10
Mount Pleasant *Tenn., U.S.A.* 35°32N 87°12W 315 D11
Mount Pleasant *Tex., U.S.A.* 33°9N 94°58W 314 E7
Mount Pleasant *Utah, U.S.A.* 39°33N 111°27W 304 G8
Mount Pleasant ✕ (MPN) *Falk. Is.* 51°49S 58°23W 153 f
Mount Pocono *U.S.A.* 41°7N 75°22W 313 E9
Mount Pulaski *U.S.A.* 40°1N 89°17W 310 D7
Mount Pulog △ *Phil.* 16°35N 120°57E 232 C3
Mount Rainier *U.S.A.* 38°56N 76°57W 143 B3
Mount Rainier △ *U.S.A.* 46°55N 121°50W 306 D5
Mount Remarkable △ *Australia* 32°47S 138°3E 282 B3
Mount Revelstoke △ *Canada* 51°5N 118°30W 296 C5
Mount Robson △ *Canada* 53°0N 119°0W 296 C5
Mount St. Helens △ *U.S.A.* 46°14N 122°11W 306 D4
Mount Selinda *Zimbabwe* 20°24S 32°43E 271 B5
Mount Shasta *U.S.A.* 41°19N 122°19W 304 F2
Mount Signal *U.S.A.* 32°39N 115°37W 307 N11
Mount Somers *N.Z.* 43°45S 171°27E 285 D6
Mount Sterling *Ill., U.S.A.* 39°59N 90°45W 310 E6
Mount Sterling *Ky., U.S.A.* 38°4N 83°56W 311 F13
Mount Sterling *Ohio, U.S.A.* 39°43N 83°16W 311 E13
Mount Surprise *Australia* 18°10S 144°17E 280 B3
Mount Union *U.S.A.* 40°23N 77°53W 312 F7
Mount Upton *U.S.A.* 42°26N 75°23W 313 D9
Mount Vernon *Australia* 32°11N 82°36W 316 C7
Mount Vernon *Ill., U.S.A.* 38°19N 88°55W 310 F8
Mount Vernon *Ind., U.S.A.* 37°56N 87°54W 311 G9
Mount Vernon *Iowa, U.S.A.* 41°55N 91°23W 310 C5
Mount Vernon *N.Y., U.S.A.* 40°54N 73°49W 132 A3
Mount Vernon *Ohio, U.S.A.* 40°23N 82°29W 312 F2
Mount Vernon *Wash., U.S.A.* 48°25N 122°20W 306 B4

**Mount Vernon Square** *Washington, D.C., U.S.A.* **143** a2
**Mount Victor** *Australia* 32°11S 139°44E **282** B3
**Mount Washington** *U.S.A.* 39°5N 84°24W **311** F11
**Mount Wellington** *N.Z.* 36°55S 174°52E **284** C3
**Mount William △** *Australia* 40°56S 148°14E **281** G4
**Mount Wynne** *St. Vincent* 13°14N 61°16W **323** n
**Mount Zion = Har Tsiyon** *Jerusalem* **123** b3
**Mount Zion** *U.S.A.* 39°46N 88°53W **311** E8
**Mounta, Akra** *Greece* 38°3N 20°47E **207** C2
**Mountain □** *Phil.* 17°20N 121°10E **232** C3
**Mountain Ash** *U.K.* 51°40N 3°23W **169** F4
**Mountain Center** *U.S.A.* 33°42N 116°44W **307** M10
**Mountain City** *Nev., U.S.A.* 41°50N 115°58W **304** F6
**Mountain City** *Tenn., U.S.A.* 36°29N 81°48W **315** C14
**Mountain Dale** *U.S.A.* 41°41N 74°32W **313** E10
**Mountain Grove** *U.S.A.* 37°8N 92°16W **308** G7
**Mountain Home** *Ark., U.S.A.* 36°20N 92°23W **314** C8
**Mountain Home** *Idaho, U.S.A.* 43°8N 115°41W **304** E6
**Mountain Iron** *U.S.A.* 47°32N 92°37W **308** B7
**Mountain Pass** *U.S.A.* 35°29N 115°35W **307** K11
**Mountain View** *Ark., U.S.A.* 35°52N 92°7W **314** D8
**Mountain View** *Calif., U.S.A.* 37°23N 122°5W **306** H4
**Mountain View** *Hawai'i, U.S.A.* 19°33N 155°7W **302** D6
**Mountain Village** *U.S.A.* 62°5N 163°43W **303** E7
**Mountain Zebra △** *S. Africa* 32°14S 25°27E **270** D4
**Mountainair** *U.S.A.* 34°31N 106°15W **305** J10
**Mountbellew** *Ireland* 53°28N 8°31W **166** C3
**Mountlake Terrace** *U.S.A.* 47°47N 122°18W **306** C4
**Mountmellick** *Ireland* 53°7N 7°20W **166** C4
**Mountrath** *Ireland* 53°0N 7°28W **166** D4
**Moura** *Queens., Australia* 24°35S 149°58E **280** C4
**Moura** *Brazil* 1°32S 61°38W **329** D5
**Moura** *Portugal* 38°7N 7°30W **195** G3
**Mourão** *Portugal* 38°22N 7°22W **195** G3
**Mourdi, Dépression du** *Chad* 18°10N 23°0E **259** E4
**Mourdiah** *Mali* 14°35N 7°25W **262** C3
**Mourenx** *France* 43°22N 0°38W **174** E3
**Mouri** *Ghana* 5°6N 1°14W **263** D4
**Mourilyan** *Australia* 17°35S 146°3E **280** B4
**Mourmelon-le-Grand** *France* 49°8N 4°22E **173** C11
**Mourne →** *U.K.* 54°52N 7°26W **166** B4
**Mourne Mts.** *U.K.* 54°10N 6°0W **166** B5
**Mournies** *Greece* 35°29N 24°1E **207** E5
**Mouscron** *Belgium* 50°45N 3°12E **170** D3
**Mousgougou** *Chad* 10°47N 16°9E **259** F3
**Moussa 'Ali** *Djibouti* 12°27N 42°24E **267** B5
**Moussoro** *Chad* 13°41N 16°35E **259** F3
**Moustique, Morne** *Guadeloupe* 16°7N 61°44W **322** e
**Mouthe** *France* 46°44N 6°12E **173** F13
**Moutier** *Switz.* 47°16N 7°21E **179** H3
**Moûtiers** *France* 45°29N 6°32E **175** C10
**Moutong** *Indonesia* 0°28N 121°13E **231** D6
**Mouy** *France* 49°18N 2°20E **173** C9
**Mouydir, Monts du** *Algeria* 25°30N 4°10E **261** C5
**Mouyondzi** *Congo* 4°1S 13°59E **264** C2
**Mouzaki** *Greece* 39°25N 21°37E **204** B3
**Mouzarak** *Chad* 13°17N 15°58E **259** F3
**Mouzon** *France* 49°36N 5°3E **173** C12
**Movas** *Mexico* 28°10N 109°25W **318** B3
**Moville** *Ireland* 55°11N 7°3W **166** A4
**Mowandjum** *Australia* 17°22S 123°40E **278** C3
**Moweaqua** *U.S.A.* 39°38N 89°1W **310** E7
**Moxico □** *Angola* 12°0S 20°30E **265** E4
**Moxotó →** *Brazil* 9°19S 38°14W **332** C4
**Moy →** *Ireland* 54°8N 9°8W **166** B2
**Moya** *Comoros Is.* 12°18S 44°18E **272** a
**Moyale** *Ethiopia* 3°34N 39°5E **266** D4
**Moyale** *Kenya* 3°30N 39°4E **257** G4
**Moyamba** *S. Leone* 8°4N 12°30W **262** D2
**Moyen Atlas** *Morocco* 33°0N 5°0W **260** B4
**Moyen-Cavally □** *Ivory C.* 6°45N 7°30W **262** D3
**Moyen-Chari □** *Chad* 9°0N 18°0E **259** G3
**Moyen-Comoé □** *Ivory C.* 6°40N 3°25W **262** D4
**Moyen-Ogooué □** *Gabon* 0°30S 11°0E **264** C2
**Moyo** *Indonesia* 8°10S 117°40E **235** D5
**Moyobamba** *Peru* 6°0S 77°0W **330** B2
**Moyowosi △** *Tanzania* 3°50S 31°0E **268** C3
**Møysalen △** *Norway* 68°32N 15°29E **160** B16
**Moyto** *Chad* 12°35N 16°33E **259** F3
**Moyu** *China* 37°15N 79°44E **217** E9
**Moyyero →** *Russia* 68°44N 103°42E **215** C11
**Moyynqum** *Zhambyl, Kazakhstan* 44°17N 72°57E **217** D8
**Moyynqum** *Zhambyl, Kazakhstan* 44°12N 71°0E **217** D8
**Moyynty** *Kazakhstan* 47°10N 73°18E **217** C8
**Mozambique = Moçambique** *Mozam.* 15°3S 40°42E **269** F5
**Mozambique ■** *Africa* 19°0S 35°0E **269** F4
**Mozambique Basin** *Ind. Oc.* 30°0S 40°0E **273** G2
**Mozambique Chan.** *Africa* 17°30S 42°30E **271** A7
**Mozarthaus** *Vienna, Austria* **142** b2
**Mozdok** *Russia* 43°45N 44°48E **191** J7
**Mozdūrān** *Iran* 36°9N 60°35E **247** B9
**Mozhaysk** *Russia* 55°30N 36°2E **188** E9
**Mozhga** *Russia* 56°26N 52°15E **190** B11
**Mozhnābād** *Iran* 34°7N 60°6E **247** C9
**Mozirje** *Slovenia* 46°22N 14°58E **199** B11
**Mozyr = Mazyr** *Belarus* 51°59N 29°15E **177** B15
**Mpanda** *Tanzania* 6°23S 31°1E **268** D3
**Mpé** *Congo* 2°58S 14°38E **264** C2
**Mpese** *Dem. Rep. of the Congo* 5°16S 15°30E **265** D3
**Mpésoba** *Mali* 12°31N 5°39W **262** C3
**Mphoeng** *Zimbabwe* 21°10S 27°51E **269** G2
**Mpika** *Zambia* 11°51S 31°25E **269** E3
**Mpoko →** *C.A.R.* 4°19N 18°33E **264** B3
**Mpouya** *Congo* 2°38S 16°13E **264** C3
**Mpulungu** *Zambia* 8°51S 31°5E **269** D3
**Mpumalanga** *S. Africa* 29°50S 30°33E **271** C5
**Mpumalanga □** *S. Africa* 26°0S 30°0E **271** C5
**Mpwapwa** *Tanzania* 6°23S 36°30E **268** D4
**Mqabba** *Malta* 35°51N 14°28E **206** F7
**Mqanduli** *S. Africa* 31°49S 28°45E **271** D4
**Mqinvartsveri = Kazbek** *Russia* 42°42N 44°30E **191** J7
**Mragowo** *Poland* 53°52N 21°18E **184** E8
**M'ramani** *Comoros Is.* 12°20S 44°31E **272** a
**Mramor** *Serbia* 43°20N 21°45E **202** C5
**Mrauk-u = Myohaung** *Burma* 20°35N 93°11E **241** E4
**Mrimina** *Morocco* 29°50N 7°9W **260** C3
**Mrkonjić Grad** *Bos.-H.* 44°26N 17°4E **182** F2
**Mrkopalj** *Croatia* 45°21N 14°52E **199** C11
**Mrocza** *Poland* 53°16N 17°35E **185** E4
**Msaken** *Tunisia* 35°49N 10°33E **258** A2
**Msambansovu** *Zimbabwe* 15°50S 30°3E **269** F3
**Msida** *Malta* 35°54N 14°29E **206** F7
**M'sila** *Algeria* 35°46N 4°30E **261** A5
**M'sila □** *Algeria* 35°20N 4°20E **261** A5
**Msoro** *Zambia* 13°35S 31°50E **269** E3
**Msta →** *Russia* 58°25N 31°20E **188** C6
**Mstislavl = Mstsislaw** *Belarus* 54°0N 31°50E **177** A16
**Mstsislaw** *Belarus* 54°0N 31°50E **177** A16
**Mszana Dolna** *Poland* 49°41N 20°5E **185** J7
**Mszczonów** *Poland* 51°58N 20°33E **185** G7
**Mtama** *Tanzania* 10°17S 39°21E **269** E4
**Mtamvuna = Mthamvuna →** *S. Africa* 31°6S 30°12E **271** D5
**Mthamvuna →** *S. Africa* 31°6S 30°12E **271** D5
**Mthatha** *S. Africa* 31°36S 28°49E **271** D4
**Mtilikwe →** *Zimbabwe* 21°9S 31°30E **269** G3
**Mtima** *Congo* 3°49S 12°7E **264** C2
**Mtirala △** *Georgia* 41°50N 42°2E **191** K6
**Mtito Andei** *Kenya* 2°41S 38°10E **268** C4
**Mtsamboro** *Mayotte* 12°42S 45°4E **272** b
**Mtsamboro, Î.** *Mayotte* 12°38S 45°2E **272** b
**Mtsangamouji** *Mayotte* 12°45S 45°5E **272** b
**Mtsapéré** *Mayotte* 12°46S 45°11E **272** b
**Mtsensk** *Russia* 53°17N 36°36E **188** F9
**Mtskheta** *Georgia* 41°52N 44°45E **191** K7
**Mtubatuba** *S. Africa* 28°30S 32°8E **271** C5
**Mtwalume** *S. Africa* 30°30S 30°38E **271** D5
**Mtwara-Mikindani** *Tanzania* 10°20S 40°20E **269** E5
**Mu →** *Burma* 21°56N 95°38E **241** E5
**Mu Gia, Deo** *Vietnam* 17°40N 105°47E **236** D5
**Mu Ko Chang △** *Thailand* 11°59N 102°22E **237** G4
**Mu Ko Surin** *Thailand* 9°30N 97°55E **237** H1
**Mu-se** *Burma* 23°59N 97°54E **241** D6
**Mu Us Shamo** *China* 39°0N 109°0E **226** E5
**Muacandala** *Angola* 10°2S 19°40E **265** E3
**Muan** *S. Korea* 34°59N 126°28E **224** E3
**Muaná** *Brazil* 1°25S 49°15W **332** B2
**Muanda** *Dem. Rep. of the Congo* 6°0S 12°20E **265** D2
**Muang Beng** *Laos* 20°23N 101°46E **228** G3
**Muang Chiang Rai = Chiang Rai** *Thailand* 19°52N 99°50E **228** H2
**Muang Et** *Laos* 20°49N 104°1E **236** B5
**Muang Hiam** *Laos* 20°5N 103°22E **236** B4
**Muang Hongsa** *Laos* 19°43N 101°20E **236** C3
**Muang Houn** *Laos* 20°8N 101°23E **228** G3
**Muang Kau** *Laos* 15°6N 105°47E **236** E5
**Muang Khao** *Laos* 19°38N 103°32E **236** C4
**Muang Khong** *Laos* 14°7N 105°51E **236** E5
**Muang Khoua** *Laos* 21°5N 102°31E **228** G4
**Muang Liap** *Laos* 18°29N 101°40E **236** C3
**Muang Mai** *Thailand* 8°5N 98°21E **237** a
**Muang May** *Laos* 14°49N 106°56E **236** E6
**Muang Na Mo** *Laos* 21°3N 101°49E **228** G3
**Muang Ngeun** *Laos* 20°36N 101°3E **228** G3
**Muang Ngoi** *Laos* 20°43N 102°41E **228** G4
**Muang Nong** *Laos* 16°22N 106°30E **236** D6
**Muang Ou Neua** *Laos* 22°18N 101°48E **228** F3
**Muang Ou Tay** *Laos* 22°7N 101°48E **228** F3
**Muang Pak Beng** *Laos* 19°54N 101°8E **228** H3
**Muang Phalane** *Laos* 16°39N 105°34E **236** D5
**Muang Phiang** *Laos* 19°6N 101°32E **236** C3
**Muang Phine** *Laos* 16°32N 106°2E **236** D6
**Muang Phonhong** *Laos* 18°30N 102°25E **236** C4
**Muang Saiapoun** *Laos* 18°24N 101°31E **236** C3
**Muang Sing** *Laos* 21°11N 101°9E **228** G3
**Muang Son** *Laos* 20°27N 103°19E **236** B4
**Muang Soui** *Laos* 19°33N 102°52E **236** C4
**Muang Va** *Laos* 21°53N 102°19E **228** G4
**Muang Va** *Laos* 18°18N 101°20E **236** C3
**Muang Xai** *Laos* 20°42N 101°59E **228** G3
**Muang Xamteu** *Laos* 19°59N 104°38E **236** C5
**Muanga** *Angola* 12°32S 19°55E **265** E3
**Muar** *Malaysia* 2°3N 102°34E **237** L4
**Muara Takus** *Indonesia* 0°20N 100°39E **234** B2
**Muaraaman** *Indonesia* 3°7S 102°12E **234** C2
**Muarabadak** *Indonesia* 0°20S 117°26E **235** C5
**Muarabeliti** *Indonesia* 3°15S 103°1E **234** C2
**Muarabungo** *Indonesia* 1°28S 102°52E **234** C2
**Muaradua** *Indonesia* 4°31S 104°4E **234** C2
**Muaraenim** *Indonesia* 3°40S 103°50E **234** C2
**Muarajambi** *Indonesia* 1°28S 103°40E **234** C2
**Muarajuloi** *Indonesia* 0°12S 114°3E **235** C4
**Muarakaman** *Indonesia* 0°2S 116°45E **235** C5
**Muarakupit** *Indonesia* 2°43S 102°54E **234** C2
**Muaras, Tanjung** *Indonesia* 1°7S 103°51E **234** C2
**Muarasiberut** *Indonesia* 1°35S 99°12E **234** C1
**Muaratebo** *Indonesia* 1°30S 102°26E **234** C2
**Muaratembesi** *Indonesia* 1°42S 103°8E **234** C2
**Muaraeweh** *Indonesia* 0°58S 114°52E **235** C4
**Muarawahau** *Indonesia* 1°1N 116°52E **235** B5
**Mubarakpur** *India* 26°6N 83°18E **243** F10
**Mubarraz = Al Mubarraz** *Si. Arabia* 25°30N 49°40E **247** E6
**Mubende** *Uganda* 0°33N 31°22E **268** B3
**Mubi** *Nigeria* 10°18N 13°16E **263** C7
**Mucaba, Sa. de** *Angola* 7°12S 15°0E **265** D3
**Mucajá** *Brazil* 3°57S 57°50W **329** D6
**Mucajaí →** *Brazil* 2°25N 60°52W **329** C5
**Mucajaí, Serra do** *Brazil* 2°23N 61°10W **329** C5
**Mucari** *Angola* 9°30S 16°54E **265** D3
**Muchachos, Roque de los** *Canary Is.* 28°44N 17°52W **153** e1
**Mücheln** *Germany* 51°17N 11°47E **178** D7
**Muchinga □** *Zambia* 12°0S 31°30E **269** E3
**Muchinga Mts.** *Zambia* 11°30S 31°30E **269** E3
**Muchkapskiy** *Russia* 51°52N 42°28E **190** E6
**Muchuan** *China* 28°57N 103°55E **228** C4
**Muck** *U.K.* 56°50N 6°15W **167** E2
**Muckadilla** *Australia* 26°35S 148°23E **281** D4
**Muckalee Cr. →** *U.S.A.* 31°38N 84°9W **316** D5
**Muckaty ✪** *Australia* 18°37S 133°52E **280** B1
**Muckle Flugga** *U.K.* 60°51N 0°54W **167** A8
**Muco →** *Colombia* 4°15N 70°21W **328** C3
**Mucoma** *Angola* 15°18S 13°39E **265** F2
**Muconda** *Angola* 10°31S 21°15E **265** E4
**Mucope** *Angola* 16°24S 14°52E **265** F2
**Mucuguê** *Brazil* 13°0S 41°23W **333** D3
**Mucuim →** *Brazil* 6°33S 64°18W **331** B5
**Mucur** *Turkey* 39°3N 34°22E **212** C6
**Mucura** *Brazil* 2°31S 62°43W **329** D5
**Mucuri** *Brazil* 18°0S 39°36W **333** E4
**Mucurici** *Brazil* 18°6S 40°31W **333** E3
**Mucusso** *Angola* 18°1S 21°25E **265** F4
**Mucusso △** *Angola* 17°27S 21°0E **265** F4
**Mucussueje** *Angola* 11°1S 21°56E **265** E4
**Muda** *Canary Is.* 28°34N 13°57W **153** e2
**Mudanjiang** *China* 44°38N 129°30E **227** B15
**Mudanya** *Turkey* 40°25N 28°50E **203** F12
**Muddebihal** *India* 16°20N 76°8E **245** F3
**Muddus △** *Sweden* 66°58N 20°15E **160** C19
**Muddy Cr. →** *U.S.A.* 38°24N 110°42W **304** G8
**Mudgee** *Australia* 32°32S 149°31E **283** B8
**Mudhol** *Andhra Pradesh, India* 18°58N 77°55E **244** E3
**Mudhol** *Karnataka, India* 16°21N 75°17E **245** F2
**Mudiatta** *Dem. Rep. of the Congo* 7°15S 22°1E **265** D4
**Mudigere** *India* 13°8N 75°38E **245** H2
**Mūdīyah** *Yemen* 13°56N 46°57E **248** D4
**Mudjatik →** *Canada* 56°1N 107°36W **297** B7
**Mudon** *Burma* 16°15N 97°44E **241** G6
**Mudug □** *Somalia* 7°0N 48°0E **267** C6
**Mudukulattur** *India* 9°21N 78°31E **245** K4
**Mudumu △** *Namibia* 18°5S 23°29E **270** A3
**Mudurnu** *Turkey* 40°27N 31°12E **212** B4
**Muecate** *Mozam.* 14°55S 39°40E **269** E4
**Mueda** *Mozam.* 11°36S 39°28E **269** E4
**Mueller Ranges** *Australia* 18°18S 126°46E **278** C4
**Muende** *Mozam.* 14°28S 33°0E **269** E3
**Muerto, Mar** *Mexico* 16°10N 94°10W **319** D6
**Mufu Shan** *China* 29°20N 114°30E **229** C10
**Mufulira** *Zambia* 12°32S 28°15E **269** E2
**Mufuma** *Angola* 9°12S 16°29E **265** D3
**Mufumbiro Range** *Africa* 1°25S 29°30E **268** C2
**Mugardos** *Spain* 43°27N 8°15W **194** B2
**Muge →** *Portugal* 39°8N 8°44W **195** F2
**Müggelberge** *Germany* 52°25N 13°37E **115** B4
**Müggelheim** *Germany* 52°24N 13°40E **115** B5
**Múggia** *Italy* 45°36N 13°46E **199** C10
**Muggiò** *Italy* 45°35N 9°13E **128** A2
**Mughal Gardens** *Delhi, India* **120** c1
**Mughal Sarai** *India* 25°18N 83°7E **243** G10
**Mughalzhar Taūy** *Kazakhstan* 49°0N 58°40E **216** C5
**Mughayrā'** *Si. Arabia* 29°17N 37°41E **246** D3
**Mugi** *Japan* 33°40N 134°25E **222** D6
**Mugia = Muxía** *Spain* 43°3N 9°10W **194** B1
**Mugila, Mts.** *Dem. Rep. of the Congo* 7°0S 28°50E **268** D2
**Muginga** *Angola* 8°21S 17°36E **265** D3
**Muğla** *Turkey* 37°15N 28°22E **205** D10
**Muğla □** *Turkey* 37°15N 28°0E **205** D10
**Muglad** *Sudan* 11°1N 27°50E **257** E2
**Müglizh** *Bulgaria* 42°37N 25°32E **203** D9
**Mugodzhary = Mughalzhar Taūy** *Kazakhstan* 49°0N 58°40E **216** C5
**Mugu** *Nepal* 29°45N 82°30E **243** E10
**Mugu Karnali →** *Nepal* 29°38N 81°51E **243** E9
**Muhagiriya** *Sudan* 12°0N 25°38E **259** F5
**Muhala** *Congo* 5°40S 28°43E **268** D2
**Muhammad, Râs** *Egypt* 27°44N 34°16E **251** L5
**Muhammad Qol** *Sudan* 20°53N 37°9E **256** C4
**Muhammadabad** *India* 26°4N 83°25E **243** F10
**Muḥāyil** *Si. Arabia* 18°33N 42°3E **248** C3
**Muḥayriqah** *Si. Arabia* 23°59N 45°4E **248** B4
**Muhesi →** *Tanzania* 7°0S 35°20E **268** D4
**Mühlacker** *Germany* 48°57N 8°51E **179** G4
**Mühldorf** *Germany* 48°14N 12°32E **179** G8
**Mühleiten** *Austria* 48°10N 16°33E **142** A3
**Mühlenfliess →** *Germany* 52°32N 13°42E **115** A5
**Mühlhausen = Milevsko** *Czech Rep.* 49°27N 14°21E **180** B7
**Mühlhausen** *Germany* 51°12N 10°27E **178** D6
**Mühlig Hofmann fjell** *Antarctica* 72°30S 5°0E **151** D3
**Mühlviertel** *Austria* 48°30N 14°10E **180** C7
**Muhoro** *Kenya* 1°1S 34°7E **266** E3
**Muhos** *Finland* 64°47N 25°59E **160** D21
**Muḥradah** *Syria* 35°15N 36°35E **250** C7
**Muhu** *Estonia* 58°36N 23°11E **188** C2
**Muhutwe** *Tanzania* 1°35S 31°45E **268** C3
**Mui Wo** *Hong Kong, China* 22°16N 114°0E **122** B1
**Muiden** *Neths.* 52°20N 5°4E **112** A3
**Muie** *Angola* 14°23S 20°25E **265** E4
**Muileann gCearr, An = Mullingar** *Ireland* 53°31N 7°21W **166** C4
**Muine Bheag = Bagenalstown** *Ireland* 52°42N 6°58W **166** D5
**Muineachán = Monaghan** *Ireland* 54°15N 6°57W **166** B5
**Muir, L.** *Australia* 34°30S 116°40E **279** F2
**Muir of Ord** *U.K.* 57°32N 4°28W **167** D4
**Muisné** *Ecuador* 0°36N 80°2W **328** C1
**Muizenberg** *S. Africa* 34°5S 18°27E **118** B1
**Mujahidpur** *India* 28°33N 77°14E **120** B2
**Mujeres, I.** *Mexico* 21°13N 86°43W **320** B2
**Mujuí dos Campos** *Brazil* 2°35S 54°41W **329** D7
**Muka, Tanjung** *Malaysia* 5°28N 100°11E **237** c
**Mukacheve** *Ukraine* 48°27N 22°45E **182** B7
**Mukachevo = Mukacheve** *Ukraine* 48°27N 22°45E **182** B7
**Mukah** *Malaysia* 2°55N 112°5E **235** B4
**Mukandpur** *India* 28°44N 77°11E **120** A2
**Mukandwara** *India* 24°49N 75°59E **242** G6
**Mukawa** *Papua N. G.* 9°38S 149°59E **286** E5
**Mukawwa, Geziret** *Egypt* 23°55N 35°53E **246** F2
**Mukawwar** *Sudan* 20°50N 37°17E **256** C4
**Mukaylah** *Si. Arabia* 19°16N 41°48E **248** C3
**Mukdahan** *Thailand* 16°32N 104°43E **236** D5
**Mukdahan △** *Thailand* 16°26N 104°45E **236** D5
**Mukden = Shenyang** *China* 41°48N 123°27E **224** B1
**Mukerian** *India* 31°57N 75°37E **242** D6
**Mukhavyets →** *Belarus* 52°5N 23°39E **185** F10
**Mukher** *India* 18°42N 77°22E **244** E3
**Mukhmas** *West Bank* 31°52N 35°17E **123** A2
**Mukhtolovo** *Russia* 55°29N 43°15E **190** C6
**Mukhtuya = Lensk** *Russia* 60°48N 114°55E **215** C12
**Mukinbudin** *Australia* 30°55S 118°5E **279** F2
**Mukishi** *Kasai-Occ., Dem. Rep. of the Congo* 5°39S 21°3E **265** D4
**Mukishi** *Katanga, Dem. Rep. of the Congo* 8°30S 24°44E **265** D4
**Muko** *Japan* 34°55N 135°40E **223** C7
**Muko →** *Japan* 34°48N 135°22E **133** A1
**Muko Phetra △** *Thailand* 6°57N 99°33E **237** J2
**Mukojima** *Japan* 35°43N 139°49E **140** A3
**Mukomuko** *Indonesia* 2°30S 101°10E **234** C2
**Mukomwenze** *Dem. Rep. of the Congo* 6°49S 27°15E **268** D2
**Mukono** *Uganda* 0°21N 32°45E **268** B3
**Muktinath** *Nepal* 28°49N 83°53E **243** E10
**Muktsar** *India* 30°30N 74°30E **242** D6
**Mukur = Moqor** *Afghan.* 32°50N 67°42E **242** C2
**Mukutuwa →** *Canada* 53°10N 97°24W **297** C9
**Mukwela** *Zambia* 17°0S 26°40E **269** F2
**Mukwonago** *U.S.A.* 42°52N 88°20W **311** B8
**Mul** *India* 20°4N 79°40E **244** D4
**Mula** *Spain* 38°3N 1°33W **197** G3
**Mula →** *India* 18°34N 74°21E **244** E2
**Mula →** *Pakistan* 27°57N 67°36E **242** F2
**Mulaku Atoll** *Maldives* 3°0N 73°30E **272** d
**Mulamba** *Dem. Rep. of the Congo* 6°21S 21°13E **265** D4
**Mulanay** *Phil.* 13°31N 122°24E **232** E4
**Mulange** *Dem. Rep. of the Congo* 3°40S 27°10E **268** C2
**Mulanje, Mt.** *Malawi* 16°2S 35°33E **269** F4
**Mulâtre, Pte.** *Dominica* 15°17N 61°15W **323** k
**Mulatupo Sasardi** *Panama* 8°57N 77°45W **328** B2
**Mulbagal** *India* 13°10N 78°24E **245** H4
**Mulbarton** *S. Africa* 26°17S 28°3E **121** B2
**Mulberry** *U.S.A.* 27°54N 81°59W **317** H8
**Mulberry Grove** *U.S.A.* 38°56N 89°16W **310** F7
**Mulchatna →** *U.S.A.* 59°40N 157°7W **303** G8
**Mulchén** *Chile* 37°45S 72°20W **334** D1
**Mulde →** *Germany* 51°53N 12°15E **178** D8
**Muldraugh** *U.S.A.* 37°56N 85°59W **311** G11
**Mule Creek Junction** *U.S.A.* 43°23N 104°13W **304** E11
**Muleba** *Tanzania* 1°50S 31°37E **268** C3
**Mulegé** *Mexico* 26°53N 111°59W **318** B2
**Muleshoe** *U.S.A.* 34°13N 102°43W **314** D3
**Muletta, Gara** *Ethiopia* 9°15N 41°44E **257** F5
**Mulgrave** *Canada* 45°38N 61°31W **299** C7
**Mulgrave I. = Badu** *Australia* 10°7S 142°11E **280** a
**Mulhacén** *Spain* 37°4N 3°20W **195** H7
**Mülheim** *Germany* 51°25N 6°54E **178** D2
**Mulhouse** *France* 47°40N 7°20E **173** E14
**Muli** *Sichuan, China* 27°52N 101°8E **228** D3
**Muli** *Maldives* 2°55N 73°34E **272** d
**Mulifanua** *Samoa* 13°50S 171°59W **287** V20
**Muling** *China* 44°35N 130°10E **227** B16
**Mulki** *India* 13°6N 74°48E **245** H2
**Mull** *U.K.* 56°25N 5°56W **167** E3
**Mull, Sound of** *U.K.* 56°30N 5°50W **167** E3
**Mullach Íde = Malahide** *Ireland* 53°26N 6°9W **120** A3
**Mullaittivu** *Sri Lanka* 9°15N 80°49E **245** K5
**Mullen** *U.S.A.* 42°3N 101°1W **308** D3
**Mullengudgery** *Australia* 31°43S 147°23E **281** B4
**Mullens** *U.S.A.* 37°35N 81°23W **309** G13
**Muller, Pegunungan** *Indonesia* 0°30N 113°30E **235** B4
**Muller Ra.** *Papua N. G.* 5°35S 142°20E **286** C2
**Mullet Pen.** *Ireland* 54°13N 10°2W **166** B1
**Mulletbaai** *St.-Maarten* 18°4N 63°7W **322** a
**Mullewa** *Australia* 28°29S 115°30E **279** E2
**Müllheim** *Germany* 47°47N 7°36E **179** H3
**Mulligan →** *Australia* 25°0S 139°0E **280** D2
**Mullingar** *Ireland* 53°31N 7°21W **166** C4
**Mullins** *U.S.A.* 34°12N 79°15W **315** D15
**Mullsjö** *Sweden* 57°56N 13°55E **163** G7
**Mullumbimby** *Australia* 28°30S 153°30E **281** D5
**Mulobezi** *Zambia* 16°45S 25°7E **269** F2
**Mulondo** *Angola* 15°41S 15°12E **265** F3
**Mulonga Plain** *Zambia* 16°20S 22°40E **265** F4
**Mulroy B.** *Ireland* 55°15N 7°46W **166** A4
**Mulshi L.** *India* 18°30N 73°48E **244** E1
**Multai** *India* 21°50N 78°21E **244** D4
**Multan** *Pakistan* 30°15N 71°36E **242** D4
**Mulu, Gunung** *Malaysia* 4°3N 114°56E **235** B4
**Mulug** *India* 18°11N 79°57E **244** E4
**Mulumbe, Mts.** *Dem. Rep. of the Congo* 8°40S 27°30E **269** D2
**Mulundu** *Dem. Rep. of the Congo* 6°40S 20°33E **265** D4
**Mulungushi Dam** *Zambia* 14°48S 28°48E **269** E2
**Mulurulu L.** *Australia* 33°15S 143°30E **282** B5
**Mulvane** *U.S.A.* 37°29N 97°15W **308** G5
**Mulwad** *Sudan* 18°45N 30°39E **256** D3
**Mulwala** *Australia* 35°59S 146°0E **283** C7
**Mulwala, L.** *Australia* 35°59S 146°1E **281** C4
**Muma** *Dem. Rep. of the Congo* 3°25N 23°21E **264** B4
**Mumbai** *India* 18°56N 72°50E **130** B2
**Mumbai Chhatrapati Shivaji Int. ✈ (BOM)** *India* 19°5N 72°51E **130** A2
**Mumbai Harbour** *India* 18°58N 72°55E **130** B2
**Mumbeji** *Zambia* 13°51S 23°39E **265** E4
**Mumbondo** *Angola* 10°9S 14°15E **265** E2
**Mumbwa** *Zambia* 15°0S 27°0E **269** F2
**Mumeng** *Papua N. G.* 7°1S 146°37E **286** D4
**Mumias** *Kenya* 0°20N 34°29E **268** C4
**Mummel Gulf △** *Australia* 31°17S 151°51E **283** A9
**Mumra** *Russia* 45°45N 47°41E **191** H8
**Mun →** *Thailand* 15°19N 105°30E **236** E5
**Mun-gyeong** *S. Korea* 36°35N 128°12E **224** D4
**Muna** *Indonesia* 5°0S 122°30E **231** F6
**Munabao** *India* 25°45N 70°17E **242** G4
**Munakata** *Japan* 33°48N 130°38E **222** D2
**Munamagi** *Estonia* 57°43N 27°4E **188** D4
**Munaung** *Burma* 18°45N 93°40E **241** F4
**Munaung I. = Cheduba I.** *Burma* 18°45N 93°40E **241** F4
**Muncan** *Indonesia* 8°34S 115°11E **231** K18
**Muncar** *Indonesia* 8°26S 114°20E **231** J17
**Munch-museum** *Norway* 59°55N 10°46E **133** A3
**Münchberg** *Germany* 50°11N 11°47E **179** E7
**Müncheberg** *Germany* 52°30N 14°9E **178** C10
**Münchehofe** *Germany* 52°29N 13°40E **115** B5
**München** *Germany* 48°8N 11°34E **131** B2
**München Franz Josef Strauss Int. ✈ (MUC)** *Germany* 48°21N 11°47E **131** A2
**Munchen-Gladbach = Mönchengladbach** *Germany* 51°11N 6°27E **178** D2
**Munchique △** *Colombia* 2°44N 77°1W **328** C2
**Muncho Lake** *Canada* 59°0N 125°50W **296** B3
**Munch'ŏn** *N. Korea* 39°14N 127°19E **224** C3
**Muncie** *U.S.A.* 40°12N 85°23W **311** D11
**Muncoonie L. West** *Australia* 25°12S 138°40E **280** D2
**Munda** *Solomon Is.* 8°20S 157°16E **287** M9
**Mundabbera** *Australia* 25°36S 151°18E **281** D5
**Mundakayam** *India* 9°30N 76°50E **245** K3
**Mundal** *Sri Lanka* 7°48N 79°48E **245** L4
**Munday** *U.S.A.* 33°27N 99°38W **314** E5
**Mundelein** *U.S.A.* 42°16N 88°0W **311** B8
**Mundemba** *Cameroon* 4°57N 8°52E **264** B1
**Münden** *Germany* 51°25N 9°38E **178** D5
**Münden △** *Germany* 51°28N 9°42E **178** D5
**Mundiwindi** *Australia* 23°47S 120°9E **278** D3
**Mundo →** *Spain* 38°30N 2°15W **197** G2
**Mundo Novo** *Brazil* 11°50S 40°29W **333** D3
**Mundo Nuevo** *Trin. & Tob.* 10°28N 61°15W **323** t
**Mundra** *India* 22°54N 69°48E **242** H3
**Mundrabilla** *Australia* 31°52S 127°51E **279** F4
**Munenga** *Angola* 10°2S 14°41E **265** E2
**Munera** *Spain* 39°2N 2°29W **197** F2
**Muneru →** *India* 16°45N 80°3E **244** F5
**Mungallala** *Australia* 26°28S 147°34E **281** D4
**Mungallala Cr. →** *Australia* 28°53S 147°5E **281** D4
**Mungana** *Australia* 17°8S 144°27E **280** B3
**Mungaoli** *India* 24°24N 78°7E **242** G8
**Mungari** *Mozam.* 17°12S 33°30E **269** F3
**Mungbere** *Dem. Rep. of the Congo* 2°36N 28°28E **268** B2
**Mungeli** *India* 22°4N 81°41E **243** H9
**Munger** *India* 25°23N 86°30E **243** G12
**Mungerannie** *Australia* 28°1S 138°39E **281** A2
**Mungilli ✪** *Australia* 25°14S 124°17E **279** E3
**Mungkan Kandju △** *Australia* 13°35S 142°52E **280** A3
**Mungkarta ✪** *Australia* 20°22S 134°2E **280** C1
**Mungo** *Angola* 11°49S 16°16E **265** E3
**Mungo, L.** *Australia* 33°45S 143°0E **282** B5
**Mungo △** *Australia* 33°44S 143°6E **282** B5
**Munhango** *Angola* 12°10S 18°38E **265** E3
**Munhango →** *Angola* 11°17S 19°44E **265** E4
**Munich = München** *Germany* 48°8N 11°34E **131** B2
**Munising** *U.S.A.* 46°25N 86°40W **308** B10
**Munka-Ljungby** *Sweden* 56°16N 12°58E **163** H6
**Munkebo** *Denmark* 55°27N 10°34E **163** J4
**Munkedal** *Sweden* 58°28N 11°40E **163** F5
**Munkfors** *Sweden* 59°47N 13°30E **162** E7
**Munkkiniemi** *Finland* 60°11N 24°52E **121** B2
**Munku-Sardyk** *Russia* 51°45N 100°20E **215** D11
**Münnerstadt** *Germany* 50°14N 10°12E **179** E6
**Munnsville** *U.S.A.* 42°58N 75°35W **313** D9
**Muñoz** *Phil.* 15°43N 120°54E **232** D3
**Muñoz Gamero, Pen.** *Chile* 52°30S 73°5W **336** D2
**Munro** *Argentina* 34°31S 58°31W **117** B1
**Munroe L.** *Canada* 59°13N 98°35W **297** B9
**Munsan** *S. Korea* 37°51N 126°48E **224** D3
**Munshiganj** *Bangla.* 23°33N 90°32E **241** D3
**Munson** *U.S.A.* 30°52N 86°52W **317** E3
**Munster** *Haut-Rhin, France* 48°2N 7°8E **173** D14
**Münster** *Niedersachsen, Germany* 52°58N 10°5E **178** C6
**Münster** *Nordrhein-Westfalen, Germany* 51°58N 7°37E **178** D3
**Munster □** *Ireland* 52°18N 8°44W **166** D3
**Münsterberg = Ziębice** *Poland* 50°37N 17°2E **185** H4
**Muntadgin** *Australia* 31°45S 118°33E **279** F2
**Muntele Mare, Vf.** *Romania* 46°30N 23°12E **183** D8
**Muntinlupa** *Phil.* 14°27N 121°2E **127** C2
**Muntok** *Indonesia* 2°5S 105°10E **234** C3
**Munzur Dağları** *Turkey* 39°30N 39°10E **213** C8
**Muong Nhie** *Vietnam* 22°12N 102°28E **228** F4
**Muong Sen** *Vietnam* 19°24N 104°8E **236** C5
**Muong Te** *Vietnam* 22°24N 102°49E **228** F4
**Muong Xia** *Vietnam* 20°19N 104°50E **236** B5
**Muonio** *Finland* 67°57N 23°40E **160** C20
**Muonio älv = Muonionjoki →** *Finland* 67°11N 23°34E **160** C20
**Muonioälven = Muonionjoki →** *Finland* 67°11N 23°34E **160** C20
**Muonionjoki →** *Finland* 67°11N 23°34E **160** C20
**Mupa** *Angola* 16°5S 15°50E **265** F3
**Mupa →** *Mozam.* 18°58S 35°54E **269** F4
**Mupa △** *Angola* 15°55S 15°35E **265** F3
**Muping** *China* 37°22N 121°36E **227** F11
**Mupoi** *South Sudan* 5°28N 27°40E **257** F2
**Muqaddam, Wadi →** *Sudan* 18°4N 31°30E **256** D3
**Muqaybirah** *Yemen* 13°20N 46°5E **248** D4
**Muqdisho** *Somalia* 2°2N 45°25E **267** D6
**Muqshin** *Oman* 19°35N 54°55E **249** C6
**Muqshin, W. →** *Oman* 19°44N 55°14E **249** C6
**Muquequete** *Angola* 14°50S 14°16E **265** E2
**Mur →** *Austria* 47°18N 16°52E **181** E9
**Mûr-de-Bretagne** *France* 48°12N 3°0W **172** D4
**Muradiye** *Manisa, Turkey* 38°39N 27°21E **205** C9
**Muradiye** *Van, Turkey* 39°0N 43°44E **213** C10
**Murai Res.** *Singapore* 1°23N 103°40E **138** A2
**Murakami** *Japan* 38°14N 139°29E **220** E9
**Muralag = Prince of Wales I.** *Australia* 10°40S 142°10E **286** F2
**Murallón, Cerro** *Chile* 49°48S 73°30W **336** C2
**Muranda** *Rwanda* 1°52S 29°20E **268** C2
**Murang'a** *Kenya* 0°45S 37°9E **268** C4
**Murano** *Venice, Italy* **142** a4
**Muranów** *Poland* 52°14N 20°58E **143** B1
**Murashi** *Russia* 59°30N 49°0E **190** A9
**Murat** *France* 45°7N 2°53E **174** C6
**Murat →** *Turkey* 38°46N 40°0E **213** C9
**Murat Bay = Ceduna** *Australia* 32°7S 133°46E **281** E1
**Murat Dağı** *Turkey* 38°55N 29°43E **205** C11
**Muratlı** *Turkey* 41°10N 27°29E **203** E11
**Murato** *France* 42°35N 9°20E **175** F13
**Murau** *Austria* 47°6N 14°10E **180** D7
**Murava** *Belarus* 52°39N 24°15E **185** F11
**Muravera** *Italy* 39°25N 9°34E **200** C2
**Muravyevo = Mažeikiai** *Lithuania* 56°20N 22°20E **184** B9
**Muravyovsky = Korsakov** *Russia* 46°36N 142°42E **215** E15
**Murayama** *Japan* 38°30N 140°25E **220** E10
**Murça** *Portugal* 41°24N 7°28W **194** D3
**Murcaayo** *Somalia* 11°41N 50°34E **267** B7
**Murchison** *N.Z.* 41°49S 172°21E **285** B4
**Murchison →** *Australia* 27°45S 114°0E **279** E1
**Murchison, Mt.** *Antarctica* 73°25S 166°20E **151** D11
**Murchison, Mt.** *N.Z.* 43°0S 171°22E **285** D6
**Murchison Falls** *Uganda* 2°15N 31°30E **268** B3
**Murchison Falls △** *Uganda* 2°17N 31°48E **268** B3
**Murchison Mts.** *N.Z.* 45°13S 167°23E **285** F2
**Murchison Ra.** *Australia* 20°0S 134°10E **280** C1
**Murchison Rapids** *Malawi* 15°55S 34°35E **269** F3
**Murchison Roadhouse** *Australia* 27°39S 116°14E **279** E2
**Murcia** *Spain* 38°5N 1°10W **197** G3
**Murcia □** *Spain* 37°50N 1°30W **197** H3
**Murdo** *U.S.A.* 43°53N 100°43W **308** D3
**Murdoch Pt.** *Australia* 14°37S 144°55E **280** A3
**Mürefte** *Turkey* 40°40N 27°14E **203** F11
**Mureş □** *Romania* 46°45N 24°40E **183** D9
**Mureş →** *Romania* 46°15N 20°13E **182** D5
**Mureşul = Mureş →** *Romania* 46°15N 20°13E **182** D5
**Muret** *France* 43°30N 1°20E **174** E5
**Murewa** *Zimbabwe* 17°39S 31°47E **271** A5
**Murfreesboro** *N.C., U.S.A.* 36°27N 77°6W **315** C16
**Murfreesboro** *Tenn., U.S.A.* 35°51N 86°24W **315** D11
**Murgap** *Tajikistan* 38°10N 74°2E **217** E8
**Murgap →** *Turkmenistan* 38°18N 61°12E **247** B9
**Murgenella** *Australia* 11°34S 132°56E **278** B5
**Murgeni** *Romania* 46°12N 28°1E **183** D13
**Murgha Kibzai** *Pakistan* 30°44N 69°25E **242** D3
**Murghob = Murgap** *Tajikistan* 38°10N 74°2E **217** E8
**Murgon** *Australia* 26°15S 151°54E **281** D5
**Muri** *Cook Is.* 21°15S 159°43W **289** h
**Muri** *India* 23°22N 85°52E **243** H11
**Muria** *Indonesia* 6°36S 110°53E **235** G14
**Muriaé** *Brazil* 21°8S 42°23W **333** F3
**Murias de Paredes** *Spain* 42°52N 6°11W **194** C4
**Murici** *Brazil* 9°19S 35°56W **332** C4
**Muriége** *Angola* 9°58S 21°11E **265** D4
**Murilo** *Micronesia* 8°40N 152°11E **288** F7
**Murien △** *India* 23°45N 93°20E **241** D4
**Murila** *Angola* 10°44S 20°20E **265** E4
**Murino** *Russia* 59°59N 30°29E **137** B2
**Müritz** *Germany* 53°25N 12°42E **178** B8
**Müritz △** *Germany* 53°22N 12°55E **178** B8
**Muriwai Beach** *N.Z.* 36°50S 174°26E **284** C3
**Murkong Selek** *India* 27°44N 95°18E **241** B5
**Murliganj** *India* 25°54N 86°59E **243** G12
**Murmansk** *Russia* 68°57N 33°10E **160** B25
**Murmashi** *Russia* 68°47N 32°42E **160** B25
**Murnau** *Germany* 47°40N 11°12E **179** H7
**Muro** *Haute-Corse, France* 42°34N 8°54E **175** F12
**Muro** *Spain* 39°44N 3°3E **206** B4
**Muro, C. di** *France* 41°44N 8°37E **175** G12
**Muro de Alcoy** *Spain* 38°46N 0°26W **197** G4
**Muro Lucano** *Italy* 40°45N 15°29E **201** B8
**Murom** *Russia* 55°35N 42°3E **190** C6
**Muroran** *Japan* 42°25N 141°0E **220** C10
**Muros** *Spain* 42°45N 9°5W **194** C1
**Muros e Noya, Ría de →** *Spain* 42°45N 9°0W **194** C1
**Muroto** *Japan* 33°18N 134°9E **222** D6
**Muroto-Misaki** *Japan* 33°15N 134°10E **222** D6
**Murovani Kurylivtsi** *Ukraine* 48°44N 27°31E **183** B12
**Murowana Goślina** *Poland* 52°35N 17°0E **185** F4
**Murphy** *U.S.A.* 43°13N 116°33W **304** E5
**Murphys** *U.S.A.* 38°8N 120°28W **306** G6
**Murphy's Station = Sunnyvale** *U.S.A.* 37°23N 122°2W **306** H4
**Murphysboro** *U.S.A.* 37°46N 89°20W **310** G7
**Murrat** *Sudan* 18°51N 29°33E **256** D2
**Murrat Wells** *Sudan* 21°3N 32°55E **256** C3
**Murray** *Queens., Australia* 9°56S 144°2E **280** a
**Murray** *Iowa, U.S.A.* 41°3N 93°57W **310** C3
**Murray** *Ky., U.S.A.* 36°37N 88°19W **308** G9
**Murray** *Utah, U.S.A.* 40°40N 111°53W **304** F8
**Murray →** *Australia* 35°20S 139°22E **282** C3
**Murray →** *Canada* 55°58N 123°13W **296** B4
**Murray, L.** *Papua N. G.* 7°0S 141°35E **286** D1
**Murray, L.** *S.C., U.S.A.* 34°3N 81°13W **316** A8
**Murray Bridge** *Australia* 35°6S 139°14E **282** C3
**Murray Fracture Zone** *Pac. Oc.* 35°0N 130°0W **289** D14
**Murray Harbour** *Canada* 46°0N 62°28W **299** C7
**Murray River △** *Australia* 34°23S 140°32E **281** C3
**Murray-Sunset △** *Australia* 34°45S 141°30E **282** C4
**Murrayfield** *U.K.* 55°57N 3°15W **121** B2
**Murraysburg** *S. Africa* 31°58S 23°47E **270** D3
**Murrayville** *U.S.A.* 39°35N 90°15W **310** E6
**Murree** *Pakistan* 33°56N 73°28E **242** C5
**Murrieta** *U.S.A.* 33°33N 117°13W **307** M9
**Murro di Porco, Capo** *Italy* 37°0N 15°20E **201** F8
**Murrumbateman** *Australia* 34°58S 149°0E **283** C8
**Murrumbidgee →** *Australia* 34°43S 143°12E **282** C5
**Murrumburrah** *Australia* 34°32S 148°22E **283** C8
**Murrurundi** *Australia* 31°42S 150°51E **283** A9
**Murshid** *Sudan* 21°40N 31°10E **256** C3
**Murshidabad** *India* 24°11N 88°19E **243** G13
**Murska Sobota** *Slovenia* 46°39N 16°12E **199** B13
**Murtala Mohammed Int. ✈ (LOS)** *Nigeria* 6°34N 3°19E **124** A1
**Murtazapur** *India* 20°40N 77°25E **244** D3
**Murtle L.** *Canada* 52°8N 119°38W **296** C5
**Murtoa** *Australia* 36°35S 142°28E **282** D5
**Murtosa** *Portugal* 40°44N 8°40W **194** E2
**Muru →** *Brazil* 8°9S 70°45W **330** B3
**Murud** *India* 18°19N 72°58E **244** E1
**Murung →** *Indonesia* 0°12N 114°3E **235** B4
**Murungu** *Tanzania* 4°12S 31°10E **268** C3
**Murupara** *N.Z.* 38°28S 176°42E **284** E5
**Mururoa** *French Polynesia* 21°52S 138°55W **289** f
**Murwara** *India* 23°46N 80°28E **243** H9
**Murwillumbah** *Australia* 28°18S 153°27E **281** D5
**Mürz →** *Austria* 47°30N 15°25E **180** D8
**Murzūq** *Libya* 25°53N 13°57E **258** C2
**Murzūq □** *Libya* 25°0N 16°0E **258** D3
**Murzūq, Idehān** *Libya* 24°50N 13°51E **258** D2
**Mürzzuschlag** *Austria* 47°36N 15°41E **180** D8
**Mus** *India* 9°14N 92°47E **245** K11
**Muş** *Turkey* 38°45N 41°30E **213** C9
**Muş □** *Turkey* 38°45N 41°30E **213** C9
**Musa** *Dem. Rep. of the Congo* 2°40N 19°18E **264** B3
**Musa →** *Papua N. G.* 9°3S 148°55E **286** E5
**Mûsa, Gebel** *Egypt* 28°33N 33°59E **251** K4
**Musa Khel** *Pakistan* 30°59N 69°52E **242** D3
**Mūsa Qal'eh** *Afghan.* 32°20N 64°50E **240** B2
**Musabeyli** *Turkey* 36°53N 36°55E **250** B7
**Musadi** *Dem. Rep. of the Congo* 2°31S 22°50E **264** C4
**Musafirkhana** *India* 26°22N 81°48E **243** F9
**Musala** *Bulgaria* 42°13N 23°37E **202** D7
**Musala** *Indonesia* 1°41N 98°28E **234** B1
**Musan** *N. Korea* 42°12N 129°12E **224** A4
**Musandam □** *Oman* 26°0N 56°20E **249** A7
**Musandam, Ra's** *Oman* 26°20N 56°20E **249** A7
**Musangu** *Dem. Rep. of the Congo* 10°28S 23°55E **265** E4
**Musasa** *Tanzania* 3°25S 31°30E **268** C3
**Musashino** *Japan* 35°42N 139°33E **140** A2
**Musaymīr** *Yemen* 13°27N 44°37E **248** D4
**Muscat = Masqat** *Oman* 23°37N 58°36E **249** B7
**Muscat & Oman = Oman ■** *Asia* 23°0N 58°0E **249** B7
**Muscatatuck →** *U.S.A.* 38°46N 86°10W **311** F10
**Muscatine** *U.S.A.* 41°25N 91°3W **310** C5
**Muschu I.** *Papua N. G.* 3°25S 143°35E **286** B2
**Muscle Shoals** *U.S.A.* 34°45N 87°40W **315** D11
**Muscoda** *U.S.A.* 43°11N 90°27W **310** A6
**Musengezi = Unsengedsi →** *Zimbabwe* 15°43S 31°14E **269** F3
**Museumquartier** *Vienna, Austria* **142** c1
**Museumsinsel** *Germany* 52°30N 13°25E **115** A3
**Musgrave Harbour** *Canada* 49°27N 53°58W **299** C9
**Musgrave Ranges** *Australia* 26°0S 132°0E **279** E5
**Mushie** *Dem. Rep. of the Congo* 2°56S 16°55E **264** C3
**Mushima** *Zambia* 14°10S 24°56E **265** E4
**Mushin** *Nigeria* 6°31N 3°21E **124** A2
**Musi →** *India* 16°41N 79°40E **244** F4
**Musi →** *Indonesia* 2°20S 104°56E **234** C2
**Musiektheater** *Amsterdam, Neths.* **112** b3
**Musina** *S. Africa* 22°20S 30°5E **271** B5
**Musiri** *India* 10°56N 78°27E **245** J4
**Muskauer Park** *Europe* 51°34N 14°43E **178** D10
**Muskeg →** *Canada* 60°20N 123°20W **296** A4
**Muskego** *U.S.A.* 42°55N 88°8W **311** B8
**Muskegon** *U.S.A.* 43°14N 86°16W **311** A10
**Muskegon →** *U.S.A.* 43°14N 86°21W **308** D10
**Muskegon Heights** *U.S.A.* 43°12N 86°16W **311** A10
**Muskogee** *U.S.A.* 35°45N 95°22W **314** D7
**Muskoka, L.** *Canada* 45°0N 79°25W **312** B5
**Muskoka Falls** *Canada* 44°59N 79°17W **312** B5
**Muskwa →** *Canada* 58°47N 122°48W **296** B4
**Muslim Mindanao □** *Phil.* 8°0N 123°0E **233** H3
**Muslim Quarter** *Jerusalem* **123** a3
**Muslimīyah** *Syria* 36°19N 37°12E **246** B3
**Musmar** *Sudan* 18°13N 35°40E **256** D4
**Musocco** *Italy* 45°29N 9°8E **128** B1
**Musofu** *Zambia* 13°30S 29°0E **269** E2
**Musoma** *Tanzania* 1°30S 33°48E **268** C3
**Musquaro, L.** *Canada* 50°38N 61°5W **299** B7
**Musquodoboit Harbour** *Canada* 44°50N 63°9W **299** D7
**Mussau I.** *Papua N. G.* 1°30S 149°40E **286** A5
**Musselburgh** *U.K.* 55°57N 3°2W **167** F5
**Musselshell →** *U.S.A.* 47°21N 107°57W **304** C10
**Mussende** *Angola* 10°32S 16°5E **265** E3
**Musserra** *Angola* 7°37S 13°2E **265** D2
**Mussidan** *France* 45°2N 0°22E **174** C4
**Mussolinea di Sardegna = Arborèa** *Italy* 39°46N 8°35E **200** C1
**Mussolo** *Angola* 9°59S 17°19E **265** D3
**Mussomeli** *Italy* 37°35N 13°45E **200** E6
**Mussoorie** *India* 30°27N 78°6E **242** D8
**Mussuco** *Angola* 17°2S 19°3E **265** F3
**Mustafakemalpaşa** *Turkey* 40°2N 28°24E **203** F12
**Mustahil** *Ethiopia* 5°16N 44°45E **267** C5
**Mustang** *Nepal* 29°10N 83°55E **243** E10
**Mustansiriya** *Iraq* 33°22N 44°24E **113** A2
**Musters, L.** *Argentina* 45°20S 69°25W **336** C3
**Mustique I.** *St. Vincent* 12°52N 61°11W **323** n
**Musturud** *Egypt* 30°8N 31°17E **117** A2
**Musudan** *N. Korea* 40°50N 129°43E **224** B4
**Muswell Hill** *U.K.* 51°35N 0°8W **125** A3
**Muswellbrook** *Australia* 32°16S 150°56E **283** B9
**Muszyna** *Poland* 49°22N 20°55E **185** J7
**Mût** *Egypt* 25°28N 28°58E **256** B2
**Mut** *Turkey* 36°40N 33°28E **250** B4
**Mutalau** *Cook Is.* 18°56S 169°50W **289** g
**Mutanabi** *Iraq* 33°19N 44°21E **113** B2
**Mutanda** *Dem. Rep. of the Congo* 5°17S 16°34E **265** D3
**Mutanda** *Mozam.* 21°0S 33°34E **271** B5
**Mutanda** *Zambia* 12°24S 26°13E **269** E2
**Mutankiang = Mudanjiang** *China* 44°38N 129°30E **227** B15
**Mutanshe** *Taiwan* 22°9N 120°48E **225** D2
**Mutare** *Zimbabwe* 18°58S 32°38E **269** F3
**Mutawintji △** *Australia* 31°10S 142°30E **281** E3
**Mutha** *Kenya* 1°48S 38°26E **268** C4
**Muthana** *Iraq* 33°19N 44°27E **113** B2
**Muting** *Indonesia* 7°23S 140°20E **231** F10
**Mutki = Mirtağ** *Turkey* 38°23N 41°56E **213** C9
**Mutoko** *Zimbabwe* 17°24S 32°13E **271** A5
**Mutomo** *Kenya* 1°51S 38°12E **268** C4
**Mutoray** *Russia* 60°56N 101°0E **215** C11
**Mutoto** *Dem. Rep. of the Congo* 5°42S 22°42E **265** D4
**Mutoxo** *Angola* 12°17S 21°40E **265** E4
**Mutsamudu** *Comoros Is.* 12°10S 44°25E **272** a
**Mutshatsha** *Dem. Rep. of the Congo* 10°35S 24°20E **265** E4
**Mutsu** *Japan* 41°5N 140°55E **220** D10
**Mutsu-Wan** *Japan* 41°5N 140°55E **220** D10
**Muttaburra** *Australia* 22°38S 144°29E **280** C3

**Muttalip** *Turkey* 39°50N 30°32E **205** B12
**Mutton I.** *Ireland* 52°49N 9°32W **166** D2
**Muttra = Mathura** *India* 27°30N 77°40E **242** F7
**Muttukuru** *India* 14°16N 80°6E **245** G5
**Mutuáli** *Mozam.* 14°55S 37°0E **269** E4
**Mutum Biyu** *Nigeria* 8°40N 10°50E **263** D7
**Mutumba** *Burundi* 3°25S 29°21E **268** C2
**Mutunópolis** *Brazil* 13°40S 49°15W **333** D2
**Mutur** *Sri Lanka* 8°27N 81°16E **245** K5
**Muweilih** *Egypt* 30°42N 34°19E **251** H5
**Muxaluando** *Angola* 8°8S 14°18E **265** D2
**Muxía** *Spain* 43°3N 9°10W **194** B1
**Muxima** *Angola* 9°33S 13°58E **265** D2
**Muy Muy** *Nic.* 12°39N 85°36W **320** D2
**Muyinga** *Burundi* 3°14S 30°33E **268** C3
**Muynak** *Uzbekistan* 43°44N 59°10E **216** D5
**Muyua = Woodlark I.** *Papua N. G.* 9°10S 152°50E **286** E7
**Muyunkum, Peski = Moyynqum** *Kazakhstan* 44°12N 71°0E **217** D8
**Muz Tag** *China* 36°25N 87°25E **217** E11
**Muzaffarabad** *Pakistan* 34°25N 73°30E **243** B5
**Muzaffargarh** *Pakistan* 30°5N 71°14E **242** D4
**Muzaffarnagar** *India* 29°26N 77°40E **242** E7
**Muzaffarpur** *India* 26°7N 85°23E **243** F11
**Muzafirpur** *Pakistan* 30°58N 69°9E **242** D3
**Mużakowski, Park = Muskauer Park** *Europe* 51°34N 14°43E **178** D10
**Muzeze** *Angola* 15°3S 17°43E **265** F3
**Muzhi** *Russia* 65°25N 64°40E **186** A11
**Muzillac** *France* 47°35N 2°30W **172** E4
**Muzon, C.** *U.S.A.* 54°40N 132°42W **303** J14
**Muztagh-Ata** *China* 38°17N 75°7E **217** E9
**Muztor = Toktogul** *Kyrgyzstan* 41°50N 72°50E **217** D8
**Muzūra** *Egypt* 28°53N 30°48E **256** J7
**Mvadhi-Ousyé** *Gabon* 1°13N 13°12E **264** B2
**Mvam** *Gabon* 0°13S 9°39E **264** C1
**Mvangan** *Cameroon* 2°17N 11°43E **264** B2
**Mvolo** *South Sudan* 6°2N 29°53E **257** F2
**Mvuma** *Zimbabwe* 19°16S 30°30E **269** F3
**Mvurwi** *Zimbabwe* 17°0S 30°57E **269** F3
**Mwabvi** ⌂ *Malawi* 16°42S 35°0E **269** F3
**Mwadi-Kalumbu** *Dem. Rep. of the Congo* 7°53S 18°43E **265** D3
**Mwadui** *Tanzania* 3°26S 33°32E **268** C3
**Mwali = Mohéli** *Comoros Is.* 12°20S 43°40E **272** a
**Mwambo** *Tanzania* 10°30S 40°22E **269** E5
**Mwandi** *Zambia* 17°30S 24°51E **269** F1
**Mwanza** *Katanga, Dem. Rep. of the Congo* 7°55S 26°43E **265** D5
**Mwanza** *Tanzania* 2°30S 32°58E **268** C3
**Mwanza** *Zambia* 16°58S 24°28E **265** F4
**Mwanza** □ *Tanzania* 2°0S 33°0E **268** C3
**Mwaya** *Tanzania* 9°32S 33°55E **269** D3
**Mweelrea** *Ireland* 53°39N 9°49W **166** C2
**Mweka** *Dem. Rep. of the Congo* 4°50S 21°34E **265** C4
**Mwendjila** *Dem. Rep. of the Congo* 7°12S 18°51E **265** D3
**Mwene-Ditu** *Dem. Rep. of the Congo* 6°35S 22°27E **265** D4
**Mwenezi** *Zimbabwe* 21°15S 30°48E **269** G3
**Mwenezi** ➜ *Mozam.* 22°40S 31°50E **269** G3
**Mwenga** *Dem. Rep. of the Congo* 3°1S 28°28E **268** C2
**Mweru, L.** *Zambia* 9°0S 28°40E **269** D2
**Mweru Wantipa** △ *Zambia* 8°39S 29°25E **269** D2
**Mwetshi** *Dem. Rep. of the Congo* 4°50S 22°38E **265** C4
**Mweza Range** *Zimbabwe* 21°0S 30°0E **269** G3
**Mwilambwe** *Dem. Rep. of the Congo* 8°7S 25°5E **265** D5
**Mwimbi** *Tanzania* 8°38S 31°39E **269** D3
**Mwingi** *Kenya* 0°56S 38°4E **268** C4
**Mwinilunga** *Zambia* 11°43S 24°25E **265** E4
**My Son** *Vietnam* 15°48N 108°7E **236** E7
**My Tho** *Vietnam* 10°29N 106°23E **237** G6
**Mya, O.** ➜ *Algeria* 30°46N 4°54E **261** B5
**Myajlar** *India* 26°15N 70°20E **242** F4
**Myakka** ➜ *U.S.A.* 26°56N 82°11W **317** J7
**Myall Lakes** △ *Australia* 32°25S 152°30E **283** B10
**Myanaung** *Burma* 18°18N 95°22E **241** F5
**Myanmar = Burma** ■ *Asia* 21°0N 96°30E **241** E6
**Myaung** *Burma* 21°50N 95°25E **241** E5
**Myaungmya** *Burma* 16°30N 94°40E **241** G5
**Mycenæ = Mikines** *Greece* 37°43N 22°46E **204** D4
**Myebon** *Burma* 20°3N 93°22E **241** E4
**Myedna** *Belarus* 51°52N 23°42E **185** G10
**Myeik = Mergui** *Burma* 12°26N 98°34E **236** F2
**Myeik Kyunzu** *Burma* 11°30N 97°30E **237** G1
**Myerstown** *U.S.A.* 40°22N 76°19W **313** F8
**Myingyan** *Burma* 21°30N 95°20E **241** E5
**Myitkyina** *Burma* 25°24N 97°26E **241** C6
**Myitson** *Burma* 23°16N 96°34E **241** D6
**Myittha** *Burma* 21°25N 96°8E **241** E6
**Myittha** ➜ *Burma* 23°12N 94°17E **241** D5
**Myjava** *Slovak Rep.* 48°41N 17°37E **181** C10
**Mykhaylivka** *Ukraine* 47°12N 35°15E **189** J8
**Mykines** *Færoe Is.* 62°7N 7°35W **160** E9
**Myking** *Norway* 60°41N 5°19E **164** D2
**Mykolayiv** *Ukraine* 46°58N 32°0E **189** J7
**Mykolayiv** □ *Ukraine* 47°20N 31°50E **189** J6
**Mykonos** *Greece* 37°30N 25°25E **205** D7
**Mylius Erichsen Land** *Greenland* 81°30N 27°0W **154** A8
**Myllypuro** *Finland* 60°13N 25°3E **121** B3
**Mymensingh** *Bangla.* 24°45N 90°24E **241** C3
**Mynydd Du** *U.K.* 51°52N 3°50W **169** F4
**Myo-gyi** *Burma* 21°27N 96°22E **241** E6
**Myohaung** *Burma* 20°35N 93°11E **241** E4
**Myohla** *Burma* 19°16N 95°25E **241** F5
**Myotha** *Burma* 21°41N 95°43E **241** E5
**Myothit** *Kachin, Burma* 24°24N 97°24E **241** C6
**Myothit** *Magwe, Burma* 20°12N 95°27E **241** E5
**Myrasýsla** *Iceland* 64°45N 21°30W **155** C5
**Mýrdalsjökull** *Iceland* 63°40N 19°6W **155** D7
**Myrhorod** *Ukraine* 49°58N 33°37E **189** H7
**Mýri** *Iceland* 65°23N 17°23W **155** B9
**Myrtle Beach** *U.S.A.* 33°42N 78°53W **315** E15
**Myrtle Creek** *U.S.A.* 43°1N 123°17W **304** E2
**Myrtle Grove** *U.S.A.* 30°23N 87°17W **317** E2
**Myrtle Point** *U.S.A.* 43°4N 124°8W **304** E1
**Myrtleford** *Australia* 36°34S 146°44E **283** D7
**Myrtoan Sea = Mirtoo Sea** *Greece* 37°0N 23°20E **204** D5
**Myrtou** *Cyprus* 35°18N 33°4E **207** E9
**Myrviken** *Sweden* 62°58N 14°20E **162** B8
**Mysen** *Norway* 59°33N 11°20E **164** E8
**Mysia** *Turkey* 39°50N 27°0E **203** G11
**Myślenice** *Poland* 49°51N 19°57E **185** J6
**Myślibórz** *Poland* 52°55N 14°50E **185** F1
**Mysłowice** *Poland* 50°15N 19°12E **185** H6
**Myslowitz = Mysłowice** *Poland* 50°15N 19°12E **185** H6
**Mysore = Karnataka** □ *India* 13°15N 77°0E **245** H3
**Mysore** *India* 12°17N 76°41E **245** H3
**Mystic** *Conn., U.S.A.* 41°21N 71°58W **313** E13
**Mystic** *Iowa, U.S.A.* 40°47N 92°57W **310** D4
**Mystic** ➜ *U.S.A.* 42°22N 71°3W **116** A2
**Mystras** *Greece* 37°4N 22°22E **204** D4
**Mysuru = Mysore** *India* 12°17N 76°41E **245** H3
**Myszków** *Poland* 50°45N 19°22E **185** H6
**Myszyniec** *Poland* 53°23N 21°21E **184** E8
**Mytishchi** *Russia* 55°50N 37°50E **188** E9
**Mývatn** *Iceland* 65°36N 17°0W **155** B10
**M'zab, Oued** ➜ *Algeria* 32°15N 5°0E **261** B6
**M'Zab Valley = M'zab, Oued** ➜ *Algeria* 32°15N 5°0E **261** B6
**Mže** ➜ *Czech Rep.* 49°46N 13°24E **180** B6
**Mzimba** *Malawi* 11°55S 33°39E **269** E3
**Mzimkulu** ➜ *S. Africa* 30°44S 30°28E **271** D5
**Mzimvubu** ➜ *S. Africa* 31°38S 29°33E **271** D4
**Mzuzu** *Malawi* 11°30S 33°55E **269** E3

# N

**N.S.C.B. Int.** ✕ **(CCU)** *India* 22°38N 88°26E **124** B2
**Na Clocha Liatha = Greystones** *Ireland* 53°9N 6°5W **166** C5
**Na Haeo** △ *Thailand* 17°31N 100°58E **236** D3
**Na Hearadh = Harris** *U.K.* 57°50N 6°55W **167** D2
**Na Hearadh, Caolas = Harris, Sd. of** *U.K.* 57°44N 7°6W **167** D1
**Na-lang** *Burma* 22°42N 97°33E **241** D6
**Na Noi** *Thailand* 18°19N 100°43E **236** C3
**Na Phao** *Laos* 17°35N 105°44E **236** D5
**Na Sam** *Vietnam* 22°3N 106°37E **228** F6
**Na Sceirí = Skerries** *Ireland* 53°35N 6°8W **166** C5
**Na Thon** *Thailand* 9°32N 99°56E **237** b
**Naab** ➜ *Germany* 49°1N 12°2E **179** F8
**Nä'älehu** *U.S.A.* 19°4N 155°35W **302** D6
**Na'am** *Sudan* 9°42N 28°27E **257** F2
**Na'am** ➜ *South Sudan* 6°48N 29°57E **257** F2
**Naama** *Algeria* 33°16N 0°19E **261** B5
**Naama** □ *Algeria* 33°15N 0°45E **261** B5
**Naantali** *Finland* 60°29N 22°2E **188** B1
**Naas** *Ireland* 53°12N 6°40W **166** C5
**Nababeep** *S. Africa* 29°36S 17°46E **270** C2
**Nabadwip = Navadwip** *India* 23°34N 88°20E **243** H13
**Nabari** *Japan* 34°37N 136°5E **223** C8
**Nabawa** *Australia* 28°30S 114°48E **279** E1
**Nabberu, L.** *Australia* 25°50S 120°30E **279** E3
**Nabburg** *Germany* 49°27N 12°11E **179** F8
**Naberezhnaya Tower** *Russia* 55°45N 37°32E **129** B2
**Naberezhnyye Chelny** *Russia* 55°42N 52°19E **190** C11
**Nabesna** *U.S.A.* 62°22N 143°0W **303** E12
**Nabeul** *Tunisia* 36°30N 10°44E **258** A2
**Nabeul** □ *Tunisia* 36°30N 10°40E **261** A7
**Nabha** *India* 30°26N 76°14E **242** D7
**Nabi Sâlih** *Egypt* 28°37N 33°59E **251** K4
**Nabīd** *Iran* 29°40N 57°38E **247** D8
**Nabire** *Indonesia* 3°15S 135°26E **231** E9
**Nabisar** *Pakistan* 25°8N 69°40E **242** G3
**Nabisipi** ➜ *Canada* 50°14N 62°13W **299** B7
**Nabiswera** *Uganda* 1°27N 32°15E **268** B3
**Nāblus = Nābulus** *West Bank* 32°14N 35°15E **251** F6
**Naboomspruit** *S. Africa* 24°32S 28°40E **271** B4
**Nabou** *Burkina Faso* 11°25N 2°50W **262** C4
**Nabouwalu** *Fiji* 17°0S 178°45E **287** A2
**Nabq** *Egypt* 28°6N 34°25E **251** K5
**Nabua** *Phil.* 13°24N 123°22E **232** E4
**Nābulus** *West Bank* 32°14N 35°15E **251** F6
**Nabunturan** *Phil.* 7°35N 125°58E **233** H5
**Nacala** *Mozam.* 14°32S 40°34E **269** E5
**Nacaome** *Honduras* 13°31N 87°30W **320** D2
**Nacaroa** *Mozam.* 14°22S 39°56E **269** E4
**Naches** *U.S.A.* 46°44N 120°42W **304** C3
**Naches** ➜ *U.S.A.* 46°38N 120°31W **306** D6
**Nachicapau, L.** *Canada* 56°40N 68°5W **299** A6
**Nachikatsuura** *Japan* 33°33N 135°58E **223** D7
**Nachingwea** *Tanzania* 10°23S 38°49E **269** E4
**Nachna** *India* 27°34N 71°41E **242** F4
**Náchod** *Czech Rep.* 50°25N 16°8E **180** A9
**Nachuge** *India* 10°47N 92°21E **245** J11
**Nacimiento, L.** *U.S.A.* 35°46N 120°53W **306** K6
**Nacka** *Sweden* 59°19N 18°10E **139** B3
**Nackara** *Australia* 32°48S 139°12E **282** B3
**Naco** *Mexico* 31°19N 109°56W **318** A3
**Nacogdoches** *U.S.A.* 31°36N 94°39W **314** F7
**Nácori Chico** *Mexico* 29°40N 108°57W **318** B3
**Nacozari de García** *Mexico* 30°25N 109°38W **318** A3
**Nacula** *Fiji* 16°54S 177°27E **287** A1
**Nada = Danzhou** *China* 19°31N 109°33E **229** a
**Nådendal = Naantali** *Finland* 60°29N 22°2E **188** B1
**Nadezhdinsky = Serov** *Russia* 59°29N 60°35E **186** C11
**Nadi** *Fiji* 17°42S 177°20E **287** A1
**Nadi** *Sudan* 18°40N 33°41E **256** D3
**Nadiad** *India* 22°41N 72°56E **242** H5
**Nădlac** *Romania* 46°10N 20°50E **182** D5
**Nador** *Morocco* 35°14N 2°58W **261** A4
**Nadur** *Malta* 35°54N 14°22E **206** F7
**Nadur** *Gozo, Malta* 36°2N 14°18E **206** E7
**Nadūshan** *Iran* 32°2N 53°35E **247** C7
**Nadvirna** *Ukraine* 48°37N 24°30E **183** B9
**Nadvoitsy** *Russia* 63°52N 34°14E **186** B5
**Nadvornaya = Nadvirna** *Ukraine* 48°37N 24°30E **183** B9
**Nadym** *Russia* 65°35N 72°42E **214** C8
**Nadym** ➜ *Russia* 66°12N 72°0E **214** C8
**Nærbø** *Norway* 58°40N 5°39E **164** F2
**Nærøyfjorden** *Norway* 60°55N 6°55E **164** D3
**Nærsnes** *Norway* 59°45N 10°27E **133** B1
**Næstved** *Denmark* 55°13N 11°44E **163** J5
**Nafada** *Nigeria* 11°8N 11°20E **263** C7
**Nafarroa = Navarra** □ *Spain* 42°40N 1°40W **196** C3
**Nafpaktos** *Greece* 38°24N 21°50E **204** C3
**Nafplio** *Greece* 37°33N 22°50E **204** D4
**Naft-e Safīd** *Iran* 31°40N 49°17E **247** D6
**Naftan Pt.** *N. Marianas* 15°5N 145°45E **302** e
**Naftshahr** *Iran* 34°0N 45°30E **213** E11
**Nafud Desert = An Nafūd** *Si. Arabia* 28°15N 41°0E **246** D4
**Nafūsah, Jabal** *Libya* 32°12N 12°30E **258** B2
**Nag Hammâdi** *Egypt* 26°2N 32°18E **256** B3
**Naga** *Japan* 26°34N 127°43E **288** a
**Naga** *Camarines S., Phil.* 13°38N 123°15E **232** E4
**Naga** *Cebu, Phil.* 10°13N 123°45E **233** F4
**Naga** *Zamboanga del S., Phil.* 7°46N 122°45E **233** H4
**Naga, Kreb en** *Africa* 24°12N 6°0W **260** D3
**Naga Hills = Nagaland** □ *India* 26°0N 94°30E **241** C5
**Naga-Shima** *Kagoshima, Japan* 32°10N 130°9E **222** E2
**Naga-Shima** *Yamaguchi, Japan* 33°49N 132°5E **222** D4
**Nagagami** *Canada* 50°23N 84°20W **298** B3
**Nagahama** *Ehime, Japan* 33°36N 132°29E **222** D4
**Nagahama** *Shiga, Japan* 35°23N 136°16E **223** B8
**Nagai** *Japan* 38°6N 140°2E **220** E10
**Nagai I.** *U.S.A.* 55°5N 160°0W **303** J8
**Nagaland** □ *India* 26°0N 94°30E **241** C5
**Nagambie** *Australia* 36°47S 145°10E **283** D6
**Nagano** *Japan* 36°40N 138°10E **223** A10
**Nagano** □ *Japan* 36°15N 138°0E **223** A10
**Nagaoka** *Japan* 37°27N 138°51E **221** F9
**Nagaon** *India* 26°20N 92°50E **241** B4
**Nagappattinam** *India* 10°46N 79°51E **245** J4
**Nagar** ➜ *Bangla.* 24°27N 89°12E **241** C2
**Nagar Karnul** *India* 16°29N 78°20E **245** F4
**Nagar Parkar** *Pakistan* 24°28N 70°46E **242** G4
**Nagara-Gawa** ➜ *Japan* 35°40N 136°43E **223** B8
**Nagaram** *India* 18°21N 80°26E **244** E5
**Nagarhole** △ *India* 12°0N 76°10E **245** J3
**Nagari Hills** *India* 13°3N 79°45E **245** H4
**Nagarjuna Sagar** *India* 16°30N 79°13E **245** F4
**Nagasaki** *Japan* 32°47N 129°50E **222** E1
**Nagasaki** □ *Japan* 32°50N 129°40E **222** E1
**Nagato** *Japan* 34°19N 131°5E **222** C3
**Nagatsuta** *Japan* 35°32N 139°31E **140** B2
**Nagaur** *India* 27°15N 73°45E **242** F5
**Nagayo** *Japan* 32°48N 129°50E **222** E1
**Nagbhir** *India* 20°34N 79°55E **244** D4
**Nagda** *India* 23°27N 75°25E **242** H6
**Nagercoil** *India* 8°12N 77°26E **245** K3
**Nagina** *India* 29°30N 78°30E **243** E8
**Nagīneh** *Iran* 34°20N 57°15E **247** C8
**Naginimara** *India* 26°49N 94°50E **241** B5
**Nagir** *Pakistan* 36°12N 74°42E **243** A6
**Naglarby** *Sweden* 60°25N 15°34E **162** D9
**Nagles Mts.** *Ireland* 52°8N 8°30W **166** D3
**Nago-wan** *Japan* 26°34N 127°57E **288** a
**Nagod** *India* 24°34N 80°36E **243** G9
**Nagold** *Germany* 48°32N 8°43E **179** G4
**Nagold** ➜ *Germany* 48°52N 8°42E **179** G4
**Nagoorin** *Australia* 24°17S 151°15E **280** C5
**Nagorno-Karabakh** □ *Azerbaijan* 39°55N 46°45E **213** C12
**Nagornyy** *Russia* 55°58N 124°57E **215** D13
**Nagoya** *Indonesia* 1°15N 104°5E **234** B2
**Nagoya** *Japan* 35°10N 136°50E **223** B8
**Nagoya** ✕ **(NGO)** *Japan* 34°53N 136°45E **223** C8
**Nagpartian = Burgos** *Phil.* 18°31N 120°39E **232** B3
**Nagpur** *India* 21°8N 79°10E **244** D4
**Nagqu** *China* 31°29N 92°3E **218** E7
**Nags Head** *St. Kitts & Nevis* 17°13N 62°38W **322** d
**Nagua** *Dom. Rep.* 19°23N 69°50W **321** C6
**Naguabo** *Puerto Rico* 18°13N 65°44W **321** b
**Nagurunguru** ◎ *Australia* 16°45S 129°45E **278** C4
**Nagyatád** *Hungary* 46°14N 17°22E **182** D2
**Nagyecsed** *Hungary* 47°53N 22°24E **182** C7
**Nagykálló** *Hungary* 47°53N 21°51E **182** C6
**Nagykanizsa** *Hungary* 46°28N 17°0E **182** D2
**Nagykáta** *Hungary* 47°25N 19°45E **182** C4
**Nagykőrös** *Hungary* 47°5N 19°48E **182** C4
**Nagyszombat = Trnava** *Slovak Rep.* 48°23N 17°35E **181** C10
**Nagytétény** *Hungary* 47°23N 18°59E **117** B1
**Nagyvárad = Oradea** *Romania* 47°2N 21°58E **182** C6
**Naha** *Japan* 26°13N 127°42E **288** a
**Nahabuan** *Indonesia* 0°49N 114°4E **235** B4
**Nahalin** *West Bank* 31°41N 35°7E **123** B1
**Nahan** *India* 30°33N 77°18E **242** D7
**Nahanni** △ *Canada* 61°36N 125°41W **296** A4
**Nahanni Butte** *Canada* 61°2N 123°31W **296** A4
**Nahargarh** *Mad. P., India* 24°10N 75°14E **242** G6
**Nahargarh** *Raj., India* 24°55N 76°50E **242** G7
**Nahariyya** *Israel* 33°1N 35°5E **250** F6
**Nahāvand** *Iran* 34°10N 48°22E **213** E13
**Nahe** ➜ *Germany* 49°58N 7°54E **179** F3
**Nahirne** *Ukraine* 45°26N 28°27E **183** E13
**Nahîya, W.** ➜ *Egypt* 28°55N 31°0E **256** B3
**Nahuel Huapi, L.** *Argentina* 41°0S 71°32W **336** B2
**Nahuel Huapi** △ *Argentina* 41°3S 71°59W **336** B2
**Nahuelbuta** △ *Chile* 37°44S 72°57W **334** D1
**Nahunta** *U.S.A.* 31°12N 81°59W **316** D8
**Nai Yong** *Thailand* 8°14N 98°22E **237** a
**Naic** *Phil.* 14°19N 120°46E **232** D3
**Naicá** *Mexico* 27°53N 105°31W **318** B3
**Naicam** *Canada* 52°30N 104°30W **297** C8
**Naifaru** *Maldives* 5°26N 73°20E **272** d
**Naikoon** ⌂ *Canada* 53°55N 131°55W **296** C2
**Naikul** *India* 21°20N 84°58E **244** D7
**Naila** *Germany* 50°19N 11°42E **179** E7
**Naimisharanya** *India* 27°21N 80°30E **243** F9
**Naimona'nyi Feng** *China* 30°26N 81°18E **243** D9
**Nain** *Nfld. & L., Canada* 56°34N 61°40W **299** A7
**Nā'īn** *Iran* 32°54N 53°0E **247** C7
**Nain** *Jamaica* 17°57N 77°38W **320** a
**Naini Tal** *India* 29°30N 79°30E **243** E8
**Nainpur** *India* 22°30N 80°10E **243** H9
**Naintré** *France* 46°46N 0°29E **172** F7
**Nainwa** *India* 25°46N 75°51E **242** G6
**Naipu** *Romania* 44°12N 25°47E **183** F10
**Nairai** *Fiji* 17°49S 179°15E **287** A2
**Nairn** *U.K.* 57°35N 3°53W **167** D5
**Nairobi** *Kenya* 1°17S 36°48E **268** C4
**Nairobi** △ *Kenya* 1°22S 36°50E **268** C4
**Naissaar** *Estonia* 59°34N 24°29E **188** C3
**Naita, Mt.** *Ethiopia* 5°30N 35°18E **257** F4
**Naitaba** *Fiji* 17°0S 179°16W **287** A3
**Naivasha** *Kenya* 0°40S 36°30E **268** C4
**Naivasha, L.** *Kenya* 0°48S 36°20E **268** C4
**Najac** *France* 44°14N 1°58E **174** D5
**Najaf = An Najaf** *Iraq* 32°3N 44°15E **213** G11
**Najafābād** *Iran* 32°40N 51°15E **247** C6
**Najafgarh Drain** ➜ *India* 28°39N 77°4E **120** B1
**Najd** *Si. Arabia* 26°30N 42°0E **248** A3
**Nájera** *Spain* 42°26N 2°48W **196** C2
**Najerilla** ➜ *Spain* 42°32N 2°48W **196** C2
**Najibabad** *India* 29°40N 78°20E **242** E8
**Najin** *N. Korea* 42°12N 130°15E **224** A5
**Najmah** *Si. Arabia* 26°42N 50°6E **247** E6
**Najrān** *Si. Arabia* 17°34N 44°18E **248** C4
**Najrān** □ *Si. Arabia* 18°30N 45°50E **248** C4
**Naju** *S. Korea* 35°3N 126°43E **224** E3
**Naka** *Japan* 36°30N 140°35E **223** A12
**Naka-Gawa** ➜ *Japan* 36°20N 140°36E **223** A12
**Nakadōri-Shima** *Japan* 32°57N 129°4E **221** H4
**Nakagusuku-wan** *Japan* 26°14N 127°53E **288** a
**Nakahara** *Japan* 35°33N 139°37E **140** B2
**Nakal = Nakło nad Notecią** *Poland* 53°9N 17°38E **185** E4
**Nakalagba** *Dem. Rep. of the Congo* 2°50N 27°58E **268** B2
**Nakalele Pt.** *U.S.A.* 21°2N 156°35W **302** B5
**Nakama** *Japan* 33°56N 130°43E **222** D2
**Nakambé = White Volta** ➜ *Ghana* 9°10N 1°15W **263** D4
**Nakaminato** *Japan* 36°21N 140°36E **223** A12
**Nakamura = Shimanto** *Japan* 32°59N 132°56E **222** E4
**Nakanai Mts.** *Papua N. G.* 5°40S 151°0E **286** C6
**Nakano** *Nagano, Japan* 36°45N 138°22E **223** A10
**Nakano** *Tōkyō, Japan* 35°42N 139°39E **140** A2
**Nakano-Shima** *Japan* 29°51N 129°52E **221** K4
**Nakanojō** *Japan* 36°35N 138°51E **223** A10
**Nakashibetsu** *Japan* 43°33N 144°59E **220** C12
**Nakatsu** *Japan* 33°34N 131°15E **222** D3
**Nakatsugawa** *Japan* 35°29N 137°30E **223** B9
**Nakfa** *Eritrea* 16°40N 38°32E **257** D4
**Nakfa** ⌂ *Eritrea* 17°28N 38°55E **257** D4
**Nakha Yai, Ko** *Thailand* 8°3N 98°28E **237** a
**Nakhichevan = Naxçıvan** *Azerbaijan* 39°12N 45°15E **213** C11
**Nakhichevan Rep. = Naxçıvan** □ *Azerbaijan* 39°25N 45°26E **213** C11
**Nakhl** *Egypt* 29°55N 33°43E **251** J4
**Nakhl-e Taqī** *Iran* 27°28N 52°36E **247** E7
**Nakhodka** *Russia* 42°53N 132°54E **220** C6
**Nakhon Nayok** *Thailand* 14°12N 101°13E **236** E3
**Nakhon Pathom** *Thailand* 13°49N 100°3E **236** F3
**Nakhon Phanom** *Thailand* 17°23N 104°43E **236** D5
**Nakhon Ratchasima** *Thailand* 14°59N 102°12E **236** E4
**Nakhon Sawan** *Thailand* 15°35N 100°10E **236** E3
**Nakhon Si Thammarat** *Thailand* 8°29N 100°0E **237** H3
**Nakhon Thai** *Thailand* 17°5N 100°44E **236** D3
**Nakhtarana** *India* 23°20N 69°15E **242** H3
**Nakijin** *Japan* 26°40N 127°58E **288** a
**Nakina** *Canada* 50°10N 86°40W **298** B2
**Nakło nad Notecią** *Poland* 53°9N 17°38E **185** E4
**Naknek** *U.S.A.* 58°44N 157°1W **303** G8
**Nako** *Burkina Faso* 10°40N 3°4W **262** C4
**Nakodar** *India* 31°8N 75°31E **242** D6
**Nakskov** *Denmark* 54°50N 11°8E **163** K5
**Naktong** ➜ *S. Korea* 35°7N 128°57E **227** G15
**Nakuru** *Kenya* 0°15S 36°4E **268** C4
**Nakuru, L.** *Kenya* 0°23S 36°5E **268** C4
**Nakusp** *Canada* 50°20N 117°45W **296** C5
**Nal** *Pakistan* 27°40N 66°12E **242** F2
**Nal** ➜ *Pakistan* 25°20N 65°30E **242** G1
**Nalázi** *Mozam.* 24°3S 33°20E **271** B5
**Nalchik** *Russia* 43°30N 43°33E **191** J6
**Nałęczów** *Poland* 51°17N 22°9E **185** G9
**Nalerigu** *Ghana* 10°35N 0°25W **263** C4
**Nalgonda** *India* 17°6N 79°15E **244** F4
**Nalhati** *India* 24°17N 87°52E **243** G12
**Naliya** *India* 23°16N 68°50E **242** H3
**Nallamalai Hills** *India* 15°30N 78°50E **245** G4
**Nallıhan** *Turkey* 40°11N 31°20E **212** B4
**Nalolo** *Zambia* 15°33S 23°7E **265** F4
**Nalón** ➜ *Spain* 43°32N 6°4W **194** B4
**Nalong** *Burma* 24°44N 97°28E **241** C6
**Nalubaale Dam** *Uganda* 0°30N 33°5E **268** B3
**Nalumasortoq** *Greenland* 60°23N 44°28W **154** E6
**Nālūt** *Libya* 31°54N 11°0E **258** B2
**Nālūt** □ *Libya* 31°52N 10°58E **258** B2
**Nam Can** *Vietnam* 8°46N 104°59E **237** H5
**Nam-ch'on** *N. Korea* 38°15N 126°26E **224** C3
**Nam Co** *China* 30°30N 90°45E **218** E7
**Nam Dinh** *Vietnam* 20°25N 106°5E **228** G6
**Nam Du, Quan Dao** *Vietnam* 9°41N 104°21E **237** H5
**Nam Hka** ➜ *Burma* 21°34N 95°41E **228** G2
**Nam Loi** ➜ *Burma* 21°3N 98°27E **228** G3
**Nam Nao** △ *Thailand* 16°44N 101°32E **236** D3
**Nam Ngum Res.** *Laos* 18°35N 102°34E **236** C4
**Nam-Phan** *Vietnam* 10°30N 106°0E **237** G6
**Nam Phong** *Thailand* 16°42N 102°52E **236** D4
**Nam Theun Res.** *Laos* 17°51N 105°3E **236** D5
**Nam Tok** *Thailand* 14°21N 99°4E **236** E2
**Nam Un Res.** *Thailand* 17°13N 103°44E **236** D4
**Namachire** *Angola* 11°26S 22°43E **265** E4
**Namacunde** *Angola* 17°18S 15°50E **265** F3
**Namacurra** *Mozam.* 17°30S 36°50E **271** A6
**Namadgi** △ *Australia* 35°42S 149°0E **283** C8
**Namai B.** *Palau* 7°31N 134°38E **288** c
**Namak, Daryācheh-ye** *Iran* 34°30N 52°0E **247** C7
**Namak, Kavir-e** *Iran* 34°30N 57°30E **247** C8
**Namakkal** *India* 11°13N 78°13E **245** J4
**Namakzār, Daryācheh-ye** *Iran* 34°0N 60°30E **240** B1
**Namaland** *Namibia* 26°0S 17°0E **270** B2
**Namanga** *Kenya* 2°33S 36°47E **268** C4
**Namangan** *Uzbekistan* 41°0N 71°40E **217** D8
**Namangan** □ *Uzbekistan* 41°0N 71°15E **217** D8
**Namapa** *Mozam.* 13°43S 39°50E **269** E4
**Namaqua** △ *S. Africa* 30°0S 17°30E **270** D2
**Namaqualand** *S. Africa* 30°0S 17°25E **270** D2
**Namasagali** *Uganda* 1°2N 33°0E **268** B3
**Namatanai** *Papua N. G.* 3°40S 152°29E **286** B7
**Namber** *Indonesia* 1°2S 134°49E **231** E8
**Nambour** *Australia* 26°32S 152°58E **281** D5
**Nambouwalu = Nabouwalu** *Fiji* 17°0S 178°45E **287** A2
**Nambuangongo** *Angola* 8°1S 14°12E **265** D2
**Nambucca Heads** *Australia* 30°37S 153°0E **283** A10
**Nambung** △ *Australia* 30°30S 115°5E **279** F2
**Namcha Barwa** *China* 29°40N 95°10E **218** F8
**Namche Bazar** *Nepal* 27°51N 86°47E **243** F12
**Namchonjŏm = Nam-ch'on** *N. Korea* 38°15N 126°26E **224** C3
**Namdapha** △ *India* 27°30N 96°50E **241** B6
**Namecunda** *Mozam.* 14°54S 37°37E **269** E4
**Nameh** *Indonesia* 2°34N 116°21E **235** B5
**Namen = Namur** *Belgium* 50°27N 4°52E **170** D4
**Namenalala** *Fiji* 17°8S 179°9E **287** A2
**Nameponda** *Mozam.* 15°50S 39°50E **269** F4
**Nameri** △ *India* 26°55N 92°55E **241** B4
**Namerikawa** *Japan* 36°46N 137°20E **223** A9
**Náměšť nad Oslavou** *Czech Rep.* 49°12N 16°10E **181** B9
**Námestovo** *Slovak Rep.* 49°24N 19°25E **181** B12
**Nametil** *Mozam.* 15°40S 39°21E **269** F4
**Namew L.** *Canada* 54°14N 101°56W **297** C8
**Namgia** *India* 31°48N 78°40E **243** D8
**Namhkam** *Burma* 23°50N 97°41E **228** E1
**Namhsan** *Burma* 22°48N 97°2E **241** D6
**Namialo** *Mozam.* 14°55S 39°59E **269** E4
**Namib Desert** *Namibia* 22°30S 15°0E **270** B2
**Namib-Naukluft** ⌂ *Namibia* 24°40S 15°16E **270** B2
**Namibe** *Angola* 15°7S 12°11E **265** F2
**Namibe** □ *Angola* 16°35S 12°30E **265** F2
**Namibe** ⌂ *Angola* 16°35S 12°20E **265** F2
**Namibia** ■ *Africa* 22°0S 18°9E **270** B2
**Namibia Abyssal Plain** *Atl. Oc.* 30°0S 5°30E **152** J12
**Namibwoestyn = Namib Desert** *Namibia* 22°30S 15°0E **270** B2
**Namīn** *Iran* 38°25N 48°30E **213** C13
**Namjeju** *S. Korea* 33°14N 126°33E **224** a
**Namlan** *Burma* 22°15N 97°24E **241** D6
**Namlea** *Indonesia* 3°18S 127°5E **231** E7
**Namoi** ➜ *Australia* 30°12S 149°30E **283** A9
**Namous, O. en** ➜ *Algeria* 31°0N 0°15W **261** B4
**Nampa** *U.S.A.* 43°34N 116°34W **304** E5
**Nampala** *Mali* 15°20N 5°30W **262** B3
**Namp'o** *N. Korea* 38°52N 125°10E **224** C2
**Namp'o** □ *N. Korea* 38°52N 125°25E **224** C2
**Nampō-Shotō** *Japan* 32°0N 140°0E **221** J10
**Nampula** *Mozam.* 15°6S 39°15E **269** F4
**Namrole** *Indonesia* 3°46S 126°46E **231** E7
**Namsan Park** *S. Korea* 37°32N 126°59E **137** B1
**Namse Shankou** *China* 30°0N 82°25E **243** E10
**Namsen** ➜ *Norway* 64°28N 11°37E **160** D14
**Namslau = Namysłów** *Poland* 51°6N 17°42E **185** G4
**Namsos** *Norway* 64°29N 11°30E **160** D14
**Namtok Chat Trakan** △ *Thailand* 17°17N 100°40E **236** D3
**Namtok Huay Yang** △ *Thailand* 11°35N 99°30E **237** G2
**Namtok Mae Surin** △ *Thailand* 18°55N 98°2E **236** C2
**Namtok Ngao** △ *Thailand* 9°58N 98°46E **237** H2
**Namtok Phlew** △ *Thailand* 12°32N 102°13E **236** F4
**Namtok Yong** △ *Thailand* 8°15N 98°45E **237** H2
**Namtsy** *Russia* 62°43N 129°37E **215** C13
**Namtu** *Burma* 23°5N 97°28E **241** D6
**Namtumbo** *Tanzania* 10°30S 36°4E **269** E4
**Namu** *Canada* 51°52N 127°50W **296** C3
**Namuka-i-Lau** *Fiji* 18°53S 178°37W **287** B3
**Namukulu** *Cook Is.* 18°57S 169°54W **289** g
**Namumea** *Tuvalu* 5°41S 176°9E **277** B14
**Namur** *Belgium* 50°27N 4°52E **170** D4
**Namur** □ *Belgium* 50°17N 5°0E **170** D4
**Namuruputh** *Kenya* 4°34N 35°57E **268** B4
**Namutoni** *Namibia* 18°49S 16°55E **270** A2
**Namwala** *Zambia* 15°44S 26°30E **269** F2
**Namwon** *Jeju-do, S. Korea* 33°16N 126°43E **224** a
**Namwon** *Jeollabuk-do, S. Korea* 35°23N 127°23E **224** E3
**Namyang** *N. Korea* 42°57N 129°52E **224** A4
**Namyangju** *S. Korea* 37°38N 127°12E **224** D3
**Namyeong** *S. Korea* 37°32N 126°57E **137** B1
**Namyit I.** *S. China Sea* 10°11N 114°22E **230** C4
**Namysłów** *Poland* 51°6N 17°42E **185** G4
**Nan** *Thailand* 18°48N 100°46E **236** C3
**Nan** ➜ *Thailand* 15°42N 100°9E **236** E3
**Nan-ch'ang = Nanchang** *China* 28°42N 115°55E **229** C10
**Nan Ling** *China* 25°0N 112°30E **229** E9
**Nan Xian** *China* 29°20N 112°22E **229** C9
**Nana** *C.A.R.* 5°0N 15°50E **264** A3
**Nana** *Romania* 44°17N 26°34E **183** F11
**Nana-Barya** ⌂ *C.A.R.* 7°40N 17°29E **264** A3
**Nana-Grébizi** □ *C.A.R.* 7°0N 19°0E **264** A3
**Nana Kru** *Liberia* 4°55N 8°45W **262** E3
**Nana-Mambéré** □ *C.A.R.* 5°30N 15°30E **264** A3
**Nanaimo** *Canada* 49°10N 124°0W **296** D4
**Nänäkuli** *U.S.A.* 21°24N 158°9W **302** K13
**Nanam** *N. Korea* 41°44N 129°40E **224** B4
**Nan'an** *China* 24°59N 118°21E **229** E12
**Nanango** *Australia* 26°40S 152°0E **281** D5
**Nan'ao** *Guangdong, China* 23°28N 117°5E **229** F11
**Nanao** *Japan* 37°0N 137°0E **221** F8
**Nanao** *Taiwan* 24°28N 121°48E **225** B3
**Nanbiancun** *China* 23°4N 113°10E **121** B1
**Nanbu** *China* 31°18N 106°3E **228** B6
**Nanchang** *China* 28°42N 115°55E **229** C10
**Nanchang He** ➜ *China* 39°58N 116°14E **114** B1
**Nancheng** *China* 27°33N 116°35E **229** D11
**Nanching = Nanjing** *China* 32°2N 118°47E **229** A12
**Nanchong** *China* 30°43N 106°2E **228** B6
**Nanchuan** *China* 29°9N 107°6E **228** C6
**Nanchung = Nanchong** *China* 30°43N 106°2E **228** B6
**Nancowry** *India* 7°59N 93°32E **245** L11
**Nancy** *France* 48°42N 6°12E **173** D13
**Nanda Devi** *India* 30°23N 79°59E **243** D8
**Nanda Devi** △ *India* 30°30N 79°50E **243** D8
**Nanda Kot** *India* 30°17N 80°5E **243** D9
**Nandan = Minamiawaji** *Japan* 34°10N 134°42E **222** C6
**Nandan** *China* 24°58N 107°29E **228** E6
**Nandang** *China* 23°6N 113°12E **121** B2
**Nanded** *India* 19°10N 77°20E **244** E3
**Nandewar Ra.** *Australia* 30°15S 150°35E **281** E5
**Nandgaon** *India* 20°19N 74°39E **244** D2
**Nandi = Nadi** *Fiji* 17°42S 177°20E **287** A1
**Nandi** *Zimbabwe* 20°58S 31°44E **269** G3
**Nandigama** *India* 16°47N 80°18E **244** F5
**Nandigram** *India* 22°1N 87°58E **243** H12
**Nandikotkur** *India* 15°52N 78°18E **245** G4
**Nandura** *India* 20°52N 76°25E **244** D3
**Nandurbar** *India* 21°20N 74°15E **244** D2
**Nandyal** *India* 15°30N 78°30E **245** G4
**Nanfeng** *Guangdong, China* 23°45N 111°47E **229** F8
**Nanfeng** *Jiangxi, China* 27°12N 116°28E **229** D11
**Nang Rong** *Thailand* 14°38N 102°48E **236** E4
**Nanga-Eboko** *Cameroon* 4°41N 12°22E **263** E7
**Nanga Parbat** *Pakistan* 35°10N 74°35E **243** B6
**Nangade** *Mozam.* 11°5S 39°36E **269** E4
**Nangal Dewat** *India* 28°33N 77°5E **120** B1
**Nangalao I.** *Phil.* 11°26N 120°10E **233** F3
**Nangamau** *Indonesia* 0°6S 111°55E **235** C4
**Nangamentebah** *Indonesia* 0°33N 112°46E **235** B4
**Nangapinoh** *Indonesia* 0°20S 111°44E **235** C4
**Nangar** △ *Australia* 33°23S 148°3E **283** B8
**Nangarhār** □ *Afghan.* 34°20N 70°0E **240** B3
**Nangatayap** *Indonesia* 1°32S 110°34E **235** C4
**Nangbéto, L. de** *Togo* 7°26N 1°25E **263** D5
**Nangeya Mts.** *Uganda* 3°30N 33°30E **268** B3
**Nangis** *France* 48°33N 3°1E **173** D10
**Nangnim-sanmaek** *N. Korea* 40°13N 126°51E **224** B3
**Nangong** *China* 37°23N 115°22E **226** F8
**Nangtud, Mt.** *Phil.* 11°17N 122°11E **233** F4
**Nanguneri** *India* 8°29N 77°40E **245** K3
**Nangwarry** *Australia* 37°33S 140°48E **282** D4
**Nanhua** *Yunnan, China* 25°13N 101°21E **228** E3
**Nanhua** *Taiwan* 23°2N 120°28E **225** C2
**Nanhuang** *China* 36°58N 121°48E **227** F11
**Nanhui** *China* 31°5N 121°44E **229** B13
**Nanhunan Shan** *Taiwan* 24°21N 121°26E **225** B3
**Nanisivik** *Canada* 73°2N 84°33W **295** C15
**Naniwa** *Japan* 34°39N 135°29E **133** B1
**Nanjangud** *India* 12°6N 76°43E **245** H3
**Nanji Shan** *China* 27°27N 121°4E **229** D13
**Nanjian** *China* 25°2N 100°25E **228** E3
**Nanjiang** *China* 32°28N 106°51E **228** A6
**Nanjing** *Fujian, China* 24°25N 117°20E **229** E11
**Nanjing** *Jiangsu, China* 32°2N 118°47E **229** A12
**Nanjirinji** *Tanzania* 9°41S 39°5E **269** D4
**Nankana Sahib** *Pakistan* 31°27N 73°38E **242** D5
**Nankang** *Jiangxi, China* 25°40N 114°45E **229** E10
**Nankang** *Taiwan* 25°3N 121°35E **225** A3
**Nanking = Nanjing** *China* 32°2N 118°47E **229** A12
**Nankoku** *Japan* 33°39N 133°44E **222** D5
**Nanlang** *China* 22°30N 113°32E **219** a
**Nanliao** *Taiwan* 24°50N 120°55E **225** B2
**Nanling** *China* 30°55N 118°20E **229** B12
**Nannial** *India* 19°4N 79°38E **244** E4
**Nanning** *China* 22°48N 108°20E **228** F7
**Nannup** *Australia* 33°59S 115°48E **279** F2
**Nanole** *India* 19°0N 72°55E **130** A2
**Nanortalik** *Greenland* 60°10N 45°17W **154** E6
**Nanpan Jiang** ➜ *China* 25°10N 106°5E **228** E6
**Nanpara** *India* 27°52N 81°33E **243** F9
**Nanping** *Fujian, China* 26°38N 118°10E **229** D12
**Nanping** *Henan, China* 29°55N 112°3E **229** C9
**Nanpu Bridge** *China* 31°12N 121°30E **138** B2
**Nanri Dao** *China* 25°15N 119°25E **229** E12
**Nansang** *Burma* 20°53N 97°43E **241** E6
**Nansei-Shotō = Ryūkyū-Rettō** *Japan* 26°0N 126°0E **221** M3
**Nansen Basin** *Arctic* 84°0N 50°0E **150** A10
**Nansen Land** *Greenland* 83°0N 43°0W **154** A6
**Nansen Sd.** *Canada* 81°0N 91°0W **295** A13
**Nansha** *China* 22°45N 113°34E **219** a
**Nansha Port** *China* 22°40N 113°40E **219** a
**Nanshan** *China* 18°19N 109°10E **229** a
**Nanshan I.** *S. China Sea* 10°45N 115°49E **230** B5
**Nanshi** *China* 31°12N 121°29E **138** B1
**Nansio** *Tanzania* 2°3S 33°4E **268** C3
**Nant** *France* 44°1N 3°18E **174** D7
**Nantan** *Japan* 35°6N 135°28E **223** B7
**Nantawarrinna** ◎ *Australia* 30°49S 138°58E **281** B2
**Nanterre** *France* 48°53N 2°12E **134** A2
**Nantes** *France* 47°12N 1°33W **172** E5
**Nantiat** *France* 46°1N 1°11E **174** B5
**Nanticoke** *U.S.A.* 41°12N 76°0W **313** E8
**Nanton** *Canada* 50°21N 113°46W **296** C6
**Nanton Pt.** *Antigua & B.* 17°0N 61°45W **322** b
**Nantong** *China* 32°1N 120°52E **229** A13
**Nantou** *China* 22°32N 113°55E **219** a
**Nant'ou** *Taiwan* 23°55N 120°41E **225** C2
**Nant'ou** □ *Taiwan* 23°50N 121°0E **225** C3
**Nantua** *France* 46°10N 5°35E **173** F12
**Nantucket** *U.S.A.* 41°17N 70°6W **309** E18
**Nantucket I.** *U.S.A.* 41°16N 70°5W **309** E18
**Nantulo** *Mozam.* 12°32S 38°45E **269** E4
**Nantung = Nantong** *China* 32°1N 120°52E **229** A13
**Nantwich** *U.K.* 53°4N 2°31W **168** D5
**Nanty Glo** *U.S.A.* 40°28N 78°50W **312** F6
**Nantzu** *Taiwan* 22°44N 120°19E **225** D2
**Nanuku Passage** *Fiji* 16°45S 179°15W **287** A3
**Nanumanga** *Pac. Oc.* 6°18S 176°20E **277** B14
**Nanuque** *Brazil* 17°50S 40°21W **333** E3
**Nanusa, Kepulauan** *Indonesia* 4°45N 127°1E **231** D7
**Nanutarra Roadhouse** *Australia* 22°32S 115°30E **278** D2
**Nanwan** *Taiwan* 21°57N 120°46E **225** E2
**Nanxi** *China* 28°54N 104°59E **228** C5
**Nanxiong** *China* 25°6N 114°15E **229** E10
**Nanyang** *China* 33°11N 112°30E **226** H7
**Nanyi Hu** *China* 31°5N 119°0E **229** B12
**Nanyuan** *China* 39°47N 116°24E **226** E9
**Nanyuki** *Kenya* 0°2N 37°4E **268** B4
**Nanzhang** *China* 31°45N 111°50E **229** B8
**Nanzhao** *China* 33°30N 112°20E **226** H7
**Nanzi = Nantzu** *Taiwan* 22°44N 120°19E **225** D2
**Nao, C. de la** *Spain* 38°44N 0°14E **197** G5
**Naococane, L.** *Canada* 52°50N 70°45W **299** B5
**Naogaon** *Bangla.* 24°52N 88°52E **241** C2
**Naoné** *Vanuatu* 15°0S 168°8E **287** E6
**Naoussa** *Cyclades, Greece* 37°7N 25°14E **205** D7
**Naoussa** *Imathia, Greece* 40°42N 22°9E **202** F6
**Naozhou Dao** *China* 20°55N 110°20E **229** G8
**Napa** *U.S.A.* 38°18N 122°17W **306** G4
**Napa** ➜ *U.S.A.* 38°10N 122°19W **306** G4
**Napaimiut** *U.S.A.* 61°33N 158°42W **303** F8
**Napakiak** *U.S.A.* 60°42N 161°57W **303** F7
**Näpali Coast** *U.S.A.* 22°11N 159°39W **302** A2
**Napanee** *Canada* 44°15N 77°0W **312** B8
**Napanoch** *U.S.A.* 41°44N 74°22W **313** E10
**Napaskiak** *U.S.A.* 60°43N 161°55W **303** F7
**Nape** *Laos* 18°18N 105°6E **236** C5
**Nape Pass = Keo Neua, Deo** *Vietnam* 18°23N 105°10E **236** C5
**Naperville** *U.S.A.* 41°46N 88°9W **311** C8
**Napier** *N.Z.* 39°30S 176°56E **284** F5
**Napier Broome B.** *Australia* 14°2S 126°37E **278** B4
**Napier Mole** *Pakistan* 24°49N 66°58E **123** B1
**Napier Pen.** *Australia* 12°4S 135°43E **280** A2
**Napierville** *Canada* 45°11N 73°25W **313** A11
**Napili-Honokowai** *U.S.A.* 20°58N 156°39W **302** C5
**Naples = Nápoli** *Italy* 40°50N 14°15E **201** B7
**Naples** *U.S.A.* 26°8N 81°48W **317** J8
**Naples Park** *U.S.A.* 26°17N 81°46W **317** J8
**Napo** *China* 23°22N 105°50E **228** F5
**Napo** □ *Ecuador* 0°30S 77°0W **328** D2
**Napo** ➜ *Peru* 3°20S 72°40W **328** D3
**Napoleon** *N. Dak., U.S.A.* 46°30N 99°46W **308** B4
**Napoleon** *Ohio, U.S.A.* 41°23N 84°8W **311** C12
**Napoleon's Tomb** *St. Helena* 15°56S 5°42W **153** h
**Nápoli** *Italy* 40°50N 14°15E **201** B7
**Nápoli, G. di** *Italy* 40°43N 14°10E **201** B7
**Nápoli Capodichino** ✕ **(NAP)** *Italy* 40°53N 14°16E **201** B7
**Napopo** *Dem. Rep. of the Congo* 4°15N 28°0E **268** B2
**Nappanee** *U.S.A.* 41°27N 86°0W **311** C11
**Napperby** *Australia* 33°9S 138°7E **282** B3
**Naqadeh** *Iran* 36°57N 45°23E **213** D11
**Naqb, Ra's an** *Jordan* 29°48N 35°44E **251** J6
**Naqqāsh** *Iran* 35°40N 49°6E **247** C6
**När** *Sweden* 57°15N 18°35E **163** G10
**Nara** *Japan* 34°40N 135°49E **223** C7
**Nara** *Mali* 15°10N 7°20W **262** B3
**Nara** □ *Japan* 34°30N 136°0E **223** C8
**Nara Canal** *Pakistan* 24°30N 69°20E **242** G3
**Nara Visa** *U.S.A.* 35°37N 103°6W **305** J12
**Naracoorte** *Australia* 36°58S 140°45E **282** D4
**Naradhan** *Australia* 33°34S 146°17E **283** B7
**Naraina** *India* 28°36N 77°8E **120** B1
**Naraini** *India* 25°11N 80°29E **243** G9
**Naranjos** *Mexico* 21°21N 97°41W **319** C5
**Narasannapeta** *India* 18°25N 84°3E **244** E7
**Narasapur** *India* 16°26N 81°40E **245** F5
**Narasaraopet** *India* 16°14N 80°4E **245** F5
**Narathiwat** *Thailand* 6°30N 101°48E **237** J3
**Narayanapatnam** *India* 18°53N 83°10E **244** E6
**Narayangadh = Bharatpur** *Nepal* 27°34N 84°10E **243** F11
**Narayanganj** *Bangla.* 23°40N 90°33E **241** D3
**Narayanpet** *India* 16°45N 77°30E **244** F3
**Narbada = Narmada** ➜ *India* 21°38N 72°36E **242** J5
**Narberth** *U.K.* 51°47N 4°44W **169** F3
**Narbonne** *France* 43°11N 3°0E **174** E7
**Narborough, I. = Fernandina, I.** *Ecuador* 0°25S 91°30W **330** a
**Narbuvoll** *Norway* 62°21N 11°27E **164** B8
**Narcea** ➜ *Spain* 43°33N 6°44W **194** B4
**Narcondam I.** *India* 13°20N 94°16E **245** H12
**Nardīn** *Iran* 37°3N 55°59E **247** B7
**Nardò** *Italy* 40°11N 18°2E **201** B11
**Narembeen** *Australia* 32°7S 118°24E **279** F2
**Nares Abyssal Plain** *Atl. Oc.* 22°0N 67°0W **152** D5
**Nares Str.** *Arctic* 80°0N 70°0W **154** B3
**Naretha** *Australia* 31°0S 124°45E **279** F3
**Narew** ➜ *Poland* 52°26N 20°41E **185** F7
**Nari** ➜ *Pakistan* 28°0N 67°40E **242** F2
**Nariman Pt.** *Mumbai, India* **130** c1
**Narin** *Afghan.* 36°5N 69°0E **240** A3
**Narindra, Helodranon' i** *Madag.* 14°55S 47°30E **272** A2
**Narino** □ *Colombia* 1°30N 78°0W **328** C2
**Narita** *Japan* 35°47N 140°19E **223** B12
**Narita, Tōkyō** ✕ **(NRT)** *Japan* 35°45N 140°25E **223** B12
**Nariva** ➜ *Trin. & Tob.* 10°24N 61°4W **323** t
**Nariva Swamp** *Trin. & Tob.* 10°26N 61°4W **323** t
**Närke** *Sweden* 59°10N 15°0E **162** E8
**Narmada** ➜ *India* 21°38N 72°36E **242** J5
**Narmada Canal** *India* 22°20N 73°45E **244** C1
**Nārmak** *Iran* 35°42N 51°28E **141** A2
**Narman** *Turkey* 40°26N 41°57E **213** B9
**Narnaul** *India* 28°5N 76°11E **242** E7
**Narni** *Italy* 42°30N 12°30E **199** F9
**Naro** *Ghana* 10°22N 2°27W **262** C4
**Naro Fominsk** *Russia* 55°23N 36°43E **188** E9
**Narochanski** △ *Belarus* 54°55N 26°50E **188** E4
**Narodnaya** *Russia* 65°5N 59°58E **186** A10
**Narodowy, Stadion** *Warsaw, Poland* **143** b3
**Narok** *Kenya* 1°55S 35°52E **268** C4
**Narón** *Spain* 43°32N 8°9W **194** B2
**Narooma** *Australia* 36°14S 150°4E **283** D9
**Narowal** *Pakistan* 32°6N 74°52E **242** C6
**Narrabri** *Australia* 30°19S 149°46E **281** E4
**Narran** ➜ *Australia* 28°37S 148°12E **281** D4
**Narrandera** *Australia* 34°42S 146°31E **283** C7
**Narrogin** *Australia* 32°58S 117°14E **279** F2
**Narromine** *Australia* 32°12S 148°12E **283** B8
**Narrow Hills** ⌂ *Canada* 54°0N 104°37W **297** C8
**Narrows, The** *St. Kitts & Nevis* 17°12N 62°40W **322** d
**Narsampet** *India* 17°57N 79°58E **244** F4
**Narsaq** *Greenland* 60°57N 46°4W **154** E6
**Narsimhapur** *India* 22°54N 79°14E **243** H8
**Narsingdi** *Bangla.* 23°55N 90°43E **241** D3
**Narsinghgarh** *India* 23°45N 76°40E **242** H7
**Narsinghpur** *India* 20°28N 85°5E **244** D7
**Narsipatnam** *India* 17°40N 82°37E **244** F6
**Nartes, L. e** *Albania* 40°32N 19°25E **202** F3
**Nartkala** *Russia* 43°33N 43°51E **191** J6

Naruo *Japan* 34°43N 135°22E **133** A1
Narutō = Sanmu *Kantō, Japan* 34°11N 134°37E **222** C6
Narutō = Sanmu *Shikoku, Japan* 35°36N 140°25E **223** B12
Naruto-Kaikyō *Japan* 34°14N 134°39E **222** C6
Narva *Estonia* 59°23N 28°12E **188** C5
Narva → *Russia* 59°27N 28°2E **188** C4
Narva Bay = Narva Laht *Estonia* 59°35N 27°35E **161** G22
Narva Laht *Estonia* 59°35N 27°35E **161** G22
Narvacan *Phil.* 17°25N 120°28E **232** C3
Narvik *Norway* 68°28N 17°26E **160** B17
Narvskoye Vdkhr. *Russia* 59°18N 28°14E **188** C5
Narwana *India* 29°39N 76°6E **242** E7
Narwiański △ *Poland* 52°5N 22°53E **185** F9
Narwinbi ❂ *Australia* 16°7S 136°17E **280** B2
Naryan-Mar *Russia* 67°42N 53°12E **186** A9
Narym *Russia* 59°0N 81°30E **214** D9
Naryn *Kyrgyzstan* 41°26N 75°58E **217** D9
Naryn □ *Kyrgyzstan* 41°26N 75°58E **217** D9
Naryn → *Uzbekistan* 40°52N 71°36E **217** D8
Naryn Qum *Kazakhstan* 47°30N 49°0E **191** G9
Nás, An = Naas *Ireland* 53°12N 6°40W **166** C5
Nasa *Norway* 66°29N 15°23E **160** C16
Nasau *Fiji* 17°19S 179°27E **287** A2
Năsăud *Romania* 47°19N 24°29E **183** C9
Nasawa *Vanuatu* 15°12S 168°9E **287** E6
Naşb, W. → *Egypt* 28°29N 34°31E **251** K5
Näsby *Sweden* 59°25N 18°5E **139** A2
Näsbypark *Sweden* 59°25N 18°5E **139** A2
Nasca *Peru* 14°50S 74°57W **330** C3
Nasca Ridge *Pac. Oc.* 20°0S 80°0W **289** K19
Naseby *N.Z.* 45°1S 170°10E **285** F5
Naselle *U.S.A.* 46°22N 123°49W **306** D3
Naser, Buheirat en *Egypt* 23°0N 32°30E **256** C3
Nashik = Nasik *India* 19°58N 73°50E **244** E1
Nashua *Iowa, U.S.A.* 42°57N 92°32W **310** B4
Nashua *Mont., U.S.A.* 48°8N 106°22W **304** B10
Nashua *N.H., U.S.A.* 42°45N 71°28W **313** D13
Nashville *Ark., U.S.A.* 33°57N 93°51W **314** E8
Nashville *Ga., U.S.A.* 31°12N 83°15W **316** D6
Nashville *Ill., U.S.A.* 38°21N 89°23W **310** F7
Nashville *Ind., U.S.A.* 39°12N 86°15W **311** E10
Nashville *Mich., U.S.A.* 42°36N 85°5W **311** B11
Nashville *Tenn., U.S.A.* 36°10N 86°47W **315** C11
Našice *Croatia* 45°32N 18°4E **182** E3
Nasielsk *Poland* 52°35N 20°50E **185** F7
Nasik *India* 19°58N 73°50E **244** E1
Nasinu *Fiji* 18°4S 178°30E **287** A2
Nasipit *Phil.* 8°57N 125°19E **233** G5
Nasir *South Sudan* 8°36N 33°4E **257** F3
Nasirabad = Mymensingh *Bangla.* 24°45N 90°24E **241** C3
Nasirabad *India* 26°15N 74°45E **242** F6
Nasirabad *Pakistan* 28°23N 68°24E **242** E3
Nasiri = Ahvāz *Iran* 31°20N 48°40E **247** D6
Nasiriyah = An Nāşirīyah *Iraq* 31°0N 46°15E **246** D5
Naskaupi → *Canada* 53°47N 60°51W **299** B7
Naso *Italy* 38°7N 14°47E **201** D7
Naso Pt. *Phil.* 10°25N 121°57E **233** F3
Naşrābād *Iran* 34°8N 51°26E **247** C6
Naşriān-e Pā'īn *Iran* 32°52N 46°52E **246** C5
Nass → *Canada* 55°0N 129°40W **296** C3
Nassarawa *Nigeria* 8°32N 7°41E **263** D6
Nassarawa □ *Nigeria* 8°30N 8°20E **263** D6
Nassau *Bahamas* 25°5N 77°20W **153** b
Nassau *N.Y., U.S.A.* 42°31N 73°37W **313** D11
Nassau, B. *Chile* 55°20S 68°0W **336** E3
Nassau Int. ✈ (NAS) *Bahamas* 25°3N 77°28W **153** b
Nasser, L. = Naser, Buheirat en *Egypt* 23°0N 32°30E **256** C3
Nasser City = Kôm Ombo *Egypt* 24°25N 32°52E **256** C3
Nassian *Ivory C.* 8°28N 3°28W **262** D4
Nässjö *Sweden* 57°39N 14°42E **163** G8
Nastapoka → *Canada* 56°55N 76°33W **298** A4
Nastapoka, Is. *Canada* 56°55N 76°50W **298** A4
Nasugbu *Phil.* 14°5N 120°38E **232** D3
Näsum *Sweden* 56°10N 14°29E **163** H8
Nasushiobara *Japan* 36°58N 140°3E **221** F10
Näsviken *Sweden* 61°46N 16°52E **162** C10
Nat Ma Taung △ *Burma* 21°30N 93°35E **241** E4
Nata *Botswana* 20°12S 26°12E **270** B4
Nata → *Botswana* 20°14S 26°10E **270** B4
Natagaima *Colombia* 3°37N 75°6W **328** C2
Natal *Brazil* 5°47S 35°13W **332** C4
Natal *Indonesia* 0°35N 99°7E **234** B1
Natal Drakensberg = uKhahlamba Drakensberg ⌓ *S. Africa* 29°27S 29°30E **271** C4
Natalinci *Serbia* 44°15N 20°49E **182** F5
Naţanz *Iran* 33°30N 51°55E **247** C6
Natashquan *Canada* 50°14N 61°46W **299** B7
Natashquan → *Canada* 50°7N 61°50W **299** B7
Natchez *U.S.A.* 31°34N 91°24W **314** F9
Natchitoches *U.S.A.* 31°46N 93°5W **314** F8
Natewa B. *Fiji* 16°35S 179°40E **287** A2
Nathalia *Australia* 36°1S 145°13E **283** D6
Nathan Philips Square *Toronto, Canada* **141** b2
Nathdwara *India* 24°55N 73°50E **242** G5
Nathu La *Asia* 27°24N 88°49E **241** B2
Nati, Pta. *Spain* 40°3N 3°50E **206** A4
Natimuk *Australia* 36°42S 142°0E **282** D5
Nation → *Canada* 55°30N 123°32W **296** B4
National Arboretum *Washington, D.C., U.S.A.* 38°54N 76°59W **143** B2
National Art Gallery *Beijing, China* **114** b2
National Capital District □ *Papua N. G.* 9°25S 147°10E **286** E4
National City *U.S.A.* 32°40N 117°5W **307** N9
National Grand Theatre *Beijing, China* **114** c2
National Maritime Museum *London, U.K.* 51°29N 0°0 **125** B3
National September 11 Memorial and Museum *New York, U.S.A.* **132** e1
National University (N.U.S.) *Singapore* 1°19N 103°46E **138** B2
National Zoological Park *Washington, D.C., U.S.A.* 38°55N 77°4W **143** B2
Nationals Park *U.S.A.* 38°53N 77°1W **143** B2
Natitingou *Benin* 10°20N 1°26E **263** C5
Natividad, I. *Mexico* 27°52N 115°11W **318** B1
Natividade *Brazil* 11°43S 47°47W **333** D2
Nativity, Basilica of *West Bank* 31°42N 35°12E **123** B2
Natkyizin *Burma* 14°57N 97°59E **236** E1
Natmauk *Burma* 20°20N 95°24E **241** E5
Natogyi *Burma* 21°25N 95°39E **241** E5
Natolin *Poland* 52°8N 21°4E **143** C2
Natonin *Phil.* 17°6N 121°18E **232** C3
Nator *Bangla.* 24°21N 89°5E **241** C2
Natron, L. *Tanzania* 2°20S 36°0E **268** C4
Natrona Heights *U.S.A.* 40°37N 79°44W **312** F5
Natrûn, W. el → *Egypt* 30°25N 30°13E **256** H7
Nattai △ *Australia* 34°12S 150°22E **283** C9
Nättraby *Sweden* 56°13N 15°31E **163** H9
Natukanaoka Pan *Namibia* 18°40S 15°45E **270** A2
Natuna Besar, Kepulauan *Indonesia* 4°0N 108°15E **235** B3
Natuna Is. = Natuna Besar, Kepulauan *Indonesia* 4°0N 108°15E **235** B3
Natuna Selatan, Kepulauan *Indonesia* 2°45N 109°0E **235** B3
Natural Bridge *U.S.A.* 44°5N 75°30W **313** B9
Natural Bridges ⌓ *U.S.A.* 37°36N 110°0W **305** H9
Naturaliste, C. *Tas., Australia* 40°50S 148°15E **281** G4
Naturaliste, C. *W. Austral., Australia* 33°32S 115°0E **279** F2
Naturaliste Plateau *Ind. Oc.* 34°0S 112°0E **276** G1
Nau Qala *Afghan.* 34°5N 68°5E **242** B3
Naucalpan de Juárez *Mexico* 19°28N 99°14W **128** B1
Naucelle *France* 44°13N 2°20E **174** D6
Nauders *Austria* 46°54N 10°30E **180** E3
Nauen *Germany* 52°36N 12°52E **178** C8
Naugard = Nowogard *Poland* 53°41N 15°10E **184** E2
Naugatuck *U.S.A.* 41°30N 73°3W **313** E11
Naujaat = Repulse Bay *Canada* 66°30N 86°30W **295** D14
Naujan *Phil.* 13°20N 121°18E **232** E3
Naujan Lake △ *Phil.* 13°9N 121°20E **232** E3
Naujoji Akmenė *Lithuania* 56°19N 22°54E **184** B9
Naulila *Angola* 17°13S 14°39E **265** F2
Naumburg *Germany* 51°9N 11°47E **178** D7
Naumburg am Queis = Nowogrodziec *Poland* 51°12N 15°24E **185** G2
Naupada *Andhra Pradesh, India* 18°34N 84°18E **244** E7
Naupada *Maharashtra, India* 19°3N 72°50E **130** A2
Nā'ūr *Jordan* 31°53N 35°50E **251** G6
Nauru ■ *Pac. Oc.* 1°0S 166°0E **288** H8
Naushahra = Nowshera *Pakistan* 34°0N 72°0E **240** B4
Naushahro *Pakistan* 26°50N 68°7E **242** F3
Naushon I. *U.S.A.* 41°29N 70°45W **313** E14
Nausori *Fiji* 18°2S 178°32E **287** B2
Naustdal *Norway* 61°31N 5°43E **164** C2
Nauta *Peru* 4°31S 73°35W **328** D3
Nautanwa *India* 27°20N 83°25E **243** F10
Naute ⌓ *Namibia* 26°55S 17°57E **270** C2
Nautla *Mexico* 20°13N 96°47W **319** C5
Nauvoo *U.S.A.* 40°33N 91°23W **310** D5
Nava *Coahuila, Mexico* 28°25N 100°45W **318** B4
Nava *Spain* 43°21N 5°31W **194** B5
Nava del Rey *Spain* 41°22N 5°6W **194** D5
Navadwip *India* 23°34N 88°20E **243** H13
Navahermosa *Spain* 39°41N 4°28W **195** F6
Navahrudak *Belarus* 53°40N 25°50E **177** B13
Navai *Fiji* 17°36S 177°57E **287** A1
Navajo Res. *U.S.A.* 36°48N 107°36W **305** H10
Naval *Phil.* 11°34N 124°23E **233** F5
Navalcarnero *Spain* 40°17N 4°5W **194** E6
Navalgund *India* 15°34N 75°22E **245** G2
Navalmoral de la Mata *Spain* 39°52N 5°33W **194** F5
Navalvillar de Pela *Spain* 39°9N 5°24W **195** F5
Navan *Ireland* 53°39N 6°41W **166** C5
Navanagar = Jamnagar *India* 22°30N 70°6E **242** H4
Navapolatsk *Belarus* 55°32N 28°37E **188** E5
Navarin, Mys *Russia* 62°15N 179°5E **215** C18
Navarino, I. *Chile* 55°0S 67°40W **336** E3
Navarra □ *Spain* 42°40N 1°40W **196** C3
Navarre *Fla., U.S.A.* 30°24N 86°52W **317** E3
Navarre *Ohio, U.S.A.* 40°43N 81°31W **312** F3
Navarro → *U.S.A.* 39°11N 123°45W **306** F3
Navas de San Juan *Spain* 38°30N 3°19W **195** G7
Navasota *U.S.A.* 30°23N 96°5W **314** F6
Navassa I. *W. Indies* 18°30N 75°0W **321** C5
Nävekvarn *Sweden* 58°38N 16°49E **163** F10
Naver → *U.K.* 58°32N 4°14W **167** C4
Navet *Trin. & Tob.* 10°21N 61°10W **323** t
Navet → *Trin. & Tob.* 10°24N 61°5W **323** t
Navet Res. *Trin. & Tob.* 10°24N 61°15W **323** t
Navi Mumbai *India* 19°5N 73°0E **130** A2
Navia *Spain* 43°35N 6°42W **194** B4
Navia → *Spain* 43°15N 6°50W **194** B4
Navia de Suarna = A Pobre *Spain* 42°58N 7°3W **194** C3
Navibandar *India* 21°26N 69°48E **242** J3
Navidad *Chile* 33°57S 71°50W **334** C1
Navidad Bank *W. Indies* 20°0N 68°58W **321** B6
Navíglio di Pavia *Italy* 45°24N 9°9E **128** B1
Navíglio Grande *Italy* 45°25N 9°5E **128** B1
Naviraí *Brazil* 23°8S 54°13W **335** A5
Naviti *Fiji* 17°7S 177°15E **287** A1
Navlakhi *India* 22°58N 70°28E **242** H4
Navlya *Russia* 52°53N 34°30E **189** F8
Năvodari *Romania* 44°19N 28°36E **183** F13
Navoi *Uzbekistan* 40°9N 65°22E **216** D7
Navojoa *Mexico* 27°6N 109°26W **318** B3
Navolato *Mexico* 24°47N 107°42W **318** C3
Navona, Piazza *Rome, Italy* **136** b2
Navotas *Phil.* 14°39N 120°56E **127** B1
Navrongo *Ghana* 10°51N 1°3W **263** C4
Navsari *India* 20°57N 72°59E **244** D1
Navua *Fiji* 18°12S 178°11E **287** B2
Navy Pier *Chicago, U.S.A.* **119** b3
Nawa Kot *Pakistan* 28°21N 71°24E **242** E4
Nawab Khan *Pakistan* 30°17N 69°12E **242** D3
Nawabganj *Bangla.* 24°35N 88°14E **241** C2
Nawabganj *Ut. P., India* 26°56N 81°14E **243** F9
Nawabganj *Ut. P., India* 28°32N 79°40E **243** E8
Nawabshah *Pakistan* 26°15N 68°25E **242** F3
Nawada *India* 24°50N 85°33E **243** G11
Nāwah *Afghan.* 32°19N 67°53E **240** B2
Nawakot *Nepal* 27°55N 85°10E **243** F11
Nawalgarh *India* 27°50N 75°15E **242** F6
Nawanshahr *India* 32°33N 74°48E **243** C6
Nawapara *India* 20°46N 82°33E **244** D6
Nawar, Dasht-i- *Afghan.* 33°52N 68°0E **242** C3
Nawāsīf, Ḩarrat *Si. Arabia* 21°20N 42°10E **248** B3
Nawi *Sudan* 18°32N 30°50E **256** D3
Nawng Hpa *Burma* 22°30N 98°30E **241** D7
Nawoiy = Navoi *Uzbekistan* 40°9N 65°22E **216** D7
Nawş, Ra's *Oman* 17°15N 55°16E **249** C6
Naxçıvan *Azerbaijan* 39°12N 45°15E **213** C11
Naxçıvan □ *Azerbaijan* 39°25N 45°26E **213** C11
Naxos *Greece* 37°8N 25°25E **205** D7
Naxxar *Malta* 35°55N 14°27E **206** F7
Nay *France* 43°10N 0°18W **174** E3
Nay, Mui *Vietnam* 12°54N 109°26E **236** F7
Nāy Band *Būshehr, Iran* 27°20N 52°40E **247** E7
Nāy Band *Khorāsān, Iran* 32°20N 57°34E **247** C8
Nay Pyi Taw = Naypyidaw *Burma* 19°44N 96°12E **241** F6
Naya → *Colombia* 3°13N 77°22W **328** C2
Nayagarh *India* 20°8N 85°6E **244** D7
Nayakhan *Russia* 61°56N 159°0E **215** C16
Nayarit □ *Mexico* 22°0N 105°0W **318** C4
Nayé *Senegal* 14°28N 12°12W **262** C2
Nayong *China* 26°50N 105°20E **228** D5
Nayoro *Japan* 44°21N 142°28E **220** B11
Naypyidaw *Burma* 19°44N 96°12E **241** F6
Nayudupeta *India* 13°54N 79°54E **245** H4
Nayyāl, W. → *Si. Arabia* 28°35N 39°4E **246** D3
Nazal Hikmat Beg *Iraq* 33°23N 44°25E **113** A2
Nazar Kahrizi *Iran* 37°20N 46°45E **213** D12
Nazaré *Bahia, Brazil* 13°2S 39°0W **333** D4
Nazaré *Pará, Brazil* 6°25S 52°29W **331** B7
Nazaré *Tocantins, Brazil* 6°23S 47°40W **332** C2
Nazaré *Portugal* 39°36N 9°4W **195** F1
Nazareth = Nazerat *Israel* 32°42N 35°17E **250** F6
Nazareth *U.S.A.* 40°44N 75°19W **313** F9
Nazarovo *Russia* 57°2N 90°40E **215** D10
Nazas *Mexico* 25°14N 104°8W **318** B4
Nazas → *Mexico* 25°12N 104°12W **318** B4
Nazca = Nasca *Peru* 14°50S 74°57W **330** C3
Naze, The *U.K.* 51°53N 1°18E **169** F9
Nazerat *Israel* 32°42N 35°17E **250** F6
Nāzīk *Iran* 39°1N 45°4E **213** C11
Nazilli *Turkey* 37°55N 28°15E **205** D10
Nazimabad *Pakistan* 24°54N 67°1E **123** A2
Nazinon = Red Volta → *Africa* 10°34N 0°30W **263** C4
Nazir Hat *Bangla.* 22°35N 91°49E **241** D3
Nazko *Canada* 53°1N 123°37W **296** C4
Nazko → *Canada* 53°7N 123°34W **296** C4
Nazlet el Simmân *Egypt* 29°59N 31°9E **117** B1
Nāzlu *Iran* 37°41N 45°0E **213** D11
Nazret *Ethiopia* 8°32N 39°22E **257** F4
Ncama *Eq. Guin.* 1°55N 10°56E **264** B2
Nchanga *Zambia* 12°30S 27°49E **269** E2
Ncheu *Malawi* 14°50S 34°47E **269** E3
Ncue *Eq. Guin.* 2°1N 10°28E **264** B2
Ndala *Tanzania* 4°45S 33°15E **268** C3
Ndalatando *Angola* 9°12S 14°48E **265** D2
Ndali *Benin* 9°50N 2°46E **263** D5
Ndareda *Tanzania* 4°12S 35°30E **268** C4
Ndélé *C.A.R.* 8°25N 20°36E **264** A4
Ndendé *Gabon* 2°22S 11°23E **264** C2
Ndiael ⌓ *Senegal* 16°15N 16°0W **262** B1
Ndikinimeki *Cameroon* 4°46N 10°50E **263** E7
Ndim *Cameroon* 5°10N 10°41E **264** A2
Ndindi *Gabon* 3°46S 11°9E **264** C2
N'Dioum *Senegal* 16°31N 14°39W **262** B2
Ndjamena *Chad* 12°10N 15°0E **259** F3
Ndjolé *Gabon* 0°10S 10°45E **264** C2
Ndogo, Lagune *Gabon* 2°35S 10°0E **264** C2
Ndok *Cameroon* 7°57N 14°42E **264** A2
Ndoki-Nouabalé ⌓ *Congo* 2°32N 16°32E **264** B3
Ndola *Zambia* 13°0S 28°34E **269** E2
Ndomo ⌓ *S. Africa* 26°52S 32°15E **271** C5
Ndoto Mts. *Kenya* 2°0N 37°0E **268** B4
Ndoua, C. *N. Cal.* 22°24S 166°56E **288** d
Ndouba *Congo* 0°9S 14°4E **264** C2
Ndoukou *C.A.R.* 4°33N 20°39E **264** B4
Nduguti *Tanzania* 4°18S 34°41E **268** C3
Nea → *Norway* 63°15N 11°0E **164** A8
Nea Alexandria *Greece* 37°52N 23°46E **112** B2
Nea Alikarnassos *Greece* 35°18N 25°13E **205** F7
Nea Anchialos *Greece* 39°16N 22°49E **204** B4
Nea Epidavros *Greece* 37°40N 23°7E **204** D5
Nea Ionia *Athina, Greece* 38°3N 23°45E **112** A2
Nea Ionia *Magnisia, Greece* 39°21N 22°56E **204** B4
Nea Kalikratia *Greece* 40°21N 23°3E **202** F7
Nea Liosia *Greece* 38°3N 23°43E **112** A2
Nea Makri *Greece* 38°5N 23°59E **204** C5
Nea Moudania *Greece* 40°15N 23°17E **202** F7
Nea Peramos *Attiki, Greece* 38°0N 23°26E **204** C5
Nea Peramos *Kavala, Greece* 40°50N 24°18E **203** F8
Nea Samsounda *Greece* 39°5N 20°45E **207** A2
Nea Smirni *Greece* 37°54N 23°43E **112** B2
Nea Visa *Greece* 41°34N 26°33E **203** E10
Nea Zichni *Greece* 41°2N 23°49E **202** E7
Neagari = Nomi *Japan* 36°26N 136°25E **223** A8
Neagh, Lough *U.K.* 54°37N 6°25W **166** B5
Neah Bay *U.S.A.* 48°22N 124°37W **306** B2
Neale, L. *Australia* 24°15S 130°0E **278** D5
Neales → *Australia* 28°8S 136°47E **281** D2
Neamati *India* 26°50N 94°20E **241** B5
Neamţ □ *Romania* 47°0N 26°20E **183** C11
Neapoli *Athens, Greece* **112** a3
Neapoli *Kozani, Greece* 40°20N 21°24E **202** F5
Neapoli *Kriti, Greece* 35°15N 25°37E **207** E6
Neapoli *Lakonia, Greece* 36°27N 23°8E **204** E5
Near Is. *U.S.A.* 52°30N 174°0E **303** K1
Near North *Chicago, U.S.A.* **119** b1
Neath *U.K.* 51°39N 3°48W **169** F4
Neath Port Talbot □ *U.K.* 51°42N 3°45W **169** F4
Nebbi *Uganda* 2°28N 31°6E **268** B3
Nebbou *Burkina Faso* 11°9N 1°51W **263** C4
Nebelat el Hagana *Sudan* 13°13N 29°2E **257** E2
Nebine Cr. → *Australia* 29°27S 146°56E **281** D4
Nebitdag = Balkanabat *Turkmenistan* 39°30N 54°22E **247** B7
Nebka *Algeria* 27°28N 3°12W **260** C4
Neblina, Pico da *Brazil* 0°48N 66°0W **328** C4
Nebo *Australia* 21°42S 148°42E **280** C4
Nebolchy *Russia* 59°8N 33°18E **188** C7
Nebraska □ *U.S.A.* 41°30N 99°30W **308** E4
Nebraska City *U.S.A.* 40°41N 95°52W **308** E6
Nébrodi, Monti *Italy* 37°54N 14°35E **201** E7
Nebušice *Czech Rep.* 50°6N 14°19E **135** B1
Necedah *U.S.A.* 44°2N 90°4W **308** C8
Nechako → *Canada* 53°55N 122°42W **296** C4
Neches → *U.S.A.* 29°58N 93°51W **314** G8
Nechisar △ *Ethiopia* 5°58N 37°55E **257** F4
Neckar → *Germany* 49°27N 8°29E **179** F4
Neckartal-Odenwald ⌓ *Germany* 49°30N 9°5E **179** F5
Necker I. *U.S.A.* 23°35N 164°42W **302** G11
Necochea *Argentina* 38°30S 58°50W **334** D4
Nectar Brook *Australia* 32°43S 137°57E **282** B2
Neda *Spain* 43°30N 8°9W **194** B2
Neda → *Greece* 37°25N 21°45E **204** D3
Nedalshytta *Norway* 62°59N 12°3E **164** B9
Nedelino *Bulgaria* 41°27N 25°3E **203** E9
Nedelišće *Croatia* 46°23N 16°22E **199** B13
Nederhorst *Neths.* 52°16N 5°3E **112** B3
Nederland = Netherlands ■ *Europe* 52°0N 5°30E **170** C5
Nedlitz *Germany* 52°25N 13°3E **115** B1
Nedoboyivtsi *Ukraine* 48°26N 26°21E **183** B11
Nedreberg *Norway* 60°59N 11°41E **164** D8
Nedroma *Algeria* 35°1N 1°45W **261** A4
Nedstrand *Norway* 59°21N 5°49E **164** E2
Nee Soon *Singapore* 1°24N 103°49E **138** A2
Needham *U.S.A.* 42°17N 71°14W **116** B1
Needham Heights *U.S.A.* 42°17N 71°14W **116** B1
Needles *B.C., Canada* 49°53N 118°7W **296** D5
Needles *Calif., U.S.A.* 34°51N 114°37W **307** L12
Needles, The *U.K.* 50°39N 1°35W **169** G6
Needles Pt. *N.Z.* 36°3S 175°25E **284** C4
Neembucú □ *Paraguay* 27°0S 58°0W **334** B4
Neemuch = Nimach *India* 24°30N 74°56E **242** G6
Neenah *U.S.A.* 44°11N 88°28W **308** C9
Neepawa *Canada* 50°15N 99°30W **297** C9
Neeses *U.S.A.* 33°33N 81°7W **316** B8
Nefta *Tunisia* 33°53N 7°50E **258** B1
Neftçala *Azerbaijan* 39°19N 49°12E **213** C13
Neftechala = Neftçala *Azerbaijan* 39°19N 49°12E **213** C13
Neftegorsk *Krasnodar, Russia* 44°25N 39°45E **191** H4
Neftegorsk *Sakhalin, Russia* 53°1N 142°58E **215** D15
Neftekumsk *Russia* 44°46N 44°50E **191** H7
Nefteyugansk *Russia* 61°5N 72°42E **214** C8
Nefyn *U.K.* 52°56N 4°31W **168** E3
Négala *Mali* 12°52N 8°30W **262** C3
Negapatam = Nagappattinam *India* 10°46N 79°51E **245** J4
Negara *Indonesia* 8°22S 114°37E **231** J17
Negaunee *U.S.A.* 46°30N 87°36W **308** B10
Negele *Oromiya, Ethiopia* 5°20N 39°36E **257** F4
Negele *Oromiya, Ethiopia* 7°21N 38°42E **266** C4
Negeri Sembilan □ *Malaysia* 2°45N 102°10E **237** L4
Negev Desert = Hanegev *Israel* 30°50N 35°0E **251** H6
Negoiul, Vf. *Romania* 45°38N 24°35E **183** E9
Negombo *Sri Lanka* 7°12N 79°50E **245** L4
Negotin *Serbia* 44°16N 22°37E **202** B6
Negotino *Macedonia* 41°29N 22°7E **202** E6
Negra, Peña *Spain* 42°11N 6°30W **194** C4
Negra, Pta. *Mauritania* 22°54N 16°18W **260** D1
Negra, Pta. *Peru* 6°6S 81°10W **330** B1
Negra Pt. *Phil.* 18°40N 120°50E **232** B3
Negra Pt. *Trin. & Tob.* 10°4N 61°23W **323** t
Negrais, C. = Maudin Sun *Burma* 16°0N 94°30E **241** G5
Nègres, Pte. des *Martinique* 14°35N 61°5W **322** j
Negreşti *Romania* 46°50N 27°30E **183** D12
Negreşti-Oaş *Romania* 47°52N 23°26E **183** C8
Negril *Jamaica* 18°22N 78°20W **320** a
Négrine *Algeria* 34°30N 7°30E **261** B6
Negro → *Argentina* 41°2S 62°47W **336** B4
Negro → *Bolivia* 14°11S 63°7W **331** C5
Negro → *Brazil* 3°0S 60°0W **329** D6
Negro → *Uruguay* 33°24S 58°22W **334** C4
Negro, C. = Tarf, Ras *Morocco* 35°40N 5°11W **260** A3
Negro, C. *Venezuela* 11°11N 63°53W **329** a
Negros *Phil.* 9°30N 122°40E **233** G4
Negros Occidental □ *Phil.* 10°0N 122°55E **233** F4
Negros Oriental □ *Phil.* 9°45N 123°0E **233** G4
Negru Vodă *Romania* 43°47N 28°21E **183** G13
Neguac *Canada* 47°15N 65°5W **299** C6
Nehalem → *U.S.A.* 45°40N 123°56W **306** E3
Nehāvand *Iran* 35°56N 49°31E **247** C6
Nehbandān *Iran* 31°35N 60°5E **247** D9
Nehe *China* 48°29N 124°50E **219** B13
Nehoiu *Romania* 45°24N 26°20E **183** E11
Nei Mongol Zizhiqu □ *China* 42°0N 112°0E **226** D7
Neiafu *Tonga* 18°39S 173°59W **287** P14
Neidenburg = Nidzica *Poland* 53°25N 20°28E **185** E7
Neiges, Piton des *Réunion* 21°5S 55°29E **272** f
Neijiang *China* 29°35N 104°55E **228** C5
Neikiang = Neijiang *China* 29°35N 104°55E **228** C5
Neilingding Dao *China* 22°25N 113°48E **219** a
Neill I. *India* 11°50N 93°3E **245** J11
Neillsville *U.S.A.* 44°34N 90°36W **308** C8
Neilson, Récif *Pac. Oc.* 27°1S 146°2W **289** f
Neilton *U.S.A.* 47°25N 123°53W **306** C3
Neipu *Taiwan* 22°37N 120°33E **225** D2
Neiqiu *China* 37°15N 114°30E **226** F8
Neisse = Nysa → *Europe* 52°4N 14°46E **178** C10
Neiva *Colombia* 2°56N 75°18W **328** C2
Neiwan *Taiwan* 24°42N 121°10E **225** B3
Neixiang *China* 33°10N 111°52E **226** H6
Nejanilini L. *Canada* 59°33N 97°48W **297** B9
Nejd = Najd *Si. Arabia* 26°30N 42°0E **248** A3
Nejo *Ethiopia* 9°30N 35°28E **257** F4
Nejrab *Afghan.* 34°58N 69°34E **240** B3
Nekā *Iran* 36°39N 53°19E **247** B7
Nekemte *Ethiopia* 9°4N 36°30E **257** F4
Nêkheb *Egypt* 25°10N 32°48E **256** B3
Neksø *Denmark* 55°4N 15°8E **163** J9
Nelamangala *India* 13°6N 77°24E **245** H3
Nelas *Portugal* 40°32N 7°52W **194** E3
Nelaug *Norway* 58°39N 8°40E **164** F5
Nelia *Australia* 20°39S 142°12E **280** C3
Nelidovo *Russia* 56°13N 32°49E **188** D7
Neligh *U.S.A.* 42°8N 98°2W **308** D4
Nelkan *Russia* 57°40N 136°4E **215** D14
Nellikuppam *India* 11°46N 79°43E **245** J4
Nellis Air Force Base ✈ (LSV) *U.S.A.* 36°14N 115°2W **124** A2
Nellore *India* 14°27N 79°59E **245** G4
Nelson *B.C., Canada* 49°30N 117°20W **296** D5
Nelson *N.Z.* 41°18S 173°16E **285** B8
Nelson *Lancs., U.K.* 53°50N 2°13W **168** D5
Nelson *Ariz., U.S.A.* 35°31N 113°19W **305** J7
Nelson *Nev., U.S.A.* 35°42N 114°49W **307** K12
Nelson □ *N.Z.* 41°20S 173°20E **285** B8
Nelson → *Canada* 54°33N 98°2W **297** C9
Nelson, C. *Vic., Australia* 38°26S 141°32E **282** E4
Nelson, C. *Papua N. G.* 9°0S 149°20E **286** E5
Nelson, Estrecho *Chile* 51°30S 75°0W **336** D2
Nelson Bay *Australia* 32°43S 152°9E **283** B10
Nelson Forks *Canada* 59°30N 124°0W **296** B4
Nelson House *Canada* 55°47N 98°51W **297** B9
Nelson L. *Canada* 55°48N 100°7W **297** B8
Nelson Lakes △ *N.Z.* 41°55S 172°44E **285** B7
Nelson Mandela = Praia ✈ (RAI) *C. Verde Is.* 14°55N 23°30W **153** j
Nelson's Dockyard *Antigua & B.* 17°1N 61°46W **322** b
Nelspoort *S. Africa* 32°7S 23°0E **270** D3
Nelspruit = Mbombela *S. Africa* 25°29S 30°59E **271** C5
Néma *Mauritania* 16°40N 7°15W **262** B3
Neman = Nemunas → *Lithuania* 55°25N 21°10E **184** C8
Neman *Russia* 55°2N 22°2E **184** C9
N'ematābād *Iran* 35°38N 51°21E **141** B2
Nembe *Nigeria* 4°32N 6°24E **263** E6
Nembrala *Indonesia* 10°53S 122°50E **278** B3
Nemea *Greece* 37°49N 22°40E **204** D4
Nemecký Brod = Havlíčkův Brod *Czech Rep.* 49°36N 15°33E **180** B8
Nemeiben L. *Canada* 55°20N 105°20W **297** B7
Nemërçkë, Mal *Albania* 40°15N 20°15E **202** F4
Nemira, Vf. *Romania* 46°17N 26°19E **183** D11
Nemiscau *Canada* 51°18N 76°54W **298** B4
Nemiscau, L. *Canada* 51°25N 76°40W **298** B4
Nemours = Ghazaouet *Algeria* 35°8N 1°50W **261** A4
Nemours *France* 48°16N 2°40E **173** D9
Nemrut Daği △ *Turkey* 38°0N 38°55E **213** C8
Nemšová *Slovak Rep.* 48°58N 18°7E **181** C11
Nemunas → *Lithuania* 55°25N 21°10E **184** C8
Nemuro *Japan* 43°20N 145°35E **220** C12
Nemuro-Kaikyō *Japan* 43°30N 145°30E **220** C12
Nemyriv *Ukraine* 50°7N 23°27E **185** H10
Nen Jiang → *China* 45°28N 124°30E **227** B13
Nenagh *Ireland* 52°52N 8°11W **166** D3
Nenana *U.S.A.* 64°34N 149°5W **303** D10
Nenasi *Malaysia* 3°9N 103°23E **237** L4
Nendo *Pac. Oc.* 10°45S 165°54E **277** C12
Nene → *U.K.* 52°49N 0°11E **169** E8
Nengkao Shan *Taiwan* 23°58N 121°16E **225** C3
Nengonengo *French Polynesia* 18°47S 141°48W **289** f
Nenita *Greece* 38°14N 26°6E **205** C8
Nenjiang *China* 49°10N 125°10E **219** B14
Neno *Malawi* 15°25S 34°40E **269** F3
Neo Chori *Greece* 38°25N 21°17E **204** C3
Neochori *Greece* 39°4N 21°0E **204** B2
Neodesha *U.S.A.* 37°25N 95°41W **308** G6
Neoga *U.S.A.* 39°19N 88°27W **311** E8
Neon Petritsi *Greece* 41°16N 23°15E **202** E7
Neópolis *Brazil* 10°18S 36°35W **332** D4
Neora Valley △ *India* 27°0N 88°45E **241** B2
Neosho *U.S.A.* 36°52N 94°22W **308** G6
Neosho → *U.S.A.* 36°48N 95°18W **314** C7
Nepal ■ *Asia* 28°0N 84°30E **243** F11
Nepalganj *Nepal* 28°5N 81°40E **243** E9
Nepalganj Road *India* 28°1N 81°41E **243** E9
Nepean B. *Australia* 35°42S 137°37E **282** C2
Nephi *U.S.A.* 39°43N 111°50W **304** G8
Nephin *Ireland* 54°1N 9°22W **166** B2
Nephin Beg Range *Ireland* 54°0N 9°40W **166** C2
Nepi *Italy* 42°14N 12°21E **199** F9
Nepomuk *Czech Rep.* 49°29N 13°35E **180** B6
Neppel = Moses Lake *U.S.A.* 47°8N 119°17W **304** C4
Neptune *U.S.A.* 40°13N 74°2W **313** F10
Neptune Is. *Australia* 35°17S 136°10E **282** C2
Neqāb *Iran* 36°42N 57°25E **247** B8
Nera → *Italy* 42°26N 12°24E **199** F9
Nera → *Romania* 44°48N 21°25E **182** F6
Nérac *France* 44°8N 0°21E **174** D4
Nerang *Australia* 27°58S 153°20E **281** D5
Nerastro, Sarīr *Libya* 24°20N 20°37E **258** D4
Neratovice *Czech Rep.* 50°16N 14°31E **180** A7
Nerchinsk *Russia* 52°0N 116°39E **215** D12
Nereju *Romania* 45°43N 26°43E **183** E11
Nerekhta *Russia* 57°26N 40°38E **188** D11
Neresnytsya *Ukraine* 48°7N 23°46E **183** B8
Néret, L. *Canada* 54°45N 70°44W **299** B5
Neretvanski Kanal *Croatia* 43°7N 17°10E **199** E14
Nerima *Japan* 35°44N 139°40E **140** A3
Neringa *Lithuania* 55°20N 21°5E **184** C8
Neris → *Lithuania* 55°8N 24°16E **188** E3
Nerja *Spain* 36°43N 3°55W **195** J7
Nerl → *Russia* 56°11N 40°34E **188** D11
Nerpio *Spain* 38°11N 2°16W **197** G2
Nerva *Spain* 37°42N 6°30W **195** H4
Nervi *Italy* 44°23N 9°2E **198** D6
Neryungri *Russia* 57°38N 124°28E **215** D13
Nes *Iceland* 65°53N 17°24W **155** B9
Nes *Buskerud, Norway* 60°34N 9°59E **164** D6
Nesbyen *Norway* 60°34N 9°8E **164** D6
Nescopeck *U.S.A.* 41°3N 76°12W **313** E8
Nesebŭr *Bulgaria* 42°41N 27°46E **203** D11
Neset *Norway* 61°53N 10°7E **164** C7
Nesflaten *Norway* 59°38N 6°48E **164** E3
Nesjahverfi *Iceland* 64°20N 15°15W **155** C11
Neskantaga *Canada* 52°14N 87°53W **298** B2
Neskaupstaður *Iceland* 65°9N 13°42W **155** B13
Nesland *Norway* 59°31N 7°59E **164** E4
Neslandsvatn *Norway* 58°57N 9°10E **164** F6
Nesodden *Norway* 59°48N 10°41E **133** B3
Nesoddtangen *Norway* 59°48N 10°40E **133** A3
Nesøya *Norway* 59°52N 10°31E **133** A2
Ness, L. *U.K.* 57°15N 4°32W **167** D4
Ness City *U.S.A.* 38°27N 99°54W **308** F4
Nessebar = Nesebŭr *Bulgaria* 42°41N 27°46E **203** D11
Nesterov = Zhovkva *Ukraine* 50°4N 23°58E **177** C12
Nesterov *Russia* 54°38N 22°41E **184** D9
Nestorio *Greece* 40°24N 21°5E **202** F5
Nestos → *Europe* 40°54N 24°49E **203** F8
Nesttun *Norway* 60°19N 5°20E **164** D2
Nesvady *Slovak Rep.* 47°56N 18°7E **181** D11
Nesvizh = Nyasvizh *Belarus* 53°14N 26°38E **177** B14
Netaji Subhash Chandra Bose Int. ✈ (CCU) *India* 22°38N 88°26E **124** B2
Netanya *Israel* 32°20N 34°51E **251** F5
Netarhat *India* 23°29N 84°16E **243** H11
Nete → *Belgium* 51°7N 4°14E **170** C4
Netherdale *Australia* 21°10S 148°33E **280** b
Netherlands ■ *Europe* 52°0N 5°30E **170** C5
Netherlands Antilles = ABC Islands *W. Indies* 12°15N 69°0W **322** g
Netherlands East Indies = Indonesia ■ *Asia* 5°0S 115°0E **235** C4
Netherlands Guiana = Suriname ■ *S. Amer.* 4°0N 56°0W **329** C6
Neto → *Italy* 39°12N 17°9E **201** C10
Netrakona *Bangla.* 24°53N 90°47E **241** C3
Netrang *India* 21°39N 73°21E **242** J5
Nettancourt *France* 48°51N 4°57E **173** D11
Nettetal *Germany* 51°19N 6°12E **178** D2
Nettilling L. *Canada* 66°30N 71°0W **295** D17
Nettuno *Italy* 41°27N 12°39E **200** A5
Netzahualcóyotl, Presa *Mexico* 17°8N 93°35W **319** D6
Neu Aubing *Germany* 48°8N 11°25E **131** B1
Neu-Bentschen = Zbąszynek *Poland* 52°16N 15°51E **185** F2
Neu Buch *Germany* 52°37N 13°31E **115** A4
Neu Buchhorst *Germany* 52°24N 13°44E **115** B5
Neu Fahrland *Germany* 52°26N 13°3E **115** B1
Neu-Isenburg *Germany* 50°3N 8°42E **179** E4
Neu-Langenburg = Tukuyu *Tanzania* 9°17S 33°35E **269** D3
Neu Lindenberg *Germany* 52°36N 13°33E **115** A4
Neu-Mecklenberg = New Ireland *Papua N. G.* 3°20S 151°50E **286** B6
Neu Pommern = New Britain *Papua N. G.* 5°50S 150°20E **286** C6
Neu-Sandec = Nowy Sącz *Poland* 49°40N 20°41E **185** J7
Neu Sandez = Nowy Sącz *Poland* 49°40N 20°41E **185** J7
Neu-Ulm *Germany* 48°22N 10°0E **179** G6
Neubiberg *Germany* 48°4N 11°40E **131** B3
Neubrandenburg *Germany* 53°33N 13°15E **178** B9
Neubukow *Germany* 54°2N 11°39E **178** A7
Neuburg *Germany* 48°44N 11°11E **179** G7
Neuchâtel *Switz.* 47°0N 6°55E **179** J2
Neuchâtel □ *Switz.* 47°0N 6°55E **179** J2
Neuchâtel, Lac de *Switz.* 46°53N 6°50E **179** J2
Neudau *Austria* 47°11N 16°6E **180** D9
Neuenberg an der Elbe = Nymburk *Czech Rep.* 50°10N 15°1E **180** A8
Neuenhagen *Germany* 52°32N 13°38E **115** A4
Neuenhaus *Germany* 52°30N 6°58E **178** C2
Neuessling *Austria* 48°15N 16°32E **142** A3
Neuf-Brisach *France* 48°1N 7°30E **173** D14
Neufahrn *Bayern, Germany* 48°41N 12°11E **179** G8
Neufahrn *Bayern, Germany* 48°18N 11°40E **179** G7
Neufchâteau *Belgium* 49°50N 5°25E **170** E5
Neufchâteau *Vosges, France* 48°21N 5°40E **173** D12
Neufchâtel-en-Bray *France* 49°44N 1°26E **172** C8
Neufchâtel-sur-Aisne *France* 49°26N 4°1E **173** C11
Neuhaus = Jindřichův Hradec *Czech Rep.* 49°10N 15°2E **180** B8
Neuhaus *Germany* 53°17N 10°55E **178** B6
Neuhäusel = Nové Zámky *Slovak Rep.* 48°2N 18°8E **181** C11
Neuhausen *Germany* 48°9N 11°32E **131** B2
Neuherberg *Germany* 48°13N 11°35E **131** A2
Neuhönow *Germany* 52°34N 13°44E **115** A5
Neuillé-Pont-Pierre *France* 47°33N 0°33E **172** E7
Neuilly-Plaisance *France* 48°51N 2°30E **134** A4
Neuilly-St-Front *France* 49°10N 3°15E **173** C10
Neuilly-sur-Marne *France* 48°51N 2°31E **134** A4
Neuilly-sur-Seine *France* 48°53N 2°15E **134** A2
Neukagran *Austria* 48°14N 16°27E **142** A2
Neukalen *Germany* 53°49N 12°46E **178** B8
Neukettenhof *Austria* 48°7N 16°28E **142** B2
Neukölln *Germany* 52°28N 13°25E **115** B3
Neumarkt = Nowy Targ *Poland* 49°29N 20°2E **185** J7
Neumarkt = Środa Śląska *Poland* 51°10N 16°36E **185** G3
Neumarkt *Germany* 49°26N 11°27E **179** F7
Neumarktl = Tržič *Slovenia* 46°22N 14°18E **199** B11
Neumayer *Antarctica* 71°0S 68°30W **151** D17
Neumittelwalde = Międzybórz *Poland* 51°25N 17°34E **185** G4
Neumünster *Germany* 54°4N 9°58E **178** A5
Neung-sur-Beuvron *France* 47°30N 1°50E **173** E8
Neunkirchen *Austria* 47°43N 16°4E **180** D9
Neunkirchen *Saarland, Germany* 49°20N 7°9E **179** F3
Neuperlach *Germany* 48°6N 11°37E **131** B2
Neuquén *Argentina* 38°55S 68°0W **336** A3
Neuquén □ *Argentina* 38°0S 69°50W **334** D2
Neuquén → *Argentina* 38°59S 68°0W **336** A3
Neuried *Germany* 48°5N 11°27E **131** B1
Neuruppin *Germany* 52°55N 12°48E **178** C8
Neusalz an der Oder = Nowa Sól *Poland* 51°48N 15°44E **185** G2
Neusäss *Germany* 48°24N 10°50E **179** G6
Neusatz = Novi Sad *Serbia* 45°18N 19°52E **182** E4
Neuse → *U.S.A.* 35°6N 76°29W **315** D16
Neusiedl *Austria* 47°57N 16°50E **181** D9
Neusiedler See *Austria* 47°50N 16°47E **181** D9
Neusiedler See-Seewinkel △ *Austria* 47°50N 16°45E **181** D9
Neusohl = Banská Bystrica *Slovak Rep.* 48°46N 19°14E **181** C12
Neuss *Germany* 51°11N 6°42E **178** D2
Neussargues-Moissac *France* 45°9N 3°0E **174** C7
Neustadt = Lwówek *Poland* 52°28N 16°10E **185** F3
Neustadt = Prudnik *Poland* 50°20N 17°38E **185** H4
Neustadt = Wejherowo *Poland* 54°35N 18°12E **184** D5
Neustadt *Bayern, Germany* 49°44N 12°10E **179** F8
Neustadt *Bayern, Germany* 48°48N 11°46E **179** G7
Neustadt *Bayern, Germany* 49°34N 10°37E **179** F6
Neustadt *Bayern, Germany* 50°19N 11°7E **179** E7
Neustadt *Brandenburg, Germany* 52°50N 12°27E **178** C8
Neustadt *Hessen, Germany* 50°51N 9°9E **178** E5
Neustadt *Niedersachsen, Germany* 52°30N 9°30E **178** C5
Neustadt *Rhld-Pfz., Germany* 49°21N 8°10E **179** F4
Neustadt *Sachsen, Germany* 51°2N 14°12E **178** D10
Neustadt *Schleswig-Holstein, Germany* 54°6N 10°49E **178** A6
Neustadt *Thüringen, Germany* 50°45N 11°43E **178** E7
Neustädtel = Nowe Miasteczko *Poland* 51°42N 15°42E **185** G2
Neustädtl = Novo Mesto *Slovenia* 45°47N 15°12E **199** C12
Neustettin = Szczecinek *Poland* 53°43N 16°41E **184** E3
Neustift am Walde *Austria* 48°14N 16°17E **142** A1
Neustrelitz *Germany* 53°21N 13°4E **178** B9
Neusüssenbrunn *Austria* 48°16N 16°29E **142** A2
Neutitschein = Nový Jičín *Czech Rep.* 49°30N 18°2E **181** B11
Neuvic *France* 45°23N 2°16E **174** C6
Neuville-sur-Saône *France* 45°52N 4°51E **175** C8
Neuvy-le-Roi *France* 47°36N 0°36E **172** E7
Neuvy-St-Sépulchre *France* 46°35N 1°48E **173** F8
Neuvy-sur-Barangeon *France* 47°20N 2°15E **173** E9
Neuwaldegg *Austria* 48°14N 16°17E **142** A1
Neuwedell = Drawno *Poland* 53°13N 15°46E **185** E2
Neuwerk *Germany* 53°55N 8°30E **178** B4
Neuwied *Germany* 50°26N 7°29E **178** E3
Neva → *Russia* 59°56N 30°20E **188** C6
Nevada *Iowa, U.S.A.* 42°1N 93°27W **310** B3
Nevada *Mo., U.S.A.* 37°51N 94°22W **310** G2
Nevada □ *U.S.A.* 39°0N 117°0W **304** G5
Nevada City *U.S.A.* 39°16N 121°1W **306** F6
Nevado, Cerro *Argentina* 35°30S 68°32W **334** D2
Nevado de Colima = Volcán de Colima △ *Mexico* 19°30N 103°40W **318** D4
Nevado de Tres Cruces △ *Chile* 27°13S 69°5W **334** B2
Nevado del Huila △ *Colombia* 3°5N 75°58W **328** C2
Nevasa *India* 19°34N 75°0E **244** E2
Neve, Sa. da *Angola* 13°43S 13°10E **265** E2
Neve Ya'akov *West Bank* 31°50N 35°14E **123** A2
Nevel *Russia* 56°0N 29°55E **188** D5
Nevelsk *Russia* 46°40N 141°51E **215** E15
Nevers *France* 47°0N 3°9E **173** F10
Nevertire *Australia* 31°50S 147°44E **283** A7
Neves *Brazil* 22°51S 43°5W **135** B2
Nevesinje *Bos.-H.* 43°14N 18°6E **202** C2
Neville *Canada* 49°58N 107°39W **297** D7
Nevinnomyssk *Russia* 44°40N 42°0E **191** H6
Nevis *St. Kitts & Nevis* 17°0N 62°30W **322** d
Nevis Pk. *St. Kitts & Nevis* 17°9N 62°34W **322** d
Nevlunghavn *Norway* 58°58N 9°53E **164** F6
Nevoso, Mte. = Snežnik *Slovenia* 45°36N 14°35E **199** C11
Nevrokop = Gotse Delchev *Bulgaria* 41°36N 23°46E **202** E7
Nevşehir *Turkey* 38°33N 34°40E **212** C6
Nevşehir □ *Turkey* 38°50N 34°40E **212** C6
Nevskoye *Russia* 54°32N 22°39E **184** D9
Nevyansk *Russia* 57°30N 60°13E **186** C11
New → *Guyana* 3°20N 57°37W **329** C6
New → *W. Va., U.S.A.* 38°10N 81°12W **309** F13
New Aiyansh *Canada* 55°12N 129°4W **296** B3
New Albany *Ind., U.S.A.* 38°18N 85°49W **311** F11
New Albany *Miss., U.S.A.* 34°29N 89°0W **315** D10
New Albany *Pa., U.S.A.* 41°36N 76°27W **313** E8
New Amsterdam *Guyana* 6°15N 57°36W **329** B6
New Athens *U.S.A.* 38°19N 89°53W **310** F7
New Atlas = Akhali Atoni *Georgia* 43°7N 40°50E **191** J5
New Baghdād *Iraq* 33°18N 44°28E **113** B2
New Baltimore *U.S.A.* 42°41N 82°44W **312** D2
New Barakpur *India* 22°40N 88°26E **124** A2
New Barbadoes = Hackensack *U.S.A.* 40°52N 74°4W **132** A1
New Bedford *U.S.A.* 41°38N 70°56W **313** E14
New Berlin = North Canton *U.S.A.* 40°53N 81°24W **312** F3
New Berlin *Ill., U.S.A.* 39°44N 89°55W **310** E7
New Berlin *N.Y., U.S.A.* 42°37N 75°20W **313** D9
New Berlin *Pa., U.S.A.* 40°50N 76°57W **312** F8
New Berlin *Wis., U.S.A.* 42°59N 88°6W **311** B8
New Bern *U.S.A.* 35°7N 77°3W **315** D16
New Bethlehem *U.S.A.* 41°0N 79°20W **312** F5
New Bight *Bahamas* 24°19N 75°24W **321** B4
New Bloomfield *U.S.A.* 40°25N 77°11W **312** F7
New Boston *U.S.A.* 33°28N 94°25W **314** E7
New Braunfels *U.S.A.* 29°42N 98°8W **314** G5
New Brighton *N.Z.* 43°29S 172°43E **285** D7
New Brighton *N.Y., U.S.A.* 40°38N 74°5W **132** C1
New Brighton *Pa., U.S.A.* 40°42N 80°19W **312** F4
New Britain *Papua N. G.* 5°50S 150°20E **286** C6
New Britain *Conn., U.S.A.* 41°40N 72°47W **313** E12
New Britain Trench *Pac. Oc.* 6°0S 153°0E **276** J3
New Brockton *U.S.A.* 31°23N 85°56W **316** D4
New Brookland = West Columbia *U.S.A.* 33°59N 81°4W **316** B8
New Brunswick *U.S.A.* 40°30N 74°27W **313** F10
New Brunswick □ *Canada* 46°50N 66°30W **299** C6
New Buffalo *U.S.A.* 41°47N 86°45W **311** C10
New Bussa *Nigeria* 9°53N 4°31E **263** D5
New Caledonia ☒ *Pac. Oc.* 21°0S 165°0E **288** d
New Caledonia Trough *Pac. Oc.* 30°0S 165°0E **288** L8
New Canada *S. Africa* 26°12S 27°56E **123** B1
New Canada Dam *S. Africa* 26°12S 27°56E **123** B1
New Carlisle *Ind., U.S.A.* 41°45N 86°32W **311** C10
New Carlisle *Ohio, U.S.A.* 39°56N 84°2W **311** E12
New Castile = Castilla-La Mancha □ *Spain* 39°30N 3°30W **195** F7

New Castle Ind., U.S.A. 39°55N 85°22W 311 E11
New Castle Ky., U.S.A. 38°26N 85°10W 311 F11
New Castle Pa., U.S.A. 41°0N 80°21W 312 F4
New City U.S.A. 41°9N 73°59W 313 E11
New Concord U.S.A. 39°59N 81°54W 312 G3
New Cross U.K. 51°28N 0°1W 125 B3
New Cumberland U.S.A. 40°30N 80°36W 312 F4
New Cuyama U.S.A. 34°57N 119°38W 307 L7
New Delhi India 28°36N 77°11E 120 B2
New Denver Canada 50°0N 117°25W 296 D5
New Don Pedro Res. U.S.A. 37°43N 120°24W 306 H6
New Dorp U.S.A. 40°34N 74°7W 132 C1
New Dorp Beach U.S.A. 40°33N 74°6W 132 C1
New Ellenton U.S.A. 33°28N 81°41W 316 B8
New England U.S.A. 43°0N 71°0W 301 G25
New England N. Dak., U.S.A. 46°32N 102°52W 308 B2
New England △ Australia 30°25S 152°30E 283 A10
New England Aquarium Boston, U.S.A. 116 b3
New England Ra. Australia 30°20S 151°45E 281 E5
New England Seamounts Atl. Oc. 38°0N 63°0W 152 C5
New Forest △ U.K. 50°53N 1°34W 169 G6
New Franklin U.S.A. 39°1N 92°44W 310 E4
New Galloway U.K. 55°5N 4°9W 167 F4
New Georgia Is. Solomon Is. 8°15S 157°30E 287 M9
New Georgia Sound Solomon Is. 8°0S 158°20E 287 L9
New Glarus U.S.A. 42°49N 89°38W 310 B7
New Glasgow Canada 45°35N 62°36W 299 C7
New Grant Trin. & Tob. 10°17N 61°19W 323 t
New Guinea Oceania 4°0S 136°0E 276 B7
New Halfa = Halfa al Jadidah Sudan 15°20N 35°35E 266 A4
New Hamburg Canada 43°23N 80°42W 312 C4
New Hampshire □ U.S.A. 44°0N 71°30W 313 C13
New Hampton U.S.A. 43°3N 92°19W 310 A4
New Hanover Papua N. G. 2°30S 150°10E 286 B6
New Hanover KwaZulu Natal, S. Africa 29°22S 30°31E 271 C5
New Harmony U.S.A. 38°8N 87°56W 311 F9
New Hartford U.S.A. 43°4N 75°18W 313 C9
New Haven Conn., U.S.A. 41°18N 72°55W 313 E12
New Haven Ill., U.S.A. 37°55N 88°8W 311 G8
New Haven Ind., U.S.A. 41°4N 85°1W 311 C11
New Haven Mich., U.S.A. 42°44N 82°48W 312 D2
New Haven Mo., U.S.A. 38°37N 91°13W 310 F5
New Haven N.Y., U.S.A. 43°28N 76°18W 313 C8
New Hazelton Canada 55°20N 127°30W 296 B3
New Hebrides = Vanuatu ■ Pac. Oc. 15°0S 168°0E 287 E6
New Holland U.S.A. 40°6N 76°5W 313 F8
New Iberia U.S.A. 30°1N 91°49W 314 F9
New Ireland Papua N. G. 3°20S 151°50E 286 B6
New Ireland □ Papua N. G. 3°0S 151°30E 286 B6
New Jersey □ U.S.A. 40°0N 74°30W 309 F16
New Kensington U.S.A. 40°34N 79°46W 312 F5
New Lexington U.S.A. 39°43N 82°13W 309 F12
New Liskeard Canada 47°31N 79°41W 298 C4
New London Conn., U.S.A. 41°22N 72°6W 313 E12
New London Iowa, U.S.A. 40°55N 91°24W 310 D5
New London Mo., U.S.A. 39°35N 91°24W 310 E5
New London Ohio, U.S.A. 41°5N 82°24W 312 E2
New London Wis., U.S.A. 44°23N 88°45W 308 C9
New Madrid U.S.A. 36°36N 89°32W 308 G9
New Malden U.K. 51°24N 0°15W 125 B2
New Martinsville U.S.A. 39°39N 80°52W 309 F13
New Meadows U.S.A. 44°58N 116°18W 304 D5
New Melones L. U.S.A. 37°57N 120°31W 306 H6
New Mexico □ U.S.A. 34°30N 106°0W 305 J11
New Miami U.S.A. 39°26N 84°32W 311 E12
New Milford Conn., U.S.A. 41°35N 73°25W 313 E11
New Milford N.Y., U.S.A. 40°56N 74°0W 132 A1
New Milford Pa., U.S.A. 41°52N 75°44W 313 E9
New Mumbai = Navi Mumbai India 19°5N 73°0E 130 A2
New Norcia Australia 30°57S 116°13E 279 F2
New Norfolk Australia 42°46S 147°2E 281 G4
New Orleans U.S.A. 29°57N 90°4W 131 B2
New Orleans Int. ✈ (MSY) U.S.A. 30°0N 90°15W 131 B1
New Palestine U.S.A. 39°45N 85°52W 311 E11
New Paris U.S.A. 39°51N 84°48W 311 E12
New Pekin U.S.A. 38°30N 86°0W 311 F10
New Philadelphia U.S.A. 40°30N 81°27W 312 F3
New Plymouth N.Z. 39°4S 174°5E 284 F3
New Plymouth Idaho, U.S.A. 43°58N 116°49W 304 E5
New Pomerania = New Britain Papua N. G. 5°50S 150°20E 286 C6
New Port Richey U.S.A. 28°16N 82°43W 317 G7
New Providence Bahamas 25°25N 77°35W 153 b
New Quay U.K. 52°13N 4°21W 169 E3
New Radnor U.K. 52°15N 3°9W 169 E4
New Richmond Qué., Canada 48°15N 65°45W 299 C6
New Richmond Ohio, U.S.A. 38°57N 84°17W 311 F12
New Richmond Wis., U.S.A. 45°7N 92°32W 308 C7
New River → U.S.A. 26°6N 80°6W 129 B3
New River Gorge ⌓ U.S.A. 37°53N 81°5W 309 G13
New Roads U.S.A. 30°42N 91°26W 314 F9
New Rochelle U.S.A. 40°55N 73°46W 313 F11
New Rockford U.S.A. 47°41N 99°8W 308 B4
New Romney U.K. 50°59N 0°57E 169 G8
New Ross Ireland 52°23N 6°57W 166 D5
New Salem U.S.A. 46°51N 101°25W 308 B3
New Scone = Scone U.K. 56°25N 3°24W 167 E5
New Sharon U.S.A. 41°28N 92°39W 310 C4
New Siberian I. = Novaya Sibir, Ostrov Russia 75°10N 150°0E 215 B16
New Siberian Is. = Novosibirskiye Ostrova Russia 75°0N 142°0E 215 B15
New Smyrna Beach U.S.A. 29°1N 80°56W 317 F9
New South Wales □ Australia 33°0S 146°0E 283 B7
New Stuyahok U.S.A. 59°29N 157°20W 303 G8
New Tecumseth = Alliston Canada 44°9N 79°52W 312 B5
New Territories Hong Kong, China 22°23N 114°5E 122 A2
New Toronto Canada 43°35N 79°30W 141 B1
New Town = Nowe Miasto Warsaw, Poland 143 a2
New Town Edinburgh, U.K. 121 a2
New Town N. Dak., U.S.A. 47°59N 102°30W 308 B2
New Tredegar U.K. 51°44N 3°16W 169 F4
New Ulm U.S.A. 44°19N 94°28W 308 C6
New Utrecht U.S.A. 40°36N 73°59W 132 C2
New Vienna U.S.A. 39°19N 83°42W 311 E13
New Washington Phil. 11°39N 122°26E 233 F4
New Waterford Canada 46°13N 60°4W 299 C7
New Westminster Canada 49°13N 122°55W 306 A4
New York U.S.A. 40°43N 74°0W 132 B2
New York □ U.S.A. 43°0N 75°0W 313 D9
New York Avenue Washington, D.C., U.S.A. 143 a2
New York J.F. Kennedy Int. ✈ (JFK) U.S.A. 40°38N 73°47W 313 F11
New York La Guardia ✈ (LGA) U.S.A. 40°46N 73°52W 132 B2
New York University New York, U.S.A. 132 d2
New Zealand ■ Oceania 40°0S 176°0E 284 G5
Newaj → India 24°24N 76°49E 242 G7
Newala Tanzania 10°58S 39°18E 269 E4
Newark Del., U.S.A. 39°41N 75°46W 309 F16
Newark N.J., U.S.A. 40°44N 74°10W 313 F10
Newark N.Y., U.S.A. 43°3N 77°6W 312 C7
Newark Ohio, U.S.A. 40°3N 82°24W 312 F2
Newark B. U.S.A. 40°40N 74°8W 132 B1
Newark Liberty Int. ✈ (EWR) U.S.A. 40°42N 74°10W 313 F10
Newark-on-Trent U.K. 53°5N 0°48W 168 D7
Newark Valley U.S.A. 42°14N 76°11W 313 D8
Newbattle U.K. 55°53N 3°4W 121 B3
Newberg U.S.A. 45°18N 122°58W 304 D2
Newberry Fla., U.S.A. 29°39N 82°37W 317 F7
Newberry Mich., U.S.A. 46°21N 85°30W 309 B11
Newberry S.C., U.S.A. 34°17N 81°37W 315 D14
Newberry Springs U.S.A. 34°50N 116°41W 307 L10
Newboro L. Canada 44°38N 76°20W 313 B8
Newbridge Ireland 53°11N 6°48W 166 C5
Newburg U.S.A. 37°55N 91°54W 310 G5
Newburgh Ont., Canada 44°19N 76°52W 312 B8
Newburgh Ind., U.S.A. 37°57N 87°24W 311 G9
Newburgh N.Y., U.S.A. 41°30N 74°1W 313 E10
Newbury W. Berkshire, U.K. 51°24N 1°20W 169 F6
Newbury N.H., U.S.A. 43°19N 72°3W 313 B12
Newbury Vt., U.S.A. 44°5N 72°4W 313 B12
Newbury Park U.K. 51°34N 0°5E 125 A4
Newburyport U.S.A. 42°49N 70°53W 313 D14
Newcastle N.S.W., Australia 33°0S 151°46E 283 B9
Newcastle N.B., Canada 47°1N 65°38W 299 C6
Newcastle Ont., Canada 43°55N 78°35W 298 D4
Newcastle Limerick, Ireland 52°27N 9°3W 166 D2
Newcastle St. Kitts & Nevis 17°14N 62°42W 322 d
Newcastle KwaZulu Natal, S. Africa 27°45S 29°58E 271 C4
Newcastle Down, U.K. 54°13N 5°54W 166 B6
Newcastle Calif., U.S.A. 38°53N 121°8W 306 G5
Newcastle Wyo., U.S.A. 43°50N 104°11W 304 E11
Newcastle Emlyn U.K. 52°2N 4°28W 169 E3
Newcastle Ra. Australia 15°45S 130°15E 278 C5
Newcastle-under-Lyme U.K. 53°1N 2°14W 168 D5
Newcastle-upon-Tyne U.K. 54°58N 1°36W 168 C6
Newcastle Waters Australia 17°30S 133°28E 280 B1
Newcomb U.S.A. 43°58N 74°10W 313 C10
Newcomerstown U.S.A. 40°16N 81°36W 312 F3
Newcraighall U.K. 55°56N 3°5W 121 B3
Newdegate Australia 33°6S 119°0E 279 F2
Newell Queens., Australia 16°20S 145°16E 280 B4
Newell Iowa, U.S.A. 42°36N 95°0W 310 B1
Newell S. Dak., U.S.A. 44°43N 103°25W 308 C2
Newenham, C. U.S.A. 58°39N 162°11W 303 G7
Newfane U.S.A. 43°17N 78°43W 312 C6
Newfield U.S.A. 42°18N 76°33W 313 D8
Newfound L. U.S.A. 43°40N 71°47W 313 C13
Newfoundland Canada 49°0N 55°0W 299 C8
Newfoundland Pa., U.S.A. 41°18N 75°19W 313 E9
Newfoundland & Labrador □ Canada 52°0N 58°0W 299 B8
Newhalen U.S.A. 59°43N 154°54W 303 G9
Newham □ U.K. 51°31N 0°3E 125 A4
Newhaven E. Sussex, U.K. 50°47N 0°3E 169 G8
Newhaven Edinburgh, U.K. 55°59N 3°11W 121 B2
Newington Edinburgh, U.K. 55°56N 3°10W 121 B2
Newington London, U.K. 125 c5
Newington Ga., U.S.A. 32°35N 81°30W 316 C8
Newkirk U.S.A. 36°53N 97°3W 314 C6
Newlands S. Africa 26°10S 27°57E 123 B1
Newlyn U.K. 50°6N 5°34W 169 G2
Newman W. Austral., Australia 23°18S 119°45E 278 D2
Newman Calif., U.S.A. 37°19N 121°1W 306 H5
Newman Ill., U.S.A. 39°48N 87°59W 311 E9
Newmarket Ont., Canada 44°3N 79°28W 312 B5
Newmarket Cork, Ireland 52°13N 9°0W 166 D2
Newmarket Jamaica 18°9N 77°55W 320 a
Newmarket Suffolk, U.K. 52°15N 0°25E 169 E8
Newmarket N.H., U.S.A. 43°5N 70°56W 313 C14
Newnan U.S.A. 33°23N 84°48W 316 B5
Newport = Nieuwpoort Curaçao 12°3N 68°49W 322 g
Newport Vic., Australia 37°50S 144°51E 128 B1
Newport Mayo, Ireland 53°53N 9°33W 166 C2
Newport I. of W., U.K. 50°42N 1°17W 169 G6
Newport Newport, U.K. 51°35N 3°0W 169 F5
Newport Ark., U.S.A. 35°37N 91°16W 314 D9
Newport Fla., U.S.A. 30°11N 84°10W 316 E5
Newport Ind., U.S.A. 39°53N 87°25W 311 E9
Newport Ky., U.S.A. 39°5N 84°29W 311 E12
Newport N.H., U.S.A. 43°22N 72°10W 313 C12
Newport N.Y., U.S.A. 43°11N 75°1W 313 C9
Newport Oreg., U.S.A. 44°39N 124°3W 304 D1
Newport Pa., U.S.A. 40°29N 77°8W 312 F7
Newport R.I., U.S.A. 41°29N 71°19W 313 E13
Newport Tenn., U.S.A. 35°58N 83°11W 315 D13
Newport Vt., U.S.A. 44°56N 72°13W 313 B12
Newport Wash., U.S.A. 48°11N 117°3W 304 B5
Newport □ U.K. 51°33N 3°1W 169 F4
Newport Beach U.S.A. 33°37N 117°56W 307 M9
Newport News U.S.A. 36°58N 76°25W 309 G15
Newport Pagnell U.K. 52°5N 0°43W 169 E7
Newquay U.K. 50°25N 5°6W 169 G2
Newry U.K. 54°11N 6°21W 166 B5
Newry Islands △ Australia 20°51S 148°56E 280 b
Newtok U.S.A. 60°56N 164°38W 303 F6
Newton Ga., U.S.A. 31°19N 84°20W 316 D5
Newton Ill., U.S.A. 38°59N 88°10W 311 F8
Newton Iowa, U.S.A. 41°42N 93°3W 310 C3
Newton Kans., U.S.A. 38°3N 97°21W 308 F5
Newton Mass., U.S.A. 42°21N 71°12W 116 B1
Newton Miss., U.S.A. 32°19N 89°10W 315 E10
Newton N.C., U.S.A. 35°40N 81°13W 315 D14
Newton N.J., U.S.A. 41°3N 74°45W 313 E10
Newton Tex., U.S.A. 30°51N 93°46W 314 F8
Newton Abbot U.K. 50°32N 3°37W 169 G4
Newton Aycliffe U.K. 54°37N 1°34W 168 C6
Newton Falls N.Y., U.S.A. 44°12N 74°59W 313 B10
Newton Falls Ohio, U.S.A. 41°11N 80°59W 312 E4
Newton L. U.S.A. 38°55N 88°15W 311 F8
Newton Stewart U.K. 54°57N 4°30W 167 G4
Newton Terrace Barbados 13°4N 59°32W 323 r
Newtonbrook Canada 43°47N 79°24W 141 A2
Newtongrange U.K. 55°53N 3°3W 121 B3
Newtonmore U.K. 57°4N 4°8W 167 D4
Newtontoppen Svalbard 79°0N 17°30E 154 B12
Newtonville U.S.A. 42°20N 71°11W 116 A1
Newtown N.S.W., Australia 33°54S 151°11E 139 B2
Newtown Powys, U.K. 52°31N 3°19W 169 E4
Newtown Ind., U.S.A. 40°13N 87°9W 311 D9
Newtown Mo., U.S.A. 40°22N 93°20W 310 D3
Newtownabbey U.K. 54°40N 5°56W 166 B6
Newtownards U.K. 54°36N 5°42W 166 B6
Newtownbarry = Bunclody Ireland 52°39N 6°40W 166 D5
Newtownstewart U.K. 54°43N 7°23W 166 B4
Newville U.S.A. 40°10N 77°24W 312 F7
Nexon France 45°41N 1°11E 174 C5
Neya Russia 58°21N 43°49E 190 A6
Neyrīz Iran 29°15N 54°19E 247 D7
Neyshābūr Iran 36°10N 58°50E 247 B8
Neyveli India 11°32N 79°29E 245 J4
Neyyattinkara India 8°26N 77°5E 245 K3
Nezametny = Aldan Russia 58°40N 125°30E 215 D13
Nezhin = Nizhyn Ukraine 51°5N 31°55E 189 G6
Nezperce U.S.A. 46°14N 116°14W 304 C5
Nezvysko Ukraine 48°46N 25°15E 183 B10
Nga, Laem Thailand 7°55N 98°27E 237 a
Ngaanyatjarra ☼ Australia 22°40S 127°0E 278 D4
Ngabang Indonesia 0°23N 109°55E 235 B3
Ngabe Congo 3°12S 16°12E 264 C3
Ngabordamlu, Tanjung Indonesia 6°56S 134°11E 231 F8
N'Gage Angola 7°46S 15°15E 265 D3
Ngaiphaipi Burma 22°14N 93°15E 241 D4
Ngala Nigeria 12°20N 14°11E 263 C7
Ngaliwurru Nungali ☼ Australia 15°42S 130°4E 278 C5
Ngalurrtju ☼ Australia 22°44S 132°5E 278 D5
Ngama Chad 11°45N 17°6E 259 F3
Ngambé Centre, Cameroon 5°48N 11°29E 263 D7
Ngambé Littoral, Cameroon 4°21N 10°40E 263 E7
Ngami Depression Botswana 20°30S 22°46E 270 B3
Ngamo Zimbabwe 19°3S 27°32E 269 F2
Ngamring China 29°14N 87°10E 218 F6
Nganbéto, L. de Togo 7°26N 1°25E 263 D5
Ngangala South Sudan 4°42N 31°55E 257 G3
Nganglong Kangri China 33°0N 81°0E 243 C9
Ngao Thailand 18°46N 99°59E 236 C2
Ngaoundéré Cameroon 7°15N 13°35E 264 A2
Ngapali Burma 18°26N 94°19E 241 F5
Ngapara N.Z. 44°57S 170°46E 285 E5
Ngape Burma 20°2N 94°28E 241 E5
Ngara Tanzania 2°29S 30°40E 268 C3
Ngardmau Palau 7°37N 134°34E 288 c
Ngardmau B. Palau 7°38N 134°34E 288 c
Ngardololok Palau 7°0N 134°14E 288 c
Ngaregur Palau 7°45N 134°37E 288 c
Ngarluma ☼ Australia 21°30S 118°30E 278 D2
Ngaruawahia N.Z. 37°42S 175°11E 284 D4
Ngaruroro → N.Z. 39°34S 176°55E 284 F5
Ngatangiia Cook Is. 21°14S 159°43W 289 h
Ngatapa N.Z. 38°32S 177°45E 284 E6
Ngathainggyaung Burma 17°24N 95°5E 241 G5
Ngau Chi Wan Hong Kong, China 22°20N 114°12E 122 A3
Ngau Tau Kok Hong Kong, China 22°19N 114°12E 122 B3
Ngauruhoe, Mt. N.Z. 39°13S 175°45E 284 F4
Ngawi Indonesia 7°24S 111°26E 235 D4
Ngcobo S. Africa 31°37S 28°0E 271 D4
Ngele Dem. Rep. of the Congo 0°30S 20°22E 264 C4
Ngelebok Cameroon 4°16N 14°3E 264 B2
Ngeregong Palau 7°6N 134°21E 288 c
Ngergoi Palau 7°5N 134°15E 288 c
Ngeru Uganda 0°27N 33°10E 268 B3
Ngerulmud = Melekeok Palau 7°27N 134°38E 288 c
Ngesebus I. Palau 7°3N 134°15E 288 c
Nggatokae Solomon Is. 8°45S 158°15E 287 M10
Nggela Pile Solomon Is. 9°5S 160°20E 287 M11
Nggela Sule Solomon Is. 9°2S 160°12E 287 M11
Nghia Lo Vietnam 21°33N 104°28E 228 G5
Ngidinga Dem. Rep. of the Congo 5°37S 15°17E 265 D3
Ngo Congo 2°29S 15°45E 264 C3
Ngoap Cameroon 4°9N 12°51E 264 B2
Ngobasangel Palau 7°16N 134°19E 288 c
Ngoboli South Sudan 4°57N 32°37E 257 G3
Ngol = Raqaba ez Zarqa → South Sudan 9°14N 29°44E 257 F2
N'Gola Angola 14°10S 14°30E 265 E2
Ngoma Malawi 13°8S 33°45E 269 E3
Ngomahura Zimbabwe 20°26S 30°43E 269 G3
Ngomba Tanzania 8°20S 32°53E 269 D3
Ngomeni, Ras Kenya 2°59S 40°14E 268 C5
Ngong Kenya 1°22S 36°39E 268 C4
Ngong Ping Hong Kong, China 22°15N 113°54E 122 B1
Ngong Shuen Chau = Stonecutters I. Hong Kong, China 22°19N 114°8E 122 B2
Ngongotaha N.Z. 38°5S 176°12E 284 E5
Ngonye Falls Zambia 16°40S 23°25E 265 F4
Ngop South Sudan 6°17N 30°9E 257 F3
Ngoring Hu China 34°55N 97°5E 218 E8
Ngorkou Mali 15°40N 3°41W 262 B4
Ngorongoro Tanzania 3°11S 35°32E 268 C4
Ngorongoro ⌓ Tanzania 2°40S 35°30E 268 C4
Ngoto C.A.R. 3°59N 17°19E 264 B3
Ngounié □ Gabon 2°0S 11°0E 264 C2
Ngounie → Gabon 0°37S 10°18E 264 C2
Ngouo, Dj. C.A.R. 7°55N 24°38E 264 A4
Ngoura Chad 12°44N 16°21E 259 F3
Ngouri Chad 13°38N 15°22E 259 F3
Ngourti Niger 15°19N 13°12E 259 E2
Ngoussou Gabon 3°0S 11°7E 264 C2
Ngozi Burundi 2°54S 29°50E 268 C2
Ngua Kok Wan Hong Kong, China 22°21N 114°5E 122 A2
Ngudu Tanzania 2°58S 33°25E 268 C3
Nguigmi Niger 14°20N 13°20E 259 F2
Nguila Cameroon 4°41N 11°43E 263 E7
Nguiu Australia 11°46S 130°38E 278 B5
Ngukurr Australia 14°44S 134°44E 280 A1
Ngum → Laos 18°31N 102°32E 236 C4
Nguna Vanuatu 17°26S 168°22E 287 G6
Ngundu Zimbabwe 18°11S 31°15E 269 F3
Ngunga Tanzania 3°37S 33°37E 268 C3
Nguru Nigeria 12°56N 10°29E 263 C7
Nguru Mts. Tanzania 6°0S 37°30E 268 D4
Ngusi Malawi 14°0S 34°50E 269 E3
Nguyen Binh Vietnam 22°39N 105°56E 228 F5
Ngwaketse □ Botswana 25°0S 25°0E 270 C3
Ngwedaung Burma 19°31N 97°9E 241 F6
Nha Bang Vietnam 10°37N 105°0E 237 G5
Nha Trang Vietnam 12°16N 109°10E 237 F7
Nhacoongo Mozam. 24°18S 35°14E 271 B6
Nhamaabué Mozam. 17°25S 35°5E 269 F4
Nhambiquara Brazil 12°50S 59°49W 331 C6
Nhamundá Brazil 2°14S 56°43W 329 D6
Nhamundá → Brazil 2°12S 56°41W 329 D6
Nhangulaze, L. Mozam. 24°0S 34°30E 271 B5
Nharêa Angola 11°38S 16°58E 265 E3
Nharnuwangga, Wajarri and Ngarlawangga ☼ Australia 24°50S 118°0E 279 D2
Nhava Sheva India 18°58N 72°55E 130 B2
Nhecolândia Brazil 19°17S 56°58W 331 D6
Nhill Australia 36°18S 141°40E 282 D4
Nho Quan Vietnam 20°18N 105°45E 228 G5
Nhulunbuy Australia 12°10S 137°20E 280 A2
Nhundo Angola 14°25S 21°23E 265 E4
Nia-nia Dem. Rep. of the Congo 1°30N 27°40E 268 B2
Niafounké Mali 16°0N 4°5W 262 B4
Niagara Falls Ont., Canada 43°7N 79°5W 312 C5
Niagara Falls N.Y., U.S.A. 43°5N 79°4W 312 C6
Niagara-on-the-Lake Canada 43°15N 79°4W 312 C5
Niah Malaysia 3°58N 113°46E 235 B4
Nialaha'u Pt. Solomon Is. 9°47S 161°34E 287 M11
Niamey Niger 13°27N 2°6E 263 C5
Niamtougou Togo 9°46N 1°6E 263 D5
Niandan-Koro Guinea 11°5N 9°15W 262 C3
Nianforando Guinea 9°37N 10°36W 262 D2
Niangara Dem. Rep. of the Congo 3°42N 27°50E 268 B2
Niangay, L. Mali 15°50N 3°0W 262 B4
Niangbo Ivory C. 8°49N 5°10W 262 D3
Niangoloko Burkina Faso 10°15N 4°55W 262 C4
Niangua → U.S.A. 38°58N 92°48W 310 G4
Niantic U.S.A. 41°20N 72°11W 313 E12
Niari Congo 4°9S 14°9E 264 C2
Niari □ Congo 3°30S 12°0E 264 C2
Niaro Sudan 10°38N 31°31E 257 E3
Nias Indonesia 1°0N 97°30E 234 B1
Niassa □ Mozam. 13°30S 36°0E 269 E4
Niassa ⌓ Mozam. 12°4S 36°57E 269 E4
Nīāvarān Iran 35°47N 51°29E 141 A2
Nibāk Si. Arabia 24°25N 50°50E 247 E7
Nibe Denmark 56°59N 9°38E 163 H3
Nibra India 22°36N 88°15E 124 B1
Nicaragua ■ Cent. Amer. 11°40N 85°30W 320 D2
Nicaragua, L. de Nic. 12°0N 85°30W 320 D2
Nicastro Italy 38°59N 16°19E 201 D9
Nice France 43°42N 7°14E 175 E11
Nice-Côte-d'Azur ✈ (NCE) France 43°41N 7°12E 175 E11
Niceville U.S.A. 30°31N 86°30W 317 E3
Nichicun, L. Canada 53°5N 71°0W 299 B5
Nichinan Japan 31°38N 131°23E 222 F3
Nicholás, Canal Caribbean 23°30N 80°5W 320 B3
Nicholas Channel = Nicholás, Canal Caribbean 23°30N 80°5W 320 B3
Nicholasville U.S.A. 37°53N 84°34W 311 G12
Nicholls U.S.A. 31°31N 82°38W 316 D7
Nichols U.S.A. 42°1N 76°22W 313 D8
Nicholson W. Austral., Australia 18°2S 128°54E 278 C4
Nicholson Pa., U.S.A. 41°37N 75°47W 313 E9
Nicholson → Australia 17°31S 139°36E 280 B2
Nicholson L. Canada 62°40N 102°40W 297 A8
Nicholson Ra. Australia 27°15S 116°45E 279 E2
Nicholville U.S.A. 44°41N 74°39W 313 B10
Nickerie → Suriname 5°58N 57°0W 329 B6
Nico Pérez = José Batlle y Ordóñez Uruguay 33°20S 55°10W 335 C4
Nicobar Is. Ind. Oc. 8°0N 93°30E 245 L11
Nicola Canada 50°12N 120°40W 296 C4
Nicolls Town Bahamas 25°8N 78°0W 320 A4
Nicosia Cyprus 35°10N 33°25E 207 E9
Nicosia Italy 37°45N 14°24E 201 E7
Nicótera Italy 38°33N 15°56E 201 D8
Nicoya Costa Rica 10°9N 85°27W 320 D2
Nicoya, G. de Costa Rica 10°0N 85°0W 320 E3
Nicoya, Pen. de Costa Rica 9°45N 85°40W 320 E2
Nictheroy = Niterói Brazil 22°53S 43°7W 135 B2
Nida Lithuania 55°20N 21°4E 184 C8
Nidāl Iraq 33°19N 44°25E 113 B2
Nidaros = Trondheim Norway 63°36N 10°25E 164 A7
Nidd → U.K. 53°59N 1°23W 168 D6
Nidda Germany 50°23N 9°1E 179 E5
Nidda → Germany 50°17N 8°48E 179 E4
Niddrie Vic., Australia 37°44S 144°51E 128 A1
Niddrie Edinburgh, U.K. 55°56N 3°7W 121 B3
Nidri Greece 38°43N 20°42E 207 B2
Nidwalden □ Switz. 46°50N 8°25E 179 J4
Nidzica Poland 53°25N 20°28E 185 E7
Niebüll Germany 54°46N 8°48E 178 A4
Nied → Germany 49°23N 6°40E 173 C13
Nieder Neuendorf Germany 52°36N 13°12E 115 A2
Niederaula Germany 50°47N 9°36E 178 E5
Niederbayern □ Germany 48°40N 12°50E 179 G8
Niederbronn-les-Bains France 48°57N 7°39E 173 D14
Niedere Tauern Austria 47°20N 14°0E 180 D7
Niederlausitz Germany 51°42N 13°59E 178 D9
Niederösterreich □ Austria 48°25N 15°40E 180 C8
Niedersachsen □ Germany 52°50N 9°0E 178 C4
Niedersächsisches Wattenmeer △ Germany 53°45N 7°30E 178 B3
Niederschöneweide Germany 52°27N 13°30E 115 B3
Niederschönhausen Germany 52°35N 13°25E 115 A3
Niefang Eq. Guin. 1°50N 10°14E 264 B2
Niekerkshoop S. Africa 29°19S 22°51E 270 C3
Niellé Ivory C. 10°5N 5°38W 262 C3
Niellim Chad 9°42N 17°49E 259 G3
Niem C.A.R. 6°12N 15°14E 264 A3
Niemba Dem. Rep. of the Congo 5°58S 28°24E 268 D2
Niemen = Nemunas → Lithuania 55°25N 21°10E 184 C8
Niemeyer Brazil 22°59S 43°16W 135 B1
Niemodlin Poland 50°38N 17°38E 185 H4
Niemur Australia 35°17S 144°9E 282 C6
Nienburg Germany 52°39N 9°13E 178 C5
Niepołomice Poland 50°3N 20°13E 185 H7
Niers → Germany 51°43N 5°57E 178 D1
Niesky Germany 51°17N 14°49E 178 D10
Nieszawa Poland 52°52N 18°50E 185 F5
Nieu Bethesda S. Africa 31°51S 24°34E 270 D3
Nieuw Amsterdam Suriname 5°53N 55°5W 329 B6
Nieuw Nickerie Suriname 6°0N 56°59W 329 B6
Nieuwe Kerk Amsterdam, Neths. 112 a2
Nieuwendam Neths. 52°23N 4°57E 112 A2
Nieuwoudtville S. Africa 31°23S 19°7E 270 D2
Nieuwpoort Belgium 51°8N 2°45E 170 C2
Nieuwpoort Curaçao 12°3N 68°49W 322 g
Nieves, Pico de las Canary Is. 27°57N 15°35W 153 e1
Nièvre □ France 47°10N 3°40E 173 E10
Nif Micronesia 9°28N 138°4E 287 S16
Niga Mali 13°38N 5°27W 262 C3
Niğde Turkey 37°58N 34°40E 212 D6
Niğde □ Turkey 38°0N 34°30E 212 D6
Nigel S. Africa 26°27S 28°25E 271 C4
Niger □ Nigeria 10°0N 5°30E 263 D6
Niger ■ W. Afr. 17°30N 10°0E 259 E2
Niger → W. Afr. 5°33N 6°33E 263 D6
Niger Delta Africa 5°0N 6°0E 263 E6
Nigeria ■ W. Afr. 8°30N 8°0E 263 D6
Nighasin India 28°14N 80°52E 243 E9
Nightcaps N.Z. 45°57S 168°2E 285 F3
Nightmute U.S.A. 60°29N 164°44W 303 F6
Nigrita Greece 40°56N 23°29E 202 F7
Nihoa U.S.A. 23°6N 161°58W 302 G11
Nihon = Japan ■ Asia 36°0N 136°0E 221 G8
Nihonbashi Tokyo, Japan 140 b5
Nii-Jima Japan 34°20N 139°15E 223 C11
Niigata Japan 37°58N 139°0E 220 F9
Niigata □ Japan 37°15N 138°45E 221 F9
Niihama Japan 33°55N 133°16E 222 D5
Ni'ihau U.S.A. 21°54N 160°9W 302 B1
Niimi Japan 34°59N 133°28E 222 C5
Niipperi Finland 60°18N 24°45E 121 B1
Niislel Khureheh = Ulaanbaatar Mongolia 47°55N 106°53E 218 B10
Niitsu Japan 37°48N 139°7E 220 F9
Nij Laluk India 27°7N 93°56E 241 B4
Níjar Spain 36°53N 2°15W 197 J2
Nijil Jordan 30°32N 35°33E 251 H6
Nijkerk Neths. 52°13N 5°30E 170 B5
Nijmegen Neths. 51°50N 5°52E 170 C5
Nijverdal Neths. 52°22N 6°28E 170 B6
Nīk Pey Iran 36°50N 48°10E 213 D13
Nikao Cook Is. 21°12S 159°48W 289 h
Nikaweratiya Sri Lanka 7°45N 80°7E 245 L5
Nike Nigeria 6°26N 7°29E 263 D6
Nikea Greece 37°57N 23°38E 112 B1
Nikel Russia 69°24N 30°13E 160 B24
Nikiboko Bonaire 12°9N 68°16W 322 h
Nikiniki Indonesia 9°49S 124°30E 278 A3
Nikisiani Greece 40°57N 24°9E 203 F8
Nikiski U.S.A. 61°41N 151°18W 303 F10
Nikiti Greece 40°13N 23°43E 202 F7
Nikitinskiye promysly = Kirovskiy Russia 45°51N 48°11E 191 H9
Nikki Benin 9°58N 3°12E 263 D5
Nikkō Japan 36°45N 139°35E 223 A11
Nikkō △ Japan 36°56N 139°37E 221 F9
Nikolai U.S.A. 62°58N 154°10W 303 E9
Nikolainkaupunki = Vaasa Finland 63°6N 21°38E 160 E19
Nikolaistad = Vaasa Finland 63°6N 21°38E 160 E19
Nikolassee Germany 52°25N 13°12E 115 B2
Nikolayev = Mykolayiv Ukraine 46°58N 32°0E 189 J7
Nikolayevsk Russia 50°0N 45°35E 190 E7
Nikolayevsk-na-Amur Russia 53°8N 140°44E 215 D15
Nikolsburg = Mikulov Czech Rep. 48°48N 16°39E 181 C9
Nikolsk Russia 53°49N 46°4E 190 D8
Nikolsk-Ussuriysky = Ussuriysk Russia 43°48N 131°59E 220 C5
Nikolskaya Pestravka = Nikolsk Russia 53°49N 46°4E 190 D8
Nikolski U.S.A. 52°56N 168°52W 303 K5
Nikolskiy Russia 55°49N 37°29E 129 B1
Nikolskoye = Ussuriysk Russia 43°48N 131°59E 220 C5
Nikolskoye Russia 55°12N 166°0E 215 D17
Nikolsky Khutor = Sursk Russia 53°3N 45°40E 190 D7
Nikopol Bulgaria 43°43N 24°54E 203 C8
Nikopol Ukraine 47°35N 34°25E 189 J8
Nikopolis Greece 39°5N 20°43E 207 A2
Niksar Turkey 40°31N 37°2E 212 B7
Nīkshahr Iran 26°15N 60°10E 247 E9
Nikšić Montenegro 42°50N 18°57E 202 D2
Nikumaroro Kiribati 4°40S 174°32W 277 A16
Nikunau Kiribati 1°22S 176°28E 277 A14
Nîl, Nahr en → Africa 30°10N 31°6E 256 H7
Nîl el Abyad → Sudan 15°38N 32°31E 257 D3
Nîl el Azraq → Sudan 15°38N 32°31E 257 D3
Nila Indonesia 6°44S 129°31E 231 F7
Nilakkottai India 10°10N 77°52E 245 J3
Niland U.S.A. 33°14N 115°31W 307 M11
Nilanga India 18°6N 76°46E 244 E3
Nile = Nîl, Nahr en → Africa 30°10N 31°6E 256 H7
Nile Delta Egypt 31°40N 31°0E 256 H7
Niles Ill., U.S.A. 42°1N 87°48W 119 A2
Niles Mich., U.S.A. 41°50N 86°15W 311 C10
Niles Ohio, U.S.A. 41°11N 80°46W 312 E4
Niles Center = Skokie U.S.A. 42°2N 87°43W 119 A2
Nileshwar India 12°15N 75°6E 245 H2
Nilgiri Hills India 11°30N 76°30E 245 J3
Nilo Peçanha Brazil 13°37S 39°6W 333 D4
Nilsebu Norway 59°11N 6°39E 164 E3
Nilüfer → Turkey 40°18N 28°27E 203 F12
Nim Ka Thana India 27°44N 75°48E 242 F6
Nimach India 24°30N 74°56E 242 G6
Nimba, Mt. Africa 7°37N 8°25W 262 D3
Nimbahera India 24°37N 74°45E 242 G6
Nîmes France 43°50N 4°23E 175 E8
Nimfaíon, Ákra = Pines, Akra Greece 40°5N 24°20E 203 F8
Nimmitabel Australia 36°29S 149°15E 283 D8
Nīmrūz □ Afghan. 30°0N 62°0E 240 C1
Nimta India 22°40N 88°24E 124 A2
Nimule South Sudan 3°32N 32°3E 257 G3
Nimule △ South Sudan 3°38N 32°2E 257 G3
Nin Croatia 44°16N 15°12E 199 D12
Nīnawá Iraq 36°25N 43°10E 213 D10
Nīnawá □ Iraq 36°15N 43°0E 246 B4
Ninda Angola 14°47S 21°24E 265 E4
Nindigully Australia 28°21S 148°50E 281 D4
Nine Degree Channel India 9°0N 73°0E 245 K1
Ninepin Group China 22°16N 114°21E 219 a
Ninety Mile Beach N.Z. 34°48S 173°0E 284 A2
Ninety Mile Beach, The Australia 38°15S 147°24E 283 E7
Ninety Six U.S.A. 34°11N 82°1W 316 A7
Ninetyeast Ridge Ind. Oc. 1°0S 90°0E 273 E7
Nineveh = Nīnawá Iraq 36°25N 43°10E 213 D10
Ning Xian China 35°30N 107°58E 226 G4
Ningaloo Marine ⌓ Australia 22°23S 113°32E 278 D1
Ning'an China 44°22N 129°20E 227 B15
Ningbo China 29°51N 121°28E 229 C13
Ningcheng China 41°32N 119°53E 227 D10
Ningde China 26°38N 119°23E 229 D12
Ningdu China 26°25N 115°59E 229 D10
Ningerum Papua N. G. 5°41S 141°8E 286 C1
Ninggang China 26°42N 113°55E 229 D9
Ningguo China 30°35N 119°0E 229 B12
Ninghai China 29°15N 121°27E 229 C13
Ninghua China 26°14N 116°45E 229 D11
Ningi Nigeria 10°55N 9°30E 263 C6
Ningjin China 37°35N 114°57E 226 F8
Ningjing Shan China 31°0N 98°20E 228 C2
Ninglang China 27°20N 100°55E 228 D3
Ningling China 34°25N 115°22E 226 G8
Ningming China 22°8N 107°4E 228 F6
Ningnan China 27°5N 102°36E 228 D4
Ningpo = Ningbo China 29°51N 121°28E 229 C13
Ningqiang China 32°47N 106°15E 226 H4
Ningshan China 33°21N 108°21E 228 A7
Ningsia Hui A.R. = Ningxia Huizu Zizhiqu □ China 38°0N 106°0E 226 F4
Ningwu China 39°0N 112°18E 226 E7
Ningxia Huizu Zizhiqu □ China 38°0N 106°0E 226 F4
Ningxiang China 28°15N 112°30E 229 C9
Ningyang China 35°47N 116°45E 226 G9
Ningyuan China 25°37N 111°57E 229 E8
Ninh Binh Vietnam 20°15N 105°55E 228 G5
Ninh Giang Vietnam 20°44N 106°24E 236 B6
Ninh Hoa Vietnam 12°30N 109°7E 236 F7
Ninh Ma Vietnam 12°48N 109°21E 236 F7
Nini-Suhien △ Ghana 5°20N 2°34W 262 D4
Ninigo Group Papua N. G. 1°22S 144°17E 286 A3
Ninove Belgium 50°51N 4°2E 170 D4
Ninoy Aquino Int. ✈ (MNL) Phil. 14°31N 121°0E 127 B2
Nioaque Brazil 21°5S 55°50W 335 A4
Niobrara U.S.A. 42°45N 98°2W 308 D4
Niobrara → U.S.A. 42°46N 98°3W 308 D4
Nioki Dem. Rep. of the Congo 2°47S 17°40E 264 C3
Niokolo-Koba △ Senegal 13°3N 13°2W 262 C2
Niono Mali 14°15N 6°0W 262 C3
Nionsamoridougou Guinea 8°45N 8°50W 262 D3
Nioro du Rip Senegal 13°40N 15°50W 262 C1
Nioro du Sahel Mali 15°15N 9°30W 262 B3
Niort France 46°19N 0°29W 174 B3
Nioumachoua Comoros Is. 12°21S 43°42E 272 a
Nipa Papua N. G. 6°9S 143°29E 286 D2
Nipani India 16°20N 74°25E 245 F2
Nipawin Canada 53°20N 104°0W 297 C8
Nipfjället Sweden 61°59N 12°50E 162 C6
Nipigon Canada 49°0N 88°17W 298 C2
Nipigon, L. Canada 49°50N 88°30W 298 C2
Nipishish L. Canada 54°12N 60°45W 299 B7
Nipissing, L. Canada 46°20N 80°0W 298 C4
Nipomo U.S.A. 35°3N 120°29W 307 K6
Nippa Japan 35°31N 139°36E 140 B2
Nippon = Japan ■ Asia 36°0N 136°0E 221 G8
Nippori Japan 35°43N 139°45E 140 A3
Nipton U.S.A. 35°28N 115°16W 307 K11
Niquelândia Brazil 14°33S 48°23W 333 D2
Nīr Iran 38°2N 47°59E 213 C12
Nira → India 17°58N 75°8E 244 F2
Nirasaki Japan 35°42N 138°27E 223 B10
Nirayama = Izunokuni Japan 35°2N 138°55E 223 B10
Nirmal India 19°3N 78°20E 244 E4
Nirmali India 26°20N 86°35E 243 F12
Niš Serbia 43°19N 21°58E 202 C5
Nisa = Nysa → Europe 52°4N 14°46E 178 C10
Nisa Portugal 39°30N 7°41W 195 F3
Nisa Turkmenistan 37°59N 58°11E 247 B8
Nişāb Si. Arabia 29°11N 44°43E 246 D5
Nişāb Yemen 14°25N 46°29E 248 D4
Nišava → Serbia 43°20N 21°46E 202 C5
Niscemi Italy 37°9N 14°23E 201 E7
Nishi Japan 34°40N 135°28E 133 A1
Nishi-Sonogi-Hantō Japan 32°55N 129°45E 222 E1
Nishi-Tosa Japan 33°13N 132°46E 222 D4
Nishinari Japan 34°37N 135°28E 133 B1
Nishinomiya Japan 34°45N 135°20E 133 A1
Nishino'omote Japan 30°43N 130°59E 221 J5
Nishio Japan 34°52N 137°3E 223 C9
Nishiwaki Japan 34°59N 134°58E 222 C6
Nishiyodogawa Japan 34°41N 135°24E 133 A1
Nishtūn Yemen 15°49N 52°14E 249 D6
Nisibin = Nusaybin Turkey 37°3N 41°10E 213 D9
Niška Banja Serbia 43°18N 22°1E 202 C6
Niskibi → Canada 56°29N 88°9W 298 A2
Nisko Poland 50°35N 22°7E 185 H9
Nisporeni Moldova 47°4N 28°10E 183 C13
Nisqually → U.S.A. 47°7N 122°42W 306 C4
Nissaki Greece 39°43N 19°52E 206 B9
Nissan → Sweden 56°40N 12°51E 163 H6
Nissedal Norway 59°10N 8°30E 164 E5
Nisser Norway 59°7N 8°28E 164 E5
Nissiros Greece 36°35N 27°12E 205 E9
Nissum Bredning Denmark 56°40N 8°20E 163 H2
Nissum Fjord Denmark 56°20N 8°11E 163 H2
Nistru = Dnister → Europe 46°18N 30°17E 177 E16
Nisutlin → Canada 60°14N 132°34W 296 A2
Nitchequon Canada 53°10N 70°58W 299 B5
Niterói Brazil 22°53S 43°7W 135 B2
Nith → Ont., Canada 43°12N 80°23W 312 C4
Nith → Dumf. & Gall., U.K. 55°14N 3°33W 167 F5
Nitmiluk △ Australia 14°6S 132°15E 278 B5
Nitra Slovak Rep. 48°19N 18°4E 181 C11
Nitra → Slovak Rep. 47°46N 18°10E 181 D11
Nitriansky □ Slovak Rep. 48°10N 18°30E 181 C11
Nittenau Germany 49°12N 12°16E 179 F8
Niu Valley U.S.A. 21°19N 157°44W 302 K14
Niua Group Tonga 15°57S 173°45W 277 D16
Niuafo'ou Tonga 15°30S 175°58W 277 D15
Niuatoputapu Tonga 15°57S 173°45W 277 D16
Niue ☒ Pac. Oc. 19°2S 169°54W 289 g
Niulakita Pac. Oc. 10°45S 179°30E 277 C14
Niulan Jiang → China 27°30N 103°5E 228 D4
Niulantsun Taiwan 25°1N 121°2E 225 A3
Niur Indonesia 0°26S 103°30E 234 C2
Niut Indonesia 0°55N 109°54E 235 B4
Niutao Pac. Oc. 6°7S 177°18E 277 B14
Niutou Shan China 29°5N 121°59E 229 C13
Niuzhuang China 40°58N 122°28E 224 B1
Nivala Finland 63°56N 24°57E 160 E21
Nivelles Belgium 50°35N 4°20E 170 D4
Nivernais France 47°15N 3°30E 173 E10
Niverville Canada 49°36N 97°3W 297 D9
Niwas India 23°3N 80°26E 243 H9
Nixa U.S.A. 37°3N 93°18W 308 G7
Nixon U.S.A. 29°16N 97°46W 314 G6
Nizam Sagar India 18°10N 77°58E 244 E3
Nizamabad India 18°45N 78°7E 244 E4
Nizamghat India 28°20N 95°45E 241 A5
Nizhne-Kolymsk Russia 68°34N 160°55E 215 C17
Nizhne-Svirskiy ⌓ Russia 60°30N 32°55E 188 B7
Nizhnegorskiy = Nyzhnohirskyy Ukraine 45°27N 34°38E 189 K8
Nizhnekamsk Russia 55°38N 51°49E 190 C10
Nizhneudinsk Russia 54°54N 99°3E 215 D10
Nizhnevartovsk Russia 60°56N 76°38E 214 C8
Nizhniy Bestyakh Russia 61°57N 129°54E 215 C13
Nizhniy Chir Russia 48°22N 43°5E 191 F6
Nizhniy Lomov Russia 53°34N 43°38E 190 D6
Nizhniy Novgorod Russia 56°20N 44°0E 190 B7
Nizhniy Novgorod □ Russia 56°30N 44°20E 190 B7
Nizhniy Tagil Russia 57°55N 59°57E 186 C10
Nizhniye Kresty = Cherskiy Russia 68°45N 161°18E 215 C17
Nizhyn Ukraine 51°5N 31°55E 189 G6
Nizina Mazowiecka Poland 52°30N 21°0E 185 F8
Nizip Turkey 37°5N 37°50E 212 D7
Nízké Tatry Slovak Rep. 48°55N 19°30E 181 C12
Nízké Tatry △ Slovak Rep. 48°55N 19°37E 181 C12
Nízký Jeseník Czech Rep. 49°50N 17°30E 181 B10
Nizwá Oman 22°56N 57°32E 249 B7
Nizza Monferrato Italy 44°46N 8°21E 198 D5
Njakwa Malawi 11°1S 33°56E 269 E3
Njarðvíkur Iceland 63°59N 22°32W 155 D4
Njazidja = Grande Comore Comoros Is. 11°35S 43°20E 272 a
Njegoš Montenegro 42°53N 18°45E 202 D2
Njinjo Tanzania 8°48S 38°54E 269 D4
Njoko → Zambia 17°8S 24°4E 265 F4
Njombe Tanzania 9°20S 34°50E 269 D3
Njombe → Tanzania 6°56S 35°6E 268 D4
Njurundabommen Sweden 62°15N 17°25E 162 B11
Nkambe Cameroon 6°35N 10°40E 263 D7
Nkana Zambia 12°50S 28°8E 269 E2
Nkandla S. Africa 28°37S 31°5E 271 C5
Nkawkaw Ghana 6°36N 0°49W 263 D4
Nkayi Congo 4°9S 13°17E 264 C2
Nkayi Zimbabwe 19°41S 29°20E 269 F2
Nkhotakota Malawi 12°56S 34°15E 269 E3
Nkhotakota ⌓ Malawi 12°50S 34°0E 269 E3
Nkolabona Gabon 1°14N 11°43E 264 B2
Nkomi, Lagune Gabon 1°35S 9°17E 264 C1
Nkondwe Tanzania 5°51S 30°51E 268 D3
Nkone Dem. Rep. of the Congo 1°2S 22°20E 264 C4
Nkongsamba Cameroon 4°55N 9°55E 263 E6
Nkoteng Cameroon 4°31N 12°2E 264 B2
Nkunga Dem. Rep. of the Congo 4°41S 18°34E 265 C3
Nkurenkuru Namibia 17°42S 18°32E 270 A2
Nkwanta Ghana 6°10N 2°10W 262 D4
Nmai → Burma 25°30N 97°25E 228 F2
Noakhali Bangla. 22°48N 91°10E 241 D3
Noatak U.S.A. 67°34N 162°58W 303 C7
Noatak ⌓ U.S.A. 68°10N 160°0W 303 B8
Nob Hill San Francisco, U.S.A. 136 b1
Nobel Canada 45°25N 80°6W 312 A4

Nobeoka *Japan* 32°36N 131°41E **222** E3
Noble *U.S.A.* 38°42N 88°14W **311** F8
Noblejas *Spain* 39°58N 3°26W **194** F7
Noblesville *U.S.A.* 40°3N 86°1W **311** D11
Noboribetsu *Japan* 42°24N 141°6E **220** C10
Nocatee *U.S.A.* 27°10N 81°53W **317** H8
Noccundra *Australia* 27°50S 142°36E **281** D3
Noce → *Italy* 46°9N 11°4E **198** B8
Nocera Inferiore *Italy* 40°44N 14°38E **201** B7
Nocera Umbra *Italy* 43°5N 12°47E **199** E9
Noci *Italy* 40°48N 17°7E **201** B10
Nockeby *Sweden* 59°19N 17°56E **139** B1
Nocona *U.S.A.* 33°47N 97°44W **314** E6
Nocrich *Romania* 45°55N 24°26E **183** E9
Noda *Japan* 35°56N 139°52E **223** B11
Nodeland *Norway* 58°8N 7°51E **164** F4
Noel Kempff Mercado △ *Bolivia* 14°9S 60°49W **331** C5
Noel Park *U.K.* 51°35N 0°5W **125** A3
Nogal Valley = Nugaaleed, Dooxo *Somalia* 8°35N 48°35E **267** C6
Nogales *Sonora, Mexico* 31°19N 110°56W **318** A2
Nogales *Ariz., U.S.A.* 31°21N 110°56W **305** L8
Nogaro *France* 43°45N 0°2W **174** E3
Nogat → *Poland* 54°17N 19°17E **184** D6
Nōgata *Japan* 33°48N 130°44E **222** D2
Nogatino *Russia* 55°41N 37°41E **129** B3
Nogaysk = Prymorske *Ukraine* 46°48N 36°20E **189** J9
Nogent *France* 48°1N 5°20E **173** D12
Nogent-le-Rotrou *France* 48°20N 0°50E **172** D7
Nogent-sur-Marne *France* 48°50N 2°28E **134** A3
Nogent-sur-Seine *France* 48°30N 3°30E **173** D10
Noggara *Ethiopia* 13°54N 36°35E **257** E4
Noggerup *Australia* 33°32S 116°5E **279** F2
Noginsk *Russia* 64°30N 90°50E **215** C10
Nogliki *Russia* 51°50N 143°10E **215** D15
Nogoa → *Australia* 23°40S 147°55E **280** C4
Nogoyá *Argentina* 32°24S 59°48W **334** C4
Nógrád □ *Hungary* 48°0N 19°30E **182** C4
Noguera Pallaresa → *Spain* 41°55N 0°55E **196** D5
Noguera Ribagorçana → *Spain* 41°40N 0°43E **196** D5
Nohar *India* 29°11N 74°49E **242** E6
Nohfelden *Germany* 49°35N 7°7E **179** F3
Nohili Pt. *U.S.A.* 22°4N 159°47W **302** A2
Nohta *India* 23°40N 79°34E **243** H8
Nohwa *S. Korea* 34°10N 126°34E **224** E3
Nohwado *S. Korea* 34°12N 126°35E **224** E3
Noia *Spain* 42°48N 8°53W **194** C2
Noichi *Japan* 33°33N 133°42E **222** D5
Noida *India* 28°36N 77°19E **120** B2
Noipuos *Papua N. G.* 2°25S 150°7E **286** B6
Noire, Montagne *France* 43°28N 2°18E **174** E6
Noires, Mts. *France* 48°11N 3°40W **172** D3
Noirétable *France* 45°48N 3°46E **174** C7
Noirmoutier, Î. de *France* 46°58N 2°10W **172** F4
Noirmoutier-en-l'Île *France* 47°0N 2°14W **172** F4
Noiseau *France* 48°46N 2°32E **134** B4
Noisiel *France* 48°51N 2°37E **134** A4
Noisy-le-Grand *France* 48°50N 2°33E **134** A4
Noisy-le-Roi *France* 48°50N 2°3E **134** A1
Noisy-le-Sec *France* 48°53N 2°27E **134** A3
Nojane *Botswana* 23°15S 20°14E **270** B3
Nojima-Zaki *Japan* 34°54N 139°53E **223** C11
Nok Kundi *Pakistan* 28°50N 62°45E **240** C1
Nok Ta Phao, Ko *Thailand* 9°23N 99°40E **237** b
Nokaneng *Botswana* 19°40S 22°17E **270** A3
Nokia *Finland* 61°30N 23°30E **188** B2
Nokkala *Finland* 60°8N 24°45E **121** C1
Nokkeushi = Kitami *Japan* 43°48N 143°54E **220** C11
Nokomis *Sask., Canada* 51°35N 105°0W **297** C8
Nokomis *Fla., U.S.A.* 27°7N 82°27W **317** H7
Nokomis *Ill., U.S.A.* 39°18N 89°18W **310** E7
Nokomis L. *Canada* 57°0N 103°0W **297** B8
Nokou *Chad* 14°35N 14°47E **259** F2
Nokuku *Vanuatu* 14°54S 166°35E **287** D4
Nola *C.A.R.* 3°35N 16°4E **264** B3
Nola *Italy* 40°55N 14°33E **201** B7
Nolay *France* 46°58N 4°35E **173** F11
Noli, C. di *Italy* 44°12N 8°25E **198** D5
Nolinsk *Russia* 57°28N 49°57E **190** B9
Noma *U.S.A.* 30°59N 85°37W **316** E4
Noma Omuramba → *Namibia* 18°52S 20°53E **270** A3
Noma-Saki *Japan* 31°25N 130°7E **222** F2
Nomad *Papua N. G.* 6°19S 142°13E **286** D2
Nombre de Dios *Panama* 9°34N 79°28W **320** E4
Nome *U.S.A.* 64°30N 165°25W **303** D6
Nomentano *Italy* 41°55N 12°30E **136** B2
Nomgon *Mongolia* 42°50N 105°8E **226** C3
Nomi *Japan* 36°26N 136°25E **223** A8
Nomo-Zaki *Japan* 32°35N 129°44E **222** E1
Nomoneas *Micronesia* 7°24N 151°53E **287** T18
Nomuka *Tonga* 20°17S 174°48W **287** Q13
Nomuka Group *Tonga* 20°20S 174°48W **287** Q13
Nonacho L. *Canada* 61°42N 109°40W **297** A7
Nonakashinden *Japan* 35°44N 139°30E **140** A2
Nonancourt *France* 48°47N 1°11E **172** D8
Nonda *Australia* 20°40S 142°28E **280** C3
Nondalton *U.S.A.* 60°0N 154°51W **303** F9
None *Italy* 44°56N 7°32E **198** D4
Nong Chang *Thailand* 15°23N 99°51E **236** E2
Nong Han Res. *Thailand* 17°11N 104°9E **236** D5
Nong Het *Laos* 19°29N 103°59E **236** C4
Nong Khai *Thailand* 17°50N 102°46E **236** D4
Nong'an *China* 44°25N 125°5E **227** B13
Nongjrong *India* 25°29N 92°6E **241** C4
Nongminyundong Jiangxisuo *China* 23°7N 113°15E **121** B2
Nongoma *S. Africa* 27°58S 31°35E **271** C5
Nongpoh *India* 25°54N 91°53E **241** C3
Nongsa *Indonesia* 1°11N 104°8E **237** d
Nongstoin *India* 25°31N 91°16E **241** C3
Nonhyeon *S. Korea* 37°30N 127°1E **137** B2
Nono *Ethiopia* 8°32N 37°26E **266** C4
Nonoava *Mexico* 27°28N 106°44W **318** B3
Nonoc I. *Phil.* 9°51N 125°37E **233** G5
Nonoichi *Japan* 36°35N 136°35E **223** A8
Nonsan *S. Korea* 36°12N 127°5E **224** D3
Nonsuch B. *Antigua & B.* 17°3N 61°42W **322** b
Nonthaburi *Thailand* 13°50N 100°29E **113** A1
Nontron *France* 45°31N 0°40E **174** C4
Nonza *France* 42°47N 9°21E **175** F13
Noon Gun *Cape Town, S. Africa* **118** b1
Noonamah *Australia* 12°40S 131°4E **278** B5
Noondie, L. *Australia* 28°30S 119°30E **279** E2
Noonkanbah ☼ *Australia* 18°30S 124°50E **278** C3
Noord *Aruba* 12°34N 70°1W **322** f
Noord Brabant □ *Neths.* 51°40N 5°0E **170** C5
Noord Holland □ *Neths.* 52°30N 4°45E **170** B4
Noord Saliña *Bonaire* 12°11N 68°16W **322** h
Noordbeveland *Neths.* 51°35N 3°50E **170** C3
Noorderkerk *Amsterdam, Neths.* **112** a1
Noordgesig *S. Africa* 26°13S 27°56E **123** B1
Noordkaap *Aruba* 12°34N 70°1W **322** f
Noordoostpolder *Neths.* 52°45N 5°45E **170** B5
Noordpunt *Bonaire* 12°18N 68°23W **322** h
Noordpunt *Curaçao* 12°24N 69°10W **322** g
Noordwijk *Neths.* 52°14N 4°26E **170** B4
Noordzeekanaal *Neths.* 52°28N 4°47E **112** A1
Noorvik *U.S.A.* 66°50N 161°3W **303** C7
Noosa Heads *Australia* 26°25S 153°6E **281** D5
Nootka I. *Canada* 49°32N 126°42W **296** D3
Nopiming ⌓ *Canada* 50°30N 95°37W **297** C9
Nóqui *Angola* 5°55S 13°30E **265** D2
Nor-Bayzzet = Kamo *Armenia* 40°21N 45°7E **191** K7
Nora *Eritrea* 16°6N 40°4E **257** D5
Nora *Sweden* 59°32N 15°2E **162** E9
Nora Springs *U.S.A.* 43°9N 93°0W **310** A4
Norala *Phil.* 6°32N 124°40E **233** H5
Noralee *Canada* 53°59N 126°26W **296** C3
Noranda = Rouyn-Noranda *Canada* 48°20N 79°0W **298** C4
Norberg *Sweden* 60°4N 15°56E **162** D9
Norborne *U.S.A.* 39°18N 93°40W **310** E3
Nórcia *Italy* 42°48N 13°5E **199** F10
Norco *U.S.A.* 33°56N 117°33W **307** M9
Norcross *U.S.A.* 33°56N 84°13W **316** B5
Nord □ *Cameroon* 8°30N 14°0E **263** D7
Nord □ *France* 50°15N 3°30E **173** B10
Nord, Gare du *Paris, France* **134** a4
Nord, Pt. *Comoros Is.* 11°22S 43°19E **272** a
Nord-Kivu □ *Dem. Rep. of the Congo* 1°0S 29°0E **268** C2
Nord-Ostsee-Kanal *Germany* 54°12N 9°32E **178** A5
Nord-Ouest □ *Cameroon* 6°20N 10°30E **263** D7
Nord-Pas-de-Calais □ *France* 50°30N 2°50E **173** B9
Nordagutu *Norway* 59°25N 9°20E **164** E6
Nordaustlandet *Svalbard* 79°14N 23°0E **150** B9
Nordberg *Norway* 61°54N 8°10E **164** C5
Nordborg *Denmark* 55°5N 9°50E **163** J3
Nordby *Denmark* 55°27N 8°24E **163** J2
Norddeich *Germany* 53°36N 7°9E **178** B3
Nordegg *Canada* 52°29N 116°5W **296** C5
Norden *Germany* 53°35N 7°12E **178** B3
Nordenham *Germany* 53°30N 8°30E **178** B4
Nordenskjöld Sea = Laptev Sea *Russia* 76°0N 125°0E **215** B13
Norderhov *Norway* 60°7N 10°17E **164** D7
Norderney *Germany* 53°42N 7°9E **178** B3
Norderstedt *Germany* 53°42N 10°1E **178** B6
Nordeste *Azores* 37°50N 25°10W **153** d3
Nordfjord *Norway* 61°55N 5°30E **164** C2
Nordfjordeid *Norway* 61°54N 6°0E **164** C2
Nordfriesische Inseln *Germany* 54°40N 8°20E **178** A4
Nordhausen *Germany* 51°30N 10°47E **178** D6
Nordhorn *Germany* 52°26N 7°4E **178** C3
Norðoyar *Færoe Is.* 62°17N 6°35W **160** E9
Norðtunga *Iceland* 64°44N 21°24W **155** C5
Norður-múlasýsla *Iceland* 65°30N 15°0W **155** B11
Norðurbotn *Iceland* 65°36N 23°46W **155** B3
Norðurland Eystra □ *Iceland* 65°30N 17°0W **155** B9
Norðurland Vestra □ *Iceland* 65°30N 20°0W **155** B6
Nördinge-Nol *Sweden* 57°56N 12°5E **163** G6
Nordingrå *Sweden* 62°56N 18°17E **162** B12
Nordjylland □ *Denmark* 57°0N 9°30E **163** G3
Nordkapp *Finnmark, Norway* 71°10N 25°50E **160** A21
Nordkapp *Svalbard* 80°31N 20°0E **150** A9
Nordkinn *Norway* 71°8N 27°40E **160** A22
Nordkinnhalvøya *Norway* 70°55N 27°40E **160** A22
Nördlicher Teutoburger Wald-Wiehengebirge ⌓ *Germany* 52°18N 8°10E **178** C4
Nördlingen *Germany* 48°48N 10°30E **179** G6
Nordmarka *Norway* 59°58N 10°41E **133** A3
Nordmøre *Norway* 63°6N 8°15E **164** B4
Nordostrundingen *Greenland* 81°22N 11°40W **154** A9
Nordøyane *Norway* 62°40N 6°0E **164** B3
Nordrand-Siedlung *Austria* 48°16N 16°26E **142** A2
Nordre Bergenhus = Sogn og Fjordane □ *Norway* 61°40N 6°45E **164** C3
Nørdre Osa *Norway* 61°18N 11°45E **164** C8
Nordre Strømfjord *Greenland* 67°10N 53°35W **154** D5
Nordrhein-Westfalen □ *Germany* 51°45N 7°30E **178** D3
Nordsinni *Norway* 60°50N 9°57E **164** D6
Nørdstedalssæter *Norway* 61°40N 7°48E **164** C4
Nordstrand *Schleswig-Holstein, Germany* 54°30N 8°52E **178** A4
Nordstrand *Oslo, Norway* 59°52N 10°48E **133** A3
Nordvik *Russia* 74°2N 111°32E **215** B12
Nore → *Ireland* 52°25N 6°58W **166** D4
Norefjell *Norway* 60°16N 9°29E **164** D6
Noreland *Canada* 44°43N 78°48W **312** B6
Noresund *Norway* 60°11N 9°37E **164** D6
Norfolk = Simcoe *Canada* 42°50N 80°23W **312** D4
Norfolk *N.Y., U.S.A.* 44°48N 74°59W **313** B10
Norfolk *Nebr., U.S.A.* 42°2N 97°25W **308** D5
Norfolk *Va., U.S.A.* 36°50N 76°17W **309** G15
Norfolk □ *U.K.* 52°39N 0°54E **169** E8
Norfolk Basin *Pac. Oc.* 32°0S 170°0E **277** G13
Norfolk Broads △ *U.K.* 52°45N 1°30E **169** E9
Norfolk I. *Pac. Oc.* 28°58S 168°3E **277** F12
Norfolk Ridge *Pac. Oc.* 29°0S 168°0E **288** K8
Norfork L. *U.S.A.* 36°15N 92°14W **314** C8
Norge = Norway ■ *Europe* 63°0N 11°0E **160** E14
Norheimsund *Norway* 60°23N 6°6E **164** D3
Norilsk *Russia* 69°20N 88°6E **215** C9
Norland *U.S.A.* 25°57N 80°12W **129** C2
Norma, Mt. *Australia* 20°55S 140°42E **280** C3
Normal *U.S.A.* 40°31N 88°59W **310** D8
Norman *U.S.A.* 35°13N 97°26W **314** D6
Norman → *Australia* 19°18S 141°51E **280** B3
Norman Manley Int. ✈ (KIN) *Jamaica* 17°56N 76°47W **320** a
Norman Park *U.S.A.* 31°16N 83°41W **316** D6
Norman Wells *Canada* 65°17N 126°51W **294** D6
Normanby *N.Z.* 39°32S 174°18E **284** F3
Normanby → *Australia* 14°23S 144°10E **280** A3
Normanby I. *Papua N. G.* 10°5S 151°5E **286** F6
Normandie *France* 48°45N 0°10E **171** B4
Normandie-Maine ⌓ *France* 48°30N 0°20W **172** D6
Normandin *Canada* 48°49N 72°31W **298** C5
Normandy = Normandie *France* 48°45N 0°10E **171** B4
Normanhurst, Mt. *Australia* 25°4S 122°30E **279** E3
Normanton *Australia* 17°40S 141°10E **280** B3
Normanville *Australia* 35°27S 138°18E **282** C3
Normétal *Canada* 49°0N 79°22W **298** C4
Norquay *Canada* 51°53N 102°5W **297** C8
Norquinco *Argentina* 41°51S 70°55W **336** B2
Norra Kvill △ *Sweden* 57°46N 15°35E **163** G9
Norra Ulvön *Sweden* 63°3N 18°40E **162** A12
Norrahammar *Sweden* 57°43N 14°7E **163** G8
Norrbottens län □ *Sweden* 66°50N 20°0E **160** C19
Norrdellen *Sweden* 61°53N 16°43E **162** C10
Nørre Åby *Denmark* 55°27N 9°52E **163** J3
Nørre Alslev *Denmark* 54°54N 11°52E **163** K5
Nørrebro *Copenhagen, Denmark* **118** a1
Nørresundby *Denmark* 57°5N 9°52E **163** G3
Norrhult-Klavreström *Sweden* 57°7N 15°10E **163** G9
Norridge *U.S.A.* 41°57N 87°49W **119** B2
Norris City *U.S.A.* 37°59N 88°20W **311** G8
Norris Point *Canada* 49°31N 57°53W **299** C8
Norristown *Ga., U.S.A.* 32°30N 82°30W **316** C7
Norristown *Pa., U.S.A.* 40°7N 75°21W **313** F9
Norrköping *Sweden* 58°37N 16°11E **163** F10
Norrland *Sweden* 62°15N 15°45E **160** E16
Norrmalm *Stockholm, Sweden* **139** a1
Norrsundet *Sweden* 60°56N 17°8E **162** D11
Norrtälje *Sweden* 59°46N 18°42E **162** E12
Norseman *Australia* 32°8S 121°43E **279** F3
Norsewood *N.Z.* 40°3S 176°13E **284** G5
Norsjø *Norway* 59°18N 9°20E **164** E6
Norsk *Russia* 52°30N 130°5E **215** D14
Norsup *Vanuatu* 16°3S 167°24E **287** F5
Norte, C. *Chile* 27°3S 109°24W **330** b
Norte, Canal do → *Brazil* 0°40N 50°20W **329** C7
Norte, Pta. *Argentina* 42°5S 63°46W **336** B4
Norte, Pta. *Chile* 33°36S 78°54W **330** c
Norte, Pta. del *Canary Is.* 27°51N 17°57W **153** e1
Norte, Pta. do *Azores* 37°1N 25°4W **153** d4
Norte, Serra do *Brazil* 11°20S 59°0W **331** C6
Norte de Santander □ *Colombia* 8°0N 73°0W **328** B3
Norte Grande *Azores* 38°40N 28°4W **153** d1
Nortelândia *Brazil* 14°25S 56°48W **331** C6
North *U.S.A.* 33°37N 81°6W **316** B8
North, C. *Canada* 47°2N 60°20W **299** C7
North Adams *U.S.A.* 42°42N 73°7W **313** D11
North America 40°0N 100°0W **292** F10
North Andaman I. *India* 13°15N 92°55E **245** H11
North Arlington *U.S.A.* 40°47N 74°7W **132** B1
North Arm *Canada* 62°0N 114°30W **296** A5
North Atlanta *U.S.A.* 33°53N 84°19W **113** A3
North Augusta *U.S.A.* 33°30N 81°59W **316** B8
North Australian Basin *Ind. Oc.* 14°30S 116°30E **276** C2
North Ayrshire □ *U.K.* 55°45N 4°44W **167** F4
North Balabac Str. *Phil.* 8°8N 117°4E **233** G1
North Baltimore *U.S.A.* 41°11N 83°41W **311** C13
North Bass I. *U.S.A.* 41°40N 82°56W **312** E2
North Battleford *Canada* 52°50N 108°17W **297** C7
North Bay *Canada* 46°20N 79°30W **298** C4
North Bay Village *U.S.A.* 25°50N 80°9W **129** C3
North Beach *San Francisco, U.S.A.* **136** a2
North Belcher Is. *Canada* 56°50N 79°50W **298** A4
North Bend *Oreg., U.S.A.* 43°24N 124°14W **304** E1
North Bend *Pa., U.S.A.* 41°20N 77°42W **312** E7
North Bend *Wash., U.S.A.* 47°30N 121°47W **306** C5
North Bennington *U.S.A.* 42°56N 73°15W **313** D11
North Bergen *U.S.A.* 40°48N 74°0W **132** B1
North Berwick *E. Loth., U.K.* 56°4N 2°42W **167** E6
North Berwick *Maine, U.S.A.* 43°18N 70°44W **313** C14
North Borneo = Sabah □ *Malaysia* 6°0N 117°0E **235** A5
North Breakers *Midway Is.* 28°13N 177°24W **302** c
North Brother I. *India* 10°59N 92°40E **245** J11
North Bruce *Canada* 44°22N 81°26W **312** B3
North Bull I. *Ireland* 53°22N 6°9W **120** A3
North C. *N.B., Canada* 47°5N 64°0W **299** C7
North C. *N.Z.* 34°23S 173°4E **284** A2
North C. *Papua N. G.* 2°32S 150°50E **286** B6
North Canadian → *U.S.A.* 35°22N 95°37W **314** D7
North Canton *U.S.A.* 40°53N 81°24W **312** F3
North Cape = Nordkapp *Norway* 71°10N 25°50E **160** A21
North Caribou L. *Canada* 52°50N 90°40W **298** B1
North Carolina □ *U.S.A.* 35°30N 80°0W **315** D15
North Cascades △ *U.S.A.* 48°45N 121°10W **304** B3
North Cay *Bahamas* 25°6N 77°26W **153** b
North Channel *Ont., Canada* 46°0N 83°0W **298** C3
North Channel *U.K.* 55°13N 5°52W **167** F3
North Charleston *U.S.A.* 32°53N 79°58W **316** C10
North Cheam *U.K.* 51°22N 0°11W **125** B2
North Chicago *U.S.A.* 42°19N 87°51W **311** B9
North College Hill *U.S.A.* 39°13N 84°33W **311** E12
North Collins *U.S.A.* 42°35N 78°56W **312** D6
North Comino Channel *Malta* 36°1N 14°20E **206** E7
North Cotabato □ *Phil.* 7°10N 125°0E **233** H5
North Cray *U.K.* 51°25N 0°8E **125** B4
North Creek *U.S.A.* 43°42N 73°59W **313** C11
North Dakota □ *U.S.A.* 47°30N 100°15W **308** B3
North Decatur *U.S.A.* 33°48N 84°17W **113** B3
North Downs *U.K.* 51°19N 0°21E **169** F8
North Druid Hills *U.S.A.* 33°49N 84°17W **113** B3
North East *U.S.A.* 42°13N 79°50W **312** D5
North East □ *Botswana* 20°45S 27°30E **271** B4
North East B. *Ascension I.* 7°55S 14°21W **153** g
North East Frontier Agency = Arunachal Pradesh □ *India* 28°0N 95°0E **241** B5
North East Lincolnshire □ *U.K.* 53°34N 0°2W **168** D7
North Eastern □ *Kenya* 1°30N 40°0E **268** B5
North End *Boston, U.S.A.* **116** a3
North Esk → *Angus, U.K.* 56°46N 2°24W **167** E6
North Esk → *Midloth., U.K.* 55°54N 3°4W **121** B2
North European Plain *Europe* 55°0N 25°0E **158** E10
North Fabius → *U.S.A.* 39°54N 91°30W **310** E5
North Foreland *U.K.* 51°22N 1°28E **169** F9
North Fork *U.S.A.* 37°14N 119°21W **306** H7
North Fork, Salt → *U.S.A.* 39°26N 91°53W **310** E5
North Fork American → *U.S.A.* 38°57N 120°59W **306** G5
North Fork Edisto → *U.S.A.* 33°16N 80°54W **316** B9
North Fork Feather → *U.S.A.* 38°33N 121°30W **306** F5
North Fork Grand → *U.S.A.* 45°47N 102°16W **308** C2
North Fork Red → *U.S.A.* 34°24N 99°14W **314** D5
North Fort Myers *U.S.A.* 26°41N 81°53W **317** J8
North Frisian Is. = Nordfriesische Inseln *Germany* 54°40N 8°20E **178** A4
North Gower *Canada* 45°8N 75°43W **313** A9
North Greenfield = West Allis *U.S.A.* 43°1N 88°0W **311** B8
North Gyle *U.K.* 55°57N 3°19W **121** B2
North Hackensack *U.S.A.* 40°54N 74°2W **132** A1
North Harbor *Phil.* 14°37N 120°57E **127** B1
North Hd. *N.S.W., Australia* 33°49S 151°18E **139** A2
North Hd. *W. Austral., Australia* 30°14S 114°59E **279** F1
North Henik L. *Canada* 61°45N 97°40W **297** A9
North Highlands *U.S.A.* 38°40N 121°23W **306** G5
North Hollywood *U.S.A.* 34°9N 118°22W **126** B2
North Horr *Kenya* 3°20N 37°8E **268** B4
North I. *India* 10°8N 72°20E **245** J1
North I. *Rift Valley, Kenya* 4°5N 36°5E **268** B4
North I. *N.Z.* 38°0S 175°0E **284** E4
North I. *Seychelles* 4°25S 55°13E **272** c
North Judson *U.S.A.* 41°13N 86°46W **311** C10
North Kingsville *U.S.A.* 41°54N 80°42W **312** E4
North Kitui ⌓ *Kenya* 0°15S 38°29E **268** C4
North Knife → *Canada* 58°53N 94°45W **297** B10
North Koel → *India* 24°45N 83°50E **243** G10
North Korea ■ *Asia* 40°0N 127°0E **224** C3
North L. *Australia* 32°30S 143°5E **282** B5
North Lakhimpur *India* 27°14N 94°7E **241** B5
North Lanarkshire □ *U.K.* 55°52N 3°56W **167** F5
North Las Vegas *U.S.A.* 36°11N 115°7W **124** A1
North Las Vegas ✈ (VGT) *U.S.A.* 36°12N 115°11W **124** A1
North Lexington *U.S.A.* 42°27N 71°14W **116** A1
North Liberty *Ind., U.S.A.* 41°32N 86°26W **311** C10
North Liberty *Iowa, U.S.A.* 41°46N 91°35W **310** C5
North Lincolnshire □ *U.K.* 53°36N 0°30W **168** D7
North Little Rock *U.S.A.* 34°45N 92°16W **314** D8
North Loup → *U.S.A.* 41°17N 98°24W **308** E4
North Luangwa △ *Zambia* 11°49S 32°9E **269** E3
North Magnetic Pole *Arctic* 85°6N 134°0W **150** A1
North Malé Atoll *Maldives* 4°25N 73°30E **272** d
North Malosmadulu Atoll *Maldives* 5°37N 72°55E **272** d
North Manchester *U.S.A.* 41°0N 85°46W **311** D11
North Mankato *U.S.A.* 44°10N 94°2W **308** C6
North Miami *U.S.A.* 25°53N 80°11W **129** C2
North Miami Beach *U.S.A.* 25°55N 80°9W **129** C2
North Minch *U.K.* 58°5N 5°55W **167** C3
North Moose L. *Canada* 54°4N 100°12W **297** C8
North Myrtle Beach *U.S.A.* 33°48N 78°42W **315** E15
North Nahanni → *Canada* 62°15N 123°20W **296** A4
North Naples *U.S.A.* 26°12N 81°48W **317** J8
North Nazimabad *Pakistan* 24°55N 67°3E **123** A2
North New River Canal *U.S.A.* 26°30N 80°30W **317** J9
North Nilandu Atoll *Maldives* 3°14N 72°56E **272** d
North Olmsted *U.S.A.* 41°25N 81°56W **312** E3
North Ossetia-Alaniya □ *Russia* 43°30N 44°30E **191** J7
North Pagai, I. = Pagai Utara, Pulau *Indonesia* 2°35S 100°0E **234** C2
North Palisade *U.S.A.* 37°6N 118°31W **306** H8
North Perry ✈ (HWO) *U.S.A.* 26°0N 80°14W **129** B2
North Platte *U.S.A.* 41°8N 100°46W **308** E3
North Platte → *U.S.A.* 41°7N 100°42W **308** E3
North Point *Hong Kong, China* 22°17N 114°12E **122** B3
North Point *Fla., U.S.A.* 27°4N 82°10W **317** H7
North Point Park *Boston, U.S.A.* **116** a1
North Pole *Arctic* 90°0N 0°0 **150** A
North Pole *Alaska, U.S.A.* 64°45N 147°21W **303** D11
North Portal *Canada* 49°0N 102°33W **297** D8
North Powder *U.S.A.* 45°2N 117°55W **304** D5
North Pt. *Ascension I.* 7°53S 14°23W **153** g
North Pt. *Barbados* 13°20N 59°37W **323** r
North Pt. *Mich., U.S.A.* 45°2N 83°16W **312** A1
North Pt. *Vanuatu* 14°56S 168°6E **287** D6
North Queensferry *U.K.* 56°1N 3°24W **121** A1
North Quincy *U.S.A.* 42°16N 71°1W **116** B2
North Reef I. *India* 13°5N 92°43E **245** H11
North Res. *U.S.A.* 42°27N 71°6W **116** A2
North Rhine Westphalia = Nordrhein-Westfalen □ *Germany* 51°45N 7°30E **178** D3
North River *Canada* 53°49N 57°6W **299** B8
North Riverside *U.S.A.* 41°50N 87°48W **119** B2
North Ronaldsay *U.K.* 59°22N 2°26W **167** B6
North Salem *U.S.A.* 39°52N 86°39W **311** E10
North Saskatchewan → *Canada* 53°15N 105°5W **297** C7
North Saugus *U.S.A.* 42°29N 71°0W **116** A2
North Sea *Europe* 56°0N 4°0E **158** D6
North Seal → *Canada* 58°50N 98°7W **297** B9
North Sentinel I. *India* 11°33N 92°15E **245** J11
North Shields *Australia* 34°38S 135°52E **282** C1
North Shore *U.S.A.* 21°39N 158°30W **302** J13
North Shore Channel → *U.S.A.* 41°58N 87°42W **119** B2
North Slope *U.S.A.* 69°15N 152°0W **300** B9
North Solomons □ *Papua N. G.* 4°0S 155°0E **286** B8
North Somerset □ *U.K.* 51°24N 2°45W **169** F5
North Station *Boston, U.S.A.* **116** a2
North Sydney *N.S.W., Australia* 33°50S 151°13E **139** B2
North Sydney *N.S., Canada* 46°12N 60°15W **299** C7
North Syracuse *U.S.A.* 43°8N 76°7W **313** C8
North Taranaki Bight *N.Z.* 38°50S 174°15E **284** E3
North Thompson → *Canada* 50°40N 120°20W **296** C4
North Tonawanda *U.S.A.* 43°2N 78°53W **312** C6
North Troy *U.S.A.* 45°0N 72°24W **313** B12
North Twin I. *Canada* 53°20N 80°0W **298** B4
North Tyne → *U.K.* 55°0N 2°8W **168** B5
North Ubian I. *Phil.* 6°9N 120°27E **233** H3
North Uist *U.K.* 57°40N 7°15W **167** D1
North Union = Shaker Heights *U.S.A.* 41°28N 81°32W **312** E3
North Union *St. Vincent* 13°13N 61°8W **323** n
North Vancouver *Canada* 49°19N 123°4W **306** A3
North Vernon *U.S.A.* 39°0N 85°38W **311** F11
North Wabasca L. *Canada* 56°0N 113°55W **296** B6
North Walsham *U.K.* 52°50N 1°22E **168** E9
North Webster *U.S.A.* 41°25N 85°48W **311** C11
North West = Severo-Zapadnyy □ *Russia* 65°0N 40°0E **214** C4
North West □ *Botswana* 19°0S 22°30E **270** A3
North-West □ *S. Africa* 27°0S 25°0E **270** C4
North West Bluff *Montserrat* 16°49N 62°12W **323** p
North West C. *Australia* 21°45S 114°9E **278** D1
North West Frontier = Khyber Pakhtunkhwa □ *Pakistan* 34°0N 72°0E **242** C4
North West Highlands *U.K.* 57°33N 4°58W **167** D4
North West Pt. *Jamaica* 18°27N 78°13W **320** a
North West River *Canada* 53°30N 60°10W **299** B7
North Western □ *Zambia* 13°30S 25°30E **269** E2
North-Western Provinces and Oudh = Uttar Pradesh □ *India* 27°0N 80°0E **243** F9
North Wildwood *U.S.A.* 39°0N 74°48W **309** F16
North Woolwich *U.K.* 51°30N 0°3E **125** A4
North Yakima = Yakima *U.S.A.* 46°36N 120°31W **304** C3
North York *Canada* 43°45N 79°27W **141** A2
North York Moors *U.K.* 54°23N 0°53W **168** C7
North York Moors △ *U.K.* 54°27N 0°51W **168** C7
North Yorkshire □ *U.K.* 54°15N 1°25W **168** C6
Northallerton *U.K.* 54°20N 1°26W **168** C6
Northam *W. Austral., Australia* 31°35S 116°42E **279** F2
Northam *Limpopo, S. Africa* 24°56S 27°18E **270** B4
Northampton *W. Austral., Australia* 28°27S 114°33E **279** E1
Northampton *Northants., U.K.* 52°15N 0°53W **169** E7
Northampton *Mass., U.S.A.* 42°19N 72°38W **313** D12
Northampton *Pa., U.S.A.* 40°41N 75°30W **313** F9
Northamptonshire □ *U.K.* 52°16N 0°55W **169** E7
Northbridge *N.S.W., Australia* 33°49S 151°15E **139** A2
Northbridge *Mass., U.S.A.* 42°9N 71°39W **313** D13
Northbridge Park *Australia* 33°49S 151°15E **139** A2
Northbrook *Ont., Canada* 44°44N 77°9W **312** B7
Northbrook *Ill., U.S.A.* 42°7N 87°50W **119** A2
Northcliff *S. Africa* 26°8S 27°58E **123** A1
Northcliffe *Australia* 34°39S 116°7E **279** F2
Northcote *Australia* 37°46S 145°0E **128** A2
Northeast C. *U.S.A.* 63°18N 168°42W **303** E5
Northeast Pacific Basin *Pac. Oc.* 32°0N 145°0W **289** D13
Northeast Providence Channel *W. Indies* 26°0N 76°0W **320** A4
Northeastern Univ. *U.S.A.* 42°20N 71°4W **116** A2
Northeim *Germany* 51°42N 10°0E **178** D6
Northern = Limpopo □ *S. Africa* 24°5S 29°0E **271** B4
Northern □ *Ghana* 9°30N 1°0W **263** D4
Northern □ *Malawi* 11°0S 34°0E **269** E3
Northern □ *Papua N. G.* 9°0S 148°30E **286** E5
Northern □ *S. Leone* 9°15N 11°30W **262** D2
Northern □ *Zambia* 10°30S 30°30E **269** E3
Northern Aral Sea *Kazakhstan* 46°20N 60°30E **216** C6
Northern Areas = Gilgit-Baltistan □ *Pakistan* 36°30N 73°0E **243** A5
Northern Bahr el Ghazal □ *South Sudan* 8°0N 27°30E **257** F2
Northern Cape □ *S. Africa* 30°0S 20°0E **270** C3
Northern Circars *India* 17°30N 82°30E **244** F6
Northern Dvina = Dvina, Severnaya → *Russia* 64°32N 40°30E **186** B7
Northern Indian L. *Canada* 57°20N 97°20W **297** B9
Northern Ireland □ *U.K.* 54°45N 7°0W **166** B5
Northern Lau Group *Fiji* 17°30S 178°59W **287** A3
Northern Light L. *Canada* 48°15N 90°39W **298** C1
Northern Marianas ☒ *Pac. Oc.* 17°0N 145°0E **302** a
Northern Province □ *S. Africa* 24°0S 29°0E **271** B4
Northern Range *Trin. & Tob.* 10°46N 61°15W **323** t
Northern Rhodesia = Zambia ■ *Africa* 15°0S 28°0E **269** F2
Northern Samar □ *Phil.* 12°30N 124°40E **232** E5
Northern Sporades = Voreios Sporades *Greece* 39°15N 23°30E **204** B5
Northern Territory □ *Australia* 20°0S 133°0E **278** D5
Northfield *Ill., U.S.A.* 42°5N 87°47W **119** A2
Northfield *Minn., U.S.A.* 44°27N 93°9W **308** C7
Northfield *Vt., U.S.A.* 44°9N 72°40W **313** B12
Northgate *Canada* 49°0N 102°16W **297** D8
Northland □ *N.Z.* 35°30S 173°30E **284** B2
Northmount *Canada* 43°46N 79°23W **141** A2
Northolt *U.K.* 51°32N 0°22W **125** A1
Northome *U.S.A.* 47°52N 94°17W **308** B6
Northport *Ala., U.S.A.* 33°14N 87°35W **315** E11
Northport *Wash., U.S.A.* 48°55N 117°48W **304** B5
Northumberland □ *U.K.* 55°12N 2°0W **168** B6
Northumberland, C. *Australia* 38°5S 140°40E **282** E4
Northumberland Heath *U.K.* 51°28N 0°10E **125** B5
Northumberland Is. *Australia* 21°30S 149°50E **280** C4
Northumberland Str. *Canada* 46°20N 64°0W **299** C7
Northville *Ont., Canada* 43°10N 81°56W **312** C3
Northville *N.Y., U.S.A.* 43°13N 74°11W **313** C10
Northway *U.S.A.* 62°58N 141°56W **303** E12
Northwest Atlantic Mid-Ocean Canyon *Atl. Oc.* 54°0N 48°0W **152** A7
Northwest Pacific Basin *Pac. Oc.* 32°0N 165°0E **288** D8
Northwest Providence Channel *W. Indies* 26°0N 78°0W **320** A4
Northwest Pt. *Bahamas* 25°4N 77°31W **153** b
Northwest Territories □ *Canada* 63°0N 118°0W **294** E8
Northwestern Hawaiian Is. Marine Nat. Monument = Papahänaumokuäkea Marine Nat. Monument ⌓ *U.S.A.* 25°25N 170°35W **302** F9
Northwestern Univ. *U.S.A.* 42°3N 87°40W **119** A2
Northwich *U.K.* 53°15N 2°31W **168** D5
Northwood *London, U.K.* 51°36N 0°25W **125** A1
Northwood *Iowa, U.S.A.* 43°27N 93°13W **308** D7
Northwood *N. Dak., U.S.A.* 47°44N 97°34W **308** B5
Northwood Park *Canada* 43°45N 79°30W **141** A1
Norton *Kans., U.S.A.* 39°50N 99°53W **308** F4
Norton *Zimbabwe* 17°52S 30°40E **269** F3
Norton B. *U.S.A.* 64°45N 161°15W **303** D7
Norton Sd. *U.S.A.* 63°50N 164°0W **303** E7
Norton Shores *U.S.A.* 43°10N 86°16W **311** A10
Nortorf *Germany* 54°10N 9°50E **178** A5
Norwalk *Calif., U.S.A.* 33°54N 118°4W **307** M8
Norwalk *Conn., U.S.A.* 41°7N 73°22W **313** E11
Norwalk *Iowa, U.S.A.* 41°29N 93°41W **310** C3
Norwalk *Ohio, U.S.A.* 41°15N 82°37W **312** E2
Norway *Maine, U.S.A.* 44°13N 70°32W **309** C18
Norway *Mich., U.S.A.* 45°47N 87°55W **308** C10
Norway ■ *Europe* 63°0N 11°0E **160** E14
Norway House *Canada* 53°59N 97°50W **297** C9
Norwegian B. *Canada* 77°30N 90°0W **295** B14
Norwegian Basin *Atl. Oc.* 68°0N 2°0W **150** C7
Norwegian Sea *Atl. Oc.* 66°0N 1°0E **158** B6
Norwich *Ont., Canada* 42°59N 80°36W **312** D4
Norwich *Norfolk, U.K.* 52°38N 1°18E **169** E9
Norwich *Conn., U.S.A.* 41°31N 72°5W **313** E12
Norwich *N.Y., U.S.A.* 42°32N 75°32W **313** D9
Norwood *Ont., Canada* 44°23N 77°59W **312** B7
Norwood *Gauteng, S. Africa* 26°9S 28°4E **123** A2
Norwood *N.Y., U.S.A.* 44°45N 75°0W **313** B10
Norwood *Ohio, U.S.A.* 39°9N 84°27W **311** E12
Norwood Park *U.S.A.* 41°59N 87°48W **119** B2
Noryangjin *S. Korea* 37°30N 126°56E **137** B1
Nosappu-Misaki *Japan* 45°26N 141°39E **220** C12
Noshaq *Pakistan* 36°24N 71°49E **240** A3
Noshiro *Japan* 40°12N 140°0E **220** D10
Nosivka *Ukraine* 50°50N 31°37E **189** G6
Nosovka = Nosivka *Ukraine* 50°50N 31°37E **189** G6
Noşratābād *Iran* 29°55N 60°0E **247** D8
Noss Hd. *U.K.* 58°28N 3°3W **167** C5
Nossa Senhora da Glória *Brazil* 10°14S 37°25W **332** D4
Nossa Senhora das Dores *Brazil* 10°29S 37°13W **332** D4
Nossa Senhora de Candelária *Rio de J., Brazil* **135** a2
Nossa Senhora do Livramento *Brazil* 15°48S 56°22W **331** D6
Nossa Senhora do Ó *Brazil* 23°30S 46°41W **137** B1
Nossa Senhora do Socorro *Brazil* 10°52S 37°7W **332** D4
Nossebro *Sweden* 58°12N 12°43E **163** F6
Nossegem *Belgium* 50°53N 4°30E **116** A3
Nossob → *S. Africa* 26°55S 20°45E **270** C3
Nossombougou *Mali* 13°5N 7°55W **262** C3
Nosy Varika *Madag.* 20°35S 48°32E **272** C2
Notasulga *U.S.A.* 32°34N 85°41W **316** C4
Noteć → *Poland* 52°44N 15°26E **185** F2
Notikewin → *Canada* 57°2N 117°38W **296** B5
Notio Aigaio □ *Greece* 36°52N 25°34E **205** E7
Notios Aiyaíon = Notio Aigaio □ *Greece* 36°52N 25°34E **205** E7
Notios Evvoikos Kolpos *Greece* 38°20N 24°0E **204** C5
Noto *Italy* 36°53N 15°4E **201** F8
Noto, G. di *Italy* 36°50N 15°12E **201** F8
Noto, Val di *Italy* 37°14N 14°31E **201** E7
Noto-Hantō *Japan* 37°15N 136°40E **221** F8
Notodden *Norway* 59°35N 9°17E **164** E6
Notre-Dame *Paris, France* **134** c4
Notre-Dame, Basilique *Montréal, Canada* **130** c3
Notre-Dame, Bois *France* 48°45N 2°34E **134** B4
Notre Dame B. *Canada* 49°45N 55°30W **299** C8
Notre-Dame-de-Grace *Canada* 45°28N 73°38W **130** B2
Notre-Dame-de-Koartac = Quaqtaq *Canada* 60°55N 69°40W **295** E18
Notre-Dame-des-Bois *Canada* 45°24N 71°4W **313** A13
Notre-Dame-d'Ivugivic = Ivujivik *Canada* 62°24N 77°55W **295** E16
Notre-Dame-du-Nord *Canada* 47°36N 79°30W **298** C4
Notsé *Togo* 7°0N 1°17E **263** D5
Nottawasaga B. *Canada* 44°35N 80°15W **312** B4
Nottaway = Senneterre *Canada* 48°25N 77°15W **298** C4
Nottaway → *Canada* 51°22N 78°55W **298** B4
Notting Hill *London, U.K.* **125** b1
Nottingham *U.K.* 52°58N 1°10W **168** E6
Nottingham, City of □ *U.K.* 52°58N 1°10W **168** E6
Nottingham I. *Canada* 63°20N 77°55W **295** E16
Nottinghamshire □ *U.K.* 53°10N 1°3W **168** D6
Nottoway → *U.S.A.* 36°33N 76°55W **309** G15
Notwane → *Botswana* 23°35S 26°58E **270** B4
Nouâdhibou *Mauritania* 20°54N 17°0W **260** D1
Nouâdhibou, Dakhlet *Mauritania* 20°55N 16°52W **260** D1
Nouâdhibou, Râs *Mauritania* 20°50N 17°0W **260** D1
Nouakchott *Mauritania* 18°9N 15°58W **262** B1
Nouâmghâr *Mauritania* 19°20N 16°20W **262** B1
Nouméa *N. Cal.* 22°17S 166°30E **288** d
Nouna *Burkina Faso* 12°45N 3°52W **262** C4
Noupoort *S. Africa* 31°10S 24°57E **270** D3
Nouveau Comptoir = Wemindji *Canada* 53°0N 78°49W **298** B4
Nouvelle Amsterdam, Î. *Ind. Oc.* 38°30S 77°30E **273** H6
Nouvelle-Calédonie = New Caledonia ☒ *Pac. Oc.* 21°0S 165°0E **288** d
Nouvelle France *Mauritius* 20°22S 57°33E **272** e
Nouzonville *France* 49°48N 4°44E **173** C11
Nová Baňa *Slovak Rep.* 48°28N 18°39E **181** C11
Nová Bystřice *Czech Rep.* 49°2N 15°8E **180** B8
Nova Cruz *Brazil* 6°28S 35°25W **332** C4
Nova Era *Brazil* 19°45S 43°3W **333** E3
Nova Esperança *Brazil* 23°8S 52°24W **335** A5
Nova Fontesvila = Vila Machado *Mozam.* 19°15S 34°14E **269** F3
Nova-Freixo = Cuamba *Mozam.* 14°45S 36°22E **269** E4
Nova Friburgo *Brazil* 22°16S 42°30W **333** F3
Nova Gaia = Cambundi-Catembo *Angola* 10°10S 17°35E **265** E3
Nova Gorica *Slovenia* 45°57N 13°39E **199** C10
Nova Gradiška *Croatia* 45°17N 17°28E **182** E2
Nova Granada *Brazil* 20°30S 49°20W **333** F2
Nova Iguaçu *Brazil* 22°45S 43°28W **333** F3
Nova Iorque *Brazil* 7°0S 44°5W **332** C3
Nova Kakhovka *Ukraine* 46°42N 33°27E **189** J7
Nova Lamego *Guinea-Biss.* 12°19N 14°11W **262** C2
Nova Lisboa = Huambo *Angola* 12°42S 15°54E **265** E3
Nova Lusitânia *Mozam.* 19°50S 34°34E **269** F3
Nova Mambone *Mozam.* 21°0S 35°3E **271** B6
Nova Milanese *Italy* 45°35N 9°12E **128** A2
Nova Odesa *Ukraine* 47°19N 31°47E **189** J6
Nova Olinda do Norte *Brazil* 3°45S 59°3W **329** D6
Nová Paka *Czech Rep.* 50°29N 15°30E **180** A8
Nova Pavova *Serbia* 44°56N 20°14E **182** F5
Nova Ponte *Brazil* 19°8S 47°41W **333** E2
Nova Russas *Brazil* 4°42S 40°34W **332** B3
Nova Scotia □ *Canada* 45°10N 63°0W **299** C7
Nova Siri *Italy* 40°10N 16°35E **201** B9
Nova Sofala *Mozam.* 20°7S 34°42E **271** B5
Nova Ushytsya *Ukraine* 48°50N 27°17E **183** B12
Nova Varoš *Serbia* 43°29N 19°48E **202** C3
Nova Venécia *Brazil* 18°45S 40°24W **333** E3
Nova Vida *Brazil* 10°11S 62°47W **331** C5
Nova Zagora *Bulgaria* 42°32N 26°1E **203** D10
Novaci *Macedonia* 41°5N 21°29E **202** E5
Novaci *Romania* 45°10N 23°42E **183** E8
Novaféltria *Italy* 43°53N 12°17E **199** E9
Novannenskiy = Novoannenskiy *Russia* 50°32N 42°39E **190** E6
Novar *Canada* 45°27N 79°15W **312** A5
Novara *Italy* 45°28N 8°38E **198** C5
Novate Milanese *Italy* 45°30N 9°8E **128** A1
Novato *U.S.A.* 38°6N 122°35W **306** G4
Novaya Aleksandriya = Puławy *Poland* 51°23N 21°59E **185** G8
Novaya Bukhara = Kogon *Uzbekistan* 39°43N 64°33E **216** E6
Novaya Derevnya *Russia* 60°0N 30°19E **137** A1
Novaya Kakhovka = Nova Kakhovka *Ukraine* 46°42N 33°27E **189** J7
Novaya Kazanka = Zhangaqala *Kazakhstan* 48°56N 49°36E **191** F9
Novaya Ladoga *Russia* 60°7N 32°16E **188** B7
Novaya Lyalya *Russia* 59°4N 60°45E **186** C11
Novaya Pismyanka = Ridder *Kazakhstan* 50°20N 83°30E **217** B10
Novaya Sibir, Ostrov *Russia* 75°10N 150°0E **215** B16
Novaya Zemlya *Russia* 75°0N 56°0E **214** B6
Nové Město *Praha, Czech Rep.* 50°4N 14°25E **135** B2
Nové Město *Slovak Rep.* 48°45N 17°50E **181** C10
Nové Město na Moravě *Czech Rep.* 49°34N 16°5E **180** B9
Nové Město nad Metují *Czech Rep.* 50°20N 16°10E **181** A9
Nové Zámky *Slovak Rep.* 48°2N 18°8E **181** C11
Novelda *Spain* 38°24N 0°45W **197** G4
Novellara *Italy* 44°51N 10°44E **198** D7
Novelty *U.S.A.* 40°1N 92°12W **310** D4
Noventa Vicentina *Italy* 45°17N 11°32E **199** C8
Novgorod = Velikiy Novgorod *Russia* 58°30N 31°25E **188** C6
Novgorod □ *Russia* 58°50N 32°30E **188** C7
Novgorod-Severskiy = Novhorod-Siverskyy *Ukraine* 52°2N 33°10E **189** G7
Novgradets = Suvorovo *Bulgaria* 43°20N 27°35E **203** C11
Novhorod-Siverskyy *Ukraine* 52°2N 33°10E **189** G7
Novi Bečej *Serbia* 45°36N 20°10E **182** E5
Novi Iskar *Bulgaria* 42°48N 23°21E **202** D7
Novi Kneževac *Serbia* 46°4N 20°8E **182** D5
Novi Lígure *Italy* 44°46N 8°47E **198** D5
Novi Pazar *Bulgaria* 43°25N 27°15E **203** C11
Novi Pazar *Serbia* 43°12N 20°28E **202** C4
Novi Sad *Serbia* 45°18N 19°52E **182** E4
Novi Slankamen *Serbia* 45°8N 20°15E **182** E5
Novi Travnik *Bos.-H.* 44°10N 17°40E **182** F2

**Novi Vinodolski** *Croatia* 45°10N 14°48E **199** C11
**Novigrad** *Istra, Croatia* 45°19N 13°33E **199** C10
**Novigrad** *Zadar, Croatia* 44°10N 15°32E **199** D12
**Novigradsko More** *Croatia* 44°12N 15°33E **199** D12
**Novinger** *U.S.A.* 40°14N 92°43W **310** D4
**Novo Acôrdo** *Brazil* 10°10S 46°48W **332** D2
**Novo Airão** *Brazil* 2°40S 60°59W **329** D5
**Novo Aripuanã** *Brazil* 5°8S 60°22W **329** E5
**Novo Cruzeiro** *Brazil* 17°29S 41°53W **333** E3
**Novo Hamburgo** *Brazil* 29°37S 51°7W **335** B5
**Novo Horizonte** *Brazil* 21°25S 49°10W **333** F2
**Novo Ivanivka** *Ukraine* 45°55N 29°5E **183** E14
**Novo-Mariinsk = Anadyr** *Russia* 64°35N 177°20E **215** C18
**Novo Mesto** *Slovenia* 45°47N 15°12E **199** C12
**Novo Miloševo** *Serbia* 45°42N 20°20E **182** E5
**Novo Nikolaevsk = Novosibirsk** *Russia* 55°0N 83°5E **217** B10
**Novo Paraiso** *Brazil* 1°17N 60°28W **329** C5
**Novo-Starobinsk = Salihorsk** *Belarus* 52°51N 27°27E **177** B14
**Novo Urgench = Urganch** *Uzbekistan* 41°40N 60°41E **216** D6
**Novoaleksandrovsk = Zarasai** *Lithuania* 55°40N 26°20E **188** E4
**Novoaleksandrovsk** *Russia* 45°29N 41°17E **191** H5
**Novoaleksandrovskaya = Novoaleksandrovsk** *Russia* 45°29N 41°17E **191** H5
**Novoaleksandrovskoye** *Russia* 59°50N 30°31E **137** B2
**Novoaltaysk** *Russia* 53°30N 84°0E **217** B10
**Novoannenskiy** *Russia* 50°32N 42°39E **190** E6
**Novoazovsk** *Ukraine* 47°15N 38°4E **189** J10
**Novocheboksarsk** *Russia* 56°5N 47°27E **190** B8
**Novocherkassk** *Russia* 47°27N 40°15E **191** G5
**Novodevichy Convent** *Russia* 55°43N 37°34E **129** B2
**Novodevichye** *Russia* 53°37N 48°50E **190** D9
**Novodvinsk** *Russia* 64°25N 40°42E **186** B7
**Novogireyevo** *Russia* 55°45N 37°46E **129** B3
**Novogrudok = Navahrudak** *Belarus* 53°40N 25°50E **177** B13
**Novohrad-Volynskyy** *Ukraine* 50°34N 27°35E **177** C14
**Novokachalinsk** *Russia* 45°5N 132°0E **220** B5
**Novokazalinsk = Zhangaqazaly** *Kazakhstan* 45°48N 62°6E **216** C6
**Novokhopersk** *Russia* 51°5N 41°39E **190** E5
**Novokiyevskoye = Kraskino** *Russia* 42°44N 130°48E **220** C5
**Novokuybyshevsk** *Russia* 53°7N 49°58E **190** D9
**Novokuznetsk** *Russia* 53°45N 87°10E **217** B11
**Novolazarevskaya** *Antarctica* 71°0S 12°0E **151** D3
**Novolyalinsky = Novaya Lyalya** *Russia* 59°4N 60°45E **186** C11
**Novomoskovsk** *Russia* 54°5N 38°15E **188** E10
**Novomoskovsk** *Ukraine* 48°33N 35°17E **189** H8
**Novomyrhorod** *Ukraine* 48°45N 31°33E **189** H6
**Novonikolayevka = Novoazovsk** *Ukraine* 47°15N 38°4E **189** J10
**Novopolotsk = Navapolatsk** *Belarus* 55°32N 28°37E **188** E5
**Novorossiysk** *Russia* 44°43N 37°46E **189** K9
**Novorybnoye** *Russia* 72°50N 105°50E **215** B11
**Novorzhev** *Russia* 57°3N 29°25E **188** D5
**Novosaratovka** *Russia* 59°50N 30°32E **137** B3
**Novosej** *Albania* 41°56N 20°35E **202** E4
**Novoselytsya** *Ukraine* 48°14N 26°15E **183** B11
**Novoshakhtinsk** *Russia* 47°46N 39°58E **189** J10
**Novosibirsk** *Russia* 55°0N 83°5E **217** B10
**Novosibirskiye Ostrova** *Russia* 75°0N 142°0E **215** B15
**Novosibirskoye Vdkhr.** *Russia* 54°35N 82°35E **217** B10
**Novosil** *Russia* 52°59N 37°2E **189** F9
**Novosokolniki** *Russia* 56°20N 30°5E **188** D6
**Novotitarovskaya** *Russia* 45°17N 39°2E **191** H4
**Novotroitsk** *Russia* 51°10N 58°15E **186** D10
**Novotroitskoye = Töle Bī** *Kazakhstan* 43°42N 73°46E **217** D8
**Novoukrayinka** *Ukraine* 48°25N 31°30E **189** H6
**Novoulyanovsk** *Russia* 54°8N 48°24E **190** C9
**Novouzensk** *Russia* 50°32N 48°17E **190** E9
**Novovolynsk** *Ukraine* 50°45N 24°4E **185** H11
**Novovoronezhskiy** *Russia* 51°19N 39°13E **189** G10
**Novoyavoriske** *Ukraine* 49°53N 23°33E **185** J10
**Novozybkov** *Russia* 52°30N 32°0E **189** F6
**Novska** *Croatia* 45°19N 17°0E **199** C14
**Nový Bor** *Czech Rep.* 50°46N 14°35E **180** A7
**Novy Bug = Novyy Buh** *Ukraine* 47°34N 32°29E **189** J7
**Nový Bydžov** *Czech Rep.* 50°14N 15°29E **180** A8
**Novy Dvor** *Belarus* 52°50N 24°21E **185** F11
**Nowy Dwór Mazowiecki** *Poland* 52°26N 20°44E **185** F7
**Nový Jičín** *Czech Rep.* 49°30N 18°2E **181** B11
**Novy Margelan = Farghona** *Uzbekistan* 40°23N 71°19E **217** D8
**Novyy Bor** *Russia* 66°43N 52°19E **186** A9
**Novyy Buh** *Ukraine* 47°34N 32°29E **189** J7
**Novyy Oskol** *Russia* 50°44N 37°55E **189** G9
**Novyy Port** *Russia* 67°40N 72°30E **214** C8
**Novyy Urengoy** *Russia* 65°48N 76°52E **214** C8
**Nowa Deba** *Poland* 50°26N 21°41E **185** H8
**Nowa Nowa** *Australia* 37°44S 148°3E **283** D8
**Nowa Ruda** *Poland* 50°35N 16°30E **185** H3
**Nowa Sarzyna** *Poland* 50°21N 22°21E **185** H9
**Nowa Sól** *Poland* 51°48N 15°44E **185** G2
**Nowata** *U.S.A.* 36°42N 95°38W **314** C7
**Nowbarān** *Iran* 35°8N 49°42E **247** C6
**Nowe** *Poland* 53°41N 18°44E **184** E5
**Nowe-Babice** *Poland* 52°15N 20°51E **143** B1
**Nowe Miasteczko** *Poland* 51°42N 15°42E **185** G2
**Nowe Miasto** *Mazowieckie, Poland* 51°38N 20°34E **185** G7
**Nowe Miasto** *Warsaw, Poland* **143** a2
**Nowe Miasto Lubawskie** *Poland* 53°27N 19°33E **184** E6
**Nowe Skalmierzyce** *Poland* 51°43N 18°0E **185** G4
**Nowe Warpno** *Poland* 53°42N 14°18E **184** E1
**Nowendoc** *Australia* 31°32S 151°44E **283** A9
**Nowendoc △** *Australia* 31°33S 151°45E **283** A9
**Nowghāb** *Iran* 33°53N 59°4E **247** C8
**Nowgong = Nagaon** *India* 26°20N 92°50E **241** B4
**Nowgong** *India* 25°4N 79°27E **243** G8
**Nowitna Nat. Wildlife Refuge ⌓** *U.S.A.* 64°40N 154°16W **303** D9
**Nowogard** *Poland* 53°41N 15°10E **184** E2
**Nowogród** *Poland* 53°14N 21°53E **185** E8
**Nowogród Bobrzanski** *Poland* 51°48N 15°15E **185** G2
**Nowogrodziec** *Poland* 51°12N 15°24E **185** G2
**Noworadomsk = Radomsko** *Poland* 51°5N 19°28E **185** G6
**Nowra** *Australia* 34°53S 150°35E **283** C9
**Nowrangapur** *India* 19°14N 82°33E **244** E6
**Nowshāk = Noshaq** *Pakistan* 36°24N 71°49E **240** A3
**Nowshera** *Pakistan* 34°0N 72°0E **240** B4
**Nowy Dwór Gdański** *Poland* 54°13N 19°7E **184** D6
**Nowy Sącz** *Poland* 49°40N 20°41E **185** J7
**Nowy Staw** *Poland* 54°13N 19°2E **184** D6
**Nowy Targ** *Poland* 49°29N 20°2E **185** J7
**Nowy Tomyśl** *Poland* 52°19N 16°10E **185** F3
**Nowy Wiśnicz** *Poland* 49°55N 20°28E **185** J7
**Noxen** *U.S.A.* 41°25N 76°4W **313** E8
**Noyabr'sk** *Russia* 64°34N 76°21E **214** C8
**Noyant** *France* 47°30N 0°6E **172** E7
**Noyers** *France* 47°40N 4°0E **173** E10
**Nöykkiö** *Finland* 60°10N 24°42E **121** B1
**Noyon** *Oise, France* 49°34N 2°59E **173** C9
**Noyon** *Mongolia* 43°2N 102°4E **226** C2
**Nozay** *France* 47°34N 1°38W **172** E5
**Nqutu** *S. Africa* 28°13S 30°32E **271** C5
**Nsa** *Congo* 2°22S 15°19E **264** C3
**Nsa, O. en →** *Algeria* 32°28N 5°24E **261** B6
**Nsa, Plateau de** *Congo* 2°26S 15°20E **264** C3
**Nsanje** *Malawi* 16°55S 35°12E **269** F4
**Nsawam** *Ghana* 5°50N 0°24W **263** D4
**Nseluka** *Zambia* 9°58S 31°16E **269** D3
**Nsok** *Eq. Guin.* 1°10N 11°19E **264** B2
**Nsomba** *Zambia* 10°45S 29°51E **269** E2
**Nsontin** *Dem. Rep. of the Congo* 3°7S 17°56E **264** C3
**Nsopzup** *Burma* 25°51N 97°30E **241** C6
**Nsukka** *Nigeria* 6°51N 7°29E **263** D6
**Ntaria ✪** *Australia* 24°0S 132°41E **278** D5
**Ntem →** *Cameroon* 2°21N 9°49E **264** B2
**Ntingui, Mt.** *Comoros Is.* 12°12S 44°25E **272** a
**Ntoum** *Gabon* 0°22N 9°47E **264** B1
**N'Tsama** *Congo* 0°53S 14°44E **264** C2
**Ntsaouéni** *Comoros Is.* 11°27S 43°15E **272** a
**Ntsoudjini** *Comoros Is.* 11°39S 43°15E **272** a
**Ntui** *Cameroon* 4°27N 11°38E **263** E7
**Ntungamo** *Uganda* 0°56S 30°17E **268** C3
**Nu Jiang →** *China* 29°58N 97°25E **228** E2
**Nu Shan** *China* 26°0N 99°20E **228** E2
**Nuakata I.** *Papua N. G.* 10°17S 151°2E **286** F6
**Nuba Mts. = Nubah, Jibalan** *Sudan* 12°0N 31°0E **257** E3
**Nubah, Jibalan** *Sudan* 12°0N 31°0E **257** E3
**Nubia** *Africa* 21°0N 32°0E **254** D7
**Nubian Desert = Nûbîya, Es Sahrâ en** *Sudan* 21°30N 33°30E **256** C3
**Nûbîya, Es Sahrâ en** *Sudan* 21°30N 33°30E **256** C3
**Nubl** *Syria* 36°22N 36°59E **250** B7
**Nubledo** *Spain* 43°31N 5°52W **194** B5
**Nuboai** *Indonesia* 2°10S 136°30E **231** E9
**Nubra →** *India* 34°35N 77°35E **243** B7
**Nucet** *Romania* 46°28N 22°35E **182** D7
**Nueces →** *U.S.A.* 27°51N 97°30W **314** H6
**Nueltin L.** *Canada* 60°30N 99°30W **297** A9
**Nuestra Señora del Rosario de Caá-Catí** *Argentina* 27°45S 57°36W **334** B4
**Nueva, I.** *Chile* 55°13S 66°30W **336** H3
**Nueva Antioquia** *Colombia* 6°5N 69°26W **328** B4
**Nueva Atzacoalco** *Mexico* 19°29N 99°4W **128** B2
**Nueva Carteya** *Spain* 37°35N 4°28W **195** H6
**Nueva Ciudad Guerrero** *Mexico* 26°34N 99°12W **319** B5
**Nueva Ecija □** *Phil.* 15°35N 121°0E **232** D3
**Nueva Esparta □** *Venezuela* 11°0N 64°0W **329** A5
**Nueva Gerona** *Cuba* 21°53N 82°49W **320** B3
**Nueva Imperial** *Chile* 38°45S 72°58W **336** A2
**Nueva Loja = Lago Agrio** *Ecuador* 0°5N 76°52W **328** C2
**Nueva Palmira** *Uruguay* 33°52S 58°20W **334** C4
**Nueva Pompeya** *Argentina* 34°40S 58°25W **117** C2
**Nueva Rosita** *Mexico* 27°57N 101°13W **318** B4
**Nueva San Salvador** *El Salv.* 13°40N 89°18W **320** D2
**Nueva Tabarca** *Spain* 38°17N 0°30W **197** G4
**Nueva Tenochtitlán** *Mexico* 19°27N 99°5W **128** B2
**Nueva Vizcaya □** *Phil.* 16°20N 121°20E **232** C3
**Nuéve de Julio** *Argentina* 35°30S 61°0W **334** D3
**Nuevitas** *Cuba* 21°30N 77°20W **320** B4
**Nuevo, G.** *Argentina* 43°0S 64°30W **336** B4
**Nuevo Casas Grandes** *Mexico* 30°25N 107°55W **318** A3
**Nuevo Laredo** *Mexico* 27°30N 99°31W **319** B5
**Nuevo León □** *Mexico* 25°20N 100°0W **318** C5
**Nuevo Mundo, Cerro** *Bolivia* 21°55S 66°53W **330** E4
**Nuevo Rocafuerte** *Ecuador* 0°55S 75°27W **328** D2
**Nugaal □** *Somalia* 8°10N 49°0E **267** C6
**Nugaal →** *Somalia* 8°0N 49°47E **267** C6
**Nugaaleed, Dooxo** *Somalia* 8°35N 48°35E **267** C6
**Nugget Pt.** *N.Z.* 46°27S 169°50E **285** G4
**Nugrus, Gebel** *Egypt* 24°47N 34°35E **256** C3
**Nuguria Is.** *Papua N. G.* 3°20S 154°45E **286** B8
**Nuhaka** *N.Z.* 39°3S 177°45E **284** F6
**Nui** *Pac. Oc.* 7°15S 177°10E **277** B14
**Nuijala** *Finland* 60°12N 24°46E **121** B1
**Nuits-St-Georges** *France* 47°10N 4°56E **173** E11
**Nukey Bluff** *Australia* 32°26S 135°29E **281** E2
**Nukha = Şaki** *Azerbaijan* 41°10N 47°5E **191** K8
**Nukhayb** *Iraq* 32°4N 42°3E **213** F10
**Nukheila** *Sudan* 19°1N 26°21E **256** D2
**Nukiki** *Solomon Is.* 6°46S 156°35E **287** L9
**Nuku** *Papua N. G.* 3°41S 142°28E **286** B2
**Nuku Hiva** *French Polynesia* 8°54S 140°6W **289** f
**Nuku'alofa** *Tonga* 21°10S 175°12W **287** Q13
**Nukuhu** *Papua N. G.* 5°34S 149°22E **286** C5
**Nukulaelae** *Tuvalu* 9°23S 179°52E **277** B14
**Nukunonu** *Pac. Oc.* 9°12S 171°54W **277** B16
**Nukus** *Uzbekistan* 42°27N 59°41E **216** D5
**Nulato** *U.S.A.* 64°43N 158°6W **303** D8
**Nules** *Spain* 39°51N 0°9W **196** F4
**Nullagine** *Australia* 21°53S 120°7E **278** D3
**Nullagine →** *Australia* 21°20S 120°20E **278** D3
**Nullarbor** *Australia* 31°28S 130°55E **279** F5
**Nullarbor △** *Australia* 32°39S 130°0E **279** F4
**Nullarbor Plain** *Australia* 31°10S 129°0E **279** F4
**Numabukuro** *Japan* 35°43N 139°39E **140** A2
**Numalla, L.** *Australia* 28°43S 144°20E **281** D3
**Numan** *Nigeria* 9°29N 12°3E **263** D7
**Numanuma** *Papua N. G.* 9°41S 150°55E **286** E6
**Numata** *Japan* 36°45N 139°4E **223** A11
**Numatinna →** *South Sudan* 7°38N 27°20E **257** F2
**Numaykoos Lake ⌓** *Canada* 57°52N 95°58W **297** B9
**Numazu** *Japan* 35°7N 138°51E **223** B10
**Numbulwar** *Australia* 14°15S 135°45E **280** A2
**Numedal** *Norway* 60°6N 9°6E **164** D6
**Numfoor** *Indonesia* 1°0S 134°50E **231** E8
**Numurkah** *Australia* 36°5S 145°26E **283** D6
**Nunaksaluk I.** *Canada* 55°49N 60°20W **299** A7
**Nunap Isua** *Greenland* 59°48N 43°55W **154** F6
**Nunavik** *Greenland* 71°50N 54°25W **154** C5
**Nunavut □** *Canada* 66°0N 85°0W **295** D15
**Nunda** *U.S.A.* 42°35N 77°56W **312** D7
**Nuneaton** *U.K.* 52°32N 1°27W **169** E6
**Nuñez** *Argentina* 34°32S 58°27W **117** B2
**Nungarin** *Australia* 31°12S 118°6E **279** F2
**Nungo** *Mozam.* 13°23S 37°43E **269** E4
**Nungwe** *Tanzania* 2°48S 32°2E **268** C3
**Nunhead** *U.K.* 51°27N 0°3W **125** B3
**Nunivak I.** *U.S.A.* 60°10N 166°30W **303** F6
**Nunkun** *India* 33°57N 76°2E **243** C7
**Ñuñoa** *Chile* 33°27S 70°35W **137** B2
**Nunukan** *Indonesia* 4°4N 117°40E **235** D5
**Nùoro** *Italy* 40°20N 9°20E **200** B2
**Nuozhadu Dam** *China* 22°39N 100°25E **228** F3
**Núpur** *Iceland* 65°56N 23°36W **155** B3
**Nuqayy, Jabal** *Libya* 23°11N 19°30E **258** D3
**Nuqūb** *Yemen* 14°59N 45°48E **248** D4
**Nuquí** *Colombia* 5°42N 77°17W **328** B2
**Nūr** *Iran* 36°33N 52°1E **247** B7
**Nur Dağı** *Turkey* 36°54N 35°39E **250** B6
**Nur Dağları** *Turkey* 36°50N 36°23E **250** B7
**Nura →** *Kazakhstan* 50°30N 69°59E **217** B7
**Nūrābād** *Hormozgān, Iran* 27°47N 57°12E **247** E8
**Nūrābād** *Lorestān, Iran* 34°4N 47°58E **213** E12
**Nurabad** *Uzbekistan* 39°36N 66°17E **217** E7
**Nure →** *Italy* 45°3N 9°49E **198** C6
**Nuremberg = Nürnberg** *Germany* 49°27N 11°3E **179** F7
**Nuri** *Sonora, Mexico* 28°5N 109°22W **318** B3
**Nuri** *Sudan* 18°29N 31°59E **256** D3
**Nuriootpa** *Australia* 34°27S 139°0E **282** C3
**Nūristān □** *Afghan.* 35°20N 71°0E **217** E8
**Nurlat** *Russia* 54°29N 50°45E **190** C10
**Nurmes** *Finland* 63°33N 29°10E **160** E23
**Nürnberg** *Germany* 49°27N 11°3E **179** F7
**Nurpur** *Pakistan* 31°53N 71°54E **242** D4
**Nurra, La** *Italy* 40°45N 8°15E **200** B1
**Nurran, L. = Terewah, L.** *Australia* 29°52S 147°35E **281** D4
**Nurrari Lakes** *Australia* 29°1S 130°5E **279** E5
**Nurri** *Italy* 39°43N 9°14E **200** C2
**Nürtingen** *Germany* 48°37N 9°19E **179** G5
**Nurzec →** *Poland* 52°37N 22°25E **185** F9
**Nus** *Italy* 45°45N 7°28E **198** C4
**Nusa Dua** *Indonesia* 8°48S 115°14E **231** K18
**Nusa Tenggara Barat □** *Indonesia* 8°50S 117°30E **235** D5
**Nusa Tenggara Timur □** *Indonesia* 9°30S 122°0E **231** F6
**Nusaybin** *Turkey* 37°3N 41°10E **213** D9
**Nuşayrīyah, J. an** *Syria* 35°20N 36°13E **250** C7
**Nuşeirat** *Gaza Strip* 31°27N 34°24E **251** G5
**Nushki** *Pakistan* 29°35N 66°0E **242** E2
**Nusle** *Czech Rep.* 50°3N 14°26E **135** B2
**Nussdorf** *Austria* 48°15N 16°21E **142** A2
**Nuuk** *Greenland* 64°10N 51°35W **154** E5
**Nuupere, Pte.** *Moorea* 17°36S 149°47W **289** e
**Nuussauq** *Greenland* 74°8N 57°3W **154** C5
**Nu'uuli** *Amer. Samoa* 14°19S 170°42W **302** f
**Nuwakot** *Nepal* 28°10N 83°55E **243** E10
**Nuwara Eliya** *Sri Lanka* 6°58N 80°48E **245** L5
**Nuwayb'ī, W. an →** *Si. Arabia* 29°18N 34°57E **251** J5
**Nuweiba'** *Egypt* 28°59N 34°39E **251** K5
**Nuweiberg** *S. Africa* 31°8S 18°24E **270** D2
**Nuweveldberge** *S. Africa* 32°10S 21°45E **270** D3
**Nuyts, Pt.** *Australia* 35°4S 116°38E **279** G2
**Nuyts Arch.** *Australia* 32°35S 133°20E **281** E1
**N'Vinda** *Angola* 13°8S 19°2E **265** E3
**Nxai Pan △** *Botswana* 19°50S 24°46E **270** A3
**Nxaunxau** *Botswana* 18°57S 21°4E **270** A3
**Nyaake** *Liberia* 4°52N 7°37W **262** E3
**Nyabessan** *Cameroon* 2°28N 10°24E **264** B2
**Nyabing** *Australia* 33°33S 118°9E **279** F2
**Nyack** *U.S.A.* 41°5N 73°55W **313** E11
**Nyagan** *Russia* 62°30N 65°38E **214** C7
**Nyah West** *Australia* 35°16S 143°21E **282** C5
**Nyahanga** *Tanzania* 2°20S 33°37E **268** C3
**Nyahua** *Tanzania* 5°25S 33°23E **268** D3
**Nyahururu** *Kenya* 0°2N 36°27E **268** B4
**Nyainqêntanglha Shan** *China* 30°0N 90°0E **218** F7
**Nyakanazi** *Tanzania* 3°2S 31°10E **268** C3
**Nyakrom** *Ghana* 5°40N 0°50W **263** D4
**Nyâlâ** *Sudan* 12°2N 24°58E **257** E1
**Nyalam** *China* 28°32N 86°4E **218** F6
**Nyamandhlovu** *Zimbabwe* 19°55S 28°16E **269** F2
**Nyambiti** *Tanzania* 2°48S 33°27E **268** C3
**Nyamira** *Kenya* 0°36S 34°52E **268** B4
**Nyamlell** *South Sudan* 9°7N 26°59E **257** F2
**Nyamwaga** *Tanzania* 1°27S 34°33E **268** C3
**Nyandekwa** *Tanzania* 3°57S 32°32E **268** C3
**Nyanding →** *South Sudan* 8°40N 32°41E **257** F3
**Nyandoma** *Russia* 61°40N 40°12E **188** B11
**Nyanga** *Congo* 2°52S 11°57E **264** C2
**Nyanga** *Western Cape, S. Africa* 33°59S 18°35E **118** A2
**Nyanga →** *Gabon* 2°58S 10°15E **264** C2
**Nyanga △** *Zimbabwe* 18°17S 32°46E **269** F3
**Nyangana** *Namibia* 18°0S 20°40E **270** A3
**Nyanguge** *Tanzania* 2°30S 33°12E **268** C3
**Nyanji** *Zambia* 14°25S 31°46E **269** E3
**Nyankpala** *Ghana* 9°21N 0°58W **263** D4
**Nyanza** *Rwanda* 2°20S 29°42E **268** C2
**Nyanza □** *Gabon* 3°30S 11°0E **264** C2
**Nyanza □** *Kenya* 0°10S 34°15E **268** C3
**Nyanza-Lac** *Burundi* 4°21S 29°36E **268** C2
**Nyaponges** *South Sudan* 5°5N 33°45E **257** F3
**Nyasa, L. = Malawi, L.** *Africa* 12°30S 34°30E **269** E3
**Nyasaland = Malawi ■** *Africa* 11°55S 34°0E **269** E3
**Nyasvizh** *Belarus* 53°14N 26°38E **177** B14
**Nyaungdon = Yandoon** *Burma* 17°0N 95°40E **241** G5
**Nyaunglebin** *Burma* 17°52N 96°42E **241** G6
**Nyazepetrovsk** *Russia* 56°3N 59°36E **186** C10
**Nyazura** *Zimbabwe* 18°40S 32°16E **269** F3
**Nyazwidzi →** *Zimbabwe* 20°0S 31°17E **269** G3
**Nybergsund** *Norway* 61°15N 12°19E **164** C9
**Nyborg** *Denmark* 55°18N 10°47E **163** J4
**Nybro** *Sweden* 56°44N 15°55E **163** H9
**Nyda** *Russia* 66°40N 72°58E **214** C8
**Nyeboe Land** *Greenland* 82°0N 57°0W **154** A5
**Nyengo Swamp** *Zambia* 14°51S 22°7E **265** E4
**Nyeri** *Kenya* 0°23S 36°56E **268** C4
**Nyerol** *South Sudan* 8°41N 32°1E **257** F3
**Nyhammar** *Sweden* 60°17N 14°58E **162** D8
**Nyika △** *Malawi* 10°30S 33°53E **269** E3
**Nyimba** *Zambia* 14°33S 30°50E **269** E3
**Nyinahin** *Ghana* 6°43N 2°3W **262** D4
**Nyingchi** *China* 29°32N 94°25E **218** F7
**Nyirbátor** *Hungary* 47°41N 21°55E **182** C6
**Nyiragongo** *Dem. Rep. of the Congo* 1°30S 29°15E **268** C2
**Nyírbátor** *Hungary* 47°49N 22°9E **182** C7
**Nyíregyháza** *Hungary* 47°58N 21°47E **182** C6
**Nyiru, Mt.** *Kenya* 2°8N 36°50E **268** B4
**Nykarleby = Uusikaarlepyy** *Finland* 63°32N 22°31E **160** E20
**Nykirke** *Norway* 60°54N 10°19E **164** D7
**Nykøbing** *Nordjylland, Denmark* 56°48N 8°51E **163** H2
**Nykøbing** *Sjælland, Denmark* 54°56N 11°52E **163** K5
**Nykøbing** *Sjælland, Denmark* 55°55N 11°40E **163** J5
**Nyköping** *Sweden* 58°45N 17°1E **163** F11
**Nykroppa** *Sweden* 59°37N 14°18E **162** E8
**Nykvarn** *Sweden* 59°11N 17°25E **162** E11
**Nyland** *Sweden* 63°1N 17°45E **162** A11
**Nylstroom = Modimolle** *S. Africa* 24°42S 28°22E **271** B4
**Nymagee** *Australia* 32°7S 146°20E **283** B7
**Nymboida △** *Australia* 29°38S 152°26E **281** D5
**Nymburk** *Czech Rep.* 50°10N 15°1E **180** A8
**Nymphenburg** *Germany* 48°9N 11°30E **131** B2
**Nymphenburg, Schloss** *Germany* 48°9N 11°30E **131** B2
**Nynäshamn** *Sweden* 58°54N 17°57E **163** F11
**Nyngan** *Australia* 31°30S 147°8E **283** A7
**Nyoma Rap** *India* 33°10N 78°40E **243** C8
**Nyoman = Nemunas →** *Lithuania* 55°25N 21°10E **184** C8
**Nyon** *Switz.* 46°23N 6°14E **179** J2
**Nyong →** *Cameroon* 3°17N 9°54E **263** E6
**Nyons** *France* 44°22N 5°10E **175** D9
**Nyou** *Burkina Faso* 12°42N 2°1W **263** C4
**Nýrsko** *Czech Rep.* 49°18N 13°9E **180** B6
**Nysa** *Poland* 50°30N 17°22E **185** H4
**Nysa →** *Europe* 52°4N 14°46E **178** C10
**Nysa Kłodzka →** *Poland* 50°49N 17°40E **185** H4
**Nysætre** *Norway* 62°2N 8°20E **164** B5
**Nysäter** *Sweden* 59°17N 12°47E **162** E6
**Nyslott = Savonlinna** *Finland* 61°52N 28°53E **188** B5
**Nyssa** *U.S.A.* 43°53N 117°0W **304** E5
**Nystad = Uusikaupunki** *Finland* 60°47N 21°25E **188** B1
**Nysted** *Denmark* 54°40N 11°44E **163** K5
**Nyunzu** *Dem. Rep. of the Congo* 5°57S 27°58E **268** D2
**Nyurba** *Russia* 63°17N 118°28E **215** C12
**Nyzhankovychi** *Ukraine* 49°40N 22°49E **185** J9
**Nyzhnohirskyy** *Ukraine* 45°27N 34°38E **189** K8
**Nyzhny Vorota** *Ukraine* 48°46N 23°6E **182** B8
**Nzébéla** *Guinea* 8°9N 9°7W **262** D3
**Nzega** *Tanzania* 4°10S 33°12E **268** C3
**Nzérékoré** *Guinea* 7°49N 8°48W **262** D3
**Nzeto** *Angola* 7°10S 12°52E **265** D2
**N'zi-Comoé □** *Ivory C.* 7°0N 4°30W **262** D4
**Nzilo, Chutes de** *Dem. Rep. of the Congo* 10°18S 25°27E **265** E5
**Nzilo, L.** *Dem. Rep. of the Congo* 10°35S 25°39E **265** E5
**N'zo →** *Ivory C.* 6°15N 7°3W **262** D3
**N'zo △** *Ivory C.* 6°15N 7°15W **262** D3
**Nzubuka** *Tanzania* 4°45S 32°50E **268** C3
**Nzwani = Anjouan** *Comoros Is.* 12°15S 44°20E **272** a

# O

**O Barco** *Spain* 42°23N 6°58W **194** C4
**O Carballiño** *Spain* 42°26N 8°5W **194** C2
**O Castro de Ferreira** *Spain* 42°31N 7°37W **194** C3
**O Convento** *Spain* 42°28N 8°41W **194** C2
**O Corgo** *Spain* 42°56N 7°25W **194** C3
**O Le Pupū Pu'e △** *Samoa* 13°59S 171°43W **287** V20
**O Pedrouzo** *Spain* 42°56N 8°20W **194** C2
**O Pino = O Pedrouzo** *Spain* 42°56N 8°20W **194** C2
**O Porriño** *Spain* 42°10N 8°37W **194** C2
**O Real** *Spain* 43°20N 8°19W **194** B2
**O Seixo** *Spain* 41°59N 8°46W **194** D2
**Ō-Shima** *Hokkaidō, Japan* 41°30N 139°22E **220** D9
**Ō-Shima** *Nagasaki, Japan* 33°29N 129°33E **222** D1
**Ō-Shima** *Shizuoka, Japan* 34°44N 139°24E **223** C11
**O.R. Tambo Int. ✈ (JNB)** *S. Africa* 27°7S 29°16E **123** A2
**Oa, Mull of** *U.K.* 55°35N 6°20W **167** F2
**Oacoma** *U.S.A.* 43°48N 99°24W **308** D4
**Oahe, L.** *U.S.A.* 44°27N 100°24W **308** C3
**Oahe Dam** *U.S.A.* 44°27N 100°24W **308** C3
**O'ahu** *U.S.A.* 21°28N 157°58W **302** K14
**Oak Creek** *U.S.A.* 42°52N 87°55W **311** B9
**Oak Forest** *U.S.A.* 41°37N 87°47W **119** D2
**Oak Grove** *U.S.A.* 33°50N 84°18W **113** A3
**Oak Harbor** *U.S.A.* 48°18N 122°39W **306** B4
**Oak Hill** *Fla., U.S.A.* 28°52N 80°51W **317** G9
**Oak Hill** *Mass., U.S.A.* 42°18N 71°10W **116** B1
**Oak Hill** *W. Va., U.S.A.* 37°59N 81°9W **309** G13
**Oak Island** *U.S.A.* 33°55N 78°10W **315** E15
**Oak Lawn** *U.S.A.* 41°42N 87°45W **119** C2
**Oak Park** *Ga., U.S.A.* 32°22N 82°19W **316** C7
**Oak Park** *Ill., U.S.A.* 41°52N 87°47W **119** B2
**Oak Ridge** *U.S.A.* 36°1N 84°16W **315** C12
**Oak Street Beach** *Chicago, U.S.A.* **119** a2
**Oak View** *Calif., U.S.A.* 34°24N 119°18W **307** L7
**Oak View** *Md., U.S.A.* 39°1N 76°58W **143** A3
**Oakan-Dake** *Japan* 43°27N 144°10E **220** C12
**Oakbank** *Australia* 33°4S 140°33E **282** B4
**Oakdale** *Calif., U.S.A.* 37°46N 120°51W **306** H6
**Oakdale** *Georgia, U.S.A.* 33°51N 84°30W **113** A2
**Oakdale** *La., U.S.A.* 30°49N 92°40W **314** F8
**Oakes** *U.S.A.* 46°8N 98°6W **308** B4
**Oakesdale** *U.S.A.* 47°8N 117°15W **304** C5
**Oakey** *Australia* 27°25S 151°43E **281** D5
**Oakfield** *Ga., U.S.A.* 31°47N 83°58W **316** D6
**Oakfield** *N.Y., U.S.A.* 43°4N 78°16W **312** C6
**Oakford** *U.S.A.* 40°6N 89°58W **310** D7
**Oakham** *U.K.* 52°40N 0°43W **169** E7
**Oakhurst** *U.S.A.* 37°19N 119°40W **306** H7
**Oakland** *Calif., U.S.A.* 37°48N 122°18W **136** B3
**Oakland** *Ill., U.S.A.* 39°39N 88°2W **311** E8
**Oakland** *Pa., U.S.A.* 41°57N 75°36W **313** E9
**Oakland City** *U.S.A.* 38°20N 87°21W **311** F9
**Oakland Park** *U.S.A.* 26°10N 80°7W **129** A3
**Oaklands** *Australia* 35°34S 146°10E **283** C7
**Oaklawn** *U.S.A.* 38°46N 76°56W **143** C3
**Oakleigh** *Australia* 37°54S 145°5E **128** B2
**Oakley** *Idaho, U.S.A.* 42°15N 113°53W **304** E7
**Oakley** *Kans., U.S.A.* 39°8N 100°51W **308** F3
**Oakover →** *Australia* 21°0S 120°40E **278** D3
**Oakridge** *U.S.A.* 43°45N 122°28W **304** E2
**Oaks, The** *Australia* 34°3S 150°34E **283** C9
**Oaktown** *U.S.A.* 38°52N 87°27W **311** F9
**Oakville** *Ont., Canada* 43°27N 79°41W **312** C5
**Oakville** *Wash., U.S.A.* 46°51N 123°14W **306** D3
**Oakwood** *U.S.A.* 41°6N 84°23W **311** C12
**Oakwood Beach** *U.S.A.* 40°33N 74°7W **132** C1
**Oamaru** *N.Z.* 45°5S 170°59E **285** F5
**Ōamishirasato** *Japan* 35°31N 140°18E **223** B12
**Oancea** *Romania* 45°21N 27°42E **183** E12
**Oarai** *Japan* 36°21N 140°34E **223** A12
**Oasis** *Calif., U.S.A.* 37°29N 117°55W **306** H9
**Oasis** *Calif., U.S.A.* 33°28N 116°6W **307** M10
**Oates Land** *Antarctica* 69°0S 160°0E **151** C11
**Oatley** *Australia* 33°59S 151°4E **139** B1
**Oatman** *U.S.A.* 35°1N 114°19W **307** K12
**Oaxaca** *Mexico* 17°3N 96°43W **319** D5
**Oaxaca □** *Mexico* 17°0N 96°30W **319** D5
**Ob →** *Russia* 66°45N 69°30E **214** C7
**Oba** *Canada* 49°4N 84°7W **298** C3
**Obala** *Cameroon* 4°9N 11°32E **263** E7
**Obalende** *Nigeria* 6°26N 3°25E **124** B2
**Obama** *Fukui, Japan* 35°30N 135°45E **223** B7
**Obama** *Nagasaki, Japan* 32°43N 130°13E **222** E2
**Obama, Mt.** *Antigua & B.* 17°2N 61°52W **322** b
**Oban** *Nigeria* 5°17N 8°33E **263** D6
**Oban** *Argyll & Bute, U.K.* 56°25N 5°29W **167** E3
**Oba's Palace** *Nigeria* 6°26N 3°22E **124** B2
**Obbia = Hobyo** *Somalia* 5°25N 48°30E **267** C6
**Obdorsk = Salekhard** *Russia* 66°30N 66°35E **214** C7
**Oberá** *Argentina* 27°21S 55°2W **335** B4
**Oberammergau** *Germany* 47°36N 11°4E **179** H7
**Oberasbach** *Germany* 49°25N 10°57E **179** F6
**Oberbayern □** *Germany* 48°5N 11°50E **179** G7
**Oberburg = Gornji Grad** *Slovenia* 46°20N 14°52E **199** B11
**Oberdonau = Oberösterreich □** *Austria* 48°10N 14°0E **180** C7
**Oberdrauburg** *Austria* 46°44N 12°58E **180** E5
**Obere Donau ⌓** *Germany* 48°5N 9°0E **179** G5
**Oberer Bayerischer Wald ⌓** *Germany* 49°15N 12°40E **179** F8
**Oberföhring** *Germany* 48°10N 11°37E **131** B2
**Oberfranken □** *Germany* 50°10N 11°20E **179** E7
**Oberglogau = Głogówek** *Poland* 50°21N 17°53E **185** H4
**Oberhaching** *Germany* 48°1N 11°35E **131** B2
**Oberhausen** *Germany* 51°28N 6°51E **178** D2
**Oberkirch** *Germany* 48°31N 8°4E **179** G4
**Oberlaa** *Austria* 48°8N 16°24E **142** B2
**Oberlaibach = Vrhnika** *Slovenia* 45°58N 14°15E **199** C11
**Oberlausitz** *Germany* 51°16N 14°18E **178** D10
**Oberlin** *Kans., U.S.A.* 39°49N 100°32W **308** F3
**Oberlin** *La., U.S.A.* 30°37N 92°46W **314** F8
**Oberlin** *Ohio, U.S.A.* 41°18N 82°13W **312** E2
**Oberlisse** *Austria* 48°17N 16°26E **142** A2
**Obermenzing** *Germany* 48°10N 11°28E **131** A1
**Obermoos Schwaige** *Germany* 48°14N 11°27E **131** A1
**Obernai** *France* 48°28N 7°30E **173** D14
**Oberndorf** *Germany* 48°17N 8°34E **179** G4
**Obernigk = Oborniki Śląskie** *Poland* 51°17N 16°53E **185** G3
**Oberon** *Australia* 33°45S 149°52E **283** B8
**Oberösterreich □** *Austria* 48°10N 14°0E **180** C7
**Oberpfalz □** *Germany* 49°20N 12°10E **179** F8
**Oberpfälzer Wald** *Germany* 49°30N 12°30E **179** F8
**Oberpfälzer Wald ⌓** *Germany* 49°40N 12°20E **179** F8
**Oberschleissheim** *Germany* 48°15N 11°33E **131** A2
**Oberschöneweide** *Germany* 52°27N 13°31E **115** B4
**Oberstdorf** *Germany* 47°24N 10°15E **179** H6
**Oberting** *Gabon* 0°22S 9°46E **264** C1
**Obertyn** *Ukraine* 48°42N 25°10E **183** B10
**Oberursel** *Germany* 50°11N 8°35E **179** E4
**Oberwart** *Austria* 47°17N 16°12E **181** D9
**Obi, Kepulauan** *Indonesia* 1°23S 127°45E **231** E7
**Obiaruku** *Nigeria* 5°51N 6°9E **263** D6
**Óbidos** *Brazil* 1°50S 55°30W **329** D6
**Óbidos** *Portugal* 39°19N 9°10W **195** F1
**Obihiro** *Japan* 42°56N 143°12E **220** C11
**Obilatu** *Indonesia* 1°25S 127°20E **231** E7
**Obilnoye** *Russia* 47°32N 44°30E **191** G7
**Obing** *Germany* 48°0N 12°24E **179** G8
**Objat** *France* 45°16N 1°24E **174** C5
**Oblong** *U.S.A.* 39°0N 87°55W **311** F9
**Obluchye** *Russia* 49°1N 131°4E **215** E14
**Obninsk** *Russia* 55°8N 36°37E **188** E9
**Obo** *C.A.R.* 5°20N 26°32E **264** A5
**Obock** *Djibouti* 12°0N 43°20E **257** E5
**Obodivka** *Ukraine* 48°24N 29°15E **183** B14
**Oborniki** *Poland* 52°39N 16°50E **185** F3
**Oborniki Śląskie** *Poland* 51°17N 16°53E **185** G3
**Obouya** *Congo* 0°56S 15°43E **264** C3
**Oboyan** *Russia* 51°15N 36°21E **189** G9
**Obozerskaya = Obozerskiy** *Russia* 63°34N 40°21E **186** B7
**Obozerskiy** *Russia* 63°34N 40°21E **186** B7
**Obrenovac** *Serbia* 44°40N 20°11E **202** B4
**O'Brien** *U.S.A.* 30°2N 82°57W **316** E7
**Obrovac** *Croatia* 44°11N 15°41E **199** D12
**Obruk** *Turkey* 38°7N 33°12E **212** C5
**Obrzycko** *Poland* 52°42N 16°32E **185** F3
**Observatory** *Sydney, Australia* **139** a1
**Observatory** *Gauteng, S. Africa* 26°10S 28°4E **123** B2
**Observatory Inlet** *Canada* 55°10N 129°54W **296** B3
**Obshchi Syrt** *Russia* 52°0N 53°0E **158** E16
**Obskaya Guba** *Russia* 69°0N 73°0E **214** C8
**Obu** *Japan* 35°0N 136°58E **223** B8
**Obuasi** *Ghana* 6°17N 1°40W **263** D4
**Obubra** *Nigeria* 6°8N 8°20E **263** D6
**Óbuda** *Hungary* 47°33N 19°2E **117** A2
**Obudu** *Nigeria* 6°38N 9°5E **263** D6
**Obukhovo** *Russia* 59°53N 30°22E **137** B2
**Obura** *Papua N. G.* 6°33S 145°58E **286** D3
**Obvodnyy Kanal** *Russia* 59°54N 30°20E **137** B1
**Obwalden □** *Switz.* 46°55N 8°15E **179** J4
**Obzor** *Bulgaria* 42°50N 27°52E **203** D11
**Ocala** *U.S.A.* 29°11N 82°8W **317** F7
**Ocamo →** *Venezuela* 2°48N 65°14W **329** C4
**Ocampo** *Chihuahua, Mexico* 28°11N 108°23W **318** B3
**Ocampo** *Tamaulipas, Mexico* 22°50N 99°20W **319** C5
**Ocaña** *Colombia* 8°15N 73°20W **328** B3
**Ocaña** *Spain* 39°55N 3°30W **194** F7
**Occidental, Cordillera** *Colombia* 5°0N 76°0W **328** C2
**Occidental, Cordillera** *Peru* 14°0S 74°0W **330** C3
**Occidental, Grand Erg** *Algeria* 30°20N 1°0E **261** B5
**Ocean City** *Md., U.S.A.* 38°20N 75°5W **309** F16
**Ocean City** *N.J., U.S.A.* 39°17N 74°35W **309** F16
**Ocean City** *Wash., U.S.A.* 47°4N 124°10W **306** C2
**Ocean Falls** *Canada* 52°18N 127°48W **296** C3
**Ocean I. = Banaba** *Kiribati* 0°45S 169°50E **288** H8
**Ocean Park** *Hong Kong, China* 22°13N 114°10E **122** B3
**Ocean Park** *Wash., U.S.A.* 46°30N 124°3W **306** D2
**Oceano** *U.S.A.* 35°6N 120°37W **307** K6
**Oceanport** *U.S.A.* 40°19N 74°3W **313** F10
**Oceanside** *U.S.A.* 33°12N 117°23W **307** M9
**Ochagavía** *Spain* 42°55N 1°5W **196** C3
**Ochakiv** *Ukraine* 46°37N 31°33E **189** J6
**Ochamchire** *Georgia* 42°46N 41°32E **191** J5
**Ochi, Oros** *Greece* 38°5N 24°25E **204** C6
**Ochiai** *Japan* 35°1N 133°45E **222** B5
**Ochil Hills** *U.K.* 56°14N 3°40W **167** E5
**Ochlocknee** *U.S.A.* 30°58N 84°3W **316** E5
**Ochlockonee →** *U.S.A.* 29°59N 84°26W **316** F5
**Ocho Rios** *Jamaica* 18°24N 77°6W **320** a
**Ochopee** *U.S.A.* 25°54N 81°18W **317** K8
**Ochota** *Poland* 52°13N 20°58E **143** B1
**Ochsenfurt** *Germany* 49°40N 10°4E **179** F6
**Ochsenhausen** *Germany* 48°4N 9°57E **179** G5
**Ocilla** *U.S.A.* 31°36N 83°15W **316** D6
**Ockelbo** *Sweden* 60°54N 16°45E **162** D10
**Ocmulgee →** *U.S.A.* 31°58N 82°33W **316** D7
**Ocmulgee ⌓** *U.S.A.* 32°49N 83°37W **316** C6
**Ocna Mureş** *Romania* 46°23N 23°55E **183** D8
**Ocna Sibiului** *Romania* 45°52N 24°2E **183** E9
**Ocnele Mari** *Romania* 45°8N 24°18E **183** E9
**Ocniţa** *Moldova* 48°25N 27°30E **183** B12
**Ocoee** *U.S.A.* 28°34N 81°32W **133** A1
**Ocoña** *Peru* 16°26S 73°8W **330** D3
**Ocoña →** *Peru* 16°28S 73°8W **330** D3
**Oconee →** *U.S.A.* 31°58N 82°33W **316** D7
**Oconee, L.** *U.S.A.* 33°28N 83°15W **316** B6
**O'Connell Street** *Dublin, Ireland* **120** b2
**Oconomowoc** *U.S.A.* 43°7N 88°30W **311** A8
**Oconto** *U.S.A.* 44°53N 87°52W **308** C10
**Oconto Falls** *U.S.A.* 44°52N 88°9W **308** C9
**Ocosingo** *Mexico* 16°53N 92°6W **319** D6
**Ocotal** *Nic.* 13°41N 86°31W **320** D2
**Ocotlán** *Jalisco, Mexico* 20°21N 102°46W **318** C4
**Ocotlán** *Oaxaca, Mexico* 16°48N 96°40W **319** D5
**Ocreza →** *Portugal* 39°32N 7°50W **195** F3
**Ócsa** *Hungary* 47°17N 19°15E **182** C4
**Ocumare del Tuy** *Venezuela* 10°7N 66°46W **328** A4
**Ocurí** *Bolivia* 18°45S 65°50W **331** D4
**Oda** *Ghana* 5°50N 0°51W **263** D4
**Ōda** *Shimane, Japan* 35°11N 132°30E **222** B4
**Oda, J.** *Sudan* 20°21N 36°39E **256** C4
**Ódáðahraun** *Iceland* 65°5N 17°0W **155** B9
**Ōdaejin** *N. Korea* 41°34N 129°40E **224** B4
**Odaesan △** *S. Korea* 37°40N 128°30E **224** D4
**Odaiba** *Japan* 35°38N 139°47E **140** B3
**Ödåkra** *Sweden* 56°7N 12°45E **163** H6
**Odana** *Japan* 35°33N 139°35E **140** B2
**Odate** *Japan* 40°16N 140°34E **220** D10
**Odawara** *Japan* 35°20N 139°6E **223** B11
**Odda** *Norway* 60°3N 6°35E **164** D3
**Odder = Xuddur** *Somalia* 4°11N 43°52E **267** D5
**Odder** *Denmark* 55°58N 10°10E **163** J4
**Odei →** *Canada* 56°6N 96°54W **297** B9
**Odell** *U.S.A.* 41°0N 88°31W **311** C8
**Odemira** *Portugal* 37°35N 8°40W **195** H2
**Ödemiş** *Turkey* 38°15N 28°0E **205** C9
**Öden-Stockach** *Germany* 48°5N 11°41E **131** B3
**Ödenburg = Sopron** *Hungary* 47°45N 16°32E **182** C1
**Odendaalsrus** *S. Africa* 27°48S 26°45E **270** C4
**Odensbacken** *Sweden* 59°10N 15°32E **162** E9
**Odense** *Denmark* 55°22N 10°23E **163** J4
**Odenwald = Neckartal-Odenwald ⌓** *Germany* 49°30N 9°5E **179** F5
**Odenwald** *Germany* 49°35N 9°0E **179** F5
**Oder →** *Europe* 53°33N 14°38E **178** B10
**Oder-Havel Kanal** *Germany* 52°52N 14°2E **178** C10
**Oderzo** *Italy* 45°47N 12°29E **199** C9
**Odesa** *Ukraine* 46°30N 30°45E **189** J6
**Odesa □** *Ukraine* 47°20N 29°55E **189** J5
**Ödeshög** *Sweden* 58°14N 14°39E **163** F8
**Odessa = Odesa** *Ukraine* 46°30N 30°45E **189** J6
**Odessa** *Ont., Canada* 44°17N 76°43W **313** B8
**Odessa** *Mo., U.S.A.* 39°0N 93°57W **310** F3
**Odessa** *Tex., U.S.A.* 31°52N 102°23W **314** F3
**Odessa** *Wash., U.S.A.* 47°20N 118°41W **304** C4
**Odiakwe** *Botswana* 20°12S 25°17E **270** B4
**Odiel →** *Spain* 37°10N 6°55W **195** H4
**Odienné** *Ivory C.* 9°30N 7°34W **262** D3
**Odilampi** *Finland* 60°18N 24°45E **121** A2
**Odimba** *Gabon* 2°2S 9°33E **264** C2
**Odintsovo** *Russia* 55°40N 37°16E **188** E9
**Odiongan** *Phil.* 12°24N 121°59E **232** E3
**Odisha □** *India* 20°0N 84°0E **244** E7
**Odivelas** *Portugal* 38°47N 9°10W **126** A1
**Odobeşti** *Romania* 45°43N 27°4E **183** E12
**Odolanów** *Poland* 51°34N 17°40E **185** G4
**Odolany** *Poland* 52°13N 20°55E **143** B1
**O'Donnell** *U.S.A.* 32°58N 101°50W **314** E4
**O'Donnell Pt.** *Canada* 45°5N 80°5W **312** A4
**Odorheiu Secuiesc** *Romania* 46°21N 25°21E **183** D10
**Odoyevo** *Russia* 53°56N 36°42E **188** F9
**Odra = Oder →** *Europe* 53°33N 14°38E **178** B10
**Odra →** *Spain* 42°14N 4°17W **194** C6
**Odum** *U.S.A.* 31°40N 82°2W **316** D7
**Odžaci** *Serbia* 45°30N 19°17E **182** E4
**Odžak** *Bos.-H.* 45°3N 18°18E **182** E3
**Odzala** *Congo* 0°37N 14°37E **264** B2
**Odzala △** *Congo* 0°55N 14°55E **264** B2
**Odzi** *Zimbabwe* 19°0S 32°20E **271** A5
**Odzi →** *Zimbabwe* 19°45S 32°23E **271** A5
**Oebisfelde** *Germany* 52°27N 10°57E **178** C6
**Oecussi = Pante Macassar** *E. Timor* 9°30S 123°58E **231** F6
**Oedong** *S. Korea* 35°42N 129°14E **224** E4
**Oeiras** *Brazil* 7°0S 42°8W **332** C3
**Oeiras** *Portugal* 38°41N 9°18W **126** A1
**Oeiras do Para** *Brazil* 1°58S 49°51W **329** D8
**Oelrichs** *U.S.A.* 43°11N 103°14W **308** D2
**Oels in Schlesien = Oleśnica** *Poland* 51°13N 17°22E **185** G4
**Oelsnitz** *Germany* 50°24N 12°10E **179** E8
**Oelwein** *U.S.A.* 42°41N 91°55W **310** B5
**Oenarodo** *S. Korea* 34°26N 127°30E **224** F3
**Oeno I.** *Pac. Oc.* 24°0S 131°0W **289** K14
**Oenpelli = Gunbalanya** *Australia* 12°20S 133°4E **278** B5
**Oetz** *Austria* 47°13N 10°53E **180** D3
**Of** *Turkey* 40°59N 40°23E **213** B9
**O'Fallon** *U.S.A.* 38°49N 90°43W **310** F6
**Ofanto →** *Italy* 41°22N 16°13E **201** A9
**Offa** *Nigeria* 8°13N 4°42E **263** D5
**Offaly □** *Ireland* 53°15N 7°30W **166** C4
**Offenbach** *Germany* 50°6N 8°44E **179** E4
**Offenburg** *Germany* 48°28N 7°56E **179** G3
**Officer Cr. →** *Australia* 27°46S 132°30E **279** E5
**Offida** *Italy* 42°56N 13°41E **199** F10
**Offoué →** *Gabon* 0°4S 11°44E **264** C2
**Ofidousa** *Greece* 36°33N 26°8E **205** E8
**Ofin** *Nigeria* 6°32N 3°30E **124** A3
**Ofolanga** *Tonga* 19°38S 174°27W **287** P13
**Ofotfjorden** *Norway* 68°27N 17°0E **160** B17
**Ofte** *Norway* 59°30N 8°12E **164** E5
**Ofu** *Amer. Samoa* 14°11S 169°41W **302** g
**Ōfunato** *Japan* 39°4N 141°43E **220** E10
**Oga** *Japan* 39°55N 139°50E **220** E9
**Oga-Hantō** *Japan* 39°58N 139°47E **220** E9
**Ogaden** *Ethiopia* 7°30N 45°30E **267** C6
**Ōgaki** *Japan* 35°21N 136°37E **223** B8
**Ogallala** *U.S.A.* 41°8N 101°43W **308** E3
**Ogan →** *Indonesia* 3°1S 104°44E **234** C2
**Ogasawara Gunto** *Pac. Oc.* 27°0N 142°0E **288** E6
**Ogawa** *Japan* 35°44N 139°28E **140** A1
**Ogbomosho** *Nigeria* 8°1N 4°11E **263** D5
**Ogden** *Iowa, U.S.A.* 42°2N 94°2W **310** B2
**Ogden** *Utah, U.S.A.* 41°13N 111°58W **304** F8
**Ogden Park** *U.S.A.* 41°46N 87°39W **119** C2
**Ogden Slip** *Chicago, U.S.A.* **119** b3
**Ogdensburg** *U.S.A.* 44°42N 75°30W **313** B9
**Ogea Driki** *Fiji* 19°12S 178°27W **287** B3
**Ogea Levu** *Fiji* 19°8S 178°24W **287** B3
**Ogeechee →** *U.S.A.* 31°50N 81°3W **316** D8
**Ogi** *Japan* 33°20N 130°15E **222** D2
**Ogikubo** *Japan* 35°42N 139°37E **140** A2
**Ogilby** *U.S.A.* 32°49N 114°50W **307** N12
**Ogilvie Transportation Center** *Chicago, U.S.A.* 41°52N 87°38W **119** B3
**Oglat Beraber** *Algeria* 30°15N 3°30W **260** B4
**Oglat el Khnâchich** *Mali* 21°51N 3°58W **260** D4
**Oglesby** *U.S.A.* 41°18N 89°4W **310** C7
**Oglethorpe** *U.S.A.* 32°18N 84°4W **316** C5
**Ogliastra □** *Italy* 39°50N 9°35E **200** C2
**Òglio →** *Italy* 45°2N 10°39E **198** C7
**Òglio Nord ⌓** *Italy* 45°22N 9°54E **198** C6
**Òglio Sud ⌓** *Italy* 45°7N 10°24E **198** C7
**Ogmore** *Australia* 22°37S 149°35E **280** C4
**Ognon →** *France* 47°16N 5°28E **173** E12
**Ogogoro** *Nigeria* 6°24N 3°35E **124** B2
**Ogoja** *Nigeria* 6°38N 8°39E **263** D6
**Ogoki** *Canada* 51°38N 85°58W **298** B2
**Ogoki →** *Canada* 51°38N 85°57W **298** B2
**Ogoki L.** *Canada* 50°50N 87°10W **298** B2
**Ogoki Res.** *Canada* 50°45N 88°15W **298** B2
**Ogooué →** *Gabon* 1°0S 9°0E **264** C1
**Ogooué-Ivindo □** *Gabon* 1°0N 13°30E **264** B2
**Ogooué-Lolo □** *Gabon* 1°0S 12°30E **264** C2
**Ogooué-Maritime □** *Gabon* 1°0S 9°0E **264** C1
**Ogōri** *Fukuoka, Japan* 33°25N 130°30E **222** D2
**Ogōri** *Yamaguchi, Japan* 34°6N 131°24E **222** C3
**Ograźden** *Macedonia* 41°30N 22°50E **202** E6
**Ogre** *Latvia* 56°49N 24°36E **188** D3
**Ogrein** *Sudan* 17°55N 34°50E **256** D3
**Ogudu** *Nigeria* 6°34N 3°24E **124** A2
**Ogosta →** *Bulgaria* 43°48N 23°55E **202** C7
**Ogou →** *Togo* 7°50N 1°19E **263** D5
**Ogoueilten Nmâdi** *Mauritania* 19°46N 11°1W **260** E2
**Ogowe = Ogooué →** *Gabon* 1°0S 9°0E **264** C1
**Ogoyo** *Nigeria* 6°25N 3°29E **124** B2
**Ogr = Sharafa** *Sudan* 11°59N 27°7E **257** E2

Ogulin *Croatia* 45°16N 15°16E **199** C12
Ogun □ *Nigeria* 7°0N 3°0E **263** D5
Oguni *Japan* 33°11N 131°8E **222** D3
Ögur *Iceland* 66°2N 22°44W **155** A4
Ogurja Ada *Turkmenistan* 38°55N 53°2E **247** B7
Oguta *Nigeria* 5°44N 6°44E **263** D6
Oğuzeli *Turkey* 36°57N 37°30E **250** B8
Ogwashi-Uku *Nigeria* 6°15N 6°30E **263** D6
Ogwe *Nigeria* 5°0N 7°14E **263** E6
Ohai *N.Z.* 45°55S 168°0E **285** F3
Ohakune *N.Z.* 39°24S 175°24E **284** F4
Ohanet *Algeria* 28°44N 8°46E **261** C6
Ohangwena □ *Namibia* 17°30S 17°0E **270** A2
Ōhara *Japan* 35°15N 140°23E **223** B12
O'Hare Int., Chicago ✈ (ORD) *U.S.A.* 41°59N 87°54W **311** C9
Ohata *Japan* 41°24N 141°10E **220** D10
Ohatchee *U.S.A.* 33°47N 86°0W **316** B4
Ohau, L. *N.Z.* 44°15S 169°53E **285** E4
Ohaupo *N.Z.* 37°56S 175°20E **284** D4
O'Higgins, C. *Chile* 27°5S 109°15W **330** b
O'Higgins, Parque *Chile* 33°27S 70°40W **137** B2
O'Higgins, Pta. *Chile* 33°41S 79°0W **330** c
Ohio □ *U.S.A.* 40°15N 82°45W **312** F2
Ohio → *U.S.A.* 36°59N 89°8W **308** G9
Ohio City *U.S.A.* 40°46N 84°37W **311** D12
Ohiwa Harbour *N.Z.* 37°59S 177°10E **284** D6
Ohlau = Oława *Poland* 50°57N 17°20E **185** H4
Ohře → *Czech Rep.* 50°30N 14°10E **180** A7
Ohre → *Sachsen-Anhalt, Germany* 52°18N 11°46E **178** C7
Ohrid *Macedonia* 41°8N 20°52E **202** E4
Ohridsko Jezero *Macedonia* 41°8N 20°52E **202** E4
Ohrigstad *S. Africa* 24°39S 30°36E **271** B5
Öhringen *Germany* 49°12N 9°31E **179** F5
Ohura *N.Z.* 38°51S 174°59E **284** E3
Oi Qu → *China* 28°37N 98°16E **228** C2
Oiapoque *Brazil* 3°50N 51°50W **329** C7
Oiapoque → *S. Amer.* 4°8N 51°40W **329** C7
Oikou *China* 38°35N 117°42E **227** E9
Oil City *U.S.A.* 41°26N 79°42W **312** E5
Oil Springs *Canada* 42°47N 82°7W **312** D2
Oildale *U.S.A.* 35°25N 119°1W **307** K7
Ōimachi *Japan* 35°35N 139°43E **140** B3
Oinousa = Inousses *Greece* 38°33N 26°14E **205** C8
Oise □ *France* 49°28N 2°30E **173** C9
Oise → *France* 49°0N 2°4E **173** C9
Oistins *Barbados* 13°4N 59°33W **323** r
Ōita *Japan* 33°14N 131°36E **222** D3
Ōita □ *Japan* 33°15N 131°30E **222** D3
Oiticica *Brazil* 5°3S 41°5W **332** C3
Ojai *U.S.A.* 34°27N 119°15W **307** L7
Ojcowski △ *Poland* 50°15N 19°50E **185** H6
Ojhar *India* 20°6N 73°56E **244** D1
Ojinaga *Mexico* 29°34N 104°25W **318** B4
Ojiya *Japan* 37°18N 138°48E **221** F9
Ojo Caliente *Mexico* 22°34N 102°15W **318** C4
Ojo de Liebre, L. *Mexico* 27°45N 114°15W **318** B2
Ojos del Salado, Cerro *Argentina* 27°0S 68°40W **334** B2
Ojota *Nigeria* 6°35N 3°23E **124** A2
Ojus *U.S.A.* 25°26N 80°9W **129** C3
Oka *Nigeria* 7°9N 3°38E **263** D5
Oka → *Russia* 56°20N 43°59E **190** B7
Okaba *Indonesia* 8°6S 139°42E **231** F9
Okahandja *Namibia* 22°0S 16°59E **270** B2
Okahukura *N.Z.* 38°48S 175°14E **284** E4
Okaihau *N.Z.* 35°19S 173°47E **284** B2
Okakarara *Namibia* 20°35S 17°27E **270** B2
Okalataka *Congo* 0°18S 14°54E **264** C2
Okanagan L. *Canada* 50°0N 119°30W **296** D5
Okandja *Gabon* 0°35S 13°45E **264** C2
Okano → *Gabon* 0°5S 10°57E **264** C2
Okanogan *U.S.A.* 48°22N 119°35W **304** B4
Okanogan → *U.S.A.* 48°6N 119°44W **304** B4
Okanogan Range *N. Amer.* 49°0N 119°55W **296** D5
Okány *Hungary* 46°52N 21°21E **182** D6
Okapa *Papua N. G.* 6°38S 145°39E **286** D3
Okapi ⌂ *Dem. Rep. of the Congo* 2°30N 27°20E **268** B2
Okaputa *Namibia* 20°5S 17°0E **270** B2
Okara *Pakistan* 30°50N 73°31E **242** D5
Okarito *N.Z.* 43°15S 170°9E **285** D5
Okato *N.Z.* 39°12S 173°53E **284** F2
Okau *Micronesia* 9°32N 138°6E **287** R16
Okaukuejo *Namibia* 19°10S 16°0E **270** A2
Okavango □ *Namibia* 18°0S 19°30E **270** A2
Okavango Delta *Botswana* 18°45S 22°45E **270** A3
Okavango Swamp = Okavango Delta *Botswana* 18°45S 22°45E **270** A3
Ōkawa *Japan* 33°9N 130°21E **222** D2
Okawville *U.S.A.* 38°26N 89°33W **310** F7
Okaya *Japan* 36°5N 138°10E **223** A10
Okayama *Japan* 34°40N 133°54E **222** C5
Okayama □ *Japan* 35°0N 133°50E **222** C5
Okazaki *Japan* 34°57N 137°10E **223** C9
Oke-Iho *Nigeria* 8°1N 3°18E **263** D5
Oke-Ira *Nigeria* 6°29N 3°22E **124** B2
Okęcie *Poland* 52°11N 20°56E **143** B1
Okęcie, Warszawa ✈ (WAW) *Poland* 52°9N 20°59E **143** B1
Okeechobee *U.S.A.* 27°15N 80°50W **317** H9
Okeechobee, L. *U.S.A.* 27°0N 80°50W **317** J9
Okefenokee ⌂ *U.S.A.* 30°45N 82°18W **316** E7
Okefenokee Swamp *U.S.A.* 30°40N 82°20W **316** E7
Okehampton *U.K.* 50°44N 4°0W **169** G4
Okemos *U.S.A.* 42°43N 84°26W **311** B12
Okene *Nigeria* 7°32N 6°11E **263** D6
Okeogbe *Nigeria* 6°24N 3°23E **124** B2
Oker → *Germany* 52°32N 10°22E **178** C6
Okha *Gujarat, India* 22°27N 69°4E **242** H3
Okha *Russia* 53°40N 143°0E **215** D15
Okhla *India* 28°33N 77°16E **120** B2
Okhotsk *Russia* 59°20N 143°10E **215** D15
Okhotsk, Sea of *Asia* 55°0N 145°0E **215** D15
Okhotskiy Perevoz *Russia* 61°52N 135°35E **215** C14
Okhta → *Russia* 59°56N 30°25E **137** B2
Okhtyrka *Ukraine* 50°25N 35°0E **189** G8
Oki-no-Shima *Japan* 32°44N 132°33E **222** E4
Oki-Shotō *Japan* 36°5N 133°15E **222** A5
Okiep *S. Africa* 29°39S 17°53E **270** C2
Okigwi *Nigeria* 5°52N 7°20E **263** D6
Okija *Nigeria* 5°54N 6°55E **263** D6
Okinawa *Japan* 26°19N 127°46E **288** a
Okinawa □ *Japan* 26°40N 128°0E **288** a
Okinawa-Guntō *Japan* 26°40N 128°0E **221** L4
Okinawa-Jima *Japan* 26°32N 128°0E **221** L4
Okino-erabu-Shima *Japan* 27°21N 128°33E **221** L4
Okitipupa *Nigeria* 6°31N 4°50E **263** D5
Okkervil → *Russia* 59°56N 30°30E **137** B2
Oklahoma □ *U.S.A.* 35°20N 97°30W **314** D6
Oklahoma City *U.S.A.* 35°30N 97°30W **314** D6
Oklawaha → *U.S.A.* 29°28N 81°41W **317** F8
Okmulgee *U.S.A.* 35°37N 95°58W **314** D7
Oknitsa = Ocnița *Moldova* 48°25N 27°30E **183** B12
Oko, W. → *Sudan* 21°15N 35°56E **256** C4
Okolo *Uganda* 2°37N 31°8E **268** B3
Okolona *Ky., U.S.A.* 38°8N 85°41W **311** F11
Okolona *Miss., U.S.A.* 34°0N 88°45W **315** E10
Okombahe *Namibia* 21°23S 15°22E **270** B2
Okonek *Poland* 53°32N 16°51E **184** E3
Okotoks *Canada* 50°43N 113°58W **296** C6
Okoyo *Congo* 1°28S 15°0E **264** C3
Okrika *Nigeria* 4°40N 7°10E **263** E6
Okrzeszyn *Poland* 52°8N 21°8E **143** C2
Oksapmin *Papua N. G.* 5°17S 142°15E **286** C2
Øksendalsøra *Norway* 62°42N 8°27E **164** B5
Oksovskiy *Russia* 62°33N 39°57E **186** B6
Oksval *Norway* 59°51N 10°40E **133** A3
Oktwin *Burma* 18°49N 96°26E **241** F6
Oktyabrsk = Qandyaghash *Kazakhstan* 49°28N 57°25E **187** E10
Oktyabrsk *Russia* 53°11N 48°40E **190** D9
Oktyabrskiy = Aktsyabrski *Belarus* 52°38N 28°53E **177** B15
Oktyabrskiy *Bashkortostan, Russia* 54°28N 53°28E **186** D9
Oktyabrskiy *Kamchatka, Russia* 52°39N 156°14E **215** D16
Oktyabrskiy *Moskva, Russia* 55°41N 37°35E **129** B2
Oktyabrskiy *Rostov, Russia* 47°30N 40°4E **191** G5
Oktyabrskoy Revolyutsii, Ostrov *Russia* 79°30N 97°0E **215** B10
Oktyabrskoye = Zhovtneve *Ukraine* 46°54N 32°3E **189** J7
Ōkubo *Tokyo, Japan* **140** a2
Ōkuchi *Japan* 32°4N 130°37E **222** E2
Okulovka *Russia* 58°25N 33°19E **188** C7
Ōkura *Japan* 35°35N 139°27E **140** B1
Okuru *N.Z.* 43°55S 168°55E **285** D3
Okushiri-Tō *Japan* 42°15N 139°30E **220** C9
Okuta *Nigeria* 9°14N 3°12E **263** D5
Okwa → *Botswana* 22°30S 23°0E **270** B3
Ola *Russia* 59°35N 151°17E **215** D16
Ola *Ark., U.S.A.* 35°2N 93°13W **314** D8
Ólafsfjörður *Iceland* 66°4N 18°39W **155** A8
Ólafsvík *Iceland* 64°53N 23°43W **155** C3
Olaine *Latvia* 56°48N 23°59E **184** B10
Olancha *U.S.A.* 36°17N 118°1W **307** J8
Olancha Pk. *U.S.A.* 36°16N 118°7W **307** J8
Olanchito *Honduras* 15°30N 86°30W **320** C2
Öland *Sweden* 56°45N 16°38E **163** H10
Ölands norra udde *Sweden* 57°22N 17°5E **163** G11
Ölands södra udde *Sweden* 56°12N 16°23E **163** H10
Olanta *U.S.A.* 33°56N 79°56W **316** B10
Olar *U.S.A.* 33°11N 81°11W **316** B8
Olargues *France* 43°34N 2°53E **174** E6
Olari *Finland* 60°10N 24°44E **121** B1
Olaria *Brazil* 22°50S 43°16W **135** B1
Olary *Australia* 32°18S 140°19E **282** B4
Olascoaga *Argentina* 35°15S 60°39W **334** D3
Olathe *U.S.A.* 38°53N 94°49W **308** F6
Olavarría *Argentina* 36°55S 60°20W **334** D3
Oława *Poland* 50°57N 17°20E **185** H4
Olbernhau *Germany* 50°40N 13°19E **178** E9
Ólbia *Italy* 40°55N 9°31E **200** B2
Ólbia, G. di *Italy* 40°55N 9°39E **200** B2
Olching *Germany* 48°12N 11°21E **179** G7
Olcott *U.S.A.* 43°20N 78°42W **312** C6
Old Admiralty *Saint Petersburg, Russia* 59°55N 30°20E **137** B1
Old Bahama Chan. = Bahama, Canal Viejo de *W. Indies* 22°10N 77°30W **320** B4
Old Baldy Pk. = San Antonio, Mt. *U.S.A.* 34°17N 117°38W **307** L9
Old Bar *Australia* 31°58S 152°35E **283** A10
Old Bridge *U.S.A.* 40°25N 74°22W **313** F10
Old Castile = Castilla y Leon □ *Spain* 42°0N 5°0W **194** D6
Old City *Shanghai, China* 31°13N 121°29E **138** B1
Old City *Delhi, India* **120** a3
Old City *Jerusalem* **123** b3
Old Crow *Canada* 67°30N 139°55W **294** D4
Old Dale *U.S.A.* 34°8N 115°47W **307** L11
Old Forge *N.Y., U.S.A.* 43°43N 74°58W **313** C10
Old Forge *Pa., U.S.A.* 41°22N 75°45W **313** E9
Old Fort = Purana Qila *Delhi, India* **120** c3
Old Fort B. *Bahamas* 25°3N 77°32W **153** b
Old Fort Pt. *Montserrat* 16°40N 62°11W **323** p
Old Fort York *Canada* 43°39N 79°24W **141** B2
Old Harbor *Alaska, U.S.A.* 57°12N 153°18W **303** H9
Old Harbor *Mass., U.S.A.* 42°19N 71°1W **116** B2
Old Harbour *Jamaica* 17°56N 77°7W **320** a
Old Harbour Bay *Jamaica* 17°54N 77°6W **320** a
Old Ironsides = U.S.S. Constitution *Boston, U.S.A.* **116** a3
Old Mapoon ◎ *Australia* 11°5S 142°22E **280** A3
Old Panamao *Phil.* 5°59N 121°13E **233** J3
Old Perlican *Canada* 48°5N 53°1W **299** C9
Old Road Bluff *Antigua & B.* 16°59N 61°50W **322** b
Old Road Town *St. Kitts & Nevis* 17°17N 62°47W **322** d
Old Roundhouse *Toronto, Canada* **141** c2
Old Shinyanga *Tanzania* 3°33S 33°27E **268** C3
Old Speck Mt. *U.S.A.* 44°34N 70°57W **313** B14
Old Town = Stare Miasto *Warsaw, Poland* **143** a2
Old Town *Edinburgh, U.K.* **121** b2
Old Town *Fla., U.S.A.* 29°36N 82°59W **317** F7
Old Town *Ill., U.S.A.* 41°54N 87°37W **119** B3
Old Town *Maine, U.S.A.* 44°56N 68°39W **309** C19
Old Town Hall = Altes Rathaus *Munich, Germany* **131** b3
Old Town Square *Warsaw, Poland* **143** a2
Old U.S. Mint *New Orleans, U.S.A.* **131** a3
Old Washington *U.S.A.* 40°2N 81°27W **312** F3
Old Wives L. *Canada* 50°5N 106°0W **297** C7
Oldbawn *Ireland* 53°17N 6°21W **120** B1
Oldbury *U.K.* 51°38N 2°33W **169** F5
Oldcastle *Ireland* 53°46N 7°10W **166** C4
Oldeani *Tanzania* 3°22S 35°35E **268** C4
Olden *Norway* 61°49N 6°49E **164** C3
Oldenburg *Niedersachsen, Germany* 53°9N 8°13E **178** B4
Oldenburg *Schleswig-Holstein, Germany* 54°17N 10°52E **178** A6
Oldenzaal *Neths.* 52°19N 6°53E **170** B6
Oldham *U.K.* 53°33N 2°7W **168** D5
Oldman → *Canada* 49°57N 111°42W **296** D6
Oldmeldrum *U.K.* 57°20N 2°19W **167** D6
Olds *Canada* 51°50N 114°10W **296** C6
Oldsmar *U.S.A.* 28°2N 82°39W **317** G7
Olduvai Gorge *Tanzania* 2°57S 35°23E **268** C4
Öldziyt *Mongolia* 44°40N 109°1E **226** B5
Ole Rømer Land *Greenland* 74°10N 24°30W **154** C8
Olean *U.S.A.* 42°5N 78°26W **312** D6
Oleby *Sweden* 60°8N 13°2E **162** D7
Olecko *Poland* 54°2N 22°31E **184** D9
Oléggio *Italy* 45°36N 8°38E **198** C5
Oleiros = O Real *Spain* 43°20N 8°19W **194** B2
Oleiros *Portugal* 39°56N 7°56W **194** F3
Olekma → *Russia* 60°22N 120°42E **215** C13
Olekminsk *Russia* 60°25N 120°30E **215** C13
Oleksandrivka *Ukraine* 48°55N 32°20E **189** H7
Oleksandriya *Kirovohrad, Ukraine* 48°42N 33°3E **189** H7
Oleksandriya *Rivne, Ukraine* 50°37N 26°19E **177** C14
Olema *U.S.A.* 38°3N 122°47W **306** G4
Ølen *Norway* 59°36N 5°48E **164** E2
Olenegorsk *Russia* 68°9N 33°18E **160** B25
Olenek *Russia* 68°28N 112°18E **215** C12
Olenek → *Russia* 73°0N 120°10E **215** B13
Olenino *Russia* 56°15N 33°30E **188** D7
Olenya = Olenegorsk *Russia* 68°9N 33°18E **160** B25
Oléron, Î. d' *France* 45°55N 1°15W **174** C2
Olesk *Ukraine* 51°6N 24°11E **185** G11
Oleśnica *Poland* 51°13N 17°22E **185** G4
Olesno *Poland* 50°51N 18°26E **185** H5
Oleta River State Rec. Area *U.S.A.* 25°55N 80°8W **129** C3
Olevsk *Ukraine* 51°12N 27°39E **177** C14
Olga, L. *Canada* 49°47N 77°15W **298** C4
Olgas, The = Kata Tjuta *Australia* 25°20S 130°50E **279** E5
Olgino *Russia* 60°0N 30°10E **137** B1
Ölgiy *Mongolia* 48°56N 89°57E **217** C11
Ølgod *Denmark* 55°49N 8°36E **163** J2
Olhão *Portugal* 37°3N 7°48W **195** H3
Olhopil *Ukraine* 48°12N 29°30E **183** B14
Olhovatka *Russia* 54°30N 22°18E **184** D9
Olib *Croatia* 44°23N 14°44E **199** D11
Oliena *Italy* 40°16N 9°24E **200** B2
Oliete *Spain* 41°1N 0°41W **196** D4
Olifants = Elefantes → *Africa* 24°10S 32°40E **271** B5
Olifants → *Namibia* 25°30S 19°30E **270** B2
Olifantshoek *S. Africa* 27°57S 22°42E **270** C3
Ólimbos *Greece* 35°44N 27°11E **205** F9
Ólimbos, Óros = Olymbos Oros *Greece* 40°6N 22°23E **202** F6
Olímpia *Brazil* 20°44S 48°54W **335** A6
Olimpico, Estadio *Mexico* 19°20N 99°11W **128** C1
Olimpos-Beydaglari △ *Turkey* 36°36N 30°30E **205** E12
Olin *U.S.A.* 42°0N 91°9W **310** B5
Olinda *Brazil* 8°1S 34°51W **332** C5
Olite *Spain* 42°29N 1°40W **196** C3
Oliva *Argentina* 32°0S 63°38W **334** C3
Oliva *Spain* 38°58N 0°9W **197** G4
Oliva de la Frontera *Spain* 38°17N 6°54W **195** G4
Olivais *Portugal* 38°45N 9°7W **126** A2
Olivar de los Padres *Mexico* 19°21N 99°14W **128** B1
Olivar del Conde *Mexico* 19°22N 99°12W **128** B1
Olivares, Cerro los *Argentina* 30°18S 69°55W **334** C2
Olivares de Júcar *Spain* 39°46N 2°20W **196** F2
Olive Branch *U.S.A.* 34°57N 89°49W **315** D10
Olive Hill *U.S.A.* 38°18N 83°13W **311** F13
Olive Park *Chicago, U.S.A.* **119** b3
Olivehurst *U.S.A.* 39°6N 121°34W **306** F5
Oliveira *Brazil* 20°39S 44°50W **333** F3
Oliveira de Azeméis *Portugal* 40°49N 8°29W **194** E2
Oliveira do Douro *Portugal* 41°5N 8°2W **194** D2
Oliveira dos Brejinhos *Brazil* 12°19S 42°54W **333** D3
Olivenza *Spain* 38°41N 7°9W **195** G3
Oliver *Canada* 49°13N 119°37W **296** D5
Oliver L. *Canada* 56°56N 103°22W **297** B8
Olives, Mt. of *West Bank* 31°46N 35°15E **123** B2
Olivet *Loiret, France* 47°51N 1°55E **173** E8
Olivet *Mich., U.S.A.* 42°27N 84°56W **311** B12
Olivia, L. *U.S.A.* 28°31N 81°31W **133** A1
Olivine Ra. *N.Z.* 44°15S 168°30E **285** E3
Olivos *Argentina* 34°30S 58°28W **117** B2
Olkhovka *Russia* 49°48N 44°32E **190** F7
Olkusz *Poland* 50°18N 19°33E **185** H6
Ollachea *Peru* 13°49S 70°29W **330** C3
Ollagüe *Chile* 21°15S 68°10W **334** A2
Ollombo *Congo* 1°18S 15°53E **264** C3
Olloua *Congo* 0°54S 14°34E **264** C2
Olmaliq *Uzbekistan* 40°50N 69°35E **217** D7
Olmedo *Spain* 41°20N 4°43W **194** D6
Olmeto *France* 41°43N 8°55E **175** G12
Olmos *Peru* 5°59S 79°46W **330** B2
Olmütz = Olomouc *Czech Rep.* 49°38N 17°12E **181** B10
Olney *Ill., U.S.A.* 38°44N 88°5W **311** F8
Olney *Tex., U.S.A.* 33°22N 98°45W **314** E5
Olofström *Sweden* 56°17N 14°32E **163** H8
Oloitokitok *Kenya* 2°56S 37°30E **268** C4
Ololi *Congo* 0°15S 14°36E **264** C2
Oloma *Cameroon* 3°29N 11°19E **263** E7
Olomane → *Canada* 50°14N 60°37W **299** B7
Olomouc *Czech Rep.* 49°38N 17°12E **181** B10
Olomoucký □ *Czech Rep.* 49°45N 17°15E **181** B10
Olona → *Italy* 45°29N 9°6E **128** B1
Olonets *Russia* 61°0N 32°54E **188** B7
Olongapo *Phil.* 14°50N 120°18E **232** D3
Olonne-sur-Mer *France* 46°32N 1°47W **174** B2
Oloron, Gave d' → *France* 43°33N 1°5W **174** E2
Oloron-Ste-Marie *France* 43°11N 0°38W **174** E3
Olosega *Amer. Samoa* 14°10S 169°37W **302** g
Olosenga = Swains I. *Amer. Samoa* 11°11S 171°4W **289** J11
Olot *Spain* 42°11N 2°30E **196** C7
Olovo *Bos.-H.* 44°8N 18°35E **182** F3
Olovyannaya *Russia* 50°58N 115°35E **215** D12
Oloy → *Russia* 66°29N 159°29E **215** C16
Olsberg *Germany* 51°21N 8°31E **178** D4
Olshammar *Sweden* 58°45N 14°48E **163** F8
Olshanka *Ukraine* 48°16N 30°58E **189** H6
Olshany *Ukraine* 50°3N 35°53E **189** G8
Olsztyn *Poland* 53°48N 20°29E **184** E7
Olsztynek *Poland* 53°34N 20°19E **184** E7
Olt □ *Romania* 44°20N 24°30E **183** F9
Olt → *Romania* 43°43N 24°51E **183** G9
Oltedal *Norway* 58°49N 6°2E **164** F3
Olten *Switz.* 47°21N 7°53E **179** H3
Olteniţa *Romania* 44°7N 26°42E **183** F11
Olton *U.S.A.* 34°11N 102°8W **314** D3
Oltu *Turkey* 40°35N 41°58E **213** B9
Oluan Pi *Taiwan* 21°53N 120°51E **225** E2
Oluanpi *Taiwan* 21°54N 120°51E **225** E2
Olula del Río *Spain* 37°21N 2°18W **197** H2
Olur *Turkey* 40°49N 42°8E **213** B10
Olustee *U.S.A.* 30°12N 82°26W **316** E7
Olutanga *Phil.* 7°26N 122°54E **233** H4
Olutanga I. *Phil.* 7°22N 122°52E **233** H4
Olvega *Spain* 41°47N 2°0W **196** D2
Olvera *Spain* 36°55N 5°18W **195** J5
Olymbos *Cyprus* 35°21N 33°45E **207** E9
Olymbos Oros *Greece* 40°6N 22°23E **202** F6
Olympia *Greece* 37°39N 21°39E **204** D3
Olympia *London, U.K.* **125** c1
Olympia *Wash., U.S.A.* 47°3N 122°53W **306** D4
Olympia, L. *U.S.A.* 28°34N 81°31W **133** A1
Olympic △ *U.S.A.* 47°45N 123°43W **306** C3
Olympic Dam *Australia* 30°30S 136°55E **282** A2
Olympic Green *China* 39°59N 116°23E **114** B2
Olympic Mts. *U.S.A.* 47°55N 123°45W **306** C3
Olympic Stadium = Turner Field *Atlanta, U.S.A.* 33°44N 84°23W **113** B2
Olympic Stadium *Beijing, China* 39°59N 116°23E **114** B2
Olympic Stadium *Helsinki, Finland* 60°11N 24°55E **121** B2
Olympique, Stade *Montréal, Canada* 45°33N 73°33W **130** A2
Olympus *Cyprus* 34°56N 32°52E **207** E8
Olympus, Mt. = Olymbos Oros *Greece* 40°6N 22°23E **202** F6
Olympus, Mt. = Uludağ *Turkey* 40°4N 29°13E **203** F13
Olympus, Mt. *U.S.A.* 47°48N 123°43W **306** C3
Olyphant *U.S.A.* 41°27N 75°36W **313** E9
Olyutorskiy, Mys *Russia* 59°55N 170°27E **215** D18
Om → *Russia* 54°59N 73°22E **217** B8
Om Hajer *Eritrea* 14°20N 36°41E **257** E4
Om Koi *Thailand* 17°48N 98°22E **236** D2
Ōma *Japan* 41°45N 141°5E **220** D10
Ōmachi *Japan* 36°30N 137°50E **223** A9
Omae-Zaki *Japan* 34°36N 138°14E **223** C10
Ōmagari = Daisen *Japan* 39°27N 140°29E **220** E10
Omagh *U.K.* 54°36N 7°19W **166** B4
Omagh □ *U.K.* 54°35N 7°15W **166** B4
Omaha *U.S.A.* 41°17N 95°58W **308** E6
Omaheke □ *Namibia* 21°30S 19°0E **270** B2
Omak *U.S.A.* 48°25N 119°31W **304** B4
Omalos *Greece* 35°19N 23°55E **207** E4
Omalur *India* 11°44N 78°4E **245** J4
Oman ■ *Asia* 23°0N 58°0E **249** B7
Oman, G. of *Asia* 24°30N 58°30E **247** E8
Omapere *N.Z.* 35°37S 173°25E **284** B2
Omar Combon *Somalia* 3°10N 45°47E **267** D6
Omaruru *Namibia* 21°26S 16°0E **270** B2
Omaruru → *Namibia* 22°7S 14°15E **270** B1
Omate *Peru* 16°45S 71°0W **330** D3
Ombai, Selat *Indonesia* 8°30S 124°50E **231** F6
Ombella-Mpoko □ *C.A.R.* 5°30N 17°30E **264** A3
Omboué *Gabon* 1°35S 9°15E **264** C1
Ombrone → *Italy* 42°42N 11°5E **198** F8
Omchi *Chad* 21°22N 17°53E **259** D3
Omdurmân *Sudan* 15°40N 32°28E **257** D3
Ōme *Japan* 35°47N 139°15E **223** B11
Omega *U.S.A.* 31°21N 83°36W **316** D6
Omegna *Italy* 45°53N 8°24E **198** C5
Omemee *Canada* 44°18N 78°33W **312** B6
Omeo *Australia* 37°6S 147°36E **283** D7
Omeonga *Dem. Rep. of the Congo* 3°40S 24°22E **264** C4
Ometepe, I. de *Nic.* 11°32N 85°35W **320** D2
Ometepec *Mexico* 16°41N 98°25W **319** D5
Ōmi-Shima *Ehime, Japan* 34°15N 133°0E **222** C5
Ōmi-Shima *Yamaguchi, Japan* 34°25N 131°9E **222** C3
Omihachiman *Japan* 35°7N 136°3E **223** B8
Omin *Micronesia* 9°36N 138°9E **287** R16
Ominato *Japan* 41°17N 141°10E **220** D10
Omineca → *Canada* 56°3N 124°16W **296** B4
Omineca Mts. *Canada* 56°30N 125°30W **296** B3
Omiš *Croatia* 43°28N 16°40E **199** E13
Omišalj *Croatia* 45°13N 14°32E **199** C11
Omitara *Namibia* 22°16S 18°2E **270** B2
Ōmiya = Saitama *Japan* 35°54N 139°38E **223** B11
Ommaney, C. *U.S.A.* 56°10N 134°40W **303** H14
Omme Å → *Denmark* 55°56N 8°32E **163** J2
Ommen *Neths.* 52°31N 6°26E **170** B6
Ömnögovĭ □ *Mongolia* 43°15N 104°0E **226** C3
Omo → *Ethiopia* 6°25N 36°10E **257** F4
Omo △ *Ethiopia* 5°54N 35°55E **257** F4
Omo Valley *Ethiopia* 5°7N 36°0E **257** F4
Omodeo, L. *Italy* 40°8N 8°56E **200** B1
Omodhos *Cyprus* 34°51N 32°48E **207** E11
Omoï *Congo* 2°56S 13°13E **264** C2
Omoko *Nigeria* 5°19N 6°40E **263** D6
Omolon → *Russia* 68°42N 158°36E **215** C16
Omona *Solomon Is.* 7°30S 158°43E **287** L10
Omonia Square *Athens, Greece* **112** b1
Omono-Gawa → *Japan* 39°46N 140°3E **220** E10
Ōmori *Japan* 35°34N 139°43E **140** B3
Ompha *Canada* 45°0N 76°50W **313** B8
Omsk *Russia* 55°0N 73°12E **217** B8
Omsukchan *Russia* 62°32N 155°48E **215** C16
Ōmu *Japan* 44°34N 142°58E **220** B11
Omul, Vf. *Romania* 45°27N 25°29E **183** E10
Omulew → *Poland* 53°5N 21°33E **185** E8
Ōmura *Japan* 32°56N 129°57E **222** E1
Ōmura-Wan *Japan* 32°57N 129°52E **222** E1
Omuramba Omatako → *Namibia* 17°45S 20°25E **270** A2
Omuramba Ovambo → *Namibia* 18°45S 16°59E **270** A2
Omurtag *Bulgaria* 43°8N 26°26E **203** C10
Omusati □ *Namibia* 18°30S 15°0E **270** A1
Ōmuta *Japan* 33°5N 130°26E **222** D2
Omuthiya *Namibia* 17°43S 16°13E **270** A2
On-ma-thi *Burma* 22°17N 96°41E **241** D6
On-Take *Japan* 31°35N 130°39E **222** F2
Oña *Spain* 42°43N 3°25W **194** C7
Ona *Fla., U.S.A.* 27°29N 81°55W **317** H8
Ona Dikonde *Dem. Rep. of the Congo* 3°51S 24°11E **264** C4
Onaga *U.S.A.* 39°29N 96°10W **308** F5
Onalaska *U.S.A.* 43°53N 91°14W **308** D8
Onancock *U.S.A.* 37°43N 75°45W **309** G16
Onangue, L. *Gabon* 0°57S 10°4E **264** C1
Onaping L. *Canada* 47°3N 81°30W **298** C3
Onarga *U.S.A.* 40°43N 88°1W **310** D8
Oñati *Spain* 43°3N 2°25W **196** B2
Onavas *Mexico* 28°31N 109°35W **318** B3
Onawa *U.S.A.* 42°2N 96°6W **308** D5
Oncócua *Angola* 16°30S 13°25E **265** F2
Onda *Spain* 39°55N 0°17W **196** F4
Ondangwa *Namibia* 17°57S 16°4E **270** A2
Ondarroa *Spain* 43°19N 2°25W **196** B2
Ondas → *Brazil* 12°8S 44°55W **333** D3
Ondava → *Slovak Rep.* 48°27N 21°48E **181** C14
Ondjiva *Angola* 16°48S 15°50E **265** F3
Ondo *Japan* 34°11N 132°32E **222** C4
Ondo *Nigeria* 7°4N 4°47E **263** D5
Ondo □ *Nigeria* 6°45N 5°0E **263** D6
Öndörhaan *Mongolia* 47°19N 110°39E **219** B11
Öndverðarnes *Iceland* 64°52N 24°0W **155** C2
One and a Half Degree Channel *Maldives* 1°30N 73°20E **272** d
One Arm Point *Australia* 16°26S 123°3E **278** C3
One Arm Point ◎ *Australia* 16°31S 122°53E **278** C3
One Prudential Plaza *Chicago, U.S.A.* **119** c2
One Tree *Australia* 34°11S 144°43E **281** E3
One World Trade Center *New York, U.S.A.* 40°43N 74°1W **132** e1
Oneata *Fiji* 18°26S 178°25W **287** B3
Oneco *U.S.A.* 27°25N 82°31W **317** H7
Onega *Russia* 64°0N 38°10E **186** B6
Onega → *Russia* 63°58N 38°2E **186** B6
Onega, G. of = Onezhskaya Guba *Russia* 64°24N 36°38E **186** B6
Onega, L. = Onezhskoye Ozero *Russia* 61°44N 35°22E **188** B8
Onehunga *N.Z.* 36°55S 174°48E **284** C3
Oneida *Ill., U.S.A.* 41°4N 90°13W **310** C6
Oneida *N.Y., U.S.A.* 43°6N 75°39W **313** C9
Oneida L. *U.S.A.* 43°12N 75°54W **313** C9
O'Neill *U.S.A.* 42°27N 98°39W **308** D4
Onekotan, Ostrov *Russia* 49°25N 154°45E **215** E16
Onema *Dem. Rep. of the Congo* 4°35S 24°30E **265** C4
Oneonta *U.S.A.* 42°27N 75°4W **313** D9
Onerahi *N.Z.* 35°45S 174°22E **284** B3
Oneroa *Cook Is.* 21°15S 159°43W **289** h
Onești *Romania* 46°17N 26°47E **183** D11
Onezhskaya Guba *Russia* 64°24N 36°38E **186** B6
Onezhskoye Ozero *Russia* 61°44N 35°22E **188** B8
Ongarue *N.Z.* 38°42S 175°19E **284** E4
Ongea Levu = Ogea Levu *Fiji* 19°8S 178°24W **287** B3
Ongers → *S. Africa* 31°4S 23°13E **270** D3
Ongerup *Australia* 33°58S 118°28E **279** F2
Ongi *Mongolia* 45°27N 103°54E **226** B3
Ongjin *N. Korea* 37°56N 125°21E **224** D2
Ongkharak *Thailand* 14°8N 101°1E **236** E3
Ongniud Qi *China* 43°0N 118°38E **227** C10
Ongoka *Dem. Rep. of the Congo* 1°20S 26°0E **268** C2
Ongole *India* 15°33N 80°2E **245** G5
Ongon = Havirga *Mongolia* 45°41N 113°5E **226** B7
Ongouendjo *Gabon* 1°23S 9°5E **264** C1
Ongoujou *Comoros Is.* 12°18S 44°30E **272** a
Ongtüstik Qazaqstan □ *Kazakhstan* 43°0N 68°0E **217** D7
Ongwediva *Namibia* 17°47S 15°46E **270** A2
Oni *Georgia* 42°33N 43°26E **191** J6
Onida *U.S.A.* 44°42N 100°4W **308** C3
Onilahy → *Madag.* 23°34S 43°45E **272** C1
Onima *Bonaire* 12°15N 68°19W **322** h
Onisigun *Nigeria* 6°35N 3°24E **124** A2
Onitsha *Nigeria* 6°6N 6°42E **263** D6
Onna *Japan* 26°29N 127°51E **288** a
Ono *Fiji* 18°55S 178°29E **287** B2
Ono *Fukui, Japan* 35°59N 136°29E **223** B8
Ono *Hyōgo, Japan* 34°51N 134°56E **222** C6
Onoda *Japan* 33°59N 131°11E **222** C3
Onohara *Japan* 34°5N 133°40E **222** C5
Onoke, L. *N.Z.* 41°22S 175°8E **284** H4
Onomichi *Japan* 34°25N 133°12E **222** C5
Onotoa *Kiribati* 1°52S 175°34E **277** A14
Ons, I. de *Spain* 42°23N 8°55W **194** C2
Onsala *Sweden* 57°26N 12°0E **163** G6
Onslow *Australia* 21°40S 115°12E **278** D2
Onslow B. *U.S.A.* 34°20N 77°15W **315** D16
Ontake-San *Japan* 35°53N 137°29E **223** B9
Ontar *Vanuatu* 14°17S 167°27E **287** D5
Ontario *Calif., U.S.A.* 34°4N 117°39W **307** L9
Ontario *Oreg., U.S.A.* 44°2N 116°58W **304** D5
Ontario □ *Canada* 48°0N 83°0W **298** B2
Ontario, L. *N. Amer.* 43°20N 78°0W **312** C7
Ontario Science Centre *Canada* 43°43N 79°20W **141** A2
Ontinyent *Spain* 38°50N 0°35W **197** G4
Ontonagon *U.S.A.* 46°52N 89°19W **308** B9
Ontong Java Plateau *Pac. Oc.* 1°0N 157°0E **277** A10
Ontur *Spain* 38°38N 1°29W **197** G3
Onverwacht *Suriname* 5°35N 55°11W **329** B6
Onyx *U.S.A.* 35°41N 118°14W **307** K8
Oodaaq *Greenland* 83°40N 30°40W **154** A8
Oodnadatta *Australia* 27°33S 135°30E **281** D2
Oodweyne *Somalia* 9°25N 45°4E **267** C6
'Ō'ōkala *U.S.A.* 20°1N 155°17W **302** C6
Ōokayama *Japan* 35°36N 139°40E **140** B3
Ooku = Ōma *Japan* 41°45N 141°5E **220** D10
Ooldea *Australia* 30°27S 131°50E **279** F5
Oombulgurri *Australia* 15°15S 127°45E **278** C4
Oombulgurri ◎ *Australia* 15°10S 127°50E **278** C4
Oorindi *Australia* 20°40S 141°1E **280** C3
Oost-Vlaanderen □ *Belgium* 51°5N 3°50E **170** C3
Oostende *Belgium* 51°15N 2°54E **170** C2
Oosterhout *Neths.* 51°39N 4°47E **170** C4
Oosterschelde → *Neths.* 51°33N 4°0E **170** C4
Oosterwolde *Neths.* 53°0N 6°17E **170** B6
Oosteschelde △ *Neths.* 51°40N 3°40E **170** C3
Oostpunt *Curaçao* 12°2N 68°44W **322** g
Oostzaan Tuindorp *Neths.* 52°25N 4°54E **112** A2
Ootacamund = Udagamandalam *India* 11°30N 76°44E **245** J3
Ootha *Australia* 33°6S 147°29E **283** B7
Ootsa L. *Canada* 53°50N 126°2W **296** C3
Ooty = Udagamandalam *India* 11°30N 76°44E **245** J3
Op Luang △ *Thailand* 18°12N 98°32E **236** C2
Opa-Locka *U.S.A.* 25°54N 80°15W **129** C1
Opa-Locka ✈ (OPF) *U.S.A.* 25°54N 80°16W **129** C1
Opacz *Poland* 52°10N 20°53E **143** B1
Opaka *Bulgaria* 43°28N 26°10E **203** C10
Opala *Dem. Rep. of the Congo* 0°40S 24°20E **264** C4
Opâle, Côte d' *France* 50°30N 1°30E **172** B8
Opalenica *Poland* 52°18N 16°24E **185** F3
Opan *Bulgaria* 42°13N 25°41E **203** D9
Opanake *Sri Lanka* 6°35N 80°40E **245** L5
Opapa *N.Z.* 39°47S 176°42E **284** F5
Opasatika *Canada* 49°30N 82°50W **298** C3
Opasquia ⌂ *Canada* 53°33N 93°5W **298** B1
Opatija *Croatia* 45°21N 14°17E **199** C11
Opatów *Poland* 50°50N 21°27E **185** H8
Opava *Czech Rep.* 49°57N 17°58E **181** B10
Opelika *U.S.A.* 32°39N 85°23W **316** C4
Opelousas *U.S.A.* 30°32N 92°5W **314** F8
Opémisca, L. *Canada* 49°56N 74°52W **298** C5
Opera House *Sydney, Australia* **139** a2
Opheim *U.S.A.* 48°51N 106°24W **304** B10
Ophir *U.S.A.* 63°10N 156°31W **303** E8
Ophirton *S. Africa* 26°13S 28°1E **123** B2
Ophthalmia Ra. *Australia* 23°15S 119°30E **278** D2
Opi *Nigeria* 6°36N 7°28E **263** D6
Opihikao *U.S.A.* 19°26N 154°53W **302** D7
Opinaca → *Canada* 52°15N 78°2W **298** B4
Opinaca, Rés. *Canada* 52°39N 76°20W **298** B4
Opinnagau → *Canada* 54°12N 82°25W **298** B3
Opiscotéo, L. *Canada* 53°10N 68°10W **299** B6
Opobo *Nigeria* 4°35N 7°34E **263** E6
Opochka *Russia* 56°42N 28°45E **188** D5
Opoczno *Poland* 51°22N 20°18E **185** G7
Opol *Phil.* 8°31N 124°34E **233** G5
Opole *Poland* 50°42N 17°58E **185** H4
Opole Lubelskie *Poland* 51°9N 21°58E **185** G8
Opolskie □ *Poland* 50°30N 18°0E **185** H5
Opon = Lapu-Lapu *Phil.* 10°20N 123°55E **233** F4
Oponono L. *Namibia* 18°8S 15°45E **270** A2
Opornyy = Borankul *Kazakhstan* 46°11N 54°25E **216** C4
Oporto = Porto *Portugal* 41°8N 8°40W **194** D2
Opotiki *N.Z.* 38°1S 177°19E **284** E6
Opp *U.S.A.* 31°17N 86°16W **316** D3
Oppdal *Norway* 62°35N 9°41E **164** B6
Oppegård *Norway* 59°45N 10°49E **133** B3
Oppeln = Opole *Poland* 50°42N 17°58E **185** H4
Oppem *Belgium* 50°57N 4°18E **116** A1
Óppido Mamertina *Italy* 38°16N 15°59E **201** D8
Oppland □ *Norway* 61°15N 9°40E **164** C6
Opportunity *U.S.A.* 47°39N 117°15W **304** C5
Oppsal *Norway* 59°53N 10°50E **133** A4
Oprişor *Romania* 44°17N 23°5E **182** F8
Oprtalj *Croatia* 45°23N 13°50E **199** C10
Opua *N.Z.* 35°19S 174°9E **284** B3
Opunake *N.Z.* 39°26S 173°52E **284** F2
Opuwo *Namibia* 18°3S 13°45E **270** A1
Opuzen *Croatia* 43°1N 17°34E **199** E14
Oquawka *U.S.A.* 40°56N 90°57W **310** D6
Or → *Kazakhstan* 51°11N 58°32E **216** B5
Or, Côte d' *France* 47°10N 4°50E **173** E11
Ora *Cyprus* 34°51N 33°12E **207** F9
Ora *Israel* 31°45N 35°9E **123** B1
Oracabessa *Jamaica* 18°24N 76°57W **320** a
Oracle *U.S.A.* 32°37N 110°46W **305** K8
Oracuzar *Peru* 4°42S 78°6W **328** D2
Oradea *Romania* 47°2N 21°58E **182** C6
Oradell *U.S.A.* 40°57N 74°2W **132** A1
Oradell Res. *U.S.A.* 40°57N 74°1W **132** A1
Öræfajökull *Iceland* 64°2N 16°39W **155** C10
Orahovac = Rahovec *Kosovo* 42°24N 20°40E **202** D4
Orahovica *Croatia* 45°35N 17°52E **182** E2
Orai *India* 25°58N 79°30E **243** G8
Oraison *France* 43°55N 5°55E **175** E9
Oral = Zhayyq → *Kazakhstan* 47°0N 51°48E **187** E9
Oral *Kazakhstan* 51°20N 51°20E **190** E10
Oran *Algeria* 35°45N 0°39W **261** A4
Oran □ *Algeria* 35°0N 0°45W **261** A4
Orang △ *India* 26°37N 92°29E **241** B4
Orange *N.S.W., Australia* 33°15S 149°7E **283** B8
Orange *Vaucluse, France* 44°8N 4°47E **175** D8
Orange *Calif., U.S.A.* 33°47N 117°51W **307** M9
Orange *Mass., U.S.A.* 42°35N 72°19W **313** D12
Orange *Tex., U.S.A.* 30°6N 93°44W **314** F8
Orange *Va., U.S.A.* 38°15N 78°7W **309** F14
Orange → *S. Africa* 28°41S 16°28E **270** C2
Orange, C. *Brazil* 4°20N 51°30W **329** C7
Orange City *U.S.A.* 28°57N 81°18W **317** G8
Orange Cove *U.S.A.* 36°38N 119°19W **306** J7
Orange Free State = Free State □ *S. Africa* 28°30S 27°0E **270** C4
Orange Grove *U.S.A.* 27°58N 97°56W **314** H6
Orange Hill *Barbados* 13°12N 59°36W **323** r
Orange Hill *Jamaica* 18°16N 77°59W **320** a
Orange Hill *St. Vincent* 13°19N 61°7W **323** n
Orange L. *U.S.A.* 29°25N 82°13W **317** F7
Orange Park *U.S.A.* 30°10N 81°42W **316** E8
Orange River Colony = Free State □ *S. Africa* 28°30S 27°0E **270** C4
Orange Walk *Belize* 18°6N 88°33W **319** D7
Orangeburg *U.S.A.* 33°30N 80°52W **316** B9
Orangeville *Ont., Canada* 43°55N 80°5W **312** C4
Orangeville *Ill., U.S.A.* 42°28N 89°39W **310** B7
Orangi *Pakistan* 24°54N 67°0E **123** A2
Orango *Guinea-Biss.* 11°5N 16°0W **262** C1
Orani *Italy* 40°15N 9°11E **200** B2
Orani *Phil.* 14°49N 120°32E **232** D3
Oranienburg *Germany* 52°45N 13°14E **178** C9
Oranje = Orange → *S. Africa* 28°41S 16°28E **270** C2
Oranjemund *Namibia* 28°38S 16°29E **270** C2
Oranjerivier *S. Africa* 29°40S 24°12E **270** C3
Oranjestad *Aruba* 12°32N 70°2W **322** f
Oranjestad *St. Eustatius* 17°28N 62°59W **322** a
Orap *Vanuatu* 15°58S 167°20E **287** E5
Oras *Phil.* 12°9N 125°28E **232** E5
Orašje *Bos.-H.* 45°1N 18°42E **182** E3
Orăştie *Romania* 45°50N 23°10E **183** E8
Orava → *Slovak Rep.* 49°9N 19°8E **181** B12
Orava, Vodna nádrž *Slovak Rep.* 49°25N 19°35E **181** B12
Oraviţa *Romania* 45°2N 21°43E **182** E6
Orawia *N.Z.* 46°1S 167°50E **285** G2
Orb → *France* 43°15N 3°18E **174** E7
Orba → *Italy* 44°53N 8°37E **198** D5
Ørbæk *Denmark* 55°17N 10°39E **163** J4
Orbe *Switz.* 46°43N 6°32E **179** J2
Orbec *France* 49°1N 0°23E **172** C7
Orbetello *Italy* 42°27N 11°13E **199** F8
Órbigo → *Spain* 42°5N 5°42W **194** C5
Orbisonia *U.S.A.* 40°15N 77°54W **312** F7
Orbost *Australia* 37°40S 148°29E **283** D8
Örbyhus *Sweden* 60°15N 17°43E **162** D11
Orcadas *Antarctica* 60°44S 44°37W **151** C18
Orcas I. *U.S.A.* 48°42N 122°56W **306** B4
Orce *Spain* 37°44N 2°28W **197** H2
Orce → *Spain* 37°44N 2°28W **197** H2
Orchard City *U.S.A.* 38°50N 107°58W **304** G10
Orchard Homes *U.S.A.* 46°55N 114°4W **304** C6
Orchard Road *Singapore* **138** a1
Orchid I. = Lan Yü *Taiwan* 22°4N 121°25E **225** D3
Orchies *France* 50°28N 3°14E **173** B10
Orchila, I. *Venezuela* 11°48N 66°10W **321** D6
Orcia → *Italy* 42°58N 11°21E **199** F8
Orco → *Italy* 45°10N 7°52E **198** C4
Orcopampa *Peru* 15°20S 72°23W **330** D3
Orcutt *U.S.A.* 34°52N 120°27W **307** L6
Ord *U.S.A.* 41°36N 98°56W **308** E4
Ord → *Australia* 15°33S 128°15E **278** C4
Ord, Mt. *Australia* 17°20S 125°34E **278** C4
Ord Mts. *U.S.A.* 34°39N 116°45W **307** L10
Ordenes = Ordes *Spain* 43°5N 8°29W **194** B2
Orderville *U.S.A.* 37°17N 112°38W **305** H7
Ordes *Spain* 43°5N 8°29W **194** B2
Ordesa y Monte Perido △ *Spain* 42°40N 0°10W **196** C4
Ording = Sankt Peter-Ording *Germany* 54°20N 8°36E **178** A4
Ordos = Mu Us Shamo *China* 39°0N 109°0E **226** E5
Ordrup *Denmark* 55°45N 12°34E **118** A3
Ordu *Turkey* 40°55N 37°53E **212** B7
Ordu □ *Turkey* 41°0N 37°50E **212** B7
Ordubad *Azerbaijan* 38°54N 46°1E **213** C12
Orduña *Álava, Spain* 42°58N 2°58W **196** C2
Orduña *Granada, Spain* 37°20N 3°30W **195** H7
Ordway *U.S.A.* 38°13N 103°46W **304** G12
Ordzhonikidze = Denisovka *Kazakhstan* 52°27N 61°39E **216** B6
Ordzhonikidze = Vladikavkaz *Russia* 43°0N 44°35E **191** J7
Ordzhonikidze = Yenakiyeve *Ukraine* 48°15N 38°15E **189** H10
Ordzhonikidze *Ukraine* 47°39N 34°3E **189** J8
Ore *Dem. Rep. of the Congo* 3°17N 29°30E **268** B2
Ore Mts. = Erzgebirge *Germany* 50°27N 12°55E **178** E8
Orealla *Guyana* 5°15N 57°23W **329** B6
Orebić *Croatia* 43°0N 17°11E **199** F14
Örebro *Sweden* 59°20N 15°18E **162** E9
Örebro län □ *Sweden* 59°27N 15°0E **162** E8
Orecchiella △ *Italy* 44°16N 10°22E **198** D7
Ořech *Czech Rep.* 50°1N 14°17E **135** B1
Oregon *Ill., U.S.A.* 42°1N 89°20W **310** B7
Oregon *Ohio, U.S.A.* 41°38N 83°25W **311** C13
Oregon *Wis., U.S.A.* 42°56N 89°23W **310** B7
Oregon □ *U.S.A.* 44°0N 121°0W **304** E3
Oregon City *U.S.A.* 45°21N 122°36W **306** E4
Oregon Dunes ⌂ *U.S.A.* 43°40N 124°10W **304** E1
Öregrund *Sweden* 60°21N 18°30E **162** D12
Öregrundsgrepen *Sweden* 60°25N 18°15E **162** D12
Oregun *Nigeria* 6°35N 3°22E **124** A2
Orekhov = Orikhiv *Ukraine* 47°30N 35°48E **189** J8
Orekhovo-Zuyevo *Russia* 55°50N 38°55E **188** E10
Orel *Russia* 52°57N 36°3E **189** F9
Orel □ *Russia* 52°30N 36°40E **189** F9
Orellana □ *Ecuador* 0°45S 76°25W **328** D2
Orellana, Canal de *Spain* 39°2N 6°0W **195** F5
Orellana, Embalse de *Spain* 39°5N 5°10W **195** F5
Orellana la Vieja *Spain* 39°1N 5°32W **195** F5
Orem *U.S.A.* 40°19N 111°42W **304** F8
Ören *Turkey* 37°3N 27°57E **205** D9
Orenburg *Russia* 51°45N 55°6E **187** D10
Örencik *Turkey* 39°16N 29°33E **205** B11
Orense = Ourense *Spain* 42°19N 7°55W **194** C3
Orepuki *N.Z.* 46°19S 167°46E **285** G2
Orestad *Denmark* 55°38N 12°35E **118** B3
Orestes Pereyra *Mexico* 26°30N 105°39W **318** B3
Orestiada *Greece* 41°30N 26°33E **203** E10
Øresund *Europe* 55°45N 12°40E **163** J6
Oretana, Cordillera = Toledo, Montes de *Spain* 39°33N 4°20W **195** F6
Oreti → *N.Z.* 46°28S 168°14E **285** G3
Orfanos Kolpos *Greece* 40°33N 24°0E **202** F7
Orford Ness *U.K.* 52°5N 1°35E **169** E9
Organ Pipe Cactus ⌂ *U.S.A.* 32°0N 112°52W **305** K7
Organos, Pta. de los *Canary Is.* 28°12N 17°17W **153** e1

Organyà Spain 42°13N 1°20E 196 C6
Orgaz Spain 39°39N 3°53W 195 F7
Ørgenvika Norway 60°17N 9°42E 164 D6
Orgeyev = Orhei
Moldova 47°24N 28°50E 183 C13
Orgiva Spain 36°53N 3°24W 195 J7
Orgūn Afghan. 32°55N 69°12E 240 B3
Orhaneli Turkey 39°54N 28°59E 203 G12
Orhaneli → Turkey 39°50N 28°55E 203 G12
Orhangazi Turkey 40°29N 29°18E 203 F13
Orhei Moldova 47°24N 28°50E 183 C13
Orhon Gol → Mongolia 50°21N 106°0E 218 A10
Ória Italy 40°30N 17°38E 201 B10
Orida Niger 21°20N 12°15E 261 D7
Orient Heights U.S.A. 42°23N 70°59W 116 A3
Oriental □ Morocco 33°0N 2°0W 261 B4
Oriental, Cordillera Bolivia 17°0S 66°0W 331 D4
Oriental, Cordillera Colombia 6°0N 73°0W 328 B3
Oriental, Grand Erg Algeria 30°0N 6°30E 261 B6
Oriental Pearl Tower
Shanghai, China 31°14N 121°30E 138 B2
Orientale □
Dem. Rep. of the Congo 2°20N 26°0E 268 B2
Oriente Argentina 38°44S 60°37W 334 D3
Orihuela Spain 38°7N 0°55W 197 G4
Orihuela del Tremedal
Spain 40°33N 1°39W 196 E3
Orikhiv Ukraine 47°30N 35°48E 189 J8
Orikum Albania 40°20N 19°26E 202 F3
Oril → Ukraine 48°40N 34°39E 189 H8
Orillia Canada 44°40N 79°24W 312 B5
Orinduik Guyana 4°40N 60°3W 329 C5
Orinoco → Venezuela 9°15N 61°30W 329 B5
Orinoco, Delta del
Venezuela 9°0N 61°30W 329 B5
Orion Canada 49°27N 110°49W 297 D6
Orion Ala., U.S.A. 31°58N 86°0W 316 D4
Orion Ill., U.S.A. 41°21N 90°23W 310 C6
Oriskany U.S.A. 43°10N 75°20W 313 C9
Orissa = Odisha □ India 20°0N 84°0E 244 E7
Orissaare Estonia 58°34N 23°5E 188 C2
Oristano Italy 39°54N 8°36E 200 C1
Oristano, G. di Italy 39°50N 8°29E 200 C1
Orituco → Venezuela 8°45N 67°27W 328 B4
Oriximiná Brazil 1°45S 55°52W 329 D6
Orizaba Mexico 18°51N 97°6W 319 D5
Orizaba, Pico de Mexico 18°58N 97°15W 319 D5
Orizare Bulgaria 42°44N 27°39E 203 D11
Orizona Brazil 17°3S 48°18W 333 E2
Ørje Norway 59°29N 11°39E 164 E8
Orjen Bos.-H. 42°35N 18°34E 202 D2
Orjiva = Orgiva Spain 36°53N 3°24W 195 J7
Orkanger Norway 63°18N 9°52E 164 A6
Örkelljunga Sweden 56°17N 13°17E 163 H7
Örken Sweden 57°6N 15°1E 163 G9
Örkény Hungary 47°9N 19°26E 182 C4
Orkhaniye = Botevgrad
Bulgaria 42°55N 23°47E 202 D7
Orkhon = Orhon Gol →
Mongolia 50°21N 106°0E 218 A10
Orkla → Norway 63°18N 9°51E 164 A6
Orkney S. Africa 26°58S 26°40E 270 C4
Orkney □ U.K. 59°2N 3°13W 167 B5
Orkney Is. U.K. 59°0N 3°0W 167 B6
Orland Calif., U.S.A. 39°45N 122°12W 306 F4
Orland Ind., U.S.A. 41°47N 85°12W 311 C11
Orland Park U.S.A. 41°38N 87°52W 119 D2
Orlando U.S.A. 28°32N 81°22W 133 A2
Orlando, C. d' Italy 38°10N 14°43E 201 D7
Orlando Dam S. Africa 26°15S 27°55E 123 B1
Orlando East S. Africa 26°14S 27°55E 123 B1
Orlando Executive ✕ (ORL)
U.S.A. 28°32N 81°20W 133 A2
Orlando Int. ✕ (MCO)
U.S.A. 28°26N 81°19W 133 B3
Orléanais France 48°0N 2°0E 173 E9
Orléans Loiret, France 47°54N 1°52E 173 E8
Orleans Ind., U.S.A. 38°40N 86°27W 311 F10
Orleans Vt., U.S.A. 44°49N 72°12W 313 B12
Orléans, Î. d' Canada 46°54N 70°58W 299 C5
Orléansville = Ech Chéliff
Algeria 36°10N 1°20E 261 A5
Orlice → Czech Rep. 50°13N 15°50E 180 A8
Orlivka Ukraine 45°19N 28°27E 183 E13
Orlov = Khalturin Russia 58°40N 48°50E 186 C8
Orlov Slovak Rep. 49°17N 20°51E 181 B13
Orlov Gay Russia 50°56N 48°19E 190 E9
Orlová Czech Rep. 49°51N 18°26E 181 B11
Orlovat Serbia 45°14N 20°33E 182 E5
Orlovista U.S.A. 28°32N 81°27W 133 A2
Orlovskoye Polesye △
Russia 58°30N 35°30E 188 F8
Orly France 48°45N 2°23E 134 B3
Orly, Paris ✕ (ORY) France 48°44N 2°23E 134 B3
Ormara Pakistan 25°16N 64°33E 240 D2
Ormea Italy 44°9N 7°54E 198 D4
Ormesson-sur-Marne
France 48°47N 2°32E 134 B4
Ormilia Greece 40°16N 23°39E 202 F7
Ormoc Phil. 11°0N 124°37E 233 F5
Ormond Vic., Australia 37°54S 145°1E 128 B2
Ormond N.Z. 38°33S 177°56E 284 E6
Ormond Beach U.S.A. 29°17N 81°3W 317 F8
Ormond-by-the-Sea
U.S.A. 29°21N 81°4W 317 F8
Ormondville N.Z. 40°5S 176°19E 284 G5
Ormøya Norway 59°52N 10°45E 133 A3
Ormož Slovenia 46°25N 16°10E 199 B13
Ormskirk U.K. 53°35N 2°54W 168 D5
Ormstown Canada 45°8N 74°0W 313 A11
Ormtjernkampen △
Norway 61°12N 9°48E 164 C6
Ornans France 47°7N 6°10E 173 E13
Orne □ France 48°40N 0°5E 172 D7
Orne → France 49°18N 0°15W 172 C6
Orneta Poland 54°8N 20°9E 184 D7
Ornö Sweden 59°4N 18°24E 162 E12
Örnsköldsvik Sweden 63°17N 18°40E 162 A12
Oro = Northern □
Papua N. G. 9°0S 148°30E 286 E5
Oro N. Korea 40°1N 127°27E 224 B3
Oro → Mexico 25°35N 105°2W 318 B3
Oro Grande U.S.A. 34°36N 117°20W 307 L9
Oro Valley U.S.A. 32°26N 110°58W 305 K8
Orobie, Alpi Italy 46°7N 10°0E 198 B6
Orobie Bergamasche ⌓
Italy 46°0N 9°45E 198 C6
Orobie Valtellinesi ⌓ Italy 46°5N 9°45E 198 B6
Orocué Colombia 4°48N 71°20W 328 C3
Orodara Burkina Faso 11°0N 4°55W 262 C4
Orodo Nigeria 5°34N 7°4E 263 D6
Orofino U.S.A. 46°29N 116°15W 304 C5
Orohena, Mt. Tahiti 17°37S 149°28W 289 e
Orol Dengizi = Aral Sea
Asia 45°0N 58°20E 216 C5
Oromiya □ Ethiopia 7°0N 40°0E 257 F5
Oromocto Canada 45°54N 66°29W 299 C6
Oron Nigeria 4°48N 8°14E 263 E6
Orona Kiribati 4°31S 172°11W 277 A16
Orongo Chile 27°11S 109°24W 330 b
Orono Ont., Canada 43°59N 78°37W 312 C6
Orono Maine, U.S.A. 44°53N 68°40W 309 C19
Oronsay U.K. 56°1N 6°15W 167 E2
Oropesa Spain 39°57N 5°10W 194 F5
Oropuche → Trin. & Tob. 10°36N 61°6W 323 t
Oropuche Lagoon
Trin. & Tob. 10°14N 61°31W 323 t
Oroquieta Phil. 8°32N 123°44E 233 G4
Orós Brazil 6°15S 38°55W 332 C4
Orosei Italy 40°23N 9°42E 200 B2
Orosei, G. di Italy 40°15N 9°44E 200 B2
Orosháza Hungary 46°32N 20°42E 182 D5
Oroszlány Hungary 47°29N 18°19E 182 C3
Orote Pen. Guam 13°26N 144°38E 302 d
Orotukan Russia 62°16N 151°42E 215 C16
Oroville Calif., U.S.A. 39°31N 121°33W 306 F5
Oroville Wash., U.S.A. 48°56N 119°26W 304 B4
Oroville, L. U.S.A. 39°33N 121°29W 306 F5
Orpington U.K. 51°22N 0°6E 125 B4
Orrefors Sweden 56°50N 15°45E 163 H9
Orrick U.S.A. 39°13N 94°7W 310 E2
Orroroo Australia 32°43S 138°38E 282 B3
Orrviken Sweden 63°6N 14°26E 162 A8
Orrville U.S.A. 40°50N 81°46W 312 F3
Orsa Sweden 61°7N 14°37E 162 C8
Orsara di Púglia Italy 41°17N 15°16E 201 A8
Orsasjön Sweden 61°7N 14°37E 162 C8
Orsay, Musée d' Paris, France 134 b3
Orsha Belarus 54°30N 30°25E 188 E6
Örsjö Sweden 56°42N 15°45E 163 H9
Orsk Russia 51°12N 58°34E 216 B5
Orşova Romania 44°41N 22°25E 182 F7
Ørsta Norway 62°13N 6°8E 164 B3
Ørsted Denmark 56°30N 10°20E 163 H4
Örsundsbro Sweden 59°44N 17°18E 162 E11
Országos Levétár Budapest, Hungary 117 b1
Orta Turkey 40°38N 33°6E 212 B5
Orta, L. d' Italy 45°49N 8°24E 198 C5
Orta Nova Italy 41°19N 15°42E 201 A8
Ortaca Turkey 36°49N 28°45E 205 E10
Ortakent Turkey 37°5N 27°21E 205 D9
Ortaklar Turkey 37°53N 27°30E 205 D9
Ortaköy Çorum, Turkey 40°16N 35°15E 212 B6
Ortaköy İstanbul, Turkey 41°3N 29°1E 122 B2
Ortaköy Niğde, Turkey 38°44N 34°3E 212 C6
Orte Italy 42°27N 12°23E 199 F9
Ortegal, C. Spain 43°43N 7°52W 194 B3
Orteguaza → Colombia 0°43N 75°16W 328 C2
Ortelsburg = Szczytno
Poland 53°33N 21°0E 184 E7
Orthez France 43°29N 0°48W 174 E3
Ortica Italy 45°28N 9°16E 128 B2
Ortigueira Spain 43°40N 7°50W 194 B3
Ortigueira, Ría de Spain 43°44N 7°45W 194 B3
Orting U.S.A. 47°6N 122°12W 306 C4
Ortisei Italy 46°34N 11°40E 199 B8
Ortles Italy 46°31N 10°33E 198 B7
Ortnevik Norway 61°6N 6°7E 164 C3
Ortoire → Trin. & Tob. 10°20N 61°0W 323 t
Ortón → Bolivia 10°50S 67°0W 330 C4
Ortona Italy 42°21N 14°24E 199 F11
Ortonville U.S.A. 45°19N 96°27W 308 C5
Oruba Nigeria 6°34N 3°24E 124 A2
Orukuizu Palau 7°10N 134°15E 288 c
Orūmīyeh Iran 37°40N 45°0E 213 D11
Orūmīyeh, Daryācheh-ye
Iran 37°50N 45°30E 213 D11
Orune Italy 40°24N 9°22E 200 B2
Oruro Bolivia 18°0S 67°9W 330 D4
Oruro □ Bolivia 18°40S 67°30W 330 D4
Orust Sweden 58°10N 11°40E 163 F5
Oruzgān □ Afghan. 33°0N 66°0E 240 B2
Orvault France 47°17N 1°38W 172 E5
Orvieto Italy 42°43N 12°7E 199 F9
Orwell N.Y., U.S.A. 43°35N 75°50W 313 C9
Orwell Ohio, U.S.A. 41°32N 80°52W 312 E4
Orwell → U.K. 51°59N 1°18E 169 F9
Orwigsburg U.S.A. 40°38N 76°6W 313 F8
Oryakhovo Bulgaria 43°40N 23°57E 202 C7
Orynyn Ukraine 48°46N 26°24E 183 B11
Oryol = Orel Russia 52°57N 36°3E 189 F9
Orzinuovi Italy 45°24N 9°55E 198 C6
Orzyc → Poland 52°46N 21°14E 185 F8
Orzysz Poland 53°50N 21°58E 184 E8
Os Norway 62°30N 11°14E 164 B8
Osa Russia 57°17N 55°26E 186 C10
Osa → Poland 53°33N 18°46E 184 E5
Osa, Pen. de Costa Rica 8°0N 84°0W 320 E3
Osage U.S.A. 43°17N 92°49W 308 D7
Osage → U.S.A. 38°36N 91°57W 310 F5
Osage City U.S.A. 38°38N 95°50W 308 F6
Ōsaka Japan 34°42N 135°30E 133 B2
Ōsaka □ Japan 34°30N 135°30E 223 C7
Ōsaka Castle Japan 34°41N 135°30E 133 A2
Ōsaka Harbour Japan 34°38N 135°25E 133 B1
Ōsaka Itami Int. ✕ (ITM)
Japan 34°46N 135°26E 133 A1
Ōsaka Kansai Int. ✕ (KIX)
Japan 34°27N 135°12E 133 B2
Ōsaka-Wan Japan 34°30N 135°18E 223 C7
Osakarovka Kazakhstan 50°33N 72°34E 217 B8
Ōsaki Kagoshima, Japan 31°25N 131°2E 222 F2
Ōsaki Miyagi, Japan 38°34N 140°58E 220 E10
Ōsaki Tōkyō, Japan 35°36N 139°42E 140 B3
Osan S. Korea 37°11N 127°4E 224 D3
Osasco Brazil 23°31S 46°46W 137 B1
Osawatomie U.S.A. 38°31N 94°57W 308 F6
Osborn Plateau Ind. Oc. 14°45S 87°0E 273 F7
Osborne U.S.A. 39°26N 98°42W 308 F4
Osby Sweden 56°23N 13°59E 163 H7
Osceola Ark., U.S.A. 35°42N 89°58W 315 D10
Osceola Iowa, U.S.A. 41°2N 93°46W 310 C3
Osceola Mo., U.S.A. 38°3N 93°42W 310 F3
Oschatz Germany 51°17N 13°6E 178 D9
Oschersleben Germany 52°2N 11°14E 178 C7
Óschiri Italy 40°43N 9°6E 200 B2
Oscoda U.S.A. 44°26N 83°20W 312 B1
Osdorf Germany 52°24N 13°20E 115 B3
Osdorp Neths. 52°22N 4°47E 112 A1
Osečina Serbia 44°23N 19°34E 202 B3
Ösel = Saaremaa Estonia 58°30N 22°30E 188 C2
Osensjøen Norway 61°13N 11°50E 164 C8
Osery Russia 54°52N 38°28E 188 E10
Osgood U.S.A. 39°8N 85°18W 311 E11
Osgoode Canada 45°8N 75°36W 313 A9
Osgoode Hall Toronto, Canada 141 b2
Osh Kyrgyzstan 40°37N 72°49E 217 D8
Osh □ Kyrgyzstan 40°0N 73°0E 217 E8
Oshana □ Namibia 17°50S 15°40E 270 A2
Oshawa Canada 43°50N 78°50W 312 C6
Oshigambo Namibia 17°45S 16°5E 270 A2
Oshika-Hantō Japan 38°20N 141°30E 220 E10
Oshikoto □ Namibia 18°30S 17°0E 270 A2
Oshivelo Namibia 18°37S 17°10E 270 A2
Oshkosh Nebr., U.S.A. 41°24N 102°21W 308 E2
Oshkosh Wis., U.S.A. 44°1N 88°33W 308 C9
Oshmyany = Ashmyany
Belarus 54°26N 25°52E 177 A13
Oshnovīyeh Iran 37°2N 45°6E 213 D11
Oshodi Nigeria 6°33N 3°21E 124 A2
Oshogbo Nigeria 7°48N 4°37E 263 D5
Oshtorīnān Iran 34°1N 48°38E 213 E13
Oshwe
Dem. Rep. of the Congo 3°25S 19°28E 264 C3
Osi Nigeria 8°8N 5°14E 263 D6
Osieczna Poland 51°55N 16°40E 185 G3
Osijek Croatia 45°34N 18°41E 182 E3
Osilo Italy 40°45N 8°40E 200 B1
Ósimo Italy 43°28N 13°29E 199 E10
Osintorf Belarus 54°40N 30°39E 188 E6
Osipenko = Berdyansk
Ukraine 46°45N 36°50E 189 J9
Osipovichi = Asipovichy
Belarus 53°19N 28°33E 177 B15
Osiyan India 26°43N 72°55E 242 F5
Osizweni S. Africa 27°49S 30°7E 271 C5
Oskaloosa U.S.A. 41°18N 92°39W 310 C4
Oskarshamn Sweden 57°15N 16°27E 163 G10
Oskarström Sweden 56°48N 12°58E 163 H6
Oskélanéo Canada 48°5N 75°15W 298 C4
Öskemen Kazakhstan 50°0N 82°36E 217 C10
Oskol → Ukraine 49°6N 37°25E 189 H9
Osku Iran 37°54N 46°8E 213 D12
Oslo Norway 59°54N 10°43E 133 A3
Oslo □ Norway 59°54N 10°43E 164 D7
Oslo ✕ (OSL) Norway 60°11N 11°6E 133 A4
Oslob Phil. 9°31N 123°26E 233 G4
Oslofjorden Norway 59°20N 10°35E 164 E7
Osmanabad India 18°5N 76°10E 244 E3
Osmancık Turkey 40°58N 34°47E 212 B6
Osmaniye Turkey 37°5N 36°10E 250 A7
Osmanlı Turkey 41°35N 26°51E 203 E10
Osmannagar India 18°32N 79°20E 244 E4
Ösmo Sweden 58°58N 17°55E 162 F11
Osnabrück Germany 52°17N 8°3E 178 C4
Ośno Lubuskie Poland 52°28N 14°51E 185 F1
Osoblaha Czech Rep. 50°17N 17°44E 181 A10
Osogbo = Oshogbo Nigeria 7°48N 4°37E 263 D5
Osogovska Planina
Macedonia 42°10N 22°30E 202 D6
Ōsone Japan 35°31N 139°37E 140 B2
Osor Italy 44°42N 14°24E 199 D11
Osório Brazil 29°53S 50°17W 335 B5
Osório da Fonseca Brazil 3°52S 58°14W 329 D6
Osorno Chile 40°25S 73°0W 336 B2
Osorno Spain 42°24N 4°22W 194 C6
Osorno □ Chile 40°34S 73°9W 336 B2
Osorno, Vol. Chile 41°0S 72°30W 336 B2
Osorun Nigeria 6°33N 3°29E 124 A2
Osoyoos Canada 49°0N 119°30W 296 D5
Osøyro Norway 60°9N 5°30E 164 D2
Óspakseyri Iceland 65°27N 21°26W 155 B5
Ospiate Italy 45°32N 9°6E 128 A1
Ospika → Canada 56°20N 124°0W 296 B4
Osprey U.S.A. 27°12N 82°29W 317 H7
Osprey Reef Australia 13°52S 146°36E 280 A4
Oss Neths. 51°46N 5°32E 170 C5
Ossa, Mt. Australia 41°52S 146°3E 281 G4
Ossa, Oros Greece 39°47N 22°42E 204 B4
Ossa de Montiel Spain 38°58N 2°45W 197 G2
Ossabaw I. U.S.A. 31°50N 81°5W 316 D8
Ossabaw Sd. U.S.A. 31°50N 81°6W 316 D8
Osse → Lot-et-Garonne,
France 44°7N 0°17E 174 D4
Osse → Nigeria 6°10N 5°20E 263 D6
Ossersee = Zarasai
Lithuania 55°40N 26°20E 188 E4
Ossi Italy 40°40N 8°35E 200 B1
Ossining U.S.A. 41°10N 73°55W 313 E11
Ossipee U.S.A. 43°41N 71°7W 313 C13
Ossokmanuan L. Canada 53°25N 65°0W 299 B7
Ossora Russia 59°20N 163°13E 215 D17
Ostankino Russia 55°49N 37°37E 129 B2
Ostashkov Russia 57°4N 33°2E 188 D7
Östavall Sweden 62°26N 15°29E 162 B9
Østby Norway 61°15N 12°33E 164 C9
Oste → Germany 53°49N 9°2E 178 B5
Ostenburg = Pultusk
Poland 52°43N 21°6E 185 F8
Ostend = Oostende
Belgium 51°15N 2°54E 170 C2
Ostend N.Z. 36°48S 175°2E 284 C4
Oster Ukraine 50°57N 30°53E 177 C16
Österbotten = Pohjanmaa □
Finland 62°58N 22°50E 160 E20
Østerbro Copenhagen, Denmark 118 a1
Osterburg Sachsen-Anhalt,
Germany 52°47N 11°45E 178 C7
Osterburg Pa., U.S.A. 40°16N 78°31W 312 F6
Osterburken Germany 49°25N 9°26E 179 F5
Österbybruk Sweden 60°13N 17°55E 162 D11
Österbymo Sweden 57°49N 15°15E 163 G9
Österdalälven → Sweden 60°30N 15°7E 162 C7
Østerdalen Norway 61°40N 10°50E 164 C7
Österfärnebo Sweden 60°19N 16°48E 162 D10
Österforse Sweden 63°9N 17°3E 162 A11
Östergötlands län □
Sweden 58°35N 15°45E 163 F9
Osterholz-Scharmbeck
Germany 53°13N 8°47E 178 B4
Østerild Denmark 57°2N 8°51E 163 G2
Osterley U.K. 51°28N 0°21W 125 B1
Osterley Park U.K. 51°29N 0°20W 125 B1
Östermalm Stockholm, Sweden 139 a3
Östermyra = Seinäjoki
Finland 62°40N 22°51E 160 E20
Osterode Germany 51°43N 10°15E 178 D6
Osterode in Ostpreussen = Ostróda
Poland 53°42N 19°58E 184 E6
Österreich = Austria ■
Europe 47°0N 14°0E 180 E7
Österreich ober der Ems =
Oberösterreich □
Austria 48°10N 14°0E 180 C7
Österskär Sweden 59°26N 18°16E 139 A3
Östersund Sweden 63°10N 14°38E 162 A8
Östervåla Sweden 60°11N 17°11E 162 D11
Østfold □ Norway 59°25N 11°25E 164 E8
Ostfriesische Inseln
Germany 53°42N 7°0E 178 B3
Ostfriesland Germany 53°20N 7°30E 178 B3
Östhammar Sweden 60°16N 18°22E 162 D12
Óstia, Lido di Italy 41°43N 12°17E 199 G9
Óstia Malpasso Italy 41°47N 12°26E 136 C1
Ostiense Italy 41°51N 12°29E 136 B1
Ostíglia Italy 45°4N 11°8E 199 C8
Östmark Sweden 60°17N 12°45E 162 D6
Østmarkkapellet Norway 59°52N 10°51E 133 A4
Østøya Norway 59°52N 10°34E 133 A2
Östra Husby Sweden 58°35N 16°33E 163 F10
Ostrava Czech Rep. 49°51N 18°18E 181 B11
Ostravský □ Czech Rep. 49°55N 17°58E 181 B10
Ostróda Poland 53°42N 19°58E 184 E6
Ostrogozhsk Russia 50°55N 39°7E 189 G10
Ostroh Ukraine 50°20N 26°30E 177 C14
Ostrołęka Poland 53°4N 21°32E 185 E8
Ostrov Bulgaria 43°40N 24°9E 203 C8
Ostrov Czech Rep. 50°18N 12°57E 180 A5
Ostrov Romania 44°6N 27°24E 183 F12
Ostrov Russia 57°25N 28°20E 188 D5
Ostrów Lubelski Poland 51°29N 22°51E 185 G9
Ostrów Mazowiecka
Poland 52°50N 21°51E 185 F8
Ostrów Wielkopolski
Poland 51°36N 17°44E 185 G4
Ostrowiec-Świętokrzyski
Poland 50°55N 21°22E 185 H8
Ostrowo = Ostrów Wielkopolski
Poland 51°36N 17°44E 185 G4
Ostrožac Bos.-H. 43°43N 17°49E 182 G2
Ostrzeszów Poland 51°25N 17°52E 185 G4
Ostseebad Kühlungsborn
Germany 54°8N 11°44E 178 A7
Osttirol □ Austria 46°50N 12°30E 180 E5
Ostuni Italy 40°44N 17°35E 201 B10
Ostyako-Vogulsk =
Khanty-Mansiysk Russia 61°0N 69°0E 214 C7
Osum → Albania 40°40N 20°10E 202 F4
Osŭm → Bulgaria 43°40N 24°50E 203 C8
Ōsumi-Hantō Japan 31°20N 130°55E 222 F2
Ōsumi-Kaikyō Japan 30°55N 131°0E 221 J5
Ōsumi-Shotō Japan 30°30N 130°0E 221 J5
Osun □ Nigeria 7°30N 4°30E 263 D5
Osuna Spain 37°14N 5°8W 195 H5
Oswegatchie → U.S.A. 44°42N 75°30W 313 B9
Oswego Ill., U.S.A. 41°41N 88°21W 311 C8
Oswego N.Y., U.S.A. 43°27N 76°31W 313 C8
Oswego → U.S.A. 43°27N 76°30W 313 C8
Oswestry U.K. 52°52N 3°3W 168 E4
Oświęcim Poland 50°2N 19°11E 185 H6
Ōta Fukui, Japan 35°57N 136°3E 223 B8
Ōta Gunma, Japan 36°18N 139°22E 223 A11
Ōta Tōkyō, Japan 35°34N 139°41E 140 B3
Ōta-Gawa → Japan 34°21N 132°18E 222 C4
Otaci Moldova 48°27N 27°47E 183 B12
Otago □ N.Z. 45°15S 170°0E 285 F5
Otago Harbour N.Z. 45°47S 170°42E 285 F5
Otago Pen. N.Z. 45°48S 170°39E 285 F5
Otaheite B. Trin. & Tob. 10°15N 61°30W 323 t
Otahuhu N.Z. 36°56S 174°51E 284 C3
Ōtake Japan 34°12N 132°13E 222 C4
Ōtaki Japan 35°17N 140°15E 223 B12
Otaki N.Z. 40°45S 175°10E 284 G4
Otane N.Z. 39°54S 176°39E 284 F5
Otaniemi Finland 60°11N 24°49E 121 B1
Otaru Japan 43°10N 141°0E 220 C10
Otaru-Wan = Ishikari-Wan
Japan 43°25N 141°1E 220 C10
Otautau N.Z. 46°9S 168°1E 285 G3
Otava → Czech Rep. 49°26N 14°12E 180 B7
Otavalo Ecuador 0°13N 78°20W 328 C2
Otavi Namibia 19°40S 17°24E 270 A2
Ōtawara Japan 36°50N 140°5E 221 F10
Otchinjau Angola 16°30S 13°56E 265 F2
Otego U.S.A. 42°23N 75°10W 313 D9
Oteiza = Marihatag Phil. 8°48N 126°18E 233 G6
Otelec Romania 45°36N 20°50E 182 E5
Otelnuk, L. Canada 56°9N 68°12W 299 A6
Oţelu Roşu Romania 45°32N 22°22E 182 E7
Otero de Rey = Outeiro de Rei
Spain 43°6N 7°36W 194 B3
Othello U.S.A. 46°50N 119°10W 304 C4
Othoni Greece 39°52N 19°22E 206 B9
Othris, Oros Greece 39°2N 22°37E 204 B4
Oti → Africa 7°48N 0°8E 263 D5
Oti ⌓ Togo 10°40N 0°35E 263 C5
Otira N.Z. 42°49S 171°35E 285 C6
Otira Gorge N.Z. 42°53S 171°33E 285 C6
Otish, Mts. Canada 52°22N 70°30W 299 B5
Otishi △ Peru 11°40S 73°59W 330 C3
Otjinene Namibia 21°8S 18°46E 270 B2
Otjiwarongo Namibia 20°30S 16°33E 270 B2
Otjozondjupa □ Namibia 21°0S 17°0E 270 B2
Otmuchów Poland 50°28N 17°10E 185 H4
Oto Tolu Group Tonga 20°21S 174°32W 287 Q13
Otočac Croatia 44°53N 15°12E 199 D12
Otoineppu Japan 44°44N 142°16E 220 B11
Otok Croatia 43°42N 16°44E 199 E13
Otomavi = Korsakov
Russia 46°36N 142°42E 215 E15
Oton Phil. 10°42N 122°29E 233 F4
Otopeni, Bucureşti ✕ (OTP)
Romania 44°30N 26°11E 183 F11
Otorohanga N.Z. 38°12S 175°14E 284 E4
Otoskwin → Canada 52°13N 88°6W 298 B2
Ōtoyo Japan 33°43N 133°45E 222 D5
Otpor = Zabaykalsk
Russia 49°40N 117°25E 215 E12
Otra → Norway 58°9N 8°1E 164 F5
Otradnyy Russia 53°22N 51°21E 190 D10
Otranto Italy 40°9N 18°28E 201 B11
Otranto, C. d' Italy 40°7N 18°30E 201 B11
Otranto, Str. of Italy 40°15N 18°40E 201 B11
Otrobanda Curaçao 12°7N 68°57W 322 g
Otrokovice Czech Rep. 49°12N 17°32E 181 B10
Otse S. Africa 25°2S 25°45E 270 C4
Otsego U.S.A. 42°27N 85°42W 311 B11
Otsego L. U.S.A. 42°45N 74°53W 313 D10
Ōtsu Japan 35°0N 135°50E 223 C7
Ōtsuka Japan 35°43N 139°44E 140 A3
Ōtsuki Japan 35°36N 138°57E 223 B10
Otta Norway 61°46N 9°32E 164 C6
Otta → Norway 61°46N 9°31E 164 C6
Ottakring Austria 48°12N 16°18E 142 A1
Ottapalam India 10°46N 76°23E 245 J3
Ottávia Italy 41°57N 12°24E 136 B1
Ottawa = Outaouais →
Canada 45°27N 74°8W 298 C5
Ottawa Ont., Canada 45°26N 75°42W 313 A9
Ottawa Ill., U.S.A. 41°21N 88°51W 311 C8
Ottawa Kans., U.S.A. 38°37N 95°16W 308 F6
Ottawa Ohio, U.S.A. 41°1N 84°3W 311 C12
Ottawa Is. Canada 59°35N 80°10W 295 F15
Ottélé Cameroon 3°38N 11°19E 263 E7
Ottensheim Austria 48°21N 14°12E 180 C7
Otter Cr. → U.S.A. 44°13N 73°17W 313 B11
Otter Creek U.S.A. 29°19N 82°46W 317 F7
Otter Lake Canada 45°17N 79°56W 312 A5
Otterbäcken Sweden 58°57N 14°3E 163 F8
Otterbein U.S.A. 40°29N 87°6W 311 D9
Otterndorf Germany 53°48N 8°53E 178 B4
Otterøya Norway 62°45N 6°50E 164 B3
Otterup Denmark 55°30N 10°22E 163 J4
Otterville Ont., Canada 42°55N 80°36W 312 D4
Otterville Mo., U.S.A. 38°42N 93°0W 310 F4
Ottery S. Africa 34°1S 18°32E 118 B2
Ottery St. Mary U.K. 50°44N 3°17W 169 G4
Ottilien Reef Papua N. G. 4°33S 148°49E 286 C5
Ottmachau = Otmuchów
Poland 50°28N 17°10E 185 H4
Otto Beit Bridge Zimbabwe 15°59S 28°56E 269 F2
Ottobrunn Germany 48°3N 11°40E 131 B3
Ottosdal S. Africa 26°46S 25°59E 270 C4
Ottoville U.S.A. 40°57N 84°22W 311 D12
Ottumwa U.S.A. 41°1N 92°25W 310 D4
Otukpa Nigeria 7°9N 7°41E 263 D6
Otuquis △ Bolivia 19°45S 58°44W 331 D6
Oturkpo Nigeria 7°16N 8°8E 263 D6
Otvazhnoye = Zhigulevsk
Russia 53°28N 49°30E 190 D9
Otvazhny = Zhigulevsk
Russia 53°28N 49°30E 190 D9
Otway, B. Chile 53°30S 74°0W 336 D2
Otway, C. Australia 38°52S 143°30E 282 E5
Otway, Seno de Chile 53°5S 71°30W 336 D2
Otway △ Australia 38°47S 143°34E 282 E5
Otwock Poland 52°5N 21°20E 185 F8
Otyniya Ukraine 48°44N 24°51E 183 B9
Ötztaler Ache → Austria 47°14N 10°50E 180 D3
Ötztaler Alpen Austria 46°56N 11°0E 180 E3
Ou → Laos 20°4N 102°13E 236 B4
Ou-Sammyaku Japan 39°20N 140°35E 220 E10
Ouachita → U.S.A. 31°38N 91°49W 314 F9
Ouachita, L. U.S.A. 34°34N 93°12W 314 D8
Ouachita Mts. U.S.A. 34°30N 94°30W 314 D7
Ouadâne Mauritania 20°50N 11°40W 260 D2
Ouadda C.A.R. 8°15N 22°20E 264 A4
Ouaddaï □ Chad 13°0N 21°0E 259 F4
Ouagadougou
Burkina Faso 12°25N 1°30W 263 C4
Ouahigouya Burkina Faso 13°31N 2°25W 262 C4
Ouahran = Oran Algeria 35°45N 0°39W 261 A4
Ouaka □ C.A.R. 6°30N 21°0E 264 A4
Ouaka → C.A.R. 4°59N 19°56E 264 B3
Oualâta Mauritania 17°20N 6°55W 262 B3
Ouallah Comoros Is. 12°19S 43°39E 272 a
Ouallam Niger 14°23N 2°10E 263 C5
Ouallene Algeria 24°41N 1°11E 261 D5
Ouanary Fr. Guiana 4°13N 51°40W 329 C7
Ouanda Djallé C.A.R. 8°55N 22°53E 264 A4
Ouandago C.A.R. 7°13N 18°50E 264 A3
Ouandja C.A.R. 8°28N 23°17E 264 A4
Ouandjia, Bahr → C.A.R. 9°35N 21°43E 264 A4
Ouandjia-Vakaga ⌓ C.A.R. 9°2N 22°18E 264 A4
Ouangani Mayotte 12°50S 45°8E 272 b
Ouango C.A.R. 4°19N 22°30E 264 B4
Ouani Comoros Is. 12°9S 44°18E 272 a
Ouantonou C.A.R. 7°19N 15°18E 264 A3
Ouarâne Mauritania 21°0N 10°30W 260 D2
Ouargaye Burkina Faso 11°40N 0°5E 263 C5
Ouargla Algeria 31°59N 5°16E 261 B6
Ouargla □ Algeria 30°30N 6°10E 261 B6
Ouarkoye Burkina Faso 12°5N 3°40W 262 C4
Ouarkziz, Jebel Algeria 28°50N 8°0W 260 C3
Ouarra → C.A.R. 5°5N 24°26E 264 A4
Ouarzazate Morocco 30°55N 6°50W 260 B3
Ouassouas Mali 16°10N 1°23E 263 B5
Ouatagouna Mali 15°11N 0°43E 263 B5
Ouatere C.A.R. 5°30N 19°8E 264 A3
Oubangi →
Dem. Rep. of the Congo 0°30S 17°50E 264 C3
Oubarakai, O. → Algeria 27°20N 9°0E 261 C6
Ouche → France 47°6N 5°16E 173 E12
Oud Zuid Amsterdam, Neths. 112 c1
Ouddorp Neths. 51°50N 3°57E 170 C3
Oude Kerk Amsterdam, Neths. 112 a2
Oude Rijn → Neths. 52°12N 4°24E 170 B4
Oudeïka Mali 17°30N 1°40W 263 B4
Oudenaarde Belgium 50°50N 3°37E 170 D3
Ouderkerk Neths. 52°18N 4°55E 112 B2
Oudon → France 47°41N 0°53W 172 E6
Oudtshoorn S. Africa 33°35S 22°14E 270 D3
Oued Zem Morocco 32°52N 6°34W 260 B3
Ouégoa N. Cal. 20°20S 164°26E 288 d
Oueita Chad 17°47N 20°39E 259 E4
Ouella Niger 14°48N 3°38E 263 C5
Ouellé Ivory C. 7°26N 4°1W 262 D4
Ouémé → Benin 6°30N 2°30E 263 D5
Ouenza Algeria 35°57N 8°4E 261 A6
Ouessa Burkina Faso 11°4N 2°47W 262 C4
Ouessant, Î. d' France 48°28N 5°6W 172 D1
Ouesso Congo 1°37N 16°5E 264 B3
Ouest □ Cameroon 5°30N 10°30E 263 D7
Ouest, Pte. de l' Canada 49°52N 64°40W 299 C7
Ouezzane Morocco 34°51N 5°35W 260 B3
Ougarou Burkina Faso 12°10N 0°58E 263 C5
Oughter, L. Ireland 54°1N 7°28W 166 B4
Oughterard Ireland 53°26N 9°18W 166 C2
Ouham □ C.A.R. 7°0N 17°30E 264 A3
Ouham → C.A.R. 6°35N 15°12E 264 A3
Ouham-Pendé □ C.A.R. 7°0N 16°0E 264 A3
Ouham → Chad 9°18N 18°14E 259 G3
Ouidah Benin 6°25N 2°0E 263 D5
Ouidi Niger 14°10N 13°0E 259 F2
Ouistreham France 49°17N 0°18W 172 C6
Oujda Morocco 34°41N 1°55W 261 B4
Oujeft Mauritania 20°2N 13°0W 260 D2
Oulad-Teïma Morocco 30°24N 9°12W 260 B3
Oulainen Finland 64°17N 24°47E 160 D21
Oulanka ⌓ Finland 66°26N 29°25E 160 C23
Ould Yenjé Mauritania 15°38N 12°16W 262 B2
Ouled Djellal Algeria 34°28N 5°2E 261 B6
Ouled Naïl, Mts. des
Algeria 34°30N 3°30E 261 B5
Ouli Cameroon 5°12N 14°33E 264 A2
Oullins France 45°43N 4°49E 175 C8
Oulmès Morocco 33°17N 6°0W 260 B3
Oulou, Bahr → C.A.R. 9°48N 21°32E 264 A4
Oulu Finland 65°1N 25°29E 160 D21
Oulujärvi Finland 64°25N 27°15E 160 D22
Oulujoki → Finland 65°1N 25°30E 160 D21
Oulunkylä Finland 60°13N 24°58E 121 B2
Oulx Italy 45°2N 6°50E 198 C3
Oum Chalouba Chad 15°48N 20°46E 259 E4
Oum-el-Bouaghi Algeria 35°55N 7°6E 261 A6
Oum-el-Bouaghi □ Algeria 35°50N 7°5E 261 A6
Oum el Ksi Algeria 29°4N 6°59W 260 C3
Oum-er-Rbia, O. →
Morocco 33°19N 8°21W 260 B3
Oum Hadjer Chad 13°18N 19°41E 259 F3
Oum Hadjer, O. → Chad 16°38N 20°14E 259 E4
Oumé Ivory C. 6°21N 5°27W 262 D3
Oumm ed Droûs Guebli, Sebkhet
Mauritania 24°3N 11°45W 260 D2
Oumm ed Droûs Telli, Sebkhet
Mauritania 24°20N 11°30W 260 D2
Ounane, Dj. Algeria 25°4N 7°19E 261 C6
Ounasjoki → Finland 66°31N 25°40E 160 C21
Ounguati Namibia 22°0S 15°46E 270 B2
Ounianga Kébir Chad 19°4N 20°29E 259 E4
Ounianga Sérir Chad 18°54N 20°51E 259 E4
Ounissoui Niger 17°34N 12°13E 259 E2
Our → Lux. 49°55N 6°5E 170 E6
Oura, Akra Greece 38°10N 26°2E 205 C8
Oura-wan Japan 26°32N 128°4E 288 a
Ouranoupoli Greece 40°20N 23°59E 202 F7
Ourârene Niger 19°30N 7°10E 263 B6
Ourari, Tarso Chad 21°27N 17°27E 259 D3
Ouray U.S.A. 38°1N 107°40W 305 G10
Ourcq → France 49°1N 3°1E 173 C10
Ourcq, Canal de l' France 48°54N 2°28E 134 A3
Ourém Brazil 1°33S 47°6W 332 B2
Ourém Portugal 39°40N 8°35W 194 F2
Ourense Spain 42°19N 7°55W 194 C3
Ourense □ Spain 42°15N 7°51W 194 C3
Ouricuri Brazil 7°53S 40°5W 332 C3
Ourinhos Brazil 23°0S 49°54W 335 A6
Ourique Portugal 37°38N 8°16W 195 H2
Ouro Fino Brazil 22°16S 46°25W 335 A6
Ouro-Ndia Mali 15°8N 4°35W 262 B4
Ouro Prêto Brazil 20°20S 43°30W 333 F3
Ouro Prêto do Oeste
Brazil 10°40S 62°18W 331 C5
Ouro Sogui Senegal 15°36N 13°19W 262 B2
Oursi Burkina Faso 14°41N 0°27W 263 C4
Ourthe → Belgium 50°29N 5°35E 170 D5
Ouse → E. Sussex, U.K. 50°47N 0°4E 169 G8
Ouse → N. Yorks., U.K. 53°44N 0°55W 168 D7
Oust France 42°52N 1°13E 174 F5
Oust → France 47°35N 2°6W 172 E4
Outamba-Kilimi △
S. Leone 9°50N 12°40W 262 D2
Outaouais → Canada 45°27N 74°8W 298 C5
Outapi Namibia 17°30S 15°0E 270 A2
Outardes → Canada 49°24N 69°30W 299 C6
Outat Oulad el Haj
Morocco 33°22N 3°42W 261 B4
Outeiro de Rei Spain 43°6N 7°36W 194 B3
Outer Hebrides U.K. 57°30N 7°15W 167 D1
Outer Mission U.S.A. 37°43N 122°26W 136 B2
Outes = A Serra de Outes
Spain 42°52N 8°55W 194 C2
Outjo Namibia 20°5S 16°7E 270 B2
Outlook Canada 51°30N 107°0W 297 C7
Outokumpu Finland 62°43N 29°1E 160 E23
Outreau France 50°40N 1°36E 173 B8
Outremont Canada 45°31N 73°36W 130 A2
Ouvéa, Î. N. Cal. 20°35S 166°35E 288 d
Ouvèze → France 43°59N 4°51E 175 E8
Ouyen Australia 35°1S 142°22E 282 C5
Ouzinkie U.S.A. 57°56N 152°30W 303 H9
Ouzouer-le-Marché France 47°54N 1°32E 173 E8
Ovacık Turkey 36°11N 33°40E 250 B4
Ovada Italy 44°38N 8°38E 198 D5
Ovahe Chile 27°5S 109°19W 330 b
Ovalau Fiji 17°40S 178°48E 287 A2
Ovalle Chile 30°33S 71°18W 334 C1
Ovamboland Namibia 18°30S 16°0E 270 A2
Ovan Gabon 0°19N 12°10E 264 B2
Ovanåker Sweden 61°22N 15°53E 162 C9
Ovar Portugal 40°51N 8°40W 194 E2
Ovau Solomon Is. 6°40S 156°8E 287 L9
Overath Germany 50°56N 7°17E 178 E3
Overflakkee Neths. 51°44N 4°10E 170 C4
Overijse Belgium 50°47N 4°32E 116 B3
Overijssel □ Neths. 52°25N 6°35E 170 B6
Overland U.S.A. 38°42N 90°21W 310 F6
Overland Park U.S.A. 38°58N 94°40W 308 F6
Overlander Roadhouse
Australia 26°19S 114°28E 279 E1
Overton U.S.A. 36°33N 114°27W 307 J12
Övertorneå Sweden 66°23N 23°38E 160 C20
Överum Sweden 58°0N 16°20E 163 F10
Ovid Mich., U.S.A. 43°1N 84°22W 311 A12
Ovid N.Y., U.S.A. 42°41N 76°49W 313 D8
Ovidiopol Ukraine 46°15N 30°30E 189 J6
Ovidiu Romania 44°16N 28°34E 183 F13
Oviedo Spain 43°25N 5°50W 194 B5
Oviedo Fla., U.S.A. 28°40N 81°13W 317 G8
Oviksfjällen Sweden 63°0N 13°49E 162 A7
Ovišrags Latvia 57°33N 21°44E 184 A8
Ovoot Mongolia 45°21N 113°45E 226 B7
Övör Hangay □ Mongolia 45°0N 102°30E 226 B2
Ovoro Nigeria 5°26N 7°16E 263 D6
Øvre Anárjohka △
Norway 68°30N 24°40E 160 B21
Øvre Årdal Norway 61°19N 7°48E 164 C4
Øvre Dividal ⌓ Norway 68°43N 19°50E 160 B18
Övre Fryken Sweden 60°0N 13°7E 162 E7
Øvre Pasvik ⌓ Norway 69°6N 28°54E 160 B23
Øvre Rendal Norway 61°54N 11°4E 164 C8
Øvre Rindal Norway 63°6N 9°10E 164 A6
Øvre Sirdal Norway 58°48N 6°43E 164 F3
Ovruch Ukraine 51°25N 28°45E 177 C15
Owaka N.Z. 46°27S 169°40E 285 G4
Owambo = Ovamboland
Namibia 18°30S 16°0E 270 A2
Owando Congo 0°29S 15°55E 264 C3
Owariasahi Japan 35°10N 137°5E 223 B9
Owasco L. U.S.A. 42°50N 76°31W 313 D8
Owase Japan 34°7N 136°12E 223 C8
Owatonna U.S.A. 44°5N 93°14W 308 C7
Owbeh Afghan. 34°28N 63°10E 240 B1
Owego U.S.A. 42°6N 76°16W 313 D8
Owen Australia 34°15S 138°32E 282 C3
Owen, Mt. N.Z. 41°35S 172°33E 285 B7
Owen Falls Dam = Nalubaale Dam
Uganda 0°30N 33°5E 268 B3
Owen Sound Canada 44°35N 80°55W 312 B4
Owen Stanley Ra.
Papua N. G. 8°30S 147°0E 286 E4
Owendo Gabon 0°17N 9°30E 264 B1
Oweniny → Ireland 54°8N 9°34W 166 B2
Owens → U.S.A. 36°32N 117°59W 306 J9
Owens L. U.S.A. 36°26N 117°57W 307 J9
Owensboro U.S.A. 37°46N 87°7W 311 G9
Owensville Ind., U.S.A. 38°16N 87°41W 311 F9
Owensville Mo., U.S.A. 38°21N 91°30W 310 F5
Owenteik Guyana 4°27N 59°55W 329 C6
Owenton U.S.A. 38°32N 84°50W 311 F12
Owerri Nigeria 5°29N 7°0E 263 D6
Owhango N.Z. 39°0S 175°23E 284 F4
Owingsville U.S.A. 38°9N 83°46W 311 F13
Owl → Canada 57°51N 92°44W 297 B10
Owo Nigeria 7°10N 5°39E 263 D6
Oworonsoki Nigeria 6°32N 3°24E 124 A2
Owosso U.S.A. 43°0N 84°10W 311 B12
Owyhee U.S.A. 41°57N 116°6W 304 F5
Owyhee → U.S.A. 43°49N 117°2W 304 E5
Owyhee, L. U.S.A. 43°38N 117°14W 304 E5
Ox Mts. = Slieve Gamph
Ireland 54°6N 9°0W 166 B3
Oxapampa Peru 10°33S 75°26W 330 C2
Öxarfjörður Iceland 66°15N 16°45W 155 A10
Oxbow Canada 49°14N 102°10W 297 D8
Oxelösund Sweden 58°43N 17°5E 163 F11
Oxford N.Z. 43°18S 172°11E 285 D7
Oxford Oxon., U.K. 51°46N 1°15W 169 F6
Oxford Ala., U.S.A. 33°36N 85°51W 316 B4
Oxford Iowa, U.S.A. 41°43N 91°47W 310 C5
Oxford Mass., U.S.A. 42°7N 71°52W 313 D13
Oxford Mich., U.S.A. 42°49N 83°16W 311 B13
Oxford Miss., U.S.A. 34°22N 89°31W 315 D10
Oxford N.C., U.S.A. 36°19N 78°35W 315 C15
Oxford N.Y., U.S.A. 42°27N 75°36W 313 D9
Oxford Ohio, U.S.A. 39°31N 84°45W 311 E12
Oxford L. Canada 54°51N 95°37W 297 C9
Oxford Street London, U.K. 125 b3
Oxfordshire □ U.K. 51°48N 1°16W 169 F6
Oxgangs U.K. 55°54N 3°13W 121 B2
Oxia Greece 38°18N 21°6E 207 C3
Oxie Sweden 55°33N 13°6E 163 J7
Oxilithos Greece 38°35N 24°7E 204 C6
Oxley Australia 34°11S 144°6E 282 C6
Oxley Wild Rivers △
Australia 30°57S 152°12E 283 A10
Oxnard U.S.A. 34°12N 119°11W 307 L7
Oxon Hill U.S.A. 38°48N 76°59W 143 C3
Oxsjövålen Sweden 62°34N 13°57E 162 B7
Oxus = Amudarya →
Uzbekistan 43°58N 59°34E 216 D5
Oya Malaysia 2°55N 111°55E 235 B4
Oyabe Japan 36°47N 136°56E 223 A8
Oyama Japan 36°18N 139°48E 223 A11
Oyambre ⌓ Spain 43°22N 4°21W 194 B6
Oyapock → Fr. Guiana 4°8N 51°40W 329 C7
Øye Norway 58°16N 6°49E 164 F3
Oyem Gabon 1°34N 11°31E 264 B2
Oyen Canada 51°22N 110°28W 297 C6
Øyer Norway 61°16N 10°25E 164 C7
Øyeren Norway 59°50N 11°15E 164 E8
Oykel → U.K. 57°56N 4°26W 167 D4
Oymyakon Russia 63°25N 142°44E 215 C15
Oyo Congo 0°0 15°51E 264 C3
Oyo Nigeria 7°46N 3°56E 263 D5
Oyo Sudan 21°58N 36°10E 256 C4
Oyo □ Nigeria 8°15N 3°30E 263 D5
Oyodo Japan 34°42N 135°29E 133 A1
Oyón Peru 10°37S 76°47W 330 C2
Oyonnax France 46°16N 5°40E 173 F12
Oyrot = Gorno-Altay □
Russia 51°0N 86°0E 217 B11
Oyrot-Tura = Gorno-Altaysk
Russia 51°50N 86°5E 217 B11
Øyslebø Norway 58°9N 7°34E 164 F4
Oyster Bay U.S.A. 40°52N 73°32W 313 F11
Oyster Harbour = Ladysmith
Canada 49°0N 123°49W 306 B3
Oyster Rock India 18°54N 72°49E 130 B1
Oyster Rocks Pakistan 24°48N 66°59E 123 B2
Øystese Norway 60°22N 6°9E 164 D3
Ōyūbari Japan 43°1N 142°5E 220 C11
Oyyl → Kazakhstan 49°4N 54°40E 216 C4
Özalp Turkey 38°39N 43°59E 213 C10
Ozamiz Phil. 8°15N 123°50E 233 G4
Ozar = Ojhar India 20°6N 73°56E 244 D1
Ozark Ala., U.S.A. 31°28N 85°39W 316 D4
Ozark Ark., U.S.A. 35°29N 93°50W 314 D8
Ozark Mo., U.S.A. 37°1N 93°12W 308 G7
Ozark Plateau U.S.A. 37°20N 91°40W 308 G8
Ozarks, L. of the U.S.A. 38°12N 92°38W 310 F4
Ożarów Poland 50°53N 21°40E 185 H8
Ózd Hungary 48°14N 20°15E 182 B5
Ozernovskiy Russia 51°30N 156°31E 215 D16
Ozernoye Russia 51°46N 51°28E 190 E10
Ozersk Russia 54°25N 22°0E 184 D8
Ozette, L. U.S.A. 48°6N 124°38W 306 B2

Ozieri Italy 40°35N 9°0E 200 B2
Ozimek Poland 50°41N 18°11E 185 H5
Ozinki Russia 51°12N 49°44E 190 E9
Ozoir-la-Ferrière France 48°46N 2°40E 134 B4
Ozona U.S.A. 30°43N 101°12W 314 F4
Ozone Park U.S.A. 40°40N 73°50W 132 B2
Ozorków Poland 51°57N 19°16E 185 G6
Ozren Bos.-H. 43°55N 18°29E 182 G3
Ōzu Ehime, Japan 33°30N 132°33E 222 D4
Ōzu Kumamoto, Japan 32°52N 130°52E 222 E2
Ozuluama Mexico 21°40N 97°51W 319 C5
Ozun Romania 45°47N 25°50E 183 E10
Ozurgeti Georgia 41°55N 42°0E 191 K5

# P

Pa Burkina Faso 11°33N 3°19W 262 C4
Pa-an Burma 16°51N 97°40E 241 G6
Pa Mong Dam Thailand 18°0N 102°22E 236 D4
Pa Sak → Thailand 15°30N 101°0E 236 E3
Paama Vanuatu 16°28S 168°14E 287 F6
Paamiut Greenland 62°0N 49°43W 154 E6
Paanayarvi △ Russia 66°16N 30°10E 160 C24
Paar → Germany 48°46N 11°36E 179 G7
Paarl S. Africa 33°45S 18°56E 270 D2
Pa'auilo U.S.A. 20°2N 155°22W 302 C6
Pab Hills Pakistan 26°30N 66°45E 242 F2
Pabaidh = Pabbay U.K. 57°46N 7°14W 167 D1
Pabbay U.K. 57°46N 7°14W 167 D1
Pabean Indonesia 6°49S 115°19E 235 D5
Pabianice Poland 51°40N 19°20E 185 G6
Pabna Bangla. 24°1N 89°18E 241 C2
Pabo Uganda 3°1N 32°10E 268 B3
Pacaás Novos, Serra dos Brazil 10°45S 64°15W 331 C5
Pacaás Novos △ Brazil 11°0S 63°0W 331 C5
Pacaipampa Peru 5°35S 79°39W 330 B2
Pacaja → Brazil 1°56S 50°50W 332 B1
Pacajus Brazil 4°10S 38°31W 332 B4
Pacaraima, Sa. S. Amer. 4°0N 62°30W 329 C5
Pacarán Peru 12°50S 76°3W 330 C2
Pacaraos Peru 11°12S 76°42W 330 C2
Pacasmayo Peru 7°20S 79°35W 330 B2
Pace U.S.A. 30°36N 87°10W 317 E2
Paceco Italy 37°59N 12°33E 200 E5
Pachacamac Peru 12°14S 77°53W 330 C2
Pachang Hsi → Taiwan 23°20N 120°7E 225 C2
Pachao Yü Taiwan 23°22N 119°29E 225 C1
Pachia Greece 36°17N 25°50E 205 E7
Pachino Italy 36°43N 15°5E 201 F8
Pachitea → Peru 8°46S 74°33W 330 B3
Pachiza Peru 7°16S 76°46W 330 B2
Pachmarhi India 22°28N 78°26E 243 H8
Pachnai India 26°57N 92°19E 241 B4
Pachnes Greece 35°16N 24°4E 207 E5
Pacho Colombia 5°8N 74°10W 328 B3
Pachora India 20°38N 75°29E 244 D2
Pachpadra India 25°58N 72°10E 242 G5
Pachuca Mexico 20°7N 98°44W 319 C5
Pacific U.S.A. 38°29N 90°45W 310 F6
Pacific Antarctic Ridge Pac. Oc. 43°0S 115°0W 151 B13
Pacific City = Huntington Beach U.S.A. 33°40N 118°5W 307 M9
Pacific Grove U.S.A. 36°38N 121°56W 306 J5
Pacific Heights U.S.A. 37°47N 122°26W 136 B2
Pacific Manor U.S.A. 37°38N 122°27W 136 C2
Pacific Ocean 10°0N 140°0W 289 G14
Pacific Palisades Calif., U.S.A. 34°2N 118°32W 126 B1
Pacific Palisades Hawai'i, U.S.A. 21°25N 157°58W 302 K14
Pacific Rim △ Canada 48°40N 124°45W 306 B2
Pacifica U.S.A. 37°37N 122°27W 136 C2
Pacitan Indonesia 8°12S 111°7E 235 D4
Packsaddle Australia 30°36S 141°58E 282 A4
Packwood U.S.A. 46°36N 121°40W 306 D5
Paco Phil. 14°35N 120°59E 127 B1
Paco de Arcos Portugal 38°41N 9°17W 126 A1
Paço Imperial Rio de J., Brazil 135 a2
Pacov Czech Rep. 49°27N 15°0E 180 B8
Pacoval Brazil 2°40S 54°11W 329 D7
Pacuí → Brazil 16°46S 45°1W 333 E2
Pacy-sur-Eure France 49°1N 1°23E 172 C8
Padaido, Kepulauan Indonesia 1°15S 136°30E 231 E9
Padali = Amursk Russia 50°14N 136°54E 215 D14
Padampur India 20°59N 83°4E 244 D6
Padang Kalimantan Barat, Indonesia 1°39S 108°55E 235 C3
Padang Riau, Indonesia 1°30N 102°30E 237 M4
Padang Sumatera Barat, Indonesia 1°0S 100°20E 234 C2
Padang Endau Malaysia 2°40N 103°38E 237 L4
Padang Lawas Indonesia 1°40N 99°56E 234 B1
Padangpanjang Indonesia 0°40S 100°20E 234 C2
Padangsidempuan Indonesia 1°30N 99°15E 234 B1
Padangtikar Indonesia 0°44S 109°15E 235 C3
Padauari → Brazil 0°15S 64°5W 329 D5
Padaung Burma 18°43N 95°9E 241 F5
Padborg Denmark 54°49N 9°21E 163 K3
Padcaya Bolivia 21°52S 64°48W 331 E5
Paddington N.S.W., Australia 33°53S 151°14E 139 B2
Paddington London, U.K. 125 b2
Paddle Prairie Canada 57°57N 117°29W 296 B5
Paderborn Germany 51°42N 8°45E 178 D4
Paderno Italy 45°33N 9°9E 128 A1
Paderoo India 18°5N 82°40E 244 E6
Padeş, Vf. Romania 45°40N 22°22E 182 E7
Padilla Bolivia 19°19S 64°20W 331 D5
Padina Romania 44°50N 27°8E 183 F12
Padjelanta △ Sweden 67°20N 16°35E 160 C17
Padma India 24°12N 85°22E 243 G11
Padma → Bangla. 23°22N 90°32E 241 D3
Pádova Italy 45°25N 11°53E 199 C8
Padra India 22°15N 73°7E 242 H5
Padrão, Pta. Angola 6°5S 12°20E 265 D2
Padrauna India 26°54N 83°59E 243 F10
Padre I. U.S.A. 27°10N 97°25W 314 H6
Padre Island ⌓ U.S.A. 27°0N 97°25W 314 H6
Padrón Spain 42°41N 8°39W 194 C2
Padstow U.K. 50°33N 4°58W 169 G3
Padthaway Australia 36°36S 140°31E 282 D4
Padua = Pádova Italy 45°25N 11°53E 199 C8
Paducah Ky., U.S.A. 37°5N 88°37W 308 G9
Paducah Tex., U.S.A. 34°1N 100°18W 314 D4
Padukka Sri Lanka 6°50N 80°5E 245 L5
Padul Spain 37°1N 3°38W 195 H7
Padwa India 18°27N 82°47E 244 E6
Paea Tahiti 17°41S 149°35W 289 e
Paekakariki N.Z. 40°59S 174°58E 284 G3
Paektu-san N. Korea 41°59N 128°4E 224 B4
Paengaroa N.Z. 37°49S 176°29E 284 D5
Paeroa N.Z. 37°23S 175°41E 284 D4
Paesana Italy 44°41N 7°16E 198 D4
Paete Phil. 14°23N 121°29E 232 D3
Pafúri Mozam. 22°28S 31°17E 271 B5
Pag Croatia 44°25N 15°3E 199 D12
Paga Gabon 0°45S 10°21E 264 C2
Paga Ghana 11°1N 1°8W 263 C4
Pagadian Phil. 7°55N 123°30E 233 H4
Pagai Selatan, Pulau Indonesia 3°0S 100°15E 234 C2
Pagai Utara, Pulau Indonesia 2°35S 100°0E 234 C2
Pagalu = Annobón Atl. Oc. 1°25S 5°36E 255 G4
Pagalungan Phil. 7°4N 124°41E 233 H5
Pagan Burma 21°10N 94°52E 241 E5
Pagan N. Marianas 18°7N 145°46E 302 a
Pagara India 24°22N 80°1E 243 G9
Pagaralam Indonesia 4°1S 103°16E 234 C2
Pagasa I. = Thitu I. S. China Sea 11°3N 114°17E 230 B4
Pagastikos Kolpos Greece 39°15N 23°0E 204 B5
Pagatan Indonesia 3°33S 115°59E 235 C5
Page U.S.A. 36°57N 111°27W 305 H8
Pagėgiai Lithuania 55°9N 21°54E 184 C8
Pagei Papua N. G. 3°2S 141°10E 286 B1
Pageri South Sudan 4°0N 32°0E 257 G3
Paget, Mt. S. Georgia 54°26S 36°31W 326 H6
Paget I. India 13°26N 92°50E 245 H11
Pagewood Australia 33°56S 151°14E 139 B2
Pago B. Guam 13°25N 144°47E 302 d
Pago Pago Amer. Samoa 14°16S 170°43W 302 f
Pago Pago Harbor Amer. Samoa 14°17S 170°40W 302 f
Pagosa Springs U.S.A. 37°16N 107°1W 305 H10
Pagote India 18°53N 72°59E 130 B2
Pagri China 27°45N 89°10E 218 F6
Pagsanjan Phil. 14°16N 121°27E 232 D3
Pagua B. Dominica 15°32N 61°17W 323 k
Pagudpud Phil. 18°34N 120°47E 232 B3
Pagwa River Canada 50°2N 85°14W 298 B2
Pagwi Papua N. G. 4°4S 143°2E 286 C2
Pāhala U.S.A. 19°12N 155°29W 302 D6
Pahang □ Malaysia 3°30N 102°45E 237 L4
Pahang → Malaysia 3°30N 103°9E 237 L4
Paharpur Bangla. 24°51N 88°44E 241 C2
Pahia Pt. N.Z. 46°20S 167°41E 285 G2
Pahiatua N.Z. 40°27S 175°50E 284 G4
Pāhoa U.S.A. 19°30N 154°57W 302 D7
Pahokee U.S.A. 26°50N 80°40W 317 J9
Pahrump U.S.A. 36°12N 115°59W 307 J11
Pahute Mesa U.S.A. 37°20N 116°45W 306 H10
Pai Thailand 19°19N 98°27E 236 C2
Pai, I. do Brazil 22°59S 43°5W 135 B2
Paia U.S.A. 20°54N 156°22W 302 C5
Paichuan Liehtao Taiwan 25°58N 119°57E 225 b
Paicines U.S.A. 36°44N 121°17W 306 J5
Paide Estonia 58°53N 25°33E 188 C3
Paignton U.K. 50°26N 3°35W 169 G4
Paihia N.Z. 35°17S 174°6E 284 B3
Paiho Taiwan 23°21N 120°25E 225 C2
Paiján Peru 7°42S 79°20W 330 B2
Päijänne Finland 61°30N 25°30E 188 B3
Pailani India 25°45N 80°26E 243 G9
Pailin Cambodia 12°46N 102°36E 236 F4
Pailolo Channel U.S.A. 21°0N 156°40W 302 B5
Paimpol France 48°48N 3°4W 172 D3
Painan Indonesia 1°21S 100°34E 234 C2
Paine Grande, Cerro Chile 50°59S 73°4W 336 D2
Painesville U.S.A. 41°43N 81°15W 312 E3
Paint Hills = Wemindji Canada 53°0N 78°49W 298 B4
Paint L. Canada 55°28N 97°57W 297 B9
Painted Desert U.S.A. 36°0N 111°0W 305 H8
Paintsville U.S.A. 37°49N 82°48W 309 G12
País Vasco □ Spain 42°50N 2°45W 196 C2
Paisha Taiwan 23°40N 119°35E 225 C1
Paisley Ont., Canada 44°18N 81°16W 312 B3
Paisley Renf., U.K. 55°50N 4°25W 167 F4
Paisley Oreg., U.S.A. 42°42N 120°32W 304 E3
Païta N. Cal. 22°8S 166°22E 288 d
Paita Peru 5°11S 81°9W 330 B1
Paithan India 19°29N 75°23E 244 E2
Paiva → Portugal 41°4N 8°16W 194 D2
Paizhou China 30°12N 113°55E 229 B9
Paja, Cerro Ecuador 1°17S 90°26W 330 a
Pájara Canary Is. 28°21N 14°6W 153 e2
Pajares Spain 43°1N 5°46W 194 B5
Pajares, Puerto de Spain 42°58N 5°46W 194 C5
Pajarito Colombia 5°17N 72°43W 328 B3
Pajęczno Poland 51°10N 19°0E 185 G5
Paju S. Korea 37°45N 126°46E 224 D3
Pak Kok Hong Kong, China 22°14N 114°7E 122 B2
Pak Kong Hong Kong, China 22°22N 114°15E 122 A3
Pak Lay Laos 18°15N 101°27E 236 C3
Pak Ou Laos 20°3N 102°12E 236 B4
Pak Phanang Thailand 8°21N 100°12E 237 H3
Pak Sane Laos 18°22N 103°39E 236 C4
Pak Song Laos 15°11N 106°14E 236 E6
Pak Suang Laos 19°58N 102°15E 228 H4
Pak Tam Hong Kong, China 22°25N 114°19E 122 A3
Pak Tam Chung China 22°24N 114°19E 219 a
Pak Thong Chai Thailand 14°43N 102°1E 236 E4
Pakala India 13°29N 79°8E 245 H4
Pakaraima Mts. Guyana 5°15N 60°0W 329 B6
Pakaur India 24°38N 87°51E 243 G12
Pakch'ŏn N. Korea 39°44N 125°35E 224 C2
Pakenham Vic., Australia 38°6S 145°30E 283 E6
Pakenham Ont., Canada 45°18N 76°18W 313 A8
Pakhoi = Beihai China 21°28N 109°6E 228 G7
Pakhuis S. Africa 32°9S 19°5E 270 D2
Pakila Finland 60°15N 24°55E 121 B2
Pakistan ■ Asia 30°0N 70°0E 242 E4
Pakkading Laos 18°19N 103°59E 236 C4
Paklay = Sayaboury Laos 19°15N 101°45E 236 C3
Paklenica △ Croatia 44°20N 15°39E 199 D12
Pakokku Burma 21°20N 95°0E 241 E5
Pakość Poland 52°48N 18°6E 185 F5
Pakowki L. Canada 49°20N 111°0W 297 D6
Pakpattan Pakistan 30°25N 73°27E 242 D5
Pakrac Croatia 45°27N 17°12E 182 E2
Pakruojis Lithuania 55°58N 23°52E 184 C10
Paks Hungary 46°38N 18°55E 182 D3
Paktīā □ Afghan. 33°30N 69°15E 240 B3
Paktīkā □ Afghan. 32°30N 69°0E 240 B3
Paku, Tanjung Indonesia 3°6S 106°31E 234 C3
Pakwach Uganda 2°28N 31°27E 268 B3
Pakxe Laos 15°5N 105°52E 236 E5
Pal Lahara India 21°27N 85°11E 243 J11
Pala Chad 9°25N 15°5E 259 G3
Pala Dem. Rep. of the Congo 6°45S 29°30E 268 D2
Pala Calif., U.S.A. 33°22N 117°5W 307 M9
Palabek Uganda 3°22N 32°33E 268 B3
Palacio Real Madrid, Spain 127 b1
Palacios U.S.A. 28°42N 96°13W 314 G6
Palafrugell Spain 41°55N 3°10E 196 D8
Palagiano Italy 40°35N 17°2E 201 B10
Palagonía Italy 37°19N 14°45E 201 E7
Palagruža Croatia 42°24N 16°15E 199 F13
Palais Royal Brussels, Belgium 116 b3
Palaiseau France 48°42N 2°14E 134 B2
Palakkad India 10°46N 76°42E 245 J3
Palakol India 16°31N 81°46E 245 F5
Palalankwe India 10°52N 92°29E 245 J11
Palam India 19°0N 77°0E 244 E3
Palamas Greece 39°26N 22°4E 204 B4
Palamós Spain 41°50N 3°10E 196 D8
Palampur India 32°10N 76°30E 242 C7
Palamut Turkey 38°59N 27°41E 205 C9
Palana Tas., Australia 39°45S 147°55E 281 F4
Palana Russia 59°10N 159°59E 215 D16
Palanan Phil. 17°8N 122°29E 232 C4
Palanan B. Phil. 17°9N 122°27E 232 C4
Palanan Pt. Phil. 17°17N 122°30E 232 C4
Palandri Pakistan 33°42N 73°40E 243 C5
Palanga Lithuania 55°58N 21°3E 184 C8
Palanganene Dem. Rep. of the Congo 6°32S 18°52E 265 D3
Palangkaraya Indonesia 2°16S 113°56E 235 C4
Palani India 10°30N 77°30E 245 J3
Palani Hills India 10°14N 77°33E 245 J3
Palanpur India 24°10N 72°25E 242 G5
Palaoa Pt. U.S.A. 20°44N 156°58W 302 C5
Palapag Phil. 12°33N 125°7E 232 E5
Palapye Botswana 22°30S 27°7E 270 B4
Palar → India 12°27N 80°13E 245 H5
Palas Pakistan 35°4N 73°14E 243 B5
Palas de Rei Spain 42°52N 7°52W 194 C3
Palasan I. Phil. 14°51N 122°2E 232 D4
Palasponga India 21°47N 85°34E 243 J11
Palatine U.S.A. 42°7N 88°3W 311 B8
Palatka Russia 60°6N 150°54E 215 C16
Palatka Fla., U.S.A. 29°39N 81°38W 316 F8
Palau Italy 41°11N 9°23E 200 A2
Palau ■ Palau 7°30N 134°30E 288 c
Palaui I. Phil. 18°32N 122°8E 232 B4
Palauk Burma 13°10N 98°40E 236 F2
Palaw Burma 12°58N 98°39E 236 F2
Palawan Phil. 9°30N 118°30E 233 G2
Palawan □ Phil. 10°0N 119°0E 233 G2
Palawan Passage Phil. 10°0N 118°0E 233 G2
Palayan Phil. 15°36N 121°8E 232 D3
Palayankottai India 8°45N 77°45E 245 K3
Palazzo, Pte. France 42°28N 8°30E 175 F12
Palazzo San Gervásio Italy 40°56N 15°59E 201 B8
Palazzolo Italy 45°34N 9°9E 128 A1
Palazzolo Acréide Italy 37°4N 14°54E 201 E7
Palca Chile 19°7S 69°9W 330 D4
Paldiski Estonia 59°23N 24°9E 188 C3
Pale Bos.-H. 43°50N 18°38E 182 G3
Palekastro Greece 35°12N 26°15E 207 E7
Paleleh Indonesia 1°10N 121°50E 231 D6
Palembang Indonesia 3°0S 104°50E 234 C2
Palena → Chile 43°50S 73°50W 336 B2
Palena, L. Chile 43°55S 71°40W 336 B2
Palencia Spain 42°1N 4°34W 194 C6
Palencia □ Spain 42°31N 4°33W 194 C6
Paleng Taiwan 24°41N 121°23E 225 B3
Palenque Mexico 17°29N 92°1W 319 D6
Paleo Faliro Greece 37°53N 23°42E 112 B2
Paleochora Greece 35°16N 23°39E 207 E4
Paleokastritsa Greece 39°40N 19°41E 206 B9
Paleometokho Cyprus 35°7N 33°11E 207 E9
Paleopoli Greece 37°49N 24°50E 204 D6
Palermo B. Aires, Argentina 34°35S 58°24W 117 B2
Palermo Colombia 2°54N 75°26W 328 C2
Palermo Italy 38°7N 13°22E 200 D6
Palermo Calif., U.S.A. 39°26N 121°33W 306 F5
Palermo ✕ (PMO) Italy 38°11N 13°5E 200 D6
Paleros Greece 38°47N 20°53E 207 B2
Palestina = Jordânia Brazil 15°55S 40°11W 333 E3
Palestina Chile 23°50S 69°47W 334 A2
Palestine Asia 32°0N 35°0E 251 G6
Palestine Ill., U.S.A. 39°0N 87°37W 311 F9
Palestine Tex., U.S.A. 31°46N 95°38W 314 F7
Palestrina Italy 41°50N 12°53E 199 G9
Paletwa Burma 21°10N 92°50E 241 E4
Palghat = Palakkad India 10°46N 76°42E 245 J3
Palgrave, Mt. Australia 23°22S 115°58E 278 D2
Palhais Portugal 38°37N 9°2W 126 B2
Palhoça Brazil 27°38S 48°40W 335 B6
Pali India 25°50N 73°20E 242 G5
Pali Taiwan 25°8N 121°23E 225 A3
Pali-Aike △ Chile 52°6S 69°44W 336 D3
Palikea U.S.A. 21°26N 158°6W 302 K13
Palikir Micronesia 6°55N 158°9E 288 G7
Palimbang Phil. 6°12N 124°12E 233 H5
Palin, Mt. Malaysia 6°10N 117°10E 235 A5
Palinuro Italy 40°2N 15°17E 201 B8
Palinuro, C. Italy 40°2N 15°16E 201 B8
Paliouri, Akra Greece 39°57N 23°45E 202 G7
Palisades Park U.S.A. 40°50N 74°1W 132 A1
Palisades Res. U.S.A. 43°20N 111°12W 304 E8
Palisadoes, The Jamaica 17°57N 76°48W 320 a
Paliseul Belgium 49°54N 5°8E 170 E5
Palitana India 21°32N 71°49E 242 J4
Palizada Mexico 18°15N 92°5W 319 D6
Palk Bay Asia 9°30N 79°15E 245 K4
Palk Strait Asia 10°0N 79°45E 245 K4
Palkānah Iraq 35°49N 44°26E 246 C5
Palkonda India 18°36N 83°48E 244 E6
Palkonda Ra. India 13°50N 79°20E 245 H4
Palkot India 22°53N 84°39E 243 H11
Palla Road = Dinokwe Botswana 23°29S 26°37E 270 B4
Pallanza = Verbánia Italy 45°56N 8°33E 198 C5
Pallarenda Australia 19°12S 146°46E 280 B4
Pallas-Ylläastunturi △ Finland 68°8N 24°15E 160 B21
Pallasovka Russia 50°4N 47°0E 190 E8
Palleru → India 16°45N 80°2E 244 F5
Pallës, Bishti i Albania 41°24N 19°24E 202 E3
Pallinup → Australia 34°27S 118°50E 279 F2
Pallisa Uganda 1°12N 33°43E 268 B3
Palliser, C. N.Z. 41°37S 175°14E 284 H4
Palliser, Îs. French Polynesia 15°30S 146°30W 289 f
Palliser B. N.Z. 41°26S 175°5E 284 H4
Pallu India 28°59N 74°14E 242 E6
Palm Bay U.S.A. 28°2N 80°35W 317 G9
Palm Beach Aruba 12°34N 70°2W 322 f
Palm Beach Fla., U.S.A. 26°43N 80°2W 317 J9
Palm Coast U.S.A. 29°35N 81°12W 317 F8
Palm Deira, The U.A.E. 25°17N 55°15E 119 A2
Palm Desert U.S.A. 33°43N 116°22W 307 M10
Palm-Grove △ Australia 24°57S 149°21E 280 C4
Palm Harbor U.S.A. 28°5N 82°46W 317 G7
Palm Is. Australia 18°40S 146°35E 280 B4
Palm Jumeirah, The U.A.E. 25°11N 55°11E 119 B1
Palm Springs U.S.A. 33°50N 116°33W 307 M10
Palm Valley U.S.A. 30°11N 81°23W 316 E8
Palma = Paraná Brazil 12°30S 47°48W 333 D2
Palma Mozam. 10°46S 40°29E 269 E5
Palma → Brazil 12°33S 47°52W 333 D2
Palma, B. de Spain 39°30N 2°39E 206 B3
Palma de Mallorca Spain 39°35N 2°39E 206 B3
Palma de Mallorca ✕ (PMI) Spain 39°34N 2°43E 197 F7
Palma del Río Spain 37°43N 5°17W 195 H5
Palma di Montechiaro Italy 37°11N 13°46E 200 E6
Palma Nova = Palmanova Spain 39°32N 2°34E 206 B3
Palma Soriano Cuba 20°15N 76°0W 320 B4
Palmaner India 13°12N 78°45E 245 H4
Palmanova Spain 39°32N 2°34E 206 B3
Palmares Brazil 8°41S 35°28W 332 C4
Palmarito Venezuela 7°37N 70°10W 328 B3
Palmarola Italy 40°56N 12°51E 200 B5
Palmas Paraná, Brazil 26°29S 52°0W 335 B5
Palmas Tocantins, Brazil 10°13S 48°16W 332 D2
Palmas, C. Liberia 4°27N 7°46W 262 E3
Pálmas, G. di Italy 39°0N 8°30E 200 D1
Palmas de Monte Alto Brazil 14°16S 43°10W 333 D3
Palmdale Calif., U.S.A. 34°35N 118°7W 307 L8
Palmdale Fla., U.S.A. 26°57N 81°19W 317 J8
Palmeira Brazil 25°25S 50°0W 333 G2
Palmeira das Missões Brazil 27°55S 53°17W 335 B5
Palmeira dos Índios Brazil 9°25S 36°37W 332 C4
Palmeirais Brazil 6°0S 43°0W 332 C3
Palmeiras Brazil 12°31S 41°34W 333 D3
Palmeiras → Brazil 12°22S 47°8W 333 D2
Palmeirinhas, Pta. das Angola 9°2S 12°57E 265 D2
Palmela Portugal 38°32N 8°57W 195 G2
Palmelo Brazil 17°20S 48°27W 333 E2
Palmer Antarctica 64°35S 65°0W 151 C17
Palmer Alaska, U.S.A. 61°36N 149°7W 303 F10
Palmer → Australia 16°0S 142°26E 280 B3
Palmer Arch. Antarctica 64°15S 65°0W 151 C17
Palmer Lake U.S.A. 39°7N 104°55W 304 G11
Palmer Land Antarctica 73°0S 63°0W 151 D18
Palmerston = Darwin Australia 12°25S 130°51E 278 B5
Palmerston N. Terr., Australia 12°31S 130°59E 278 B5
Palmerston Ont., Canada 43°50N 80°51W 312 C4
Palmerston Dublin, Ireland 53°20N 6°22W 120 A1
Palmerston N.Z. 45°29S 170°43E 285 F5
Palmerston North N.Z. 40°21S 175°39E 284 G4
Palmerton U.S.A. 40°48N 75°37W 313 F9
Palmetto Fla., U.S.A. 27°31N 82°34W 317 H7
Palmetto Ga., U.S.A. 33°31N 84°40W 316 B5
Palmetto Pt. Antigua & B. 17°37N 61°51W 322 c
Palmetto Pt. St. Kitts & Nevis 17°18N 62°46W 322 d
Palmi Italy 38°21N 15°51E 201 D8
Palmira Argentina 32°59S 68°34W 334 C2
Palmira Colombia 3°32N 76°16W 328 C2
Palms U.S.A. 34°1N 118°24W 126 B2
Palmyra = Tudmur Syria 34°36N 38°15E 213 E8
Palmyra Ill., U.S.A. 39°26N 90°0W 310 E7
Palmyra Mo., U.S.A. 39°48N 91°32W 310 E5
Palmyra N.J., U.S.A. 40°0N 75°1W 313 F9
Palmyra N.Y., U.S.A. 43°5N 77°18W 312 C7
Palmyra Pa., U.S.A. 40°18N 76°36W 313 F8
Palmyra Wis., U.S.A. 42°52N 88°36W 311 B8
Palmyra Is. Pac. Oc. 5°52N 162°5W 289 G11
Palmyras = Santos Dumont Brazil 22°55S 43°10W 333 F3
Palmyras Pt. India 20°46N 87°1E 244 D8
Palo Phil. 11°10N 124°59E 233 F5
Palo Alto U.S.A. 37°27N 122°10W 306 H4
Palo Seco Trin. & Tob. 10°4N 61°36W 323 t
Palo Verde U.S.A. 33°26N 114°44W 307 M12
Palo Verde △ Costa Rica 10°21N 85°21W 320 D2
Paloh Indonesia 1°43N 109°18E 235 B3
Paloheinä Finland 60°15N 24°56E 121 B2
Paloich South Sudan 10°28N 32°32E 257 E3
Palomar Mt. U.S.A. 33°22N 116°50W 307 M10
Palomeras Spain 40°22N 3°39W 127 B2
Palompon Phil. 11°3N 124°23E 233 F5
Palopo Indonesia 3°0S 120°16E 231 E6
Palos, C. de Spain 37°38N 0°40W 197 H4
Palos de la Frontera Spain 37°14N 6°53W 195 H4
Palos Heights U.S.A. 41°39N 87°47W 119 D2
Palos Hills U.S.A. 41°42N 87°49W 119 C2
Palos Park U.S.A. 41°40N 87°50W 119 C1
Palos Verdes, Pt. U.S.A. 33°46N 118°25W 307 M8
Palos Verdes Estates U.S.A. 33°48N 118°23W 307 M8
Palpa Peru 14°30S 75°15W 330 C2
Palpara India 22°38N 88°22E 124 B2
Pålsboda Sweden 59°3N 15°22E 162 E9
Palu Indonesia 1°0S 119°52E 235 C5
Palu Turkey 38°45N 40°0E 213 C9
Paluan Phil. 13°26N 120°29E 232 E3
Paluke Liberia 5°2N 8°5W 262 D3
Paluma Ra. Australia 19°9S 146°22E 280 B4
Paluzza Italy 46°32N 13°1E 199 B10
Palwal India 28°8N 77°19E 242 E7
Pama Burkina Faso 11°19N 0°44E 263 C5
Pama → C.A.R. 4°23N 18°43E 264 B3
Pama ⌓ Burkina Faso 11°27N 0°40E 263 C5
Pamandzi Mayotte 12°47S 45°16E 272 b
Pamanukan Indonesia 6°16S 107°49E 235 D3
Pamban I. India 9°15N 79°20E 245 K4
Pamekasan Indonesia 7°10S 113°28E 235 D4
Pamenang Indonesia 8°24S 116°6E 231 J19
Pameungpeuk Indonesia 7°37S 107°43E 235 D3
Pamiers France 43°7N 1°39E 174 E5
Pamir Tajikistan 37°40N 73°0E 217 E8
Pamirsky Post = Murgap Tajikistan 38°10N 74°2E 217 E8
Pamlico → U.S.A. 35°20N 76°28W 315 D16
Pamlico Sd. U.S.A. 35°20N 76°0W 315 D17
Pampa U.S.A. 35°32N 100°58W 314 D4
Pampa de Agma Argentina 43°45S 69°40W 336 B3
Pampa de las Salinas Argentina 32°1S 66°58W 334 C2
Pampa Grande Bolivia 18°5S 64°6W 331 D5
Pampa Hermosa Peru 7°7S 75°4W 330 B2
Pampanga □ Phil. 15°4N 120°40E 232 D3
Pampanua Indonesia 4°16S 120°8E 231 E6
Pampas Argentina 35°0S 63°0W 334 D3
Pampas Peru 12°20S 74°50W 330 C3
Pampas → Peru 13°24S 73°12W 330 C3
Pampatar Venezuela 11°11N 63°48W 329 a
Pamphylia Turkey 37°0N 31°20E 250 B2
Pamplemousses Mauritius 20°6S 57°34E 272 e
Pamplona Colombia 7°23N 72°39W 328 B3
Pamplona Phil. 18°31N 121°20E 232 B3
Pamplona-Iruña Spain 42°48N 1°38W 196 C3
Pampoenpoort S. Africa 31°3S 22°40E 270 D3
Pamuk → Turkey 37°2N 34°49E 250 A5
Pamukçu Turkey 39°30N 27°54E 205 B9
Pamukkale Turkey 37°55N 29°8E 205 D11
Pan de Azúcar Chile 24°5S 68°10W 334 A2
Pan de Azúcar △ Chile 26°0S 70°40W 334 B1
Pan Xian China 25°46N 104°38E 228 E5
Pana U.S.A. 39°23N 89°5W 310 E7
Panabo Phil. 7°19N 125°42E 233 H5
Panaca U.S.A. 37°47N 114°23W 305 H6
Panacea U.S.A. 30°2N 84°23W 316 E5
Panadura Sri Lanka 6°47N 79°53E 245 L4
Panagyurishte Bulgaria 42°30N 24°15E 203 D8
Panaitan Indonesia 6°36S 105°12E 234 D3
Panajam Indonesia 1°15S 116°46E 235 C5
Panaji India 15°25N 73°50E 245 G1
Panamá Panama 9°0N 79°25W 320 c
Panama Sri Lanka 6°45N 81°48E 245 L5
Panama ■ Cent. Amer. 8°48N 79°55W 320 E4
Panamá, G. de Panama 8°4N 79°20W 320 E4
Panama, Isthmus of Cent. Amer. 9°0N 79°0W 292 J12
Panama Basin Pac. Oc. 5°0N 83°30W 289 G19
Panama Canal Panama 9°10N 79°37W 320 c
Panama City U.S.A. 30°10N 85°40W 316 E4
Panama City Beach U.S.A. 30°11N 85°48W 316 E4
Panamint Range U.S.A. 36°20N 117°20W 307 J9
Panamint Springs U.S.A. 36°20N 117°28W 307 J9
Panão Peru 9°55S 75°55W 330 B2
Panaon I. Phil. 9°50N 125°13E 233 G5
Panare Thailand 6°51N 101°30E 237 J3
Panarea Italy 38°38N 15°4E 201 D8
Panaro → Italy 44°55N 11°25E 199 D8
Panay Phil. 11°10N 122°30E 233 F4
Panay G. Phil. 11°0N 122°30E 233 F4
Pančevo Serbia 44°52N 20°41E 182 F5
Panch'iao Taiwan 25°1N 121°27E 225 A3
Panchur India 22°32N 88°16E 124 B1
Panciu Romania 45°54N 27°8E 183 E12
Pancol Phil. 10°52N 119°25E 233 F2
Pancorbo, Desfiladero Spain 42°32N 3°5W 194 C7
Pâncota Romania 46°20N 21°45E 182 D6
Panda Mozam. 24°2S 34°45E 271 B5
Pandacan Phil. 14°35N 121°0E 127 B2
Pandan Malaysia 1°32N 103°46E 237 d
Pandan Antique, Phil. 11°45N 122°10E 233 F4
Pandan Catanduanes, Phil. 14°3N 124°10E 232 D5
Pandan, Selat Singapore 1°15N 103°44E 138 B2
Pandan B. Phil. 11°43N 122°0E 233 F4
Pandan Res. Singapore 1°18N 103°44E 138 B2
Pandan Tampoi = Tampoi Malaysia 1°30N 103°39E 237 d
Pandanan I. Phil. 8°17N 117°13E 233 G1
Pandegelang Indonesia 6°25S 106°5E 234 D3
Pandhana India 21°42N 76°13E 242 J7
Pandharkawada India 20°1N 78°32E 244 D4
Pandharpur India 17°41N 75°20E 244 F2
Pandhurna India 21°36N 78°35E 244 D4
Pando Uruguay 34°44S 56°0W 335 C4
Pando □ Bolivia 11°20S 67°40W 330 C4
Pando, L. = Hope, L. Australia 28°24S 139°18E 281 D2
Pandokratoras Greece 39°45N 19°50E 206 B9
Pandora Costa Rica 9°43N 83°3W 320 E3
Pandrup Denmark 57°14N 9°40E 163 G3
Pandu Dem. Rep. of the Congo 4°59N 19°16E 264 B3
Panepistimio Athens, Greece 112 b2
Panevéggio-Pale di San Martino ⌓ Italy 46°14N 11°46E 199 B8
Panevėžys Lithuania 55°42N 24°25E 188 E3
Panfilov = Zharkent Kazakhstan 44°10N 80°0E 217 D10
Panfilovo Russia 50°25N 42°46E 190 E6
Pang Sida △ Thailand 14°5N 102°17E 236 E4
Panga Dem. Rep. of the Congo 1°52N 26°18E 268 B2
Pangai Tonga 19°48S 174°21W 287 P13
Pangaíon Óros Greece 40°50N 24°0E 203 F8
Pangala Congo 3°16S 14°34E 264 C2
Pangalanes, Canal des = Ampangalana, Lakandranon' Madag. 22°48S 47°50E 272 C2
Pangandaran Indonesia 7°40S 108°39E 235 D3
Pangandaran △ Indonesia 7°43S 108°42E 235 D3
Pangani Tanzania 5°25S 38°58E 268 D4
Pangani → Tanzania 5°26S 38°58E 268 D4
Pangantocan Phil. 7°50N 124°49E 233 H5
Pangar Djeréme ⌓ Cameroon 5°50N 13°10E 263 D7
Pangasinan □ Phil. 15°55N 120°20E 232 D3
Pangfou = Bengbu China 32°58N 117°20E 229 A11
Pangga, Tanjung Indonesia 8°54S 116°2E 231 K19
Panghsang = Bangkang Burma 22°4N 99°1E 228 F2
Pangil Dem. Rep. of the Congo 3°10S 26°35E 268 C2
Pangjiabu China 40°38N 115°26E 226 D8
Pangkah, Tanjung Indonesia 6°51S 112°33E 235 D4
Pangkai Burma 22°49N 98°39E 228 F2
Pangkajene Indonesia 4°46S 119°34E 235 C5
Pangkalanbrandan Indonesia 4°1N 98°20E 234 B1
Pangkalanbuun Indonesia 2°41S 111°37E 235 C4
Pangkalansusu Indonesia 4°2N 98°13E 234 B1
Pangkalpinang Indonesia 2°10S 106°10E 234 C3
Pangkoh Indonesia 3°5S 114°8E 235 C4
Pangkor, Pulau Malaysia 4°13N 100°34E 237 K3
Panglao Phil. 9°35N 123°45E 233 G4
Panglao I. Phil. 9°35N 123°48E 233 G4
Pangniqtuuq = Pangnirtung Canada 66°8N 65°43W 295 D18
Pangnirtung Canada 66°8N 65°43W 295 D18
Pango Alucuem Angola 8°43S 14°33E 265 D2
Pangody Russia 65°52N 74°27E 214 C8
Pangong Tso = Bangong Co China 33°45N 78°43E 243 C8
Pangrati Greece 37°56N 23°45E 112 B2
Pangsau Pass Asia 27°15N 96°10E 241 B6
Pangsua, Sungei → Singapore 1°25N 103°45E 138 A2
Pangtara Burma 20°57N 96°40E 241 E6
Panguipulli Chile 39°38S 72°20W 336 A2
Panguitch U.S.A. 37°50N 112°26W 305 H7
Panguna Papua N. G. 6°21S 155°25E 286 D8
Pangururan Indonesia 2°37N 98°42E 234 B1
Pangutaran Phil. 6°18N 120°35E 233 H3
Pangutaran Group Phil. 6°18N 120°34E 233 H3
Panhala India 16°49N 74°7E 244 F2
Panhandle U.S.A. 35°21N 101°23W 314 D4
Pani Mines India 22°29N 73°50E 242 H5
Pania-Mutombo Dem. Rep. of the Congo 5°11S 23°51E 265 D4
Pānī'au U.S.A. 21°56N 160°5W 302 B1
Panié, Mt. N. Cal. 20°36S 164°46E 288 d
Panihati India 22°41N 88°22E 124 A2
Panikota I. India 20°46N 71°21E 242 J4
Panipat India 29°25N 77°2E 242 E7
Paniqui Phil. 15°40N 120°34E 232 D3
Panitan Phil. 11°28N 122°46E 233 F4
Panj = Pyandzh → Asia 37°6N 68°20E 240 A2
Panjab Afghan. 34°23N 67°1E 240 B2
Panjakent Tajikistan 39°29N 67°37E 217 E7
Panjal Range = Pir Panjal Range India 32°30N 76°50E 242 C7
Panjang Kepulauan Riau, Indonesia 4°15N 108°12E 235 B3
Panjang Lampung, Indonesia 5°25S 105°20E 234 D3
Panjang, Bukit Singapore 1°22N 103°45E 138 A2
Panjgur Pakistan 27°0N 64°5E 240 D2
Panjhra → India 21°13N 74°57E 244 D2
Panjim = Panaji India 15°25N 73°50E 245 G1
Panjin China 41°3N 122°2E 227 D12
Panjnad → Pakistan 28°57N 70°30E 242 E4
Panjnad Barrage Pakistan 29°22N 71°15E 242 E4
Panjshīr □ Afghan. 35°50N 69°45E 240 B3
Panjwai Afghan. 31°26N 65°27E 242 D1
Panke → Germany 52°31N 13°22E 115 A3
Pankisi Gorge = Pankisis Kheoba Georgia 42°7N 45°15E 191 J7
Pankisis Kheoba Georgia 42°7N 45°15E 191 J7
Pankow Germany 52°34N 13°23E 115 A3
Pankshin Nigeria 9°16N 9°25E 263 D6
Panmunjŏm N. Korea 37°59N 126°38E 224 D3
Panna India 24°40N 80°15E 243 G9
Panna △ India 24°40N 80°0E 243 G8
Panna Hills India 24°40N 81°15E 243 G9
Pannawonica Australia 21°39S 116°19E 278 D2
Panngi Vanuatu 15°58S 168°12E 287 E6
Pano Akil Pakistan 27°51N 69°7E 242 F3
Pano Lefkara Cyprus 34°53N 33°20E 207 F9
Pano Panayia Cyprus 34°55N 32°38E 207 F8
Panopah Indonesia 1°55S 111°10E 235 C4
Panora U.S.A. 41°42N 94°22W 310 C2
Panorama Brazil 21°21S 51°51W 335 A5
Panormos Greece 35°25N 24°41E 207 E5
Panruti India 11°46N 79°35E 245 J4
Pansemal India 21°39N 74°42E 242 J6
Panshan = Panjin China 41°3N 122°2E 227 D12
Panshi China 42°58N 126°5E 227 C14
Pantabangan L. Phil. 15°50N 121°9E 232 D3
Pantanal Matogrossense △ Brazil 17°35S 57°27W 331 D6
Pantanaw Burma 16°59N 95°28E 241 G5
Pantanos de Centla ⌓ Mexico 18°25N 92°25W 319 D6
Pantar Indonesia 8°28S 124°10E 231 F6
Pante Macassar E. Timor 9°30S 123°58E 231 F6
Pantelleria Italy 36°50N 11°57E 200 F4
Panthéon Paris, France 134 c4
Pantheon Rome, Italy 136 b2
Panthersville U.S.A. 33°43N 84°16W 113 B3
Panti Indonesia 0°22N 100°3E 234 B2
Pantin France 48°53N 2°24E 134 A3
Pantin Sakan Burma 18°38N 97°33E 241 F6
Pantitlán Mexico 19°24N 99°4W 128 B2
Pantoja Peru 0°58S 75°10W 328 D2
Pantón = O Castro de Ferreira Spain 42°31N 7°37W 194 C3
Pantukan Phil. 7°9N 125°54E 233 H5
Panu Dem. Rep. of the Congo 3°50S 19°10E 264 C3
Pánuco Mexico 22°3N 98°10W 319 C5
Panuitan I. Phil. 19°26N 121°30E 232 B3
Panukulan Phil. 14°56N 121°49E 232 D3
Panvel India 18°59N 73°4E 244 E1
Panyabungan Indonesia 0°51N 99°33E 234 B1
Panyam Nigeria 9°27N 9°8E 263 D6
Panyu = Guangzhou China 23°6N 113°13E 121 B2
Panyu China 23°1N 113°21E 121 B2
Panzhihua China 26°33N 101°44E 228 D3
Panzi Dem. Rep. of the Congo 7°17S 18°1E 265 D3
Pao → Anzoátegui, Venezuela 8°6N 64°17W 329 B5
Pao → Apure, Venezuela 8°33N 68°1W 328 B4
Paoay Phil. 18°3N 120°30E 232 B3
Paochi = Baoji China 34°20N 107°5E 226 G4
Paoki = Baoji China 34°20N 107°5E 226 G4
Páola Italy 39°21N 16°2E 201 C9
Paola Malta 35°52N 14°30E 206 F8
Paola Kans., U.S.A. 38°35N 94°53W 308 F6
Paoli U.S.A. 38°33N 86°28W 311 F10
Paonia U.S.A. 38°52N 107°36W 304 G10
Paopao Moorea 17°30S 149°49W 289 e
Paoting = Baoding China 38°50N 115°28E 226 E8
Paot'ou = Baotou China 40°32N 110°2E 226 D6
Paoua C.A.R. 7°9N 16°20E 264 A3
Pápa Hungary 47°22N 17°30E 182 C2
Päpä Hawai'i, U.S.A. 19°13N 155°52W 302 D6
Papa Stour U.K. 60°20N 1°42W 167 A7
Papa Westray U.K. 59°20N 2°55W 167 B6
Päpa'aloa U.S.A. 19°59N 155°13W 302 D6
Papadopoli, Palazzo Venice, Italy 142 b2
Papagayo → Mexico 16°46N 99°43W 319 D5
Papagayo, G. de Costa Rica 10°30N 85°50W 320 D2
Papagni → India 15°35N 77°45E 245 G3
Papahänaumokuäkea Marine Nat. Monument ⌓ U.S.A. 25°25N 170°35W 302 F9
Papaïchton Fr. Guiana 3°48N 54°10W 329 C7
Päpa'ikou U.S.A. 19°47N 155°6W 302 D6
Papakura N.Z. 37°4S 174°59E 284 D3
Papantla Mexico 20°27N 97°19W 319 C5
Papar Malaysia 5°45N 116°0E 235 A5
Papara Tahiti 17°43S 149°31W 289 e
Paparoa N.Z. 36°6S 174°16E 284 C3
Paparoa △ N.Z. 42°7S 171°26E 285 C6
Paparoa Ra. N.Z. 42°5S 171°35E 285 C6
Papas, Akra Greece 38°13N 21°20E 204 C3
Papatoetoe N.Z. 36°59S 174°51E 284 C3
Papatura Solomon Is. 7°32S 158°47E 287 L10
Papeete Tahiti 17°32S 149°34W 289 e
Papenburg Germany 53°5N 7°23E 178 B3
Papenoo Tahiti 17°30S 149°25W 289 e
Papenoo → Tahiti 17°30S 149°25W 289 e
Papetoai Moorea 17°29S 149°52W 289 e
Paphlagonia Turkey 41°30N 33°0E 212 B5
Paphos Cyprus 34°46N 32°25E 207 F8
Paphos ✕ (PFO) Cyprus 34°43N 32°30E 207 F8
Papien Chiang = Da → Vietnam 21°15N 105°20E 228 G5
Papikio Oros Greece 41°15N 25°13E 203 E9
Papiol Spain 41°25N 2°0E 114 A1
Paposo Chile 25°0S 70°30W 334 B1
Papoutsa Cyprus 34°54N 33°4E 207 F9
Papua □ Indonesia 4°0S 137°0E 231 E9
Papua, G. of Papua N. G. 9°0S 144°50E 286 E3
Papua New Guinea ■ Oceania 8°0S 145°0E 286 E3
Papudo Chile 32°29S 71°27W 334 C1
Papuk Croatia 45°30N 17°30E 182 E2
Papun Burma 18°2N 97°30E 241 F6
Papunya Australia 23°15S 131°54E 278 D5
Pará = Belém Brazil 1°20S 48°30W 332 B2
Pará □ Brazil 3°20S 52°0W 331 A7
Paraburdoo Australia 23°14S 117°32E 278 D2
Paracale Phil. 14°17N 122°48E 232 D4
Paracas, Pen. de Peru 13°53S 76°20W 330 C2
Paracatu Brazil 17°10S 46°50W 333 E2
Paracatu → Brazil 16°30S 45°4W 333 E2
Paracel Is. S. China Sea 15°50N 112°0E 230 A4
Parachilna Australia 31°10S 138°21E 282 A3
Parachinar Pakistan 33°55N 70°5E 242 C4
Paraćin Serbia 43°54N 21°27E 202 C5
Paracuru Brazil 3°24S 39°4W 332 B4
Parada, Punta Peru 15°22S 75°11W 330 D2
Paradas Spain 37°18N 5°29W 195 H5
Paradela Spain 42°44N 7°37W 194 C3
Paradera Aruba 12°32N 70°0W 322 f
Paradip India 20°15N 86°35E 244 D8
Paradise Calif., U.S.A. 39°46N 121°37W 306 F5
Paradise Nev., U.S.A. 36°5N 115°8W 124 B2
Paradise → Canada 53°27N 57°19W 299 B8
Paradise Hill Canada 53°32N 109°28W 297 C7
Paradise I. Bahamas 25°6N 77°19W 153 b
Paradise River Canada 53°27N 57°17W 299 B8
Paradise Valley U.S.A. 41°30N 117°32W 304 F5
Paradisi Greece 36°18N 28°7E 206 E12
Paragould U.S.A. 36°3N 90°29W 315 C9
Paragua = Palawan Phil. 9°30N 118°30E 233 G2
Paraguá → Bolivia 13°34S 61°53W 331 C5
Paragua → Venezuela 6°55N 62°55W 329 B5
Paraguaçu = Paraguaçu Paulista Brazil 22°22S 50°35W 335 A5
Paraguaçú → Brazil 12°45S 38°54W 333 D4
Paraguaçu Paulista Brazil 22°22S 50°35W 335 A5
Paraguaipoa Venezuela 11°21N 71°57W 328 A3
Paraguaná, Pen. de Venezuela 12°0N 70°0W 328 A4
Paraguarí Paraguay 25°36S 57°0W 334 B4
Paraguarí □ Paraguay 26°0S 57°10W 334 B4
Paraguay ■ S. Amer. 23°0S 57°0W 334 A4
Paraguay → Paraguay 27°18S 58°38W 334 B4
Paraíba = João Pessoa Brazil 7°10S 34°52W 332 C5
Paraíba □ Brazil 7°0S 36°0W 332 C4
Paraíba do Sul → Brazil 21°37S 41°3W 333 F3
Paraíso Brazil 19°3S 52°59W 331 D7
Paraíso Tabasco, Mexico 18°24N 93°14W 319 D6
Paraíso Panama 9°3N 79°38W 320 c
Parak Iran 27°38N 52°25E 247 E7
Parakhino Paddubye Russia 58°26N 33°10E 188 C7
Parakou Benin 9°25N 2°40E 263 D5
Parakylia Australia 30°24S 136°25E 282 A2
Paralimni Cyprus 35°2N 33°58E 207 E9
Paralio Astros Greece 37°25N 22°45E 204 D4
Paralkote India 19°47N 80°41E 244 E5
Param I. Micronesia 7°21N 151°47E 287 T18
Parama I. Papua N. G. 9°0S 143°25E 286 E2
Paramaribo Suriname 5°50N 55°10W 329 B6
Parambu Brazil 6°13S 40°43W 332 C3
Paramillo, Cerro Colombia 7°4N 75°55W 328 B2
Paramillo △ Colombia 7°37N 76°13W 328 B2
Paramirim Brazil 13°26S 42°15W 333 D3

Paramirim → Brazil 11°34S 43°18W 333 D3
Paramithia Greece 39°30N 20°35E 204 B2
Paramonga Peru 10°40S 77°50W 330 C2
Paramount Studios U.S.A. 34°5N 118°19W 126 B3
Paramus U.S.A. 40°56N 74°2W 132 A1
Paramushir, Ostrov Russia 50°24N 156°0E 215 D16
Paran → Israel 30°20N 35°10E 251 H6
Paraná Argentina 31°45S 60°30W 334 C3
Paraná Brazil 12°30S 47°48W 333 D2
Paraná □ Brazil 24°30S 51°0W 335 A5
Paraná → Argentina 33°43S 59°15W 334 C4
Paraná → Brazil 12°30S 48°14W 333 D2
Paranaguá Brazil 25°30S 48°30W 335 B6
Paranaíba Brazil 19°40S 51°11W 331 D7
Paranaíba → Brazil 20°6S 51°4W 333 F1
Paranapanema → Brazil 22°40S 53°9W 335 A5
Paranapiacaba, Serra do Brazil 24°31S 48°35W 335 A6
Paranaque Phil. 14°30N 120°59E 127 B1
Paranas Phil. 11°42N 125°2E 233 F5
Paranavaí Brazil 23°4S 52°56W 335 A5
Parang Maguindanao, Phil. 7°23N 124°16E 233 H5
Parang Sulu, Phil. 5°55N 120°54E 233 J3
Parangippettai India 11°30N 79°38E 245 J4
Parângul Mare, Vf. Romania 45°20N 23°37E 183 E8
Paranthan Sri Lanka 9°26N 80°24E 245 K5
Paraoa French Polynesia 19°9S 140°43W 289 f
Paraparaumu N.Z. 40°57S 175°3E 284 G4
Parapetí → Bolivia 18°58S 62°21W 331 D5
Paraspori, Akra Greece 35°55N 27°15E 205 F9
Parate Bueno Venezuela 10°59N 64°22W 329 a
Paratinga Brazil 12°40S 43°10W 333 D3
Paratoo Australia 32°42S 139°20E 282 B3
Parauapebas Brazil 6°4S 49°54W 332 C2
Paraúna Brazil 16°55S 50°26W 333 E1
Paray-le-Monial France 46°27N 4°7E 173 F11
Paray-Vieille-Poste France 48°42N 2°20E 134 B3
Parbati → Mad. P., India 25°50N 76°30E 242 G7
Parbati → Raj., India 26°54N 77°53E 242 F7
Parbatipur Bangla. 25°39N 88°55E 241 C2
Parbhani India 19°8N 76°52E 244 E3
Parc des Princes Paris, France 48°50N 2°15E 134 A2
Parchim Germany 53°26N 11°52E 178 B7
Parchwitz = Prochowice Poland 51°17N 16°20E 185 G3
Parco = Sinclair U.S.A. 41°47N 107°7W 304 F10
Parczew Poland 51°40N 22°52E 185 G9
Pardes Hanna-Karkur Israel 32°28N 34°57E 251 F5
Pardilla Spain 41°33N 3°43W 194 D7
Pardisān Nature Park Iran 35°44N 51°22E 141 A2
Pardo → Bahia, Brazil 15°40S 39°0W 333 E4
Pardo → Mato Grosso, Brazil 21°46S 52°9W 335 A5
Pardo → Minas Gerais, Brazil 15°48S 44°48W 333 E3
Pardo → São Paulo, Brazil 20°10S 48°38W 333 F2
Pardoo Roadhouse Australia 20°6S 119°3E 278 D2
Pardubice Czech Rep. 50°3N 15°45E 180 A8
Pardubický □ Czech Rep. 49°50N 16°0E 180 B8
Pardubitz = Pardubice Czech Rep. 50°3N 15°45E 180 A8
Pare Indonesia 7°43S 112°12E 231 G15
Pare Mts. Tanzania 4°0S 37°45E 268 C4
Parecis, Serra dos Brazil 13°0S 60°0W 331 C6
Paredes de Nava Spain 42°9N 4°42W 194 C6
Parel India 18°59N 72°49E 130 B1
Parelhas Brazil 6°41S 36°39W 332 C4
Paren Russia 62°30N 163°15E 215 C17
Parenda India 18°16N 75°28E 244 E2
Parengarenga Harbour N.Z. 34°31S 173°0E 284 A2
Parent Canada 47°55N 74°35W 298 C5
Parent, L. Canada 48°31N 77°1W 298 C4
Parentis-en-Born France 44°21N 1°4W 174 D2
Parepare Indonesia 4°0S 119°40E 235 C5
Parfino Russia 57°59N 31°34E 188 D6
Parga Greece 39°15N 20°29E 204 B2
Pargas = Länsi-Turunmaa Finland 60°18N 22°18E 188 B2
Pargi India 17°11N 77°53E 244 E3
Pargo, Pta. do Madeira 32°49N 17°17W 153 c
Parguera Puerto Rico 17°59N 67°3W 321 b
Parham Canada 44°39N 76°43W 313 B8
Pari Brazil 23°32S 46°36W 137 B2
Paria → U.S.A. 36°52N 111°36W 305 H8
Paria, G. de Venezuela 10°30N 61°40W 323 t
Paria, Pen. de Venezuela 10°50N 62°30W 329 A5
Pariaguán Venezuela 8°51N 64°34W 329 B5
Pariaman Indonesia 0°47S 100°11E 234 C2
Paricatuba Brazil 4°26S 61°53W 329 D5
Paricutín, Cerro Mexico 19°28N 102°15W 318 D4
Parigi Indonesia 0°50S 120°5E 231 E6
Parika Guyana 6°50N 58°20W 329 B6
Parikia Greece 37°6N 25°11E 205 D7
Parikkala Finland 61°33N 29°31E 188 B5
Parima, Serra Brazil 2°30N 64°0W 329 C5
Parinari Peru 4°35S 74°25W 330 A3
Pariñas, Pta. Peru 4°30S 82°0W 330 A1
Parincea Romania 46°27N 27°9E 183 D12
Paringa Australia 34°10S 140°46E 282 C4
Parintins Brazil 2°40S 56°50W 329 D6
Parioli Italy 41°55N 12°29E 136 B1
Pariparit Kyun Burma 14°52N 93°41E 245 G11
Paris Ont., Canada 43°12N 80°25W 312 C4
Paris France 48°53N 2°20E 134 A3
Paris Idaho, U.S.A. 42°14N 111°24W 304 E8
Paris Ill., U.S.A. 39°36N 87°42W 311 E9
Paris Ky., U.S.A. 38°13N 84°15W 311 F12
Paris Mo., U.S.A. 39°29N 92°0W 310 E5
Paris Tenn., U.S.A. 36°18N 88°19W 315 C10
Paris Tex., U.S.A. 33°40N 95°33W 314 E7
Paris, Ville de □ France 48°50N 2°20E 173 D9
Paris Charles de Gaulle ✈ (CDG) France 49°0N 2°32E 173 D9
Paris Orly ✈ (ORY) France 48°44N 2°23E 134 B3
Parish U.S.A. 43°25N 76°8W 313 C8
Parishville U.S.A. 44°38N 74°49W 313 B10
Pariti Indonesia 10°1S 123°45E 278 B3
Parje India 18°54N 72°57E 130 B2
Park U.S.A. 48°45N 122°18W 306 B4
Park City U.S.A. 37°48N 97°20W 308 G5
Pārk-e Āzādegān Iran 35°37N 51°28E 141 B2
Pārk-e Mellat Iran 35°47N 51°24E 141 A2
Park Falls U.S.A. 45°56N 90°27W 308 C8
Park Forest U.S.A. 41°29N 87°40W 311 C9
Park Head Canada 44°36N 81°9W 312 B3
Park Hills U.S.A. 37°51N 90°51W 310 G6
Park Range U.S.A. 40°41N 106°41W 304 F10
Park Rapids U.S.A. 46°55N 95°4W 308 B6
Park Ridge U.S.A. 42°2N 87°51W 119 A1
Park River U.S.A. 48°24N 97°45W 308 A5
Park Royal U.K. 51°31N 0°16W 125 A2
Park Rynie S. Africa 30°25S 30°45E 271 D5
Parkā Bandar Iran 25°55N 59°35E 247 E8
Parkal India 18°12N 79°43E 244 E4
Parkán = Štúrovo Slovak Rep. 47°48N 18°41E 181 D11
Parkano Finland 62°1N 23°0E 188 A2
Parkchester U.S.A. 40°49N 73°50W 132 B2
Parkdale Canada 43°38N 79°25W 141 B2
Parkent Uzbekistan 41°18N 69°40E 217 D7
Parker Ariz., U.S.A. 34°9N 114°17W 307 L12
Parker Pa., U.S.A. 41°5N 79°41W 312 E5
Parker Center Los Angeles, U.S.A. 127 b2
Parker Dam U.S.A. 34°18N 114°8W 307 L12
Parkersburg Iowa, U.S.A. 42°35N 92°47W 310 B4
Parkersburg W. Va., U.S.A. 39°16N 81°34W 309 F13
Parkes Australia 33°9S 148°11E 283 B8
Parkfield U.S.A. 35°54N 120°26W 306 K6
Parkhill Canada 43°15N 81°38W 312 C3
Parkhurst S. Africa 26°8S 28°1E 123 A2
Parkland U.S.A. 47°9N 122°26W 306 C4
Parklawn U.S.A. 38°50N 77°7W 143 B2
Parkmore S. Africa 26°5S 28°2E 123 A2
Parkside U.S.A. 37°44N 122°29W 136 B2
Parkston U.S.A. 43°24N 97°59W 308 D5
Parksville Canada 49°20N 124°21W 296 D4
Parktown S. Africa 26°10S 28°2E 123 B2
Parkview S. Africa 26°9S 28°1E 123 A2
Parkville U.S.A. 40°38N 73°57W 132 C2
Parkway U.S.A. 38°32N 121°26W 306 G5
Parkwood Gauteng, S. Africa 26°9S 28°2E 123 A2
Parkwood Western Cape, S. Africa 34°2S 18°30E 118 B1
Parla Spain 40°14N 3°46W 194 E7
Parlakimidi India 18°45N 84°5E 244 E7
Parlatuvier Trin. & Tob. 11°18N 60°39W 323 s
Parli India 18°50N 76°35E 244 E3
Parliament Budapest, Hungary 117 b2
Pârliţa Moldova 47°19N 27°52E 183 C12
Parma Italy 44°48N 10°20E 198 D7
Parma Idaho, U.S.A. 43°47N 116°57W 304 E5
Parma Ohio, U.S.A. 41°24N 81°43W 312 E3
Parma → Italy 44°56N 10°26E 198 D7
Parnaguá Brazil 10°10S 44°38W 332 D3
Parnaíba Brazil 2°54S 41°47W 332 B3
Parnaíba → Brazil 3°0S 41°50W 332 B3
Parnamirim Pernambuco, Brazil 8°5S 39°34W 332 C4
Parnamirim Rio Grande do N., Brazil 5°55S 35°15W 332 C4
Parnarama Brazil 5°31S 43°6W 332 C3
Parnassos Greece 38°35N 22°30E 204 C4
Parnassus N.Z. 42°42S 173°23E 285 C8
Parndana Australia 35°48S 137°12E 282 C2
Parner India 19°0N 74°26E 244 E2
Parnitha Greece 38°14N 23°45E 204 C5
Parnitha △ Greece 38°12N 23°44E 204 C5
Parnonas Oros Greece 37°15N 22°45E 204 D4
Pärnu Estonia 58°28N 24°33E 188 C3
Pärnu → Estonia 58°28N 24°33E 188 C3
Paro Dzong Bhutan 27°32N 89°53E 241 B2
Parola India 20°47N 75°7E 244 D2
Paroo → Australia 31°28S 143°32E 282 A5
Paros Greece 37°5N 25°12E 205 D7
Parow S. Africa 33°53S 18°37E 118 A2
Parowan U.S.A. 37°51N 112°50W 305 H7
Parpaillon France 44°30N 6°40E 175 D10
Parque Chacabuco Argentina 34°39S 58°26W 117 B2
Parque Patricios Argentina 34°39S 58°23W 117 B2
Parral Chile 36°10S 71°52W 334 D1
Parramatta Australia 33°48S 151°1E 283 B9
Parramatta → Australia 33°49S 151°3E 139 A1
Parras Mexico 25°25N 102°11W 318 B4
Parrett → U.K. 51°12N 3°1W 169 F4
Parris I. U.S.A. 32°20N 80°41W 316 C9
Parrish U.S.A. 27°35N 82°26W 317 H7
Parrott U.S.A. 31°54N 84°31W 316 D5
Parrsboro Canada 45°30N 64°25W 299 C7
Parry Channel Canada 74°15N 94°0W 295 C13
Parry I. Canada 45°18N 80°10W 312 A4
Parry Is. Canada 77°0N 110°0W 295 B10
Parry Sound Canada 45°20N 80°0W 312 A5
Parsābād Iran 39°39N 47°50E 213 C12
Parsaloi Kenya 1°16N 36°51E 268 B4
Parsberg Germany 49°10N 11°43E 179 F7
Parsęta → Poland 54°11N 15°34E 184 D2
Parsnip → Canada 55°10N 123°2W 296 B4
Parsons U.S.A. 37°20N 95°16W 308 G6
Parsons Ra. Australia 13°30S 135°15E 280 A2
Partabpur India 20°0N 80°42E 244 E5
Partanna Italy 37°43N 12°53E 200 E5
Partenio ⌓ Italy 40°56N 14°38E 201 B7
Parthenay France 46°38N 0°16W 172 F6
Parthenon Athens, Greece 112 c2
Partinico Italy 38°3N 13°7E 200 D6
Partizansk Russia 43°8N 133°9E 215 E14
Partizánske Slovak Rep. 48°38N 18°23E 181 C11
Partridge I. Canada 55°59N 87°37W 298 A2
Partry Mts. Ireland 53°40N 9°28W 166 C2
Partur India 19°40N 76°14E 244 E3
Paru → Brazil 1°33S 52°38W 329 D7
Parú → Venezuela 4°20N 66°27W 328 C4
Paru de Oeste → Brazil 1°30N 56°0W 329 C6
Parucito → Venezuela 5°18N 65°59W 328 B4
Parur India 10°13N 76°14E 245 J3
Paruro Peru 13°45S 71°50W 330 C3
Parvān □ Afghan. 35°0N 69°0E 240 B3
Parvatipuram India 18°50N 83°25E 244 E6
Parvatsar India 26°52N 74°49E 242 F6
Påryd Sweden 56°34N 15°55E 163 H9
Parys S. Africa 26°52S 27°29E 270 C4
Pas, Pta. des Spain 38°46N 1°26E 206 D1
Pas, The Canada 53°45N 101°15W 297 C8
Pas-de-Calais □ France 50°30N 2°10E 173 B9
Paşabahçe Turkey 41°6N 29°5E 122 B2
Pasada Spain 43°23N 5°40W 194 B5
Pasadena Nfld. & L., Canada 49°1N 57°36W 299 C8
Pasadena Calif., U.S.A. 34°9N 118°8W 126 B4
Pasadena Tex., U.S.A. 29°43N 95°13W 314 G7
Pasaje Ecuador 3°23S 79°50W 328 D2
Pasaje → Argentina 25°39S 63°56W 334 B3
Paşalimanı Turkey 40°29N 27°36E 203 F11
Pasar Indonesia 8°27S 114°54E 231 J17
Pasar Minggu Indonesia 6°16S 106°49E 122 B1
Pasargadae Iran 30°11N 53°10E 247 D7
Pasarkuok Indonesia 1°27S 100°36E 234 C2
Pasarsibuhuan Indonesia 1°3N 99°43E 234 B1
Pasay Phil. 14°32N 120°59E 127 B1
Pascagoula U.S.A. 30°21N 88°33W 315 F10
Pascagoula → U.S.A. 30°23N 88°37W 315 F10
Paşcani Romania 47°14N 26°45E 183 C11
Paschimbanga □ India 23°0N 88°0E 243 H13
Pasco U.S.A. 46°14N 119°6W 304 C4
Pasco □ Peru 10°40S 75°0W 330 C3
Pasco I. Australia 20°57S 115°20E 278 D2
Pascoag U.S.A. 41°57N 71°42W 313 E13
Pascoe Vale Australia 37°43S 144°55E 128 A1
Pascua, I. de Chile 27°7S 109°23W 330 b
Paseo de la Reforma Mexico City, Mexico 128 b2
Pasewalk Germany 53°30N 13°58E 178 B9
Pasfield L. Canada 58°24N 105°20W 297 B7
Pasha → Russia 60°29N 32°55E 188 B7
Pashmakli = Smolyan Bulgaria 41°36N 24°38E 203 E8
Pasig Phil. 14°33N 121°4E 127 B2
Pasig → Phil. 14°31N 121°6E 127 B2
Pasighat India 28°4N 95°21E 241 A5
Pasila Finland 60°12N 24°56E 121 B2
Pasing Germany 48°8N 11°28E 131 B1
Pasinler Turkey 39°59N 41°41E 213 C9
Pasir Mas Malaysia 6°2N 102°8E 237 J4
Pasir Panjang Singapore 1°18N 103°46E 138 B2
Pasir Putih Malaysia 5°50N 102°24E 237 K4
Pasir Ris Singapore 1°22N 103°56E 138 A3
Pasirian Indonesia 8°13S 113°8E 235 D4
Pasirkuning = Dabo Indonesia 0°30S 104°33E 234 C2
Pasirpengarayan Indonesia 0°51N 100°16E 234 B2
Påskallavik Sweden 57°10N 16°26E 163 G10
Paskūh Iran 27°34N 61°39E 247 E9
Pasłęk Poland 54°3N 19°41E 184 D6
Pasłęka → Poland 54°26N 19°46E 184 D6
Pasley, C. Australia 33°52S 123°35E 279 F3
Pašman Croatia 43°58N 15°20E 199 E12
Pasmore → Australia 31°5S 139°49E 282 A3
Pasni Pakistan 25°15N 63°27E 240 D1
Paso Bravo △ Paraguay 22°32S 57°5W 334 A4
Paso Cantinela Mexico 32°33N 115°47W 307 N11
Paso de Indios Argentina 43°55S 69°0W 336 B3
Paso de los Indios Argentina 38°32S 69°25W 336 A3
Paso de los Libres Argentina 29°44S 57°10W 334 B4
Paso de los Toros Uruguay 32°45S 56°30W 334 C4
Paso Flores Argentina 40°35S 70°38W 336 B2
Paso Robles U.S.A. 35°38N 120°41W 306 K6
Pasorapa Bolivia 18°16S 64°37W 331 D5
Paspébiac Canada 48°3N 65°17W 299 C6
Pasrur Pakistan 32°16N 74°43E 242 C6
Passage East Ireland 52°14N 7°0W 166 D5
Passage West Ireland 51°52N 8°21W 166 E3
Passaic U.S.A. 40°51N 74°7W 132 A1
Passaic → U.S.A. 40°42N 74°10W 132 B1
Passam Papua N. G. 3°41S 143°38E 286 B2
Passau Germany 48°34N 13°28E 179 G9
Passenheim = Pasym Poland 53°48N 20°49E 184 E7
Passero, C. Italy 36°41N 15°10E 201 F8
Passi Phil. 11°6N 122°38E 233 F4
Passirana Italy 45°32N 9°2E 128 A1
Passo Fundo Brazil 28°10S 52°20W 335 B5
Passos Brazil 20°45S 46°37W 333 F2
Passow Germany 53°8N 14°6E 178 B10
Passy France 45°55N 6°41E 175 C10
Pastavy Belarus 55°4N 26°50E 188 E4
Pastaza □ Ecuador 2°0S 77°0W 328 D2
Pastaza → Peru 4°50S 76°52W 328 D2
Pasto Colombia 1°13N 77°17W 328 C2
Pastol B. U.S.A. 63°7N 163°15W 303 E7
Pastos Bons Brazil 6°36S 44°5W 332 C3
Pastrana Spain 40°27N 2°53W 196 E2
Pasuquin Phil. 18°20N 120°37E 232 B3
Pasuruan Indonesia 7°40S 112°44E 235 D4
Pasym Poland 53°48N 20°49E 184 E7
Pásztó Hungary 47°52N 19°43E 182 C4
Pata Phil. 5°51N 121°10E 233 J3
Pata I. Phil. 5°49N 121°10E 233 J3
Patag I. = Flat I. S. China Sea 10°49N 115°49E 230 B5
Patagonia Argentina 45°0S 69°0W 336 C3
Patagonia Ariz., U.S.A. 31°33N 110°45W 305 L8
Patambar Iran 29°45N 60°17E 247 D9
Patan = Lalitpur Nepal 27°40N 85°20E 243 F11
Patan = Somnath India 20°53N 70°22E 242 J4
Patan Gujarat, India 23°54N 72°14E 242 H5
Patan Maharashtra, India 17°22N 73°57E 244 F1
Patani Indonesia 0°20N 128°50E 231 D7
Pătârlagele Romania 45°19N 26°21E 183 E11
Pataudi India 28°18N 76°48E 242 E7
Patchewollock Australia 35°22S 142°12E 282 C5
Patchogue U.S.A. 40°46N 73°1W 313 F11
Pate Coast, Kenya 2°10S 41°0E 268 C5
Pate Taiwan 24°56N 121°17E 225 B3
Patea N.Z. 39°45S 174°30E 284 F3
Pategi Nigeria 8°50N 5°45E 263 D6
Patel Nagar India 28°39N 77°10E 120 B1
Patensie S. Africa 33°46S 24°49E 270 D3
Paterna Spain 39°30N 0°26W 197 F4
Paternion Austria 46°43N 13°38E 180 E6
Paternò Italy 37°34N 14°54E 201 E7
Pateros Manila, Phil. 14°32N 121°3E 127 B2
Pateros Wash., U.S.A. 48°3N 119°54W 304 B4
Paterson N.S.W., Australia 32°35S 151°36E 283 B9
Paterson N.J., U.S.A. 40°54N 74°9W 313 F10
Paterson Inlet N.Z. 46°56S 168°12E 285 G3
Paterson Ra. Australia 21°45S 122°10E 278 D3
Pathankot India 32°18N 75°45E 242 C6
Pathardi India 19°10N 75°11E 244 E2
Patharghata Bangla. 22°2N 89°58E 241 D2
Pathein = Bassein Burma 16°45N 94°30E 241 G5
Pathfinder Res. U.S.A. 42°28N 106°51W 304 E10
Pathiu Thailand 10°42N 99°19E 237 G2
Pathri India 19°15N 76°27E 244 E3
Pathum Thani Thailand 14°1N 100°32E 236 E3
Pathumwan Thailand 13°44N 100°31E 113 B2
Pati Indonesia 6°45S 111°1E 235 D4
Pati Pt. Guam 13°35N 144°57E 302 d
Patía Colombia 2°4N 77°4W 328 C2
Patía → Colombia 2°13N 78°40W 328 C2
Patiala Punjab, India 30°23N 76°26E 242 D7
Patiala Ut. P., India 27°43N 79°1E 243 F8
Patine Kouka Senegal 12°45N 13°45W 262 C2
Patipukur India 22°36N 88°24E 124 B2
Patisia Greece 38°2N 23°45E 112 A2
Patitiri Greece 39°8N 23°50E 204 B5
Patkai Bum India 27°0N 95°30E 241 B5
Patmos Greece 37°21N 26°36E 205 D8
Patna India 25°35N 85°12E 243 G11
Patnagarh India 20°43N 83°9E 244 D6
Patnanongan I. Phil. 14°48N 122°11E 232 D4
Patnongon Phil. 10°55N 122°0E 233 F4
Patnos Turkey 39°13N 42°51E 213 C10
Pato Branco Brazil 26°13S 52°40W 335 B5
Patoka L. U.S.A. 38°20N 86°40W 311 F10
Patong, Ao Thailand 7°54N 98°17E 237 a
Patonga Uganda 2°45N 33°15E 268 B3
Patos Albania 40°42N 19°38E 202 F3
Patos Brazil 6°55S 37°16W 332 C4
Patos, L. dos Brazil 31°20S 51°0W 335 C5
Patos, Río de los → Argentina 31°18S 69°25W 334 C2
Patos de Minas Brazil 18°35S 46°32W 333 E2
Patquía Argentina 30°2S 66°55W 334 C2
Patra Greece 38°14N 21°47E 204 C3
Patraikos Kolpos Greece 38°17N 21°30E 204 C3
Patras = Patra Greece 38°14N 21°47E 204 C3
Patreksfjörður Iceland 65°35N 24°0W 155 B2
Patriarsheye = Donskoy Russia 53°55N 38°15E 188 F10
Patricio Lynch, I. Chile 48°35S 75°30W 336 C1
Patriot Hills Antarctica 82°20S 81°25W 151 E16
Patrocínio Brazil 18°57S 47°0W 333 E2
Pattada Italy 40°35N 9°6E 200 B2
Pattadakal India 16°1N 75°42E 245 F2
Pattallassang Indonesia 5°26S 119°26E 235 D5
Pattani Thailand 6°48N 101°15E 237 J3
Pattaya Thailand 12°52N 100°55E 236 F3
Patten U.S.A. 46°0N 68°38W 309 B19
Patterson Calif., U.S.A. 37°28N 121°8W 306 H5
Patterson Ga., U.S.A. 31°23N 82°8W 316 D7
Patterson La., U.S.A. 29°42N 91°18W 314 G9
Patterson, Mt. U.S.A. 38°29N 119°20W 306 G7
Patteson, Passage Vanuatu 15°26S 168°12E 287 E6
Patti Punjab, India 31°17N 74°54E 242 D6
Patti Ut. P., India 25°55N 82°12E 243 G10
Patti Italy 38°8N 14°58E 201 D7
Pattoki Pakistan 31°5N 73°52E 242 D5
Patton = Monroeville U.S.A. 40°26N 79°45W 312 F5
Patton U.S.A. 40°38N 78°39W 312 F6
Pattonsburg U.S.A. 40°3N 94°8W 310 D2
Pattukkattai India 10°25N 79°20E 245 J4
Patu Brazil 6°6S 37°38W 332 C4
Patuakhali Bangla. 22°20N 90°25E 241 D3
Patuanak Canada 55°55N 107°43W 297 B7
Patuca → Honduras 15°50N 84°18W 320 C3
Patuca, Punta Honduras 15°49N 84°14W 320 C3
Patuca △ Honduras 14°30N 85°30W 320 D2
Pătulele Romania 44°21N 22°47E 182 F7
Patur India 20°27N 76°56E 244 D3
Patvinsuo △ Finland 63°7N 30°45E 160 E24
Pátzcuaro Mexico 19°31N 101°38W 318 D4
Pau France 43°19N 0°25W 174 E3
Pau, Gave de → France 43°33N 1°12W 174 E2
Pau d'Arco Brazil 7°30S 49°22W 332 C2
Pau dos Ferros Brazil 6°7S 38°10W 332 C4
Pauanui N.Z. 37°1S 175°52E 284 D4
Paucartambo Peru 13°19S 71°35W 330 C3
Paudash Canada 44°59N 77°58W 312 B7
Pauillac France 45°11N 0°46W 174 C3
Pauini Brazil 7°40S 66°58W 330 B4
Pauini → Brazil 1°42S 62°50W 329 D5
Pauk Burma 21°27N 94°30E 241 E5
Paukkaung Burma 18°54N 95°33E 241 F5
Pauktaw Burma 20°11N 93°4E 241 E4
Paul I. Canada 56°30N 61°20W 299 A7
Paul Isnard Fr. Guiana 4°47N 54°1W 329 C7
Paul Revere Park Boston, U.S.A. 116 a2
Paul Smiths U.S.A. 44°26N 74°15W 313 B10
Paulatuk Canada 69°25N 124°0W 294 D7
Paulding U.S.A. 41°8N 84°35W 311 C12
Paulding Bay S. Ocean 66°0S 118°0E 151 C8
Paulhan France 43°33N 3°28E 174 E7
Paulis = Isiro Dem. Rep. of the Congo 2°53N 27°40E 268 B2
Paulista = Paulistana Brazil 8°9S 41°9W 332 C3
Paulista Brazil 7°57S 34°53W 332 C5
Paulistana Brazil 8°9S 41°9W 332 C3
Pauliström Sweden 57°28N 15°31E 163 G9
Paulo Afonso Brazil 9°21S 38°15W 332 C4
Paulo de Faria Brazil 20°2S 49°24W 333 F2
Paulo E. Virginia, Gruta Brazil 22°56S 43°16W 135 B1
Paulpietersburg S. Africa 27°23S 30°50E 271 C5
Pauls Valley U.S.A. 34°44N 97°13W 314 D6
Paulshof Germany 52°34N 13°42E 115 A5
Pauma Valley U.S.A. 33°16N 116°58W 307 M10
Paung Burma 16°37N 94°28E 241 G5
Paungde Burma 18°29N 95°30E 241 F5
Pauni India 20°48N 79°40E 244 D4
Pauri India 30°9N 78°47E 243 D8
Pausa Peru 15°16S 73°22W 330 D3
Pauto → Colombia 5°9N 70°55W 328 B3
Pavagada India 14°6N 77°16E 245 G3
Pāveh Iran 35°3N 46°22E 213 E12
Pavelets Russia 53°49N 39°14E 188 F10
Pavia Italy 45°7N 9°8E 198 C6
Pavilion U.S.A. 42°52N 78°1W 312 D6
Pavilly France 49°34N 0°57E 172 C7
Pāvilosta Latvia 56°53N 21°14E 184 B8
Pavlikeni Bulgaria 43°14N 25°20E 203 C9
Pavlodar Kazakhstan 52°33N 77°0E 217 B9
Pavlograd = Pavlohrad Ukraine 48°30N 35°52E 189 H8
Pavlohrad Ukraine 48°30N 35°52E 189 H8
Pavlovo Russia 55°58N 43°5E 190 C6
Pavlovsk Russia 50°26N 40°5E 190 E5
Pavlovskaya Russia 46°17N 39°47E 191 G4
Pavlovskiy-Posad Russia 55°47N 38°42E 188 E10
Pavo U.S.A. 30°58N 83°45W 316 E6
Pavullo nel Frignano Italy 44°20N 10°50E 198 D7
Pavuvu Solomon Is. 9°4S 159°8E 287 M10
Paw Paw Ill., U.S.A. 41°41N 88°59W 310 C8
Paw Paw Mich., U.S.A. 42°13N 85°53W 311 B11
Pawahku Burma 26°11N 98°40E 241 B7
Pawai, Pulau Singapore 1°11N 103°44E 237 d
Pawan → Indonesia 1°55S 110°0E 235 C4
Pawayan India 28°4N 80°6E 243 E9
Pawhuska U.S.A. 36°40N 96°20W 314 C6
Pawling U.S.A. 41°34N 73°36W 313 E11
Pawnee Ill., U.S.A. 39°36N 89°35W 310 E7
Pawnee Okla., U.S.A. 36°20N 96°48W 314 C6
Pawnee City U.S.A. 40°7N 96°9W 308 E5
Pawtucket U.S.A. 41°53N 71°23W 313 E13
Paxi Greece 39°14N 20°12E 206 C10
Paximadia Greece 35°0N 24°35E 207 F5
Paxson U.S.A. 63°2N 145°30W 303 E11
Paxton U.S.A. 40°27N 88°6W 311 D8
Paya Lebar Singapore 1°21N 103°52E 138 A3
Payagyi Burma 17°29N 96°32E 241 G6
Payakumbuh Indonesia 0°20S 100°35E 234 C2
Payapa = General Tinio Phil. 15°39N 121°10E 232 D3
Payas = Yakacık Turkey 36°46N 36°11E 250 B7
Payerne Switz. 46°49N 6°56E 179 J2
Payette U.S.A. 44°5N 116°56W 304 D5
Paymogo Spain 37°44N 7°21W 195 H3
Payne U.S.A. 41°5N 84°44W 311 C12
Payne Bay = Kangirsuk Canada 60°0N 70°0W 295 F18
Payne L. Canada 59°30N 74°30W 295 F17
Payne Pt. Ascension I. 7°57S 14°25W 153 g
Paynes Find Australia 29°15S 117°42E 279 E2
Paynesville Liberia 6°20N 10°45W 262 D2
Paynesville Minn., U.S.A. 45°23N 94°43W 308 C6
Payo Obispo = Chetumal Mexico 18°30N 88°20W 319 D7
Pays de la Loire □ France 47°45N 0°25W 172 E6
Paysandú Uruguay 32°19S 58°8W 334 C4
Payson Ariz., U.S.A. 34°14N 111°20W 305 J8
Payson Utah, U.S.A. 40°3N 111°44W 304 F8
Paz → Guatemala 13°44N 90°10W 320 D1
Paz, B. de la Mexico 24°9N 110°25W 318 C2
Pāzanān Iran 30°35N 49°59E 247 D6
Pazar Turkey 41°10N 40°50E 213 B9
Pazarcık Turkey 37°30N 37°17E 212 D7
Pazardzhik Bulgaria 42°12N 24°20E 203 D8
Pazardzhik □ Bulgaria 42°12N 24°20E 203 D8
Pazarköy Turkey 39°51N 27°24E 205 B9
Pazarlar Turkey 39°0N 29°7E 205 C11
Pazaryeri Turkey 40°0N 29°56E 205 B11
Pazaryolu Turkey 40°21N 40°47E 213 B9
Pazin Croatia 45°14N 13°56E 199 C10
Pazña Bolivia 18°36S 66°55W 330 D4
Pčinja → Macedonia 41°50N 21°45E 202 E5
Pe Ell U.S.A. 46°34N 123°18W 306 D3
Pea → U.S.A. 31°1N 85°51W 316 D4
Peabody U.S.A. 42°31N 70°56W 313 D14
Peace → Alta., Canada 59°0N 111°25W 296 B6
Peace → Fla., U.S.A. 26°56N 82°6W 317 J7
Peace Point Canada 59°7N 112°27W 296 B6
Peace River Canada 56°15N 117°18W 296 B5
Peach Springs U.S.A. 35°32N 113°25W 305 J7
Peachland Canada 49°47N 119°45W 296 D5
Peachtree City U.S.A. 33°25N 84°35W 316 B5
Peacock Pt. Wake I. 19°16N 166°37E 302 b
Peak, The = Kinder Scout U.K. 53°24N 1°52W 168 D6
Peak, The Ascension I. 7°57S 14°20W 153 g
Peak Charles △ Australia 32°42S 121°10E 279 F3
Peak District △ U.K. 53°24N 1°46W 168 D6
Peak Hill Australia 32°47S 148°11E 283 B8
Peak Ra. Australia 22°50S 148°20E 280 C4
Peake Australia 35°25S 139°55E 282 C3
Peake Cr. → Australia 28°2S 136°7E 281 D2
Peakhurst Australia 33°57S 151°3E 139 B1
Peal de Becerro Spain 37°55N 3°7W 195 H7
Peale, Mt. U.S.A. 38°26N 109°14W 304 G9
Peale I. Wake I. 19°18N 166°37E 302 b
Peania Greece 37°56N 23°50E 112 B3
Pearblossom U.S.A. 34°30N 117°55W 307 L9
Pearl U.S.A. 39°28N 90°38W 310 E6
Pearl → U.S.A. 30°11N 89°32W 315 F10
Pearl and Hermes Reef U.S.A. 27°55N 175°45W 302 F8
Pearl Banks Sri Lanka 8°45N 79°45E 245 K4
Pearl City U.S.A. 21°24N 157°59W 302 K14
Pearl Harbor U.S.A. 21°21N 157°57W 302 K14
Pearl Harbor Nat. Wildlife Refuge ⌓ U.S.A. 21°23N 157°59W 302 K14
Pearl River = Zhu Jiang → China 22°45N 113°37E 229 F9
Pearl River U.S.A. 41°4N 74°2W 313 E10
Pearl River Bridge China 22°15N 113°48E 219 a
Pearls Grenada 12°9N 61°37W 323 q
Pearls Rock Grenada 12°9N 61°36W 323 q
Pearsall U.S.A. 28°54N 99°6W 314 G5
Pearson U.S.A. 31°18N 82°51W 316 D7
Pearson Int. Toronto ✈ (YYZ) Canada 43°46N 79°35W 141 A1
Peary Chan. Canada 79°40N 101°30W 295 B11
Peary Land Greenland 82°40N 33°0W 154 A7
Pease → U.S.A. 34°12N 99°2W 314 D5
Peawanuck Canada 55°15N 85°12W 298 A2
Pebane Mozam. 17°10S 38°8E 269 F4
Pebas Peru 3°10S 71°46W 328 D3
Pebble, I. Falk. Is. 51°20S 59°40W 153 f
Pebble Beach U.S.A. 36°34N 121°57W 306 J5
Peć = Pejë Kosovo 42°40N 20°17E 202 D4
Peçanha Brazil 18°33S 42°34W 333 E3
Pecatonica U.S.A. 42°19N 89°22W 310 B7
Pecatonica → U.S.A. 42°26N 89°12W 310 B7
Péccioli Italy 43°33N 10°43E 198 E7
Pechea Romania 45°36N 27°49E 183 E12
Pechenga Russia 69°29N 31°4E 160 B24
Pechenizhyn Ukraine 48°30N 24°48E 183 B9
Pechiguera, Pta. Canary Is. 28°51N 13°53W 153 e2
Pechnezhskoye Vdkhr. Ukraine 50°5N 36°54E 189 G9
Pechora Russia 65°10N 57°11E 186 A10
Pechora → Russia 68°13N 54°15E 186 A9
Pechorskaya Guba Russia 68°40N 54°0E 186 A9
Pechory Russia 57°48N 27°40E 188 D4
Pecica Romania 46°10N 21°3E 182 D6
Pecka Serbia 44°18N 19°33E 202 B3
Peckham U.K. 51°28N 0°3W 125 B3
Pécora, C. Italy 39°27N 8°23E 200 C1
Pecos N. Mex., U.S.A. 35°35N 105°41W 305 J11
Pecos Tex., U.S.A. 31°26N 103°30W 314 F3
Pecos → U.S.A. 29°42N 101°22W 314 G4
Pécs Hungary 46°5N 18°15E 182 D3
Pedasí Panama 7°32N 80°2W 320 E3
Pedda Bellala India 19°4N 78°49E 244 E4
Peddapalli India 18°40N 79°24E 244 E4
Peddapuram India 17°6N 82°8E 244 F6
Pedder, L. Australia 42°55S 146°10E 281 G4
Peddie S. Africa 33°14S 27°7E 271 D4
Pedernales Dom. Rep. 18°2N 71°44W 321 C5
Pedernales Ecuador 0°5N 80°3W 328 C1
Pederstrup Denmark 55°44N 12°20E 118 A2
Pedieos → Cyprus 35°10N 33°54E 207 E9
Pedirka Desert Australia 26°47S 134°11E 281 A1
Pedra Azul Brazil 16°2S 41°17W 333 E3
Pedra Branca Brazil 0°51N 51°58W 329 C7
Pedra Grande, Recifes de Brazil 17°45S 38°58W 333 E4
Pedra Lume C. Verde Is. 16°40N 22°52W 153 j
Pedralbes Spain 41°23N 2°7E 114 A1
Pedras Negras Brazil 12°51S 62°54W 331 C5
Pedras Tinhosas, I. São Tomé & Príncipe 1°22N 7°17E 265 a
Pedregal de San Angel, Jardines del Mexico 19°19N 99°12W 128 C1
Pedreguer Spain 38°48N 0°3E 197 G5
Pedreiras Brazil 4°32S 44°40W 332 B3
Pedro Afonso Brazil 9°0S 48°10W 332 C2
Pedro Bank Caribbean 17°5N 78°20W 320 C4
Pedro Bay U.S.A. 59°47N 154°7W 303 G9
Pedro Cays Jamaica 17°5N 77°48W 320 C4
Pedro Chico Colombia 1°4N 70°25W 328 C3
Pedro de Valdivia Chile 22°55S 69°38W 334 A2
Pedro Dorado Colombia 1°0N 70°14W 328 C3
Pedro González Venezuela 11°7N 63°56W 329 a
Pedro Juan Caballero Paraguay 22°30S 55°40W 335 A4
Pedro Miguel Locks Panama 9°1N 79°36W 320 c
Pedro Muñoz Spain 39°25N 2°56W 195 F8
Pedro Pt. = North West Pt. Jamaica 18°27N 78°13W 320 a
Pedrógão Grande Portugal 39°55N 8°9W 194 F2
Pee Dee = Great Pee Dee → U.S.A. 33°21N 79°10W 315 E15
Peebinga Australia 34°52S 140°57E 282 C4
Peebles Borders, U.K. 55°40N 3°11W 167 F5
Peebles Ohio, U.S.A. 38°57N 83°24W 311 F13
Peekskill U.S.A. 41°17N 73°55W 313 E11
Peel I. of Man 54°13N 4°40W 168 C3
Peel → N.S.W., Australia 30°50S 150°29E 283 A9
Peel → N.W.T., Canada 67°0N 135°0W 294 D5
Peel Sd. Canada 73°0N 96°0W 294 C12
Peene → Germany 54°9N 13°46E 178 A9
Peera Peera Poolanna L. Australia 26°30S 138°0E 281 D2
Peerless Lake Canada 56°37N 114°40W 296 B6
Peers Canada 53°40N 116°0W 296 C5
Peery L. Australia 30°45S 143°35E 282 A5
Pegasus Bay N.Z. 43°20S 173°10E 285 D8
Peggau Austria 47°12N 15°21E 180 D8
Peggy Guggenheim, Collezione Venice, Italy 142 b2
Pegnitz Germany 49°44N 11°31E 179 F7
Pegnitz → Germany 49°30N 10°59E 179 F6
Pego Spain 38°51N 0°8W 197 G4
Pegu Burma 17°20N 96°29E 241 G6
Pegu □ Burma 17°30N 96°30E 241 G6
Pegu Yoma Burma 19°0N 96°0E 241 F6
Peguera Spain 39°32N 2°26E 206 B3
Pehčevo Macedonia 41°41N 22°55E 202 E6
Pehlıvanköy Turkey 41°20N 26°55E 203 E10
Pehuajó Argentina 35°45S 62°0W 334 D3
Pei Xian China 34°44N 116°55E 226 G9
Peian = Bei'an China 48°10N 126°20E 219 B14
Peihai = Beihai China 21°28N 109°6E 228 G7
Peikang Taiwan 23°34N 120°18E 225 C2
Peikang Hsi → Taiwan 24°2N 120°50E 225 B2
Peikant'ang Taiwan 26°13N 120°0E 225 b
Peimen Taiwan 23°16N 120°7E 225 C2
Peinan Taiwan 22°47N 121°7E 225 D3
Peinan Hsi → Taiwan 22°46N 121°10E 225 D3
Peinanchu Shan Taiwan 23°3N 120°52E 225 C2
Peine Chile 23°45S 68°8W 334 A2
Peine Niedersachsen, Germany 52°19N 10°14E 178 C6
Peip'ing = Beijing China 39°53N 116°21E 114 B1
Peipu Taiwan 24°2N 121°36E 225 B3
Peipus, L. = Chudskoye, Ozero Russia 58°13N 27°30E 188 C4
Peissenberg Germany 47°48N 11°4E 179 H7
Peitawu Shan Taiwan 22°38N 120°46E 225 D2
Peitou Changhua, Taiwan 23°52N 120°30E 225 C2
Peitou T'aipei, Taiwan 25°11N 121°27E 225 A3
Peitun Taiwan 24°10N 120°41E 225 B2
Peitz Germany 51°51N 14°24E 178 D10
Peixe Brazil 12°0S 48°40W 333 D2
Peixe → Brazil 21°31S 51°58W 333 F1
Peixoto de Azeredo → Brazil 10°6S 55°31W 331 C6
Pejantan, Pulau Indonesia 0°7N 107°13E 234 B3
Pejë Kosovo 42°40N 20°17E 202 D4
Pek → Serbia 44°45N 21°29E 202 B5
Pekalongan Indonesia 6°53S 109°40E 235 D3
Pekan Malaysia 3°30N 103°25E 237 L4
Pekan Nenas Malaysia 1°31N 103°31E 237 d
Pekanbaru Indonesia 0°30N 101°15E 234 B2
Pekin U.S.A. 40°35N 89°40W 310 D7
Peking = Beijing China 39°53N 116°21E 114 B1
Pekutatan Indonesia 8°25S 114°49E 231 J17
Pela Greece 40°46N 22°23E 202 F6
Pelabuhan Ratu, Teluk Indonesia 7°5S 106°30E 234 D3
Pelabuhanratu Indonesia 7°0S 106°32E 234 D3
Pélagos = Kira Panagia Greece 39°17N 24°4E 204 B6
Pelaihari Indonesia 3°55S 114°45E 235 C4
Pelat, Mt. France 44°16N 6°42E 175 D10
Pelcowizna Poland 52°17N 21°0E 143 B2
Pełczyce Poland 53°3N 15°16E 185 E2
Peleaga, Vf. Romania 45°22N 22°55E 182 E7
Pelechuco Bolivia 14°48S 69°4W 330 C4
Pelée, Mt. Martinique 14°48N 61°10W 322 j
Pelee, Pt. Canada 41°54N 82°31W 298 D3
Pelee I. Canada 41°47N 82°40W 312 E2
Pelejo Peru 6°10S 75°49W 330 B2
Pelekech Kenya 3°52N 35°8E 268 B4
Peleliu I. Palau 7°1N 134°15E 288 c
Peleng Indonesia 1°20S 123°30E 231 E6
Pelenge Dem. Rep. of the Congo 2°44S 22°39E 264 C4
Pelentong Malaysia 1°32N 103°49E 237 d
Pélézi Ivory C. 7°17N 6°54W 262 D3
Pelham U.S.A. 31°8N 84°9W 316 D5
Pelhřimov Czech Rep. 49°24N 15°12E 180 B8
Pelican U.S.A. 57°58N 136°14W 296 B1
Pelican L. Canada 52°28N 100°20W 297 C8
Pelican Narrows Canada 55°10N 102°56W 297 B8
Pelion U.S.A. 33°46N 81°15W 316 B8
Pelister △ Macedonia 41°0N 21°10E 202 F5
Pelješac Croatia 42°55N 17°25E 199 F14
Pelkosenniemi Finland 67°6N 27°28E 160 C22
Pell City U.S.A. 33°35N 86°17W 316 B3
Pella Greece 40°52N 22°0E 202 F6
Pella Northern Cape, S. Africa 29°1S 19°6E 270 C2
Pella Iowa, U.S.A. 41°25N 92°55W 310 C4
Pello Finland 66°47N 23°59E 160 C20
Pellworm Germany 54°31N 8°39E 178 A4
Pelly → Canada 62°47N 137°19W 296 A1
Pelly Bay Canada 68°38N 89°50W 295 D14
Peloponnesos □ Greece 37°10N 22°0E 204 D4
Peloponnisos Station Athens, Greece 112 a1
Peloritani, Monti Italy 38°3N 15°20E 201 D8
Pelorus → N.Z. 41°16S 173°45E 285 B8
Pelorus Sd. N.Z. 40°59S 173°59E 285 A8
Pelotas Brazil 31°42S 52°23W 335 C5
Pelotas → Brazil 27°28S 51°55W 335 B5
Pelovo Bulgaria 43°26N 24°17E 203 C8
Pelplin Poland 53°55N 18°42E 184 E5
Pelvoux, Massif du France 44°52N 6°20E 175 D10
Pemalang Indonesia 6°53S 109°23E 235 D3
Pemanggil, Pulau Malaysia 2°37N 104°21E 237 L5
Pematangsiantar Indonesia 2°57N 99°5E 234 B1
Pemba Mozam. 12°58S 40°30E 269 E5
Pemba Zambia 16°30S 27°28E 269 F2
Pemba Channel Tanzania 5°0S 39°37E 268 D4
Pemba I. Tanzania 5°0S 39°45E 268 D4
Pemberton W. Austral., Australia 34°30S 116°0E 279 F2
Pemberton B.C., Canada 50°25N 122°50W 296 C4
Pembina → Canada 54°45N 114°17W 296 C6
Pembroke Ont., Canada 45°50N 77°7W 298 C4
Pembroke Trin. & Tob. 11°13N 60°37W 323 s
Pembroke Pembs., U.K. 51°41N 4°55W 169 F3
Pembroke Ga., U.S.A. 32°8N 81°37W 316 C8
Pembroke Park U.S.A. 25°59N 80°10W 129 C2
Pembroke Pines U.S.A. 26°0N 80°13W 129 B1
Pembrokeshire □ U.K. 51°52N 4°56W 169 F3
Pembrokeshire Coast △ U.K. 51°50N 5°2W 169 F2
Pembuang → Indonesia 3°24S 112°33E 235 C4
Pen India 18°45N 73°5E 244 E1
Pen-y-bont ar Ogwr = Bridgend U.K. 51°30N 3°34W 169 F4
Pen-y-Ghent U.K. 54°10N 2°14W 168 C5
Peña, Sierra de la Spain 42°32N 0°45W 196 C4
Peña de Francia, Sierra de la Spain 40°32N 6°10W 194 E4
Penafiel Portugal 41°12N 8°17W 194 D2
Peñafiel Spain 41°35N 4°7W 194 D6
Peñaflor Spain 37°43N 5°21W 195 H5
Penal Trin. & Tob. 10°9N 61°29W 323 t
Peñalara Spain 40°51N 3°57W 194 E7
Peñalolén Chile 33°28S 70°32W 137 B2
Penalva Brazil 3°18S 45°10W 332 B2
Penal/Debe □ Trin. & Tob. 10°14N 61°27W 323 t
Penamacôr Portugal 40°10N 7°10W 194 E3
Penang = Pinang Malaysia 5°25N 100°15E 237 c
Penápolis Brazil 21°30S 50°0W 335 A6
Peñaranda de Bracamonte Spain 40°53N 5°13W 194 E5
Peñarroya Spain 40°25N 0°40W 196 E4
Peñarroya-Pueblonuevo Spain 38°19N 5°16W 195 G5
Penarth U.K. 51°26N 3°11W 169 F4
Peñas, C. de Spain 43°42N 5°52W 194 B5
Peñas, G. de Chile 47°0S 75°0W 336 C2
Peñas, Pta. Venezuela 11°17N 62°0W 329 A5
Peñas de San Pedro Spain 38°44N 2°0W 197 G3
Peñas del Chache Canary Is. 29°6N 13°33W 153 e2
Peñausende Spain 41°17N 5°52W 194 D5
Pench → India 21°17N 79°10E 244 D4
Pench △ India 21°45N 79°20E 243 J8
Pench'i = Benxi China 41°20N 123°48E 224 B1
Pend Oreille → U.S.A. 49°4N 117°37W 304 B5
Pend Oreille, L. U.S.A. 48°10N 116°21W 304 B5
Pendalofos Greece 40°14N 21°12E 202 F5
Pendé → C.A.R. 7°55N 16°36E 264 A3
Pendembu Eastern, S. Leone 8°10N 10°42W 262 D2
Pendembu Northern, S. Leone 9°7N 11°14W 262 D2
Pendências Brazil 5°15S 36°43W 332 C4
Pender B. Australia 16°45S 122°42E 278 C3
Pendik Turkey 40°53N 29°13E 203 F13
Pendjari → Benin 10°55N 0°50E 263 C5
Pendjari △ Benin 11°15N 1°32E 263 C5
Pendleton Ind., U.S.A. 40°0N 85°45W 311 E11
Pendleton Oreg., U.S.A. 45°40N 118°47W 304 D4
Pendopo Indonesia 3°16S 103°52E 234 C2
Pendra India 22°46N 81°57E 243 H9
Pendzhikent = Panjakent Tajikistan 39°29N 67°37E 217 E7
Penebangan Indonesia 1°13S 109°15E 235 C3
Peneda-Gerês △ Portugal 41°57N 8°15W 194 D2
Penedo Brazil 10°15S 36°36W 332 D4
Penelokan Indonesia 8°17S 115°22E 231 J18
Penetanguishene Canada 44°50N 79°55W 312 B5
Penfield U.S.A. 41°13N 78°35W 312 E6
Penfro = Pembroke U.K. 51°41N 4°55W 169 F3
Peng Chau Hong Kong, China 22°17N 114°2E 122 B2

Peng Siang → Singapore 1°24N 103°43E 138 A2
Peng'an China 31°2N 106°22E 228 B6
Penganga → India 19°53N 79°9E 244 E4
Penge Kasai-Or., Dem. Rep. of the Congo 5°30S 24°33E 265 D4
Penge Sud-Kivu, Dem. Rep. of the Congo 4°27S 28°25E 268 C2
Penge London, U.K. 51°24N 0°3W 125 B3
P'enghu □ Taiwan 23°30N 119°30E 225 C1
P'enghu Ch'üntou Taiwan 23°34N 119°30E 225 C1
P'enghu Tao Taiwan 23°34N 119°37E 225 C1
Penglai China 37°48N 120°42E 227 F11
Pengshan China 30°14N 103°58E 228 B4
Pengshui China 29°17N 108°12E 228 C7
Penguin Australia 41°8S 146°6E 281 G4
Pengxi China 30°44N 105°45E 228 B5
Pengze China 29°52N 116°32E 229 C11
Pengzhou China 31°4N 103°32E 228 B4
Penha Brazil 22°49S 43°17W 135 A1
Penhalonga Zimbabwe 18°52S 32°40E 269 F3
Peniche Portugal 39°19N 9°22W 195 F1
Penicuik U.K. 55°50N 3°13W 121 B2
Penida, Nusa Indonesia 8°45S 115°30E 231 K18
Penninnes, Alpes = Pennine, Alpi Alps 46°4N 7°30E 179 J3
Peninsular Malaysia □ Malaysia 4°0N 102°0E 237 L4
Peñíscola Spain 40°22N 0°24E 196 E5
Penitente, Serra do Brazil 8°45S 46°20W 332 C2
Penjaringan Indonesia 6°7S 106°48E 122 A1
Pënjwin Iraq 35°37N 45°56E 213 E11
Penki = Benxi China 41°20N 123°48E 224 B1
Penkridge U.K. 52°44N 2°6W 168 E5
Penmarch France 47°49N 4°21W 172 E2
Penmarch, Pte. de France 47°48N 4°22W 172 E2
Penn = Penn Hills U.S.A. 40°28N 79°52W 312 F5
Penn Hills U.S.A. 40°28N 79°52W 312 F5
Penn Station New York, U.S.A. 132 c2
Penn Yan U.S.A. 42°40N 77°3W 312 D7
Penna, Punta della Italy 42°10N 14°43E 199 F11
Pennant Canada 50°32N 108°14W 297 C7
Penne Italy 42°27N 13°55E 199 F10
Penner → India 14°35N 80°10E 245 G5
Penneshaw Australia 35°44S 137°56E 282 C2
Pennine, Alpi Alps 46°4N 7°30E 179 J3
Pennines U.K. 54°45N 2°27W 168 C5
Pennington U.S.A. 39°15N 121°47W 306 F5
Pennington → Nigeria 4°45N 5°35E 263 E6
Pennino, Mte. Italy 43°6N 12°53E 199 E9
Pennsburg U.S.A. 40°23N 75°29W 313 F9
Pennsylvania □ U.S.A. 40°45N 77°30W 309 E15
Pennsylvania Avenue Washington, D.C., U.S.A. 143 b2
Pennville U.S.A. 40°30N 85°9W 311 D11
Penny Canada 53°51N 121°20W 296 C4
Peno Russia 57°2N 32°49E 188 D7
Penobscot → U.S.A. 44°30N 68°48W 309 C19
Penobscot B. U.S.A. 44°35N 68°50W 309 C19
Penola Australia 37°25S 140°48E 282 D4
Penong Australia 31°56S 133°1E 279 F5
Penonomé Panama 8°31N 80°21W 320 E3
Penot, Mt. Vanuatu 16°20S 167°31E 287 F5
Penrhyn Cook Is. 9°0S 158°0W 289 H12
Penrith N.S.W., Australia 33°43S 150°38E 283 B9
Penrith Cumb., U.K. 54°40N 2°45W 168 C5
Penryn U.K. 50°9N 5°7W 169 G2
Pensacola U.S.A. 30°25N 87°13W 317 E2
Pensacola B. U.S.A. 30°25N 87°5W 317 E2
Pensacola Mts. Antarctica 84°0S 40°0W 151 E1
Pense Canada 50°25N 104°59W 297 C8
Penshurst Australia 37°49S 142°20E 282 D5
Pensiangan Malaysia 4°33N 116°19E 235 B5
Pentadaktylos Cyprus 35°20N 33°20E 207 E9
Pentagon U.S.A. 38°53N 77°3W 143 B2
Pentecost Vanuatu 15°42S 168°10E 287 E6
Pentecostes Brazil 3°48S 39°17W 332 B4
Pentecôte = Pentecost Vanuatu 15°42S 168°10E 287 E6
Penticton Canada 49°30N 119°38W 296 D5
Pentland Australia 20°32S 145°25E 280 C4
Pentland Firth U.K. 58°43N 3°10W 167 C5
Pentland Hills U.K. 55°48N 3°25W 167 F5
Penukonda India 14°5N 77°38E 245 G3
Penza Russia 53°15N 45°5E 190 D7
Penza □ Russia 52°50N 44°50E 190 D7
Penzance U.K. 50°7N 5°33W 169 G2
Penzberg Germany 47°45N 11°22E 179 H7
Penzhino Russia 63°30N 167°55E 215 C17
Penzhinskaya Guba Russia 61°30N 163°0E 215 C17
Penzing Austria 48°11N 16°18E 142 A1
Penzlin Germany 53°30N 13°5E 178 B9
People's Park China 31°13N 121°28E 138 B1
People's Square China 31°13N 121°28E 138 B1
Peoria Ariz., U.S.A. 33°43N 112°14W 305 K7
Peoria Ill., U.S.A. 40°42N 89°36W 310 D7
Peoria Heights U.S.A. 40°45N 89°35W 310 D7
Peotone U.S.A. 41°20N 87°48W 311 C9
Pepacton Res. U.S.A. 42°5N 74°58W 313 D10
Pepani → S. Africa 25°49S 22°47E 270 C3
Pepeekeo U.S.A. 19°51N 155°6W 302 D6
Pepel S. Leone 8°40N 13°5W 262 D2
Peqin Albania 41°3N 19°44E 202 E3
Pera Hd. Australia 12°55S 141°37E 280 A3
Perabumulih Indonesia 3°27S 104°15E 234 C2
Perachora Greece 38°2N 22°56E 204 C4
Perachori Greece 38°21N 20°43E 207 C2
Perak □ Malaysia 5°0N 101°0E 237 K3
Perak → Malaysia 4°0N 100°50E 237 K3
Perales del Alfambra Spain 40°38N 1°0W 196 E4
Perales del Puerto Spain 40°10N 6°40W 194 E4
Perales del Rio Spain 40°18N 3°38W 127 C2
Peralta Spain 42°20N 1°48W 196 C3
Perama Kerkyra, Greece 39°34N 19°54E 206 B9
Perama Kriti, Greece 35°20N 24°40E 207 E5
Perämeri △ Finland 65°35N 24°22E 160 D21
Perancak Indonesia 8°24S 114°37E 231 J17
Peräpohjola Finland 66°16N 26°10E 160 C22
Perast Montenegro 42°31N 18°47E 202 D2
Peratia Greece 38°49N 20°45E 207 B2
Peravillo Mexico City, Mexico 128 a3
Percé Canada 48°31N 64°13W 299 C7
Perche France 48°31N 1°1E 172 D8
Perche, Collines du France 48°30N 0°40E 171 B4
Perche ⌂ France 48°24N 0°46E 172 D7
Perchtoldsdorf Austria 48°7N 16°17E 142 B1
Percival Lakes Australia 21°25S 125°0E 278 D4
Percy Manche, France 48°55N 1°11W 172 D5
Percy Ill., U.S.A. 38°5N 89°41W 310 F7
Percy Is. Australia 21°39S 150°16E 280 C5
Perdido → Argentina 42°55S 67°0W 336 B3
Perdido, Mte. Spain 42°40N 0°5E 196 C5
Perdizes Brazil 23°32S 46°39W 137 B2
Perdu, Mt. = Perdido, Mte. Spain 42°40N 0°5E 196 C5
Perechyn Ukraine 48°44N 22°28E 182 B7
Perehinske Ukraine 48°49N 24°11E 183 B9
Pereira Colombia 4°49N 75°43W 328 C2
Perejil Spain 35°55N 5°29W 195 K5
Perelazovskiy Russia 49°8N 42°35E 191 F6
Peremul Par India 11°10N 72°4E 245 J1
Peremyshl = Przemyśl Poland 49°50N 22°45E 185 J9
Perené → Peru 11°9S 74°14W 330 C3
Perenjori Australia 29°26S 116°16E 279 E2
Peresecina Moldova 47°16N 28°46E 183 C13
Pereslavl-Zalesskiy Russia 56°45N 38°50E 188 D10
Peretu Romania 44°3N 25°5E 183 F10
Pereyaslav-Khmelnytskyy Ukraine 50°3N 31°28E 189 G6
Pereyma Ukraine 48°4N 29°30E 183 B14
Pérez, I. Mexico 22°24N 89°42W 319 C7
Perg Austria 48°15N 14°38E 180 C7
Pergamino Argentina 33°52S 60°30W 334 C3
Pergamon Museum Berlin, Germany 115 a4
Pergau → Malaysia 5°23N 102°2E 237 K3
Perge Turkey 37°3N 30°56E 250 A1
Pérgine Valsugana Italy 46°4N 11°14E 199 B8
Pérgola Italy 43°34N 12°50E 199 E9
Perham U.S.A. 46°36N 95°34W 308 B6
Perhentian, Kepulauan Malaysia 5°54N 102°42E 237 K4
Peri → Turkey 38°53N 39°52E 213 C8
Periam Romania 46°2N 20°52E 182 D5
Péribonka → Canada 48°45N 72°5W 299 C5
Péribonka, L. Canada 50°1N 71°10W 299 B5
Péribonka, La Centrale de Canada 49°30N 71°10W 299 C5
Perico Argentina 24°20S 65°5W 334 A2
Pericos Mexico 25°3N 107°42W 318 B3
Périers France 49°11N 1°25W 172 C5
Périgord France 45°0N 0°40E 174 D4
Périgord-Limousin ⌂ France 45°40N 0°50E 174 C4
Périgueux France 45°10N 0°42E 174 C4
Perijá, Sierra de Colombia 9°30N 73°3W 328 B3
Perijá △ Venezuela 9°30N 72°55W 328 B3
Peringat Malaysia 6°2N 102°17E 237 J4
Perisher Valley Australia 36°27S 148°25E 283 D8
Peristera Greece 39°15N 23°58E 204 B5
Peristeri Greece 38°1N 23°42E 112 A2
Peristerona → Cyprus 35°8N 33°5E 207 E9
Perito Moreno Argentina 46°36S 70°56W 336 C2
Perito Moreno △ Argentina 47°49S 72°17W 336 C2
Peritoró Brazil 4°20S 44°18W 332 B3
Perivale U.K. 51°31N 0°18W 125 A2
Perivol = Dragovishtitsa Bulgaria 42°22N 22°39E 202 D6
Periyakulam India 10°5N 77°30E 245 J3
Periyar → India 10°15N 76°10E 245 J3
Periyar, L. India 9°25N 77°10E 245 K3
Periyar △ India 9°25N 77°10E 245 K3
Perk Belgium 50°56N 4°30E 116 A2
Perkasie U.S.A. 40°22N 75°18W 313 F9
Perković Croatia 43°41N 16°10E 199 E13
Perlach Germany 48°5N 11°37E 131 B2
Perlacher Forst Germany 48°4N 11°34E 131 B2
Perlas, Arch. de las Panama 8°41N 79°7W 320 E4
Perlas, Punta de Nic. 12°30N 83°30W 320 D3
Perleberg Germany 53°5N 11°52E 178 B7
Perlez Serbia 45°11N 20°22E 182 E5
Perlis □ Malaysia 6°30N 100°15E 237 J2
Perm Russia 58°0N 56°10E 186 C10
Përmet Albania 40°15N 20°21E 202 F4
Permskoye = Komsomolsk-na-Amur Russia 50°30N 137°0E 219 A16
Pernambuco = Recife Brazil 8°0S 35°0W 332 C5
Pernambuco □ Brazil 8°0S 37°0W 332 C4
Pernambuco Abyssal Plain Atl. Oc. 5°0S 24°0W 152 G9
Pernatty Lagoon Australia 31°30S 137°12E 282 A2
Pernik Bulgaria 42°35N 23°2E 202 D7
Pernik □ Bulgaria 42°35N 23°2E 202 D7
Pernov = Pärnu Estonia 58°28N 24°33E 188 C3
Pero Italy 45°30N 9°5E 128 A1
Peron Is. Australia 13°9S 130°4E 278 B5
Peron Pen. Australia 26°0S 113°10E 279 E1
Péronne France 49°55N 2°57E 173 C9
Peropok, Bukit Singapore 1°19N 103°42E 138 B2
Perosa Argentina Italy 44°58N 7°10E 198 D4
Perovo Russia 55°44N 37°45E 129 B3
Perovsk = Qyzylorda Kazakhstan 44°48N 65°28E 216 D7
Perow Canada 54°35N 126°10W 296 C3
Perparim = Pogradec Albania 40°54N 20°37E 202 F4
Perpignan France 42°42N 2°53E 174 F6
Perrégaux = Mohammadia Algeria 35°33N 0°3E 261 A5
Perrine U.S.A. 25°36N 80°21W 317 K9
Perris U.S.A. 33°47N 117°14W 307 M9
Perros-Guirec France 48°49N 3°28W 172 D3
Perry Fla., U.S.A. 30°7N 83°35W 316 E6
Perry Ga., U.S.A. 32°28N 83°44W 316 C6
Perry Iowa, U.S.A. 41°51N 94°6W 310 C2
Perry Mich., U.S.A. 42°50N 84°13W 311 B12
Perry Mo., U.S.A. 39°26N 91°40W 310 E5
Perry N.Y., U.S.A. 42°42N 78°0W 312 D7
Perry Okla., U.S.A. 36°17N 97°14W 314 C6
Perrysburg U.S.A. 41°34N 83°38W 311 C13
Perryton U.S.A. 36°24N 100°48W 314 C4
Perryville Alaska, U.S.A. 55°55N 159°9W 303 J8
Perryville Mo., U.S.A. 37°43N 89°52W 310 G7
Persan France 49°9N 2°16E 173 C9
Persberg Sweden 59°47N 14°15E 162 E8
Perşembe Turkey 41°5N 37°46E 212 B7
Persepolis Iran 29°55N 52°50E 247 D7
Perseverancia Bolivia 14°44S 62°48W 331 C5
Pershing Square Los Angeles, U.S.A. 127 c1
Pershotravensk Ukraine 50°13N 27°40E 177 C14
Pershotravnevoye = Pershotravensk Ukraine 50°13N 27°40E 177 C14
Persia = Iran ■ Asia 33°0N 53°0E 247 C7
Persian Gulf Asia 27°0N 50°0E 247 E6
Perstorp Sweden 56°10N 13°25E 163 H7
Pertek Turkey 38°51N 39°19E 213 C8
Perth W. Austral., Australia 31°57S 115°52E 279 F2
Perth Ont., Canada 44°55N 76°15W 313 B8
Perth Perth & Kinr., U.K. 56°24N 3°26W 167 E5
Perth & Kinross □ U.K. 56°45N 3°55W 167 E5
Perth Amboy U.S.A. 40°30N 74°15W 313 F10
Perth-Andover Canada 46°44N 67°42W 299 C6
Pertuis France 43°42N 5°30E 175 E9
Pertusato, C. France 41°21N 9°11E 175 G13
Pertusella Italy 45°35N 9°3E 128 A1
Peru Ill., U.S.A. 41°20N 89°8W 310 C7
Peru Ind., U.S.A. 40°45N 86°4W 311 D10
Peru N.Y., U.S.A. 44°35N 73°32W 313 B11
Peru ■ S. Amer. 4°0S 75°0W 328 D3
Peru Basin Pac. Oc. 20°0S 95°0W 289 J18
Peru-Chile Trench Pac. Oc. 20°0S 72°0W 326 E3
Perúgia Italy 43°7N 12°23E 199 E9
Perušić Croatia 44°40N 15°22E 199 D12
Peruvian Vale St. Vincent 13°11N 61°12W 323 n
Pervomaysk Russia 54°56N 43°58E 190 C6
Pervomaysk Ukraine 48°10N 30°46E 189 H6
Pervomayskīy Kazakhstan 50°16N 82°0E 217 B10
Pervouralsk Russia 56°59N 59°59E 186 C10
Pervouralsky = Pervouralsk Russia 56°59N 59°59E 186 C10
Pesada Greece 38°7N 20°35E 207 C2
Pesagot West Bank 31°54N 35°13E 123 A2
Pesanggrahag, Kali → Indonesia 6°10S 106°44E 122 B1
Pésaro Italy 43°54N 12°55E 199 E9
Pésaro e Urbino □ Italy 43°45N 12°40E 199 E9
Pescadores = P'enghu Ch'üntou Taiwan 23°34N 119°30E 225 C1
Pescara Italy 42°28N 14°13E 199 F11
Pescara → Italy 42°28N 14°13E 199 F11
Peschanokopskoye Russia 46°14N 41°4E 191 G5
Peschanoye = Yashkul Russia 46°11N 45°21E 191 G7
Peschiera Borromeo Italy 45°26N 9°19E 128 B2
Pescia Italy 43°54N 10°41E 198 E7
Pescina Italy 42°2N 13°39E 199 F10
Pesek, Pulau Singapore 1°17N 103°41E 138 B2
Peshawar Pakistan 34°2N 71°37E 242 B4
Peshkopi Albania 41°41N 20°25E 202 E4
Peshtera Bulgaria 42°2N 24°18E 203 D8
Peshtigo U.S.A. 45°3N 87°45W 308 C10
Peski Russia 51°14N 42°29E 190 E6
Peski Turkmenistan 38°11N 62°59E 216 E6
Pêso da Régua Portugal 41°10N 7°47W 194 D3
Pesochnya = Kirov Russia 54°3N 34°20E 188 E8
Pesqueira Brazil 8°20S 36°42W 332 C4
Pessac France 44°48N 0°37W 174 D3
Pest Hungary 47°29N 19°4E 117 B2
Pest □ Hungary 47°29N 19°5E 182 C4
Pesterzsébet Hungary 47°26N 19°6E 117 B2
Pesthidegkút Hungary 47°33N 18°57E 117 A1
Pestimre Hungary 47°24N 19°11E 117 B3
Pestlőrinc Hungary 47°26N 19°11E 117 B3
Pestovo = Zavolzhye Russia 56°37N 43°26E 190 B6
Pestovo Russia 58°33N 35°42E 188 C8
Pestravka Russia 52°28N 49°57E 190 D9
Pestújhely Hungary 47°32N 19°7E 117 A2
Petah Tiqwa Israel 32°6N 34°53E 251 F5
Petalas Greece 38°25N 21°5E 207 C3
Petalidi Greece 36°57N 21°55E 204 E3
Petaling Jaya Malaysia 3°4N 101°42E 237 L3
Petaloudes Greece 36°18N 28°5E 206 E12
Petaluma U.S.A. 38°14N 122°39W 306 G4
Pétange Lux. 49°33N 5°55E 170 E5
Petare Venezuela 10°29N 66°49W 321 D6
Petaro Pakistan 25°31N 68°18E 242 G3
Petas Helsinki, Finland 60°15N 24°50E 121 B2
Petas Greece 39°10N 21°2E 204 B3
Petatlán Mexico 17°31N 101°16W 318 D4
Petauke Zambia 14°14S 31°20E 269 E3
Petawawa Canada 45°54N 77°17W 298 C4
Petén Itzá, L. Guatemala 16°58N 89°50W 320 C2
Peter I. Br. Virgin Is. 18°22N 64°35W 321 b
Peter I. Øy Antarctica 69°0S 91°0W 151 C16
Peter Pond L. Canada 55°55N 108°44W 297 B7
Peterbell Canada 48°36N 83°21W 298 C3
Peterborough S. Austral., Australia 32°58S 138°51E 282 B3
Peterborough Ont., Canada 44°20N 78°20W 312 B6
Peterborough Peterborough, U.K. 52°35N 0°15W 169 E7
Peterborough N.H., U.S.A. 42°53N 71°57W 313 D13
Peterborough □ U.K. 52°35N 0°15W 169 E7
Peterculter U.K. 57°6N 2°16W 167 D6
Peterhead U.K. 57°31N 1°48W 167 D7
Peterhof = Petrodvorets Russia 59°52N 29°54E 188 C5
Peterlee U.K. 54°47N 1°20W 168 C6
Petermann ◎ Australia 24°58S 130°0E 279 E4
Petermann Bjerg Greenland 73°7N 28°25W 154 C8
Petermann Gletscher Greenland 80°30N 60°0W 154 A4
Petermann Ranges Australia 26°0S 130°30E 279 E5
Peter's Mine Guyana 6°14N 59°20W 329 B6
Petersburg = Peterborough Australia 32°58S 138°51E 282 B3
Petersburg Alaska, U.S.A. 56°48N 132°58W 303 H14
Petersburg Ill., U.S.A. 40°1N 89°51W 310 D7
Petersburg Ind., U.S.A. 38°30N 87°17W 311 F9
Petersburg Mich., U.S.A. 41°54N 83°43W 311 C13
Petersburg Pa., U.S.A. 40°34N 78°3W 312 F6
Petersburg Va., U.S.A. 37°14N 77°24W 309 G15
Petersburg W. Va., U.S.A. 39°1N 79°5W 309 F14
Petersfield U.K. 51°1N 0°56W 169 F7
Petershagen Germany 52°23N 8°58E 178 C4
Petília Policastro Italy 39°7N 16°48E 201 C9
Petilla de Aragón Spain 42°28N 1°6W 196 C3
Petit Batanga Cameroon 3°15N 9°54E 264 B1
Petit-Bourg Guadeloupe 16°11N 61°37W 322 e
Petit-Canal Guadeloupe 16°25N 61°31W 322 e
Petit Cul-de-Sac Marin Guadeloupe 16°12N 61°33W 322 e
Petit Dominique Grenada 12°30N 61°24W 323 q
Petit-Goâve Haiti 18°27N 72°51W 321 C5
Petit Lac Manicouagan Canada 51°25N 67°40W 299 B6
Petit Loango △ Gabon 2°20S 9°40E 264 C1
Petit-Mécatina → Canada 50°40N 59°30W 299 B8
Petit-Mécatina, Î. du Canada 50°30N 59°25W 299 B8
Petit Piton St. Lucia 13°51N 61°5W 323 m
Petit Raffray Mauritius 20°0S 57°36E 272 e
Petit-Saguenay Canada 48°15N 70°4W 299 C5
Petit Saint Bernard, Col du Italy 45°40N 6°52E 175 C10
Petit Saut, Barrage de Fr. Guiana 5°0N 53°10W 329 C7
Petit Soufrière B. Dominica 15°23N 61°15W 323 k
Petitcodiac Canada 45°57N 65°11W 299 C6
Petite Anse Martinique 14°28N 61°4W 322 j
Petite-Île Réunion 21°20S 55°35E 272 f
Petite Martinique Grenada 12°31N 61°23W 323 q
Petite Rivière Mauritius 20°11S 57°26E 272 e
Petite Savane Dominica 15°15N 61°17W 323 k
Petite Terre = Pamandzi Mayotte 12°47S 45°16E 272 b
Petite Terre, Îles de la Guadeloupe 16°13N 61°9W 322 e
Petites-Anses Guadeloupe 15°51N 61°38W 322 e
Petitjean = Sidi Kacem Morocco 34°12N 5°42W 260 B3
Petitot → Canada 60°14N 123°29W 296 A4
Petitsikapau L. Canada 54°37N 66°25W 299 B6
Petlad India 22°30N 72°45E 242 H5
Peto Mexico 20°8N 88°55W 319 C7
Petone N.Z. 41°13S 174°53E 284 H3
Petorca Chile 32°15S 70°56W 334 C1
Petoskey U.S.A. 45°22N 84°57W 309 C11
Petra Jordan 30°20N 35°22E 251 H6
Petra Spain 39°37N 3°6E 206 B4
Petra, Ostrov Russia 76°15N 118°30E 215 B12
Petra Velikogo, Zaliv Russia 42°40N 132°0E 220 C6
Petre, Pt. Canada 43°50N 77°9W 312 C7
Petrel = Petrer Spain 38°30N 0°46W 197 G4
Petrella, Monte Italy 41°18N 13°40E 200 A6
Petrer Spain 38°30N 0°46W 197 G4
Petreto-Bicchisano France 41°47N 8°58E 175 G12
Petrich Bulgaria 41°24N 23°13E 202 E7
Petrified Forest △ U.S.A. 35°0N 109°30W 305 J9
Petrijanec Croatia 46°23N 16°17E 199 B13
Petrikov = Pyetrikaw Belarus 52°11N 28°29E 177 B15
Petrila Romania 45°29N 23°29E 183 E8
Petrillo Music Shell Chicago, U.S.A. 119 c2
Petrinja Croatia 45°28N 16°18E 199 C13
Petrodvorets Russia 59°52N 29°54E 188 C5
Petrograd = Sankt-Peterburg Russia 59°55N 30°20E 137 B1
Petrogradskaya Storona Russia 59°56N 30°20E 137 B2
Petrolândia Brazil 9°5S 38°20W 332 C4
Petrolia Canada 42°54N 82°9W 312 D2
Petrolina Brazil 9°24S 40°30W 332 C3
Petromaryevka = Pervomaysk Ukraine 48°10N 30°46E 189 H6
Petropavl Kazakhstan 54°53N 69°13E 217 B7
Petropavlovsk = Petropavl Kazakhstan 54°53N 69°13E 217 B7
Petropavlovsk-Kamchatskiy Russia 53°3N 158°43E 215 D16
Petropavlovskiy = Akhtubinsk Russia 48°13N 46°7E 191 F8
Petropavlovsky = Severouralsk Russia 60°9N 59°57E 186 B10
Petrópolis Brazil 22°33S 43°9W 333 F3
Petroşani Romania 45°28N 23°20E 183 E8
Petroupoli Greece 38°3N 23°40E 112 A2
Petrova Gora Croatia 45°15N 15°45E 199 C12
Petrovac Montenegro 42°13N 18°57E 202 D2
Petrovac Serbia 44°22N 21°26E 202 B5
Petrovaradin Serbia 45°16N 19°55E 182 E4
Petrovgrad = Zrenjanin Serbia 45°22N 20°23E 182 E5
Petrovice Czech Rep. 50°2N 14°33E 115 B3
Petrovsk Russia 52°22N 45°19E 190 D7
Petrovsk-Port = Makhachkala Russia 43°0N 47°30E 191 J8
Petrovsk-Zabaykalskiy Russia 51°20N 108°55E 215 D11
Petrovskaya Russia 45°25N 37°58E 189 K9
Petrovskiy Park Russia 55°47N 37°34E 129 B2
Petrovsko-Razumovskoye Russia 55°49N 37°34E 129 B2
Petrovskoye = Svetlograd Russia 45°25N 42°58E 191 H6
Petrovsky Stadium Saint Petersburg, Russia 59°57N 30°19E 137 B1
Petrovsky Zavod = Petrovsk-Zabaykalskiy Russia 51°20N 108°55E 215 D11
Petrozavodsk Russia 61°41N 34°20E 188 B8
Petrus Steyn S. Africa 27°38S 28°8E 271 C4
Petrusburg S. Africa 29°4S 25°26E 270 C4
Petsamo = Pechenga Russia 69°29N 31°4E 160 B24
Pettycur U.K. 56°4N 3°10W 121 A2
Petukhovo Russia 55°6N 67°58E 217 A7
Petuna = Fuyu China 45°12N 124°43E 227 B13
Petzeck Austria 46°57N 12°48E 180 E5
Peumo Chile 34°21S 71°12W 334 C1
Peureulak Indonesia 4°48N 97°45E 234 B1
Peusangan → Indonesia 5°16N 96°51E 234 A1
Peutie Belgium 50°56N 4°27E 116 A2
Pevek Russia 69°41N 171°19E 215 C18
Pevely U.S.A. 38°17N 90°24W 310 F6
Peveragno Italy 44°20N 7°37E 198 D4
Peyrehorade France 43°34N 1°7W 174 E2
Peyruis France 44°1N 5°56E 175 D9
Pézenas France 43°28N 3°24E 174 E7
Pezinok Slovak Rep. 48°17N 17°17E 181 C10
Pfaffenhofen Germany 48°31N 11°31E 179 G7
Pfälzerwald ⌂ Germany 49°18N 9°55E 179 F5
Pfarrkirchen Germany 48°25N 12°56E 179 G8
Pfaueninsel Germany 52°26N 13°7E 115 B1
Pfeffenhausen Germany 48°39N 11°58E 179 G7
Pforzheim Germany 48°52N 8°41E 179 G4
Pfullendorf Germany 47°55N 9°15E 179 H5
Pfungstadt Germany 49°48N 8°35E 179 F4
Pha Taem △ Thailand 15°32N 105°30E 236 E5
Phaestos Greece 35°2N 24°50E 207 E5
Phagwara India 31°10N 75°40E 242 D6
Phala Botswana 23°45S 26°50E 270 B4
Phalaborwa S. Africa 23°57S 31°7E 271 B5
Phalera = Phulera India 26°52N 75°16E 242 F6
Phalodi India 27°12N 72°24E 242 F5
Phalsbourg France 48°46N 7°15E 173 D14
Phaltan India 17°59N 74°26E 244 F2
Phaluai, Ko Thailand 9°32N 99°41E 237 b
Phan Thailand 19°28N 99°43E 236 C2
Phan Rang-Thap Cham Vietnam 11°34N 109°0E 237 G7
Phan Ri Cua Vietnam 11°16N 108°40E 237 G7
Phan Si Pan Vietnam 22°18N 103°46E 236 A4
Phan Thiet Vietnam 11°1N 108°9E 237 G7
Phan Thiet, Vinh Vietnam 10°53N 108°5E 237 G7
Phan Wa, Laem Thailand 7°47N 98°25E 237 a
Phanae Greece 38°8N 25°57E 205 C7
Phanat Nikhom Thailand 13°27N 101°11E 236 F3
Phangan, Ko Thailand 9°45N 100°0E 237 H3
Phangnga Thailand 8°28N 98°30E 237 H2
Phangnga, Ao Thailand 8°16N 98°33E 237 a
Phanom Sarakham Thailand 13°45N 101°21E 236 F3
Phaphund India 26°36N 79°28E 243 F8
Pharenda India 27°5N 83°17E 243 F10
Pharr U.S.A. 26°12N 98°11W 314 H5
Phatthalung Thailand 7°39N 100°6E 237 J3
Phawngpui Blue Mountain △ India 22°45N 93°5E 241 D4
Phaya Thai Thailand 13°45N 100°37E 113 B2
Phayam, Ko Thailand 9°44N 98°25E 237 H2
Phayao Thailand 19°11N 99°55E 236 C2
Phelps U.S.A. 42°58N 77°3W 312 D7
Phelps L. Canada 59°15N 103°15W 297 B8
Phenix City U.S.A. 32°28N 85°1W 316 C4
Phet Buri = Phetchaburi Thailand 13°1N 99°55E 236 F2
Phetchabun Thailand 16°25N 101°8E 236 D3
Phetchabun, Thiu Khao Thailand 16°0N 101°20E 236 E3
Phetchaburi Thailand 13°1N 99°55E 236 F2
Phi Phi, Ko Thailand 7°45N 98°46E 237 J2
Phiafay Laos 14°48N 106°0E 236 E6
Phibun Mangsahan Thailand 15°14N 105°14E 236 E5
Phichai Thailand 17°22N 100°10E 236 D3
Phichit Thailand 16°26N 100°22E 236 D3
Phihai Pakistan 24°50N 67°8E 123 A2
Philadelphia Miss., U.S.A. 32°46N 89°7W 315 E10
Philadelphia N.Y., U.S.A. 44°9N 75°43W 313 B9
Philadelphia Pa., U.S.A. 39°57N 75°9W 313 G9
Philip U.S.A. 44°2N 101°40W 308 C3
Philip Smith Mts. U.S.A. 68°0N 148°0W 303 C10
Philipi Greece 41°1N 24°16E 203 E8
Philippeville = Skikda Algeria 36°50N 6°58E 261 A6
Philippeville Belgium 50°12N 4°33E 170 D4
Philippi U.S.A. 39°9N 80°3W 309 F13
Philippi L. Australia 24°20S 138°55E 280 C2
Philippine Basin Pac. Oc. 17°0N 132°0E 288 F5
Philippine Sea Pac. Oc. 18°0N 125°0E 288 F4
Philippine Trench = Mindanao Trench Pac. Oc. 12°0N 126°6E 232 E5
Philippines ■ Asia 12°0N 123°0E 232 E4
Philippolis S. Africa 30°15S 25°16E 270 D4
Philippopolis = Plovdiv Bulgaria 42°8N 24°44E 203 D8
Philipsburg Qué., Canada 45°2N 73°5W 313 A11
Philipsburg St.-Maarten 18°3N 63°5W 322 a
Philipsburg Mont., U.S.A. 46°20N 113°18W 304 C7
Philipsburg Pa., U.S.A. 40°54N 78°13W 312 F6
Philipstown = Daingean Ireland 53°18N 7°17W 166 C4
Philipstown S. Africa 30°28S 24°30E 270 D3
Phillip B. Australia 33°58S 151°14E 139 B2
Phillip I. Australia 38°30S 145°12E 283 E6
Phillips U.S.A. 45°42N 90°24W 308 C8
Phillipsburg Ga., U.S.A. 31°25N 83°30W 316 D6
Phillipsburg Kans., U.S.A. 39°45N 99°19W 308 F4
Phillipsburg N.J., U.S.A. 40°42N 75°12W 313 F9
Philmont U.S.A. 42°15N 73°39W 313 D11
Philomath Ga., U.S.A. 33°44N 82°59W 316 B7
Philomath Oreg., U.S.A. 44°32N 123°22W 304 D2
Phimai Thailand 15°13N 102°30E 236 E4
Phitsanulok Thailand 16°50N 100°12E 236 D3
Phnom Kulen △ Cambodia 13°38N 104°15E 236 F5
Phnom Penh Cambodia 11°33N 104°55E 237 G5
Phnum Penh = Phnom Penh Cambodia 11°33N 104°55E 237 G5
Pho, Laem Thailand 6°55N 101°19E 237 J3
Phocis = Fokida Greece 38°30N 22°15E 204 C4
Phoenicia U.S.A. 42°5N 74°14W 313 D10
Phoenix Mauritius 20°17S 57°30E 272 e
Phoenix Ariz., U.S.A. 33°26N 112°4W 305 K7
Phoenix Ill., U.S.A. 41°36N 87°37W 119 D3
Phoenix N.Y., U.S.A. 43°14N 76°18W 313 C8
Phoenix Is. Kiribati 3°30S 172°0W 277 A16
Phoenix Park Ireland 53°21N 6°20W 120 A2
Phoenixville U.S.A. 40°8N 75°31W 313 F9
Phon Thailand 15°49N 102°36E 236 E4
Phong → Thailand 16°23N 102°56E 236 D4
Phong Nha -Ke Bang △ Vietnam 17°30N 106°10E 236 D6
Phong Saly Laos 21°42N 102°9E 236 B4
Phong Tho Vietnam 22°32N 103°21E 236 A4
Phonsavan Laos 19°27N 103°10E 236 C4
Phonum Thailand 8°49N 98°48E 237 H2
Phosphate Hill Australia 21°53S 139°58E 280 C2
Photharam Thailand 13°41N 99°51E 236 F2
Phra Kaeo Bangkok, Thailand 113 b1
Phra Khanong Thailand 13°40N 100°36E 113 B2
Phra Nakhon Thailand 13°45N 100°30E 113 B2
Phra Nakhon Si Ayutthaya Thailand 14°25N 100°30E 236 E3
Phra Pradaeng Thailand 13°39N 100°33E 113 C2
Phra Thong, Ko Thailand 9°5N 98°17E 237 H2
Phrae Thailand 18°7N 100°9E 236 C3
Phranakhon Thailand 13°44N 100°29E 113 B1
Phrom Phiram Thailand 17°2N 100°12E 236 D3
Phrom Thep, Laem Thailand 7°45N 98°19E 237 a
Phrygia Turkey 38°40N 30°0E 212 C4
Phthiotis = Fthiotida Greece 38°50N 22°25E 204 C4
Phu Bia Laos 19°10N 103°0E 236 C4
Phu Chong -Na Yoi △ Thailand 14°25N 105°30E 236 E5
Phu Hin Rong Kla △ Thailand 17°0N 100°59E 236 D3
Phu Kao -Phu Phan Kham △ Thailand 16°53N 102°31E 236 D4
Phu Kradung △ Thailand 17°2N 101°44E 236 D3
Phu Loi Laos 20°14N 103°14E 236 B4
Phu Luang △ Thailand 17°15N 101°29E 236 D3
Phu Ly Vietnam 20°35N 105°50E 228 G5
Phu My Vietnam 14°15N 109°5E 236 E7
Phu Pha Man △ Thailand 16°44N 101°50E 236 D3
Phu Phan △ Thailand 17°0N 103°56E 236 D4
Phu Quoc, Dao Vietnam 10°20N 104°0E 237 G4
Phu Sa Dok Bua △ Thailand 16°11N 104°45E 236 D5
Phu Sang △ Thailand 19°35N 100°19E 236 C3
Phu Tho Vietnam 21°24N 105°13E 228 G5
Phu Wiang △ Thailand 16°39N 102°23E 236 D4
Phuc Yen Vietnam 21°16N 105°45E 228 G5
Phuket Thailand 7°53N 98°24E 237 a
Phuket, Ko Thailand 8°0N 98°22E 237 a
Phul India 30°19N 75°14E 242 D6
Phulad India 25°38N 73°49E 242 G5
Phulbani India 20°28N 84°14E 244 D7
Phulchari Bangla. 25°11N 89°37E 241 C2
Phulera India 26°52N 75°16E 242 F6
Phulpur India 25°31N 82°49E 243 G10
Phunphin Thailand 9°7N 99°12E 237 H2
Phuntsholing Bhutan 26°51N 89°23E 243 F13
Phuphrabat Thailand 17°40N 102°45E 236 D4
Phuthaditjhaba S. Africa 28°29S 28°48E 271 C4
Phyu = Pyu Burma 18°30N 96°28E 241 F6
Pia ◎ Australia 27°7S 116°23E 279 E2
Piaçabuçu Brazil 10°24S 36°25W 332 D4
Piacenza Italy 45°1N 9°40E 198 C6
Piai, Tanjung Malaysia 1°17N 103°30E 237 d
Piako → N.Z. 37°12S 175°30E 284 D4
Pian Cr. → Australia 30°2S 148°12E 281 E4
Pian-Upe ⌂ Uganda 1°44N 34°20E 268 B3
Piana France 42°15N 8°34E 175 F12
Pianella Italy 42°24N 14°2E 199 F11
Piangil Australia 35°5S 143°20E 282 C5
Pianosa Puglia, Italy 42°12N 15°44E 199 F12
Pianosa Toscana, Italy 42°35N 10°5E 198 F7
Piao'ertun China 41°50N 123°47E 227 D12
Piapot Canada 49°59N 109°8W 297 D7
Piarco Trin. & Tob. 10°35N 61°20W 323 t
Piarco Int. ✕ (POS) Trin. & Tob. 10°36N 61°20W 323 t
Pias Portugal 38°1N 7°29W 195 G3
Piaseczno Poland 52°5N 21°2E 185 F8
Piaski Poland 51°8N 22°52E 185 G9
Piastów Poland 52°12N 20°48E 185 F7
Piatã Brazil 13°9S 41°48W 333 D3
Piatra Romania 43°51N 25°9E 183 G10
Piatra Craiului △ Romania 45°30N 25°12E 183 E10
Piatra Neamţ Romania 46°56N 26°21E 183 D11
Piatra Olt Romania 44°22N 24°16E 183 F9
Piauí □ Brazil 7°0S 43°0W 332 C3
Piauí → Brazil 6°38S 42°42W 332 C3
Piave → Italy 45°32N 12°44E 199 C9
Piazza Ármerina Italy 37°21N 14°20E 201 E7
Pibor → South Sudan 7°35N 33°0E 257 F3
Pibor Post South Sudan 6°47N 33°3E 257 F3
Pic St-Loup France 43°47N 3°48E 174 E7
Pica Chile 20°35S 69°25W 330 E4
Picardie □ France 49°50N 3°0E 173 C10
Picardie, Plaine de France 50°0N 2°0E 173 C9
Picardy = Picardie □ France 49°50N 3°0E 173 C10
Picasso, Museu Barcelona, Spain 114 c2
Picayune U.S.A. 30°32N 89°41W 315 F10
Piccadilly London, U.K. 125 b3
Picerno Italy 40°38N 15°38E 201 B8
Pichhor India 25°58N 78°20E 243 G8
Pichilemu Chile 34°22S 72°0W 334 C1
Pichincha, □ Ecuador 0°10S 78°40W 328 D2
Pichor India 25°11N 78°11E 242 G8
Pickerel L. Canada 48°40N 91°25W 298 C1
Pickering U.K. 54°15N 0°46W 168 C7
Pickering, Vale of U.K. 54°14N 0°45W 168 C7
Pickle Lake Canada 51°30N 90°12W 298 B1
Pickwick L. U.S.A. 35°4N 88°15W 315 D10
Picnic B. Hong Kong, China 22°13N 114°10E 122 B2
Pico Azores 38°28N 28°20W 153 d1
Pico, Ponta do Azores 38°28N 28°25W 153 d1
Pico Bonito △ Honduras 15°34N 86°48W 320 C2
Pico da Neblina △ Brazil 0°19N 66°28W 328 C4
Pico Rivera U.S.A. 33°59N 118°5W 126 C4
Pico Truncado Argentina 46°40S 68°0W 336 C3
Picos = Colinas Brazil 6°0S 44°10W 332 C3
Picos Brazil 7°5S 41°28W 332 C3
Picos, Pta. dos Spain 41°52N 8°53W 194 D2
Picos de Europa △ Spain 43°14N 4°59W 194 B6
Picota Peru 6°54S 76°24W 330 B2
Picton N.S.W., Australia 34°12S 150°34E 283 C9
Picton Canada 44°1N 77°9W 312 B7
Picton N.Z. 41°18S 174°3E 285 B9
Picton, I. Chile 55°2S 66°57W 336 E3
Pictou Canada 45°41N 62°42W 299 C7
Picture Butte Canada 49°55N 112°45W 296 D6
Pictured Rocks ⌂ U.S.A. 46°30N 86°30W 308 B10
Picuí Brazil 6°31S 36°21W 332 C4
Picún Leufú Argentina 39°30S 69°5W 336 A3
Pidbuzh Ukraine 49°19N 23°14E 185 J10
Pidurutalagala Sri Lanka 7°10N 80°50E 245 L5
Piechowice Poland 50°51N 15°36E 185 H2
Piedade Rio de J., Brazil 22°52S 43°18W 135 B1
Piedade Lisboa, Portugal 38°49N 9°16W 126 A1
Piedade, Cova da Portugal 38°40N 9°8W 126 A2
Piedecuesta Colombia 6°59N 73°3W 328 B3
Piedimonte Matese Italy 41°22N 14°22E 201 A7
Piedmont = Piemonte □ Italy 45°0N 8°0E 198 D5
Piedmont Ala., U.S.A. 33°55N 85°37W 316 B4
Piedmont S.C., U.S.A. 34°42N 76°28W 292 F11
Piedmont Park U.S.A. 33°47N 84°22W 113 B2
Piedra → Spain 41°18N 1°47W 196 D3
Piedra del Águila Argentina 40°2S 70°4W 336 B2
Piedra del Águila, Embalse Argentina 40°15S 70°4W 336 B2
Piedra Lais Venezuela 3°10N 65°50W 328 C4
Piedrabuena Spain 39°0N 4°10W 195 G6
Piedrahita Spain 40°28N 5°23W 194 E5
Piedralaves Spain 40°19N 4°42W 194 E6
Piedras, R. de las → Peru 12°30S 69°15W 330 C4
Piedras Blancas Spain 43°33N 5°58W 194 B5
Piedras Negras Mexico 28°42N 100°31W 318 B4
Piedras Pt. Phil. 10°11N 118°48E 233 F2
Piekar = Piekary Śląskie Poland 50°24N 18°57E 185 H5
Piekary Śląskie Poland 50°24N 18°57E 185 H5
Pieksämäki Finland 62°18N 27°10E 188 A4
Pielinen Finland 63°15N 29°40E 160 E23
Pieljekaise △ Sweden 66°20N 16°45E 160 C17
Piemonte □ Italy 45°0N 8°0E 198 D5
Pienaarsrivier S. Africa 25°15S 28°18E 271 C4
Pieniężno Poland 54°14N 20°8E 184 D7
Pieninský △ Europe 49°25N 20°28E 181 B13
Pieńsk Poland 51°16N 15°2E 185 G2
Pienza Italy 43°4N 11°40E 199 E8
Piercefield U.S.A. 44°13N 74°35W 313 B10
Pierceland Canada 54°20N 109°46W 297 C7
Pieria Greece 40°13N 22°25E 202 F6
Pierpont U.S.A. 41°45N 80°34W 312 E4
Pierre U.S.A. 44°22N 100°21W 308 C3
Pierre-Buffière France 45°41N 1°22E 174 C5
Pierre-de-Bresse France 46°54N 5°13E 173 F12
Pierre Elliott Trudeau ✕ (YUL) Canada 45°28N 73°44W 130 B1
Pierrefonds Canada 45°29N 73°51W 313 A11
Pierrefontaine-les-Varans France 47°14N 6°32E 173 E13
Pierrefort France 44°55N 2°50E 174 D6
Pierrelatte France 44°23N 4°43E 175 D8
Pierson U.S.A. 29°14N 81°28W 317 F8
Piešťany Slovak Rep. 48°38N 17°55E 181 C10
Piesting → Austria 48°6N 16°40E 181 C9
Pieszyce Poland 50°43N 16°33E 185 H3
Piet Retief S. Africa 27°1S 30°50E 271 C5
Pietarsaari Finland 63°40N 22°43E 160 E20
Pieter Both Mauritius 20°11S 57°32E 272 e
Pietermaritzburg S. Africa 29°35S 30°25E 271 C5
Pietersburg = Polokwane S. Africa 23°54S 29°25E 271 B4
Pietragalla Italy 40°45N 15°53E 201 B8
Pietralata Italy 41°55N 12°33E 136 B2
Pietrasanta Italy 43°57N 10°14E 198 E7
Pietroşiţa Romania 45°11N 25°26E 183 E10
Pietrosul, Vf. Maramureş, Romania 47°35N 24°43E 183 C9
Pietrosul, Vf. Suceava, Romania 47°12N 25°18E 183 C10
Pieve di Cadore Italy 46°26N 12°22E 199 B9
Pieve di Teco Italy 44°3N 7°56E 198 D4
Pievepélago Italy 44°12N 10°37E 198 D7
Pigaditsa Greece 39°59N 21°23E 202 G5
Pigeon Guadeloupe 16°9N 61°46W 322 e
Pigeon I. India 14°2N 74°20E 245 G2
Pigeon I. St. Lucia 14°6N 60°58W 323 m
Pigeon L. Canada 44°27N 78°30W 312 B6
Piges Greece 39°17N 21°25E 204 B3
Piggott U.S.A. 36°23N 90°11W 315 C9
Pigna Italy 43°56N 7°40E 198 E4
Pigüe Argentina 37°36S 62°25W 334 D3
Piha N.Z. 36°57S 174°28E 284 C3
Pihani India 27°36N 80°15E 243 F9
Pihlajamäki Finland 60°14N 24°58E 121 B2
Pihlajasaari Finland 60°8N 24°55E 121 C2
Pihlajavesi Finland 61°45N 28°45E 188 B5
Pijijiapan Mexico 15°42N 93°14W 319 D6
Pikalevo Russia 59°37N 34°9E 188 C8
Pikangikum Canada 51°49N 94°0W 297 C10
Pikes Peak U.S.A. 38°50N 105°3W 304 G11
Piketberg S. Africa 32°55S 18°40E 270 D2
Pikeville U.S.A. 37°29N 82°31W 309 G12
Pikit Phil. 7°4N 124°41E 233 H5
Pikou China 39°18N 122°22E 227 E12
Pikounda Congo 0°30N 16°44E 264 B3
Pikwitonei Canada 55°35N 97°9W 297 B9
Pila Poland 53°10N 16°48E 185 E3
Pila Spain 38°16N 1°11W 197 G3
Pili Phil. 13°33N 123°19E 232 E4
Pilibhit India 28°40N 79°50E 243 E8
Pilica → Poland 51°52N 21°17E 185 G8
Pilio, Oros Greece 39°27N 23°3E 204 B5
Pilipinas = Philippines ■ Asia 12°0N 123°0E 232 E4
Pilis Hungary 47°17N 19°35E 182 C4
Pilisvörösvár Hungary 47°38N 18°56E 182 C3
Pilkhawa India 28°43N 77°42E 242 E7
Pillar B. Ascension I. 7°59S 14°21W 153 g
Pillaro Ecuador 1°10S 78°32W 328 D2
Pillau = Baltiysk Russia 54°41N 19°58E 184 D6
Pilliga Australia 30°21S 148°54E 281 E4
Pilos Greece 36°55N 21°42E 204 E3
Pilot Grove U.S.A. 38°53N 92°55W 310 F4
Pilot Mound Canada 49°15N 98°54W 297 D9
Pilot Point Alaska, U.S.A. 57°34N 157°35W 303 H8
Pilot Point Tex., U.S.A. 33°24N 96°58W 314 E6
Pilot Rock U.S.A. 45°29N 118°50W 304 D4
Pilot Station U.S.A. 61°56N 162°53W 303 F7
Pilote → Martinique 14°28N 60°55W 322 j
Pilsen = Pilzno Poland 49°58N 21°16E 185 J8
Pilsen = Plzeň Czech Rep. 49°45N 13°22E 180 B6
Pilštanj Slovenia 46°8N 15°39E 199 B12
Piltene Latvia 57°13N 21°40E 184 A8

Pilton U.K. 55°58N 3°13W 121 B2
Pilzno Poland 49°58N 21°16E 185 J8
Pima U.S.A. 32°54N 109°50W 305 K9
Pimba Australia 31°18S 136°46E 282 A2
Pimenta Bueno Brazil 11°35S 61°10W 331 C5
Pimenteiras Brazil 13°40S 60°58W 331 C5
Pimentel Peru 6°45S 79°55W 330 B2
Pimlico London, U.K. 125 c3
Pimpri Chinchwad India 18°37N 73°47E 244 E1
Pimu Dem. Rep. of the Congo 1°42N 20°58E 264 B4
Pin Valley △ India 31°50N 77°50E 242 D7
Pina de Ebro Spain 41°29N 0°33W 196 D4
Pinamalayan Phil. 13°2N 121°29E 232 E3
Pinang Malaysia 5°25N 100°15E 237 c
Pinang □ Malaysia 5°20N 100°20E 237 K3
Pinar, C. des Spain 39°53N 3°12E 206 B4
Pinar del Río Cuba 22°26N 83°40W 320 B3
Pınarbaşı Çanakkale, Turkey 39°53N 26°15E 205 B8
Pınarbaşı Kayseri, Turkey 38°43N 36°23E 212 C7
Pınarhisar Turkey 41°37N 27°30E 203 E11
Pinatubo, Mt. Phil. 15°8N 120°21E 232 D3
Pinawa Canada 50°9N 95°50W 297 C9
Pincehely Hungary 46°41N 18°27E 182 D3
Pinchang China 31°36N 107°3E 228 B6
Pincher Creek Canada 49°30N 113°57W 296 D6
Pinchi L. Canada 54°38N 124°30W 296 C4
Pinckard U.S.A. 31°19N 85°33W 316 D4
Pinckneyville U.S.A. 38°5N 89°23W 310 F7
Pińczów Poland 50°32N 20°32E 185 H7
Pind Dadan Khan Pakistan 32°36N 73°7E 217 F8
Pindar Australia 28°30S 115°47E 279 E2
Pindaré ➔ Brazil 3°17S 44°47W 332 B3
Pindaré-Mirim Brazil 3°37S 45°21W 332 B2
Pindera Downs ◎ Australia 29°24S 142°37E 281 A3
Pindi Gheb Pakistan 33°14N 72°21E 242 C5
Pindiga Nigeria 9°58N 10°53E 263 D7
Pindobal Brazil 3°16S 48°25W 332 B2
Pindos △ Greece 39°52N 21°11E 204 B3
Pindos Oros Greece 40°0N 21°0E 204 B3
Pindus Mts. = Pindos Oros Greece 40°0N 21°0E 204 B3
Pine ➔ B.C., Canada 56°8N 120°43W 296 B4
Pine ➔ Sask., Canada 58°50N 105°38W 297 B7
Pine Bluff U.S.A. 34°13N 92°1W 314 D8
Pine Bluffs U.S.A. 41°11N 104°4W 304 F11
Pine Castle U.S.A. 28°28N 81°22W 133 B2
Pine City U.S.A. 45°50N 92°59W 308 C7
Pine Cr. ➔ U.S.A. 41°10N 77°16W 312 E7
Pine Creek Australia 13°50S 131°50E 278 B5
Pine Falls Canada 50°34N 96°11W 297 C9
Pine Flat L. U.S.A. 36°50N 119°20W 306 J7
Pine Grove Ont., Canada 43°47N 79°35W 141 A1
Pine Grove Pa., U.S.A. 40°33N 76°23W 313 F8
Pine Hill Australia 23°38S 146°57E 280 C4
Pine Hills U.S.A. 28°33N 81°27W 133 A2
Pine I. U.S.A. 26°36N 82°7W 317 J7
Pine Island U.S.A. 26°5N 80°16W 129 B1
Pine Island Glacier Antarctica 76°0S 100°0W 151 D15
Pine Level U.S.A. 32°4N 86°4W 316 C3
Pine Mountain U.S.A. 32°49N 84°51W 316 C5
Pine Pass Canada 55°25N 122°42W 296 B4
Pine Ridge N.S.W., Australia 31°30S 150°28E 283 A9
Pine Ridge S. Dak., U.S.A. 43°2N 102°33W 308 D2
Pine River Man., Canada 51°45N 100°30W 297 C8
Pine River Minn., U.S.A. 46°43N 94°24W 308 B6
Pine Valley U.S.A. 32°50N 116°32W 307 N10
Pinecrest Calif., U.S.A. 38°12N 120°1W 306 G6
Pinecrest Fla., U.S.A. 25°40N 80°18W 129 D1
Pineda de Mar Spain 41°37N 2°42E 196 D7
Pinedale Calif., U.S.A. 36°50N 119°48W 306 J7
Pinedale Wyo., U.S.A. 42°52N 109°52W 304 E9
Pinega ➔ Russia 64°30N 44°19E 186 B8
Pinehouse L. Canada 55°32N 106°35W 297 B7
Pineimuta ➔ Canada 52°8N 88°33W 298 B1
Pinellas Park U.S.A. 27°50N 82°41W 317 H7
Pinerolo Italy 44°53N 7°21E 198 D4
Pines, Akra Greece 40°5N 24°20E 203 F8
Pineto Italy 42°36N 14°4E 199 F11
Pinetop-Lakeside U.S.A. 34°9N 109°58W 305 J9
Pinetown S. Africa 29°48S 30°54E 271 C5
Pinetta U.S.A. 30°36N 83°21W 316 E6
Pineview U.S.A. 32°7N 83°30W 316 C6
Pineville La., U.S.A. 31°19N 92°26W 314 F8
Pineville S.C., U.S.A. 33°26N 80°1W 316 B9
Pinewood U.S.A. 33°44N 80°27W 316 B9
Pinewood Park U.S.A. 25°52N 80°13W 129 C2
Piney France 48°22N 4°21E 173 D11
Ping ➔ Thailand 15°42N 100°9E 236 E3
Pingaring Australia 32°40S 118°32E 279 F2
Pingba China 26°23N 106°12E 228 D6
Pingbian China 23°0N 103°45E 228 F4
Pingchuan China 27°35N 101°55E 228 D3
Pingding China 37°47N 113°38E 226 F7
Pingdingshan China 33°43N 113°27E 226 H7
Pingdu China 36°42N 119°59E 227 F10
Pingelly Australia 32°32S 117°5E 279 F2
Pingguo China 23°19N 107°36E 228 F6
Pinghe China 24°17N 117°21E 229 E11
Pinghu China 30°40N 121°2E 229 B13
Pingjiang China 28°45N 113°36E 229 C9
Pingle China 24°40N 110°40E 229 E8
Pingli China 32°27N 109°22E 228 A7
Pingliang China 35°35N 106°31E 226 G4
Pinglin Taiwan 24°56N 121°42E 225 B3
Pinglu China 39°31N 112°30E 226 E7
Pingluo China 38°52N 106°30E 226 E4
Pingnan Fujian, China 26°55N 119°0E 229 D12
Pingnan Guangxi Zhuangzu, China 23°33N 110°22E 229 F8
Pingo Gabon 1°19S 10°55E 264 C2
Pingquan China 41°1N 118°37E 227 D10
Pingrup Australia 33°32S 118°29E 279 F2
Pingshan China 28°39N 104°3E 228 C5
Pingtan China 25°31N 119°47E 229 E12
Pingtang China 25°49N 107°17E 228 E6
P'ingtung Taiwan 22°38N 120°30E 225 D2
P'ingtung □ Taiwan 22°30N 120°40E 225 D2
Pingwu China 32°25N 104°30E 226 H3
Pingxiang Guangxi Zhuangzu, China 22°6N 106°46E 228 F6
Pingxiang Jiangxi, China 27°43N 113°48E 229 D9
Pingyao China 37°12N 112°10E 226 F7
Pingyi China 35°30N 117°35E 227 G9
Pingyin China 36°20N 116°25E 226 F9
Pingyuan Guangdong, China 24°37N 115°57E 229 E10
Pingyuan Shandong, China 37°10N 116°22E 226 F9
Pingyuanjie China 23°45N 103°48E 228 F4
Pingzhou China 23°1N 113°11E 122 B1
Pinhal Novo Portugal 38°38N 8°55W 195 G2
Pinheiro Brazil 2°31S 45°5W 332 B2
Pinheiro Machado Brazil 31°34S 53°23W 335 C5
Pinheiros ➔ Brazil 23°37S 46°44W 137 B1
Pinhel Portugal 40°50N 7°1W 194 E3
Pinhuá ➔ Brazil 6°21S 65°0W 331 B5
Pini Indonesia 0°10N 98°40E 234 B1
Pinios ➔ Ilia, Greece 37°48N 21°20E 204 D3
Pinios ➔ Trikala, Greece 39°55N 22°41E 204 B4
Pinjarra Australia 32°37S 115°52E 279 F2
Pinjrapur Pakistan 24°53N 67°4E 123 A2
Pink Beach Bonaire 12°5N 68°17W 322 h
Pink Mountain Canada 57°3N 122°52W 296 B4
Pinkafeld Austria 47°22N 16°9E 181 D9
Pinlaung Burma 20°8N 96°47E 241 E6
Pinlebu Burma 24°5N 95°22E 241 C5
Pinnacle Is. = Senkaku-Shotō E. China Sea 25°45N 123°30E 221 M1
Pinnacles △ U.S.A. 36°25N 121°12W 306 J5
Pinnaroo Australia 35°17S 140°53E 282 C4
Pinneberg Germany 53°40N 9°48E 178 B5
Pinner U.K. 51°35N 0°22W 125 A1
Pinner Green U.K. 51°35N 0°23W 125 A1
Pino Hachado, Paso S. Amer. 38°39S 70°54W 336 A2
Pinon Hills U.S.A. 34°26N 117°39W 307 L9
Pinos Mexico 22°18N 101°34W 318 C4
Pinos, Mt. U.S.A. 34°49N 119°8W 307 L7
Pinos Pt. U.S.A. 36°38N 121°57W 305 H3
Pinos Puente Spain 37°15N 3°45W 195 H7
Pinrang Indonesia 3°46S 119°41E 235 C5
Pins, Î. des N. Cal. 22°37S 167°30E 288 d
Pins, Pte. aux Canada 42°15N 81°51W 312 D3
Pinsk Belarus 52°10N 26°1E 177 B14
Pinta, Canal de Ecuador 0°27N 90°38W 330 a
Pinta, I. Ecuador 0°35N 90°44W 330 a
Pintados Chile 20°35S 69°40W 330 E4
Pinturas ➔ Argentina 46°30S 70°20W 336 C2
Pintuyan Phil. 9°57N 125°15E 233 G5
Pinukpuk Phil. 17°35N 121°22E 232 C3
Pinyang China 27°42N 120°31E 229 D13
Pinyug Russia 60°5N 48°0E 186 B8
Pio Duran Phil. 13°2N 123°25E 232 E4
Pio V. Corpuz Phil. 11°55N 124°2E 233 F5
Pio XII Brazil 3°53S 45°17W 332 B2
Pioche U.S.A. 37°56N 114°27W 305 H6
Pioltello Italy 45°30N 9°19E 128 A2
Piombino Italy 42°55N 10°32E 198 F7
Piombino, Canale di Italy 42°53N 10°30E 198 F7
Pioner, Ostrov Russia 79°50N 92°0E 215 B10
Pionerskiy Russia 54°56N 20°14E 184 D7
Pionki Poland 51°29N 21°28E 185 G8
Piopiotaki = Milford Sd. N.Z. 44°41S 167°47E 285 E2
Piorini ➔ Brazil 3°23S 63°30W 329 D5
Piorini, L. Brazil 3°15S 62°35W 329 D5
Piotrków Trybunalski Poland 51°23N 19°43E 185 G6
Piove di Sacco Italy 45°18N 12°2E 199 C9
Pīp Iran 26°45N 60°10E 247 E9
Pipar India 26°25N 73°31E 242 F5
Pipar Road India 26°27N 73°27E 242 F5
Piparia Mad. P., India 22°45N 78°23E 242 H8
Piparia Mad. P., India 21°49N 77°37E 242 J7
Piparo Trin. & Tob. 10°20N 61°20W 323 f
Pipas Angola 14°57S 12°11E 265 E2
Piperi Greece 39°20N 24°19E 204 B6
Piperno = Priverno Italy 41°28N 13°11E 200 A6
Pipestone U.S.A. 44°0N 96°19W 308 D5
Pipestone ➔ Canada 52°53N 89°23W 298 B2
Pipestone Cr. ➔ Canada 49°38N 100°15W 297 D8
Pipiriki N.Z. 39°28S 175°5E 284 F4
Piplan Pakistan 32°17N 71°21E 242 C4
Piploda India 23°37N 74°56E 242 H6
Pipmuacan, Rés. Canada 49°45N 70°30W 299 C5
Pippingarra Australia 20°27S 118°42E 278 D2
Pipriac France 47°59N 1°58W 172 E5
Piqua U.S.A. 40°9N 84°15W 311 D12
Piquet Carneiro Brazil 5°48S 39°25W 332 C4
Piquiri ➔ Brazil 24°3S 54°14W 335 A5
Pir Panjal Range India 32°30N 76°50E 242 C7
Pīr Sohrāb Iran 25°44N 60°54E 247 E9
Pira Benin 8°28N 1°48E 263 D5
Piracanjuba Brazil 17°18S 49°1W 333 E2
Piracicaba Brazil 22°45S 47°40W 335 A6
Piracuruca Brazil 3°50S 41°50W 332 B3
Pirae Tahiti 17°31S 149°32W 289 e
Piræus = Pireas Greece 37°57N 23°42E 112 B1
Piraiévs = Pireas Greece 37°57N 23°42E 112 B1
Pirajuçara ➔ Brazil 23°33S 46°42W 137 B1
Pirajuí Brazil 21°59S 49°29W 335 A6
Piram I. India 21°36N 72°21E 242 J5
Piran Slovenia 45°31N 13°33E 199 C10
Pirané Argentina 25°42S 59°6W 334 B4
Piranhas Brazil 9°27S 37°46W 332 C4
Pirano = Piran Slovenia 45°31N 13°33E 199 C10
Pīrānshahr Iran 36°41N 45°8E 213 D11
Pirapemas Brazil 3°43S 44°14W 332 B3
Pirapora Brazil 17°20S 44°56W 333 E3
Pirara Guyana 3°37N 59°40W 329 C6
Pirawa India 24°10N 76°2E 242 G7
Piray ➔ Bolivia 16°32S 63°45W 331 D5
Pirdop Bulgaria 42°40N 24°10E 203 D8
Pireas Greece 37°57N 23°42E 112 B1
Pires do Rio Brazil 17°18S 48°17W 333 E2
Pirganj Bangla. 25°51N 88°24E 241 C2
Pirgi Greece 38°13N 25°59E 205 C7
Pirgos Ilia, Greece 37°40N 21°27E 204 D3
Pirgos Kriti, Greece 35°0N 25°9E 207 E6
Pirgovo Bulgaria 43°44N 25°43E 203 C9
Piribebuy Paraguay 25°26S 57°2W 334 B4
Pirimapun Indonesia 6°20S 138°24E 231 F9
Pirin △ Bulgaria 41°48N 23°22E 202 E7
Pirin Planina Bulgaria 41°40N 23°30E 202 E7
Pirinççi Turkey 41°10N 28°52E 122 B1
Pírineos = Pyrénées Europe 42°45N 0°18E 174 F4
Piripiri Brazil 4°15S 41°46W 332 B3
Piritu Venezuela 9°23N 69°12W 328 B4
Pirituba Brazil 23°29S 46°44W 137 A1
Pirkkola Finland 60°14N 24°55E 121 B2
Pirlangimpi Australia 11°24S 130°26E 278 B5
Pirmasens Germany 49°12N 7°36E 179 F3
Pirna Germany 50°57N 13°56E 178 E9
Pirojpur Bangla. 22°35N 90°1E 241 D3
Pirot Serbia 43°9N 22°33E 202 C6
Piru Indonesia 3°4S 128°12E 231 E7
Piru Calif., U.S.A. 34°25N 118°48W 307 L8
Piryatin = Pyryatyn Ukraine 50°15N 32°25E 189 G7
Pisa Italy 43°43N 10°23E 198 E7
Pisa ➔ Poland 53°14N 21°52E 185 E8
Pisa, Firenze ✕ (PSA) Italy 43°40N 10°22E 198 E7
Pisa Ra. N.Z. 44°52S 169°12E 285 E4
Pisac Peru 13°25S 71°50W 330 C3
Pisagua Chile 19°40S 70°15W 330 D3
Pisarovina Croatia 45°35N 15°50E 199 C12
Pisau, Tanjong Malaysia 6°4N 117°59E 235 A5
Pisba △ Colombia 10°39N 74°30W 328 A3
Pisco Peru 13°50S 76°12W 330 C2
Piscu Romania 45°30N 27°43E 183 E12
Písek Czech Rep. 49°19N 14°10E 180 B7
Pisgat O'mer West Bank 31°49N 35°14E 123 B2
Pisgat Ze'ev West Bank 31°49N 35°14E 123 B2
Pishan China 37°30N 78°33E 217 E9
Pishcha Ukraine 51°35N 23°50E 185 G10
Pishchanka Ukraine 48°12N 28°54E 183 B13
Pīshīn Iran 26°6N 61°47E 247 E9
Pishin Pakistan 30°35N 67°0E 242 D2
Pishin Lora ➔ Pakistan 29°9N 64°5E 242 E1
Pishpek = Bishkek Kyrgyzstan 42°54N 74°46E 217 D8
Pisidia Turkey 37°30N 31°40E 212 D4
Pising Indonesia 5°8S 121°53E 231 F6
Pisiou, Pte. Guadeloupe 15°59N 61°13W 322 e
Pismo Beach U.S.A. 35°9N 120°38W 307 K6
Písnice Czech Rep. 49°59N 14°28E 135 C2
Piso, L. Liberia 6°50N 11°15W 262 D2
Pisogne Italy 45°45N 10°10E 198 C7
Pissila Burkina Faso 13°7N 0°50W 263 C4
Pissis, Cerro Argentina 27°45S 68°48W 334 B2
Pissos France 44°19N 0°49W 174 D3
Pissouri Cyprus 34°40N 32°42E 207 F8
Pisticci Italy 40°23N 16°33E 201 B9
Pistóia Italy 43°55N 10°54E 198 E7
Pistol B. Canada 62°25N 92°37W 297 A10
Pisuerga ➔ Spain 41°33N 4°52W 194 D6
Pisz Poland 53°38N 21°49E 184 E8
Pit ➔ U.S.A. 40°47N 122°6W 304 F2
Pita Guinea 11°5N 12°15W 262 C2
Pitalito Colombia 1°51N 76°2W 328 C2
Pitampura India 28°41N 77°7E 120 A1
Pitanga Brazil 24°46S 51°44W 333 F1
Pitangui Brazil 19°40S 44°54W 333 E3
Pitarpunga L. Australia 34°24S 143°30E 282 C5
Pitcairn I. Pac. Oc. 25°5S 130°5W 289 K14
Pitch Pt. Trin. & Tob. 10°15N 61°37W 323 t
Piteå Sweden 65°20N 21°25E 160 D19
Piteälven ➔ Sweden 65°20N 21°25E 160 D19
Piterka Russia 50°41N 47°29E 190 E8
Pitești Romania 44°52N 24°54E 183 F9
Pithapuram India 17°10N 82°15E 244 F6
Pithara Australia 30°20S 116°35E 279 F2
Pithio Greece 41°24N 26°40E 203 E10
Pithiviers France 48°10N 2°13E 173 D9
Pithora India 21°16N 82°31E 244 D6
Pithoragarh India 29°35N 80°13E 243 E9
Pithoro Pakistan 25°31N 69°23E 242 G3
Piti Guam 13°28N 144°41E 302 d
Pitigliano Italy 42°38N 11°40E 199 F8
Pitkäjärvi Finland 60°15N 24°45E 121 B1
Pitkyaranta Russia 61°34N 31°37E 188 B6
Pitlochry U.K. 56°42N 3°44W 167 E5
Pitnak = Drujba Uzbekistan 41°13N 61°18E 216 D6
Pitoa Cameroon 9°23N 13°32E 264 A2
Pitogo Phil. 13°47N 122°5E 232 E4
Piton, Pte. du Guadeloupe 16°30N 61°26W 322 e
Piton de la Petite Rivière Noire Mauritius 20°24S 57°23E 272 e
Pitons, Anses des St. Lucia 13°49N 61°4W 323 m
Pitou Taiwan 23°53N 120°27E 225 C2
Pitou Chiao Taiwan 25°8N 121°55E 225 A3
Pitrufquén Chile 38°59S 72°39W 336 A2
Pitschen = Byczyna Poland 51°7N 18°12E 185 G5
Pitsilia Cyprus 34°55N 33°0E 207 F9
Pitsunda = Bichvinta Georgia 43°9N 40°21E 191 J5
Pitt, Pta. Ecuador 0°43S 89°14W 330 a
Pitt I. B.C., Canada 53°30N 129°50W 296 C3
Pitt I. N.Z. 44°15S 176°15W 285 c
Pitti I. India 10°50N 72°38E 245 J1
Pittsburg Calif., U.S.A. 38°2N 121°53W 306 G5
Pittsburg Kans., U.S.A. 37°25N 94°42W 308 G6
Pittsburg Tex., U.S.A. 33°0N 94°59W 314 E7
Pittsburgh U.S.A. 40°26N 79°58W 312 F5
Pittsfield Ill., U.S.A. 39°36N 90°49W 310 E6
Pittsfield Maine, U.S.A. 44°47N 69°23W 309 C19
Pittsfield Mass., U.S.A. 42°27N 73°15W 313 D11
Pittsfield N.H., U.S.A. 43°18N 71°20W 313 C13
Pittston U.S.A. 41°19N 75°47W 313 E9
Pittsview U.S.A. 32°11N 85°10W 316 C4
Pittsworth Australia 27°41S 151°37E 281 D5
Pituri ➔ Australia 22°35S 138°30E 280 C2
Pium Brazil 10°27S 49°11W 332 D2
Piumafua Mt. Amer. Samoa 14°11S 169°37W 302 f
Piumhi Brazil 20°28S 45°58W 333 F2
Piura Peru 5°15S 80°38W 330 B1
Piura □ Peru 5°10S 80°0W 330 B2
Piuthan Nepal 28°7N 82°56E 243 E10
Piva ➔ Montenegro 43°20N 18°50E 202 C2
Pivijay Colombia 10°28N 74°37W 328 A3
Piwniczna Poland 49°27N 20°42E 185 J7
Pixian China 30°48N 103°52E 228 B4
Pixley U.S.A. 35°58N 119°18W 306 K7
Pizarra Spain 36°36N 4°42W 195 J6
Pizarro Colombia 4°58N 77°22W 328 C2
Pizhou = Pei Xian China 34°44N 116°55E 226 G9
Pizhou China 34°18N 117°57E 227 G9
Pizzo Italy 38°44N 16°10E 201 D9
Placentia Canada 47°20N 54°0W 299 C9
Placentia B. Canada 47°0N 54°40W 299 C9
Placer Masbate, Phil. 11°52N 123°55E 233 F4
Placer Surigao N., Phil. 9°36N 125°38E 233 G5
Placerville U.S.A. 38°44N 120°48W 306 G6
Placetas Cuba 22°15N 79°44W 320 B4
Plácido de Castro Brazil 10°20S 67°11W 330 C4
Plačkovica Macedonia 41°45N 22°30E 202 E6
Plaine des Jarres Laos 19°27N 103°10E 236 C4
Plaine Magnien Mauritius 20°25S 57°39E 272 e
Plaines des Papayes Mauritius 20°3S 57°34E 272 e
Plainfield Ill., U.S.A. 41°37N 88°12W 311 C8
Plainfield Ind., U.S.A. 39°42N 86°24W 311 E10
Plainfield N.J., U.S.A. 40°37N 74°25W 313 F10
Plainfield Ohio, U.S.A. 40°13N 81°43W 312 F3
Plainfield Vt., U.S.A. 44°17N 72°26W 313 B12
Plains Ga., U.S.A. 32°2N 84°24W 316 C5
Plains Mont., U.S.A. 47°28N 114°53W 304 C6
Plains Tex., U.S.A. 33°11N 102°50W 314 E3
Plainview Nebr., U.S.A. 42°21N 97°47W 308 D5
Plainview Tex., U.S.A. 34°11N 101°43W 314 D4
Plainwell U.S.A. 42°27N 85°38W 311 B11
Plaisance France 43°36N 0°3E 174 E4
Plaistow U.S.A. 42°50N 71°6W 313 D13
Plaju Indonesia 2°58S 104°49E 234 C2
Plaka Greece 40°0N 25°24E 205 B7
Plaka, Akra Greece 35°11N 26°19E 207 E7
Plakenska Planina Macedonia 41°14N 21°2E 202 E5
Plampang Indonesia 8°47S 117°46E 235 D5
Planá Czech Rep. 49°50N 12°44E 180 B5
Plana Cays Bahamas 22°38N 73°30W 321 B5
Planada U.S.A. 37°16N 120°19W 306 H6
Planchón Peru 12°14S 69°11W 330 C4
Plancoët France 48°32N 2°13W 172 D4
Plandište Serbia 45°16N 21°10E 182 E6
Planegg Germany 48°6N 11°25E 131 B1
Planeta Rica Colombia 8°25N 75°36W 328 B2
Plano Ill., U.S.A. 41°40N 88°32W 311 C8
Plano Tex., U.S.A. 33°1N 96°42W 314 E6
Plant City U.S.A. 28°1N 82°7W 317 G7
Plantation U.S.A. 26°7N 80°14W 129 B2
Plantation Isles U.S.A. 26°6N 80°14W 129 B2
Plaquemine U.S.A. 30°17N 91°14W 314 F9
Plaridel Phil. 8°37N 123°43E 233 G4
Plasencia Spain 40°3N 6°8W 194 E4
Plaški Croatia 45°4N 15°22E 199 C12
Plassen Norway 61°9N 12°30E 164 C9
Plast Russia 54°22N 60°50E 216 B6
Plaster City U.S.A. 32°47N 115°51W 307 N11
Plaster Rock Canada 46°53N 67°22W 299 C6
Plastun Russia 44°45N 136°19E 220 B8
Plasy Czech Rep. 49°56N 13°24E 180 B6
Plata, Río de la ➔ S. Amer. 34°45S 57°30W 334 C4
Plátani ➔ Italy 37°23N 13°16E 200 E6
Platanos Greece 35°28N 23°33E 207 E4
Plataria Greece 39°27N 20°16E 206 C10
Plateau □ Nigeria 8°30N 9°0E 263 D6
Plateau d'Ipassa ⌓ Gabon 0°26N 12°40E 264 B2
Plateaux □ Congo 2°30S 15°30E 264 C3
Plathe = Płoty Poland 53°48N 15°18E 184 E2
Platinum U.S.A. 59°1N 161°49W 303 G7
Platja d'Aro Spain 41°49N 3°4E 196 D8
Plato Colombia 9°47N 74°47W 328 B3
Platte U.S.A. 43°23N 98°51W 308 D4
Platte ➔ Mo., U.S.A. 39°16N 94°50W 310 E2
Platte ➔ Nebr., U.S.A. 41°4N 95°53W 308 E6
Platte City U.S.A. 39°22N 94°47W 310 E2
Platteville U.S.A. 42°44N 90°29W 310 B6
Plattling Germany 48°46N 12°53E 179 G8
Plattsburg U.S.A. 39°34N 94°27W 310 E2
Plattsburgh U.S.A. 44°42N 73°28W 313 B11
Plattsmouth U.S.A. 41°1N 95°53W 308 E6
Plau Germany 53°27N 12°15E 178 B8
Plauen Germany 50°30N 12°8E 178 E8
Plauer See Germany 53°28N 12°17E 178 B8
Plav Montenegro 42°38N 19°57E 202 D3
Plavinas Latvia 56°35N 25°46E 188 D3
Plavnica Montenegro 42°20N 19°13E 202 D3
Plavno Croatia 44°9N 16°10E 199 D13
Plavsk Russia 53°40N 37°18E 188 F9
Playa Blanca Canary Is. 28°51N 13°50W 153 e2
Playa de las Americas Canary Is. 28°5N 16°43W 153 e1
Playa de Mogán Canary Is. 27°48N 15°47W 153 e1
Playa del Carmen Mexico 20°37N 87°4W 319 C7
Playa del Inglés Canary Is. 27°45N 15°33W 153 e1
Playas Ecuador 2°38S 80°23W 328 D1
Playgreen L. Canada 54°0N 98°15W 297 C9
Plaza Mayor Madrid, Spain 127 b2
Pleasant Bay Canada 46°51N 60°48W 299 C7
Pleasant Hill Calif., U.S.A. 37°57N 122°4W 306 H4
Pleasant Hill Ill., U.S.A. 39°27N 90°52W 310 E6
Pleasant Hill Mo., U.S.A. 38°47N 94°16W 310 F2
Pleasant Mount U.S.A. 41°44N 75°26W 313 E9
Pleasant Point N.Z. 44°16S 171°9E 285 c
Pleasant Prairie U.S.A. 42°33N 87°56W 311 B9
Pleasanton Calif., U.S.A. 37°39N 121°52W 306 H5
Pleasanton Tex., U.S.A. 28°58N 98°29W 314 G5
Pleasantville Iowa, U.S.A. 41°23N 93°18W 310 C3
Pleasantville N.J., U.S.A. 39°24N 74°32W 309 F16
Pleasantville Pa., U.S.A. 41°35N 79°34W 312 E5
Pleasure Island U.S.A. 28°21N 81°31W 133 B1
Pleasure Ridge Park U.S.A. 38°9N 85°50W 311 F11
Pléaux France 45°8N 2°13E 174 C6
Plei Ku Vietnam 13°57N 108°0E 236 F7
Plélan-le-Grand France 48°0N 2°7W 172 D4
Plenița Romania 44°14N 23°10E 183 F8
Plenty ➔ Australia 23°25S 136°31E 280 C2
Plenty, B. of N.Z. 37°45S 177°0E 284 D6
Plentywood U.S.A. 48°47N 104°34W 304 B11
Plérin France 48°32N 2°46W 172 D4
Plesetsk Russia 62°43N 40°20E 186 B7
Pleshcheyevko Ozero △ Russia 56°45N 38°50E 188 D10
Pleskau = Pskov Russia 57°50N 28°25E 188 D5
Plessisville Canada 46°14N 71°47W 299 C5
Plestin-les-Grèves France 48°40N 3°39W 172 D3
Pleszew Poland 51°53N 17°47E 185 G4
Pleternica Croatia 45°17N 17°48E 182 E2
Plétipi, L. Canada 51°44N 70°6W 299 B5
Pleven Bulgaria 43°26N 24°37E 203 C8
Pleven □ Bulgaria 43°26N 24°37E 203 C8
Plevna Canada 44°58N 76°59W 312 B8
Plitvice Lakes = Plitvička Jezera △ Croatia 44°54N 15°35E 199 D12
Plitvička Jezera △ Croatia 44°54N 15°35E 199 D12
Plješevica Croatia 44°45N 15°45E 199 D12
Pljevlja Montenegro 43°21N 19°21E 202 C3
Ploaghe Italy 40°40N 8°45E 200 B1
Ploče Croatia 43°4N 17°26E 199 E14
Płock Poland 52°32N 19°40E 185 F6
Plöckenpass Italy 46°37N 12°57E 199 B9
Plöckenstein Germany 48°46N 13°51E 179 G9
Ploemeur France 47°44N 3°26W 172 E3
Ploërmel France 47°55N 2°26W 172 E4
Plöhnen = Płońsk Poland 52°37N 20°21E 185 F7
Ploiești Romania 44°57N 26°5E 183 F11
Plomari Greece 38°59N 26°22E 205 C8
Plombières-les-Bains France 47°58N 6°27E 173 E13
Plomin Croatia 45°8N 14°10E 199 C11
Plön Germany 54°9N 10°24E 178 A6
Plonge, Lac la Canada 55°8N 107°20W 297 B7
Płońsk Poland 52°37N 20°21E 185 F7
Plopeni Romania 45°4N 25°59E 183 E10
Plopișului, Munții Romania 47°5N 22°30E 182 C7
Plotsk = Płock Poland 52°32N 19°40E 185 F6
Płoty Poland 53°48N 15°18E 184 E2
Plouaret France 48°37N 3°28W 172 D3
Plouay France 47°55N 3°21W 172 E3
Ploučnice ➔ Czech Rep. 50°46N 14°13E 180 A7
Ploudalmézeau France 48°34N 4°41W 172 D2
Plouescat France 48°39N 4°10W 172 D2
Plougasnou France 48°42N 3°49W 172 D3
Plougastel-Daoulas France 48°22N 4°17W 172 D2
Plouguerneau France 48°36N 4°30W 172 D2
Plouha France 48°41N 2°57W 172 D4
Plouhinec France 48°0N 4°29W 172 E2
Plovdiv Bulgaria 42°8N 24°44E 203 D8
Plovdiv □ Bulgaria 42°15N 24°30E 203 D8
Plover Cove Res. China 22°28N 114°15E 219 a
Pluies, R. des ➔ Réunion 20°52S 55°31E 272 f
Plum U.S.A. 40°29N 79°47W 312 F5
Plum I. U.S.A. 41°11N 72°12W 313 E12
Plumas U.S.A. 39°45N 120°4W 306 F6
Plummer U.S.A. 47°20N 116°53W 304 C5
Plumridge Lakes Australia 29°26S 125°16E 279 E4
Plumstead Western Cape, S. Africa 34°1S 18°28E 118 B1
Plumstead London, U.K. 51°29N 0°5E 125 B4
Plumtree Zimbabwe 20°27S 27°55E 269 G2
Plungė Lithuania 55°53N 21°59E 184 C8
Pluvigner France 47°46N 3°1W 172 E3
Plužine Montenegro 43°8N 18°51E 202 C2
Plymouth Montserrat 16°41N 62°12W 323 p
Plymouth Trin. & Tob. 11°14N 60°48W 323 s
Plymouth Plymouth, U.K. 50°22N 4°10W 169 G3
Plymouth Calif., U.S.A. 38°29N 120°51W 306 G6
Plymouth Ill., U.S.A. 40°18N 90°58W 310 D6
Plymouth Ind., U.S.A. 41°21N 86°19W 311 C10
Plymouth Mass., U.S.A. 41°57N 70°40W 313 E14
Plymouth N.C., U.S.A. 35°52N 76°43W 315 D16
Plymouth N.H., U.S.A. 43°46N 71°41W 313 C13
Plymouth Pa., U.S.A. 41°14N 75°57W 313 E9
Plymouth Wis., U.S.A. 43°45N 87°59W 308 D10
Plympton-Wyoming = Wyoming Canada 42°57N 82°7W 312 D2
Plynlimon = Pumlumon Fawr U.K. 52°28N 3°46W 169 E4
Plyusa Russia 58°28N 29°27E 188 C5
Plyusa ➔ Russia 59°4N 28°6E 188 C5
Plyushchevo Russia 55°44N 37°45E 129 B3
Plzeň Czech Rep. 49°45N 13°22E 180 B6
Plzeňský □ Czech Rep. 49°35N 13°0E 180 B6
Pmere Nyente ◎ Australia 24°15S 136°10E 280 C2
Pniewy Poland 52°31N 16°16E 185 F3
Pnika Athens, Greece 112 c1
Pnyx = Pnika Athens, Greece 112 c1
Pô Burkina Faso 11°14N 1°5W 263 C4
Po ➔ Italy 44°57N 12°4E 199 D9
Po, Delta del Italy 44°55N 12°30E 199 D9
Pô △ Burkina Faso 11°25N 1°5W 263 C4
Po Hai = Bo Hai China 39°0N 119°0E 227 E10
Po Toi China 22°10N 114°16E 219 a
Po Toi Is. Hong Kong, China 22°10N 114°16E 122 B3
Po Toi O Hong Kong, China 22°16N 114°17E 122 B3
Poasco Italy 45°24N 9°16E 128 B2
Pobé Benin 7°0N 2°56E 263 D5
Pobé Burkina Faso 13°53N 1°42W 263 C4
Pobeda Russia 65°12N 146°12E 215 C15
Pobedy, Pik Kyrgyzstan 42°0N 79°58E 217 D9
Pobiedziska Poland 52°29N 17°11E 185 F4
Pobladura del Valle Spain 42°6N 5°44W 194 C5
Poblet, Monasterio de Spain 41°22N 1°4E 196 D6
Pobra de Trives Spain 42°20N 7°10W 194 C3
Pocahontas Ark., U.S.A. 36°16N 90°58W 315 C9
Pocahontas Ill., U.S.A. 38°50N 89°33W 310 F7
Pocahontas Iowa, U.S.A. 42°44N 94°40W 310 B2
Pocatello U.S.A. 42°52N 112°27W 304 E7
Počátky Czech Rep. 49°15N 15°14E 180 B8
Pocheon S. Korea 37°53N 127°13E 224 D3
Pochep Russia 52°58N 33°29E 189 F7
Pochinki Russia 54°41N 44°59E 190 C7
Pochinok Russia 54°28N 32°29E 188 E7
Pöchlarn Austria 48°12N 15°12E 180 C8
Poci Venezuela 5°57N 61°29W 329 B5
Pocinhos Brazil 7°4S 36°3W 332 C4
Pocking Germany 48°23N 13°19E 179 G9
Pocklington Reef Papua N. G. 10°51S 155°44E 286 F8
Poções Brazil 14°31S 40°21W 333 D3
Pocomoke City U.S.A. 38°5N 75°34W 309 F16
Poconé Brazil 16°15S 56°37W 331 D6
Poços de Caldas Brazil 21°50S 46°33W 335 A6
Podbaba Czech Rep. 50°7N 14°22E 135 B2
Podbořany Czech Rep. 50°14N 13°25E 180 A6
Poddębice Poland 51°54N 18°58E 185 G5
Poděbrady Czech Rep. 50°9N 15°8E 180 A8
Podensac France 44°40N 0°22W 174 D3
Podenzano Italy 44°57N 9°41E 198 D6
Podgorač Croatia 45°27N 18°13E 182 E3
Podgorica Montenegro 42°30N 19°19E 202 D3
Podgorie Albania 40°49N 20°48E 202 F4
Podile India 15°37N 79°37E 245 G4
Podilska Vysochyna Ukraine 49°0N 28°0E 183 B13
Podkarpackie □ Poland 50°0N 22°10E 185 H9
Podkova Bulgaria 41°24N 25°24E 203 E9
Podlapača Croatia 44°37N 15°47E 199 D12
Podlaskie □ Poland 53°10N 23°0E 185 E10
Podocarpus △ Ecuador 4°13S 79°2W 328 D2
Podoleni Romania 46°46N 26°39E 183 D11
Podoli Czech Rep. 50°2N 14°25E 135 B2
Podolínec Slovak Rep. 49°16N 20°31E 181 B13
Podolsk Russia 55°25N 37°30E 188 E9
Podor Senegal 16°40N 15°2W 262 B1
Podporozhye Russia 60°55N 34°2E 188 B8
Podu Iloaiei Romania 47°13N 27°16E 183 C12
Podu Turcului Romania 46°11N 27°25E 183 D12
Podujevo = Besianë Kosovo 42°54N 21°10E 202 D5
Podyji △ Czech Rep. 48°51N 15°57E 180 C8
Poechos Peru 4°41S 80°34W 328 D1
Poel Germany 54°0N 11°25E 178 B6
Pofadder S. Africa 29°10S 19°22E 270 C2
Poggiardo Italy 40°3N 18°23E 201 B11
Poggibonsi Italy 43°28N 11°9E 198 E8
Póggio Mirteto Italy 42°16N 12°41E 199 F9
Pogoanele Romania 44°55N 27°0E 183 F12
Pogorzela Poland 51°50N 17°12E 185 G4
Pogoso Dem. Rep. of the Congo 6°46S 17°12E 265 D3
Pogradec Albania 40°54N 20°37E 202 F4
Pogranichnyy Russia 44°25N 131°24E 220 B5
Poh Indonesia 0°46S 122°51E 231 E6
Pohang S. Korea 36°1N 129°23E 224 D4
Pohjanmaa □ Finland 62°58N 22°50E 160 E20
Pohjois-Pirkkala = Nokia Finland 61°30N 23°30E 188 B2
Pohnpei Micronesia 6°55N 158°10E 288 G7
Pohorelá Slovak Rep. 48°50N 20°2E 181 C13
Pohořelice Czech Rep. 48°59N 16°31E 181 C9
Pohorje Slovenia 46°30N 15°20E 199 B12
Pohri India 25°32N 77°22E 242 G6
Pöhue B. U.S.A. 19°0N 155°48W 302 E6
Poi Solomon Is. 10°9S 161°42E 287 N11
Poiana Mare Romania 43°57N 23°5E 182 G8
Poiana Ruscăi, Munții Romania 45°45N 22°25E 182 E7
Poiana Stampei Romania 47°19N 25°8E 183 C10
Poie Dem. Rep. of the Congo 2°50S 23°14E 264 C4
Poike, Península Chile 27°6S 109°15W 330 b
Poindimié N. Cal. 20°56S 165°20E 288 d
Poinsett, C. Antarctica 65°42S 113°18E 151 C8
Point Arena U.S.A. 38°55N 123°41W 306 G3
Point Baker U.S.A. 56°21N 133°37W 296 B2
Point Calimere India 10°17N 79°49E 245 J4
Point Fortin Trin. & Tob. 10°10N 61°42W 323 t
Point Hope U.S.A. 68°21N 166°47W 303 B6
Point L. Canada 65°15N 113°4W 294 D9
Point Lay U.S.A. 69°46N 163°3W 303 B7
Point Lisas Trin. & Tob. 10°24N 61°29W 323 t
Point Pedro Sri Lanka 9°50N 80°15E 245 K5
Point Pelee △ Canada 41°57N 82°31W 312 E2
Point Pleasant N.J., U.S.A. 40°5N 74°4W 313 F10
Point Pleasant W. Va., U.S.A. 38°51N 82°8W 309 F12
Point Reyes ⌓ U.S.A. 38°10N 122°55W 306 G2
Point Salines Int. ✕ (GND) Grenada 12°0N 61°46W 323 q
Pointe-à-Pierre Trin. & Tob. 10°19N 61°28W 323 t
Pointe-à-Pitre Guadeloupe 16°15N 61°32W 322 e
Pointe-au-Pic = La Malbaie Canada 47°40N 70°10W 299 C5
Pointe-Aux-Trembles Canada 45°38N 73°30W 130 A2
Pointe-Claire Canada 45°26N 73°50W 313 A11
Pointe-Gatineau Canada 45°27N 75°41W 313 A9
Pointe Michel Dominica 15°15N 61°23W 323 k
Pointe-Noire Congo 4°48S 11°53E 265 C2
Pointe-Noire Guadeloupe 16°14N 61°47W 322 e
Poio = O Convento Spain 42°28N 8°41W 194 C2
Poipet Cambodia 13°39N 102°33E 236 F4
Poirino Italy 44°56N 7°48E 198 D4
Poisonbush Ra. Australia 22°30S 121°30E 278 D3
Poissonnier Pt. Australia 19°57S 119°10E 278 C2
Poissy France 48°55N 2°2E 134 A1
Poitiers France 46°35N 0°20E 172 F7
Poitou France 46°40N 0°10W 174 B3
Poitou-Charentes □ France 46°10N 0°15E 174 B4
Poix-de-Picardie France 49°47N 1°58E 173 C8
Poix-Terron France 49°38N 4°38E 173 C11
Pojoaque U.S.A. 35°54N 106°1W 305 J10
Pok Fu Lam Hong Kong, China 22°16N 114°7E 122 B2
Pöka'ī B. U.S.A. 21°27N 158°12W 302 K13
Pokaran India 27°0N 71°50E 242 F4
Pokataroo Australia 29°30S 148°36E 281 D4
Pokcheong S. Korea 37°28N 127°8E 137 C2
Pokhara Nepal 28°14N 83°58E 243 E10
Pokhvistnevo Russia 53°36N 52°0E 190 D11
Pokigron Suriname 4°30N 55°22W 329 C6
Poko Dem. Rep. of the Congo 3°7N 26°52E 268 B2
Poko South Sudan 5°41N 31°55E 257 F3
Pokrov Russia 55°55N 39°7E 188 E10
Pokrovka = Kyzyl-Suu Kyrgyzstan 42°20N 78°0E 217 D9
Pokrovsk = Engels Russia 51°28N 46°6E 190 E8
Pokrovsk Russia 61°29N 129°0E 215 C13
Pokrovskoy = Priazovskoye Ukraine 46°44N 35°40E 189 J8
Pokrovskoye Russia 47°25N 38°54E 189 J10
Pol-e Dokhtar Iran 33°9N 47°42E 213 F12
Pol-e Khomri Afghan. 35°56N 68°42E 240 B3
Pol-e Zahāb Iran 34°27N 45°51E 213 E11
Pola = Istra Croatia 45°10N 14°0E 199 C10
Pola = Pula Croatia 44°54N 13°57E 199 D10
Pola Russia 57°55N 32°0E 188 D7
Pola de Allande Spain 43°16N 6°37W 194 B4
Pola de Lena Spain 43°10N 5°49W 194 B5
Pola de Siero Spain 43°24N 5°39W 194 B5
Pola de Somiedo Spain 43°5N 6°15W 194 B4
Pola I. Amer. Samoa 14°14S 170°40W 302 f
Polacca U.S.A. 35°50N 110°23W 305 J8
Polan Iran 25°30N 61°10E 247 E9
Pol'ana Slovak Rep. 48°38N 19°29E 181 C12
Poland U.S.A. 43°13N 75°3W 313 C9
Poland ■ Europe 52°0N 20°0E 185 G3
Polanica-Zdrój Poland 50°24N 16°32E 185 H3
Połaniec Poland 50°26N 21°17E 185 H8
Polanów Poland 54°7N 16°41E 184 D3
Polar Bear ⌓ Canada 55°0N 83°45W 298 A2
Polatlı Turkey 39°36N 32°9E 212 C5
Polatsk Belarus 55°30N 28°50E 188 E5
Polavaram India 17°15N 81°38E 244 F5
Polcura Chile 37°17S 71°43W 334 D1
Połczyn-Zdrój Poland 53°47N 16°5E 184 E3
Poldasht Iran 39°20N 45°4E 213 C11
Poleski △ Poland 51°29N 23°5E 185 G10
Polessk Russia 54°50N 21°8E 184 D8
Polesye = Pripet Marshes Europe 52°10N 27°10E 177 B15
Polevskoy Russia 56°26N 60°11E 186 C11
Polewali Indonesia 3°25S 119°20E 235 C5
Polgar Hungary 47°54N 21°6E 182 C6
Poli Cameroon 8°34N 13°15E 263 C7
Policastro, G. di Italy 40°0N 15°35E 201 C8
Police Poland 53°33N 14°33E 184 E1
Police, Pte. Seychelles 4°51S 55°32E 272 c
Polichnitos Greece 39°6N 26°10E 205 B8
Polička Czech Rep. 49°43N 16°15E 181 B9
Policoro Italy 40°13N 16°41E 201 B9
Poliegos Greece 36°45N 24°38E 204 E6
Poligiros Greece 40°23N 23°25E 202 F7
Polignano a Mare Italy 41°0N 17°13E 201 A9
Poligny France 46°50N 5°42E 173 F12
Polillo Phil. 14°43N 121°56E 232 D3
Polillo Is. Phil. 14°56N 122°0E 232 D4
Polillo Str. Phil. 14°44N 121°51E 232 D3
Polis Cyprus 35°2N 32°26E 207 E8
Polístena Italy 38°24N 16°4E 201 D9
Pölitz = Police Poland 53°33N 14°33E 184 E1
Polk U.S.A. 41°22N 79°56W 312 E5
Polkowice Poland 51°29N 16°3E 185 G3
Polkwitz = Polkowice Poland 51°29N 16°3E 185 G3
Polla Italy 40°31N 15°29E 201 B8
Pollachi India 10°35N 77°0E 245 J3
Pollença Spain 39°54N 3°1E 206 B4
Pollença, B. de Spain 39°53N 3°8E 206 B4
Pollfoss Norway 61°58N 7°54E 164 C4
Póllica Italy 40°11N 15°3E 201 B8
Pollino, Mte. Italy 39°55N 16°11E 201 C9
Pollino △ Italy 40°0N 16°12E 201 C9
Polna Russia 58°31N 28°5E 188 C5
Polnovat Russia 63°50N 65°54E 214 C7
Polo Ill., U.S.A. 41°59N 89°35W 310 C7
Polo Mo., U.S.A. 39°33N 94°3W 310 E2
Pology Ukraine 47°29N 36°15E 189 J9
Polokwane S. Africa 23°54S 29°25E 271 B4
Polokwane ➔ S. Africa 22°25S 30°5E 271 B5
Polomolok Phil. 6°13N 125°3E 233 H5
Polonnaruwa Sri Lanka 7°56N 81°0E 245 L5
Polonne Ukraine 50°6N 27°30E 177 C14
Polonnoye = Polonne Ukraine 50°6N 27°30E 177 C14
Polski Trŭmbesh Bulgaria 43°20N 25°38E 203 C9
Polsko Kosovo Bulgaria 43°23N 25°38E 203 C9
Polson U.S.A. 47°41N 114°9W 304 C6
Poltár Slovak Rep. 48°26N 19°48E 181 C12
Poltava Ukraine 49°35N 34°35E 189 H8
Poltava □ Ukraine 50°15N 33°15E 189 G7
Polton U.K. 55°52N 3°7W 121 B3
Poltoratsk = Ashgabat Turkmenistan 37°58N 58°24E 247 B8
Põltsamaa Estonia 58°39N 25°58E 188 C3
Polunochnoye Russia 60°52N 60°25E 214 C7
Polur India 12°32N 79°11E 245 H4
Põlva Estonia 58°3N 27°3E 188 C4
Polvoranca, Parque de Spain 40°19N 3°48W 127 C1
Polyana Ukraine 48°38N 22°58E 182 B7
Polyarny Russia 69°8N 33°20E 160 B25
Polyarnyye Zori Russia 67°22N 32°30E 160 C25
Polynesia Pac. Oc. 10°0S 162°0W 289 F11
Polynesian Cultural Center U.S.A. 21°38N 157°55W 302 J14
Polynésie française = French Polynesia ☑ Pac. Oc. 20°0S 145°0W 289 f
Polyustrovo Russia 59°57N 30°25E 137 B2
Pomabamba = Azurduy Bolivia 19°59S 64°29W 331 D5
Pomabamba Peru 8°50S 77°28W 330 B2
Pomarance Italy 43°18N 10°52E 198 E7
Pombal Brazil 6°45S 37°50W 332 C4
Pombal Portugal 39°55N 8°40W 194 F2
Pombia Greece 35°0N 24°51E 207 F5
Pombos, B. dos Angola 11°40S 13°47E 265 E2
Pomene Mozam. 22°53S 35°33E 271 B6
Pomeroy Ohio, U.S.A. 39°2N 82°2W 309 F12
Pomeroy Wash., U.S.A. 46°28N 117°36W 304 C5
Pomézia Italy 41°40N 12°30E 200 A5
Pomichna Ukraine 48°13N 31°36E 189 H6
Pomio Papua N. G. 5°32S 151°33E 286 C6
Pomme de Terre L. U.S.A. 37°54N 93°19W 310 G3
Pomme Rose Grenada 12°3N 61°39W 323 q
Pomona Queens., Australia 26°22S 152°52E 281 D5
Pomona Calif., U.S.A. 34°4N 117°45W 307 L9
Pomona Park U.S.A. 29°30N 81°36W 317 F8
Pomorie Bulgaria 42°32N 27°41E 203 D11
Pomorskie □ Poland 54°30N 18°0E 184 D5
Pomorskie, Pojezierze Poland 53°40N 16°37E 184 E3
Pomos Cyprus 35°9N 32°33E 207 E8
Pomos, C. Cyprus 35°10N 32°33E 207 E8
Pompano Beach U.S.A. 26°14N 80°7W 129 A3
Pompei Italy 40°45N 14°30E 201 B7
Pompey France 48°46N 6°6E 173 D13
Pompeys Pillar U.S.A. 45°59N 107°57W 304 D10
Pompeys Pillar ⌓ U.S.A. 46°0N 108°0W 304 D10
Pompidou, Centre Paris, France 134 b4
Pomprap Thailand 13°44N 100°30E 113 B2
Pompton Lakes U.S.A. 41°0N 74°17W 313 F10
Ponape = Pohnpei Micronesia 6°55N 158°10E 288 G7
Ponask L. Canada 54°0N 92°41W 298 B1
Ponca U.S.A. 42°34N 96°43W 308 D5
Ponca City U.S.A. 36°42N 97°5W 314 C6
Ponce Puerto Rico 18°1N 66°37W 321 C6
Ponce de Leon U.S.A. 30°44N 85°56W 316 E4
Ponce de Leon B. U.S.A. 25°15N 81°10W 317 K8
Ponchatoula U.S.A. 30°26N 90°26W 315 F9
Poncheville, L. Canada 50°10N 76°55W 298 B4
Pond U.S.A. 35°43N 119°20W 307 K7
Pond Inlet Canada 72°40N 77°0W 295 C16
Pondicherry = Puducherry India 11°59N 79°50E 245 J4
Pondo Papua N. G. 4°33S 151°38E 286 C6
Pondok Gede Indonesia 6°17S 106°55E 122 A2
Pondok Indah Indonesia 6°16S 106°46E 122 B1

Ponds, I. of Canada 53°27N 55°52W 299 B8
Ponérihouen N. Cal. 21°5S 165°24E 288 d
Ponferrada Spain 42°32N 6°35W 194 C4
Pongo, Wadi → South Sudan 8°42N 27°40E 257 F2
Poniatowa Poland 51°11N 22°3E 185 G9
Poniec Poland 51°48N 16°50E 185 G3
Ponikva Slovenia 46°16N 15°26E 199 B12
Ponizovkino = Krasnyy Profintern Russia 57°45N 40°27E 188 D11
Ponnaiyar → India 11°50N 79°45E 245 J4
Ponnani India 10°45N 75°59E 245 J2
Ponneri India 13°20N 80°15E 245 H5
Ponnuru India 16°5N 80°34E 245 F5
Ponoka Canada 52°42N 113°40W 296 C6
Ponorogo Indonesia 7°52S 111°27E 235 D4
Ponot Phil. 8°25N 123°0E 233 G4
Ponoy Russia 67°0N 41°13E 186 A7
Ponoy → Russia 66°59N 41°17E 186 A7
Pons = Ponts Spain 41°55N 1°12E 196 D6
Pons France 45°35N 0°34W 174 C3
Ponsul → Portugal 39°40N 7°31W 194 F3
Pont-à-Mousson France 48°54N 6°1E 173 D13
Pont-Audemer France 49°21N 0°30E 172 C7
Pont-Aven France 47°51N 3°47W 172 E3
Pont Canavese Italy 45°25N 7°36E 198 C4
Pont Casse Dominica 15°22N 61°21W 323 k
Pont-d'Ain France 46°3N 5°21E 173 F12
Pont-de-Roide France 47°23N 6°45E 173 E13
Pont-de-Salars France 44°18N 2°44E 174 D6
Pont-de-Vaux France 46°26N 4°56E 173 F11
Pont-de-Veyle France 46°17N 4°53E 173 F11
Pont-du-Château France 45°47N 3°15E 173 G10
Pont du Gard France 43°57N 4°32E 175 E8
Pont-l'Abbé France 47°52N 4°15W 172 E2
Pont-l'Évêque France 49°18N 0°11E 172 C7
Pont-St-Esprit France 44°16N 4°40E 175 D8
Pont-St-Martin Italy 45°36N 7°48E 198 C4
Pont-Ste-Maxence France 49°18N 2°36E 173 C9
Pont-sur-Yonne France 48°18N 3°10E 173 D10
Pont-Viau Canada 45°35N 73°41W 130 A1
Ponta de Pedras Brazil 1°23S 48°52W 332 B2
Ponta Delgada Flores, Azores 39°31N 31°13W 153 d2
Ponta Delgada São Miguel, Azores 37°44N 25°40W 153 d3
Ponta Delgada ✕ (PDL) Azores 37°44N 25°41W 153 d3
Ponta do Pargo Madeira 32°49N 17°15W 153 c
Ponta do Sol Madeira 32°42N 17°7W 153 c
Ponta Grossa Brazil 25°7S 50°10W 335 B5
Ponta Porã Brazil 22°20S 55°35W 335 A4
Pontacq France 43°11N 0°8W 174 E3
Pontailler-sur-Saône France 47°13N 5°25E 173 E12
Pontal → Brazil 9°8S 40°12W 332 C3
Pontalina Brazil 17°31S 49°27W 333 E2
Pontarlier France 46°54N 6°20E 173 F13
Pontassieve Italy 43°46N 11°26E 199 E8
Pontault-Combault France 48°47N 2°36E 134 B4
Pontaumur France 45°52N 2°40E 174 C6
Pontcharra France 45°26N 6°1E 175 C10
Pontchartrain, L. U.S.A. 30°5N 90°5W 315 F9
Pontchâteau France 47°25N 2°5W 172 E4
Ponte Alta, Serra do Brazil 19°42S 47°40W 333 E2
Ponte Alta do Norte Brazil 10°45S 47°34W 332 D2
Ponte Branca Brazil 16°27S 52°40W 331 D7
Ponte da Barca Portugal 41°48N 8°25W 194 D2
Ponte de Lima Portugal 41°46N 8°35W 194 D2
Ponte de Sor Portugal 39°17N 8°1W 195 F2
Ponte dell'Ólio Italy 44°52N 9°39E 198 D6
Ponte di Legno Italy 46°16N 10°31E 198 B7
Ponte do Pungué Mozam. 19°30S 34°33E 269 F3
Ponte-Leccia France 42°28N 9°13E 175 F13
Ponte nelle Alpi Italy 46°11N 12°16E 199 B9
Ponte Nova Brazil 20°25S 42°54W 333 F3
Ponte Vedra Beach U.S.A. 30°15N 81°23W 316 E8
Ponteareas Spain 42°10N 8°28W 194 C2
Pontebba Italy 46°30N 13°18E 199 B10
Ponteceso Spain 43°15N 8°54W 194 B2
Pontecorvo Italy 41°27N 13°40E 200 A6
Pontedeume Spain 43°24N 8°10W 194 B2
Ponteix Canada 49°46N 107°29W 297 D7
Pontes e Lacerda Brazil 15°12S 59°22W 331 D6
Pontevedra Capiz, Phil. 11°29N 122°50E 233 F4
Pontevedra Neg. Occ., Phil. 10°22N 122°52E 233 F4
Pontevedra Spain 42°26N 8°40W 194 C2
Pontevedra □ Spain 42°25N 8°39W 194 C2
Pontevedra, R. de → Spain 42°22N 8°45W 194 C2
Pontevico Italy 45°16N 10°5E 198 C7
Pontiac Ill., U.S.A. 40°53N 88°38W 311 D8
Pontiac Mich., U.S.A. 42°38N 83°18W 311 B13
Pontian Kechil Malaysia 1°29N 103°23E 237 d
Pontianak Indonesia 0°3S 109°15E 235 C3
Pontine Is. = Ponziane, Ísole Italy 40°55N 12°57E 200 B5
Pontine Mts. = Kuzey Anadolu Dağları Turkey 41°0N 36°45E 212 B7
Pontinha Portugal 38°45N 9°11W 126 A1
Pontínia Italy 41°25N 13°2E 200 A6
Pontivy France 48°5N 2°58W 172 D4
Pontoise France 49°3N 2°5E 173 C9
Ponton → Canada 58°27N 116°11W 296 B5
Pontorson France 48°34N 1°30W 172 D5
Pontrémoli Italy 44°22N 9°53E 198 D6
Pontrieux France 48°42N 3°10W 172 D3
Ponts Spain 41°55N 1°12E 196 D6
Pontypool Ont., Canada 44°6N 78°38W 312 B6
Pontypool Torf., U.K. 51°42N 3°2W 169 F4
Pontypridd U.K. 51°36N 3°20W 169 F4
Ponza Italy 40°54N 12°58E 200 B5
Ponziane, Ísole Italy 40°55N 12°57E 200 B5
Poochera Australia 32°43S 134°51E 281 E1
Pool □ Congo 3°30S 15°0E 264 C2
Poole Trin. & Tob. 10°17N 61°14W 323 t
Poole Poole, U.K. 50°43N 1°59W 169 G6
Poole □ U.K. 50°43N 1°59W 169 G6
Poole → Trin. & Tob. 10°15N 61°5W 323 t
Pooler U.S.A. 32°7N 81°15W 316 C8
Poona = Pune India 18°29N 73°57E 244 E1
Poonamallee India 13°3N 80°10E 245 H5
Pooncarie Australia 33°22S 142°31E 282 B5
Poopelloe L. Australia 31°40S 144°0E 283 A6
Poopó Bolivia 18°23S 66°59W 330 D4
Poopó, L. de Bolivia 18°30S 67°35W 330 D4
Poor Knights Is. N.Z. 35°29S 174°43E 284 B3
Poorman U.S.A. 64°5N 155°33W 303 D9
Popa Gabon 1°35S 12°32E 264 C2
Popa, Mt. Burma 20°55N 95°15E 241 E5
Popayán Colombia 2°27N 76°36W 328 C2
Poperinge Belgium 50°51N 2°42E 170 D2
Popiltah L. Australia 33°10S 141°42E 282 B4
Popina Bulgaria 44°7N 26°57E 203 B10
Popio L. Australia 33°10S 141°52E 282 B4
Poplar London, U.K. 51°30N 0°0 125 A3
Poplar Mont., U.S.A. 48°7N 105°12W 304 B11
Poplar → Canada 53°0N 97°19W 297 C9
Poplar Bluff U.S.A. 36°46N 90°24W 308 G8
Poplar Head = Dothan U.S.A. 31°13N 85°24W 316 D4
Poplarville U.S.A. 30°51N 89°32W 315 F10
Popocatépetl, Volcán Mexico 19°2N 98°38W 319 D5
Popokabaka Dem. Rep. of the Congo 5°41S 16°40E 265 D3
Pópoli Italy 42°10N 13°50E 199 F10
Popolo Dem. Rep. of the Congo 2°22N 21°8E 264 B4
Popolo, Porta del Rome, Italy 136 a2
Popomanaseu, Mt. Solomon Is. 9°40S 160°1E 287 M11
Popondetta Papua N. G. 8°48S 148°17E 286 E5
Popovača Croatia 45°30N 16°41E 199 C13
Popovo Bulgaria 43°21N 26°18E 203 C10
Poppberg Germany 49°26N 11°37E 179 F7
Poppi Italy 43°43N 11°46E 199 E8
Poppintree Ireland 53°23N 6°17W 120 A2
Poprad Slovak Rep. 49°3N 20°18E 181 B13
Poprad → Slovak Rep. 49°38N 20°42E 181 B13
Poradaha Bangla. 23°51N 89°1E 241 D2
Porali → Pakistan 25°58N 66°26E 242 G2
Porangaba Brazil 8°48S 70°36W 330 B3
Porangahau N.Z. 40°17S 176°37E 284 G5
Porangatu Brazil 13°26S 49°10W 333 D2
Porbandar India 21°44N 69°43E 242 J3
Porce → Colombia 7°28N 74°53W 328 B3
Porcher I. Canada 53°50N 130°30W 296 C2
Porco Bolivia 19°50S 65°59W 331 D4
Porcos → Brazil 12°42S 45°7W 333 D2
Porcuna Spain 37°52N 4°11W 195 H6
Porcupine → Sask., Canada 59°11N 104°46W 297 B8
Porcupine → Alaska, U.S.A. 66°34N 145°19W 303 C11
Porcupine Abyssal Plain Atl. Oc. 48°0N 8°0W 152 B10
Porcupine Gorge △ Australia 20°22S 144°26E 280 C3
Pordenone Italy 45°57N 12°39E 199 C9
Pordim Bulgaria 43°23N 24°51E 203 C8
Pore Colombia 5°43N 72°0W 328 B3
Poreč Croatia 45°14N 13°36E 199 C10
Porecatu Brazil 22°43S 51°24W 333 F1
Porechye = Demidov Russia 55°16N 31°30E 188 E6
Poretskoye Russia 55°9N 46°21E 190 C8
Porgera Papua N. G. 5°28S 143°12E 286 C2
Pori Finland 61°29N 21°48E 188 B1
Pori Greece 35°58N 23°13E 204 F5
Porkhov Russia 57°45N 29°38E 188 D5
Porlamar Venezuela 10°57N 63°51W 329 a
Porlezza Italy 46°2N 9°7E 198 B6
Porma → Spain 42°49N 5°28W 194 C5
Pormpuraaw Australia 14°59S 141°26E 280 A3
Pormpuraaw © Australia 14°55S 141°47E 280 A3
Pornic France 47°7N 2°5W 172 E4
Poronaysk Russia 49°13N 143°0E 219 B17
Poros Attiki, Greece 37°30N 23°30E 204 D5
Poros Kefalonia, Greece 38°9N 20°47E 207 C2
Poros Lefkada, Greece 38°38N 20°43E 207 B2
Poroshiri-Dake Japan 42°41N 142°52E 220 C11
Poroszló Hungary 47°39N 20°40E 182 C5
Poroto Mts. Tanzania 9°0S 33°30E 269 D3
Porpoise B. Antarctica 66°0S 127°0E 151 C9
Porpoise Pt. Ascension I. 7°54S 14°21W 153 g
Porquerolles, Î. de France 43°0N 6°13E 175 F10
Porrentruy Switz. 47°25N 7°6E 179 H3
Porreres Spain 39°31N 3°2E 206 B10
Porsangerfjorden Norway 70°40N 25°40E 160 A21
Porsgrunn Norway 59°10N 9°40E 164 E6
Port Adelaide Australia 34°50S 138°30E 282 C3
Port Alberni Canada 49°14N 124°50W 296 D4
Port Albert Australia 38°42S 146°42E 283 F7
Port Alexander U.S.A. 56°15N 134°38W 303 H14
Port Alfred S. Africa 33°36S 26°55E 270 D4
Port Alice Canada 50°20N 127°25W 296 C3
Port Allegany U.S.A. 41°48N 78°17W 312 E6
Port Allen U.S.A. 30°27N 91°12W 314 F9
Port Alma Queens., Australia 23°38S 150°53E 280 C5
Port Alma Ont., Canada 42°10N 82°14W 312 D2
Port Angeles U.S.A. 48°7N 123°27W 306 B3
Port Antonio Jamaica 18°10N 76°26W 320 a
Port Aransas U.S.A. 27°50N 97°4W 314 H6
Port Arthur Tas., Australia 43°7S 147°50E 281 G4
Port Arthur Tex., U.S.A. 29°54N 93°56W 314 G8
Port au Choix Canada 50°43N 57°22W 299 B8
Port au Port B. Canada 48°40N 58°50W 299 C8
Port-au-Prince Haiti 18°40N 72°20W 321 C5
Port Augusta Australia 32°30S 137°50E 282 B2
Port Austin U.S.A. 44°3N 83°1W 312 B2
Port Authority Bus Terminal New York, U.S.A. 132 c2
Port-aux-Français Kerguelen 49°21S 70°13E 273 J6
Port Bergé Vaovao Madag. 15°33S 47°40E 272 B2
Port Blair India 11°40N 92°45E 245 J11
Port Blandford Canada 48°20N 54°10W 299 C9
Port Botany Australia 33°58S 151°13E 139 B2
Port-Bouët Ivory C. 5°16N 3°57W 262 D4
Port Bradshaw Australia 12°30S 137°20E 280 A2
Port Broughton Australia 33°37S 137°56E 282 B2
Port Bruce Canada 42°39N 81°0W 312 D4
Port Burwell Canada 42°40N 80°48W 312 D4
Port Byron U.S.A. 41°36N 90°20W 310 C6
Port Campbell Vic., Australia 38°37S 143°1E 282 E5
Port Campbell India 11°56N 92°37E 245 J11
Port Campbell △ Australia 38°8S 143°6E 282 E5
Port Canning India 22°23N 88°40E 243 H13
Port Carling Canada 45°7N 79°35W 312 A5
Port-Cartier Canada 50°2N 66°50W 299 B6
Port Chalmers N.Z. 45°49S 170°30E 285 F5
Port Charles N.Z. 36°33S 175°30E 284 C4
Port Charlotte U.S.A. 26°59N 82°6W 317 J7
Port Chester U.S.A. 41°0N 73°40W 313 F11
Port Clements Canada 53°40N 132°10W 296 C2
Port Clinton U.S.A. 41°31N 82°56W 311 C14
Port Colborne Canada 42°50N 79°10W 312 D5
Port Coquitlam Canada 49°15N 122°45W 306 A4
Port Cornwallis India 13°17N 93°5E 245 H11
Port Credit Canada 43°33N 79°35W 312 C5
Port-Cros △ France 43°0N 6°24E 175 F10
Port Curtis Australia 23°57S 151°20E 280 C5
Port d'Alcúdia Spain 39°50N 3°7E 206 B4
Port Dalhousie Canada 43°13N 79°16W 312 C5
Port d'Andratx Spain 39°32N 2°23E 206 B3
Port Darwin N. Terr., Australia 12°24S 130°45E 278 B5
Port Darwin Falk. Is. 51°50S 59°0W 153 f
Port Davey Australia 43°16S 145°55E 281 G4
Port-de-Bouc France 43°24N 4°59E 175 E8
Port-de-Paix Haiti 19°50N 72°50W 321 C5
Port de Pollença Spain 39°54N 3°4E 206 B4
Port de Sóller Spain 39°48N 2°42E 206 B3
Port Dickson Malaysia 2°30N 101°49E 237 L3
Port Douglas Australia 16°30S 145°30E 280 B4
Port Dover Canada 42°47N 80°12W 312 D4
Port Edward Canada 54°12N 130°10W 296 C2
Port Elgin Canada 44°25N 81°25W 312 B3
Port Elizabeth S. Africa 33°58S 25°40E 270 D4
Port Ellen U.K. 55°38N 6°11W 167 F2
Port Elliot Australia 35°32S 138°41E 282 C3
Port-en-Bessin-Huppain France 49°21N 0°45W 172 C6
Port Erin I. of Man 54°5N 4°45W 168 C3
Port Essington Australia 11°15S 132°10E 278 B5
Port Etienne = Nouâdhibou Mauritania 20°54N 17°0W 260 D1
Port Ewen U.S.A. 41°54N 73°59W 313 E11
Port Fairy Australia 38°22S 142°12E 282 E5
Port Fitzroy N.Z. 36°8S 175°20E 284 C4
Port Florence = Kisumu Kenya 0°3S 34°45E 268 C3
Port Fouâd = Bûr Fuad Egypt 31°15N 32°20E 256 H8
Port Francqui = Ilebo Dem. Rep. of the Congo 4°17S 20°55E 265 C4
Port Gamble U.S.A. 47°51N 122°34W 306 C4
Port-Gentil Gabon 0°40S 8°50E 264 C1
Port Germein Australia 33°1S 138°1E 281 E2
Port Ghalib Egypt 25°20N 34°50E 246 E2
Port Gibson U.S.A. 31°58N 90°59W 314 F9
Port Glasgow U.K. 55°56N 4°41W 167 F4
Port-Gueydon = Azeffoun Algeria 36°51N 4°26E 261 A5
Port Harcourt Nigeria 4°40N 7°10E 263 E6
Port Hardy Canada 50°41N 127°30W 296 C3
Port Harrison = Inukjuak Canada 58°25N 78°15W 295 F16
Port Hawkesbury Canada 45°36N 61°22W 299 C7
Port Hedland Australia 20°25S 118°35E 278 D2
Port Heiden U.S.A. 56°55N 158°41W 303 H8
Port Henry U.S.A. 44°3N 73°28W 313 B11
Port Herald = Nsanje Malawi 16°55S 35°12E 269 F4
Port Hood Canada 46°0N 61°32W 299 C7
Port Hope Ont., Canada 43°56N 78°20W 312 C6
Port Hope Mich., U.S.A. 43°57N 82°43W 312 C2
Port Hope Simpson Canada 52°33N 56°18W 299 B8
Port Hueneme U.S.A. 34°7N 119°12W 307 L7
Port Huron U.S.A. 42°58N 82°26W 312 D2
Port Ilıç Azerbaijan 38°53N 48°47E 213 C13
Port Jefferson U.S.A. 40°57N 73°3W 313 F11
Port Jervis U.S.A. 41°22N 74°41W 313 E10
Port-Joinville France 46°45N 2°23W 172 F4
Port Katon Russia 46°52N 38°46E 189 J10
Port Kembla Australia 34°52S 150°49E 283 C9
Port Kenny Australia 33°10S 134°41E 281 E1
Port-la-Nouvelle France 43°1N 3°3E 174 E7
Port Láirge = Waterford Ireland 52°15N 7°8W 166 D4
Port Lavaca U.S.A. 28°37N 96°38W 314 G6
Port Leyden U.S.A. 43°35N 75°21W 313 C9
Port Lincoln Australia 34°42S 135°52E 282 C1
Port Lions U.S.A. 57°52N 152°53W 303 H9
Port Loko S. Leone 8°48N 12°46W 262 D2
Port Louis Morbihan, France 47°42N 3°22W 172 E3
Port-Louis Guadeloupe 16°28N 61°32W 322 e
Port Louis Mauritius 20°10S 57°30E 272 e
Port Lyautey = Kenitra Morocco 34°15N 6°40W 260 B3
Port MacDonnell Australia 38°5S 140°48E 282 E4
Port McNeill Canada 50°35N 127°6W 296 C3
Port Macquarie Australia 31°25S 152°25E 283 A10
Port Maria Jamaica 18°22N 76°54W 320 a
Port Mathurin Rodrigues 19°41S 63°25E 273 F5
Port Matilda U.S.A. 40°48N 78°3W 312 F6
Port Mayaca U.S.A. 26°59N 80°36W 317 J9
Port McNicoll Canada 44°44N 79°48W 312 B5
Port Mearnóg = Portmarnock Ireland 53°26N 6°8W 120 A3
Port Melbourne Australia 37°50S 144°54E 128 B1
Port Mellon Canada 49°32N 123°31W 296 D4
Port-Menier Canada 49°51N 64°15W 299 C7
Port Moller U.S.A. 55°59N 160°34W 303 J7
Port Moody Canada 49°17N 122°51W 306 A4
Port Morant Jamaica 17°54N 76°19W 320 a
Port Moresby Papua N. G. 9°24S 147°8E 286 E4
Port Mourant Guyana 6°15N 57°20W 329 B6
Port Muhammed Bin Qasim = Port Qasim Pakistan 24°46N 67°20E 242 G2
Port Musgrave Australia 11°55S 141°50E 280 A3
Port Narevin = Potnarvin Vanuatu 18°45S 169°10E 287 H7
Port-Navalo France 47°34N 2°54W 172 E4
Port Neches U.S.A. 30°0N 93°59W 314 G8
Port Nicholson N.Z. 41°20S 174°52E 284 H3
Port Nolloth S. Africa 29°17S 16°52E 270 C2
Port Nouveau-Québec = Kangiqsualujjuaq Canada 58°30N 65°59W 295 F18
Port of Climax Canada 49°10N 108°20W 297 D7
Port of Coronach Canada 49°7N 105°31W 297 D7
Port of Spain Trin. & Tob. 10°40N 61°31W 323 t
Port Olry Vanuatu 15°1S 167°4E 287 E5
Port Orange U.S.A. 29°9N 80°59W 317 F9
Port Orchard U.S.A. 47°32N 122°38W 306 C4
Port Orford U.S.A. 42°45N 124°30W 304 E1
Port Pegasus N.Z. 47°12S 167°41E 285 H2
Port Perry Canada 44°6N 78°56W 312 B6
Port Phillip B. Australia 38°10S 144°50E 283 E6
Port Pirie Australia 33°10S 138°1E 282 B3
Port Qasim Pakistan 24°46N 67°20E 242 G2
Port Rashid U.A.E. 25°16N 55°17E 119 B2
Port Renfrew Canada 48°30N 124°20W 306 B2
Port Richmond U.S.A. 40°38N 74°7W 132 C1
Port Roper Australia 14°45S 135°25E 280 A2
Port Rowan Canada 42°40N 80°30W 312 D4
Port Royal Jamaica 17°56N 76°51W 320 a
Port Royal Sd. U.S.A. 32°15N 80°40W 316 C9
Port Saeed U.A.E. 25°15N 55°20E 119 B2
Port Safaga = Bûr Safâga Egypt 26°43N 33°57E 246 E2
Port Said = Bûr Sa'îd Egypt 31°16N 32°18E 256 H8
Port St. Joe U.S.A. 29°49N 85°18W 316 F4
Port St. John U.S.A. 28°29N 80°47W 317 G9
Port St. Johns = Umzimvubu S. Africa 31°38S 29°33E 271 D4
Port-St-Louis-du-Rhône France 43°23N 4°49E 175 E8
Port St. Lucie U.S.A. 27°18N 80°21W 317 H9
Port-Ste-Marie France 44°15N 0°25E 174 D4
Port Salerno U.S.A. 27°9N 80°12W 317 H9
Port Sanilac U.S.A. 43°26N 82°33W 312 C2
Port Severn Canada 44°48N 79°43W 312 B5
Port Shelter Hong Kong, China 22°20N 114°17E 122 A3
Port Shepstone S. Africa 30°44S 30°28E 271 D5
Port Simpson Canada 54°30N 130°20W 296 C2
Port Stanley = Stanley Falk. Is. 51°40S 59°51W 153 f
Port Stanley Canada 42°40N 81°10W 312 D3
Port Sudan = Bûr Sûdân Sudan 19°32N 37°9E 256 D4
Port Sulphur U.S.A. 29°29N 89°42W 315 G10
Port-sur-Saône France 47°42N 6°2E 173 E13
Port Talbot U.K. 51°35N 3°47W 169 F4
Port Taufiq = Bûr Taufiq Egypt 29°54N 32°32E 256 J8
Port Townsend U.S.A. 48°7N 122°45W 306 B4
Port Union Canada 43°47N 79°7W 141 A4
Port-Vato Vanuatu 16°20S 168°7E 287 F6
Port-Vendres France 42°32N 3°8E 174 F7
Port Victoria Australia 34°30S 137°29E 282 C2
Port Vila Vanuatu 17°45S 168°18E 287 G6
Port Vladimir Russia 69°25N 33°6E 160 B25
Port Wakefield Australia 34°12S 138°10E 282 C3
Port Washington U.S.A. 43°23N 87°53W 308 D10
Port Weld = Kuala Sepetang Malaysia 4°49N 100°28E 237 K3
Port Wentworth U.S.A. 32°9N 81°10W 316 C8
Porta Orientalis Romania 45°6N 22°18E 177 F12
Portachuelo Bolivia 17°10S 63°20W 331 D5
Portacloy Ireland 54°20N 9°46W 166 B2
Portadown U.K. 54°25N 6°27W 166 B5
Portaferry U.K. 54°23N 5°33W 166 B6
Portage Ind., U.S.A. 41°34N 87°11W 311 C10
Portage Mich., U.S.A. 42°12N 85°35W 311 B11
Portage Pa., U.S.A. 40°23N 78°41W 312 F6
Portage Wis., U.S.A. 43°33N 89°28W 308 D9
Portage → U.S.A. 41°31N 83°5W 311 C14
Portage la Prairie Canada 49°58N 98°18W 297 D9
Portage Park U.S.A. 41°56N 87°45W 119 B2
Portageville U.S.A. 36°26N 89°42W 308 G9
Portal U.S.A. 32°33N 81°56W 316 C8
Portal de la Pau, Plaza Barcelona, Spain 114 c2
Portalegre Portugal 39°19N 7°25W 195 F3
Portalegre □ Portugal 39°20N 7°40W 195 F3
Portales U.S.A. 34°11N 103°20W 305 J12
Portarlington Ireland 53°9N 7°14W 166 C4
Portbou Spain 42°25N 3°9E 196 C8
Porteira Brazil 1°5S 57°4W 329 D6
Porteirinha Brazil 15°44S 43°2W 333 E3
Portel Brazil 1°57S 50°49W 332 B1
Portel Portugal 38°19N 7°41W 195 G3
Portela, Lisboa ✕ (LIS) Portugal 38°46N 9°8W 126 A2
Porter U.S.A. 41°36N 87°4W 311 C9
Porter, L. U.S.A. 28°30N 81°19W 133 A3
Porter L. N.W.T., Canada 61°41N 108°5W 297 A7
Porter L. Sask., Canada 56°20N 107°20W 297 B7
Porterville Western Cape, S. Africa 33°0S 19°0E 270 D2
Porterville Calif., U.S.A. 36°4N 119°1W 306 J8
Portes-lès-Valence France 44°52N 4°54E 175 D8
Porth Tywyn = Burry Port U.K. 51°41N 4°15W 169 F3
Porthcawl U.K. 51°29N 3°42W 169 F4
Porthill U.S.A. 48°59N 116°30W 304 B5
Porthmadog U.K. 52°55N 4°8W 168 E3
Portile de Fier Europe 44°44N 22°30E 182 F7
Portimão Portugal 37°8N 8°32W 195 H2
Portishead U.K. 51°29N 2°46W 169 F5
Portiţei, Gura Romania 44°41N 29°0E 183 F14
Portknockie U.K. 57°42N 2°51W 167 D6
Portland N.S.W., Australia 33°20S 150°0E 283 B9
Portland Vic., Australia 38°20S 141°35E 282 E4
Portland Ont., Canada 44°42N 76°12W 313 B8
Portland Conn., U.S.A. 41°34N 72°38W 313 E12
Portland Fla., U.S.A. 30°31N 86°12W 316 E3
Portland Ind., U.S.A. 40°26N 84°59W 311 D12
Portland Maine, U.S.A. 43°39N 70°16W 309 D18
Portland Mich., U.S.A. 42°52N 84°54W 311 B12
Portland Oreg., U.S.A. 45°32N 122°37W 306 E4
Portland Pa., U.S.A. 40°55N 75°6W 313 F9
Portland Tex., U.S.A. 27°53N 97°20W 314 H6
Portland, I. of U.K. 50°33N 2°26W 169 G5
Portland, Récif French Polynesia 23°42S 134°30W 289 f
Portland B. Australia 38°15S 141°45E 282 E4
Portland Bight Jamaica 17°52N 77°5W 320 a
Portland Bill U.K. 50°31N 2°28W 169 G5
Portland Canal U.S.A. 55°56N 130°0W 296 B2
Portland Int. ✕ (PDX) U.S.A. 45°35N 122°36W 306 E4
Portland Pt. Ascension I. 7°59S 14°25W 153 g
Portland Pt. Jamaica 17°42N 77°11W 320 a
Portlaoise Ireland 53°2N 7°18W 166 C4
Portmadoc = Porthmadog U.K. 52°55N 4°8W 168 E3
Portmarnock Ireland 53°26N 6°8W 120 A3
Portmore Jamaica 17°53N 76°53W 320 a
Porto Brazil 3°54S 42°42W 332 B3
Porto Corse-du-Sud, France 42°16N 8°42E 175 F12
Porto Portugal 41°8N 8°40W 194 D2
Porto □ Portugal 41°8N 8°20W 194 D2
Porto, G. de France 42°17N 8°34E 175 F12
Porto Acre Brazil 9°34S 67°31W 330 B4
Pôrto Alegre = Luzilândia Brazil 3°28S 42°22W 332 B3
Pôrto Alegre Pará, Brazil 4°22S 52°44W 329 D7
Pôrto Alegre Rio Grande do S., Brazil 30°5S 51°10W 335 C5
Porto Alegre São Tomé & Príncipe 0°2N 6°32E 265 a
Porto Amboim = Gunza Angola 10°50S 13°50E 265 E2
Porto Amélia = Pemba Mozam. 12°58S 40°30E 269 E5
Porto Azzurro Italy 42°46N 10°24E 198 F7
Porto Brandão Portugal 38°40N 9°12W 126 A1
Pôrto Cajueiro Brazil 11°3S 55°53W 331 C6
Porto Cervo Italy 41°8N 9°33E 200 A2
Porto Colom Spain 39°26N 3°15E 206 B4
Porto Cristo Spain 39°33N 3°20E 206 B4
Pôrto da Fôlha Brazil 9°55S 37°17W 332 C4
Pôrto de Moz Brazil 1°41S 52°13W 329 D7
Porto de Pedras Brazil 9°10S 35°17W 332 C4
Pôrto des Meinacos Brazil 12°33S 53°7W 331 C7
Pôrto dos Gaúchos Brazil 11°32S 57°16W 331 C6
Porto Empédocle Italy 37°17N 13°32E 200 E6
Porto Esperança Brazil 19°37S 57°29W 331 D6
Porto Espirdão Brazil 15°51S 58°28W 331 D6
Porto Formoso Azores 37°49N 25°25W 153 d3
Porto Franco Brazil 6°20S 47°24W 332 C2
Porto Grande Brazil 0°42N 51°24W 329 C7
Porto Inglês = Vila do Maio C. Verde Is. 15°21N 23°10W 153 j
Porto Jofre Brazil 17°20S 56°48W 331 D6
Porto Lengone = Porto Azzurro Italy 42°46N 10°24E 198 F7
Porto Maurizio = Impéria Italy 43°53N 8°3E 198 E5
Porto Mendes Brazil 24°30S 54°15W 335 A5
Porto Moniz Madeira 32°52N 17°11W 153 c
Porto Murtinho Brazil 21°45S 57°55W 331 E6
Porto Nacional Brazil 10°40S 48°30W 332 D2
Porto-Novo Benin 6°23N 2°42E 263 D5
Porto Novo Rio de J., Brazil 22°50S 43°7W 135 A2
Porto Novo Cr. → Nigeria 6°25N 3°22E 124 B2
Porto Primavera, Represa Brazil 22°10S 52°45W 335 A5
Porto San Giórgio Italy 43°11N 13°48E 199 E10
Porto Sant' Elpídio Italy 43°15N 13°45E 199 E10
Porto Santana Brazil 0°3S 51°11W 329 D7
Porto Santo, I. de Madeira 33°45N 16°25W 260 B1
Porto Santo Stéfano Italy 42°26N 11°7E 198 F8
Porto São José Brazil 22°43S 53°10W 335 A5
Porto Seguro = Guadalupe Brazil 6°44S 43°47W 332 C3
Porto Seguro Brazil 16°26S 39°5W 333 E4
Porto Tolle Italy 44°56N 12°22E 199 D9
Porto Tórres Italy 40°50N 8°24E 200 B1
Porto União Brazil 26°10S 51°10W 335 B5
Porto-Vecchio France 41°35N 9°16E 175 G13
Porto Velho Brazil 8°46S 63°54W 331 B5
Porto Viro Italy 45°1N 12°13E 199 C9
Porto Walter Brazil 8°15S 72°40W 330 B3
Portobello U.K. 55°57N 3°7W 121 B3
Portobelo Panama 9°35N 79°42W 320 E4
Portoferráio Italy 42°48N 10°20E 198 F7
Portofino Italy 44°18N 9°12E 198 D6
Portogruaro Italy 45°47N 12°50E 199 C9
Portola U.S.A. 39°49N 120°28W 306 F6
Portomaggiore Italy 44°42N 11°48E 199 D8
Portopetro Spain 39°22N 3°13E 206 B4
Portør Norway 58°48N 9°28E 164 F6
Portoscuso Italy 39°12N 8°24E 200 C1
Portoviejo Ecuador 1°7S 80°28W 328 D1
Portpatrick U.K. 54°51N 5°7W 167 G3
Portree U.K. 57°25N 6°12W 167 D2
Portrero U.S.A. 37°46N 122°25W 136 B3
Portrush U.K. 55°12N 6°40W 166 A5
Portsmouth Dominica 15°34N 61°27W 323 k
Portsmouth Portsmouth, U.K. 50°48N 1°6W 169 G6
Portsmouth N.H., U.S.A. 43°5N 70°45W 313 C14
Portsmouth Ohio, U.S.A. 38°44N 82°57W 309 F12
Portsmouth R.I., U.S.A. 41°36N 71°15W 313 E13
Portsmouth Va., U.S.A. 36°58N 76°23W 309 G15
Portsmouth □ U.K. 50°48N 1°6W 169 G6
Portsoy U.K. 57°41N 2°41W 167 D6
Portstewart U.K. 55°11N 6°43W 166 A5
Porttipahdan tekojärvi Finland 68°5N 26°40E 160 B22
Portugal ■ Europe 40°0N 8°0W 194 F3
Portugalete Spain 43°19N 3°4W 196 B1
Portuguesa □ Venezuela 9°10N 69°15W 328 B4
Portuguese East Africa = Mozambique ■ Africa 19°0S 35°0E 269 F4
Portuguese Guinea = Guinea-Bissau ■ Africa 12°0N 15°0W 262 C2
Portuguese Timor = East Timor ■ Asia 8°50S 126°0E 231 F7
Portuguese West Africa = Angola ■ Africa 12°0S 18°0E 265 E3
Portumna Ireland 53°6N 8°14W 166 C3
Portville U.S.A. 42°3N 78°20W 312 D6
Poruma Australia 10°2S 143°4E 280 a
Porus Jamaica 18°2N 77°25W 320 a
Porvenir Bolivia 11°10S 68°50W 330 C4
Porvenir Chile 53°10S 70°16W 336 D2
Porvoo Finland 60°24N 25°40E 188 B3
Porzuna Spain 39°9N 4°9W 195 F6
Pos Chiquito Aruba 12°27N 69°57W 322 f
Posada Italy 40°38N 9°43E 200 B2
Posada → Italy 40°39N 9°45E 200 B2
Posadas Argentina 27°30S 55°50W 335 B4
Posadas Spain 37°47N 5°11W 195 H5
Poschiavo Switz. 46°19N 10°4E 179 J6
Posen = Poznań Poland 52°25N 16°55E 185 F3
Posen U.S.A. 41°38N 87°42W 119 D2
Posets Spain 42°39N 0°25E 196 C5
Poseyville U.S.A. 38°10N 87°47W 311 F9
Poshan = Boshan China 36°28N 117°49E 227 F9
Posht-e Badam Iran 33°2N 55°23E 247 C7
Posidium Greece 35°30N 27°10E 205 F9
Poso Indonesia 1°20S 120°55E 231 E6
Poso, Danau Indonesia 1°52S 120°35E 231 E6
Posoegroenoe Suriname 4°23N 55°43W 329 C6
Posof Turkey 41°30N 42°43E 213 B10
Pospelikha Russia 51°57N 81°46E 217 B10
Posse Brazil 14°4S 46°18W 333 D2
Possedimenti Italiani dell'Egeo = Dodekanisa Greece 36°35N 27°0E 205 E8
Possel C.A.R. 5°5N 19°10E 264 A3
Possession I. Antarctica 72°4S 172°0E 151 D11
Pössneck Germany 50°42N 11°35E 178 E7
Possum Kingdom L. U.S.A. 32°52N 98°26W 314 E5
Post U.S.A. 33°12N 101°23W 314 E4
Post Falls U.S.A. 47°43N 116°57W 304 C5
Postavy = Pastavy Belarus 55°4N 26°50E 188 E4
Poste, R. du Mauritius 20°29S 57°36E 272 e
Poste de Flacq Mauritius 20°9S 57°43E 272 e
Poste de Flacq → Mauritius 20°9S 57°44E 272 e
Poste-de-la-Baleine = Kuujjuarapik Canada 55°20N 77°35W 298 A4
Postmasburg S. Africa 28°18S 23°5E 270 C3
Postojna Slovenia 45°46N 14°12E 199 C11
Poston U.S.A. 34°0N 114°24W 307 M12
Postumia = Postojna Slovenia 45°46N 14°12E 199 C11
Postville Nfld. & L., Canada 54°54N 59°47W 299 B8
Postville Iowa, U.S.A. 43°5N 91°34W 310 A5
Posyet Russia 42°39N 130°48E 220 C5
Potamos Antikythira, Greece 35°52N 23°15E 204 F5
Potamos Kythira, Greece 36°15N 22°58E 204 E4
Potchefstroom S. Africa 26°41S 27°7E 270 C4
Potcoava Romania 44°30N 24°39E 183 F9
Poté Brazil 17°49S 41°49W 333 E3
Poteau U.S.A. 35°3N 94°37W 314 D7
Poteet U.S.A. 29°2N 98°35W 314 G5
Potenza Italy 40°38N 15°48E 201 B8
Potenza → Italy 43°25N 13°40E 199 E10
Potenza Picena Italy 43°22N 13°37E 199 E10
Poteriteri, L. N.Z. 46°5S 167°10E 285 G2
Potgietersrus = Mokopane S. Africa 24°10S 28°55E 271 B4
Poti Georgia 42°10N 41°38E 191 J5
Potiraguá Brazil 15°36S 39°53W 333 E4
Potiskum Nigeria 11°39N 11°2E 263 C7
Potlogi Romania 44°34N 25°34E 183 F10
Potnarvin Vanuatu 18°45S 169°10E 287 H7
Potomac → U.S.A. 38°0N 76°23W 309 F14
Potomac Overlook Reg. Park ⌂ U.S.A. 38°55N 77°6W 143 B2
Potomac Park Washington, D.C., U.S.A. 143 c1
Potosí Bolivia 19°38S 65°50W 331 D4
Potosi Mo., U.S.A. 37°56N 90°47W 310 G6
Potosí □ Bolivia 20°31S 67°0W 330 E4
Potosi Mt. U.S.A. 35°57N 115°29W 307 K11
Pototan Phil. 10°54N 122°38E 233 F4
Potrerillos Chile 26°30S 69°30W 334 B2
Potrero Pt. U.S.A. 37°45N 122°22W 136 B2
Potsdam Brandenburg, Germany 52°23N 13°3E 115 B1
Potsdam N.Y., U.S.A. 44°40N 74°59W 313 B10
Potsdamer Platz Berlin, Germany 115 b3
Pottangi India 18°34N 82°58E 244 E6
Pottenstein Germany 49°46N 11°24E 179 F7
Potters Village Antigua & B. 17°5N 61°49W 322 b
Pottersville U.S.A. 43°43N 73°50W 313 C11
Pottery Hill = Abû Ballas Egypt 24°26N 27°36E 256 C2
Pottstown U.S.A. 40°15N 75°39W 313 F9
Pottsville U.S.A. 40°41N 76°12W 313 F8
Pottuvil Sri Lanka 6°55N 81°50E 245 L5
Potzham Germany 48°1N 11°36E 131 B2
Pötzleinsdorf Austria 48°14N 16°17E 142 A1
P'otzu Taiwan 23°28N 120°15E 225 C2
Pouancé France 47°44N 1°10W 172 E5
Pouce Coupé Canada 55°40N 120°10W 296 B4
Pouébo N. Cal. 20°24S 164°34E 288 d
Poughkeepsie U.S.A. 41°42N 73°56W 313 E11
Pouilly-sur-Loire France 47°17N 2°57E 173 E9
Poulan U.S.A. 31°31N 83°47W 316 D6
Poulaphouca Res. Ireland 53°8N 6°30W 166 C5
Poulsbo U.S.A. 47°44N 122°38W 306 C4
Poultney U.S.A. 43°31N 73°14W 313 C11
Poulton-le-Fylde U.K. 53°51N 2°58W 168 D5
Poum N. Cal. 20°14S 164°2E 288 d
Pounga-Nganda Gabon 2°58S 10°51E 264 C2
Pouso Alegre Mato Grosso, Brazil 11°46S 57°16W 331 C6
Pouso Alegre Minas Gerais, Brazil 22°14S 45°57W 335 A6
Pouso Alto = Piracanjuba Brazil 17°18S 49°1W 333 E2
Pout Senegal 14°45N 17°0W 262 C1
Pouthisat Cambodia 12°34N 103°50E 236 F4
Pouytenga Burkina Faso 12°15N 0°25W 263 C4
Pouzauges France 46°47N 0°50W 172 F6
Považská Bystrica Slovak Rep. 49°8N 18°27E 181 B11
Povenets Russia 62°50N 34°50E 186 B5
Poverty B. N.Z. 38°43S 178°2E 284 E7
Povlen Serbia 44°9N 19°44E 202 B3
Póvoa de Lanhosa Portugal 41°33N 8°15W 194 D2
Póvoa de Santa Iria Portugal 38°51N 9°4W 195 G1
Póvoa de Santo Adriao Portugal 38°47N 9°9W 126 A2
Póvoa de Varzim Portugal 41°25N 8°46W 194 D2
Povoação Azores 37°45N 25°15W 153 d3
Povorino Russia 51°12N 42°5E 190 E6
Povorotnyy, Mys Russia 42°40N 133°2E 220 C6
Povungnituk = Puvirnituq Canada 60°2N 77°10W 295 E16
Powassan Canada 46°5N 79°25W 298 C4
Poway U.S.A. 32°58N 117°2W 307 N9
Powązki Poland 52°15N 20°58E 143 B1
Powder → U.S.A. 46°45N 105°26W 304 C11
Powder River U.S.A. 43°2N 106°59W 304 E10
Powder Springs U.S.A. 33°52N 84°41W 316 B5
Powell U.S.A. 44°45N 108°46W 304 D9
Powell, L. U.S.A. 36°57N 111°29W 305 H8
Powell River Canada 49°50N 124°35W 296 D4
Powelton U.S.A. 33°26N 82°52W 316 B7
Power House = Drayton Valley Canada 53°12N 114°58W 296 C6
Powers U.S.A. 45°41N 87°32W 308 C10
Powiśle Poland 52°14N 21°1E 143 B2
Pownal U.S.A. 42°45N 73°14W 313 D11
Powsin Poland 52°8N 21°6E 143 C2
Powsinek Poland 52°9N 21°6E 143 C2
Powys □ U.K. 52°20N 3°20W 169 E4
Poxoréo Brazil 15°50S 54°23W 331 D7
Poya N. Cal. 21°19S 165°7E 288 d
Poyan Res. Singapore 1°22N 103°40E 138 A2
Poyang Hu China 29°5N 116°20E 229 C11
Poyarkovo Russia 49°36N 128°41E 215 E13
Poysdorf Austria 48°40N 16°37E 181 C9
Poza de la Sal Spain 42°35N 3°31W 196 C1
Poza Rica Mexico 20°33N 97°27W 319 C5
Pozantı Turkey 37°25N 34°50E 212 D6
Požarevac Serbia 44°35N 21°18E 202 B5
Pozazal, Puerto Spain 42°56N 4°10W 194 C6
Požega Croatia 45°20N 17°40E 182 E2
Požega Serbia 43°53N 20°2E 202 C4
Poznań Poland 52°25N 16°55E 185 F3
Poznań ✕ (POZ) Poland 52°26N 16°45E 185 F3
Pozo U.S.A. 35°20N 120°24W 307 K6
Pozo Alcón Spain 37°42N 2°56W 195 H8
Pozo Almonte Chile 20°10S 69°50W 330 E4
Pozo Colorado Paraguay 23°30S 58°45W 334 A4
Pozo Negro Canary Is. 28°19N 13°55W 153 e2
Pozoblanco Spain 38°23N 4°51W 195 G6
Pozorrubio Phil. 16°7N 120°33E 232 C3
Pozuelo de Alarcón Spain 40°24N 3°49W 127 B1
Pozuzo Peru 10°5S 75°35W 330 C2
Pozzallo Italy 36°43N 14°51E 201 F7
Pozzomaggiore Italy 40°24N 8°39E 200 B1
Pozzuoli Italy 40°49N 14°7E 201 B7
Pra → Ghana 5°1N 1°37W 263 D4
Prabuty Poland 53°47N 19°15E 184 E6
Prača Bos.-H. 43°47N 18°43E 182 G3
Prachatice Czech Rep. 49°1N 14°0E 180 B6
Prachin Buri Thailand 14°0N 101°25E 236 F3
Prachuap Khirikhan Thailand 11°49N 99°48E 237 G2
Pradelles France 44°46N 3°52E 174 D7
Pradera Colombia 3°25N 76°15W 328 C2
Prades France 42°38N 2°23E 174 F6
Prado Brazil 17°20S 39°13W 333 E4
Prado, Museo del Madrid, Spain 127 b3
Prado Churubusco Mexico 19°20N 99°8W 128 B2
Prado del Rey Spain 36°48N 5°33W 195 J5
Præstø Denmark 55°8N 12°2E 163 J6
Praga Poland 52°15N 21°2E 143 B2
Pragersko Slovenia 46°27N 15°42E 199 B12
Prague = Praha Czech Rep. 50°4N 14°25E 135 B2
Praha Czech Rep. 50°4N 14°25E 135 B2
Praha ✕ (PRG) Czech Rep. 50°6N 14°16E 135 B1
Prahecq France 46°19N 0°26W 174 B3
Prahita → India 19°0N 79°55E 244 E4
Prahova □ Romania 45°10N 26°0E 183 E10
Prahova → Romania 44°50N 25°50E 183 F10
Prahovo Serbia 44°18N 22°39E 202 B6
Praia Azores 39°3N 27°58W 153 d1
Praia C. Verde Is. 15°2N 23°34W 153 j
Praia ✕ (RAI) C. Verde Is. 14°55N 23°30W 153 j
Praia a Mare Italy 39°50N 15°45E 201 C8
Praia da Vitória Azores 38°44N 27°4W 153 d1
Praia do Norte Azores 38°36N 28°46W 153 d1
Praia Grande Brazil 24°0S 46°24W 333 F2
Praid Romania 46°32N 25°10E 183 D10
Prainha Azores 38°27N 28°12W 153 d1
Prainha Pará, Brazil 1°45S 53°30W 329 D7
Prainha Nova Brazil 7°10S 60°30W 331 B5
Prairies, R. des → Canada 45°38N 73°36W 130 A2
Prairie Australia 20°50S 144°35E 280 C3
Prairie City U.S.A. 44°28N 118°43W 304 D4
Prairie Dog Town Fork Red → U.S.A. 34°34N 99°58W 314 D5
Prairie du Chien U.S.A. 43°3N 91°9W 310 A5
Prairie du Rocher U.S.A. 38°5N 90°6W 310 F6
Prairie Village U.S.A. 38°58N 94°38W 310 F2
Prairies, L. of the Canada 51°16N 101°32W 297 C8
Pramanda Greece 39°32N 21°8E 204 B3
Prambanan Indonesia 7°45S 110°29E 235 D4
Prambanan △ Indonesia 7°45S 110°28E 231 G14
Prampram Ghana 5°43N 0°8E 263 D5
Pran Buri Thailand 12°23N 99°55E 236 F2
Prándarjökull Iceland 64°40N 14°55W 155 C12
Prang Ghana 8°1N 0°56W 263 D4
Prapat Indonesia 2°41N 98°58E 234 B1
Praslin St. Lucia 13°52N 60°54W 323 m
Praslin Seychelles 4°18S 55°45E 272 c
Prasonisi, Akra Greece 35°42N 27°46E 206 F11
Prassberg = Mozirje Slovenia 46°22N 14°58E 199 B11
Praszka Poland 51°5N 18°31E 185 G5
Prata Brazil 19°25S 48°54W 333 E2
Pratabpur India 23°28N 83°15E 243 H10
Pratapgarh Raj., India 24°2N 74°40E 242 G6
Pratapgarh Ut. P., India 25°56N 81°59E 243 G9
Pratas I. = Dongsha Dao S. China Sea 20°45N 116°43E 219 G12
Prater Austria 48°12N 16°25E 142 A2
Prato Italy 43°53N 11°6E 198 E8
Prátola Peligna Italy 42°6N 13°52E 199 F10
Prats-de-Mollo-la-Preste France 42°25N 2°27E 174 F6
Pratt U.S.A. 37°39N 98°44W 308 G4
Prattville U.S.A. 32°28N 86°29W 315 E11
Praust = Pruszcz Gdański Poland 54°17N 18°40E 184 D5
Pravara → India 19°35N 74°45E 244 E2
Pravdinsk Kaliningrad, Russia 54°27N 21°1E 184 D8
Pravdinsk Nizhniy Novgorod, Russia 56°29N 43°28E 190 B6
Pravets Bulgaria 42°53N 23°55E 202 D7
Pravia Spain 43°30N 6°12W 194 B4
Praya Indonesia 8°39S 116°17E 235 D5
Prayag = Allahabad India 25°25N 81°58E 243 G9
Pre-delta △ Argentina 32°10S 60°40W 334 C3
Pré-en-Pail France 48°28N 0°12W 172 D6
Preah Vihear Cambodia 14°23N 104°41E 236 E5
Preau Trin. & Tob. 10°12N 61°19W 323 t
Preble U.S.A. 42°44N 76°8W 313 D8
Prêcheur Martinique 14°48N 61°14W 322 c
Precipice △ Australia 25°18S 150°5E 281 D5
Precordillera Argentina 30°0S 69°1W 334 C2

Precotto *Italy* 45°30N 9°13E **128** A2
Predáppio *Italy* 44°6N 11°59E **199** D8
Predazzo *Italy* 46°19N 11°36E **199** B8
Predeal *Romania* 45°30N 25°34E **183** E10
Predejane *Serbia* 42°51N 22°9E **202** D6
Preeceville *Canada* 51°57N 102°40W **297** C8
Preetz *Germany* 54°14N 10°18E **178** A6
Pregolya → *Russia* 54°41N 20°22E **184** D7
Pregrada *Croatia* 46°11N 15°45E **199** B12
Preiļi *Latvia* 56°18N 26°43E **188** D4
Preko *Croatia* 44°7N 15°10E **199** D12
Prelog *Croatia* 46°18N 16°32E **199** B13
Premer *Australia* 31°29S 149°56E **283** A8
Prémery *France* 47°10N 3°18E **173** E10
Premià de Mar *Spain* 41°29N 2°22E **196** D7
Premont *U.S.A.* 27°22N 98°7W **314** H5
Premuda *Croatia* 44°20N 14°36E **199** D11
Prenestino Labicano *Italy* 41°53N 12°33E **136** B2
Prentice *U.S.A.* 45°33N 90°17W **308** C8
Prenzlau *Germany* 53°19N 13°50E **178** B9
Prenzlauerberg *Germany* 52°32N 13°24E **115** A3
Preobrazheniye *Russia* 42°54N 133°54E **220** C6
Preparis I. = Pariparit Kyun
*Burma* 14°52N 93°41E **245** G11
Preparis North Channel
*Ind. Oc.* 15°27N 94°5E **245** G11
Preparis South Channel
*Ind. Oc.* 14°33N 93°30E **245** G11
Přerov *Czech Rep.* 49°28N 17°27E **181** B10
Prescott *Ont., Canada* 44°45N 75°30W **313** B9
Prescott *Ariz., U.S.A.* 34°33N 112°28W **305** J7
Prescott *Ark., U.S.A.* 33°48N 93°23W **314** E8
Prescott Valley *U.S.A.* 34°40N 112°18W **305** J7
Preservation Inlet *N.Z.* 46°8S 166°35E **285** G1
Preševo *Serbia* 42°19N 21°39E **202** D5
Presho *U.S.A.* 43°54N 100°3W **308** D3
Presicce *Italy* 39°54N 18°16E **201** C11
Presidencia de la Plaza
*Argentina* 27°0S 59°50W **334** B4
Presidencia Roque Saenz Peña
*Argentina* 26°45S 60°30W **334** B3
Président-Thiers, Récif
*French Polynesia* 24°30S 146°0W **289** f
Presidente Dutra *Brazil* 5°15S 44°30W **332** C3
Presidente Epitácio *Brazil* 21°56S 52°6W **333** F1
Presidente Figueiredo
*Brazil* 1°57S 60°3W **329** D5
Presidente Hayes □
*Paraguay* 24°0S 59°0W **334** A4
Presidente Juán Perón = Chaco □
*Argentina* 26°30S 61°0W **334** B3
Presidente Médici *Brazil* 11°17S 61°55W **331** C5
Presidente Prudente *Brazil* 22°5S 51°25W **335** A5
Presidente Ríos, L. *Chile* 46°28S 74°25W **336** C2
Presidente Vargas = Nova Era
*Brazil* 19°45S 43°3W **333** E3
Presidio *U.S.A.* 29°34N 104°22W **314** G2
Preslav *Bulgaria* 43°10N 26°52E **203** C10
Preslavska Planina
*Bulgaria* 43°10N 26°45E **203** C10
Prešov *Slovak Rep.* 49°0N 21°15E **181** B14
Prešovský □ *Slovak Rep.* 49°10N 21°0E **181** B13
Prespa *Bulgaria* 41°44N 24°55E **203** E8
Prespa, L. = Prespansko Jezero
*Macedonia* 40°55N 21°0E **202** F5
Prespa △ *Greece* 40°48N 21°4E **202** F5
Prespansko Jezero
*Macedonia* 40°55N 21°0E **202** F5
Presque I. *U.S.A.* 42°10N 80°6W **312** D4
Presque Isle *U.S.A.* 46°41N 68°1W **309** B19
Pressburg = Bratislava
*Slovak Rep.* 48°10N 17°7E **181** C10
Prestatyn *U.K.* 53°20N 3°24W **168** D4
Prestea *Ghana* 5°22N 2°7W **262** D4
Presteigne *U.K.* 52°17N 3°0W **169** E5
Přeštice *Czech Rep.* 49°34N 13°20E **180** B6
Presto *Bolivia* 18°55S 64°56W **331** D5
Preston *Vic., Australia* 37°44S 145°0E **128** A1
Preston *Ont., Canada* 43°23N 80°21W **312** C4
Preston *Lancs., U.K.* 53°46N 2°42W **168** D5
Preston *Ga., U.S.A.* 32°4N 84°32W **316** C5
Preston *Idaho, U.S.A.* 42°6N 111°53W **304** E8
Preston *Iowa, U.S.A.* 42°3N 90°24W **310** B6
Preston *Minn., U.S.A.* 43°40N 92°5W **308** D7
Preston *Mo., U.S.A.* 37°56N 93°13W **310** G3
Preston, C. *Australia* 20°51S 116°12E **278** D2
Prestonsburg *U.S.A.* 37°40N 82°47W **309** G12
Prestranda *Norway* 59°6N 9°4E **162** E3
Prestwick *U.K.* 55°29N 4°37W **167** F4
Prêto → *Amazonas, Brazil* 0°8S 64°6W **329** D5
Prêto → *Bahia, Brazil* 11°21S 43°52W **332** D3
Prêto do Igapó-Açu →
*Brazil* 4°26S 59°48W **329** D6
Pretoria *S. Africa* 25°44S 28°12E **271** C4
Pretos Forros, Sa. dos
*Brazil* 22°54S 43°17W **135** B1
Preuilly-sur-Claise *France* 46°51N 0°56E **172** F7
Preussisch-Eylau = Bagrationovsk
*Russia* 54°23N 20°39E **184** D7
Preussisch Friedland = Debrzno
*Poland* 53°31N 17°14E **184** E4
Preussisch Holland = Pasłęk
*Poland* 54°3N 19°41E **184** D6
Preussisch-Stargard = Starogard
Gdański *Poland* 53°59N 18°30E **184** E5
Preveza *Greece* 38°57N 20°45E **207** B2
Preveza-Lefkada ✕ (PVK)
*Greece* 38°57N 20°45E **207** B2
Préville *Canada* 45°28N 73°29W **130** B3
Prey Veng *Cambodia* 11°35N 105°29E **237** G5
Přezletice *Czech Rep.* 50°9N 14°34E **135** B3
Priazovskoye *Ukraine* 46°44N 35°40E **189** J8
Pribalkhash = Balqash
*Kazakhstan* 46°50N 74°50E **214** E8
Pribaykalsky △ *Russia* 52°30N 106°0E **215** D11
Pribilof Is. *U.S.A.* 57°0N 170°0W **303** H5
Priboj *Serbia* 43°35N 19°32E **202** C3
Příbram *Czech Rep.* 49°41N 14°2E **180** B7
Price *U.S.A.* 39°36N 110°49W **304** G8
Price, C. *India* 13°34N 93°3E **245** H11
Price I. *Canada* 52°23N 128°41W **296** C3
Prichard *U.S.A.* 30°44N 88°5W **315** F10
Prickly Pear Cays *Anguilla* 18°16N 63°11W **322** a
Prickly Pt. *Grenada* 11°59N 61°45W **323** q
Priego *Spain* 40°26N 2°21W **196** E2
Priego de Córdoba *Spain* 37°27N 4°12W **195** H6
Priekule *Latvia* 56°26N 21°35E **188** B8
Priekule *Lithuania* 55°33N 21°19E **184** C8
Prielbrusye △ *Russia* 43°20N 42°37E **191** J6
Prien *Germany* 47°51N 12°20E **179** H8
Prienai *Lithuania* 54°38N 23°57E **184** D10
Prieska *S. Africa* 29°40S 22°42E **270** C3
Priest L. *U.S.A.* 48°35N 116°52W **304** B5
Priest River *U.S.A.* 48°11N 116°55W **304** B5
Priest Valley *U.S.A.* 36°10N 120°39W **306** J6
Prieto Diaz *Phil.* 13°2N 124°12E **232** E5
Prievidza *Slovak Rep.* 48°46N 18°36E **181** C11
Prignitz *Germany* 53°6N 11°45E **178** B7
Prijedor *Bos.-H.* 44°58N 16°41E **199** D13
Prijepolje *Serbia* 43°27N 19°40E **202** C3
Prikaspiyskaya Nizmennost =
Caspian Depression
*Eurasia* 47°0N 48°0E **191** G9
Prikro *Ivory C.* 7°40N 3°59W **262** D4
Prikubanskaya Nizmennost
*Russia* 45°39N 38°33E **191** H4
Prilep *Macedonia* 41°21N 21°32E **202** E5
Priluki = Pryluky *Ukraine* 50°30N 32°24E **189** G7
Prima Porta *Italy* 42°0N 12°30E **136** B1
Primavalle *Italy* 41°55N 12°25E **136** B1
Prime Seal I. *Australia* 40°3S 147°43E **281** G4
Primeira Cruz *Brazil* 2°30S 43°26W **332** B3
Primkenau = Przemków
*Poland* 51°31N 15°48E **185** G2
Primo Tapia *Mexico* 32°16N 116°54W **307** N10
Primorsk *Kaliningrad, Russia* 54°44N 20°0E **184** D6
Primorsk *St. Petersburg, Russia* 60°22N 28°37E **188** B5
Primorskiy Kray □ *Russia* 45°0N 135°0E **220** B7
Primorsko *Bulgaria* 42°15N 27°44E **203** D11
Primorsko-Akhtarsk
*Russia* 46°2N 38°10E **189** J10
Primrose *S. Africa* 26°11S 28°9E **123** B2
Primrose L. *Canada* 54°55N 109°45W **297** C7
Prince Albert *Sask., Canada* 53°15N 105°50W **297** C7
Prince Albert *Western Cape, S. Africa* 33°12S 22°2E **270** D3
Prince Albert △ *Canada* 54°0N 106°25W **297** C7
Prince Albert Mts.
*Antarctica* 76°0S 161°30E **151** D11
Prince Albert Pen.
*Canada* 72°30N 116°0W **294** C8
Prince Albert Sd. *Canada* 70°25N 115°0W **294** C9
Prince Alfred, C. *Canada* 74°20N 124°40W **150** B1
Prince Charles I. *Canada* 67°47N 76°12W **295** D16
Prince Charles Mts.
*Antarctica* 72°0S 67°0E **151** D6
Prince Edward Fracture Zone
*Ind. Oc.* 46°0S 35°0E **151** A4
Prince Edward I. □
*Canada* 46°20N 63°20W **299** C7
Prince Edward Is. *Ind. Oc.* 46°35S 38°0E **273** J2
Prince George *Canada* 53°55N 122°50W **296** C4
Prince of Wales, C.
*U.S.A.* 65°36N 168°5W **303** D5
Prince of Wales I. *Queens., Australia* 10°40S 142°10E **286** F2
Prince of Wales I. *Nunavut, Canada* 73°0N 99°0W **294** C12
Prince of Wales I. *Alaska, U.S.A.* 55°47N 132°50W **303** J14
Prince of Wales Icefield
*Canada* 78°15N 79°0W **295** B16
Prince of Wales Str.
*Canada* 73°0N 117°0W **294** C8
Prince Patrick I. *Canada* 77°0N 120°0W **295** B8
Prince Regent Inlet
*Canada* 73°0N 90°0W **295** C14
Prince Rupert *Canada* 54°20N 130°20W **296** C2
Prince Rupert B. *Dominica* 15°34N 61°29W **323** k
Prince Rupert Bluff Pt.
*Dominica* 15°35N 61°29W **323** k
Prince William Sd.
*U.S.A.* 60°40N 147°0W **303** F11
Princes Street *Edinburgh, U.K.* **121** b2
Princes Town *Trin. & Tob.* 10°16N 61°23W **323** t
Princesa Isabel *Brazil* 7°44S 38°0W **332** C4
Princess Charlotte B.
*Australia* 14°25S 144°0E **280** A3
Princess Elizabeth Trough
*S. Ocean* 64°10S 83°0E **151** C7
Princess May Ranges
*Australia* 15°30S 125°30E **278** C4
Princess Royal I. *Canada* 53°0N 128°40W **296** C3
Princeton *B.C., Canada* 49°27N 120°30W **296** D4
Princeton *Calif., U.S.A.* 39°24N 122°1W **306** F4
Princeton *Ill., U.S.A.* 41°23N 89°28W **310** C7
Princeton *Ind., U.S.A.* 38°21N 87°34W **311** F9
Princeton *Ky., U.S.A.* 37°7N 87°53W **308** G10
Princeton *Mo., U.S.A.* 40°24N 93°35W **310** D3
Princeton *N.J., U.S.A.* 40°21N 74°39W **313** F10
Princeton *W. Va., U.S.A.* 37°22N 81°6W **309** G13
Princeville *Hawai'i, U.S.A.* 22°13N 159°29W **302** A2
Princeville *Ill., U.S.A.* 40°56N 89°46W **310** D7
Príncipe *São Tomé & Príncipe* 1°37N 7°25E **265** a
Principe da Beira *Brazil* 12°20S 64°30W **331** C5
Prineville *U.S.A.* 44°18N 120°51W **304** D3
Pringles Bay *Dominica* 15°21N 61°25W **323** k
Pringsewu *Indonesia* 5°24S 104°55E **234** D2
Prins Christian Sund
*Greenland* 60°4N 43°10W **154** E6
Prins Harald Kyst *Antarctica* 70°0S 35°1E **151** D4
Prins Karls Forland
*Svalbard* 78°30N 11°0E **154** B12
Prinsesse Astrid Kyst
*Antarctica* 70°45S 12°30E **151** D3
Prinsesse Ragnhild Kyst
*Antarctica* 70°15S 27°30E **151** D4
Printer's Row *Chicago, U.S.A.* **119** d2
Prinzapolca *Nic.* 13°20N 83°35W **320** D3
Prior, C. *Spain* 43°34N 8°17W **194** B2
Priozersk *Russia* 61°2N 30°7E **188** B6
Pripet = Prypyat →
*Europe* 51°20N 30°15E **177** C16
Pripet Marshes *Europe* 52°10N 27°10E **177** B15
Pripyat Marshes = Pripet Marshes
*Europe* 52°10N 27°10E **177** B15
Pripyats = Prypyat →
*Europe* 51°20N 30°15E **177** C16
Prishib = Leninsk *Russia* 48°40N 45°15E **191** F7
Prishtinë *Kosovo* 42°40N 21°13E **202** D5
Prislop, Pasul *Romania* 47°37N 24°48E **183** C9
Pristen *Russia* 51°15N 36°44E **189** G9
Priština = Prishtinë
*Kosovo* 42°40N 21°13E **202** D5
Pritzwalk *Germany* 53°9N 12°10E **178** B8
Privas *France* 44°45N 4°37E **175** D8
Priverno *Italy* 41°28N 13°11E **200** A6
Privolzhsk *Russia* 57°23N 41°16E **190** B5
Privolzhskaya Vozvyshennost
*Russia* 51°0N 46°0E **190** E7
Privolzhskiy *Russia* 51°25N 46°3E **190** E8
Privolzhskiy □ *Russia* 56°0N 50°0E **214** D6
Privolzhye *Russia* 52°52N 48°33E **190** D9
Priyutnoye *Russia* 46°12N 43°40E **191** G6
Prizren *Kosovo* 42°13N 20°45E **202** D4
Prizzi *Italy* 37°43N 13°26E **200** E6
Prnjavor *Bos.-H.* 44°52N 17°43E **182** F2
Probolinggo *Indonesia* 7°46S 113°13E **235** D4
Prochowice *Poland* 51°17N 16°20E **185** G3
Proctor *U.S.A.* 43°40N 73°2W **313** C11
Proddatur *India* 14°45N 78°30E **245** G4
Prodhromos *Cyprus* 34°57N 32°50E **207** F8
Proença-a-Nova *Portugal* 39°45N 7°54W **194** F3
Profilia *Greece* 36°5N 27°51E **206** E11
Profondeville *Belgium* 50°23N 4°52E **170** D4
Progreso *Coahuila, Mexico* 27°28N 100°59W **318** B4
Progreso *Yucatán, Mexico* 21°20N 89°40W **319** C7
Progreso Nacional *Mexico* 19°30N 99°9W **128** A2
Progress *Antarctica* 66°22S 76°22E **151** C12
Progress *Russia* 49°45N 129°37E **215** E13
Prokhladnyy *Russia* 43°50N 44°2E **191** J7
Prokhorovka *Russia* 51°2N 36°44E **190** E3
Prokletije *Albania* 42°30N 19°45E **202** D3
Prokopyevsk *Russia* 54°0N 86°45E **217** B11
Prokuplje *Serbia* 43°16N 21°36E **202** C5
Proletarsk *Russia* 46°42N 41°50E **191** G5
Prome *Burma* 18°49N 95°13E **241** F5
Promise City *U.S.A.* 40°45N 93°9W **310** D3
Promzino = Surskoye
*Russia* 54°30N 46°44E **190** C8
Prophet → *Canada* 58°48N 122°40W **296** B4
Prophet River *Canada* 58°6N 122°43W **296** B4
Prophetstown *U.S.A.* 41°40N 89°56W **310** C7
Propriá *Brazil* 10°13S 36°51W **332** D4
Propriano *France* 41°41N 8°52E **175** G12
Prosek *Czech Rep.* 50°7N 14°30E **135** B3
Proserpine *Australia* 20°21S 148°36E **280** b
Proskurov = Khmelnytskyy
*Ukraine* 49°23N 27°0E **177** D14
Prosna → *Poland* 52°6N 17°44E **185** F4
Prospect *N.Y., U.S.A.* 43°18N 75°9W **313** C9
Prospect *Ohio, U.S.A.* 40°27N 83°11W **311** D13
Prospect Hill Park *U.S.A.* 42°23N 71°13W **116** A1
Prosperidad *Phil.* 8°34N 125°52E **233** G5
Prosperity *U.S.A.* 30°51N 85°56W **316** E4
Prosperous B. *St. Helena* 15°56S 5°39W **153** h
Prosser *U.S.A.* 46°12N 119°46W **304** C4
Prossnitz = Prostějov
*Czech Rep.* 49°30N 17°9E **181** B10
Prostějov *Czech Rep.* 49°30N 17°9E **181** B10
Prostki *Poland* 53°42N 22°25E **184** E9
Proston *Australia* 26°8S 151°32E **281** D5
Proszowice *Poland* 50°13N 20°16E **185** H7
Proti *Greece* 37°5N 21°32E **204** D3
Provadiya *Bulgaria* 43°12N 27°30E **203** C11
Provadiyska → *Bulgaria* 43°12N 27°42E **203** C11
Provence *France* 43°40N 5°46E **175** E9
Provence-Alpes-Côte d'Azur □
*France* 44°0N 6°15E **175** D10
Providence *Ky., U.S.A.* 37°24N 87°46W **308** G10
Providence *R.I., U.S.A.* 41°49N 71°24W **313** E13
Providence, C. *N.Z.* 45°59S 166°29E **285** F1
Providence Bay *Canada* 45°41N 82°15W **298** C3
Providence Mts. *U.S.A.* 35°10N 115°15W **307** K11
Providencia *Chile* 33°25S 70°36W **137** B2
Providencia, I. de
*Colombia* 13°25N 81°26W **320** D3
Provideniya *Russia* 64°23N 173°18W **215** C19
Provincetown *U.S.A.* 42°3N 70°11W **309** D18
Provins *France* 48°33N 3°15E **173** D10
Provo *U.S.A.* 40°14N 111°39W **304** F8
Provost *Canada* 52°25N 110°20W **297** C6
Prozor *Bos.-H.* 43°50N 17°34E **182** G2
Prrenjas *Albania* 41°4N 20°32E **202** E4
Prudentópolis *Brazil* 25°12S 50°57W **333** G1
Prudhoe Bay *U.S.A.* 70°18N 148°22W **303** A10
Prudhoe I. *Australia* 21°19S 149°41E **280** C4
Prud'homme *Canada* 52°20N 105°54W **297** C7
Prudnik *Poland* 50°20N 17°38E **185** H4
Průhonice *Czech Rep.* 50°0N 14°33E **135** C3
Prüm *Germany* 50°12N 6°25E **179** E2
Prundu *Romania* 44°6N 26°14E **183** F11
Prundu Bârgăului
*Romania* 47°13N 24°46E **183** C9
Pruszcz Gdański *Poland* 54°17N 18°40E **184** D5
Pruszków *Poland* 52°9N 20°49E **185** F7
Prut → *Romania* 45°28N 28°10E **183** E13
Pruzhany *Belarus* 52°33N 24°28E **177** B13
Prvič *Croatia* 44°55N 14°47E **199** D11
Prydz B. *Antarctica* 69°0S 74°0E **151** C6
Pryluky *Ukraine* 50°30N 32°24E **189** G7
Prymorske *Ukraine* 46°48N 36°20E **189** J9
Pryor *U.S.A.* 36°19N 95°19W **314** C7
Prypyat → *Europe* 51°20N 30°15E **177** C16
Prypyatsky △ *Belarus* 52°0N 28°0E **177** C14
Przasnysz *Poland* 53°2N 20°54E **185** E7
Przedbórz *Poland* 51°6N 19°53E **185** G6
Przedecz *Poland* 52°20N 18°53E **185** F5
Przemków *Poland* 51°31N 15°48E **185** G2
Przemyśl *Poland* 49°50N 22°45E **185** J9
Przeworsk *Poland* 50°6N 22°32E **185** H9
Przewóz *Poland* 51°28N 14°57E **185** G1
Przhevalsk = Karakol
*Kyrgyzstan* 42°30N 78°20E **217** D9
Przysucha *Poland* 51°22N 20°38E **185** G7
Psachna *Greece* 38°34N 23°35E **204** C5
Psara *Greece* 38°37N 25°38E **205** C7
Psathoura *Greece* 39°30N 24°12E **204** B6
Pserimos *Greece* 36°56N 27°8E **205** E9
Psichiko *Greece* 38°1N 23°46E **112** A2
Psiloritis, Oros *Greece* 35°15N 24°45E **207** E5
Psira *Greece* 35°12N 25°52E **207** E6
Pskov *Russia* 57°50N 28°25E **188** D5
Pskov □ *Russia* 57°20N 29°0E **188** D5
Pskovskoye, Ozero *Russia* 58°0N 27°58E **188** C5
Psol → *Ukraine* 49°10N 33°37E **189** H7
Psunj *Croatia* 45°25N 17°19E **182** E2
Pteleos *Greece* 39°3N 22°57E **204** B4
Ptich = Ptsich → *Belarus* 52°9N 28°52E **177** B15
Ptichia = Vidos *Greece* 39°38N 19°55E **206** B9
Ptolemaida *Greece* 40°30N 21°43E **202** F5
Ptsich → *Belarus* 52°9N 28°52E **177** B15
Ptuj *Slovenia* 46°28N 15°50E **199** B12
Ptujska Gora *Slovenia* 46°23N 15°47E **199** B12
Pu Xian *China* 36°24N 111°6E **226** F6
Pua *Thailand* 19°11N 100°55E **236** C3
Pua'ena Pt. *U.S.A.* 21°36N 158°6W **302** J13
Puán *Argentina* 37°30S 62°45W **334** D3
Pu'an *Guizhou, China* 25°46N 104°57E **228** E5
Pu'apu'a *Samoa* 13°34S 172°9W **287** V19
Pubei *China* 22°16N 109°31E **228** F7
Pucacuro → *Peru* 3°20S 74°58W **328** D3
Pucallpa *Peru* 8°25S 74°30W **330** B3
Pucará *Bolivia* 18°43S 64°11W **331** D5
Pucará *Cajamarca, Peru* 6°0S 79°7W **330** B2
Pucará *Puno, Peru* 15°5S 70°24W **330** D3
Pucarani *Bolivia* 16°23S 68°30W **330** D4
Pucheng *China* 27°59N 118°31E **229** D12
Pucheni *Romania* 45°12N 25°17E **183** E10
Puchheim *Germany* 48°9N 11°21E **179** G7
Puch'on = Bucheon
*S. Korea* 37°28N 126°45E **224** D3
Púchov *Slovak Rep.* 49°8N 18°20E **181** B11
Pucio Pt. *Phil.* 11°46N 121°51E **233** F3
Pucioasa *Romania* 45°5N 25°25E **183** E10
Pučišća *Croatia* 43°22N 16°43E **199** E13
Puck *Poland* 54°45N 18°23E **184** D5
Pucka, Zatoka *Poland* 54°30N 18°40E **184** D5
Puçol *Spain* 39°37N 0°18W **197** F4
Pudasjärvi *Finland* 65°23N 26°53E **160** D22
Puding *China* 26°18N 105°44E **228** D5
Pudong New Area *China* 31°13N 121°30E **138** B2
Pudozh *Russia* 61°48N 36°32E **188** B9
Pudu = Suizhou *China* 31°42N 113°24E **229** B9
Puducherry *India* 11°59N 79°50E **245** J4
Pudukkottai *India* 10°28N 78°47E **245** J4
Pue *Cook Is.* 21°12S 159°45W **289** h
Puebla *Mexico* 19°3N 98°12W **319** D5
Puebla □ *Mexico* 18°50N 98°0W **319** D5
Puebla de Alcocer *Spain* 38°59N 5°14W **195** G5
Puebla de Don Fadrique
*Spain* 37°58N 2°25W **197** H2
Puebla de Don Rodrigo
*Spain* 39°5N 4°37W **195** F6
Puebla de Guzmán *Spain* 37°37N 7°15W **195** H3
Puebla de la Calzada *Spain* 38°54N 6°37W **195** G4
Puebla de Sanabria *Spain* 42°4N 6°38W **194** C4
Puebla de Trives = Pobra de Trives
*Spain* 42°20N 7°10W **194** C3
Pueblo *U.S.A.* 38°16N 104°37W **308** F2
Pueblo Libre *Peru* 12°5S 77°4W **124** B2
Pueblo Nuevo = El Poblenou
*Spain* 41°23N 2°11E **114** A2
Pueblo Nuevo *Spain* 40°25N 3°37W **127** B2
Puelches *Argentina* 38°5S 65°51W **334** D2
Puelén *Argentina* 37°32S 67°38W **334** D2
Puente Alto *Chile* 33°32S 70°35W **334** C1
Puente-Genil *Spain* 37°22N 4°47W **195** H6
Puente la Reina *Spain* 42°40N 1°49W **196** C3
Puente San Miguel *Spain* 43°21N 4°5W **194** B6
Puentearenas = Ponteareas
*Spain* 42°10N 8°28W **194** C2
Puentedeume = Pontedeume
*Spain* 43°24N 8°10W **194** B2
Puentes de Garcia Rodriguez = As Pontes de Garcia Rodriguez
*Spain* 43°27N 7°50W **194** B3
Pu'er *China* 23°0N 101°15E **228** F3
Puerca, Pta. *Puerto Rico* 18°13N 65°36W **321** b
Puerco → *U.S.A.* 34°22N 107°50W **305** J10
Puerta del Sol, Plaza *Madrid, Spain* **127** b2
Puerto Acosta *Bolivia* 15°32S 69°15W **330** D4
Puerto Aisén *Chile* 45°27S 73°0W **336** C2
Puerto Ángel *Mexico* 15°40N 96°29W **319** D5
Puerto Arista *Mexico* 15°56N 93°48W **319** D6
Puerto Armuelles *Panama* 8°20N 82°51W **320** E3
Puerto Asís *Colombia* 0°30N 76°30W **328** C2
Puerto Ayacucho
*Venezuela* 5°40N 67°35W **328** B4
Puerto Ayora *Ecuador* 0°45S 90°19W **330** a
Puerto Baquerizo Moreno
*Ecuador* 0°54S 89°36W **330** a
Puerto Barrios *Guatemala* 15°40N 88°32W **320** C2
Puerto Bermejo *Argentina* 26°55S 58°34W **334** B4
Puerto Bermúdez *Peru* 10°20S 74°58W **330** C3
Puerto Bolívar *Ecuador* 3°19S 79°55W **328** D2
Puerto Cabello *Venezuela* 10°28N 68°1W **328** A4
Puerto Cabezas *Nic.* 14°0N 83°30W **320** D3
Puerto Cabo Gracias á Dios
*Nic.* 15°0N 83°10W **320** D3
Puerto Capaz = El Jebha
*Morocco* 35°11N 4°43W **260** A4
Puerto Carreño *Colombia* 6°12N 67°22W **328** B4
Puerto Castilla *Honduras* 16°0N 86°0W **320** C2
Puerto Chicama *Peru* 7°45S 79°20W **330** B2
Puerto Cisnes *Chile* 44°45S 72°42W **336** B2
Puerto Coig *Argentina* 50°54S 69°15W **336** D3
Puerto Cortés *Honduras* 15°51N 88°0W **320** C2
Puerto Cumarebo
*Venezuela* 11°29N 69°30W **328** A4
Puerto de Alcudia = Port d'Alcúdia
*Spain* 39°50N 3°7E **206** B4
Puerto de Cabras = Puerto del Rosario *Canary Is.* 28°30N 13°52W **153** e2
Puerto de Cabrera *Spain* 39°8N 2°56E **206** B3
Puerto de la Cruz
*Canary Is.* 28°24N 16°32W **153** e1
Puerto de los Angeles ⌂
*Mexico* 23°39N 105°45W **318** C3
Puerto de Mazarrón *Spain* 37°34N 1°15W **197** H3
Puerto de Sóller = Port de Sóller
*Spain* 39°48N 2°42E **206** B3
Puerto de Somosierra *Spain* 41°9N 3°35W **194** D7
Puerto del Carmen
*Canary Is.* 28°55N 13°38W **153** e2
Puerto del Rosario
*Canary Is.* 28°30N 13°52W **153** e2
Puerto Deseado *Argentina* 47°55S 66°0W **336** C3
Puerto Escondido *Mexico* 15°50N 97°3W **319** D5
Puerto Gaitán *Colombia* 4°19N 72°4W **328** C3
Puerto Galera *Phil.* 13°30N 120°57E **232** E3
Puerto Guarani *Paraguay* 21°18S 57°55W **331** E6
Puerto Heath *Bolivia* 12°34S 68°39W **330** C4
Puerto Huitoto *Colombia* 0°18N 74°3W **328** C3
Puerto Inca *Peru* 9°22S 74°54W **330** B3
Puerto Inírida *Colombia* 3°53N 67°52W **328** C4
Puerto Juárez *Mexico* 21°11N 86°49W **319** C7
Puerto La Cruz *Venezuela* 10°13N 64°38W **329** A5
Puerto Leguízamo
*Colombia* 0°12S 74°46W **328** D3
Puerto Lempira *Honduras* 15°16N 83°46W **320** C3
Puerto Libertad *Mexico* 29°55N 112°43W **318** B2
Puerto Limón *Colombia* 3°23N 73°30W **328** C3
Puerto Lobos *Argentina* 42°0S 65°3W **336** B3
Puerto López *Colombia* 4°5N 72°58W **328** C3
Puerto Lumbreras *Spain* 37°34N 1°48W **197** H3
Puerto Madero *Argentina* 34°37S 58°21W **117** B2
Puerto Madryn *Argentina* 42°48S 65°4W **336** B3
Puerto Maldonado *Peru* 12°30S 69°10W **330** C4
Puerto Manatí *Cuba* 21°22N 76°50W **320** B4
Puerto Mariti *Colombia* 1°10S 69°59W **328** D4
Puerto Mercedes *Colombia* 1°11N 72°53W **328** C3
Puerto Mexico = Coatzacoalcos
*Mexico* 18°7N 94°25W **319** D6
Puerto Miraña *Colombia* 1°20S 70°19W **328** D3
Puerto Montt *Chile* 41°28S 73°0W **336** B2
Puerto Morazán *Nic.* 12°51N 87°11W **320** D2
Puerto Morelos *Mexico* 20°50N 86°52W **319** C7
Puerto Nariño *Colombia* 4°56N 67°48W **328** C4
Puerto Natales *Chile* 51°45S 72°15W **336** D2
Puerto Nuevo *Colombia* 5°53N 69°56W **328** B4
Puerto Ordaz *Venezuela* 8°16N 62°44W **329** B5
Puerto Oscuro *Chile* 31°24S 71°35W **334** C1
Puerto Padre *Cuba* 21°13N 76°35W **320** B4
Puerto Páez *Venezuela* 6°13N 67°28W **328** B4
Puerto Peñasco *Mexico* 31°20N 113°33W **318** A2
Puerto Pinasco *Paraguay* 22°36S 57°50W **334** A4
Puerto Pirámides
*Argentina* 42°35S 64°20W **336** B4
Puerto Piritu *Venezuela* 10°4N 65°3W **329** A4
Puerto Plata *Dom. Rep.* 19°48N 70°45W **321** C5
Puerto Pollensa = Port de Pollença
*Spain* 39°54N 3°4E **206** B4
Puerto Portillo *Peru* 9°45S 72°42W **330** B3
Puerto Princesa *Phil.* 9°46N 118°45E **233** G2
Puerto Princesa Subterranean River △ *Phil.* 10°10N 118°55E **233** F2
Puerto Quepos *Costa Rica* 9°29N 84°6W **320** E3
Puerto Real *Spain* 36°33N 6°12W **195** J4
Puerto Rico *Bolivia* 11°5S 67°38W **330** C4
Puerto Rico *Canary Is.* 27°47N 15°42W **153** e1
Puerto Rico □ *W. Indies* 18°15N 66°45W **321** C6
Puerto Rico Trench
*Atl. Oc.* 19°50N 66°0W **321** C6
Puerto Rondón *Colombia* 6°17N 71°6W **328** B3
Puerto Saavedra *Chile* 38°47S 73°24W **336** A2
Puerto San Julián
*Argentina* 49°15S 67°45W **336** C3
Puerto Santa Cruz
*Argentina* 50°0S 68°32W **336** D3
Puerto Sastre *Paraguay* 22°2S 57°55W **334** A4
Puerto Serrano *Spain* 36°56N 5°33W **195** J5
Puerto Siles *Bolivia* 12°48S 65°5W **331** C4
Puerto Suárez *Bolivia* 18°58S 57°52W **331** D6
Puerto Supe *Peru* 11°0S 77°30W **330** C2
Puerto Tejada *Colombia* 3°14N 76°24W **328** C2
Puerto Umbría *Colombia* 0°52N 76°33W **328** C2
Puerto Vallarta *Mexico* 20°37N 105°15W **318** C3
Puerto Varas *Chile* 41°19S 72°59W **336** B2
Puerto Velasco Ibarra
*Ecuador* 1°17S 90°29W **330** a
Puerto Villamil *Ecuador* 0°56S 91°1W **330** a
Puerto Villazón *Bolivia* 13°32S 61°57W **331** C5
Puerto Wilches *Colombia* 7°21N 73°54W **328** B3
Puerto Williams *Chile* 54°56S 67°37W **336** D3
Puertollano *Spain* 38°43N 4°7W **195** G6
Puesto Cunambo *Peru* 2°10S 76°0W **328** D2
Pueu *Tahiti* 17°44S 149°13W **289** e
Pueyrredón, L. *Argentina* 47°20S 72°0W **336** C2
Púez Odle ⌂ *Italy* 46°37N 11°48E **199** B8
Puffin I. *Ireland* 51°50N 10°24W **166** E1
Pugachev *Russia* 52°0N 48°49E **190** D9
Pugal *India* 28°30N 72°48E **242** E5
Puge *Sichuan, China* 27°20N 102°31E **228** D4
Puge *Tanzania* 4°45S 33°11E **268** C3
Puget Sound *U.S.A.* 47°50N 122°30W **306** C4
Puget-Théniers *France* 43°58N 6°53E **175** E10
Púglia □ *Italy* 41°15N 16°15E **201** A9
Pugŏdong *N. Korea* 42°5N 130°0E **224** A5
Pugu *Tanzania* 6°55S 39°4E **268** D4
Pūgūnzī *Iran* 25°49N 59°10E **247** E8
Puha *N.Z.* 38°30S 177°50E **284** E6
Puhuangyu *China* 39°50N 116°22E **114** B2
Pui *Romania* 45°30N 23°4E **182** E8
Pui O Wan
*Hong Kong, China* 22°15N 113°58E **122** B1
Puica *Peru* 15°0S 72°33W **330** D3
Puiești *Romania* 46°25N 27°33E **183** D12
Puig Major *Spain* 39°48N 2°47E **206** B3
Puigcerdà *Spain* 42°24N 1°50E **196** C6
Puigmal *Spain* 42°23N 2°7E **196** C7
Puigpunyent *Spain* 39°38N 2°32E **206** B3
Puijiang *China* 30°14N 103°30E **228** B4
Puisaye, Collines de la
*France* 47°37N 3°20E **173** E10
Puiseaux *France* 48°11N 2°30E **173** D9
Puistola *Finland* 60°16N 25°2E **121** B3
Pujehun *S. Leone* 7°23N 11°45W **262** D2
Pujiang *China* 29°29N 119°54E **229** C12
Pujili *Ecuador* 0°57S 78°41W **328** D2
Pujols *France* 44°48N 0°2W **174** D3
Pujon *Indonesia* 1°19S 114°19E **235** C4
Pujon-ho *N. Korea* 40°35N 127°35E **224** B3
Puka Puka
*French Polynesia* 14°49S 138°48W **289** f
Puka Ruha
*French Polynesia* 18°20S 137°2W **289** f
Pukaki, L. *N.Z.* 44°4S 170°1E **285** E5
Pukalani *U.S.A.* 20°51N 156°20W **302** C5
Pukapuka *Cook Is.* 10°53S 165°49W **289** J11
Pukaskwa △ *Canada* 48°20N 86°0W **298** C2
Pukatawagan *Canada* 55°45N 101°20W **297** B8
Pukchin *N. Korea* 40°12N 125°45E **224** B2
Pukch'ŏng *N. Korea* 40°14N 128°10E **224** D4
Pukë *Albania* 42°2N 19°53E **202** D3
Pukearuhe *N.Z.* 38°55S 174°31E **284** E3
Pukekohe *N.Z.* 37°12S 174°55E **284** D3
Puketeraki Ra. *N.Z.* 42°58S 172°13E **285** C7
Puketoi Ra. *N.Z.* 40°30S 176°5E **284** G5
Pukeuri *N.Z.* 45°4S 171°2E **285** F6
Pukhrayan *India* 26°14N 79°51E **243** F8
Pukinmäki *Finland* 60°15N 24°57E **121** B2
Puksubaek-san *N. Korea* 40°42N 127°45E **224** B3
Pula *Croatia* 44°54N 13°57E **199** D10
Pula *Italy* 39°1N 9°0E **200** C1
Pulacayo *Bolivia* 20°25S 66°41W **330** E4
Pulandian *China* 39°25N 121°58E **227** E11
Pulanduta Pt. *Phil.* 11°54N 123°9E **233** F4
Pulangpisau *Indonesia* 2°46S 114°13E **235** C4
Pulaski *N.Y., U.S.A.* 43°34N 76°8W **313** C8
Pulaski *Tenn., U.S.A.* 35°12N 87°2W **315** D11
Pulaski *Va., U.S.A.* 37°3N 80°47W **309** G13
Pulau → *Indonesia* 5°50S 138°15E **231** F9
Pulau Gili *Indonesia* 8°21S 116°1E **231** J19
Pulau Miangas *Indonesia* 5°35N 126°34E **233** J6
Puławy *Poland* 51°23N 21°59E **185** G8
Pulga *U.S.A.* 39°48N 121°29W **306** F5
Pulgaon *India* 20°44N 78°21E **244** D4
Puli *Taiwan* 23°58N 120°57E **225** C2
Pulicat *India* 13°25N 80°19E **245** H5
Pulicat L. *India* 13°40N 80°15E **245** H5
Pulivendla *India* 14°25N 78°14E **245** G4
Puliyangudi *India* 9°11N 77°24E **245** K3
Pulkovo Int. ✕ (LED)
*Russia* 59°48N 30°18E **137** C1
Pullach *Germany* 48°3N 11°31E **131** B1
Pullman *U.S.A.* 46°44N 117°10W **304** C5
Pullman Historic District
*U.S.A.* 41°41N 87°36W **119** C3
Pulo Gadung *Indonesia* 6°11S 106°54E **122** B2
Pulog, Mt. *Phil.* 16°40N 120°50E **232** C3
Pulpí *Spain* 37°24N 1°44W **197** H3
Pułtusk *Poland* 52°43N 21°6E **185** F8
Pülümür *Turkey* 39°30N 39°51E **213** C8
Pumlumon Fawr *U.K.* 52°28N 3°46W **169** E4
Puna *Bolivia* 19°45S 65°28W **331** D4
Puná, I. *Ecuador* 2°55S 80°5W **328** D1
Punaauia *Tahiti* 17°37S 149°34W **289** e
Pūnak *Iran* 35°46N 51°20E **141** A2
Punakha Dzong *Bhutan* 27°42N 89°52E **241** B2
Punalur *India* 9°0N 76°56E **245** K3
Punalu'u *U.S.A.* 21°35N 157°53W **302** J14
Punasar *India* 27°6N 73°6E **242** F5
Punata *Bolivia* 17°32S 65°50W **331** D4
Punch *India* 33°48N 74°4E **243** C6
Punch → *Pakistan* 33°12N 73°40E **242** C5
Punchbowl *Australia* 33°55S 151°3E **139** B1
Punda *Curaçao* 12°6N 68°55W **322** g
Punda Maria *S. Africa* 22°40S 31°5E **271** B5
Punde *India* 18°53N 72°57E **130** B2
Pune *India* 18°29N 73°57E **244** E1
Punggol *Singapore* 1°23N 103°54E **138** A3
Punggol, Sungei →
*Singapore* 1°24N 103°54E **138** A3
Punggol Pt. *Singapore* 1°24N 103°54E **138** A3
Pungo Andongo *Angola* 9°44S 15°35E **265** D3
P'ungsan *N. Korea* 40°50N 128°9E **224** B4
Pungsan *S. Korea* 36°34N 128°34E **224** D4
Pungue, Ponte de *Mozam.* 19°0S 34°0E **269** F3
Puning *China* 23°20N 116°12E **229** F11
Punjab □ *India* 31°0N 76°0E **242** D7
Punjab □ *Pakistan* 32°0N 72°30E **242** E6
Punjabi Bagh *India* 28°40N 77°6E **120** A1
Puno *Peru* 15°55S 70°3W **330** D3
Puno □ *Peru* 15°0S 70°0W **330** C3
Punpun → *India* 25°31N 85°18E **243** G11
Punta, Cerro de
*Puerto Rico* 18°10N 66°37W **321** b
Punta Alta *Argentina* 38°53S 62°4W **336** A4
Punta Arenas *Chile* 53°10S 71°0W **336** D2
Punta Cana ✕ (PUJ)
*Dom. Rep.* 18°34N 68°21W **321** C6
Punta Cardón *Venezuela* 11°38N 70°14W **328** A3
Punta Coles *Peru* 17°43S 71°23W **330** D3
Punta de Bombón *Peru* 17°10S 71°48W **330** D3
Punta de Piedras *Venezuela* 10°54N 64°5W **329** a
Punta del Díaz *Chile* 28°0S 70°45W **334** B1
Punta del Hidalgo
*Canary Is.* 28°33N 16°19W **153** e1
Punta Delgado *Argentina* 42°43S 63°38W **336** B4
Punta Gorda *Belize* 16°10N 88°45W **320** C2
Punta Gorda *Fla., U.S.A.* 26°56N 82°3W **317** J7
Punta Prieta *Mexico* 28°58N 114°17W **318** B2
Punta Prima *Spain* 39°48N 4°16E **206** B5
Punta Umbría *Spain* 37°10N 6°56W **195** H4
Puntarenas *Costa Rica* 10°0N 84°50W **320** E3
Puntland *Somalia* 9°0N 50°0E **267** C6
Punto Fijo *Venezuela* 11°50N 70°13W **328** A3
Punxsutawney *U.S.A.* 40°57N 78°59W **312** F6
Punyu = Guangzhou
*China* 23°6N 113°13E **121** B2
Puotila *Finland* 60°13N 25°5E **121** B3
Pupuan *Indonesia* 8°19S 115°0E **231** J18
Pūpūkea *U.S.A.* 21°40N 158°3W **302** J13
Puqi *China* 29°40N 113°50E **229** C9
Puquio *Peru* 14°45S 74°10W **330** C3
Pur → *Russia* 67°31N 77°55E **214** C8
Puracé, Vol. *Colombia* 2°21N 76°23W **328** C2
Puracé △ *Colombia* 2°10N 76°21W **328** C2
Puračić *Bos.-H.* 44°33N 18°28E **182** F3
Puralia = Puruliya *India* 23°17N 86°24E **243** H12
Purana Qila *Delhi, India* **120** c3
Puranpur *India* 28°31N 80°9E **243** E9
Purari → *Papua N. G.* 7°49S 145°0E **286** D3
Purbalingga *Indonesia* 7°23S 109°21E **235** D3
Purbeck, Isle of *U.K.* 50°39N 1°59W **169** G5
Purcell *U.S.A.* 35°1N 97°22W **314** D6
Purcell Mts. *Canada* 49°55N 116°15W **296** D5
Purdy *Canada* 45°19N 77°44W **312** A7
Puri *India* 19°50N 85°58E **244** E7
Purificación *Colombia* 3°51N 74°55W **328** C3
Purmerend *Neths.* 52°32N 4°58E **170** B4
Purna → *India* 19°6N 77°2E **244** E3
Purnia *India* 25°45N 87°31E **243** G12
Purnululu △ *Australia* 17°20S 128°20E **278** C4
Pursat = Pouthisat
*Cambodia* 12°34N 103°50E **236** F4
Purukcahu *Indonesia* 0°35S 114°35E **235** C4
Puruliya *India* 23°17N 86°24E **243** H12
Purus → *Brazil* 3°42S 61°28W **329** D5
Purutu I. *Papua N. G.* 8°24S 143°27E **286** E2
Puruvesi *Finland* 61°50N 29°30E **188** B5
Purvis *U.S.A.* 31°9N 89°25W **315** F10
Pŭrvomay *Bulgaria* 42°8N 25°17E **203** D9
Purwa *India* 26°28N 80°47E **243** F9
Purwakarta *Indonesia* 6°35S 107°29E **235** D3
Purwo, Tanjung
*Indonesia* 8°44S 114°21E **231** K18
Purwodadi *Indonesia* 7°7S 110°55E **235** D4
Purwokerto *Indonesia* 7°25S 109°14E **235** D3
Purworejo *Indonesia* 7°43S 110°2E **235** D4
Puryŏng *N. Korea* 42°5N 129°43E **224** A4
Pus → *India* 19°55N 77°55E **244** E3
Pusa *India* 25°59N 85°41E **243** G11
Pusad *India* 19°56N 77°36E **244** E3
Pusan = Busan *S. Korea* 35°5N 129°0E **224** E4
Pushkin *Russia* 59°45N 30°25E **188** C6
Pushkino *Moskva, Russia* 56°2N 37°49E **188** D9
Pushkino *Saratov, Russia* 51°16N 47°0E **190** E8
Püspökladány *Hungary* 47°19N 21°6E **182** C6
Pustoshka *Russia* 56°20N 29°30E **188** D5
Puszczykowo *Poland* 52°18N 16°49E **185** F3
Put-in-Bay *U.S.A.* 41°39N 82°49W **312** E2
Putahow L. *Canada* 59°54N 100°40W **297** B8
Putai *Taiwan* 23°23N 120°9E **225** C2
Putao *Burma* 27°28N 97°30E **241** B6
Putaruru *N.Z.* 38°2S 175°50E **284** E4
Putatan *Malaysia* 5°53N 116°3E **235** A5
Putbus *Germany* 54°22N 13°28E **178** A9
Puteaux *France* 48°53N 2°14E **134** A2
Puteran *Indonesia* 7°5S 114°0E **235** D4
Putian *China* 25°23N 119°0E **229** E12
Putignano *Italy* 40°51N 17°7E **201** B10
Putina *Peru* 14°55S 69°55W **330** C4
Puting, Tanjung *Indonesia* 3°31S 111°46E **235** C4
Putlitz *Germany* 53°15N 12°2E **178** B8
Putna *Romania* 47°50N 25°33E **183** C10
Putna → *Romania* 45°42N 27°26E **183** E12
Putnam *U.S.A.* 41°55N 71°55W **313** E13
Putney *London, U.K.* 51°27N 0°13W **125** B2
Putney *Ga., U.S.A.* 31°29N 84°8W **316** D5
Putnok *Hungary* 48°18N 20°26E **182** B5
Putorana, Gory *Russia* 69°0N 95°0E **215** C10
Putorino *N.Z.* 39°4S 176°58E **284** F5
Putrajaya *Malaysia* 2°55N 101°40E **237** L3
Putre *Chile* 18°12S 69°35W **330** D4
Puttalam *Sri Lanka* 8°1N 79°55E **245** K5
Puttalam Lagoon *Sri Lanka* 8°15N 79°45E **245** K4
Puttegga *Norway* 62°13N 6°36E **164** B4
Puttgarden *Germany* 54°30N 11°10E **178** A7
Püttlingen *Germany* 49°17N 6°53E **179** F2
Puttur *Andhra Pradesh, India* 13°27N 79°33E **245** H4
Puttur *Karnataka, India* 12°46N 75°12E **245** H2
Putty *Australia* 32°57S 150°42E **283** B9
Putumayo → *S. Amer.* 3°7S 67°58W **328** D4
Putuo *Shanghai, China* 31°15N 121°24E **138** B1
Putuo *Zhejiang, China* 29°56N 122°20E **229** C14
Putussibau *Indonesia* 0°50N 112°56E **235** B4
Pututahi *N.Z.* 38°39S 177°53E **284** E6
Putxet *Spain* 41°24N 2°8E **114** A1
Putyla *Ukraine* 48°0N 25°5E **183** B10
Pu'uanahulu *U.S.A.* 19°49N 155°51W **302** D6
Pu'uhonua o Hōnaunau ⌂
*U.S.A.* 19°25N 155°54W **302** D6
Pu'uka'aumakua
*U.S.A.* 21°30N 157°54W **302** J14
Pu'ukeahiakahoe
*U.S.A.* 21°23N 157°49W **302** K14
Pu'ukoholā Heiau ⌂
*U.S.A.* 20°1N 155°49W **302** C6
Pu'ula'ula *U.S.A.* 20°42N 156°15W **302** C5
Pu'u'oke'oke'o *U.S.A.* 19°13N 155°44W **302** D6
Pu'uwai *U.S.A.* 21°54N 160°12W **302** B1
Puvirnituq *Canada* 60°2N 77°10W **295** E16
Puxi *China* 31°12N 121°30E **138** B1
Puy-de-Dôme *France* 45°46N 2°57E **174** C6
Puy-de-Dôme □ *France* 45°40N 3°5E **174** C7
Puy-l'Évêque *France* 44°31N 1°9E **174** D5
Puyallup *U.S.A.* 47°12N 122°18W **306** C4
Puyang *China* 35°40N 115°1E **226** G8
Puyehue *Chile* 40°40S 72°37W **336** B2
Puyehue △ *Chile* 40°27S 72°6W **336** B2
Puylaurens *France* 43°35N 2°0E **174** E6
Puyo *Ecuador* 1°28S 77°59W **328** D2
Puysegur Pt. *N.Z.* 46°9S 166°37E **285** G1
Pūzeh Rīg *Iran* 27°20N 58°40E **247** E8
Puzhaykove *Ukraine* 48°7N 29°50E **183** B14
Puzi = P'otzu *Taiwan* 23°28N 120°15E **225** C2
Pwani = Coast □ *Kenya* 2°40S 39°45E **268** C4
Pwani □ *Tanzania* 7°0S 39°0E **268** D4
Pweto *Dem. Rep. of the Congo* 8°25S 28°51E **269** D2
Pwinbyu *Burma* 20°23N 94°40E **241** E5
Pwllheli *U.K.* 52°53N 4°25W **168** E3
Pyana → *Russia* 55°43N 46°1E **190** C8
Pyandzh → *Asia* 37°6N 68°20E **240** A2
Pyaozero, Ozero *Russia* 66°5N 30°58E **160** C24
Pyapon *Burma* 16°20N 95°40E **241** G5
Pyasina → *Russia* 73°30N 87°0E **215** B9
Pyatigorsk *Russia* 44°2N 43°6E **191** H6
Pyatykhatky *Ukraine* 48°28N 33°38E **189** H7
Pyawbwe *Burma* 20°35N 96°2E **241** E6
Pyay = Prome *Burma* 18°49N 95°13E **241** F5
Pyaye *Burma* 19°12N 95°10E **241** F5
Pydhuni *Mumbai, India* **130** b2
Pydna *Greece* 40°20N 22°34E **202** F6
Pye = Prome *Burma* 18°49N 95°13E **241** F5
Pyeonghae *S. Korea* 36°43N 129°26E **224** D4
Pyeongtaek *S. Korea* 37°1N 127°4E **224** D3
Pyetrikaw *Belarus* 52°11N 28°29E **177** B15
Pyhäjoki → *Finland* 64°28N 24°14E **160** D21
Pyhätunturi △ *Finland* 66°53N 27°5E **160** C22
Pyin-Oo-Lwin = Maymyo
*Burma* 22°2N 96°28E **236** A1
Pyinbauk *Burma* 19°10N 95°12E **241** F5
Pyingaing *Burma* 23°9N 94°50E **241** D5
Pyinkayaing *Burma* 15°53N 94°24E **241** H5
Pyinmana *Burma* 19°45N 96°12E **241** F6
Pyinyaung *Burma* 20°49N 96°25E **241** E6
Pyla *Cyprus* 35°1N 33°41E **250** C4
Pyla, C. *Cyprus* 34°56N 33°51E **207** F9
Pymatuning Res. *U.S.A.* 41°30N 80°28W **312** E4
Pyŏktong *N. Korea* 40°50N 125°50E **224** B2
P'yŏnganbuk-do □
*N. Korea* 40°0N 125°15E **224** C2
P'yŏngannam-do □
*N. Korea* 39°30N 126°24E **224** C3
P'yŏnggang *N. Korea* 38°24N 127°17E **224** C3
P'yŏngsong *N. Korea* 39°14N 125°52E **224** C2
P'yŏngyang *N. Korea* 39°0N 125°30E **224** C2
P'yŏngyang □ *N. Korea* 39°4N 125°45E **224** C2
Pyote *U.S.A.* 31°32N 103°8W **314** F3
Pyramid L. *U.S.A.* 40°1N 119°35W **304** F4

Pyramid Pk. U.S.A. 36°25N 116°37W 307 J10
Pyramid Pt. Ascension I. 7°55S 14°24W 153 g
Pyramids Egypt 29°58N 31°9E 117 B1
Pyrénées Europe 42°45N 0°18E 174 F4
Pyrénées △ France 42°52N 0°10W 174 F3
Pyrénées-Atlantiques □ France 43°10N 0°50W 174 E3
Pyrénées-Orientales □ France 42°35N 2°26E 174 F6
Pyry Poland 52°8N 21°0E 143 C1
Pyryatyn Ukraine 50°15N 32°25E 189 G7
Pyrzyce Poland 53°10N 14°55E 185 E1
Pyskowice Poland 50°24N 18°38E 185 H5
Pytalovo Russia 57°5N 27°55E 188 D4
Pyttegga = Puttegga Norway 62°13N 7°42E 164 B4
Pyu Burma 18°30N 96°28E 241 F6
Pyzdry Poland 52°11N 17°42E 185 F4


# Q


Qaanaaq Greenland 77°30N 69°10W 154 B4
Qaasuitsup □ Greenland 74°0N 52°0W 154 C5
Qäbälä Azerbaijan 40°58N 47°47E 191 K8
Qabanbay Kazakhstan 45°50N 80°37E 217 C10
Qabirri → Azerbaijan 41°3N 46°17E 191 K8
Qabr Hūd Yemen 16°9N 49°34E 249 C5
Qachasnek S. Africa 30°6S 28°42E 271 D4
Qādisiyah, Buhayrat al Iraq 34°20N 42°12E 213 E10
Qādub Yemen 12°37N 53°57E 249 D6
Qa'el Jafr Jordan 30°20N 36°25E 251 H7
Qa'emābād Iran 31°44N 60°2E 247 D9
Qā'emshahr Iran 36°30N 52°53E 247 B7
Qagan Nur Jilin, China 45°15N 124°18E 227 B13
Qagan Nur Nei Monggol Zizhiqu, China 43°30N 114°55E 226 C8
Qahar Youyi Zhongqi China 41°12N 112°40E 226 D7
Qahremānshahr = Kermānshāh Iran 34°23N 47°0E 213 E12
Qaidam Pendi China 37°0N 95°0E 218 D8
Qaiyara Iraq 35°48N 43°17E 213 E10
Qajarīyeh Iran 31°1N 48°22E 247 D6
Qala Malta 36°2N 14°19E 206 E7
Qala, Ras il Malta 36°2N 14°20E 206 E7
Qala-i-Jadid = Spīn Būldak Afghan. 31°1N 66°25E 242 D2
Qala Point = Qala, Ras il Malta 36°2N 14°20E 206 E7
Qala Viala Pakistan 30°49N 67°17E 242 D2
Qala Yangi Afghan. 34°20N 66°30E 242 B2
Qalācheh Afghan. 35°30N 67°43E 240 B2
Qalaikhum = Kalaikhum Tajikistan 38°28N 70°46E 217 E8
Qalandiya West Bank 31°52N 35°12E 123 A2
Qalansīyah Yemen 12°41N 53°29E 249 D6
Qal'at al Akhḑar Si. Arabia 28°4N 37°9E 251 K8
Qal'at Bīshah Si. Arabia 20°0N 42°36E 248 C3
Qal'at Dīzah Iraq 36°11N 45°7E 213 D11
Qalāt-i-Ghilzai Afghan. 32°15N 66°58E 240 B2
Qal'at Salah el Din Syria 34°46N 36°15E 250 D7
Qal'at Şāliḩ Iraq 31°31N 47°16E 246 D5
Qal'at Sukkar Iraq 31°51N 46°5E 213 G12
Qal'eh Morghī Iran 35°38N 51°22E 141 B2
Qal'eh-ye Bost Afghan. 31°30N 64°21E 240 C2
Qal'eh-ye Now Afghan. 35°0N 63°5E 240 B1
Qal'eh-ye Panjeh Afghan. 37°0N 72°35E 240 A4
Qal'eh-ye Sarkari Afghan. 35°54N 67°17E 240 B2
Qal'eh-ye Valī Afghan. 35°46N 63°45E 240 B1
Qalyûb Egypt 30°12N 31°11E 251 H2
Qalyûbîya □ Egypt 30°18N 31°18E 251 H2
Qamani'tuaq = Baker Lake Canada 64°20N 96°3W 294 E12
Qamar, Ghubbat al Yemen 16°20N 52°30E 249 C6
Qamar, Jabal al Oman 16°48N 53°15E 249 C6
Qamdo China 31°15N 97°6E 228 B1
Qamea Fiji 16°45S 179°45W 287 A3
Qamīnis Libya 31°40N 20°1E 258 B4
Qammieh Point Malta 35°58N 14°19E 206 F7
Qamruddin Karez Pakistan 31°45N 68°20E 242 D3
Qandahār = Kandahār Afghan. 31°32N 65°43E 240 C2
Qandahār = Kandahār □ Afghan. 31°0N 65°0E 240 C2
Qandala Somalia 11°30N 49°58E 267 B6
Qandyaghash Kazakhstan 49°28N 57°25E 187 E10
Qapān Iran 37°40N 55°47E 247 B7
Qapqal China 43°48N 81°5E 217 D10
Qapshaghay Kazakhstan 43°51N 77°14E 217 D9
Qapshaghay Bögeni Kazakhstan 43°45N 77°50E 217 D9
Qaqortoq Greenland 60°43N 46°0W 154 E6
Qâra Egypt 29°38N 26°30E 256 B2
Qarā', Jabal al Oman 17°15N 54°15E 249 C6
Qara Dāgh Iraq 35°18N 45°18E 213 E11
Qara Qash → China 35°0N 78°30E 243 B8
Qarabalyq Kazakhstan 53°45N 62°2E 216 B6
Qarabutaq Kazakhstan 50°0N 60°14E 216 C6
Qaraçala Azerbaijan 39°45N 48°53E 191 L9
Qaraçuxar Azerbaijan 40°25N 50°1E 191 K10
Qaraghandy Kazakhstan 49°50N 73°10E 217 C8
Qaraghayly Kazakhstan 49°26N 76°0E 214 E8
Qārah Si. Arabia 29°55N 40°3E 246 D4
Qarah Āghāj Iran 37°8N 46°58E 213 D12
Qarakol Uzbekistan 39°32N 63°50E 216 E6
Qaraoba Kazakhstan 47°6N 56°15E 216 C5
Qaraqīya Oyysy Kazakhstan 43°27N 51°45E 216 D4
Qaraqosh Iraq 36°16N 43°22E 213 D10
Qarataū Ongtüstik Qazaqstan, Kazakhstan 43°30N 69°30E 217 D7
Qarataū Zhambyl, Kazakhstan 43°10N 70°28E 217 D8
Qarāvol Afghan. 37°14N 68°46E 240 A3
Qarazhal Kazakhstan 48°2N 70°49E 214 E8
Qarchak Iran 35°25N 51°34E 247 C6
Qardho Somalia 9°30N 49°6E 267 C6
Qardud Sudan 10°20N 29°56E 257 E2
Qareh → Iran 39°25N 47°22E 213 C12
Qareh Tekān Iran 36°38N 49°29E 247 B6
Qarnein U.A.E. 24°56N 52°52E 247 E7
Qarokŭl = Karakul, Ozero Tajikistan 39°5N 73°25E 217 E8
Qarqan He → China 39°30N 88°30E 217 E11
Qarqaraly Kazakhstan 49°26N 75°30E 217 C9
Qarqin Afghan. 37°24N 66°4E 240 A2
Qarrasa Sudan 14°38N 32°5E 257 E3
Qarshi Uzbekistan 38°53N 65°48E 217 E7
Qartabā Lebanon 34°4N 35°50E 250 D6
Qārūh Kuwait 28°49N 48°46E 247 D6
Qaryat al Gharab Iraq 31°27N 44°48E 246 D5
Qaryat al 'Ulyā Si. Arabia 27°33N 47°42E 246 E5
Qarynzharyq Oyysy Kazakhstan 42°55N 54°25E 216 D4
Qaşbah, Râs al Si. Arabia 28°2N 34°38E 251 K5
Qāsemābād Iran 35°46N 51°30E 141 A3
Qashqadaryo □ Uzbekistan 38°35N 66°0E 217 E7
Qasigiannguit Greenland 68°50N 51°18W 154 D5
Qasr 'Amra Jordan 31°48N 36°35E 246 D3
Qaşr Bū Hadi Libya 31°1N 16°45E 258 B3
Qasr-e Fīrūzeh Iran 35°29N 51°31E 141 B3
Qaşr-e Qand Iran 26°15N 60°45E 247 E9
Qaşr-e Shīrīn Iran 34°31N 45°35E 213 E11
Qasr Farâfra Egypt 27°0N 28°1E 256 B2
Qaşr Larocu Libya 26°32N 13°19E 258 C2
Qasuittuq = Resolute Canada 74°42N 94°54W 295 C13
Qa'ţabah Yemen 13°51N 44°42E 248 D4
Qatanā Syria 33°26N 36°4E 250 E7
Qaţānan, Ra's Yemen 12°21N 53°33E 249 D6
Qatane West Bank 31°50N 35°6E 123 B1
Qatar ■ Asia 25°30N 51°15E 247 E6
Qatlīsh Iran 37°50N 57°19E 247 B8
Qattâra Egypt 30°12N 27°3E 256 A2
Qattâra, Munkhafed el Egypt 29°30N 27°30E 256 B2
Qattâra Depression = Qattâra, Munkhafed el Egypt 29°30N 27°30E 256 B2
Qawām al Ḩamzah = Al Ḩamzah Iraq 31°43N 44°58E 246 D5
Qawra Point Malta 35°58N 14°26E 206 F7
Qāyen Iran 33°40N 59°10E 247 C8
Qaynar Kazakhstan 49°12N 77°22E 217 C9
Qazaly Kazakhstan 45°45N 62°6E 216 C6
Qazaqstan = Kazakhstan ■ Asia 50°0N 70°0E 217 C8
Qazaqtyng Usaqshogylyghy Kazakhstan 50°0N 72°0E 217 C8
Qazax Azerbaijan 41°5N 45°21E 191 K7
Qazımämmäd Azerbaijan 40°3N 49°0E 191 K9
Qazvīn Iran 36°15N 50°0E 247 B6
Qazvīn □ Iran 36°20N 50°0E 247 B6
Qazyghurt Kazakhstan 41°45N 69°23E 217 D7
Qeisari = Caesarea Israel 32°30N 34°53E 251 F5
Qeissan Sudan 11°4N 34°40E 257 E3
Qena Egypt 26°10N 32°43E 256 B3
Qena, W. → Egypt 26°12N 32°44E 256 B3
Qeqertarsuaq Qaasuitsup, Greenland 69°45N 53°30W 154 D5
Qeqertarsuaq Qaasuitsup, Greenland 69°15N 53°38W 154 D5
Qeqertarsuatsiaat Greenland 63°5N 50°45W 154 E5
Qeqqata □ Greenland 66°30N 48°0W 154 D6
Qeshlāq Iran 34°55N 46°28E 213 E12
Qeshm Iran 26°55N 56°10E 247 E8
Qeydār Iran 36°6N 48°35E 213 D13
Qeys Iran 26°32N 53°58E 249 A6
Qezel Owzen → Iran 36°45N 49°22E 247 B6
Qezi'ot Israel 30°52N 34°26E 251 H5
Qi Xian China 34°40N 114°48E 226 G8
Qian Gorlos China 45°5N 124°42E 227 B13
Qian Hai China 22°32N 113°54E 219 a
Qian Xian China 34°31N 108°15E 226 G5
Qian'an China 40°0N 118°41E 227 E10
Qiancheng China 27°12N 109°50E 228 D7
Qianjiang Guangxi Zhuangzu, China 23°38N 108°58E 228 F7
Qianjiang Hubei, China 30°24N 112°55E 229 B9
Qianjiang Sichuan, China 29°33N 108°47E 228 C7
Qianjin China 47°34N 133°4E 219 B15
Qianmen China 39°51N 116°21E 114 B2
Qianshan Anhui, China 30°37N 116°35E 229 B11
Qianshan Guangdong, China 22°15N 113°31E 219 a
Qianwei China 29°13N 103°56E 228 C4
Qianxi China 27°3N 106°3E 228 D6
Qianyang Hunan, China 27°18N 110°10E 229 D8
Qianyang Shaanxi, China 34°40N 107°8E 226 G4
Qianyang Zhejiang, China 30°11N 119°25E 229 B12
Qi'ao China 22°25N 113°39E 219 a
Qi'ao Dao China 22°25N 113°38E 219 a
Qiaocun China 39°56N 112°55E 226 E7
Qiaojia China 26°56N 102°58E 228 D4
Qichun China 30°18N 115°25E 229 B10
Qidong Hunan, China 26°49N 112°7E 229 D9
Qidong Jiangsu, China 31°48N 121°38E 229 B13
Qiemo China 38°8N 85°32E 217 E11
Qijiang China 28°57N 106°35E 228 C6
Qijiaojing China 43°28N 91°36E 217 D12
Qikiqtarjuaq Canada 67°33N 63°0W 295 D19
Qila Saifullāh Pakistan 30°45N 68°17E 242 D3
Qilian Shan China 38°30N 96°0E 218 D8
Qimei = Ch'imei Taiwan 23°12N 119°25E 225 C1
Qimen China 29°50N 117°42E 229 C11
Qin He → China 35°1N 113°22E 226 G7
Qin Jiang → Guangxi Zhuangzu, China 21°53N 108°35E 228 F7
Qin Jiang → Jiangxi, China 26°15N 115°55E 229 D10
Qin Ling = Qinling Shandi China 33°50N 108°10E 226 H5
Qināb, W. → Yemen 17°55N 49°59E 249 C5
Qin'an China 34°48N 105°40E 226 G3
Qing Xian China 38°35N 116°45E 226 E9
Qingcheng China 37°15N 117°40E 227 F9
Qingcheng Shan China 30°58N 103°31E 228 B4
Qingchuan China 32°36N 105°9E 226 H3
Qingdao China 36°5N 120°20E 227 F11
Qingfeng China 35°52N 115°8E 226 G8
Qinghai □ China 36°0N 98°0E 218 D8
Qinghai Hu China 36°40N 100°10E 218 D9
Qinghe China 46°37N 90°25E 217 C12
Qinghecheng China 41°28N 124°15E 224 B2
Qinghemen China 41°48N 121°25E 227 D11
Qinghuayuan China 39°59N 116°19E 114 B1
Qingjian China 37°8N 110°8E 226 F6
Qingjiang = Huaiyin China 33°30N 119°2E 227 H10
Qingliu China 26°11N 116°48E 229 D11
Qinglong China 25°49N 105°12E 228 E5
Qingningsi China 31°16N 121°33E 138 B2
Qingping China 26°39N 107°47E 228 D6
Qingshui China 34°48N 106°8E 226 G4
Qingshuihe China 39°55N 111°35E 226 E6
Qingtian China 28°12N 120°15E 229 C13
Qingtongxia China 38°2N 106°3E 226 E4
Qingtongxia Shuiku China 37°50N 105°58E 226 F3
Qingxi China 27°8N 108°43E 228 D7
Qingxu China 37°34N 112°22E 226 F7
Qingyang Anhui, China 30°38N 117°50E 229 B11
Qingyang Gansu, China 36°2N 107°55E 226 F4
Qingyi Jiang → China 29°32N 103°44E 228 C4
Qingyuan Guangdong, China 23°40N 112°59E 229 F9
Qingyuan Liaoning, China 42°10N 124°55E 224 A2
Qingyuan Zhejiang, China 27°36N 119°3E 229 D12
Qingyun China 37°45N 117°20E 227 F9
Qingzhen China 26°31N 106°25E 228 D6
Qinhuangdao China 39°56N 119°30E 227 E10
Qinling Shandi China 33°50N 108°10E 226 H5
Qinshui = Ch'ingshui Taiwan 24°16N 120°34E 225 B2
Qinshui China 35°40N 112°8E 226 G7
Qinyang = Jiyuan China 35°7N 112°57E 226 G7
Qinyang China 35°5N 112°56E 226 G7
Qinyuan China 36°29N 112°20E 226 F7
Qinzhou China 21°58N 108°38E 228 G7
Qionghai China 19°15N 110°26E 229 a
Qionglai China 30°25N 103°31E 228 B4
Qionglai Shan China 31°0N 102°30E 228 B4
Qiongshan China 19°51N 110°26E 229 a
Qiongzhou Haixia China 20°10N 110°15E 229 a
Qiqihar China 47°26N 124°0E 219 B13
Qira China 37°0N 80°48E 217 E10
Qiraîya, W. → Egypt 30°27N 34°0E 251 H5
Qiryat Ata Israel 32°47N 35°6E 250 F6
Qiryat Gat Israel 31°32N 34°46E 251 G5
Qiryat Mal'akhi Israel 31°44N 34°44E 251 G5
Qiryat Shemona Israel 33°13N 35°35E 250 E6
Qiryat Yam Israel 32°51N 35°4E 250 F6
Qirzah, W. → Libya 30°56N 14°31E 258 B2
Qishan = Ch'ishan Taiwan 22°44N 120°31E 225 D2
Qishan China 34°25N 107°38E 226 G4
Qishn Yemen 15°26N 51°40E 249 D5
Qitai China 44°2N 89°35E 217 D11
Qitaihe China 45°48N 130°51E 220 B5
Qitbīt, W. → Oman 19°15N 54°23E 249 C6
Qiubei China 24°2N 104°12E 228 E5
Qixia China 37°17N 120°52E 227 F11
Qiyang China 26°35N 111°50E 229 D8
Qızılağac Körfäzi Azerbaijan 39°9N 49°0E 213 C13
Qobda Kazakhstan 50°55N 54°31E 216 B4
Qods Iran 35°45N 51°15E 247 C6
Qojūr Iran 36°12N 47°55E 246 B5
Qolhak Iran 35°45N 51°26E 141 A2
Qom Iran 34°40N 51°0E 247 C6
Qom □ Iran 34°40N 51°0E 247 C6
Qomolangma Feng = Everest, Mt. Nepal 28°5N 86°58E 243 E12
Qomsheh Iran 32°0N 51°55E 247 D6
Qong Muztag China 35°42N 82°22E 217 E10
Qoqek = Tacheng China 46°40N 82°58E 217 C10
Qoqon = Qŭqon Uzbekistan 40°31N 70°56E 217 D8
Qoraqalpoghistan □ Uzbekistan 43°0N 58°0E 216 D5
Qorghalzhyn Kazakhstan 50°25N 69°11E 217 B7
Qormi Malta 35°53N 14°28E 206 F7
Qorveh Iran 35°10N 47°48E 213 E12
Qosshaghyl Kazakhstan 46°40N 54°0E 187 E9
Qostanay Kazakhstan 53°10N 63°35E 216 B6
Qotanqaraghay Kazakhstan 49°10N 85°36E 217 C11
Qoţūr Iran 38°28N 44°25E 213 C11
Qoz Salsilgo C.A.R. 10°45N 22°54E 264 A4
Qrejten Point Malta 35°57N 14°27E 206 F7
Qu Jiang → China 30°1N 106°24E 228 B6
Qu Xian China 30°48N 106°58E 228 B6
Quabbin Res. U.S.A. 42°20N 72°20W 313 D12
Quadraro Italy 41°51N 12°33E 136 B2
Quaid-i-Azam Pakistan 24°50N 66°59E 123 A1
Quairading Australia 32°0S 117°21E 279 F2
Quakenbrück Germany 52°41N 7°57E 178 C3
Quakertown U.S.A. 40°26N 75°21W 313 F9
Qualicum Beach Canada 49°22N 124°26W 296 D4
Quambatook Australia 35°49S 143°34E 282 C5
Quambone Australia 30°57S 147°53E 283 A7
Quamby Australia 20°22S 140°17E 280 C3
Quan Long = Ca Mau Vietnam 9°7N 105°8E 237 H5
Quanah U.S.A. 34°18N 99°44W 314 D5
Quandialla Australia 34°1S 147°47E 283 C7
Quang Ngai Vietnam 15°13N 108°58E 236 E7
Quang Tri Vietnam 16°45N 107°13E 236 D6
Quang Yen Vietnam 20°56N 106°52E 228 G6
Quannan China 24°45N 114°33E 229 E10
Quantock Hills U.K. 51°8N 3°10W 169 F4
Quanyang China 42°21N 127°32E 227 C14
Quanzhou Fujian, China 24°55N 118°34E 229 E12
Quanzhou Guangxi Zhuangzu, China 25°57N 111°5E 229 E8
Qu'Appelle → Canada 50°33N 103°53W 297 C8
Quaqtaq Canada 60°55N 69°40W 295 E18
Quaraí Brazil 30°15S 56°20W 334 C4
Quarré-les-Tombes France 47°21N 4°0E 173 E11
Quarteira Portugal 37°4N 8°6W 195 H2
Quarter, The Anguilla 18°13N 63°3W 322 a
Quartier D'Orléans St.-Martin 18°5N 63°2W 322 a
Quartier Militaire Mauritius 20°14S 57°35E 272 e
Quartiere Zingone Italy 45°25N 9°3E 128 B1
Quartu Sant'Élena Italy 39°15N 9°10E 200 C2
Quartzsite U.S.A. 33°40N 114°13W 307 M12
Quatre, I. à St. Vincent 12°59N 61°15W 323 n
Quatre Bornes Mauritius 20°15S 57°28E 272 e
Quatsino Sd. Canada 50°25N 127°58W 296 C3
Quba Azerbaijan 41°21N 48°32E 191 K9
Qubeiba West Bank 31°50N 35°8E 123 A1
Qūchān Iran 37°10N 58°27E 247 B8
Quds Iraq 33°23N 44°24E 113 A2
Queanbeyan Australia 35°17S 149°14E 283 C8
Québec Canada 46°52N 71°13W 299 C5
Québec □ Canada 48°0N 74°0W 298 B6
Quebo Guinea-Biss. 11°20N 14°56W 262 C2
Quebrada del Condorito △ Argentina 31°49S 64°40W 334 C3
Quebradillas Puerto Rico 18°29N 66°56W 321 b
Quedlinburg Germany 51°47N 11°8E 178 D7
Queen Alexandra Ra. Antarctica 85°0S 170°0E 151 E11
Queen Charlotte B. Falk. Is. 51°50S 60°40W 153 f
Queen Charlotte City Canada 53°15N 132°2W 296 C2
Queen Charlotte Is. = Haida Gwaii Canada 53°20N 132°10W 296 C2
Queen Charlotte Sd. B.C., Canada 51°0N 128°0W 296 C3
Queen Charlotte Sd. N.Z. 41°10S 174°15E 285 B9
Queen Charlotte Strait Canada 50°45N 127°10W 296 C3
Queen City U.S.A. 40°25N 92°34W 310 D4
Queen Elizabeth △ Uganda 0°0 30°0E 268 C3
Queen Elizabeth Is. Canada 76°0N 95°0W 295 B13
Queen Elizabeth Land Antarctica 85°0S 60°0W 151 E17
Queen Elizabeth Nat. Park = Ruwenzori △ Uganda 0°20N 30°0E 268 B2
Queen Elizabeth Olympic Park London, U.K. 51°33N 0°0 125 A3
Queen Mary Land Antarctica 70°0S 95°0E 151 D7
Queen Mary Res. U.K. 51°24N 0°27W 125 B1
Queen Maud G. Canada 68°15N 102°30W 294 D11
Queen Maud Land = Dronning Maud Land Antarctica 72°30S 12°0E 151 D3
Queen Maud Mts. Antarctica 86°0S 160°0W 151 E12
Queen Street Edinburgh, U.K. 121 a1
Queen Victoria Market Australia 37°47S 144°57W 128 A1
Queens Channel Australia 15°0S 129°30E 278 C4
Queens-Midtown Tunnel New York, U.S.A. 132 d2
Queen's Quay Terminal Toronto, Canada 141 c2
Queensboro Bridge New York, U.S.A. 132 c3
Queensbury U.K. 51°35N 0°16W 125 A2
Queenscliff Australia 38°16S 144°39E 282 E6
Queenscliffe Australia 33°47S 151°17E 139 A2
Queensferry U.K. 55°59N 3°23W 121 B1
Queensland U.S.A. 31°46N 83°14W 316 D6
Queensland □ Australia 22°0S 142°0E 280 C3
Queensland Plateau Pac. Oc. 17°0S 150°0E 276 D8
Queenstown = Cobh Ireland 51°51N 8°17W 166 E3
Queenstown Tas., Australia 42°4S 145°35E 281 G4
Queenstown N.Z. 45°1S 168°40E 285 F3
Queenstown Singapore 1°18N 103°48E 138 B2
Queenstown Eastern Cape, S. Africa 31°52S 26°52E 270 D4
Queets U.S.A. 47°32N 124°19W 306 C2
Queguay Grande → Uruguay 32°9S 58°9W 334 C4
Queimada, Pta. da Azores 38°23N 28°14W 153 d1
Queimadas Brazil 11°0S 39°38W 332 D4
Queiros, C. Vanuatu 14°55S 167°1E 287 D5
Quela Angola 9°10S 16°56E 265 D3
Quelimane Mozam. 17°53S 36°58E 269 F4
Quellerina S. Africa 26°9S 27°56E 123 A1
Quellón Chile 43°7S 73°37W 336 B2
Quelo Angola 6°29S 12°36E 265 D2
Quelpart = Jeju-do S. Korea 33°29N 126°34E 224 a
Queluz Portugal 38°45N 9°14W 126 A1
Quemado N. Mex., U.S.A. 34°20N 108°30W 305 J9
Quemado Tex., U.S.A. 28°56N 100°37W 314 G4
Quemoy = Chinmen Taiwan 24°26N 118°19E 225 a
Quemú-Quemú Argentina 36°3S 63°36W 334 D3
Quepem India 15°13N 74°3E 245 G2
Quequén Argentina 38°30S 58°30W 334 D4
Querco Peru 13°50S 74°52W 330 C3
Querétaro Mexico 20°36N 100°23W 318 C4
Querétaro □ Mexico 21°0N 99°55W 318 C5
Querfurt Germany 51°23N 11°35E 178 D7
Quérigut France 42°42N 2°6E 174 F6
Querqueville France 49°40N 1°42W 172 C5
Quesada Spain 37°51N 3°4W 195 H7
Queshan China 32°55N 114°2E 229 A10
Quesnel Canada 53°0N 122°30W 296 C4
Quesnel → Canada 52°58N 122°29W 296 C4
Quesnel L. Canada 52°30N 121°20W 296 C4
Questa U.S.A. 36°42N 105°36W 305 H11
Questembert France 47°40N 2°28W 172 E4
Quetena Bolivia 22°10S 67°25W 330 E4
Quetico ⌂ Canada 48°30N 91°45W 298 C1
Quetrequile Argentina 41°33S 69°22W 336 B3
Quetta Pakistan 30°15N 66°55E 242 D2
Quetzaltenango Guatemala 14°50N 91°30W 320 D1
Queulat △ Chile 44°29S 72°24W 336 B2
Quevedo Ecuador 1°2S 79°29W 328 D2
Queyras ⌂ France 44°45N 6°50E 175 D10
Quezon Phil. 9°15N 117°59E 233 G1
Quezon □ Phil. 14°40N 121°30E 232 D3
Quezon △ Phil. 14°0N 121°55E 232 D3
Quezon City Phil. 14°37N 121°2E 127 B2
Qufār Si. Arabia 27°26N 41°37E 246 E4
Qufu China 35°36N 116°58E 226 G9
Qui Nhon Vietnam 13°40N 109°13E 236 F7
Quibala Angola 10°46S 14°59E 265 E2
Quibaxe Angola 8°24S 14°27E 265 D2
Quibdó Colombia 5°42N 76°40W 328 B2
Quiberon France 47°29N 3°9W 172 E3
Quiberon, Presqu'île de France 47°30N 3°8W 172 E3
Quiçama △ Angola 9°41S 13°35E 265 D2
Quickborn Germany 53°42N 9°52E 178 B5
Quiet L. Canada 61°5N 133°5W 296 A2
Quiindy Paraguay 25°58S 57°14W 334 B4
Quilá Mexico 24°23N 107°13W 318 C3
Quilán, C. Chile 43°15S 74°30W 336 B2
Quilcene U.S.A. 47°49N 122°53W 306 C4
Quilenda Angola 10°39S 14°23E 265 E2
Quilengues Angola 14°12S 14°12E 265 E2
Quilicura Chile 33°22S 70°43W 137 B1
Quilimarí Chile 32°5S 71°30W 334 C1
Quilino Argentina 30°14S 64°29W 334 C3
Quill, The St. Eustatius 17°28N 62°57W 322 a
Quillabamba Peru 12°50S 72°50W 330 C3
Quillacollo Bolivia 17°26S 66°17W 330 D4
Quillagua Chile 21°40S 69°40W 334 A2
Quillan France 42°53N 2°10E 174 F6
Quillota Chile 32°54S 71°16W 334 C1
Quilmes Argentina 34°43S 58°15W 334 C4
Quilon = Kollam India 8°50N 76°38E 245 K3
Quilpie Australia 26°35S 144°11E 281 D3
Quilpué Chile 33°5S 71°33W 334 C1
Quilua Mozam. 16°17S 39°54E 269 F4
Quimbele Angola 6°17S 16°41E 265 D3
Quimbo Angola 14°4S 16°11E 265 E3
Quimbonge Angola 8°36S 18°30E 265 D3
Quime Bolivia 17°2S 67°15W 330 D4
Quimilí Argentina 27°40S 62°30W 334 B3
Quimper France 48°0N 4°9W 172 E2
Quimperlé France 47°53N 3°33W 172 E3
Quinam B. Trin. & Tob. 10°4N 61°30W 323 t
Quinault → U.S.A. 47°21N 124°18W 306 C2
Quince Mil Peru 13°15S 70°40W 330 C3
Quincy Calif., U.S.A. 39°56N 120°57W 306 F6
Quincy Fla., U.S.A. 30°35N 84°34W 316 E5
Quincy Ill., U.S.A. 39°56N 91°23W 310 E5
Quincy Mass., U.S.A. 42°14N 71°0W 116 B2
Quincy Mich., U.S.A. 41°57N 84°53W 311 C12
Quincy Wash., U.S.A. 47°14N 119°51W 304 C4
Quincy B. U.S.A. 42°16N 70°59W 116 B3
Quines Argentina 32°13S 65°48W 334 C2
Quinga Mozam. 15°49S 40°15E 269 F5
Quingey France 47°7N 5°52E 173 E12
Quingombe Angola 6°38S 13°1E 265 D2
Quinhagak U.S.A. 59°45N 161°54W 303 G7
Quinhámel Guinea-Biss. 11°53N 15°51W 262 C1
Quiniluban Group Phil. 11°27N 120°48E 233 F3
Quinta Normal Chile 33°26S 70°42W 137 B1
Quintana de la Serena Spain 38°45N 5°40W 195 G5
Quintana Roo □ Mexico 19°40N 88°30W 319 D7
Quintanar de la Orden Spain 39°36N 3°5W 195 F7
Quintanar de la Sierra Spain 41°57N 2°55W 196 D2
Quintanar del Rey Spain 39°21N 1°56W 197 F3
Quintero Chile 32°45S 71°30W 334 C1
Quintin France 48°26N 2°56W 172 D4
Quinto Spain 41°25N 0°32W 196 D4
Quinto de Stampi Italy 45°24N 9°10E 128 B2
Quinto Romano Italy 45°28N 9°7E 128 B1
Quinzáu Angola 6°51S 12°44E 265 D2
Quípar → Spain 38°15N 1°40W 197 G3
Quipeio Angola 12°27S 15°30E 265 E3
Quirihue Chile 36°15S 72°35W 334 D1
Quirima Angola 10°47S 18°6E 265 E3
Quirimbas △ Mozam. 12°30S 40°15E 269 E5
Quirimbo Angola 10°36S 14°12E 265 E2
Quirinale Italy 41°53N 12°29E 136 B1
Quirinale, Palazzo dei Rome, Italy 136 b3
Quirindi Australia 31°28S 150°40E 283 A9
Quirino □ Phil. 16°15N 121°40E 232 C3
Quirinópolis Brazil 18°32S 50°30W 333 E1
Quiroga Spain 42°28N 7°18W 194 C3
Quiruvilca Peru 8°1S 78°19W 330 B2
Quissac France 43°55N 4°0E 175 E8
Quissanga Mozam. 12°24S 40°28E 269 E5
Quissico Mozam. 24°42S 34°44E 271 B5
Quissongo Angola 10°2S 15°5E 265 E3
Quitapa Angola 10°20S 18°19E 265 E3
Quitilipi Argentina 26°50S 60°13W 334 B3
Quitman U.S.A. 30°47N 83°34W 316 E6
Quito Ecuador 0°15S 78°35W 328 D2
Quitralco △ Chile 45°43S 73°25W 336 C2
Quixadá Brazil 4°55S 39°0W 332 B4
Quixaxe Mozam. 15°17S 40°4E 269 F5
Quixeramobim Brazil 5°12S 39°17W 332 C4
Quixico Angola 7°59S 14°25E 265 D2
Quixinge Angola 9°52S 14°23E 265 D2
Quizenga Angola 9°21S 15°28E 265 D3
Qujing China 25°32N 103°41E 228 E4
Qulan Kazakhstan 42°55N 72°43E 214 E8
Qul'ân, Jazâ'ir Egypt 24°22N 35°31E 246 E2
Qulsary Kazakhstan 46°59N 54°1E 187 E9
Qumbu S. Africa 31°10S 28°48E 271 D4
Qunayyin, Sabkhat al Libya 30°10N 21°0E 258 B4
Quneitra = Al Qunayţirah Syria 33°5N 35°45E 250 F6
Qŭnghirot Uzbekistan 43°2N 58°50E 216 D5
Qu'nyido China 31°15N 98°6E 228 B2
Quoin I. Australia 14°54S 129°32E 278 B4
Quoin Pt. S. Africa 34°46S 19°37E 270 D2
Quorn Australia 32°25S 138°5E 282 B3
Qŭqon Uzbekistan 40°31N 70°56E 217 D8
Qurein Sudan 13°30N 34°50E 257 E3
Qŭrghonteppa Tajikistan 37°50N 68°47E 217 E7
Qurimbas △ Mozam. 12°20S 40°10E 269 E5
Qurnat as Sawdā' Lebanon 34°18N 36°6E 250 D7
Quryq Kazakhstan 43°12N 51°39E 216 D4
Qûs Egypt 25°55N 32°50E 256 B3
Qusar Azerbaijan 41°25N 48°26E 191 K9
Quşaybā' Si. Arabia 26°53N 43°35E 246 E4
Qusaybah Iraq 34°24N 40°59E 213 E9
Quşay'ir Yemen 14°55N 50°20E 249 D5
Quseir Egypt 26°7N 34°16E 246 E2
Quseir Amra = Qasr 'Amra Jordan 31°48N 36°35E 246 D3
Qūshchī Iran 37°59N 45°3E 213 D11
Qusmuryn Kazakhstan 52°27N 64°36E 216 B6
Qusmuryn Köli Kazakhstan 52°41N 64°48E 216 B6
Qutang Gorge = Qutang Xia China 31°0N 109°40E 228 B7
Qutang Xia China 31°0N 109°40E 228 B7
Qutb Minar India 28°31N 77°11E 120 B2
Quthing Lesotho 30°25S 27°36E 271 D4
Qūţīābād Iran 35°47N 48°30E 213 E13
Quttinirpaaq △ Canada 82°13N 72°13W 295 A17
Quwayq → Syria 36°20N 37°10E 250 B8
Quweisna Egypt 30°34N 31°9E 251 H2
Quwo China 35°38N 111°25E 226 G6
Quyang China 38°35N 114°40E 226 E8
Quynh Nhai Vietnam 21°49N 103°33E 236 B4
Quyon Canada 45°31N 76°14W 313 A8
Quzhou China 28°57N 118°54E 229 C12
Quzi China 36°20N 107°20E 226 F4
Qvareli Georgia 41°57N 45°47E 191 K7
Qytet Stalin = Kuçovë Albania 40°47N 19°57E 202 F3
Qyzylorda Kazakhstan 44°48N 65°28E 216 D7
Qyzylorda □ Kazakhstan 45°0N 65°0E 216 D6
Qyzylzhar Kazakhstan 48°17N 69°38E 217 C7


# R


R.F.K. Memorial Stadium U.S.A. 38°52N 76°58W 143 B3
Ra, Ko Thailand 9°13N 98°16E 237 H2
Raab Austria 48°21N 13°39E 180 C6
Raahe Finland 64°40N 24°28E 160 D21
Raalte Neths. 52°23N 6°16E 170 B6
Ra'ananna Israel 32°10N 34°52E 251 F5
Raas Indonesia 7°8S 114°33E 235 D4
Raasay U.K. 57°25N 6°4W 167 D2
Raasay, Sd. of U.K. 57°30N 6°8W 167 D2
Raasdorf Austria 48°14N 16°33E 142 A3
Raasepori Finland 60°0N 23°26E 188 B2
Rab Croatia 44°45N 14°45E 199 D11
Raba Indonesia 8°36S 118°55E 235 D5
Rába → Hungary 47°38N 17°38E 182 C2
Raba → Poland 50°8N 20°30E 185 H7
Rabaçal → Portugal 41°30N 7°12W 194 D3
Rabah Nigeria 13°5N 5°30E 263 C6
Rabai Kenya 3°50S 39°31E 268 C4
Rabak Sudan 13°9N 32°44E 257 E3
Rabaraba Papua N. G. 9°58S 149°49E 286 E5
Rabastens France 43°50N 1°43E 174 E5
Rabastens-de-Bigorre France 43°23N 0°9E 174 E4
Rabat = Victoria Malta 36°3N 14°14E 206 E6
Rabat Malta 35°53N 14°24E 206 F7
Rabat Morocco 34°2N 6°48W 260 B3
Rabat □ Morocco 34°10N 6°45W 260 B3
Rabaul Papua N. G. 4°24S 152°18E 286 C7
Rabbit Flat Australia 20°11S 130°1E 278 D5
Rabbit Lake Mine Canada 58°4N 104°5W 297 B8
Rabi Fiji 16°30S 179°59W 287 A3
Rābigh Si. Arabia 22°50N 39°5E 248 B2
Rabka Poland 49°37N 19°59E 185 J6
Râbniţa Moldova 47°45N 29°0E 183 C14
Rābor Iran 29°17N 56°55E 247 D8
Rabwah = Chenab Nagar Pakistan 31°45N 72°55E 242 D5
Rača Serbia 44°14N 21°0E 202 B4
Răcăciuni Romania 46°20N 26°59E 183 D11
Răcăşdia Romania 44°59N 21°36E 182 F6
Racconigi Italy 44°46N 7°46E 198 D4
Raccoon → U.S.A. 41°35N 93°37W 310 C3
Raccoon Cr. → U.S.A. 39°47N 87°23W 311 E9
Race, C. Canada 46°40N 53°5W 299 C9
Race Course Jamaica 17°51N 77°20W 320 a
Race Pond U.S.A. 31°1N 82°8W 316 D7
Rach Gia Vietnam 10°5N 105°5E 237 G5
Rach Soi Vietnam 9°57N 105°7E 237 H5
Racha Noi, Ko Thailand 7°30N 98°19E 237 J2
Racha Yai, Ko Thailand 7°36N 98°21E 237 J2
Rachid Mauritania 18°45N 11°35W 262 B2
Raciąż Poland 52°46N 20°10E 185 F7
Racibórz Poland 50°7N 18°18E 185 H5
Racichy Belarus 53°44N 23°42E 184 E10
Racine U.S.A. 42°44N 87°47W 311 B9
Račisdorf = Rača Serbia 44°14N 21°0E 202 B4
Rackerby U.S.A. 39°26N 121°22W 306 F5
Råda Sweden 60°0N 13°36E 162 E7
Radama, Nosy Madag. 14°0S 47°47E 272 A2
Radama, Saikanosy Madag. 14°16S 47°53E 272 A2
Radan Serbia 42°59N 21°29E 202 D5
Rădăuţi Romania 47°50N 25°59E 183 C10
Rădăuţi-Prut Romania 48°14N 26°48E 183 B11
Radbuza → Czech Rep. 49°45N 13°22E 180 B6
Radcliff U.S.A. 37°51N 85°57W 311 G11
Radcliffe College U.S.A. 42°22N 71°7W 116 A2
Radeberg Germany 51°7N 13°55E 178 D9
Radebeul Germany 51°6N 13°39E 178 D9
Radeče Slovenia 46°5N 15°14E 199 B12
Radekhiv Ukraine 50°25N 24°32E 177 C13
Radekhov = Radekhiv Ukraine 50°25N 24°32E 177 C13
Radenthein Austria 46°48N 13°43E 180 E6
Radew → Poland 54°2N 15°52E 184 D2
Radford U.S.A. 37°8N 80°34W 309 G13
Radhanpur India 23°50N 71°38E 242 H4
Rådhus Oslo, Norway 133 b1
Radhwa, Jabal Si. Arabia 24°34N 38°18E 246 E3
Radika → Macedonia 41°38N 20°37E 202 E4
Radisson Qué., Canada 53°47N 77°37W 298 B4
Radisson Sask., Canada 52°30N 107°20W 297 C7
Radium Hot Springs Canada 50°35N 116°2W 296 C5
Radlice Czech Rep. 50°3N 14°23E 135 B2
Radlje ob Dravi Slovenia 46°38N 15°13E 199 B12
Radmannsdorf = Radovljica Slovenia 46°22N 14°12E 199 B11
Radnevo Bulgaria 42°17N 25°58E 203 D9
Radnice Czech Rep. 49°51N 13°35E 180 B6
Radnor Forest U.K. 52°17N 3°10W 169 E4
Radolfzell Germany 47°45N 8°59E 179 H4
Radom Poland 51°23N 21°12E 185 G8
Radom △ Sudan 9°20N 23°50E 264 A4
Radomir Bulgaria 42°37N 22°59E 202 D6
Radomka → Poland 51°43N 21°28E 185 G8
Radomsko Poland 51°5N 19°28E 185 G6
Radomyshl Ukraine 50°30N 29°12E 177 C15
Radomyśl Wielki Poland 50°14N 21°15E 185 H8
Radość Poland 52°11N 21°11E 143 B3
Radoszyce Poland 51°4N 20°15E 185 G7
Radotín Czech Rep. 49°59N 14°21E 135 C2
Radoviš Macedonia 41°38N 22°28E 202 E6
Radovljica Slovenia 46°22N 14°12E 199 B11
Radstadt Austria 47°24N 13°28E 180 D6
Radstock, C. Australia 33°12S 134°20E 281 E1
Răducăneni Romania 46°58N 27°54E 183 D12
Raduša Macedonia 42°7N 21°15E 202 D5
Raduzhnyy Russia 62°5N 77°28E 214 C8
Radvanichy Belarus 52°1N 24°0E 185 F11
Radviliškis Lithuania 55°49N 23°33E 184 C10
Radville Canada 49°30N 104°15W 297 D8
Raḑwá, J. Si. Arabia 24°34N 38°18E 256 C4
Radymno Poland 49°59N 22°52E 185 J9
Radzanów Poland 52°56N 20°8E 185 F7
Radziejów Poland 52°40N 18°30E 185 F5
Radzyń Chełmiński Poland 53°23N 18°55E 184 E5
Radzyń Podlaski Poland 51°47N 22°37E 185 G9
Rae Canada 62°50N 116°3W 296 A5
Rae Bareli India 26°18N 81°20E 243 F9
Rae Isthmus Canada 66°40N 87°30W 295 D14
Raeren Belgium 50°41N 6°7E 170 D6
Raeside, L. Australia 29°20S 122°0E 279 E3
Raetihi N.Z. 39°25S 175°17E 284 F4
Rafaela Argentina 31°10S 61°30W 334 C3
Rafah Gaza Strip 31°18N 34°14E 251 G5
Rafai C.A.R. 4°59N 23°58E 264 B4
Rafat West Bank 31°52N 35°11E 123 A2
Raffadali Italy 37°24N 13°32E 200 E6
Raffili South Sudan 6°50N 28°0E 257 F2
Raffles Hotel Singapore 138 b3
Raffles Park Singapore 1°19N 103°48E 138 B2
Rafḩā Si. Arabia 29°35N 43°35E 246 D4
Rafina Greece 38°2N 24°0E 204 C6
Rafsanjān Iran 30°30N 56°5E 247 D8
Raft Pt. Australia 16°4S 124°26E 278 C3
Raga South Sudan 8°28N 25°41E 257 F2
Raga → South Sudan 8°41N 25°52E 257 F2
Ragachow Belarus 53°8N 30°5E 177 B16
Ragag Sudan 10°59N 24°40E 257 E1
Ragang, Mt. Phil. 7°43N 124°32E 233 H5
Ragay Phil. 13°49N 122°47E 232 E4
Ragay G. Phil. 13°30N 122°45E 232 E4
Ragged, Mt. Australia 33°27S 123°25E 279 F3
Rāgh Afghan. 37°32N 70°27E 240 A3
Raghunathpalli India 22°14N 84°48E 243 H11
Raghunathpur India 23°33N 86°40E 243 H12
Raglan N.Z. 37°55S 174°55E 284 D3
Raglan Harbour N.Z. 37°47S 174°50E 284 D3
Ragland U.S.A. 33°45N 86°9W 316 B3
Ragnit = Neman Russia 55°2N 22°2E 184 C9
Raguda, Ghubbet Somalia 10°43N 46°22E 267 B6
Ragusa = Dubrovnik Croatia 42°39N 18°6E 202 D2
Ragusa Italy 36°55N 14°44E 201 F7
Raha Indonesia 4°55S 123°0E 231 E6
Rahad, Nahr ed → Sudan 14°28N 33°31E 257 E3
Rahad al Bardī Sudan 11°20N 23°40E 259 F4
Rahaeng = Tak Thailand 16°52N 99°8E 236 D2
Rahat Israel 31°24N 34°45E 251 G5
Rahat, Ḩarrat Si. Arabia 23°0N 40°5E 256 C5
Rahatgarh India 23°47N 78°22E 243 H8
Rahden Germany 52°26N 8°36E 178 C4
Raheb, Ras ir- Malta 35°54N 14°20E 206 F7
Raheita Eritrea 12°46N 43°4E 257 E5
Raheng = Tak Thailand 16°52N 99°8E 236 D2
Raheny Ireland 53°22N 6°10W 120 A3
Rahimyar Khan Pakistan 28°30N 70°25E 242 E4
Rāhjerd Iran 34°22N 50°22E 247 C6
Rahnsdorf Germany 52°25N 13°41E 115 B5
Rahole ⌂ Kenya 0°5N 38°57E 268 B4
Råholt Norway 60°16N 11°11E 164 D8
Rahon India 31°3N 76°7E 242 D7
Rahotu N.Z. 39°20S 173°49E 284 F2
Rahovec Kosovo 42°24N 20°40E 202 D4
Rahuri India 19°23N 74°39E 244 E2
Rai, Hon Vietnam 9°48N 104°38E 237 H5
Raiatéa, Î. French Polynesia 16°50S 151°25W 289 f
Raichur India 16°10N 77°20E 245 F3
Raiford U.S.A. 30°4N 82°14W 316 E7
Raiganj India 25°37N 88°10E 243 G13
Raigarh India 21°56N 83°25E 244 D6
Raighar India 19°51N 82°6E 244 E6
Raijua Indonesia 10°37S 121°36E 231 F6
Raikot India 30°41N 75°42E 242 D6
Railton Australia 41°25S 146°28E 281 G4
Rainbow Bridge ⌂ U.S.A. 37°5N 110°58W 305 H8
Rainbow City U.S.A. 33°57N 86°5W 316 B3
Rainbow Lake Canada 58°30N 119°23W 296 B5
Rainier U.S.A. 46°53N 122°41W 306 D4
Rainier, Mt. U.S.A. 46°52N 121°46W 306 D5
Rainy L. Canada 48°42N 93°10W 297 D10
Rainy River Canada 48°43N 94°29W 297 D10
Raippaluoto Finland 63°13N 21°14E 160 E19
Raipur India 21°17N 81°45E 244 D5
Rairakhol India 21°4N 84°21E 244 D7
Ra'is Si. Arabia 23°33N 38°43E 256 C4
Raisen India 23°20N 77°48E 242 H8
Raisio Finland 60°28N 22°11E 188 B2
Raivavae French Polynesia 23°52S 147°40W 289 f
Raj Ghat Delhi, India 120 b3
Raj Nandgaon India 21°5N 81°5E 244 D5
Raj Nilgiri India 21°28N 86°46E 243 J12
Raja, Ujung Indonesia 3°40N 96°25E 234 B1
Raja Ampat, Kepulauan Indonesia 0°30S 130°0E 231 E8
Rajah Sikatuna △ Phil. 9°40N 124°20E 233 G5
Rajahmundry India 17°1N 81°48E 244 F5
Rajaji △ India 30°10N 78°20E 242 D8
Rajakylä Finland 60°15N 25°5E 121 B3
Rajampet India 14°11N 79°10E 245 G4
Rajang → Malaysia 2°30N 112°0E 235 B4
Rajang Mangroves △ Malaysia 2°6N 111°16E 235 B4
Rajanpur Pakistan 29°6N 70°19E 242 E4
Rajapalaiyam India 9°25N 77°35E 245 K3
Rajapur India 16°40N 73°31E 244 F1
Rajasthan □ India 26°45N 73°30E 242 F5
Rajasthan Canal = Indira Gandhi Canal India 28°0N 72°0E 242 F5
Rajauri India 33°25N 74°21E 243 C6
Rajbari Bangla. 23°47N 89°41E 241 D2
Rajendranagar India 17°18N 78°27E 244 F4
Rajgarh Mad. P., India 24°2N 76°45E 242 G7
Rajgarh Raj., India 27°14N 76°38E 242 F7
Rajgarh Raj., India 28°40N 75°25E 242 E6
Rajghat Dam India 24°45N 78°20E 244 B4
Rajgir India 25°2N 85°25E 243 G11
Rajgród Poland 53°42N 22°42E 184 E9
Rajim India 20°58N 81°53E 244 D5
Rajkot India 22°15N 70°56E 242 H4
Rajmahal Hills India 24°30N 87°30E 243 G12
Rajpath Delhi, India 120 c2
Rajpipla India 21°50N 73°30E 244 D1
Rajpur India 22°18N 74°21E 242 H6
Rajpura Delhi, India 28°41N 77°12E 120 A2
Rajpura Punjab, India 30°25N 76°32E 242 D7
Rajputana = Rajasthan □ India 26°45N 73°30E 242 F5
Rajsamand = Kankroli India 25°4N 73°53E 242 G5

Rajshahi Bangla. 24°22N 88°39E 241 C2
Rajshahi □ Bangla. 25°0N 89°0E 241 C2
Rājū Syria 36°40N 36°40E 250 B7
Rajula India 21°3N 71°26E 242 J4
Rajur India 20°7N 78°55E 244 D4
Rajura India 19°47N 79°22E 244 E4
Rakaia N.Z. 43°45S 172°1E 285 D7
Rakaia → N.Z. 43°36S 172°15E 285 D7
Rakan, Ra's Qatar 26°10N 51°20E 247 E6
Rakaposhi Pakistan 36°10N 74°25E 243 A6
Rakata, Pulau Indonesia 6°10S 105°20E 234 D3
Rakbah, Sahl Si. Arabia 22°15N 41°0E 256 C5
Rakhine □ Burma 19°0N 94°15E 241 F5
Rakhiv Ukraine 48°3N 24°12E 183 B9
Rakhni Pakistan 30°4N 69°56E 242 D3
Rakhni → Pakistan 29°31N 69°36E 242 E3
Rakhny-Lisovi Ukraine 48°47N 28°29E 183 B13
Rakhyūt Oman 16°44N 53°20E 249 C6
Rakiraki Fiji 17°22S 178°11E 287 A2
Rakitnoye Russia 45°36N 134°17E 220 B7
Rakitovo Bulgaria 41°59N 24°5E 203 E8
Rakiura = Stewart I. N.Z. 46°58S 167°54E 285 G2
Rakkestad Norway 59°25N 11°21E 164 E8
Rakoniewice Poland 52°10N 16°16E 185 F3
Rakops Botswana 21°1S 24°28E 270 B3
Rákos-patak → Hungary 47°29N 19°12E 117 B3
Rákoshegy Hungary 47°27N 19°14E 117 B3
Rákoskeresztúr Hungary 47°29N 19°15E 117 B3
Rákoskert Hungary 47°27N 19°18E 117 B3
Rákosliget Hungary 47°29N 19°16E 117 B3
Rákospalota Hungary 47°34N 19°7E 117 A2
Rákosszentmihály Hungary 47°31N 19°8E 117 A2
Rakovica Croatia 44°59N 15°38E 199 D12
Rakovník Czech Rep. 50°6N 13°42E 180 A6
Rakovski Bulgaria 42°21N 24°57E 203 D8
Raków Poland 52°11N 20°56E 143 B1
Rakshan → Pakistan 27°10N 63°25E 240 D1
Rakvere Estonia 59°20N 26°25E 188 C4
Raleigh Fla., U.S.A. 29°25N 82°32W 317 F7
Raleigh N.C., U.S.A. 35°47N 78°39W 315 D15
Ralik Chain Pac. Oc. 8°0N 168°0E 288 G8
Ralja Serbia 44°33N 20°34E 202 B4
Rälla Sweden 56°40N 16°30E 163 H10
Ralls U.S.A. 33°41N 101°24W 314 E4
Ralston U.S.A. 41°30N 76°57W 312 E8
Ram West Bank 31°51N 35°14E 123 A2
Ram → Canada 62°1N 123°41W 296 A4
Rām Allāh West Bank 31°55N 35°10E 123 A2
Rama Nic. 12°9N 84°15W 320 D3
Ramacca Italy 37°23N 14°42E 201 E7
Ramachandrapuram India 16°50N 82°4E 244 F6
Ramadān Iraq 33°19N 44°20E 113 B2
Ramagiri Udayagiri India 19°5N 84°18E 244 E7
Ramagundam India 18°55N 79°15E 244 E4
Ramakona India 21°43N 78°50E 243 J8
Ramakrishna Puram India 28°32N 77°10E 120 B1
Ramalho, Serra do Brazil 13°45S 44°0W 333 D3
Rāmallāh = Rām Allāh West Bank 31°55N 35°10E 123 A2
Raman Thailand 6°29N 101°18E 237 J3
Ramanathapuram India 9°25N 78°55E 245 K4
Ramanathpur India 22°41N 88°14E 124 A1
Ramanujganj India 23°48N 83°42E 243 H10
Ramas C. India 15°5N 73°55E 245 G1
Ramat Allon West Bank 31°49N 35°12E 123 B2
Ramat Eshkol West Bank 31°48N 35°13E 123 B2
Ramat Gan Israel 32°4N 34°48E 251 F5
Ramat Razi'el Israel 31°46N 35°4E 123 B1
Ramat Shelomo West Bank 31°48N 35°12E 123 B2
Ramatlhabama S. Africa 25°37S 25°33E 270 C4
Ramban India 33°14N 75°12E 243 C6
Rambervillers France 48°20N 6°38E 173 D13
Rambi = Rabi Fiji 16°30S 179°59W 287 A3
Rambipuji Indonesia 8°12S 113°37E 235 D4
Rambler Channel Hong Kong, China 22°21N 114°6E 122 A2
Rambouillet France 48°39N 1°50E 173 D8
Rambrai India 25°40N 91°19E 241 C3
Rambutyo I. Papua N. G. 2°18S 147°49E 286 B4
Ramdurg India 15°58N 75°22E 245 G2
Rame Hd. Australia 37°47S 149°30E 283 D8
Ramechhap Nepal 27°25N 86°10E 243 F12
Ramenki Russia 55°41N 37°28E 129 B1
Ramenskoye Russia 55°32N 38°15E 188 E10
Ramer U.S.A. 32°3N 86°13W 316 C3
Ramersdorf Germany 48°6N 11°35E 131 B2
Rameses Station Egypt 30°3N 31°15E 117 A2
Rameswaram India 9°17N 79°18E 245 K4
Ramganga → India 27°5N 79°58E 243 F8
Ramgarh Bangla. 22°59N 91°44E 241 D3
Ramgarh Jharkhand, India 23°40N 85°35E 243 H11
Ramgarh Raj., India 27°16N 75°14E 242 F6
Ramgarh Raj., India 27°30N 70°36E 242 F4
Rāmhormoz Iran 31°15N 49°35E 247 D6
Ramiān Iran 37°3N 55°16E 247 B7
Ramiers Haiti 19°34N 72°14W 321 C5
Ramingining Australia 12°19S 135°3E 280 A2
Ramla Israel 31°55N 34°52E 251 G5
Ramlat Zalṭan Libya 28°30N 19°30E 258 C3
Ramlu Eritrea 13°32N 41°40E 257 E5
Ramm = Rum Jordan 29°39N 35°26E 251 J6
Râmna → Romania 45°36N 27°3E 183 E12
Ramnad = Ramanathapuram India 9°25N 78°55E 245 K4
Ramnagar Jammu & Kashmir, India 32°47N 75°18E 243 C6
Ramnagar Uttarakhand, India 29°24N 79°7E 243 E8
Ramnäs Sweden 59°46N 16°12E 162 E10
Râmnicu Sărat Romania 45°26N 27°3E 183 E12
Râmnicu Vâlcea Romania 45°9N 24°21E 183 E9
Ramnous Greece 38°12N 24°3E 204 C6
Ramon Isabela, Phil. 16°50N 121°31E 232 C3
Ramon Russia 51°55N 39°21E 189 G10
Ramona U.S.A. 33°2N 116°52W 307 M10
Ramonville-St-Agne France 43°33N 1°28E 174 E5
Ramore Canada 48°30N 80°25W 298 C3
Ramos Brazil 22°50S 43°14W 135 B1
Ramos → Nigeria 5°8N 5°22E 263 D6
Ramos I. Phil. 8°6N 117°1E 233 G1
Ramos Mejía Argentina 34°39S 58°33W 117 B1
Ramot West Bank 31°48N 35°13E 123 B2
Ramotswa Botswana 24°50S 25°52E 270 B4
Rampanalgas Trin. & Tob. 10°44N 60°59W 323 t
Rampart U.S.A. 65°30N 150°10W 303 D10
Rampur H.P., India 31°26N 77°43E 242 D7
Rampur Mad. P., India 23°25N 73°53E 242 H5
Rampur Odisha, India 21°48N 83°58E 244 D6
Rampur Ut. P., India 28°44N 77°18E 120 A2
Rampur Ut. P., India 28°50N 79°5E 243 E8
Rampur Hat India 24°10N 87°50E 243 G12
Rampura India 24°30N 75°27E 242 G6
Ramrama Tola India 21°52N 79°55E 243 J8
Ramree I. Burma 19°0N 93°40E 241 F5
Ramsagar △ Bangla. 25°33N 88°37E 241 C2
Rāmsar Iran 36°53N 50°41E 247 B6
Ramsey I. of Man 54°20N 4°22W 168 C3
Ramsey Ill., U.S.A. 39°8N 89°7W 310 E7
Ramsey N.J., U.S.A. 41°4N 74°9W 313 E10
Ramsey L. Canada 47°13N 82°15W 298 C3
Ramsgate N.S.W., Australia 33°58S 151°8E 139 B1
Ramsgate Kent, U.K. 51°20N 1°25E 169 F9
Ramshai India 26°44N 88°51E 241 B2
Ramsjö Sweden 62°11N 15°37E 162 B9
Ramstein Germany 49°27N 7°32E 179 F3
Ramtek India 21°20N 79°15E 244 D4
Ramu Kenya 3°55N 41°10E 268 B5
Ramu → Papua N. G. 4°0S 144°41E 286 C3
Ramvik Sweden 62°49N 17°51E 162 B11
Ramville, Î. = Chancel, Î. Martinique 14°41N 60°53W 322 j
Rana Pratap Sagar Dam India 24°58N 75°38E 242 G6
Ranaghat India 23°15N 88°35E 243 H13
Ranahu Pakistan 25°55N 69°45E 242 G3
Ranai Indonesia 3°55N 108°22E 235 B3
Ranau Malaysia 6°2N 116°40E 235 A5
Ranau, Danau Indonesia 4°49S 103°55E 234 C2
Rancagua Chile 34°10S 70°50W 334 C1
Rance → France 48°34N 1°59W 172 D5
Rancharia Brazil 22°15S 50°55W 333 F1
Rancheria → Canada 60°13N 129°7W 296 A3
Ranchester U.S.A. 44°54N 107°10W 304 D10
Ranchi India 23°19N 85°27E 243 H11
Rancho Cordova U.S.A. 38°36N 121°18W 306 G5
Rancho Cucamonga U.S.A. 34°10N 117°30W 307 L9
Rancho Park U.S.A. 34°3N 118°26W 126 B2
Ranco, L. Chile 40°15S 72°25W 336 B2
Rand Australia 35°33S 146°32E 283 C7
Rand ✕ (QRA) S. Africa 26°14S 28°8E 123 B2
Randaberg Norway 59°1N 5°36E 164 E2
Randabygda Norway 61°51N 6°20E 164 C3
Randalls I. U.S.A. 40°47N 73°55W 132 B2
Randalstown U.K. 54°45N 6°19W 166 B5
Randan France 46°2N 3°21E 173 F10
Randazzo Italy 37°53N 14°57E 201 E7
Randburg S. Africa 26°5S 27°57E 123 A1
Rander India 21°14N 72°47E 244 D1
Randers Denmark 56°29N 10°1E 163 H4
Randers Fjord Denmark 56°37N 10°20E 163 H4
Randfontein S. Africa 26°8S 27°45E 271 C4
Randhart S. Africa 26°16S 28°7E 123 B2
Randle U.S.A. 46°32N 121°57W 306 D5
Randolph Mass., U.S.A. 42°10N 71°2W 313 D13
Randolph N.Y., U.S.A. 42°10N 78°59W 312 D6
Randolph Utah, U.S.A. 41°40N 111°11W 304 F8
Randolph Vt., U.S.A. 43°55N 72°40W 313 C12
Randpark Ridge S. Africa 26°6S 27°58E 123 A1
Randsburg U.S.A. 35°22N 117°39W 307 K9
Randsfjorden Norway 60°25N 10°24E 164 D7
Randsverk Norway 61°44N 9°3E 164 C6
Randwick Australia 33°54S 151°14E 139 B2
Rånealven → Sweden 65°50N 22°20E 160 D20
Ranelagh Ireland 53°20N 6°15W 120 A2
Ranenburg = Chaplygin Russia 53°15N 40°0E 188 F11
Ranfurly N.Z. 45°7S 170°6E 285 F5
Rangae Thailand 6°19N 101°44E 237 J3
Rangamati Bangla. 22°38N 92°12E 241 D4
Rangapara India 26°49N 92°39E 241 B4
Rangárvallasýsla Iceland 63°55N 20°0W 155 D7
Rangataua N.Z. 39°26S 175°28E 284 F4
Rangaunu B. N.Z. 34°51S 173°15E 284 A2
Range, The Zimbabwe 19°2S 31°2E 269 F3
Rangeley U.S.A. 44°58N 70°39W 313 B14
Rangeley L. U.S.A. 44°55N 70°43W 313 B14
Rangely U.S.A. 40°5N 108°48W 304 F9
Ranger U.S.A. 32°28N 98°41W 314 E5
Rangia India 26°28N 91°38E 241 B3
Rangiora N.Z. 43°19S 172°36E 285 D7
Rangiroa French Polynesia 15°10S 147°35W 289 f
Rangitaiki N.Z. 38°52S 176°24E 284 E5
Rangitaiki → N.Z. 37°54S 176°49E 284 D5
Rangitata → N.Z. 43°45S 171°15E 285 D6
Rangitikei → N.Z. 40°17S 175°15E 284 G4
Rangitoto ke te tonga = D'Urville I. N.Z. 40°50S 173°55E 285 A8
Rangitoto Ra. N.Z. 38°25S 175°35E 284 E4
Rangkasbitung Indonesia 6°21S 106°15E 234 D3
Rangoon Burma 16°45N 96°20E 241 G6
Rangoon □ Burma 17°0N 96°10E 241 G6
Rangoon → Burma 16°28N 96°40E 241 G6
Rangpur Bangla. 25°42N 89°22E 241 C2
Rangpuri India 28°32N 77°8E 120 B1
Rangsang Indonesia 1°20N 103°5E 237 M4
Rangwe Kenya 0°36S 34°35E 266 E3
Ranibennur India 14°35N 75°30E 245 G2
Raniganj India 23°40N 87°5E 243 H12
Ranikhet India 29°39N 79°25E 243 E8
Ranippettai India 12°56N 79°23E 245 H4
Ranirawa India 24°50N 72°10E 242 G5
Rāniyah Iraq 36°15N 44°53E 213 D11
Ranka India 23°59N 83°47E 243 H10
Ranken → Australia 20°31S 137°36E 280 C2
Rankin Ill., U.S.A. 40°28N 87°54W 311 D9
Rankin Tex., U.S.A. 31°13N 101°56W 314 F4
Rankin Inlet Canada 62°30N 93°0W 294 E13
Rankins Springs Australia 33°49S 146°14E 283 B7
Rankovicevo = Kraljevo Serbia 43°44N 20°41E 202 C4
Rankweil Austria 47°17N 9°39E 180 D2
Rannersdorf Austria 48°7N 16°27E 142 B2
Rannoch, L. U.K. 56°41N 4°20W 167 E4
Rannoch Moor U.K. 56°38N 4°48W 167 E4
Rano Kau Chile 27°11S 109°26W 330 b
Rano Raraku, Volcán Chile 27°7S 109°17W 330 b
Ranobe → Madag. 17°10S 44°58E 272 B1
Ranobe, Helodranon' i Madag. 23°3S 43°33E 272 C1
Ranohira Madag. 22°29S 45°24E 272 C2
Ranomafana Toamasina, Madag. 18°57S 48°50E 272 B2
Ranomafana Toliara, Madag. 24°34S 47°0E 272 C2
Ranomafana △ Madag. 21°16S 47°25E 272 C2
Ranomena Madag. 23°25S 47°17E 272 C2
Ranon Vanuatu 16°8S 168°7E 287 E6
Ranong Thailand 9°56N 98°40E 237 H2
Ranongga Solomon Is. 8°5S 156°35E 287 M9
Ranotsara Nord Madag. 22°48S 46°36E 272 C2
Ranpur India 20°5N 85°20E 244 D7
Rānsa Iran 33°39N 48°18E 247 C6
Ransbèche Belgium 50°56N 4°27E 116 B2
Ransborg Neths. 52°24N 5°0E 112 A2
Ransiki Indonesia 1°30S 134°10E 231 E8
Ransom U.S.A. 41°9N 88°39W 311 C8
Rantabe Madag. 15°42S 49°39E 272 B2
Rantau Indonesia 2°56S 115°9E 235 C5
Rantau Abang Malaysia 4°52N 103°24E 237 K4
Rantauparang Kalimantan Tengah, Indonesia 1°22S 112°4E 235 C4
Rantaupanjang Kalimantan Timur, Indonesia 2°9N 117°25E 235 B5
Rantauprapat Indonesia 2°15N 99°50E 234 B1
Rantaupulut Indonesia 1°55S 112°12E 235 C4
Rantemario Indonesia 3°15S 119°57E 231 E5
Ranthambore △ India 26°10N 76°30E 242 F7
Rantoul U.S.A. 40°19N 88°9W 311 D8
Ranum Denmark 56°54N 9°14E 163 H3
Ranvad India 24°50N 69°45E 242 G3
Ranyah, W. → Si. Arabia 21°18N 43°20E 248 B3
Raohe China 46°47N 134°0E 220 A7
Raon l'Étape France 48°24N 6°50E 173 D13
Raoping China 23°42N 117°1E 229 F11
Raoui, Erg er Algeria 29°0N 2°0W 261 C4
Raoul I. Pac. Oc. 29°16S 177°54W 278 E11
Raoyang China 38°15N 115°45E 226 E8
Rap, Ko Thailand 9°19N 99°58E 237 b
Rapa French Polynesia 27°35S 144°20W 289 f
Rapa Nui = Pascua, I. de Chile 27°7S 109°23W 330 b
Rapallo Italy 44°21N 9°14E 198 D6
Rapar India 23°34N 70°38E 242 H4
Rāpch Iran 25°40N 59°15E 247 E8
Rapel, Lago Chile 34°20S 71°14W 334 C1
Raper, C. Canada 69°44N 67°24W 295 D18
Rapid City U.S.A. 44°5N 103°14W 308 C2
Rapid River U.S.A. 45°55N 86°58W 308 C10
Rapla Estonia 59°1N 24°52E 188 C3
Raposo Portugal 38°40N 9°11W 126 A1
Rapti → India 26°18N 83°41E 243 F10
Rapu Rapu I. Phil. 13°12N 124°9E 232 E5
Raqaba ez Zarqa → South Sudan 9°14N 29°44E 257 F2
Rāqūbah Libya 28°58N 19°2E 258 C3
Raquette → U.S.A. 45°0N 74°42W 313 B10
Raquette Lake U.S.A. 43°49N 74°40W 313 C10
Rara △ Nepal 29°30N 82°10E 243 E10
Raraka French Polynesia 16°10S 144°54W 289 f
Raroia French Polynesia 16°1S 142°27W 289 f
Rarotonga Cook Is. 21°30S 160°0W 289 h
Ra's al 'Ayn Syria 36°45N 40°12E 213 D9
Ras al Hadd Oman 22°30N 59°50E 249 B7
Ra's al Khaymah U.A.E. 25°50N 55°59E 247 E7
Ra's at Tib Tunisia 37°1N 11°2E 258 A2
Râs el Ma Algeria 34°26N 0°50W 261 B4
Râs el Mâ Mali 16°35N 4°30W 262 B4
Râs el Oued Algeria 35°57N 5°2E 261 A6
Râs Ghârib Egypt 28°6N 33°18E 256 B3
Râs Kôh Pakistan 28°43N 64°55E 240 C2
Ra's Lānūf Libya 30°46N 18°11E 258 B3
Râs Muhammad △ Egypt 27°45N 34°16E 256 B3
Ra's Shamrah Syria 35°35N 35°45E 250 C6
Râs Sudr Egypt 29°40N 32°42E 256 B3
Rasa, Pta. B. Aires, Argentina 36°20S 56°41W 334 D4
Rasa, Pta. Río Negro, Argentina 40°50S 62°15W 336 B4
Rasa I. Phil. 9°13N 118°26E 233 G2
Rasca, Pta. de la Canary Is. 27°59N 16°41W 153 e1
Rășcani Moldova 47°58N 27°33E 183 C12
Rasdhoo Maldives 4°17N 72°58E 272 d
Rasdu Atoll Maldives 4°18N 72°58E 272 d
Raseiniai Lithuania 55°25N 23°5E 184 C10
Rashad Sudan 11°55N 31°0E 257 E3
Rashid Egypt 31°21N 30°22E 256 H7
Rashîd, Masabb Egypt 31°22N 30°17E 256 H7
Rashin = Najin N. Korea 42°12N 130°15E 224 A5
Rashmi India 25°4N 74°22E 242 G6
Rasht Iran 37°20N 49°40E 213 D13
Rashtrapati Bhawan Delhi, India 120 c1
Rasi Salai Thailand 15°20N 104°9E 236 E5
Rasipuram India 11°30N 78°15E 245 J4
Raška Serbia 43°19N 20°39E 202 C4
Raskot Nepal 29°14N 81°39E 243 E9
Râsnov Romania 45°35N 25°27E 183 E10
Rasŏn □ N. Korea 42°21N 130°23E 224 A5
Rason L. Australia 28°45S 124°25E 279 E3
Rașova Romania 44°15N 27°55E 183 F12
Rasovo Bulgaria 43°42N 23°17E 202 C7
Rasra India 25°50N 83°50E 243 G10
Rasskazovo Russia 52°35N 41°50E 190 D5
Rast Romania 43°53N 23°16E 183 G8
Rastaala Finland 60°15N 24°47E 121 B1
Rastatt Germany 48°50N 8°11E 179 G4
Rastede Germany 53°15N 8°12E 178 B4
Rastenburg = Kętrzyn Poland 54°7N 21°22E 184 D8
Rastila Finland 60°12N 25°7E 121 B3
Rästolița Romania 46°59N 24°58E 183 D9
Rastyapino = Dzerzhinsk Russia 56°14N 43°30E 190 B6
Rasua Garhi Nepal 28°17N 85°23E 243 E11
Rasul Pakistan 32°42N 73°34E 242 C5
Raszków Poland 51°43N 17°40E 185 G4
Raszyn Poland 52°9N 20°54E 143 C1
Rat → Canada 49°35N 97°10W 297 D9
Rat Buri = Ratchaburi Thailand 13°30N 99°54E 236 F2
Rat I. = Hawadax U.S.A. 51°48N 178°15E 303 L2
Rat I. St. Lucia 14°2N 60°58W 323 m
Rat Islands U.S.A. 52°0N 178°0E 303 L2
Rat L. Canada 56°10N 99°40W 297 B9
Ratak Chain Pac. Oc. 1°0N 170°0E 288 G8
Rätan Sweden 62°29N 14°33E 162 B8
Ratangarh India 28°5N 74°35E 242 E6
Raṭāwī Iraq 30°38N 47°13E 246 D5
Ratcatchers L. Australia 32°38S 143°12E 282 B5
Ratchaburi Thailand 13°30N 99°54E 236 F2
Rath India 25°36N 79°37E 243 G8
Rath Luirc = Charleville Ireland 52°21N 8°40W 166 D3
Rathangan Ireland 53°14N 7°0W 166 C4
Rathbun L. U.S.A. 40°54N 93°5W 310 D4
Rathdrum Ireland 52°56N 6°14W 166 D5
Rathedaung Burma 20°29N 92°45E 241 E4
Rathenow Germany 52°37N 12°19E 178 C8
Rathfarnham Ireland 53°18N 6°16W 120 B2
Rathkeale Ireland 52°32N 8°56W 166 D3
Rathlin I. U.K. 55°18N 6°14W 166 A5
Rathmelton Ireland 55°2N 7°39W 166 A4
Ratho U.K. 55°55N 3°23W 121 B1
Ratho Station U.K. 55°56N 3°23W 121 B1
Ratibor = Racibórz Poland 50°7N 18°18E 185 H5
Rätikon Austria 47°0N 9°55E 180 D2
Ratingen Germany 51°18N 6°52E 178 D2
Ratlam India 23°20N 75°0E 242 H6
Ratmanova Ostrov Russia 65°46N 169°6W 300 B6
Ratnagiri India 16°57N 73°18E 244 F1
Ratnapura Sri Lanka 6°40N 80°20E 245 L5
Rato Portugal 38°43N 9°8W 126 A2
Ratodero Pakistan 27°48N 68°18E 242 F3
Raton U.S.A. 36°54N 104°24W 305 H11
Ratschach = Radeče Slovenia 46°5N 15°14E 199 B12
Rattaphum Thailand 7°8N 100°16E 237 J3
Ratten Austria 47°28N 15°44E 180 D8
Rattray Hd. U.K. 57°38N 1°50W 167 D7
Rättvik Sweden 60°52N 15°7E 162 D9
Ratz, Mt. Canada 57°23N 132°12W 296 B2
Ratzebuhr = Okonek Poland 53°32N 16°51E 184 E3
Ratzeburg Germany 53°40N 10°46E 178 B6
Rau Indonesia 0°34N 100°1E 234 B2
Raub Malaysia 3°47N 101°52E 237 L3
Rauch Argentina 36°45S 59°5W 334 D4
Raudales Mexico 17°27N 93°39W 319 D6
Raudeberg Norway 61°59N 5°7E 164 C2
Raufarhöfn Iceland 66°27N 15°57W 155 A11
Raufoss Norway 60°44N 10°37E 164 D7
Rauhellern Norway 60°15N 7°50E 164 D5
Raukumara Ra. N.Z. 38°5S 177°55E 284 E6
Raul Soares Brazil 20°5S 42°22W 333 F3
Rauma Finland 61°10N 21°30E 188 B1
Rauma → Norway 62°34N 7°43E 164 B4
Raumo = Rauma Finland 61°10N 21°30E 188 B1
Raung, Gunung Indonesia 8°8S 114°3E 231 J17
Raurkela India 22°14N 84°50E 243 H11
Rausu-Dake Japan 44°4N 145°7E 220 B12
Răut → Moldova 47°15N 29°9E 183 C14
Rava-Ruska Ukraine 50°15N 23°42E 185 H10
Rava Russkaya = Rava-Ruska Ukraine 50°15N 23°42E 185 H10
Ravahere French Polynesia 18°14S 142°9W 289 f
Ravalli U.S.A. 47°17N 114°11W 304 C6
Ravānsar Iran 34°43N 46°40E 213 E12
Ravanusa Italy 37°16N 13°58E 200 E6
Rāvar Iran 31°20N 56°51E 247 D8
Ravelston U.K. 55°57N 3°14W 121 B2
Ravena U.S.A. 42°28N 73°49W 313 D11
Ravenel U.S.A. 32°46N 80°15W 316 C9
Ravenna Italy 44°25N 12°12E 199 D9
Ravenna Ky., U.S.A. 37°41N 83°57W 311 G13
Ravenna Nebr., U.S.A. 41°1N 98°55W 308 E4
Ravenna Ohio, U.S.A. 41°9N 81°15W 312 E3
Ravensburg Germany 47°46N 9°36E 179 H5
Ravenshoe Australia 17°37S 145°29E 280 B4
Ravensthorpe Australia 33°35S 120°2E 279 F3
Ravenswood Queens., Australia 20°6S 146°54E 280 C4
Ravenswood W. Va., U.S.A. 38°57N 81°46W 309 F13
Ravensworth Australia 32°26S 151°4E 283 B9
Ravenwood U.S.A. 40°22N 94°41W 310 D2
Raver India 21°15N 76°2E 244 D3
Ravi → Pakistan 30°35N 71°49E 242 D4
Ravine Chaude Guadeloupe 16°14N 61°40W 322 e
Ravna Gora Croatia 45°24N 14°50E 199 C11
Ravna Reka Serbia 44°1N 21°35E 202 B5
Ravne na Koroškem Slovenia 46°36N 14°59E 199 B11
Rawa Mazowiecka Poland 51°46N 20°12E 185 G7
Rawaki Kiribati 3°43S 170°43W 277 A16
Rawalpindi Pakistan 33°38N 73°8E 242 C5
Rawamangun Indonesia 6°11S 106°52E 122 B2
Rawang Malaysia 3°20N 101°35E 237 L3
Rawene N.Z. 35°25S 173°32E 284 B2
Rawi, Ko Thailand 6°33N 99°14E 237 J2
Rawicz Poland 51°36N 16°52E 185 G3
Rawitsch = Rawicz Poland 51°36N 16°52E 185 G3
Rawka → Poland 52°9N 20°8E 185 F7
Rawlinna Australia 30°58S 125°28E 279 F4
Rawlins U.S.A. 41°47N 107°14W 304 F10
Rawlinson Ra. Australia 24°40S 128°30E 279 D4
Rawson Argentina 43°15S 65°5W 336 B3
Raxaul India 26°59N 84°51E 243 F11
Ray U.S.A. 48°21N 103°10W 308 A2
Ray, C. Canada 47°33N 59°15W 299 C8
Ray City U.S.A. 31°5N 83°11W 316 D6
Ray Mts. U.S.A. 66°0N 152°0W 303 D10
Raya Ring, Ko Thailand 8°18N 98°29E 237 a
Rayachoti India 14°4N 78°50E 245 G4
Rayadurg India 14°40N 76°50E 245 G3
Rayagada India 19°15N 83°20E 244 E6
Raychikhinsk Russia 49°46N 129°25E 215 E13
Rāyen Iran 29°34N 57°26E 247 D8
Rayle U.S.A. 33°48N 82°54W 316 B7
Rayleigh U.K. 51°36N 0°37E 169 F8
Raymond Alta., Canada 49°30N 112°35W 296 D6
Raymond Calif., U.S.A. 37°13N 119°54W 306 H7
Raymond Ill., U.S.A. 39°19N 89°34W 310 E7
Raymond N.H., U.S.A. 43°2N 71°11W 313 C13
Raymond Wash., U.S.A. 46°41N 123°44W 306 D3
Raymond Terrace Australia 32°45S 151°44E 283 B9
Raymondville U.S.A. 26°29N 97°47W 314 H6
Raymore Canada 51°25N 104°31W 297 C8
Raynes Lane U.K. 51°34N 0°23W 125 A1
Raynes Park U.K. 51°24N 0°12W 125 B2
Rayón Mexico 29°43N 110°35W 318 B2
Rayong Thailand 12°40N 101°20E 236 F3
Raypur India 22°28N 88°22E 124 C2
Raystown L. U.S.A. 40°25N 78°5W 312 F6
Raysūt Oman 16°56N 53°59E 249 C6
Raytown U.S.A. 39°1N 94°28W 310 E2
Rayville U.S.A. 32°29N 91°46W 314 E9
Raz, Pte. du France 48°2N 4°47W 172 D2
Razan Iran 35°23N 49°2E 213 E13
Ražana Serbia 44°6N 19°55E 202 B3
Ražanj Serbia 43°40N 21°31E 202 C5
Razāzah, Buḥayrat ar Iraq 32°40N 43°35E 213 F10
Razazah, L. = Razāzah, Buḥayrat ar Iraq 32°40N 43°35E 213 F10
Razdelna Bulgaria 43°13N 27°41E 203 C11
Razdel'naya = Rozdilna Ukraine 46°50N 30°2E 183 D15
Razdolnoye Russia 43°30N 131°52E 220 C5
Razdolnoye Ukraine 45°46N 33°29E 189 K7
Razeh Iran 32°47N 48°9E 247 C6
Razgrad Bulgaria 43°33N 26°34E 203 C10
Razgrad □ Bulgaria 43°35N 26°35E 203 C10
Razim, Lacul Romania 44°50N 29°0E 183 F14
Razlog Bulgaria 41°53N 23°28E 202 E7
Razmak Pakistan 32°45N 69°50E 242 C3
Răznas Ezers △ Latvia 56°30N 27°30E 188 D4
Re, Cu Lao Vietnam 15°22N 109°8E 236 E7
Ré, Î. de France 46°12N 1°30W 174 B2
Reach Falls Jamaica 18°2N 76°18W 320 a
Reading Reading, U.K. 51°27N 0°58W 169 F7
Reading Mich., U.S.A. 41°50N 84°45W 311 C12
Reading Ohio, U.S.A. 39°13N 84°26W 311 E12
Reading Pa., U.S.A. 40°20N 75°56W 313 F9
Reading □ U.K. 51°27N 0°58W 169 F7
Real, Cordillera Bolivia 17°0S 67°10W 330 D4
Real Felipe, Fuerte Peru 12°4S 77°9W 124 B2
Realejo Alto Canary Is. 28°22N 16°34W 153 e1
Realicó Argentina 35°0S 64°15W 334 D3
Réalmont France 43°48N 2°10E 174 E6
Ream Cambodia 10°34N 103°39E 237 G4
Ream △ Cambodia 10°30N 103°45E 237 G4
Reams, L. U.S.A. 28°26N 81°34W 133 B1
Reao French Polynesia 18°31S 136°23W 289 f
Reay Forest U.K. 58°22N 4°55W 167 C4
Rebais France 48°50N 3°10E 173 D10
Rebecca, L. Australia 30°0S 122°15E 279 F3
Rebi Indonesia 6°23S 134°7E 231 F8
Rebiana Libya 24°12N 22°10E 258 D4
Rebiana, Sahrâ' Libya 24°30N 21°0E 258 D3
Reboly Russia 63°49N 30°47E 160 E24
Rebun-Tō Japan 45°23N 141°2E 220 B10
Recanati Italy 43°24N 13°32E 199 E10
Recaş Romania 45°46N 21°30E 182 E6
Recco Italy 44°22N 9°9E 198 D6
Recherche, Arch. of the Australia 34°15S 122°50E 279 F3
Rechna Doab Pakistan 31°35N 73°30E 242 D5
Rechytsa Belarus 52°21N 30°24E 177 B16
Recife Brazil 8°0S 35°0W 332 C4
Recife Seychelles 4°36S 55°42E 272 c
Recklinghausen Germany 51°37N 7°12E 178 D3
Reckong Peo India 31°32N 78°16E 242 D8
Reclining Buddha = Wat Pho Bangkok, Thailand 113 b1
Recoleta B. Aires, Argentina 34°36S 58°24W 117 B2
Recoleta Santiago, Chile 33°25S 70°40W 137 B2
Reconquista Argentina 29°10S 59°45W 334 B4
Recreio Brazil 8°0S 58°25W 331 B6
Recreo Argentina 29°25S 65°10W 334 B2
Recuay Peru 9°43S 77°28W 330 B2
Recz Poland 53°16N 15°31E 185 E2
Red = Hong → Vietnam 20°16N 106°34E 236 B5
Red → U.S.A. 31°1N 91°45W 314 F9
Red Bank U.S.A. 40°21N 74°5W 313 F10
Red Bay Canada 51°44N 56°25W 299 B8
Red Bluff U.S.A. 40°11N 122°15W 304 F2
Red Bluff Res. U.S.A. 31°54N 103°55W 305 L12
Red Bud U.S.A. 38°13N 89°59W 310 F7
Red Cliffs Australia 34°19S 142°11E 282 C5
Red Cloud U.S.A. 40°5N 98°32W 308 E4
Red Creek U.S.A. 43°14N 76°45W 313 C8
Red Deer Canada 52°20N 113°50W 296 C6
Red Deer → Alta., Canada 50°58N 110°0W 297 C7
Red Deer → Man., Canada 52°53N 101°1W 297 C8
Red Deer L. Canada 52°55N 101°20W 297 C8
Red Devil U.S.A. 61°46N 157°19W 303 F8
Red Fort = Lal Qila Delhi, India 120 a3
Red Hook U.S.A. 41°55N 73°53W 313 E11
Red Indian L. Canada 48°35N 57°0W 299 C8
Red L. Canada 51°3N 93°49W 297 C10
Red Lake Canada 51°3N 93°49W 297 C10
Red Lake Falls U.S.A. 47°53N 96°16W 308 B5
Red Lake Road Canada 49°59N 93°25W 297 C10
Red Lodge U.S.A. 45°11N 109°15W 304 D9
Red Mountain U.S.A. 35°37N 117°38W 307 K9
Red Oak U.S.A. 41°1N 95°14W 308 E6
Red River of the North → N. Amer. 49°0N 97°15W 308 A5
Red Rock Canada 48°55N 88°15W 298 C2
Red Rock, L. U.S.A. 41°22N 92°59W 310 C3
Red Rocks Pt. Australia 32°13S 127°32E 279 F4
Red Sea Asia 25°0N 36°0E 238 E3
Red Slate Mt. U.S.A. 37°31N 118°52W 306 H8
Red Square Moscow, Russia 129 b2
Red Sucker L. Canada 54°9N 93°40W 298 B1
Red Tower Pass = Turnu Roșu, P. Romania 45°33N 24°17E 183 E9
Red Volta → Africa 10°34N 0°30W 263 C4
Red Wing U.S.A. 44°34N 92°31W 310 C3
Reda Poland 54°40N 18°19E 184 D5
Redang, Pulau Malaysia 5°49N 103°2E 237 K4
Redange Lux. 49°46N 5°52E 170 E5
Redbridge □ U.K. 51°35N 0°7E 125 A4
Redcar U.K. 54°37N 1°4W 168 C6
Redcar & Cleveland □ U.K. 54°29N 1°0W 168 C7
Redcliff Canada 50°10N 110°50W 304 A8
Redcliffe Australia 27°12S 153°6E 281 D5
Redcliffe, Mt. Australia 28°30S 121°30E 279 E3
Reddersburg S. Africa 29°41S 26°10E 270 C4
Reddick Fla., U.S.A. 29°22N 82°12W 317 F7
Reddick Ill., U.S.A. 41°6N 88°15W 311 C8
Redding Calif., U.S.A. 40°35N 122°24W 304 F2
Redding Iowa, U.S.A. 40°36N 94°23W 310 D2
Redditch U.K. 52°18N 1°55W 169 E6
Redenção Brazil 4°13S 38°43W 332 B4
Redentore, Chiesa del Venice, Italy 142 c2
Redfern Australia 33°54S 151°12E 139 B2
Redfield U.S.A. 44°53N 98°31W 308 C4
Redford U.S.A. 44°38N 73°48W 313 B11
Redhead Trin. & Tob. 10°44N 60°58W 323 t
Redkey U.S.A. 40°21N 85°9W 311 D11
Redkino Russia 56°39N 36°16E 188 D9
Redlands U.S.A. 34°4N 117°11W 307 M9
Redmond Oreg., U.S.A. 44°17N 121°11W 304 D3
Redmond Wash., U.S.A. 47°40N 122°7W 306 C4
Redon France 47°40N 2°6W 172 E4
Redonda Antigua & B. 16°58N 62°19W 321 C7
Redonda, Pta. Chile 27°10S 109°22W 330 b
Redondela Spain 42°15N 8°38W 194 C2
Redondo Portugal 38°39N 7°37W 195 G3
Redondo Beach U.S.A. 33°50N 118°23W 307 M8
Redoubt Volcano U.S.A. 60°29N 152°45W 303 F9
Redpath Sugar Museum Toronto, Canada 141 c3
Redruth U.K. 50°14N 5°14W 169 G2
Redvers Canada 49°35N 101°40W 297 D8
Redwater Canada 53°55N 113°6W 296 C6
Redwood U.S.A. 44°18N 75°48W 313 B9
Redwood △ U.S.A. 41°40N 124°5W 304 F1
Redwood City U.S.A. 37°30N 122°15W 306 H4
Redwood Falls U.S.A. 44°32N 95°7W 308 C6
Ree, L. Ireland 53°35N 8°0W 166 C3
Reed City U.S.A. 43°53N 85°31W 309 D11
Reed L. Canada 54°38N 100°30W 297 C8
Reedley U.S.A. 36°36N 119°27W 306 J7
Reedsburg U.S.A. 43°32N 90°0W 308 D8
Reedsport U.S.A. 43°42N 124°6W 304 E1
Reedsville U.S.A. 40°39N 77°35W 312 F7
Reedy Creek Australia 36°58S 140°2E 282 D4
Reef Is. Pac. Oc. 10°15S 166°10E 277 C12
Reefton N.Z. 42°6S 171°51E 285 C6
Rees Germany 51°46N 6°24E 178 D2
Reese → U.S.A. 40°48N 117°4W 304 F5
Reetz = Recz Poland 53°16N 15°31E 185 E2
Refahiye Turkey 39°54N 38°47E 213 C8
Reflecting Pool Washington, D.C., U.S.A. 143 b1
Refshaleøen Denmark 55°41N 12°36E 118 A3
Reftele Sweden 57°11N 13°35E 163 G7
Refugio U.S.A. 28°18N 97°17W 314 G6
Rega → Poland 54°10N 15°18E 184 D2
Regalbuto Italy 37°39N 14°38E 201 E7
Regana, C. de Spain 39°25N 2°43E 206 B3
Regar = Tursunzoda Tajikistan 38°30N 68°14E 217 E7
Regen Germany 48°58N 13°8E 179 G9
Regen → Germany 49°1N 12°6E 179 F8
Regeneração Brazil 6°15S 42°41W 332 C3
Regensburg Germany 49°1N 12°6E 179 F8
Regenstauf Germany 49°7N 12°8E 179 F8
Regents Park Gauteng, S. Africa 26°14S 28°3E 123 B2
Regent's Park London, U.K. 125 a2
Regenwalde = Resko Poland 53°47N 15°25E 184 E2
Reggâne = Zaouiet Reggâne Algeria 26°32N 0°3E 261 C5
Reggello Italy 43°41N 11°32E 199 E8
Réggio di Calàbria Italy 38°6N 15°39E 201 D8
Réggio nell'Emilia Italy 44°43N 10°36E 198 D7
Reghin Romania 46°46N 24°42E 183 D9
Regina Sask., Canada 50°27N 104°35W 297 C8
Régina Fr. Guiana 4°19N 52°8W 329 C7
Regina Beach Canada 50°47N 105°0W 297 C8
Register U.S.A. 32°22N 81°53W 316 C8
Registro Brazil 24°29S 47°49W 335 A6
Rego Park U.S.A. 40°43N 73°51W 132 B2
Reguengos de Monsaraz Portugal 38°25N 7°32W 195 G3
Rehar → India 23°55N 82°40E 243 H10
Rehli India 23°38N 79°5E 243 H8
Rehoboth Namibia 23°15S 17°4E 270 B2
Rehovot Israel 31°54N 34°48E 251 G5
Rei, Costa Italy 39°15N 9°40E 200 C2
Reibell = Ksar Chellala Algeria 35°13N 2°19E 261 A5
Reichenau = Rychnov nad Kněžnou Czech Rep. 50°10N 16°17E 181 A9
Reichenbach = Dzierżoniów Poland 50°45N 16°39E 185 H3
Reichenbach Germany 50°37N 12°17E 178 E8
Reichenberg = Liberec Czech Rep. 50°47N 15°7E 180 A8
Reichshof = Rzeszów Poland 50°5N 21°58E 185 H8
Reichstag Berlin, Germany 115 a3
Reid Australia 30°49S 128°26E 279 F4
Reidsville Ga., U.S.A. 32°6N 82°7W 316 C7
Reidsville N.C., U.S.A. 36°21N 79°40W 315 C15
Reifnig = Ribnica Slovenia 45°45N 14°45E 199 C11
Reigate U.K. 51°14N 0°12W 169 F7
Reillo Spain 39°54N 1°53W 196 F3
Reims France 49°15N 4°1E 173 C11
Reina Adelaida, Arch. Chile 52°20S 74°0W 336 D2
Reina Beatrix Int. ✕ (AUA) Aruba 12°30N 70°1W 322 f
Reina Sofía, Centro de Arte Madrid, Spain 127 c3
Reina Sofía, Tenerife ✕ (TFS) Canary Is. 28°3N 16°33W 153 e1
Reinbeck U.S.A. 42°19N 92°36W 310 B4
Reinbek Germany 53°30N 10°16E 178 B6
Reindeer → Canada 55°36N 103°11W 297 B8
Reindeer I. Canada 52°30N 98°0W 297 C9
Reindeer L. Canada 57°15N 102°15W 297 B8
Reinga, C. N.Z. 34°25S 172°43E 284 A1
Reinheimen △ Norway 62°10N 7°45E 164 B4
Reinickendorf Germany 52°34N 13°22E 115 A3
Reinosa Spain 43°2N 4°15W 194 B6
Reinsvoll Norway 60°40N 10°36E 164 D7
Reitan Norway 62°49N 11°22E 164 B8
Reitz S. Africa 27°48S 28°29E 271 C4
Reivilo S. Africa 27°36S 24°8E 270 C3
Rejaf South Sudan 4°45N 31°35E 257 G3
Rejmyre Sweden 58°50N 15°55E 163 F9
Rejowiec Fabryczny Poland 51°5N 23°17E 185 G10
Reka → Slovenia 45°40N 14°0E 199 C11
Rekohu = Chatham I. N.Z. 43°50S 176°20W 285 a
Rekola Finland 60°15N 25°4E 121 B3
Rekovac Serbia 43°51N 21°3E 202 C5
Relámpago, Pta. Venezuela 11°3N 64°23W 329 a
Reliance Canada 63°0N 109°20W 297 A7
Relizane Algeria 35°44N 0°31E 261 A5
Relizane □ Algeria 35°45N 0°55E 261 A5
Remad, Oued → Algeria 33°28N 1°20W 261 B4
Rémalard France 48°26N 0°47E 172 D7
Remanso Brazil 9°41S 42°4W 332 C3
Remarkable, Mt. Australia 32°48S 138°10E 282 B3
Remarkables, The N.Z. 45°10S 168°50E 285 F3
Rembang Indonesia 6°42S 111°21E 235 D4
Rembau Malaysia 2°35N 102°6E 234 B2
Rembert U.S.A. 34°6N 80°32W 316 A9
Rembertów Poland 52°15N 21°9E 143 B2
Rembrandthuis Amsterdam, Neths. 112 b3
Rembrandtpark Neths. 52°22N 4°51E 112 A2
Rembrandtplein Amsterdam, Neths. 112 b2
Remchi Algeria 35°2N 1°26W 261 A4
Remedios Colombia 7°2N 74°41W 328 B3
Remedios Panama 8°15N 81°50W 320 E3
Remedios de Escalada Argentina 34°43S 58°24W 117 C2
Remeshk Iran 26°55N 58°50E 247 E8
Remetea Romania 46°45N 25°29E 183 D10
Remich Lux. 49°32N 6°22E 170 E6
Remington U.S.A. 40°46N 87°9W 311 D9
Rémire Fr. Guiana 4°53N 52°17W 329 C7
Remiremont France 48°2N 6°36E 173 D13
Remo Ethiopia 6°48N 41°20E 257 F5
Rémola, Estany del Spain 41°6N 2°4E 114 B1
Remontnoye Russia 46°34N 43°37E 191 G6
Remoulins France 43°55N 4°35E 175 E8
Rempang Indonesia 0°51N 104°10E 234 B2
Rempart → Mauritius 20°13S 57°22E 272 e
Remparts → Réunion 21°22S 55°37E 272 f
Remscheid Germany 51°11N 7°12E 178 D3
Ren Xian China 37°8N 114°40E 226 F8
Rena Norway 61°8N 11°20E 164 C8
Rena → Norway 61°8N 11°23E 164 C8
Renascença Brazil 3°50S 66°21W 328 D4
Renca Chile 33°24S 70°42W 137 B1
Rend Lake U.S.A. 38°2N 88°58W 310 F8
Rendang Indonesia 8°26S 115°25E 231 J18
Rende Italy 39°20N 16°11E 201 C9
Rendezvous Barbados 13°4N 59°35W 323 r
Rendina Greece 39°4N 21°58E 204 B3
Rendova Solomon Is. 8°33S 157°17E 287 M9
Rendsburg Germany 54°17N 9°39E 178 A5
Renfrew Canada 45°30N 76°40W 313 A8
Renfrewshire □ U.K. 55°49N 4°38W 167 F4
Renfroe U.S.A. 32°14N 84°43W 316 C5
Rengat Indonesia 0°30S 102°45E 234 C2
Rengo Chile 34°24S 70°50W 334 C1
Renhua China 25°5N 113°40E 229 E9
Renhuai China 27°48N 106°24E 228 D6
Reni = Taranagar India 28°43N 74°50E 242 E6
Reni Ukraine 45°28N 28°15E 183 E13
Renigunta India 13°38N 79°30E 245 H4
Renk South Sudan 11°50N 32°50E 257 E3
Renland Greenland 71°10N 26°30W 154 C8
Renmark Australia 34°11S 140°43E 282 C4
Rennebu Norway 62°52N 9°49E 164 B6
Rennell Solomon Is. 11°40S 160°10E 287 N11
Rennell Sd. Canada 53°23N 132°35W 296 C2
Rennemoulin France 48°50N 2°2E 134 A1
Renner Springs Australia 18°20S 133°47E 280 B1
Rennes France 48°7N 1°41W 172 D5
Rennick Glacier Antarctica 70°30S 161°45E 151 D11
Rennie L. Canada 61°32N 105°35W 297 A7
Reno U.S.A. 39°31N 119°48W 306 F7
Reno → Italy 44°38N 12°16E 199 D9
Renovo U.S.A. 41°20N 77°45W 312 E7
Renqiu China 38°43N 116°5E 226 E9
Rens Denmark 54°54N 9°5E 163 K3
Renshou China 29°59N 104°9E 228 C5
Rensselaer Ind., U.S.A. 40°57N 87°9W 311 D9
Rensselaer N.Y., U.S.A. 42°38N 73°45W 313 D11
Renton U.S.A. 47°28N 122°12W 306 C4
Renukoot India 24°12N 83°2E 243 G10
Renwick N.Z. 41°30S 173°51E 285 B8
Renwick Gallery Washington, D.C., U.S.A. 143 a1
Renwu = Jenwu Taiwan 22°42N 120°20E 225 D2
Réo Burkina Faso 12°28N 2°35W 262 C4
Reocín = Puente San Miguel Spain 43°21N 4°5W 194 B6
Reotipur India 25°33N 83°45E 243 G10
Repalle India 16°2N 80°45E 245 F5
Répcelak Hungary 47°24N 17°1E 182 C2
Řeporyje Czech Rep. 50°1N 14°18E 135 B1
Reppen = Rzepin Poland 52°20N 14°49E 185 F1
Republic Mo., U.S.A. 37°7N 93°29W 308 G7
Republic Wash., U.S.A. 48°39N 118°44W 304 B4
Republican → U.S.A. 39°4N 96°48W 308 F5
Republiek Suriname 5°30N 55°13W 329 B6
Republika Srpska □ Bos.-H. 44°56N 17°11E 199 D14
République, Place de la Paris, France 134 b5
Repulse B. Australia 20°35S 148°46E 280 b
Repulse Bay Nunavut, Canada 66°30N 86°30W 295 D14
Repulse Bay Hong Kong, China 22°13N 114°10E 122 B3
Repy Czech Rep. 50°4N 14°17E 135 B1
Requena Peru 5°5S 73°52W 330 B3
Requena Spain 39°30N 1°4W 197 F3
Requin Bay Grenada 12°2N 61°39W 323 q
Réquista France 44°1N 2°32E 174 D6
Reşadiye Muğla, Turkey 36°45N 27°39E 205 E9
Reşadiye Tokat, Turkey 40°23N 37°20E 212 B7
Reşadiye Yarımadası Turkey 36°40N 27°45E 205 E9
Resavica Serbia 44°4N 21°30E 202 B5
Resen Macedonia 41°5N 21°0E 202 E5
Reserve U.S.A. 33°43N 108°45W 305 K9
Resht = Rasht Iran 37°20N 49°40E 213 D13
Residenz Germany 48°8N 11°34E 131 B2
Residenzmuseum Munich, Germany 131 b3
Resistencia Argentina 27°30S 59°0W 334 B4
Reşiţa Romania 45°18N 21°53E 182 E6
Resko Poland 53°47N 15°25E 184 E2

Reso = Raisio *Finland* 60°28N 22°11E **188** B2
Resolute *Canada* 74°42N 94°54W **295** C13
Resolution I. *Nunavut, Canada* 61°30N 65°0W **295** E19
Resolution I. *N.Z.* 45°40S 166°40E **285** F1
Resplandes *Brazil* 6°17S 45°13W **332** C2
Resplendor *Brazil* 19°20S 41°15W **333** E3
Ressano Garcia *Mozam.* 25°25S 32°0E **271** C5
Restinga, L. de la *Venezuela* 10°59N 64°8W **329** a
Restinga de Jurubatiba △ *Brazil* 22°5S 41°20W **333** F3
Reston *Canada* 49°33N 101°6W **297** D8
Resulayn = Ceylanpınar *Turkey* 36°50N 40°2E **213** D9
Reszel *Poland* 54°4N 21°10E **184** D8
Retalhuleu *Guatemala* 14°33N 91°46W **320** D1
Retenue, L. de *Dem. Rep. of the Congo* 11°0S 27°0E **269** E2
Retezat, Munţii *Romania* 45°25N 23°0E **182** E8
Retezat △ *Romania* 45°23N 22°56E **182** E7
Retford *U.K.* 53°19N 0°56W **168** D7
Rethel *France* 49°30N 4°20E **173** C11
Rethem *Germany* 52°47N 9°22E **178** C5
Rethimno *Greece* 35°18N 24°30E **207** E5
Reti *Pakistan* 28°5N 69°48E **242** E3
Retiche, Alpi *Switz.* 46°30N 10°0E **179** J6
Retiers *France* 47°55N 1°23W **172** E5
Retiro *B. Aires, Argentina* 34°35S 58°23W **117** B2
Retiro *Madrid, Spain* 40°24N 3°40W **124** B2
Retiro, Puerto *Argentina* 34°36S 58°21W **117** B2
Retortillo *Spain* 40°48N 6°21W **194** E4
Retournac *France* 45°12N 4°2E **175** C8
Retreat *S. Africa* 34°4S 18°28E **118** B1
Rétság *Hungary* 47°58N 19°10E **182** C4
Réunion ☒ *Ind. Oc.* 21°0S 56°0E **272** f
Reus *Spain* 41°10N 1°5E **196** D6
Reusam *Indonesia* 2°11N 96°38E **234** B1
Reuterstadt Stavenhagen *Germany* 53°42N 12°54E **178** B8
Reutlingen *Germany* 48°29N 9°12E **179** G5
Reutov *Russia* 55°45N 37°50E **129** B4
Reutte *Austria* 47°29N 10°42E **180** D3
Reval = Tallinn *Estonia* 59°22N 24°48E **188** C3
Revda *Russia* 56°48N 59°57E **186** C10
Réveillon → *France* 48°42N 2°30E **134** B4
Revel = Tallinn *Estonia* 59°22N 24°48E **188** C3
Revel *France* 43°28N 2°1E **174** E6
Revelganj *India* 25°50N 84°40E **243** G11
Revelstoke *Canada* 51°0N 118°10W **296** C5
Reventazón *Peru* 6°10S 80°58W **330** B1
Revere *U.S.A.* 42°25N 71°0W **116** A2
Revere House *Boston, U.S.A.* **116** b3
Revigny-sur-Ornain *France* 48°49N 4°59E **173** D11
Revillagigedo, Is. de *Pac. Oc.* 18°40N 112°0W **318** D2
Revin *France* 49°55N 4°39E **173** C11
Revúca *Slovak Rep.* 48°41N 20°7E **181** C13
Revuè → *Mozam.* 19°50S 34°0E **269** F3
Rewa *India* 24°33N 81°25E **243** G9
Rewa → *Guyana* 3°19N 58°42W **329** C6
Rewari *India* 28°15N 76°40E **242** E7
Rexburg *U.S.A.* 43°49N 111°47W **304** E8
Rexdale *Canada* 43°43N 79°35W **141** A1
Rey *Iran* 35°35N 51°25E **216** E4
Rey, I. del *Panama* 8°20N 78°30W **320** E4
Rey, L. del *Mexico* 27°1N 103°26W **318** B4
Rey, Mayo → *Cameroon* 8°47N 14°1E **264** A2
Rey, Rio-del- → *Cameroon* 4°31N 8°45E **264** B1
Rey Bouba *Cameroon* 8°40N 14°15E **264** A2
Rey Malabo *Eq. Guin.* 3°45N 8°50E **263** E6
Reyðarfjörður *Iceland* 65°2N 14°13W **155** B12
Reyes *Bolivia* 14°19S 67°23W **330** C4
Reyes, Pt. *U.S.A.* 38°0N 123°0W **306** H3
Reyhanlı *Turkey* 36°16N 36°35E **250** B7
Reykhólar *Iceland* 65°27N 22°12W **155** B4
Reykholt *Suðurnes Iceland* 64°40N 21°18W **155** C5
Reykholt *Vesturland Iceland* 64°10N 20°25W **155** C6
Reykjahlið *Iceland* 65°40N 16°55W **155** B10
Reykjanes *Iceland* 63°48N 22°40W **155** D4
Reykjanes Ridge *Atl. Oc.* 59°0N 31°0W **152** A8
Reykjavik *Iceland* 64°10N 21°57W **155** C5
Reykjavik Keflavik ✈ (KEF) *Iceland* 64°0N 22°45W **155** C4
Reynolds *Ga., U.S.A.* 32°33N 84°6W **316** C5
Reynolds *Ill., U.S.A.* 41°20N 90°40W **310** C6
Reynolds Ra. *Australia* 22°30S 133°0E **278** D5
Reynoldsville *Ga., U.S.A.* 30°51N 84°47W **316** E5
Reynoldsville *Pa., U.S.A.* 41°6N 78°53W **312** E6
Reynosa *Mexico* 26°7N 98°18W **319** B5
Reynosa Tamaulipas *Mexico* 19°30N 99°10W **128** A1
Reza'iyeh = Orūmīyeh *Iran* 37°40N 45°0E **213** D11
Reza'iyeh, L. = Orūmīyeh, Daryācheh-ye *Iran* 37°50N 45°30E **213** D11
Rēzekne *Latvia* 56°30N 27°17E **188** D4
Rezhitsa = Rēzekne *Latvia* 56°30N 27°17E **188** D4
Rezina *Moldova* 47°45N 28°58E **183** C13
Rezovo *Bulgaria* 42°0N 28°0E **203** E12
Rezvān *Iran* 27°34N 56°6E **247** E8
Rezvānshahr *Iran* 37°32N 49°7E **213** D13
Rgotina *Serbia* 44°1N 22°17E **202** B6
Rharbi, Zahrez *Algeria* 34°50N 2°55E **261** B5
Rharis, O. → *Algeria* 26°0N 5°4E **261** C5
Rhayader *U.K.* 52°18N 3°29W **169** E4
Rheda-Wiedenbrück *Germany* 51°50N 8°20E **178** D4
Rhede *Germany* 51°50N 6°42E **178** D2
Rhein → *Europe* 51°52N 6°2E **170** C6
Rhein-Main-Donau-Kanal *Germany* 49°1N 11°27E **179** F7
Rhein-Ruhr, Düsseldorf ✈ (DUS) *Germany* 51°17N 6°46E **178** D2
Rhein-Taunus △ *Germany* 50°10N 8°10E **179** E4
Rhein-Westerwald △ *Germany* 50°32N 7°20E **178** E3
Rheinbach *Germany* 50°38N 6°57E **178** E2
Rheine *Germany* 52°17N 7°26E **178** C3
Rheinfelden *Germany* 47°33N 7°47E **179** H3
Rheinland-Pfalz □ *Germany* 50°0N 7°0E **179** E2
Rheinsberg *Germany* 53°6N 12°54E **178** B8
Rheris, Oued → *Morocco* 30°50N 4°34W **260** B4
Rhin = Rhein → *Europe* 51°52N 6°2E **170** C6
Rhine = Rhein → *Europe* 51°52N 6°2E **170** C6
Rhine *U.S.A.* 31°59N 83°12W **316** D6
Rhinebeck *U.S.A.* 41°56N 73°55W **313** E11
Rhineland-Palatinate = Rheinland-Pfalz □ *Germany* 50°0N 7°0E **179** E2
Rhinelander *U.S.A.* 45°38N 89°25W **308** C9
Rhinns Pt. *U.K.* 55°40N 6°29W **167** F2
Rhino Camp *Uganda* 3°0N 31°22E **268** B3
Rhir, Cap *Morocco* 30°38N 9°54W **260** B3
Rho *Italy* 45°31N 9°2E **128** A1
Rhode Island □ *U.S.A.* 41°40N 71°30W **313** E13
Rhodes *N.S.W., Australia* 33°49S 151°6E **139** A1
Rhodes *Greece* 36°15N 28°10E **206** E12
Rhodes ✈ (RHO) *Greece* 36°23N 28°12E **205** E10
Rhodesia = Zimbabwe ■ *Africa* 19°0S 30°0E **269** F3
Rhodon *France* 48°42N 2°3E **134** B1
Rhodon → *France* 48°42N 2°4E **134** B1
Rhodope Mts. = Rhodopi Planina *Bulgaria* 41°40N 24°20E **203** E8
Rhodopi Planina *Bulgaria* 41°40N 24°20E **203** E8
Rhön *Germany* 50°24N 9°58E **178** E5
Rhondda *U.K.* 51°39N 3°31W **169** F4
Rhondda Cynon Taff □ *U.K.* 51°42N 3°27W **169** F4
Rhône □ *France* 45°54N 4°35E **175** C8
Rhône → *France* 43°28N 4°42E **175** E8
Rhône-Alpes □ *France* 45°40N 6°0E **175** C9
Rhum = Rùm *U.K.* 57°0N 6°20W **167** E2
Rhydaman = Ammanford *U.K.* 51°48N 3°59W **169** F4
Rhyl *U.K.* 53°20N 3°29W **168** D4
Ri-Aba *Eq. Guin.* 3°28N 8°40E **263** E6
Ria Formosa △ *Portugal* 37°1N 7°48W **195** H3
Riachão *Brazil* 7°20S 46°37W **332** C2
Riacho de Santana *Brazil* 13°37S 42°57W **333** D3
Rialma *Brazil* 15°18S 49°34W **333** E2
Rialto, Ponte di *Venice, Italy* **138** b2
Rialto Towers *Australia* 37°49S 144°57W **128** A1
Riam *Indonesia* 1°49S 111°54E **235** C4
Riang *India* 27°31N 92°56E **241** B4
Riang, Laem *Thailand* 8°7N 98°27E **237** a
Riangnom *South Sudan* 9°55N 30°1E **257** F3
Riaño *Spain* 42°59N 4°59W **194** C6
Rians *France* 43°37N 5°44E **175** E9
Riansáres → *Spain* 39°32N 3°18W **195** F7
Riasi *India* 33°10N 74°50E **243** C6
Riau □ *Indonesia* 0°0 102°35E **234** B2
Riau, Kepulauan □ *Indonesia* 0°30N 104°20E **234** B2
Riau Arch. = Riau, Kepulauan □ *Indonesia* 0°30N 104°20E **234** B2
Riaza *Spain* 41°18N 3°30W **194** D7
Riaza → *Spain* 41°42N 3°55W **194** D7
Riba de Saelices *Spain* 40°55N 2°17W **196** E2
Riba-roja de Túria *Spain* 39°33N 0°34W **197** F4
Ribadavia *Spain* 42°17N 8°8W **194** C2
Ribadeo *Spain* 43°35N 7°5W **194** B3
Ribadesella *Spain* 43°30N 5°7W **194** B5
Ribado *Nigeria* 9°16N 12°47E **263** D7
Ribamar *Brazil* 2°33S 44°3W **332** B3
Ribao *Cameroon* 6°32N 11°30E **263** D7
Ribas = Ribes de Freser *Spain* 42°19N 2°15E **196** C7
Ribas do Rio Pardo *Brazil* 20°27S 53°46W **331** E7
Ribauè *Mozam.* 14°57S 38°17E **269** E4
Ribble → *U.K.* 53°52N 2°25W **168** D5
Ribe *Denmark* 55°19N 8°44E **163** J2
Ribeauvillé *France* 48°10N 7°20E **173** D14
Ribécourt-Dreslincourt *France* 49°30N 2°55E **173** C9
Ribeira *Rio de J., Brazil* 22°49S 43°10W **135** A1
Ribeira *Spain* 42°36N 8°58W **194** C2
Ribeira Brava *Madeira* 32°41N 17°4W **153** c
Ribeira do Pombal *Brazil* 10°50S 38°32W **332** D4
Ribeira Grande *Azores* 37°49N 25°31W **153** d3
Ribeira Grande *C. Verde Is.* 17°0N 25°4W **153** j
Ribeira Grande *C. Verde Is.* 14°54N 23°36W **153** j
Ribeirão Prêto *Brazil* 21°10S 47°50W **335** A6
Ribeirão Gonçalves *Brazil* 7°32S 45°14W **332** C2
Ribemont *France* 49°47N 3°27E **173** C10
Ribera *Italy* 37°30N 13°16E **200** E6
Ribérac *France* 45°15N 0°20E **174** C4
Riberalta *Bolivia* 11°0S 66°0W **331** C4
Ribes de Freser *Spain* 42°19N 2°15E **196** C7
Ribnica *Slovenia* 45°45N 14°45E **199** C11
Ribnitz-Damgarten *Germany* 54°15N 12°27E **178** A8
Říčany *Czech Rep.* 50°0N 14°40E **180** B7
Ricarda, Estany de la *Spain* 41°17N 2°6E **114** B1
Riccarton *N.Z.* 43°32S 172°37E **285** D7
Riccia *Italy* 41°30N 14°50E **201** A7
Riccione *Italy* 43°59N 12°39E **199** E9
Rice *U.S.A.* 34°5N 114°51W **307** L12
Rice L. *Canada* 44°12N 78°10W **312** B6
Rice Lake *U.S.A.* 45°30N 91°44W **308** C8
Riceboro *U.S.A.* 31°44N 81°26W **316** D8
Rich, C. *Canada* 44°43N 80°38W **312** B4
Richard Toll *Senegal* 16°25N 15°42W **262** B1
Richards Bay *S. Africa* 28°48S 32°6E **271** C5
Richardson → *Canada* 58°25N 111°14W **297** B6
Richardson Lakes *U.S.A.* 44°46N 70°58W **309** C18
Richardson Mts. *N.Z.* 44°49S 168°34E **285** E3
Richardson Springs *U.S.A.* 39°51N 121°46W **306** F5
Riche, C. *Australia* 34°36S 118°47E **279** F2
Richelieu *France* 47°1N 0°20E **172** E7
Richey *U.S.A.* 47°39N 105°4W **304** C11
Richfield *U.S.A.* 38°46N 112°5W **304** G7
Richfield Springs *U.S.A.* 42°51N 74°59W **313** D10
Richford *U.S.A.* 45°0N 72°40W **313** B12
Richibucto *Canada* 46°42N 64°54W **299** C7
Richland *Ga., U.S.A.* 32°5N 84°40W **316** C5
Richland *Iowa, U.S.A.* 41°13N 92°0W **310** C5
Richland *Mo., U.S.A.* 37°51N 92°26W **310** G4
Richland *Wash., U.S.A.* 46°17N 119°18W **304** C4
Richland Center *U.S.A.* 43°21N 90°23W **308** D8
Richlands *U.S.A.* 37°6N 81°48W **309** G13
Richmond *N.S.W., Australia* 33°35S 150°42E **283** B9
Richmond *Queens., Australia* 20°43S 143°8E **280** C3
Richmond *Vic., Australia* 37°48S 145°0E **128** A2
Richmond *Nelson-Marlborough, N.Z.* 41°20S 173°12E **285** B8
Richmond *N. Yorks., U.K.* 54°25N 1°43W **168** C6
Richmond *Calif., U.S.A.* 37°46N 122°27W **136** B2
Richmond *Calif., U.S.A.* 37°56N 122°21W **306** H4
Richmond *Ind., U.S.A.* 39°50N 84°53W **311** E12
Richmond *Ky., U.S.A.* 37°45N 84°18W **311** G12
Richmond *Mich., U.S.A.* 42°49N 82°45W **312** D2
Richmond *Mo., U.S.A.* 39°17N 93°58W **310** E3
Richmond *Tex., U.S.A.* 29°35N 95°46W **314** G7
Richmond *Utah, U.S.A.* 41°56N 111°48W **304** F8
Richmond *Va., U.S.A.* 37°33N 77°27W **309** G15
Richmond *Vt., U.S.A.* 44°24N 72°59W **313** B12
Richmond, Mt. *N.Z.* 41°32S 173°22E **285** B8
Richmond Hill *Ont., Canada* 43°52N 79°27W **312** C5
Richmond Hill *Ga., U.S.A.* 31°56N 81°18W **316** D8
Richmond Hill *N.Y., U.S.A.* 40°41N 73°51W **132** B2
Richmond Park *U.K.* 51°26N 0°16W **125** B2
Richmond Peak *St. Vincent* 13°17N 61°13W **323** n
Richmond Ra. *N.S.W., Australia* 29°0S 152°45E **281** D5
Richmond Ra. *N.Z.* 41°32S 173°22E **285** B8
Richmond-upon-Thames □ *U.K.* 51°27N 0°17W **125** B2
Richmondville *U.S.A.* 42°38N 74°33W **313** D10
Richtersveld △ *S. Africa* 28°15S 17°10E **270** C2
Richville *U.S.A.* 44°25N 75°23W **313** B9
Richwood *Ohio, U.S.A.* 40°26N 83°18W **311** D13
Richwood *W. Va., U.S.A.* 38°14N 80°32W **309** F13
Ricla *Spain* 41°31N 1°24W **196** D3
Ricupe *Angola* 14°37S 21°25E **265** E4
Ridā' *Yemen* 14°25N 44°50E **248** D4
Riddarholmen *Stockholm, Sweden* **139** c1
Riddarhuset *Stockholm, Sweden* **139** c2
Ridder *Kazakhstan* 50°20N 83°30E **217** B10
Riddlesburg *U.S.A.* 40°9N 78°15W **312** F6
Rideau → *Canada* 45°27N 75°42W **313** A9
Ridge, The *India* 28°37N 77°10E **120** B2
Ridge Farm *U.S.A.* 39°54N 87°39W **311** E9
Ridge Spring *U.S.A.* 33°51N 81°40W **316** B8
Ridgecrest *U.S.A.* 35°38N 117°40W **307** K9
Ridgefield *Conn., U.S.A.* 41°17N 73°30W **313** E11
Ridgefield *N.J., U.S.A.* 40°49N 74°0W **132** B1
Ridgefield *Wash., U.S.A.* 45°49N 122°45W **306** E4
Ridgefield Park *U.S.A.* 40°52N 74°1W **132** A1
Ridgeland *Miss., U.S.A.* 32°26N 90°8W **315** E9
Ridgeland *S.C., U.S.A.* 32°29N 80°59W **316** C9
Ridgetown *Canada* 42°26N 81°52W **312** D3
Ridgeville *Ind., U.S.A.* 40°18N 85°2W **311** D11
Ridgeville *S.C., U.S.A.* 33°6N 80°19W **316** B9
Ridgewood *N.J., U.S.A.* 40°59N 74°7W **313** F10
Ridgewood *N.Y., U.S.A.* 40°42N 73°53W **132** B2
Ridgway *Ill., U.S.A.* 37°48N 88°16W **311** G8
Ridgway *Pa., U.S.A.* 41°25N 78°44W **312** E6
Riding Mountain △ *Canada* 50°50N 100°0W **297** C9
Ridley, Mt. *Australia* 33°12S 122°7E **279** F3
Riebeek-Oos *S. Africa* 33°10S 26°10E **270** D4
Ried *Austria* 48°14N 13°30E **180** C6
Riedlingen *Germany* 48°9N 9°28E **179** G5
Riedstadt *Germany* 49°45N 8°30E **179** F4
Riem *Germany* 48°8N 11°41E **131** B3
Riemst *Belgium* 50°48N 5°36E **176** D5
Rienza → *Italy* 46°49N 11°47E **199** B8
Riesa *Germany* 51°17N 13°17E **178** D9
Riesco, I. *Chile* 52°55S 72°40W **336** D2
Riesenburg = Prabuty *Poland* 53°47N 19°15E **184** E6
Riesenrad *Austria* 48°14N 16°23E **142** A2
Riesi *Italy* 37°17N 14°5E **201** E7
Riet → *S. Africa* 29°0S 23°54E **270** C3
Rietavas *Lithuania* 55°44N 21°56E **184** C8
Rietbron *S. Africa* 32°54S 23°10E **270** D3
Rietfontein *Namibia* 21°58S 20°58E **270** B3
Rieti *Italy* 42°24N 12°51E **199** F9
Rieupeyroux *France* 44°19N 2°12E **174** D6
Riez *France* 43°49N 6°6E **175** E10
Rif = Er Rif *Morocco* 35°1N 4°1W **261** A4
Rif *Iceland* 64°56N 23°49W **155** C3
Riffe L. *U.S.A.* 46°32N 122°26W **306** D4
Rifle *U.S.A.* 39°32N 107°47W **304** G10
Rifstangi *Iceland* 66°32N 16°12W **155** A10
Rift Valley *Africa* 7°0N 30°0E **254** G7
Rift Valley □ *Kenya* 0°20N 36°0E **268** B4
Rig Rig *Chad* 14°13N 14°25E **259** F2
Riga *India* 28°26N 95°2E **241** A5
Riga *Latvia* 56°53N 24°8E **184** B11
Riga ✈ (RIX) *Latvia* 56°54N 23°59E **184** B10
Riga, G. of *Latvia* 57°40N 23°45E **184** A10
Rigacikun *Nigeria* 10°40N 7°28E **263** C6
Rīgān *Iran* 28°37N 58°58E **247** D8
Rīgas Jūras Līcis = Riga, G. of *Latvia* 57°40N 23°45E **184** A10
Rigaud *Canada* 45°29N 74°18W **313** A10
Rigby *U.S.A.* 43°40N 111°55W **304** E8
Rigestān *Afghan.* 30°15N 65°0E **240** C2
Riggins *U.S.A.* 45°25N 116°19W **304** D5
Rignac *France* 44°25N 2°16E **174** D6
Rigolet *Canada* 54°10N 58°23W **299** B8
Rigu *Ghana* 9°59N 0°48W **263** D4
Rihand Dam *India* 24°9N 83°2E **243** G10
Riihimäki *Finland* 60°45N 24°48E **188** B3
Riiser-Larsen-halvøya *Antarctica* 68°0S 35°0E **151** C4
Riiser-Larsen Ice Shelf *S. Ocean* 74°0S 19°0W **151** D2
Riiser-Larsen Sea *S. Ocean* 67°30S 22°0E **151** C4
Riisitunturi △ *Finland* 66°27N 28°27E **160** C23
Rijau *Nigeria* 11°8N 5°17E **263** C6
Rijeka *Croatia* 45°20N 14°21E **199** C11
Rijeka Crnojevića *Montenegro* 42°24N 19°1E **202** D3
Rijksmuseum *Amsterdam, Neths.* **112** c1
Rijssen *Neths.* 52°19N 6°31E **170** B6
Rika → *Ukraine* 48°11N 23°16E **183** B8
Rikā', W. ar → *Si. Arabia* 22°25N 44°50E **248** B4
Rike *Ethiopia* 10°50N 39°53E **257** E4
Rikers I. *U.S.A.* 40°47N 73°53W **132** B2
Riksdagshuset *Stockholm, Sweden* **139** b2
Rikuchū-Kaigan △ *Japan* 39°20N 142°0E **220** E11
Rikuzentakada *Japan* 39°0N 141°40E **220** E10
Rila *Bulgaria* 42°7N 23°7E **202** D7
Rila Planina *Bulgaria* 42°10N 23°20E **202** D7
Riley *U.S.A.* 43°32N 119°28W **304** E4
Rima → *Nigeria* 13°4N 5°10E **263** C6
Rimac *Peru* 12°2S 77°2W **124** B2
Rimāf *Yemen* 17°30N 50°35E **249** C5
Rimah, Wadi ar → *Si. Arabia* 26°5N 41°30E **246** E4
Rimatara *French Polynesia* 22°38S 152°51W **289** f
Rimau, Pulau *Malaysia* 5°15N 100°16E **237** c
Rimavská Sobota *Slovak Rep.* 48°22N 20°2E **181** C13
Rimbey *Canada* 52°35N 114°15W **296** C6
Rimbo *Sweden* 59°44N 18°21E **162** E12
Rimé, O. → *Chad* 14°2N 18°3E **259** F3
Rimersburg *U.S.A.* 41°3N 79°30W **312** E5
Rimforsa *Sweden* 58°6N 15°43E **163** F9
Rimini *Italy* 44°3N 12°33E **199** D9
Rimouski *Canada* 48°27N 68°30W **299** C6
Rimrock *U.S.A.* 46°40N 121°7W **306** D5
Rinca *Indonesia* 8°45S 119°35E **235** D5
Rincon *Bonaire* 12°14N 68°20W **322** h
Rincon *Puerto Rico* 18°20N 67°15W **321** b
Rincon *Ga., U.S.A.* 32°18N 81°14W **316** C8
Rincón de Anchuras = Anchuras *Spain* 39°29N 4°50W **195** F6
Rincón de la Victoria *Spain* 36°43N 4°18W **195** J6
Rincón de Romos *Mexico* 22°14N 102°18W **318** C4
Rincon Falls *Trin. & Tob.* 10°46N 61°24W **323** t
Rinconada *Argentina* 22°26S 66°10W **334** A2
Rind → *India* 25°53N 80°33E **243** G9
Rindal *Norway* 63°3N 9°13E **164** E3
Ringarum *Sweden* 58°21N 16°26E **163** F10
Ringas *India* 27°21N 75°34E **242** F6
Ringdove *Vanuatu* 16°40S 168°10E **287** F6
Ringe *Denmark* 55°13N 10°28E **163** J4
Ringebu *Norway* 61°32N 10°7E **164** C7
Ringgold Is. *Solomon Is.* 8°5S 157°10E **287** M9
Ringgold Is. *Fiji* 16°15S 179°25W **287** A3
Ringim *Nigeria* 12°13N 9°10E **263** C6
Ringkøbing *Denmark* 56°5N 8°15E **163** H2
Ringkøbing Fjord *Denmark* 56°0N 8°15E **163** J2
Ringoma *Angola* 12°25S 17°32E **265** E3
Ringsaker *Norway* 60°54N 10°45E **164** D7
Ringsend *Ireland* 53°20N 6°12W **120** A2
Ringsjön *Sweden* 55°55N 13°30E **163** J7
Ringsted *Denmark* 55°25N 11°46E **163** J5
Ringvassøya *Norway* 69°56N 19°15E **160** B18
Ringwood *U.S.A.* 41°7N 74°15W **313** E10
Rinia *Greece* 37°23N 25°13E **207** D7
Rinjani, Gunung *Indonesia* 8°24S 116°28E **235** D5
Rinjani △ *Indonesia* 8°26S 116°23E **235** D5
Rinkeby *Sweden* 59°23N 17°55E **139** A1
Rinteln *Germany* 52°11N 9°8E **178** C5
Rio, Punta del *Spain* 36°49N 2°24W **197** J2
Rio Bonito = Caiapônia *Brazil* 16°57S 51°49W **331** D7
Rio Branco = Arcoverde *Brazil* 8°25S 37°4W **332** C4
Rio Branco = Paratinga *Brazil* 12°40S 43°10W **333** D3
Rio Branco = Roraima □ *Brazil* 2°0N 61°30W **329** C5
Rio Branco *Brazil* 9°58S 67°49W **330** B4
Rio Branco *Uruguay* 32°40S 53°40W **335** C5
Rio Bravo *Mexico* 25°59N 98°6W **319** B5
Rio Bravo △ *N. Amer.* 29°2N 102°45W **318** B4
Rio Bravo del Norte → *Mexico* 25°57N 97°9W **319** B5
Rio Brilhante *Brazil* 21°48S 54°33W **335** A5
Rio Bueno *Chile* 40°19S 72°58W **336** B2
Rio Bueno *Jamaica* 18°28N 77°28W **320** a
Rio Caribe *Venezuela* 10°42N 63°7W **329** A5
Rio Chico *Venezuela* 10°19N 65°59W **328** A4
Rio Claro *Brazil* 22°19S 47°35W **335** A6
Rio Claro *Trin. & Tob.* 10°20N 61°10W **323** t
Rio Cobre → *Jamaica* 17°59N 76°52W **320** a
Rio Colorado *Argentina* 39°0S 64°0W **336** A4
Rio Comprido *Brazil* 22°55S 43°13W **135** B1
Rio Cuarto *Argentina* 33°10S 64°25W **334** C3
Rio das Pedras *Mozam.* 23°8S 35°28E **271** B6
Rio de Contas *Brazil* 13°36S 41°48W **333** D3
Rio de Janeiro *Brazil* 22°54S 43°12W **135** B1
Rio de Janeiro □ *Brazil* 22°50S 43°0W **333** F3
Rio de Janeiro Galeão ✈ (GIG) *Brazil* 22°49S 43°15W **135** A1
Rio de Mouro *Portugal* 38°46N 9°15W **126** A1
Rio de Oro, B. de *W. Sahara* 23°45N 15°50W **260** D1
Rio do Prado *Brazil* 16°35S 40°34W **333** E3
Rio do Sul *Brazil* 27°13S 49°37W **335** B6
Rio Dulce △ *Guatemala* 15°43N 88°50W **320** C2
Rio Gallegos *Argentina* 51°35S 69°15W **336** D3
Rio Grande *Argentina* 53°50S 67°45W **336** D3
Rio Grande *Bolivia* 20°51S 67°17W **330** E4
Rio Grande *Brazil* 32°0S 52°20W **335** C5
Rio Grande *Zacatecas, Mexico* 23°50N 103°2W **318** C4
Rio Grande *Puerto Rico* 18°23N 65°50W **321** b
Rio Grande → *N. Amer.* 25°58N 97°9W **314** J6
Rio Grande City *U.S.A.* 26°23N 98°49W **314** H5
Rio Grande de Santiago → *Mexico* 21°36N 105°26W **318** C3
Rio Grande do Norte □ *Brazil* 5°40S 36°0W **332** C4
Rio Grande do Sul □ *Brazil* 30°0S 53°0W **335** C5
Rio Grande Rise *Atl. Oc.* 31°0S 35°0W **152** K8
Rio Hato *Panama* 8°22N 80°10W **320** E3
Rio Lagartos *Mexico* 21°36N 88°10W **319** C7
Rio Largo *Brazil* 9°28S 35°50W **332** C4
Rio Maior *Portugal* 39°19N 8°57W **195** F2
Rio Marina *Italy* 42°49N 10°25E **198** F7
Rio Mayo *Argentina* 45°40S 70°15W **336** C2
Rio Mulatos *Bolivia* 19°40S 66°50W **330** D4
Rio Muni □ *Eq. Guin.* 1°30N 10°0E **264** B2
Rio Negro *Brazil* 26°0S 49°55W **335** B6
Rio Negro *Chile* 40°47S 73°14W **336** B2
Rio Negro, Pantanal do *Brazil* 19°0S 56°0W **331** D6
Rio Novo = Ipiaú *Brazil* 14°8S 39°44W **333** D4
Rio Pardo = Ribas do Rio Pardo *Brazil* 20°27S 53°46W **331** E7
Rio Pardo *Brazil* 30°0S 52°30W **335** C5
Rio Pico *Argentina* 44°0S 70°22W **336** B2
Rio Pilcomayo △ *Argentina* 25°5S 58°5W **334** B4
Rio Prêto = Santa Rita de Cássia *Brazil* 11°0S 44°32W **332** D3
Rio Preto da Eva *Brazil* 2°46S 59°41W **329** D6
Rio Rancho *U.S.A.* 35°14N 106°41W **305** J10
Rio Real *Brazil* 11°28S 37°56W **333** D4
Rio Seco = Villa de María *Argentina* 29°55S 63°43W **334** B3
Rio Segundo *Argentina* 31°40S 63°59W **334** C3
Rio Simpson △ *Chile* 45°27S 73°30W **336** C2
Rio Tercero *Argentina* 32°15S 64°8W **334** C3
Rio Tinto *Brazil* 6°48S 35°5W **332** C4
Rio Tinto *Portugal* 41°11N 8°34W **194** D2
Rio Tuba *Phil.* 8°31N 117°26E **233** G1
Rio Turbio *Argentina* 51°32S 72°18W **336** D2
Rio Verde *Brazil* 17°50S 51°0W **333** E1
Rio Verde *San Luis Potosí, Mexico* 21°56N 99°59W **319** C5
Rio Verde de Mato Grosso *Brazil* 18°56S 54°52W **331** D7
Rio Viejo △ *Venezuela* 7°15N 71°20W **328** B3
Rio Vista *U.S.A.* 38°10N 121°42W **306** G5
Riobamba *Ecuador* 1°50S 78°45W **328** D2
Riohacha *Colombia* 11°33N 72°55W **328** A3
Rioja *Peru* 6°11S 77°5W **330** B2
Riom *France* 45°54N 3°7E **174** C7
Riom-ès-Montagnes *France* 45°17N 2°39E **174** C6
Rion-des-Landes *France* 43°55N 0°56W **174** E3
Rionegro *Antioquia, Colombia* 6°9N 75°22W **328** B2
Rionegro *Santander, Colombia* 7°15N 73°9W **328** B3
Rionero in Vúlture *Italy* 40°55N 15°40E **201** B8
Rioni → *Georgia* 42°14N 41°44E **191** J5
Riós *Spain* 41°58N 7°16W **194** D3
Riosinho → *Brazil* 7°5S 51°39W **331** B7
Riosucio *Caldas, Colombia* 5°30N 75°40W **328** B2
Riosucio *Choco, Colombia* 7°27N 77°7W **328** B2
Riou L. *Canada* 59°7N 106°25W **297** B7
Rioz *France* 47°26N 6°5E **173** E13
Riozinho → *Brazil* 2°55S 67°7W **328** D4
Ripatransone *Italy* 42°59N 13°46E **199** F10
Ripley *Ont., Canada* 44°4N 81°35W **312** B3
Ripley *Calif., U.S.A.* 33°32N 114°39W **307** M12
Ripley *N.Y., U.S.A.* 42°16N 79°43W **312** D5
Ripley *Ohio, U.S.A.* 38°45N 83°51W **311** F13
Ripley *Tenn., U.S.A.* 35°45N 89°32W **315** D10
Ripley *W. Va., U.S.A.* 38°49N 81°43W **309** F13
Ripoll *Spain* 42°15N 2°13E **196** C7
Ripollet *Spain* 41°26N 2°10E **114** A1
Ripon *N. Yorks., U.K.* 54°9N 1°31W **168** C6
Ripon *Calif., U.S.A.* 37°44N 121°7W **306** H5
Ripon *Wis., U.S.A.* 43°51N 88°50W **308** D9
Riposto *Italy* 37°44N 15°12E **201** E8
Rippin = Rypin *Poland* 53°3N 19°25E **185** E6
Ris *Norway* 59°56N 10°41E **133** A3
Risan *Montenegro* 42°32N 18°42E **202** D2
Risaralda □ *Colombia* 5°0N 76°10W **328** C2
Risby *Denmark* 55°41N 12°19E **118** A1
Riscle *France* 43°39N 0°5W **174** E3
Rishā', W. ar → *Si. Arabia* 25°33N 44°5E **246** E5
Rishikesh *India* 30°7N 78°19E **242** D8
Rishiri-Rebun-Sarobetsu △ *Japan* 45°26N 141°30E **220** B10
Rishiri-Tō *Japan* 45°11N 141°15E **220** B10
Rishon le Ẕiyyon *Israel* 31°58N 34°48E **251** G5
Rishra *India* 22°42N 88°20E **124** A2
Rising Sun *U.S.A.* 38°57N 84°51W **311** F12
Risle → *France* 49°26N 0°23E **172** C7
Risnjak △ *Croatia* 45°25N 14°36E **199** C11
Rison *U.S.A.* 33°58N 92°11W **314** E8
Risør *Norway* 58°43N 9°13E **164** F6
Rissani *Morocco* 31°18N 4°12W **260** B4
Rita Blanca Cr. → *U.S.A.* 35°40N 102°29W **314** D3
Ritchie's Arch. *India* 12°14N 93°10E **245** H11
Rithala *India* 28°42N 77°6E **120** A1
Riti *Nigeria* 7°57N 9°41E **263** D6
Ritidian Pt. *Guam* 13°39N 144°51E **302** d
Ritter, Mt. *U.S.A.* 37°41N 119°12W **306** H7
Rittman *U.S.A.* 40°58N 81°47W **312** F3
Ritzville *U.S.A.* 47°8N 118°23W **304** C4
Riu *India* 28°19N 95°3E **241** A5
Riva del Garda *Italy* 45°53N 10°50E **198** C7
Riva Ligure *Italy* 43°50N 7°50E **198** E4
Rivadavia *B. Aires, Argentina* 35°29S 62°59W **334** D3
Rivadavia *Mendoza, Argentina* 33°13S 68°30W **334** C2
Rivadavia *Salta, Argentina* 24°5S 62°54W **334** A3
Rivadavia *Chile* 29°57S 70°35W **334** B1
Rivarolo Canavese *Italy* 45°19N 7°43E **198** C4
Rivas *Nic.* 11°30N 85°50W **320** D2
Rivash *Iran* 35°28N 58°26E **247** C8
Rive-de-Gier *France* 45°32N 4°37E **175** C8
Rive Sud, Canal de la *Canada* 45°24N 73°31W **130** B2
River Cess *Liberia* 5°30N 9°32W **262** D3
River Edge *U.S.A.* 40°56N 74°1W **132** A1
River Estate & Waterwheel *Trin. & Tob.* 10°41N 61°33W **323** t
River Forest *U.S.A.* 41°53N 87°49W **119** B2
River Grove *U.S.A.* 41°55N 87°50W **119** B1
River Jordan *Canada* 48°26N 124°3W **306** B2
River North *Chicago, U.S.A.* **119** b1
River Ridge *U.S.A.* 29°57N 90°12W **131** B1
Rivera *Argentina* 37°12S 63°14W **334** D3
Rivera *Uruguay* 31°0S 55°50W **335** C4
Riverbank *U.S.A.* 37°44N 120°56W **306** H6
Riverdale *Calif., U.S.A.* 36°26N 119°52W **306** J7
Riverdale *Ga., U.S.A.* 33°34N 84°25W **316** B5
Riverdale *Ill., U.S.A.* 41°38N 87°37W **119** D3
Riverdale *Md., U.S.A.* 38°57N 76°54W **143** B3
Riverdale *N.Y., U.S.A.* 40°59N 74°17W **132** A2
Riverdale Park *Canada* 43°40N 79°21W **141** A2
Riverhead *U.S.A.* 40°55N 72°40W **313** F12
Riverhurst *Canada* 50°55N 106°50W **297** C7
Riverlea *S. Africa* 26°12S 27°58E **123** B1
Rivers *Canada* 50°2N 100°14W **297** C8
Rivers □ *Nigeria* 4°30N 7°10E **263** E6
Rivers Inlet *Canada* 51°42N 127°15W **296** C3
Riversdale *Ont., Canada* 44°5N 81°20W **312** B3
Riversdale *N.Z.* 45°54S 168°44E **285** F3
Riversdale *Western Cape, S. Africa* 34°7S 21°15E **270** D3
Riverside *Calif., U.S.A.* 33°59N 117°22W **307** M9
Riverside *Ill., U.S.A.* 41°49N 87°49W **119** C2
Riversleigh *Australia* 19°5S 138°40E **280** B2
Riverton *S. Austral., Australia* 34°10S 138°46E **282** C3
Riverton *Man., Canada* 51°1N 97°0W **297** C9
Riverton *N.Z.* 46°21S 168°0E **285** G3
Riverton *Ill., U.S.A.* 39°51N 89°33W **310** E7
Riverton *Wyo., U.S.A.* 43°2N 108°23W **304** E9
Riverview *Fla., U.S.A.* 27°52N 82°20W **317** H7
Riverview *Fla., U.S.A.* 30°32N 87°12W **317** E2
Riverwood *Australia* 33°57S 151°3E **139** B1
Rives *France* 45°21N 5°31E **175** C9
Rivesaltes *France* 42°47N 2°50E **174** F6
Riviera = Azur, Côte d' *France* 43°25N 7°10E **175** E11
Riviera *U.S.A.* 35°4N 114°35W **307** K12
Riviera Beach *U.S.A.* 26°47N 80°3W **317** J9
Riviera di Levante *Italy* 44°15N 9°30E **198** D6
Riviera di Ponente *Italy* 44°10N 8°20E **198** D5
Rivière à Goyave, Pte. de la *Guadeloupe* 16°8N 61°33W **322** e
Rivière-au-Renard *Canada* 48°59N 64°23W **299** C7
Rivière des Anguilles *Mauritius* 20°29S 57°33E **272** e
Rivière-des-Prairies *Canada* 45°38N 73°34W **130** A2
Rivière-du-Loup *Canada* 47°50N 69°30W **299** C6
Rivière du Rempart *Mauritius* 20°6S 57°41E **272** e
Rivière-Pentecôte *Canada* 49°57N 67°1W **299** C6
Rivière-Pilote *Martinique* 14°26N 60°53W **322** j
Rivière St-Paul *Canada* 51°28N 57°45W **299** B8
Rivière-Salée *Martinique* 14°31N 61°0W **322** j
Rivne *Odesa, Ukraine* 46°1N 29°10E **183** D14
Rivne *Rivne, Ukraine* 50°40N 26°10E **177** C14
Rivne □ *Ukraine* 51°15N 26°30E **177** C14
Rivoli *Italy* 45°3N 7°31E **198** C4
Rivoli B. *Australia* 37°32S 140°3E **282** D4
Riwaka *N.Z.* 41°5S 172°59E **285** B7
Rixensart *Belgium* 50°43N 4°32E **116** B3
Rixheim *France* 47°40N 7°24E **173** E14
Riyad *Iraq* 33°18N 44°27E **113** B2
Riyadh = Ar Riyāḍ *Si. Arabia* 24°41N 46°42E **246** E5
Riza *Greece* 40°31N 23°15E **202** F7
Rizal *Cagayan, Phil.* 17°51N 121°21E **232** C3
Rizal *Nueva Ecija, Phil.* 15°43N 121°6E **232** D3
Rizal *Zamboanga del N., Phil.* 8°35N 123°26E **233** G4
Rizal Park *Phil.* 14°35N 120°58E **127** B1
Rizal Stadium *Phil.* 14°34N 120°59E **127** B1
Rize *Turkey* 41°0N 40°30E **213** B9
Rize □ *Turkey* 41°0N 40°30E **213** B9
Rizhao *China* 35°25N 119°30E **227** G10
Rizokarpaso *Cyprus* 35°36N 34°23E **207** E10
Rizzuto, C. *Italy* 38°53N 17°5E **201** D10
Rjukan *Norway* 59°54N 8°33E **164** E5
Rjuven *Norway* 59°9N 7°8E **164** E4
Rkîz, L. *Mauritania* 16°50N 15°23W **262** B1
Ro *Greece* 36°9N 29°33E **205** E11
Roa *Dem. Rep. of the Congo* 3°49N 24°56E **264** B4
Roa *Oppland, Norway* 60°17N 10°37E **164** D7
Roa *Oslo, Norway* 59°57N 10°39E **133** A2
Roa *Spain* 41°41N 3°56W **194** D7
Roachdale *U.S.A.* 39°51N 86°48W **311** E10
Road Town *Br. Virgin Is.* 18°27N 64°37W **321** C7
Roan Plateau *U.S.A.* 39°20N 109°20W **304** G9
Roanne *France* 46°3N 4°4E **173** F11
Roanoke *Ala., U.S.A.* 33°9N 85°22W **316** B4
Roanoke *Ind., U.S.A.* 40°58N 85°22W **311** D11
Roanoke *Va., U.S.A.* 37°16N 79°56W **309** G14
Roanoke → *U.S.A.* 35°57N 76°42W **315** D16
Roanoke I. *U.S.A.* 35°53N 75°39W **315** D17
Roanoke Rapids *U.S.A.* 36°28N 77°40W **315** C16
Roatán *Honduras* 16°18N 86°35W **320** C2
Rob Roy *Solomon Is.* 7°23S 157°36E **287** L9
Robāt *Iran* 34°16N 46°47E **213** E12
Robāt Sang *Iran* 35°35N 59°10E **247** C8
Robāṭkarīm *Iran* 35°25N 50°59E **247** C6
Robben I. *S. Africa* 33°46S 18°22E **270** D2
Robbins *U.S.A.* 41°38N 87°42W **119** D2
Robbins I. *Australia* 40°42S 145°0E **281** G4
Róbbio *Italy* 45°17N 8°35E **198** C5
Robe *Australia* 37°11S 139°45E **282** D3
Robe → *Australia* 21°42S 116°15E **278** D2
Röbel *Germany* 53°22N 12°35E **178** B8
Robert, Havre du *Martinique* 14°40N 60°55W **322** j
Robert Bourassa, Rés. *Canada* 53°40N 76°55W **298** B4
Robert Lee *U.S.A.* 31°54N 100°29W **314** F4
Roberta *U.S.A.* 32°43N 84°1W **316** C5
Roberts *U.S.A.* 40°37N 88°11W **311** D8
Roberts, Mt. *Trin. & Tob.* 10°47N 61°10W **323** t
Roberts, Mt. *Alaska, U.S.A.* 60°2N 166°16W **303** D6
Robertsdale *U.S.A.* 40°11N 78°6W **312** F6
Robertsganj *India* 24°44N 83°4E **243** G10
Robertsham *S. Africa* 26°15S 28°1E **123** B2
Robertson *S. Africa* 33°46S 19°50E **270** D2
Robertson I. *Antarctica* 65°15S 59°30W **151** C18
Robertson Ra. *Australia* 23°15S 121°0E **278** D3
Robertsport *Liberia* 6°45N 11°26W **262** D2
Robertstown *Australia* 33°58S 139°5E **282** B3
Roberval *Canada* 48°32N 72°15W **299** C5
Robeson Chan. *N. Amer.* 82°0N 61°30W **154** A4
Robesonia *U.S.A.* 40°21N 76°8W **312** F8
Robi *Ethiopia* 7°52N 39°38E **257** F4
Robinson *U.S.A.* 39°0N 87°44W **311** F9
Robinson → *Australia* 16°3S 137°16E **280** B2
Robinson Crusoe I. *Pac. Oc.* 33°38S 78°52W **330** c
Robinson Ra. *Australia* 25°40S 119°0E **279** E2
Robinvale *Australia* 34°40S 142°45E **282** C5
Robledal *Venezuela* 11°2N 64°22W **329** a
Robledo *Spain* 38°46N 2°26W **197** G2
Roblin *Canada* 51°14N 101°21W **297** C8
Roboré *Bolivia* 18°10S 59°45W **331** D6
Robson, Mt. *Canada* 53°10N 119°10W **296** C5
Robstown *U.S.A.* 27°47N 97°40W **314** H6
Roca, C. da *Portugal* 38°40N 9°31W **195** G1
Roca Partida, I. *Mexico* 19°1N 112°2W **318** D2
Rocamadour *France* 44°48N 1°37E **174** D5
Rocas, Atol das *Brazil* 4°0S 34°1W **152** G8
Rocca San Casciano *Italy* 44°3N 11°50E **199** D8
Roccadàspide *Italy* 40°27N 15°10E **201** B8
Roccastrada *Italy* 43°0N 11°10E **199** F8
Roccella Iónica *Italy* 38°19N 16°24E **201** D9
Rocciamelone, Mte. *Italy* 45°12N 7°5E **175** C11
Rocha *Uruguay* 34°30S 54°25W **335** C5
Rochdale *U.K.* 53°38N 2°9W **168** D5
Roche Melon = Rocciamelone, Mte. *Italy* 45°12N 7°5E **175** C11
Rochechouart *France* 45°50N 0°49E **174** C4
Rochedo *Brazil* 19°57S 54°52W **331** D7
Rochefort *Belgium* 50°9N 5°12E **170** D5
Rochefort *Charente-Maritime, France* 45°56N 0°57W **174** C3
Rochefort-en-Terre *France* 47°42N 2°22W **172** E4
Rochelle *Ga., U.S.A.* 31°57N 83°27W **316** D6
Rochelle *Ill., U.S.A.* 41°56N 89°4W **310** C7
Rochelle Park *U.S.A.* 40°54N 74°4W **132** A1
Rocher River *Canada* 61°23N 112°44W **296** A6
Roches, R. des → *Réunion* 21°0S 55°42E **272** f
Roche's Bluff *Montserrat* 16°42N 62°9W **323** p
Roches Noires *Mauritius* 20°5S 57°42E **272** e
Rocheservière *France* 46°57N 1°30W **172** F5
Rochester *Vic., Australia* 36°22S 144°42E **282** D6
Rochester *Medway, U.K.* 51°23N 0°31E **169** F8
Rochester *Ind., U.S.A.* 41°4N 86°13W **311** C10
Rochester *Minn., U.S.A.* 44°1N 92°28W **308** C7
Rochester *N.H., U.S.A.* 43°18N 70°59W **313** C14
Rochester *N.Y., U.S.A.* 43°10N 77°37W **312** C7
Rochester Hills *U.S.A.* 42°41N 83°8W **311** B13
Rociu *Romania* 44°43N 25°2E **183** F10
Rock → *Yukon, Canada* 60°7N 127°7W **296** A3
Rock → *Ill., U.S.A.* 41°29N 90°37W **310** C6
Rock, The *Australia* 35°15S 147°2E **283** C7
Rock Cr. → *U.S.A.* 38°54N 77°3W **143** B2
Rock Creek *U.S.A.* 41°40N 80°52W **312** E4
Rock Creek Park *U.S.A.* 38°56N 77°2W **143** B2
Rock Falls *U.S.A.* 41°47N 89°41W **310** C7
Rock Flat *Australia* 36°21S 149°13E **283** D8
Rock Hall *Barbados* 13°11N 59°36W **323** r
Rock Hill *U.S.A.* 34°56N 81°1W **315** D14
Rock Island *U.S.A.* 41°30N 90°34W **310** C6
Rock Port *U.S.A.* 40°25N 95°31W **308** E6
Rock Rapids *U.S.A.* 43°26N 96°10W **308** D5
Rock Sound *Bahamas* 24°54N 76°12W **320** B4
Rock Springs *Mont., U.S.A.* 46°49N 106°15W **304** C10
Rock Springs *Wyo., U.S.A.* 41°35N 109°14W **304** F9
Rock Valley *U.S.A.* 43°12N 96°18W **308** D5
Rockall *Atl. Oc.* 57°37N 13°42W **158** D3
Rockall Trough *Atl. Oc.* 57°0N 12°0W **152** A10
Rockaway Beach *U.S.A.* 40°34N 73°49W **132** C3
Rockaway Pt. *U.S.A.* 40°33N 73°54W **132** C2
Rockdale *N.S.W., Australia* 33°57S 151°8E **139** B1
Rockdale *Tex., U.S.A.* 30°39N 97°0W **314** F6
Rockdale *Wash., U.S.A.* 47°22N 121°28W **306** C5
Rockeby = Mungkan Kandju △ *Australia* 13°35S 142°52E **280** A3
Rockefeller Center *New York, U.S.A.* **132** c2
Rockefeller Plateau *Antarctica* 76°0S 130°0W **151** E14
Rockford *Ala., U.S.A.* 32°53N 86°13W **316** C3
Rockford *Ill., U.S.A.* 42°16N 89°6W **310** B7
Rockford *Iowa, U.S.A.* 43°3N 92°57W **310** A4
Rockford *Mich., U.S.A.* 43°7N 85°34W **311** A11
Rockford *Ohio, U.S.A.* 40°41N 84°39W **311** D12
Rockglen *Canada* 49°11N 105°57W **297** D7
Rockhampton *Australia* 23°22S 150°32E **280** C5
Rockingham *W. Austral., Australia* 32°15S 115°38E **279** F2
Rockingham *N.C., U.S.A.* 34°57N 79°46W **315** D15
Rockingham *Vt., U.S.A.* 43°11N 72°29W **313** C12
Rockingham B. *Australia* 18°5S 146°10E **280** B4
Rocklake *U.S.A.* 48°47N 99°15W **308** A4
Rockland *Ont., Canada* 45°33N 75°17W **313** A9
Rockland *Idaho, U.S.A.* 42°34N 112°53W **304** E7
Rockland *Maine, U.S.A.* 44°6N 69°7W **309** C19
Rockland *Mich., U.S.A.* 46°44N 89°11W **308** B9
Rocklands Bird Sanctuary *Jamaica* 18°24N 77°55W **320** a
Rocklands Reservoir *Australia* 37°15S 142°5E **282** D5
Rockledge *U.S.A.* 28°20N 80°43W **317** G9
Rocklin *U.S.A.* 38°48N 121°14W **306** G5
Rockly B. *Trin. & Tob.* 11°9N 60°46W **323** s
Rockmart *U.S.A.* 34°1N 85°3W **316** A4
Rockport *Ind., U.S.A.* 37°53N 87°3W **311** G9
Rockport *Mass., U.S.A.* 42°39N 70°37W **313** D14
Rockport *Tex., U.S.A.* 28°2N 97°3W **314** G6
Rocksprings *U.S.A.* 30°1N 100°13W **314** F4
Rockstone *Guyana* 5°59N 58°33W **329** B6
Rockville *Conn., U.S.A.* 41°52N 72°28W **313** E12
Rockville *Ind., U.S.A.* 39°46N 87°14W **311** E9
Rockville *Md., U.S.A.* 39°5N 77°9W **309** F15
Rockwall *U.S.A.* 32°56N 96°28W **314** E6
Rockwell City *U.S.A.* 42°24N 94°38W **310** B2
Rockwood *Ont., Canada* 43°37N 80°8W **312** C4
Rockwood *Maine, U.S.A.* 45°41N 69°45W **309** C19
Rockwood *Tenn., U.S.A.* 35°52N 84°41W **315** D12
Rocky Ford *U.S.A.* 38°3N 103°43W **304** G12
Rocky Fork L. *U.S.A.* 39°11N 83°26W **311** E13
Rocky Gully *Australia* 34°30S 116°57E **279** F2
Rocky Harbour *Canada* 49°36N 57°55W **299** C8
Rocky Island L. *Canada* 46°55N 83°0W **298** C3
Rocky Lane *Canada* 58°31N 116°22W **296** B5
Rocky Mount *U.S.A.* 35°57N 77°48W **315** D16
Rocky Mountain △ *U.S.A.* 40°25N 105°45W **304** F11
Rocky Mountain House *Canada* 52°22N 114°55W **296** C6
Rocky Mts. *N. Amer.* 49°0N 115°0W **304** B6
Rocky Point *Namibia* 19°3S 12°30E **270** A2
Rocroi *France* 49°55N 4°30E **173** C11
Rod *Pakistan* 28°10N 63°5E **240** C1
Roda = Stadtroda *Germany* 50°52N 11°44E **178** E7
Roda *Greece* 39°48N 19°46E **206** B9
Roda, Gezîret el *Egypt* 30°1N 31°13E **117** A2
Roda I. = Roda, Gezîret el *Egypt* 30°1N 31°13E **117** A2
Rodaun *Austria* 48°8N 16°16E **142** B1
Rødberg *Norway* 60°17N 8°56E **164** D5
Rødby *Denmark* 54°41N 11°23E **163** K5
Rødbyhavn *Denmark* 54°39N 11°22E **163** K5
Roddickton *Canada* 50°51N 56°8W **299** B8
Rødding *Denmark* 55°23N 9°3E **163** J3
Rödeby *Sweden* 56°15N 15°37E **163** H9
Rødekro *Denmark* 55°4N 9°20E **163** J3
Rodenkirchen *Germany* 53°23N 8°26E **178** B4
Rodez *France* 44°21N 2°33E **174** D6
Ródhos = Rhodes *Greece* 36°15N 28°10E **206** E12
Rodi Garganico *Italy* 41°55N 15°53E **199** G12
Rodia *Greece* 35°22N 25°1E **207** E6
Rodina *Kazakhstan* 50°16N 66°53E **217** B7
Rodna *Romania* 47°25N 24°50E **183** C9

Rodna ◎ Australia 23°45S 132°4E 278 D5
Rodnei, Munţii Romania 47°35N 24°35E 183 C9
Rodney Canada 42°34N 81°41W 312 D3
Rodney, C. N.Z. 36°17S 174°50E 284 C3
Rodney B. St. Lucia 14°5N 60°58W 323 m
Rodniki Russia 57°7N 41°47E 190 B5
Rodolivos Greece 40°55N 24°0E 202 F7
Rodonit, Kepi i Albania 41°35N 19°27E 202 E3
Rodopi Greece 41°5N 25°30E 203 E9
Rodopos Greece 35°34N 23°45E 207 E4
Rødovre Denmark 55°40N 12°26E 118 A2
Rodrigo de Freitas, L. Brazil 22°58S 43°12W 135 B1
Rodrigues Ind. Oc. 19°45S 63°20E 273 F5
Roe → U.K. 55°6N 6°59W 166 A5
Roebling U.S.A. 40°7N 74°47W 313 F10
Roebourne Australia 20°44S 117°9E 278 D2
Roebuck B. Australia 18°5S 122°20E 278 C3
Roebuck Roadhouse Australia 17°59S 122°36E 278 C3
Roehampton U.K. 51°27N 0°15W 125 B2
Roermond Neths. 51°12N 6°0E 170 C6
Roes Welcome Sd. Canada 65°0N 87°0W 295 E14
Roeselare Belgium 50°57N 3°7E 170 D3
Rogachev = Ragachow Belarus 53°8N 30°5E 177 B16
Rogačica Serbia 44°4N 19°40E 202 B3
Rogagua, L. Bolivia 13°43S 66°50W 330 C4
Rogaland □ Norway 59°12N 6°20E 164 E3
Rogaška Slatina Slovenia 46°15N 15°42E 199 B12
Rogatec Slovenia 46°15N 15°46E 199 B12
Rogatica Bos.-H. 43°47N 19°0E 182 G4
Rogatyn Ukraine 49°24N 24°36E 177 D13
Rogen Sweden 62°20N 12°20E 162 B6
Rogers U.S.A. 36°20N 94°7W 314 C7
Rogers Centre Toronto, Canada 141 c1
Rogers City U.S.A. 45°25N 83°49W 309 C12
Rogers Park U.S.A. 42°0N 87°40W 119 A3
Rogersville Canada 46°44N 65°26W 299 C6
Roggan → Canada 54°24N 79°25W 298 B4
Roggan L. Canada 54°8N 77°50W 298 B4
Roggeveen Basin Pac. Oc. 31°30S 95°30W 289 L18
Roggeveldberge S. Africa 32°10S 20°10E 270 D3
Roggiano Gravina Italy 39°37N 16°9E 201 C9
Rogliano Haute-Corse, France 42°57N 9°30E 175 F13
Rogliano Italy 39°10N 16°19E 201 C9
Rogoaguado, L. Bolivia 13°0S 65°30W 332 B4
Rogojampi Indonesia 8°19S 114°17E 231 J17
Rogoźno Poland 52°45N 16°59E 185 F3
Rogue → U.S.A. 42°26N 124°26W 304 E1
Roha India 18°26N 73°7E 244 E1
Rohan France 48°4N 2°45W 172 D4
Rohnert Park U.S.A. 38°16N 122°40W 306 G4
Rohri Pakistan 27°45N 68°51E 242 F3
Rohri Canal Pakistan 26°15N 68°27E 242 F3
Rohtak India 28°55N 76°43E 242 E7
Rohtisch-Sauerbrunn = Rogaška Slatina Slovenia 46°15N 15°42E 199 B12
Roi Et Thailand 16°4N 103°40E 236 D4
Roi-Georges, Îs. du French Polynesia 14°32S 145°8W 289 f
Roihuvuori Finland 60°11N 25°2E 121 B3
Roing India 28°9N 95°51E 241 A5
Roissy-en-Brie France 48°48N 2°39E 134 B4
Roja Latvia 57°29N 22°43E 184 A9
Rojas Argentina 34°10S 60°45W 334 C3
Rojište Romania 44°4N 23°56E 183 F8
Rojo, C. Mexico 21°33N 97°20W 319 C5
Rokan → Indonesia 2°0N 100°50E 234 B2
Rokel → S. Leone 8°30N 12°48W 262 D2
Rokin Amsterdam, Neths. 112 b2
Rokiškis Lithuania 55°55N 25°35E 188 E3
Rokitno Russia 50°57N 35°56E 189 G8
Rokua △ Finland 64°30N 26°15E 160 D22
Rokycany Czech Rep. 49°43N 13°35E 180 B6
Rokytka → Czech Rep. 50°6N 14°27E 135 B3
Roland Garros Paris, France 48°51N 2°15E 134 A2
Rolândia Brazil 23°18S 51°23W 335 A5
Røldal Norway 59°47N 6°50E 164 E3
Rolfe U.S.A. 42°49N 94°31W 310 B2
Rolla Mo., U.S.A. 37°57N 91°46W 310 G5
Rolla N. Dak., U.S.A. 48°52N 99°37W 308 A4
Rolleston Queens., Australia 24°28S 148°35E 280 C4
Rolleston N.Z. 43°35S 172°24E 285 D7
Rolling Fork → U.S.A. 37°55N 85°50W 311 G11
Rollingstone Australia 19°2S 146°24E 280 B4
Rom Vest-Agder, Norway 58°8N 7°56E 164 F4
Rom South Sudan 9°54N 32°16E 257 F3
Roma Queens., Australia 26°32S 148°49E 281 D4
Roma Italy 41°54N 12°28E 136 B1
Roma Sweden 57°32N 18°26E 163 G12
Roma, Piazzale Venice, Italy 142 b2
Roma Fiumicino ✈ (FCO) Italy 41°48N 12°15E 199 G9
Roma-Los Saenz U.S.A. 26°24N 99°1W 314 H5
Roma Urbe ✈ Italy 41°57N 12°30E 136 B2
Római-Fürdő Hungary 47°34N 19°4E 117 A2
Romain, C. U.S.A. 33°0N 79°22W 315 E15
Romaine → Canada 50°18N 63°47W 299 B7
Romainville France 48°52N 2°26E 134 A3
Roman Bulgaria 43°8N 23°57E 202 C7
Roman Romania 46°57N 26°55E 183 D11
Roman Forum = Foro Romano Rome, Italy 136 c3
Roman-Kosh, Gora Ukraine 44°37N 34°15E 189 K8
Romanche → France 45°5N 5°43E 175 C9
Romang Indonesia 7°30S 127°20E 231 F7
Români Egypt 30°59N 32°38E 251 H3
Romania ■ Europe 46°0N 25°0E 183 D10
Romanija Bos.-H. 43°50N 18°45E 182 G3
Romano, C. U.S.A. 25°51N 81°41W 317 K8
Romano, Cayo Cuba 22°0N 77°30W 320 B4
Romano Banco Italy 45°25N 9°6E 128 B1
Romanov-Borisoglebsk = Tutayev Russia 57°53N 39°32E 188 D10
Romanovka = Basarabeasca Moldova 46°21N 28°58E 183 D13
Romanovna-Murmane = Murmansk Russia 68°57N 33°10E 160 B25
Romanovsk = Kropotkin Russia 45°28N 40°28E 191 H5
Romanovskiy Khutor = Kropotkin Russia 45°28N 40°28E 191 H5
Romans-sur-Isère France 45°3N 5°3E 175 C9
Romanshorn Switz. 47°33N 9°22E 179 H5
Romanzof C. U.S.A. 61°49N 166°6W 303 F6
Rombari South Sudan 4°33N 31°2E 257 G3
Romblon Phil. 12°33N 122°17E 232 E4
Romblon □ Phil. 12°30N 122°15E 232 E4
Romblon Pass. Phil. 12°27N 122°12E 232 E4
Rome = Roma Italy 41°54N 12°28E 136 B1
Rome Ga., U.S.A. 34°15N 85°10W 315 D12
Rome N.Y., U.S.A. 43°13N 75°27W 313 C9
Rome Pa., U.S.A. 41°51N 76°21W 313 E8
Romema Israel 31°48N 35°12E 123 B2
Romeoville U.S.A. 41°39N 88°3W 311 C8
Rometta Italy 38°10N 15°25E 201 D8
Romford U.K. 51°34N 0°11E 125 A5
Romilly-sur-Seine France 48°31N 3°44E 173 D10
Romiton Uzbekistan 39°56N 64°23E 216 E6
Rommani Morocco 33°31N 6°40W 260 B3
Romney U.S.A. 39°21N 78°45W 309 F14
Romney Marsh U.K. 51°2N 0°54E 169 F8
Romny Ukraine 50°48N 33°28E 189 G7
Rømø Denmark 55°10N 8°30E 163 J2
Romodan Ukraine 49°55N 33°15E 189 G7
Romodanovo Russia 54°26N 45°23E 190 C7
Romont Switz. 46°42N 6°54E 179 J2
Romorantin-Lanthenay France 47°21N 1°45E 173 E8
Rompin → Malaysia 2°49N 103°29E 237 L4
Romsdalen Norway 62°25N 7°52E 164 B4
Romsdalsfjorden Norway 62°38N 7°20E 164 B4
Romsey U.K. 51°0N 1°29W 169 G6
Ron India 15°40N 75°44E 245 G2
Ron Vietnam 17°53N 106°27E 236 D6
Rona U.K. 57°34N 5°59W 167 D3
Ronald Reagan Nat. Washington ✈ (DCA) U.S.A. 38°51N 77°2W 143 B2
Ronan U.S.A. 47°32N 114°6W 304 C6
Roncador, Cayos Colombia 13°32N 80°4W 320 D3
Roncador, Serra do Brazil 12°30S 52°30W 333 D1
Ronciglione Italy 42°17N 12°13E 199 F9
Ronco → Italy 44°24N 12°12E 199 D9
Ronda Spain 36°46N 5°12W 195 J5
Ronda, Serranía de Spain 36°44N 5°3W 195 J5
Rondane Norway 61°57N 9°50E 164 C6
Rondane △ Norway 61°55N 9°44E 164 C6
Ronde, Pt. Dominica 15°33N 61°29W 323 k
Ronde I. Grenada 12°29N 61°36W 323 q
Rondebosch S. Africa 33°58S 18°28E 118 A1
Rondón Colombia 6°17N 71°6W 328 B3
Rondônia Brazil 10°52S 61°57W 331 C5
Rondônia □ Brazil 11°0S 63°0W 331 C5
Rondonópolis Brazil 16°28S 54°38W 331 D7
Rondslottet Norway 61°55N 9°45E 164 C6
Rondu Pakistan 35°32N 75°10E 243 B6
Rong, Koh Cambodia 10°45N 103°15E 237 G4
Rong Jiang → China 24°35N 109°20E 228 E7
Rong Xian China 22°50N 110°31E 229 F8
Rong'an China 25°14N 109°22E 228 E7
Rongchang China 29°20N 105°32E 228 C5
Rongcheng China 37°9N 122°23E 227 F12
Ronge, L. la Canada 55°6N 105°17W 297 B7
Rongjiang China 25°57N 108°28E 228 E7
Rongotea N.Z. 40°19S 175°25E 284 G4
Rongshui China 25°5N 109°12E 228 E7
Rongxian China 29°23N 104°22E 228 C5
Rønne Denmark 55°6N 14°43E 163 J8
Ronne Ice Shelf Antarctica 77°30S 60°0W 151 D18
Ronneby Sweden 56°12N 15°17E 163 H9
Ronnebyån → Sweden 56°11N 15°18E 163 H9
Rönneshytta Sweden 58°56N 15°2E 163 F9
Ronsard, C. Australia 24°46S 113°10E 279 D1
Ronse Belgium 50°45N 3°35E 170 D3
Ronuro → Brazil 11°56S 53°33W 331 C7
Roodepoort S. Africa 26°11S 27°54E 271 C4
Roodhouse U.S.A. 39°29N 90°24W 310 E6
Roof Butte U.S.A. 36°28N 109°5W 305 H9
Rooiboklaagte → Namibia 20°50S 21°0E 270 B3
Rooniu, Mt. Tahiti 17°49S 149°12W 289 e
Roopville U.S.A. 33°27N 85°8W 316 B4
Roorkee India 29°52N 77°59E 242 E7
Roosendaal Neths. 51°32N 4°29E 170 C4
Roosevelt U.S.A. 40°18N 109°59W 304 F9
Roosevelt → Brazil 7°35S 60°20W 331 B5
Roosevelt, Mt. Canada 58°26N 125°20W 296 B3
Roosevelt I. Antarctica 79°30S 162°0W 151 D12
Roosevelt I. New York, U.S.A. 132 c3
Ropczyce Poland 50°4N 21°38E 185 H8
Roper → Australia 14°43S 135°27E 280 A2
Roper Bar Australia 14°44S 134°44E 280 A1
Roper River = St. Vidgeon's ◎ Australia 14°47S 134°53E 280 A1
Roppongi Tokyo, Japan 140 c3
Roque Pérez Argentina 35°25S 59°24W 334 D4
Roquefort France 44°2N 0°20W 174 D3
Roquemaure France 44°3N 4°48E 175 D8
Roquetas de Mar Spain 36°46N 2°36W 197 J2
Roquetes Spain 40°50N 0°30E 196 E5
Roquevaire France 43°20N 5°36E 175 E9
Roraima □ Brazil 2°0N 61°30W 329 C5
Roraima, Mt. Venezuela 5°10N 60°40W 329 B5
Røros Norway 62°35N 11°23E 164 B8
Rorschach Switz. 47°28N 9°28E 179 H5
Ros Comáin = Roscommon Ireland 53°38N 8°11W 166 C3
Ros Mhic Thriúin = New Ross Ireland 52°23N 6°57W 166 D5
Rosa Zambia 9°33S 31°15E 269 D3
Rosa, C. Algeria 37°0N 8°16E 261 A6
Rosa, C. Galápagos Is., Ecuador 1°4S 91°10W 330 a
Rosa, Monte Europe 45°57N 7°53E 198 C4
Rosais, Pta. dos Azores 38°45N 28°19W 153 d1
Rosal de la Frontera Spain 37°59N 7°13W 195 H3
Rosales Phil. 15°54N 120°38E 232 D3
Rosalia U.S.A. 47°14N 117°22W 304 C5
Rosalie Dominica 15°22N 61°16W 323 k
Rosalie → Dominica 15°22N 61°15W 323 k
Rosalind Bank Caribbean 16°30N 80°30W 320 C3
Rosamond U.S.A. 34°52N 118°10W 307 L8
Rosans France 44°24N 5°29E 175 D9
Rosário Argentina 33°0S 60°40W 334 C3
Rosário Maranhão, Brazil 3°0S 44°15W 332 B3
Rosário Sinaloa, Mexico 22°58N 105°53W 318 C3
Rosário Paraguay 24°30S 57°35W 334 A4
Rosário Agusan del S., Phil. 8°24N 125°59E 233 G5
Rosário Batangas, Phil. 13°50N 121°12E 232 E3
Rosário, Villa del Venezuela 10°19N 72°19W 328 A3
Rosário de la Frontera Argentina 25°50S 65°0W 334 B3
Rosário de Lerma Argentina 24°59S 65°35W 334 A2
Rosario del Tala Argentina 32°20S 59°10W 334 C4
Rosário do Sul Brazil 30°15S 54°55W 335 C5
Rosário Oeste Brazil 14°50S 56°25W 331 C6
Rosarito Baja Calif., Mexico 32°20N 117°2W 307 N9
Rosarito Baja Calif., Mexico 28°38N 114°1W 318 B2
Rosarno Italy 38°29N 15°58E 201 D8
Rosas = Roses Spain 42°19N 3°10E 196 C8
Roscoe Mo., U.S.A. 37°58N 93°48W 310 G3
Roscoe N.Y., U.S.A. 41°56N 74°55W 313 E10
Roscoff France 48°44N 3°58W 172 D3
Roscommon Ireland 53°38N 8°11W 166 C3
Roscommon □ Ireland 53°49N 8°23W 166 C3
Roscrea Ireland 52°57N 7°49W 166 D4
Rose → Australia 14°16S 135°45E 280 A2
Rose, L. Bahamas 21°0N 73°30W 321 B5
Rose, L. Fla., U.S.A. 28°32N 81°30W 133 A1
Rose Belle Mauritius 20°24S 57°36E 273 d
Rose Blanche Canada 47°38N 58°45W 299 C8
Rose Bowl U.S.A. 34°9N 118°10W 126 B4
Rose Hall Great House Jamaica 18°31N 77°49W 320 a
Rose Hill = Port Mourant Guyana 6°15N 57°20W 329 B6
Rose Hill Mauritius 20°14S 57°27E 272 e
Rose Hill Va., U.S.A. 38°47N 77°6W 143 C2
Rose Pt. Canada 54°11N 131°39W 296 C2
Rose Rock Grenada 12°24N 61°28W 323 q
Rose Valley Canada 52°19N 103°49W 297 C8
Roseau Dominica 15°17N 61°24W 323 k
Roseau Minn., U.S.A. 48°51N 95°46W 308 A6
Rosebank Gauteng, S. Africa 26°8S 28°2E 123 A2
Rosebank N.Y., U.S.A. 40°36N 74°4W 132 C1
Rosebery N.S.W., Australia 33°55S 151°12E 139 B2
Rosebery Tas., Australia 41°46S 145°33E 281 G4
Rosebud Vic., Australia 38°21S 144°54E 282 E6
Rosebud S. Dak., U.S.A. 43°14N 100°51W 308 D3
Rosebud Tex., U.S.A. 31°4N 96°59W 314 F6
Roseburg U.S.A. 43°13N 123°20W 304 E2
Rosedal La Candelaria Mexico 19°20N 99°10W 128 B2
Rosedale U.S.A. 33°51N 91°2W 315 E9
Rosehearty U.K. 57°42N 2°7W 167 D6
Roseires Res. Sudan 11°51N 34°23E 266 B3
Roseland Calif., U.S.A. 38°25N 122°43W 306 G4
Roseland Ill., U.S.A. 41°42N 87°37W 119 C3
Rosemary Canada 50°46N 112°5W 296 C6
Rosemead U.S.A. 34°4N 118°4W 126 B4
Rosemont Qué., Canada 45°34N 73°33W 130 A2
Rosemont Ill., U.S.A. 41°59N 87°53W 119 B1
Rosenberg = Olesno Poland 50°51N 18°26E 185 H5
Rosenberg = Susz Poland 53°44N 19°20E 184 E6
Rosenberg U.S.A. 29°34N 95°49W 314 G7
Rosenborg Slot Copenhagen, Denmark 118 b2
Rosendaël France 51°3N 2°24E 173 A9
Rosendal Norway 59°59N 6°0E 164 E3
Rosendale U.S.A. 40°4N 94°51W 310 D2
Rosenheim Germany 47°51N 12°7E 179 H8
Rosenthal Germany 52°35N 13°22E 115 A3
Roses Spain 42°19N 3°10E 196 C8
Roses, G. de Spain 42°10N 3°15E 196 C8
Roseto degli Abruzzi Italy 42°41N 14°1E 199 F11
Rosetown Canada 51°35N 107°59W 297 C7
Rosetta = Rashîd Egypt 31°21N 30°22E 256 H7
Rosettenville S. Africa 26°15S 28°3E 123 B2
Roseville Calif., U.S.A. 38°45N 121°17W 306 G5
Roseville Ill., U.S.A. 40°44N 90°40W 310 D6
Roseville Mich., U.S.A. 42°30N 82°56W 312 D2
Roseville Pa., U.S.A. 41°51N 76°57W 313 E8
Rosewell U.K. 55°51N 3°8W 121 B3
Rosewood Australia 27°38S 152°36E 281 D5
Rosherville Dam S. Africa 26°13S 28°6E 123 B2
Roshkhvār Iran 34°58N 59°37E 247 C8
Rosières-en-Santerre France 49°49N 2°42E 173 C9
Rosignano Marittimo Italy 43°24N 10°28E 198 E7
Rosignol Guyana 6°15N 57°30W 329 B6
Roşiori de Vede Romania 44°9N 25°0E 183 F10
Rositsa Bulgaria 43°57N 27°57E 203 C11
Rositsa → Bulgaria 43°10N 25°30E 203 C9
Rosjön Sweden 59°26N 18°0E 139 A2
Roskilde Denmark 55°38N 12°3E 163 J6
Roskovec Albania 40°44N 19°43E 202 F3
Roslags-Näsby Sweden 59°25N 18°2E 139 A2
Roslavl Russia 53°57N 32°55E 188 F7
Roslin U.K. 55°51N 3°11W 121 B3
Roslindale U.S.A. 42°17N 71°7W 116 B2
Rosmaninhal Portugal 39°44N 7°5W 194 F3
Rosmead S. Africa 31°29S 25°8E 270 D4
Røsnæs Denmark 55°44N 10°55E 163 J4
Rosny-sous-Bois France 48°52N 2°30E 134 A4
Rosolini Italy 36°49N 14°57E 201 F7
Rosporden France 47°57N 3°50W 172 E3
Ross Tas., Australia 42°2S 147°30E 281 G4
Ross N.Z. 42°53S 170°49E 285 C5
Ross Béthio Mauritania 16°15N 16°8W 262 B1
Ross Dependency Antarctica 76°0S 170°0W 151 D12
Ross I. Antarctica 77°30S 168°0E 151 D11
Ross Ice Shelf Antarctica 80°0S 180°0E 151 E12
Ross L. U.S.A. 48°44N 121°4W 304 B3
Ross-on-Wye U.K. 51°54N 2°34W 169 F5
Ross River N. Terr., Australia 23°44S 134°30E 280 C1
Ross River Yukon, Canada 62°30N 131°30W 296 A2
Ross Sea Antarctica 74°0S 178°0E 151 D11
Rossall Pt. U.K. 53°55N 3°3W 168 D4
Rossan Pt. Ireland 54°42N 8°47W 166 B3
Rossano Italy 39°36N 16°39E 201 C9
Rossburn Canada 50°40N 100°49W 297 C8
Rosseau Canada 45°16N 79°39W 312 A5
Rosseau, L. Canada 45°10N 79°35W 312 A5
Rössel = Reszel Poland 54°4N 21°10E 184 D8
Rossel I. Papua N. G. 11°21S 154°9E 286 F8
Rosses, The Ireland 55°2N 8°20W 166 A3
Rossford U.S.A. 41°36N 83°34W 311 C13
Rossignol, L. Canada 52°43N 73°40W 298 B5
Rossignol L. Canada 44°12N 65°10W 299 D6
Rossiya = Russia ■ Eurasia 62°0N 105°0E 215 C11
Rosskreppfjorden Norway 59°4N 7°10E 164 E4
Rossland Canada 49°6N 117°50W 296 D5
Rosslare Ireland 52°17N 6°24W 166 D5
Rosslare Europort = Rosslare Harbour Ireland 52°15N 6°20W 166 D5
Rosslare Harbour Ireland 52°15N 6°20W 166 D5
Rosslau Germany 51°52N 12°15E 178 D8
Rosslyn U.S.A. 38°53N 77°4W 143 B2
Rossmore Canada 44°8N 77°23W 312 B7
Rosso Mauritania 16°40N 15°45W 262 B1
Rosso, C. France 42°13N 8°32E 175 F12
Rossosh Russia 50°15N 39°28E 189 G10
Rossvatnet Norway 65°45N 14°5E 160 D16
Rossville Ill., U.S.A. 40°23N 87°40W 311 D9
Rossville Ind., U.S.A. 40°25N 86°36W 311 D10
Røst Norway 67°32N 12°10E 160 C15
Rostaq = Ar Rustāq Oman 23°23N 57°26E 249 B7
Rostāq Afghan. 37°7N 69°49E 240 A3
Rosthern Canada 52°40N 106°20W 297 C7
Rostock Germany 54°5N 12°8E 178 A8
Rostov Don, Russia 47°15N 39°45E 189 J10
Rostov Yaroslavl, Russia 57°14N 39°25E 188 D10
Rostov □ Russia 48°50N 41°10E 191 F5
Rostrenen France 48°14N 3°21W 172 D3
Roswell Ga., U.S.A. 34°2N 84°22W 316 A5
Roswell N. Mex., U.S.A. 33°24N 104°32W 305 K11
Rosyth U.K. 56°2N 3°25W 121 A1
Rot-Front = Dobropole Ukraine 48°25N 37°2E 189 H9
Rota N. Marianas 14°9N 145°12E 302 a
Rota Spain 36°37N 6°20W 195 J4
Rotan U.S.A. 32°51N 100°28W 314 E4
Rote Indonesia 10°50S 123°0E 231 F6
Rotenburg Hessen, Germany 50°59N 9°44E 178 E5
Rotenburg Niedersachsen, Germany 53°6N 9°25E 178 B5
Roth Germany 49°15N 11°5E 179 F7
Rothaargebirge Germany 51°2N 8°13E 178 D4
Rothaargebirge △ Germany 51°0N 8°15E 178 E4
Rothenburg ob der Tauber Germany 49°23N 10°11E 179 F6
Rother → U.K. 50°59N 0°45E 169 G8
Rothera Antarctica 67°34S 68°8W 151 C17
Rotherham U.K. 53°26N 1°20W 168 D6
Rotherhithe U.K. 51°29N 0°2W 125 B3
Rothes U.K. 57°32N 3°13W 167 D5
Rothesay N.B., Canada 45°23N 66°0W 299 C6
Rothesay Argyll & Bute, U.K. 55°50N 5°3W 167 F3
Rothneusiedl Austria 48°8N 16°23E 142 B2
Rothschmaige Germany 48°14N 11°27E 131 A1
Roti = Rote Indonesia 10°50S 123°0E 231 F6
Rotja, Pta. Spain 38°38N 1°35E 206 D2
Rotnes Norway 60°3N 10°51E 164 D7
Roto Australia 33°0S 145°30E 283 B6
Rotoaira, L. N.Z. 39°3S 175°45E 284 F4
Rotoehu, L. N.Z. 38°1S 176°32E 284 E5
Rotoiti, L. Bay of Plenty, N.Z. 38°2S 176°26E 284 E5
Rotoiti, L. W. Coast, N.Z. 41°51S 172°49E 285 B7
Rotoma, L. N.Z. 38°2S 176°35E 284 E5
Rotondo, Mte. France 42°14N 9°8E 175 F13
Rotoroa, L. N.Z. 41°55S 172°39E 285 B7
Rotorua N.Z. 38°9S 176°16E 284 E5
Rotorua, L. N.Z. 38°5S 176°18E 284 E5
Rott → Germany 48°27N 13°25E 179 G9
Rottenburg Germany 48°28N 8°55E 179 G4
Rottenmann Austria 47°31N 14°22E 180 D7
Rotterdam Neths. 51°55N 4°30E 170 C4
Rotterdam N.Y., U.S.A. 42°48N 74°1W 313 D10
Rottne Sweden 57°1N 14°54E 163 G8
Rottnest I. Australia 32°0S 115°27E 279 F2
Rottumeroog Neths. 53°33N 6°34E 170 A6
Rottweil Germany 48°9N 8°37E 179 G4
Rotuma Fiji 12°25S 177°5E 277 C14
Roubaix France 50°40N 3°10E 173 B10
Rouche Island St. Lucia 13°57N 60°52W 323 m
Roudnice nad Labem Czech Rep. 50°25N 14°15E 180 A7
Rouen France 49°27N 1°4E 172 C8
Rouergue France 44°15N 2°0E 174 D5
Rouge Hill Canada 43°48N 79°6W 141 A4
Rough Ridge N.Z. 45°10S 169°55E 285 F4
Rouillac France 45°47N 0°4W 174 C3
Rouissat Algeria 31°55N 5°20E 261 B6
Rouleau Canada 50°10N 104°56W 297 C8
Roulers = Roeselare Belgium 50°57N 3°7E 170 D3
Roulpmaulpma ◎ Australia 23°52S 133°0E 278 D5
Round Hill Jamaica 17°50N 77°23W 320 a
Round Hill St. Kitts & Nevis 17°11N 62°36W 322 d
Round I. Hong Kong, China 22°13N 114°11E 122 B3
Round Mountain U.S.A. 38°43N 117°4W 304 G5
Round Mt. Australia 30°26S 152°16E 283 A10
Round Rock U.S.A. 30°31N 97°41W 314 F6
Roundhouse Park Toronto, Canada 141 c2
Roundup U.S.A. 46°27N 108°33W 304 C9
Roura Fr. Guiana 4°44N 52°20W 329 C7
Rousay U.K. 59°10N 3°2W 167 B5
Rouses Point U.S.A. 44°59N 73°22W 313 B11
Rouseville U.S.A. 41°28N 79°42W 312 E5
Rousse = Ruse Bulgaria 43°48N 25°59E 203 C9
Roussenski Lom △ Bulgaria 43°40N 26°10E 203 C10
Roussillac Swamp Trin. & Tob. 10°14N 61°35W 323 t
Roussillon Isère, France 45°24N 4°49E 175 C8
Roussillon Pyrénées-Or., France 42°30N 2°35E 174 F6
Rouxville S. Africa 30°25S 26°50E 270 D4
Rouyn-Noranda Canada 48°20N 79°0W 298 C4
Rovaniemi Finland 66°29N 25°41E 160 C21
Rovato Italy 45°34N 10°0E 198 C7
Rovenki Ukraine 48°5N 39°21E 189 H10
Rovereto Italy 45°53N 11°3E 198 C8
Roverud Norway 60°15N 12°3E 164 D9
Rovigno = Rovinj Croatia 45°5N 13°40E 199 C10
Rovigo Italy 45°4N 11°47E 199 C8
Rovinj Croatia 45°5N 13°40E 199 C10
Rovira Colombia 4°15N 75°20W 328 C2
Rovno = Rivne Ukraine 50°40N 26°10E 177 C14
Rovnoye Russia 50°52N 46°3E 190 E8
Rovuma = Ruvuma → Tanzania 10°29S 40°28E 269 E5
Row'ān Iran 35°8N 48°51E 247 C6
Rowena Australia 29°48S 148°55E 281 D4
Rowley I. Canada 69°6N 77°52W 295 D16
Rowley Shoals Australia 17°30S 119°0E 278 C2
Roxa Guinea-Biss. 11°15N 15°45W 262 C1
Roxas Capiz, Phil. 11°36N 122°49E 233 F4
Roxas Isabela, Phil. 17°8N 121°36E 232 C3
Roxas Mind. Or., Phil. 12°35N 121°31E 232 E3
Roxas Palawan, Phil. 10°20N 119°21E 233 F2
Roxboro U.S.A. 36°24N 78°59W 315 C15
Roxborough Trin. & Tob. 11°15N 60°35W 323 s
Roxburgh N.Z. 45°33S 169°19E 285 F4
Roxbury Mass., U.S.A. 42°19N 71°5W 116 B2
Roxbury N.Y., U.S.A. 42°17N 74°33W 313 D10
Roxbury Pa., U.S.A. 40°6N 77°39W 312 F7
Roxby Downs Australia 30°43S 136°46E 281 E2
Roxen Sweden 58°30N 15°40E 163 F9
Roxeth U.K. 51°33N 0°20W 125 A1
Roy Mont., U.S.A. 47°20N 108°58W 304 C9
Roy N. Mex., U.S.A. 35°57N 104°12W 305 J11
Roy Utah, U.S.A. 41°10N 112°2W 304 F7
Roy Thomson Hall Toronto, Canada 141 c2
Royal △ Australia 34°5S 151°5E 283 C9
Royal Bardia △ Nepal 28°20N 81°20E 243 E9
Royal Botanic Gardens Sydney, Australia 139 b2
Royal Botanic Gardens Edinburgh, U.K. 55°58N 3°12W 121 B2
Royal Canal Ireland 53°30N 7°13W 166 C4
Royal Center U.S.A. 40°52N 86°30W 311 D10
Royal Chitawan △ Nepal 26°30N 84°30E 243 F11
Royal Exhibition Building Australia 37°48S 144°58E 128 A1
Royal Geographical Society U.K. 125 b1
Royal Geographical Society Is. Canada 68°56N 100°15W 294 D11
Royal Leamington Spa U.K. 52°18N 1°31W 169 E6
Royal Manas △ Bhutan 26°45N 90°50E 241 B3
Royal Natal △ S. Africa 28°43S 28°51E 271 C4
Royal Oak U.S.A. 42°30N 83°9W 311 B13
Royal Observatory U.K. 55°55N 3°12W 121 B2
Royal Palace = Koninklijk Paleis Amsterdam, Neths. 112 a2
Royal Palace = Kungliga Slottet Stockholm, Sweden 139 b2
Royal Palace = Palacio Real Madrid, Spain 127 b1
Royal Palace = Palais Royal Brussels, Belgium 116 b3
Royal Palace = Slottet Oslo, Norway 133 a1
Royal Palm Beach U.S.A. 26°42N 80°14W 317 J9
Royal Park Australia 37°46S 144°57E 128 A1
Royal Tunbridge Wells U.K. 51°7N 0°16E 169 F8
Royal Turf Club Bangkok, Thailand 113 b2
Royale, Isle U.S.A. 48°0N 88°54W 308 B9
Royalla Australia 35°30S 149°9E 283 C8
Royan France 45°37N 1°2W 174 C2
Roye France 49°42N 2°48E 173 C9
Röylä Finland 60°18N 24°42E 121 B1
Royston U.K. 52°3N 0°0 169 E7
Royal Montenegro 42°50N 20°11E 202 D4
Rożan Poland 52°52N 21°25E 185 F8
Rozas, Portilleros de las Spain 40°29N 3°49W 127 B1
Rozay-en-Brie France 48°41N 2°58E 173 D9
Rozdilna Ukraine 46°50N 30°2E 183 D15
Rozhnyativ Ukraine 48°56N 24°9E 183 B9
Rozhyshche Ukraine 50°54N 25°15E 177 C13
Rožmitál pod Třemšínem Czech Rep. 49°36N 13°53E 180 B6
Rožňava Slovak Rep. 48°37N 20°35E 181 C13
Rozogi Poland 53°28N 21°19E 184 E8
Rozoy-sur-Serre France 49°40N 4°8E 173 C11
Roztoczański △ Poland 50°37N 23°0E 185 H10
Rozstoky Czech Rep. 50°9N 14°23E 135 B2
Rozzano Italy 45°22N 9°10E 128 B1
Rrëshen Albania 41°47N 19°49E 202 E3
Rrogozhinë Albania 41°4N 19°50E 202 E3
Rtanj Serbia 43°45N 21°50E 202 C5
Rtem, O. er → Algeria 33°29N 5°38E 261 B6
Rtishchevo Russia 52°18N 43°46E 190 D6
Rúa = A Rúa Spain 42°24N 7°6W 194 C3
Ruacaná Namibia 17°27S 14°21E 265 F2
Ruaha △ Tanzania 7°41S 34°30E 268 D3
Ruahine Ra. N.Z. 39°55S 176°2E 284 F5
Ruamahanga → N.Z. 41°24S 175°8E 284 H4
Ruapehu N.Z. 39°17S 175°35E 284 F4
Ruapuke I. N.Z. 46°46S 168°31E 285 G3
Ruâq, W. → Egypt 30°0N 33°49E 251 J4
Ruatoria N.Z. 37°55S 178°20E 284 D7
Ruavatu Solomon Is. 9°26S 160°26E 287 M11
Ruawai N.Z. 36°8S 173°59E 284 C2
Rub' al Khālī Si. Arabia 19°0N 48°0E 249 C5
Rubeho Mts. Tanzania 6°50S 36°25E 268 D4
Rubezhnoye = Rubizhne Ukraine 49°6N 38°25E 189 H10
Rubh a' Mhail U.K. 55°56N 6°8W 167 F2
Rubha Hunish U.K. 57°42N 6°20W 167 D2
Rubha Robhanais = Lewis, Butt of U.K. 58°31N 6°16W 167 C2
Rubí Spain 41°29N 2°2E 196 D7
Rubi → Dem. Rep. of the Congo 2°48N 23°54E 264 B4
Rubí → Barcelona, Spain 41°26N 2°0E 114 A1
Rubiataba Brazil 15°8S 49°48W 333 E2
Rubicon → U.S.A. 38°53N 121°4W 306 G5
Rubicone → Italy 44°8N 12°28E 199 D9
Rubik Albania 41°46N 19°47E 202 E3
Rubinéia Brazil 20°13S 51°2W 333 F1
Rubino Ivory C. 6°4N 4°18W 262 D4
Rubio Venezuela 7°43N 72°22W 328 B3
Rubizhne Ukraine 49°6N 38°25E 189 H10
Rubondo △ Tanzania 2°18S 31°58E 268 C3
Rubtsovsk Russia 51°30N 81°10E 217 B10
Ruby U.S.A. 64°45N 155°30W 303 D9
Ruby Beach = Jacksonville Beach U.S.A. 30°17N 81°24W 316 E8
Ruby L. U.S.A. 40°10N 115°28W 304 F6
Ruby Mts. U.S.A. 40°30N 115°20W 304 F6
Rubyvale Australia 23°25S 147°42E 280 C4
Rucheng China 25°33N 113°38E 229 E9
Ruciane-Nida Poland 53°40N 21°32E 184 E8
Rūd Sar Iran 37°8N 50°18E 247 B6
Ruda Sweden 57°6N 16°7E 163 G10
Ruda Śląska Poland 50°16N 18°50E 185 H5
Rudall Australia 33°43S 136°17E 282 B2
Rudall → Australia 22°34S 122°13E 278 D3
Rudall River △ Australia 22°38S 122°30E 278 D3
Rūdbār Afghan. 30°9N 62°36E 240 C1
Rudbar Iran 36°48N 49°23E 247 B6
Rüdersdorf Germany 52°27N 13°47E 178 C9
Rudewa Tanzania 10°7S 34°40E 269 E3
Rudkøbing Denmark 54°56N 10°41E 163 K4
Rudky Ukraine 49°38N 23°29E 185 J10
Rudna Poland 51°30N 16°17E 185 G3
Rudnik Bulgaria 42°36N 27°30E 203 D11
Rudnik Poland 50°26N 22°15E 185 H9
Rudnik Serbia 44°7N 20°35E 202 B4
Rudnya Russia 54°55N 31°7E 188 E6
Rudnytsa Ukraine 48°16N 28°54E 183 B13
Rudnyy Kazakhstan 52°57N 63°7E 216 B6
Rudo Bos.-H. 43°41N 19°23E 182 G4
Rudolfa, Ostrov Russia 81°45N 58°30E 214 A6
Rudolfsheim Austria 48°12N 16°20E 142 A2
Rudolfshöhe Germany 52°37N 13°44E 115 A5
Rudolstadt Germany 50°44N 11°19E 178 E7
Rudong China 32°20N 121°12E 229 A13
Rudow Germany 52°24N 13°29E 115 B3
Rudozem Bulgaria 41°29N 24°51E 203 E8
Rudrapur India 28°59N 79°24E 243 E8
Rudyard U.S.A. 46°14N 84°36W 309 B11
Rue France 50°15N 1°40E 173 B8
Rueil-Malmaison France 48°52N 2°11E 134 A2
Ruenya → Africa 16°24S 33°48E 269 F3
Rufa'a Sudan 14°44N 33°22E 257 E3
Rufflin U.S.A. 33°0N 80°49W 316 B9
Ruffling Pt. Br. Virgin Is. 18°44N 64°27W 321 b
Rufiji → Tanzania 7°50S 39°15E 268 D4
Rufino Argentina 34°20S 62°50W 334 C3
Rufisque Senegal 14°40N 17°15W 262 C1
Rufunsa Zambia 15°4S 29°34E 269 F2
Rugao China 32°23N 120°31E 229 A13
Rugby Warks., U.K. 52°23N 1°16W 169 E6
Rugby N. Dak., U.S.A. 48°22N 100°0W 308 A4
Rügen Germany 54°22N 13°24E 178 A9
Rügen △ Germany 54°25N 13°25E 178 A9
Rugles France 48°50N 0°40E 172 D7
Ruhea Bangla. 26°10N 88°25E 241 B2
Ruhengeri Rwanda 1°30S 29°36E 268 C2
Ruhla Germany 50°54N 10°23E 178 E6
Ruhland Germany 51°27N 13°51E 178 D9
Ruhnu Estonia 57°48N 23°15E 184 A10
Ruhr → Germany 51°27N 6°43E 178 D2
Ruhuhu → Tanzania 10°31S 34°34E 269 E3
Rui Barbosa Brazil 12°18S 40°27W 333 D3
Rui'an China 27°47N 120°40E 229 D13
Ruichang China 29°40N 115°39E 229 C10
Ruidoso U.S.A. 33°20N 105°41W 305 K11
Ruifang = Juifang Taiwan 25°7N 121°48E 225 A3
Ruijin China 25°48N 116°0E 229 E10
Ruili China 24°6N 97°46E 241 C6
Ruiru Kenya 1°9S 36°58E 268 C4
Ruisbroek Belgium 50°47N 4°18E 116 B1
Ruislip U.K. 51°34N 0°24W 125 A1
Ruivo, Pico Madeira 32°45N 16°56W 153 c
Ruj Bulgaria 42°52N 22°34E 202 D6
Rujen Macedonia 42°9N 22°30E 202 D6
Rujm Tal'at al Jamā'ah Jordan 30°24N 35°30E 251 H6
Ruk Pakistan 27°50N 68°42E 242 F3
Rukan-sho Japan 26°6N 127°32E 288 a
Rukhla Pakistan 32°27N 71°57E 242 C4
Rukumkot Nepal 28°37N 82°37E 243 E10
Rukwa □ Tanzania 7°0S 31°30E 268 D3
Rukwa, L. Tanzania 8°0S 32°20E 268 D3
Rulenge Burundi 2°43S 30°37E 268 C3
Rulhieres, C. Australia 13°56S 127°22E 278 B4
Rum Jordan 29°39N 35°26E 251 J6
Rum Highl., U.K. 57°0N 6°20W 167 E2
Rum Cay Bahamas 23°40N 74°58W 321 B5
Rum Jungle Australia 13°0S 130°59E 278 B5
Ruma Serbia 45°0N 19°50E 182 E4
Ruma △ Kenya 0°39S 34°18E 268 C3
Rumāḥ Si. Arabia 25°29N 47°10E 246 E5
Rumah Kulit Malaysia 2°9N 114°14E 235 B4
Rumania = Romania ■ Europe 46°0N 25°0E 183 D10
Rumaylah Iraq 30°47N 47°37E 246 D5
Rumaylah, 'Urūq ar Si. Arabia 22°0N 48°30E 249 B5
Rumbek South Sudan 6°54N 29°37E 257 F2
Rumburk Czech Rep. 50°57N 14°32E 180 A7
Rumelihisarı Turkey 41°4N 29°2E 122 B2
Rumford U.S.A. 44°33N 70°33W 313 B14
Rumia Poland 54°37N 18°25E 184 D5
Rumilly France 45°53N 5°56E 175 C9
Rummelsburg = Miastko Poland 54°0N 16°58E 184 E3
Rumoi Japan 43°56N 141°39E 220 C10
Rumonge Burundi 3°59S 29°26E 268 C2
Rumphi Malaysia 11°1S 33°52E 269 E3
Rumson U.S.A. 40°23N 74°0W 313 F11
Rumung Micronesia 9°37N 138°9E 287 R16
Rumuruti Kenya 0°17N 36°32E 268 B4
Runan China 33°0N 114°30E 229 A10
Runanga N.Z. 42°25S 171°15E 285 C6
Runaway, C. N.Z. 37°32S 177°59E 284 D6
Runaway Bay Jamaica 18°27N 77°20W 320 a
Runaway B. Antigua & B. 17°9N 61°51W 322 b
Runcorn U.K. 53°21N 2°44W 168 D5
Rundu Namibia 17°52S 19°43E 270 A2
Rungis France 48°44N 2°20E 134 B3
Rungwa Tanzania 6°55S 33°32E 268 D3
Rungwa → Tanzania 7°36S 31°50E 268 D3
Rungwa △ Tanzania 6°53S 34°2E 268 D3
Rungwe Tanzania 9°11S 33°32E 269 D3
Runka Nigeria 12°28N 7°20E 263 C6
Runn Sweden 60°30N 15°40E 162 D9
Runton Ra. Australia 23°31S 123°6E 278 D3
Runu Micronesia 9°35N 138°8E 287 R16
Ruo Shui → China 41°0N 100°16E 218 C9
Ruokolahti Finland 61°17N 28°50E 188 B5
Ruoqiang China 38°55N 88°10E 217 E11
Rupa India 27°15N 92°21E 241 B4
Rupar India 31°2N 76°38E 242 D7
Rupat Indonesia 1°45N 101°40E 234 B2
Rupea Romania 46°2N 25°13E 183 D10
Rupen → India 23°28N 71°31E 242 H4
Rupert U.S.A. 42°37N 113°41W 304 E7
Rupert → Canada 51°29N 78°45W 298 B4
Rupert B. Canada 51°35N 79°0W 298 B4
Rupert House = Waskaganish Canada 51°30N 78°40W 298 B4
Rupsa India 21°37N 87°1E 243 J12
Rupununi → Guyana 4°3N 58°35W 329 C6
Rur → Germany 51°11N 5°59E 178 D1
Rurópolis Brazil 4°5S 54°59W 329 D7
Rurrenabaque Bolivia 14°30S 67°32W 330 C4
Rurutu French Polynesia 22°26S 151°20W 289 f
Rus → Spain 39°30N 2°30W 197 F2
Rusāfa Iraq 33°21N 44°23E 113 A2
Rusambo Zimbabwe 16°30S 32°4E 269 F3
Rusape Zimbabwe 18°35S 32°8E 269 F3
Ruschuk = Ruse Bulgaria 43°48N 25°59E 203 C9
Ruse Bulgaria 43°48N 25°59E 203 C9
Ruse □ Bulgaria 43°35N 25°40E 203 C9
Ruşeţu Romania 44°57N 27°14E 183 F12
Rush Ireland 53°31N 6°6W 166 C5
Rush Green U.K. 51°33N 0°10E 125 A5
Rushan China 36°56N 121°30E 227 F11
Rushden U.K. 52°18N 0°35W 169 E7
Rushikulya → India 19°23N 85°5E 244 E7
Rushmore, Mt. U.S.A. 43°53N 103°28W 308 D2
Rushville Ill., U.S.A. 40°7N 90°34W 310 D6
Rushville Ind., U.S.A. 39°37N 85°27W 311 E11
Rushville Nebr., U.S.A. 42°43N 102°28W 308 D2
Rushworth Australia 36°32S 145°1E 283 D6
Ruskin U.S.A. 27°43N 82°26W 317 H7
Russa India 22°29N 88°21E 124 C2
Russas Brazil 4°55S 37°50W 332 B4
Russell Man., Canada 50°50N 101°20W 297 C8
Russell N.Z. 35°16S 174°10E 284 B3
Russell Fla., U.S.A. 30°3N 81°45W 316 E8
Russell Kans., U.S.A. 38°54N 98°52W 308 F4
Russell N.Y., U.S.A. 44°27N 75°9W 313 B9
Russell Pa., U.S.A. 41°56N 79°8W 312 E5
Russell Cave △ U.S.A. 34°59N 85°49W 315 D12
Russell Is. Solomon Is. 9°4S 159°12E 287 M10
Russell L. Man., Canada 56°15N 101°30W 297 B8
Russell L. N.W.T., Canada 63°5N 115°44W 296 A5
Russellkonda India 19°57N 84°42E 244 E7
Russells Point U.S.A. 40°28N 83°54W 311 D13
Russellville Ala., U.S.A. 34°30N 87°44W 315 D11
Russellville Ark., U.S.A. 35°17N 93°8W 314 D8
Russellville Ky., U.S.A. 36°51N 86°53W 308 G10
Rüsselsheim Germany 49°59N 8°23E 179 F4
Russi Italy 44°22N 12°2E 199 D9
Russia ■ Eurasia 62°0N 105°0E 215 C11
Russian → U.S.A. 38°27N 123°8W 306 G3
Russian Hill San Francisco, U.S.A. 136 a1
Russian Mission U.S.A. 61°47N 161°19W 303 F7
Russiaville U.S.A. 40°25N 86°16W 311 D10
Russkaya Arktika △ Russia 73°40N 55°55E 214 B6
Russkiy, Ostrov Russia 43°0N 131°50E 220 C5
Russky Sever △ Russia 59°57N 38°34E 188 B10
Rust Austria 47°49N 16°42E 181 D9
Rustam Shahr Pakistan 26°58N 66°6E 242 F2
Rustavi Georgia 41°30N 45°0E 191 K7
Rustenburg S. Africa 25°41S 27°14E 270 C4
Ruston U.S.A. 32°32N 92°38W 314 E8
Rutana Burundi 3°55S 30°0E 268 C3
Rute Spain 37°19N 4°23W 195 H6
Ruteng Indonesia 8°35S 120°30E 231 F6
Rutenga Zimbabwe 21°15S 30°44E 269 G3
Ruth U.S.A. 43°42N 82°45W 312 C2
Rutherford Calif., U.S.A. 38°26N 122°24W 306 G4
Rutherford N.J., U.S.A. 40°49N 74°6W 132 B1
Rutherglen Australia 36°5S 146°29E 283 D7
Rutland U.S.A. 43°37N 72°58W 313 C12
Rutland □ U.K. 52°38N 0°40W 169 E7
Rutland I. India 11°25N 92°10E 245 J11
Rutland Water U.K. 52°39N 0°38W 169 E7
Rutledalen Norway 61°4N 5°10E 164 C2
Rutledge U.S.A. 33°38N 83°37W 316 B6
Rutledge → Canada 61°4N 112°0W 297 A6
Rutledge L. Canada 61°33N 110°47W 297 A6
Rutog China 33°27N 79°42E 217 F9
Rutqa, W. → Syria 34°30N 41°3E 213 E9
Rutshuru Dem. Rep. of the Congo 1°13S 29°25E 268 C2
Ruvo di Púglia Italy 41°7N 16°29E 201 A9
Ruvu Tanzania 6°49S 38°43E 268 D4
Ruvu → Tanzania 6°23S 38°52E 268 D4
Ruvubu △ Burundi 3°3S 29°33E 268 C2
Ruvuma □ Tanzania 10°20S 36°0E 269 E4
Ruvuma → Tanzania 10°29S 40°28E 269 E5
Ruwais U.A.E. 24°5N 52°50E 247 E7
Ruwenzori Africa 0°30N 29°55E 268 B2
Ruwenzori △ Uganda 0°20N 30°0E 268 B2
Ruya → Zimbabwe 16°27S 32°5E 271 A5
Ruyang China 34°9N 112°27E 226 G7
Ruyigi Burundi 3°29S 30°15E 268 C3
Ruyuan China 24°46N 113°16E 229 E9
Rūzaevka Kazakhstan 52°49N 66°56E 217 B7
Ruzayevka Russia 54°4N 45°0E 190 C7
Růžkovo Konare Bulgaria 42°23N 24°46E 203 D8
Ruzhou China 34°11N 112°52E 226 G7
Ružomberok Slovak Rep. 49°3N 19°17E 181 B12
Ruzyně Czech Rep. 50°5N 14°17E 135 B1
Ruzyně, Praha ✈ (PRG) Czech Rep. 50°6N 14°16E 135 B1
Rwanda ■ Africa 2°0S 30°0E 268 C3
Ryakhovo Bulgaria 43°58N 26°18E 203 C10
Ryan, L. U.K. 55°0N 5°2W 167 G3
Ryazan Russia 54°40N 39°40E 188 E10
Ryazan □ Russia 54°5N 39°30E 190 C4
Ryazhsk Russia 53°45N 40°3E 188 F11
Rybachiy Russia 55°10N 20°50E 184 C7
Rybachiy Poluostrov Russia 69°43N 32°0E 160 B25
Rybachye = Balykchy Kyrgyzstan 42°26N 76°12E 217 D9
Rybatskaya Russia 59°59N 30°29E 137 B2
Rybinsk Russia 58°5N 38°50E 188 C10
Rybinskoye Vdkhr. Russia 58°30N 38°25E 188 C10
Rybnik Poland 50°6N 18°32E 185 H5
Rybnitsa = Râbniţa Moldova 47°45N 29°0E 183 C14
Rybnoye Russia 54°45N 39°30E 188 E10
Rychnov nad Kněžnou Czech Rep. 50°10N 16°17E 181 A9
Rychwał Poland 52°4N 18°10E 185 F5
Rycroft Canada 55°45N 118°40W 296 B5
Ryd Sweden 56°27N 14°42E 163 H8
Rydaholm Sweden 56°59N 14°18E 163 H8
Rydboholm Sweden 59°26N 18°12E 139 A3

Ryde N.S.W., Australia 33°48S 151°6E 139 A1
Ryde I. of W., U.K. 50°43N 1°9W 169 G6
Ryderwood U.S.A. 46°23N 123°3W 306 D3
Rydzyna Poland 51°47N 16°39E 185 G3
Rye U.K. 50°57N 0°45E 169 G8
Rye → U.K. 54°11N 0°44W 168 C7
Rye Bay U.K. 50°52N 0°49E 169 G8
Rye Patch Res. U.S.A. 40°28N 118°19W 304 F4
Ryegate U.S.A. 46°18N 109°15W 304 C9
Ryerson University Toronto, Canada 141 a3
Ryfylke Norway 59°25N 6°25E 164 E3
Rykene Norway 58°24N 8°37E 164 F5
Ryki Poland 51°38N 21°56E 185 G8
Rykovo = Yenakiyeve Ukraine 48°15N 38°15E 189 H10
Ryley Canada 53°17N 112°26W 296 C6
Rylsk Russia 51°36N 34°43E 189 G8
Rylstone Australia 32°46S 149°58E 283 B8
Rymanów Poland 49°35N 21°51E 185 J8
Ryn Poland 53°57N 21°34E 184 E8
Ryn Peski = Naryn Qum Kazakhstan 47°30N 49°0E 191 G9
Ryogoku Japan 35°40N 139°48E 140 A3
Ryōhaku-Sanchi Japan 36°9N 136°49E 223 A8
Ryojun = Lüshun China 38°45N 121°15E 227 E11
Ryōtsu Japan 38°5N 138°26E 220 E9
Rypin Poland 53°3N 19°25E 185 E6
Ryssby Sweden 56°52N 14°10E 163 H8
Rysy Europe 49°10N 20°4E 181 B13
Ryūgasaki Japan 35°54N 140°11E 223 B12
Ryukyu Is. = Ryūkyū-Rettō Japan 26°0N 126°0E 221 M3
Ryūkyū-Rettō Japan 26°0N 126°0E 221 M3
Ryūō = Kai Japan 35°42N 138°30E 223 B10
Rzepin Poland 52°20N 14°49E 185 F1
Rzeszów Poland 50°5N 21°58E 185 H8
Rzhev Russia 56°20N 34°20E 188 D8
Rzhevka Russia 59°59N 30°31E 137 B3


# S


Sa Cabaneta Spain 39°37N 2°45E 206 B3
Sa Canal Spain 38°51N 1°23E 206 D1
Sa Conillera Spain 38°59N 1°13E 206 D1
Sa Dec Vietnam 10°20N 105°46E 237 G5
Sa Dragonera Spain 39°35N 2°19E 206 B3
Sa Kaeo Thailand 13°49N 102°4E 236 F4
Sa-koi Burma 19°54N 97°3E 241 F6
Sa Mesquida Spain 39°55N 4°16E 206 B5
Sa Pa Vietnam 22°20N 103°47E 236 A4
Sa Pobla Spain 39°46N 3°1E 206 B4
Sa Savina Spain 38°44N 1°25E 206 D1
Sa'a Solomon Is. 9°43S 161°35E 287 M11
Sa'ādat Shahr Iran 30°10N 53°5E 247 D7
Sa'ādatābād Hormozgān, Iran 28°3N 55°53E 247 D7
Sa'ādatābād Kermān, Iran 29°40N 55°51E 247 D7
Sa'ādatābād Tehrān, Iran 35°47N 51°22E 141 A2
Saadūn Iraq 33°19N 44°25E 113 B2
Saale → Germany 51°56N 11°54E 178 D7
Saaler Bodden Germany 54°20N 12°27E 178 A8
Saalfeld Germany 50°38N 11°21E 178 E7
Saalfelden Austria 47°25N 12°51E 180 D5
Saane → Switz. 47°8N 7°10E 179 H3
Saanich Canada 48°29N 123°26W 306 B3
Saar → Europe 49°41N 6°32E 170 E6
Saar-Hunsrück ⌓ Germany 49°30N 6°50E 179 F2
Saar in Mähren = Ždár nad Sázavov Czech Rep. 49°34N 15°57E 180 B8
Saarbrücken Germany 49°14N 6°59E 179 F2
Saarburg Germany 49°36N 6°32E 179 F2
Saaremaa Estonia 58°30N 22°30E 188 C2
Saarijärvi Finland 62°43N 25°16E 160 E21
Saarland □ Germany 49°20N 7°0E 179 F2
Saarlautern = Saarlouis Germany 49°18N 6°45E 179 F2
Saarlouis Germany 49°18N 6°45E 179 F2
Saatlı Azerbaijan 39°55N 48°22E 213 C13
Saavedra Argentina 34°33S 58°29W 117 B2
Saaz = Žatec Czech Rep. 50°20N 13°32E 180 A6
Sab 'Ābar Syria 33°46N 37°41E 212 F7
Saba W. Indies 17°38N 63°14W 322 a
Šabac Serbia 44°48N 19°42E 202 B3
Sabadell Spain 41°28N 2°7E 196 D7
Sabae Japan 35°57N 136°11E 223 B8
Sabah □ Malaysia 6°0N 117°0E 235 A5
Şabāḩ, Wadi → Si. Arabia 23°50N 48°30E 249 B5
Sabak Bernam Malaysia 3°46N 100°58E 237 L3
Sabalān, Kūhhā-ye Iran 38°15N 47°45E 213 C12
Sabalana, Kepulauan Indonesia 6°45S 118°50E 231 F5
Sabalana, Kepuluauan Indonesia 6°45S 118°49E 235 D5
Sabana, Arch. de Cuba 23°0N 80°0W 320 B3
Sabana de la Mar Dom. Rep. 19°7N 69°24W 321 C6
Sabana Grande Puerto Rico 18°5N 66°58W 321 b
Sabana Westpunt = Westpunt Curaçao 12°22N 69°10W 322 g
Sábanalarga Colombia 10°38N 74°55W 328 A3
Sabaneta Pt. N. Marianas 15°17N 145°49E 302 e
Sabang Indonesia 5°50N 95°15E 234 A1
Şabanözü Turkey 40°28N 33°16E 212 B5
Săbăoani Romania 47°1N 26°51E 183 C11
Sabari → India 17°35N 81°16E 244 F5
Sabarmati → India 22°18N 72°22E 242 H5
Sab'atayn, Ramlat as Yemen 15°30N 46°10E 248 D4
Sabattis U.S.A. 44°6N 74°40W 313 B10
Sabáudia Italy 41°18N 13°1E 200 A6
Sabaya Bolivia 19°1S 68°23W 330 D4
Şābāyā, Jaza'ir Si. Arabia 18°35N 41°3E 248 C3
Saberania Indonesia 2°5S 138°18E 231 E9
Sabhā Libya 27°9N 14°29E 258 C2
Sabhar Bangla. 23°50N 90°15E 241 D3
Sabi → India 28°29N 76°44E 242 E7
Sabi Game Reserve = Kruger △ S. Africa 24°50S 26°10E 271 B4
Sabidana, J. Sudan 18°4N 36°50E 256 D4
Sabie S. Africa 25°10S 30°48E 271 C5
Sabina U.S.A. 39°29N 83°38W 311 E13
Sabinal U.S.A. 29°19N 99°28W 314 G5
Sabiñánigo Spain 42°31N 0°22W 196 C4
Sabinar, Punta del Spain 36°43N 2°44W 197 J2
Sabinas Mexico 27°51N 101°7W 318 B4
Sabinas → Mexico 27°37N 100°42W 318 B4
Sabinas Hidalgo Mexico 26°30N 100°10W 318 B4
Sabine → U.S.A. 29°59N 93°47W 314 G8
Sabine L. U.S.A. 29°53N 93°51W 314 G8
Sabine Pass U.S.A. 29°44N 93°54W 314 G8
Sabinópolis Brazil 18°40S 43°6W 333 E3
Sabinov Slovak Rep. 49°6N 21°5E 181 B14
Sabirabad Azerbaijan 40°5N 48°30E 191 K9
Sabka Chad 19°15N 16°35E 259 E3
Sablayan Phil. 12°50N 120°50E 232 E3
Sable Canada 55°30N 68°21W 299 A6
Sable, C. N.S., Canada 43°29N 65°38W 299 D6
Sable, C. Fla., U.S.A. 25°9N 81°8W 317 K8
Sable I. N.S., Canada 44°0N 60°0W 299 D8
Sable I. Papua N. G. 3°38S 154°42E 286 B8
Sablé-sur-Sarthe France 47°50N 0°20W 172 E6
Saboeiro Brazil 6°32S 39°54W 332 C4
Saboli India 28°42N 77°18E 120 A2
Sabonkafi Niger 14°40N 8°45E 259 F1
Sabor → Portugal 41°10N 7°7W 194 D3
Sabou Burkina Faso 12°1N 2°15W 262 C4
Sabres France 44°9N 0°43W 174 D3
Sabrina Coast Antarctica 68°0S 120°0E 151 C9
Sabtang I. Phil. 20°19N 121°52E 232 A3
Sabugal Portugal 40°20N 7°5W 194 E3
Sabugo Portugal 38°49N 9°17W 126 A1
Sabula U.S.A. 42°4N 90°10W 310 B6
Sabulubek Indonesia 1°36S 98°40E 234 C1
Sabuncu Turkey 39°33N 30°12E 205 B12
Şabyā Si. Arabia 17°9N 42°37E 248 C3
Sabzevār Iran 36°15N 57°40E 247 B8
Sabzi Mand India 28°40N 77°12E 120 A2
Sabzvārān = Jiroft Iran 28°45N 57°50E 247 D8
Sac City U.S.A. 42°25N 95°0W 310 B2
Sacaolo Angola 12°58S 22°28E 265 E4
Sacatengo Angola 13°16S 21°20E 265 E4
Sacavém Portugal 38°47N 9°5W 126 A2
Sacca Fisola Venice, Italy 142 c1
Sacca San Biágio Venice, Italy 142 c1
Sacedón Spain 40°29N 2°41W 196 E2
Săcele Romania 45°37N 25°41E 183 E10
Sacheon S. Korea 35°0N 128°6E 224 E4
Sachigo → Canada 55°6N 88°58W 298 A2
Sachigo, L. Canada 53°50N 92°12W 298 B1
Sachimbo Angola 9°14S 20°16E 265 D4
Sachin India 21°5N 72°53E 244 D1
Sachkhere Georgia 42°25N 43°28E 191 J6
Sachsen □ Germany 50°55N 13°10E 178 E9
Sachsen-Anhalt □ Germany 52°0N 12°0E 178 D7
Sächsische Schweiz △ Germany 50°55N 14°10E 178 E10
Sacile Italy 45°57N 12°30E 199 C9
Sackets Harbor U.S.A. 43°57N 76°7W 313 C8
Sackville Canada 45°54N 64°22W 299 C7
Saclay France 48°43N 2°10E 134 B2
Saclay, Étang de France 48°44N 2°9E 134 B1
Saco Maine, U.S.A. 43°30N 70°27W 313 C14
Saco Mont., U.S.A. 48°28N 107°21W 304 B10
Sacol I. Phil. 6°58N 122°13E 233 H4
Sacomã Brazil 23°36S 46°35W 137 B2
Sacramento = Itatupã Brazil 0°37S 51°12W 329 D7
Sacramento Brazil 19°53S 47°27W 333 E2
Sacramento Calif., U.S.A. 38°35N 121°29W 306 G5
Sacramento → U.S.A. 38°3N 121°56W 306 G5
Sacramento Mts. U.S.A. 32°30N 105°30W 305 K11
Sacramento Valley U.S.A. 39°30N 122°0W 306 G5
Sacratif, C. Spain 36°42N 3°28W 195 J7
Sacré Cœur Paris, France 134 a4
Sacrow Germany 52°25N 13°6E 115 B1
Sacrower See Germany 52°26N 13°6E 115 B1
Săcueni Romania 47°20N 22°5E 182 C7
Sada Mayotte 12°51S 45°6E 272 b
Sada Spain 43°22N 8°15W 194 B2
Sada-Misaki Japan 33°20N 132°5E 222 D4
Sada-Misaki-Hantō Japan 33°22N 132°1E 222 D4
Sádaba Spain 42°19N 1°12W 196 C3
Sadabad India 27°27N 78°3E 242 F8
Şa'dah Yemen 16°15N 43°37E 248 C3
Şa'dah □ Yemen 16°15N 43°37E 248 C3
Sadang S. Korea 37°29N 126°58E 137 C1
Sadani Tanzania 5°58S 38°35E 268 D4
Sadani ⌓ Tanzania 6°3S 38°47E 268 D4
Sadao Thailand 6°38N 100°26E 237 J3
Sadar Bazar Delhi, India 120 a1
Sadaseopet India 17°38N 77°59E 244 F3
Sadd el Aali Egypt 23°54N 32°54E 256 C3
Saddle → U.S.A. 40°51N 74°6W 132 A1
Saddle Brook U.S.A. 40°53N 74°5W 132 A1
Saddle Hill St. Kitts & Nevis 17°7N 62°33W 322 d
Saddle Mt. U.S.A. 45°58N 123°41W 306 E3
Saddle Pk. India 13°9N 93°1E 245 H11
Saddle Pt. St. Helena 15°57S 5°38W 153 h
Sade Nigeria 11°22N 10°45E 263 C7
Şadḩ Oman 17°3N 55°4E 249 C6
Sadhoowa Trin. & Tob. 10°8N 61°27W 323 t
Sadimi Dem. Rep. of the Congo 9°25S 23°32E 265 D4
Sadiola Mali 13°50N 11°40W 262 C2
Sadiya India 27°50N 95°40E 241 B5
Sa'dīyah, Hawr as Iraq 32°15N 46°30E 213 F12
Sadlers St. Kitts & Nevis 17°24N 62°47W 322 d
Sado Japan 38°0N 138°25E 220 F9
Sado → Portugal 38°29N 8°55W 195 G2
Sadon Russia 42°52N 43°58E 191 J6
Sadovoye Russia 47°47N 44°31E 191 G7
Sadowara Japan 32°2N 131°26E 222 E3
Sadr Pakistan 24°51N 67°2E 123 A2
Sadr City Iraq 33°23N 44°27E 113 A2
Sadra India 23°21N 72°43E 242 H5
Sadrazamköy = Liveras Cyprus 35°23N 32°57E 207 E8
Sadri India 25°11N 73°26E 242 G5
Sadyba Poland 52°11N 21°3E 143 B2
Sæbøvik Norway 59°47N 5°40E 164 E2
Sæby Denmark 57°21N 10°30E 163 G4
Saegertown U.S.A. 41°43N 80°9W 312 E4
Saelices Spain 39°55N 2°49W 196 F2
Sætre Norway 59°41N 10°33E 164 E7
Sævareid Norway 60°11N 5°46E 164 D2
Safaalan Turkey 41°26N 28°6E 203 E12
Şafājah Si. Arabia 26°25N 39°0E 246 E3
Šafárikovo = Tornal'a Slovak Rep. 48°25N 20°20E 181 C13
Safata B. Samoa 14°0S 171°50W 287 W20
Safdar Jang's Tomb India 28°35N 77°12E 120 B2
Safed Koh Afghan. 34°0N 70°0E 240 B3
Säffle Sweden 59°8N 12°55E 162 E6
Safford U.S.A. 32°50N 109°43W 305 K9
Saffron Walden U.K. 52°1N 0°16E 169 E8
Safi Morocco 32°18N 9°20W 260 B3
Safia Papua N. G. 9°35S 148°38E 286 E5
Safia, Hamada Mali 23°10N 4°15W 260 D4
Şafīābād Iran 36°45N 57°58E 247 B8
Safīd Dasht Iran 33°27N 48°11E 247 C6
Safīd Kūh Afghan. 34°45N 63°0E 240 B1
Safīd Rūd → Iran 37°23N 50°11E 247 B6
Safipur India 26°44N 80°21E 243 F9
Şāfītā Syria 34°48N 36°7E 250 D7
Safonovo Russia 55°4N 33°16E 188 E7
Safranbolu Turkey 41°15N 32°41E 212 B5
Saft el Laban Egypt 30°1N 31°10E 117 A2
Saft Rashîn Egypt 28°58N 30°55E 256 J7
Safune Samoa 13°25S 172°21W 287 V19
Şafwān Iraq 30°7N 47°43E 246 D5
Sag Harbor U.S.A. 41°0N 72°18W 313 F12
Sag Sag Papua N. G. 5°32S 148°23E 286 C5
Saga Kōchi, Japan 33°5N 133°6E 222 D5
Saga Saga, Japan 33°15N 130°16E 222 D2
Saga □ Japan 33°15N 130°20E 222 D2
Sagae Japan 38°22N 140°17E 220 E10
Sagaing Burma 21°52N 95°59E 241 E5
Sagaing □ Burma 23°55N 95°56E 241 D5
Sagala Mali 14°9N 6°38W 262 C3
Sagami-Nada Japan 34°58N 139°30E 223 C11
Sagami-Wan Japan 35°15N 139°25E 223 B11
Sagamihara Japan 35°33N 139°25E 223 B11
Sagamore U.S.A. 40°46N 79°14W 312 F5
Sagan = Żagań Poland 51°39N 15°22E 185 G2
Saganaga L. Canada 48°14N 90°52W 308 A8
Saganoseki Japan 33°15N 131°53E 222 D3
Saganthit Kyun Burma 11°56N 98°29E 237 G2
Sagar Karnataka, India 16°38N 76°48E 244 F3
Sagar Karnataka, India 14°14N 75°6E 245 G2
Sagar Mad. P., India 23°50N 78°44E 243 H8
Sagara Japan 34°41N 138°12E 223 C10
Sagara, L. Tanzania 5°20S 31°0E 268 D3
Sagarejo Georgia 41°44N 45°19E 191 K7
Sagarmatha = Everest, Mt. Nepal 28°5N 86°58E 243 E12
Sagarmatha △ Nepal 27°55N 86°45E 243 F12
Sagavanirktok → U.S.A. 70°19N 147°53W 303 A11
Sagay Phil. 10°57N 123°25E 233 F4
Sagene Norway 59°55N 10°46E 133 A3
Saghîr, El Bahr el → Egypt 31°8N 31°54E 251 G2
Sagiada Greece 39°38N 20°12E 206 B10
Saginaw U.S.A. 43°26N 83°56W 309 D12
Saginaw B. U.S.A. 43°50N 83°40W 309 D12
Sagleipie Liberia 7°0N 8°52W 262 D3
Saglouc = Salluit Canada 62°14N 75°38W 295 E16
Sagone France 42°7N 8°42E 175 F12
Sagone, G. de France 42°4N 8°40E 175 F12
Sagrada Família, Templo de Barcelona, Spain 114 a2
Sagres Portugal 37°0N 8°58W 195 J2
Sagu Burma 20°13N 94°46E 241 E5
Sagua la Grande Cuba 22°50N 80°10W 320 B3
Saguache U.S.A. 38°5N 106°8W 304 G10
Saguaro △ U.S.A. 32°12N 110°38W 305 K8
Saguenay → Canada 48°22N 71°0W 299 C5
Saguia el Hamra → W. Sahara 27°24N 13°43W 260 C2
Sagunt Spain 39°42N 0°18W 196 F4
Sagunto = Sagunt Spain 39°42N 0°18W 196 F4
Sagvåg Norway 59°46N 5°25E 164 E2
Sagwara India 23°41N 74°1E 242 H6
Sahaba Sudan 18°57N 30°25E 256 D3
Sahagún Colombia 8°57N 75°27W 328 B2
Sahagún Spain 42°18N 5°2W 194 C5
Saḩam al Jawlān Syria 32°45N 35°55E 250 F6
Sahamandrevo Madag. 23°15S 45°35E 272 C2
Sahand, Kūh-e Iran 37°44N 46°27E 213 D12
Sahar, Mumbai ✕ (BOM) India 19°5N 72°51E 130 A2
Sahara Africa 23°0N 5°0E 254 D4
Saḩara, G. Egypt 28°2N 34°8E 251 K5
Saharan Atlas = Saharien, Atlas Algeria 33°30N 1°0E 261 B5
Saharan Seamounts Atl. Oc. 25°30N 19°50W 152 D10
Saharanpur India 29°58N 77°33E 242 E7
Saharien, Atlas Algeria 33°30N 1°0E 261 B5
Saharsa India 25°53N 86°36E 243 G12
Sahasinaka Madag. 21°49S 47°49E 272 C2
Sahaswan India 28°5N 78°45E 243 E8
Saheira, W. el → Egypt 30°5N 33°25E 251 H4
Sahel Africa 16°0N 5°0E 254 E3
Sahel, Canal du Mali 14°20N 6°0W 262 C3
Sahibganj India 25°12N 87°40E 243 G12
Sāḩilīyah Iraq 33°43N 42°42E 213 F10
Sahiwal Pakistan 30°45N 73°8E 242 D5
Şaḩneh Iran 34°29N 47°41E 213 E12
Sahrawi = Western Sahara ■ Africa 25°0N 13°0W 260 D2
Sahuaripa Mexico 29°3N 109°14W 318 B3
Sahuarita U.S.A. 31°57N 110°58W 305 L8
Sahuayo de Díaz Mexico 20°4N 102°43W 318 C4
Šahy Slovak Rep. 48°4N 18°55E 181 C11
Sai → India 25°39N 82°47E 243 G10
Sai Buri Thailand 6°43N 101°45E 237 J3
Sai-Cinza Brazil 6°17S 57°42W 331 B6
Sai Kung Hong Kong, China 22°23N 114°16E 122 A3
Sai Thong △ Thailand 15°56N 101°10E 236 E3
Sai Tso Wan Hong Kong, China 22°16N 113°53E 122 B1
Sai Wan Ho Hong Kong, China 22°17N 114°12E 122 B3
Sai Ying Pun Hong Kong, China 22°17N 114°8E 122 B2
Sai Yok △ Thailand 14°25N 98°40E 236 E2
Saibai I. Australia 9°25S 142°40E 280 a
Sa'id Bundâs South Sudan 8°24N 24°48E 259 G4
Saïda Algeria 34°50N 0°11E 261 B5
Saïda □ Algeria 34°40N 0°20E 261 B5
Sa'īdābād = Sīrjān Iran 29°30N 55°45E 247 D7
Sa'īdābād Iran 36°8N 54°11E 247 B7
Saidaiji Japan 34°39N 134°2E 222 C6
Saïdia Morocco 35°5N 2°14W 261 A4
Saidor Papua N. G. 5°40S 146°29E 286 C4
Saidpur Bangla. 25°48N 89°0E 241 C2
Saidpur India 25°33N 83°11E 243 G10
Saidu Sharif Pakistan 34°43N 72°24E 243 B5
Saignes France 45°20N 2°31E 174 C6
Saigō Japan 36°12N 133°20E 222 A5
Saigon = Thanh Pho Ho Chi Minh Vietnam 10°58N 106°40E 237 G6
Saiha India 22°29N 92°58E 241 D4
Saijō Japan 33°55N 133°11E 222 D5
Saikai △ Japan 33°12N 129°36E 222 D1
Saikhoa Ghat India 27°50N 95°40E 241 B5
Saiki Japan 32°58N 131°51E 222 E3
Sailana India 23°28N 74°55E 242 H6
Saillans France 44°42N 5°12E 175 D9
Sailolof Indonesia 1°15S 130°46E 231 E8
Sailu India 19°28N 76°28E 244 E3
Saimaa Finland 61°15N 28°15E 188 B5
Saimbeyli Turkey 37°59N 36°6E 212 D7
Saimen = Saimaa Finland 61°15N 28°15E 188 B5
Şa'in Dezh Iran 36°40N 46°25E 213 D12
St. Abb's Head U.K. 55°55N 2°8W 167 F6
St-Affrique France 43°57N 2°53E 174 E6
St-Agrève France 45°0N 4°23E 175 C8
St-Aignan France 47°16N 1°22E 172 E8
St. Alban's Nfld. & L., Canada 47°51N 55°50W 299 C8
St. Albans Herts., U.K. 51°45N 0°19W 169 F7
St. Albans Vt., U.S.A. 44°49N 73°5W 313 B11
St. Albans W. Va., U.S.A. 38°23N 81°50W 309 F13
St. Alban's Head U.K. 50°34N 2°4W 169 G5
St. Albert Canada 53°37N 113°32W 296 C6
St-Amand-en-Puisaye France 47°32N 3°5E 173 E10
St-Amand-les-Eaux France 50°27N 3°25E 173 B10
St-Amand-Montrond France 46°43N 2°30E 173 F9
St-Amarin France 47°54N 7°2E 173 E14
St-Amour France 46°26N 5°21E 173 F12
St-André Montréal, Canada 130 c1
St-André Réunion 20°57S 55°39E 272 f
St-André-de-Cubzac France 44°59N 0°26W 174 D3
St-André-les-Alpes France 43°58N 6°30E 175 E10
St. Andrew Sd. U.S.A. 30°58N 81°25W 316 E8
St. Andrew's Nfld. & L., Canada 47°45N 59°15W 299 C8
St. Andrews N.Z. 44°33S 171°10E 285 E6
St. Andrews Fife, U.K. 56°20N 2°47W 167 E6
St. Andrews S.C., U.S.A. 32°47N 80°0W 316 C9
St-Anicet Canada 45°8N 74°22W 313 A10
St. Anne U.S.A. 41°1N 87°43W 311 C9
St. Annes Canada 49°40N 96°39W 297 D9
St. Anns B. Canada 46°22N 60°25W 299 C7
St. Ann's Bay Jamaica 18°26N 77°12W 320 a
St. Anthony Nfld. & L., Canada 51°22N 55°35W 299 B8
St. Anthony Idaho, U.S.A. 43°58N 111°41W 304 E8
St-Antoine Canada 46°22N 64°45W 299 C7
St-Antonin-Noble-Val France 44°10N 1°45E 174 D5
St-Arnaud = El Eulma Algeria 36°9N 5°42E 261 A6
St. Arnaud Australia 36°40S 143°16E 282 D5
St. Arnaud Ra. N.Z. 42°1S 172°53E 285 C7
St-Astier France 45°8N 0°31E 174 C4
St-Aubin France 48°44N 2°8E 134 B1
St-Aubin-du-Cormier France 48°15N 1°26W 172 D5
St-Augustin Canada 51°13N 58°38W 299 B8
St-Augustin → Canada 51°16N 58°40W 299 B8
St. Augustine U.S.A. 29°54N 81°19W 316 F8
St. Augustine Beach U.S.A. 29°51N 81°16W 316 F8
St-Aulaye France 45°12N 0°9E 174 C4
St. Austell U.K. 50°20N 4°47W 169 G3
St-Avold France 49°6N 6°43E 173 C13
St. Barbe Canada 51°12N 56°46W 299 B8
St-Barthélemy ⧄ W. Indies 17°50N 62°50W 322 a
St-Barthélemy Channel St.-Martin 18°0N 63°0W 322 a
St. Barts = St-Barthélemy ⧄ W. Indies 17°50N 62°50W 322 a
St. Basil's Cathedral Moscow, Russia 129 b3
St. Bathans N.Z. 44°53S 169°50E 285 E4
St. Bathan's, Mt. N.Z. 44°45S 169°45E 285 E4
St-Béat France 42°55N 0°41E 174 F4
St. Bees Hd. U.K. 54°31N 3°38W 168 C4
St. Bees I. Australia 20°56S 149°26E 280 b
St-Benoît Réunion 21°2S 55°43E 272 f
St-Benoît-du-Sault France 46°26N 1°24E 174 B5
St-Bonnet-en-Champsaur France 44°40N 6°5E 175 D10
St-Brevin-les-Pins France 47°14N 2°10W 172 E4
St-Brice-en-Coglès France 48°25N 1°22W 172 D5
St. Bride's Canada 46°56N 54°10W 299 C9
St. Brides B. U.K. 51°49N 5°9W 169 F2
St-Brieuc France 48°30N 2°46W 172 D4
St-Calais France 47°55N 0°45E 172 E7
St-Cast-le-Guildo France 48°37N 2°18W 172 D4
St. Catharines Canada 43°10N 79°15W 312 C5
St. Catherine, Mt. Grenada 12°10N 61°40W 323 q
St. Catherine Pt. Bermuda 32°23N 64°40W 153 a
St. Catherines I. U.S.A. 31°40N 81°10W 316 D8
St. Catherine's Monastery Egypt 28°34N 33°58E 251 K4
St. Catherine's Pt. U.K. 50°34N 1°18W 169 G6
St-Céré France 44°51N 1°54E 174 D5
St-Cergue Switz. 46°27N 6°10E 179 J2
St-Cernin France 45°5N 2°25E 174 C6
St-Chamond France 45°28N 4°31E 175 C8
St. Charles Ill., U.S.A. 41°54N 88°19W 311 C8
St. Charles Md., U.S.A. 38°36N 76°56W 309 F15
St. Charles Mo., U.S.A. 38°47N 90°29W 310 F6
St. Charles Va., U.S.A. 36°48N 83°4W 309 G12
St-Chély-d'Apcher France 44°48N 3°17E 174 D7
St-Chinian France 43°25N 2°56E 174 E6
St. Christopher = St. Kitts W. Indies 17°20N 62°40W 322 d
St. Christopher-Nevis = St. Kitts & Nevis ■ W. Indies 17°20N 62°40W 322 d
St-Ciers-sur-Gironde France 45°17N 0°37W 174 C3
St. Clair Ga., U.S.A. 33°9N 82°13W 316 B7
St. Clair Mich., U.S.A. 42°50N 82°30W 312 D2
St. Clair Mo., U.S.A. 38°21N 90°59W 310 F6
St. Clair Pa., U.S.A. 40°43N 76°12W 313 F8
St. Clair → U.S.A. 42°38N 82°31W 312 D2
St. Clair, L. S. Austral., Australia 37°20S 139°55E 282 D3
St. Clair, L. N. Amer. 42°27N 82°39W 312 D2
St. Clair Shores U.S.A. 42°30N 82°53W 311 B14
St. Clairsville U.S.A. 40°5N 80°54W 312 F4
St-Claud France 45°54N 0°28E 174 C4
St. Claude Canada 49°40N 98°20W 297 D9
St-Claude Jura, France 46°22N 5°52E 173 F12
St-Claude Guadeloupe 16°3N 61°42W 322 e
St. Clears U.K. 51°49N 4°31W 169 F3
St-Clet Canada 45°21N 74°13W 313 A10
St-Cloud France 48°50N 2°12E 134 A2
St. Cloud Fla., U.S.A. 28°15N 81°17W 317 G8
St. Cloud Minn., U.S.A. 45°34N 94°10W 308 C6
St. Cricq, C. Australia 25°17S 113°6E 279 E1
St. Croix U.S. Virgin Is. 17°45N 64°45W 321 C7
St. Croix → U.S.A. 44°45N 92°48W 308 C7
St. Croix Falls U.S.A. 45°24N 92°38W 308 C7
St-Cyprien France 42°37N 3°2E 174 F7
St-Cyr-l'École France 48°47N 2°4E 134 B1
St-Cyr-l'École ✕ France 48°48N 2°4E 134 B1
St-Cyr-sur-Mer France 43°11N 5°43E 175 E9
St. David U.S.A. 40°30N 90°3W 310 D6
St. David's Nfld. & L., Canada 48°12N 58°52W 299 C8
St. David's Grenada 12°2N 61°40W 323 q
St. David's Pembs., U.K. 51°53N 5°16W 169 F2
St. David's Head U.K. 51°54N 5°19W 169 F2
St. David's I. Bermuda 32°21N 64°39W 153 a
St-Denis = Sig Algeria 35°32N 0°12W 261 A4
St-Denis Seine-St-Denis, France 48°56N 2°20E 134 A3
St-Denis Réunion 20°52S 55°27E 272 f
St-Denis → Réunion 20°52S 55°27E 272 f
St-Denis ✕ (RUN) Réunion 20°53S 55°32E 272 f
St-Dié-en-Vosges France 48°17N 6°56E 173 D13
St-Dizier France 48°38N 4°56E 173 D11
St-Égrève France 45°14N 5°41E 175 C9
St. Elias, Mt. U.S.A. 60°18N 140°56W 303 F12
St. Elias Mts. N. Amer. 60°33N 139°28W 296 A1
St-Élie Fr. Guiana 4°49N 53°17W 329 C7
St. Elmo U.S.A. 39°2N 88°51W 311 E8
St-Eloy-les-Mines France 46°10N 2°51E 173 F9
St-Émilion France 44°53N 0°9W 174 D3
St-Étienne France 45°27N 4°22E 175 C8
St-Étienne → Réunion 21°17S 55°25E 272 f
St-Étienne-de-Tinée France 44°16N 6°56E 175 D10
St-Étienne-du-Rouvray France 49°23N 1°6E 172 C8
St. Eugène Canada 45°30N 74°28W 313 A10
St. Eustatius W. Indies 17°20N 63°0W 322 a
St-Exupery, Lyon ✕ (LYS) France 45°44N 5°2E 175 C9
St-Fargeau France 47°39N 3°4E 173 E10
St-Félicien Canada 48°40N 72°25W 298 C5
St. Ferdinand = Florissant U.S.A. 38°47N 90°19W 310 F6
St-Florent France 42°41N 9°18E 175 F13
St-Florent, G. de France 42°47N 9°12E 175 F13
St-Florent-sur-Cher France 46°59N 2°15E 173 F9
St-Florentin France 48°0N 3°45E 173 E10
St-Flour France 45°2N 3°6E 174 C7
St. Francis U.S.A. 39°47N 101°48W 308 F3
St. Francis → U.S.A. 34°38N 90°36W 315 D9
St. Francis, C. S. Africa 34°14S 24°49E 270 D3
St. Francisville Ill., U.S.A. 38°36N 87°39W 311 F9
St. Francisville La., U.S.A. 30°47N 91°23W 314 F9
St-François Guadeloupe 16°16N 61°18W 322 e
St-François, L. Canada 45°10N 74°22W 313 A10
St-Fulgent France 46°50N 1°10W 172 F5
St-Gabriel Canada 46°17N 73°24W 298 C5
St. Gallen = Sankt Gallen Switz. 47°26N 9°22E 179 H5
St-Galmier France 45°35N 4°19E 173 G11
St-Gaudens France 43°6N 0°44E 174 E4
St-Gaultier France 46°39N 1°26E 172 F8
St-Gengoux-le-National France 46°37N 4°40E 173 F11
St-Geniez-d'Olt France 44°27N 2°58E 174 D6
St. George Queens., Australia 28°1S 148°30E 281 D4
St. George Bermuda 32°22N 64°40W 153 a
St. George N.B., Canada 45°11N 66°50W 299 C6
St. George Ont., Canada 43°15N 80°15W 312 C4
St. George Ga., U.S.A. 30°31N 82°2W 316 E7
St. George S.C., U.S.A. 33°11N 80°35W 316 B9
St. George Utah, U.S.A. 37°6N 113°35W 305 H7
St. George, C. Nfld. & L., Canada 48°30N 59°16W 299 C8
St. George, C. Papua N. G. 4°49S 152°53E 286 C7
St. George, C. Fla., U.S.A. 29°40N 85°5W 316 F4
St. George I. Alaska, U.S.A. 56°35N 169°35W 303 H5
St. George I. Fla., U.S.A. 29°35N 84°55W 316 F5
St. George Ra. Australia 18°40S 125°0E 278 C4
St. George's Canada 48°26N 58°31W 299 C8
St-Georges Qué., Canada 46°8N 70°40W 299 C5
St-Georges Fr. Guiana 3°53N 51°50W 329 C7
St. George's Grenada 12°5N 61°43W 323 q
St. George's B. Canada 48°24N 58°53W 299 C8
St. Georges Basin N.S.W., Australia 35°7S 150°36E 283 C9
St. Georges Basin W. Austral., Australia 15°23S 125°2E 278 C4
St. George's Channel Europe 52°0N 6°0W 166 E6
St. George's Channel India 7°15N 93°43E 245 L11
St. George's Channel Papua N. G. 4°10S 152°20E 286 C7
St. Georges Harbour Bermuda 32°33N 64°42W 153 a
St. Georges Hd. Australia 35°12S 150°42E 283 C9
St. Georges I. Bermuda 32°23N 64°40W 153 a
St-Georges-lès-Baillargeaux France 46°41N 0°22E 174 B4
St-Germain, Forêt de France 48°57N 2°5E 134 A1
St-Germain-de-Calberte France 44°13N 3°48E 174 D7
St-Germain-en-Laye France 48°53N 2°4E 134 A1
St-Germain-Lembron France 45°27N 3°14E 174 C7
St-Gervais-d'Auvergne France 46°4N 2°50E 173 F9
St-Gervais-les-Bains France 45°53N 6°42E 175 C10
St-Gildas, Pte. de France 47°8N 2°14W 172 E4
St. Giles Cathedral Edinburgh, U.K. 121 b2
St-Gilles Brussels, Belgium 50°49N 4°20E 116 B2
St-Gilles Gard, France 43°40N 4°26E 175 E8
St-Gilles-les-Bains Réunion 21°2S 55°14E 272 f
St-Gilles-les-Hauts Réunion 21°2S 55°15E 272 f
St-Girons France 42°59N 1°8E 174 F5
St. Gotthard P. = San Gottardo, P. del Switz. 46°33N 8°33E 179 J4
St. Helena Atl. Oc. 15°58S 5°42W 153 h
St. Helena Calif., U.S.A. 38°30N 122°28W 306 G4
St. Helena, Mt. U.S.A. 38°40N 122°36W 306 G4
St. Helena B. S. Africa 32°40S 18°10E 270 D2
St. Helena Sd. U.S.A. 32°15N 80°25W 316 C9
St. Helens Tas., Australia 41°20S 148°15E 281 G4
St. Helens Mersey., U.K. 53°27N 2°44W 168 D5
St. Helens Oreg., U.S.A. 45°52N 122°48W 306 E4
St. Helens, Mt. U.S.A. 46°12N 122°12W 306 D4
St. Helier Chan. Is., U.K. 49°10N 2°7W 169 H5
St. Helier London, U.K. 51°23N 0°11W 125 B2
St-Herblain France 47°13N 1°40W 172 E5
St-Hilaire-du-Harcouët France 48°35N 1°5W 172 D5
St-Hillaire-de-Riez France 46°43N 1°57W 174 B2
St-Hippolyte France 47°19N 6°50E 173 E13
St-Hippolyte-du-Fort France 43°58N 3°52E 174 E7
St-Honoré-les-Bains France 46°54N 3°50E 173 F10
St-Hubert Canada 45°29N 73°25W 130 B3
St-Hubert, Galeries Royales Brussels, Belgium 116 b2
St-Hyacinthe Canada 45°40N 72°58W 298 C5
St. Ignace U.S.A. 45°52N 84°44W 309 C11
St. Ignace I. Canada 48°45N 88°0W 298 C2
St. Ignatius U.S.A. 47°19N 114°6W 304 C6
St-Imier Switz. 47°9N 6°58E 179 H2
St. Isaac's Cathedral Russia 59°55N 30°19E 137 B1
St. Ives Cambs., U.K. 52°20N 0°4W 169 E7
St. Ives Corn., U.K. 50°12N 5°30W 169 G2
St-Jacques Montréal, Canada 130 a2
St-Jacques → Canada 45°26N 73°29W 130 B3
St-James France 48°31N 1°20W 172 D5
St. James Minn., U.S.A. 43°59N 94°38W 308 D6
St. James Mo., U.S.A. 38°0N 91°37W 310 G5
St. James Cathedral Toronto, Canada 141 b3
St. James's London, U.K. 125 b3
St-Jean St. Barts 17°53N 62°50W 322 a
St-Jean → Canada 50°17N 64°20W 299 B7
St-Jean, L. Canada 48°40N 72°0W 299 C5
St-Jean Baptiste Montréal, Canada 130 a1
St-Jean-d'Angély France 45°57N 0°31W 174 C3
St-Jean-de-Braye France 47°53N 1°58E 173 E8
St-Jean-de-Luz France 43°23N 1°39W 174 E2
St-Jean-de-Maurienne France 45°16N 6°21E 175 C10
St-Jean-de-Monts France 46°47N 2°4W 172 F4
St-Jean-du-Gard France 44°7N 3°52E 174 D7
St-Jean-en-Royans France 45°1N 5°18E 175 C9
St-Jean-Pied-de-Port France 43°10N 1°14W 174 E2
St-Jean-Port-Joli Canada 47°15N 70°13W 299 C5
St-Jean-sur-Richelieu Canada 45°20N 73°20W 313 A11
St-Jérôme Canada 45°47N 74°0W 298 C5
St. Joe U.S.A. 41°19N 84°54W 311 C12
St. John N.B., Canada 45°20N 66°8W 299 C6
St. John Kans., U.S.A. 38°0N 98°46W 308 F4
St. John → Liberia 6°40N 9°10W 262 D2
St. John → N. Amer. 45°12N 66°5W 309 C20
St. John, C. Canada 50°0N 55°32W 299 C8
St. John I. U.S. Virgin Is. 18°20N 64°42W 321 b
St. John's Antigua & B. 17°6N 61°51W 322 b
St. John's Nfld. & L., Canada 47°35N 52°40W 299 C9
St. Johns Montserrat 16°46N 62°11W 323 p
St. Johns Ariz., U.S.A. 34°30N 109°22W 305 J9
St. Johns Mich., U.S.A. 43°0N 84°33W 311 B12
St. Johns → U.S.A. 30°24N 81°24W 316 E8
St. John's Pt. Ireland 54°34N 8°27W 166 B3
St. Johnsbury U.S.A. 44°25N 72°1W 313 B12
St. Johnston Village Antigua & B. 17°7N 61°50W 322 b
St. Johnsville U.S.A. 43°0N 74°43W 313 C10
St-Joost-Ten-Node Belgium 50°51N 4°21E 116 A2
St. Joseph Ont., Canada 43°24N 81°42W 312 C3
St. Joseph Dominica 15°24N 61°26W 323 k
St-Joseph Martinique 14°39N 61°4W 322 j
St-Joseph Réunion 21°22S 55°37E 272 f
St. Joseph Mayaro, Trin. & Tob. 10°18N 60°59W 323 t
St. Joseph Tunapuna, Trin. & Tob. 10°40N 61°25W 323 t
St. Joseph Ill., U.S.A. 40°7N 88°2W 311 D8
St. Joseph La., U.S.A. 31°55N 91°14W 314 F9
St. Joseph Mich., U.S.A. 42°6N 86°29W 311 B10
St. Joseph Mo., U.S.A. 39°46N 94°50W 310 E2
St. Joseph → U.S.A. 42°7N 86°29W 311 B10
St. Joseph, I. Canada 46°12N 83°58W 298 C3
St. Joseph, L. Canada 51°10N 90°35W 298 B1
St. Joseph Pt. U.S.A. 29°52N 85°24W 316 F4
St-Juéry France 43°57N 2°12E 174 E6
St. Julian's Malta 35°55N 14°29E 206 F7
St-Julien-Chapteuil France 45°2N 4°4E 175 C8
St-Julien-de-Vouvantes France 47°38N 1°13W 172 E5
St-Julien-en-Genevois France 46°9N 6°5E 173 F13
St-Junien France 45°53N 0°55E 174 C4
St-Just-en-Chaussée France 49°30N 2°25E 173 C9
St-Just-en-Chevalet France 45°55N 3°50E 174 C7
St. Kilda Vic., Australia 37°51S 144°58E 128 B1
St. Kilda N.Z. 45°53S 170°31E 285 F5
St. Kilda W. Isles, U.K. 57°49N 8°34W 165 C2
St. Kitts W. Indies 17°20N 62°40W 322 d
St. Kitts & Nevis ■ W. Indies 17°20N 62°40W 322 d
St-Lambert Qué., Canada 45°30N 73°29W 130 A3
St-Lambert Yvelines, France 48°43N 2°1E 134 B1
St. Laurent Canada 50°25N 97°58W 297 C9
St-Laurent Canada 45°30N 73°43W 130 A1
St-Laurent-de-la-Salanque France 42°46N 2°59E 174 F6
St-Laurent du Maroni Fr. Guiana 5°29N 54°3W 329 B7
St-Laurent-du-Pont France 45°23N 5°45E 175 C9
St-Laurent-en-Grandvaux France 46°35N 5°58E 173 F12
St-Laurent-Médoc France 45°8N 0°49W 174 C3
St. Lawrence Queens., Australia 22°16S 149°31E 280 C4
St. Lawrence Nfld. & L., Canada 46°54N 55°23W 299 C8
St. Lawrence → Canada 49°30N 66°0W 299 C6
St. Lawrence, Gulf of Canada 48°25N 62°0W 299 C7
St. Lawrence I. U.S.A. 63°30N 170°30W 303 E5
St. Lawrence Islands △ Canada 44°27N 75°52W 313 B9
St. Lawrence Market Toronto, Canada 141 b3
St-Lazare, Gare Paris, France 134 a3
St. Léonard Canada 47°12N 67°58W 299 C6
St-Léonard Canada 45°35N 73°34W 130 A2
St-Léonard-de-Noblat France 45°49N 1°29E 174 C5
St-Leu Réunion 21°9S 55°18E 272 f
St. Lewis → Canada 52°26N 56°11W 299 B8
St-Lô France 49°7N 1°5W 172 C5
St-Louis Montréal, Canada 130 b2
St-Louis Haut-Rhin, France 47°30N 7°34E 173 E14
St-Louis Guadeloupe 15°56N 61°19W 322 e
St-Louis Réunion 21°16S 55°25E 272 f
St-Louis Senegal 16°8N 16°27W 262 B1
St. Louis U.S.A. 38°37N 90°11W 310 F6
St-Louis □ Senegal 16°20N 15°0W 262 B2
St. Louis → U.S.A. 46°44N 92°9W 308 B7
St. Louis Lambert Int. ✕ (STL) U.S.A. 38°45N 90°22W 310 F6
St-Loup-sur-Semouse France 47°53N 6°16E 173 E13
St-Luc Canada 45°22N 73°18W 313 A11
St. Lucia ■ W. Indies 14°0N 60°57W 323 m
St. Lucia, L. S. Africa 28°5S 32°30E 271 C5
St. Lucia ⌓ S. Africa 28°6S 32°27E 271 C5
St. Lucia Channel W. Indies 14°15N 61°0W 321 D7
St. Lucie U.S.A. 27°29N 80°20W 317 H9
St. Lucie Canal U.S.A. 27°10N 80°18W 317 H9
St. Maarten ⧄ W. Indies 18°2N 63°5W 322 a
St. Magnus B. U.K. 60°25N 1°35W 167 A7
St-Maixent-l'École France 46°24N 0°12W 174 B3
St-Malo France 48°39N 2°1W 172 D4
St-Malo, G. de France 48°50N 2°30W 172 D4
St-Mandé France 48°50N 2°24E 134 A3
St-Mandrier-sur-Mer France 43°4N 5°57E 175 E9
St-Marc Haiti 19°10N 72°41W 321 C5
St-Marcellin France 45°9N 5°20E 175 C9
St-Marcouf, Îs. France 49°30N 1°10W 172 C5
St. Margaret's Ireland 53°25N 6°18W 120 A2
St. Maries U.S.A. 47°19N 116°35W 304 C5
St. Mark B. Grenada 12°11N 61°42W 323 q
St. Marks U.S.A. 30°9N 84°12W 316 E5
St. Mark's Square = San Marco, Piazza Venice, Italy 142 b3
St-Martin ⧄ W. Indies 18°5N 63°5W 322 a
St-Martin, Bois France 48°48N 2°35E 134 B4
St-Martin, C. Martinique 14°52N 61°14W 322 j
St. Martin, L. Canada 51°40N 98°30W 297 C9
St-Martin-de-Crau France 43°38N 4°48E 175 E8
St-Martin-de-Ré France 46°12N 1°21W 174 B2
St-Martin-d'Hères France 45°9N 5°45E 175 C9
St-Martin-Vésubie France 44°4N 7°15E 175 D11
St. Martin's I. Bangla. 20°36N 92°20E 241 E4
St-Martory France 43°9N 0°56E 174 E4
St. Mary U.S.A. 37°53N 89°57W 310 G7
St. Mary, Mt. Papua N. G. 8°8S 147°2E 286 E4
St. Mary Cray U.K. 51°23N 0°7E 125 B4
St. Mary Is. India 13°20N 74°35E 245 H2
St. Mary Pk. Australia 31°32S 138°34E 282 A3
St. Marys Tas., Australia 41°35S 148°11E 281 G4
St. Marys Ont., Canada 43°20N 81°10W 312 C3
St. Mary's Trin. & Tob. 10°14N 61°33W 323 t
St. Mary's Corn., U.K. 49°55N 6°18W 169 H1
St. Mary's Orkney, U.K. 58°54N 2°54W 167 C6
St. Mary's Alaska, U.S.A. 62°4N 163°10W 303 E7
St. Marys Ga., U.S.A. 30°44N 81°33W 316 E8
St. Marys Ohio, U.S.A. 40°33N 84°24W 311 D12
St. Marys Pa., U.S.A. 41°26N 78°34W 312 E6
St. Marys → U.S.A. 30°43N 81°27W 316 E8
St. Mary's, C. Canada 46°50N 54°12W 299 C9
St. Mary's B. Canada 46°50N 53°50W 299 C9
St. Mary's Bay Canada 44°25N 66°10W 299 D6
St. Mary's Cathedral San Francisco, U.S.A. 136 c1
St-Mathieu, Pte. France 48°20N 4°45W 172 D2
St. Matthew I. U.S.A. 60°24N 172°42W 303 F4
St. Matthews Ky., U.S.A. 38°15N 85°39W 311 F11
St. Matthews S.C., U.S.A. 33°40N 80°46W 316 B9
St. Matthews, I. = Zadetkyi Kyun Burma 10°0N 98°25E 237 G2
St. Matthias Group Papua N. G. 1°30S 150°0E 286 A6
St-Maur-des-Fossés France 48°48N 2°29E 134 B3
St-Maurice France 48°49N 2°24E 134 B3
St-Maurice → Canada 46°21N 72°31W 298 C5
St. Mawes U.K. 50°10N 5°2W 169 G2
St-Maximin-la-Ste-Baume France 43°27N 5°52E 175 E9
St-Médard-en-Jalles France 44°53N 0°43W 174 D3
St-Méen-le-Grand France 48°11N 2°12W 172 D4
St. Meinrad U.S.A. 38°10N 86°49W 311 F10
St. Michael U.S.A. 63°29N 162°2W 303 E7
St. Michael's Cathedral Toronto, Canada 141 a3
St-Michel Canada 45°34N 73°37W 130 A2
St-Mihiel France 48°54N 5°32E 173 D12
St-Nazaire France 47°17N 2°12W 172 E4
St. Neots U.K. 52°14N 0°15W 169 E7
St-Nicolas-de-Port France 48°38N 6°18E 173 D13
St-Omer France 50°45N 2°15E 173 B9
St-Ouen France 48°56N 2°20E 134 A3
St-Palais-sur-Mer France 45°38N 1°5W 174 C2
St-Pamphile Canada 46°58N 69°48W 299 C6
St. Pancras International London, U.K. 125 a4
St-Pardoux-la-Rivière France 45°29N 0°45E 174 C4
St. Paris U.S.A. 40°8N 83°58W 311 D13
St-Pascal Canada 47°32N 69°48W 299 C6
St. Patricks Barbados 13°6N 59°30W 323 r
St. Patrick's Cathedral Dublin, Ireland 120 c1
St. Patrick's Cathedral New York, U.S.A. 132 c2
St. Patrick's Church Toronto, Canada 141 a1
St. Paul Canada 54°0N 111°17W 296 C6
St-Paul Réunion 20°59S 55°17E 272 f

St. Paul Alaska, U.S.A. 57°7N 170°17W 303 H5
St. Paul Ind., U.S.A. 39°26N 85°38W 311 E11
St. Paul Minn., U.S.A. 44°56N 93°5W 308 C7
St. Paul Nebr., U.S.A. 41°13N 98°27W 308 E4
St-Paul → Canada 51°27N 57°42W 299 B8
St. Paul → Liberia 6°25N 10°48W 262 D2
St. Paul, Î. Ind. Oc. 38°55S 77°34E 273 H6
St-Paul-de-Fenouillet France 42°48N 2°30E 174 F6
St. Paul I. N.S., Canada 47°12N 60°9W 299 C7
St. Paul I. Alaska, U.S.A. 57°10N 170°15W 303 H5
St-Paul-lès-Dax France 43°44N 1°3W 174 E2
St-Paul-sur-Ubaye France 44°31N 6°45E 175 D10
St. Pauls St. Helena 15°57S 5°43W 153 h
St. Paul's Bay Malta 35°57N 14°24E 206 F7
St. Paul's Cathedral London, U.K. 125 b4
St. Paul's Cray U.K. 51°23N 0°6E 125 B4
St-Péray France 44°57N 4°50E 175 D8
St. Pete Beach U.S.A. 27°43N 82°44W 317 H7
St. Peter U.S.A. 44°20N 93°57W 308 C7
St. Peter & St. Paul San Francisco, U.S.A. 136 a2
St. Peter Port U.K. 49°26N 2°33W 169 H5
St. Peters N.S.W., Australia 33°55S 151°11E 139 B2
St. Peters N.S., Canada 45°40N 60°53W 299 C7
St. Peters P.E.I., Canada 46°25N 62°35W 299 C7
St. Peters Montserrat 16°43N 62°13W 323 p
St. Peters Mo., U.S.A. 38°48N 90°37W 310 F6
St. Peter's Square = San Pietro, Piazza Rome, Italy 136 b1
St. Petersburg = Sankt-Peterburg Russia 59°55N 30°20E 137 B1
St. Petersburg U.S.A. 27°46N 82°40W 317 H7
St. Petersburg Pulkovo Int. ✈ (LED) Russia 59°48N 30°18E 137 C1
St-Philbert-de-Grand-Lieu France 47°2N 1°39W 172 E5
St-Phillippe Réunion 21°21S 55°44E 272 f
St-Pie Canada 45°30N 72°54W 313 A12
St-Pierre Qué., Canada 45°27N 73°38W 130 B2
St-Pierre Martinique 14°45N 61°10W 322 j
St. Pierre Mauritius 20°13S 57°31E 272 e
St-Pierre Réunion 21°19S 55°28E 272 f
St-Pierre St-P. & M. 46°46N 56°12W 299 C8
St-Pierre, L. Canada 46°12N 72°52W 298 C5
St-Pierre, Rade de Martinique 14°44N 61°11W 322 j
St-Pierre-de-la-Pointe-aux-Esquimaux = Havre-St.-Pierre Canada 50°18N 63°33W 299 B7
St-Pierre-d'Oléron France 45°57N 1°19W 174 C2
St-Pierre-en-Port France 49°48N 0°30E 172 C7
St-Pierre-et-Miquelon ☒ N. Amer. 46°55N 56°10W 299 C8
St-Pierre-le-Moûtier France 46°47N 3°7E 173 F10
St-Pierre-sur-Dives France 49°2N 0°1W 172 C6
St-Pieters Leew Belgium 50°47N 4°16E 116 B1
St-Pol-de-Léon France 48°41N 4°0W 172 D3
St-Pol-sur-Mer France 51°1N 2°20E 173 A9
St-Pol-sur-Ternoise France 50°23N 2°20E 173 B9
St-Pons France 43°30N 2°45E 174 E6
St-Pourçain-sur-Sioule France 46°18N 3°18E 173 F10
St-Priest France 45°42N 4°57E 175 C8
St-Quay-Portrieux France 48°39N 2°51W 172 D4
St-Quentin N.B., Canada 47°30N 67°23W 299 C6
St-Quentin Aisne, France 49°50N 3°16E 173 C10
St-Quentin, Étang de France 48°47N 2°0E 134 B1
St-Rambert-d'Albon France 45°17N 4°49E 175 C8
St-Raphaël France 43°25N 6°46E 175 E10
St. Regis U.S.A. 47°18N 115°6W 304 C6
St. Regis Falls U.S.A. 44°40N 74°32W 313 B10
St-Renan France 48°26N 4°37W 172 D2
St. Robert U.S.A. 37°50N 92°11W 310 G4
St-Saëns France 49°41N 1°16E 172 C8
St-Savin France 46°34N 0°53E 174 B4
St-Savinien France 45°53N 0°42W 174 C3
St. Sebastien, Tanjon' i Madag. 12°26S 48°44E 272 A2
St-Seine-l'Abbaye France 47°26N 4°47E 173 E11
St-Sernin-sur-Rance France 43°54N 2°35E 174 E6
St-Sever France 43°45N 0°35W 174 E3
St-Siméon Canada 47°51N 69°54W 299 C6
St. Simons I. U.S.A. 31°12N 81°15W 316 D8
St. Simons Island U.S.A. 31°9N 81°22W 316 D8
St. Stephen N.B., Canada 45°16N 67°17W 299 C6
St. Stephen S.C., U.S.A. 33°24N 79°55W 316 B10
St. Stephen's Basilica Budapest, Hungary 117 b2
St. Stephen's Cathedral = Stephansdom Vienna, Austria 142 b2
St. Stephen's Green Dublin, Ireland 120 c3
St-Stevens-Woluwe Belgium 50°52N 4°26E 116 A2
St-Sulpice France 43°46N 1°41E 174 E5
St-Sulpice-Laurière France 46°3N 1°29E 174 B5
St-Sulpice-les-Feuilles France 46°19N 1°21E 174 B5
St-Syprien = St-Cyprien France 42°37N 3°2E 174 F7
St. Teresa U.S.A. 29°55N 84°27W 316 F5
St-Thégonnec France 48°31N 3°57W 172 D3
St. Thomas = Charlotte Amalie U.S. Virgin Is. 18°21N 64°56W 321 C7
St. Thomas Canada 42°45N 81°10W 312 D3
St. Thomas Bay Malta 35°51N 14°34E 206 F8
St. Thomas I. U.S. Virgin Is. 18°20N 64°55W 321 C7
St-Tite Canada 46°45N 72°34W 298 C5
St-Trond = Sint-Truiden Belgium 50°48N 5°10E 170 D5
St-Tropez France 43°17N 6°38E 175 E10
St-Vaast-la-Hougue France 49°35N 1°17W 172 C5
St-Valery-en-Caux France 49°52N 0°43E 172 C7
St-Valéry-sur-Somme France 50°11N 1°38E 173 B8
St-Vallier France 46°38N 4°22E 173 F11
St-Vallier-de-Thiey France 43°42N 6°51E 175 E10
St-Varent France 46°53N 0°13W 172 F6
St-Vaury France 46°12N 1°46E 174 B5
St. Vidgeon's ✿ Australia 14°47S 134°53E 280 A1
St. Vincent = São Vicente C. Verde Is. 17°0N 25°0W 153 j
St. Vincent Italy 45°45N 7°39E 198 C4
St. Vincent W. Indies 13°15N 61°10W 323 n
St. Vincent, G. Australia 35°0S 138°0E 282 C3
St. Vincent & the Grenadines ■ W. Indies 13°0N 61°10W 323 n
St-Vincent-de-Paul Canada 45°36N 73°39W 130 A2
St-Vincent-de-Tyrosse France 43°39N 1°19W 174 E2
St. Vincent I. U.S.A. 29°42N 85°3W 317 F4
St. Vincent Passage W. Indies 13°30N 61°0W 321 D7
St-Vith Belgium 50°17N 6°9E 170 D6
St-Vivien-de-Médoc France 45°25N 1°2W 174 C2
St. Walburg Canada 53°39N 109°12W 297 C7
St. Xavier Univ. U.S.A. 41°42N 87°42W 119 C2
St-Yrieix-la-Perche France 45°31N 1°12E 174 C5
Saintala India 20°26N 83°20E 244 D6
Ste-Adresse France 49°31N 0°5E 172 C7
Ste-Agathe-des-Monts Canada 46°3N 74°17W 298 C5
Ste-Anne Guadeloupe 16°13N 61°24W 322 e
Ste-Anne Martinique 14°25N 60°54W 322 j
Ste-Anne Réunion 21°4S 55°45E 272 f
Ste-Anne Seychelles 4°36S 55°31E 272 c
Ste-Anne, L. Canada 50°0N 67°42W 299 B6
Ste-Anne-des-Monts Canada 49°8N 66°30W 299 C6
Ste-Catherine Canada 45°24N 73°34W 130 B2
Ste-Croix Switz. 46°49N 6°34E 179 J2
Ste-Enimie France 44°22N 3°26E 174 D7
Ste-Foy-la-Grande France 44°50N 0°13E 174 D4
Ste. Genevieve U.S.A. 37°59N 90°2W 310 G6
Ste-Hélène, Î. Canada 45°31N 73°32W 130 A2
Ste-Hermine France 46°32N 1°4W 174 B2
Ste-Livrade-sur-Lot France 44°24N 0°36E 174 D4
Ste-Luce Martinique 14°28N 60°55W 322 j
Ste. Madeleine Trin. & Tob. 10°16N 61°26W 323 t
Ste-Marguerite Guadeloupe 16°23N 61°24W 322 e
Ste-Marguerite → Canada 50°9N 66°36W 299 B6
Ste-Marie Canada 46°26N 71°0W 299 C5
Ste. Marie Gabon 3°48S 11°1E 264 C2
Ste-Marie Guadeloupe 16°6N 61°33W 322 e
Ste-Marie Martinique 14°48N 61°1W 322 j
Ste-Marie Réunion 20°53S 55°33E 272 f
Ste-Marie, Ile = Boraha, Nosy Madag. 16°50S 49°55E 272 B2
Ste-Marie-aux-Mines France 48°15N 7°12E 173 D14
Ste-Marthe Guadeloupe 16°15N 61°15W 322 e
Ste-Maure-de-Touraine France 47°7N 0°37E 172 E7
Ste-Maxime France 43°19N 6°39E 175 E10
Ste-Menehould France 49°5N 4°54E 173 C11
Ste-Mère-Église France 49°24N 1°19W 172 C5
Ste-Rose Guadeloupe 16°20N 61°45W 322 e
Ste-Rose Réunion 21°8S 55°45E 272 f
Ste. Rose du Lac Canada 51°4N 99°30W 297 C9
Ste-Savine France 48°18N 4°3E 173 D11
Ste-Sigolène France 45°15N 4°14E 175 C8
Ste-Suzanne Réunion 20°54S 55°36E 272 f
Saintes France 45°45N 0°37W 174 C3
Saintes, Canal des Guadeloupe 15°55N 61°40W 322 e
Saintes, Îs. des Guadeloupe 15°50N 61°35W 322 e
Stes-Maries-de-la-Mer France 43°26N 4°26E 175 E8
Saintfield U.K. 54°28N 5°49W 166 B6
Saintonge France 45°40N 0°50W 174 C3
Saipal Nepal 29°50N 81°40E 243 E9
Saipan N. Marianas 15°12N 145°45E 302 e
Saipan Channel N. Marianas 15°5N 145°41E 302 e
Sairang India 23°50N 92°45E 241 D4
Sairecábur, Cerro Bolivia 22°43S 67°54W 334 A2
Sāitah Si. Arabia 16°36N 42°56E 248 C3
Saitama Japan 35°54N 139°38E 223 B11
Saitama ☐ Japan 36°25N 139°30E 223 A11
Saiteli = Kadınhanı Turkey 38°14N 32°13E 212 C5
Saiți Moldova 46°30N 29°24E 183 D14
Saito Japan 32°3N 131°24E 222 E3
Saiwai Japan 35°32N 139°41E 140 B3
Saiyid Pakistan 33°7N 73°2E 242 C5
Saja-Besaya ⌂ Spain 43°10N 4°9W 194 B6
Sajama Bolivia 18°7S 69°0W 330 D4
Sajama, Nevado Bolivia 18°6S 68°54W 330 D4
Sajan Serbia 45°50N 20°20E 182 E5
Sajó → Hungary 47°56N 21°7E 182 C6
Sajókazinc = Kazincbarcika Hungary 48°17N 20°36E 182 B5
Sajószentpéter Hungary 48°12N 20°44E 182 B5
Sajum India 33°20N 79°0E 243 C8
Sak → S. Africa 30°52S 20°25E 270 D3
Saka Kenya 0°9S 39°20E 268 B4
Saka Kalat Pakistan 27°3N 65°3E 240 D2
Sakaba Nigeria 11°4N 5°35E 263 C6
Sakai Fukui, Japan 36°9N 136°16E 223 A8
Sakai Ōsaka, Japan 34°34N 135°27E 133 B1
Sakai Harbour Japan 34°36N 135°26E 133 B1
Sakaide Japan 34°19N 133°50E 222 C5
Sakaiminato Japan 35°38N 133°11E 222 B5
Sakākah Si. Arabia 30°0N 40°8E 246 D4
Sakakawea, L. U.S.A. 47°30N 101°25W 308 B3
Sakami → Canada 53°40N 76°40W 298 B4
Sakami, L. Canada 53°15N 77°0W 298 B4
Sâkâne, 'Erg i-n Mali 20°30N 1°30W 260 D4
Sakania Dem. Rep. of the Congo 12°43S 28°30E 269 E2
Sakar I. Papua N. G. 5°25S 148°6E 286 C5
Sakaraha Madag. 22°55S 44°32E 272 C1
Sakartvelo = Georgia ■ Asia 42°0N 43°0E 191 J6
Sakarya Turkey 40°48N 30°25E 212 B4
Sakarya ☐ Turkey 40°45N 30°25E 212 B4
Sakarya → Turkey 41°7N 30°39E 212 B4
Sakashima-Guntō Japan 24°46N 124°0E 221 M2
Sakassou Ivory C. 7°29N 5°19W 262 D3
Sakata Japan 38°55N 139°50E 220 E9
Sakawa Japan 33°28N 133°11E 222 D5
Sakchu N. Korea 40°23N 125°2E 224 B2
Sakeny → Madag. 20°0S 45°25E 272 C2
Sakété Benin 6°40N 2°45E 263 D5
Sakha ☐ Russia 66°0N 130°0E 215 C14
Sakhalin Russia 51°0N 143°0E 215 D15
Sakhalinskiy Zaliv Russia 54°0N 141°0E 215 D15
Sakhi Gopal India 19°58N 85°50E 244 E7
Şaki Azerbaijan 41°10N 47°5E 191 K8
Šakiai Lithuania 54°59N 23°2E 184 D10
Sakiz-Adasi = Chios Greece 38°27N 26°9E 205 C8
Sakmara → Russia 51°46N 55°1E 216 B5
Sakoli India 21°5N 79°59E 244 D4
Sakon Nakhon Thailand 17°10N 104°9E 236 D5
Sakra, Pulau Singapore 1°15N 103°41E 138 B2
Sakrand Pakistan 26°10N 68°15E 242 F3
Sakri Maharashtra, India 26°13N 86°5E 243 F12
Sakri Maharashtra, India 21°2N 74°20E 244 D2
Sakrivier S. Africa 30°54S 20°28E 270 D3
Sakskøbing Denmark 54°49N 11°39E 163 K5
Sakti India 22°2N 82°58E 243 H10
Saku Japan 36°17N 138°31E 223 A10
Sakuma Japan 35°3N 137°49E 223 B9
Sakura Japan 35°43N 140°14E 223 B12
Sakurai Japan 34°30N 135°51E 223 C7
Sakurajima = On-Take Japan 31°35N 130°39E 222 F2
Saky Ukraine 45°9N 33°34E 189 K7
Sal → Russia 47°31N 40°45E 191 G5
Sal Rei C. Verde Is. 16°11N 22°53W 153 j
Sala Eritrea 16°53N 37°36E 257 D4
Šal'a Slovak Rep. 48°10N 17°50E 181 C10
Sala Sweden 59°58N 16°35E 162 E10
Sala → Eritrea 16°53N 37°36E 257 D4
Sala, O. → Chad 17°0N 20°53E 259 E4
Sala Consilina Italy 40°23N 15°36E 201 B8
Sala-y-Gómez Pac. Oc. 26°28S 105°28W 289 K17
Sala-y-Gómez Ridge Pac. Oc. 25°0S 98°0W 289 K18
Salaberry-de-Valleyfield Canada 45°15N 74°8W 313 A10
Salacgrīva Latvia 57°45N 24°21E 184 A11
Salada, L. Mexico 32°20N 115°40W 305 K6
Saladas Argentina 28°15S 58°40W 334 B4
Saladillo Argentina 35°40S 59°55W 334 D4
Saladin's Castle = Qal'at Salah el Din Syria 34°46N 36°15E 250 D7
Salado → B. Aires, Argentina 35°44S 57°22W 334 D4
Salado → La Pampa, Argentina 37°30S 67°0W 336 A3
Salado → Río Negro, Argentina 41°34S 65°3W 336 B3
Salado → Santa Fe, Argentina 31°40S 60°41W 334 C3
Salado → Tamaulipas, Mexico 26°52N 99°19W 314 H5
Salaga Ghana 8°31N 0°31W 263 D4
Sālah Syria 32°40N 36°45E 250 F7
Şalāḩ ad Dīn ☐ Iraq 34°35N 43°35E 246 C4
Salahin Somalia 2°57N 46°26E 267 D6
Sălaj ☐ Romania 47°15N 23°0E 182 C8
Salakos Greece 36°17N 27°57E 206 E11
Salal Chad 14°48N 17°12E 259 F3
Salala Liberia 6°42N 10°7W 262 D2
Salala Sudan 21°17N 36°16E 256 C4
Salālah Oman 16°56N 53°59E 249 C6
Salam Iraq 33°20N 44°20E 113 A2
Salamajärvi △ Finland 63°12N 24°50E 160 E21
Salamanca Chile 31°46S 70°59W 334 C1
Salamanca Madrid, Spain 40°25N 3°41W 127 B1
Salamanca Salamanca, Spain 40°58N 5°39W 194 E5
Salamanca N.Y., U.S.A. 42°10N 78°43W 312 D6
Salamanca ☐ Spain 40°57N 5°40W 194 E5
Salamat ☐ Chad 11°0N 20°30E 259 F4
Salamat, Bahr → Chad 9°20N 18°0E 259 G3
Salāmatābād Iran 35°39N 47°50E 246 C5
Salamina Colombia 5°25N 75°29W 328 B2
Salamina Greece 37°56N 23°30E 204 D5
Salamis Cyprus 35°11N 33°54E 207 E9
Salamonie L. U.S.A. 40°46N 85°37W 311 D11
Salar de Atacama Chile 23°30S 68°25W 334 A2
Salar de Uyuni Bolivia 20°30S 67°45W 330 E4
Sălard Romania 47°12N 22°3E 182 C7
Salas Spain 43°25N 6°15W 194 B4
Salas de los Infantes Spain 42°2N 3°17W 194 C7
Salatiga Indonesia 7°19S 110°30E 235 D4
Salavat Russia 53°21N 55°55E 186 D10
Salaverry Peru 8°15S 79°0W 330 B2
Salawati Indonesia 1°7S 130°52E 231 E8
Salawin △ Thailand 18°18N 97°40E 236 C1
Salay Phil. 8°52N 124°47E 233 G5
Salaya India 22°19N 69°35E 242 H3
Salayar Indonesia 6°7S 120°30E 231 F6
Salazar → Spain 42°40N 1°20W 196 C3
Salazie Réunion 21°2S 55°32E 272 f
Salazie, Cirque de Réunion 21°3S 55°30E 272 f
Salbris France 47°25N 2°3E 173 E9
S'Albufera Spain 39°47N 3°7E 206 B4
S'Albufera d'es Grau Spain 39°56N 4°16E 206 B5
Salcantay, Nevado Peru 13°19S 72°33W 330 C3
Salcedo Phil. 11°9N 125°40E 233 F5
Salcia Romania 43°56N 24°55E 183 G9
Sălciua Romania 46°24N 23°26E 183 D8
Salcombe U.K. 50°14N 3°47W 169 G4
Saldaña Spain 42°32N 4°48W 194 C6
Saldanha S. Africa 33°0S 17°58E 270 D2
Saldanha B. S. Africa 33°6S 18°0E 270 D2
Saldus Latvia 56°38N 22°30E 184 B9
Saldus ☐ Latvia 56°35N 22°30E 184 B9
Sale Vic., Australia 38°6S 147°6E 283 E7
Sale Burma 20°50N 94°45E 241 E5
Sale Italy 44°59N 8°48E 198 D5
Salé Morocco 34°3N 6°48W 260 B3
Sale Gt. Man., U.K. 53°26N 2°19W 168 D5
Sale City U.S.A. 31°16N 84°1W 316 D5
Salée, Rivière Guadeloupe 16°17N 61°33W 322 e
Salegard = Salekhard Russia 66°30N 66°35E 214 C7
Saleh, Teluk Indonesia 8°34S 117°57E 235 D5
Salekhard Russia 66°30N 66°35E 214 C7
Salelologa Samoa 13°41S 172°11W 287 V19
Salem India 11°40N 78°11E 245 J4
Salem Montserrat 16°45N 62°13W 323 p
Salem Fla., U.S.A. 29°53N 83°25W 316 F6
Salem Ill., U.S.A. 38°38N 88°57W 310 F8
Salem Ind., U.S.A. 38°36N 86°6W 311 F10
Salem Mass., U.S.A. 42°31N 70°53W 313 D14
Salem Mo., U.S.A. 37°39N 91°32W 308 G8
Salem N.H., U.S.A. 42°45N 71°12W 313 D13
Salem N.J., U.S.A. 39°34N 75°28W 309 F16
Salem N.Y., U.S.A. 43°10N 73°20W 313 C11
Salem Ohio, U.S.A. 40°54N 80°52W 312 F4
Salem Oreg., U.S.A. 44°56N 123°2W 304 D2
Salem S. Dak., U.S.A. 43°44N 97°23W 308 D5
Salem Va., U.S.A. 37°18N 80°3W 309 G13
Salemi Italy 37°49N 12°48E 200 E5
Sälen Sweden 61°20N 13°10E 162 C7
Salernes France 43°34N 6°15E 175 E10
Salerno Italy 40°41N 14°47E 201 B7
Salerno, G. di Italy 40°32N 14°42E 201 B7
Sales Brazil 4°2S 63°40W 329 D5
Salford U.K. 53°30N 2°18W 168 D5
Salgótarján Hungary 48°5N 19°47E 182 B4
Salgueiro Brazil 8°4S 39°6W 332 C4
Salher India 20°40N 73°55E 244 D1
Salhus Norway 60°30N 5°15E 164 D2
Salhyr → Ukraine 45°38N 35°1E 189 K8
Salibabu Indonesia 3°51N 126°40E 231 D7
Salibea = Salybia Trin. & Tob. 10°43N 61°2W 323 t
Salibia Dominica 15°30N 61°16W 323 k
Salida U.S.A. 38°32N 106°0W 304 G11
Salies-de-Béarn France 43°28N 0°56W 174 E3
Salihli Turkey 38°28N 28°8E 212 C3
Salihorsk Belarus 52°51N 27°27E 177 B14
Salin Burma 20°35N 94°40E 241 E5
Salina Italy 38°34N 14°50E 201 D7
Salina Kans., U.S.A. 38°50N 97°37W 308 F5
Salina Utah, U.S.A. 38°58N 111°51W 304 G8
Salina Cruz Mexico 16°10N 95°12W 319 D5
Salina di Margherita di Savóia ⌂ Italy 41°23N 16°4E 201 A9
Salinas = Salinópolis Brazil 0°40S 47°20W 332 B2
Salinas Brazil 16°10S 42°10W 333 E3
Salinas Ecuador 2°10S 80°58W 328 D1
Salinas Calif., U.S.A. 36°40N 121°39W 306 J5
Salinas → Guatemala 16°28N 90°31W 319 D6
Salinas → Calif., U.S.A. 36°45N 121°48W 306 J5
Salinas, B. das Angola 14°11S 12°21E 265 E2
Salinas, B. de Nic. 11°4N 85°45W 320 D2
Salinas, Pampa de las Argentina 31°58S 66°42W 334 C2
Salinas Ambargasta Argentina 29°0S 65°0W 334 B3
Salinas de Hidalgo Mexico 22°38N 101°43W 318 C4
Salinas Grandes Argentina 30°0S 65°0W 334 C3
Salinas Pueblo Missions ⌂ U.S.A. 34°6N 106°4W 305 J10
Salinas Valley U.S.A. 36°15N 121°15W 306 J5
Saline U.S.A. 42°10N 83°47W 311 B13
Saline → Ark., U.S.A. 33°10N 92°8W 314 E8
Saline → Kans., U.S.A. 38°52N 97°30W 308 F5
Saline B. Trin. & Tob. 10°42N 61°2W 323 t
Saline di Trapani e Paceco ⌂ Italy 37°59N 12°28E 200 E5
Saline I. Grenada 12°26N 61°28W 323 q
Salines, C. de ses Spain 39°16N 3°4E 206 B4
Salines, Étang des Martinique 14°24N 60°52W 322 j
Salines, Pt. Grenada 12°0N 61°48W 323 q
Salines, Pte. de Martinique 14°23N 60°53W 322 j
Salinópolis Brazil 0°40S 47°20W 332 B2
Salins-les-Bains France 46°58N 5°52E 173 F12
Salir Portugal 37°14N 8°2W 195 H2
Salisbury = Harare Zimbabwe 17°43S 31°2E 269 F3
Salisbury S. Austral., Australia 34°46S 138°38E 282 C3
Salisbury Dominica 15°26N 61°27W 323 k
Salisbury Wilts., U.K. 51°4N 1°47W 169 F6
Salisbury Md., U.S.A. 38°22N 75°36W 309 F16
Salisbury Mo., U.S.A. 39°25N 92°48W 310 E4
Salisbury N.C., U.S.A. 35°40N 80°29W 315 D14
Salisbury I. Canada 63°30N 77°0W 295 E16
Salisbury Plain U.K. 51°14N 1°55W 169 F6
Săliște Romania 45°45N 23°56E 183 E8
Salitre → Brazil 9°29S 40°39W 332 C3
Salkehatchie → U.S.A. 32°37N 80°53W 316 C9
Şalkhad Syria 32°29N 36°43E 251 F7
Salkove Ukraine 48°15N 29°59E 183 B14
Salla Finland 66°50N 28°49E 160 C23
Sallanches France 45°55N 6°38E 175 C10
Sallent Spain 41°49N 1°54E 196 D6
Salles France 44°33N 0°52W 174 D3
Salles-Curan France 44°11N 2°48E 174 D6
Salling Denmark 56°40N 8°55E 163 H2
Salliq = Coral Harbour Canada 64°8N 83°10W 295 E15
Sallisaw U.S.A. 35°28N 94°47W 314 D7
Sallom Sudan 19°17N 37°6E 256 D4
Salluit Canada 62°14N 75°38W 295 E16
Sallyana Nepal 28°22N 82°10E 243 E10
Sallynoggin Ireland 53°17N 6°8W 120 B3
Salmān Pak Iraq 33°6N 44°34E 213 G11
Salmannsdorf Austria 48°14N 16°14E 142 A1
Salmās Iran 38°11N 44°47E 213 C11
Salmedina Spain 40°18N 3°35W 127 C2
Salmerón Spain 40°33N 2°29W 196 E2
Salmo Canada 49°10N 117°20W 296 D5
Salmon U.S.A. 45°11N 113°54W 304 D7
Salmon → B.C., Canada 54°3N 122°40W 296 C4
Salmon → Idaho, U.S.A. 45°51N 116°47W 304 D5
Salmon Arm Canada 50°40N 119°15W 296 C5
Salmon Gums Australia 32°59S 121°38E 279 F3
Salmon Pt. Canada 43°52N 77°15W 312 C7
Salmon River Mts. U.S.A. 44°50N 115°30W 304 D6
Salmon River Res. U.S.A. 43°32N 75°55W 313 C9
Salo C.A.R. 3°10N 16°8E 264 B3
Salo Finland 60°22N 23°10E 188 B2
Salò Italy 45°36N 10°31E 198 C7
Salobreña Spain 36°44N 3°35W 195 J7
Salome U.S.A. 33°47N 113°37W 307 M13
Salomea Poland 52°11N 20°55E 143 B1
Salomon, C. Martinique 14°30N 61°6W 322 j
Salon India 26°2N 81°27E 243 F9
Salon-de-Provence France 43°39N 5°6E 175 E9
Salonga → Dem. Rep. of the Congo 0°10S 19°50E 264 C4
Salonga-Nord △ Dem. Rep. of the Congo 1°55S 21°45E 264 C4
Salonga-Sud △ Dem. Rep. of the Congo 2°25S 21°0E 264 C4
Salonica = Thessaloniki Greece 40°38N 22°58E 202 F6
Salonta Romania 46°49N 21°42E 182 D6
Salop = Shropshire ☐ U.K. 52°36N 2°45W 169 E5
Salor → Spain 39°39N 7°3W 195 F3
Salou Spain 41°4N 1°8E 196 D6
Salou, C. de Spain 41°3N 1°10E 196 D6
Saloum → Senegal 13°50N 16°45W 262 C1
Salpausselkä Finland 61°3N 26°15E 188 B4
Salsacate Argentina 31°20S 65°5W 334 C2
Salses France 42°50N 2°55E 174 F6
Salsette I. India 19°2N 72°53E 130 A2
Salsk Russia 46°28N 41°30E 191 G5
Salso → Italy 37°6N 13°57E 200 E6
Salsomaggiore Terme Italy 44°49N 9°59E 198 D6
Salt Spain 41°59N 2°47E 196 D7
Salt → Alta., Canada 60°0N 112°25W 296 B6
Salt → Ariz., U.S.A. 33°23N 112°19W 305 K7
Salt → Mo., U.S.A. 39°28N 91°4W 310 E5
Salt Cay Bahamas 25°6N 77°18W 153 b
Salt Flats = Witte Pan Bonaire 12°3N 68°17W 322 h
Salt Fork Red → U.S.A. 34°27N 99°21W 314 D5
Salt L. N.S.W., Australia 30°6S 142°8E 281 E3
Salt L. Hawai'i, U.S.A. 21°21N 157°55W 302 K14
Salt Lake City = Bidhan Nagar India 22°35N 88°25E 124 B2
Salt Lake City U.S.A. 40°45N 111°53W 304 F8
Salt Lake Stadium Kolkata, India 22°34N 88°25E 124 B2
Salt Range Pakistan 32°30N 72°25E 242 C5
Salt River S. Africa 34°6S 18°28E 118 A1
Salt Springs U.S.A. 29°21N 81°44W 317 F8
Salt Water L. India 22°33N 88°26E 124 B2
Salta Argentina 24°57S 65°25W 334 A2
Salta ☐ Argentina 24°48S 65°30W 334 A2
Saltara Italy 43°45N 12°50E 199 E9
Saltash U.K. 50°24N 4°14W 169 G3
Saltburn by the Sea U.K. 54°35N 0°58W 168 C7
Saltcoats U.K. 55°38N 4°47W 167 F4
Saltee Is. Ireland 52°7N 6°37W 166 D5
Salters U.S.A. 33°36N 79°51W 316 B10
Saltfjellet Norway 66°40N 15°15E 160 C16
Saltfjellet-Svartisen △ Norway 66°45N 15°10E 160 C16
Saltfjorden Norway 67°15N 14°10E 160 C16
Saltholm Denmark 55°38N 12°43E 163 J6
Salthólmavík Iceland 65°24N 21°57W 155 B5
Saltillo Mexico 25°25N 101°0W 318 B4
Salto Argentina 34°20S 60°15W 334 C3
Salto Uruguay 31°27S 57°50W 334 C4
Salto da Divisa Brazil 16°0S 39°57W 333 E4
Salto del Guaíra Paraguay 24°3S 54°17W 335 A5
Salton City U.S.A. 33°18N 115°57W 307 M11
Salton Sea U.S.A. 33°15N 115°45W 307 M11
Saltpond Ghana 5°15N 1°3W 263 D4
Saltrød Norway 58°30N 8°49E 164 F5
Saltsburg U.S.A. 40°29N 79°27W 312 F5
Saltsjö-Duvnäs Sweden 59°18N 18°12E 139 B3
Saltsjöbaden Sweden 59°15N 18°20E 162 E12
Saluda U.S.A. 34°0N 81°46W 316 A8
Saluda → U.S.A. 34°1N 81°4W 316 A8
Salue Timpaus, Selat Indonesia 1°50S 123°50E 231 E6
Salug Phil. 8°7N 122°47E 233 G4
Salûm Egypt 31°31N 25°7E 256 A2
Salûm, Khâlig el Egypt 31°35N 25°24E 256 A2
Salur India 18°27N 83°18E 244 E6
Salut, Is. du Fr. Guiana 5°15N 52°35W 329 B7
Saluzzo Italy 44°39N 7°29E 198 D4
Salvación, B. Chile 50°50S 75°10W 336 D1
Salvador Brazil 13°0S 38°30W 333 D4
Salvador Sask., Canada 52°10N 109°32W 297 C7
Salvador, El ■ Cent. Amer. 13°50N 89°0W 320 D2
Salvador, L. U.S.A. 29°43N 90°15W 315 G9
Salvaterra Brazil 0°46S 48°31W 332 B2
Salvaterra de Magos Portugal 39°1N 8°47W 195 F2
Salvisa U.S.A. 37°54N 84°51W 311 G12
Sálvora, I. de Spain 42°30N 8°58W 194 C2
Salween → Burma 16°31N 97°37E 241 G6
Salyan Azerbaijan 39°33N 48°59E 213 C13
Salybia Trin. & Tob. 10°43N 61°2W 323 t
Salza → Austria 47°40N 14°43E 180 D7
Salzach → Austria 48°12N 12°56E 180 C5
Salzburg Austria 47°48N 13°2E 180 D6
Salzburg ☐ Austria 47°15N 13°0E 180 D6
Salzburgen = Château-Salins France 48°50N 6°30E 173 D13
Salzgitter Germany 52°9N 10°19E 178 C6
Salzkotten Germany 51°40N 8°37E 178 D4
Salzwedel Germany 52°52N 11°10E 178 C7
Sam Gabon 0°58N 11°16E 264 B2
Sam India 26°50N 70°31E 242 F4
Sam Neua Laos 20°29N 104°5E 228 G5
Sam Ngao Thailand 17°18N 99°0E 236 D2
Sam Rayburn Res. U.S.A. 31°4N 94°5W 314 F7
Sam Rong, Laem Thailand 9°35N 100°4E 237 b
Sam Son Vietnam 19°44N 105°54E 236 C5
Sama de Langreo = Langreo Spain 43°18N 5°40W 194 B5
Samacimbo Angola 13°33S 16°59E 265 E3
Şamad Oman 22°48N 58°9E 249 B7
Samagaltay Russia 50°36N 95°3E 217 B13
Samā'il Oman 23°40N 57°50E 249 B7
Samaipata Bolivia 18°9S 63°52W 331 D5
Samal Phil. 7°5N 125°42E 233 H5
Samal I. Phil. 7°3N 125°44E 233 H5
Samales Group Phil. 6°0N 122°0E 233 J3
Samalga Pass U.S.A. 52°50N 169°0W 300 E6
Samalkot India 17°3N 82°13E 244 F6
Samâlût Egypt 28°20N 30°42E 256 B3
Samana India 30°10N 76°13E 242 D7
Samana Cays Bahamas 23°3N 73°45W 321 B5
Samandağ Turkey 36°5N 35°59E 250 B6
Samandıra Turkey 40°59N 29°13E 203 F13
Samanga Tanzania 8°20S 39°13E 269 D4
Samangān ☐ Afghan. 36°15N 68°3E 240 A3
Samangwa Dem. Rep. of the Congo 4°23S 24°10E 265 C4
Samani Japan 42°7N 142°56E 220 C11
Samanli Dağları Turkey 40°32N 29°10E 203 F13
Samannûd Egypt 30°57N 31°14E 251 H2
Samar Phil. 12°0N 125°0E 233 F5
Samar ☐ Phil. 11°50N 125°0E 233 F5
Samar Sea Phil. 12°0N 124°15E 232 E5
Samara Russia 53°8N 50°6E 190 D10
Samara → Russia 53°10N 50°4E 190 D10
Samara → Ukraine 48°28N 35°7E 189 H8
Samarai Papua N. G. 10°39S 150°41E 286 F6
Samaria = Shōmrōn West Bank 32°15N 35°13E 251 F6
Samaria West Bank 32°17N 35°12E 251 F6
Samaria △ Greece 35°17N 23°58E 207 E4
Samariapo Venezuela 5°15N 67°48W 328 B4
Samarinda Indonesia 0°30S 117°9E 235 C5
Samarkand = Samarqand Uzbekistan 39°40N 66°55E 217 E7
Samarkandsky = Temirtau Kazakhstan 50°5N 72°56E 217 B8
Samarqand Uzbekistan 39°40N 66°55E 217 E7
Samarqand ☐ Uzbekistan 39°35N 66°35E 217 E7
Sāmarrā' Iraq 34°12N 43°52E 213 E10
Samarskaya Luka △ Russia 53°30N 49°30E 190 D9
Samastipur India 25°50N 85°50E 243 G11
Samatya Turkey 40°59N 28°55E 122 C1
Samaúma Brazil 7°50S 60°2W 331 B5
Şamaxı Azerbaijan 40°38N 48°37E 191 K9
Samba Équateur, Dem. Rep. of the Congo 0°13N 21°25E 264 B4
Samba Maniema, Dem. Rep. of the Congo 4°38S 26°22E 265 C5
Samba Jammu & Kashmir, India 32°32N 75°10E 243 C6
Samba Caju Angola 8°46S 15°24E 265 D3
Sambaíba Brazil 7°8S 45°21W 332 C2
Sambalpur India 21°28N 84°4E 244 D7
Sambar, Tanjung Indonesia 2°59S 110°19E 235 C4
Sambas Indonesia 1°20N 109°20E 235 B3
Sambava Madag. 14°16S 50°10E 272 A3
Sambawizi Zimbabwe 18°24S 26°13E 269 F2
Sambhajinagar = Aurangabad India 19°50N 75°23E 244 E2
Sambhal India 28°35N 78°37E 243 E8
Sambhar India 26°52N 75°6E 242 F6
Sambhar L. India 26°55N 75°12E 242 F6
Sambiase Italy 38°58N 16°17E 201 D9
Sambir Ukraine 49°30N 23°10E 185 J10
Sambo Angola 13°3S 16°8E 265 E3
Sambo Indonesia 3°22S 118°52E 235 C5
Samboja Indonesia 1°1S 117°1E 235 C5
Sambor Cambodia 12°46N 106°0E 236 F6
Sambor Prei Kuk Cambodia 12°46N 105°58E 236 F5
Samborombón, B. Argentina 36°5S 57°20W 334 D4
Sambuca di Sicília Italy 37°39N 13°7E 200 E6
Samburu ⌂ Kenya 0°37N 37°31E 268 B4
Samcheok S. Korea 37°30N 129°10E 224 D4
Same Tanzania 4°2S 37°38E 268 C4
Samer France 50°38N 1°44E 173 B8
Samet, Ko Thailand 12°34N 101°27E 236 F3
Samfya Zambia 11°22S 29°31E 269 E2
Samḩah Yemen 12°15N 53°5E 249 D6
Samḩān, Jabal Oman 17°12N 54°55E 249 C6
Sami Greece 38°15N 20°39E 207 C2
Samka Burma 20°9N 96°57E 241 E6
Şämkir Azerbaijan 40°50N 46°0E 191 K8
Samland = Zemlandskiy Poluostrov Russia 54°50N 20°20E 184 D7
Şamlı Turkey 39°48N 27°51E 205 B9
Sammanturai Sri Lanka 7°36N 81°39E 245 L5
Samnah Si. Arabia 25°10N 37°15E 246 E3
Samnū Libya 27°15N 14°55E 258 C2
Samo Alto Chile 30°22S 71°0W 334 C1
Samoa ■ Pac. Oc. 14°0S 172°0W 287 V20
Samoan Is. Pac. Oc. 14°0S 171°0W 287 V20
Samobor Croatia 45°47N 15°44E 199 C12
Samoëns France 46°5N 6°45E 173 F13
Samokov Bulgaria 42°18N 23°35E 202 D7
Šamorín Slovak Rep. 48°2N 17°19E 181 C10
Samorogouan Burkina Faso 11°21N 4°57W 262 C4
Samos Greece 37°45N 26°50E 205 D8
Samoš Serbia 45°13N 20°46E 182 E5
Samos Spain 42°44N 7°20W 194 C3
Samoset U.S.A. 27°28N 82°33W 317 H7
Samosir Indonesia 2°55N 98°50E 234 B1
Samothráki = Mathraki Greece 39°48N 19°31E 206 B9
Samothraki Greece 40°28N 25°28E 203 F9
Samoylovka Russia 51°12N 43°43E 190 E6
Sampa Angola 10°38S 18°56E 265 E3
Sampa Ghana 8°0N 2°36W 262 D4
Sampacho Argentina 33°20S 64°50W 334 C3
Sampalan Indonesia 8°41S 115°34E 231 K18
Sampaloc Phil. 14°36N 120°59E 127 B1
Sampang Indonesia 7°11S 113°13E 235 D4
Samper de Calanda Spain 41°11N 0°28W 196 D4
Sampéyre Italy 44°34N 7°11E 198 D4
Samphan Thawong Thailand 13°44N 100°31E 113 B2
Sampit Indonesia 2°34S 113°0E 235 C4
Sampit → Indonesia 2°44S 112°54E 235 C4
Sampit, Teluk Indonesia 3°5S 113°3E 235 C4
Sampun Papua N. G. 5°21S 152°8E 286 C7
Samrong Cambodia 14°15N 103°30E 236 E4
Samseon S. Korea 37°34N 127°0E 137 B2
Samsø Denmark 55°50N 10°35E 163 J4
Samsø Bælt Denmark 55°45N 10°45E 163 J4
Samson U.S.A. 31°7N 86°3W 316 D3
Samsun Turkey 41°15N 36°22E 212 B7
Samsun ☐ Turkey 41°10N 36°10E 212 B7
Samtah Si. Arabia 16°36N 42°56E 248 C3
Samtredia Georgia 42°7N 42°24E 191 J6
Samuel Smith Park Canada 43°35N 79°30W 141 B1
Samui, Ko Thailand 9°30N 100°0E 237 b
Samur → Russia 41°53N 48°32E 191 K9
Samurskiy Khrebet Russia 41°55N 47°11E 191 K8
Samusole Dem. Rep. of the Congo 10°2S 24°0E 265 E4
Samut Prakan Bangkok, Thailand 13°40N 100°36E 113 B2
Samut Sakhon Thailand 13°32N 100°17E 236 F3
Samut Songkhram Thailand 13°24N 100°1E 236 F3
Samwari Pakistan 28°30N 66°46E 242 E2
San Mali 13°15N 4°57W 262 C4
San → Cambodia 13°32N 105°57E 236 F5
San → Poland 50°45N 21°51E 185 H8
San Adrián Spain 42°20N 1°56W 196 C3
San Adrián, C. de Spain 43°21N 8°50W 194 B2
San Agustín Colombia 1°53N 76°16W 328 C2
San Agustin Romblon, Phil. 12°34N 122°6E 232 E4
San Agustin, C. Phil. 6°20N 126°13E 233 H6
San Agustín de Valle Fértil Argentina 30°35S 67°30W 334 C2
San Ambrosio Pac. Oc. 26°28S 79°53W 326 F3
San Andreas U.S.A. 38°12N 120°41W 306 G6
San Andres Catanduanes, Phil. 13°36N 124°6E 232 E5
San Andres Romblon, Phil. 13°19N 122°41E 232 E4
San Andres Romblon, Phil. 12°31N 122°2E 232 E4
San Andrés Barcelona, Spain 41°26N 2°11E 114 A2
San Andrés, I. de Caribbean 12°42N 81°46W 320 D3
San Andrés del Rabanedo Spain 42°37N 5°36W 194 C5
San Andres Mts. U.S.A. 33°0N 106°30W 305 K10
San Andres Pt. Phil. 13°34N 121°52E 232 E3
San Andrés Tuxtla Mexico 18°27N 95°13W 319 D5
San Angel Mexico 19°20N 99°11W 128 B1
San Angelo U.S.A. 31°28N 100°26W 314 F4
San Angelo Raffaele Venice, Italy 142 b2
San Anselmo U.S.A. 37°59N 122°34W 306 H4
San Antonio Belize 16°15N 89°2W 320 C2
San Antonio Chile 33°40S 71°40W 334 C1
San Antonio Phil. 14°57N 120°5E 232 D3
San Antonio N. Mex., U.S.A. 33°55N 106°52W 305 K10
San Antonio Tex., U.S.A. 29°25N 98°29W 314 G5
San Antonio Amazonas, Venezuela 3°30N 66°44W 328 C4
San Antonio Nueva Esparta, Venezuela 10°57N 63°54W 329 a
San Antonio → U.S.A. 28°30N 96°54W 314 G6
San Antonio, C. Argentina 36°15S 56°40W 334 D4
San Antonio, C. de Cuba 21°50N 84°57W 320 B3
San Antonio, C. de Spain 38°48N 0°12E 197 G5
San Antonio, Mt. U.S.A. 34°17N 117°38W 307 L9
San Antonio B. Phil. 8°38N 117°35E 233 G1
San Antonio de los Baños Cuba 22°54N 82°31W 320 B3
San Antonio de los Cobres Argentina 24°10S 66°17W 334 A2
San Antonio Oeste Argentina 40°40S 65°0W 336 B4
San Arcángelo Italy 40°14N 16°14E 201 B9
San Ardo U.S.A. 36°1N 120°54W 306 J6
San Augustín Canary Is. 27°47N 15°32W 153 e1
San Augustine U.S.A. 31°32N 94°7W 314 F7
San Bartolomé Canary Is. 28°59N 13°37W 153 e2
San Bartolomé de Tirajana Canary Is. 27°54N 15°34W 153 e1
San Bartolomeo in Galdo Italy 41°24N 15°1E 201 A8
San Basilio Italy 41°56N 12°35E 136 B2
San Benedetto del Tronto Italy 42°57N 13°53E 199 F10
San Benedetto Po Italy 45°2N 10°55E 198 C7
San Benedicto, I. Mexico 19°18N 110°49W 318 D2
San Benito U.S.A. 26°8N 97°38W 314 H6
San Benito → U.S.A. 36°53N 121°34W 306 J5
San Benito Mt. U.S.A. 36°22N 120°37W 306 J6
San Bernardino U.S.A. 34°7N 117°19W 307 L9
San Bernardino Mts. U.S.A. 34°10N 116°45W 307 L10
San Bernardino Str. Phil. 12°30N 124°10E 232 E5
San Bernardo Chile 33°40S 70°50W 334 C1
San Bernardo, I. de Colombia 9°45N 75°50W 328 B2
San-Beyse = Choybalsan Mongolia 48°4N 114°30E 219 B11
San Biagio Venice, Italy 142 b4
San Blas Mexico 26°5N 108°46W 318 B3
San Blas, Arch. de Panama 9°50N 78°31W 320 E4
San Blas, C. U.S.A. 29°40N 85°21W 316 F4
San Bonifacio Italy 45°24N 11°16E 199 C8
San Borja Bolivia 14°50S 66°52W 330 C4
San Borja Lima, Peru 12°6S 76°59W 124 B3
San Bóvio Italy 45°27N 9°18E 128 B2
San Bruno, Pt. U.S.A. 37°39N 122°22W 136 C2
San Bruno Mountain State Park ⌂ U.S.A. 37°41N 122°26W 136 B2
San Buenaventura = Ventura U.S.A. 34°17N 119°18W 307 L7
San Buenaventura Bolivia 14°28S 67°35W 330 C4
San Buenaventura Coahuila, Mexico 27°5N 101°32W 318 B4
San Carlos = Butuku-Luba Eq. Guin. 3°29N 8°33E 263 E6
San Carlos = Sant Carles Spain 39°3N 1°34E 206 C2
San Carlos Argentina 33°50S 69°0W 334 C2
San Carlos Bolivia 17°24S 63°45W 331 D5
San Carlos Chile 36°10S 72°0W 334 D1
San Carlos Baja Calif. S., Mexico 24°47N 112°7W 318 C2
San Carlos Coahuila, Mexico 29°1N 100°51W 318 B4
San Carlos Nic. 11°12N 84°50W 320 D3
San Carlos Neg. Occ., Phil. 10°29N 123°25E 233 F4
San Carlos Pangasinan, Phil. 15°55N 120°20E 232 D3
San Carlos Uruguay 34°46S 54°58W 335 C5
San Carlos Ariz., U.S.A. 33°21N 110°27W 305 K8
San Carlos Amazonas, Venezuela 1°55N 67°4W 328 C4
San Carlos Cojedes, Venezuela 9°40N 68°36W 328 B4
San Carlos de Bariloche Argentina 41°10S 71°25W 336 B2
San Carlos de Bolívar Argentina 36°15S 61°6W 334 D3
San Carlos de la Rápita = Sant Carles de la Ràpita Spain 40°37N 0°35E 196 E5
San Carlos de Río Negro Venezuela 1°55N 67°4W 328 C4
San Carlos del Zulia Venezuela 9°1N 71°55W 328 B3
San Carlos L. U.S.A. 33°11N 110°32W 305 K8
San Carlos Park U.S.A. 26°28N 81°49W 317 J8
San Cataldo Italy 37°29N 13°59E 200 E6
San Celoni = Sant Celoni Spain 41°42N 2°30E 196 D7
San Clemente Chile 35°30S 71°29W 334 D1
San Clemente Spain 39°24N 2°25W 197 F2
San Clemente Calif., U.S.A. 33°26N 117°37W 307 M9
San Clemente I. U.S.A. 32°53N 118°29W 307 N8

San Cristóbal = Es Migjorn Gran *Spain* 39°57N 4°3E **206** B5
San Cristóbal *B. Aires, Argentina* 34°38S 58°23W **117** B2
San Cristóbal *Santa Fe, Argentina* 30°20S 61°10W **334** C3
San Cristóbal *Colombia* 2°18S 73°2W **328** D3
San Cristóbal *Dom. Rep.* 18°25N 70°6W **321** C5
San Cristóbal *Solomon Is.* 10°30S 161°0E **287** N11
San Cristóbal *Madrid, Spain* 40°25N 3°35W **127** B2
San Cristóbal *Venezuela* 7°46N 72°14W **328** B3
San Cristóbal, Cerro *Chile* 33°25S 70°38W **137** B2
San Cristóbal, I. *Ecuador* 0°50S 89°26W **330** a
San Cristóbal, Virgen del *Chile* 33°25S 70°38W **137** B2
San Cristóbal de La Laguna *Canary Is.* 28°28N 16°18W **153** e1
San Cristóbal de las Casas *Mexico* 16°45N 92°38W **319** D6
San Cristoforo *Italy* 45°26N 9°9E **128** B1
San Damiano d'Asti *Italy* 44°50N 8°4E **198** D5
San Daniele del Friuli *Italy* 46°9N 13°1E **199** B10
San Diego *Calif., U.S.A.* 32°42N 117°9W **307** N9
San Diego *Tex., U.S.A.* 27°46N 98°14W **314** H5
San Diego, C. *Argentina* 54°40S 65°10W **336** D3
San Diego de la Unión *Mexico* 21°28N 100°52W **318** C4
San Diego Int. ✕ (SAN) *U.S.A.* 32°44N 117°11W **307** N9
San Dimitri, Ras *Malta* 36°4N 14°11E **206** E6
San Dimitri Point = San Dimitri, Ras *Malta* 36°4N 14°11E **206** E6
San Donà di Piave *Italy* 45°38N 12°34E **199** C9
San Donato Milanese *Italy* 45°24N 9°16E **128** B2
Sân el Hagar *Egypt* 30°58N 31°52E **251** H2
San Estanislao *Paraguay* 24°39S 56°26W **334** A4
San Esteban △ *Venezuela* 10°24N 67°58W **328** A4
San Esteban de Gormaz *Spain* 41°34N 3°13W **196** D1
San Eugenio = Artigas *Uruguay* 30°20S 56°30W **334** C4
San Felice Circeo *Italy* 41°14N 13°5E **200** A6
San Felice sul Panaro *Italy* 44°50N 11°8E **199** D8
San Felipe *Chile* 32°43S 70°42W **334** C1
San Felipe *Colombia* 1°55N 67°6W **328** C4
San Felipe *Baja Calif., Mexico* 31°1N 114°52W **318** A2
San Felipe *Phil.* 15°4N 120°4E **232** D3
San Felipe *Venezuela* 10°20N 68°44W **328** A4
San Felipe → *U.S.A.* 33°10N 115°49W **307** M11
San Félix *Chile* 28°56S 70°28W **334** B1
San Félix *Pac. Oc.* 26°23S 80°0W **326** F2
San Fernando = Sant Ferran *Spain* 38°42N 1°28E **206** D1
San Fernando *Chile* 34°30S 71°0W **334** C1
San Fernando *Tamaulipas, Mexico* 24°51N 98°10W **319** C5
San Fernando *Cebu, Phil.* 10°10N 123°42E **233** F4
San Fernando *La Union, Phil.* 16°40N 120°23E **232** C3
San Fernando *Pampanga, Phil.* 15°5N 120°37E **232** D3
San Fernando *Romblon, Phil.* 12°18N 122°36E **232** E4
San Fernando *Cádiz, Spain* 36°28N 6°17W **195** J4
San Fernando *Trin. & Tob.* 10°16N 61°28W **323** t
San Fernando *Calif., U.S.A.* 34°17N 118°26W **307** L8
San Fernando de Apure *Venezuela* 7°54N 67°15W **328** B4
San Fernando de Atabapo *Venezuela* 4°3N 67°42W **328** C4
San Fernando di Púglia *Italy* 41°18N 16°5E **201** A9
San Francesco di Paola *Venice, Italy* **142** b4
San Francique = Erin *Trin. & Tob.* 10°5N 61°39W **323** t
San Francisco *Córdoba, Argentina* 31°30S 62°5W **334** C3
San Francisco *Bolivia* 15°16S 65°31W **331** D4
San Francisco *Peru* 12°36S 73°49W **330** C3
San Francisco *Agusan del S., Phil.* 8°30N 125°56E **233** G5
San Francisco *Cebu, Phil.* 10°39N 124°23E **233** F5
San Francisco *Quezon, Phil.* 13°21N 122°31E **232** E4
San Francisco *S. Leyte, Phil.* 10°4N 125°9E **233** F5
San Francisco *Calif., U.S.A.* 37°46N 122°23W **136** B2
San Francisco → *U.S.A.* 32°59N 109°22W **305** K9
San Francisco, C. de *Colombia* 6°18N 77°29W **328** B2
San Francisco, Paso de *S. Amer.* 27°0S 68°0W **334** B2
San Francisco B. *U.S.A.* 37°39N 122°14W **136** B3
San Francisco Culhuacán *Mexico* 19°19N 99°8W **128** C2
San Francisco de Macanao *Venezuela* 11°1N 64°17W **329** a
San Francisco de Macorís *Dom. Rep.* 19°19N 70°15W **321** C5
San Francisco del Monte de Oro *Argentina* 32°36S 66°8W **334** C2
San Francisco del Oro *Mexico* 26°52N 105°51W **318** B3
San Francisco della Vigna *Venice, Italy* **142** b3
San Francisco Int. ✕ (SFO) *U.S.A.* 37°37N 122°22W **306** H4
San Francisco Javier = Sant Francesc de Formentera *Spain* 38°42N 1°26E **206** D1
San Fratello *Italy* 38°1N 14°36E **201** D7
San Fruttuoso *Italy* 45°34N 9°14E **128** A2
San Gabriel *Chile* 33°47S 70°15W **334** C1
San Gabriel *Ecuador* 0°36N 77°49W **328** C2
San Gabriel *Calif., U.S.A.* 34°5N 118°5W **126** B4
San Gabriel → *U.S.A.* 33°58N 118°5W **126** C4
San Gabriel Chilac *Mexico* 18°19N 97°21W **319** D5
San Gabriel Mts. *U.S.A.* 34°17N 117°38W **307** L9
San Gavino Monreale *Italy* 39°33N 8°47E **200** C1
San Gerardo *Venice, Italy* **142** c1
San Geremia *Venice, Italy* **142** a2
San German *Puerto Rico* 18°4N 67°4W **321** b
San Giacomo dall'Orio *Venice, Italy* **142** b2
San Gil *Colombia* 6°33N 73°8W **328** B3
San Giljan = St. Julian's *Malta* 35°55N 14°29E **206** F7
San Gimignano *Italy* 43°28N 11°2E **198** E8
San Giobbe *Venice, Italy* **142** a2
San Giorgio degli Schiavoni, Scuola di *Venice, Italy* **142** b3
San Giórgio di Nogaro *Italy* 45°50N 13°13E **199** C10
San Giórgio Iónico *Italy* 40°27N 17°23E **201** B10
San Giorgio Maggiore *Venice, Italy* **142** c3
San Giorgio Maggiore, Isola di *Venice, Italy* **142** c3
San Giovanni e Paolo *Venice, Italy* **142** b3
San Giovanni Bianco *Italy* 45°52N 9°39E **198** C6
San Giovanni in Bragora *Venice, Italy* **142** b3
San Giovanni in Fiore *Italy* 39°15N 16°42E **201** C9
San Giovanni in Persiceto *Italy* 44°38N 11°11E **199** D8
San Giovanni Rotondo *Italy* 41°42N 15°44E **199** G12
San Giovanni Valdarno *Italy* 43°34N 11°32E **199** E8
San Giuliano Milanese *Italy* 45°24N 9°17E **128** B2
San Giuliano Terme *Italy* 43°46N 10°26E **198** E7
San Gorgonio Mt. *U.S.A.* 34°6N 116°50W **307** L10
San Gottardo, P. del *Switz.* 46°33N 8°33E **179** J4
San Gregorio *Uruguay* 32°37S 55°40W **335** C4
San Gregorio *Calif., U.S.A.* 37°20N 122°23W **306** H4
San Guillermo △ *Argentina* 27°50S 69°45W **334** B2
San Guiseppe Jato *Italy* 37°57N 13°11E **200** E6
San Ignacio *Belize* 17°10N 89°5W **320** C2
San Ignacio *Beni, Bolivia* 14°53S 65°36W **331** C4
San Ignacio *Santa Cruz, Bolivia* 16°20S 60°55W **331** D5
San Ignacio *Baja Calif. S., Mexico* 27°27N 112°51W **318** B2
San Ignacio *Paraguay* 26°52S 57°3W **334** B4
San Ignacio *Peru* 5°8S 78°59W **330** B2
San Ignacio, L. *Mexico* 26°54N 113°13W **318** B2
San Ildefonso *Phil.* 15°4N 120°56E **232** D3
San Ildefonso, C. *Phil.* 16°0N 122°1E **232** C4
San Ildefonso Pen. *Phil.* 16°9N 122°5E **232** C4
San Isidro *Argentina* 34°29S 58°31W **334** C4
San Isidro *Lima, Peru* 12°5S 77°2W **124** B2
San Isidro *Phil.* 6°50N 126°5E **233** H6
San Isidro de Potot = Burgos *Phil.* 16°4N 119°52E **232** C2
San Jacinto *Colombia* 9°50N 75°8W **328** B2
San Jacinto *Phil.* 12°34N 123°44E **232** E4
San Jacinto *Calif., U.S.A.* 33°47N 116°57W **307** M10
San Jaime = Sant Jaume *Spain* 39°54N 4°4E **206** B5
San Javier *Misiones, Argentina* 27°55S 55°5W **335** B4
San Javier *Santa Fe, Argentina* 30°40S 59°55W **334** C4
San Javier *Beni, Bolivia* 14°34S 64°42W **331** C5
San Javier *Santa Cruz, Bolivia* 16°18S 62°30W **331** D5
San Javier *Chile* 35°40S 71°45W **334** D1
San Javier *Spain* 37°49N 0°50W **197** H4
San Jerónimo Lidice *Mexico* 19°19N 99°14W **128** C1
San Jerónimo Taviche *Mexico* 16°44N 96°35W **319** D5
San Joaquin *Bolivia* 13°4S 64°49W **331** C5
San Joaquín *Santiago, Chile* 33°29S 70°35W **137** B2
San Joaquin *Phil.* 10°35N 122°8E **233** F4
San Joaquin *Calif., U.S.A.* 36°36N 120°11W **306** J6
San Joaquin → *Bolivia* 13°8S 63°41W **331** C5
San Joaquin → *Calif., U.S.A.* 38°4N 121°51W **306** G5
San Joaquin, Cerro *Ecuador* 0°53S 89°30W **330** a
San Joaquin Valley *U.S.A.* 37°20N 121°0W **306** J6
San Jon *U.S.A.* 35°6N 103°20W **305** J12
San Jordi = Sant Jordi *Spain* 39°33N 2°46E **206** B3
San Jorge *Argentina* 31°54S 61°50W **334** C3
San Jorge *Solomon Is.* 8°28S 159°38E **287** M10
San Jorge, B. *Mexico* 31°20N 113°20W **318** A2
San Jorge, G. *Argentina* 46°0S 66°0W **336** C3
San José = San Josep *Spain* 38°55N 1°18E **206** D1
San José *Argentina* 32°12S 58°15W **334** C4
San José *Costa Rica* 9°55N 84°2W **320** E3
San José *Guatemala* 14°0N 90°50W **320** D1
San Jose *N. Marianas* 14°58N 145°37E **302** e
San Jose *Mind. Occ., Phil.* 12°27N 121°4E **232** E3
San Jose *Nueva Ecija, Phil.* 15°45N 120°55E **232** D3
San Jose *Calif., U.S.A.* 37°20N 121°53W **306** H5
San Jose *Ill., U.S.A.* 40°18N 89°36W **310** D7
San Jose → *U.S.A.* 34°25N 106°45W **305** J10
San José, G. *Argentina* 42°20S 64°18W **336** B4
San José, I. *Mexico* 25°0N 110°38W **318** C2
San Jose de Buenavista *Phil.* 10°45N 121°56E **233** F3
San José de Chiquitos *Bolivia* 17°53S 60°50W **331** D5
San José de Feliciano *Argentina* 30°26S 58°46W **334** C4
San José de Guanipa *Venezuela* 8°53N 64°9W **329** B5
San José de Jáchal *Argentina* 30°15S 68°46W **334** C2
San José de Mayo *Uruguay* 34°27S 56°40W **334** C4
San José de Ocuné *Colombia* 4°15N 70°20W **328** C3
San José de Uchapiamonas *Bolivia* 14°13S 68°5W **330** C4
San José del Cabo *Mexico* 23°3N 109°41W **318** C3
San José del Guaviare *Colombia* 2°35N 72°38W **328** C3
San Jose del Monte *Phil.* 14°49N 121°3E **232** D3
San José do Anauá *Brazil* 0°58N 61°22W **329** C5
San José Río Hondo *Mexico* 19°26N 99°14W **128** B1
San Josep *Spain* 38°55N 1°18E **206** D1
San Juan *Argentina* 31°30S 68°30W **334** C2
San Juan *Antioquia, Colombia* 8°46N 76°32W **328** B2
San Juan *Curaçao* 12°15N 69°6W **322** g
San Juan *Ica, Peru* 15°22S 75°7W **330** D2
San Juan *Batangas, Phil.* 13°50N 121°24E **232** E3
San Juan *S. Leyte, Phil.* 10°16N 125°10E **233** F5
San Juan *Puerto Rico* 18°28N 66°7W **321** C6
San Juan *Trin. & Tob.* 10°39N 61°29W **323** t
San Juan □ *Argentina* 31°9S 69°0W **334** C2
San Juan → *Argentina* 32°20S 67°25W **334** C2
San Juan → *Bolivia* 21°2S 65°19W **331** E4
San Juan → *Colombia* 4°3N 77°27W **328** C2
San Juan → *Nic.* 10°56N 83°42W **320** D3
San Juan → *Manila, Phil.* 14°35N 121°0E **127** B2
San Juan → *Utah, U.S.A.* 37°16N 110°26W **305** H8
San Juan → *Nueva Esparta, Venezuela* 10°56N 63°57W **329** a
San Juan → *Sucre, Venezuela* 10°14N 62°38W **329** A5
San Juan, C. *Argentina* 54°44S 63°44W **336** D4
San Juan, C. *Eq. Guin.* 1°5N 9°20E **264** B1
San Juan Bautista = Sant Joan de Labritja *Spain* 39°5N 1°31E **206** C2
San Juan Bautista = Villahermosa *Mexico* 17°59N 92°55W **319** D6
San Juan Bautista *Chile* 33°37S 78°50W **330** c
San Juan Bautista *Paraguay* 26°37S 57°6W **334** B4
San Juan Bautista *Calif., U.S.A.* 36°51N 121°32W **306** J5
San Juan Bautista *Venezuela* 11°1N 63°56W **329** a
San Juan Capistrano *U.S.A.* 33°30N 117°40W **307** M9
San Juan Cr. → *U.S.A.* 35°40N 120°22W **306** J5
San Juan de Aragón *Mexico* 19°28N 99°4W **128** B2
San Juan de Aragón, Parque *Mexico* 19°27N 99°4W **128** B2
San Juan de Guadelupe *Mexico* 24°38N 102°44W **318** C4
San Juan de Guía, Cabo de *Colombia* 11°21N 73°59W **328** A3
San Juan de la Costa *Mexico* 24°20N 110°41W **318** C2
San Juan de los Lagos *Mexico* 21°15N 102°18W **318** C4
San Juan de los Morros *Venezuela* 9°55N 67°21W **328** B4
San Juan de Lurigancho *Peru* 11°59S 77°0W **124** A2
San Juan de Manapiare *Venezuela* 5°15N 66°5W **328** B4
San Juan de Villa Hermosa = Villahermosa *Mexico* 17°59N 92°55W **319** D6
San Juan del César *Colombia* 10°46N 73°1W **328** A3
San Juan del Monte *Phil.* 14°36N 121°1E **127** B2
San Juan del Norte *Nic.* 10°58N 83°40W **320** D3
San Juan del Norte, B. de *Nic.* 11°0N 83°40W **320** D3
San Juan del Río *Mexico* 20°23N 100°0W **319** C5
San Juan del Sur *Nic.* 11°20N 85°51W **320** D2
San Juan I. *U.S.A.* 48°32N 123°5W **306** B3
San Juan Island △ *U.S.A.* 48°35N 123°8W **306** B4
San Juan Ixtacala *Mexico* 19°31N 99°10W **128** A1
San Juan Mts. *U.S.A.* 37°30N 107°0W **305** H10
San Julian *Phil.* 11°45N 125°27E **233** F5
San Just, Sierra de *Spain* 40°45N 0°49W **196** E4
San Just Desvern *Spain* 41°22N 2°4E **114** A1
San Justo *B. Aires, Argentina* 34°40S 58°33W **117** C1
San Justo *Santa Fe, Argentina* 30°47S 60°30W **334** C3
San Kamphaeng *Thailand* 18°45N 99°8E **236** C2
San Lázaro, C. *Mexico* 24°50N 112°18W **318** C2
San Leandro *U.S.A.* 37°42N 122°9W **306** H4
San Leonardo de Yagüe *Spain* 41°51N 3°5W **196** D1
San Lorenzo = Sant Llorenç des Cardassar *Spain* 39°37N 3°17E **206** B4
San Lorenzo *Argentina* 32°45S 60°45W **334** C3
San Lorenzo *Beni, Bolivia* 15°22S 65°48W **331** D4
San Lorenzo *Tarija, Bolivia* 21°26S 64°47W **331** E5
San Lorenzo *Ecuador* 1°15N 78°50W **328** C2
San Lorenzo *Venice, Italy* **142** b3
San Lorenzo *Paraguay* 25°20S 57°32W **334** B4
San Lorenzo → *Mexico* 24°15N 107°24W **318** C3
San Lorenzo, I. *Baja Calif., Mexico* 28°38N 112°51W **318** B2
San Lorenzo, I. *Peru* 12°7S 77°15W **330** C2
San Lorenzo, Mte. *Argentina* 47°40S 72°20W **336** C2
San Lorenzo de la Parrilla *Spain* 39°51N 2°22W **196** F2
San Lorenzo de Morunys = Sant Llorenç de Morunys *Spain* 42°8N 1°35E **196** C6
San Lorenzo Tezonco *Mexico* 19°19N 99°3W **128** C2
San Lucas = Cabo San Lucas *Mexico* 22°53N 109°54W **318** C3
San Lucas *Bolivia* 20°5S 65°7W **331** E4
San Lucas *Baja Calif. S., Mexico* 27°10N 112°14W **318** B2
San Lucas *Calif., U.S.A.* 36°8N 121°1W **306** J5
San Lucas, C. *Mexico* 22°52N 109°53W **318** C3
San Lúcido *Italy* 39°18N 16°3E **201** C9
San Luis = Entre Ríos *Bolivia* 21°30S 64°25W **334** A3
San Luis = Sevilla *Colombia* 4°16N 75°57W **328** C2
San Luis *Argentina* 33°20S 66°20W **334** C2
San Luis *Pinar del Río, Cuba* 22°17N 83°46W **320** B3
San Luis *Guatemala* 16°14N 89°27W **320** C2
San Luis *Lima, Peru* 12°4S 77°0W **124** B2
San Luis *Ariz., U.S.A.* 32°29N 114°47W **305** K6
San Luis *Colo., U.S.A.* 37°12N 105°25W **305** H11
San Luis □ *Argentina* 34°0S 66°0W **334** C2
San Luis, I. *Mexico* 29°58N 114°26W **318** B2
San Luis, L. de *Bolivia* 13°45S 64°0W **331** C5
San Luis, Sierra de *Argentina* 32°30S 66°10W **334** C2
San Luis de la Paz *Mexico* 21°18N 100°31W **318** C4
San Luis Obispo *U.S.A.* 35°17N 120°40W **307** K6
San Luis Potosí *Mexico* 22°9N 100°59W **318** C4
San Luis Potosí □ *Mexico* 23°0N 101°0W **318** C4
San Luis Res. *U.S.A.* 37°4N 121°5W **306** H5
San Luis Río Colorado *Mexico* 32°29N 114°58W **318** A2
San Manuel *Phil.* 16°4N 120°40E **232** C3
San Manuel *Ariz., U.S.A.* 32°36N 110°38W **305** K8
San Marco *Venice, Italy* **142** b3
San Marco, C. *Italy* 39°51N 8°26E **200** C1
San Marco, Canale di *Venice, Italy* **142** b3
San Marco, Piazza *Venice, Italy* **142** b3
San Marco Argentano *Italy* 39°33N 16°7E **201** C9
San Marco in Lámis *Italy* 41°43N 15°38E **199** G12
San Marcos *Colombia* 8°39N 75°8W **328** B2
San Marcos *Calif., U.S.A.* 33°9N 117°10W **307** M9
San Marcos *Tex., U.S.A.* 29°53N 97°56W **314** G6
San Marcos, I. *Mexico* 27°13N 112°6W **318** B2
San Mariano *Phil.* 17°0N 122°2E **232** C4
San Marino *San Marino* 43°55N 12°30E **199** E9
San Marino *Calif., U.S.A.* 34°7N 118°5W **126** B4
San Marino ■ *Europe* 43°56N 12°25E **199** E9
San Martín = Tarapoto *Peru* 6°30S 76°20W **330** B2
San Martín *Antarctica* 68°11S 67°0W **151** C17
San Martín *Argentina* 33°5S 68°28W **334** C2
San Martín *Colombia* 3°42N 73°42W **328** C3
San Martín *Barcelona, Spain* 41°24N 2°11E **114** A2
San Martín □ *Peru* 7°0S 76°50W **330** B2
San Martín → *Bolivia* 13°8S 63°43W **331** C5
San Martín, L. *Argentina* 48°50S 72°50W **336** C2
San Martín de la Vega *Spain* 40°13N 3°34W **194** E7
San Martín de los Andes *Argentina* 40°10S 71°20W **336** B2
San Martín de Porras *Peru* 12°1S 77°5W **124** B2
San Martín de Valdeiglesias *Spain* 40°21N 4°24W **194** E6
San Mateo = Sant Mateu *Baleares, Spain* 39°3N 1°23E **206** C1
San Mateo = Sant Mateu *Valencia, Spain* 40°28N 0°10E **196** E5
San Mateo *Isabela, Phil.* 16°54N 121°33E **232** C3
San Mateo *Calif., U.S.A.* 37°34N 122°19W **306** H4
San Mateo Tlaltenango *Mexico* 19°20N 99°16W **128** B1
San Matías *Bolivia* 16°25S 58°20W **331** D6
San Matías, G. *Argentina* 41°30S 64°0W **336** B4
San Michele, Isola di *Venice, Italy* **142** a3
San Miguel = Linapacan *Phil.* 11°30N 119°52E **233** F2
San Miguel = Sant Miquel *Spain* 39°3N 1°26E **206** C1
San Miguel = Sarrat *Phil.* 18°9N 120°39E **232** B3
San Miguel *Bolivia* 16°42S 61°1W **331** C5
San Miguel *Santiago, Chile* 33°29S 70°39W **137** B2
San Miguel *El Salv.* 13°30N 88°12W **320** D2
San Miguel *Panama* 8°27N 78°55W **320** E4
San Miguel *Lima, Peru* 12°5S 77°6W **124** B2
San Miguel *Bulacan, Phil.* 15°9N 120°59E **232** D3
San Miguel *Palawan, Phil.* 11°30N 119°51E **233** F2
San Miguel *Surigao S., Phil.* 9°3N 125°59E **233** G5
San Miguel *Calif., U.S.A.* 35°45N 120°42W **306** K6
San Miguel → *Bolivia* 13°52S 63°56W **331** C5
San Miguel → *Ecuador* 0°25N 76°30W **328** C2
San Miguel, Golfo de *Panama* 8°22N 78°17W **328** B2
San Miguel B. *Phil.* 13°51N 123°11E **232** E4
San Miguel de Huachi *Bolivia* 15°40S 67°15W **330** D4
San Miguel de Tucumán *Argentina* 26°50S 65°20W **334** B2
San Miguel del Monte *Argentina* 35°23S 58°50W **334** D4
San Miguel I. *U.S.A.* 34°2N 120°23W **307** L6
San Miguel Is. *Phil.* 7°45N 118°28E **233** H2
San Miguelito *Panama* 9°2N 79°30W **320** c
San Millán de la Cogolla *Spain* 42°19N 2°51W **196** C2
San Miniato *Italy* 43°41N 10°51E **198** E7
San Narciso *Phil.* 13°34N 122°34E **232** E4
San Nicandro Gargánico *Italy* 41°50N 15°34E **199** G12
San Nicolas = Sint Nicolaas *Curaçao* 12°17N 69°8W **322** g
San Nicolás *B. Aires, Argentina* 34°36S 58°22W **117** B2
San Nicolás *Canary Is.* 27°58N 15°47W **153** e1
San Nicolas *Phil.* 18°10N 120°36E **232** B3
San Nicolás de los Arroyos *Argentina* 33°25S 60°10W **334** C3
San Nicolas I. *U.S.A.* 33°15N 119°30W **307** M7
San Nicolo dei Mendicoli *Venice, Italy* **142** b1
San Onofre *Colombia* 9°44N 75°32W **328** B2
San Onofre *Calif., U.S.A.* 33°22N 117°34W **307** M9
San Onófrio *Italy* 41°57N 12°25E **136** B1
San Pablo *Bolivia* 21°43S 66°38W **334** A2
San Pablo *Isabela, Phil.* 17°27N 121°48E **232** C3
San Pablo *Laguna, Phil.* 14°11N 121°31E **232** D3
San Pablo *Calif., U.S.A.* 37°58N 122°21W **306** H4
San Pablo de Manta = Manta *Ecuador* 1°0S 80°40W **328** D1
San Pantalon *Venice, Italy* **142** b2
San Páolo di Civitate *Italy* 41°44N 15°15E **199** G12
San Pascual *Phil.* 13°8N 122°59E **232** E4
San Pedro *B. Aires, Argentina* 33°40S 59°40W **334** C4
San Pedro *Misiones, Argentina* 26°30S 54°10W **335** B5
San Pedro *Chile* 33°54S 71°28W **334** C1
San Pedro *Colombia* 4°56N 71°53W **328** C3
San Pedro *Ivory C.* 4°50N 6°33W **262** E3
San Pedro *Baja Calif. S., Mexico* 23°55N 110°17W **318** C2
San Pedro *Peru* 14°49S 74°5W **330** C3
San Pedro □ *Paraguay* 24°0S 57°0W **334** A4
San Pedro → *Chihuahua, Mexico* 28°21N 105°25W **318** B3
San Pedro → *Nayarit, Mexico* 21°45N 105°30W **318** C3
San Pedro → *Ariz., U.S.A.* 32°59N 110°47W **305** K8
San Pedro, Pta. *Chile* 25°30S 70°38W **334** B1
San Pedro, Sierra de *Spain* 39°18N 6°40W **195** F4
San Pedro B. *Phil.* 11°10N 125°6E **233** F5
San Pedro Channel *U.S.A.* 33°30N 118°25W **307** M8
San Pedro de Arimena *Colombia* 4°37N 71°42W **328** C3
San Pedro de Atacama *Chile* 22°55S 68°15W **334** A2
San Pedro de Coche *Venezuela* 10°47N 64°0W **329** a
San Pedro de Jujuy *Argentina* 24°12S 64°55W **334** A3
San Pedro de las Colonias *Mexico* 25°45N 102°59W **318** B4
San Pedro de Lloc *Peru* 7°15S 79°28W **330** B2
San Pedro de Macorís *Dom. Rep.* 18°30N 69°18W **321** C6
San Pedro del Norte *Nic.* 13°4N 84°33W **320** D3
San Pedro del Paraná *Paraguay* 26°43S 56°13W **334** B4
San Pedro del Pinatar *Spain* 37°50N 0°50W **197** H4
San Pedro Mártir *Spain* 41°23N 2°6E **114** A1
San Pedro Mártir, Sa. de *Mexico* 30°45N 115°13W **318** A1
San Pedro Ocampo = Melchor Ocampo *Mexico* 24°51N 101°39W **318** C4
San Pedro Pochutla *Mexico* 15°44N 96°28W **319** D5
San Pedro Sula *Honduras* 15°30N 88°0W **320** C2
San Pedro Tututepec *Mexico* 16°9N 97°38W **319** D5
San Pedro Zacatenco *Mexico* 19°30N 99°6W **128** A2
San Pietro *Italy* 39°8N 8°17E **200** C1
San Pietro, Isola di *Venice, Italy* **142** b4
San Pietro, Piazza *Rome, Italy* **136** b1
San Pietro di Castello *Venice, Italy* **142** b4
San Pietro Vernótico *Italy* 40°29N 18°0E **201** B11
San Po Kong *Hong Kong, China* 22°20N 114°11E **122** B3
San Polo *Venice, Italy* **142** b2
San Rafael *Argentina* 34°40S 68°21W **334** C2
San Rafael *Bolivia* 16°45S 60°34W **331** D5
San Rafael *Trin. & Tob.* 10°34N 61°16W **323** t
San Rafael *Calif., U.S.A.* 37°58N 122°32W **306** H4
San Rafael *N. Mex., U.S.A.* 35°7N 107°53W **305** J10
San Rafael *Venezuela* 10°58N 71°46W **328** A3
San Rafael Chamapa *Mexico* 19°27N 99°15W **128** B1
San Rafael Hills *U.S.A.* 34°10N 118°12W **126** A3
San Rafael Mt. *U.S.A.* 34°41N 119°52W **307** L7
San Rafael Mts. *U.S.A.* 34°40N 119°50W **307** L7
San Ramón *Bolivia* 13°17S 64°43W **331** C5
San Ramón de la Nueva Orán *Argentina* 23°10S 64°20W **334** A3
San Remo *Italy* 43°49N 7°46E **198** E4
San Román, C. *Venezuela* 12°12N 70°0W **328** A4
San Roque *Argentina* 28°25S 58°45W **334** B4
San Roque *Manila, Phil.* 14°37N 121°5E **127** B2
San Roque *N. Samar, Phil.* 12°37N 124°52E **232** E5
San Roque *Spain* 36°17N 5°21W **195** J5
San Rosendo *Chile* 37°16S 72°43W **334** D1
San Saba *U.S.A.* 31°12N 98°43W **314** F5
San Salvador *El Salv.* 13°40N 89°10W **320** D2
San Salvador *Venice, Italy* **142** b3
San Salvador, Canal de *Ecuador* 0°25S 90°30W **330** a
San Salvador, I. *Ecuador* 0°16S 90°42W **330** a
San Salvador de Jujuy *Argentina* 24°10S 64°48W **334** A3
San Salvador I. *Bahamas* 24°0N 74°30W **321** B5
San Salvo *Italy* 42°3N 14°44E **199** F11
San Sebastián = Donostia-San Sebastián *Spain* 43°17N 1°58W **196** B3
San Sebastián *Argentina* 53°10S 68°30W **336** D3
San Sebastián *Puerto Rico* 18°20N 66°59W **321** b
San Sebastián de la Gomera *Canary Is.* 28°5N 17°7W **153** e1
San Sebastiano *Venice, Italy* **142** b2
San Serra = Son Serra *Spain* 39°43N 3°13E **206** B4
San Serverino Marche *Italy* 43°13N 13°10E **199** E10
San Severo *Italy* 41°41N 15°23E **199** G12
San Simeon *U.S.A.* 35°39N 121°11W **306** K5
San Simeon Grande *Venice, Italy* **142** b2
San Simon *U.S.A.* 32°16N 109°14W **305** K9
San Siro *Italy* 45°28N 9°7E **128** B1
San Souci *Australia* 33°59S 151°8E **139** B1
San Stefano *Venice, Italy* **142** b2
San Stéfano di Cadore *Italy* 46°34N 12°33E **199** B9
San Stino di Livenza *Italy* 45°44N 12°41E **199** C9
San Tau *Hong Kong, China* 22°17N 113°55E **122** B1
San Telmo = Sant Elm *Spain* 39°35N 2°21E **206** B3
San Telmo *B. Aires, Argentina* 34°37S 58°23W **117** B2
San Telmo *Baja Calif., Mexico* 30°58N 116°6W **318** A1
San Teodoro *Italy* 40°46N 9°40E **200** B2
San Teodoro *Phil.* 13°26N 121°1E **232** E3
San Tiburcio *Mexico* 24°8N 101°32W **318** C4
San Trovaso *Venice, Italy* **142** c2
San Valentin, Mte. *Chile* 46°30S 73°30W **336** C2
San Vicenç dels Horts *Spain* 41°23N 2°0E **114** A1
San Vicente de Alcántara *Spain* 39°22N 7°8W **195** F3
San Vicente de Cañete *Peru* 13°8S 76°30W **330** C2
San Vicente de la Barquera *Spain* 43°23N 4°29W **194** B6
San Vicente del Caguán *Colombia* 2°7N 74°46W **328** C3
San Vicenzo *Spain* 42°58N 8°46W **194** C2
San Vincenzo *Italy* 43°6N 10°32E **198** E7
San Vito *Costa Rica* 8°50N 82°58W **320** E3
San Vito *Italy* 39°26N 9°32E **200** C2
San Vito, C. *Italy* 38°11N 12°41E **200** D5
San Vito al Tagliamento *Italy* 45°54N 12°52E **199** C9
San Vito Chietino *Italy* 42°18N 14°27E **199** F11
San Vito dei Normanni *Italy* 40°39N 17°42E **201** B10
San Yanaro *Colombia* 2°47N 69°42W **328** C4
San Zaccaria *Venice, Italy* **142** b3
Sana' = Ṣan'ā' *Yemen* 15°27N 44°12E **248** D4
Saña *Peru* 6°54S 79°36W **330** B2
Ṣan'ā' *Yemen* 15°27N 44°12E **248** D4
Ṣan'ā' □ *Yemen* 15°27N 44°12E **248** D4
Sana → *Bos.-H.* 45°3N 16°23E **199** C13
Sanaa = Ṣan'ā' *Yemen* 15°27N 44°12E **248** D4
Sanaag □ *Somalia* 10°30N 48°0E **267** B6
Sanaba *Burkina Faso* 12°25N 3°47W **262** C4
Sanae IV *Antarctica* 70°20S 9°0W **151** D2
Ṣanāfīr *Si. Arabia* 27°56N 34°42E **251** L5
Sanaga → *Cameroon* 3°35N 9°38E **263** E6
Sanak I. *U.S.A.* 54°25N 162°40W **303** J7
Sanalona, Presa *Mexico* 24°49N 107°7W **318** C3
Sanām *Si. Arabia* 23°40N 44°45E **248** B4
Sanana *Indonesia* 2°4S 125°58E **231** E7
Sanand *India* 22°59N 72°25E **242** H5
Sanandaj *Iran* 35°18N 47°1E **213** E12
Sanandita *Bolivia* 21°40S 63°45W **334** A3
Sanaroa I. *Papua N. G.* 9°37S 151°0E **286** E6
Sanary-sur-Mer *France* 43°7N 5°49E **175** E9
Sanāw *Yemen* 17°50N 51°5E **249** C5
Sanawad *India* 22°11N 76°5E **242** H7
Sanbancho *Tokyo, Japan* **140** a3
Sanbe-San *Japan* 35°6N 132°38E **222** B4
Sancellas = Sencelles *Spain* 39°39N 2°54E **206** B3
Sancergues *France* 47°10N 2°54E **173** E9
Sancerre *France* 47°20N 2°50E **173** E9
Sancerrois, Collines du *France* 47°20N 2°40E **173** E9
Sancha He → *China* 26°48N 106°7E **228** D6
Sanchahe *China* 44°50N 126°2E **227** B14
Sánchez *Dom. Rep.* 19°15N 69°36W **321** C6
Sanchez Mira *Phil.* 18°34N 121°14E **232** B3
Sanchi *India* 23°28N 77°44E **242** H7
Sanchih *Taiwan* 25°15N 121°30E **225** A3
Sanchor *India* 24°45N 71°55E **242** G4
Sanch'ung *Taiwan* 25°4N 121°30E **225** A3
Sancho Pt. *Phil.* 8°15N 126°27E **233** G6
Sancoins *France* 46°47N 2°55E **173** F9
Sancti Spíritus *Cuba* 21°52N 79°33W **320** B4
Sancy, Puy de *France* 45°32N 2°50E **174** C6
Sand = Polokwane → *S. Africa* 22°25S 30°5E **271** B5
Sand *Norway* 59°29N 6°16E **164** E3
Sand Bank B. *St. Kitts & Nevis* 17°15N 62°38W **322** d
Sand Cr. → *U.S.A.* 39°3N 85°51W **311** E11
Sand Hills *Guyana* 6°27N 58°19W **329** B6
Sand Hills *Nebr., U.S.A.* 42°10N 101°30W **308** D3
Sand I. *Midway Is.* 28°12N 177°23W **302** c
Sand I. *Hawai'i, U.S.A.* 21°19N 157°53W **302** K14
Sand Islet *Midway Is.* 28°16N 177°22W **302** c
Sand Lakes △ *Canada* 57°51N 98°32W **297** B9
Sand Point *U.S.A.* 55°20N 160°30W **303** J7
Sand Springs *U.S.A.* 36°9N 96°7W **314** C6
Sanda *Japan* 34°53N 135°14E **223** C7
Sandai *Indonesia* 1°15S 110°31E **235** C4
Sandakan *Malaysia* 5°53N 118°4E **235** A5
Sandalwood *Australia* 34°55S 140°9E **282** C4
Sandan = Sambor *Cambodia* 12°46N 106°0E **236** F6
Sandane *Norway* 61°46N 6°13E **164** C3
Sandanski *Bulgaria* 41°35N 23°16E **202** E7
Sandaré *Mali* 14°40N 10°15W **262** C2
Sandared *Sweden* 57°43N 12°47E **163** G6
Sandarne *Sweden* 61°16N 17°9E **162** C11
Sandaun = West Sepik □ *Papua N. G.* 3°30S 142°0E **286** B2
Sanday *U.K.* 59°16N 2°31W **167** B6
Sande *Møre og Romsdal, Norway* 62°15N 5°27E **164** B2
Sande *Sogn og Fjordane, Norway* 61°20N 5°47E **164** C2
Sande *Vestfold, Norway* 59°36N 10°12E **162** E4
Sandefjord *Norway* 59°10N 10°15E **164** E7
Sandeid *Norway* 59°33N 5°52E **164** E2
Sanders *Ariz., U.S.A.* 35°13N 109°20W **305** J9
Sanders *Ky., U.S.A.* 38°40N 84°56W **311** F12
Sanderson *Fla., U.S.A.* 30°15N 82°16W **316** E7
Sanderson *Tex., U.S.A.* 30°9N 102°24W **314** F3
Sandersville *U.S.A.* 32°59N 82°48W **316** C7
Sandfire Roadhouse *Australia* 19°45S 121°15E **278** C3
Sandfloegga *Norway* 59°58N 7°10E **164** E4
Sandfly L. *Canada* 55°43N 106°6W **297** B7
Sandfontein *Namibia* 23°48S 19°1E **270** B2
Sandhammaren *Sweden* 55°23N 14°14E **163** J8
Sandheads, The *India* 21°10N 88°20E **241** E2
Sandgerði *Iceland* 64°3N 22°42W **155** C4
Sandía *Peru* 14°10S 69°30W **330** C4
Sandıklı *Turkey* 38°28N 30°17E **205** C12
Sandila *India* 27°5N 80°31E **243** F9
Sandilands *Bahamas* 25°3N 77°19W **153** b
Sanding *Indonesia* 3°28S 100°40E **234** C2
Sanding, Selat *Indonesia* 3°24S 100°34E **234** C2
Sandnes *Aust-Agder, Norway* 58°53N 7°45E **164** F4
Sandnes *Rogaland, Norway* 58°50N 5°45E **164** F2
Sandnessjøen *Norway* 66°2N 12°38E **160** C15
Sandoa *Dem. Rep. of the Congo* 9°41S 23°0E **265** D4
Sandomierz *Poland* 50°40N 21°43E **185** H8
Sândominic *Romania* 46°35N 25°47E **183** D10
Sandona *Colombia* 1°17N 77°28W **328** C2
Sandongo *Angola* 15°30S 21°28E **265** E4
Sandoval *U.S.A.* 38°37N 89°7W **310** F7
Sandover → *Australia* 21°43S 136°32E **280** C2
Sandoway = Thandwe *Burma* 18°20N 94°30E **241** F5
Sandown *S. Africa* 26°5S 28°4E **123** A2
Sandown Park Races *U.K.* 51°22N 0°21W **125** B1
Sandoy *Færoe Is.* 61°52N 6°46W **160** F9
Sandpoint *U.S.A.* 48°17N 116°33W **304** B5
Sandray *U.K.* 56°53N 7°31W **167** E1
Sandringham *U.K.* 52°51N 0°31E **168** E8
Sandstone *Australia* 27°59S 119°16E **279** E2
Sandton *S. Africa* 26°5S 28°4E **123** A2
Sandu *China* 26°0N 107°52E **228** E6
Sandumba *Angola* 13°45S 17°34E **265** E3
Sandur *India* 15°6N 76°33E **245** F3
Sandusky *Mich., U.S.A.* 43°25N 82°50W **312** C2
Sandusky *Ohio, U.S.A.* 41°27N 82°42W **312** E2
Sandusky → *U.S.A.* 41°27N 83°0W **311** C14
Sandveld *Namibia* 21°25S 20°0E **270** B3
Sandvig *Denmark* 55°18N 14°47E **163** J8
Sandvika *Norway* 59°54N 10°31E **133** A2
Sandviken *Sweden* 60°38N 16°46E **162** D10
Sandwich *U.S.A.* 41°39N 88°37W **311** C8
Sandwich, C. *Australia* 18°14S 146°18E **280** B4
Sandwich B. *Nfld. & L., Canada* 53°40N 57°15W **299** B8
Sandwich B. *Namibia* 23°25S 14°20E **270** B1
Sandwip I. *Bangla.* 22°30N 91°25E **241** D3
Sandy *Oreg., U.S.A.* 45°24N 122°16W **306** E4
Sandy *Pa., U.S.A.* 41°6N 78°46W **312** E6
Sandy *Utah, U.S.A.* 40°32N 111°50W **304** F8
Sandy B. *St. Helena* 16°0S 5°43W **153** h
Sandy Bay *Canada* 55°31N 102°19W **297** B8
Sandy Bight *Australia* 33°50S 123°20E **279** F3
Sandy C. *Queens., Australia* 24°42S 153°15E **280** C5
Sandy C. *Tas., Australia* 41°25S 144°45E **281** G3
Sandy Cay *Bahamas* 23°13N 75°18W **321** B4
Sandy Cr. → *N.S.W., Australia* 31°54S 145°18E **281** B4
Sandy Cr. → *Wyo., U.S.A.* 41°51N 109°47W **304** F9
Sandy Creek *U.S.A.* 43°38N 76°5W **313** C8
Sandy Ground Village *Anguilla* 18°12N 63°6W **322** a
Sandy Hill B. *Anguilla* 18°13N 63°1W **322** a
Sandy I. *Anguilla* 18°13N 63°7W **322** a
Sandy I. *Grenada* 12°29N 61°29W **323** q
Sandy I. *Grenada* 12°13N 61°35W **323** q
Sandy L. *Canada* 53°2N 93°0W **298** B1
Sandy Lake *Canada* 53°0N 93°15W **298** B1
Sandy Point *India* 10°32N 92°22E **245** J11
Sandy Point Town *St. Kitts & Nevis* 17°22N 62°51W **322** d
Sandy Springs *U.S.A.* 33°56N 84°23W **316** B7
Sandy Valley *U.S.A.* 35°49N 115°38W **307** K11
Sandyford *Ireland* 53°17N 6°13W **120** B2
Sandymount *Ireland* 53°20N 6°13W **120** B2
Sånfjället △ *Sweden* 62°17N 13°35E **162** B7
Sanford *Fla., U.S.A.* 28°48N 81°16W **317** G8
Sanford *Maine, U.S.A.* 43°27N 70°47W **313** C14
Sanford *N.C., U.S.A.* 35°29N 79°10W **315** D15
Sanford → *Australia* 27°22S 115°53E **279** E2
Sanford, Mt. *U.S.A.* 62°13N 144°8W **303** E11
Sang-i-Masha *Afghan.* 33°8N 67°27E **242** C2
Sanga *Angola* 11°9S 15°21E **265** E3
Sanga *Mozam.* 12°22S 35°21E **269** E4
Sanga → *Congo* 1°5S 17°0E **264** C3
Sangaie *Dem. Rep. of the Congo* 6°48S 22°46E **265** D4
Sangamner *India* 19°37N 74°15E **244** E2
Sangamon → *U.S.A.* 40°1N 90°26W **310** D6
Sangān *Iran* 34°23N 60°15E **247** C9
Sanganeb Atoll △ *Sudan* 19°33N 37°11E **256** D4
Sangar *Afghan.* 32°56N 65°30E **242** C1
Sangar *Russia* 64°2N 127°31E **215** C13
Sangar Sarai *Afghan.* 34°27N 70°35E **242** B4
Sangareddi *India* 17°38N 78°7E **244** F4
Sangaredi *Guinea* 11°7N 13°52W **262** C2
Sangarh → *Pakistan* 30°43N 70°44E **242** D4
Sangasanga *Indonesia* 0°36S 117°13E **235** C5
Sangasso *Mali* 12°5N 5°35W **262** C3
Sangatte *France* 50°56N 1°44E **173** B8
Sangaw *Iraq* 35°17N 45°10E **213** E11
Sangay *Ecuador* 2°0S 78°20W **328** D2
Sangay △ *Ecuador* 2°15S 78°20W **328** D2
Sangbé *Cameroon* 6°3N 12°28E **264** A2
Sangchris L. *U.S.A.* 39°39N 89°29W **310** E7
Sangdong *S. Korea* 37°7N 128°49E **224** D4
Sange *Dem. Rep. of the Congo* 6°58S 28°21E **268** D2
Sangeang *Indonesia* 8°12S 119°6E **235** D5
Sangenjaya *Japan* 35°37N 139°39E **140** B2
Sângeorz-Băi *Romania* 47°22N 24°41E **183** C9
Sanger *U.S.A.* 36°42N 119°33W **306** J7
Sângera *Moldova* 46°55N 28°58E **183** D13
Sangerhausen *Germany* 51°28N 11°18E **178** D7
Sanggan He → *China* 38°12N 117°15E **226** E9
Sanggau *Kalimantan Barat, Indonesia* 0°5N 110°30E **235** B4
Sanggau *Kalimantan Barat, Indonesia* 1°7N 109°36E **235** B3
Sanggye *S. Korea* 37°38N 127°3E **137** B2
Sangha □ *Congo* 1°0N 15°30E **264** B3
Sangha-Mbaéré □ *C.A.R.* 4°30N 16°30E **264** B3
Sanghar *Pakistan* 26°2N 68°57E **242** F3
Sangihe, Kepulauan *Indonesia* 3°0N 125°30E **231** D7
Sangihe, Pulau *Indonesia* 3°35N 125°30E **231** D7
Sangin *Afghan.* 32°4N 64°50E **240** B2
Sangiran *Indonesia* 7°25S 110°55E **235** D4
Sangiran △ *Indonesia* 7°27S 110°50E **231** G14
Sangju *S. Korea* 36°25N 128°10E **224** D4
Sangkapura *Indonesia* 5°52S 112°40E **235** D4
Sangkha *Thailand* 14°37N 103°52E **236** E4
Sangkhla Buri *Thailand* 14°57N 98°28E **236** E2
Sangkulirang *Indonesia* 0°59N 117°58E **235** B5
Sangla *Pakistan* 31°43N 73°23E **242** D5
Sangley Pt. *Phil.* 14°29N 120°54E **127** C1
Sangli *India* 16°55N 74°33E **244** F2
Sangmélima *Cameroon* 2°57N 12°1E **263** E7
Sango *Angola* 9°51S 15°44E **265** D2
Sango *Zimbabwe* 18°44S 31°44E **269** F3
Sangod *India* 24°55N 76°17E **242** G7
Sangole *India* 17°26N 75°12E **244** F2
Sangorodok = Ust-Vorkuta *Russia* 67°24N 64°0E **186** A11
Sangpang Bum *Burma* 26°30N 95°50E **241** B5
Sangre de Cristo Mts. *U.S.A.* 37°30N 105°20W **305** H11
Sangre Grande *Trin. & Tob.* 10°35N 61°8W **323** t
Sangro → *Italy* 42°14N 14°32E **199** F11
Sangrur *India* 30°14N 75°50E **242** D6
Sangudo *Canada* 53°50N 114°54W **296** C6
Sangue → *Brazil* 11°1S 58°39W **331** C6
Sangüesa *Spain* 42°37N 1°17W **196** C3
Sanguinaires, Îs. *France* 41°51N 8°36E **175** G12
Sangzhi *China* 29°25N 110°12E **229** C8
Sanhala *Ivory C.* 10°3N 6°51W **262** C3
Sanhsia *Taiwan* 24°56N 121°22E **225** B3
Sanhsien *Hualien, Taiwan* 23°8N 121°25E **225** C3
Sanhsien *T'aitung, Taiwan* 23°24N 121°19E **225** C3
Sanhsing *Taiwan* 24°40N 121°36E **225** B3
Sani *Taiwan* 24°24N 120°46E **225** B2
Sanibel *U.S.A.* 26°27N 82°1W **317** J7
Sanibel I. *U.S.A.* 26°26N 82°6W **317** J7
Sanikiluaq *Canada* 56°32N 79°14W **298** A4
Sanin-Kaigan △ *Japan* 35°39N 134°37E **222** B6
Sanirajak = Hall Beach *Canada* 68°46N 81°12W **295** D15
Sanjawi *Pakistan* 30°17N 68°21E **242** D3
Sanje *Uganda* 0°49S 31°30E **268** C3
Sanjiang *China* 25°48N 109°37E **228** E7

Sanjo *Japan* 37°37N 138°57E 220 F9
Sankarankovil *India* 9°10N 77°35E 245 K3
Sankeshwar *India* 16°23N 74°32E 245 F2
Sankh → *India* 22°15N 84°48E 243 H11
Sankosh → *India* 26°24N 89°47E 241 B2
Sankrail *India* 22°33N 88°13E 124 B1
Sankt Andrä *Austria* 46°46N 14°50E 180 E7
Sankt Anton *Austria* 47°8N 10°16E 179 H6
Sankt Augustin *Germany* 50°45N 7°10E 178 E3
Sankt Blasien *Germany* 47°47N 8°7E 179 H4
Sankt Gallen *Switz.* 47°26N 9°22E 179 H5
Sankt Gallen □ *Switz.* 47°25N 9°22E 179 H5
Sankt Goar *Germany* 50°12N 7°43E 179 E3
Sankt Ingbert *Germany* 49°16N 7°6E 179 F3
Sankt Johann im Pongau *Austria* 47°22N 13°12E 180 D6
Sankt Johann in Tirol *Austria* 47°30N 12°25E 180 D5
Sankt Marein = Smarje *Slovenia* 46°15N 15°34E 199 B12
Sankt Michel = Mikkeli *Finland* 61°43N 27°15E 188 B4
Sankt Moritz *Switz.* 46°30N 9°51E 179 J5
Sankt Peter-Ording *Germany* 54°20N 8°36E 178 A4
Sankt-Peterburg *Russia* 59°55N 30°20E 137 B1
Sankt Pölten *Austria* 48°12N 15°38E 180 C8
Sankt Ulrich = Ortisei *Italy* 46°34N 11°40E 199 B8
Sankt Valentin *Austria* 48°11N 14°33E 180 C7
Sankt Veit *Austria* 48°11N 16°16E 142 A1
Sankt Veit an der Glan *Austria* 46°47N 14°22E 180 E7
Sankt Wendel *Germany* 49°27N 7°9E 179 F3
Sankt Wolfgang *Austria* 47°43N 13°27E 180 D6
Sankuru → *Dem. Rep. of the Congo* 4°17S 20°25E 265 C4
Sanlihe *China* 39°53N 116°18E 114 B1
Sanlin *China* 31°9N 121°29E 138 C1
Sanlintang *China* 31°9N 121°29E 138 C1
Sanliurfa *Turkey* 37°12N 38°50E 213 D8
Sanliurfa □ *Turkey* 37°0N 39°0E 213 D8
Sanlúcar de Barrameda *Spain* 36°46N 6°21W 195 J4
Sanluri *Italy* 39°34N 8°54E 200 C1
Sânmartin *Romania* 46°19N 25°58E 183 D10
Sanmen *China* 29°5N 121°35E 229 C13
Sanmenxia *China* 34°47N 111°12E 226 G6
Sanming *China* 26°15N 117°40E 229 D11
Sanmu *Kantō, Japan* 34°11N 134°37E 222 C6
Sanmu *Shikoku, Japan* 35°36N 140°25E 223 B12
Sannan *Japan* 35°2N 135°1E 223 B7
Sannat *Malta* 36°1N 14°15E 206 E6
Sanndraigh = Sandray *U.K.* 56°53N 7°31W 167 E1
Sânnicolau Mare *Romania* 46°5N 20°39E 182 D5
Sannieshof *S. Africa* 26°30S 25°47E 270 C4
Sannīn, J. *Lebanon* 33°57N 35°52E 250 E6
Sanniquellie *Liberia* 7°19N 8°38W 262 D3
Sannûr *Egypt* 28°58N 31°3E 251 K2
Sannûr, W. → *Egypt* 28°59N 31°3E 251 K2
Sano *Japan* 36°19N 139°35E 223 A11
Sanok *Poland* 49°35N 22°10E 185 J9
Sanqingshan △ *China* 28°54N 118°3E 229 C12
Sanquhar *U.K.* 55°22N 3°54W 167 F5
Sanquianga △ *Colombia* 2°33N 78°14W 328 C2
Sans *Spain* 41°22N 2°7E 114 A1
Sans Souci *St. Vincent* 13°13N 61°7W 323 n
Sans Souci *Trin. & Tob.* 10°50N 61°0W 323 t
Sansanding *Mali* 13°48N 6°0W 262 C3
Sansané *Niger* 13°50N 1°36E 263 C5
Sansepolcro *Italy* 43°34N 12°8E 199 E9
Sansha *China* 26°58N 120°12E 229 D13
Sanshui *China* 23°10N 112°56E 229 F9
Sanski Most *Bos.-H.* 44°46N 16°40E 199 D13
Sanssouci *Germany* 52°23N 13°2E 115 B1
Sansui *China* 26°58N 108°39E 228 D7
Sant Agusti *Barcelona, Spain* 114 c2
Sant Ambrogio, Basilica di *Italy* 45°27N 9°10E 128 B2
Sant' Andrea *Venice, Italy* 142 b1
Sant Antoni de Portmany *Spain* 38°59N 1°19E 206 D1
Sant Boi de Llobregat *Spain* 41°20N 2°2E 114 A1
Sant Carles *Spain* 39°3N 1°34E 206 C2
Sant Carles de la Ràpita *Spain* 40°37N 0°35E 196 E5
Sant Celoni *Spain* 41°42N 2°30E 196 D7
Sant Cugat *Spain* 41°28N 2°5E 114 A1
Sant' Elena *Venice, Italy* 142 c4
Sant' Elena, Darsena di *Venice, Italy* 142 c4
Sant' Elena, Isola di *Venice, Italy* 142 c4
Sant Elm *Spain* 39°35N 2°21E 206 B3
Sant Feliu de Guíxols *Spain* 41°45N 3°1E 196 D8
Sant Feliu de Llobregat *Spain* 41°22N 2°2E 114 A1
Sant Ferran *Spain* 38°42N 1°28E 206 D1
Sant Francesc de Formentera *Spain* 38°42N 1°26E 206 D1
Sant Jaume *Spain* 39°54N 4°4E 206 B5
Sant Joan *Spain* 39°36N 3°4E 206 B4
Sant Joan d'Alacant *Spain* 38°24N 0°26W 197 G4
Sant Joan de Labritja *Spain* 39°5N 1°31E 206 C2
Sant Joan Despi *Spain* 41°22N 2°2E 114 A1
Sant Jordi *Ibiza, Spain* 38°53N 1°24E 206 D1
Sant Jordi *Mallorca, Spain* 39°33N 2°46E 206 B3
Sant Jordi, G. de *Spain* 40°53N 1°2E 196 E6
Sant Llorenç de Morunys *Spain* 42°8N 1°35E 196 C6
Sant Llorenç del Munt y l'Obac ⌓ *Spain* 41°39N 1°55W 196 D3
Sant Llorenç des Cardassar *Spain* 39°37N 3°17E 206 B4
Sant Maria del Mar *Barcelona, Spain* 114 b3
Sant Mateu *Baleares, Spain* 39°3N 1°23E 206 C1
Sant Mateu *Valencia, Spain* 40°28N 0°10E 196 E5
Sant Miquel *Spain* 39°3N 1°26E 206 C1
Sant Pau del Camp *Barcelona, Spain* 114 c2
Sant Pere de Ribes *Spain* 41°16N 1°46E 196 D6
Sant Salvador *Spain* 39°27N 3°11E 206 B4
Sant Vicent del Raspeig *Spain* 38°24N 0°31W 197 G4
Santa *Peru* 8°59S 78°40W 330 B2
Sant' Ágata Militello *Italy* 38°2N 14°8E 201 D7
Santa Agnés *Spain* 39°3N 1°21E 206 C1
Santa Ana *Beni, Bolivia* 13°50S 65°40W 331 C4
Santa Ana *La Paz, Bolivia* 15°31S 67°30W 330 D4
Santa Ana *Santa Cruz, Bolivia* 18°43S 58°44W 331 D6
Santa Ana *Santa Cruz, Bolivia* 16°37S 60°43W 331 D5
Santa Ana *Ecuador* 1°16S 80°20W 328 D1
Santa Ana *El Salv.* 14°0N 89°31W 320 D2
Santa Ana *Guam* 13°32N 145°46E 302 d
Santa Ana *Sonora, Mexico* 30°33N 111°7W 318 A2
Santa Ana *Cagayan, Phil.* 18°28N 122°20E 232 B4
Santa Ana *Manila, Phil.* 14°34N 121°0E 127 B2
Santa Ana *Solomon Is.* 10°50S 162°30E 287 N12
Santa Ana *Calif., U.S.A.* 33°46N 117°52W 307 M9
Santa Ana → *Venezuela* 9°30N 71°57W 328 B3
Santa Ana de los Ríos de Cuenca = Cuenca *Ecuador* 2°50S 79°9W 328 D2
Sant' Ángelo Lodigiano *Italy* 45°14N 9°25E 198 C6
Santa Anita Park *U.S.A.* 34°8N 118°5W 126 B4
Sant' Antíoco *Italy* 39°4N 8°27E 200 C1
Santa Bárbara *Santa Maria, Azores* 36°59N 25°4W 153 d4
Santa Bárbara *Terciera, Azores* 38°41N 27°20W 153 d1
Santa Bárbara *Chile* 37°40S 72°1W 334 D1
Santa Bárbara *Colombia* 5°53N 75°35W 328 B2
Santa Barbara *Curaçao* 12°5N 68°51W 322 g
Santa Bárbara *Honduras* 14°53N 88°14W 320 D2
Santa Bárbara *Chihuahua, Mexico* 26°48N 105°49W 318 B3
Santa Barbara *Phil.* 10°50N 122°32E 233 F4
Santa Bárbara *Spain* 40°42N 0°29E 196 E5
Santa Barbara *Calif., U.S.A.* 34°25N 119°42W 307 L7
Santa Bárbara *Amazonas, Venezuela* 3°57N 67°6W 328 C4
Santa Bárbara *Barinas, Venezuela* 7°47N 71°10W 328 B3
Santa Bárbara, Mt. *Spain* 37°23N 2°50W 197 H2
Santa Bárbara, Serra de *Azores* 38°44N 27°19W 153 d1
Santa Barbara Channel *U.S.A.* 34°15N 120°0W 307 L7
Santa Barbara I. *U.S.A.* 33°29N 119°2W 307 M7
Santa Catalina *Colombia* 10°36N 75°17W 328 A2
Santa Catalina *Neg. Or., Phil.* 9°20N 122°52E 233 G4
Santa Catalina *Solomon Is.* 10°53S 162°29E 287 N12
Santa Catalina, Gulf of *U.S.A.* 33°10N 117°50W 307 N9
Santa Catalina, I. *Mexico* 25°40N 110°47W 318 B2
Santa Cataliña de Armada *Spain* 43°2N 8°49W 194 B2
Santa Catalina I. *U.S.A.* 33°23N 118°25W 307 M8
Santa Catarina □ *Brazil* 27°25S 48°30W 335 B6
Santa Catarina, I. de *Brazil* 27°30S 48°40W 335 B6
Santa Caterina *Venice, Italy* 142 a3
Santa Caterina di Pittinuri *Italy* 40°6N 8°27E 200 B1
Santa Caterina Villarmosa *Italy* 37°35N 14°2E 201 E7
Santa Cecília *Brazil* 26°56S 50°18W 335 B5
Santa Clara *Cuba* 22°20N 80°0W 320 B4
Santa Clara *Calif., U.S.A.* 37°21N 121°57W 306 H5
Santa Clara *N.Y., U.S.A.* 44°38N 74°27W 313 B10
Santa Clara *Utah, U.S.A.* 37°8N 113°39W 305 H7
Santa Clara → *Mexico* 29°51N 107°6W 318 A3
Santa Clara, I. *Chile* 33°42S 79°0W 330 c
Santa Clara de Olimar *Uruguay* 32°50S 54°54W 335 C5
Santa Clara Valley *U.S.A.* 36°50N 121°30W 306 J5
Santa Clarita *U.S.A.* 34°24N 118°33W 307 L8
Santa Clotilde *Peru* 2°33S 73°45W 328 D3
Santa Coloma de Farners *Spain* 41°50N 2°39E 196 D7
Santa Coloma de Gramenet *Spain* 41°27N 2°13E 114 A2
Santa Comba = Santa Cataliña de Armada *Spain* 43°2N 8°49W 194 B2
Santa Croce *Venice, Italy* 142 b2
Santa Croce Camerina *Italy* 36°50N 14°31E 201 F7
Santa Croce di Magliano *Italy* 41°42N 14°59E 199 G11
Santa Cruz *Aruba* 12°30N 69°59W 322 f
Santa Cruz *Bolivia* 17°43S 63°10W 331 D5
Santa Cruz *Brazil* 6°13S 36°1W 332 C4
Santa Cruz *Chile* 34°38S 71°27W 334 C1
Santa Cruz *Costa Rica* 10°15N 85°35W 320 D2
Santa Cruz *Curaçao* 12°18N 69°7W 322 g
Santa Cruz *Maharashtra, India* 19°4N 72°51E 130 A1
Santa Cruz *Jamaica* 18°3N 77°43W 320 a
Santa Cruz *Madeira* 32°42N 16°46W 153 c
Santa Cruz *Peru* 5°40S 75°56W 330 B2
Santa Cruz *Davao del S., Phil.* 6°50N 125°25E 233 H5
Santa Cruz *Laguna, Phil.* 14°20N 121°24E 232 D3
Santa Cruz *Manila, Phil.* 14°36N 120°58E 127 B1
Santa Cruz *Marinduque, Phil.* 13°28N 122°2E 232 E4
Santa Cruz *Mind. Occ., Phil.* 13°4N 120°43E 232 E3
Santa Cruz *Zambales, Phil.* 15°46N 119°55E 232 D2
Santa Cruz *Calif., U.S.A.* 36°58N 122°1W 306 J4
Santa Cruz *Venezuela* 8°3N 64°27W 329 B5
Santa Cruz □ *Argentina* 49°0S 70°0W 336 C3
Santa Cruz □ *Bolivia* 17°43S 63°10W 331 D5
Santa Cruz → *Argentina* 50°10S 68°20W 336 D3
Santa Cruz, B. *Curaçao* 12°18N 69°10W 322 g
Santa Cruz, I. *Ecuador* 0°38S 90°23W 330 a
Santa Cruz, I. de *Brazil* 22°51S 43°7W 135 B2
Santa Cruz Cabrália *Brazil* 16°17S 39°2W 333 E4
Santa Cruz da Graciosa *Azores* 39°5N 28°1W 153 d1
Santa Cruz das Flores *Azores* 39°27N 31°7W 153 d2
Santa Cruz de Bravo = Felipe Carrillo Puerto *Mexico* 19°38N 88°3W 319 D7
Santa Cruz de la Palma *Canary Is.* 28°41N 17°46W 153 e1
Santa Cruz de la Palma ✈ (SPC) *Canary Is.* 28°40N 17°45W 153 e1
Santa Cruz de Mompox = Mompós *Colombia* 9°14N 74°26W 328 B3
Santa Cruz de Mudela *Spain* 38°39N 3°28W 195 G7
Santa Cruz de Olorde *Spain* 41°25N 2°3E 114 A1
Santa Cruz de Tenerife *Canary Is.* 28°28N 16°15W 153 e1
Santa Cruz del Norte *Cuba* 23°9N 81°55W 320 B3
Santa Cruz del Retamar *Spain* 40°8N 4°14W 194 E6
Santa Cruz del Sur *Cuba* 20°44N 78°0W 320 B4
Santa Cruz do Rio Pardo *Brazil* 22°54S 49°37W 335 A6
Santa Cruz do Sul *Brazil* 29°42S 52°25W 335 B5
Santa Cruz I. *U.S.A.* 34°1N 119°43W 307 M7
Santa Cruz Is. *Solomon Is.* 10°30S 166°0E 277 C12
Santa Cruz la Vieja △ *Bolivia* 17°55S 60°50W 331 D5
Santa Cruz Mts. *Jamaica* 17°58N 77°43W 320 a
Santa Efigénia *Brazil* 23°32S 46°38W 137 B2
Sant' Egídio alla Vibrata *Italy* 42°49N 13°42E 199 F10
Santa Elena *Argentina* 30°58S 59°47W 334 C4
Santa Elena *Ecuador* 2°16S 80°52W 328 D1
Santa Elena *Camarines N., Phil.* 14°12N 122°24E 232 D4
Santa Elena *Manila, Phil.* 14°38N 121°5E 127 B2
Santa Elena, C. *Costa Rica* 10°54N 85°56W 320 D2
Santa Elena del Gomero *Chile* 33°28S 70°45W 137 B1
Sant' Eufémia, G. di *Italy* 38°51N 16°4E 201 D9
Santa Eulalia *Spain* 41°25N 2°10E 114 A2
Santa Eulària des Riu *Spain* 38°59N 1°32E 206 D2
Santa Fé *Argentina* 31°35S 60°41W 334 C3
Santa Fe *Nueva Viscaya, Phil.* 16°10N 120°57E 232 C3
Santa Fe *Romblon, Phil.* 12°10N 122°0E 232 E4
Santa Fé *Spain* 37°11N 3°43W 195 H7
Santa Fe *N. Mex., U.S.A.* 35°41N 105°57W 305 J11
Santa Fé □ *Argentina* 31°50S 60°55W 334 C3
Santa Fé, Canal de *Ecuador* 0°48S 89°55W 330 a
Santa Fé, I. *Ecuador* 0°49S 90°5W 330 a
Santa Fé do Sul *Brazil* 20°13S 50°56W 333 F1
Santa Fe Springs *U.S.A.* 33°56N 118°3W 126 C4
Santa Filomena *Brazil* 9°6S 45°50W 332 C2
Santa Fiora *Italy* 42°50N 11°35E 199 F8
Santa Gertrudis *Spain* 39°0N 1°26E 206 C1
Santa Giulia *France* 41°32N 9°17E 175 G13
Santa Giustina *Italy* 46°10N 12°5E 199 B9
Santa Helena *Brazil* 2°14S 45°18W 332 B2
Santa Helena de Goiás *Brazil* 17°53S 50°35W 333 E1
Santa Inês *Bahia, Brazil* 13°17S 39°48W 333 D4
Santa Inês *Maranhão, Brazil* 3°39S 45°20W 332 B2
Santa Inés *Extremadura, Spain* 38°32N 5°37W 195 G5
Santa Inés, I. *Chile* 54°0S 73°0W 336 D2
Santa Iria da Azóia *Portugal* 38°49N 9°5W 126 A2
Santa Isabel = Rey Malabo *Eq. Guin.* 3°45N 8°50E 263 E6
Santa Isabel *Argentina* 36°10S 66°54W 334 D2
Santa Isabel *Puerto Rico* 17°58N 66°24W 321 b
Santa Isabel *Solomon Is.* 8°0S 159°0E 287 M10
Santa Isabel do Araguaia *Brazil* 6°7S 48°19W 332 C2
Santa Isabel do Morro *Brazil* 11°34S 50°40W 333 D1
Santa Isabel do Río Negro *Brazil* 0°24S 65°2W 329 D4
Santa Julia *Chile* 33°30S 70°35W 137 C2
Santa Lucía *Corrientes, Argentina* 28°58S 59°5W 334 B4
Santa Lucía *San Juan, Argentina* 31°30S 68°30W 334 C2
Santa Lucia *Phil.* 17°7N 120°27E 232 C3
Santa Lucía *Spain* 37°35N 0°58W 197 H4
Santa Lucía *Uruguay* 34°27S 56°24W 334 C4
Santa Lucia, Stazione *Venice, Italy* 142 a2
Santa Lucía de Tirajana *Canary Is.* 27°55N 5°32W 153 e1
Santa Lucia Range *U.S.A.* 36°0N 121°20W 306 K5
Santa Luzia = Luziânia *Brazil* 16°20S 48°0W 333 E2
Santa Luzia *Brazil* 19°47S 43°52W 333 E3
Santa Luzia *C. Verde Is.* 16°50N 24°35W 153 j
Santa Margalida *Spain* 39°42N 3°6E 206 B4
Santa Margarita *Argentina* 38°28S 61°35W 334 D3
Santa Margarita *Calif., U.S.A.* 35°23N 120°37W 306 K6
Santa Margarita → *U.S.A.* 33°13N 117°23W 307 M9
Santa Margarita, I. *Mexico* 24°27N 111°50W 318 C2
Santa Margherita *Italy* 38°58N 8°58E 200 D1
Santa Margherita Ligure *Italy* 44°20N 9°11E 198 D6
Santa María *Argentina* 26°40S 66°0W 334 B2
Santa Maria *Azores* 36°58N 25°6W 153 d4
Santa Maria *Brazil* 29°40S 53°48W 335 B5
Santa Maria *C. Verde Is.* 16°31N 22°53W 153 j
Santa María *Mexico City, Mexico* 128 a1
Santa Maria *Ilocos S., Phil.* 17°22N 120°29E 232 C3
Santa Maria *Isabela, Phil.* 17°28N 121°45E 232 C3
Santa Maria *Calif., U.S.A.* 34°57N 120°26W 307 L6
Santa María → *Mexico* 31°0N 107°14W 318 A3
Santa María, B. de *Mexico* 25°4N 108°6W 318 B3
Santa Maria, C. de *Portugal* 36°58N 7°53W 195 J3
Santa María, I. *Ecuador* 1°17S 90°26W 330 a
Santa María, Vol. *Guatemala* 14°45N 91°33W 320 D1
Santa Maria Cápua Vétere *Italy* 41°5N 14°15E 201 A7
Santa Maria da Feira *Portugal* 40°55N 8°35W 194 E2
Santa Maria da Vitória *Brazil* 13°24S 44°12W 333 D3
Santa María de Guadalupe = Guadalupe *Spain* 39°27N 5°17W 195 F5
Santa María de Ipire *Venezuela* 8°49N 65°19W 329 B4
Santa Maria dei Frari *Venice, Italy* 142 b2
Santa Maria dei Miracoli *Venice, Italy* 142 b3
Santa María del Camí *Spain* 39°38N 2°47E 206 B3
Santa Maria della Misericórdia *Venice, Italy* 142 a3
Santa Maria della Pianto *Venice, Italy* 142 b3
Santa Maria della Salute *Venice, Italy* 142 c2
Santa Maria della Visitazione *Venice, Italy* 142 b3
Santa Maria delle Penitenti *Venice, Italy* 142 a2
Santa Maria di Léuca, C. *Italy* 39°47N 18°22E 201 C11
Santa Maria do Boiaçu *Brazil* 0°25S 61°48W 329 D5
Santa Maria do Suaçuí *Brazil* 18°12S 42°25W 333 E3
Santa Maria dos Marmelos *Brazil* 6°7S 61°51W 331 B5
Santa Maria Formosa *Venice, Italy* 142 b3
Santa María la Real de Nieva *Spain* 41°4N 4°24W 194 D6
Santa Maria Maggiore, Ex Chiesa di *Venice, Italy* 142 b1
Santa Marinella *Italy* 42°2N 11°52E 199 F8
Santa Marta *Colombia* 11°15N 74°13W 328 A3
Santa Marta, Sierra Nevada de *Colombia* 10°55N 73°50W 328 A3
Santa Marta de Tormes *Spain* 40°57N 5°38W 194 E5
Santa Marta Grande, C. *Brazil* 28°43S 48°50W 335 B6
Santa Martabaai = Sint Marthabaai *Curaçao* 12°17N 69°8W 322 g
Santa Maura = Lefkada *Greece* 38°40N 20°43E 207 B2
Santa Monica *U.S.A.* 34°1N 118°29W 126 B2
Santa Monica Mts. *U.S.A.* 34°6N 118°29W 126 B2
Santa Monica Mts. ⌓ *U.S.A.* 34°4N 118°44W 307 L8
Santa Olalla *Spain* 40°2N 4°25W 194 E6
Santa Olalla del Cala *Spain* 37°54N 6°14W 195 H4
Santa Paula *U.S.A.* 34°21N 119°4W 307 L7
Santa Pola *Spain* 38°13N 0°35W 197 G4
Santa Ponça *Spain* 39°30N 2°28E 206 B3
Santa Quitéria *Brazil* 4°20S 40°10W 332 B3
Santa Rita = Itumbiara *Brazil* 18°20S 49°10W 333 E2
Santa Rita *Amazonas, Brazil* 3°29S 69°19W 328 D4
Santa Rita *Paraíba, Brazil* 7°8S 34°58W 332 C5
Santa Rita *Colombia* 4°53N 68°24W 328 C4
Santa Rita *Guam* 13°23N 144°40E 302 d
Santa Rita *Samar, Phil.* 11°27N 124°56E 233 F5
Santa Rita *Zulia, Venezuela* 10°32N 71°32W 328 A3
Santa Rita de Cássia *Brazil* 11°0S 44°32W 332 D3
Santa Rita do Araguaia = Guiratinga *Brazil* 16°21S 53°45W 331 D7
Santa Rita do Araguaia *Brazil* 17°20S 53°12W 331 D7
Santa Rosa = Bella Unión *Uruguay* 30°15S 57°40W 334 C4
Santa Rosa *La Pampa, Argentina* 36°40S 64°17W 334 D3
Santa Rosa *San Luis, Argentina* 32°21S 65°10W 334 C2
Santa Rosa *Beni, Bolivia* 14°10S 66°53W 330 C4
Santa Rosa *Pando, Bolivia* 10°36S 67°20W 330 C4
Santa Rosa *Santa Cruz, Bolivia* 17°7S 63°35W 331 D5
Santa Rosa *Brazil* 27°52S 54°29W 335 B5
Santa Rosa *Colombia* 3°32N 69°48W 328 C4
Santa Rosa *Curaçao* 12°7N 68°53W 322 g
Santa Rosa *El Oro, Ecuador* 3°27S 79°58W 328 D2
Santa Rosa *Galápagos Is., Ecuador* 0°40S 90°25W 330 a
Santa Rosa *Puno, Peru* 14°30S 70°50W 330 C3
Santa Rosa *San Martin, Peru* 6°41S 76°37W 330 B2
Santa Rosa *Phil.* 15°25N 120°57E 232 D3
Santa Rosa *Calif., U.S.A.* 38°26N 122°43W 306 G4
Santa Rosa *N. Mex., U.S.A.* 34°57N 104°41W 305 J11
Santa Rosa *Amazonas, Venezuela* 1°29N 66°55W 328 C4
Santa Rosa, Mt. *Guam* 13°32N 144°55E 302 d
Santa Rosa and San Jacinto Mts. ⌓ *U.S.A.* 33°28N 116°20W 307 M10
Santa Rosa Beach *U.S.A.* 30°22N 86°14W 316 E3
Santa Rosa de Amanadona *Venezuela* 1°29N 66°55W 328 C4
Santa Rosa de Cabal *Colombia* 4°52N 75°38W 328 C2
Santa Rosa de Copán *Honduras* 14°47N 88°46W 320 D2
Santa Rosa de la Roca *Bolivia* 16°3S 61°34W 331 D5
Santa Rosa de Locobe *Chile* 33°25S 70°33W 137 B2
Santa Rosa de Osos *Colombia* 6°39N 75°28W 328 B2
Santa Rosa de Río Primero *Argentina* 31°8S 63°20W 334 C3
Santa Rosa de Viterbo *Colombia* 5°53N 72°59W 328 B3
Santa Rosa del Palmar *Bolivia* 16°54S 62°24W 331 D5
Santa Rosa I. *Calif., U.S.A.* 33°58N 120°6W 307 M6
Santa Rosa I. *Fla., U.S.A.* 30°20N 86°50W 317 E3
Santa Rosa Range *U.S.A.* 41°45N 117°40W 304 F5
Santa Rosalía *Mexico* 27°19N 112°17W 318 B2
Santa Stae *Venice, Italy* 142 b2
Santa Sylvina *Argentina* 27°50S 61°10W 334 B3
Santa Tecla = Nueva San Salvador *El Salv.* 13°40N 89°18W 320 D2
Santa Teresa *Argentina* 33°25S 60°47W 334 C3
Santa Teresa *N. Terr., Australia* 24°8S 134°22E 280 C1
Santa Teresa *Brazil* 19°55S 40°36W 333 E3
Santa Teresa *Tamaulipas, Mexico* 25°17N 97°51W 319 B5
Santa Teresa *Venezuela* 4°43N 61°4W 329 C5
Santa Teresa △ *Uruguay* 33°57S 53°31W 335 C5
Santa Teresa de la Ovalle *Chile* 33°22S 70°44W 137 B1
Santa Teresa di Riva *Italy* 37°57N 15°22E 201 E8
Santa Teresa Gallura *Italy* 41°14N 9°11E 200 A2
Santa Teresinha *Brazil* 10°28S 50°31W 332 D1
Santa Teresita *Argentina* 36°32S 56°41W 334 D4
Santa Uxía de Ribeira = Ribeira *Spain* 42°36N 8°58W 194 C2
Santa Vitória *Brazil* 18°50S 50°8W 333 E1
Santa Vitória do Palmar *Brazil* 33°32S 53°25W 335 C5
Santa Ynez → *U.S.A.* 34°41N 120°36W 307 L6
Santa Ynez Mts. *U.S.A.* 34°30N 120°0W 307 L6
Santa Ysabel *U.S.A.* 33°7N 116°40W 307 M10
Santadi *Italy* 39°5N 8°43E 200 C1
Santaella *Spain* 37°34N 4°51W 195 H6
Santahamina *Finland* 60°8N 25°2E 121 C3
Santahar *Bangla.* 24°48N 88°59E 241 C2
Santai *China* 31°5N 104°58E 228 B5
Santaluz *Brazil* 11°15S 39°22W 332 D4
Santan *Indonesia* 0°3S 117°28E 235 C5
Santana = Uruaçu *Brazil* 14°30S 49°10W 333 D2
Santana *Bahia, Brazil* 13°2S 44°5W 333 D3
Santana *São Paulo, Brazil* 23°29S 46°36W 137 A2
Santana *Madeira* 32°48N 16°52W 153 c
Sântana *Romania* 46°20N 21°30E 182 D6
Santana, Coxilha de *Brazil* 30°50S 55°35W 335 C4
Santana do Ipanema *Brazil* 9°22S 37°14W 332 C4
Santana do Livramento *Brazil* 30°55S 55°30W 335 C4
Santana do Paranaíba = Paranaíba *Brazil* 19°40S 51°11W 331 D7
Santander *Colombia* 3°1N 76°28W 328 C2
Santander *Phil.* 9°25N 123°20E 233 G4
Santander *Spain* 43°27N 3°51W 194 B7
Santander □ *Colombia* 7°0N 73°15W 328 B3
Santander Jiménez *Mexico* 24°13N 98°28W 319 C5
Sant'Angelo, Castel *Rome, Italy* 136 b1
Santanilla, Is. *Honduras* 17°22N 83°57W 320 C3
Santanyí *Spain* 39°20N 3°5E 206 B4
Santaquin *U.S.A.* 39°59N 111°47W 304 G8
Santarcángelo di Romagna *Italy* 44°4N 12°26E 199 D9
Santarém *Brazil* 2°25S 54°42W 329 D7
Santarém *Portugal* 39°12N 8°42W 195 F2
Santarém □ *Portugal* 39°10N 8°40W 195 F2
Santaren Channel *W. Indies* 24°0N 79°30W 320 B4
Santee *U.S.A.* 32°50N 116°58W 307 N10
Santee → *U.S.A.* 33°7N 79°17W 315 E15
Santeny *France* 48°43N 2°34E 134 B4
Santéramo in Colle *Italy* 40°49N 16°45E 201 B9
Santerno → *Italy* 44°34N 11°58E 199 D8
Santhià *Italy* 45°22N 8°10E 198 C5
Santi *Taiwan* 22°43N 120°39E 225 D2
Santi-Quaranta = Sarandë *Albania* 39°52N 19°55E 206 B9
Santiago = Río Grande de Santiago → *Mexico* 21°36N 105°26W 318 C3
Santiago = São Tiago *C. Verde Is.* 15°0N 23°40W 153 j
Santiago *Brazil* 29°11S 54°52W 335 B5
Santiago *Canary Is.* 28°2N 17°12W 153 e1
Santiago *Chile* 33°26S 70°40W 137 B2
Santiago *Panama* 8°0N 81°0W 320 E3
Santiago *Peru* 14°11S 75°43W 330 C2
Santiago *Ilocos S., Phil.* 17°18N 120°27E 232 C3
Santiago *Isabela, Phil.* 16°41N 121°33E 232 C3
Santiago → *Peru* 4°27S 77°38W 328 D2
Santiago, C. *Chile* 50°46S 75°27W 336 D1
Santiago, I. = San Salvador, I. *Ecuador* 0°16S 90°42W 330 a
Santiago, Punta de *Eq. Guin.* 3°12N 8°40E 263 E6
Santiago, Sierra de *Bolivia* 18°25S 59°25W 331 D6
Santiago Benítez ✈ (SCL) *Santiago, Chile* 33°33S 70°42W 137 B1
Santiago de Chiquitos *Bolivia* 18°19S 59°34W 331 D6
Santiago de Chuco *Peru* 8°9S 78°11W 330 B2
Santiago de Compostela *Spain* 42°52N 8°37W 194 C2
Santiago de Cuba *Cuba* 20°0N 75°49W 320 C4
Santiago de los Caballeros *Dom. Rep.* 19°30N 70°40W 321 C5
Santiago de Surco *Peru* 12°9S 77°0W 124 B2
Santiago del Estero *Argentina* 27°50S 64°15W 334 B3
Santiago del Estero □ *Argentina* 27°40S 63°15W 334 B3
Santiago del Teide *Canary Is.* 28°17N 16°48W 153 e1
Santiago do Boqueirão = Santiago *Brazil* 29°11S 54°52W 335 B5
Santiago do Cacém *Portugal* 38°1N 8°42W 195 G2
Santiago I. *Phil.* 16°23N 119°56E 232 C2
Santiago Ixcuintla *Mexico* 21°49N 105°13W 318 C3
Santiago Jamiltepec *Mexico* 16°17N 97°49W 319 D5
Santiago Papasquiaro *Mexico* 25°3N 105°25W 318 C3
Santiago Pinotepa Nacional *Mexico* 16°19N 98°1W 319 D5
Santiaguillo, L. de *Mexico* 24°48N 104°48W 318 C4
Santialing *Taiwan* 25°5N 121°51E 225 A3
Santiao Chiao *Taiwan* 25°1N 122°0E 225 A3
Santiaolun *Taiwan* 23°39N 120°9E 225 C2
Santiguila *Mali* 12°42N 7°25W 262 C3
Santillana del Mar *Spain* 43°24N 4°6W 194 B6
Santisteban del Puerto *Spain* 38°17N 3°15W 195 G7
Santo → *Peru* 8°56S 78°37W 330 B2
Santo Amaro *Bahia, Brazil* 12°30S 38°43W 333 D4
Santo Amaro *São Paulo, Brazil* 23°39S 46°42W 137 B1
Santo Amaro *Lisboa, Portugal* 38°42N 9°11W 126 A1
Santo Anastácio *Brazil* 21°58S 51°39W 335 A5
Santo André *Brazil* 23°39S 46°29W 335 A6
Santo André *Lisboa, Portugal* 38°38N 9°3W 126 B2
Santo Ângelo *Brazil* 28°15S 54°15W 335 B5
Santo Antão *C. Verde Is.* 16°52N 25°10W 153 j
Santo Antão do Tojal *Portugal* 38°49N 9°9W 126 A2
Santo Antônia *São Tomé & Príncipe* 1°37N 7°27E 265 a
Santo Antônio *Brazil* 2°24S 60°58W 329 D5
Santo Antônio, Qta. de *Portugal* 38°39N 9°15W 126 B1
Santo Antônio da Cachoeira = Itaguatins *Brazil* 5°47S 47°29W 332 C2
Santo Antônio de Jesus *Brazil* 12°58S 39°16W 333 D4
Santo Antônio do Abaixo = Santo Antônio do Leverger *Brazil* 15°52S 56°5W 331 D6
Santo Antônio do Içá *Brazil* 3°5S 67°57W 328 D4
Santo Antônio do Leverger *Brazil* 15°52S 56°5W 331 D6
Santo Corazón *Bolivia* 18°0S 58°45W 331 D6
Santo Cosimo e Damiano, Ex Chiesa di *Venice, Italy* 142 c2
Santo Domingo *Dom. Rep.* 18°30N 69°59W 321 C6
Santo Domingo *Baja Calif. S., Mexico* 25°29N 111°55W 318 B2
Santo Domingo *Nic.* 12°14N 84°59W 320 D3
Santo Domingo, Cay *Bahamas* 21°25N 75°45W 320 B4
Santo Domingo de la Calzada *Spain* 42°26N 2°57W 196 C2
Santo Domingo de los Colorados *Ecuador* 0°15S 79°9W 328 D2
Santo Domingo Pueblo *U.S.A.* 35°31N 106°22W 305 J10
Santo Domingo Tehuantepec = Tehuantepec *Mexico* 16°21N 95°13W 319 D5
Santo Nino I. *Phil.* 11°54N 124°26E 233 F5
Santo Stéfano di Camastro *Italy* 38°1N 14°22E 201 D7
Santo Tirso *Portugal* 41°21N 8°28W 194 D2
Santo Tomás *Galápagos Is., Ecuador* 0°51S 91°2W 330 a
Santo Tomás *Baja Calif., Mexico* 31°33N 116°24W 318 A1
Santo Tomás *Peru* 14°26S 72°8W 330 C3
Santo Tomas *Phil.* 7°32N 125°37E 233 H5
Santo Tomas, Univ. of *Phil.* 14°36N 120°59E 127 B1
Santo Tomás, Volcán *Ecuador* 0°48S 91°7W 330 a
Santo Tomé *Argentina* 28°40S 56°5W 335 B4
Santo Tomé de Guayana = Ciudad Guayana *Venezuela* 8°0N 62°30W 329 B5
Santomera *Spain* 38°4N 1°3W 197 G3
Santoña *Spain* 43°29N 3°27W 194 B7
Santorini *Greece* 36°23N 25°27E 205 E7
Santos *Brazil* 24°0S 46°20W 335 A6
Santos, Sierra de los *Spain* 38°7N 5°12W 195 G5
Santos Dumont *Brazil* 22°55S 43°10W 333 F3
Santos Dumont ✈ (SDU) *Brazil* 22°54S 43°9W 135 B2
Santoshpur *India* 22°31N 88°16E 124 B1
Santragachi *India* 22°35N 88°17E 124 B1
Santry *Ireland* 53°24N 6°15W 120 A2
Santuario de Aves Laguna Colorada △ *Bolivia* 22°10S 67°45W 334 A2
Sanuki *Japan* 34°19N 134°10E 222 C6
Sanur *Indonesia* 8°41S 115°15E 231 K18
Sanwan *Taiwan* 24°39N 120°57E 225 B2
Sanwer *India* 22°59N 75°50E 242 H6
Sanxenxo *Spain* 42°24N 8°49W 194 C2
Sanxia = Sanhsia *Taiwan* 24°56N 121°22E 225 B3
Sanxia Shuiku *China* 30°3N 107°58E 228 B6
Sanxiang *China* 22°21N 113°25E 219 a
Sanxing = Sanhsing *Taiwan* 24°40N 121°36E 225 B3
Sanya *China* 18°14N 109°29E 229 a
San'yō *Japan* 34°2N 131°5E 222 C3
Sanyuan *China* 34°35N 108°58E 226 G5
Sanyuanli *China* 23°8N 113°14E 121 B2
Sanyuki-Sammyaku *Japan* 34°5N 134°0E 222 C6
Sanza Pombo *Angola* 7°18S 15°56E 265 D3
São Bartolomeu de Messines *Portugal* 37°15N 8°17W 195 H2
São Benedito = Beneditinos *Brazil* 5°27S 42°22W 332 C3
São Benedito *Brazil* 4°3S 40°53W 332 B3
São Benedito → *Brazil* 9°11S 57°2W 331 B6
São Bento *Brazil* 2°42S 44°50W 332 B3
São Bento do Norte *Brazil* 5°4S 36°2W 332 C4
São Bernardo do Campo *Brazil* 23°45S 46°34W 333 F2
São Borja *Brazil* 28°39S 56°0W 335 B4
São Brás de Alportel *Portugal* 37°8N 7°37W 195 H3
São Braz, C. de *Angola* 9°58S 13°19E 265 D2
São Caetano do Sul *Brazil* 23°37S 46°34W 137 B2
São Caitano *Brazil* 8°21S 36°6W 332 C4
São Carlos *Brazil* 22°0S 47°50W 335 A6
São Conrado *Brazil* 23°0S 43°17W 135 B1
São Cristóvão *Rio de J., Brazil* 22°53S 43°13W 135 B1
São Cristóvão *Sergipe, Brazil* 11°1S 37°15W 332 D4
São Domingos *Brazil* 13°25S 46°19W 333 D2
São Domingos *Guinea-Biss.* 12°19N 16°13W 262 C1
São Domingos da Boa Vista = São Domingos do Capim *Brazil* 1°41S 47°47W 332 B2
São Domingos do Capim *Brazil* 1°41S 47°47W 332 B2
São Domingos do Maranhão *Brazil* 5°42S 44°22W 332 C3
São Felipe = Eirunepé *Brazil* 6°35S 69°53W 330 B4
São Felipe = Içana *Brazil* 0°21N 67°19W 328 C4
São Félix *Brazil* 11°36S 50°39W 333 D1
São Félix do Xingu *Brazil* 6°38S 51°59W 331 B7
São Filipe *C. Verde Is.* 15°2N 24°30W 153 j
São Francisco = Itapagé *Brazil* 3°41S 39°34W 332 B4
São Francisco *Brazil* 16°0S 44°50W 333 E3
São Francisco → *Brazil* 10°30S 36°24W 332 D4
São Francisco do Maranhão *Brazil* 6°15S 42°52W 332 C3
São Francisco do Sul *Brazil* 26°15S 48°36W 335 B6
São Francisco Penitência *Rio de J., Brazil* 135 b1
São Gabriel *Brazil* 30°20S 54°20W 335 C5
São Gabriel da Cachoeira *Brazil* 0°8S 67°5W 328 D4
São Gabriel da Palha *Brazil* 18°47S 40°39W 333 E3
São Gonçalo = Araripina *Brazil* 7°33S 40°34W 332 C3
São Gonçalo *Brazil* 22°48S 43°5W 333 F3
São Gotardo *Brazil* 19°19S 46°3W 333 E2
Sao Hill *Tanzania* 8°20S 35°12E 269 D4
São João *Guinea-Biss.* 11°32N 15°25W 262 C1
São João da Baliza *Brazil* 0°52N 59°52W 329 C6
São João da Barra *Brazil* 21°38S 41°3W 333 F3
São João da Boa Vista *Brazil* 22°0S 46°52W 335 A6
São João da Madeira *Portugal* 40°54N 8°30W 194 E2
São João da Pesqueira *Portugal* 41°8N 7°24W 194 D3
São João da Ponte *Brazil* 15°56S 44°1W 333 E3
São João de Meriti *Brazil* 22°48S 43°21W 333 F3
São João de Montenegro = Montenegro *Brazil* 29°39S 51°29W 335 B5
São João del Rei *Brazil* 21°8S 44°15W 333 F3
São João do Araguaia *Brazil* 5°23S 48°46W 332 C2
São João do Paraíso *Brazil* 15°19S 42°1W 333 E3
São João do Piauí *Brazil* 8°21S 42°15W 332 C3
São João do Sul *Angola* 15°46S 12°0E 265 F2
São João dos Patos *Brazil* 6°30S 43°42W 332 C3
São Joaquim *Amazonas, Brazil* 0°1S 67°16W 328 D4
São Joaquim *Sta. Catarina, Brazil* 28°18S 49°56W 335 B6
São Joaquim △ *Brazil* 28°12S 49°37W 335 B6
São Joaquim da Barra *Brazil* 20°35S 47°53W 333 F2
São Jorge *Azores* 38°38N 28°3W 153 d1
São Jorge, Canal de *Azores* 38°30N 28°0W 153 d1
São Jorge, Castelo de *Portugal* 38°42N 9°8W 126 A2
São Jorge, Pta. de *Azores* 38°42N 27°3W 153 d1
São Jorge, Pta. de *Madeira* 32°50N 16°53W 153 c
São José *Brazil* 27°38S 48°39W 335 B5
São José, B. de *Brazil* 2°38S 44°4W 332 B3
São José da Lagoa = Nova Era *Brazil* 19°45S 43°3W 333 E3
São José da Laje *Brazil* 9°1S 36°3W 332 C4
São José de Mipibu *Brazil* 6°5S 35°15W 332 C4
São José de Tocantins = Niquelândia *Brazil* 14°33S 48°23W 333 D2
São José do Norte *Brazil* 32°1S 52°3W 335 C5
São José do Peixe *Brazil* 7°24S 42°34W 332 C3
São José do Rio Preto *Brazil* 20°50S 49°20W 335 A6
São José dos Campos *Brazil* 23°7S 45°52W 335 A6
São José dos Cocais = Nossa Senhora do Livramento *Brazil* 15°48S 56°22W 331 D6
São José dos Matões = Parnarama *Brazil* 5°31S 43°6W 332 C3
São Juliao do Tojal *Portugal* 38°49N 9°8W 126 A2
São Leopoldo *Brazil* 29°50S 51°10W 335 B5
São Lourenço *Brazil* 22°7S 45°3W 333 F2
São Lourenço → *Brazil* 17°53S 57°27W 331 D6
São Lourenço, Pantanal do *Brazil* 17°30S 56°20W 331 D6
São Lourenço, Pta. de *Madeira* 32°44N 16°39W 153 c
São Lourenço do Sul *Brazil* 31°22S 51°58W 335 C5
São Luís *Brazil* 2°39S 44°15W 332 B3
São Luís do Curu *Brazil* 3°40S 39°14W 332 B4
São Luís do Tapajós *Brazil* 4°25S 56°12W 329 D6
São Luís Gonzaga = Ipixuna *Brazil* 7°0S 71°40W 330 B3
São Luís Gonzaga *Brazil* 28°25S 55°0W 335 B5
São Marcos → *Brazil* 18°15S 47°37W 333 E2
São Marcos, B. de *Brazil* 2°0S 44°0W 332 B3
São Martinho da Cortiça *Portugal* 40°18N 8°8W 194 E2
São Mateus *Azores* 38°26N 28°27W 153 d1
São Mateus *Brazil* 18°44S 39°50W 333 E4
São Mateus → *Brazil* 18°35S 39°44W 333 E4
São Mateus do Sul *Brazil* 25°52S 50°23W 335 B5
São Miguel *Azores* 37°47N 25°30W 153 d3
São Miguel do Araguaia *Brazil* 13°19S 50°13W 333 D1
São Miguel do Guamá *Brazil* 1°37S 47°29W 332 B2
São Miguel do Oeste *Brazil* 26°45S 53°34W 335 B5
São Miguel dos Campos *Brazil* 9°47S 36°5W 332 C4
São Nicolau *C. Verde Is.* 16°20N 24°20W 153 j
São Nicolau → *Angola* 14°16S 12°22E 265 E2
São Nicolau → *Brazil* 5°45S 42°2W 332 C3
São Paulo *Atl. Oc.* 0°56N 29°22W 152 F9
São Paulo *Brazil* 23°32S 46°38W 137 B2
São Paulo □ *Brazil* 22°0S 49°0W 335 A6
São Paulo Congonhas ✈ (CGH) *Brazil* 23°38S 46°39W 137 B2
São Paulo de Olivença *Brazil* 3°27S 68°48W 328 D4
São Pedro *Atl. Oc.* 0°56N 29°22W 152 F9
São Pedro do Sul *Portugal* 40°46N 8°4W 194 E2
São Rafael *Brazil* 5°47S 36°55W 332 C4
São Raimundo das Mangabeiras *Brazil* 7°1S 45°29W 332 C2
São Raimundo Nonato *Brazil* 9°1S 42°42W 332 C3
São Romão *Brazil* 16°22S 45°4W 333 E2
São Roque *Madeira* 32°46N 16°48W 153 c
São Roque, C. de *Brazil* 5°30S 35°16W 332 C4
São Roque do Pico *Azores* 38°31N 28°19W 153 d1
São Salvador do Congo = Mbanza Congo *Angola* 6°18S 14°16E 265 D2
São Sebastião *Azores* 38°39N 27°6W 153 d1
São Sebastião, I. de *Brazil* 23°50S 45°18W 335 A6

São Sebastião do Paraíso *Brazil* 20°54S 46°59W 335 A6
São Simão *Brazil* 18°56S 50°30W 333 E1
São Teotónio *Portugal* 37°30N 8°42W 195 H2
São Tiago *C. Verde Is.* 15°0N 23°40W 153 j
São Tomé *Brazil* 5°58S 36°4W 332 C4
São Tomé *São Tomé & Príncipe* 0°10N 6°39E 265 a
São Tomé, C. de *Brazil* 22°0S 40°59W 333 F3
São Tomé, Pico de *São Tomé & Príncipe* 0°16N 6°33E 265 a
São Tomé & Príncipe ■ *Africa* 0°12N 6°39E 265 a
São Vicente = Araguatins *Brazil* 5°38S 48°7W 332 C2
São Vicente *Brazil* 23°57S 46°23W 335 A6
São Vicente *C. Verde Is.* 17°0N 25°0W 153 j
São Vicente *Madeira* 32°48N 17°3W 153 c
São Vicente, C. de *Portugal* 37°0N 9°0W 195 H1
Saona, I. *Dom. Rep.* 18°10N 68°40W 321 C6
Saône → *France* 45°44N 4°50E 173 G11
Saône-et-Loire □ *France* 46°30N 4°50E 173 F11
Saonek *Indonesia* 0°22S 130°55E 231 E8
Saoura, O. → *Algeria* 29°0N 0°55W 261 C4
Sapa *India* 22°30N 88°15E 124 B1
Sapam, Ao *Thailand* 8°0N 98°26E 237 a
Sapanca *Turkey* 40°41N 30°16E 212 B4
Sapanjang *Indonesia* 7°10S 115°50E 235 D5
Sapão → *Brazil* 11°1S 45°32W 332 D2
Saparua *Indonesia* 3°33S 128°40E 231 E7
Sapateiro, Cor. do → *Brazil* 23°35S 46°41W 137 B1
Sapé *Brazil* 7°6S 35°13W 332 C4
Sape *Indonesia* 8°34S 118°59E 235 D5
Sape, Teluk *Indonesia* 8°32S 119°4E 235 D5
Sapele *Nigeria* 5°50N 5°40E 263 D6
Sapelo I. *U.S.A.* 31°25N 81°12W 316 D8
Sapelo Sound *U.S.A.* 31°30N 81°10W 316 D8
Sapes *Greece* 41°2N 25°43E 203 E9
Şaphane *Turkey* 39°1N 29°13E 205 B11
Sapi ⌂ *Zimbabwe* 15°48S 29°42E 269 F2
Sapienza *Greece* 36°45N 21°43E 204 E3
Sapindji *Dem. Rep. of the Congo* 9°39S 23°12E 265 D4
Sapo △ *Liberia* 5°15N 8°30W 262 D3
Sapone *Burkina Faso* 12°3N 1°35W 263 C4
Saposoa *Peru* 6°55S 76°45W 330 B2
Sapotskina *Belarus* 53°49N 23°40E 184 E10
Sapouy *Burkina Faso* 11°34N 1°44W 263 C4
Sapozhok *Russia* 53°59N 40°41E 190 D5
Sapphire *Australia* 23°28S 147°43E 280 C4
Sappho *U.S.A.* 48°4N 124°16W 306 B2
Sapporo *Japan* 43°0N 141°21E 220 C10
Sapri *Italy* 40°4N 15°38E 201 B8
Sapt Kosi → *Nepal* 26°32N 86°56E 243 F12
Sapu *Angola* 12°8S 19°26E 265 E3
Sapudi *Indonesia* 7°6S 114°20E 235 D4
Sapulpa *U.S.A.* 35°59N 96°5W 314 D6
Sapulut *Malaysia* 4°42N 116°28E 235 B5
Saqqez *Iran* 36°15N 46°20E 213 D12
Sar Dasht *Āzarbāyjān-e Gharbī, Iran* 36°9N 45°28E 213 D11
Sar Dasht *Khuzestān, Iran* 32°32N 48°52E 247 C6
Sar-e Pol *Afghan.* 36°10N 66°0E 240 A2
Sar-e Pol □ *Afghan.* 36°20N 65°50E 240 A2
Sar Gachīneh = Yāsūj *Iran* 30°31N 51°31E 247 D6
Sar Passage *Palau* 7°12N 134°22E 288 c
Sar Planina *Macedonia* 42°0N 21°0E 202 E4
Sara *Burkina Faso* 11°40N 3°53W 262 C4
Sara *Niger* 20°46N 12°35E 259 D2
Sara *Phil.* 11°16N 123°1E 233 F4
Šara △ *Serbia* 42°12N 21°0E 202 D5
Sara Buri = Saraburi *Thailand* 14°30N 100°55E 236 E3
Sarāb *Iran* 37°55N 47°40E 213 D12
Sarābādī *Iraq* 33°1N 44°48E 246 C5
Sarâbît el Khâdim *Egypt* 29°2N 33°25E 251 J4
Sarableh *Iran* 33°44N 46°34E 213 F12
Saraburi *Thailand* 14°30N 100°55E 236 E3
Saradiya *India* 21°34N 70°2E 242 J4
Saraféré *Mali* 15°50N 3°40W 262 B4
Saragossa = Zaragoza *Spain* 41°39N 0°53W 196 D4
Saraguro *Ecuador* 3°35S 79°16W 328 D2
Sarahs *Turkmenistan* 36°32N 61°13E 247 B9
Sarai Naurang *Pakistan* 32°50N 70°47E 242 C4
Saraikela *India* 22°42N 85°56E 243 H11
Saraipali *India* 21°20N 82°59E 244 D6
Saraiu *Romania* 44°43N 28°10E 183 F13
Sarajevo *Bos.-H.* 43°52N 18°26E 182 G3
Sarakhs = Sarahs *Turkmenistan* 36°32N 61°13E 247 B9
Sarakhs *Iran* 36°32N 61°9E 216 E6
Saramacca → *Suriname* 5°50N 55°55W 329 B6
Saramati *Burma* 25°44N 95°2E 241 C5
Saran, Gunung *Indonesia* 0°30S 111°25E 235 C4
Saranac *U.S.A.* 42°56N 85°13W 311 B11
Saranac Lake *U.S.A.* 44°20N 74°10W 313 B10
Saranac Lakes *U.S.A.* 44°20N 74°28W 313 B10
Saranda *Tanzania* 5°45S 34°59E 268 D3
Sarandë *Albania* 39°52N 19°55E 206 B9
Sarandí *Argentina* 34°40S 58°20W 117 C2
Sarandí del Yí *Uruguay* 33°18S 55°38W 335 C4
Sarandí Grande *Uruguay* 33°44S 56°20W 334 C4
Sarangani □ *Phil.* 5°45N 125°20E 233 J5
Sarangani B. *Phil.* 6°0N 125°13E 233 J5
Sarangani I. *Phil.* 5°26N 125°28E 233 J5
Sarangani Is. *Phil.* 5°25N 125°25E 233 J5
Sarangarh *India* 21°30N 83°5E 244 D6
Saranovo = Septemvri *Bulgaria* 42°13N 24°6E 203 D8
Saransk *Russia* 54°10N 45°10E 190 C7
Sarapul *Russia* 56°28N 53°48E 186 C9
Sarāqib *Syria* 35°52N 36°47E 250 C7
Sarar Plain = Bannaanka Saraar *Somalia* 9°25N 46°17E 267 C6
Sarasota *U.S.A.* 27°20N 82°32W 317 H7
Saraswati → *India* 22°46N 88°15E 124 A1
Sarata *Ukraine* 46°1N 29°40E 183 D14
Sarata → *Ukraine* 45°51N 29°41E 183 E14
Saratoga *Calif., U.S.A.* 37°16N 122°2W 306 H4
Saratoga *Wyo., U.S.A.* 41°27N 106°49W 304 F10
Saratoga ⌂ *U.S.A.* 43°0N 73°38W 313 D11
Saratoga L. *U.S.A.* 43°1N 73°44W 313 C11
Saratoga Springs *U.S.A.* 43°5N 73°47W 313 C11
Saratok *Malaysia* 1°55N 111°17E 235 B4
Saratov *Russia* 51°30N 46°2E 190 E7
Saratov □ *Russia* 51°50N 46°20E 190 E8
Saratovskoye Vdkhr. *Russia* 53°10N 48°35E 190 D9
Sarāvān *Iran* 27°25N 62°15E 247 E9
Saravane *Laos* 15°43N 106°25E 236 E6
Sarawak □ *Malaysia* 2°0N 113°0E 235 B4
Saray *Tekirdağ, Turkey* 41°26N 27°55E 203 E11
Saray *Van, Turkey* 38°38N 44°9E 213 C11
Saraya *Senegal* 12°50N 11°45W 262 C2
Sarayçık *Turkey* 39°1N 29°49E 205 B11
Sarayköy *Turkey* 37°55N 28°54E 205 D10
Saraylar *Turkey* 40°39N 27°40E 203 F11
Sarayönü *Turkey* 38°16N 32°24E 212 C5
Sarbāz *Iran* 26°38N 61°19E 247 E9
Sarbīsheh *Iran* 32°30N 59°40E 247 C8
Sárbogárd *Hungary* 46°50N 18°40E 182 D3
Sarca → *Italy* 45°52N 10°52E 198 C7
Sarcelles *France* 49°1N 2°23E 173 D9
Sarda → *India* 27°21N 81°23E 243 F9
Sardalas *Libya* 25°50N 10°34E 258 C2
Sardar Sarovar Dam *India* 21°50N 73°50E 244 D1
Sardarshahr *India* 28°30N 74°29E 242 E6
Sardegna □ *Italy* 40°0N 9°0E 200 B1
Sardhana *India* 29°9N 77°39E 242 E7
Sardina, Pta. *Canary Is.* 28°9N 15°44W 153 e1
Sardinata *Colombia* 8°5N 72°48W 328 B3
Sardinia = Sardegna □ *Italy* 40°0N 9°0E 200 B1
Sardinia *U.S.A.* 39°0N 83°49W 311 F13
Sardis *Turkey* 38°28N 27°58E 205 C10
Sardis *Ga., U.S.A.* 32°58N 81°46W 316 C8
Sardūīyeh = Dar Mazār *Iran* 29°14N 57°20E 247 D8
Sarecky potok → *Czech Rep.* 50°7N 14°23E 135 B2
Sarek △ *Sweden* 67°22N 17°35E 160 C17
Saren *Indonesia* 8°26S 115°34E 231 J18
S'Arenal *Spain* 39°30N 2°45E 206 B3
Sarentino *Italy* 46°38N 11°21E 199 B8
Saréyamou *Mali* 16°7N 3°10W 262 B4
Sargasso Sea *Atl. Oc.* 27°0N 72°0W 292 G13
Sargent *U.S.A.* 33°26N 84°52W 316 B5
Sargodha *Pakistan* 32°10N 72°40E 242 C5
Sarh *Chad* 9°5N 18°23E 259 G3
Sarhala *Ivory C.* 8°22N 6°8W 262 D3
Sarhro, Jebel *Morocco* 31°6N 5°0W 260 B4
Sārī *Iran* 36°30N 53°4E 247 B7
Sari d'Orcino *France* 42°3N 8°49E 175 F12
Saria *Greece* 35°54N 27°17E 205 F9
Saria *India* 21°38N 83°22E 243 J10
Sariab *Pakistan* 30°6N 66°59E 242 D2
Sarıbeyler *Turkey* 39°24N 27°35E 205 B9
Saricumbe *Angola* 12°12S 19°46E 265 E3
Sarigan *N. Marianas* 16°43N 145°47E 302 a
Sarıgöl *Turkey* 38°14N 28°41E 212 C3
Sarıkamış *Turkey* 40°22N 42°35E 213 B10
Sarıkaya *Turkey* 39°29N 35°22E 212 C6
Sarikei *Malaysia* 2°8N 111°30E 235 B4
Sarıköy *Turkey* 40°12N 27°37E 203 F11
Sarila *India* 25°46N 79°41E 243 G8
Sarimbun *Singapore* 1°24N 103°41E 138 A2
Sarimbun Res. *Singapore* 1°25N 103°41E 138 A2
Sarina *Australia* 21°22S 149°13E 280 C4
Sariñena *Spain* 41°47N 0°10W 196 D4
Sarinleey *Somalia* 2°22N 42°17E 267 D5
Sarıoğlan *Turkey* 39°5N 35°59E 212 C6
Sariri *Papua N. G.* 9°11S 148°35E 286 E5
Sarita *U.S.A.* 27°13N 97°47W 314 H6
Sarıveliler *Turkey* 36°41N 32°37E 250 B3
Sariwŏn *N. Korea* 38°31N 125°46E 224 C2
Sariyar Barajı *Turkey* 40°2N 31°33E 212 B4
Sarıyer *Turkey* 41°10N 29°3E 122 A2
Sarız *Turkey* 38°28N 36°30E 212 C7
Sarju → *India* 27°21N 81°23E 243 F9
Sark *U.K.* 49°25N 2°22W 169 H5
Sarkad *Hungary* 46°47N 21°23E 182 D6
Sarkari Tala *India* 27°39N 70°52E 242 F4
Şarkışla *Turkey* 39°21N 36°25E 212 C7
Şarköy *Turkey* 40°36N 27°6E 203 F11
Sarlat-la-Canéda *France* 44°54N 1°13E 174 D5
Sărmăşag *Romania* 47°21N 22°50E 182 C7
Sărmaşu *Romania* 46°45N 24°13E 183 D9
Sarmi *Indonesia* 1°49S 138°44E 231 E9
Sarmiento *Argentina* 45°35S 69°5W 336 C3
Sarmiento, Mt. *Chile* 54°27S 70°50W 336 D2
Sarmizegetusa *Romania* 45°31N 22°47E 182 E7
Särna *Sweden* 61°41N 13°8E 162 C7
Sarnano *Italy* 43°2N 13°18E 199 E10
Sarnen *Switz.* 46°53N 8°13E 179 J4
Sarnia *Canada* 42°58N 82°23W 312 D2
Sarno *Italy* 40°49N 14°37E 201 B7
Sarnthein = Sarentino *Italy* 46°38N 11°21E 199 B8
Sårö *Sweden* 57°31N 11°57E 163 G5
Sarolangun *Indonesia* 2°19S 102°42E 234 C2
Saronikos Kolpos *Greece* 37°45N 23°45E 204 D5
Saronno *Italy* 45°38N 9°2E 198 C6
Saros Körfezi *Turkey* 40°30N 26°15E 203 F10
Sárospatak *Hungary* 48°18N 21°33E 182 B6
Sarowbi *Afghan.* 34°36N 69°44E 240 B3
Sarpsborg *Norway* 59°16N 11°7E 164 E8
Sarqan *Kazakhstan* 45°24N 79°55E 217 C9
Sarracín *Spain* 42°15N 3°45W 194 C7
Sarralbe *France* 49°0N 7°1E 173 D14
Sarrat *Phil.* 18°9N 120°39E 232 B3
Sarre = Saar → *Europe* 49°41N 6°32E 176 C6
Sarre *France* 45°40N 7°15E 198 C4
Sarre-Union *France* 48°57N 7°4E 173 D14
Sarrebourg *France* 48°43N 7°3E 173 D14
Sarreguemines *France* 49°5N 7°4E 173 C14
Sarrià *Barcelona, Spain* 41°22N 2°8E 114 A1
Sarria *Galicia, Spain* 42°49N 7°29W 194 C3
Sarrión *Spain* 40°9N 0°49W 196 E4
Sarro *Mali* 13°40N 5°15W 262 C3
Sarroch *Italy* 39°4N 9°1E 200 C2
Sarsing *Iraq* 37°2N 43°20E 213 D10
Sarstedt *Germany* 52°14N 9°52E 178 C5
Sarsuna *India* 22°28N 88°17E 124 C1
Sartell *U.S.A.* 45°37N 94°12W 308 C6
Sartène *France* 41°38N 8°58E 175 G12
Sarthe □ *France* 47°58N 0°10E 172 D7
Sarthe → *France* 47°33N 0°31W 172 E6
Sartilly *France* 48°45N 1°28W 172 D5
Sartrouville *France* 48°56N 2°10E 134 A2
Saruhanlı *Turkey* 38°44N 27°36E 205 C9
Sărulești *Romania* 44°25N 26°39E 183 F11
Saruna → *Pakistan* 26°31N 67°7E 242 F2
Sarupeta *India* 26°30N 91°55E 241 B3
Särur *Azerbaijan* 39°22N 45°5E 213 C11
Saruwaged Ra. *Papua N. G.* 6°13S 146°45E 286 D4
Sárvár *Hungary* 47°15N 16°56E 182 C1
Sarvar *India* 26°4N 75°0E 242 F6
Sarvestān *Iran* 29°20N 53°10E 247 D7
Särvfjället *Sweden* 62°42N 13°30E 162 B7
Sárvíz → *Hungary* 46°24N 18°41E 182 D3
Sary-Tash *Kyrgyzstan* 39°44N 73°15E 217 E8
Sarych, Mys *Ukraine* 44°25N 33°45E 189 K7
Saryesik-Atyraū Qumy *Kazakhstan* 45°30N 76°0E 217 C9
Sarykamyshskoye, Ozero = Saryqamysh Köli *Turkmenistan* 41°56N 57°25E 216 D5
Sarykemer *Kazakhstan* 43°0N 71°30E 217 D8
Sarykenggir → *Kazakhstan* 48°22N 67°59E 217 C7
Saryköl *Kazakhstan* 53°20N 65°12E 216 B7
Sarykolskiy Khrebet *Tajikistan* 38°30N 74°30E 217 E8
Saryözek *Kazakhstan* 44°22N 77°59E 217 D9
Saryqamysh Köli *Turkmenistan* 41°56N 57°25E 216 D5
Saryshaghan *Kazakhstan* 46°12N 73°38E 217 C8
Sarysū → *Kazakhstan* 45°12N 66°36E 217 C7
Sarzana *Italy* 44°7N 9°58E 198 D6
Sarzeau *France* 47°31N 2°48W 172 E4
Sasabeneh *Ethiopia* 7°59N 44°43E 267 C5
Sasad *Hungary* 47°28N 19°0E 117 B2
Sasamungga *Solomon Is.* 7°0S 156°50E 287 L9
Sasan Gir *India* 21°10N 70°36E 242 J4
Sasaram *India* 24°57N 84°5E 243 G11
Sasari, Mt. *Solomon Is.* 8°10S 159°30E 287 M10
Sasayama *Japan* 35°4N 135°13E 223 B7
Sasebo *Japan* 33°10N 129°43E 222 D1
Saser Kangri *India* 34°50N 77°50E 243 B7
Sashalom *Hungary* 47°30N 19°10E 117 A3
Saska *Poland* 52°14N 21°3E 143 B2
Saskatchewan □ *Canada* 54°40N 106°0W 297 C7
Saskatchewan → *Canada* 53°37N 100°40W 297 C8
Saskatoon *Canada* 52°10N 106°38W 297 C7
Saskylakh *Russia* 71°55N 114°1E 215 B12
Sasolburg *S. Africa* 26°46S 27°49E 271 C4
Sason *Turkey* 38°19N 41°24E 213 C9
Sasovo *Russia* 54°25N 41°55E 190 C5
Sassandra *Ivory C.* 4°55N 6°8W 262 E3
Sassandra → *Ivory C.* 4°58N 6°5W 262 E3
Sássari *Italy* 40°43N 8°34E 200 B1
Sassie *Australia* 10°2S 142°51E 280 a
Sassnitz *Germany* 54°29N 13°39E 178 A9
Sasso Marconi *Italy* 44°24N 11°15E 199 D8
Sassocorvaro *Italy* 43°47N 12°30E 199 E9
Sassoferrato *Italy* 43°26N 12°51E 199 E9
Sassuolo *Italy* 44°33N 10°47E 198 D7
Sástago *Spain* 41°19N 0°21W 196 D4
Sastamala *Finland* 61°20N 22°54E 188 B2
Sastown *Liberia* 4°45N 8°27W 262 E3
Sasvad *India* 18°20N 74°2E 244 E2
Sasyk, Ozero *Ukraine* 45°45N 29°40E 183 E14
Sasyqköl *Kazakhstan* 46°35N 81°0E 217 C10
Sata-Misaki *Japan* 31°0N 130°40E 222 F2
Satadougou *Mali* 12°25N 11°25W 262 C2
Satakunta □ *Finland* 61°45N 23°0E 160 F20
Satalice *Czech Rep.* 50°7N 14°34E 135 B3
Satama-Soukoura *Ivory C.* 7°55N 4°27W 262 D4
Satara *India* 17°44N 73°58E 244 F1
Satara *S. Africa* 24°29S 31°47E 271 B5
Sätbaev *Kazakhstan* 48°10N 67°31E 217 C7
Satbarwa *India* 23°55N 84°16E 243 H11
Satellite Beach *U.S.A.* 28°10N 80°36W 317 G9
Säter *Sweden* 60°21N 15°45E 162 D9
Satevó *Mexico* 27°57N 106°7W 318 B3
Satgachi *India* 22°37N 88°25E 124 B2
Satilla → *U.S.A.* 30°59N 81°29W 316 E8
Satipo *Peru* 11°15S 74°25W 330 C3
Satka *Russia* 55°3N 59°1E 186 C10
Satkania *Bangla.* 22°4N 92°3E 241 D4
Satkhira *Bangla.* 22°43N 89°8E 241 D2
Satmala Hills *Andhra Pradesh, India* 19°45N 78°45E 244 E4
Satmala Hills *Maharashtra, India* 20°15N 74°40E 244 D2
Satna *India* 24°35N 80°50E 243 G9
Šator *Bos.-H.* 44°11N 16°37E 199 D13
Sátoraljaújhely *Hungary* 48°25N 21°41E 182 B6
Satpukur *India* 22°37N 88°24E 124 B2
Satpura △ *India* 22°40N 78°15E 242 H8
Satpura Ra. *India* 21°25N 76°10E 244 D3
Satrup *Germany* 54°41N 9°36E 178 A5
Satsuma-Hantō *Japan* 31°25N 130°25E 222 F2
Satsuma-Sendai *Japan* 31°50N 130°20E 222 F2
Satsunan-Shotō *Japan* 30°0N 130°0E 221 K5
Sattahip *Thailand* 12°41N 100°54E 236 F3
Sattenapalle *India* 16°25N 80°6E 245 F5
Sattru Phai *Bangkok, Thailand* 113 b2
Satu Mare *Romania* 47°46N 22°55E 182 C7
Satu Mare □ *Romania* 47°45N 23°0E 182 C8
Satui *Indonesia* 3°50S 115°27E 235 C5
Satun *Thailand* 6°43N 100°2E 237 J3
Satupa'itea *Samoa* 13°45S 172°18W 287 V19
Saturnina → *Brazil* 12°15S 58°10W 331 C6
Sauce = Juan L. Lacaze *Uruguay* 34°26S 57°25W 334 C4
Sauce *Argentina* 30°5S 58°46W 334 C4
Sauceda *Mexico* 25°46N 101°19W 318 B4
Saucillo *Mexico* 28°1N 105°17W 318 B3
Sauda *Norway* 59°40N 6°20E 164 E3
Saudasjøen *Norway* 59°38N 6°17E 164 E3
Saúde *Bahia, Brazil* 10°56S 40°24W 332 D3
Saúde *São Paulo, Brazil* 23°36S 46°37W 137 B2
Sauðárkrókur *Iceland* 65°45N 19°40W 155 B7
Saudi Arabia ■ *Asia* 26°0N 44°0E 246 B3
Sauerland *Germany* 51°12N 7°59E 176 C8
Saugatuck *U.S.A.* 42°40N 86°12W 311 B10
Saugeen → *Canada* 44°30N 81°22W 312 B3
Saugerties *U.S.A.* 42°5N 73°57W 313 D11
Saugues *France* 44°58N 3°32E 174 D7
Saugus *Calif., U.S.A.* 34°25N 118°32W 307 L8
Saugus *Mass., U.S.A.* 42°28N 71°0W 116 A2
Saugus → *U.S.A.* 42°27N 70°58W 116 A2
Saujbulagh = Mahābād *Iran* 36°50N 45°45E 213 D11
Saujon *France* 45°41N 0°55W 174 C3
Sauk Centre *U.S.A.* 45°44N 94°57W 308 C6
Sauk City *U.S.A.* 43°17N 89°43W 310 A7
Sauk Rapids *U.S.A.* 45°35N 94°10W 308 C6
Saül *Fr. Guiana* 3°37N 53°12W 329 C7
Sauland *Norway* 59°37N 8°56E 164 E5
Saulgau *Germany* 48°1N 9°29E 179 G5
Saulieu *France* 47°17N 4°14E 173 E11
Sault *France* 44°6N 5°24E 175 D9
Sault-au-Récollet *Canada* 45°35N 73°39W 130 A2
Sault Ste. Marie *Ont., Canada* 46°30N 84°20W 298 C3
Sault Ste. Marie *Mich., U.S.A.* 46°30N 84°21W 309 B11
Saūmalköl *Kazakhstan* 53°17N 68°6E 217 B7
Saumlaki *Indonesia* 7°55S 131°20E 231 F8
Saumur *France* 47°15N 0°5W 172 E6
Saundatti *India* 15°47N 75°7E 245 G2
Saunders, C. *N.Z.* 45°53S 170°45E 285 F5
Saunders I. *Antarctica* 57°48S 26°28W 151 B1
Saunders Pt. *Australia* 27°52S 125°38E 279 E4
Saunemin *U.S.A.* 40°54N 88°24W 311 D8
Saupite *Angola* 13°54S 17°43E 265 E3
Saurbær *Norðurland Eystra, Iceland* 65°27N 18°13W 155 B8
Saurbær *Vesturland, Iceland* 64°24N 21°35W 155 C5
Sauri *Nigeria* 11°42N 6°44E 263 C6
Saurimo *Angola* 9°40S 20°12E 265 D4
Sausalito *U.S.A.* 37°51N 122°29W 136 A2
Sautatá *Colombia* 7°50N 77°4W 328 B2
Sauteurs *Grenada* 12°14N 61°38W 323 q
Sauvage, Côte *France* 45°50N 1°30W 174 C2
Sauveterre-de-Béarn *France* 43°24N 0°57W 174 E3
Sauzé-Vaussais *France* 46°8N 0°8E 174 B4
Savá *Honduras* 15°32N 86°15W 320 C2
Sava *Italy* 40°24N 17°33E 201 B10
Sava → *Serbia* 44°50N 20°26E 182 F5
Savage *U.S.A.* 47°27N 104°21W 304 C11
Savage I. = Niue ☑ *Pac. Oc.* 19°2S 169°54W 289 g
Savage River *Australia* 41°31S 145°14E 281 G4
Savai'i *Samoa* 13°28S 172°24W 287 V19
Savalou *Benin* 7°57N 1°58E 263 D5
Savane *Mozam.* 19°37S 35°8E 269 F4
Savanes □ *Ivory C.* 9°30N 6°0W 262 D3
Savaneta *Aruba* 12°27N 69°56W 322 f
Savanna *U.S.A.* 42°5N 90°8W 310 B6
Savanna-la-Mar *Jamaica* 18°10N 78°10W 320 a
Savannah *Ga., U.S.A.* 32°5N 81°6W 316 C8
Savannah *Mo., U.S.A.* 39°56N 94°50W 308 E6
Savannah *Tenn., U.S.A.* 35°14N 88°15W 315 D10
Savannah → *U.S.A.* 32°2N 80°53W 316 C9
Savannah Beach = Tybee Island *U.S.A.* 32°1N 80°51W 316 C9
Savannakhet *Laos* 16°30N 104°49E 236 D5
Savanne, Piton *Mauritius* 20°26S 57°29E 272 e
Savannes B. *St. Lucia* 13°45N 60°56W 323 m
Savant L. *Canada* 50°16N 90°44W 298 B1
Savant Lake *Canada* 50°14N 90°40W 298 B1
Savantvadi *India* 15°55N 73°54E 245 G1
Savanur *India* 14°59N 75°21E 245 G2
Savarkundla = Kundla *India* 21°21N 71°25E 242 J4
Săvârșin *Romania* 46°1N 22°14E 182 D7
Savaştepe *Turkey* 39°22N 27°42E 205 B9
Savda *India* 21°9N 75°56E 244 D2
Savé *Benin* 8°2N 2°29E 263 D5
Save → *Haute-Garonne, France* 43°47N 1°17E 174 E5
Save → *Mozam.* 21°16S 34°0E 271 B5
Sāveh *Iran* 35°2N 50°20E 247 C6
Savelugu *Ghana* 9°38N 0°54W 263 D4
Savenay *France* 47°20N 1°55W 172 E5
Săveni *Romania* 47°57N 26°52E 183 C11
Saverdun *France* 43°14N 1°34E 174 E5
Saverne *France* 48°43N 7°20E 173 D14
Savigliano *Italy* 44°38N 7°40E 198 D4
Savigny-sur-Braye *France* 47°53N 0°49E 172 E7
Sávio → *Italy* 44°19N 12°20E 199 D9
Šavnik *Montenegro* 42°59N 19°10E 202 D3
Savo *Finland* 62°45N 27°30E 160 E22
Savo *Solomon Is.* 9°8S 159°48E 287 M10
Savoie □ *France* 45°26N 6°25E 175 C10
Savolax = Savo *Finland* 62°45N 27°30E 160 E22
Savona *Italy* 44°17N 8°30E 198 D5
Savona *N.Y., U.S.A.* 42°17N 77°13W 312 D7
Savonet *Curaçao* 12°21N 69°7W 322 g
Savonlinna *Finland* 61°52N 28°53E 188 B5
Savoonga *U.S.A.* 63°42N 170°29W 303 E5
Savoy = Savoie □ *France* 45°26N 6°25E 175 C10
Şavşat *Turkey* 41°15N 42°20E 213 B10
Sävsjö *Sweden* 57°20N 14°40E 163 G8
Savur *Turkey* 37°34N 40°53E 246 B4
Savusavu *Fiji* 16°34S 179°15E 287 A2
Savusavu B. *Fiji* 16°45S 179°15E 287 A2
Sawah Besar *Indonesia* 6°8S 106°49E 122 A1
Sawahlunto *Indonesia* 0°40S 100°52E 234 C2
Sawai *Indonesia* 3°0S 129°5E 231 E7
Sawai Madhopur *India* 26°0N 76°25E 242 G7
Sawaleke *Fiji* 17°59S 179°18E 287 A2
Sawang Daen Din *Thailand* 17°28N 103°28E 236 D4
Sawankhalok *Thailand* 17°19N 99°50E 236 D2
Sawara *Japan* 35°55N 140°30E 223 B12
Sawatch Range *U.S.A.* 39°0N 106°30W 304 G10
Sawdā', Jabal as *Libya* 28°51N 15°12E 258 C3
Sawel Mt. *U.K.* 54°50N 7°2W 166 B4
Sawfajjin, W. → *Libya* 31°41N 14°44E 258 B2
Sawi *Thailand* 10°14N 99°5E 237 G2
Sawla *Ghana* 9°17N 2°25W 262 D4
Sawmills *Zimbabwe* 19°30S 28°2E 269 F2
Şawqirah *Oman* 18°7N 56°32E 249 C7
Şawqirah, Ghubbat *Oman* 18°35N 57°0E 249 C7
Sawtell *Australia* 30°19S 153°6E 283 A10
Sawtelle *U.S.A.* 34°2N 118°27W 126 B2
Sawtooth ⌂ *U.S.A.* 44°0N 114°50W 304 D6
Sawtooth Range *U.S.A.* 44°3N 114°58W 304 D6
Sawu *Indonesia* 10°35S 121°50E 231 F6
Sawu Sea *Indonesia* 9°30S 121°50E 231 F6
Saxby → *Australia* 18°25S 140°53E 280 B3
Saxmundham *U.K.* 52°13N 1°30E 169 E9
Saxon Switzerland = Sächsische Schweiz △ *Germany* 50°55N 14°10E 178 E10
Saxony = Sachsen □ *Germany* 50°55N 13°10E 178 E9
Saxony, Lower = Niedersachsen □ *Germany* 52°50N 9°0E 178 C4
Saxton *U.S.A.* 40°13N 78°15W 312 F6
Say *Mali* 13°50N 4°57W 262 C4
Say *Niger* 13°8N 2°22E 263 C5
Saya *Nigeria* 9°30N 3°18E 263 D5
Sayabec *Canada* 48°35N 67°41W 299 C6
Sayaboury *Laos* 19°15N 101°45E 236 C3
Sayán *Peru* 11°8S 77°12W 330 C2
Sayan, Vostochnyy *Russia* 54°0N 96°0E 215 D10
Sayan, Zapadnyy *Russia* 52°30N 94°0E 217 B12
Sayanogorsk *Russia* 53°5N 91°23E 215 D10
Saydā *Lebanon* 33°35N 35°25E 250 E6
Sayghān *Afghan.* 35°10N 67°55E 240 B2
Sayhandulaan = Öldziyt *Mongolia* 44°40N 109°1E 226 B5
Şayhūt *Yemen* 15°12N 51°10E 249 D5
Saykhin *Kazakhstan* 48°50N 46°47E 191 F8
Saylac *Somalia* 11°21N 43°30E 267 B5
Saylorville L. *U.S.A.* 41°48N 93°46W 310 C3
Saynshand = Buyant-Uhaa *Mongolia* 44°55N 110°11E 226 B6
Sayō *Japan* 34°59N 134°22E 222 C6
Sayre *Okla., U.S.A.* 35°18N 99°38W 314 D5
Sayre *Pa., U.S.A.* 41°59N 76°32W 313 E8
Sayreville *U.S.A.* 40°28N 74°22W 313 F10
Sayula *Mexico* 19°52N 103°36W 318 D4
Say'ūn *Yemen* 15°56N 48°47E 249 D4
Sayward *Canada* 50°21N 125°55W 296 C3
Saza *Japan* 33°14N 129°36E 222 D1
Sazanit *Albania* 40°30N 19°20E 202 F3
Sázava → *Czech Rep.* 49°53N 14°24E 180 B7
Sazin *Pakistan* 35°35N 73°30E 243 B5
Sazlika → *Bulgaria* 41°59N 25°50E 203 E9
Sbeïtla *Tunisia* 35°12N 9°7E 258 A1
Scaër *France* 48°2N 3°42W 172 D3
Scafell Pike *U.K.* 54°27N 3°14W 168 C4
Scald Law *U.K.* 55°50N 3°17W 121 B2
Scalea *Italy* 39°49N 15°47E 201 C8
Scalloway *U.K.* 60°9N 1°17W 167 A7
Scalpay *U.K.* 57°18N 6°0W 167 D3
Scalzi, Ponte degli *Venice, Italy* 142 b2
Scammon Bay *U.S.A.* 61°51N 165°35W 303 F6
Scandia *Canada* 50°20N 112°2W 296 C6
Scandiano *Italy* 44°36N 10°43E 198 D7
Scandicci *Italy* 43°45N 11°11E 199 E8
Scandinavia *Europe* 64°0N 12°0E 160 E15
Scansano *Italy* 42°41N 11°20E 199 F8
Scapa Flow *U.K.* 58°53N 3°3W 167 C5
Scappoose *U.S.A.* 45°45N 122°53W 306 E4
Scarámia, Capo *Italy* 36°47N 14°29E 201 F7
Scarba *U.K.* 56°11N 5°43W 167 E3
Scarborough *Ont., Canada* 43°44N 79°14W 141 A3
Scarborough *Trin. & Tob.* 11°11N 60°42W 323 s
Scarborough *N. Yorks., U.K.* 54°17N 0°24W 168 C7
Scarborough Bluffs *Canada* 43°42N 79°14W 141 A3
Scarborough Shoal *S. China Sea* 15°0N 117°50E 232 D1
Scargill *N.Z.* 42°56S 172°58E 285 C7
Scariff I. *Ireland* 51°44N 10°15W 166 E1
Scarp *U.K.* 58°1N 7°8W 167 C1
Scarpanto = Karpathos *Greece* 35°37N 27°10E 205 F9
Scarpe-Escaut ⌂ *France* 50°26N 3°23E 173 B10
Scarsdale *Australia* 37°41S 143°39E 282 D5
Sceaux *France* 48°46N 2°17E 134 B2
Scebeli = Shabeelle → *Somalia* 2°0N 44°0E 267 D5
Šćedro *Croatia* 43°6N 16°43E 199 E13
Scenery, Mt. *Saba* 17°38N 63°14W 322 a
Schaal See *Germany* 53°36N 10°55E 178 B6
Schaalsee ⌂ *Germany* 53°40N 10°59E 178 B6
Schaerbeek *Belgium* 50°52N 4°22E 116 A2
Schaffhausen *Switz.* 47°42N 8°39E 179 H4
Schagen *Neths.* 52°49N 4°48E 170 B4
Schaghticoke *U.S.A.* 42°54N 73°35W 313 D11
Schärding *Austria* 48°27N 13°27E 180 C6
Scharfenberg *Germany* 52°35N 13°15E 115 A2
Scharfenwiese = Ostrołęka *Poland* 53°4N 21°32E 185 E8
Scharhörn *Germany* 53°57N 8°24E 178 B4
Schässburg = Sighişoara *Romania* 46°12N 24°50E 183 D9
Scheessel *Germany* 53°10N 9°29E 178 B5
Schefferville *Canada* 54°48N 66°50W 299 B6
Scheibbs *Austria* 48°1N 15°9E 180 C8
Scheidt = Schelde → *Belgium* 51°15N 4°16E 170 C4
Schelde → *Belgium* 51°15N 4°16E 170 C4
Schell City *U.S.A.* 38°1N 94°7W 310 F2
Schell Creek Ra. *U.S.A.* 39°25N 114°40W 304 G6
Schellsburg *U.S.A.* 40°3N 78°39W 312 F6
Schemnitz = Banská Štiavnica *Slovak Rep.* 48°25N 18°55E 181 C11
Schenectady *U.S.A.* 42°49N 73°57W 313 D11
Schenevus *U.S.A.* 42°33N 74°50W 313 D10
Scherfede *Germany* 51°32N 9°2E 178 D5
Schesslitz *Germany* 49°58N 11°1E 179 F7
Schiavoni, Riva degli *Venice, Italy* 142 b3
Schiedam *Neths.* 51°55N 4°25E 170 C4
Schieratz = Sieradz *Poland* 51°37N 18°41E 185 G5
Schiermonnikoog *Neths.* 53°30N 6°15E 170 A6
Schiermonnikoog △ *Neths.* 53°30N 6°15E 170 A6
Schiller Woods *U.S.A.* 41°57N 87°51W 119 B1
Schiltigheim *France* 48°35N 7°45E 173 D14
Schinousa *Greece* 36°53N 25°31E 205 E7
Schio *Italy* 45°43N 11°21E 199 C8
Schiphol, Amsterdam ✈ (AMS) *Neths.* 52°18N 4°45E 112 B1
Schippenbeil = Sępopol *Poland* 54°16N 21°2E 184 D8
Schivelbein = Świdwin *Poland* 53°47N 15°49E 184 E2
Schlachtensee *Germany* 52°26N 13°13E 115 B2
Schladming *Austria* 47°23N 13°41E 180 D6
Schlanders = Silandro *Italy* 46°38N 10°46E 198 B7
Schlawa = Sława *Poland* 51°52N 16°2E 185 G3
Schlei → *Germany* 54°40N 10°0E 178 A5
Schleiden *Germany* 50°31N 6°28E 178 E2
Schleinitz Ra. *Papua N. G.* 3°0S 151°30E 286 B6
Schleiz *Germany* 50°35N 11°49E 178 E7
Schlesiersee = Sława *Poland* 51°52N 16°2E 185 G3
Schleswig *Germany* 54°31N 9°34E 178 A5
Schleswig-Holstein □ *Germany* 54°30N 9°30E 178 A5
Schlettstadt = Sélestat *France* 48°16N 7°26E 173 D14
Schlichtingsheim = Szlichtyngowa *Poland* 51°42N 16°15E 185 G3
Schlochau = Człuchów *Poland* 53°41N 17°22E 184 E4
Schloppe = Człopa *Poland* 53°6N 16°6E 185 E3
Schlossgarten *Germany* 52°31N 13°18E 115 A2
Schlüchtern *Germany* 50°20N 9°32E 179 E5
Schmalkalden *Germany* 50°44N 10°26E 178 E6
Schmargendorf *Germany* 52°28N 13°17E 115 B2
Schmölln *Germany* 50°54N 12°19E 178 E8
Schneeberg *Austria* 47°47N 15°48E 180 D8
Schneeberg *Sachsen, Germany* 50°35N 12°38E 178 E8
Schneidemühl = Piła *Poland* 53°10N 16°48E 185 E3
Schneider *U.S.A.* 41°13N 87°28W 311 C9
Schneverdingen *Germany* 53°7N 9°48E 178 B5
Schœlcher *Martinique* 14°36N 61°7W 322 j
Schofield Barracks *U.S.A.* 21°29N 158°7W 302 K13
Schoharie *U.S.A.* 42°40N 74°19W 313 D10
Schoharie Cr. → *U.S.A.* 42°57N 74°18W 313 D10
Schokland *Neths.* 52°38N 5°46E 170 B5
Scholls *U.S.A.* 45°24N 122°56W 306 E4
Schönau = Świerzawa *Poland* 51°1N 15°54E 185 G2
Schönberg *Mecklenburg-Vorpommern, Germany* 53°52N 10°56E 178 B6
Schönberg *Schleswig-Holstein, Germany* 54°23N 10°22E 178 A6
Schönblick *Germany* 52°27N 13°43E 115 B5
Schönbrunn *Austria* 48°10N 16°19E 142 A1
Schönbuch ⌂ *Germany* 48°35N 9°2E 179 G5
Schönebeck *Germany* 52°2N 11°44E 178 C7
Schöneberg *Germany* 52°28N 13°20E 115 B3
Schönefeld *Germany* 52°22N 13°33E 115 B4
Schöneiche *Germany* 52°28N 13°41E 115 B5
Schöngau *Germany* 47°47N 10°53E 179 H6
Schöningen *Germany* 52°8N 10°58E 178 C6
Schönlanke = Trzcianka *Poland* 53°3N 16°25E 185 E3
Schönstein = Šoštanj *Slovenia* 46°23N 15°4E 199 B12
Schönwalde *Germany* 52°37N 13°7E 115 A1
Schoolcraft *U.S.A.* 42°7N 85°38W 311 B11
Schopfheim *Germany* 47°38N 7°50E 179 H3
Schorndorf *Germany* 48°47N 9°32E 179 G5
Schortens *Germany* 53°31N 7°56E 178 B3
Schotschekloof *Cape Town, S. Africa* 118 b1
Schottegat *Curaçao* 12°7N 68°55W 322 g
Schouten I. *Australia* 42°20S 148°20E 281 G4
Schouten Is. = Supiori *Indonesia* 1°0S 136°0E 231 E9
Schouten Is. *Papua N. G.* 3°30S 144°30E 286 B3
Schouwen *Neths.* 51°43N 3°45E 170 C3
Schramberg *Germany* 48°13N 8°22E 179 G4
Schrankogel *Austria* 47°3N 11°7E 180 D4
Schreiber *Canada* 48°45N 87°20W 298 C2
Schrems *Austria* 48°47N 15°4E 180 C8
Schrobenhausen *Germany* 48°34N 11°16E 179 G7
Schroffenstein *Namibia* 27°11S 18°42E 270 C2
Schroon Lake *U.S.A.* 43°50N 73°46W 313 C11
Schröttersberg = Płock *Poland* 52°32N 19°40E 185 F6
Schruns *Austria* 47°5N 9°56E 180 D2
Schuchye = Shchūchīnsk *Kazakhstan* 52°56N 70°12E 217 B8
Schuler *Canada* 50°20N 110°6W 297 C6
Schulzendorf *Germany* 52°30N 13°16E 115 A2
Schumacher *Canada* 48°30N 81°16W 298 C3
Schurz *U.S.A.* 38°57N 118°49W 304 G4
Schuyler *U.S.A.* 41°27N 97°4W 308 E5
Schuylerville *U.S.A.* 43°6N 73°35W 313 C11
Schuylkill → *U.S.A.* 39°53N 75°12W 313 G9
Schuylkill Haven *U.S.A.* 40°37N 76°11W 313 F8
Schwabach *Germany* 49°19N 11°2E 179 F7
Schwaben □ *Germany* 48°15N 10°30E 179 G6
Schwabing *Germany* 48°10N 11°35E 131 B2
Schwäbisch-Fränkischer Wald ⌂ *Germany* 49°0N 9°30E 179 G5
Schwäbisch Gmünd *Germany* 48°48N 9°47E 179 G5
Schwäbisch Hall *Germany* 49°6N 9°44E 179 F5
Schwäbische Alb *Germany* 48°20N 9°30E 179 G5
Schwabmünchen *Germany* 48°10N 10°46E 179 G6
Schwalmstadt *Germany* 50°55N 9°10E 178 E5
Schwandorf *Germany* 49°20N 12°7E 179 F8
Schwanebeck *Germany* 52°37N 13°32E 115 A4
Schwanenwerder *Germany* 52°26N 13°10E 115 B2
Schwaner, Pegunungan *Indonesia* 1°0S 112°30E 235 C4
Schwanewede *Germany* 53°14N 8°35E 178 B4
Schwarmstedt *Germany* 52°39N 9°38E 178 C5
Schwarze Elster → *Germany* 51°48N 12°50E 178 D8
Schwarzenberg *Germany* 50°32N 12°47E 178 E8
Schwarzlackenau *Austria* 48°16N 16°22E 142 A2
Schwarzrand *Namibia* 25°37S 16°50E 270 C2
Schwarzwald *Germany* 48°30N 8°20E 179 G4
Schwatka Mts. *U.S.A.* 67°20N 156°30W 303 C8
Schwaz *Austria* 47°20N 11°44E 180 D4
Schwechat *Austria* 48°8N 16°28E 142 B2
Schwechat, Wien ✈ (VIE) *Austria* 48°7N 16°35E 142 B3
Schwedt *Germany* 53°3N 14°16E 178 B10
Schweidnitz = Świdnica *Poland* 50°50N 16°30E 185 H3
Schweinfurt *Germany* 50°3N 10°14E 179 E6
Schweiz = Switzerland ■ *Europe* 46°30N 8°0E 179 J4
Schweizer-Reneke *S. Africa* 27°11S 25°18E 270 C4
Schwenningen = Villingen-Schwenningen *Germany* 48°3N 8°26E 179 G4
Schwerin = Skwierzyna *Poland* 52°33N 15°30E 185 F2
Schwerin *Germany* 53°36N 11°22E 178 B7
Schweriner See *Germany* 53°43N 11°28E 178 B7
Schwetzingen *Germany* 49°23N 8°35E 179 F4
Schwiebus = Świebodzin *Poland* 52°15N 15°31E 185 F2
Schwyz *Switz.* 47°2N 8°39E 179 H4
Schwyz □ *Switz.* 47°2N 8°39E 179 H4
Sciacca *Italy* 37°31N 13°3E 200 E6
Scicli *Italy* 36°47N 14°42E 201 F7
Science and Industry, Museum of *U.S.A.* 41°47N 87°34W 119 C3
Sciliar-Catinaccio ⌂ *Italy* 46°28N 11°35E 199 B8
Scilla *Italy* 38°15N 15°43E 201 D8
Scilly, Isles of *U.K.* 49°56N 6°22W 169 H1
Ścinawa *Poland* 51°25N 16°26E 185 G3
Scione *Greece* 39°57N 23°36E 202 G7
Scioto → *U.S.A.* 38°44N 83°1W 311 D13
Scituate *U.S.A.* 42°12N 70°44W 313 D14
Scobey *U.S.A.* 48°47N 105°25W 304 B11
Scomenzera, Canale *Venice, Italy* 142 b1
Scone *N.S.W., Australia* 32°5S 150°52E 283 B9
Scone *Perth & Kinr., U.K.* 56°25N 3°24W 167 E5
Scopus, Mt. *West Bank* 31°48N 35°14E 123 B2
Scordia *Italy* 37°18N 14°51E 201 E7
Scoresby Sund *Greenland* 70°28N 21°46W 154 C8
Scoresbysund = Ittoqqortoormiit *Greenland* 70°20N 23°0W 154 C8
Scorniceşti *Romania* 44°34N 24°33E 183 F9
Scotia *Calif., U.S.A.* 40°29N 124°6W 304 F1
Scotia *N.Y., U.S.A.* 42°50N 73°58W 313 D11
Scotia Sea *Antarctica* 56°5S 56°0W 151 B18
Scotland *Canada* 43°1N 80°22W 312 C4
Scotland □ *U.K.* 57°0N 4°0W 167 E5
Scott *Antarctica* 77°50S 166°45E 151 D11
Scott, C. *Australia* 13°30S 129°49E 278 B4
Scott Circle *Washington, D.C., U.S.A.* 143 a1
Scott City *U.S.A.* 38°29N 100°54W 308 F3
Scott Glacier *Antarctica* 66°15S 100°5E 151 C8
Scott I. *Antarctica* 67°0S 179°0E 151 C11
Scott Is. *Canada* 50°48N 128°40W 296 C3
Scott L. *Canada* 59°55N 106°18W 297 B7
Scott Monument *Edinburgh, U.K.* 121 b2
Scott Reef *Australia* 14°0S 121°50E 278 B3
Scottburgh *S. Africa* 30°15S 30°47E 271 D5
Scottdale *Georgia, U.S.A.* 33°47N 84°16W 113 B3
Scottdale *Pa., U.S.A.* 40°6N 79°35W 312 F5
Scottish Borders □ *U.K.* 55°35N 2°50W 167 F6
Scottish Parliament *Edinburgh, U.K.* 55°57N 3°10W 121 B2
Scotts Head *N.S.W., Australia* 30°45S 153°0E 283 A10
Scotts Head *Dominica* 15°13N 61°23W 323 k
Scotts Head Village *Dominica* 15°12N 61°22W 323 k
Scotts Valley *U.S.A.* 37°3N 122°1W 306 H4
Scottsbluff *U.S.A.* 41°52N 103°40W 308 E2
Scottsboro *U.S.A.* 34°40N 86°2W 315 D11
Scottsburg *U.S.A.* 38°41N 85°47W 311 F11
Scottsdale *Tas., Australia* 41°9S 147°31E 281 G4
Scottsdale *Ariz., U.S.A.* 33°40N 111°53W 305 K8
Scottsville *Ky., U.S.A.* 36°45N 86°11W 308 G10
Scottsville *N.Y., U.S.A.* 43°2N 77°47W 312 C7
Scottville *U.S.A.* 43°58N 86°17W 308 D10
Scranton *U.S.A.* 41°25N 75°40W 313 E9
Screven *U.S.A.* 31°29N 82°1W 316 D7
Scrub I. *Anguilla* 18°19N 62°55W 322 a
Scugog, L. *Canada* 44°10N 78°55W 312 B6
Sculeni *Moldova* 47°20N 27°37E 183 C12
Scunthorpe *U.K.* 53°36N 0°39W 168 D7
Scuol Schuls *Switz.* 46°48N 10°17E 179 J6
Scutari = Shkodër *Albania* 42°4N 19°32E 202 D3
Scutari = Üsküdar *Turkey* 41°1N 29°0E 122 B2
Sea Is. *U.S.A.* 31°30N 81°7W 316 D9
Sea Lake *Australia* 35°28S 142°55E 282 C5
Sea Point *S. Africa* 34°55S 18°23E 118 A1
Seabra = Tarauacá *Brazil* 8°6S 70°48W 330 B3
Seabra *Brazil* 12°25S 41°46W 333 D3
Seabrook, L. *Australia* 30°55S 119°40E 279 F2
Seacliff *U.S.A.* 37°47N 122°28W 136 B2
Seaford *E. Sussex, U.K.* 50°47N 0°7E 169 G8
Seaford *Del., U.S.A.* 38°39N 75°37W 309 F16
Seaforth *N.S.W., Australia* 33°48S 151°15E 139 A2
Seaforth *Queens., Australia* 20°55S 148°57E 280 b
Seaforth *Ont., Canada* 43°35N 81°25W 312 C3
Seaforth, L. *U.K.* 57°52N 6°36W 167 D2
Seagate *U.S.A.* 40°34N 74°0W 132 C1
Seagraves *U.S.A.* 32°57N 102°34W 314 E3
Seaham *U.K.* 54°50N 1°20W 168 C6
Seal → *Canada* 59°4N 94°48W 297 B10
Seal I. *Anguilla* 18°16N 63°9W 322 a
Seal L. *Canada* 54°20N 61°30W 299 B7
Seale *U.S.A.* 32°18N 85°10W 316 C4
Sealy *U.S.A.* 29°47N 96°9W 314 G6
Seaman *U.S.A.* 38°57N 83°34W 311 F13
Searchlight *U.S.A.* 35°28N 114°55W 307 K12
Searcy *U.S.A.* 35°15N 91°44W 314 D9
Searles L. *U.S.A.* 35°44N 117°21W 307 K9
Sears Tower = Willis Tower *Chicago, U.S.A.* 119 c1
Seascale *U.K.* 54°24N 3°29W 168 C4
Seaside *Calif., U.S.A.* 36°37N 121°50W 306 J5
Seaside *Oreg., U.S.A.* 46°0N 123°56W 306 E3
Seaspray *Australia* 38°25S 147°15E 283 E7
Seattle *U.S.A.* 47°36N 122°19W 306 C4
Seattle-Tacoma Int. ✈ (SEA) *U.S.A.* 47°27N 122°18W 306 C4
Seaward Kaikoura Ra. *N.Z.* 42°10S 173°44E 285 C8
SeaWorld *U.S.A.* 28°24N 81°28W 113 C2
Seba *Indonesia* 10°29S 121°50E 278 B3
Sebago L. *U.S.A.* 43°52N 70°34W 313 C14
Sebago Lake *U.S.A.* 43°51N 70°34W 313 C14
Sebakung *Indonesia* 1°37S 116°25E 235 C5
Sebangau △ *Indonesia* 2°34S 113°38E 235 C4
Sebangka *Indonesia* 0°7N 104°36E 234 B2
Sebastian *U.S.A.* 27°49N 80°28W 317 G9
Sebastián Vizcaíno, B. *Mexico* 28°0N 114°30W 318 B2
Sebastopol = Sevastopol *Ukraine* 44°35N 33°30E 189 K7
Sebastopol *U.S.A.* 38°24N 122°49W 306 G4
Sebatik *Asia* 4°10N 117°45E 235 B5
Sebba *Burkina Faso* 13°35N 0°32E 263 C5
Sebderat *Eritrea* 15°26N 36°42E 257 D4
Sebdou *Algeria* 34°38N 1°19W 261 B4
Sébé → *Gabon* 1°2S 13°6E 264 C2
Sébékoro *Mali* 12°58N 9°0W 262 C3
Seben *Turkey* 40°24N 31°34E 212 B4
Šeberov *Czech Rep.* 50°0N 14°30E 135 B3
Sebeș *Romania* 45°58N 23°34E 183 E8
Sebeşului, Munţii *Romania* 45°36N 23°40E 183 E8

Sebewaing U.S.A. 43°44N 83°27W 309 D12
Sebezh Russia 56°14N 28°22E 188 D5
Sebezhsky △ Russia 56°16N 28°30E 188 D5
Sebha = Sabhā Libya 27°9N 14°29E 258 C2
Sébi Mali 15°50N 4°12W 262 B4
Şebinkarahisar Turkey 40°22N 38°28E 213 B8
Sebino, L. di = Iseo, L. d' Italy 45°43N 10°4E 198 C7
Sebiş Romania 46°23N 22°13E 182 D7
Seblat Indonesia 3°14S 101°38E 234 C2
Sebnitz Germany 50°58N 14°15E 178 E10
Sebou, Oued → Morocco 34°16N 6°40W 260 B3
Sebring Fla., U.S.A. 27°30N 81°27W 317 H8
Sebring Ohio, U.S.A. 40°55N 81°2W 312 F3
Sebringville Canada 43°24N 81°4W 312 C3
Sebta = Ceuta N. Afr. 35°52N 5°18W 260 A3
Sebuku Indonesia 3°30S 116°25E 235 C5
Sebuku, Teluk Indonesia 4°0N 118°10E 235 B5
Sečanj Serbia 45°25N 20°47E 182 E5
Secaucus U.S.A. 40°47N 74°3W 132 B1
Secchia → Italy 45°4N 11°0E 198 C8
Sechelt Canada 49°25N 123°42W 296 D4
Sechura Peru 5°39S 80°50W 330 B1
Sechura, Desierto de Peru 6°0S 80°30W 330 B1
Seclin France 50°33N 3°2E 173 B10
Second World War Memorial Washington, D.C., U.S.A. 143 b1
Secondigny France 46°37N 0°26W 172 F6
Sečovce Slovak Rep. 48°42N 21°40E 181 C14
Secretary I. N.Z. 45°15S 166°56E 285 F1
Secunderabad India 17°28N 78°30E 244 F4
Sécure → Bolivia 15°10S 64°52W 331 D5
Security U.S.A. 38°45N 104°45W 304 G11
Sedalia U.S.A. 38°42N 93°14W 310 F3
Sedam India 17°11N 77°17E 244 E3
Sedan S. Austral., Australia 34°34S 139°19E 282 C3
Sedan Ardennes, France 49°43N 4°57E 173 C11
Sedan Kans., U.S.A. 37°8N 96°11W 308 G5
Sedano Spain 42°43N 3°49W 194 C7
Sedaw Burma 22°19N 96°19E 241 D6
Sedbergh U.K. 54°20N 2°31W 168 C5
Seddinsee Germany 52°23N 13°41E 115 B5
Seddon N.Z. 41°40S 174°7E 285 B9
Seddonville N.Z. 41°33S 172°1E 285 B7
Sedé Boqér Israel 30°52N 34°47E 251 H5
Sedeh Fārs, Iran 30°45N 52°11E 247 D7
Sedeh Khorāsān, Iran 33°20N 59°14E 247 C8
Séderon France 44°12N 5°32E 175 D9
Sederot Israel 31°32N 34°37E 251 G5
Sédhiou Senegal 12°44N 15°30W 262 C1
Sedico Italy 46°8N 12°6E 199 B9
Sedlčany Czech Rep. 49°40N 14°25E 180 B7
Sedley Canada 50°10N 104°0W 297 C8
Sedom Israel 31°5N 35°20E 251 G6
Sedona U.S.A. 34°52N 111°46W 305 J8
Sedova, Pik Russia 73°29N 54°58E 214 B6
Sedrata Algeria 36°7N 7°31E 261 A6
Sedro-Woolley U.S.A. 48°30N 122°14W 306 B4
Šeduva Lithuania 55°45N 23°45E 184 C10
Sędziszów Poland 50°35N 20°4E 185 H7
Sędziszów Małapolski Poland 50°5N 21°45E 185 H8
Seebad Ahlbeck Germany 53°56N 14°10E 178 B10
Seeberg Germany 52°33N 13°41E 115 A5
Seeburg = Jeziorany Poland 53°58N 20°46E 184 E7
Seeburg Germany 52°30N 13°7E 115 A1
Seefeld Germany 52°37N 13°40E 115 A5
Seefeld in Tirol Austria 47°19N 11°13E 180 D4
Seegefeld Germany 52°33N 13°5E 115 A1
Seehausen Germany 52°54N 11°45E 178 C7
Seeheim Namibia 26°50S 17°45E 270 C2
Seeheim-Jugenheim Germany 49°49N 8°40E 179 F4
Seehof Germany 52°24N 13°17E 115 B2
Seeis Namibia 22°29S 17°39E 270 B2
Seekoei → S. Africa 30°18S 25°1E 270 D4
Seeley's Bay Canada 44°29N 76°14W 313 B8
Seelow Germany 52°32N 14°23E 178 C10
Sées France 48°38N 0°10E 172 D7
Seesen Germany 51°54N 10°10E 178 D6
Seevetal Germany 53°26N 10°1E 178 B6
Seewinkel = Neusiedler See-Seewinkel △ Austria 47°50N 16°45E 181 D9
Şefaatli Turkey 39°30N 34°45E 212 C6
Seferihisar Turkey 38°10N 26°50E 205 C8
Séféto Mali 14°8N 9°49W 262 C3
Sefophe Botswana 22°11S 27°58E 271 B4
Sefrou Morocco 33°52N 4°52W 260 B4
Sefton N.Z. 43°15S 172°41E 285 D7
Sefuri-San Japan 33°28N 130°18E 222 D2
Sefwi Bekwai Ghana 6°10N 2°25W 262 D4
Seg-ozero Russia 63°20N 33°46E 186 B5
Segag Ethiopia 7°39N 42°50E 267 C5
Segamat Malaysia 2°30N 102°50E 237 L4
Şegarcea Romania 44°6N 23°43E 183 F8
Ségbana Benin 10°55N 3°42E 263 C5
Segbwema S. Leone 8°0N 11°0W 262 D2
Segeltorp Sweden 59°16N 17°56E 139 B1
Segersta Sweden 61°16N 16°39E 162 C10
Segesta Italy 37°56N 12°50E 200 E5
Seget Indonesia 1°24S 130°58E 231 E8
Segewold = Sigulda Latvia 57°10N 24°55E 188 D3
Segezha Russia 63°44N 34°19E 186 B5
Segueur, O. → Algeria 32°14N 1°48E 261 B5
Seghe Solomon Is. 8°32S 157°54E 287 M9
Segmon Sweden 59°17N 13°3E 162 E7
Segonzac France 45°36N 0°14W 174 C3
Segorbe Spain 39°50N 0°30W 196 F4
Ségou Mali 13°30N 6°16W 262 C3
Ségou □ Mali 14°0N 6°0W 262 C3
Segovia = Coco → Cent. Amer. 15°0N 83°8W 320 D3
Segovia Colombia 7°7N 74°42W 328 B3
Segovia Spain 40°57N 4°10W 194 E6
Segovia □ Spain 40°55N 4°10W 194 E6
Segrate Italy 45°29N 9°17E 128 B2
Segré France 47°40N 0°52W 172 E6
Segre → Spain 41°40N 0°43E 196 D5
Seguam I. U.S.A. 52°19N 172°30W 303 K4
Seguam Pass U.S.A. 52°0N 172°30W 303 K4
Séguédine Niger 20°9N 12°55E 259 D2
Séguéla Ivory C. 7°55N 6°40W 262 D3
Séguélon Ivory C. 9°13N 7°7W 262 D3
Séguénéga Burkina Faso 13°25N 1°58W 263 C4
Seguin U.S.A. 29°34N 97°58W 314 G6
Segundo → Argentina 30°53S 62°44W 334 C3
Segura → Spain 38°3N 0°44W 197 G4
Segura, Sierra de Spain 38°5N 2°45W 197 G2
Seguro Italy 45°28N 9°3E 128 B1
Seh Konj, Kūh-e Iran 30°6N 57°30E 247 D8
Seh Qal'eh Iran 33°40N 58°24E 247 C8
Sehitwa Botswana 20°30S 22°30E 270 B3
Sehlabathebe △ Lesotho 29°53S 29°7E 271 C4
Sehore India 23°10N 77°5E 242 H7
Sehulea Papua N. G. 9°58S 151°10E 286 E6
Sehwan Pakistan 26°28N 67°53E 242 F2
Seia Portugal 40°25N 7°42W 194 E3
Şeica Mare Romania 46°1N 24°7E 183 D9
Seikan Tunnel Japan 41°28N 140°10E 220 D10
Seikpyu Burma 20°54N 94°48E 241 E5
Seil U.K. 56°18N 5°38W 167 E3
Seiland Norway 70°25N 23°15E 160 A20
Seilhac France 45°22N 1°43E 174 C5
Seiling U.S.A. 36°9N 98°56W 314 C5
Seille → Moselle, France 49°7N 6°11E 173 C13
Seille → Saône-et-Loire, France 46°31N 4°57E 173 F11
Sein, Î. de France 48°2N 4°52W 172 D2
Seinäjoki Finland 62°40N 22°51E 160 E20
Seine → France 49°26N 0°26E 172 C7
Seine, B. de la France 49°40N 0°40W 172 C6
Seine-et-Marne □ France 48°45N 3°0E 173 D10
Seine-Inférieure = Seine-Maritime □ France 49°40N 1°0E 172 C7
Seine-Maritime □ France 49°40N 1°0E 172 C7
Seine-St-Denis □ France 48°58N 2°24E 173 D9
Seini Romania 47°44N 23°21E 183 C8
Seirijai Lithuania 54°14N 23°49E 184 D10
Seis de Septiembre = Moron Argentina 34°39S 58°37W 334 C4
Seistan = Sīstān Asia 30°50N 61°0E 247 D9
Seistan, Daryācheh-ye = Sīstān, Daryācheh-ye Iran 31°0N 61°0E 247 D9
Seitler = Nyzhnohirskyy Ukraine 45°27N 34°38E 189 K8
Seitseminen △ Finland 61°55N 23°25E 160 F20
Seixal Madeira 32°48N 17°7W 153 c
Seixal Lisboa, Portugal 38°38N 9°5W 126 B2
Sejerø Denmark 55°54N 11°9E 163 J5
Sejerø Bugt Denmark 55°53N 11°15E 163 J5
Sejny Poland 54°6N 23°21E 184 D10
Seka Ethiopia 8°10N 36°52E 257 F4
Sekadau Indonesia 0°1N 110°54E 235 C4
Sekayu Indonesia 2°51S 103°51E 234 C2
Seke Tanzania 3°20S 33°31E 268 C3
Seke-Banza Dem. Rep. of the Congo 5°20S 13°16E 265 D2
Sekenke Tanzania 4°18S 34°11E 268 C3
Sekhira Tunisia 34°20N 10°5E 258 B2
Seki Japan 35°29N 136°55E 223 B8
Seki Turkey 36°48N 29°33E 205 E11
Sekigahara Japan 35°22N 136°28E 223 B8
Sekondi-Takoradi Ghana 4°58N 1°45W 262 E4
Sekota Ethiopia 12°40N 39°2E 257 E4
Sekseüil Kazakhstan 47°5N 61°9E 216 C6
Seksna Russia 59°13N 38°30E 188 C10
Sekudai Malaysia 1°32N 103°39E 237 d
Sekuma Botswana 24°36S 23°50E 270 B3
Selah U.S.A. 46°39N 120°32W 304 C3
Selama Malaysia 5°12N 100°42E 237 K3
Selangor □ Malaysia 3°10N 101°30E 237 L3
Selārgius Italy 39°16N 9°10E 200 C2
Selaru Indonesia 8°9S 131°0E 231 F8
Selatan, Selat Malaysia 5°15N 100°20E 237 c
Selatpanjang Indonesia 1°0N 102°43E 234 B2
Selawik U.S.A. 66°36N 160°0W 303 C8
Selawik L. U.S.A. 66°30N 160°45W 303 C7
Selawik Nat. Wildlife Refuge ⌓ U.S.A. 66°35N 159°10W 303 C8
Selb Germany 50°10N 12°7E 179 E8
Selbusjøen Norway 63°15N 10°50E 164 A7
Selby Gauteng, S. Africa 26°12S 28°2E 123 B2
Selby N. Yorks., U.K. 53°47N 1°5W 168 D6
Selby S. Dak., U.S.A. 45°31N 100°2W 308 C3
Selca Croatia 43°20N 16°50E 199 E13
Selçuk Turkey 37°56N 27°22E 205 D9
Selden U.S.A. 39°33N 100°34W 308 F3
Seldovia U.S.A. 59°26N 151°43W 303 G10
Sele → Italy 40°29N 14°56E 201 B7
Selebi-Phikwe Botswana 21°58S 27°48E 271 B4
Selemdzha → Russia 51°42N 128°53E 215 D13
Selendi Manisa, Turkey 38°43N 28°50E 205 C10
Selendi Manisa, Turkey 38°46N 27°53E 205 C9
Selenga = Selenge Mörön → Asia 52°16N 106°16E 218 A10
Selenge Dem. Rep. of the Congo 1°58S 18°11E 264 C3
Selenge Mörön → Asia 52°16N 106°16E 218 A10
Selenicë Albania 40°33N 19°39E 202 F3
Selenter See Germany 54°18N 10°26E 178 A6
Sélestat France 48°16N 7°26E 173 D14
Seletan, Tanjung Indonesia 4°10S 114°40E 235 C4
Seletar Singapore 1°22N 103°53E 138 A3
Seletar, Pulau Singapore 1°26N 103°51E 138 A3
Seletar Hills Singapore 1°23N 103°52E 138 A3
Seletar Res. Singapore 1°24N 103°48E 138 A2
Selevac Serbia 44°28N 20°52E 202 B4
Selfoss Iceland 63°56N 21°0W 155 D6
Selhurst U.K. 51°23N 0°5W 125 B3
Sélibabi Mauritania 15°10N 12°15W 262 B2
Seliger, Ozero Russia 57°15N 33°0E 188 D7
Seligman U.S.A. 35°20N 112°53W 305 J7
Şelim Turkey 40°30N 42°46E 213 B10
Selîma Sudan 21°22N 29°19E 256 C2
Selimiye Turkey 37°24N 27°40E 205 D9
Selinda Spillway → Botswana 18°35S 23°10E 270 A3
Sélingué, L. de Mali 11°37N 8°14W 262 C3
Selinsgrove U.S.A. 40°48N 76°52W 312 F8
Selizharovo Russia 56°51N 33°27E 188 D7
Selje Norway 62°3N 5°22E 164 B2
Seljord Norway 59°30N 8°40E 164 E5
Selkirk Man., Canada 50°10N 96°55W 297 C9
Selkirk Ont., Canada 42°49N 79°56W 312 D5
Selkirk Borders, U.K. 55°33N 2°50W 167 F6
Selkirk I. = Horse I. Canada 53°20N 99°6W 297 C9
Selkirk Mts. Canada 51°15N 117°40W 294 G8
Sellafield U.K. 54°25N 3°29W 168 C4
Sellama Sudan 12°51N 29°46E 257 E2
Sellia Greece 35°12N 24°23E 207 E5
Sellières France 46°50N 5°32E 173 F12
Sells U.S.A. 31°55N 111°53W 305 L8
Sellye Hungary 45°52N 17°51E 182 E2
Selma Ala., U.S.A. 32°25N 87°1W 315 E11
Selma Calif., U.S.A. 36°34N 119°37W 306 J7
Selma N.C., U.S.A. 35°32N 78°17W 315 D15
Selmer U.S.A. 35°10N 88°36W 315 D10
Selong Indonesia 8°39S 116°32E 235 D5
Selongey France 47°36N 5°11E 173 E12
Selouane Morocco 35°7N 2°57W 261 A4
Selous ⌓ Tanzania 8°37S 37°42E 269 D4
Selowandoma Falls Zimbabwe 21°15S 31°50E 269 G3
Selpele Indonesia 0°1S 130°5E 231 E8
Selsey Bill U.K. 50°43N 0°47W 169 G7
Seltso Russia 53°22N 34°4E 188 F8
Seltz France 48°54N 8°4E 173 D15
Selu Indonesia 7°32S 130°55E 231 F8
Sélune → France 48°38N 1°22W 172 D5
Selva = La Selva del Camp Spain 41°13N 1°8E 196 D6
Selva Argentina 29°50S 62°0W 334 B3
Selva Mallorca, Spain 39°46N 2°54E 206 B9
Selva Lancandona = Montes Azules ⌓ Mexico 16°21N 91°3W 319 D6
Selvagens, Ilhas Madeira 30°5N 15°55W 260 B1
Selvas Brazil 6°30S 67°0W 330 B4
Selwyn L. Canada 60°0N 104°30W 297 B8
Selwyn Mts. Canada 63°0N 130°0W 294 E5
Selwyn Passage Vanuatu 16°3S 168°12E 287 F6
Selwyn Ra. Australia 21°10S 140°0E 280 C3
Selyatyn Ukraine 47°50N 25°12E 183 C10
Sem Norway 59°14N 10°17E 164 E7
Sem Kolodezey = Lenine Ukraine 45°17N 35°46E 189 K8
Semadrek = Samothraki Greece 40°28N 25°28E 203 F9
Seman → Albania 40°47N 19°30E 202 F3
Semangka, Teluk Indonesia 5°36S 104°42E 234 D2
Semarang Indonesia 7°0S 110°26E 235 D4
Semarapura = Klungkung Indonesia 8°32S 115°24E 231 K18
Sematan Malaysia 1°48N 109°46E 235 B3
Semayang, Danau Indonesia 0°14S 116°28E 235 C5
Sembabule Uganda 0°4S 31°25E 268 C3
Sembawang Singapore 1°27N 103°50E 138 A2
Sembé Congo 1°39N 14°36E 264 B2
Sembilang △ Indonesia 1°59S 104°34E 234 C2
Sembung Indonesia 8°28S 115°11E 231 J18
Şemdinli Turkey 37°18N 44°35E 213 D11
Sémé Senegal 15°4N 13°41W 262 B2
Semeih Sudan 12°43N 30°53E 257 E3
Semendua Dem. Rep. of the Congo 3°10S 18°6E 264 C3
Semenic-Cheile Caraşului △ Romania 45°8N 22°5E 182 E7
Semenivka Chernihiv, Ukraine 52°8N 32°36E 189 F7
Semenivka Kremenchuk, Ukraine 49°37N 33°10E 189 H7
Semenov Russia 56°43N 44°30E 190 B7
Semenuv Indonesia 8°4S 112°55E 235 D4
Semey Kazakhstan 50°30N 80°10E 217 B10
Semichi Is. U.S.A. 52°42N 174°0E 303 K1
Semikarakorskiy Russia 47°31N 40°48E 191 G5
Semiluki Russia 51°41N 39°2E 189 G10
Seminoe Res. U.S.A. 42°9N 106°55W 304 E10
Seminole Fla., U.S.A. 27°50N 82°47W 317 H7
Seminole Okla., U.S.A. 35°14N 96°41W 314 D6
Seminole Tex., U.S.A. 32°43N 102°39W 314 E3
Seminole, L. U.S.A. 30°43N 84°52W 316 E5
Seminole Draw → U.S.A. 32°27N 102°20W 314 E3
Semipalatinsk = Semey Kazakhstan 50°30N 80°10E 217 B10
Semirara I. Phil. 12°4N 121°23E 232 E3
Semirara Is. Phil. 12°0N 121°20E 233 F3
Semisopochnoi I. U.S.A. 51°55N 179°36E 303 L2
Semitau Indonesia 0°29N 111°57E 235 B4
Semliki △ Uganda 0°49N 30°4E 268 B3
Semlin = Zemun Serbia 44°51N 20°25E 202 B4
Semmelweis Museum Budapest, Hungary 117 c2
Semmering P. Austria 47°41N 15°45E 180 D8
Semnān Iran 35°40N 53°23E 247 C7
Semnān □ Iran 36°0N 54°0E 247 C7
Sempang Mengayou, Tanjong Malaysia 7°0N 116°40E 235 A5
Semporna Malaysia 4°30N 118°33E 235 B5
Semuda Indonesia 2°51S 112°58E 235 C4
Semur-en-Auxois France 47°30N 4°20E 173 E11
Semyonovka = Arsenev Russia 44°10N 133°15E 220 B6
Semyonovskoye = Bereznik Russia 62°51N 42°40E 186 B7
Sen → Cambodia 12°32N 104°28E 236 F5
Sena Bolivia 11°32S 67°11W 330 C4
Senā Iran 28°27N 51°36E 247 D6
Sena Mozam. 17°25S 35°0E 269 F4
Sena → Bolivia 11°31S 67°11W 330 C4
Sena Madureira Brazil 9°5S 68°45W 330 B4
Senachwine L. U.S.A. 41°10N 89°18W 310 C7
Senador José Porfírio Brazil 2°35S 51°55W 329 D7
Senador Pompeu Brazil 5°40S 39°20W 332 C4
Senago Italy 45°34N 9°7E 128 A1
Senaja Malaysia 6°45N 117°3E 235 A5
Senaki Georgia 42°15N 42°1E 191 J6
Senang, Pulau Singapore 1°11N 103°52E 237 d
Senanga Zambia 16°7S 23°16E 265 F4
Senatobia U.S.A. 34°37N 89°58W 315 D10
Senayan Stadium = Gelora Bung Karno Stadium Jakarta, Indonesia 6°13S 106°47E 122 B1
Sencelles Spain 39°39N 2°54E 206 B3
Sendafa Ethiopia 9°11N 39°3E 257 F4
Sendai = Satsuma-Sendai Japan 31°50N 130°20E 222 F2
Sendai Japan 38°15N 140°53E 220 E10
Sendai-Wan Japan 38°15N 141°0E 220 E10
Senden Bayern, Germany 48°19N 10°4E 179 G6
Senden Nordrhein-Westfalen, Germany 51°52N 7°22E 178 D3
Sendhwa India 21°41N 75°6E 242 J6
Sendling Germany 48°7N 11°31E 131 B2
Sendlinger Tor Platz Munich, Germany 131 c1
Sendurjana India 21°32N 78°17E 244 D4
Sene → Ghana 7°30N 0°33W 263 D4
Senec Slovak Rep. 48°12N 17°23E 181 C10
Seneca Ill., U.S.A. 41°19N 88°37W 311 C8
Seneca S.C., U.S.A. 34°41N 82°57W 315 D13
Seneca Falls U.S.A. 42°55N 76°48W 313 D8
Seneca L. U.S.A. 42°40N 76°54W 312 D8
Senecaville L. U.S.A. 39°55N 81°25W 312 G3
Senegal ■ W. Afr. 14°30N 14°30W 262 C2
Sénégal → W. Afr. 15°48N 16°32W 262 B1
Senegambia Africa 12°45N 12°0W 254 E2
Senegambia & Niger = Mali ■ Africa 17°0N 3°0W 262 B4
Senekal S. Africa 28°20S 27°36E 271 C4
Senftenberg Germany 51°32N 14°0E 178 D10
Senga Hill Zambia 9°19S 31°11E 269 D3
Senge Khambab = Indus → Pakistan 24°20N 67°47E 242 G2
Sengerema Tanzania 2°42S 32°35E 268 C3
Sengeti Indonesia 1°28S 103°31E 234 C2
Senggigi Indonesia 8°29S 116°2E 231 J19
Sengiley Russia 53°58N 48°46E 190 D9
Sengua → Zimbabwe 17°7S 28°5E 269 F2
Senguerr → Argentina 45°35S 68°50W 336 C3
Senhor-do-Bonfim Brazil 10°30S 40°10W 332 D3
Senica Slovak Rep. 48°41N 17°25E 181 C10
Senigállia Italy 43°43N 13°13E 199 E10
Seniku Burma 25°32N 97°48E 241 C6
Senio → Italy 44°35N 12°15E 199 D9
Senirkent Turkey 38°6N 30°33E 205 C12
Senise Italy 40°9N 16°17E 201 B9
Senj Croatia 45°0N 14°58E 199 D11
Senja Norway 69°25N 17°30E 160 B17
Senju Japan 35°44N 139°48E 140 A3
Senkaku-Shotō E. China Sea 25°45N 123°30E 221 M1
Senkang Singapore 1°23N 103°53E 138 A3
Senlis France 49°13N 2°35E 173 C9
Senmonorom Cambodia 12°27N 107°12E 236 F6
Sennâr Sudan 13°30N 33°35E 257 E3
Sennâr □ Sudan 13°0N 34°0E 257 E3
Senneterre Canada 48°25N 77°15W 298 C4
Senno Belarus 54°45N 29°43E 188 E5
Sènnori Italy 40°47N 8°35E 200 B1
Seno Laos 16°35N 104°50E 236 D5
Senoia U.S.A. 33°18N 84°33W 316 B5
Senonches France 48°34N 1°2E 172 D8
Senorbì Italy 39°32N 9°8E 200 C2
Senožeče Slovenia 45°43N 14°3E 199 C11
Senqu = Orange → S. Africa 28°41S 16°28E 270 C2
Senriyama Japan 34°47N 135°30E 133 A2
Sens France 48°11N 3°15E 173 D10
Senta Serbia 45°55N 20°3E 182 E5
Sentarum, Danau Indonesia 0°51N 112°6E 235 B4
Sentery = Lubao Dem. Rep. of the Congo 5°17S 25°42E 265 D5
Sentinel U.S.A. 32°52N 113°13W 305 K7
Šentjur Slovenia 46°14N 15°24E 199 B12
Sentosa Singapore 1°16N 103°50E 138 B2
Sentry Hill St.-Maarten 18°2N 63°4W 322 a
Senwabarana S. Africa 23°17S 29°7E 271 B4
Senya Beraku Ghana 5°28N 0°31W 263 D4
Seo de Urgel = La Seu d'Urgell Spain 42°22N 1°23E 196 C6
Seobinggo S. Korea 37°31N 126°58E 137 B1
Seocho S. Korea 37°28N 127°0E 137 C1
Seodaemun S. Korea 37°34N 126°55E 137 B1
Seogwipo S. Korea 33°13N 126°34E 224 a
Seohara India 29°15N 78°33E 243 E8
Seokgeuram Grotto S. Korea 35°46N 129°20E 224 E4
Seokkwan S. Korea 37°35N 127°2E 137 B2
Seonath → India 21°44N 82°28E 243 J10
Seondha India 26°9N 78°48E 243 F8
Seongbuk S. Korea 37°35N 127°0E 137 B2
Seongdong S. Korea 37°33N 127°3E 137 B2
Seongmodo S. Korea 37°41N 126°19E 224 D3
Seongnam S. Korea 37°26N 127°8E 224 D3
Seongsu S. Korea 37°32N 127°2E 137 B2
Seoni India 22°5N 79°30E 243 H8
Seoni Malwa India 22°27N 77°28E 242 H8
Seonsan S. Korea 36°14N 128°17E 224 D4
Seonyudo S. Korea 35°49N 126°24E 224 E3
Seoraksan S. Korea 38°7N 128°27E 224 C4
Seoraksan △ S. Korea 38°10N 128°25E 224 C4
Seoriuarayan India 21°45N 82°34E 244 D6
Seosan S. Korea 36°47N 126°27E 224 D3
Seoul S. Korea 37°31N 126°58E 137 B1
Seoul Nat. Univ. S. Korea 37°28N 126°57E 137 C1
Seoul Tower S. Korea 37°32N 126°59E 137 B1
Separation Pt. N.Z. 40°47S 172°59E 285 A7
Sepasu Indonesia 0°43N 117°34E 235 B5
Sepatini → Brazil 7°36S 65°24W 330 B4
Sepi Solomon Is. 8°31S 159°52E 287 M10
Sepīdān Iran 30°20N 52°5E 247 D7
Sepik → Papua N. G. 3°49S 144°30E 286 B3
Sepo-ri N. Korea 38°57N 127°25E 224 C3
Sepolia Greece 38°1N 23°42E 112 A2
Sępólno Krajeńskie Poland 53°26N 17°30E 184 E4
Sepone Laos 16°45N 106°13E 236 D6
Sepopol Poland 54°16N 21°2E 184 D8
Seppa India 27°16N 92°54E 241 B4
Sept-Îles Canada 50°13N 66°22W 299 B6
Septemvri Bulgaria 42°13N 24°6E 203 D8
Sepúlveda Spain 41°18N 3°45W 194 D7
Sepulveda Dam Rec. Area ⌓ U.S.A. 34°10N 118°28W 126 A2
Sequeros Spain 40°31N 6°2W 194 E4
Sequim U.S.A. 48°5N 123°6W 306 B3
Sequoia △ U.S.A. 36°30N 118°30W 306 J8
Serafimovich Russia 49°36N 42°43E 190 F6
Seraing Belgium 50°35N 5°32E 170 D5
Serakhis → Cyprus 35°13N 32°55E 207 E8
Seram Indonesia 3°10S 129°0E 231 E7
Seram Sea Indonesia 2°30S 128°30E 231 E7
Serampore = Shrirampur India 22°44N 88°21E 243 H13
Seranantsara Madag. 18°30S 49°55E 272 B2
Serang Indonesia 6°8S 106°10E 234 D3
Serangoon Singapore 1°23N 103°54E 138 A3
Serangoon, Pulau Singapore 1°23N 103°55E 138 A3
Serangoon, Sungei → Singapore 1°23N 103°55E 138 A3
Serangoon Harbour Singapore 1°23N 103°57E 138 A3
Serasan Indonesia 2°29N 109°4E 235 B3
Serasan, Selat Indonesia 2°20N 109°0E 235 B3
Seravezza Italy 43°59N 10°13E 198 E7
Seraya, Pulau Singapore 1°16N 103°43E 138 B2
Serbâl, G. Egypt 28°40N 33°39E 251 K4
Şerbettar Turkey 41°27N 26°46E 203 E10
Serbia ■ Europe 43°20N 20°0E 202 C4
Şercaia Romania 45°49N 25°9E 183 E10
Serchhip India 23°18N 92°51E 241 D4
Serdar Turkmenistan 39°4N 56°23E 247 B8
Serdo Ethiopia 11°56N 41°14E 257 E5
Serdobol = Sortavala Russia 61°42N 30°41E 188 B6
Serdobsk Russia 52°28N 44°10E 190 D7
Serebryanka → Russia 55°47N 37°44E 129 B3
Serebryansk Kazakhstan 49°41N 83°17E 217 C10
Sereď Slovak Rep. 48°17N 17°44E 181 C10
Sereda = Furmanov Russia 57°10N 41°9E 190 B5
Seredka Russia 58°12N 28°10E 188 C5
Serednye Ukraine 48°32N 22°30E 182 B7
Şereflikoçhisar Turkey 38°56N 33°32E 212 C5
Seregno Italy 45°39N 9°12E 198 C6
Seremban Malaysia 2°43N 101°53E 237 L3
Serengeti △ Tanzania 2°11S 35°0E 268 C3
Serengeti Plain Tanzania 2°40S 35°0E 268 C4
Serenje Zambia 13°14S 30°15E 269 E3
Sereth = Siret → Romania 45°24N 28°1E 183 E12
Sergach Russia 55°30N 45°30E 190 C7
Sergeevka Kazakhstan 53°52N 67°24E 217 B7
Sergen Turkey 41°41N 27°42E 203 E11
Sergeya Kirova, Ostrova Russia 77°30N 89°0E 215 B10
Sergino Russia 62°25N 65°12E 214 C7
Sergiopol = Ayakōz Kazakhstan 48°10N 80°10E 217 C10
Sergipe □ Brazil 10°30S 37°30W 332 D4
Sergiyev Posad Russia 56°20N 38°10E 188 D10
Sergo = Stakhanov Ukraine 48°35N 38°40E 189 H10
Serhetabat Turkmenistan 35°20N 62°18E 247 C9
Seria Brunei 4°37N 114°23E 235 B4
Serian Malaysia 1°10N 110°31E 235 B4
Seriate Italy 45°41N 9°43E 198 C6
Seribu △ Indonesia 5°32S 106°33E 234 D3
Seribudolok Indonesia 2°55N 98°37E 234 B1
Sericho Kenya 1°5N 39°5E 268 B4
Sérifontaine France 49°20N 1°45E 173 C8
Serifos Greece 37°9N 24°30E 204 D6
Sérignan France 43°17N 3°17E 174 E7
Sérigny → Canada 56°47N 66°0W 299 A6
Serik Turkey 36°55N 31°7E 250 B2
Seringapatam Reef Australia 13°38S 122°5E 278 B3
Serinhisar Turkey 37°36N 29°18E 205 D11
Seririt Indonesia 8°12S 114°56E 231 J17
Serishābād Iran 35°14N 47°36E 213 E12
Serkout Algeria 23°56N 6°47E 261 D6
Sermaize-les-Bains France 48°47N 4°54E 173 D11
Sermata Indonesia 8°15S 128°50E 231 F7
Sermersooq □ Greenland 68°0N 40°0W 154 D7
Sermersuaq Greenland 79°30N 62°0W 154 B4
Sèrmide Italy 45°0N 11°18E 199 D8
Sernovodsk Russia 53°58N 51°16E 190 D10
Sernur Russia 56°52N 49°2E 190 B9
Serock Poland 52°31N 21°4E 185 F8
Serove Colorado Aruba 12°25N 69°52W 322 f
Serón Spain 37°20N 2°29W 197 H2
Serós Spain 41°27N 0°24E 196 D5
Serouenout Algeria 24°18N 7°25E 261 D6
Serov Russia 59°29N 60°35E 186 C11
Serowe Botswana 22°25S 26°43E 270 B4
Serpa Portugal 37°57N 7°38W 195 H3
Serpeddi, Pta. Italy 39°22N 9°18E 200 C2
Serpentara Italy 39°8N 9°36E 200 C2
Serpentine Lakes Australia 28°30S 129°10E 279 E4
Serpent's Mouth = Sierpe, Bocas de la Venezuela 10°0N 61°30W 329 G9
Serpis → Spain 38°59N 0°9W 197 G4
Serpneve Ukraine 46°18N 29°1E 183 D14
Serpukhov Russia 54°55N 37°28E 188 E9
Serra Brazil 20°7S 40°18W 333 F3
Serra da Bocaina △ Brazil 23°0S 44°40W 333 F3
Serra da Canastra △ Brazil 20°3S 46°50W 333 F2
Serra da Capivara △ Brazil 8°42S 42°15W 332 C3
Serra da Estrela △ Portugal 40°27N 7°33W 194 E3
Serra das Confusões △ Brazil 8°50S 43°50W 332 C3
Serra de Mesa, Barragem de Brazil 14°30S 48°30W 333 D2
Serra do Cipó △ Brazil 19°14S 43°29W 333 E3
Serra do Divisor △ Brazil 8°3S 73°29W 330 B3
Serra do Navio Brazil 0°59N 52°3W 329 C7
Serra do Salitre Brazil 19°6S 46°41W 333 E2
Serra dos Orgãos △ Brazil 22°25S 43°8W 333 F3
Serra San Bruno Italy 38°35N 16°20E 201 D9
Serra Talhada Brazil 7°59S 38°18W 332 C4
Serradilla Spain 39°50N 6°9W 194 F4
Serramanna Italy 39°25N 8°55E 200 C1
Serramonte U.S.A. 37°39N 122°28W 136 C2
Serranía de la Neblina △ Venezuela 1°5N 65°51W 328 C4
Serranía San Luís △ Paraguay 22°35S 57°22W 334 A4
Serranía San Rafael △ Paraguay 26°30S 56°0W 335 B4
Serranilla Bank Caribbean 15°50N 80°0W 320 C4
Serranópolis Brazil 18°16S 52°0W 331 D7
Serras d'Aire e Candeeiros ⌓ Portugal 39°31N 8°48W 195 F2
Serrat, C. Tunisia 37°14N 9°10E 261 A6
Serravalle Scrivia Italy 44°43N 8°51E 198 D5
Serre-Ponçon, L. de France 44°22N 6°20E 175 D10
Serrejón Spain 39°49N 5°48W 194 F5
Serres Hautes-Alpes, France 44°26N 5°43E 175 D9
Serres Greece 41°5N 23°31E 202 E7
Serrezuela Argentina 30°40S 65°20W 334 C2
Serrinha Brazil 11°39S 39°0W 332 D4
Serrita Brazil 7°56S 39°19W 332 C4
Sersale Italy 39°1N 16°43E 201 C9
Sertã Portugal 39°48N 8°6W 194 F2
Sertânia Brazil 8°5S 37°20W 332 C4
Sertanópolis Brazil 23°4S 51°2W 335 A5
Sêrtar China 32°20N 100°41E 228 A3
Serua Indonesia 6°18S 130°1E 231 F8
Serui Indonesia 1°53S 136°10E 231 E9
Serule Botswana 21°57S 27°20E 270 B4
Serutu Indonesia 1°42S 108°45E 235 C3
Servia Greece 40°11N 22°0E 202 F6
Serzedelo Portugal 41°24N 8°14W 194 D2
Ses Salines Spain 39°21N 3°3E 206 B4
Sesayap → Indonesia 3°36N 117°15E 235 B5
Sese Is. Uganda 0°20S 32°20E 268 C3
Seseko-shima Japan 26°39N 127°52E 288 a
Sesepe Indonesia 1°30S 127°59E 231 E7
Sesfontein Namibia 19°7S 13°39E 270 A1
Sesheke Zambia 17°29S 24°13E 270 A3
Sésia → Italy 45°5N 8°37E 198 C5
Sesimbra Portugal 38°28N 9°6W 195 G1
S'Espalmador Spain 38°47N 1°26E 206 D1
S'Espardell Spain 38°48N 1°29E 206 D1
Sessa Angola 13°56S 20°38E 265 E4
Sessa Aurunca Italy 41°14N 13°56E 200 A6
Sesser U.S.A. 38°5N 89°1W 310 F7
S'Estanyol Spain 39°22N 2°54E 206 B3
Sestao Spain 43°18N 3°0W 196 B2
Sesto Calende Italy 45°44N 8°37E 198 C5
Sesto San Giovanni Italy 45°31N 9°13E 128 A2
Sesto Ulteriano Italy 45°24N 9°16E 128 B2
Sestri Levante Italy 44°16N 9°24E 198 D6
Sestriere Italy 44°57N 6°53E 198 D3
Sestroretsk Russia 60°5N 29°58E 188 B6
Sestrunj Croatia 44°10N 15°0E 199 D11
Sestu Italy 39°18N 9°5E 200 C2
Setagaya Japan 35°37N 139°36E 140 B2
Setaka Japan 33°9N 130°28E 222 D2
Setana Japan 42°26N 139°51E 220 C9
Sète France 43°25N 3°42E 174 E7
Sete Cidades △ Brazil 4°0S 41°37W 332 B3
Sete Lagoas Brazil 19°27S 44°16W 333 E3
Setermoen Norway 59°52N 10°47E 133 A3
Setesdalsheiene = Suldalsheiene Norway 59°28N 7°10E 164 E3
Seti → Nepal 28°59N 81°8E 243 E9
Setia Budi Indonesia 6°12S 106°49E 122 B1
Sétif Algeria 36°9N 5°26E 261 A6
Sétif □ Algeria 36°10N 5°0E 261 A6
Setit → Sudan 14°20N 35°50E 257 E4
Seto Japan 35°14N 137°6E 223 B9
Setonaikai Japan 34°20N 133°30E 222 C5
Setonaikai △ Japan 34°15N 133°15E 222 C5
Setsan Burma 16°3N 95°23E 241 G5
Settat Morocco 33°0N 7°40W 260 B3
Setté-Cama Gabon 2°32S 9°45E 264 C1
Settebagni Italy 42°0N 12°31E 136 A2
Settecamini Italy 41°57N 12°38E 136 B2
Séttimo Milanese Italy 45°28N 9°3E 128 B1
Séttimo Torinese Italy 45°9N 7°46E 198 C4
Setting L. Canada 55°0N 98°38W 297 C9
Settle U.K. 54°5N 2°16W 168 C5
Settlement Wake I. 19°18N 166°38E 302 b
Settlement, The Br. Virgin Is. 18°43N 64°22W 321 b
Settlers S. Africa 25°2S 28°30E 271 C4
Settsu Japan 34°47N 135°33E 133 A2
Setúbal Portugal 38°30N 8°58W 195 G2
Setúbal □ Portugal 38°25N 8°35W 195 G2
Setúbal, B. de Portugal 38°40N 8°56W 195 G2
Seugne → France 45°42N 0°32W 174 C3
Seul, Lac Canada 50°20N 92°30W 298 B1
Seulimeum Indonesia 5°27N 95°15E 234 A1
Seurre France 47°0N 5°8E 173 F12
Seutula Finland 60°20N 24°52E 121 A2
Sevan Armenia 40°33N 44°56E 191 K7
Sevan, Ozero = Sevana Lich Armenia 40°30N 45°20E 191 K7
Sevana Lich Armenia 40°30N 45°20E 191 K7
Sevastopol Ukraine 44°35N 33°30E 189 K7
Seven Corners U.S.A. 38°53N 77°9W 143 B2
Seven Islands = Sept-Îles Canada 50°13N 66°22W 299 B6
Seven Kings U.K. 51°33N 0°5E 125 A4
Seven Sisters Canada 54°56N 128°10W 296 C3
Seventeen Street Canal U.S.A. 30°3N 90°7W 131 A2
Sever → Spain 39°40N 7°32W 195 F3
Sévérac-le-Château France 44°20N 3°5E 174 D7
Severn → Ont., Canada 56°2N 87°36W 298 A2
Severn → U.K. 51°35N 2°40W 169 F5
Severnaya Zemlya Russia 79°0N 100°0E 215 B11
Severno Kosovo Kosovo 43°0N 21°27E 202 C4
Severnyye Uvaly Russia 60°0N 50°0E 186 C8
Severo-Kurilsk Russia 50°40N 156°8E 215 D16
Severo-Yeniseyskiy Russia 60°22N 93°1E 215 C10
Severo-Zapadnyy □ Russia 65°0N 40°0E 214 C4
Severobaykalsk Russia 55°39N 109°19E 215 D11
Severočeský □ Czech Rep. 50°30N 14°0E 180 A7
Severodonetsk = Syeverodonetsk Ukraine 48°58N 38°35E 189 H10
Severodvinsk Russia 64°27N 39°58E 186 B6
Severomoravský □ Czech Rep. 49°38N 17°40E 181 B10
Severomorsk Russia 69°5N 33°27E 160 B25
Severouralsk Russia 60°9N 59°57E 186 B10
Seversk Russia 56°36N 84°49E 214 D9
Sévesco → Italy 45°35N 9°35E 128 A1
Sevier → U.S.A. 39°4N 113°6W 304 G7
Sevier Desert U.S.A. 39°40N 112°45W 304 G7
Sevier L. U.S.A. 38°54N 113°9W 304 G7
Sevilla Colombia 4°16N 75°57W 328 C2
Sevilla Spain 37°23N 5°58W 195 H5
Sevilla □ Spain 37°25N 5°30W 195 H5
Seville = Sevilla Spain 37°23N 5°58W 195 H5
Seville Fla., U.S.A. 29°19N 81°30W 317 F8
Seville Ga., U.S.A. 31°58N 83°36W 316 D6
Sevlievo Bulgaria 43°2N 25°6E 203 C9
Sevnica Slovenia 46°2N 15°19E 199 B12
Sevran France 48°56N 2°31E 134 A4
Sèvre-Nantaise → France 47°12N 1°33W 172 E5
Sèvre-Niortaise → France 46°28N 0°50W 174 B3
Sèvres Paris, France 48°49N 2°12E 134 B2
Sevsk Russia 52°10N 34°30E 189 F8
Sewa → S. Leone 7°20N 12°10W 262 D2
Sewani India 28°58N 75°39E 242 E6
Seward Alaska, U.S.A. 60°7N 149°27W 303 F10
Seward Nebr., U.S.A. 40°55N 97°6W 308 E5
Seward Pa., U.S.A. 40°25N 79°1W 312 F5
Seward Peninsula U.S.A. 65°30N 166°0W 303 D6
Sewell Chile 34°10S 70°23W 334 C1
Sewer Indonesia 5°53S 134°40E 231 F8
Sewickley U.S.A. 40°32N 80°12W 312 F4
Sewri India 18°59N 72°50E 130 B2
Sexsmith Canada 55°21N 118°47W 296 B5
Seychelles ■ Ind. Oc. 5°0S 56°0E 272 c
Seyðisfjörður Iceland 65°16N 13°57W 155 B13
Seydişehir Turkey 37°25N 31°51E 212 D4
Seydvān Iran 38°34N 45°2E 213 C11
Seyhan → Turkey 36°43N 34°53E 250 B5
Seyhan Barajı Turkey 37°2N 35°18E 212 D6
Seyitgazi Turkey 39°27N 30°43E 205 B12
Seyitömer Turkey 39°34N 29°52E 205 B11
Seym → Ukraine 51°27N 32°34E 189 G7
Seymen Turkey 41°6N 27°57E 203 E11
Seymour Vic., Australia 37°2S 145°10E 283 D6
Seymour Eastern Cape, S. Africa 32°33S 26°46E 271 D4
Seymour Conn., U.S.A. 41°24N 73°4W 313 E11
Seymour Ind., U.S.A. 38°58N 85°53W 311 F11
Seymour Tex., U.S.A. 33°35N 99°16W 314 E5
Seyne France 44°21N 6°22E 175 D10
Seyssel France 45°57N 5°50E 175 C9
Sežana Slovenia 45°43N 13°41E 199 C10
Sézanne France 48°40N 3°40E 173 D10
Sezze Italy 41°30N 13°3E 200 A6
Sfântu Gheorghe Covasna, Romania 45°52N 25°48E 183 E10
Sfântu Gheorghe Tulcea, Romania 44°53N 29°36E 183 F14
Sfântu Gheorghe, Braţul → Romania 44°51N 29°36E 183 F14
Sfax Tunisia 34°49N 10°48E 258 B2
Sfax □ Tunisia 34°40N 10°20E 261 B7
Sforzesco, Castello Italy 45°28N 9°10E 128 B2
Sha Chau Hong Kong, China 22°21N 113°53E 122 A1
Sha Kok Mei Hong Kong, China 22°23N 114°16E 122 A3
Sha Lo Wan Hong Kong, China 22°17N 113°54E 122 B1
Sha Tau Kok China 22°33N 114°13E 219 a
Sha Tin Hong Kong, China 22°23N 114°12E 122 A3
Sha Xi → China 26°35N 118°0E 229 D12
Sha Xian China 26°23N 117°45E 229 D11
Shaanxi □ China 35°0N 109°0E 226 G5
Sha'ar Binyamin West Bank 31°52N 35°16E 123 A2
Shaba = Katanga □ Dem. Rep. of the Congo 8°0S 25°0E 268 D2
Shaba ⌓ Kenya 0°38N 37°48E 268 B4
Shabeellaha Dhexe □ Somalia 3°0N 46°0E 267 D6
Shabeellaha Hoose □ Somalia 1°0N 44°0E 267 D5
Shabeelle → Somalia 2°0N 44°0E 267 D5
Shabestar Iran 38°11N 45°41E 213 C11
Shabla Bulgaria 43°31N 28°32E 203 C12
Shabogamo L. Canada 53°15N 66°30W 299 B6
Shabrâmant Egypt 29°56N 31°11E 117 B2
Shabunda Dem. Rep. of the Congo 2°40S 27°16E 268 C2
Shabwah Yemen 15°22N 47°1E 248 D4
Shabwah □ Yemen 15°22N 47°1E 248 D4
Shache China 38°20N 77°10E 217 E9
Shackleton Fracture Zone S. Ocean 60°0S 60°0W 151 B18
Shackleton Ice Shelf Antarctica 66°0S 100°0E 151 C8
Shackleton Inlet Antarctica 83°0S 160°0E 151 E11
Shādegān Iran 30°40N 48°38E 247 D6
Shadi Jiangxi, China 26°7N 114°47E 229 D10
Shadi Jammu & Kashmir, India 33°24N 77°14E 243 C7
Shadrinsk Russia 56°5N 63°32E 214 D7
Shady Dale U.S.A. 33°24N 83°36W 316 B6
Shady Grove U.S.A. 30°17N 83°38W 316 E6
Shadyside U.S.A. 39°58N 80°45W 312 G4
Shafer, L. U.S.A. 40°46N 86°46W 311 D10
Shaffa Nigeria 10°30N 12°6E 263 C7
Shafter U.S.A. 35°30N 119°16W 307 K7
Shaftesbury U.K. 51°0N 2°11W 169 F5
Shaftsbury U.S.A. 43°0N 73°11W 313 D11
Shag Pt. N.Z. 45°29S 170°52E 285 F5
Shag Rocks Atl. Oc. 53°0S 41°0W 152 M7
Shagamu Nigeria 6°51N 3°39E 263 D5
Shageluk U.S.A. 62°41N 159°34W 303 E8
Shagram Pakistan 36°24N 72°20E 243 A5
Shah Alam Malaysia 3°5N 101°32E 237 L3
Shah Alizai Pakistan 29°25N 66°33E 242 E2
Shah Bunder Pakistan 24°13N 67°56E 242 G2
Shāh Jūy Afghan. 32°31N 67°25E 242 C2
Shah Mosque Iran 35°41N 51°25E 141 A2
Shahabad Karnataka, India 17°10N 76°54E 244 F3
Shahabad Punjab, India 30°10N 76°55E 242 D7
Shahabad Raj., India 25°15N 77°11E 242 G7
Shahabad Ut. P., India 27°36N 79°56E 243 F8
Shahada India 21°33N 74°30E 244 D2
Shahadpur Pakistan 25°55N 68°35E 242 G3
Shahapur India 15°50N 74°34E 245 G2
Shahbā' Syria 32°52N 36°38E 250 F7
Shahbazpur I. Bangla. 22°30N 90°45E 241 D3
Shahdād Iran 30°30N 57°40E 247 D8
Shahdād, Namakzār-e Iran 30°20N 58°20E 247 D8
Shahdadkot Pakistan 27°50N 67°55E 242 F2
Shahdara India 28°40N 77°18E 124 C2
Shahdol India 23°19N 81°26E 243 H9
Shahe Guangdong, China 23°9N 113°19E 121 B2
Shahe Hebei, China 37°0N 114°32E 226 F8
Shahganj India 26°3N 82°44E 243 F10
Shahgarh India 27°15N 69°50E 242 F3
Shaḥḥāt Libya 32°48N 21°54E 258 B4
Shahid Rajaee Port = Bandar Shahid Rajaee Iran 27°7N 56°4E 247 E8
Shahīdān Afghan. 36°42N 67°49E 240 A2
Shāhīn Shahr Iran 32°49N 51°32E 247 C6
Shahjahanpur India 27°54N 79°57E 243 F8
Shahpur = Salmās Iran 38°11N 44°47E 213 C11
Shahpur Karnataka, India 16°40N 76°48E 244 F3
Shahpur Mad. P., India 22°12N 77°58E 242 H7
Shahpur Baluchistan, Pakistan 28°46N 68°27E 242 E3

Shahpur Punjab, Pakistan 32°17N 72°26E 242 C5
Shahpur Chakar Pakistan 26°9N 68°39E 242 F3
Shahpura Mad. P., India 23°10N 80°45E 243 H9
Shahpura Raj., India 25°38N 74°56E 242 G6
Shahr-e Bābak Iran 30°7N 55°9E 247 D7
Shahr-e Kord Iran 32°15N 50°55E 247 C6
Shahr-e Rey Iran 35°36N 51°25E 141 B2
Shahrak-e Golshahr Iran 35°37N 51°18E 141 B1
Shahrak-e Qods Iran 35°47N 51°22E 141 A2
Shāhrakht Iran 33°38N 60°16E 247 C9
Shāhrezā = Qomsheh Iran 32°0N 51°55E 247 D6
Shahrig Pakistan 30°15N 67°40E 242 D2
Shahrisabz Uzbekistan 39°3N 66°50E 217 E7
Shāhrud = Emāmrūd Iran 36°30N 55°0E 247 B7
Shahukou China 40°20N 112°18E 226 D7
Shaikh Aomar Iraq 33°20N 44°23E 113 A2
Shaikhabad Afghan. 34°2N 68°45E 242 B3
Shajapur India 23°27N 76°21E 242 H7
Shajing China 22°44N 113°48E 219 a
Shajuwan Taiwan 23°13N 121°23E 225 C3
Shakargarh Pakistan 32°17N 75°10E 242 C6
Shakawe Botswana 18°28S 21°49E 270 A3
Shakenge Dem. Rep. of the Congo 6°14S 18°41E 265 D3
Shaker Heights U.S.A. 41°28N 81°32W 312 E3
Shakhrisyabz = Shahrisabz Uzbekistan 39°3N 66°50E 217 E7
Shakhtersk Russia 49°10N 142°8E 215 E15
Shakhtīnsk Kazakhstan 49°42N 72°35E 217 C8
Shakhty Russia 47°40N 40°16E 191 G5
Shakhtyorskoye = Pershotravensk Ukraine 50°13N 27°40E 177 C14
Shakhunya Russia 57°40N 46°46E 190 B8
Shaki Nigeria 8°41N 3°21E 263 D5
Shākir Egypt 27°30N 33°59E 256 B3
Shakotan-Hantō Japan 43°10N 140°30E 220 C10
Shaksam Valley Asia 36°0N 76°20E 243 A7
Shaktoolik U.S.A. 64°20N 161°9W 303 D7
Shakurbasti India 28°41N 77°6E 120 A1
Shala, L. Ethiopia 7°30N 38°30E 257 F4
Shali Russia 43°9N 45°55E 191 J7
Shalim Oman 18°7N 55°38E 249 C6
Shalkar Köli Kazakhstan 50°35N 51°47E 190 E10
Shalkiya India 22°36N 88°21E 124 B2
Shallow Lake Canada 44°36N 81°5W 312 B3
Shalqar Kazakhstan 47°48N 59°39E 216 C5
Shalqar Köli Kazakhstan 50°33N 51°40E 216 B4
Shalskiy Russia 61°48N 35°58E 188 B8
Shalu Taiwan 24°14N 120°34E 225 B2
Shaluli Shan China 30°40N 99°55E 228 B2
Shām Iran 26°39N 57°21E 247 E8
Shām, Bādiyat ash Asia 32°0N 40°0E 246 C3
Shām, J. ash Oman 23°14N 57°16E 249 B7
Sham Shui Po Hong Kong, China 22°19N 114°9E 122 B2
Sham Tseng Hong Kong, China 22°22N 114°3E 122 A2
Sham Wat Hong Kong, China 22°16N 113°53E 122 B1
Shamâl Bahr el Ghazal = Northern Bahr el Ghazal □ South Sudan 8°0N 27°30E 257 F2
Shamâl Dârfûr □ Sudan 15°0N 25°0E 257 E2
Shamâl Kordofân □ Sudan 15°0N 30°0E 257 E3
Shamâl Sînî □ Egypt 30°30N 33°30E 251 H4
Shamapur India 28°44N 77°8E 120 A1
Shamattawa Canada 55°51N 92°5W 298 A1
Shamattawa → Canada 55°1N 85°23W 298 A2
Shambe South Sudan 7°8N 30°46E 257 F3
Shambe △ South Sudan 6°57N 30°50E 257 F3
Shambu Ethiopia 9°32N 37°3E 257 F4
Shamgong Dzong Bhutan 27°13N 90°35E 241 B3
Shamian China 23°6N 113°13E 121 B2
Shamīl Iran 27°30N 56°55E 247 E8
Shamkhor = Şämkir Azerbaijan 40°50N 46°0E 191 K8
Shāmkūh Iran 35°47N 57°50E 247 C8
Shamli India 29°32N 77°18E 242 E7
Shammar, Jabal Si. Arabia 27°40N 41°0E 246 E4
Shamo = Gobi Asia 44°0N 110°0E 226 C6
Shamo, L. Ethiopia 5°45N 37°30E 257 F4
Shamokin U.S.A. 40°47N 76°34W 313 F8
Shamrock Ont., Canada 45°23N 76°50W 313 A8
Shamrock Tex., U.S.A. 35°13N 100°15W 314 D4
Shamva Zimbabwe 17°20S 31°32E 269 F3
Shan □ Burma 21°30N 98°30E 241 E7
Shan Mei Hong Kong, China 22°23N 114°11E 122 A3
Shan Xian China 34°50N 116°5E 226 G9
Shana = Kurilsk Russia 45°14N 147°53E 215 E15
Shanan → Ethiopia 8°0N 40°20E 257 F5
Shanchengzhen China 42°20N 125°20E 224 A2
Shāndak Iran 28°28N 60°27E 247 D9
Shandan China 38°45N 101°15E 218 D9
Shandon U.S.A. 35°39N 120°23W 306 K6
Shandong □ China 36°0N 118°0E 227 G10
Shandong Bandao China 37°0N 121°0E 227 F11
Shandur Pass Pakistan 36°4N 72°31E 243 A5
Shang Xian = Shangzhou China 33°50N 109°58E 226 H5
Shangalowe Dem. Rep. of the Congo 10°50S 26°30E 269 E2
Shangani Zimbabwe 19°41S 29°20E 271 A4
Shangani → Zimbabwe 18°41S 27°10E 269 F2
Shangbancheng China 40°50N 118°1E 227 D10
Shangcheng China 31°47N 115°26E 229 B10
Shangchuan Dao China 21°40N 112°50E 229 G9
Shangdu China 41°30N 113°30E 226 D7
Shanggao China 28°17N 114°55E 229 C10
Shanghai China 31°15N 121°26E 138 B2
Shanghai Hongqiao Int. ✈ (SHA) China 31°12N 121°20E 138 B1
Shanghai Pudong Int. ✈ (PVG) China 31°9N 121°47E 138 B2
Shanghai Shi □ China 31°0N 121°30E 229 B13
Shanghang China 25°2N 116°23E 229 E11
Shanghe China 37°20N 117°10E 227 F9
Shangjao = Shangrao China 28°25N 117°59E 229 C11
Shanglin China 23°27N 108°33E 228 F7
Shangnan China 33°32N 110°50E 226 H6
Shangqiu China 34°26N 115°36E 226 G8
Shangrao China 28°25N 117°59E 229 C11
Shangri-La = Zhongdian China 27°48N 99°42E 228 D2
Shangshui China 33°32N 114°35E 226 H8
Shangsi China 22°8N 107°58E 228 F6
Shangyi China 41°4N 113°57E 226 D7
Shangyou China 25°48N 114°32E 229 E10
Shangyu China 30°3N 120°52E 229 B13
Shangzhi China 45°22N 127°56E 227 B14
Shangzhou China 33°50N 109°58E 226 H5
Shanhetun China 44°33N 127°15E 227 B14
Shanhu Tan Taiwan 23°12N 120°23E 225 C2
Shanhua Taiwan 23°8N 120°17E 225 C2
Shani Nigeria 10°14N 12°2E 263 C7
Shānidar Iraq 36°48N 44°14E 213 D11
Shankill Ireland 53°14N 6°7W 120 B3
Shanklin U.K. 50°38N 1°11W 169 G6
Shanlin Taiwan 23°0N 120°32E 225 C2
Shannon N.Z. 40°33S 175°25E 284 G4
Shannon → Ireland 52°35N 9°30W 166 D2
Shannon ✈ (SNN) Ireland 52°42N 8°57W 166 D3
Shannon, Mouth of the Ireland 52°30N 9°55W 166 D2
Shannon △ Australia 34°35S 116°25E 279 F2
Shannon Ø Greenland 75°10N 18°30W 154 B9
Shannonbridge Ireland 53°17N 8°3W 166 C3
Shannontown U.S.A. 33°53N 80°21W 316 B9
Shanshan China 42°52N 90°10E 217 D12
Shanshang Taiwan 23°6N 120°21E 225 C2
Shansi = Shanxi □ China 37°0N 112°0E 226 F7
Shantar, Ostrov Bolshoy Russia 55°9N 137°40E 215 D14
Shantipur India 23°17N 88°25E 243 H13
Shantou China 23°18N 116°40E 229 F11
Shantung = Shandong □ China 36°0N 118°0E 227 G10
Shanwei China 22°48N 115°22E 229 F10
Shanxi □ China 37°0N 112°0E 226 F7
Shanyang China 33°31N 109°55E 226 H5
Shanyin China 39°25N 112°56E 226 E7
Shaodong China 27°15N 111°43E 229 D8
Shaoguan China 24°48N 113°35E 229 E9
Shaohing = Shaoxing China 30°0N 120°35E 229 C13
Shaoshan China 27°55N 112°33E 229 D9
Shaowu China 27°22N 117°28E 229 D11
Shaoxing China 30°0N 120°35E 229 C13
Shaoyang Hunan, China 26°59N 111°20E 229 D8
Shaoyang Hunan, China 27°14N 111°25E 229 D8
Shap U.K. 54°32N 2°40W 168 C5
Shapinsay U.K. 59°3N 2°51W 167 B6
Shaqlāwah Iraq 36°23N 44°20E 213 D11
Shaqq el Gi'eifer → Sudan 15°16N 26°0E 257 D2
Shaqra' Si. Arabia 25°15N 45°16E 246 E5
Shar Kazakhstan 49°35N 81°2E 217 C10
Sharafa Sudan 11°59N 27°7E 257 E2
Sharafkhāneh Iran 38°11N 45°29E 213 C11
Sharashova Belarus 52°34N 24°12E 185 F11
Sharavati → India 14°20N 74°25E 245 G2
Sharbaqty Kazakhstan 51°23N 78°17E 217 B9
Sharbithāt, Ra's ash Oman 17°56N 56°21E 249 C7
Sharbot Lake Canada 44°46N 76°41W 313 B8
Shard Building London, U.K. 125 b5
Shardara, Step Kazakhstan 42°20N 68°0E 217 D7
Sharhorod Ukraine 48°45N 28°5E 183 B13
Shari Japan 43°55N 144°40E 220 C12
Shariff Aguak = Maganoy Phil. 6°51N 124°31E 233 H5
Shariff Kabunsuan □ Phil. 7°5N 124°5E 233 H5
Sharjah = Ash Shāriqah U.A.E. 25°23N 55°26E 247 E7
Shark B. Australia 25°30S 113°32E 279 E1
Shark Bay △ Australia 25°30S 113°30E 279 E1
Sharm el Sheikh Egypt 27°53N 34°18E 251 L5
Sharon Ont., Canada 44°6N 79°26W 312 B5
Sharon Mass., U.S.A. 42°7N 71°11W 313 D13
Sharon Pa., U.S.A. 41°14N 80°31W 312 E4
Sharon Wis., U.S.A. 42°30N 88°44W 311 B8
Sharon Springs Kans., U.S.A. 38°54N 101°45W 308 F3
Sharon Springs N.Y., U.S.A. 42°48N 74°37W 313 D10
Sharonville U.S.A. 39°16N 84°25W 311 E12
Sharp I. Hong Kong, China 22°21N 114°17E 122 A3
Sharp Pk. Phil. 5°58N 125°31E 233 J5
Sharp Pt. Australia 10°58S 142°43E 286 F2
Sharpe L. Canada 54°24N 93°40W 298 B1
Sharpes U.S.A. 28°26N 80°46W 317 G9
Sharpsville U.S.A. 41°15N 80°29W 312 E4
Sharq el Istiwa'iya = Eastern Equatoria □ South Sudan 5°0N 33°0E 257 G3
Sharqi, Al Jabal ash Lebanon 33°40N 36°10E 250 E7
Sharqîya □ Egypt 30°48N 31°48E 251 H2
Sharr Kosovo 42°5N 20°41E 202 D4
Sharya Russia 58°22N 45°20E 190 A7
Shasha Ethiopia 6°29N 35°59E 257 F4
Shashemene Ethiopia 7°13N 38°33E 257 F4
Shashi Botswana 21°15S 27°27E 271 B4
Shashi → Africa 21°14S 29°20E 269 G2
Shasta, Mt. U.S.A. 41°25N 122°12W 304 F2
Shasta L. U.S.A. 40°43N 122°25W 304 F2
Shastrinagar India 28°40N 77°10E 120 A2
Shatawi Sudan 14°39N 32°6E 257 E3
Shāţi', Wādī ash → Libya 27°30N 15°0E 258 C3
Shatilki = Svyetlahorsk Belarus 52°38N 29°46E 177 B15
Shatsk Russia 54°5N 41°45E 190 C5
Shatsk Ukraine 51°29N 23°55E 185 G10
Shatsky Rise Pac. Oc. 34°0N 157°0E 288 D7
Shatskyy ⌂ Ukraine 51°30N 23°52E 185 G10
Shatt al Arab Asia 29°57N 48°34E 247 D6
Shatura Russia 55°33N 39°21E 188 E10
Shaturtof = Shatura Russia 55°33N 39°21E 188 E10
Shau Kei Wan Hong Kong, China 22°16N 114°13E 122 B3
Shaumyani = Shulaveri Georgia 41°22N 44°45E 191 K7
Shaunavon Canada 49°35N 108°25W 297 D7
Shaver L. U.S.A. 37°9N 119°18W 306 H7
Shavgar = Türkistan Kazakhstan 43°17N 68°16E 217 D7
Shavli = Šiauliai Lithuania 55°56N 23°15E 184 C10
Shaw → Australia 20°21S 119°17E 278 D2
Shaw I. Australia 20°30S 149°2E 280 b
Shawanaga Canada 45°31N 80°17W 312 A4
Shawangunk Mts. U.S.A. 41°35N 74°30W 313 E10
Shawano U.S.A. 44°47N 88°36W 308 C9
Shawinigan Canada 46°35N 72°50W 298 C5
Shawmari, J. ash Jordan 30°35N 36°35E 251 H7
Shawnee Ga., U.S.A. 32°29N 81°25W 316 C8
Shawnee Kans., U.S.A. 39°1N 94°43W 310 E2
Shawnee Okla., U.S.A. 35°20N 96°55W 314 D6
Shawocun China 39°53N 116°13E 114 B1
Shay Gap Australia 20°30S 120°10E 278 D3
Shayang China 30°42N 112°29E 229 B9
Shaybārā Si. Arabia 25°26N 36°47E 246 E3
Shayib el Banat, Gebel Egypt 26°59N 33°29E 256 B3
Shaykh, J. ash Lebanon 33°25N 35°50E 250 E6
Shaykh Miskīn Syria 32°49N 36°9E 250 F7
Shaykh Sa'd Iraq 32°34N 46°17E 213 F12
Shaykh 'Uthmān Yemen 12°52N 44°59E 248 D4
Shaytansky Zavod = Pervouralsk Russia 56°59N 59°59E 186 C10
Shayuan China 23°5N 113°15E 121 B2
Shāzand Iran 33°56N 49°24E 247 C6
Shazud Tajikistan 37°45N 72°25E 217 E8
Shcheglovo = Kemerovo Russia 55°20N 86°5E 214 D9
Shchekino Russia 54°1N 37°34E 188 E9
Shcherbakov = Rybinsk Russia 58°5N 38°50E 188 C10
Shchigry Russia 51°55N 36°58E 189 G9
Shchors Ukraine 51°48N 31°56E 189 G6
Shchūchīnsk Kazakhstan 52°56N 70°12E 217 B8
She Xian Anhui, China 29°50N 118°25E 229 C12
She Xian Hebei, China 36°30N 113°40E 226 F7
Shea Guyana 2°48N 59°4W 329 C6
Shebekino Russia 50°28N 36°54E 189 G9
Shebela → Ethiopia 7°32N 45°43E 267 C6
Shebele = Shabeelle → Somalia 2°0N 44°0E 267 D5
Shebele Ethiopia 8°8N 42°40E 267 C5
Sheberghān Afghan. 36°40N 65°45E 240 A2
Sheboygan U.S.A. 43°46N 87°45W 308 D10
Shebshi Mts. Nigeria 8°30N 12°0E 263 D7
Shediac Canada 46°14N 64°32W 299 C7
Sheelin, L. Ireland 53°48N 7°20W 166 C4
Sheen, L. U.S.A. 28°25N 81°31W 133 B1
Sheenjek → U.S.A. 66°45N 144°33W 303 C11
Sheep Haven Ireland 55°11N 7°52W 166 A4
Sheep Range U.S.A. 36°35N 115°15W 307 J11
Sheepshead Bay U.S.A. 40°35N 73°55W 132 C2
Sheerness U.K. 51°26N 0°47E 169 F8
Sheet Harbour Canada 44°56N 62°31W 299 D7
Sheffield N.Z. 43°23S 172°1E 285 D7
Sheffield S. Yorks., U.K. 53°23N 1°28W 168 D6
Sheffield Ala., U.S.A. 34°46N 87°41W 315 D11
Sheffield Ill., U.S.A. 41°21N 89°44W 310 C7
Sheffield Iowa, U.S.A. 42°54N 93°13W 310 B3
Sheffield Mass., U.S.A. 42°5N 73°21W 313 D11
Sheffield Pa., U.S.A. 41°42N 79°3W 312 E5
Shegaon India 20°48N 76°47E 244 D3
Shehojele Ethiopia 10°40N 35°9E 257 E4
Shehong China 30°54N 105°18E 228 B5
Shehuen → Argentina 49°35S 69°34W 336 C3
Shei-Pa △ Taiwan 24°36N 121°22E 225 B3
Shei Shan Taiwan 24°22N 121°15E 225 B3
Sheikh, W. el → Egypt 28°41N 33°41E 251 K4
Sheikh Zayed Canal Egypt 23°30N 30°15E 256 C3
Sheikh Zayed Road U.A.E. 25°11N 55°15E 119 B2
Sheikhpura India 25°9N 85°53E 243 G11
Shek Hasan Ethiopia 12°5N 35°58E 257 E4
Shek Kong Hong Kong, China 22°26N 114°6E 122 A2
Shek Kwu Chau Hong Kong, China 22°12N 113°59E 122 B1
Shek O Hong Kong, China 22°13N 114°15E 122 B3
Shek O Country Park ⌂ Hong Kong, China 22°16N 114°14E 122 B3
Shek Pik Hong Kong, China 22°14N 113°53E 122 B1
Shek Pik Res. Hong Kong, China 22°14N 113°54E 122 B1
Shekhupura Pakistan 31°42N 73°58E 242 D5
Sheki = Şaki Azerbaijan 41°10N 47°5E 191 K8
Shekki = Zhongshan China 22°26N 113°20E 229 F9
Shekou China 22°30N 113°55E 219 a
Shelbina U.S.A. 39°47N 92°2W 310 E4
Shelburn U.S.A. 39°11N 87°24W 311 E9
Shelburne N.S., Canada 43°47N 65°20W 299 D6
Shelburne Ont., Canada 44°4N 80°15W 312 B4
Shelburne Vt., U.S.A. 44°23N 73°14W 313 B11
Shelburne B. Australia 11°50S 142°50E 286 F2
Shelburne Falls U.S.A. 42°36N 72°45W 313 D12
Shelby Mich., U.S.A. 43°37N 86°22W 308 D10
Shelby Miss., U.S.A. 33°57N 90°46W 315 E9
Shelby Mont., U.S.A. 48°30N 111°51W 304 B8
Shelby N.C., U.S.A. 35°17N 81°32W 315 D14
Shelby Ohio, U.S.A. 40°53N 82°40W 312 F2
Shelbyville Ill., U.S.A. 39°24N 88°48W 311 E8
Shelbyville Ind., U.S.A. 39°31N 85°47W 311 E11
Shelbyville Ky., U.S.A. 38°13N 85°14W 311 F11
Shelbyville Mo., U.S.A. 39°48N 92°2W 310 E4
Shelbyville Tenn., U.S.A. 35°29N 86°28W 315 D11
Shelbyville, L. U.S.A. 39°26N 88°46W 311 E8
Sheldon Ill., U.S.A. 40°46N 87°34W 311 D9
Sheldon Iowa, U.S.A. 43°11N 95°51W 308 D6
Sheldon Mo., U.S.A. 37°40N 94°18W 310 G2
Sheldon S.C., U.S.A. 32°36N 80°48W 316 C9
Sheldon Point U.S.A. 62°32N 164°52W 303 E6
Sheldrake Canada 50°20N 64°51W 299 B7
Shelek Kazakhstan 43°33N 78°17E 217 D9
Shelengo, Khawr → Sudan 10°33N 28°40E 257 E2
Shelikhova, Zaliv Russia 59°30N 157°0E 215 D16
Shelikof Strait U.S.A. 57°30N 155°0W 303 H9
Shell Beach = Huntington Beach U.S.A. 33°40N 118°5W 307 M9
Shell Lakes Australia 29°20S 127°30E 279 E4
Shellbrook Canada 53°13N 106°24W 297 C7
Shellharbour Australia 34°31S 150°51E 283 C9
Shellman U.S.A. 31°46N 84°37W 316 D5
Shellsburg U.S.A. 42°6N 91°52W 310 B5
Shelon → Russia 58°13N 30°47E 188 C6
Shelter Bay = Port-Cartier Canada 50°2N 66°50W 299 B6
Shelter I. Hong Kong, China 22°19N 114°17E 122 B3
Shelter I. N.Y., U.S.A. 41°4N 72°20W 313 E12
Shelton Conn., U.S.A. 41°19N 73°5W 313 E11
Shelton Wash., U.S.A. 47°13N 123°6W 306 C3
Shemakha = Şamaxı Azerbaijan 40°38N 48°37E 191 K9
Shemonaīkha Kazakhstan 50°37N 81°54E 217 B10
Shëmri Albania 42°7N 20°13E 202 D4
Shemsi Sudan 19°2N 29°57E 256 D2
Shen Xian China 36°15N 115°40E 226 F8
Shenandoah Iowa, U.S.A. 40°46N 95°22W 308 E6
Shenandoah Pa., U.S.A. 40°49N 76°12W 313 F8
Shenandoah Va., U.S.A. 38°29N 78°37W 309 F14
Shenandoah → U.S.A. 39°19N 77°44W 309 F15
Shenandoah △ U.S.A. 38°35N 78°22W 309 F14
Shenchi China 39°8N 112°10E 226 E7
Shencottah India 8°59N 77°18E 245 K3
Shendam Nigeria 8°49N 9°30E 263 D6
Shendî Sudan 16°46N 33°22E 257 D3
Shendurni India 20°39N 75°36E 244 D2
Shengang = Shenkang Taiwan 24°9N 120°39E 225 B2
Shenge S. Leone 7°54N 12°55W 262 D2
Shengfang China 39°3N 116°42E 226 E9
Shëngjergj Albania 41°17N 20°10E 202 E4
Shëngjin Albania 41°50N 19°35E 202 E3
Shengzhou China 29°35N 120°50E 229 C13
Shenjingzi China 44°40N 124°30E 227 B13
Shenkang Taiwan 24°9N 120°39E 225 B2
Shenmu China 38°50N 110°29E 226 E6
Shennongjia China 31°43N 110°44E 229 B8
Shenqiu China 33°25N 115°5E 226 H8
Shensi = Shaanxi □ China 35°0N 109°0E 226 G5
Shenyang China 41°48N 123°27E 224 B1
Shenzhen China 22°32N 114°5E 229 F10
Shenzhen Bao'an Int. ✈ (SZX) China 22°41N 113°49E 219 a
Shenzhen Shuiku China 22°34N 114°8E 219 a
Shenzhen Wan China 22°27N 113°55E 219 a
Sheo India 26°11N 71°15E 242 F4
Sheopur Kalan India 25°40N 76°40E 242 G7
Shepetivka Ukraine 50°10N 27°10E 177 C14
Shepherd Is. Vanuatu 16°55S 168°36E 287 F6
Shepherds Bush U.K. 51°30N 0°13W 125 A2
Shepherdsville U.S.A. 37°59N 85°43W 311 G11
Shepparton Australia 36°23S 145°26E 283 D6
Shepperton U.K. 51°23N 0°26W 125 B1
Sheppey, I. of U.K. 51°25N 0°48E 169 F8
Shepton Mallet U.K. 51°11N 2°33W 169 F5
Sheqi China 33°12N 112°57E 226 H7
Sher Khan Qala Afghan. 29°53N 66°13E 240 C2
Sher Qila Pakistan 36°7N 74°2E 243 A6
Sherab Sudan 10°44N 24°41E 257 E1
Sherabad Uzbekistan 37°40N 67°1E 217 E7
Sherborne U.K. 50°57N 2°31W 169 G5
Sherbro → S. Leone 7°45N 12°55W 262 D2
Sherbro I. S. Leone 7°30N 12°40W 262 D2
Sherbrooke N.S., Canada 45°8N 61°59W 299 C7
Sherbrooke Qué., Canada 45°28N 71°57W 313 A13
Sherburne U.S.A. 42°41N 75°30W 313 D9
Sherburne Reef Papua N. G. 3°20S 148°0E 286 B5
Sherda Chad 20°7N 16°46E 259 D3
Shereik Sudan 18°44N 33°47E 256 D3
Sheremetyevo ✈ (SVO) Russia 55°58N 37°25E 129 A1
Shergaon India 27°7N 92°16E 241 B4
Shergarh India 26°20N 72°18E 242 F5
Sherghati India 24°34N 84°47E 243 G11
Sheridan Ark., U.S.A. 34°19N 92°24W 314 D8
Sheridan Ill., U.S.A. 41°32N 88°41W 311 C8
Sheridan Ind., U.S.A. 40°8N 86°13W 311 D10
Sheridan Wyo., U.S.A. 44°48N 106°58W 304 D10
Sheringham U.K. 52°56N 1°13E 168 E9
Sherkin I. Ireland 51°28N 9°26W 166 E2
Sherkot India 29°22N 78°35E 243 E8
Sherlovaya Gora Russia 50°34N 116°15E 215 D12
Sherman N.Y., U.S.A. 42°9N 79°35W 312 D5
Sherman Tex., U.S.A. 33°38N 96°36W 314 E6
Sherman Oaks U.S.A. 34°8N 118°29W 126 B2
Sherman Park U.S.A. 41°47N 87°39W 119 C2
Sherpur Bangla. 25°0N 90°0E 241 C3
Sherpur India 25°34N 83°47E 243 G10
Sherridon Canada 55°8N 101°5W 297 B8
Sherriffs St. Kitts & Nevis 17°10N 62°32W 322 d
Shertallai = Cherthala India 9°42N 76°20E 245 K3
Sherwood U.S.A. 41°17N 84°33W 311 C12
Sherwood, L. U.S.A. 28°33N 81°29W 133 A2
Sherwood Forest U.K. 53°6N 1°7W 168 D6
Sherwood Park Canada 53°31N 113°19W 296 C6
Sheslay → Canada 58°48N 132°5W 296 B2
Shet Bandar India 18°57N 72°55E 130 B2
Shethanei L. Canada 58°48N 97°50W 297 B9
Shetland □ U.K. 60°30N 1°30W 167 A7
Shetland Is. U.K. 60°30N 1°30W 167 A7
Shetou Taiwan 23°53N 120°35E 225 C2
Shetpe Kazakhstan 44°10N 52°7E 216 D4
Shetrunji → India 21°19N 72°7E 242 J5
Sheung Fa Shan Hong Kong, China 22°23N 114°5E 122 A2
Sheung Lau Wan Hong Kong, China 22°16N 114°16E 122 B3
Sheung Shui China 22°31N 114°7E 219 a
Sheung Wan Hong Kong, China 22°16N 114°9E 122 B2
Sheva India 18°56N 72°57E 130 B2
Sheva Nhava India 18°57N 72°57E 130 B2
Shevaroy Hills India 11°58N 78°12E 245 J4
Shevchenkovo = Dolynska Ukraine 48°6N 32°46E 189 H7
Shevchenkovo Ukraine 45°33N 29°20E 183 E14
Shevgaon India 19°21N 75°14E 244 E2
Shevisheh Iran 35°21N 46°40E 213 E12
Shewa Ethiopia 9°33N 38°10E 257 F4
Shewa Gimira Ethiopia 7°4N 35°51E 257 F4
Shey-Phoksundo △ Nepal 29°30N 82°45E 243 E10
Sheyang China 33°48N 120°29E 227 H11
Sheyenne → U.S.A. 47°2N 96°50W 308 B5
Shiashkotan, Ostrov Russia 48°49N 154°6E 215 E16
Shiba Tokyo, Japan 140 c4
Shibām Yemen 15°59N 48°36E 249 D5
Shibata Japan 37°57N 139°20E 220 F9
Shibecha Japan 43°17N 144°36E 220 C12
Shibetsu Hokkaidō, Japan 43°30N 145°10E 220 C12
Shibetsu Hokkaidō, Japan 44°10N 142°23E 220 B11
Shibîn el Kôm Egypt 30°31N 30°55E 256 H7
Shibîn el Qanâtir Egypt 30°19N 31°19E 256 H7
Shibing China 27°2N 108°7E 228 D7
Shibogama L. Canada 53°35N 88°15W 298 B2
Shibpur India 22°34N 88°19E 124 B1
Shibukawa Japan 36°29N 139°0E 223 A11
Shibushi Japan 31°25N 131°8E 222 F3
Shibushi-Wan Japan 31°24N 131°8E 222 F3
Shibuya Tokyo, Japan 140 c1
Shicheng China 26°22N 116°20E 229 D11
Shicheng Dao China 39°31N 122°59E 224 C1
Shickshinny U.S.A. 41°9N 76°9W 313 E8
Shickshock Mts. = Chic-Chocs, Mts. Canada 48°55N 66°0W 299 C6
Shidād Si. Arabia 21°19N 40°3E 248 B3
Shidao China 36°50N 122°25E 227 F12
Shiderti → Kazakhstan 52°32N 74°50E 217 B8
Shidian China 24°40N 99°5E 228 E2
Shido = Sanuki Japan 34°19N 134°10E 222 C6
Shiel, L. U.K. 56°48N 5°34W 167 E3
Shield, C. Australia 13°20S 136°20E 280 A2
Shīeli Kazakhstan 44°20N 66°15E 217 D7
Shifang China 31°8N 104°10E 228 B5
Shiga □ Japan 35°20N 136°0E 223 B8
Shigaib Sudan 15°5N 23°35E 259 E4
Shigu China 26°51N 99°56E 228 D2
Shiguaigou China 40°52N 110°15E 226 D6
Shihan Yemen 17°42N 52°27E 249 C6
Shihan, W. → Yemen 17°24N 51°26E 249 C5
Shihchiachuangi = Shijiazhuang China 38°2N 114°28E 226 E8
Shihezi China 44°15N 86°2E 217 D11
Shihiu Taiwan 24°38N 121°10E 225 B3
Shihkangkeng Taiwan 24°1N 120°57E 225 B2
Shihmen Taiwan 25°17N 121°33E 225 A3
Shihmen Shuiku Taiwan 24°49N 121°21E 225 B3
Shihtan Taiwan 24°32N 120°55E 225 B2
Shiiba Japan 32°29N 131°4E 222 E3
Shiikh Somalia 9°56N 45°13E 267 C6
Shijak Albania 41°21N 19°33E 202 E3
Shijiazhuang China 38°2N 114°28E 226 E8
Shijiu Hu China 31°25N 118°50E 229 B12
Shikarpur India 28°17N 78°7E 242 E8
Shikarpur Pakistan 27°57N 68°39E 242 F3
Shikhrany = Kanash Russia 55°30N 47°32E 190 C8
Shikine-Jima Japan 34°19N 139°13E 223 C11
Shikohabad India 27°6N 78°36E 243 F8
Shikokochūō Japan 34°1N 133°34E 222 C5
Shikoku Japan 33°30N 133°30E 222 D5
Shikoku □ Japan 33°30N 133°30E 222 D5
Shikoku-Sanchi Japan 33°30N 133°30E 222 D5
Shikotan, Ostrov Asia 43°47N 146°44E 215 E15
Shikotsu-Ko Japan 42°45N 141°25E 220 C10
Shikotsu-Tōya △ Japan 44°4N 145°8E 220 C10
Shikuka = Poronaysk Russia 49°13N 143°0E 219 B17
Shilabo Ethiopia 6°5N 44°46E 267 C5
Shiliguri India 26°45N 88°25E 241 B2
Shilihe China 39°50N 116°25E 114 B2
Shiliu = Changjiang China 19°20N 108°55E 229 a
Shilka Russia 52°0N 115°55E 215 D12
Shilka → Russia 53°20N 121°26E 215 D13
Shillelagh Ireland 52°45N 6°32W 166 D5
Shillington U.S.A. 40°18N 75°58W 313 F9
Shillong India 25°35N 91°53E 241 C3
Shilo West Bank 32°4N 35°18E 251 F6
Shilong China 23°5N 113°52E 229 F9
Shilou China 37°0N 110°48E 226 F6
Shilovo Russia 54°25N 40°57E 190 C5
Shima-Hantō Japan 34°22N 136°45E 223 C8
Shimabara Japan 32°48N 130°20E 222 E2
Shimada Japan 34°49N 138°10E 223 C10
Shimane □ Japan 35°0N 132°30E 222 C4
Shimane-Hantō Japan 35°30N 133°0E 222 B5
Shimanovsk Russia 52°15N 127°30E 215 D13
Shimanto Kōchi, Japan 33°12N 133°8E 222 D5
Shimanto Kōchi, Japan 32°59N 132°56E 222 E4
Shimba Hills ⌂ Kenya 4°14S 39°25E 268 C4
Shimbiris Somalia 10°44N 47°14E 267 B6
Shimen China 29°35N 111°20E 229 C8
Shimenjie China 29°29N 116°48E 229 C11
Shimian China 29°17N 102°23E 228 C4
Shimizu Japan 35°0N 138°30E 223 C10
Shimla India 31°2N 77°9E 242 D7
Shimo-Jima Japan 32°15N 130°7E 222 E2
Shimo-Koshiki-Jima Japan 31°40N 129°43E 222 F1
Shimoda Japan 34°40N 138°57E 223 C10
Shimodate Japan 36°20N 139°55E 223 A11
Shimoga India 13°57N 75°32E 245 H2
Shimogawara Japan 35°39N 139°27E 140 B1
Shimokita-Hantō Japan 41°20N 141°0E 220 D10
Shimoni Kenya 4°38S 39°20E 268 C4
Shimonita Japan 36°13N 138°47E 223 A10
Shimonoseki Japan 33°58N 130°55E 222 D2
Shimosalo Japan 35°45N 139°31E 140 A2
Shimoshakujii Japan 35°43N 139°35E 140 A2
Shimotsuma Japan 36°11N 139°58E 223 A11
Shimpuru Rapids Namibia 17°45S 19°55E 265 F3
Shimsha → India 13°15N 77°10E 245 H3
Shimsk Russia 58°15N 30°50E 188 C6
Shin, L. U.K. 58°5N 4°30W 167 C4
Shin-Nan'yō Japan 34°3N 131°49E 222 C3
Shin-Tone-Gawa → Japan 35°44N 140°51E 223 B12
Shinagawa Japan 35°36N 139°44E 140 B3
Shinan China 22°44N 109°53E 228 F7
Shinano-Gawa → Japan 36°50N 138°30E 221 F9
Shināş Oman 24°46N 56°28E 247 E8
Shīndand Afghan. 33°12N 62°8E 240 B1
Shing Mun Country Park ⌂ Hong Kong, China 22°23N 114°8E 122 A2
Shing Mun Res. Hong Kong, China 22°23N 114°8E 122 A2
Shingbwiyang Burma 26°41N 96°13E 241 B6
Shinglehouse U.S.A. 41°58N 78°12W 312 E6
Shingū Japan 33°40N 135°55E 223 D7
Shingwidzi S. Africa 23°5S 31°25E 271 B5
Shinji Japan 35°24N 132°54E 222 B4
Shinji-Ko Japan 35°26N 132°57E 222 B4
Shinjō Japan 38°46N 140°18E 220 E10
Shinjuku Tokyo, Japan 140 a1
Shinjuku Nat. Garden Tokyo, Japan 140 a2
Shinkafe Nigeria 13°8N 6°29E 263 C6
Shinkoiwa Japan 35°43N 139°51E 140 A4
Shinminato = Imizu Japan 36°47N 137°4E 223 A9
Shinnakano Japan 35°41N 139°40E 140 A3
Shinshār Syria 34°36N 36°43E 250 D7
Shinshiro Japan 34°54N 137°30E 223 C9
Shintuya Peru 12°41S 71°15W 330 C3
Shinyanga Tanzania 3°45S 33°27E 268 C3
Shinyanga □ Tanzania 3°50S 34°0E 268 C3
Shio-no-Misaki Japan 33°25N 135°45E 223 D7
Shiogama Japan 38°19N 141°1E 220 E10
Shiojiri Japan 36°6N 137°58E 223 A9
Shipai China 23°8N 113°20E 121 B3
Shipchenski Prokhod Bulgaria 42°45N 25°15E 203 D9
Shiphoirt, L. = Seaforth, L. U.K. 57°52N 6°36W 167 D2
Shiping China 23°45N 102°23E 228 F4
Shippagan Canada 47°45N 64°45W 299 C7
Shippensburg U.S.A. 40°3N 77°31W 312 F7
Shippenville U.S.A. 41°15N 79°28W 312 E5
Shiprock U.S.A. 36°47N 108°41W 305 H9
Shiqian China 27°32N 108°13E 228 D7
Shiqma, N. → Israel 31°37N 34°30E 251 G5
Shiquan China 33°5N 108°15E 228 A7
Shiquan He = Indus → Pakistan 24°20N 67°47E 242 G2
Shīr Khān Afghan. 37°11N 68°36E 240 A3
Shīr Kūh Iran 31°39N 54°3E 247 D7
Shira'awh Qatar 25°2N 52°14E 247 E7
Shirabad = Sherabad Uzbekistan 37°40N 67°1E 217 E7
Shiragami-Misaki Japan 41°24N 140°12E 220 D10
Shirahama Japan 33°41N 135°20E 223 D7
Shirakawa Fukushima, Japan 37°7N 140°13E 221 F10
Shirakawa Gifu, Japan 36°17N 136°56E 223 A8
Shirane-San Gumma, Japan 36°48N 139°22E 223 A11
Shirane-San Yamanashi, Japan 35°42N 138°9E 223 B10
Shiraoi Japan 42°33N 141°21E 220 C10
Shirati Tanzania 1°8S 33°59E 266 E3
Shīrāz Iran 29°42N 52°30E 247 D7
Shirbīn Egypt 31°11N 31°32E 256 H7
Shire → Africa 17°42S 35°19E 269 F4
Shiren China 41°57N 126°34E 227 D14
Shiretoko △ Japan 44°15N 145°15E 220 B12
Shiretoko-Misaki Japan 44°21N 145°20E 220 B12
Shirinab → Pakistan 30°15N 66°28E 242 D2
Shirinashi → Japan 34°38N 135°27E 133 B1
Shiriya-Zaki Japan 41°25N 141°30E 220 D10
Shirley U.S.A. 39°53N 85°35W 311 E11
Shirogane Japan 35°37N 139°44E 140 B3
Shiroishi Japan 38°0N 140°37E 220 F10
Shirol India 16°47N 74°41E 244 F2
Shiroro Res. Nigeria 9°56N 6°54E 263 D6
Shirpur India 21°21N 74°57E 244 D2
Shirshov Ridge Pac. Oc. 58°0N 170°0E 288 B8
Shīrvān Iran 37°30N 57°50E 247 B8
Shirwa, L. = Chilwa, L. Malawi 15°15S 35°40E 269 F4
Shishaldin Volcano U.S.A. 54°45N 163°58W 303 J7
Shishi China 24°44N 118°37E 229 E12
Shishmaref U.S.A. 66°15N 166°4W 303 C6
Shishou China 29°38N 112°22E 229 C9
Shisur Oman 18°15N 53°39E 249 C6
Shitai China 30°12N 117°25E 229 B11
Shitata South Sudan 4°30N 30°10E 257 G3
Shitennoji Temple Japan 34°39N 135°31E 133 B2
Shithāthah Iraq 32°34N 43°28E 213 G10
Shivamogga = Shimoga India 13°57N 75°32E 245 H2
Shively U.S.A. 38°12N 85°49W 311 F11
Shivpuri India 25°26N 77°42E 242 G7
Shiweitang China 23°6N 113°12E 121 B2
Shixian China 43°5N 129°50E 227 C15
Shixing China 24°46N 114°5E 229 E10
Shiyan Guangdong, China 22°42N 113°56E 219 a
Shiyan Hubei, China 32°35N 110°45E 229 A8
Shiyan Shuiku China 22°42N 113°54E 219 a
Shiyata Egypt 29°25N 25°7E 256 B2
Shizhu China 29°58N 108°7E 228 C7
Shizong China 24°50N 104°0E 228 E5
Shizuishan China 39°15N 106°50E 226 E4
Shizuoka Japan 34°57N 138°24E 223 C10
Shizuoka □ Japan 35°15N 138°40E 223 B10
Shkhara Georgia 43°0N 43°8E 213 A10
Shklov = Shklow Belarus 54°16N 30°15E 177 A16
Shklow Belarus 54°16N 30°15E 177 A16
Shkodër Albania 42°4N 19°32E 202 D3
Shkodra = Shkodër Albania 42°4N 19°32E 202 D3
Shkumbini → Albania 41°2N 19°31E 202 E3
Shmidta, Ostrov Russia 81°0N 91°0E 215 A10
Shō-Gawa → Japan 36°47N 137°4E 223 A9
Shoal Cr. → U.S.A. 39°44N 93°32W 310 E3
Shoal L. Canada 49°33N 95°1W 297 D9
Shoal Lake Canada 50°30N 100°35W 297 C8
Shoalhaven → Australia 34°54S 150°42E 283 C9
Shoals U.S.A. 38°40N 86°47W 311 F10
Shōbara Japan 34°51N 133°1E 222 C5
Shōdo-Shima Japan 34°30N 134°15E 222 C6
Shogunle Nigeria 6°34N 3°20E 124 A2
Sholapur = Solapur India 17°43N 75°56E 244 F2
Shomolu Nigeria 6°32N 3°22E 124 A2
Shōmrōn West Bank 32°15N 35°13E 251 F6
Shonian Harb. Palau 7°10N 134°23E 288 c
Shonzhy Kazakhstan 43°32N 79°28E 217 D9
Shooters Hill U.K. 51°28N 0°4E 125 B4
Shoranur India 10°46N 76°19E 245 J3
Shorapur India 16°31N 76°48E 245 F3
Shoreditch London, U.K. 125 a5
Shoreham U.S.A. 43°53N 73°18W 313 C11
Shoreham by Sea U.K. 50°50N 0°16W 169 G7
Shorewood U.S.A. 43°5N 87°53W 311 A9
Shori → Pakistan 28°29N 69°44E 242 E3
Shorkot Pakistan 30°50N 72°0E 242 D4
Shorkot Road Pakistan 30°47N 72°15E 242 D5
Shorsky △ Russia 52°40N 88°0E 217 B11
Shorter U.S.A. 32°24N 85°57W 316 C4
Shorterville U.S.A. 31°34N 85°6W 316 D4
Shortland I. Solomon Is. 7°0S 155°45E 287 L8
Shortland Is. Solomon Is. 7°0S 156°0E 287 L8
Shortlands U.K. 51°23N 0°0 125 B4
Shortt's I. India 20°47N 87°4E 244 D8
Shoshone Calif., U.S.A. 35°58N 116°16W 307 K10
Shoshone Idaho, U.S.A. 42°56N 114°25W 304 E6
Shoshone L. U.S.A. 44°22N 110°43W 304 D8
Shoshone Mts. U.S.A. 39°20N 117°25W 304 G5
Shoshong Botswana 22°56S 26°31E 270 B4
Shoshoni U.S.A. 43°14N 108°7W 304 E9
Shostka Ukraine 51°57N 33°32E 189 G7
Shot Iran 39°12N 44°49E 213 C11
Shotor Khūn Afghan. 34°19N 64°56E 240 B2
Shotover → N.Z. 44°59S 168°41E 285 E3
Shou Xian China 32°37N 116°42E 229 A11
Shouchang China 29°18N 119°12E 229 C12
Shouchia Taiwan 22°14N 120°50E 225 D2
Shoufeng Taiwan 23°52N 121°30E 225 C3
Shouguang China 37°52N 118°45E 227 F10
Shouning China 27°27N 119°31E 229 D12
Shouyang China 37°54N 113°8E 226 F7
Show Low U.S.A. 34°15N 110°2W 305 J8
Showa Japan 35°36N 138°29E 223 B10
Showak Sudan 14°23N 35°52E 257 E4
Shpola Ukraine 49°1N 31°30E 189 H6
Shpykiv Ukraine 48°47N 28°34E 183 B13
Shqipëria = Albania ■ Europe 41°0N 20°0E 202 E4
Shreveport U.S.A. 32°31N 93°45W 314 E8
Shrewsbury U.K. 52°43N 2°45W 169 E5
Shri Mohangarh India 27°17N 71°18E 242 F4
Shrigonda India 18°37N 74°41E 244 E2
Shrirampur India 22°44N 88°21E 243 H13
Shropshire □ U.K. 52°36N 2°45W 169 E5
Shtërpcë Kosovo 42°14N 21°1E 202 D5
Shū Kazakhstan 43°36N 73°42E 217 D8
Shū → Kazakhstan 45°0N 67°44E 217 D7
Shu'afat West Bank 31°49N 35°14E 123 B2
Shuangbai China 24°42N 101°38E 228 E3
Shuangcheng China 45°20N 126°15E 227 B14
Shuangfeng China 27°29N 112°11E 229 D9
Shuanggou China 34°2N 117°30E 227 G9
Shuangjiang China 23°26N 99°58E 228 F2
Shuangliao China 43°29N 123°30E 227 C12
Shuangshanzi China 40°20N 119°8E 227 D10
Shuangyang China 43°28N 125°40E 227 C13
Shuangyashan China 46°28N 131°5E 219 B15
Shu'b, Ra's Yemen 12°30N 53°25E 249 D6
Shubarqudyq Kazakhstan 49°13N 56°34E 216 C5
Shubarshī Kazakhstan 48°39N 57°11E 216 C5
Shubrâ Egypt 30°5N 31°14E 117 A2
Shubrâ el Kheima Egypt 30°4N 31°14E 117 A2
Shubrâ Khit Egypt 31°2N 30°42E 256 H7
Shucheng China 31°28N 116°57E 229 B11
Shugozero Russia 59°54N 34°10E 188 C8
Shuguri Falls Tanzania 8°33S 37°22E 269 D4
Shuḩayr Yemen 14°41N 49°23E 249 D5
Shui Hau Hong Kong, China 22°13N 113°55E 122 B1
Shuiding = Huocheng China 44°0N 80°48E 217 D10
Shuiji China 27°13N 118°20E 229 D12
Shuikuo China 23°10N 113°10E 121 A2
Shuili Taiwan 23°49N 120°51E 225 C2
Shuilien Taiwan 23°47N 121°34E 225 C3
Shuishang Taiwan 23°25N 120°23E 225 C2
Shuitiliao Taiwan 22°23N 120°35E 225 D2
Shujalpur India 23°18N 76°46E 242 H7
Shukpa Kunzang India 34°22N 78°22E 243 B8
Shulan China 44°28N 127°0E 227 B14
Shulaveri Georgia 41°22N 44°45E 191 K7
Shule China 39°25N 76°3E 217 E9
Shule He → China 40°20N 92°50E 218 C7
Shullsburg U.S.A. 42°35N 90°13W 310 B6
Shumagin Is. U.S.A. 55°7N 160°30W 303 J7
Shumanay Uzbekistan 42°38N 58°55E 216 D5
Shumen Bulgaria 43°18N 26°55E 203 C10
Shumerlya Russia 55°30N 46°25E 190 C8
Shumikha Russia 55°10N 63°15E 214 D7
Shûna, W. el → Egypt 29°38N 32°6E 251 J3
Shunān Japan 34°3N 131°50E 222 C3
Shunchang China 26°54N 117°48E 229 D11
Shunde China 22°42N 113°14E 229 F9
Shungay Kazakhstan 48°30N 46°45E 191 F8
Shungnak U.S.A. 66°52N 157°9W 303 C8
Shuo Xian = Shuozhou China 39°20N 112°33E 226 E7
Shuozhou China 39°20N 112°33E 226 E7
Shuqrā' Yemen 13°22N 45°44E 248 D4
Shūr → Fārs, Iran 28°30N 55°0E 247 D7
Shūr → Kermān, Iran 30°52N 57°37E 247 D8
Shūr → Yazd, Iran 31°45N 55°15E 247 D7
Shūr Āb Iran 34°23N 51°11E 247 C6
Shūr Gaz Iran 29°10N 59°20E 247 D8
Shūrāb Iran 33°43N 56°29E 247 C8
Shuri Japan 26°13N 127°43E 288 a
Shūrjestān Iran 31°24N 52°25E 247 D7
Shurkhua Burma 22°15N 93°38E 241 D4
Shurugwi Zimbabwe 19°40S 30°0E 269 F3
Shūsf Iran 31°50N 60°5E 247 D9
Shūsh Iran 32°11N 48°15E 213 F13
Shusha Azerbaijan 39°46N 46°45E 213 C12
Shushenskoye Russia 53°19N 91°56E 217 B12
Shushensky Bor △ Russia 52°40N 91°15E 217 B12
Shūshtar Iran 32°0N 48°50E 247 D6
Shuswap L. Canada 50°55N 119°3W 296 C5
Shute Harbour △ Australia 20°17S 148°47E 280 b
Shuya Russia 56°50N 41°28E 190 B5
Shuyak I. U.S.A. 58°31N 152°30W 303 G9
Shuyang China 34°10N 118°42E 227 G10
Shuzenji = Izu Japan 34°58N 138°56E 223 C10
Shūzū Iran 29°52N 54°30E 247 D7
Shwangliao = Liaoyuan China 42°58N 125°2E 227 C13
Shwebo Burma 22°30N 95°45E 241 D5
Shwegu Burma 24°15N 96°26E 241 C6
Shwegun Burma 17°9N 97°39E 241 G6
Shwegyin Burma 17°55N 96°53E 241 G6
Shweli → Burma 23°45N 96°45E 241 D6
Shwenyaung Burma 20°46N 96°57E 241 E6
Shyamnagar India 13°21N 92°57E 245 H11
Shyghanaq Kazakhstan 45°6N 73°59E 217 C8
Shyghys Qazaqstan □ Kazakhstan 48°30N 82°0E 217 D10
Shymkent Kazakhstan 42°18N 69°36E 217 D7
Shyok India 34°13N 78°12E 243 B8
Shyok → Pakistan 35°13N 75°53E 243 B6
Shyroke Odesa, Ukraine 45°59N 30°5E 183 E15
Shyroke Ternopil, Ukraine 48°13N 23°6E 182 B8
Si Kiang = Xi Jiang → China 22°5N 113°20E 229 F9
Si Lanna △ Thailand 19°17N 99°12E 236 C2

Si Nakarin Res. Thailand 14°35N 99°0E 236 E2
Si-ngan = Xi'an China 34°15N 109°0E 226 G5
Si Phangnga Thailand 9°8N 98°29E 237 H2
Si Prachan Thailand 14°37N 100°9E 236 E3
Si Racha Thailand 13°10N 100°48E 236 F3
Si Sa Ket Thailand 15°8N 104°23E 236 E5
Siachen Glacier Asia 35°20N 77°30E 243 B7
Sīah Chashmeh Iran 39°3N 44°25E 213 C11
Siahaf → Pakistan 29°3N 68°57E 242 E3
Siahan Range Pakistan 27°30N 64°40E 240 D2
Siak → Indonesia 1°13N 102°9E 234 B2
Siak Sri Indrapura Indonesia 0°51N 102°0E 234 B2
Sialkot Pakistan 32°32N 74°30E 242 C6
Sialum Papua N. G. 6°5S 147°36E 286 D4
Siam = Thailand ■ Asia 16°0N 102°0E 236 E4
Sian = Xi'an China 34°15N 109°0E 226 G5
Sian Ka'an ⌓ Mexico 19°35N 87°40W 319 D7
Siangtan = Xiangtan China 27°51N 112°54E 229 D9
Sianów Poland 54°13N 16°18E 184 D3
Siantan Indonesia 3°10N 106°15E 234 B3
Siaolanyu = Hsiaohungt'ou Hsü Taiwan 21°57N 121°36E 225 E3
Siàpo → Venezuela 2°7N 66°28W 328 C4
Sīāreh Iran 28°5N 60°14E 247 D9
Siargao I. Phil. 9°52N 126°3E 233 G6
Siasi Phil. 5°34N 120°50E 233 J3
Siasi I. Phil. 5°33N 120°51E 233 J3
Siassi Papua N. G. 5°40S 147°51E 286 C4
Siatista Greece 40°15N 21°33E 202 F5
Siaton Phil. 9°4N 123°2E 233 G4
Siau Indonesia 2°50N 125°25E 231 D7
Šiauliai Lithuania 55°56N 23°15E 184 C10
Šiauliai □ Lithuania 55°56N 23°19E 184 C10
Siavonga Zambia 16°33S 28°42E 271 A4
Siazan = Siyäzän Azerbaijan 41°3N 49°10E 191 K9
Sibâi, Gebel el Egypt 25°45N 34°10E 246 E2
Sibang Gabon 0°25N 9°31E 264 B1
Sibang Bali, Indonesia 8°34S 115°13E 231 K18
Sibay Russia 52°42N 58°39E 186 D10
Sibay I. Phil. 11°51N 121°29E 233 F3
Sibayi, L. S. Africa 27°20S 32°45E 271 C5
Sibdu Sudan 10°57N 26°17E 257 E2
Šibenik Croatia 43°48N 15°54E 199 E12
Siberia = Sibirskiy □ Russia 58°0N 90°0E 215 D10
Siberia Russia 60°0N 100°0E 210 B12
Siberië Curaçao 12°14N 69°3W 322 g
Siberut Indonesia 1°30S 99°0E 234 C1
Siberut, Selat Indonesia 0°42S 98°35E 234 C1
Siberut △ Indonesia 1°17S 98°45E 234 C1
Sibi Pakistan 29°30N 67°54E 242 E2
Sibigo Indonesia 2°50N 95°54E 234 B1
Sibiloi △ Kenya 4°0N 36°20E 268 B4
Sibirskiy □ Russia 58°0N 90°0E 215 D10
Sibirtsevo Russia 44°12N 132°26E 220 B5
Sibiti Congo 3°38S 13°19E 264 C2
Sibiu Romania 45°45N 24°9E 183 E9
Sibiu □ Romania 45°50N 24°15E 183 E9
Sibium Mts. Papua N. G. 9°19S 148°25E 286 E5
Sibley Ill., U.S.A. 40°35N 88°23W 311 D8
Sibley Iowa, U.S.A. 43°24N 95°45W 308 D6
Sibo Sweden 61°13N 16°37E 162 C10
Sibolga Indonesia 1°42N 98°45E 234 B1
Siborongborong Indonesia 2°13N 98°58E 237 L2
Sibsagar India 27°0N 94°36E 241 B5
Sibu Malaysia 2°18N 111°49E 235 B4
Sibuco Phil. 7°20N 122°10E 233 H4
Sibuguey B. Phil. 7°50N 122°45E 233 H4
Sibut C.A.R. 5°46N 19°10E 264 A3
Sibutu Phil. 4°45N 119°30E 235 B5
Sibutu Group Phil. 4°45N 119°20E 233 J2
Sibutu I. Phil. 4°47N 119°29E 233 J2
Sibutu Passage E. Indies 4°50N 120°0E 233 J3
Sibuyan I. Phil. 12°25N 122°40E 232 E4
Sibuyan Sea Phil. 12°30N 122°20E 232 E4
Sic Romania 46°56N 23°53E 183 D8
Sicamous Canada 50°49N 119°0W 296 C5
Sicapoo, Mt. Phil. 18°1N 120°56E 232 B3
Sicasica Bolivia 17°22S 67°45W 330 D4
Siccus → Australia 31°55S 139°17E 282 A3
Sichelberg = Sierpc Poland 52°55N 19°43E 185 F6
Sichon Thailand 9°0N 99°54E 237 H2
Sichuan □ China 30°30N 103°0E 228 B5
Sichuan Pendi China 31°0N 105°0E 228 B5
Sicilia Italy 37°30N 14°30E 201 E7
Sicily = Sicilia Italy 37°30N 14°30E 201 E7
Sicily, Str. of Medit. S. 37°35N 11°56E 200 E4
Sico → Honduras 15°58N 84°58W 320 C3
Sicuani Peru 14°21S 71°10W 330 C3
Šid Serbia 45°8N 19°14E 182 E4
Sidamo Ethiopia 5°0N 37°50E 257 G4
Sidaouet Niger 18°34N 8°3E 259 E1
Sidari Greece 39°47N 19°41E 206 B9
Sidcup U.K. 51°25N 0°6E 125 B4
Siddapur India 14°20N 74°53E 245 G2
Siddhapur India 23°56N 72°25E 242 H5
Siddipet India 18°5N 78°51E 244 E4
Side Turkey 36°45N 31°23E 250 B2
Sidensjö Sweden 63°18N 18°17E 162 A12
Sidéradougou Burkina Faso 10°42N 4°12W 262 C4
Siderno Italy 38°16N 16°18E 201 D9
Sideros, Akra Greece 35°19N 26°19E 207 E7
Sidhauli India 27°17N 80°50E 243 F9
Sidhi India 24°25N 81°53E 243 G9
Sîdi Abd el Rahmân Egypt 30°55N 29°44E 256 A2
Sîdi Barrâni Egypt 31°38N 25°58E 256 A2
Sidi-bel-Abbès Algeria 35°13N 0°39W 261 A4
Sidi-bel-Abbès □ Algeria 34°50N 0°30W 261 B4
Sidi Bennour Morocco 32°40N 8°25W 260 B3
Sidi Bou Zid Tunisia 35°1N 9°16E 258 B1
Sidi Bou Zid □ Tunisia 35°0N 9°30E 258 B1
Sidi Boubekeur Algeria 35°1N 0°4E 261 A5
Sîdi Haneish Egypt 31°10N 27°35E 256 A2
Sidi Ifni Morocco 29°29N 10°12W 260 C2
Sidi Kacem Morocco 34°12N 5°42W 260 B3
Sîdi Omar Egypt 31°24N 24°57E 256 A1
Sidi Slimane Morocco 34°16N 5°56W 260 B3
Sidi Smaïl Morocco 32°50N 8°31W 260 B3
Sīdī 'Uzayz Libya 31°41N 24°55E 258 B4
Sidikalang Indonesia 2°45N 98°19E 237 L2
Sidimo Somalia 2°27N 41°58E 267 D5
Siding No 14 = Ponoka Canada 52°42N 113°40W 296 C6
Sidirokastro Greece 41°13N 23°24E 202 E7
Sidlaw Hills U.K. 56°32N 3°2W 167 E5
Sidley, Mt. Antarctica 77°2S 126°2W 151 D14
Sidmouth U.K. 50°40N 3°15W 169 G4
Sidmouth, C. Australia 13°25S 143°36E 280 A3
Sidney B.C., Canada 48°39N 123°24W 306 B3
Sidney Mont., U.S.A. 47°43N 104°9W 304 C11
Sidney N.Y., U.S.A. 42°19N 75°24W 313 D9
Sidney Nebr., U.S.A. 41°8N 102°59W 308 E2
Sidney Ohio, U.S.A. 40°17N 84°9W 311 D12
Sidney Lanier, L. U.S.A. 34°10N 84°4W 316 A5
Sido Mali 11°37N 7°29W 262 C3
Sidoarjo Indonesia 7°27S 112°43E 235 D4
Sidoktaya Burma 20°27N 94°15E 241 E5
Sidon = Saydā Lebanon 33°35N 35°25E 250 E6
Sidra = Surt Libya 31°11N 16°39E 258 B3
Sidra, G. of = Surt, Khalīj Libya 31°40N 18°30E 258 B3
Sidrolândia Brazil 20°55S 54°58W 331 E7
Siebenhirten Austria 48°8N 16°17E 142 B1
Siedlce Poland 52°10N 22°20E 185 F9
Siedlung Germany 52°35N 13°7E 115 A1
Sieg → Germany 50°46N 7°6E 178 E3
Siegburg Germany 50°47N 7°12E 178 E3
Siegen Germany 50°51N 8°0E 178 E4
Siekierki Poland 52°12N 21°4E 143 B2
Sielce Poland 52°12N 21°2E 143 B2
Siem Pang Cambodia 14°7N 106°23E 236 E6
Siem Reap = Siemreab Cambodia 13°20N 103°52E 236 F4
Siemensstadt Germany 52°32N 13°16E 115 A2
Siemiatycze Poland 52°27N 22°53E 185 F9
Siemreab Cambodia 13°20N 103°52E 236 F4
Siena Italy 43°19N 11°21E 199 E8
Sieniawa Poland 50°11N 22°38E 185 H9
Sienyang = Xianyang China 34°20N 108°40E 226 G5
Sieradz Poland 51°37N 18°41E 185 G5
Sieraków Poland 52°39N 16°2E 185 F3
Sierck-les-Bains France 49°26N 6°20E 173 C13
Sierning Austria 48°2N 14°18E 180 C7
Sierpc Poland 52°55N 19°43E 185 F6
Sierpe, Bocas de la Venezuela 10°0N 61°30W 329 G9
Sierra Blanca U.S.A. 31°11N 105°22W 314 F2
Sierra Blanca Peak U.S.A. 33°23N 105°49W 305 K11
Sierra City U.S.A. 39°34N 120°38W 306 F6
Sierra Colorada Argentina 40°35S 67°50W 336 B3
Sierra de Agalta △ Honduras 15°1N 85°48W 320 C2
Sierra de Andújar ⌓ Spain 38°20N 3°50W 195 G7
Sierra de Aracena y Picos de Aroche ⌓ Spain 37°53N 6°41W 195 H4
Sierra de Bahoruco △ Dom. Rep. 18°10N 71°25W 321 C5
Sierra de Baza ⌓ Spain 37°20N 2°48W 197 H2
Sierra de Castril ⌓ Spain 37°54N 2°50W 197 H2
Sierra de Espuña ⌓ Spain 37°50N 1°31W 197 H3
Sierra de Grazalema ⌓ Spain 36°31N 5°28W 195 J5
Sierra de Gredos ⌓ Spain 40°17N 5°17W 194 E5
Sierra de Hornachuelos ⌓ Spain 37°56N 5°14W 195 H5
Sierra de Huétor ⌓ Spain 37°14N 3°30W 195 H7
Sierra de la Culata △ Venezuela 8°48N 70°56W 328 B3
Sierra de la Macarena △ Colombia 11°19N 74°1W 328 A3
Sierra de las Nieves ⌓ Spain 36°42N 5°0W 195 J6
Sierra de las Quijadas △ Argentina 32°29S 67°5W 334 C2
Sierra de María-Los Vélez ⌓ Spain 37°41N 2°10W 197 H2
Sierra de San Luis △ Venezuela 11°11N 69°33W 328 A4
Sierra de San Pedro Mártir △ Mexico 31°10N 115°30W 318 A1
Sierra de Yeguas Spain 37°7N 4°52W 195 H6
Sierra del São Mamede ⌓ Portugal 39°17N 7°18W 195 F3
Sierra Gorda Chile 22°50S 69°15W 334 A2
Sierra Grande Argentina 41°36S 65°22W 336 B3
Sierra Leone ■ W. Afr. 9°0N 12°0W 262 D2
Sierra Leone Basin Atl. Oc. 5°0N 17°0W 152 F10
Sierra Leone Rise Atl. Oc. 7°0N 22°0W 152 F9
Sierra Madre Mexico 16°0N 93°0W 319 D6
Sierra Madre Calif., U.S.A. 34°9N 118°3W 126 B4
Sierra Madre Occidental Mexico 27°0N 107°0W 318 B3
Sierra Madre Oriental Mexico 25°0N 100°0W 318 C5
Sierra Mágina ⌓ Spain 37°44N 3°28W 195 H7
Sierra Mojada Mexico 27°18N 103°41W 318 B4
Sierra Nevada Spain 37°3N 3°15W 195 H7
Sierra Nevada Calif., U.S.A. 39°0N 120°30W 306 H8
Sierra Nevada ⌓ Spain 37°4N 3°7W 195 H7
Sierra Norte de Sevilla ⌓ Spain 37°55N 5°46W 195 H5
Sierra Subbéticas ⌓ Spain 37°26N 4°18W 195 H6
Sierra Vista U.S.A. 31°33N 110°18W 305 L8
Sierras de Cardeña y Montoro ⌓ Spain 38°13N 4°15W 195 G6
Sierras de Cazorla, Segura y las Villas ⌓ Spain 37°0N 2°45W 197 J2
Sierraville U.S.A. 39°36N 120°22W 306 F6
Sierre Switz. 46°17N 7°31E 179 J3
Sievering Austria 48°15N 16°20E 142 A2
Sīf Yemen 15°19N 48°20E 249 D5
Sifani Ethiopia 12°18N 40°19E 257 E5
Sifié Ivory C. 8°0N 7°5W 262 D3
Sifnos Greece 37°0N 24°45E 204 E6
Sifton Canada 51°21N 100°8W 297 C8
Sifton Pass Canada 57°52N 126°15W 296 B3
Sig Algeria 35°32N 0°12W 261 A4
Sigaboy = Governor Generoso Phil. 6°39N 126°5E 233 H6
Sigatoka Fiji 18°8S 177°32E 287 B1
Sigdal Norway 60°3N 9°38E 164 D6
Sigean France 43°2N 2°58E 174 E6
Siggiewi Malta 35°51N 14°26E 206 F7
Sighetu-Marmației Romania 47°57N 23°52E 183 C8
Sighișoara Romania 46°12N 24°50E 183 D9
Sighthill U.K. 55°56N 3°17W 121 B2
Sigiriya Sri Lanka 7°57N 80°45E 245 L5
Sigli Indonesia 5°25N 96°0E 234 A1
Siglufjörður Iceland 66°12N 18°55W 155 A8
Siglunes Iceland 66°12N 18°50W 155 A8
Sigmaringen Germany 48°5N 9°12E 179 G5
Signa Italy 43°45N 11°10E 198 E8
Signakhi = Tsnori Georgia 41°40N 45°57E 191 K7
Signal de Botrang Belgium 50°29N 6°4E 170 D6
Signal Hill S. Africa 34°5S 18°24E 118 A1
Signal Pk. U.S.A. 33°20N 114°2W 307 M12
Signy I. Antarctica 60°43S 45°36W 151 C18
Signy-l'Abbaye France 49°40N 4°25E 173 C11
Sigourney U.S.A. 41°20N 92°12W 310 C4
Sigsbee U.S.A. 31°16N 83°52W 316 D6
Sigsbee Deep Gulf of Mexico 25°0N 92°0W 152 D1
Sígsig Ecuador 3°0S 78°50W 328 D2
Sigtuna Sweden 59°36N 17°44E 162 E11
Sigüenza Spain 41°3N 2°40W 196 D2
Siguiri Guinea 11°31N 9°10W 262 C3
Sigulda Latvia 57°10N 24°55E 188 D3
Siguniangshan China 31°15N 103°10E 228 B4
Sihanoukville = Kampong Saom Cambodia 10°38N 103°30E 237 G4
Sihawa India 20°19N 81°55E 244 D5
Siheung Gyeonggi-do, S. Korea 37°25N 126°47E 224 D3
Siheung Seoul, S. Korea 37°28N 126°54E 137 C1
Sihong China 33°27N 118°16E 227 H10
Sihora India 23°29N 80°6E 243 H9
Sihu = Ssuhu Taiwan 23°38N 120°13E 225 C2
Sihuas Peru 8°40S 77°40W 330 B2
Sihui China 23°20N 112°40E 229 F9
Siikajoki → Finland 64°50N 24°43E 160 D21
Siilinjärvi Finland 63°4N 27°39E 160 E22
Siirt Turkey 37°57N 41°55E 213 D9
Siirt □ Turkey 37°55N 41°55E 213 D9
Sijarira Ra. = Chizarira Zimbabwe 17°36S 27°45E 269 F2
Sijungjung Indonesia 0°42S 100°58E 234 C2
Sika India 22°26N 69°47E 242 H3
Sikanni Chief → Canada 57°47N 122°15W 296 B4
Sikao Thailand 7°34N 99°21E 237 J2
Sikar India 27°33N 75°10E 242 F6
Sikasso Mali 11°18N 5°35W 262 C3
Sikasso □ Mali 10°55N 7°0W 262 C3
Sikátorpuszta Hungary 47°34N 19°10E 117 A3
Sikelenge Zambia 14°53S 24°14E 265 E4
Sikeston U.S.A. 36°53N 89°35W 308 G9
Sikhote Alin, Khrebet Russia 45°0N 136°0E 220 B8
Sikhote Alin Ra. = Sikhote Alin, Khrebet Russia 45°0N 136°0E 220 B8
Sikia Greece 40°2N 23°56E 202 F7
Sikinos Greece 36°40N 25°8E 205 E7
Sikkim □ India 27°50N 88°30E 241 B2
Siklós Hungary 45°50N 18°19E 182 E3
Sil → Spain 42°27N 7°43W 194 C3
Silacayoapan Mexico 17°30N 98°9W 319 D5
Šilalė Lithuania 55°28N 22°12E 184 C9
Silampur India 28°39N 77°16E 120 B2
Silandro Italy 46°38N 10°46E 198 B7
Silang Phil. 14°14N 120°58E 232 D3
Silawad India 21°54N 74°54E 242 J6
Silay Phil. 10°47N 122°58E 233 F4
Silba Croatia 44°24N 14°41E 199 D11
Silchar India 24°49N 92°48E 241 C4
Sildegapet Norway 62°5N 5°0E 164 B2
Şile Turkey 41°10N 29°37E 203 E13
Silent Valley △ India 11°10N 76°20E 245 J3
Siler City U.S.A. 35°44N 79°28W 315 D15
Sileru → India 17°49N 81°24E 244 F5
Silesia = Śląsk Poland 51°0N 16°30E 176 C9
Silet Algeria 22°44N 4°37E 261 D5
Siletitengiz Köli Kazakhstan 53°20N 73°10E 217 B8
Silgarhi Doti Nepal 29°15N 81°0E 243 E9
Silghat India 26°35N 93°0E 241 B4
Silhouette Seychelles 4°29S 55°12E 272 c
Sili Burkina Faso 11°37N 2°30W 262 C4
Siliana Tunisia 36°5N 9°22E 261 A6
Siliana □ Tunisia 36°0N 9°20E 261 A6
Silicon Valley = Santa Clara Valley U.S.A. 36°50N 121°30W 306 J5
Silifke Turkey 36°22N 33°58E 250 B4
Siliguri = Shiliguri India 26°45N 88°25E 241 B2
Silil Somalia 11°0N 43°26E 267 B5
Siling Co China 31°50N 89°20E 218 E6
Silisili, Mt. Samoa 13°37S 172°29W 287 V19
Silistea Nouă Romania 44°23N 25°1E 183 F10
Silistra Bulgaria 44°6N 27°19E 203 B11
Silistra □ Bulgaria 44°6N 27°19E 203 B11
Silivri Turkey 41°4N 28°14E 203 E12
Siljan Telemark, Norway 59°18N 9°42E 164 E6
Siljan Sweden 60°55N 14°45E 162 D8
Siljansnäs Sweden 60°47N 14°52E 162 D8
Silkeborg Denmark 56°10N 9°32E 163 H3
Silkwood Australia 17°45S 146°2E 280 B4
Silla Spain 39°22N 0°25W 197 F4
Sillajhuay, Cordillera Chile 19°46S 68°40W 330 D4
Sillamäe Estonia 59°24N 27°45E 188 C4
Sillé-le-Guillaume France 48°10N 0°8W 172 D6
Silleda Spain 42°42N 8°14W 194 C2
Sillein = Žilina Slovak Rep. 49°12N 18°42E 181 B11
Sillim S. Korea 37°28N 126°56E 137 C1
Sillod India 20°18N 75°39E 244 D2
Silloth U.K. 54°52N 3°23W 168 C4
Sillustani Peru 15°50S 70°7W 330 D3
Silo Greece 41°10N 25°53E 203 E9
Siloam Springs U.S.A. 36°11N 94°32W 314 C7
Silopi Turkey 37°15N 42°27E 213 D10
Siltou Chad 16°46N 15°33E 259 E3
Siluko Nigeria 6°35N 5°10E 263 D6
Siluo = Hsilo Taiwan 23°48N 120°27E 225 C2
Šilutė Lithuania 55°21N 21°33E 184 C8
Silva Porto = Kuito Angola 12°22S 16°55E 265 E3
Silvan Turkey 38°7N 41°2E 213 C9
Silvani India 23°18N 78°25E 243 H8
Silvassa India 20°16N 73°1E 244 D1
Silver, L. U.S.A. 28°35N 81°23W 133 A2
Silver Bank W. Indies 20°30N 69°45W 321 B6
Silver Bank Passage W. Indies 20°0N 70°0W 321 B5
Silver City U.S.A. 32°46N 108°17W 305 K9
Silver Cr. → U.S.A. 43°16N 119°13W 304 E4
Silver Creek U.S.A. 42°33N 79°10W 312 D5
Silver Grove U.S.A. 39°2N 84°23W 311 E12
Silver Hill Montserrat 16°49N 62°11W 323 p
Silver Hill Md., U.S.A. 38°49N 76°55W 143 B3
Silver L. U.S.A. 38°39N 120°6W 306 G6
Silver Lake Calif., U.S.A. 34°5N 118°15W 126 B3
Silver Lake Calif., U.S.A. 35°21N 116°7W 307 K10
Silver Lake Ind., U.S.A. 41°4N 85°53W 311 C11
Silver Lake Oreg., U.S.A. 43°8N 121°3W 304 E3
Silver Lake Wis., U.S.A. 42°33N 88°13W 311 B8
Silver Mine B. Hong Kong, China 22°16N 114°0E 122 B2
Silver Spring U.S.A. 38°59N 77°2W 143 A2
Silver Springs U.S.A. 29°13N 82°3W 317 F7
Silverdalen Sweden 57°32N 15°45E 163 G9
Silvermine Mts. Ireland 52°47N 8°15W 166 D3
Silvermine Nature Reserve S. Africa 34°6S 18°27E 118 B1
Silverstrand Hong Kong, China 22°19N 114°16E 122 B3
Silverton N.S.W., Australia 31°52S 141°10E 282 A4
Silverton Colo., U.S.A. 37°49N 107°40W 305 H10
Silverton Tex., U.S.A. 34°28N 101°19W 314 D4
Silves Brazil 2°54S 58°27W 329 D6
Silves Portugal 37°11N 8°26W 195 H2
Silvi Marina Italy 42°34N 14°5E 199 F11
Silvia Colombia 2°37N 76°21W 328 C2
Silvies → U.S.A. 43°34N 119°2W 304 E4
Silvolantekojärvi Finland 60°17N 24°54E 121 B2
Silvrettahorn Switz. 46°50N 10°6E 198 B7
Silwa Bahari Egypt 24°45N 32°55E 256 C3
Silz Austria 47°16N 10°56E 180 D3
Sim, C. Morocco 31°26N 9°51W 260 B3
Simakumba Zambia 14°12S 23°16E 265 E4
Simaltala India 24°43N 86°33E 243 G12
Simaluguri India 26°55N 94°46E 241 B5
Sim'ān, J. Syria 36°25N 36°53E 250 B7
Simanggang = Bandar Sri Aman Malaysia 1°15N 111°32E 235 B4
Simao China 22°47N 101°5E 228 F3
Simão Dias Brazil 10°44S 37°49W 332 D4
Simara I. Phil. 12°48N 122°3E 232 E4
Simard, L. Canada 47°40N 78°40W 298 C4
Şīmareh → Iran 33°9N 47°41E 213 F12
Simav Turkey 39°4N 28°58E 205 B10
Simav → Turkey 40°23N 28°31E 203 F12
Simav Dağları Turkey 39°10N 28°30E 205 B10
Simba Dem. Rep. of the Congo 0°38N 22°59E 264 B4
Simba Tanzania 2°10S 37°36E 268 C4
Simbach Germany 48°16N 13°2E 179 G9
Simberi I. Papua N. G. 2°38S 152°0E 286 B7
Simbirsk = Ulyanovsk Russia 54°20N 48°25E 190 C9
Simbo Solomon Is. 8°16S 156°33E 287 M9
Simbo Tanzania 4°51S 29°41E 268 C2
Simbu = Chimbu □ Papua N. G. 6°15S 144°50E 286 D3
Simcoe Canada 42°50N 80°23W 312 D4
Simcoe, L. Canada 44°25N 79°20W 312 B5
Simdega India 22°37N 84°31E 243 H11
Simei Singapore 1°20N 103°47E 138 A3
Simeonovgrad Bulgaria 42°1N 25°50E 203 D9
Simeria Romania 45°51N 23°1E 182 E8
Simeto → Italy 37°24N 15°6E 201 E8
Simeulue Indonesia 2°45N 95°45E 234 B1
Simferopol Ukraine 44°55N 34°3E 189 K8
Simi Greece 36°35N 27°50E 205 E9
Simi Valley U.S.A. 34°16N 118°47W 307 L8
Simien △ Ethiopia 13°19N 38°0E 257 E4
Simikot Nepal 30°0N 81°50E 243 E9
Similajau △ Malaysia 3°27N 113°15E 235 B4
Simineh → Iran 36°59N 45°54E 213 D11
Simití Colombia 7°58N 73°57W 328 B3
Simitli Bulgaria 41°52N 23°7E 202 E7
Simla = Shimla India 31°2N 77°9E 242 D7
Simla India 22°35N 88°22E 124 B2
Simlångsdalen Sweden 56°43N 13°6E 163 H7
Şimleu-Silvaniei Romania 47°17N 22°50E 182 C7
Simlipal △ India 21°45N 86°30E 243 J12
Simmering Austria 48°10N 16°24E 142 A2
Simmering Heide Austria 48°10N 16°26E 142 A2
Simmern Germany 49°58N 7°30E 179 F3
Simmie Canada 49°56N 108°6W 297 D7
Simmler U.S.A. 35°21N 119°59W 307 K7
Simnas Lithuania 54°24N 23°39E 184 D10
Simo älv = Simojoki → Finland 65°35N 25°1E 160 D21
Simões Brazil 7°36S 40°49W 332 C3
Simojoki → Finland 65°35N 25°1E 160 D21
Simojovel Mexico 17°12N 92°38W 319 D6
Simonette → Canada 55°9N 118°15W 296 B5
Simonière, Plaine de la Guadeloupe 16°16N 61°19W 322 e
Simonkylä Finland 60°18N 25°1E 121 B3
Šimonovany = Partizánske Slovak Rep. 48°38N 18°23E 181 C11
Simonstown S. Africa 34°14S 18°26E 270 D2
Simontornya Hungary 46°45N 18°33E 182 D3
Simpang Indonesia 1°16S 104°4E 234 C2
Simpang Empat Malaysia 5°27N 100°29E 237 c
Simpangkiri → Indonesia 2°50N 97°40E 234 B1
Simplício Mendes Brazil 7°51S 41°54W 332 C3
Simplonpass Switz. 46°15N 8°3E 179 J4
Simplontunnel Switz. 46°15N 8°7E 179 J4
Simpson, Mt. Papua N. G. 10°2S 149°34E 286 F5
Simpson Bay Lagoon St.-Martin 18°3N 63°6W 322 a
Simpson Desert Australia 25°0S 137°0E 280 D2
Simpson Desert △ Australia 24°59S 138°21E 280 C2
Simpson Pen. Canada 68°34N 88°45W 295 D14
Simrishamn Sweden 55°33N 14°22E 163 J8
Simsbury U.S.A. 41°53N 72°48W 313 E12
Simsonbaai St.-Maarten 18°2N 63°7W 322 a
Simuk Indonesia 0°4S 97°52E 234 C1
Simunjan Malaysia 1°25N 110°45E 235 B4
Simunul Phil. 4°54N 119°51E 233 J2
Simushir, Ostrov Russia 46°50N 152°30E 215 E16
Sin Cowe I. S. China Sea 9°53N 114°19E 230 C4
Sin-do N. Korea 39°52N 124°14E 224 C2
Sina → India 17°30N 75°55E 244 F2
Sina Dhago Somalia 5°50N 47°0E 267 C6
Sinabang Indonesia 2°30N 96°24E 234 B1
Sinabung Indonesia 3°10N 98°23E 234 B1
Sinai = Es Sînâ' Egypt 29°0N 34°0E 246 D2
Sinai, Mt. = Mûsa, Gebel Egypt 28°33N 33°59E 251 K4
Sinai, Mt. Grenada 12°4N 61°42W 323 q
Sinai Peninsula Egypt 29°30N 34°0E 251 J5
Sinaia Romania 45°21N 25°38E 183 E10
Sinait Phil. 17°52N 120°27E 232 C3
Sinako, Mt. Phil. 7°30N 125°17E 233 H5
Sinaloa □ Mexico 25°0N 107°30W 318 C3
Sinaloa de Leyva Mexico 25°50N 108°14W 318 B3
Sinalunga Italy 43°12N 11°44E 199 E8
Sinan China 27°56N 108°13E 228 D7
Sînandrei Romania 45°52N 21°13E 182 E6
Sinarades Greece 39°34N 19°51E 206 B9
Sīnāwan Libya 31°0N 10°37E 258 B2
Sinbaungwe Burma 19°43N 95°10E 241 F5
Sinbo Burma 24°46N 97°3E 241 C6
Sincan Turkey 40°0N 32°36E 212 B5
Sincanlı Turkey 38°45N 30°15E 205 C12
Sincé Colombia 9°15N 75°9W 328 B2
Sincelejo Colombia 9°18N 75°24W 328 B2
Sinch'ang N. Korea 40°7N 128°28E 224 B4
Sincheorwon S. Korea 38°8N 127°18E 224 C3
Sinch'ŏn N. Korea 38°17N 125°21E 224 C2
Sinchon Seoul, S. Korea 37°34N 126°57E 137 B1
Sinclair U.S.A. 41°47N 107°7W 304 F10
Sinclair, L. U.S.A. 33°8N 83°12W 316 B6
Sinclair Mills Canada 54°5N 121°40W 296 C4
Sinclair's B. U.K. 58°31N 3°5W 167 C5
Sinclairville U.S.A. 42°16N 79°16W 312 D5
Sincorá, Serra do Brazil 13°10S 41°20W 333 D3
Sind = Sindh □ Pakistan 26°0N 69°0E 242 G3
Sind → Jammu & Kashmir, India 34°18N 74°45E 243 B6
Sind → Mad. P., India 26°26N 79°13E 243 F8
Sind Sagar Doab Pakistan 32°0N 71°30E 242 D4
Sindal Denmark 57°28N 10°10E 163 G4
Sindang S. Korea 37°35N 127°2E 137 B2
Sindangan Phil. 8°10N 123°5E 233 G4
Sindangan B. Phil. 8°11N 122°50E 233 G4
Sindangbarang Indonesia 7°27S 107°1E 234 D3
Sindara Gabon 1°7S 10°41E 264 C2
Sinde Zambia 17°28S 25°51E 269 F2
Sindelfingen Germany 48°42N 9°0E 179 G4
Sindewahi India 20°17N 79°39E 244 D4
Sindgi India 16°55N 76°14E 244 F3
Sindh = Indus → Pakistan 24°20N 67°47E 242 G2
Sindh □ Pakistan 26°0N 69°0E 242 G3
Sindhnur India 15°47N 76°46E 245 F3
Sindhuli Garhi Nepal 27°16N 85°58E 243 F11
Sindi India 20°48N 78°52E 244 D4
Sındırgı Turkey 39°13N 28°10E 205 B10
Sindou Burkina Faso 10°35N 5°4W 262 C3
Sindri India 23°45N 86°42E 243 H12
Sine → Senegal 14°10N 16°28W 262 C1
Sinegorskiy Russia 47°55N 40°52E 191 G5
Sinekli Turkey 41°14N 28°12E 203 E12
Sinelnikovo = Synelnykove Ukraine 48°25N 35°30E 189 H8
Sinendé Benin 10°20N 2°22E 263 C5
Sines Portugal 37°56N 8°51W 195 H2
Sines, C. de Portugal 37°58N 8°53W 195 H2
Sineu Spain 39°38N 3°1E 206 B4
Sinewit, Mt. Papua N. G. 4°44S 152°2E 286 C7
Sinfra Ivory C. 6°35N 5°56W 262 D3
Sing Buri Thailand 14°53N 100°25E 236 E3
Sing Sing = Ossining U.S.A. 41°10N 73°55W 313 E11
Singa Sudan 13°10N 33°57E 257 E3
Singako Chad 9°50N 19°24E 259 G3
Singalila △ India 27°10N 88°5E 241 B2
Singanallur India 11°2N 77°1E 245 J3
Singapore ■ Asia 1°17N 103°51E 138 B3
Singapore, Straits of Asia 1°15N 104°0E 237 d
Singapore Changi ✕ (SIN) Singapore 1°23N 103°59E 138 A3
Singaraja Indonesia 8°7S 115°6E 231 J18
Singatoka = Sigatoka Fiji 18°8S 177°32E 287 B1
Singen Germany 47°45N 8°50E 179 H4
Singida Tanzania 4°49S 34°48E 268 C3
Singida □ Tanzania 6°0S 34°30E 268 D3
Singkang Indonesia 4°8S 120°1E 231 E6
Singkarak, Danau Indonesia 0°36S 100°32E 234 C2
Singkawang Indonesia 1°0N 108°57E 235 B3
Singkep Indonesia 0°30S 104°25E 234 C2
Singkil Indonesia 2°17N 97°49E 237 L1
Singkuang Indonesia 1°3N 98°55E 237 L2
Singleton Australia 32°33S 151°10E 283 B9
Singleton, Mt. N. Terr., Australia 22°0S 130°46E 278 D5
Singleton, Mt. W. Austral., Australia 29°27S 117°15E 279 E2
Singö Sweden 60°12N 18°45E 162 D12
Singoli India 25°0N 75°22E 242 G6
Singora = Songkhla Thailand 7°13N 100°37E 237 J3
Singrauli India 24°7N 82°23E 243 G10
Singri India 26°36N 92°29E 241 B4
Singsås Norway 62°56N 10°37E 164 B7
Singu Burma 22°33N 96°0E 241 D6
Sinh Ton, Dao = Sin Cowe I. S. China Sea 9°53N 114°19E 230 C4
Sinharaja Sri Lanka 6°25N 80°30E 245 L5
Sinhgarh India 18°22N 73°45E 244 E1
Sinhŭng Hamgyŏngnam-do, N. Korea 40°11N 127°34E 224 B3
Sinhŭng Hamgyŏngnam-do, N. Korea 41°8N 127°31E 224 B3
Siniloan Phil. 14°25N 121°27E 232 D3
Sining = Xining China 36°34N 101°40E 218 D9
Sínis Italy 38°55N 8°25E 200 C1
Siniscóla Italy 40°34N 9°41E 200 B2
Sinj Croatia 43°42N 16°39E 199 E13
Sinjai Indonesia 5°7S 120°20E 231 F6
Sinjajevina Montenegro 42°57N 19°22E 202 D3
Sinjār Iraq 36°19N 41°52E 213 D9
Sinjār Syria 35°35N 37°0E 250 C8
Sinjār, Jabal Iraq 36°23N 41°47E 213 D9
Sinkat Sudan 18°55N 36°49E 256 D4
Sinki, Selat Singapore 1°15N 103°42E 138 B2
Sinkiang = Xinjiang Uygur Zizhiqu □ China 42°0N 86°0E 217 D11
Sinko Guinea 8°53N 8°16W 262 D3
Sinlumkaba Burma 24°16N 97°31E 241 C6
Sinmak N. Korea 38°25N 126°14E 224 C3
Sinmi-do N. Korea 39°33N 124°53E 224 C2
Sínnai Italy 39°18N 9°13E 200 C2
Sinnar India 19°48N 74°0E 244 E2
Sinni → Italy 40°8N 16°41E 201 B9
Sinnuris Egypt 29°26N 30°31E 256 J7
Sinoie, Lacul Romania 44°35N 28°50E 183 F13
Sinop Turkey 42°1N 35°11E 212 A6
Sinop □ Turkey 42°0N 35°0E 212 B6
Sinor India 21°55N 73°20E 242 J5
Sinp'o N. Korea 40°0N 128°13E 224 C4
Sinsa S. Korea 37°31N 127°0E 137 B2
Sinsang N. Korea 39°38N 127°24E 224 C3
Sinsheim Germany 49°15N 8°52E 179 F4
Sinsiang = Xinxiang China 35°18N 113°50E 226 G7
Sinsk Russia 61°8N 126°48E 215 C13
Sint Annabaai Curaçao 12°6N 68°55W 322 g
Sint Christoffelberg Curaçao 12°20N 69°8W 322 g
Sint-Genesius-Rode Belgium 50°45N 4°22E 116 B2
Sint-Hubert Belgium 50°2N 5°23E 170 D5
Sint Jorisbaai Curaçao 12°7N 68°48W 322 g
Sint Marie, K. Curaçao 12°11N 69°3W 322 g
Sint Marthabaai Curaçao 12°17N 69°8W 322 g
Sint Michiel Curaçao 12°8N 69°0W 322 g
Sint Nicolaas Aruba 12°27N 69°54W 322 f
Sint Nicolaas Curaçao 12°17N 69°8W 322 g
Sint-Niklaas Belgium 51°10N 4°8E 170 C4
Sint-Truiden Belgium 50°48N 5°10E 170 D5
Sint Willibrordus Curaçao 12°12N 69°4W 322 g
Sintang Indonesia 0°5N 111°35E 235 B4
Sinton U.S.A. 28°2N 97°31W 314 G6
Sintra Portugal 38°47N 9°25W 195 G1
Sintra-Cascais ⌓ Portugal 38°50N 9°25W 195 G1
Sinŭiju N. Korea 40°5N 124°24E 224 B2
Sinujif Somalia 8°33N 48°59E 267 C6
Sinyukha → Ukraine 48°3N 30°51E 189 H6
Sinzig Germany 50°32N 7°14E 178 E3
Sio → Hungary 46°20N 18°53E 182 D3
Siocon Phil. 7°40N 122°10E 233 H4
Siófok Hungary 46°54N 18°3E 182 D3
Sioma Zambia 16°40S 23°32E 265 F4
Sioma Ngwezi △ Zambia 17°14S 23°26E 265 F4
Sion Maharashtra, India 19°3N 72°52E 130 A2
Sion Switz. 46°14N 7°20E 179 J3
Sion Mills U.K. 54°48N 7°29W 166 B4
tSionainn, An = Shannon → Ireland 52°35N 9°30W 166 D2
Sioux Center U.S.A. 43°5N 96°11W 308 D5
Sioux City U.S.A. 42°30N 96°24W 308 D5
Sioux Falls U.S.A. 43°33N 96°44W 308 D5
Sioux Lookout Canada 50°10N 91°50W 298 B1
Sioux Narrows Canada 49°25N 94°10W 297 D10
Sipadan Malaysia 4°6N 118°38E 235 B5
Sipalay Phil. 9°45N 122°24E 233 G4
Šipan Croatia 42°45N 17°52E 202 D1
Sipang, Tanjong Malaysia 1°48N 110°20E 235 B4
Siparia Trin. & Tob. 10°8N 61°31W 323 t
Siparia □ Trin. & Tob. 10°9N 61°28W 323 t
Sipil Daği △ Turkey 38°35N 27°30E 205 C9
Siping China 43°8N 124°21E 227 C13
Sipitang Malaysia 5°5N 115°33E 235 A5
Sipiwesk L. Canada 55°5N 97°35W 297 B9
Siple I. Antarctica 73°40S 125°10W 151 D14
Sipocot Phil. 13°46N 122°58E 232 E4
Šipovo Bos.-H. 44°16N 17°6E 182 F2
Sipra → India 23°55N 75°28E 242 H6
Sipson U.K. 51°29N 0°26W 125 B1
Sipsongpanna = Xishuangbanna China 22°5N 101°1E 228 F3
Sipur India 21°11N 85°9E 244 D7
Sipura Indonesia 2°18S 99°40E 234 C1
Sipura, Selat Indonesia 2°27S 99°54E 234 C1
Siqeil Egypt 30°7N 31°10E 117 A1
Siqirah Yemen 12°37N 54°20E 249 D6
Siqueira Campos Brazil 23°42S 49°50W 333 F2
Siquia → Nic. 12°10N 84°20W 320 D3
Siquijor Phil. 9°12N 123°35E 233 G4
Siquijor □ Phil. 9°11N 123°35E 233 G4
Siquirres Costa Rica 10°6N 83°30W 320 D3
Siquisique Venezuela 10°34N 69°42W 328 A4
Şīr Abu Nu'ayr U.A.E. 25°20N 54°20E 247 E7
Şīr Banī Yās U.A.E. 24°19N 52°37E 247 E7
Sir Edward Pellew Group Australia 15°40S 137°10E 280 B2
Sir Graham Moore Is. Australia 13°53S 126°34E 278 B4
Sir James MacBrien, Mt. Canada 62°7N 127°41W 294 E6
Sira India 13°41N 76°49E 245 H3
Sira Vest-Agder, Norway 58°24N 6°40E 164 F3
Sira → Norway 58°23N 6°34E 164 F3
Siracusa Italy 37°4N 15°17E 201 E8
Sirajganj Bangla. 24°25N 89°47E 241 C2
Sirakoro Mali 12°41N 9°14W 262 C3
Şiran Turkey 40°11N 39°7E 213 B8
Sirasso Ivory C. 9°16N 6°6W 262 D3
Sirathu India 25°39N 81°19E 243 G9
Siraway Phil. 7°34N 122°8E 233 H4
Sirdalsvatnet Norway 58°34N 6°43E 164 F3
Sīrdān Iran 36°39N 49°12E 213 D13
Sirdaryo □ Uzbekistan 40°30N 68°45E 217 D7
Sire Ethiopia 6°55N 35°36E 257 F4
Siren U.S.A. 45°47N 92°24W 308 C7
Sirente-Velino ⌓ Italy 42°10N 13°32E 199 F10
Sirer Spain 38°56N 1°22E 206 D1
Siret Romania 47°55N 26°5E 183 C11
Siret → Romania 45°24N 28°1E 183 E12
Sirevåg Norway 58°30N 5°48E 164 F2
Sirghāyā Syria 33°51N 36°8E 250 E7
Şiria Romania 46°16N 21°38E 182 D6
Sirik, Tanjong Malaysia 2°47N 111°15E 235 B4
Sirikit Res. Thailand 17°45N 100°34E 236 C3
Sirinat △ Thailand 8°6N 98°17E 237 a
Sirino, Mte. Italy 40°7N 15°50E 201 B8
Sīrjān Iran 29°30N 55°45E 247 D7
Sirkali = Sirkazhi India 11°15N 79°41E 245 J4
Sirkazhi India 11°15N 79°41E 245 J4
Sirmans U.S.A. 30°21N 83°39W 316 E6
Sirmaur India 24°51N 81°23E 243 G9
Sirmilik △ Canada 72°50N 80°35W 295 C15
Sirmione Italy 45°30N 10°36E 198 C7
Sirna Greece 36°22N 26°42E 205 E8
Şirnak Turkey 37°32N 42°28E 213 D10
Sirohi India 24°52N 72°53E 242 G5
Sirombu Indonesia 0°57N 97°25E 234 B1
Sironj India 24°5N 77°39E 242 G7
Síros = Ermoupoli Greece 37°28N 24°57E 204 D6
Siroz = Serres Greece 41°5N 23°31E 202 E7
Sirpur India 19°29N 79°36E 244 E4
Sirr, Nafud as Si. Arabia 25°33N 44°35E 246 E5
Sirrayn Si. Arabia 19°38N 40°36E 248 C3
Sirretta Pk. U.S.A. 35°56N 118°19W 307 K8
Sīrrī Iran 25°55N 54°32E 247 E7
Sirsa India 29°33N 75°4E 242 E6
Sirsa → India 26°51N 79°4E 243 F8
Sirsi India 14°40N 74°49E 245 G2
Sirsilla India 18°23N 78°50E 244 E4
Sirte = Surt Libya 31°11N 16°39E 258 B3
Siruela Spain 38°58N 5°3W 195 G5
Siruguppa India 15°38N 76°54E 245 F3
Sirur India 18°50N 74°23E 244 E2
Şirvan Azerbaijan 39°59N 48°52E 191 L9
Sirvān → Iran 35°4N 46°50E 213 E12
Sisak Croatia 45°30N 16°21E 199 C13
Sisante Spain 39°25N 2°12W 197 F2
Sisargas, Is. Spain 43°21N 8°50W 194 B2
Sishen S. Africa 27°47S 22°59E 270 C3
Sishui China 35°42N 117°18E 227 G9
Sisian Armenia 39°31N 46°1E 213 C12
Sisiga Solomon Is. 7°54S 159°10E 287 L10
Sisimiut Greenland 66°40N 53°30W 154 D5
Sisipuk L. Canada 55°45N 101°50W 297 B8
Şişli Turkey 41°3N 28°58E 122 B1
Sisophon Cambodia 13°38N 102°59E 236 F4
Sissano Papua N. G. 3°0S 142°3E 286 B2
Sisseton U.S.A. 45°40N 97°3W 308 C5
Sisson = Mount Shasta U.S.A. 41°19N 122°19W 304 F2
Sissonne France 49°34N 3°51E 173 C10
Sīstān Asia 30°50N 61°0E 247 D9
Sīstan, Daryācheh-ye Iran 31°0N 61°0E 247 D9
Sīstān va Balūchestān □ Iran 27°0N 62°0E 247 E9
Sisteron France 44°12N 5°57E 175 D9
Sisters U.S.A. 44°18N 121°33W 304 D3
Sisters, The Grenada 12°18N 61°36W 323 q
Sisters, The Seychelles 4°16S 55°52E 272 c
Sisters Pk. Ascension I. 7°56S 14°22W 153 g
Sisters Rocks Trin. & Tob. 11°20N 60°39W 323 s
Siswa Bazar India 27°9N 83°46E 243 F10
Sitakili Mali 13°7N 11°14W 262 C2
Sitakunda Bangla. 22°37N 91°39E 241 D3
Sitamarhi India 26°37N 85°30E 243 F11
Sitampiky Madag. 16°41S 46°6E 272 B2
Sitangkai Phil. 4°40N 119°24E 233 J2
Sitapur India 27°38N 80°45E 243 F9
Siteki Swaziland 26°32S 31°58E 271 C5
Sitges Spain 41°17N 1°47E 196 D6
Sithonia Greece 40°0N 23°45E 202 F7
Sitia Greece 35°13N 26°6E 207 E7
Sitia ✕ (JSH) Greece 35°15N 26°5E 207 E7
Sítio da Abadia Brazil 14°48S 46°16W 333 D2
Sitito-Ozima Ridge Pac. Oc. 23°0N 143°0E 288 E6
Sitka U.S.A. 57°3N 135°20W 296 B1
Sitka ⌓ U.S.A. 57°3N 135°19W 303 H14
Sitkaing = Sagaing Burma 21°52N 95°59E 241 E5
Sitkinak I. U.S.A. 56°33N 154°10W 303 H9
Sitoti Botswana 23°15S 23°40E 270 B3
Sitra Egypt 28°40N 26°53E 256 B2
Sittang Myit → Burma 17°20N 96°45E 241 G6
Sittard Neths. 51°0N 5°52E 170 C5
Sittaung Burma 24°10N 94°35E 241 C5
Sittensen Germany 53°17N 9°32E 178 B5
Sittingbourne U.K. 51°21N 0°45E 169 F8
Sittona Eritrea 14°25N 37°23E 257 E4
Sittoung = Sittang Myit → Burma 17°20N 96°45E 241 G6
Sittwe Burma 20°18N 92°45E 241 E4
Situbondo Indonesia 7°42S 113°56E 235 D4
Siu Kau Yi Chau Hong Kong, China 22°17N 114°3E 122 B2
Siufaalete Pt. Amer. Samoa 14°17S 169°29W 302 f
Siulagi Pt. Amer. Samoa 14°13S 169°30W 302 g
Si'umu Samoa 14°1S 171°48W 287 W20
Siuna Nic. 13°37N 84°45W 320 D3
Siuri India 23°50N 87°34E 243 H12
Siutghiol, Lacul Romania 44°15N 28°35E 183 F13
Sivaganga India 9°50N 78°28E 245 K4
Sivagiri India 9°16N 77°26E 245 K3
Sivakasi India 9°24N 77°47E 245 K3
Sīvand Iran 30°5N 52°55E 247 D7
Sivas Turkey 39°43N 36°58E 212 C7
Sivas □ Turkey 39°45N 37°0E 212 C7
Sivasamudram India 12°16N 77°10E 245 H3
Sivaslı Turkey 38°31N 29°42E 205 C11
Siverek Turkey 37°50N 39°19E 213 D8
Sivomaskinskiy Russia 66°40N 62°35E 186 A11
Sivota Greece 39°24N 20°13E 206 C10
Sivrihisar Turkey 39°30N 31°35E 212 C4
Sivros Greece 38°40N 20°39E 207 B2
Sîwa Egypt 29°11N 25°31E 256 B2
Sîwa, El Wâhât es Egypt 29°10N 25°30E 256 B2
Siwa Oasis = Sîwa, El Wâhât es Egypt 29°10N 25°30E 256 B2
Siwalik Range Nepal 28°0N 83°0E 243 F10
Siwan India 26°13N 84°21E 243 F11
Siwana India 25°38N 72°25E 242 G5
Six Cross Roads Barbados 13°7N 59°28W 323 r
Six-Fours-les-Plages France 43°6N 5°49E 175 E9
Sixian China 33°30N 117°50E 227 H9
Sixmilebridge Ireland 52°44N 8°46W 166 D3
Sixth Cataract Sudan 16°20N 32°42E 257 D3
Siyabuswa S. Africa 25°7S 29°3E 271 C4
Siyah Kuh, Kavīr-e Iran 32°55N 53°55E 247 C7
Siyâl, Jazâ'ir Egypt 22°49N 36°12E 256 C4
Siyang China 33°42N 118°40E 227 H10
Siyäzän Azerbaijan 41°3N 49°10E 191 K9
Siziwang Qi China 41°25N 111°40E 226 D6
Sjælland Denmark 55°30N 11°30E 163 J5
Sjælland □ Denmark 55°30N 11°30E 163 J5
Sjællands Odde Denmark 55°58N 11°24E 163 J5
Sjenica Serbia 43°16N 20°0E 202 C3
Sjoa Norway 61°41N 9°33E 164 C6
Sjöbo Sweden 55°37N 13°45E 163 J7
Sjøholt Norway 62°27N 6°52E 164 B3
Sjølisand Norway 61°29N 11°18E 164 C8
Sjötofta Sweden 57°22N 13°17E 163 G7
Sjötorp Sweden 58°50N 14°0E 163 F8
Sjumen = Shumen Bulgaria 43°18N 26°55E 203 C10
Sjuntorp Sweden 58°12N 12°13E 163 F6
Skåbu Norway 61°32N 9°24E 164 C6
Skadarsko Jezero Europe 42°10N 19°20E 202 D3
Skadarsko Jezero △ Montenegro 42°10N 19°20E 202 D3

Skadovsk Ukraine 46°17N 32°52E 189 J7
Skælskør Denmark 55°15N 11°18E 163 J5
Skærbæk Denmark 55°9N 8°45E 163 J2
Skaftafell Iceland 64°1N 17°0W 155 C9
Skaftafell △ Iceland 64°9N 16°50W 155 C9
Skagafjarðarsýsla Iceland 65°30N 19°0W 155 B7
Skagafjörður Iceland 65°54N 19°35W 155 B7
Skagastølstindane Norway 61°28N 7°52E 164 C4
Skagaströnd Iceland 65°50N 20°19W 155 B6
Skagatá Iceland 66°7N 20°6W 155 A6
Skagen Denmark 57°43N 10°35E 163 G4
Skagern Sweden 59°0N 14°20E 162 E8
Skagerrak Denmark 57°30N 9°0E 163 G2
Skagit ➔ U.S.A. 48°23N 122°22W 306 B4
Skagway U.S.A. 59°28N 135°19W 303 G14
Skala Greece 38°5N 20°47E 207 C2
Skala nad Zbruczem = Skala-Podilska Ukraine 48°50N 26°15E 183 B11
Skala-Podilska Ukraine 48°50N 26°15E 183 B11
Skalat Ukraine 49°23N 25°55E 177 D13
Skálavík Iceland 66°11N 23°29W 155 A3
Skalbmierz Poland 50°20N 20°25E 185 H7
Skälderviken Sweden 56°22N 12°30E 163 H6
Skålevik Norway 58°5N 8°1E 164 F5
Skalica Slovak Rep. 48°50N 17°15E 181 C10
Skallingen Denmark 55°32N 8°13E 163 J2
Skalni Dol = Kamenyak Bulgaria 43°24N 26°57E 203 C10
Skanderborg Denmark 56°2N 9°55E 163 H3
Skåne Sweden 55°59N 13°30E 163 J7
Skåne län □ Sweden 56°15N 14°0E 163 H7
Skaneateles U.S.A. 42°57N 76°26W 313 D8
Skaneateles L. U.S.A. 42°51N 76°22W 313 D8
Skånevik Norway 59°43N 5°53E 164 E2
Skänninge Sweden 58°24N 15°5E 163 F9
Skanör med Falsterbo Sweden 55°24N 12°50E 163 J6
Skansen Sweden 59°19N 18°7E 139 B2
Skantzoura Greece 39°5N 24°6E 204 B6
Skara Sweden 58°25N 13°30E 163 F7
Skärblacka Sweden 58°35N 15°54E 163 F9
Skarð Iceland 65°17N 22°19W 155 B4
Skardu Pakistan 35°20N 75°44E 243 B6
Skare Hordaland, Norway 59°55N 6°36E 164 E3
Skåre Sweden 59°26N 13°26E 162 E7
Skärhamn Sweden 57°59N 11°34E 163 G5
Skärholmen Sweden 59°16N 17°53E 139 B1
Skarnes Norway 60°15N 11°41E 164 D8
Skarpäng Sweden 59°26N 18°0E 139 A2
Skarpnäck Sweden 59°16N 18°7E 139 B2
Skarszewy Poland 54°4N 18°25E 184 D5
Skarvan og Roltdalen △ Norway 63°16N 11°31E 160 E14
Skaryszew Poland 51°19N 21°15E 185 G8
Skaryszewski, Park Poland 52°15N 21°3E 143 B2
Skarżysko-Kamienna Poland 51°7N 20°52E 185 G7
Skattkärr Sweden 59°25N 13°40E 162 E7
Skattungbyn Sweden 61°10N 14°56E 162 C8
Skawina Poland 49°59N 19°50E 185 J6
Skebobruk Sweden 59°58N 18°36E 162 E12
Skee Sweden 58°56N 11°19E 163 F5
Skeena ➔ Canada 54°9N 130°5W 296 C2
Skeena Mts. Canada 56°40N 128°30W 296 B3
Skegness U.K. 53°9N 0°20E 168 D8
Skei Norway 61°34N 6°28E 164 C3
Skeiðarársandur Iceland 63°54N 17°14W 155 D9
Skeiðflötur Iceland 63°26N 19°11W 155 D7
Skeleton Coast ⌓ Namibia 20°0S 13°20E 270 B1
Skellefteå Sweden 64°45N 20°50E 160 D19
Skellefteälven ➔ Sweden 64°45N 21°10E 160 D19
Skelleftehamn Sweden 64°40N 21°9E 160 D19
Skellig Michael = Great Skellig Ireland 51°47N 10°33W 166 E1
Skender Vakuf Bos.-H. 44°29N 17°22E 182 F2
Skënderaj Kosovo 42°45N 20°47E 202 D4
Skeppsholmen Stockholm, Sweden 139 c3
Skerries Ireland 53°35N 6°8W 166 C5
Skerries, The U.K. 53°25N 4°36W 168 D3
Skhidnytsya Ukraine 49°13N 23°20E 185 J10
Skhiza Greece 36°41N 21°40E 204 E3
Ski Norway 59°43N 10°52E 164 E7
Skiathos Greece 39°12N 23°30E 204 B5
Skibbereen Ireland 51°33N 9°16W 166 E2
Skiddaw U.K. 54°39N 3°9W 168 C4
Skidegate Canada 53°15N 132°1W 296 C2
Skidra Greece 40°46N 22°10E 202 F6
Skien Norway 59°12N 9°35E 164 E6
Skierniewice Poland 51°58N 20°10E 185 G7
Skihist, Mt. Canada 50°12N 121°54W 296 C4
Skikda Algeria 36°50N 6°58E 261 A6
Skikda □ Algeria 36°45N 6°50E 261 A6
Skillet Fork ➔ U.S.A. 38°5N 88°5W 311 F8
Skillingaryd Sweden 57°27N 14°5E 163 G8
Skillinge Sweden 55°30N 14°16E 163 J8
Skilloura Cyprus 35°14N 33°10E 207 E9
Skinari, Akra Greece 37°56N 20°42E 207 D2
Skinnastaður Iceland 66°4N 16°27W 155 A10
Skinnskatteberg Sweden 59°50N 15°42E 162 E9
Skipton Vic., Australia 37°39S 143°40E 282 D5
Skipton N. Yorks., U.K. 53°58N 2°3W 168 D5
Skiptvet Norway 59°28N 11°11E 164 E8
Skiring, C. Senegal 12°26N 16°46W 262 C1
Skirmish Pt. Australia 11°59S 134°17E 280 A1
Skíros = Skyros Greece 38°55N 24°34E 204 C6
Skivarp Sweden 55°26N 13°34E 163 J7
Skive Denmark 56°33N 9°2E 163 H3
Skjærhalden Norway 59°2N 11°2E 164 E8
Skjálfandafljót ➔ Iceland 65°59N 17°25W 155 B9
Skjálfandi Iceland 66°5N 17°30W 155 A9
Skjeberg Norway 59°12N 11°12E 164 E8
Skjern Denmark 55°57N 8°30E 163 J2
Skjern Å △ Denmark 55°50N 8°30E 163 H2
Skjold Norway 59°31N 5°34E 164 E2
Skjolden Norway 61°29N 7°36E 164 C4
Skjöldólfsstaðir Iceland 65°19N 15°7W 155 B11
Skjønhaug Norway 59°39N 11°19E 164 E8
Skobelev = Farghona Uzbekistan 40°23N 71°19E 217 D8
Škocjanskie Jame Slovenia 45°40N 14°0E 199 C10
Skoczów Poland 49°49N 18°45E 185 J5
Skodje Norway 62°30N 6°43E 164 B3
Škofja Loka Slovenia 46°9N 14°19E 199 B11
Skógar Iceland 63°32N 19°28W 155 D7
Skógarnes Iceland 64°46N 22°34W 155 C4
Skoghall Sweden 59°20N 13°30E 162 E7
Skogskyrkogården Sweden 59°16N 18°5E 139 B2
Skogstorp Sweden 59°19N 16°29E 162 E10
Skoki Poland 52°40N 17°11E 185 F4
Skokie U.S.A. 42°2N 87°43W 119 A2
Skokie ➔ U.S.A. 42°3N 87°46W 119 A2
Skokie Heritage Museum Chicago, U.S.A. 42°2N 87°44W 119 A2
Skoklefall Norway 59°50N 10°40E 133 A3
Skole Ukraine 49°3N 23°30E 177 D12
Skollenborg Norway 59°38N 9°43E 164 E6
Sköndal Sweden 59°15N 18°6E 139 B2
Skopelos Greece 39°9N 23°47E 204 B5
Skopi Greece 35°11N 26°2E 207 E7
Skopin Russia 53°55N 39°32E 188 F10
Skopje Macedonia 42°1N 21°26E 202 D5
Skopje ✈ (SKP) Macedonia 41°59N 21°29E 202 E5
Skoppum Norway 59°23N 10°26E 164 E7
Skórcz Poland 53°47N 18°30E 184 E5
Skørping Denmark 56°50N 9°53E 163 H3
Skotfoss Norway 59°12N 9°30E 164 E6
Skotterud Norway 60°0N 12°7E 164 D9
Skövde Sweden 58°24N 13°50E 163 F7
Skovlunde Denmark 55°42N 12°25E 118 A2
Skovorodino Russia 54°0N 124°0E 215 D13
Skovshoved Denmark 55°45N 12°35E 118 A3
Skowhegan U.S.A. 44°46N 69°43W 309 C19
Skradin Croatia 43°52N 15°53E 199 E12
Skrea Sweden 56°53N 12°34E 163 H6
Skreia Norway 60°40N 10°56E 164 D7
Skrim Norway 59°31N 9°38E 164 E6
Skrunda Latvia 56°41N 22°1E 184 B9
Skrwa ➔ Poland 52°35N 19°32E 185 F6
Skudeneshavn Norway 59°10N 5°10E 164 E2
Skuleskogen △ Sweden 63°6N 18°30E 162 A12
Skull Ireland 51°32N 9°34W 166 E2
Skultorp Sweden 58°24N 13°51E 163 F7
Skultuna Sweden 59°43N 16°25E 162 E10
Skunk ➔ U.S.A. 40°42N 91°7W 310 D5
Skuodas Lithuania 56°16N 21°33E 184 B8
Skuru Sweden 59°18N 18°12E 139 B3
Skurup Sweden 55°28N 13°30E 163 J7
Skutskär Sweden 60°37N 17°25E 162 D11
Skútustaðir Iceland 65°34N 17°2W 155 B9
Skvyra Ukraine 49°44N 29°40E 177 D15
Skwierzyna Poland 52°33N 15°30E 185 F2
Sky Dome = Rogers Centre Toronto, Canada 141 c1
Sky Lake U.S.A. 28°27N 81°23W 133 B2
Skye U.K. 57°15N 6°10W 167 D2
Skykomish U.S.A. 47°42N 121°22W 304 C3
Skyring, Seno Chile 52°35S 72°0W 336 D3
Skyropoula Greece 38°50N 24°21E 204 C6
Skyros Greece 38°55N 24°34E 204 C6
Skyttorp Sweden 60°5N 17°44E 162 D11
Slade Green U.K. 51°27N 0°11E 125 B5
Slade Point Australia 21°4S 149°13E 280 b
Slade Pt. Australia 21°5S 149°13E 280 b
Slættaratindur Færoe Is. 62°18N 7°1W 160 E9
Slagelse Denmark 55°23N 11°19E 163 J5
Slamet Indonesia 7°16S 109°8E 235 D3
Slane Ireland 53°42N 6°33W 166 C5
Slaney ➔ Ireland 52°26N 6°33W 166 D5
Slangberge S. Africa 31°32S 20°48E 270 D3
Slănic Romania 45°14N 25°58E 183 E10
Slano Croatia 42°48N 17°53E 202 D1
Slantsy Russia 59°7N 28°5E 188 C5
Slaný Czech Rep. 50°13N 14°6E 180 A7
Śląsk Poland 51°0N 16°30E 176 C9
Śląskie □ Poland 50°30N 19°0E 185 H6
Slätbaken Sweden 58°25N 16°45E 163 F10
Slate Is. Canada 48°40N 87°0W 298 C2
Slater U.S.A. 39°13N 93°4W 310 E3
Slatina Croatia 45°42N 17°45E 182 E2
Slatina Romania 44°28N 24°22E 183 F9
Slatina Timiş Romania 45°15N 22°17E 182 E7
Slatington U.S.A. 40°45N 75°37W 313 F9
Slaton U.S.A. 33°26N 101°39W 314 E4
Slave ➔ Canada 61°18N 113°39W 296 A6
Slave Coast W. Afr. 6°0N 2°30E 263 D5
Slave Lake Canada 55°17N 114°43W 296 B6
Slave Pt. Canada 61°11N 115°56W 296 A5
Slavgorod Russia 53°1N 78°37E 217 B9
Slavinja Serbia 43°9N 22°50E 202 C6
Slavkov u Brna Czech Rep. 49°10N 16°52E 181 B9
Slavkovský Les ⌓ Czech Rep. 50°5N 12°44E 180 A5
Slavonija Europe 45°20N 17°40E 182 E2
Slavonski Brod Croatia 45°11N 18°1E 182 E3
Slavsk Russia 55°3N 21°41E 184 C8
Slavske Ukraine 48°51N 23°27E 183 B8
Slavskoye Russia 54°30N 20°27E 184 D7
Slavuta Ukraine 50°15N 27°2E 177 C14
Slavyanka Russia 42°53N 131°21E 220 C5
Slavyanovo Bulgaria 43°28N 24°52E 203 C8
Slavyansk = Slovyansk Ukraine 48°55N 37°36E 189 H9
Slavyansk-na-Kubani Russia 45°15N 38°11E 189 K10
Sława Poland 51°52N 16°2E 185 G3
Slawharad Belarus 53°27N 31°0E 177 B16
Sławno Poland 54°20N 16°41E 184 D3
Sławoborze Poland 53°55N 15°42E 184 E2
Slea Hd. Ireland 52°6N 10°27W 166 D1
Sleaford U.K. 53°0N 0°24W 168 D7
Sleaford B. Australia 34°55S 135°45E 281 E2
Sleat, Sd. of U.K. 57°5N 5°47W 167 D3
Sleðbrjótur Iceland 65°34N 14°30W 155 B12
Sleeper Is. Canada 58°30N 81°0W 295 F15
Sleeping Bear Dunes ⌓ U.S.A. 44°50N 86°5W 308 C10
Sleepy Eye U.S.A. 44°18N 94°43W 308 C6
Sleetmute U.S.A. 61°42N 157°10W 303 F8
Slemon L. Canada 63°13N 116°4W 296 A5
Slependen Norway 59°52N 10°30E 133 A2
Ślesin Poland 52°22N 18°14E 185 F5
Slide Mt. U.S.A. 42°0N 74°25W 313 E10
Slidell U.S.A. 30°17N 89°47W 315 F10
Slidre Norway 61°5N 8°58E 164 C5
Sliema Malta 35°55N 14°30E 206 F8
Slieve Aughty Ireland 53°4N 8°30W 166 C3
Slieve Bloom Ireland 53°4N 7°40W 166 C4
Slieve Donard U.K. 54°11N 5°55W 166 B6
Slieve Gamph Ireland 54°6N 9°0W 166 B3
Slieve Gullion U.K. 54°7N 6°26W 166 B5
Slieve League Ireland 54°40N 8°42W 166 B3
Slieve Mish Ireland 52°12N 9°50W 166 D2
Slievenamon Ireland 52°25N 7°34W 166 D4
Sligeach = Sligo Ireland 54°16N 8°28W 166 B3
Sligo Sligo, Ireland 54°16N 8°28W 166 B3
Sligo Pa., U.S.A. 41°6N 79°29W 312 E5
Sligo □ Ireland 54°8N 8°42W 166 B3
Sligo B. Ireland 54°18N 8°40W 166 B3
Slipi Indonesia 6°11S 106°47E 122 B1
Slippery Rock U.S.A. 41°4N 80°3W 312 E4
Slite Sweden 57°42N 18°48E 163 G12
Slīteres ⌓ Latvia 57°41N 22°21E 184 A9
Sliven Bulgaria 42°42N 26°19E 203 D10
Sliven □ Bulgaria 42°42N 26°19E 203 D10
Slivenec Czech Rep. 50°1N 14°21E 135 B2
Slivnitsa Bulgaria 42°50N 23°2E 202 D7
Sljeme Croatia 45°57N 15°58E 199 C12
Sloan U.S.A. 35°57N 115°13W 307 K11
Sloansville U.S.A. 42°45N 74°22W 313 D10
Slobidka Ukraine 47°54N 29°21E 183 C14
Slobodskoy Russia 58°40N 50°6E 186 C9
Slobozia Moldova 46°45N 29°42E 183 D14
Slobozia Argeş, Romania 44°30N 25°14E 183 F10
Slobozia Ialomiţa, Romania 44°34N 27°23E 183 F12
Slocan Canada 49°48N 117°28W 296 D5
Slocomb U.S.A. 31°7N 85°36W 316 D4
Slomikhino = Zhalpaqtal Kazakhstan 49°42N 49°25E 190 F9
Słomniki Poland 50°16N 20°4E 185 H7
Slonim Belarus 53°4N 25°19E 177 B13
Slot, The = New Georgia Sound Solomon Is. 8°0S 158°20E 287 L9
Sloten Neths. 52°21N 4°48E 112 A1
Sloterdijk Neths. 52°23N 4°51E 112 A1
Sloterpark Neths. 52°22N 4°49E 112 A1
Slottet Oslo, Norway 133 a1
Slough U.K. 51°30N 0°36W 169 F7
Slough □ U.K. 51°30N 0°36W 169 F7
Sloughhouse U.S.A. 38°26N 121°12W 306 G5
Slovak Rep. ■ Europe 48°30N 20°0E 181 C13
Slovakia = Slovak Rep. ■ Europe 48°30N 20°0E 181 C13
Slovakian Ore Mts. = Slovenské Rudohorie Slovak Rep. 48°45N 20°0E 181 C12
Slovenia ■ Europe 45°58N 14°30E 199 C11
Slovenija = Slovenia ■ Europe 45°58N 14°30E 199 C11
Slovenj Gradec Slovenia 46°31N 15°5E 199 B12
Slovenska = Slovak Rep. ■ Europe 48°30N 20°0E 181 C13
Slovenska Bistrica Slovenia 46°24N 15°35E 199 B12
Slovenské Konjice Slovenia 46°20N 15°28E 199 B12
Slovenské Rudohorie Slovak Rep. 48°45N 20°0E 181 C12
Slovenský Raj △ Slovak Rep. 48°53N 20°25E 181 C13
Slovyansk Ukraine 48°55N 37°36E 189 H9
Słowiński △ Poland 54°43N 17°26E 184 D4
Słubice Poland 52°22N 14°35E 185 F1
Sluch ➔ Ukraine 51°37N 26°38E 177 C14
Sluhy Czech Rep. 50°11N 14°33E 135 A3
Sluis Neths. 51°18N 3°23E 170 C3
Slŭnchev Bryag Bulgaria 42°40N 27°41E 203 D11
Slunj Croatia 45°6N 15°33E 199 C12
Słupca Poland 52°15N 17°52E 185 F4
Słupia ➔ Poland 54°35N 16°51E 184 D3
Słupsk Poland 54°30N 17°3E 184 D4
Slurry S. Africa 25°49S 25°42E 270 C4
Slutsk = Pavlovsk Russia 50°26N 40°5E 190 E5
Slutsk Belarus 53°2N 27°31E 177 B14
Służew Poland 52°10N 21°1E 143 B2
Służewiec Poland 52°10N 21°0E 143 B2
Slyne Hd. Ireland 53°25N 10°10W 166 C1
Slyudyanka Russia 51°40N 103°40E 215 D11
Smaalenene = Østfold □ Norway 59°25N 11°25E 164 E8
Småland Sweden 57°15N 15°25E 163 G9
Smålandsfarvandet Denmark 55°10N 11°20E 163 J5
Smålandsstenar Sweden 57°10N 13°25E 163 G7
Smaldeel = Theunissen S. Africa 28°26S 26°43E 270 C4
Smalltree L. Canada 61°0N 105°0W 297 A8
Smallwood Res. Canada 54°5N 64°30W 299 B7
Smara W. Sahara 26°48N 11°41W 260 C2
Smarhon Belarus 54°20N 26°24E 177 A14
Smarje Slovenia 46°15N 15°34E 199 B12
Smartt Syndicate Dam S. Africa 30°45S 23°10E 270 D3
Smartville U.S.A. 39°13N 121°18W 306 F5
Smeaton Canada 53°30N 104°49W 297 C8
Smedby Sweden 56°41N 16°13E 163 H10
Smederevo Serbia 44°40N 20°57E 202 B4
Smederevska Palanka Serbia 44°22N 20°58E 202 B4
Smedjebacken Sweden 60°8N 15°25E 162 D9
Smela = Smila Ukraine 49°15N 31°58E 189 H6
Smeralda, Costa Italy 41°5N 9°35E 200 A2
Smerwick Harbour Ireland 52°12N 10°23W 166 D1
Smethport U.S.A. 41°49N 78°27W 312 E6
Smíchov Czech Rep. 50°4N 14°23E 135 B2
Smidovich Russia 48°36N 133°49E 215 E14
Śmigiel Poland 52°1N 16°32E 185 F3
Smila Ukraine 49°15N 31°58E 189 H6
Smilyan Bulgaria 41°29N 24°46E 203 E8
Smith Canada 55°10N 114°0W 296 B6
Smith B. U.S.A. 70°30N 154°20W 303 A9
Smith Center U.S.A. 39°47N 98°47W 308 F4
Smith Forest Preserve U.S.A. 41°59N 87°45W 119 B2
Smith I. Nunavut, Canada 60°45N 78°25W 295 E16
Smith I. India 13°20N 93°4E 245 H11
Smith Islands △ Australia 20°40S 149°9E 280 b
Smith River ⌓ U.S.A. 41°55N 124°0W 304 F2
Smith Sd. N. Amer. 78°25N 74°0W 154 B3
Smithburne ➔ Australia 17°3S 140°57E 280 B3
Smithers Canada 54°45N 127°10W 296 C3
Smithfield Free State, S. Africa 30°9S 26°30E 271 D4
Smithfield N.C., U.S.A. 35°31N 78°21W 315 D15
Smithfield Utah, U.S.A. 41°50N 111°50W 304 F8
Smiths U.S.A. 32°32N 85°6W 316 C4
Smiths Falls Canada 44°55N 76°0W 313 B9
Smithsonian Institution Washington, D.C., U.S.A. 143 b2
Smithton Australia 40°53S 145°6E 281 G4
Smithville Ont., Canada 43°6N 79°33W 312 C5
Smithville Ga., U.S.A. 31°54N 84°15W 316 D5
Smithville Mo., U.S.A. 39°23N 94°35W 310 E2
Smithville Tex., U.S.A. 30°1N 97°10W 314 F6
Smoke Creek Desert U.S.A. 40°30N 119°40W 304 F4
Smoky ➔ Canada 56°10N 117°21W 296 B5
Smoky Bay Australia 32°22S 134°13E 281 E1
Smoky Hill ➔ U.S.A. 39°4N 96°48W 308 F5
Smoky Hills U.S.A. 39°15N 99°30W 308 F4
Smoky Lake Canada 54°10N 112°30W 296 C6
Smøla Norway 63°23N 8°3E 164 A5
Smolensk Russia 54°45N 32°5E 188 E7
Smolensk □ Russia 55°20N 33°0E 188 E7
Smolenskoye Poozerye △ Russia 55°35N 31°50E 188 E6
Smolikas, Oros Greece 40°9N 20°58E 202 F4
Smolník Slovak Rep. 48°43N 20°44E 181 C13
Smolny Russia 59°56N 30°25E 137 B2
Smolny △ Russia 54°50N 47°10E 190 C7
Smolny Cathedral Russia 59°56N 30°24E 137 B2
Smolyan Bulgaria 41°36N 24°38E 203 E8
Smolyan □ Bulgaria 41°36N 24°38E 203 E8
Smooth Rock Falls Canada 49°17N 81°37W 298 C3
Smoothstone L. Canada 54°40N 106°50W 297 C7
Smorgon = Smarhon Belarus 54°20N 26°24E 177 A14
Smotrych Ukraine 48°57N 26°33E 183 B11
Smotrych ➔ Ukraine 48°34N 26°39E 183 B11
Smulţi Romania 45°57N 27°44E 183 E12
Smyadovo Bulgaria 43°2N 27°1E 203 C11
Smygehamn Sweden 55°21N 13°22E 163 J7
Smygehuk Sweden 55°20N 13°20E 163 J7
Smyley I. Antarctica 72°55S 78°0W 151 D17
Smyrna = İzmir Turkey 38°25N 27°8E 205 C9
Smyrna Del., U.S.A. 39°18N 75°36W 309 F16
Smyrna Ga., U.S.A. 33°53N 84°31W 316 B5
Snæfell Iceland 64°48N 15°34W 155 C11
Snaefell I. of Man 54°16N 4°27W 168 C3
Snæfellsjökull Iceland 64°49N 23°46W 155 C3
Snæfellsnessýsla Iceland 65°0N 23°0W 155 C3
Snake ➔ U.S.A. 46°12N 119°2W 304 C4
Snake Creek Canal U.S.A. 25°57N 80°19W 129 C2
Snake I. Australia 38°47S 146°33E 283 E7
Snake Pt. Anguilla 18°17N 62°58W 322 a
Snake Range U.S.A. 39°0N 114°20W 304 G6
Snake River Plain U.S.A. 42°50N 114°0W 304 E7
Snarøya Norway 59°52N 10°33E 133 A2
Snasahögarna Sweden 63°13N 12°21E 162 A6
Snåsavatnet Norway 64°12N 12°0E 160 D15
Snättringe Sweden 59°15N 17°58E 139 B1
Snedsted Denmark 56°55N 8°32E 163 H2
Sneek Neths. 53°2N 5°40E 170 A5
Sneem Ireland 51°50N 9°54W 166 E2
Sneeuberge S. Africa 31°46S 24°20E 270 D3
Snegurovka = Tetiyev Ukraine 49°22N 29°38E 177 D15
Snejbjerg Denmark 56°8N 8°54E 163 H2
Snelling Calif., U.S.A. 37°31N 120°26W 306 H6
Snelling S.C., U.S.A. 33°15N 81°27W 316 B8
Snells Beach N.Z. 36°25S 174°44E 284 C3
Snezhnoye Ukraine 48°0N 38°58E 189 J10
Sněžka Europe 50°41N 15°50E 185 A8
Snežnik Slovenia 45°36N 14°35E 199 C11
Śniadowo Poland 53°2N 22°0E 185 E8
Śniardwy, Jezioro Poland 53°48N 21°50E 184 E8
Śnieżka Europe 50°44N 15°44E 180 A8
Snigirevka = Snihurivka Ukraine 47°2N 32°49E 189 J7
Snihurivka Ukraine 47°2N 32°49E 189 J7
Snillfjord Norway 63°24N 9°30E 164 A6
Snina Slovak Rep. 48°58N 22°9E 181 C15
Snizort, L. U.K. 57°33N 6°28W 167 D2
Snøhetta Norway 62°19N 9°16E 164 B6
Snohomish U.S.A. 47°55N 122°6W 306 C4
Snønuten Norway 59°31N 6°52E 164 E3
Snoqualmie U.S.A. 47°31N 121°49W 306 C5
Snoqualmie Pass U.S.A. 47°25N 121°25W 306 C5
Snoul Cambodia 12°4N 106°26E 237 F6
Snover U.S.A. 43°27N 82°58W 312 C2
Snovsk = Shchors Ukraine 51°48N 31°56E 189 G6
Snow Hill U.S.A. 38°11N 75°24W 309 F16
Snow Lake Canada 54°52N 100°3W 297 C8
Snow Mt. Calif., U.S.A. 39°23N 122°45W 306 F4
Snow Mt. Maine, U.S.A. 45°18N 70°48W 313 A14
Snow Shoe U.S.A. 41°2N 77°57W 312 E7
Snowbird L. Canada 60°45N 103°0W 297 A8
Snowdon U.K. 53°4N 4°5W 168 D3
Snowdonia △ U.K. 53°7N 3°59W 168 D4
Snowdoun U.S.A. 32°15N 86°18W 316 C3
Snowdrift = Łutsel K'e Canada 62°24N 110°44W 297 A6
Snowdrift ➔ Canada 62°24N 110°44W 297 A6
Snowflake U.S.A. 34°30N 110°5W 305 J8
Snowshoe Pk. U.S.A. 48°13N 115°41W 304 B6
Snowtown Australia 33°46S 138°14E 282 B3
Snowville U.S.A. 41°58N 112°43W 304 F7
Snowy ➔ Australia 37°46S 148°30E 283 D8
Snowy Mt. U.S.A. 43°42N 74°23W 313 C10
Snowy Mts. Australia 36°30S 148°20E 283 D8
Snowy River △ Australia 37°15S 147°29E 283 D7
Snug Corner Bahamas 22°33N 73°52W 321 B5
Snug Harbour Canada 45°22N 80°17W 312 A4
Snyatyn Ukraine 48°27N 25°38E 183 B10
Snyder Okla., U.S.A. 34°40N 98°57W 314 D5
Snyder Tex., U.S.A. 32°44N 100°55W 314 E4
So Kwun Wat Hong Kong, China 22°23N 114°0E 122 A2
Soacha Colombia 4°35N 74°13W 328 C3
Soahanina Madag. 18°42S 44°13E 272 B1
Soalala Madag. 16°6S 45°20E 272 B2
Soaloka Madag. 18°32S 45°15E 272 B2
Soamanonga Madag. 23°52S 44°47E 272 C1
Soan ➔ Pakistan 33°1N 71°44E 242 C4
Soanierana-Ivongo Madag. 16°55S 49°35E 272 B2
Soanindraniny Madag. 19°54S 47°14E 272 B2
Şoarş Romania 45°56N 24°55E 183 E9
Soavina Madag. 20°23S 46°56E 272 C2
Soavinandriana Madag. 19°9S 46°45E 272 B2
Soba Nigeria 10°58N 8°4E 263 C6
Sobaeksan △ S. Korea 36°50N 128°25E 224 D4
Sobat ➔ South Sudan 9°22N 31°33E 257 F3
Soběslav Czech Rep. 49°16N 14°45E 180 B7
Sobhapur India 22°47N 78°17E 242 H8
Sobinka Russia 56°0N 40°0E 188 E11
Sobo-Yama Japan 32°51N 131°22E 222 E3
Søborg Denmark 55°43N 12°29E 118 A2
Sobótka Poland 50°54N 16°44E 185 H3
Sobra Croatia 42°44N 17°34E 199 F14
Sobradinho, Represa de Brazil 9°30S 42°0W 332 C3
Sobral Brazil 3°50S 40°20W 332 B3
Sobrance Slovak Rep. 48°45N 22°11E 181 C15
Sobreda Portugal 38°39N 9°11W 126 B1
Sobreira Formosa Portugal 39°46N 7°51W 194 F3
Soc Giang Vietnam 22°54N 106°1E 228 F6
Soc Trang Vietnam 9°37N 105°50E 237 H5
Soča ➔ Europe 46°20N 13°40E 180 E6
Socastee U.S.A. 33°41N 78°59W 315 E15
Soccer City Stadium Johannesburg, S. Africa 26°14S 27°59E 123 B1
Soccsksargen □ Phil. 6°30N 125°0E 233 J5
Sochaczew Poland 52°15N 20°13E 185 F7
Soch'e = Shache China 38°20N 77°10E 217 E9
Sochi Russia 43°35N 39°40E 191 J4
Sochi ✈ (AER) Russia 43°27N 39°57E 191 J4
Sochi △ Russia 43°40N 39°35E 191 J4
Sochos Greece 40°48N 23°22E 202 F7
Social Circle U.S.A. 33°39N 83°43W 316 B6
Société, Îs. de la French Polynesia 17°0S 151°0W 289 f
Society Hill U.S.A. 32°26N 85°27W 316 C4
Society Is. = Société, Îs. de la French Polynesia 17°0S 151°0W 289 f
Socompa, Portezuelo de Chile 24°27S 68°18W 334 A2
Socorro = Fronteiras Brazil 7°5S 40°37W 332 C3
Socorro Colombia 6°29N 73°16W 328 B3
Socorro Phil. 9°37N 125°58E 233 G5
Socorro N. Mex., U.S.A. 34°4N 106°54W 305 J10
Socorro Tex., U.S.A. 31°39N 106°18W 314 F1
Socorro, I. Mexico 18°45N 110°58W 318 D2
Socotra Yemen 12°30N 54°0E 249 D6
Socovos Spain 38°20N 1°58W 197 G3
Socuéllamos Spain 39°16N 2°47W 197 F2
Soda L. U.S.A. 35°10N 116°4W 307 K10
Soda Plains India 35°30N 79°0E 243 B8
Soda Springs U.S.A. 42°39N 111°36W 304 E8
Sodankylä Finland 67°29N 26°40E 160 C22
Soddy-Daisy U.S.A. 35°17N 85°10W 315 D12
Söderala Sweden 61°17N 16°55E 162 C10
Söderåsen △ Sweden 56°2N 13°13E 163 H7
Söderbärke Sweden 60°5N 15°33E 162 D9
Söderby Sweden 59°24N 18°12E 139 A3
Söderfors Sweden 60°23N 17°25E 162 D11
Söderhamn Sweden 61°18N 17°10E 162 C11
Söderköping Sweden 58°31N 16°20E 163 F10
Södermalm Sweden 59°18N 18°4E 139 B2
Södermanland Sweden 58°56N 16°55E 161 G17
Södermanlands län □ Sweden 59°10N 16°30E 162 E10
Södertälje Sweden 59°12N 17°39E 162 E11
Sodiri Sudan 14°27N 29°0E 257 E2
Sodo Ethiopia 7°0N 37°41E 257 F4
Sodpur India 22°42N 88°24E 124 A2
Södra Finnskoga Sweden 60°42N 12°34E 162 D6
Södra Sandby Sweden 55°43N 13°21E 163 J7
Södra Ulvön Sweden 62°59N 18°38E 162 B12
Södra Vi Sweden 57°45N 15°45E 163 G9
Sodražica Slovenia 45°45N 14°39E 199 C11
Sodus U.S.A. 43°14N 77°4W 312 C7
Sodwana Bay △ S. Africa 27°35S 32°43E 271 C5
Soe Indonesia 9°52S 124°17E 278 A3
Soekmekaar = Morebeng S. Africa 23°30S 29°55E 271 B4
Soest Nordrhein-Westfalen, Germany 51°34N 8°7E 178 D4
Soest Neths. 52°9N 5°19E 170 B5
Soeurs, Î. des Canada 45°27N 73°32W 130 B2
Sofades Greece 39°20N 22°4E 204 B4
Sofaïa Guadeloupe 16°17N 61°43W 322 e
Sofala □ Mozam. 19°30S 34°30E 271 A5
Sofara Mali 13°59N 4°9W 262 C4
Sofia = Sofiya Bulgaria 42°45N 23°20E 202 D7
Sofia ➔ Madag. 15°27S 47°23E 272 B2
Sofievka Ukraine 48°6N 33°55E 189 H7
Sofiko Greece 37°47N 23°3E 204 D5
Sofiya Bulgaria 42°45N 23°20E 202 D7
Sofiya □ Bulgaria 42°15N 23°20E 202 D7
Sofiya ✈ (SOF) Bulgaria 42°46N 23°28E 202 D7
Sofrana Greece 36°5N 26°24E 205 E8
Sōfu-Gan Japan 29°49N 140°21E 221 K10
Sogakofe Ghana 6°2N 0°39E 263 D5
Sogamoso Colombia 5°43N 72°56W 328 B3
Sogār Iran 25°53N 58°6E 247 E8
Sögel Germany 52°50N 7°31E 178 C3
Sogeri Papua N. G. 9°26S 147°35E 286 E4
Sogn og Fjordane □ Norway 61°40N 6°45E 164 C3
Sogndalsfjøra Norway 61°14N 7°5E 164 C4
Søgne Norway 58°5N 7°48E 164 F4
Sognefjorden Norway 61°10N 5°50E 164 C2
Sognsvatn Norway 59°58N 10°43E 133 A3
Sogod Phil. 10°28N 124°59E 233 F5
Söğüt Bilecik, Turkey 40°2N 30°11E 205 A12
Söğüt Burdur, Turkey 37°2N 29°50E 205 D11
Söğüt Dağı Turkey 37°50N 29°55E 205 D11
Söğütköy Turkey 36°40N 28°8E 205 E10
Soh Iran 33°26N 51°27E 247 C6
Sohâg Egypt 26°33N 31°43E 256 B3
Sohagpur India 22°42N 78°12E 242 H8
Sohano Papua N. G. 5°22S 154°37E 286 C8
Sohar = Şuḩār Oman 24°20N 56°40E 247 E8
Sohela India 21°18N 83°24E 244 D6
Soheuksando S. Korea 34°4N 125°7E 224 E2
Sohm Abyssal Plain Atl. Oc. 36°0N 55°0W 152 C6
Soho London, U.K. 125 b3
Soho New York, U.S.A. 132 e1
Sohoton △ Phil. 11°22N 125°6E 233 F5
Soignes, Forêt de Belgium 50°47N 4°25E 116 B2
Soignies Belgium 50°35N 4°5E 170 D4
Soin Burkina Faso 12°47N 3°50W 262 C4
Soira Eritrea 14°45N 39°30E 257 E4
Soissons France 49°25N 3°19E 173 C10
Sōja Japan 34°40N 133°45E 222 C5
Sojat India 25°55N 73°45E 242 G5
Sok ➔ Russia 53°24N 50°8E 190 D10
Sok Kwu Wan Hong Kong, China 22°12N 114°7E 122 B2
Sokal Ukraine 50°31N 24°15E 177 C13
Sokcho S. Korea 38°12N 128°36E 224 C4
Söke Turkey 37°48N 27°28E 205 D9
Sokelo Dem. Rep. of the Congo 9°55S 24°36E 265 D4
Sokhumi Georgia 43°0N 41°0E 191 J5
Sokki, Oued In ➔ Algeria 29°30N 3°42E 261 C5
Sokna Norway 60°16N 9°58E 164 D6
Soknedal Norway 62°57N 10°13E 164 B7
Soko Banja Serbia 43°40N 21°51E 202 C5
Soko Is. Hong Kong, China 22°10N 113°54E 122 B1
Sokodé Togo 9°0N 1°11E 263 D5
Sokol Russia 59°30N 40°5E 188 C11
Sokolac Bos.-H. 43°56N 18°48E 182 G3
Sokółka Poland 53°25N 23°30E 184 E10
Sokolniki Russia 55°47N 37°40E 129 B3
Sokolniki Park Russia 55°48N 37°40E 129 B3
Sokolo Ségou, Mali 14°53N 6°8W 262 C3
Sokolo Sikasso, Mali 10°52N 6°59W 262 C3
Sokolov Czech Rep. 50°12N 12°40E 180 A5
Sokołów Poland 52°9N 20°51E 143 C1
Sokołów Małpolski Poland 50°12N 22°7E 185 H9
Sokołów Podlaski Poland 52°25N 22°15E 185 F9
Sokoły Poland 52°59N 22°42E 185 F9
Sokoto Nigeria 13°2N 5°16E 263 C6
Sokoto □ Nigeria 12°30N 6°0E 263 C6
Sokoto ➔ Nigeria 11°20N 4°10E 263 C5
Sokyrnytsya Ukraine 48°7N 23°23E 183 B8
Sokyryany Ukraine 48°27N 27°25E 183 B12
Sol, Costa del Spain 36°30N 4°30W 195 J6
Sol Iletsk Russia 51°10N 55°0E 186 D10
Sola Rogaland, Norway 58°53N 5°36E 164 F2
Sola Vanuatu 13°51S 167°33E 287 C5
Sola ➔ Poland 50°4N 19°15E 185 H6
Solai Kenya 0°2N 36°12E 268 B4
Solalinden Germany 48°5N 11°42E 131 B3
Solan India 30°55N 77°7E 242 D7
Solana Phil. 17°39N 121°41E 232 C3
Solana Beach U.S.A. 32°58N 117°16W 307 N9
Solander I. N.Z. 46°34S 166°54E 285 G1
Solano Phil. 16°31N 121°15E 232 C3
Solapur India 17°43N 75°56E 244 F2
Solca Romania 47°40N 25°50E 183 C10
Solda Gölü Turkey 37°33N 29°42E 205 D11
Soldăneşti Moldova 47°49N 28°48E 183 C13
Soldeu Andorra 42°35N 1°40E 196 C6
Soldier Pt. Antigua & B. 17°2N 61°41W 322 b
Soldin = Myślibórz Poland 52°55N 14°50E 185 F1
Soldotna U.S.A. 60°29N 151°3W 303 F10
Soléa Cyprus 35°5N 33°4E 207 E9
Solec Kujawski Poland 53°5N 18°14E 185 E5
Soledad Colombia 10°55N 74°46W 328 A3
Soledad Calif., U.S.A. 36°26N 121°20W 306 J5
Soledad Venezuela 8°10N 63°34W 329 B5
Sølen Norway 61°53N 11°31E 164 C8
Solent, The U.K. 50°45N 1°25W 169 G6
Solenzara France 41°53N 9°23E 175 G13
Solesmes France 50°10N 3°30E 173 B10
Solferino Italy 45°22N 10°34E 198 C7
Solfonntaggen Norway 60°2N 6°57E 164 D3
Solhan Turkey 38°57N 41°3E 213 C9
Solheim Norway 60°53N 5°27E 164 D2
Soligalich Russia 59°5N 42°10E 186 C7
Soligorsk = Salihorsk Belarus 52°51N 27°27E 177 B14
Solihull U.K. 52°26N 1°47W 169 E6
Solikamsk Russia 59°38N 56°50E 186 C10
Solila Madag. 21°25S 46°37E 272 C2
Solimões = Amazonas ➔ S. Amer. 0°5S 50°0W 329 D8
Solin Croatia 43°33N 16°30E 199 E13
Solingen Germany 51°10N 7°5E 178 D3
Söll Austria 47°30N 12°11E 179 H8
Sollebrunn Sweden 58°8N 12°32E 163 F6
Sollefteå Sweden 63°12N 17°20E 162 A11
Sollentuna Sweden 59°25N 17°56E 139 A1
Sóller Spain 39°46N 2°43E 206 B3
Sollerön Sweden 60°55N 14°37E 162 D8
Solling Germany 51°42N 9°38E 178 D5
Solling-Vogler ⌓ Germany 51°45N 9°32E 178 D5
Solln Germany 48°4N 11°31E 131 B2
Sollsvika Norway 60°26N 4°58E 164 D1
Solna Sweden 59°21N 17°59E 139 A1
Solnechnogorsk Russia 56°10N 36°57E 188 D9
Solo ➔ Indonesia 6°47S 112°22E 231 G15
Solofra Italy 40°50N 14°51E 201 B7
Sologne France 47°40N 1°45E 173 E8
Solok Indonesia 0°45S 100°40E 234 C2
Sololá Guatemala 14°49N 91°10W 320 D1
Sololo Kenya 3°33N 38°39E 268 B4
Solomon, N. Fork ➔ U.S.A. 39°29N 98°26W 308 F4
Solomon, S. Fork ➔ U.S.A. 39°25N 99°12W 308 F4
Solomon Is. Papua N. G. 6°0S 155°0E 286 D8
Solomon Is. ■ Pac. Oc. 6°0S 155°0E 287 L8
Solomon Rise Pac. Oc. 1°0N 157°0E 288 G7
Solomon Sea Papua N. G. 7°0S 150°0E 286 D6
Solon China 46°32N 121°10E 219 B13
Solon Springs U.S.A. 46°22N 91°49W 308 B8
Solonópole Brazil 5°44S 39°1W 332 C4
Solor Indonesia 8°27S 123°0E 231 F6
Solotcha Russia 54°48N 39°53E 188 E10
Solothurn Switz. 47°13N 7°32E 179 H3
Solothurn □ Switz. 47°18N 7°40E 179 H3
Solotvyn Ukraine 48°42N 24°25E 183 B9
Solovetskiye Ostrova Russia 65°5N 35°40E 186 B6
Solsona Phil. 18°5N 120°46E 232 B3
Solsona Spain 42°0N 1°31E 196 C6
Solt Hungary 46°45N 19°1E 182 D4
Šolta Croatia 43°24N 16°15E 199 E13
Solţānābād Khorāsān, Iran 34°13N 59°58E 247 C8
Solţānābād Khorāsān, Iran 36°29N 58°5E 247 B8
Solţānīyeh Iran 36°26N 48°47E 213 D13
Soltau Germany 52°59N 9°50E 178 C5
Soltsy Russia 58°10N 30°30E 188 C6
Soltüstik Qazaqstan □ Kazakhstan 54°0N 70°0E 217 B8
Solund Norway 61°5N 4°50E 164 C1
Solunska Glava Macedonia 41°44N 21°31E 202 E5
Solvang U.S.A. 34°36N 120°8W 307 L6
Solvay U.S.A. 43°3N 76°13W 313 C8
Sölvesborg Sweden 56°5N 14°35E 163 H8
Solvychegodsk Russia 61°21N 46°56E 186 B8
Solway Firth U.K. 54°49N 3°35W 168 C4
Solwezi Zambia 12°11S 26°21E 269 E2
Sōma Japan 37°40N 140°50E 220 F10
Soma Turkey 39°10N 27°35E 205 B9
Somabhula Zimbabwe 19°42S 29°40E 271 A4
Somali = Sumale □ Ethiopia 7°0N 45°0E 267 C6
Somali Pen. Africa 7°0N 46°0E 254 F8
Somalia ■ Africa 7°0N 47°0E 267 C6
Somaliland □ Somalia 10°0N 46°0E 267 C6
Sombe Dzong Bhutan 27°13N 89°8E 241 B2
Sombernon France 47°20N 4°40E 173 E11
Sombo Angola 8°42S 20°59E 265 D4
Sombor Serbia 45°46N 19°9E 182 E4
Sombra Canada 42°43N 82°29W 312 D2
Sombrerete Mexico 23°38N 103°39W 318 C4
Sombrero Anguilla 18°37N 63°30W 321 C7
Sombrero Channel India 7°41N 93°35E 245 L11
Şomcuta Mare Romania 47°31N 23°28E 183 C8
Somdari India 25°47N 72°38E 242 G5
Someido ⌓ Spain 43°5N 6°11W 194 B4
Somers U.S.A. 48°5N 114°13W 304 B6
Somerset Bermuda 32°17N 64°52W 153 a
Somerset Ky., U.S.A. 37°5N 84°36W 309 G11
Somerset Mass., U.S.A. 41°47N 71°8W 313 E13
Somerset Md., U.S.A. 38°57N 77°5W 143 B2
Somerset Pa., U.S.A. 40°1N 79°5W 312 F5
Somerset □ U.K. 51°9N 3°0W 169 F5
Somerset East S. Africa 32°42S 25°35E 270 D4
Somerset I. Bermuda 32°17N 64°52W 153 a
Somerset I. Nunavut, Canada 73°30N 93°0W 294 C13
Somerset West S. Africa 34°8S 18°50E 270 D2
Somersworth U.S.A. 43°16N 70°52W 313 C14
Somerton U.S.A. 32°36N 114°43W 305 K6
Somerville Mass., U.S.A. 42°22N 71°5W 116 A2
Somerville N.J., U.S.A. 40°35N 74°38W 313 F10
Someş ➔ Romania 47°49N 22°43E 182 C7
Someşul Mare ➔ Romania 47°9N 23°55E 183 C8
Somme □ France 49°57N 2°20E 173 C9
Somme ➔ France 50°11N 1°38E 173 B8
Somme, B. de la France 50°14N 1°33E 172 B8
Sommen Jönköping, Sweden 58°12N 14°58E 163 F8
Sommen Östergötland, Sweden 58°0N 15°15E 163 F9
Sommepy-Tahure France 49°15N 4°31E 173 C11
Sömmerda Germany 51°9N 11°7E 178 D7
Sommerfeld = Lubsko Poland 51°45N 14°57E 185 G1
Sommesous France 48°44N 4°12E 173 D11
Sommières France 43°47N 4°6E 175 E8
Somnath India 20°53N 70°22E 242 J4
Somogy □ Hungary 46°19N 17°30E 182 D2
Somogyszob Hungary 46°18N 17°20E 182 D2
Somosomo Fiji 16°47S 179°58W 287 A3
Somosomo Str. Fiji 16°0S 180°0E 287 A3
Somoto Nic. 13°28N 86°37W 320 D2
Sompolno Poland 52°26N 18°30E 185 F5
Somport, Túnel de Spain 42°48N 0°31W 196 C4
Somuncurá, Meseta de Argentina 41°30S 67°0W 336 B3
Somvarpet India 12°36N 75°52E 245 H2
Son Norway 59°32N 10°42E 164 E7
Son ➔ India 25°42N 84°52E 243 G11
Son, Laem Thailand 7°59N 98°16E 237 a
Son Ha Vietnam 15°3N 108°34E 236 E7
Son La Vietnam 21°20N 103°50E 228 G4
Son Morrell Spain 39°44N 3°20E 206 B4
Son Rapinya Spain 39°35N 2°37E 206 B3
Son Sardina Spain 39°37N 2°40E 206 B3
Son Serra Spain 39°43N 3°13E 206 B4
Son Servera Spain 39°37N 3°21E 206 B4
Son Tay Vietnam 21°8N 105°30E 228 G5
Son Tinh Vietnam 15°10N 108°40E 236 E7
Soná Panama 8°0N 81°20W 320 E3
Sonamarg India 34°18N 75°21E 243 B6
Sonamukhi India 23°18N 87°27E 243 H12
Sonamura India 23°29N 91°15E 241 D3
Sonar ➔ India 24°24N 79°56E 243 G8
Sonari India 18°54N 72°59E 130 B2
Sŏnch'ŏn N. Korea 39°48N 124°55E 224 C2
Sondags ➔ S. Africa 33°44S 25°51E 270 D4
Sóndalo Italy 46°20N 10°19E 198 B7
Søndeled Norway 58°46N 9°3E 164 F6
Sønder Felding Denmark 55°57N 8°47E 163 J2
Sønder Omme Denmark 55°50N 8°54E 163 J2
Sønderborg Denmark 54°55N 9°49E 163 K3
Sondershausen Germany 51°22N 10°51E 178 D6
Søndersø Denmark 55°46N 12°21E 118 A2
Søndre Bergenhaus = Hordaland □ Norway 60°25N 6°15E 164 D3
Søndre Strømfjord = Kangerlussuaq Greenland 66°59N 50°40W 154 D5
Søndre Trøndhjem = Sør-Trøndelag □ Norway 63°0N 11°0E 164 A7
Sóndrio Italy 46°10N 9°52E 198 B6
Sondur ➔ India 20°40N 82°1E 244 D6
Sone Mozam. 17°23S 34°55E 269 F3
Sonepur India 20°55N 83°50E 244 D6
Sonfim Brazil 6°0S 67°52W 330 B4
Song Nigeria 9°49N 12°39E 263 D7
Song Thailand 18°28N 100°11E 236 C3
Song Cau Vietnam 13°27N 109°18E 236 F7
Song-Köl Kyrgyzstan 41°50N 75°12E 217 D9
Song Ma Vietnam 20°56N 103°53E 228 G4
Song Qingling, Former Residence of Beijing, China 114 a2
Song Xian China 34°12N 112°8E 226 G7
Songadh India 21°9N 73°33E 244 D1
Songan Indonesia 8°13S 115°24E 231 J18
Songavatnet Norway 59°52N 7°32E 164 E4
Songea Tanzania 10°40S 35°40E 269 E4
Songeons France 49°32N 1°50E 173 C8
Sŏnggan N. Korea 40°47N 126°34E 224 B3
Songgang China 22°46N 113°50E 219 a
Songhua Hu China 43°35N 126°50E 227 C14
Songhua Jiang ➔ China 47°45N 132°30E 219 B15
Songimvelo ⌓ S. Africa 25°50S 31°2E 271 C5
Songjiang Jilin, China 42°34N 128°20E 224 A4
Songjiang Shanghai, China 31°1N 121°12E 229 B13
Songjianghe China 42°10N 127°29E 224 A3
Sŏngjin = Kimch'aek N. Korea 40°40N 129°10E 224 B4
Songkan China 28°35N 106°52E 228 C6
Songkhla Thailand 7°13N 100°37E 237 J3
Songming China 25°12N 103°2E 228 E4
Songnim N. Korea 38°45N 125°39E 224 C2
Songnisan △ S. Korea 36°28N 127°45E 224 D3
Songo Angola 7°22S 14°51E 265 D2
Songo Mozam. 15°34S 32°38E 271 A5

Songololo = Mbanza Ngungu Dem. Rep. of the Congo 5°12S 14°53E 265 D2
Songololo Dem. Rep. of the Congo 5°42S 14°2E 265 D2
Songpa S. Korea 37°30N 127°7E 137 B2
Songpan China 32°40N 103°30E 228 A4
Songtao China 28°11N 109°10E 228 C7
Songwe Dem. Rep. of the Congo 3°20S 26°16E 268 C2
Songwe → Africa 9°44S 33°58E 269 D3
Songxi China 27°31N 118°44E 229 D12
Songzi China 30°12N 111°45E 229 B8
Sonhat India 23°29N 82°31E 243 H10
Sonid Youqi China 42°45N 112°48E 226 C7
Sonid Zuoqi China 43°50N 113°42E 226 C7
Sonipat India 29°0N 77°5E 242 E7
Sonkach India 22°59N 76°21E 242 H7
Sonkovo Russia 57°50N 37°5E 188 D9
Sonmiani Pakistan 25°25N 66°40E 242 G2
Sonmiani B. Pakistan 25°15N 66°30E 242 G2
Sonnino Italy 41°25N 13°14E 200 A6
Sono → Minas Gerais, Brazil 17°2S 45°32W 333 E2
Sono → Tocantins, Brazil 9°58S 48°11W 332 C2
Sonobe = Nantan Japan 35°6N 135°28E 223 B7
Sonoma U.S.A. 38°18N 122°28W 306 G4
Sonora Calif., U.S.A. 37°59N 120°23W 306 H6
Sonora Tex., U.S.A. 30°34N 100°39W 314 F4
Sonora □ Mexico 29°20N 110°40W 318 B2
Sonora → Mexico 29°5N 110°55W 318 B2
Sonoran Desert U.S.A. 33°40N 113°30W 307 L12
Sonoyta Mexico 31°51N 112°50W 318 A2
Sonqor Iran 34°47N 47°36E 213 E12
Sonseca Spain 39°42N 3°57W 195 F7
Sonsón Colombia 5°43N 75°18W 328 B2
Sonsonate El Salv. 13°43N 89°44W 320 D2
Sonstorp Sweden 58°44N 15°38E 163 F9
Sonthofen Germany 47°30N 10°16E 179 H6
Sony Picture Studio U.S.A. 34°1N 118°4W 126 B2
Soo Japan 31°40N 131°5E 222 F3
Soochow = Suzhou China 31°19N 120°38E 229 B13
Sooke Canada 48°13N 123°43W 306 B3
Sool □ Somalia 8°40N 47°30E 267 C6
Soomaa △ Estonia 58°30N 28°5E 188 C3
Soomaaliya = Somalia ■ Africa 7°0N 47°0E 267 C6
Sop Hao Laos 20°33N 104°27E 228 G5
Sop Prap Thailand 17°53N 99°20E 236 D2
Sopachuy Bolivia 19°29S 64°31W 331 D5
Sopchoppy U.S.A. 30°4N 84°29W 316 E5
Sopelana Spain 43°23N 2°58W 196 B2
Soperton U.S.A. 32°23N 82°35W 316 C7
Sopi Indonesia 2°34N 128°28E 231 D7
Sopo, Nahr → South Sudan 8°40N 26°30E 257 F2
Sopot Bulgaria 42°39N 24°45E 203 D8
Sopot Poland 54°27N 18°31E 184 D5
Sopot Serbia 44°29N 20°36E 202 B4
Sopotnica Macedonia 41°18N 21°13E 202 E5
Sopron Hungary 47°45N 16°32E 182 C1
Sopur India 34°18N 74°27E 243 B6
Sør-Rondane Antarctica 72°0S 25°0E 151 D4
Sør-Trøndelag □ Norway 63°0N 11°0E 164 A7
Sora Italy 41°43N 13°37E 199 G10
Sorab India 14°23N 75°6E 245 G2
Sorada India 19°45N 84°26E 244 E7
Sorah Pakistan 27°13N 68°56E 242 F3
Söråker Sweden 62°30N 17°32E 162 B11
Sorang Kazakhstan 49°46N 72°51E 217 C8
Sorano Italy 42°41N 11°43E 199 F8
Soraon India 25°37N 81°51E 243 G9
Sorata Bolivia 15°50S 68°40W 330 D4
Sorbas Spain 37°6N 2°7W 197 H2
Sörbygden Sweden 62°48N 16°12E 162 B10
Sord = Swords Ireland 53°28N 6°13W 120 A2
Sordellen Sweden 61°48N 16°43E 162 C10
Sore France 44°18N 0°35W 174 D3
Søre Osa → Norway 61°18N 11°46E 164 C8
Sorel-Tracy Canada 46°0N 73°10W 298 C5
Soresina Italy 45°17N 9°51E 198 C6
Sørfjorden Norway 60°20N 6°37E 164 D3
Sörforsa Sweden 61°43N 16°58E 162 C10
Sórgono Italy 40°1N 9°6E 200 B2
Sorgues France 44°1N 4°53E 175 D8
Sorgun Turkey 39°46N 35°11E 212 C6
Sorgun → Turkey 36°36N 34°20E 250 B5
Sori Papua N. G. 1°58S 146°42E 286 A4
Soria Spain 41°43N 2°32W 196 D2
Soria □ Spain 41°46N 2°28W 196 D2
Soriano Uruguay 33°24S 58°19W 334 C4
Soriano nel Cimino Italy 42°25N 12°14E 199 F9
Sorkh, Kuh-e Iran 35°40N 58°30E 247 C8
Sorø Denmark 55°26N 11°32E 163 J5
Soro Guinea 10°9N 9°48W 262 C3
Soroca Moldova 48°8N 28°12E 183 B13
Sorocaba Brazil 23°31S 47°27W 335 A6
Sorochinsk Russia 52°26N 53°10E 186 D9
Soroka = Belomorsk Russia 64°35N 34°54E 186 B5
Soroki = Soroca Moldova 48°8N 28°12E 183 B13
Sorokino = Krasnodon Ukraine 48°17N 39°44E 189 H10
Soroksár Hungary 47°24N 19°7E 117 B2
Soroksari Duna → Hungary 47°25N 19°5E 117 B2
Sorong Indonesia 0°55S 131°15E 231 E8
Soroni Greece 36°21N 28°1E 206 E12
Soroti Uganda 1°43N 33°35E 268 B3
Sørøya Norway 70°40N 22°30E 160 A20
Sørøysane Norway 62°25N 5°32E 164 B2
Sørøysundet Norway 70°25N 23°0E 160 A20
Sorraia → Portugal 38°55N 8°53W 195 G2
Sorrell Australia 42°47S 147°34E 281 G4
Sorrento Italy 40°37N 14°22E 201 B7
Sorsele Sweden 65°31N 17°30E 160 D17
Sörsjön Sweden 61°24N 13°5E 162 C7
Sorso Italy 40°48N 8°34E 200 B1
Sorsogon Phil. 13°0N 124°0E 232 E5
Sorsogon □ Phil. 12°50N 123°55E 232 E4
Sortavala Russia 61°42N 30°41E 188 B6
Sortino Italy 37°9N 15°2E 201 E8
Sortland Norway 68°42N 15°25E 160 B16
Sortot Sudan 19°3N 30°28E 256 D3
Sørum Norway 60°30N 10°17E 164 D7
Sorvizhi Russia 57°52N 48°32E 190 B9
Sos del Rey Católico Spain 42°30N 1°13W 196 C3
Soscumica, L. Canada 50°15N 77°27W 298 B4
Sösdala Sweden 56°2N 13°41E 163 H7
Sosenka → Russia 55°46N 37°42E 129 B3
Sosna → Russia 52°42N 38°55E 189 F10
Sosnogorsk Russia 63°37N 53°51E 186 B9
Sosnovka Kirov, Russia 56°17N 51°17E 190 B10
Sosnovka St. Petersburg, Russia 60°0N 30°22E 137 B2
Sosnovka Tambov, Russia 53°13N 41°24E 190 D5
Sosnovyy Bor Russia 59°55N 29°6E 188 C5
Sosnowiec Poland 50°20N 19°10E 185 H6
Sosnowitz = Sosnowiec Poland 50°20N 19°10E 185 H6
Soso C.A.R. 3°55N 15°30E 264 B3
Sospel France 43°52N 7°27E 175 E11
Sospiri, Ponte dei Venice, Italy 142 b3
Sossus Vlei Namibia 24°40S 15°23E 270 B2
Šoštanj Slovenia 46°23N 15°4E 199 B12
Sŏsura N. Korea 42°16N 130°36E 224 A5
Sot → India 27°27N 79°37E 243 F8
Sotasæter Norway 61°49N 7°43E 164 C4
Sotavento C. Verde Is. 15°0N 24°0W 153 j
Sotik Kenya 0°41S 35°7E 268 C4
Sotkamo Finland 64°8N 28°23E 160 D23
Soto Curaçao 12°16N 69°6W 322 g
Soto Spain 43°32N 6°4W 194 B4
Soto la Marina Mexico 23°46N 98°13W 319 C5
Soto la Marina → Mexico 23°45N 97°45W 319 C5
Soto y Amío Spain 42°46N 5°53W 194 C5
Sotouboua Togo 8°34N 0°59E 263 D5
Sotrondio Spain 43°17N 5°36W 194 B5
Sotuf, Adrar W. Sahara 21°42N 15°36W 260 D1
Sotuta Mexico 20°36N 89°1W 319 C7
Souanké Congo 2°10N 14°3E 264 B2
Soubré Ivory C. 5°50N 6°35W 262 D3
Souda Greece 35°29N 24°4E 207 E5
Soudas, Ormos Greece 35°25N 24°10E 207 E5
Souderton U.S.A. 40°19N 75°19W 313 F9
Souflay Congo 2°1N 14°54E 264 B2
Soufli Greece 41°12N 26°18E 203 E10
Soufrière Dominica 15°13N 61°22W 323 k
Soufrière Guadeloupe 16°5N 61°40W 322 e
Soufrière St. Lucia 13°51N 61°3W 323 m
Soufrière Bay Dominica 15°13N 61°22W 323 k
Soufrière Bay St. Lucia 13°51N 61°4W 323 m
Soufrière Hills Volcano Montserrat 16°43N 62°10W 323 p
Souillac Lot, France 44°53N 1°29E 174 D5
Souillac Mauritius 20°31S 57°31E 272 e
Souilly France 49°3N 5°17E 173 C12
Souk-Ahras Algeria 36°23N 7°57E 261 A6
Souk-Ahras □ Algeria 36°10N 7°55E 261 A6
Souk el Arba du Rharb Morocco 34°43N 5°59W 260 B3
Soukhouma Laos 14°38N 105°48E 236 E5
Sŏul = Seoul S. Korea 37°31N 126°58E 137 B2
Soulac-sur-Mer France 45°30N 1°7W 174 C2
Soulougou Burkina Faso 13°1N 0°25E 263 C5
Soultz-sous-Forêts France 48°57N 7°52E 173 D14
Sound, The = Øresund Europe 55°45N 12°40E 163 J6
Sound, The U.K. 50°20N 4°10W 169 G3
Sound I. India 12°58N 92°59E 245 H11
Soundview U.S.A. 40°49N 73°53W 132 B2
Sounio, Akra Greece 37°37N 24°1E 204 D6
Sour el Ghozlane Algeria 36°10N 3°45E 261 A5
Sources, Mt. aux Lesotho 28°45S 28°50E 271 C4
Soure Brazil 0°35S 48°30W 332 B2
Soure Portugal 40°4N 8°38W 194 E2
Souris Man., Canada 49°40N 100°20W 297 D8
Souris P.E.I., Canada 46°21N 62°15W 299 C7
Souris → N. Amer. 49°40N 99°34W 308 A4
Sourou → Africa 12°45N 3°25W 262 C4
Sourpi Greece 39°6N 22°54E 204 B4
Sous, O. → Morocco 30°27N 9°31W 260 B3
Sous le Vent, Is. French Polynesia 16°30S 155°30W 289 f
Sous le Vent, Région Réunion 21°12S 55°20E 272 f
Sous-Massa △ Morocco 30°26N 9°35W 260 B3
Sous-Massa-Drâa □ Morocco 30°45N 6°30W 260 B3
Sousa Brazil 6°45S 38°10W 332 C4
Sousel Brazil 2°38S 52°29W 332 B1
Sousel Portugal 38°57N 7°40W 195 G3
Sousse Tunisia 35°50N 10°38E 258 A2
Sousse □ Tunisia 35°40N 10°30E 261 A7
Soustons France 43°45N 1°19W 174 E2
Sout → S. Africa 31°35S 18°24E 270 D2
South Africa ■ Africa 32°0S 23°0E 270 D3
South America 10°0S 60°0W 326 E5
South Andaman India 11°45N 92°10E 245 J11
South Aulatsivik I. Canada 56°45N 61°30W 299 A7
South Australia □ Australia 32°0S 139°0E 282 B3
South Australian Basin Ind. Oc. 38°0S 126°0E 288 L4
South Ayrshire □ U.K. 55°18N 4°41W 167 F4
South Baldy Pk. U.S.A. 34°6N 107°11W 305 J10
South Bass I. U.S.A. 41°39N 82°49W 312 E2
South Bay U.S.A. 26°40N 80°43W 317 J9
South Beach Bahamas 25°1N 77°20W 153 b
South Beach Fla., U.S.A. 25°46N 80°7W 129 D3
South Beach N.Y., U.S.A. 40°35N 74°4W 132 C1
South Beach Harbor San Francisco, U.S.A. 136 c3
South Beloit U.S.A. 42°29N 89°2W 310 B7
South Bend Ind., U.S.A. 41°41N 86°15W 311 C10
South Bend Wash., U.S.A. 46°40N 123°48W 306 D3
South Bend Park U.S.A. 33°42N 84°23W 113 B2
South Boston Mass., U.S.A. 42°20N 71°2W 116 A2
South Boston Va., U.S.A. 36°42N 78°54W 309 G14
South Branch Canada 47°55N 59°2W 299 C8
South Branch Chicago River → Chicago, U.S.A. 119 d1
South Brook Canada 49°26N 56°5W 299 C8
South Brother I. India 10°56N 92°37E 245 J11
South Bruny I. Australia 43°20S 147°15E 281 G4
South C. = Kalae U.S.A. 18°55N 155°41W 302 E6
South Carolina □ U.S.A. 34°0N 81°0W 315 E14
South Channel Phil. 14°18N 120°37E 232 D3
South Charleston U.S.A. 38°22N 81°44W 309 F13
South China Sea Asia 10°0N 113°0E 230 C4
South Comino Channel Malta 36°0N 14°20E 206 F7
South Congaree U.S.A. 33°53N 81°9W 316 B8
South Cotabato □ Phil. 6°0N 125°0E 233 J5
South Cumberland Is. △ Australia 20°42S 149°11E 280 b
South Dakota □ U.S.A. 44°15N 100°0W 308 C4
South Dayton U.S.A. 42°21N 79°3W 312 D5
South Daytona U.S.A. 29°10N 81°0W 317 F8
South Decatur U.S.A. 33°44N 84°16W 113 B3
South Deerfield U.S.A. 42°29N 72°37W 313 D12
South Deering U.S.A. 41°42N 87°33W 119 C3
South Downs U.K. 50°52N 0°25W 169 G7
South Downs △ U.K. 50°50N 0°50W 169 G7
South East □ Botswana 25°0S 25°40E 270 C4
South East B. Ascension I. 7°57S 14°18W 153 g
South East C. Australia 43°40S 146°50E 281 G4
South East Forest △ Australia 37°0S 149°30E 283 D8
South East Is. Australia 34°17S 123°30E 279 F3
South El Monte U.S.A. 34°3N 118°2W 126 B4
South Elgin U.S.A. 42°0N 88°18W 311 C8
South Esk → U.K. 56°43N 2°31W 167 E6
South Fiji Basin Pac. Oc. 26°0S 175°0E 288 K9
South Foreland U.K. 51°8N 1°24E 169 F9
South Fork American → U.S.A. 38°57N 120°59W 306 G5
South Fork Edisto → U.S.A. 33°16N 80°54W 316 B9
South Fork Feather → U.S.A. 39°17N 121°36W 306 F5
South Fork Grand → U.S.A. 45°43N 102°17W 308 C2
South Fork Licking → U.S.A. 38°40N 84°18W 311 F12
South Fork Milk → U.S.A. 48°4N 106°19W 304 B10
South Fork Republican → U.S.A. 40°3N 101°31W 308 E3
South Gate U.S.A. 33°56N 118°12W 126 C3
South Georgia Antarctica 54°30S 37°0W 151 B1
South Gloucestershire □ U.K. 51°32N 2°28W 169 F5
South Grand → U.S.A. 38°17N 93°25W 310 F3
South Hadley U.S.A. 42°16N 72°35W 313 D12
South Harbor Phil. 14°34N 120°58E 127 B1
South Harrow U.K. 51°33N 0°21W 125 A1
South Haven U.S.A. 42°24N 86°16W 311 B10
South Hd. Australia 33°50S 151°16E 139 B2
South Henik L. Canada 61°30N 97°20W 297 A9
South Hill Village Anguilla 18°11N 63°5W 322 a
South Hills S. Africa 26°14S 28°5E 123 B2
South Holland U.S.A. 41°36N 87°36W 119 D3
South Horr Kenya 2°12N 36°56E 268 B4
South I. India 10°3N 72°17E 245 J1
South I. Eastern, Kenya 2°35N 36°35E 268 B4
South I. N.Z. 44°0S 170°0E 285 E5
South Indian Lake Canada 56°47N 98°56W 297 B9
South Invercargill N.Z. 46°26S 168°23E 285 G3
South Island △ Kenya 2°39N 36°35E 268 B4
South Kensington London, U.K. 125 c2
South Kitui ⌂ Kenya 1°48S 38°46E 268 C4
South Knife → Canada 58°55N 94°37W 297 B10
South Koel → India 22°32N 85°14E 243 H11
South Korea ■ Asia 36°0N 128°0E 224 D4
South Lake Tahoe U.S.A. 38°57N 119°59W 306 G6
South Lanarkshire □ U.K. 55°37N 3°53W 167 F5
South Lawn U.S.A. 38°47N 77°0W 143 C2
South Loup → U.S.A. 41°4N 98°39W 308 E4
South Luangwa △ Zambia 13°0S 31°20E 269 E3
South Lyon U.S.A. 42°28N 83°39W 311 B13
South Magnetic Pole Antarctica 64°24S 137°12E 151 C9
South Malé Atoll Maldives 4°0N 73°25E 272 d
South Malosmadulu Atoll Maldives 5°12N 73°0E 272 d
South Miami U.S.A. 25°42N 80°17W 129 D1
South Milwaukee U.S.A. 42°55N 87°52W 311 B9
South Molton U.K. 51°1N 3°51W 169 F4
South Monroe U.S.A. 41°54N 83°26W 311 C13
South Moose L. Canada 53°49N 100°1W 297 C8
South Nahanni → Canada 61°3N 123°21W 296 A4
South Nation → Canada 45°34N 75°6W 313 A9
South Natuna Is. = Natuna Selatan, Kepulauan Indonesia 2°45N 109°0E 235 B3
South Negril Pt. Jamaica 18°16N 78°22W 320 a
South New Hebrides Trench Pac. Oc. 22°30S 170°0E 277 E13
South Newport U.S.A. 31°38N 81°24W 316 D8
South Nilandu Atoll Maldives 2°52N 72°57E 272 d
South Norwood U.K. 51°23N 0°3W 125 B3
South of Market San Francisco, U.S.A. 136 c2
South Orkney Is. Antarctica 63°0S 45°0W 151 C18
South Ossetia □ Georgia 42°21N 44°2E 191 J7
South Otselic U.S.A. 42°38N 75°46W 313 D9
South Ozone Park U.S.A. 40°41N 73°49W 132 B3
South Pagai, I. = Pagai Selatan, Pulau Indonesia 3°0S 100°15E 234 C2
South Paris U.S.A. 44°14N 70°31W 313 B14
South Pasadena U.S.A. 34°7N 118°8W 126 B4
South Pekin U.S.A. 40°30N 89°39W 310 D7
South Pittsburg U.S.A. 35°1N 85°42W 315 D12
South Platte → U.S.A. 41°7N 100°42W 308 E3
South Pole Antarctica 90°0S 0°0 151 E
South Ponte Vedra Beach U.S.A. 30°3N 81°20W 316 E8
South Porcupine Canada 48°30N 81°12W 298 C3
South Portland U.S.A. 43°38N 70°15W 309 D18
South Pt. Ascension I. 8°0S 14°24W 153 g
South Pt. Barbados 13°2N 59°32W 323 r
South Pt. Mich., U.S.A. 44°52N 83°19W 312 B1
South Res. U.S.A. 42°26N 71°6W 116 A2
South River Ont., Canada 45°52N 79°23W 298 C4
South River N.J., U.S.A. 40°27N 74°23W 313 F10
South Ronaldsay U.K. 58°48N 2°58W 167 C6
South Ruislip U.K. 51°33N 0°24W 125 A1
South Rukuru Malawi 10°44S 34°14E 269 E3
South San Francisco U.S.A. 37°38N 122°26W 136 C2
South San Gabriel U.S.A. 34°3N 118°6W 126 B4
South Sandwich Is. Antarctica 57°0S 27°0W 151 B1
South Sandwich Trench Atl. Oc. 56°0S 24°0W 151 B1
South Saskatchewan → Canada 53°15N 105°5W 297 C7
South Seal → Canada 58°48N 98°8W 297 B9
South Sentinel I. India 10°59N 92°14E 245 J11
South Shetland Is. Antarctica 62°0S 59°0W 151 C18
South Shields U.K. 55°0N 1°25W 168 C6
South Shore U.S.A. 41°45N 87°34W 119 C3
South Sioux City U.S.A. 42°28N 96°24W 308 D5
South Sister U.S.A. 44°4N 121°51W 304 D3
South Solomon Trench Pac. Oc. 11°0S 164°30E 277 C11
South Soufrière Hills Montserrat 16°41N 62°10W 323 p
South Street Boston, U.S.A. 116 c2
South Sudan ■ Africa 8°0N 30°0E 257 F2
South Taranaki Bight N.Z. 39°40S 174°5E 284 F3
South Tasman Rise S. Ocean 48°0S 146°0E 151 A10
South Thompson → Canada 50°40N 120°20W 296 C4
South Twin I. Canada 53°7N 79°52W 298 B4
South Tyne → U.K. 54°59N 2°8W 168 C5
South Ubian Phil. 5°11N 120°30E 233 J3
South Uist U.K. 57°20N 7°15W 167 D1
South Valley U.S.A. 35°1N 106°41W 305 J10
South Venice U.S.A. 27°3N 82°25W 317 H7
South Verde I. Phil. 10°4N 119°13E 233 F2
South Wayne U.S.A. 42°34N 89°53W 310 B7
South Wellesley Is. Australia 16°58S 139°17E 280 B2
South West Africa = Namibia ■ Africa 22°0S 18°9E 270 B2
South West B. Ascension I. 7°58S 14°25W 153 g
South West B. Bahamas 25°0N 77°32W 153 b
South West C. Tas., Australia 43°34S 146°3E 281 G4
South West C. N.Z. 47°17S 167°28E 285 H2
South West Pt. Papua N. G. 2°14S 146°34E 286 B4
South West Pt. St. Helena 15°59S 5°48W 153 h
South West Rocks Australia 30°52S 153°3E 283 A10
South Whitley U.S.A. 41°5N 85°38W 311 C11
South Williamsport U.S.A. 41°13N 77°0W 312 E8
South Yemen = Yemen ■ Asia 15°0N 44°0E 248 D4
South Yorkshire □ U.K. 53°27N 1°36W 168 D6
Southall U.K. 51°30N 0°22W 125 A1
Southampton Ont., Canada 44°30N 81°25W 312 B3
Southampton Southampton, U.K. 50°54N 1°23W 169 G6
Southampton N.Y., U.S.A. 40°53N 72°23W 313 F12
Southampton □ U.K. 50°54N 1°23W 169 G6
Southampton I. Canada 64°30N 84°0W 295 E15
Southaven U.S.A. 34°59N 90°0W 315 D9
Southbank Canada 54°2N 125°46W 296 C3
Southborough U.K. 51°23N 0°12E 125 B4
Southbridge N.Z. 43°48S 172°16E 285 D7
Southbridge Mass., U.S.A. 42°5N 72°2W 313 D12
Southeast C. U.S.A. 62°56N 169°39W 303 E5
Southeast Indian Ridge Ind. Oc. 43°0S 80°0E 273 J10
Southend Sask., Canada 56°19N 103°22W 297 B8
Southend London, U.K. 51°25N 0°0 125 B3
Southend-on-Sea U.K. 51°32N 0°44E 169 F8
Southend-on-Sea □ U.K. 51°32N 0°44E 169 F8
Southern = Yedebub Biheroch Bihereseboch na Hizboch □ Ethiopia 12°0N 36°0E 257 F4
Southern = Yuzhnyy □ Russia 44°0N 40°0E 214 E5
Southern □ Malawi 15°0S 35°0E 269 F4
Southern □ S. Leone 8°0N 12°30W 262 D2
Southern □ Zambia 16°20S 26°20E 269 F2
Southern △ South Sudan 6°50N 28°45E 257 F2
Southern Alps N.Z. 43°41S 170°11E 285 D5
Southern Aral Sea Asia 45°0N 58°0E 216 D5
Southern California, Univ. of U.S.A. 34°1N 118°17W 126 B3
Southern Cross Australia 31°12S 119°15E 279 F2
Southern Highlands □ Papua N. G. 6°15S 143°25E 286 D2
Southern Indian L. Canada 57°10N 98°30W 297 B9
Southern Lau Group Fiji 18°40S 178°40W 287 B3
Southern Leyte □ Phil. 10°30N 125°10E 233 F5
Southern Ocean 62°0S 60°0E 151 C6
Southern Pines U.S.A. 35°11N 79°24W 315 D15
Southern Rhodesia = Zimbabwe ■ Africa 19°0S 30°0E 269 F3
Southern Uplands U.K. 55°28N 3°52W 167 F5
Southfield U.S.A. 42°28N 83°15W 311 B13
Southfields U.K. 51°26N 0°11W 125 B2
Southington U.S.A. 41°36N 72°53W 313 E12
Southland □ N.Z. 45°30S 168°0E 285 F3
Southold U.S.A. 41°4N 72°26W 313 E12
Southport Queens., Australia 27°58S 153°25E 281 D5
Southport Mersey., U.K. 53°39N 3°0W 168 D4
Southport Fla., U.S.A. 30°17N 85°38W 316 E4
Southport La., U.S.A. 29°57N 90°8W 131 B2
Southport N.Y., U.S.A. 42°3N 76°49W 312 D8
Southwark □ U.K. 51°29N 0°6W 125 B3
Southwest △ Australia 43°8S 146°5E 281 G4
Southwest Museum Los Angeles, U.S.A. 34°6N 118°13W 126 B3
Southwest Pacific Basin Pac. Oc. 40°0S 140°0W 277 G17
Southwest Pt. U.S. Virgin Is. 17°40N 64°55W 321 b
Southwold U.K. 52°20N 1°41E 169 E9
Southwood △ Australia 27°48S 150°8E 281 D5
Soutpansberg S. Africa 23°0S 29°30E 271 B4
Souvigny France 46°33N 3°10E 173 F10
Søvang Denmark 55°34N 12°37E 118 B3
Sovata Romania 46°35N 25°3E 183 D10
Soverato Italy 38°41N 16°33E 201 D9
Sovetsk Kaliningrad, Russia 55°6N 21°50E 184 C8
Sovetsk Kirov, Russia 57°38N 48°53E 190 B9
Sovetskaya Gavan Russia 48°58N 140°18E 215 E15
Sovetskoye = Zelenokumsk Russia 44°24N 44°0E 191 H6
Sovicille Italy 43°17N 11°13E 199 E8
Søvik Norway 62°33N 6°17E 164 B3
Soweto S. Africa 26°14S 27°52E 123 B1
Sowhānak Iran 35°48N 51°31E 141 A3
Sowma'eh Sarā Iran 37°17N 49°18E 213 D13
Soya Japan 35°44N 139°55E 140 A4
Sōya-Kaikyō = La Perouse Str. Asia 45°40N 142°0E 220 B11
Sōya-Misaki Japan 45°30N 141°55E 220 B10
Soyagho S. Korea 37°57N 127°54E 224 D3
Soyaux France 45°39N 0°12E 174 C4
Søyland Norway 58°41N 5°36E 164 F2
Soyo Angola 6°13S 12°20E 265 D2
Sozaq Kazakhstan 44°8N 68°28E 217 D7
Sozh → Belarus 51°57N 30°48E 177 B16
Sozopol Bulgaria 42°23N 27°42E 203 D11
Spa Belgium 50°29N 5°53E 170 D5
Spaans Lagoen Aruba 12°28N 69°58W 322 f
Spaanse Water Curaçao 12°4N 68°51W 322 g
Spaatz I. Antarctica 73°10S 75°0W 151 D17
Spaccaforno = Ispica Italy 36°47N 14°55E 201 F7
Spagna, Piazza di Rome, Italy 136 b3
Spain ■ Europe 39°0N 4°0W 192 D3
Spalato = Split Croatia 43°31N 16°26E 199 E13
Spalding S. Austral., Australia 33°30S 138°37E 282 B3
Spalding Lincs., U.K. 52°48N 0°9W 168 E7
Spanaway U.S.A. 47°6N 122°26W 306 C4
Spandau Germany 52°33N 13°9E 115 A1
Spånga Sweden 59°23N 17°53E 139 A1
Spangler U.S.A. 40°39N 78°48W 312 F6
Spanische Reitschule Vienna, Austria 142 b1
Spanish Canada 46°12N 82°20W 298 C3
Spanish Fork U.S.A. 40°7N 111°39W 304 F8
Spanish Pt. Antigua & B. 17°33N 61°44W 322 c
Spanish Pt. Bermuda 32°18N 64°49W 153 a
Spanish Riding School = Spanische Reitschule Vienna, Austria 142 b1
Spanish Steps = Spagna, Piazza di Rome, Italy 136 b3
Spanish Town Br. Virgin Is. 18°26N 64°26W 321 b
Spanish Town Jamaica 18°0N 76°57W 320 a
Sparks Ga., U.S.A. 31°11N 83°26W 316 D6
Sparks Nev., U.S.A. 39°32N 119°45W 306 F7
Sparreholm Sweden 59°4N 16°49E 162 E10
Sparrow Bay Grenada 12°30N 61°27W 323 q
Sparta = Sparti Greece 37°5N 22°25E 204 D4
Sparta Ga., U.S.A. 33°17N 82°58W 316 B7
Sparta Ill., U.S.A. 38°8N 89°42W 310 F7
Sparta Mich., U.S.A. 43°10N 85°42W 311 A11
Sparta N.J., U.S.A. 41°2N 74°38W 313 E10
Sparta Wis., U.S.A. 43°56N 90°49W 308 D8
Spartanburg U.S.A. 34°56N 81°57W 315 D14
Spartel, C. Morocco 35°47N 5°56W 260 A3
Sparti Greece 37°5N 22°25E 204 D4
Spartivento, C. Calabria, Italy 37°55N 16°4E 201 E9
Spartivento, C. Sard., Italy 38°53N 8°50E 200 D1
Spartochori Greece 38°40N 20°46E 207 B2
Sparwood Canada 49°44N 114°53W 296 D6
Spas-Demensk Russia 54°20N 34°0E 188 E7
Spas-Klepiki Russia 55°10N 40°10E 188 E11
Spassk = Bednodemyanovsk Russia 53°55N 43°15E 190 D6
Spassk-Dalniy Russia 44°40N 132°48E 220 B6
Spassk-Ryazanskiy Russia 54°24N 40°25E 188 E11
Spatha, Akra Greece 35°42N 23°43E 207 E4
Spatsizi → Canada 57°42N 128°7W 296 B3
Spatsizi Plateau Wilderness ⌂ Canada 57°40N 128°0W 296 B3
Spean → U.K. 56°55N 4°59W 167 E4
Spearfish U.S.A. 44°30N 103°52W 308 C2
Spearman U.S.A. 36°12N 101°12W 314 C4
Spectacle I. U.S.A. 42°19N 70°59W 116 A3
Speculator U.S.A. 43°30N 74°22W 313 C10
Speed Australia 35°21S 142°27E 282 C5
Speedway U.S.A. 39°48N 86°16W 311 E10
Speery I. St. Helena 16°1S 5°46W 153 h
Speia Moldova 46°59N 29°19E 183 D14
Speicher-See Germany 48°12N 11°42E 131 A3
Speightstown Barbados 13°15N 59°39W 323 r
Speising Austria 48°10N 16°17E 142 B1
Speke Gulf Tanzania 2°20S 32°50E 268 C3
Spello Italy 42°59N 12°40E 199 F9
Spence Bay = Taloyoak Canada 69°32N 93°32W 294 D13
Spencer Idaho, U.S.A. 44°22N 112°11W 304 D7
Spencer Ind., U.S.A. 39°17N 86°46W 311 E10
Spencer Iowa, U.S.A. 43°9N 95°9W 308 D6
Spencer N.Y., U.S.A. 42°13N 76°30W 313 D8
Spencer Nebr., U.S.A. 42°53N 98°42W 308 D4
Spencer, C. Australia 35°20S 136°53E 282 C2
Spencer B. Namibia 25°30S 14°47E 270 C1
Spencer G. Australia 34°0S 137°20E 282 C2
Spencerville Ont., Canada 44°51N 75°33W 313 B9
Spencerville Ohio, U.S.A. 40°43N 84°21W 311 D12
Spences Bridge Canada 50°25N 121°20W 296 C4
Spennymoor U.K. 54°42N 1°36W 168 C6
Spenser Mts. N.Z. 42°15S 172°45E 285 E7
Spentrup Denmark 56°33N 10°2E 163 H4
Sperchios → Greece 38°57N 22°3E 204 C4
Sperillen Norway 60°28N 10°2E 164 D7
Sperrin Mts. U.K. 54°50N 7°0W 166 B5
Spessart Germany 49°56N 9°18E 179 F5
Spetalen Norway 59°18N 10°45E 164 E7
Spetses Greece 37°15N 23°10E 204 D5
Spey → U.K. 57°40N 3°6W 167 D5
Speyer Germany 49°29N 8°25E 179 F4
Speyside Trin. & Tob. 11°17N 60°32W 323 s
Spezand Pakistan 29°59N 67°0E 242 E2
Spezzano Albanese Italy 39°40N 16°19E 201 C9
Sphinx Egypt 29°58N 31°8E 117 B1
Spickard U.S.A. 40°14N 93°36W 310 D3
Spiddle Ireland 53°15N 9°18W 166 C2
Spiekeroog Germany 53°46N 7°42E 178 B3
Spiez Switz. 46°40N 7°40E 179 J3
Spili Greece 35°13N 24°31E 207 E5
Spilimbergo Italy 46°7N 12°54E 199 B9
Spīn Būldak Afghan. 31°1N 66°25E 242 D2
Spinaceto Italy 41°47N 12°27E 136 C1
Spinalonga Greece 35°18N 25°44E 207 E6
Spinazzola Italy 40°58N 16°5E 201 B9
Spineni Romania 44°43N 24°37E 183 F9
Spinifex ◎ Australia 28°30S 128°30E 279 E4
Spirding = Śniardwy, Jezioro Poland 53°48N 21°50E 184 E8
Spirit Lake U.S.A. 46°15N 122°9W 306 D4
Spirit River Canada 55°45N 118°50W 296 B5
Spiritwood Canada 53°24N 107°33W 297 C7
Spišská Nová Ves Slovak Rep. 48°58N 20°34E 181 C13
Spišské Podhradie Slovak Rep. 49°0N 20°48E 181 B13
Spit Junction Australia 33°49S 151°14E 139 A2
Spital Austria 47°42N 14°18E 180 D7
Spithead U.K. 50°45N 1°10W 169 G6
Spitsbergen = Svalbard Arctic 78°0N 17°0E 154 B12
Spittal an der Drau Austria 46°48N 13°31E 180 E6
Spjelkavik Norway 62°28N 6°22E 164 B3
Split Croatia 43°31N 16°26E 199 E13
Split ✈ (SPU) Croatia 43°33N 16°15E 199 E13
Split L. Canada 56°8N 96°15W 297 B9
Split Lake Canada 56°8N 96°15W 297 B9
Splitski Kanal Croatia 43°31N 16°20E 199 E13
Splügenpass Switz. 46°30N 9°20E 179 J5
Spofford U.S.A. 29°10N 100°25W 314 G4
Spokane U.S.A. 47°40N 117°24W 304 C5
Spoleto Italy 42°44N 12°44E 199 F9
Sponvika Norway 59°7N 11°15E 164 E8
Spoon → U.S.A. 40°19N 90°4W 310 D6
Spooner U.S.A. 45°50N 91°53W 308 C8
Spořilov Czech Rep. 50°2N 14°29E 135 B3
Sporyy Navolok, Mys Russia 75°50N 68°40E 214 B7
Spot Pond U.S.A. 42°26N 71°4W 116 A2
Spotswood Australia 37°50S 144°52E 128 B1
Sprague U.S.A. 47°18N 117°59W 304 C5
Spratly I. S. China Sea 8°38N 111°55E 230 C4
Spratly Is. S. China Sea 8°20N 112°0E 230 C4
Spray U.S.A. 44°50N 119°48W 304 D4
Spreča → Bos.-H. 44°44N 18°6E 182 F3
Spree → Germany 52°32N 13°12E 178 C9
Spreewald Germany 51°58N 13°51E 178 D9
Spremberg Germany 51°34N 14°22E 178 D10
Sprengisandur Iceland 64°52N 18°7W 155 C8
Spring City U.S.A. 40°11N 75°33W 313 F9
Spring Cr. → U.S.A. 30°54N 84°45W 316 E5
Spring Creek U.S.A. 40°44N 115°35W 304 F6
Spring Garden Guyana 6°59N 58°31W 329 B6
Spring Garden Calif., U.S.A. 39°52N 120°47W 306 F6
Spring Green U.S.A. 43°11N 90°4W 310 A6
Spring Hill Ala., U.S.A. 31°42N 85°58W 316 D4
Spring Hill Fla., U.S.A. 28°27N 82°41W 317 G7
Spring Mts. U.S.A. 36°0N 115°45W 307 J11
Spring Valley Calif., U.S.A. 32°44N 116°59W 307 N10
Spring Valley Ill., U.S.A. 41°20N 89°12W 310 C7
Spring Valley Nev., U.S.A. 36°6N 115°14W 124 B1
Springbok S. Africa 29°42S 17°54E 270 C2
Springboro U.S.A. 41°48N 80°22W 312 E4
Springdale Nfld. & L., Canada 49°30N 56°6W 299 C8
Springdale Ark., U.S.A. 36°11N 94°8W 314 C7
Springdale Ohio, U.S.A. 39°17N 84°29W 311 E12
Springe Germany 52°13N 9°33E 178 C5
Springeberg Germany 52°26N 13°43E 115 B5
Springer U.S.A. 36°22N 104°36W 305 H11
Springerville U.S.A. 34°8N 109°17W 305 J9
Springfield Ont., Canada 42°50N 80°56W 312 D4
Springfield Dominica 15°21N 61°22W 323 k
Springfield N.Z. 43°19S 171°56E 285 D6
Springfield Colo., U.S.A. 37°24N 102°37W 305 H12
Springfield Fla., U.S.A. 30°10N 85°37W 316 E4
Springfield Ga., U.S.A. 32°22N 81°18W 316 C8
Springfield Ill., U.S.A. 39°48N 89°39W 310 E7
Springfield Ky., U.S.A. 37°41N 85°13W 311 G11
Springfield Mass., U.S.A. 42°6N 72°35W 313 D12
Springfield Mo., U.S.A. 37°13N 93°17W 308 G7
Springfield Ohio, U.S.A. 39°55N 83°49W 311 E13
Springfield Oreg., U.S.A. 44°3N 123°1W 304 D2
Springfield S.C., U.S.A. 33°30N 81°17W 316 B8
Springfield Tenn., U.S.A. 36°31N 86°53W 315 C11
Springfield Va., U.S.A. 38°46N 77°10W 143 C1
Springfield Vt., U.S.A. 43°18N 72°29W 313 C12
Springfield, L. U.S.A. 39°46N 89°36W 310 E7
Springfontein S. Africa 30°15S 25°40E 270 D4
Springhill Canada 45°40N 64°4W 299 C7
Springhill La., U.S.A. 33°0N 93°28W 314 E8
Springhouse Canada 51°56N 122°7W 296 C4
Springlands = Corriverton Guyana 5°55N 57°20W 329 B6
Springs S. Africa 26°13S 28°25E 271 C4
Springsure Australia 24°8S 148°6E 280 C4
Springvale Ga., U.S.A. 31°50N 84°53W 316 D5
Springvale Maine, U.S.A. 43°28N 70°48W 313 C14
Springville Calif., U.S.A. 36°8N 118°49W 306 J8
Springville Iowa, U.S.A. 42°3N 91°27W 310 B5
Springville N.Y., U.S.A. 42°31N 78°40W 312 D6
Springville Utah, U.S.A. 40°10N 111°37W 304 F8
Springwater U.S.A. 42°38N 77°35W 312 D7
Sprottau = Szprotawa Poland 51°33N 15°35E 185 G2
Spruce-Creek U.S.A. 40°36N 78°9W 312 F6
Spruce Knob-Seneca Rocks ⌂ U.S.A. 38°50N 79°30W 309 F14
Spruce Mt. U.S.A. 44°12N 72°19W 313 B12
Sprucedale Canada 45°29N 79°28W 312 A5
Spur U.S.A. 33°28N 100°52W 314 E4
Spurn Hd. U.K. 53°35N 0°8E 168 D8
Spuž Montenegro 42°32N 19°10E 202 D3
Spuzzum Canada 49°37N 121°23W 296 D4
Spydeberg Norway 59°36N 11°5E 164 E8
Squam L. U.S.A. 43°45N 71°32W 313 C13
Squamish Canada 49°45N 123°10W 296 D4
Squantum U.S.A. 42°17N 71°0W 116 B2
Square Islands Canada 52°47N 55°47W 299 B8
Squillace, G. di Italy 38°45N 16°50E 201 D9
Squinzano Italy 40°26N 18°2E 201 B11
Squires, Mt. Australia 26°14S 127°28E 279 E4
Sragen Indonesia 7°26S 111°2E 235 D4
Srbac Bos.-H. 45°7N 17°30E 182 E2
Srbica = Skënderaj Kosovo 42°45N 20°47E 202 D4
Srbija = Serbia ■ Europe 43°20N 20°0E 202 C4
Srbobran Serbia 45°32N 19°48E 182 E4
Sre Ambel Cambodia 11°8N 103°46E 237 G4
Sre Khtum Cambodia 12°10N 106°52E 237 F6
Sre Umbell = Sre Ambel Cambodia 11°8N 103°46E 237 G4
Srebarna Bulgaria 44°6N 27°4E 203 B11
Srebrenica Bos.-H. 44°6N 19°18E 182 F4
Sredinnyy Khrebet Russia 57°0N 160°0E 215 D17
Sredinnyy Ra. = Sredinnyy Khrebet Russia 57°0N 160°0E 215 D17
Središče Slovenia 46°24N 16°17E 199 B13
Sredna Gora Bulgaria 42°40N 24°20E 203 D8
Srednaya Rogatka Russia 59°49N 30°22E 137 C2
Srednekolymsk Russia 67°27N 153°40E 215 C16
Sredni Rodopi Bulgaria 41°40N 24°45E 203 E8
Srednogorie Bulgaria 42°43N 24°10E 203 D8
Śrem Poland 52°6N 17°2E 185 F4
Sremska Mitrovica Serbia 44°59N 19°38E 182 F4
Sremski Karlovci Serbia 45°12N 19°56E 182 E4
Srepok → Cambodia 13°33N 106°16E 236 F6
Sretensk Russia 52°10N 117°40E 215 D12
Sri Aman = Bandar Sri Aman Malaysia 1°15N 111°32E 235 B4
Sri Kalahasti India 13°45N 79°44E 245 H4
Sri Lanka ■ Asia 7°30N 80°50E 245 L5
Sri Pada = Adam's Peak Sri Lanka 6°48N 80°30E 245 L5
Sriharikota I. India 13°40N 80°20E 245 H5
Srikakulam India 18°14N 83°58E 244 E6
Srinagar India 34°5N 74°50E 243 B6
Sripur Bangla. 24°14N 90°30E 241 C3
Srivardhan India 18°4N 73°3E 244 E1
Srivilliputtur India 9°31N 77°40E 245 K3
Środa Śląska Poland 51°10N 16°36E 185 G3
Środa Wielkopolski Poland 52°15N 17°19E 185 F4
Śródmieście Poland 52°13N 21°0E 143 B2
Srono Indonesia 8°24S 114°16E 231 J17
Srpska Crnja Serbia 45°38N 20°44E 182 E5
Srpski Itebej Serbia 45°35N 20°44E 182 E5
Srungavarapukota India 18°7N 83°10E 244 E6
Ssese Is. = Sese Is. Uganda 0°20S 32°20E 268 C3
Ssuhu Taiwan 23°38N 120°13E 225 C2
Staaken Germany 52°31N 13°8E 115 A1
Staaten → Australia 16°24S 141°17E 280 B3
Staaten River △ Australia 16°15S 142°40E 280 B3
Stabbursdalen △ Norway 70°5N 24°15E 160 A21
Stabekk Norway 59°54N 10°36E 133 A2
Staberhuk Germany 54°23N 11°18E 178 A7
Stade Germany 53°35N 9°29E 178 B5
Stade de France Paris, France 48°55N 2°22E 134 A3
Staðarfell Iceland 65°7N 22°12W 155 B4
Staðarhólskirkja Iceland 65°23N 21°58W 155 B5
Staðastaður Iceland 64°49N 23°1W 155 C3
Stadhavet Norway 62°13N 5°0E 164 B2
Stadhuis Amsterdam, Neths. 112 b3
Staður Norðurland Vestra Iceland 65°9N 21°3W 155 B5
Staður Vestfirðir Iceland 66°15N 22°50W 155 A4
Stadlandet Norway 62°10N 5°10E 164 B2
Stadlau Austria 48°13N 16°27E 142 A2
Stadshuset Stockholm, Sweden 139 b1
Stadskanaal Neths. 53°4N 6°55E 170 A6
Stadsschouwburg Amsterdam, Neths. 112 c1
Stadttallendorf Germany 50°48N 9°1E 178 E5
Stadthagen Germany 52°19N 9°13E 178 C5
Stadtlohn Germany 51°59N 6°55E 178 D2
Stadtroda Germany 50°52N 11°44E 178 E7
Stafafell Iceland 64°25N 14°52W 155 C12
Staffa U.K. 56°27N 6°21W 167 E2
Staffanstorp Sweden 55°39N 13°13E 163 J7
Stafford Staffs., U.K. 52°49N 2°7W 168 E5
Stafford Kans., U.S.A. 37°58N 98°36W 308 G4
Stafford, L. U.S.A. 29°20N 82°29W 317 F7
Stafford Springs U.S.A. 41°57N 72°18W 313 E12
Staffordshire □ U.K. 52°53N 2°10W 168 E5
Stagnone Italy 37°52N 12°26E 200 E5
Stagnone di Marsala ⌂ Italy 37°52N 12°26E 200 E5
Staines-upon-Thames U.K. 51°26N 0°29W 169 F7
Stains France 48°57N 2°22E 134 A3
Stainz Austria 46°53N 15°17E 180 E8
Stakhanov Ukraine 48°35N 38°40E 189 H10
Stalać Serbia 43°43N 21°28E 202 C5
Stalin = Kuçovë Albania 40°47N 19°57E 202 F3
Stalin = Varna Bulgaria 43°13N 27°56E 203 C11
Stalin Pk. = Gerlachovský štít Slovak Rep. 49°11N 20°7E 181 B13
Stalin Pk. = imeni Ismail Samani, Pik Tajikistan 39°0N 72°2E 217 E8
Stalin Pk. = Musala Bulgaria 42°13N 23°37E 202 D7
Stalinabad = Dushanbe Tajikistan 38°33N 68°48E 217 E7
Stalingrad = Volgograd Russia 48°40N 44°25E 191 F7
Staliniri = Tskhinvali Georgia 42°14N 44°1E 191 J7
Stalinogorsk = Novomoskovsk Russia 54°5N 38°15E 188 E10
Stalinogrod = Katowice Poland 50°17N 19°5E 185 H6
Stalinsk = Novokuznetsk Russia 53°45N 87°10E 217 B11
Stalinstadt = Eisenhüttenstadt Germany 52°9N 14°38E 178 C10
Stallarholmen Sweden 59°22N 17°12E 162 E11
Ställdalen Sweden 59°56N 14°56E 162 E8
Stalowa Wola Poland 50°34N 22°3E 185 H9
Stalybridge U.K. 53°28N 2°3W 168 D5
Stamford Queens., Australia 21°15S 143°46E 280 C3
Stamford Lincs., U.K. 52°39N 0°29W 169 E7
Stamford Conn., U.S.A. 41°3N 73°32W 313 E11
Stamford N.Y., U.S.A. 42°25N 74°38W 313 D10
Stamford Tex., U.S.A. 32°57N 99°48W 314 E5
Stamford Hill U.K. 51°34N 0°4W 125 A3
Stammersdorf Austria 48°18N 16°24E 142 A2
Stamnes Norway 60°40N 5°45E 164 D2
Stamping Ground U.S.A. 38°16N 84°41W 311 F12
Stampriet Namibia 24°20S 18°28E 270 B2
Stamps U.S.A. 33°22N 93°30W 314 E8
Stanberry U.S.A. 40°13N 94°35W 310 D2
Stančevo = Kalipetrovo Bulgaria 44°5N 27°14E 203 B11
Standerton S. Africa 26°55S 29°7E 271 C4

Standish *U.S.A.* 43°59N 83°57W **309** D12
Stanford *S. Africa* 34°26S 19°29E **270** D2
Stanford *Mont., U.S.A.* 47°9N 110°13W **304** C8
Stånga *Sweden* 57°17N 18°29E **163** G12
Stange *Norway* 60°43N 11°5E **164** D8
Stanger *S. Africa* 29°27S 31°14E **271** C5
Stängselåsen = Salpausselkä
*Finland* 61°3N 26°15E **188** B4
Stangvik *Norway* 62°55N 8°28E **164** B5
Stanhope *Vic., Australia* 36°27S 144°59E **283** D6
Stanhope *Iowa, U.S.A.* 42°17N 93°48W **310** B3
Stanimaka = Asenovgrad
*Bulgaria* 42°1N 24°51E **203** D8
Stanišić *Serbia* 45°56N 19°10E **182** E4
Stanislaus → *U.S.A.* 37°40N 121°14W **306** H5
Stanislav = Ivano-Frankivsk
*Ukraine* 48°40N 24°40E **183** B9
Stanisławów = Ivano-Frankivsk
*Ukraine* 48°40N 24°40E **183** B9
Stanisławów *Poland* 52°18N 21°33E **185** F8
Stanley *Tas., Australia* 40°46S 145°19E **281** G4
Stanley *Hong Kong, China* 22°13N 114°12E **122** B3
Stanley *Falk. Is.* 51°40S 59°51W **153** f
Stanley *Durham, U.K.* 54°53N 1°41W **168** C6
Stanley *Idaho, U.S.A.* 44°13N 114°56W **304** D6
Stanley *N. Dak., U.S.A.* 48°19N 102°23W **308** A2
Stanley *N.Y., U.S.A.* 42°48N 77°6W **312** D7
Stanley B.
*Hong Kong, China* 22°13N 114°13E **122** B3
Stanley Falls = Boyoma, Chutes
*Dem. Rep. of the Congo* 0°35N 25°23E **264** B5
Stanley Mission *Canada* 55°25N 104°33W **297** B8
Stanley Pen.
*Hong Kong, China* 22°12N 114°12E **122** B3
Stanley Pool = Malebo, Pool
*Africa* 4°17S 15°20E **265** C3
Stanley Res. *India* 11°50N 77°40E **245** J3
Stanleyville = Kisangani
*Dem. Rep. of the Congo* 0°35N 25°15E **268** B2
Stanmore *U.K.* 51°37N 0°18W **125** A2
Stannards *U.S.A.* 42°5N 77°55W **312** D7
Stanovoy Khrebet *Russia* 55°0N 130°0E **215** D14
Stanovoy Ra. = Stanovoy Khrebet
*Russia* 55°0N 130°0E **215** D14
Stansmore Ra. *Australia* 21°23S 128°33E **278** D4
Stansted, London ✈ (STN)
*U.K.* 51°54N 0°14E **169** F8
Stanthorpe *Australia* 28°36S 151°59E **281** D5
Stanton *Ky., U.S.A.* 37°54N 83°52W **311** G13
Stanton *Tex., U.S.A.* 32°8N 101°48W **314** E4
Stantsiya Regar = Tursunzoda
*Tajikistan* 38°30N 68°14E **217** E7
Stanwood *U.S.A.* 48°15N 122°23W **306** B4
Staples *Ont., Canada* 42°10N 82°35W **312** D2
Staples *Minn., U.S.A.* 46°21N 94°48W **308** B6
Stapleton *N.Y., U.S.A.* 40°36N 74°5W **132** C1
Stapleton *Nebr., U.S.A.* 41°29N 100°31W **308** E3
Stąporków *Poland* 51°9N 20°31E **185** G7
Star City *Canada* 52°50N 104°20W **297** C8
Star Harbour
*Solomon Is.* 10°47S 162°19E **287** N12
Star Lake *U.S.A.* 44°10N 75°2W **313** B9
Stará Ďala = Hurbanovo
*Slovak Rep.* 47°51N 18°11E **181** D11
Stará L'ubovňa
*Slovak Rep.* 49°18N 20°42E **181** B13
Stara Moravica *Serbia* 45°50N 19°30E **182** E4
Stara Pazova *Serbia* 44°58N 20°10E **182** F5
Stara Planina *Bulgaria* 43°15N 23°0E **202** C7
Stara Sil *Ukraine* 49°29N 22°58E **185** J9
Stará Turá *Slovak Rep.* 48°47N 17°42E **181** C10
Stara Ushytsya *Ukraine* 48°35N 27°8E **183** B12
Stara Zagora *Bulgaria* 42°26N 25°39E **203** D9
Stara Zagora ☐ *Bulgaria* 42°26N 25°39E **203** D9
Starachowice *Poland* 51°3N 21°2E **185** G8
Staraya Derevnya *Russia* 59°58N 30°15E **137** B1
Staraya Russa *Russia* 57°58N 31°23E **188** D6
Starbuck I. *Kiribati* 5°37S 155°55W **289** H12
Starchiojd *Romania* 45°19N 26°11E **183** E11
Starcke △ *Australia* 14°56S 145°2E **280** A4
Staré Město *Czech Rep.* 50°5N 14°25E **136** B2
Stare Miasto *Warsaw, Poland* **143** a2
Stargard in Pommern = Stargard Szczeciński *Poland* 53°20N 15°0E **184** E2
Stargard Szczeciński
*Poland* 53°20N 15°0E **184** E2
Stårheim *Norway* 61°56N 5°40E **164** C2
Stari Bar *Montenegro* 42°7N 19°10E **202** D3
Stari Bečej = Bečej *Serbia* 45°36N 20°3E **182** E5
Stari Grad *Croatia* 43°10N 16°38E **199** E13
Stari Trg *Slovenia* 45°29N 15°7E **199** C12
Staritsa *Russia* 56°33N 34°55E **188** D8
Starke *U.S.A.* 29°57N 82°7W **316** F7
Starke, L. *U.S.A.* 28°34N 81°32W **133** A1
Starkville *U.S.A.* 33°28N 88°49W **315** E10
Starnberg *Germany* 48°0N 11°21E **179** H7
Starnberger See *Germany* 47°54N 11°19E **179** H7
Staro Oryakhovo
*Bulgaria* 42°59N 27°47E **203** D11
Starobilsk *Ukraine* 49°16N 39°0E **189** H10
Starodub *Russia* 52°30N 32°50E **189** F7
Starogard Gdański *Poland* 53°59N 18°30E **184** E5
Starokonstantinov = Starokonstyantyniv
*Ukraine* 49°48N 27°10E **177** D14
Starokonstyantyniv
*Ukraine* 49°48N 27°10E **177** D14
Starokozache *Ukraine* 46°20N 29°59E **183** D14
Starominskaya *Russia* 46°33N 39°0E **191** G4
Staroshcherbinovskaya
*Russia* 46°40N 38°53E **191** G4
Starrs Mill *U.S.A.* 33°19N 84°31W **316** B5
Start Pt. *U.K.* 50°13N 3°39W **169** G4
Stary Sącz *Poland* 49°33N 20°35E **185** J7
Staryy Biryuzyak *Russia* 44°46N 46°50E **191** H8
Staryy Chartoriysk
*Ukraine* 51°15N 25°54E **177** C13
Staryy Krym *Ukraine* 45°3N 35°8E **189** K8
Staryy Margilan = Marghilon
*Uzbekistan* 40°27N 71°42E **217** D8
Staryy Oskol *Russia* 51°19N 37°55E **189** G9
Staryy Sambir *Ukraine* 49°27N 22°59E **185** J9
Stassfurt *Germany* 51°51N 11°35E **178** D7
Staszów *Poland* 50°33N 21°10E **185** H8
State Center *U.S.A.* 42°1N 93°10W **310** B3
State College *U.S.A.* 40°48N 77°52W **312** F7
State Street *Chicago, U.S.A.* **119** c2
Stateline *U.S.A.* 38°57N 119°56W **306** G7
Staten, I. = Estados, I. de Los
*Argentina* 54°40S 64°30W **336** D4
Staten I. *U.S.A.* 40°35N 74°9W **313** F10
Staten Island Zoo *U.S.A.* 40°38N 74°6W **132** C1
Staten Islands Ferry Terminal
*U.S.A.* 40°38N 74°4W **132** C1
Statenice *Czech Rep.* 50°9N 14°19E **135** B1
Statenville *U.S.A.* 30°42N 83°2W **316** E6
Statesboro *U.S.A.* 32°27N 81°47W **316** C8
Statesville *U.S.A.* 35°47N 80°53W **315** D14
Statham *U.S.A.* 33°58N 83°35W **316** B6
Stathelle *Norway* 59°3N 9°41E **164** E6
Statia = St. Eustatius
*W. Indies* 17°20N 63°0W **322** a
Stauffer *U.S.A.* 34°45N 119°3W **307** L7
Staunton *Ill., U.S.A.* 39°1N 89°47W **310** F7
Staunton *Va., U.S.A.* 38°9N 79°4W **309** F14
Stavanger = Rogaland ☐
*Norway* 59°12N 6°20E **164** E3
Stavanger *Norway* 58°57N 5°40E **164** F2
Stavelot *Belgium* 50°23N 5°55E **170** D5
Stavern *Norway* 59°0N 10°1E **164** F7
Stavoren *Neths.* 52°53N 5°22E **170** B5
Stavropol *Russia* 45°5N 42°0E **191** H6
Stavropol ☐ *Russia* 47°20N 42°50E **191** G6
Stavros *Cyprus* 35°1N 32°38E **207** E8
Stavros *Ithaki, Greece* 38°27N 20°39E **207** C2
Stavros *Kriti, Greece* 35°12N 24°45E **207** E5
Stavros *Thessaloníki, Greece* 40°39N 23°43E **202** F7
Stavros, Akra *Greece* 35°26N 24°58E **207** E5
Stavroupoli *Greece* 41°12N 24°45E **203** E8
Stawell *Australia* 37°5S 142°47E **282** D5
Stawell → *Australia* 20°20S 142°55E **280** C3
Stawiski *Poland* 53°22N 22°9E **184** E9
Stawiszyn *Poland* 51°56N 18°4E **185** G5
Stayner *Canada* 44°25N 80°5W **312** B4
Stayton *U.S.A.* 44°48N 122°48W **304** D2
Steamboat Springs
*U.S.A.* 40°29N 106°50W **304** F10
Stean *Norway* 59°16N 8°33E **164** E5
Stebbins *U.S.A.* 63°31N 162°17W **303** E7
Steblevë *Albania* 41°23N 20°33E **202** E4
Stedelijk Museum *Neths.* 52°21N 4°52E **112** A2
Steele *Ala., U.S.A.* 33°56N 86°12W **316** B3
Steele *N. Dak., U.S.A.* 46°51N 99°55W **308** B4
Steele Creek *Australia* 37°44S 144°52E **128** A1
Steelton *U.S.A.* 40°14N 76°50W **312** F8
Steelville *U.S.A.* 37°58N 91°22W **310** G5
Steen River *Canada* 59°40N 117°12W **296** B5
Steenkool = Bintuni
*Indonesia* 2°7S 133°32E **231** E8
Steenokkerzeel *Belgium* 50°55N 4°31E **116** A2
Steens Mt. *U.S.A.* 42°35N 118°40W **304** E4
Steenstrup Gletscher
*Greenland* 75°15N 57°0W **154** B5
Steenwijk *Neths.* 52°47N 6°7E **170** B6
Steep Pt. *Australia* 26°8S 113°8E **279** E1
Steep Rock *Canada* 51°30N 98°48W **297** C9
Steer, L. *U.S.A.* 28°31N 81°30W **133** A2
Ştefan Vodă *Moldova* 46°27N 29°42E **183** D14
Ştefăneşti *Romania* 47°44N 27°15E **183** C12
Stefanie L. = Chew Bahir
*Ethiopia* 4°40N 36°50E **257** G4
Stefanie L. △ *Ethiopia* 4°55N 36°55E **257** G4
Stefansson Bay *Antarctica* 67°20S 59°8E **151** C5
Stefansson I. *Canada* 73°20N 105°45W **295** C10
Stege *Denmark* 54°59N 12°18E **163** K6
Stegi = Siteki *Swaziland* 26°32S 31°58E **271** C5
Steglitz *Germany* 52°27N 13°19E **115** B2
Stegman = Artesia
*U.S.A.* 32°51N 104°24W **305** K11
Ştei *Romania* 46°32N 22°27E **182** D7
Steiermark ☐ *Austria* 47°26N 15°0E **180** D8
Steigerwald *Germany* 49°44N 10°26E **179** F6
Steigerwald △ *Germany* 49°50N 10°30E **179** F6
Steilacoom *U.S.A.* 47°10N 122°36W **306** C4
Steilrandberge *Namibia* 17°45S 13°20E **270** A1
Stein = Kamnik *Slovenia* 46°14N 14°37E **199** B11
Steinbach *Canada* 49°32N 96°40W **297** D9
Steinfurt *Germany* 52°9N 7°20E **178** C3
Steinhatchee *U.S.A.* 29°40N 83°23W **316** F6
Steinhausen *Namibia* 21°49S 18°20E **270** B2
Steinheim *Germany* 51°51N 9°5E **178** D5
Steinhuder Meer *Germany* 52°29N 9°21E **178** C5
Steinhuder Meer ⌂
*Germany* 52°30N 9°16E **178** C5
Steinkjer *Norway* 64°1N 11°31E **160** D14
Steinkopf *S. Africa* 29°18S 17°43E **270** C2
Steinshamn *Norway* 62°47N 6°28E **164** B3
Steinwald ⌂ *Germany* 49°55N 12°8E **179** F8
Stellarton *Canada* 45°32N 62°30W **299** C7
Stellenbosch *S. Africa* 33°58S 18°50E **270** D2
Stélvio, Paso dello *Italy* 46°32N 10°27E **198** B7
Stenay *France* 49°29N 5°12E **173** C12
Stendal *Germany* 52°36N 11°53E **178** C7
Stende *Latvia* 57°11N 22°33E **184** A9
Stenen Koraal *Curaçao* 12°10N 68°56W **322** g
Stenhamra *Sweden* 59°20N 17°41E **162** E11
Stenshuvud △ *Sweden* 55°39N 14°15E **163** J8
Stenstorp *Sweden* 58°17N 13°45E **163** F7
Stenungsund *Sweden* 58°6N 11°50E **163** F5
Steornabhaigh = Stornoway
*U.K.* 58°13N 6°23W **167** C2
Stepanakert = Xankändi
*Azerbaijan* 39°52N 46°49E **213** C12
Stepanavan *Armenia* 41°1N 44°23E **191** K7
Stepaside *Ireland* 53°15N 6°12W **120** B2
Stephansdom *Vienna, Austria* **142** b2
Stephens, C. *N.Z.* 40°42S 173°58E **285** A8
Stephens Creek *Australia* 31°50S 141°30E **282** A4
Stephens I. *B.C., Canada* 54°10N 130°45W **296** C2
Stephens I. *N.Z.* 40°40S 174°1E **285** A9
Stephens L. *Canada* 56°32N 95°0W **297** B9
Stephenville *Nfld. & L., Canada* 48°31N 58°35W **299** C8
Stephenville *Tex., U.S.A.* 32°13N 98°12W **314** E5
Stepney *U.K.* 51°30N 0°3W **125** A3
Stepnica *Poland* 53°38N 14°36E **184** E1
Stepnogorsk *Kazakhstan* 52°21N 71°53E **217** B8
Stepnoi = Elista *Russia* 46°16N 44°14E **191** G7
Steppe *Asia* 50°0N 50°0E **210** C7
Steps Pt. *Amer. Samoa* 14°23S 170°45W **302** f
Sterea Ellas ☐ *Greece* 38°50N 23°0E **204** C4
Sterkstroom *S. Africa* 31°32S 26°32E **270** D4
Sterling *Alaska, U.S.A.* 60°32N 150°46W **303** F10
Sterling *Colo., U.S.A.* 40°37N 103°13W **304** F12
Sterling *Ill., U.S.A.* 41°48N 89°42W **310** C7
Sterling *Kans., U.S.A.* 38°13N 98°12W **308** F4
Sterling City *U.S.A.* 31°51N 101°0W **314** F4
Sterling Heights *U.S.A.* 42°35N 83°2W **311** B13
Sterling Park *U.S.A.* 37°41N 122°27W **136** B2
Sterling Run *U.S.A.* 41°25N 78°12W **312** E6
Sterlitamak *Russia* 53°40N 56°0E **186** D10
Sternberg *Germany* 53°42N 11°50E **178** B7
Šternberk *Czech Rep.* 49°45N 17°15E **181** B10
Sternes *Greece* 35°30N 24°9E **207** E5
Sterzing = Vipiteno *Italy* 46°54N 11°26E **199** B8
Stettin = Szczecin *Poland* 53°27N 14°27E **184** E1
Stettiner Haff *Germany* 53°47N 14°15E **178** B10
Stettler *Canada* 52°19N 112°40W **296** C6
Steubenville *U.S.A.* 40°22N 80°37W **312** F4
Stevenage *U.K.* 51°55N 0°13W **169** F7
Stevens Point *U.S.A.* 44°31N 89°34W **308** C9
Stevens Pottery *U.S.A.* 32°57N 83°17W **316** C6
Stevens Village *U.S.A.* 66°1N 149°6W **303** C10
Stevenson *U.S.A.* 45°42N 121°53W **306** E5
Stevenson → *Australia* 27°6S 135°33E **281** D2
Stevenson L. *Canada* 53°55N 96°0W **297** C9
Stevensville *U.S.A.* 46°30N 114°5W **304** C6
Stevns Klint *Denmark* 55°17N 12°28E **163** J6
Steward *U.S.A.* 41°51N 89°1W **310** C7
Stewardson *U.S.A.* 39°16N 88°38W **311** E8
Stewart *B.C., Canada* 55°56N 129°57W **296** B3
Stewart *Ga., U.S.A.* 33°25N 83°52W **316** B6
Stewart *Nev., U.S.A.* 39°5N 119°46W **306** F7
Stewart → *Canada* 63°19N 139°26W **294** E4
Stewart, C. *Australia* 11°57S 134°56E **280** A1
Stewart, I. *Chile* 54°50S 71°15W **336** D2
Stewart I. *N.Z.* 46°58S 167°54E **285** G2
Stewarts Point *U.S.A.* 38°39N 123°24W **306** G3
Stewartsville *U.S.A.* 39°45N 94°30W **310** E2
Stewartville *U.S.A.* 43°51N 92°29W **308** D7
Stewiacke *Canada* 45°9N 63°22W **299** C7
Steynsburg *S. Africa* 31°15S 25°49E **270** D4
Steyr *Austria* 48°3N 14°25E **180** C7
Steyr → *Austria* 48°3N 14°25E **180** C7
Steytlerville *S. Africa* 33°17S 24°19E **270** D3
Stia *Italy* 43°48N 11°42E **199** E8
Sticklinge udde *Sweden* 59°23N 18°6E **139** A2
Stickney *U.S.A.* 41°49N 87°46W **119** C2
Stigler *U.S.A.* 35°15N 95°8W **314** D7
Stigliano *Italy* 40°24N 16°14E **201** B9
Stigtomta *Sweden* 58°47N 16°48E **163** F10
Stikine → *Canada* 56°40N 132°30W **296** B2
Stilfontein *S. Africa* 26°51S 26°50E **270** C4
Stilida *Greece* 38°55N 22°47E **204** C4
Stillmore *U.S.A.* 32°27N 82°13W **316** C7
Stillorgan *Ireland* 53°17N 6°11W **120** B2
Stillwater *N.Y., U.S.A.* 42°55N 73°41W **313** D11
Stillwater *Okla., U.S.A.* 36°7N 97°4W **314** C6
Stillwater Range *U.S.A.* 39°50N 118°5W **304** G4
Stillwater Res. *U.S.A.* 43°54N 75°3W **313** C9
Stilo, Pta. *Italy* 38°25N 16°35E **201** D9
Stilwell *U.S.A.* 35°49N 94°38W **314** D7
Stînga Nistrului ☐
*Moldova* 47°20N 29°15E **183** C14
Štip *Macedonia* 41°42N 22°10E **202** E6
Stira *Greece* 38°9N 24°14E **204** C6
Stirling *Ont., Canada* 44°18N 77°33W **312** B7
Stirling *N.Z.* 46°14S 169°49E **285** G4
Stirling *Stirling, U.K.* 56°8N 3°57W **167** E5
Stirling ☐ *U.K.* 56°12N 4°18W **167** E4
Stirling Ra. *Australia* 34°23S 118°0E **279** F2
Stirling Range △
*Australia* 34°26S 118°20E **279** F2
Stittsville *Canada* 45°15N 75°55W **313** A9
Stjernøya *Norway* 70°20N 22°40E **160** A20
Stjørdalshalsen *Norway* 63°29N 10°51E **164** A7
Stock Island *U.S.A.* 24°32N 81°34W **317** L8
Stocka *Sweden* 61°53N 17°20E **162** C11
Stockach *Germany* 47°50N 9°1E **179** H5
Stockaryd *Sweden* 57°19N 14°36E **163** G8
Stockbridge *Ga., U.S.A.* 33°33N 84°14W **316** B5
Stockbridge *Mich., U.S.A.* 42°27N 84°11W **311** B12
Stockerau *Austria* 48°24N 16°13E **181** C9
Stockholm *Sweden* 59°19N 18°4E **139** B2
Stockholm Arlanda ✈ (ARN)
*Sweden* 59°41N 17°56E **139** A1
Stockholms län ☐
*Sweden* 59°30N 18°20E **162** E12
Stockport *U.K.* 53°25N 2°9W **168** D5
Stocksbridge *U.K.* 53°29N 1°35W **168** D6
Stocksund *Sweden* 59°23N 18°3E **139** A2
Stockton *Calif., U.S.A.* 37°58N 121°17W **306** H5
Stockton *Ill., U.S.A.* 42°21N 90°1W **310** B6
Stockton *Kans., U.S.A.* 39°26N 99°16W **308** F4
Stockton *Mo., U.S.A.* 37°42N 93°48W **310** G3
Stockton-on-Tees *U.K.* 54°35N 1°19W **168** C6
Stockton-on-Tees ☐ *U.K.* 54°35N 1°19W **168** C6
Stockton Plateau *U.S.A.* 30°30N 102°30W **314** F3
Stoclet, Palais *Belgium* 50°50N 4°24E **116** B2
Stoczek Łukowski *Poland* 51°58N 21°58E **185** G8
Stöde *Sweden* 62°28N 16°35E **162** B10
Stöðvarfjörður *Iceland* 64°49N 13°52W **155** D13
Stodůlky *Czech Rep.* 50°3N 14°19E **135** B1
Stoeng Treng *Cambodia* 13°31N 105°58E **236** F5
Stoer, Pt. of *U.K.* 58°16N 5°23W **167** C3
Stogovo *Macedonia* 41°31N 20°38E **202** E4
Stoholm *Denmark* 56°30N 9°8E **163** H3
Stoke *N.Z.* 41°19S 173°14E **285** B8
Stoke Newington *U.K.* 51°33N 0°4W **125** A3
Stoke-on-Trent *U.K.* 53°1N 2°11W **168** D5
Stoke-on-Trent ☐ *U.K.* 53°1N 2°11W **168** D5
Stokes △ *Australia* 33°45S 121°11E **279** F3
Stokes Bay *Canada* 45°0N 81°28W **312** B3
Stokes Pt. *Australia* 40°10S 143°56E **281** G3
Stokes Ra. *Australia* 15°50S 130°50E **278** C5
Stokkseyri *Iceland* 63°50N 21°2W **155** D3
Stokksnes *Iceland* 64°14N 14°58W **155** C12
Stokmarknes *Norway* 68°34N 14°54E **160** B16
Stolac *Bos.-H.* 43°5N 17°59E **202** C1
Stolberg *Germany* 50°47N 6°13E **178** E2
Stolbovoy, Ostrov
*Russia* 74°44N 135°14E **215** B14
Stolbtsy = Stowbtsy
*Belarus* 53°30N 26°43E **177** B14
Stolin *Belarus* 51°53N 26°50E **177** C14
Stöllet *Sweden* 60°26N 13°15E **162** D7
Stolnici *Romania* 44°31N 24°48E **183** F9
Stolp = Słupsk *Poland* 54°30N 17°3E **184** D4
Stolpmünde = Ustka
*Poland* 54°35N 16°55E **184** D3
Stomio *Greece* 35°21N 23°32E **207** E4
Ston *Croatia* 42°51N 17°43E **199** F14
Stone *U.K.* 52°55N 2°9W **168** E5
Stone Canyon Res.
*U.S.A.* 34°6N 118°27W **126** B2
Stone Mountain *U.S.A.* 33°49N 84°10W **316** B5
Stone Zoo *U.S.A.* 42°28N 71°6W **116** A2
Stoneboro *U.S.A.* 41°20N 80°7W **312** E4
Stonebridge *U.K.* 51°32N 0°16W **125** A2
Stonecutters I.
*Hong Kong, China* 22°19N 114°8E **122** B2
Stoneham *U.S.A.* 42°29N 71°5W **116** A2
Stonehaven *U.K.* 56°59N 2°12W **167** E6
Stonehenge *Queens., Australia* 24°22S 143°17E **280** C3
Stonehenge *Wilts., U.K.* 51°9N 1°45W **169** F6
Stonewall *Canada* 50°10N 97°19W **297** C9
Stongfjorden *Norway* 61°26N 5°10E **164** C2
Stonington *U.S.A.* 39°44N 89°12W **310** E7
Stony Brook Res. *U.S.A.* 42°15N 71°8W **116** B2
Stony Creek → *U.S.A.* 41°38N 87°41W **119** C2
Stony Hill *Jamaica* 18°5N 76°48W **320** a
Stony I. *U.S.A.* 43°53N 76°19W **313** C8
Stony L. *Man., Canada* 58°51N 98°40W **297** B9
Stony L. *Ont., Canada* 44°30N 78°5W **312** B6
Stony Point *U.S.A.* 41°14N 73°59W **313** E11
Stony Pt. *U.S.A.* 43°50N 76°18W **313** C8
Stony Rapids *Canada* 59°16N 105°50W **297** B7
Stony River *U.S.A.* 61°47N 156°35W **303** F8
Stony Tunguska = Tunguska, Podkamennaya →
*Russia* 61°50N 90°13E **215** C10
Stonyford *U.S.A.* 39°23N 122°33W **306** F4
Stopnica *Poland* 50°27N 20°57E **185** H7
Storå *Sweden* 59°42N 15°6E **162** E9
Storå → *Denmark* 56°20N 8°19E **163** H2
Stora Gla *Sweden* 59°30N 12°30E **162** E6
Stora Le *Sweden* 59°5N 11°55E **162** E5
Stora Lulevatten *Sweden* 67°10N 19°30E **160** C18
Stora Sjöfallet △ *Sweden* 67°36N 17°45E **160** C17
Stora Värtan *Sweden* 59°25N 18°7E **139** A2
Stóra-Vatnshorn *Iceland* 65°4N 21°33W **155** B3
Storavan *Sweden* 65°45N 18°10E **160** D18
Stord *Norway* 59°52N 5°23E **164** E2
Stordalen *Norway* 59°2N 7°13E **164** E4
Store Bælt *Denmark* 55°20N 11°0E **163** J4
Store Hareskov *Denmark* 55°46N 12°23E **118** A2
Store Heddinge *Denmark* 55°18N 12°23E **163** J6
Store Jukleggi = Høgeloft
*Norway* 61°3N 8°12E **164** C5
Store Koldewey *Greenland* 76°30N 19°0W **154** B9
Store Magleby *Denmark* 55°35N 12°35E **118** B3
Store Mosse △ *Sweden* 57°18N 13°55E **163** G7
Store Sotra *Norway* 60°18N 5°4E **164** D1
Storebro *Sweden* 57°35N 15°52E **163** G9
Støren *Norway* 63°3N 10°18E **164** A7
Storerikvollen *Norway* 63°7N 11°58E **164** A8
Storfjellsætra *Norway* 61°40N 10°30E **164** C7
Storfjorden *Norway* 62°28N 6°35E **164** B3
Storfors *Sweden* 59°32N 14°17E **162** E8
Storholmen *Sweden* 59°23N 18°8E **139** A2
Storico Navale, Museo *Venice, Italy* **142** b3
Störidalur *Iceland* 63°38N 19°57W **155** D7
Stórinúpur *Iceland* 64°3N 20°10W **155** C6
Storkersen Pen.
*Canada* 72°30N 106°30W **294** C10
Storkyrkan *Stockholm, Sweden* **139** c2
Storli *Norway* 62°42N 9°5E **164** B6
Storlien *Sweden* 63°19N 12°6E **162** A6
Storm B. *Australia* 43°10S 147°30E **281** G4
Storm Lake *U.S.A.* 42°39N 95°13W **308** D6
Stormberge *S. Africa* 31°16S 26°17E **270** D4
Stormsrivier *S. Africa* 33°59S 23°52E **270** D3
Stornoway *U.K.* 58°13N 6°23W **167** C2
Storo *Italy* 45°51N 10°35E **198** C7
Storozhinets = Storozhynets
*Ukraine* 48°14N 25°45E **183** B10
Storozhynets *Ukraine* 48°14N 25°45E **183** B10
Storrs *U.S.A.* 41°49N 72°15W **313** E12
Storsjøen *Hedmark, Norway* 60°20N 11°40E **164** D8
Storsjøen *Hedmark, Norway* 61°30N 11°14E **164** C8
Storsjön *Gävleborg, Sweden* 60°35N 16°45E **162** D10
Storsjön *Jämtland, Sweden* 62°48N 13°7E **162** B7
Storsjön *Jämtland, Sweden* 63°9N 14°30E **162** A8
Storsølnkletten *Norway* 61°59N 10°16E **164** C7
Storstrømmen *Greenland* 76°17N 22°25W **154** B8
Storuman *Sweden* 65°5N 17°10E **160** D17
Storuman, L. *Sweden* 65°13N 16°50E **160** D17
Stóruvellir *Iceland* 65°30N 17°29W **155** B9
Storvättershägna *Sweden* 62°6N 12°30E **162** B6
Storviglen *Norway* 62°32N 12°2E **164** B9
Storvik *Sweden* 60°35N 16°33E **162** D10
Storvreta *Sweden* 59°58N 17°44E **162** E11
Story City *U.S.A.* 42°11N 93°36W **310** B3
Stouffville *Canada* 43°58N 79°15W **312** C5
Stoughton *Sask., Canada* 49°40N 103°0W **297** D8
Stoughton *Wis., U.S.A.* 42°55N 89°13W **310** B8
Stour → *Dorset, U.K.* 50°43N 1°47W **169** G6
Stour → *Kent, U.K.* 51°18N 1°22E **169** F9
Stour → *Suffolk, U.K.* 51°57N 1°4E **169** F9
Stourbridge *U.K.* 52°28N 2°8W **169** E5
Stout L. *Canada* 52°0N 94°40W **297** C10
Stove Pipe Wells Village
*U.S.A.* 36°35N 117°11W **307** J9
Støvring *Denmark* 56°54N 9°50E **163** H3
Stow *U.S.A.* 41°10N 81°27W **312** E3
Stowbtsy *Belarus* 53°30N 26°43E **177** B14
Stowmarket *U.K.* 52°12N 1°0E **169** E9
Stoyka *Russia* 59°57N 30°25E **137** B2
Strabane *U.K.* 54°50N 7°27W **166** B4
Stracin *Macedonia* 42°13N 22°2E **202** D6
Stradella *Italy* 45°5N 9°18E **198** C6
Strahan *Australia* 42°9S 145°20E **281** G4
Straiton *U.K.* 55°53N 3°9W **121** B3
Strajitsa *Bulgaria* 43°14N 25°58E **203** C9
Strakonice *Czech Rep.* 49°15N 13°53E **180** B6
Straldzha *Bulgaria* 42°35N 26°40E **203** D10
Stralsund *Germany* 54°18N 13°4E **178** A9
Strand *Hedmark, Norway* 61°17N 11°17E **164** C8
Strand *Western Cape, S. Africa* 34°9S 18°48E **270** D2
Strand *London, U.K.* **125** b4
Stranda *Møre og Romsdal, Norway* 62°19N 6°58E **164** B3
Stranda *Nord-Trøndelag, Norway* 63°33N 10°14E **160** E14
Strandasýsla *Iceland* 65°45N 21°45W **155** B5
Strandby *Denmark* 57°30N 10°29E **163** G4
Strandfontein *S. Africa* 34°4S 18°34E **118** B2
Strangford L. *U.K.* 54°30N 5°37W **166** B6
Strängnäs *Sweden* 59°23N 17°2E **162** E11
Stranorlar *Ireland* 54°48N 7°46W **166** B4
Stranraer *U.K.* 54°54N 5°1W **167** G3
Strasbourg *Sask., Canada* 51°4N 104°55W **297** C8
Strasbourg *Bas-Rhin, France* 48°35N 7°42E **173** D14
Strasburg *Germany* 53°30N 13°43E **178** B9
Străşeni *Moldova* 47°8N 28°36E **183** C13
Strašnice *Czech Rep.* 50°4N 14°28E **135** B2
Stråssa *Sweden* 59°44N 15°12E **162** E9
Strassburg = Aiud
*Romania* 46°19N 23°44E **183** D8
Strassstrudering *Germany* 48°6N 11°41E **131** B3
Stratford *N.S.W., Australia* 32°7S 151°55E **283** B9
Stratford *Vic., Australia* 37°59S 147°7E **283** D7
Stratford *Ont., Canada* 43°23N 81°0W **312** C4
Stratford *N.Z.* 39°20S 174°19E **284** F3
Stratford *London, U.K.* 51°33N 0°0 **125** A4
Stratford *Calif., U.S.A.* 36°11N 119°49W **306** J7
Stratford *Conn., U.S.A.* 41°12N 73°8W **313** E11
Stratford *Tex., U.S.A.* 36°20N 102°4W **314** C3
Stratford-upon-Avon *U.K.* 52°12N 1°42W **169** E6
Strath Spey *U.K.* 57°9N 3°49W **167** D5
Strathalbyn *Australia* 35°13S 138°53E **282** C3
Strathaven *U.K.* 55°40N 4°5W **167** F4
Strathcona △ *Canada* 49°38N 125°40W **296** D3
Strathfield *Australia* 33°52S 151°5E **139** B1
Strathmore *Alta., Canada* 51°5N 113°18W **296** C6
Strathmore *Angus, U.K.* 56°37N 3°7W **167** E5
Strathmore *Calif., U.S.A.* 36°9N 119°4W **306** J7
Strathnaver *Canada* 53°20N 122°33W **296** C4
Strathpeffer *U.K.* 57°35N 4°32W **167** D4
Strathroy *Canada* 42°58N 81°38W **312** D3
Strathy Pt. *U.K.* 58°36N 4°1W **167** C4
Strattanville *U.S.A.* 41°12N 79°19W **312** E5
Stratton *U.S.A.* 45°8N 70°26W **313** A14
Stratton Mt. *U.S.A.* 43°4N 72°55W **313** C12
Straubing *Germany* 48°52N 12°34E **179** G8
Straumnes *Iceland* 66°26N 23°8W **155** A3
Strausberg *Germany* 52°35N 13°54E **178** C9
Strawberry → *U.S.A.* 40°10N 110°24W **304** F8
Strawberry Point *U.S.A.* 42°41N 91°32W **310** B5
Strážnice *Czech Rep.* 48°54N 17°19E **181** C10
Streaky B. *Australia* 32°48S 134°13E **281** E1
Streaky Bay *Australia* 32°51S 134°18E **281** E1
Streatham *U.K.* 51°25N 0°7W **125** B3
Streatham Vale *U.K.* 51°24N 0°8W **125** B3
Streator *U.S.A.* 41°8N 88°50W **311** C8
Strebersdorf *Austria* 48°17N 16°23E **142** A2
Středočeský ☐ *Czech Rep.* 49°55N 14°30E **180** B7
Streetsboro *U.S.A.* 41°14N 81°21W **312** E3
Streetsville *Canada* 43°35N 79°42W **312** C5
Strehaia *Romania* 44°37N 23°10E **183** F8
Strehlen = Strzelin *Poland* 50°46N 17°2E **185** H4
Strelcha *Bulgaria* 42°25N 24°19E **203** D8
Streng → *Cambodia* 13°12N 103°37E **236** F4
Stresa *Italy* 45°52N 8°28E **198** C5
Střešovice *Czech Rep.* 50°5N 14°23E **135** B2
Streymoy *Færoe Is.* 62°8N 7°5W **160** E9
Strezhevoy *Russia* 60°42N 77°34E **214** C8
Stříbro *Czech Rep.* 49°44N 13°0E **180** A6
Strickland → *Papua N. G.* 7°35S 141°36E **286** D1
Striegau = Strzegom
*Poland* 50°58N 16°20E **185** H3
Strilky *Ukraine* 49°20N 22°59E **185** J9
Strimonas → *Greece* 40°46N 23°51E **202** F7
Strip, The *U.S.A.* 36°7N 115°10W **124** B2
Střížkov *Czech Rep.* 50°7N 14°28E **135** B2
Stroeder *Argentina* 40°12S 62°37W **336** B4
Strofades *Greece* 37°15N 21°0E **204** D3
Strokestown *Ireland* 53°47N 8°5W **166** C3
Stroma *U.K.* 58°41N 3°7W **167** C5
Strombeek-Bever *Belgium* 50°54N 4°21E **116** A2
Stromberg-Heuchelberg ⌂
*Germany* 49°2N 8°50E **179** F4
Strómboli *Italy* 38°47N 15°13E **201** D8
Stromeferry *U.K.* 57°21N 5°33W **167** D3
Strommen *Norway* 59°57N 11°0E **164** E7
Stromness *U.K.* 58°58N 3°17W **167** C5
Stromovka *Czech Rep.* 50°6N 14°25E **135** B2
Strömsbruk *Sweden* 61°52N 17°18E **162** C11
Stromsburg *U.S.A.* 41°7N 97°36W **308** E5
Strömsnäsbruk *Sweden* 56°35N 13°45E **163** H7
Strömstad *Sweden* 58°56N 11°10E **163** F5
Strömsund *Sweden* 63°51N 15°33E **160** E16
Strongburst *U.S.A.* 40°45N 90°55W **310** D6
Strongilí *Greece* 36°6N 29°42E **205** E11
Strongoli *Italy* 39°16N 17°3E **201** C10
Strongsville *U.S.A.* 41°19N 81°50W **312** E3
Stronie Śląskie *Poland* 50°18N 16°53E **185** H3
Stronsay *U.K.* 59°7N 2°35W **167** B6
Stropkov *Slovak Rep.* 49°13N 21°39E **181** B14
Stroud *U.K.* 51°45N 2°13W **169** F5
Stroud Road *Australia* 32°18S 151°57E **283** B9
Stroudsburg *U.S.A.* 40°59N 75°12W **313** F9
Stroumbi *Cyprus* 34°53N 32°29E **207** F8
Štrpce = Shtërpcë *Kosovo* 42°14N 21°1E **202** D5
Struer *Denmark* 56°30N 8°35E **163** H2
Struga *Macedonia* 41°11N 20°44E **202** E4
Strugi Krasnyye *Russia* 58°21N 29°1E **188** C5
Strumica *Macedonia* 41°28N 22°41E **202** E6
Strumica → *Europe* 41°20N 23°22E **202** E7
Strumok *Ukraine* 45°43N 29°27E **183** E14
Struthers *U.S.A.* 41°4N 80°39W **312** E4
Stryama *Bulgaria* 42°16N 24°54E **203** D8
Stryker *U.S.A.* 43°41N 114°46W **304** B6
Stryków *Poland* 51°55N 19°33E **185** G6
Stryn *Norway* 61°54N 6°43E **164** C3
Stryy *Ukraine* 49°16N 23°48E **177** D12
Strzegom *Poland* 50°58N 16°20E **185** H3
Strzelce Krajeńskie *Poland* 52°52N 15°33E **185** F2
Strzelce Opolskie *Poland* 50°31N 18°18E **185** H5
Strzelecki Cr. →
*Australia* 29°37S 139°59E **281** D2
Strzelecki Desert *Australia* 29°30S 140°0E **281** D3
Strzelin *Poland* 50°46N 17°2E **185** H4
Strzelno *Poland* 52°35N 18°9E **185** F5
Strzybnica *Poland* 50°28N 18°48E **185** H5
Strzyżów *Poland* 49°52N 21°47E **185** J8
Stuart *Fla., U.S.A.* 27°12N 80°15W **317** H9
Stuart *Iowa, U.S.A.* 41°30N 94°19W **310** C2
Stuart *Nebr., U.S.A.* 42°36N 99°8W **308** D4
Stuart → *Canada* 54°0N 123°35W **296** C4
Stuart Bluff Ra. *Australia* 22°50S 131°52E **278** D5
Stuart I. *U.S.A.* 63°35N 162°30W **303** E7
Stuart L. *Canada* 54°30N 124°30W **296** C4
Stuart Mts. *N.Z.* 45°2S 167°39E **285** F2
Stuart Ra. *Australia* 29°10S 134°56E **281** D1
Stubbekøbing *Denmark* 54°53N 12°9E **163** K6
Stubbs *St. Vincent* 13°7N 61°9W **323** n
Stuben *Austria* 47°10N 10°8E **180** D3
Štubnianske Teplice = Turčianske Teplice *Slovak Rep.* 48°52N 18°52E **181** C11
Studen Kladenets, Yazovir
*Bulgaria* 41°37N 25°30E **203** E9
Studenica *Serbia* 43°29N 20°32E **202** C4
Studenka *Czech Rep.* 49°44N 18°5E **181** B11
Studholme *N.Z.* 44°42S 171°9E **285** E6
Studio City *U.S.A.* 34°8N 118°23W **126** B2
Studley Park *Trin. & Tob.* 11°11N 60°40W **323** s
Stugudalen *Norway* 62°53N 11°53E **164** B8
Stugun *Sweden* 63°10N 15°40E **162** A9
Stuhlweissenburg = Székesfehérvár
*Hungary* 47°15N 18°25E **182** C3
Stuhm = Sztum *Poland* 53°55N 19°1E **184** E6
Stuhr *Germany* 53°5N 8°44E **178** B4
Stull L. *Canada* 54°24N 92°34W **298** B1
Stung Treng = Stoeng Treng
*Cambodia* 13°31N 105°58E **236** F5
Stupart → *Canada* 56°0N 93°25W **298** A1
Stupava *Slovak Rep.* 48°17N 17°2E **181** C10
Stupino *Russia* 54°57N 38°2E **188** E10
Stureby *Sweden* 59°15N 18°4E **139** B2
Sturge I. *Antarctica* 67°26S 164°47E **151** C11
Sturgeon B. *Canada* 52°0N 97°50W **297** C9
Sturgeon Bay *U.S.A.* 44°50N 87°23W **308** C10
Sturgeon Falls *Canada* 46°25N 79°57W **298** C4
Sturgeon L. *Alta., Canada* 55°6N 117°32W **296** B5
Sturgeon L. *Ont., Canada* 50°0N 90°45W **298** B1
Sturgeon L. *Ont., Canada* 44°28N 78°43W **312** B6
Sturgis *Sask., Canada* 51°56N 102°36W **297** C8
Sturgis *Mich., U.S.A.* 41°48N 85°25W **311** C11
Sturgis *S. Dak., U.S.A.* 44°25N 103°31W **308** C2
Sturkö *Sweden* 56°5N 15°42E **163** H9
Štúrovo *Slovak Rep.* 47°48N 18°41E **181** D11
Sturt △ *Australia* 29°17S 141°37E **281** D3
Sturt Cr. → *Australia* 19°8S 127°50E **278** C4
Sturt Stony Desert
*Australia* 28°30S 141°0E **281** D3
Sturts Meadows
*Australia* 31°18S 141°42E **282** A4
Stutterheim *S. Africa* 32°33S 27°28E **270** D4
Stuttgart *Baden-W., Germany* 48°48N 9°11E **179** G5
Stuttgart *Ark., U.S.A.* 34°30N 91°33W **314** D9
Stuttgart Echterdingen ✈ (STR)
*Germany* 48°42N 9°11E **179** G5
Stutthof = Sztutowo
*Poland* 54°20N 19°15E **184** D6
Stuvsta *Sweden* 59°15N 18°0E **139** B2
Stuyvesant *U.S.A.* 42°23N 73°45W **313** D11
Stuyvesant Town *New York, U.S.A.* **132** d2
Stykkishólmur *Iceland* 65°2N 22°40W **155** B4
Styria = Steiermark ☐
*Austria* 47°26N 15°0E **180** D8
Styrsö *Sweden* 57°37N 11°46E **163** G5
Su-no-Saki *Japan* 34°58N 139°45E **223** C11
Su Xian = Suzhou *China* 33°41N 116°59E **226** H9
Suakin *Sudan* 19°8N 37°20E **256** D4
Suakin Archipelago
*Sudan* 18°42N 38°30E **256** D4
Suamico *U.S.A.* 44°38N 88°2W **308** C9
Suan *N. Korea* 38°42N 126°22E **224** C3
Suana *Indonesia* 8°44S 115°36E **237** J18
Süanhwa = Xuanhua
*China* 40°40N 115°2E **226** D8
Suao *Taiwan* 24°36N 121°51E **225** B3
Suape *Brazil* 8°24S 35°0W **332** G5
Suapure → *Venezuela* 6°48N 67°1W **328** B4
Suar *India* 29°2N 79°3E **243** E8
Suau *Papua N. G.* 0°37S 150°2E **286** F6
Suavanao *Solomon Is.* 7°35S 158°47E **287** L10
Şubā *Si. Arabia* 27°10N 35°40E **246** E2
Subang *Indonesia* 6°34S 107°45E **235** D3
Subankhata *India* 26°48N 91°25E **241** B3
Subansiri → *India* 26°48N 93°50E **241** B5
Subarnagiri *India* 19°50N 83°51E **244** E6
Subarnarekha → *India* 22°34N 87°24E **243** H12
Subay', Urūq *Si. Arabia* 22°15N 43°5E **256** C5
Subayhah *Si. Arabia* 30°2N 38°50E **246** D3
Subcetate *Romania* 45°36N 23°0E **182** E8
Subhepur *India* 22°58N 77°15E **120** A3
Subi *Indonesia* 2°58N 108°50E **235** B3
Subiaco *Italy* 41°56N 13°5E **199** G10
Sublette *U.S.A.* 37°29N 100°51W **314** C4
Subotica *Serbia* 46°6N 19°39E **182** D4
Subraman Canal *U.S.A.* 40°20N 90°11W **131** B1
Suca *Ethiopia* 6°31N 39°40E **257** F4
Sucat *Phil.* 14°27N 121°2E **127** C2
Suceava *Romania* 47°38N 26°16E **183** C11
Suceava ☐ *Romania* 47°37N 25°40E **183** C10
Suceava → *Romania* 47°32N 26°32E **183** C11
Sucha-Beskidzka *Poland* 49°44N 19°35E **185** J6
Suchan = Partizansk
*Russia* 43°8N 133°9E **215** E14
Suchań *Poland* 53°18N 15°18E **185** E2
Suchdol *Czech Rep.* 50°8N 14°22E **135** B2
Suchedniów *Poland* 51°3N 20°49E **185** G7
Suchil *Mexico* 23°39N 103°54W **318** C4
Suchou = Suzhou *China* 31°19N 120°38E **229** B13
Süchow = Xuzhou *China* 34°18N 117°10E **227** G9
Suchowola *Poland* 53°33N 23°3E **184** E10
Sucio → *Colombia* 7°27N 77°7W **328** B2
Suck → *Ireland* 53°17N 8°3W **166** C3
Suckling, Mt. *Papua N. G.* 9°49S 148°53E **286** E5
Sucre *Bolivia* 19°0S 65°15W **331** D4
Sucre *Colombia* 8°49N 74°44W **328** B3
Sucre ☐ *Colombia* 8°50N 75°40W **328** B2
Sucre ☐ *Venezuela* 10°25N 63°30W **329** A5
Sucuaro *Colombia* 4°34N 68°50W **328** C4
Sucumbíos ☐ *Ecuador* 0°6S 76°52W **328** D2
Sućuraj *Croatia* 43°10N 17°8E **199** E14
Sucuriju *Brazil* 1°39N 49°57W **332** A2
Sucuriú → *Brazil* 20°47S 51°38W **331** E7
Sucy-en-Brie *France* 48°46N 2°31E **134** B4
Sud ☐ *Cameroon* 2°30N 11°45E **263** E7
Sud, Pte. *Comoros Is.* 11°53S 43°29E **272** a
Sud, Pte. du *Canada* 49°3N 62°14W **299** C7
Sud-Bandama ☐ *Ivory C.* 6°0N 5°15W **262** D3
Sud-Comoé ☐ *Ivory C.* 5°30N 3°0W **262** D4
Sud-Kivu ☐
*Dem. Rep. of the Congo* 3°0S 28°30E **268** C2
Sud-Ouest ☐ *Cameroon* 5°25N 9°20E **263** D6
Sud-Ouest, Pte. *Qué., Canada* 49°23N 63°36W **299** C7
Sud Ouest, Pte. *Mauritius* 20°28S 57°18E **272** e
Suda → *Russia* 59°0N 37°40E **188** C9
Sudak *Ukraine* 44°51N 34°57E **189** K8
Sudan *U.S.A.* 34°4N 102°31W **314** D3
Sudan ■ *Africa* 15°0N 30°0E **257** E3
Sudauen = Suwałki *Poland* 54°8N 22°59E **184** D9
Sudbury *Ont., Canada* 46°30N 81°0W **298** C3
Sudbury *Suffolk, U.K.* 52°2N 0°45E **169** E8
Sudd *South Sudan* 8°20N 30°0E **257** F3
Suddie *Guyana* 7°8N 58°29W **329** B6
Sudeifel =
Deutsch-Luxemburgischer ⌂
*Germany* 49°58N 6°12E **179** F2
Süderbrarup *Germany* 54°38N 9°45E **178** A5
Süderlügum *Germany* 54°52N 8°54E **178** A4
Süderoogsand *Germany* 54°27N 8°28E **178** A4
Sudeten Mts. = Sudety
*Europe* 50°20N 16°45E **181** A9
Sudety *Europe* 50°20N 16°45E **181** A9
Súðavík *Iceland* 66°2N 23°0W **155** A3
Südheide ⌂ *Germany* 52°46N 10°11E **178** C6
Suður-múlasýsla *Iceland* 65°0N 14°30W **155** C12
Suður-þingeyjarsýsla
*Iceland* 65°30N 17°0W **155** B9
Suðureyri *Iceland* 66°7N 23°32W **155** A3
Suðurland ☐ *Iceland* 64°30N 19°30W **155** C7
Suðurnes ☐ *Iceland* 63°50N 22°30W **155** D4
Suðuroy *Færoe Is.* 61°32N 6°50W **160** F9
Sudi *Tanzania* 10°11S 39°57E **269** E4
Sudirman, Pegunungan
*Indonesia* 4°30S 137°0E **231** E9
Sudiți *Romania* 44°35N 27°38E **183** F12
Sudogda *Russia* 55°55N 40°50E **190** C5
Sudong, Pulau *Singapore* 1°13N 103°44E **237** d
Sudostroy = Severodvinsk
*Russia* 64°27N 39°58E **186** B6
Sudova Vyshnya *Ukraine* 49°46N 23°22E **185** J10
Sudzha *Russia* 51°14N 35°17E **189** G8
Sue → *South Sudan* 7°41N 28°3E **257** F2
Sue, L. *U.S.A.* 28°34N 81°21W **133** A2
Sueca *Spain* 39°12N 0°21W **197** F4
Suedinenie *Bulgaria* 42°16N 24°33E **203** D8
Suemez I. *U.S.A.* 55°15N 133°20W **296** B2
Sueyoshi = Soo *Japan* 31°40N 131°5E **222** F3
Suez = El Suweis *Egypt* 29°58N 32°31E **256** B3
Suez, G. of = Suweis, Khalîg el
*Egypt* 28°40N 33°0E **256** J8
Suez Canal = Suweis, Qanâ es
*Egypt* 31°0N 32°20E **256** H8
Suffield *Canada* 50°12N 111°10W **296** C6
Suffolk *U.S.A.* 36°44N 76°35W **309** G15
Suffolk ☐ *U.K.* 52°16N 1°0E **169** E9
Şufiān *Iran* 38°16N 45°58E **213** C11
Suga-no-Sen *Japan* 35°25N 134°25E **222** B6
Şugag *Romania* 45°47N 23°37E **183** E8
Sugaing = Sagaing *Burma* 21°52N 95°59E **241** E5
Sugamo *Japan* 35°44N 139°43E **140** A3
Sugar → *U.S.A.* 42°26N 89°12W **310** B7
Sugar Cr. → *Ill., U.S.A.* 40°9N 89°38W **310** D7
Sugar Cr. → *Ind., U.S.A.* 39°51N 87°21W **311** E9
Sugar Grove *U.S.A.* 41°59N 79°20W **312** E5
Sugar Hill *U.S.A.* 34°6N 84°2W **316** A5
Sugar Loaf *Grenada* 12°13N 61°36W **323** q
Sugar Loaf Mt. = Açúcar, Pão de
*Brazil* 22°56S 43°9W **135** B2
Sugar Loaf Pt. *St. Helena* 15°54S 5°42W **153** h
Sugarcreek *U.S.A.* 41°25N 79°52W **312** E5
Sugarive → *India* 26°16N 86°24E **243** F12
Sugbai Passage *Phil.* 5°22N 120°33E **233** J3
Suge *Japan* 35°37N 139°32E **140** B2
Sughd ☐ *Tajikistan* 40°0N 69°0E **217** E7
Sughwaras *Indonesia* 4°1S 103°46E **234** C2
Suginami *Japan* 35°41N 139°37E **140** A2
Suğla Gölü *Turkey* 37°20N 32°0E **212** D5
Sugluk = Salluit *Canada* 62°14N 75°38W **295** E16
Sugō *Japan* 35°34N 139°33E **140** B2
Sugun *China* 39°53N 76°47E **217** E9
Suha Reke = Therandë
*Kosovo* 42°21N 20°50E **202** D4
Suhaia, Lacul *Romania* 43°45N 25°15E **183** G10
Şuḩār *Oman* 24°20N 56°40E **247** E8
Sühbaatar *Mongolia* 50°17N 106°10E **218** A10
Sühbaatar ☐ *Mongolia* 45°30N 114°0E **226** B8
Suheli Par *India* 10°5N 72°17E **245** J1
Suhl *Germany* 50°36N 10°42E **178** E6
Şuhut *Turkey* 38°31N 30°32E **205** C12
Sui *Pakistan* 28°37N 69°19E **242** E3
Sui Sai Wan
*Hong Kong, China* 22°16N 114°14E **122** B3
Sui Xian *China* 34°25N 115°2E **226** G8
Suiá Missu → *Brazil* 11°13S 53°15W **331** C7
Šuica *Bos.-H.* 43°52N 17°11E **182** G2
Suichang *China* 28°29N 119°15E **229** C12
Suichuan *China* 26°20N 114°32E **229** D10
Suide *China* 37°30N 110°12E **226** F6
Suifenhe *China* 44°25N 131°10E **227** B16
Suihua *China* 46°32N 126°55E **219** B14
Suijiang *China* 28°40N 103°59E **228** C4
Suining *Hunan, China* 26°35N 110°10E **229** D8
Suining *Jiangsu, China* 33°56N 117°58E **227** H9
Suining *Sichuan, China* 30°26N 105°35E **228** B5
Suiping *China* 33°10N 113°59E **226** H7
Suippes *France* 49°8N 4°30E **173** C11
Suir → *Ireland* 52°16N 7°9W **166** D4
Suisse = Switzerland ■
*Europe* 46°30N 8°0E **179** J4
Suisun City *U.S.A.* 38°15N 122°2W **306** G4
Suita *Japan* 34°45N 135°32E **133** A2
Suitland *U.S.A.* 38°50N 76°55W **143** B3
Suixi *China* 21°19N 110°18E **229** G8
Suiyang *Guizhou, China* 27°58N 107°18E **228** D6
Suiyang *Heilongjiang, China* 44°30N 130°56E **227** B16
Suizhong *China* 40°21N 120°20E **227** D11
Suizhou *China* 31°42N 113°24E **229** B9
Sujangarh *India* 27°42N 74°31E **242** F6
Sujiatun *China* 41°39N 123°20E **227** D12
Sukabumi *Indonesia* 6°56S 106°50E **234** D3

Sukadana Kalimantan Barat, Indonesia 1°10S 110°0E 235 C4
Sukadana Lampung, Indonesia 5°5S 105°33E 234 D3
Sukadana, Teluk Indonesia 1°24S 109°50E 235 C3
Sukagawa Japan 37°17N 140°23E 221 F10
Sukamade Indonesia 8°30S 113°52E 235 D4
Sukamara Indonesia 2°43S 111°10E 235 C4
Sukaraja Indonesia 2°28S 110°25E 235 C4
Sukarnapura = Jayapura Indonesia 2°28S 140°38E 231 E10
Sukarno, Puntjak = Jaya, Puncak Indonesia 3°57S 137°17E 231 E9
Sukau Malaysia 5°32N 118°17E 235 A5
Sukawati Indonesia 8°35S 115°17E 231 K18
Sukchar India 22°42N 88°22E 124 A2
Sukch'ŏn N. Korea 39°22N 125°35E 224 C2
Sukhindol Bulgaria 43°11N 25°10E 203 C9
Sukhinichi Russia 54°8N 35°10E 188 E8
Sukhona → Russia 61°15N 46°39E 186 C6
Sukhothai Thailand 17°1N 99°49E 236 D2
Sukhumi = Sokhumi Georgia 43°0N 41°0E 191 J5
Sukkertoppen = Maniitsoq Greenland 65°26N 52°55W 154 D5
Sukkur Pakistan 27°42N 68°54E 242 F3
Sukkur Barrage Pakistan 27°40N 68°50E 242 F3
Sukma India 18°24N 81°45E 244 E5
Sukovo Serbia 43°4N 22°37E 202 C6
Sukri → India 25°4N 71°43E 242 G4
Sukumo Japan 32°56N 132°44E 222 E4
Sukunka → Canada 55°45N 121°15W 296 B4
Sul, Canal do Brazil 0°10S 48°30W 332 B2
Sula Norway 61°7N 4°54E 164 C1
Sula → Ukraine 49°40N 32°41E 189 H7
Sula, Kepulauan Indonesia 1°45S 125°0E 231 E7
Sulaco → Honduras 15°2N 87°44W 320 C2
Sulaiman Range Pakistan 30°30N 69°50E 242 D3
Sulaiman-Too Kyrgyzstan 40°31N 72°46E 217 D8
Sulak → Russia 43°20N 47°34E 191 J8
Sulakyurt Turkey 40°9N 33°43E 212 B5
Sūlār Iran 31°53N 51°54E 247 D6
Sulawesi Indonesia 2°0S 120°0E 235 C5
Sulawesi Barat □ Indonesia 3°0S 119°0E 235 C5
Sulawesi Sea = Celebes Sea Indonesia 3°0N 123°0E 231 D6
Sulawesi Selatan □ Indonesia 2°30S 120°0E 231 E6
Sulawesi Tengah □ Indonesia 1°30S 121°0E 231 E6
Sulawesi Tenggara □ Indonesia 3°50S 122°0E 231 E6
Sulawesi Utara □ Indonesia 1°0N 124°0E 231 D6
Suldalsheiene Norway 59°28N 7°10E 164 E3
Suldalsosen Norway 59°29N 6°29E 164 E3
Sulechów Poland 52°5N 15°40E 185 F2
Sulęcin Poland 52°26N 15°10E 185 F2
Sulei Solomon Is. 8°3S 159°34E 287 M10
Suleja Nigeria 9°10N 7°10E 263 D6
Sulejów Poland 51°26N 19°53E 185 G6
Sulejówek Poland 52°13N 21°17E 185 F8
Süleymanlı Turkey 38°58N 27°47E 205 C9
Sulima S. Leone 6°58N 11°32W 262 D2
Sulina Romania 45°10N 29°40E 183 E14
Sulina, Braţul → Romania 45°10N 29°40E 183 E14
Sulingen Germany 52°41N 8°48E 178 C4
Suliţa Romania 47°39N 26°59E 183 C11
Sulitjelma Norway 67°9N 16°3E 160 C17
Sułkowice Poland 49°50N 19°49E 185 J6
Sullana Peru 4°52S 80°39W 330 A1
Süller Turkey 38°9N 29°29E 205 C11
Sullivan Ill., U.S.A. 39°36N 88°37W 311 E8
Sullivan Ind., U.S.A. 39°6N 87°24W 311 E9
Sullivan Mo., U.S.A. 38°13N 91°10W 310 F5
Sullivan Bay Canada 50°55N 126°50W 296 C3
Sullivan I. = Lanbi Kyun Burma 10°50N 98°20E 237 G2
Sullom Voe U.K. 60°27N 1°20W 167 A7
Sullorsuaq Greenland 70°5N 53°0W 154 C5
Sully U.S.A. 41°34N 92°50W 310 C4
Sully-sur-Loire France 47°45N 2°20E 173 E9
Sulmierzyce Poland 51°37N 17°32E 185 G4
Sulmona Italy 42°3N 13°55E 199 F10
Süloğlu Turkey 41°44N 26°53E 203 E10
Sulphur La., U.S.A. 30°14N 93°23W 314 F8
Sulphur Okla., U.S.A. 34°31N 96°58W 314 D6
Sulphur Channel Hong Kong, China 22°15N 114°7E 122 B2
Sulphur Pt. Canada 60°56N 114°48W 296 A6
Sulphur Springs U.S.A. 33°8N 95°36W 314 E7
Sulsul Ethiopia 5°5N 44°50E 267 C5
Sultan Ont., Canada 47°36N 82°47W 298 C3
Sultan Wash., U.S.A. 47°52N 121°49W 306 C5
Sultan Dağları Turkey 38°20N 31°20E 212 C4
Sultan Hamud Kenya 2°1S 37°22E 268 C4
Sultan Kudarat Phil. 7°16N 124°18E 233 H5
Sultan Kudarat □ Phil. 6°30N 124°10E 233 H5
Sultan Naga Dimaporo Phil. 7°55N 123°44E 233 H4
Sultan sa Barongis Phil. 6°45N 124°35E 233 H5
Sultanābād = Arāk Iran 34°0N 49°40E 247 C6
Sultanahme Camil Turkey 41°0N 28°58E 122 B1
Sultanhisar Turkey 37°53N 28°9E 205 D10
Sultaniça Turkey 40°37N 26°8E 203 F10
Sultaniye Turkey 40°11N 28°12E 203 F12
Sultanpur Mad. P., India 23°9N 77°56E 242 H8
Sultanpur Punjab, India 31°13N 75°11E 242 D6
Sultanpur Ut. P., India 26°18N 82°4E 243 F10
Sulu □ Phil. 5°30N 120°30E 233 J3
Sulu Arch. Phil. 6°0N 121°0E 233 J3
Sulu Sea E. Indies 8°0N 120°0E 233 G3
Sülüklü Turkey 38°53N 32°20E 212 C5
Sululta Ethiopia 9°10N 38°43E 257 F4
Suluova Turkey 40°46N 35°32E 212 B6
Sulūq Libya 31°44N 20°14E 258 B4
Suluru India 13°42N 80°1E 245 H5
Sulzbach Germany 49°18N 7°3E 179 F3
Sulzbach-Rosenberg Germany 49°30N 11°44E 179 F7
Sulzberger Ice Shelf Antarctica 78°0S 150°0W 151 E13
Sumaco -Napo Galeras △ Ecuador 0°34S 77°38W 328 D2
Sumalata Indonesia 1°0N 122°31E 231 D6
Sumale □ Ethiopia 7°0N 45°0E 267 C6
Sumampa Argentina 29°25S 63°29W 334 B3
Sumapaz △ Colombia 3°49N 74°13W 328 C3
Sumaré Brazil 22°48S 47°17W 333 F2
Sumatera Indonesia 0°40N 100°20E 234 B2
Sumatera Barat □ Indonesia 1°0S 101°0E 234 B1
Sumatera Selatan □ Indonesia 3°0S 104°0E 234 C2
Sumatera Utara □ Indonesia 2°30N 98°0E 234 B1
Sumatra = Sumatera Indonesia 0°40N 100°20E 234 B2
Sumatra U.S.A. 30°1N 84°59W 316 E5
Sumava △ Czech Rep. 49°0N 13°49E 180 C6
Sumba Angola 6°15S 12°38E 265 D2
Sumba Indonesia 9°45S 119°35E 231 F5
Sumba, Selat Indonesia 9°0S 118°40E 231 F5
Sumbawa Indonesia 8°26S 117°30E 235 D5
Sumbawa Besar Indonesia 8°30S 117°26E 235 D5
Sumbe Angola 11°10S 13°48E 265 E2
Sumbu △ Zambia 8°43S 30°22E 269 D3
Sumburgh Hd. U.K. 59°52N 1°17W 167 B7
Sumdeo India 31°26N 78°44E 243 D8
Sumdo China 35°6N 78°41E 243 B8
Sumé Brazil 7°39S 36°55W 332 C4
Sumedang Indonesia 6°52S 107°55E 235 D3
Sümeg Hungary 46°59N 17°20E 182 D2
Sumeih Sudan 9°50N 27°39E 257 F2
Šumen = Shumen Bulgaria 43°18N 26°55E 203 C10
Sumenep Indonesia 7°1S 113°52E 235 D4
Sumgait = Sumqayıt Azerbaijan 40°34N 49°38E 191 K9
Sumida Japan 35°42N 139°49E 140 A3
Sumida → Japan 35°39N 139°45E 140 A3
Sumisu-Jima Japan 31°27N 140°3E 223 F12
Sumiyoshi Japan 34°36N 135°30E 133 B2
Sumiyoshi Shrine Japan 34°36N 135°30E 133 B1
Summer L. U.S.A. 42°50N 120°45W 304 E3
Summerland Canada 49°32N 119°41W 296 D5
Summerland Key U.S.A. 24°40N 81°27W 317 L8
Summerside Canada 46°24N 63°47W 299 C7
Summersville U.S.A. 38°17N 80°51W 309 F13
Summerton U.S.A. 33°36N 80°20W 316 B9
Summertown U.S.A. 32°45N 82°16W 316 C7
Summerville Ont., Canada 43°37N 79°33W 141 B1
Summerville Ga., U.S.A. 34°29N 85°21W 315 D12
Summerville S.C., U.S.A. 33°1N 80°11W 316 B9
Summit Alaska, U.S.A. 63°20N 149°7W 303 E10
Summit Ill., U.S.A. 41°47N 87°47W 119 C2
Summit Lake Canada 54°20N 122°40W 296 C4
Summit Peak U.S.A. 37°21N 106°42W 305 H10
Sumner N.Z. 43°35S 172°48E 285 D7
Sumner Ill., U.S.A. 38°42N 87°53W 311 F9
Sumner Iowa, U.S.A. 42°51N 92°6W 310 B4
Sumner Wash., U.S.A. 47°12N 122°14W 306 C4
Sumner, L. N.Z. 42°42S 172°15E 285 C7
Sumner Tunnel Boston, U.S.A. 116 a3
Sumoto Japan 34°21N 134°54E 222 C6
Sumpangbinangae Indonesia 4°24S 119°36E 235 C5
Šumperk Czech Rep. 49°59N 16°59E 181 B9
Sumprabum Burma 26°33N 97°36E 241 B6
Sumqayıt Azerbaijan 40°34N 49°38E 191 K9
Sumter U.S.A. 33°55N 80°21W 316 B9
Sumxi China 34°35N 80°22E 217 F10
Sumy Ukraine 50°57N 34°50E 189 G8
Sumy □ Ukraine 50°50N 33°50E 189 G7
Sun City S. Africa 25°17S 27°3E 270 C4
Sun City Center U.S.A. 27°43N 82°21W 317 H7
Sun Kosi → Nepal 26°59N 87°8E 243 F12
Sun Lakes U.S.A. 33°10N 111°52W 305 K8
Sun Prairie U.S.A. 43°11N 89°13W 310 A7
Sun Valley U.S.A. 43°42N 114°21W 304 E6
Sunagawa Japan 43°29N 141°55E 220 C10
Sunamachi Japan 35°40N 139°50E 140 A4
Sunamganj Bangla. 25°4N 91°24E 241 C3
Sunan N. Korea 39°15N 125°40E 224 C2
Sunart, L. U.K. 56°42N 5°43W 167 E3
Sunburst U.S.A. 48°53N 111°55W 304 B8
Sunbury Vic., Australia 37°35S 144°44E 283 D6
Sunbury Pa., U.S.A. 40°52N 76°48W 313 F8
Sunbury-on-Thames U.K. 51°25N 0°26W 125 B1
Sunchales Argentina 30°58S 61°35W 334 C3
Suncheon S. Korea 34°52N 127°31E 224 E3
Suncho Corral Argentina 27°55S 63°27W 334 B3
Sunch'on N. Korea 39°25N 125°56E 224 C2
Suncook U.S.A. 43°8N 71°27W 313 C13
Sunda, Selat Indonesia 6°20S 105°30E 234 D3
Sunda Is. Indonesia 5°0S 105°0E 288 H2
Sunda Str. = Sunda, Selat Indonesia 6°20S 105°30E 234 D3
Sunda Trench = Java Trench Ind. Oc. 9°0S 105°0E 234 D2
Sundance Man., Canada 56°32N 94°4W 297 B10
Sundance Wyo., U.S.A. 44°24N 104°23W 304 D11
Sundar Nagar India 31°32N 76°53E 242 D7
Sundarbans Asia 22°0N 89°0E 241 E2
Sundarbans △ India 22°0N 88°45E 241 E2
Sundargarh India 22°4N 84°5E 244 C7
Sundays = Sondags → S. Africa 33°44S 25°51E 270 D4
Sundbyberg Sweden 59°22N 17°57E 139 A1
Sundbyerne Denmark 55°39N 12°36E 118 B3
Sunderland Ont., Canada 44°16N 79°4W 312 B5
Sunderland Tyne & W., U.K. 54°55N 1°23W 168 C6
Sundi Lutete Dem. Rep. of the Congo 4°34S 14°14E 265 C2
Sundown △ Australia 28°49S 151°38E 281 D5
Sundre Canada 51°49N 114°38W 296 C6
Sunds Denmark 56°13N 9°1E 163 H3
Sundsvall Sweden 62°23N 17°17E 162 B11
Sundsvallsbukten Sweden 62°21N 17°25E 162 B11
Sungai Acheh Malaysia 5°8N 100°30E 237 c
Sungai Kolok Thailand 6°2N 101°58E 237 J3
Sungai Lembing Malaysia 3°55N 103°3E 237 L4
Sungai Petani Malaysia 5°37N 100°30E 237 K3
Sungai Siput Malaysia 4°49N 101°4E 234 B2
Sungaidurian Indonesia 0°6S 109°21E 235 C3
Sungaigerong Indonesia 2°59S 104°52E 234 C2
Sungailiat Indonesia 1°51S 106°8E 234 C3
Sungaipakning Indonesia 1°19N 102°8E 234 B2
Sungaipenuh Indonesia 2°1S 101°20E 234 C2
Sungari = Songhua Jiang → China 47°45N 132°30E 219 B15
Sungei Kadut Industrial Estate Singapore 1°24N 103°44E 138 A2
Sungei Selatar Res. Singapore 1°24N 103°51E 138 A3
Sungguminasa Indonesia 5°17S 119°30E 235 D5
Sunghua Chiang = Songhua Jiang → China 47°45N 132°30E 219 B15
Sungikai Sudan 12°20N 29°51E 257 E2
Sungsang Indonesia 2°22S 104°55E 234 C2
Sungu Dem. Rep. of the Congo 1°5S 17°21E 264 C3
Sungurlu Turkey 40°12N 34°21E 212 B6
Sunja Croatia 45°21N 16°35E 199 C13
Sunland Park U.S.A. 31°50N 106°40W 305 L10
Sunnansjö Sweden 60°13N 14°58E 162 D8
Sunndalsøra Norway 62°40N 8°33E 164 B5
Sunne Sweden 59°52N 13°5E 162 E7
Sunnemo Sweden 59°53N 13°44E 162 E7
Sunnfjord Norway 61°35N 5°45E 164 C2
Sunnmøre Norway 62°35N 6°30E 164 B3
Sunny Bay Hong Kong, China 22°20N 114°1E 122 B1
Sunny Isles Beach U.S.A. 25°55N 80°7W 129 C3
Sunnyside U.S.A. 46°20N 120°0W 304 C4
Sunnyvale U.S.A. 37°23N 122°2W 306 H4
Sunrise U.S.A. 26°8N 80°14W 129 B2
Sunrise Manor U.S.A. 36°12N 115°4W 124 A2
Sunrise Mountain Natural Area U.S.A. 36°12N 114°58W 124 A2
Sunset Beach U.S.A. 21°40N 158°3W 302 J13
Sunset Park N.Y., U.S.A. 40°38N 73°59W 132 C2
Sunset Park Nev., U.S.A. 36°3N 115°6W 124 B2
Sunset Peak Hong Kong, China 22°15N 113°57E 122 B1
Sunshine Coast Australia 26°30S 153°0E 276 F9
Sunshine I. Hong Kong, China 22°16N 114°3E 122 B2
Sunshine Park U.S.A. 26°2N 80°13W 129 B2
Suntar Russia 62°15N 117°30E 215 C12
Sunter Indonesia 6°7S 106°51E 122 A2
Sunter, Kali → Indonesia 6°10S 106°53E 122 B2
Suntrana U.S.A. 63°52N 148°51W 303 E10
Sunwi-do N. Korea 37°43N 125°16E 224 D2
Sunyani Ghana 7°21N 2°22W 262 D4
Suō-Nada Japan 33°50N 131°30E 222 D3
Suomenlinna Finland 60°9N 24°59E 121 C2
Suomenselkä Finland 62°52N 24°0E 160 E21
Suomi = Finland ■ Europe 63°0N 27°0E 160 E22
Suomussalmi Finland 64°54N 29°10E 160 D23
Suoyarvi Russia 62°3N 32°20E 188 A7
Supai U.S.A. 36°15N 112°41W 305 H7
Supamo → Venezuela 6°48N 61°50W 329 B5
Supaul India 26°10N 86°40E 243 F12
Superagüi △ Brazil 25°6S 48°18W 333 G2
Superior Ariz., U.S.A. 33°18N 111°6W 305 K8
Superior Mont., U.S.A. 47°12N 114°53W 304 C6
Superior Nebr., U.S.A. 40°1N 98°4W 308 E4
Superior Wis., U.S.A. 46°44N 92°6W 308 B7
Superior, L. N. Amer. 47°0N 87°0W 298 C2
Supetar Croatia 43°25N 16°32E 199 E13
Suphan Buri Thailand 14°14N 100°10E 236 E3
Suphan Dağı Turkey 38°54N 42°48E 213 C10
Supiori Indonesia 1°0S 136°0E 231 E9
Supraśl Poland 53°13N 23°19E 185 E10
Supraśl → Poland 53°11N 22°57E 185 E9
Supreme Court Washington, D.C., U.S.A. 143 b3
Supsa Georgia 42°2N 41°49E 191 J5
Supung N. Korea 40°27N 124°54E 224 B2
Supung Shuiku China 40°35N 124°50E 224 B2
Sūq 'Abs Yemen 16°0N 43°12E 248 D3
Sūq al Jarraḩī Yemen 14°10N 43°20E 248 D3
Sūq ash Shuyūkh Iraq 30°53N 46°28E 246 D5
Sūq Suwayq Si. Arabia 24°23N 38°27E 246 E3
Şuqaylabīyah Syria 35°23N 36°23E 250 C7
Suqian China 33°54N 118°8E 227 H10
Suquţra = Socotra Yemen 12°30N 54°0E 249 D6
Sūr Lebanon 33°19N 35°16E 250 E6
Şūr Oman 22°34N 59°32E 249 B7
Sur, C. Chile 27°12S 109°26W 330 b
Sur, Pt. U.S.A. 36°18N 121°54W 306 J5
Sur Bahr West Bank 31°44N 35°13E 123 B2
Sura India 22°33N 88°24E 124 B2
Sura → Russia 56°6N 46°0E 190 C8
Surab Pakistan 28°25N 66°15E 242 E2
Surabaja = Surabaya Indonesia 7°17S 112°45E 235 D4
Surabaya Indonesia 7°17S 112°45E 235 D4
Surahammar Sweden 59°43N 16°13E 162 E10
Suraia Romania 45°40N 27°25E 183 E12
Surakarta Indonesia 7°35S 110°48E 235 D4
Suraksan S. Korea 37°40N 127°4E 137 A2
Surallah Phil. 6°22N 124°44E 233 H5
Šurany Slovak Rep. 48°6N 18°10E 181 C11
Surat Queens., Australia 27°10S 149°6E 281 D4
Surat India 21°12N 72°55E 244 D1
Surat Thani Thailand 9°6N 99°20E 237 H2
Suratgarh India 29°18N 73°55E 242 E5
Surathkal India 12°58N 74°46E 245 H2
Suraxanı = Qaraçuxar Azerbaijan 40°25N 50°1E 191 K10
Şuraymilā Si. Arabia 25°7N 46°7E 246 E5
Suraż Poland 52°57N 22°57E 185 F9
Surazh Belarus 55°25N 30°44E 188 E6
Surazh Russia 53°5N 32°27E 189 F7
Surbiton U.K. 51°23N 0°17W 125 B2
Surduc Romania 47°15N 23°25E 183 C8
Surduc Pasul Romania 45°21N 23°23E 183 E8
Surdulica Serbia 42°41N 22°11E 202 D6
Surendranagar India 22°45N 71°40E 242 H4
Suresnes France 48°52N 2°13E 134 A2
Surf U.S.A. 34°41N 120°36W 307 L6
Surfers Paradise Australia 28°0S 153°25E 281 D5
Surfside U.S.A. 25°52N 80°7W 129 C3
Surgana India 20°34N 73°37E 244 D1
Surgères France 46°7N 0°47W 174 B3
Surgut Russia 61°14N 73°20E 214 C8
Sùria Spain 41°50N 1°45E 196 D6
Surian, Palazzo Venice, Italy 142 a2
Suriapet India 17°10N 79°40E 244 F4
Suribachi Yama Iwo Jima 24°45N 141°17E 288 b
Surigao Phil. 9°47N 125°29E 233 G5
Surigao del Norte □ Phil. 9°40N 125°40E 233 G5
Surigao del Sur □ Phil. 8°45N 126°0E 233 G6
Surigao Str. Phil. 10°15N 125°23E 233 F5
Surin Thailand 14°50N 103°34E 236 E4
Surinam = Suriname ■ S. Amer. 4°0N 56°0W 329 C6
Surinam Mauritius 20°30S 57°30E 272 e
Suriname ■ S. Amer. 4°0N 56°0W 329 C6
Suriname → Suriname 5°50N 55°15W 329 B6
Surjagarh India 19°36N 80°25E 244 E5
Surma → Bangla. 24°34N 91°14E 241 C3
Sūrmaq Iran 31°3N 52°48E 247 D7
Sürmene Turkey 41°0N 40°1E 213 B9
Surna → Norway 62°59N 8°40E 164 B5
Surnadalsøra Norway 62°58N 8°40E 164 B5
Surovikino Russia 48°32N 42°55E 191 F6
Surprise U.S.A. 33°38N 112°19W 305 K7
Surquillo Peru 12°6S 77°1W 124 B2
Surrency U.S.A. 31°44N 82°12W 316 D7
Surrey Canada 49°7N 122°45W 306 A4
Surrey □ Jamaica 18°5N 76°34W 320 a
Surrey □ U.K. 51°15N 0°31W 169 F7
Surrey Hills Australia 33°53S 151°13E 139 B2
Sursand India 26°39N 85°43E 243 F11
Sursar → India 26°14N 87°3E 243 F12
Sursee Switz. 47°11N 8°6E 179 H4
Sursk Russia 53°3N 45°40E 190 D7
Surskoye Russia 54°30N 46°44E 190 C8
Surt Libya 31°11N 16°39E 258 B3
Surt □ Libya 30°0N 17°30E 258 B3
Surt, Al Ḩamādah al Libya 30°0N 17°50E 258 C3
Surt, Khalīj Libya 31°40N 18°30E 258 B3
Surtanahu Pakistan 26°22N 70°0E 242 F4
Surte Sweden 57°50N 12°1E 163 G6
Surtsey Iceland 63°20N 20°30W 155 D6
Surubim Brazil 7°50S 35°45W 332 C4
Sürüç Turkey 36°58N 38°25E 213 D8
Surud, Ras Somalia 11°10N 47°30E 267 B6
Surud Ad Somalia 10°42N 47°9E 267 B6
Suruga-Wan Japan 34°45N 138°30E 223 C10
Surulangun Indonesia 2°37S 102°45E 234 C2
Surulere Nigeria 6°29N 3°21E 124 B2
Surumu → Brazil 3°22N 60°19W 329 C5
Surxondaryo □ Uzbekistan 38°0N 67°30E 217 E7
Susa = Sousse Tunisia 35°50N 10°38E 258 A2
Susa Italy 45°8N 7°3E 198 C4
Suså → Denmark 55°12N 11°42E 163 J5
Sušac Croatia 42°46N 16°30E 199 F13
Susaek S. Korea 37°34N 126°54E 137 B1
Sūsah Libya 32°52N 21°59E 258 B4
Susak Croatia 44°30N 14°18E 199 D11
Susaki Japan 33°22N 133°17E 222 D5
Susam-Adasi = Samos Greece 37°45N 26°50E 205 D8
Sūsangerd Iran 31°35N 48°6E 213 G13
Susanville U.S.A. 40°25N 120°39W 304 F3
Susch Switz. 46°46N 10°5E 179 J6
Suşehri Turkey 40°10N 38°6E 213 B8
Sušice Czech Rep. 49°17N 13°30E 180 B6
Susleni Moldova 47°25N 28°59E 183 C13
Susner India 23°57N 76°5E 242 H7
Susong China 30°10N 116°5E 229 B11
Susono Japan 35°10N 138°55E 223 B10
Susquehanna U.S.A. 41°57N 75°36W 313 E9
Susquehanna → U.S.A. 39°33N 76°5W 313 G8
Susques Argentina 23°35S 66°25W 334 A2
Süssenbrunn Austria 48°16N 16°29E 142 A2
Sussex N.B., Canada 45°45N 65°37W 299 C6
Sussex N.J., U.S.A. 41°13N 74°37W 313 E10
Sussex, East □ U.K. 51°0N 0°20E 169 G8
Sussex, West □ U.K. 51°0N 0°30W 169 G7
Sussex Inlet Australia 35°10S 150°36E 283 C9
Sustut → Canada 56°20N 127°30W 296 B3
Susuman Russia 62°47N 148°10E 215 C15
Susunu Indonesia 3°7S 133°39E 231 E8
Susurluk Turkey 39°54N 28°8E 205 B10
Susuz Turkey 40°46N 43°8E 213 B10
Susz Poland 53°44N 19°20E 184 E6
Sutay Uul Asia 46°35N 93°38E 218 B7
Sütçüler Turkey 37°29N 30°57E 212 D4
Şuţeşti Romania 45°13N 27°27E 183 E12
Sutherland N.S.W., Australia 34°2S 151°4E 283 C9
Sutherland Northern Cape, S. Africa 32°24S 20°40E 270 D3
Sutherland Highl., U.K. 58°12N 4°50W 167 C4
Sutherland Nebr., U.S.A. 41°10N 101°8W 308 E3
Sutherland Falls N.Z. 44°48S 167°46E 285 E2
Sutherland Road Barbados 13°16N 59°39W 323 r
Sutherlin U.S.A. 43°23N 123°19W 304 E2
Suthri India 23°3N 68°55E 242 H3
Sutjeska △ Bos.-H. 43°50N 18°32E 182 G3
Sutlej → Pakistan 29°23N 71°3E 242 E4
Sutter U.S.A. 39°10N 121°45W 306 F5
Sutter Buttes U.S.A. 39°12N 121°49W 306 F5
Sutter Creek U.S.A. 38°24N 120°48W 306 G6
Sutton Qué., Canada 45°6N 72°37W 313 A12
Sutton Dublin, Ireland 53°23N 6°7W 120 A3
Sutton N.Z. 45°34S 170°8E 285 F5
Sutton London, U.K. 51°21N 0°11W 125 B2
Sutton Nebr., U.S.A. 40°36N 97°52W 308 E5
Sutton W. Va., U.S.A. 38°40N 80°43W 309 F13
Sutton → Canada 55°15N 83°45W 298 A3
Sutton Coldfield U.K. 52°35N 1°49W 169 E6
Sutton in Ashfield U.K. 53°8N 1°16W 168 D6
Sutton L. Canada 54°15N 84°42W 298 B3
Suttor → Australia 21°36S 147°2E 280 C4
Suttsu Japan 42°48N 140°14E 220 C10
Sutwik I. U.S.A. 56°34N 157°12W 303 H8
Suva Fiji 18°6S 178°30E 287 B2
Suva Gora Macedonia 41°45N 21°3E 202 E5
Suva Planina Serbia 43°10N 22°5E 202 C6
Suva Reka = Therandë Kosovo 42°21N 20°50E 202 D4
Suvorov Russia 54°7N 36°30E 188 E9
Suvorov Is. = Suwarrow Is. Cook Is. 13°15S 163°5W 289 J11
Suvorove Ukraine 45°35N 28°59E 183 E13
Suvorovo Bulgaria 43°20N 27°35E 203 C11
Suwa Japan 36°2N 138°8E 223 A10
Suwa-Ko Japan 36°3N 138°5E 223 A10
Suwałki Poland 54°8N 22°59E 184 D9
Suwannaphum Thailand 15°33N 103°47E 236 E4
Suwannee U.S.A. 29°20N 83°9W 317 F6
Suwannee → U.S.A. 29°17N 83°10W 317 F6
Suwannee Sd. U.S.A. 29°20N 83°15W 317 F6
Suwanose-Jima Japan 29°38N 129°43E 221 K4
Suwarrow Is. Cook Is. 13°15S 163°5W 289 J11
Suwayqīyah, Hawr as Iraq 32°40N 46°3E 213 G12
Suweis, Khalîg el Egypt 28°40N 33°0E 256 J8
Suweis, Qanâ es Egypt 31°0N 32°20E 256 H8
Suwon S. Korea 37°17N 127°1E 224 D3
Suyu S. Korea 37°37N 127°0E 137 B2
Suzaka Japan 36°39N 138°19E 223 A10
Suzdal Russia 56°29N 40°26E 188 D11
Suzhou Anhui, China 33°41N 116°59E 226 H9
Suzhou Jiangsu, China 31°19N 120°38E 229 B13
Suzu Japan 37°25N 137°17E 221 F8
Suzu-Misaki Japan 37°31N 137°21E 221 F8
Suzuka Japan 34°55N 136°36E 223 C8
Suzuka-Sammyaku Japan 35°5N 136°30E 223 B8
Suzukishinden Japan 35°43N 139°31E 140 A2
Suzun Russia 53°47N 82°18E 217 B10
Suzzara Italy 44°59N 10°45E 198 D7
Svalbard Arctic 78°0N 17°0E 154 B12
Svalbard Radio = Longyearbyen Svalbard 78°13N 15°40E 150 B8
Svalbarð Iceland 66°12N 15°43W 155 A11
Svalbarðseyri Iceland 65°45N 18°5W 155 B8
Svalöv Sweden 55°57N 13°8E 163 J7
Svalyava Ukraine 48°33N 22°59E 182 B7
Svaneke Denmark 55°8N 15°8E 163 J9
Svanemøllen Denmark 55°43N 12°34E 118 A3
Svaneti Georgia 42°50N 42°45E 213 A10
Svängsta Sweden 56°16N 14°47E 163 H8
Svanskog Sweden 59°11N 12°33E 162 E6
Svappavaara Sweden 67°40N 21°3E 160 C19
Svärdsjö Sweden 60°45N 15°54E 162 D9
Svarstad Norway 59°27N 9°56E 164 E6
Svartå Sweden 59°8N 14°32E 162 E8
Svartárkot Iceland 65°20N 17°15W 155 B9
Svartevatn Norway 59°10N 6°56E 164 E3
Svartisen Norway 66°40N 13°59E 160 C15
Svartvik Sweden 62°19N 17°24E 162 B11
Svatove Ukraine 49°22N 38°15E 189 H10
Svatovo = Svatove Ukraine 49°22N 38°15E 189 H10
Svatsum Norway 61°20N 9°50E 164 C6
Svay Chek Cambodia 13°48N 102°58E 236 F4
Svay Rieng Cambodia 11°9N 105°45E 237 G5
Sveaborg = Suomenlinna Finland 60°9N 24°59E 121 C2
Svealand Sweden 60°20N 15°0E 162 D9
Svedala Sweden 55°30N 13°15E 163 J7
Sveg Sweden 62°2N 14°21E 162 B8
Sveindal Norway 58°29N 7°30E 164 F4
Sveinseyri Iceland 65°38N 23°51W 155 B3
Sveio Norway 59°33N 5°23E 164 E2
Svelgen Norway 61°46N 5°17E 164 C2
Svelvik Norway 59°37N 10°24E 164 E7
Svendborg Denmark 55°4N 10°35E 163 J4
Svene Norway 59°45N 9°31E 164 E6
Svenljunga Sweden 57°29N 13°5E 163 G7
Svenstavik Sweden 62°45N 14°26E 162 B8
Svenstrup Denmark 56°58N 9°50E 163 H3
Svenyhorodka Ukraine 49°4N 30°56E 189 H6
Sverdlov Russia 55°46N 37°36E 129 B2
Sverdlovsk = Yekaterinburg Russia 56°50N 60°30E 214 D7
Sverdlovsk Ukraine 48°5N 39°47E 189 H10
Sverdrup Chan. Canada 79°56N 96°25W 295 B12
Sverdrup Is. Canada 79°0N 97°0W 292 B10
Sverige = Sweden ■ Europe 57°0N 15°0E 161 H16
Sveshtari Bulgaria 43°40N 26°40E 203 C10
Svestad Norway 59°46N 10°36E 133 B2
Svetac Croatia 43°3N 15°43E 199 E12
Sveti Ivan = Zelina Croatia 45°57N 16°16E 199 C13
Sveti Nikola, Prokhad Europe 43°27N 22°6E 202 C6
Sveti Nikole Macedonia 41°51N 21°56E 202 E5
Sveti Rok Croatia 44°22N 15°39E 199 D12
Sveti Vrach = Sandanski Bulgaria 41°35N 23°16E 202 E7
Svetlaya Russia 46°33N 138°18E 220 A9
Svetlogorsk = Svyetlahorsk Belarus 52°38N 29°46E 177 B15
Svetlogorsk Russia 54°56N 20°10E 184 D7
Svetlograd Russia 45°25N 42°58E 191 H6
Svetlovodsk = Svitlovodsk Ukraine 49°2N 33°13E 189 H7
Svetlyy Kaliningrad, Russia 54°41N 20°8E 184 D7
Svetlyy Orenburg, Russia 50°48N 60°51E 216 B6
Svidník Slovak Rep. 49°20N 21°37E 181 B14
Svignaskarð Iceland 64°40N 21°42W 155 C5
Svilaja Planina Croatia 43°49N 16°31E 199 E13
Svilajnac Serbia 44°15N 21°11E 202 B5
Svilengrad Bulgaria 41°49N 26°12E 203 E10
Svinafell Iceland 63°59N 16°51W 155 D10
Svinö Finland 60°7N 24°44E 121 C1
Svir → Russia 60°30N 32°48E 188 B7
Sviritsa Russia 60°29N 32°51E 188 B7
Svishtov Bulgaria 43°36N 25°23E 203 C9
Svislach Belarus 53°3N 24°2E 185 E11
Svitava → Czech Rep. 49°11N 16°37E 181 B9
Svitavy Czech Rep. 49°47N 16°28E 181 B9
Svitlovodsk Ukraine 49°2N 33°13E 189 H7
Svityaz, Ozero Ukraine 51°30N 23°50E 185 G10
Svizzera = Switzerland ■ Europe 46°30N 8°0E 179 J4
Svobodnyy Russia 51°20N 128°0E 215 D13
Svoge Bulgaria 42°59N 23°23E 202 D7
Svolvær Norway 68°15N 14°34E 160 B16
Svorkmo Norway 63°10N 9°46E 164 A6
Svoronata Greece 38°7N 20°31E 207 C2
Svratka → Czech Rep. 49°11N 16°38E 181 B9
Svrljig Serbia 43°25N 22°6E 202 C6
Svullrya Norway 60°25N 12°23E 164 D9
Svyatogorovsky Rudnik = Dobropole Ukraine 48°25N 37°2E 189 H9
Svyetlahorsk Belarus 52°38N 29°46E 177 B15
Swa Burma 19°15N 96°17E 241 F6
Swa Tende Dem. Rep. of the Congo 7°9S 17°7E 265 D3
Swabian Alps = Schwäbische Alb Germany 48°20N 9°30E 179 G5
Swaffham U.K. 52°39N 0°42E 169 E8
Swains I. Amer. Samoa 11°11S 171°4W 289 J11
Swainsboro U.S.A. 32°36N 82°20W 316 C7
Swakop → Namibia 22°38S 14°36E 270 B2
Swakopmund Namibia 22°37S 14°30E 270 B1
Swale → U.K. 54°5N 1°20W 168 C6
Swamihalli India 14°52N 76°38E 245 G3
Swan → W. Austral., Australia 32°3S 115°45E 279 F2
Swan → Man., Canada 52°30N 100°45W 297 C8
Swan Hill Australia 35°20S 143°33E 282 C5
Swan Hills Canada 54°43N 115°24W 296 C5
Swan Is. = Santanilla, Is. Honduras 17°22N 83°57W 320 C3
Swan L. Man., Canada 52°30N 100°40W 297 C8
Swan L. Ont., Canada 54°16N 91°11W 298 B1
Swan Ra. U.S.A. 48°0N 113°45W 304 C7
Swan Reach Australia 34°35S 139°37E 282 C3
Swan River Canada 52°10N 101°16W 297 C8
Swanage U.K. 50°36N 1°58W 169 G6
Swanley U.K. 51°23N 0°11E 125 B4
Swansea N.S.W., Australia 33°3S 151°35E 283 B9
Swansea Tas., Australia 42°8S 148°4E 281 G4
Swansea Ont., Canada 43°38N 79°28W 141 B2
Swansea Swansea, U.K. 51°37N 3°57W 169 F4
Swansea S.C., U.S.A. 33°44N 81°6W 316 B8
Swansea □ U.K. 51°38N 4°3W 169 F3
Swanton U.S.A. 41°35N 83°53W 311 C13
Swartberge S. Africa 33°20S 22°0E 270 D3
Swartmodder S. Africa 28°1S 20°32E 270 C3
Swartnossob → Namibia 23°8S 18°42E 270 B2
Swartruggens S. Africa 25°39S 26°42E 270 C4
Swarzędz Poland 52°25N 17°4E 185 F4
Swastika Canada 48°7N 80°6W 298 C3
Swat → Pakistan 34°40N 72°5E 243 B5
Swatow = Shantou China 23°18N 116°40E 229 F11
Swaziland ■ Africa 26°30S 31°30E 271 C5
Sweden ■ Europe 57°0N 15°0E 161 H16
Swedru Ghana 5°32N 0°41W 263 D4
Sweet Grass U.S.A. 48°59N 111°58W 304 B8
Sweet Home U.S.A. 44°24N 122°44W 304 D2
Sweet Springs U.S.A. 38°58N 93°25W 310 F3
Sweetwater Nev., U.S.A. 38°27N 119°9W 306 G7
Sweetwater Tenn., U.S.A. 35°36N 84°28W 315 D12
Sweetwater Tex., U.S.A. 32°28N 100°25W 314 E4
Sweetwater → U.S.A. 42°31N 107°2W 304 E10
Swellendam S. Africa 34°1S 20°26E 270 D3
Swider → Poland 52°6N 21°14E 185 F8
Świdnica Poland 50°50N 16°30E 185 H3
Świdnik Poland 51°13N 22°39E 185 G9
Świdwin Poland 53°47N 15°49E 184 E2
Świebodzice Poland 50°51N 16°20E 185 H3
Świebodzin Poland 52°15N 15°31E 185 F2
Świecie Poland 53°25N 18°30E 184 E5
Świerzawa Poland 51°1N 15°54E 185 G2
Świętokrzyski △ Poland 50°53N 20°59E 185 H7
Świętokrzyskie □ Poland 50°45N 20°45E 185 H7
Świętokrzyskie, Góry Poland 51°0N 20°30E 185 H7
Swift Current Canada 50°20N 107°45W 297 C7
Swift Current → Canada 50°38N 107°44W 297 C7
Swifts Creek Australia 37°17S 147°44E 283 D7
Swilly, L. Ireland 55°12N 7°33W 166 A4
Swinburne I. U.S.A. 40°33N 74°3W 132 C1
Swindon U.K. 51°34N 1°46W 169 F6
Swindon □ U.K. 51°34N 1°46W 169 F6
Swinemünde = Świnoujście Poland 53°54N 14°16E 184 E1
Swinford Ireland 53°57N 8°58W 166 C3
Świnoujście Poland 53°54N 14°16E 184 E1
Switzerland ■ Europe 46°30N 8°0E 179 J4
Swords Ireland 53°28N 6°13W 120 A2
Swoyerville U.S.A. 41°18N 75°53W 313 E9
Syasstroy Russia 60°9N 32°33E 188 B7
Sycamore Ill., U.S.A. 41°59N 88°41W 311 C8
Sycamore Ohio, U.S.A. 40°57N 83°10W 311 D13
Sychevka Russia 55°59N 34°16E 188 E8
Syców Poland 51°19N 17°40E 185 G4
Syddanmark □ Denmark 55°30N 9°0E 163 J2
Sydenham S. Africa 26°9S 28°5E 123 A2
Sydenham → Canada 42°33N 82°25W 312 D2
Sydney N.S.W., Australia 33°52S 151°12E 139 B2
Sydney N.S., Canada 46°7N 60°7W 299 C7
Sydney, Univ. of Australia 33°54S 151°11E 139 B2
Sydney Harbour △ Australia 33°50S 151°14E 139 B2
Sydney Harbour Bridge Australia 33°51S 151°12E 139 B2
Sydney Kingsford Smith ✈ (SYD) Australia 33°57S 151°11E 139 B2
Sydney L. Canada 50°41N 94°25W 297 C10
Sydney Mines Canada 46°18N 60°15W 299 C7
Sydprøven = Alluitsup Paa Greenland 60°30N 45°35W 154 E6
Sydra, G. of = Surt, Khalīj Libya 31°40N 18°30E 258 B3
Sydstranden Denmark 55°34N 12°38E 118 B3
Syeverodonetsk Ukraine 48°58N 38°35E 189 H10
Syfteland Norway 60°14N 5°27E 164 D2
Syke Germany 52°55N 8°50E 178 C4
Sykesville U.S.A. 41°3N 78°50W 312 E6
Sykkylven Norway 62°23N 6°35E 164 B3
Syktyvkar Russia 61°45N 50°40E 186 B9
Sylacauga U.S.A. 33°10N 86°15W 316 B3
Sylarna Sweden 63°2N 12°13E 164 A9
Sylhet Bangla. 24°54N 91°52E 241 C3
Sylhet □ Bangla. 24°50N 91°50E 241 C3
Sylt Germany 54°54N 8°22E 178 A4
Sylte Norway 62°18N 7°17E 164 B4
Sylvan Beach U.S.A. 43°12N 75°44W 313 C9
Sylvan Lake Canada 52°20N 114°3W 296 C6
Sylvania N.S.W., Australia 34°0S 151°7E 139 C1
Sylvania Ga., U.S.A. 32°45N 81°38W 316 C8
Sylvania Ohio, U.S.A. 41°43N 83°42W 311 C13
Sylvester U.S.A. 31°32N 83°50W 316 D6
Sym Russia 60°20N 88°18E 214 C9
Symphony Hall San Francisco, U.S.A. 136 c1
Synelnykove Ukraine 48°25N 35°30E 189 H8
Synevyr △ Ukraine 48°30N 23°40E 183 B8
Synevyrska Polyana Ukraine 48°35N 23°41E 183 B8
Synnervika Norway 62°25N 11°54E 164 B8
Synnfjell Norway 61°5N 9°46E 164 C6
Synnot Ra. Australia 16°30S 125°20E 278 C4
Syntagma Square Athens, Greece 112 b2
Synyak Ukraine 48°35N 22°51E 182 B7
Syon Park U.K. 51°28N 0°18W 125 B2
Syöte △ Finland 65°44N 27°58E 160 D22
Syowa Antarctica 68°50S 12°0E 151 C5
Syracuse = Siracusa Italy 37°4N 15°17E 201 E8
Syracuse Ind., U.S.A. 41°26N 85°45W 311 C11
Syracuse Kans., U.S.A. 37°59N 101°45W 308 G3
Syracuse N.Y., U.S.A. 43°3N 76°9W 313 C8
Syracuse Nebr., U.S.A. 40°39N 96°11W 308 E5
Syrdarya → Kazakhstan 46°3N 61°0E 216 C6
Syria ■ Asia 35°0N 38°0E 213 E8
Syriam Burma 16°44N 96°19E 241 G6
Syrian Desert = Shām, Bādiyat ash Asia 32°0N 40°0E 246 C3
Syros = Ermoupoli Greece 37°28N 24°57E 204 D6
Sysslebäck Sweden 60°44N 12°52E 162 D6
Syvden Norway 62°5N 5°44E 164 B2
Syzran Russia 53°12N 48°30E 190 D9
Szabolcs-Szatmár-Bereg □ Hungary 48°2N 21°45E 182 B6
Szadek Poland 51°41N 18°59E 185 G5
Szamocin Poland 53°2N 17°7E 185 E4
Szamos → Hungary 48°7N 22°20E 182 B7
Szamotuły Poland 52°37N 16°33E 185 F3
Száraz → Hungary 46°10N 21°15E 182 D6
Szarvas Hungary 46°50N 20°38E 182 D5
Százhalombatta Hungary 47°20N 18°58E 182 C3
Szczawnica Poland 49°26N 20°30E 185 J7
Szczebrzeszyn Poland 50°42N 22°59E 185 H9
Szczecin Poland 53°27N 14°27E 184 E1
Szczecinek Poland 53°43N 16°41E 184 E3
Szczeciński, Zalew = Stettiner Haff Germany 53°47N 14°15E 178 B10
Szczekociny Poland 50°38N 19°48E 185 H6
Szczęśliwice Poland 52°12N 20°57E 143 B1
Szczucin Poland 50°18N 21°4E 185 H8
Szczuczyn Poland 53°36N 22°19E 184 E9
Szczyrk Poland 49°43N 19°2E 185 J6
Szczytna Poland 50°25N 16°28E 185 H3
Szczytno Poland 53°33N 21°0E 184 E7
Széchnenyi-hegy Hungary 47°29N 18°57E 117 B1
Szechuan = Sichuan □ China 30°30N 103°0E 228 B5
Szechuan Basin = Sichuan Pendi China 31°0N 105°0E 228 B5
Szécsény Hungary 48°7N 19°30E 182 B4
Szeged Hungary 46°16N 20°10E 182 D5
Szeghalom Hungary 47°1N 21°10E 182 C6
Székesfehérvár Hungary 47°15N 18°25E 182 C3
Szekszárd Hungary 46°22N 18°42E 182 D3
Szendrő Hungary 48°24N 20°41E 182 B5
Szentendre Hungary 47°39N 19°4E 182 C4
Szentes Hungary 46°39N 20°21E 182 D5
Szentgotthárd Hungary 46°58N 16°19E 182 D1
Szentlőrinc Hungary 46°3N 18°1E 182 D3
Széphalom Hungary 47°34N 18°57E 117 A1
Szeping = Siping China 43°8N 124°21E 227 C13
Szerencs Hungary 48°10N 21°12E 182 B6
Szigetszentmiklós Hungary 47°21N 19°3E 182 C4
Szigetvár Hungary 46°3N 17°46E 182 D2
Szikszó Hungary 48°12N 20°56E 182 B5
Szklarska Poreba Poland 50°50N 15°33E 185 H2
Szkwa → Poland 53°11N 21°43E 185 E8
Szlichtyngowa Poland 51°42N 16°15E 185 G3
Szob Hungary 47°48N 18°53E 182 C3
Szolnok Hungary 47°10N 20°15E 182 C5
Szombathely Hungary 47°14N 16°38E 182 C1
Szprotawa Poland 51°33N 15°35E 185 G2
Sztálinváros = Dunaújváros Hungary 46°58N 18°57E 182 D3
Sztum Poland 53°55N 19°1E 184 E6
Sztutowo Poland 54°20N 19°15E 184 D6
Szubin Poland 53°1N 17°45E 185 E4
Szydłowiec Poland 51°15N 20°51E 185 G7
Szypliszki Poland 54°17N 23°2E 184 D10

## T

Ta Khli Thailand 15°15N 100°21E 236 E3
Ta Lai Vietnam 11°24N 107°23E 237 G6
Ta Phraya △ Thailand 14°11N 102°49E 236 E4
Ta Pieh Shan = Dabie Shan China 31°20N 115°20E 229 B10
Taakoka Cook Is. 21°15S 159°43W 289 h
Taal, L. Phil. 13°56N 121°0E 232 E3
Taal Volcano Phil. 14°7N 120°59E 231 B6
Taal Volcano △ Phil. 14°1N 120°59E 232 D3
Taamisaari = Raasepori Finland 60°0N 23°26E 188 B2
Taan Taiwan 24°22N 120°35E 225 B2
Taastrup Denmark 55°39N 12°18E 118 B1
Tab Hungary 46°44N 18°2E 182 D3
Tabacal Argentina 23°15S 64°15W 334 A3
Tabaco Phil. 13°22N 123°44E 232 E4
Tabagné Ivory C. 7°59N 3°4W 262 D4
Ţābah Si. Arabia 26°55N 42°38E 246 E4
Tabajara Brazil 8°56S 62°8W 331 B5
Tabalo Papua N. G. 1°24S 149°40E 286 A5
Tabalos Peru 6°26S 76°37W 330 B2
Tabanan Indonesia 8°32S 115°8E 231 K18
Tabang Indonesia 0°34N 116°1E 235 B5
Tabankort Niger 17°44N 0°20E 263 B5
Tabaquite Trin. & Tob. 10°23N 61°18W 323 t
Tabaquite/Talparo □ Trin. & Tob. 10°28N 61°18W 323 t
Tabar I. Papua N. G. 2°56S 152°0E 286 B7
Tabar Is. Papua N. G. 2°50S 152°0E 286 B7
Tabarka Tunisia 36°56N 8°46E 258 A1
Ţabas Khorāsān, Iran 32°48N 60°12E 247 C9
Ţabas Yazd, Iran 33°35N 56°55E 247 C8
Tabasará, Serranía de Panama 8°35N 81°40W 320 E3
Tabasco □ Mexico 18°0N 92°40W 319 D6
Tabāsīn Iran 31°12N 57°54E 247 D8
Tabata Japan 35°44N 139°46E 140 A3
Tabatinga Brazil 4°16S 69°56W 330 A4
Tabatinga, Serra da Brazil 10°30S 44°0W 332 D3
Tabayin Burma 22°42N 95°20E 241 D5
Tabelbala Algeria 29°24N 3°15W 260 C4
Tabelbala, Kahal de Algeria 28°47N 2°0W 261 C4
Tabelembila Algeria 24°43N 4°16E 261 D5
Taber Canada 49°47N 112°8W 296 D6
Taberg Sweden 57°40N 14°6E 163 G8
Tabernacle St. Kitts & Nevis 17°23N 62°46W 322 d
Tabi Angola 8°10S 13°18E 265 D2
Tabina Phil. 7°28N 123°24E 233 H4
Tabira Brazil 7°35S 37°33W 332 C4
Tabiteuea Kiribati 1°25S 174°50E 277 A13
Tabla Niger 13°46N 3°1E 263 C5
Tablada Argentina 34°41S 58°32W 117 C1
Tablas de Daimiel △ Spain 39°9N 3°40W 195 F7
Tablas I. Phil. 12°25N 122°2E 232 E4
Tablas Str. Phil. 12°40N 121°48E 232 E3
Table, Pte. de la Réunion 21°14S 55°48E 272 f
Table B. Nfld. & L., Canada 53°40N 56°25W 299 B8
Table B. Western Cape, S. Africa 33°35S 18°25E 118 A1
Table C. N.Z. 39°6S 178°0E 284 F7

Table Grove U.S.A. 40°20N 90°27W 310 D6
Table I. Burma 14°12N 93°22E 245 G11
Table Mountain △ S. Africa 33°58S 18°28E 118 A1
Table Mt. S. Africa 33°58S 18°26E 118 A1
Table Rock L. U.S.A. 36°36N 93°19W 308 G7
Tableland Trin. & Tob. 10°16N 61°16W 323 t
Tabletop, Mt. Australia 23°24S 147°11E 280 C4
Taboão da Serra Brazil 23°36S 46°45W 137 B1
Tabocal Brazil 2°42S 57°40W 329 D6
Tabon Cave Complex Phil. 9°17N 118°5E 233 G2
Tábor Czech Rep. 49°25N 14°39E 180 B7
Tabora Tanzania 5°2S 32°50E 268 D3
Tabora □ Tanzania 5°0S 33°0E 268 D3
Tabou Ivory C. 4°30N 7°20W 262 E3
Tabrīz Iran 38°7N 46°20E 213 C12
Tabuaeran Kiribati 3°51N 159°22W 289 G12
Tabubil Papua N. G. 5°20S 141°15E 286 C1
Tabuenca Spain 41°42N 1°33W 196 D3
Tabuk Phil. 17°24N 121°25E 232 C3
Tabūk Si. Arabia 28°23N 36°36E 251 K7
Tabūk □ Si. Arabia 27°40N 36°50E 246 E3
Tabunifi Micronesia 9°28N 138°4E 287 S16
Taburno-Camposauro ⌂ Italy 41°8N 14°37E 201 A7
Tabwemasana, Mt. Vanuatu 15°20S 166°44E 287 E4
Täby Sweden 59°26N 18°2E 139 A2
Tacámbaro de Codallos Mexico 19°14N 101°28W 318 D4
Tacarigua Trin. & Tob. 10°38N 61°22W 323 t
Tacarigua Venezuela 11°3N 63°54W 329 a
Tacarigua, Laguna de Venezuela 10°15N 65°50W 328 A4
Tacheng Xinjiang Uygur, China 46°40N 82°58E 217 C10
Tacheng Taiwan 23°51N 120°19E 225 C2
Tach'i Taiwan 24°53N 121°17E 225 B3
Tachia Taiwan 24°25N 120°28E 225 B2
Tachia Hsi → Taiwan 24°20N 120°33E 225 B3
Tachibana-Wan Japan 32°45N 130°7E 222 E2
Tachikawa Japan 35°42N 139°25E 223 B11
Tachilek Burma 20°26N 99°52E 236 B2
Tach'ing Shan = Daqing Shan China 40°40N 111°0E 226 D6
Táchira □ Venezuela 8°7N 72°15W 328 B3
Tachiumet Libya 26°19N 10°3E 258 C2
Tachoshui Taiwan 24°20N 121°44E 225 B3
Tachov Czech Rep. 49°47N 12°39E 180 B5
Tácina → Italy 38°57N 16°55E 201 D9
Tacloban Phil. 11°15N 124°58E 233 F5
Tacna Peru 18°0S 70°20W 330 D3
Tacna □ Peru 17°40S 70°20W 330 D3
Tacoma U.S.A. 47°14N 122°26W 306 C4
Tacopaya = Zudañez Bolivia 19°6S 64°44W 331 D5
Tacuarembó Uruguay 31°45S 56°0W 335 C4
Tacuba Mexico 19°26N 99°11W 128 B1
Tacubaya Mexico 19°24N 99°10W 128 B1
Tacurong Phil. 6°40N 124°41E 233 H5
Tacutu = Takutu → Guyana 3°30N 60°29W 329 C5
Tada-u Burma 21°49N 95°58E 241 E5
Tadahadi Solomon Is. 10°18S 161°35E 287 N11
Tademaït, Plateau du Algeria 28°30N 2°30E 261 C5
Tādepallegudem India 16°50N 81°30E 244 F5
Tadéra Niger 20°29N 8°18E 261 D6
Tadine N. Cal. 21°33S 167°52E 288 d
Tadio, L. Ivory C. 5°10N 5°15W 262 D3
Tadjerdjeri, O. → Algeria 26°0N 8°0E 261 C6
Tadjerouna Algeria 33°3N 2°3E 261 B5
Tadjettaret, O. → Algeria 21°20N 7°22E 261 D6
Tadjmout Laghouat, Algeria 33°52N 2°30E 261 B5
Tadjmout Saoura, Algeria 25°37N 3°48E 261 C5
Tadjoura Djibouti 11°50N 42°55E 257 E5
Tadjoura, Golfe de Djibouti 11°50N 43°0E 257 E5
Tadla-Azilal □ Morocco 32°0N 6°30W 260 B3
Tadmor N.Z. 41°27S 172°45E 285 B7
Tadoba △ India 20°30N 78°20E 244 D4
Tadotsu Japan 34°16N 133°45E 222 C5
Tadoule L. Canada 58°36N 98°20W 297 B9
Tadoussac Canada 48°11N 69°42W 299 C6
Tadpatri India 14°55N 78°1E 245 G4
Tadrés ⌂ Niger 16°0N 7°10E 263 B6
Tadzhikistan = Tajikistan ■ Asia 38°30N 70°0E 217 E8
Tae-an S. Korea 36°45N 126°17E 224 D3
Tae-an △ S. Korea 36°40N 126°0E 224 D3
Taebaek S. Korea 37°10N 128°59E 224 D4
Taebaeksan △ S. Korea 37°5N 128°54E 224 D4
T'aebaeksanmaek S. Korea 37°40N 128°50E 224 D4
Taedong-gang → N. Korea 38°41N 125°15E 224 C2
Taedong-man N. Korea 38°48N 125°7E 224 C2
Taegu = Daegu S. Korea 35°50N 128°37E 224 E4
Taegwan N. Korea 40°13N 125°12E 224 B2
Taehung N. Korea 40°5N 126°56E 224 B3
Taehwa-do N. Korea 39°26N 124°36E 224 C2
Taejŏn = Daejeon S. Korea 36°20N 127°28E 224 D3
Tælavåg Norway 60°15N 4°58E 164 D1
Taen, Ko Thailand 9°22N 99°57E 237 b
Tafalla Spain 42°30N 1°41W 196 C3
Tafar South Sudan 6°52N 28°15E 257 F2
Tafassasset, O. → Algeria 22°0N 9°57E 261 D6
Tafelbaai = Table B. S. Africa 33°35S 18°25E 118 A1
Tafelberg Curaçao 12°4N 68°50W 322 g
Tafelney, C. Morocco 31°3N 9°51W 260 B3
Tafermaar Indonesia 6°47S 134°10E 231 F8
Taffermit Morocco 29°37N 9°15W 260 C3
Tafí Viejo Argentina 26°43S 65°17W 334 B2
Tafihān Iran 29°25N 52°39E 247 D7
Tafilalet Morocco 31°20N 4°45W 260 B4
Tafiré Ivory C. 9°4N 5°4W 262 D3
Tafjord Norway 62°14N 7°24E 164 B4
Tafnidilt Morocco 28°47N 10°58W 260 C2
Tafo Ghana 6°15N 0°20W 263 D4
Tafraoute Morocco 29°50N 8°58W 260 C3
Tafresh Iran 34°45N 49°57E 247 C6
Taft Iran 31°45N 54°14E 247 D7
Taft Phil. 11°57N 125°30E 233 F5
Taft Calif., U.S.A. 35°8N 119°28W 307 K7
Taft Fla., U.S.A. 28°25N 81°21W 133 B2
Taftan Pakistan 29°0N 61°30E 240 C1
Taftān, Kūh-e Iran 28°40N 61°0E 247 D9
Tafu Taiwan 23°37N 121°23E 225 C3
Tafwap India 7°23N 93°42E 245 L11
Taga Samoa 13°46S 172°28W 287 V19
Taga Dzong Bhutan 27°5N 89°55E 241 B2
Tagana-an Phil. 9°42N 125°35E 233 G5
Taganay △ Russia 55°15N 59°48E 216 B5
Taganrog Russia 47°12N 38°50E 189 J10
Taganrogskiy Zaliv Russia 47°0N 38°30E 189 J10
Tagânt □ Mauritania 19°0N 10°0W 260 E3
Tagap Ga Burma 26°56N 96°13E 241 B6
Tagauayan I. Phil. 10°58N 121°13E 232 F3
Tagaung Burma 23°30N 96°2E 241 D6
Tagawa Japan 33°38N 130°51E 222 D2
Tagaytay Phil. 14°6N 120°56E 232 D3
Tagbilaran Phil. 9°39N 123°51E 233 G4
Tagdempt = Tiaret Algeria 35°20N 1°21E 261 A5
Tage Papua N. G. 6°19S 143°20E 286 D2
Tageren Canal Micronesia 9°33N 138°8E 287 R16
Tággia Italy 43°52N 7°51E 198 E4
Taghit Algeria 30°58N 2°0W 261 B4
Tagig → Phil. 14°31N 121°5E 127 B2
Tagish Canada 60°19N 134°16W 296 A2
Tagish L. Canada 60°10N 134°20W 296 A2
Tagkawayan Phil. 13°58N 122°32E 232 E4
Tagliacozzo Italy 42°4N 13°14E 199 F10
Tagliamento → Italy 45°38N 13°6E 199 C10
Táglio di Po Italy 45°0N 12°12E 199 D9
Tagna Colombia 2°24S 70°37W 328 D3
Tago Phil. 9°2N 126°13E 233 G6
Tago, Mt. Phil. 8°23N 125°5E 233 G5
Tagomago Spain 39°2N 1°39E 206 C2
Tagourãret Mauritania 17°45N 7°45W 262 B3
Tagpochau, Mt. N. Marianas 15°11N 145°44E 302 e
Taguatinga Distrito Federal, Brazil 15°51S 48°4W 333 E2
Taguatinga Tocantins, Brazil 12°27S 46°22W 333 D2
Tagudin Phil. 16°56N 120°27E 232 C3
Taguenout Chagguéret Mali 21°14N 0°48W 261 D4
Taguig Phil. 14°31N 121°4E 127 B2
Tagula Papua N. G. 11°22S 153°15E 286 F7
Tagula I. Papua N. G. 11°30S 153°30E 286 F7
Tagum Phil. 7°33N 125°53E 233 H5
Tagus = Tejo → Europe 38°40N 9°24W 195 F2
Tahakopa N.Z. 46°30S 169°23E 285 G4
Tahala Morocco 34°0N 4°28W 260 B4
Tahan, Gunung Malaysia 4°34N 102°17E 237 K4
Tahānah-ye sūr Gol Afghan. 31°43N 67°53E 240 C2
Tahara Japan 34°40N 137°16E 223 C9
Tahat Algeria 23°18N 5°33E 261 D6
Tāherī Iran 27°43N 52°20E 247 E7
Tahgong Pt. N. Marianas 15°6N 145°39E 302 e
Tahifet Algeria 22°58N 6°0E 261 D6
Tahiti French Polynesia 17°37S 149°27W 289 e
Tahlab → Pakistan 28°9N 62°45E 240 C1
Tahlequah U.S.A. 35°55N 94°58W 314 D7
Tahoe, L. U.S.A. 39°6N 120°2W 306 G6
Tahoe City U.S.A. 39°10N 120°9W 306 F6
Tahoka U.S.A. 33°10N 101°48W 314 E4
Taholah U.S.A. 47°21N 124°17W 306 C2
Tahora N.Z. 39°2S 174°49E 284 F3
Tahoua Niger 14°57N 5°16E 263 C6
Tahrir Square Egypt 30°2N 31°14E 117 A2
Tahrūd Iran 29°26N 57°49E 247 D8
Tahsis Canada 49°55N 126°40W 296 D3
Tahta Egypt 26°44N 31°32E 256 B3
Tahtaköprü Turkey 39°57N 29°39E 203 G13
Tahtalı Dağları Turkey 38°20N 36°0E 212 C7
Tahu Taiwan 24°26N 120°52E 225 B2
Tahuamanú → Bolivia 11°6S 67°36W 330 C4
Tahuata, I. French Polynesia 9°57S 139°5W 289 f
Tahulandang Indonesia 2°27N 125°23E 231 D7
Tahuna Indonesia 3°38N 125°30E 231 D7
Taï Ivory C. 5°55N 7°30W 262 D3
Taï △ Ivory C. 5°25N 7°5W 262 D3
Tai Ho Hong Kong, China 22°17N 113°58E 122 B1
Tai Hu China 31°5N 120°10E 229 B13
Tai Lam Chung Res. Hong Kong, China 22°23N 114°1E 122 A2
Tai Lam Country Park ⌂ Hong Kong, China 22°23N 114°0E 122 A2
Tai Lo Shan Hong Kong, China 22°21N 114°13E 122 A3
Tai Long Wan Tsuen Hong Kong, China 22°13N 113°53E 122 B1
Tai Mo Shan Hong Kong, China 22°25N 114°7E 122 A2
Tai O Hong Kong, China 22°15N 113°52E 122 B1
Tai Pang Wan China 22°33N 114°24E 219 a
Tai Po China 22°27N 114°10E 219 a
Tai Po Tsai Hong Kong, China 22°20N 114°15E 122 A3
Tai Rom Yen △ Thailand 8°45N 99°30E 237 H2
Tai Seng Singapore 1°20N 103°53E 138 A3
Tai Shui Hang Hong Kong, China 22°24N 114°12E 122 A3
Tai Tam B. Hong Kong, China 22°12N 114°13E 122 B3
Tai Tam Country Park ⌂ Hong Kong, China 22°15N 114°12E 122 B3
Tai Tam Tuk Res. Hong Kong, China 22°14N 114°13E 122 B3
Tai Wai Hong Kong, China 22°22N 114°10E 122 A3
Tai Wan Tau Hong Kong, China 22°17N 114°17E 122 B3
Tai Wo Hau Hong Kong, China 22°21N 114°7E 122 A2
Tai Yue Shan = Lantau I. Hong Kong, China 22°15N 113°56E 122 B1
Tai'an China 36°12N 117°8E 227 F9
Taiarapu, Presqu'île de Tahiti 17°47S 149°14W 289 e
Taibai Shan China 33°57N 107°45E 226 H4
Taibei = T'aipei Taiwan 25°4N 121°29E 225 A3
Taibique Canary Is. 27°42N 17°58W 153 e1
Taibus Qi China 41°54N 115°22E 226 D8
Taicang China 31°30N 121°5E 229 B13
Taichow = Taizhou China 32°28N 119°55E 229 A12
T'aichung Taiwan 24°9N 120°37E 225 B2
Taieri → N.Z. 46°3S 170°12E 285 G5
Taigu China 37°28N 112°30E 226 F7
Taihang Shan China 36°0N 113°30E 226 G7
Taihape N.Z. 39°41S 175°48E 284 F4
Taihe Anhui, China 33°20N 115°42E 226 H8
Taihe Jiangxi, China 26°47N 114°52E 229 D10
Taihoku = T'aipei Taiwan 25°4N 121°29E 225 A3
Taihsi Taiwan 23°51N 120°16E 225 C2
Taihu China 30°22N 116°20E 229 B11
Taijiang China 26°39N 108°21E 228 D7
Taikang China 34°5N 114°50E 226 G8
Taikkyi Burma 17°20N 96°0E 241 G6
Tailem Bend Australia 35°12S 139°29E 282 C3
Tailfingen Germany 48°15N 9°1E 179 G5
T'ailuko Taiwan 24°9N 121°37E 225 B3
T'aimali Taiwan 22°36N 121°0E 225 D3
Taimyr Peninsula = Taymyr, Poluostrov Russia 75°0N 100°0E 215 B11
Tain U.K. 57°49N 4°4W 167 D4
Tainaka Japan 34°36N 135°35E 133 B2
T'ainan Taiwan 23°0N 120°10E 225 D2
T'ainan □ Taiwan 23°15N 120°20E 225 C2
Tainggyo Burma 17°49N 94°29E 241 G5
Taining China 26°54N 117°9E 229 D11
Taiobeiras Brazil 15°49S 42°14W 333 E3
Taipa China 22°10N 113°35E 219 a
T'aipei Taiwan 25°4N 121°29E 225 A3
T'aipei □ Taiwan 24°50N 121°35E 225 B3
Taiping Anhui, China 30°15N 118°6E 229 B12
Taiping Malaysia 4°51N 100°44E 237 K3
Taiping Dao = Itu Aba I. S. China Sea 10°23N 114°21E 230 B4
Taipingchuan China 44°23N 123°11E 227 B12
Taipingzhen China 33°35N 111°42E 226 H6
Taipu Brazil 5°37S 35°36W 332 C4
Tairenpokpi India 24°39N 93°40E 241 C4
Tairua N.Z. 37°0S 175°51E 284 D4
Tais Indonesia 4°6S 102°34E 234 C2
Taisha Japan 35°24N 132°40E 222 B4
Taishan Guangdong, China 22°14N 112°41E 229 F9
Taishan Shandong, China 36°25N 117°20E 227 F9
Taishō Japan 34°38N 135°27E 133 B1
Taishun China 27°30N 119°42E 229 D12
Taita Hills Kenya 3°25S 38°15E 268 C4
Taitao, C. Chile 45°53S 75°5W 336 C1
Taitao, Pen. de Chile 46°30S 75°0W 336 C2
T'aitung Taiwan 22°43N 121°4E 225 D3
T'aitung □ Taiwan 23°0N 121°0E 225 D3
Taivalkoski Finland 65°33N 28°12E 160 D23
Taiwan ■ Asia 23°30N 121°0E 225 C3
Taiwan Strait Asia 24°40N 120°0E 229 E12
Taixi = Taihsi Taiwan 23°51N 120°16E 225 C2
Taixing China 32°11N 120°0E 229 A13
Taiyara Sudan 13°12N 30°47E 257 E3
Taiyiba Israel 32°36N 35°27E 250 F6
Taiyuan China 37°52N 112°33E 226 F7
Taizhong = T'aichung Taiwan 24°9N 120°37E 225 B2
Taizhou Jiangsu, China 32°28N 119°55E 229 A12
Taizhou Zhejiang, China 28°40N 121°24E 229 C13
Taizhou Liedao China 28°30N 121°55E 229 C13
Ta'izz Yemen 13°35N 44°2E 248 D4
Ta'izz □ Yemen 13°35N 44°2E 248 D4
Taj Mahal India 27°10N 78°2E 242 F8
Tājābād Iran 30°2N 54°24E 247 D7
Tajapuru, Furo do Brazil 1°50S 50°25W 332 B1
Tajarhī Libya 24°21N 14°28E 258 D2
Tajen Taiwan 22°17N 120°53E 225 D2
Tajikistan ■ Asia 38°30N 70°0E 217 E8
Tajima = Minamiaizu Japan 37°12N 139°46E 221 F9
Tajimi Japan 35°19N 137°8E 223 B9
Tajo = Tejo → Europe 38°40N 9°24W 195 F2
Tajrīsh Iran 35°48N 51°25E 141 A2
Tajumulco, Vol. Guatemala 15°2N 91°55W 320 C1
Tājūrā Libya 32°51N 13°21E 258 B2
Tak Thailand 16°52N 99°8E 236 D2
Takāb Iran 36°24N 47°7E 213 D12
Takabanare-shima Japan 26°22N 127°59E 288 a
Takabba Kenya 3°21N 40°13E 267 D5
Takachiho Japan 32°42N 131°18E 222 E3
Takachu Botswana 22°37S 21°58E 270 B3
Takada Japan 37°7N 138°15E 221 F9
Takahagi Japan 36°43N 140°45E 221 F10
Takahashi Japan 34°51N 133°39E 222 C5
Takaido Japan 35°40N 139°37E 140 A2
Takaishi Japan 35°36N 139°31E 140 B2
Takaka N.Z. 40°51S 172°50E 285 A7
Takaki = Yamato Japan 35°27N 139°25E 223 B11
Takalar Indonesia 5°28S 119°24E 235 D5
Takalous, O. → Algeria 22°36N 7°21E 261 D6
Takamaka Seychelles 4°50S 55°30E 272 c
Takamatsu Japan 34°20N 134°5E 222 C6
Takanabe Japan 32°8N 131°30E 222 E3
Takangkou Taiwan 23°28N 121°29E 225 C3
Takaoka Japan 36°47N 137°0E 223 A9
Takapau N.Z. 40°2S 176°21E 284 G5
Takapuna N.Z. 36°47S 174°47E 284 C3
Takarazuka Japan 34°47N 135°20E 133 A1
Takaroa French Polynesia 14°28S 144°58W 289 f
Takasago Japan 35°44N 139°52E 140 A4
Takasaki Japan 36°20N 139°0E 223 A11
Takashima Japan 35°24N 136°2E 223 B8
Takatsu Japan 35°36N 139°37E 140 B2
Takatsuki Japan 34°51N 135°37E 223 C7
Takaungu Kenya 3°38S 39°52E 268 C4
Takayama Japan 36°18N 137°11E 223 A9
Takayama-Bonchi Japan 36°0N 137°18E 223 B9
Take-Shima Japan 30°49N 130°26E 221 J5
Takefu = Echizen Japan 35°50N 136°10E 223 B8
Takehara Japan 34°21N 132°55E 222 C4
Takengon Indonesia 4°45N 96°50E 234 B1
Takeo Cambodia 10°59N 104°47E 237 G5
Takeo Japan 33°12N 130°1E 222 D2
Tåkern Sweden 58°22N 14°45E 163 F8
Takeshima = Liancourt Rocks Asia 37°15N 131°52E 221 F5
Takeshita Japan 35°33N 139°32E 140 B2
Tākestān Iran 36°0N 49°40E 247 C6
Taketa Japan 32°58N 131°24E 222 E3
Takh India 33°6N 77°32E 243 C7
Takhār □ Afghan. 36°40N 70°0E 240 A3
Takhiatash Uzbekistan 42°20N 59°33E 216 D5
Takhmau Cambodia 11°29N 104°57E 237 G5
Takht-e Soleyman Iran 36°36N 47°14E 213 D12
Takht-Sulaiman Pakistan 31°40N 69°58E 242 D3
Taki Papua N. G. 6°29S 155°52E 286 D8
Takiéta Niger 13°41N 8°32E 263 C6
Takikawa Japan 43°33N 141°54E 220 C10
Takinegawa Japan 35°45N 139°44E 140 A3
Takla L. Canada 55°15N 125°45W 296 B3
Takla Landing Canada 55°30N 125°50W 296 B3
Taklamakan China 38°0N 83°0E 217 E10
Taklamakan Shamo = Taklamakan China 38°0N 83°0E 217 E10
Takoma Park U.S.A. 38°58N 77°0W 143 B2
Takotna U.S.A. 62°59N 156°4W 303 E8
Taksim Turkey 41°2N 28°58E 122 B1
Taksimo Russia 56°20N 114°52E 215 D12
Taku Japan 33°18N 130°3E 222 D2
Taku → Canada 58°30N 133°50W 296 B2
Takua Thung Thailand 8°24N 98°27E 237 a
Takum India 27°47N 93°37E 241 B4
Takum Nigeria 7°18N 9°36E 263 D6
Takume French Polynesia 15°49S 142°12W 289 f
Takundi Dem. Rep. of the Congo 4°45S 16°34E 265 C3
Takutu → Guyana 3°30N 60°29W 329 C5
Tal Halāl Iran 28°54N 55°1E 247 D7
Tala Uruguay 34°21S 55°46W 335 C4
Talachyn Belarus 54°25N 29°42E 188 E5
Talacogan Phil. 8°32N 125°39E 233 G5
Talagang Pakistan 32°55N 72°25E 242 C5
Talagante Chile 33°40S 70°50W 334 C1
Talahouhait Algeria 24°52N 1°5E 261 D5
Talaide Portugal 38°44N 9°18W 126 A1
Talaimannar Sri Lanka 9°6N 79°43E 245 K4
Talaïnt Morocco 29°41N 9°40W 260 C3
Talak Niger 18°0N 5°0E 263 B6
Talakag Phil. 8°16N 124°37E 233 G5
Talamanca, Cordillera de Cent. Amer. 9°20N 83°20W 320 E3
Talampaya △ Argentina 29°43S 67°42W 334 B2
Talangbetutu Indonesia 2°53S 104°41E 234 C2
Talant France 47°19N 4°58E 173 E11
Talara Peru 4°38S 81°18W 330 A1
Talas Kyrgyzstan 42°30N 72°13E 217 D8
Talas Turkey 38°41N 35°33E 212 C6
Talas □ Kyrgyzstan 42°20N 72°0E 217 D8
Talas → Kazakhstan 44°0N 70°20E 217 D8
Talas Ala Too Kyrgyzstan 42°15N 72°0E 217 D8
Talasea Papua N. G. 5°20S 150°2E 286 C6
Talasskiy Alatau = Talas Ala Too Kyrgyzstan 42°15N 72°0E 217 D8
Talâta Egypt 30°36N 32°20E 251 H3
Talata Mafara Nigeria 12°38N 6°4E 263 C6
Talaud, Kepulauan Indonesia 4°30N 126°50E 231 D7
Talaud Is. = Talaud, Kepulauan Indonesia 4°30N 126°50E 231 D7
Talavera de la Reina Spain 39°55N 4°46W 194 F6
Talavera la Real Spain 38°53N 6°46W 195 G4
Talawgyi Burma 25°4N 97°19E 241 C6
Talayan Phil. 6°52N 124°24E 233 H5
Talayuela Spain 39°59N 5°36W 194 F5
Talbandh India 22°3N 86°20E 243 H12
Talbert, Sillon de France 48°53N 3°5W 172 D3
Talbot Australia 37°10S 143°44E 282 D5
Talbot, C. Australia 13°48S 126°43E 278 B4
Talbotton U.S.A. 32°41N 84°32W 316 C5
Talbragar → Australia 32°12S 148°37E 283 B8
Talca Chile 35°28S 71°40W 334 D1
Talcahuano Chile 36°40S 73°10W 334 D1
Talcher India 21°0N 85°18E 244 D7
Talcho Niger 14°44N 3°28E 263 C5
Taldy Kurgan = Taldyqorghan Kazakhstan 45°10N 78°45E 217 C9
Taldyqorghan Kazakhstan 45°10N 78°45E 217 C9
Tālesh Iran 37°58N 48°58E 213 D13
Tālesh, Kūhhā-ye Iran 37°42N 48°55E 213 D13
Talgar = Talghar Kazakhstan 43°19N 77°15E 217 D9
Talghar Kazakhstan 43°19N 77°15E 217 D9
Talguharai Sudan 18°19N 35°56E 256 D4
Talguppa India 14°13N 74°56E 245 G2
Tali Post South Sudan 5°55N 30°44E 257 F3
Taliabu Indonesia 1°50S 125°0E 231 E6
Taliao Taiwan 22°36N 120°23E 225 D2
Talibon Phil. 10°9N 124°20E 233 F5
Talichien Taiwan 24°58N 121°55E 225 B3
Taliganga India 22°30N 88°22E 124 B2
Talihina U.S.A. 34°45N 95°3W 314 D7
Talikota India 16°29N 76°17E 245 F3
Talikud I. Phil. 6°56N 125°41E 233 H5
Talin Taiwan 23°36N 120°27E 225 C2
Talipapa Phil. 14°41N 121°1E 127 A2
Talipaw Phil. 5°59N 121°7E 233 J3
Talipparamba India 12°3N 75°21E 245 H2
Talisay Phil. 10°44N 122°58E 233 F4
Talisayan Phil. 9°0N 124°55E 233 G5
Taliwang Indonesia 8°50S 116°55E 235 D5
Talkeetna U.S.A. 62°20N 150°6W 303 E10
Talkha Egypt 31°3N 31°22E 251 G2
Tálknafjörður Iceland 65°34N 24°0W 155 B2
Talkot Nepal 29°37N 81°19E 243 E9
Tall 'Afar Iraq 36°22N 42°27E 213 D10
Tall Kalakh Syria 34°41N 36°15E 250 D7
Tall Kayf Iraq 36°29N 43°7E 213 D10
Talla Egypt 28°5N 30°43E 256 B3
Talladega U.S.A. 33°26N 86°6W 316 B3
Tallaganda △ Australia 35°29S 149°37E 283 C8
Tallaght Ireland 53°17N 6°22W 120 B1
Tallahassee U.S.A. 30°27N 84°17W 316 E5
Tallangatta Australia 36°15S 147°19E 283 D7
Tallapoosa U.S.A. 33°45N 85°17W 316 B4
Tallapoosa → U.S.A. 32°30N 86°16W 316 C3
Tallard France 44°28N 6°3E 175 D10
Tallarook Australia 37°5S 145°6E 283 D6
Tallassee U.S.A. 32°32N 85°54W 316 C4
Tällberg Sweden 60°51N 15°2E 162 D9
Tallering Pk. Australia 28°6S 115°37E 279 E2
Talli Pakistan 29°32N 68°8E 242 E3
Tallinn Estonia 59°22N 24°48E 188 C3
Tallkrogen Sweden 59°16N 18°4E 139 B2
Tallmadge U.S.A. 41°6N 81°27W 312 E3
Tallulah U.S.A. 32°25N 91°11W 314 E9
Tălmaciu Romania 45°38N 24°19E 183 E9
Talmest Morocco 31°48N 9°21W 260 B3
Talmont-St-Hilaire France 46°27N 1°37W 174 B2
Talnakh Russia 69°29N 88°22E 215 C9
Talne Ukraine 48°50N 30°44E 189 H6
Talnoye = Talne Ukraine 48°50N 30°44E 189 H6
Taloda India 21°34N 74°11E 244 D2
Talodi Sudan 10°35N 30°22E 257 E3
Talofofo Guam 13°21N 144°45E 302 d
Tāloqān Afghan. 36°44N 69°33E 240 A3
Talovaya Russia 51°6N 40°45E 190 E5
Taloyoak Canada 69°32N 93°32W 294 D13
Talpa de Allende Mexico 20°23N 104°51W 318 C4
Talparo Trin. & Tob. 10°30N 61°17W 323 t
Talparo → Trin. & Tob. 10°34N 61°17W 323 t
Talquin, L. U.S.A. 30°23N 84°39W 316 E5
Talsi Latvia 57°10N 22°30E 184 A9
Talsi □ Latvia 57°20N 22°40E 184 A9
Talsinnt Morocco 32°33N 3°27W 261 B4
Taltal Chile 25°23S 70°33W 334 B1
Taltson → Canada 61°24N 112°46W 296 A6
Talu Indonesia 0°13N 99°58E 234 B1
Taluk Indonesia 0°31S 101°34E 234 C2
Talwood Australia 28°29S 149°29E 281 D4
Talyawalka Cr. → Australia 32°28S 142°22E 282 B5
Tam Dao △ Vietnam 21°45N 105°45E 236 B5
Tam Ky Vietnam 15°34N 108°29E 236 E7
Tam Quan Vietnam 14°35N 109°3E 236 E7
Tama Tōkyō, Japan 35°38N 139°26E 140 B1
Tama Iowa, U.S.A. 41°58N 92°35W 310 C4
Tama → Japan 35°32N 139°39E 140 B2
Tama ⌂ Ethiopia 5°55N 36°5E 257 F4
Tama Abu, Banjaran Malaysia 3°50N 115°5E 235 B5
Tama Kyūryō Japan 35°34N 139°30E 140 B2
Tamada Algeria 21°34N 3°20E 261 D5
Tamaden Japan 35°39N 139°38E 140 B2
Tamagawa-josui → Japan 35°41N 139°47E 140 A1
Tamakautoga Cook Is. 19°5S 169°55W 289 g
Tamalameque Colombia 8°52N 73°49W 328 B3
Tamale Ghana 9°22N 0°50W 263 D4
Taman Russia 45°14N 36°41E 189 K9
Taman Negara △ Malaysia 4°38N 102°26E 237 K4
Taman Sari Indonesia 6°8S 106°48E 122 A1
T'aman Shan Taiwan 24°42N 121°27E 225 B3
Tamana Japan 32°58N 130°32E 222 E2
Tamana Kiribati 2°30S 175°59E 277 A14
Tamana, Mt. Trin. & Tob. 10°28N 61°12W 323 t
Tamanar Morocco 31°1N 9°46W 260 B3
Tamanduateí → Brazil 23°37S 46°38W 137 B2
Tamanhint Libya 27°13N 14°37E 258 C2
Tamani Mali 13°20N 6°50W 262 C3
Tamano Japan 34°29N 133°59E 222 C5
Tamanrasset Algeria 22°50N 5°30E 261 D6
Tamanrasset □ Algeria 23°45N 4°40E 261 D5
Tamanrasset, O. → Algeria 22°0N 2°0E 261 D5
Tamanthi Burma 25°19N 95°17E 241 C5
Tamaqua U.S.A. 40°48N 75°58W 313 F9
Tamar → U.K. 50°27N 4°15W 169 G3
Támara Colombia 5°50N 72°10W 328 B3
Tamarac U.S.A. 26°12N 80°15W 129 A1
Tamarin Mauritius 20°19S 57°20E 272 e
Tamarinda Spain 39°55N 3°49E 206 B4
Tamarite de Litera Spain 41°52N 0°25E 196 D5
Tamaroa U.S.A. 38°8N 89°14W 310 F7
Tamashima Japan 34°32N 133°40E 222 C5
Tamási Hungary 46°40N 18°18E 182 D3
Tamaské Niger 14°49N 5°43E 263 C6
Tamatave = Toamasina Madag. 18°10S 49°25E 272 B2
Tamaulipas □ Mexico 24°0N 98°45W 319 C5
Tamaulipas, Sierra de Mexico 23°30N 98°20W 319 C5
Tamazula Mexico 24°57N 106°57W 318 C3
Tamazunchale Mexico 21°16N 98°47W 319 C5
Tamba-Dabatou Guinea 11°50N 10°40W 262 C2
Tambach Kenya 0°36N 35°31E 268 B4
Tambacounda Senegal 13°45N 13°40W 262 C2
Tambacounda □ Senegal 14°0N 13°0W 262 C2
Tambaram India 12°55N 80°7E 245 H5
Tambea Solomon Is. 9°16S 159°41E 287 M10
Tambelan, Kepulauan Indonesia 1°0N 107°30E 235 B3
Tambellup Australia 34°4S 117°37E 279 F2
Tambo Queens., Australia 24°54S 146°14E 280 C4
Tambo Peru 12°57S 74°1W 330 C3
Tambo → Peru 10°42S 73°47W 330 C3
Tambo de Mora Peru 13°30S 76°8W 330 C2
Tambobamba Peru 13°54S 72°8W 330 C3
Tamboerskloof S. Africa 33°56S 18°25E 118 A1
Tambohorano Madag. 17°30S 43°58E 272 B1
Tambopata → Peru 13°21S 69°36W 330 C4
Tambora Jakarta, Indonesia 6°8S 106°47E 122 A1
Tambora Nusa Tenggara Barat, Indonesia 8°12S 118°5E 235 D5
Tamboritha, Mt. Australia 37°31S 146°40E 283 D7
Tamboura C.A.R. 5°10N 25°12E 264 A5
Tambov Russia 52°45N 41°28E 190 D5
Tambov □ Russia 52°50N 41°20E 190 D5
Tambre → Spain 42°49N 8°53W 194 C2
Tambuku Indonesia 7°8S 113°40E 235 D4
Tambul Papua N. G. 5°54S 143°54E 286 C2
Tambunar Malaysia 5°43N 116°24E 235 A5
Tambura South Sudan 5°40N 27°25E 257 F2
Tambuyukan, Gunong Malaysia 6°13N 116°39E 235 A5
Tâmchekket Mauritania 17°25N 10°40W 262 B2
Tame Colombia 6°28N 71°44W 328 B3
Tâmega → Portugal 41°5N 8°21W 194 D2
Tamegroute Morocco 30°15N 5°39W 260 B3
Tamelelt Morocco 31°50N 7°32W 260 B3
Tamenglong India 25°0N 93°35E 241 C4
Tamerza Tunisia 34°23N 7°58E 258 B1
Tamgak, Adrar Niger 19°12N 8°35E 259 E1
Tamgué, Massif du Guinea 12°0N 12°18W 262 C2
Tami Is. Papua N. G. 6°46S 147°55E 286 D4
Tamiahua, L. de Mexico 21°35N 97°35W 319 C5
Tamiami Canal U.S.A. 25°50N 81°0W 317 K8
Tamianglayang Indonesia 2°7S 115°10E 235 C5
Tamil Nadu □ India 11°0N 77°0E 245 J3
Tamis → Serbia 44°51N 20°39E 182 F5
Tamiya Egypt 29°29N 30°58E 256 J7
Tamlelt, Plaine de Morocco 32°30N 2°20W 261 B4
Tamluk India 22°18N 87°58E 243 H12
Tammerfors = Tampere Finland 61°30N 23°50E 188 B2
Tammisalo Finland 60°11N 25°5E 121 B3
Tammūh Egypt 29°55N 31°15E 117 B2
Tämnaren Sweden 60°10N 17°25E 162 D11
Tampa Angola 15°30S 13°27E 265 F2
Tampa Fla., U.S.A. 27°56N 82°27W 317 H7
Tampa, Tanjung Indonesia 8°55S 116°12E 231 K19
Tampa B. U.S.A. 27°50N 82°30W 317 H7
Tampa Int. ✈ (TPA) U.S.A. 27°59N 82°32W 317 H7
Tamparan Phil. 7°53N 124°20E 233 H5
Tampere Finland 61°30N 23°50E 188 B2
Tampico Tamaulipas, Mexico 22°13N 97°51W 319 C5
Tampico Ill., U.S.A. 41°38N 89°47W 310 C7
Tampin Malaysia 2°28N 102°13E 237 L4
Tampines Singapore 1°21N 103°56E 138 A3
Tampoi Malaysia 1°30N 103°39E 237 d
Tamrah Si. Arabia 20°24N 45°25E 248 B4
Tamri Morocco 30°49N 9°50W 260 B3
Tamrida = Qādub Yemen 12°37N 53°57E 249 D6
Tamsagbulag Mongolia 47°14N 117°21E 219 B12
Tamsweg Austria 47°7N 13°49E 180 D6
Tamu Burma 24°13N 94°12E 241 C5
Tamuja → Spain 39°38N 6°29W 195 F4
Tamuning Guam 13°29N 144°47E 302 d
Tamworth N.S.W., Australia 31°7S 150°58E 283 A9
Tamworth Ont., Canada 44°29N 77°0W 312 B8
Tamworth Staffs., U.K. 52°39N 1°41W 169 E6
Tan An Vietnam 10°32N 106°25E 237 G6
Tan Chau Vietnam 10°48N 105°12E 237 G5
T'an-do N. Korea 39°30N 124°41E 224 C2
Tan Hiep Vietnam 10°27N 106°21E 237 G6
Tan Iddah Algeria 26°33N 9°42E 261 C6
Tan-Tan Morocco 28°29N 11°1W 260 C2
Tan Yen Vietnam 22°4N 105°3E 236 A5
Tana → Coast, Kenya 2°32S 40°31E 268 C5
Tana → Finnmark, Norway 70°30N 28°14E 160 A23
Tana, L. Ethiopia 13°5N 37°30E 257 E4
Tana River Primate ⌂ Kenya 1°55S 40°7E 268 C5
Tanabe Japan 33°44N 135°22E 223 D7
Tanabi Brazil 20°37S 49°37W 333 F2
Tanacross U.S.A. 63°23N 143°21W 303 E12
Tanafjorden Norway 70°45N 28°25E 160 A23
Tanaga I. U.S.A. 51°48N 177°53W 303 L3
Tanaga Volcano U.S.A. 51°53N 178°8W 303 L3
Tanah Abang Indonesia 6°12S 106°48E 122 B1
Tanah Kusir Indonesia 6°15S 106°46E 122 B1
Tanah Merah Malaysia 5°48N 102°9E 237 K4
Tanahbala Indonesia 0°30S 98°30E 234 C1
Tanahgrogot Indonesia 1°55S 116°15E 235 C5
Tanahjampea Indonesia 7°10S 120°35E 231 F6
Tanahmasa Indonesia 0°12S 98°39E 234 C1
Tanahmerah Indonesia 6°5S 140°16E 231 F10
Tanahputih Indonesia 1°40N 101°3E 234 B2
Tanakpur India 29°5N 80°7E 243 E9
Tanamalwila Sri Lanka 6°26N 81°8E 245 L5
Tanami Desert Australia 18°50S 132°0E 278 C5
Tanana U.S.A. 65°10N 152°4W 303 D9
Tanana → U.S.A. 65°10N 151°58W 303 D10
Tananarive = Antananarivo Madag. 18°55S 47°31E 272 B2
Tananger Norway 58°57N 5°37E 164 F2
Tanant Morocco 31°54N 6°56W 260 B3
Tanapag N. Marianas 15°14N 145°45E 302 e
Tànaro → Italy 44°55N 8°40E 198 D5
Tanauan Phil. 14°5N 121°10E 232 D3
Tanay Phil. 14°30N 121°17E 232 D3
Tanba-Sanchi Japan 35°7N 135°48E 223 B7
Tancheng China 34°25N 118°20E 227 G10
Tanch'ŏn N. Korea 40°27N 128°54E 224 B4
Tanda Ut. P., India 26°33N 82°35E 243 F10
Tanda Ut. P., India 28°57N 78°56E 243 E8
Tanda Ivory C. 7°48N 3°10W 262 D4
Tandag Phil. 9°4N 126°9E 233 G6
Tandaia Tanzania 9°25S 34°15E 269 D3
Tăndărei Romania 44°39N 27°40E 183 F12
Tandaué Angola 16°58S 18°5E 265 F3
Tandil Argentina 37°15S 59°6W 334 D4
Tandil, Sa. del Argentina 37°30S 59°0W 334 D4
Tandin Burma 19°33N 93°58E 241 F4
Tandjilé □ Chad 9°30N 16°30E 259 G3
Tandjilé → Chad 9°45N 15°50E 259 G3
Tandlianwala Pakistan 31°3N 73°9E 242 D5
Tando Adam Pakistan 25°45N 68°40E 242 G3
Tando Allahyar Pakistan 25°28N 68°43E 242 G3
Tando Bago Pakistan 24°47N 68°58E 242 G3
Tando Mohommed Khan Pakistan 25°8N 68°32E 242 G3
Tando-Zinze Angola 5°22S 12°30E 265 D2
Tandou-Bengou Congo 3°50S 11°44E 264 C2
Tandou L. Australia 32°40S 142°5E 282 B5
Tandoureh △ Iran 37°50N 59°0E 247 B8
Tandragee U.K. 54°21N 6°24W 166 B5
Tandsjöborg Sweden 61°42N 14°43E 162 C8
Tandubas Phil. 5°8N 120°20E 233 J3
Tandula → India 21°6N 81°14E 244 D5
Tandula Tank India 20°40N 81°12E 244 D5
Tandur Andhra Pradesh, India 19°11N 79°30E 244 E4
Tandur Andhra Pradesh, India 17°14N 77°35E 244 F3
Tane-Ga-Shima Japan 30°30N 131°0E 221 J5
Taneatua N.Z. 38°4S 177°1E 284 E6
Tanen Tong Dan = Dawna Ra. Burma 16°30N 98°30E 236 D2
Tanew → Poland 50°29N 22°16E 185 H9
Tanezrouft Algeria 23°9N 0°11E 261 D5
Tanezzuft, W. → Libya 25°51N 10°19E 258 C2
Tang, Koh Cambodia 10°16N 103°7E 237 G4
Tang, Ra's-e Iran 25°21N 59°52E 247 E8
Tang Krasang Cambodia 12°34N 105°3E 236 F5
Tanga Tanzania 5°5S 39°2E 268 D4
Tanga □ Tanzania 5°20S 38°0E 268 D4
Tanga Is. Papua N. G. 3°20S 153°15E 286 B7
Tanga Langua Grenada 12°14N 61°39W 323 q
Tangail Bangla. 24°15N 89°55E 241 C2
Tangalla Sri Lanka 6°1N 80°48E 245 L5
Tanganyika = Tanzania ■ Africa 6°0S 34°0E 268 D3
Tanganyika, L. Africa 6°40S 30°0E 268 D3
Tangará da Serra Brazil 14°50S 57°47W 331 C6
Tangarare Solomon Is. 9°36S 159°41E 287 M10
Tangasseri India 8°53N 76°35E 245 K3
Tangaza Nigeria 13°19N 4°55E 263 C5
Tangelo Park U.S.A. 28°27N 81°26W 133 B2
Tangen Norway 60°37N 11°15E 164 D8
Tanger Morocco 35°50N 5°49W 260 A3
Tanger-Med Morocco 35°53N 5°30W 195 K5
Tanger-Tétouan □ Morocco 35°50N 5°50W 260 A3
Tangerang Indonesia 6°11S 106°37E 234 D3
Tangerhütte Germany 52°26N 11°48E 178 C7
Tangermünde Germany 52°33N 11°58E 178 C7
Tanggu China 39°2N 117°40E 227 E9
Tanggula Shan China 32°40N 92°10E 218 E7
Tanggula Shankou China 32°42N 92°27E 218 E7
Tanghe China 32°47N 112°50E 229 A9
Tanghla Range = Tanggula Shan China 32°40N 92°10E 218 E7
Tangi India 19°56N 85°24E 244 E7
Tangier = Tanger Morocco 35°50N 5°49W 260 A3
Tangjia China 22°22N 113°35E 219 a
Tangjia Wan China 22°21N 113°36E 219 a
Tango-Hantō Japan 35°45N 135°10E 223 B7
Tangorin Australia 21°47S 144°12E 280 C3
Tangorombohitr'i Makay Madag. 21°0S 45°15E 272 C2
Tangra Yumco China 31°0N 86°38E 218 E6
Tangshan China 39°38N 118°10E 227 E10
Tangtou China 35°28N 118°30E 227 G10
Tangub Phil. 8°3N 123°44E 233 G4
Tanguen-Dassouri Burkina Faso 12°16N 1°42W 263 C4
Tanguiéta Benin 10°35N 1°21E 263 C5
Tangxi China 29°3N 119°25E 229 C12
Tangyan He → China 28°54N 108°19E 228 C7
Tangyin China 35°54N 114°21E 226 G8
Taniantaweng Shan China 31°20N 98°0E 228 B2
Tanimbar, Kepulauan Indonesia 7°30S 131°30E 231 F8
Tanimbar Is. = Tanimbar, Kepulauan Indonesia 7°30S 131°30E 231 F8
Tanintharyi = Tenasserim Burma 12°6N 99°3E 237 F2
Tanis Egypt 31°0N 31°54E 251 H2
Tanjay Phil. 9°30N 123°5E 233 G4
Tanjong Pelepas Malaysia 1°21N 103°33E 237 d
Tanjong Po Malaysia 1°45N 110°30E 235 B4
Tanjore = Thanjavur India 10°48N 79°12E 245 J4
Tanjung Kalimantan Selatan, Indonesia 2°10S 115°25E 235 C5
Tanjung Nusa Tenggara Barat, Indonesia 8°21S 116°9E 231 J19
Tanjung Datu △ Malaysia 2°13N 109°3E 235 B3
Tanjung Duren Indonesia 6°10S 106°46E 122 B1
Tanjung Malim Malaysia 3°42N 101°31E 237 L3
Tanjung Priok Indonesia 6°6S 106°52E 122 A2
Tanjung Putung △ Indonesia 2°54S 111°59E 235 C4
Tanjung Tokong Malaysia 5°28N 100°18E 237 c
Tanjungbalai Kepulauan Riau, Indonesia 1°0N 103°25E 234 B2
Tanjungbalai Sumatera Utara, Indonesia 2°55N 99°44E 234 B1
Tanjungbatu Kalimantan Selatan, Indonesia 3°0S 116°13E 235 C5
Tanjungbatu Kalimantan Timur, Indonesia 2°23N 118°3E 235 B5
Tanjungbatu Kepulauan Riau, Indonesia 0°37N 103°25E 234 B2
Tanjungkarang Telukbetung = Bandar Lampung Indonesia 5°20S 105°10E 234 D3
Tanjungpandan Indonesia 2°43S 107°38E 234 C3
Tanjungpinang Indonesia 1°5N 104°30E 234 B2
Tanjungpriok Indonesia 6°8S 106°55E 234 D3
Tanjungraja Indonesia 3°21S 104°46E 234 C2
Tanjungredeb Indonesia 2°9N 117°29E 235 B5
Tanjungselor Indonesia 2°55N 117°25E 235 B5
Tank Pakistan 32°14N 70°25E 242 C4
Tankhala India 21°58N 73°47E 242 J5
Tankwa-Karoo △ S. Africa 32°14S 19°50E 270 D2
Tanlu Taiwan 22°12N 120°44E 225 D2
Tanna Vanuatu 19°30S 169°20E 287 J7
Tännäs Sweden 62°26N 12°42E 162 B6
Tannersville U.S.A. 41°3N 75°18W 313 E9
Tannis Bugt Denmark 57°40N 10°15E 163 G4
Tannu Ola Asia 51°0N 94°0E 217 B12
Tannum Sands Australia 23°57S 151°22E 280 C5
Tano → Ghana 5°7N 2°56W 262 D4
Tanombella Algeria 25°30N 5°49E 261 C6
Tanon Str. Phil. 10°20N 123°30E 233 F4
Tanout Niger 14°50N 8°55E 259 F1
Tanquinho Brazil 11°58S 39°6W 333 D4
Tanshui Taiwan 25°10N 121°28E 225 A3
Tanshui Kang → Taiwan 25°10N 121°28E 225 A3
Tansilla Burkina Faso 12°25N 4°23W 262 C4
Tansing Nepal 27°52N 83°33E 243 F10
Tanta Egypt 30°45N 30°57E 256 H7
Tantabin Burma 17°1N 95°59E 241 G5
Tantoyuca Mexico 21°21N 98°14W 319 C5
Tantung = Dandong China 40°10N 124°20E 224 B2
T'antzu Taiwan 24°13N 120°42E 225 B2
Tanuku India 16°45N 81°44E 244 F5
Tanum Norway 59°53N 10°28E 133 A1
Tanūmah Si. Arabia 18°58N 42°10E 248 C3
Tanumshede Sweden 58°42N 11°20E 163 F5
Tanunda Australia 34°30S 139°0E 282 C3
Tanur India 11°1N 75°52E 245 J2
Tanus France 44°8N 2°19E 174 D6
Tanzania ■ Africa 6°0S 34°0E 268 D3
Tanzawa-Sanchi Japan 35°27N 139°0E 223 B11
Tanzhou China 22°16N 113°28E 219 a
Tanzi = T'antzu Taiwan 24°13N 120°42E 225 B2
Tanzilla → Canada 58°8N 130°43W 296 B2
Tao, Ko Thailand 10°5N 99°52E 237 G2
Tao'an = Taonan China 45°22N 122°40E 227 B12
Tao'er He → China 45°45N 124°5E 227 B13
Taohua Dao China 29°50N 122°20E 229 C14
Taolanaro Madag. 25°2S 47°0E 272 D2
Taole China 38°48N 106°40E 226 E4
Taonan China 45°22N 122°40E 227 B12
Taora Solomon Is. 7°21S 157°20E 287 L9
Taormina Italy 37°51N 15°17E 201 E8
Taos U.S.A. 36°24N 105°35W 305 H11
Taoudenni Mali 22°40N 3°55W 260 D4
Taoudrart, Adrar Algeria 24°25N 2°24E 261 D5
Taounate Morocco 34°25N 4°41W 260 B3
Taourirt Algeria 26°37N 0°20E 261 C5
Taourirt Morocco 34°20N 2°53W 261 B4
Taouz Morocco 30°53N 4°0W 260 B4

Taoyuan *Hunan, China* 28°55N 111°16E **229** C8
T'aoyüan *Kaohsiung, Taiwan* 23°9N 120°46E **225** C2
T'aoyüan *Yünlin, Taiwan* 25°0N 121°4E **225** B3
T'aoyüan □ *Taiwan* 24°55N 121°15E **225** B3
**Tap Shek Kok** *Hong Kong, China* 22°23N 113°55E **122** A1
**Tapa** *Estonia* 59°15N 25°50E **161** G21
**Tapa Shan = Daba Shan** *China* 32°0N 109°0E **228** B7
**Tapachula** *Mexico* 14°54N 92°17W **319** E6
**Tapada** *Portugal* 38°49N 9°16W **126** A1
**Tapah** *Malaysia* 4°12N 101°15E **237** K3
**Tapajós** → *Brazil* 2°24S 54°41W **329** D7
**Tapaktuan** *Indonesia* 3°15N 97°10E **234** B1
**Tapanahoni** → *Suriname* 4°20N 54°25W **329** C7
**Tapanila** *Finland* 60°15N 25°2E **121** B3
**Tapanui** *N.Z.* 45°56S 169°18E **285** F4
**Taparo Pt.** *Trin. & Tob.* 10°3N 61°38W **323** t
**Tapauá** *Brazil* 5°40S 64°20W **331** B5
**Tapauá** → *Brazil* 5°40S 64°21W **331** B5
**Tapaz** *Phil.* 11°16N 122°32E **233** F4
**Tapes** *Brazil* 30°40S 51°23W **335** C5
**Tapeta** *Liberia* 6°29N 8°52W **262** D3
**Taphan Hin** *Thailand* 16°13N 100°26E **236** D3
**Tapia de Casariego** *Spain* 43°34N 6°56W **194** B4
**Tapiales** *Argentina* 34°42S 58°30W **117** C1
**Tapiantana Channel** *Phil.* 6°22N 122°1E **233** H4
**Tapiantana Group** *Phil.* 6°20N 122°0E **233** H4
**Tapiau = Gvardeysk** *Russia* 54°39N 21°5E **184** D8
**Tapilon = Daanbantayan** *Phil.* 11°17N 124°2E **233** F5
**Taping** *Taiwan* 24°6N 120°53E **225** B2
**Tapini** *Papua N. G.* 8°19S 147°0E **286** E4
**Tapiola** *Finland* 60°10N 24°48E **121** B1
**Tapiraí** *Brazil* 19°52S 46°1W **333** E2
**Tapirapé** → *Brazil* 10°41S 50°38W **332** D1
**Tapirapecó, Serra** *Venezuela* 1°10N 65°0W **329** C5
**Taplan** *Australia* 34°33S 140°52E **282** C4
**Taplejung** *Nepal* 27°1N 86°16E **243** F12
**Tapo-Capara** △ *Venezuela* 7°55N 71°15W **328** B3
**Tapoeripa** *Suriname* 5°22N 56°34W **329** B6
**Tapolca** *Hungary* 46°53N 17°29E **182** D2
**Tapsia** *India* 22°32N 88°23E **124** B2
**Tapti** → *India* 21°8N 72°41E **244** D1
**Tapu** *Taiwan* 23°18N 120°35E **225** C2
**Tapuae-o-Uenuku** *N.Z.* 42°0S 173°39E **285** C8
**Tapul** *Phil.* 5°42N 120°55E **233** J3
**Tapul Group** *Phil.* 5°35N 120°50E **233** J3
**Tapul I.** *Phil.* 5°43N 120°55E **233** J3
**Tapun** *India* 27°35N 96°22E **241** B6
**Tapurucuará** *Brazil* 0°24S 65°2W **329** D4
**Taputapu, C.** *Amer. Samoa* 14°20S 170°51W **302** f
**Taputimu** *Amer. Samoa* 14°21S 170°46W **302** f
**Ţaqţaq** *Iraq* 35°53N 44°35E **213** E11
**Taquara** *Brazil* 29°36S 50°46W **335** B5
**Taquari** → *Brazil* 19°15S 57°17W **331** D6
**Taquaritinga** *Brazil* 21°24S 48°30W **333** F2
**Tara** *Queens., Australia* 27°17S 150°31E **281** D5
**Tara** *Ont., Canada* 44°28N 81°9W **312** B3
**Tara** *Maharashtra, India* 19°5N 72°49E **130** A1
**Tara** *Japan* 33°2N 130°11E **222** D2
**Tara** *Russia* 56°55N 74°24E **214** D8
**Tara** *Zambia* 16°58S 26°45E **269** F2
**Tara** → *Montenegro* 43°21N 18°51E **202** C2
**Tara** △ *Serbia* 43°55N 19°30E **202** C3
**Tara-Dake** *Japan* 32°58N 130°6E **222** E2
**Taraba** □ *Nigeria* 8°0N 10°30E **263** D7
**Taraba** → *Nigeria* 8°30N 10°15E **263** D7
**Tarabuco** *Bolivia* 19°10S 64°57W **331** D5
**Tarābulus** *Lebanon* 34°31N 35°50E **250** D6
**Tarābulus** *Libya* 32°49N 13°7E **258** B2
**Tarābulus** *Libya* 31°0N 13°0E **258** B2
**Tarabya** *Turkey* 41°8N 29°3E **122** B2
**Taraclia** *Taraclia, Moldova* 45°54N 28°40E **183** E13
**Taraclia** *Tighina, Moldova* 46°34N 29°7E **183** D14
**Taradale** *N.Z.* 39°33S 176°53E **284** F5
**Taradehi** *India* 23°18N 79°21E **243** H8
**Tarāghin** *Libya* 26°0N 14°30E **258** C2
**Taragi** *Japan* 32°16N 130°56E **222** E2
**Tarahouahout** *Algeria* 22°41N 5°59E **261** D6
**Tarajalejo** *Canary Is.* 28°12N 14°7W **153** e2
**Tarakan** *Indonesia* 3°20N 117°35E **235** B5
**Tarakit, Mt.** *Kenya* 2°2N 35°10E **268** B4
**Taralga** *Australia* 34°26S 149°52E **283** C8
**Tarama-Jima** *Japan* 24°39N 124°42E **221** M2
**Taramakau** → *N.Z.* 42°34S 171°8E **285** C6
**Taran, Mys** *Russia* 54°56N 19°59E **184** D6
**Taranagar** *India* 28°43N 74°50E **242** E6
**Taranaki** □ *N.Z.* 39°25S 174°30E **284** F3
**Taranaki, Mt.** *N.Z.* 39°17S 174°5E **284** F3
**Tarancón** *Spain* 40°1N 3°1W **196** E1
**Tarangire** △ *Tanzania* 4°21S 36°7E **268** C4
**Taransay** *U.K.* 57°54N 7°0W **167** D1
**Táranto** *Italy* 40°28N 17°14E **201** B10
**Táranto, G. di** *Italy* 40°8N 17°20E **201** B10
**Tarapacá** *Colombia* 2°56S 69°46W **328** D4
**Tarapacá** □ *Chile* 20°45S 69°30W **334** A2
**Tarapoto** *Peru* 6°30S 76°20W **330** B2
**Taraquá** *Brazil* 0°6N 68°28W **328** C4
**Tarare** *France* 45°54N 4°26E **175** C8
**Tararua Ra.** *N.Z.* 40°45S 175°25E **284** G4
**Tarasag** *Vanuatu* 14°12S 167°36E **287** D5
**Tarasaigh = Taransay** *U.K.* 57°54N 7°0W **167** D1
**Tarascon** *France* 43°48N 4°39E **175** E8
**Tarascon-sur-Ariège** *France* 42°50N 1°36E **174** F5
**Tarashcha** *Ukraine* 49°30N 30°31E **177** D16
**Tarata** *Peru* 17°27S 70°2W **330** D3
**Tarauacá** *Brazil* 8°6S 70°48W **330** B3
**Tarauacá** → *Brazil* 6°42S 69°48W **330** B4
**Taravao** *Tahiti* 17°43S 149°18W **289** e
**Taravao, Isthme de** *Tahiti* 17°43S 149°19W **289** e
**Taravo** → *France* 41°42N 8°49E **175** G12
**Tarawa** *Kiribati* 1°30N 173°0E **288** G9
**Tarawai I.** *Papua N. G.* 3°13S 143°15E **286** B2
**Tarawera** *N.Z.* 39°2S 176°36E **284** F5
**Tarawera, L.** *N.Z.* 38°13S 176°27E **284** E5
**Tarawera, Mt.** *N.Z.* 38°14S 176°32E **284** E5
**Taraz** *Kazakhstan* 42°54N 71°22E **217** D8
**Tarazona** *Spain* 41°55N 1°43W **196** D3
**Tarazona de la Mancha** *Spain* 39°16N 1°55W **197** F3
**Tårbæk** *Denmark* 55°46N 12°35E **118** A3
**Tarbagatay, Khrebet** *Kazakhstan* 48°0N 83°0E **217** C10
**Tarbaj** *Kenya* 2°12N 40°8E **267** D5
**Tarbat Ness** *U.K.* 57°52N 3°47W **167** D5
**Tarbela Dam** *Pakistan* 34°8N 72°52E **242** B5
**Tarbert** *Kerry, Ireland* 52°34N 9°22W **166** D2
**Tarbert** *Argyll & Bute, U.K.* 55°52N 5°25W **167** F3
**Tarbert** *W. Isles, U.K.* 57°54N 6°49W **167** D2
**Tarbes** *France* 43°15N 0°3E **174** E4
**Tarboro** *U.S.A.* 35°54N 77°32W **315** D16
**Tărcău, Munţii** *Romania* 46°39N 26°7E **183** D11
**Tarcento** *Italy* 46°13N 13°13E **199** B10
**Tarchomin** *Poland* 52°19N 20°58E **143** B1
**Tarcoola** *Australia* 30°44S 134°36E **281** E1
**Tarcoon** *Australia* 30°15S 146°43E **281** E4
**Tarcutta** *Australia* 35°16S 147°44E **283** C7
**Tardeo** *India* 18°57N 72°48E **130** B1
**Tardets-Sorholus** *France* 43°8N 0°52W **174** E3
**Tardoire** → *France* 45°52N 0°14E **174** C4
**Taredjerdja** *Algeria* 25°12N 2°32E **261** C5
**Taree** *Australia* 31°50S 152°30E **283** A10
**Tarella** *Australia* 31°2S 143°2E **282** A5
**Tarf, Ras** *Morocco* 35°40N 5°11W **260** A3
**Ţarfā, Ra's aţ** *Si. Arabia* 17°2N 42°22E **248** C3
**Tarfa, W. el** → *Egypt* 28°25N 30°50E **256** B3
**Tarfaya** *Morocco* 27°55N 12°55W **260** C2
**Târgovişte** *Romania* 44°55N 25°27E **183** F10
**Targówek** *Poland* 52°16N 21°3E **143** B2
**Târgu Bujor** *Romania* 45°52N 27°54E **183** E12
**Târgu Cărbuneşti** *Romania* 44°57N 23°31E **183** F8
**Târgu Frumos** *Romania* 47°12N 27°2E **183** C12
**Târgu Jiu** *Romania* 45°5N 23°19E **183** E8
**Târgu Lăpuş** *Romania* 47°27N 23°52E **183** C8
**Târgu Mureş** *Romania* 46°31N 24°38E **183** D9
**Târgu Neamţ** *Romania* 47°12N 26°25E **183** C11
**Târgu Ocna** *Romania* 46°16N 26°39E **183** D11
**Târgu Secuiesc** *Romania* 46°0N 26°10E **183** E11
**Targuist** *Morocco* 34°59N 4°14W **260** B4
**Târguşor** *Romania* 44°27N 28°25E **183** F13
**Tarhăus, Vf.** *Romania* 46°40N 26°8E **183** D11
**Tarhbalt** *Morocco* 30°39N 5°20W **260** B3
**Tarhūnah** *Libya* 32°27N 13°36E **258** B2
**Tari** *Papua N. G.* 5°54S 142°59E **286** C2
**Táriba** *Venezuela* 7°49N 72°13W **328** B3
**Tarif** *U.A.E.* 24°3N 53°46E **247** E7
**Tarifa** *Spain* 36°1N 5°36W **195** J5
**Tarigtig Pt.** *Phil.* 16°25N 122°14E **232** C4
**Tarija** *Bolivia* 21°30S 64°40W **334** A3
**Tarija** □ *Bolivia* 21°30S 63°30W **334** A3
**Tarik I.** *Micronesia* 7°20N 151°46E **287** T18
**Tariku** → *Indonesia* 2°55S 138°26E **231** E9
**Tarīm** *Yemen* 16°3N 49°0E **249** C5
**Tarim Basin = Tarim Pendi** *China* 40°0N 84°0E **217** E10
**Tarim He** → *China* 39°30N 88°30E **217** E11
**Tarim Pendi** *China* 40°0N 84°0E **217** E10
**Tarime** *Tanzania* 1°21S 34°22E **266** E3
**Taritatu** → *Indonesia* 2°54S 138°27E **231** E9
**Tarka** → *S. Africa* 32°10S 26°0E **270** D4
**Tarka La** *Bhutan* 27°12N 89°44E **243** F13
**Tarkastad** *S. Africa* 32°0S 26°16E **270** D4
**Tarkhankut, Mys** *Ukraine* 45°25N 32°30E **189** K7
**Tarko Sale** *Russia* 64°55N 77°50E **214** C8
**Tarkwa** *Ghana* 5°20N 2°0W **262** D4
**Tarlac** *Phil.* 15°29N 120°35E **232** D3
**Tarlac** □ *Phil.* 15°30N 120°30E **232** D3
**Tarm** *Denmark* 55°56N 8°31E **163** J2
**Tarma** *Peru* 11°25S 75°45W **330** C2
**Tarmiya** *Iraq* 33°40N 44°23E **213** G11
**Tarn** □ *France* 43°49N 2°8E **174** E6
**Tarn** → *France* 44°5N 1°6E **174** D5
**Tarn-et-Garonne** □ *France* 44°8N 1°20E **174** D5
**Tarna** → *Hungary* 47°31N 19°59E **182** C4
**Târnava Mare** → *Romania* 46°10N 23°43E **183** D8
**Târnava Mică** → *Romania* 46°9N 23°55E **183** D8
**Târnăveni** *Romania* 46°19N 24°13E **183** D9
**Tårnby** *Denmark* 55°37N 12°35E **118** B3
**Tarnica** *Poland* 49°4N 22°44E **185** J9
**Tarnobrzeg** *Poland* 50°35N 21°41E **185** H8
**Tarnogród** *Poland* 50°22N 22°45E **185** H9
**Tarnopol = Ternopil** *Ukraine* 49°30N 25°40E **177** D13
**Tarnos** *France* 43°32N 1°28W **174** E2
**Târnova** *Moldova* 48°10N 27°40E **183** B12
**Târnova** *Romania* 45°23N 21°59E **182** E6
**Tarnów** *Poland* 50°3N 21°0E **185** H8
**Tarnowitz = Tarnowskie Góry** *Poland* 50°27N 18°54E **185** H5
**Tarnowskie Góry** *Poland* 50°27N 18°54E **185** H5
**Tärnsjö** *Sweden* 60°9N 16°56E **162** D10
**Taro** *Solomon Is.* 6°43S 156°24E **287** L9
**Táro** → *Italy* 45°2N 10°15E **198** C7
**Taroko** △ *Taiwan* 24°10N 121°33E **225** B3
**Ţārom** *Iran* 28°11N 55°46E **247** D7
**Taroom** *Australia* 25°36S 149°48E **281** D4
**Taroudannt** *Morocco* 30°30N 8°52W **260** B3
**Taroume** *Cook Is.* 21°15S 159°45W **289** h
**Tarp** *Germany* 54°39N 9°24E **178** A5
**Tarpeena** *Australia* 37°37S 140°47E **282** D4
**Tarpon Springs** *U.S.A.* 28°9N 82°45W **317** G7
**Tarqua Bay** *Nigeria* 6°24N 3°23E **124** B2
**Tarquinia** *Italy* 42°15N 11°45E **199** F8
**Tarra Bulga** △ *Australia* 38°24S 146°32E **283** E7
**Tarrafal** *C. Verde Is.* 15°18N 23°39W **153** j
**Tarragona** *Spain* 41°5N 1°17E **196** D6
**Tarragona** □ *Spain* 41°5N 1°0E **196** D6
**Tarraleah** *Australia* 42°17S 146°26E **281** G4
**Tarrasa = Terrassa** *Spain* 41°34N 2°1E **196** D7
**Tàrrega** *Spain* 41°39N 1°9E **196** D6
**Tarrytown** *Ga., U.S.A.* 32°19N 82°34W **316** C7
**Tarrytown** *N.Y., U.S.A.* 41°4N 73°52W **313** E11
**Tårs** *Denmark* 57°23N 10°7E **163** G4
**Tarsus** *Turkey* 36°58N 34°55E **250** B5
**Tarsus** → *Turkey* 36°46N 34°52E **250** B5
**Tartagal** *Argentina* 22°30S 63°50W **334** A3
**Tartane** *Martinique* 14°45N 60°55W **322** j
**Tärtär** *Azerbaijan* 40°20N 46°58E **191** K8
**Tärtär** → *Azerbaijan* 40°26N 47°20E **191** K8
**Tartas** *France* 43°50N 0°49W **174** E3
**Tartu** *Estonia* 58°20N 26°44E **188** C4
**Ţarţūs** *Syria* 34°55N 35°55E **250** D6
**Ţarţūs** □ *Syria* 35°0N 36°0E **250** D7
**Tarumirim** *Brazil* 19°16S 41°59W **333** E3
**Tarumizu** *Japan* 31°29N 130°42E **222** F2
**Tarussa** *Russia* 54°44N 37°10E **188** E9
**Tarutao = Ko Tarutao** △ *Thailand* 6°31N 99°26E **237** J2
**Tarutao, Ko** *Thailand* 6°33N 99°40E **237** J2
**Tarutung** *Indonesia* 2°0N 98°54E **234** B1
**Tarutyne** *Ukraine* 46°12N 29°9E **183** D14
**Tarvisio** *Italy* 46°30N 13°35E **199** B10
**Tarxien** *Malta* 35°52N 14°31E **206** F8
**Taşağıl** *Turkey* 36°55N 31°14E **250** B2
**Tasahku** *Burma* 27°33N 97°52E **241** B6
**Tasaret, O.** → *Algeria* 26°25N 1°59E **261** C5
**Tasāwah** *Libya* 26°0N 13°30E **258** C2
**Tasböget** *Kazakhstan* 44°46N 65°33E **216** D7
**Tasek Merimbun** △ *Brunei* 4°31N 114°41E **235** B4
**Taseko** → *Canada* 52°8N 123°45W **296** C4
**Tasgaon** *India* 17°2N 74°39E **244** F2
**Tash-Kömür** *Kyrgyzstan* 41°40N 72°10E **217** D8
**Tashauz = Daşoguz** *Turkmenistan* 41°49N 59°58E **216** D5
**Tashi Chho Dzong = Thimphu** *Bhutan* 27°31N 89°45E **241** B2
**Tashino = Pervomaysk** *Russia* 54°56N 43°58E **190** C6
**Ţashk, Daryācheh-ye** *Iran* 29°45N 53°35E **247** D7
**Tashkent = Toshkent** *Uzbekistan* 41°20N 69°10E **217** D7
**Tashtagol** *Russia* 52°47N 87°53E **217** B11
**Tashu** *Taiwan* 22°41N 120°25E **225** D2
**Tasiilaq** *Greenland* 65°40N 37°20W **154** D7
**Tasik Bera** *Malaysia* 3°5N 102°38E **234** B2
**Tasik Kenyir** *Malaysia* 5°5N 102°45E **234** A2
**Tasikmalaya** *Indonesia* 7°18S 108°12E **235** D3
**Tåsinge** *Denmark* 55°0N 10°36E **163** J4
**Tåsjön** *Sweden* 64°15N 15°40E **160** D16
**Task** *Niger* 14°56N 10°46E **259** F2
**Taskan** *Russia* 62°59N 150°20E **215** C16
**Taşkent** *Turkey* 36°55N 32°29E **250** B3
**Taşköprü** *Turkey* 41°30N 34°15E **212** B6
**Taskul** *Papua N. G.* 2°32S 150°27E **286** B6
**Taşlâc** *Moldova* 47°4N 29°24E **183** C14
**Taşliçay** *Turkey* 39°38N 43°22E **213** C10
**Tasman** □ *N.Z.* 41°30S 172°40E **285** B7
**Tasman** → *N.Z.* 43°48S 170°8E **285** D5
**Tasman, Mt.** *N.Z.* 43°34S 170°12E **285** D5
**Tasman Abyssal Plain** *Pac. Oc.* 34°30S 153°15E **276** G9
**Tasman B.** *N.Z.* 40°59S 173°25E **285** A8
**Tasman Basin** *Pac. Oc.* 46°0S 158°0E **288** M7
**Tasman Glacier** *N.Z.* 43°37S 170°12E **285** D5
**Tasman Mts.** *N.Z.* 41°3S 172°25E **285** B7
**Tasman Pen.** *Australia* 43°10S 148°0E **281** G4
**Tasman Sea** *Pac. Oc.* 36°0S 160°0E **277** H10
**Tasmania** □ *Australia* 42°0S 146°30E **281** G4
**Tasmanian Wilderness World Heritage Area** △ *Australia* 43°0S 146°0E **281** G4
**Tăşnad** *Romania* 47°30N 22°33E **182** C7
**Taşova** *Turkey* 40°45N 36°19E **212** B7
**Tassili n'Ajjer** *Algeria* 25°47N 8°1E **261** C6
**Tassili n'Ajjer** △ *Algeria* 26°5N 6°0E **258** C1
**Tassili-Oua-n-Ahaggar** *Algeria* 20°41N 5°30E **261** D6
**Tassili Tin-Rerhoh** *Algeria* 20°5N 3°55E **261** D5
**Taşucu** *Turkey* 36°19N 33°52E **250** B4
**Taşucu Körfezi** *Turkey* 36°16N 33°56E **250** B4
**Tasuj** *Iran* 38°18N 45°23E **213** C11
**Tat Ton** △ *Thailand* 15°57N 102°2E **236** E4
**Tata** *Hungary* 47°37N 18°19E **182** C3
**Tata** *Morocco* 29°46N 7°56W **260** C3
**Tatabánya** *Hungary* 47°32N 18°25E **182** C3
**Tatakoto** *French Polynesia* 17°20S 138°23W **289** f
**Tatamá** △ *Colombia* 5°5N 76°9W **328** B2
**Tatamba** *Solomon Is.* 8°21S 159°51E **287** M10
**Tataouine** *Tunisia* 32°57N 10°29E **258** B2
**Tataouine** □ *Tunisia* 32°0N 10°0E **261** B7
**Tatar-Pazardzhik = Pazardzhik** *Bulgaria* 42°12N 24°20E **203** D8
**Tatar Republic = Tatarstan** □ *Russia* 55°30N 51°30E **190** C10
**Tatarbunary** *Ukraine* 45°50N 29°39E **183** E14
**Tatarsk** *Russia* 55°14N 76°0E **217** A9
**Tatarskiy Proliv** *Russia* 50°0N 141°0E **215** E15
**Tatarstan** □ *Russia* 55°30N 51°30E **190** C10
**Tatatóváros = Tata** *Hungary* 47°37N 18°19E **182** C3
**Tatatua, Pte.** *Tahiti* 17°44S 149°8W **289** e
**Tatau** *Malaysia* 2°53N 112°51E **235** B4
**Tatau I.** *Papua N. G.* 2°48S 151°57E **286** B6
**Tatebayashi** *Japan* 36°15N 139°32E **223** A11
**Tateshina-Yama** *Japan* 36°8N 138°11E **223** A10
**Tateyama** *Chiba, Japan* 35°0N 139°50E **223** C11
**Tateyama** *Toyama, Japan* 36°40N 137°35E **223** A9
**Tathlina L.** *Canada* 60°33N 117°39W **296** A5
**Tathlīth** *Si. Arabia* 19°32N 43°30E **248** C3
**Tathlīth, W.** → *Si. Arabia* 20°35N 44°20E **248** B4
**Tathong Channel** *Hong Kong, China* 22°15N 114°16E **122** B3
**Tathong Pt.** *Hong Kong, China* 22°14N 114°17E **122** B3
**Tathra** *Australia* 36°44S 149°59E **283** D8
**Tatinnai L.** *Canada* 60°55N 97°40W **297** A9
**Tatitlek** *U.S.A.* 60°52N 146°41W **303** F11
**Tatkon** *Burma* 20°7N 96°13E **241** E6
**Tatla Lake** *Canada* 52°0N 124°20W **296** C4
**Tatlısu = Akanthou** *Cyprus* 35°22N 33°45E **207** E9
**Tatlısu** *Turkey* 40°24N 27°55E **203** F11
**Tatnam, C.** *Canada* 57°16N 91°0W **297** B10
**Tatra = Tatry** *Slovak Rep.* 49°20N 20°0E **181** B13
**Tatranský** △ *Slovak Rep.* 49°10N 20°0E **181** B13
**Tatry** *Slovak Rep.* 49°20N 20°0E **181** B13
**Tatshenshini** → *Canada* 59°28N 137°45W **296** B1
**Tatshenshini-Alsek** ⌂ *Canada* 59°55N 137°45W **296** B1
**Tatsuno** *Hyōgo, Japan* 34°52N 134°33E **222** C6
**Tatsuno** *Nagano, Japan* 35°58N 138°0E **223** B10
**Tatta = Thatta** *Pakistan* 24°42N 67°55E **242** G2
**Tatuapé** *Brazil* 23°31S 46°33W **137** B2
**Tatuí** *Brazil* 23°25S 47°53W **335** A6
**Tatum** *U.S.A.* 33°16N 103°19W **305** K12
**Tat'ung = Datong** *China* 40°6N 113°18E **226** D7
**Tatura** *Australia* 36°29S 145°16E **283** D6
**Tatvan** *Turkey* 38°31N 42°15E **213** C10
**Ta'ū** *Amer. Samoa* 14°15S 169°30W **302** g
**Tau** *Rogaland, Norway* 59°3N 5°55E **164** E2
**Tauá** *Brazil* 6°1S 40°26W **332** C3
**Taubaté** *Brazil* 23°0S 45°36W **335** A6
**Tauberbischofsheim** *Germany* 49°37N 9°39E **179** F5
**Taucha** *Germany* 51°23N 12°29E **178** D8
**Tauern** *Austria* 47°15N 12°40E **176** E7
**Tauern-tunnel** *Austria* 47°0N 13°12E **180** D6
**Taufikia** *South Sudan* 9°24N 31°37E **257** F3
**Taufkirchen** *Germany* 48°2N 11°36E **131** B2
**Taulé** *France* 48°37N 3°55W **172** D3
**Taumarunui** *N.Z.* 38°53S 175°15E **284** E4
**Taumaturgo** *Brazil* 8°54S 72°51W **330** B3
**Taung** *S. Africa* 27°33S 24°47E **270** C3
**Taungdwingyi** *Burma* 20°1N 95°40E **241** E5
**Taunggyi** *Burma* 20°50N 97°0E **241** E6
**Taungoo = Tounggoo** *Burma* 19°0N 96°30E **241** F6
**Taungtha** *Burma* 21°12N 95°25E **241** E5
**Taungup** *Burma* 18°51N 94°14E **241** F5
**Taungup Pass** *Burma* 18°40N 94°45E **241** F5
**Taunsa** *Pakistan* 30°42N 70°39E **242** D4
**Taunsa Barrage** *Pakistan* 30°42N 70°50E **242** D4
**Taunton** *Somst., U.K.* 51°1N 3°5W **169** F4
**Taunton** *Mass., U.S.A.* 41°54N 71°6W **313** E13
**Taunus** *Germany* 50°13N 8°34E **179** E4
**Taupo** *N.Z.* 38°41S 176°7E **284** E5
**Taupo, L.** *N.Z.* 38°46S 175°55E **284** E4
**Tauragė** *Lithuania* 55°14N 22°16E **184** C9
**Tauragė** □ *Lithuania* 55°15N 22°17E **184** C9
**Tauranga** *N.Z.* 37°42S 176°11E **284** D5
**Tauranga Harb.** *N.Z.* 37°30S 176°5E **284** D5
**Taureau, Rés.** *Canada* 46°46N 73°50W **298** C5
**Tauri** → *Papua N. G.* 8°8S 146°8E **286** E4
**Taurianova** *Italy* 38°21N 16°1E **201** D9
**Tauroa Pt.** *N.Z.* 35°10S 173°4E **284** B2
**Taurus Mts. = Toros Dağları** *Turkey* 37°0N 32°30E **250** B3
**Taus = Domažlice** *Czech Rep.* 49°28N 12°58E **180** B5
**Tauste** *Spain* 41°58N 1°18W **196** D3
**Tautira** *Tahiti* 17°44S 149°9W **289** e
**Tauyskaya Guba** *Russia* 59°20N 150°20E **215** D16
**Tauz = Tovuz** *Azerbaijan* 41°0N 45°40E **191** K7
**Tavan Bogd Uul** *Mongolia* 49°10N 87°49E **217** C11
**Tavares** *U.S.A.* 28°48N 81°44W **317** G8
**Tavares, I. dos** *Brazil* 22°49S 43°6W **135** A2
**Tavas** *Turkey* 37°34N 29°4E **205** D11
**Tavastehus = Hämeenlinna** *Finland* 61°0N 24°28E **188** B3
**Tavda** *Russia* 58°7N 65°8E **214** D7
**Tavda** → *Russia* 57°47N 67°18E **214** D7
**Taverner B.** *Canada* 67°12N 72°25W **295** D17
**Tavernes de la Valldigna** *Spain* 39°5N 0°13W **197** F4
**Tavernier** *U.S.A.* 25°1N 80°31W **317** K9
**Taveta** *Kenya* 3°23S 37°37E **268** C4
**Taveuni** *Fiji* 16°51S 179°58W **287** A3
**Taviano** *Italy* 39°59N 18°5E **201** C11
**Tavignano** → *France* 42°7N 9°33E **175** F13
**Tavira** *Portugal* 37°8N 7°40W **195** H3
**Tavistock** *Ont., Canada* 43°19N 80°50W **312** C4
**Tavistock** *Devon, U.K.* 50°33N 4°9W **169** G3
**Tavolara** *Italy* 40°54N 9°42E **200** B2
**Távora** → *Portugal* 41°8N 7°35W **194** D3
**Tavoy** *Burma* 14°2N 98°12E **236** E2
**Tavoy Pt.** *Burma* 13°32N 98°10E **236** F2
**Tavrichanka** *Russia* 43°18N 131°59E **220** C5
**Tavropos** → *Greece* 39°10N 21°45E **204** B3
**Tavros** *Greece* 37°57N 23°43E **112** B2
**Tavşanlı** *Turkey* 39°32N 29°30E **205** B11
**Tavua** *Fiji* 17°37S 177°5E **287** A1
**Tavuki** *Fiji* 19°7S 178°8E **287** B2
**Taw** → *U.K.* 51°4N 4°4W **169** F3
**Tawa** → *India* 22°48N 77°48E **242** H8
**Tawa Res.** *India* 22°35N 78°5E **244** C4
**Tawa Tawa Mal Reef** *Papua N. G.* 11°3S 152°55E **286** F7
**Tawai** *India* 27°48N 96°47E **241** B6
**Tawang** *India* 27°35N 91°52E **241** B3
**Tawas City** *U.S.A.* 44°16N 83°31W **309** C12
**Tawau** *Malaysia* 4°20N 117°55E **235** B5
**Tawau Hills** △ *Malaysia* 4°20N 117°54E **235** B5
**Taweisha** *Sudan* 12°19N 26°40E **257** E2
**Tawi-tawi** □ *Phil.* 5°0N 120°0E **233** J3
**Tawi-tawi I.** *Phil.* 5°10N 120°15E **233** J3
**Tawngche** *Burma* 26°34N 95°38E **241** B5
**Tawu** *Taiwan* 22°22N 120°54E **225** D2
**Tāwūq** *Iraq* 35°8N 44°26E **213** E11
**Tāwurghā'** *Libya* 32°1N 15°2E **258** B3
**Tāwurghā', Sabkhat** *Libya* 31°51N 15°15E **258** B3
**Taxco** *Mexico* 18°33N 99°36W **319** D5
**Taxila** *Pakistan* 33°42N 72°52E **242** C5
**Taxkorgan Tajik Zizhixian** *China* 37°49N 75°14E **217** E9
**Tay** → *U.K.* 56°37N 3°38W **167** E5
**Tay, Firth of** *U.K.* 56°25N 3°8W **167** E5
**Tay, L.** *W. Austral., Australia* 32°55S 120°48E **279** F3
**Tay, L.** *Perth & Kinr., U.K.* 56°32N 4°8W **167** E4
**Tay** ⌂ *U.K.* 56°43N 3°59W **167** E5
**Tay Ninh** *Vietnam* 11°20N 106°5E **237** G6
**Tayabamba** *Peru* 8°15S 77°16W **330** B2
**Tayabas = Quezon** *Phil.* 9°15N 117°59E **233** G1
**Tayabas** *Phil.* 14°1N 121°35E **232** D3
**Tayabas B.** *Phil.* 13°45N 121°45E **232** E3
**Tayan** *Indonesia* 0°1S 110°7E **235** C4
**Taygetos Oros** *Greece* 37°0N 22°23E **204** D4
**Taylakova** *Russia* 59°13N 74°0E **214** D8
**Taylor** *B.C., Canada* 56°13N 120°40W **296** B4
**Taylor** *Fla., U.S.A.* 30°26N 82°18W **316** E7
**Taylor** *Mich., U.S.A.* 42°14N 83°16W **311** B13
**Taylor** *Nebr., U.S.A.* 41°46N 99°23W **308** E4
**Taylor** *Pa., U.S.A.* 41°23N 75°43W **313** E9
**Taylor** *Tex., U.S.A.* 30°34N 97°25W **314** F6
**Taylor, Mt.** *N.Z.* 43°30S 171°20E **285** D6
**Taylor, Mt.** *N. Mex., U.S.A.* 35°14N 107°37W **305** J10
**Taylorsville** *U.S.A.* 38°2N 85°21W **311** F11
**Taylorsville L.** *U.S.A.* 38°0N 85°15W **311** G11
**Taylorville** *U.S.A.* 39°33N 89°18W **310** E7
**Taymā** *Si. Arabia* 27°35N 38°45E **246** E3
**Taymyr, Oz.** *Russia* 74°20N 102°0E **215** B11
**Taymyr, Poluostrov** *Russia* 75°0N 100°0E **215** B11
**Taypaq** *Kazakhstan* 49°0N 51°47E **187** E9
**Tayport** *U.K.* 56°27N 2°52W **167** E6
**Tayrona** △ *Colombia* 11°20N 74°2W **328** A3
**Tayshet** *Russia* 55°58N 98°1E **215** D10
**Taytay** *Phil.* 10°45N 119°30E **233** F2
**Taytay B.** *Phil.* 10°55N 119°35E **233** F2
**Tayuan** *Taiwan* 25°3N 121°11E **225** A3
**Tayug** *Phil.* 16°2N 120°45E **232** C3
**Tayüling** *Taiwan* 24°11N 121°18E **225** B3
**Tāyyebād** *Iran* 34°45N 60°45E **247** C9
**Tāyyebād** □ *Iran* 34°44N 60°44E **247** C9
**Tayynsha** *Kazakhstan* 53°50N 69°45E **217** B7
**Taz** → *Russia* 67°32N 78°40E **214** C8
**Taza** *Morocco* 34°16N 4°6W **260** B4
**Taza-Al Hoceïma-Taounate** □ *Morocco* 34°15N 3°20W **261** B4
**Tāza Khurmātū** *Iraq* 35°18N 44°20E **213** E11
**Taza-Taou** □ *Morocco* 34°15N 4°10W **260** B4
**Tazawa-Ko** *Japan* 39°43N 140°40E **220** E10
**Taze** *Burma* 22°57N 95°24E **241** D5
**Tazenakht** *Morocco* 30°35N 7°12W **260** B3
**Tazerbo** *Libya* 25°45N 21°0E **258** C4
**Tazin** → *Canada* 59°48N 109°55W **297** B7
**Tazin L.** *Canada* 59°44N 108°42W **297** B7
**Tazlina** *U.S.A.* 62°4N 146°27W **303** E11
**Tazouikert** *Mali* 21°27N 1°16W **261** D4
**Tazoult** *Algeria* 35°29N 6°11E **261** A6
**Tazovskiy** *Russia* 67°30N 78°44E **214** C8
**Tazrouk** *Algeria* 23°24N 6°15E **261** D6
**Tbilisi** *Georgia* 41°43N 44°50E **191** K7
**Tchad = Chad** ■ *Africa* 15°0N 17°15E **259** F3
**Tchad, L.** *Chad* 13°30N 14°30E **259** F2
**Tchaourou** *Benin* 8°58N 2°40E **263** D5
**Tch'eng-tou = Chengdu** *China* 30°38N 104°2E **228** B5
**Tchentlo L.** *Canada* 55°15N 125°0W **296** B4
**Tchetti** *Benin* 7°50N 1°40E **263** D5
**Tchibanga** *Gabon* 2°45S 11°0E **264** C2
**Tchien** *Liberia* 5°59N 8°15W **262** D3
**Tchin Tabaraden** *Niger* 15°58N 5°56E **263** B6
**Tchogha Zanbil = Choghā Zanbīl** *Iran* 32°1N 48°32E **247** C6
**Tcholliré** *Cameroon* 8°24N 14°10E **264** A2
**Tch'ong-k'ing = Chongqing** *China* 29°35N 106°25E **228** C6
**Tchoupitoulas Street** *New Orleans, U.S.A.* **131** b2
**Tczew** *Poland* 54°8N 18°50E **184** D5
**TD Garden** *Boston, U.S.A.* **116** a2
**Te Anau** *N.Z.* 45°25S 167°43E **285** F2
**Te Anau, L.** *N.Z.* 45°15S 167°45E **285** F2
**Te Araroa** *N.Z.* 37°39S 178°25E **284** D7
**Te Aroha** *N.Z.* 37°32S 175°44E **284** D4
**Te Awamutu** *N.Z.* 38°1S 175°20E **284** E4
**Te Ika a Maui = North I.** *N.Z.* 38°0S 175°0E **284** E4
**Te Kaha** *N.Z.* 37°44S 177°52E **284** D6
**Te Karaka** *N.Z.* 38°26S 177°53E **284** E6
**Te Kauwhata** *N.Z.* 37°25S 175°9E **284** D4
**Te Kopuru** *N.Z.* 36°2S 173°56E **284** C2
**Te Kou** *Cook Is.* 21°14S 159°46W **289** h
**Te Kuiti** *N.Z.* 38°20S 175°11E **284** E4
**Te Manga** *Cook Is.* 21°14S 159°45W **289** h
**Te-n-Dghâmcha, Sebkhet** *Mauritania* 18°30N 15°55W **262** B1
**Te Nggano, L.** *Solomon Is.* 11°40S 160°19E **287** N11
**Te Puke** *N.Z.* 37°46S 176°22E **284** D5
**Te Teko** *N.Z.* 38°2S 176°48E **284** E5
**Te Waewae B.** *N.Z.* 46°13S 167°33E **285** G2
**Te Wai Pounamu = South I.** *N.Z.* 44°0S 170°0E **285** E5
**Tea** → *Brazil* 0°30S 65°9W **328** D4
**Teaca** *Romania* 46°55N 24°30E **183** D9
**Teague** *U.S.A.* 31°38N 96°17W **314** F6
**Teahupoo** *Tahiti* 17°50S 149°16W **289** e
**Teaneck** *U.S.A.* 40°53N 74°1W **132** a1
**Teano** *Italy* 41°15N 14°4E **201** A7
**Teapa** *Mexico* 17°33N 92°57W **319** D6
**Teba** *Spain* 36°59N 4°55W **195** J6
**Tebakang** *Malaysia* 1°6N 110°30E **235** B4
**Tébarat** *Niger* 14°49N 4°27E **263** C5
**Teberau** → *Malaysia* 1°33N 103°42E **237** d
**Teberda** *Russia* 43°30N 41°46E **191** J5
**Tébessa** *Algeria* 35°22N 8°8E **261** A6
**Tébessa** □ *Algeria* 35°0N 7°50E **261** B6
**Tebet** *Indonesia* 6°14S 106°50E **122** B2
**Tebicuary** → *Paraguay* 26°36S 58°16W **334** B4
**Tebingtinggi** *Riau, Indonesia* 1°0N 102°45E **234** B2
**Tebingtinggi** *Sumatera Selatan, Indonesia* 3°36S 103°4E **234** C2
**Tebingtinggi** *Sumatera Utara, Indonesia* 3°20N 99°9E **234** B1
**Tebourba** *Tunisia* 36°49N 9°51E **258** A1
**Téboursouk** *Tunisia* 36°29N 9°10E **258** A1
**Tebulos** *Georgia* 42°36N 45°17E **191** J7
**Tecamachalco** *Mexico* 19°25N 99°14W **128** B1
**Tecate** *Mexico* 32°34N 116°38W **307** N10
**Tecer Dağları** *Turkey* 39°27N 37°27E **212** C7
**Tech** → *France* 42°36N 3°3E **174** F7
**Techiman** *Ghana* 7°35N 1°58W **262** D4
**Techirghiol** *Romania* 44°4N 28°32E **183** F13
**Techou = Dezhou** *China* 37°26N 116°18E **226** F9
**Teckla** *Argentina* 43°29S 70°48W **336** B2
**Tecomán** *Mexico* 18°55N 103°53W **318** D4
**Tecopa** *U.S.A.* 35°51N 116°13W **307** K10
**Tecoripa** *Mexico* 28°37N 109°57W **318** B3
**Tecuala** *Mexico* 22°23N 105°27W **318** C3
**Tecuci** *Romania* 45°51N 27°27E **183** E12
**Tecumseh** *Ont., Canada* 42°19N 82°54W **312** D2
**Tecumseh** *Mich., U.S.A.* 42°0N 83°57W **311** B13
**Tecumseh** *Okla., U.S.A.* 35°15N 96°56W **314** D6
**Ted** *Somalia* 4°24N 43°55E **267** D5
**Ted Williams Tunnel** *U.S.A.* 42°21N 71°1W **116** A2
**Teddington** *U.K.* 51°25N 0°20W **125** B1
**Tedjert** *Algeria* 21°23N 6°25E **261** D6
**Tedzhen = Tejen** *Turkmenistan* 37°23N 60°31E **216** E6
**Tees** → *U.K.* 54°37N 1°10W **168** C6
**Tees B.** *U.K.* 54°40N 1°9W **168** C6
**Teeswater** *Canada* 43°59N 81°17W **312** C3
**Tefé** *Brazil* 3°25S 64°50W **329** D5
**Tefé** → *Brazil* 3°35S 64°47W **329** D5
**Tefenni** *Turkey* 37°18N 29°45E **205** D11
**Tegal** *Indonesia* 6°52S 109°8E **235** D3
**Tegallalang** *Indonesia* 8°27S 115°17E **231** J18
**Tegalsari** *Indonesia* 8°25S 114°8E **231** J17
**Tegano, L. = Te Nggano, L.** *Solomon Is.* 11°40S 160°19E **287** N11
**Tegel** *Germany* 52°34N 13°16E **115** A2
**Tegeler See** *Germany* 52°34N 13°15E **115** A2
**Tegelort** *Germany* 52°34N 13°13E **115** A2
**Tegernsee** *Germany* 47°43N 11°46E **179** H7
**Teggiano** *Italy* 40°23N 15°32E **201** B8
**Tegid, L. = Bala, L.** *U.K.* 52°53N 3°37W **168** E4
**Tegina** *Nigeria* 10°5N 6°11E **263** C6
**Tegua** *Vanuatu* 13°15S 166°37E **287** C4
**Tegucigalpa** *Honduras* 14°5N 87°14W **320** D2
**Teguidda i-n-Tessoum** *Niger* 17°25N 6°37E **263** B6
**Teguise** *Canary Is.* 29°3N 13°33W **153** e2
**Tehachapi** *U.S.A.* 35°8N 118°27W **307** K8
**Tehachapi Mts.** *U.S.A.* 35°0N 118°30W **307** L8
**Tehamiyam** *Sudan* 18°20N 36°32E **256** D4
**Teheran = Tehrān** *Iran* 35°41N 51°25E **141** A2
**Tehilla** *Sudan* 17°42N 36°6E **256** D4
**Téhini** *Ivory C.* 9°39N 3°40W **262** D4
**Tehoru** *Indonesia* 3°23S 129°30E **231** E7
**Tehrān** *Iran* 35°41N 51°25E **141** A2
**Tehrān** □ *Iran* 35°30N 51°30E **247** C6
**Tehrān Mehrābād** ✕ (THR) *Iran* 35°41N 51°18E **141** A1
**Tehrān Pārs** *Iran* 35°44N 51°32E **141** A3
**Tehri** *India* 30°23N 78°29E **243** D8
**Tehuacán** *Mexico* 18°27N 97°23W **319** D5
**Tehuantepec** *Mexico* 16°21N 95°13W **319** D5
**Tehuantepec, G. de** *Mexico* 15°50N 95°12W **319** D5
**Tehuantepec, Istmo de** *Mexico* 17°15N 94°30W **319** D6
**Tehuantepec Fracture Zone** *Pac. Oc.* 13°0N 97°0W **289** F18
**Tei Tong Tsui** *Hong Kong, China* 22°16N 114°17E **122** B3
**Teide, Pico del** *Canary Is.* 28°15N 16°38W **153** e1
**Teifi** → *U.K.* 52°5N 4°41W **169** E3
**Teigebyen** *Norway* 60°12N 11°0E **162** D5
**Teign** → *U.K.* 50°32N 3°32W **169** G4
**Teignmouth** *U.K.* 50°33N 3°31W **169** G4
**Teinainano = Tarawa** *Kiribati* 1°30N 173°0E **288** G9
**Teiuş** *Romania* 46°12N 23°40E **183** D8
**Teixeira** *Brazil* 7°13S 37°15W **332** C4
**Teixeira Pinto** *Guinea-Biss.* 12°3N 16°0W **262** C1
**Tejakula** *Indonesia* 8°8S 115°20E **231** J18
**Tejen** *Turkmenistan* 37°23N 60°31E **216** E6
**Tejen** → *Turkmenistan* 37°24N 60°38E **247** B9
**Tejo** → *Europe* 38°40N 9°24W **195** F2
**Tejo, Rio** → *Portugal* 38°45N 9°3W **126** A2
**Tejon Pass** *U.S.A.* 34°49N 118°53W **307** L8
**Tekamah** *U.S.A.* 41°47N 96°13W **308** E5
**Tekapo** → *N.Z.* 44°13S 170°21E **285** E5
**Tekapo, L.** *N.Z.* 43°53S 170°33E **285** D5
**Tekax** *Mexico* 20°12N 89°17W **319** C7
**Teke** *Turkey* 41°4N 29°39E **203** E13
**Tekeli** *Kazakhstan* 44°50N 79°0E **217** D9
**Tekeze** → *Ethiopia* 14°20N 35°50E **257** E4
**Tekeze Dam** *Ethiopia* 13°10N 38°45E **257** E4
**Tekija** *Serbia* 44°42N 22°26E **202** B6
**Tekirdağ** *Turkey* 40°58N 27°30E **203** F11
**Tekirdağ** □ *Turkey* 41°0N 27°0E **203** E11
**Tekirova** *Turkey* 36°30N 30°32E **205** E12
**Tekkali** *India* 18°37N 84°15E **244** E7
**Tekke** *Turkey* 40°42N 36°12E **212** B7
**Tekman** *Turkey* 39°38N 41°29E **213** C9
**Teknaf** *Bangla.* 20°52N 92°18E **241** E4
**Tekoa** *U.S.A.* 47°14N 117°4W **304** C5
**Tekokota** *French Polynesia* 17°18S 142°34W **289** f
**Tekong Besar, Pulau** *Singapore* 1°25N 104°3E **237** d
**Tekouiàt, O.** → *Algeria* 22°25N 2°35E **261** D5
**Tèkro** *Chad* 19°32N 20°56E **259** E4
**Tekstilshchik** *Russia* 55°42N 37°41E **129** B3
**Tel** → *India* 20°50N 83°54E **244** D6
**Tel Aviv-Yafo** *Israel* 32°4N 34°48E **251** F5
**Tel Lakhish** *Israel* 31°34N 34°51E **251** G5
**Tel Megiddo** *Israel* 32°35N 35°11E **250** F6
**Tela** *Honduras* 15°40N 87°28W **320** C2
**Télagh** *Algeria* 34°51N 0°32W **261** B4
**Telanaipura = Jambi** *Indonesia* 1°38S 103°30E **234** C2
**Telangana** *India* 17°30N 78°30E **244** F4
**Telašćica** ⌂ *Croatia* 43°55N 15°10E **199** E12
**Telavi** *Georgia* 42°0N 45°30E **191** J7
**Telč** *Czech Rep.* 49°11N 15°28E **180** B8
**Telciu** *Romania* 47°25N 24°24E **183** C9
**Telde** *Canary Is.* 27°59N 15°25W **153** e1
**Tele** → *Dem. Rep. of the Congo* 2°48N 23°54E **264** B4
**Telefomin** *Papua N. G.* 5°10S 141°31E **286** C1
**Telegraph Creek** *Canada* 58°0N 131°10W **296** B2
**Telegraph Hill** *San Francisco, U.S.A.* **136** a2
**Telekhany = Tsyelyakhany** *Belarus* 52°30N 25°46E **177** B13
**Telemark** *Norway* 59°15N 7°40E **161** G12
**Telemark** □ *Norway* 59°25N 8°30E **164** E5
**Télemsès** *Niger* 15°37N 4°44E **263** B5
**Telén** *Argentina* 36°15S 65°31W **334** D2
**Telen** → *Indonesia* 0°10S 117°20E **235** C5
**Teleneşti** *Moldova* 47°30N 28°22E **183** C13
**Teleng** *Iran* 25°47N 61°3E **247** E9
**Teleno** *Spain* 42°23N 6°22W **194** C4
**Teleorman** □ *Romania* 44°0N 25°0E **183** G10
**Teleorman** → *Romania* 43°52N 25°26E **183** G10
**Telerhteba, Djebel** *Algeria* 24°10N 6°51E **261** D6
**Teles Pires** → *Brazil* 7°21S 58°3W **331** B6
**Telescope Pk.** *U.S.A.* 36°10N 117°5W **307** J9
**Telescope Pt.** *Grenada* 12°7N 61°36W **323** q
**Teletaye** *Mali* 16°31N 1°30E **263** B5
**Teletskoye, Oz.** *Russia* 51°40N 87°30E **217** B11
**Telford** *U.K.* 52°40N 2°27W **169** E5
**Telford and Wrekin** □ *U.K.* 52°45N 2°27W **168** E5
**Telfs** *Austria* 47°19N 11°4E **180** D4
**Telhal** *Portugal* 38°48N 9°18W **126** A1
**Telida** *U.S.A.* 63°23N 153°16W **303** E9
**Télimélé** *Guinea* 10°54N 13°2W **262** C2
**Teljo, J.** *Sudan* 14°42N 25°26E **257** E2
**Telkwa** *Canada* 54°41N 127°5W **296** C3
**Tell City** *U.S.A.* 37°57N 86°46W **311** G10
**Teller** *U.S.A.* 65°16N 166°22W **303** D6
**Tellicherry = Thalassery** *India* 11°45N 75°30E **245** J2
**Telluride** *U.S.A.* 37°56N 107°49W **305** H10
**Telok Blangah** *Singapore* 1°17N 103°49E **138** B2
**Teloloapán** *Mexico* 18°21N 99°51W **319** D5
**Telpos Iz** *Russia* 63°16N 59°13E **186** B10
**Telsen** *Argentina* 42°30S 66°50W **336** B3
**Telšiai** *Lithuania* 55°59N 22°14E **184** C9
**Telšiai** □ *Lithuania* 55°59N 22°15E **184** C9
**Teltow** *Germany* 52°23N 13°17E **115** B2
**Teltow kanal** *Germany* 52°26N 13°29E **115** B3
**Teluk Anson = Teluk Intan** *Malaysia* 4°3N 101°0E **237** K3
**Teluk Bahang** *Malaysia* 5°28N 100°13E **237** c
**Teluk Betung = Bandar Lampung** *Indonesia* 5°20S 105°10E **234** D3
**Teluk Intan** *Malaysia* 4°3N 101°0E **237** K3
**Teluk Kumbar** *Malaysia* 5°18N 100°14E **237** c
**Telukbatang** *Indonesia* 1°10S 109°46E **235** C3
**Telukbayur** *Kalimantan Timur, Indonesia* 2°9N 117°24E **235** B5
**Telukbayur** *Sumatera Barat, Indonesia* 0°59S 100°23E **234** C2
**Telukbutun** *Indonesia* 4°13N 108°12E **235** B3
**Telukdalam** *Indonesia* 0°33N 97°50E **234** B1
**Tema** *Ghana* 5°41N 0°0 **263** D5
**Temagami, L.** *Canada* 47°0N 80°10W **298** C3
**Temasint** *Algeria* 23°18N 7°40E **261** D6
**Tematangi** *French Polynesia* 21°41S 140°40W **289** f
**Temax** *Mexico* 21°9N 88°56W **319** C7
**Temba** *S. Africa* 25°20S 28°17E **271** C4
**Tembagapura** *Indonesia* 4°20S 137°0E **231** E9
**Tembe** *Dem. Rep. of the Congo* 0°16S 28°14E **268** C2
**Tembe** ⌂ *S. Africa* 26°51S 32°24E **271** C5
**Tembesi** → *Indonesia* 1°43S 103°6E **234** C2
**Tembilahan** *Indonesia* 0°19S 103°9E **234** C2
**Temblador** *Venezuela* 8°59N 62°44W **329** B5
**Tembleque** *Spain* 39°41N 3°30W **194** F7
**Temblor Range** *U.S.A.* 35°20N 119°50W **307** K7
**Tembo Aluma** *Angola* 7°42S 17°17E **265** D3
**Teme** → *U.K.* 52°11N 2°13W **169** E5
**Temecula** *U.S.A.* 33°30N 117°9W **307** M9
**Temengor, Tasik** *Malaysia* 5°24N 101°18E **237** K3
**Temerloh** *Malaysia* 3°27N 102°25E **237** L4
**Temiang** *Indonesia* 0°19N 104°23E **234** B2
**Teminabuan** *Indonesia* 1°26S 132°1E **231** E8
**Temir** *Kazakhstan* 49°1N 57°14E **187** E10
**Temir-Khan-Shura = Buynaksk** *Russia* 42°48N 47°7E **191** J8
**Temirtau** *Kazakhstan* 50°5N 72°56E **217** B8
**Temirtau** *Russia* 53°10N 87°30E **217** B11
**Témiscamie** → *Canada* 50°59N 73°5W **299** B5
**Témiscaming** *Canada* 46°44N 79°5W **298** C4
**Témiscamingue, L.** *Canada* 47°10N 79°25W **298** C4
**Temnikov** *Russia* 54°40N 43°11E **190** C6
**Temo** → *Italy* 40°17N 8°28E **200** B1
**Temora** *Australia* 34°30S 147°30E **283** C7
**Temosachic** *Mexico* 28°57N 107°51W **318** B3
**Tempe** *U.S.A.* 33°24N 111°54W **305** K8
**Tempelburg = Czaplinek** *Poland* 53°34N 16°14E **184** E3
**Tempelhof** *Germany* 52°27N 13°23E **115** B3
**Temperance** *U.S.A.* 41°47N 83°34W **311** C13
**Tempino** *Indonesia* 1°46S 103°30E **234** C2
**Témpio Pausània** *Italy* 40°54N 9°6E **200** B2
**Tempiute** *U.S.A.* 37°39N 115°38W **306** H11
**Temple Bank** *S. China Sea* 9°0N 117°30E **233** F1
**Temple** *U.S.A.* 31°6N 97°21W **314** F6
**Temple B.** *Australia* 12°15S 143°3E **286** G2
**Temple City** *U.S.A.* 34°6N 118°3W **126** B4
**Temple Hills** *U.S.A.* 38°48N 76°56W **143** C3
**Temple Mount** *Jerusalem* **123** b3
**Temple of Heaven** *China* 39°52N 116°23E **114** B2
**Temple of the Dawn = Arun** *Bangkok, Thailand* **113** b1
**Temple Terrace** *U.S.A.* 28°2N 82°23W **317** G7
**Templemore** *Ireland* 52°47N 7°51W **166** D4
**Templeogue** *Ireland* 53°18N 6°18W **120** B2
**Templeton** *U.S.A.* 35°33N 120°42W **306** K6
**Templeton** → *Australia* 21°0S 138°40E **280** C2
**Templin** *Germany* 53°7N 13°28E **178** B9
**Templo Mayor** *Mexico City, Mexico* **128** b3
**Tempoal de Sánchez** *Mexico* 21°31N 98°23W **319** C5
**Temppeliaukio Church** *Finland* 60°10N 24°56E **121** B2
**Tempué** *Angola* 13°27S 18°49E **265** E3
**Temryuk** *Russia* 45°15N 37°24E **189** K9
**Temska** → *Serbia* 43°17N 22°33E **202** C6
**Temuco** *Chile* 38°45S 72°40W **336** A2
**Temuka** *N.Z.* 44°14S 171°17E **285** E6
**Ten Degree Channel** *India* 10°0N 92°30E **245** K11
**Ten Thousand Is.** *U.S.A.* 25°55N 81°45W **317** K8
**Tena** *Ecuador* 0°59S 77°49W **328** D2
**Tenabo** *Mexico* 20°3N 90°14W **319** C6
**Tenafly** *U.S.A.* 40°54N 73°58W **132** A2
**Tenaha** *U.S.A.* 31°57N 94°15W **314** F7
**Tenakee Springs** *U.S.A.* 57°47N 135°13W **296** B1
**Tenali** *India* 16°15N 80°35E **245** F5
**Tenancingo** *Mexico* 18°58N 99°38W **319** D5
**Tenango del Valle** *Mexico* 19°7N 99°33W **319** D5
**Tenaro, Akra** *Greece* 36°22N 22°27E **204** E4
**Tenasserim** *Burma* 12°6N 99°3E **237** F2
**Tenasserim** □ *Burma* 14°0N 98°30E **236** F2
**Tenasserim** → *Burma* 12°24N 98°37E **236** F2
**Tenayuca, Piramide de** *Mexico* 19°31N 99°10W **128** A1
**Tenby** *U.K.* 51°40N 4°42W **169** F3
**Tenda, Colle di** *France* 44°7N 7°36E **175** D11
**Tendaho** *Ethiopia* 11°48N 40°54E **257** E5
**Tende** *France* 44°5N 7°35E **175** D11
**Tendelti** *Sudan* 13°1N 31°55E **257** E3
**Tendjedi, Adrar** *Algeria* 23°41N 7°32E **261** D6
**Tendō** *Japan* 38°20N 140°30E **220** E10
**Tendrara** *Morocco* 33°3N 1°58W **261** B4
**Tendrovskaya Kosa** *Ukraine* 46°16N 31°35E **189** J6
**Tendukhera** *India* 23°24N 79°33E **243** H8
**Teneguía, Volcán** *Canary Is.* 28°28N 17°51W **153** e1
**Teneida** *Egypt* 25°30N 29°19E **256** B2
**Tenenkou** *Mali* 14°28N 4°55W **262** C4
**Tenente Marques** → *Brazil* 11°10S 59°56W **331** C6
**Ténéré** *Niger* 19°0N 10°30E **259** E2
**Ténéré, Erg du** *Niger* 17°35N 10°55E **259** E2
**Tenerife** *Canary Is.* 28°15N 16°35W **153** e1
**Tenerife, Pico** *Canary Is.* 27°43N 18°1W **153** e1

Tenerife Norte ✕ (TFN) Canary Is. 28°28N 16°17W 153 e1
Tenerife Sur ✕ (TFS) Canary Is. 28°3N 16°33W 153 e1
Ténès Algeria 36°31N 1°14E 261 A5
Teng Xian Guangxi Zhuangzu, China 23°21N 110°56E 229 F8
Teng Xian Shandong, China 35°5N 117°10E 227 G9
Tengah → Singapore 1°23N 103°43E 138 A2
Tengah, Kepulauan Indonesia 7°5S 118°15E 235 D5
Tengchong China 25°0N 98°28E 228 E2
Tengchowfu = Penglai China 37°48N 120°42E 227 F11
Tenggarong Indonesia 0°24S 116°58E 235 C5
Tengger Feng China 43°12N 86°48E 217 D11
Tengger Shamo China 38°0N 104°10E 226 F3
Tenggol, Pulau Malaysia 4°48N 103°41E 237 K4
Tengiz Köli Kazakhstan 50°30N 69°0E 217 B7
Tengzhou China 35°4N 117°9E 227 G9
Tenhult Sweden 57°41N 14°20E 163 G8
Teniente Enciso △ Paraguay 21°5S 61°8W 334 A3
Tenille U.S.A. 29°46N 83°19W 316 F6
Tenino U.S.A. 46°51N 122°51W 306 D4
Tenkasi India 8°55N 77°20E 245 K3
Tenke Katanga, Dem. Rep. of the Congo 11°22S 26°40E 269 E2
Tenke Katanga, Dem. Rep. of the Congo 10°32S 26°7E 269 E2
Tenkodogo Burkina Faso 11°54N 0°19W 263 C4
Tenna → Italy 43°14N 13°47E 199 E10
Tennant Creek Australia 19°30S 134°15E 280 B1
Tennessee □ U.S.A. 36°0N 86°30W 315 D11
Tennessee → U.S.A. 37°4N 88°34W 315 C10
Tennille U.S.A. 32°56N 82°48W 316 C7
Tennoji Japan 34°39N 135°30E 133 B2
Teno, Pta. de Canary Is. 28°21N 16°55W 153 e1
Tenojoki = Tana → Norway 70°30N 28°14E 160 A23
Tenom Malaysia 5°4N 115°57E 235 A5
Tenosique Mexico 17°29N 91°26W 319 D6
Tenri Japan 34°39N 135°49E 223 C7
Tenryū Japan 34°52N 137°49E 223 C9
Tenryū-Gawa → Japan 35°39N 137°48E 223 B9
Tensift, Oued → Morocco 32°3N 9°28W 260 B3
Tente Indonesia 8°35S 118°41E 235 D5
Tenterden U.K. 51°4N 0°42E 169 F8
Tenterfield Australia 29°0S 152°0E 281 D5
Tenuaiur, Uad → W. Sahara 21°36N 16°0W 260 D1
Teo = A Ramallosa Spain 42°54N 8°30W 194 C2
Teófilo Otoni Brazil 17°50S 41°30W 333 E3
Tepa Indonesia 7°52S 129°31E 231 F7
Tepa Pt. Cook Is. 19°6S 169°55W 289 g
Tepalcatepec → Mexico 18°35N 101°59W 318 D4
Tepalcates Mexico 19°23N 99°3W 128 B2
Tepecik Bursa, Turkey 40°7N 28°25E 203 F12
Tepecik Kütahya, Turkey 39°32N 29°28E 205 B11
Tepehuanes Mexico 25°21N 105°44W 318 B3
Tepelenë Albania 40°17N 20°2E 202 F4
Tepequem, Serra Brazil 3°45N 61°45W 329 C5
Tepetongo Mexico 22°28N 103°9W 318 C4
Tepeyac △ Mexico 19°30N 99°7W 128 B2
Tepic = Nayarit □ Mexico 22°0N 105°0W 318 C4
Tepic Mexico 21°30N 104°54W 318 C4
Teplá Czech Rep. 49°59N 12°52E 180 B5
Teplice Czech Rep. 50°40N 13°48E 180 A6
Teplitz = Teplice Czech Rep. 50°40N 13°48E 180 A6
Teplyk Ukraine 48°40N 29°44E 183 B14
Tequila Mexico 20°54N 103°47W 318 C4
Ter → Spain 42°2N 3°12E 196 C8
Ter Apel Neths. 52°53N 7°5E 170 B7
Téra Niger 14°0N 0°45E 263 C5
Tera → Spain 41°54N 5°44W 194 D5
Tera Kora Bonaire 12°11N 68°16W 322 h
Teraina Kiribati 4°43N 160°25W 289 G12
Terakeka South Sudan 5°26N 31°45E 257 F3
Téramo Italy 42°39N 13°42E 199 F10
Terang Australia 38°15S 142°55E 282 E5
Terang, Teluk Indonesia 8°44S 116°0E 231 K19
Terawhiti, C. N.Z. 41°16S 174°38E 284 H3
Terazit, Massif de Niger 20°2N 8°30E 259 D1
Tercan Turkey 39°47N 40°23E 213 C9
Terceira Azores 38°43N 27°13W 153 d1
Tercero → Argentina 32°58S 61°47W 334 C3
Terdal India 16°33N 75°3E 244 F2
Terebovlya Ukraine 49°18N 25°44E 177 D13
Teregova Romania 45°10N 22°16E 182 E7
Tereida Sudan 10°35N 31°17E 257 E3
Terek → Russia 44°0N 47°30E 191 J8
Terengganu □ Malaysia 4°55N 103°0E 237 K4
Terenos Brazil 20°26S 54°50W 331 E7
Terepaima △ Venezuela 9°58N 69°17W 328 B4
Tereshka → Russia 51°48N 46°26E 190 E8
Teresina Brazil 5°9S 42°45W 332 C3
Teresinha Brazil 0°58N 52°2W 329 C7
Terespol Poland 52°5N 23°37E 185 F10
Teressa India 8°15N 93°10E 245 K11
Teresva Ukraine 48°0N 23°42E 183 B8
Terewah, L. Australia 29°52S 147°35E 281 D4
Terges → Portugal 37°49N 7°41W 195 H3
Tergnier France 49°40N 3°17E 173 C10
Terhazza Mali 23°38N 5°22W 260 D3
Teridgerie Cr. → Australia 30°25S 148°50E 283 A8
Terijoki = Zelenogorsk Russia 60°12N 29°43E 188 B5
Terlizzi Italy 41°8N 16°32E 201 A9
Termas de Río Hondo Argentina 27°29S 64°52W 334 B3
Terme Turkey 41°11N 37°0E 212 B7
Términi Imerese Italy 37°59N 13°42E 200 E6
Términos, L. de Mexico 18°37N 91°33W 319 D6
Termit, Massif de Niger 16°2N 11°20E 259 E2
Termiz Uzbekistan 37°15N 67°15E 217 E7
Térmoli Italy 42°0N 15°0E 199 F12
Ternate Indonesia 0°45N 127°25E 231 D7
Terneuzen Neths. 51°20N 3°50E 170 C3
Terney Russia 45°3N 136°37E 220 B8
Terni Italy 42°34N 12°37E 199 F9
Ternitz Austria 47°43N 16°2E 180 D9
Ternivka Ukraine 48°32N 29°58E 183 B14
Ternopil Ukraine 49°30N 25°40E 177 D13
Ternopil □ Ukraine 48°10N 25°10E 177 D13
Ternopol = Ternopil Ukraine 49°30N 25°40E 177 D13
Terowie Australia 33°8S 138°55E 282 B3
Terpni Greece 40°55N 23°26E 202 F7
Terra Bella U.S.A. 35°58N 119°3W 307 K7
Terra Nova △ Canada 48°33N 53°55W 299 C9
Terrace Canada 54°30N 128°35W 296 C3
Terrace Bay Canada 48°47N 87°5W 298 C2
Terracina Italy 41°17N 13°15E 200 A6
Terralba Italy 39°43N 8°39E 200 C1
Terranova di Sicilia = Gela Italy 37°4N 14°15E 201 E7
Terranova Pausania = Ólbia Italy 40°55N 9°31E 200 B2
Terrasini Italy 38°10N 13°4E 200 D6
Terrassa Spain 41°34N 2°1E 196 D7
Terrasson-la-Villedieu France 45°8N 1°18E 174 C5
Terrazzano Italy 45°32N 9°4E 128 A1
Terre-de-Bas Guadeloupe 15°51N 61°38W 322 e
Terre-de-Bas Guadeloupe 16°10N 61°7W 322 e
Terre-de-Haut Guadeloupe 15°52N 61°34W 322 e
Terre des Hommes Canada 45°31N 73°32W 130 A2
Terre Haute U.S.A. 39°28N 87°25W 311 E9
Terre Rouge Mauritius 20°7S 57°31E 272 e
Terrebonne B. U.S.A. 29°5N 90°35W 315 G9
Terrecht Mali 19°35N 0°22E 261 D4
Terrell U.S.A. 32°44N 96°17W 314 E6
Terrenceville Canada 47°40N 54°44W 299 C9
Terrick Terrick △ Australia 36°8S 144°13E 282 D6
Terrugem Portugal 38°41N 9°17W 126 A1
Terry U.S.A. 46°47N 105°19W 304 C11
Terrytown U.S.A. 29°54N 90°1W 131 B2
Terryville U.S.A. 41°41N 73°3W 313 E11
Terschelling Neths. 53°25N 5°20E 170 A5
Tersko-Kumskiy Kanal Russia 44°32N 44°38E 191 H7
Tertenia Italy 39°42N 9°34E 200 C2
Terter = Tärtär → Azerbaijan 40°26N 47°20E 191 K8
Teruel Spain 40°22N 1°8W 196 E3
Teruel □ Spain 40°48N 1°0W 196 E4
Tervel Bulgaria 43°45N 27°28E 203 C11
Tervola Finland 66°6N 24°49E 160 C21
Tervuren Belgium 50°49N 4°31E 116 B3
Tervuren, Park van Belgium 50°49N 4°31E 116 B3
Teryaweynya L. Australia 32°18S 143°22E 282 B5
Tešanj Bos.-H. 44°38N 18°1E 182 F3
Teschen = Cieszyn Poland 49°45N 18°35E 185 J5
Teseney Eritrea 15°5N 36°42E 257 D4
Tesha → Russia 55°38N 42°9E 190 C6
Teshekpuk L. U.S.A. 70°35N 153°26W 303 A9
Teshio Japan 44°53N 141°44E 220 B10
Teshio-Gawa → Japan 44°53N 141°45E 220 B10
Tešica Serbia 43°27N 21°45E 202 C5
Tesiyn Gol → Mongolia 50°40N 93°20E 218 A7
Teslić Bos.-H. 44°37N 17°54E 182 F2
Teslin Canada 60°10N 132°43W 296 A2
Teslin → Canada 61°34N 134°35W 296 A2
Teslin L. Canada 60°15N 132°57W 296 A2
Tesouro Brazil 16°4S 53°34W 331 D7
Tessalit Mali 20°12N 1°0E 261 D5
Tessaoua Niger 13°47N 7°56E 259 F1
Tessin Germany 54°2N 12°26E 178 A8
Tessit Mali 15°13N 0°18E 263 B5
Tessounfat Mali 22°53N 0°32E 261 D5
Test → U.K. 50°56N 1°29W 169 G6
Testa del Gargano Italy 41°50N 16°10E 199 G13
Testigos, Is. Los Venezuela 11°23N 63°7W 321 D7
Tét Hungary 47°30N 17°33E 182 C2
Têt → France 42°44N 3°2E 174 F7
Tetachuck L. Canada 53°18N 125°55W 296 C3
Tetas, Pta. Chile 23°31S 70°38W 334 A1
Tete Mozam. 16°13S 33°33E 269 F3
Tete □ Mozam. 15°15S 32°40E 269 F3
Tetenga, Caleta Chile 27°9S 109°19W 330 b
Tetepare Solomon Is. 8°45S 157°35E 287 M9
Teterev → Ukraine 51°1N 30°5E 177 C16
Teterow Germany 53°46N 12°34E 178 B8
Teteven Bulgaria 42°58N 24°17E 203 D8
Tethul → Canada 60°35N 112°12W 296 A6
Tetiyev Ukraine 49°22N 29°38E 177 D15
Tetlin U.S.A. 63°8N 142°31W 303 E12
Tetlin Junction U.S.A. 63°19N 142°36W 303 E12
Tetlin Nat. Wildlife Refuge △ U.S.A. 62°40N 141°50W 303 E12
Tetlit Zheh = Fort McPherson Canada 67°30N 134°55W 294 D5
Teton → U.S.A. 47°56N 110°31W 304 C8
Tétouan Morocco 35°35N 5°21W 260 A3
Tetovo Macedonia 42°1N 20°59E 202 D4
Tetschen = Děčín Czech Rep. 50°47N 14°12E 180 A7
Tetuán Spain 40°27N 3°42W 127 B1
Tetufera, Mt. Tahiti 17°40S 149°26W 289 e
Tetyukhe = Dalnegorsk Russia 44°32N 135°33E 220 B7
Tetyushi Russia 54°55N 48°49E 190 C9
Teuco → Argentina 25°35S 60°11W 334 B3
Teufelsberg Germany 52°29N 13°14E 115 B2
Teulada Italy 38°58N 8°46E 200 D1
Teulon Canada 50°23N 97°16W 297 C9
Teun Indonesia 6°59S 129°8E 231 F7
Teuri-Tō Japan 44°26N 141°19E 220 B10
Teutoburger Wald Germany 52°5N 8°22E 178 C4
Teutopolis U.S.A. 39°8N 88°29W 311 E8
Tevere → Italy 41°44N 12°14E 199 G9
Tevere △ Italy 42°46N 12°14E 199 F9
Teverya Israel 32°47N 35°32E 250 F6
Teviot → U.K. 55°29N 2°38W 167 F6
Tewantin Australia 26°27S 153°3E 281 D5
Teweh → Indonesia 0°58N 114°54E 235 C5
Tewkesbury U.K. 51°59N 2°9W 169 F5
Texada I. Canada 49°40N 124°25W 296 D4
Texarkana Ark., U.S.A. 33°26N 94°2W 314 E7
Texarkana Tex., U.S.A. 33°26N 94°3W 314 E7
Texas Australia 28°49S 151°9E 281 D5
Texas □ U.S.A. 31°40N 98°30W 314 F5
Texas City U.S.A. 29°24N 94°54W 314 G7
Texel Neths. 53°5N 4°50E 170 A4
Texline U.S.A. 36°23N 103°2W 314 C3
Texoma, L. U.S.A. 33°50N 96°34W 314 E6
Teykovo Russia 56°55N 40°30E 188 D11
Teyvareh Afghan. 33°30N 64°24E 240 B2
Teza → Russia 56°32N 41°53E 190 B5
Tezin Afghan. 34°24N 69°30E 242 B3
Teziutlán Mexico 19°49N 97°21W 319 D5
Tezpur India 26°40N 92°45E 241 B4
Tezu India 27°55N 96°10E 241 B6
Tezzeron L. Canada 54°43N 124°30W 296 C4
Tha-anne → Canada 60°31N 94°37W 297 A10
Tha Deua Laos 17°57N 102°53E 236 D4
Tha Deua Laos 19°26N 101°50E 236 C3
Tha Li Thailand 17°37N 101°25E 236 D3
Tha Pla Thailand 17°48N 100°32E 236 D3
Tha Rua Thailand 14°34N 100°44E 236 E3
Tha Sala Thailand 8°40N 99°56E 237 H2
Tha Song Yang Thailand 17°34N 97°55E 236 D1
Thaba Putsoa Lesotho 29°45S 28°0E 271 C4
Thaba-Tseka Lesotho 29°32S 28°36E 271 C4
Thabana Ntlenyana Lesotho 29°30S 29°16E 271 C4
Thabaung Burma 17°2N 94°48E 241 G5
Thabazimbi S. Africa 24°40S 27°21E 271 B4
Thabeikkyin Burma 22°53N 95°59E 241 H5
Thabt, G. el Egypt 28°17N 34°1E 251 K5
Thādiq Si. Arabia 25°18N 45°52E 246 E5
Thai Binh Vietnam 20°35N 106°1E 228 G6
Thai Muang Thailand 8°24N 98°16E 237 H2
Thai Nguyen Vietnam 21°35N 105°55E 228 G5
Thailand ■ Asia 16°0N 102°0E 236 E4
Thailand, G. of Asia 11°30N 101°0E 237 G3
Thakhek Laos 17°25N 104°45E 236 D5
Thakurgaon Bangla. 26°2N 88°34E 241 B2
Thal Pakistan 33°28N 70°33E 242 C4
Thal Desert Pakistan 31°10N 71°30E 242 D4
Thala Tunisia 35°35N 8°40E 258 A1
Thala La = Hkakabo Razi Burma 28°25N 97°23E 228 C1
Thalabarivat Cambodia 13°33N 105°57E 236 F5
Thalang = Amphoe Thalang Thailand 8°1N 98°20E 237 a
Thalang Thailand 8°2N 98°20E 237 H2
Thalara Nepal 29°29N 80°59E 243 E9
Thalassery India 11°45N 75°30E 245 J2
Thale Sap Songkhla Thailand 7°12N 100°28E 237 J3
Thalkirchen Germany 48°6N 11°32E 131 B2
Thallon Australia 28°39S 148°49E 281 D4
Thalu, Ko Thailand 9°26N 99°54E 237 b
Thalwil Switz. 47°17N 8°35E 179 H4
Tham Lot Thailand 19°34N 98°16E 236 C2
Thamarīt Oman 17°39N 54°2E 249 C5
Thames N.Z. 37°7S 175°34E 284 D4
Thames → Ont., Canada 42°20N 82°25W 312 D2
Thames → U.K. 51°29N 0°34E 169 F8
Thames → Conn., U.S.A. 41°18N 72°5W 313 E12
Thames, Firth of N.Z. 37°0S 175°25E 284 D4
Thames Ditton U.K. 51°23N 0°20W 125 B1
Thames Estuary U.K. 51°29N 0°52E 169 F8
Thamesford Canada 43°4N 81°0W 312 C4
Thamesmead U.K. 51°30N 0°7E 125 A4
Thamesville Canada 42°33N 81°59W 312 D3
Thāmit, W. → Libya 31°11N 16°8E 258 B3
Thamūd Yemen 17°18N 49°55E 249 C5
Than India 22°34N 71°11E 242 H4
Than Kyun Burma 9°49N 98°4E 237 H1
Than Uyen Vietnam 22°0N 103°54E 236 B4
Thana Cr. → India 19°4N 72°54E 130 A2
Thana Gazi India 27°25N 76°19E 242 F7
Thanbyuzayat Burma 15°58N 97°44E 241 G6
Thandaung Burma 19°4N 96°41E 241 F6
Thandla India 23°0N 74°34E 242 H6
Thandwe Burma 18°20N 94°30E 241 F5
Thane India 19°12N 72°59E 244 E1
Thanesar India 30°1N 76°52E 242 D7
Thanet, I. of U.K. 51°21N 1°20E 169 F9
Thangool Australia 24°38S 150°42E 280 C5
Thanh Hoa Vietnam 19°48N 105°46E 236 C5
Thanh Hung Vietnam 9°55N 105°43E 237 H5
Thanh Pho Ho Chi Minh Vietnam 10°58N 106°40E 237 G6
Thanh Thuy Vietnam 22°55N 104°51E 236 A5
Thanjavur India 10°48N 79°12E 245 J4
Thanlwin = Salween → Burma 16°31N 97°37E 241 G6
Thanlyin = Syriam Burma 16°44N 96°19E 241 G6
Thann France 47°48N 7°5E 173 E14
Thano Bula Khan Pakistan 25°22N 67°50E 242 G2
Thanya Buri Thailand 14°1N 100°45E 236 E3
Thaoge → Botswana 20°27S 22°36E 270 B3
Thaolintoa L. Canada 61°30N 96°25W 297 A9
Thaon-les-Vosges France 48°15N 6°24E 173 D13
Thap Lan △ Thailand 14°15N 102°16E 236 E4
Thap Sakae Thailand 11°30N 99°37E 237 G2
Thap Than Thailand 15°27N 99°54E 236 E2
Thar Desert India 28°0N 72°0E 242 F5
Tharad India 24°30N 71°44E 242 G4
Thargomindah Australia 27°58S 143°46E 281 D3
Tharp Fracture Zone S. Ocean 54°0S 135°0W 151 B14
Tharrawaddy Burma 17°38N 95°48E 241 G5
Tharrawaw Burma 17°41N 95°28E 241 G5
Tharthār, Buḩayrat ath Iraq 34°0N 43°15E 213 E10
Tharthar, L. = Tharthār, Buḩayrat ath Iraq 34°0N 43°15E 213 E10
Tharthār, W. ath → Iraq 34°32N 43°4E 213 E10
Thasopoula Greece 40°49N 24°45E 203 F8
Thasos Greece 40°40N 24°40E 203 F8
That Khe Vietnam 22°16N 106°28E 228 F6
Thatcher Ariz., U.S.A. 32°51N 109°46W 305 K9
Thatcher Colo., U.S.A. 37°33N 104°7W 305 H11
Thaton Burma 16°55N 97°22E 241 G6
Thatta Pakistan 24°42N 67°55E 242 G2
Thau, Bassin de France 43°23N 3°36E 174 E7
Thaungdut Burma 24°30N 94°40E 241 C5
Thawatti Burma 19°32N 96°16E 241 E6
Thayawthadangy Kyun Burma 12°19N 98°0E 236 F1
Thayer U.S.A. 36°31N 91°33W 308 G8
Thayetmyo Burma 19°20N 95°10E 241 F5
Thazi Magwe, Burma 19°59N 95°3E 241 F5
Thazi Mandalay, Burma 21°0N 96°5E 241 E6
Thbeng Meanchey Cambodia 13°49N 104°58E 236 F5
The Bahamas ■ N. Amer. 24°0N 75°0W 321 B5
The Broads U.K. 52°45N 1°30E 168 E9
The Everglades U.S.A. 25°50N 81°0W 317 K9
The Gambia ■ W. Afr. 13°25N 16°0W 262 C1
The Gulf = Persian Gulf Asia 27°0N 50°0E 247 E6
The Hague = 's-Gravenhage Neths. 52°7N 4°17E 170 B4
The Pas Canada 53°45N 101°15W 297 C8
The Wash U.K. 52°58N 0°20E 168 E8
The Weald U.K. 51°4N 0°20E 169 F8
Thebes = Thiva Greece 38°19N 23°19E 204 C5
Thebes Egypt 25°40N 32°35E 256 B3
Thedford U.S.A. 41°59N 100°35W 308 E3
Theebine Australia 25°57S 152°34E 281 D5
Thègon Burma 18°39N 95°25E 241 F5
Thekulthili L. Canada 61°3N 110°0W 297 A7
Thelon → Canada 64°16N 96°4W 297 A8
Thénezay France 46°44N 0°2W 172 F6
Thenon France 45°9N 1°4E 174 C5
Theodore Queens., Australia 24°55S 150°3E 280 C5
Theodore Sask., Canada 51°26N 102°55W 297 C8
Theodore Ala., U.S.A. 30°33N 88°10W 315 F10
Theodore Roosevelt △ U.S.A. 47°0N 103°25W 308 B2
Theodore Roosevelt L. U.S.A. 33°40N 111°10W 305 K8
Thepha Thailand 6°52N 100°58E 237 J3
Thérain → France 49°15N 2°27E 173 C9
Therandë Kosovo 42°21N 20°50E 202 D4
Theresa U.S.A. 44°13N 75°48W 313 B9
Theressa U.S.A. 29°50N 82°4W 317 F7
Therma = Eagle Nest U.S.A. 36°33N 105°16W 305 H11
Thermopolis U.S.A. 43°39N 108°13W 304 E9
Thermopylae Greece 38°48N 22°35E 204 C4
Thesprotia Greece 39°27N 20°22E 204 B2
Thessalon Canada 46°20N 83°30W 298 C3
Thessalonica, Gulf of = Thessaloniki Kolpos Greece 40°15N 22°45E 202 F6
Thessaloniki Greece 40°38N 22°58E 202 F6
Thessaloniki ✕ (SKG) Greece 40°30N 23°0E 202 F7
Thessaloniki Kolpos Greece 40°15N 22°45E 202 F6
Thessaly □ Greece 39°25N 22°0E 204 B4
Thetford U.K. 52°25N 0°45E 169 E8
Thetford Mines Canada 46°8N 71°18W 299 C5
Theun → Laos 18°19N 104°0E 236 C5
Theunissen S. Africa 28°26S 26°43E 270 C4
Thevenard Australia 32°9S 133°38E 281 E1
Thiais France 48°46N 2°23E 134 B3
Thiamis → Greece 39°15N 20°6E 204 B2
Thibaud Dominica 15°36N 61°24W 323 k
Thiberville France 49°8N 0°27E 172 C7
Thibodaux U.S.A. 29°48N 90°49W 315 G9
Thicket Portage Canada 55°19N 97°42W 297 B9
Thief River Falls U.S.A. 48°7N 96°10W 308 A5
Thiel Mts. Antarctica 85°15S 91°0W 151 E16
Thiene Italy 45°42N 11°29E 199 C8
Thiérache France 49°51N 3°45E 173 C10
Thiers France 45°52N 3°33E 174 C7
Thiès Senegal 14°50N 16°51W 262 C1
Thiès □ Senegal 14°45N 16°50W 262 C1
Thiesi Italy 40°31N 8°43E 200 B1
Thika Kenya 1°1S 37°5E 268 C4
Thille-Boubacar Senegal 16°31N 15°5W 262 B1
Thimân, W. → Egypt 28°4N 33°45E 251 K4
Thimphu Bhutan 27°31N 89°45E 241 B2
Thina → S. Africa 31°18S 29°13E 271 D4
Thinadhoo Maldives 0°32N 72°56E 272 d
Thingangyun Burma 16°49N 96°12E 241 G6
Þingeyjarsýsla Iceland 65°40N 16°30W 155 B10
Þingeyri Iceland 65°52N 23°30W 155 B3
Þingmúli Iceland 65°2N 14°37W 155 B12
Þingvallavatn Iceland 64°11N 21°9W 155 C5
Þingvellir Iceland 64°15N 21°7W 155 C5
Þingvellir △ Iceland 64°16N 21°5W 155 C5
Thio N. Cal. 21°37S 166°14E 288 d
Thionville France 49°20N 6°10E 173 C13
Thira = Santorini Greece 36°23N 25°27E 205 E7
Thirasia Greece 36°26N 25°21E 205 E7
Third Cataract Sudan 19°42N 30°20E 256 D3
Thirsk U.K. 54°14N 1°19W 168 C6
Thiruvananthapuram India 8°41N 77°0E 245 K3
Thiruvarur India 10°46N 79°38E 245 J4
Thisio Athens, Greece 112 c1
Thisted Denmark 56°58N 8°40E 163 H2
Þistilfjörður Iceland 66°18N 15°24W 155 A11
Thistle I. Australia 35°0S 136°8E 282 C2
Thistletown Canada 43°44N 79°34W 141 A1
Thitgy Burma 18°15N 96°13E 241 F6
Thithia = Cicia Fiji 17°45S 179°18W 287 A3
Thitpokpin Burma 19°24N 95°58E 241 F5
Thitu I. S. China Sea 11°3N 114°17E 230 B4
Thiva Greece 38°19N 23°19E 204 C5
Thiviers France 45°25N 0°54E 174 C4
Thizy France 46°2N 4°18E 173 F11
Þjórsá → Iceland 63°47N 20°48W 155 D6
Thlewiaza → Canada 60°29N 94°40W 297 A10
Thmar Puok Cambodia 13°57N 103°4E 236 F4
Tho Chu, Dao Vietnam 9°20N 103°28E 237 H4
Tho Vinh Vietnam 19°16N 105°42E 236 C5
Thoa → Canada 60°31N 109°47W 297 A7
Thoen Thailand 17°43N 99°12E 236 D2
Thoeng Thailand 19°41N 100°12E 236 C3
Thomas U.S.A. 35°45N 98°45W 314 D5
Thomas, L. Australia 26°4S 137°58E 281 D2
Thomas Circle Washington, D.C., U.S.A. 143 a1
Thomas Hill Res. U.S.A. 39°34N 92°39W 310 E4
Thomas Hubbard, C. Canada 82°0N 94°25W 295 A13
Thomaston U.S.A. 32°53N 84°20W 316 C5
Thomastown Australia 37°40S 145°2E 128 A2
Thomasville Ala., U.S.A. 31°55N 87°44W 315 F11
Thomasville Ga., U.S.A. 30°50N 83°59W 316 E6
Thomasville N.C., U.S.A. 35°53N 80°5W 315 D14
Thompson Man., Canada 55°45N 97°52W 297 B9
Thompson Pa., U.S.A. 41°52N 75°31W 313 E9
Thompson → B.C., Canada 50°15N 121°24W 296 C4
Thompson → Mo., U.S.A. 39°46N 93°37W 310 E3
Thompson Falls U.S.A. 47°36N 115°21W 304 C6
Thompson I. U.S.A. 42°19N 70°59W 116 B3
Thompson Pk. U.S.A. 41°0N 123°2W 304 F2
Thompson Sd. N.Z. 45°8S 166°46E 285 F1
Thompson Springs U.S.A. 38°58N 109°43W 304 G9
Thompsontown U.S.A. 40°33N 77°14W 312 F7
Thomson Ga., U.S.A. 33°28N 82°30W 316 B7
Thomson Ill., U.S.A. 41°58N 90°6W 310 C6
Thomson → Australia 25°11S 142°53E 280 C3
Thomson's Falls = Nyahururu Kenya 0°2N 36°27E 268 B4
Thon Buri Thailand 13°45N 100°29E 113 B1
Thônes France 45°54N 6°18E 175 C10
Thong Yang Thailand 9°28N 99°56E 237 b
Thongwa Burma 16°45N 96°33E 241 G6
Thonon-les-Bains France 46°22N 6°29E 173 F13
Thonze Burma 17°38N 95°47E 241 G5
Thoothukudi = Tuticorin India 8°50N 78°12E 245 K4
Thorez Ukraine 48°4N 38°34E 189 H10
Þórisjökull Iceland 64°32N 20°43W 155 C6
Þórisvatn Iceland 64°20N 18°55W 155 C8
Þórkötlustaðir Iceland 63°50N 22°24W 155 D4
Þorlákshöfn Iceland 63°51N 21°22W 155 D5
Thorn = Toruń Poland 53°2N 18°39E 185 E5
Thornaby on Tees U.K. 54°33N 1°18W 168 C6
Thornbury Vic., Australia 37°44S 145°1E 128 A2
Thornbury Ont., Canada 44°34N 80°26W 312 B4
Thornbury N.Z. 46°17S 168°9E 285 G3
Thorncliffe Canada 43°42N 79°20W 141 A2
Thorne U.K. 53°37N 0°57W 168 D7
Thornhill Canada 43°48N 79°25W 141 A2
Thornton Ont., Canada 44°16N 79°43W 312 B5
Thornton Western Cape, S. Africa 33°55S 18°32E 118 A2
Thornton Colo., U.S.A. 39°52N 104°58W 304 G11
Thornton Iowa, U.S.A. 42°57N 93°23W 310 B3
Thornton Heath U.K. 51°23N 0°6W 125 B3
Thorntown U.S.A. 40°8N 86°36W 311 D10
Thorold Canada 43°7N 79°12W 312 C5
Thorpes Barbados 13°9N 59°37W 323 r
Þórshöfn Iceland 66°12N 15°20W 155 A11
Thouarcé France 47°17N 0°30W 172 E6
Thouars France 47°0N 0°15W 172 F6
Thoubal India 24°38N 94°1E 241 C5
Thouet → France 47°17N 0°6W 172 E6
Thouin, C. Australia 20°20S 118°10E 278 D2
Thousand Islands U.S.A. 44°20N 76°0W 313 B9
Thousand Oaks U.S.A. 34°10N 118°50W 307 L8
Thrace Turkey 41°0N 27°0E 203 F10
Thrace, Sea of Greece 40°30N 25°0E 203 F8
Thredbo Australia 36°31S 148°20E 283 D8
Three Fathoms Cove Hong Kong, China 22°25N 114°16E 122 A3
Three Forks U.S.A. 45°54N 111°33W 304 D8
Three Gorges Dam China 30°45N 111°15E 229 B8
Three Gorges Res. = Sanxia Shuiku China 30°3N 107°58E 228 B6
Three Hills Canada 51°43N 113°15W 296 C6
Three Hummock I. Australia 40°25S 144°55E 281 G3
Three Oaks U.S.A. 41°48N 86°36W 311 C10
Three Pagodas Pass Asia 15°20N 98°30E 236 E2
Three Points, C. Ghana 4°42N 2°6W 262 E4
Three Rivers Calif., U.S.A. 36°26N 118°54W 306 J8
Three Rivers Mich., U.S.A. 41°57N 85°38W 311 C11
Three Rivers Tex., U.S.A. 28°28N 98°11W 314 G5
Three Sisters Is. Solomon Is. 10°10S 161°57E 287 N11
Three Springs Australia 29°32S 115°45E 279 E2
Threipmuir Res. U.K. 55°51N 3°19W 124 B2
Thrissur India 10°30N 76°18E 245 J3
Throg's Neck U.S.A. 40°48N 73°49W 132 B5
Throssell, L. Australia 27°33S 124°10E 279 E3
Throssell Ra. Australia 22°3S 121°43E 278 D3
Thrumshing △ Bhutan 27°25N 90°50E 241 B3
Thrushton △ Australia 27°47S 147°40E 281 D4
Thu Dau Mot Vietnam 10°58N 106°39E 237 G6
Thua → Kenya 1°31S 39°30E 268 C4
Thuamal Rampur India 19°23N 82°56E 244 E6
Thuan Hoa Vietnam 8°58N 105°30E 237 H5
Thubun Lakes Canada 61°30N 112°0W 297 A6
Thueyts France 44°41N 4°9E 175 D8
Thugga = Dougga Tunisia 36°25N 9°13E 258 A1
Thuin Belgium 50°20N 4°17E 170 D4
Thuir France 42°38N 2°45E 174 F6
Thule = Qaanaaq Greenland 77°30N 69°10W 154 B4
Thule Air Base = Uummannaq Greenland 77°33N 68°52W 154 B4
Thun Switz. 46°45N 7°38E 179 J3
Thunder B. U.S.A. 45°0N 83°20W 312 B1
Thunder Bay Canada 48°20N 89°15W 298 C2
Thunderbolt U.S.A. 32°3N 81°4W 316 C8
Thunersee Switz. 46°43N 7°39E 179 J3
Thung Salaeng Luang △ Thailand 16°43N 100°50E 236 D3
Thung Song Thailand 8°10N 99°40E 237 H2
Thungyai △ Thailand 15°20N 98°55E 236 E2
Thunkar Bhutan 27°55N 91°0E 241 B3
Thuong Tra Vietnam 16°2N 107°42E 236 D6
Thur → Switz. 47°32N 9°10E 179 H5
Thurgau □ Switz. 47°34N 9°10E 179 H5
Thüringen □ Germany 51°0N 11°0E 178 D6
Thüringer Wald Germany 50°35N 11°0E 178 E6
Thuringowa △ Australia 19°18S 146°43E 280 B4
Thurles Ireland 52°41N 7°49W 166 D4
Thurn P. Austria 47°20N 12°25E 180 D5
Thurrock □ U.K. 51°31N 0°23E 169 F8
Thursday I. Australia 10°30S 142°3E 286 F2
Thurso Qué., Canada 45°36N 75°15W 298 C4
Thurso Highl., U.K. 58°36N 3°32W 167 C5
Thurso → U.K. 58°36N 3°32W 167 C5
Thurston I. Antarctica 72°0S 100°0W 151 D16
Thury-Harcourt France 48°59N 0°30W 172 D6
Thutade L. Canada 57°0N 126°55W 296 B3
Thy Denmark 56°52N 8°25E 163 H2
Thy △ Denmark 56°55N 8°25E 163 H2
Thyborøn Denmark 56°42N 8°12E 163 H2
Þykkvabæjarklaustur Iceland 63°30N 18°22W 155 D8
Þykkvibær Iceland 63°45N 20°37W 155 D6
Thyolo Malawi 16°7S 35°5E 269 F4
Thyssen-Bornemisza, Museo Madrid, Spain 127 b3
Ti-n-Amzi → Niger 18°20N 4°32E 263 B5
Ti-n-Barraouene, O. → Africa 18°40N 4°5E 261 E5
Ti-n-Rerhoh Algeria 20°44N 4°2E 261 D5
Ti-n-Tanetfirt Algeria 24°49N 3°48E 261 D5
Ti-n-Tarabine, O. → Algeria 21°16N 7°25E 261 D6
Ti-n-Toumma Niger 16°4N 12°40E 259 E2
Ti-n-Zaouatene Algeria 19°55N 2°55E 261 E5
Ti-Tree Australia 22°5S 133°22E 280 C1
Tiadiaye Senegal 14°25N 16°40W 262 C1
Tiahuanaco Bolivia 16°33S 68°42W 330 D4
Tian Shan Asia 40°30N 76°0E 217 D9
Tian Tan Buddha = Big Buddha Hong Kong, China 22°15N 113°54E 122 B1
Tian'anmen Square Beijing, China 114 c2
Tianchang China 32°40N 119°0E 229 A12
Tiancun China 39°54N 116°12E 114 B1
Tiandeng China 23°6N 107°7E 228 F6
Tiandong China 23°36N 107°8E 228 F6
Tian'e China 25°1N 107°9E 228 E6
Tianguá Brazil 3°44S 40°59W 332 B3
Tianhe Guangdong, China 23°7N 113°21E 121 B3
Tianhe Guangxi Zhuangzu, China 24°48N 108°40E 228 E7
Tianjin China 39°7N 117°12E 227 E9
Tianjin Shi □ China 39°8N 117°10E 227 E9
Tianjun China 38°0N 98°30E 218 D8
Tiankoura Burkina Faso 10°47N 3°17W 262 C4
Tianlin China 24°21N 106°12E 228 E6
Tianmen China 30°39N 113°9E 229 B9
Tianquan China 30°7N 102°43E 228 B4
Tianshifu China 41°17N 124°22E 224 B2
Tianshui China 34°32N 105°40E 226 G3
Tiantai China 29°10N 121°2E 229 C13
Tiantan Park Beijing, China 114 c3
Tianya China 18°18N 109°20E 229 a
Tianyang China 23°42N 106°53E 228 F6
Tianyar Indonesia 8°12S 115°30E 231 J18
Tianzhen China 40°24N 114°5E 226 D8
Tianzhong = T'ienchung Taiwan 23°52N 120°35E 225 C2
Tianzhu China 26°54N 109°11E 228 D7
Tianzhuangtai China 40°43N 122°5E 227 D12
Tiarei Tahiti 17°32S 149°20W 289 e
Tiaret Algeria 35°20N 1°21E 261 A5
Tiaret □ Algeria 34°30N 1°30E 261 B5
Tias Canary Is. 28°57N 13°39W 153 e2
Tiassalé Ivory C. 5°58N 4°57W 262 D4
Tibagi Brazil 24°30S 50°24W 335 A5
Tibagi → Brazil 22°47S 51°1W 335 A5
Tibastī, Sarīr Libya 22°50N 18°30E 258 D3
Tibati Cameroon 6°22N 12°30E 263 D7
Tibe Ethiopia 9°2N 37°12E 257 F4
Tiber = Tevere → Italy 41°44N 12°14E 199 G9
Tiber Res. U.S.A. 48°19N 111°6W 304 B8
Tiberias = Teverya Israel 32°47N 35°32E 250 F6
Tiberias, L. = Yam Kinneret Israel 32°45N 35°35E 250 F6
Tibesti Chad 21°0N 17°30E 259 D3
Tibet = Xizang Zizhiqu □ China 32°0N 88°0E 218 E6
Tibet, L. U.S.A. 28°27N 81°31W 133 B1
Tibet, Plateau of Asia 32°0N 86°0E 210 E10
Tibiao Phil. 11°17N 122°2E 233 F4
Tibidabo Spain 41°25N 2°6E 114 A1
Tibiri Niger 13°34N 7°4E 263 C6
Țibleș, Vf. Romania 47°32N 24°15E 183 C9
Țibleșului, Munții Romania 47°38N 24°5E 183 C9
Tibnī Syria 35°36N 39°50E 213 E8
Tibooburra Australia 29°26S 142°1E 281 D3
Tibradden Mt. Ireland 53°15N 6°16W 120 B2
Tibrikot Nepal 29°3N 82°48E 243 E10
Tibro Sweden 58°28N 14°10E 163 F8
Tiburon U.S.A. 37°52N 122°27W 136 A2
Tiburón, I. Mexico 29°0N 112°25W 318 B2
Tiburtino Italy 41°53N 12°30E 136 B2
Ticao I. Phil. 12°31N 123°42E 232 E4
Tice U.S.A. 26°40N 81°49W 317 J8
Tichît Mauritania 18°21N 9°29W 262 B3
Tichla Mauritania 21°36N 14°58W 260 D2
Ticho Ethiopia 7°50N 39°32E 257 F4
Ticino □ Switz. 46°20N 8°45E 179 J4
Ticino → Italy 45°9N 9°14E 198 C6
Ticleni Romania 44°53N 23°24E 183 F8
Ticomán Mexico 19°31N 99°8W 128 A2
Ticonderoga U.S.A. 43°51N 73°26W 313 C11
Ticul Mexico 20°24N 89°32W 319 C7
Tidaholm Sweden 58°12N 13°58E 163 F7
Tidal Basin Washington, D.C., U.S.A. 143 c1
Tidan Sweden 58°34N 14°1E 163 F8
Tiddim Burma 23°28N 93°45E 241 D4
Tiden India 7°15N 93°33E 245 L11
Tiderïdjaouine, Adrar Algeria 22°0N 2°15E 261 D5
Tidikelt Algeria 26°58N 1°30E 261 C5
Tidioute U.S.A. 41°41N 79°24W 312 E5
Tidjikja Mauritania 18°29N 11°35W 262 B2
Tidmore = Seminole U.S.A. 35°14N 96°41W 314 D6
Tidore Indonesia 0°40N 127°25E 231 D7
Tiébissou Ivory C. 7°9N 5°10W 262 D3
Tiéboro Chad 21°20N 17°7E 259 D3
Tiefa China 42°28N 123°26E 224 A1
Tiefersee Germany 52°24N 13°5E 115 B1
Tiegang Shuiku China 22°37N 113°53E 219 a
Tiel Neths. 51°53N 5°26E 170 C5
Tiel Senegal 14°55N 15°5W 262 C1
Tieli China 46°57N 128°3E 219 B14
Tieling China 42°20N 123°55E 224 A1
Tielt Belgium 51°0N 3°20E 170 C3
Tien Shan = Tian Shan Asia 40°30N 76°0E 217 D9
Tien-tsin = Tianjin China 39°7N 117°12E 227 E9
Tien Yen Vietnam 21°20N 107°24E 236 B6
T'ienching = Tianjin China 39°7N 117°12E 227 E9
T'ienchung Taiwan 23°52N 120°35E 225 C2
Tienen Belgium 50°48N 4°57E 170 D4
Tiénigbé Ivory C. 8°11N 5°43W 262 D3
Tientsin = Tianjin China 39°7N 117°12E 227 E9
Tiergarten Germany 52°31N 13°20E 115 A3
Tieri Australia 23°2S 148°21E 280 C4
Tieroko, Tarso Chad 20°45N 17°52E 259 D3
Tierp Sweden 60°20N 17°30E 162 D11
Tierra Amarilla Chile 27°28S 70°18W 334 B1
Tierra Amarilla N. Mex., U.S.A. 36°42N 106°33W 305 H10
Tierra Colorada Mexico 17°11N 99°32W 319 D5
Tierra de Barros Spain 38°40N 6°30W 195 G4
Tierra de Campos Spain 42°10N 4°50W 194 C6
Tierra del Fuego □ Argentina 54°0S 67°45W 336 D3
Tierra del Fuego, I. Grande de Argentina 54°0S 69°0W 336 D3
Tierra del Fuego △ Argentina 54°50S 68°23W 336 D3
Tierradentro Colombia 2°35N 76°2W 328 C2
Tierralta Colombia 8°11N 76°4W 328 B2
Tiétar → Spain 39°50N 6°1W 194 F4
Tietê → Brazil 20°40S 51°35W 335 A5
Tifariti W. Sahara 26°9N 10°33W 260 C2
Tiffin U.S.A. 41°7N 83°11W 311 C13
Tiffin → U.S.A. 41°17N 84°23W 311 C12
Tiflèt Morocco 33°54N 6°20W 260 B3
Tiflis = Tbilisi Georgia 41°43N 44°50E 191 K7
Tifton U.S.A. 31°27N 83°31W 316 D6
Tifu Indonesia 3°39S 126°24E 231 E7
Tiga, Î. N. Cal. 21°7S 167°49E 288 d
Tiga Res. Nigeria 11°35N 8°30E 263 C6
Tigalda I. U.S.A. 54°6N 165°5W 303 J6
Tigaon Phil. 13°38N 123°30E 232 E4
Tigbauan Phil. 10°41N 122°27E 233 F4
Tiger Leaping Gorge = Hutiao Xia China 27°13N 100°9E 228 D3
Tighina Moldova 46°50N 29°30E 183 D14
Tigil Russia 57°49N 158°40E 215 D16
Tigiria India 20°29N 85°31E 244 D7
Tignall U.S.A. 33°52N 82°44W 316 B7
Tignish Canada 46°58N 64°2W 299 C7
Tigray □ Ethiopia 13°35N 39°15E 257 E4
Tigre → Peru 4°30S 74°10W 328 D3
Tigre → Venezuela 9°20N 62°30W 329 B5
Tigre, Pta. de Venezuela 11°5N 64°11W 329 a
Tigris = Dijlah, Nahr → Asia 31°0N 47°25E 246 D5
Tiguentourine Algeria 27°52N 9°8E 261 C6
Tigveni Romania 45°10N 24°31E 183 E9
Tigyaing Burma 23°45N 96°10E 241 D6
Tigzerte, O. → Morocco 28°10N 9°37W 260 C3
Tîh, Gebel el Egypt 29°32N 33°26E 256 B3
Tihodaine, Erg de Algeria 25°15N 7°15E 261 C6
Tihwa = Ürümqi China 43°45N 87°45E 217 D11
Tiilikka △ Finland 63°40N 28°15E 160 E23
Tijara India 27°56N 76°31E 242 F7
Tijgerhof S. Africa 33°53S 18°30E 118 A2
Tijī Libya 32°0N 11°18E 258 B2
Tijuana Mexico 32°32N 117°1W 307 N9
Tijuca Brazil 22°56S 43°13W 135 B1
Tijuca, Pico da Brazil 22°56S 43°15W 135 B1
Tijuca △ Brazil 22°56S 43°14W 135 B1
Tikahau French Polynesia 15°0S 148°10W 289 f
Tikal Guatemala 17°13N 89°24W 320 C2
Tikamgarh India 24°44N 78°50E 243 G8
Tikaré Burkina Faso 13°15N 1°43W 263 C4
Tikchik Lakes U.S.A. 60°0N 159°0W 303 G8
Tikéi French Polynesia 14°58S 144°32W 289 f
Tikhonkaya = Birobidzhan Russia 48°50N 132°50E 219 B15
Tikhoretsk Russia 45°56N 40°5E 191 H5
Tikhvin Russia 59°35N 33°30E 188 C7
Tikirarjuaq = Whale Cove Canada 62°10N 92°34W 297 A10
Tikkadouine, Adrar Algeria 24°28N 1°30E 261 D5
Tikkurila Finland 60°17N 25°1E 121 B3
Tīkmehdāsh Iran 37°16N 46°54E 213 D12
Tiko Cameroon 4°4N 9°20E 263 E6
Tikopia Pac. Oc. 12°19S 168°49E 277 C12
Tikrīt Iraq 34°35N 43°37E 213 E10
Tiksi Russia 71°40N 128°45E 215 B13
Tilā' al 'Alī Jordan 32°0N 35°52E 251 G6
Tiladummati Atoll Maldives 7°0N 73°20E 272 d
Tilak Nagar India 28°38N 77°5E 120 B1
Tilamuta Indonesia 0°32N 122°23E 231 D6
Tilanqiao China 31°15N 121°29E 138 B1
Tilburg Neths. 51°31N 5°6E 170 C5
Tilbury Ont., Canada 42°17N 82°23W 312 D2
Tilbury Essex, U.K. 51°27N 0°22E 169 F8
Tilcara Argentina 23°36S 65°23W 334 A2
Tilden U.S.A. 42°3N 97°50W 308 D5
Tilemsi, Vallée du Mali 17°42N 0°15E 263 B5
Tilhar India 28°0N 79°45E 243 F8
Tilia, O. → Algeria 27°32N 0°55E 261 C5
Tilichiki Russia 60°27N 166°5E 215 C17
Tililane Algeria 27°49N 0°6W 261 C4
Tilin Burma 21°41N 94°6E 241 E5
Tilissos Greece 35°20N 25°1E 207 E6
Till → U.K. 55°41N 2°13W 168 B5
Tillabéri Niger 14°28N 1°28E 263 C5
Tillamook U.S.A. 45°27N 123°51W 304 D2
Tillanchong I. India 8°30N 93°37E 245 K11
Tillberga Sweden 59°40N 16°39E 162 E10
Tillia Niger 16°8N 4°47E 263 B5
Tillman U.S.A. 32°28N 81°6W 316 C8
Tillsonburg Canada 42°53N 80°44W 312 D4
Tillyeria Cyprus 35°6N 32°40E 207 E8
Tilogne Senegal 16°0N 13°40W 262 B2
Tilos Greece 36°27N 27°27E 205 E9
Tilpa Australia 30°57S 144°24E 282 A6
Tilrhemt Algeria 33°9N 3°22E 261 B5
Tilsit = Sovetsk Russia 55°6N 21°50E 184 C8
Tilt → U.K. 56°46N 3°51W 167 E5
Tilton U.S.A. 43°27N 71°36W 313 C13
Tiltonsville U.S.A. 40°10N 80°41W 312 F4
Tim Denmark 56°12N 8°19E 163 H2
Tima Egypt 26°54N 31°25E 256 B3
Timah, Bukit Singapore 1°21N 103°46E 138 A2
Timanah Asia 19°0N 41°0E 248 C3
Timanfaya △ Canary Is. 29°0N 13°46W 153 e2
Timanskiy Kryazh Russia 65°58N 50°5E 186 A9
Timaru N.Z. 44°23S 171°14E 285 E6
Timashevo Russia 53°22N 51°9E 190 D10
Timashevsk Russia 45°35N 39°0E 191 H4
Timau Kenya 0°4N 37°15E 268 B4
Timbaki Greece 35°4N 24°45E 207 E6
Timbaúba Brazil 7°31S 35°19W 332 C4
Timbedgha Mauritania 16°17N 8°16W 262 B3
Timber Creek Australia 15°40S 130°29E 278 C5
Timber Lake U.S.A. 45°26N 101°5W 308 C3
Timber Mt. U.S.A. 37°6N 116°28W 306 H10
Timbio Colombia 2°20N 76°40W 328 C2
Timbiqui Colombia 2°46N 77°42W 328 C2
Timbo Guinea 10°35N 11°50W 262 C2
Timbo Liberia 5°35N 9°45W 262 D3
Timboon Australia 38°30S 142°58E 282 E5
Timbué, Ponta Mozam. 18°47S 36°22E 269 F4
Timbuktu = Tombouctou Mali 16°50N 3°0W 262 B4
Timdjaouine Algeria 21°37N 4°30E 261 D5
Timéïaouine Algeria 20°27N 1°50E 261 D5

Timellouline Algeria 29°22N 8°55E 261 C6
Times Square New York, U.S.A. 132 c2
Timétrin Mali 19°19N 0°34W 263 B4
Timétrine, Mts. Mali 19°25N 1°0W 263 B4
Timfi Oros Greece 39°59N 20°45E 204 B2
Timfristos, Oros Greece 38°57N 21°50E 204 C3
Timgad Algeria 35°29N 6°28E 261 A6
Timhadit Morocco 33°15N 5°4W 260 B3
Timi Cyprus 34°44N 32°31E 207 F8
Timia Niger 18°4N 8°40E 259 E1
Timika Indonesia 4°47S 136°32E 231 E9
Timimoun Algeria 29°14N 0°16E 261 C5
Timimoun, Sebkha de Algeria 28°50N 0°46E 261 C5
Timiris, Râs Mauritania 19°21N 16°30W 262 B1
Timiryazev Park Russia 55°49N 37°33E 129 B2
Timiş = Tamis ➔ Serbia 44°51N 20°39E 182 F5
Timiş ☐ Romania 45°40N 21°30E 182 E6
Timiskaming, L. = Témiscamingue, L. Canada 47°10N 79°25W 298 C4
Timişoara Romania 45°43N 21°15E 182 E6
Timmersdala Sweden 58°32N 13°46E 163 F7
Timmins Canada 48°28N 81°25W 298 C3
Timmonsville U.S.A. 34°8N 79°57W 316 A10
Timok ➔ Serbia 44°10N 22°40E 202 B6
Timoleague Ireland 51°39N 8°46W 166 E3
Timon Brazil 5°8S 42°52W 332 C3
Timor Asia 9°0S 125°0E 231 F7
Timor Leste = East Timor ■ Asia 8°50S 126°0E 231 F7
Timor Sea Ind. Oc. 12°0S 127°0E 278 B4
Timrå Sweden 62°29N 17°18E 162 B11
Timucuan ⌓ U.S.A. 30°28N 81°27W 316 E8
Tīn, Ra's at Libya 32°37N 23°8E 258 B4
Tin Alkoum Algeria 24°42N 10°17E 261 D7
Tin Amzi, O. ➔ Algeria 18°20N 4°32E 261 D6
Tin Atanai Algeria 25°52N 1°37E 261 C5
Tin Can Bay Australia 25°56S 153°0E 281 D5
Tin Can I. Nigeria 6°26N 3°21E 124 B2
Tin Ethisane Mali 19°3N 0°52W 263 B4
Tin Gornai Mali 16°38N 0°38W 263 B4
Tin Mt. U.S.A. 36°50N 117°10W 306 J9
Tin Shui Wai China 22°28N 114°0E 219 a
Tina = Thina ➔ S. Africa 31°18S 29°13E 271 D4
Tîna, Khalîg el Egypt 31°10N 32°40E 251 G3
Tinaca Pt. Phil. 5°30N 125°25E 233 J5
Tinaco Venezuela 9°42N 68°26W 328 B4
Tinajo Canary Is. 29°4N 13°42W 153 e2
Tinca Romania 46°46N 21°58E 182 D6
Tindal Australia 14°31S 132°22E 278 B5
Tindivanam India 12°15N 79°41E 245 H4
Tindouf Algeria 27°42N 8°10W 260 C3
Tindouf ☐ Algeria 27°25N 5°50W 260 C3
Tinée ➔ France 43°55N 7°11E 175 E11
Tineo Spain 43°21N 6°27W 194 B4
Tinerhir Morocco 31°29N 5°31W 260 B3
Tinfouchi Algeria 28°52N 5°49W 260 C3
Tinfunque △ Paraguay 23°55S 60°17W 334 A3
Ting Jiang ➔ China 24°45N 116°35E 229 E11
Ting Kau Hong Kong, China 22°22N 114°4E 122 A2
Tinggi, Pulau Malaysia 2°18N 104°7E 237 L5
Tinghert, Ḥamādat Libya 29°0N 11°0E 258 C2
Tingi Mts. S. Leone 8°55N 10°47W 262 D2
Tingkan Taiwan 23°48N 120°52E 225 C2
Tingkawk Sakan Burma 26°4N 96°44E 241 B6
Tinglayan Phil. 17°15N 121°9E 232 C3
Tinglev Denmark 54°57N 9°13E 163 K3
Tingmerkpuk Mt. U.S.A. 68°34N 162°28W 303 B7
Tingo Maria Peru 9°10S 75°54W 330 B2
Tingrela Ivory C. 10°27N 6°25W 262 C3
Tingri China 28°34N 86°38E 218 F6
Tingsryd Sweden 56°31N 15°0E 163 H9
Tingstäde Sweden 57°44N 18°37E 163 G12
Tingvoll Norway 62°55N 8°12E 164 B5
Tingwon Group Papua N. G. 2°37S 149°42E 286 B5
Tinh Bien Vietnam 10°36N 104°57E 237 G5
Tinharé, I. de Brazil 13°30S 38°58W 333 D4
Tinian N. Marianas 15°0N 145°38E 302 e
Tinian Channel N. Marianas 14°54N 145°36E 302 e
Tinigua △ Colombia 2°30N 74°8W 328 C3
Tiniguiban Phil. 11°22N 119°30E 233 F2
Tinjar ➔ Malaysia 4°4N 114°18E 235 B4
Tinkisso ➔ Guinea 11°21N 9°10W 262 C3
Tinn = Atrå Norway 59°59N 8°45E 164 E5
Tinnevelly = Tirunelveli India 8°45N 77°45E 245 K3
Tinnoset Norway 59°43N 9°3E 164 E6
Tinnsjå Norway 59°55N 8°54E 164 E5
Tinogasta Argentina 28°5S 67°32W 334 B2
Tinos Greece 37°33N 25°8E 205 D7
Tiñoso, C. Spain 37°32N 1°6W 197 H3
Tinpahar India 24°59N 87°44E 243 G12
Tinputz Papua N. G. 5°33S 155°0E 286 C8
Tinrhert, Plateau du Algeria 29°30N 9°0E 258 C1
Tinsukia India 27°29N 95°20E 241 B5
Tinta Peru 14°3S 71°20W 330 C3
Tintamarre, Île St.-Martin 18°7N 63°2W 322 a
Tintâne Mauritania 16°18N 10°10W 262 B2
Tintina Argentina 27°2S 62°45W 334 B3
Tintinara Australia 35°48S 140°2E 282 C4
Tintioulé Guinea 10°13N 9°12W 262 C3
Tinto ➔ Spain 37°12N 6°55W 195 H4
Tinui N.Z. 40°52S 176°5E 284 G5
Tinwald N.Z. 43°55S 171°43E 285 D6
Tiobraid Árann = Tipperary Ireland 52°28N 8°10W 166 D3
Tioga N. Dak., U.S.A. 48°24N 102°56W 308 A2
Tioga Pa., U.S.A. 41°55N 77°8W 312 E7
Tioman, Pulau Malaysia 2°50N 104°10E 237 L5
Tione di Trento Italy 46°2N 10°43E 198 B7
Tionesta U.S.A. 41°30N 79°28W 312 E5
Tior South Sudan 6°26N 31°11E 257 F3
Tiouliline Algeria 27°1N 0°2W 261 C4
Tipaza Algeria 36°35N 2°26E 261 A5
Tipaza ☐ Algeria 36°35N 2°25E 261 A5
Tipitapa Nic. 12°12N 86°5W 320 D2
Tipp City U.S.A. 39°58N 84°11W 311 E12
Tippecanoe ➔ U.S.A. 40°30N 86°45W 311 D10
Tipperary Ireland 52°28N 8°10W 166 D3
Tipperary ☐ Ireland 52°37N 7°55W 166 D4
Tipton Calif., U.S.A. 36°4N 119°19W 306 J7
Tipton Ind., U.S.A. 40°17N 86°2W 311 D10
Tipton Iowa, U.S.A. 41°46N 91°8W 310 C5
Tipton Mo., U.S.A. 38°39N 92°47W 310 F4
Tipton Mt. U.S.A. 35°32N 114°12W 307 K12
Tiptonville U.S.A. 36°23N 89°29W 315 C10
Tiptur India 13°15N 76°26E 245 H3
Tiquié ➔ Brazil 0°5N 68°25W 328 C4
Tiquina Bolivia 16°13S 68°50W 330 D4
Tira West Bank 31°52N 35°7E 123 A1
Tiracambu, Serra do Brazil 3°15S 46°30W 332 B2
Tirad Pass △ Phil. 17°3N 120°38E 232 C3
Tirahart, O. ➔ Algeria 23°45N 3°10E 261 D5
Tīrān Iran 32°45N 51°8E 247 C6
Tīrān Si. Arabia 27°57N 34°32E 251 L5
Tīrān, Maḍīq Egypt 27°55N 34°30E 251 L5
Tiranë Albania 41°18N 19°49E 202 E3
Tiranë ✕ (TIA) Albania 41°57N 19°42E 202 E3
Tirano Italy 46°13N 10°10E 198 B7
Tirari Desert Australia 28°22S 138°7E 281 D2
Tiraspol Moldova 46°55N 29°35E 183 D14
Tiratimine Algeria 25°56N 3°37E 261 C5
Tirau N.Z. 37°58S 175°46E 284 D4
Tirdout Mali 16°7N 1°5W 263 B4
Tire Turkey 38°5N 27°45E 205 C9
Tirebolu Turkey 40°58N 38°45E 213 B8
Tiree U.K. 56°31N 6°55W 167 E2
Tiree, Passage of U.K. 56°30N 6°30W 167 E2
Tîrgovişte = Târgovişte Romania 44°55N 25°27E 183 F10
Tîrgu Jiu = Târgu Jiu Romania 45°5N 23°19E 183 E8
Tîrgu Mureş = Târgu Mureş Romania 46°31N 24°38E 183 D9
Tirgua △ Venezuela 10°5N 68°48W 328 A4
Tirich Mir Pakistan 36°15N 71°55E 240 A3
Tiriolo Italy 38°57N 16°30E 201 D9
Tiririca, Serra da Brazil 17°6S 47°6W 333 E2
Tiriro Guinea 10°27N 8°40W 262 C3
Tiris Zemmour ☐ Mauritania 24°0N 9°0W 260 D3
Tiritiri o te Moana = Southern Alps N.Z. 43°41S 170°11E 285 D5
Tirna ➔ India 18°4N 76°57E 244 E3
Tirnavos Greece 39°45N 22°18E 204 B4
Tirodi India 21°40N 79°44E 244 D4
Tirol ☐ Austria 47°3N 10°43E 180 D3
Tiros Brazil 19°0S 45°58W 333 E2
Tirrukkovil Sri Lanka 7°7N 81°51E 245 L5
Tirsa Egypt 29°57N 31°12E 117 B2
Tirschenreuth Germany 49°53N 12°19E 179 F8
Tirschtiegel = Trzciel Poland 52°23N 15°50E 185 F2
Tirso ➔ Italy 39°53N 8°32E 200 C1
Tirstrup Denmark 56°18N 10°42E 163 H4
Tirtagangga Indonesia 8°24S 115°35E 231 J18
Tirthahalli India 13°42N 75°14E 245 H2
Tirua Pt. N.Z. 38°25S 174°40E 284 E3
Tiruchchendur India 8°30N 78°11E 245 K4
Tiruchchirappalli India 10°45N 78°45E 245 J4
Tirukkoyilur India 11°57N 79°12E 245 J4
Tirumangalam India 9°49N 77°58E 245 K3
Tirumayam India 10°14N 78°45E 245 J4
Tirunelveli India 8°45N 77°45E 245 K3
Tirupati India 13°39N 79°25E 245 H4
Tiruppattur Tamil Nadu, India 10°8N 78°37E 245 J4
Tiruppattur Tamil Nadu, India 12°30N 78°30E 245 H4
Tiruppur India 11°5N 77°22E 245 J3
Tirur India 10°54N 75°55E 245 J2
Tiruttani India 13°11N 79°58E 245 H4
Tirutturaippundi India 10°32N 79°41E 245 J4
Tiruvadaimarudur India 11°2N 79°27E 245 J4
Tiruvalla India 9°23N 76°34E 245 K3
Tiruvallar India 13°9N 79°57E 245 H4
Tiruvannamalai India 12°15N 79°5E 245 H4
Tiruvettipuram India 12°39N 79°33E 245 H4
Tiruvottiyur India 13°10N 80°22E 245 H5
Tis Issat Ethiopia 11°25N 37°45E 257 E4
Tisa India 32°50N 76°9E 242 C7
Tisa ➔ Serbia 45°15N 20°17E 182 E5
Tisdale Canada 52°50N 104°0W 297 C8
Tishomingo U.S.A. 34°14N 96°41W 314 D6
Tishrīyaa Iraq 33°18N 44°24E 112 B2
Tisjön Sweden 60°56N 13°0E 162 D7
Tisnaren Sweden 58°58N 15°56E 163 F9
Tišnov Czech Rep. 49°21N 16°25E 181 B9
Tisovec Slovak Rep. 48°41N 19°56E 181 C12
Tissamaharama Sri Lanka 6°17N 81°17E 245 L5
Tissemsilt Algeria 35°35N 1°50E 261 A5
Tissemsilt ☐ Algeria 35°45N 1°45E 261 A5
Tissint Morocco 29°57N 7°16W 260 C3
Tista ➔ India 25°23N 89°43E 241 C2
Tistedal Norway 59°8N 11°27E 164 E8
Tisza = Tisa ➔ Serbia 45°15N 20°17E 182 E5
Tiszaföldvár Hungary 46°58N 20°14E 182 D5
Tiszafüred Hungary 47°38N 20°50E 182 C5
Tiszalök Hungary 48°1N 21°20E 182 B6
Tiszavasvári Hungary 47°58N 21°18E 182 C6
Tit Ahaggar, Algeria 23°0N 5°10E 261 D6
Tit Tademait, Algeria 27°0N 1°29E 261 C5
Tit-Ary Russia 71°55N 127°2E 215 B13
Titabar India 26°36N 94°12E 241 B5
Titaguas Spain 39°53N 1°6W 196 F3
Titao Burkina Faso 13°45N 2°5W 263 C4
Titel Serbia 45°10N 20°18E 182 E5
Tithwal Pakistan 34°21N 73°50E 243 B5
Titicaca, L. S. Amer. 15°30S 69°30W 330 D4
Titikaveka Cook Is. 21°16S 159°45W 289 h
Titisee Germany 47°54N 8°10E 179 H4
Tititira Hd. N.Z. 43°36S 169°25E 285 D4
Tititut Burma 18°54N 95°16E 241 F5
Titiwa Nigeria 12°14N 12°53E 263 C7
Titlagarh India 20°15N 83°11E 244 D6
Tito Italy 40°35N 15°40E 201 B8
Titograd = Podgorica Montenegro 42°30N 19°19E 202 D3
Titova Korenica Croatia 44°45N 15°41E 199 D12
Titu Romania 44°39N 25°32E 183 F10
Titule Dem. Rep. of the Congo 3°15N 25°31E 268 B2
Titusville Fla., U.S.A. 28°37N 80°49W 317 G9
Titusville Pa., U.S.A. 41°38N 79°41W 312 E5
Tiu Keng Leng Hong Kong, China 22°18N 114°15E 122 B3
Tivaouane Senegal 14°56N 16°45W 262 C1
Tivat Montenegro 42°28N 18°43E 202 D2
Tivedens △ Sweden 58°45N 14°35E 163 F8
Tiverton Ont., Canada 44°16N 81°32W 312 B3
Tiverton Devon, U.K. 50°54N 3°29W 169 G4
Tivoli Grenada 12°10N 61°37W 323 q
Tivoli Italy 41°58N 12°45E 199 G9
Tiwanaku = Tiahuanaco Bolivia 16°33S 68°42W 330 D4
Tiwī Oman 22°45N 59°12E 249 B7
Tiwi ☼ Australia 11°33S 130°42E 278 B5
Tiyo Eritrea 14°41N 40°15E 257 E5
Tizapán Mexico 19°19N 99°13W 128 C2
Tizga Morocco 32°1N 5°9W 260 B3
Ti'zi N'Isli Morocco 32°28N 5°47W 260 B3
Tizi-Ouzou Algeria 36°42N 4°3E 261 A5
Tizi-Ouzou ☐ Algeria 36°35N 4°5E 261 A5
Tizimín Mexico 21°9N 88°9W 319 C7
Tiznados ➔ Venezuela 8°16N 67°47W 328 B4
Tiznap He ➔ China 38°21N 77°26E 217 E9
Tiznit Morocco 29°48N 9°45W 260 C3
Tjæreborg Denmark 55°28N 8°36E 163 J2
Tjällmo Sweden 58°43N 15°21E 163 F9
Tjeggelvas Sweden 66°37N 17°45E 160 C17
Tjeggelvas = Tjeggelvas Sweden 66°37N 17°45E 160 C17
Tjirebon = Cirebon Indonesia 6°45S 108°32E 235 D3
Tjirrkarli ☼ Australia 26°0S 125°28E 279 E4
Tjluring Indonesia 8°25S 114°13E 231 J17
Tjøme Norway 59°8N 10°26E 164 E7
Tjörn Sweden 58°0N 11°35E 163 G5
Tjukayirla Roadhouse Australia 27°9S 124°34E 279 E3
Tjurabalan ☼ Australia 19°50S 128°0E 278 C4
Tkibuli = Tqibuli Georgia 42°26N 43°0E 191 J6
Tkvarcheli = Tqvarcheli Georgia 42°47N 41°42E 191 J5
Tlacotalpan Mexico 18°37N 95°40W 319 D5
Tlahualilo de Zaragoza Mexico 26°7N 103°27W 318 B4
Tlalnepantla ➔ Mexico 19°30N 99°18W 128 A1
Tlalpan Mexico 19°18N 99°10W 128 C2
Tlaquepaque Mexico 20°39N 103°19W 318 C4
Tlaxcala Mexico 19°19N 98°14W 319 D5
Tlaxcala ☐ Mexico 19°25N 98°10W 319 D5
Tlaxiaco Mexico 17°25N 97°35W 319 D5
Tlemcen Algeria 34°52N 1°21W 261 B4
Tlemcen ☐ Algeria 34°38N 1°30W 261 B4
Tleta Sidi Bouguedra Morocco 32°16N 9°59W 260 B3
Tlokweng Botswana 24°40S 25°58E 270 B4
Tlumach Ukraine 48°51N 25°0E 183 B10
Tłuszcz Poland 52°25N 21°25E 185 F8
Tlyarata Russia 42°9N 46°26E 191 J8
Tmassah Libya 26°19N 15°51E 258 C3
To Bong Vietnam 12°45N 109°16E 236 F7
To Kwa Wan Hong Kong, China 22°18N 114°11E 122 B3
To-Shima Japan 34°31N 139°17E 223 C11
Toa Payoh Singapore 1°20N 103°51E 138 A3
Toad ➔ Canada 59°25N 124°57W 296 B4
Toad River Canada 58°51N 125°14W 296 B3
Toamasina Madag. 18°10S 49°25E 272 B2
Toamasina ☐ Madag. 18°0S 49°0E 272 B2
Toay Argentina 36°43S 64°38W 334 D3
Toba China 31°19N 97°42E 228 B1
Toba Japan 34°30N 136°51E 223 C8
Toba, Danau Indonesia 2°30N 98°30E 234 B1
Toba Kakar Pakistan 31°30N 69°0E 242 D3
Toba Tek Singh Pakistan 30°55N 72°25E 242 D5
Tobago Trin. & Tob. 11°10N 60°30W 323 s
Tobarra Spain 38°37N 1°44W 197 G3
Tobelo Indonesia 1°45N 127°56E 231 D7
Tobercurry Ireland 54°3N 8°44W 166 B3
Tobermory Ont., Canada 45°12N 81°40W 312 A3
Tobermory Argyll & Bute, U.K. 56°38N 6°5W 167 E2
Tobi Palau 2°40N 131°10E 231 D8
Tobi-Shima Japan 41°12N 139°34E 220 D9
Tobias Fornier = Dao Phil. 10°30N 121°57E 233 F3
Tobiishi Hana Iwo Jima 24°45N 141°17E 288 b
Tobin, L. Australia 21°45S 125°49E 278 D4
Tobin L. Canada 53°35N 103°30W 297 C8
Toblach = Dobbiaco Italy 46°44N 12°14E 199 B9
Toboali Indonesia 3°0S 106°25E 234 C3
Tobol ➔ Russia 58°10N 68°12E 214 D7
Toboli Indonesia 0°38S 120°5E 231 E6
Tobolsk Russia 58°15N 68°10E 214 D7
Tobor Senegal 12°40N 16°15W 262 C1
Toboso Phil. 10°43N 123°31E 233 F4
Tobruk = Tubruq Libya 32°7N 23°55E 258 B4
Tobyhanna U.S.A. 41°11N 75°25W 313 E9
Tobyl = Tobol ➔ Russia 58°10N 68°12E 214 D7
Tobyl Kazakhstan 52°41N 62°34E 216 B6
Tocache Nuevo Peru 8°9S 76°26W 330 B2
Tocantínia Brazil 9°33S 48°22W 332 C2
Tocantinópolis Brazil 6°20S 47°25W 332 C2
Tocantins ☐ Brazil 10°0S 48°0W 332 D2
Tocantins ➔ Brazil 1°45S 49°10W 332 B2
Toccoa U.S.A. 34°35N 83°19W 315 D13
Toce ➔ Italy 45°56N 8°29E 198 C5
Tochi ➔ Pakistan 32°49N 70°41E 242 C4
Tochigi Japan 36°25N 139°45E 223 A11
Tochigi ☐ Japan 36°45N 139°45E 223 A11
Tocina Spain 37°37N 5°44W 195 H5
Töcksfors Sweden 59°31N 11°52E 162 E5
Točná Czech Rep. 49°58N 14°25E 135 C2
Toco Chile 22°5S 69°35W 334 A2
Toco Trin. & Tob. 10°49N 60°57W 323 t
Toco Hills U.S.A. 33°49N 84°20W 113 B2
Toconao Chile 23°11S 68°1W 334 A2
Tocopilla Chile 22°5S 70°10W 334 A2
Tocqueville = Râs el Oued Algeria 35°57N 5°2E 261 A6
Tocumwal Australia 35°51S 145°31E 283 C6
Tocuyo ➔ Venezuela 11°3N 68°23W 328 A4
Tocuyo de la Costa Venezuela 11°2N 68°23W 328 A4
Todalen Norway 62°49N 8°44E 164 B5
Todd ➔ Australia 24°52S 135°48E 280 C2
Todds Road Trin. & Tob. 10°28N 61°20W 323 t
Toddu Atoll Maldives 4°25N 72°57E 272 d
Todeli Indonesia 1°40S 124°29E 231 E6
Todenyang Kenya 4°35N 35°56E 268 B4
Todgarh India 25°42N 73°58E 242 G5
Todi Italy 42°47N 12°24E 199 F9
Todos os Santos, B. de Brazil 12°48S 38°38W 333 D4
Todos Santos Mexico 23°26N 110°13W 318 C2
Todt Hill U.S.A. 40°36N 74°6W 132 C1
Todtnau Germany 47°49N 7°56E 179 H3
Toe Hd. U.K. 57°50N 7°8W 167 D1
Toecé Burkina Faso 11°50N 1°16W 263 C4
Toetoes B. N.Z. 46°42S 168°41E 285 G3
Tofield Canada 53°25N 112°40W 296 C6
Tofino Canada 49°11N 125°55W 296 D3
Töfsingdalen △ Sweden 62°10N 12°28E 162 B6
Tofte Norway 59°33N 10°34E 164 E7
Tofua Tonga 19°45S 175°5W 287 P13
Toga Vanuatu 13°26S 166°42E 287 C4
Togane Japan 35°33N 140°22E 223 B12
Togba Mauritania 17°26N 10°12W 262 B2
Togbo C.A.R. 6°0N 17°27E 264 A3
Togdheer ☐ Somalia 9°20N 45°25E 267 C6
Togdheer ➔ Somalia 9°20N 46°39E 267 C6
Togiak U.S.A. 59°4N 160°24W 303 G7
Togiak Nat. Wildlife Refuge ⌓ U.S.A. 59°20N 160°15W 303 G7
Togian, Kepulauan Indonesia 0°20S 121°50E 231 E6
Togliatti Russia 53°32N 49°24E 190 D9
Togo ■ W. Afr. 8°30N 1°35E 263 D5
Togo Wichale Somalia 9°22N 43°40E 267 C5
Togrög Mongolia 47°25N 92°13E 217 C12
Togtoh China 40°15N 111°10E 226 D6
Tohiea, Mt. Moorea 17°33S 149°49W 289 e
Tohma ➔ Turkey 38°29N 38°23E 212 C8
Tōhoku ☐ Japan 39°50N 141°45E 220 E10
Töhöm Mongolia 44°27N 108°2E 226 B5
Tohopekaliga, East L. U.S.A. 28°18N 81°15W 317 G8
Tohopekaliga, L. U.S.A. 28°12N 81°24W 317 G8
Toi Cook Is. 18°57S 169°51W 289 g
Toi Japan 34°54N 138°47E 223 C10
Toibalewe India 10°32N 92°30E 245 J11
Toiny St.-Martin 17°53N 62°47W 322 a
Toinya South Sudan 6°17N 29°46E 257 F2
Toiyabe Range U.S.A. 39°30N 117°0W 304 G5
Tojikiston = Tajikistan ■ Asia 38°30N 70°0E 217 E8
Tōjō Japan 34°53N 133°16E 222 C5
Tok U.S.A. 63°20N 142°59W 303 E12
Toka Guyana 3°58N 59°17W 329 C6
Tokaanu N.Z. 38°58S 175°46E 284 E4
Tokachi-Dake Japan 43°17N 142°5E 220 C11
Tokachi-Gawa ➔ Japan 42°44N 143°42E 220 C11
Tōkagi Japan 35°42N 139°55E 140 A4
Tokai Japan 35°2N 136°55E 223 B8
Tokai Plantation S. Africa 34°3S 18°24E 118 B1
Tōkaichiba Japan 35°31N 139°30E 140 B2
Tokaj Hungary 48°8N 21°27E 182 B6
Tokala Indonesia 1°30S 121°40E 231 E6
Tōkamachi Japan 37°8N 138°43E 221 F9
Tokanui N.Z. 46°34S 168°56E 285 G3
Tokar Sudan 18°27N 37°56E 256 D4
Tokara-Rettō Japan 29°37N 129°43E 221 K4
Tokarahi N.Z. 44°56S 170°39E 285 E5
Tokashiki-Shima Japan 26°11N 127°21E 221 L3
Tokat Turkey 40°22N 36°35E 212 B7
Tokat ☐ Turkey 40°15N 36°30E 212 B7
Tŏkch'ŏn N. Korea 39°45N 126°18E 224 C3
Tokdo = Liancourt Rocks Asia 37°15N 131°52E 221 F5
Tokeland U.S.A. 46°42N 123°59W 306 D3
Tokelau Is. ☒ Pac. Oc. 9°0S 171°45W 277 B16
Toki Japan 35°18N 137°8E 223 B9
Toki Pt. Wake I. 19°19N 166°35E 302 b
Tokmak Kyrgyzstan 42°49N 75°15E 217 D9
Tokmak Ukraine 47°16N 35°42E 189 J8
Toko Ra. Australia 23°5S 138°20E 280 C2
Tokomaru Bay N.Z. 38°8S 178°22E 284 E7
Tokoname Japan 34°53N 136°51E 223 C8
Tokoro-Gawa ➔ Japan 44°7N 144°5E 220 B12
Tokoroa N.Z. 38°13S 175°50E 284 E4
Tokorozawa Japan 35°47N 139°28E 223 B11
Toksook Bay U.S.A. 60°32N 165°0W 303 F6
Toksun China 42°47N 88°38E 217 D11
Toktogul Kyrgyzstan 41°50N 72°50E 217 D8
Toku Tonga 18°10S 174°11W 287 P13
Tokuji Japan 34°11N 131°42E 222 C3
Tokuno-Shima Japan 27°56N 128°55E 221 L4
Tokushima Japan 34°4N 134°34E 222 C6
Tokushima ☐ Japan 33°55N 134°0E 222 D6
Tokuyama = Shunān Japan 34°3N 131°50E 222 C3
Tōkyō Japan 35°43N 139°45E 140 B3
Tōkyō ☐ Japan 35°40N 139°30E 223 B11
Tōkyō B. = Tōkyō-Wan Japan 35°25N 139°50E 140 B4
Tōkyō Haneda ✕ (HND) Japan 35°33N 139°46E 140 B3
Tōkyō Harbour Japan 35°38N 139°46E 140 B3
Tōkyō Narita ✕ (NRT) Japan 35°45N 140°25E 223 B12
Tōkyō Sky Tree Japan 35°42N 139°49E 140 A3
Tōkyō-Wan Japan 35°25N 139°50E 140 B4
Tokzār Afghan. 35°52N 66°26E 240 B2
Tol I. Micronesia 7°20N 151°37E 287 U17
Tolaga Bay N.Z. 38°21S 178°20E 284 E7
Tolageak U.S.A. 70°3N 162°37W 303 A7
Tolbo Mongolia 48°25N 90°17E 217 C12
Tolbukhin = Dobrich Bulgaria 43°37N 27°49E 203 C11
Tolé C.A.R. 6°34N 16°1E 264 A3
Tole Bī Kazakhstan 43°42N 73°46E 217 D8
Toledo Brazil 24°44S 53°45W 335 A5
Toledo Phil. 10°23N 123°38E 233 F4
Toledo Spain 39°50N 4°2W 194 F6
Toledo Ill., U.S.A. 39°16N 88°15W 311 E8
Toledo Iowa, U.S.A. 42°0N 92°35W 310 C4
Toledo Ohio, U.S.A. 41°39N 83°33W 311 C13
Toledo Oreg., U.S.A. 44°37N 123°56W 304 D2
Toledo Wash., U.S.A. 46°26N 122°51W 306 D4
Toledo, Montes de Spain 39°33N 4°20W 195 F6
Toledo Bend Res. U.S.A. 31°11N 93°34W 314 F8
Tolentino Italy 43°12N 13°17E 199 E10
Tolfa Italy 42°9N 11°56E 199 F8
Tolga Algeria 34°40N 5°22E 261 B6
Tolga Queens., Australia 17°15S 145°29E 280 B4
Tolga Hedmark, Norway 62°26N 11°1E 164 B8
Tolhuaca △ Chile 38°15S 71°50W 336 A2
Toli China 45°57N 83°37E 217 C10
Toliara Madag. 23°21S 43°40E 272 C1
Toliara ☐ Madag. 21°0S 45°0E 272 C2
Tolima Colombia 4°40N 75°19W 328 C2
Tolima ☐ Colombia 3°45N 75°15W 328 C2
Tolitoli Indonesia 1°5N 120°50E 231 D6
Tolka ➔ Ireland 53°21N 6°14W 120 A1
Tolkmicko Poland 54°19N 19°31E 184 D6
Tollarp Sweden 55°55N 13°58E 163 J7
Tollensesee Germany 53°30N 13°13E 178 B9
Tollhouse U.S.A. 37°1N 119°24W 306 H7
Tollygunge = Taliganga India 22°30N 88°22E 124 B2
Tolmachevo Russia 58°56N 29°51E 188 C5
Tolmezzo Italy 46°24N 13°1E 199 B10
Tolmin Slovenia 46°11N 13°45E 199 B10
Tolna Hungary 46°25N 18°48E 182 D3
Tolna ☐ Hungary 46°30N 18°30E 182 D3
Tolo Dem. Rep. of the Congo 2°55S 18°34E 264 C3
Tolo, Teluk Indonesia 2°20S 122°10E 231 E6
Tolo Harbour Hong Kong, China 22°25N 114°13E 122 A3
Tolochin = Talachyn Belarus 54°25N 29°42E 188 E5
Tolokiwa I. Papua N. G. 5°19S 147°37E 286 C4
Tolong B. Phil. 9°20N 122°49E 233 G4
Tolono U.S.A. 39°59N 88°16W 311 E8
Tolosa Spain 43°8N 2°5W 196 B2
Tolox Spain 36°41N 4°54W 195 J6
Toltén Chile 39°13S 74°14W 336 A2
Toluca México, Mexico 19°17N 99°40W 319 D5
Toluca Ill., U.S.A. 41°0N 89°8W 310 C7
Tolworth U.K. 51°22N 0°17W 125 B2
Tolyatti = Togliatti Russia 53°32N 49°24E 190 D9
Tom Burke S. Africa 23°5S 28°0E 271 B4
Tom Price Australia 22°40S 117°48E 278 D2
Toma Burkina Faso 12°45N 2°53W 262 C4
Tomah U.S.A. 43°59N 90°30W 308 D8
Tomahawk U.S.A. 45°28N 89°44W 308 C9
Tomai Moldova 46°34N 28°19E 183 D13
Tomakomai Japan 42°38N 141°36E 220 C10
Tomales U.S.A. 38°15N 122°53W 306 G4
Tomales B. U.S.A. 38°15N 123°58W 306 G3
Tomanivi Fiji 17°37S 178°1E 287 A2
Tomar Portugal 39°36N 8°25W 195 F2
Tomaros, Oros Greece 39°29N 20°48E 204 B2
Tomarza Turkey 38°27N 35°48E 212 C6
Tomás Barrón Bolivia 17°35S 67°31W 330 D4
Tomashevka Belarus 51°33N 23°36E 185 G10
Tomashpil Ukraine 48°32N 28°31E 183 B13
Tomaszów Lubelski Poland 50°27N 23°25E 185 H10
Tomaszów Mazowiecki Poland 51°30N 20°2E 185 G7
Tomatlán Mexico 19°56N 105°15W 318 D3
Tomb of the Kings Jerusalem 123 a2
Tomba di Nerone Italy 41°58N 12°26E 136 B1
Tombadonkéa Guinea 11°0N 14°25W 262 C2
Tombador, Serra do Brazil 12°0S 58°0W 331 C6
Tombe South Sudan 5°53N 31°40E 257 F3
Tombeau Bay Mauritius 20°6S 57°30E 272 e
Tombel Cameroon 4°45N 9°40E 264 B1
Tombigbee ➔ U.S.A. 31°8N 87°57W 315 F11
Tomboco Angola 6°48S 13°18E 265 D2
Tombouctou Mali 16°50N 3°0W 262 B4
Tombouctou ☐ Mali 20°0N 3°0W 262 B4
Tombstone U.S.A. 31°43N 110°4W 305 L8
Tombua Angola 15°55S 11°55E 265 F2
Tomé Chile 36°36S 72°57W 334 D1
Tome Japan 38°40N 141°20E 220 E10
Tomé-Açu Brazil 2°25S 48°9W 332 B2
Tomelilla Sweden 55°33N 13°58E 163 J7
Tomelloso Spain 39°10N 3°2W 195 F7
Tomil Micronesia 9°31N 138°9E 287 R16
Tomil Harbor Pac. Oc. 9°30N 138°10E 287 R16
Tomingley Australia 32°26S 148°16E 283 B8
Tomini Indonesia 0°30N 120°30E 231 D6
Tomini, Teluk Indonesia 0°10S 121°0E 231 E6
Tominian Mali 13°17N 4°35W 262 C4
Tomiño = O Seixo Spain 41°59N 8°46W 194 D2
Tomintoul U.K. 57°15N 3°23W 167 D5
Tomioka Japan 36°15N 138°54E 223 A10
Tomislavgrad Bos.-H. 43°42N 17°13E 182 G2
Tomkinson Ranges Australia 26°11S 129°5E 279 E4
Tommot Russia 59°4N 126°20E 215 D13
Tommy Thompson Park Canada 43°38N 79°20W 141 B3
Tomnop Ta Suos Cambodia 11°20N 104°15E 237 G5
Tomo Colombia 2°38N 67°32W 328 C4
Tomo ➔ Colombia 5°20N 67°48W 328 B4
Tomobe Japan 36°20N 140°20E 223 A12
Tomra Norway 62°34N 6°56E 164 B3
Toms Place U.S.A. 37°34N 118°41W 306 H8
Toms River U.S.A. 39°58N 74°12W 313 G10
Tomsk Russia 56°30N 85°5E 214 D9
Tomtabacken Sweden 57°30N 14°30E 163 G8
Tömük Turkey 36°42N 34°23E 212 D6
Tona Spain 41°51N 2°14E 196 D7
Tonalá Chiapas, Mexico 16°4N 93°45W 319 D6
Tonalá Jalisco, Mexico 20°37N 103°14W 318 C4
Tonale, Passo del Italy 46°16N 10°35E 198 B7
Tonami Japan 36°40N 136°58E 223 A8
Tonantins Brazil 2°45S 67°45W 328 D4
Tonasket U.S.A. 48°42N 119°26W 304 B4
Tonate Fr. Guiana 5°0N 52°28W 329 C7
Tonawanda U.S.A. 43°1N 78°53W 312 D6
Tonb Iran 26°15N 55°15E 247 E7
Tonbo Burma 18°31N 95°25E 241 F5
Tonbridge U.K. 51°11N 0°17E 169 F8
Tondano Indonesia 1°35N 124°54E 231 D6
Tondela Portugal 40°31N 8°5W 194 E2
Tønder Denmark 54°58N 8°50E 163 K2
Tondern = Tønder Denmark 54°58N 8°50E 163 K2
Tondi India 9°45N 79°4E 245 K4
Tondi Kiwindi Niger 14°28N 2°2E 263 C5
Tondibi Mali 16°39N 0°14W 263 B4
Tondo Phil. 14°36N 120°57E 127 B1
Tondoro Namibia 17°45S 18°50E 270 A2
Tone ➔ Australia 34°25S 116°25E 279 F2
Tone-Gawa ➔ Japan 35°44N 140°51E 223 B12
Tonekābon Iran 36°45N 51°12E 247 B6
Tong Fuk Hong Kong, China 22°14N 113°56E 122 B1
Tong I. Papua N. G. 2°2S 147°47E 286 B4
Tong Xian China 39°55N 116°35E 226 E9
Tong-yeong S. Korea 34°50N 128°20E 224 E4
Tonga Cameroon 4°58N 10°42E 264 B2
Tonga South Sudan 9°28N 31°3E 257 F3
Tonga ■ Pac. Oc. 19°50S 174°30W 287 P13
Tonga Trench Pac. Oc. 18°0S 173°0W 277 D16
Tongaat S. Africa 29°33S 31°9E 271 C5
Tongala Australia 36°14S 144°56E 283 D6
Tong'an China 24°37N 118°8E 229 E12
Tongareva = Penrhyn Cook Is. 9°0S 158°0W 289 H12
Tongariro, Mt. N.Z. 39°8S 175°38E 284 F4
Tongariro △ N.Z. 39°8S 175°33E 284 F4
Tongass Nat. Forest U.S.A. 54°45N 133°0W 303 J14
Tongatapu Tonga 21°10S 175°10W 287 Q13
Tongatapu Group Tonga 21°0S 175°0W 287 Q13
Tongbai China 32°20N 113°23E 229 A9
Tongbinggo S. Korea 37°31N 126°58E 137 B1
Tongcheng Anhui, China 31°4N 116°56E 229 B11
Tongcheng Hubei, China 29°15N 113°50E 229 C9
Tongchuan China 35°6N 109°3E 226 G5
Tongdao China 26°10N 109°42E 228 D7
Tongeren Belgium 50°47N 5°28E 170 D5
Tonggu China 28°31N 114°20E 229 C10
Tonggu Jiao China 22°22N 113°37E 219 a
Tongguan China 34°40N 110°25E 226 G6
Tonghai China 24°10N 102°53E 228 E4
Tonghua China 41°42N 125°58E 224 B2
Tongi = Tungi Bangla. 23°53N 90°24E 241 D3
Tongjiang Heilongjiang, China 47°40N 132°27E 219 B15
Tongjiang Sichuan, China 31°58N 107°11E 228 B6
Tongjosŏn Man N. Korea 39°30N 128°0E 224 C4
Tongking, G. of = Tonkin, G. of Asia 20°0N 108°0E 236 C7
Tongliang China 29°50N 106°3E 228 C6
Tongliao China 43°38N 122°18E 227 C12
Tongling China 30°55N 117°48E 229 B11
Tonglu China 29°45N 119°37E 229 C12
Tongnan = Anyue China 30°9N 105°50E 228 B5
Tongoa Vanuatu 16°54S 168°34E 287 F6
Tongobory Madag. 23°32S 44°20E 272 C1
Tongoy Chile 30°16S 71°31W 334 C1
Tongqiao China 31°21N 121°22E 138 A1
Tongquil I. Phil. 6°2N 121°51E 233 H3
Tongren Guizhou, China 27°43N 109°11E 228 D7
Tongren Qinghai, China 35°25N 102°5E 218 D9
Tongres = Tongeren Belgium 50°47N 5°28E 170 D5
Tongsa Dzong Bhutan 27°31N 90°31E 241 B3
Tongsha Tao Taiwan 26°12N 128°28E 225 b
Tongshi China 18°30N 109°20E 229 a
Tongue U.K. 58°29N 4°25W 167 C4
Tongue ➔ U.S.A. 46°25N 105°52W 304 C11
Tongwei China 35°0N 105°5E 226 G3
Tongxiang China 30°39N 120°34E 229 B13
Tongxiao = T'unghsiao Taiwan 24°29N 120°40E 225 B2
Tongxin China 36°59N 105°58E 226 F3
Tongyang N. Korea 39°9N 126°53E 224 C3
Tongyu China 44°45N 123°4E 227 B12
Tongzhou China 32°12N 121°2E 229 A13
Tongzi China 28°9N 106°49E 228 C6
Tonica U.S.A. 41°13N 89°4W 310 C7
Tonj South Sudan 7°20N 28°44E 257 F2
Tonj ➔ South Sudan 7°31N 28°55E 257 F2
Tonk India 26°6N 75°54E 242 F6
Tonkawa U.S.A. 36°41N 97°18W 314 C6
Tonkin = Bac Phan Vietnam 22°0N 105°0E 228 G5
Tonkin, G. of Asia 20°0N 108°0E 236 C7
Tonlé Sap Cambodia 13°0N 104°0E 236 F5
Tonnay-Charente France 45°56N 0°55W 174 C3
Tonneins France 44°23N 0°19E 174 D4
Tonnerre France 47°51N 3°59E 173 E10
Tönning Germany 54°19N 8°56E 178 A4
Tono Japan 39°19N 141°32E 220 E10
Tonoas I. Micronesia 7°22N 151°52E 287 T18
Tonopah U.S.A. 38°4N 117°14W 305 G5
Tonoshō Japan 34°29N 134°11E 222 C6
Tonosí Panama 7°20N 80°20W 320 E3
Tons ➔ Haryana, India 30°30N 77°39E 242 D7
Tons ➔ Ut. P., India 26°1N 83°33E 243 F10
Tønsberg Norway 59°19N 10°25E 164 E7
Tonsina U.S.A. 61°39N 145°11W 303 F11
Tonstad Norway 58°40N 6°45E 164 F3
Tonto △ U.S.A. 33°39N 111°7W 305 K8
Tonumea Tonga 20°30S 174°30W 287 Q13
Tonya Turkey 40°53N 39°16E 213 B8
Tonzang Burma 23°36N 93°42E 241 D4
Tonzi Burma 24°39N 94°57E 241 C5
Toobanna Australia 18°42S 146°9E 280 B4
Toodyay Australia 31°34S 116°28E 279 F2
Tooele U.S.A. 40°32N 112°18W 304 F7
Toompine Australia 27°15S 144°19E 281 D3
Toomsboro U.S.A. 32°50N 83°5W 316 C6
Toora Australia 38°39S 146°23E 283 E7
Toora-Khem Russia 52°28N 96°17E 217 B13
Toorak Australia 37°50S 145°1E 128 B2
Tootias Somalia 3°57N 43°57E 267 D5
Toowoomba Australia 27°32S 151°56E 281 D5
Top Springs Australia 16°37S 131°51E 278 C5
Topalu Romania 44°31N 28°3E 183 F13
Topanga State Park ⌓ U.S.A. 34°7N 118°31W 126 B1
Topaz U.S.A. 38°41N 119°30W 306 G7
Topeka U.S.A. 39°3N 95°40W 308 F6
Topkapı Turkey 41°1N 28°55E 122 B1
Topkapı Palaca Turkey 41°1N 28°59E 122 B1
Topľa ➔ Slovak Rep. 48°45N 21°45E 181 C14
Topley Canada 54°49N 126°18W 296 C3
Toplica ➔ Serbia 43°15N 21°49E 202 C5
Toplița Romania 46°55N 25°20E 183 D10
Topo Azores 38°33N 27°45W 153 d1
Topo, Pta. do Azores 38°33N 27°46W 153 d1
Topocalma, Pta. Chile 34°10S 72°2W 334 C1
Topock U.S.A. 34°46N 114°29W 307 L12
Topola Serbia 44°17N 20°41E 202 B4
Topolčani Macedonia 41°14N 21°25E 202 E5
Topoľčany Slovak Rep. 48°35N 18°12E 181 C11
Topolnitsa ➔ Bulgaria 42°11N 24°18E 203 D8
Topolobampo Mexico 25°36N 109°3W 318 B3
Topoloveni Romania 44°49N 25°5E 183 F10
Topolovgrad Bulgaria 42°5N 26°20E 203 D10
Topolvățu Mare Romania 45°46N 21°41E 182 E6
Topozero, Ozero Russia 65°35N 32°0E 160 D25
Toppenish U.S.A. 46°23N 120°19W 304 C3
Topraisar Romania 44°1N 28°27E 183 F13
Toprakkale Turkey 37°5N 36°8E 250 A7
Topusko Croatia 45°18N 15°59E 199 C12
Toquepala Peru 17°24S 70°25W 330 D3
Toqyraūyn ➔ Kazakhstan 46°48N 75°24E 217 C9
Tor Di Quinto Italy 41°56N 12°27E 136 B1
Tor Pignattara Italy 41°53N 12°31E 136 B2
Tor Sapienza Italy 41°53N 12°35E 136 B2
Torà Spain 41°49N 1°25E 196 D6
Tora Kit South Sudan 11°2N 32°36E 257 E3
Toranomon Tokyo, Japan 140 c3
Torata Peru 17°23S 70°1W 330 D3
Torbalı Turkey 38°10N 27°21E 205 C9
Torbat-e Heydārīyeh Iran 35°15N 59°12E 247 C8
Torbat-e Jām Iran 35°16N 60°35E 247 C9
Torbay Canada 47°40N 52°42W 299 C9
Torbay ☐ U.K. 50°26N 3°31W 169 G4
Torberget Norway 61°8N 12°7E 164 C9
Torbjörntorp Sweden 58°12N 13°36E 163 F7
Torcy France 48°51N 2°39E 134 A4
Tordesillas Spain 41°30N 5°0W 194 D6
Töreboda Sweden 58°41N 14°7E 163 F8
Torekov Sweden 56°26N 12°37E 163 H6
Torellò Spain 42°3N 2°16E 196 C7
Toreno Spain 42°42N 6°30W 194 C4
Torfaen ☐ U.K. 51°43N 3°3W 169 F4
Torfajökull Iceland 63°54N 19°0W 155 D7
Torgau Germany 51°34N 13°0E 178 D8
Torgelow Germany 53°37N 14°1E 178 B10
Torghay Kazakhstan 49°38N 63°29E 216 C6
Torghay ➔ Kazakhstan 48°1N 62°45E 216 C6
Torghay Ustirti Asia 51°0N 63°0E 216 B6
Torghay Zhylghasy Kazakhstan 52°0N 64°30E 216 B6
Torgovaya = Salsk Russia 46°28N 41°30E 191 G5
Torhamn Sweden 56°6N 15°50E 163 H9
Torhout Belgium 51°5N 3°7E 170 C3
Torhovytsya Ukraine 48°36N 25°26E 183 B10
Tori Ethiopia 7°53N 33°35E 257 F3
Tori-Shima Japan 30°29N 140°19E 221 J10
Torigni-sur-Vire France 49°3N 0°58W 172 C6
Torija Spain 40°44N 3°2W 196 E1
Torilla Pen. Australia 22°29S 150°5E 280 C5
Torino Italy 45°3N 7°40E 198 C4
Torit South Sudan 4°27N 32°31E 257 G3
Torkamān Iran 37°35N 47°23E 213 D12
Torkovichi Russia 58°51N 30°21E 188 C6
Tormac Romania 45°30N 21°30E 182 E6
Tormes ➔ Spain 41°18N 6°29W 194 D4
Tornado Mt. Canada 49°55N 114°40W 296 D6
Tornal'a Slovak Rep. 48°25N 20°20E 181 C13
Torneå = Tornio Finland 65°50N 24°12E 160 D21
Torneälven ➔ Europe 65°50N 24°12E 160 D21
Torneträsk Sweden 68°24N 19°15E 160 B18
Torngat Mountains Nat. Park △ Canada 59°0N 63°40W 295 F19
Torngat Mts. Canada 59°0N 63°40W 295 F19
Tornio Finland 65°50N 24°12E 160 D21
Tornionjoki = Torneälven ➔ Europe 65°50N 24°12E 160 D21
Tornquist Argentina 38°8S 62°15W 334 D3
Toro Baleares, Spain 39°59N 4°8E 206 B5
Toro Zamora, Spain 41°35N 5°24W 194 D5
Torö Sweden 58°48N 17°50E 163 F11
Toro, Cerro del Chile 29°10S 69°50W 334 B2
Toro △ Uganda 1°5N 30°22E 268 C3
Toro Pk. U.S.A. 33°34N 116°24W 307 M10
Torodi Niger 13°7N 1°47E 263 C5
Torokina Papua N. G. 6°14S 155°3E 286 D8
Törökszentmiklós Hungary 47°11N 20°27E 182 C5
Toronto N.S.W., Australia 33°0S 151°30E 283 B9
Toronto Ont., Canada 43°39N 79°20W 141 B2
Toronto Ohio, U.S.A. 40°28N 80°36W 312 F4
Toronto, Univ. of Canada 43°39N 79°23W 141 B2
Toronto City Centre ✕ (YTZ) Canada 43°38N 79°24W 141 B2
Toronto Harbour Canada 43°38N 79°21W 141 B2
Toronto I. Canada 43°37N 79°23W 141 B2
Toronto Lester B. Pearson Int. ✕ (YYZ) Canada 43°46N 79°35W 141 A1
Toropets Russia 56°30N 31°40E 188 D6
Tororo Uganda 0°45N 34°12E 268 B3
Toros Dağları Turkey 37°0N 32°30E 250 B3
Toros Monumental, Templo de Barcelona, Spain 114 a3
Torotoro Bolivia 18°7S 65°46W 331 D4
Torotoro △ Bolivia 18°8S 65°46W 331 D4
Torpa India 22°57N 85°6E 243 H11
Torpo Norway 60°40N 8°43E 164 D5
Torquay Vic., Australia 38°20S 144°19E 282 E6
Torquay Torbay, U.K. 50°27N 3°32W 169 G4
Torquemada Spain 42°2N 4°19W 194 C6
Torrais, Pta. Azores 39°43N 31°7W 153 d2
Torrance U.S.A. 33°50N 118°20W 307 M8
Torrão Portugal 38°16N 8°11W 195 G2
Torre Annunziata Italy 40°45N 14°27E 201 B7
Torre de Moncorvo Portugal 41°12N 7°8W 194 D3
Torre del Campo Spain 37°46N 3°53W 195 H7
Torre del Greco Italy 40°47N 14°22E 201 B7
Torre del Mar Spain 36°44N 4°6W 195 J6
Torre Latino-Americana Mexico City, Mexico 128 b2
Torre Lupara Italy 41°59N 12°39E 136 B2
Torre Nova Italy 41°51N 12°36E 136 B2
Torre-Pacheco Spain 37°44N 0°57W 197 H4
Torre Pellice Italy 44°49N 7°13E 198 D4
Torreblanca Spain 40°14N 0°12E 196 E5
Torrecampo Spain 38°29N 4°41W 195 G6
Torrecilla en Cameros Spain 42°15N 2°38W 196 C2
Torredembarra Spain 41°9N 1°24E 196 D6
Torredonjimeno Spain 37°46N 3°57W 195 H7
Torrejón de Ardoz Spain 40°27N 3°29W 194 E7
Torrejoncillo Spain 39°54N 6°28W 194 F4
Torrelaguna Spain 40°50N 3°38W 194 E7
Torrelavega Spain 43°20N 4°5W 194 B6
Torrellas ➔ Spain 41°23N 2°1E 114 A1
Torremaggiore Italy 41°41N 15°17E 199 G12
Torremolinos Spain 36°38N 4°30W 195 J6
Torrens, L. Australia 31°0S 137°50E 282 A2
Torrens Cr. ➔ Australia 22°23S 145°9E 280 C4
Torrens Creek Australia 20°48S 145°3E 280 C4
Torrent Spain 39°27N 0°28W 197 F4
Torrenueva Spain 38°38N 3°22W 195 G7
Torreón Mexico 25°33N 103°26W 318 B4
Torreperogil Spain 38°2N 3°17W 195 G7
Torres Brazil 29°21S 49°44W 335 B5

Torres Mexico 28°46N 110°47W 318 B2
Torres, Is. Vanuatu 13°15S 166°37E 287 C4
Torres del Paine △ Chile 51°3S 72°58W 336 D2
Torres Novas Portugal 39°27N 8°33W 195 F2
Torres Strait Australia 9°50S 142°20E 280 a
Torres Vedras Portugal 39°5N 9°15W 195 F1
Torrevécchia Italy 41°55N 12°25E 136 B1
Torrevieja Spain 37°59N 0°42W 197 H4
Torrey U.S.A. 38°18N 111°25W 304 G8
Torricelli Mts. Papua N. G. 3°23S 142°15E 286 B2
Torridge → U.K. 51°0N 4°13W 169 G3
Torridon, L. U.K. 57°35N 5°50W 167 D3
Torrijos Phil. 13°19N 122°5E 232 E4
Torrijos Spain 39°59N 4°18W 194 F6
Tørring Denmark 55°52N 9°29E 163 J3
Torrington Conn., U.S.A. 41°48N 73°7W 313 E11
Torrington Wyo., U.S.A. 42°4N 104°11W 304 E11
Torroella de Montgrí Spain 42°2N 3°8E 196 C8
Torrox Spain 36°46N 3°57W 195 J7
Torsås Sweden 56°24N 16°0E 163 H9
Torsby Sweden 60°7N 13°0E 162 D6
Torshälla Sweden 59°25N 16°28E 162 E10
Tórshavn Færoe Is. 62°5N 6°56W 160 E9
Torslanda Sweden 57°44N 11°45E 163 G5
Torsö Sweden 58°48N 13°45E 163 F7
Tortola Br. Virgin Is. 18°19N 64°45W 321 C7
Tórtoles de Esgueva Spain 41°49N 4°2W 194 D6
Tortolì Italy 39°55N 9°39E 200 C2
Tortona Italy 44°54N 8°52E 198 D5
Tortorici Italy 38°2N 14°49E 201 D7
Tortosa Spain 40°49N 0°31E 196 E5
Tortosa, C. Spain 40°41N 0°52E 196 E5
Tortosendo Portugal 40°15N 7°31W 194 E3
Tortue, Î. de la Haiti 20°5N 72°57W 321 B5
Tortuga Trin. & Tob. 10°22N 61°24W 323 t
Tortuguero △ Costa Rica 10°31N 83°29W 320 D3
Tortum Turkey 40°19N 41°35E 213 B9
Ţorūd Iran 35°25N 55°5E 247 C7
Torul Turkey 40°34N 39°18E 213 B8
Toruń Poland 53°2N 18°39E 185 E5
Torun Ukraine 48°40N 23°34E 183 B8
Tory Hill Canada 44°58N 78°16W 312 B6
Tory I. Ireland 55°16N 8°14W 166 A3
Torysa → Slovak Rep. 48°39N 21°21E 181 C14
Torzhok Russia 57°5N 34°55E 188 D8
Torzym Poland 52°19N 15°5E 185 F2
Tosa Japan 33°24N 133°23E 222 D5
Tosa-Shimizu Japan 32°52N 132°58E 222 E4
Tosa-Wan Japan 33°15N 133°30E 222 D5
Tosa-Yamada = Kami Japan 33°36N 133°38E 222 D5
Toscana □ Italy 43°25N 11°0E 198 E8
Toscanella = Tuscánia Italy 42°25N 11°52E 199 F8
Toscano, Arcipelago Italy 42°30N 10°30E 198 F7
Toshima Japan 35°43N 139°43E 140 A3
Toshimaen Japan 35°43N 139°38E 140 A2
Toshka Egypt 22°30N 31°53E 256 C3
Toshka Lakes Egypt 22°50N 31°0E 256 C3
Toshkent Uzbekistan 41°20N 69°10E 217 D7
Toshkent □ Uzbekistan 41°0N 69°40E 217 D7
Tosno Russia 59°38N 30°46E 188 C6
Tossa de Mar Spain 41°43N 2°56E 196 D7
Tösse Sweden 58°58N 12°39E 163 F6
Tostado Argentina 29°15S 61°50W 334 B3
Tostedt Germany 53°17N 9°42E 178 B5
Tostón, Pta. de Canary Is. 28°42N 14°2W 153 e2
Tosu Japan 33°22N 130°31E 222 D2
Tosya Turkey 41°1N 34°2E 212 B6
Toszek Poland 50°27N 18°32E 185 H5
Totak Norway 59°40N 8°0E 164 E5
Totana Spain 37°45N 1°30W 197 H3
Totebo Sweden 57°38N 16°12E 163 G10
Toteng Botswana 20°22S 22°58E 270 B3
Tôtes France 49°41N 1°2E 172 C8
Tótkomlós Hungary 46°24N 20°45E 182 D5
Totland Norway 61°56N 5°23E 164 C2
Totma Russia 60°0N 42°40E 186 C7
Totnes U.K. 50°26N 3°42W 169 G4
Totness Suriname 5°53N 56°19W 329 B6
Toto Angola 7°9S 14°16E 265 D2
Toto Nigeria 8°26N 7°5E 263 D6
Totonicapán Guatemala 14°58N 91°12W 320 D1
Totora Bolivia 17°42S 65°9W 331 D4
Totoya, I. Fiji 18°57S 179°50W 287 B3
Totten Glacier Antarctica 66°45S 116°10E 151 C8
Tottenham N.S.W., Australia 32°14S 147°21E 283 B7
Tottenham Vic., Australia 37°48S 144°51E 128 A1
Tottenham Ont., Canada 44°1N 79°49W 312 B5
Tottenham London, U.K. 51°35N 0°4W 125 A3
Tottori Japan 35°30N 134°15E 222 B6
Tottori □ Japan 35°30N 134°12E 222 B6
Touáret Niger 20°17N 7°8E 261 D6
Touat Algeria 27°27N 0°30E 261 C5
Touba Ivory C. 8°22N 7°40W 262 D3
Touba Senegal 14°50N 15°55W 262 C1
Toubkal, Djebel Morocco 31°0N 8°0W 260 B3
Toubkal △ Morocco 31°0N 8°2W 260 B3
Touboro Cameroon 7°47N 15°22E 264 A3
T'ouch'eng Taiwan 24°52N 121°49E 225 B3
Toucy France 47°44N 3°15E 173 E10
T'oufen Taiwan 24°41N 120°54E 225 B2
Tougan Burkina Faso 13°11N 2°58W 262 C4
Touggourt Algeria 33°6N 6°4E 261 B6
Tougouri Burkina Faso 13°20N 0°30W 263 C4
Tougué Guinea 11°25N 11°50W 262 C2
Toukoto Mali 13°27N 9°52W 262 C3
Toul France 48°40N 5°53E 173 D12
Toulepleu Ivory C. 6°32N 8°24W 262 D3
Touliu Taiwan 23°42N 120°31E 225 C2
Toulon Var, France 43°10N 5°55E 175 E9
Toulon Ill., U.S.A. 41°6N 89°52W 310 C7
Toulouse France 43°37N 1°27E 174 E5
Toulouse Blagnac ✈ (TLS) France 43°37N 1°22E 174 E5
Toulouse Street New Orleans, U.S.A. 131 b2
Toummo Niger 22°45N 14°8E 258 D2
Toummo, Mts. de Africa 22°43N 14°12E 258 D2
Toumodi Ivory C. 6°32N 5°4W 262 D3
Tounan Taiwan 23°41N 120°28E 225 C2
Tounassine, Hamada Algeria 28°48N 5°0W 260 C4
Tounggoo Burma 19°0N 96°30E 241 F6
Toungo Nigeria 8°20N 12°3E 263 D7
Touques → France 49°22N 0°8E 172 C7
Touraine France 47°20N 0°30E 172 E7
Touran = Tūrān △ Iran 35°45N 56°30E 247 C8
Tourane = Da Nang Vietnam 16°4N 108°13E 236 D7
Tourcoing France 50°42N 3°10E 173 B10
Touriñán, C. Spain 43°3N 9°18W 194 B1
Tourîne Mauritania 22°23N 11°50W 260 D2
Tournai Belgium 50°35N 3°25E 170 D3
Tournan-en-Brie France 48°44N 2°46E 173 D9
Tournay France 43°13N 0°13E 174 E4
Tournon-St-Martin France 46°45N 0°58E 172 F7
Tournon-sur-Rhône France 45°4N 4°50E 175 C8
Tournus France 46°35N 4°54E 173 F11
Touros Brazil 5°12S 35°28W 332 C4
Tours France 47°22N 0°40E 172 E7
Tousidé, Pic Chad 21°1N 16°29E 259 D3
Toussoro, Mt. C.A.R. 9°7N 23°14E 264 A4
Toussus-le-Noble France 48°44N 2°6E 134 B1
Toussus-le-Noble ✈ (TNF) France 48°44N 2°6E 134 B1
Touws → S. Africa 33°45S 21°11E 270 D3
Touwsrivier S. Africa 33°20S 20°2E 270 D3
Tovar Venezuela 8°20N 71°46W 328 B3
Tovarkovskiy Russia 53°40N 38°14E 188 F10
Tovdal Norway 58°47N 8°10E 164 F5
Tovdalselva → Norway 58°11N 8°7E 164 F5
Tovste Ukraine 48°50N 25°44E 183 B10
Tovuz Azerbaijan 41°0N 45°40E 191 K7
Towada Japan 40°37N 141°13E 220 D10
Towada-Hachimantai △ Japan 40°20N 140°55E 220 D10
Towada-Ko Japan 40°28N 140°55E 220 D10
Towanda Ill., U.S.A. 40°36N 88°53W 311 D8
Towanda Pa., U.S.A. 41°46N 76°27W 313 E8
Towarri △ Australia 31°50S 150°37E 283 A9
Towchāl Cable Car Iran 35°49N 51°24E 141 A2
Tower U.S.A. 47°48N 92°17W 308 B7
Tower, I. = Genovesa, I. Ecuador 0°20N 89°58W 330 a
Tower Bridge London, U.K. 125 b5
Tower Hamlets □ U.K. 51°32N 0°2W 125 A3
Tower of London U.K. 51°30N 0°4W 125 A3
Towerhill Cr. → Australia 22°28S 144°35E 280 C3
Towner U.S.A. 48°21N 100°25W 308 A3
Townsend Ga., U.S.A. 31°33N 81°31W 316 D8
Townsend Mont., U.S.A. 46°19N 111°31W 304 C8
Townshend I. Australia 22°10S 150°31E 280 C5
Townsville Australia 19°15S 146°45E 280 B4
Towot South Sudan 6°12N 34°25E 257 F3
Towra Pt. Australia 34°0S 151°10E 139 C2
Towraghondī Afghan. 35°13N 62°16E 240 B1
Towson U.S.A. 39°24N 76°36W 309 F15
Towuti, Danau Indonesia 2°45S 121°32E 231 E6
Toxkan He → China 41°8N 80°11E 217 D10
Tōya-Ko Japan 42°35N 140°51E 220 C10
Toyama Japan 36°40N 137°15E 223 A9
Toyama □ Japan 36°45N 137°30E 223 A9
Toyama-Wan Japan 37°0N 137°30E 221 F8
Toyapakeh Indonesia 8°41S 115°29E 231 K18
Tøyen Norway 59°55N 10°47E 133 A3
Tōyō Ehime, Japan 33°56N 133°5E 222 D5
Tōyō Kōchi, Japan 33°26N 134°16E 222 D6
Toyohara = Yuzhno-Sakhalinsk Russia 46°58N 142°45E 219 B17
Toyohashi Japan 34°45N 137°25E 223 C9
Toyokawa Japan 34°48N 137°27E 223 C9
Toyonaka Japan 34°46N 135°28E 133 A1
Toyooka Japan 35°35N 134°48E 222 B6
Toyota Japan 35°3N 137°7E 223 B9
Toyoura Japan 34°6N 130°57E 222 C2
Tozeur Tunisia 33°56N 8°8E 258 B1
Tozeur □ Tunisia 34°0N 8°5E 261 B6
Tqibuli Georgia 42°26N 43°0E 191 J6
Tqvarcheli Georgia 42°47N 41°42E 191 J5
Trá Lí = Tralee Ireland 52°16N 9°42W 166 D2
Trá Mhór = Tramore Ireland 52°10N 7°10W 166 D4
Tra On Vietnam 9°58N 105°55E 237 H5
Tra Vinh Vietnam 9°50N 106°15E 237 H6
Trabancos → Spain 41°36N 5°15W 194 D5
Traben-Trarbach Germany 49°57N 7°7E 179 F3
Trabzon Turkey 41°0N 39°45E 213 B8
Trabzon □ Turkey 41°10N 39°45E 213 B8
Tracadie Canada 47°30N 64°55W 299 C7
Trachenburg = Żmigród Poland 51°28N 16°53E 185 G3
Tracy Qué., Canada 46°1N 73°9W 298 C5
Tracy Calif., U.S.A. 37°44N 121°26W 306 H5
Tracy Minn., U.S.A. 44°14N 95°37W 308 C6
Tradate Italy 45°43N 8°54E 198 C5
Trade Town Liberia 5°40N 9°50W 262 D3
Traer U.S.A. 42°12N 92°28W 310 B4
Trafalgar Vic., Australia 38°14S 146°12E 283 E7
Trafalgar Dominica 15°19N 61°21W 323 k
Trafalgar, C. Spain 36°10N 6°2W 195 J4
Trafalgar Square London, U.K. 125 b3
Trafaria Portugal 38°40N 9°13W 126 A1
Tragonhsi Greece 37°27N 25°29E 205 D7
Traian Brăila, Romania 45°11N 27°44E 183 E12
Traian Tulcea, Romania 45°2N 28°15E 183 E13
Traição, Cor. → Brazil 23°35S 46°41W 137 B2
Traiguén Chile 38°15S 72°41W 336 A2
Trail Canada 49°5N 117°40W 296 D5
Traill Ø Greenland 72°30N 23°0W 154 C8
Traimit Bangkok, Thailand 113 c2
Trainor L. Canada 60°24N 120°17W 296 A4
Traíra → Brazil 1°4S 69°26W 328 D4
Trakai △ Lithuania 54°30N 25°10E 161 J21
Trákhonas Cyprus 35°12N 33°21E 207 E9
Tralee Ireland 52°16N 9°42W 166 D2
Tralee B. Ireland 52°17N 9°55W 166 D2
Tram Chim △ Vietnam 10°43N 105°31E 237 G5
Tramore Ireland 52°10N 7°10W 166 D4
Tramore B. Ireland 52°9N 7°10W 166 D4
Tramuntana, Serra de Spain 39°48N 2°54E 206 B3
Tran Ninh, Cao Nguyen Laos 19°30N 103°10E 236 C4
Tranås Sweden 58°3N 14°59E 163 F8
Tranbjerg Denmark 56°6N 10°9E 163 H4
Tranby Norway 59°49N 10°15E 164 E7
Trancas Argentina 26°11S 65°20W 334 B2
Trancoso Portugal 40°49N 7°21W 194 E3
Tranebjerg Denmark 55°51N 10°36E 163 J4
Tranegilde Denmark 55°37N 12°20E 118 B2
Tranemo Sweden 57°30N 13°20E 163 G7
Trang Thailand 7°33N 99°38E 237 J2
Trangahy Madag. 19°7S 44°31E 272 B1
Trangan Indonesia 6°40S 134°20E 231 F8
Trangie Australia 32°4S 148°0E 283 B8
Trångsund Sweden 59°13N 18°8E 139 B2
Trångsviken Sweden 63°19N 13°59E 162 A7
Trani Italy 41°17N 16°25E 201 A9
Tranoroa Madag. 24°42S 45°4E 272 C2
Tranqueras Uruguay 31°13S 55°45W 335 C4
Trans-Alaska Pipeline U.S.A. 70°11N 148°27W 303 A10
Transamerica Pyramid San Francisco, U.S.A. 136 b2
Transantarctic Mts. Antarctica 85°0S 170°0W 151 E12
Transbay Terminal San Francisco, U.S.A. 136 b3
Transcarpathia = Zakarpattya □ Ukraine 48°20N 23°20E 183 B8
Transilvania Romania 46°30N 24°0E 183 D9
Transilvanian Alps = Carpaţii Meridionali Romania 45°30N 25°0E 183 E9
Transjordan = Jordan ■ Asia 31°0N 36°0E 251 H7
Transnistria = Stînga Nistrului □ Moldova 47°20N 29°15E 183 C14
Transtrand Sweden 61°6N 13°20E 162 C7
Transtrandsfjällen Sweden 61°8N 13°0E 162 C6
Transylvania = Transilvania Romania 46°30N 24°0E 183 D9
Trants Bay Montserrat 16°46N 62°9W 323 p
Trápani Italy 38°1N 12°29E 200 D5
Trappenfelde Germany 52°34N 13°39E 115 A4
Trapper Pk. U.S.A. 45°54N 114°18W 304 D6
Traralgon Australia 38°12S 146°34E 283 E7
Traryd Sweden 56°35N 13°45E 163 H7
Trarza □ Mauritania 18°0N 15°0W 260 E2
Trás-os-Montes = Cucumbi Angola 10°17S 19°5E 265 E3
Trasacco Italy 41°57N 13°32E 199 G10
Trăscău, Munţii Romania 46°14N 23°14E 183 D8
Trasimeno, L. Italy 43°8N 12°6E 199 E9
Träslövsläge Sweden 57°4N 12°16E 163 G6
Trastévere Italy 41°53N 12°28E 136 B1
Trasvase Tajo-Segura, Canal de Spain 40°15N 2°55W 196 E2
Trat Thailand 12°14N 102°33E 237 F4
Tratani → Pakistan 29°19N 68°20E 242 E3
Traun Austria 48°14N 14°15E 180 C7
Traunreut Germany 47°57N 12°36E 179 H8
Traunsee Austria 47°55N 13°50E 180 D6
Traunstein Germany 47°52N 12°37E 179 H8
Travellers L. Australia 33°20S 142°0E 282 B5
Travemünde Germany 53°57N 10°52E 178 B6
Travers, Mt. N.Z. 42°1S 172°45E 285 C7
Traverse City U.S.A. 44°46N 85°38W 309 C11
Travis, L. U.S.A. 30°24N 97°55W 314 F6
Travnik Bos.-H. 44°17N 17°39E 182 F2
Trawbreaga B. Ireland 55°20N 7°25W 166 A4
Trbovlje Slovenia 46°12N 15°5E 199 B12
Treasure I. U.S.A. 37°49N 122°22W 136 B2
Treasure Island U.S.A. 27°46N 82°46W 317 H7
Treasury Is. Solomon Is. 7°22S 155°37E 287 L8
Trébbia → Italy 45°4N 9°41E 198 C6
Trebel → Germany 53°54N 13°2E 178 B9
Trébeurden France 48°46N 3°35W 172 D3
Trebević △ Bos.-H. 43°20N 18°45E 182 G3
Třebíč Czech Rep. 49°14N 15°55E 180 B8
Trebinje Bos.-H. 42°44N 18°22E 202 D2
Trebisacce Italy 39°52N 16°32E 201 C9
Trebišnjica → Bos.-H. 42°47N 18°8E 202 D2
Trebišov Slovak Rep. 48°38N 21°41E 181 C14
Trebitsch = Třebíč Czech Rep. 49°14N 15°55E 180 B8
Trebižat → Bos.-H. 43°15N 17°30E 199 E14
Trebnitz = Trzebnica Poland 51°20N 17°1E 185 G4
Trebnje Slovenia 45°54N 15°1E 199 C12
Třeboň Czech Rep. 49°1N 14°48E 180 B7
Trebonne Australia 18°37S 146°5E 280 B4
Třeboňsko ⌓ Czech Rep. 49°1N 14°49E 180 B7
Třeboradice Czech Rep. 50°9N 14°31E 135 B3
Třebotov Czech Rep. 49°58N 14°17E 135 C1
Trebujena Spain 36°52N 6°11W 195 J4
Trecate Italy 45°26N 8°44E 198 C5
Tree Tops Park U.S.A. 26°4N 80°16W 129 B1
Trefaldwyn = Montgomery U.K. 52°34N 3°8W 169 E4
Trefynwy = Monmouth U.K. 51°48N 2°42W 169 F5
Tregaron U.K. 52°14N 3°56W 169 E4
Tregnago Italy 45°31N 11°10E 199 C8
Tregrosse Is. Australia 17°41S 150°43E 280 B5
Tréguier France 48°47N 3°16W 172 D3
Trégunc France 47°51N 3°51W 172 E3
Treherne Canada 49°38N 98°42W 297 D9
Tréia Italy 43°19N 13°19E 199 E10
Treignac France 45°32N 1°48E 174 C5
Treinta y Tres Uruguay 33°16S 54°17W 335 C5
Treis-karden Germany 50°10N 7°18E 179 E3
Treklyano Bulgaria 42°33N 22°36E 202 D6
Trelawney Zimbabwe 17°30S 30°30E 271 A5
Trélazé France 47°26N 0°30W 172 E6
Trelew Argentina 43°10S 65°20W 336 B3
Trélissac France 45°11N 0°47E 174 C4
Trelleborg Sweden 55°20N 13°10E 163 J7
Tremadog Bay U.K. 52°51N 4°18W 168 E3
Tremblay-en-France France 48°56N 2°35E 134 A4
Tremblet Réunion 21°17S 55°48E 272 f
Trembowla = Terebovlya Ukraine 49°18N 25°44E 177 D13
Tremedal = Monte Azul Brazil 15°9S 42°53W 333 E3
Tremembe → Brazil 23°27S 46°34W 137 A2
Trémiti Italy 42°8N 15°30E 199 F12
Tremont U.S.A. 40°50N 73°52W 132 A2
Tremonton U.S.A. 41°43N 112°10W 304 F7
Tremp Spain 42°10N 0°52E 196 C5
Trenche → Canada 47°46N 72°53W 298 C5
Trenčiansky □ Slovak Rep. 48°45N 18°20E 181 C11
Trenčín Slovak Rep. 48°52N 18°4E 181 C11
Trengereid Norway 60°26N 5°37E 164 D2
Trenggalek Indonesia 8°3S 111°43E 235 D4
Trenno Italy 45°29N 9°6E 128 B1
Trenque Lauquen Argentina 36°5S 62°45W 334 D3
Trent → Ont., Canada 44°6N 77°34W 312 B7
Trent → England, U.K. 53°41N 0°42W 168 D7
Trentino-Alto Adige □ Italy 46°30N 11°20E 199 B8
Trento Italy 46°4N 11°8E 198 B8
Trento Agusan del S., Phil. 8°3N 126°2E 233 G6
Trenton Ont., Canada 44°10N 77°34W 312 B7
Trenton Fla., U.S.A. 29°37N 82°49W 317 F7
Trenton Mich., U.S.A. 42°8N 83°11W 311 B13
Trenton Mo., U.S.A. 40°5N 93°37W 310 D3
Trenton N.J., U.S.A. 40°14N 74°46W 313 F10
Trenton Nebr., U.S.A. 40°11N 101°1W 308 E3
Trenton Ohio, U.S.A. 39°29N 84°28W 311 E12
Trenton S.C., U.S.A. 33°45N 81°51W 316 B8
Trepassey Canada 46°43N 53°25W 299 C9
Treptow Germany 52°29N 13°27E 115 B3
Treptow an der Rega = Trzebiatów Poland 54°3N 15°18E 184 D2
Trepuzzi Italy 40°24N 18°4E 201 B11
Tres Arroyos Argentina 38°26S 60°20W 334 D3
Três Casas Brazil 6°59S 62°41W 331 B5
Três Corações Brazil 21°44S 45°15W 333 F2
Tres Equinas Colombia 0°43N 75°16W 328 C2
Três Lagoas Brazil 20°50S 51°43W 333 F1
Tres Lagos Argentina 49°35S 71°25W 336 C2
Tres Lomas Argentina 36°27S 62°51W 334 D3
Três Marias, Represa Brazil 18°12S 45°15W 333 E2
Tres Montes, C. Chile 46°50S 75°30W 336 C1
Tres Pinos U.S.A. 36°48N 121°19W 306 J5
Três Pontas Brazil 21°23S 45°29W 333 F2
Três Pontas, C. das Angola 10°28S 13°32E 265 E2
Tres Puentes Chile 27°50S 70°15W 334 B1
Tres Puntas, C. Argentina 47°0S 66°0W 336 C3
Três Rios Brazil 22°6S 43°15W 333 F3
Três Rios, Sa. dos Brazil 22°56S 43°17W 135 B1
Tres Valles Mexico 18°15N 96°8W 319 D5
Tresco U.K. 49°57N 6°20W 169 H1
Tresfjord Norway 62°31N 7°7E 164 B4
Treska → Macedonia 42°0N 21°20E 202 E5
Treskavica Bos.-H. 43°40N 18°20E 182 G3
Trespaderne Spain 42°47N 3°24W 194 C7
Tresticklan △ Sweden 59°0N 11°42E 163 F5
Trets France 43°27N 5°41E 175 E9
Treuburg = Olecko Poland 54°2N 22°31E 184 D9
Treuchtlingen Germany 48°58N 10°54E 179 G6
Treuenbrietzen Germany 52°5N 12°52E 178 C8
Treungen Norway 59°1N 8°31E 164 E5
Trèves = Trier Germany 49°45N 6°38E 179 F2
Trevi Italy 42°52N 12°45E 199 F9
Trevi, Fontana di Rome, Italy 136 b3
Treviglio Italy 45°31N 9°35E 198 C6
Trevinca, Peña Spain 42°15N 6°46W 194 C4
Treviño Spain 42°44N 2°45W 194 C8
Treviso Italy 45°40N 12°15E 199 C9
Trévoux France 45°57N 4°47E 175 C8
Trezzano sul Navíglio Italy 45°24N 9°4E 128 B1
Trgovište Serbia 42°20N 22°10E 202 D6
Triabunna Australia 42°30S 147°55E 281 G4
Trianda = Ialissos Greece 36°24N 28°10E 206 E12
Triangle Zimbabwe 21°2S 31°28E 271 B5
Triaucourt-en-Argonne France 48°59N 5°2E 173 D12
Tribal Areas □ Pakistan 33°0N 70°0E 242 C4
Tribsees Germany 54°5N 12°44E 178 A8
Tribugá, G. de Colombia 5°45N 77°20W 328 B2
Tribulation, C. Australia 16°5S 145°29E 280 B4
Tribune U.S.A. 38°28N 101°45W 308 F3
Tribune Tower Chicago, U.S.A. 119 b2
Tricárico Italy 40°37N 16°9E 201 B9
Tricase Italy 39°56N 18°22E 201 C11
Trichinopoly = Tiruchchirappalli India 10°45N 78°45E 245 J4
Trichonida, L. Greece 38°34N 21°30E 204 C3
Trichur = Thrissur India 10°30N 76°18E 245 J3
Trichy = Tiruchchirappalli India 10°45N 78°45E 245 J4
Trida Australia 33°1S 145°1E 283 B6
Trier Germany 49°45N 6°38E 179 F2
Trieste Lazio, Italy 41°55N 12°30E 136 B2
Trieste Trieste, Italy 45°40N 13°46E 199 C10
Trieste, G. di Italy 45°40N 13°35E 199 C10
Trieux → France 48°43N 3°9W 172 D3
Triggiano Italy 41°4N 16°55E 201 A9
Triglav Slovenia 46°21N 13°50E 199 B10
Triglavski △ Slovenia 46°20N 13°50E 199 B10
Trigno → Italy 42°4N 14°48E 199 F11
Trigo de Morais = Guijá Mozam. 24°27S 33°0E 271 B5
Trigueros Spain 37°24N 6°50W 195 H4
Trikala Greece 39°34N 21°47E 204 B3
Trikeri Greece 39°6N 23°5E 204 B5
Trikomo Cyprus 35°17N 33°52E 207 E9
Trikora, Puncak Indonesia 4°15S 138°45E 231 E9
Trilby U.S.A. 28°28N 82°12W 317 G7
Trilj Croatia 43°38N 16°42E 199 E13
Trillo Spain 40°42N 2°35W 196 E2
Trim Ireland 53°33N 6°48W 166 C5
Trimbak India 19°56N 73°33E 244 E1
Trimmu Dam Pakistan 31°10N 72°8E 242 D5
Trincomalee Sri Lanka 8°38N 81°15E 245 K5
Trindade Atl. Oc. 20°20S 29°50W 152 J9
Trindade Brazil 16°40S 49°30W 333 E2
Třinec Czech Rep. 49°41N 18°39E 181 B11
Trinidad = Jose Abad Santos Phil. 5°55N 125°39E 233 J5
Trinidad Bolivia 14°46S 64°50W 331 C5
Trinidad Colombia 5°25N 71°40W 328 B3
Trinidad Cuba 21°48N 80°0W 320 B4
Trinidad Trin. & Tob. 10°30N 61°15W 323 t
Trinidad Uruguay 33°30S 56°50W 334 C4
Trinidad Colo., U.S.A. 37°10N 104°31W 305 H11
Trinidad D.C., U.S.A. 38°54N 76°59W 143 B3
Trinidad, G. Chile 49°55S 75°25W 336 C1
Trinidad, I. Argentina 39°10S 62°0W 336 A4
Trinidad & Tobago ■ W. Indies 10°30N 61°20W 323 t
Trinitápoli Italy 41°21N 16°5E 201 A9
Trinité, Havre de Martinique 14°44N 60°58W 322 j
Trinity Nfld. & L., Canada 48°59N 53°55W 299 C9
Trinity Edinburgh, U.K. 55°58N 3°12W 121 B2
Trinity Tex., U.S.A. 30°57N 95°22W 314 F7
Trinity → Calif., U.S.A. 41°11N 123°42W 304 F2
Trinity → Tex., U.S.A. 29°45N 94°43W 314 G7
Trinity B. Canada 48°20N 53°10W 299 C9
Trinity Church New York, U.S.A. 132 f1
Trinity College Dublin, Ireland 120 c3
Trinity Hills Trin. & Tob. 10°7N 61°7W 323 t
Trinity Is. U.S.A. 56°33N 154°25W 303 H9
Trinity Range U.S.A. 40°10N 118°40W 304 F4
Trinkat India 8°5N 93°30E 245 K11
Trinkitat Sudan 18°45N 37°51E 256 D4
Trino Italy 45°12N 8°18E 198 C5
Trinway U.S.A. 40°9N 82°1W 312 F2
Triolet Mauritius 20°4S 57°32E 272 e
Trionfale Italy 41°54N 12°26E 136 B1
Trionto, C. Italy 39°37N 16°43E 201 C9
Triora Italy 44°1N 7°46E 198 D4
Tripoli = Tarābulus Lebanon 34°31N 35°50E 250 D6
Tripoli = Tarābulus Libya 32°49N 13°7E 258 B2
Tripoli Greece 37°31N 22°25E 204 D4
Tripoli Iowa, U.S.A. 42°49N 92°16W 310 B4
Tripolitania = Tarābulus Libya 31°0N 13°0E 258 B2
Tripura □ India 24°0N 92°0E 241 D4
Tripylos Cyprus 34°59N 32°41E 207 F8
Trischen Germany 54°4N 8°40E 178 A4
Tristan da Cunha Atl. Oc. 37°6S 12°20W 255 K2
Trisul India 30°19N 79°47E 243 D8
Triton I. S. China Sea 15°47N 111°12E 230 A4
Triulzo Italy 45°25N 9°16E 128 B2
Trivandrum = Thiruvananthapuram India 8°41N 77°0E 245 K3
Trivento Italy 41°47N 14°33E 199 G11
Trizin Greece 37°25N 23°15E 204 D5
Trnava Slovak Rep. 48°23N 17°35E 181 C10
Trnavský □ Slovak Rep. 48°30N 17°45E 181 C10
Troarn France 49°11N 0°11W 172 C6
Trobriand Is. Papua N. G. 8°30S 151°0E 286 E6
Trocadero Paris, France 134 b1
Trochu Canada 51°50N 113°13W 296 C6
Trodely I. Canada 52°15N 79°26W 298 B4
Troebratskīy Kazakhstan 54°25N 66°4E 217 B7
Trogir Croatia 43°32N 16°15E 199 E13
Troglav Croatia 43°56N 16°36E 199 E13
Tróia Italy 41°22N 15°18E 201 A8
Troilus, L. Canada 50°50N 74°35W 298 B5
Troina Italy 37°47N 14°36E 201 E7
Trois Boutiques Mauritius 20°26S 57°38E 272 e
Trois Fourches, Cap des Morocco 35°26N 2°58W 261 A4
Trois-Pistoles Canada 48°5N 69°10W 299 C6
Trois Pitons, Morne Dominica 15°22N 61°20W 323 k
Trois-Rivières Qué., Canada 46°25N 72°34W 298 C5
Trois-Rivières Guadeloupe 15°57N 61°40W 322 e
Trois Rivières Martinique 14°28N 60°58W 322 j
Troisdorf Germany 50°48N 7°11E 178 E3
Troitsk Russia 54°10N 61°35E 216 B6
Troitsko Pechorsk Russia 62°40N 56°10E 186 B10
Troitskosavsk = Kyakhta Russia 50°30N 106°25E 215 D11
Troitskoye Russia 46°26N 44°15E 191 G7
Troitsky = Troitsk Russia 54°10N 61°35E 216 B6
Troja Czech Rep. 50°7N 14°25E 135 B2
Troll Antarctica 72°0S 2°30E 151 D3
Trölladyngja Iceland 64°54N 17°16W 155 C9
Trollbäcken Sweden 59°14N 18°12E 139 B3
Trollhättan Sweden 58°17N 12°20E 163 F6
Trollheimen Norway 62°46N 9°1E 164 B6
Trombay India 19°2N 72°56E 130 A2
Trombetas → Brazil 1°55S 55°35W 329 D6
Tromelin I. Ind. Oc. 15°52S 54°25E 273 F4
Tromøy Norway 58°27N 8°51E 164 F5
Tromsø Norway 69°40N 18°56E 160 B18
Tron Thailand 17°28N 100°7E 236 D3
Trona U.S.A. 35°46N 117°23W 307 K9
Tronador, Mte. Argentina 41°10S 71°50W 336 B2
Tronchetto Venice, Italy 142 b1
Trøndelag Norway 64°17N 11°50E 160 D14
Trondheim Norway 63°36N 10°25E 164 A7
Trondheimsfjorden Norway 63°35N 10°30E 160 E14
Trondheimsleia Norway 63°25N 8°30E 164 A5
Trondhjem = Trondheim Norway 63°36N 10°25E 164 A7
Trönninge Sweden 56°37N 12°51E 163 H6
Tronto → Italy 42°54N 13°55E 199 F10
Troodos Cyprus 34°55N 32°52E 207 F8
Troon U.K. 55°33N 4°39W 167 F4
Troparevo Russia 55°39N 37°29E 129 C1
Tropea Italy 38°41N 15°54E 201 D8
Tropic U.S.A. 37°37N 112°5W 305 H7
Tropojë Albania 42°23N 20°10E 202 D4
Troppau = Opava Czech Rep. 49°57N 17°58E 181 B10
Trosa Sweden 58°54N 17°33E 163 F11
Trostan U.K. 55°3N 6°10W 166 A5
Trostberg Germany 48°1N 12°33E 179 G8
Trostyanets Sumy, Ukraine 50°33N 34°59E 189 G8
Trostyanets Vinnyts'ka, Ukraine 48°31N 29°11E 183 B14
Trotsk = Chapayevsk Russia 53°0N 49°40E 190 D9
Trotsk = Gatchina Russia 59°35N 30°9E 188 C6
Trou Gras Pt. St. Lucia 13°51N 60°53W 323 m
Troumaka St. Vincent 13°16N 61°17W 323 n
Trout → Canada 61°19N 119°51W 296 A5
Trout L. N.W.T., Canada 60°40N 121°14W 296 A4
Trout L. Ont., Canada 51°20N 93°15W 297 C10
Trout Lake N.W.T., Canada 56°30N 114°32W 296 B6
Trout Lake Wash., U.S.A. 46°0N 121°32W 306 E5
Trout River Canada 49°29N 58°8W 299 C8
Trout Run U.S.A. 41°23N 77°3W 312 E7
Trouville-sur-Mer France 49°21N 0°5E 172 C7
Trowbridge U.K. 51°18N 2°12W 169 F5
Troy Turkey 39°57N 26°12E 205 B8
Troy Ala., U.S.A. 31°48N 85°58W 316 D4
Troy Ill., U.S.A. 38°44N 89°54W 310 F7
Troy Ind., U.S.A. 37°59N 86°55W 311 G10
Troy Kans., U.S.A. 39°47N 95°5W 308 F6
Troy Mich., U.S.A. 42°37N 83°9W 311 B13
Troy Mo., U.S.A. 38°59N 90°59W 310 F6
Troy Mont., U.S.A. 48°28N 115°53W 304 B6
Troy N.Y., U.S.A. 42°44N 73°41W 313 D11
Troy Ohio, U.S.A. 40°2N 84°12W 311 D12
Troy Pa., U.S.A. 41°47N 76°47W 313 E8
Troyan Bulgaria 42°57N 24°43E 203 D8
Troyes France 48°19N 4°3E 173 D11
Trpanj Croatia 43°1N 17°15E 199 E14
Trstenik Serbia 43°36N 21°0E 202 C5
Trubchevsk Russia 52°33N 33°47E 189 F7
Truchas Pk. U.S.A. 35°58N 105°39W 305 J11
Trucial States = United Arab Emirates ■ Asia 23°50N 54°0E 247 F7
Truckee U.S.A. 39°20N 120°11W 306 F6
Trudeau, Montréal ✈ (YUL) Canada 45°28N 73°44W 130 B1
Trudfront Russia 45°56N 47°40E 191 H8
Trudovoye Russia 43°17N 132°5E 220 C6
Trudyashchikhsya, Ostrov Russia 59°58N 30°18E 137 B1
Trujillo Colombia 4°10N 76°19W 328 C2
Trujillo Honduras 16°0N 86°0W 320 C2
Trujillo Peru 8°6S 79°0W 330 B2
Trujillo Spain 39°28N 5°55W 195 F5
Trujillo N. Mex., U.S.A. 35°32N 104°42W 305 J11
Trujillo Venezuela 9°22N 70°38W 328 B3
Trujillo □ Venezuela 9°25N 70°30W 328 B3
Trujillo, Mte. = Duarte, Pico Dom. Rep. 19°2N 70°59W 321 C5
Trujillo Alto Puerto Rico 18°21N 66°1W 321 b
Truk Micronesia 7°25N 151°46E 287 T17
Trumann U.S.A. 35°41N 90°31W 315 D9
Trumansburg U.S.A. 42°33N 76°40W 313 D8
Trumbull, Mt. U.S.A. 36°25N 113°19W 305 H7
Trump Tower Chicago, U.S.A. 119 b2
Trŭn Bulgaria 42°51N 22°38E 202 D6
Trun Orne, France 48°50N 0°2E 172 D7
Trundle Australia 32°53S 147°35E 283 B7
Trung Lon, Hon Vietnam 8°36N 106°8E 237 H6
Trung-Phan Vietnam 17°0N 109°0E 236 D6
Truong Sa, Dao = Spratly I. S. China Sea 8°38N 111°55E 230 C4
Truro S. Austral., Australia 34°24S 139°9E 282 C3
Truro N.S., Canada 45°21N 63°14W 299 C7
Truro Corn., U.K. 50°16N 5°4W 169 G2
Trus Madi, Gunung Malaysia 5°33N 116°31E 235 A5
Truskavets Ukraine 49°17N 23°30E 177 D12
Trŭstenik Bulgaria 43°31N 24°28E 203 C8
Trustrup Denmark 56°20N 10°46E 163 H4
Trutch Canada 57°44N 122°57W 296 B4
Truth or Consequences U.S.A. 33°8N 107°15W 305 K10
Trutnov Czech Rep. 50°37N 15°54E 180 A8
Truyère → France 44°38N 2°34E 174 D6
Tryavna Bulgaria 42°54N 25°25E 203 D9
Tryonville U.S.A. 41°42N 79°48W 312 E5
Tryphena N.Z. 36°18S 175°28E 284 C4
Trysilelva → Norway 61°2N 12°35E 164 C9
Tryvasshøgda Norway 59°59N 10°40E 133 A3
Trzcianka Poland 53°3N 16°25E 185 E3
Trzciel Poland 52°23N 15°50E 185 F2
Trzcińsko Zdrój Poland 52°58N 14°35E 185 F1
Trzebiatów Poland 54°3N 15°18E 184 D2
Trzebiez Poland 53°38N 14°31E 184 E1
Trzebnica Poland 51°20N 17°1E 185 G4
Trzemeszno Poland 52°33N 17°48E 185 F4
Tržič Slovenia 46°22N 14°18E 199 B11
Tsagaannur Mongolia 49°32N 89°42E 217 C11
Tsagan Aman Russia 47°34N 46°43E 191 G8
Tsala Apopka L. U.S.A. 28°53N 82°19W 317 G7
Tsamandas Greece 39°46N 20°21E 204 B2
Tsamkong = Zhanjiang China 21°15N 110°20E 229 G8
Tsandi Namibia 17°42S 14°50E 270 A1
Tsangpo = Brahmaputra → Asia 23°40N 90°35E 241 D3
Tsaochiao Taiwan 24°39N 120°51E 225 B2
Ts'aot'un Taiwan 23°58N 120°41E 225 C2
Tsaratanana Madag. 16°47S 47°39E 272 B2
Tsaratanana, Mt. de = Maromokotro Madag. 14°0S 49°0E 272 A2
Tsaratanana ⌓ Madag. 13°57S 48°52E 272 A2
Tsarekonstantinovka = Kuybyshevo Ukraine 47°25N 36°40E 189 J9
Tsarevo = Michurin Bulgaria 42°9N 27°51E 203 D11
Tsarevo Bulgaria 42°28N 25°52E 203 D9
Tsaribrod = Dimitrovgrad Serbia 43°2N 22°48E 202 C6
Tsaritsani Greece 39°53N 22°14E 204 B4
Tsarkasianos Greece 38°10N 20°40E 207 C2
Tsarskoye Selo = Pushkin Russia 59°45N 30°25E 188 C6
Tsaryovokokshaysk = Yoshkar Ola Russia 56°38N 47°55E 190 B8
Tsau Botswana 20°8S 22°22E 270 B3
Tsavo Kenya 2°59S 38°28E 268 C4
Tsavo East △ Kenya 2°44S 38°47E 268 C4
Tsavo West △ Kenya 3°19S 37°57E 268 C4
Tsawlaw Burma 26°9N 98°17E 241 B7
Tselinograd = Astana Kazakhstan 51°10N 71°30E 217 B8
Tsementny = Fokino Russia 53°30N 34°22E 188 F8
Tseng Lan Shue Hong Kong, China 22°20N 114°14E 122 B3
Tsengwen Hsi → Taiwan 23°8N 120°19E 225 C2
Tsengwen Shuiku Taiwan 23°16N 120°34E 225 C2
Tsentralen Balkan △ Bulgaria 42°40N 24°45E 203 D8
Tsentralnyy □ Russia 52°0N 40°0E 214 D4
Tses Namibia 25°58S 18°8E 270 C2
Tsetserleg Mongolia 47°36N 101°32E 218 B9
Tseung Kwan Hong Kong, China 22°19N 114°15E 122 B3
Tsévié Togo 6°25N 1°20E 263 D5
Tshabong Botswana 26°2S 22°29E 270 C3
Tshabuta Dem. Rep. of the Congo 7°42S 23°7E 265 D4
Tshane Botswana 24°5S 21°54E 270 B3
Tshela Dem. Rep. of the Congo 4°57S 13°4E 265 C2
Tshesebe Botswana 21°51S 27°32E 271 B4
Tshibeke Dem. Rep. of the Congo 2°40S 28°35E 268 C2
Tshibinda Dem. Rep. of the Congo 2°23S 28°43E 268 C2
Tshikapa Dem. Rep. of the Congo 6°28S 20°48E 265 D4
Tshilenge Dem. Rep. of the Congo 6°17S 23°48E 265 D4
Tshindjambo Dem. Rep. of the Congo 10°52S 22°43E 265 E4
Tshinota Dem. Rep. of the Congo 7°2S 20°58E 265 D4
Tshinsenda Dem. Rep. of the Congo 12°20S 28°0E 269 E2
Tshitadi Dem. Rep. of the Congo 6°46S 21°43E 265 D4
Tshofa Dem. Rep. of the Congo 5°13S 25°16E 265 D5
Tshuapa → Dem. Rep. of the Congo 0°14S 20°42E 264 C4
Tshumbiri Dem. Rep. of the Congo 2°38S 16°18E 264 C3
Tshwane = Pretoria S. Africa 25°44S 28°12E 271 C4
Tshwane Botswana 22°24S 22°1E 270 B3
Tsiaotso = Jiaozuo China 35°16N 113°12E 226 G7
Tsibirihina → Madag. 19°42S 44°31E 272 B1
Tsigara Botswana 20°22S 25°54E 270 B4
Tsihombe Madag. 25°10S 45°41E 272 D2
Tsiigehtchic Canada 67°15N 134°0W 294 D5
Ts'il-os ⌓ Canada 51°9N 123°59W 296 C4
Tsim Sha Tsui Hong Kong, China 22°18N 114°10E 122 B3
Tsimlyansk Russia 47°40N 42°6E 191 G6
Tsimlyansk Res. = Tsimlyanskoye Vdkhr. Russia 48°0N 43°0E 191 F6
Tsimlyanskoye Vdkhr. Russia 48°0N 43°0E 191 F6
Tsinan = Jinan China 36°38N 117°1E 226 F9
Tsineng S. Africa 27°5S 23°5E 270 C3
Tsing Lung Tau Hong Kong, China 22°22N 114°3E 122 A2
Tsing Yi Hong Kong, China 22°21N 114°6E 122 A2
Tsinghai = Qinghai □ China 36°0N 98°0E 218 D8
Tsingshih = Jinshi China 29°40N 111°50E 229 C8
Tsingtao = Qingdao China 36°5N 120°20E 227 F11
Tsingy de Bemaraha ⌓ Madag. 18°35S 44°55E 272 B2
Tsingy de Namoraka ⌓ Madag. 16°29S 45°25E 272 B2
Tsining = Jining China 35°22N 116°34E 226 G9
Tsinjoarivo Madag. 19°37S 47°40E 272 B2
Tsinjomitondraka Madag. 15°40S 47°8E 272 B2
Tsinling Shan = Qinling Shandi China 33°50N 108°10E 226 H5
Tsirigo = Kythira Greece 36°8N 23°0E 204 E5
Tsiroanomandidy Madag. 18°46S 46°2E 272 B2
Tsis I. Micronesia 7°17N 151°49E 287 U18
Tsiteli-Tsqaro = Dedopolis Tsqaro Georgia 41°33N 46°0E 191 K8
Tsitondroina Madag. 21°19S 46°0E 272 C2
Tsitsihar = Qiqihar China 47°26N 124°0E 219 B13
Tsitsikamma △ S. Africa 34°3S 23°40E 270 D3
Tsivilsk Russia 55°50N 47°25E 190 C8
Tsivory Madag. 24°4S 46°5E 272 C2
Tskhinvali Georgia 42°14N 44°1E 191 J7
Tsna → Russia 54°55N 41°58E 190 C6
Tsnori Georgia 41°40N 45°57E 191 K7
Tso Moriri, L. India 32°50N 78°20E 243 C8
Tsobis Namibia 19°27S 17°30E 270 A2
Tsodilo Hills Botswana 18°49S 21°43E 270 A3
Tsogni Gabon 2°48S 10°10E 264 C2
Tsogttsetsiy = Baruunsuu Mongolia 43°43N 105°35E 226 C3
Tsolo S. Africa 31°18S 28°37E 271 D4
Tsomo S. Africa 32°0S 27°42E 271 D4
Tsoukalades Greece 38°41N 20°47E 207 B2
Tsova West Bank 31°47N 35°6E 123 B1
Tsoying Taiwan 22°41N 120°17E 225 D2
Tsu Japan 34°45N 136°25E 223 C8
Tsu L. Canada 60°40N 111°52W 296 A6
Tsubata Japan 36°40N 136°44E 223 A8
Tsuchiura Japan 36°5N 140°15E 223 A12
Tsuen Wan Hong Kong, China 22°22N 114°6E 122 A2
Tsugaru-Hantō Japan 41°0N 140°30E 220 D10
Tsugaru-Kaikyō Japan 41°35N 141°0E 220 D10
Tsuken-jima Japan 26°15N 127°56E 288 a
Tsukiji Tokyo, Japan 140 c5
Tsukuba Japan 36°2N 140°4E 223 A12
Tsukumi Japan 33°4N 131°52E 222 D3
Tsukushi-Sanchi Japan 33°25N 130°30E 222 D2
Tsumeb Namibia 19°9S 17°44E 270 A2
Tsumis Namibia 23°39S 17°29E 270 B2
Tsuna = Awaji Japan 34°28N 134°56E 222 C6
Tsuno-Shima Japan 34°21N 130°52E 222 C2
Tsur Hadassa Israel 31°43N 35°6E 123 B1
Tsuru Japan 35°31N 138°57E 223 B10
Tsuruga Japan 35°45N 136°2E 223 B8
Tsuruga-Wan Japan 35°50N 136°3E 223 B8
Tsurugi Japan 36°29N 136°37E 223 A8
Tsurugi-San Japan 33°51N 134°6E 222 D6
Tsurumi → Japan 35°32N 139°40E 140 B3
Tsurumi-Saki Japan 32°56N 132°5E 222 E4
Tsuruoka Japan 38°44N 139°50E 220 E9
Tsurusaki Japan 33°14N 131°41E 222 D3
Tsushima Ehime, Japan 33°7N 132°32E 222 D4
Tsushima Gifu, Japan 35°10N 136°43E 223 B8
Tsushima Nagasaki, Japan 34°20N 129°20E 222 C1
Tsuyama Japan 35°3N 134°0E 222 B6
Tsvetkovo Ukraine 49°8N 31°33E 189 H6
Tsyelyakhany Belarus 52°30N 25°46E 177 B13
Tsz Wan Shan Hong Kong, China 22°20N 114°11E 122 A3
Tu → Burma 21°50N 96°15E 241 E6
Tua Dem. Rep. of the Congo 3°38S 16°38E 264 C3
Tua → Papua N. G. 6°30S 144°28E 286 D3
Tua → Portugal 41°13N 7°26W 194 D3
Tuaheni Pt. N.Z. 38°43S 178°4E 284 E7
Tuai N.Z. 38°47S 177°10E 284 E6
Tuaim = Tuam Ireland 53°31N 8°51W 166 C3
Tuakau N.Z. 37°16S 174°59E 284 D3
Tual Indonesia 5°38S 132°44E 231 F8
Tualatin U.S.A. 45°23N 122°45W 306 E4
Tuam Ireland 53°31N 8°51W 166 C3
Tuamarina N.Z. 41°25S 173°59E 285 B8
Tuamotu, Îs. French Polynesia 17°0S 144°0W 289 f
Tuamotu Arch. = Tuamotu, Îs. French Polynesia 17°0S 144°0W 289 f
Tuamotu Ridge Pac. Oc. 20°0S 138°0W 289 K14
Tuan Giao Vietnam 21°35N 103°25E 236 B4
Tuanfeng China 30°38N 114°52E 229 B10

Tuangku *Indonesia* 2°10N 97°16E 234 B1
Tuanxi *China* 27°28N 107°8E 228 D6
Tuao *Phil.* 17°45N 121°22E 232 C3
Tuapa *Cook Is.* 18°57S 169°54W 289 g
Tuapse *Russia* 44°5N 39°10E 191 H4
Tuaran *Malaysia* 6°10N 116°13E 235 A5
Tuas *Singapore* 1°19N 103°39E 138 B1
Tuatapere *N.Z.* 46°8S 167°41E 285 G2
Tuba City *U.S.A.* 36°8N 111°14W 305 H8
Tuban *Indonesia* 6°54S 112°3E 235 D4
Tubani *Botswana* 24°46S 24°18E 270 B3
Tubarão *Brazil* 28°30S 49°0W 335 B6
Tūbās *West Bank* 32°20N 35°22E 251 F6
Tubas → *Namibia* 22°54S 14°35E 270 B2
Tubau *Malaysia* 3°10N 113°40E 235 B4
Tubbataha Reefs ⌓ *Phil.* 8°53N 119°53E 233 G2
Tubigon *Phil.* 9°57N 123°58E 233 G4
Tübingen *Germany* 48°31N 9°4E 179 G5
Tubod *Phil.* 8°3N 123°48E 233 G4
Tubou *Fiji* 18°13S 178°48W 287 B3
Tubruq *Libya* 32°7N 23°55E 258 B4
Tubuaï *French Polynesia* 23°18S 149°30W 289 f
Tubuaï, Îs. *French Polynesia* 25°0S 150°0W 289 f
Tuburan *Basilan, Phil.* 6°39N 122°16E 233 H4
Tuburan *Cebu, Phil.* 10°44N 123°49E 233 F4
Tuc Trung *Vietnam* 11°1N 107°12E 237 G6
Tucacas *Venezuela* 10°48N 68°19W 328 A4
Tucano *Brazil* 10°58S 38°48W 332 D4
T'uch'ang *Taiwan* 24°35N 121°29E 225 B3
Tuchitua *Canada* 60°55N 129°13W 296 A3
Tuchodi → *Canada* 58°17N 123°42W 296 B4
Tuchola *Poland* 53°33N 17°52E 184 E4
Tuchoměřice *Czech Rep.* 50°7N 14°16E 135 B1
Tuchów *Poland* 49°54N 21°1E 185 J8
Tuckahoe *U.S.A.* 40°56N 73°49W 132 A3
Tuckanarra *Australia* 27°7S 118°5E 279 E2
Tucker *U.S.A.* 33°51N 84°13W 316 B5
Tuckers Town *Bermuda* 32°20N 64°42W 153 a
Tucson *U.S.A.* 32°13N 110°58W 305 K8
Tucumán □ *Argentina* 26°48S 66°2W 334 B2
Tucumcari *U.S.A.* 35°10N 103°44W 305 J12
Tucunaré *Brazil* 5°18S 55°51W 331 B6
Tucupido *Venezuela* 9°17N 65°47W 328 B4
Tucupita *Venezuela* 9°2N 62°3W 329 B5
Tucuruí *Brazil* 3°42S 49°44W 332 B2
Tucuruí, Represa de *Brazil* 4°0S 49°30W 332 B2
Tucuruvi *Brazil* 23°28S 46°35W 137 A2
Tuczno *Poland* 53°13N 16°10E 185 E3
Tuddal *Norway* 59°46N 8°49E 164 E5
Tudela *Spain* 42°4N 1°39W 196 C3
Tudmur *Syria* 34°36N 38°15E 213 E8
Tudor, L. *Canada* 55°50N 65°25W 299 A6
Tudora *Romania* 47°31N 26°45E 183 C11
Tuella → *Portugal* 41°30N 7°12W 194 D3
Tuen Mun *Hong Kong, China* 22°23N 113°57E 122 A1
Tuensang *India* 26°17N 94°50E 241 B5
Tueré → *Brazil* 2°48S 50°59W 332 B1
Tufanbeyli *Turkey* 38°15N 36°13E 212 C7
Tufello *Italy* 41°56N 12°32E 136 B2
Tüffer = Laško *Slovenia* 46°10N 15°16E 199 B12
Tufi *Papua N. G.* 9°8S 149°19E 286 E5
Tufnell Park *U.K.* 51°33N 0°8W 125 A3
Tufsingdal *Norway* 62°18N 11°44E 164 B8
Tufts Abyssal Plain *Pac. Oc.* 47°0N 140°0W 289 C14
Tufts Univ. *U.S.A.* 42°24N 71°7W 116 A2
Tufu Pt. *Amer. Samoa* 14°13S 169°30W 302 g
Tug Hill Plateau *U.S.A.* 43°45N 75°50W 313 C9
Tugaya *Phil.* 7°53N 124°10E 233 H5
Tugela → *S. Africa* 29°14S 31°30E 271 C5
Tugela Falls *S. Africa* 28°42S 29°51E 271 C4
Tughlakabad *India* 28°30N 77°16E 120 B2
Tugidak I. *U.S.A.* 56°30N 154°40W 303 H9
Tuguegarao *Phil.* 17°35N 121°42E 232 C3
Tugur *Russia* 53°44N 136°45E 215 D14
Tui *Spain* 42°3N 8°39W 194 C2
Tuileries, Jardin des *Paris, France* 134 b3
Tuineje *Canary Is.* 28°19N 14°3W 153 e2
Tukangbesi, Kepulauan *Indonesia* 6°0S 124°0E 231 F6
Tukarak I. *Canada* 56°15N 78°45W 298 A4
Tukayyid *Iraq* 29°47N 45°36E 246 D5
Tûkh *Egypt* 30°21N 31°12E 256 H7
Tukhlya *Ukraine* 48°55N 23°28E 183 B8
Tukituki → *N.Z.* 39°36S 176°56E 284 F5
Tukobo *Ghana* 5°1N 2°47W 262 D4
Tūkrah *Libya* 32°30N 20°37E 258 B4
Tuktoyaktuk *Canada* 69°27N 133°2W 294 D5
Tuktuk *Indonesia* 2°37N 98°54E 234 B1
Tuktut Nogait △ *Canada* 69°15N 122°0W 294 D7
Tuku *Taiwan* 23°41N 120°23E 225 C2
Tukums *Latvia* 56°58N 23°10E 184 B10
Tukums □ *Latvia* 56°55N 23°0E 184 B10
Tukuran *Phil.* 7°51N 123°34E 233 H4
Tukuyu *Tanzania* 9°17S 33°35E 269 D3
Tula *Amer. Samoa* 14°15S 170°34W 302 f
Tula *Hidalgo, Mexico* 20°3N 99°21W 319 C5
Tula *Tamaulipas, Mexico* 23°0N 99°43W 319 C5
Tula *Nigeria* 9°51N 11°27E 263 D7
Tula *Russia* 54°13N 37°38E 188 E9
Tula □ *Russia* 53°45N 37°30E 188 F9
Tulach Mhór = Tullamore *Ireland* 53°16N 7°31W 166 C4
Tulagi *Solomon Is.* 9°5S 160°10E 287 M11
Tūlak *Afghan.* 33°55N 63°40E 240 B1
Tulan *Taiwan* 22°53N 121°13E 225 D3
Tulancingo *Mexico* 20°5N 98°22W 319 C5
Tulangbawang → *Indonesia* 4°24S 105°52E 234 C3
Tulare *Serbia* 42°48N 21°28E 202 D5
Tulare *Calif., U.S.A.* 36°13N 119°21W 306 J7
Tulare Lake Bed *U.S.A.* 36°0N 119°48W 306 K7
Tularosa *U.S.A.* 33°5N 106°1W 305 K10
Tulbagh *S. Africa* 33°16S 19°6E 270 D2
Tulcán *Ecuador* 0°48N 77°43W 328 C2
Tulcea *Romania* 45°13N 28°46E 183 E13
Tulcea □ *Romania* 45°0N 28°30E 183 E13
Tulchyn *Ukraine* 48°41N 28°49E 183 B13
Tüledi Araldary *Kazakhstan* 45°2N 50°16E 191 H10
Tūleh *Iran* 34°35N 52°33E 247 C7
Tulemalu L. *Canada* 62°58N 99°25W 297 A9
Tulgheş *Romania* 46°58N 25°45E 183 D10
Tuli *Zimbabwe* 21°58S 29°13E 269 G2
Tulia *U.S.A.* 34°32N 101°46W 314 D4
Tuliszków *Poland* 52°5N 18°18E 185 F5
Tulita *Canada* 64°57N 125°30W 294 E6
Ţūlkarm *West Bank* 32°19N 35°2E 251 F6
Tulla *Ireland* 52°53N 8°46W 166 D3
Tullahoma *U.S.A.* 35°22N 86°13W 315 D11
Tullamarine *Australia* 37°41S 144°50E 128 A1
Tullamore *N.S.W., Australia* 32°39S 147°36E 283 B7
Tullamore *Offaly, Ireland* 53°16N 7°31W 166 C4
Tulle *France* 45°16N 1°46E 174 C5
Tulln *Austria* 48°20N 16°4E 180 C9
Tullow *Ireland* 52°49N 6°45W 166 D5
Tullus *Sudan* 11°7N 24°31E 257 E1
Tully *Queens., Australia* 17°56S 145°55E 280 B4
Tully *N.Y., U.S.A.* 42°48N 76°7W 313 D8
Ţulmaythah *Libya* 32°40N 20°55E 258 B4
Tulnici *Romania* 45°51N 26°38E 183 E11
Tulovo *Bulgaria* 42°33N 25°32E 203 D9
Tulsa *U.S.A.* 36°10N 95°55W 314 C7
Tulse Hill *U.K.* 51°26N 0°6W 125 B3
Tulsequah *Canada* 58°39N 133°35W 296 B2
Tulu Milki *Ethiopia* 9°55N 38°20E 257 F4
Tulu Welel *Ethiopia* 8°56N 34°47E 257 F3
Tuluá *Colombia* 4°6N 76°11W 328 C2
Tuluceşti *Romania* 45°34N 28°2E 183 E13
Tuluksak *U.S.A.* 61°6N 160°58W 303 F7
Tulum *Mexico* 20°13N 87°28W 319 C7
Tulun *Russia* 54°32N 100°35E 215 D11
Tulungagung *Indonesia* 8°5S 111°54E 235 D4
Tuluran I. *Phil.* 10°58N 119°16E 233 F2
Tuma *Russia* 55°10N 40°30E 188 E11
Tuma → *Nic.* 13°6N 84°35W 320 D3
Tumacacori ⌓ *U.S.A.* 31°35N 111°6W 305 L8
Tumaco *Colombia* 1°50N 78°45W 328 C2
Tumaco, Ensenada *Colombia* 1°55N 78°45W 328 C2
Tumakuru = Tumkur *India* 13°18N 77°6E 245 H3
Tumatumari *Guyana* 5°20N 58°55W 329 B6
Tumauini *Phil.* 17°17N 121°49E 232 C3
Tumba *Dem. Rep. of the Congo* 3°10S 23°36E 264 C4
Tumba *Sweden* 59°12N 17°48E 162 E11
Tumba, L. *Dem. Rep. of the Congo* 0°50S 18°0E 264 C3
Tumbangsamba *Indonesia* 1°27S 113°7E 235 C4
Tumbarumba *Australia* 35°44S 148°0E 283 C8
Tumbaya *Argentina* 23°50S 65°26W 334 A2
Tumbes *Peru* 3°37S 80°27W 330 A1
Tumbes □ *Peru* 3°50S 80°30W 330 A1
Tumbler Ridge *Canada* 55°8N 121°0W 296 B4
Tumbur *South Sudan* 4°20N 31°34E 257 G3
Tumbwe *Dem. Rep. of the Congo* 11°25S 27°15E 269 E2
Tumby Bay *Australia* 34°21S 136°8E 282 C2
Tumd Youqi *China* 40°30N 110°30E 226 D6
Tumen *China* 43°0N 129°50E 224 A4
Tumen Jiang → *China* 42°20N 130°35E 224 A5
Tumeremo *Venezuela* 7°18N 61°30W 329 B5
Tumindao I. *Phil.* 4°41N 119°24E 233 J2
Tumiritinga *Brazil* 18°58S 41°38W 333 E3
Tumkur *India* 13°18N 77°6E 245 H3
Tumon B. *Guam* 13°31N 144°48E 302 d
Tump *Pakistan* 26°7N 62°16E 240 D1
Tumpat *Malaysia* 6°11N 102°10E 237 J4
Tumsar *India* 21°26N 79°45E 244 D4
Tumu *Ghana* 10°56N 1°56W 262 C4
Tumucumaque, Serra *Brazil* 2°0N 55°0W 329 C7
Tumupasa *Bolivia* 14°9S 67°55W 330 C4
Tumut *Australia* 35°16S 148°13E 283 C8
Tumwater *U.S.A.* 47°1N 122°54W 306 C4
Tun *Sweden* 58°26N 12°43E 163 F6
Tuna *India* 22°59N 70°5E 242 H4
Tunapuna *Trin. & Tob.* 10°38N 61°24W 323 t
Tunas de Zaza *Cuba* 21°39N 79°34W 320 B4
Tunbridge Wells = Royal Tunbridge Wells *U.K.* 51°7N 0°16E 169 F8
Tunçbilek *Turkey* 39°37N 29°29E 205 B11
Tunceli *Turkey* 39°6N 39°31E 213 C8
Tunceli □ *Turkey* 39°5N 39°35E 213 C8
Tunchang *China* 19°21N 110°5E 229 a
Tuncurry *Australia* 32°17S 152°29E 283 B10
Tundla *India* 27°12N 78°17E 242 F8
Tundubai *Sudan* 18°36N 28°35E 256 D2
Tunduru *Tanzania* 11°8S 37°25E 269 E4
Tundzha → *Bulgaria* 41°40N 26°35E 203 E10
Tung Chung *Hong Kong, China* 22°17N 113°57E 122 B1
Tung Lung Chau *Hong Kong, China* 22°15N 114°17E 122 B3
Tung O *Hong Kong, China* 22°11N 114°8E 122 B2
Tunga → *India* 15°0N 75°50E 245 G2
Tunga Pass *Asia* 29°0N 94°14E 241 A5
Tungabhadra → *India* 15°57N 78°15E 245 G4
Tungabhadra Dam *India* 15°0N 75°50E 245 G2
Tungao *Taiwan* 24°31N 121°50E 225 B3
Tungaru *Sudan* 10°9N 30°52E 257 E3
Tungawan *Phil.* 7°30N 122°20E 233 H4
Tungchi Yü *Taiwan* 23°15N 119°40E 225 C1
Tungch'uan = Dongchuan *China* 26°8N 103°1E 228 D4
Tungho *Taiwan* 22°58N 121°18E 225 D3
T'unghsiao *Taiwan* 24°29N 120°40E 225 B2
Tunghwa = Tonghua *China* 41°42N 125°58E 224 B2
Tungi *Bangla.* 23°53N 90°24E 241 D3
Tungkang *Taiwan* 22°27N 120°26E 225 D2
Tungku *Malaysia* 5°1N 118°53E 235 A5
Tungla *Nic.* 13°24N 84°21W 320 D3
T'unglo *Taiwan* 24°30N 120°47E 225 B2
Tungnafellsjökull *Iceland* 64°45N 17°55W 155 C9
Tungsha Tao = Dongsha Dao *S. China Sea* 20°45N 116°43E 219 G12
Tungshan *Taiwan* 24°38N 121°47E 225 B3
Tungshih *Changhua, Taiwan* 24°12N 120°43E 225 B2
Tungshih *Chiai, Taiwan* 23°27N 120°8E 225 C2
Tungsten *Canada* 61°57N 128°16W 296 A3
Tungufell *Iceland* 64°17N 20°10W 155 C6
Tungurahua □ *Ecuador* 1°15S 78°35W 328 D2
Tunguska, Nizhnyaya → *Russia* 65°48N 88°4E 215 C9
Tunguska, Podkamennaya → *Russia* 61°50N 90°13E 215 C10
Tungyin Tao *Taiwan* 26°22N 128°29E 225 b
Tuni *India* 17°22N 82°36E 244 F6
Tunia *Colombia* 2°41N 76°31W 328 C2
Tunica *U.S.A.* 34°41N 90°23W 315 D9
Tunis *Baghdād, Iraq* 33°23N 44°21E 113 A2
Tunis *Tunisia* 36°50N 10°11E 258 A2
Tunis □ *Tunisia* 36°46N 10°10E 261 A7
Tunis ✈ (TUN) *Tunisia* 36°52N 10°14E 200 F3
Tunis, Golfe de *Tunisia* 37°0N 10°30E 258 A2
Tunisia ■ *Africa* 33°30N 9°10E 258 B1
Tunja *Colombia* 5°33N 73°25W 328 B3
Tunkhannock *U.S.A.* 41°32N 75°57W 313 E9
Tunkinsky △ *Russia* 51°30N 102°0E 215 D11
Tunliu *China* 36°13N 112°52E 226 F7
Tunnel Creek △ *Australia* 17°41S 125°18E 278 C4
Tunnsjøen *Norway* 64°45N 13°25E 160 D15
Tunø *Denmark* 55°57N 10°27E 163 J4
Tuntutuliak *U.S.A.* 60°22N 162°38W 303 F7
Tununak *U.S.A.* 60°37N 165°15W 303 F6
Tunungayualok I. *Canada* 56°0N 61°0W 299 A7
Tunuyán *Argentina* 33°35S 69°0W 334 C2
Tunuyán → *Argentina* 33°33S 67°30W 334 C2
Tunxi = Huangshan *China* 30°8N 118°9E 229 B12
Tuo Jiang → *China* 28°50N 105°35E 228 C5
Tuolumne *U.S.A.* 37°58N 120°15W 306 H6
Tuolumne → *U.S.A.* 37°36N 121°13W 306 H5
Tuomarila *Finland* 60°11N 24°41E 121 B1
Tüp *Kyrgyzstan* 42°45N 78°20E 217 D9
Tūp Āghāj *Iran* 36°3N 47°50E 213 D12
Tupã *Brazil* 21°57S 50°28W 335 A5
Tupaciguara *Brazil* 18°35S 48°42W 333 E2
Tupelo *U.S.A.* 34°16N 88°43W 315 D10
Tupik *Russia* 55°42N 33°22E 188 E7
Tupinambarana, I. *Brazil* 3°0S 58°0W 329 D6
Tupirama *Brazil* 8°58S 48°12W 332 C2
Tupiratins *Brazil* 8°23S 48°8W 332 C2
Tupiza *Bolivia* 21°30S 65°40W 334 A2
Tupižnica *Serbia* 43°43N 22°10E 202 C6
Tupman *U.S.A.* 35°18N 119°21W 307 K7
Tupper *Canada* 55°32N 120°1W 296 B4
Tupper L. *U.S.A.* 44°10N 74°32W 313 B10
Tupper Lake *U.S.A.* 44°14N 74°28W 313 B10
Tüpqarghan Muyis *Kazakhstan* 44°40N 50°19E 191 H10
Tupungato, Cerro *S. Amer.* 33°15S 69°50W 334 C2
Tuquan *China* 45°18N 121°38E 227 B11
Túquerres *Colombia* 1°5N 77°37W 328 C2
Tura *India* 25°30N 90°16E 241 C3
Tura *Russia* 64°20N 100°17E 215 C11
Turabah *Ḥā'il, Si. Arabia* 28°20N 43°15E 246 D4
Turabah *Makkah, Si. Arabia* 21°15N 41°34E 248 B3
Turagua, Serranía *Venezuela* 7°20N 64°35W 329 B5
Turakina *N.Z.* 40°3S 175°16E 284 G4
Turakina → *N.Z.* 40°5S 175°8E 284 G4
Turakirae Hd. *N.Z.* 41°26S 174°56E 284 H3
Turama → *Papua N. G.* 7°40S 143°50E 286 D2
Tūrān *Iran* 35°39N 56°42E 247 C8
Turan *Russia* 51°55N 94°0E 217 B12
Tūrān △ *Iran* 35°45N 56°30E 247 C8
Turan Lowland *Asia* 43°30N 62°0E 216 D6
Turangi *N.Z.* 38°59S 175°48E 284 E4
Ţurayf *Si. Arabia* 31°41N 38°39E 246 D3
Turbaco *Colombia* 10°21N 75°25W 328 A2
Turbacz *Poland* 49°30N 20°8E 185 J7
Turbat *Pakistan* 25°59N 63°4E 240 D1
Turbe *Bos.-H.* 44°15N 17°35E 182 F2
Turbeville *U.S.A.* 33°54N 80°1W 316 B9
Turbo *Colombia* 8°6N 76°43W 328 B2
Turčianske Teplice *Slovak Rep.* 48°52N 18°52E 181 C11
Turco *Bolivia* 18°10S 68°11W 330 D4
Turcoaia *Romania* 45°7N 28°11E 183 E13
Turda *Romania* 46°34N 23°47E 183 D8
Tureberg *Sweden* 59°25N 17°55E 139 A1
Turéia *French Polynesia* 20°50S 138°32W 289 f
Turek *Poland* 52°3N 18°30E 185 F5
Turfan = Turpan *China* 43°58N 89°10E 217 D11
Turfan Basin = Turpan Pendi *China* 42°40N 89°25E 217 D11
Turfan Depression = Turpan Pendi *China* 42°40N 89°25E 217 D11
Turffontein *S. Africa* 26°14S 28°2E 123 B2
Turgayskaya Stolovaya Strana = Torghay Ustirti *Asia* 51°0N 63°0E 216 B6
Turgeon → *Canada* 50°0N 78°56W 298 C4
Tŭrgovishte *Bulgaria* 43°17N 26°38E 203 C10
Tŭrgovishte □ *Bulgaria* 43°17N 26°38E 203 C10
Turgut *Turkey* 37°22N 28°4E 205 D10
Turgutlu *Turkey* 38°30N 27°43E 205 C9
Turgwe → *Zimbabwe* 21°31S 32°15E 271 B5
Turhal *Turkey* 40°24N 36°5E 212 B7
Turia → *Spain* 39°27N 0°19W 197 F4
Turiaçu *Brazil* 1°40S 45°19W 332 B2
Turiaçu → *Brazil* 1°36S 45°19W 332 B2
Turiec → *Slovak Rep.* 49°7N 18°55E 181 B11
Turin = Torino *Italy* 45°3N 7°40E 198 C4
Turinskaya Kultbaza = Tura *Russia* 64°20N 100°17E 215 C11
Türk Telekom Arena *Istanbul, Turkey* 41°5N 28°59E 122 B1
Turka *Ukraine* 49°10N 23°2E 185 J10
Turkana, L. *Africa* 3°30N 36°5E 268 B4
Turkayel *Ethiopia* 8°7N 45°21E 267 C6
Türkeli *Turkey* 40°30N 27°30E 203 F11
Turkestan = Türkistan *Kazakhstan* 43°17N 68°16E 217 D7
Turkestan Range *Asia* 39°35N 69°0E 217 E7
Túrkeve *Hungary* 47°6N 20°44E 182 C5
Turkey ■ *Eurasia* 39°0N 36°0E 212 C7
Turkey → *U.S.A.* 42°43N 91°2W 310 B5
Turkey Creek = Warmun *Australia* 17°2S 128°12E 278 C4
Turkey L. *U.S.A.* 28°30N 81°28W 133 A2
Turkey Lake Park *U.S.A.* 28°30N 81°28W 133 A2
Turki *Russia* 52°0N 43°15E 190 D6
Türkistan *Kazakhstan* 43°17N 68°16E 217 D7
Türkmenabat *Turkmenistan* 39°6N 63°34E 247 B9
Türkmenbashi *Turkmenistan* 40°5N 53°5E 247 A7
Turkmenistan ■ *Asia* 39°0N 59°0E 216 E5
Türkmenli *Turkey* 39°45N 26°30E 205 B8
Türkoğlu *Turkey* 37°23N 36°50E 212 D7
Turks & Caicos Is. ☒ *W. Indies* 21°20N 71°20W 321 B5
Turks Island Passage *Turks & Caicos* 21°25N 71°19W 321 B5
Turku *Finland* 60°30N 22°19E 188 B2
Turkwel → *Kenya* 3°6N 36°6E 268 B4
Turlock *U.S.A.* 37°30N 120°51W 306 H6
Turnagain *Australia* 9°34S 142°17E 280 a
Turnagain → *Canada* 59°12N 127°35W 296 B3
Turnagain, C. *N.Z.* 40°28S 176°38E 284 G5
Turneffe Is. *Belize* 17°20N 87°50W 320 C2
Turner *U.S.A.* 48°51N 108°24W 304 B9
Turner Field *Atlanta, U.S.A.* 33°44N 84°23W 113 B2
Turner Pt. *Australia* 11°47S 133°32E 280 A1
Turner Valley *Canada* 50°40N 114°17W 296 C6
Turners Falls *U.S.A.* 42°36N 72°33W 313 D12
Turner's Pen. *S. Leone* 7°22N 12°24W 262 D2
Turnham Green *U.K.* 51°29N 0°16W 125 B2
Turnhouse *U.K.* 55°57N 3°20W 121 B1
Turnhout *Belgium* 51°19N 4°57E 170 C4
Türnitz *Austria* 47°55N 15°29E 180 D8
Turnor L. *Canada* 56°35N 108°35W 297 B7
Turnov *Czech Rep.* 50°34N 15°10E 180 A8
Tŭrnovo = Veliko Tŭrnovo *Bulgaria* 43°5N 25°41E 203 C9
Turnu Măgurele *Romania* 43°46N 24°56E 183 G9
Turnu Roşu, P. *Romania* 45°33N 24°17E 183 E9
Turobin *Poland* 50°50N 22°44E 185 H9
Tuross Head *Australia* 36°3S 150°8E 283 D9
Turpan *China* 43°58N 89°10E 217 D11
Turpan Pendi *China* 42°40N 89°25E 217 D11
Turrawan *Australia* 30°28S 149°53E 283 A8
Turrës, Kala e *Albania* 41°10N 19°28E 202 E3
Turriff *U.K.* 57°32N 2°27W 167 D6
Tursāq *Iraq* 33°27N 45°47E 213 F11
Tursi *Italy* 40°15N 16°28E 201 B9
Tursunzoda *Tajikistan* 38°30N 68°14E 217 E7
Turtle Head I. *Australia* 10°56S 142°37E 286 F2
Turtle Is. *Phil.* 6°7N 118°14E 233 H2
Turtle Is. *S. Leone* 7°40N 13°0W 262 D2
Turtle Islands *Phil.* 6°13N 118°6E 235 A5
Turtle L. *Canada* 53°36N 108°38W 297 C7
Turtle Lake *U.S.A.* 47°31N 100°53W 308 B3
Turtleford *Canada* 53°23N 108°57W 297 C7
Turtucaia = Tutrakan *Bulgaria* 44°2N 26°40E 203 B10
Turua *N.Z.* 37°14S 175°35E 284 D4
Turukhansk *Russia* 65°21N 88°5E 215 C9
Turyinskiye Rudniki = Krasnoturinsk *Russia* 59°46N 60°12E 186 C11
Turzovka *Slovak Rep.* 49°25N 18°35E 181 B11
Tuscaloosa *U.S.A.* 33°12N 87°34W 315 E11
Tuscánia *Italy* 42°25N 11°52E 199 F8
Tuscany = Toscana □ *Italy* 43°25N 11°0E 198 E8
Tuscarawas → *U.S.A.* 40°24N 81°25W 312 F3
Tuscarora Mt. *U.S.A.* 40°55N 77°55W 312 F7
Tuscola *Ill., U.S.A.* 39°48N 88°17W 311 E8
Tuscola *Tex., U.S.A.* 32°12N 99°48W 314 E5
Tuscolana, Via *Italy* 41°52N 12°31E 136 B2
Tuscumbia *Ala., U.S.A.* 34°44N 87°42W 315 D11
Tuscumbia *Mo., U.S.A.* 38°14N 92°28W 310 F4
Tuskegee *U.S.A.* 32°25N 85°42W 316 C4
Tusket Wedge = Wedgeport *Canada* 43°44N 65°59W 299 D6
Tustna *Norway* 63°10N 8°5E 164 A5
Tuszyn *Poland* 51°36N 19°33E 185 G6
Tutak *Turkey* 39°31N 42°46E 213 C10
Tutayev *Russia* 57°53N 39°32E 188 D10
Tuticorin *India* 8°50N 78°12E 245 K4
Tutin *Serbia* 42°58N 20°20E 202 D4
Tutóia *Brazil* 2°45S 42°20W 332 B3
Tutong *Brunei* 4°47N 114°40E 235 B4
Tutova → *Romania* 46°7N 27°30E 183 D12
Tutrakan *Bulgaria* 44°2N 26°40E 203 B10
Tuttle Creek L. *U.S.A.* 39°15N 96°36W 308 F5
Tuttlingen *Germany* 47°58N 8°48E 179 H4
Tutuala *E. Timor* 8°25S 127°15E 231 F7
Tutuba *Vanuatu* 15°33S 167°16E 287 E5
Tutubeia *Papua N. G.* 9°34S 150°40E 286 E6
Tutuila *Amer. Samoa* 14°19S 170°50W 302 f
Tutuko, Mt. *N.Z.* 44°35S 168°1E 285 E3
Tutun *Egypt* 29°9N 30°46E 256 J7
Tütz = Tuczno *Poland* 53°13N 16°10E 185 E3
Tuul Gol → *Mongolia* 48°30N 104°25E 218 B9
Tuva □ *Russia* 51°30N 95°0E 217 B12
Tuvalu ■ *Pac. Oc.* 8°0S 178°0E 277 B14
Tuvuca *Fiji* 17°40S 178°48W 287 A3
Tūwal *Si. Arabia* 22°17N 39°6E 248 B2
Tuxer Alpen *Austria* 47°10N 11°45E 180 D4
Tuxpan *Mexico* 20°57N 97°24W 319 C5
Tuxtla Gutiérrez *Mexico* 16°45N 93°7W 319 D6
Tuy = Tui *Spain* 42°3N 8°39W 194 C2
Tuy Duc *Vietnam* 12°15N 107°27E 237 F6
Tuy Phong *Vietnam* 11°14N 108°43E 237 G7
Tuya L. *Canada* 59°7N 130°35W 296 B2
Tuyen Hoa *Vietnam* 17°50N 106°10E 236 D6
Tuyen Quang *Vietnam* 21°50N 105°10E 228 G5
Tuymazy *Russia* 54°36N 53°42E 216 B4
Tūysarkān *Iran* 34°33N 48°27E 213 E13
Tuyün = Duyun *China* 26°18N 107°29E 228 D6
Tuz Gölü *Turkey* 38°42N 33°18E 212 C5
Ţūz Khurmātū *Iraq* 34°56N 44°38E 213 E11
Tuzi *Montenegro* 42°22N 19°20E 202 D3
Tuzigoot △ *U.S.A.* 34°46N 112°2W 305 J7
Tuzla *Bos.-H.* 44°34N 18°41E 182 F3
Tuzla *Turkey* 36°42N 35°6E 250 B6
Tuzlov → *Russia* 47°17N 39°57E 189 J10
Tuzluca *Turkey* 40°3N 43°39E 213 B10
Tuzly *Ukraine* 45°54N 30°6E 183 E15
Tvååker *Sweden* 57°4N 12°25E 163 G6
Tvardiţa *Moldova* 46°9N 28°58E 183 D13
Tvedestrand *Norway* 58°38N 8°58E 164 F5
Tver *Russia* 56°55N 35°59E 188 D8
Tver □ *Russia* 56°50N 35°0E 188 D8
Tvrdošin *Slovak Rep.* 49°21N 19°35E 181 B12
Tvrdošovce *Slovak Rep.* 48°6N 18°4E 181 C11
Tvŭrditsa *Bulgaria* 42°42N 25°53E 203 D9
Twain *U.S.A.* 40°1N 121°3W 306 E5
Twain Harte *U.S.A.* 38°2N 120°14W 306 G6
Twardogóra *Poland* 51°23N 17°28E 185 G4
Twee River *Namibia* 25°27S 19°27E 270 C2
Tweed *Canada* 44°29N 77°19W 312 B7
Tweed → *U.K.* 55°45N 2°0W 167 F6
Tweed Heads *Australia* 28°10S 153°31E 281 D5
Tweedsmuir ⌓ *Canada* 53°0N 126°20W 296 C3
Twelve Apostles *S. Africa* 33°58S 18°23E 118 A1
Twentieth Century Fox Studios *U.S.A.* 34°4N 118°25W 126 B2
Twentynine Palms *U.S.A.* 34°8N 116°3W 307 L10
Tweya *Dem. Rep. of the Congo* 0°54S 18°58E 264 C3
Twickenham *U.K.* 51°26N 0°20W 125 B1
Twickenham Rugby Ground *U.K.* 51°27N 0°20W 125 B1
Twillingate *Canada* 49°42N 54°45W 299 C9
Twin Bridges *U.S.A.* 45°33N 112°20W 304 D7
Twin City *U.S.A.* 32°35N 82°10W 316 C7
Twin Falls *Canada* 53°30N 64°32W 299 B7
Twin Falls *Idaho, U.S.A.* 42°34N 114°28W 304 E6
Twin Hills *U.S.A.* 59°23N 159°58W 303 G8
Twin Lakes *U.S.A.* 30°43N 83°13W 316 E6
Twin Peaks *U.S.A.* 37°45N 122°26W 136 B2
Twin Valley *U.S.A.* 47°16N 96°16W 308 B5
Twinnge *Burma* 23°10N 96°2E 241 D6
Twins, The *Hong Kong, China* 22°15N 114°12E 122 B3
Twinsburg *U.S.A.* 41°19N 81°26W 312 E3
Twistringen *Germany* 52°48N 8°37E 178 C4
Twitchell Res. *U.S.A.* 34°59N 120°19W 307 L6
Two Boats Village *Ascension I.* 7°56S 14°22W 153 g
Two Harbors *U.S.A.* 47°2N 91°40W 308 B8
Two Hills *Canada* 53°43N 111°52W 296 C6
Two Rivers *U.S.A.* 44°9N 87°34W 308 C10
Two Rock Mt. *Ireland* 53°15N 6°14W 120 B2
Two Rocks *Australia* 31°30S 115°35E 279 F2
Two Thumb Ra. *N.Z.* 43°45S 170°44E 285 D5
Twofold B. *Australia* 37°8S 149°59E 283 D8
Twyfelfontein *Namibia* 20°34S 14°22E 270 B1
Ty Ty *U.S.A.* 31°28N 83°39W 316 D6
Tyachiv *Ukraine* 48°1N 23°35E 177 D12
Tybee Island *U.S.A.* 32°1N 80°51W 316 C9
Tychy *Poland* 50°9N 18°59E 185 H5
Tyczyn *Poland* 49°58N 22°2E 185 J9
Tydal *Norway* 63°4N 11°34E 164 A8
Tyin *Norway* 61°18N 8°15E 164 C5
Tykocin *Poland* 53°13N 22°46E 185 E9
Tyler *Minn., U.S.A.* 44°17N 96°8W 308 C5
Tyler *Tex., U.S.A.* 32°21N 95°18W 314 E7
Tyligul → *Ukraine* 47°4N 30°57E 189 J6
Tylldal *Norway* 62°8N 10°48E 164 B7
Tymanivka *Ukraine* 48°34N 28°50E 183 B13
Tymon North *Ireland* 53°18N 6°20W 120 B1
Týn nad Vltavou *Czech Rep.* 49°13N 14°26E 180 B7
Tynda *Russia* 55°10N 124°43E 215 D13
Tyndall *U.S.A.* 43°0N 97°50W 308 D5
Tyndinsky = Tynda *Russia* 55°10N 124°43E 215 D13
Tyne → *U.K.* 54°59N 1°32W 168 C6
Tyne & Wear □ *U.K.* 55°6N 1°17W 168 B6
Týnec nad Sázavou *Czech Rep.* 49°50N 14°36E 180 B7
Tynemouth *U.K.* 55°1N 1°26W 168 B6
Tynset *Norway* 62°17N 10°47E 164 B7
Tyonek *U.S.A.* 61°4N 151°8W 303 F10
Tyre = Sūr *Lebanon* 33°19N 35°16E 250 E6
Tyresta △ *Sweden* 59°12N 18°14E 162 E12
Tyrifjorden *Norway* 60°2N 10°8E 164 D7
Tyringe *Sweden* 56°9N 13°35E 163 H7
Tyristrand *Norway* 60°4N 10°6E 164 D7
Tyrnyauz *Russia* 43°21N 42°45E 191 J6
Tyrol = Tirol □ *Austria* 47°3N 10°43E 180 D3
Tyrone *U.S.A.* 40°40N 78°14W 312 F6
Tyrone □ *U.K.* 54°38N 7°11W 166 B4
Tyrrel Bay *Grenada* 12°27N 61°28W 323 q
Tyrrell → *Australia* 35°26S 142°51E 282 C5
Tyrrell, L. *Australia* 35°20S 142°50E 282 C5
Tyrrell L. *Canada* 63°7N 105°27W 297 A7
Tyrrhenian Sea *Medit. S.* 40°0N 12°30E 192 D6
Tysfjorden *Norway* 68°7N 16°25E 160 B17
Tysmenytsya *Ukraine* 48°54N 24°51E 183 B9
Tysnes *Norway* 60°1N 5°30E 164 D2
Tysnesøya *Norway* 60°0N 5°35E 164 D2
Tysse *Norway* 60°23N 5°47E 164 D2
Tyssedal *Norway* 60°7N 6°35E 164 D3
Tystberga *Sweden* 58°51N 17°15E 163 F11
Tytuvėnai *Lithuania* 55°36N 23°12E 184 C10
Tyub Karagan, Mys = Tüpqarghan Muyis *Kazakhstan* 44°40N 50°19E 191 H10
Tyuleni, Ostrova = Tüledi Araldary *Kazakhstan* 45°2N 50°16E 191 H10
Tyuleniy *Russia* 44°28N 47°30E 191 H8
Tyuleniy, Mys *Azerbaijan* 40°12N 50°22E 191 K10
Tyulgan *Russia* 52°22N 56°12E 186 D10
Tyumen *Russia* 57°11N 65°29E 214 D7
Tyup = Tüp *Kyrgyzstan* 42°45N 78°20E 217 D9
Tywi → *U.K.* 51°48N 4°21W 169 F3
Tywyn *U.K.* 52°35N 4°5W 169 E3
Tzaneen *S. Africa* 23°47S 30°9E 271 B5
Tzermiado *Greece* 35°12N 25°29E 207 E6
Tzia = Kea *Greece* 37°35N 24°22E 204 D6
Tzoumérka, Óros = Athamanon Oros *Greece* 39°30N 21°26E 204 B3
Tzukong = Zigong *China* 29°15N 104°48E 228 C5
Tzukuan *Taiwan* 22°46N 120°16E 225 D2
Tzupo = Boshan *China* 36°28N 117°49E 227 F9
Tzutung *Taiwan* 23°45N 120°30E 225 C2

# U

U.S.A. = United States of America ■ *N. Amer.* 37°0N 96°0W 301 H20
U.S. Capitol *Washington, D.C., U.S.A.* 143 b3
U.S. Cellular Field *Chicago, U.S.A.* 41°50N 87°37W 119 C3
U.S.S. Arizona ⌓ *U.S.A.* 21°22N 157°57W 302 K14
U.S.S. Constitution *Boston, U.S.A.* 116 a3
U.S. Virgin Is. ☒ *W. Indies* 18°20N 65°0W 321 C7
Ua Huka *French Polynesia* 8°55S 139°32W 289 f
Ua Pu *French Polynesia* 9°25S 140°0W 289 f
Uachadi, Sierra = Uasadi-jidi *Venezuela* 4°54N 65°18W 329 C4
Uad Atui → *W. Sahara* 20°4N 15°59W 260 D2
Uad el Jat → *W. Sahara* 26°47N 13°3W 260 C2
Uaimh, An = Navan *Ireland* 53°39N 6°41W 166 C5
Uainambi *Colombia* 1°43N 69°51W 328 C4
Uamba *Angola* 7°21S 16°10E 265 D3
Uanle Uen = Wanleweyne *Somalia* 2°37N 44°54E 267 D5
Uasadi-jidi *Venezuela* 4°54N 65°18W 329 C4
Uati-Paraná → *Brazil* 1°51S 65°37W 328 D4
Uatumã → *Brazil* 2°26S 57°37W 329 D6
Uauá *Brazil* 9°50S 39°28W 332 C4
Uaupés *Brazil* 0°8S 67°5W 328 D4
Uaupés → *Brazil* 0°2N 67°16W 328 C4
Uaxactún *Guatemala* 17°25N 89°29W 320 C2
Ub *Serbia* 44°28N 20°6E 202 B4
Ubá *Brazil* 21°8S 43°0W 333 F3
Uba *Nigeria* 10°29N 13°13E 263 C7
Ubai *Papua N. G.* 5°39S 150°38E 286 C6
Ubaitaba *Brazil* 14°18S 39°20W 333 D4
Ubajara △ *Brazil* 3°55S 40°50W 332 B3
Ubangi = Oubangi → *Dem. Rep. of the Congo* 0°30S 17°50E 264 C3
Ubaté *Colombia* 5°19N 73°49W 328 B3
Ubauro *Pakistan* 28°15N 69°45E 242 E3
Ubay *Phil.* 10°3N 124°28E 233 F5
Ubaye → *France* 44°28N 6°18E 175 D10
Ubayyiḍ, W. al → *Iraq* 32°34N 43°48E 213 F10
Ube *Japan* 33°56N 131°15E 222 D3
Úbeda *Spain* 38°3N 3°23W 195 G7
Ubeidiya *West Bank* 31°43N 35°17E 123 B2
Uberaba *Brazil* 19°50S 47°55W 333 E2
Uberaba → *Brazil* 23°35S 46°41W 137 B2
Uberaba, L. *Brazil* 17°30S 57°50W 331 D6
Uberlândia *Minas Gerais, Brazil* 19°0S 48°20W 333 E2
Uberlândia *Roraïma, Brazil* 0°48N 59°20W 329 C6
Überlingen *Germany* 47°46N 9°10E 179 H5
Ubiaja *Nigeria* 6°41N 6°22E 263 D6
Ubin, Pulau *Singapore* 1°24N 103°57E 138 A3
Ubly *U.S.A.* 43°42N 82°55W 312 C2
Ubolratna Res. *Thailand* 16°45N 102°30E 236 D4
Ubombo *S. Africa* 27°31S 32°4E 271 C5
Ubon Ratchathani *Thailand* 15°15N 104°50E 236 E5
Ubondo *Dem. Rep. of the Congo* 0°55S 25°42E 268 C2
Ubort → *Belarus* 52°6N 28°30E 177 B15
Ubrique *Spain* 36°41N 5°27W 195 J5
Ubud *Indonesia* 8°30S 115°16E 231 J18
Ubuna *Solomon Is.* 10°11S 161°24E 287 N11
Ubundu *Dem. Rep. of the Congo* 0°22S 25°30E 264 C5
Ucar *Azerbaijan* 40°31N 47°39E 191 K8
Ucayali → *Peru* 4°30S 73°30W 328 D3
Uccle *Belgium* 50°48N 4°22E 116 B2
Uchab *Namibia* 19°47S 17°42E 270 A2
Uchiko *Japan* 33°33N 132°39E 222 D4
Uchiura-Wan *Japan* 42°25N 140°40E 220 C10
Uchiza *Peru* 8°25S 76°20W 330 B2
Uchquduq *Uzbekistan* 41°50N 62°50E 216 D6
Uchte *Germany* 52°30N 8°54E 178 C4
Uchur → *Russia* 58°48N 130°35E 215 D14
Uckermark *Germany* 53°5N 13°30E 178 B9
Ucluelet *Canada* 48°57N 125°32W 296 D3
Úcua *Angola* 8°43S 14°8E 265 D2
Uda → *Russia* 54°42N 135°14E 215 D14
Uda Walawe △ *Sri Lanka* 6°20N 81°0E 245 L5
Udachnyy *Russia* 66°25N 112°24E 215 C12
Udagamandalam *India* 11°30N 76°44E 245 J3
Udainagar *India* 22°33N 76°13E 242 H7
Udaipur *Raj., India* 24°36N 73°44E 242 G5
Udaipur *Tripura, India* 23°32N 91°30E 241 D3
Udaipur Garhi *Nepal* 27°0N 86°35E 243 F12
Udala *India* 21°35N 86°34E 243 J12
Udalguri *India* 26°46N 92°8E 241 B4
Udayagiri *Andhra Pradesh, India* 14°52N 79°19E 245 G4
Udayagiri *Odisha, India* 20°8N 84°23E 244 D7
Udbina *Croatia* 44°31N 15°47E 199 D12
Uddeholm *Sweden* 60°1N 13°38E 162 D7
Uddevalla *Sweden* 58°21N 11°55E 163 F5
Uddheden *Sweden* 59°57N 12°54E 162 E6
Uddjaure *Sweden* 65°56N 17°49E 160 D17
Udegeyskaya Legenda △ *Russia* 45°45N 135°30E 220 B7
Udelnaya *Russia* 60°0N 30°21E 137 A2
Udelnoe *Russia* 59°58N 30°20E 137 B1
Uden *Neths.* 51°40N 5°37E 170 C5
Udgir *India* 18°25N 77°5E 244 E3
Udhampur *India* 33°0N 75°5E 243 C6
Udi *Nigeria* 6°17N 7°21E 263 D6
Údine *Italy* 46°3N 13°14E 199 B10
Udintsev Fracture Zone *S. Ocean* 57°0S 145°0W 151 B13
Udlding *Germany* 48°15N 11°25E 131 A1
Udmurtia □ *Russia* 57°30N 52°30E 186 C9
Udon Thani *Thailand* 17°29N 102°46E 236 D4
Udong *Cambodia* 11°48N 104°45E 237 G5
Udot I. *Micronesia* 7°22N 151°42E 287 T17
Udskaya Guba *Russia* 54°50N 135°45E 215 D14
Udu Pt. *Fiji* 16°9S 179°57W 287 A3
Udumalaippettai *India* 10°35N 77°15E 245 J3
Udupi *India* 13°25N 74°42E 245 H2
Udva *India* 20°5N 73°0E 244 D1
Udvoy Balkan *Bulgaria* 42°50N 26°50E 203 D10
Udzungwa △ *Tanzania* 7°52S 36°35E 268 D4
Udzungwa Range *Tanzania* 9°30S 35°10E 269 D4
Ueckermünde *Germany* 53°44N 14°1E 178 B10
Ueda *Japan* 36°24N 138°16E 223 A10
Uedineniya, Os. *Russia* 78°0N 85°0E 150 B12
Uele → *Dem. Rep. of the Congo* 3°45N 24°45E 264 B4
Uelen *Russia* 66°10N 170°0W 215 C19
Uelzen *Germany* 52°57N 10°32E 178 C6
Ueno *Mie, Japan* 34°45N 136°8E 223 C8
Ueno *Tōkyō, Japan* 35°42N 139°46E 140 A3
Uetersen *Germany* 53°40N 9°40E 178 B5
Uetze *Germany* 52°28N 10°11E 178 C6
Ufa *Russia* 54°45N 55°55E 186 D10
Ufa → *Russia* 54°40N 56°0E 186 D10
Uffenheim *Germany* 49°33N 10°14E 179 F6
Ugab → *Namibia* 20°55S 13°30E 270 B1
Ugalla → *Tanzania* 5°8S 30°42E 268 D3
Ugalla River ⌓ *Tanzania* 5°50S 31°54E 268 D3
Uganda ■ *Africa* 2°0N 32°0E 268 B3
Ugento *Italy* 39°56N 18°10E 201 C11
Ugep *Nigeria* 5°53N 8°2E 263 D6
Ughelli *Nigeria* 5°33N 6°0E 263 D6
Ugie *S. Africa* 31°10S 28°13E 271 D4
Ugíjar *Spain* 36°58N 3°7W 195 J7
Ugine *France* 45°45N 6°25E 175 C10
Uglegorsk *Russia* 49°5N 142°2E 215 E15
Uglich *Russia* 57°33N 38°20E 188 D10
Ugljan *Croatia* 44°12N 15°10E 199 D12
Ugljane *Croatia* 43°35N 16°46E 199 E13
Ugolny = Beringovskiy *Russia* 63°3N 179°19E 215 C18
Ugolny = Karpinsk *Russia* 59°45N 60°1E 186 C11
Ugolnye Kopi = Kopeysk *Russia* 55°7N 61°37E 216 A6
Ugolnye Kopi *Russia* 64°44N 177°42E 215 C18
Ugoofaaru *Maldives* 5°40N 73°0E 272 d
Ugra → *Russia* 54°30N 36°7E 188 E9
Ugra △ *Russia* 54°45N 35°30E 188 E8
Ugŭrchin *Bulgaria* 43°6N 24°26E 203 C8
Uh → *Slovak Rep.* 48°37N 22°0E 181 C15
Uherské Hradiště *Czech Rep.* 49°4N 17°30E 181 B10
Uherský Brod *Czech Rep.* 49°1N 17°40E 181 B10
Úhlava → *Czech Rep.* 49°45N 13°24E 180 B6
Uhlenhorst *Namibia* 23°45S 17°55E 270 B2
Uhniv *Ukraine* 50°22N 23°45E 185 H10
Üholičky *Czech Rep.* 50°9N 14°19E 135 B1
Uhrichsville *U.S.A.* 40°24N 81°21W 312 F3
Uhříněves *Czech Rep.* 50°2N 14°35E 135 B3
Uibhist a Deas = South Uist *U.K.* 57°20N 7°15W 167 D1
Uibhist a Tuath = North Uist *U.K.* 57°40N 7°15W 167 D1
Uiche *Angola* 12°2S 20°51E 265 E4
Uido *S. Korea* 34°36N 125°50E 224 E2
Uig *U.K.* 57°35N 6°21W 167 D2
Uíge *Angola* 7°30S 14°40E 265 D2
Uíge □ *Angola* 7°0S 16°0E 265 D3
Uiha *Tonga* 19°54S 174°25W 287 P13
Uijeongbu *S. Korea* 37°44N 127°2E 224 D3
Ŭiju *N. Korea* 40°15N 124°35E 224 B2
Uinta Mts. *U.S.A.* 40°45N 110°30W 304 F8
Uiryeong *S. Korea* 35°19N 128°15E 224 E4
Uis *Namibia* 21°8S 14°49E 270 B1
Uiseong *S. Korea* 36°21N 128°45E 224 D4
Uitenhage *S. Africa* 33°40S 25°28E 270 D4
Uithoorn *Neths.* 52°14N 4°50E 112 B1
Uithuizen *Neths.* 53°24N 6°41E 170 A6
Ujazd *Poland* 50°23N 18°21E 185 H5
Ujazdów *Poland* 52°13N 21°1E 143 B2
Ujazdowski Castle *Warsaw, Poland* 143 c3
Újfehértó *Hungary* 47°49N 21°41E 182 C6
Ujh → *India* 32°10N 75°18E 242 C6
Ujhani *India* 28°0N 79°6E 243 F8
Uji *Japan* 34°53N 135°48E 223 C7
Uji-guntō *Japan* 31°15N 129°25E 221 J4
Ujiyamada = Ise *Japan* 34°25N 136°45E 223 C8
Ujjain *India* 23°9N 75°43E 242 H6
Újpalota *Hungary* 47°32N 19°8E 117 A2
Újpest *Hungary* 47°35N 19°4E 117 A2
Ujście *Poland* 53°3N 16°45E 185 E3
Ujście Warty △ *Poland* 52°35N 14°44E 185 F1
Újszász *Hungary* 47°19N 20°7E 182 C5
Ujung Kulon △ *Indonesia* 6°46S 105°19E 234 D3
Ujung Pandang = Makassar *Indonesia* 5°10S 119°20E 235 D5
Uka *Russia* 57°50N 162°0E 215 D17
Ukai Sagar *India* 21°20N 73°43E 244 D1
Ukara I. *Tanzania* 1°50S 33°0E 268 C3
Uke-Shima *Japan* 28°2N 129°14E 221 K4
Ukerewe I. *Tanzania* 2°0S 33°0E 268 C3
uKhahlamba Drakensberg ⌓ *S. Africa* 29°27S 29°30E 271 C4
Ukholovo *Russia* 53°47N 40°30E 190 D5
Ukhrul *India* 25°10N 94°25E 241 C5
Ukhta *Russia* 63°34N 53°41E 186 B9
Uki Ni Masi *Solomon Is.* 10°15S 161°47E 287 N11
Ukiah *U.S.A.* 39°9N 123°13W 306 F3
Ukita *Japan* 35°40N 139°51E 140 A4
Ukkusiksalik △ *Canada* 65°20N 89°30W 294 D14
Ukmergė *Lithuania* 55°15N 24°45E 188 E3
Ukraine ■ *Europe* 49°0N 32°0E 189 H7
Uku *Angola* 11°24S 14°22E 265 E2
Ukwi *Botswana* 23°29S 20°30E 270 B3
Ula *Turkey* 37°6N 28°25E 212 D3
Ulaan Nuur *Mongolia* 44°30N 103°40E 226 B2
Ulaan-Uul *Mongolia* 46°4N 100°49E 218 B9
Ulaanbaatar *Mongolia* 47°55N 106°53E 218 B10
Ulaangom *Mongolia* 50°5N 92°10E 217 B12
Ulaanjirem *Mongolia* 45°5N 105°30E 226 B3
Ulak I. *U.S.A.* 51°22N 178°57W 303 L3
Ulala = Gorno-Altaysk *Russia* 51°50N 86°5E 217 B11
Ulalu I. *Micronesia* 7°23N 151°41E 287 T17
Ulamambri *Australia* 31°19S 149°23E 283 A8
Ulamba *Dem. Rep. of the Congo* 9°3S 23°38E 265 D4
Ulamona *Papua N. G.* 5°0S 151°15E 286 C6
Ulan Bator = Ulaanbaatar *Mongolia* 47°55N 106°53E 218 B10
Ulan Erge *Russia* 46°19N 44°53E 191 G7
Ulan Khol *Russia* 45°18N 47°4E 191 H8
Ulan Ude *Russia* 51°45N 107°40E 219 A10
Ulanhad = Chifeng *China* 42°18N 118°58E 227 C10
Ulanhot = Horqin Youyi Qianqi *China* 46°5N 122°3E 227 A12
Ulanów *Poland* 50°30N 22°16E 185 H9
Ulansuhai Nur *China* 40°53N 108°51E 226 D5
Ulaş *Sivas, Turkey* 39°26N 37°2E 212 C7
Ulaş *Tekirdağ, Turkey* 41°14N 27°42E 203 E11
Ulawa *Solomon Is.* 9°46S 161°57E 287 M11
Ulawun, Mt. *Papua N. G.* 5°3S 151°20E 286 C6
Ulaya *Morogoro, Tanzania* 7°3S 36°55E 268 D4
Ulaya *Tabora, Tanzania* 4°25S 33°30E 268 C3
Ulcinj *Montenegro* 41°58N 19°10E 202 E3
Ulco *S. Africa* 28°21S 24°15E 270 C3
Ule älv = Oulujoki → *Finland* 65°1N 25°30E 160 D21
Ule träsk = Oulujärvi *Finland* 64°25N 27°15E 160 D22
Uleåborg = Oulu *Finland* 65°1N 25°29E 160 D21
Ulefoss *Norway* 59°17N 9°16E 164 E6
Uleta *U.S.A.* 25°27N 80°10W 129 C2
Ulëz *Albania* 41°46N 19°54E 202 E3
Ulfborg *Denmark* 56°16N 8°20E 163 H2
Ulhasnagar *India* 19°15N 73°10E 244 E1
Uliastay *Mongolia* 47°56N 97°28E 218 B8
Uljin *S. Korea* 36°59N 129°24E 224 D4
Uljma *Serbia* 45°2N 21°10E 182 E6
Ülken *Kazakhstan* 45°12N 73°58E 217 C8
Ülken Borsyq Qumy *Kazakhstan* 47°0N 59°11E 216 C5
Ulla → *Spain* 42°39N 8°44W 194 C2
Ulladulla *Australia* 35°21S 150°29E 283 C9
Ullal *India* 12°48N 74°51E 245 H2
Ullapool *U.K.* 57°54N 5°9W 167 D3

Ullared Sweden 57°8N 12°42E 163 G6
Ulldecona Spain 40°36N 0°20E 196 E5
Ullerup Denmark 55°34N 12°36E 118 B3
Ulleungdo S. Korea 37°30N 130°30E 224 D5
Ullevål Norway 59°56N 10°46E 133 A3
Ullswater Ont., Canada 45°12N 79°29W 312 A5
Ullswater Cumb., U.K. 54°34N 2°52W 168 C5
Ulm Germany 48°23N 9°58E 179 G5
Ulmarra Australia 29°37S 153°4E 281 D5
Ulmeni Buzău, Romania 45°4N 26°40E 183 E11
Ulmeni Maramureş, Romania 47°28N 23°18E 183 C8
Ulonguè Mozam. 14°37S 34°19E 269 E3
Ulricehamn Sweden 57°46N 13°26E 163 G7
Ulrika Sweden 58°5N 15°23E 163 F9
Ulriksdal Sweden 59°23N 17°59E 139 A1
Ulsan S. Korea 35°20N 129°15E 224 E4
Ulsberg Norway 62°45N 10°0E 164 B6
Ulsta U.K. 60°30N 1°9W 167 A7
Ulsteinvik Norway 62°21N 5°53E 164 B2
Ulster □ U.K. 54°35N 6°30W 166 B5
Ulstrem Bulgaria 42°1N 26°27E 203 D10
Ultima Australia 35°30S 143°18E 282 C5
Ulu Temburong △ Brunei 4°27N 115°15E 235 B5
Ulubat Gölü Turkey 40°9N 28°35E 203 F12
Ulubey Turkey 38°25N 29°18E 205 C11
Uluborlu Turkey 38°4N 30°28E 205 C12
Uluçinar Turkey 36°24N 35°53E 250 B6
Uludağ Turkey 40°4N 29°13E 203 F13
Uludağ △ Turkey 40°5N 29°12E 203 F13
Uludere Turkey 37°28N 42°42E 213 D10
Ulugqat China 39°48N 74°15E 217 E8
Uluguru Mts. Tanzania 7°15S 37°40E 268 D4
Ulukışla = Marathóvounos Cyprus 35°13N 33°37E 207 E9
Ulukışla Turkey 37°33N 34°28E 212 D6
Ulundi S. Africa 28°20S 31°25E 271 C5
Ulungur He → China 47°1N 87°24E 217 C11
Ulungur Hu China 47°20N 87°10E 217 C11
Ulupalakua U.S.A. 20°39N 156°24W 302 C5
Uluru Australia 25°23S 131°5E 279 E5
Uluru-Kata Tjuta △ Australia 25°19S 131°1E 279 E5
Ulutau Kazakhstan 48°39N 67°1E 217 C7
Uluwatu Indonesia 8°50S 115°5E 231 K18
Ulva U.K. 56°29N 6°13W 167 E2
Ulverston U.K. 54°13N 3°5W 168 C4
Ulverstone Australia 41°11S 146°11E 281 G4
Ulvik Norway 60°35N 6°54E 164 D3
Ulya Russia 59°10N 142°0E 215 D15
Ulyanka Russia 59°50N 30°14E 137 B1
Ulyanovo Russia 54°50N 22°6E 184 D9
Ulyanovsk Russia 54°20N 48°25E 190 C9
Ulyanovsk □ Russia 54°5N 48°5E 190 C9
Ulyasutay = Uliastay Mongolia 47°56N 97°28E 218 B8
Ulysses Kans., U.S.A. 37°35N 101°22W 308 G3
Ulysses Pa., U.S.A. 41°54N 77°46W 312 E7
Ulysses, Mt. Canada 57°20N 124°5W 296 B4
Ulysses S. Grant Nat. Historic Site ⌂ U.S.A. 38°33N 90°28W 310 F6
Ulyzhylanshyq → Kazakhstan 48°51N 63°46E 216 C6
Um Al Khanazir I. Iraq 33°17N 44°22E 113 B2
Umag Croatia 45°26N 13°31E 199 C10
Umala Bolivia 17°25S 68°5W 330 D4
'Umān = Oman ■ Asia 23°0N 58°0E 249 B7
Uman Ukraine 48°40N 30°12E 177 D16
Uman I. Micronesia 7°17N 151°52E 287 U18
Umaria India 23°35N 80°50E 243 H9
Umarkhed India 19°37N 77°46E 244 E3
Umarkot Pakistan 25°15N 69°40E 242 G3
Umarpada India 21°27N 73°30E 242 J5
Umatac Guam 13°18N 144°39E 302 d
Umatilla U.S.A. 45°55N 119°21W 304 D4
Umba Russia 66°42N 34°11E 186 A5
Umbagog L. U.S.A. 44°46N 71°3W 313 B13
Umbakumba Australia 13°47S 136°50E 280 A2
Umbértide Italy 43°18N 12°20E 199 E9
Umboi I. Papua N. G. 5°40S 148°0E 286 C5
Umbrella Mts. N.Z. 45°35S 169°5E 285 F4
Umbria □ Italy 42°53N 12°30E 199 F9
Umeå Sweden 63°45N 20°20E 160 E19
Umeälven → Sweden 63°45N 20°20E 160 E19
Umeda Japan 34°41N 135°29E 133 A1
Umera Indonesia 0°12S 129°37E 231 E7
Umerkhadi Mumbai, India 130 b2
Umfuli → Zimbabwe 17°30S 29°23E 269 F2
Umfurudzi ⌂ Zimbabwe 17°6S 31°40E 269 F3
Umgusa Zimbabwe 19°29S 27°52E 269 F2
Umgwenya → Mozam. 25°14S 32°18E 271 C5
Umiat U.S.A. 69°22N 152°8W 303 B9
Umiray Phil. 15°13N 121°25E 232 D3
Umiujaq Canada 56°33N 76°33W 298 A4
Umka Serbia 44°40N 20°19E 202 B4
Umkomaas S. Africa 30°13S 30°48E 271 D5
Umm ad Daraj, J. Jordan 32°18N 35°48E 251 F6
Umm al Arānib Libya 26°10N 14°43E 258 C2
Umm al Khashab Si. Arabia 17°23N 42°32E 256 D5
Umm al Qaywayn U.A.E. 25°30N 55°35E 247 E7
Umm al Qittayn Jordan 32°18N 36°40E 251 F7
Umm al Rasas Jordan 31°30N 35°55E 251 G6
Umm al Sheif U.A.E. 25°9N 55°13E 119 B1
Umm al'Abīd Libya 27°31N 15°2E 258 C3
Umm Arda Sudan 15°17N 32°31E 257 D3
Umm Bāb Qatar 25°12N 50°48E 247 E6
Umm Badr Sudan 14°13N 27°58E 257 E2
Umm Bel Sudan 13°35N 28°0E 257 E2
Umm Birkah Si. Arabia 27°44N 36°31E 256 B4
Umm Boim Sudan 11°43N 25°27E 257 E2
Umm Dam Sudan 13°45N 30°59E 257 E3
Umm Debi Sudan 14°37N 30°23E 257 E3
Umm Dubban Sudan 15°23N 32°52E 257 D3
Umm Durman = Omdurmân Sudan 15°40N 32°28E 257 D3
Umm el Fahm Israel 32°31N 35°9E 251 F6
Umm Gafala Sudan 13°22N 27°15E 257 E2
Umm Gimala Sudan 11°27N 28°12E 257 E2
Umm Inderaba Sudan 17°30N 33°13E 256 D3
Umm Isheirât, G. Egypt 28°21N 34°18E 251 K5
Umm Keddada Sudan 13°33N 26°35E 257 E2
Umm Koweika Sudan 13°10N 32°16E 257 E3
Umm Lajj Si. Arabia 25°0N 37°23E 246 E3
Umm Merwa Sudan 18°4N 32°30E 256 D3
Umm Qantur Sudan 14°17N 31°22E 257 E3
Umm Qasr Iraq 30°1N 47°58E 246 D5
Umm Qurein Sudan 9°58N 28°55E 257 F2
Umm Ruwaba Sudan 12°50N 31°20E 257 E3
Umm Sa'id Qatar 25°0N 51°33E 247 E6
Umm Saiyala Sudan 14°25N 31°10E 257 E3
Umm Shanqa Sudan 13°14N 27°14E 266 B2
Umm Shugeira Sudan 13°34N 29°37E 266 B2
Umm Shutur South Sudan 7°17N 33°14E 257 F3
Umm Sidr Sudan 14°29N 25°10E 257 E2
Umm Suqeim U.A.E. 25°11N 55°14E 119 B1
Umm Tais △ Qatar 26°7N 51°15E 247 E6
Umm Urūmah Si. Arabia 25°43N 36°35E 256 B4
Umm Zehetir Egypt 28°48N 32°31E 256 J8
Umnak I. U.S.A. 53°15N 168°20W 303 K5
Umniati → Zimbabwe 16°49S 28°45E 269 F2
Umpqua → U.S.A. 43°40N 124°12W 304 E1
Umpulo Angola 12°38S 17°42E 265 E3
Ümraniye Turkey 41°1N 29°4E 122 B2
Umred India 20°51N 79°18E 244 D4
Umreth India 22°41N 73°4E 242 H5
Umri India 19°2N 77°39E 244 E3
Umtata = Mthatha S. Africa 31°36S 28°49E 271 D4
Umuahia Nigeria 5°31N 7°26E 263 D6
Umuarama Brazil 23°45S 53°20W 335 A5
Umuda I. Papua N. G. 8°29S 143°46E 286 E2
Umurbey Turkey 40°13N 26°36E 203 F10
Umvukwe Ra. Zimbabwe 16°45S 30°45E 269 F3
Umzimvubu S. Africa 31°38S 29°33E 271 D4
Umzingwane → Zimbabwe 22°12S 29°56E 269 G2
Umzinto = eMuziwezinto S. Africa 30°15S 30°45E 271 D5
Una India 20°46N 71°8E 242 J4
Una → Bos.-H. 45°0N 16°20E 199 D13
Unac → Bos.-H. 44°30N 16°9E 199 D13
Unaðsdalur Iceland 66°7N 22°36W 155 A4
Unadilla Ga., U.S.A. 32°16N 83°44W 316 C6
Unadilla N.Y., U.S.A. 42°20N 75°19W 313 D9
Unaí Brazil 16°23S 46°53W 333 E2
Unalakleet U.S.A. 63°52N 160°47W 303 E7
Unalaska U.S.A. 53°53N 166°32W 303 K6
Unalaska I. U.S.A. 53°35N 166°50W 303 K6
'Unayzah Si. Arabia 26°6N 43°58E 246 E4
'Unayzah, J. Asia 32°12N 39°18E 213 F8
Uncastillo Spain 42°21N 1°8W 196 C3
Uncía Bolivia 18°25S 66°40W 330 D4
Uncompahgre Peak U.S.A. 38°4N 107°28W 304 G10
Uncompahgre Plateau U.S.A. 38°20N 108°15W 304 G9
Undara Volcanic △ Australia 18°14S 144°41E 280 B3
Unden Sweden 58°45N 14°25E 163 F8
Underbool Australia 35°10S 141°51E 282 C4
Underground Atlanta U.S.A. 33°45N 84°24W 113 B2
Underhill, L. U.S.A. 28°32N 81°20W 133 A3
Undersaker Sweden 63°19N 13°21E 162 A7
Underwood Canada 44°18N 81°29W 312 B3
Undredal Norway 60°57N 7°6E 164 D4
Unea I. Papua N. G. 4°53S 149°9E 286 C5
Unecha Russia 52°50N 32°37E 189 F7
Uneiuxi → Brazil 0°37S 65°34W 328 D4
Unětický potok → Czech Rep. 50°9N 14°24E 135 B2
Unga I. U.S.A. 55°15N 160°40W 303 J7
Ungarie Australia 33°38S 146°56E 283 B7
Ungarisch-Hradisch = Uherské Hradiště Czech Rep. 49°4N 17°30E 181 B10
Ungarisch-Ostra = Uherský Brod Czech Rep. 49°1N 17°40E 181 B10
Ungarra Australia 34°12S 136°2E 282 C2
Ungat Papua N. G. 2°40S 150°15E 286 B6
Ungava, Pén. d' Canada 60°0N 74°0W 295 F17
Ungava B. Canada 59°30N 67°30W 295 F18
Ungeny = Ungheni Moldova 47°11N 27°51E 183 C12
Unggi N. Korea 42°16N 130°28E 224 A5
Ungheni Moldova 47°11N 27°51E 183 C12
Unguala → Ethiopia 8°6N 41°9E 257 F5
Ungvár = Uzhhorod Ukraine 48°36N 22°18E 182 B7
Ungwana B. Kenya 2°45S 40°20E 268 C5
Ungwatiri Sudan 16°52N 36°10E 257 D4
Unhos Portugal 38°49N 9°7W 126 A2
Uni Russia 57°46N 51°31E 190 B10
União Brazil 4°35S 42°52W 332 B3
União da Vitória Brazil 26°13S 51°5W 335 B5
União dos Palmares Brazil 9°10S 36°2W 332 C4
Uničov Czech Rep. 49°46N 17°8E 181 B10
Unidad Santa Fe Mexico 19°23N 99°13W 128 B1
Uniejów Poland 51°59N 18°46E 185 G5
Unije Croatia 44°40N 14°15E 199 D11
Unimak I. U.S.A. 54°45N 164°0W 303 J7
Unimak Pass. U.S.A. 54°15N 164°30W 303 J6
Unini → Brazil 1°41S 61°31W 329 D5
Union Miss., U.S.A. 32°34N 89°7W 315 E10
Union Mo., U.S.A. 38°27N 91°0W 310 F6
Union Ohio, U.S.A. 39°55N 84°12W 311 E12
Union S.C., U.S.A. 34°43N 81°37W 315 D14
Union City Calif., U.S.A. 37°36N 122°1W 306 H4
Union City Ga., U.S.A. 33°35N 84°33W 316 B5
Union City New York, U.S.A. 132 b1
Union City Ohio, U.S.A. 40°12N 84°48W 311 D12
Union City Pa., U.S.A. 41°54N 79°51W 312 E5
Union City Tenn., U.S.A. 36°26N 89°3W 315 C10
Union Dale U.S.A. 41°43N 75°29W 313 E9
Union Gap U.S.A. 46°33N 120°28W 304 C3
Union Grove U.S.A. 42°41N 88°3W 311 B8
Union I. St. Vincent 12°36N 61°26W 323 n
Union Park U.S.A. 28°34N 81°17W 317 G8
Union Passenger Terminal New Orleans, U.S.A. 131 b1
Union Point U.S.A. 33°37N 83°4W 316 B6
Union Port U.S.A. 40°48N 73°51W 132 B2
Union Springs Ala., U.S.A. 32°9N 85°43W 316 C4
Union Springs N.Y., U.S.A. 42°50N 76°41W 313 D8
Union Square Hong Kong, China 22°19N 114°9E 122 B2
Union Square San Francisco, U.S.A. 136 b2
Union Star U.S.A. 39°59N 94°36W 310 E2
Union Station Toronto, Canada 141 c2
Union Station Chicago, U.S.A. 119 c1
Union Station Washington, D.C., U.S.A. 143 b3
Union Station Los Angeles, U.S.A. 127 b3
Union Station Plaza Washington, D.C., U.S.A. 143 b3
Uniondale S. Africa 33°39S 23°7E 270 D3
Uniontown Ky., U.S.A. 37°47N 87°56W 311 G9
Uniontown Pa., U.S.A. 39°54N 79°44W 309 F14
Unionville Ga., U.S.A. 31°26N 83°30W 316 D6
Unionville Mo., U.S.A. 40°29N 93°1W 310 D3
Unirea Romania 44°15N 27°35E 183 F12
United Arab Emirates ■ Asia 23°50N 54°0E 247 F7
United Arab Republic = Egypt ■ Africa 28°0N 31°0E 256 B3
United Center U.S.A. 41°53N 87°41W 119 B2
United Kingdom ■ Europe 53°0N 2°0W 165 E6
United Nations Headquarters New York, U.S.A. 132 c3
United Provinces = Uttar Pradesh □ India 27°0N 80°0E 243 F9
United States of America ■ N. Amer. 37°0N 96°0W 301 H20
Unity Canada 52°30N 109°5W 297 C7
Unity □ South Sudan 8°30N 30°0E 257 F3
Universal Studios Calif., U.S.A. 34°9N 118°21W 126 B2
Universal Studios Fla., U.S.A. 28°29N 81°29W 133 B2
Universales, Mtes. Spain 40°18N 1°33W 196 E3
Universidad Spain 40°27N 3°44W 127 B1
University City U.S.A. 38°39N 90°18W 310 F6
University Park Md., U.S.A. 38°58N 76°56W 143 B3
University Park N. Mex., U.S.A. 32°17N 106°45W 305 K10
University Place U.S.A. 47°14N 122°33W 306 C4
Unjha India 23°46N 72°24E 242 H5
Unmet Vanuatu 16°8S 167°15E 287 F5
Unna Germany 51°32N 7°42E 178 D3
Unnao India 26°35N 80°30E 243 F9
Uno, Ilha Guinea-Biss. 11°15N 16°13W 262 C1
Unruhstadt = Kargowa Poland 52°5N 15°51E 185 F2
Unsan N. Korea 40°6N 125°54E 224 B2
Unsengedsi → Zimbabwe 15°43S 31°14E 269 F3
Unst U.K. 60°44N 0°53W 167 A8
Unstrut → Germany 51°10N 11°48E 178 D7
Unter den Linden Berlin, Germany 115 a4
Unterbiberg Germany 48°6N 11°38E 131 B2
Unterdrauburg = Dravograd Slovenia 46°36N 15°5E 199 B12
Unterföhring Germany 48°11N 11°38E 131 A3
Unterfranken □ Germany 50°0N 10°0E 179 F5
Unterhaching Germany 48°3N 11°37E 131 B2
Unterlaa Austria 48°8N 16°24E 142 B2
Untermenzing Germany 48°10N 11°28E 131 A1
Unterschleissheim Germany 48°17N 11°34E 179 G7
Unuk → Canada 56°5N 131°3W 296 B2
Ünye Turkey 41°5N 37°15E 212 B7
Unzen-Amakusa △ Japan 32°15N 130°10E 222 E2
Unzen-Dake Japan 32°45N 130°17E 222 E2
Unzha Russia 58°0N 44°0E 190 A7
Unzha → Russia 57°49N 43°47E 190 B6
Uong Bi Vietnam 21°2N 106°47E 236 B6
Uotsuri-Shima E. China Sea 25°45N 123°29E 221 M1
Uozu Japan 36°48N 137°24E 223 A9
Upata Venezuela 8°1N 62°24W 329 B5
Upatoi Cr. → U.S.A. 32°22N 84°58W 316 C5
Upemba, L. Dem. Rep. of the Congo 8°30S 26°20E 269 D2
Upemba △ Dem. Rep. of the Congo 9°0S 26°35E 269 D2
Upernavik Greenland 72°49N 56°20W 154 C5
Upington S. Africa 28°25S 21°15E 270 C3
Upleta India 21°46N 70°16E 242 J4
'Upolu Samoa 13°58S 172°0W 287 V20
Upolu Pt. U.S.A. 20°16N 155°52W 302 C6
Upongkor Vanuatu 18°50S 168°59E 287 H6
Upper Alkali L. U.S.A. 41°47N 120°8W 304 F3
Upper Arlington U.S.A. 40°0N 83°4W 311 E13
Upper Arrow L. Canada 50°30N 117°50W 296 C5
Upper Austria = Oberösterreich □ Austria 48°10N 14°0E 180 C7
Upper B. U.S.A. 40°40N 74°3W 132 C1
Upper Daly ✿ Australia 14°26S 131°3E 278 B5
Upper Darby U.S.A. 39°55N 75°16W 309 F16
Upper East □ Ghana 10°30N 1°0W 263 C4
Upper East Side New York, U.S.A. 132 b3
Upper Elmers End U.K. 51°23N 0°1W 125 B3
Upper Foster L. Canada 56°47N 105°20W 297 B7
Upper Hutt N.Z. 41°8S 175°5E 284 H4
Upper Klamath L. U.S.A. 42°25N 121°55W 304 E3
Upper Lake U.S.A. 39°10N 122°54W 306 F4
Upper Liard Canada 60°3N 128°54W 296 A3
Upper Manilla Australia 30°38S 150°40E 283 A9
Upper Manzanilla Trin. & Tob. 10°31N 61°4W 323 t
Upper Missouri Breaks ⌂ U.S.A. 47°50N 109°55W 304 C9
Upper Musquodoboit Canada 45°10N 62°58W 299 C7
Upper New York B. = Upper B. U.S.A. 40°40N 74°3W 132 C1
Upper Nile □ South Sudan 9°30N 33°0E 257 F3
Upper Norwood U.K. 51°24N 0°6W 125 B3
Upper Peirce Res. Singapore 1°22N 103°47E 138 A2
Upper Red L. U.S.A. 48°8N 94°45W 308 A6
Upper Sandusky U.S.A. 40°50N 83°17W 311 D13
Upper Senegal & Niger = Mali ■ Africa 17°0N 3°0W 262 B4
Upper Sydenham U.K. 51°26N 0°4W 125 B3
Upper Tooting U.K. 51°25N 0°9W 125 B3
Upper Volta = Burkina Faso ■ Africa 12°0N 1°0W 262 C4
Upper West □ Ghana 10°30N 2°20W 262 C4
Upper West Side New York, U.S.A. 132 a2
Upphärad Sweden 58°9N 12°19E 163 F6
Uppland Sweden 59°59N 17°48E 162 D12
Upplands-Väsby Sweden 59°31N 17°54E 162 E11
Uppsala Sweden 59°53N 17°38E 162 E11
Uppsala län □ Sweden 60°0N 17°30E 162 D11
Upshi India 33°48N 77°52E 243 C7
Upton London, U.K. 51°32N 0°1E 125 A4
Upton Wyo., U.S.A. 44°6N 104°38W 304 D11
Uptown U.S.A. 41°58N 87°40W 119 B2
Uqsuqtuuq = Gjoa Haven Canada 68°38N 95°53W 294 D12
Ur Iraq 30°55N 46°25E 246 D5
Ur Kut Somalia 3°31N 42°47E 267 D5
Ura-Tyube = Istaravshān Tajikistan 39°55N 69°1E 217 E7
Urabá, G. de Colombia 8°25N 76°53W 328 B2
Urad Qianqi China 40°40N 108°30E 226 D5
Uraga-Suidō Japan 35°13N 139°45E 223 B11
Urahoro Japan 42°50N 143°40E 220 C11
Urakawa Japan 42°9N 142°47E 220 C11
Ural = Uralskiy □ Russia 64°0N 70°0E 214 C7
Ural = Zhayyq → Kazakhstan 47°0N 51°48E 187 E9
Ural Australia 33°21S 146°12E 283 B7
Ural Mts. = Uralskie Gory Eurasia 60°0N 59°0E 186 C10
Uralla Australia 30°37S 151°29E 283 A9
Uralmedstroy = Krasnouralsk Russia 58°21N 60°3E 186 C11
Uralsk = Oral Kazakhstan 51°20N 51°20E 190 E10
Uralskie Gory Eurasia 60°0N 59°0E 186 C10
Uralskiy □ Russia 64°0N 70°0E 214 C7
Urambo Tanzania 5°4S 32°0E 268 D3
Uran India 18°53N 72°56E 130 B2
Urana Australia 35°15S 146°21E 283 C7
Urana, L. Australia 35°16S 146°10E 283 C7
Urandangi Australia 21°32S 138°14E 280 C2
Uranga Australia 30°31S 153°1E 283 A10
Uranium City Canada 59°34N 108°37W 297 B7
Urapuntja = Utopia Australia 22°14S 134°33E 280 C1
Uraricaá → Brazil 3°20N 61°56W 329 C5
Uraricoera Brazil 3°27N 60°59W 329 C5
Uraricoera → Brazil 3°2N 60°30W 329 C5
Urasoe Japan 26°15N 127°43E 288 a
Uravakonda India 14°57N 77°12E 245 G3
Urawa = Saitama Japan 35°54N 139°38E 223 B11
Uray Russia 60°5N 65°15E 214 C7
Urayasu Japan 35°39N 139°53E 140 B4
'Uray'irah Si. Arabia 25°57N 48°53E 247 E6
Urbakh = Pushkino Russia 51°16N 47°0E 190 E8
Urbana Ill., U.S.A. 40°7N 88°12W 311 D8
Urbana Ohio, U.S.A. 40°7N 83°45W 311 D13
Urbandale U.S.A. 41°38N 93°43W 310 C3
Urbánia Italy 43°40N 12°31E 199 E9
Urbano Santos Brazil 3°12S 43°23W 332 B3
Urbe ✈ Italy 41°57N 12°30E 136 B2
Urbel → Spain 42°21N 3°40W 194 C7
Urbino Italy 43°43N 12°38E 199 E9
Urbión, Picos de Spain 42°1N 2°52W 196 C2
Urca Brazil 22°56S 43°9W 135 B2
Urcos Peru 13°40S 71°38W 330 C3
Urdaneta Phil. 15°59N 120°34E 232 D3
Urdinarrain Argentina 32°37S 58°52W 334 C4
Urdos France 42°51N 0°35W 174 F3
Ure → U.K. 54°5N 1°20W 168 C6
Uren Russia 57°35N 45°55E 190 B7
Urengoy Russia 65°58N 78°22E 214 C8
Ureparapara Vanuatu 13°32S 167°20E 287 C5
Ures Mexico 29°26N 110°24W 318 B2
Ureshino Japan 33°6N 129°59E 222 D1
Urewera △ N.Z. 38°29S 177°7E 284 E6
Urfa = Sanliurfa Turkey 37°12N 38°50E 213 D8
Urga = Ulaanbaatar Mongolia 47°55N 106°53E 218 B10
Urganch Uzbekistan 41°40N 60°41E 216 D6
Urgench = Urganch Uzbekistan 41°40N 60°41E 216 D6
Ürgüp Turkey 38°38N 34°56E 212 C6
Urho Kekkonen △ Finland 68°20N 27°40E 160 B22
Uri India 34°8N 74°2E 243 B6
Uri □ Switz. 46°43N 8°35E 179 J4
Uribante → Venezuela 7°25N 71°50W 328 B3
Uribe Colombia 3°13N 74°24W 328 C3
Uribia Colombia 11°43N 72°16W 328 A3
Uricani Romania 45°20N 23°9E 182 E8
Urimba Angola 10°56S 16°32E 265 E3
Uriondo Bolivia 21°41S 64°41W 334 A3
Urique Mexico 27°13N 107°55W 318 B3
Urique → Mexico 26°29N 107°58W 318 B3
Uritsk Russia 59°49N 30°10E 137 C1
Urk Neths. 52°39N 5°36E 170 B5
Urkiola ⌂ Spain 43°6N 1°2W 196 B3
Urla Turkey 38°20N 26°47E 205 C8
Urlaţi Romania 44°59N 26°15E 183 F11
Urmia = Orūmīyeh Iran 37°40N 45°0E 213 D11
Urmia, L. = Orūmīyeh, Daryācheh-ye Iran 37°50N 45°30E 213 D11
Urmston Road Hong Kong, China 22°22N 113°55E 122 A1
Üröm Hungary 47°35N 19°1E 117 A2
Uromi Nigeria 6°42N 6°20E 263 D6
Uroševac = Ferizaj Kosovo 42°23N 21°10E 202 D5
Ŭroteppa = Istaravshān Tajikistan 39°55N 69°1E 217 E7
Uroyan, Montanas de Puerto Rico 18°12N 66°50W 321 b
Urrampinyi Iltjiltarri ✿ Australia 24°20S 132°10E 278 D5
Urrao Colombia 6°20N 76°11W 328 B2
Urshult Sweden 56°31N 14°50E 163 H8
Ursus Poland 52°11N 20°52E 143 B1
Ursvik Sweden 59°23N 17°57E 139 A1
Uru Uru, L. Bolivia 18°6S 67°8W 330 D4
Uruaçu Brazil 14°30S 49°10W 333 D2
Uruanã Brazil 15°30S 49°41W 333 E2
Uruapan Mexico 19°24N 102°3W 318 D4
Uruará Brazil 3°42S 53°51W 329 D7
Uruará → Brazil 2°6S 53°38W 329 D7
Urubamba Peru 13°20S 72°10W 330 C3
Urubamba → Peru 10°43S 73°48W 330 C3
Urubaxi → Brazil 0°31S 64°50W 329 D5
Urubu → Brazil 2°55S 58°25W 329 D6
Urucará Brazil 2°32S 57°45W 329 D6
Uruçuí Brazil 7°20S 44°28W 332 C3
Uruçuí, Serra do Brazil 9°0S 44°45W 332 C3
Uruçuí Prêto → Brazil 7°20S 44°38W 332 C3
Urucuia → Brazil 16°8S 45°5W 333 E2
Uruguai → Brazil 26°0S 53°30W 335 B5
Uruguaiana Brazil 29°50S 57°0W 334 B4
Uruguay ■ S. Amer. 32°30S 56°30W 334 C4
Uruguay → S. Amer. 34°12S 58°18W 334 C4
Urukthapel I. Palau 7°17N 134°25E 288 c
Uruma Japan 26°21N 127°52E 288 a
Urumchi = Ürümqi China 43°45N 87°45E 217 D11
Ürümqi China 43°45N 87°45E 217 D11
Uruna ✿ Australia 24°3S 133°1E 278 D5
Urundi = Burundi ■ Africa 3°15S 30°0E 268 C3
Urup → Russia 45°0N 41°10E 191 H5
Urup, Ostrov Russia 46°0N 151°0E 215 E16
Urutaí Brazil 17°28S 48°12W 333 E2
Uryupinsk Russia 50°45N 41°58E 190 E5
Ürzhar Kazakhstan 47°5N 81°38E 217 C10
Urzhum Russia 57°10N 49°56E 190 B9
Urziceni Romania 44°40N 26°42E 183 F11
Usa Japan 33°31N 131°21E 222 D3
Usa → Russia 66°16N 59°49E 186 A10
Uşak Turkey 38°43N 29°28E 205 C11
Uşak □ Turkey 38°30N 29°0E 205 C11
Usakos Namibia 21°54S 15°31E 270 B2
Usborne, Mt. Falk. Is. 51°40S 59°55W 153 f
Ušće Serbia 43°30N 20°39E 202 C4
Usedom Germany 53°55N 14°2E 178 B10
Usedom ⌂ Germany 53°55N 14°0E 178 B10
Useless Loop Australia 26°8S 113°23E 279 E1
Usera Spain 40°22N 3°42W 127 B1
'Usfān Si. Arabia 21°58N 39°27E 248 B2
Ushakova, Ostrov Russia 82°0N 80°0E 215 A8
Ushakovo Russia 54°37N 20°16E 184 D7
Ushant = Ouessant, Î. d' France 48°28N 5°6W 172 D1
Üsharal Kazakhstan 46°10N 80°56E 217 C10
Ushashi Tanzania 1°59S 33°57E 268 C3
Ushat South Sudan 7°59N 29°28E 257 F2
'Ushayrah Ar Riyāḑ, Si. Arabia 25°35N 45°47E 246 E5
'Ushayrah Makkah, Si. Arabia 21°46N 40°42E 256 C5
Ushibuka Japan 32°11N 130°1E 222 E2
Ushigome Japan 35°42N 139°44E 140 A3
Üshtöbe Kazakhstan 45°16N 78°0E 217 C9
Ushuaia Argentina 54°50S 68°23W 336 D3
Ushumun Russia 52°47N 126°32E 215 D13
Ushytsya → Ukraine 48°35N 27°8E 183 B12
Usina Brazil 22°57S 43°17W 135 B1
Usino Papua N. G. 5°32S 145°23E 286 C3
Usinsk Russia 65°57N 57°27E 186 A10
Usk Canada 54°38N 128°26W 296 C3
Usk → U.K. 51°33N 2°58W 169 F5
Uska India 27°12N 83°7E 243 F10
Uskedalen Norway 59°56N 5°53E 164 E2
Üsküb = Skopje Macedonia 42°1N 21°26E 202 D5
Üsküdar Turkey 41°1N 29°0E 122 B2
Uslar Germany 51°39N 9°38E 178 D5
Usman Russia 52°5N 39°48E 189 F10
Usoke Tanzania 5°8S 32°24E 268 D3
Usolye-Sibirskoye Russia 52°48N 103°40E 215 D11
Usolye-Solikamskoye = Berezniki Russia 59°24N 56°46E 186 C10
Usoro Nigeria 5°33N 6°11E 263 D6
Uspallata, P. de Argentina 32°37S 69°22W 334 C2
Uspenka = Kirovskiy Russia 45°7N 133°30E 220 B6
Ussel France 45°32N 2°18E 174 C6
Usson-du-Poitou France 46°16N 0°31E 174 B4
Ussuriysk Russia 43°48N 131°59E 220 C5
Ussurka Russia 45°12N 133°31E 220 B6
Ust-Aldan = Batamay Russia 63°30N 129°15E 215 C13
Ust-Amginskoye = Khandyga Russia 62°42N 135°35E 215 C14
Ust-Buzulukskaya Russia 50°8N 42°11E 190 E6
Ust-Chaun Russia 68°47N 170°30E 215 C18
Ust-Chorna Ukraine 48°19N 23°56E 183 B8
Ust-Donetskiy Russia 47°35N 40°55E 191 G5
Ust-Ilimpeya = Yukta Russia 63°26N 105°42E 215 C11
Ust-Ilimsk Russia 58°3N 102°39E 215 D11
Ust-Ishim Russia 57°45N 71°10E 214 D8
Ust-Kamchatsk Russia 56°10N 162°28E 215 D17
Ust-Kamenogorsk = Öskemen Kazakhstan 50°0N 82°36E 217 C10
Ust-Khayryuzovo Russia 57°15N 156°45E 215 D16
Ust-Kut Russia 56°50N 105°42E 215 D11
Ust-Kuyga Russia 70°1N 135°43E 215 B14
Ust-Labinsk Russia 45°15N 39°41E 191 H4
Ust-Luga Russia 59°35N 28°20E 188 C5
Ust-Maya Russia 60°30N 134°28E 215 C14
Ust-Medveditskaya = Serafimovich Russia 49°36N 42°43E 190 F6
Ust-Mil Russia 59°40N 133°11E 215 D14
Ust-Nera Russia 64°35N 143°15E 215 C15
Ust-Nyukzha Russia 56°34N 121°37E 215 D13
Ust-Olenek Russia 73°0N 120°5E 215 B12
Ust-Omchug Russia 61°9N 149°38E 215 C15
Ust-Port Russia 69°40N 84°26E 214 C9
Ust-Slavyanka Russia 59°51N 30°32E 137 C3
Ust-Sysolsk = Syktyvkar Russia 61°45N 50°40E 186 B9
Ust-Tsilma Russia 65°28N 52°11E 186 A9
Ust-Urt = Ustyurt Plateau Asia 44°0N 55°0E 216 D5
Ust-Usa Russia 66°2N 56°57E 186 A10
Ust-Vorkuta Russia 67°24N 64°0E 186 A11
Ust-Zhuya = Chara Russia 56°54N 118°20E 215 D12
Ustaoset Norway 60°30N 8°2E 164 D5
Ustaritz France 43°24N 1°27W 174 E2
Ustecký □ Czech Rep. 50°30N 14°0E 180 A7
Uster Switz. 47°22N 8°43E 179 H4
Ústí nad Labem Czech Rep. 50°41N 14°3E 180 A7
Ústí nad Orlicí Czech Rep. 49°58N 16°24E 181 B9
Ústica Italy 38°42N 13°11E 200 D6
Ustinov = Izhevsk Russia 56°51N 53°14E 186 C9
Ustka Poland 54°35N 16°55E 184 D3
Ustroń Poland 49°43N 18°48E 185 J5
Ustrzyki Dolne Poland 49°27N 22°40E 185 J9
Ustupo Panama 9°27N 78°34W 328 B2
Ustyluh Ukraine 50°51N 24°10E 185 H11
Ustyurt Plateau Asia 44°0N 55°0E 216 D5
Ustyuzhna Russia 58°50N 36°32E 188 C9
Usu China 44°27N 84°40E 217 D10
Usuki Japan 33°8N 131°49E 222 D3
Usulután El Salv. 13°25N 88°28W 320 D2
Usumacinta → Mexico 18°24N 92°38W 319 D6
Usumbura = Bujumbura Burundi 3°16S 29°18E 268 C2
Usure Tanzania 4°40S 34°22E 268 C3
Usutuo → Mozam. 26°48S 32°7E 271 C5
Uta Indonesia 4°33S 136°0E 231 E9
Utah □ U.S.A. 39°20N 111°30W 304 G8
Utah L. U.S.A. 40°12N 111°48W 304 F8
Utansjö Sweden 62°46N 17°55E 162 B11
Utara, Selat Malaysia 5°28N 100°20E 237 c
Utarni India 26°5N 71°58E 242 F4
Utatlan Guatemala 15°2N 91°11W 320 C1
Ute Creek → U.S.A. 35°21N 103°50W 305 J12
Utebo Spain 41°43N 1°0W 196 D3
Utegi Tanzania 1°19S 34°13E 266 E3
Uteke Sweden 59°24N 18°15E 139 A3
Utena Lithuania 55°27N 25°40E 188 E3
Utete Tanzania 8°0S 38°45E 268 D4
Uthai Thani Thailand 15°22N 100°3E 236 E3
Uthal Pakistan 25°44N 66°40E 242 G2
Utiariti Brazil 13°0S 58°10W 331 C6
Utica N.Y., U.S.A. 43°6N 75°14W 313 C9
Utica Ohio, U.S.A. 40°14N 82°27W 312 F2
Utiel Spain 39°37N 1°11W 197 F3
Utikuma L. Canada 55°50N 115°30W 296 B5
Utila Honduras 16°6N 86°56W 320 C2
Utinga Brazil 12°6S 41°5W 333 D3
Utkela India 20°6N 83°10E 244 D6
Utlängen Sweden 56°2N 15°48E 163 H9
Utne Norway 60°25N 6°37E 164 D3
Utnur India 19°22N 78°46E 244 E4
Uto Japan 32°41N 130°40E 222 E2
Utö Sweden 58°56N 18°16E 162 F12
Utopia Australia 22°14S 134°33E 280 C1
Utrata Poland 52°15N 21°4E 143 B2
Utraula India 27°19N 82°25E 243 F10
Utrecht Neths. 52°5N 5°8E 170 B5
Utrecht KwaZulu Natal, S. Africa 27°38S 30°20E 271 C5
Utrecht □ Neths. 52°6N 5°7E 170 B5
Utrera Spain 37°12N 5°48W 195 H5
Utría △ Colombia 5°57N 77°21W 328 B2
Utsira Norway 59°19N 4°53E 164 E1
Utsjoki → Finland 69°51N 26°59E 160 B22
Utsunomiya Japan 36°30N 139°50E 223 A11
Uttar Pradesh □ India 27°0N 80°0E 243 F9
Uttaradit Thailand 17°36N 100°5E 236 D3
Uttarakhand □ India 30°0N 79°30E 243 D8
Uttaranchal = Uttarakhand □ India 30°0N 79°30E 243 D8
Uttarpara India 22°39N 88°21E 124 B1
Utterslev Mose Denmark 55°42N 12°29E 118 A2
Utterson Canada 45°12N 79°19W 312 A5
Uttoxeter U.K. 52°54N 1°52W 168 E6
Utuado Puerto Rico 18°16N 66°42W 321 b
Uummannaq Qaasuitsup, Greenland 70°58N 52°17W 150 B5
Uummannaq Qaasuitsup, Greenland 77°33N 68°52W 154 B4
Uummannarsuaq = Nunap Isua Greenland 59°48N 43°55W 154 F6
Uunartoq Qeqertoq Greenland 71°33N 21°47W 154 C8
Uusikaarlepyy Finland 63°32N 22°31E 160 E20
Uusikaupunki Finland 60°47N 21°25E 188 B1
Uva Russia 56°59N 52°13E 190 B11
Uvá → Colombia 3°41N 70°3W 328 C3
Uvac → Serbia 43°35N 19°30E 202 C3
Uvalda U.S.A. 32°2N 82°31W 316 C7
Uvalde U.S.A. 29°13N 99°47W 314 G5
Uvarovo Russia 51°59N 42°14E 190 E6
Uvat Russia 59°5N 68°50E 214 D7
Uvdal Norway 60°17N 8°48E 164 D5
Uvéa, I. Wall. & F. Is. 13°18S 176°10W 277 C15
Uvinza Tanzania 5°5S 30°24E 268 D3
Uvira Dem. Rep. of the Congo 3°22S 29°3E 268 C2
Uvs □ Mongolia 49°38N 93°0E 217 C12
Uvs Nuur Mongolia 50°20N 92°30E 217 B12
Uwa Japan 33°22N 132°31E 222 D4
'Uwairidh, Ḩarrat al Si. Arabia 26°50N 38°0E 246 E3
Uwajima Japan 33°10N 132°35E 222 D4
Uwanda ⌂ Tanzania 7°46S 32°0E 268 D3
Uweinat, Jebel Sudan 21°54N 24°58E 256 C1
Uxbridge Canada 44°6N 79°7W 312 B5
Uxin Qi China 38°50N 109°5E 226 E5
Uxmal Mexico 20°22N 89°46W 319 C7
Uyak U.S.A. 57°38N 154°0W 303 H9
Üydzin Mongolia 44°9N 107°0E 226 B4
Uyo Nigeria 5°1N 7°53E 263 D6
Uyu → Burma 24°51N 94°57E 241 C5
Üyüklü Tepe Turkey 37°5N 27°21E 205 D9
Uyûn Mûsa Egypt 29°53N 32°40E 251 J3
Uyuni Bolivia 20°28S 66°47W 330 E4
Uzbekistan ■ Asia 41°30N 65°0E 217 D7
Uzboy → Turkmenistan 39°30N 55°0E 247 B7
Uzen, Mal → Kazakhstan 49°4N 49°44E 191 F9
Uzerche France 45°25N 1°34E 174 C5
Uzès France 44°1N 4°26E 175 D8
Uzh → Ukraine 51°15N 30°12E 177 C16
Uzhgorod = Uzhhorod Ukraine 48°36N 22°18E 182 B7
Uzhhorod Ukraine 48°36N 22°18E 182 B7
Uzhok Ukraine 48°59N 22°52E 182 B7
Užice Serbia 43°55N 19°50E 202 C3
Uzlovaya Russia 54°0N 38°5E 188 F10
Üzümlü Turkey 36°44N 29°14E 205 E11
Uzuncaburç Turkey 36°35N 33°57E 250 B4
Uzunköprü Turkey 41°16N 26°43E 203 E10
Uzunkuyu Turkey 38°17N 26°33E 205 C8

## V

V.C. Bird Int. ✈ (ANU) Antigua & B. 17°8N 61°47W 322 b
Vaal → S. Africa 29°4S 23°38E 270 C3
Vaal Dam S. Africa 27°0S 28°14E 271 C4
Vaalwater S. Africa 24°15S 28°8E 271 B4
Vaasa Finland 63°6N 21°38E 160 E19
Vabre France 43°42N 2°24E 174 E6
Vác Hungary 47°49N 19°10E 182 C4
Vacaos, Mare aux Mauritius 20°22S 57°30E 272 e
Vacaria Brazil 28°31S 50°52W 335 B5
Vacaville U.S.A. 38°21N 121°59W 306 G5
Vaccarès, Étang de France 43°32N 4°34E 175 E8
Vach = Vakh → Russia 60°45N 76°45E 214 C8
Vache, Î. à Haiti 18°2N 73°35W 321 C5
Väckelsång Sweden 56°37N 14°58E 163 H8
Vaclavské náměstí Prague, Czech Rep. 135 b2
Vacoas Mauritius 20°18S 57°29E 272 e
Vada India 19°39N 73°8E 244 E1
Vadakara India 11°35N 75°40E 245 J2
Vadaul India 19°2N 72°55E 130 A2
Väddö Sweden 60°0N 18°50E 162 D12
Vadehavet △ Denmark 55°20N 8°30E 163 J2
Väderstad Sweden 58°19N 14°55E 163 F8
Vadheim Norway 61°13N 5°49E 164 C2
Vadnagar India 23°47N 72°40E 242 H5
Vado Ligure Italy 44°17N 8°26E 198 D5
Vadodara India 22°20N 73°10E 242 H5
Vadsø Norway 70°3N 29°50E 160 A23
Vadstena Sweden 58°28N 14°54E 163 F8
Vaduj India 17°36N 74°27E 244 F2
Vaduz Liech. 47°8N 9°31E 179 H5
Vadvetjåkka △ Sweden 68°30N 18°28E 160 B18
Værlandet Norway 61°18N 4°44E 164 C1
Værøy Norway 67°40N 12°40E 160 C15
Vagalat Albania 39°44N 20°8E 206 B10
Vågåmo Norway 61°52N 9°6E 164 C6
Vágar Færoe Is. 62°5N 7°15W 160 E9
Vaggeryd Sweden 57°30N 14°10E 163 G8
Vagharshapat = Ejmiatsin Armenia 40°12N 44°19E 191 K7
Vaghena Solomon Is. 7°25S 157°45E 287 L9
Vaghia Greece 38°19N 23°11E 204 C5
Vagia, Akra Greece 36°15N 28°11E 206 E12
Vagney France 48°1N 6°43E 173 D13
Vagnhärad Sweden 58°57N 17°33E 163 F11
Vagos Portugal 40°33N 8°42W 194 E2
Vågsfjorden Norway 68°50N 16°50E 160 B17
Váh → Slovak Rep. 47°43N 18°7E 181 D11
Vahitahi French Polynesia 18°44S 138°52W 289 f
Vahsel B. Antarctica 75°0S 35°0W 151 D1
Váhtjer = Gällivare Sweden 67°9N 20°40E 160 C19
Vaï Greece 35°15N 26°18E 207 E7
Vaiaku = Fongafale Tuvalu 8°31S 179°13E 277 B14
Vaiea Cook Is. 19°6S 169°54W 289 g
Vaigai → India 9°15N 79°10E 245 K4
Vaiges France 48°2N 0°30W 172 D6
Vaihingen Germany 48°54N 8°57E 179 G4
Vaihiria, L. Tahiti 17°40S 149°25W 289 e
Vaijapur India 19°58N 74°45E 244 E2
Vaikam India 9°45N 76°25E 245 K3
Vail U.S.A. 39°40N 106°20W 304 G10
Vailala → Papua N. G. 7°57S 145°25E 286 D3
Vailhau, Récif Comoros Is. 11°48S 43°4E 272 a
Vailly-sur-Aisne France 49°24N 3°31E 173 C10
Vailoatai Amer. Samoa 14°21S 170°46W 302 f
Vaippar → India 9°0N 78°25E 245 K4
Vairaatea French Polynesia 19°19S 139°20W 289 f
Vairao Tahiti 17°47S 149°17W 289 e
Vaires-sur-Marne France 48°52N 2°38E 134 A4
Vaisali → India 26°28N 78°53E 243 F8
Vaison-la-Romaine France 44°14N 5°4E 175 D9
Vaitogi Amer. Samoa 14°24S 170°44W 302 f
Vaitupu Pac. Oc. 7°28S 178°41E 277 B14
Vajpur India 21°24N 73°17E 244 D1
Vakaga □ C.A.R. 10°0N 22°30E 264 A4
Vakaga → C.A.R. 9°48N 21°32E 264 A4
Vakarai Sri Lanka 8°8N 81°26E 245 K5
Vakarel Bulgaria 42°35N 23°40E 202 D7
Vakfikebir Turkey 41°2N 39°17E 213 B8
Vakh → Russia 60°45N 76°45E 214 C8
Vakhtan Russia 57°53N 46°47E 190 B8
Vaksdal Norway 60°29N 5°45E 164 D2
Vakuta I. Papua N. G. 8°51S 151°10E 286 E6
Vál Hungary 47°22N 18°40E 182 C3
Val Camónica Italy 45°57N 10°17E 198 C7
Val-de-Marne □ France 48°45N 2°28E 173 D9
Val-d'Isère France 45°27N 6°59E 175 C10
Val-d'Oise □ France 49°5N 2°10E 173 C9
Val-d'Or Canada 48°7N 77°47W 298 C4
Val Grande △ Italy 46°3N 8°25E 198 B5
Val Marie Canada 49°15N 107°45W 297 D7
Val Thorens France 45°20N 6°33E 175 C10
Valaam Russia 61°22N 30°57E 188 B6
Valadares Portugal 41°5N 8°38W 194 D2
Valahia Romania 44°35N 25°0E 183 F9
Valaichenai Sri Lanka 7°54N 81°32E 245 L5
Valais □ Switz. 46°12N 7°45E 179 J3
Valais, Alpes du Switz. 46°5N 7°35E 179 J3
Valandovo Macedonia 41°19N 22°34E 202 E6
Valašské Meziříčí Czech Rep. 49°29N 17°59E 181 B10
Valatie U.S.A. 42°24N 73°40W 313 D11
Valaxa Greece 38°50N 24°29E 204 C6
Vålberg Sweden 59°23N 13°11E 162 E7
Valbo Sweden 60°40N 17°0E 162 D10
Valbondione Italy 46°2N 10°1E 198 B7
Valby Denmark 55°39N 12°29E 118 B2
Valcamonica = Val Camónica Italy 45°57N 10°17E 198 C7
Vălcani Romania 46°0N 20°26E 182 D5
Valcannuta Italy 41°52N 12°25E 136 B1
Vâlcea □ Romania 45°0N 24°10E 183 F9
Valcheta Argentina 40°40S 66°8W 336 B3
Valdagno Italy 45°39N 11°18E 199 C8
Valdahon France 47°8N 6°21E 173 E13
Valdai Hills = Valdayskaya Vozvyshennost Russia 57°0N 33°30E 188 D7
Valday Russia 57°58N 33°9E 188 D7
Valdayskaya Vozvyshennost Russia 57°0N 33°30E 188 D7
Valdaysky △ Russia 57°30N 33°0E 188 D7
Valdeazogues → Spain 38°45N 4°55W 195 G6
Valdecañas, Embalse de Spain 39°45N 5°25W 194 F5
Valdelatas Spain 40°31N 3°42W 127 A1
Valdemarsvik Sweden 58°14N 16°40E 163 F10
Valdemoro Spain 40°12N 3°40W 194 E7
Valdepeñas Spain 38°43N 3°25W 195 G7
Valderaduey → Spain 41°31N 5°42W 194 D5
Valdérice Italy 38°4N 12°37E 200 D5
Valderrobres Spain 40°53N 0°9E 196 E5
Valdés, Pen. Argentina 42°30S 63°45W 336 B4
Valdez Ecuador 1°15N 79°0W 328 C2
Valdez Alaska, U.S.A. 61°7N 146°16W 303 F11
Valdgeym = Dobropole Ukraine 48°25N 37°2E 189 H9
Valdivia Chile 39°50S 73°14W 336 A2
Valdivia Colombia 7°11N 75°27W 328 B2
Valdivia Abyssal Plain S. Ocean 62°30S 70°0E 151 C6
Valdobbiádene Italy 45°54N 12°0E 199 C8
Valdosta U.S.A. 30°50N 83°17W 316 E6

Valdoviño = Aviño *Spain* 43°36N 8°8W **194** B2
Valdres *Norway* 61°5N 9°5E **164** C6
Vale *Georgia* 41°30N 42°58E **191** K6
Vale *Oreg., U.S.A.* 43°59N 117°15W **304** E5
Vale of Glamorgan □ *U.K.* 51°28N 3°25W **169** F4
Valea lui Mihai *Romania* 47°32N 22°11E **182** C7
Valea Mărului *Romania* 45°49N 27°42E **183** E12
Valemount *Canada* 52°50N 119°15W **296** C5
Valença = Valença do Piauí *Brazil* 6°20S 41°45W **332** C3
Valença *Brazil* 13°20S 39°5W **333** D4
Valença *Portugal* 42°1N 8°34W **194** C2
Valença do Piauí *Brazil* 6°20S 41°45W **332** C3
Valençay *France* 47°9N 1°34E **173** E8
Valence *France* 44°57N 4°54E **175** D8
Valence d'Agen *France* 44°6N 0°53E **174** D4
Valencia *Phil.* 7°57N 125°3E **233** H5
Valencia *Spain* 39°27N 0°23W **197** F4
Valencia *Trin. & Tob.* 10°39N 61°11W **323** t
Valencia *N. Mex., U.S.A.* 34°48N 106°43W **305** J10
Valencia *Venezuela* 10°11N 68°0W **328** A4
Valencia □ *Spain* 39°20N 0°40W **197** F4
Valencia ✕ (VLC) *Spain* 39°20N 0°26W **197** F4
Valencia, G. de *Spain* 39°30N 0°20E **197** F5
Valencia de Alcántara *Spain* 39°25N 7°14W **195** F3
Valencia de Don Juan *Spain* 42°17N 5°31W **194** C5
Valencia I. *Ireland* 51°54N 10°22W **166** E1
Valenciennes *France* 50°20N 3°34E **173** B10
Văleni *Romania* 44°15N 24°45E **183** F9
Vălenii de Munte *Romania* 45°11N 26°2E **183** E11
Valensole *France* 43°50N 5°59E **175** E9
Valentigney *France* 47°27N 6°51E **173** E13
Valentim, Sa. do *Brazil* 6°0S 43°30W **332** C3
Valentin *Russia* 43°8N 134°17E **220** C7
Valentine *Nebr., U.S.A.* 42°52N 100°33W **308** D3
Valentine *Tex., U.S.A.* 30°35N 104°30W **314** F2
Valenton *France* 48°44N 2°27E **134** B3
Valenza *Italy* 45°1N 8°38E **198** C5
Våler *Hedmark, Norway* 60°41N 11°50E **164** D8
Våler *Østfold, Norway* 59°29N 10°51E **164** E7
Valera *Piemonte, Italy* 45°33N 9°3E **128** A1
Valera *Venezuela* 9°19N 70°37W **328** B3
Valesdir *Vanuatu* 16°47S 168°10E **287** F6
Valestrand *Norway* 59°40N 5°26E **164** E2
Valga *Estonia* 57°47N 26°2E **188** D4
Valguarnera Caropepe *Italy* 37°30N 14°23E **201** E7
Valier *U.S.A.* 48°18N 112°16W **304** B7
Valinco, G. de *France* 41°40N 8°52E **175** G12
Valjevo *Serbia* 44°18N 19°53E **202** B3
Valka *Latvia* 57°46N 26°3E **188** D3
Valkeakoski *Finland* 61°16N 24°2E **188** B2
Valkenswaard *Neths.* 51°21N 5°29E **170** C5
Vall de Uxó = La Vall d'Uixó *Spain* 39°49N 0°15W **196** F4
Valla *Sweden* 59°2N 16°20E **162** E10
Valladolid *Yucatán, Mexico* 20°41N 88°12W **319** C7
Valladolid *Spain* 41°38N 4°43W **194** D6
Valladolid □ *Spain* 41°38N 4°43W **194** D6
Vallata *Italy* 41°2N 15°15E **201** A8
Vallcarca *Spain* 41°25N 2°9E **114** A1
Valldemossa *Spain* 39°43N 2°37E **206** B3
Valldoreix *Spain* 41°27N 2°3E **114** A1
Valle *Norway* 59°13N 7°33E **164** E4
Valle d'Aosta □ *Italy* 45°45N 7°15E **198** C4
Valle de la Pascua *Venezuela* 9°13N 66°0W **328** B4
Valle de las Palmas *Mexico* 32°20N 116°43W **307** N10
Valle de Santiago *Mexico* 20°23N 101°12W **318** C4
Valle de Villaverde *Spain* 43°15N 3°15W **194** B7
Valle de Zaragoza *Mexico* 27°25N 105°50W **318** B3
Valle del Cauca □ *Colombia* 3°45N 76°30W **328** C2
Valle del Ticino ⌓ *Italy* 45°22N 9°0E **198** C6
Valle Fértil, Sierra del *Argentina* 30°20S 68°0W **334** C2
Valle Gran Rey *Canary Is.* 28°5N 17°20W **153** e1
Valle Hermoso *Mexico* 25°35N 97°40W **319** B5
Valle Nacional *Mexico* 17°47N 96°18W **319** D5
Vallecas *Spain* 40°22N 3°37W **127** B2
Vallecas, Cumbres de *Spain* 40°20N 3°33W **127** B2
Valledupar *Colombia* 10°29N 73°15W **328** A3
Vallée de Mai ⌓ *Seychelles* 4°19S 55°44E **272** c
Vallée du Bandama □ *Ivory C.* 8°0N 5°0W **262** D3
Vallegrande *Bolivia* 18°30S 64°10W **331** D5
Vallehermoso *Canary Is.* 28°10N 17°15W **153** e1
Vallejo *U.S.A.* 38°7N 122°14W **306** G4
Vallenar *Chile* 28°30S 70°50W **334** B1
Vallensbæk *Denmark* 55°38N 12°21E **118** B2
Vallensbæk Strand *Denmark* 55°36N 12°23E **118** B2
Vallentuna *Sweden* 59°32N 18°5E **162** E12
Vallentunasjön *Sweden* 59°27N 18°1E **139** A2
Valleranello *Italy* 41°46N 12°29E **136** C1
Valleraugue *France* 44°6N 3°39E **174** D7
Vallet *France* 47°10N 1°15W **172** E5
Valletta *Malta* 35°54N 14°31E **206** F8
Valley, The *Anguilla* 18°13N 63°4W **322** a
Valley Center *U.S.A.* 33°13N 117°2W **307** M9
Valley City *U.S.A.* 46°55N 98°0W **308** B5
Valley Falls *Oreg., U.S.A.* 42°29N 120°17W **304** E3
Valley Falls *R.I., U.S.A.* 41°54N 71°24W **313** E13
Valley Junction = West Des Moines *U.S.A.* 41°35N 93°43W **310** C3
Valley of Flowers △ *India* 30°50N 79°40E **243** D8
Valley of the Kings *Egypt* 25°41N 32°34E **256** B3
Valley Springs *U.S.A.* 38°12N 120°50W **306** G6
Valley Station *U.S.A.* 38°6N 85°52W **311** F11
Valley View *U.S.A.* 40°39N 76°33W **313** F8
Valley Wells *U.S.A.* 35°27N 115°46W **307** K11
Valleyview *Canada* 55°5N 117°17W **296** B5
Valli di Comácchio *Italy* 44°40N 12°15E **199** D9
Vallimanca, Arroyo *Argentina* 35°40S 59°10W **334** D4
Vallisaari *Finland* 60°7N 25°0E **121** C3
Vallo della Lucánia *Italy* 40°14N 15°16E **201** B8
Vallon-Pont-d'Arc *France* 44°24N 4°24E **175** D8
Vallorbe *Switz.* 46°42N 6°20E **179** J2
Valls *Spain* 41°18N 1°15E **196** D6
Vallvidrera *Spain* 41°24N 2°6E **114** A1
Vallvik *Sweden* 61°11N 17°10E **162** C11
Valmaseda = Balmaseda *Spain* 43°11N 3°12W **196** B1
Valmeyer *U.S.A.* 38°18N 90°19W **310** F6
Valmiera *Latvia* 57°37N 25°29E **188** D3
Valnera *Spain* 43°9N 3°40W **194** B7
Valognes *France* 49°30N 1°28W **172** C5
Valona = Vlorë *Albania* 40°32N 19°28E **202** F3
Valongo *Portugal* 41°8N 8°30W **194** D2
Valozhyn *Belarus* 54°3N 26°30E **177** A14
Valpaços *Portugal* 41°36N 7°17W **194** D3
Valparai *India* 10°22N 76°58E **245** J3
Valparaíso *Chile* 33°2S 71°40W **334** C1
Valparaíso *Zacatecas, Mexico* 22°46N 103°34W **318** C4
Valparaiso *Fla., U.S.A.* 30°29N 86°30W **317** E3
Valparaiso *Ind., U.S.A.* 41°28N 87°4W **311** C9
Valparaíso □ *Chile* 33°2S 71°40W **334** C1
Valpovo *Croatia* 45°39N 18°25E **182** E3
Valpoy *India* 15°32N 74°8E **245** G2
Valréas *France* 44°24N 5°0E **175** D9
Vals *Switz.* 46°39N 9°11E **179** J5
Vals → *S. Africa* 27°23S 26°30E **270** C4
Vals, Tanjung *Indonesia* 8°26S 137°25E **231** F9
Vals-les-Bains *France* 44°42N 4°24E **175** D8
Valsad *India* 20°40N 72°58E **244** D1
Valsamata *Greece* 38°10N 20°36E **207** C2
Valtellina *Italy* 46°11N 9°55E **198** B6
Valþjofsstaður *Iceland* 65°1N 14°59W **155** B12
Valti *Greece* 38°27N 21°7E **207** C3
Valuyki *Russia* 50°10N 38°5E **189** G10
Valverde *Canary Is.* 27°48N 17°55W **153** e1
Valverde del Camino *Spain* 37°35N 6°47W **195** H4
Valverde del Fresno *Spain* 40°15N 6°51W **194** E4
Valvidrera → *Spain* 41°25N 2°0E **114** A1
Vama *Romania* 47°34N 25°42E **183** C10
Vambori *India* 19°17N 74°44E **244** E2
Vamdrup *Denmark* 55°25N 9°17E **163** J3
Våmhus *Sweden* 61°7N 14°29E **162** C8
Vamizi, I. *Mozam.* 11°2S 40°40E **269** E5
Vammala = Sastamala *Finland* 61°20N 22°54E **188** B2
Vamos *Greece* 35°24N 24°13E **207** E5
Vamsadhara → *India* 18°21N 84°8E **244** E7
Van *Turkey* 38°30N 43°20E **213** C10
Van □ *Turkey* 38°30N 43°20E **213** C10
Van, L. = Van Gölü *Turkey* 38°30N 43°0E **213** C10
Van Alstyne *U.S.A.* 33°25N 96°35W **314** E6
Van Blommestein Meer *Suriname* 4°45N 55°5W **329** C6
Van Buren = Kettering *U.S.A.* 39°41N 84°10W **311** E12
Van Buren *N.B., Canada* 47°10N 67°55W **299** C6
Van Buren *Ark., U.S.A.* 35°26N 94°21W **314** D7
Van Buren *Maine, U.S.A.* 47°10N 67°58W **309** B20
Van Buren *Mo., U.S.A.* 37°0N 91°1W **308** G8
Van Canh *Vietnam* 13°37N 109°0E **236** F7
Van Diemen, C. *N. Terr., Australia* 11°9S 130°24E **278** B5
Van Diemen, C. *Queens., Australia* 16°30S 139°46E **280** B2
Van Diemen G. *Australia* 11°45S 132°0E **278** B5
Van Gogh Museum *Amsterdam, Neths.* **112** c1
Van Gölü *Turkey* 38°30N 43°0E **213** C10
Van Horn *U.S.A.* 31°3N 104°50W **314** F2
Van Horne *U.S.A.* 42°1N 92°5W **310** B4
Van Meter *U.S.A.* 41°32N 93°57W **310** C3
Van Ninh *Vietnam* 12°42N 109°14E **236** F7
Van Rees, Pegunungan *Indonesia* 2°35S 138°15E **231** E9
Van Tivu *India* 8°51N 78°15E **245** K4
Van Wert *U.S.A.* 40°52N 84°35W **311** D12
Van Yen *Vietnam* 21°4N 104°42E **228** G5
Van Zylsrus *S. Africa* 26°52S 22°4E **270** C3
Vanadzor *Armenia* 40°48N 44°30E **191** K7
Vanak *Iran* 35°45N 51°23E **141** A2
Vanavana *French Polynesia* 20°47S 139°9W **289** f
Vanavara *Russia* 60°22N 102°16E **215** C11
Vanceburg *U.S.A.* 38°36N 83°19W **311** F13
Vancouver *B.C., Canada* 49°15N 123°7W **306** A3
Vancouver *Wash., U.S.A.* 45°38N 122°40W **306** E4
Vancouver, C. *Australia* 35°2S 118°11E **279** G2
Vancouver, Mt. *U.S.A.* 60°20N 139°41W **303** F13
Vancouver I. *Canada* 49°50N 126°0W **306** B2
Vancouver Int. ✕ (YVR) *Canada* 49°10N 123°10W **306** A3
Vanda = Vantaa *Finland* 60°18N 24°56E **121** B2
Vandalia *Ill., U.S.A.* 38°58N 89°6W **310** F7
Vandalia *Mo., U.S.A.* 39°19N 91°29W **310** E5
Vandalia *Ohio, U.S.A.* 39°54N 84°12W **311** E12
Vandavasi *India* 12°30N 79°30E **245** H4
Vandellòs *Spain* 41°0N 0°55E **196** E5
Vandeloos B. *Sri Lanka* 8°0N 81°45E **245** L5
Vandenberg Village *U.S.A.* 34°43N 120°28W **307** L6
Vandergrift *U.S.A.* 40°36N 79°34W **312** F5
Vanderhoof *Canada* 54°0N 124°0W **296** C4
Vanderkloof Dam *S. Africa* 30°4S 24°40E **270** D3
Vanderlin I. *Australia* 15°44S 137°2E **280** B2
Vänern *Sweden* 58°47N 13°30E **163** F7
Vänersborg *Sweden* 58°26N 12°19E **163** F6
Vang *Norway* 61°7N 8°34E **164** C5
Vang Vieng *Laos* 18°58N 102°32E **236** C4
Vanga *Kenya* 4°35S 39°12E **268** C4
Vangaindrano *Madag.* 23°21S 47°36E **272** C2
Vänge *Sweden* 59°50N 17°20E **162** E11
Vangede *Denmark* 55°45N 12°30E **118** A3
Vangsnes *Norway* 61°9N 6°39E **164** C3
Vanguard *Canada* 49°55N 107°20W **297** D7
Vangunu *Solomon Is.* 8°40S 158°5E **287** M10
Vanikoro *Pac. Oc.* 11°39S 166°54E **277** C12
Vaniköy *Turkey* 41°3N 29°3E **122** B2
Vanimo *Papua N. G.* 2°42S 141°21E **286** B1
Vanino *Russia* 48°50N 140°5E **215** E15
Vanivilasa Sagara *India* 13°45N 76°30E **245** H3
Vaniyambadi *India* 12°46N 78°44E **245** H4
Vânju Mare *Romania* 44°25N 22°52E **182** F7
Vankleek Hill *Canada* 45°32N 74°40W **313** A10
Vanløse *Denmark* 55°41N 12°28E **118** A2
Vännäs *Sweden* 63°58N 19°48E **160** E18
Vannes *France* 47°40N 2°47W **172** E4
Vannøya *Norway* 70°6N 19°50E **160** A18
Vanoise, Massif de la *France* 45°25N 6°40E **175** C10
Vanrhynsdorp *S. Africa* 31°36S 18°44E **270** D2
Vansada *India* 20°47N 73°25E **244** D1
Vansbro *Sweden* 60°32N 14°15E **162** D8
Vanse *Norway* 58°6N 6°41E **164** F3
Vansittart B. *Australia* 14°3S 126°17E **278** B4
Vansittart I. *Canada* 65°50N 84°0W **295** D15
Vantaa *Finland* 60°18N 24°56E **121** B2
Vantaankoski *Finland* 60°18N 24°50E **121** B2
Vantaanpuisto *Finland* 60°18N 24°53E **121** B2
Vanua Balavu *Fiji* 17°12S 178°55W **287** A3
Vanua Lava *Vanuatu* 13°50S 167°30E **287** C5
Vanua Levu *Fiji* 16°33S 179°15E **287** A2
Vanua Vatu *Fiji* 18°22S 179°15W **287** B3
Vanuatu ■ *Pac. Oc.* 15°0S 168°0E **287** E6
Vanves *France* 48°49N 2°17E **134** B2
Vanwyksvlei *S. Africa* 30°18S 21°49E **270** D3
Vao *N. Cal.* 22°39S 167°32E **288** d
Vapi *India* 20°22N 72°54E **244** D1
Vapnyarka *Ukraine* 48°32N 28°45E **183** B13
Var □ *France* 43°27N 6°18E **175** E10
Var → *France* 43°39N 7°12E **175** E11
Vara *Sweden* 58°16N 12°55E **163** F6
Vara, Pico da *Azores* 37°48N 25°13W **153** d3
Varada → *India* 15°0N 75°40E **245** G2
Varades *France* 47°25N 1°1W **172** E5
Varáita → *Italy* 44°9N 7°53E **198** D4
Varaldsøy *Norway* 60°6N 5°59E **164** D2
Varalé *Ivory C.* 9°40N 3°17W **262** D4
Varallo *Italy* 45°49N 8°15E **198** C5
Varāmīn *Iran* 35°20N 51°39E **247** C6
Varāmīn □ *Iran* 35°18N 51°35E **247** B6
Varanasi *India* 25°22N 83°0E **243** G10
Varangerfjorden *Norway* 70°3N 29°25E **160** A23
Varangerhalvøya *Norway* 70°25N 29°30E **160** A23
Varano, Lago di *Italy* 41°53N 15°45E **199** G12
Varaždin *Croatia* 46°20N 16°20E **199** B13
Varazze *Italy* 44°22N 8°34E **198** D5
Varberg *Sweden* 57°6N 12°20E **163** G6
Varcar Vakuf = Mrkonjić Grad *Bos.-H.* 44°26N 17°4E **182** F2
Vardak □ *Afghan.* 34°0N 68°0E **240** B3
Vardar = Axios → *Greece* 40°57N 22°35E **202** F6
Varde *Denmark* 55°38N 8°29E **163** J2
Varde Å → *Denmark* 55°35N 8°19E **163** J2
Vardenis *Armenia* 40°10N 45°43E **191** K7
Vardø *Norway* 70°23N 31°5E **160** A24
Varedo *Italy* 45°35N 9°8E **128** A1
Varel *Germany* 53°23N 8°8E **178** B4
Varella, Mui = Nay, Mui *Vietnam* 12°54N 109°26E **236** F7
Varėna *Lithuania* 54°12N 24°30E **188** E3
Varennes-sur-Allier *France* 46°19N 3°24E **173** F10
Varennes-Vauzelles *France* 47°3N 3°9E **173** E10
Vareš *Bos.-H.* 44°12N 18°23E **182** F3
Varese *Italy* 45°48N 8°50E **198** C5
Vârfurile *Romania* 46°19N 22°31E **182** D7
Vårgårda *Sweden* 58°2N 12°49E **163** F6
Vargem Bonita *Brazil* 20°20S 46°22W **333** F2
Vargem Grande *Brazil* 3°33S 43°56W **332** B3
Varginha *Brazil* 21°33S 45°25W **335** A6
Vargön *Sweden* 58°22N 12°20E **163** F6
Varhaug *Norway* 58°37N 5°41E **164** F2
Vari *Greece* 38°24N 20°35E **207** C2
Varillas *Chile* 24°0S 70°10W **334** A1
Varkaus *Finland* 62°19N 27°50E **188** A4
Varkiza *Greece* 37°50N 23°49E **112** C2
Värmdölandet *Sweden* 59°20N 18°33E **162** E12
Värmeln *Sweden* 59°35N 12°54E **162** E6
Värmlands län □ *Sweden* 60°0N 13°20E **162** E6
Värmlandsbro *Sweden* 59°11N 13°0E **162** E7
Varna *Bulgaria* 43°13N 27°56E **203** C11
Varna □ *Bulgaria* 43°20N 27°30E **203** C11
Varna → *India* 16°48N 74°32E **244** F2
Värnamo *Sweden* 57°10N 14°3E **163** G8
Várnjárga = Varangerhalvøya *Norway* 70°25N 29°30E **160** A23
Varnsdorf *Czech Rep.* 50°55N 14°35E **180** A7
Varnville *U.S.A.* 32°51N 81°5W **316** C8
Várpalota *Hungary* 47°12N 18°8E **182** C3
Vars *Ont., Canada* 45°21N 75°21W **313** A9
Vars *Hautes-Alpes, France* 44°37N 6°42E **175** D10
Vartdal *Norway* 62°20N 6°8E **164** B3
Vartiokylä *Finland* 60°13N 25°6E **121** B3
Vartiosaari *Finland* 60°11N 25°5E **121** B3
Varto *Turkey* 39°10N 41°27E **213** C9
Varvarin *Serbia* 43°43N 21°20E **202** C5
Varysburg *U.S.A.* 42°46N 78°19W **312** D6
Varzaneh *Iran* 32°25N 52°40E **247** C7
Varzaqān *Iran* 38°29N 46°40E **213** C12
Várzea Alegre *Brazil* 6°47S 39°17W **332** C4
Várzea da Palma *Brazil* 17°36S 44°44W **333** E3
Várzea Grande *Brazil* 15°39S 56°8W **331** D6
Varzi *Italy* 44°49N 9°12E **198** D6
Varzo *Italy* 46°12N 8°15E **198** B5
Varzy *France* 47°22N 3°20E **173** E10
Vas □ *Hungary* 47°10N 16°55E **182** C1
Vasa = Vaasa *Finland* 63°6N 21°38E **160** E19
Vasa Barris → *Brazil* 11°10S 37°10W **332** D4
Vasai-Virar *India* 19°28N 72°48E **244** E1
Vasamuseet *Stockholm, Sweden* **139** b3
Vásárosnamény *Hungary* 48°9N 22°19E **182** B7
Vascão → *Portugal* 37°31N 7°31W **195** H3
Vașcău *Romania* 46°28N 22°30E **182** D7
Vasco *S. Africa* 33°54S 18°34E **118** A2
Vascongadas = País Vasco □ *Spain* 42°50N 2°45W **196** C2
Vasfenārd *Iran* 35°38N 51°20E **141** B2
Vashi *India* 19°4N 72°59E **130** A2
Vāshīr *Afghan.* 32°16N 63°51E **240** B1
Vashkivtsi *Ukraine* 48°23N 25°31E **183** B10
Vasht = Khāsh *Iran* 28°15N 61°15E **240** C1
Vasilevichi *Belarus* 52°15N 29°50E **177** B16
Vasiliki *Greece* 38°37N 20°36E **207** B2
Vasiliko = Michurin *Bulgaria* 42°9N 27°51E **203** D11
Vasiliko *Greece* 38°25N 23°40E **204** C5
Vasilikos *Greece* 37°43N 20°59E **207** D2
Vasilkov = Vasylkiv *Ukraine* 50°7N 30°15E **177** C16
Vasilyevskiy, Ostrov *Russia* 59°55N 30°16E **137** B1
Vasilyova Sloboda = Chkolovsk *Russia* 56°50N 43°10E **190** B6
Vasilyovo = Chkolovsk *Russia* 56°50N 43°10E **190** B6
Väskinde *Sweden* 57°40N 18°20E **163** G10
Vaslui *Romania* 46°38N 27°42E **183** D12
Vaslui □ *Romania* 46°30N 27°45E **183** D12
Väsman *Sweden* 60°9N 15°5E **162** D9
Vassar *Man., Canada* 49°10N 95°55W **297** D9
Vassar *Mich., U.S.A.* 43°22N 83°35W **309** D12
Vassfaret *Norway* 60°38N 9°28E **164** D6
Västerås *Sweden* 59°37N 16°38E **162** E10
Västerbotten *Sweden* 64°36N 20°4E **160** D19
Västerdalälven → *Sweden* 60°30N 15°7E **162** D8
Västergötland *Sweden* 58°0N 13°10E **163** F7
Västerhaninge *Sweden* 59°7N 18°6E **162** E12
Västervik *Sweden* 57°43N 16°33E **163** G10
Västmanland *Sweden* 59°45N 16°20E **161** G17
Västmanlands län □ *Sweden* 59°45N 16°20E **162** E10
Vasto *Italy* 42°8N 14°40E **199** F11
Västra Götalands Län □ *Sweden* 58°0N 13°0E **163** F6
Vasvár *Hungary* 47°3N 16°47E **182** C1
Vasylivka *Ukraine* 45°38N 28°50E **183** E13
Vasylkiv *Ukraine* 50°7N 30°15E **177** C16
Vat Phou *Laos* 14°51N 105°49E **236** E5
Vatan *France* 47°4N 1°50E **173** E8
Vaté = Efate, I. *Vanuatu* 17°40S 168°25E **287** G6
Vatersay *U.K.* 56°55N 7°32W **167** E1
Vathi *Greece* 38°41N 20°47E **207** B2
Vathia *Greece* 36°29N 22°29E **204** E4
Vati *Greece* 36°3N 27°53E **206** E11
Vatia *Amer. Samoa* 14°15S 170°40W **302** f
Vatican City ■ *Europe* 41°54N 12°27E **136** B1
Vaticano, C. *Italy* 38°37N 15°50E **201** D8
Vatili *Cyprus* 35°6N 33°40E **207** E9
Vatin *Serbia* 45°12N 21°20E **182** E6
Vatiu = Atiu *Cook Is.* 20°0S 158°10W **289** J12
Vatnajökull *Iceland* 64°30N 16°48W **155** C10
Vatnajökull △ *Iceland* 64°24N 16°48W **155** C10
Vatnås *Norway* 59°58N 9°37E **164** E6
Vatnsfjörður *Iceland* 65°56N 22°30W **155** B4
Vato *Sweden* 59°50N 19°0E **162** E12
Vatolakkos *Greece* 35°27N 23°53E **207** E4
Vatoloha *Madag.* 17°52S 47°48E **272** B2
Vatomandry *Madag.* 19°20S 48°59E **272** B2
Vatra-Dornei *Romania* 47°22N 25°22E **183** C10
Vatrak → *India* 23°9N 73°2E **242** H5
Vattaru Atoll *Maldives* 3°16N 73°25E **272** d
Vättern *Sweden* 58°25N 14°30E **163** F8
Vatu Vara *Fiji* 17°26S 179°31W **287** A3
Vatulele *Fiji* 18°33S 177°37E **287** B1
Vauclin, Mt. du *Martinique* 14°33N 60°53W **322** j
Vauclin, Pte. de *Martinique* 14°34N 60°49W **322** j
Vaucluse *Australia* 33°51S 151°15E **139** B2
Vaucluse □ *France* 43°50N 5°20E **175** E9
Vaucluse House *Australia* 33°51S 151°15E **139** B2
Vaucouleurs *France* 48°37N 5°40E **173** D12
Vaucresson *France* 48°50N 2°9E **134** A1
Vaud □ *Switz.* 46°35N 6°30E **179** J2
Vaudreuil-Dorion *Canada* 45°23N 74°3W **313** A10
Vaughan *Canada* 43°50N 79°32W **141** A1
Vaughn *Mont., U.S.A.* 47°33N 111°33W **304** C8
Vaughn *N. Mex., U.S.A.* 34°36N 105°13W **305** J11
Vauhallan *France* 48°44N 2°12E **134** B2
Vaujours *France* 48°56N 2°34E **134** A4
Vaujours L. *Canada* 55°27N 74°15W **298** A5
Vaupés = Uaupés → *Brazil* 0°2N 67°16W **328** C4
Vaupés □ *Colombia* 1°0N 71°0W **328** C3
Vauvert *France* 43°42N 4°17E **175** E8
Vauxhall *Alta., Canada* 50°5N 112°9W **296** C6
Vauxhall *London, U.K.* **125** c4
Vav *India* 24°22N 71°31E **242** G4
Vavatenina *Madag.* 17°28S 49°12E **272** B2
Vava'u *Tonga* 18°36S 174°0W **287** P14
Vava'u Group *Tonga* 18°40S 174°0W **287** P14
Vavoua *Ivory C.* 7°23N 6°29W **262** D3
Vavuniya *Sri Lanka* 8°45N 80°30E **245** K5
Vawkavysk *Belarus* 53°9N 24°30E **177** B13
Vaxholm *Sweden* 59°25N 18°20E **162** E12
Växjö *Sweden* 56°52N 14°50E **163** H8
Våxtorp *Sweden* 56°25N 13°8E **163** H7
Vayalpad *India* 13°39N 78°38E **245** H4
Vayenga = Severomorsk *Russia* 69°5N 33°27E **160** B25
Vaygach, Ostrov *Russia* 70°0N 60°0E **214** C7
Veadeiros *Brazil* 14°7S 47°31W **333** D2
Veaikevárri = Svappavaara *Sweden* 67°40N 21°3E **160** C19
Vechelde *Germany* 52°16N 10°22E **178** C6
Vechta *Germany* 52°44N 8°17E **178** C4
Vechte → *Neths.* 52°34N 6°6E **170** B6
Vecsés *Hungary* 47°26N 19°19E **117** B3
Vedaranniyam *India* 10°25N 79°50E **245** J4
Vedavågen *Norway* 59°17N 5°12E **164** E2
Veddige *Sweden* 57°17N 12°20E **163** G6
Vedea → *Romania* 43°42N 25°41E **183** G10
Vedi *Armenia* 39°54N 44°43E **213** C11
Vedia *Argentina* 34°30S 61°31W **334** C3
Vedrette di Ries-Aurina ⌓ *Italy* 46°54N 12°5E **199** B9
Vedum *Sweden* 58°11N 13°0E **163** F7
Veedersburg *U.S.A.* 40°7N 87°16W **311** D9
Veendam *Neths.* 53°5N 6°52E **170** A6
Veenendaal *Neths.* 52°2N 5°34E **170** B5
Vefsna → *Norway* 65°48N 13°10E **160** D15
Vega *Nordland, Norway* 65°40N 11°55E **160** D14
Vega *Tex., U.S.A.* 35°15N 102°26W **314** D3
Vega Alta *Puerto Rico* 18°25N 66°20W **321** b
Vega Baja *Puerto Rico* 18°27N 66°23W **321** b
Vega de Ribadeo = Vegadeo *Spain* 43°27N 7°4W **194** B3
Vegadeo *Spain* 43°27N 7°4W **194** B3
Vegårshei *Norway* 58°44N 8°51E **164** F5
Vegas Verde = North Las Vegas *U.S.A.* 36°11N 115°7W **124** A1
Veggli *Norway* 60°3N 9°9E **164** D6
Veglia = Krk *Croatia* 45°8N 14°40E **199** C11
Vegoritida, L. *Greece* 40°45N 21°45E **202** F5
Vegreville *Canada* 53°30N 112°5W **296** C6
Veiholmen *Norway* 63°31N 7°58E **164** A4
Veimandu Channel *Maldives* 2°10N 73°20E **272** d
Veinge *Sweden* 56°33N 13°4E **163** H7
Veisiejai *Lithuania* 54°6N 23°42E **184** D10
Vejbystrand *Sweden* 56°19N 12°45E **163** H6
Vejen *Denmark* 55°30N 9°9E **163** J3
Vejer de la Frontera *Spain* 36°15N 5°59W **195** J5
Vejle *Denmark* 55°43N 9°30E **163** J3
Vejle Fjord *Denmark* 55°40N 9°50E **163** J3
Vela Luka *Croatia* 42°59N 16°44E **199** F13
Velachha *India* 21°26N 73°1E **244** D1
Velanai I. *Sri Lanka* 9°45N 79°45E **245** K4
Velas *Azores* 38°41N 28°13W **153** d1
Velas, C. *Costa Rica* 10°21N 85°52W **320** D2
Velasco, Sierra de *Argentina* 29°20S 67°10W **334** B2
Velay, Mts. du *France* 45°0N 3°40E **174** D7
Velbert *Germany* 51°20N 7°3E **178** D3
Velddrif *S. Africa* 32°42S 18°11E **270** D2
Velebit ⌓ *Croatia* 44°30N 15°15E **199** D12
Velebit Planina *Croatia* 44°50N 15°20E **199** D12
Velebitski Kanal *Croatia* 44°45N 14°55E **199** D11
Veleka → *Bulgaria* 42°4N 27°58E **203** D11
Veleň *Czech Rep.* 50°10N 14°33E **135** A3
Velencei-tó *Hungary* 47°13N 18°36E **182** C3
Velenje *Slovenia* 46°23N 15°8E **199** B12
Veles *Macedonia* 41°46N 21°47E **202** E5
Veleslavin *Czech Rep.* 50°5N 14°21E **135** B2
Velestino *Greece* 39°23N 22°43E **204** B4
Vélez *Colombia* 6°1N 73°41W **328** B3
Vélez-Málaga *Spain* 36°48N 4°5W **195** J6
Vélez Rubio *Spain* 37°41N 2°5W **197** H2
Velhas → *Brazil* 17°13S 44°49W **333** E3
Velika *Croatia* 45°27N 17°40E **182** E2
Velika Gorica *Croatia* 45°44N 16°5E **199** C13
Velika Kapela *Croatia* 45°10N 15°5E **199** C12
Velika Kikinda = Kikinda *Serbia* 45°50N 20°30E **182** E5
Velika Kladuša *Bos.-H.* 45°11N 15°48E **199** C12
Velika Kruša = Krushë e Madhe *Kosovo* 42°19N 20°39E **202** D4
Velika Morava → *Serbia* 44°43N 21°3E **202** B5
Velika Plana *Serbia* 44°20N 21°4E **202** B5
Velikaya → *Russia* 57°48N 28°10E **188** D5
Velikaya Kema *Russia* 45°30N 137°12E **220** B8
Velikaya Lepetikha *Ukraine* 47°2N 33°58E **189** J7
Velike Lašče *Slovenia* 45°49N 14°45E **199** C11
Veliki Jastrebac *Serbia* 43°25N 21°30E **202** C5
Veliki Kanal *Serbia* 45°45N 19°15E **182** E4
Veliki Popović *Serbia* 44°8N 21°18E **202** B5
Velikiy Ustyug *Russia* 60°47N 46°20E **186** B8
Velikiy Novgorod *Russia* 58°30N 31°25E **188** C6
Velikiye Luki *Russia* 56°25N 30°32E **188** D6
Veliko Gradište *Serbia* 44°46N 21°29E **202** B5
Veliko Tŭrnovo *Bulgaria* 43°5N 25°41E **203** C9
Veliko Tŭrnovo □ *Bulgaria* 43°5N 25°41E **203** C9
Velikonda Range *India* 14°45N 79°10E **245** G4
Vélingara *Kolda, Senegal* 13°12N 14°5W **262** C2
Vélingara *Louga, Senegal* 15°0N 14°40W **262** B2
Velingrad *Bulgaria* 42°4N 23°58E **202** D7
Velino, Mte. *Italy* 42°9N 13°23E **199** F10
Velizh *Russia* 55°36N 31°11E **188** E6
Vélizy-Villacoublay *France* 48°47N 2°11E **134** B2
Velka-Chuchle *Czech Rep.* 50°0N 14°23E **135** B2
Vel'ké Kapušany *Slovak Rep.* 48°34N 22°5E **181** C15
Velké Karlovice *Czech Rep.* 49°20N 18°17E **181** B11
Velké Meziříčí *Czech Rep.* 49°21N 16°1E **180** B9
Velké Přílepy *Czech Rep.* 50°9N 14°19E **135** B1
Vel'ký Javorník *Slovak Rep.* 49°19N 18°22E **181** B11
Vel'ký Krtíš *Slovak Rep.* 48°12N 19°21E **181** C12
Vel'ký Meder *Slovak Rep.* 47°52N 17°46E **181** D10
Vel'ký Tribeč *Slovak Rep.* 48°28N 18°15E **181** C11
Vella G. *Solomon Is.* 8°0S 156°50E **287** M9
Vella Lavella *Solomon Is.* 7°45S 156°40E **287** L9
Vellar → *India* 11°30N 79°36E **245** J4
Velletri *Italy* 41°41N 12°47E **200** A5
Vellinge *Sweden* 55°29N 13°2E **163** J6
Vellmar *Germany* 51°22N 9°28E **178** D5
Vellore *India* 12°57N 79°10E **245** H4
Velopoula *Greece* 36°55N 23°27E **204** E5
Velsk *Russia* 61°10N 42°0E **188** B11
Velten *Germany* 52°42N 13°10E **178** C9
Veluwezoom △ *Neths.* 52°5N 6°0E **170** B6
Velva *U.S.A.* 48°4N 100°56W **308** A3
Velvendos *Greece* 40°15N 22°6E **202** F6
Velyka Mykhaylivka *Ukraine* 47°4N 29°52E **183** C14
Velyki Luchky *Ukraine* 48°25N 22°34E **182** B7
Velykyy Bereznyy *Ukraine* 48°54N 22°28E **182** B7
Velykyy Bychkiv *Ukraine* 47°58N 24°1E **183** C9
Vemb *Denmark* 56°21N 8°21E **163** H2
Vembanad L. *India* 9°36N 76°15E **245** K3
Vemdalen *Sweden* 62°27N 13°51E **162** B7
Ven *Sweden* 55°55N 12°45E **163** J6
Venaco *France* 42°14N 9°11E **175** F13
Venado *Mexico* 22°56N 101°6W **318** C4
Venado Tuerto *Argentina* 33°50S 62°0W **334** C3
Venafro *Italy* 41°29N 14°2E **201** A7
Venarey-les-Laumes *France* 47°32N 4°26E **173** E11
Venaría *Italy* 45°8N 7°38E **198** C4
Venčane *Serbia* 44°24N 20°28E **202** B4
Vence *France* 43°43N 7°6E **175** E11
Venda Seca *Portugal* 38°46N 9°15W **126** A1
Vendas Novas *Portugal* 38°39N 8°27W **195** G2
Vendée □ *France* 46°50N 1°35W **172** F5
Vendée → *France* 46°20N 1°10W **172** F5
Vendéen, Bocage *France* 46°40N 1°20W **174** B2
Vendeuvre-sur-Barse *France* 48°14N 4°28E **173** D11
Vendicari ⌓ *Italy* 36°49N 15°6E **201** F8
Vendôme *France* 47°47N 1°3E **172** E8
Vendramin Calergi, Palazzo *Venice, Italy* **142** a2
Vendrell = El Vendrell *Spain* 41°10N 1°30E **196** D6
Vendsyssel *Denmark* 57°22N 10°0E **163** G4
Vendychany *Ukraine* 48°38N 27°48E **183** B12
Venelles *France* 43°35N 5°28E **175** E9
Véneta, L. *Italy* 45°23N 12°25E **199** C9
Venetian Islands *U.S.A.* 25°47N 80°9W **129** D3
Venetie *U.S.A.* 67°1N 146°25W **303** C11
Véneto □ *Italy* 45°30N 12°0E **199** C9
Venev *Russia* 54°22N 38°17E **188** E10
Venézia *Italy* 45°27N 12°21E **199** C9
Venézia, G. di *Italy* 45°15N 13°0E **199** C10
Venézia, Palazzo *Rome, Italy* **136** c2
Venézia Lido *Italy* 45°25N 12°22E **199** C9
Venézia Tridentina = Trentino-Alto Adige □ *Italy* 46°30N 11°20E **199** B8
Venezuela ■ *S. Amer.* 8°0N 66°0W **328** B4
Venezuela, G. de *Venezuela* 11°30N 71°0W **328** A3
Venezuelan Basin *Cent. Amer.* 14°0N 68°0W **321** C6
Vengurla *India* 15°53N 73°45E **245** G1
Vengurla Rocks *India* 15°55N 73°22E **245** G1
Venice = Venézia *Italy* 45°27N 12°21E **199** C9
Venice *Calif., U.S.A.* 33°59N 118°27W **126** C2
Venice *Fla., U.S.A.* 27°6N 82°27W **317** H7
Vénissieux *France* 45°42N 4°53E **175** C8
Venjan *Sweden* 60°57N 13°55E **162** D7
Venjansjön *Sweden* 60°54N 14°0E **162** D8
Venkatagiri *India* 14°0N 79°35E **245** H4
Venkatapuram *India* 18°20N 80°30E **244** E5
Venlo *Neths.* 51°22N 6°11E **170** C6
Vennachar Junction *Canada* 45°5N 77°14W **312** A7
Vennesla *Norway* 58°15N 7°59E **164** F4
Venosa *Italy* 40°58N 15°49E **201** B8
Venray *Neths.* 51°31N 6°0E **170** C6
Vent, Îs. du *French Polynesia* 17°30S 149°30W **289** f
Venta *Lithuania* 56°12N 22°42E **184** B9
Venta → *Latvia* 57°24N 21°33E **184** A8
Venta de Baños *Spain* 41°55N 4°30W **194** D6
Venta de Cardeña = Cardeña *Spain* 38°16N 4°20W **195** G6
Ventana, Sa. de la *Argentina* 38°0S 62°30W **334** D3
Ventas *Spain* 40°26N 3°40W **127** B1
Ventersburg *S. Africa* 28°7S 27°9E **270** C4
Ventersburgweg = Hennenman *S. Africa* 27°59S 27°1E **270** C4
Venterstad *S. Africa* 30°47S 25°48E **270** D4
Ventimíglia *Italy* 43°47N 7°36E **198** E4
Ventnor *U.K.* 50°36N 1°12W **169** G6
Ventorro del Cano *Spain* 40°23N 3°49W **127** B1
Ventoténe *Italy* 40°47N 13°25E **200** B6
Ventoux, Mt. *France* 44°10N 5°17E **175** D9
Ventspils *Latvia* 57°25N 21°32E **184** A8
Ventspils □ *Latvia* 57°20N 21°50E **184** A8
Ventuarí → *Venezuela* 3°58N 67°2W **328** C4
Ventucopa *U.S.A.* 34°50N 119°29W **307** L7
Ventura *U.S.A.* 34°17N 119°18W **307** L7
Venus *U.S.A.* 27°4N 81°22W **317** H8
Vénus, Pte. *Tahiti* 17°29S 149°29W **289** e
Venus B. *Australia* 38°40S 145°42E **283** E6
Venustiano Carranza *Baja Calif., Mexico* 30°25N 115°53W **318** A1
Venustiano Carranza *Distrito Federal, Mexico* 19°25N 99°5W **128** B2
Venustiano Carranza, Presa *Mexico* 27°30N 100°37W **318** B4
Vera *Argentina* 29°30S 60°20W **334** B3
Vera *Spain* 37°15N 1°51W **197** H3
Veracruz *Mexico* 19°11N 96°8W **319** D5
Veracruz □ *Mexico* 19°0N 96°15W **319** D5
Veraval *India* 20°53N 70°27E **242** J4
Verbánia *Italy* 45°56N 8°33E **198** C5
Verbano, L. di = Maggiore, L. *Italy* 45°57N 8°39E **198** B5
Verbano Cusio Ossola ⌓ *Italy* 46°15N 8°20E **198** B5
Verbicaro *Italy* 39°45N 15°55E **201** C8
Verbier *Switz.* 46°6N 7°13E **179** J3
Vercelli *Italy* 45°19N 8°25E **198** C5
Verchovchevo *Ukraine* 48°32N 34°10E **189** H8
Vercors ⌓ *France* 45°0N 5°25E **175** D9
Verdalsøra *Norway* 63°48N 11°30E **160** E14
Verde → *Argentina* 41°56S 65°5W **336** B3
Verde → *Goiás, Brazil* 19°11S 50°44W **333** E1
Verde → *Goiás, Brazil* 18°1S 50°14W **333** E1
Verde → *Mato Grosso, Brazil* 11°54S 55°48W **331** C6
Verde → *Mato Grosso do Sul, Brazil* 21°25S 52°20W **331** E7
Verde → *São Paulo, Brazil* 23°29S 46°27W **137** A1
Verde → *Chihuahua, Mexico* 26°39N 107°11W **318** B3
Verde → *Jalisco, Mexico* 20°42N 103°14W **318** C4
Verde → *Oaxaca, Mexico* 15°59N 97°50W **319** D5
Verde → *Paraguay* 23°9S 57°37W **334** A4
Verde → *Ariz., U.S.A.* 33°33N 111°40W **305** K8
Verde, Cay *Bahamas* 23°0N 75°5W **321** B4
Verde Grande → *Brazil* 16°13S 43°49W **333** E3
Verde I. *Phil.* 13°33N 121°5E **232** E3
Verde Island Pass. *Phil.* 13°34N 120°51E **232** E3
Verde Pequeno → *Brazil* 14°48S 43°31W **333** D3
Verden *Germany* 52°55N 9°14E **178** C5
Verdi *Athina, Greece* 38°2N 23°40E **112** A2
Verdi *Nev., U.S.A.* 39°31N 119°59W **306** F7
Verdikoussa *Greece* 39°47N 21°59E **204** B3
Verdon → *France* 43°43N 5°46E **175** E9
Verdon ⌓ *France* 43°50N 6°5E **175** E10
Verdugo Mts. *U.S.A.* 34°10N 118°16W **126** A2
Verdun *Qué., Canada* 45°27N 73°35W **130** B2
Verdun *Meuse, France* 49°9N 5°24E **173** C12
Verdun-sur-le-Doubs *France* 46°54N 5°2E **173** F12
Vereeniging *S. Africa* 26°38S 27°57E **271** C4
Verga, C. *Guinea* 10°30N 14°10W **262** C2
Vergara = Bergara *Spain* 43°9N 2°28W **196** B2
Vergara *Uruguay* 32°56S 53°57W **335** C5
Vergato *Italy* 44°17N 11°7E **198** D8
Vergemont Cr. → *Australia* 24°16S 143°16E **280** C3
Vergennes *U.S.A.* 44°10N 73°15W **313** B11
Vergina = Aigai *Greece* 40°28N 22°19E **202** F6
Vergt *France* 45°2N 0°43E **174** C4
Vérhalom *Hungary* 47°31N 19°1E **117** A2
Veria *Greece* 40°34N 22°12E **202** F6
Verín *Spain* 41°57N 7°27W **194** D3
Verkhnedvinsk = Vyerkhnyadzvinsk *Belarus* 55°45N 27°58E **188** E4
Verkhnetulomskoye Vdkhr. *Russia* 68°36N 31°12E **160** B24
Verkhnevilyuysk *Russia* 63°27N 120°18E **215** C13
Verkhniy Baskunchak *Russia* 48°14N 46°44E **191** F8
Verkhovye *Russia* 52°55N 37°15E **189** F9
Verkhovyna *Ukraine* 48°9N 24°47E **183** B9
Verkhoyansk *Russia* 67°35N 133°25E **215** C14
Verkhoyansk Ra. = Verkhoyanskiy Khrebet *Russia* 66°0N 129°0E **215** C13
Verkhoyanskiy Khrebet *Russia* 66°0N 129°0E **215** C13
Verma *Norway* 62°21N 8°3E **164** B5
Vermeille, Côte *France* 42°50N 3°20E **174** F7
Vermelho → *Brazil* 23°30S 46°46W **137** B1
Vermenton *France* 47°40N 3°42E **173** E10
Vermilion *Alta., Canada* 53°20N 110°50W **297** C6
Vermilion *Ohio, U.S.A.* 41°25N 82°22W **312** E2
Vermilion → *Alta., Canada* 53°22N 110°51W **297** C6
Vermilion → *Ill., U.S.A.* 41°19N 89°4W **310** C7
Vermilion B. *U.S.A.* 29°42N 92°0W **314** G9
Vermilion Bay *Canada* 49°51N 93°34W **297** D10
Vermilion L. *U.S.A.* 47°53N 92°26W **308** B7
Vermillion *U.S.A.* 42°47N 96°56W **308** D5
Vermillion → *Canada* 47°38N 72°56W **298** C5
Vermont *U.S.A.* 40°18N 90°26W **310** D6
Vermont □ *U.S.A.* 44°0N 73°0W **313** C12
Vermont Knolls *U.S.A.* 33°57N 118°21W **126** C3
Vermosh *Albania* 42°35N 19°42E **202** D3
Verna *U.S.A.* 27°23N 82°16W **317** H7
Vernadsky *Antarctica* 65°0S 64°0W **151** C17
Vernal *U.S.A.* 40°27N 109°32W **304** F9
Vernalis *U.S.A.* 37°36N 121°17W **306** H5
Vernazza *Italy* 44°10N 9°45E **198** D6
Verner *Canada* 46°25N 80°8W **298** C3
Verneuil-sur-Avre *France* 48°45N 0°55E **172** D7
Verneukpan *S. Africa* 30°0S 21°0E **270** D3
Vernier *Switz.* 46°11N 6°12E **179** J2
Vérnio *Italy* 44°3N 11°9E **198** D8
Vernon *B.C., Canada* 50°20N 119°15W **296** C5
Vernon *Eure, France* 49°5N 1°30E **172** C8
Vernon *Calif., U.S.A.* 34°0N 118°13W **126** B3
Vernon *Ill., U.S.A.* 38°48N 89°5W **310** F7
Vernon *Ind., U.S.A.* 38°59N 85°36W **311** F11
Vernon *Tex., U.S.A.* 34°9N 99°17W **314** D5
Vernonia *U.S.A.* 45°52N 123°11W **306** E3
Vernou *Guadeloupe* 16°11N 61°39W **322** e
Verny = Almaty *Kazakhstan* 43°15N 76°57E **217** D9
Vero Beach *U.S.A.* 27°38N 80°24W **317** H9
Véroia = Veria *Greece* 40°34N 22°12E **202** F6
Véroli *Italy* 41°41N 13°25E **199** G10
Verona *Ont., Canada* 44°29N 76°42W **313** B8
Verona *Italy* 45°27N 10°59E **198** C7
Verona *Wis., U.S.A.* 42°59N 89°32W **310** B7
Verrès *Italy* 45°40N 7°42E **198** C4
Verrières-le-Buisson *France* 48°44N 2°16E **134** B2
Verron Ra. *Papua N. G.* 4°21S 152°46E **286** C7
Versailles *B. Aires, Argentina* 34°38S 58°31W **117** B1
Versailles *Yvelines, France* 48°48N 2°7E **134** B1
Versailles *Ill., U.S.A.* 39°53N 90°39W **310** E6
Versailles *Ind., U.S.A.* 39°4N 85°15W **311** E11
Versailles *Ky., U.S.A.* 38°3N 84°44W **311** F12
Versailles *Mo., U.S.A.* 38°26N 92°51W **310** F4
Versailles *Ohio, U.S.A.* 40°13N 84°29W **311** D12
Versalles *Bolivia* 12°44S 63°18W **331** C5
Versmold *Germany* 52°2N 8°9E **178** C4
Vert, C. *Senegal* 14°45N 17°30W **262** C1
Vertou *France* 47°10N 1°28W **172** E5
Vertus *France* 48°54N 4°2E **173** D11
Verulam *S. Africa* 29°38S 31°2E **271** C5
Verviers *Belgium* 50°37N 5°52E **170** D5
Vervins *France* 49°50N 3°53E **173** C10
Veržej *Slovenia* 46°34N 16°13E **199** B13
Verzy *France* 49°9N 4°10E **173** C11
Vescovato *France* 42°30N 9°27E **175** F13
Veselí nad Lužnicí *Czech Rep.* 49°12N 14°43E **180** B7
Veselie *Bulgaria* 42°18N 27°38E **203** D11
Veselovskoye Vdkhr. *Russia* 46°58N 41°25E **191** G5
Veshenskaya *Russia* 49°35N 41°44E **190** F5
Veshnyaki *Russia* 55°43N 37°48E **129** B3
Vesle → *France* 49°23N 3°28E **173** C10
Vesolyy Posolok *Russia* 59°53N 30°28E **137** B2
Vesoul *France* 47°40N 6°11E **173** E13
Vessigebro *Sweden* 56°58N 12°40E **163** H6
Vest-Agder □ *Norway* 58°30N 7°15E **164** F4
Vestale, Toraka *Madag.* 16°20S 43°58E **272** B1
Vestbygd *Norway* 58°6N 6°34E **164** F3
Vesterålen *Norway* 68°45N 15°0E **160** B16
Vestfirðir □ *Iceland* 65°45N 22°30W **155** B4
Vestfjorden *Norway* 67°55N 14°0E **160** C16
Vestfold □ *Norway* 59°15N 10°0E **164** E7
Vestfossen *Norway* 59°44N 9°52E **164** E6
Vestmannaeyjar *Iceland* 63°27N 20°15W **155** D6
Vestnes *Norway* 62°39N 7°5E **164** B4
Vestra *Finland* 60°19N 24°46E **121** B1
Vestre Gausdal *Norway* 61°12N 10°8E **164** C7
Vestskoven *Denmark* 55°41N 12°23E **118** A2
Vestur-skaftafellssýsla *Iceland* 63°50N 18°30W **155** D8
Vesturland □ *Iceland* 64°50N 22°0W **155** C5
Vestvågøya *Norway* 68°18N 13°50E **160** B15
Vesuvio *Italy* 40°49N 14°26E **201** B7
Vesuvius, Mt. = Vesuvio *Italy* 40°49N 14°26E **201** B7
Vesyegonsk *Russia* 58°40N 37°16E **188** C9
Veszprém *Hungary* 47°8N 17°57E **182** C2
Veszprém □ *Hungary* 47°5N 17°55E **182** C2
Vésztő *Hungary* 46°55N 21°16E **182** D6
Vetapalem *India* 15°47N 80°18E **245** G5
Vetlanda *Sweden* 57°24N 15°3E **163** G9
Vetluga *Russia* 57°53N 45°45E **190** B7
Vetlugu → *Russia* 56°36N 46°4E **190** B8
Vetluzhskiy *Kostroma, Russia* 58°23N 45°26E **190** A7
Vetluzhskiy *Nizhniy Novgorod, Russia* 57°17N 45°12E **190** B7
Vetovo *Bulgaria* 43°42N 26°16E **203** C10
Vetralla *Italy* 42°20N 12°2E **199** F9
Vetren *Bulgaria* 42°15N 24°3E **203** D8
Vettore, Mte. *Italy* 42°49N 13°16E **199** F10
Veurne *Belgium* 51°5N 2°40E **170** C2
Vevay *U.S.A.* 38°45N 85°4W **311** F11
Veveno → *South Sudan* 6°40N 32°58E **257** F3
Vevey *Switz.* 46°28N 6°51E **179** J2
Vevi *Greece* 40°47N 21°38E **202** F5
Veynes *France* 44°32N 5°49E **175** D9
Veys *Iran* 31°30N 49°0E **247** D6
Vézelay *France* 47°27N 3°45E **173** E10
Vézelise *France* 48°30N 6°5E **173** D13
Vézère → *France* 44°53N 0°53E **174** D4
Vezhen *Bulgaria* 42°50N 24°20E **203** D8
Vezirköprü *Turkey* 41°8N 35°27E **212** B6
Vezzani *France* 42°10N 9°15E **175** F13
Vi Thanh *Vietnam* 9°42N 105°26E **237** H5
Viacha *Bolivia* 16°39S 68°18W **330** D4
Viadana *Italy* 44°56N 10°31E **198** D7
Vialar = Tissemsilt *Algeria* 35°35N 1°50E **261** A5
Viamão *Brazil* 30°5S 51°0W **335** C5
Viana *Brazil* 3°13S 44°55W **332** B3

Viana Spain 42°31N 2°22W 196 C2
Viana do Alentejo Portugal 38°17N 7°59W 195 G3
Viana do Bolo Spain 42°11N 7°6W 194 C3
Viana do Castelo Portugal 41°42N 8°50W 194 D2
Viana do Castelo □ Portugal 41°50N 8°30W 194 D2
Vianden Lux. 49°56N 6°12E 170 E6
Viangchan = Vientiane Laos 17°58N 102°36E 236 D4
Vianópolis Brazil 16°40S 48°35W 333 E2
Vianos Greece 35°2N 25°21E 207 E6
Viar → Spain 37°36N 5°50W 195 H5
Viaréggio Italy 43°52N 10°14E 198 E7
Viaur → France 44°8N 1°58E 174 D5
Vibble Sweden 57°37N 18°16E 163 G12
Vibo Valéntia Italy 38°40N 16°6E 201 D9
Viborg Denmark 56°27N 9°23E 163 H3
Vibraye France 48°3N 0°44E 172 D7
Vic Spain 41°58N 2°19E 196 D7
Vic, Étang de France 43°29N 3°50E 174 E7
Vic-en-Bigorre France 43°24N 0°3E 174 E4
Vic-Fezensac France 43°47N 0°19E 174 E4
Vic-le-Comte France 45°39N 3°14E 173 G10
Vic-sur-Cère France 44°59N 2°38E 174 D6
Vicálvaro Spain 40°24N 3°36W 127 B2
Vícar Spain 36°50N 2°38W 197 J2
Vicente Lopez Argentina 34°31S 58°30W 117 B2
Vicente Pérez Rosales △ Chile 41°11S 72°12W 336 B2
Vicenza Italy 45°33N 11°33E 199 C8
Vich = Vic Spain 41°58N 2°19E 196 D7
Vichada □ Colombia 5°0N 69°30W 328 C4
Vichada → Colombia 4°55N 67°50W 328 C4
Vichuga Russia 57°12N 41°55E 190 B5
Vichy France 46°9N 3°26E 173 F10
Vicksburg Ariz., U.S.A. 33°45N 113°45W 307 M13
Vicksburg Mich., U.S.A. 42°7N 85°32W 311 B11
Vicksburg Miss., U.S.A. 32°21N 90°53W 315 E9
Vico France 42°10N 8°49E 175 F12
Vico, L. di Italy 42°19N 12°10E 199 F9
Vico del Gargano Italy 41°54N 15°57E 199 G12
Viçosa Brazil 9°28S 36°14W 332 C4
Viçosa do Ceará Brazil 3°34S 41°5W 332 B3
Vicovu de Sus Romania 47°56N 25°41E 183 C10
Victor India 21°0N 71°30E 242 J4
Victor Emanuel Ra. Papua N. G. 5°20S 142°15E 286 C2
Victor Harbor Australia 35°30S 138°37E 282 C3
Victor Hugo = Hamadia Algeria 35°28N 1°57E 261 A5
Victoria = Bandar Labuan Malaysia 5°20N 115°14E 235 A5
Victoria Argentina 32°40S 60°10W 334 C3
Victoria B.C., Canada 48°30N 123°25W 306 B3
Victoria Chile 38°13S 72°20W 336 A2
Victoria Hong Kong, China 22°17N 114°11E 122 B2
Victoria Grenada 12°12N 61°42W 323 q
Victoria Guinea 10°50N 14°32W 262 C2
Victoria Gozo, Malta 36°3N 14°14E 206 E6
Victoria Mind. Or., Phil. 13°12N 121°12E 232 E3
Victoria Tarlac, Phil. 15°35N 120°41E 232 D3
Victoria Romania 45°44N 24°41E 183 E9
Victoria Seychelles 4°38S 55°28E 272 c
Victoria London, U.K. 125 c3
Victoria Kans., U.S.A. 38°52N 99°9W 308 F4
Victoria Tex., U.S.A. 28°48N 97°0W 314 G6
Victoria □ Australia 37°0S 144°0E 282 D6
Victoria → Australia 15°10S 129°40E 278 C4
Victoria, Grand L. Canada 47°31N 77°30W 298 C4
Victoria, L. Africa 1°0S 33°0E 268 C3
Victoria, L. N.S.W., Australia 33°57S 141°15E 282 B4
Victoria, Mt. = Tomanivi Fiji 17°37S 178°1E 287 A2
Victoria, Mt. Burma 21°14N 93°55E 241 E4
Victoria, Mt. Papua N. G. 8°55S 147°32E 286 E4
Victoria, Pont Canada 45°29N 73°32W 130 B2
Victoria and Alfred Waterfront Cape Town, S. Africa 118 a1
Victoria Beach Canada 50°40N 96°35W 297 C9
Victoria de Durango = Durango Mexico 24°3N 104°39W 318 C4
Victoria de las Tunas = Las Tunas Cuba 20°58N 76°59W 320 B4
Victoria Falls Zimbabwe 17°58S 25°52E 269 F2
Victoria Fjord Greenland 82°10N 46°0W 154 A6
Victoria Gardens India 18°58N 72°50E 130 B2
Victoria Harbour Ont., Canada 44°45N 79°45W 312 B5
Victoria Harbour Hong Kong, China 22°17N 114°10E 122 B3
Victoria I. Canada 71°0N 111°0W 294 C9
Victoria Island Nigeria 6°25N 3°25E 124 B2
Victoria L. Nfld. & L., Canada 48°20N 57°27W 299 C8
Victoria L. Gauteng, S. Africa 26°13S 28°9E 123 B2
Victoria Lawn Tennis Courts Australia 37°50S 145°1E 128 B2
Victoria Ld. Antarctica 75°0S 160°0E 151 D11
Victoria Nile → Uganda 2°14N 31°26E 268 B3
Victoria Park Singapore 1°19N 103°49E 138 B2
Victoria Peak Hong Kong, China 22°16N 114°8E 122 B2
Victoria Peaks Phil. 9°22N 118°20E 233 G2
Victoria Pk. Belize 16°48N 88°37W 319 D7
Victoria Ra. N.Z. 42°12S 172°7E 285 C7
Victoria River Australia 16°25S 131°0E 278 C5
Victoria Str. Canada 69°31N 100°30W 294 D11
Victoria Terminus = Chhatrapati Shivaji Terminus India 18°56N 72°50E 130 B2
Victoria West S. Africa 31°25S 23°4E 270 D3
Victoria Wharf Cape Town, S. Africa 118 a2
Victorias Phil. 10°54N 123°5E 233 F4
Victoriaville Canada 46°4N 71°56W 299 C5
Victorica Argentina 36°20S 65°30W 334 D2
Victorville U.S.A. 34°32N 117°18W 307 L9
Vicuña Chile 30°0S 70°50W 334 C1
Vicuña Mackenna Argentina 33°53S 64°25W 334 C3
Vidal U.S.A. 34°7N 114°31W 307 L12
Vidalia U.S.A. 32°13N 82°25W 316 C7
Vidamlya Belarus 52°19N 23°47E 185 F10
Vidauban France 43°25N 6°27E 175 E10
Viddolatno = Vindelälven → Sweden 63°55N 19°50E 160 E18
Videbæk Denmark 56°6N 8°38E 163 H2
Videle Romania 44°17N 25°31E 183 F10
Videsæter Norway 61°57N 7°14E 164 C4
Vidette U.S.A. 33°2N 82°15W 316 B7
Vidigueira Portugal 38°12N 7°48W 195 G3
Vidin Bulgaria 43°59N 22°50E 202 C6
Vidin □ Bulgaria 43°59N 22°50E 202 C6
Vidio, C. Spain 43°35N 6°14W 194 B4
Vidisha India 23°28N 77°53E 242 H7
Vidos Greece 39°38N 19°55E 206 B9
Vidra Romania 45°56N 26°55E 183 E11
Viduša Bos.-H. 42°55N 18°21E 202 D2
Vidzy Belarus 55°23N 26°37E 188 E4
Viechtach Germany 49°4N 12°53E 179 F8
Viedma Argentina 40°50S 63°0W 336 B4
Viedma, L. Argentina 49°30S 72°30W 336 C2
Vieille Case Dominica 15°36N 61°24W 323 k
Vieira do Minho Portugal 41°38N 8°8W 194 D2
Vielha Spain 42°43N 0°44E 196 C5
Viella = Vielha Spain 42°43N 0°44E 196 C5
Vielle St-Girons France 43°56N 1°18W 174 E2
Vielsalm Belgium 50°17N 5°54E 170 D5
Vienenburg Germany 51°57N 10°34E 178 D6
Vieng Pou Kha Laos 20°41N 101°4E 228 G3
Vienna = Wien Austria 48°12N 16°22E 142 A2
Vienna Ont., Canada 42°41N 80°48W 312 D4
Vienna Ga., U.S.A. 32°6N 83°47W 316 C6
Vienna Ill., U.S.A. 37°25N 88°54W 308 G9
Vienna Mo., U.S.A. 38°11N 91°57W 310 F5
Vienne France 45°31N 4°53E 175 C8
Vienne □ France 46°30N 0°42E 174 B4
Vienne → France 47°13N 0°5E 172 E7
Vientiane Laos 17°58N 102°36E 236 D4
Vientos, Paso de los Caribbean 20°0N 74°0W 321 C5
Vieques Puerto Rico 18°8N 65°25W 321 b
Vierge Pt. St. Lucia 13°49N 60°53W 323 m
Vierkant Pt. Bonaire 12°7N 68°17W 322 h
Viernheim Germany 49°31N 8°35E 179 F4
Viersen Germany 51°15N 6°23E 178 D2
Vierwaldstättersee Switz. 47°0N 8°30E 179 J4
Vierzon France 47°13N 2°5E 173 E9
Vieste Italy 41°53N 16°10E 199 G13
Viet Quang Vietnam 22°30N 104°48E 228 F5
Viet Tri Vietnam 21°18N 105°25E 236 B5
Vietnam ■ Asia 19°0N 106°0E 236 C6
Vietnam Veterans Memorial Washington, D.C., U.S.A. 38°53N 77°2W 143 B2
Vietz = Witnica Poland 52°40N 14°54E 185 F1
Vieux-Boucau-les-Bains France 43°48N 1°23W 174 E2
Vieux Bourg Guadeloupe 16°20N 61°36W 322 e
Vieux Carré = French Quarter New Orleans, U.S.A. 131 a2
Vieux Fort Guadeloupe 15°57N 61°41W 322 e
Vieux Fort Marie-Galante, Guadeloupe 15°59N 61°17W 322 e
Vieux Fort St. Lucia 13°46N 60°58W 323 m
Vieux Fort, Pte. du Guadeloupe 15°57N 61°42W 322 e
Vieux Fort, R. du → Guadeloupe 15°59N 61°17W 322 e
Vieux Grand Port Mauritius 20°22S 57°42E 272 e
Vieux-Habitants Guadeloupe 16°4N 61°46W 322 e
Vieux-Habitants, Rivière des → Guadeloupe 16°3N 61°46W 322 e
Vieux-Montréal Montréal, Canada 130 b3
View Park U.S.A. 34°0N 118°20W 126 B3
Vif France 45°5N 5°41E 175 C9
Viga Phil. 13°52N 124°18E 232 E5
Vigan Phil. 17°35N 120°28E 232 C3
Vigário Geral Brazil 22°48S 43°18W 135 A1
Vigeland Norway 58°5N 7°18E 164 F4
Vigentino Italy 45°26N 9°13E 128 B2
Vigévano Italy 45°19N 8°51E 198 C5
Viggbyholm Sweden 59°26N 18°7E 139 A2
Vighignolo Italy 45°29N 9°2E 128 B1
Vigia = Almenara Brazil 16°11S 40°42W 333 E3
Vigia Brazil 0°50S 48°5W 332 B2
Vigla Greece 39°7N 20°50E 207 A2
Viglas, Akra Greece 35°54N 27°51E 206 F11
Vignemalle France 42°47N 0°10W 174 F3
Vigneulles-lès-Hattonchâtel France 48°59N 5°43E 173 D12
Vignola Italy 44°29N 11°1E 198 D8
Vigo Spain 42°12N 8°41W 194 C2
Vigo, Ría de Spain 42°15N 8°45W 194 C2
Vigrestad Norway 58°34N 5°42E 164 F2
Vigsø Bugt Denmark 57°8N 8°47E 163 G2
Vihiers France 47°10N 0°30W 172 E6
Vihowa Pakistan 31°8N 70°30E 242 D4
Vihowa → Pakistan 31°8N 70°41E 242 D4
Viikki Finland 60°13N 25°1E 121 B3
Viipuri = Vyborg Russia 60°43N 28°47E 188 B5
Vijayadurg India 16°30N 73°25E 244 F1
Vijayawada India 16°31N 80°39E 244 F5
Vijosë → Albania 40°37N 19°24E 202 F3
Vík Iceland 63°25N 19°1W 155 D7
Vik Sogn og Fjordane, Norway 61°21N 6°6E 164 C3
Vika Sweden 60°57N 14°28E 162 D8
Vikarabad India 17°20N 77°54E 244 E3
Vikarbyn Sweden 60°55N 15°1E 162 D9
Vike Norway 60°42N 5°35E 164 D2
Vikedal Norway 59°30N 5°55E 164 E2
Vikeke = Viqueque E. Timor 8°52S 126°23E 231 F7
Vikeland = Vigeland Norway 58°5N 7°18E 164 F4
Viken Skåne, Sweden 56°9N 12°34E 163 H6
Viken Västra Götaland, Sweden 58°39N 14°20E 163 F8
Vikersund Norway 59°58N 9°59E 164 E6
Vikeså Norway 58°38N 6°3E 164 F3
Vikevåg Norway 59°5N 5°41E 164 E2
Vikhammer Norway 63°26N 10°37E 164 A7
Vikhroli India 19°6N 72°55E 130 A2
Viking Canada 53°7N 111°50W 296 C6
Vikmanshyttan Sweden 60°18N 15°50E 162 D9
Vikna Norway 64°55N 10°58E 160 D14
Vikos-Aoos △ Greece 40°0N 20°45E 204 B2
Vikøyri Norway 61°4N 6°34E 164 C3
Vila Alferes Chamusca = Guijá Mozam. 24°27S 33°0E 271 B5
Vila António Enes = Angoche Mozam. 16°8S 39°55E 269 F4
Vila Baleira Madeira 33°4N 16°20W 260 B1
Vila Bela da Santissima Trindade Brazil 15°0S 59°57W 331 C6
Vila Cabral = Lichinga Mozam. 13°13S 35°11E 269 E4
Vila Cabral = Niassa □ Mozam. 13°30S 36°0E 269 E4
Vila da Maganja Mozam. 17°18S 37°30E 269 F4
Vila da Ribeira Brava C. Verde Is. 16°32N 24°25W 153 j
Vila de Rei Portugal 39°41N 8°9W 194 F2
Vila do Bispo Portugal 37°5N 8°53W 195 H2
Vila do Conde Portugal 41°21N 8°45W 194 D2
Vila do Maio C. Verde Is. 15°21N 23°10W 153 j
Vila do Porto Azores 36°56N 25°9W 153 d4
Vila Franca de Xira Portugal 38°57N 8°59W 195 G2
Vila Franca do Campo Azores 37°43N 25°26W 153 d3
Vila Gamito Mozam. 14°12S 33°0E 269 E3
Vila Gomes da Costa Mozam. 24°20S 33°37E 271 B5
Vila Guilherme Brazil 23°30S 46°38W 137 B2
Vila Isabel Brazil 22°54S 43°15W 135 B1
Vila Jaguára Brazil 23°30S 46°45W 137 B1
Vila Machado Mozam. 19°15S 34°14E 269 F3
Vila Madalena Brazil 23°32S 46°41W 137 B1
Vila Maria Brazil 23°31S 46°36W 137 B2
Vila Mariana Brazil 23°34S 46°36W 137 B2
Vila Mouzinho Mozam. 14°48S 34°25E 269 E3
Vila Nova de Famalicão Portugal 41°25N 8°32W 194 D2
Vila Nova de Foz Côa Portugal 41°5N 7°9W 194 D3
Vila Nova de Gaia Portugal 41°8N 8°37W 194 D2
Vila Nova de Gaza = Xai-Xai Mozam. 25°6S 33°31E 271 C5
Vila Nova do Corvo Azores 39°40N 31°8W 153 d2
Vila Nova Sintra C. Verde Is. 14°52N 24°42W 153 j
Vila Pereira de Eça = Ondjiva Angola 16°48S 15°50E 265 F3
Vila Pery = Manica Mozam. 18°58S 32°59E 271 A5
Vila Pouca de Aguiar Portugal 41°30N 7°38W 194 D3
Vila Prudente Brazil 23°35S 46°33W 137 B2
Vila Real Portugal 41°17N 7°48W 194 D3
Vila-Real Spain 39°55N 0°3W 196 F4
Vila Real □ Portugal 41°36N 7°35W 194 D3
Vila Real de Santo António Portugal 37°10N 7°28W 195 H3
Vila-seca Spain 41°7N 1°9E 196 D6
Vila Texeira da Silva = Luau Angola 10°40S 22°10E 265 E4
Vila Vasco da Gama Mozam. 14°54S 32°14E 269 E3
Vila Velha Amapá, Brazil 3°13N 51°13W 329 C7
Vila Velha Espirito Santo, Brazil 20°20S 40°17W 333 F3
Vila Velha Sergipe, Brazil 11°20S 38°9W 332 D4
Vila Viçosa Portugal 38°45N 7°27W 195 G3
Viladecans Spain 41°18N 2°1E 114 B1
Vilafranca del Maestrat = Villafranca del Cid Spain 40°26N 0°16W 196 E4
Vilafranca del Penedès Spain 41°21N 1°40E 196 D6
Vilagarcía de Arousa Spain 42°34N 8°46W 194 C2
Vilaine → France 47°30N 2°27W 172 E4
Vilakalaka Vanuatu 15°25S 167°42E 287 E5
Vilanandro, Tanjona Madag. 16°11S 44°27E 272 B1
Vilanculos Mozam. 22°1S 35°17E 271 B6
Vilanova i la Geltrú Spain 41°13N 1°40E 196 D6
Vilar Formoso Portugal 40°38N 6°45W 194 E4
Vilaseca-Salou = Vila-seca Spain 41°7N 1°9E 196 D6
Vilbjerg Denmark 56°12N 8°46E 163 H2
Vilcabamba, Cordillera Peru 13°0S 73°0W 330 C3
Vilcanchos Peru 13°40S 74°25W 330 C3
Vilcheka, Ostrov Russia 80°0N 58°31E 214 B6
Vilcheka, Zemlya Russia 80°30N 60°30E 150 A11
Vilches Spain 38°12N 3°30W 195 G7
Vile Parle India 19°6N 72°51E 130 A2
Vileyka Belarus 54°30N 26°53E 177 A14
Vilhelmina Sweden 64°35N 16°39E 160 D17
Vilhena Brazil 12°40S 60°5W 331 C5
Viliya = Neris → Lithuania 55°8N 24°16E 188 E3
Viljandi Estonia 58°28N 25°30E 188 C3
Viljoensdorp = Newcastle S. Africa 27°45S 29°58E 271 C4
Vilkaviškis Lithuania 54°39N 23°2E 184 D10
Vilkija Lithuania 55°3N 23°35E 184 C10
Vilkitskogo, Proliv Russia 78°0N 103°0E 215 B11
Vilkomir = Ukmergė Lithuania 55°15N 24°45E 188 E3
Vilkovo = Vylkove Ukraine 45°28N 29°32E 183 E14
Villa Abecia Bolivia 21°0S 68°18W 334 A2
Villa Adelina Argentina 34°31S 58°33W 117 B1
Villa Ana Argentina 28°28S 59°40W 334 B4
Villa Angela Argentina 27°34S 60°45W 334 B3
Villa Ballester Argentina 34°33S 58°33W 117 B1
Villa Barilari Argentina 34°42S 58°20W 117 C2
Villa Bella = Serra Talhada Brazil 7°59S 38°18W 332 C4
Villa Bella Bolivia 10°25S 65°22W 331 C4
Villa Borghese Rome, Italy 136 a3
Villa Bosch Argentina 34°35S 58°33W 117 B1
Villa Bruzual Venezuela 9°20N 69°6W 328 C4
Villa C. Colon Argentina 34°41S 58°21W 117 C2
Villa Cañás Argentina 34°0S 61°35W 334 C3
Villa Cecilia = Ciudad Madero Mexico 22°19N 97°50W 319 C5
Villa Cisneros = Dakhla W. Sahara 23°50N 15°53W 260 D1
Villa Ciudadela Argentina 34°38S 58°33W 117 B1
Villa Constitución Argentina 33°15S 60°20W 334 C3
Villa de Arriaga Mexico 21°56N 101°20W 318 C4
Villa de Cura Venezuela 10°2N 67°29W 328 A4
Villa de Guadalupe Mexico 19°29N 99°6W 128 B2
Villa de María Argentina 29°55S 63°43W 334 B3
Villa de Méndez Mexico 25°7N 98°34W 319 B5
Villa del Nevoso = Ilirska-Bistrica Slovenia 45°34N 14°14E 199 C11
Villa del Rio Spain 37°59N 4°17W 195 H6
Villa del Rosario Venezuela 10°19N 72°19W 328 A3
Villa Devoto Argentina 34°36S 58°31W 117 B1
Villa Diamante Argentina 34°41S 58°25W 117 C2
Villa Dolores Argentina 31°58S 65°15W 334 C2
Villa Dominico Argentina 34°41S 58°19W 117 C3
Villa Gesell Argentina 37°15S 56°55W 334 D4
Villa Grove U.S.A. 39°52N 88°10W 311 E8
Villa Guillermina Argentina 28°15S 59°29W 334 B4
Villa Hayes Paraguay 25°5S 57°20W 334 B4
Villa Hidalgo Mexico 24°15N 99°26W 319 C5
Villa Iris Argentina 38°12S 63°12W 334 D3
Villa Lugano Argentina 34°41S 58°27W 117 C2
Villa Lynch Argentina 34°35S 58°31W 117 B1
Villa Madero Argentina 34°41S 58°30W 117 C1
Villa María Argentina 32°20S 63°10W 334 C3
Villa Mazán Argentina 28°40S 66°30W 334 B2
Villa Minozzo Italy 44°22N 10°28E 198 D7
Villa Montes Bolivia 21°10S 63°30W 334 A3
Villa Ocampo Argentina 28°30S 59°20W 334 B4
Villa Ocampo Durango, Mexico 26°27N 105°31W 318 B3
Villa Ojo de Agua Argentina 29°30S 63°44W 334 B3
Villa Regina Argentina 39°6S 67°4W 336 A3
Villa Rica U.S.A. 33°44N 84°55W 316 B5
Villa Sáenz Pena Argentina 34°37S 58°32W 117 B1
Villa San Giovanni Italy 38°13N 15°38E 201 D8
Villa San Martín Argentina 28°15S 64°9W 334 B3
Villa Sanjurjo = Al Hoceïma Morocco 35°8N 3°58W 261 A4
Villa Santina Italy 46°24N 12°55E 199 B9
Villa Unión Mexico 23°12N 106°14W 318 C3
Villa Urquiza Argentina 34°34S 58°28W 117 B2
Villaba Phil. 11°13N 124°24E 233 F5
Villablino Spain 42°57N 6°19W 194 C4
Villacarlos Spain 39°53N 4°17E 206 B5
Villacarriedo Spain 43°14N 3°48W 194 B7
Villacarrillo Spain 38°7N 3°3W 195 G7
Villacastín Spain 40°46N 4°25W 194 E6
Villach Austria 46°37N 13°51E 180 E6
Villacidro Italy 39°27N 8°44E 200 C1
Villada Spain 42°15N 4°59W 194 C6
Villadiego Spain 42°31N 4°1W 194 C6
Villadóssola Italy 46°4N 8°16E 198 B5
Villafeliche Spain 41°10N 1°30W 196 D3
Villafranca Spain 42°17N 1°46W 196 C3
Villafranca de los Barros Spain 38°35N 6°18W 195 G4
Villafranca de los Caballeros Spain 39°26N 3°21W 195 F7
Villafranca del Cid Spain 40°26N 0°16W 196 E4
Villafranca del Panadés = Vilafranca del Penedès Spain 41°21N 1°40E 196 D6
Villafranca di Verona Italy 45°21N 10°50E 198 C7
Villafranca Tirrena Italy 38°20N 15°25E 201 D8
Villagio Mussolini = Arboréa Italy 39°46N 8°35E 200 C1
Villagrán Mexico 24°29N 99°29W 319 C5
Villaguay Argentina 32°0S 59°0W 334 C4
Villaharta Spain 38°9N 4°54W 195 G6
Villahermosa Tabasco, Mexico 17°59N 92°55W 319 D6
Villahermosa Spain 38°46N 2°52W 197 G2
Villaines-la-Juhel France 48°21N 0°20W 172 D6
Villajoyosa Spain 38°30N 0°12W 197 G4
Villalba Puerto Rico 18°8N 66°30W 321 b
Villalba Spain 43°22N 7°40W 194 B3
Villalba de Guardo Spain 42°42N 4°49W 194 C6
Villalón de Campos Spain 42°5N 5°4W 194 C5
Villalpando Spain 41°51N 5°25W 194 D5
Villaluenga de la Sagra Spain 40°2N 3°54W 194 E7
Villamanán Spain 42°19N 5°35W 194 C5
Villamartín Spain 36°52N 5°38W 195 J5
Villamayor de Santiago Spain 39°50N 2°59W 196 F2
Villamblard France 45°2N 0°32E 174 C4
Villanova Monteleone Italy 40°30N 8°28E 200 B1
Villanueva Colombia 10°37N 72°59W 328 A3
Villanueva N. Mex., U.S.A. 35°16N 105°22W 305 J11
Villanueva de Castellón Spain 39°5N 0°31W 197 F4
Villanueva de Córdoba Spain 38°20N 4°38W 195 G6
Villanueva de la Fuente Spain 38°42N 2°42W 197 G2
Villanueva de la Serena Spain 38°59N 5°50W 195 G5
Villanueva de la Sierra Spain 40°12N 6°24W 194 E4
Villanueva de los Castillejos Spain 37°30N 7°15W 195 H3
Villanueva de los Infantes Spain 38°43N 3°1W 195 G7
Villanueva del Arzobispo Spain 38°10N 3°0W 197 G2
Villanueva del Fresno Spain 38°23N 7°10W 195 G3
Villanueva y Geltrú = Vilanova i la Geltrú Spain 41°13N 1°40E 196 D6
Villaputzu Italy 39°26N 9°34E 200 C2
Villaquilambre Spain 42°39N 5°33W 194 C5
Villar del Arzobispo Spain 39°44N 0°50W 196 F4
Villar del Rey Spain 39°7N 6°50W 195 F4
Villard-de-Lans France 45°3N 5°33E 175 C9
Villarramiel Spain 42°2N 4°55W 194 C6
Villarreal = Vila-Real Spain 39°55N 0°3W 196 F4
Villarrica Chile 39°15S 72°15W 336 A2
Villarrica Paraguay 25°40S 56°30W 334 B4
Villarrica △ Chile 39°24S 71°46W 336 A2
Villarrobledo Spain 39°18N 2°36W 197 F2
Villarroya de la Sierra Spain 41°27N 1°46W 196 D3
Villarrubia de los Ojos Spain 39°14N 3°36W 195 F7
Villars-les-Dombes France 46°0N 5°3E 173 F12
Villasayas Spain 41°24N 2°39W 196 D2
Villaseco de los Gamitos Spain 41°2N 6°7W 194 D4
Villasimíus Italy 39°8N 9°31E 200 C2
Villastar Spain 40°17N 1°9W 196 E3
Villatobas Spain 39°54N 3°20W 194 F7
Villaverde Spain 40°21N 3°42W 127 B1
Villaverde Bajo Spain 40°20N 3°40W 127 B1
Villavicencio Argentina 32°28S 69°0W 334 C2
Villavicencio Colombia 4°9N 73°37W 328 C3
Villaviciosa Spain 43°32N 5°27W 194 B5
Villazón Bolivia 22°0S 65°35W 334 A2
Ville-d'Avray France 48°49N 2°11E 134 B2
Ville-Marie Canada 47°20N 79°30W 298 C4
Ville Platte U.S.A. 30°41N 92°17W 314 F8
Villecresnes France 48°43N 2°31E 134 B4
Villedieu-les-Poêles France 48°50N 1°13W 172 D5
Villefort France 44°28N 3°56E 174 D7
Villefranche-de-Lauragais France 43°25N 1°44E 174 E5
Villefranche-de-Rouergue France 44°21N 2°2E 174 D6
Villefranche-du-Périgord France 44°38N 1°5E 174 D5
Villefranche-sur-Saône France 45°59N 4°43E 175 C8
Villejuif France 48°47N 2°21E 134 B3
Villel Spain 40°14N 1°12W 196 E3
Villemomble France 48°52N 2°30E 134 A4
Villemur-sur-Tarn France 43°51N 1°31E 174 E5
Villena Spain 38°39N 0°52W 197 G4
Villenauxe-la-Grande France 48°35N 3°33E 173 D10
Villenave-d'Ornon France 44°46N 0°33W 174 D3
Villeneuve-d'Ascq France 50°38N 3°9E 173 B10
Villeneuve-la-Garenne France 48°56N 2°19E 134 A2
Villeneuve-l'Archevêque France 48°14N 3°32E 173 D10
Villeneuve-le-Roi France 48°43N 2°24E 134 B3
Villeneuve-lès-Avignon France 43°58N 4°49E 175 E8
Villeneuve-St-Georges France 48°43N 2°27E 134 B3
Villeneuve-sur-Allier France 46°40N 3°13E 173 F10
Villeneuve-sur-Lot France 44°24N 0°42E 174 D4
Villeneuve-sur-Yonne France 48°5N 3°18E 173 D10
Villeparisis France 48°56N 2°36E 134 A4
Villeréal France 44°38N 0°45E 174 D4
Villers-Bocage France 49°3N 0°40W 172 C6
Villers-Cotterêts France 49°15N 3°4E 173 C10
Villers-sur-Mer France 49°21N 0°2W 172 C6
Villersexel France 47°33N 6°26E 173 E13
Villerupt France 49°28N 5°55E 173 C12
Villeurbanne France 45°46N 4°55E 175 C8
Villevaudé France 48°55N 2°39E 134 A4
Villiers S. Africa 27°2S 28°36E 271 C4
Villiers-le-Bâcle France 48°44N 2°8E 134 B1
Villiers-sur-Marne France 48°49N 2°32E 134 B4
Villingen-Schwenningen Germany 48°3N 8°26E 179 G4
Villinki Finland 60°9N 25°6E 121 C3
Villisca U.S.A. 40°56N 94°59W 310 D2
Villmanstrand = Lappeenranta Finland 61°3N 28°12E 188 B5
Villoresi, Canale Italy 45°33N 9°9E 128 A1
Villupuram India 11°59N 79°31E 245 J4
Vilna = Vilnius Lithuania 54°38N 25°19E 188 E3
Vilna Canada 54°7N 111°55W 296 C6
Vilnius Lithuania 54°38N 25°19E 188 E3
Vils Austria 47°33N 10°38E 180 D3
Vils → Bayern, Germany 48°37N 13°11E 179 G9
Vils → Bayern, Germany 49°10N 11°57E 179 F7
Vilsandi △ Estonia 58°23N 21°52E 188 C1
Vilsbiburg Germany 48°26N 12°22E 179 G8
Vilshofen Germany 48°37N 13°11E 179 G9
Vilusi Montenegro 42°44N 18°34E 202 D2
Vilvoorde Belgium 50°56N 4°26E 116 A2
Vilyuchinsk Russia 52°55N 158°24E 215 D16
Vilyuy → Russia 64°24N 126°26E 215 C13
Vilyuysk Russia 63°40N 121°35E 215 C13
Vilyuyskoye Vdkhr. Russia 63°0N 112°0E 215 C12
Vimianzo Spain 43°7N 9°2W 194 B1
Vimioso Portugal 41°35N 6°31W 194 D4
Vimmerby Sweden 57°40N 15°55E 163 G9
Vimodrone Italy 45°30N 9°16E 128 A2
Vimont Canada 45°36N 73°43W 130 A1
Vimoutiers France 48°57N 0°10E 172 D7
Vimperk Czech Rep. 49°3N 13°46E 180 B6
Vina → Cameroon 7°45N 15°36E 264 A3
Viña del Mar Chile 33°0S 71°30W 334 C1
Vinanmek Mansion Bangkok, Thailand 113 a2
Vinarós Spain 40°30N 0°27E 196 E5
Vincendo Réunion 21°21S 55°41E 272 f
Vincennes Val-de-Marne, France 48°51N 2°26E 134 A3
Vincennes Ind., U.S.A. 38°41N 87°32W 311 F9
Vincennes, Bois de France 48°49N 2°26E 134 B3
Vincennes Bay S. Ocean 66°0S 109°0E 151 C8
Vincent U.S.A. 34°33N 118°11W 307 L8
Vinces Ecuador 1°32S 79°45W 328 D2
Vinchina Argentina 28°45S 68°15W 334 B2
Vindava = Ventspils Latvia 57°25N 21°32E 184 A8
Vindelälven → Sweden 63°55N 19°50E 160 E18
Vindeln Sweden 64°12N 19°43E 160 D18
Vinderup Denmark 56°29N 8°45E 163 H2
Vindhya Ra. India 22°50N 77°0E 242 H7
Vine Grove U.S.A. 37°49N 85°59W 311 G11
Vineland Fla., U.S.A. 28°23N 81°30W 133 B1
Vineland N.J., U.S.A. 39°29N 75°2W 309 F16
Vineuil France 47°35N 1°22E 172 E8
Vinga Romania 46°1N 21°14E 182 D6
Vingåker Sweden 59°2N 15°52E 162 E9
Vingelen Norway 62°25N 10°52E 164 B7
Vingnes Norway 61°7N 10°26E 164 C7
Vinh Vietnam 18°45N 105°38E 236 C5
Vinh Loi = Bac Lieu Vietnam 9°17N 105°43E 237 H5
Vinh Long Vietnam 10°16N 105°57E 237 G5
Vinh Moc Vietnam 21°18N 105°1E 236 B5
Vinh Yen Vietnam 21°21N 105°35E 228 G5
Vinhais Portugal 41°50N 7°5W 194 D3
Vinica Croatia 46°20N 16°9E 199 B13
Vinica Macedonia 41°53N 22°30E 202 E6
Vinica Slovenia 45°28N 15°16E 199 C12
Vinings U.S.A. 33°53N 84°29W 113 A2
Vinita U.S.A. 36°39N 95°9W 314 C7
Vinje Sør-Trøndelag, Norway 63°12N 9°0E 164 A5
Vinje Telemark, Norway 59°37N 7°51E 164 E4
Vinjo Norway 60°48N 6°30E 164 D3
Vinkovci Croatia 45°19N 18°48E 182 E3
Vinnitsa = Vinnytsya Ukraine 49°15N 28°30E 177 D15
Vinnytsya Ukraine 49°15N 28°30E 177 D15
Vinnytsya □ Ukraine 49°20N 28°15E 177 D15
Vinodelnoye = Ipatovo Russia 45°45N 42°50E 191 H6
Vinohrady Prague, Czech Rep. 135 c3
Vinoř Czech Rep. 50°8N 14°34E 135 B3
Vinslöv Sweden 56°7N 13°55E 163 H7
Vinson Massif Antarctica 78°35S 85°25W 151 D16
Vinstra Norway 61°37N 9°44E 164 C6
Vinstra → Norway 61°37N 9°44E 164 C6
Vintar Phil. 18°14N 120°39E 232 B3
Vintjärn Sweden 60°50N 16°4E 162 D10
Vinton Calif., U.S.A. 39°48N 120°10W 306 F6
Vinton Iowa, U.S.A. 42°10N 92°1W 310 B4
Vinton La., U.S.A. 30°11N 93°35W 314 F8
Vințu de Jos Romania 46°0N 23°30E 183 D8
Vinukonda India 16°4N 79°45E 245 F4
Viöl Germany 54°34N 9°11E 178 A5
Viola U.S.A. 41°12N 90°35W 310 C6
Violet Hill Hong Kong, China 22°15N 114°11E 122 B3
Violet Town Australia 36°38S 145°42E 283 D6
Violet Valley ۞ Australia 17°10S 127°55E 278 C4
Vioolsdrif S. Africa 28°46S 17°39E 270 C2
Viotia Greece 38°20N 23°0E 204 C5
Vipacco = Vipava Slovenia 45°51N 13°58E 199 C10
Vipava Slovenia 45°51N 13°58E 199 C10
Vipiteno Italy 46°54N 11°26E 199 B8
Viqueque E. Timor 8°52S 126°23E 231 F7
Vir Croatia 44°17N 15°3E 199 D12
Virac Phil. 13°30N 124°20E 232 E5
Virachey Cambodia 13°59N 106°49E 236 F6
Virachey △ Cambodia 14°14N 106°55E 236 E6
Virago Sd. Canada 54°0N 132°30W 296 C2
Virajpet = Virarajendrapet India 12°10N 75°50E 245 H2
Viramgam India 23°5N 72°0E 242 H5
Viranansehir Turkey 37°13N 39°45E 213 D8
Virányos Hungary 47°31N 18°59E 117 A1
Virarajendrapet India 12°10N 75°50E 245 H2
Virawah Pakistan 24°31N 70°46E 242 G4
Virbalis Lithuania 54°39N 22°49E 184 D9
Virden Man., Canada 49°50N 100°56W 297 D8
Virden Ill., U.S.A. 39°30N 89°46W 310 E7
Vire France 48°50N 0°53W 172 D6
Vire → France 49°20N 1°7W 172 C5
Virei Angola 15°43S 12°52E 265 F2
Virgem da Lapa Brazil 16°49S 42°21W 333 E3
Vírgenes, C. Argentina 52°19S 68°21W 336 D3
Virgin → U.S.A. 36°28N 114°21W 305 H6
Virgin Gorda Br. Virgin Is. 18°30N 64°26W 321 C7
Virgin Is. (British) ☑ W. Indies 18°30N 64°30W 321 C7
Virgin Is. (U.S.) ☑ W. Indies 18°20N 65°0W 321 C7
Virgin Islands △ U.S. Virgin Is. 18°21N 64°43W 321 b
Virginia Free State, S. Africa 28°8S 26°55E 270 C4
Virginia Ill., U.S.A. 39°57N 90°13W 310 E6
Virginia Minn., U.S.A. 47°31N 92°32W 308 B7
Virginia □ U.S.A. 37°30N 78°45W 309 G14
Virginia, L. U.S.A. 28°35N 81°20W 133 A2
Virginia Beach U.S.A. 36°49N 76°9W 309 F16
Virginia City Mont., U.S.A. 45°18N 111°56W 304 D8
Virginia City Nev., U.S.A. 39°19N 119°39W 306 F7
Virginia Falls Canada 61°38N 125°42W 296 A3
Virginia Gardens U.S.A. 25°48N 80°18W 129 D1
Virginia Key U.S.A. 25°44N 80°8W 129 D3
Virginiatown Canada 48°9N 79°36W 298 C4
Virje Croatia 46°4N 16°59E 199 B13
Viroflay France 48°48N 2°10E 134 B2
Vironas Greece 37°55N 23°46E 112 B2
Viroqua U.S.A. 43°34N 90°53W 308 D8
Virovitica Croatia 45°51N 17°21E 182 E2
Virpazar Montenegro 42°14N 19°6E 202 D3
Virpur India 21°51N 70°42E 242 J4
Virsbo Sweden 59°52N 16°2E 162 E10
Virserum Sweden 57°20N 15°35E 163 G9
Virton Belgium 49°35N 5°32E 170 E5
Virú Peru 8°25S 78°45W 330 B2
Virudunagar India 9°30N 77°58E 245 K3
Virum Denmark 55°47N 12°27E 118 A2
Virunga △ Dem. Rep. of the Congo 0°5N 29°38E 268 B2
Vis Croatia 43°4N 16°10E 199 E13
Visalia U.S.A. 36°20N 119°18W 306 J7
Visayan Sea Phil. 11°30N 123°30E 233 F4
Visayas □ Phil. 9°30N 122°45E 233 G4
Visby Sweden 57°37N 18°18E 163 G12
Viscount Melville Sd. Canada 74°10N 108°0W 295 C10
Visé Belgium 50°44N 5°41E 170 D5
Vise, Ostrov Russia 79°33N 76°50E 214 B8
Višegrad Bos.-H. 43°47N 19°17E 182 G4
Viseu Brazil 1°10S 46°5W 332 B2
Viseu Portugal 40°40N 7°55W 194 E3
Viseu □ Portugal 40°40N 7°55W 194 E3
Vişeu de Sus Romania 47°45N 24°25E 183 C9
Vishakhapatnam India 17°45N 83°20E 244 F6
Vişina Romania 43°52N 24°27E 183 G9
Vişineşti Moldova 46°20N 28°27E 183 D13
Visingsö Sweden 58°2N 14°20E 163 F8
Visitacion Valley U.S.A. 37°42N 122°23W 136 B2
Viskafors Sweden 57°37N 12°50E 163 G6
Viskan → Sweden 57°14N 12°12E 163 G6
Viški Kanal Croatia 43°4N 16°5E 199 E13
Vislanda Sweden 56°46N 14°30E 163 H8
Visnagar India 23°45N 72°32E 242 H5
Višnja Gora Slovenia 45°58N 14°45E 199 C11
Viso, Mte. Italy 44°38N 7°5E 198 D4
Viso del Marqués Spain 38°32N 3°34W 195 G7
Visoko Bos.-H. 43°58N 18°10E 182 G3
Visokoi I. Antarctica 56°43S 27°15W 151 B1
Visp Switz. 46°17N 7°52E 179 J3
Vissefjärda Sweden 56°32N 15°35E 163 H9
Visselhövede Germany 52°59N 9°34E 178 C5
Vissenbjerg Denmark 55°23N 10°7E 163 J4
Vista U.S.A. 33°12N 117°14W 307 M9
Vista Alegre Santiago, Chile 33°30S 70°43W 137 C1
Vista Alegre Lima, Peru 12°9S 76°59W 124 B3
Vista Grove U.S.A. 33°51N 84°16W 113 A3
Vistabella Trin. & Tob. 10°17N 61°27W 323 t
Vistonida, L. Greece 41°0N 25°7E 203 E9
Vistonikos, Ormos = Vistonida, L. Greece 41°0N 25°7E 203 E9
Vistula = Wisła → Poland 54°22N 18°55E 184 D5
Vistula Lagoon = Zalew Wiślany Poland 54°20N 19°50E 184 D6
Vit → Bulgaria 43°30N 24°30E 203 C8
Vita India 17°17N 74°33E 244 F2
Vitacura Chile 33°23S 70°35W 137 B2
Vitanje Slovenia 46°25N 15°18E 199 B12
Vitebsk = Vitsyebsk Belarus 55°10N 30°15E 188 E6
Viterbo Italy 42°25N 12°6E 199 F9
Vitez Bos.-H. 44°10N 17°48E 182 F2
Viti Levu Fiji 17°30S 177°30E 287 A1
Vitiaz Str. Papua N. G. 5°40S 147°10E 286 C4
Vitiaz Trench Pac. Oc. 10°0S 170°0E 277 C13
Vitigudino Spain 41°1N 6°26W 194 D4
Vitim Russia 59°28N 112°35E 215 D12
Vitim → Russia 59°26N 112°34E 215 D12
Vitina Bos.-H. 43°17N 17°29E 199 E14
Vitina Greece 37°40N 22°10E 204 D4
Vitínia Italy 41°47N 12°24E 136 C1
Vítkov Czech Rep. 49°46N 17°45E 181 B10
Vitória = Vitória de Santo Antão Brazil 8°10S 35°20W 332 C4
Vitória Espirito Santo, Brazil 20°20S 40°22W 333 F3
Vitória Pará, Brazil 2°54S 52°1W 329 D7
Vitória da Conquista Brazil 14°51S 40°51W 333 D3
Vitória de Santo Antão Brazil 8°10S 35°20W 332 C4
Vitoria-Gasteiz Spain 42°50N 2°41W 196 C2
Vitória Seamount Atl. Oc. 20°0S 44°0W 152 J8
Vitorino Freire Brazil 4°4S 45°10W 332 B2
Vitosha △ Bulgaria 42°36N 23°18E 202 D7
Vitré France 48°8N 1°12W 172 D5
Vitry-le-François France 48°43N 4°33E 173 D11
Vitry-sur-Seine France 48°47N 2°23E 134 B3
Vitsand Sweden 60°20N 13°0E 162 D7
Vitsi, Oros Greece 40°40N 21°25E 202 F5
Vitsyebsk Belarus 55°10N 30°15E 188 E6
Vitsyebsk □ Belarus 55°10N 28°50E 188 E5
Vittaryd Sweden 56°58N 13°57E 163 H7
Vitteaux France 47°24N 4°30E 173 E11
Vittel France 48°12N 5°57E 173 D12
Vittória Italy 36°57N 14°32E 201 F7
Vittório = Vittório Véneto Italy 45°59N 12°18E 199 C9
Vittório Véneto Italy 45°59N 12°18E 199 C9
Vittoriosa Malta 35°54N 14°31E 206 F8
Vittsjö Sweden 56°20N 13°40E 163 H7
Viveiro Spain 43°39N 7°38W 194 B3
Vivian U.S.A. 32°53N 93°59W 314 E8
Viviers France 44°30N 4°40E 175 D8
Vivonne S. Austral., Australia 35°59S 137°9E 282 C2
Vivonne Vienne, France 46°25N 0°15E 174 B4
Vivonne B. Australia 35°59S 137°9E 282 C2
Viwa Fiji 17°10S 177°58E 287 A1
Vizagapatam = Vishakhapatnam India 17°45N 83°20E 244 F6
Vizandino, Moussio Athens, Greece 112 b3
Vizcaíno, Desierto de Mexico 27°30N 113°45W 318 B2
Vizcaíno, Sierra Mexico 27°30N 114°0W 318 B2
Vizcaya □ Spain 43°15N 2°45W 196 B2
Vize Turkey 41°34N 27°45E 203 E11
Vizianagaram India 18°6N 83°30E 244 E6
Vizille France 45°5N 5°46E 175 C9
Viziñada Croatia 45°20N 13°46E 199 C10
Viziru Romania 45°0N 27°43E 183 E12
Vizlinsky Zaliv = Zalew Wiślany Poland 54°20N 19°50E 184 D6
Vizzini Italy 37°10N 14°45E 201 E7
Vlaardingen Neths. 51°55N 4°21E 170 C4
Vlachiotis Greece 36°52N 22°42E 204 E4
Vlădeasa, Vf. Romania 46°47N 22°50E 182 D7
Vladičin Han Serbia 42°42N 22°1E 202 D6
Vladikavkaz Russia 43°0N 44°35E 191 J7
Vladimir Russia 56°15N 40°30E 188 D11
Vladimir □ Russia 56°5N 40°10E 190 B5
Vladimir Volynskiy = Volodymyr-Volynskyy Ukraine 50°50N 24°18E 177 C13
Vladimirci Serbia 44°36N 19°50E 202 B3
Vladimirovac Serbia 45°1N 20°53E 182 E5
Vladimirovka = Yuzhno-Sakhalinsk Russia 46°58N 142°45E 219 B17
Vladimirovka Russia 48°27N 46°10E 191 F8
Vladimirovo Bulgaria 43°32N 23°22E 202 C7
Vladislavovka Ukraine 45°12N 35°29E 189 K8
Vladivostok Russia 43°10N 131°53E 220 C5
Vladykino Russia 55°51N 37°35E 129 A2
Vlăhiţa Romania 46°21N 25°31E 183 D10
Vlasenica Bos.-H. 44°11N 18°59E 182 F3
Vlašić Bos.-H. 44°19N 17°37E 182 F2
Vlašim Czech Rep. 49°40N 14°53E 180 B7
Vlasinsko Jezero Serbia 42°44N 22°22E 202 D6
Vlasotince Serbia 42°59N 22°7E 202 D6
Vlieland Neths. 53°16N 4°55E 170 A4
Vlissingen Neths. 51°26N 3°34E 170 C3
Vlkolínec Slovak Rep. 49°1N 19°16E 181 B12
Vlorë Albania 40°32N 19°28E 202 F3
Vlorës, Gjiri i Albania 40°29N 19°27E 202 F3
Vltava → Czech Rep. 50°21N 14°30E 180 A7
Vo Dat Vietnam 11°9N 107°31E 237 G6
Voćin Croatia 45°37N 17°33E 182 E2
Vöcklabruck Austria 48°1N 13°39E 180 C6
Vodice Croatia 43°47N 15°47E 199 E12
Vodlozersky △ Russia 62°40N 37°5E 214 C1
Vodňany Czech Rep. 49°9N 14°11E 180 B7
Vodnjan Croatia 44°59N 13°52E 199 D10
Vodopyanovo = Donskoy Russia 53°55N 38°15E 188 F10
Voe U.K. 60°21N 1°16W 167 A7
Vogan Togo 6°23N 1°30E 263 D5
Vogar Iceland 63°58N 22°22W 155 D4
Vogel Pk. Nigeria 8°24N 11°47E 263 D7
Vogelkop = Doberai, Jazirah Indonesia 1°25S 133°0E 231 E8
Vogelsberg Germany 50°31N 9°12E 178 E5
Voghera Italy 44°59N 9°1E 198 D6
Voh N. Cal. 20°58S 164°42E 288 d
Vohibinany Madag. 18°49S 49°4E 272 B2
Vohilava Madag. 21°4S 48°0E 272 C2
Vohimarina = Iharana Madag. 13°25S 50°0E 272 A3
Vohimena, Tanjon' i Madag. 25°36S 45°8E 272 D2

Vohipeno *Madag.* 22°22S 47°51E 272 C2
Voi *Kenya* 3°25S 38°32E 268 C4
Void-Vacon *France* 48°40N 5°36E 173 D12
Voineşti *Iaşi, Romania* 47°5N 27°27E 183 C12
Voineşti *Prahova, Romania* 45°5N 25°14E 183 E10
Voinjama *Liberia* 8°25N 9°44W 262 D3
Voiron *France* 45°22N 5°35E 175 C9
Voisey B. *Canada* 56°15N 61°50W 299 A7
Voitsberg *Austria* 47°3N 15°9E 180 D8
Vojens *Denmark* 55°16N 9°18E 163 J3
Vojmsjön *Sweden* 65°0N 16°24E 160 D17
Vojnić *Croatia* 45°19N 15°43E 199 C12
Vojnik *Italy* 46°18N 15°19E 199 B12
Vojvodina □ *Serbia* 45°20N 20°0E 182 E5
Vokeo I. *Papua N. G.* 3°14S 144°2E 286 B3
Vokhtoga *Russia* 58°46N 41°8E 188 C11
Vokovice *Czech Rep.* 50°5N 14°21E 135 B2
Volary *Czech Rep.* 48°54N 13°52E 180 C6
Volborg *U.S.A.* 45°51N 105°41W 304 D11
Volcán de Colima △ *Mexico* 19°30N 103°40W 318 D4
Volcano *U.S.A.* 19°26N 155°14W 302 D6
Volcano Is. = Kazan-Rettō *Pac. Oc.* 25°0N 141°0E 288 E6
Volcans △ *Rwanda* 1°30S 29°26E 268 C2
Volcans d'Auvergne ⌓ *France* 45°20N 2°40E 174 C6
Volchansk = Vovchansk *Ukraine* 50°17N 36°58E 189 G9
Volchikha *Russia* 52°2N 80°23E 217 B10
Volchya → *Ukraine* 48°32N 36°0E 189 H8
Volda *Norway* 62°9N 6°5E 164 B3
Volga = Privolzhskiy □ *Russia* 56°0N 50°0E 214 D6
Volga *Russia* 57°58N 38°16E 188 C10
Volga → *Russia* 46°0N 48°30E 191 G9
Volga Hts. = Privolzhskaya Vozvyshennost *Russia* 51°0N 46°0E 190 E7
Volgelsdorf *Germany* 52°30N 13°44E 115 B5
Volgo-Baltiyskiy Kanal *Russia* 60°0N 38°0E 188 B9
Volgo-Donskoy Kanal *Russia* 48°40N 43°37E 191 F7
Volgodonsk *Russia* 47°33N 42°5E 191 G6
Volgograd *Russia* 48°40N 44°25E 191 F7
Volgograd □ *Russia* 49°40N 44°30E 190 F7
Volgogradskoye Vdkhr. *Russia* 50°0N 45°20E 190 E8
Volgorechensk *Russia* 57°28N 41°14E 190 B5
Volimes *Greece* 37°52N 20°39E 207 D2
Volintiri *Moldova* 46°26N 29°37E 183 D14
Volissos *Greece* 38°29N 25°54E 205 C7
Volkach *Germany* 49°52N 10°14E 179 F6
Völkermarkt *Austria* 46°39N 14°39E 180 E7
Volkhonka-Zil *Russia* 55°39N 37°37E 129 C2
Volkhov *Russia* 59°55N 32°15E 188 C7
Volkhov → *Russia* 60°8N 32°20E 188 B7
Volkhovstroy = Volkhov *Russia* 59°55N 32°15E 188 C7
Völklingen *Germany* 49°15N 6°50E 179 F2
Volkovysk = Vawkavysk *Belarus* 53°9N 24°30E 177 B13
Volksrust *S. Africa* 27°24S 29°53E 271 C4
Voll *Norway* 62°31N 7°27E 164 B4
Vollen *Norway* 59°48N 10°27E 133 B1
Volnovakha *Ukraine* 47°35N 37°30E 189 J9
Volochanka *Russia* 71°0N 94°28E 215 B10
Volodarsk *Russia* 56°12N 43°15E 190 B6
Volodarskoye *Russia* 59°54N 30°23E 137 B2
Volodymyr-Volynskyy *Ukraine* 50°50N 24°18E 177 C13
Vologda *Russia* 59°10N 39°45E 188 C10
Vologda □ *Russia* 60°15N 39°0E 188 B10
Volokolamsk *Russia* 56°5N 35°57E 188 D8
Volokonovka *Russia* 50°33N 37°52E 189 G9
Volos *Greece* 39°24N 22°59E 204 B4
Vološinovo = Novi Bečej *Serbia* 45°36N 20°10E 182 E5
Volosovo *Russia* 59°27N 29°32E 188 C5
Volovets *Ukraine* 48°43N 23°11E 183 B8
Volovo *Russia* 53°35N 38°1E 188 F10
Volozhin = Valozhyn *Belarus* 54°3N 26°30E 177 A14
Volsk *Russia* 52°5N 47°22E 190 D8
Volta □ *Ghana* 7°0N 0°30E 263 D5
Volta → *Ghana* 5°46N 0°41E 263 D5
Volta, L. *Ghana* 7°30N 0°0 263 D5
Volta Blanche = White Volta → *Ghana* 9°10N 1°15W 263 D4
Volta Redonda *Brazil* 22°31S 44°5W 333 F3
Voltaire, C. *Australia* 14°16S 125°35E 278 B4
Volterra *Italy* 43°24N 10°51E 198 E7
Voltri *Italy* 44°26N 8°45E 198 D5
Volturno → *Italy* 41°1N 13°55E 200 A6
Volubilis *Morocco* 34°2N 5°33W 260 B3
Volvi, L. *Greece* 40°40N 23°34E 202 F7
Volyn □ *Ukraine* 51°15N 24°30E 177 C13
Volyně *Czech Rep.* 49°10N 13°53E 180 B6
Volynkina-Derevnya *Russia* 59°53N 30°18E 137 B1
Volzhsk *Russia* 55°57N 48°23E 190 C9
Volzhskiy *Russia* 48°56N 44°46E 191 F7
Vomo *Fiji* 17°30S 177°15E 287 A1
Vonavona *Solomon Is.* 8°15S 157°5E 287 M9
Vondelpark *Neths.* 52°21N 4°52E 112 A2
Vondrozo *Madag.* 22°49S 47°20E 272 C2
Vonitsa *Greece* 38°55N 20°53E 207 B2
Vopnafjörður *Iceland* 65°45N 14°50W 155 B12
Vorarlberg □ *Austria* 47°20N 10°0E 180 D2
Voras Oros *Greece* 40°57N 21°45E 202 F5
Vorbasse *Denmark* 55°39N 9°6E 163 J3
Vorchdorf *Austria* 48°0N 13°55E 180 C6
Vorderrhein → *Switz.* 46°49N 9°25E 179 J5
Vordingborg *Denmark* 55°0N 11°54E 163 J5
Vorë *Albania* 41°23N 19°40E 202 E3
Voreio Aigaio □ *Greece* 38°50N 25°30E 205 C7
Voreios Sporades *Greece* 39°15N 23°30E 204 B5
Voreppe *France* 45°18N 5°39E 175 C9
Vori *Greece* 35°4N 24°49E 207 E5
Vorios Evoikos Kolpos *Greece* 38°45N 23°15E 204 C5
Vorkuta *Russia* 67°48N 64°20E 186 A11
Vorma → *Norway* 60°9N 11°29E 164 D8
Vormsi *Estonia* 59°1N 23°13E 188 C2
Vorona → *Russia* 51°22N 42°3E 190 E6
Voronezh *Russia* 51°40N 39°10E 189 G10
Voronezh *Ukraine* 51°47N 33°28E 189 G7
Voronezh □ *Russia* 51°30N 39°30E 190 E4
Voronezh → *Russia* 51°32N 39°10E 189 G10
Vorontsovo-Aleksandrovskoye = Zelenokumsk *Russia* 44°24N 44°0E 191 H6
Voroshilov = Ussuriysk *Russia* 43°48N 131°59E 220 C5
Voroshilovgrad = Luhansk *Ukraine* 48°38N 39°15E 189 H10
Voroshilovsk = Alchevsk *Ukraine* 48°30N 38°45E 189 H10
Voroshilovsk = Stavropol *Russia* 45°5N 42°0E 191 H6
Vorpommersche Boddenlandschaft △ *Germany* 54°25N 12°32E 178 A8
Vorskla → *Ukraine* 48°50N 34°10E 189 H8
Võrts järv *Estonia* 58°16N 26°3E 188 C4
Vöru *Estonia* 57°48N 26°54E 188 D4
Vösendorf *Austria* 48°7N 16°20E 142 B2
Vosges *France* 48°20N 7°10E 173 D14
Vosges □ *France* 48°12N 6°20E 173 D13
Vosges du Nord ⌓ *France* 49°0N 7°30E 173 D14
Voskopojë *Albania* 40°35N 20°33E 202 F4
Voskresensk *Russia* 55°19N 38°43E 188 E10
Voskresenskoye *Russia* 56°51N 45°30E 190 B7
Voss *Norway* 60°38N 6°26E 164 D3
Vostochnyy Port *Russia* 42°44N 133°4E 220 C6
Vostok = Neftegorsk *Russia* 44°25N 39°45E 191 H4
Vostok *Antarctica* 78°30S 106°50E 151 D8
Vostok I. *Kiribati* 10°5S 152°23W 289 J12
Votice *Czech Rep.* 49°38N 14°39E 180 B7
Votkinsk *Russia* 57°0N 53°55E 186 C9
Votkinskoye Vdkhr. *Russia* 57°22N 55°12E 186 C10
Votuporanga *Brazil* 20°24S 49°59W 333 F2
Vouga → *Portugal* 40°41N 8°40W 194 E2
Vouillé *France* 46°38N 0°10E 172 F7
Voula *Greece* 37°49N 23°45E 112 C2
Vouliagmeni *Greece* 37°50N 23°46E 112 C2
Voulkaria, L. *Greece* 38°52N 20°50E 207 B2
Voulou *C.A.R.* 8°33N 22°36E 264 A4
Vouxa, Akra *Greece* 35°37N 23°32E 207 E4
Vouzela *Portugal* 40°43N 8°7W 194 E2
Vouziers *France* 49°22N 4°40E 173 C11
Vovchansk *Ukraine* 50°17N 36°58E 189 G9
Vovodo → *C.A.R.* 5°40N 24°21E 264 A4
Vowchyn *Belarus* 52°18N 23°18E 185 F10
Voyageurs △ *U.S.A.* 48°32N 93°0W 308 A7
Voynitsa *Russia* 65°10N 30°20E 160 D24
Voyvozh *Russia* 62°56N 54°56E 186 B9
Vozhe, Ozero *Russia* 60°45N 39°0E 188 B10
Vozhega *Russia* 60°29N 40°12E 188 B11
Voznesensk *Ukraine* 47°35N 31°21E 189 J6
Voznesenye *Russia* 61°0N 35°28E 188 B8
Vrå *Denmark* 57°21N 9°56E 163 G3
Vráble *Slovak Rep.* 48°15N 18°16E 181 C11
Vraćevšnica *Serbia* 44°2N 20°34E 202 B4
Vrachneika *Greece* 38°10N 21°40E 204 C3
Vrådal *Norway* 59°20N 8°25E 164 E5
Vrancea □ *Romania* 45°50N 26°45E 183 E11
Vrancei, Munţii *Romania* 46°0N 26°30E 183 E11
Vrangel *Russia* 42°43N 133°5E 220 C6
Vrangelya, Ostrov *Russia* 71°0N 180°0E 215 B18
Vranica *Bos.-H.* 43°55N 17°50E 182 G2
Vranje *Serbia* 42°34N 21°54E 202 D5
Vranjska Banja *Serbia* 42°34N 22°1E 202 D6
Vranov nad Topl'ou *Slovak Rep.* 48°53N 21°40E 181 C14
Vransko *Slovenia* 46°17N 14°58E 199 B11
Vransko Jezero *Croatia* 43°53N 15°34E 199 E12
Vrapčište *Macedonia* 41°50N 20°53E 202 E4
Vratsa *Bulgaria* 43°15N 23°30E 202 C7
Vratsa □ *Bulgaria* 43°15N 23°30E 202 C7
Vråvatn *Norway* 59°20N 8°8E 164 E5
Vrbas *Serbia* 45°40N 19°40E 182 E4
Vrbas → *Bos.-H.* 45°8N 17°29E 182 E2
Vrbnik *Croatia* 45°4N 14°40E 199 C11
Vrbovec *Croatia* 45°53N 16°28E 199 C13
Vrbovsko *Croatia* 45°24N 15°5E 199 C12
Vrchlabí *Czech Rep.* 50°38N 15°37E 180 A8
Vrede *S. Africa* 27°24S 29°6E 271 C4
Vredefort *S. Africa* 27°0S 27°22E 270 C4
Vredehoek *S. Africa* 33°57S 18°25E 118 A1
Vreden *Germany* 52°2N 6°50E 178 C2
Vredenburg *S. Africa* 32°56S 18°0E 270 D2
Vredendal *S. Africa* 31°41S 18°35E 270 D2
Vretstorp *Sweden* 59°1N 14°53E 162 E8
Vrgorac *Croatia* 43°12N 17°20E 199 E14
Vrhnika *Slovenia* 45°58N 14°15E 199 C11
Vriddhachalam *India* 11°30N 79°20E 245 J4
Vrïdi *Ivory C.* 5°15N 4°3W 262 D4
Vrigstad *Sweden* 57°22N 14°28E 163 G8
Vrindavan *India* 27°37N 77°40E 242 F7
Vrisses *Greece* 35°23N 24°13E 207 E5
Vrnograč *Bos.-H.* 45°10N 15°57E 199 C12
Vrondados *Greece* 38°25N 26°7E 205 C8
Vrpolje *Croatia* 45°13N 18°24E 182 E3
Vršac *Serbia* 45°8N 21°20E 182 E6
Vrsacki Kanal *Serbia* 45°15N 21°0E 182 E5
Vršovice *Czech Rep.* 50°4N 14°28E 135 B2
Vrútky *Slovak Rep.* 49°7N 18°55E 181 B11
Vryburg *S. Africa* 26°55S 24°45E 270 C3
Vryheid *S. Africa* 27°45S 30°47E 271 C5
Vsetín *Czech Rep.* 49°20N 18°0E 181 B11
Vu Liet *Vietnam* 18°43N 105°23E 236 C5
Vŭcha → *Bulgaria* 42°10N 24°26E 203 D8
Vučitrn = Vushtrri *Kosovo* 42°49N 20°59E 202 D4
Vuga *South Sudan* 5°21N 29°40E 257 F2
Vukovar *Croatia* 45°21N 18°59E 182 E3
Vuktyl *Russia* 63°52N 57°20E 214 C6
Vulcan *Alta., Canada* 50°25N 113°15W 296 C6
Vulcan *Romania* 45°23N 23°17E 183 E8
Vulcaneşti *Moldova* 45°41N 28°18E 183 E13
Vulcano *Italy* 38°24N 14°58E 201 D7
Vŭlchedruma *Bulgaria* 43°42N 23°27E 202 C7
Vulkaneshty = Vulcaneşti *Moldova* 45°41N 28°18E 183 E13
Vunduzi → *Mozam.* 18°56S 34°1E 269 F3
Vung Tau *Vietnam* 10°21N 107°4E 237 G6
Vunidawa *Fiji* 17°50S 178°21E 287 A2
Vunisea *Fiji* 19°3S 178°10E 287 B2
Vuntut △ *Canada* 68°25N 139°41W 294 D4
Vuranggo *Solomon Is.* 6°39S 156°38E 287 L9
Vŭrbitsa *Bulgaria* 42°59N 26°40E 203 D10
Vurshets *Bulgaria* 43°13N 23°23E 202 C7
Vushtrri *Kosovo* 42°49N 20°59E 202 D4
Vutcani *Romania* 46°26N 27°59E 183 D12
Vuzlove *Ukraine* 48°22N 22°24E 182 B7
Vwaza ⌓ *Malawi* 10°58S 33°25E 269 E3
Vyara *India* 21°8N 73°28E 244 D1
Vyartsilya *Russia* 62°8N 30°45E 188 A6
Vyatka = Kirov *Russia* 58°35N 49°40E 186 C8
Vyatka → *Russia* 55°37N 51°28E 190 C10
Vyatskiye Polyany *Russia* 56°14N 51°5E 190 B10
Vyazemskiy *Russia* 47°32N 134°45E 215 E14
Vyazma *Russia* 55°10N 34°15E 188 E8
Vyazniki *Russia* 56°10N 42°10E 190 B6
Vyborg *Russia* 60°43N 28°47E 188 B5
Vyborgskaya Storona *Russia* 59°57N 30°22E 137 B2
Vychegda → *Russia* 61°18N 46°36E 186 B8
Vychodné Beskydy *Europe* 49°20N 22°0E 181 B15
Vyerkhnyadzvinsk *Belarus* 55°45N 27°58E 188 E4
Vyg-ozero *Russia* 63°47N 34°29E 186 B5
Vyhoda *Ukraine* 48°56N 23°55E 183 B8
Vykhino *Russia* 55°42N 37°48E 129 B3
Vyksa *Russia* 55°19N 42°11E 190 C6
Vylkove *Ukraine* 45°28N 29°32E 183 E14
Vylok *Ukraine* 48°6N 22°50E 182 B7
Vynohradiv *Ukraine* 48°9N 23°2E 182 B8
Vypin *India* 10°10N 76°15E 245 J3
Vyrnwy, L. *U.K.* 52°48N 3°31W 168 E4
Vyšehrad *Czech Rep.* 50°3N 14°25E 135 B2
Vyshkiv *Ukraine* 48°44N 23°39E 183 B8
Vyshkove *Ukraine* 48°3N 23°25E 183 B8
Vyshniy Volochek *Russia* 57°30N 34°30E 188 D8
Vyshzha = imeni 26 Bakinskikh Komissarov *Turkmenistan* 39°22N 54°10E 247 B7
Vyškov *Czech Rep.* 49°17N 17°0E 181 B9
Vysokaye *Belarus* 52°22N 23°22E 185 F10
Vysoké Mýto *Czech Rep.* 49°58N 16°10E 181 B9
Vysokovsk *Russia* 56°22N 36°30E 188 D9
Vyšší Brod *Czech Rep.* 48°37N 14°19E 180 C7
Vytegra *Russia* 61°0N 36°27E 188 B9
Vyzhnytsya *Ukraine* 48°15N 25°11E 183 B10
Vyzhnytsya ⌓ *Ukraine* 48°7N 25°15E 183 B10

# W

W du Benin △ *Benin* 11°57N 2°43E 263 C5
W du Burkina Faso △ *Burkina Faso* 11°52N 2°50E 263 C5
W du Niger △ *Niger* 13°31N 2°28E 263 C5
W.A.C. Bennett Dam *Canada* 56°2N 122°6W 296 B4
Wa *Ghana* 10°7N 2°25W 262 C4
Waag *Amsterdam, Neths.* 112 b3
Waal → *Neths.* 51°37N 5°0E 170 C5
Waalwijk *Neths.* 51°42N 5°4E 170 C5
Waanyi-Garawa ☼ *Australia* 18°2S 137°33E 280 B2
Waat *South Sudan* 8°10N 32°7E 257 F3
Wabag *Papua N. G.* 5°32S 143°40E 286 C2
Wabakimi △ *Canada* 50°43N 89°29W 298 B2
Wabana *Canada* 47°40N 53°0W 299 C9
Wabasca → *Canada* 58°22N 115°20W 296 B5
Wabasca-Desmarais *Canada* 55°57N 113°56W 296 B6
Wabash *U.S.A.* 40°48N 85°49W 311 D11
Wabash → *U.S.A.* 37°48N 88°2W 311 G8
Wabasso *U.S.A.* 27°45N 80°26W 317 H9
Wabawng *Burma* 26°20N 97°25E 241 B6
Wabi → *Ethiopia* 7°45N 40°50E 257 F5
Wabigoon L. *Canada* 49°44N 92°44W 297 D10
Wabowden *Canada* 54°55N 98°38W 297 C9
Wąbrzeźno *Poland* 53°16N 18°57E 185 E5
Wabu Hu *China* 32°20N 116°50E 229 A11
Wabuda I. *Papua N. G.* 8°23S 143°37E 286 E2
Wabuk Pt. *Canada* 55°20N 85°5W 298 A2
Wabush *Canada* 52°55N 66°52W 299 B6
Waccasassa B. *U.S.A.* 29°10N 82°50W 317 F7
Wachau *Austria* 48°21N 15°26E 180 C8
Wąchock *Poland* 51°4N 21°1E 185 G8
Wachterhof *Germany* 48°2N 11°42E 131 B3
Wächtersbach *Germany* 50°14N 9°17E 179 E5
Wacissa *U.S.A.* 30°22N 83°59W 316 E6
Waco *U.S.A.* 31°33N 97°9W 314 F6
Waconichi, L. *Canada* 50°8N 74°0W 298 B5
Wad Ban Naqa *Sudan* 16°32N 33°9E 257 D3
Wad Banda *Sudan* 13°10N 27°56E 257 E2
Wad el Haddad *Sudan* 13°50N 33°30E 257 E3
Wad en Nau *Sudan* 14°10N 33°34E 257 E3
Wad Hamid *Sudan* 16°30N 32°45E 257 D3
Wad Medanî *Sudan* 14°28N 33°30E 257 E3
Wad Thana *Pakistan* 27°22N 66°23E 242 F2
Wadai = Ouaddaï □ *Chad* 13°0N 21°0E 259 F4
Wadala *India* 19°1N 72°51E 130 A2
Wadayama *Japan* 35°19N 134°52E 222 B6
Wadbilliga △ *Australia* 36°25S 149°35E 283 D8
Waddān *Libya* 29°9N 16°10E 258 C3
Waddeneilanden *Neths.* 53°25N 5°10E 170 A5
Waddenzee *Neths.* 53°6N 5°10E 170 A5
Waddi, Chappal *Nigeria* 7°2N 11°43E 263 D7
Waddington *U.S.A.* 44°52N 75°12W 313 B9
Waddington, Mt. *Canada* 51°23N 125°15W 296 C3
Waddy Pt. *Australia* 24°58S 153°21E 281 C5
Wadebridge *U.K.* 50°31N 4°51W 169 G3
Wadena *Sask., Canada* 51°57N 103°47W 297 C8
Wadena *Minn., U.S.A.* 46°26N 95°8W 308 B6
Wädenswil *Switz.* 47°14N 8°40E 179 H4
Wadern *Germany* 49°32N 6°53E 179 F2
Wadeye *Australia* 14°28S 129°52E 278 B4
Wadgaon *India* 18°44N 73°39E 244 E1
Wadhams *Canada* 51°30N 127°30W 296 C3
Wadhwan *India* 22°42N 71°41E 242 H4
Wadi *India* 17°4N 76°59E 244 F3
Wadi al-Arayis *West Bank* 31°43N 35°15E 123 B2
Wādī al Ḩayāt □ *Libya* 26°26N 12°30E 258 C2
Wādī as Sīr *Jordan* 31°56N 35°49E 251 G6
Wādī ash Shāţi □ *Libya* 27°27N 13°37E 258 C2
Wâdi Feirân *Egypt* 28°42N 33°19E 251 K4
Wadi Fira □ *Chad* 15°0N 21°0E 259 F4
Wadi Fukin *West Bank* 31°42N 35°6E 123 B1
Wâdi Gemâl, J. *Egypt* 24°35N 35°10E 256 C4
Wadi Halfa *Sudan* 21°53N 31°19E 256 C3
Wādī Mūsá *Jordan* 30°19N 35°29E 251 H6
Wādī Rum △ *Jordan* 29°30N 35°20E 251 J6
Wadian *China* 32°42N 112°29E 229 A9
Wadlew *Poland* 51°31N 19°23E 185 G6
Wadley *Ala., U.S.A.* 33°7N 85°34W 316 B4
Wadley *Ga., U.S.A.* 32°52N 82°24W 316 C7
Wadowice *Poland* 49°52N 19°30E 185 J6
Wadsworth *Nev., U.S.A.* 39°38N 119°17W 304 G4
Wadsworth *Ohio, U.S.A.* 41°2N 81°44W 312 E3
Waduk Pluit *Indonesia* 6°5S 106°46E 122 A1
Waegwan *S. Korea* 35°59N 128°23E 224 E4
Wafangdian *China* 39°38N 121°58E 227 E11
Wafania *Dem. Rep. of the Congo* 1°23S 20°22E 264 C4
Wafrah *Kuwait* 28°33N 47°56E 246 D5
Wagadugu = Ouagadougou *Burkina Faso* 12°25N 1°30W 263 C4
Wagait ☼ *Australia* 13°1S 130°5E 278 B5
Wageima = Wakema *Burma* 16°30N 95°11E 241 G5
Wagener *U.S.A.* 33°39N 81°22W 316 B8
Wageningen *Neths.* 51°58N 5°40E 170 C5
Wageningen *Suriname* 5°50N 56°50W 329 B6
Wager B. *Canada* 65°26N 88°40W 295 D14
Wagga Wagga *Australia* 35°7S 147°24E 283 C7
Waggaman *U.S.A.* 29°55N 90°12W 131 B1
Waghai *India* 20°46N 73°29E 244 D1
Waghete *Indonesia* 4°10S 135°50E 231 E9
Wagin *Australia* 33°17S 117°25E 279 F2
Wagner *U.S.A.* 43°5N 98°18W 308 D4
Wagon Mound *U.S.A.* 36°1N 104°42W 305 H11
Wagoner *U.S.A.* 35°58N 95°22W 314 D7
Wągrowiec *Poland* 52°48N 17°11E 185 F4
Wah *Pakistan* 33°45N 72°40E 242 C5
Wah Fu *Hong Kong, China* 22°15N 114°8E 122 B2
Wahai *Indonesia* 2°48S 129°35E 231 E7
Waharoa *N.Z.* 37°46S 175°45E 284 D4
Wahda = Unity □ *South Sudan* 8°30N 30°0E 257 F3
Wahda *Iraq* 33°18N 44°26E 113 B2
Wahiawā *U.S.A.* 21°30N 158°2W 302 K13
Wahiawā District *U.S.A.* 21°31N 157°58W 302 J14
Wahiawā Res. *U.S.A.* 21°30N 158°3W 302 K13
Wahībah, Ramlat al *Oman* 21°15N 58°45E 249 B7
Wâḩid *Egypt* 30°48N 32°21E 251 H3
Wahnai *Afghan.* 32°40N 65°50E 242 C1
Wahni *Ethiopia* 12°40N 36°39E 257 E4
Wahoo *U.S.A.* 41°13N 96°37W 308 E5
Wahpeton *U.S.A.* 46°16N 96°36W 308 B5
Währing *Austria* 48°14N 16°20E 142 A2
Wahx, Ras il- *Malta* 35°56N 14°20E 206 F7
Wai *India* 17°56N 73°57E 244 F1
Wai'ale'ale *U.S.A.* 22°4N 159°30W 302 A2
Waiale'e *U.S.A.* 21°41N 158°1W 302 J13
Waialua *U.S.A.* 21°34N 158°8W 302 J13
Waialua B. *U.S.A.* 21°35N 158°5W 302 J13
Waialua District *U.S.A.* 21°35N 158°5W 302 J13
Wai'anae *U.S.A.* 21°27N 158°11W 302 K13
Wai'anae Coast *U.S.A.* 21°26N 158°11W 302 K13
Wai'anae District *U.S.A.* 21°28N 158°10W 302 K13
Wai'anae Range *U.S.A.* 21°30N 158°10W 302 K13
Waiao *Taiwan* 24°54N 121°51E 225 B3
Waiapu → *N.Z.* 37°47S 178°29E 284 D7
Waiau *N.Z.* 42°39S 173°5E 285 C8
Waiau → *Canterbury, N.Z.* 42°47S 173°22E 285 C8
Waiau → *Southland, N.Z.* 46°12S 167°38E 285 G2
Waiawa → *U.S.A.* 21°23N 157°59W 302 K14
Waiawe Ganga → *Sri Lanka* 6°15N 81°0E 245 L5
Waibeem *Indonesia* 0°30S 132°59E 231 E8
Waiblingen *Germany* 48°49N 9°18E 179 G5
Waidhofen an der Thaya *Austria* 48°49N 15°17E 180 C8
Waidhofen an der Ybbs *Austria* 47°57N 14°46E 180 D7
Waidmannslust *Germany* 52°36N 13°20E 115 A3
Waigeo *Indonesia* 0°20S 130°40E 231 E8
Waihao → *N.Z.* 44°47S 171°10E 285 E6
Waihao Downs *N.Z.* 44°48S 170°55E 285 E5
Waiheke I. *N.Z.* 36°48S 175°6E 284 C4
Waihi *N.Z.* 37°23S 175°52E 284 D4
Waihi Beach *N.Z.* 37°25S 175°57E 284 D4
Waihola *N.Z.* 46°1S 170°8E 285 G5
Waihola L. *N.Z.* 45°59S 170°8E 285 F5
Waihou → *N.Z.* 37°15S 175°40E 284 D4
Waika *Dem. Rep. of the Congo* 2°22S 25°42E 264 C5
Waikabubak *Indonesia* 9°45S 119°25E 231 F5
Waikaia *N.Z.* 45°44S 168°51E 285 F3
Waikaka *N.Z.* 45°55S 169°1E 285 F4
Waikane *U.S.A.* 21°30N 157°51W 302 J14
Waikare, L. *N.Z.* 37°26S 175°13E 284 D4
Waikareiti, L. *N.Z.* 38°43S 177°10E 284 E6
Waikaremoana *N.Z.* 38°42S 177°12E 284 E6
Waikaremoana, L. *N.Z.* 38°49S 177°9E 284 E6
Waikari *N.Z.* 42°58S 172°41E 285 C7
Waikato → *N.Z.* 37°23S 174°43E 284 D3
Waikelo *Indonesia* 9°24S 119°19E 278 A2
Waikerie *Australia* 34°9S 140°0E 282 C4
Waikiekie *N.Z.* 35°57S 174°16E 284 B3
Waikīkī *U.S.A.* 21°17N 157°50W 302 K14
Waikokopu *N.Z.* 39°3S 177°52E 284 F6
Waikoloa Village *U.S.A.* 19°55N 155°49W 302 D6
Waikouaiti *N.Z.* 45°36S 170°41E 285 F5
Waikouaiti Downs *N.Z.* 45°30S 170°30E 285 F5
Wailea-Makena *U.S.A.* 20°40N 156°27W 302 C5
Wailing Wall = Western Wall *Jerusalem* 123 b3
Wailua *U.S.A.* 22°3N 159°20W 302 A2
Wailuku *U.S.A.* 20°53N 156°30W 302 C5
Waimakariri → *N.Z.* 43°24S 172°42E 285 D7
Waimalu *U.S.A.* 21°24N 157°57W 302 K14
Waimānalo *U.S.A.* 21°21N 157°43W 302 K14
Waimānalo B. *U.S.A.* 21°20N 157°40W 302 K14
Waimānalo Beach *U.S.A.* 21°21N 157°42W 302 K14
Waimangaroa *N.Z.* 41°43S 171°46E 285 B6
Waimano → *U.S.A.* 21°25N 157°58W 302 K14
Waimarie *N.Z.* 41°35S 171°58E 285 B6
Waimate *N.Z.* 44°45S 171°3E 285 E6
Waimea *Hawai'i, U.S.A.* 21°58N 159°40W 302 B2
Waimea *Hawai'i, U.S.A.* 21°39N 158°3W 302 J13
Waimea B. *U.S.A.* 21°40N 158°5W 302 J13
Waimea Plain *N.Z.* 45°55S 168°35E 285 F3
Wainganga → *India* 18°50N 79°55E 244 E4
Waingapu *Indonesia* 9°35S 120°11E 231 F6
Waingmaw *Burma* 25°21N 97°26E 241 C6
Waini → *Guyana* 8°20N 59°50W 329 B6
Wainuiomata *N.Z.* 41°17S 174°56E 284 H3
Wainwright *Alta., Canada* 52°50N 110°50W 297 C6
Wainwright *Alaska, U.S.A.* 70°38N 160°2W 303 A7
Waiotapu *N.Z.* 38°21S 176°25E 284 E5
Waiouru *N.Z.* 39°28S 175°41E 284 F4
Waipa → *N.Z.* 38°16S 175°21E 284 E4
Waipahi *N.Z.* 46°6S 169°15E 285 G4
Waipahu *U.S.A.* 21°23N 158°1W 302 K13
Waipapa Pt. *N.Z.* 46°40S 168°51E 285 G3
Waipara *N.Z.* 43°3S 172°46E 285 D7
Waipawa *N.Z.* 39°56S 176°38E 284 F5
Waipi'o *U.S.A.* 21°25N 158°0W 302 K14
Waipi'o Acres *U.S.A.* 21°28N 158°1W 302 K13
Waipi'o Peninsula *U.S.A.* 21°20N 158°0W 302 K14
Waipiro *N.Z.* 38°2S 178°22E 284 E7
Waipiro Bay *N.Z.* 38°1S 178°21E 284 E7
Waipoua Forest *N.Z.* 35°39S 173°33E 284 B2
Waipu *N.Z.* 35°59S 174°29E 284 B3
Waipukurau *N.Z.* 40°1S 176°33E 284 G5
Wairakei *N.Z.* 38°37S 176°6E 284 E5
Wairarapa, L. *N.Z.* 41°14S 175°15E 284 H4
Wairau → *N.Z.* 41°32S 174°7E 285 B9
Wairio *N.Z.* 45°59S 168°3E 285 F3
Wairoa *N.Z.* 39°3S 177°25E 284 F6
Wairoa → *Hawke's Bay, N.Z.* 39°4S 177°25E 284 F6
Wairoa → *Northland, N.Z.* 36°5S 173°59E 284 C2
Waisantiang *Taiwan* 23°29N 120°1E 225 C2
Waïsisi *Vanuatu* 19°32S 169°22E 287 J7
Waitaki → *N.Z.* 44°56S 171°7E 285 E6
Waitaki Plains *N.Z.* 44°22S 170°0E 285 E5
Waitangi *N.Z.* 35°16S 174°5E 284 B3
Waitara *N.Z.* 38°59S 174°15E 284 E3
Waitara → *N.Z.* 38°59S 174°14E 284 E3
Waitiki Landing *N.Z.* 34°31S 172°50E 284 A1
Waitoa *N.Z.* 37°37S 175°35E 284 D4
Waitomo Caves *N.Z.* 38°16S 175°7E 284 E4
Waitotara *N.Z.* 39°49S 174°44E 284 F3
Waitotara → *N.Z.* 39°51S 174°41E 284 F3
Waitsburg *U.S.A.* 46°16N 118°9W 304 C4
Waitzen = Vác *Hungary* 47°49N 19°10E 182 C4
Waiuku *N.Z.* 37°15S 174°45E 284 D3
Wajima *Japan* 37°30N 137°0E 221 F8
Wajir *Kenya* 1°42N 40°5E 268 B5
Waka *Dem. Rep. of the Congo* 1°1N 20°13E 264 B4
Waka *Ethiopia* 7°2N 37°20E 257 F4
Waka-Kungo *Angola* 11°21S 15°7E 265 E3
Wakarusa *U.S.A.* 41°32N 86°1W 311 C10
Wakasa *Japan* 35°20N 134°24E 222 B6
Wakasa-Wan *Japan* 35°40N 135°30E 223 B7
Wakatipu, L. *N.Z.* 45°5S 168°33E 285 F3
Wakaw *Canada* 52°39N 105°44W 297 C7
Wakaya *Fiji* 17°37S 179°0E 287 A2
Wakayama *Japan* 34°15N 135°15E 223 C7
Wakayama □ *Japan* 33°50N 135°30E 223 D7
Wake *Japan* 34°48N 134°8E 222 C6
Wake Forest *U.S.A.* 35°59N 78°30W 315 D15
Wake I. *Pac. Oc.* 19°18N 166°36E 302 b
WaKeeney *U.S.A.* 39°1N 99°53W 308 F4
Wakefield *Jamaica* 18°26N 77°42W 320 a
Wakefield *N.Z.* 41°24S 173°5E 285 B8
Wakefield *W. Yorks., U.K.* 53°41N 1°29W 168 D6
Wakefield *Mass., U.S.A.* 42°30N 71°5W 116 A2
Wakefield *Mich., U.S.A.* 46°29N 89°56W 308 B9
Wakema *Burma* 16°30N 95°11E 241 G5
Wākhān *Afghan.* 37°8N 73°4E 240 A4
Waki = Mima *Japan* 34°4N 134°9E 222 C6
Wakkanai *Japan* 45°28N 141°35E 220 B10
Wakkerstroom *S. Africa* 27°24S 30°10E 271 C5
Wakool *Australia* 35°28S 144°23E 282 C6
Wakool → *Australia* 35°5S 143°33E 282 C5
Wakre *Indonesia* 0°19S 131°5E 231 E8
Waku *Papua N. G.* 6°5S 149°9E 286 D5
Wakuach, L. *Canada* 55°34N 67°32W 299 A6
Wakulla *U.S.A.* 30°14N 84°14W 316 E5
Wakunai *Papua N. G.* 5°52S 155°13E 286 C8
Walagunya ☼ *Australia* 23°10S 120°50E 278 D3
Walamba *Zambia* 13°30S 28°42E 269 E2
Wałbrzych *Poland* 50°45N 16°18E 185 H3
Walbury Hill *U.K.* 51°21N 1°28W 169 F6
Walcha *Australia* 30°55S 151°31E 283 A9
Walcheren *Neths.* 51°30N 3°35E 170 C3
Walcott *U.S.A.* 41°46N 106°51W 304 F10
Wałcz *Poland* 53°17N 16°27E 185 E3
Waldbröl *Germany* 50°52N 7°37E 178 E3
Waldburg Ra. *Australia* 24°40S 117°35E 279 D2
Waldeck *Germany* 51°12N 9°4E 178 D5
Walden *Colo., U.S.A.* 40°44N 106°17W 304 F10
Walden *N.Y., U.S.A.* 41°34N 74°11W 313 E10
Waldenberg = Wałbrzych *Poland* 50°45N 16°18E 185 H3
Waldesruh *Germany* 52°28N 13°37E 115 B4
Waldkirch *Germany* 48°5N 7°58E 179 G3
Waldkirchen *Germany* 48°43N 13°36E 179 G9
Waldkraiburg *Germany* 48°11N 12°24E 179 G8
Waldo *U.S.A.* 29°48N 82°10W 316 F7
Waldperlach *Germany* 48°4N 11°40E 131 B3
Waldport *U.S.A.* 44°26N 124°4W 304 D1
Waldron *U.S.A.* 34°54N 94°5W 314 D7
Waldtrudering *Germany* 48°6N 11°42E 131 B3
Waldviertel *Austria* 48°30N 15°30E 180 C8
Walebing *Australia* 30°41S 116°13E 279 F2
Walembele *Ghana* 10°30N 1°58W 262 C4
Walensee *Switz.* 47°7N 9°13E 179 H5
Wales *U.S.A.* 65°37N 168°5W 303 D5
Wales □ *U.K.* 52°19N 4°43W 169 E3
Wales I. *Canada* 68°1N 86°40W 295 D14
Walewale *Ghana* 10°21N 0°50W 263 C4
Walgett *Australia* 30°0S 148°5E 281 E4
Walgreen Coast *Antarctica* 75°15S 105°0W 151 D15
Walhalla *Australia* 37°56S 146°29E 283 D7
Walis I. *Papua N. G.* 3°14S 143°18E 286 B2
Walker *Mich., U.S.A.* 42°58N 85°46W 311 B11
Walker *Minn., U.S.A.* 47°6N 94°35W 308 B6
Walker, L. *Canada* 50°20N 67°11W 299 B6
Walker L. *Man., Canada* 54°42N 95°57W 297 C9
Walker L. *Nev., U.S.A.* 38°42N 118°43W 304 G4
Walkerston *Australia* 21°11S 149°8E 280 b
Walkerton *Ont., Canada* 44°10N 81°10W 312 B3
Walkerton *Ind., U.S.A.* 41°28N 86°29W 311 C10
Walkinstown *Ireland* 53°19N 6°20W 120 B1
Wall *U.S.A.* 44°0N 102°8W 308 C2
Wall Street *New York, U.S.A.* 132 f1
Walla Walla *N.S.W., Australia* 35°45S 146°54E 283 C7
Walla Walla *Wash., U.S.A.* 46°4N 118°20W 304 C4
Wallabout Bay *New York, U.S.A.* 132 f2
Wallace *Idaho, U.S.A.* 47°28N 115°56W 304 C6
Wallace *N.C., U.S.A.* 34°44N 77°59W 315 D16
Wallaceburg *Canada* 42°34N 82°23W 312 D2
Wallacetown *N.Z.* 46°21S 168°19E 285 G3
Wallachia = Valahia *Romania* 44°35N 25°0E 183 F9
Wallal *Australia* 26°32S 146°7E 281 D4
Wallam Cr. → *Australia* 28°40S 147°20E 281 D4
Wallambin, L. *Australia* 30°57S 117°35E 279 F2
Wallan *Australia* 37°26S 144°59E 283 D6
Wallangarra *Australia* 28°56S 151°58E 281 D5
Wallaroo *Australia* 33°56S 137°39E 282 B2
Walldürn *Germany* 49°34N 9°22E 179 F5
Wallenhorst *Germany* 52°21N 8°1E 178 C4
Wallenpaupack, L. *U.S.A.* 41°25N 75°15W 313 E9
Wallerawang *Australia* 33°25S 150°4E 283 B9
Wallingat △ *Australia* 32°14S 152°25E 283 B10
Wallingford *Conn., U.S.A.* 41°27N 72°50W 313 E12
Wallingford *Vt., U.S.A.* 43°28N 72°58W 313 C12
Wallis & Futuna, Îs. ☑ *Pac. Oc.* 13°18S 176°10W 277 C15
Wallowa *U.S.A.* 45°34N 117°32W 304 D5
Wallowa Mts. *U.S.A.* 45°20N 117°30W 304 D5
Walls *U.K.* 60°14N 1°33W 167 A7
Walls of Jerusalem △ *Australia* 41°56S 146°15E 281 G4
Wallsend *Australia* 32°55S 151°40E 283 B9
Wallula *U.S.A.* 46°5N 118°54W 304 C4
Wallumbilla *Australia* 26°33S 149°9E 281 D4
Walmsley L. *Canada* 63°25N 108°36W 297 A7
Walney, I. of *U.K.* 54°6N 3°15W 168 C4
Walnut *U.S.A.* 41°33N 89°36W 310 C7
Walnut Canyon ⌓ *U.S.A.* 35°15N 111°20W 305 J8
Walnut Creek *U.S.A.* 37°54N 122°4W 306 H4
Walnut Grove *U.S.A.* 34°4N 86°18W 316 A3
Walnut Hill *U.S.A.* 30°53N 87°30W 317 E2
Walnut Ridge *U.S.A.* 36°4N 90°57W 315 C9
Walpeup *Australia* 35°7S 142°2E 282 C5
Walpole *W. Austral., Australia* 34°58S 116°44E 279 F2
Walpole *Mass., U.S.A.* 42°9N 71°15W 313 D13
Walpole-Nornalup △ *Australia* 35°0S 116°45E 279 G2
Wals *Austria* 47°47N 12°58E 180 D5
Walsall *U.K.* 52°35N 1°58W 169 E6
Walsenburg *U.S.A.* 37°38N 104°47W 305 H11
Walsh *U.S.A.* 37°23N 102°17W 305 H12
Walsh → *Australia* 16°31S 143°42E 280 B3
Walsingham *Canada* 42°40N 80°31W 312 D4
Walsrode *Germany* 52°51N 9°35E 178 C5
Walt Disney Concert Hall *Los Angeles, U.S.A.* 127 b1
Walt Disney World *U.S.A.* 28°22N 81°33W 133 B1
Waltair *India* 17°44N 83°23E 244 F6
Walter F. George Res. *U.S.A.* 31°38N 85°4W 316 D4
Walterboro *U.S.A.* 32°55N 80°40W 316 C9
Walters *U.S.A.* 34°22N 98°19W 314 D5
Waltershausen *Germany* 50°54N 10°33E 178 E6
Waltershausen Gletscher *Greenland* 73°54N 24°25W 154 C8
Waltham *U.S.A.* 42°23N 71°14W 116 A1
Waltham Forest □ *U.K.* 51°35N 0°0 125 A3
Walthamstow *U.K.* 51°34N 0°1W 125 A3
Waltman *U.S.A.* 43°4N 107°12W 304 E10
Walton *Ky., U.S.A.* 38°52N 84°37W 311 F12
Walton *N.Y., U.S.A.* 42°10N 75°8W 313 D9
Walton-on-Thames *U.K.* 51°23N 0°24W 125 B1
Walton-on-the-Naze *U.K.* 51°51N 1°17E 169 F9
Waltonville *U.S.A.* 38°13N 89°2W 310 F7
Walu *Burma* 26°28N 98°2E 241 B7
Walvis Bay *Namibia* 23°0S 14°28E 270 B1
Walvis Ridge *Atl. Oc.* 26°0S 5°0E 152 J12
Walvisbaai = Walvis Bay *Namibia* 23°0S 14°28E 270 B1
Walwa *Australia* 35°59S 147°44E 283 C7
Wamba *Équateur, Dem. Rep. of the Congo* 1°37S 22°30E 264 C4
Wamba *Orientale, Dem. Rep. of the Congo* 2°10N 27°57E 268 B2
Wamba *Rift Valley, Kenya* 0°58N 37°19E 268 B4
Wamba *Nigeria* 8°57N 8°42E 263 D6
Wamba → *Dem. Rep. of the Congo* 3°56S 17°12E 265 C3
Wambardi ☼ *Australia* 16°2S 130°55E 278 C5
Wambeek *Belgium* 50°55N 4°30E 116 A3
Wamego *U.S.A.* 39°12N 96°18W 308 F5
Wamena *Indonesia* 4°4S 138°57E 231 E9
Wampana Karlantijpa ☼ *Australia* 17°45S 132°10E 278 C5
Wampaya ☼ *Australia* 17°20S 135°0E 280 B2
Wampsville *U.S.A.* 43°4N 75°42W 313 C9
Wamsutter *U.S.A.* 41°40N 107°58W 304 F10
Wamulan *Indonesia* 3°27S 126°7E 231 E7
Wan Chai *Hong Kong, China* 22°16N 114°10E 122 B3
Wan Hat *Burma* 20°14N 97°53E 241 E6
Wan Kinghao *Burma* 21°34N 98°17E 241 E7
Wan Lai-kam *Burma* 21°21N 98°22E 241 E7
Wan Tup *Burma* 21°13N 98°42E 228 G2
Wan Xian *China* 38°47N 115°7E 226 E8
Wana *Pakistan* 32°20N 69°32E 242 C3
Wanaaring *Australia* 29°38S 144°9E 281 D3
Wanaka *N.Z.* 44°42S 169°9E 285 E4
Wanaka, L. *N.Z.* 44°33S 169°7E 285 E4
Wan'an *China* 26°26N 114°49E 229 D10
Wanani *Comoros Is.* 12°20S 43°47E 272 a
Wanapa *Bonaire* 12°7N 68°14W 322 h
Wanapitei L. *Canada* 46°45N 80°40W 298 C3
Wanbi *Australia* 34°46S 140°17E 282 C4
Wandaik *Guyana* 4°27N 59°35W 329 C6
Wandan = Wantan *Taiwan* 22°35N 120°29E 225 D2
Wandel Sea = McKinley Sea *Arctic* 82°0N 0°0 154 A11
Wandérama *Ivory C.* 8°37N 4°25W 262 D4
Wandhari *Pakistan* 27°42N 66°48E 242 F2
Wanding *China* 24°5N 98°4E 228 E2
Wandle → *U.K.* 51°27N 0°12W 125 B2
Wando *S. Korea* 34°21N 126°41E 224 E3
Wandoan *Australia* 26°5S 149°55E 281 D4
Wandsworth □ *U.K.* 51°27N 0°11W 125 B2
Wandur Marine △ *India* 11°30N 92°30E 245 J11
Wanfu *China* 40°8N 122°38E 224 B1
Wang → *Thailand* 17°8N 99°2E 236 D2
Wang Kai *South Sudan* 9°3N 29°23E 257 F2
Wang Noi *Thailand* 14°13N 100°44E 236 E3
Wang Saphung *Thailand* 17°18N 101°46E 236 D3
Wang Thong *Thailand* 16°50N 100°26E 236 D3
Wanga *Dem. Rep. of the Congo* 2°58N 29°12E 268 B2
Wangan *Taiwan* 23°21N 119°29E 225 C1
Wanganella *Australia* 35°6S 144°49E 283 C6
Wanganui *N.Z.* 39°56S 175°3E 284 F4
Wanganui → *W. Coast, N.Z.* 43°3S 170°26E 285 D5
Wanganui → *Wanganui-Manawatu, N.Z.* 39°55S 175°4E 284 F4
Wangaratta *Australia* 36°21S 146°19E 283 D7
Wangary *Australia* 34°35S 135°29E 281 E2
Wangcang *China* 32°18N 106°20E 228 A6
Wangcheng *China* 28°22N 112°49E 229 C9
Wangcun *China* 36°41N 117°41E 227 F9
Wangdu *China* 38°40N 115°7E 226 E8
Wangdu Phodrang *Bhutan* 27°28N 89°54E 241 B2
Wangen *Germany* 47°41N 9°50E 179 H5
Wangerin = Węgorzyno *Poland* 53°32N 15°33E 184 E2
Wangerooge *Germany* 53°47N 7°54E 178 B3
Wangiwangi *Indonesia* 5°22S 123°37E 231 F6
Wangjiang *China* 30°10N 116°42E 229 B11
Wangjing *China* 40°0N 116°28E 114 B2
Wangkung *Taiwan* 23°57N 120°20E 225 C2
Wangmo *China* 25°11N 106°5E 228 E6
Wangolodougou *Ivory C.* 9°55N 5°10W 262 D3
Wangqing *China* 43°12N 129°42E 227 C15
Wani *India* 20°5N 78°55E 244 D4
Wanigela *Papua N. G.* 9°21S 149°9E 286 E5
Wanimiyn ☼ *Australia* 15°55S 130°49E 278 C5
Wanjina Wunggurr Wilinggin ☼ *Australia* 16°0S 127°0E 278 C4
Wanjung *Taiwan* 23°43N 121°25E 225 C3
Wankaner *India* 22°35N 71°0E 242 H4
Wankhede Stadium *Mumbai, India* 130 c2
Wanless *Canada* 54°11N 101°21W 297 C8
Wanleweyne *Somalia* 2°37N 44°54E 267 D5
Wanli *Taiwan* 25°10N 121°41E 225 A3
Wanluan *Taiwan* 22°34N 120°34E 225 D2
Wanneroo *Australia* 31°42S 115°46E 279 F2
Wannian *China* 28°42N 117°4E 229 C11
Wanning *China* 18°48N 110°22E 229 a
Wannoo Billabong Roadhouse *Australia* 27°25S 115°49E 279 E2
Wannsee *Germany* 52°25N 13°9E 115 B1
Wanon Niwat *Thailand* 17°38N 103°46E 236 D4
Wanqinsha *China* 22°43N 113°33E 219 a
Wanquan *China* 40°50N 114°40E 226 D8
Wanrong *China* 35°25N 110°50E 226 G6
Wansdorf *Germany* 52°38N 13°5E 115 A1
Wansen = Wiązów *Poland* 50°50N 17°10E 185 H4
Wanshan *China* 27°30N 109°12E 228 D7
Wanshan Qundao *China* 21°57N 113°45E 219 a
Wansheng *China* 28°57N 106°53E 228 C6
Wanstead *N.Z.* 40°8S 176°30E 284 G5
Wanstead *London, U.K.* 51°34N 0°1E 125 A4
Wantage *U.K.* 51°35N 1°25W 169 F6
Wantan *Taiwan* 22°35N 120°29E 225 D2
Wantouliu *Taiwan* 24°1N 120°41E 225 B2
Wanxian *China* 30°42N 108°20E 228 B7
Wanyin *Burma* 20°23N 97°15E 241 E6
Wanyuan *China* 32°4N 108°3E 228 A7
Wanzai *Guangdong, China* 22°12N 113°31E 219 a
Wanzai *Jiangxi, China* 28°7N 114°30E 229 C10
Wapakoneta *U.S.A.* 40°34N 84°12W 311 D12
Wapato *U.S.A.* 46°27N 120°25W 304 C3
Wapawekka L. *Canada* 54°55N 104°40W 297 C8
Wapello *U.S.A.* 41°11N 91°11W 310 C5
Wapikopa L. *Canada* 52°56N 87°53W 298 B2
Wapinda *Dem. Rep. of the Congo* 3°41N 22°48E 264 B4
Wapiti → *Canada* 55°5N 118°18W 296 B5
Wapping *U.K.* 51°30N 0°3W 125 A3
Wappingers Falls *U.S.A.* 41°36N 73°55W 313 E11
Wapsipinicon → *U.S.A.* 41°44N 90°19W 310 C6
Wapusk △ *Canada* 57°46N 93°22W 297 B10
War Galoh *Somalia* 6°17N 47°31E 267 C6
War in the Pacific Nat. Hist. Park △ *Guam* 13°24N 144°39E 302 d
Warab *South Sudan* 8°8N 28°37E 257 F2
Warab □ *South Sudan* 7°30N 28°30E 257 F2
Warabi *Japan* 35°49N 139°41E 223 B11
Warakurna *Australia* 24°59S 128°17E 279 D4
Warangal *India* 17°58N 79°35E 244 F4
Waraseoni *India* 21°45N 80°2E 243 J9
Waratah *Australia* 41°30S 145°30E 281 G4
Waratah B. *Australia* 38°54S 146°5E 283 E7
Warburg *Germany* 51°28N 9°11E 178 D5
Warburton *Vic., Australia* 37°47S 145°42E 283 D6
Warburton *W. Austral., Australia* 26°8S 126°35E 279 E4
Warburton ☼ *Australia* 26°7S 126°34E 279 E4
Warburton → *Australia* 28°4S 137°28E 281 D2
Warburton Groove *Australia* 28°18S 137°8E 281 A2
Warburton Ra. *Australia* 25°55S 126°28E 279 E4
Ward *N.Z.* 41°49S 174°11E 285 B9
Ward → *Australia* 26°28S 146°6E 281 D4
Ward Hunt, C. *Papua N. G.* 8°2S 148°10E 286 E5
Ward Hunt Str. *Papua N. G.* 9°30S 150°0E 286 E6
Ward Mt. *U.S.A.* 37°12N 118°54W 306 H8
Wardang I. *Australia* 34°30S 137°20E 282 C2
Warden *S. Africa* 27°50S 29°0E 271 C4
Wardha *India* 20°45N 78°39E 244 D4
Wardha → *India* 19°57N 79°11E 244 E4
Wardija Point *Malta* 36°2N 14°11E 206 E6
Wards I. *U.S.A.* 40°47N 73°55W 132 B2
Wardsville *Canada* 42°39N 81°45W 312 D3
Ware *Herts., U.K.* 51°49N 0°0 169 F8
Ware *Mass., U.S.A.* 42°16N 72°14W 313 D12
Waregem *Belgium* 50°53N 3°27E 170 D3
Wareham *U.S.A.* 41°46N 70°43W 313 E14
Waremme *Belgium* 50°43N 5°15E 170 D5
Waren *Germany* 53°31N 12°40E 178 B8
Warendorf *Germany* 51°57N 8°1E 178 D4
Waresboro *U.S.A.* 31°15N 82°29W 316 D7

Waria → Papua N. G. 7°49S 147°41E 286 D4
Warialda Australia 29°29S 150°33E 281 D5
Warin Chamrap Thailand 15°12N 104°53E 236 E5
Warka Poland 51°47N 21°12E 185 G8
Warkopi Indonesia 1°12S 134°9E 231 E8
Warkworth N.Z. 36°24S 174°41E 284 C3
Warm Baths = Bela Bela S. Africa 24°51S 28°19E 271 B4
Warm Springs Ga., U.S.A. 32°53N 84°41W 316 C5
Warm Springs Nev., U.S.A. 38°10N 116°20W 305 G5
Warman Canada 52°19N 106°30W 297 C7
Warmbad = Bela Bela S. Africa 24°51S 28°19E 271 B4
Warmbad Namibia 28°25S 18°42E 270 C2
Warming I. = Uunartoq Qeqertoq Greenland 71°33N 21°47W 154 C8
Warmińsko-Mazurskie ☐ Poland 54°0N 21°0E 184 D8
Warminster Wilts., U.K. 51°12N 2°10W 169 F5
Warminster Pa., U.S.A. 40°12N 75°6W 313 F9
Warmun Australia 17°2S 128°12E 278 C4
Warnberg Germany 48°4N 11°31E 131 B2
Warnemünde Germany 54°10N 12°4E 178 A8
Warner Brothers Studios U.S.A. 34°9N 118°20W 126 B2
Warner Mts. U.S.A. 41°40N 120°15W 304 F3
Warner Robins U.S.A. 32°37N 83°36W 316 C6
Warnes Bolivia 17°30S 63°10W 331 D5
Warnow → Germany 54°6N 12°9E 178 A8
Waroona Australia 32°50S 115°58E 279 F2
Warora India 20°14N 79°1E 244 D4
Warrabah △ Australia 30°31S 150°56E 283 A10
Warrabri ☼ Australia 21°1S 134°19E 280 C1
Warracknabeal Australia 36°9S 142°26E 282 D5
Warragul Australia 38°10S 145°58E 283 E6
Warrâq el 'Arab Egypt 30°4N 31°11E 117 A2
Warrego → Australia 30°24S 145°21E 281 E4
Warrego Ra. Australia 24°58S 146°0E 280 C4
Warren N.S.W., Australia 31°42S 147°51E 283 A7
Warren Ark., U.S.A. 33°37N 92°4W 314 E8
Warren Ill., U.S.A. 42°29N 90°0W 310 B7
Warren Ind., U.S.A. 40°41N 85°26W 311 D11
Warren Mich., U.S.A. 42°28N 83°1W 311 B13
Warren Minn., U.S.A. 48°12N 96°46W 308 A5
Warren Ohio, U.S.A. 41°14N 80°49W 312 E4
Warren Pa., U.S.A. 41°51N 79°9W 312 E5
Warrenpoint U.K. 54°6N 6°15W 166 B5
Warrensburg Ill., U.S.A. 39°56N 89°4W 310 E7
Warrensburg Mo., U.S.A. 38°46N 93°44W 310 F3
Warrensburg N.Y., U.S.A. 43°29N 73°46W 313 C11
Warrenton Northern Cape, S. Africa 28°9S 24°47E 270 C3
Warrenton Ga., U.S.A. 33°24N 82°40W 316 B7
Warrenton Mo., U.S.A. 38°49N 91°9W 310 F5
Warrenton Oreg., U.S.A. 46°10N 123°56W 306 D3
Warrenville U.S.A. 33°33N 81°48W 316 B8
Warri Nigeria 5°30N 5°41E 263 D6
Warringal Park Australia 37°45S 145°4E 128 A2
Warrington N.Z. 45°43S 170°35E 285 F5
Warrington Warrington, U.K. 53°24N 2°35W 168 D5
Warrington Fla., U.S.A. 30°23N 87°17W 317 E2
Warrington ☐ U.K. 53°24N 2°35W 168 D5
Warriston U.K. 55°58N 3°11W 121 B2
Warrnambool Australia 38°25S 142°30E 282 E5
Warroad U.S.A. 48°54N 95°19W 308 A6
Warrumbungle △ Australia 31°18S 149°1E 283 A8
Warruwi Australia 11°36S 133°20E 280 A1
Warsak Dam Pakistan 34°11N 71°19E 242 B4
Warsaw = Warszawa Poland 52°14N 21°0E 143 B2
Warsaw Ill., U.S.A. 40°22N 91°26W 310 D5
Warsaw Ind., U.S.A. 41°14N 85°51W 311 C11
Warsaw Ky., U.S.A. 38°47N 84°54W 311 F12
Warsaw Mo., U.S.A. 38°15N 93°23W 310 F3
Warsaw N.Y., U.S.A. 42°45N 78°8W 312 D6
Warsaw Ohio, U.S.A. 40°20N 82°0W 312 F3
Warshiikh Somalia 2°28N 45°55E 267 D6
Warstein Germany 51°26N 8°22E 178 D4
Warszawa Poland 52°14N 21°0E 143 B2
Warszawa ✈ (WAW) Poland 52°9N 20°59E 143 B1
Warta Poland 51°43N 18°38E 185 G5
Warta → Poland 52°35N 14°39E 185 F1
Wartenberg Germany 52°34N 13°31E 115 A4
Wartenburg = Barczewo Poland 53°50N 20°42E 184 E7
Warthbrücken = Koło Poland 52°14N 18°40E 185 F5
Warthe = Warta → Poland 52°35N 14°39E 185 F1
Warthen U.S.A. 33°6N 82°48W 316 B7
Warthenau = Zawiercie Poland 50°30N 19°24E 185 H6
Waru Indonesia 3°30S 130°36E 231 E8
Warud India 21°30N 78°16E 244 D4
Warumungu ☼ Australia 19°15S 134°44E 280 B1
Warwick Queens., Australia 28°10S 152°1E 281 D5
Warwick Warks., U.K. 52°18N 1°35W 169 E6
Warwick Ga., U.S.A. 31°50N 83°57W 316 D6
Warwick N.Y., U.S.A. 41°16N 74°22W 313 E10
Warwick R.I., U.S.A. 41°42N 71°28W 313 E13
Warwickshire ☐ U.K. 52°14N 1°38W 169 E6
Wasaga Beach Canada 44°31N 80°1W 312 B4
Wasagaming Canada 50°39N 99°58W 297 C9
Wasatch Ra. U.S.A. 40°0N 111°30W 304 F8
Wasbank S. Africa 28°15S 30°9E 271 C5
Wasco Calif., U.S.A. 35°36N 119°20W 307 K7
Wasco Oreg., U.S.A. 45°36N 120°42W 304 D3
Wase Nigeria 9°4N 9°54E 263 D6
Waseca U.S.A. 44°5N 93°30W 308 C7
Wasekamio L. Canada 56°45N 108°45W 297 B7
Wasgomura △ Sri Lanka 7°45N 81°0E 245 L5
Wash, The U.K. 52°58N 0°20E 168 E8
Washago Canada 44°45N 79°20W 312 B5
Washburn Ill., U.S.A. 40°55N 89°17W 310 D7
Washburn N. Dak., U.S.A. 47°17N 101°2W 308 B3
Washburn Wis., U.S.A. 46°40N 90°54W 308 B8
Washim India 20°3N 77°0E 244 D3
Washington Bonaire 12°17N 68°23W 322 h
Washington Tyne & W., U.K. 54°55N 1°30W 168 C6
Washington D.C., U.S.A. 38°53N 77°2W 143 B2
Washington Ga., U.S.A. 33°44N 82°44W 316 B7
Washington Ill., U.S.A. 40°42N 89°24W 310 D7
Washington Ind., U.S.A. 38°40N 87°10W 311 F9
Washington Iowa, U.S.A. 41°18N 91°42W 310 C5
Washington Mo., U.S.A. 38°33N 91°1W 310 F5
Washington N.C., U.S.A. 35°33N 77°3W 315 D16
Washington N.J., U.S.A. 40°46N 74°59W 313 F10
Washington Pa., U.S.A. 40°10N 80°15W 312 F4
Washington Utah, U.S.A. 37°8N 113°31W 305 H7
Washington ☐ U.S.A. 47°30N 120°30W 304 C3
Washington, Mt. U.S.A. 44°16N 71°18W 313 B13
Washington Court House U.S.A. 39°32N 83°26W 311 E13
Washington Heights U.S.A. 40°51N 73°56W 132 A2
Washington I. U.S.A. 45°23N 86°54W 308 C10
Washington Land Greenland 80°30N 66°0W 154 A4
Washington Monument Washington, D.C., U.S.A. 143 b1
Washington Park U.S.A. 41°47N 87°36W 119 C3
Washington Ronald Reagan Nat. ✈ (DCA) U.S.A. 38°51N 77°2W 143 B2
Washington Slagbaai △ Bonaire 12°16N 68°23W 322 h
Washougal U.S.A. 45°35N 122°21W 306 E4
Washpool △ Australia 29°22S 152°20E 281 D5
Washuk Pakistan 27°42N 64°45E 240 D2
Wasian Indonesia 1°47S 133°19E 231 E8
Wasilków Poland 53°12N 23°13E 185 E10
Wasilla U.S.A. 61°35N 149°26W 303 F10
Wasini Marine ⌓ Kenya 4°33S 39°14E 268 C4
Wasior Indonesia 2°43S 134°30E 231 E8
Wasiri Indonesia 7°30S 126°30E 231 F7
Wāsiṭ ☐ Iraq 32°50N 45°50E 213 F11
Wasjabo Suriname 5°13N 57°11W 329 B6
Waskaganish Canada 51°30N 78°40W 298 B4
Waskaiowaka L. Canada 56°33N 96°23W 297 B9
Waskesiu Lake Canada 53°55N 106°5W 297 C7
Wassaw I. U.S.A. 31°53N 80°58W 316 D9
Wassaw Sd. U.S.A. 31°55N 80°55W 316 D9
Wasserburg Germany 48°3N 12°14E 179 G8
Wasserkuppe Germany 50°29N 9°55E 178 E5
Wassy France 48°30N 4°58E 173 D11
Wasu Papua N. G. 5°58S 147°12E 286 C4
Wasua Papua N. G. 8°18S 142°52E 286 E2
Waswanipi Canada 49°40N 76°29W 298 C4
Waswanipi, L. Canada 49°35N 76°40W 298 C4
Wat Pho Bangkok, Thailand 113 b1
Watagans △ Australia 33°0S 151°28E 283 B9
Watam Papua N. G. 3°55S 144°33E 286 B3
Watampone Indonesia 4°29S 120°25E 231 E6
Watamu Kenya 3°23S 40°0E 268 C5
Watansoppeng Indonesia 4°10S 119°56E 235 C5
Watarrka △ Australia 24°20S 131°30E 278 D5
Watee Solomon Is. 10°30S 162°2E 287 N12
Watenstadt-Salzgitter = Salzgitter Germany 52°9N 10°19E 178 C6
Water of Leith → U.K. 55°59N 3°10W 121 B1
Water Park Pt. Australia 22°56S 150°47E 280 C5
Water Tower Place Chicago, U.S.A. 119 a2
Water Valley U.S.A. 34°10N 89°38W 315 D10
Waterberg Plateau ⌓ Namibia 20°25S 17°18E 270 B2
Waterberge S. Africa 24°10S 28°0E 271 B4
Waterbury Conn., U.S.A. 41°33N 73°3W 313 E11
Waterbury Vt., U.S.A. 44°20N 72°46W 313 B12
Waterbury L. Canada 58°10N 104°22W 297 B8
Waterdown Canada 43°20N 79°53W 312 C5
Wateree → U.S.A. 33°45N 80°37W 316 B9
Waterford Ont., Canada 42°56N 80°17W 312 D4
Waterford Waterford, Ireland 52°15N 7°8W 166 D4
Waterford Calif., U.S.A. 37°38N 120°46W 306 H6
Waterford Mich., U.S.A. 42°45N 83°32W 311 B13
Waterford Pa., U.S.A. 41°57N 79°59W 312 E5
Waterford Wis., U.S.A. 42°46N 88°13W 311 B8
Waterford ☐ Ireland 52°10N 7°40W 166 D4
Waterford Harbour Ireland 52°8N 6°58W 166 D5
Watergraafsmeer Neths. 52°21N 4°56E 112 A2
Waterhen L. Canada 52°10N 99°40W 297 C9
Waterland Neths. 52°26N 4°58E 112 A2
Waterloo Belgium 50°43N 4°25E 116 B2
Waterloo Ont., Canada 43°30N 80°32W 312 C4
Waterloo Qué., Canada 45°22N 72°32W 313 A12
Waterloo S. Leone 8°26N 13°8W 262 D2
Waterloo Trin. & Tob. 10°28N 61°28W 323 t
Waterloo London, U.K. 125 b4
Waterloo Ill., U.S.A. 38°20N 90°9W 310 F6
Waterloo Ind., U.S.A. 41°26N 85°1W 311 C11
Waterloo Iowa, U.S.A. 42°30N 92°21W 310 B4
Waterloo N.Y., U.S.A. 42°54N 76°52W 312 D8
Waterloo Wis., U.S.A. 43°11N 88°59W 310 A8
Waterman U.S.A. 41°46N 88°47W 311 C8
Watermeal-Boitsfort Belgium 50°48N 4°25E 116 B2
Watersmeet U.S.A. 46°16N 89°11W 308 B9
Waterton Lakes △ Canada 48°45N 115°0W 296 D6
Watertown Conn., U.S.A. 41°36N 73°7W 313 E11
Watertown Fla., U.S.A. 30°11N 82°36W 316 E7
Watertown Mass., U.S.A. 42°22N 71°10W 116 A1
Watertown N.Y., U.S.A. 43°59N 75°55W 313 C9
Watertown S. Dak., U.S.A. 44°54N 97°7W 308 C5
Watertown Wis., U.S.A. 43°12N 88°43W 311 A8
Waterval-Boven = Emgwenya S. Africa 25°40S 30°18E 271 C5
Waterville Qué., Canada 45°16N 71°54W 313 A13
Waterville Maine, U.S.A. 44°33N 69°38W 309 C19
Waterville N.Y., U.S.A. 42°56N 75°23W 313 D9
Waterville Pa., U.S.A. 41°19N 77°21W 312 E7
Waterville Wash., U.S.A. 47°39N 120°4W 304 C3
Watervliet Mich., U.S.A. 42°11N 86°18W 311 B10
Watervliet N.Y., U.S.A. 42°44N 73°42W 313 D11
Wates Indonesia 7°51S 110°10E 235 D4
Watford Ont., Canada 42°57N 81°53W 312 D3
Watford Herts., U.K. 51°40N 0°24W 169 F7
Watford City U.S.A. 47°48N 103°17W 308 B2
Wathaman → Canada 57°16N 102°59W 297 B8
Wathaman L. Canada 56°58N 103°44W 297 B8
Watheroo Australia 30°15S 116°5E 279 F2
Watheroo △ Australia 30°19S 115°48E 279 F2
Wating China 35°40N 106°38E 226 G4
Watîr, W. → Egypt 29°0N 34°40E 251 K5
Watkins Glen U.S.A. 42°23N 76°52W 312 D8
Watkinsville U.S.A. 33°52N 83°25W 316 B6
Watling I. = San Salvador I. Bahamas 24°0N 74°30W 321 B5
Watom I. Papua N. G. 4°7S 152°4E 286 C7
Watonga U.S.A. 35°51N 98°25W 314 D5
Watrous Sask., Canada 51°40N 105°25W 297 C7
Watrous N. Mex., U.S.A. 35°48N 104°59W 305 J11
Watsa Dem. Rep. of the Congo 3°4N 29°30E 268 B2
Watseka U.S.A. 40°47N 87°44W 311 D9
Watsi Kenga Dem. Rep. of the Congo 0°49S 20°34E 264 C4
Watson Canada 52°10N 104°30W 297 C8
Watson Lake Canada 60°6N 128°49W 296 A3
Watsonia Australia 37°43S 145°6E 128 A2
Watsontown U.S.A. 41°5N 76°52W 312 E8
Watsonville U.S.A. 36°55N 121°45W 306 J5
Watt Mt. Dominica 15°19N 61°19W 323 k
Wattiwarriganna Cr. → Australia 28°57S 136°10E 281 D2
Watts U.S.A. 33°56N 118°15W 126 C3
Wattwil Switz. 47°18N 9°6E 179 H5
Watu Dem. Rep. of the Congo 3°18S 20°3E 264 C4
Watuata = Batuata Indonesia 6°12S 122°42E 231 F6
Watubela, Kepulauan Indonesia 4°28S 131°35E 231 E8
Watubela Is. = Watubela, Kepulauan Indonesia 4°28S 131°35E 231 E8
Wau Papua N. G. 7°21S 146°47E 286 D4
Wau South Sudan 7°45N 28°1E 257 F2
Waubamik Canada 45°27N 80°1W 312 A4
Waubay U.S.A. 45°20N 97°18W 308 C5
Waubra Australia 37°21S 143°39E 282 D5
Wauchope N.S.W., Australia 31°28S 152°45E 283 A10
Wauchope N. Terr., Australia 20°36S 134°15E 280 C1
Wauchula U.S.A. 27°33N 81°49W 317 H8
Waukarlycarly, L. Australia 21°18S 121°56E 278 D3
Waukeenah U.S.A. 30°25N 83°57W 316 E6
Waukegan U.S.A. 42°22N 87°50W 311 B9
Waukesha U.S.A. 43°1N 88°14W 311 B8
Waukon U.S.A. 43°16N 91°29W 308 D8
Waunakee U.S.A. 43°11N 89°27W 310 A7
Waupaca U.S.A. 44°21N 89°5W 308 C9
Waupun U.S.A. 43°38N 88°44W 308 D9
Waurika U.S.A. 34°10N 98°0W 314 D6
Wausau Fla., U.S.A. 30°38N 85°35W 316 E4
Wausau Wis., U.S.A. 44°58N 89°38W 308 C9
Wauseon U.S.A. 41°33N 84°8W 311 C12
Wautoma U.S.A. 44°4N 89°18W 308 C9
Wauwatosa U.S.A. 43°2N 88°0W 311 A9
Wave Hill = Kalkarindji Australia 17°30S 130°47E 278 C5
Wave Rock ⌓ Australia 32°26S 118°53E 279 F2
Waveland U.S.A. 39°53N 87°3W 311 E9
Waveney → U.K. 52°35N 1°39E 169 E9
Waverley N.S.W., Australia 33°53S 151°15E 139 B2
Waverley N.Z. 39°46S 174°37E 284 F3
Waverley Gauteng, S. Africa 26°7S 28°4E 123 A2
Waverley Mass., U.S.A. 42°23N 71°10W 116 A1
Waverley Station Edinburgh, U.K. 121 b3
Waverly Ala., U.S.A. 32°44N 85°35W 316 C4
Waverly Fla., U.S.A. 27°59N 81°37W 317 H8
Waverly Ga., U.S.A. 31°6N 81°43W 316 D8
Waverly Ill., U.S.A. 39°36N 89°57W 310 E7
Waverly Iowa, U.S.A. 42°44N 92°29W 310 B4
Waverly Mo., U.S.A. 39°13N 93°31W 310 E3
Waverly N.Y., U.S.A. 42°1N 76°32W 313 E8
Waverly Hall U.S.A. 32°41N 84°44W 316 C5
Wavre Belgium 50°43N 4°38E 170 D4
Wâw = Wau South Sudan 7°45N 28°1E 257 F2
Waw Burma 17°28N 96°41E 241 G6
Wāw al Kabīr Libya 25°20N 16°43E 258 C3
Wāw an Nāmūs Libya 24°55N 17°46E 258 D3
Wawa Ont., Canada 47°59N 84°47W 298 C3
Wawa Nigeria 9°54N 4°27E 263 D5
Wawa Sudan 20°30N 30°22E 256 C3
Wawanesa Canada 49°36N 99°40W 297 D9
Wawasee, L. U.S.A. 41°24N 85°42W 311 C11
Wawer Poland 52°13N 21°8E 143 B2
Wawoi → Papua N. G. 7°48S 143°16E 286 D2
Wawona U.S.A. 37°32N 119°39W 306 H7
Wawrzyszew Poland 52°17N 20°53E 143 B1
Waxahachie U.S.A. 32°24N 96°51W 314 E6
Waxxari China 38°42N 87°19E 217 E11
Way, L. Australia 26°45S 120°16E 279 E3
Way Kambas △ Indonesia 4°54S 105°43E 234 C3
Waya Fiji 17°19S 177°10E 287 A1
Waycross U.S.A. 31°13N 82°21W 316 D7
Wayi South Sudan 5°8N 30°10E 257 F3
Wayland Mich., U.S.A. 42°40N 85°39W 311 B11
Wayland N.Y., U.S.A. 42°34N 77°35W 312 D7
Wayne Nebr., U.S.A. 42°14N 97°1W 308 D5
Wayne W. Va., U.S.A. 38°13N 82°27W 309 F12
Wayne City U.S.A. 38°21N 88°35W 311 F8
Wayne County, Detroit ✈ (DTW) U.S.A. 42°13N 83°21W 311 B13
Wayne Lakes U.S.A. 40°1N 84°40W 311 D12
Waynesboro Ga., U.S.A. 33°6N 82°1W 316 B7
Waynesboro Miss., U.S.A. 31°40N 88°39W 315 F10
Waynesboro Pa., U.S.A. 39°45N 77°35W 309 F15
Waynesboro Va., U.S.A. 38°4N 78°53W 309 F14
Waynesburg U.S.A. 39°54N 80°11W 309 F13
Waynesville Mo., U.S.A. 37°50N 92°12W 310 G4
Waynesville N.C., U.S.A. 35°28N 82°58W 315 D13
Waynesville Ohio, U.S.A. 39°32N 84°5W 311 E12
Waynoka U.S.A. 36°35N 98°53W 314 C5
Wayside U.S.A. 33°4N 83°37W 316 B6
Waza Afghan. 33°22N 69°26E 240 B3
Waza △ Cameroon 11°15N 14°38E 259 F2
Wazikhwah Afghan. 32°11N 68°21E 240 B3
Wāzin Libya 31°58N 10°40E 258 B2
Wazirabad Delhi, India 28°43N 77°13E 120 A2
Wazirabad Pakistan 32°30N 74°8E 242 C6
Waziristan Pakistan 33°0N 70°0E 242 C4
Wazīrīya Iraq 33°22N 44°23E 113 A2
Wazirpur India 28°41N 77°10E 120 A2
Wda → Poland 53°25N 18°29E 184 E5
We Indonesia 5°51N 95°18E 234 A1
Wé N. Cal. 20°55S 167°16E 288 d
Weald, The U.K. 51°4N 0°20E 169 F8
Wealdstone U.K. 51°35N 0°17W 125 A1
Weam Papua N. G. 8°37S 141°8E 286 E1
Wear → U.K. 54°55N 1°23W 168 C6
Weatherford Okla., U.S.A. 35°32N 98°43W 314 D5
Weatherford Tex., U.S.A. 32°46N 97°48W 314 E6
Weaubleau U.S.A. 37°54N 93°32W 310 G3
Weaverville U.S.A. 40°44N 122°56W 304 F2
Webb City U.S.A. 37°9N 94°28W 308 G6
Webequie Canada 52°59N 87°21W 298 B2
Weber N.Z. 40°24S 176°20E 284 G5
Weber Basin Indonesia 6°0S 131°0E 276 B5
Webo = Nyaake Liberia 4°52N 7°37W 262 E3
Webster Mass., U.S.A. 42°3N 71°53W 313 D13
Webster N.Y., U.S.A. 43°13N 77°26W 312 C7
Webster S. Dak., U.S.A. 45°20N 97°31W 308 C5
Webster City U.S.A. 42°28N 93°49W 310 B3
Webster Springs U.S.A. 38°29N 80°25W 309 F13
Webuye Kenya 0°37N 34°46E 268 B3
Weda Indonesia 0°21N 127°50E 231 D7
Weda, Teluk Indonesia 0°20N 128°0E 231 D7
Weddell Abyssal Plain S. Ocean 65°0S 20°0W 151 C2
Weddell I. Falk. Is. 51°50S 61°0W 153 f
Weddell Sea Antarctica 72°30S 40°0W 151 D1
Wedderburn Australia 36°26S 143°33E 282 D5
Weddin Mts. △ Australia 33°59S 148°0E 283 C8
Wedding Germany 52°32N 13°21E 115 A3
Wedel Germany 53°34N 9°42E 178 B5
Wedemark Germany 52°32N 9°43E 178 C5
Wedgeport Canada 43°44N 65°59W 299 D6
Wednesday I. Australia 10°31S 142°16E 286 F2
Wedowee U.S.A. 33°19N 85°29W 316 B4
Wedza Zimbabwe 18°40S 31°33E 269 F3
Wee Waa Australia 30°11S 149°26E 281 E4
Weed U.S.A. 41°25N 122°23W 304 F2
Weed Heights U.S.A. 38°59N 119°13W 306 G7
Weedsport U.S.A. 43°2N 76°33W 313 C8
Weedville U.S.A. 41°17N 78°30W 312 E6
Weehawken New York, U.S.A. 132 b1
Weeki Wachee U.S.A. 28°32N 82°35W 317 G7
Weel Shimbirro Somalia 2°23N 44°14E 267 D5
Weenen S. Africa 28°48S 30°7E 271 C5
Weener Germany 53°9N 7°20E 178 B3
Weerribben △ Neths. 52°47N 5°58E 170 B5
Weert Neths. 51°15N 5°43E 170 C5
Weesp Neths. 52°18N 5°2E 112 B3
Węgierska-Górka Poland 49°36N 19°7E 185 J6
Węgliniec Poland 51°18N 15°10E 185 G2
Węgorzewo Poland 54°13N 21°43E 184 D8
Węgorzyno Poland 53°32N 15°33E 184 E2
Węgrów Poland 52°24N 22°0E 185 F9
Wei He → Hebei, China 36°10N 115°45E 226 F8
Wei He → Shaanxi, China 34°38N 110°15E 226 G6
Weichang China 41°58N 117°49E 227 D9
Weichuan China 34°20N 113°59E 226 G7
Weida Germany 50°46N 12°2E 178 E8
Weiden Germany 49°41N 12°10E 179 F8
Weidling Austria 48°17N 16°18E 142 A1
Weidlingbach Austria 48°16N 16°15E 142 A1
Weifang China 36°44N 119°7E 227 F10
Weihai China 37°30N 122°6E 227 F12
Weihui China 35°25N 114°3E 226 G8
Weil Germany 47°35N 7°37E 179 H3
Weilburg Germany 50°28N 8°17E 178 E4
Weilheim Germany 47°50N 11°9E 179 H7
Weimar Germany 50°58N 11°19E 178 E7
Weinan China 34°31N 109°29E 226 G5
Weingarten Germany 49°3N 8°31E 179 F4
Weinheim Germany 49°32N 8°39E 179 F4
Weining China 26°50N 104°17E 228 D5
Weipa Australia 12°40S 141°50E 280 A3
Weir → Queens., Australia 28°20S 149°50E 281 D4
Weir → Man., Canada 56°54N 93°21W 297 B10
Weir, L. U.S.A. 29°0N 81°57W 317 F8
Weir River Canada 56°49N 94°6W 297 B10
Weirsdale U.S.A. 28°59N 81°55W 317 G8
Weirton U.S.A. 40°24N 80°35W 312 F4
Weiser U.S.A. 44°15N 116°58W 304 D5
Weishan Shandong, China 34°47N 117°5E 227 G9
Weishan Yunnan, China 25°12N 100°20E 228 E3
Weishan Hu China 34°35N 117°14E 227 G9
Weissenburg Germany 49°2N 10°58E 179 F6
Weissenfels Germany 51°11N 12°0E 178 D7
Weissensee Germany 52°33N 13°27E 115 A3
Weisskirchen = Hranice Czech Rep. 49°34N 17°45E 181 B10
Weisswasser Germany 51°30N 14°36E 178 D10
Weistritz = Bystrzyca → Dolnośląskie, Poland 51°12N 16°55E 185 G3
Weistritz = Bystrzyca → Lubelskie, Poland 51°21N 22°46E 185 G9
Wéitra Austria 48°41N 14°54E 180 C7
Weixi China 27°10N 99°10E 228 D2
Weixin China 27°48N 105°3E 228 D5
Weiyuan Gansu, China 35°7N 104°10E 226 G3
Weiyuan Sichuan, China 29°35N 104°36E 228 C5
Weiz Austria 47°13N 15°39E 180 D8
Weizhou Dao China 21°0N 109°5E 228 G7
Wejherowo Poland 54°35N 18°12E 184 D5
Wekoewa Pt. Bonaire 12°13N 68°24W 322 h
Wekusko L. Canada 54°40N 99°50W 297 C9
Welch U.S.A. 37°26N 81°35W 309 G13
Welchman Hall Barbados 13°11N 59°34W 323 r
Weldya Ethiopia 11°50N 39°34E 257 E4
Welega Ethiopia 9°25N 34°20E 257 F3
Welford △ Australia 25°5S 143°16E 280 D3
Weligama Sri Lanka 5°58N 80°25E 245 M5
Welkite Ethiopia 8°15N 37°42E 257 F4
Welkom S. Africa 28°0S 26°46E 270 C4
Welland Canada 43°0N 79°15W 312 D5
Welland → U.K. 52°51N 0°5W 169 E7
Wellawaya Sri Lanka 6°44N 81°6E 245 L5
Welles Harbor Midway Is. 28°13N 177°25W 302 c
Wellesley Hills U.S.A. 42°18N 71°16W 116 B1
Wellesley Is. Australia 16°42S 139°30E 280 B2
Wellesley Islands ☼ Australia 16°32S 139°23E 280 B2
Welling U.K. 51°27N 0°6E 125 B4
Wellingborough U.K. 52°19N 0°41W 169 E7
Wellington N.S.W., Australia 32°35S 148°59E 283 B8
Wellington Ont., Canada 43°57N 77°20W 312 C7
Wellington N.Z. 41°19S 174°46E 284 H3
Wellington Western Cape, S. Africa 33°38S 19°1E 270 D2
Wellington Somst., U.K. 50°58N 3°13W 169 G4
Wellington Telford & Wrekin, U.K. 52°42N 2°30W 169 E5
Wellington Colo., U.S.A. 40°42N 105°0W 304 F11
Wellington Fla., U.S.A. 26°39N 80°15W 317 J9
Wellington Kans., U.S.A. 37°16N 97°24W 308 G5
Wellington Mass., U.S.A. 42°24N 71°5W 116 A2
Wellington Mo., U.S.A. 39°8N 93°59W 310 E3
Wellington Nev., U.S.A. 38°45N 119°23W 306 G7
Wellington Ohio, U.S.A. 41°10N 82°13W 312 E2
Wellington Tex., U.S.A. 34°51N 100°13W 314 D4
Wellington ☐ N.Z. 41°0S 175°30E 284 H4
Wellington, I. Chile 49°30S 75°0W 336 C2
Wellington, L. Australia 38°6S 147°20E 283 E7
Wellington Chan. Canada 75°0N 93°0W 295 C13
Wellman U.S.A. 41°28N 91°50W 310 C5
Wells Somst., U.K. 51°13N 2°39W 169 F5
Wells Maine, U.S.A. 43°20N 70°35W 313 C14
Wells N.Y., U.S.A. 43°24N 74°17W 313 C10
Wells Nev., U.S.A. 41°7N 114°58W 304 F6
Wells, L. Australia 26°44S 123°15E 279 E3
Wells, Mt. Australia 17°25S 127°8E 278 C4
Wells Fargo Center Los Angeles, U.S.A. 127 b1
Wells Gray ⌓ Canada 52°30N 120°15W 296 C4
Wells-next-the-Sea U.K. 52°57N 0°51E 168 E8
Wells River U.S.A. 44°9N 72°4W 313 B12
Wellsboro U.S.A. 41°45N 77°18W 312 E7
Wellsburg U.S.A. 40°16N 80°37W 312 F4
Wellsford N.Z. 36°16S 174°32E 284 C3
Wellston = Warner Robins U.S.A. 32°37N 83°36W 316 C6
Wellsville Mo., U.S.A. 39°4N 91°34W 310 E5
Wellsville N.Y., U.S.A. 42°7N 77°57W 312 D7
Wellsville Ohio, U.S.A. 40°36N 80°39W 312 F4
Wellsville Utah, U.S.A. 41°38N 111°56W 304 F8
Wellton U.S.A. 32°40N 114°8W 305 K6
Welmel, Wabi → Ethiopia 5°38N 40°47E 257 F5
Welo Ethiopia 11°50N 39°48E 257 E4
Welo Somalia 9°25N 48°55E 267 C6
Wels Austria 48°9N 14°1E 180 C7
Welshpool Vic., Australia 38°42S 146°26E 283 E7
Welshpool Powys, U.K. 52°39N 3°8W 169 E4
Weltevreden Park S. Africa 26°7S 27°56E 123 A1
Welungen = Wieluń Poland 51°15N 18°34E 185 G5
Welwitschia = Khorixas Namibia 20°16S 14°59E 270 B1
Welwyn Garden City U.K. 51°48N 0°12W 169 F7
Wem U.K. 52°52N 2°44W 168 E5
Wembere → Tanzania 4°10S 34°15E 268 C3
Wembley U.K. 51°33N 0°17W 125 A2
Wemindji Canada 53°0N 78°49W 298 B4
Wemmel Belgium 50°55N 4°18E 116 A1
Wemmer Pan S. Africa 26°13S 28°3E 123 B2
Wemyss Canada 44°52N 76°23W 313 B8
Wen Xian Gansu, China 32°43N 104°36E 226 H3
Wen Xian Henan, China 34°55N 113°5E 226 G7
Wenatchee U.S.A. 47°25N 120°19W 304 C3
Wenceslas Square = Vaclavské náměstí Prague, Czech Rep. 135 b2
Wenchang China 19°38N 110°42E 229 a
Wencheng China 27°46N 120°4E 229 D13
Wenchi Ghana 7°46N 2°8W 262 D4
Wenchow = Wenzhou China 28°0N 120°38E 229 D13
Wenchuan China 31°22N 103°35E 228 B4
Wenden U.S.A. 33°49N 113°33W 307 M13
Wendeng China 37°15N 122°5E 227 F12
Wendenschloss Germany 52°24N 13°35E 115 B4
Wendesi Indonesia 2°30S 134°17E 231 E8
Wendo Ethiopia 6°40N 38°27E 257 F4
Wendover U.S.A. 40°44N 114°2W 304 F6
Weng'an China 27°5N 107°25E 228 D6
Wengcheng China 24°22N 113°50E 229 E9
Wengen Switz. 46°37N 7°55E 173 F14
Wengyuan China 24°20N 114°9E 229 E10
Wenling China 28°21N 121°20E 229 C13
Wenlock → Australia 12°2S 141°55E 286 G1
Wennington U.K. 51°30N 0°12E 125 A5
Weno Pac. Oc. 7°27N 151°52E 287 T18
Wenona U.S.A. 41°3N 89°3W 310 C7
Wenshan China 23°20N 104°18E 228 F5
Wenshang China 35°45N 116°30E 226 G9
Wenshui China 37°26N 112°1E 226 F7
Wensleydale U.K. 54°17N 2°0W 168 C6
Wensu China 41°15N 80°10E 217 D10
Wensum → U.K. 52°40N 1°15E 168 E8
Wentworth Australia 34°2S 141°54E 282 C4
Wentzel L. Canada 59°2N 114°28W 296 B6
Wentzville U.S.A. 38°49N 90°51W 310 F6
Wenut Indonesia 3°11S 133°19E 231 E8
Wenxi China 35°20N 111°10E 226 G6
Wenzhou China 28°0N 120°38E 229 D13
Weott U.S.A. 40°20N 123°55W 304 F2
Wepener S. Africa 29°42S 27°3E 270 C4
Werda Botswana 25°24S 23°15E 270 C3
Werdau Germany 50°44N 12°22E 178 E8
Werder Ethiopia 6°58N 45°1E 267 C6
Werder Brandenburg, Germany 52°23N 12°55E 178 C8
Werdohl Germany 51°15N 7°46E 178 D3
Wereilu Ethiopia 10°40N 39°28E 257 E4
Weri Indonesia 3°10S 132°38E 231 E8
Werneck Germany 49°58N 10°5E 179 F6
Werneuchen Germany 52°38N 13°44E 115 A5
Wernigerode Germany 51°50N 10°47E 178 D6
Werra → Germany 51°24N 9°39E 178 D5
Werribee Australia 37°54S 144°40E 282 D6
Werrikimbe △ Australia 31°11S 152°15E 283 A10
Werrimull Australia 34°25S 141°38E 282 C4
Werris Creek Australia 31°18S 150°38E 283 A9
Werschetz = Vršac Serbia 45°8N 21°20E 182 E6
Wertach → Germany 48°22N 10°54E 179 G6
Wertheim Germany 49°45N 9°32E 179 F5
Wertingen Germany 48°33N 10°41E 179 G6
Wesel Germany 51°39N 6°37E 178 D2
Weser → Germany 53°36N 8°28E 178 B4
Weserbergland Germany 52°12N 9°7E 178 C5
Weserbergland Schaumburg Hameln ⌓ Germany 52°8N 9°20E 178 C5
Wesermünde = Bremerhaven Germany 53°33N 8°36E 178 B4
Weslaco U.S.A. 26°10N 97°58W 314 H6
Weslemkoon L. Canada 45°2N 77°25W 312 A7
Wesley Dominica 15°33N 61°18W 323 k
Wesleyville Nfld. & L., Canada 49°9N 53°33W 299 C9
Wesleyville Pa., U.S.A. 42°9N 80°1W 312 D4
Wessel, C. Australia 10°59S 136°46E 280 A2
Wessel Is. Australia 11°10S 136°45E 280 A2
Wesselburen Germany 54°13N 8°54E 178 A4
Wessex U.K. 51°0N 2°0W 169 F5
Wessington Springs U.S.A. 44°5N 98°34W 308 C4
West U.S.A. 31°48N 97°6W 314 F6
West → U.S.A. 42°52N 72°33W 313 D12
West Allis U.S.A. 43°1N 88°0W 311 B8
West Antarctica Antarctica 80°0S 90°0W 151 D15
West Baines → Australia 15°38S 129°59E 278 C4
West Bank ■ Asia 32°6N 35°13E 251 F6
West Bend U.S.A. 43°25N 88°11W 308 D9
West Bengal = Paschimbanga ☐ India 23°0N 88°0E 243 H13
West Berkshire ☐ U.K. 51°25N 1°17W 169 F6
West Beskids = Západné Beskydy Europe 49°30N 19°0E 181 B12
West Branch U.S.A. 44°17N 84°14W 309 C11
West Branch Susquehanna → U.S.A. 40°53N 76°48W 313 F8
West Bromwich U.K. 52°32N 1°59W 169 E6
West Burra U.K. 60°5N 1°21W 167 A7
West Canada Cr. → U.S.A. 43°1N 74°58W 313 C10
West Caroline Basin Pac. Oc. 4°0N 138°0E 288 G5
West Carrollton U.S.A. 39°40N 84°17W 311 E12
West Chazy U.S.A. 44°49N 73°28W 313 B11
West Chester U.S.A. 39°58N 75°36W 313 G9
West Chicago U.S.A. 41°53N 88°12W 311 C8
West Coast ☐ N.Z. 43°15S 170°30E 285 D5
West Coast ⌓ Namibia 21°53S 14°14E 270 B1
West Coast △ S. Africa 33°13S 18°0E 270 D2
West Columbia S.C., U.S.A. 33°59N 81°4W 316 B8
West Columbia Tex., U.S.A. 29°9N 95°39W 314 G7
West Covina U.S.A. 34°4N 117°54W 307 L9
West Des Moines U.S.A. 41°35N 93°43W 310 C3
West Don → Canada 43°44N 79°24W 141 A2
West Drayton U.K. 51°30N 0°28W 125 A1
West Dunbartonshire ☐ U.K. 55°59N 4°30W 167 F4
West End Bahamas 26°41N 78°58W 320 A4
West End Boston, U.S.A. 116 b1
West End Village Anguilla 18°10N 63°10W 322 a
West Falkland Falk. Is. 51°40S 60°0W 153 f
West Fargo U.S.A. 46°52N 96°54W 308 B5
West Fiji Basin Pac. Oc. 17°0S 173°0E 288 J9
West Fjord = Vestfjorden Norway 67°55N 14°0E 160 C16
West Fork Trinity → U.S.A. 32°48N 96°54W 314 E6
West Frankfort U.S.A. 37°54N 88°55W 310 G8
West Grand L. U.S.A. 45°14N 67°51W 309 C20
West Green U.S.A. 31°37N 82°44W 316 D7
West Ham U.K. 51°31N 0°1E 125 A4
West Harrow U.K. 51°34N 0°21W 125 A1
West Hartford U.S.A. 41°45N 72°44W 313 E12
West Haven U.S.A. 41°17N 72°57W 313 E12
West Hazleton U.S.A. 40°58N 76°0W 313 F9
West Heath U.K. 51°29N 0°7E 125 B4
West Hill Canada 43°46N 79°10W 141 A3
West Hollywood U.S.A. 34°5N 118°21W 126 B2
West Hurley U.S.A. 41°59N 74°7W 313 E10
West I. India 13°35N 92°54E 245 H11
West Ice Shelf Antarctica 67°0S 85°0E 151 C7
West Indies Cent. Amer. 15°0N 65°0W 321 D7
West Jefferson U.S.A. 39°57N 83°17W 311 E13
West Jordan U.S.A. 40°36N 111°56W 304 F8
West Kensington London, U.K. 125 c1
West Kilburn London, U.K. 125 a1
West Lafayette U.S.A. 40°27N 86°55W 311 D10
West Lamma Channel Hong Kong, China 22°14N 114°4E 122 B2
West Liberty Iowa, U.S.A. 41°34N 91°16W 310 C5
West Liberty Ky., U.S.A. 37°55N 83°16W 311 G13
West Liberty Ohio, U.S.A. 40°15N 83°45W 311 D13
West Linn U.S.A. 45°21N 122°36W 306 E4
West Lorne Canada 42°36N 81°36W 312 D3
West Los Angeles, Univ. of U.S.A. 34°7N 118°23W 126 C2
West Lothian ☐ U.K. 55°54N 3°36W 167 F5
West Lunga → Zambia 13°6S 24°39E 265 E4
West Lunga △ Zambia 12°49S 24°47E 265 E4
West MacDonnell △ Australia 23°38S 132°59E 278 D5
West Mariana Basin Pac. Oc. 15°0N 137°0E 288 F5
West Medford U.S.A. 42°25N 71°7W 116 A2
West Memphis U.S.A. 35°8N 90°10W 315 D9
West Miami U.S.A. 25°45N 80°17W 129 D1
West Midlands ☐ U.K. 52°26N 2°0W 169 E6
West Mifflin U.S.A. 40°21N 79°52W 312 F5
West Milford U.S.A. 41°8N 74°22W 313 E10
West Milton Ohio, U.S.A. 39°58N 84°20W 311 E12
West Milton Pa., U.S.A. 41°1N 76°50W 312 E8
West Molesey U.K. 51°24N 0°22W 125 B1
West Monroe U.S.A. 32°31N 92°9W 314 E8
West New Britain ☐ Papua N. G. 5°0S 149°30E 286 C5
West New York New York, U.S.A. 132 a1
West Newton U.S.A. 40°14N 79°46W 312 F5
West Nicholson Zimbabwe 21°2S 29°20E 269 G2
West Odessa U.S.A. 31°50N 102°30W 314 F3
West of Twin Peaks U.S.A. 37°43N 122°27W 136 B2
West Palm Beach U.S.A. 26°43N 80°3W 317 J9
West Palm Beach Canal U.S.A. 26°40N 80°15W 317 J9
West Park Gauteng, S. Africa 26°9S 27°59E 123 A1
West Park Fla., U.S.A. 25°59N 80°12W 129 C2
West Pensacola U.S.A. 30°25N 87°16W 317 E2
West Plains U.S.A. 36°44N 91°51W 308 G8
West Point Ga., U.S.A. 32°53N 85°11W 316 C4
West Point Iowa, U.S.A. 40°43N 91°27W 310 D5
West Point Ky., U.S.A. 37°59N 85°57W 311 G11
West Point Miss., U.S.A. 33°36N 88°39W 315 E10
West Point N.Y., U.S.A. 41°24N 73°58W 313 E11
West Point Nebr., U.S.A. 41°51N 96°43W 308 E5
West Point Va., U.S.A. 37°32N 76°48W 309 G15
West Point L. U.S.A. 33°8N 85°0W 316 B4
West Pt. = Ouest, Pte. de l' Canada 49°52N 64°40W 299 C7
West Pt. Australia 35°1S 135°56E 282 C1
West Ra. Papua N. G. 4°15S 141°30E 286 C1
West Road → Canada 53°18N 122°53W 296 C4
West Rouge Canada 43°48N 79°7W 141 A4
West Roxbury U.S.A. 42°16N 71°9W 116 B2
West Rutland U.S.A. 43°36N 73°3W 313 C11
West Salem U.S.A. 38°31N 88°1W 311 F8
West Schelde = Westerschelde → Neths. 51°25N 3°25E 170 C3
West Seneca U.S.A. 42°51N 78°48W 312 D6
West Sepik ☐ Papua N. G. 3°30S 142°0E 286 B2
West Siberian Plain Russia 62°0N 75°0E 210 B9
West Sussex ☐ U.K. 50°55N 0°30W 169 G7
West Terre Haute U.S.A. 39°28N 87°27W 311 E9
West-Terschelling Neths. 53°22N 5°13E 170 A5
West Town U.S.A. 41°53N 87°42W 119 B2
West Union Iowa, U.S.A. 42°57N 91°49W 310 B5
West Union Ohio, U.S.A. 38°48N 83°33W 311 F13
West Unity U.S.A. 41°35N 84°26W 311 C12
West Valley City U.S.A. 40°42N 111°58W 304 F8
West Virginia ☐ U.S.A. 38°45N 80°30W 309 F13
West-Vlaanderen ☐ Belgium 51°0N 3°0E 170 D2
West Walker → U.S.A. 38°54N 119°9W 306 G7
West Wharf Pakistan 24°49N 66°58E 123 B1
West Wyalong Australia 33°56S 147°10E 283 B7
West Yellowstone U.S.A. 44°40N 111°6W 304 D8
West Yorkshire ☐ U.K. 53°45N 1°40W 168 D6
Westall, Pt. Australia 32°55S 134°4E 281 E1
Westbay U.S.A. 30°18N 85°52W 316 E4
Westbourne Green London, U.K. 125 a1
Westbrook U.S.A. 43°41N 70°22W 309 D18
Westbury Australia 41°30S 146°51E 281 G4
Westby U.S.A. 48°52N 104°3W 304 B11
Westchester Calif., U.S.A. 33°57N 118°23W 126 C2
Westchester N.Y., U.S.A. 40°51N 73°51W 132 A2
Westcliff S. Africa 26°10S 28°1E 123 B2
Westdene S. Africa 26°10S 27°59E 123 B1
Westend Helsinki, Finland 60°9N 24°48E 121 C1
Westend Calif., U.S.A. 35°42N 117°24W 307 K9
Wester Hailes U.K. 55°55N 3°16W 121 B2
Westerham Germany 48°3N 11°36E 131 B2
Westerland Germany 54°54N 8°17E 178 A4
Westerly U.S.A. 41°22N 71°50W 313 E13
Western ☐ Ghana 5°30N 2°30W 262 D4
Western ☐ Kenya 0°30N 34°30E 268 B3
Western ☐ Papua N. G. 7°30S 142°0E 286 D2
Western ☐ S. Leone 8°30N 13°20W 262 D2
Western ☐ Zambia 15°0S 24°4E 265 F4
Western Addition U.S.A. 37°47N 122°25W 136 B2
Western Australia ☐ Australia 25°0S 118°0E 279 E2
Western Bahr el Ghazâl ☐ South Sudan 7°30N 25°30E 257 F2
Western Cape ☐ S. Africa 34°0S 20°0E 270 D3
Western Dvina = Daugava → Latvia 57°4N 24°3E 188 D3
Western Equatoria ☐ South Sudan 5°0N 30°0E 257 G3
Western Ghats India 14°0N 75°0E 245 H2
Western Highlands ☐ Papua N. G. 5°45S 144°30E 286 C3
Western Isles = Eilean Siar ☐ U.K. 57°30N 7°10W 167 D1
Western Sahara ■ Africa 25°0N 13°0W 260 D2
Western Samoa = Samoa ■ Pac. Oc. 14°0S 172°0W 287 V20
Western Sierra Madre = Madre Occidental, Sierra Mexico 27°0N 107°0W 318 B3
Western Wall Jerusalem 123 b3
Westernport U.S.A. 39°29N 79°3W 309 F14
Westerschelde → Neths. 51°25N 3°25E 170 C3
Westerstede Germany 53°15N 7°55E 178 B3
Westerwald Germany 50°38N 7°56E 178 E3
Westfield Ill., U.S.A. 39°27N 88°0W 311 E8
Westfield Ind., U.S.A. 40°2N 86°8W 311 D10
Westfield Mass., U.S.A. 42°7N 72°45W 313 D12
Westfield N.Y., U.S.A. 42°20N 79°35W 312 D5
Westfield Pa., U.S.A. 41°55N 77°32W 312 E7
Westgate La., U.S.A. 30°0N 90°13W 131 A1
Westgate Md., U.S.A. 38°57N 77°6W 143 B2
Westhill U.K. 57°9N 2°19W 167 D6
Westhope U.S.A. 48°55N 101°1W 308 A3
Westlake Western Cape, S. Africa 34°4S 18°26E 118 B1
Westlake Calif., U.S.A. 34°4N 118°15W 126 B3
Westlake Calif., U.S.A. 37°42N 122°29W 136 B2
Westland U.S.A. 42°15N 83°20W 311 B13
Westland △ N.Z. 43°16S 170°16E 285 D5
Westland Bight N.Z. 42°55S 170°5E 285 C5
Westlock Canada 54°9N 113°55W 296 C6
Westmar Australia 27°55S 149°44E 281 D4
Westmeath ☐ Ireland 53°33N 7°34W 166 C4
Westminster London, U.K. 51°30N 0°7W 125 A3
Westminster Calif., U.S.A. 33°45N 118°0W 307 M8
Westminster Colo., U.S.A. 39°50N 105°2W 304 G11
Westminster Md., U.S.A. 39°34N 76°59W 309 F15
Westmont U.S.A. 40°19N 78°58W 312 F6
Westmorland U.S.A. 33°2N 115°37W 307 M11
Westmount Canada 45°29N 73°35W 130 B2
Weston Ont., Canada 43°42N 79°30W 141 A1
Weston Ohio, U.S.A. 41°21N 83°47W 311 C13
Weston Oreg., U.S.A. 45°49N 118°26W 304 D4
Weston W. Va., U.S.A. 39°2N 80°28W 309 F13
Weston I. Canada 52°33N 79°36W 298 B4
Weston-super-Mare U.K. 51°21N 2°58W 169 F5
Westover U.S.A. 40°45N 78°40W 312 F6
Westphalia U.S.A. 38°26N 92°0W 310 F5
Westport Ont., Canada 44°40N 76°25W 313 B8
Westport Mayo, Ireland 53°48N 9°31W 166 C2
Westport N.Z. 41°46S 171°37E 285 B6
Westport Ind., U.S.A. 39°11N 85°34W 311 E11
Westport N.Y., U.S.A. 44°11N 73°26W 313 B11
Westport Oreg., U.S.A. 46°8N 123°23W 306 D3
Westport Wash., U.S.A. 46°53N 124°6W 306 D2
Westpunt Curaçao 12°22N 69°10W 322 g
Westray Man., Canada 53°36N 101°24W 297 C8
Westray Orkney, U.K. 59°18N 3°0W 167 B5
Westree Canada 47°26N 81°34W 298 C3
Westville Calif., U.S.A. 39°8N 120°42W 306 F6
Westville Fla., U.S.A. 30°46N 85°51W 316 E4
Westville Ill., U.S.A. 40°2N 87°38W 311 D9
Westville Ind., U.S.A. 41°32N 86°54W 311 C10
Westwego U.S.A. 29°54N 90°8W 131 B2
Westwood U.S.A. 40°18N 121°0W 304 F3
Westwood Lake U.S.A. 25°44N 80°23W 317 K9
Westwood Village U.S.A. 34°3N 118°26W 126 B2
Westzaan Neths. 52°28N 4°46E 112 A1
Wetar Indonesia 7°48S 126°30E 231 F7
Wetaskiwin Canada 52°55N 113°24W 296 C6
Wetherby U.K. 53°56N 1°23W 168 D6
Wethersfield U.S.A. 41°42N 72°40W 313 E12

Wetlet Burma 22°20N 95°53E 241 D5
Wetteren Belgium 51°0N 3°53E 170 D3
Wetton S. Africa 34°0S 18°31E 118 B2
Wetumpka U.S.A. 32°32N 86°13W 316 C3
Wetzlar Germany 50°32N 8°31E 178 E4
Wevok U.S.A. 68°53N 166°13W 303 B6
Wewahitchka U.S.A. 30°7N 85°12W 316 E4
Wewak Papua N. G. 3°38S 143°41E 286 B2
Wewoka U.S.A. 35°9N 96°30W 314 D6
Wexford Ont., Canada 43°45N 79°18W 141 A3
Wexford Wexford, Ireland 52°20N 6°28W 166 D5
Wexford □ Ireland 52°20N 6°25W 166 D5
Wexford Harbour Ireland 52°20N 6°25W 166 D5
Weybridge U.K. 51°22N 0°27W 125 B1
Weyburn Canada 49°40N 103°50W 297 D8
Weyer Markt Austria 47°51N 14°40E 180 D7
Weyhe Germany 52°58N 8°49E 178 C4
Weyib → Ethiopia 7°15N 40°15E 257 F5
Weymouth N.S., Canada 44°30N 66°1W 299 D6
Weymouth Dorset, U.K. 50°37N 2°28W 169 G5
Weymouth Mass., U.S.A. 42°13N 70°58W 313 D14
Weymouth, C. Australia 12°37S 143°27E 280 A3
Wezembeek-Oppem Belgium 50°51N 4°29E 116 A2
Wha Ti Canada 63°8N 117°16W 294 E8
Whakaari N.Z. 37°30S 177°13E 284 D6
Whakamaru N.Z. 38°23S 175°50E 284 E4
Whakatane N.Z. 37°57S 177°1E 284 D6
Whakatane → N.Z. 37°57S 177°1E 284 D6
Whale = Baleine → Canada 58°15N 67°40W 299 A6
Whale B. Burma 11°37N 98°38E 237 G2
Whale Cove Canada 62°10N 92°34W 297 A10
Whale Pt. Ascension I. 7°57S 14°18W 153 g
Whale Valley = Hitan, W. el Egypt 29°19N 30°10E 256 J7
Whales, B. of Antarctica 78°0S 160°0W 151 D12
Whalsay U.K. 60°22N 0°59W 167 A8
Whangaehu → N.Z. 40°3S 175°6E 284 G4
Whangamata N.Z. 37°12S 175°53E 284 D4
Whangamomona N.Z. 39°8S 174°44E 284 F3
Whanganui △ N.Z. 39°17S 174°53E 284 F3
Whangaparaoa Pen. N.Z. 36°40S 174°45E 284 C3
Whangarei N.Z. 35°43S 174°21E 284 B3
Whangarei Harb. N.Z. 35°45S 174°28E 284 B3
Whangaroa Harb. N.Z. 35°4S 173°46E 284 B2
Whangaruru Harb. N.Z. 35°24S 174°23E 284 B3
Wharanui N.Z. 41°55S 174°6E 285 B9
Wharekauri = Chatham Is. Pac. Oc. 44°0S 176°40W 285 a
Wharfe → U.K. 53°51N 1°9W 168 D6
Wharfedale U.K. 54°6N 2°1W 168 C5
Wharton N.J., U.S.A. 40°54N 74°35W 313 F10
Wharton Pa., U.S.A. 41°31N 78°1W 312 E6
Wharton Tex., U.S.A. 29°19N 96°6W 314 G6
Wharton Basin Ind. Oc. 22°0S 99°0E 273 G9
Whataroa N.Z. 43°18S 170°24E 285 D5
Whataroa → N.Z. 43°7S 170°16E 285 D5
Whatcom = Bellingham U.S.A. 48°46N 122°29W 306 B4
Wheatfield U.S.A. 41°13N 87°4W 311 C9
Wheatland Calif., U.S.A. 39°1N 121°25W 306 F5
Wheatland Ind., U.S.A. 38°40N 87°19W 311 F9
Wheatland Wyo., U.S.A. 42°3N 104°58W 304 E11
Wheatley Canada 42°6N 82°27W 312 D2
Wheaton Ill., U.S.A. 41°52N 88°6W 311 C8
Wheaton Md., U.S.A. 39°3N 77°3W 309 F15
Wheaton Minn., U.S.A. 45°48N 96°30W 308 C5
Wheelbarrow Pk. U.S.A. 37°26N 116°5W 306 H10
Wheeler Oreg., U.S.A. 45°41N 123°53W 304 D2
Wheeler Tex., U.S.A. 35°27N 100°16W 314 D4
Wheeler → Canada 57°2N 67°13W 299 A6
Wheeler L. U.S.A. 34°48N 87°23W 315 D11
Wheeler Pk. N. Mex., U.S.A. 36°34N 105°25W 305 H11
Wheeler Pk. Nev., U.S.A. 38°57N 114°15W 304 G6
Wheeler Ridge U.S.A. 35°0N 118°57W 307 L8
Wheelersburg U.S.A. 38°44N 82°51W 309 F12
Wheeling U.S.A. 40°4N 80°43W 312 F4
Whernside U.K. 54°14N 2°24W 168 C5
Whiddy I. Ireland 51°41N 9°31W 166 E2
Whim Creek Australia 20°50S 117°49E 278 D2
Whirlwind Reef Papua N. G. 4°42S 148°16E 286 C5
Whiskey Jack L. Canada 58°23N 101°55W 297 B8
Whiskeytown-Shasta-Trinity △ U.S.A. 40°45N 122°15W 304 F2
Whistleduck Cr. → Australia 20°15S 135°18E 280 C2
Whistler Canada 50°7N 122°58W 296 C4
Whitby Ont., Canada 43°52N 78°56W 312 C6
Whitby N. Yorks., U.K. 54°29N 0°37W 168 C7
Whitcombe Pass N.Z. 43°13S 170°55E 285 D5
White → Ark., U.S.A. 33°57N 91°5W 314 E9
White → Ind., U.S.A. 38°25N 87°45W 311 F9
White → S. Dak., U.S.A. 43°42N 99°27W 308 D4
White → Tex., U.S.A. 33°14N 100°56W 314 E4
White → Utah, U.S.A. 40°4N 109°41W 304 F9
White → Vt., U.S.A. 43°37N 72°20W 313 C12
White → Wash., U.S.A. 47°12N 122°15W 306 C4
White, L. Australia 21°9S 128°56E 278 D4
White B. Canada 50°0N 56°35W 299 C8
White Bird U.S.A. 45°46N 116°18W 304 D5
White Butte U.S.A. 46°23N 103°18W 308 B2
White City Fla., U.S.A. 29°53N 85°13W 316 F4
White City Oreg., U.S.A. 42°26N 122°51W 304 E2
White Cliffs Australia 30°50S 143°10E 282 A5
White Cloud Hill = Baiyun Mountain Scenic Area China 23°11N 113°17E 121 A2
White Desert = Es Sahrâ al Beida Egypt 27°50N 28°45E 256 B2
White Hall U.S.A. 39°26N 90°24W 310 E6
White Haven U.S.A. 41°4N 75°47W 313 E9
White Horse, Vale of U.K. 51°37N 1°30W 169 F6
White House, The Washington, D.C., U.S.A. 143 b1
White I. = Whakaari N.Z. 37°30S 177°13E 284 D6
White I. Grenada 12°26N 61°28W 323 q
White L. Ont., Canada 45°18N 76°31W 313 A8
White L. La., U.S.A. 29°44N 92°30W 314 G8
White Lake Canada 45°21N 76°29W 313 A8
White Mountain U.S.A. 64°41N 163°24W 303 D7
White Mountain Peak U.S.A. 37°38N 118°15W 306 H8
White Mountains Nat. Recr. Area △ U.S.A. 65°30N 147°40W 303 D11
White Mts. Alaska, U.S.A. 65°30N 146°30W 303 D11
White Mts. Calif., U.S.A. 37°30N 118°15W 306 H8
White Mts. N.H., U.S.A. 44°15N 71°15W 313 B13
White Mts. △ Australia 20°43S 145°12E 280 C4
White Nile = Nîl el Abyad → Sudan 15°38N 32°31E 257 D3
White Nile Dam = Khazzān Jabal al Awliyā Sudan 15°24N 32°20E 257 D3
White Oak U.S.A. 31°2N 81°43W 316 D8
White Otter L. Canada 49°5N 91°55W 298 C1
White Pass U.S.A. 46°38N 121°24W 306 D5
White Pigeon U.S.A. 41°48N 85°39W 311 C11
White Plains Ga., U.S.A. 33°28N 83°1W 316 B6
White Plains N.Y., U.S.A. 41°2N 73°46W 313 E11
White River Canada 48°35N 85°20W 298 C2
White River S. Dak., U.S.A. 43°34N 100°45W 308 D3
White Rock B.C., Canada 49°2N 122°48W 306 A4
White Rock N. Mex., U.S.A. 35°50N 106°12W 305 J10
White Russia = Belarus ■ Europe 53°30N 27°0E 177 B14
White Sands △ U.S.A. 32°46N 106°20W 305 K10
White Sea = Beloye More Russia 66°30N 38°0E 186 A6
White Springs U.S.A. 30°20N 82°45W 316 E7
White Sulphur Springs Mont., U.S.A. 46°33N 110°54W 304 C8
White Sulphur Springs W. Va., U.S.A. 37°48N 80°18W 309 G13
White Swan U.S.A. 46°23N 120°44W 306 D6
White Volta → Ghana 9°10N 1°15W 263 D4
Whitechapel U.K. 51°31N 0°3W 125 A3
Whitecliffs N.Z. 43°26S 171°55E 285 D6
Whitecourt Canada 54°10N 115°45W 296 C5
Whiteface Mt. U.S.A. 44°22N 73°54W 313 B11
Whitefield U.S.A. 44°23N 71°37W 313 B13
Whitefish U.S.A. 48°25N 114°20W 304 B6
Whitefish B. U.S.A. 46°40N 84°55W 298 C3
Whitefish Bay U.S.A. 43°6N 87°54W 311 A9
Whitefish L. Canada 62°41N 106°48W 297 A7
Whitefish Pt. U.S.A. 46°45N 84°59W 309 B11
Whitegull, L. = Goélands, L. aux Canada 55°27N 64°17W 299 A7
Whitehall Dublin, Ireland 53°22N 6°16W 120 A2
Whitehall London, U.K. 125 b3
Whitehall Mich., U.S.A. 43°24N 86°21W 308 D10
Whitehall Mont., U.S.A. 45°52N 112°6W 304 D7
Whitehall N.Y., U.S.A. 43°33N 73°24W 313 C11
Whitehall Wis., U.S.A. 44°22N 91°19W 308 C8
Whitehaven U.K. 54°33N 3°35W 168 C4
Whitehorse Canada 60°43N 135°3W 296 A1
Whiteman Ra. Papua N. G. 5°55S 150°0E 286 C6
Whitemark Australia 40°7S 148°3E 281 G4
Whiteplains Liberia 6°28N 10°40W 262 D2
Whiteriver U.S.A. 33°50N 109°58W 305 K9
Whitesand → Canada 60°9N 115°45W 296 A5
Whitesands S. Africa 34°23S 20°50E 270 D3
Whitesboro N.Y., U.S.A. 43°7N 75°18W 313 C9
Whitesboro Tex., U.S.A. 33°39N 96°54W 314 E6
Whiteshell △ Canada 50°0N 95°40W 297 D9
Whiteside, Canal Chile 53°55S 70°15W 336 D2
Whiteville U.S.A. 34°20N 78°42W 315 D15
Whitewater U.S.A. 42°50N 88°44W 311 B8
Whitewater B. U.S.A. 25°15N 81°0W 317 K9
Whitewater Baldy U.S.A. 33°20N 108°39W 305 K9
Whitewater L. Canada 50°50N 89°10W 298 B2
Whitewood Queens., Australia 21°28S 143°30E 280 C3
Whitewood Sask., Canada 50°20N 102°20W 297 C8
Whitfield Australia 36°42S 146°24E 283 D7
Whithorn U.K. 54°44N 4°26W 167 G4
Whitianga N.Z. 36°47S 175°41E 284 C4
Whiting U.S.A. 41°41N 87°30W 311 C9
Whitman U.S.A. 42°5N 70°56W 313 D14
Whitmore Mts. Antarctica 82°35S 104°30W 151 E15
Whitmore Village U.S.A. 21°31N 158°1W 302 J13
Whitney Ont., Canada 45°31N 78°14W 312 A6
Whitney Nev., U.S.A. 36°4N 115°5W 124 B2
Whitney, Mt. U.S.A. 36°35N 118°18W 306 J8
Whitney Point U.S.A. 42°20N 75°58W 313 D9
Whitstable U.K. 51°21N 1°3E 169 F9
Whitsunday I. Australia 20°15S 149°4E 280 b
Whitsunday Islands △ Australia 20°15S 149°0E 280 b
Whittemore U.S.A. 43°4N 94°26W 310 A2
Whittier Alaska, U.S.A. 60°47N 148°41W 303 F10
Whittier Calif., U.S.A. 33°58N 118°2W 126 C4
Whittier Narrows Recreation Area △ U.S.A. 34°2N 118°4W 126 B4
Whittlesea Australia 37°27S 145°9E 283 D6
Whitton U.K. 51°27N 0°21W 125 B1
Wholdaia L. Canada 60°43N 104°20W 297 A8
Whyalla Australia 33°2S 137°30E 282 B2
Wiang Kosai △ Thailand 17°54N 99°29E 236 D2
Wiang Sa Thailand 18°34N 100°45E 236 C3
Wiarton Canada 44°40N 81°10W 312 B3
Wiawso Ghana 6°10N 2°25W 262 D4
Wiay U.K. 57°24N 7°13W 167 D1
Wiązów Poland 50°50N 17°10E 185 H4
Wibaux U.S.A. 46°59N 104°11W 304 C11
Wichabai Guyana 2°57N 59°35W 329 C6
Wichian Buri Thailand 15°39N 101°7E 236 E3
Wichita U.S.A. 37°42N 97°20W 308 G5
Wichita Falls U.S.A. 33°54N 98°30W 314 E5
Wick U.K. 58°26N 3°5W 167 C5
Wickenburg U.S.A. 33°58N 112°44W 305 K7
Wickepin Australia 32°50S 117°30E 279 F2
Wickham Australia 20°42S 117°11E 278 D2
Wickham, C. Australia 39°35S 143°57E 281 F3
Wickliffe U.S.A. 41°36N 81°28W 312 E3
Wicklow Ireland 52°59N 6°3W 166 D5
Wicklow □ Ireland 52°57N 6°25W 166 D5
Wicklow Hd. Ireland 52°58N 6°0W 166 D6
Wicklow Mts. Ireland 52°58N 6°26W 166 C5
Wicklow Mts. △ Ireland 53°6N 6°21W 166 C5
Widawa Poland 51°27N 18°51E 185 G5
Widawka → Poland 51°27N 18°52E 185 G5
Wide B. Papua N. G. 5°5S 152°5E 286 C7
Wideawake = Ascension I. ✕ (ASI) Ascension I. 7°58S 14°23W 153 g
Widgeegoara Cr. → Australia 28°51S 146°34E 281 D4
Widgiemooltha Australia 31°30S 121°34E 279 F3
Widnes U.K. 53°23N 2°45W 168 D5
Wido S. Korea 35°35N 126°17E 224 E3
Więcbork Poland 53°21N 17°30E 185 E4
Wieden Austria 48°11N 16°22E 142 A2
Wiehengebirge = Nördlicher Teutoburger Wald-Wiehengebirge △ Germany 52°18N 8°10E 178 C4
Wiehl Germany 50°56N 7°34E 178 E3
Wiek Germany 54°37N 13°17E 178 A9
Wielbark Poland 53°24N 20°55E 184 E7
Wieleń Poland 52°53N 16°9E 185 F3
Wielichowo Poland 52°7N 16°22E 185 F3
Wieliczka Poland 50°0N 20°5E 185 J7
Wielkopolski △ Poland 52°18N 16°45E 185 F3
Wielkopolskie □ Poland 52°10N 17°30E 185 F4
Wieluń Poland 51°15N 18°34E 185 G5
Wien Austria 48°12N 16°22E 142 A2
Wien-Schwechat ✕ (VIE) Austria 48°7N 16°35E 142 B3
Wiener Neustadt Austria 47°49N 16°16E 181 D9
Wienerberg Austria 48°9N 16°21E 142 B2
Wieprz → Poland 51°34N 21°49E 185 G8
Wieprza → Poland 54°26N 16°25E 184 D3
Wieruszów Poland 51°19N 18°9E 185 G5
Wierzbno Poland 52°11N 21°1E 143 B2
Wiesbaden Germany 50°4N 8°14E 179 E4
Wiesental Germany 49°13N 8°31E 179 F4
Wiesloch Germany 49°18N 8°41E 179 F4
Wiesmoor Germany 53°24N 7°47E 178 B3
Wieżyca Poland 54°14N 18°8E 184 D5
Wigan U.K. 53°33N 2°38W 168 D5
Wiggins Colo., U.S.A. 40°14N 104°4W 304 F11
Wiggins Miss., U.S.A. 30°51N 89°8W 315 F10
Wight, I. of U.K. 50°41N 1°17W 169 G6
Wigierski △ Poland 54°5N 23°5E 184 D10
Wigry, Jezioro Poland 54°2N 23°8E 184 D10
Wigston U.K. 52°35N 1°6W 169 E6
Wigton U.K. 54°50N 3°10W 168 C4
Wigtown U.K. 54°53N 4°27W 167 G4
Wigtown B. U.K. 54°46N 4°15W 167 G4
Wijde Wormer Neths. 52°28N 4°52E 112 A2
Wik and Wikway People ⊙ Australia 13°55S 142°28E 280 A3
Wil Switz. 47°28N 9°3E 179 H5
Wilamowice Poland 49°55N 19°9E 185 J6
Wilanów Poland 52°10N 21°4E 143 B2
Wilanówka → Poland 52°13N 21°6E 143 C2
Wilber U.S.A. 40°29N 96°58W 308 E5
Wilberforce Canada 45°2N 78°13W 312 A6
Wilberforce, C. Australia 11°54S 136°35E 280 A2
Wilburton U.S.A. 34°55N 95°19W 314 D7
Wilcannia Australia 31°30S 143°26E 282 A5
Wilcox U.S.A. 41°35N 78°41W 312 E6
Wildbad Germany 48°44N 8°33E 179 G4
Wildcat Cr. → U.S.A. 40°28N 86°52W 311 D10
Wildenschwert = Ústí nad Orlicí Czech Rep. 49°58N 16°24E 181 B9
Wildeshausen Germany 52°54N 8°27E 178 C4
Wildeshauser Geest △ Germany 52°54N 8°30E 178 C4
Wildomar U.S.A. 33°36N 117°16W 307 M9
Wildon Austria 46°52N 15°31E 180 E8
Wildrose U.S.A. 36°14N 117°11W 307 J9
Wilds, The S. Africa 26°10S 28°2E 123 B2
Wildspitze Austria 46°53N 10°53E 180 E3
Wildwood U.S.A. 28°52N 82°2W 317 G7
Wilga → Poland 51°52N 21°18E 185 G8
Wilge → S. Africa 27°3S 28°20E 271 C4
Wilhelm, Mt. Papua N. G. 5°50S 145°1E 286 C3
Wilhelm II Coast Antarctica 68°0S 90°0E 151 C7
Wilhelmina Geb. Suriname 3°50N 56°30W 329 C6
Wilhelmina Top = Trikora, Puncak Indonesia 4°15S 138°45E 231 E9
Wilhelmsburg Austria 48°6N 15°36E 180 C8
Wilhelmshagen Germany 52°26N 13°42E 115 B5
Wilhelmshaven Germany 53°31N 8°7E 178 B4
Wilhelmstal Namibia 21°58S 16°21E 270 B2
Wilis Indonesia 7°51S 111°48E 235 D4
Wilkes-Barre U.S.A. 41°15N 75°53W 313 E9
Wilkes I. Wake I. 19°18N 166°34E 302 b
Wilkes Land Antarctica 69°0S 120°0E 151 D9
Wilket Creek Park Canada 43°43N 79°21W 141 A2
Wilkie Canada 52°27N 108°42W 297 C7
Wilkieston U.K. 55°54N 3°24W 121 B1
Wilkins Ice Shelf Antarctica 70°30S 72°0W 151 C17
Wilkinsburg U.S.A. 40°26N 79°52W 312 F5
Wilkinson Lakes Australia 29°40S 132°39E 279 E5
Will Rogers State Historical Park △ U.S.A. 34°2N 118°30W 126 B1
Willacoochee U.S.A. 31°20N 83°3W 316 D6
Willandra △ Australia 33°12S 145°0E 283 B6
Willandra Creek → Australia 33°22S 145°52E 283 B6
Willapa B. U.S.A. 46°40N 124°0W 306 D3
Willapa Hills U.S.A. 46°35N 123°25W 306 D3
Willard U.S.A. 41°3N 82°44W 312 E2
Willare Bridge Roadhouse Australia 17°43S 123°38E 278 C3
Willaumez Pen. Papua N. G. 5°15S 150°2E 286 C6
Willbriggie Australia 34°28S 146°2E 283 C7
Willbrook Ireland 53°17N 6°16W 120 B2
Willcox U.S.A. 32°15N 109°50W 305 K9
Willemstad Curaçao 12°5N 68°55W 322 g
Willenberg = Wielbark Poland 53°24N 20°55E 184 E7
Willesden U.K. 51°32N 0°15W 125 A2
Willesden Green U.K. 51°32N 0°13W 125 A2
Willi Willi △ Australia 30°57S 152°27E 283 A10
William → Canada 59°8N 109°19W 297 B7
William, Mt. Australia 37°17S 142°35E 282 D5
William 'Bill' Dannelly Res. U.S.A. 32°6N 87°24W 315 E11
William Creek Australia 28°58S 136°22E 281 D2
Williamnagar India 25°31N 90°37E 241 C3
Williams W. Austral., Australia 33°2S 116°52E 279 F2
Williams Ariz., U.S.A. 35°15N 112°11W 305 J7
Williams Calif., U.S.A. 39°9N 122°9W 306 F4
Williams Harbour Canada 52°33N 55°47W 299 B8
Williams Lake Canada 52°10N 122°10W 296 C4
Williamsbridge U.S.A. 40°52N 73°51W 132 A2
Williamsburg Fla., U.S.A. 28°24N 81°26W 133 B2
Williamsburg Iowa, U.S.A. 41°40N 92°1W 310 C4
Williamsburg Ky., U.S.A. 36°44N 84°10W 309 G11
Williamsburg New York, U.S.A. 132 f3
Williamsburg Pa., U.S.A. 40°28N 78°12W 312 F6
Williamsburg Va., U.S.A. 37°16N 76°43W 309 G15
Williamsburg Bridge New York, U.S.A. 132 e2
Williamsfield U.S.A. 40°55N 90°1W 310 D6
Williamson N.Y., U.S.A. 43°14N 77°11W 312 C7
Williamson W. Va., U.S.A. 37°41N 82°17W 309 G12
Williamsport Ind., U.S.A. 40°17N 87°17W 311 D9
Williamsport Pa., U.S.A. 41°15N 77°1W 312 E7
Williamston Mich., U.S.A. 42°41N 84°17W 311 B12
Williamston N.C., U.S.A. 35°51N 77°4W 315 D16
Williamstown Vic., Australia 37°51S 144°52E 128 B1
Williamstown Ky., U.S.A. 38°38N 84°34W 311 F12
Williamstown Mass., U.S.A. 42°43N 73°12W 313 D11
Williamstown N.Y., U.S.A. 43°26N 75°53W 313 C9
Williamsville U.S.A. 39°57N 89°33W 310 E7
Willikies Antigua & B. 17°3N 61°42W 322 b
Willimantic U.S.A. 41°43N 72°13W 313 E12
Willingboro U.S.A. 40°3N 74°54W 309 E16
Willis, L. U.S.A. 28°23N 81°28W 133 B2
Willis Tower Chicago, U.S.A. 119 c1
Willisburg U.S.A. 37°49N 85°8W 311 G11
Williston Northern Cape, S. Africa 31°20S 20°53E 270 D3
Williston Fla., U.S.A. 29°23N 82°27W 317 F7
Williston N. Dak., U.S.A. 48°9N 103°37W 308 A2
Williston S.C., U.S.A. 33°24N 81°25W 316 B8
Williston L. Canada 56°0N 124°0W 296 B4
Willits U.S.A. 39°25N 123°21W 304 G2
Willmar U.S.A. 45°7N 95°3W 308 C6
Willmore Wilderness △ Canada 53°45N 119°30W 296 C5
Willoughby N.S.W., Australia 33°48S 151°12E 139 A2
Willoughby Ohio, U.S.A. 41°39N 81°24W 312 E3
Willoughby B. Antigua & B. 17°2N 61°44W 322 b
Willow U.S.A. 61°45N 150°3W 303 F10
Willow Bunch Canada 49°20N 105°35W 297 D7
Willow L. Canada 62°10N 119°8W 296 A5
Willow Tree Australia 31°40S 150°45E 283 A9
Willow Wall, The China 42°10N 122°0E 227 C12
Willowdale Ont., Canada 43°46N 79°25W 141 A2
Willowdale La., U.S.A. 30°0N 90°12W 131 A1
Willowick U.S.A. 41°38N 81°28W 312 E3
Willowlake → Canada 62°42N 123°8W 296 A4
Willowmore S. Africa 33°15S 23°30E 270 D3
Willows U.S.A. 39°31N 122°12W 306 F4
Willowvale = Gatyana S. Africa 32°16S 28°31E 271 D4
Wills, L. Australia 21°25S 128°51E 278 D4
Wills Cr. → Australia 22°43S 140°2E 280 C3
Willsboro U.S.A. 44°21N 73°24W 313 B11
Willunga Australia 35°15S 138°30E 282 C3
Wilma U.S.A. 30°9N 84°58W 316 E5
Wilmersdorf Berlin, Germany 115 c1
Wilmette U.S.A. 42°4N 87°42W 119 A2
Wilmington S. Austral., Australia 32°39S 138°7E 282 B3
Wilmington Kent, U.K. 51°25N 0°12E 125 B5
Wilmington Del., U.S.A. 39°45N 75°33W 309 F16
Wilmington Ill., U.S.A. 41°18N 88°9W 311 C8
Wilmington N.C., U.S.A. 34°14N 77°55W 315 D16
Wilmington Ohio, U.S.A. 39°27N 83°50W 311 E13
Wilmington Vt., U.S.A. 42°52N 72°52W 313 D12
Wilmslow U.K. 53°19N 2°13W 168 D5
Wilna = Vilnius Lithuania 54°38N 25°19E 188 E3
Wilpattu △ Sri Lanka 8°20N 79°50E 245 K4
Wilpena Australia 31°31S 138°37E 282 A3
Wilpena Cr. → Australia 31°25S 139°29E 282 A3
Wilsall U.S.A. 45°59N 110°38W 304 D8
Wilson N.C., U.S.A. 35°44N 77°55W 315 D16
Wilson N.Y., U.S.A. 43°19N 78°50W 312 C6
Wilson Pa., U.S.A. 40°41N 75°15W 313 F9
Wilson → Australia 16°48S 128°16E 278 C4
Wilson Bluff Australia 31°41S 129°0E 279 F4
Wilson Inlet Australia 35°0S 117°22E 279 G2
Wilson Str. Solomon Is. 8°0S 156°39E 287 M9
Wilsons Promontory Australia 38°59S 146°23E 283 E7
Wilsons Promontory △ Australia 38°59S 146°23E 283 D7
Wilster Germany 53°55N 9°23E 178 B5
Wilton Iowa, U.S.A. 41°35N 91°1W 310 C5
Wilton N. Dak., U.S.A. 47°10N 100°47W 308 B3
Wilton → Australia 14°45S 134°33E 280 A1
Wilton Manors U.S.A. 26°9N 80°8W 129 B3
Wiltshire □ U.K. 51°18N 1°53W 169 F6
Wiltz Lux. 49°57N 5°55E 170 E5
Wiluna Australia 26°36S 120°14E 279 E3
Wimbledon U.K. 51°25N 0°13W 125 B2
Wimbledon Common U.K. 51°26N 0°14W 125 B2
Wimbledon Park U.K. 51°25N 0°11W 125 B2
Wimbledon Tennis Ground U.K. 51°25N 0°12W 125 B2
Wimborne Minster U.K. 50°48N 1°59W 169 G6
Wimereux France 50°45N 1°37E 173 B8
Wimmera → Australia 36°8S 141°56E 282 D4
Winam G. Kenya 0°20S 34°15E 268 C3
Winamac U.S.A. 41°3N 86°36W 311 C10
Winburg S. Africa 28°30S 27°2E 270 C4
Winchelsea Australia 38°10S 144°1E 282 E6
Winchendon U.S.A. 42°41N 72°3W 313 D12
Winchester N.Z. 44°11S 171°17E 285 E6
Winchester Hants., U.K. 51°4N 1°18W 169 F6
Winchester Conn., U.S.A. 41°53N 73°9W 313 E11
Winchester Idaho, U.S.A. 46°14N 116°38W 304 C5
Winchester Ill., U.S.A. 39°38N 90°27W 310 E6
Winchester Ind., U.S.A. 40°10N 84°59W 311 D12
Winchester Ky., U.S.A. 37°59N 84°11W 311 G12
Winchester Mass., U.S.A. 42°26N 71°8W 116 A2
Winchester N.H., U.S.A. 42°46N 72°23W 313 D12
Winchester Nev., U.S.A. 36°7N 115°7W 124 B2
Winchester Ohio, U.S.A. 38°56N 83°39W 311 F13
Winchester Tenn., U.S.A. 35°11N 86°7W 315 D11
Winchester Va., U.S.A. 39°11N 78°10W 309 F14
Wind → U.S.A. 43°12N 108°12W 304 E9
Wind Cave △ U.S.A. 43°32N 103°17W 308 D2
Wind Point U.S.A. 42°47N 87°46W 311 B9
Wind River Range U.S.A. 43°0N 109°30W 304 E9
Windamere, L. Australia 32°48S 149°51E 283 B8
Windau = Ventspils Latvia 57°25N 21°32E 184 A8
Windber U.S.A. 40°14N 78°50W 312 F6
Winder U.S.A. 34°0N 83°45W 316 A6
Windermere Western Cape, S. Africa 33°55S 18°30E 118 A2
Windermere Cumb., U.K. 54°23N 2°55W 168 C5
Windermere Fla., U.S.A. 28°29N 81°32W 133 B1
Windfall U.S.A. 40°22N 85°57W 311 D11
Windhoek Namibia 22°35S 17°4E 270 B2
Windidda ⊙ Australia 26°23S 122°12E 279 E3
Windisch-Feistritz = Slovenska Bistrica Slovenia 46°24N 15°35E 199 B12
Windischgarsten Austria 47°42N 14°21E 180 D7
Windischgratz = Slovenj Gradec Slovenia 46°31N 15°5E 199 B12
Windjana Gorge △ Australia 17°51S 125°0E 278 C3
Windom U.S.A. 43°52N 95°7W 308 D6
Windorah Australia 25°24S 142°36E 280 D3
Window Rock U.S.A. 35°41N 109°3W 305 J9
Windrush → U.K. 51°43N 1°24W 169 F6
Windsor N.S.W., Australia 33°37S 150°50E 283 B9
Windsor N.S., Canada 44°59N 64°5W 299 D7
Windsor Ont., Canada 42°18N 83°0W 312 D2
Windsor N.Z. 44°59S 170°49E 285 E5
Windsor Gauteng, S. Africa 26°7S 27°59E 123 A1
Windsor Windsor & Maidenhead, U.K. 51°29N 0°36W 169 F7
Windsor Calif., U.S.A. 38°33N 122°49W 306 G4
Windsor Colo., U.S.A. 40°29N 104°54W 304 F11
Windsor Conn., U.S.A. 41°50N 72°39W 313 E12
Windsor Ill., U.S.A. 39°26N 88°36W 311 E8
Windsor Mo., U.S.A. 38°32N 93°31W 310 F3
Windsor N.Y., U.S.A. 42°5N 75°37W 313 D9
Windsor Vt., U.S.A. 43°29N 72°24W 313 C12
Windsor, Gare Montréal, Canada 130 c2
Windsor & Maidenhead □ U.K. 51°29N 0°40W 169 F7
Windsor Caves Jamaica 18°21N 77°39W 320 a
Windsor Hills U.S.A. 33°59N 118°22W 126 C2
Windsorton S. Africa 28°16S 24°44E 270 C3
Windward Grenada 12°31N 61°26W 323 q
Windward Is. W. Indies 13°0N 61°0W 321 D7
Windward Passage = Vientos, Paso de los Caribbean 20°0N 74°0W 321 C5
Windward Side Saba 17°38N 63°14W 322 a
Windy Arbour Ireland 53°18N 6°14W 120 B2
Winefred L. Canada 55°30N 110°30W 297 B6
Winejok South Sudan 9°1N 27°30E 257 F2
Winfield Iowa, U.S.A. 41°7N 91°26W 310 C5
Winfield Kans., U.S.A. 37°15N 96°59W 308 G5
Winfield Mo., U.S.A. 39°0N 90°44W 310 F6
Wingate Mts. Australia 14°25S 130°40E 278 B5
Wingellina = Irrunytju Australia 26°3S 128°56E 279 E4
Wingham N.S.W., Australia 31°48S 152°22E 283 A10
Wingham Ont., Canada 43°55N 81°20W 312 C3
Winisk → Canada 55°17N 85°5W 298 A2
Winisk L. Canada 52°55N 87°22W 298 B2
Wink U.S.A. 31°45N 103°9W 314 F3
Winkler Canada 49°10N 97°56W 297 D9
Winklern Austria 46°52N 12°52E 180 E5
Winlock U.S.A. 46°30N 122°56W 306 D4
Winneba Ghana 5°25N 0°36W 263 D4
Winnebago U.S.A. 42°16N 89°15W 310 B7
Winnebago, L. U.S.A. 44°0N 88°26W 308 D9
Winnecke Cr. → Australia 18°35S 131°34E 278 C5
Winnemucca U.S.A. 40°58N 117°44W 304 F5
Winnemucca L. U.S.A. 40°7N 119°21W 304 F4
Winner U.S.A. 43°22N 99°52W 308 D4
Winnetka U.S.A. 42°6N 87°45W 119 A2
Winnett U.S.A. 47°0N 108°21W 304 C9
Winnfield U.S.A. 31°56N 92°38W 314 F8
Winnibigoshish, L. U.S.A. 47°27N 94°13W 308 B6
Winning Germany 48°2N 11°37E 131 B2
Winnipeg Canada 49°54N 97°9W 297 D9
Winnipeg → Canada 50°38N 96°19W 297 C9
Winnipeg, L. Canada 52°0N 97°0W 297 C9
Winnipeg Beach Canada 50°30N 96°58W 297 C9
Winnipegosis Canada 51°39N 99°55W 297 C9
Winnipegosis L. Canada 52°30N 100°0W 297 C9
Winnipesaukee, L. U.S.A. 43°38N 71°21W 313 C13
Winnisquam L. U.S.A. 43°33N 71°31W 313 C13
Winnsboro La., U.S.A. 32°10N 91°43W 314 E9
Winnsboro S.C., U.S.A. 34°23N 81°5W 315 D14
Winnsboro Tex., U.S.A. 32°58N 95°17W 314 E7
Winokapau, L. Canada 53°15N 62°50W 299 B7
Winona Minn., U.S.A. 44°3N 91°39W 308 C8
Winona Miss., U.S.A. 33°29N 89°44W 315 E10
Winooski U.S.A. 44°29N 73°11W 313 B11
Winooski → U.S.A. 44°32N 73°17W 313 B11
Winschoten Neths. 53°9N 7°3E 170 A7
Winsen Germany 53°22N 10°13E 178 B6
Winsford U.K. 53°12N 2°31W 168 D5
Winslow = Bainbridge Island U.S.A. 47°38N 122°32W 306 C4
Winslow Ariz., U.S.A. 35°2N 110°42W 305 J8
Winslow Ind., U.S.A. 38°23N 87°13W 311 F9
Winslow Reef Kiribati 1°36S 174°57W 277 A16
Winsted U.S.A. 41°55N 73°4W 313 E11
Winston-Salem U.S.A. 36°6N 80°15W 315 C14
Winter Garden U.S.A. 28°34N 81°35W 317 G8
Winter Haven U.S.A. 28°1N 81°44W 317 G8
Winter Park U.S.A. 28°36N 81°20W 317 G8
Winterberg Germany 51°11N 8°33E 178 D4
Winterhaven U.S.A. 32°44N 114°38W 307 N12
Winters U.S.A. 38°32N 121°58W 306 G5
Winterset U.S.A. 41°20N 94°1W 310 C3
Wintersville U.S.A. 40°23N 80°42W 312 F4
Winterswijk Neths. 51°58N 6°43E 170 C6
Winterthur Switz. 47°30N 8°44E 179 H4
Winthrop U.S.A. 48°28N 120°10W 304 B3
Winton Queens., Australia 22°24S 143°3E 280 C3
Winton N.Z. 46°8S 168°20E 285 G3
Wintua Vanuatu 16°30S 167°26E 287 F5
Wipper → Germany 51°16N 11°12E 178 D7
Wirlyajarrayi ⊙ Australia 21°45S 132°35E 278 D5
Wirraminna Australia 31°12S 136°13E 282 A2
Wirrulla Australia 32°24S 134°31E 281 E1
Wisbech U.K. 52°41N 0°9E 169 E8
Wisconsin □ U.S.A. 44°45N 89°30W 308 C9
Wisconsin → U.S.A. 43°0N 91°15W 310 A5
Wisconsin Rapids U.S.A. 44°23N 89°49W 308 C9
Wisdom U.S.A. 45°37N 113°27W 304 D7
Wiseman U.S.A. 67°25N 150°6W 303 C10
Wishaw U.K. 55°46N 3°54W 167 F5
Wishek U.S.A. 46°16N 99°33W 308 B4
Wisła Poland 49°38N 18°53E 185 J5
Wisła → Poland 54°22N 18°55E 184 D5
Wisłok → Poland 50°13N 22°32E 185 H9
Wisłoka → Poland 50°27N 21°23E 185 H8
Wismar Mecklenburg-Vorpommern, Germany 53°54N 11°29E 178 B7
Wismar Guyana 5°59N 58°18W 329 B6
Wisner U.S.A. 41°59N 96°55W 308 E5
Wissant France 50°52N 1°40E 173 B8
Wissembourg France 49°2N 7°57E 173 C14
Wissous France 48°44N 2°19E 134 B2
Wisznice Poland 51°48N 23°13E 185 G10
Witbank = eMalahleni S. Africa 25°51S 29°14E 271 C4
Witches Gorge = Wu Xia China 31°2N 110°10E 229 B8
Witdraai S. Africa 26°58S 20°48E 270 C3
Witham U.K. 51°48N 0°40E 169 F8
Witham → U.K. 52°59N 0°2W 168 E7
Withernsea U.K. 53°44N 0°1E 168 D8
Withlacoochee → Fla., U.S.A. 30°24N 83°10W 316 E6
Withlacoochee → Fla., U.S.A. 29°0N 82°45W 317 G7
Witjira △ Australia 26°22S 135°37E 281 D2
Witkowo Poland 52°26N 17°45E 185 F4
Witless Bay Canada 47°17N 52°50W 299 C9
Witney U.K. 51°48N 1°28W 169 F6
Witnica Poland 52°40N 14°54E 185 F1
Witnossob → Namibia 23°55S 18°45E 270 C3
Witriver S. Africa 25°20S 31°0E 271 C5
Wittdün Germany 54°38N 8°23E 178 A4
Witte Pan Bonaire 12°3N 68°17W 322 h
Wittelsheim France 47°48N 7°14E 173 E14
Witten Germany 51°26N 7°20E 178 D3
Wittenau Germany 52°35N 13°19E 115 A2
Wittenberge Germany 53°0N 11°45E 178 B7
Wittenburg Germany 53°31N 11°4E 178 B7
Wittenoom Australia 22°15S 118°20E 278 D2
Witti, Banjaran Malaysia 5°11N 116°29E 235 A5
Wittingau = Třeboň Czech Rep. 49°1N 14°48E 180 B7
Wittingen Germany 52°44N 10°44E 178 C6
Wittlich Germany 49°59N 6°53E 179 F2
Wittmund Germany 53°34N 7°46E 178 B3
Wittow Germany 54°38N 13°20E 178 A9
Wittstock Germany 53°10N 12°28E 178 B8
Witu Kenya 2°23S 40°26E 268 C5
Witu Is. Papua N. G. 4°50S 149°25E 286 C5
Witvlei Namibia 22°23S 18°32E 270 B2
Witwatersrand, Univ. of S. Africa 26°11S 28°1E 123 B2
Witzenhausen Germany 51°20N 9°51E 178 D5
Wiwon N. Korea 40°54N 126°3E 224 B3
Wixom U.S.A. 42°32N 83°32W 311 B13
Wkra → Poland 52°27N 20°44E 185 F7
Władysławowo Poland 54°48N 18°25E 184 D5
Wleń Poland 51°2N 15°39E 185 G2
Wlingi Indonesia 8°5S 112°25E 235 D4
Włochy Poland 52°12N 20°54E 143 B1
Włocławek Poland 52°40N 19°3E 185 F6
Włodawa Poland 51°33N 23°31E 185 G10
Włoszczowa Poland 50°50N 19°55E 185 H6
Wo Mei Hong Kong, China 22°21N 114°15E 122 A3
Wo Yi Hop Hong Kong, China 22°23N 114°8E 122 A2
Woburn Ont., Canada 43°46N 79°12W 141 A3
Woburn Mass., U.S.A. 42°29N 71°9W 116 A2
Wodian China 32°50N 112°35E 226 H7
Wodonga Australia 36°5S 146°50E 283 D7
Wodzisław Śląski Poland 50°1N 18°26E 185 H5
Wœrth France 48°57N 7°45E 173 D14
Wohlau = Wołów Poland 51°20N 16°38E 185 G3
Woinbogoin China 32°51N 98°39E 228 A2
Woippy France 49°10N 6°8E 173 C13
Woitape Papua N. G. 8°33S 147°15E 286 E4
Wojcieszow Poland 50°58N 15°55E 185 H2
Wokam Indonesia 5°45S 134°28E 231 F8
Wokha India 26°6N 94°16E 241 B5
Woking U.K. 51°19N 0°34W 169 F7
Wokingham U.K. 51°24N 0°49W 169 F7
Wokingham □ U.K. 51°25N 0°51W 169 F7
Woko △ Australia 31°46S 151°49E 283 A9
Wola Poland 52°14N 20°57E 143 B1
Wolbrom Poland 50°24N 19°45E 185 H6
Wolcottville U.S.A. 41°32N 85°22W 311 C11
Wołczyn Poland 51°1N 18°3E 185 G5
Woldegk Germany 53°27N 13°34E 178 B9
Woldenberg = Dobiegniew Poland 52°59N 15°45E 185 F2
Woldenberg Park New Orleans, U.S.A. 131 b3
Woleu-Ntem □ Gabon 2°0N 12°30E 264 B2
Wolf → Canada 60°17N 132°33W 296 A2
Wolf, Volcán Ecuador 0°2N 91°20W 330 a
Wolf Creek U.S.A. 47°0N 112°4W 304 C7
Wolf L. Canada 60°24N 131°40W 296 A2
Wolf Point U.S.A. 48°5N 105°39W 304 B11
Wolfe Creek Crater △ Australia 19°10S 127°47E 278 C4
Wolfe I. Canada 44°7N 76°20W 313 B8
Wolfeboro U.S.A. 43°35N 71°13W 313 C13
Wolfen Germany 51°39N 12°15E 178 D8
Wolfenbüttel Germany 52°10N 10°33E 178 C6
Wolfratshausen Germany 47°54N 11°24E 179 H7
Wolfsberg Austria 46°50N 14°52E 180 E7
Wolfsburg Germany 52°25N 10°48E 178 C6
Wolgast Germany 54°3N 13°44E 178 A9
Wolgok S. Korea 37°35N 127°1E 137 B2
Wolhusen Switz. 47°4N 8°4E 179 H4
Wolica Poland 52°7N 20°51E 143 C1
Wolin Poland 53°50N 14°37E 184 E1
Woliński △ Poland 53°57N 14°28E 184 E1
Wollaston U.S.A. 42°15N 71°2W 116 B2
Wollaston, Is. Chile 55°40S 67°30W 336 E3
Wollaston Forland Greenland 74°25N 19°40W 154 C9
Wollaston L. Canada 58°7N 103°10W 297 B8
Wollaston Lake Canada 58°3N 103°33W 297 B8
Wollaston Pen. Canada 69°30N 115°0W 294 D9
Wollemi △ Australia 33°0S 150°30E 283 B9
Wollongong Australia 34°25S 150°54E 283 C9
Wolmar = Valmiera Latvia 57°37N 25°29E 188 D3
Wolmaransstad S. Africa 27°12S 25°59E 270 C4
Wolmirstedt Germany 52°14N 11°37E 178 C7
Wołomin Poland 52°19N 21°15E 185 F8
Wołów Poland 51°20N 16°38E 185 G3
Wolseley S. Austral., Australia 36°23S 140°54E 282 D4
Wolseley Western Cape, S. Africa 33°26S 19°7E 270 D2
Wolsey U.S.A. 44°25N 98°28W 308 C4
Wolstenholme, C. Canada 62°35N 77°30W 292 C12
Wolsztyn Poland 52°8N 16°5E 185 F3
Woltersdorf Germany 52°27N 13°44E 115 B5
Woluwe-St-Lambert Belgium 50°50N 4°24E 116 A2
Woluwe-St-Pierre Belgium 50°50N 4°25E 116 A2
Wolvega Neths. 52°52N 6°0E 170 B6
Wolverhampton U.K. 52°35N 2°7W 169 E5
Wondai Australia 26°20S 151°49E 281 D5
Wonenara Papua N. G. 6°48S 145°53E 286 D3
Wong Chuk Hang Hong Kong, China 22°15N 114°10E 122 B3
Wong Chuk Wan Hong Kong, China 22°23N 114°17E 122 A3
Wong Chuk Yeung Hong Kong, China 22°24N 114°15E 122 A3
Wonga Wongué △ Gabon 0°29S 9°25E 264 C1
Wongalarroo L. Australia 31°32S 144°0E 282 A6
Wongan Hills Australia 30°51S 116°37E 279 F2
Wonju S. Korea 37°22N 127°58E 224 D3
Wonosari Indonesia 7°58S 110°36E 231 G14
Wonosobo Indonesia 7°22S 109°54E 235 D3
Wonowon Canada 56°44N 121°48W 296 B4
Wŏnsan N. Korea 39°11N 127°27E 224 C3
Wonthaggi Australia 38°37S 145°37E 283 E6
Wood Buffalo △ Canada 59°0N 113°41W 296 B6
Wood Green U.K. 51°36N 0°6W 125 A3
Wood Is. Australia 16°24S 123°19E 278 C3
Wood L. Canada 55°17N 103°17W 297 B8
Wood Ridge U.S.A. 40°50N 74°4W 132 A1
Wood River U.S.A. 38°52N 90°5W 310 F6
Wood-Tikchik State Park △ U.S.A. 59°30N 158°30W 303 G8
Woodah, I. Australia 13°27S 136°10E 280 A2
Woodbine U.S.A. 30°58N 81°44W 316 E8
Woodbine Race Track Canada 43°43N 79°36W 141 A1
Woodbourne U.S.A. 41°46N 74°36W 313 E10
Woodbridge Ont., Canada 43°47N 79°36W 141 A1
Woodbridge Suffolk, U.K. 52°6N 1°20E 169 E9
Woodbridge B. Dominica 15°19N 61°25W 323 k
Woodburn N.S.W., Australia 29°6S 153°23E 281 A5
Woodburn Oreg., U.S.A. 45°9N 122°51W 304 D2
Woodbury U.S.A. 32°59N 83°45W 316 C5
Woodenbong Australia 28°24S 152°39E 281 D5
Woodend Australia 37°20S 144°33E 282 D6
Woodford Queens., Australia 26°58S 152°47E 281 D5
Woodford London, U.K. 51°36N 0°1E 125 A4
Woodford Bridge U.K. 51°36N 0°3E 125 A4
Woodford Green U.K. 51°36N 0°1E 125 A4
Woodfords U.S.A. 38°47N 119°50W 306 G7
Woodhaven U.S.A. 40°41N 73°51W 132 B2
Woodhouselee U.K. 55°52N 3°13W 121 B2
Woodlake U.S.A. 36°25N 119°6W 306 J7
Woodland Calif., U.S.A. 38°41N 121°46W 306 G5
Woodland Maine, U.S.A. 45°9N 67°25W 309 C20
Woodland Pa., U.S.A. 41°0N 78°21W 312 F6
Woodland Wash., U.S.A. 45°54N 122°45W 306 E4
Woodland Caribou △ Canada 51°0N 94°45W 297 C10
Woodlands Singapore 1°26N 103°46E 138 A2
Woodlands, The U.S.A. 30°9N 95°29W 314 F7
Woodlark I. Papua N. G. 9°10S 152°50E 286 E7
Woodmont U.S.A. 38°59N 77°5W 143 B2
Woodonga Australia 36°10S 146°50E 281 F4
Woodridge Canada 49°20N 96°9W 297 D9
Woodroffe, Mt. Australia 26°20S 131°45E 279 E5
Woods, L. Australia 17°50S 133°30E 280 B1
Woods, L. of the N. Amer. 49°15N 94°45W 297 D10
Woods Bay Canada 45°8N 79°59W 312 A5
Woodside S. Austral., Australia 34°58S 138°52E 282 C3
Woodside Vic., Australia 38°31S 146°52E 283 E7
Woodside London, U.K. 51°23N 0°4W 125 B3
Woodside N.Y., U.S.A. 40°44N 73°54W 132 B2
Woodson U.S.A. 39°37N 90°14W 310 E6
Woodstock N.S.W., Australia 33°45S 148°53E 283 B8
Woodstock Queens., Australia 19°35S 146°50E 280 B4
Woodstock N.B., Canada 46°11N 67°37W 299 C6
Woodstock Ont., Canada 43°10N 80°45W 312 C4
Woodstock Western Cape, S. Africa 33°55S 18°27E 118 A1
Woodstock Oxon., U.K. 51°51N 1°20W 169 F6
Woodstock Ill., U.S.A. 42°19N 88°27W 311 B8
Woodstock N.Y., U.S.A. 42°2N 74°7W 313 D10
Woodstock Vt., U.S.A. 43°37N 72°31W 313 C12
Woodsville U.S.A. 44°9N 72°2W 313 B12
Woodview Canada 44°35N 78°8W 312 B6
Woodville N.Z. 40°20S 175°53E 284 G4
Woodville Fla., U.S.A. 30°19N 84°15W 316 E5
Woodville Ga., U.S.A. 33°40N 83°7W 316 B6
Woodville Miss., U.S.A. 31°6N 91°18W 314 F9
Woodville Ohio, U.S.A. 41°27N 83°22W 311 C13
Woodville Tex., U.S.A. 30°47N 94°25W 314 F7
Woodward U.S.A. 36°26N 99°24W 314 C5
Woody U.S.A. 35°42N 118°50W 307 K8
Woody → Canada 52°31N 100°51W 297 C8
Woody I. S. China Sea 16°50N 112°20E 230 A4
Woolacombe U.K. 51°10N 4°13W 169 F3
Woolamai, C. Australia 38°30S 145°23E 283 E6
Woolbrook Australia 30°56S 151°25E 283 A9
Wooler U.K. 55°33N 2°1W 168 B5
Woolgoolga Australia 30°6S 153°11E 281 E5
Woollahra Australia 33°53S 151°15E 139 B2

Woolloomooloo Sydney, Australia 139 b2
Woolooware B. Australia 34°1S 151°8E 139 C1
Woolwich U.K. 51°29N 0°4E 125 B4
Woolworth Building New York, U.S.A. 132 e1
Woomargama △ Australia 35°50S 147°15E 283 C7
Woomera Australia 31°5S 136°50E 282 A2
Woonsocket R.I., U.S.A. 42°0N 71°31W 313 E13
Woonsocket S. Dak., U.S.A. 44°3N 98°17W 308 C4
Wooramel → Australia 25°47S 114°10E 279 E1
Wooramel Roadhouse Australia 25°45S 114°17E 279 E1
Wooroonooran △ Australia 16°25S 146°1E 280 B4
Wooster U.S.A. 40°48N 81°56W 312 F3
Woqooyi Bari = North Eastern □ Kenya 1°30N 40°0E 268 B5
Woqooyi Galbeed □ Somalia 10°0N 44°30E 267 C5
Woraksan △ S. Korea 36°50N 128°5E 224 D4
Worcester Western Cape, S. Africa 33°39S 19°27E 270 D2
Worcester Worcs., U.K. 52°11N 2°12W 169 E5
Worcester Mass., U.S.A. 42°16N 71°48W 313 D13
Worcester N.Y., U.S.A. 42°36N 74°45W 313 D10
Worcestershire □ U.K. 52°13N 2°10W 169 E5
Worden U.S.A. 38°56N 89°50W 310 F7
Wörgl Austria 47°29N 12°3E 180 D5
Worker's Stadium China 39°55N 116°25E 114 B2
Workington U.K. 54°39N 3°33W 168 C4
Worksop U.K. 53°18N 1°7W 168 D6
Workum Neths. 52°59N 5°26E 170 B5
Worland U.S.A. 44°1N 107°57W 304 D10
World Bank Washington, D.C., U.S.A. 143 b1
World Financial Center New York, U.S.A. 132 e1
World Financial Centre Shanghai, China 31°14N 121°30E 138 B2
World Trade Center, Site of former = National September 11 Memorial and Museum New York, U.S.A. 132 e1
World War Two Memorial Washington, D.C., U.S.A. 143 b1
Worli India 19°1N 72°49E 130 A1
Wormhout France 50°52N 2°28E 173 B9
Worms Germany 49°37N 8°21E 179 F4
Worodougou □ Ivory C. 8°0N 6°0W 262 D3
Worsley Canada 56°31N 119°8W 296 B5
Wörth Bayern, Germany 49°1N 12°24E 179 F8
Worth Ill., U.S.A. 41°41N 87°47W 119 C2
Wortham U.S.A. 31°47N 96°28W 314 F6
Wörther See Austria 46°37N 14°10E 180 E7
Worthing U.K. 50°49N 0°21W 169 G7
Worthington Ind., U.S.A. 39°7N 86°59W 311 E10
Worthington Minn., U.S.A. 43°37N 95°36W 308 D6
Worthington Ohio, U.S.A. 40°5N 83°1W 311 D13
Worthington Pa., U.S.A. 40°50N 79°38W 312 F5
Wosi Indonesia 0°15S 128°0E 231 E7
Wote Kenya 1°47S 37°38E 268 C4
Wotjalum ☼ Australia 16°30S 123°45E 278 C3
Wotjobaluk ☼ Australia 37°0S 142°0E 281 C3
Wou-han = Wuhan China 30°31N 114°18E 229 B10
Wour Chad 21°14N 16°0E 259 D3
Wousi = Wuxi China 31°33N 120°18E 229 B13
Wowoni Indonesia 4°5S 123°5E 231 E6
Woy Woy Australia 33°30S 151°19E 283 B9
Wrangel I. = Vrangelya, Ostrov Russia 71°0N 180°0E 215 B18
Wrangell U.S.A. 56°28N 132°23W 296 B2
Wrangell Mts. U.S.A. 61°30N 142°0W 303 F12
Wrangell-St. Elias △ U.S.A. 61°0N 142°0W 303 F12
Wrath, C. U.K. 58°38N 5°1W 167 C3
Wray U.S.A. 40°5N 102°13W 304 F12
Wrekin, The U.K. 52°41N 2°32W 169 E5
Wrens U.S.A. 33°12N 82°23W 316 B7
Wren's Nest U.S.A. 33°44N 84°25W 113 B2
Wrexham U.K. 53°3N 3°0W 168 D4
Wrexham □ U.K. 53°1N 2°58W 168 D5
Wriezen Germany 52°42N 14°7E 178 C10
Wright = Paranas Phil. 11°42N 125°2E 233 F5
Wright Fla., U.S.A. 30°27N 86°38W 317 E3
Wright Wyo., U.S.A. 43°45N 105°28W 304 E11
Wright Pt. Canada 43°48N 81°44W 312 C3
Wrightmyo India 11°47N 92°43E 245 J11
Wrightson, Mt. U.S.A. 31°42N 110°51W 305 L8
Wrightsville U.S.A. 32°44N 82°43W 316 C7
Wrightwood U.S.A. 34°22N 117°38W 307 L9
Wrigley Canada 63°16N 123°37W 294 E7
Wrigley Building Chicago, U.S.A. 119 b2
Wrigley Field U.S.A. 41°56N 87°39W 119 B3
Wrocław Poland 51°5N 17°5E 185 G4
Wronki Poland 52°41N 16°21E 185 F3
Września Poland 52°21N 17°36E 185 F4
Wschowa Poland 51°48N 16°20E 185 G3
Wu Hsi → Taiwan 24°9N 120°31E 225 B2
Wu Jiang → China 29°40N 107°20E 228 C6
Wu Kau Tang China 22°30N 114°14E 219 a
Wu Xia China 31°2N 110°10E 229 B8
Wu'an China 36°40N 114°15E 226 F8
Wubalawun ☼ Australia 15°28S 133°1E 278 C5
Wubin Australia 30°6S 116°37E 279 F2
Wubu China 37°28N 110°42E 226 F6
Wuchang China 44°55N 127°5E 227 B14
Wucheng China 37°12N 116°20E 226 F9
Wuch'i Taiwan 24°16N 120°31E 225 B2
Wuchieh Taiwan 24°41N 121°47E 225 B3
Wuchow = Wuzhou China 23°30N 111°18E 229 F8
Wuchuan Guangdong, China 21°33N 110°43E 229 G8
Wuchuan Guizhou, China 28°25N 108°3E 228 C7
Wuchuan Nei Monggol Zizhiqu, China 41°5N 111°28E 226 D6
Wuda China 39°29N 106°42E 226 E4
Wudang Shan China 32°23N 111°2E 229 A8
Wuday'ah Si. Arabia 17°2N 47°7E 248 C4
Wudi China 37°40N 117°35E 227 F9
Wuding China 25°24N 102°21E 228 E4
Wuding He → China 37°2N 110°23E 226 F6
Wudinna Australia 33°0S 135°22E 281 E2
Wudongde Dam China 26°20N 102°15E 228 D4
Wudu China 33°22N 104°54E 226 H3
Wufeng Henan, China 30°12N 110°42E 229 B8
Wufeng Taiwan 24°4N 120°42E 225 B2
Wugang China 26°44N 110°35E 229 D8
Wugong Shan China 27°30N 114°0E 229 D9
Wuguishan China 22°25N 113°25E 219 a
Wugullar = Beswick Australia 14°34S 132°53E 278 B5
Wuhai China 39°39N 106°48E 226 E4
Wuhan China 30°31N 114°18E 229 B10
Wuhe China 33°10N 117°50E 227 H9
Wuhlgarten Germany 52°31N 13°34E 115 A4
Wuhsi = Wuxi China 31°33N 120°18E 229 B13
Wuhu China 31°22N 118°21E 229 B12
Wujiang China 31°10N 120°38E 229 B13
Wujiaochang China 31°18N 121°31E 138 B2
Wujie = Wuchieh Taiwan 24°41N 121°47E 225 B3
Wujih Taiwan 24°6N 120°38E 225 B2
Wukari Nigeria 7°51N 9°42E 263 D6
Wulai Taiwan 24°52N 121°33E 225 B3
Wulajie China 44°6N 126°33E 227 B14
Wulanbulang China 41°5N 110°55E 226 D6
Wular L. India 34°20N 74°30E 243 B6
Wulehe Ghana 8°39N 0°0 263 D5
Wulff Land Greenland 82°0N 49°0W 154 A6
Wulian China 35°40N 119°12E 227 G10
Wulian Feng China 27°48N 103°36E 228 D4
Wuliang Shan China 24°30N 100°40E 228 E3
Wuliaru Indonesia 7°27S 131°0E 231 F8
Wulicheng Taiwan 23°47N 121°0E 225 C3
Wuling Shan China 30°0N 110°0E 228 C7
Wulingyuan ⌓ China 29°20N 110°30E 229 C8
Wulong China 29°22N 107°43E 228 C6
Wulong △ China 31°8N 103°5E 228 B4
Wulu Taiwan 23°10N 121°2E 225 C3
Wulumuchi = Ürümqi China 43°45N 87°45E 217 D11
Wum Cameroon 6°24N 10°2E 263 D7
Wumeng Shan China 26°48N 104°0E 228 D5
Wuming China 23°12N 108°18E 228 F7
Wun Rog South Sudan 9°0N 28°20E 257 F2
Wundanyi Kenya 3°24S 38°22E 268 C4
Wundwin Burma 21°5N 96°4E 241 E6
Wuning China 29°17N 115°5E 229 C10
Wunna → India 20°18N 78°48E 244 D4
Wunnummin L. Canada 52°55N 89°10W 298 B2
Wunsiedel Germany 50°2N 12°0E 179 E8
Wunstorf Germany 52°25N 9°26E 178 C5
Wuntho Burma 23°55N 95°45E 241 D5
Wupatki ⌓ U.S.A. 35°35N 111°20W 305 J8
Wuping China 25°5N 116°5E 229 E11
Wuppertal Nordrhein-Westfalen, Germany 51°16N 7°12E 178 D3
Wuppertal Western Cape, S. Africa 32°13S 19°12E 270 D2
Wuqi = Wuch'i Taiwan 24°16N 120°31E 225 B2
Wuqia China 39°40N 75°7E 217 E9
Wuqing China 39°23N 117°4E 227 E9
Wuri = Wujih Taiwan 24°6N 120°38E 225 B2
Würm → Germany 48°8N 11°27E 131 B1
Würm-kanal Germany 48°13N 11°29E 131 A1
Wurralibi ☼ Australia 15°43S 137°1E 280 B2
Wurtsboro U.S.A. 41°35N 74°29W 313 E10
Würzburg Germany 49°46N 9°55E 179 F5
Wurzen Germany 51°22N 12°44E 178 D8
Wushan China 34°43N 104°53E 226 G3
Wushi China 41°9N 79°13E 217 D9
Wushishi Nigeria 9°46N 6°7E 263 D6
Wusi Vanuatu 15°21S 166°40E 287 E4
Wusih = Wuxi China 31°33N 120°18E 229 B13
Wusong China 31°22N 121°29E 138 A1
Wutach → Germany 47°37N 8°15E 179 H4
Wutai China 38°40N 113°12E 226 E7
Wutai Shan China 39°3N 113°32E 226 E7
Wuting = Huimin China 37°27N 117°28E 227 F9
Wutong China 25°24N 110°4E 229 E8
Wutonghaolai China 42°50N 120°5E 227 C11
Wutongqiao China 29°22N 103°50E 228 C4
Wutung Papua N. G. 2°37S 141°1E 286 B1
Wuwei Anhui, China 31°18N 117°54E 229 B11
Wuwei Gansu, China 37°57N 102°34E 218 D9
Wuxi Jiangsu, China 31°33N 120°18E 229 B13
Wuxi Sichuan, China 31°23N 109°35E 228 B7
Wuxiang China 36°49N 112°50E 226 F7
Wuxuan China 23°34N 109°38E 228 F7
Wuxue China 29°52N 115°30E 229 C10
Wuyang China 33°25N 113°35E 226 H7
Wuyi Hebei, China 37°46N 115°56E 226 F8
Wuyi Zhejiang, China 28°52N 119°50E 229 C12
Wuyi Shan China 27°0N 117°0E 229 D11
Wuyishan China 27°45N 118°0E 229 D12
Wuyishan △ China 27°55N 117°54E 229 D11
Wuyo Nigeria 10°23N 11°50E 263 C7
Wuyuan Jiangxi, China 29°15N 117°50E 229 C11
Wuyuan Nei Monggol Zizhiqu, China 41°2N 108°20E 226 D5
Wuzhai China 38°54N 111°48E 226 E6
Wuzhi Shan China 18°45N 109°45E 229 a
Wuzhishan = Tongshi China 18°30N 109°20E 229 a
Wuzhong China 38°2N 106°12E 226 E4
Wuzhou China 23°30N 111°18E 229 F8
Wyaaba Cr. → Australia 16°27S 141°35E 280 B3
Wyalkatchem Australia 31°8S 117°22E 279 F2
Wyalusing U.S.A. 41°40N 76°16W 313 E8
Wyandotte U.S.A. 42°12N 83°9W 311 B13
Wyandra Australia 27°12S 145°56E 281 D4
Wyangala, L. Australia 33°54S 149°0E 283 B8
Wyara, L. Australia 28°42S 144°14E 281 D3
Wycheproof Australia 36°5S 143°17E 282 D5
Wycliffe Well Australia 20°48S 134°14E 280 C1
Wyczółki Poland 52°9N 20°59E 143 C1
Wye → U.K. 51°38N 2°40W 169 F5
Wyemandoo Australia 28°28S 118°29E 279 E2
Wygoda Poland 52°15N 21°7E 143 B2
Wyk Germany 54°41N 8°33E 178 A4
Wymondham U.K. 52°35N 1°7E 169 E9
Wymore U.S.A. 40°7N 96°40W 308 E5
Wynberg S. Africa 34°2S 18°28E 118 B1
Wyndham W. Austral., Australia 15°33S 128°3E 278 C4
Wyndham N.Z. 46°20S 168°51E 285 G3
Wynne U.S.A. 35°14N 90°47W 315 D9
Wynyard Tas., Australia 41°5S 145°44E 281 G4
Wynyard Sask., Canada 51°45N 104°10W 297 C8
Wyola L. Australia 29°8S 130°17E 279 E5
Wyoming Ont., Canada 42°57N 82°7W 312 D2
Wyoming Ill., U.S.A. 41°4N 89°47W 310 C7
Wyoming Iowa, U.S.A. 42°4N 91°0W 310 B6
Wyoming Mich., U.S.A. 42°54N 85°42W 311 B11
Wyoming □ U.S.A. 43°0N 107°30W 304 E10
Wyomissing U.S.A. 40°20N 75°59W 313 F9
Wyong Australia 33°14S 151°24E 283 B9
Wyperfeld △ Australia 35°35S 141°42E 282 C4
Wyrzysk Poland 53°10N 17°17E 185 E4
Wyśmierzyce Poland 51°37N 20°50E 185 G7
Wysoka Poland 53°13N 17°2E 185 E4
Wysokie Poland 50°55N 22°40E 185 H9
Wysokie Mazowieckie Poland 52°55N 22°30E 185 F9
Wyszków Poland 52°36N 21°25E 185 F8
Wyszogród Poland 52°23N 20°9E 185 F7
Wytheville U.S.A. 36°57N 81°5W 309 G13
Wyżyna Małopolska Poland 50°45N 20°0E 185 H7

# X

Xa-Cassau Angola 9°5S 20°15E 265 D4
Xa-Muteba Angola 9°34S 17°50E 265 D3
Xaafuun Somalia 10°25N 51°16E 267 B7
Xaafuun, Ras Somalia 10°27N 51°24E 267 B7
Xàbia = Jávea Spain 38°48N 0°10E 197 G5
Xabregas Portugal 38°43N 9°6W 126 A2
Xaçmaz Azerbaijan 41°31N 48°42E 191 K9
Xaghra Malta 36°3N 14°16E 206 E7
Xai-Xai Mozam. 25°6S 33°31E 271 C5
Xaidulla China 36°28N 77°59E 217 E9
Xaignabouri = Sayaboury Laos 19°15N 101°45E 236 C3
Xainza China 30°58N 88°35E 218 E6
Xalapa Mexico 19°32N 96°55W 319 D5
Xalin Somalia 9°6N 48°37E 267 C6
Xallas → Spain 42°54N 9°8W 194 C1
Xambioá Brazil 6°25S 48°40W 332 C2
Xangongo Angola 16°45S 15°5E 265 F3
Xankändi Azerbaijan 39°52N 46°49E 213 C12
Xanlar = Goygöl Azerbaijan 40°37N 46°12E 191 K8
Xanten Germany 51°39N 6°26E 178 D2
Xanthi Greece 41°10N 24°58E 203 E8
Xanthos Turkey 36°19N 29°18E 205 E11
Xanxerê Brazil 26°53S 52°23W 335 B5
Xapuri Brazil 10°35S 68°35W 330 C4
Xar Moron He → China 43°25N 120°35E 227 C11
Xarardheere Somalia 4°33N 47°38E 267 D6
Xarrë Albania 39°44N 20°3E 206 B10
Xátiva Spain 38°59N 0°32W 197 G4
Xau, L. Botswana 21°15S 24°44E 270 B3
Xavantina Brazil 21°15S 52°48W 335 A5
Xayar China 41°13N 82°48E 217 D10
Xebert China 44°2N 122°0E 227 B12
Xenia U.S.A. 39°41N 83°56W 311 E13
Xeraco Spain 39°2N 0°13W 197 F4
Xeropotamos → Cyprus 34°42N 32°33E 207 F8
Xertigny France 48°3N 6°24E 173 D13
Xewkija Malta 36°2N 14°15E 206 E7
Xhora S. Africa 31°55S 28°38E 271 D4
Xhumo Botswana 21°7S 24°35E 270 B3
Xi Jiang → China 22°5N 113°20E 229 F9
Xi Ujimqin Qi China 44°32N 117°40E 227 B9
Xi Xian Henan, China 32°20N 114°43E 229 A10
Xi Xian Shanxi, China 36°41N 110°58E 226 F6
Xia Xian China 35°8N 111°12E 226 G6
Xiachengzi China 44°40N 130°18E 227 B16
Xiachuan Dao China 21°40N 112°40E 229 G9
Xiaguan China 25°32N 100°16E 218 F9
Xiajiang China 27°30N 115°10E 229 D10
Xiajin China 36°56N 116°0E 226 F9
Xiamen China 24°25N 118°4E 229 E12
Xi'an China 34°15N 109°0E 226 G5
Xian Xian China 38°12N 116°6E 226 E9
Xianfeng China 29°40N 109°8E 228 C7
Xiang Jiang → China 28°55N 112°50E 229 C9
Xiang Khouang Laos 19°17N 103°25E 236 C4
Xiangcheng Henan, China 33°50N 113°27E 226 H7
Xiangcheng Sichuan, China 28°53N 99°47E 228 C2
Xiangdu China 23°13N 106°58E 228 F6
Xiangfan China 32°2N 112°8E 229 A9
Xianggang = Hong Kong □ China 22°11N 114°14E 219 a
Xianghuang Qi China 42°2N 113°50E 226 C7
Xiangjiaba Dam China 28°37N 104°17E 228 C5
Xiangning China 35°58N 110°50E 226 G6
Xiangquan China 36°30N 113°1E 226 F7
Xiangquan He = Sutlej → Pakistan 29°23N 71°3E 242 E4
Xiangshan = Hsiangshan Taiwan 24°48N 120°54E 225 B2
Xiangshan China 29°29N 121°51E 229 C13
Xiangshui China 34°12N 119°33E 227 G10
Xiangtan China 27°51N 112°54E 229 D9
Xiangxiang China 27°43N 112°28E 229 D9
Xiangyin China 28°38N 112°54E 229 C9
Xiangyun China 25°34N 100°35E 228 E3
Xiangzhou China 23°58N 109°40E 228 F7
Xianju China 28°51N 120°44E 229 C13
Xianning China 29°51N 114°16E 229 C10
Xianshui He → China 30°10N 100°59E 228 B3
Xiantao China 30°25N 113°25E 229 B9
Xianyang China 34°20N 108°40E 226 G5
Xianyou China 25°22N 118°38E 229 E12
Xiao Hinggan Ling China 49°0N 127°0E 219 B14
Xiao Xian China 34°15N 116°55E 226 G9
Xiaofeng China 30°35N 119°32E 229 B12
Xiaogan China 30°52N 113°55E 229 B9
Xiaogang = Hsiaokang Taiwan 22°34N 120°20E 225 D2
Xiaogang Park China 23°6N 113°16E 121 B2
Xiaojin China 30°59N 102°21E 228 B4
Xiaolan China 22°38N 113°13E 229 F9
Xiaoping China 23°12N 113°13E 121 A2
Xiaoshan China 30°12N 120°18E 229 B13
Xiaowan Dam China 24°42N 100°5E 228 E3
Xiaowutai Shan China 39°51N 114°59E 226 E8
Xiaoyi China 37°8N 111°48E 226 F6
Xiapu China 26°54N 119°59E 229 D12
Xiashachong China 23°8N 113°9E 121 B1
Xiashan = Zhanjiang China 21°15N 110°20E 229 G8
Xiawa China 42°35N 120°38E 227 C11
Xiayi China 34°15N 116°10E 226 G9
Xichang Guangdong, China 23°9N 113°13E 121 B2
Xichang Sichuan, China 27°51N 102°19E 228 D4
Xicheng Beijing, China 114 b1
Xichong China 30°57N 105°54E 228 B5
Xichou China 23°25N 104°42E 228 E5
Xichuan China 33°0N 111°30E 229 A8
Xidan China 39°52N 116°20E 114 B2
Xide China 28°8N 102°19E 228 C4
Xiemahe China 31°38N 111°12E 229 B8
Xifei He → China 32°45N 116°40E 229 A11
Xifeng Gansu, China 35°40N 107°40E 226 G4
Xifeng Guizhou, China 27°7N 106°42E 228 D6
Xifeng Liaoning, China 42°42N 124°45E 227 C13
Xifengzhen = Xifeng China 35°40N 107°40E 226 G4
Xigang = Hsikang Taiwan 23°7N 120°12E 225 C2
Xigazê China 29°5N 88°45E 218 F6
Xihe China 34°2N 105°20E 226 G3
Xihua China 33°45N 114°30E 226 H8
Xilagani Greece 40°58N 25°28E 203 F9
Xili Shuiku China 22°36N 113°57E 219 a
Xiliao He → China 43°32N 123°35E 227 C12
Xilin China 24°30N 105°6E 228 E5
Xiling Gorge = Xiling Xia China 30°54N 110°48E 229 B8
Xiling Xia China 30°54N 110°48E 229 B8
Xilinhot China 43°52N 116°2E 226 C9
Xilokastro Greece 38°5N 22°38E 204 C4
Xiluodu Dam China 28°12N 103°34E 228 C4
Ximana Mozam. 19°24S 33°58E 269 F3
Xime Guinea-Biss. 11°59N 14°57W 262 C2
Ximeng China 22°50N 99°27E 228 F2
Ximiao China 40°59N 100°12E 218 C9
Xin Jiang → China 28°45N 116°35E 229 C11
Xin Xian = Xinzhou China 38°22N 112°46E 226 E7
Xin'anjiang Shuiku China 29°33N 118°56E 229 C12
Xinavane Mozam. 25°2S 32°47E 271 C5
Xinbin China 41°40N 125°2E 224 B2
Xincai China 32°43N 114°58E 229 A10
Xinchang China 29°28N 120°52E 229 C13
Xincheng = Hsinch'eng Taiwan 24°8N 121°39E 225 B3
Xincheng Guangxi Zhuangzu, China 24°5N 108°39E 228 E7
Xincheng Jiangxi, China 26°48N 114°6E 229 D10
Xinchengzi China 42°2N 123°30E 224 A1
Xindian = Hsintien Taiwan 24°57N 121°32E 225 B3
Xinfeng = Hsinfeng Taiwan 24°54N 120°59E 225 B2
Xinfeng Guangdong, China 24°5N 114°16E 229 E10
Xinfeng Jiangxi, China 27°7N 116°11E 229 D11
Xinfeng Jiangxi, China 25°27N 114°58E 229 E10
Xinfengjiang Shuiku China 23°52N 114°30E 229 F10
Xing Xian China 38°27N 111°7E 226 E6
Xing'an Guangxi Zhuangzu, China 25°38N 110°40E 229 E8
Xingan Jiangxi, China 27°46N 115°20E 229 D10
Xingcheng China 40°40N 120°45E 227 D11
Xingguo China 26°21N 115°21E 229 D10
Xinghe China 40°55N 113°55E 226 D7
Xinghua China 32°58N 119°48E 229 A12
Xinghua Wan China 25°15N 119°20E 229 E12
Xinglong China 40°25N 117°30E 227 D9
Xingning China 24°3N 115°42E 229 E10
Xingping China 34°20N 108°28E 226 G5
Xingren China 25°24N 105°11E 228 E5
Xingshan China 31°15N 110°45E 229 B8
Xingtai China 37°3N 114°32E 226 F8
Xingu → Brazil 1°30S 51°53W 329 D7
Xingwen China 28°22N 104°50E 228 C5
Xingxingxia China 41°47N 95°0E 218 C7
Xingyang China 34°45N 112°52E 226 G7
Xingyi China 25°3N 104°59E 228 E5
Xinhe Hebei, China 37°30N 115°15E 226 F8
Xinhe Xinjiang Uygur, China 41°33N 82°37E 217 D10
Xinhua = Hsinhua Taiwan 23°2N 120°18E 225 C2
Xinhua China 27°42N 111°13E 229 D8
Xinhuang China 27°21N 109°12E 228 D7
Xinhui China 22°25N 113°0E 229 F9
Xining China 36°34N 101°40E 218 D9
Xinji China 37°55N 115°13E 226 F8
Xinjian China 28°37N 115°46E 229 C10
Xinjiang China 35°34N 111°11E 226 G6
Xinjiang Uygur Zizhiqu □ China 42°0N 86°0E 217 D11
Xinjin = Pulandian China 39°25N 121°58E 227 E11
Xinjin China 30°24N 103°47E 228 B4
Xinkai He → China 43°32N 123°35E 227 C12
Xinken China 22°39N 113°36E 219 a
Xinle China 38°25N 114°40E 226 E8
Xinlitun China 42°0N 122°8E 227 D12
Xinlong China 30°57N 100°12E 228 B3
Xinmi China 34°30N 113°25E 226 G7
Xinmin China 41°59N 122°50E 224 B1
Xinning China 26°28N 110°50E 229 D8
Xinping China 24°5N 101°59E 228 E3
Xinshao China 27°21N 111°26E 229 D8
Xinshi = Hsinshih Taiwan 23°4N 120°17E 225 C2
Xintai China 35°55N 117°45E 227 G9
Xintian China 25°55N 112°13E 229 E9
Xinwan China 22°47N 113°40E 219 a
Xinwu = Hsinwu Taiwan 24°59N 121°6E 225 B3
Xinxiang China 35°18N 113°50E 226 G7
Xinxing China 22°35N 112°15E 229 F9
Xinyang China 32°6N 114°3E 229 A10
Xinye China 32°30N 112°21E 229 A9
Xinyi Guangdong, China 22°25N 111°0E 229 F8
Xinyi Nei Monggol Zizhiqu, China 34°23N 118°21E 227 G10
Xinyin = Hsinying Taiwan 23°21N 120°17E 225 C2
Xinyu China 27°49N 114°58E 229 D10
Xinyuan = Hsinyuan Taiwan 22°32N 120°27E 225 D2
Xinzhan China 43°50N 127°18E 227 C14
Xinzheng China 34°20N 113°45E 226 G7
Xinzhou Hainan, China 19°43N 109°17E 229 a
Xinzhou Hubei, China 30°50N 114°48E 229 B10
Xinzhou Shanxi, China 38°22N 112°46E 226 E7
Xinzhuang = Hsinchuang Taiwan 25°2N 121°27E 225 A3
Xinzo de Limia Spain 42°3N 7°47W 194 C3
Xiongyuecheng China 40°12N 122°5E 227 D12
Xiping Henan, China 33°22N 114°5E 226 H8
Xiping Henan, China 33°25N 111°8E 226 H6
Xiping Zhejiang, China 28°16N 119°29E 229 C12
Xique-Xique Brazil 10°50S 42°40W 332 D3
Xiruá → Brazil 6°3S 67°50W 330 B4
Xisha Qundao = Paracel Is. S. China Sea 15°50N 112°0E 230 A4
Xishuangbanna China 22°5N 101°1E 228 F3
Xishui Guizhou, China 28°19N 106°9E 228 C6
Xishui Hubei, China 30°30N 115°15E 229 B10
Xitole Guinea-Biss. 11°43N 14°50W 262 C2
Xiu Shui → China 29°13N 116°0E 229 C10
Xiuning China 29°45N 118°10E 229 C12
Xiuren China 24°27N 110°12E 229 E8
Xiushan China 28°25N 108°57E 228 C7
Xiushui China 29°2N 114°33E 229 C10
Xiuwen China 26°49N 106°32E 228 D6
Xiuyan China 40°18N 123°11E 224 B1
Xiva Uzbekistan 41°30N 60°18E 216 D6
Xixabangma Feng China 28°20N 85°40E 243 E11
Xixia China 33°25N 111°29E 226 H6
Xixiang Guangdong, China 22°34N 113°52E 219 a
Xixiang Shaanxi, China 33°0N 107°44E 226 H4
Xixón = Gijón Spain 43°32N 5°42W 194 B5
Xiyang China 37°38N 113°38E 226 F7
Xizang Zizhiqu □ China 32°0N 88°0E 218 E6
Xizhi = Hsichih Taiwan 25°4N 121°39E 225 A3
Xizhimen China 39°55N 116°19E 114 B1
Xlendi Malta 36°1N 14°12E 206 E6
Xochimilco, Parque Ecológico Mexico 19°18N 99°5W 128 C2
Xochob Mexico 19°21N 89°48W 319 D7
Xo'jayli Uzbekistan 42°29N 59°31E 216 D5
Xorazm □ Uzbekistan 43°0N 60°0E 216 D6
Xu Beihong Memorial Hall Beijing, China 114 a2
Xu Jiang → China 28°0N 116°25E 229 D11
Xuan Loc Vietnam 10°56N 107°14E 237 G6
Xuan'en China 30°0N 109°30E 228 C7
Xuanhan China 31°18N 107°38E 228 B6
Xuanhua China 40°40N 115°2E 226 D8
Xuanwei China 26°15N 103°59E 228 C5
Xuanwu Beijing, China 114 c1
Xuanzhou China 30°56N 118°43E 229 B12
Xuchang China 34°2N 113°48E 226 G7
Xudat Azerbaijan 41°38N 48°41E 191 K9
Xuddur Somalia 4°11N 43°52E 267 D5
Xuefeng Shan China 27°5N 110°35E 229 D8
Xuejia = Hsüehchia Taiwan 23°14N 120°10E 225 C2
Xuejiaping China 31°39N 110°16E 229 B8
Xuhui China 31°11N 121°26E 138 B1
Xujiahui China 31°11N 121°25E 138 B1
Xun Jiang → China 23°35N 111°30E 229 F8
Xun Xian China 35°42N 114°33E 226 G8
Xundian China 25°36N 103°15E 228 E4
Xunwu China 24°54N 115°37E 229 E10
Xunyang China 32°48N 109°22E 226 H5
Xunyi China 35°8N 108°20E 226 G5
Xupu China 27°53N 110°32E 229 D8
Xúquer → Spain 39°5N 0°10W 197 F4
Xushui China 39°2N 115°40E 226 E8
Xuwen China 20°20N 110°10E 229 G8
Xuyi China 32°55N 118°32E 229 A12
Xuyong China 28°10N 105°22E 228 C5
Xuzhou China 34°18N 117°10E 227 G9
Xylophagou Cyprus 34°54N 33°51E 207 F9

# Y

Y Drenewydd = Newtown U.K. 52°31N 3°19W 169 E4
Y Fenni = Abergavenny U.K. 51°49N 3°1W 169 F4
Y Gelli Gandryll = Hay-on-Wye U.K. 52°5N 3°8W 169 E4
Y Trallwng = Welshpool U.K. 52°39N 3°8W 169 E4
Y.S. Falls Jamaica 18°9N 77°49W 320 a
Ya Xian = Sanya China 18°14N 109°29E 229 a
Yaamba Australia 23°8S 150°22E 280 C5
Ya'an China 29°58N 103°5E 228 C4
Yaapeet Australia 35°45S 142°3E 282 C5
Yaba Nigeria 6°30N 3°22E 124 A2
Yabassi Cameroon 4°30N 9°57E 263 E6
Yabayo Ivory C. 5°56N 6°36W 262 D3
Yabelo Ethiopia 4°50N 38°8E 257 G4
Yabelo ⌓ Ethiopia 6°0N 37°50E 257 F4
Yablanitsa Bulgaria 43°2N 24°5E 203 C8
Yablonovyy Khrebet Russia 53°0N 114°0E 215 D12
Yablonovyy Ra. = Yablonovyy Khrebet Russia 53°0N 114°0E 215 D12
Yabluniv Ukraine 48°24N 24°57E 183 B9
Yablunytsya Ukraine 48°19N 24°29E 183 B9
Yabrai Shan China 39°40N 103°0E 226 E2
Yabrūd Syria 33°58N 36°39E 250 E7
Yabucoa Puerto Rico 18°3N 65°53W 321 b
Yacambú △ Venezuela 9°42N 69°27W 328 B4
Yacata Fiji 17°15S 179°31W 287 A3
Yacheng China 18°22N 109°6E 229 a
Yackandandah Australia 36°18S 146°52E 283 D7
Yacuiba Bolivia 22°0S 63°43W 334 A3
Yacuma → Bolivia 13°38S 65°23W 331 C4
Yacurí △ Ecuador 4°42S 79°20W 330 A2
Yadgir India 16°45N 77°5E 244 F3
Yadkin → U.S.A. 35°23N 80°4W 315 D14
Yadong China 27°26N 88°56E 241 B2
Yadrin Russia 55°57N 46°12E 190 C8
Yadua Fiji 16°49S 178°18E 287 A2
Yaeyama-Rettō Japan 24°30N 123°40E 221 M1
Yafran Libya 32°4N 12°31E 258 B2
Yaftābād Iran 35°37N 51°17E 141 B1
Yagaba Ghana 10°14N 1°20W 263 C4
Yagaji-shima Japan 26°39N 128°0E 288 a
Yagasa Cluster Fiji 18°57S 178°28W 287 B3
Yağcılar Turkey 39°25N 28°23E 205 B10
Yagodnoye Russia 62°33N 149°40E 215 C15
Yagoua Cameroon 10°20N 15°13E 259 F3
Yaguas → Peru 2°45S 70°10W 328 D3
Yahara Japan 35°44N 139°37E 140 A2
Yahila Orientale, Dem. Rep. of the Congo 0°13N 24°28E 264 B4
Yahila Orientale, Dem. Rep. of the Congo 1°48N 23°37E 264 B4
Yahk Canada 49°6N 116°10W 296 D5
Yaho Japan 35°40N 139°26E 140 A1
Yahotyn Ukraine 50°17N 31°46E 189 G6
Yahuma Dem. Rep. of the Congo 1°0N 23°10E 264 B4
Yahyalı Turkey 38°5N 35°2E 212 C6
Yaita Japan 36°48N 139°56E 221 F9
Yaiza Canary Is. 28°57N 13°46W 153 e2
Yaizu Japan 34°52N 138°20E 223 C10
Yajiang China 30°2N 100°57E 228 B3
Yajua Nigeria 11°27N 12°49E 263 C7
Yakacık Turkey 36°46N 36°11E 250 B7
Yakage Japan 34°37N 133°35E 222 C5
Yakamba Dem. Rep. of the Congo 2°42N 19°38E 264 B3
Yakapınar Turkey 36°57N 35°36E 250 B6
Yakeshi China 49°17N 120°44E 219 B13
Yakima U.S.A. 46°36N 120°31W 304 C3
Yakima → U.S.A. 46°15N 119°14W 304 C4
Yakire Japan 35°45N 139°54E 140 A4
Yakishiri-Jima Japan 44°26N 141°25E 220 B10
Yako Burkina Faso 12°59N 2°15W 262 C4
Yakobi I. U.S.A. 58°0N 136°30W 296 B1
Yakoma Dem. Rep. of the Congo 4°5N 22°27E 264 B4
Yakoruda Bulgaria 42°1N 23°39E 202 D7
Yakossi C.A.R. 5°37N 23°19E 264 A4
Yakovlevka Russia 44°26N 133°28E 220 B6
Yakovlevskoye = Privolzhsk Russia 57°23N 41°16E 190 B5
Yaksu S. Korea 37°34N 127°1E 137 B2
Yaku-Shima Japan 30°20N 130°30E 221 J5
Yakumo Japan 42°15N 140°16E 220 C10
Yakutat U.S.A. 59°33N 139°44W 303 G13
Yakutat B. U.S.A. 59°45N 140°45W 303 G12
Yakutia = Sakha □ Russia 66°0N 130°0E 215 C14
Yakutsk Russia 62°5N 129°50E 215 C13
Yakymivka Ukraine 46°44N 35°0E 189 J8
Yala Thailand 6°33N 101°18E 237 J3
Yala △ Sri Lanka 6°20N 81°30E 245 L5
Yalata Australia 31°59S 132°26E 279 F5
Yalata ☼ Australia 31°35S 132°7E 279 F5
Yalboroo Australia 20°50S 148°40E 280 b
Yale U.S.A. 43°8N 82°48W 312 C2
Yalgorup △ Australia 32°39S 115°38E 279 F2
Yali Dem. Rep. of the Congo 0°4N 21°3E 264 B4
Yaligimba Dem. Rep. of the Congo 2°13N 22°56E 264 B4
Yalikanda Dem. Rep. of the Congo 0°23N 24°47E 264 B4
Yalinga C.A.R. 6°33N 23°10E 264 A4
Yalkabul, Pta. Mexico 21°32N 88°37W 319 C7
Yallahs Jamaica 17°53N 76°35W 320 a
Yallahs Hill Jamaica 17°54N 76°30W 320 a
Yalleroi Australia 24°3S 145°42E 280 C4
Yalobusha → U.S.A. 33°33N 90°10W 315 E9
Yaloké C.A.R. 5°19N 17°5E 264 A3
Yalong China 18°12N 109°42E 229 a
Yalong Jiang → China 26°40N 101°55E 228 D3
Yalova Turkey 40°41N 29°15E 203 F13
Yalpirakinu ☼ Australia 22°24S 132°15E 278 D5
Yalpuh, Ozero Ukraine 45°30N 28°41E 183 E13
Yalta Ukraine 44°30N 34°10E 189 K8
Yalu Jiang → China 39°55N 124°19E 224 C2
Yalvaç Turkey 38°17N 31°10E 212 C4
Yam Australia 9°54S 142°46E 280 a
Yam Ha Melaḫ = Dead Sea Asia 31°30N 35°30E 251 G6
Yam Kinneret Israel 32°45N 35°35E 250 F6
Yamada = Kama Japan 33°33N 130°49E 222 D2
Yamada Kanagawa, Japan 35°33N 139°37E 140 B2
Yamada Ōsaka, Japan 34°47N 135°32E 133 A2
Yamaga Japan 33°1N 130°41E 222 D2
Yamagata Japan 38°15N 140°15E 220 E10
Yamagata □ Japan 38°30N 140°0E 220 E10
Yamagawa Japan 31°12N 130°39E 222 F2
Yamaguchi Japan 34°10N 131°32E 222 C3
Yamaguchi □ Japan 34°20N 131°40E 222 C3
Yamal, Poluostrov Russia 71°0N 70°0E 214 B8
Yamal Pen. = Yamal, Poluostrov Russia 71°0N 70°0E 214 B8
Yamanaka Japan 36°15N 136°22E 223 A8
Yamanashi Japan 35°41N 138°40E 223 B10
Yamanashi □ Japan 35°40N 138°40E 223 B10
Yamantau, Gora Russia 54°15N 58°6E 186 D10
Yamasaki Japan 35°0N 134°32E 222 C6
Yamato Japan 35°27N 139°25E 223 B11
Yamato → Japan 34°36N 135°26E 133 B1
Yamato Ridge Sea of Japan 39°20N 135°0E 220 E7
Yamatotakada Japan 34°31N 135°45E 223 C7
Yamba Australia 29°26S 153°23E 281 D5
Yambarran Ra. Australia 15°10S 130°25E 278 C5
Yambata Dem. Rep. of the Congo 2°26N 21°58E 264 B4
Yambéring Guinea 11°50N 12°18W 262 C2
Yambio South Sudan 4°35N 28°16E 257 G2
Yambol Bulgaria 42°30N 26°30E 203 D10
Yambol □ Bulgaria 42°30N 26°30E 203 D10
Yamboyo Dem. Rep. of the Congo 0°40N 22°18E 264 B4
Yamburg Russia 68°21N 77°8E 214 C8
Yambuya Dem. Rep. of the Congo 1°17N 24°34E 264 B4
Yamdena Indonesia 7°45S 131°20E 231 F8
Yame Japan 33°13N 130°35E 222 D2
Yamethin Burma 20°29N 96°18E 241 E6
Y'Ami I. Phil. 21°6N 121°57E 232 A3
Yamma Yamma, L. Australia 26°16S 141°20E 281 D3
Yamoussoukro Ivory C. 6°49N 5°17W 262 D3
Yampa → U.S.A. 40°32N 108°59W 304 F9
Yampi Sd. Australia 16°8S 123°38E 278 C3
Yampil Moldova 48°15N 28°15E 177 D15
Yampol = Yampil Moldova 48°15N 28°15E 177 D15
Yamrat Nigeria 10°11N 9°55E 263 C6
Yamrukchal = Botev Bulgaria 42°44N 24°52E 203 D8
Yamu, Laem Thailand 7°59N 98°26E 237 a
Yamuna → India 25°30N 81°53E 243 G9
Yamunanagar India 30°7N 77°17E 242 D7
Yamzho Yumco China 28°48N 90°35E 218 F7
Yan Nigeria 10°5N 12°11E 263 C7
Yan Kit Singapore 1°21N 103°58E 138 A3
Yan Oya → Sri Lanka 9°0N 81°10E 245 K5
Yana → Russia 71°30N 136°0E 215 B14
Yanagawa Japan 33°10N 130°24E 222 D2
Yanahara Japan 34°58N 134°2E 222 C6
Yanai Japan 33°58N 132°7E 222 D4
Yan'an China 36°35N 109°26E 226 F5
Yanaul Russia 56°25N 55°0E 186 C10
Yanbian China 26°47N 101°31E 228 D3
Yanbu China 23°5N 113°9E 121 B1
Yanbu 'al Baḥr Si. Arabia 24°5N 38°5E 246 E3
Yanchang China 36°43N 110°1E 226 F6
Yanchao = Yenchao Taiwan 22°46N 120°21E 225 D2
Yancheng Henan, China 33°35N 114°0E 226 H8
Yancheng Jiangsu, China 33°23N 120°8E 227 H11
Yanchep Australia 31°33S 115°37E 279 F2
Yanchi China 37°48N 107°20E 226 F4
Yanchuan China 36°51N 110°10E 226 F6
Yanco Australia 34°38S 146°27E 283 C7
Yanco Cr. → Australia 35°14S 145°35E 283 C6
Yandang Shan China 28°0N 120°25E 229 D13
Yandeyarra ☼ Australia 21°17S 118°24E 278 D2
Yandicoogina Australia 22°49S 119°12E 278 D2
Yandina Solomon Is. 9°7S 159°13E 287 M10
Yandja Dem. Rep. of the Congo 1°41S 17°43E 264 C3
Yandongi Dem. Rep. of the Congo 2°51N 22°16E 264 B4
Yandoon Burma 17°0N 95°40E 241 G5
Yanfeng China 25°52N 101°8E 228 E3
Yanfolila Mali 11°11N 8°9W 262 C3
Yang Xian China 33°15N 107°30E 228 A6
Yang-yang S. Korea 38°4N 128°38E 224 C4
Yang-Yang Senegal 15°30N 15°20W 262 B1
Yangambi Dem. Rep. of the Congo 0°47N 24°24E 264 B4
Yangbi China 25°41N 99°58E 228 E2
Yangcheng China 35°28N 112°22E 226 G7
Yangcheon S. Korea 37°30N 126°51E 137 B1
Yangchow = Yangzhou China 32°21N 119°26E 229 A12
Yangch'ü = Taiyuan China 37°52N 112°33E 226 F7
Yangchüan = Yangquan China 37°58N 113°31E 226 F7
Yangchun China 22°11N 111°48E 229 F8
Yangdok N. Korea 39°13N 126°38E 224 C3
Yanggang-do □ N. Korea 41°15N 128°0E 224 B4
Yanggao China 40°21N 113°55E 226 D7
Yanggu China 36°8N 115°43E 226 F8
Yanghuayuan China 39°49N 116°18E 114 C1
Yangiyul Uzbekistan 41°0N 69°3E 217 D7
Yangjae S. Korea 37°29N 127°2E 137 C2
Yangjiang China 21°50N 111°59E 229 G8
Yangjiazhuang China 31°22N 121°25E 138 A1
Yangjing China 31°15N 121°32E 138 B2
Yangju S. Korea 37°47N 127°7E 224 D3
Yangliuqing China 39°2N 117°5E 227 E9
Yangmei Taiwan 24°55N 121°8E 225 B3
Yangmingshan △ Taiwan 25°9N 121°32E 225 A3
Yangon = Rangoon Burma 16°45N 96°20E 241 G6
Yangonde Dem. Rep. of the Congo 0°3N 22°43E 264 B4
Yangping China 31°12N 111°25E 229 B8
Yangpingguan China 32°58N 106°5E 228 A6
Yangpu China 31°16N 121°32E 138 B2
Yangpu Park China 31°17N 121°31E 138 B2
Yangquan China 37°58N 113°31E 226 F7
Yangsan S. Korea 35°20N 129°2E 224 E4
Yangshan Guangdong, China 24°30N 112°40E 229 E9
Yangshan Shanghai, China 30°37N 122°4E 229 B14
Yangshuo China 24°48N 110°29E 229 E8
Yangtse = Chang Jiang → China 31°48N 121°10E 229 B13
Yangtze Kiang = Chang Jiang → China 31°48N 121°10E 229 B13
Yangudi Rassa △ Ethiopia 10°50N 40°42E 257 E5
Yangxin China 29°50N 115°12E 229 C10
Yangyuan China 40°1N 114°10E 226 D8
Yangzhong China 32°22N 119°22E 229 A12
Yangzhou China 32°21N 119°26E 229 A12
Yanhe China 28°31N 108°29E 228 C7
Yanji China 42°59N 129°30E 227 C15
Yanjin China 28°5N 104°18E 228 C5
Yanjing China 29°7N 98°33E 228 C2
Yankari △ Nigeria 9°50N 10°28E 259 G2
Yankton U.S.A. 42°53N 97°23W 308 D5
Yankunytjatjara-Antakirinja ☼ Australia 27°20S 134°30E 281 A1
Yannawa Thailand 13°43N 100°32E 113 B2
Yanonge Dem. Rep. of the Congo 0°35N 24°38E 264 B4
Yanov = Ivanava Belarus 52°7N 25°29E 177 B13
Yanpu = Yenpu Taiwan 22°45N 120°35E 225 D2
Yanqi China 42°5N 86°35E 217 D11
Yanqing China 40°30N 115°58E 226 D8
Yanshan Hebei, China 38°4N 117°22E 227 E9
Yanshan Jiangxi, China 28°15N 117°41E 229 C11
Yanshan Yunnan, China 23°35N 104°20E 228 F5
Yanshou China 45°28N 128°22E 227 B15
Yanshui = Yenshui Taiwan 23°19N 120°16E 225 C2
Yantabulla Australia 29°21S 145°0E 281 D4
Yantai China 37°34N 121°22E 227 F11
Yantarnyy Russia 54°52N 19°57E 184 D6
Yantian China 22°35N 114°16E 219 a
Yanting China 31°11N 105°24E 228 B5
Yantongshan China 43°17N 126°0E 227 C14
Yantra → Bulgaria 43°40N 25°37E 203 C9
Yanuca Fiji 18°24S 178°0E 287 B1
Yanununbeyan △ Australia 35°29S 149°24E 283 C8
Yanwa China 27°35N 98°55E 228 D2
Yanyuan China 27°25N 101°30E 228 D3
Yanzhou China 35°35N 116°49E 226 G9
Yao Chad 12°56N 17°33E 259 F3
Yao Japan 34°37N 135°36E 223 C7
Yao Xian China 34°55N 108°59E 226 G5
Yao Yai, Ko Thailand 8°7N 98°37E 237 a
Yao'an China 25°31N 101°18E 228 E3
Yaoundé Cameroon 3°50N 11°35E 263 E7
Yaowan China 34°15N 118°3E 227 G10
Yap Pac. Oc. 9°30N 138°10E 287 R16
Yapacana △ Venezuela 3°49N 66°44W 328 C4

Yapehe
Dem. Rep. of the Congo 0°13S 24°28E 264 C4
Yapei Ghana 9°10N 1°10W 263 D4
Yapen Indonesia 1°50S 136°0E 231 E9
Yapen, Selat Indonesia 1°20S 136°10E 231 E9
Yapero Indonesia 4°59S 137°11E 231 E9
Yappar → Australia 18°22S 141°16E 280 B3
Yapuparra ✪ Australia 27°15S 126°20E 279 E4
Yaqaga Fiji 16°35S 178°36E 287 A2
Yaqui → Mexico 27°37N 110°39W 318 B2
Yar-Sale Russia 66°50N 70°50E 214 C8
Yaracuy □ Venezuela 10°20N 68°45W 328 A4
Yaracuy → Venezuela 10°33N 68°15W 328 A4
Yaraka Australia 24°53S 144°3E 280 C3
Yaransk Russia 57°22N 47°49E 190 B8
Yarbasan Turkey 38°59N 28°49E 205 C10
Yardımcı Burnu Turkey 36°13N 30°25E 205 E12
Yare → U.K. 52°35N 1°38E 169 E9
Yaremcha Ukraine 48°27N 24°33E 183 B9
Yaren Nauru 0°33S 166°55E 288 H8
Yarensk Russia 62°11N 49°15E 186 B8
Yarfa Si. Arabia 24°37N 38°35E 256 C4
Yarí → Colombia 0°20S 72°20W 328 D3
Yarīm Yemen 14°20N 44°22E 248 D4
Yaritagua Venezuela 10°5N 69°8W 328 A4
Yarkand = Shache China 38°20N 77°10E 217 E9
Yarkant He → China 40°26N 80°59E 217 D10
Yarker Canada 44°23N 76°46W 313 B8
Yarkhun → Pakistan 36°17N 72°30E 243 A5
Yarlung Ziangbo Jiang =
Brahmaputra → Asia 23°40N 90°35E 241 D3
Yarmouth Canada 43°50N 66°7W 299 D6
Yarmūk Iraq 33°18N 44°19E 113 B1
Yarmūk → Syria 32°42N 35°40E 250 F6
Yaroslavl Russia 57°35N 39°55E 188 D10
Yaroslavl □ Russia 59°20N 38°50E 188 C10
Yarra → Trin. & Tob. 10°48N 61°21W 323 t
Yarra Bend Park Australia 37°47S 145°0E 128 A2
Yarra Ranges △ Australia 37°40S 146°3E 283 D7
Yarra Yarra Lakes
Australia 29°40S 115°45E 279 E2
Yarram Australia 38°29S 146°39E 283 E7
Yarraman Australia 26°50S 152°0E 281 D5
Yarras Australia 31°25S 152°20E 283 A10
Yarraville Australia 37°48S 144°53E 128 A1
Yarrawonga Australia 36°0S 146°0E 283 D7
Yarrie Australia 20°40S 120°12E 278 D3
Yartsevo Sib., Russia 60°20N 90°0E 215 C10
Yartsevo Smolensk, Russia 55°6N 32°43E 188 E7
Yarumal Colombia 6°58N 75°24W 328 B2
Yasa Dem. Rep. of the Congo 3°50S 21°25E 264 C4
Yasawa Fiji 16°47S 177°31E 287 A1
Yasawa Group Fiji 17°0S 177°23E 287 A1
Yaselda Belarus 52°7N 26°28E 177 B14
Yasen Ukraine 48°45N 24°10E 183 B9
Yashbum Yemen 14°19N 46°56E 248 D4
Yashi Nigeria 12°23N 7°54E 263 C6
Yashikera Nigeria 9°44N 3°29E 263 D5
Yashiro-Jima Japan 33°55N 132°15E 222 D4
Yashkul Russia 46°11N 45°21E 191 G7
Yasi = Türkistan
Kazakhstan 43°17N 68°16E 217 D7
Yasin Pakistan 36°24N 73°23E 243 A5
Yasinovataya Ukraine 48°7N 37°57E 189 H9
Yasinski, L. Canada 53°16N 77°35W 298 B4
Yasinya Ukraine 48°16N 24°21E 183 B9
Yasnyy Russia 51°1N 59°58E 216 B5
Yasothon Thailand 15°50N 104°10E 236 E5
Yass Australia 34°49S 148°54E 283 C8
Yasugi Japan 35°26N 133°15E 222 B5
Yāsūj Iran 30°31N 51°31E 247 D6
Yasuní △ Ecuador 1°19S 76°3W 328 D2
Yat Niger 20°28N 13°27E 259 D2
Yata → Bolivia 10°29S 65°26W 331 C4
Yata → C.A.R. 10°23N 22°45E 264 A4
Yata-Ngaya △ C.A.R. 9°15N 23°25E 264 A4
Yatağan Turkey 37°20N 28°10E 205 D10
Yatakala Niger 14°50N 0°22E 263 C5
Yaté N. Cal. 22°9S 166°57E 288 d
Yates Center U.S.A. 37°53N 95°44W 308 G6
Yates Pt. N.Z. 44°29S 167°49E 285 E2
Yathkyed L. Canada 62°40N 98°0W 297 A9
Yathong Australia 32°37S 145°33E 283 B6
Yatolemu
Dem. Rep. of the Congo 0°25N 24°35E 264 B4
Yatsuo Japan 36°34N 137°8E 223 A9
Yatsushiro Japan 32°30N 130°40E 222 E2
Yatsushiro-Kai Japan 32°30N 130°25E 222 E2
Yatta Plateau Kenya 2°0S 38°0E 268 C4
Yatua → Venezuela 1°30N 66°30W 328 C4
Yauca Peru 15°39S 74°35W 330 D3
Yauco Puerto Rico 18°2N 66°51W 321 b
Yauri Peru 14°47S 71°25W 330 C3
Yauya Peru 8°59S 77°17W 330 B2
Yauyos Peru 12°19S 75°50W 330 C2
Yauza → Russia 55°54N 37°43E 129 B4
Yaval India 21°10N 75°42E 244 D2
Yavari → Peru 4°21S 70°2W 330 A3
Yávaros Mexico 26°42N 109°31W 318 B3
Yavatmal India 20°20N 78°15E 244 D4
Yavero → Peru 12°6S 72°57W 330 C3
Yavne Israel 31°52N 34°45E 251 G5
Yavoriv Ukraine 49°55N 23°20E 177 D12
Yavorov = Yavoriv
Ukraine 49°55N 23°20E 177 D12
Yavuzeli Turkey 37°18N 37°24E 212 D7
Yawatahama Japan 33°27N 132°24E 222 D4
Yawnghwe Burma 20°39N 96°56E 241 E6
Yawri B. S. Leone 8°22N 13°0W 262 D2
Yaxi China 27°33N 106°41E 228 D6
Yaxian = Sanya China 18°14N 109°29E 229 a
Yayama
Dem. Rep. of the Congo 1°16S 23°7E 264 C4
Yayladağı Turkey 35°54N 36°3E 250 C7
Yazd Iran 31°55N 54°27E 247 D7
Yazd □ Iran 32°0N 55°0E 247 D7
Yazd-e Khvāst Iran 31°31N 52°7E 247 D7
Yazdān Iran 33°30N 60°50E 240 B1
Yazıköy Turkey 36°40N 27°20E 205 E9
Yazman Pakistan 29°8N 71°45E 242 E4
Yazoo → U.S.A. 32°22N 90°54W 315 E9
Yazoo City U.S.A. 32°51N 90°25W 315 E9
Ybbs Austria 48°12N 15°4E 180 C8
Ybycuí △ Paraguay 26°5S 56°46W 334 B4
Ybytyruzú △ Paraguay 25°51S 56°11W 335 B4
Ye Burma 15°15N 97°15E 236 E1
Ye-ngan Burma 21°9N 96°27E 241 E6
Ye-u Burma 22°46N 95°26E 241 D5
Ye Xian = Laizhou China 37°8N 119°57E 227 F10
Ye Xian China 33°35N 113°25E 226 H7
Yea Australia 37°14S 145°26E 283 D6
Yeading U.K. 51°31N 0°23W 125 A1
Yebawmi Burma 25°15N 95°45E 241 C5
Yebbi-Souma Chad 21°7N 17°54E 259 D3
Yebyu Burma 14°15N 98°13E 236 E2
Yecheng China 37°54N 77°26E 217 E9
Yecheon S. Korea 36°39N 128°27E 224 D4
Yecla Spain 38°35N 1°5W 197 G3
Yécora Mexico 28°20N 108°58W 318 B3
Yedashe Burma 19°10N 96°20E 241 F6
Yedebub Biheroch Bihereseboch na
Hizboch □ Ethiopia 12°10N 36°0E 257 F4
Yedigöller △ Turkey 40°55N 31°55E 212 B4
Yedikule Turkey 40°59N 28°55E 122 C1
Yedintsy = Edineț
Moldova 48°9N 27°18E 183 B12
Yedri Chad 22°25N 17°30E 259 D3
Yedseram → Nigeria 12°30N 14°5E 263 C7
Yeed Somalia 4°33N 43°2E 267 D5
Yefremov Russia 53°8N 38°3E 188 F10
Yegguéba Niger 19°59N 12°52E 259 E2
Yeghegnadzor Armenia 39°44N 45°19E 213 C11
Yegorlyk → Russia 46°35N 41°57E 191 G5
Yegorlykskaya Russia 46°35N 40°35E 191 G5
Yegoryevsk Russia 55°27N 38°55E 188 E10
Yegri-Dere = Ardino
Bulgaria 41°34N 25°9E 203 E9
Yegros Paraguay 26°20S 56°25W 334 B4
Yehbuah Indonesia 8°23S 114°45E 231 J17
Yehuda, Midbar Israel 31°35N 35°15E 251 G6
Yei South Sudan 4°9N 30°40E 257 G3
Yei, Nahr → South Sudan 6°15N 30°13E 257 F3
Yeji Ghana 8°13N 0°39W 263 D4
Yejmiadzin = Ejmiatsin
Armenia 40°12N 44°19E 191 K7
Yekaterinburg Russia 56°50N 60°30E 214 D7
Yekaterinenshtadt = Marks
Russia 51°45N 46°50E 190 E8
Yekaterinodar = Krasnodar
Russia 45°5N 39°0E 191 H4
Yekateriny, Proliv
Russia 44°30N 146°30E 215 E15
Yekumbe
Dem. Rep. of the Congo 1°2S 23°27E 264 C4
Yelabuga Russia 55°46N 52°2E 190 C11
Yelan Russia 50°55N 43°43E 190 E6
Yelandur India 12°6N 77°0E 245 H3
Yelarbon Australia 28°33S 150°38E 281 D5
Yelatma Russia 55°0N 41°45E 190 C5
Yelcho, L. Chile 43°18S 72°18W 336 B2
Yelenovka = Sevan
Armenia 40°33N 44°56E 191 K7
Yelenovskiye Karyery =
Dokuchayevsk Ukraine 47°44N 37°40E 189 J9
Yelets Russia 52°40N 38°30E 189 F10
Yélimané Mali 15°9N 10°34W 262 B2
Yelin = Lingshui China 18°27N 110°0E 229 a
Yelizavetgrad = Kirovohrad
Ukraine 48°35N 32°20E 189 H7
Yelizovo Russia 53°11N 158°23E 215 D16
Yell U.K. 60°35N 1°5W 167 A7
Yell Sd. U.K. 60°33N 1°15W 167 A7
Yellamanchilli = Elamanchili
India 17°33N 82°50E 244 F6
Yellandu India 17°39N 80°23E 244 F5
Yellapur India 14°58N 74°43E 245 G2
Yellareddi India 18°12N 78°2E 244 E4
Yellow = Huang He →
China 37°55N 118°50E 227 F10
Yellow → U.S.A. 30°30N 87°0W 317 E3
Yellow Sea China 35°0N 123°0E 227 G12
Yellowhead Pass Canada 52°53N 118°25W 296 C5
Yellowknife Canada 62°27N 114°29W 296 A6
Yellowknife → Canada 62°31N 114°19W 296 A6
Yellowstone → U.S.A. 47°59N 103°59W 304 C12
Yellowstone △ U.S.A. 44°40N 110°30W 304 D8
Yellowstone L. U.S.A. 44°27N 110°22W 304 D8
Yelnya Russia 54°35N 33°15E 188 E7
Yelsk Belarus 51°50N 29°10E 177 C15
Yelwa Nigeria 10°49N 4°41E 263 C5
Yemanzhelinsk Russia 54°58N 61°18E 216 B6
Yemassee U.S.A. 32°41N 80°51W 316 C9
Yembongo
Dem. Rep. of the Congo 3°12N 19°2E 264 B3
Yemen ■ Asia 15°0N 44°0E 248 D4
Yemin Moshe Jerusalem 123 b2
Yemmiganur India 15°44N 77°29E 245 G3
Yen Bai Vietnam 21°42N 104°52E 228 G5
Yenagoa Nigeria 4°58N 6°16E 263 E6
Yenakiyeve Ukraine 48°15N 38°15E 189 H10
Yenakiyevo = Yenakiyeve
Ukraine 48°15N 38°15E 189 H10
Yenangyat Burma 21°6N 94°48E 241 E5
Yenangyaung Burma 20°30N 95°0E 241 E5
Yenanma Burma 19°46N 94°49E 241 F5
Yenbo = Yanbu 'al Baḥr
Si. Arabia 24°5N 38°5E 246 E3
Yenchao Taiwan 22°46N 120°21E 225 E2
Yenda Australia 34°13S 146°14E 283 C7
Yende Millimou Guinea 8°55N 10°10W 262 D2
Yendéré Burkina Faso 10°12N 4°59W 262 C4
Yendi Ghana 9°29N 0°1W 263 D4
Yengisar China 38°56N 76°9E 217 E9
Yengo Congo 0°22N 15°29E 264 B3
Yengo △ Australia 33°0S 150°55E 283 B9
Yéni Niger 13°30N 3°1E 263 C5
Yeni Erenköy = Yialousa
Cyprus 35°32N 34°10E 207 E10
Yeni-Pazar = Novi Pazar
Serbia 43°12N 20°28E 202 C4
Yenibogaziçi = Áyios Seryios
Cyprus 35°12N 33°53E 207 E9
Yenice Ankara, Turkey 39°14N 32°42E 212 C5
Yenice Aydın, Turkey 37°49N 28°35E 205 D10
Yenice Çanakkale, Turkey 39°55N 27°17E 205 B9
Yenice Edirne, Turkey 40°42N 26°9E 203 F10
Yenice Kahramanmaraş,
Turkey 37°0N 35°4E 250 B6
Yenice → Turkey 37°37N 35°33E 212 D6
Yenifoça Turkey 38°44N 26°51E 205 C8
Yenihisar = Didim Turkey 37°22N 27°16E 205 D9
Yenikapı Turkey 41°0N 28°56E 122 B1
Yeniköy Bursa, Turkey 40°31N 29°22E 203 F13
Yeniköy Çanakkale, Turkey 39°55N 26°10E 205 B8
Yeniköy İstanbul, Turkey 41°6N 29°3E 122 B2
Yeniköy Kütahya, Turkey 38°52N 29°17E 205 C11
Yenipazar Turkey 37°49N 28°11E 205 D10
Yenişehir Turkey 40°16N 29°38E 203 F13
Yenisey → Russia 71°50N 82°40E 214 B9
Yeniseysk Russia 58°27N 92°13E 215 D10
Yeniseyskiy Zaliv Russia 72°20N 81°0E 214 B9
Yenki = Yanji China 42°59N 129°30E 227 C15
Yenne France 45°43N 5°44E 175 C9
Yenotayevka Russia 47°15N 47°0E 191 G8
Yenpu Taiwan 22°45N 120°35E 225 D2
Yenshui Taiwan 23°19N 120°16E 225 D2
Yenyuka Russia 57°57N 121°15E 215 D13
Yeo → U.K. 51°2N 2°49W 169 G5
Yeo, L. Australia 28°0S 124°30E 279 E3
Yeo I. Canada 45°24N 81°48W 312 A3
Yeoju S. Korea 37°20N 127°35E 224 D3
Yeola India 20°2N 74°30E 244 D2
Yeon-gi S. Korea 36°35N 127°15E 224 D3
Yeoncheon S. Korea 38°5N 127°4E 224 C3
Yeong-am S. Korea 34°47N 126°42E 224 E3
Yeong-ilman S. Korea 36°4N 129°28E 224 D5
Yeong-wol S. Korea 37°11N 128°28E 224 D4
Yeong-yang S. Korea 36°39N 129°7E 224 D4
Yeongcheon S. Korea 35°58N 128°56E 224 D4
Yeongdeok S. Korea 36°24N 129°22E 224 D5
Yeongdeungpo S. Korea 37°31N 126°54E 137 B1
Yeongdong Chungcheongbuk-do,
S. Korea 36°10N 127°46E 224 D3
Yeongdong Seoul, S. Korea 37°30N 127°1E 137 B2
Yeonggwang S. Korea 35°18N 126°34E 224 D3
Yeongheungdo S. Korea 37°15N 126°27E 224 D3
Yeongju S. Korea 36°50N 128°40E 224 D4
Yeongju △ S. Korea 35°45N 129°20E 224 D4
Yeonpyeongdo S. Korea 37°40N 125°45E 224 D2
Yeonsu S. Korea 34°47N 127°45E 224 E3
Yeotmal = Yavatmal
India 20°20N 78°15E 244 D4
Yeouido S. Korea 37°31N 126°55E 137 B1
Yeovil U.K. 50°57N 2°38W 169 G5
Yepes Spain 39°55N 3°39W 194 F7
Yeppoon Australia 23°5S 150°47E 280 C5
Yerba Buena I. U.S.A. 37°48N 122°21W 136 B2
Yerbent Turkmenistan 39°19N 58°36E 247 B8
Yerbogachen Russia 61°16N 108°0E 215 C11
Yerevan Armenia 40°10N 44°31E 191 K7
Yerington U.S.A. 38°59N 119°10W 304 G4
Yerkesik Turkey 37°7N 28°19E 205 D10
Yerköy Turkey 39°38N 34°28E 212 C6
Yerla → India 16°50N 74°30E 244 F2
Yermo U.S.A. 34°54N 116°50W 307 L10
Yerolakkos Cyprus 35°11N 33°15E 207 E9
Yeropol Russia 65°15N 168°40E 215 C17
Yeroskipos Cyprus 34°46N 32°28E 207 F8
Yerres France 48°43N 2°30E 134 B4
Yershov Russia 51°23N 48°27E 190 E9
Yerushalayim = Jerusalem
Israel/West Bank 31°47N 35°10E 123 B2
Yerville France 49°40N 0°53E 172 C7
Yes Tor U.K. 50°41N 4°0W 169 G4
Yesagyo Burma 21°38N 95°14E 241 E5
Yesan S. Korea 36°41N 126°51E 224 D3
Yeshin Burma 23°43N 95°6E 241 D5
Yeşikent = Erzin Turkey 36°57N 36°11E 250 B7
Yeşil → Turkey 37°20N 33°16E 250 A4
Yeşildere Turkey 37°9N 33°31E 250 A4
Yeşilhisar Turkey 38°20N 35°5E 212 C6
Yeşilırmak → Turkey 41°22N 36°37E 212 B7
Yeşilkent Turkey 36°57N 36°12E 212 D7
Yeşilköy Turkey 40°57N 28°49E 203 F12
Yeşilova Turkey 37°31N 29°46E 205 D11
Yeşilyurt Manisa, Turkey 38°22N 28°40E 205 C10
Yeşilyurt Muğla, Turkey 37°10N 28°20E 205 D10
Yeski Dzhumaya = Târgovişte
Romania 44°55N 25°27E 183 F10
Yessentuki Russia 44°5N 42°53E 191 H6
Yessey Russia 68°29N 102°10E 215 C11
Yeste Spain 38°22N 2°19W 197 G2
Yetman Australia 28°56S 150°48E 281 D5
Yetti Mauritania 26°10N 7°50W 260 C3
Yeu, Î. d' France 46°42N 2°20W 172 F4
Yevdokimovskoye =
Krasnogvardeyskoye
Russia 45°52N 41°33E 191 H5
Yevlax Azerbaijan 40°39N 47°7E 191 K8
Yevpatoriya Ukraine 45°15N 33°20E 189 K7
Yeya → Russia 46°40N 38°40E 191 G4
Yeysk Russia 46°40N 38°12E 189 J10
Yezd = Yazd Iran 31°55N 54°27E 247 D7
Yezerishche Belarus 55°50N 30°0E 188 E5
Ygatimi Paraguay 24°5S 55°40W 335 A4
Yhati Paraguay 25°45S 56°35W 334 B4
Yhú Paraguay 25°0S 56°0W 335 B4
Yí → Uruguay 33°7S 57°8W 334 C4
Yi 'Allaq, G. Egypt 30°21N 33°31E 251 H4
Yi He → China 34°10N 118°8E 227 G10
Yi O San Tsuen
Hong Kong, China 22°14N 113°51E 122 B1
Yi Xian Anhui, China 29°55N 117°57E 229 C11
Yi Xian Hebei, China 39°20N 115°30E 226 E8
Yi Xian Liaoning, China 41°30N 121°22E 227 D11
Yialiás → Cyprus 35°9N 33°44E 207 E9
Yialousa Cyprus 35°32N 34°10E 207 E10
Yibin China 28°45N 104°32E 228 C5
Yichang China 30°40N 111°20E 229 B8
Yicheng Henan, China 31°41N 112°12E 229 B9
Yicheng Shanxi, China 35°42N 111°40E 226 G6
Yichuan China 36°2N 110°10E 226 F6
Yichun Heilongjiang,
China 47°44N 128°52E 219 B14
Yichun Jiangxi, China 27°48N 114°22E 229 D10
Yidu China 36°43N 118°28E 227 F10
Yidun China 30°22N 99°21E 228 B2
Yifag Ethiopia 12°4N 37°46E 257 E4
Yifeng China 28°22N 114°45E 229 C10
Yigo Guam 13°32N 144°53E 302 d
Yiheyuan China 39°59N 116°15E 114 B1
Yihuang China 27°30N 116°12E 229 D11
Yijun China 35°28N 109°8E 226 G5
Yilan = Ilan Taiwan 24°45N 121°44E 225 B3
Yılanlıkale Turkey 36°59N 35°47E 250 B6
Yıldız Dağları Turkey 41°48N 27°36E 203 E11
Yıldız Park Turkey 41°2N 29°1E 122 B2
Yıldızeli Turkey 39°51N 36°36E 212 C7
Yilehuli Shan China 51°20N 124°20E 219 A13
Yiliang Yunnan, China 27°38N 104°2E 228 D5
Yiliang Yunnan, China 24°56N 103°11E 228 E4
Yılmazköy = Skilloura
Cyprus 35°14N 33°10E 207 E9
Yilong China 31°34N 106°23E 228 B6
Yima China 34°44N 111°53E 226 G6
Yimen China 24°40N 102°10E 228 E4
Yimianpo China 45°7N 128°2E 227 B15
Yin Xu China 36°7N 114°18E 226 F8
Yi'nan China 35°31N 118°24E 227 G10
Yinchuan China 38°30N 106°15E 226 E4
Yindaik Burma 23°35N 95°22E 241 D5
Yindarlgooda, L.
Australia 30°40S 121°52E 279 F3
Yindjibarndi ✪ Australia 22°0S 118°35E 278 D2
Ying He → China 32°30N 116°30E 229 A11
Ying Xian China 39°32N 113°10E 226 E7
Yingcheng China 30°56N 113°35E 229 B9
Yingde China 24°10N 113°25E 229 E9
Yingjiang China 24°41N 97°55E 228 E1
Yingjing China 29°41N 102°52E 228 C4
Yingkiong India 28°37N 95°3E 241 A5
Yingkou China 40°37N 122°18E 224 B1
Yingkow = Yingkou
China 40°37N 122°18E 224 B1
Yingpanshui China 37°26N 104°18E 226 F3
Yingshan Hubei, China 30°41N 115°32E 229 B10
Yingshan Sichuan, China 31°4N 106°35E 228 B6
Yingshang China 32°38N 116°12E 229 A11
Yingtan China 28°12N 117°0E 229 C11
Yingualyalya ✪ Australia 18°49S 129°12E 278 C4
Yinhangzhen China 31°20N 121°31E 138 A2
Yining China 43°58N 81°10E 217 D10
Yiningarra ✪ Australia 20°53S 129°27E 278 D4
Yinjiang China 28°1N 108°21E 228 C7
Yinmabin Burma 22°10N 94°55E 241 D5
Yioura = Giaros Greece 37°32N 24°40E 204 D6
Yipinglang China 25°10N 101°52E 228 E3
Yirba Muda Ethiopia 6°12N 38°42E 257 F4
Yirga Alem Ethiopia 6°48N 38°22E 257 F4
Yirol South Sudan 6°33N 30°30E 257 F3
Yirrkala Australia 12°14S 136°56E 280 A2
Yishan China 24°28N 108°38E 228 E7
Yishui China 35°47N 118°30E 227 G10
Yishun Singapore 1°26N 103°51E 138 A3
Yitong China 43°13N 125°20E 227 C13
Yiwu China 29°20N 120°3E 229 C13
Yixing China 31°21N 119°48E 229 B12
Yiyang Henan, China 34°27N 112°10E 226 G7
Yiyang Hunan, China 28°35N 112°18E 229 C9
Yiyang Jiangxi, China 28°22N 117°20E 229 C11
Yizhang China 25°27N 112°57E 229 E9
Yizheng China 32°18N 119°10E 229 A12
Yizhu = Ichu Taiwan 23°20N 120°14E 225 C2
Ylästö Finland 60°17N 24°54E 126 A2
Yli-Kitka Finland 66°8N 28°30E 160 C23
Yliki, L. Greece 38°24N 23°15E 204 C5
Ylitornio Finland 66°19N 23°39E 160 C20
Ylivieska Finland 64°4N 24°28E 160 D21
Ymer Ø Greenland 73°9N 24°20W 154 C8
Yngaren Sweden 58°50N 16°35E 163 F10
Yoakum U.S.A. 29°17N 97°9W 314 G6
Yob △ Eritrea 17°15N 37°50E 257 D4
Yobe □ Nigeria 12°0N 11°30E 263 C7
Yoboki Djibouti 11°30N 42°6E 267 B5
Yobuko Japan 33°32N 129°54E 222 D1
Yodo → Japan 34°45N 135°35E 133 A2
Yog Pt. Phil. 14°6N 124°12E 232 D5
Yoğuntaş Turkey 41°50N 27°4E 203 E11
Yogyakarta Indonesia 7°49S 110°22E 235 D4
Yogyakarta □ Indonesia 7°48S 110°22E 235 D4
Yoho △ Canada 51°25N 116°30W 296 C5
Yojoa, L. de Honduras 14°53N 88°0W 320 D2
Yok Don △ Vietnam 12°50N 107°40E 236 F6
Yokadouma Cameroon 3°26N 14°55E 264 B2
Yōkaichi Japan 35°6N 136°12E 223 B8
Yōkaichiba Japan 35°42N 140°33E 223 B12
Yokkaichi Japan 34°55N 136°38E 223 C8
Yoko Cameroon 5°32N 12°20E 263 D7
Yokohama Japan 35°27N 139°28E 223 B11
Yokosuka Japan 35°20N 139°40E 223 B11
Yokote Japan 39°20N 140°30E 220 E10
Yola Nigeria 9°10N 12°29E 263 D7
Yolaina, Cordillera de Nic. 11°30N 84°0W 320 D3
Yolombo
Dem. Rep. of the Congo 1°36S 23°12E 264 C4
Yölöten Turkmenistan 37°18N 62°21E 247 B9
Yom → Thailand 15°35N 100°1E 236 E3
Yombi Gabon 1°26S 10°37E 264 C2
Yona Guam 13°25N 144°46E 302 d
Yonago Japan 35°25N 133°19E 222 B5
Yonaguni-Jima Japan 24°27N 123°0E 221 M1
Yōnan N. Korea 37°55N 126°11E 224 D3
Yonezawa Japan 37°57N 140°4E 220 F10
Yong-in S. Korea 37°14N 127°12E 224 D3
Yong Peng Malaysia 2°0N 103°3E 237 M4
Yong Sata Thailand 7°8N 99°41E 237 J2
Yongama
Dem. Rep. of the Congo 0°2N 24°35E 264 B4
Yongampo N. Korea 39°56N 124°23E 224 C2
Yong'an China 25°59N 117°25E 229 E11
Yongchang China 38°17N 102°7E 218 D9
Yongcheng China 33°55N 116°20E 226 H9
Yongchuan China 29°17N 105°55E 228 C5
Yongchun China 25°16N 118°20E 229 E12
Yongde China 24°5N 99°25E 228 E2
Yongdeng China 36°38N 103°25E 226 F2
Yongding China 24°43N 116°45E 229 E11
Yongdingman China 39°50N 116°20E 114 B2
Yonge Street Toronto, Canada 141 b3
Yongfeng China 27°20N 115°22E 229 D10
Yongfu China 24°59N 109°59E 228 E7
Yongfucun China 23°8N 113°17E 121 B2
Yonggyap Pass Asia 29°17N 95°37E 241 A5
Yonghe China 36°46N 110°38E 226 F6
Yonghong India 26°28N 94°58E 241 B5
Yŏnghŭng N. Korea 39°31N 127°18E 224 C3
Yŏnghŭng-man N. Korea 39°14N 127°30E 224 C3
Yongji Jilin, China 43°33N 126°13E 227 C14
Yongji Shanxi, China 34°52N 110°28E 226 G6
Yongjia China 28°10N 120°45E 229 C13
Yongkang = Yungk'ang
Taiwan 23°2N 120°15E 225 C2
Yongkang Yunnan, China 24°9N 99°20E 228 E2
Yongkang Zhejiang, China 28°55N 120°2E 229 C13
Yongnian China 36°47N 114°29E 226 F8
Yongning Guangxi Zhuangzu,
China 22°44N 108°28E 228 F7
Yongning Ningxia Huizu,
China 38°15N 106°14E 226 E4
Yongping China 25°27N 99°38E 228 E2
Yongren China 26°4N 101°40E 228 D3
Yongsan S. Korea 37°32N 126°58E 137 B1
Yongshan China 28°11N 103°35E 228 C4
Yongsheng China 26°38N 100°46E 228 D3
Yongshun China 29°2N 109°51E 228 C7
Yongtai China 25°49N 118°58E 229 E12
Yongxin = Jinggangshan
China 26°58N 114°15E 229 D10
Yongxing China 26°9N 113°8E 229 D9
Yongxing Dao = Woody I.
S. China Sea 16°50N 112°20E 230 A4
Yongxiu China 29°2N 115°42E 229 C10
Yongzhou China 26°17N 111°37E 229 D8
Yonibana S. Leone 8°30N 12°19W 262 D2
Yonkers U.S.A. 40°56N 73°52W 132 A2
Yonne □ France 47°50N 3°40E 173 E10
Yonne → France 48°23N 2°58E 173 D9
Yopal Colombia 5°21N 72°23W 328 B3
York W. Austral., Australia 31°52S 116°47E 279 F2
York Ont., Canada 43°40N 79°26W 141 A2
York York, U.K. 53°58N 1°6W 168 D6
York Ala., U.S.A. 32°29N 88°18W 315 E10
York Nebr., U.S.A. 40°52N 97°36W 308 E5
York Pa., U.S.A. 39°58N 76°44W 309 F15
York, C. Australia 10°42S 142°31E 286 F2
York, City of □ U.K. 53°58N 1°6W 168 D6
York, Kap Greenland 75°55N 66°25W 154 B4
York, Vale of U.K. 54°15N 1°25W 168 C6
York I. Antigua & B. 17°2N 61°40W 322 b
York Mills Canada 43°45N 79°22W 141 A2
York Sd. Australia 15°0S 125°5E 278 C4
York Univ. Canada 43°43N 79°29W 141 A1
Yorke Pen. Australia 34°50S 137°40E 282 C2
Yorketown Australia 35°2S 137°33E 282 C2
Yorkshire Dales △ U.K. 54°12N 2°10W 168 C5
Yorkshire Wolds U.K. 54°8N 0°31W 168 C7
Yorkton Canada 51°11N 102°28W 297 C8
Yorkville Calif., U.S.A. 38°52N 123°13W 306 G3
Yorkville Ga., U.S.A. 33°55N 84°58W 316 B5
Yorkville Ill., U.S.A. 41°38N 88°27W 311 C8
Yoro Honduras 15°9N 87°7W 320 C2
Yoron-Jima Japan 27°2N 128°26E 221 L4
Yorosso Mali 12°17N 4°55W 262 C4
Yos Sudarso, Pulau = Dolak, Pulau
Indonesia 8°0S 138°30E 231 F9
Yosemite △ U.S.A. 37°45N 119°40W 306 H7
Yosemite Village U.S.A. 37°45N 119°35W 306 H7
Yoshida Japan 34°40N 132°42E 222 C4
Yoshimatsu Japan 32°0N 130°47E 222 F2
Yoshino-Kumano △
Japan 34°12N 135°55E 223 C7
Yoshinogawa Japan 34°4N 134°21E 222 C6
Yoshkar Ola Russia 56°38N 47°55E 190 B8
Yotala Bolivia 19°10S 65°17W 331 D4
Yotsuya Tokyo, Japan 140 a2
Yotvata Israel 29°55N 35°2E 251 J6
You Jiang → China 22°50N 108°6E 228 F7
You Xian China 27°1N 113°17E 229 D9
You'anmen China 39°51N 116°21E 114 B2
Youbou Canada 48°53N 124°13W 306 B2
Youghal Ireland 51°56N 7°52W 166 E4
Youghal B. Ireland 51°55N 7°49W 166 E4
Youkounkoun Guinea 12°35N 13°11W 262 C2
Young N.S.W., Australia 34°19S 148°18E 283 C8
Young Sask., Canada 51°47N 105°45W 297 C7
Young Uruguay 32°44S 57°36W 334 C4
Young I. Antarctica 66°25S 162°24E 151 C11
Young Ra. N.Z. 44°10S 169°30E 285 E4
Younghusband, L.
Australia 30°50S 136°5E 282 A2
Younghusband Pen.
Australia 36°0S 139°25E 282 D3
Youngsfield S. Africa 34°0S 18°30E 118 B1
Youngstown Alta.,
Canada 51°35N 111°10W 297 C6
Youngstown Fla., U.S.A. 30°22N 85°26W 316 E4
Youngstown N.Y., U.S.A. 43°15N 79°3W 312 C5
Youngstown Ohio, U.S.A. 41°6N 80°39W 312 E4
Youngsville U.S.A. 41°51N 79°19W 312 E5
Youngwood U.S.A. 40°14N 79°34W 312 F5
Youssoufia Morocco 32°16N 8°31W 260 B3
Youxi China 26°10N 118°13E 229 D12
Youyang China 28°47N 108°42E 228 C7
Youyu China 40°10N 112°20E 226 D7
Yozgat Turkey 39°51N 34°47E 212 C6
Yozgat □ Turkey 39°30N 35°0E 212 C6
Ypacaraí △ Paraguay 25°18S 57°19W 334 B4
Ypané → Paraguay 23°29S 57°19W 334 A4
Yport France 49°45N 0°15E 172 C7
Ypres = Ieper Belgium 50°51N 2°53E 170 D2
Ypsilanti U.S.A. 42°14N 83°37W 311 B13
Yr Wyddgrug = Mold U.K. 53°9N 3°8W 168 D4
Yreka U.S.A. 41°44N 122°38W 304 F2
Yrghyz Kazakhstan 48°37N 61°16E 216 C6
Yrghyz → Kazakhstan 48°6N 62°30E 216 C6
Ysabel Chan. Papua N. G. 2°0S 150°0E 286 B6
Yssingeaux France 45°9N 4°8E 175 C8
Ystabohamn Norway 59°3N 5°23E 164 E2
Ystad Sweden 55°26N 13°50E 163 J7
Ysyk-Köl = Balykchy
Kyrgyzstan 42°26N 76°12E 217 D9
Ysyk-Köl Kyrgyzstan 42°25N 77°15E 217 D9
Ysyk-Köl □ Kyrgyzstan 42°0N 78°0E 217 D9
Ythan → U.K. 57°19N 1°59W 167 D7
Ytre Arna Norway 60°27N 5°25E 164 D2
Ytre Enebakk Norway 59°44N 11°0E 164 E8
Ytre Rendal Norway 61°46N 11°23E 164 C8
Ytteran Sweden 63°16N 14°7E 162 A8
Ytterhogdal Sweden 62°12N 14°56E 162 B8
Yttermalung Sweden 60°35N 13°51E 162 D7
Ytyk-Kyuyel Russia 62°30N 133°45E 215 C14
Yu Jiang → China 23°22N 110°3E 228 F7
Yü Shan Taiwan 23°25N 120°52E 225 C2
Yü Shan △ Taiwan 24°45N 121°12E 225 C3
Yu Xian = Yuzhou China 34°10N 113°28E 226 G7
Yu Xian Hebei, China 39°50N 114°35E 226 E8
Yu Xian Shanxi, China 38°5N 113°20E 226 E7
Yuan Jiang → Hunan,
China 28°55N 111°50E 229 C8
Yuan Jiang → Yunnan,
China 22°20N 103°59E 228 F4
Yuan'an China 31°3N 111°34E 229 B8
Yüanch'ang Taiwan 23°39N 120°18E 225 C2
Yuanjiang Hunan, China 28°47N 112°21E 229 C9
Yuanjiang Yunnan, China 23°32N 102°0E 228 F4
Yüanli Taiwan 24°27N 120°39E 225 B2
Yüanlin Taiwan 23°58N 120°30E 225 C2
Yuanling China 28°29N 110°22E 229 C8
Yuanmingyuan Park
China 40°0N 116°17E 114 A1
Yuanmou China 25°42N 101°53E 228 E3
Yuanping China 38°42N 112°46E 226 E7
Yuanqu China 35°18N 111°40E 226 G6
Yuanshan Taiwan 24°45N 121°43E 225 B3
Yuanxiatian China 23°12N 113°17E 121 A2
Yuanyang Henan, China 35°3N 113°58E 226 G7
Yuanyang Yunnan, China 23°10N 102°43E 228 F4
Yuat → Papua N. G. 4°10S 143°52E 286 C2
Yuba → U.S.A. 39°8N 121°36W 306 F5
Yuba City U.S.A. 39°8N 121°37W 306 F5
Yūbari Japan 43°4N 141°59E 220 C10
Yubdo Ethiopia 8°58N 35°24E 257 F4
Yūbetsu Japan 44°13N 143°50E 220 B11
Yucatán □ Mexico 20°50N 89°0W 319 C7
Yucatán, Canal de
Caribbean 22°0N 86°30W 320 B2
Yucatán, Península de
Mexico 19°30N 89°0W 292 H11
Yucatan Basin Cent. Amer. 19°0N 86°0W 320 C3
Yucatan Channel = Yucatán, Canal
de Caribbean 22°0N 86°30W 320 B2
Yucca U.S.A. 34°52N 114°9W 307 L12
Yucca Valley U.S.A. 34°8N 116°27W 307 L10
Yucheng China 36°55N 116°32E 226 F9
Yüch'ih Taiwan 23°54N 120°56E 225 C2
Yuching Taiwan 23°7N 120°27E 225 C2
Yuci = Jinzhong China 37°42N 112°46E 226 F7
Yudu China 25°59N 115°30E 229 E10
Yuechi China 30°34N 106°25E 228 B6
Yuen Long China 22°26N 114°2E 219 a
Yuendumu Australia 22°16S 131°49E 278 D5
Yuendumu ✪ Australia 22°21S 131°40E 278 D5
Yueqing China 28°9N 120°59E 229 C13
Yueqing Wan China 28°5N 121°20E 229 C13
Yuexi Anhui, China 30°50N 116°20E 229 B11
Yuexi Sichuan, China 28°37N 102°26E 228 C4
Yuexiu China 23°8N 113°16E 121 B2
Yuexiu Park China 23°8N 113°16E 121 B2
Yueyang China 29°21N 113°5E 229 C9
Yufu-Dake Japan 33°17N 131°33E 222 D3
Yugan China 28°43N 116°37E 229 C11
Yuğluk Dağı Turkey 36°59N 33°50E 250 B4
Yugo-Zapad Russia 55°40N 37°30E 129 B2
Yugorenok Russia 59°47N 137°40E 215 D14
Yugyd Va △ Russia 62°25N 58°45E 214 C6
Yuhuan China 28°9N 121°12E 229 C13
Yühuan Dao China 28°5N 121°15E 229 C13
Yujiang China 28°10N 116°43E 229 C11
Yukhary Askipara
Azerbaijan 41°4N 45°1E 213 B11
Yukhnov Russia 54°44N 35°15E 188 E8
Yūki Japan 36°18N 139°53E 223 A11
Yukon U.S.A. 35°31N 97°45W 314 D6
Yukon → U.S.A. 62°32N 163°54W 303 E7
Yukon-Charley Rivers △
U.S.A. 65°15N 144°0W 303 D12
Yukon Delta Nat. Wildlife Refuge △
U.S.A. 61°0N 163°0W 303 F7
Yukon Flats U.S.A. 66°40N 145°45W 303 C11
Yukon Territory □ Canada 63°0N 135°0W 294 E5
Yüksekova Turkey 37°34N 44°16E 213 D11
Yukta Russia 63°26N 105°42E 215 C11
Yukuhashi Japan 33°44N 130°59E 222 D2
Yulara Australia 25°10S 130°55E 279 E5
Yule → Australia 20°41S 118°17E 278 D2
Yuleba Australia 26°37S 149°24E 281 D4
Yulee U.S.A. 30°38N 81°36W 316 D8
Yuli China 41°19N 86°15E 217 D11
Yuli Nigeria 9°44N 10°12E 263 D7
Yüli Taiwan 23°20N 121°18E 225 C3
Yulin Guangxi Zhuangzu,
China 22°40N 110°8E 229 F8
Yulin Hainan, China 18°10N 109°31E 229 a
Yulin Shaanxi, China 38°20N 109°30E 226 E5
Yulong Xueshan China 27°6N 100°10E 228 D3
Yuma Ariz., U.S.A. 32°43N 114°37W 307 N12
Yuma Colo., U.S.A. 40°8N 102°43W 304 F12
Yuma, B. de Dom. Rep. 18°20N 68°35W 321 C6
Yumali Australia 35°32S 139°45E 282 C3
Yumbe Uganda 3°28N 31°15E 268 B3
Yumbi Equateur,
Dem. Rep. of the Congo 1°53S 16°34E 264 C3
Yumbi Maniema,
Dem. Rep. of the Congo 1°12S 26°15E 268 C2
Yumbo Colombia 3°35N 76°28W 328 C2
Yumen China 39°50N 97°30E 218 D8
Yumurtalık Turkey 36°45N 35°48E 250 B6
Yun Gui Gaoyuan China 26°0N 104°0E 228 E3
Yun Ling Shan China 27°0N 99°20E 228 D2
Yun Xian Hubei, China 32°50N 110°46E 229 A8
Yun Xian Yunnan, China 24°27N 100°8E 228 E3
Yuna Australia 28°20S 115°0E 279 E2
Yunak Turkey 38°49N 31°43E 212 C4
Yunan China 23°12N 111°30E 229 F8
Yunaska I. U.S.A. 52°38N 170°40W 303 K5
Yuncheng Henan, China 35°36N 115°57E 226 G8
Yuncheng Shanxi, China 35°2N 111°0E 226 G6
Yunfu China 22°50N 112°5E 229 F9
Yung Shue Wan
Hong Kong, China 22°13N 114°6E 122 B2
Yungan Taiwan 22°49N 120°12E 225 D2
Yungang Shiku China 40°6N 113°7E 226 D7
Yungas Bolivia 17°0S 66°0W 331 D4
Yungay Chile 37°10S 72°5W 334 D1
Yungay Peru 9°2S 77°45W 330 B2
Yungk'ang Taiwan 23°2N 120°15E 225 C2
Yungki = Jilin China 43°44N 126°30E 227 C14
Yungning = Nanning
China 22°48N 108°20E 228 F7
Yunhe China 28°8N 119°33E 229 C12
Yunkai Dashan China 22°30N 111°0E 229 F8
Yunkanjini ✪ Australia 22°33S 131°6E 278 D5
Yünlin □ Taiwan 23°40N 120°20E 225 C2
Yunling Shan China 28°30N 98°50E 218 F8
Yunlong China 25°57N 99°13E 228 E2
Yunmeng China 31°2N 113°43E 229 B9
Yunnan □ China 25°0N 102°0E 228 E4
Yunotsu Japan 35°5N 132°21E 222 B4
Yunquera de Henares
Spain 40°47N 3°11W 196 E1
Yunshui Taiwan 23°23N 120°31E 225 C2
Yunt Dağı Turkey 38°56N 27°13E 205 C9
Yunta Australia 32°34S 139°36E 281 E2
Yunxi China 33°0N 110°22E 229 A8
Yunxiao China 23°59N 117°18E 229 F11
Yunyang Chongqing, China 31°2N 108°51E 228 B7
Yunyang Henan, China 33°26N 112°42E 229 A9
Yupanqui Basin Pac. Oc. 19°0S 101°0W 289 J17
Yuping China 27°13N 108°56E 228 D7
Yupukarri Guyana 3°45N 59°20W 329 C6
Yuqing China 27°13N 107°53E 228 D6
Yuraygir △ Australia 29°45S 153°15E 281 D5
Yurga Russia 55°42N 84°51E 214 D9
Yurihonjō Japan 39°23N 140°3E 220 E10
Yurimaguas Peru 5°55S 76°7W 330 B2
Yurkiyka Ukraine 48°42N 28°35E 183 B13
Yurubí △ Venezuela 10°26N 68°42W 321 E6
Yurungkax He → China 38°5N 80°34E 217 E10
Yuryev = Tartu Estonia 58°20N 26°44E 188 C4
Yuryev-Polskiy Russia 56°30N 39°40E 188 D10
Yuryevets Russia 57°25N 43°2E 190 B6
Yuscarán Honduras 13°58N 86°45W 320 D2
Yūsef, Bahr → Egypt 28°25N 30°35E 256 B3
Yushan China 28°42N 118°10E 229 C12
Yushanzhen China 29°28N 108°22E 228 C7
Yushe China 37°4N 112°58E 226 F7
Yushu Jilin, China 44°43N 126°38E 227 B14
Yushu Qinghai, China 33°5N 96°55E 218 E8
Yūsofābād Iran 35°43N 51°24E 141 A2
Yusufeli Turkey 40°50N 41°33E 213 B9
Yutai China 35°0N 116°45E 226 G9
Yutian Hebei, China 39°53N 117°45E 227 E9
Yutian Sinkiang-Uigur,
China 36°52N 81°42E 217 E10
Yütze = Jinzhong China 37°42N 112°46E 226 F7
Yüweng Tao Taiwan 23°36N 119°30E 225 C1
Yuxarı Qarabağ =
Nagorno-Karabakh □
Azerbaijan 39°55N 46°45E 213 C12
Yuxi China 24°30N 102°35E 228 E4
Yuyao China 30°3N 121°10E 229 B13
Yuzawa Japan 39°10N 140°30E 220 E10
Yuzha Russia 56°34N 42°1E 190 B6
Yuzhno-Kurilsk Russia 44°1N 145°51E 215 E15
Yuzhno-Sakhalinsk
Russia 46°58N 142°45E 219 B17
Yuzhno-Sukhokumsk
Russia 44°40N 45°35E 191 H7
Yuzhnouralsk Russia 54°26N 61°15E 216 B6
Yuzhnyy □ Russia 44°0N 40°0E 214 E5
Yuzhou China 34°10N 113°28E 226 G7
Yuzovka = Donetsk
Ukraine 48°0N 37°45E 189 J9
Yvelines □ France 48°40N 1°45E 173 D8
Yverdon-les-Bains Switz. 46°47N 6°39E 179 J2
Yvetot France 49°37N 0°44E 172 C7
Yzeure France 46°33N 3°22E 173 F10

## Z

Za'abeel U.A.E. 25°13N 55°19E 119 B2
Zaandam Neths. 52°26N 4°49E 112 A1
Zaandijk Neths. 52°28N 4°49E 112 A1
Zaanstad Neths. 52°27N 4°50E 112 A1
Zab, Monts du Algeria 34°55N 5°0E 261 B6
Zāb al Kabīr → Iraq 36°1N 43°24E 213 D10
Zāb aş Şaghīr → Iraq 35°17N 43°29E 213 E10
Žabalj Serbia 45°21N 20°5E 182 E5
Žabari Serbia 44°22N 21°15E 202 B5
Zabarjad Egypt 23°40N 36°12E 256 C4
Zabaykalsk Russia 49°40N 117°25E 215 E12
Zabaykalsky △ Russia 53°40N 109°0E 215 D11
Zabbar Malta 35°53N 14°32E 206 F8
Zábřehlice Czech Rep. 50°3N 14°29E 135 B2
Zabid Yemen 14°0N 43°10E 248 D3
Zabīd, W. → Yemen 14°7N 43°6E 248 D3
Ząbki Poland 52°17N 21°6E 143 B2
Ząbkowice Śląskie Poland 50°35N 16°50E 185 H3
Žabljak Montenegro 43°18N 19°5E 202 C3
Zabłudów Poland 53°0N 23°19E 185 F9
Żabno Poland 50°9N 20°53E 185 H7
Zābol Iran 31°0N 61°32E 247 D9
Zābol □ Afghan. 32°0N 67°0E 240 C2
Zābolī Iran 27°10N 61°35E 247 E9
Zabolotiv Ukraine 48°28N 25°18E 183 B10
Zabolottya Ukraine 51°38N 24°16E 185 G11
Zabré Burkina Faso 11°12N 0°36W 263 C4
Zábřeh Czech Rep. 49°53N 16°52E 181 B9
Zabrze Poland 50°18N 18°50E 185 H5
Zabuzhzhya Ukraine 51°21N 23°42E 185 G10
Zabzuga Ghana 9°20N 0°30E 263 D5
Zacapa Guatemala 14°59N 89°31W 320 D2
Zacapu Mexico 19°50N 101°43W 318 D4
Zacatecas Mexico 22°47N 102°35W 318 C4
Zacatecas □ Mexico 23°0N 103°0W 318 C4
Zacatecoluca El Salv. 13°29N 88°51W 320 D2
Zacharo Greece 37°30N 21°39E 204 D3
Zachary U.S.A. 30°39N 91°9W 314 F9
Zachodnio-Pomorskie □
Poland 53°40N 15°50E 184 E2
Żacisze Poland 52°17N 21°4E 143 B2
Zacoalco de Torres
Mexico 20°14N 103°35W 318 C4
Zacualtipán Mexico 20°39N 98°36W 319 C5
Zadar Croatia 44°8N 15°14E 199 D12
Zadawa Nigeria 11°33N 10°19E 263 C7
Zadetkyi Kyun Burma 10°0N 98°25E 237 G2
Zadonsk Russia 52°25N 38°56E 189 F10
Zafarqand Iran 33°11N 52°29E 247 C7
Zafra Spain 38°26N 6°30W 195 G4
Żagań Poland 51°39N 15°22E 185 G2
Zagaoua Chad 16°0N 21°10E 259 E4
Žagarė Lithuania 56°21N 23°15E 184 B10
Zagazig Egypt 30°40N 31°30E 256 H7
Zāgheh Iran 33°30N 48°42E 247 C6
Zaghouan Tunisia 36°23N 10°10E 258 A2
Zaghouan □ Tunisia 36°20N 10°0E 261 A7
Zaglou Algeria 27°17N 0°3W 261 C4
Zagnanado Benin 7°18N 2°28E 263 D5
Zagora Greece 39°27N 23°6E 204 B5
Zagora Morocco 30°22N 5°51W 260 B3
Zagorje Slovenia 46°8N 15°0E 199 B11
Zagórów Poland 52°10N 17°54E 185 F4

Zagorsk = Sergiyev Posad Russia 56°20N 38°10E 188 D10
Zagorsky = Krasnozavodsk Russia 56°27N 38°25E 188 D10
Zagórz Poland 49°30N 22°14E 185 J9
Zagreb Croatia 45°50N 15°58E 199 C12
Zagreb ✈ (ZAG) Croatia 45°45N 16°4E 199 C13
Zāgros, Kūhhā-ye Iran 33°45N 48°5E 247 C6
Zagros Mts. = Zāgros, Kūhhā-ye Iran 33°45N 48°5E 247 C6
Žagubica Serbia 44°15N 21°47E 202 B5
Zaguinaso Ivory C. 10°1N 6°14W 262 C3
Zagyva → Hungary 47°5N 20°4E 182 C5
Zahamena ⌓ Madag. 17°37S 48°49E 272 B2
Zāhedān Fārs, Iran 28°46N 53°52E 247 D7
Zāhedān Sīstān va Balūchestān, Iran 29°30N 60°50E 247 D9
Zahirabad India 17°43N 77°37E 244 F3
Zahlah Lebanon 33°52N 35°50E 250 E6
Zahna Germany 51°55N 12°49E 178 D8
Záhony Hungary 48°25N 22°11E 182 B7
Zahrā Iraq 33°22N 44°19E 113 A1
Ẓahrān al Janub Si. Arabia 17°40N 43°30E 248 C3
Zainsk Russia 55°18N 52°4E 190 C11
Zaïre = Congo → Africa 6°4S 12°24E 265 D2
Zaïre = Congo, Dem. Rep. of the ■ Africa 3°0S 23°0E 265 C4
Zaire □ Angola 7°0S 14°0E 265 D2
Zaječar Serbia 43°53N 22°18E 202 C6
Zaka Zimbabwe 20°20S 31°29E 271 B5
Zakamensk Russia 50°23N 103°17E 215 D11
Zakani Dem. Rep. of the Congo 2°33N 23°16E 264 B4
Zakarpattya □ Ukraine 48°20N 23°20E 183 B8
Zakataly = Zaqatala Azerbaijan 41°38N 46°35E 191 K8
Zakbayemé Cameroon 4°2N 10°34E 264 B2
Zakhodnaya Dzvina = Daugava → Latvia 57°4N 24°3E 188 D3
Zākhū Iraq 37°10N 42°50E 213 D10
Zakinthos = Zakynthos Greece 37°47N 20°54E 207 D2
Zakinthos, Diavlos Greece 37°50N 21°0E 207 D2
Zakopane Poland 49°18N 19°57E 185 J6
Zakouma Chad 10°54N 19°49E 259 F3
Zakouma △ Chad 10°52N 19°45E 259 F3
Zakroczym Poland 52°26N 20°38E 185 F7
Zakros Greece 35°6N 26°10E 207 E7
Zakynthos Greece 37°47N 20°54E 207 D2
Zakynthos ✈ (ZTH) Greece 37°45N 20°50E 207 D2
Zala Angola 7°52S 13°42E 265 D2
Zala Ethiopia 6°28N 37°13E 257 F4
Zala □ Hungary 46°42N 16°50E 182 D1
Zala → Hungary 46°43N 17°16E 182 D2
Zalaegerszeg Hungary 46°53N 16°47E 182 D1
Zalakomár Hungary 46°33N 17°10E 182 D2
Zalalövő Hungary 46°51N 16°35E 182 D1
Zalamea de la Serena Spain 38°40N 5°38W 195 G5
Zalamea la Real Spain 37°41N 6°38W 195 H4
Zalantun China 48°0N 122°43E 219 B13
Zalari Russia 53°33N 102°30E 215 D11
Zalău Romania 47°12N 23°3E 182 C8
Žalec Slovenia 46°16N 15°10E 199 B12
Zaleshchiki = Zalishchyky Ukraine 48°45N 25°45E 183 B10
Zalesye Russia 54°50N 21°31E 184 D8
Zalew Wiślany Poland 54°20N 19°50E 184 D6
Zalewo Poland 53°50N 19°41E 184 E6
Ẓalīm Si. Arabia 22°43N 42°10E 248 B3
Zalingei Sudan 12°51N 23°29E 259 F4
Zalishchyky Ukraine 48°45N 25°45E 183 B10
Zalmah, J. az Libya 25°30N 24°40E 258 C4
Žalov Czech Rep. 50°10N 14°22E 135 A2
Zalṭan Al Wāḥāt, Libya 28°51N 19°52E 258 C3
Zalṭan An Nuqāt al Khams, Libya 32°57N 11°52E 258 B2
Zalun Burma 17°29N 95°34E 241 G5
Załuski Poland 52°9N 20°55E 143 C1
Zama L. Canada 58°45N 119°5W 296 B5
Zambales □ Phil. 15°20N 120°10E 232 D3
Zambales Mts. Phil. 15°45N 120°5E 232 D3
Zambeke Dem. Rep. of the Congo 2°8N 25°17E 268 B2
Zambeze → Africa 18°35S 36°20E 269 F4
Zambezi = Zambeze → Africa 18°35S 36°20E 269 F4
Zambezi Zambia 13°30S 23°15E 265 E4
Zambezi △ Zimbabwe 17°54S 25°41E 269 F2
Zambezia □ Mozam. 16°15S 37°30E 269 F4
Zambia ■ Africa 15°0S 28°0E 269 F2
Zamboanga Phil. 6°59N 122°3E 233 H4
Zamboanga del Norte □ Phil. 8°0N 123°0E 233 G4
Zamboanga del Sur □ Phil. 7°40N 123°0E 233 H4
Zamboanga Pen. Phil. 7°32N 122°16E 233 H4
Zamboanguita Phil. 9°6N 123°11E 233 G4
Zambrano Colombia 9°45N 74°49W 328 B3
Zambrów Poland 52°59N 22°14E 185 F9
Zamdorf Germany 48°8N 11°35E 131 B2
Zametchino Russia 53°30N 42°30E 190 D6
Zamfara □ Nigeria 12°10N 6°0E 263 C6
Zamfara → Nigeria 12°5N 4°2E 263 C5
Zamora Ecuador 4°4S 78°58W 328 D2
Zamora Michoacan, Mexico 19°59N 102°16W 318 D4
Zamora Spain 41°30N 5°45W 194 D5
Zamora □ Spain 41°30N 5°46W 194 D5
Zamora → Ecuador 2°59S 78°13W 328 D2
Zamora-Chinchipe □ Ecuador 4°15S 78°50W 328 D2
Zamość Poland 50°43N 23°15E 185 H10
Zamtang China 32°26N 101°6E 228 A3
Zamuro, Sierra del Venezuela 4°0N 62°30W 329 C5
Zamzam, W. → Libya 30°58N 14°48E 258 B2
Zan Ghana 9°26N 0°17W 263 D4
Zanaga Congo 2°48S 13°48E 264 C2
Záncara → Spain 39°18N 3°18W 197 F1
Zanda China 31°32N 79°50E 218 E4
Zanderij Suriname 5°20N 55°16W 329 B6
Zandu Dem. Rep. of the Congo 5°11S 18°16E 265 D3
Zandvoort Neths. 52°22N 4°32E 170 B4
Zanesville U.S.A. 39°56N 82°1W 312 G2
Zanevka Russia 59°55N 30°31E 137 B3
Zangābād Iran 38°26N 46°44E 246 B5
Zangliveri Greece 40°36N 23°15E 202 F7
Zangoza = Sangüesa Spain 42°37N 1°17W 196 C3
Zangue → Mozam. 17°50S 35°21E 269 F4
Zanjān Iran 36°40N 48°35E 213 D13
Zanjān □ Iran 37°20N 49°30E 247 B6
Zanjān → Iran 37°8N 47°47E 247 B6
Zannone Italy 40°58N 13°3E 200 B6
Zanow = Sianów Poland 54°13N 16°18E 184 D3
Zante = Zakynthos Greece 37°47N 20°54E 207 D2
Zanthus Australia 31°2S 123°34E 279 F3
Zanzan □ Ivory C. 8°30N 3°30W 262 D4
Zanzibar Tanzania 6°12S 39°12E 268 D4
Zanzūr Libya 32°55N 13°1E 258 B2
Zaouatallaz Algeria 24°52N 8°30E 261 D6
Zaouiet El-Kala = Bordj Omar Driss Algeria 28°10N 6°40E 261 C6
Zaouiet Reggâne Algeria 26°32N 0°3E 261 C5
Zaoyang China 32°10N 112°45E 229 A9
Zaozernyy Kazakhstan 53°6N 71°9E 217 B8
Zaozhuang China 34°50N 117°35E 227 G9
Zap Suyu = Zāb al Kabīr → Iraq 36°1N 43°24E 213 D10
Zapadna Morava → Serbia 43°38N 21°30E 202 C5
Zapadnaya Dvina = Daugava → Latvia 57°4N 24°3E 188 D3
Zapadnaya Dvina Russia 56°15N 32°3E 188 D7
Západné Beskydy Europe 49°30N 19°0E 181 B12
Zapadni Rodopi Bulgaria 41°50N 24°0E 202 E7
Západočeský □ Czech Rep. 49°35N 13°0E 180 B6
Zapala Argentina 39°0S 70°5W 336 A2
Zapaleri, Cerro Bolivia 22°49S 67°11W 334 A2
Zapata U.S.A. 26°55N 99°16W 314 H5
Zapatón → Spain 39°0N 6°49W 195 F4
Zapiga Chile 19°40S 69°55W 330 D4
Zapolyarnyy Russia 69°26N 30°51E 160 B24
Zapopán Mexico 20°43N 103°24W 318 C4
Zaporizhzhya Ukraine 47°50N 35°10E 189 J8
Zaporizhzhya □ Ukraine 46°55N 35°50E 189 J8
Zaporozhye = Zaporizhzhya Ukraine 47°50N 35°10E 189 J8
Zapote Phil. 14°27N 120°56E 127 C1
Zappeion Athens, Greece 112 c2
Zaqatala Azerbaijan 41°38N 46°35E 191 K8
Zara Turkey 39°58N 37°43E 212 C7
Zarafshon Uzbekistan 41°34N 64°12E 216 D6
Zaragoza Colombia 7°30N 74°52W 328 B3
Zaragoza Coahuila, Mexico 28°29N 100°55W 318 B4
Zaragoza Nuevo León, Mexico 23°58N 99°46W 319 C5
Zaragoza Spain 41°39N 0°53W 196 D4
Zaragoza □ Spain 41°35N 1°0W 196 D4
Zarand Kermān, Iran 30°46N 56°34E 247 D8
Zarand Markazī, Iran 35°18N 50°25E 247 C6
Zărandului, Munţii Romania 46°14N 22°7E 182 D7
Zaranj Afghan. 30°55N 61°55E 240 C1
Zarasai Lithuania 55°40N 26°20E 188 E4
Zárate Argentina 34°7S 59°0W 334 C4
Zarautz Spain 43°17N 2°10W 196 B2
Zaraysk Russia 54°48N 38°53E 188 E10
Zaraza Venezuela 9°21N 65°19W 329 B4
Zard, Kūh-e Iran 32°22N 50°4E 247 C6
Zāreh Iran 35°7N 49°9E 247 C6
Zari Nigeria 13°4N 12°45E 263 C7
Zaria Nigeria 11°0N 7°40E 263 C6
Zarineh → Iran 36°17N 46°26E 213 D12
Zarinsk Russia 53°43N 84°55E 217 B10
Żarki Poland 50°38N 19°23E 185 H6
Zarko Greece 39°38N 22°6E 204 B4
Zarneh Iran 33°55N 46°10E 246 C5
Zărneşti Romania 45°33N 25°18E 183 E10
Zaros Greece 35°8N 24°54E 207 E5
Żarów Poland 50°56N 16°29E 185 H3
Zarqā', Nahr az → Jordan 32°10N 35°37E 251 F6
Zarrīn Iran 32°46N 54°37E 247 C7
Zarrinābād Iran 36°25N 48°17E 213 D13
Zaruma Ecuador 3°40S 79°38W 328 D2
Żary Poland 51°37N 15°10E 185 G2
Zarza de Granadilla Spain 40°14N 6°3W 194 E4
Zarzaïtine Algeria 28°15N 9°34E 261 C6
Zarzal Colombia 4°24N 76°4W 328 C2
Zarzis Tunisia 33°31N 11°2E 258 B2
Zas Spain 43°4N 8°53W 194 B2
Zashaghan Kazakhstan 51°11N 51°20E 216 B4
Zaskar → India 34°13N 77°20E 243 B7
Zaskar Mts. India 33°15N 77°30E 243 C7
Zastavna Ukraine 48°31N 25°51E 183 B10
Zastron S. Africa 30°18S 27°7E 270 D4
Žatec Czech Rep. 50°20N 13°32E 180 A6
Zaterechnyy Russia 44°48N 45°11E 191 H7
Zatishye = Elektrostal Russia 55°41N 38°32E 188 E10
Zator Poland 49°59N 19°28E 185 J6
Zatyshshya Ukraine 47°20N 29°51E 183 C14
Zavala Bos.-H. 42°50N 17°59E 202 D1
Zavāreh Iran 33°29N 52°28E 247 C7
Zave Zimbabwe 17°6S 30°1E 271 A5
Zaventem Belgium 50°53N 4°28E 116 A2
Zavetnoye Russia 47°13N 43°50E 191 G6
Zavidovići Bos.-H. 44°27N 18°10E 182 F3
Zavitaya = Zavitinsk Russia 50°10N 129°20E 215 D13
Zavitinsk Russia 50°10N 129°20E 215 D13
Zavodovski I. Antarctica 56°0S 27°45W 151 B1
Zavodskoy = Komsomolskiy Russia 54°27N 45°33E 190 C7
Zavolzhsk Russia 57°30N 42°3E 190 B6
Zavolzhye = Zavolzhsk Russia 57°30N 42°3E 190 B6
Zavolzhye Russia 56°37N 43°26E 190 B6
Zawady Poland 52°10N 21°6E 143 B2
Zawadzkie Poland 50°37N 18°28E 185 H5
Zawichost Poland 50°48N 21°51E 185 H8
Zawidów Poland 51°1N 15°1E 185 G2
Zawiercie Poland 50°30N 19°24E 185 H6
Zāwīyah, J. az Syria 35°45N 36°35E 250 C7
Zāwiyat al Bayḍā = Al Bayḍā Libya 32°50N 21°44E 258 B4
Zāwiyat Masūs Libya 31°35N 21°1E 258 B4
Zâwiyet Abû Musallam Egypt 29°56N 31°9E 117 B1
Zawrā' Park Iraq 33°18N 44°23E 113 B2
Zâwyet Shammas Egypt 31°30N 26°37E 256 A2
Zâwyet Um el Rakham Egypt 31°18N 27°1E 256 A2
Zâwyet Ungeîla Egypt 31°23N 26°42E 256 A2
Zāyā Iraq 33°33N 44°13E 246 C5
Zāyandeh → Iran 32°35N 52°0E 247 C7
Ẓaymah Si. Arabia 21°37N 40°6E 248 B3
Zaysan Kazakhstan 47°28N 84°52E 217 C10
Zaysan Köli Kazakhstan 48°0N 83°0E 217 C10
Zayü China 28°48N 97°27E 218 F8
Zazafotsy Madag. 21°11S 46°21E 272 C2
Zāzamt, W. → Libya 30°29N 14°30E 258 B2
Zazir, O. → Algeria 22°0N 5°40E 261 D6
Zázrivá Slovak Rep. 49°16N 19°7E 181 B12
Zbarazh Ukraine 49°43N 25°44E 177 D13
Zbąszyń Poland 52°14N 15°56E 185 F2
Zbąszynek Poland 52°16N 15°51E 185 F2
Zblewo Poland 53°56N 18°19E 184 E5
Zbraslav Czech Rep. 49°58N 14°23E 135 C2
Zbruch → Ukraine 48°32N 26°27E 183 B11
Zbuzany Czech Rep. 50°1N 14°17E 135 B1
Žďár nad Sázavov Czech Rep. 49°34N 15°57E 180 B8
Zdiby Czech Rep. 50°9N 14°27E 135 B2
Zdolbuniv Ukraine 50°30N 26°15E 177 C14
Ždrelo Serbia 44°16N 21°28E 202 B5
Zduńska Wola Poland 51°37N 18°59E 185 G5
Zduny Poland 51°39N 17°21E 185 G4
Zearing U.S.A. 42°10N 93°18W 310 B3
Zeballos Canada 49°59N 126°50W 296 D3
Zebbug Malta 35°52N 14°26E 206 F7
Zebbug Gozo, Malta 36°4N 14°14E 206 E6
Zebediela S. Africa 24°20S 29°17E 271 B4
Zebila Ghana 10°55N 0°30W 263 C4
Zebulon U.S.A. 33°6N 84°21W 316 B5
Zeebrugge Belgium 51°19N 3°12E 170 C3
Zeehan Australia 41°52S 145°25E 281 G4
Zeekoevlei S. Africa 34°4S 18°31E 118 B2
Zeeland U.S.A. 42°49N 86°1W 311 B10
Zeeland □ Neths. 51°30N 3°50E 170 C3
Zeelandia St. Eustatius 17°30N 62°59W 322 a
Zeerust S. Africa 25°31S 26°4E 270 C4
Zefat Israel 32°58N 35°29E 250 F6
Zegdou Algeria 29°51N 4°45W 260 C4
Zege Ethiopia 11°43N 37°18E 257 E4
Zeggerene, Iracher Mali 16°49N 2°16E 263 B5
Zégoua Mali 10°32N 5°35W 262 C3
Zehak Iran 30°53N 61°42E 247 D9
Zehden = Cedynia Poland 52°53N 14°12E 185 F1
Zehdenick Germany 52°58N 13°20E 178 C9
Zehlendorf Germany 52°26N 13°16E 115 B2
Zeigler U.S.A. 37°54N 89°3W 310 G7
Zeil, Mt. Australia 23°30S 132°23E 278 D5
Zeila = Saylac Somalia 11°21N 43°30E 267 B5
Zeist Neths. 52°5N 5°15E 170 B5
Zeitz Germany 51°2N 12°7E 178 D8
Zejtun Malta 35°51N 14°32E 206 F8
Żelechów Poland 51°49N 21°54E 185 G8
Zelena Ukraine 48°3N 24°45E 183 B9
Zelená Hora Czech Rep. 49°34N 15°56E 180 B8
Zelengora Bos.-H. 43°22N 18°30E 202 C2
Zelenodolsk Russia 55°55N 48°30E 190 C9
Zelenogorsk Russia 60°12N 29°43E 188 B5
Zelenograd Russia 56°1N 37°12E 188 D9
Zelenogradsk Russia 54°53N 20°29E 184 D7
Zelenokumsk Russia 44°24N 44°0E 191 H6
Zeleqa, W. → Egypt 29°7N 34°31E 251 J5
Železná Ruda Czech Rep. 49°8N 13°15E 180 B6
Železnik Serbia 44°43N 20°23E 202 B4
Zelfana Algeria 32°27N 4°15E 261 B5
Zelienople U.S.A. 40°48N 80°8W 312 F4
Želiezovce Slovak Rep. 48°3N 18°40E 181 C11
Zelina Croatia 45°57N 16°16E 199 C13
Zell Baden-W., Germany 47°42N 7°52E 179 H3
Zell Rhld-Pfz., Germany 50°1N 7°10E 179 E3
Zell am See Austria 47°19N 12°47E 180 D5
Zella-Mehlis Germany 50°39N 10°40E 178 E6
Zelmen = Rovnoye Russia 50°52N 46°3E 190 E8
Zelów Poland 51°28N 19°14E 185 G6
Zeltweg Austria 47°11N 14°45E 180 D7
Zelyony Dol = Zelenodolsk Russia 55°55N 48°30E 190 C9
Žemaitijos △ Lithuania 56°2N 21°55E 184 B8
Zembra, I. Tunisia 37°5N 10°56E 258 A2
Zemgale = Jelgava Latvia 56°41N 23°49E 184 B10
Zémio C.A.R. 5°2N 25°5E 264 A5
Zemlandskiy Poluostrov Russia 54°50N 20°20E 184 D7
Zemlya Imperatora Nikolaya II = Severnaya Zemlya Russia 79°0N 100°0E 215 B11
Zemmora Algeria 35°44N 0°51E 261 A5
Zemmur W. Sahara 25°5N 12°0W 260 C2
Zemongo ⌓ C.A.R. 6°45N 25°5E 264 A5
Zemoul, O. → Algeria 29°15N 7°0W 260 C3
Zempelburg = Sępólno Krajeńskie Poland 53°26N 17°30E 184 E4
Zempléni-hegység Hungary 48°25N 21°25E 182 B6
Zemplínska šírava Slovak Rep. 48°48N 22°0E 181 C15
Zempoala Mexico 19°27N 96°23W 319 D5
Zemun Serbia 44°51N 20°25E 202 B4
Zendeh Jān Afghan. 34°21N 61°45E 240 B1
Zengbé Cameroon 5°46N 13°4E 263 D7
Zengcheng China 23°13N 113°52E 229 F9
Zenica Bos.-H. 44°10N 17°57E 182 F2
Zenne → Belgium 51°4N 4°26E 116 A2
Zentsūji Japan 34°14N 133°47E 222 C5
Zenza → Angola 8°45S 13°24E 265 D2
Zenza do Itombe Angola 9°16S 14°13E 265 D2
Žepče Bos.-H. 44°28N 18°2E 182 F3
Zephyr Field U.S.A. 29°58N 90°12W 131 B1
Zephyrhills U.S.A. 28°14N 82°11W 317 G7
Zepu China 38°11N 77°16E 217 E9
Zeraf, Bahr ez → South Sudan 9°42N 30°52E 257 F3
Żerań Poland 52°18N 20°58E 143 B1
Zerbst Germany 51°58N 12°5E 178 D8
Zerhamra Algeria 29°58N 2°30W 261 C4
Żerków Poland 52°4N 17°32E 185 F4
Zermatt Switz. 46°2N 7°46E 179 J3
Zernez Switz. 46°42N 10°7E 179 J6
Zernograd Russia 46°52N 40°19E 191 G5
Zernovoy = Zernograd Russia 46°52N 40°19E 191 G5
Zero Milestone Washington, D.C., U.S.A. 143 b1
Zerqan Albania 41°27N 20°20E 202 E4
Zerzeń Poland 52°12N 21°7E 143 B2
Zestaponi Georgia 42°6N 43°0E 191 J6
Zetel Germany 53°25N 7°58E 178 B3
Zetland = Shetland □ U.K. 60°30N 1°30W 167 A7
Zeulenroda Germany 50°39N 11°59E 178 E7
Zévallos Guadeloupe 16°18N 61°17W 322 e
Zeven Germany 53°17N 9°16E 178 B5
Zevenaar Neths. 51°56N 6°5E 170 C6
Zévio Italy 45°22N 11°8E 198 C8
Zeya Russia 53°48N 127°14E 215 D13
Zeya → Russia 51°42N 128°53E 215 D13
Zeyne Turkey 36°25N 33°31E 250 B4
Zeyskoye Vdkhr. Russia 54°30N 127°30E 215 D13
Zeytinbaği Turkey 40°24N 28°47E 203 F12
Zeytinburnu Turkey 40°58N 28°53E 122 C1
Zeytindağ Turkey 38°58N 27°4E 205 C9
Zghartā Lebanon 34°21N 35°53E 250 D6
Zgierz Poland 51°50N 19°27E 185 G6
Zgorzelec Poland 51°10N 15°0E 185 G2
Zgurița Moldova 48°8N 28°1E 183 B13
Zhabei China 31°16N 121°26E 138 B1
Zhabinka Belarus 52°13N 24°2E 185 F11
Zhabokrych Ukraine 48°23N 28°59E 183 B13
Zhalaghash Kazakhstan 45°5N 64°40E 216 C6
Zhalpaqtal Kazakhstan 49°42N 49°25E 190 F9
Zhaltyr Kazakhstan 51°37N 69°49E 217 B7
Zhambyl = Taraz Kazakhstan 42°54N 71°22E 217 D8
Zhambyl □ Kazakhstan 44°0N 72°0E 217 D8
Zhanatas Kazakhstan 43°35N 69°35E 217 D7
Zhangaly Kazakhstan 47°1N 50°37E 191 G10
Zhangaözen Kazakhstan 43°18N 52°48E 187 F9
Zhangaqala Kazakhstan 48°56N 49°36E 191 F9
Zhangaqazaly Kazakhstan 45°48N 62°6E 216 C6
Zhangatas = Zhanatas Kazakhstan 43°35N 69°35E 217 D7
Zhangbei China 41°10N 114°45E 226 D8
Zhangguangcai Ling China 45°0N 129°0E 227 B15
Zhangjiabian China 22°33N 113°28E 219 a
Zhangjiagang China 31°55N 120°30E 229 B13
Zhangjiakou China 40°48N 114°55E 226 D8
Zhangping China 25°17N 117°23E 229 E11
Zhangpu China 24°8N 117°35E 229 E11
Zhangshu China 28°4N 115°29E 229 C10
Zhangye China 38°50N 100°23E 218 D9
Zhangzhou China 24°30N 117°35E 229 E11
Zhanhua China 37°40N 118°8E 227 F10
Zhänibek Kazakhstan 49°25N 46°50E 190 F8
Zhanjiang China 21°15N 110°20E 229 G8
Zhannetty, Ostrov Russia 76°43N 158°0E 215 B16
Zhanyi China 25°38N 103°48E 228 E4
Zhanyu China 44°30N 122°30E 227 B12
Zhao Xian China 37°43N 114°45E 226 F8
Zhao'an China 23°41N 117°10E 229 F11
Zhaocheng China 36°22N 111°38E 226 F6
Zhaodong China 46°4N 125°59E 219 B13
Zhaojue China 28°1N 102°49E 228 C4
Zhaoping China 24°11N 110°48E 229 E8
Zhaoqing China 23°0N 112°20E 229 F9
Zhaotong China 27°20N 103°44E 228 D4
Zhaoyang Hu China 35°4N 116°47E 226 G9
Zhaoyuan Heilongjiang, China 45°27N 125°0E 227 B13
Zhaoyuan Shandong, China 37°20N 120°23E 227 F11
Zhar, Mali Kosovo 42°20N 21°0E 202 D5
Zhari Namco China 31°6N 85°36E 218 E6
Zharkent Kazakhstan 44°10N 80°0E 217 D10
Zharkovskiy Russia 55°56N 32°19E 188 E7
Zhashkiv Ukraine 49°15N 30°5E 177 D16
Zhashui China 33°40N 109°8E 226 H5
Zhaslyk Uzbekistan 43°58N 57°10E 216 D5
Zhayrang Kazakhstan 48°20N 70°10E 217 C8
Zhayylma Kazakhstan 51°37N 61°33E 216 B6
Zhayyq → Kazakhstan 47°0N 51°48E 187 E9
Zhdanov = Mariupol Ukraine 47°5N 37°31E 189 J9
Zhdanov Russia 55°44N 37°41E 129 B3
Zhecheng China 34°7N 115°20E 226 G8
Zhegao China 31°46N 117°45E 229 B11
Zhejiang □ China 29°0N 120°0E 229 C13
Zheleznodorozhnyy = Qŭnghirot Uzbekistan 43°2N 58°50E 216 D5
Zheleznodorozhnyy Kaliningrad, Russia 54°22N 21°19E 184 D8
Zheleznodorozhnyy Komi, Russia 62°35N 50°55E 186 B9
Zheleznogorsk Russia 52°22N 35°23E 189 F8
Zheleznogorsk-Ilimskiy Russia 56°34N 104°8E 215 D11
Zheltyye Vody = Zhovti Vody Ukraine 48°21N 33°31E 189 H7
Zhen'an China 33°27N 109°9E 228 A7
Zhenba China 32°34N 107°58E 228 A6
Zhenfeng China 25°22N 105°40E 228 E5
Zheng'an China 28°32N 107°27E 228 C6
Zhengding China 38°8N 114°32E 226 E8
Zhenghe China 27°20N 118°50E 229 D12
Zhengyang China 32°37N 114°22E 229 A10
Zhengyangguan China 32°30N 116°29E 229 A11
Zhengzhou China 34°45N 113°34E 226 G7
Zhenhai China 29°59N 121°42E 229 C13
Zhenjiang China 32°11N 119°26E 229 A12
Zhenkang China 23°58N 99°0E 228 F2
Zhenlai China 45°50N 123°5E 227 B12
Zhenning China 26°4N 105°45E 228 D5
Zhenping Henan, China 33°10N 112°16E 226 H7
Zhenping Shaanxi, China 31°59N 109°31E 228 B7
Zhenru China 31°16N 121°22E 138 B1
Zhenxiong China 27°27N 104°50E 228 D5
Zhenyuan Gansu, China 35°35N 107°30E 226 G4
Zhenyuan Guizhou, China 27°4N 108°21E 228 D7
Zhenyuan Yunnan, China 23°51N 100°59E 228 F3
Zherdevka Russia 51°56N 41°29E 190 E5
Zherebkove Ukraine 47°50N 29°52E 183 C14
Zhernovka Russia 59°56N 30°30E 137 B2
Zherong China 27°15N 119°52E 229 D12
Zhetiqara Kazakhstan 52°11N 61°12E 216 B6
Zhezdi Kazakhstan 48°3N 67°3E 217 C7
Zhezqazghan Kazakhstan 47°44N 67°40E 217 C7
Zhicheng China 30°25N 111°27E 229 B8
Zhicun China 23°0N 113°18E 121 B2
Zhidan China 36°48N 108°48E 226 F5
Zhigansk Russia 66°48N 123°27E 215 C13
Zhigulevsk Russia 53°28N 49°30E 190 D9
Zhijiang Hubei, China 30°28N 111°45E 229 B8
Zhijiang Hunan, China 27°27N 109°42E 228 D7
Zhijin China 26°37N 105°45E 228 D5
Zhilinda Russia 70°0N 114°20E 215 C12
Zhilino Russia 54°54N 21°54E 184 D8
Zhingli = Chungli Taiwan 24°57N 121°13E 225 B3
Zhirnovsk Russia 50°57N 44°49E 190 E7
Zhirnovsky = Zhirnovsk Russia 50°57N 44°49E 190 E7
Zhirnoye = Zhirnovsk Russia 50°57N 44°49E 190 E7
Zhitomir = Zhytomyr Ukraine 50°20N 28°40E 177 C15
Zhizdra Russia 53°45N 34°40E 188 F8
Zhlobin Belarus 52°55N 30°0E 177 B16
Zhmerynka Ukraine 49°2N 28°2E 177 D15
Zhob Pakistan 31°20N 69°31E 242 D3
Zhob → Pakistan 32°4N 69°50E 242 C3
Zhodzina Belarus 54°5N 28°17E 177 A15
Zhokhova, Ostrov Russia 76°4N 152°40E 215 B16
Zholkev = Zhovkva Ukraine 50°4N 23°58E 177 C12
Zholkva = Zhovkva Ukraine 50°4N 23°58E 177 C12
Zhongba China 29°39N 84°10E 218 F5
Zhongdian China 27°48N 99°42E 228 D2
Zhongdong China 22°48N 107°47E 228 F6
Zhongdu China 24°40N 109°40E 228 E7
Zhongguancun China 39°59N 116°18E 114 B1
Zhonghe = Chungho Taiwan 25°0N 121°28E 225 A3
Zhongjian Dao = Triton I. S. China Sea 15°47N 111°12E 230 A4
Zhongjiang China 30°53N 104°46E 228 B5
Zhongning China 37°29N 105°40E 226 F3
Zhongpu = Chungpu Taiwan 23°26N 120°31E 225 C2
Zhongsha Qundao = Macclesfield Bank S. China Sea 16°0N 114°30E 230 A4
Zhongshan Antarctica 69°0S 39°50E 151 C6
Zhongshan Guangdong, China 22°26N 113°20E 229 F9
Zhongshan Guangxi Zhuangzu, China 24°29N 111°18E 229 E8
Zhongshan Park Beijing, China 114 c3
Zhongshan Park Shanghai, China 31°13N 121°24E 138 B1
Zhongshankong China 22°35N 113°29E 219 a
Zhongtiao Shan China 35°0N 111°10E 226 G6
Zhongwei China 37°30N 105°12E 226 F3
Zhongxian China 30°18N 107°58E 228 B6
Zhongxiang China 31°12N 112°34E 229 B9
Zhongyang China 37°20N 111°11E 226 F6
Zhorany Ukraine 51°19N 23°58E 185 G10
Zhosaly Kazakhstan 45°29N 64°4E 216 C6
Zhoucun Guangdong, China 23°11N 113°11E 121 A2
Zhoucun Shandong, China 36°47N 117°48E 227 F9
Zhoujiadu China 31°11N 121°29E 138 B1
Zhoujiazhen China 31°16N 121°33E 138 B2
Zhoukou China 33°38N 114°38E 226 H8
Zhoukoudian China 39°41N 115°56E 226 E8
Zhouning China 27°12N 119°20E 229 D12
Zhoushan China 30°1N 122°6E 229 B14
Zhoushan Dao China 30°5N 122°10E 229 B14
Zhouzhi China 34°10N 108°12E 226 G5
Zhouzhuangzi China 39°51N 116°16E 114 B1
Zhovkva Ukraine 50°4N 23°58E 177 C12
Zhovti Vody Ukraine 48°21N 33°31E 189 H7
Zhovtneve Lubelskie, Ukraine 50°42N 24°12E 185 H11
Zhovtneve Mykolayiv, Ukraine 46°54N 32°3E 189 J7
Zhu Jiang → China 22°45N 113°37E 229 F9
Zhuanghe China 39°40N 123°0E 224 C1
Zhuangwei = Chuangwei Taiwan 24°45N 121°47E 225 B3
Zhubei = Chupei Taiwan 24°50N 121°0E 225 B3
Zhucheng China 36°0N 119°27E 227 G10
Zhudong = Chutung Taiwan 24°44N 121°5E 225 B3
Zhugqu China 33°40N 104°30E 226 H3
Zhuhai China 22°17N 113°34E 229 F9
Zhuji China 29°40N 120°10E 229 C13
Zhujiang Kou China 22°20N 113°45E 219 a
Zhukovka Russia 53°35N 33°50E 188 F7
Zhulebino Russia 55°42N 37°50E 129 B4
Zhumadian China 32°59N 114°2E 229 A10
Zhunan = Chunan Taiwan 24°41N 120°52E 225 B2
Zhuo Xian = Zhuozhou China 39°28N 115°58E 226 E8
Zhuolu China 40°20N 115°12E 226 D8
Zhuozhou China 39°28N 115°58E 226 E8
Zhuozi China 41°0N 112°25E 226 D7
Zhuqi = Chuch'i Taiwan 23°31N 120°33E 225 C2
Zhur Kosovo 42°13N 20°34E 202 D4
Zhushadi China 23°11N 113°22E 121 A3
Zhushan = Chushan Taiwan 23°45N 120°40E 225 C2
Zhushan China 32°15N 110°13E 229 A8
Zhuxi China 32°25N 109°40E 228 A7
Zhuzhou China 27°49N 113°12E 229 D9
Zhvanets Ukraine 48°33N 26°30E 183 B11
Zhympīty Kazakhstan 50°16N 52°35E 216 B4
Zhytomyr Ukraine 50°20N 28°40E 177 C15
Zhytomyr □ Ukraine 50°50N 28°10E 177 C14
Zi Shui → China 28°40N 112°40E 229 C9
Žiar nad Hronom Slovak Rep. 48°35N 18°53E 181 C11
Ziarat Pakistan 30°25N 67°49E 242 D2
Zibo China 36°47N 118°3E 227 F10
Zichang China 37°18N 109°40E 226 F5
Zidarovo Bulgaria 42°20N 27°24E 203 D11
Zidi = Wandhari Pakistan 27°42N 66°48E 242 F2
Ziębice Poland 50°37N 17°2E 185 H4
Ziebingen = Cybinka Poland 52°12N 14°46E 185 F1
Ziegenhals = Głuchołazy Poland 50°19N 17°24E 185 H4
Zielenzig = Sulęcin Poland 52°26N 15°10E 185 F2
Zielona Poland 52°14N 21°11E 143 B3
Zielona Góra Poland 51°57N 15°31E 185 G2
Zielonka Poland 52°18N 21°9E 143 B2
Zierikzee Neths. 51°40N 3°55E 170 C3
Ziesar Germany 52°16N 12°17E 178 C8
Zifta Egypt 30°43N 31°14E 256 H7
Zīghan Libya 25°29N 22°8E 258 C4
Zigon Burma 18°20N 95°37E 241 F5
Zigong China 29°15N 104°48E 228 C5
Ziguéy Chad 14°43N 15°50E 259 F3
Ziguinchor Senegal 12°35N 16°20W 262 C1
Ziguinchor □ Senegal 12°45N 16°20W 262 C1
Zihuatanejo Mexico 17°39N 101°33W 318 D4
Zijin China 23°33N 115°8E 229 F10
Zile Turkey 40°15N 35°52E 212 B6
Žilina Slovak Rep. 49°12N 18°42E 181 B11
Žilinský □ Slovak Rep. 49°10N 19°0E 181 B12
Zillah Libya 28°30N 17°33E 258 C3
Zillertaler Alpen Austria 47°6N 11°45E 180 D4
Zima Russia 54°0N 102°5E 215 D11
Zimapán Mexico 20°45N 99°21W 319 C5
Zimba Zambia 17°20S 26°11E 269 F2
Zimbabwe Zimbabwe 20°16S 30°54E 269 G3
Zimbabwe ■ Africa 19°0S 30°0E 269 F3
Zimmi S. Leone 7°20N 11°20W 262 D2
Zimnicea Romania 43°40N 25°22E 183 G10
Zimovniki Russia 47°10N 42°25E 191 G6
Zina Cameroon 11°19N 14°54E 259 F2
Zinave △ Mozam. 21°35S 33°40E 271 B5
Zinder Niger 13°48N 9°0E 259 F1
Zinder □ Niger 15°0N 10°30E 263 C7
Zinga C.A.R. 3°49N 18°34E 264 B3
Zinga Tanzania 9°16S 38°49E 269 D4
Zingaro ⌓ Italy 38°6N 12°53E 200 D5
Zingst Germany 54°26N 12°39E 178 A8
Ziniaré Burkina Faso 12°35N 1°18W 263 C4
Zinjibār Yemen 13°7N 45°23E 248 D4
Zinnowitz Germany 54°4N 13°54E 178 A9
Zinovyevsk = Kirovohrad Ukraine 48°35N 32°20E 189 H7
Zion St. Kitts & Nevis 17°8N 62°33W 322 d
Zion Ill., U.S.A. 42°27N 87°50W 311 B9
Zion △ U.S.A. 37°15N 113°5W 305 H7
Zionsville U.S.A. 39°57N 86°16W 311 E10
Zipaquirá Colombia 5°0N 74°0W 328 C3
Zirbitzkogel Austria 47°4N 14°34E 180 D7
Zirc Hungary 47°17N 17°52E 182 C2
Žiri Slovenia 46°5N 14°5E 199 B11
Žirje Croatia 43°39N 15°42E 199 E12
Zirke = Sieraków Poland 52°39N 16°2E 185 F3
Zirl Austria 47°17N 11°14E 180 D4
Zirndorf Germany 49°27N 10°57E 179 F6
Ziro India 27°37N 93°44E 241 B4
Ziros Greece 35°5N 26°8E 207 E7
Zirreh, Gowd-e Afghan. 29°45N 62°0E 240 C1
Zisterdorf Austria 48°33N 16°45E 181 C9
Zitácuaro Mexico 19°24N 100°22W 318 D4
Žitava → Slovak Rep. 48°14N 18°21E 181 C11
Zitelle, Chiesa delle Venice, Italy 142 c3
Žitište Serbia 45°30N 20°32E 182 E5
Zitong China 31°37N 105°10E 228 B5
Zitsa Greece 39°47N 20°40E 204 B2
Zittau Germany 50°53N 14°48E 178 E10
Zitundo Mozam. 26°48S 32°47E 271 C5
Živinice Bos.-H. 44°27N 18°36E 182 F3
Ziwa Maghariba = Kagera □ Tanzania 2°0S 31°30E 268 C3
Ziway Ethiopia 7°56N 38°43E 266 C4
Ziway, L. Ethiopia 8°0N 38°50E 257 F4
Zixi China 27°45N 117°4E 229 D11
Zixing China 25°59N 113°21E 229 E9
Ziyamet = Leonárisso Cyprus 35°28N 34°8E 207 E10
Ziyang Shaanxi, China 32°32N 108°31E 226 H5
Ziyang Sichuan, China 30°6N 104°40E 228 B5
Ziyuan China 26°2N 110°40E 229 D8
Ziyun China 25°45N 106°5E 228 E6
Ziz, Oued → Morocco 31°40N 4°15W 260 B4
Zizhong China 29°48N 104°47E 228 C5
Zizhou = Ch'ich'ou Taiwan 23°45N 120°33E 225 C2
Zizhuyuan Park China 39°54N 116°18E 114 B1
Žižkov Czech Rep. 50°5N 14°28E 135 B2
Zizur Mayor Spain 42°47N 1°41W 196 C3
Zlarin Croatia 43°42N 15°49E 199 E12
Zlatar Croatia 46°5N 16°3E 199 B13
Zlatar Serbia 43°25N 19°47E 202 C3
Zlataritsa Bulgaria 43°2N 25°55E 203 C9
Zlaté Moravce Slovak Rep. 48°23N 18°24E 181 C11
Zlatibor Serbia 43°45N 19°43E 202 C3
Zlatitsa Bulgaria 42°41N 24°7E 203 D8
Zlatna Romania 46°8N 23°11E 183 D8
Zlatna Panega Bulgaria 43°5N 24°9E 203 C8
Zlatni Pyasŭtsi Bulgaria 43°17N 28°3E 203 C12
Zlatograd Bulgaria 41°22N 25°7E 203 E9
Zlatoust Russia 55°10N 59°40E 186 C10
Zletovo Macedonia 41°59N 22°17E 202 E6
Zličín Czech Rep. 50°3N 14°17E 135 B1
Zlín Czech Rep. 49°14N 17°40E 181 B10
Zlínský □ Czech Rep. 49°20N 17°40E 181 B10
Ẓlītan Libya 32°32N 14°35E 258 B2
Złocieniec Poland 53°30N 16°1E 184 E3
Złoczew Poland 51°24N 18°35E 185 G5
Zlot Serbia 44°1N 21°58E 202 B5
Złotoryja Poland 51°8N 15°55E 185 G2
Złotów Poland 53°22N 17°2E 184 E4
Zmeinogorsk Kazakhstan 51°10N 82°13E 217 B10
Żmigród Poland 51°28N 16°53E 185 G3
Zmiyev Ukraine 49°39N 36°27E 189 H9
Znamenka = Znamyanka Ukraine 48°45N 32°30E 189 H7
Znamensk Russia 54°36N 21°16E 184 D8
Znamyanka Ukraine 48°45N 32°30E 189 H7
Żnin Poland 52°51N 17°44E 185 F4
Znojmo Czech Rep. 48°50N 16°2E 180 C9
Zobeyrī Iran 34°10N 46°40E 246 C5
Zobia Dem. Rep. of the Congo 3°0N 25°59E 268 B2
Zobten = Sobótka Poland 50°54N 16°44E 185 H3
Zócalo Mexico City, Mexico 128 b3
Zoetermeer Neths. 52°3N 4°30E 170 B4
Zogang China 29°55N 97°42E 228 C1
Zogno Italy 45°48N 9°40E 198 C6
Zografou Greece 37°58N 23°47E 112 B2
Zohreh → Iran 30°16N 51°15E 247 D6
Zolfo Springs U.S.A. 27°30N 81°48W 317 H8
Żoliborz Poland 52°16N 20°57E 143 B1
Zolochiv Ukraine 49°45N 24°51E 177 D13
Zolotonosha Ukraine 49°39N 32°5E 189 H7
Zolotyy Potik Ukraine 48°54N 25°20E 183 B10
Zomba Malawi 15°22S 35°19E 269 F4
Zongo Dem. Rep. of the Congo 4°20N 18°35E 264 B3
Zonguldak Turkey 41°28N 31°50E 212 B4
Zonguldak □ Turkey 41°20N 31°45E 212 B4
Zongyang China 30°42N 117°12E 229 B11
Zonnebloem S. Africa 33°56S 18°26E 118 A1
Zonqor Pt. Malta 35°52N 14°34E 206 F8
Zonza France 41°45N 9°11E 175 G13
Zoo Baba Niger 18°13N 13°2E 259 E2
Zorgo Burkina Faso 12°15N 0°35W 263 C4
Zorita Spain 39°17N 5°39W 195 F5
Zorleni Romania 46°14N 27°44E 183 D12
Zornitsa Bulgaria 42°23N 26°58E 203 D10
Zorritos Peru 3°43S 80°40W 330 A1
Żory Poland 50°3N 18°44E 185 H5
Zorzor Liberia 7°46N 9°28W 262 D3
Zossen Germany 52°13N 13°27E 178 C9
Zou Xiang China 35°30N 116°58E 226 G9
Zouan-Hounien Ivory C. 6°55N 8°15W 262 D3
Zouar Chad 20°30N 16°32E 259 D3
Zouérate = Zouîrât Mauritania 22°44N 12°21W 260 D2
Zouîrât Mauritania 22°44N 12°21W 260 D2
Zouri Gabon 1°1S 8°53E 264 C1
Zourika Niger 19°16N 7°52E 259 E1
Zourma Burkina Faso 11°20N 0°50W 263 C4
Zousfana, O. → Algeria 31°28N 2°17W 261 B4
Zoutkamp Neths. 53°20N 6°18E 170 A6
Zov Tigra △ Russia 43°25N 134°10E 220 C7
Zrenjanin Serbia 45°22N 20°23E 182 E5
Zuatá → Venezuela 7°52N 65°22W 329 B4
Zuba Nigeria 9°11N 7°12E 263 D6
Zubayr Yemen 15°3N 42°10E 248 D3
Zubin Potok Kosovo 42°54N 20°41E 202 D4
Zubtsov Russia 56°10N 34°34E 188 D8
Zudañez Bolivia 19°6S 64°44W 331 D5
Zuénoula Ivory C. 7°34N 6°3W 262 D3
Zuera Spain 41°51N 0°49W 196 D4
Zuetina = Az Zuwaytīnah Libya 30°58N 20°7E 258 B4
Ẓufār Oman 17°40N 54°0E 249 C6
Ẓufār □ Oman 18°0N 54°0E 249 C6
Zug Switz. 47°10N 8°31E 179 H4
Zug W. Sahara 21°36N 14°9W 260 D2
Zugdidi Georgia 42°30N 41°55E 191 J5
Zugersee Switz. 47°7N 8°35E 179 H4
Zugliget Hungary 47°30N 18°59E 117 B1
Zugló Hungary 47°31N 19°8E 117 A2
Zugspitze Germany 47°25N 10°59E 179 H6
Zuhd, J. az Si. Arabia 28°20N 35°17E 251 K6
Zuid-Holland □ Neths. 52°0N 4°35E 170 C4
Zuidbeveland Neths. 51°30N 3°50E 170 C3
Zuiderwoude Neths. 52°26N 5°2E 112 A3
Zuidhorn Neths. 53°15N 6°23E 170 A6
Zújar Spain 37°34N 2°50W 195 H8
Zújar → Spain 39°1N 5°47W 195 G5
Żukowo Poland 54°21N 18°22E 184 D5
Zula Eritrea 15°17N 39°40E 257 D4
Zulia □ Venezuela 10°0N 72°10W 328 B3
Züllichau = Sulechów Poland 52°5N 15°40E 185 F2
Zülpich Germany 50°41N 6°39E 178 E2
Zülz = Biała Poland 50°24N 17°40E 185 H4
Zumaia Spain 43°19N 2°15W 196 B2
Zumárraga Spain 43°5N 2°19W 196 B2
Zumbi Brazil 22°49S 43°10W 135 A1
Zumbo Mozam. 15°35S 30°26E 269 F3
Zummo Nigeria 9°51N 12°59E 263 D7
Zumpango Mexico 19°48N 99°6W 319 D5
Zunderdorp Neths. 52°24N 4°58E 112 A2
Zundi Angola 10°28S 16°48E 265 E3
Zungeru Nigeria 9°48N 6°8E 263 D6
Zunheboto India 25°58N 94°31E 241 C5
Zunhua China 40°18N 117°58E 227 D9
Zuni Pueblo U.S.A. 35°4N 108°51W 305 J9
Zunyi China 27°42N 106°53E 228 D6
Zuo Jiang → China 22°50N 108°6E 228 F6
Zuoquan China 37°1N 113°27E 226 F7
Zuoying = Tsoying Taiwan 22°41N 120°17E 225 D2
Zuozhou China 22°42N 107°27E 228 F6
Županja Croatia 45°4N 18°43E 182 E3
Zurbātīyah Iraq 33°9N 46°3E 213 F12
Zürich Switz. 47°22N 8°32E 179 H4
Zürich □ Switz. 47°26N 8°40E 179 H4
Zürichsee Switz. 47°18N 8°40E 179 H4
Żuromin Poland 53°4N 19°51E 185 E6
Zurrieq Malta 35°50N 14°28E 206 F7
Žut Croatia 43°52N 15°17E 199 E12
Zutphen Neths. 52°9N 6°12E 170 B6
Zuurberg △ S. Africa 33°12S 25°32E 270 D4
Zuvuvu → Brazil 23°40S 46°42W 137 C1
Zuwārah Libya 32°58N 12°1E 258 B2
Zūzan Iran 34°22N 59°53E 247 C8
Žužemberk Slovenia 45°52N 14°56E 199 C11
Zvanka = Volkhov Russia 59°55N 32°15E 188 C7
Zvečan Kosovo 42°54N 20°50E 202 D4
Zvenigorodka = Svenyhorodka Ukraine 49°4N 30°56E 189 H6
Zvezdets Bulgaria 42°6N 27°26E 203 D11
Zvishavane Zimbabwe 20°17S 30°2E 269 G3
Zvolen Slovak Rep. 48°33N 19°10E 181 C12
Zvonce Serbia 42°57N 22°34E 202 D6
Zvornik Bos.-H. 44°26N 19°5E 182 F4
Zwanenburg Neths. 52°23N 4°45E 112 A1
Zwedru = Tchien Liberia 5°59N 8°15W 262 D3
Zweibrücken Germany 49°15N 7°21E 179 F3
Zwenkau Germany 51°13N 12°20E 178 D8
Zwettl Austria 48°35N 15°9E 180 C8
Zwickau Germany 50°44N 12°30E 178 E8
Zwierzyniec Poland 50°36N 22°58E 185 H9
Zwiesel Germany 49°1N 13°13E 179 F9
Zwittau = Svitavy Czech Rep. 49°47N 16°28E 181 B9
Zwoleń Poland 51°21N 21°36E 185 G8
Zwölfaxing Austria 48°6N 16°28E 142 B2
Zwolle Neths. 52°31N 6°6E 170 B6
Zwolle La., U.S.A. 31°38N 93°39W 314 F8
Żychlin Poland 52°15N 19°37E 185 F6
Żyrardów Poland 52°3N 20°28E 185 F7
Zyryan Kazakhstan 49°43N 84°20E 217 C10
Zyryanka Russia 65°45N 150°51E 215 C16
Zyryanovsk = Zyryan Kazakhstan 49°43N 84°20E 217 C10
Zyuratkul △ Russia 54°50N 58°56E 216 B5
Żywiec Poland 49°42N 19°10E 185 J6

# KEY TO EUROPEAN MAP PAGES

Large scale maps (>1:3 900 000)

Medium scale maps (1:4 000 000 – 1:7 900 000)

Small scale maps (<1:8 000 000)

Paris p134 City maps

155
Arctic Circle
ICELAND

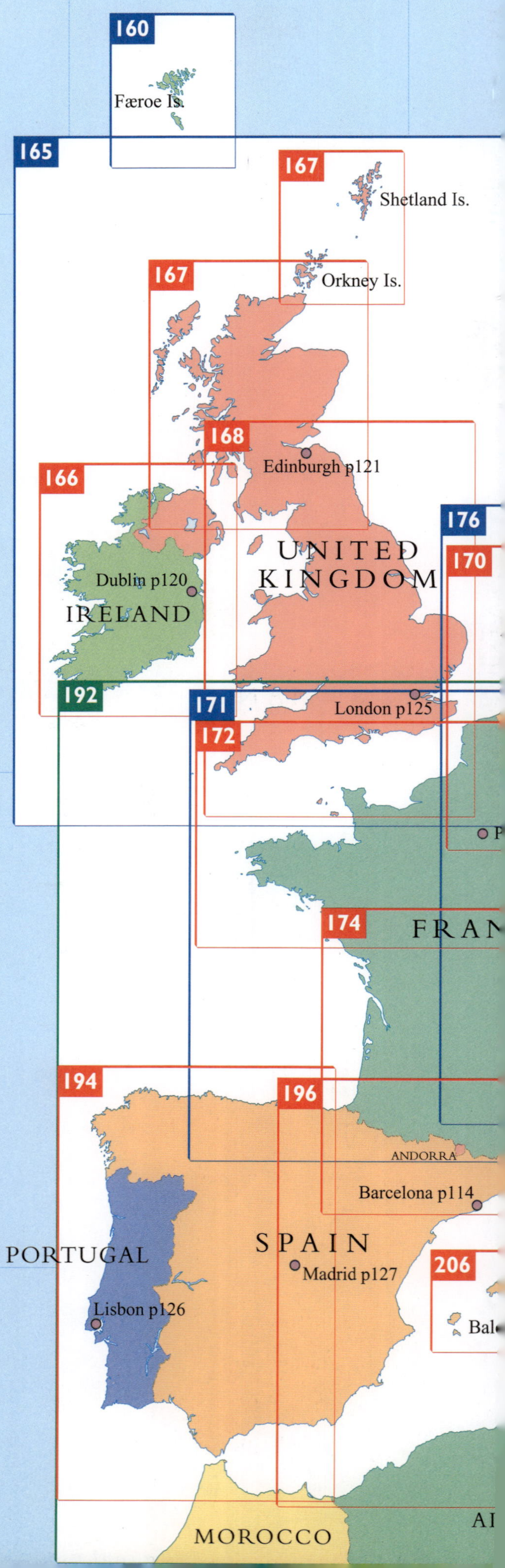
160
Færoe Is.
165
167
Shetland Is.
167
Orkney Is.
168
Edinburgh p121
166
176
UNITED KINGDOM
170
Dublin p120
IRELAND
192
171
London p125
172
174
FRAN
194
196
ANDORRA
Barcelona p114
PORTUGAL
SPAIN
Madrid p127
206
Lisbon p126
Bal
MOROCCO
Al

# WORLD COUNTRY INDEX


Afghanistan 240
Albania 202
Algeria 260–261
Angola 265
Argentina 334, 336
Armenia 213
Australia 278–283
Austria 180–181
Azerbaijan 213
Azores 153

Bahamas 320–321
Bahrain 249
Bangladesh 241
Barbados 322
Belarus 188–189
Belgium 170
Belize 320
Benin 263
Bhutan 241
Bolivia 330–331
Bosnia-Herzegovina 198, 202
Botswana 270
Brazil 328–335
Brunei 235
Bulgaria 202–203
Burkina Faso 262–263
Burma (Myanmar) 236–237, 241
Burundi 268

Cambodia 236–237
Canary Is. 153
Cameroon 259, 264
Canada 294–299
Cape Verde Is. 153
Central African Republic 264
Chad 259
Chile 330, 334, 336
China 218–219, 226–229
Colombia 328
Comoros 272
Congo 264–265
Congo, Dem. Rep. of the 264–265, 268–269
Costa Rica 320
Croatia 182, 199
Cuba 320–321
Cyprus 207
Czech Republic 180–181

Denmark 163
Djibouti 267
Dominican Republic 321

Ecuador 328
Egypt 256
El Salvador 320
England 168–169
Equatorial Guinea 264
Eritrea 266–267
Estonia 188
Ethiopia 266–267

Fiji 287
Finland 160–161
France 172–175
French Guiana 329

Gabon 264
Gambia 262
Georgia 213
Germany 178–179
Ghana 262–263
Greece 202–205
Greenland 154
Guadeloupe 322
Guatemala 320
Guinea 262
Guinea-Bissau 262
Guyana 329

Haiti 321
Honduras 320
Hungary 182

Iceland 155
India 241, 242–245
Indonesia 230–231, 234–235
Iran 246–247
Iraq 246–247
Irish Republic 166
Israel 250–251
Italy 198–201
Ivory Coast 262

Jamaica 320
Japan 220–223
Jordan 251

Kazakhstan 216–217
Kenya 268
Korea, North 224
Korea, South 224
Kosovo 202
Kuwait 246–247
Kyrgyzstan 217

Laos 236
Latvia 188
Lebanon 250
Lesotho 271
Liberia 262
Libya 258
Lithuania 188
Luxembourg 170

Macedonia 202
Madagascar 272
Malawi 269
Malaysia 234–235
Mali 260–263
Malta 206
Martinique 322
Mauritania 260, 262
Mauritius 272
Mexico 318–319
Moldova 183
Mongolia 218–219
Montenegro 202
Morocco 260–261
Mozambique 269, 271

Namibia 270
Nepal 243
Netherlands 170
New Zealand 284–285
Nicaragua 320
Niger 259, 263
Nigeria 263
Northern Ireland 166
Norway 160–161, 164

Oman 249

Pakistan 240
Panama 320
Papua New Guinea 286
Paraguay 334–335
Peru 328, 330
Philippines 232–233
Poland 184–185
Portugal 194–195
Puerto Rico 321

Qatar 249

Réunion 272
Romania 182–183
Russia 186–191, 214–215
Rwanda 268

Samoa 287
Saudi Arabia 246–249
Scotland 167
Senegal 262
Serbia 182, 202
Seychelles 272
Sierra Leone 262
Singapore 237
Slovak Republic 181
Slovenia 199
Solomon Is. 287
Somali Republic 267
South Africa 270–271
Spain 194–197
Sri Lanka 245
Sudan 256–257
Sudan, South 257
Suriname 329
Swaziland 271
Sweden 160–163
Switzerland 179
Syria 212–213

Taiwan 225
Tajikistan 217
Tanzania 268–269
Thailand 236–237
Togo 263
Tonga 287
Trinidad and Tobago 323
Tunisia 261
Turkey 212–213
Turkmenistan 216–217

Uganda 268
Ukraine 189
United Arab Emirates 249
United Kingdom 166–169
USA 300–317
Uruguay 334–335
Uzbekistan 216–217

Vanuatu 287
Venezuela 328–329
Vietnam 236–237

Wales 168–169

Yemen 248–249

Zambia 265, 269
Zimbabwe 269